KJV

STUDY BIBLE

JOEL R. BEEKE,
GENERAL EDITOR

MICHAEL P.V. BARRETT,
OLD TESTAMENT EDITOR

GERALD M. BILKES,
NEW TESTAMENT EDITOR

PAUL M. SMALLEY,
EDITORIAL ASSISTANT

KJV Study Bible

Published by:
Christian Art Gifts
359 Longview Dr.
Bloomingdale, IL 60108
www.christianartgifts.com

Previously Published in 2014 as The Reformation Heritage KJV Study Bible by:
Reformation Heritage Books
3070 29th St. SE
Grand Rapids, MI 49512
www.heritagebooks.org in 2014.

Covers and interiors designed by Brad Miedema.

Cover and interior images used under license from Shutterstock.com.

Printed in China

ISBN 978-1-64272-552-0 KJV130
ISBN 978-1-64272-890-3 KJV196
ISBN 978-1-63952-217-0 KJV216
ISBN 978-1-63952-218-7 KJV217
ISBN 978-1-63952-220-0 KJV219
ISBN 978-1-63952-223-1 KJV222
ISBN 978-1-63952-225-5 KJV224

22 23 24 25 26 27 28 29 30 31 – 11 10 9 8 7 6 5 4 3 2

KJV

STUDY BIBLE

Presented to

____

____

By

____

____

Date

____

____

THIS CERTIFIES THAT

&

WERE UNITED IN

Holy Matrimony

ON

AT

OFFICIATING

WITNESSES

The FAMILY RECORD

Marriages

NAMES	DATE

Births

NAMES	DATE

Deaths

NAMES	DATE

Occasions TO REMEMBER

EVENT	DATE

KJV

STUDY BIBLE

The

KING JAMES VERSION

OLD AND NEW TESTAMENT

Scriptures

CHRISTIAN ART PUBLISHERS

TABLE OF

CONTENTS

THE OLD TESTAMENT

THE NEW TESTAMENT

STUDY HELPS

LIST OF IN-TEXT

ARTICLES

ALPHABETICAL LIST OF THE

BOOKS OF THE BIBLE

BIBLICAL BOOK NAMES AND

ABBREVIATIONS

THE OLD TESTAMENT

Gen.	1 Kings	Eccl.	Obad.
Ex.	2 Kings	Song	Jonah
Lev.	1 Chron.	Isa.	Mic.
Num.	2 Chron.	Jer.	Nah.
Deut.	Ezra	Lam.	Hab.
Josh.	Neh.	Ezek.	Zeph.
Judg.	Est.	Dan.	Hag.
Ruth	Job	Hos.	Zech.
1 Sam.	Ps.	Joel	Mal.
2 Sam.	Prov.	Amos	

THE NEW TESTAMENT

Matt.	2 Cor.	1 Tim.	2 Peter
Mark	Gal.	2 Tim.	1 John
Luke	Eph.	Titus	2 John
John	Phil.	Philem.	3 John
Acts	Col.	Heb.	Jude
Rom.	1 Thess.	James	Rev.
1 Cor.	2 Thess.	1 Peter	

ADDITIONAL ABBREVIATIONS

For ease of reading, we have generally tried to avoid the use of additional abbreviations, with the exception of v. (verse), vv. (verses), ch. (chapter), and chs. (chapters).

WELCOME

TO THE REFORMATION HERITAGE KJV STUDY BIBLE

God has spoken, and His written Word is the Bible. In an age of uncertainty, this is good news. His Word is light in our darkness. You can know God and hear His voice today by reading the pages of His Book. Here is pure truth—truth you can trust. The Lord Jesus Christ, the living Word, still speaks in the written Word by His Spirit. His words are life, and the Holy Spirit can make them life for you too.

What you hold in your hands is both the Bible and tools to help you understand the Bible. The words of the Bible appear in the top half of the page in larger print. These are the very words of God, breathed out by Him (2 Tim. 3:16), given to us through the prophets and apostles as they were infallibly moved by the Spirit (2 Peter 1:21), and faithfully translated into English. All they say is true. On the bottom half of the page, and also in separate articles throughout the book, appear the words of Bible teachers to help you understand and obey God's Word. The risen Christ gives us teachers, and though they are not perfect, God still uses them to explain and apply the Holy Scriptures.

In particular, this is the *Reformation Heritage KJV (King James Version) Study Bible*. All of the words in this title represent something special about this edition of the Bible.

The words *Reformation Heritage* are more than the name of the publisher. These words remind us that the Lord granted a theological and spiritual revival in the sixteenth and seventeenth centuries that resulted in a rich legacy of Bible truth for the church. Located in this Bible at key places throughout the text of Scripture are short articles about key teachings of the Christian faith, some drawn from the writings of the Reformers and Puritans, and others by modern theologians who stand in the same stream of thought. At the end, you will also find an overview of church history and a collection of classic creeds and confessions—declarations from the church of its living faith in the Lord Jesus Christ.

The Reformation's legacy consists not only of theological truths but also of vibrant personal godliness and experience of the Lord's grace that is built on the truth. To help you know the Lord and grow in His grace, this Bible includes a unique feature titled "Thoughts for Personal / Family Worship" at the end of each chapter's notes. Regular times of reading the Bible by yourself and with your family are crucial for Christian spirituality. We are hoping that this feature will particularly assist busy heads of households to prepare some helpful thoughts for daily family worship; even a glance at these thoughts should be of considerable assistance. These sections aim to help you take what you just read and turn it into fruitful meditation and discussion in other private and public settings as well. You will also find at the end of the Bible a collection of articles on practical Christian living that touch on topics such as prayer, pride, parenting, and living positively in a negative world.

The *King James Version* is the classic translation that God has used to nourish English-speaking Christians for more than four hundred years. The work of godly and highly educated Bible scholars, the KJV, or Authorized Version, remains useful, reliable, and widely read. The care of the translators is reflected in their placing in *italics* any words not found in the original manuscripts that were added for the reader's understanding. Though sometimes viewed as quaint, the use of "thee" and "thou" actually reveals that the original text designated the singular as opposed to the plural "ye" or "you," a clarity of expression no longer in use in modern English. It is true that the meanings of some words have changed over the centuries, but to help the modern reader, the study notes of this Bible define difficult words and phrases so that the whole is quite understandable.

Finally, this is a *study Bible*. Each book of the Bible is prefaced by an introduction that discusses questions of the book's authorship, date, theme, and purpose and gives a synopsis of its message. In some cases, difficult questions of interpretation are also addressed in the introduction. Below the text of Holy Scripture, thousands of study notes explain the meaning of individual words and phrases in their original context. Cross-references to other relevant Scriptures are integrated into the study notes, allowing you to investigate a theme or teaching.

A map section at the end will help you to visualize the location of various events described in the Bible. (Note that Map 3 tracing the route of the Exodus is incorrect. See the comment on Exodus 13:18 that properly identifies the general location of the miraculous crossing of the Red Sea.) And a concordance will assist you in finding some of the most important scriptural references to a large variety of words.

So here is the *Reformation Heritage KJV Study Bible*. We are glad that you have opened it, but always remember that simply owning a Bible does you no good. Read the Bible, pray over it, believe it, love it, and obey it in dependency on the Holy Spirit. And use the study helps with discretion, never placing them on par with the Scriptures, but remembering always to subject fallible notes, articles, and confessional documents to them. May the God and Father of our Lord Jesus Christ open your eyes by His Spirit that you may behold wondrous things in His law and gospel, incline your heart to His Son and His testimonies, and give you life in His ways. Pray with us that this study Bible be used by the Holy Spirit to the salvation of many people, the spiritual maturation of believers, and the building up of God's truth and church for generations to come—all to the honor and glory of the Triune God.

JOEL R. BEEKE
General Editor

READING
THE BIBLE EXPERIENTIALLY

To read the Bible experientially simply means to read it with all of our heart, soul, mind, and strength. That is how the Bible is intended to be read. The reason we even have to use the word "experientially" is simply because people imagine they are reading the Bible when they are only reading the Bible in a superficial way.

For instance, many people read the Bible only for tidbits of information, or to gain more head-knowledge. They are interested in facts, history, or even doctrine, but their study of the Bible stops at that level. Sometimes such people read just to confirm what they already know or believe. They read only certain sections of the Bible or if they read through the Bible, they pick out what they find interesting, relevant, or helpful.

Other people read the Bible in order to walk away with an emotional feeling of well-being. They want an emotional fix or shot in the arm to help them through another day or week.

Again, others read the Bible simply because they want to do something. They want practical tips or directives to guide them in their every day life, or as vision for their church or organization.

Each of these groups are marked by this significant flaw: They are not reading the Bible on its own terms. They are not reading the Bible as the revelation of God, His truth, His Word, in all its breadth, depth, and height.

A test as to whether you are reading the Bible experientially is whether in the process of reading the Bible, the Bible reads *you*. No doubt, this will sound like a peculiar way of thinking. "How can a passage read me?" you might wonder. "Words on a page have neither eyes nor a mind that they could read me. Besides, I am not a book full of pages with words to be read."

Admittedly, we do not typically think or talk like this. Yet, we miss something important as a result. Think of what happened when the prophet Nathan came to David the king with the parable of the young lamb (2 Sam. 12:1–6). It ended up revealing the sin in David's life that, until that point, he had not seen as he should have. Nathan's parable acted as a searchlight on David's heart and uncovered something that David had been concealing beneath layers of excuses and attempts to suppress his guilt. David grasped the Word of God that day. But, more importantly, the Word of God grasped him.

Without a doubt, the Holy Spirit was working in David to produce accurate self-knowledge. But the word that Nathan brought was the means God used to that end. It should be no surprise that the Spirit loves to use the Word that way. After all, He has inspired it (2 Peter 1:21). He is pleased to use it to bring sinners to a true and saving knowledge of themselves and of God (John 16:8–14).

Yet, many today are content to read the Bible in a way in which the Word of God is subject to them, rather than that *they* are subject to the Word. They study the Bible—so they think—but do not realize that the Bible needs to study us. We need to *search* the Scriptures, but it is a blessing when we discover that the Scriptures are *searching* us, teaching us both how matters should go in our lives and how they often do go, which always falls short of how they should go (Rom. 7:14–25).

When God uses His Word to search and change us, we have what theologians have called the experiential approach to the Scriptures. In fact, when you come to Scripture truly believing it to be what it claims to be—the Word of God—and submitting to its scrutiny of all of your life, then you are reading the Word experientially. In its entirely Psalm 119 is one glorious expression of experiential reading, and verse 130 states it succinctly: "The entrance of thy words giveth light; it giveth understanding to the simple."

By nature everything is out of order in our lives. We do not see things as they truly are. Sin has drawn a veil over our hearts, and we love this darkness rather than the light (John 3:19). We have lost the sense of being subject to God and accountable to him. Actually, it is even worse than that. We actively rebel against His authority and transgress His laws (Rom. 8:7). We imagine we can make God submit to us. We make His Word the object of our scrutiny, rather than submitting ourselves to its scrutiny. Many Bible students and teachers think they understand the Bible, and yet they do not subject their lives to it. As we read in the Word: "The natural man receiveth not the things of the Spirit of God" (1 Cor. 2:14).

Sometimes people will tell you that reading the Bible experientially means superimposing something on Scripture. They imagine it as an "extra" that comes from mystically inclined minds, those who are not content with the plain meaning of Scripture. Admittedly, there has been a stream of interpreters throughout the centuries who have done a lot to give credence to this charge. But the abuse of experiential interpretation does not mean it is not necessary or useful when done properly.

How can I read the Bible experientially? Prayerfully consider the following biblical pointers.

1. *Respect the Bible as the single and complete authority over your whole life.* Isaiah says it like this: "To the law and to the testimony: if they speak not according to this word, it is because there is no light in them" (Isa. 8:20). That means we cannot depart even ever so little from the Bible. We are not the judges of whether the Bible is valid or relevant at some point. Nor can any other books or human traditions share the authority over our lives with the Bible.
2. *Do not doubt that the Bible is accurate at every point.* David says in Psalm 19:7: "The law of the LORD is perfect, converting the soul: the testimony of the LORD is sure, making wise the simple." David believed it with his whole heart. What it says is wrong or lacking, is truly wrong or lacking. What it says God hates, God truly does hate. What it says God loves, God truly does love.
3. *Submit your heart and life fully to the scrutiny of the Bible.* Psalm 119:80 say, "Let my heart be sound in thy statutes: that I be not ashamed." For the Psalmist to say this, he does not hold back anything from the Word of God.
4. *Prayerfully meditate on the truth of Scripture, carrying it with you wherever you go and whatever you do.* The Bible frequently stresses meditation as an essential part of living godly in this world (Josh. 1:8; Ps. 1:2; Eph. 4:17–18).
5. *Never forget that it is God who is speaking to you through His Word.* Throughout His Word, God reminds us frequently of His majestic character and speech (Gen. 1:1; Ex. 20:1; Ps. 50:1-6). The Scriptures speak to us like a father to his children and like a revered friend writing a letter to us.
6. *Gather with God's people for worship to hear God's Word faithfully preached.* Private Bible reading and study, important though it is, is not substitute for the official and faithful proclamation of the Word of God by His servants. In Ps. 87:2 we read: "The LORD loveth the gates of Zion more than all the dwellings of Jacob." That means that the place where God's people meet for corporate worship and the exposition of God's truth is more precious to the Lord than all the separate dwellings of the people of God, where we are to worship God in our families. Hebrews 10:25 makes the same point. We will be immensely helped when we are companions of others of those who fear the Lord and keep His precepts (Ps. 119:63).
7. *Depend absolutely on grace so that your heart may profit from the Word of God.* To read the Bible experientially means that we receive the Word with meekness. We need humble hearts. Pride keeps us from receiving the Word as we should. Of course, we cannot cure ourselves of pride, but we need earnestly to seek the Holy Spirit to make us teachable. Remember, God's Word is what God uses to save sinners by uniting them to Christ (James 1:20).
8. *Look to the triune God to transcribe God's truth on your heart.* Paul rejoiced that he could say of those Christians he pastored: "Ye are manifestly declared to be the epistle of Christ ministered by us, written not with ink, but with the Spirit of the living God; not in tables of stone, but in fleshy tables of the heart" (2 Cor. 3:3).
9. *Do not be content to simply "hear" the Word; be by grace a doer of the Word.* James is emphatic: "But whoso looketh into the perfect law of liberty, and continueth therein, he being not a forgetful hearer, but a doer of the work, this man shall be blessed in his deed" (James 1:25).
10. *Be ready to sing the Word of God.* Singing helps solidify truth in our minds and hearts (Deut. 31:19). For example, when we sing the Psalms, the God-given book of praise, we help give voice to our desires in a way that, with God's blessing, endears the Word to us even further. David says in Psalm 108:7: "God hath spoken in his holiness: I will rejoice." Ask yourself which of the Psalms echoes what you are reading or gives you a way to respond to what you are reading, and then sing it.

KING JAMES VERSION

ITS TRADITION, TEXT, AND TRANSLATION

The year 2011 marked the four hundredth anniversary of the first edition of the King James Version (KJV) or Authorized Version (AV) of the Bible. From its inception to the present, the King James Version has testified to the unfailing providence of God in preserving His Word and in providing a vehicle for disseminating that Word to the entire English-speaking world.

The influence of the KJV has been incalculable. It helped shape the very language into which it was translated. The KJV's mark on the English language is immeasurable in terms of its use in classic literature and its origination of idioms so commonly used even in everyday speech. It became the principal primer for learning; for many, to read the Bible was the chief reason for learning to read. Although the incentive to literacy is now more secular than sacred, familiarity with the language of the KJV is still an important component in literary education. In addition, and most significantly, the King James Version served the advance of Christ's kingdom wherever English was spoken and read.

Faith comes by hearing and hearing by the Word of God (Rom. 10:17). For centuries, for English-speakers, the KJV was the Word heard. Although aspects of the English language have changed over four hundred years, causing many today to regard the AV as a venerated but irrelevant relic, its value, influence, accuracy, beauty, and understandability remain. Notwithstanding its age, there is no good reason to disregard it or to relegate it to the past. So, reflection on the history, influence, and reliability of the Authorized Version is in order. Its tradition is rich; its textual basis is verifiably sure; and its translation is accurate. In every way, the KJV is an outstanding version of the Scriptures, worthy of continued use as well as historic respect.

ITS TRADITION

As is so often the case regarding the workings of divine providence, events and circumstances affirm God's control in using obstacles and opposition to accomplish His purpose in such a way that all glory is His. The history of the English Bible that culminated in the publication of the KJV is checkered with human hindrances and divine superintendence.

The KJV translators stood on the shoulders of those who, often in peril of their lives, labored to bring God's Word to the public domain from the secrecy and seclusion of Romish control. The Word of God fueled the Reformation, and as the fires of Reformation spread, so did the desire for the Scriptures. William Tyndale's work indisputably laid the foundation upon which others built, including the translators of the King James Version. Tyndale was charged with heresy and warned not to preach in public, but he was driven by his desire to see the Bible translated into English so that every man could read God's Word for himself. In response to a priest attacking his doctrine, Tyndale uttered his now-famous words: "If God spare my life, before long I shall cause a ploughboy to know the scriptures better than you do." God did not spare his life long enough for him to see his prophecy fulfilled, but the Lord did spare him long enough for him to set in motion the means whereby his desire was fulfilled exceedingly abundantly, more than he could ever have dreamed. His translation (1526, 1534) influenced the Coverdale Bible (1535), the Matthew Bible (1537), the Great Bible (1539), the Geneva Bible (1560), the Bishop's Bible (1586), and the King James Version (1611). It is commonly calculated that ninety percent of Tyndale's Bible has been preserved in the Authorized Version. With the widespread acceptance and use of the KJV, Tyndale's hope was fulfilled beyond his dreams to every place on the planet where English is spoken or read. A work begun under the threat of persecution (the human hindrance) prospered because it was preserved and blessed by God (the divine superintendence).

Although each of the antecedent English Bibles has its own story generating praise for God's good providence in making His Word accessible, the production of the King James Version is a testimony to the way God uses men's hostility to accomplish His purpose. If not a matter of overturning outright hostility, it certainly illustrates God's ability to turn a king's heart to achieve an end not in the mind of the king himself. In many ways, King James I was an unlikely character to be associated with a Bible so singularly blessed by God. The son of Mary, Queen of Scots, James was awkward as a youth and not particularly regal as an adult. Worse yet, James was in some ways an opponent to the cause of Christ and an immoral man. But regardless of his less-than-commanding appearance and demeanor, he followed his mother's rival, Queen Elizabeth I, to the throne of England. Behind his back, of course, it was murmured around England that "King Elizabeth" was to be followed by "Queen James." However, what he lacked in regal bearing, he made up for in intellectual accomplishment. He was well trained in the classics, and even had hands-on experience in biblical studies, including translation.

The relationship between church and state was a pressing issue from the beginning of James's monarchy. At the beginning of his reign, a group of Puritan ministers presented him with a petition requesting that certain concerns about the church be resolved. After a delay caused by a deadly epidemic in the country, the Hampton Court Conference convened in 1604 to address the concerns. For the most part, the conference failed to resolve any issues. But on the last day, John Rainolds made a most unexpected proposal. Rainolds was a Puritan, a Hebrew scholar, the president of Corpus Christi College at Oxford, and not particularly liked by the king. He proposed a new translation of the Scriptures that would be acceptable to all Protestants. Some summarily dismissed the suggestion because there were already multiple versions available, some of which were remarkably good. Surprisingly, however, James was favorable to the proposal and gave it his moral but not financial support.

He did so with a couple of caveats that give some insight into the reason for his support. He had a deep disdain for the Geneva Bible, which he considered to be the worst of all the English translations. His dislike was not so much for the translation as for the notes, some of which he interpreted to be subversive to the monarchy and the state church administered by bishops. Consequently, he sanctioned the new translation project so long as there would be no notes and nothing that would promote Puritan doctrine. So, ironically, the king's hatred of doctrines that we hold dear led to the translation of the Bible we cherish. What an example this is of God turning the heart of a king!

The operation of divine providence is evident in the entire project; without that divine superintendence, the work would never have been completed. The planned procedure, humanly speaking, did not have much prospect for success; it was going to be a committee project. Whereas earlier English versions had been the works of individuals, who often labored in secrecy because they were in peril of their lives, this was going to be a collaborative effort of forty-seven scholars and churchmen divided into six groups: two at Oxford, two at Cambridge, and two at Westminster. The results defy the platitude that assigning something to a committee is a death sentence. Together with the Heidelberg Catechism and the Westminster Standards, the KJV translation stands as a testimony of how God can bring together Christians in joint efforts that are very productive for His glory.

Notwithstanding the official sanction and amazing circumstances associated with the production of this new English version, the KJV did not receive immediate widespread acceptance. Particularly, the Geneva Bible, with its strongly Calvinistic and anti-monarchal comments, remained the popular choice among most Puritans—at least until the mid-seventeenth century. Significantly, the Geneva Bible, packed by the Pilgrims on the *Mayflower*, was the first English version to reach North America. But before long, the KJV, though its final form was never officially authorized by the throne, was accepted both by the clergy and the people.

From that time, the KJV became the standard text of the English Bible, and its history and tradition cannot be separated from the history of the church in the English-speaking community throughout the world. The KJV enjoyed that rich tradition until relatively recently, when its language and text have been questioned by a new generation of scholars and churchmen. Many, while recognizing the significant history of the KJV, contend that it has no future. The translation that has done so much in shaping and influencing the English language and its literature is now regarded as archaic, antiquated, and inadequate for communicating to the contemporary English-speaking community.

We reject this assessment and argue that there is no good reason to abandon the use of this version that owns such a celebrated heritage and tradition. We admit that the plethora of modern English versions, some produced by liberal critics and some by evangelicals, has destroyed the monopoly held by the KJV for centuries, but we do not believe the KJV will soon be dethroned as the standard English Bible to which all others will be compared and by which all others will be evaluated. Just as modern versions use contemporary language to give expression to God's Word, so the KJV translators were committed to putting the Bible into the common language. But the KJV alone had and has the kind of weight that has affected the language itself. Expressions and idioms from the KJV abound in current usage and are employed even by those who are clueless regarding their origin. "Feet of clay," "reaping the whirlwind," "scapegoat," "thorn in the flesh," "labor of love," "my brother's keeper," "lamb to the slaughter," "fly in the ointment," "powers that be," "salt of the earth," "sour grapes," "a law unto themselves," "falling flat on one's face," "a broken heart," "a drop in the bucket," "seeing eye to eye," "putting words in one's mouth," "the root of the matter"—these are just a few of the KJV-originated words and phrases that come to mind, and the list could go on and on. It is hard to determine the KJV's range of influence objectively, but there is enough evidence to suggest that accusations against its readability may be exaggerated.

Undeniably, some of the vocabulary and syntax patterns are archaic. This is not surprising, for it is the nature of language to evolve over time. Four hundred years is ample time for semantic shifts to occur and for grammatical conventions to change. But these changes are neither severe nor incomprehensible; they serve to aid the church, particularly in public worship. In some cases the older language aids in communicating the dignity of the church's worship as the Bible is read to the congregation. So much of contemporary worship today is brought down to common levels. When pressures from popular culture define so much of public worship, it is imperative to promote and maintain in worship a distinction, dignity, and reverence that directs our hearts and minds to the majesty and uniqueness of our God. The beauty, elegance, and cadence of the KJV—not to speak of its translation accuracy—create dignity and contribute to our perception of the matchlessness of God's Word.

The supposed difficulty in understanding the language of the KJV can be remedied by habitual exposure to it. Understanding anything requires a circle of knowledge that includes specialized jargon. To someone unfamiliar with baseball, the statement "the batter drew a walk" is incomprehensible. Similarly, a stranger to baseball's rules might find it odd that fans would jeer a pitcher for throwing balls when throwing a ball is his job. But it does not take long to figure out the language and rules of the game. For an older person, listening to younger people talking about computer technology or techniques is confusing. But if you listen long enough, you can figure out what it means to blog, even if you do not know the derivation of the word.

So, there is a jargon with which we must be familiar if we are to understand the Bible. This is not a unique phenomenon caused by the age of the KJV. The Septuagint, the Greek translation of the Hebrew Old Testament, created a biblical jargon understandable to those who knew the Bible but liable to misunderstanding by those who did not. There are several instances in which the translators infused a Greek word with un-Greek significance to include the nuances of the Hebrew word it translated. This practice resulted in word meanings that would have been understood in the biblical context but misunderstood in a secular context. Similarly, the language of the KJV is understandable if given the chance. It does not take much exposure to figure out that "to wit" means "to know," "to prevent" means "to precede," "quick" means "alive," or "conversation" means "behavior."

Learning the language of the KJV requires thought, but that is never a bad thing when coming to the Word of God. It is better to retain a translation that has influenced culture positively, as has the KJV, than to dumb down a translation to reflect the culture. Even more significant than cultural or literary influence is the contribution the AV has made to the sober worship of the Lord. The KJV remains the best liturgical text to meet the needs of the sanctuary. Let the tradition continue.

ITS TEXT

In evaluating any version of the Scriptures, the text from which it is translated is a crucial factor. In the providence of God, the Hebrew and Greek Testaments used by the translators of the KJV have proven to be the most accurate and verifiably reliable texts available both then and now. The Masoretic text printed in the Rabbinic edition of Daniel Bomberg (1524/25) was the basis for the Old Testament, and the Greek text of Theodore Beza (1598), designated as the *Textus Receptus* or Received Text, was the basis for the New Testament.

But these published editions did not fall from heaven into the hands of the translators. They represent a long history of transmission from the original inspired manuscripts through multiple copies and finally to the printed text. All along the way, God guarded and ensured the preservation of His Word. This divine preservation is the necessary and logical corollary to divine inspiration. Foundational to confidence in Scripture as the Word of God, whether in the texts of the original languages or in the texts of versions, is the fact that God inspired His Word. Divine inspiration involves both a process and a consequent product. Peter describes the process: "Knowing this first, that no prophecy of the scripture is of any private interpretation. For the prophecy came not in old time by the will of man: but holy men of God spake as they were moved by the Holy Ghost" (2 Peter 1:20–21). Peter's remark does not concern the interpretation of the meaning of Scripture but rather its origin. In another well-known passage, Paul describes the consequent product of the supernatural process of inspiration: "All scripture is given by inspiration of God, and is profitable for doctrine, for reproof, for correction, for instruction in righteousness: that the man of God may be perfect, thoroughly furnished unto all good works" (2 Tim. 3:16–17). God used men as His instruments of communication, but the words communicated were formed by the Holy Spirit bearing the human authors along in such a supernatural manner that what they wrote was the "breathed-out" Word of God. We cannot explain the mechanics of inspiration, but neither can we deny its fact.

The process of inspiration is past and finished. It was a supernatural operation of God's Spirit limited to those men, beginning with Moses and ending with John, whom God selected to be His instruments in the writing of the biblical books. The process of inspiration ceased at the close of the canon. This is a vital truth for those of us who are cessationists, for so long as there is inspiration, the door is open for continuing revelation. The product of inspiration, the infallible, inerrant corpus of truth—the divinely breathed-out words of Scripture—is the starting point for the progression of preservation that leads to the Bible we possess.

Whereas inspiration involved an extraordinary, supernatural work of God, preservation involves the operation of God's providence—His ordinary work, but His work nonetheless. Inspiration guarantees the preservation and recognition of both the canon and text. Books are not canonical because the church recognized them as such; the church recognized them as canonical because they were, immediately in consequence of their inspiration. Likewise, the text of Scripture has been preserved because of its inspiration. The church has not determined the text; it has been the means through which God has protected His Word and ensured its perpetuation, just as Israel, the Old Testament church, received and safeguarded the laws and promises given at first (Rom. 9:4). Although thousands of years separate us from the past process of inspiration, in God's providence we have a massive amount of evidence that assures the recognition of the words breathed out by the Holy Spirit. God's Word was inspired in terms of process; it is inspired in terms of the product.

We do not possess the actual documents written by the human authors of Scripture, but we do possess thousands of witnesses to the original texts—manuscripts, ancient versions, and patristic writings. How that evidence is interpreted is crucial. Our principal reason for retaining the KJV after all these years is the text from which it is translated. We believe that the extant evidence justifies the conclusion that the Greek edition used by the KJV translators represents the best tradition preserved in the majority of witnesses to the text of the New Testament. The KJV's predecessors were based on the same basic text, but with the exception of the New King James Version, its successors have used a different textual basis. In the providence of God, which text to use was not an issue for the seventeenth-century translators; they used the only text available to them. But what was the only text then remains the best text tradition now. That is not surprising, since it represents the text perpetuated by the church, to whom God entrusted His Word.

Confessedly, our conclusion rests on our opinion as to how to account for the evidence. Others who believe in inspiration and preservation as dogmatically as we have a different opinion as to how and where God preserved His Word. The principal difference of opinion concerns the New Testament text. The history and transmission of the Old Testament text is interesting and important but not as controversial as that of the New Testament. Virtually all scholars regard the Masoretic text of the Old Testament to be authoritative, and it is the text used by most of the modern translations. The New Testament text is another story.

The AV translators used the Greek edition of Theodore Beza. But there was a long history of transmission before the Greek New Testament was published and printed. As late as AD

200, Tertullian wrote that the originals of some of the New Testament letters were still located in the churches to whom they were written, which implies that there were already copies of those letters elsewhere. In fact, we have portions of the New Testament dating to Tertullian's day and one fragment from about seventy years earlier. On the one hand, that is amazing; on the other hand, it is not. The desire for the dissemination of the Word accompanied the spread of the church. But until the invention of the printing press in the fifteenth century, every new manuscript was a handmade copy of another. Notwithstanding how tedious the process was, it produced thousands of Greek manuscripts of the New Testament in the Greek-speaking world. For many years, that Greek-speaking world was the world of the New Testament, and presumably the Bible spread wherever the church was. However, in time Latin replaced Greek in the West, which led to Latin translations, culminating in Jerome's Vulgate in AD 404. The Latin version in the West meant practically that there was little reason to continue copying the Greek text. Greek, however, remained the language in the East, and consequently, Greek manuscripts continued to proliferate in what became the Byzantine Empire. It is not surprising, therefore, that the majority of extant Greek manuscripts come from these locations, where the Greek-speaking church continued the preservation of the Word in the form in which it was originally given. Some manuscripts have been discovered that date earlier than many of those coming from the Byzantine Empire and have readings differing significantly from those in the church-used and church-preserved text, but discovery is not preservation. Preservation implies continuity and unbroken tradition. Genuine readings can be traced throughout the history of the church.

For centuries, partly due to Rome's idolatrous elevation of the Vulgate, the West had neither interest in nor access to the Greek New Testament. The providence of God changed that. The Renaissance generated the interest, and the rise and dominance of Islam afforded the access. Studying the originals behind the classics was an earmark of the Renaissance; this included study of the Scriptures. Hebrew and Greek scholars began to proliferate. The spread of Islam in the East caused churchmen to migrate to the West, taking the Scriptures with them. So, providentially, the Greek text that had prevailed from the early church was the text that entered Europe at the time when God was about to initiate the Reformation, that epic movement that was going to direct the course of the church from that time on.

In addition, God's providence put in place a mechanism that made hand copying obsolete and opened the way for the effusive spread of His Word, both in the original languages and in translation. The printing press served God's purpose in the advance of the Reformation. It also gave birth to a new business: publication. Publishers knew the importance of being the first to the press in order to secure the advantage in the marketplace.

In the early sixteenth century, the race was on to publish the first Greek New Testament. The forerunner appeared to be Cardinal Francisco Ximenes from Spain with the Complutensian Polyglot (Hebrew, Aramaic, Latin, and Greek). It was printed in 1514 but not published until 1522. Forben, a printer in Basel, Switzerland, was aware of the Polyglot and was determined to beat it to publication. He approached Desiderius Erasmus, a learned Greek scholar, and commissioned him to prepare a text for publication. Erasmus agreed, and using the few manuscripts kept in the library at Basel, he won the race to publication in 1516. The edition went through various printings and edits until it was standardized by the French printer Robertus Stephanus in 1546/49. Then John Calvin's successor, Beza, produced a Greek Testament (1565) that was essentially the same as that of Stephanus's; it became the standard Greek Testament used by Protestants, including the translators of the KJV. It was not until an edition published in 1633 by the Elzevir Brothers that the expression *Textus Receptus* was used. Included in the introduction were these words: "Therefore you have the text that is now received by all." That designation then attached itself anachronistically to the earlier editions.

From a purely human perspective, the production of the Greek Testament was a successful business venture. But God ruled over the entire process. The few manuscripts available to Erasmus represented the text tradition that had prevailed from the early church and had been preserved in what we now know to be the vast majority of witnesses to the inspired text of the New Testament. When compared with the majority of extant Greek manuscripts, the Received Text agrees ninety-nine percent of the time. What a testimony this is to the providence of God in preserving His Word! The few manuscripts available for use in the sixteenth century to produce the edition used in the seventeenth century to translate the KJV just happen to reflect the text tradition that is verifiably sure. This is a good and important reason for retaining the use of the AV. Ultimately, the merit of any translation of the Bible depends on the text from which it is translated.

We have not addressed the technicalities of textual criticism except to emphasize the importance of widespread and unbroken tradition in determining the superiority of readings. That the Received Text agrees with the majority text in the majority of places is significant. It represents the Greek text that was preserved throughout the Greek-speaking church for centuries. It is the basis of the English, French, Dutch, and German translations so vital in the Reformation churches. All of this ecclesiastical recognition is hard to ignore. The textual foundation of the KJV is verifiably sure.

ITS TRANSLATION

The beauty of language is that the message communicated in one language can be communicated in another. Language, like everything else, is subject to divine providence, and this has significant implications regarding the Scriptures. Although the biblical authors did not write in English, we can assuredly affirm our English Bible to be God's Word. Indeed, the translators of the AV affirmed "that the very meanest translation of the Bible in English… containeth the word of God, nay, is the Word of God."[1] The words are not the same, but the message expressed in the Hebrew, Aramaic, and Greek words of the Old and New Testaments can be conveyed in English and indeed in any other tongue. God breathed out every Hebrew, Aramaic, and Greek word in the Scriptures, but the message He revealed through those words is not so intrinsically subsumed in those words as to prevent the message from being expressed and understood with words of another language. Scripture's message is so important that the original languages "are to be translated into the vulgar language of every nation unto which they come" (Westminster Confession of Faith, 1.8).

Equally important to the need for translation is the manner of translation. Given the magnitude of the message, it is imperative that the message of the original and the message of the translation be the same. Translating accurately and faithfully requires that the translator be proficient in both the original and target languages. The six committees engaged in the project commissioned by King James were comprised of competent scholars in biblical languages and men most capable of crafting the English language.

The translators operated under a set of fifteen rules designed to ensure uniformity and to achieve illusive consensus regarding each part before final approval of the whole. The rules detailed the procedures they would follow in the translation process and created safeguards to guarantee agreement, accuracy, and acceptability. The number of required "hoops" seemed to doom the project from the beginning, but contrary to expectation, the process worked well to produce an English Bible that became the standard by which and to which all other translations would be compared.

The first rule governing the committees was that they were to use the Bishop's Bible as the basis of their revision, deviating from it only when absolutely necessary. Rule fourteen allowed them to consult and use other versions that were judged to be superior to the Bishop's. Rule fourteen consistently trumped rule one; the Tyndale, Coverdale, Great, Geneva, and even the Rheims-Douay Bibles were consulted along with the Bishop's. Tyndale's version had the greatest impact. The translators said, "we never thought from the beginning, that we should need to make a new translation, nor yet to make of a bad one a good one…but to make a good one better, or out of many good ones, one principal good one."[2] But although the KJV is a revision of earlier English versions, the committees relied heavily on the Hebrew and Greek testaments as well. In their address to the readers, the translators frequently reference the importance of the original languages. It is appropriate to refer to them as translators and to their work as translation.

Without knowledge of all the issues of differing translation philosophies and techniques that are currently prevalent and part of academic disciplines, the translators employed methods

1 "An Answer to the Imputations of Our Adversaries," in "The Translators to the Reader," *The Holy Bible: Conteyning the Old Testament and the New. Newly Translated out of the Original Tongues: and with the Former Translations Diligently Compared and Revised, by His Maiesties Speciall Commandement* (London: Robert Barker, 1611), no pagination.

2 "The Purpose of the Translators," in "The Translators to the Reader," *The Holy Bible*, no pagination.

that can be evaluated and labeled by modern criteria. We argue that the KJV is in the category sometimes referred to as complete equivalency. Simply stated, this means that the translation was as literal as possible— giving due regard to the words, grammar, figures of speech, etc. of the original, yet as free as necessary—ensuring that the message intended by the original was not obscured.

For instance, by using italics to identify words in the translation that have no counterpart in the original, the translators revealed their high regard for the original text as well as their desire to help the reader by smoothing out passages that otherwise would be awkward. Even the use of what are now the archaic second-person pronouns (thee, thou, ye) allows the reader to see something that is clear in the original texts but obscured by the modern usage of "you." Thee, thou, and ye may sound outdated, but they reflect the original Hebrew and Greek precisely and often have interpretative significance, which readers of modern English versions will miss. Giving the readers of a translation the same opportunity of understanding and response as the readers of the original should be the goal of translation and is a mark of a good one. We think that is why, too, the KJV translators from time to time put alternative translations of difficult or ambiguous statements in the margins. These alternatives give the readers the opportunity to think through the obscurities inherent in the originals.

The merit of any translation is determined by how well it achieves the purpose of translation: conveying the message recorded in one language into another. A good version translates without explaining, maintains the original's content and intent, retains interpretation issues, and permits an equivalence of response between the original and target audiences. It is accurate in regard to lexical and grammatical fidelity. It is sensitive to and reflective of the various styles of biblical writers. And in addition to faithfulness to the original, it is readable, both in terms of private devotion and study, and public worship. If these are the marks of a good translation, then the KJV is an indisputably good translation. It has served its purpose well for four hundred years. It continues to serve its purpose well.

CONCLUSION

The publication of the King James Version in 1611 was a landmark. The version has left its mark for four hundred years on literature, speech, culture, religion, and, most significantly, the hearts of millions. It has earned its place as the most influential book ever printed, and with the passing of its four-hundredth-anniversary year, venerating it is appropriate. It is old, but it is not outdated.

BEHOLD
THE DAYS COME
Saith
THE LORD
THAT I WILL MAKE A
New
COVENANT
with
THE HOUSE OF
ISRAEL
&
WITH THE HOUSE OF
JUDAH

JEREMIAH 31:31

The OLD TESTAMENT

SCRIPTURES

God

SAW

EVERY THING

THAT HE HAD MADE

&

BEHOLD

IT WAS

very good

GENESIS 1:31

INTRODUCTION TO THE PENTATEUCH

The Hebrew Bible consists of three parts: the Law, the Prophets, and the Writings, often referred to as the *Tanakh*, a word formed by the first letters of the Hebrew words for law, prophets, and writings. Jesus, in His post-resurrection conversation with the two disciples on the road to Emmaus, alluded to this tripartite division when He spoke of the law of Moses, the prophets, and the psalms (Luke 24:44). In so doing, He referred to all of what we call the Old Testament.

The first division, the Law, is the translation of the Hebrew word *torah*, which means "instruction." It is, in fact, the most general word in the Old Testament to refer to God's special revelation. The Law consists of the first five books, Genesis–Deuteronomy, and is commonly designated as the Pentateuch. Pentateuch is from the Greek, meaning "five scrolls." The Old Testament itself refers to these five books as "the book of the law of Moses" (2 Kings 14:6), the "book of the law" (Josh. 1:8), "the law of Moses" (Josh. 8:31), or the "book of Moses" (Ezra 6:18). Christ spoke of both the law and the book of Moses (Mark 12:26; Luke 24:44). Indeed, occasionally He referred to the whole corpus simply as "Moses" (Luke 16:29; 24:27). The apostles did the same (Acts 15:21; 2 Cor. 3:15).

The biblical evidence, which includes the very words of Jesus Christ, attributes the authorship of these books to Moses. The evidence is overwhelming and unequivocal. The Scripture states that Moses recorded God's words and deeds in writing, as the Lord had commanded him (Ex. 17:14; 24:4; 34:27; Num. 33:2; Deut. 31:9). The Lord Jesus affirmed that Moses wrote the law: "For had ye believed Moses, ye would have believed me: for he wrote of me. But if ye believe not his writings, how shall ye believe my words?" (John 5:46–47; see also Mark 1:44; 7:10; 10:3–5; Luke 5:14; 20:37; John 7:19). The apostles testified to the Mosaic authorship of the Pentateuch (John 1:17,45; Acts 3:22; 7:37; 26:22; Rom. 10:5,19; 2 Cor. 3:15; Heb. 7:14). There is collaborating evidence in the Pentateuch itself that points to Moses as the author. Deuteronomy 31:24 says explicitly, "And it came to pass, when Moses had made an end of writing the words of this law in a book, until they were finished" (also 31:22; see similar commands for Moses to write, Ex. 17:14; 34:27). Certainly, Moses had the qualifications: he was educated; he would have been familiar with the geography, as well as the flora and fauna of both Egypt and the Sinai. The Bible settles the question, and it has been the consensus of Christian tradition throughout the history of the church that Moses is in fact the author.

However, critical, rationalistic scholarship has categorically denied Mosaic authorship of the Pentateuch. Alternative theories have proliferated and evolved, especially from the eighteenth century until the present, with the result that the Pentateuch is viewed as a composite from various traditions, redactors, and editors that did not take its final shape until a thousand years after Moses. No other portion of the Old Testament as been subjected to as much disintegrative criticism as has the Pentateuch. Such an assessment undermines the authority of Scripture and must be categorically rejected.

Dating the life and career of Moses and thus the dating of the Pentateuch is inseparably linked to the dating of the exodus. The key chronological clue comes from 1 Kings 6:1, which states that the exodus occurred 480 years before Solomon's fourth year. Since the dates of Solomon (ca. 970–931 BC) are not disputed, this puts the exodus event in the mid-fifteenth century BC at about 1446, followed by the forty-year trek through the wilderness, ending in 1406. Consequently, Moses wrote each of the five books during that forty-year span from 1446–1406 BC. The specific dates are discussed in each of the respective introductions.

What the four Gospels are to the New Testament, the Pentateuch is to the Old. In addition to key theological themes and life applications, they both record the historical facts upon which the whole message of the Bible rests. The Pentateuch is foundational to the rest of the Old Testament, indeed to the whole of Scripture, since the New Testament is the continuation of God's gracious communication that began in Eden. If the history and theology in the

Pentateuch are brought under suspicion, then the authority and veracity of the rest of the Bible, including the gospel itself, crumble. Unquestionably, this is why so much rationalist criticism focuses its attack on the Pentateuch. God's redemptive plan progresses through time and history; therefore, if the history is not trustworthy the gospel message is reduced to tradition and religious folklore. This is why Bible believers must affirm and defend the Mosaic authorship and the historicity of all the events detailed in the Pentateuch.

The Pentateuch reveals the origins and early development of God's redemptive plan in terms of historical narrative interspersed with poetic sections but is essentially a self-contained story. The doctrines of divine sovereignty and providence, fallen humanity, gracious salvation, and the demand for holiness are on the surface, yet run deep, throughout the narrative. Genesis focuses on God's absolute sovereignty in creation and in His plan to redeem a fallen race through the seed of the woman, who is further identified as the seed of Abraham. Consequently, it traces the development of Abraham's seed, beginning history's trek to the fullness of time when the ultimate and Ideal Seed would appear (Gal. 4:4). Exodus focuses on God's covenant love and redeeming power in delivering Abraham's seed from bondage and slavery. God's rescuing Israel vouchsafed the Seed promise and became a paradigm in the rest of Scripture for God's redeeming grace. Leviticus focuses on God's sanctity and the absolute uniqueness of the holiness of His Person. God sets the terms and conditions of fellowshipping with Him, as His people are to imitate His holiness. Numbers focuses on the severity and providence of God as He leads them to the Promised Land. There is severity evidenced through the multiple disciplines designed to keep the faithless from inheriting the blessing. His providence is evidenced in His leading and providing for the people every day through those forty years. Deuteronomy focuses on the principles and requirements of covenant obedience. The conditions required for blessing and the warnings of curse for disobedience became the texts from which virtually every following prophet preached. Simply said, the Pentateuch defines the context for the Bible, both theologically and historically.

Admittedly, as you read through the Pentateuch much will seem to be outdated and irrelevant to the church corporately and to Christian individually. In fact, if we repeat literally some of the Pentateuch's directives, we will violate Hebrew's warnings about returning again to animal sacrifices, which would repudiate the once-for-all sacrifice of Christ. Remember that the Pentateuch records the first installments of God's redemptive revelation. What Moses preached about the gospel was exactly what Paul preached in terms of content, although different in presentation. In contrasting his ministry with that of Moses, Paul said, "We use great plainness of speech" (2 Cor. 3:12). Through Moses God gave the people pictures and object lessons to point them to the reality the perfect Lamb of God. So even though we no longer implement the object lessons, we can still profit from looking at them to direct us to Christ. That was Moses' intent. Paul gives us the interpretational clue for reading the Pentateuch: the veil of misunderstanding that sometimes affects the reading of the Old Testament is "done away in Christ" (2 Cor. 3:14–16). So as you read the Pentateuch, do so with a view to Christ. You will discover in the Pentateuch a visible paradigm of the gospel, both in terms of initial salvation and of progressive sanctification.

INTRODUCTION TO THE BOOK OF GENESIS

Authorship and Date: See the Introduction to the Pentateuch.

Theme: God's sovereignty over man and all creation and events, and His faithfulness to His covenant despite man's corruption and unfaithfulness.

Purpose: Moses wrote Genesis most likely while leading Israel through the wilderness (see Introduction to the Pentateuch above). For centuries, the people had lived as slaves under the oppressive rule of Egypt, where many gods were worshiped; now they lived in dependence upon the Lord who was leading them to the Promised Land. Genesis reminds Israel of her noble identity under the one true God by teaching her historical roots in Adam, Noah, and Abraham.

The purpose of Genesis is thus theological, historical, and covenantal. It is theological because all mankind should know the Lord is Creator; thus God is the central figure in the book from beginning to end (1:1; 50:20,25). It is historical because it is the only record of the true history of Adam and the human race, and the true history of Israel and who God is in relation to them. In contrast to other ancient writings, the Bible contains straightforward accounts of real historical events, not myths and legends. It is covenantal because God's mighty works for His people throughout the book (including His establishing covenant with them) were proofs of His faithfulness, and because His people are required to trust Him.

Ultimately Genesis fosters the hope of the church, beginning with God's first great promise of the Messiah and His rich revelation to His ancient people Israel. The great promise in Genesis is that of the "seed" who will redeem mankind from sin and Satan through Christ's suffering (3:15). This promise is foundational to the book, as each successive covenantal revelation revolves around "seed" (9:9; 17:7; 26:3; 28:4; 48:4). It also illuminates the meaning of the sacrifices, which appear immediately after the fall (4:4; cf. 3:21), showing that animal sacrifices were mere shadows of Christ, the promised Seed and the one perfect sacrifice for sin. This protected Israel from resting upon the ceremonies revealed in the law, guarding them from formalistic, external religion and pointing them to trust in the coming Christ. Believers today are warned of the same dangers (Gal. 3).

Issues of Interpretation: *Genesis and the History of Origins*

The stakes are high when interpreting this book because Genesis is fundamental to the rest of the Bible—indeed, to the entire Christian faith. A plain and straightforward reading of the text has led many believers to view it as the real, historical, authoritative narrative of the origins of the universe, biological life, the human race, and the beginning of the nation of Israel. This literal understanding of Genesis is the one taken in the notes of this study Bible.

However, this reading of Genesis contradicts the views of many modern scientists and historians. To avoid this conflict, people have made various proposals, especially concerning the opening chapters of the book. For example, some authors say that "create" does not mean to make something but to give it a new function. Others argue that "day" need not indicate an actual day or that the early parts of Genesis are a literary framework, more like symbolic poetry than a historical account. Adam, we are told by others, was not literally made by God from the dust but from some apelike creature. Some even say that not all mankind came from Adam or that Adam never existed as an individual man in history as Genesis describes him. Others deny that the seven days of creation are ordinary days and still others try to put gaps in the week of creation.

The aim of most of these proposals is to accommodate Genesis to theories about the evolution of mankind from simple forms of life and ultimately from inanimate matter. Some of their authors still affirm orthodox Christian beliefs, but their ideas tend to take many away from biblical faith.

Scripture is like a tapestry with truths running throughout it. We cannot unravel one book of the Bible and think that it will not harm our faith. Many doctrines find their roots in the early chapters of Genesis. The Trinity is involved in creation (1:2,26), with Christ preeminent over all things (John 1:3; Col. 1:15–18). Man is made in the image of God, different from the animals (Gen. 1:27; 1 Cor. 11:7), and at the beginning of creation (Matt. 19:4). The first woman is not made from dust as Adam, but from the side of Adam (Gen. 1:27–28; 2:18,22–24; 1 Tim. 2:13). Marriage is defined as one man to one woman (Gen. 2:23; Matt. 19:4–6; Eph. 5:31). Sorrow and death come from Satan and Adam's sin (Gen. 3; John 8:44; Rom. 5:12; 1 Cor. 15:22). Adam brought suffering and death upon the whole of the human race; there was no death prior to the fall (Rom. 5; 1 Cor. 15). Sin has brought hardship in work for men and in childbearing for women (1 Tim. 2:14–15). Blood sacrifice is essential to atone for sin (Gen. 3:21; 4:4; Heb. 9:22). Clothing is needed as a direct consequence of the fall (Gen. 3:21; 1 Tim. 2:9). The worldwide flood is a type of the final judgment to come (Luke 17:26–27); just as the second coming of Christ is universal to all men, so the flood was universal to the whole world (Gen. 6–9; Luke 17; 2 Peter 3). The Seed of the woman would come and bruise the serpent's head; Christ would be born of a virgin and gain the victory over the serpent and his seed (Gen. 3:15; Isa. 7:14; Luke 2).

All of these doctrines are rooted in Genesis. For example, consider the effects of denying that Adam was a real, historical man who did what Genesis relates, but instead is a symbol of mankind's origins through evolution. We lose, *first*, the basis of mankind's nobility above the animals (1:26–28; 9:1–6; Ps. 8); *second*, the root of mankind's unity despite all our colors and cultures (Gen. 3:20; Acts 17:26); *third*, the divine institution of our distinctive identities and relationships as men and women (Matt. 19:3–6; 1 Cor. 11:8–9; 1 Tim. 2:13–14); *fourth*, the theology of Christ as our last and greater Adam (Luke 3:22–23,38; Rom. 5:14–19; 1 Cor. 15:21–22,45,47); and *fifth*, the explanation of death as not original to God's creation but the consequence of sin (Gen. 2:17; Rom. 5:12).

This last point of the theology of death due to sin is particularly important because it is linked to the theology of the atonement taught in the New Testament (Rom. 5; 1 Cor. 15:3). The theistic evolution position (which seeks to accommodate evolution within Scripture) attempts unsuccessfully to have pre-Adamic creatures evolving (and physically dying) before Adam and his fall. Consequently, they try to suggest Adam only spiritually dies at the fall. If the penalty for sin was only spiritual death, then why did Jesus physically die on the cross? Ultimately, theistic evolution undermines the gospel.

In the midst of such confusion, we need to remember that unless the genre of particular portions of Scripture indicates otherwise, Scripture is best read in a straightforward fashion with confidence that God will teach those who seek Him. The evangelical doctrine of Holy Scripture gives us freedom to receive whatever the Bible teaches. The *perspicuity* (clarity) of Scripture means that the Bible is clear in all the major teachings of the faith. We do not need an interpretation that requires convoluted arguments or advanced learning to squeeze Scripture into an evolutionary mold. For example, when the creation account speaks of six days with mornings and evenings, we exegete the word *yom* (Hebrew for the word "day") consistently with the whole of the Old Testament where *yom*, mentioned with morning or evening, always refers to ordinary days, not ages.

The *sufficiency* of Scripture declares that the Bible gives us all we need in order to know the true God and His will. We do not need new scientific insights in order to know what God's ways really are. The *authority* of Scripture reminds us that whenever the Bible conflicts with human ideas, God's Word must rule. Other forms of study, such as science and history, are valuable and worthy of a Christian's labors; they contribute to our service of our neighbor and stewardship of creation. Indeed Scripture gives the framework for such studies. But for all our learning, we must humbly listen whenever God speaks. This is not turning off our mind, but using it in the most reasonable fashion. What is more reasonable than to believe the words of One who is infinitely wiser than us?

Synopsis: *The Contribution of Genesis to Redemptive Revelation*

Genesis offers four main contributions to the revelation of Holy Scripture, each of which points to the glory of God in Christ. Each of these contributions finds its major expression in one part of the book (see outline below), but also permeates the book as a whole.

First, Genesis presents the doctrine of *creation*. God called into being all that exists by His Word and Spirit (1:1–3). Whereas other creation stories in the Ancient Near East spoke of the world arising out of a conflict between various supernatural powers, Genesis unfolds the forces of the universe coming into existence in a peaceful and orderly fashion according to the will of one Creator, who then pronounced them "very good" (v. 31). The process of creation over six days displays God's perfect wisdom and power. Particularly in His creation of man, God revealed that He is a God of relationships. He has relationships within Himself ("Let us make man," v. 26), and He made man in His image (v. 27) to reflect His glory as the good ruler of the world (v. 28) and to relate to Him as children relate to the father who begot them (5:1–3). All mankind shares this common root in Adam (3:20) and all nations come from the offspring of Noah after the flood as recorded in the table of nations (ch. 10). True cosmology and anthropology are only understood through the lens of Genesis.

Second, Genesis teaches the doctrine of *corruption*. God warned that death would follow disobedience immediately (2:17). Though physical death was mercifully delayed (3:19; 5:5), spiritual death fell on Adam and Eve immediately, replacing openness with shame, boldness with fear, and love with hatred (3:7–12). God drove the king and queen of creation out of His presence and barred the way to Paradise with hostile angels and fiery death (3:24). Their children manifested the bitter fruits of their sin in unacceptable worship, jealousy, murder, lying, and polygamy (ch. 4). While the human race still showed some fragments of the image of God in its skill in agriculture, architecture, music, industry, and poetry (4:17–24), their souls were so corrupt that every notion of their hearts was always evil (6:5), even from their youth (8:21). All of this corruption offended the Lord (6:6–7). God made His judgment against sinners plain when He wiped all humanity off the face of the earth with the sole exception of Noah's family (7:21–23). After the flood, corruption spread again and God deliberately confused the one-world system under Nimrod with different languages at the Tower of Babel (ch. 11), and later yet again when He destroyed the cities of Sodom and Gomorrah (ch. 19).

Third, Genesis introduces the doctrine of *covenants*. In chs. 2–3, God appears nineteen times as "the LORD God," where the first word is His covenant name, Jehovah. He imposed His law of obedience upon Adam with the threat of death and the promise of life sealed in the sacramental signs of the two trees (2:9,15–17; 3:11,22). He later used this same name when revealing Himself to Moses as the sovereign and faithful covenant God of Israel (Ex. 3:13–18). The word "covenant" appears repeatedly in God's dealings with Noah (Gen. 6:18; 9:9–17) and Abraham (15:18; 17:1–21)—sealed with a rainbow (9:13–16) and circumcision, respectively (17:10–14). The covenant is implied also in expressions like "the God of Abraham," Isaac, or Jacob (24:12,27,42,48; 26:24; 28:13; 31:5,29,42,53; 32:9; 43:23; 46:1,3; 49:24–25; 50:17). But whereas Adam was placed under a law of works before he fell, Abraham and His covenant seed were placed under God's grace—His kindness, mercy, truth, and faithfulness (24:12,14,27; 32:10; 39:21). They were not justified by their works, being deeply flawed men, but by faith in the promise (15:6).

Fourth, Genesis announces the inevitable *crisis* when man's corruption and strange providences conflict with God's covenants, and God's people must live by faith. Abel worshiped God acceptably but was martyred for his faithfulness. Abraham received God's promise of a multitude of offspring, but stumbled at times as he waited for decades to receive just one son in the covenant. Then he died without seeing the Promised Land in his possession. Jacob was foreordained to be blessed (25:23), but his deceit sent him fleeing into exile that lasted for years, while he himself suffered the tricks of another until God brought him home. The life of Joseph is the supreme example of this crisis, and Genesis devotes over a fifth of its chapters to his humiliation because of his brothers and his exaltation to save the same brothers, and by extension, God's chosen people.

These four themes come to a focal point in Christ. As the eternal, divine Son, Jesus Christ is the great image of God who cooperated with His Father to create all things (Col. 1:15–17; Heb. 1:2–3). He did this so that He could come as the incarnate image of God and rule the universe with the sons and daughters of God re-created in His likeness (Rom. 8:17–23,29). The promise given in the covenants centers upon Him, the Seed that crushed the head of the tempter at great cost to Himself and through whom all nations were and are blessed (Gen. 3:15; 12:3; Gal. 3:8,13–14,16). He was humiliated even unto death on the cross, but was lifted up to save sinners (Acts 5:30–31; Phil. 2:5–11). Just as the Hebrew lord of Egypt fed thousands and rescued them from death, so the Son of God will feed people beyond numbering and rescue them from eternal death.

Outline:

- I. The Creation and Corruption of the World (1:1—11:32)
  - A. The Creation of All Things with Adam as Head (1:1—2:25)
  - B. The Fall of Mankind into Sin and Death (3:1—5:32)
  - C. The Worldwide Flood and the Rainbow Promise (6:1—9:29)
  - D. The Division of Nations and Languages (10:1—11:32)
- II. The Covenant with Abraham, Isaac, and Jacob (12:1—36:43)
  - A. The Promises of God to Abraham (12:1—25:18)
  - B. The Grace of God to Isaac and Jacob (25:19—36:43)
- III. The Crisis of Israel Regarding Joseph and Judah (37:1—50:26)
  - A. The Humiliation of Joseph and Sin of Judah (37:1—40:23)
  - B. The Exaltation of Joseph and Nobility of Judah (41:1—45:28)
  - C. The Sojourning of Israel in Egypt (46:1—50:26)

THE FIRST BOOK OF MOSES CALLED GENESIS

CHAPTER 1

IN the beginning God created the heaven and the
earth.
2 And the earth was without form, and void; and
darkness *was* upon the face of the deep. And the
Spirit of God moved upon the face of the waters.
3 And God said, Let there be light: and there was
light.
4 And God saw the light, that *it was* good: and
God divided the light from the darkness.
5 And God called the light Day, and the darkness
he called Night. And the evening and the morning
were the first day.
6 ¶ And God said, Let there be a firmament in the
midst of the waters, and let it divide the waters
from the waters.
7 And God made the firmament, and divided the
waters which *were* under the firmament from the
waters which *were* above the firmament: and it
was so.
8 And God called the firmament Heaven. And
the evening and the morning were the second day.
9 ¶ And God said, Let the waters under the
heaven be gathered together unto one place, and
let the dry *land* appear: and it was so.
10 And God called the dry *land* Earth; and the
gathering together of the waters called he Seas:
and God saw that *it was* good.
11 And God said, Let the earth bring forth grass,
the herb yielding seed, *and* the fruit tree yielding
fruit after his kind, whose seed *is* in itself, upon
the earth: and it was so.
12 And the earth brought forth grass, *and* herb
yielding seed after his kind, and the tree yielding
fruit, whose seed *was* in itself, after his kind: and
God saw that *it was* good.
13 And the evening and the morning were the
third day.
14 ¶ And God said, Let there be lights in the fir-
mament of the heaven to divide the day from the
night; and let them be for signs, and for seasons,
and for days, and years:

THE CREATION AND CORRUPTION OF THE WORLD (1:1—11:32)

The Creation of All Things with Adam as Head (1:1—2:25)

Chapter 1: *God creates the universe as a good and orderly home where mankind, created in God's image, could live and serve Him.*

1:1 *In the beginning God.* The beginning of time, space, and matter. All came from Him and is under His control. The Hebrew word *created* means "to create new." This is uniquely divine activity; God is the only subject of the verb. Creation testifies to divine power, ownership, and authority.

1:2 *without form, and void.* What the original creation was at the beginning, not what it became. The gap theory tries to argue original creation became corrupt, but the expression means empty or uninhabited (Job 26:7; Jer. 4:23). Isaiah 45:18 proves the world was made to be inhabited. Also v. 31 shows there was no death or corruption before the fall.

1:3 *Let there be light.* Creation is by the spoken word of God. Christ spoke everything into existence (John 1:3; Col. 1:16), which power He displayed in the many miracles He performed. Paul drew an analogy between the creation of light and the regeneration of the believer (2 Cor. 4:6). The wonder of being born again of God's Holy Spirit is equal to the power displayed on the first day of creation. That is surely awesome!

1:4 *it was good.* Another repeated phrase—see note at v. 31. Even the inanimate creation is declared good.

1:5 *God called the light Day, and the darkness he called Night.* All one needs is a rotating globe and a directional aspect to the light to produce day and night, and God could have directly produced the light, as He will in the heavenly city (Rev. 21:23). *first day.* Literally, "day one." Though the numeral is translated *first* (ordinal), the word here is primarily cardinal and defines the usage here of *day* as one cycle of *evening* and *morning.* Thereafter (vv. 8,13, etc.) the counting is ordinal.

1:6–8 *firmament.* This word means "expanse" and includes outer space. It is not just the sky since God calls the firmament *Heaven* (v. 8) and the stars are put in the firmament (v. 14). This is the expanse which God stretches out (Job 9:8; Ps. 104:2; Isa. 40:22; 42:5; 44:24; 45:12; 48:13; 51:13; Jer. 10:12; Zech. 12:1).

1:9 *Let the waters under the heaven be gathered together unto one place, and let the dry land appear.* Second Peter 3:5 refers to this separation of water and land and confirms that the land appeared with some under water and some above.

1:11 *whose seed is in itself.* The first living things are made: plants and trees with "seed in itself," a mark of living things.

1:14–19 *lights in the firmament.* The momentous creation of the sun, the moon, and the stars whose light takes over from the light sources of the first three days. *the stars also.* God calls them all by their names (Ps. 147:4; Isa. 40:26). There are an estimated 200 billion stars in the Milky Way galaxy alone and an estimated 100 billion galaxies in the universe. The stars are the work of His fingers (Ps. 8:3).

15 And let them be for lights in the firmament
of the heaven to give light upon the earth: and it
was so.
16 And God made two great lights; the greater
light to rule the day, and the lesser light to rule the
night: *he made* the stars also.
17 And God set them in the firmament of the
heaven to give light upon the earth,
18 And to rule over the day and over the night,
and to divide the light from the darkness: and
God saw that *it was* good.
19 And the evening and the morning were the
fourth day.
20 And God said, Let the waters bring forth
abundantly the moving creature that hath life,
and fowl *that* may fly above the earth in the open
firmament of heaven.
21 And God created great whales, and every
living creature that moveth, which the waters
brought forth abundantly, after their kind, and
every winged fowl after his kind: and God saw
that *it was* good.
22 And God blessed them, saying, Be fruitful, and
multiply, and fill the waters in the seas, and let
fowl multiply in the earth.
23 And the evening and the morning were the
fifth day.
24 ¶ And God said, Let the earth bring forth the
living creature after his kind, cattle, and creeping
thing, and beast of the earth after his kind: and it
was so.
25 And God made the beast of the earth after his
kind, and cattle after their kind, and every thing
that creepeth upon the earth after his kind: and
God saw that *it was* good.
26 ¶ And God said, Let us make man in our im-
age, after our likeness: and let them have domin-
ion over the fish of the sea, and over the fowl of
the air, and over the cattle, and over all the earth,
and over every creeping thing that creepeth upon
the earth.
27 So God created man in his *own* image, in the
image of God created he him; male and female
created he them.
28 And God blessed them, and God said unto
them, Be fruitful, and multiply, and replenish the
earth, and subdue it: and have dominion over the
fish of the sea, and over the fowl of the air, and over
every living thing that moveth upon the earth.
29 ¶ And God said, Behold, I have given you every
herb bearing seed, which *is* upon the face of all the
earth, and every tree, in the which *is* the fruit of a
tree yielding seed; to you it shall be for meat.
30 And to every beast of the earth, and to every
fowl of the air, and to every thing that creepeth
upon the earth, wherein *there is* life, *I have given*
every green herb for meat: and it was so.
31 And God saw every thing that he had made,

1:20–23 *the waters brought forth abundantly, after their kind, and every winged fowl after his kind.* Swimming creatures as well as flying creatures were all made on day five of creation. Notice that evolution would have flying animals come after land creatures.

1:21 *great whales.* These differ from both fish and seagoing reptiles (like crocodiles). This word here is translated elsewhere as serpent, dragon, sea monster, and leviathan. The exact identification is uncertain, but certainly indicates that God made very large sea creatures.

1:25 *the beast of the earth.* Wild animals. *cattle.* Animals subject to domestication. *every thing that creepeth upon the earth.* Reptiles like crocodiles and lizards as well as insects that crawl on the ground. All the land creatures are made on the sixth day—this includes dinosaurs which we know from fossils existed in the past. *God saw that it was good.* This is the sixth of seven pronouncements by God concerning the goodness of creation (vv. 4,10,12,18,21,25,31). There can be no doubt that God made an originally perfect creation.

1:26 *Let us make man.* The verb form highlights the uniqueness of man's creation. The impersonal verb, "Let there be," occurs with the rest of creation, but here it is personal, *Let us.* The plurality of God is stressed. Relationship lies at the heart of God's very being, so man is created in relationship first with God. *in our image, after our likeness.* God is spirit (John 4:24) and thus invisible (1 Tim. 1:17). He created man to be His visible, living *image* on earth (2 Cor. 4:4; Col. 1:15) with qualities such as knowledge, righteousness, and holiness (Eph. 4:24; Col. 3:10) that give man unique value (9:6), capacity for familiar relationship to God (5:1–3; Rom. 8:29), and dominion over the world as God's representative (1:26,28; Ps. 8:4–8).

1:27 *male and female.* The first mention of female is in the context that both man and woman were created in God's image. This is creation, not development from existing creatures.

1:28 *Be fruitful, and multiply, and replenish the earth, and subdue it.* The dominion mandate given to man is clear. Having made man in His own image, God delegated authority to man over the world and the animals. The verb *replenish* is literally, "fill."

1:29–30 *I have given you every herb bearing seed.* Man and the animals at this stage were vegetarian. After the flood man is allowed to eat meat (9:3). *meat.* Here, food of any kind.

1:31 *And God saw every thing that he had made, and, behold, it was very good.* The seventh and final statement that all was good. There was nothing out of place in all creation, including the extraterrestrial universe—the planets, stars, and galaxies. It also must include the angels since these are created beings. Consequently the fall of Satan must be after day six of creation.

Thoughts for Personal/Family Worship: Chapter 1

1. **Consider the power of God in creation. If a computer were observing 10 million stars per second, it would still take 63 million years to count all the stars! Such is the power of the Almighty. Remarkably, the stars are the work of His fingers (Ps. 8:3) but salvation is the work of His right hand (Ps. 98:1). In a wonderful way God's work in making believers new creations in Christ Jesus demonstrates a power greater than commanding the world into existence. Let us be amazed at the wonder of creation; let us be overwhelmed with the wonder of grace. How does saving grace display even greater glory than creation?**
2. **Stand in awe of the power of God's word. God's word**

CREATION AND GOD'S GLORY

Whether it is in the beauty, power, or complexity of creation, a taste of God's wonder is engraved on all things as an unmistakable testament of His incomprehensible glory. The glory of God has been disclosed in the whole workmanship of the universe: "The heavens declare the glory of God" (Ps. 19:1) and "the whole earth is full of his glory" (Isa. 6:3).

There are two helpful ways to express the presentation of God's glory in creation. *First*, His glory is like a brilliant light shed abroad—even to the darkest reaches of the earth. This flashing light penetrates all men's minds (Rom. 1:19–20). It radiates richly throughout all the heavens, where the Lord's majesty is shed forth (Ps. 104:2). There is no place where the sparks of His glory cannot be discerned. *Second*, the glory of God is revealed in creation like an image in a mirror. The glory of the invisible God is reflected visibly by His creation (Heb. 11:3). This allows all to gaze upon the invisible nature of God, as portrayed in His creation. Whether God's glory appears like a light or like an image in a mirror, truly men cannot open their eyes without being compelled to see Him.

Though God's whole creation displays His glory, it is man himself, as the pinnacle of creation, who reveals God's glory most explicitly. He is a rare spectacle of God's power, goodness, and wisdom. Infants have tongues so eloquent to preach God's glory that there is no need at all for other orators (cf. Ps. 8:2). The human body—from its mouth and eyes to its very toenails—exhibits exquisite workmanship. Man's soul, in intelligence, imagination, memory, and even in dreaming, speaks of his Creator. The image of God has been so fully stamped upon men that, as all are adorned with an air of His glory, God readily testifies that He is the Father of all (Acts 17:28). God has made man His masterpiece, surpassing all else in creation. Further, as the church is conformed to the express image of the invisible God, Jesus Christ (Col. 1:15; Heb. 1:3), the glory of God becomes more distinct.

For the unbeliever, the expression of God in creation cannot be missed, even if the darkness of his mind causes the image to appear clouded. For him, the glory of God displayed in creation is a testimony against unbelief (Rom. 1:19–20). In addition to the inward witness of the heart, God has provided innumerable evidences in the world of His existence and of man's duty to submit to his Creator (cf. Acts 14:16–17). The glory of God is inscribed in creation with bold letters, yet the unbeliever has exchanged the glory of the incorruptible for images of corruptible things (Rom. 1:23). This confusion of the creation with the Creator supplants the true God with a shadow deity, depriving God of His right as Creator and denying creation's proper place as an announcement of the glories of its Maker. Though God sweetly attracts men with semblances of His glory, man's rashness and superficiality, joined with ignorance and darkness, have led to disdain for creation's testimony and, ultimately, to a rejection of the Creator Himself.

For the believer, the beauty of creation speaks of the majestic beauty of his God. With Scripture's revelation and the Spirit's work, the believer is able rightly to understand and appreciate the glory of God displayed in creation. He hears God's awesome voice upon the waters, breaking the cedars, shaking the wilderness, and causing new birth; thus, the believer worships the Lord in the beauty of holiness (Ps. 29). Examining creation brings him to praise and submit to his sovereign Creator—who sustains the mass of heaven and earth by His Word. God's nod alone shakes the heavens with thunderbolts; kindles the air with flashes; disturbs the earth with storms, and then silences them; and compels the sea to hang as though in midair, only to make it calm again. All of this incites reverential awe and adoration in the heart of every believer for the glorious God heralded by creation.

—adapted from John Calvin, *Institutes of the Christian Religion*, 1.5.1–3, 13–14; 1.6.14

and, behold, *it was* very good. And the evening
and the morning were the sixth day.

CHAPTER 2

THUS the heavens and the earth were finished,
and all the host of them.
2 And on the seventh day God ended his work
which he had made; and he rested on the seventh
day from all his work which he had made.
3 And God blessed the seventh day, and sancti-
fied it: because that in it he had rested from all his
work which God created and made.
4 ¶ These *are* the generations of the heavens
and of the earth when they were created, in the
day that the LORD God made the earth and the
heavens,
5 And every plant of the field before it was in the
earth, and every herb of the field before it grew:
for the LORD God had not caused it to rain upon
the earth, and *there was* not a man to till the
ground.
6 But there went up a mist from the earth, and
watered the whole face of the ground.
7 And the LORD God formed man *of* the dust
of the ground, and breathed into his nostrils the
breath of life; and man became a living soul.
8 ¶ And the LORD God planted a garden eastward
in Eden; and there he put the man whom he had
formed.
9 And out of the ground made the LORD God to
grow every tree that is pleasant to the sight, and
good for food; the tree of life also in the midst
of the garden, and the tree of knowledge of good
and evil.
10 And a river went out of Eden to water the gar-
den; and from thence it was parted, and became
into four heads.
11 The name of the first *is* Pison: that *is* it which
compasseth the whole land of Havilah, where
there is gold;
12 And the gold of that land *is* good: there *is* bdel-
lium and the onyx stone.
13 And the name of the second river *is* Gihon:
the same *is* it that compasseth the whole land of
Ethiopia.
14 And the name of the third river *is* Hiddekel:
that *is* it which goeth toward the east of Assyria.
And the fourth river *is* Euphrates.
15 And the LORD God took the man, and put him
into the garden of Eden to dress it and to keep it.
16 And the LORD God commanded the man,

is the agency of creation. God said, "Let there be . . ." Christ demonstrated this power in the miracles both with people such as raising Lazarus from the dead (John 11) and with the inanimate creation such as calming the storm (Mark 4:35–40). God's word still is powerful today through the Scriptures. It is by the word of His power as well that He bears His created world along according to His purpose of providence (Heb. 1:3). The fact that God created gives Him the right to govern and to use His creation as He sees fit (Ps. 24:1–2; 95:5). Since creation, including man, belongs to God, all of creation, including man, is dependent on Him and accountable to Him. The theological implications of creation are far-reaching.

Chapter 2: *Having described the creation of all things, the focus shifts to retell the creation of man in more detail, revealing God as the Lord of man's life, law, and love.*

2:2 *he rested.* Literally, God "sabbathed," the same root later used for the Sabbath (Ex. 16:30; 20:8–11; 23:12).

2:3 *God blessed the seventh day, and sanctified it.* The principle of setting apart one day in seven for rest and devotion to God is a creation ordinance. It is a day that God Himself rested, not because He needed to, but as an example for man and for man's good (Mark 2:27). The establishment of the Sabbath at creation shows that its moral obligation was not limited to the law of Moses but abides as long as creation.

2:4 *These are the generations.* Many regard this phrase which occurs throughout Genesis as the narrator's introduction to the next section. The Hebrew word *generations* (*toledot*) is used in 2:4 (*heavens* and *earth*); 5:1 ("Adam"); 6:9 ("Noah"); 10:1 ("sons of Noah"); 11:10 ("Shem"); 11:27 ("Terah"); 25:12 ("Ishmael"); 25:19 ("Isaac"); 36:1,9 ("Esau"); and 37:2 ("Jacob").

2:5–6 *the LORD God had not caused it to rain upon the earth.* There was no violent rainfall before the flood. *till.* Serve or work. *there went up a mist from the earth.* There was a well-watered system of rivers and dew arising by condensation.

2:7 *the LORD God formed man.* This is not a separate creation account, but a detailed account of humanity's creation after ch. 1 gave the big picture. *of the dust of the ground.* The first man was not formed of creatures already made—no evolutionary process. God made Adam from dust—the literal dust to which he must return since the fall (3:19). *man.* Hebrew, *adam*, meaning "from the earth, ruddy," linking his name to his origin. *God . . . breathed into his nostrils the breath of life.* The life of man was produced directly from the breath or Spirit of God (Job 32:8; 33:4). Because he is made in God's image there is a direct action of God in his creation. *man became a living soul.* Literally, "a living entity" or "being."

2:8 *God planted a garden.* There was order and beauty in God's original creation, and all that man could need was provided.

2:9 The *tree of life* is first mentioned here at the beginning of creation and at the end of Scripture (Rev. 22:2,14). Christ, "the way, the truth, and the life" (John 14:6) was pierced on a tree for His people's sins (Acts 5:30; 10:39; 13:29; Gal. 3:13) and became their Tree of Life (John 3:14–15). The *tree of knowledge of good and evil* was not of itself evil; evil came by disobedience to God's command.

2:10–14 Four rivers came out of the original Edenic *river*: *Pison, Gihon, Hiddekel,* and *Euphrates*. These mean respectively, "increase," "bursting forth," "rapid," and "fruitfulness." They are not the same as any rivers today since Eden was buried under a mass of sediment along with all the other original land at the worldwide flood. *compasseth.* Surrounds or borders.

2:15 *to dress it and to keep it.* Literally, "to serve it and to guard it." Even in the prefall world Adam had work to do. When again man is without sin in the new heavens and new earth to come, he will not be idle. Work only became a drudgery after the fall (3:19).

saying, Of every tree of the garden thou mayest
freely eat:
17 But of the tree of the knowledge of good and
evil, thou shalt not eat of it: for in the day that
thou eatest thereof thou shalt surely die.
18 ¶ And the LORD God said, *It is* not good that
the man should be alone; I will make him an help
meet for him.
19 And out of the ground the LORD God formed
every beast of the field, and every fowl of the air;
and brought *them* unto Adam to see what he
would call them: and whatsoever Adam called ev-
ery living creature, that *was* the name thereof.
20 And Adam gave names to all cattle, and to the
fowl of the air, and to every beast of the field; but
for Adam there was not found an help meet for him.
21 And the LORD God caused a deep sleep to fall
upon Adam, and he slept: and he took one of his
ribs, and closed up the flesh instead thereof;
22 And the rib, which the LORD God had taken
from man, made he a woman, and brought her
unto the man.
23 And Adam said, This *is* now bone of my bones,
and flesh of my flesh: she shall be called Woman,
because she was taken out of Man.
24 Therefore shall a man leave his father and his
mother, and shall cleave unto his wife: and they
shall be one flesh.
25 And they were both naked, the man and his
wife, and were not ashamed.

CHAPTER 3

NOW the serpent was more subtil than any beast
of the field which the LORD God had made. And
he said unto the woman, Yea, hath God said, Ye
shall not eat of every tree of the garden?
2 And the woman said unto the serpent, We may
eat of the fruit of the trees of the garden:
3 But of the fruit of the tree which *is* in the midst
of the garden, God hath said, Ye shall not eat of it,
neither shall ye touch it, lest ye die.
4 And the serpent said unto the woman, Ye shall
not surely die:
5 For God doth know that in the day ye eat
thereof, then your eyes shall be opened, and ye
shall be as gods, knowing good and evil.
6 And when the woman saw that the tree *was*
good for food, and that it *was* pleasant to the eyes,
and a tree to be desired to make *one* wise, she took

2:16 *God commanded.* The first solemn charge that God gives to Adam. Man had choice and only in his prefall condition did he have perfect liberty to do that which is good. The first man received this positive command alone, a sign of his sole headship in representing mankind before God in the covenant of works. Positively, Adam could eat of the trees in the garden freely.
2:17 *But of the tree of the knowledge of good and evil, thou shalt not eat of it.* The negative covenant command was a test of obedience but also a test of man's trust in God—that God knew what was right for man better than Adam did. *in the day that thou eatest thereof thou shalt surely die.* Death, first mentioned here in the Bible, was not part of God's original creation (1:29–31), but came through the violation of God's law by Adam (Rom. 5:12).
2:18 *It is not good that the man should be alone.* Man, created in God's image, should be in relationship with God and his fellow human beings. *help meet for him.* A capable and needed assistant well suited for man, created in God's image (1:27) to support man in his calling to fill and subdue the earth in obedience to God's law (1:28; 2:15–17).
2:19–20 *whatsoever Adam called every living creature, that was the name thereof.* He named the cattle, fowl of the air, and the beasts of the field. Naming is a sign of his authority (1:5, 8,10) as God's image and ruling representative on earth (1:26).
2:21–22 *rib.* Or "side" (same word in Job 18:12; Ezek. 41:15). *from man, made he a woman.* This is the climax of ch. 2. The mode of creation of woman is vital in understanding the nature of woman: God made woman after man as under his authority (1 Tim. 2:11–13), and from man to share his nature yet not to be independent from him but to be for him (1 Cor. 11:7–9). The word *made* (not the same as 1:26–27; 2:7) means "built" and is often used of architecture, implying that woman is intricately crafted and balanced to complement man.
2:23–25 *bone of my bones, and flesh of my flesh.* An intimate and lasting bond (*one flesh*, Matt. 19:5–6; 1 Cor. 6:16). *she shall be called Woman.* Again, naming implies authority (vv. 19–20), yet her name implies union and equality of essence. Adam's reaction has a spiritual parallel in the relationship of the church to Christ, for marriage is a picture of Christ and the church (Eph. 5:25–33).

Thoughts for Personal/Family Worship: Chapter 2

1. **Keep and cherish the Lord's Day (Isa. 58:13–14). The term "sabbath" means "cessation"; thus the Sabbath is a day where normal activity is to stop. In the New Testament, Christ's resurrection marked the end of His meriting salvation for His people; thus the term "Sabbath" is most appropriate to commemorate that momentous day. So the Sabbath has now moved to Sunday and is still blessed by God, as the "market day of the soul." How can we guard this day as a special day of rest and communion with God?**
2. **Honor marriage as a divine institution and picture of Christ and His church. Our marriages should reflect the different roles that the Lord made for man and woman. The woman was made of the man and for the man. Her calling is to assist and support him in submission to his authority. Man was created first and received the commission and commandment of God. His calling is to lead the family in doing God's will, and to love his wife as Christ loved the church—with humble and glad self-sacrifice for her good.**

The Fall of Mankind into Sin and Death (3:1—5:32)

Chapter 3: *Satan tempts the woman and man, and they rebel against God, provoking Him to pronounce judgment and yet to promise salvation.*

3:1–6 *serpent.* An evil spirit, Satan, the Devil (Isa. 27:1; Rev. 12:9). *subtil.* Cunning. *hath God said, Ye shall not eat of every tree of the garden?* The woman listened to the serpent's voice and the questioning of God's word. She then conversed with the serpent. She was now being drawn into his deceit, by which she now conceived evil in her own heart. She *saw* in a different way: as *a tree to be desired to make one wise.* She *desired,*

THE FALL OF MAN

No event has cast a darker shadow over human life throughout the centuries than the fall of our first parents from their state of original righteousness, life, and communion with God into the state of sin, death, and corruption in all faculties and parts of soul and body. No aspect of human experience is more crucial for understanding the world we live in, the desperation of its plight, and how necessary it was for God to intervene by sending His Son into the world, "that the world through him might be saved" (John 3:17).

The fall of man was a major turning point for humanity. In Eden, Adam and Eve lived a life far different from ours. They were at home in their world, happy in their marriage, blessed in their life and work, and at peace with their God. Guilt and shame, disease and death, lust and longing, heartache and loss, and enmity and danger were unknown. There was no thorn to prick them, no thistle to mar the beauty of their garden home, no sweat upon their brow. Everything changed when they succumbed to the lies of the serpent and defied the law of God.

Trivial questions can detract from rightly understanding the fall of man. Was the serpent real? He was real enough to serve Satan's purposes! Did the serpent actually speak, or was Satan simply voicing thoughts in Eve's mind? Either way, she got the message. Did Adam really join with Eve to sin against God? The tragic truth is simple: the evidence that he did is incontrovertible.

The imputation of Adam's sin to all his natural offspring is a presupposition of the gospel. Human beings are lost from conception and birth, even before they begin their personal careers of sin. The Son of God became the Son of Man to atone for sin by dying in the place of sinners. To deny the fall of man into sin is to rob the death of Christ of its redemptive meaning and saving power.

The reality of the fall as historical fact is demonstrated by its many bitter and persistent effects on human beings today:

> There is none righteous, no, not one: there is none that understandeth, there is none that seeketh after God. They are all gone out of the way, they are together become unprofitable; there is none that doeth good, no, not one. Their throat is an open sepulcher; with their tongues they have used deceit; the poison of asps is under their lips: whose mouth is full of cursing and bitterness: their feet are swift to shed blood: destruction and misery are in their ways: and the way of peace they have not known: there is no fear of God before their eyes. (Rom. 3:10–18)

Every line of this passage was taken from the Hebrew Bible. Paul did not need to do any original thinking about man's fallen state; it was all attested in Scripture long before his time.

Theologians describe fallen man as being totally depraved or corrupted. Some understand the term to mean that men and women are as bad as they can be, something human experience refutes. Thanks to God's restraining hand, men and nations seldom realize their full potential for sin. There have been Herods and Hitlers throughout history, but far fewer than we might have expected. The Roman Empire was idolatrous and debauched, but not beyond the power of the gospel to transform it into the world's first Christian superpower.

Limiting the extent of the fall by exempting some aspect of man's being from its effects opens the way for fallen man to be his own savior. If his intellect is not darkened, then he can find salvation by the use of reason and improve himself through education. If his will is not enslaved, then man has the final say in his salvation, quite apart from God's will. If man's body does not bear the marks of the fall, then defects, deformities, disease, aging, and death are natural and normal for our race, not evils to be opposed and overcome or enemies Christ died to defeat. Let us ask God to show us ever more profoundly the tragic results of our fall, that we might understand ever more profoundly the amazing wonders of the gospel.

of the fruit thereof, and did eat, and gave also
unto her husband with her; and he did eat.
7 And the eyes of them both were opened, and
they knew that they *were* naked; and they sewed
fig leaves together, and made themselves aprons.
8 And they heard the voice of the LORD God
walking in the garden in the cool of the day: and
Adam and his wife hid themselves from the pres-
ence of the LORD God amongst the trees of the
garden.
9 And the LORD God called unto Adam, and said
unto him, Where *art* thou?
10 And he said, I heard thy voice in the garden,
and I was afraid, because I *was* naked; and I hid
myself.
11 And he said, Who told thee that thou *wast* na-
ked? Hast thou eaten of the tree, whereof I com-
manded thee that thou shouldest not eat?
12 And the man said, The woman whom thou
gavest *to be* with me, she gave me of the tree, and
I did eat.
13 And the LORD God said unto the woman,
What *is* this *that* thou hast done? And the woman
said, The serpent beguiled me, and I did eat.
14 And the LORD God said unto the serpent, Be-
cause thou hast done this, thou *art* cursed above
all cattle, and above every beast of the field; upon
thy belly shalt thou go, and dust shalt thou eat all
the days of thy life:
15 And I will put enmity between thee and the
woman, and between thy seed and her seed; it shall
bruise thy head, and thou shalt bruise his heel.
16 Unto the woman he said, I will greatly multi-
ply thy sorrow and thy conception; in sorrow thou
shalt bring forth children; and thy desire *shall be*
to thy husband, and he shall rule over thee.
17 And unto Adam he said, Because thou hast
hearkened unto the voice of thy wife, and hast
eaten of the tree, of which I commanded thee,
saying, Thou shalt not eat of it: cursed *is* the
ground for thy sake; in sorrow shalt thou eat *of* it
all the days of thy life;
18 Thorns also and thistles shall it bring forth to
thee; and thou shalt eat the herb of the field;
19 In the sweat of thy face shalt thou eat bread,
till thou return unto the ground; for out of it wast
thou taken: for dust thou *art*, and unto dust shalt
thou return.

---

and she *took*. The Devil did not need to tempt Adam directly, for Eve would influence her husband to do the same. Adam took the fruit knowingly, in deliberate rebellion (1 Tim. 2:14), whereas Eve was tricked by the deceit of the Devil.

3:7 *the eyes of them both were opened*. The immediate effect of sin was the awareness of their nakedness before God—guilt and shame (contrast 2:25). They experienced the beginnings of death. Death is separation from life, and their souls were now cut off from communion with God's Spirit. Spiritual death had come immediately (Eph. 2:1). Physical death (separation of soul from body) would come nine hundred or so years later to Adam. Eternal death threatened to punish body and soul in hell forever (Rev. 20:14). *and he did eat*. Adam tragically broke covenant with God for himself and all human posterity whom he represented (Rom. 5).

3:8 *Adam and his wife hid themselves from the presence of the LORD God*. As with all sin, their first thought was to cover it up. The consequence of their sin was that they first tried to cover themselves with fig leaves. But the next consequence was that they tried to hide themselves from the presence of God. Both were pitiful and futile attempts.

3:9 *Adam . . . Where art thou?* This is the second question recorded in Genesis (v. 1). God knew where they were, but He asked the question in order that they might acknowledge their sin. God asks the same question down the centuries to all mankind, "Where are you?"

3:10 *I heard thy voice . . . I was afraid*. The voice of God brings fear to the sinner. This is an important first stage in dealing with sin. There is hope when men and women have a fear of God.

3:11 *Hast thou eaten of the tree*. The question was asked by God, not because He did not know, but that Adam and Eve might admit their guilt. There can be no restoration without confession (1 John 1:7–9).

3:12 *The woman whom thou gavest to be with me*. Adam blames Eve and by implication he also blames God. This was grievous indeed as Adam does not take full responsibility for his own sin.

3:13 *The serpent beguiled me*. Eve blames the serpent and his deception. God does not ask the serpent, "What have you done?" There is no redemption for the Devil and his angels, and no bringing to repentance.

3:14 *dust shalt thou eat all the days of thy life*. Snakes have the Jacobson's organ in the roof of their mouths that helps the snake to smell by the forked tongue constantly sampling bits of dust. Licking the dust is also a metaphor for humiliating defeat (Ps. 72:9; Isa. 49:23; Mic. 7:17), a statement of God's curse on Satan.

3:15 *enmity*. Hostility, hatred. God would turn the woman's heart against the Devil: the gift of repentance (2 Tim. 2:25–26). *her seed*. Her offspring, particularly her spiritual offspring who stand against the wicked world, the children (*thy seed*) of the Devil (John 8:44; see note at 4:8). This promise is the foundation of all the other *seed* promises in the covenants of Genesis (9:9; 12:7; etc.). *shall bruise thy head*. The first promise of the Redeemer to come to rescue man. The singular *seed* points to one man (4:25; cf. Gal. 3:16), the champion of God's people who will bring them victory over Satan by His grace (Rom. 16:20). But the serpent would nevertheless strike Him (*bruise his heel*) so that salvation comes through suffering (see note at v. 21).

3:16 *I will greatly multiply thy sorrow and thy conception*. Until modern medical procedures, many women died in childbirth. Though mammals in the animal kingdom can also die in childbirth, there is generally greater pain, difficulty, and danger in human childbirth. *thy desire shall be to thy husband*. Previously Eve naturally followed Adam's lead, but now collision of wills is bound to take place.

3:17–18 *hearkened*. Listened. *cursed is the ground for thy sake*. Adam was to know difficulty in providing for his wife and family. The ground which previously grew produce with little difficulty was now cursed, and *thorns* and *thistles* would throttle plants grown for food (cf. Matt. 13:7). Thorns would be upon the brow of the Savior as He took the curse for sin upon Himself (Mark 15:17).

3:19 *In the sweat of thy face shalt thou eat bread*. Whereas beforehand the work that Adam did was easy and light, now life would be very difficult and he would be constantly reminded

20 And Adam called his wife's name Eve; because
she was the mother of all living.
21 Unto Adam also and to his wife did the LORD
God make coats of skins, and clothed them.
22 ¶ And the LORD God said, Behold, the man is
become as one of us, to know good and evil: and
now, lest he put forth his hand, and take also of
the tree of life, and eat, and live for ever:
23 Therefore the LORD God sent him forth
from the garden of Eden, to till the ground from
whence he was taken.
24 So he drove out the man; and he placed at
the east of the garden of Eden Cherubims, and
a flaming sword which turned every way, to keep
the way of the tree of life.

CHAPTER 4

AND Adam knew Eve his wife; and she conceived,
and bare Cain, and said, I have gotten a man from
the LORD.
2 And she again bare his brother Abel. And Abel
was a keeper of sheep, but Cain was a tiller of the
ground.
3 And in process of time it came to pass, that
Cain brought of the fruit of the ground an offer-
ing unto the LORD.
4 And Abel, he also brought of the firstlings of
his flock and of the fat thereof. And the LORD had
respect unto Abel and to his offering:
5 But unto Cain and to his offering he had
not respect. And Cain was very wroth, and his
countenance fell.
6 And the LORD said unto Cain, Why art thou
wroth? and why is thy countenance fallen?
7 If thou doest well, shalt thou not be accepted?
and if thou doest not well, sin lieth at the door.
And unto thee *shall be* his desire, and thou shalt
rule over him.
8 And Cain talked with Abel his brother: and it
came to pass, when they were in the field, that Cain
rose up against Abel his brother, and slew him.

---

that the ground he was tilling was cursed. His livelihood would now depend on his success. *unto dust shalt thou return.* Death is the curse and penalty for sin (Rom. 5:12; 6:23).

3:20 *the mother of all living. Eve* literally means "life." Her name expresses Adam's hope in God's promise (v. 15).

3:21 *the LORD God make coats of skins.* The first recorded instance of a sacrifice, since to have coats made of animal skins implies that an animal was killed. God thus provides a sacrifice symbolic of the Lamb to come (John 1:29), the Lord Jesus Christ, whose death would cover the shame of sinners.

3:22 *lest he . . . take also of the tree of life . . . and live for ever.* Before the fall, the Tree of Life was a symbol of everlasting life. Now man is denied it because of sin. Life now could come only through the seed of the woman (v. 15), who alone could reverse the curse.

3:23–24 *till.* Serve or work. *So he drove out the man.* Adam now has to gain his bread outside Eden. Only in the new Jerusalem does the Tree of Life become accessible again for the healing of the nations with the curse finally removed (Rev. 22:2–3). *Cherubims.* Heavenly spirits pictured as winged creatures (Ex. 25:20; Ps. 18:10) that attend God (Ezek. 1:5–14; 10:1). The angels now are ministers of judgment shutting out sinners from God's presence (Matt. 13:41–42; 25:31).

Thoughts for Personal/Family Worship: Chapter 3

1. **Believe in the historic fall. The fall of man is just as literal as the rest of Genesis. Without a real Adam, a real garden, and a real serpent, there is no reason to believe in a real Christ, a real cross, and a real resurrection. The theology of Rom. 5 and 1 Cor. 15 in this regard is inescapable. These are real historical events. Redemption in Christ is predicated upon a literal fall of man in the garden of Eden.**
2. **Resist temptation. Like Eve we are tempted to sin by first listening to the lie of Satan, conversing in our minds with the thought of sin, which is then conceived (James 1:15). We look, we desire, and we take. It is not a matter of eating, but of the heart (Matt. 15:11,18). So begin the battle there.**
3. **Consider the horrible effects of the fall. Immediately, there was shame (v. 7), separation from God (v. 8), and guilt (v. 10). Consequently, according to God's sentence on the guilty, man now knows toil and hardship in work and women know suffering in childbearing. But yet, in the very statement of curse, God announces the first gospel message of a coming Seed who will reverse the curse itself. As soon as man needs a word of grace, God gives the word of grace. Only Christ can reverse this for He took the curse for sin. How believers should thank the Lord that He did not banish us as He has banished the angels that sinned! We have a Redeemer!**

Chapter 4: ***From Adam and Eve come two kinds of people, the one worshiping God rightly, and the other hating God and persecuting the godly.***

4:1 *bare.* Gave birth. *I have gotten a man from the LORD.* The first birth is recorded. No doubt she longed for the promised Seed (3:15) to reverse the effects of the fall. But she in fact gives birth to Cain who refuses to walk in God's way and is hostile to God.

4:3–4 *Cain brought of the fruit of the ground* for the worship of God, but *Abel* brought a blood sacrifice from the best (*firstlings . . . fat*) of his livestock, which the Lord respected. This shows that (a) God requires a blood sacrifice which is implied by the earlier covering of Adam and Eve (see note at 3:21), and (b) Adam had taught both brothers that this was required, since Abel offered his sacrifice by faith (Heb. 11:4), and faith comes by hearing the word of God (Rom. 10:17). God had revealed the way of acceptable worship.

4:5 *Cain was very wroth* because his offering was not accepted and his anger is expressed against God directly. *wroth.* Angry.

4:6 *Why art thou wroth?* As the Lord dealt with Adam and Eve when they sinned, so the Lord deals with Cain with a question. He confronts him with his sin.

4:7 *sin lieth at the door.* Like a predatory animal ready to pounce. Alternatively the Hebrew word for *sin* is the same as "sin offering" (Lev. 4:3), so perhaps God appeals to him to bring the sin offering and he will be accepted. *unto thee shall be his desire, and thou shalt rule over him.* Similar expression as that used of Eve (3:16). The interpretation is disputed. Possibly that Abel would still be subject to Cain as his elder brother or that sin desired Cain but he could gain victory over sin

9 ¶ And the LORD said unto Cain, Where *is* Abel
thy brother? And he said, I know not: *Am* I my
brother's keeper?
10 And he said, What hast thou done? the voice
of thy brother's blood crieth unto me from the
ground.
11 And now *art* thou cursed from the earth,
which hath opened her mouth to receive thy
brother's blood from thy hand;
12 When thou tillest the ground, it shall not
henceforth yield unto thee her strength; a fugitive
and a vagabond shalt thou be in the earth.
13 And Cain said unto the LORD, My punishment
is greater than I can bear.
14 Behold, thou hast driven me out this day from
the face of the earth; and from thy face shall I be
hid; and I shall be a fugitive and a vagabond in
the earth; and it shall come to pass, *that* every one
that findeth me shall slay me.
15 And the LORD said unto him, Therefore who-
soever slayeth Cain, vengeance shall be taken on
him sevenfold. And the LORD set a mark upon
Cain, lest any finding him should kill him.
16 ¶ And Cain went out from the presence of the
LORD, and dwelt in the land of Nod, on the east
of Eden.
17 And Cain knew his wife; and she conceived, and
bare Enoch: and he builded a city, and called the
name of the city, after the name of his son, Enoch.
18 And unto Enoch was born Irad: and Irad begat
Mehujael: and Mehujael begat Methusael: and
Methusael begat Lamech.
19 ¶ And Lamech took unto him two wives: the
name of the one *was* Adah, and the name of the
other Zillah.
20 And Adah bare Jabal: he was the father of such
as dwell in tents, and *of such as have* cattle.
21 And his brother's name *was* Jubal: he was the
father of all such as handle the harp and organ.
22 And Zillah, she also bare Tubal-cain, an
instructer of every artificer in brass and iron: and
the sister of Tubal-cain *was* Naamah.
23 And Lamech said unto his wives, Adah and
Zillah, Hear my voice; ye wives of Lamech,
hearken unto my speech: for I have slain a man
to my wounding, and a young man to my hurt.
24 If Cain shall be avenged sevenfold, truly
Lamech seventy and sevenfold.
25 ¶ And Adam knew his wife again; and she bare
a son, and called his name Seth: For God, *said she*,
hath appointed me another seed instead of Abel,
whom Cain slew.
26 And to Seth, to him also there was born a son;
and he called his name Enos: then began men to
call upon the name of the LORD.

---

through the gospel (Rom. 6:14).

4:8 *Cain rose up against Abel . . . and slew him.* Cain refused the grace that God had offered freely to him. Sin now takes its course and brings forth death (James 1:15). Cain's hatred against his righteous brother showed that he was the seed of the serpent (3:15; 1 John 3:12).

4:9 *Where is Abel thy brother?* Yet again God deals with sin by asking questions. Like the first question of God to Adam (3:9), this question, "Where is your brother?" echoes down the generations to us. We cannot expect the forgiveness of God, if we do not love our brother (1 John 4:20). *Am I my brother's keeper?* One would have expected this famous retort by Cain to provoke God's immediate judgment by the death penalty, but God was patient.

4:10 *the voice of thy brother's blood crieth unto me from the ground.* The Lord Jesus Himself spoke of Abel's blood (Matt. 23:35). God does not forget the death of the innocents. Thankfully, there is blood that speaks better things than Abel's, the saving blood of Jesus (Heb. 12:24).

4:11–12 *cursed from the earth.* The Lord is constantly alluding to the earth that was cursed at the first sin. The earth has now absorbed Abel's blood. It would eventually receive the blood of the pure Lamb of God who took the curse of sin in our place. Cain was cursed from the earth and would now become a fugitive and a wanderer (*vagabond*).

4:13–15 *My punishment is greater than I can bear.* The common mercy of God is such that God still hears Cain's cries. The Lord sets a *mark upon Cain*, so that no one can take his life without severe punishment. God takes vengeance seriously (Deut. 32:35; Rom. 12:19).

4:16 *Cain went out from the presence of the LORD.* Such is the fate of the one who refuses the grace of God, as Judas later did (John 13:30; Acts 1:25). *Nod.* Literally, "wandering."

4:17 *Cain knew his wife.* Cain probably married his sister (or possibly his niece). The first recorded city is of Cain's line. Cities often lead to concentration of evil (10:11–12; 11:1–8; 13:12).

4:19 *Lamech took unto him two wives.* The first mention of polygamy which shows the departure of Cain's line from God's pathway of marriage of one man to one woman (2:24).

4:20–22 *have cattle . . . handle the harp and organ . . . instructer of every artificer in brass.* Remnants of the image of God were still visible in the ungodly through skill in agriculture, music, and metalwork. Knowledge was well advanced so that the massive undertaking of building the ark later in the time of Noah is perfectly feasible.

4:23–24 *I have slain a man.* Lamech is bragging in proud and presumptuous self-confidence rather than having any sense of remorse. *to my wounding . . . to my hurt.* In revenge for wounding and hurting me.

4:25 *appointed me another seed instead of Abel.* Eve continues to hope in the promise of the coming Seed (3:15; 4:1). *Seth* means "appointed" or "compensation," and he headed the godly line.

4:26 *men to call upon the name of the LORD.* After a downward spiral of sin and sadness, this shows that God always has a remnant who love Him and seek His grace in prayer.

Thoughts for Personal/Family Worship: Chapter 4

1. **Grieve at the results of the fall. Chapter 4 reveals the horrible consequences of Adam's sin—his children are infected with the pride, hatred, and deception of the serpent. Yet there is hope, for we also see here the fruit of God's promise (3:15). Satan has his seed among men, but God moves some to trust His promise and worship Him acceptably. Though the godly seed suffers persecution, it will triumph at last.**
2. **Marvel at God's patience. It is remarkable that God**

CHAPTER 5

THIS *is* the book of the generations of Adam. In
the day that God created man, in the likeness of
God made he him;
2 Male and female created he them; and blessed
them, and called their name Adam, in the day
when they were created.
3 ¶ And Adam lived an hundred and thirty years,
and begat *a son* in his own likeness, after his
image; and called his name Seth:
4 And the days of Adam after he had begotten
Seth were eight hundred years: and he begat sons
and daughters:
5 And all the days that Adam lived were nine
hundred and thirty years: and he died.
6 And Seth lived an hundred and five years, and
begat Enos:
7 And Seth lived after he begat Enos eight
hundred and seven years, and begat sons and
daughters:
8 And all the days of Seth were nine hundred and
twelve years: and he died.
9 ¶ And Enos lived ninety years, and begat
Cainan:
10 And Enos lived after he begat Cainan eight
hundred and fifteen years, and begat sons and
daughters:
11 And all the days of Enos were nine hundred
and five years: and he died.
12 ¶ And Cainan lived seventy years, and begat
Mahalaleel:
13 And Cainan lived after he begat Mahalaleel
eight hundred and forty years, and begat sons and
daughters:
14 And all the days of Cainan were nine hundred
and ten years: and he died.
15 ¶ And Mahalaleel lived sixty and five years,
and begat Jared:
16 And Mahalaleel lived after he begat Jared eight
hundred and thirty years, and begat sons and
daughters:
17 And all the days of Mahalaleel were eight
hundred ninety and five years: and he died.
18 ¶ And Jared lived an hundred sixty and two
years, and he begat Enoch:
19 And Jared lived after he begat Enoch eight
hundred years, and begat sons and daughters:
20 And all the days of Jared were nine hundred
sixty and two years: and he died.
21 ¶ And Enoch lived sixty and five years, and
begat Methuselah:
22 And Enoch walked with God after he begat
Methuselah three hundred years, and begat sons
and daughters:
23 And all the days of Enoch were three hundred
sixty and five years:
24 And Enoch walked with God: and he *was* not;
for God took him.
25 And Methuselah lived an hundred eighty and
seven years, and begat Lamech:
26 And Methuselah lived after he begat Lamech
seven hundred eighty and two years, and begat
sons and daughters:
27 And all the days of Methuselah were nine
hundred sixty and nine years: and he died.
28 ¶ And Lamech lived an hundred eighty and
two years, and begat a son:
29 And he called his name Noah, saying, This

---

converses patiently with Cain and gives him ample opportunity to repent of his jealousy. Even though his offering has been refused, Cain should have listened to the warnings, but refused. Murder is always in the human heart. "For out of the heart proceed evil thoughts, murders, adulteries, fornications, thefts, false witness, blasphemies" (Matt. 15:19).

3. Beware of the growth of sin. Once we harbor sin, it leads to worse sin, which affects others. Cain's initial sin leads to worse in his descendants, such as Lamech bragging about his murders. Like the godly line of Seth, we need to call upon the name of the Lord. What sins does this chapter teach us to pray against, and what graces should we seek from the Lord?

Chapter 5: ***The line of Adam and Seth shows evidence of its godliness and yet suffers death as the bitter consequence of the fall.***

5:1–3 *generations*. See note at 2:4. *in the likeness of God made he him . . . begat a son in his own likeness*. The parallel implies that God created man in His image to be His son (Luke 3:38). However, Adam fathering a child *in his own likeness* also implies that he passed on to his children not the pure image of God but an image broken and ruined by sin. *called their name Adam*. God named the entire race "Man," because both men and women were under a male head.

5:5 *nine hundred and thirty years*. The possibilities of later generations having direct communication with Adam are striking. Adam was still alive when his son of the eighth generation (Lamech) was a mature man. *and he died*. The grim consequence of the fall resonates eight times through this chapter.

5:21 *Methuselah*. Meaning, "when he is dead it will come," or "his death will bring," possibly a prophecy of the flood. *Enoch* was a prophet who foretold the coming of the Lord for judgment (Jude 14–15).

5:22–24 *Enoch walked with God*. To walk with God is to live in friendship with Him by daily trusting His promises and keeping His commandments (6:9; 17:1; 24:40; 48:15). *God took him*. God translated him without death to heaven (Heb. 11:5), the only other person to experience this being Elijah (2 Kings 2:9–12). In a chapter full of death, God revealed the hope of eternal life (Ps. 49:15; 73:24; "receive" is the same word as *took*).

5:29 The *name Noah* means *comfort* or "rest." He is a type of Christ since in his day he builds the place of rescue from the impending judgment.

5:32 *Shem, Ham, and Japheth*. Likely the birth order was Japheth, Shem, and Ham (9:22–24; 10:21; 11:10).

Thoughts for Personal/Family Worship: Chapter 5

1. By God's grace, strive to imitate Enoch. Enoch walked with God. Surely the secret of our Christian life is to abide in Christ: "Without me ye can do nothing" (John 15:5).

same shall comfort us concerning our work and toil of our hands, because of the ground which the LORD hath cursed.
30 And Lamech lived after he begat Noah five hundred ninety and five years, and begat sons and daughters:
31 And all the days of Lamech were seven hundred seventy and seven years: and he died.
32 And Noah was five hundred years old: and Noah begat Shem, Ham, and Japheth.

CHAPTER 6

AND it came to pass, when men began to multiply on the face of the earth, and daughters were born unto them,
2 That the sons of God saw the daughters of men that they *were* fair; and they took them wives of all which they chose.
3 And the LORD said, My spirit shall not always strive with man, for that he also *is* flesh: yet his days shall be an hundred and twenty years.
4 There were giants in the earth in those days; and also after that, when the sons of God came in
unto the daughters of men, and they bare *children* to them, the same *became* mighty men which *were* of old, men of renown.
5 ¶ And GOD saw that the wickedness of man *was* great in the earth, and *that* every imagination of the thoughts of his heart *was* only evil continually.
6 And it repented the LORD that he had made man on the earth, and it grieved him at his heart.
7 And the LORD said, I will destroy man whom I have created from the face of the earth; both man, and beast, and the creeping thing, and the fowls of the air; for it repenteth me that I have made them.
8 But Noah found grace in the eyes of the LORD.
9 ¶ These *are* the generations of Noah: Noah was a just man *and* perfect in his generations, *and* Noah walked with God.
10 And Noah begat three sons, Shem, Ham, and Japheth.
11 The earth also was corrupt before God, and the earth was filled with violence.
12 And God looked upon the earth, and, behold, it was corrupt; for all flesh had corrupted his way upon the earth.
13 And God said unto Noah, The end of all flesh

Spend time in the Word of God, praying, meditating, repenting of sin, and obeying God's laws. Just as God took Enoch to heaven, so walking with God on earth is the best assurance that we will walk with God in heaven. The children of God must bear their Father's image.

2. **The repentance and faith of the godly does not exempt them from death, unless the Lord should come and take them home first (1 Thess. 4:16–17). Every generation from Adam onward has seen death as the bitter fruit of the fall. Though most people try to ignore death, we are not ready to live until we are ready to die. What is the best way to face death?**

The Worldwide Flood and the Rainbow Promise (6:1—9:29)

Chapter 6: *Man's corrupt heart and violent acts provoke God to destroy the world with a flood, but the Lord calls Noah to preserve his family and the animals and birds in the ark.*

6:1 *when men began to multiply on the face of the earth.* The suggestion is that there was a large population in the world immediately prior to the flood.

6:2 *the sons of God saw the daughters of men that they were fair; and they took them wives of all which they chose.* Outward physical attraction without the fear of God led to ungodly unions. The identity of the *sons of God* is not clear, and has been variously interpreted to mean angels (Job 1:6)—though angels have no relations with women (Mark 12:25); or powerful men (Ps. 82:6) taking harems; or the union of the line of Seth with the line of Cain (chs. 4–5), the forbidden intermarriage of the godly with the wicked (Ex. 34:16; Deut. 7:3–4).

6:3 *his days shall be an hundred and twenty years.* From this we deduce that the warning to Noah was 120 years before the flood. Noah preached righteousness for over a century to a lost world that would not listen (2 Peter 2:5).

6:4 The offspring of the ungodly unions were *giants*. The Hebrew word comes from the Hebrew verb which means "to fall." These giants were thus associated with violence and rebellion.

6:5 *God saw . . . the wickedness of man.* There is nothing that God does not see, though sinners pretend He is blind (1 Chron. 28:9; Ps. 94:5–9). This statement is a stark contrast to the statement that "God saw" that man and all creation were "very good" (1:31). *every imagination of the thoughts of his heart was only evil continually.* The first mention in Scripture of the *heart* (the entirety of inner self: mind, will, and emotions). The heart of fallen man is totally corrupt from the youngest age, ruled by sinful thoughts and desires, and unable to produce anything pleasing to God apart from His saving grace (8:21; Ps. 14:1–3; 51:5; 58:3; Jer. 17:1,9; Rom. 1:21; 3:10–12; 8:6–8; Eph. 2:1–3; 4:17–18).

6:6 *it repented the LORD . . . it grieved him at his heart.* God and His decree do not change, but God does grieve over sin and His relationships change (1 Sam. 15:11,29,35). The Lord's heart is deeply concerned about man's heart.

6:7 *I will destroy man whom I have created.* The word *destroy* is a very strong word; it can be translated "blot out" or "exterminate." The Creator of man became the Destroyer of man because of man's sin. The Lord Jesus warned that this destruction foreshadowed the sudden and complete destruction Christ will bring when He returns (Luke 17:26–30; 2 Peter 3:3–6).

6:8 *Noah found grace in the eyes of the LORD.* It is only of the Lord's grace that anyone is saved, and that through faith—just as Noah was (Heb. 11:7).

6:9 *Just* refers to his legal standing of justification, and *perfect,* meaning "complete," refers to his wholehearted dedication to God or his sanctification. Noah is a spiritually saved person, not by his own righteousness but by God's grace upon him. *walked with God.* See note at 5:22–24.

6:11 *corrupt before God . . . filled with violence.* The corruption and violence flows from the corrupt imagination of the thoughts of [the] heart" (v. 5; cf. Prov. 23:7; Matt. 15:19).

6:12 Man's sin is counted against the "earth" (v. 11) and *all flesh*—words that include animal flesh throughout the flood account (vv. 13,17,19; 7:15–16,21; 8:17; 9:11,15,–17).

6:13 *I will destroy them.* A repeat of the essence of v. 7 but using the word "corrupt" of v. 12 ("corrupted his way") as part

is come before me; for the earth is filled with
violence through them; and, behold, I will destroy
them with the earth.
14 ¶ Make thee an ark of gopher wood; rooms
shalt thou make in the ark, and shalt pitch it
within and without with pitch.
15 And this *is the fashion* which thou shalt make
it *of*: The length of the ark *shall be* three hundred
cubits, the breadth of it fifty cubits, and the height
of it thirty cubits.
16 A window shalt thou make to the ark, and in
a cubit shalt thou finish it above; and the door
of the ark shalt thou set in the side thereof; *with*
lower, second, and third *stories* shalt thou make it.
17 And, behold, I, even I, do bring a flood of
waters upon the earth, to destroy all flesh, wherein
is the breath of life, from under heaven; *and* every
thing that *is* in the earth shall die.
18 But with thee will I establish my covenant; and
thou shalt come into the ark, thou, and thy sons,
and thy wife, and thy sons' wives with thee.
19 And of every living thing of all flesh, two of every *sort* shalt thou bring into the ark, to keep *them*
alive with thee; they shall be male and female.
20 Of fowls after their kind, and of cattle after
their kind, of every creeping thing of the earth
after his kind, two of every *sort* shall come unto
thee, to keep *them* alive.
21 And take thou unto thee of all food that is
eaten, and thou shalt gather *it* to thee; and it shall
be for food for thee, and for them.
22 Thus did Noah; according to all that God
commanded him, so did he.

CHAPTER 7

AND the LORD said unto Noah, Come thou and
all thy house into the ark; for thee have I seen
righteous before me in this generation.
2 Of every clean beast thou shalt take to thee by
sevens, the male and his female: and of beasts that
are not clean by two, the male and his female.
3 Of fowls also of the air by sevens, the male and
the female; to keep seed alive upon the face of all
the earth.
4 For yet seven days, and I will cause it to rain

---

of the judgment: "I will ruin them for ruining themselves." *With the earth* shows that the earth would also be destroyed with all its living creatures (vv. 7,17).

6:14 *Make thee an ark.* Noah is to make the ark in obedience to God's instructions (v. 22)—a picture of Christ's work of salvation by His perfect obedience. *gopher wood.* The identity of this wood is not clear.

6:15 Caricatures of the ark in children's literature do great damage to this impressive work of construction that took about 120 years to build. The ark was roughly 450 feet (137.1 meters) long, 75 feet (22.9 meters) wide, and 45 feet (13.7 meters) tall. The ark was about twice the length of a Boeing 747 (232 feet; 70.7 meters). Ancient peoples were advanced engineers and could certainly construct such an object.

6:16 The ark was designed with three levels and a window opening of approximately 1.5 feet (0.5 meters). Note that the ark described in the Mesopotamian Epic of Gilgamesh is a perfect cube with a side dimension of 200 feet (70 meters) and seven stories high. Such a craft could roll on the open sea, and it is obvious to a nautical engineer that the account in Genesis is using seagoing proportions while the Gilgamesh version is a fanciful corruption.

6:17 The word *flood* is the first mention of the Hebrew word translated in the Septuagint with the word from which we get the English "cataclysmic" which underlines the huge nature of this event. The possible mechanisms of this worldwide event are discussed in 7:11. *every thing that is in the earth shall die.* This is a worldwide event (v. 7; 7:4). One might well ask if the flood was a local flood, then what is the point of building a huge boat if all one had to do was go to the nearest high mountain or leave the area?

6:18 *with thee will I establish my covenant.* As with Abraham later (15:18; 17:2), God makes a covenant with Noah (9:9–17). God's grace is sealed in His covenant agreements.

6:19 *of every living thing of all flesh, two of every sort shalt thou bring . . . male and female.* Estimates of the capacity of the ark are for about 125,000 animals with an average size of a sheep. Estimates of the number of land animals would be not more than 50,000 that Noah would need in total on the ark. The food (v. 21) and Noah's living quarters would take up the remainder.

6:20 *two of every sort shall come unto thee.* God brings all the animals to Noah.

6:22 *according to all that God commanded him.* The salvation of some of mankind from destruction depended upon the obedience of one righteous man (7:1,5); this is a type of Christ (Rom. 5:15–19).

Thoughts for Personal/Family Worship: Chapter 6

1. **From Noah we learn patience and faith. Noah took more than a hundred years to build the ark. He patiently worked and witnessed to the people who rejected his message (2 Peter 2:5). We live in similar days (Luke 17:26) and need to preach faithfully despite the mocking of men against the gospel. The only safe place from the flood was the ark being built. The only safe place from God's eternal judgment is Christ.**
2. **Noah found grace in the eyes of the Lord and walked with God. Significantly, Noah found grace before he was described as just and perfect. It is grace that enables faith, and God regarded Noah as just in consequence of that grace that caused him to believe and obey. May the Lord help us to walk with Him. Trust in Christ and obey Him, for then you will abide in His love (John 15:10).**

Chapter 7: ***In obedience to the Lord, Noah and his family enter the ark with the animals, and God destroys all other human and animal life on earth through the flood.***

7:1 *Come thou and all thy house into the ark.* This invitation is echoed in Matt. 11:28, "Come unto me, all ye that labour and are heavy laden, and I will give you rest." *thee have I seen righteous.* There is a similarity to Job who is righteous in his generation (Job 1:1). Ultimately Noah's righteousness points to Christ, God's righteous servant (Isa. 53:11; 1 John 2:1).

7:2–3 *by sevens.* Most take this to mean seven pairs (*the male and the female*) of *clean* animals.

7:4 *yet seven days.* The animals and Noah had come into the ark a week before the flood began. There was still time for

upon the earth forty days and forty nights; and
every living substance that I have made will I
destroy from off the face of the earth.
5 And Noah did according unto all that the LORD
commanded him.
6 And Noah *was* six hundred years old when the
flood of waters was upon the earth.
7 ¶ And Noah went in, and his sons, and his wife,
and his sons' wives with him, into the ark, because
of the waters of the flood.
8 Of clean beasts, and of beasts that *are* not clean,
and of fowls, and of every thing that creepeth
upon the earth,
9 There went in two and two unto Noah into
the ark, the male and the female, as God had
commanded Noah.
10 And it came to pass after seven days, that the
waters of the flood were upon the earth.
11 ¶ In the six hundredth year of Noah's life, in
the second month, the seventeenth day of the
month, the same day were all the fountains of the
great deep broken up, and the windows of heaven
were opened.
12 And the rain was upon the earth forty days
and forty nights.
13 In the selfsame day entered Noah, and Shem,
and Ham, and Japheth, the sons of Noah, and
Noah's wife, and the three wives of his sons with
them, into the ark;
14 They, and every beast after his kind, and all the
cattle after their kind, and every creeping thing
that creepeth upon the earth after his kind, and
every fowl after his kind, every bird of every sort.
15 And they went in unto Noah into the ark, two
and two of all flesh, wherein *is* the breath of life.
16 And they that went in, went in male and
female of all flesh, as God had commanded him:
and the LORD shut him in.
17 And the flood was forty days upon the earth;
and the waters increased, and bare up the ark, and
it was lift up above the earth.
18 And the waters prevailed, and were increased
greatly upon the earth; and the ark went upon the
face of the waters.
19 And the waters prevailed exceedingly upon the
earth; and all the high hills, that *were* under the
whole heaven, were covered.
20 Fifteen cubits upward did the waters prevail;
and the mountains were covered.
21 And all flesh died that moved upon the earth,
both of fowl, and of cattle, and of beast, and of
every creeping thing that creepeth upon the earth,
and every man:
22 All in whose nostrils *was* the breath of life, of
all that *was* in the dry *land*, died.
23 And every living substance was destroyed
which was upon the face of the ground, both
man, and cattle, and the creeping things, and the
fowl of the heaven; and they were destroyed from
the earth: and Noah only remained *alive*, and they
that *were* with him in the ark.
24 And the waters prevailed upon the earth an
hundred and fifty days.

---

repentance in that final week with the door open and the way of escape from the impending doom still available. *forty days and forty nights.* This is the first mention of the number forty, often associated with testing and difficulty (Ex. 24:18; 34:28; Num. 14:33–34; 32:13; Deut. 9:11,18,25; 10:10; 1 Sam 17:16; 1 Kings 9:18; Luke 4:2).

7:5 *Noah did according unto all that the LORD commanded him.* This was the secret of God's blessing upon him.

7:10 *the waters of the flood were upon the earth.* Some have suggested that the flood was a scouring of the earth and that the waters then came after this. This verse does not support such a concept. The waters themselves flood across the world and drown all land creatures in their path (Matt. 24:39).

7:11 *six hundredth year of Noah's life, in the second month, the seventeenth day of the month.* The exact days are now recorded, which strongly suggests Noah himself is recording the events as a diary. *the fountains of the great deep broken up.* Possibly referring to underground reservoirs or superheated water which shot up into the atmosphere due to the splitting of the continental plates.

7:12 Worldwide *rain* for *forty days and forty nights* requires more than atmospheric moisture, which is why most do not think this is a collapse of a vapor canopy. Rather it is thought this is the downpour of water that has been ejected first up into the atmosphere as superheated steam.

7:13 The word *selfsame* stresses that it was foreordained and definite.

7:16 *the LORD shut him in.* When Noah, his family, and the animals were all in the ark, God shut the door. He secures the ark and keeps them from danger. One is reminded of Matt. 25:10, "the door was shut."

7:18 *the waters prevailed . . . increased greatly upon the earth.* The flood waters now rose up even after the forty days of rain. This is the second period of the flood year after the initial destruction of the first forty days.

7:19 *the waters prevailed exceedingly . . . all the high hills.* The waters now can never cover the earth, so this means that the mountains and high hills were much lower before the flood. Peter states, "the world that then was, being overflowed with water, perished" (2 Peter 3:6).

7:20 *Fifteen cubits upward did the waters prevail.* The maximum depth above the highest hills was about twenty-two feet or half the height of the ark and thus probably approximately the draft of the ship. This can be no local flood as it is repeated that *the mountains were covered.*

7:23 *every living substance was destroyed.* As one would expect, the sedimentary rocks all over the globe carry abundant evidence of creatures buried quickly and fossilized. *Noah only remained alive, and they that were with him.* God's purposes were achieved just as He had said. The destruction was total and only those in the ark survived.

7:24 *the waters prevailed . . . an hundred and fifty days.* This is the end of the second stage of the flood before the assuaging of the waters takes place.

Thoughts for Personal/Family Worship: Chapter 7

1. God's judgment upon the world of sinners is fearsome. The thought of millions of people drowning while water

CHAPTER 8

AND God remembered Noah, and every living
thing, and all the cattle that *was* with him in the
ark: and God made a wind to pass over the earth,
and the waters asswaged;
2 The fountains also of the deep and the windows
of heaven were stopped, and the rain from heaven
was restrained;
3 And the waters returned from off the earth
continually: and after the end of the hundred and
fifty days the waters were abated.
4 And the ark rested in the seventh month, on the
seventeenth day of the month, upon the moun-
tains of Ararat.
5 And the waters decreased continually until the
tenth month: in the tenth *month*, on the first *day*
of the month, were the tops of the mountains
seen.
6 ¶ And it came to pass at the end of forty days,
that Noah opened the window of the ark which
he had made:
7 And he sent forth a raven, which went forth to
and fro, until the waters were dried up from off
the earth.
8 Also he sent forth a dove from him, to see if
the waters were abated from off the face of the
ground;
9 But the dove found no rest for the sole of her
foot, and she returned unto him into the ark, for
the waters *were* on the face of the whole earth:
then he put forth his hand, and took her, and
pulled her in unto him into the ark.
10 And he stayed yet other seven days; and again
he sent forth the dove out of the ark;
11 And the dove came in to him in the evening;
and, lo, in her mouth *was* an olive leaf pluckt off:
so Noah knew that the waters were abated from
off the earth.
12 And he stayed yet other seven days; and sent
forth the dove; which returned not again unto
him any more.
13 ¶ And it came to pass in the six hundredth
and first year, in the first *month*, the first *day* of
the month, the waters were dried up from off the
earth: and Noah removed the covering of the ark,
and looked, and, behold, the face of the ground
was dry.
14 And in the second month, on the seven and
twentieth day of the month, was the earth dried.
15 ¶ And God spake unto Noah, saying,
16 Go forth of the ark, thou, and thy wife, and thy
sons, and thy sons' wives with thee.
17 Bring forth with thee every living thing that *is*
with thee, of all flesh, *both* of fowl, and of cattle,
and of every creeping thing that creepeth upon
the earth; that they may breed abundantly in
the earth, and be fruitful, and multiply upon the
earth.
18 And Noah went forth, and his sons, and his
wife, and his sons' wives with him:
19 Every beast, every creeping thing, and every
fowl, *and* whatsoever creepeth upon the earth,
after their kinds, went forth out of the ark.
20 ¶ And Noah builded an altar unto the LORD;

sweeps away all human constructions is horrifying. Yet it is a small thing compared to the burning wrath of God yet to come when the Lord Jesus appears with His holy angels. The flood brought death, but judgment day will bring eternal punishment in hell. Let us give sober consideration to this awesome and inevitable reality. How does the flood teach us to fear the Lord?

2. The Lord calls men, women, and children through the gospel to come into the ark of safety, Jesus Christ the Righteous One (Matt. 11:28; Luke 14:17). Just as the Lord shut Noah and his family into the ark and protected them during the flood, so the Lord will save all who trust in Christ alone from the wrath that is to come. After the flood came, no one was left except those in the ark. In the same way, the living church of Jesus Christ will be the only people to escape God's wrath. Therefore come to Christ now, and place your entire trust in Him.

Chapter 8: *God preserves Noah and the ark, the waters go down, they disembark, and Noah offers the Lord a pleasing sacrifice.*

8:1 *God remembered Noah.* This does not refer to a return of lapsed memory, but to God acting with faithful love according to His covenant promise (6:18; cf. 9:15–16; 19:29; Ex. 2:24; 6:5; Lev. 26:42,45; Ps.105:8; 106:45; 111:5; Ezek. 16:60; Luke 1:72). *the waters asswaged.* They decreased. This third stage of the flood led to the world surface as we know it being formed. Major erosion pathways were formed as the waters raced to the new ocean beds (Ps. 104:6–9).

8:3 *The waters returned from off the earth continually.* The scouring effect of the water runoff is seen all across the continents today. E.g., many regard the mile-deep Grand Canyon to have been formed by the powerful cutting action of fast moving waters into previously laid down sediments.

8:4 *the ark rested . . . upon the mountains of Ararat.* Notice the diary-like entry. There is no conclusive proof that the remnants of the ark are still extant. The wood was likely used for building, though we should be open to the possibility some remains may still be found.

8:5 *tops of the mountains.* The three months of waters abating until the tops of the mountains were seen and the caution in waiting forty days to open the window of the ark is again consistent with the flood not being local in extent, coupled with the necessity to check using the raven and the dove (vv. 7–8) for a dry location to disembark.

8:11–12 Another week and the *dove* comes back with an *olive leaf.* Yet another week and the dove does not return at all meaning there is land available and plants are growing.

8:14 *was the earth dried.* One year and ten days since the beginning of the flood.

8:16 *Go forth of the ark.* Noah awaited God's instruction to leave the ark. It was almost five months between seeing the tops of the mountains until Noah and his family finally left the ark. Noah was careful to still honor God after the major catastrophe is over.

8:20–21 *Noah builded an altar.* Noah looked to the Lord very firmly in these momentous days at the beginning of the new

and took of every clean beast, and of every clean
fowl, and offered burnt offerings on the altar.
21 And the LORD smelled a sweet savour; and the
LORD said in his heart, I will not again curse the
ground any more for man's sake; for the imagina-
tion of man's heart *is* evil from his youth; neither
will I again smite any more every thing living, as
I have done.
22 While the earth remaineth, seedtime and har-
vest, and cold and heat, and summer and winter,
and day and night shall not cease.

CHAPTER 9

AND God blessed Noah and his sons, and said
unto them, Be fruitful, and multiply, and replen-
ish the earth.
2 And the fear of you and the dread of you shall
be upon every beast of the earth, and upon every
fowl of the air, upon all that moveth *upon* the
earth, and upon all the fishes of the sea; into your
hand are they delivered.
3 Every moving thing that liveth shall be meat for
you; even as the green herb have I given you all
things.
4 But flesh with the life thereof, *which is* the blood
thereof, shall ye not eat.
5 And surely your blood of your lives will I re-
quire; at the hand of every beast will I require
it, and at the hand of man; at the hand of every
man's brother will I require the life of man.
6 Whoso sheddeth man's blood, by man shall his
blood be shed: for in the image of God made he
man.
7 And you, be ye fruitful, and multiply; bring
forth abundantly in the earth, and multiply
therein.
8 ¶ And God spake unto Noah, and to his sons
with him, saying,
9 And I, behold, I establish my covenant with
you, and with your seed after you;
10 And with every living creature that *is* with you,
of the fowl, of the cattle, and of every beast of the
earth with you; from all that go out of the ark, to
every beast of the earth.
11 And I will establish my covenant with you;
neither shall all flesh be cut off any more by the
waters of a flood; neither shall there any more be
a flood to destroy the earth.
12 And God said, This *is* the token of the covenant
which I make between me and you and every
living creature that *is* with you, for perpetual
generations:
13 I do set my bow in the cloud, and it shall be for
a token of a covenant between me and the earth.
14 And it shall come to pass, when I bring a cloud
over the earth, that the bow shall be seen in the
cloud:

---

world. *burnt offerings.* Sacrifices to atone for sin and please the Lord (*sweet savour*, cf. Lev. 1:4,9,13,17). This was costly worship given the limited number of clean animals (7:2). *I will not again curse the ground any more for man's sake.* This shows that the flood itself was global, as local floods have happened since. Just as Noah's sacrifice resulted in God's promise not to send another flood, so Christ's sacrifice resulted in God's promise not to punish His people in wrath (Isa. 53:10–11; 54:9–10). God refers to the flood as a *curse* on the *ground*, showing the curse from the fall (3:17) was still in operation and ultimately led to worldwide destruction. *for the imagination of man's heart is evil from his youth.* The flood could not remove man's corrupt nature (see note at 6:5).

8:22 *While the earth remaineth.* The Lord promises the continuity of predictable annual seasons and the rhythm of day and night (Jer. 31:35–36; 33:20,25).

Thoughts for Personal/Family Worship: Chapter 8

1. **In the midst of overwhelming sorrows and dangers, we tend to think that God has forgotten us. But when the ark was a tiny speck floating in a vast sea of destruction, God remembered Noah. If we are in covenant with Him, He will certainly remember us too. Do not fear that God has abandoned you. His mercies will never forsake the one who belongs to Him, for His people are forever united to Christ. Christ is righteous; Christ has offered all-pleasing sacrifice to satisfy God's justice; Christ will save His own.**
2. **The appropriate response to deliverance from trouble is worship. Noah might well have said to himself that he could not afford the time or resources to worship God after leaving the ark, but instead he built an altar and offered up sacrifices. From what evils, either physical or spiritual, has God delivered you? How are you worshiping Him for it?**

Chapter 9: *God renews His creation mandate through a covenant with Noah, his seed, and all living creatures; tragically, Noah and his family fall into sin.*

9:1 *Be fruitful, and multiply, and replenish the earth.* A similar command to what the Lord said in the beginning to Adam (1:28). Salvation brings a new creation.

9:3 *Every moving thing that liveth shall be meat for you.* Whereas before man was vegetarian (1:29), now he is allowed to eat animal meat. This may be due to harsher and more rigorous conditions in the postflood climate that necessitate high-energy protein intake.

9:5–6 *your blood of your lives will I require.* This indicates how serious the bloodshed was before the flood. Now strict rules are given concerning the sanctity of human life. The blood of man represents his life. Since he alone is made in *the image of God*, his blood is not to be shed lightly. *Whoso sheddeth man's blood, by man shall his blood be shed.* The law of capital punishment to be administered by man has never been revoked by God (Rom. 13:4).

9:9 *I establish my covenant with you, and with your seed.* God had made a covenant with Noah (6:18). This is now extended to Noah's descendants. The promise not to destroy the world again with another flood is repeated (8:22; 9:11). The postflood cosmos will be kept in a regular and predictable cycle of seasons and will end by fire (2 Peter 3:7).

9:13 *I do set my bow in the cloud.* God now brings a sign of His covenant mercy to the new human population. The rainbow which God produces is new, so we see that this confirms that

15 And I will remember my covenant, which *is*
between me and you and every living creature of
all flesh; and the waters shall no more become a
flood to destroy all flesh.
16 And the bow shall be in the cloud; and I will
look upon it, that I may remember the everlasting
covenant between God and every living creature
of all flesh that *is* upon the earth.
17 And God said unto Noah, This *is* the token of
the covenant, which I have established between
me and all flesh that *is* upon the earth.
18 ¶ And the sons of Noah, that went forth of the
ark, were Shem, and Ham, and Japheth: and Ham
is the father of Canaan.
19 These *are* the three sons of Noah: and of them
was the whole earth overspread.
20 And Noah began *to be* an husbandman, and he
planted a vineyard:
21 And he drank of the wine, and was drunken;
and he was uncovered within his tent.
22 And Ham, the father of Canaan, saw the
nakedness of his father, and told his two brethren
without.
23 And Shem and Japheth took a garment, and
laid *it* upon both their shoulders, and went back-
ward, and covered the nakedness of their father;
and their faces *were* backward, and they saw not
their father's nakedness.
24 And Noah awoke from his wine, and knew
what his younger son had done unto him.
25 And he said, Cursed *be* Canaan; a servant of
servants shall he be unto his brethren.
26 And he said, Blessed *be* the LORD God of Shem;
and Canaan shall be his servant.
27 God shall enlarge Japheth, and he shall dwell
in the tents of Shem; and Canaan shall be his
servant.
28 ¶ And Noah lived after the flood three hundred
and fifty years.
29 And all the days of Noah were nine hundred
and fifty years: and he died.

CHAPTER 10

NOW these *are* the generations of the sons of
Noah, Shem, Ham, and Japheth: and unto them
were sons born after the flood.
2 The sons of Japheth; Gomer, and Magog, and
Madai, and Javan, and Tubal, and Meshech, and
Tiras.
3 And the sons of Gomer; Ashkenaz, and Riphath,
and Togarmah.

---

there was no rain before the flood (2:5) in the sense of the downpours that we now experience.

9:19 *of them was the whole earth overspread.* The whole of the human population in the postflood world has come from the three sons of Noah and their wives.

9:21 *And he drank of the wine, and was drunken.* This sad event shows that even godly Noah fell. Drunkenness is a sin (Prov. 23:29–35; Isa. 5:11–12,20–24; Eph. 5:18), and habitual drunks have no place in God's kingdom (1 Cor. 6:10; Gal. 5:21).

9:22 *Ham . . . saw the nakedness of his father.* An honorable son would have respectfully covered his father as his elder brothers did, but he *told his two brethren.*

9:24 *what his younger son had done unto him.* It is possible that Ham or Canaan committed some unspoken sin against their father.

9:25–27 Noah saw prophetically what would happen to his three sons, from whom the whole human race would develop. *Cursed be Canaan.* Canaan was the father of the Canaanites who later would be driven out by Joshua and enslaved (*servant of servants*) by Israel and other nations. As in ch. 3, a blessing accompanies the curse. God would *enlarge Japheth.* God would make a covenant with the descendants of Shem (*God of Shem*) and *dwell in the tents of Shem* (an anticipation of tabernacle, temple, and incarnation of the Son of God).

Thoughts for Personal/Family Worship: Chapter 9

1. **Thank God for the rainbow promise that God will never again flood the world. These are days of grace where God "now commandeth all men every where to repent" (Acts 17:30). The covenant with Noah guards the first gospel promise of the Redeemer coming into the human race (Gen. 3:15). The flood destroyed humanity except for Noah's family, and it seemed like the promise was in jeopardy. But God assured the continuation of the human race. Not even the judgment of sin will frustrate God's redemptive purpose in Christ.**
2. **Beware of the danger of drunkenness. We personally need to be very careful with strong drink. It is a stumbling block to many. Alcoholic drink is not wrong *per se*, but the Bible does clearly teach that drunkenness is a sin. It shows that drunkenness makes one unaware of what is happening. We must not misuse our bodies. Drunkenness is often linked to immorality and unseemly behavior. Therefore, diligently heed the biblical warnings, and guard yourself against ever becoming intoxicated (Gal. 5:21).**

The Division of Nations and Languages (10:1—11:32)

Chapter 10: *Noah's sons multiply into the nations of the world.*

10:1 Another list of *generations* (see note at 2:4) closes off the period of the flood and moves to the origin of the nations from the three sons of Noah.

10:2–5 The descendants of Japheth.

10:2 *Gomer* may be linked to the Celts (the Welsh language is Cymraeg or Gymraeg), Cimmeria, the Crimea, Galatia (part of Turkey), Gaul (France), and Galicia (northwest Spain). *Magog* lived in the north (Ezek. 38:15) and may be linked to Scythia (Romania and the Ukraine). *Madai.* The ancestor to the Medes, who later settled parts of India. *Javan* may refer to Greece (Dan. 8:21). *Tubal* is probably connected to Caucasian Iberia (Georgia), peopled by the Thobelites with the capital Tbilisi. *Meshech* is probably connected to the Meschera lowland. *Tiras* is linked to Thrace and Macedonia.

10:3 *Ashkenaz* is present Germany. *Riphath* is associated by Josephus with Paphlagonia (northern Turkey). The Armenians have a tradition that they are descended from *Togarmah.*

10:4 *Elishah* is linked to one of the Greek peoples named in the *Iliad,* "the Eilesians." *Tarshish* is on the Mediterranean coast, variously with Tarsus (Turkey), Carthage (north Africa), or southern Spain. *Kittim* is Cyprus.

4 And the sons of Javan; Elishah, and Tarshish,
Kittim, and Dodanim.
5 By these were the isles of the Gentiles divided in
their lands; every one after his tongue, after their
families, in their nations.
6 ¶ And the sons of Ham; Cush, and Mizraim,
and Phut, and Canaan.
7 And the sons of Cush; Seba, and Havilah, and
Sabtah, and Raamah, and Sabtecha: and the sons
of Raamah; Sheba, and Dedan.
8 And Cush begat Nimrod: he began to be a
mighty one in the earth.
9 He was a mighty hunter before the LORD:
wherefore it is said, Even as Nimrod the mighty
hunter before the LORD.
10 And the beginning of his kingdom was Babel,
and Erech, and Accad, and Calneh, in the land of
Shinar.
11 Out of that land went forth Asshur, and build-
ed Nineveh, and the city Rehoboth, and Calah,
12 And Resen between Nineveh and Calah: the
same *is* a great city.
13 And Mizraim begat Ludim, and Anamim, and
Lehabim, and Naphtuhim,
14 And Pathrusim, and Casluhim, (out of whom
came Philistim,) and Caphtorim.
15 ¶ And Canaan begat Sidon his firstborn, and
Heth,
16 And the Jebusite, and the Amorite, and the
Girgasite,
17 And the Hivite, and the Arkite, and the Sinite,
18 And the Arvadite, and the Zemarite, and the
Hamathite: and afterward were the families of the
Canaanites spread abroad.
19 And the border of the Canaanites was from
Sidon, as thou comest to Gerar, unto Gaza; as thou
goest, unto Sodom, and Gomorrah, and Admah,
and Zeboim, even unto Lasha.
20 These *are* the sons of Ham, after their fami-
lies, after their tongues, in their countries, *and* in
their nations.
21 ¶ Unto Shem also, the father of all the children
of Eber, the brother of Japheth the elder, even to
him were *children* born.
22 The children of Shem; Elam, and Asshur, and
Arphaxad, and Lud, and Aram.
23 And the children of Aram; Uz, and Hul, and
Gether, and Mash.
24 And Arphaxad begat Salah; and Salah begat Eber.
25 And unto Eber were born two sons: the name
of one *was* Peleg; for in his days was the earth di-
vided; and his brother's name *was* Joktan.
26 And Joktan begat Almodad, and Sheleph, and
Hazarmaveth, and Jerah,
27 And Hadoram, and Uzal, and Diklah,
28 And Obal, and Abimael, and Sheba,
29 And Ophir, and Havilah, and Jobab: all these
were the sons of Joktan.
30 And their dwelling was from Mesha, as thou
goest unto Sephar a mount of the east.
31 These *are* the sons of Shem, after their fami-
lies, after their tongues, in their lands, after their
nations.
32 These *are* the families of the sons of Noah,

10:5 *The isles of the Gentiles* primarily refers to the sons of Japheth and the European dispersion, but later it refers to all non-Israelites.

10:6–20 The descendants of Ham.

10:6 The Scriptures refer to Egypt as the land of *Ham* (Ps. 105:23,27; 106:22). *Cush* is Ethiopia. *Mizraim* is Egypt (50:11). Josephus records that *Phut* is the old name for Libya, and the ancient river Phut was in Libya. *Canaan* settled in what is today modern Israel and Jordan.

10:8 The name *Nimrod* means "rebellion" or "let us rebel." His name is preserved in many legends from Babylonia and he is undoubtedly the first great emperor. After his death legends state he was deified and worshiped as Merodach or Marduk and possibly the Egyptian god Osiris and the Hindu god Shiva.

10:9 *a mighty hunter*. Nimrod is associated with feats of great physical valor in hunting.

10:10 *the beginning of his kingdom was Babel*. The might of Nimrod is seen in the building of Babel as his capital city and the Tower of Babel in the land of Shinar (11:1–4) in the Tigris-Euphrates valley.

10:11 *Asshur* is a son of Shem (v. 22) so it is reckoned that this verse is showing Asshur had settled in the area two hundred miles north of Babylon in *Nineveh* but Nimrod went forth into Asshur and invaded it, annexing it to his own kingdom. Eventually this would later become Assyria. The city of Nineveh is named after Nimrod's son Ninus.

10:13–14 Here are listed the descendants of *Mizraim* (Egypt). Most of them are difficult to trace in secular records since they migrated deeper into Africa. It is known that the *Pathrusim* dwelt in Pathros which is Upper Egypt, and the *Caphtorim* are identified with the *Philistim* (Philistines) in the Bible.

10:15 *Sidon*. Firstborn of Canaan. Sidon still exists today and was the chief city of the Phoenicians. *Heth* is the ancestor of the Hittites who were a great empire in Asia Minor for over eight hundred years. When that empire crumbled, many went east, possibly to China or Mongolia.

10:16 The *Amorite* was referred to in secular records as the Amurru.

10:17 The *Sinite* may be connected to the wilderness of Sin, Mount Sinai, an Assyrian god Sin, and Sinim or China (Isa. 49:12).

10:21–31 The descendants of Shem.

10:21 *Shem also, the father of all the children of Eber.* Some suggest that *Eber* is the origin of the term "Hebrews," but that is not likely.

10:22 *Elam* is part of Persia (now Iran). *Asshur* became Assyria, but his settlement was taken over by Nimrod (see v. 11). *Arphaxad* is linked to the Chaldeans. *Lud* is the origin of Lydia in what is now western Turkey, and *Aram* is the old name for Syria. The language Aramaic was used very widely across the ancient world (2 Kings 18:26, and Christ speaking on the cross in Mark 15:34).

10:23 *Uz* is the name for Job's homeland (Job 1:1).

10:25 *Peleg* means "division" and probably means that the division of Babel took place in his lifetime (*for in his days was the earth divided*).

10:32 *after their generations, in their nations*. This chapter has given the true origin of the nations of the world. Not all details are there but there is sufficient structure for all to see what our true origins are as a human race after the flood.

after their generations, in their nations: and by these were the nations divided in the earth after the flood.

CHAPTER 11

AND the whole earth was of one language, and of
one speech.
2 And it came to pass, as they journeyed from the
east, that they found a plain in the land of Shinar;
and they dwelt there.
3 And they said one to another, Go to, let us make
brick, and burn them throughly. And they had
brick for stone, and slime had they for morter.
4 And they said, Go to, let us build us a city and a
tower, whose top *may reach* unto heaven; and let
us make us a name, lest we be scattered abroad
upon the face of the whole earth.
5 And the LORD came down to see the city and
the tower, which the children of men builded.
6 And the LORD said, Behold, the people *is* one,
and they have all one language; and this they begin to do: and now nothing will be restrained
from them, which they have imagined to do.
7 Go to, let us go down, and there confound their
language, that they may not understand one another's speech.
8 So the LORD scattered them abroad from thence
upon the face of all the earth: and they left off to
build the city.
9 Therefore is the name of it called Babel; because the LORD did there confound the language
of all the earth: and from thence did the LORD
scatter them abroad upon the face of all the earth.
10 ¶ These *are* the generations of Shem: Shem
was an hundred years old, and begat Arphaxad
two years after the flood:
11 And Shem lived after he begat Arphaxad five
hundred years, and begat sons and daughters.
12 And Arphaxad lived five and thirty years, and
begat Salah:
13 And Arphaxad lived after he begat Salah four
hundred and three years, and begat sons and
daughters.
14 And Salah lived thirty years, and begat Eber:
15 And Salah lived after he begat Eber four
hundred and three years, and begat sons and
daughters.
16 And Eber lived four and thirty years, and begat Peleg:
17 And Eber lived after he begat Peleg four
hundred and thirty years, and begat sons and
daughters.
18 And Peleg lived thirty years, and begat Reu:

Thoughts for Personal/Family Worship: Chapter 10

1. **God sovereignly distributes the human race among the nations (Acts 17:26). All the nations come from the three sons of Noah. No man is an island. We are all part of the family of man. There is really only one race: the human race, various colors and cultures notwithstanding. How then should we view other peoples and nations?**
2. **The Bible is not the property of one particular nation, but God's Word for all mankind. The Lord is the God of all flesh (Jer. 32:27). Jesus is the Lord of all (Acts 10:36; Rom. 10:12). Therefore we must not arrogantly exclude people of other nations and ethnicities from the church. Nor may we foolishly say that every nation has its own way to God.**

Chapter 11: ***The Lord frustrates man's attempt to glorify himself by dividing men into different languages and focuses His purposes upon the line of Shem.***

11:1 The people were all of *one language* (Hebrew, "lip") and *one speech* (Hebrew, "word"). The double statement gives great force and emphasis to what Nimrod had done in establishing a one-world dictatorship under himself.

11:2 *plain . . . of Shinar*. Southern Iraq in the valley where the Tigris and Euphrates flow.

11:3 *let us make brick*. God's altars were never made of brick but always natural stone (Ex. 20:25). God's house later (the temple) was made of shaped stone but even then the working of the stone was not done at the temple site (1 Kings 6:7).

11:4 *let us build us a city and a tower . . . let us make us a name*. The emphasis is *us*. It is man making a name for himself; it is not for the glory of God but is for man-centered worship. *lest we be scattered abroad upon the face of the whole earth*. Rebellion against God's command (9:1).

11:6 *one language*. Unity of purpose is invariably aided greatly by a common language. *nothing will be restrained . . . which they have imagined to do*. The warning here is similar to what the Lord said of man before the flood (6:5). These verses underline that man's heart is profoundly wicked and naturally in rebellion against God. The scattering of the people is to diminish the concentration of evil which the tower represented.

11:7 *confound their language*. This is a miraculous act of God and implies that the basic language units did not naturally evolve from each other. Some have suggested that the seventy names of ch. 10 represent the languages that the Lord created in ch. 11.

11:8 *the Lord scattered them abroad*. They are now forced to do what God had originally intended. No doubt Nimrod remained with his immediate tribe and probably the Sumerian civilization is the remnant of his empire.

11:9 *the name of it called Babel*. Some have identified the tower as a ziggurat, an ancient pagan temple shaped like an artificial tiered mountain. Remnants of one are in the vicinity of ancient Babylon. Although of a different Hebrew root, *Babel* is similar in sound to the word translated *confound*.

11:10–26 The *generations of Shem* (see note at 2:4) marks the end of the section describing the time of the Babel dispersion and introduces the genealogy of Shem's offspring. The years each patriarch lived now reduces steadily after the flood. This was probably due to the large climatic changes to harsher conditions afterward. This genealogy is similar in construction to that in ch. 5. The names are repeated in 1 Chron. 1:17–27 (cf. Luke 3:34–36).

11:16 *Peleg*. See note at 10:25.

11:27 *These are the generations of Terah* marks the end of the list of descendants from Shem and introduces the family of *Abram*. The theme of *generations* links this history back to the promise of the Seed who would redeem mankind.

19 And Peleg lived after he begat Reu two hundred
and nine years, and begat sons and daughters.
20 And Reu lived two and thirty years, and begat
Serug:
21 And Reu lived after he begat Serug two
hundred and seven years, and begat sons and
daughters.
22 And Serug lived thirty years, and begat Nahor:
23 And Serug lived after he begat Nahor two hun-
dred years, and begat sons and daughters.
24 And Nahor lived nine and twenty years, and
begat Terah:
25 And Nahor lived after he begat Terah an hun-
dred and nineteen years, and begat sons and
daughters.
26 And Terah lived seventy years, and begat
Abram, Nahor, and Haran.
27 ¶ Now these *are* the generations of Terah:
Terah begat Abram, Nahor, and Haran; and Ha-
ran begat Lot.
28 And Haran died before his father Terah in the
land of his nativity, in Ur of the Chaldees.
29 And Abram and Nahor took them wives: the
name of Abram's wife *was* Sarai; and the name of
Nahor's wife, Milcah, the daughter of Haran, the
father of Milcah, and the father of Iscah.
30 But Sarai was barren; she *had* no child.
31 And Terah took Abram his son, and Lot the
son of Haran his son's son, and Sarai his daughter
in law, his son Abram's wife; and they went forth
with them from Ur of the Chaldees, to go into the
land of Canaan; and they came unto Haran, and
dwelt there.
32 And the days of Terah were two hundred and
five years: and Terah died in Haran.

CHAPTER 12

NOW the LORD had said unto Abram, Get thee out
of thy country, and from thy kindred, and from
thy father's house, unto a land that I will shew
thee:
2 And I will make of thee a great nation, and I
will bless thee, and make thy name great; and
thou shalt be a blessing:
3 And I will bless them that bless thee, and curse
him that curseth thee: and in thee shall all families
of the earth be blessed.
4 So Abram departed, as the LORD had spoken
unto him; and Lot went with him: and Abram
was seventy and five years old when he departed
out of Haran.
5 And Abram took Sarai his wife, and Lot his
brother's son, and all their substance that they had
gathered, and the souls that they had gotten in
Haran; and they went forth to go into the land of
Canaan; and into the land of Canaan they came.
6 ¶ And Abram passed through the land unto the
place of Sichem, unto the plain of Moreh. And the
Canaanite *was* then in the land.
7 And the LORD appeared unto Abram, and
said, Unto thy seed will I give this land: and there

11:29 *Abram and Nahor took them wives.* Abram married his half sister (20:12) and Nahor marries his niece (*Milcah, the daughter of Haran*). These are close marriages but not yet genetically dangerous enough for prohibition which came later (Lev. 18:6).

11:31 *And Terah took Abram his son . . . and they went forth with them from Ur of the Chaldees.* God had called Abram when he was yet in Ur, and some of his family went part of the way with him to *Haran* (see note at 12:1–3).

Thoughts for Personal/Family Worship: Chapter 11

1. **God judges pride. How wicked and rebellious is the natural heart of man! It is not long since the flood, and yet man is again rebelling. Our own hearts will always naturally turn from the Lord's love and grace to our own schemes of self-exaltation. Yet such schemes always set us in opposition to God's purposes and lead to frustration and dishonor. How can we recognize and defeat this satanic impulse of pride in our hearts?**
2. **We must never assume that large gatherings of people and great accomplishments by human ingenuity are good or pleasing to God. Concentrations of people may simply result in concentrations of evil. Though men seek outward glory, God often chooses to work through an unlikely individual following an apparently foolish call—like Abram. Pray for God to teach you how to live by faith and not by sight.**

THE COVENANT WITH ABRAHAM, ISAAC, AND JACOB (12:1—36:43)

The Promises of God to Abraham (12:1—25:18)

Chapter 12: *The Lord called Abram to walk by faith in the promise, and he responded with sincere but imperfect faith.*

12:1–3 *the LORD had said.* Abram, Terah, and Lot left Ur and its idols after the Lord chose to reveal Himself to Abram (15:7; Josh. 24:2–3; Neh. 9:7; Acts 7:1–4). Abram was a prophet (20:7), receiving direct revelation from God. *kindred.* Extended family. God gave two commands: a calling to the inheritance (*Get thee out . . . unto a land*) and a mission to the world (*be a blessing*). The central promise is that *I will bless thee*, implying a reversal of the curse due to sin (3:17) and restoration of creation to God's intention (1:28). This blessing brings justification by faith and the gift of the Spirit (Gal. 3:8–9,14). Specifically, the Lord promised guidance to the inheritance (*I will shew*), multiplication of offspring (*great nation*), honor and glory (*make thy name great*), protection and vindication (*bless them . . . and curse*), and salvation to all nations (*all families of the earth*). The repeated *I will* emphasizes that God would do this as an act of sovereign grace. Yet the call demanded faith (Heb. 11:8).

12:4–9 Abram responded to God's word with obedience (v. 4), public prayer, and praise (vv. 7–8).

12:5 *souls that they had gotten.* People acquired as servants. *Haran.* Spoken of in ancient texts as an important city in culture and commerce.

12:6 *Sichem.* Shechem. Abram had traveled over five hundred miles from Haran after previously traveling from Ur.

12:7 *the LORD appeared.* In a visible way, whether in a dream,

builded he an altar unto the LORD, who appeared
unto him.
8 And he removed from thence unto a moun-
tain on the east of Beth-el, and pitched his tent,
having Beth-el on the west, and Hai on the east:
and there he builded an altar unto the LORD, and
called upon the name of the LORD.
9 And Abram journeyed, going on still toward
the south.
10 ¶ And there was a famine in the land: and
Abram went down into Egypt to sojourn there;
for the famine *was* grievous in the land.
11 And it came to pass, when he was come near to
enter into Egypt, that he said unto Sarai his wife,
Behold now, I know that thou *art* a fair woman
to look upon:
12 Therefore it shall come to pass, when the
Egyptians shall see thee, that they shall say, This
is his wife: and they will kill me, but they will save
thee alive.
13 Say, I pray thee, thou *art* my sister: that it may
be well with me for thy sake; and my soul shall live
because of thee.
14 ¶ And it came to pass, that, when Abram
was come into Egypt, the Egyptians beheld the
woman that she *was* very fair.
15 The princes also of Pharaoh saw her, and com-
mended her before Pharaoh: and the woman was
taken into Pharaoh's house.
16 And he entreated Abram well for her sake: and
he had sheep, and oxen, and he asses, and men-
servants, and maidservants, and she asses, and
camels.
17 And the LORD plagued Pharaoh and his house
with great plagues because of Sarai Abram's wife.
18 And Pharaoh called Abram, and said, What *is*
this *that* thou hast done unto me? why didst thou
not tell me that she *was* thy wife?
19 Why saidst thou, She *is* my sister? so I might
have taken her to me to wife: now therefore
behold thy wife, take *her*, and go thy way.
20 And Pharaoh commanded *his* men concern-
ing him: and they sent him away, and his wife, and
all that he had.

CHAPTER 13

AND Abram went up out of Egypt, he, and his
wife, and all that he had, and Lot with him, into
the south.
2 And Abram *was* very rich in cattle, in silver, and
in gold.
3 And he went on his journeys from the south
even to Beth-el, unto the place where his tent had
been at the beginning, between Beth-el and Hai;
4 Unto the place of the altar, which he had made
there at the first: and there Abram called on the
name of the LORD.
5 ¶ And Lot also, which went with Abram, had
flocks, and herds, and tents.
6 And the land was not able to bear them, that
they might dwell together: for their substance was
great, so that they could not dwell together.
7 And there was a strife between the herdmen of
Abram's cattle and the herdmen of Lot's cattle:
and the Canaanite and the Perizzite dwelled then
in the land.
8 And Abram said unto Lot, Let there be no strife,

---

vision, or earthly form (17:1; 18:1; 26:2,24; 32:30; 35:9; 48:3). *seed.* Offspring, a key term in God's promises (3:15; 4:25; 9:9; 22:17). The singular term *seed* points to Christ, and in Him all believers as heirs of God's promise of grace (Gal. 3:16,29). By faith, Abram was like a priest, worshiping at an *altar*.

12:10 *the famine was grievous.* A great trial for Abram, threatening to take his wealth and even his life—a surprise after he traveled there trusting in God's blessing. *went down into Egypt.* Perhaps out of a lack of faith in God's promises (26:1–3). *sojourn.* Dwell for a time as a foreigner in another land.

12:11 *fair.* Beautiful.

12:12–13 Although a believer, Abram responded to this trial with cowardice and telling a half-truth (20:12) instead of protecting his wife.

12:16 *entreated.* Treated. Archaeology has discovered evidence of the domestication of *camels* well before 2000 BC.

12:17 *plagues.* Same word used of final plague on Egypt (Ex. 11:1), perhaps foreshadowing God's judgments on Israel's future slave-masters. Remarkably, God still saved Abram even when his faith was weak and his love was compromised by fear.

Thoughts for Personal/Family Worship: Chapter 12

1. **God's covenant motivates missions. God called Abram to receive His blessing in order to be a blessing to all nations. How much more the new covenant in Christ's blood calls the church to make disciples of all nations. God's covenant people must be willing to give themselves away to reach the world for Christ.**
2. **God blesses only believers. We must walk in the footsteps of Abram by following Christ in faith, obedience, and public worship. Abraham's faith sometimes faltered and he sinned; therefore we should not demand a great faith of ourselves before we can rest assured that Christ has saved us. Let us rather trust Christ to save us even through a weak faith and pray, "Lord, increase our faith."**

Chapter 13: *Abram and Lot respond to conflict in two ways, representing humble faith and selfish worldliness.*

13:2 *very rich.* Abram was a nomadic sheikh, without land yet owning great wealth, large herds of livestock, and hundreds of servants caring for his possessions (14:14).

13:4 *called on the name of the LORD.* Abram prayed for grace from the God of promise (4:26; 12:8; 21:33; 26:25; Ps. 116:4). Mention of the *altar* indicates prayer in public worship with his family and servants, probably with the offering of sacrifices. The life of faith is a life of prayer and worship, including family worship.

13:7 *herdmen.* Men who care for livestock.

13:8–9 Abram went directly to Lot to resolve the conflict (Matt. 5:23–24; 18:15). *I pray thee.* Please. Though he was older than Lot, Abram showed courtesy and deference to his nephew

I pray thee, between me and thee, and between my
herdmen and thy herdmen; for we *be* brethren.
9 *Is* not the whole land before thee? separate thy-
self, I pray thee, from me: if *thou wilt take* the left
hand, then I will go to the right; or if *thou depart*
to the right hand, then I will go to the left.
10 And Lot lifted up his eyes, and beheld all the
plain of Jordan, that it *was* well watered every
where, before the LORD destroyed Sodom and
Gomorrah, *even* as the garden of the LORD, like
the land of Egypt, as thou comest unto Zoar.
11 Then Lot chose him all the plain of Jordan;
and Lot journeyed east: and they separated them-
selves the one from the other.
12 Abram dwelled in the land of Canaan, and Lot
dwelled in the cities of the plain, and pitched *his*
tent toward Sodom.
13 But the men of Sodom *were* wicked and
sinners before the LORD exceedingly.
14 ¶ And the LORD said unto Abram, after that
Lot was separated from him, Lift up now thine
eyes, and look from the place where thou art
northward, and southward, and eastward, and
westward:
15 For all the land which thou seest, to thee will I
give it, and to thy seed for ever.
16 And I will make thy seed as the dust of the
earth: so that if a man can number the dust of the
earth, *then* shall thy seed also be numbered.
17 Arise, walk through the land in the length of it
and in the breadth of it; for I will give it unto thee.
18 Then Abram removed *his* tent, and came and
dwelt in the plain of Mamre, which *is* in Hebron,
and built there an altar unto the LORD.

CHAPTER 14

AND it came to pass in the days of Amraphel king
of Shinar, Arioch king of Ellasar, Chedorlaomer
king of Elam, and Tidal king of nations;
2 *That these* made war with Bera king of Sodom,
and with Birsha king of Gomorrah, Shinab king
of Admah, and Shemeber king of Zeboiim, and
the king of Bela, which is Zoar.
3 All these were joined together in the vale of
Siddim, which is the salt sea.
4 Twelve years they served Chedorlaomer, and in
the thirteenth year they rebelled.
5 And in the fourteenth year came Chedor-
laomer, and the kings that *were* with him, and
smote the Rephaims in Ashteroth Karnaim, and
the Zuzims in Ham, and the Emims in Shaveh
Kiriathaim,
6 And the Horites in their mount Seir, unto El-
paran, which *is* by the wilderness.
7 And they returned, and came to En-mishpat,
which *is* Kadesh, and smote all the country of the
Amalekites, and also the Amorites, that dwelt in
Hazezon-tamar.
8 And there went out the king of Sodom, and the
king of Gomorrah, and the king of Admah, and
the king of Zeboiim, and the king of Bela (the
same *is* Zoar;) and they joined battle with them
in the vale of Siddim;

and offered a practical solution to the problem, allowing Lot to take the better portion.

13:10 *well watered . . . even as the garden of the LORD.* See 2:8–14. Genesis treats the garden of Eden as a real location, not a mythical story.

13:11 Lot acted in selfishness and greed with eyes dazzled by worldly gain.

13:13 Lot turned a blind eye to the danger of taking his household near to Sodom, whose men were *wicked and sinners before the LORD exceedingly*.

13:14–17 The Lord blessed Abram with a restatement of the promise of an inheritance (v. 14; 12:1,7), and multiplication of offspring (v. 16; 12:2). *seed.* See note at 12:7. *dust of the earth.* Ironically, this reminder of man's humble origin and death because of sin (2:7; 3:19; 18:27) also becomes an image of the vast numbers (Isa. 40:12) of the covenant offspring (28:14). This promise was fulfilled, at least in part, in the kingdom of Solomon (2 Chron. 1:9).

13:18 Again, Abram responded to God's promises with worship (v. 4).

Thoughts for Personal/Family Worship: Chapter 13

1. **Abram is a model of peacemaking. Like him, we should respond to conflict by speaking directly and courteously to the other person, offering a reasonable solution to the problem, and deferring largely to his preferences. Such peacemaking is possible only when we exercise faith in God's promises and regularly look to Him in prayer and worship; then we can let go of earthly gain because we have the Lord.**
2. **God's promises to multiply Abram's offspring and give them dominion over the land found partial fulfillment in the days of Solomon. But they point further to the kingdom of Jesus Christ. Those who follow in the footsteps of Abram's faith are being multiplied in every nation and will one day inherit the earth. Christians may therefore claim these promises and be optimistic about the church's future. Following Christ may result in worldly losses and suffering injustice, but one day a great multitude that no one can number will reign with Christ in the new heavens and earth.**

Chapter 14: ***War engulfs the region so that Abram must rescue Lot, receiving the blessing of Salem's priest-king, Melchizedek.***

14:1 *Shinar.* Babylon (in modern Iraq), site of the Tower of Babel (10:10; 11:2). *Ellasar.* City of Larsa by the Euphrates River in southeast Mesopotamia (also in Iraq). *Elam.* Nation east of Babylon (in modern Iran). *Tidal.* Perhaps Tudhaliya, a king of the Hittites (modern Turkey). This then was a coalition of the major powers north and east of the land of Canaan.

14:2 These cities were in the region immediately east and south of the present Dead Sea.

14:5 *Rephaims . . . Emims.* Sometimes translated "giants"; ethnic groups noted for their large size (Deut. 2:10–11,20–21; 3:11,13). The victories of vv. 5–8, especially over such strong

9 With Chedorlaomer the king of Elam, and with Tidal king of nations, and Amraphel king of Shinar, and Arioch king of Ellasar; four kings with five.

10 And the vale of Siddim *was full of* slimepits; and the kings of Sodom and Gomorrah fled, and fell there; and they that remained fled to the mountain.

11 And they took all the goods of Sodom and Gomorrah, and all their victuals, and went their way.

12 And they took Lot, Abram's brother's son, who dwelt in Sodom, and his goods, and departed.

13 ¶ And there came one that had escaped, and told Abram the Hebrew; for he dwelt in the plain of Mamre the Amorite, brother of Eshcol, and brother of Aner: and these *were* confederate with Abram.

14 And when Abram heard that his brother was taken captive, he armed his trained *servants*, born in his own house, three hundred and eighteen, and pursued *them* unto Dan.

15 And he divided himself against them, he and his servants, by night, and smote them, and pursued them unto Hobah, which *is* on the left hand of Damascus.

16 And he brought back all the goods, and also brought again his brother Lot, and his goods, and the women also, and the people.

17 ¶ And the king of Sodom went out to meet him after his return from the slaughter of Chedorlaomer, and of the kings that *were* with him, at the valley of Shaveh, which *is* the king's dale.

18 And Melchizedek king of Salem brought forth bread and wine: and he *was* the priest of the most high God.

19 And he blessed him, and said, Blessed *be* Abram of the most high God, possessor of heaven and earth:

20 And blessed be the most high God, which hath delivered thine enemies into thy hand. And he gave him tithes of all.

21 And the king of Sodom said unto Abram, Give me the persons, and take the goods to thyself.

22 And Abram said to the king of Sodom, I have lift up mine hand unto the LORD, the most high God, the possessor of heaven and earth,

23 That I will not *take* from a thread even to a shoelatchet, and that I will not take any thing that *is* thine, lest thou shouldest say, I have made Abram rich:

24 Save only that which the young men have eaten, and the portion of the men which went with me, Aner, Eshcol, and Mamre; let them take their portion.

CHAPTER 15

AFTER these things the word of the LORD came unto Abram in a vision, saying, Fear not, Abram: I *am* thy shield, *and* thy exceeding great reward.

2 And Abram said, Lord GOD, what wilt thou

---

people, show the great power of the forces of *Chedorlaomer*.

14:10 *slimepits*. Pits of natural tar and oily asphalt. Asphalt is still found at the Dead Sea. People or animals falling into such pits are caught in the thick, sticky fluid and die.

14:11 *victuals*. Food.

14:13 *confederate*. In an alliance with Abram by covenant.

14:14 Abram was like a king, leading his people in war. *Dan* is probably the city in the far north of Israel (1 Sam. 3:20) which was named Laish at this time, and renamed after being conquered by the tribe of Dan (Judg. 18:29). In that case, a later scribe updated the text after Moses died so readers would understand. *Dan* may also be another city, perhaps Danjaan (2 Sam. 24:6).

14:15 Abram pursued the four kings for no less than 120 miles. Attacking from different directions *by night* to gain surprise shows Abram's wisdom. Faith in God does not hinder wise strategies and tactics. To drive away his defeated enemies, he chased them another 50 miles beyond *Damascus*.

14:18 *Melchizedek*. Literally, "king of righteousness." *Salem*. "Peace." Perhaps Jerusalem, capital city of David's kingdom and God's temple (Ps. 76:2), but references to a Salem occur in various texts from the Ancient Near East. *bread and wine*. Not a sacrifice, but a meal of thanksgiving. *priest*. As king and priest, he foreshadowed Christ (Ps. 110:4; Heb. 7).

14:20 Abram's victory came *from the most high God* who rules over all things and to Him went the glory. *tithes*. A tenth of the spoils of his victory, a sign of giving honor (28:22; Heb. 7:4–10).

14:21 *persons*. Servants captured in battle.

14:23 *shoelatchet*. Strap of a sandal. Abram was moved not by greed, but love.

14:24 *Save*. Except. Abram saw to it that his servants (*young men*) and allies received fair pay for their military service, even though he refused any reward from Sodom.

Thoughts for Personal/Family Worship: Chapter 14

1. **Faith and love draw believers into combat with evil. Though a Christian may at times fall into cowardice, he is not ruled by a spirit of fear but of power, love, and self-control. He is a soldier in the Lord's army. Therefore, believers, let us act like men and engage in the battle between good and evil with courageous action.**
2. **The church faces overwhelming odds but overcomes. How? First, our God is the Most High, the Creator and Possessor of all things. His power guarantees our victory. Second, believers have a Priest and King to bless us, Jesus Christ, after the order of Melchizedek. His intercession guarantees that God will bless His people despite their sins and not curse them as they deserve. This makes them more than overcomers in Christ Jesus.**

Chapter 15: *The Lord renews His promise, counts Abram righteous by faith, and confirms the promise in a solemn covenant.*

15:1 *word of the LORD . . . vision*. See note at 12:7. *Fear not, Abram*. The Lord promised that He would be his protection (*shield*) from evil and his all-sufficient good (*exceeding great reward*).

give me, seeing I go childless, and the steward of
my house *is* this Eliezer of Damascus?
3 And Abram said, Behold, to me thou hast given
no seed: and, lo, one born in my house is mine
heir.
4 And, behold, the word of the LORD *came* unto
him, saying, This shall not be thine heir; but he
that shall come forth out of thine own bowels
shall be thine heir.
5 And he brought him forth abroad, and said,
Look now toward heaven, and tell the stars, if
thou be able to number them: and he said unto
him, So shall thy seed be.
6 And he believed in the LORD; and he counted it
to him for righteousness.
7 And he said unto him, I *am* the LORD that
brought thee out of Ur of the Chaldees, to give
thee this land to inherit it.
8 And he said, Lord GOD, whereby shall I know
that I shall inherit it?
9 And he said unto him, Take me an heifer of
three years old, and a she goat of three years old,
and a ram of three years old, and a turtledove, and
a young pigeon.
10 And he took unto him all these, and divided
them in the midst, and laid each piece one against
another: but the birds divided he not.
11 And when the fowls came down upon the car-
cases, Abram drove them away.
12 And when the sun was going down, a deep
sleep fell upon Abram; and, lo, an horror of great
darkness fell upon him.
13 And he said unto Abram, Know of a surety
that thy seed shall be a stranger in a land *that is*
not theirs, and shall serve them; and they shall af-
flict them four hundred years;
14 And also that nation, whom they shall serve,
will I judge: and afterward shall they come out
with great substance.
15 And thou shalt go to thy fathers in peace; thou
shalt be buried in a good old age.
16 But in the fourth generation they shall come
hither again: for the iniquity of the Amorites *is*
not yet full.
17 And it came to pass, that, when the sun went
down, and it was dark, behold a smoking furnace,
and a burning lamp that passed between those
pieces.
18 In the same day the LORD made a covenant
with Abram, saying, Unto thy seed have I given
this land, from the river of Egypt unto the great
river, the river Euphrates:
19 The Kenites, and the Kenizzites, and the
Kadmonites,
20 And the Hittites, and the Perizzites, and the
Rephaims,
21 And the Amorites, and the Canaanites, and the
Girgashites, and the Jebusites.

15:2 *LORD GOD*. In Hebrew, *Adonai-Jehovah*. Abram exercised faith by praying titles of God's Lordship (Jer. 32:17). *steward*. Literally, "son of possession," Abram's anticipated heir (v. 3).
15:4 *out of thine own bowels*. A child begotten of Abram's body.
15:5 *abroad*. Outside. *tell the stars*. Count them; same Hebrew word as *number*. God repeated the promise of multiplied offspring (12:2; 13:16; Heb. 11:12).
15:6 *he believed in the LORD*. Despite his own inability to produce a child, Abram trusted that God would fulfill His promise by His supernatural power (Rom. 4:18–21). Ultimately, his faith rested in the promise of Christ (John 8:56; see note at 12:7). *counted it to him for righteousness*. The Lord, as righteous Judge (18:25), did not impute or count Abram's sins against him, but gave him a verdict of righteous. He was justified solely through his faith in the promise, not his works, which could merit nothing, nor circumcision, which came later (Rom. 4:1–12). Even faith itself was not Abram's righteousness, for his faith was imperfect (12:1–20); rather, faith receives the righteousness of Christ as a free gift from God (Rom. 3:24; 4:4; 5:17). Believers are Abraham's children and share the same righteousness by faith in Christ alone (Gal. 3:6–14).
15:7 *I am the LORD that brought thee out*. Abram's Redeemer (Isa. 29:22). The same expression is used of the Lord's redemption of Israel from Egypt (Ex. 13:9; 20:2; 29:46; Ps. 81:10).
15:10–11 Cutting the sacrifices in two and exposing them to birds of prey was a sign that death and humiliation would fall on anyone who broke the covenant (Jer. 34:18–20).
15:13 *Know of a surety*. Know for sure. God's covenant confirmed His promises so that believers might have a stron g consolation (Heb. 6:13–20).
15:14 *great substance*. Many possessions. God planned the details of Israel's exodus centuries before it took place (Isa. 46:10).
15:16 *hither*. To here.
15:17 *furnace . . . lamp*. A firepot for a portable stove and a torch for light. These visible signs of God's holy presence in Christ passed between the sacrifices while Abram slept, showing that the covenant would be fulfilled by grace alone, not human efforts. The Son of God Himself would die so that the covenant would stand firm.
15:18 *made a covenant*. Literally, "cut a covenant," an allusion to the sacrifices (v. 10). *given this land*. God later gave the land to Israel through Joshua and especially Solomon (2 Kings 4:21,24). In Christ God's promise expands to include inheriting the whole earth in Christ's kingdom, of which the land of Canaan was a type (Matt. 5:3–5; Rom. 4:13; Heb. 11:8–16).

Thoughts for Personal/Family Worship: Chapter 15

1. **God's promise of salvation comes to us in our hopeless inability to save ourselves. In our own strength, we are as spiritually barren as Abram and Sarai. But, by the Spirit's grace, if we trust in the promise of Christ in the gospel, the righteous Judge will declare us righteous in His sight. You have warrant to trust Christ, for the Lord has established His promise in a covenant. It depends not on your worthiness—not even on how strong your faith and deep your repentance is—but on the Lord alone, who shed His own blood to save the church.**
2. **Theologians have often said that God's gracious covenant is one-sided in its establishment, and two-sided in its outworking. Based on this chapter, how can we confirm that God establishes His covenant with His people out of pure one-sided grace? Why is the covenant two-sided in its outworking?**

FAITH IN GOD

Faith is the resting of the heart on God, the Author of life and eternal salvation, so that we may be saved from all evil through Him and may follow all good unto Him (Ps. 37:5; Isa. 10:20; Jer. 17:7). Faith welcomes a sweet exchange of sins for righteousness, wherein a sinful man is credited as righteous in Christ, Christ having been made sin for him (Rom. 3:21–26). Faith then follows with outward evidences of itself, which are commonly called "good works."

Faith is comprised of two distinct but inseparable tenets: an act of understanding and an act of will. *First*, faith involves an act of understanding wherein the mind gives assent to evidence. This is a knowledge of the declarations in Scripture regarding the gospel of Christ (1 Cor. 1:23; 2:2; 2 Cor. 5:19). However, the message itself is not the object of faith (John 20:31). The true object of faith is the Person in whom faith is placed—that is, God Himself through Jesus Christ (1 Tim. 4:10). Man not only believes *about* God but *in* God. Moreover, God is the ultimate object of faith, while Christ is the mediate object of faith (Rom. 6:11; 2 Cor. 3:4; 1 Peter 1:21). This means that true, saving faith is an understanding placed in God through Jesus Christ.

However, bare belief in God through Christ divorced from an act of will is not saving faith (John 7:17; 8:31,32; 1 John 2:3). This act of will is the second necessary aspect of saving faith. Not a mere act of intellect, the exercising of faith involves an act of choice by the whole man. Faith is a determined resolve. It is a genuine turning of the will away from reliance on self toward dependence on God. This entails surrender by a consent of the will (John 6:35). To believe in God through Christ, then, is to cling to God, to lean on God, and to rest in God as our all-sufficient life and salvation (Deut. 30:20; Pss. 37:3–5; 62:7; Prov. 3:5; Isa. 10:20; 31:1; 50:10; Rom. 10:11).

Faith is a genuine receiving (John 1:12)—a *sure* dependence upon God (Prov. 3:5). Accordingly, faith is not uncertain and doubtful, a result of man's imperfect knowledge of a testimony alone. Though scriptural testimony is sure in itself (John 9:29; Rom. 3:4; 1 Cor. 2:5; 2 Peter 1:20–21), faith is most certain because it unites itself to God's Person. He who is infallible lends infallibility to true, saving faith itself. Faith lays hold of the power of the whole triune God in salvation (Mark 11:23; Luke 17:6; Rom. 1:16–17). Unfortunately, due to man's imperfect inclinations, the surety of true faith often feels debilitated. This is why man supposes that the assurance of his faith is questionable—and why he needs the inner persuasion and strengthening of faith by the Holy Spirit (1 Cor. 12:3; cf. Mark 9:24). Nonetheless, true faith, whether a feeble hand or a strong grasp, is faith *in God*—and therein lies assurance (cf. Matt. 9:21; Heb. 11). Therefore, faith so certainly unites man to God in Christ that none can remove him or separate him from God (John 10:28–29; Rom. 8:35–39).

In addition, though, general intellectual assent and reliance without any life is no saving faith (James 2:24). Faith is an assent based on knowledge whereby *man lives to God in Christ*. Faith entails declaring God our God in Christ; this is known as submission to the Sovereign. While it is the first act whereby we are saved by God in Christ, faith evokes many resultant acts of good works. Faith brings with itself man's living to God. From the spring of faith flow sincere resolutions to a life of obedience. Furthermore, because faith in God guarantees a progressive holiness—both a separation from sin and a clinging to righteousness—the test of true, saving faith is summarized simply: faith that saves is faith that works.

—adapted from William Ames, *The Marrow of Theology*, 1.3

CHAPTER 16

NOW Sarai Abram's wife bare him no children:
and she had an handmaid, an Egyptian, whose
name *was* Hagar.
2 And Sarai said unto Abram, Behold now, the
LORD hath restrained me from bearing: I pray
thee, go in unto my maid; it may be that I may
obtain children by her. And Abram hearkened to
the voice of Sarai.
3 And Sarai Abram's wife took Hagar her maid
the Egyptian, after Abram had dwelt ten years in
the land of Canaan, and gave her to her husband
Abram to be his wife.
4 ¶ And he went in unto Hagar, and she con-
ceived: and when she saw that she had conceived,
her mistress was despised in her eyes.
5 And Sarai said unto Abram, My wrong *be* upon
thee: I have given my maid into thy bosom; and
when she saw that she had conceived, I was despised
in her eyes: the LORD judge between me and thee.
6 But Abram said unto Sarai, Behold, thy maid *is*
in thy hand; do to her as it pleaseth thee. And when
Sarai dealt hardly with her, she fled from her face.
7 ¶ And the angel of the LORD found her by a
fountain of water in the wilderness, by the foun-
tain in the way to Shur.
8 And he said, Hagar, Sarai's maid, whence
camest thou? and whither wilt thou go? And she
said, I flee from the face of my mistress Sarai.
9 And the angel of the LORD said unto her, Return
to thy mistress, and submit thyself under her hands.
10 And the angel of the LORD said unto her, I will
multiply thy seed exceedingly, that it shall not be
numbered for multitude.
11 And the angel of the LORD said unto her,
Behold, thou *art* with child, and shalt bear a son,
and shalt call his name Ishmael; because the LORD
hath heard thy affliction.
12 And he will be a wild man; his hand *will be*
against every man, and every man's hand against
him; and he shall dwell in the presence of all his
brethren.
13 And she called the name of the LORD that
spake unto her, Thou God seest me: for she said,
Have I also here looked after him that seeth me?
14 Wherefore the well was called Beer-lahai-roi;
behold, *it is* between Kadesh and Bered.
15 ¶ And Hagar bare Abram a son: and Abram
called his son's name, which Hagar bare, Ishmael.
16 And Abram *was* fourscore and six years old,
when Hagar bare Ishmael to Abram.

CHAPTER 17

AND when Abram was ninety years old and nine,
the LORD appeared to Abram, and said unto him,

Chapter 16: *Sarai gives her servant to Abram to bear them a child. The resulting strife causes Hagar to flee into the wilderness, where the Lord meets her.*

16:2 *the LORD hath restrained me from bearing.* God controls the conception and birth of children (20:18; 25:21; 1 Sam. 1:5–6). *I pray thee.* Please. *hearkened.* Listened. It was culturally acceptable for a barren wife to provide a slave-concubine for her husband to get children but contrary to God's will for marriage (2:24). Sexual relations outside of monogamous marriage are sinful and sure to produce inevitable conflict.

16:6 *in thy hand.* In your power to treat as you please. Abram continues to be sadly passive, first following Sarai's bad advice and then leaving it to her to deal with resulting problems. *dealt hardly.* Hurt and humiliated her. *fled from her face.* Ran from her presence.

16:7 The *angel of the LORD* is a supernatural being sent from the Lord as His messenger. Yet the particular being who spoke to Hagar is also "the LORD" and "God" (v. 13). Therefore He is God the Son, sent from the Father prior to His incarnation to mediate grace; this is a Christophany. *fountain.* Natural spring of water. *way to Shur.* Road southwest from the land toward the Red Sea and Egypt—Hagar's roots (20:1; Ex. 15:22).

16:8–11 The divine *angel* questioned Hagar to convict her of her sin, commanded her to repent (*return . . . and submit*), and gave her a promise of mercy. *the LORD hath heard thy affliction.* Ishmael's name ("God hears") testifies that the Lord has compassion on the suffering (Ex. 3:7).

16:12 *wild man.* Literally, "a wild donkey of a man," that is, untamable. *in the presence of all his brethren.* Probably, "in defiance of" or "against all his brethren."

16:13 *Thou God seest me.* Literally, "the God of seeing." Here used as a divine name. *Have I also here looked after him that seeth me.* I have seen the One who sees me. God's sight here is not just knowledge but also His compassion and care (Ex. 2:25), "see" sometimes being translated "provide" (22:8,14). God granted Hagar, an abused, foreign slave-woman, the rare privilege of seeing His glory and experiencing His compassion.

16:14 *Kadesh.* Probably Kadesh-barnea, at the southern edge of the land toward Egypt.

16:16 *fourscore and six years.* Eighty-six years old.

Thoughts for Personal/Family Worship: Chapter 16

1. **Waiting on God requires faith. We will be tempted to take matters into our own hands when prayer and lawful means do not obtain what we desire. We must resist this and cling to God's promises. It is especially important for fathers not to be passive like Abram during such trials, but to lead their families in justice and love. Compromising God's laws may bring temporary relief, but bears bitter fruit. Let us therefore repent of our sins and face their consequences with faith in God's mercy.**
2. **God grants His precious mercies to those who have suffered oppression for their social status, gender, or ethnicity. Christ reaches out to all people of all nations in the gospel. He makes the poor rich in faith and enriches the rest of the world through their experience of God. Abram no doubt learned more about God when Hagar returned bearing news of how God met her in the wilderness. Yet God commands us to repent of rebellion and submit to proper authority. His way is not to overthrow all structures of authority and obedience but to renew His creations of marriage and family.**

Chapter 17: *The Lord gives a fuller revelation of His covenant and institutes circumcision as a sign of the covenant between Him and Abraham's seed.*

I *am* the Almighty God; walk before me, and be
thou perfect.
2 And I will make my covenant between me and
thee, and will multiply thee exceedingly.
3 And Abram fell on his face: and God talked
with him, saying,
4 As for me, behold, my covenant *is* with thee,
and thou shalt be a father of many nations.
5 Neither shall thy name any more be called
Abram, but thy name shall be Abraham; for a
father of many nations have I made thee.
6 And I will make thee exceeding fruitful, and I
will make nations of thee, and kings shall come
out of thee.
7 And I will establish my covenant between me
and thee and thy seed after thee in their gener-
ations for an everlasting covenant, to be a God
unto thee, and to thy seed after thee.
8 And I will give unto thee, and to thy seed after
thee, the land wherein thou art a stranger, all the
land of Canaan, for an everlasting possession; and
I will be their God.
9 ¶ And God said unto Abraham, Thou shalt
keep my covenant therefore, thou, and thy seed
after thee in their generations.
10 This *is* my covenant, which ye shall keep, be-
tween me and you and thy seed after thee; Every
man child among you shall be circumcised.
11 And ye shall circumcise the flesh of your
foreskin; and it shall be a token of the covenant
betwixt me and you.
12 And he that is eight days old shall be circum-
cised among you, every man child in your genera-
tions, he that is born in the house, or bought with
money of any stranger, which *is* not of thy seed.
13 He that is born in thy house, and he that is
bought with thy money, must needs be circum-
cised: and my covenant shall be in your flesh for
an everlasting covenant.
14 And the uncircumcised man child whose flesh
of his foreskin is not circumcised, that soul shall
be cut off from his people; he hath broken my
covenant.
15 ¶ And God said unto Abraham, As for Sarai
thy wife, thou shalt not call her name Sarai, but
Sarah *shall* her name *be*.
16 And I will bless her, and give thee a son also of
her: yea, I will bless her, and she shall be *a mother*
of nations; kings of people shall be of her.
17 Then Abraham fell upon his face, and laughed,
and said in his heart, Shall *a child* be born unto
him that is an hundred years old? and shall Sarah,
that is ninety years old, bear?
18 And Abraham said unto God, O that Ishmael
might live before thee!
19 And God said, Sarah thy wife shall bear thee
a son indeed; and thou shalt call his name Isaac:
and I will establish my covenant with him for an
everlasting covenant, *and* with his seed after him.
20 And as for Ishmael, I have heard thee: Behold,
I have blessed him, and will make him fruitful,
and will multiply him exceedingly; twelve princes
shall he beget, and I will make him a great nation.
21 But my covenant will I establish with Isaac,
which Sarah shall bear unto thee at this set time
in the next year.
22 And he left off talking with him, and God went
up from Abraham.
23 ¶ And Abraham took Ishmael his son, and
all that were born in his house, and all that were

17:1 *Almighty.* Hebrew, *Shaddai*, a title of God's majesty and power to bless and to judge (49:25; Job 37:22–24; Isa. 13:6). *walk before me.* See note at 5:22. *perfect.* Not sinlessness, but righteous integrity and sincerity (6:9), an Old Testament word for sanctification referring to wholehearted consecration.
17:2 *make my covenant.* Literally, "give my covenant." The covenant was officially "cut" earlier (see note at 15:18), and the Lord now revealed it in a fuller way. The word *covenant* appears more often in this chapter (thirteen times) than any other chapter in the Bible.
17:3 *Abram fell on his face.* He responded to God's word of grace with worship (12:7; 13:18).
17:4–6 God renewed His promise to multiply Abram's offspring (12:2; 13:16; 15:5), changing his name from *Abram* (exalted father) to *Abraham* (father of a multitude). He would be not only the father of a nation, namely, Israel, but the *father of many nations*, that is, people from every nation who have the same faith in God's promise (Rom. 4:16–17). Abraham's line would produce *kings* (v. 16; 35:11), a promise later applied to the tribe of Judah (49:8–12) and fulfilled ultimately in Jesus Christ.
17:7–8 *to be a God unto thee.* Or, "to be your God." *stranger.* Foreigner residing (sojourning) away from his homeland. In the covenant, God gives Himself to Abraham and his offspring (*seed*), who were pilgrims and strangers on earth (Heb. 11:16). *the land.* See note at 15:18.
17:9 *keep my covenant.* They must obey the covenant in order to receive the promises (vv. 1–2; 18:19; Ex. 19:5; Deut. 7:11–12), the opposite of which is covenant breaking (v. 14).
17:10–12 *man child.* Male (1:27). *token.* Sign or distinctive mark (1:14; 9:12–13,17), here a seal of the righteousness that Abraham had already received by faith (Rom. 4:11). *betwixt.* Between. The outward sign of covenant keeping was the circumcision of every male *eight days old* or older in Abraham's household, including the servants. The cutting of skin from the male reproductive organ represented the removal of sin from the *seed* and the placement in the heart of faithful love toward the Lord (Deut. 10:16; 30:6; Jer. 4:4; Acts 7:51; Rom. 2:29).
17:15–16 Her name would no longer be "my princess" (*Sarai*), but simply "princess" (*Sarah*), for she would become the royal mother of many *nations* and *kings*, including Christ Himself.
17:19 *Isaac.* Meaning, "he laughs." A reminder both of their doubts (v. 17; 18:12) and of the joy God gave them by His almighty grace (21:6).
17:20–21 As the son of Abraham's love and prayers, *Ishmael* received physical blessings from God and the external sign of circumcision (v. 23), but God said *my covenant will I establish with Isaac*, not Ishmael. God is free in choosing His people (Rom. 9:6–7).

bought with his money, every male among the
men of Abraham's house; and circumcised the
flesh of their foreskin in the selfsame day, as God
had said unto him.
24 And Abraham *was* ninety years old and nine,
when he was circumcised in the flesh of his
foreskin.
25 And Ishmael his son *was* thirteen years old,
when he was circumcised in the flesh of his
foreskin.
26 In the selfsame day was Abraham circumcised,
and Ishmael his son.
27 And all the men of his house, born in the
house, and bought with money of the stranger,
were circumcised with him.

CHAPTER 18

AND the LORD appeared unto him in the plains
of Mamre: and he sat in the tent door in the heat
of the day;
2 And he lift up his eyes and looked, and, lo, three
men stood by him: and when he saw *them*, he ran
to meet them from the tent door, and bowed him-
self toward the ground,
3 And said, My Lord, if now I have found favour
in thy sight, pass not away, I pray thee, from thy
servant:
4 Let a little water, I pray you, be fetched, and
wash your feet, and rest yourselves under the tree:
5 And I will fetch a morsel of bread, and com-
fort ye your hearts; after that ye shall pass on: for
therefore are ye come to your servant. And they
said, So do, as thou hast said.
6 And Abraham hastened into the tent unto
Sarah, and said, Make ready quickly three mea-
sures of fine meal, knead *it*, and make cakes upon
the hearth.
7 And Abraham ran unto the herd, and fetcht a
calf tender and good, and gave *it* unto a young
man; and he hasted to dress it.
8 And he took butter, and milk, and the calf
which he had dressed, and set *it* before them; and
he stood by them under the tree, and they did eat.
9 ¶ And they said unto him, Where *is* Sarah thy
wife? And he said, Behold, in the tent.
10 And he said, I will certainly return unto thee
according to the time of life; and, lo, Sarah thy
wife shall have a son. And Sarah heard *it* in the
tent door, which *was* behind him.
11 Now Abraham and Sarah *were* old *and* well
stricken in age; *and* it ceased to be with Sarah af-
ter the manner of women.
12 Therefore Sarah laughed within herself, say-
ing, After I am waxed old shall I have pleasure, my
lord being old also?
13 And the LORD said unto Abraham, Wherefore
did Sarah laugh, saying, Shall I of a surety bear a
child, which am old?
14 Is any thing too hard for the LORD? At the time
appointed I will return unto thee, according to
the time of life, and Sarah shall have a son.
15 Then Sarah denied, saying, I laughed not; for
she was afraid. And he said, Nay; but thou didst
laugh.
16 ¶ And the men rose up from thence, and
looked toward Sodom: and Abraham went with
them to bring them on the way.
17 And the LORD said, Shall I hide from Abraham
that thing which I do;
18 Seeing that Abraham shall surely become a
great and mighty nation, and all the nations of

17:23–26 The painful circumcision of Abraham, Ishmael, and their whole house that same day showed Abraham's wholehearted submission to God's covenant.

Thoughts for Personal/Family Worship: Chapter 17

1. **Through the covenant, the Lord creates a bond of shared life between Himself and His people. He gives Himself to the elect in sovereign love and He moves them to give themselves to Him in submissive love. Let us marvel and be filled with joy at the kindness of God—that He would lower Himself thus!**
2. **Circumcised bodies meant nothing without circumcised hearts. While we must obey God's laws in the outward forms of worship, we dare not be satisfied with external religion. Ishmael had his father's love, prayers, and circumcision, but proved to be a "wild donkey" of a man. Let us cry out to God for a truly converted heart to love Him and keep His covenant. Is this your daily prayer?**

Chapter 18: *The Lord visits Abraham in human form, declares another promise concerning Isaac, and draws Abraham out to intercede for Sodom.*

18:1 *the LORD appeared unto him.* This is the first record of the Lord appearing to Abraham in human form, a foreshadowing of the incarnation of Christ through a birth more miraculous than that of Isaac (Luke 1:26–38).

18:2–8 Abraham was eager to show humble and generous hospitality to guests. It is not clear whether he knew his guests were heavenly visitors, but it is suggested by *My Lord* (Hebrew, *adonai*, v. 3; 15:2,8; 18:27,30–32; 20:4). This form of the word refers uniquely to deity and is not the same word as Sarah's polite "my lord" (Hebrew, *adoni*, 18:12).

18:4 *wash your feet.* A common courtesy for guests in an age when people walked from place to place on dirt roads (19:2; 24:32; 43:24; Luke 7:44).

18:5 *morsel of bread.* Polite understatement for the feast of bread, butter, beef, and milk given them. *comfort ye your hearts.* Be refreshed and strengthened (Judg. 19:5).

18:6 *three measures.* Three "seahs"—seven quarts or twenty-eight cups of flour for each guest.

18:7 *dress.* Prepare or make the meal.

18:10 *according to the time of life.* About that same time next year (2 Kings 4:16–17).

18:11 *well stricken in age.* Literally, "going on in days," that is, advanced in age. *ceased . . . after the manner of women.* In menopause; beyond hope of bearing children.

18:13 *of a surety.* Surely, indeed.

18:14 *Is any thing too hard for the LORD?* The phrase often

the earth shall be blessed in him?
19 For I know him, that he will command his
children and his household after him, and they
shall keep the way of the LORD, to do justice and
judgment; that the LORD may bring upon Abra-
ham that which he hath spoken of him.
20 And the LORD said, Because the cry of Sodom
and Gomorrah is great, and because their sin is
very grievous;
21 I will go down now, and see whether they have
done altogether according to the cry of it, which is
come unto me; and if not, I will know.
22 And the men turned their faces from thence,
and went toward Sodom: but Abraham stood yet
before the LORD.
23 ¶ And Abraham drew near, and said, Wilt thou
also destroy the righteous with the wicked?
24 Peradventure there be fifty righteous within
the city: wilt thou also destroy and not spare the
place for the fifty righteous that *are* therein?
25 That be far from thee to do after this manner,
to slay the righteous with the wicked: and that the
righteous should be as the wicked, that be far from
thee: Shall not the Judge of all the earth do right?
26 And the LORD said, If I find in Sodom fifty
righteous within the city, then I will spare all the
place for their sakes.
27 And Abraham answered and said, Behold now,
I have taken upon me to speak unto the Lord,
which *am but* dust and ashes:
28 Peradventure there shall lack five of the fifty
righteous: wilt thou destroy all the city for *lack of*
five? And he said, If I find there forty and five, I
will not destroy *it*.
29 And he spake unto him yet again, and said,
Peradventure there shall be forty found there.
And he said, I will not do *it* for forty's sake.
30 And he said *unto him*, Oh let not the Lord be
angry, and I will speak: Peradventure there shall
thirty be found there. And he said, I will not do *it*,
if I find thirty there.
31 And he said, Behold now, I have taken upon
me to speak unto the Lord: Peradventure there
shall be twenty found there. And he said, I will
not destroy *it* for twenty's sake.
32 And he said, Oh let not the Lord be angry, and
I will speak yet but this once: Peradventure ten
shall be found there. And he said, I will not de-
stroy *it* for ten's sake.
33 And the LORD went his way, as soon as he had
left communing with Abraham: and Abraham re-
turned unto his place.

CHAPTER 19

AND there came two angels to Sodom at even; and
Lot sat in the gate of Sodom: and Lot seeing *them*
rose up to meet them; and he bowed himself with
his face toward the ground;
2 And he said, Behold now, my lords, turn in,
I pray you, into your servant's house, and tarry
all night, and wash your feet, and ye shall rise up
early, and go on your ways. And they said, Nay;
but we will abide in the street all night.
3 And he pressed upon them greatly; and they
turned in unto him, and entered into his house;
and he made them a feast, and did bake unleav-
ened bread, and they did eat.

---

refers to the miraculous; what is impossible to man is not to God. God promised to give a son to an old, barren woman by His power, calling her to trust His Word. By the same power He created the world out of nothing, caused His Son to be born of a virgin, and raises the dead (Luke 1:35,37; Rom. 4:17–21). Like Isaac, the children of God are created not by human power or will (John 1:12–13), but by God's Spirit working through God's promise (Rom. 9:8–9; Gal. 4:23,28–29).

18:19 *I know him.* God had chosen to form a special relationship with Abraham (Amos 3:1–2), and therefore reveals His ways to him (Ps. 25:14). *command his children . . . that the LORD may bring upon Abraham.* Training the next generation to walk in God's *way* is essential to the fulfillment of His promises to His elect. *justice and judgment.* Righteousness and justice, implying that Abraham knew God's moral law (26:5) and taught it to his family.

18:24 *Peradventure.* Perhaps.

18:25 *Shall not the Judge of all the earth do right?* Abraham interceded for Sodom (and Lot) by appealing to God's character. He is a righteous Judge (Ex. 23:7; Deut. 25:1). It is inconceivable that God would treat *the righteous* the same as *the wicked*, for the righteous are justified by faith in His promises (15:6) and walk with Him in obedience (6:9,22; 7:1).

18:27 *which am but dust and ashes.* "Though I am just dust and ashes," a humble recognition of the infinite difference between God and man.

18:33 *left communing.* Finished talking.

Thoughts for Personal/Family Worship: Chapter 18

1. **When it is hard to trust God's promises, let us remember who God is. Though your problems overwhelm you, nothing is too hard for Him. He created the universe out of nothing and raised Christ from the dead. If you fear His judgments on sin, remember that He knows how to save those who trust Him.**
2. **If God is your God, then you can pray to Him claiming His attributes by faith, for even His righteousness is your friend. Have you learned to place all your hope in His righteousness, both in terms of your justification and your sanctification?**

Chapter 19: ***God's angels rescue Lot from Sodom and destroy it, but Lot's life remained a disgraceful tragedy.***

19:1–3 Two of the "men" who visited Abraham are now called *angels. at even.* In the evening. *Lot* moved near wicked Sodom two decades earlier (13:12), taking up residence in the city (14:12) and appearing at its *gate*, the center of commercial and legal business. Yet Lot showed hospitality like Abraham (18:2–8); he too was a righteous man, though backslidden (2 Peter 2:7–8). Lot *pressed upon them greatly* to stay with him, no doubt to protect them from danger (13:13; 18:20).

19:3 *unleavened bread.* Only here in Genesis; perhaps a hint

4 ¶ But before they lay down, the men of the city,
even the men of Sodom, compassed the house
round, both old and young, all the people from
every quarter:
5 And they called unto Lot, and said unto him,
Where *are* the men which came in to thee this
night? bring them out unto us, that we may know
them.
6 And Lot went out at the door unto them, and
shut the door after him,
7 And said, I pray you, brethren, do not so
wickedly.
8 Behold now, I have two daughters which have
not known man; let me, I pray you, bring them
out unto you, and do ye to them as *is* good in your
eyes: only unto these men do nothing; for there-
fore came they under the shadow of my roof.
9 And they said, Stand back. And they said *again*,
This one *fellow* came in to sojourn, and he will
needs be a judge: now will we deal worse with thee,
than with them. And they pressed sore upon the
man, *even* Lot, and came near to break the door.
10 But the men put forth their hand, and pulled
Lot into the house to them, and shut to the door.
11 And they smote the men that *were* at the door
of the house with blindness, both small and great:
so that they wearied themselves to find the door.
12 ¶ And the men said unto Lot, Hast thou here
any besides? son in law, and thy sons, and thy
daughters, and whatsoever thou hast in the city,
bring *them* out of this place:
13 For we will destroy this place, because the
cry of them is waxen great before the face of the
LORD; and the LORD hath sent us to destroy it.
14 And Lot went out, and spake unto his sons in
law, which married his daughters, and said, Up,
get you out of this place; for the LORD will destroy
this city. But he seemed as one that mocked unto
his sons in law.
15 ¶ And when the morning arose, then the an-
gels hastened Lot, saying, Arise, take thy wife, and
thy two daughters, which are here; lest thou be
consumed in the iniquity of the city.
16 And while he lingered, the men laid hold upon
his hand, and upon the hand of his wife, and
upon the hand of his two daughters; the LORD
being merciful unto him: and they brought him
forth, and set him without the city.
17 ¶ And it came to pass, when they had brought
them forth abroad, that he said, Escape for thy
life; look not behind thee, neither stay thou in all
the plain; escape to the mountain, lest thou be
consumed.
18 And Lot said unto them, Oh, not so, my Lord:
19 Behold now, thy servant hath found grace in
thy sight, and thou hast magnified thy mercy,
which thou hast shewed unto me in saving my
life; and I cannot escape to the mountain, lest
some evil take me, and I die:
20 Behold now, this city *is* near to flee unto, and it
is a little one: Oh, let me escape thither, (*is* it not a
little one?) and my soul shall live.
21 And he said unto him, See, I have accepted thee
concerning this thing also, that I will not over-
throw this city, for the which thou hast spoken.
22 Haste thee, escape thither; for I cannot do
any thing till thou be come thither. Therefore the
name of the city was called Zoar.
23 ¶ The sun was risen upon the earth when Lot
entered into Zoar.
24 Then the LORD rained upon Sodom and upon
Gomorrah brimstone and fire from the LORD out
of heaven;
25 And he overthrew those cities, and all the
plain, and all the inhabitants of the cities, and that
which grew upon the ground.
26 ¶ But his wife looked back from behind him,
and she became a pillar of salt.
27 ¶ And Abraham gat up early in the morning to
the place where he stood before the LORD:
28 And he looked toward Sodom and Gomorrah,
and toward all the land of the plain, and beheld,

---

at Israel's deliverance from Egypt (Ex. 12:8).

19:4 *compassed the house round.* Surrounded the house to prevent escape.

19:5 *know them.* Have sex with them (4:1,17,25; 19:8; 24:16; 38:26). In addition to its sins of pride, luxury, and neglect of the poor (Ezek. 16:49), Sodom was guilty of unnatural sexual lust (Jude 7), highlighted here in its homosexual violence.

19:7–8 Lot boldly rebuked their sin and defended his guests. Tragically, however, he failed to protect his daughters but tried to use them to appease the wicked mob.

19:9 *sojourn.* Stay for a time in a foreign nation. *pressed sore.* Pressed hard. The wicked Sodomites responded to Lot's rebuke by accusing him of presuming to be their *judge* and by rejecting his misguided offer. Nothing but men would satisfy their lusts.

19:13 *the cry of them is waxen great.* The cry of those whom Sodom oppressed and abused had grown loud in God's ears (18:20), demanding His just punishment.

19:14 *as one that mocked.* His sons-in-law were so blind to God's wrath against Sodom's sins they thought Lot was joking. He betrothed his daughters to men who did not fear God.

19:16 *he lingered.* Lot came to Sodom with great wealth and yet sought more (13:5,10–12). Now his love for possessions nearly destroyed him. *the LORD being merciful unto him.* God's compassion saved His backslidden servant despite his worldliness. *without.* Outside.

19:24–25 *brimstone.* Sulphur. The destruction of Sodom points to Christ's sudden coming with fire (Luke 17:28–30). Those who reject the gospel will face judgment worse than Sodom (Matt. 10:15; 11:23–24).

19:26 Lot's *wife* disobeyed the heavenly call (v. 17) and *looked back* to her destruction (Luke 9:62), probably because she loved this world. *Salt* was part of the desolation that came on the area (Deut. 29:23). Christ said, "Remember Lot's wife," when he warned of the necessity of losing one's life in this world to escape divine judgment (Luke 17:32–33).

19:27 *gat up.* Got up.

and, lo, the smoke of the country went up as the
smoke of a furnace.
29 ¶ And it came to pass, when God destroyed the
cities of the plain, that God remembered Abra-
ham, and sent Lot out of the midst of the over-
throw, when he overthrew the cities in the which
Lot dwelt.
30 ¶ And Lot went up out of Zoar, and dwelt in
the mountain, and his two daughters with him;
for he feared to dwell in Zoar: and he dwelt in a
cave, he and his two daughters.
31 And the firstborn said unto the younger, Our
father *is* old, and *there is* not a man in the earth to
come in unto us after the manner of all the earth:
32 Come, let us make our father drink wine, and
we will lie with him, that we may preserve seed of
our father.
33 And they made their father drink wine that
night: and the firstborn went in, and lay with her
father; and he perceived not when she lay down,
nor when she arose.
34 And it came to pass on the morrow, that the
firstborn said unto the younger, Behold, I lay yes-
ternight with my father: let us make him drink
wine this night also; and go thou in, *and* lie with
him, that we may preserve seed of our father.
35 And they made their father drink wine that
night also: and the younger arose, and lay with
him; and he perceived not when she lay down,
nor when she arose.
36 Thus were both the daughters of Lot with
child by their father.
37 And the firstborn bare a son, and called his
name Moab: the same *is* the father of the Moabites
unto this day.
38 And the younger, she also bare a son, and
called his name Ben-ammi: the same *is* the father
of the children of Ammon unto this day.

CHAPTER 20

AND Abraham journeyed from thence toward the
south country, and dwelled between Kadesh and
Shur, and sojourned in Gerar.
2 And Abraham said of Sarah his wife, She *is* my
sister: and Abimelech king of Gerar sent, and took
Sarah.
3 But God came to Abimelech in a dream by
night, and said to him, Behold, thou *art but* a
dead man, for the woman which thou hast taken;
for she *is* a man's wife.
4 But Abimelech had not come near her: and he
said, Lord, wilt thou slay also a righteous nation?
5 Said he not unto me, She *is* my sister? and she,
even she herself said, He *is* my brother: in the in-
tegrity of my heart and innocency of my hands
have I done this.
6 And God said unto him in a dream, Yea, I know
that thou didst this in the integrity of thy heart;
for I also withheld thee from sinning against me:
therefore suffered I thee not to touch her.
7 Now therefore restore the man *his* wife; for he
is a prophet, and he shall pray for thee, and thou
shalt live: and if thou restore *her* not, know thou

19:29 *God remembered Abraham.* The Lord answered Abraham's prayer not by saving Sodom which did not have ten righteous people (18:32), but by having mercy on its only righteous man (v. 16).

19:30–36 Instead of starting over or returning to Abraham, Lot degenerated into fearful isolation. His daughters lured him into a drunken stupor and then incestuously abused him to gain children.

19:34 *yesternight.* Last night.

19:37–38 *Moab.* Meaning, "from father." *Ben-ammi.* Meaning, "son of my people." God provided the descendants of Lot with land (Deut. 2:9,19), but the Moabites and Ammonites became enemies of God and Israel (Deut. 23:3) with one notable exception (Ruth 1:4,16). Ultimately, these nations fell under the same wrath that consumed Sodom (Zeph. 2:9).

Thoughts for Personal/Family Worship: Chapter 19

1. **Lot shows us the bitterness of backsliding. Peter tells us that he was a righteous man, but he took one step after another into worldliness. In the end, he lost his wealth, his wife, the purity of his children, his mental health, and his own dignity—and nearly lost his life. When the world promises to please us with sin, how can we use the history of Lot and his wife to reject the world's pleasures?**
2. **The Lord is a God of both justice and mercy. He will punish sin with flaming fire that will suddenly fall on the wicked when Christ returns. He disciplines His children when they do not repent of sin. Yet He has mercy upon His children, and hears the prayers of their great intercessor, Jesus Christ. Let us therefore flee from sin and flee to Christ.**

Chapter 20: *Abraham sins again in cowardice, endangering the fulfillment of God's promise, but God defends Sarah and their future offspring.*

20:1 *Kadesh and Shur.* See notes at 16:7 and 16:14. *Gerar.* Southwest of the land, an area associated with the Philistines (26:1). Just as the famine tested Abram's faith and drove him to Egypt (12:10), so it may be that witnessing the destruction of Sodom and Gomorrah (19:28) despite his prayers (18:32) drove him to Gerar. Abraham perhaps did not know Lot's fate.

20:2 *She is my sister.* Again, Abraham's faith stumbled and he used Sarah to protect himself (12:13). *Abimelech.* Literally, "my father-king," a common name attributed to several men (26:1; Judg. 8:31; 2 Sam. 11:21; 1 Chron. 18:16; Ps. 34:1). Sarah was 90 years old, but she would live to 127 years (23:1), and so could have been like a very attractive woman in her late forties or early fifties. The giving away of Sarah threatened to defeat God's promise, for how could Abraham and Sarah have a son if she was in the arms of another man?

20:3 *But God came.* God intervened with His word and providence to protect Sarah and ensure the fulfillment of His promise of offspring.

20:6 *I also withheld thee from sinning against me: therefore suffered I thee not to touch her.* "I, even I, restrained you from sinning against me. Therefore, I did not give to you to have sex with her." God can restrain sin in unbelievers and often does to protect His people (35:5; Ex. 34:24).

that thou shalt surely die, thou, and all that *are*
thine.
8 Therefore Abimelech rose early in the morning,
and called all his servants, and told all these things
in their ears: and the men were sore afraid.
9 Then Abimelech called Abraham, and said unto
him, What hast thou done unto us? and what have
I offended thee, that thou hast brought on me and
on my kingdom a great sin? thou hast done deeds
unto me that ought not to be done.
10 And Abimelech said unto Abraham, What
sawest thou, that thou hast done this thing?
11 And Abraham said, Because I thought, Surely
the fear of God *is* not in this place; and they will
slay me for my wife's sake.
12 And yet indeed *she is* my sister; she *is* the
daughter of my father, but not the daughter of my
mother; and she became my wife.
13 And it came to pass, when God caused me to
wander from my father's house, that I said unto
her, This *is* thy kindness which thou shalt shew
unto me; at every place whither we shall come, say
of me, He *is* my brother.
14 And Abimelech took sheep, and oxen, and
menservants, and womenservants, and gave *them*
unto Abraham, and restored him Sarah his wife.
15 And Abimelech said, Behold, my land *is* before
thee: dwell where it pleaseth thee.
16 And unto Sarah he said, Behold, I have given
thy brother a thousand *pieces* of silver: behold, he *is*
to thee a covering of the eyes, unto all that *are* with
thee, and with all *other*: thus she was reproved.
17 ¶ So Abraham prayed unto God: and God
healed Abimelech, and his wife, and his maidser-
vants; and they bare *children*.
18 For the LORD had fast closed up all the wombs
of the house of Abimelech, because of Sarah
Abraham's wife.

CHAPTER 21

AND the LORD visited Sarah as he had said, and
the LORD did unto Sarah as he had spoken.
2 For Sarah conceived, and bare Abraham a son
in his old age, at the set time of which God had
spoken to him.
3 And Abraham called the name of his son that
was born unto him, whom Sarah bare to him,
Isaac.
4 And Abraham circumcised his son Isaac being
eight days old, as God had commanded him.
5 And Abraham was an hundred years old, when
his son Isaac was born unto him.
6 ¶ And Sarah said, God hath made me to laugh,
so that all that hear will laugh with me.
7 And she said, Who would have said unto Abra-
ham, that Sarah should have given children suck?
for I have born *him* a son in his old age.
8 And the child grew, and was weaned: and Abra-
ham made a great feast the *same* day that Isaac
was weaned.
9 ¶ And Sarah saw the son of Hagar the Egyptian,
which she had born unto Abraham, mocking.
10 Wherefore she said unto Abraham, Cast out

20:7 Though God appeared to Abimelech in a dream, he was not a *prophet* like Abraham, and so Abraham must pray for the healing of Abimelech's household (v. 17). Moses also was a prophet whose intercession delivered sinners from divine punishments (Ex. 10:16–19; 32:7–14).
20:8 *sore afraid.* Very afraid.
20:9 Ironically, though Abraham is a prophet, he must be rebuked for his sin by an unbeliever.
20:14 Assyrian documents attest to a custom that if a man ignorantly takes another man's wife into his company (even without sexual relations), he must pay compensation to the husband.
20:16 *she was reproved.* The verb can mean to decide a legal case (31:37), "her case was judged." He protected Sarah from shame (*covering of the eyes*) by a public legal transaction.
20:18 *the LORD had fast closed up all the wombs.* This statement of God's control over pregnancy prepares the reader for His miraculous gift of a child to His servant (ch. 21).

Thoughts for Personal/Family Worship: Chapter 20

1. **God rebukes husbands who do not trust Him enough to cherish their wives. Abimelech showed more concern for honoring Sarah than her own husband! If Christian men fail to give honor and care to their own families, they act worse than many unbelievers. God may discipline them with public embarrassment. Let men repent of their cowardice and stand up to protect and provide for their wives and children.**
2. **The Lord remains faithful despite the weak faith of believers. God could have come in judgment against Abraham's sin and failure to trust God fully, but instead He came in grace. God's promises cannot fail, for they do not depend upon man's unstable will but upon God's eternal will. Trust in the Lord; do not let the fear of man rule you.**

Chapter 21: ***Isaac is born, and conflict and divine revelation prompt Abraham to send away Hagar and Ishmael. Abimelech makes a covenant with Abraham.***
21:1–2 *as he had said . . . as he had spoken . . . at the set time of which God had spoken.* The Word of God proves true in all its details (Prov. 30:5).
21:3 *Isaac.* See note at 17:19.
21:4 *as God had commanded him.* God's covenant faithfulness was echoed in Abraham's faithfulness to keep the covenant and place its sign on his son (17:9–14).
21:5 *hundred years old.* The emphasis on Abraham's "old age" (vv. 2,7) points to the supernatural origin of the covenant seed. See note at 18:14.
21:6 *laugh.* Isaac's name became a note of triumphant joy when God fulfilled His promise. God's people sing for joy when He multiplies them despite their barrenness in sin (Isa. 54:1–8).
21:7 *given children suck.* Breastfeed children.
21:9 *mocking.* Ironically, the same verb as "laugh" (v. 6), the root of "Isaac." In this intensified form it means to joke, mock,

this bondwoman and her son: for the son of this
bondwoman shall not be heir with my son, *even*
with Isaac.
11 And the thing was very grievous in Abraham's
sight because of his son.
12 ¶ And God said unto Abraham, Let it not be
grievous in thy sight because of the lad, and be-
cause of thy bondwoman; in all that Sarah hath
said unto thee, hearken unto her voice; for in
Isaac shall thy seed be called.
13 And also of the son of the bondwoman will I
make a nation, because he *is* thy seed.
14 And Abraham rose up early in the morning,
and took bread, and a bottle of water, and gave
it unto Hagar, putting *it* on her shoulder, and the
child, and sent her away: and she departed, and
wandered in the wilderness of Beer-sheba.
15 And the water was spent in the bottle, and she
cast the child under one of the shrubs.
16 And she went, and sat her down over against
him a good way off, as it were a bowshot: for she
said, Let me not see the death of the child. And she
sat over against *him*, and lift up her voice, and wept.
17 And God heard the voice of the lad; and the
angel of God called to Hagar out of heaven, and
said unto her, What aileth thee, Hagar? fear not;
for God hath heard the voice of the lad where he *is*.
18 Arise, lift up the lad, and hold him in thine
hand; for I will make him a great nation.
19 And God opened her eyes, and she saw a well
of water; and she went, and filled the bottle with
water, and gave the lad drink.
20 And God was with the lad; and he grew, and
dwelt in the wilderness, and became an archer.
21 And he dwelt in the wilderness of Paran: and
his mother took him a wife out of the land of
Egypt.
22 ¶ And it came to pass at that time, that Abim-
elech and Phichol the chief captain of his host
spake unto Abraham, saying, God *is* with thee in
all that thou doest:
23 Now therefore swear unto me here by God
that thou wilt not deal falsely with me, nor with
my son, nor with my son's son: *but* according to
the kindness that I have done unto thee, thou shalt
do unto me, and to the land wherein thou hast
sojourned.
24 And Abraham said, I will swear.
25 And Abraham reproved Abimelech because of
a well of water, which Abimelech's servants had
violently taken away.
26 And Abimelech said, I wot not who hath done
this thing: neither didst thou tell me, neither yet
heard I *of it*, but to day.
27 And Abraham took sheep and oxen, and gave
them unto Abimelech; and both of them made a
covenant.
28 And Abraham set seven ewe lambs of the flock
by themselves.
29 And Abimelech said unto Abraham, What
mean these seven ewe lambs which thou hast set
by themselves?
30 And he said, For *these* seven ewe lambs shalt
thou take of my hand, that they may be a witness
unto me, that I have digged this well.
31 Wherefore he called that place Beer-sheba;
because there they sware both of them.
32 Thus they made a covenant at Beer-sheba:
then Abimelech rose up, and Phichol the chief
captain of his host, and they returned into the
land of the Philistines.
33 ¶ And *Abraham* planted a grove in Beer-sheba,
and called there on the name of the LORD, the
everlasting God.
34 And Abraham sojourned in the Philistines'
land many days.

or play, sometimes with sexual connotations (19:14; 26:8; Ex. 32:6; Judg. 16:25). The mockery of a teenager may have posed a real threat to a toddler, an example of the persecution of believers (Gal. 4:29).

21:10 *bondwoman.* Female slave. Ishmael is an example of merely human religion under the law because of his bondage and origins in human wisdom and strength, not God's promise and Spirit (Gal. 4:21–31).

21:12–13 *hearken unto her voice.* Listen to her and do what she says. *in Isaac shall thy seed be called.* God had promised to be the covenant God of Abraham's *seed* or "offspring" and to give them the land (12:7; 13:15; 15:18; 17:7–8). Ishmael was Abraham's physical offspring, circumcised in the flesh, but God did not choose him to be a true member of the covenant people (17:18–23; Rom. 9:6–9,11,16). Nevertheless, God gave him many physical blessings *because he is thy* (Abraham's) *seed.*

21:14 *rose up early in the morning.* He was quick to obey God's painful command, trusting in God's promise to care for Ishmael (v. 13). *bottle.* Soft canteen made of an animal skin or bladder. *wilderness of Beer-sheba.* The Negev or southern area of the land between the Dead Sea and the Mediterranean Sea (20:1).

21:17 *God heard . . . God hath heard.* A reminder of God's promise when He named Ishmael ("God hears," 16:11). The Lord is good to those who call to Him in trouble (Ps. 107:4–9).

21:21 *wilderness of Paran.* Sinai (see note at 25:18). *Egypt.* The land of Hagar's origin (16:1).

21:22 *God is with thee.* The Lord was present with him to bless and protect him. God had promised to be with His people (26:3; 28:15; 31:3; 39:2–3,21,23; 46:4).

21:26 *I wot not.* I do not know.

21:33 *the LORD, the everlasting God.* Literally, "Jehovah, God of eternity" (17:7,19; Deut. 33:27; Isa. 40:27–28).

Thoughts for Personal/Family Worship: Chapter 21

1. **The Lord is faithful. Keep trusting Him even if waiting stretches from days into decades. Though we may have to wait a lifetime, He will keep His promises. If men often keep the solemn oaths of their covenants, surely the Lord will keep His covenant forever. How can God's covenant faithfulness help us in life's daily callings?**
2. **Never mock the people of God, no matter how weak they may appear. The everlasting God is with them, and one day they will laugh with joy. Those who are wise will**

CHAPTER 22

AND it came to pass after these things, that God
did tempt Abraham, and said unto him, Abra-
ham: and he said, Behold, *here* I *am*.
2 And he said, Take now thy son, thine only *son*
Isaac, whom thou lovest, and get thee into the
land of Moriah; and offer him there for a burnt
offering upon one of the mountains which I will
tell thee of.
3 ¶ And Abraham rose up early in the morning,
and saddled his ass, and took two of his young
men with him, and Isaac his son, and clave the
wood for the burnt offering, and rose up, and
went unto the place of which God had told him.
4 Then on the third day Abraham lifted up his
eyes, and saw the place afar off.
5 And Abraham said unto his young men, Abide
ye here with the ass; and I and the lad will go yon-
der and worship, and come again to you.
6 And Abraham took the wood of the burnt of-
fering, and laid *it* upon Isaac his son; and he took
the fire in his hand, and a knife; and they went
both of them together.
7 And Isaac spake unto Abraham his father, and
said, My father: and he said, Here *am* I, my son.
And he said, Behold the fire and the wood: but
where *is* the lamb for a burnt offering?
8 And Abraham said, My son, God will provide
himself a lamb for a burnt offering: so they went
both of them together.
9 And they came to the place which God had told
him of; and Abraham built an altar there, and laid
the wood in order, and bound Isaac his son, and
laid him on the altar upon the wood.
10 And Abraham stretched forth his hand, and
took the knife to slay his son.
11 And the angel of the LORD called unto him out
of heaven, and said, Abraham, Abraham: and he
said, Here *am* I.
12 And he said, Lay not thine hand upon the lad,
neither do thou any thing unto him: for now I
know that thou fearest God, seeing thou hast not
withheld thy son, thine only *son* from me.
13 And Abraham lifted up his eyes, and looked,
and behold behind *him* a ram caught in a thicket
by his horns: and Abraham went and took the
ram, and offered him up for a burnt offering in
the stead of his son.
14 And Abraham called the name of that place
Jehovah-jireh: as it is said *to* this day, In the mount
of the LORD it shall be seen.
15 ¶ And the angel of the LORD called unto Abra-
ham out of heaven the second time,
16 And said, By myself have I sworn, saith the
LORD, for because thou hast done this thing, and
hast not withheld thy son, thine only *son*:
17 That in blessing I will bless thee, and in mul-
tiplying I will multiply thy seed as the stars of the
heaven, and as the sand which *is* upon the sea shore;
and thy seed shall possess the gate of his enemies;
18 And in thy seed shall all the nations of the earth
be blessed; because thou hast obeyed my voice.
19 So Abraham returned unto his young men,
and they rose up and went together to Beer-
sheba; and Abraham dwelt at Beer-sheba.
20 ¶ And it came to pass after these things, that
it was told Abraham, saying, Behold, Milcah, she
hath also born children unto thy brother Nahor;

---

join in covenant with them, taking them as their people and the Lord as their God.

Chapter 22: *God tests Abraham and provides a lamb to die in Isaac's place.*

22:1 *God did tempt*. In the sense of "tested." God tempts no one to sin (James 1:13). Rather, God tested Abraham's faith and obedience (Ex. 16:4).

22:2 *thy son, thine only son Isaac, whom thou lovest*. A type or shadow of the sacrifice God made of His beloved and only begotten Son (Luke 3:22; John 3:16). *Moriah*. Future location of the temple (2 Chron. 3:1). God hates child sacrifice (Lev. 20:1–5); this command seemed to contradict God's character and promises (17:19; 21:12).

22:3 *rose up early*. Again, Abraham was quick to obey God (21:14). *his young men*. His servants. *clave the wood*. Split the wood.

22:5 *lad*. Young man, a term used for boys but also fully grown young adults (1 Chron. 12:28). *and come again*. The verb form implies, "We will come again." Abraham believed that, if necessary, God would raise Isaac from the dead to keep His promises (Heb. 11:17–19).

22:8 *God will provide*. Literally, "God will see" (v. 14). Abraham trusted that the Lord of whom Hagar said, "God seest me" (16:13) would certainly look out for the covenant Seed.

22:11 *angel of the LORD*. The Son sent by the Father (see note at 16:7). God already knew Abraham's heart (15:6; Jer. 17:10) and future (Isa. 46:10). Why then test him? Because it matured his faith and demonstrated that he was a righteous man (James 1:3; 2:21–22).

22:12 The Lord was delighted (*now I know*; Ps. 37:18; Nah. 1:7) that Abraham esteemed (*fearest*) Him above all else. *thou has not withheld thy son*. The same verb used here and in v. 16 in the ancient Greek Septuagint translation appears in Rom. 8:32, "He that spared not his own Son."

22:13 Isaac would be the father of the people of God, but as a fallen sinner in Adam he deserved to die (2:17; 3:19). God provided *a ram* (male sheep) as a substitute to die in place of (*in the stead of*) the covenant people, *a burnt offering* to atone for sin (Lev. 1:4).

22:14 *mount of the LORD*. Mt. Zion, where David reigned and the temple was built (Ps. 24:3; Isa. 2:3; Zech. 8:3). There Christ would die like a lamb as the substitute for sinners (Isa. 53:5–7).

22:16–17 *By myself have I sworn, saith the LORD*. God confirmed the promises by an oath so that believers in Christ may have strong assurance (Heb. 6:13–20). *blessing I will bless . . . multiplying I will multiply*. "I will surely bless, I will surely multiply." The *gate* was the center of a city's political, legal, and commercial life (23:10; 34:20; Ruth 4:1); to *possess the gate of his enemies* is to conquer and rule them (24:60; Matt. 16:18).

22:18 *because thou hast obeyed my voice*. God's blessing to all nations comes through the obedience of His servant, and

21 Huz his firstborn, and Buz his brother, and
Kemuel the father of Aram,
22 And Chesed, and Hazo, and Pildash, and
Jidlaph, and Bethuel.
23 And Bethuel begat Rebekah: these eight
Milcah did bear to Nahor, Abraham's brother.
24 And his concubine, whose name *was* Reumah,
she bare also Tebah, and Gaham, and Thahash,
and Maachah.

CHAPTER 23

AND Sarah was an hundred and seven and twenty
years old: *these were* the years of the life of Sarah.
2 And Sarah died in Kirjath-arba; the same *is* He-
bron in the land of Canaan: and Abraham came
to mourn for Sarah, and to weep for her.
3 ¶ And Abraham stood up from before his dead,
and spake unto the sons of Heth, saying,
4 I *am* a stranger and a sojourner with you: give
me a possession of a buryingplace with you, that
I may bury my dead out of my sight.
5 And the children of Heth answered Abraham,
saying unto him,
6 Hear us, my lord: thou *art* a mighty prince
among us: in the choice of our sepulchres bury
thy dead; none of us shall withhold from thee his
sepulchre, but that thou mayest bury thy dead.
7 And Abraham stood up, and bowed himself
to the people of the land, *even* to the children of
Heth.
8 And he communed with them, saying, If it be
your mind that I should bury my dead out of my
sight; hear me, and intreat for me to Ephron the
son of Zohar,
9 That he may give me the cave of Machpelah,
which he hath, which *is* in the end of his field; for
as much money as it is worth he shall give it me
for a possession of a buryingplace amongst you.
10 And Ephron dwelt among the children of
Heth: and Ephron the Hittite answered Abraham
in the audience of the children of Heth, *even* of all
that went in at the gate of his city, saying,
11 Nay, my lord, hear me: the field give I thee, and
the cave that *is* therein, I give it thee; in the pres-
ence of the sons of my people give I it thee: bury
thy dead.
12 And Abraham bowed down himself before the
people of the land.
13 And he spake unto Ephron in the audience of
the people of the land, saying, But if thou *wilt give
it*, I pray thee, hear me: I will give thee money for
the field; take *it* of me, and I will bury my dead
there.
14 And Ephron answered Abraham, saying unto
him,
15 My lord, hearken unto me: the land *is worth*
four hundred shekels of silver; what *is* that be-
twixt me and thee? bury therefore thy dead.
16 And Abraham hearkened unto Ephron; and
Abraham weighed to Ephron the silver, which he
had named in the audience of the sons of Heth,
four hundred shekels of silver, current *money*
with the merchant.
17 ¶ And the field of Ephron, which *was* in Mach-
pelah, which *was* before Mamre, the field, and the
cave which *was* therein, and all the trees that *were*
in the field, that *were* in all the borders round
about, were made sure
18 Unto Abraham for a possession in the pres-
ence of the children of Heth, before all that went
in at the gate of his city.

---

ultimately because of the obedience of Christ unto death on the cross.

22:20–24 *Bethuel begat Rebekah.* God was already providing a wife for Isaac so that the covenant seed would continue (24:15).

Thoughts for Personal/Family Worship: Chapter 22

1. **What is your "Isaac"? What earthly relationship or possession do you treasure most? If obedience to God required you to let go of it, do you fear Him enough to make the sacrifice? Pray for grace to show the Lord that this too is His.**
2. **God made the highest sacrifice. The covenant people of God deserve eternal death in hell. To provide a substitute to take their place, God did not spare His own Son, His only begotten Son whom He loves. Christ Himself became the Lamb of God's provision. So trust in His redeeming love; trust that if God gave His Son for us, He will certainly provide us with all that is good for us.**

Chapter 23: *Sarah dies and Abraham grieves and negotiates to purchase a burial plot for her from the people dwelling in the land.*

23:2 *Kirjath-arba . . . Hebron.* West of the Dead Sea (13:18). *to mourn . . . and to weep.* To lament with wailing and tears. Abraham grieved with open and intense emotion. Sarah had faithfully walked with him for well over sixty years since their days at Ur (11:31).

23:3 *sons of Heth.* The Hittites (v. 10), descendants of Canaan (10:15; 15:20). They may have been related to the Hittite kingdom formed to the north (in modern Turkey).

23:4 *a stranger and a sojourner.* Believers are pilgrims in this world (Heb. 11:13; 1 Peter 2:11).

23:6 *mighty prince.* Literally, "prince of God," perhaps another acknowledgement that God was with him and made him great (21:22). *sepulchre.* Same word as "buryingplace" (v. 4).

23:7 *bowed himself to the people.* Abraham showed humility, courtesy, and respect for others in his business dealings (Titus 3:1–2). Though the Hittites did not worship the Lord and would one day forfeit the land for their sins (15:16–21; 26:34–35), he still honored them (1 Peter 2:17).

23:8 *communed with them.* Said to them. *intreat.* Request.

23:11 Abraham asked to buy the "cave" (v. 9), but Ephron added the *field.* Under Hittite law, he must sell the whole property in order to transfer the obligation to pay tax to the local king.

23:13 *in the audience.* In the ears or hearing.

23:15 *hearken unto me.* Listen to me. *four hundred shekels.*

19 And after this, Abraham buried Sarah his
wife in the cave of the field of Machpelah before
Mamre: the same *is* Hebron in the land of Canaan.
20 And the field, and the cave that *is* therein, were
made sure unto Abraham for a possession of a
buryingplace by the sons of Heth.

CHAPTER 24

AND Abraham was old, *and* well stricken in age:
and the LORD had blessed Abraham in all things.
2 And Abraham said unto his eldest servant of his
house, that ruled over all that he had, Put, I pray
thee, thy hand under my thigh:
3 And I will make thee swear by the LORD, the
God of heaven, and the God of the earth, that thou
shalt not take a wife unto my son of the daughters
of the Canaanites, among whom I dwell:
4 But thou shalt go unto my country, and to my
kindred, and take a wife unto my son Isaac.
5 And the servant said unto him, Peradventure
the woman will not be willing to follow me unto
this land: must I needs bring thy son again unto
the land from whence thou camest?
6 And Abraham said unto him, Beware thou that
thou bring not my son thither again.
7 ¶ The LORD God of heaven, which took me
from my father's house, and from the land of
my kindred, and which spake unto me, and that
sware unto me, saying, Unto thy seed will I give
this land; he shall send his angel before thee, and
thou shalt take a wife unto my son from thence.
8 And if the woman will not be willing to follow
thee, then thou shalt be clear from this my oath:
only bring not my son thither again.
9 And the servant put his hand under the thigh of
Abraham his master, and sware to him concern-
ing that matter.
10 ¶ And the servant took ten camels of the cam-
els of his master, and departed; for all the goods
of his master *were* in his hand: and he arose, and
went to Mesopotamia, unto the city of Nahor.
11 And he made his camels to kneel down without
the city by a well of water at the time of the evening,
even the time that women go out to draw *water*.
12 And he said, O LORD God of my master Abra-
ham, I pray thee, send me good speed this day,
and shew kindness unto my master Abraham.
13 Behold, I stand *here* by the well of water; and
the daughters of the men of the city come out to
draw water:
14 And let it come to pass, that the damsel to
whom I shall say, Let down thy pitcher, I pray
thee, that I may drink; and she shall say, Drink,
and I will give thy camels drink also: *let the same*
be she *that* thou hast appointed for thy servant
Isaac; and thereby shall I know that thou hast
shewed kindness unto my master.
15 ¶ And it came to pass, before he had done
speaking, that, behold, Rebekah came out, who
was born to Bethuel, son of Milcah, the wife of
Nahor, Abraham's brother, with her pitcher upon
her shoulder.
16 And the damsel *was* very fair to look upon, a

Not a number of coins here but a measure of weight: perhaps about ten pounds of silver, apparently a very high cost.

23:20 *possession*. Same word (vv. 4,9) used in God's promise that He would give Abraham's seed "all the land of Canaan, for an everlasting possession" (17:8). Yet Abraham had to pay a high price and even incur taxes to get a tiny portion of the land (23:11,15). He and Sarah lived by faith in the promises, not receiving the inheritance in their lifetime. This shows their hope in the resurrection and a heavenly city (Heb. 11:13–16).

Thoughts for Personal/Family Worship: Chapter 23

1. **By their union with Christ, God's people are kings and heirs of a great inheritance. Yet in this world they may have little; they must live by faith, not by sight. Pray for the God of hope to fill you with all joy and peace in believing the promises about Christ, so that by the power of the Holy Spirit, you may abound in hope.**
2. **God calls believers to live as strangers and aliens—not entangled among the wicked Sodomites and Hittites in their pursuit of this world, but pilgrims waiting for the city of God. This separation from sin does not excuse isolation or rudeness, but instead demands that we do business in this world with honor and courtesy to all. What ways can you practice this in the spheres where God has called you to live and work?**

Chapter 24: *Abraham sends his servant to find a wife for Isaac, and God leads him to Rebekah through a remarkable providence.*

24:1 *well stricken in age*. Literally, "went on in days," that is, became advanced in age.

24:3 The divine name *LORD* (Hebrew, *Jehovah*) appears nineteen times in this chapter, more than any other chapter in Genesis. The Lord is the Creator and Owner *of heaven* and *earth* (v. 7; 1:1; 14:22). He is also the God of Abraham (vv. 12,27,42,48) and will use His power over all things to bless and multiply the covenant seed. Abraham sought a wife for Isaac who was not one of the *Canaanites*, a warning to Israel not to intermarry with the wicked (26:34–35).

24:4 *kindred*. Extended family.

24:5 *Peradventure*. Perhaps.

24:6 *thither*. There.

24:7 Abraham depended upon the promises of the Lord to provide for the future of the covenant seed. *his angel*. Probably the divine angel of the Lord (16:7–13; 22:11–18).

24:10 *camels*. See note at 12:16. *to Mesopotamia, unto the city of Nahor*. To Haran by the Euphrates River (11:28; 27:43), a journey of about five hundred miles.

24:11 *without the city*. Outside the city.

24:12 *send me good speed*. Literally, "cause it to happen before me," that is, give me success (27:20). *kindness*. God's loyal love and faithful goodness (v. 14), particularly to His people.

24:14 *damsel*. Young woman. *pitcher*. Earthenware water jar. The servant's prayer and its answer imply that God controls the choices of human beings.

24:16 Since Rebekah was quite attractive (*very fair*), her sexual innocence as a *virgin* whom no man had *known* sexually (4:1) attested to her personal purity.

virgin, neither had any man known her: and she
went down to the well, and filled her pitcher, and
came up.
17 And the servant ran to meet her, and said, Let
me, I pray thee, drink a little water of thy pitcher.
18 And she said, Drink, my lord: and she hasted,
and let down her pitcher upon her hand, and gave
him drink.
19 And when she had done giving him drink, she
said, I will draw *water* for thy camels also, until
they have done drinking.
20 And she hasted, and emptied her pitcher into
the trough, and ran again unto the well to draw
water, and drew for all his camels.
21 And the man wondering at her held his peace,
to wit whether the LORD had made his journey
prosperous or not.
22 And it came to pass, as the camels had done
drinking, that the man took a golden earring of
half a shekel weight, and two bracelets for her
hands of ten *shekels* weight of gold;
23 And said, Whose daughter *art* thou? tell me, I
pray thee: is there room *in* thy father's house for
us to lodge in?
24 And she said unto him, I *am* the daughter of
Bethuel the son of Milcah, which she bare unto
Nahor.
25 She said moreover unto him, We have both
straw and provender enough, and room to lodge in.
26 And the man bowed down his head, and wor-
shipped the LORD.
27 And he said, Blessed *be* the LORD God of my
master Abraham, who hath not left destitute my
master of his mercy and his truth: I *being* in the
way, the LORD led me to the house of my master's
brethren.
28 And the damsel ran, and told *them of* her
mother's house these things.
29 ¶ And Rebekah had a brother, and his name
was Laban: and Laban ran out unto the man, unto
the well.
30 And it came to pass, when he saw the earring
and bracelets upon his sister's hands, and when he
heard the words of Rebekah his sister, saying, Thus
spake the man unto me; that he came unto the man;
and, behold, he stood by the camels at the well.
31 And he said, Come in, thou blessed of the
LORD; wherefore standest thou without? for I have
prepared the house, and room for the camels.
32 ¶ And the man came into the house: and he
ungirded his camels, and gave straw and proven-
der for the camels, and water to wash his feet, and
the men's feet that *were* with him.
33 And there was set *meat* before him to eat: but
he said, I will not eat, until I have told mine er-
rand. And he said, Speak on.
34 And he said, I *am* Abraham's servant.
35 And the LORD hath blessed my master greatly;
and he is become great: and he hath given him
flocks, and herds, and silver, and gold, and men-
servants, and maidservants, and camels, and asses.
36 And Sarah my master's wife bare a son to my
master when she was old: and unto him hath he
given all that he hath.
37 And my master made me swear, saying, Thou
shalt not take a wife to my son of the daughters of
the Canaanites, in whose land I dwell:
38 But thou shalt go unto my father's house, and
to my kindred, and take a wife unto my son.
39 And I said unto my master, Peradventure the
woman will not follow me.
40 And he said unto me, The LORD, before whom
I walk, will send his angel with thee, and prosper
thy way; and thou shalt take a wife for my son of
my kindred, and of my father's house:
41 Then shalt thou be clear from *this* my oath,
when thou comest to my kindred; and if they give
not thee *one*, thou shalt be clear from my oath.
42 And I came this day unto the well, and said, O
LORD God of my master Abraham, if now thou do
prosper my way which I go:
43 Behold, I stand by the well of water; and it
shall come to pass, that when the virgin cometh
forth to draw *water*, and I say to her, Give me, I
pray thee, a little water of thy pitcher to drink;
44 And she say to me, Both drink thou, and I
will also draw for thy camels: *let* the same *be* the
woman whom the LORD hath appointed out for
my master's son.
45 And before I had done speaking in mine heart,
behold, Rebekah came forth with her pitcher on
her shoulder; and she went down unto the well,

24:18 *hasted.* Acted quickly.
24:20 *drew for all his camels.* A camel can drink dozens of gallons of water in a few minutes, so drawing water for ten camels required many trips to the well with the water jar. Rebekah's service and hospitality (like that of Abraham, 18:2–8) showed her godly character.
24:21 *to wit.* To know.
24:22 *half a shekel weight . . . ten shekels weight.* Perhaps a fifth of an ounce of gold (6 g) and a quarter of a pound of gold (113 g)—suggesting large pieces of jewelry.
24:25 *provender.* Fodder, food for livestock.
24:27 The Lord's *mercy* (same word as "kindness," v. 12) and *truth* (or faithfulness) are at the core of His character as a covenant-keeping God (32:10; Ex. 34:6; Ps. 25:10; 86:15; Mic. 7:19–20). His goodness calls for our worship (*Blessed be the LORD*) and our imitation (v. 49).
24:28 *damsel.* Young woman.
24:31 *without.* Outside.
24:32 *ungirded.* Untied and took the gear off the camels.
24:33 *meat.* Food of any kind.
24:37–48 The repetition of the earlier part of the story (vv. 2–27) serves to reinforce the sense of wonder at how God answered the prayers of His servants, as well as the clarity of His will (v. 50).

and drew *water*: and I said unto her, Let me drink,
I pray thee.
46 And she made haste, and let down her pitcher
from her *shoulder*, and said, Drink, and I will give
thy camels drink also: so I drank, and she made
the camels drink also.
47 And I asked her, and said, Whose daughter *art*
thou? And she said, The daughter of Bethuel, Na-
hor's son, whom Milcah bare unto him: and I put
the earring upon her face, and the bracelets upon
her hands.
48 And I bowed down my head, and worshipped
the LORD, and blessed the LORD God of my mas-
ter Abraham, which had led me in the right way to
take my master's brother's daughter unto his son.
49 And now if ye will deal kindly and truly with
my master, tell me: and if not, tell me; that I may
turn to the right hand, or to the left.
50 Then Laban and Bethuel answered and said,
The thing proceedeth from the LORD: we cannot
speak unto thee bad or good.
51 Behold, Rebekah *is* before thee, take *her*, and
go, and let her be thy master's son's wife, as the
LORD hath spoken.
52 And it came to pass, that, when Abraham's ser-
vant heard their words, he worshipped the LORD,
bowing himself to the earth.
53 And the servant brought forth jewels of silver,
and jewels of gold, and raiment, and gave *them* to
Rebekah: he gave also to her brother and to her
mother precious things.
54 And they did eat and drink, he and the men
that *were* with him, and tarried all night; and they
rose up in the morning, and he said, Send me
away unto my master.
55 And her brother and her mother said, Let the
damsel abide with us *a few* days, at the least ten;
after that she shall go.
56 And he said unto them, Hinder me not, seeing
the LORD hath prospered my way; send me away
that I may go to my master.
57 And they said, We will call the damsel, and en-
quire at her mouth.
58 And they called Rebekah, and said unto her,
Wilt thou go with this man? And she said, I will go.
59 And they sent away Rebekah their sister, and
her nurse, and Abraham's servant, and his men.
60 And they blessed Rebekah, and said unto her,
Thou *art* our sister, be thou *the mother* of thou-
sands of millions, and let thy seed possess the gate
of those which hate them.
61 ¶ And Rebekah arose, and her damsels, and
they rode upon the camels, and followed the man:
and the servant took Rebekah, and went his way.
62 And Isaac came from the way of the well La-
hai-roi; for he dwelt in the south country.
63 And Isaac went out to meditate in the field at
the eventide: and he lifted up his eyes, and saw,
and, behold, the camels *were* coming.
64 And Rebekah lifted up her eyes, and when she
saw Isaac, she lighted off the camel.
65 For she *had* said unto the servant, What man
is this that walketh in the field to meet us? And
the servant *had* said, It *is* my master: therefore she
took a vail, and covered herself.
66 And the servant told Isaac all things that he
had done.
67 And Isaac brought her into his mother Sarah's
tent, and took Rebekah, and she became his wife;
and he loved her: and Isaac was comforted after
his mother's *death*.

CHAPTER 25

THEN again Abraham took a wife, and her name
was Keturah.
2 And she bare him Zimran, and Jokshan, and
Medan, and Midian, and Ishbak, and Shuah.

24:39 *Peradventure.* Perhaps.
24:53 *jewels of silver, and jewels of gold.* Silver and gold items. *raiment.* Clothing.
24:54 *tarried all night.* Stayed overnight.
24:55 *damsel.* Young woman.
24:57–58 *enquire at her mouth.* Ask her to speak for herself. Rebekah's simple but resolute response, *I will go*, echoes Abraham's faith in leaving his kindred to follow God (12:1,4), and a believer's faith when surrendering to the God-man and perfect Husband, Jesus Christ, to follow Him unconditionally.
24:59 *her nurse.* Deborah (35:8), the servant who had cared for Rebekah in her childhood and perhaps breastfed her (Ex. 2:7–9; 2 Sam. 4:4).
24:60 *possess the gate.* See note at 22:16–17.
24:62–63 Isaac *went out to meditate* (literally, "talk to himself") in the evening (*eventide*), perhaps on his mother's death (v. 67), on the faithful love of "the Living One who sees me" (Hebrew, *Lahairoi*, 16:13–14), and on His promises (Ps. 1:2; 119:148).
24:64 *lighted off.* Came down quickly.
24:67 *she became his wife; and he loved her.* The beloved son (22:2) gained a beloved wife, just as by God's grace His beloved Son will gain a beloved bride, the church.

Thoughts for Personal/Family Worship: Chapter 24

1. **Our God is the Lord of heaven and earth, controlling even the little details of a young woman's kindness to a stranger. This chapter bears strong testimony to how we should trust Him completely and show love and faithfulness to the people around us. Who knows how He will use our acts of kindness?**
2. **We can especially trust that the sovereign Lord will multiply the covenant seed and win a bride for His Son. Such faith should express itself in courageous work to increase the church, joined to confident prayer and humble praise for His great works of power.**
3. **Like Rebekah, are you willing to follow Jesus Christ unconditionally for your salvation and as Lord?**

Chapter 25: ***Abraham dies, Ishmael multiplies, and the covenant seed continues in Isaac.***

3 And Jokshan begat Sheba, and Dedan. And the
sons of Dedan were Asshurim, and Letushim, and
Leummim.
4 And the sons of Midian; Ephah, and Epher, and
Hanoch, and Abida, and Eldaah. All these *were*
the children of Keturah.
5 ¶ And Abraham gave all that he had unto Isaac.
6 But unto the sons of the concubines, which
Abraham had, Abraham gave gifts, and sent them
away from Isaac his son, while he yet lived, east-
ward, unto the east country.
7 And these *are* the days of the years of Abra-
ham's life which he lived, an hundred threescore
and fifteen years.
8 Then Abraham gave up the ghost, and died in
a good old age, an old man, and full *of years*; and
was gathered to his people.
9 And his sons Isaac and Ishmael buried him in
the cave of Machpelah, in the field of Ephron the
son of Zohar the Hittite, which *is* before Mamre;
10 The field which Abraham purchased of the
sons of Heth: there was Abraham buried, and
Sarah his wife.
11 ¶ And it came to pass after the death of Abra-
ham, that God blessed his son Isaac; and Isaac
dwelt by the well Lahai-roi.
12 ¶ Now these *are* the generations of Ishmael,
Abraham's son, whom Hagar the Egyptian, Sar-
ah's handmaid, bare unto Abraham:
13 And these *are* the names of the sons of Ishmael,
by their names, according to their generations:
the firstborn of Ishmael, Nebajoth; and Kedar,
and Adbeel, and Mibsam,
14 And Mishma, and Dumah, and Massa,
15 Hadar, and Tema, Jetur, Naphish, and
Kedemah:
16 These *are* the sons of Ishmael, and these *are*
their names, by their towns, and by their castles;
twelve princes according to their nations.
17 And these *are* the years of the life of Ishmael,
an hundred and thirty and seven years: and he
gave up the ghost and died; and was gathered
unto his people.
18 And they dwelt from Havilah unto Shur, that *is*
before Egypt, as thou goest toward Assyria: *and* he
died in the presence of all his brethren.
19 ¶ And these *are* the generations of Isaac, Abra-
ham's son: Abraham begat Isaac:
20 And Isaac was forty years old when he took
Rebekah to wife, the daughter of Bethuel the Syr-
ian of Padan-aram, the sister to Laban the Syrian.
21 And Isaac intreated the LORD for his wife, be-
cause she *was* barren: and the LORD was intreated
of him, and Rebekah his wife conceived.
22 And the children struggled together within
her; and she said, If *it be* so, why *am* I thus? And
she went to enquire of the LORD.
23 And the LORD said unto her, Two nations *are*
in thy womb, and two manner of people shall be
separated from thy bowels; and *the one* people
shall be stronger than *the other* people; and the
elder shall serve the younger.
24 ¶ And when her days to be delivered were ful-
filled, behold, *there were* twins in her womb.
25 And the first came out red, all over like an
hairy garment; and they called his name Esau.
26 And after that came his brother out, and his
hand took hold on Esau's heel; and his name was
called Jacob: and Isaac *was* threescore years old
when she bare them.
27 And the boys grew: and Esau was a cunning
hunter, a man of the field; and Jacob *was* a plain
man, dwelling in tents.
28 And Isaac loved Esau, because he did eat of *his*
venison: but Rebekah loved Jacob.
29 ¶ And Jacob sod pottage: and Esau came from
the field, and he *was* faint:
30 And Esau said to Jacob, Feed me, I pray thee,

25:3 *begat.* Fathered a child.

25:7 *hundred threescore and fifteen.* One hundred and seventy-five. See note at 50:22.

25:8 *gathered to his people.* Implies the continued existence of the spirits of the dead in another realm, but not in every case a blessed afterlife (15:15; 25:17; 35:29; 49:29,33; Num. 20:24,26; 27:13; 31:2; Deut. 32:50; Judg. 2:10; 2 Kings 22:20; 2 Chron. 17:11; 34:28; Ps. 49:19).

25:12 *these are the generations.* A marker of transition to a new focus in Genesis (2:4; 5:1; 6:9; 10:1; 11:10,27; 25:19; 36:1; 37:1). *Ishmael.* See ch. 16; 17:18–26.

25:13–18 The *sons of Ishmael* became nomadic peoples of the Arabian wilderness between Egypt and Babylon. God multiplied Ishmael into *twelve princes* as He promised (17:20).

25:16 *castles.* Either walled cities or, more likely, tent encampments.

The Grace of God to Isaac and Jacob (25:19—36:43)

25:19 *These are the generations of Isaac.* This phrase (see note at v. 12) opens a new section in Genesis, switching the focus from Abraham (11:27—25:18) to Isaac and his seed.

25:21–22 *intreated.* Prayed. *enquire.* Seek or ask. Isaac and Rebekah were people of prayer.

25:23 *two manner of people shall be separated from thy bowels.* The two children in your womb will become two distinct nations. God revealed His election of *the younger* before the two were born, showing that His calling was of grace, not works (Rom. 9:10–12). This reversed the primacy of the firstborn (v. 31); God's calling is contrary to man's wisdom (1 Cor. 1:26–29).

25:27 *cunning hunter.* Literally, "a man who knows hunting." *plain man.* A complete man, ordinarily meaning a man of integrity (Job 1:1,8), but perhaps here cultured or thoughtful.

25:28 *of his venison.* Of his hunting (same word as in v. 27). Sadly, *Isaac loved Esau* more than Jacob in disregard of God's word (v. 23). He was blinded by his love for food (27:4,9,14).

25:29 *sod pottage.* Cooked soup, literally, "stewed stew." *faint.* Weary, exhausted.

25:30 Literally, he ravenously babbled, "Let me gulp down some of the red, this red." The name *Edom* sounds like "red" in Hebrew. Edom's character was stained "red" by his unthinking

with that same red *pottage*; for I *am* faint: there-
fore was his name called Edom.
31 And Jacob said, Sell me this day thy birthright.
32 And Esau said, Behold, I *am* at the point to die:
and what profit shall this birthright do to me?
33 And Jacob said, Swear to me this day; and he
sware unto him: and he sold his birthright unto
Jacob.
34 Then Jacob gave Esau bread and pottage of
lentiles; and he did eat and drink, and rose up, and
went his way: thus Esau despised *his* birthright.

CHAPTER 26

AND there was a famine in the land, beside the
first famine that was in the days of Abraham. And
Isaac went unto Abimelech king of the Philistines
unto Gerar.
2 And the LORD appeared unto him, and said, Go
not down into Egypt; dwell in the land which I
shall tell thee of:
3 Sojourn in this land, and I will be with thee,
and will bless thee; for unto thee, and unto thy
seed, I will give all these countries, and I will per-
form the oath which I sware unto Abraham thy
father;
4 And I will make thy seed to multiply as the stars
of heaven, and will give unto thy seed all these
countries; and in thy seed shall all the nations of
the earth be blessed;
5 Because that Abraham obeyed my voice, and
kept my charge, my commandments, my statutes,
and my laws.
6 ¶ And Isaac dwelt in Gerar:
7 And the men of the place asked *him* of his wife;
and he said, She *is* my sister: for he feared to say,
She is my wife; lest, *said he*, the men of the place
should kill me for Rebekah; because she *was* fair
to look upon.
8 And it came to pass, when he had been there a
long time, that Abimelech king of the Philistines
looked out at a window, and saw, and, behold,
Isaac *was* sporting with Rebekah his wife.
9 And Abimelech called Isaac, and said, Behold,
of a surety she *is* thy wife: and how saidst thou,
She *is* my sister? And Isaac said unto him, Because
I said, Lest I die for her.
10 And Abimelech said, What *is* this thou hast
done unto us? one of the people might lightly
have lien with thy wife, and thou shouldest have
brought guiltiness upon us.
11 And Abimelech charged all *his* people, saying,
He that toucheth this man or his wife shall surely
be put to death.
12 Then Isaac sowed in that land, and received
in the same year an hundredfold: and the LORD
blessed him.
13 And the man waxed great, and went forward,
and grew until he became very great:
14 For he had possession of flocks, and possession

---

preoccupation with physical satisfaction (Heb. 12:16).

25:31 *birthright.* The right of the firstborn son to special honor (43:33) and a double portion of the inheritance (Deut. 21:17), in this case the blessing of the Lord. Jacob's demand reflects his determination to get God's blessing (32:26) and his sinful grasping after it by manipulation.

25:34 *pottage of lentiles.* Stew of red lentil beans. *did eat and drink, and rose up, and went his way.* Without regret or concern. *despised.* Regarded God's blessing as trivial.

Thoughts for Personal/Family Worship: Chapter 25

1. **We must prepare our estates and prepare our children for the time when we will die. Most of all, we must prepare ourselves for the day when our spirits will be gathered to another place. Will that place be heaven or hell?**
2. **God elected His people before they were born, apart from their works. In one family, God may select one and pass by another. Such election means that the Holy Spirit will produce a change in the sinner so that he hungers for grace. But if God does not elect and call him, then he hungers for this world and despises God's grace, and thus his condemnation is just. Do you hunger and thirst for God, or do you despise His Word?**

Chapter 26: *Isaac sojourns among the Philistines and repeats his father's sin, but the Lord reaffirms the promise of His presence.*

26:1 *the first famine.* See 12:10. *Abimelech.* Not the same man met by Abraham (see note at 20:2). This chapter showed the similarity between Abraham and Isaac in their trials, sins, and experiences of God's grace (vv. 1,3,7,18,24–25,28). Rather than the clumsy work of a hypothetical editor, as some scholars believe, this similarity reveals that God keeps the covenant with His people even as they face the same challenges as their fathers.

26:2–5 *The LORD appeared* to Isaac as He did to Abraham (12:7; 18:1; 26:24). As Abraham had to walk by faith by leaving Ur, so Isaac had to live by faith by staying in the land of famine. He had to *sojourn* as a landless foreigner while he waited for God's promised inheritance (20:1; 21:34; 23:4). God confirmed His promise to bless him and his seed (12:1–3; 22:17–18), *the oath* that He swore *unto Abraham* (22:16). The blessing came *because that Abraham obeyed* God (22:16) and taught his family to follow God's ways (18:19). *my charge, my commandments, my statutes, and my laws.* The same four Hebrew words are used of the law of Moses, for God's moral law does not change (1 Kings 2:3; cf. Ex. 24:12; Lev. 26:46; Deut. 4:40; 11:1).

26:7 *fair to look upon.* Beautiful. Isaac fell into the same cowardice as his father (12:11; 20:2).

26:8 *sporting.* Playfully "flirting" as husband and wife, an intensified form of "laugh," Isaac's name.

26:9 *of a surety.* Surely.

26:10 *lightly have lien with.* Easily could have had sexual relations with her. Abimelech shows us that even people who do not worship the Lord can be concerned about justice and mercy.

26:13 Literally, "And the man became great and walked walking and became great until he was very great." He became extremely wealthy.

26:14 *great store of servants.* Many servants.

of herds, and great store of servants: and the
Philistines envied him.
15 For all the wells which his father's servants
had digged in the days of Abraham his father,
the Philistines had stopped them, and filled them
with earth.
16 And Abimelech said unto Isaac, Go from us;
for thou art much mightier than we.
17 ¶ And Isaac departed thence, and pitched his
tent in the valley of Gerar, and dwelt there.
18 And Isaac digged again the wells of water,
which they had digged in the days of Abraham
his father; for the Philistines had stopped them
after the death of Abraham: and he called their
names after the names by which his father had
called them.
19 And Isaac's servants digged in the valley, and
found there a well of springing water.
20 And the herdmen of Gerar did strive with
Isaac's herdmen, saying, The water *is* ours: and
he called the name of the well Esek; because they
strove with him.
21 And they digged another well, and strove for
that also: and he called the name of it Sitnah.
22 And he removed from thence, and digged
another well; and for that they strove not: and he
called the name of it Rehoboth; and he said, For
now the LORD hath made room for us, and we
shall be fruitful in the land.
23 And he went up from thence to Beer-sheba.
24 And the LORD appeared unto him the same
night, and said, I *am* the God of Abraham thy fa-
ther: fear not, for I *am* with thee, and will bless
thee, and multiply thy seed for my servant Abra-
ham's sake.
25 And he builded an altar there, and called
upon the name of the LORD, and pitched his tent
there: and there Isaac's servants digged a well.
26 ¶ Then Abimelech went to him from Gerar,
and Ahuzzath one of his friends, and Phichol the
chief captain of his army.
27 And Isaac said unto them, Wherefore come ye
to me, seeing ye hate me, and have sent me away
from you?
28 And they said, We saw certainly that the LORD
was with thee: and we said, Let there be now an
oath betwixt us, *even* betwixt us and thee, and let
us make a covenant with thee;
29 That thou wilt do us no hurt, as we have not
touched thee, and as we have done unto thee noth-
ing but good, and have sent thee away in peace:
thou *art* now the blessed of the LORD.
30 And he made them a feast, and they did eat
and drink.
31 And they rose up betimes in the morning, and
sware one to another: and Isaac sent them away,
and they departed from him in peace.
32 And it came to pass the same day, that Isaac's
servants came, and told him concerning the well
which they had digged, and said unto him, We
have found water.
33 And he called it Shebah: therefore the name of
the city *is* Beer-sheba unto this day.
34 ¶ And Esau was forty years old when he took
to wife Judith the daughter of Beeri the Hittite,
and Bashemath the daughter of Elon the Hittite:
35 Which were a grief of mind unto Isaac and to
Rebekah.

CHAPTER 27

AND it came to pass, that when Isaac was old,
and his eyes were dim, so that he could not see,
he called Esau his eldest son, and said unto him,

26:15 *all the wells . . . the Philistines had stopped them, and filled them.* Cutting off access to wells and springs in an arid land threatened Isaac's family and flocks with disaster.
26:16–22 Though he was *much mightier* than the Philistines, Isaac sought peace rather than a fight, as Abraham did when he had a conflict with Lot (13:8).
26:24 *fear not, for I am with thee, and will bless thee.* Rather than rebuking Isaac for his weakness, the Lord called him to faith instead of fear. He was still the shield of Abraham (15:1).
26:25 Isaac responded to God's words with worship, just as Abraham had (12:7–8; 13:18).
26:28–31 Cutting a covenant involved swearing an oath and sharing a meal together, representing solemn commitment and joyful fellowship (Ex. 24:7–11). *betimes.* Early.
26:34–35 Abraham had been careful to seek a wife for Isaac from the worshipers of the Lord, not the Canaanites (24:3), but Esau neglected his grandfather's ways and grieved his parents. While business and political cooperation with unbelievers may be helpful, marriages with them are foolish.

Thoughts for Personal/Family Worship: Chapter 26

1. The Lord is the same yesterday, today, and forever. He still can be trusted to bless His people with physical provision and the hope of future glory. But the richest blessings that believers presently enjoy are the fruits and gifts of the Holy Spirit. In the midst of famines and other trials, let us seek these riches diligently in prayer.

2. Christians must be wise in their relationships with the world. We must not flee to worldly powers when trials come but trust the promises and obey God's moral law. Do not be surprised when the world is hostile, but do not let the fear of man lead you into lies and sin. Beware of relationships that entangle you with unbelievers.

Chapter 27: ***At his mother's instigation, Jacob tricks Isaac into giving him the blessing of the firstborn, enraging Esau but fulfilling God's prophecy.***

27:1–4 Just as Isaac's *eyes were dim*, so he was blind to Esau's ungodliness (25:34; 26:34) and failed to lead his family by God's promise to exalt Jacob (25:23). Instead he let his *love* for Esau's *savoury meat* control him (vv. 4,9,14). God's purpose to *bless* the elect seed still would prevail. The verb *bless* appears seventeen times in this chapter, and the related noun "blessing" six times.

My son: and he said unto him, Behold, *here am* I.
2 And he said, Behold now, I am old, I know not
the day of my death:
3 Now therefore take, I pray thee, thy weapons,
thy quiver and thy bow, and go out to the field,
and take me *some* venison;
4 And make me savoury meat, such as I love, and
bring *it* to me, that I may eat; that my soul may
bless thee before I die.
5 And Rebekah heard when Isaac spake to Esau
his son. And Esau went to the field to hunt *for*
venison, *and* to bring *it*.
6 ¶ And Rebekah spake unto Jacob her son, say-
ing, Behold, I heard thy father speak unto Esau
thy brother, saying,
7 Bring me venison, and make me savoury meat,
that I may eat, and bless thee before the LORD
before my death.
8 Now therefore, my son, obey my voice accord-
ing to that which I command thee.
9 Go now to the flock, and fetch me from thence
two good kids of the goats; and I will make them
savoury meat for thy father, such as he loveth:
10 And thou shalt bring *it* to thy father, that he
may eat, and that he may bless thee before his
death.
11 And Jacob said to Rebekah his mother, Be-
hold, Esau my brother *is* a hairy man, and I *am*
a smooth man:
12 My father peradventure will feel me, and I
shall seem to him as a deceiver; and I shall bring a
curse upon me, and not a blessing.
13 And his mother said unto him, Upon me *be*
thy curse, my son: only obey my voice, and go
fetch me *them*.
14 And he went, and fetched, and brought *them*
to his mother: and his mother made savoury
meat, such as his father loved.
15 And Rebekah took goodly raiment of her el-
dest son Esau, which *were* with her in the house,
and put them upon Jacob her younger son:
16 And she put the skins of the kids of the goats
upon his hands, and upon the smooth of his neck:
17 And she gave the savoury meat and the bread,
which she had prepared, into the hand of her son
Jacob.
18 ¶ And he came unto his father, and said, My
father: and he said, Here *am* I; who *art* thou, my
son?
19 And Jacob said unto his father, I *am* Esau thy
firstborn; I have done according as thou badest
me: arise, I pray thee, sit and eat of my venison,
that thy soul may bless me.
20 And Isaac said unto his son, How *is it* that thou
hast found *it* so quickly, my son? And he said,
Because the LORD thy God brought *it* to me.
21 And Isaac said unto Jacob, Come near, I pray
thee, that I may feel thee, my son, whether thou *be*
my very son Esau or not.
22 And Jacob went near unto Isaac his father; and
he felt him, and said, The voice *is* Jacob's voice,
but the hands *are* the hands of Esau.
23 And he discerned him not, because his hands
were hairy, as his brother Esau's hands: so he
blessed him.
24 And he said, *Art* thou my very son Esau? And
he said, I *am*.
25 And he said, Bring *it* near to me, and I will eat
of my son's venison, that my soul may bless thee.
And he brought *it* near to him, and he did eat: and
he brought him wine, and he drank.
26 And his father Isaac said unto him, Come near
now, and kiss me, my son.
27 And he came near, and kissed him: and he
smelled the smell of his raiment, and blessed him,
and said, See, the smell of my son *is* as the smell of
a field which the LORD hath blessed:
28 Therefore God give thee of the dew of heaven,
and the fatness of the earth, and plenty of corn
and wine:
29 Let people serve thee, and nations bow down
to thee: be lord over thy brethren, and let thy
mother's sons bow down to thee: cursed *be* ev-
ery one that curseth thee, and blessed *be* he that
blesseth thee.
30 ¶ And it came to pass, as soon as Isaac had
made an end of blessing Jacob, and Jacob was
yet scarce gone out from the presence of Isaac
his father, that Esau his brother came in from his
hunting.
31 And he also had made savoury meat, and
brought it unto his father, and said unto his father,
Let my father arise, and eat of his son's venison,
that thy soul may bless me.

27:5–6 *Isaac spake to Esau his son . . . Rebekah spake unto Jacob her son*. The family is fractured by favoritism (25:28). Rebekah called Esau *thy brother*, but called Jacob *her son*. Conversely, Isaac called Jacob *thy brother* but only Esau *his son*, not even addressing Jacob as his son when he sent him away (28:1–4). The family did not communicate openly, and only at the end did Rebekah speak directly to Isaac.

27:11–12 *peradventure*. Perhaps. Jacob feared getting caught, but not sinning (contrast with 39:9).

27:15 *goodly raiment*. Delightful clothes.

27:19 *badest*. Said.

27:20 *the LORD thy God brought it to me*. He did not shrink from blasphemy by bringing God's name into his lie. In an ironic contrast of deception against dependence, he used the same Hebrew expression that Abraham's servant did in his prayer to God (24:12).

27:21–27 Inclined to gratify his senses of touch, taste, and smell through food, Isaac was vulnerable to manipulation through those same senses.

27:28–29 *dew*. Important in an arid region (Ps. 133:3; Prov. 19:12). *fatness of the earth*. Fertile and productive soil. *corn*. General term for grain. *thy brethren*. The extended family

32 And Isaac his father said unto him, Who *art*
thou? And he said, I *am* thy son, thy firstborn
Esau.
33 And Isaac trembled very exceedingly, and said,
Who? where *is* he that hath taken venison, and
brought *it* me, and I have eaten of all before thou
camest, and have blessed him? yea, *and* he shall
be blessed.
34 And when Esau heard the words of his father,
he cried with a great and exceeding bitter cry, and
said unto his father, Bless me, *even* me also, O my
father.
35 And he said, Thy brother came with subtilty,
and hath taken away thy blessing.
36 And he said, Is not he rightly named Jacob? for
he hath supplanted me these two times: he took
away my birthright; and, behold, now he hath
taken away my blessing. And he said, Hast thou
not reserved a blessing for me?
37 And Isaac answered and said unto Esau, Behold, I have made him thy lord, and all his brethren have I given to him for servants; and with
corn and wine have I sustained him: and what
shall I do now unto thee, my son?
38 And Esau said unto his father, Hast thou but
one blessing, my father? bless me, *even* me also, O
my father. And Esau lifted up his voice, and wept.
39 And Isaac his father answered and said unto
him, Behold, thy dwelling shall be the fatness of
the earth, and of the dew of heaven from above;
40 And by thy sword shalt thou live, and shalt
serve thy brother; and it shall come to pass when
thou shalt have the dominion, that thou shalt
break his yoke from off thy neck.
41 ¶ And Esau hated Jacob because of the blessing wherewith his father blessed him: and Esau
said in his heart, The days of mourning for my father are at hand; then will I slay my brother Jacob.
42 And these words of Esau her elder son were
told to Rebekah: and she sent and called Jacob
her younger son, and said unto him, Behold, thy
brother Esau, as touching thee, doth comfort
himself, *purposing* to kill thee.
43 Now therefore, my son, obey my voice; and
arise, flee thou to Laban my brother to Haran;
44 And tarry with him a few days, until thy brother's fury turn away;
45 Until thy brother's anger turn away from thee,
and he forget *that* which thou hast done to him:
then I will send, and fetch thee from thence: why
should I be deprived also of you both in one day?
46 And Rebekah said to Isaac, I am weary of my
life because of the daughters of Heth: if Jacob
take a wife of the daughters of Heth, such as these
which are of the daughters of the land, what good
shall my life do me?

CHAPTER 28

AND Isaac called Jacob, and blessed him, and
charged him, and said unto him, Thou shalt not
take a wife of the daughters of Canaan.
2 Arise, go to Padan-aram, to the house of
Bethuel thy mother's father; and take thee a wife
from thence of the daughters of Laban thy mother's brother.
3 And God Almighty bless thee, and make thee
fruitful, and multiply thee, that thou mayest be a
multitude of people;
4 And give thee the blessing of Abraham, to thee,

(31:46). Isaac blessed him with prosperity and royalty.

27:33 *yea, and he shall be blessed.* Perhaps a father's blessing was irrevocable, but it may also be that Isaac realized that God was fulfilling His word to lift up the younger son (25:23).

27:35 *subtilty.* Deceit, fraud.

27:36 *Jacob . . . supplanted me.* One could render it, "Jacob jacobed me." The name *Jacob* means to take by the heel (25:26), suggesting to attack from behind or cheat.

27:40 *yoke.* Subjection to authority. Edom would be subjugated by David (2 Sam. 8:14), but later rebelled against Solomon, Joram, and future kings (1 Kings 11:14–22; 2 Kings 8:20–22).

27:42–45 Though Jacob received the blessing as God ordained, he and his mother paid a high price for their deceitful scheming. Despite Rebekah's hopes, Jacob would stay (*tarry*) with his uncle far from his parents not *a few days*, but for twenty years (31:38,41).

27:46 Rebekah again manipulated her husband, her last words in Genesis; she next appears in the tomb (49:31).

Thoughts for Personal/Family Worship: Chapter 27

1. **The sins of believers can hurt and divide their families. Favoritism, broken lines of communication, lies, the love of the world, nominal religion, and seeking God's blessing through sinful means can tear Christian families apart. While God's purposes of grace cannot fail, He will discipline His people, possibly through broken relationships. Let us therefore repent of our sins, speak openly with each other in love, and seek peace.**
2. **God is sovereign over sin. He does not command it or cause it, but He decreed each sin as part of His plan to fulfill His good purposes (50:20). He is in control. This gives us a powerful reason to seek His blessing by prayer rather than manipulating others.**

Chapter 28: *The Lord appears to Jacob on the road to Haran, revealing His promises of grace and moving the son of Isaac to fear and worship.*

28:1 *charged.* Commanded him, to which Jacob responded with obedience (v. 7).

28:2 *Padan-aram.* Northwest Mesopotamia near Haran (v. 10), about five hundred miles to the north. In contrast to the caravan of Abraham's servant (24:10,32,54), Jacob appears to travel alone.

28:3–4 *Almighty.* See note at 17:1. *multitude of people.* An assembly of peoples (35:11; 48:4). The word meaning "assembly" is often used of the congregation of Israel (Ps. 22:22–31); here it is many nations called together to worship the Lord. Isaac pronounced on Jacob the covenantal *blessing* given to *Abraham* by the Lord (12:1–3; 17:1–8).

and to thy seed with thee; that thou mayest in-
herit the land wherein thou art a stranger, which
God gave unto Abraham.
5 And Isaac sent away Jacob: and he went to Padan-
aram unto Laban, son of Bethuel the Syrian, the
brother of Rebekah, Jacob's and Esau's mother.
6 ¶ When Esau saw that Isaac had blessed Jacob,
and sent him away to Padan-aram, to take him a
wife from thence; and that as he blessed him he
gave him a charge, saying, Thou shalt not take a
wife of the daughters of Canaan;
7 And that Jacob obeyed his father and his
mother, and was gone to Padan-aram;
8 And Esau seeing that the daughters of Canaan
pleased not Isaac his father;
9 Then went Esau unto Ishmael, and took unto
the wives which he had Mahalath the daughter of
Ishmael Abraham's son, the sister of Nebajoth, to
be his wife.
10 ¶ And Jacob went out from Beer-sheba, and
went toward Haran.
11 And he lighted upon a certain place, and tar-
ried there all night, because the sun was set; and
he took of the stones of that place, and put *them*
for his pillows, and lay down in that place to sleep.
12 And he dreamed, and behold a ladder set up
on the earth, and the top of it reached to heaven:
and behold the angels of God ascending and de-
scending on it.
13 And, behold, the LORD stood above it, and
said, I *am* the LORD God of Abraham thy father,
and the God of Isaac: the land whereon thou liest,
to thee will I give it, and to thy seed;
14 And thy seed shall be as the dust of the earth,
and thou shalt spread abroad to the west, and to
the east, and to the north, and to the south: and
in thee and in thy seed shall all the families of the
earth be blessed.
15 And, behold, I *am* with thee, and will keep thee
in all *places* whither thou goest, and will bring
thee again into this land; for I will not leave thee,
until I have done *that* which I have spoken to thee
of.
16 ¶ And Jacob awaked out of his sleep, and he
said, Surely the LORD is in this place; and I knew
it not.
17 And he was afraid, and said, How dreadful *is*
this place! this *is* none other but the house of God,
and this *is* the gate of heaven.
18 And Jacob rose up early in the morning, and
took the stone that he had put *for* his pillows, and
set it up *for* a pillar, and poured oil upon the top
of it.
19 And he called the name of that place Beth-el:
but the name of that city *was called* Luz at the first.
20 And Jacob vowed a vow, saying, If God will be
with me, and will keep me in this way that I go, and
will give me bread to eat, and raiment to put on,
21 So that I come again to my father's house in
peace; then shall the LORD be my God:
22 And this stone, which I have set *for* a pillar,
shall be God's house: and of all that thou shalt
give me I will surely give the tenth unto thee.

CHAPTER 29

THEN Jacob went on his journey, and came into
the land of the people of the east.
2 And he looked, and behold a well in the field,
and, lo, there *were* three flocks of sheep lying by it;

28:9 *Mahalath.* See note at 36:3.

28:10–11 *lighted upon.* Happened to come to. *tarried.* Stayed. From *Beer-sheba* to Beth-el (v. 19) is about fifty miles, a few days' journey. *pillows.* Some ancient people did use hard headrests, but this may mean placed by his head (1 Kings 19:6), possibly for ready self-defense (1 Sam. 26:7).

28:12 *ladder.* Staircase or ramp. Christ implied that this bridge between heaven and earth was a type of Himself, God and man, the only way to the Father (John 1:51; cf. John 1:1,14; 14:6). *angels of God.* Powerful spirits who are messengers of the Lord (19:1,11,13,15; 32:1–3).

28:13–15 *the LORD stood above it.* Or possibly, the Lord stood "over him" on earth (v. 16). The Lord gave His promises to Jacob as He had done earlier with Isaac (26:24). *God of Abraham.* Title of covenant faithfulness (17:7; Ex. 3:13–17). *I will not leave thee.* Believers reject greedy grasping like Jacob and rest content in what we have, for we have God Himself forever (Heb. 13:5).

28:16–18 *the LORD is in this place . . . the house of God . . . the gate of heaven.* The dream of heaven joined to earth (v. 12) revealed God's intent to dwell permanently with His people (v. 15). As the *gate* was not just an entrance but the hub of a city's trade, so the Lord was bringing the very business of *heaven* to earth. God's Word develops this great theme in the tabernacle, the temple, Christ, the church, and the heavenly city of Jerusalem (Ex. 29:45; 1 Kings 8:13; Matt. 1:23; Eph. 2:22; Rev. 21:3). *dreadful.* Fearful, awe-inspiring. Even when God comes in grace, His presence inspires fear (31:42).

28:20–22 Jacob took a solemn vow that if the Lord would *be with* him, protect him in his travels, and give him the necessities of food (*bread*) and clothing (*raiment*), then he would worship the Lord as his covenant God and give Him tithes of his income (*the tenth*; cf. 14:20).

Thoughts for Personal/Family Worship: Chapter 28

1. **Man attempts to grasp heaven but his efforts fail, whether they are the proud labors of the Tower of Babel or the deceitful manipulations of Jacob. However, God bridges the gap with Jesus Christ. He is the only Mediator, the stairway to heaven. Let us repent of our pride and deceitful ways, and rest content in Christ alone as the Almighty Savior.**
2. **The church of Christ is the greatest wonder on earth. It is the assembly of many peoples, diverse nations united by the worship of the one true God. It is the house of God and the gate of heaven. Sadly, though "the LORD is in this place," many would have to confess, "I knew it not." Do you come to church with holy fear, since God dwells with His people?**

Chapter 29: ***Jacob comes to his uncle Laban, marries Leah and Rachel, and Leah begins bearing him children.***

29:1 *the people of the east.* A hint that Laban is a worshiper

for out of that well they watered the flocks: and a
great stone *was* upon the well's mouth.
3 And thither were all the flocks gathered: and
they rolled the stone from the well's mouth, and
watered the sheep, and put the stone again upon
the well's mouth in his place.
4 And Jacob said unto them, My brethren,
whence *be* ye? And they said, Of Haran *are* we.
5 And he said unto them, Know ye Laban the son
of Nahor? And they said, We know *him*.
6 And he said unto them, *Is* he well? And they
said, *He is* well: and, behold, Rachel his daughter
cometh with the sheep.
7 And he said, Lo, *it is* yet high day, neither *is it*
time that the cattle should be gathered together:
water ye the sheep, and go *and* feed *them*.
8 And they said, We cannot, until all the flocks be
gathered together, and *till* they roll the stone from
the well's mouth; then we water the sheep.
9 ¶ And while he yet spake with them, Rachel
came with her father's sheep: for she kept them.
10 And it came to pass, when Jacob saw Rachel
the daughter of Laban his mother's brother, and
the sheep of Laban his mother's brother, that
Jacob went near, and rolled the stone from the
well's mouth, and watered the flock of Laban his
mother's brother.
11 And Jacob kissed Rachel, and lifted up his
voice, and wept.
12 And Jacob told Rachel that he *was* her father's
brother, and that he *was* Rebekah's son: and she
ran and told her father.
13 And it came to pass, when Laban heard the
tidings of Jacob his sister's son, that he ran to
meet him, and embraced him, and kissed him,
and brought him to his house. And he told Laban
all these things.
14 And Laban said to him, Surely thou *art* my
bone and my flesh. And he abode with him the
space of a month.
15 ¶ And Laban said unto Jacob, Because thou *art*
my brother, shouldest thou therefore serve me for
nought? tell me, what *shall* thy wages *be*?
16 And Laban had two daughters: the name of
the elder *was* Leah, and the name of the younger
was Rachel.
17 Leah *was* tender eyed; but Rachel was beauti-
ful and well favoured.
18 And Jacob loved Rachel; and said, I will serve
thee seven years for Rachel thy younger daughter.
19 And Laban said, *It is* better that I give her to
thee, than that I should give her to another man:
abide with me.
20 And Jacob served seven years for Rachel; and
they seemed unto him *but* a few days, for the love
he had to her.
21 ¶ And Jacob said unto Laban, Give *me* my wife,
for my days are fulfilled, that I may go in unto her.
22 And Laban gathered together all the men of
the place, and made a feast.
23 And it came to pass in the evening, that he
took Leah his daughter, and brought her to him;
and he went in unto her.
24 And Laban gave unto his daughter Leah Zil-
pah his maid *for* an handmaid.
25 And it came to pass, that in the morning,
behold, it *was* Leah: and he said to Laban, What
is this thou hast done unto me? did not I serve
with thee for Rachel? wherefore then hast thou
beguiled me?
26 And Laban said, It must not be so done in our
country, to give the younger before the firstborn.
27 Fulfil her week, and we will give thee this also
for the service which thou shalt serve with me yet
seven other years.
28 And Jacob did so, and fulfilled her week: and
he gave him Rachel his daughter to wife also.
29 And Laban gave to Rachel his daughter Bilhah
his handmaid to be her maid.
30 And he went in also unto Rachel, and he loved
also Rachel more than Leah, and served with him
yet seven other years.
31 ¶ And when the LORD saw that Leah *was* hated,
he opened her womb: but Rachel *was* barren.

---

of other gods (31:19,30), as the *east* in Genesis sometimes implies away from God's presence (3:24; 4:16; 11:1–3).

29:3 *thither.* To there.

29:4 *whence be ye.* From where do you come?

29:10 Jacob was a strong man, able to roll a large stone that ordinarily required more than one man to move (vv. 2–3). The stone of ch. 28 symbolized God's grace; here the stone reveals Jacob's strength. In contrast to the servant of Abraham, who traveled to this same region but approached the well with prayer to the Lord (24:11–14), Jacob depended on his own strength.

29:11 *lifted up his voice, and wept.* Jacob was overwhelmed at God's providence leading him quickly to the daughter of Laban, exactly the person his father sent him to find (28:2).

29:15 *nought.* Nothing. Six times this chapter says that Jacob had to *serve* Laban (vv. 15,18,20,25,27,30; cf. 30:26,29; 31:6,41), a term associated with the labor of servants and slaves (15:13–14; Ex. 1:13–14). Though Isaac had blessed Jacob with supremacy so that nations would serve him (27:29), for now God forced Jacob to serve others in order to teach humility.

29:17 *tender eyed.* Leah's eyes were "soft," either weak or gentle. *beautiful and well favoured.* Literally, "attractive of form and attractive of appearance." Jacob foolishly allowed physical desires to dictate his choices (39:6–7), just as Isaac followed his appetite for food (25:28).

29:25 *wherefore then hast thou beguiled me?* Why did you trick me? Jacob who had tricked his brother and father now finds himself the target of treachery, at the cost of another seven years of his labor. Jacob the younger son had disguised himself as the older son to trick Isaac; now Laban disguised the older daughter as the younger daughter to trick Jacob. God was wrestling with Jacob to discipline him and to teach him to hate deception.

32 And Leah conceived, and bare a son, and she
called his name Reuben: for she said, Surely the
LORD hath looked upon my affliction; now there-
fore my husband will love me.
33 And she conceived again, and bare a son; and
said, Because the LORD hath heard that I *was*
hated, he hath therefore given me this *son* also:
and she called his name Simeon.
34 And she conceived again, and bare a son; and
said, Now this time will my husband be joined
unto me, because I have born him three sons:
therefore was his name called Levi.
35 And she conceived again, and bare a son: and
she said, Now will I praise the LORD: therefore she
called his name Judah; and left bearing.

CHAPTER 30

AND when Rachel saw that she bare Jacob no
children, Rachel envied her sister; and said unto
Jacob, Give me children, or else I die.
2 And Jacob's anger was kindled against Rachel:
and he said, *Am* I in God's stead, who hath with-
held from thee the fruit of the womb?
3 And she said, Behold my maid Bilhah, go in
unto her; and she shall bear upon my knees, that I
may also have children by her.
4 And she gave him Bilhah her handmaid to wife:
and Jacob went in unto her.
5 And Bilhah conceived, and bare Jacob a son.
6 And Rachel said, God hath judged me, and hath
also heard my voice, and hath given me a son:
therefore called she his name Dan.
7 And Bilhah Rachel's maid conceived again, and
bare Jacob a second son.
8 And Rachel said, With great wrestlings have I
wrestled with my sister, and I have prevailed: and
she called his name Naphtali.
9 When Leah saw that she had left bearing, she
took Zilpah her maid, and gave her Jacob to wife.
10 And Zilpah Leah's maid bare Jacob a son.
11 And Leah said, A troop cometh: and she called
his name Gad.
12 And Zilpah Leah's maid bare Jacob a second son.
13 And Leah said, Happy am I, for the daughters
will call me blessed: and she called his name Asher.
14 ¶ And Reuben went in the days of wheat
harvest, and found mandrakes in the field, and
brought them unto his mother Leah. Then Ra-
chel said to Leah, Give me, I pray thee, of thy son's
mandrakes.
15 And she said unto her, *Is it* a small matter that
thou hast taken my husband? and wouldest thou
take away my son's mandrakes also? And Rachel
said, Therefore he shall lie with thee to night for
thy son's mandrakes.
16 And Jacob came out of the field in the evening,
and Leah went out to meet him, and said, Thou
must come in unto me; for surely I have hired
thee with my son's mandrakes. And he lay with
her that night.
17 And God hearkened unto Leah, and she con-
ceived, and bare Jacob the fifth son.
18 And Leah said, God hath given me my hire,
because I have given my maiden to my husband:
and she called his name Issachar.
19 And Leah conceived again, and bare Jacob the
sixth son.
20 And Leah said, God hath endued me *with* a
good dowry; now will my husband dwell with me,

29:31–35 In the midst of the rivalry between Jacob's two wives, the Lord revealed His glory in several ways. He showed His compassion for the suffering, such as an unloved (*hated*) wife. He exercised His power over conception and birth. He demonstrated His faithfulness to keep His promises in multiplying the seed of Abraham, Isaac, and Jacob. He used His sovereignty over suffering to draw out of evil the praise of His name (*now I will praise the LORD*). And He glorified His wisdom by making the wife Jacob did not prefer into the mother of Moses, Aaron, and the priesthood (by *Levi*) and of David, the kings, and Christ Himself (by *Judah*).

Thoughts for Personal/Family Worship: Chapter 29

1. **God disciplines His children, at times with poetic justice, when the sinning Christian must suffer similar sins from others. God's faithfulness to His people should not diminish our fear of displeasing Him. He is a strong and holy Father. Let us tremble at the thought of sinning against such a God and not despise His discipline.**
2. **Are you relying on your own strength to move obstacles or crying out to the Lord? Our God has abundant compassion, power, and faithfulness. He is always at work even through human sin. Take your painful situation to Him in prayer, and give Him the praise when He answers you.**

Chapter 30: *Jacob's wives bear children in bitter rivalry, and Jacob and Laban seek to swindle each other.*

30:1–2 *in God's stead.* In the place of God. *fruit of the womb.* Children. Childlessness provoked Jacob and Rachel to quarrel, revealing the shallowness of their attraction for each other.
30:3 *upon my knees.* As Rachel's children (50:23).
30:6–8 Leah's naming of her children revolved around longing for her husband's love, but Rachel's naming of Bilhah's children smacks of self-righteousness and pride.
30:11 *troop.* Or good fortune.
30:14 *mandrakes.* Plant believed to increase sexual desire (Song 7:13).
30:15 The scenario suggests that Jacob had ceased having regular sexual relations with Leah.
30:16 Jacob did not lead his family with fatherly wisdom and love, but acted like a mere pawn or *hired* man in the struggle between Rachel and Leah.
30:17 Rachel used mandrakes, but Leah called upon the Lord and He heard (*hearkened*) Leah's request and gave her more children.
30:20 *endued me with a good dowry.* Given me a good gift.
30:22 *God remembered Rachel.* Refers to God acting according to His covenant faithfulness and love (6:18; 8:1; 9:15–16; Ex. 2:24; 6:5; Lev. 26:42,45).

because I have born him six sons: and she called
his name Zebulun.
21 And afterwards she bare a daughter, and called
her name Dinah.
22 ¶ And God remembered Rachel, and God
hearkened to her, and opened her womb.
23 And she conceived, and bare a son; and said,
God hath taken away my reproach:
24 And she called his name Joseph; and said, The
LORD shall add to me another son.
25 ¶ And it came to pass, when Rachel had born
Joseph, that Jacob said unto Laban, Send me away,
that I may go unto mine own place, and to my
country.
26 Give *me* my wives and my children, for whom I
have served thee, and let me go: for thou knowest
my service which I have done thee.
27 And Laban said unto him, I pray thee, if I
have found favour in thine eyes, *tarry: for* I have
learned by experience that the LORD hath blessed
me for thy sake.
28 And he said, Appoint me thy wages, and I will
give *it*.
29 And he said unto him, Thou knowest how I
have served thee, and how thy cattle was with me.
30 For *it was* little which thou hadst before I
came, and it is *now* increased unto a multitude;
and the LORD hath blessed thee since my com-
ing: and now when shall I provide for mine own
house also?
31 And he said, What shall I give thee? And Jacob
said, Thou shalt not give me any thing: if thou
wilt do this thing for me, I will again feed *and*
keep thy flock:
32 I will pass through all thy flock to day, re-
moving from thence all the speckled and spotted
cattle, and all the brown cattle among the sheep,
and the spotted and speckled among the goats:
and *of such* shall be my hire.
33 So shall my righteousness answer for me in
time to come, when it shall come for my hire be-
fore thy face: every one that *is* not speckled and
spotted among the goats, and brown among the
sheep, that shall be counted stolen with me.
34 And Laban said, Behold, I would it might be
according to thy word.
35 And he removed that day the he goats that
were ringstraked and spotted, and all the she
goats that were speckled and spotted, *and* every
one that had *some* white in it, and all the brown
among the sheep, and gave *them* into the hand of
his sons.
36 And he set three days' journey betwixt himself
and Jacob: and Jacob fed the rest of Laban's flocks.
37 ¶ And Jacob took him rods of green pop-
lar, and of the hazel and chesnut tree; and pilled
white strakes in them, and made the white appear
which *was* in the rods.
38 And he set the rods which he had pilled before
the flocks in the gutters in the watering troughs
when the flocks came to drink, that they should
conceive when they came to drink.
39 And the flocks conceived before the rods, and
brought forth cattle ringstraked, speckled, and
spotted.
40 And Jacob did separate the lambs, and set the
faces of the flocks toward the ringstraked, and all
the brown in the flock of Laban; and he put his
own flocks by themselves, and put them not unto
Laban's cattle.
41 And it came to pass, whensoever the stronger
cattle did conceive, that Jacob laid the rods be-
fore the eyes of the cattle in the gutters, that they
might conceive among the rods.
42 But when the cattle were feeble, he put *them*
not in: so the feebler were Laban's, and the stron-
ger Jacob's.
43 And the man increased exceedingly, and had

30:23 *reproach.* Disgrace.

30:24 Rachel learned to look not to mandrakes but to her Maker for children. God appears over a dozen times in the account of the birth of Jacob's children: *the LORD* (Hebrew, *Jehovah*) four times in 29:31–35 (Leah), "God" twice in 30:1–16 (Bilhah and Zilpah), "God" three times in 30:17–21 (Leah), "God" three times in 30:22–23 (Rachel), and *the LORD* in 30:24 (Rachel). God overruled the ugliness of polygamy and strife to multiply the covenant seed as He promised.

30:27 *experience.* Divination, the use of magic and omens to gain secret knowledge—forbidden by the Lord (Deut. 18:10–14). *blessed me for thy sake.* God's presence with His people blesses even their unbelieving family and neighbors (v. 30; 39:5).

30:32 *cattle.* Not only cows and bulls, but in the old sense of livestock in general, particularly here sheep and goats. Only a fraction of them would be of mixed colors.

30:35–36 *ringstraked.* Striped. *white.* The Hebrew word for "white" is *laban* (v. 37), a pun with the name of Laban, reminding us of Jacob's bartering with Esau or Edom whose name means "red" (25:29–34). *betwixt.* Between. Laban treacherously isolated the flocks with mixed colors from those tended by Jacob in order to rob him of his share of their bargain.

30:37–42 *hazel.* Almond tree. *chesnut.* Plane tree. *pilled.* Peeled. *strakes.* Stripes. Jacob made a foolish attempt to manipulate the breeding of the sheep through superstition, as if the colors of the wood controlled the colors of the sheep's offspring as a mandrake controlled fertility. He also employed the science of selective breeding to favor the stronger animals. The Lord later revealed to Jacob that his success came from God (31:11–12).

30:43 *increased exceedingly.* Literally, Jacob "broke out very much" or "spread out very much," exactly what the Lord had promised (28:14). Despite the oppression of Laban and their own sins, God blessed the family of Jacob with many offspring, servants, and livestock.

Thoughts for Personal/Family Worship: Chapter 30

1. **Few matters touch a woman's heart more than her children and her husband's love. Men are often driven to**

much cattle, and maidservants, and menservants,
and camels, and asses.

CHAPTER 31

AND he heard the words of Laban's sons, saying,
Jacob hath taken away all that *was* our father's;
and of *that* which *was* our father's hath he gotten
all this glory.
2 And Jacob beheld the countenance of Laban,
and, behold, it *was* not toward him as before.
3 And the LORD said unto Jacob, Return unto the
land of thy fathers, and to thy kindred; and I will
be with thee.
4 And Jacob sent and called Rachel and Leah to
the field unto his flock,
5 And said unto them, I see your father's counte-
nance, that it *is* not toward me as before; but the
God of my father hath been with me.
6 And ye know that with all my power I have
served your father.
7 And your father hath deceived me, and changed
my wages ten times; but God suffered him not to
hurt me.
8 If he said thus, The speckled shall be thy wages;
then all the cattle bare speckled: and if he said
thus, The ringstraked shall be thy hire; then bare
all the cattle ringstraked.
9 Thus God hath taken away the cattle of your
father, and given *them* to me.
10 And it came to pass at the time that the cattle
conceived, that I lifted up mine eyes, and saw in a
dream, and, behold, the rams which leaped upon
the cattle *were* ringstraked, speckled, and grisled.
11 And the angel of God spake unto me in a
dream, *saying*, Jacob: And I said, Here *am* I.
12 And he said, Lift up now thine eyes, and see,
all the rams which leap upon the cattle *are* ring-
straked, speckled, and grisled: for I have seen all
that Laban doeth unto thee.
13 I *am* the God of Beth-el, where thou anoint-
edst the pillar, *and* where thou vowedst a vow
unto me: now arise, get thee out from this land,
and return unto the land of thy kindred.
14 And Rachel and Leah answered and said unto
him, *Is there* yet any portion or inheritance for us
in our father's house?
15 Are we not counted of him strangers? for he
hath sold us, and hath quite devoured also our
money.
16 For all the riches which God hath taken from
our father, that *is* ours, and our children's: now
then, whatsoever God hath said unto thee, do.
17 ¶ Then Jacob rose up, and set his sons and his
wives upon camels;
18 And he carried away all his cattle, and all his
goods which he had gotten, the cattle of his get-
ting, which he had gotten in Padan-aram, for to
go to Isaac his father in the land of Canaan.
19 And Laban went to shear his sheep: and Rachel
had stolen the images that *were* her father's.
20 And Jacob stole away unawares to Laban the
Syrian, in that he told him not that he fled.
21 So he fled with all that he had; and he rose up,
and passed over the river, and set his face *toward*
the mount Gilead.
22 And it was told Laban on the third day that
Jacob was fled.
23 And he took his brethren with him, and
pursued after him seven days' journey; and they
overtook him in the mount Gilead.
24 And God came to Laban the Syrian in a dream
by night, and said unto him, Take heed that thou
speak not to Jacob either good or bad.

---

seek success in their work and wealth; let us beware lest these natural desires become idols and lead us into sins such as deception and injustice.

2. **Sin has consequences but can never defeat God's purposes. Multiple sexual relationships and dishonest and selfish business practices create sorrow, envy, and hatred. But the Lord uses sin to fulfill His promises and to multiply His people throughout the world. If you are in a family or business situation marred by sin, wait on the Lord and put your trust in His Word. He will bless you and build His kingdom.**

Chapter 31: *Jacob flees toward Canaan and Laban pursues him, resulting in a confrontation that again reveals God's faithful mercy.*

31:1 *glory*. Wealth.

31:2 *countenance*. Face, that is, favor and approval (v. 5; 32:20).

31:3 *Return unto the land of thy fathers*. The Lord called Jacob to Canaan like Abraham. *kindred*. Extended family. *I will be with thee*. God offered His promise and presence to overcome Jacob's fear of Laban and Esau.

31:7–9 *suffered*. Literally, "gave," as in sovereign permission. *cattle*. Livestock. *ringstraked*. Striped. Laban repeatedly changed their business agreement (vv. 31–34), but divine providence protected and prospered Jacob.

31:10 *leaped upon*. Mated with. *grisled*. Spotted.

31:11–13 *angel of God . . . I have seen*. The divine Mediator, the Living One who sees and has compassion (16:7,13–14). *God of Beth-el*. The Lord reminded Jacob of God's promise to bless him and give him the land, and of Jacob's *vow* to worship the Lord as his God (28:13–33).

31:19 *images*. Figures of household gods (vv. 30,32; Judg. 17:5; 18:14–20). Rachel may have taken them for protection, monetary value, revenge, or symbolism of owning the inheritance.

31:20 *stole away unawares*. Jacob obeyed God's call, but snuck away in fear rather than dealing openly with Laban in the fear of God (vv. 27,31).

31:21 *the mount Gilead*. Hilly country east of Jordan River.

31:24 *Take heed*. Watch yourself. *either good or bad*. The Lord did not prohibit Laban from speaking, but from passing a legal judgment over Jacob (v. 29; 2 Sam. 13:22; 1 Kings 3:9). Once the Lord reveals His verdict in a case, His judgment stands (24:50).

31:26–27 *mirth*. Gladness. *tabret*. Tambourine. Laban

25 ¶ Then Laban overtook Jacob. Now Jacob had
pitched his tent in the mount: and Laban with his
brethren pitched in the mount of Gilead.
26 And Laban said to Jacob, What hast thou done,
that thou hast stolen away unawares to me, and
carried away my daughters, as captives *taken* with
the sword?
27 Wherefore didst thou flee away secretly, and
steal away from me; and didst not tell me, that I
might have sent thee away with mirth, and with
songs, with tabret, and with harp?
28 And hast not suffered me to kiss my sons and
my daughters? thou hast now done foolishly in
so doing.
29 It is in the power of my hand to do you hurt:
but the God of your father spake unto me yester-
night, saying, Take thou heed that thou speak not
to Jacob either good or bad.
30 And now, *though* thou wouldest needs be
gone, because thou sore longedst after thy father's
house, *yet* wherefore hast thou stolen my gods?
31 And Jacob answered and said to Laban, Be-
cause I was afraid: for I said, Peradventure thou
wouldest take by force thy daughters from me.
32 With whomsoever thou findest thy gods, let
him not live: before our brethren discern thou
what *is* thine with me, and take *it* to thee. For
Jacob knew not that Rachel had stolen them.
33 And Laban went into Jacob's tent, and into
Leah's tent, and into the two maidservants' tents;
but he found *them* not. Then went he out of
Leah's tent, and entered into Rachel's tent.
34 Now Rachel had taken the images, and put
them in the camel's furniture, and sat upon them.
And Laban searched all the tent, but found *them*
not.
35 And she said to her father, Let it not displease
my lord that I cannot rise up before thee; for the
custom of women *is* upon me. And he searched,
but found not the images.
36 ¶ And Jacob was wroth, and chode with La-
ban: and Jacob answered and said to Laban, What
is my trespass? what *is* my sin, that thou hast so
hotly pursued after me?
37 Whereas thou hast searched all my stuff, what
hast thou found of all thy household stuff? set *it*
here before my brethren and thy brethren, that
they may judge betwixt us both.
38 This twenty years *have* I *been* with thee; thy
ewes and thy she goats have not cast their young,
and the rams of thy flock have I not eaten.
39 That which was torn *of beasts* I brought not
unto thee; I bare the loss of it; of my hand didst
thou require it, *whether* stolen by day, or stolen
by night.
40 *Thus* I was; in the day the drought consumed
me, and the frost by night; and my sleep departed
from mine eyes.
41 Thus have I been twenty years in thy house; I
served thee fourteen years for thy two daughters,
and six years for thy cattle: and thou hast changed
my wages ten times.
42 Except the God of my father, the God of Abra-
ham, and the fear of Isaac, had been with me,
surely thou hadst sent me away now empty. God
hath seen mine affliction and the labour of my
hands, and rebuked *thee* yesternight.
43 ¶ And Laban answered and said unto Jacob,
These daughters *are* my daughters, and *these*
children *are* my children, and *these* cattle *are* my
cattle, and all that thou seest *is* mine: and what
can I do this day unto these my daughters, or unto
their children which they have born?
44 Now therefore come thou, let us make a
covenant, I and thou; and let it be for a witness
between me and thee.
45 And Jacob took a stone, and set it up *for* a pillar.
46 And Jacob said unto his brethren, Gather
stones; and they took stones, and made an heap:
and they did eat there upon the heap.
47 And Laban called it Jegar-sahadutha: but Jacob
called it Galeed.
48 And Laban said, This heap *is* a witness between
me and thee this day. Therefore was the name of
it called Galeed;
49 And Mizpah; for he said, The LORD watch
between me and thee, when we are absent one
from another.
50 If thou shalt afflict my daughters, or if thou
shalt take *other* wives beside my daughters, no

---

hypocritically depicted Jacob as an oppressive kidnapper and himself as a loving father.

31:29 *yesternight*. Last night.

31:30 *thou wouldest needs be gone because thou sore longedst after*. You must go because you greatly desired. *wherefore*. Why.

31:31 *Peradventure*. Perhaps.

31:34 *furniture*. Saddle. These "gods" can be stolen, hidden, and sat upon!

31:35 *custom of women*. Menstruation.

31:36 *wroth*. Angry. *chode*. Literally, "contended" as in a lawsuit. *trespass*. Sin.

31:37 *betwixt*. Between.

31:38–41 *cast their young*. Miscarried. *I bare the loss of it*. Ordinarily he would not be obligated to repay Laban for animals lost to predators and thieves (Ex. 22:12–13). Jacob protested his hard work and honesty in serving Laban, who did not reward him rightly.

31:42 *God of Abraham*. The covenant Lord of Abraham and his descendants (26:24; 28:13). *fear of Isaac*. Title similar to "the Holy One of Israel" (Isa. 41:14), depicting the Lord in His majesty and faithfulness to the covenant seed. The God of Abraham rescued Jacob from the oppressor and brought him to the land, just as He later did with the nation of Israel (Ex. 3:6,15–17). *yesternight*. Last night.

31:49–50 *the LORD watch between me and thee . . . God is*

man *is* with us; see, God *is* witness betwixt me
and thee.
51 And Laban said to Jacob, Behold this heap, and
behold *this* pillar, which I have cast betwixt me
and thee;
52 This heap *be* witness, and *this* pillar *be* witness,
that I will not pass over this heap to thee, and that
thou shalt not pass over this heap and this pillar
unto me, for harm.
53 The God of Abraham, and the God of Nahor,
the God of their father, judge betwixt us. And Ja-
cob sware by the fear of his father Isaac.
54 Then Jacob offered sacrifice upon the mount,
and called his brethren to eat bread: and they did
eat bread, and tarried all night in the mount.
55 And early in the morning Laban rose up, and
kissed his sons and his daughters, and blessed
them: and Laban departed, and returned unto his
place.

CHAPTER 32

AND Jacob went on his way, and the angels of God
met him.
2 And when Jacob saw them, he said, This *is*
God's host: and he called the name of that place
Mahanaim.
3 And Jacob sent messengers before him to Esau
his brother unto the land of Seir, the country of
Edom.
4 And he commanded them, saying, Thus shall ye
speak unto my lord Esau; Thy servant Jacob saith
thus, I have sojourned with Laban, and stayed
there until now:
5 And I have oxen, and asses, flocks, and menser-
vants, and womenservants: and I have sent to tell
my lord, that I may find grace in thy sight.
6 ¶ And the messengers returned to Jacob, say-
ing, We came to thy brother Esau, and also he
cometh to meet thee, and four hundred men with
him.
7 Then Jacob was greatly afraid and distressed:
and he divided the people that *was* with him, and
the flocks, and herds, and the camels, into two
bands;
8 And said, If Esau come to the one company,
and smite it, then the other company which is left
shall escape.
9 ¶ And Jacob said, O God of my father Abra-
ham, and God of my father Isaac, the LORD which
saidst unto me, Return unto thy country, and to
thy kindred, and I will deal well with thee:
10 I am not worthy of the least of all the mercies,
and of all the truth, which thou hast shewed unto
thy servant; for with my staff I passed over this
Jordan; and now I am become two bands.
11 Deliver me, I pray thee, from the hand of my
brother, from the hand of Esau: for I fear him, lest
he will come and smite me, *and* the mother with
the children.
12 And thou saidst, I will surely do thee good, and
make thy seed as the sand of the sea, which cannot
be numbered for multitude.
13 ¶ And he lodged there that same night; and
took of that which came to his hand a present for
Esau his brother;
14 Two hundred she goats, and twenty he goats,
two hundred ewes, and twenty rams,

---

witness betwixt me and thee. Not a blessing, but a covenant curse that God would judge Jacob if he harmed Laban or his children.

Thoughts for Personal/Family Worship: Chapter 31

1. **Laban is an example of a bully, oppressor, and tyrant. He robs the righteous, envies their prosperity, breaks his promises, alienates his family, worships idols, accuses others falsely, puts on a show of kindness, uses force to take what deceit will not get him, cheats honest employees, constantly changes his words, sees everything he takes as his right, and uses religion to protect his interests. But God will rebuke and judge him. Believers may face and overcome such people with truth, justice, and faith in the Lord.**
2. **The Lord stands in stark contrast to the gods of this world. Their little idols are ridiculous and helpless, but tragically the world pursues them and treasures them. The Lord however is the fearsome and faithful God. He is with His people, and He alone is worthy of our trust. Are you one of His children and are you presently trusting Him in and for all things?**

Chapter 32: *Jacob prepares to meet a hostile Esau, and the Lord comes to wrestle with him.*

32:1–2 *angels of God.* See note at 28:12. *God's host.* Camp of God's army. The forces of heaven surround God's servants to defend them (2 Kings 6:17; Ps. 91:11; Heb. 1:14). The same word for *host* or camp appears as "band" (vv. 7,10), "company" (vv. 8,21), and "drove" (33:8).

32:3–5 *Jacob* sought reconciliation with *Esau. Seir.* Mountainous region southeast of the Dead Sea (36:6–8). Jacob used *lord-servant* language to show his humble repentance of stealing from Esau the blessing of lordship belonging to the first-born (27:29,37,40).

32:6 *four hundred men.* Esau had grown as powerful as his grandfather (14:14), but unlike Abraham he mobilized his army not to save his relative but to destroy him.

32:8 *smite.* Strike, attack.

32:9 *kindred.* Extended family. Jacob leaned on God's covenant (*God of my father*) and His specific command and promise.

32:10 *mercies . . . truth.* See note at 24:27. He sought God without self-righteousness (Luke 18:13).

32:11 *Deliver me.* Save me. *I fear him.* He poured out his heart to the Lord (1 Sam. 1:15; Ps. 62:8).

32:12 *sand of the sea.* Promised to Abraham (22:17). *cannot be numbered for multitude.* Too many to count. Jacob pleaded with the God of Abraham to keep His promises (v. 9; 31:42).

32:14–15 *milch camels.* Camels nursing their young. *kine.* Cows or heifers. Jacob sent 550 head of livestock, a gift fit for a king. Thus he made restitution for stealing the birthright.

15 Thirty milch camels with their colts, forty
kine, and ten bulls, twenty she asses, and ten foals.
16 And he delivered *them* into the hand of his
servants, every drove by themselves; and said
unto his servants, Pass over before me, and put a
space betwixt drove and drove.
17 And he commanded the foremost, saying,
When Esau my brother meeteth thee, and asketh
thee, saying, Whose *art* thou? and whither goest
thou? and whose *are* these before thee?
18 Then thou shalt say, *They be* thy servant
Jacob's; it *is* a present sent unto my lord Esau: and,
behold, also he *is* behind us.
19 And so commanded he the second, and the
third, and all that followed the droves, saying, On
this manner shall ye speak unto Esau, when ye
find him.
20 And say ye moreover, Behold, thy servant
Jacob *is* behind us. For he said, I will appease
him with the present that goeth before me, and
afterward I will see his face; peradventure he will
accept of me.
21 So went the present over before him: and him-
self lodged that night in the company.
22 And he rose up that night, and took his two
wives, and his two womenservants, and his eleven
sons, and passed over the ford Jabbok.
23 And he took them, and sent them over the
brook, and sent over that he had.
24 ¶ And Jacob was left alone; and there wrestled
a man with him until the breaking of the day.
25 And when he saw that he prevailed not against
him, he touched the hollow of his thigh; and the
hollow of Jacob's thigh was out of joint, as he
wrestled with him.
26 And he said, Let me go, for the day breaketh.
And he said, I will not let thee go, except thou
bless me.
27 And he said unto him, What *is* thy name? And
he said, Jacob.
28 And he said, Thy name shall be called no more
Jacob, but Israel: for as a prince hast thou power
with God and with men, and hast prevailed.
29 And Jacob asked *him*, and said, Tell *me*, I pray
thee, thy name. And he said, Wherefore *is* it *that*
thou dost ask after my name? And he blessed him
there.
30 And Jacob called the name of the place Pe-
niel: for I have seen God face to face, and my life
is preserved.
31 And as he passed over Penuel the sun rose
upon him, and he halted upon his thigh.
32 Therefore the children of Israel eat not *of* the
sinew which shrank, which *is* upon the hollow of
the thigh, unto this day: because he touched the
hollow of Jacob's thigh in the sinew that shrank.

CHAPTER 33

AND Jacob lifted up his eyes, and looked, and,
behold, Esau came, and with him four hundred
men. And he divided the children unto Leah, and
unto Rachel, and unto the two handmaids.
2 And he put the handmaids and their children

32:16 *betwixt drove and drove.* Between each group of livestock. The gifts would arrive one wave after another to win over the heart of Esau.
32:17 *foremost.* First. *whither.* To where.
32:20 *appease.* Propitiate or turn away anger (Prov. 16:14); same word used for sacrifices of atonement to obtain forgiveness from God (Lev. 4:20). *see his face.* Receive favor from him (Num. 6:24–26). *peradventure he will accept of me.* Literally, "perhaps he will lift up my face."
32:22 *Jabbok.* A river which flows into the Jordan River (v. 10) from the east in Gilead.
32:24 God (v. 30) appeared as *a man*, a shadow of the coming of Christ (see note at 18:1–2). He *wrestled* with Jacob; God humbles and sanctifies His elect. The Hebrew word for *wrestled* suggests "dust;" God lowered Himself in the incarnation when He came to make men holy.
32:25 *he prevailed not.* Literally, "he was not able," a surprising verb to use of the Lord (18:14). *touched.* Or possibly struck. *the hollow of his thigh.* His hip joint. The result was a limp (v. 31). God is not able to fulfill His purposes of grace for His elect without wounding them.
32:26 God defeated Jacob's trickery, so now Jacob clung tenaciously and tearfully to the Lord until He would *bless* him (Hos. 12:3–4).
32:28 He was no longer Jacob the deceiver, but *Israel* who conquered with God. Israel means both "he struggles with God," and "God struggles." On the gift of a new name, see 17:5,15.
32:29 *Wherefore.* Why. God's *name* is not just a word, but His glory, which cannot be fully known by our limited minds (Deut. 28:58; Judg. 13:17–18; Neh. 9:5; Ps. 148:13).
32:31 *halted upon his thigh.* Limping because of his hip injury, Jacob must now face Esau in weakness and pain, unable to fight or run and utterly dependent on God.

Thoughts for Personal/Family Worship: Chapter 32

1. **Like Jacob, we should call upon the covenant God and Father of Jesus Christ, pray His words back to Him, confess that we are unworthy of His grace, thank Him for His mercies, ask for salvation, pour out the fears of our hearts, and strengthen our faith with His promises. This is true prayer.**
2. **If we have sinned against other people, let us first humble ourselves before God and find peace with Him. Then let us humble ourselves before them, ask for forgiveness, and seek to pay back any losses that we caused them. Most of all, we must cling to God that He would bless us whether or not people will make peace with us.**

Chapter 33: ***Esau meets Jacob, and the brothers make peace and yet go in different directions.***

33:1–3 *handmaids.* Female servants. *foremost . . . hindermost.* First and last. That his wives and children ranked high in Jacob's affections was plain to see. Still, Jacob no longer sent them ahead of him (32:23), but *passed over before them*, sacrificially taking the most dangerous position as the first to approach Esau.

foremost, and Leah and her children after, and
Rachel and Joseph hindermost.
3 And he passed over before them, and bowed
himself to the ground seven times, until he came
near to his brother.
4 And Esau ran to meet him, and embraced him,
and fell on his neck, and kissed him: and they wept.
5 And he lifted up his eyes, and saw the women
and the children; and said, Who *are* those with
thee? And he said, The children which God hath
graciously given thy servant.
6 Then the handmaidens came near, they and
their children, and they bowed themselves.
7 And Leah also with her children came near, and
bowed themselves: and after came Joseph near
and Rachel, and they bowed themselves.
8 And he said, What *meanest* thou by all this
drove which I met? And he said, *These are* to find
grace in the sight of my lord.
9 And Esau said, I have enough, my brother; keep
that thou hast unto thyself.
10 And Jacob said, Nay, I pray thee, if now I have
found grace in thy sight, then receive my present
at my hand: for therefore I have seen thy face, as
though I had seen the face of God, and thou wast
pleased with me.
11 Take, I pray thee, my blessing that is brought
to thee; because God hath dealt graciously with
me, and because I have enough. And he urged
him, and he took *it*.
12 And he said, Let us take our journey, and let us
go, and I will go before thee.
13 And he said unto him, My lord knoweth that
the children *are* tender, and the flocks and herds
with young *are* with me: and if men should over-
drive them one day, all the flock will die.
14 Let my lord, I pray thee, pass over before his
servant: and I will lead on softly, according as the
cattle that goeth before me and the children be
able to endure, until I come unto my lord unto
Seir.
15 And Esau said, Let me now leave with thee
some of the folk that *are* with me. And he said,
What needeth it? let me find grace in the sight of
my lord.
16 ¶ So Esau returned that day on his way unto
Seir.
17 And Jacob journeyed to Succoth, and built
him an house, and made booths for his cattle:
therefore the name of the place is called Succoth.
18 ¶ And Jacob came to Shalem, a city of
Shechem, which *is* in the land of Canaan, when
he came from Padan-aram; and pitched his tent
before the city.
19 And he bought a parcel of a field, where he
had spread his tent, at the hand of the children of
Hamor, Shechem's father, for an hundred pieces
of money.
20 And he erected there an altar, and called it
El-elohe-Israel.

CHAPTER 34

AND Dinah the daughter of Leah, which she bare
unto Jacob, went out to see the daughters of the
land.

33:4 *fell on his neck.* Hugged him and held him close (46:29). A picture of reconciliation; compare the actions of the father of the prodigal son (Luke 15:20).
33:5 *God hath graciously given.* Jacob's humility is evident in how he credited God's grace for all his blessings (v. 11). Esau never mentions God in this conversation.
33:8 *all this drove.* All these livestock (see note at 32:2).
33:10 *I have seen thy face, as though I had seen the face of God.* Jacob's reconciliation with Esau was linked to his encounter with God (32:30), where he gained humility and blessing.
33:11 *Take . . . my blessing.* Jacob's gift of the livestock aimed to make up for the stolen blessing (27:36).
33:13–14 *tender.* Weak. *softly.* Gently. The *children* and *herds with young* may indeed have been weary after fleeing from Laban for ten days (31:22–23). *until I come unto my lord unto Seir.* Perhaps a lie motivated by fear, or a polite but noncommittal way of saying Jacob might visit Esau someday. God had called the seed of Abraham to live in Canaan, not Seir.
33:16–19 Esau traveled one hundred miles south to *Seir*, but *Jacob journeyed to Succoth* and then to Shechem, moving west into Canaan. He did not go immediately to Beth-el to worship God (28:19–22; 35:1), a hint of incomplete obedience. *to Shalem.* The word could be understood as a place name (as the KJV translates) or as an adverb meaning "peacefully, safely" (34:21). *bought a parcel of a field.* Piece of land given to Joseph (see note at 48:22). Jacob's purchase of property *in the land of Canaan* showed his intention to dwell in the land of God's promise.
33:20 *El-elohe-Israel.* The Lord had appeared to Abraham at Shechem, promising to give the land to his offspring (12:6–7), and Abraham built an altar there. By building another altar at Shechem and naming it "God is the God of Israel," Jacob affirmed his faith in the promises and kept part of his vow to take the Lord as his God if He would bring Jacob safely home (28:21).

Thoughts for Personal/Family Worship: Chapter 33

1. **How beautiful when God reconciles enemies and heals broken relationships! It is a picture of divine grace. Repentance is shown for sins committed, restitution is made for damages done, forgiveness is granted to the guilty, and tenderhearted friendship is renewed. Reconciliation is costly—most of all to our pride—but it is sweet and precious. Insofar as it depends upon us, let us pursue peace with all.**
2. **The best reconciliation is reconciliation with God and returning home to Him. Jacob had gone on an exile of sorts because of his sins, but the Lord brought him home to the land of promise. Perhaps you have backslidden away from the Lord, and as a result have gone far from Him. God delights to bring the exiles home. Turn back to Him today.**

Chapter 34: ***Jacob's daughter Dinah consorts with the wicked and is raped, and his sons respond with deceit and violence.***
34:1 Jacob's *daughter* (fourteen times in this chapter) went

2 And when Shechem the son of Hamor the Hivite, prince of the country, saw her, he took her, and lay with her, and defiled her.

3 And his soul clave unto Dinah the daughter of Jacob, and he loved the damsel, and spake kindly unto the damsel.

4 And Shechem spake unto his father Hamor, saying, Get me this damsel to wife.

5 And Jacob heard that he had defiled Dinah his daughter: now his sons were with his cattle in the field: and Jacob held his peace until they were come.

6 ¶ And Hamor the father of Shechem went out unto Jacob to commune with him.

7 And the sons of Jacob came out of the field when they heard *it*: and the men were grieved, and they were very wroth, because he had wrought folly in Israel in lying with Jacob's daughter; which thing ought not to be done.

8 And Hamor communed with them, saying, The soul of my son Shechem longeth for your daughter: I pray you give her him to wife.

9 And make ye marriages with us, *and* give your daughters unto us, and take our daughters unto you.

10 And ye shall dwell with us: and the land shall be before you; dwell and trade ye therein, and get you possessions therein.

11 And Shechem said unto her father and unto her brethren, Let me find grace in your eyes, and what ye shall say unto me I will give.

12 Ask me never so much dowry and gift, and I will give according as ye shall say unto me: but give me the damsel to wife.

13 And the sons of Jacob answered Shechem and Hamor his father deceitfully, and said, because he had defiled Dinah their sister:

14 And they said unto them, We cannot do this thing, to give our sister to one that is uncircumcised; for that *were* a reproach unto us:

15 But in this will we consent unto you: If ye will be as we *be*, that every male of you be circumcised;

16 Then will we give our daughters unto you, and we will take your daughters to us, and we will dwell with you, and we will become one people.

17 But if ye will not hearken unto us, to be circumcised; then will we take our daughter, and we will be gone.

18 And their words pleased Hamor, and Shechem Hamor's son.

19 And the young man deferred not to do the thing, because he had delight in Jacob's daughter: and he *was* more honourable than all the house of his father.

20 ¶ And Hamor and Shechem his son came unto the gate of their city, and communed with the men of their city, saying,

21 These men *are* peaceable with us; therefore let them dwell in the land, and trade therein; for the land, behold, *it is* large enough for them; let us take their daughters to us for wives, and let us give them our daughters.

22 Only herein will the men consent unto us for to dwell with us, to be one people, if every male among us be circumcised, as they *are* circumcised.

23 *Shall* not their cattle and their substance and every beast of theirs *be* ours? only let us consent unto them, and they will dwell with us.

24 And unto Hamor and unto Shechem his son hearkened all that went out of the gate of his city; and every male was circumcised, all that went out of the gate of his city.

25 ¶ And it came to pass on the third day, when they were sore, that two of the sons of Jacob, Simeon and Levi, Dinah's brethren, took each man his sword, and came upon the city boldly, and slew all the males.

26 And they slew Hamor and Shechem his son

---

out to socialize with *the daughters of the land*, women and girls of the wicked Canaanites (27:46; 38:1–2).

34:2 *defiled*. Humiliated, here by rape, a crime in Israel (Deut. 22:28–29).

34:3 *his soul clave*. He became attached to her after she pleased him sexually, reversing God's order for marriage of commitment and then physical union (2:24). *damsel*. Young woman.

34:5 *defiled*. Not the same word used earlier (v. 2), but a term meaning made her unclean by sexual sin, though not of her own choice (vv. 13,27; Num. 5:13; Deut. 24:4; Ezek. 18:6; 22:11). *held his peace*. Jacob remained passive and silent until the end (v. 30), perhaps because of fear or a lack of compassion for a daughter of Leah (v. 1), his unwanted wife (29:31).

34:6 *commune*. Speak.

34:7 *wroth*. Angry. *wrought folly*. Committed a crime (Isa. 32:6; Jer. 29:23), associated with sexual sins on more than one occasion (Deut. 22:21; Judg. 19:23–24; 20:6,10; 2 Sam. 13:12).

34:8 The Canaanites made no mention of, much less apology for, Shechem's horrendous crime, only a proposal of marriage. Throughout the chapter, men treated Dinah and other women as objects to be taken (vv. 2,4,9,16–17,21,26,28–29).

34:9–10 The covenant seed was often tempted to intermarry with pagans, raising the danger of becoming one people with them (v. 16) and losing their holiness as God's chosen people (Deut. 7:1–6).

34:12 *damsel*. Young woman.

34:13 *deceitfully*. They acted as Jacob had when he acted "with subtilty" (same word) and stole the blessing (27:35).

34:14–15 *uncircumcised . . . circumcised*. Jacob's sons sinned greatly against God by treating the holy sign of the Lord's covenant (17:10–11) as a means of gain, deception, and revenge.

34:17 *hearken*. Listen.

34:19 *deferred not*. Did not delay.

34:20 *gate of their city*. See note at 22:16–17.

34:22 *Only herein*. Only by this.

34:23 *substance*. Wealth.

34:24 *all that went out of the gate*. Every participant in the business of their city (23:10,18).

34:25 *boldly*. Or possibly when the city thought it was "safe" (v. 21). Simeon and Levi were liars and murderers. Jacob now knew the Lord as his God, but his sons needed redemption.

34:26 *took Dinah out of Shechem's house*. She was still a captive in the home of her rapist, some days after suffering sexual

with the edge of the sword, and took Dinah out
of Shechem's house, and went out.
27 The sons of Jacob came upon the slain, and
spoiled the city, because they had defiled their
sister.
28 They took their sheep, and their oxen, and
their asses, and that which *was* in the city, and that
which *was* in the field,
29 And all their wealth, and all their little ones,
and their wives took they captive, and spoiled
even all that *was* in the house.
30 And Jacob said to Simeon and Levi, Ye have
troubled me to make me to stink among the in-
habitants of the land, among the Canaanites and
the Perizzites: and I *being* few in number, they
shall gather themselves together against me, and
slay me; and I shall be destroyed, I and my house.
31 And they said, Should he deal with our sister
as with an harlot?

CHAPTER 35

AND God said unto Jacob, Arise, go up to Beth-
el, and dwell there: and make there an altar unto
God, that appeared unto thee when thou fleddest
from the face of Esau thy brother.
2 Then Jacob said unto his household, and to all
that *were* with him, Put away the strange gods that
are among you, and be clean, and change your
garments:
3 And let us arise, and go up to Beth-el; and I will
make there an altar unto God, who answered me
in the day of my distress, and was with me in the
way which I went.
4 And they gave unto Jacob all the strange gods
which *were* in their hand, and *all their* earrings
which *were* in their ears; and Jacob hid them
under the oak which *was* by Shechem.
5 And they journeyed: and the terror of God was
upon the cities that *were* round about them, and
they did not pursue after the sons of Jacob.
6 ¶ So Jacob came to Luz, which *is* in the land of
Canaan, that *is*, Beth-el, he and all the people that
were with him.
7 And he built there an altar, and called the place
El-beth-el: because there God appeared unto him,
when he fled from the face of his brother.
8 But Deborah Rebekah's nurse died, and she
was buried beneath Beth-el under an oak: and the
name of it was called Allon-bachuth.
9 ¶ And God appeared unto Jacob again, when he
came out of Padan-aram, and blessed him.
10 And God said unto him, Thy name *is* Jacob: thy
name shall not be called any more Jacob, but Israel
shall be thy name: and he called his name Israel.
11 And God said unto him, I *am* God Almighty:
be fruitful and multiply; a nation and a company
of nations shall be of thee, and kings shall come
out of thy loins;
12 And the land which I gave Abraham and Isaac,
to thee I will give it, and to thy seed after thee will
I give the land.
13 And God went up from him in the place where
he talked with him.
14 And Jacob set up a pillar in the place where
he talked with him, *even* a pillar of stone: and he
poured a drink offering thereon, and he poured
oil thereon.
15 And Jacob called the name of the place where
God spake with him, Beth-el.

---

assault. It was right for her brothers to rescue her, but not like this.
34:30 *make me to stink*. Made them hate me (Ex. 5:21; 2 Sam. 10:6). Even unbelievers would be outraged by treachery against an ally. Jacob's words revolve around self-centered fear (*I shall be destroyed*), not a love for righteousness.
34:31 *harlot*. Prostitute.

Thoughts for Personal/Family Worship: Chapter 34

1. **Christians should not entangle themselves with the world. Close relationships with ungodly friends may draw us into or make us the victims of their sins. Is there any such relationship alive in your life?**
2. **We must neither take revenge nor remain passive and quiet in the face of great crimes. Instead, let each person use the rightful power he has to seek justice for the oppressed.**
3. **Men often treat women as mere objects to be taken and used for their sexual pleasure. Fathers should teach their girls to avoid making themselves naive, and train their boys to honor and protect women as God's precious image bearers.**

Chapter 35: ***Jacob experiences both the blessing of God's presence at Beth-el and sin and death in his family.***

35:1 *go up to Beth-el . . . make there an altar*. God called Jacob to draw near to Him in worship and so keep his vow (28:20–22; see note at 33:20). *fleddest*. Fled.
35:2 Jacob obeyed God's call to lead his family in worship. *strange gods*. Idols worshiped by people outside Abraham's household (31:19,30–35; Deut. 31:16). Idols must be rejected to worship the Lord with all our hearts (Josh. 24:23; 1 Sam. 7:3). *be clean, and change your garments*. Ceremonial preparations to enter the holy presence of God (Ex. 19:10–11; 29:4–5).
35:4 Perhaps these *earrings* bore some idolatrous image.
35:5 God put His *terror* upon the Canaanite *cities* so they would not avenge the people of Shechem (34:30), perhaps by showing His glory in the divine angel of the Lord (Ex. 23:23,27).
35:8 *Deborah* had traveled with *Rebekah* since her departure from Mesopotamia (24:59). Deborah's presence with Jacob implies that he had visited Isaac and that Rebekah had died. The "oak of weeping" (*Allon-bachuth*) emphasizes the family's sorrow.
35:9–12 The blessing of *God Almighty*, restatement of Jacob's new *name*, and promises to *multiply* him, raise up *kings*, and give him the *land* echo God's words to Abraham (17:1–9), thus renewing the covenant. The Lord remained faithful as the God of His unworthy people.
35:14 *drink offering*. Wine poured out to God in old covenant worship (Ex. 29:40; Lev. 23:13).

16 ¶ And they journeyed from Beth-el; and there
was but a little way to come to Ephrath: and
Rachel travailed, and she had hard labour.
17 And it came to pass, when she was in hard
labour, that the midwife said unto her, Fear not;
thou shalt have this son also.
18 And it came to pass, as her soul was in depart-
ing, (for she died) that she called his name Ben-
oni: but his father called him Benjamin.
19 And Rachel died, and was buried in the way to
Ephrath, which *is* Beth-lehem.
20 And Jacob set a pillar upon her grave: that *is*
the pillar of Rachel's grave unto this day.
21 ¶ And Israel journeyed, and spread his tent be-
yond the tower of Edar.
22 And it came to pass, when Israel dwelt in that
land, that Reuben went and lay with Bilhah his
father's concubine: and Israel heard *it*. Now the
sons of Jacob were twelve:
23 The sons of Leah; Reuben, Jacob's firstborn,
and Simeon, and Levi, and Judah, and Issachar,
and Zebulun:
24 The sons of Rachel; Joseph, and Benjamin:
25 And the sons of Bilhah, Rachel's handmaid;
Dan, and Naphtali:
26 And the sons of Zilpah, Leah's handmaid; Gad,
and Asher: these *are* the sons of Jacob, which were
born to him in Padan-aram.
27 ¶ And Jacob came unto Isaac his father unto
Mamre, unto the city of Arbah, which *is* Hebron,
where Abraham and Isaac sojourned.
28 And the days of Isaac were an hundred and
fourscore years.
29 And Isaac gave up the ghost, and died, and
was gathered unto his people, *being* old and full
of days: and his sons Esau and Jacob buried him.

CHAPTER 36

Now these *are* the generations of Esau, who *is*
Edom.
2 Esau took his wives of the daughters of Canaan;
Adah the daughter of Elon the Hittite, and
Aholibamah the daughter of Anah the daughter
of Zibeon the Hivite;
3 And Bashemath Ishmael's daughter, sister of
Nebajoth.
4 And Adah bare to Esau Eliphaz; and Bashemath
bare Reuel;
5 And Aholibamah bare Jeush, and Jaalam, and
Korah: these *are* the sons of Esau, which were
born unto him in the land of Canaan.
6 And Esau took his wives, and his sons, and his
daughters, and all the persons of his house, and
his cattle, and all his beasts, and all his substance,
which he had got in the land of Canaan; and went
into the country from the face of his brother Jacob.
7 For their riches were more than that they might
dwell together; and the land wherein they were
strangers could not bear them because of their
cattle.
8 Thus dwelt Esau in mount Seir: Esau *is* Edom.

35:16 *travailed.* Went into labor to give birth.
35:18 *as her soul was in departing.* Literally, "when her soul/life went out" (1 Kings 17:22; Job 11:20; Jer. 15:9).
35:22 Reuben committed immorality (Lev. 18:8; Deut. 22:30) and dishonored his father. To *lay* sexually with his father's *concubine* was to grasp at his position of authority (2 Sam. 3:7; 16:20–22), but instead Reuben lost his right as firstborn (49:3–4; 1 Chron. 5:1).
35:23–26 Note the divisions in Jacob's family (*sons of* four mothers).
35:28 *hundred and fourscore years.* One hundred eighty years. On the life-spans of the patriarchs, see note at 50:22.
35:29 *gave up the ghost.* Expired. *gathered unto his people.* See note at 25:8. Isaac was still alive when Joseph was sold into slavery (25:26; 37:2; 41:46–47; 45:6; 47:9), but Genesis includes his death to highlight Jacob's sorrows and then to move on to the story of his sons. The sons of *Isaac* appear at his grave in peace; *Esau* did not murder *Jacob* as he once wished to do (27:41).

Thoughts for Personal/Family Worship: Chapter 35

1. **Fathers should lead their families to worship the Lord alone. God calls men to exhort their families to bury their idols and to gather their wives and children together to offer God the sacrifices of praise. Just when His people appear at their worst, the Lord surprises them with blessing. Shall we not worship and praise Him in our homes?**
2. **God's grace has not yet fully rescued us from the miseries of sin and death. It is striking how God's promises of blessing to Jacob come in the midst of weeping by the graves of three beloved family members, plus grieving over the sin of children. Grace and tears mingle together in this life; do not be surprised when believers suffer and die. Take hope that they have a great reward waiting.**

Chapter 36: *Esau departs from the Promised Land, but receives from the Lord the material blessings of children, wealth, and land.*

36:1 *these are the generations.* Just as with Ishmael and Isaac (see notes at 25:12,19), Genesis closes off its consideration of the family of Esau to focus on Jacob's sons (37:2).
36:2–3 By comparison to other Scriptures (26:34; 28:9), it appears that Esau had four wives: (1) Judith, the daughter of Beeri, who bore him no children and is omitted from this genealogy, (2) *Adah the daughter of Elon the Hittite,* who was also named Bashemath, (3) *Aholibamah the daughter of Anah,* and (4) *Bashemath Ishmael's daughter,* also known as Mahalath. Persons often have more than one name, and certain names are commonly found among a people. Bashemath means "fragrance" or "perfume" and could have been a popular name for girls.
36:6–8 Esau was in the land of *Seir* before Jacob returned (32:3), but he may have received an inheritance of livestock at Isaac's death, pastured them for a time in Canaan, and then moved back to Seir. Though at peace with Jacob, he did not remain in his presence (*face*). He left the Promised Land, like Lot (13:6,12–13), Ishmael, and Abraham's other sons (25:6). The name *Edom* reminds the reader of his contempt for his birthright (25:29–34). Yet Edom's possession of Seir was still a gift

9 ¶ And these *are* the generations of Esau the fa-
ther of the Edomites in mount Seir:
10 These *are* the names of Esau's sons; Eliphaz
the son of Adah the wife of Esau, Reuel the son of
Bashemath the wife of Esau.
11 And the sons of Eliphaz were Teman, Omar,
Zepho, and Gatam, and Kenaz.
12 And Timna was concubine to Eliphaz Esau's
son; and she bare to Eliphaz Amalek: these *were*
the sons of Adah Esau's wife.
13 And these *are* the sons of Reuel; Nahath, and
Zerah, Shammah, and Mizzah: these were the
sons of Bashemath Esau's wife.
14 ¶ And these were the sons of Aholibamah, the
daughter of Anah the daughter of Zibeon, Esau's
wife: and she bare to Esau Jeush, and Jaalam, and
Korah.
15 ¶ These *were* dukes of the sons of Esau: the
sons of Eliphaz the firstborn *son* of Esau; duke Te-
man, duke Omar, duke Zepho, duke Kenaz,
16 Duke Korah, duke Gatam, *and* duke Amalek:
these *are* the dukes *that came* of Eliphaz in the
land of Edom; these *were* the sons of Adah.
17 ¶ And these *are* the sons of Reuel Esau's son;
duke Nahath, duke Zerah, duke Shammah, duke
Mizzah: these *are* the dukes *that came* of Reuel in
the land of Edom; these *are* the sons of Bashe-
math Esau's wife.
18 ¶ And these *are* the sons of Aholibamah Esau's
wife; duke Jeush, duke Jaalam, duke Korah: these
were the dukes *that came* of Aholibamah the
daughter of Anah, Esau's wife.
19 These *are* the sons of Esau, who *is* Edom, and
these *are* their dukes.
20 ¶ These *are* the sons of Seir the Horite, who
inhabited the land; Lotan, and Shobal, and Zib-
eon, and Anah,
21 And Dishon, and Ezer, and Dishan: these *are*
the dukes of the Horites, the children of Seir in
the land of Edom.
22 And the children of Lotan were Hori and He-
mam; and Lotan's sister *was* Timna.
23 And the children of Shobal *were* these; Alvan,
and Manahath, and Ebal, Shepho, and Onam.
24 And these *are* the children of Zibeon; both
Ajah, and Anah: this *was that* Anah that found
the mules in the wilderness, as he fed the asses of
Zibeon his father.
25 And the children of Anah *were* these; Dishon,
and Aholibamah the daughter of Anah.
26 And these *are* the children of Dishon; Hemdan,
and Eshban, and Ithran, and Cheran.
27 The children of Ezer *are* these; Bilhan, and
Zaavan, and Akan.
28 The children of Dishan *are* these; Uz, and Aran.
29 These *are* the dukes *that came* of the Horites;
duke Lotan, duke Shobal, duke Zibeon, duke Anah,
30 Duke Dishon, duke Ezer, duke Dishan: these
are the dukes *that came* of Hori, among their
dukes in the land of Seir.
31 ¶ And these *are* the kings that reigned in the
land of Edom, before there reigned any king over
the children of Israel.
32 And Bela the son of Beor reigned in Edom:
and the name of his city *was* Dinhabah.
33 And Bela died, and Jobab the son of Zerah of
Bozrah reigned in his stead.
34 And Jobab died, and Husham of the land of
Temani reigned in his stead.
35 And Husham died, and Hadad the son of Be-
dad, who smote Midian in the field of Moab,
reigned in his stead: and the name of his city *was*
Avith.
36 And Hadad died, and Samlah of Masrekah
reigned in his stead.
37 And Samlah died, and Saul of Rehoboth *by* the
river reigned in his stead.
38 And Saul died, and Baal-hanan the son of
Achbor reigned in his stead.
39 And Baal-hanan the son of Achbor died, and
Hadar reigned in his stead: and the name of his
city *was* Pau; and his wife's name *was* Mehetabel,
the daughter of Matred, the daughter of Mezahab.
40 And these *are* the names of the dukes *that*

---

from the Lord (Deut. 2:5; Josh. 24:4), who gave Esau material blessings just as he did Ishmael (17:20). Indeed God gives all nations their homes (Acts 17:26).

36:9 *Edomites*. Later enemies of Israel (Num. 20:18–21; 24:18; 1 Sam. 14:47; 2 Sam. 8:14), but still counted as close relatives (Deut. 23:7) until their treachery against Israel brought them under God's wrath, as the book of Obadiah declares.

36:11 *Eliphaz . . . Teman*. Eliphaz the Temanite was the name of one of Job's friends (Job 2:11), suggesting that Job's friend was an Edomite.

36:12 *Amalek*. The tribe by this name attacked Israel and came under God's curse (Ex. 17:8,16; Num. 24:20; Deut. 25:17–19).

36:15 *dukes*. Chief men, a title particularly associated with the Edomites (Ex. 15:15; 1 Chron. 1:51–54). Also called "kings" (v. 31).

36:20–30 The area was evidently named after *Seir the Horite* whose dynasty ruled it until Esau's family conquered them by God's providence (Deut. 2:12,22).

36:33 *in his stead*. In his place.

36:40 *dukes*. Chief men.

Thoughts for Personal/Family Worship: Chapter 36

1. **The Lord reigns over all nations. We must not treat Him like a tribal god who belongs to one people or place; He is not a white god or a black god, a Jewish god or an American god. He is God over all nations. He gives every people their land and every person his life. Let us therefore give Him glory for every good thing in the entire world.**
2. **Children often reap many benefits from being raised by Christian parents. God may bless their marriages, children, and finances. He may give them property and positions of leadership. But for all this, they should never assume that they are in a saving relationship with**

came of Esau, according to their families, after
their places, by their names; duke Timnah, duke
Alvah, duke Jetheth,
41 Duke Aholibamah, duke Elah, duke Pinon,
42 Duke Kenaz, duke Teman, duke Mibzar,
43 Duke Magdiel, duke Iram: these *be* the dukes
of Edom, according to their habitations in the
land of their possession: he *is* Esau the father of
the Edomites.

CHAPTER 37

AND Jacob dwelt in the land wherein his father
was a stranger, in the land of Canaan.
2 These *are* the generations of Jacob. Joseph, *be-*
ing seventeen years old, was feeding the flock with
his brethren; and the lad *was* with the sons of
Bilhah, and with the sons of Zilpah, his father's
wives: and Joseph brought unto his father their
evil report.
3 Now Israel loved Joseph more than all his chil-
dren, because he *was* the son of his old age: and he
made him a coat of *many* colours.
4 And when his brethren saw that their father
loved him more than all his brethren, they hated
him, and could not speak peaceably unto him.
5 ¶ And Joseph dreamed a dream, and he told *it*
his brethren: and they hated him yet the more.
6 And he said unto them, Hear, I pray you, this
dream which I have dreamed:
7 For, behold, we *were* binding sheaves in the
field, and, lo, my sheaf arose, and also stood up-
right; and, behold, your sheaves stood round
about, and made obeisance to my sheaf.
8 And his brethren said to him, Shalt thou indeed
reign over us? or shalt thou indeed have dominion
over us? And they hated him yet the more for his
dreams, and for his words.
9 ¶ And he dreamed yet another dream, and told
it his brethren, and said, Behold, I have dreamed a
dream more; and, behold, the sun and the moon
and the eleven stars made obeisance to me.
10 And he told *it* to his father, and to his brethren:
and his father rebuked him, and said unto him,
What *is* this dream that thou hast dreamed? Shall
I and thy mother and thy brethren indeed come
to bow down ourselves to thee to the earth?
11 And his brethren envied him; but his father
observed the saying.
12 ¶ And his brethren went to feed their father's
flock in Shechem.
13 And Israel said unto Joseph, Do not thy breth-
ren feed *the flock* in Shechem? come, and I will send
thee unto them. And he said to him, Here *am I*.
14 And he said to him, Go, I pray thee, see whether
it be well with thy brethren, and well with the
flocks; and bring me word again. So he sent him
out of the vale of Hebron, and he came to Shechem.
15 ¶ And a certain man found him, and, behold,
he was wandering in the field: and the man asked
him, saying, What seekest thou?
16 And he said, I seek my brethren: tell me, I pray
thee, where they feed *their flocks*.
17 And the man said, They are departed hence; for
I heard them say, Let us go to Dothan. And Joseph
went after his brethren, and found them in Dothan.
18 And when they saw him afar off, even before
he came near unto them, they conspired against
him to slay him.
19 And they said one to another, Behold, this
dreamer cometh.
20 Come now therefore, and let us slay him, and

---

the Lord and the heirs of His promises. Abraham had Ishmael, and Isaac had Esau. Therefore, children, do not rest in your family privileges and covenant privileges, but seek true conversion through repentance and faith so that you rest in Christ alone.

THE CRISIS OF ISRAEL REGARDING JOSEPH AND JUDAH (37:1—50:26)

The Humiliation of Joseph and Sin of Judah (37:1—40:23)

Chapter 37: *Joseph, Jacob's favored son, receives dreams of exaltation but is captured and enslaved by his wicked brothers.*

37:1 *stranger*. Foreigner. In contrast to Esau, who departed for Seir (36:8), Jacob remained a sojourner in the Promised Land.

37:2 *the generations of Jacob*. The expected genealogy is delayed (46:8–26), and instead the reader finds the story of *Joseph*, Jacob's first son by Rachel. *sons of Bilhah . . . sons of Zilpah*. Dan, Naphtali, Gad, and Asher. *their evil report*. A bad report about them. Jacob appointed Joseph to oversee his brothers' work (v. 14), an early sign of his leadership ability.

37:3 *coat of many colours*. Perhaps a sign of royalty (2 Sam. 13:18). A mural at the palace of Mari from the eighteenth century BC shows men wearing robes of different colored panels of cloth.

37:6 *I pray you*. Please.

37:7 *binding sheaves*. Tying up cut stalks of grain in a bundle during the harvest. *made obeisance*. Bowed down. God revealed key elements of Joseph's future: interpreting dreams, gathering food, and exercising authority.

37:9 *another dream*. The doubling of the dream of exaltation indicated that it was God's fixed will and He would begin implementing it soon (41:32). Yet He would use strange means.

37:11 *observed*. Literally, "kept," that is, meditated on these revelations (Luke 1:66; 2:19).

37:12 *feed*. Shepherd or lead to pasture.

37:14 *Shechem* is fifty miles north of *Hebron*. The name is also a reminder of how murderous Jacob's sons could be (34:25–26).

37:15 God's providence secretly guided Joseph while he *was wandering* looking for his brothers, so that he met the particular *man* who could direct him to them (1 Sam. 9:1–16).

37:17 Joseph had to travel another fifteen miles or more from Shechem to *Dothan*.

37:19 *dreamer*. Literally, "master of dreams," a scornful reference to Joseph's dreams of his future reign over his brothers.

37:20 *let us slay him*. Jacob's sons were liars and murderers

cast him into some pit, and we will say, Some evil
beast hath devoured him: and we shall see what
will become of his dreams.
21 And Reuben heard *it*, and he delivered him out
of their hands; and said, Let us not kill him.
22 And Reuben said unto them, Shed no blood,
but cast him into this pit that *is* in the wilderness,
and lay no hand upon him; that he might rid him
out of their hands, to deliver him to his father
again.
23 ¶ And it came to pass, when Joseph was come
unto his brethren, that they stript Joseph out of
his coat, *his* coat of *many* colours that *was* on him;
24 And they took him, and cast him into a pit:
and the pit *was* empty, *there was* no water in it.
25 And they sat down to eat bread: and they
lifted up their eyes and looked, and, behold, a
company of Ishmeelites came from Gilead with
their camels bearing spicery and balm and myrrh,
going to carry *it* down to Egypt.
26 And Judah said unto his brethren, What profit
is it if we slay our brother, and conceal his blood?
27 Come, and let us sell him to the Ishmeelites,
and let not our hand be upon him; for he *is* our
brother *and* our flesh. And his brethren were
content.
28 Then there passed by Midianites merchant-
men; and they drew and lifted up Joseph out of
the pit, and sold Joseph to the Ishmeelites for
twenty *pieces* of silver: and they brought Joseph
into Egypt.
29 ¶ And Reuben returned unto the pit; and, be-
hold, Joseph *was* not in the pit; and he rent his
clothes.
30 And he returned unto his brethren, and said,
The child *is* not; and I, whither shall I go?
31 And they took Joseph's coat, and killed a kid of
the goats, and dipped the coat in the blood;
32 And they sent the coat of *many* colours, and
they brought *it* to their father; and said, This have
we found: know now whether it *be* thy son's coat
or no.
33 And he knew it, and said, *It is* my son's coat; an
evil beast hath devoured him; Joseph is without
doubt rent in pieces.
34 And Jacob rent his clothes, and put sackcloth
upon his loins, and mourned for his son many
days.
35 And all his sons and all his daughters rose up
to comfort him; but he refused to be comforted;
and he said, For I will go down into the grave unto
my son mourning. Thus his father wept for him.
36 And the Midianites sold him into Egypt unto
Potiphar, an officer of Pharaoh's, *and* captain of
the guard.

CHAPTER 38

AND it came to pass at that time, that Judah went
down from his brethren, and turned in to a cer-
tain Adullamite, whose name *was* Hirah.
2 And Judah saw there a daughter of a certain
Canaanite, whose name *was* Shuah; and he took
her, and went in unto her.
3 And she conceived, and bare a son; and he
called his name Er.
4 And she conceived again, and bare a son; and
she called his name Onan.
5 And she yet again conceived, and bare a son;
and called his name Shelah: and he was at Chezib,
when she bare him.
6 And Judah took a wife for Er his firstborn,
whose name *was* Tamar.
7 And Er, Judah's firstborn, was wicked in the
sight of the LORD; and the LORD slew him.
8 And Judah said unto Onan, Go in unto thy

like Cain and the serpent (3:1–5; 4:8–9; John 8:44; 1 John 3:12). They needed salvation.

37:22 *rid him out of their hands.* Snatch him out of their power.

37:25 *sat down to eat.* They were remarkably callous, eating while Joseph cried out for help (42:21). *behold, a company of Ishmeelites.* Another seemingly random encounter (v. 15) as God's providence preserved Joseph's life and sent him into Egypt. *spicery and balm and myrrh.* Gum or resin used for fragrance, cosmetics, and medicine.

37:26 *What profit.* Judah's first words in Genesis and the first display of his wickedness (ch. 38). Sadly, he cared more for a little silver than for his brother.

37:27–28 *Ishmeelites . . . Midianites.* These two words are sometimes used of the same people (Judg. 8:22–24). *twenty pieces of silver.* Also the price of a slave in Babylon c. 2000 BC.

37:29 *rent.* Tore.

37:30 *whither.* Where.

37:34 *rent his clothes.* Tore his clothes. *put sackcloth upon his loins.* Put on undergarments of rough, uncomfortable cloth. These are signs of mourning (2 Kings 19:1; Est. 4:1).

Thoughts for Personal/Family Worship: Chapter 37

1. **God promises to exalt His servants, but they must often face great humiliations and sufferings first. This was the case for Joseph, as it would later be for Jesus Christ. These experiences test our faith, but we can look back to those who suffered before us, especially the Son of God, and find hope that God has a plan for us.**
2. **God made families to be havens of love, righteousness, and safety, but sin can twist them into dens of jealousy, hatred, murder, enslavement, lies, and great grief. If you or a friend come from a family like that, have hope. God can use the horrors of an evil family background to bring great blessing, as the story of Joseph will reveal.**

Chapter 38: ***Judah's offspring are threatened by their worldliness and wickedness, but the Lord preserves his seed.***

38:1–2 *Adullamite.* Man from Canaanite city of Adullam (Josh. 12:15). Taking a friend (vv. 12,20) and a wife from the

brother's wife, and marry her, and raise up seed
to thy brother.
9 And Onan knew that the seed should not be
his; and it came to pass, when he went in unto his
brother's wife, that he spilled *it* on the ground, lest
that he should give seed to his brother.
10 And the thing which he did displeased the
LORD: wherefore he slew him also.
11 Then said Judah to Tamar his daughter in law,
Remain a widow at thy father's house, till Shelah
my son be grown: for he said, Lest peradventure
he die also, as his brethren *did*. And Tamar went
and dwelt in her father's house.
12 ¶ And in process of time the daughter of Shuah
Judah's wife died; and Judah was comforted, and
went up unto his sheepshearers to Timnath, he
and his friend Hirah the Adullamite.
13 And it was told Tamar, saying, Behold thy father
in law goeth up to Timnath to shear his sheep.
14 And she put her widow's garments off from
her, and covered her with a vail, and wrapped her-
self, and sat in an open place, which *is* by the way
to Timnath; for she saw that Shelah was grown,
and she was not given unto him to wife.
15 When Judah saw her, he thought her *to be* an
harlot; because she had covered her face.
16 And he turned unto her by the way, and said,
Go to, I pray thee, let me come in unto thee; (for
he knew not that she *was* his daughter in law.)
And she said, What wilt thou give me, that thou
mayest come in unto me?
17 And he said, I will send *thee* a kid from the
flock. And she said, Wilt thou give *me* a pledge,
till thou send *it*?
18 And he said, What pledge shall I give thee?
And she said, Thy signet, and thy bracelets, and
thy staff that *is* in thine hand. And he gave *it* her,
and came in unto her, and she conceived by him.
19 And she arose, and went away, and laid by her
vail from her, and put on the garments of her
widowhood.
20 And Judah sent the kid by the hand of his
friend the Adullamite, to receive *his* pledge from
the woman's hand: but he found her not.
21 Then he asked the men of that place, saying,
Where *is* the harlot, that *was* openly by the way side?
And they said, There was no harlot in this *place*.
22 And he returned to Judah, and said, I cannot
find her; and also the men of the place said, *that*
there was no harlot in this *place*.
23 And Judah said, Let her take *it* to her, lest we
be shamed: behold, I sent this kid, and thou hast
not found her.
24 ¶ And it came to pass about three months after,
that it was told Judah, saying, Tamar thy daughter
in law hath played the harlot; and also, behold,
she *is* with child by whoredom. And Judah said,
Bring her forth, and let her be burnt.
25 When she *was* brought forth, she sent to her
father in law, saying, By the man, whose these *are*,
am I with child: and she said, Discern, I pray thee,
whose *are* these, the signet, and bracelets, and
staff.
26 And Judah acknowledged *them*, and said, She
hath been more righteous than I; because that I
gave her not to Shelah my son. And he knew her
again no more.
27 ¶ And it came to pass in the time of her travail,
that, behold, twins *were* in her womb.
28 And it came to pass, when she travailed, that
the one put out *his* hand: and the midwife took
and bound upon his hand a scarlet thread, saying,
This came out first.
29 And it came to pass, as he drew back his hand,

Canaanites revealed Judah's worldliness (24:3; Ex. 34:14–16).

38:8–9 *seed*. Offspring. The brother-in-law of a widow with no children married her in order to produce children to carry on the name of his deceased brother (Deut. 25:5–6). Thus Onan's sin consisted of his selfish and deceptive avoidance of providing offspring for his brother's name.

38:11 *Lest peradventure*. Unless perhaps. Judah showed his spiritual blindness when he blamed Tamar for the death of his sons instead of their own wickedness.

38:13 The time for a man *to shear his sheep* was a festival (2 Sam. 13:23–24); agricultural festivals were sometimes associated with prostitution (Hos. 9:1–2).

38:14–16 *vail*. Veil. *harlot*. Prostitute. *Go to, I pray thee*. Please grant. Two interpretations of Tamar's actions are possible. She may have veiled herself to remind Judah that she should be given to *Shelah*—betrothed and married women were veiled (24:65)—but when Judah mistook her for a prostitute, she played along so that he would fulfill his son's responsibility of giving her children. Or it may be that she intentionally presented herself as a prostitute to seduce Judah in order to obtain children and preserve her husband's name. However, it appears that prostitutes generally did not wear veils, but painted their faces (Jer. 4:30; Ezek. 23:40).

38:18 *signet*. Ring or other artistically designed object used to mark writings with a personal seal. *bracelets*. Cord, probably holding the signet.

38:21–22 *harlot*. Unlike "harlot" in v. 15, the word used here refers specifically to a woman who sells sex as part of ritual worship (Deut. 23:17; Hos. 4:14), suggesting that Tamar was near a pagan temple—another reason why Judah might think she was a prostitute.

38:23 *lest we be shamed*. Judah probably did not want everyone to know he had given his signet to a prostitute, a foolish act that showed how much lust controlled him.

38:24 *whoredom*. Prostitution. *let her be burnt*. Death by fire was the penalty for immorality by the daughter of a priest because she had desecrated his holy calling (Lev. 21:8–9). Ironically, Judah was hypocritical, not holy.

38:26 *knew her again no more*. Did not have sexual relations with her again (4:1). *Judah* was humbled for his sin, for he acknowledged that Tamar was *more righteous than* he was, and confessed his specific sin in not giving her to *Shelah*. He will play a noble role later (chs. 43–44).

38:27 *travail*. Labor pains in giving birth. The wrestling of *twins* reminds us of Jacob and Esau in the womb of Rebekah, suggesting that God had a special purpose for one of the boys.

that, behold, his brother came out: and she said,
How hast thou broken forth? *this* breach *be* upon
thee: therefore his name was called Pharez.
30 And afterward came out his brother, that had
the scarlet thread upon his hand: and his name
was called Zarah.

CHAPTER 39

AND Joseph was brought down to Egypt; and Pot-
iphar, an officer of Pharaoh, captain of the guard,
an Egyptian, bought him of the hands of the Ish-
meelites, which had brought him down thither.
2 And the LORD was with Joseph, and he was a
prosperous man; and he was in the house of his
master the Egyptian.
3 And his master saw that the LORD *was* with
him, and that the LORD made all that he did to
prosper in his hand.
4 And Joseph found grace in his sight, and he
served him: and he made him overseer over his
house, and all *that* he had he put into his hand.
5 And it came to pass from the time *that* he had
made him overseer in his house, and over all that
he had, that the LORD blessed the Egyptian's house
for Joseph's sake; and the blessing of the LORD was
upon all that he had in the house, and in the field.
6 And he left all that he had in Joseph's hand; and
he knew not ought he had, save the bread which
he did eat. And Joseph was *a* goodly *person*, and
well favoured.
7 ¶ And it came to pass after these things, that his
master's wife cast her eyes upon Joseph; and she
said, Lie with me.
8 But he refused, and said unto his master's wife,
Behold, my master wotteth not what *is* with me
in the house, and he hath committed all that he
hath to my hand;
9 *There is* none greater in this house than I;
neither hath he kept back any thing from me but
thee, because thou *art* his wife: how then can I do
this great wickedness, and sin against God?
10 And it came to pass, as she spake to Joseph day
by day, that he hearkened not unto her, to lie by
her, *or* to be with her.
11 And it came to pass about this time, that *Joseph*
went into the house to do his business; and *there
was* none of the men of the house there within.
12 And she caught him by his garment, saying,
Lie with me: and he left his garment in her hand,
and fled, and got him out.
13 And it came to pass, when she saw that he had
left his garment in her hand, and was fled forth,
14 That she called unto the men of her house, and
spake unto them, saying, See, he hath brought in
an Hebrew unto us to mock us; he came in unto
me to lie with me, and I cried with a loud voice:
15 And it came to pass, when he heard that I lifted
up my voice and cried, that he left his garment
with me, and fled, and got him out.
16 And she laid up his garment by her, until his
lord came home.
17 And she spake unto him according to these
words, saying, The Hebrew servant, which thou
hast brought unto us, came in unto me to mock me:
18 And it came to pass, as I lifted up my voice and
cried, that he left his garment with me, and fled out.
19 And it came to pass, when his master heard

38:29 *breach.* Breaking out. Judah's son *Pharez* (sometimes spelled Phares or Perez) was the forefather of David (Ruth 4:18–22), and ultimately of Jesus Christ (Matt. 1:1–3).

Thoughts for Personal/Family Worship: Chapter 38

1. **Apart from grace, sin and God's wrath would destroy His covenant people, just as He killed Judah's two sons. The visible church is too easily drawn into the world. We need more than godly parents; we need grace to forgive our sins and change our hearts.**
2. **Let us humble ourselves for our sins and glorify God for His power to bring good out of evil. This is one of the most sordid chapters in the Bible, and yet through these sins the Lord preserved the line of Judah and made Tamar into the ancestor of our Savior.**

Chapter 39: *The Lord was with Joseph in his service in Egypt, and Joseph walked with God in righteousness, but he suffered from the wicked.*

39:1 *down thither.* Down to there. In God's providence, Joseph was *bought* as a slave by one of the most powerful men of Egypt and put to work not in the fields or mine, but in his household.

39:2 *the LORD was with Joseph.* God's promise to be with His people is a major theme of Scripture (vv. 21,23; see 21:22; 26:3; 28:15; 31:3; 39:2–3,21,23; 46:4).

39:6 *Joseph's hand.* His power and authority. *he knew not ought he had.* He entrusted the management of his household and property completely to Joseph. *save.* Except. *a goodly person, and well favoured.* Handsome, the same words used of his mother's physical beauty (29:17).

39:8 *he refused.* Joseph was between seventeen and twenty-eight years old (37:2; 41:1,46), single, far from family, and thus vulnerable to sexual temptation. His moral purity stands in direct contrast to the lust of Reuben and Judah (35:22; 38:15–16). *wotteth not.* Does not know or pay attention. Joseph was horrified at the thought of violating his master's trust, an attitude of gratitude and integrity.

39:9 *how then can I do this great wickedness, and sin against God?* Joseph feared the Lord and turned away from evil (Job 28:28; Prov. 3:7).

39:10 *hearkened not.* Did not listen. *or to be with her.* Joseph wisely avoided temptation as much as possible, which must have taken great thought and care since she persisted *day by day.*

39:12 *left his garment in her hand, and fled.* Joseph is a model of a man who faithfully flees youthful lusts (2 Tim. 2:22).

39:19–20 *his wrath was kindled.* His anger became hot or fierce. *put him into the prison.* Joseph lost what liberty he had and was bound in painful iron chains (Ps. 105:18). One would expect that a slave convicted of sexually assaulting his master's wife would be killed. It may be that Potiphar's anger was

the words of his wife, which she spake unto him,
saying, After this manner did thy servant to me;
that his wrath was kindled.
20 And Joseph's master took him, and put him
into the prison, a place where the king's prisoners
were bound: and he was there in the prison.
21 ¶ But the LORD was with Joseph, and shewed
him mercy, and gave him favour in the sight of
the keeper of the prison.
22 And the keeper of the prison committed to Jo-
seph's hand all the prisoners that *were* in the prison;
and whatsoever they did there, he was the doer *of it*.
23 The keeper of the prison looked not to any
thing *that was* under his hand; because the LORD
was with him, and *that* which he did, the LORD
made *it* to prosper.

CHAPTER 40

AND it came to pass after these things, *that* the
butler of the king of Egypt and *his* baker had
offended their lord the king of Egypt.
2 And Pharaoh was wroth against two *of* his
officers, against the chief of the butlers, and
against the chief of the bakers.
3 And he put them in ward in the house of the
captain of the guard, into the prison, the place
where Joseph *was* bound.
4 And the captain of the guard charged Joseph
with them, and he served them: and they contin-
ued a season in ward.
5 ¶ And they dreamed a dream both of them,
each man his dream in one night, each man ac-
cording to the interpretation of his dream, the
butler and the baker of the king of Egypt, which
were bound in the prison.
6 And Joseph came in unto them in the morning,
and looked upon them, and, behold, they *were* sad.
7 And he asked Pharaoh's officers that *were*
with him in the ward of his lord's house, saying,
Wherefore look ye *so* sadly to day?
8 And they said unto him, We have dreamed
a dream, and *there is* no interpreter of it. And
Joseph said unto them, *Do* not interpretations
belong to God? tell me *them*, I pray you.
9 And the chief butler told his dream to Joseph,
and said to him, In my dream, behold, a vine *was*
before me;
10 And in the vine *were* three branches: and it *was*
as though it budded, *and* her blossoms shot forth;
and the clusters thereof brought forth ripe grapes:
11 And Pharaoh's cup *was* in my hand: and I took
the grapes, and pressed them into Pharaoh's cup,
and I gave the cup into Pharaoh's hand.
12 And Joseph said unto him, This *is* the inter-
pretation of it: The three branches *are* three days:
13 Yet within three days shall Pharaoh lift up
thine head, and restore thee unto thy place: and
thou shalt deliver Pharaoh's cup into his hand, af-
ter the former manner when thou wast his butler.
14 But think on me when it shall be well with
thee, and shew kindness, I pray thee, unto me, and
make mention of me unto Pharaoh, and bring me
out of this house:
15 For indeed I was stolen away out of the land of
the Hebrews: and here also have I done nothing
that they should put me into the dungeon.
16 When the chief baker saw that the interpreta-

---

directed primarily at his wife, but social custom demanded that he punish Joseph (see note at 40:3–4). *a place where the king's prisoners were bound.* Not the prison for common criminals, but for persons of some rank (40:1–4).

39:21 *mercy.* Variously translated as kindness, goodness, or mercy; especially God's loyal love to those in covenant with Him (24:12,14,27; 32:10; Ex. 20:6; 34:6).

39:23 *the LORD was with him . . . the LORD made it to prosper.* Repeated from v. 3, enclosing this chapter with reminders of God's purpose and power to bless His servant.

Thoughts for Personal/Family Worship: Chapter 39

1. **Doing right may bring great pain. Few things are more painful than false accusations, but that is often how the wicked respond when we refuse to join them in sin. We must learn to fear the Lord more than we fear the slanders of men and women.**
2. **What does it mean that God is with us? It certainly does not mean that we will escape mistreatment at home and at work. Joseph experienced both, but God was with him. How? God blessed his soul with the fear of the Lord, hatred of sin, diligence in labor, and perseverance under both trial and temptation. He blessed him with wisdom and skill in his work and made him a blessing to those around him, gaining the respect of those who knew him. Though God's people suffer, God is with them in a real and powerful way.**

Chapter 40: *Joseph meets two officials of the king in prison, and God uses him to reveal their future, but he remains in prison.*

40:1 *butler.* Cupbearer (v. 21), a trusted official with direct access to the king (41:9; Neh. 1:11; 2:1–8).

40:2 *wroth.* Angry.

40:3–4 *in ward.* In custody or under arrest. *captain of the guard.* This exact phrase was used of Potiphar (37:36; 39:1), suggesting that he retained Joseph as his servant in the prison (41:12) despite his wife's accusations. Entrusting these high-level officials to his care speaks of Potiphar's continuing trust in Joseph.

40:5 *dream.* A reminder of Joseph's dreams (ch. 37) and hint that his exaltation was near. *each man according to the interpretation of his dream.* Each man's dream had its own meaning.

40:7 *Wherefore.* Why.

40:8 *interpreter.* Ancient people relied upon wise men and sorcerers to explain the meaning of strange dreams (41:8; Dan. 2:2). *interpretations belong to God.* Joseph gave glory to God, not himself, spirits, or magic as the source of wisdom (41:16; Dan. 2:20–28).

40:13 *butler.* Cupbearer.

40:15 *dungeon.* Pit; the same word used when Joseph's brothers cast him into a pit (37:20).

40:16 *white.* White bread or cake.

tion was good, he said unto Joseph, I also *was* in
my dream, and, behold, *I had* three white baskets
on my head:
17 And in the uppermost basket *there was* of all
manner of bakemeats for Pharaoh; and the birds
did eat them out of the basket upon my head.
18 And Joseph answered and said, This *is* the in-
terpretation thereof: The three baskets *are* three
days:
19 Yet within three days shall Pharaoh lift up thy
head from off thee, and shall hang thee on a tree;
and the birds shall eat thy flesh from off thee.
20 ¶ And it came to pass the third day, *which was*
Pharaoh's birthday, that he made a feast unto all
his servants: and he lifted up the head of the chief
butler and of the chief baker among his servants.
21 And he restored the chief butler unto his but-
lership again; and he gave the cup into Pharaoh's
hand:
22 But he hanged the chief baker: as Joseph had
interpreted to them.
23 Yet did not the chief butler remember Joseph,
but forgat him.

CHAPTER 41

AND it came to pass at the end of two full years,
that Pharaoh dreamed: and, behold, he stood by
the river.
2 And, behold, there came up out of the river
seven well favoured kine and fatfleshed; and they
fed in a meadow.
3 And, behold, seven other kine came up after
them out of the river, ill favoured and leanfleshed;
and stood by the *other* kine upon the brink of the
river.
4 And the ill favoured and leanfleshed kine did
eat up the seven well favoured and fat kine. So
Pharaoh awoke.
5 And he slept and dreamed the second time:
and, behold, seven ears of corn came up upon one
stalk, rank and good.
6 And, behold, seven thin ears and blasted with
the east wind sprung up after them.
7 And the seven thin ears devoured the seven
rank and full ears. And Pharaoh awoke, and,
behold, *it was* a dream.
8 And it came to pass in the morning that his spirit
was troubled; and he sent and called for all the ma-
gicians of Egypt, and all the wise men thereof: and
Pharaoh told them his dream; but *there was* none
that could interpret them unto Pharaoh.
9 ¶ Then spake the chief butler unto Pharaoh,
saying, I do remember my faults this day:
10 Pharaoh was wroth with his servants, and put
me in ward in the captain of the guard's house,
both me and the chief baker:
11 And we dreamed a dream in one night, I and
he; we dreamed each man according to the inter-
pretation of his dream.
12 And *there was* there with us a young man,
an Hebrew, servant to the captain of the guard;
and we told him, and he interpreted to us our
dreams; to each man according to his dream he
did interpret.
13 And it came to pass, as he interpreted to us, so
it was; me he restored unto mine office, and him
he hanged.
14 ¶ Then Pharaoh sent and called Joseph, and they
brought him hastily out of the dungeon: and he
shaved *himself*, and changed his raiment, and came
in unto Pharaoh.
15 And Pharaoh said unto Joseph, I have dreamed
a dream, and *there is* none that can interpret it:

40:17 *bakemeats.* Baked goods.
40:22 *as Joseph had interpreted to them.* Everything happened exactly as Joseph said, a sign that he was a true prophet of the Lord (Deut. 18:22; 1 Sam. 3:19).
40:23 *forgat him.* After this reminder that God's revelations come true and the golden opportunity for his release, one can imagine the bitter disappointment for Joseph to remain forgotten in prison. God's people not only experience injustice, but sometimes must endure it for years while they cry, "How long, O Lord?" (Ps. 6:3; 13:1; 35:17; 74:10; 79:5; 80:4; 89:46; 90:13; 94:3).

Thoughts for Personal/Family Worship: Chapter 40

1. **Though false teachers deny that God can know what people will choose to do tomorrow, in reality God knows every day of our lives before we are even born. He is able to declare the end from the beginning. We can trust Him with the future; He has plans to do good to all His redeemed people.**
2. **Painful circumstances in our lives may drag on for years. Sometimes, we must endure great disappointments when our hopes get raised only to be dashed to the ground. We must wait on the Lord. Nothing is more difficult than waiting, but nothing is more profitable for our souls. By grace, waiting cultivates faith, prayer, submission, and humility; it prepares us for greater fruitfulness in the future. Above all, it focuses our hope not on earthly things or relationships, but upon the Lord Himself. Have you, too, learned to wait actively, prayerfully, and expectantly on God?**

The Exaltation of Joseph and Nobility of Judah (41:1—45:28)

Chapter 41: *Pharaoh's dreams lead to the appointment of Joseph as lord over Egypt.*

41:1 *the river.* The Nile, the great river of Egypt.
41:2 *well favoured kine and fatfleshed.* Attractive and well-fed cows.
41:3 *ill favoured and leanfleshed.* Ugly and thin. The cow was a symbol of the Egyptian goddess of fertility, so a dream of the destruction of healthy cows would disturb the Egyptians.
41:5 *corn.* Grain, not necessarily corn (maize). *rank.* Healthy.
41:9 *butler.* Cupbearer.
41:10 *wroth.* Angry. *in ward.* In custody or under arrest.
41:14 *shaved.* Egyptian men were clean-shaven, unlike Hebrew men (2 Sam. 10:5). *raiment.* Clothing.

and I have heard say of thee, *that* thou canst
understand a dream to interpret it.
16 And Joseph answered Pharaoh, saying, *It is*
not in me: God shall give Pharaoh an answer of
peace.
17 And Pharaoh said unto Joseph, In my dream,
behold, I stood upon the bank of the river:
18 And, behold, there came up out of the river
seven kine, fatfleshed and well favoured; and they
fed in a meadow:
19 And, behold, seven other kine came up after
them, poor and very ill favoured and leanfleshed,
such as I never saw in all the land of Egypt for
badness:
20 And the lean and the ill favoured kine did eat
up the first seven fat kine:
21 And when they had eaten them up, it could
not be known that they had eaten them; but they
were still ill favoured, as at the beginning. So I
awoke.
22 And I saw in my dream, and, behold, seven
ears came up in one stalk, full and good:
23 And, behold, seven ears, withered, thin, *and*
blasted with the east wind, sprung up after them:
24 And the thin ears devoured the seven good
ears: and I told *this* unto the magicians; but *there*
was none that could declare *it* to me.
25 ¶ And Joseph said unto Pharaoh, The dream
of Pharaoh *is* one: God hath shewed Pharaoh
what he *is* about to do.
26 The seven good kine *are* seven years; and the
seven good ears *are* seven years: the dream *is* one.
27 And the seven thin and ill favoured kine that
came up after them *are* seven years; and the seven
empty ears blasted with the east wind shall be
seven years of famine.
28 This *is* the thing which I have spoken unto
Pharaoh: What God *is* about to do he sheweth
unto Pharaoh.
29 Behold, there come seven years of great plenty
throughout all the land of Egypt:
30 And there shall arise after them seven years of
famine; and all the plenty shall be forgotten in the
land of Egypt; and the famine shall consume the
land;
31 And the plenty shall not be known in the land
by reason of that famine following; for it *shall be*
very grievous.
32 And for that the dream was doubled unto Pha-
raoh twice; *it is* because the thing *is* established by
God, and God will shortly bring it to pass.
33 Now therefore let Pharaoh look out a man
discreet and wise, and set him over the land of
Egypt.
34 Let Pharaoh do *this*, and let him appoint offi-
cers over the land, and take up the fifth part of the
land of Egypt in the seven plenteous years.
35 And let them gather all the food of those good
years that come, and lay up corn under the hand
of Pharaoh, and let them keep food in the cities.
36 And that food shall be for store to the land
against the seven years of famine, which shall
be in the land of Egypt; that the land perish not
through the famine.
37 ¶ And the thing was good in the eyes of Pha-
raoh, and in the eyes of all his servants.
38 And Pharaoh said unto his servants, Can we
find *such a one* as this *is*, a man in whom the Spirit
of God *is*?
39 And Pharaoh said unto Joseph, Forasmuch as
God hath shewed thee all this, *there is* none so dis-
creet and wise as thou *art*:
40 Thou shalt be over my house, and according
unto thy word shall all my people be ruled: only
in the throne will I be greater than thou.
41 And Pharaoh said unto Joseph, See, I have set
thee over all the land of Egypt.
42 And Pharaoh took off his ring from his hand,
and put it upon Joseph's hand, and arrayed him in
vestures of fine linen, and put a gold chain about
his neck;
43 And he made him to ride in the second chariot
which he had; and they cried before him, Bow the
knee: and he made him *ruler* over all the land of
Egypt.
44 And Pharaoh said unto Joseph, I *am* Pharaoh,
and without thee shall no man lift up his hand or
foot in all the land of Egypt.
45 And Pharaoh called Joseph's name Zaphnath-
paaneah; and he gave him to wife Asenath the

41:16 *It is not in me: God shall give Pharaoh an answer.* Despite the opportunity to promote himself before Pharaoh, Joseph chose to humble himself and honor God (40:8).

41:25 *God hath shewed Pharaoh what he is about to do.* God could declare the future because He controls the future (vv. 28,32; 2 Chron. 20:6; Isa. 14:24,27). The pharaoh was an absolute dictator, called a son of the sun god. But Joseph proclaimed God to be ruler over Egypt's future.

41:33–36 *plenteous.* Abundant. *hand of Pharaoh.* Authority of Pharaoh. God had prepared Joseph with years of experience, and now his wisdom shone in his plan for the coming crisis.

41:38 *the Spirit of God.* Though this could be translated, "spirit of the gods," Pharaoh's statement in the next verse that "God hath shewed thee" confirms the KJV translation. All wisdom comes from the Spirit (Job 32:8; 33:4), especially spiritual wisdom (1 Cor. 2:9–16; 12:3).

41:39 *Forasmuch.* Since.

41:40 A pharaoh often appointed a vizier, (civil officer) in Egypt, to oversee his government, but it would be shocking for the pharaoh to promote an imprisoned slave to this position.

41:42 *vestures of fine linen.* Clothing made from flax fibers. It was cool in hot weather—a popular fabric for the rich (Ex. 28:5; 1 Chron. 15:27; Est. 8:15; Isa. 3:23; Luke 16:19).

41:45 *Poti-pherah.* Not the same as Potiphar. *On.* City in Egypt, also known as Heliopolis. A granite obelisk of the temple of the sun god from this period still stands there, some sixty-eight feet tall.

daughter of Poti-pherah priest of On. And Joseph
went out over *all* the land of Egypt.
46 ¶ And Joseph *was* thirty years old when he
stood before Pharaoh king of Egypt. And Joseph
went out from the presence of Pharaoh, and went
throughout all the land of Egypt.
47 And in the seven plenteous years the earth
brought forth by handfuls.
48 And he gathered up all the food of the seven
years, which were in the land of Egypt, and laid up
the food in the cities: the food of the field, which
was round about every city, laid he up in the same.
49 And Joseph gathered corn as the sand of the
sea, very much, until he left numbering; for *it was*
without number.
50 And unto Joseph were born two sons before
the years of famine came, which Asenath the
daughter of Poti-pherah priest of On bare unto
him.
51 And Joseph called the name of the firstborn
Manasseh: For God, *said he*, hath made me forget
all my toil, and all my father's house.
52 And the name of the second called he Ephraim:
For God hath caused me to be fruitful in the land
of my affliction.
53 ¶ And the seven years of plenteousness, that
was in the land of Egypt, were ended.
54 And the seven years of dearth began to come,
according as Joseph had said: and the dearth was
in all lands; but in all the land of Egypt there was
bread.
55 And when all the land of Egypt was famished,
the people cried to Pharaoh for bread: and Pha-
raoh said unto all the Egyptians, Go unto Joseph;
what he saith to you, do.
56 And the famine was over all the face of the
earth: And Joseph opened all the storehouses, and
sold unto the Egyptians; and the famine waxed
sore in the land of Egypt.
57 And all countries came into Egypt to Joseph
for to buy *corn*; because that the famine was *so*
sore in all lands.

CHAPTER 42

Now when Jacob saw that there was corn in
Egypt, Jacob said unto his sons, Why do ye look
one upon another?
2 And he said, Behold, I have heard that there is
corn in Egypt: get you down thither, and buy for
us from thence; that we may live, and not die.
3 ¶ And Joseph's ten brethren went down to buy
corn in Egypt.
4 But Benjamin, Joseph's brother, Jacob sent not
with his brethren; for he said, Lest peradventure
mischief befall him.
5 And the sons of Israel came to buy *corn* among
those that came: for the famine was in the land
of Canaan.
6 And Joseph *was* the governor over the land, *and*
he *it was* that sold to all the people of the land: and
Joseph's brethren came, and bowed down them-
selves before him *with* their faces to the earth.
7 And Joseph saw his brethren, and he knew
them, but made himself strange unto them, and
spake roughly unto them; and he said unto them,
Whence come ye? And they said, From the land of
Canaan to buy food.
8 And Joseph knew his brethren, but they knew
not him.
9 And Joseph remembered the dreams which
he dreamed of them, and said unto them, Ye *are*

41:46 *thirty years old.* Joseph spent thirteen years in bondage (37:2). Thirty years old was also the age inaugurating the work of the Levites, David, and Jesus Christ (Num. 4:3; 2 Sam. 5:4; Luke 3:23).
41:51–52 Joseph glorified *God* for his exaltation by Pharaoh. God's ways were mysterious, but Joseph now saw how God decreed his family's sins and his afflictions for good (50:20), so that he was able to *forget* the bitterness of the past and be *fruitful* in serving God in the present.
41:54 *dearth.* Famine.
41:56 *waxed sore.* Grew severe.

Thoughts for Personal/Family Worship: Chapter 41

1. **Wisdom comes from the Spirit of God. The Spirit gives gifts and abilities to serve, the Word of God to guide us, and experiences of suffering to sanctify us. Pray that the Spirit would fill you with wisdom, developing your knowledge, character, and skills.**
2. **God glorifies Himself by exalting His humbled servants. Christ suffered from His people's envy and false accusations. He went down into humiliation, even an accursed death on the cross. But just as Joseph's enslavement and imprisonment prepared for his service as Pharaoh's vizier, so Christ's suffering for our sins laid the foundation for His exaltation as the living Savior reigning at God's right hand. Let us praise the wisdom of God for the strange yet necessary humiliation of His Son, for without it no one would ever be saved.**

Chapter 42: *Jacob's sons go to Egypt seeking food in the famine and meet Joseph there, but they do not recognize him and he tests them.*
42:1 *corn.* Grain of any kind, not just corn (maize). *Why do ye look one upon another?* Jacob's interactions with his sons in chs. 42–43 show his exasperation. They still needed conversion.
42:2 *down thither.* Down to there. *from thence.* From there. *live, and not die.* Life-threatening famine must have raised questions in Jacob's family of whether God was displeased with them.
42:4 *Lest peradventure mischief befall him.* Perhaps something bad might happen to him. Jacob continued to show favoritism to the sons of Rachel by sending all his sons but Benjamin.
42:6 *bowed down.* Fulfilling what God revealed in Joseph's dreams (v. 9; 37:5–11).
42:7 *made himself strange.* Acted like a stranger instead of their brother.

spies; to see the nakedness of the land ye are come.
10 And they said unto him, Nay, my lord, but to
buy food are thy servants come.
11 We *are* all one man's sons; we *are* true *men*, thy
servants are no spies.
12 And he said unto them, Nay, but to see the
nakedness of the land ye are come.
13 And they said, Thy servants *are* twelve
brethren, the sons of one man in the land of
Canaan; and, behold, the youngest *is* this day with
our father, and one *is* not.
14 And Joseph said unto them, That *is it* that I
spake unto you, saying, Ye *are* spies:
15 Hereby ye shall be proved: By the life of Pha-
raoh ye shall not go forth hence, except your
youngest brother come hither.
16 Send one of you, and let him fetch your
brother, and ye shall be kept in prison, that your
words may be proved, whether *there be any* truth
in you: or else by the life of Pharaoh surely ye *are*
spies.
17 And he put them all together into ward three
days.
18 And Joseph said unto them the third day, This
do, and live; *for* I fear God:
19 If ye *be* true *men*, let one of your brethren be
bound in the house of your prison: go ye, carry
corn for the famine of your houses:
20 But bring your youngest brother unto me; so
shall your words be verified, and ye shall not die.
And they did so.
21 ¶ And they said one to another, We *are* verily
guilty concerning our brother, in that we saw the
anguish of his soul, when he besought us, and we
would not hear; therefore is this distress come
upon us.
22 And Reuben answered them, saying, Spake I
not unto you, saying, Do not sin against the child;
and ye would not hear? therefore, behold, also his
blood is required.
23 And they knew not that Joseph understood
them; for he spake unto them by an interpreter.
24 And he turned himself about from them, and
wept; and returned to them again, and com-
muned with them, and took from them Simeon,
and bound him before their eyes.
25 ¶ Then Joseph commanded to fill their sacks
with corn, and to restore every man's money into
his sack, and to give them provision for the way:
and thus did he unto them.
26 And they laded their asses with the corn, and
departed thence.
27 And as one of them opened his sack to give his
ass provender in the inn, he espied his money; for,
behold, it *was* in his sack's mouth.
28 And he said unto his brethren, My money is re-
stored; and, lo, *it is* even in my sack: and their heart
failed *them*, and they were afraid, saying one to an-
other, What *is* this *that* God hath done unto us?
29 ¶ And they came unto Jacob their father unto
the land of Canaan, and told him all that befell
unto them; saying,
30 The man, *who is* the lord of the land, spake
roughly to us, and took us for spies of the country.
31 And we said unto him, We *are* true *men*; we
are no spies:
32 We *be* twelve brethren, sons of our father; one
is not, and the youngest *is* this day with our father
in the land of Canaan.
33 And the man, the lord of the country, said unto
us, Hereby shall I know that ye *are* true *men*; leave
one of your brethren *here* with me, and take *food*
for the famine of your households, and be gone:
34 And bring your youngest brother unto me:
then shall I know that ye *are* no spies, but *that* ye
are true *men: so* will I deliver you your brother,
and ye shall traffick in the land.
35 ¶ And it came to pass as they emptied their
sacks, that, behold, every man's bundle of money
was in his sack: and when *both* they and their fa-
ther saw the bundles of money, they were afraid.
36 And Jacob their father said unto them, Me

42:9 *nakedness of the land.* Ways in which Egypt was vulnerable to attack. Spies could be killed.

42:11 *true men.* Just or honest—not an accurate statement of their overall character.

42:13 *one is not.* Joseph's questions bring to their remembrance their former sin against him.

42:15 *proved.* Tested. *By the life of Pharaoh.* An oath. *hence . . . hither.* From here . . . to here.

42:16 *fetch.* Bring. Joseph desired to see Benjamin, his only full brother, to make sure that they had not harmed him also.

42:17 *into ward.* In custody or under arrest. With poetic justice, the brothers got a small taste of the false accusation and imprisonment that Joseph suffered for years in Egypt.

42:18 *This do, and live.* Moses reported Joseph's words in a way that echoed the demands of the law (Lev. 18:5; Neh. 9:29; Luke 10:28; Rom. 10:5; Gal. 3:12). *I fear God.* Joseph reminded his brothers that God is the righteous Judge (18:25; 39:9).

42:21–22 *verily guilty.* Truly guilty. Once deaf to his cries, now the memory of the *anguish of our brother* moved their hearts. *his blood is required.* God's justice demands punishment against the oppressor. The interrogation awakened in them conviction of sin and judgment.

42:24 *wept.* Though outwardly rough with them, Joseph's heart was warm with compassion. *communed.* Talked.

42:26 *laded their asses.* Loaded their donkeys.

42:27 *provender.* Feed for livestock. *in the inn.* At a place to lodge or spend the night, perhaps just a place to camp (Josh. 4:3). *espied.* Saw.

42:28 *What is this that God hath done unto us?* The strange mercy of finding their money increased the fear of God's judgment in them (v. 35).

42:29 *befell unto them.* Happened to them.

42:34 *traffick.* Travel for business.

42:36 *Me have ye bereaved of my children: Joseph is not.* Jacob implicitly accused his sons of responsibility for Joseph's death—another arrow of conviction in their hearts.

have ye bereaved *of my children*: Joseph *is* not, and
Simeon *is* not, and ye will take Benjamin *away*: all
these things are against me.
37 And Reuben spake unto his father, saying, Slay
my two sons, if I bring him not to thee: deliver him
into my hand, and I will bring him to thee again.
38 And he said, My son shall not go down with
you; for his brother is dead, and he is left alone: if
mischief befall him by the way in the which ye go,
then shall ye bring down my gray hairs with sor-
row to the grave.

CHAPTER 43

AND the famine *was* sore in the land.
2 And it came to pass, when they had eaten up
the corn which they had brought out of Egypt,
their father said unto them, Go again, buy us a
little food.
3 And Judah spake unto him, saying, The man
did solemnly protest unto us, saying, Ye shall not
see my face, except your brother *be* with you.
4 If thou wilt send our brother with us, we will go
down and buy thee food:
5 But if thou wilt not send *him*, we will not go
down: for the man said unto us, Ye shall not see
my face, except your brother *be* with you.
6 And Israel said, Wherefore dealt ye *so* ill with
me, *as* to tell the man whether ye had yet a brother?
7 And they said, The man asked us straitly of our
state, and of our kindred, saying, *Is* your father
yet alive? have ye *another* brother? and we told
him according to the tenor of these words: could
we certainly know that he would say, Bring your
brother down?
8 And Judah said unto Israel his father, Send the
lad with me, and we will arise and go; that we may
live, and not die, both we, and thou, *and* also our
little ones.
9 I will be surety for him; of my hand shalt thou
require him: if I bring him not unto thee, and set
him before thee, then let me bear the blame for
ever:
10 For except we had lingered, surely now we had
returned this second time.
11 And their father Israel said unto them, If *it
must be* so now, do this; take of the best fruits in
the land in your vessels, and carry down the man
a present, a little balm, and a little honey, spices,
and myrrh, nuts, and almonds:
12 And take double money in your hand; and the
money that was brought again in the mouth of
your sacks, carry *it* again in your hand; peradven-
ture it *was* an oversight:
13 Take also your brother, and arise, go again
unto the man:
14 And God Almighty give you mercy before the
man, that he may send away your other brother,
and Benjamin. If I be bereaved *of my children*, I
am bereaved.
15 ¶ And the men took that present, and they
took double money in their hand, and Benjamin;
and rose up, and went down to Egypt, and stood
before Joseph.
16 And when Joseph saw Benjamin with them,
he said to the ruler of his house, Bring *these* men
home, and slay, and make ready; for *these* men
shall dine with me at noon.
17 And the man did as Joseph bade; and the man
brought the men into Joseph's house.
18 And the men were afraid, because they were
brought into Joseph's house; and they said, Be-
cause of the money that was returned in our sacks
at the first time are we brought in; that he may

42:37 *Slay my two sons.* Reuben seems to have offered Jacob the chance to avenge Joseph and Benjamin if the latter was also lost. Guilt often seeks atonement through punishing oneself.

Thoughts for Personal/Family Worship: Chapter 42

1. **The exalted lord of Egypt tested his brothers to convict them of their sins against him. Notice the similarities to the first regal act of the Lord after His ascension: He poured out the Spirit and convicted Israel of their sins against Him. Pray for the Spirit of Christ to convict the lost, so that they may begin to long for salvation and be open to hear the gospel.**
2. **When God uses the Word, the Spirit, and providence to convict us of sin, let us not avoid Him but seek His grace. We will find no help in punishing ourselves. Behind the Lord's fearsome convictions is a warm heart of mercy for all who repent.**

Chapter 43: ***Famine compels the brothers to return to Egypt with Benjamin, and Joseph receives them with surprising mercy.***

43:1 *sore.* Severe.
43:3 *protest.* Testify. *see my face.* Receive favor from me (32:20).
43:6 *Wherefore dealt ye so ill with me.* Why did you cause me harm?
43:7 *straitly.* Rigorously.
43:8 *lad.* Young man. Benjamin was in his twenties or thirties; see note at 22:5. Joseph was now thirty-nine.
43:9 *surety.* A person who promises to pay the debt or fulfill the obligation of another, like a cosigner on a loan (Prov. 6:1–5; 20:16; 22:26–27). Judah, once immoral and hypocritical (ch. 38), now took responsibility to guarantee Benjamin's safety at his own expense so that the family would have food.
43:11 *Israel* unwittingly mentioned the goods (*balm, spices,* and *myrrh*) carried by the traders to whom his sons sold Joseph as a slave (37:25)—another reminder of their sin.
43:12 *peradventure.* Perhaps.
43:14 *God Almighty.* See note at 17:1. Israel leaned on the power of his covenant God in this time of desperation.
43:16 *slay.* Butcher an animal for meat.
43:17 *bade.* Said.
43:18 *fall upon us.* Attack us. *bondmen.* Slaves, as Joseph had once been.

seek occasion against us, and fall upon us, and take us for bondmen, and our asses.

19 And they came near to the steward of Joseph's house, and they communed with him at the door of the house,

20 And said, O sir, we came indeed down at the first time to buy food:

21 And it came to pass, when we came to the inn, that we opened our sacks, and, behold, *every* man's money *was* in the mouth of his sack, our money in full weight: and we have brought it again in our hand.

22 And other money have we brought down in our hands to buy food: we cannot tell who put our money in our sacks.

23 And he said, Peace *be* to you, fear not: your God, and the God of your father, hath given you treasure in your sacks: I had your money. And he brought Simeon out unto them.

24 And the man brought the men into Joseph's house, and gave *them* water, and they washed their feet; and he gave their asses provender.

25 And they made ready the present against Joseph came at noon: for they heard that they should eat bread there.

26 ¶ And when Joseph came home, they brought him the present which *was* in their hand into the house, and bowed themselves to him to the earth.

27 And he asked them of *their* welfare, and said, *Is* your father well, the old man of whom ye spake? *Is* he yet alive?

28 And they answered, Thy servant our father *is* in good health, he *is* yet alive. And they bowed down their heads, and made obeisance.

29 And he lifted up his eyes, and saw his brother Benjamin, his mother's son, and said, *Is* this your younger brother, of whom ye spake unto me? And he said, God be gracious unto thee, my son.

30 And Joseph made haste; for his bowels did yearn upon his brother: and he sought *where* to weep; and he entered into *his* chamber, and wept there.

31 And he washed his face, and went out, and refrained himself, and said, Set on bread.

32 And they set on for him by himself, and for them by themselves, and for the Egyptians, which did eat with him, by themselves: because the Egyptians might not eat bread with the Hebrews; for that *is* an abomination unto the Egyptians.

33 And they sat before him, the firstborn according to his birthright, and the youngest according to his youth: and the men marvelled one at another.

34 And he took *and sent* messes unto them from before him: but Benjamin's mess was five times so much as any of theirs. And they drank, and were merry with him.

CHAPTER 44

AND he commanded the steward of his house, saying, Fill the men's sacks *with* food, as much as they can carry, and put every man's money in his sack's mouth.

2 And put my cup, the silver cup, in the sack's mouth of the youngest, and his corn money. And he did according to the word that Joseph had spoken.

43:19 *communed.* Talked.

43:21 *inn.* See note at 42:27.

43:23 Joseph taught wisdom to the Egyptians (Ps. 105:22), and though this servant may have known that the money was put in their sacks at Joseph's command (42:25), he rightly attributed it to God's providence over all things, as had the brothers (42:28). They had seen it as a fearful judgment, but he offered them *peace* and comfort by faith in the covenant *God of* Israel.

43:24 *gave them water, and they washed their feet.* A courtesy of ancient hospitality (18:4; 19:2; 24:32). *gave their asses provender.* Fed their donkeys.

43:25 *against Joseph came.* Until Joseph came.

43:28 *made obeisance.* Bowed low. Again, Joseph's dream was fulfilled (37:7), a reminder that the Lord rules all events according to His plan (Eph. 1:11).

43:29 *God be gracious unto thee.* Joseph could not contain his love for Benjamin, and in so doing reminded all his brothers of the grace of God.

43:30 *made haste.* Quickly left. *his bowels did yearn.* His compassion grew warm, that is, his feelings of affection were deeply stirred. This is the same word used of God's mercy (v. 14).

43:31 *refrained himself.* Controlled himself. *Set on bread.* Put out the food for the meal.

43:32 *abomination.* Something hated. Egyptian culture required separation from the Hebrews (46:34; Ex. 8:26). This suggests that they still needed reconciliation with Joseph.

43:33 There is only a 1 in 39,916,800 chance of seating eleven adult men in birth order by accident. Joseph may have intended to humble them by suggesting his supernatural knowledge (44:15) or to raise questions and thus prepare them to learn that he was their brother.

43:34 *messes.* Portions of food. *were merry.* They all had plenty to eat and drink, but Benjamin was favored, just as Joseph once was by his father—perhaps a test of their envy.

Thoughts for Personal/Family Worship: Chapter 43

1. **God uses hard times to compel us to seek Him, just as He compelled Joseph's brothers to return to Him again. What afflictions can you use as opportunities to seek God?**
2. **Whereas ch. 42 focused on the sins of the sons of Israel, ch. 43 reveals the mercy of God in His power, peace, compassion, grace, and hospitality. Though God uses conviction of sin to awaken sinners to their need for reconciliation with Him, He also wins their hearts with displays of His mercy in Christ. Let us remember this when raising our children, evangelizing our neighbors, or bringing the gospel to the lost.**

Chapter 44: ***Joseph gives his brothers a final test of their loyalty, and Judah displays a remarkable spirit of self-sacrifice.***

3 As soon as the morning was light, the men were
sent away, they and their asses.
4 *And* when they were gone out of the city, *and*
not *yet* far off, Joseph said unto his steward,
Up, follow after the men; and when thou dost
overtake them, say unto them, Wherefore have ye
rewarded evil for good?
5 *Is* not this *it* in which my lord drinketh, and
whereby indeed he divineth? ye have done evil in
so doing.
6 ¶ And he overtook them, and he spake unto
them these same words.
7 And they said unto him, Wherefore saith my
lord these words? God forbid that thy servants
should do according to this thing:
8 Behold, the money, which we found in our
sacks' mouths, we brought again unto thee out of
the land of Canaan: how then should we steal out
of thy lord's house silver or gold?
9 With whomsoever of thy servants it be found,
both let him die, and we also will be my lord's
bondmen.
10 And he said, Now also *let* it *be* according unto
your words: he with whom it is found shall be my
servant; and ye shall be blameless.
11 Then they speedily took down every man his
sack to the ground, and opened every man his
sack.
12 And he searched, *and* began at the eldest, and
left at the youngest: and the cup was found in
Benjamin's sack.
13 Then they rent their clothes, and laded every
man his ass, and returned to the city.
14 ¶ And Judah and his brethren came to Joseph's
house; for he *was* yet there: and they fell before
him on the ground.
15 And Joseph said unto them, What deed *is* this
that ye have done? wot ye not that such a man as I
can certainly divine?
16 And Judah said, What shall we say unto my
lord? what shall we speak? or how shall we clear
ourselves? God hath found out the iniquity of thy
servants: behold, we *are* my lord's servants, both
we, and *he* also with whom the cup is found.
17 And he said, God forbid that I should do so:
but the man in whose hand the cup is found, he
shall be my servant; and as for you, get you up in
peace unto your father.
18 ¶ Then Judah came near unto him, and said,
Oh my lord, let thy servant, I pray thee, speak a
word in my lord's ears, and let not thine anger
burn against thy servant: for thou *art* even as
Pharaoh.
19 My lord asked his servants, saying, Have ye a
father, or a brother?
20 And we said unto my lord, We have a father,
an old man, and a child of his old age, a little one;
and his brother is dead, and he alone is left of his
mother, and his father loveth him.
21 And thou saidst unto thy servants, Bring him
down unto me, that I may set mine eyes upon him.
22 And we said unto my lord, The lad cannot
leave his father: for *if* he should leave his father,
his father would die.
23 And thou saidst unto thy servants, Except your
youngest brother come down with you, ye shall
see my face no more.
24 And it came to pass when we came up unto
thy servant my father, we told him the words of
my lord.
25 And our father said, Go again, *and* buy us a
little food.
26 And we said, We cannot go down: if our
youngest brother be with us, then will we go
down: for we may not see the man's face, except
our youngest brother *be* with us.
27 And thy servant my father said unto us, Ye
know that my wife bare me two *sons*:

44:4 *Wherefore.* Why.
44:5 *divineth.* See note at 30:27. It is very unlikely that Joseph used the cup for divination, a magical and idolatrous practice hated by the Lord (Lev. 19:26). He believed in the sovereign providence of the God of Israel (41:25,28; 45:5,7–8; 50:20). When speaking to his steward, he simply called it his silver cup and did not mention divination (v. 2). However, it may be that Egyptians called him a diviner, having no other category to describe his supernatural wisdom and insight (41:38–39). When Joseph used such terminology, he may have used the idiom of Egypt for divine revelation or intended to deceive his brothers until revealing himself.
44:9 *bondmen.* Slaves.
44:13 *rent their clothes.* A sign of grief. *laded every man his ass.* Each man loaded his donkey. They did not hand over Benjamin and depart, but returned together, a notable act of loyalty.
44:14 Moses highlighted *Judah* for he has begun to act as the leader among *his brethren.*
44:15 *wot ye not.* Do you not know. *I can certainly divine.* See note at v. 5.
44:16 *Judah* showed his humility in his repeated use of *lord-servant* language in this chapter, the same language his father Jacob used in seeking reconciliation with Esau (chs. 32–33). *God hath found out the iniquity of thy servants.* Though only Benjamin appeared to be a thief, Judah confessed that they all were guilty, probably thinking of their sin against Joseph (42:21).
44:17 *as for you, get you up in peace.* Joseph offered his brothers an opportunity to abandon Benjamin to slavery as they had once done to him. *unto your father.* A subtle reminder that to return without their brother would break Jacob's heart again.
44:18–34 Judah interceded for Benjamin, retelling the story recorded in previous chapters in order to appeal to the Egyptian ruler's compassion for Benjamin's old father. His words reveal a dramatically changed man compared to the Judah of chs. 37–38.
44:20 *little one.* Not a reference to Benjamin's size, but to his lower age than his brothers and his father's affection for the "baby" of the house. *his brother is dead.* Twenty-two years after Joseph was sold into slavery, it was reasonable to believe he probably was dead from hard labor.

28 And the one went out from me, and I said,
Surely he is torn in pieces; and I saw him not
since:
29 And if ye take this also from me, and mischief
befall him, ye shall bring down my gray hairs with
sorrow to the grave.
30 Now therefore when I come to thy servant my
father, and the lad *be* not with us; seeing that his
life is bound up in the lad's life;
31 It shall come to pass, when he seeth that the
lad *is* not *with us*, that he will die: and thy servants
shall bring down the gray hairs of thy servant our
father with sorrow to the grave.
32 For thy servant became surety for the lad unto
my father, saying, If I bring him not unto thee,
then I shall bear the blame to my father for ever.
33 Now therefore, I pray thee, let thy servant
abide instead of the lad a bondman to my lord;
and let the lad go up with his brethren.
34 For how shall I go up to my father, and the lad
be not with me? lest peradventure I see the evil
that shall come on my father.

CHAPTER 45

THEN Joseph could not refrain himself before
all them that stood by him; and he cried, Cause
every man to go out from me. And there stood no
man with him, while Joseph made himself known
unto his brethren.
2 And he wept aloud: and the Egyptians and the
house of Pharaoh heard.
3 And Joseph said unto his brethren, I *am* Jo-
seph; doth my father yet live? And his brethren
could not answer him; for they were troubled at
his presence.
4 And Joseph said unto his brethren, Come near
to me, I pray you. And they came near. And he
said, I *am* Joseph your brother, whom ye sold into
Egypt.
5 Now therefore be not grieved, nor angry with
yourselves, that ye sold me hither: for God did
send me before you to preserve life.
6 For these two years *hath* the famine *been* in
the land: and yet *there are* five years, in the which
there shall neither *be* earing nor harvest.
7 And God sent me before you to preserve you a
posterity in the earth, and to save your lives by a
great deliverance.
8 So now *it was* not you *that* sent me hither, but
God: and he hath made me a father to Pharaoh,
and lord of all his house, and a ruler throughout
all the land of Egypt.
9 Haste ye, and go up to my father, and say unto
him, Thus saith thy son Joseph, God hath made me
lord of all Egypt: come down unto me, tarry not:
10 And thou shalt dwell in the land of Goshen,
and thou shalt be near unto me, thou, and thy
children, and thy children's children, and thy
flocks, and thy herds, and all that thou hast:

44:32–33 Out of love for his father to whom he promised to be Benjamin's *surety* (43:9), Judah asked to suffer his punishment so that his brother might go free—an act of substitution. Christ is the surety of the new covenant, the priest who, in order to please His Father, once for all suffered the punishment deserved by His people to set them free (Heb. 7:22,27; 10:5–7).

44:34 *lest peradventure*. Unless perhaps.

Thoughts for Personal/Family Worship: Chapter 44

1. **How precious is Jesus Christ, the Son of Judah, who intercedes for the condemned on the basis of His office as their Surety! He died as a substitute for sins He did not commit so that the guilty may go free. Is Christ your Surety? Have you confessed that God has found out your iniquity? Have you cried out for mercy to the Savior? He is full of mercy.**
2. **When God converts a sinner, he starts becoming like the Savior. He ceases to live for money and pleasure. He loves other people—beginning with his family. He shows a willingness to sacrifice himself in order to serve others. Does this describe you?**

Chapter 45: *Joseph stuns his brothers by revealing his identity, and sends them back to Canaan to tell Jacob and bring the family to Egypt.*

45:1 *refrain*. Control.

45:2 *wept aloud*. Or, "gave forth his voice in weeping." Now that his brothers have demonstrated their change of heart, Joseph released his pent-up emotions of love (42:24; 43:30).

45:4 *I pray you*. Please. Joseph gently invited them, *Come near to me*. Despite thirteen years of slavery and prison and twenty-two years of exile from his father, Joseph had no bitterness but loved and forgave his brothers.

45:5 *hither*. To here, that is, to Egypt. Joseph's forgiveness was empowered by the knowledge that though they were responsible for their sin (*ye sold me*), God's providence was behind it all (*God did send me*) for His good and loving purpose (*to preserve life*).

45:6 *earing*. Plowing.

45:7 Their sin against Joseph was the means by which they were saved from starvation—such is the wisdom of God. *posterity*. Descendants, literally, "a remnant." *a great deliverance*. Literally, "many survivors." The terms "remnant" and "survivors" are used in the prophets for those in Israel whom God will save from sin and misery (Isa. 4:2; 10:20; 37:32–33; 46:3–4; Jer. 23:3–6; 31:7; Joel 2:32; Mic. 7:18). Similarly, Israel's rejection of Christ was God's ordained means to save His people from sin (Acts 2:23; 4:28; 10:38–43), including the elect remnant of Israel (Rom. 9:21–24,27).

45:8 *not you . . . but God*. As the primary and sovereign cause of events, God overrules the intentions of mere men, who are but secondary and dependent causes. *father*. Not an authority over Pharaoh, but one who gave him counsel and care (Judg. 17:10; Isa. 22:21). Egyptian officials sometimes bore the title of "god's father" where Pharaoh was the "god," but scholars debate whether Joseph's words refer to this.

45:9 *Haste ye*. Hurry. *tarry not*. Do not stand (doing nothing).

45:10 *Goshen*. Probably a fertile delta area east of the Nile. In God's providence, it was ideally located for the Israelites to escape Egypt and return to Canaan.

11 And there will I nourish thee; for yet *there are*
five years of famine; lest thou, and thy household,
and all that thou hast, come to poverty.
12 And, behold, your eyes see, and the eyes of my
brother Benjamin, that *it is* my mouth that speak-
eth unto you.
13 And ye shall tell my father of all my glory in
Egypt, and of all that ye have seen; and ye shall
haste and bring down my father hither.
14 And he fell upon his brother Benjamin's neck,
and wept; and Benjamin wept upon his neck.
15 Moreover he kissed all his brethren, and wept
upon them: and after that his brethren talked
with him.
16 ¶ And the fame thereof was heard in Pharaoh's
house, saying, Joseph's brethren are come: and it
pleased Pharaoh well, and his servants.
17 And Pharaoh said unto Joseph, Say unto thy
brethren, This do ye; lade your beasts, and go, get
you unto the land of Canaan;
18 And take your father and your households,
and come unto me: and I will give you the good
of the land of Egypt, and ye shall eat the fat of
the land.
19 Now thou art commanded, this do ye; take
you wagons out of the land of Egypt for your lit-
tle ones, and for your wives, and bring your father,
and come.
20 Also regard not your stuff; for the good of all
the land of Egypt *is* yours.
21 And the children of Israel did so: and Joseph
gave them wagons, according to the commandment
of Pharaoh, and gave them provision for the way.
22 To all of them he gave each man changes of
raiment; but to Benjamin he gave three hundred
pieces of silver, and five changes of raiment.
23 And to his father he sent after this *manner*; ten
asses laden with the good things of Egypt, and ten
she asses laden with corn and bread and meat for
his father by the way.
24 So he sent his brethren away, and they
departed: and he said unto them, See that ye fall
not out by the way.
25 ¶ And they went up out of Egypt, and came
into the land of Canaan unto Jacob their father,
26 And told him, saying, Joseph *is* yet alive, and
he *is* governor over all the land of Egypt. And Ja-
cob's heart fainted, for he believed them not.
27 And they told him all the words of Joseph,
which he had said unto them: and when he saw
the wagons which Joseph had sent to carry him,
the spirit of Jacob their father revived:
28 And Israel said, *It is* enough; Joseph my son *is*
yet alive: I will go and see him before I die.

CHAPTER 46

AND Israel took his journey with all that he had,
and came to Beer-sheba, and offered sacrifices
unto the God of his father Isaac.
2 And God spake unto Israel in the visions of the
night, and said, Jacob, Jacob. And he said, Here
am I.
3 And he said, I *am* God, the God of thy father:
fear not to go down into Egypt; for I will there
make of thee a great nation:

45:13 *hither.* To here.
45:14 *fell upon his brother Benjamin's neck.* Embraced him (33:4).
45:16 *fame.* Sound, as in, news.
45:17 *lade.* Load.
45:18 *eat the fat.* Enjoy the best. Though Pharaoh did not know Joseph's family, he was eager to bless them richly because he was so pleased with Joseph. Similarly, the Father blesses those in union with Christ because He is well pleased with His Son.
45:22 *raiment.* Clothing.
45:23 *laden.* Loaded. *meat.* Food of any kind.
45:24 *fall not out by the way.* Do not get upset or quarrel on the road.
45:26 *Jacob's heart fainted.* He was shocked by the good news that *Joseph is yet alive*, just as Christ's disciples were amazed by the news of His resurrection (Mark 16:8).

Thoughts for Personal/Family Worship: Chapter 45

1. **Christ's humiliation and exaltation served the purpose of saving many people. Praise God's wisdom, for the very sins of mankind against Christ serve for our salvation. Even when His purposes seemed defeated by the murder of His Son, God was performing the plans He made in eternity to rescue wicked sinners.**
2. **When Joseph's brothers first heard Joseph identify himself, they were afraid, but when he added that he was their brother, they drew near. Today when sinners are converted, Christ's heart overflows with love and joy toward them. How does He bring them near to Him as their elder brother and welcome them with the embraces and kisses of His Spirit? Can you draw more parallels between Joseph's encounters with his brothers and a sinner's encounter with Jesus Christ?**
3. **In union with Christ, we share in His humiliation and one day will share in His exaltation. The Father will welcome us into His presence and give us His best to enjoy forever. Christians should grow in their hope and anticipation of the glory of God; in the twinkling of an eye, poor and persecuted believers will become kings forever.**

The Sojourning of Israel in Egypt (46:1—50:26)

Chapter 46: ***The Lord assures Jacob that he should go to Egypt, the whole family makes the trip, and Jacob is reunited with Joseph.***

46:1 *Beer-sheba.* City in southern Canaan along the road between Hebron (37:14) and Egypt. *offered sacrifices.* Perhaps on the altar built there by *Isaac* after the Lord appeared and made similar promises to him as He was about to do to Jacob (26:23–25).
46:4 *bring thee up again.* The Lord had revealed to Abraham that his offspring would be foreigners in another land and subject to dependence ultimately leading to slavery, but God

4 I will go down with thee into Egypt; and I will
also surely bring thee up *again*: and Joseph shall
put his hand upon thine eyes.
5 And Jacob rose up from Beer-sheba: and the
sons of Israel carried Jacob their father, and their
little ones, and their wives, in the wagons which
Pharaoh had sent to carry him.
6 And they took their cattle, and their goods,
which they had gotten in the land of Canaan, and
came into Egypt, Jacob, and all his seed with him:
7 His sons, and his sons' sons with him, his
daughters, and his sons' daughters, and all his
seed brought he with him into Egypt.
8 ¶ And these *are* the names of the children of Is-
rael, which came into Egypt, Jacob and his sons:
Reuben, Jacob's firstborn.
9 And the sons of Reuben; Hanoch, and Phallu,
and Hezron, and Carmi.
10 ¶ And the sons of Simeon; Jemuel, and Jamin,
and Ohad, and Jachin, and Zohar, and Shaul the
son of a Canaanitish woman.
11 ¶ And the sons of Levi; Gershon, Kohath, and
Merari.
12 ¶ And the sons of Judah; Er, and Onan, and
Shelah, and Pharez, and Zerah: but Er and Onan
died in the land of Canaan. And the sons of
Pharez were Hezron and Hamul.
13 ¶ And the sons of Issachar; Tola, and Phuvah,
and Job, and Shimron.
14 ¶ And the sons of Zebulun; Sered, and Elon,
and Jahleel.
15 These *be* the sons of Leah, which she bare unto
Jacob in Padan-aram, with his daughter Dinah:
all the souls of his sons and his daughters *were*
thirty and three.
16 ¶ And the sons of Gad; Ziphion, and Haggi,
Shuni, and Ezbon, Eri, and Arodi, and Areli.
17 ¶ And the sons of Asher; Jimnah, and Ishuah,
and Isui, and Beriah, and Serah their sister: and
the sons of Beriah; Heber, and Malchiel.
18 These *are* the sons of Zilpah, whom Laban
gave to Leah his daughter, and these she bare unto
Jacob, *even* sixteen souls.
19 The sons of Rachel Jacob's wife; Joseph, and
Benjamin.
20 ¶ And unto Joseph in the land of Egypt were
born Manasseh and Ephraim, which Asenath the
daughter of Poti-pherah priest of On bare unto
him.
21 ¶ And the sons of Benjamin *were* Belah, and
Becher, and Ashbel, Gera, and Naaman, Ehi, and
Rosh, Muppim, and Huppim, and Ard.
22 These *are* the sons of Rachel, which were born
to Jacob: all the souls *were* fourteen.
23 ¶ And the sons of Dan; Hushim.
24 ¶ And the sons of Naphtali; Jahzeel, and Guni,
and Jezer, and Shillem.
25 These *are* the sons of Bilhah, which Laban gave
unto Rachel his daughter, and she bare these unto
Jacob: all the souls *were* seven.
26 All the souls that came with Jacob into Egypt,
which came out of his loins, besides Jacob's sons'
wives, all the souls *were* threescore and six;
27 And the sons of Joseph, which were born him
in Egypt, *were* two souls: all the souls of the house
of Jacob, which came into Egypt, *were* threescore
and ten.
28 ¶ And he sent Judah before him unto Joseph,
to direct his face unto Goshen; and they came
into the land of Goshen.
29 And Joseph made ready his chariot, and went
up to meet Israel his father, to Goshen, and pre-
sented himself unto him; and he fell on his neck,
and wept on his neck a good while.
30 And Israel said unto Joseph, Now let me die,
since I have seen thy face, because thou *art* yet
alive.
31 And Joseph said unto his brethren, and unto his
father's house, I will go up, and shew Pharaoh, and
say unto him, My brethren, and my father's house,
which *were* in the land of Canaan, are come unto me;
32 And the men *are* shepherds, for their trade
hath been to feed cattle; and they have brought
their flocks, and their herds, and all that they have.
33 And it shall come to pass, when Pharaoh shall
call you, and shall say, What *is* your occupation?

---

would bring them out again (15:13–14). For a while they prospered but due to the generosity of the Egyptians. Since God expressly prohibited Isaac from going to Egypt during a famine (26:2), He now assured Jacob that he may rightly accept Joseph's invitation.

46:6 *seed.* Offspring.

46:8 The genealogy anticipated by, "These are the generations of Jacob" (37:2), finally appears, for Israel has now passed successfully through the crisis of chs. 37–45. There are some questions about the details of this genealogy and its numbers; it is possible that some of the people listed here were born in Egypt, such as the sons of Pharez (v. 12; 38:29) or some of the sons of Benjamin (v. 21).

46:15 *souls.* Persons.

46:26 *came out of his loins.* Were his biological children. *threescore and six.* Sixty-six.

46:27 *threescore and ten.* Seventy. Factors of seven, the number of perfection, figure prominently in this genealogy: there were forty-nine descendants of Leah and Zilpah, fourteen of Rachel, and seven of Bilhah. The whole family of Jacob (v. 6) went together into Egypt.

46:28 Again *Judah* appears as a leader. *direct his face.* Difficult to translate; probably, "to present him." *they came into the land of Goshen.* A painting in the Beni Hasan tomb of the Egyptian Khnum-Hotep (nineteenth century BC) shows a group of bearded men in multi-colored clothing coming from Canaan to trade in Egypt.

46:29 *fell on his neck.* Embraced him.

46:30 *Now let me die.* Jacob felt his life had been fulfilled in seeing Joseph, much as Simeon felt when he saw the Christ child (Luke 2:29–30).

46:34 Joseph schooled his family in how to approach the

34 That ye shall say, Thy servants' trade hath been
about cattle from our youth even until now, both
we, *and* also our fathers: that ye may dwell in the
land of Goshen; for every shepherd *is* an abomi-
nation unto the Egyptians.

CHAPTER 47

THEN Joseph came and told Pharaoh, and said,
My father and my brethren, and their flocks, and
their herds, and all that they have, are come out of
the land of Canaan; and, behold, they *are* in the
land of Goshen.
2 And he took some of his brethren, *even* five
men, and presented them unto Pharaoh.
3 And Pharaoh said unto his brethren, What *is*
your occupation? And they said unto Pharaoh,
Thy servants *are* shepherds, both we, *and* also our
fathers.
4 They said moreover unto Pharaoh, For to
sojourn in the land are we come; for thy servants
have no pasture for their flocks; for the famine *is*
sore in the land of Canaan: now therefore, we pray
thee, let thy servants dwell in the land of Goshen.
5 And Pharaoh spake unto Joseph, saying, Thy
father and thy brethren are come unto thee:
6 The land of Egypt *is* before thee; in the best of
the land make thy father and brethren to dwell;
in the land of Goshen let them dwell: and if thou
knowest *any* men of activity among them, then
make them rulers over my cattle.
7 And Joseph brought in Jacob his father, and set
him before Pharaoh: and Jacob blessed Pharaoh.
8 And Pharaoh said unto Jacob, How old *art*
thou?
9 And Jacob said unto Pharaoh, The days of the
years of my pilgrimage *are* an hundred and thirty
years: few and evil have the days of the years of
my life been, and have not attained unto the days
of the years of the life of my fathers in the days of
their pilgrimage.
10 And Jacob blessed Pharaoh, and went out
from before Pharaoh.
11 ¶ And Joseph placed his father and his breth-
ren, and gave them a possession in the land of
Egypt, in the best of the land, in the land of Ra-
meses, as Pharaoh had commanded.
12 And Joseph nourished his father, and his
brethren, and all his father's household, with
bread, according to *their* families.
13 ¶ And *there was* no bread in all the land; for
the famine *was* very sore, so that the land of Egypt
and *all* the land of Canaan fainted by reason of
the famine.
14 And Joseph gathered up all the money that
was found in the land of Egypt, and in the land
of Canaan, for the corn which they bought: and
Joseph brought the money into Pharaoh's house.
15 And when money failed in the land of Egypt,
and in the land of Canaan, all the Egyptians came
unto Joseph, and said, Give us bread: for why
should we die in thy presence? for the money
faileth.
16 And Joseph said, Give your cattle; and I will
give you for your cattle, if money fail.
17 And they brought their cattle unto Joseph: and
Joseph gave them bread *in exchange* for horses,
and for the flocks, and for the cattle of the herds,
and for the asses: and he fed them with bread for
all their cattle for that year.

---

pharaoh with diplomacy and tact. *abomination*. See note at 43:32.

Thoughts for Personal/Family Worship: Chapter 46

1. **The Lord says to His people, "Fear not." Sometimes we must travel to a strange or dangerous place or take some step into the unknown. Fear is a natural response, and it is aggravated by our sinful pride. How then can we overcome fear? We must meditate on the promise of God, "I will go with thee." If the company of a strong and competent friend gives us peace, how much more the company of the strong, covenant God?**
2. **The prosperity of Israel's family in Egypt rested entirely upon Joseph. His position and intercession with the pharaoh was their key to unlock blessing. So we too must realize that our place in the kingdom of heaven rests entirely upon Jesus Christ. We must depend upon Him, and approach the Father only through Him and according to His Word. In the Mediator we are welcome; apart from Him we are enemies of the King.**

Chapter 47: ***Joseph presents his family to Pharaoh and uses the food stored up for the famine to provide for the hungry and to increase Pharaoh's wealth and power.***

47:4 *sojourn*. Live as a foreigner for a time in another nation. *sore*. Severe.
47:6 *men of activity*. Able men, capable leaders (Ex. 18:21,25).
47:7 *Jacob blessed Pharaoh* (v. 10). Pharaoh had blessed Jacob and his family, and so Jacob pronounced God's blessing on Pharaoh. This fulfilled God's promise to Abraham that all nations would be blessed through him, particularly those who blessed him (12:3).
47:9 *pilgrimage*. Same root as "sojourn" (v. 4). See note at 23:4. *few and evil*. Ancient Egyptian literature spoke of the ideal life-span as 110 years. Though Jacob had already exceeded that by twenty years, he did not aim to impress Pharaoh, but frankly stated that his life had been hard and could not compare to the prosperity and endurance of his fathers.
47:11 *Rameses*. Located in the northeastern delta of the Nile. The name Rameses, based on a chief Egyptian god, was in use long before Rameses I of the nineteenth dynasty.
47:13 *sore*. Severe. *fainted*. Became weak.
47:14 *corn*. Grain of various kinds, not just corn (maize).
47:15 *money faileth*. They had spent all their money already.
47:20 *bought all the land . . . for Pharaoh*. Comparing biblical chronology with Egyptian dates, Joseph's rise to power might have occurred during the administration of Sesostris III of the twelfth Dynasty. Significantly, Sesostris III is credited with reunifying Egypt under a centralized administration. And even

18 When that year was ended, they came unto him the second year, and said unto him, We will not hide *it* from my lord, how that our money is spent; my lord also hath our herds of cattle; there is not ought left in the sight of my lord, but our bodies, and our lands:

19 Wherefore shall we die before thine eyes, both we and our land? buy us and our land for bread, and we and our land will be servants unto Pharaoh: and give *us* seed, that we may live, and not die, that the land be not desolate.

20 And Joseph bought all the land of Egypt for Pharaoh; for the Egyptians sold every man his field, because the famine prevailed over them: so the land became Pharaoh's.

21 And as for the people, he removed them to cities from *one* end of the borders of Egypt even to the *other* end thereof.

22 Only the land of the priests bought he not; for the priests had a portion *assigned them* of Pharaoh, and did eat their portion which Pharaoh gave them: wherefore they sold not their lands.

23 Then Joseph said unto the people, Behold, I have bought you this day and your land for Pharaoh: lo, *here is* seed for you, and ye shall sow the land.

24 And it shall come to pass in the increase, that ye shall give the fifth *part* unto Pharaoh, and four parts shall be your own, for seed of the field, and for your food, and for them of your households, and for food for your little ones.

25 And they said, Thou hast saved our lives: let us find grace in the sight of my lord, and we will be Pharaoh's servants.

26 And Joseph made it a law over the land of Egypt unto this day, *that* Pharaoh should have the fifth *part*; except the land of the priests only, *which* became not Pharaoh's.

27 ¶ And Israel dwelt in the land of Egypt, in the country of Goshen; and they had possessions therein, and grew, and multiplied exceedingly.

28 And Jacob lived in the land of Egypt seventeen years: so the whole age of Jacob was an hundred forty and seven years.

29 And the time drew nigh that Israel must die: and he called his son Joseph, and said unto him, If now I have found grace in thy sight, put, I pray thee, thy hand under my thigh, and deal kindly and truly with me; bury me not, I pray thee, in Egypt:

30 But I will lie with my fathers, and thou shalt carry me out of Egypt, and bury me in their buryingplace. And he said, I will do as thou hast said.

31 And he said, Swear unto me. And he sware unto him. And Israel bowed himself upon the bed's head.

CHAPTER 48

AND it came to pass after these things, that *one* told Joseph, Behold, thy father *is* sick: and he took with him his two sons, Manasseh and Ephraim.

2 And *one* told Jacob, and said, Behold, thy son Joseph cometh unto thee: and Israel strengthened himself, and sat upon the bed.

3 And Jacob said unto Joseph, God Almighty appeared unto me at Luz in the land of Canaan, and blessed me,

4 And said unto me, Behold, I will make thee fruitful, and multiply thee, and I will make of thee

---

more significantly, the Bible explains how that happened.

47:21 *he removed them to cities*. This, the reading of the Hebrew Masoretic text, may indicate a temporary relocation of people to centers of food distribution. However, the Greek Septuagint, Samaritan Pentateuch, and Latin Vulgate read, "he made servants of them." This reading would be obtained by a slight scribal error in copying two Hebrew letters.

47:24 *in the increase*. When the land produces again and harvest comes.

47:25 *thou hast saved our lives . . . we will be Pharaoh's servants*. This was not oppression or exploitation, but salvation for a starving people, and they were grateful. Joseph did not enslave them so much as he instituted a feudal system where the people gave a relatively small portion of their produce to the king. In this he was a type of Christ, who uses the riches of His grace to save perishing people and to make them servants of the living God.

47:29 *drew nigh*. Came near.

47:31 *Israel bowed himself.* An act of worshiping God by faith (Heb. 11:21). *the bed's head*. The Greek Septuagint reads, "the top of his staff/stick." The Hebrew words for "bed" and "staff" have the same consonants and sound very similar.

Thoughts for Personal/Family Worship: Chapter 47

1. Though we are pilgrims in this evil world, we are to be a blessing to our neighbors. We must show respect to whom respect is due, such as government officials, and we must pray for God's blessing upon those who do not yet know Him. Do you pray regularly for your leaders? Do you pray for the physical and spiritual needs of your neighbors?

2. Christ's sufferings and obedience have obtained a vast treasure of blessings for perishing sinners. Unlike Joseph, He offers them for free to all who come to Him. But like Joseph, Christ makes all whom He saves into servants of God to do His will. Praise God that our brother, the Lord Jesus, is rich in blessings and glorious in majesty. By grace, offer yourself to God through Him as a servant, ready to do His will and eager to give back some of what He gives to you.

Chapter 48: *Israel blesses Joseph and his sons, adopting them as his own, but blessing the younger over the firstborn.*

48:3 *God Almighty appeared unto me at Luz*. See 28:10–22.

48:4 *give this land*. Though they now lived in Egypt, and Canaan has been withered by years of famine, Jacob still looked by faith for the fulfillment of God's promise of a good inheritance.

a multitude of people; and will give this land to
thy seed after thee *for* an everlasting possession.
5 ¶ And now thy two sons, Ephraim and Manas-
seh, which were born unto thee in the land of Egypt
before I came unto thee into Egypt, *are* mine; as
Reuben and Simeon, they shall be mine.
6 And thy issue, which thou begettest after them,
shall be thine, *and* shall be called after the name of
their brethren in their inheritance.
7 And as for me, when I came from Padan, Ra-
chel died by me in the land of Canaan in the way,
when yet *there was* but a little way to come unto
Ephrath: and I buried her there in the way of Eph-
rath; the same *is* Beth-lehem.
8 And Israel beheld Joseph's sons, and said, Who
are these?
9 And Joseph said unto his father, They *are* my
sons, whom God hath given me in this *place.* And
he said, Bring them, I pray thee, unto me, and I
will bless them.
10 Now the eyes of Israel were dim for age, *so that*
he could not see. And he brought them near unto
him; and he kissed them, and embraced them.
11 And Israel said unto Joseph, I had not thought
to see thy face: and, lo, God hath shewed me also
thy seed.
12 And Joseph brought them out from between
his knees, and he bowed himself with his face to
the earth.
13 And Joseph took them both, Ephraim in
his right hand toward Israel's left hand, and
Manasseh in his left hand toward Israel's right
hand, and brought *them* near unto him.
14 And Israel stretched out his right hand, and
laid *it* upon Ephraim's head, who *was* the younger,
and his left hand upon Manasseh's head, guid-
ing his hands wittingly; for Manasseh *was* the
firstborn.
15 ¶ And he blessed Joseph, and said, God, before
whom my fathers Abraham and Isaac did walk, the
God which fed me all my life long unto this day,
16 The Angel which redeemed me from all evil,
bless the lads; and let my name be named on
them, and the name of my fathers Abraham and
Isaac; and let them grow into a multitude in the
midst of the earth.
17 And when Joseph saw that his father laid his
right hand upon the head of Ephraim, it dis-
pleased him: and he held up his father's hand, to
remove it from Ephraim's head unto Manasseh's
head.
18 And Joseph said unto his father, Not so, my
father: for this *is* the firstborn; put thy right hand
upon his head.
19 And his father refused, and said, I know *it*,
my son, I know *it*: he also shall become a people,
and he also shall be great: but truly his younger
brother shall be greater than he, and his seed shall
become a multitude of nations.
20 And he blessed them that day, saying, In
thee shall Israel bless, saying, God make thee as
Ephraim and as Manasseh: and he set Ephraim
before Manasseh.
21 And Israel said unto Joseph, Behold, I die: but
God shall be with you, and bring you again unto
the land of your fathers.

48:5 *thy two sons . . . are mine.* Jacob adopted his grandsons *Ephraim and Manasseh* as his own sons, increasing their honor and inheritance in the family. *as Reuben.* Jacob's firstborn lost his birthright by immorality (35:22), and Jacob gave it to Joseph's sons instead (1 Chron. 5:1).
48:6 *thy issue, which thou begettest.* Your biological children.
48:8 *Who are these?* The question might spring of his blindness, but also could be a formality in the adoption process similar to the wedding question, "Who gives this woman to this man?"
48:9 *whom God hath given me.* Joseph was full of gratitude, knowing that children are gifts from God (29:31; 30:2; Ps. 127:3).
48:11 *seed.* Offspring. Jacob also gratefully acknowledged that their blessings come from *God.*
48:12 *from between his knees.* Probably "by" his knees, as the grandsons were now grown.
48:14 *wittingly.* Intentionally.
48:15–16 *walk.* See note at 17:1. Jacob blessed Joseph and his sons by faith (Heb. 11:21), trusting in the character of the Lord. He is *God*, strong and mighty, and also the *Angel*, sent to save His people (Isa. 63:9). See notes at 16:7; 22:11. He is the shepherd (the meaning of *fed*) who daily guides and provides for them (49:24; Ps. 23:1), and the kinsman-redeemer (*redeemed me*) who pays the price to powerfully set them free *from all evil* (Ex. 6:6; 15:13; Lev. 25:48).
48:18–20 As with Jacob and Esau (25:23), God reversed the rights of the *firstborn* and placed special blessing upon the *younger* son. *Ephraim* would become such a powerful tribe that the entire northern part of Israel would take its name from him (Hos. 11:3,8). God does not give grace according to human status, but according to His freedom (1 Cor. 1:26–31).
48:21 *Behold I die: but God shall be with you.* This is the great comfort of believers when their loved ones die (50:24). God will never leave them but will *bring* them to their inheritance.
48:22 *portion.* Literally, "Shechem." Jacob had bought a field near Shechem (33:19), and now bequeathed it to Joseph, an act of faith that they would return as God promised. *with my sword and with my bow.* Jacob originally obtained the property by purchase, but it may be that he later had to recapture it from the *Amorite* after he had moved to Hebron. Centuries later, Christ met the Samaritan woman at the well there (John 4:5).

Thoughts for Personal/Family Worship: Chapter 48

1. **How beautiful it is to hear an old saint glorify God for His faithfulness! God's character is a rich feast and solid support for both old and young believers. His power gives us hope that His promises will not fail despite the darkest times. Let us seek grace to walk closely with this God all our days, so that when we are old we may give Him glory.**
2. **When death breaks our fellowship with parents, siblings, and dear friends, we must look to the God who is always there. Let us make use of times of mourning to seek a deeper communion with our Father through Christ, that His Spirit may fill us with comfort.**

22 Moreover I have given to thee one portion
above thy brethren, which I took out of the hand
of the Amorite with my sword and with my bow.

CHAPTER 49

AND Jacob called unto his sons, and said, Gather
yourselves together, that I may tell you *that* which
shall befall you in the last days.
2 Gather yourselves together, and hear, ye sons of
Jacob; and hearken unto Israel your father.
3 ¶ Reuben, thou *art* my firstborn, my might, and
the beginning of my strength, the excellency of
dignity, and the excellency of power:
4 Unstable as water, thou shalt not excel; because
thou wentest up to thy father's bed; then defiledst
thou *it*: he went up to my couch.
5 ¶ Simeon and Levi *are* brethren; instruments of
cruelty *are in* their habitations.
6 O my soul, come not thou into their secret;
unto their assembly, mine honour, be not thou
united: for in their anger they slew a man, and in
their selfwill they digged down a wall.
7 Cursed *be* their anger, for *it was* fierce; and their
wrath, for it was cruel: I will divide them in Jacob,
and scatter them in Israel.
8 ¶ Judah, thou *art he* whom thy brethren shall
praise: thy hand *shall be* in the neck of thine
enemies; thy father's children shall bow down
before thee.
9 Judah *is* a lion's whelp: from the prey, my son,
thou art gone up: he stooped down, he couched as
a lion, and as an old lion; who shall rouse him up?
10 The sceptre shall not depart from Judah, nor a
lawgiver from between his feet, until Shiloh come;
and unto him *shall* the gathering of the people *be*.
11 Binding his foal unto the vine, and his ass's
colt unto the choice vine; he washed his garments
in wine, and his clothes in the blood of grapes:
12 His eyes *shall be* red with wine, and his teeth
white with milk.
13 ¶ Zebulun shall dwell at the haven of the sea;
and he *shall be* for an haven of ships; and his border
shall be unto Zidon.
14 ¶ Issachar *is* a strong ass couching down between
two burdens:
15 And he saw that rest *was* good, and the land
that *it was* pleasant; and bowed his shoulder to
bear, and became a servant unto tribute.
16 ¶ Dan shall judge his people, as one of the
tribes of Israel.
17 Dan shall be a serpent by the way, an adder in
the path, that biteth the horse heels, so that his
rider shall fall backward.
18 I have waited for thy salvation, O LORD.
19 ¶ Gad, a troop shall overcome him: but he
shall overcome at the last.
20 ¶ Out of Asher his bread *shall be* fat, and he
shall yield royal dainties.
21 ¶ Naphtali *is* a hind let loose: he giveth goodly
words.
22 ¶ Joseph *is* a fruitful bough, *even* a fruitful
bough by a well; *whose* branches run over the wall:
23 The archers have sorely grieved him, and shot
at him, and hated him:
24 But his bow abode in strength, and the arms

Chapter 49: *Israel speaks prophetically of the future of the twelve tribes which will arise from his sons, especially Judah and Joseph.*

49:1 *that which shall befall*. What will happen.

49:2 *hearken*. Listen.

49:4 *Unstable as water*. Driven by boiling passion. *excel*. Rise above the others. *thy father's bed*. Reuben had sex with Jacob's concubine (35:22).

49:6 *their secret*. Their company or counsel, namely, their deceitful plan of murder (34:13,25). *digged down a wall*. Better, "hamstrung oxen."

49:7 *divide . . . scatter*. The tribe of Simeon would be distributed through the territory of Judah (Josh. 19:1), and the Levites throughout the whole land (Num. 35:7–8). The same prophecy was literally fulfilled in two different ways: Simeon essentially lost its identity being assimilated into Judah whereas Levi received an honored status as the priestly tribe receiving an inheritance throughout the nation.

49:8 *Judah* means *praise*, originally given to the Lord (29:35), but here directed to Judah.

49:9 *whelp*. Cub. *couched*. Crouched. *lion*. A metaphor for power. Though Joseph received the right of the firstborn, from Judah came the Davidic line of kings (1 Chron. 5:2). Christ is the Lion of the tribe of Judah, and He has overcome all the powers of the Devil (Rev. 5:5; 17:14).

49:10 *sceptre*. Rod used by a king (Num. 24:17; Ps. 2:9; 45:6). *lawgiver*. A king (Isa. 33:22), or possibly another word for rod. *Shiloh*. Difficult to translate, but could mean "him to whom [the kingdom] belongs." See the similar expression in Ezek. 21:27. *the gathering of the people*. Literally, "the obedience of the peoples," the nations who will submit to Christ the Lord.

49:11–12 *vine . . . wine . . . grapes . . . milk*. Images of prosperity and beauty in the kingdom.

49:13 *Zebulun* would settle near Phoenicia, by the Sea of Galilee on the route to the Mediterranean Sea (Isa. 9:1–2).

49:14 *couching*. Crouching.

49:17 The tribe of Dan became a center for idolatry and would massacre an unsuspecting people (Judg. 18; 1 Kings 12:28–30; 2 Kings 10:29). The words *serpent* and *heels* may allude to the ancient tempter and his violent but unsuccessful attack on the Seed of the Woman (3:1–5,15).

49:18 After declaring the serpentlike character of Dan's descendants (v. 17), Jacob cried out with words of enduring hope in God (*I have waited*). If the previous verse alludes to 3:15, then *thy salvation, O LORD* may refer to victory over Satan through the suffering Seed, Jesus Christ.

49:20 *his bread shall be fat*. His food will be rich. *royal dainties*. Fine foods enjoyed by a king.

49:21 *hind*. Female deer (Ps. 18:33; Hab. 3:19). *giveth goodly words*. The Hebrew is uncertain.

49:23 *archers*. Metaphor for the attacks Joseph and his offspring suffer from enemies.

49:24–25 *from thence*. An ancient Syriac version reads "from

of his hands were made strong by the hands of the
mighty *God* of Jacob; (from thence *is* the shep-
herd, the stone of Israel:)
25 *Even* by the God of thy father, who shall help
thee; and by the Almighty, who shall bless thee
with blessings of heaven above, blessings of the
deep that lieth under, blessings of the breasts, and
of the womb:
26 The blessings of thy father have prevailed
above the blessings of my progenitors unto the
utmost bound of the everlasting hills: they shall
be on the head of Joseph, and on the crown of the
head of him that was separate from his brethren.
27 ¶ Benjamin shall ravin *as* a wolf: in the
morning he shall devour the prey, and at night he
shall divide the spoil.
28 ¶ All these *are* the twelve tribes of Israel: and
this *is it* that their father spake unto them, and
blessed them; every one according to his blessing
he blessed them.
29 And he charged them, and said unto them, I
am to be gathered unto my people: bury me with
my fathers in the cave that *is* in the field of Ephron
the Hittite,
30 In the cave that *is* in the field of Machpelah,
which *is* before Mamre, in the land of Canaan,
which Abraham bought with the field of Ephron
the Hittite for a possession of a buryingplace.
31 There they buried Abraham and Sarah his
wife; there they buried Isaac and Rebekah his
wife; and there I buried Leah.
32 The purchase of the field and of the cave that *is*
therein *was* from the children of Heth.
33 And when Jacob had made an end of com-
manding his sons, he gathered up his feet into the
bed, and yielded up the ghost, and was gathered
unto his people.

CHAPTER 50

AND Joseph fell upon his father's face, and wept
upon him, and kissed him.
2 And Joseph commanded his servants the
physicians to embalm his father: and the
physicians embalmed Israel.
3 And forty days were fulfilled for him; for so are
fulfilled the days of those which are embalmed:
and the Egyptians mourned for him threescore
and ten days.
4 And when the days of his mourning were past,
Joseph spake unto the house of Pharaoh, saying,
If now I have found grace in your eyes, speak, I
pray you, in the ears of Pharaoh, saying,
5 My father made me swear, saying, Lo, I die: in
my grave which I have digged for me in the land
of Canaan, there shalt thou bury me. Now there-
fore let me go up, I pray thee, and bury my father,
and I will come again.
6 And Pharaoh said, Go up, and bury thy father,
according as he made thee swear.
7 ¶ And Joseph went up to bury his father: and
with him went up all the servants of Pharaoh, the
elders of his house, and all the elders of the land
of Egypt,
8 And all the house of Joseph, and his brethren,
and his father's house: only their little ones, and
their flocks, and their herds, they left in the land
of Goshen.
9 And there went up with him both chariots and
horsemen: and it was a very great company.
10 And they came to the threshingfloor of Atad,
which *is* beyond Jordan, and there they mourned
with a great and very sore lamentation: and he
made a mourning for his father seven days.
11 And when the inhabitants of the land, the
Canaanites, saw the mourning in the floor of
Atad, they said, This *is* a grievous mourning to
the Egyptians: wherefore the name of it was called
Abel-mizraim, which *is* beyond Jordan.
12 And his sons did unto him according as he
commanded them:
13 For his sons carried him into the land of Ca-
naan, and buried him in the cave of the field of
Machpelah, which Abraham bought with the field

the name of." Jacob gloried in several attributes or names of God, declaring His power (*mighty*), love (*shepherd*), dependability (*stone*), covenant faithfulness through the generations (*God of thy father*), and sufficiency to do all He promises (*Almighty*).

49:26 *progenitors*. Forefathers.

49:27 *ravin*. Tear to pieces. Strong warriors such as Ehud, Saul, and Jonathan came from Benjamin (Judg. 3:15; 1 Sam. 9:1–2; 1 Chron. 8:40; 12:2).

49:29 Jacob's request to be buried in the family tomb in Canaan (23:9–20; 25:9) showed his hope in the promise and in the resurrection (see notes at 22:5; 23:20).

49:33 *yielded up the ghost*. Expired. *gathered unto his people*. See note at 25:8.

Thoughts for Personal/Family Worship: Chapter 49

1. **Many centuries before Jesus was born, God revealed His purpose that from Judah would arise a king to rule the nations. He decreed before the creation of the world that His Son would have a kingdom. Though God's people had to wait for millennia for the Savior, their salvation was certain. How much more, then, should sinners like us have hope?**
2. **Do not grow weary in waiting upon the Lord. God's plan will not fail; Christ's kingdom will come. Make Jacob's prayer your own: "I have waited for thy salvation, O LORD."**

Chapter 50: *Joseph buries Jacob in Canaan, comforts his brothers with God's sovereignty, and dies with his own hope set upon the promise.*

50:3 *threescore and ten*. Seventy.

50:10 *sore lamentation*. Heavy grief. It is right to mourn the dead (23:2; John 11:35; Acts 8:2; 9:39), though believers need not mourn as those without hope (1 Thess. 4:13,18).

for a possession of a buryingplace of Ephron the
Hittite, before Mamre.
14 ¶ And Joseph returned into Egypt, he, and his
brethren, and all that went up with him to bury
his father, after he had buried his father.
15 ¶ And when Joseph's brethren saw that their
father was dead, they said, Joseph will peradven-
ture hate us, and will certainly requite us all the
evil which we did unto him.
16 And they sent a messenger unto Joseph, saying,
Thy father did command before he died, saying,
17 So shall ye say unto Joseph, Forgive, I pray thee
now, the trespass of thy brethren, and their sin;
for they did unto thee evil: and now, we pray thee,
forgive the trespass of the servants of the God of
thy father. And Joseph wept when they spake unto
him.
18 And his brethren also went and fell down
before his face; and they said, Behold, we *be* thy
servants.
19 And Joseph said unto them, Fear not: for *am* I
in the place of God?
20 But as for you, ye thought evil against me; *but*
God meant it unto good, to bring to pass, as *it is*
this day, to save much people alive.
21 Now therefore fear ye not: I will nourish you,
and your little ones. And he comforted them, and
spake kindly unto them.
22 ¶ And Joseph dwelt in Egypt, he, and his
father's house: and Joseph lived an hundred and
ten years.
23 And Joseph saw Ephraim's children of the third
generation: the children also of Machir the son of
Manasseh were brought up upon Joseph's knees.
24 And Joseph said unto his brethren, I die: and
God will surely visit you, and bring you out of this
land unto the land which he sware to Abraham, to
Isaac, and to Jacob.
25 And Joseph took an oath of the children of
Israel, saying, God will surely visit you, and ye
shall carry up my bones from hence.
26 So Joseph died, *being* an hundred and ten
years old: and they embalmed him, and he was
put in a coffin in Egypt.

50:15 *peradventure*. Perhaps. *requite*. Pay back.
50:17 *trespass*. Sin.
50:19–21 *Fear not.* Joseph's love and forgiveness of his brothers sprang from humility before God's majesty (*am I in the place of God?*) and faith in God's loving providence. *ye thought evil against me; but God meant it unto good*. The same Hebrew word is translated by *thought* and *meant*, signifying to think or plan. It comes from a root meaning "to skillfully weave" or "artistically design" (Ex. 26:1). The Hebrew text makes it clear that *it* in *meant it* refers to *evil*. Joseph's brothers had formed a cunning plan to destroy him, but God had planned their *evil* for the *good* not just of Joseph but *much people*. God has decreed all things, including sin and evil, to glorify Himself through the salvation of many (see notes at 45:5–8).
50:22 *hundred and ten years*. The ideal life-span mentioned often in Egyptian writings. Terah lived 205 years (11:32), Abraham 175 years (25:7), Isaac 180 years (35:28), Jacob 147 years (47:28), and Joseph 110 years.
50:23 Surrounded in old age by his children, grandchildren, and great-grandchildren, Joseph was an emblem of God's covenant to continue His blessing through the generations (17:7; Deut. 7:9).
50:24 Joseph was a high official of the mighty land where the Great Pyramid rose 481 feet into the air, but on his deathbed his mind was not on the glories of Egypt but on the inheritance of *the land which* the Lord *sware to Abraham, to Isaac, and to Jacob*. By faith in the promise, he saw what was not yet visible (Heb. 11:22).
50:26 *coffin*. Box, same word used of the "ark" of the covenant. Genesis ends on a note of death, a reminder of the consequences of the fall of man (2:17; 3:19). But it also ends on a note of anticipation that God would keep His covenant oath (v. 24). The tomb of Joseph would remind Israel of God's promises while they suffered in slavery. Joseph's bones remained in Egypt for hundreds of years; then Moses took them in the exodus and the people buried them in the plot of land that Jacob gave to Joseph (48:22; Ex. 13:19; Josh. 24:32).

Thoughts for Personal/Family Worship: Chapter 50

1. **Joseph is a model of forgiveness. A robust view of God's majesty above us, His providence over evil, and His goodness sets us free from bitterness to love the people who have hurt us. Learn to see all things under the banner of "God meant it for good."**
2. **Genesis began with an account of how God made all things good, but Satan and sin brought evil to man and his world. Surely it is no accident that Genesis ends by declaring that what sinners planned for evil, God planned for good. Furthermore, the account of Joseph's life gives us a type of how God would save many perishing sinners. The fall of man and the curse of death would lead to the humiliation of God's faithful servant, but His very suffering would become the foundation for His exaltation as the Lord of the kingdom and Savior of the nations. Thus Genesis calls us to hope in God's decree to use evil to bring salvation for His glory. Cling to that hope to your dying day.**

GOD'S COVENANTS

Looking death in the face, Joseph rallies in Genesis 50 for one final act of faith. He recalls God's promise to Abram (Gen. 15:13,14) and assures his brothers that God will bring them out of Egypt and back to the Promised Land. He commands them to "carry up my bones from hence," binding them with an oath. Accordingly, Moses takes the bones of Joseph with him when Israel goes out of Egypt (Ex. 13:19).

Why was Joseph sure that God would keep His promises? It was because he knew the promises were stipulations of God's covenant with Abraham, sealed with God's oath, "two immutable things, in which it was impossible for God to lie" (Heb. 6:18). God had spoken. That was enough for Joseph.

The notion of covenant is older than the Bible and embedded in the culture of the ancient Near East. The human authors of Scripture use the word without explanation or elaboration for their readers. The basic meaning of the Hebrew word *berith* is "agreement." The Greek word *diatheke* means "arrangement" and was applied to a will, the legal instrument by which one disposes of earthly goods and property after death. The two words have in common the binding character of what is "agreed" upon or "arranged" (Gal. 3:15). Promises must be kept and obligations performed, no matter what.

God's covenants are "agreements" between Himself and His people, defining their relationship to Him. There are two parts: *first*, what God promises to do for them, and *second*, what they are obliged to do in response. Many covenants are recorded in Scripture: the covenant of works implicit in the history of Adam and Eve, and their life in Eden as regulated by God's commandments (Gen. 1,2); the creation covenant with Noah after the destruction of the old world by the flood (Gen. 9); the covenant with Israel enacted at Sinai (Ex. 19,20); and the covenant with David and his house (2 Sam. 7).

These covenants are overshadowed by the covenant of grace made with Abraham (Gen. 17:7), confirmed and renewed as "the new covenant" in Christ's blood (Jer. 31:31–34; Matt. 26:28) and proclaimed as "the promise" by Peter at Pentecost (Acts 2:39). The other covenants are applications of the covenant of grace to particular people or to their special needs or circumstances. Some continue to bind God and man (the covenant of works, the creation covenant with Noah), but others have been fulfilled in Christ (the covenants with Israel and the house of David) and are no longer binding.

Justified by faith in Christ, Christians are the blessed seed of "faithful Abraham" (Gen. 15:6; Rom. 4:11–12; Gal. 3:7–9). Together with their children, they are bound to God as His people, and He has bound Himself to them as their God (Gen. 17:7; Acts 2:39). The children of believers, however, are not saved by the covenant relationship automatically; rather, they must personally be brought to repentance and faith in the Lord Jesus Christ. By God's grace, and through saving faith, they are heirs to all that God has promised them in Christ; they are obliged, for Christ's sake, to cleave to this one God, trusting in Him and loving Him with all their hearts, forsaking the world, crucifying the old nature, and walking in newness and holiness of life.

The New Testament gives much attention to the development and varying emphases between the old covenant made with Israel at Sinai through Moses and the new covenant established in Christ in fulfillment of the promises made to Abraham. The epistle to the Hebrews expounds this development at length, showing the superiority of Christ and His new covenant to anything given to Israel through Moses.

Noting this difference, some have argued that the moral law, summarized in the Ten Commandments (Ex. 20, Deut. 5) as part of the Mosaic covenant, is not binding on Christians under the gospel. But long before Moses, the moral law was written in the human heart (Rom. 2:14). Sin was imputed and punished by death, from Adam to Moses (Rom. 5:13–14). Christ Himself declared that He did not come to destroy the law (Matt. 5:17). As a rule of life for believers, the moral law is an essential part of the covenant of grace.

THE TEN *Commandments*

I

Thou shalt have no other gods before me

II

Thou shalt not make unto thee any graven image

III

Thou shalt not take the name of the Lord thy God in vain

IV

Remember the sabbath day, to keep it holy

V

Honour thy father and thy mother

VI

Thou shalt not kill

VII

Thou shalt not commit adultery

VIII

Thou shalt not steal

IX

Thou shalt not bear false witness against thy neighbour

X

Thou shalt not covet

INTRODUCTION TO THE BOOK OF EXODUS

Authorship and Date: On the authorship and date of the book, see Introduction to the Pentateuch. The date of Israel's exodus is debated. Some scholars propose a late date around 1290 BC based upon an interpretation of archaeological evidence. However, other archaeologists have found additional evidence that calls into question this conclusion. More importantly, the Scriptures indicate a much earlier date, c. 1446 BC, by placing the exodus about 300 years before the judge Jephthah (Judg. 11:26) and 480 years before Solomon's fourth year on the throne (1 Kings 6:1). Even if one or both of these are round numbers, they point to an exodus in the fifteenth century BC.

Theme: God keeps His covenant through the gifts of redemption, law, and divine presence.

Purpose: To reveal the Lord as the gracious and powerful God who keeps His covenant though His people are lawbreakers.

Synopsis: *The Contribution of Exodus to Redemptive Revelation*

The word "exodus," the ancient Greek title of the book, means "the way out" or "departure," referring to the Lord's deliverance of Israel out of Egypt. The book's history reaches back to the death of Joseph circa 1875 BC. However, most of its events (chs. 3–40) take place in the time of the exodus from Egypt in the mid-fifteenth century BC.

Exodus builds upon Genesis as the continuing history of God's mighty works to bless the offspring of Abraham, Isaac, and Jacob (1:1; 2:24; 3:15). It also echoes Genesis in many smaller ways. The multiplication of Israel in Egypt alludes to God's blessing upon newly created man to be fruitful and multiply (1:7; Gen. 1:28). Little Moses is set afloat in a miniature "ark" coated with tar and pitch like Noah's great ark (Gen. 6:14; Ex. 2:3;). The same God who created the "herb," "fruit," and "tree" also destroyed them in His plague of locusts on Egypt (Gen. 1:11; Ex. 10:15).

Genesis is a book of promises to Abraham and his offspring, and Exodus is a book where the God of Abraham continues fulfilling those promises. Exodus especially declares how the covenant Lord of Israel kept His promise to redeem His people and dwelt with them as their King and Lawgiver (6:2–8; 19:4–6; 29:43–46).

This message may be summed up in the following key themes.

First, God revealed His glory in His works: "I am the LORD" (20:2). In one sense, the book revolves around the revelation of the meaning of God's name, *Jehovah* or "the LORD" (3:13–14; 6:2–8). The purpose of His mighty works in Exodus is that people of all nations would know who He is (9:16; 10:1–2). Thus we find the repeated statement that God acts so that people will "know that I am the LORD" (6:7; 7:5,17; 8:22; 14:4,18; 16:12; 29:46; 31:13; also many times in Ezek.). The Lord will glorify His great name, and even His enemies will serve that purpose (Ex. 14:4,17–18).

However, His great works are meant not only to instruct people about Him intellectually, but to know Him personally and live in His presence as His covenant people (29:46). This is the essence of the eternal life given to sinners: that they know God through Christ's mediation (John 17:3). One of the core promises of the new covenant is that all of God's people will know Him experientially (Heb. 8:11) as the only real treasure (Jer. 9:23–24).

Second, the Creator waged war against the false gods of Egypt to display His sovereignty (12:12; Num. 33:4). Egypt regarded the Pharaoh as a divine being. The God of Israel opposed their "thus saith Pharaoh" with "thus saith the LORD" in a titanic contest of sovereignty (Ex. 5:1,10). In the ancient world, people worshiped many gods and believed that each god ruled a particular part of life. The Lord sent Moses and Aaron with miracles to humiliate the sorcerers of Egypt, who invoked the powers of their gods (7:8–12; 8:18–19; 9:11). The ten plagues displayed the impotence of Egypt's gods to defend their land against the Lord, with some plagues (if not all) targeting the domain of a specific idol (see notes at chs. 7–10). The Lord's total control over the river, frogs, insects, livestock, weather, light, and life of Pharaoh's own son demonstrate that He is the Creator who is sovereign over all things.

God was training His people to understand Him as the only true God. Thus Israel sang at the banks of the Red Sea, "Who is like unto thee, O LORD, among the gods? . . . The LORD shall reign for ever and ever" (15:11,18). This is the backdrop of the first commandment: "Thou shalt have no other gods before me" (20:3). It is also the thrust of the book of Revelation, which calls men to cease worshiping the pleasures and idols of this world and to give glory to Him who sits on the throne and to the Lamb. "The kingdoms of this world are become the kingdoms of our Lord, and of his Christ; and he shall reign for ever and ever" (Rev. 11:15).

Third, God revealed His righteous sovereignty over sin. The Lord not only entered into battle against sinners, but also staged and controlled the battle for His own glory. Before Pharaoh even heard the Lord's command to "let my people go," God told Moses that He would harden Pharaoh's heart so that he would not comply (4:21). Exodus uses three terms for God hardening Pharaoh's heart: eight times the Lord is said to have "hardened" his heart (4:21; 9:12; 10:20,27; 11:10; 14:4,8,17; cf. Josh. 11:20; Ps. 95:8); once He "made stubborn" his heart (Ex. 7:3; cf. Deut. 2:30); and once He "made heavy" his heart (Ex. 10:1), in the sense of making it insensitive and unresponsive (Isa. 6:10). This was not a passive permission on God's part, but an active control according to His plan, giving Pharaoh over to the power of sin.

Pharaoh is not thereby excused for his stubborn pride: three times it says that he "made heavy" his own heart (8:15,32) and so he "sinned" (9:34). Several times Exodus simply says that Pharaoh's heart was hardened without giving a cause (7:14,22; 8:19; 9:7,35). The very mention of his "heart," however, implies that Pharaoh acted as an agent with a mind and a will. Therefore, Pharaoh was not reduced to the level of a robot; he chose this course of action and was held responsible for his sin (10:16). Nor did God have any pleasure in his sin, but instead commanded him to release Israel and rebuked him for his stubbornness (10:3). God is not the author of sin.

However, the Lord's holy will ruled over Pharaoh's sinful will, so that Pharaoh's choices were set by God's decree and determined by providence: "But the LORD hardened Pharaoh's heart, and he would not [literally, "was not willing to"] let them go" (10:27). When Pharaoh hardened his heart, it was "as the LORD had said" (8:15)—man's sin fulfilling God's Word (7:13,22; 8:19; 9:35). Pharaoh's resistance against God served God's purpose to display His glory and sovereignty through His mighty works (7:3; 9:16; 10:1; 14:4). Though the Egyptians believed that the heart of Pharaoh was sovereign over the world, God held the heart of the king in His hand, turning it wherever He pleased (Prov. 21:1).

Exodus expands on the theme of the Joseph narrative in Genesis: sinners plan evil but God planned their evil for good (Gen. 50:20). The hardening of Pharaoh's heart demonstrated that God reigns over the sinful hearts of His enemies. We observe the same theme in the New Testament accounts of Christ's crucifixion, which teach that sinful men were guilty of the murder of Jesus Christ, and yet God controlled everything to fulfill the plan of redemption He had revealed in the Scriptures (Matt. 26:54,56; 27:9,35; Mark 15:28; Luke 9:22; 22:22; John 19:36; Acts 2:23; 4:27–28; 1 Cor. 15:3–4).

Fourth, the Lord redeemed sinners to be His covenant people (6:6–7). In the law, the redemption of a criminal was the payment of a compensation price to release him from punishment (21:29–30). The redemption of a slave required a kinsman to pay the price to purchase him out of bondage (Lev. 25:47–48). The Lord redeemed His people from their slavery to the Egyptians, though Israel was guilty of idol worship and deserved divine punishment (Josh. 24:14; Ezek. 20:5–9; cf. Ex. 32). When His wrath fell on Egypt, Israel was spared only because God covered them with His redemption (8:23). The blood of the Passover lamb turned away divine judgment (12:13) so that death to Egypt was freedom for Israel. Christ is our Passover sacrifice (1 Cor. 5:7), for His bloody death as the Lamb of God sets people from all nations free from their sins (John 1:29; 1 Peter 1:18–19; Rev. 1:5; 5:9).

In redemption, the Lord took Israel as His special treasure (19:5; Deut. 7:6). Their redemption was not merely for the sake of liberation from political oppression; God redeemed Israel so that they would be His people under His covenant. God said to Pharaoh, "Let my people go, that they may serve me" (Ex. 7:16; 8:1,20; 9:1,13; 10:3). Yet their service was not slavery, but worship (5:1,3)—adoration of the God who saved them (15:1–2). The Ten Commandments open with a reminder of redeeming grace: "I am the LORD thy God, which have brought thee out of the land of Egypt, out of the house of bondage" (20:2). To be sure, God's law regulated every facet of Israel's life, asserting His authority as Lord over all. Israel could not be God's holy covenant people without obedience to the covenant Lord (19:5–6). But obedience to the commandments must spring from faith in the God who already accomplished salvation and in His Mediator (4:1; 14:31; 19:9). God's grace trains us to do righteousness because Christ redeemed His people from the penalty and power of sin (Titus 2:11–14).

The physical hub of Israel's covenant relationship with the Lord was the sanctuary where God lived (25:8). Mankind lost their dwelling with God when expelled from the garden of Eden (Gen. 3:23–24). God revealed to Jacob that He intended to join heaven and earth so that He would dwell with His people in His house (Gen. 28:10–22). It was the very purpose of redemption that God should dwell with His people (Ex. 29:46). In the tabernacle, this plan advanced in a significant way. As the notes at chs. 25–31 show, the design of the tabernacle and the ordination of the priesthood reveal much about how Christ would open the way for His people to enter the holy place (Heb. 10:19–22) and bring them to a heavenly Eden (Rev. 22:2).

Fifth, God worked salvation and judgment through a human mediator. Moses was not merely a recorder of God's acts but was central to everything God did in this book. In a limited sense, we may use the word "mediator" of Moses (Gal. 3:19), for he was a type of Christ.

Moses was foremost a *prophetic* mediator of God's truth. Exodus states dozens of times that the Lord spoke to Moses, from his call at the burning bush to the refrain "as the LORD commanded Moses" that pulses like a drumbeat through the last two chapters of the book. God put His words in the prophet's mouth; he spoke only what God had given to him (4:12,15–16; 6:29; 7:1–2; Jer. 1:9; 2 Peter 1:20–21). Yet he was a man like those he served, and a human prophet was a gift of mercy because the people feared they would die when God spoke directly to them (Ex. 20:18–19). Moses experienced amazing face-to-face access to God (24:15–18; 33:9–11). His unusual ministry foreshadowed the great Prophet (Deut. 18:18; 34:10; Acts 3:22; 7:37), the Son who dwells in the heart of the Father and alone makes Him known (Matt. 11:27; John 1:18).

Moses also served as a *kingly* mediator of God's power. The Lord was with him to bring Israel out of Egypt (3:10–12) by working wonders through him (9:8–10). The "rod of God" (4:20) in the hand of Moses (and Aaron), though perhaps only a shepherd's staff, became like a king's scepter whereby God challenged the sovereignty of Pharaoh (4:2,4,17; 7:9–10,12). By this instrument the Lord sent judgment upon Egypt (7:15,17,19–20; 8:5,16–17; 9:23; 10:13) and gave salvation and life to Israel (14:16; 17:5,9). Moses became the head of a large administration of rulers over Israel (18:18–27). Later, after the debacle of the golden calf, Moses disciplined the people forcefully (32:19–29). Thus he was a type of the royal Son of God, who defends, rules, and disciplines His church (Rev. 3:7–8,19).

Lastly, Exodus reveals a *priestly* mediator of God's mercy. The priestly office of Christ was foreshadowed in the ministry of Aaron and his sons (Heb. 5:1–6). Moses did not bear a priesthood of this order, but he shared in its work (Ps. 99:6) and in some ways exceeded its privileges. Aaron could handle the holy things of God only when consecrated and clothed in sacred garments (Ex. 28–29), but Moses was the one who consecrated the first priests and holy places (Lev. 8–9). His inauguration of the tabernacle created an external way for the Lord to dwell with His people—a way superseded only when the Son became the living tabernacle, together with all united to Him (John 1:14; 1 Cor. 3:16). The priestly character of Moses' office also appears in his intercession with the Lord. His prayers ended specific plagues (Ex. 8:8–14,28–31; 9:27–33; 10:16–19), and saved Israel from the wrath of God when he offered himself to die as their substitute and obtained a marvelous revelation of God's love (chs. 32–34).

However, Moses was an imperfect mediator, and not a mediator of saving grace. In this book, he faithfully records his own unbelief and provoking of God's anger (4:13–14,24–25). His "uncircumcised lips" resulted in him delegating part of his ministry to Aaron (6:12–13). His responsibility to rule wearied him; no mere man could bear the burden of leading the people alone (18:18). Moses gave the law written on stone tablets but could not write it on their hearts. The Lord did not accept his offer to die as a substitute (32:32–33), and the priestly system instituted through him consisted of sinful men and mere animal sacrifices. In the end, Moses was only a shadow of Him who was to come, the one Mediator between God and man (1 Tim. 2:5).

God designed Exodus to be a rich book, and yet an incomplete book in two senses. *First*, it ends without a full revelation of the ritual laws necessary to instruct Israel in how to live with a holy God, thereby leading directly into Leviticus. *Second* and more significantly, Exodus is incomplete because it recounts physical redemption but reveals spiritual bondage, thereby pointing to the need for Christ. For all the glory of the old covenant, it was but moonlight waiting for the rising of the Sun of righteousness with healing in His wings (Mal. 4:2).

Outline:

I. The Lord Redeems Israel out of Egypt (1:1—18:27)
- A. The Calling of the Deliverer (1:1—7:7)
  1. The Sorrows of Israel and Moses (1:1—2:25)
  2. The Lord's Revelation of Himself to Moses (3:1—4:31)
  3. Pharaoh's Resistance and the Lord's Promise (5:1—7:7)
- B. The Lord against the Gods of Egypt (7:8—15:21)
  1. Confrontation of the Serpents (7:8–13)
  2. Plagues 1–3: No One Like the Lord (7:14—8:19)
  3. Plagues 4–6: The Lord Sets Apart His People (8:20—9:12)
  4. Plagues 7–9: Devastation from the Lord (9:13—10:29)
  5. Plague 10: Passover and Exodus from Egypt (11:1—13:22)
  6. Salvation to the Glory of God (14:1—15:21)
- C. Israel in the Wilderness with God (15:22—18:27)
  1. Tests and Crises of Faith (15:22—17:16)
  2. Jethro's Worship and Wisdom (18:1–27)

II. The Lord Takes Israel for His People (19:1—40:38)
- A. God's Gracious Covenant of Law (19:1—24:18)
  1. The Fearsome Majesty of the Lord (19:1–25)
  2. The Ten Commandments (20:1–21)
  3. The Book of the Covenant (20:22—23:33)
  4. The Cutting of the Covenant (24:1–18)
- B. God's Holy Presence in the Tabernacle (25:1—40:38)
  1. The Design of the Tabernacle (25:1—31:18)
  2. The Problem of God's Presence with Idolaters (32:1—34:35)
  3. The Construction and Filling of the Tabernacle (35:1—40:38)

[The law and ceremonies continue in Leviticus.]

THE SECOND BOOK OF MOSES CALLED EXODUS

CHAPTER 1

Now these *are* the names of the children of Israel, which came into Egypt; every man and his household came with Jacob.

2 Reuben, Simeon, Levi, and Judah,

3 Issachar, Zebulun, and Benjamin,

4 Dan, and Naphtali, Gad, and Asher.

5 And all the souls that came out of the loins of Jacob were seventy souls: for Joseph was in Egypt *already*.

6 And Joseph died, and all his brethren, and all that generation.

7 ¶ And the children of Israel were fruitful, and increased abundantly, and multiplied, and waxed exceeding mighty; and the land was filled with them.

8 Now there arose up a new king over Egypt, which knew not Joseph.

9 And he said unto his people, Behold, the people of the children of Israel *are* more and mightier than we:

10 Come on, let us deal wisely with them; lest they multiply, and it come to pass, that, when there falleth out any war, they join also unto our enemies, and fight against us, and *so* get them up out of the land.

11 Therefore they did set over them taskmasters to afflict them with their burdens. And they built for Pharaoh treasure cities, Pithom and Raamses.

12 But the more they afflicted them, the more they multiplied and grew. And they were grieved because of the children of Israel.

13 And the Egyptians made the children of Israel to serve with rigour:

14 And they made their lives bitter with hard bondage, in morter, and in brick, and in all manner of service in the field: all their service, wherein they made them serve, *was* with rigour.

15 ¶ And the king of Egypt spake to the Hebrew midwives, of which the name of the one *was* Shiphrah, and the name of the other Puah:

16 And he said, When ye do the office of a midwife to the Hebrew women, and see *them* upon the stools; if it *be* a son, then ye shall kill him: but if it *be* a daughter, then she shall live.

17 But the midwives feared God, and did not as

THE LORD REDEEMS ISRAEL OUT OF EGYPT (1:1—18:27)

The Calling of the Deliverer (1:1—7:7)

The Sorrows of Israel and Moses (1:1—2:25)

Chapter 1: *God multiplies the descendants of Israel in Egypt despite severe oppression.*

1:1 *names of the children of Israel.* The list of Jacob's sons links Exodus to the last genealogy of Genesis (Gen. 46:8–27), continuing the story of God's blessing on Abraham, Isaac, and Jacob, and the progress of history toward the promised Seed, the Savior (Gen. 3:15).

1:5 *souls.* Persons. *came out of the loins.* Were his biological children.

1:7 *children of Israel.* Adults and children from Jacob's family. *were fruitful.* God caused this (Ps. 105:24), thus fulfilling His original mandate for mankind (Gen. 1:28) and His promises to Noah, Abraham, Isaac, and Jacob (Gen. 9:1; 17:6; 28:3; 35:11). *increased abundantly.* Teem or swarm like the original creation (Gen. 1:20–21). *waxed exceeding mighty.* Became a very, very large group of people. The fulfillment of God's promise drew near (Acts 7:17).

1:8 *Joseph* has been the famous lord of Egypt who saved it from starvation (Gen. 47:25).

1:10 *falleth out.* Happens to be. Persecution often begins with propaganda depicting God's people as dangerous.

1:11 *taskmasters.* Literally, "rulers of burdens," slave masters. The tomb of Rekhmire, vizier over Egypt in the fifteenth century BC, depicts slaves making bricks with the caption, "The taskmaster says to the builders, 'The rod is in my hand; do not be lazy.'" God had foretold to Abraham that his offspring would live in dependence on others in a foreign land (Gen. 15:13). That dependence ultimately turned to the bondage of slavery. *treasure cities.* Fortified cities for storage. *Raamses.* Probably located at Qantir.

1:12 *the more they afflicted them, the more they multiplied.* God fulfilled His plan through Israel's enslavement (Ps. 105:25), as with Joseph (Gen. 45:4–5). *grieved.* Distressed.

1:13–14 *rigour.* Severe hardship. *bondage.* Slavery. *morter.* Mortar.

1:15 *midwives.* Women who assist in the birth of children, here the chief two of Israel.

1:16 *office.* Job or service. *stools.* Literally, "two stones." Perhaps a stool on which women sat to give birth, or possibly meaning, "look for the testicles" to determine the baby's gender.

1:17–18 *feared God.* Rejoiced and trembled before God's majesty so that they cared more about pleasing God than anything else. *men children.* Baby boys.

the king of Egypt commanded them, but saved the men children alive.

18 And the king of Egypt called for the midwives, and said unto them, Why have ye done this thing, and have saved the men children alive?

19 And the midwives said unto Pharaoh, Because the Hebrew women *are* not as the Egyptian women; for they *are* lively, and are delivered ere the midwives come in unto them.

20 Therefore God dealt well with the midwives: and the people multiplied, and waxed very mighty.

21 And it came to pass, because the midwives feared God, that he made them houses.

22 And Pharaoh charged all his people, saying, Every son that is born ye shall cast into the river, and every daughter ye shall save alive.

CHAPTER 2

AND there went a man of the house of Levi, and took *to wife* a daughter of Levi.

2 And the woman conceived, and bare a son: and when she saw him that he *was a* goodly *child*, she hid him three months.

3 And when she could not longer hide him, she took for him an ark of bulrushes, and daubed it with slime and with pitch, and put the child therein; and she laid *it* in the flags by the river's brink.

4 And his sister stood afar off, to wit what would be done to him.

5 ¶ And the daughter of Pharaoh came down to wash *herself* at the river; and her maidens walked along by the river's side; and when she saw the ark among the flags, she sent her maid to fetch it.

6 And when she had opened *it*, she saw the child: and, behold, the babe wept. And she had compassion on him, and said, This *is one* of the Hebrews' children.

7 Then said his sister to Pharaoh's daughter, Shall I go and call to thee a nurse of the Hebrew women, that she may nurse the child for thee?

8 And Pharaoh's daughter said to her, Go. And the maid went and called the child's mother.

9 And Pharaoh's daughter said unto her, Take this child away, and nurse it for me, and I will give *thee* thy wages. And the woman took the child, and nursed it.

10 And the child grew, and she brought him unto Pharaoh's daughter, and he became her son. And she called his name Moses: and she said, Because I drew him out of the water.

11 ¶ And it came to pass in those days, when Moses was grown, that he went out unto his brethren, and looked on their burdens: and he spied an Egyptian smiting an Hebrew, one of his brethren.

12 And he looked this way and that way, and when he saw that *there was* no man, he slew the Egyptian, and hid him in the sand.

13 And when he went out the second day, behold, two men of the Hebrews strove together: and he said to him that did the wrong, Wherefore smitest thou thy fellow?

1:19 *lively.* Vigorous. *ere.* Before. Perhaps a lie, or perhaps the midwife delayed her arrival until after the birth.

1:20 *waxed very mighty.* Became a very large or strong group of people.

1:21 *houses.* Families. Since they saved the children of others, God gave them children.

1:22 *charged.* Commanded. The killing of infants is the worst kind of murder but sadly common even in the modern world, including the scourge of abortion.

Thoughts for Personal/Family Worship: Chapter 1

1. **God will multiply His people (Matt. 16:18), sometimes even through persecution. For example, the persecution of the church in Jerusalem actually spread the gospel so that "the word of God grew and multiplied" (Acts 8:1–4; 12:1,24). If you face persecution, how can you find the courage to not fear but stand firm with other believers (Phil. 1:27–29)?**
2. **When bullies and tyrants demand that we sin, we should fear God more than men (Matt. 10:28). God rewards those who fear Him (Ps. 33:18; 34:9–10). Disobedience to civil authority is lawful when necessary to obey God (Acts 4:19; 5:29), but breaking God's laws (such as lying) because of danger is never right.**

Chapter 2: ***Moses was delivered from death and raised by the daughter of Pharaoh, but later chose the people of God over the riches of Egypt, and fled to Midian.***

2:1 *house of Levi.* Family descended from Levi. *to wife.* As a wife.

2:2 *Saw* that he was good (*goodly*) means "she found him delightful" (Gen. 3:6). It also implies that God delighted in Moses (Acts 7:20, Greek) as in a new creation (Gen. 1:4,10). *hid him.* She defied the king's decree by faith in the Lord (Heb. 11:23).

2:3 *ark.* Box. Elsewhere in Scripture this only referred to the ark of Noah, an instrument of salvation and new creation (Gen. 6–9). *bulrushes.* Papyrus, the reeds of which were used to make boats. *slime.* Tar for waterproofing, like Noah's ark (Gen. 6:14). *therein.* Into it. *flags.* Reeds to hide the child.

2:4 *wit.* Know.

2:5 *Pharaoh* probably had many children by various women, so this *daughter* and her children may not have been particularly prominent. *maidens . . . maid.* Female servants.

2:9 *nursed it.* God allowed Moses' mother to nurture him at least in his early childhood.

2:10 *he became her son.* Moses was raised in Egyptian knowledge and leadership skills (Acts 7:22). By God's providence, Pharaoh's decree to destroy the Hebrew boys resulted in the training of the future deliverer of Israel.

2:11 *Moses was grown.* Forty years old (Acts 7:23). He turned away from the glories of Egypt, and embraced the sorrows of *his brethren* to share in Christ's reward (Heb. 11:24–26). *spied.* Saw. *smiting.* Striking.

2:12 *slew.* Killed. Moses defended and avenged the oppressed, believing God would save Israel through him (Acts 7:24–25). Yet he did so without authority or commission from God.

2:13 *strove.* Fought.

14 And he said, Who made thee a prince and a
judge over us? intendest thou to kill me, as thou
killedst the Egyptian? And Moses feared, and said,
Surely this thing is known.
15 Now when Pharaoh heard this thing, he
sought to slay Moses. But Moses fled from the
face of Pharaoh, and dwelt in the land of Midian:
and he sat down by a well.
16 Now the priest of Midian had seven daugh-
ters: and they came and drew *water*, and filled the
troughs to water their father's flock.
17 And the shepherds came and drove them
away: but Moses stood up and helped them, and
watered their flock.
18 And when they came to Reuel their father, he
said, How *is it that* ye are come so soon to day?
19 And they said, An Egyptian delivered us out
of the hand of the shepherds, and also drew *water*
enough for us, and watered the flock.
20 And he said unto his daughters, And where *is*
he? why *is* it *that* ye have left the man? call him,
that he may eat bread.
21 And Moses was content to dwell with the man:
and he gave Moses Zipporah his daughter.
22 And she bare *him* a son, and he called his
name Gershom: for he said, I have been a stranger
in a strange land.
23 ¶ And it came to pass in process of time, that the
king of Egypt died: and the children of Israel sighed
by reason of the bondage, and they cried, and their
cry came up unto God by reason of the bondage.
24 And God heard their groaning, and God
remembered his covenant with Abraham, with
Isaac, and with Jacob.
25 And God looked upon the children of Israel,
and God had respect unto *them*.

CHAPTER 3

NOW Moses kept the flock of Jethro his father in
law, the priest of Midian: and he led the flock to
the backside of the desert, and came to the moun-
tain of God, *even* to Horeb.
2 And the angel of the LORD appeared unto him
in a flame of fire out of the midst of a bush: and
he looked, and, behold, the bush burned with fire,
and the bush *was* not consumed.
3 And Moses said, I will now turn aside, and see
this great sight, why the bush is not burnt.
4 And when the LORD saw that he turned aside to
see, God called unto him out of the midst of the
bush, and said, Moses, Moses. And he said, Here
am I.
5 And he said, Draw not nigh hither: put off thy
shoes from off thy feet, for the place whereon
thou standest *is* holy ground.
6 Moreover he said, I *am* the God of thy father,
the God of Abraham, the God of Isaac, and the
God of Jacob. And Moses hid his face; for he was
afraid to look upon God.
7 ¶ And the LORD said, I have surely seen the af-
fliction of my people which *are* in Egypt, and have

2:14 Israel rejected the deliverer sent by God, as they did Christ (Acts 7:25,35). But Christ, unlike Moses, did not set Himself up as an earthly ruler (Luke 12:14).
2:15 *Pharaoh.* Most likely, Thutmose II according to the widely accepted chronology of Egypt's eighteenth through twentieth dynasties. *face.* Presence. *Midian.* Desert of the Sinai peninsula and northwest Arabia.
2:17 *helped.* Saved, as a deliverer of the oppressed (v. 19). *watered their flock.* Like Jacob (Gen. 29:10).
2:18 *Reuel.* Jethro (3:1).
2:22 *stranger.* Foreigner like Abraham, Isaac, and Jacob (Gen. 23:4; 26:3; 47:9; Heb. 11:13). God prepared the deliverer by afflicting him.
2:23 *children of Israel.* Adults and children descended from Jacob. *bondage.* Slavery. God uses affliction to humble people and make them long for salvation.
2:24–25 *God heard . . . God remembered . . . God looked . . . God had respect.* The *covenant*-keeping God (Gen. 15:13–21) feels great compassion for His hurting people. *remembered.* Not recovery of lost memories, but thought that stirs a person to action (Gen. 8:1; Ps. 25:6–7). *had respect.* Or, the Lord "knew" them with love (Ps. 1:6).

Thoughts for Personal/Family Worship: Chapter 2

1. **Moses' parents are examples to us of doing what is right in an oppressive culture of death. We must trust in God's providence even when life makes no sense. Let us persevere in doing good by faith that God overrules this wicked world to save His people. He is not cold to our pain, but has warm compassion for all our sufferings.**
2. **God's servant must suffer rejection. Christ came to His own people, but they did not receive Him. Nor would we receive Him apart from a new birth (John 1:11–13). By grace, do you manifest the fruits of the new birth in your daily life? As you follow the rejected and crucified Savior, how might you suffer rejection as well?**

The Lord's Revelation of Himself to Moses (3:1—4:31)

Chapter 3: *The Lord reveals Himself to Moses and calls him to bring Israel out of Egypt.*

3:1 *Now Moses.* Forty years have passed (7:7; Acts 7:30). *kept the flock.* The son of Pharaoh's daughter was reduced to an occupation despised by Egyptians. *backside.* Distant parts. *mountain of God.* Mt. Sinai, where God would appear, traditionally identified as Jebel Musa (elev. 7,500 ft.) in the southern part of the Sinai peninsula. *Horeb.* Mt. Sinai (1 Kings 19:8).
3:2 *angel of the LORD.* God (v. 4), the Son sent by the Father (see note at Gen. 16:7). *bush.* Thorny shrub, a lowly plant. *burned.* Sign of God's glorious presence (13:21; 19:14,18; 24:17; Gen. 15:17). *not consumed.* God came not to destroy Israel in wrath but to dwell with His lowly people in grace (Deut. 33:16).
3:5 *nigh hither.* Close to here. *put off thy shoes.* A gesture of reverence (Josh. 5:15). *holy ground.* God's holy presence sets apart people, times, and things as sacred.
3:6 *I am . . . the God of Abraham.* Abraham yet lived in God's presence (Matt. 22:32) in covenant with the Lord (Gen. 17:7; 26:24). *hid his face.* As do the seraphim in heaven (Isa. 6:1–3).
3:7 *seen . . . heard . . . know.* See note at 2:24–25.

heard their cry by reason of their taskmasters; for
I know their sorrows;
8 And I am come down to deliver them out of the
hand of the Egyptians, and to bring them up out
of that land unto a good land and a large, unto a
land flowing with milk and honey; unto the place
of the Canaanites, and the Hittites, and the Amor-
ites, and the Perizzites, and the Hivites, and the
Jebusites.
9 Now therefore, behold, the cry of the children
of Israel is come unto me: and I have also seen
the oppression wherewith the Egyptians oppress
them.
10 Come now therefore, and I will send thee unto
Pharaoh, that thou mayest bring forth my people
the children of Israel out of Egypt.
11 ¶ And Moses said unto God, Who *am* I, that I
should go unto Pharaoh, and that I should bring
forth the children of Israel out of Egypt?
12 And he said, Certainly I will be with thee; and
this *shall be* a token unto thee, that I have sent
thee: When thou hast brought forth the peo-
ple out of Egypt, ye shall serve God upon this
mountain.
13 And Moses said unto God, Behold, *when* I
come unto the children of Israel, and shall say
unto them, The God of your fathers hath sent me
unto you; and they shall say to me, What *is* his
name? what shall I say unto them?
14 And God said unto Moses, I AM THAT I AM:
and he said, Thus shalt thou say unto the children
of Israel, I AM hath sent me unto you.
15 And God said moreover unto Moses, Thus
shalt thou say unto the children of Israel, The
LORD God of your fathers, the God of Abraham,
the God of Isaac, and the God of Jacob, hath sent
me unto you: this *is* my name for ever, and this *is*
my memorial unto all generations.
16 Go, and gather the elders of Israel together, and
say unto them, The LORD God of your fathers, the
God of Abraham, of Isaac, and of Jacob, appeared
unto me, saying, I have surely visited you, and
seen that which is done to you in Egypt:
17 And I have said, I will bring you up out of the
affliction of Egypt unto the land of the Canaan-
ites, and the Hittites, and the Amorites, and the
Perizzites, and the Hivites, and the Jebusites, unto
a land flowing with milk and honey.
18 And they shall hearken to thy voice: and thou
shalt come, thou and the elders of Israel, unto
the king of Egypt, and ye shall say unto him, The
LORD God of the Hebrews hath met with us: and
now let us go, we beseech thee, three days' journey
into the wilderness, that we may sacrifice to the
LORD our God.
19 ¶ And I am sure that the king of Egypt will not
let you go, no, not by a mighty hand.
20 And I will stretch out my hand, and smite
Egypt with all my wonders which I will do in the
midst thereof: and after that he will let you go.
21 And I will give this people favour in the sight
of the Egyptians: and it shall come to pass, that,
when ye go, ye shall not go empty:
22 But every woman shall borrow of her neigh-
bour, and of her that sojourneth in her house,
jewels of silver, and jewels of gold, and raiment:
and ye shall put *them* upon your sons, and upon
your daughters; and ye shall spoil the Egyptians.

3:8 *come down.* God is present in all places (Ps. 139), but this figure of speech pictures Him as the King of heaven descending to be with His people on earth (2:23), an anticipation of the incarnation (John 3:13). *flowing with milk and honey.* Rich for livestock and producing sweet luxuries. *Canaanites . . . Jebusites.* See Gen. 15:18–21.
3:9 *wherewith.* With which.
3:11–12 *Who am I . . . I will be with thee.* We must rely not on our strength but on God's covenant-keeping presence with us (Deut. 31:6). *serve.* Worship with sacrifices (v. 18; 5:1,3).
3:14 *I AM.* The name "the LORD" (Hebrew, *YHWH*) means, "He is" or "He will be." The expanded phrase *I AM THAT I AM* is very similar to "I will be gracious to whom I will be gracious" (33:19), an expression of sovereign freedom (Rom. 9:14–16). Thus when He commits Himself to Moses, "I will be [same word as *I AM*] with thee" (v. 12), nothing can make Him abandon His people or stop Him from blessing them (Num. 23:19–20; Deut. 31:6).
3:15 Like "Holy One of Israel" (Isa. 12:6), God here joins His sovereign freedom (*"the LORD,"* or, "I AM," v. 14) with His faithfulness to love His covenant people ("God of Abraham"). *memorial.* Remembrance.
3:16 *elders.* Leaders. *visited.* As promised by Joseph (Gen. 50:24–25).
3:18 *hearken.* Listen. *beseech.* Plead.
3:19 *I am sure.* God already knew that Pharaoh would resist until compelled *by a mighty hand* (6:1; 13:9; 32:11). God knows our future choices because He rules over them (4:21).
3:20 *smite.* Strike. *in the midst thereof.* In it.
3:22 *borrow.* Ask. *sojourneth.* Dwells. *jewels.* Jewelry or articles. *raiment.* Clothing. *spoil.* Plunder. The Israelite slaves would experience some justice in receiving gifts from their oppressors (11:2–3; 12:35–36), as God had promised Abraham (Gen. 15:14).

Thoughts for Personal/Family Worship: Chapter 3

1. **God's name, *YHWH* or "the LORD," reveals His eternal being, absolute independence, and freedom from all needs or limitations (Isa. 41:4; 43:10–13; 44:6–8; 48:12–13; John 8:58; Rev. 1:8). His being, will, and works are entirely from Himself. He borrows nothing from us and does not need our help (Acts 17:24–25). Yet we can be loved by Him, for He is the God and Father of our Lord Jesus Christ, the God of electing, covenant love. God desires to be known and worshiped for His lordship and love (Ps. 136:1–3).**
2. **In God's covenant compassion (Eph. 2:4), He comes to His elect in order to deliver them from the oppressive domain of darkness and transfer them into the kingdom of blessing, that is, the kingdom of His dear Son (Col. 1:13). He does not save people to live as they please, but to serve and worship Him in holiness (Eph. 1:4,6,12,14; Col. 3:12). How does salvation from sin and misery motivate Christians to serve and worship God?**

GOD'S NAMES

"God is a Spirit, infinite, eternal, and unchangeable, in His being, wisdom, power, holiness, justice, goodness, and truth" (Westminster Shorter Catechism, Q. 4). Consequently, He is incomprehensible; man is incapable of thinking about all that God is. So any self-revelation of God is a gracious act whereby God condescends to man's limited understanding.

God's names or titles are one of the key ways by which God has revealed Himself. These names are more than just labels of identification; they are propositional descriptions of some aspects of His infinite Persons. Consequently, they are not used haphazardly and should not be passed over lightly in the reading of Scripture.

There are generally three categories of God's names: (1) *propositional*, expressing some fact pertaining to the divine being, such as "God Most High" (Gen. 14:18–22) and "everlasting God" (Gen. 21:33); (2) *historical*, commemorating some encounter with God (such as *Jehovahjireh*, "the Lord will provide," Gen. 22:14; see also Gen. 16:13; Ex. 17:15); and (3) *personal*, declaring some individual experience ("the God of Abraham," "the fear of Isaac," etc.).

Here is a brief explanation of some common propositional names in the Old Testament:

Jehovah. This is God's personal name, especially linked to His covenant grace and mercy. Derived from the verb "I am" (explained at the burning bush in Exodus 3), the name declares God's self-sufficient independence, eternity, and sovereignty. Yet, amazingly, Jehovah is the principal name of God used in contexts of salvation. Although God is infinitely independent of anything outside of Himself, He is willing to have intimate fellowship with man, particularly through the covenant of grace. Jehovah, therefore, is often referred to as God's "covenant name." In the King James Version it is always translated in capital letters as "LORD" or occasionally as "GOD."

God. This is the most general term for deity. The Hebrew word can be either singular (*El*) or plural (*Elohim*). Both forms stress God's greatness. He is all-powerful; He possesses all authority; He is able to do whatever He pleases. This title also magnifies God's transcendence; He is exalted far above all creation, including man. The plural form is a plural of majesty or excellence that highlights His power and greatness with even greater emphasis. Significantly, this is His first self-revelation: "In the beginning God . . ." (Gen. 1:1; see Ps. 19:1). He is the Creator.

Lord. The title *Adonai* describes God as the supreme Owner and Master of everything. Everything belongs to Him, and He governs everything according to His own purposes for His own glory. This name declares His absolute sovereignty or kingship. Earthly kings come and go, but the heavenly King reigns supreme forever (Isa. 6:1). All men and every nation, whether or not they acknowledge Him, are subject to His authority and accountable to Him. He is the Sovereign over all the earth; all will bow before Him (2 Kings 7:6; Ps. 110:5; Dan. 1:2; Amos 1:8). In the KJV this title is translated as "Lord" to distinguish it from Jehovah, which is rendered as "LORD."

God Almighty. Although this title occurs most frequently in the patriarchal period, especially in Job, it is not limited to that period. The Hebrew is *El Shaddai*. Opinions differ regarding the translation, but most likely it means "the God who is sufficient." He is fully able to keep every word of His promises, even when the fulfillment seems impossible. Nothing is too hard for *El Shaddai*. So even though the prospect of a great nation descending from Abraham seemed unlikely, behind the promise was *El Shaddai*, and thus the promise was certain (Gen. 17:1; 35:11–12).

LORD of Hosts. This is "Jehovah of armies," a military expression identifying God as the "Commander" who has all authority and infinite rank to order His troops to accomplish His will. This title occurs most frequently during the period of the monarchy (Samuel, Kings, Chronicles, Psalms, and the Prophets). Depending on the context, the army may refer to Israel, the angels, the heavenly bodies (stars and planets), or even all of creation. The point is that God has the power, authority, and resources at His command to do and to achieve all of His plans and purposes. No matter how great the promise or how serious the threat, the LORD of hosts will command and it will be done. Notice, for instance, that Zechariah uses this expression more than fifty times in his prophecy to reinforce the certainty of the Lord's every word (see also Isa. 6:1–4).

CHAPTER 4

AND Moses answered and said, But, behold, they
will not believe me, nor hearken unto my voice:
for they will say, The LORD hath not appeared
unto thee.
2 And the LORD said unto him, What *is* that in
thine hand? And he said, A rod.
3 And he said, Cast it on the ground. And he cast
it on the ground, and it became a serpent; and
Moses fled from before it.
4 And the LORD said unto Moses, Put forth thine
hand, and take it by the tail. And he put forth his
hand, and caught it, and it became a rod in his hand:
5 That they may believe that the LORD God of their
fathers, the God of Abraham, the God of Isaac, and
the God of Jacob, hath appeared unto thee.
6 ¶ And the LORD said furthermore unto him,
Put now thine hand into thy bosom. And he put
his hand into his bosom: and when he took it out,
behold, his hand *was* leprous as snow.
7 And he said, Put thine hand into thy bosom
again. And he put his hand into his bosom again;
and plucked it out of his bosom, and, behold, it
was turned again as his *other* flesh.
8 And it shall come to pass, if they will not believe
thee, neither hearken to the voice of the first sign,
that they will believe the voice of the latter sign.
9 And it shall come to pass, if they will not be-
lieve also these two signs, neither hearken unto
thy voice, that thou shalt take of the water of the
river, and pour *it* upon the dry *land*: and the wa-
ter which thou takest out of the river shall become
blood upon the dry *land*.
10 ¶ And Moses said unto the LORD, O my Lord,
I *am* not eloquent, neither heretofore, nor since
thou hast spoken unto thy servant: but I *am* slow
of speech, and of a slow tongue.
11 And the LORD said unto him, Who hath made
man's mouth? or who maketh the dumb, or deaf,
or the seeing, or the blind? have not I the LORD?
12 Now therefore go, and I will be with thy
mouth, and teach thee what thou shalt say.
13 And he said, O my Lord, send, I pray thee, by
the hand *of him whom* thou wilt send.
14 And the anger of the LORD was kindled against
Moses, and he said, *Is* not Aaron the Levite thy
brother? I know that he can speak well. And also,
behold, he cometh forth to meet thee: and when
he seeth thee, he will be glad in his heart.
15 And thou shalt speak unto him, and put words
in his mouth: and I will be with thy mouth, and
with his mouth, and will teach you what ye shall
do.
16 And he shall be thy spokesman unto the
people: and he shall be, *even* he shall be to thee
instead of a mouth, and thou shalt be to him
instead of God.
17 And thou shalt take this rod in thine hand,
wherewith thou shalt do signs.
18 ¶ And Moses went and returned to Jethro his
father in law, and said unto him, Let me go, I pray
thee, and return unto my brethren which *are* in
Egypt, and see whether they be yet alive. And
Jethro said to Moses, Go in peace.
19 And the LORD said unto Moses in Midian, Go,
return into Egypt: for all the men are dead which
sought thy life.
20 And Moses took his wife and his sons, and set
them upon an ass, and he returned to the land
of Egypt: and Moses took the rod of God in his
hand.
21 And the LORD said unto Moses, When thou
goest to return into Egypt, see that thou do all
those wonders before Pharaoh, which I have put

Chapter 4: *The Lord gives Moses miraculous signs to work and Aaron to assist him, as Moses resists God's call to bring out Israel.*

4:1 *hearken.* Listen. Moses contradicted God's promise, not fully trusting His word (3:18).

4:3 *serpent.* Snakes were feared in Egypt and used as symbols of power. In their myths, the demonic spirit of evil and chaos was a huge serpent. The Pharaoh's crown featured the uraeus or upright cobra as a symbol of the patron goddess of Egypt who supposedly gave Pharaoh his power. The power of Egypt is sometimes portrayed as a serpent (or "dragon" in Ps. 74:13; Isa. 51:9–10; Ezek. 29:3). Turning a staff into a snake declared the sovereignty of the Lord over false gods.

4:5 *That they may believe.* Miracles confirmed that the new revelation was from God (Acts 14:3; Heb. 2:3–4).

4:6 *into thy bosom.* By your chest, that is, inside your garment. *leprous as snow.* Moses' dark skin was turned pale by a skin disease.

4:8 *hearken.* Listen.

4:9 *water of the river.* Egypt lived or died by the Nile, which it regarded as the gift of the gods. The Lord showed that He alone controls life and death.

4:10 *heretofore.* In the past. Moses set his mind on his inability instead of God's ability.

4:11 *dumb.* Unable to speak. The Lord declared His sovereignty over all human ability and disability (Dan. 2:20).

4:12 *I will be with thy mouth.* God repeated the promise of His empowering presence (3:12), applying it to the prophet's ability to speak (vv. 15–16).

4:13 *send . . . whom thou wilt send.* Polite resistance against God's call.

4:14 *kindled.* Burned. The stubborn refusal of Moses to fully trust God's promises angered God. Yet God was merciful to Moses and did not reject him.

4:15–16 *instead of.* In place of. The prophet of the Lord was divinely empowered to speak God's *words* for Him, as if the prophet were God's own *mouth*. Some Egyptian officials were titled, "the mouth of the king." The words of the prophets are the Word of God, the King of kings.

4:18 *I pray thee.* Please.

4:19 God's words to Moses were echoed in the angel's encouragement to Joseph (Matt. 2:20).

4:20 *ass.* Male donkey.

4:21 *harden.* Make strong or stubborn. See the third major

in thine hand: but I will harden his heart, that he
shall not let the people go.
22 And thou shalt say unto Pharaoh, Thus saith
the LORD, Israel *is* my son, *even* my firstborn:
23 And I say unto thee, Let my son go, that he
may serve me: and if thou refuse to let him go, be-
hold, I will slay thy son, *even* thy firstborn.
24 ¶ And it came to pass by the way in the inn,
that the LORD met him, and sought to kill him.
25 Then Zipporah took a sharp stone, and cut off
the foreskin of her son, and cast *it* at his feet, and
said, Surely a bloody husband *art* thou to me.
26 So he let him go: then she said, A bloody hus-
band *thou art*, because of the circumcision.
27 ¶ And the LORD said to Aaron, Go into the
wilderness to meet Moses. And he went, and met
him in the mount of God, and kissed him.
28 And Moses told Aaron all the words of the
LORD who had sent him, and all the signs which
he had commanded him.
29 ¶ And Moses and Aaron went and gathered
together all the elders of the children of Israel:
30 And Aaron spake all the words which the LORD
had spoken unto Moses, and did the signs in the
sight of the people.
31 And the people believed: and when they heard
that the LORD had visited the children of Israel,
and that he had looked upon their affliction, then
they bowed their heads and worshipped.

CHAPTER 5

AND afterward Moses and Aaron went in, and
told Pharaoh, Thus saith the LORD God of Israel,
Let my people go, that they may hold a feast unto
me in the wilderness.
2 And Pharaoh said, Who *is* the LORD, that I
should obey his voice to let Israel go? I know not
the LORD, neither will I let Israel go.
3 And they said, The God of the Hebrews hath
met with us: let us go, we pray thee, three days'
journey into the desert, and sacrifice unto the
LORD our God; lest he fall upon us with pesti-
lence, or with the sword.
4 And the king of Egypt said unto them, Where-
fore do ye, Moses and Aaron, let the people from
their works? get you unto your burdens.
5 And Pharaoh said, Behold, the people of the
land now *are* many, and ye make them rest from
their burdens.
6 And Pharaoh commanded the same day the
taskmasters of the people, and their officers, saying,
7 Ye shall no more give the people straw to make
brick, as heretofore: let them go and gather straw
for themselves.
8 And the tale of the bricks, which they did make
heretofore, ye shall lay upon them; ye shall not di-
minish *ought* thereof: for they *be* idle; therefore
they cry, saying, Let us go *and* sacrifice to our God.
9 Let there more work be laid upon the men, that

---

theme in the Introduction: Synopsis.

4:22–23 The Lord lovingly adopts His covenant people as His children (Deut. 14:1; Jer. 31:9; Hos. 1:10; 11:1; Rom. 8:14–16; 9:4). Here all Israel was counted corporately as *my son*, the *firstborn* or oldest male child with special rights to dignity and the inheritance. Pharaoh had been attacking God's *son*, thus God threatened to strike Pharaoh's *son* (11:5).

4:24–26 *inn*. Place to camp or lodge, not necessarily a building. *cast*. Touched. *bloody husband*. Literally, "relative of blood," possibly a positive statement of family ties to Moses or Zipporah's son. Moses' failure to circumcise his son violated the covenant with Abraham (Gen. 17:9–14).

Thoughts for Personal/Family Worship: Chapter 4

1. **Trust God's all-sufficiency. He is Lord over the natural world and Lord over all human ability and disability. We should never let our weaknesses become an excuse for disobedience. When God's Word calls us to act, trust that God will be with you.**
2. **Those who would lead God's people must be faithful in their home life. Moses' failure to circumcise his son nearly cost him his life. David resolved to walk within his house with integrity of heart (Ps. 101:2), but his adultery tore his family apart. Why is it dangerous when leaders neglect to be faithful in marriage and parenting?**

Pharaoh's Resistance and the Lord's Promise (5:1—7:7)

Chapter 5: *Moses and Aaron confront Pharaoh with the Lord's demands, but Pharaoh only increases the oppression of Israel.*

5:1 *Pharaoh*. Most likely Thutmose III according to the best Egyptian chronology for this period. The key issue is the date demanded by the biblical evidence rather than the name of the Pharaoh. Significantly, Thutmose III was the most powerful military king of the eighteenth Dynasty, putting in bold God's almighty power in the exodus event. *Thus saith*. A formula introducing the words of a king or ruler (v. 20; Num. 22:16; 1 Kings 2:30; 20:2; 22:27; 2 Kings 9:18–19; 18:19,29,31; 19:3; Ezra 1:2). As the true King the Lord addressed Pharaoh. *Let my people go, that they may hold a feast unto me*. Salvation is for worship. See the fourth major theme in the Introduction: Synopsis.

5:2 *Who is the LORD, that I should obey his voice*. Pharaoh viewed himself as a god. Egyptians claimed that Pharaoh could performs feats of amazing strength like shooting arrows that pierced through 2–3 inches of copper plate. Thus Pharaoh faced the Lord in a contest of sovereignty. However, God had already told Moses that He would harden Pharaoh's heart and he would resist the Lord (3:19; 4:21). So Pharaoh's challenge to God was itself a display of God's sovereignty.

5:3 *we pray thee*. Please. *fall upon us with pestilence*. Strike us with disease/death.

5:4 *Wherefore do ye . . . let*. Why do you make them stop?

5:6 *taskmasters*. See note at 1:11. *their officers*. Hebrew officials in the slave administration (v. 14).

5:7–8 *heretofore*. Before. *Straw* helped the clay to dry and bound it together to keep the bricks from cracking. *tale*. Number. *diminish ought thereof*. Reduce any of it.

5:9 *vain words*. Pharaoh declared the words of God to be a lie.

5:10–11 *Thus saith Pharaoh*. The word of a king against the Word of the King (see note at v. 1). *not ought . . . diminished*. None reduced.

they may labour therein; and let them not regard
vain words.
10 ¶ And the taskmasters of the people went out,
and their officers, and they spake to the people,
saying, Thus saith Pharaoh, I will not give you
straw.
11 Go ye, get you straw where ye can find it: yet
not ought of your work shall be diminished.
12 So the people were scattered abroad through-
out all the land of Egypt to gather stubble instead
of straw.
13 And the taskmasters hasted *them*, saying, Fulfil
your works, *your* daily tasks, as when there was
straw.
14 And the officers of the children of Israel,
which Pharaoh's taskmasters had set over them,
were beaten, *and* demanded, Wherefore have ye
not fulfilled your task in making brick both yes-
terday and to day, as heretofore?
15 ¶ Then the officers of the children of Israel
came and cried unto Pharaoh, saying, Wherefore
dealest thou thus with thy servants?
16 There is no straw given unto thy servants,
and they say to us, Make brick: and, behold, thy
servants *are* beaten; but the fault *is* in thine own
people.
17 But he said, Ye *are* idle, *ye are* idle: therefore ye
say, Let us go *and* do sacrifice to the LORD.
18 Go therefore now, *and* work; for there shall no
straw be given you, yet shall ye deliver the tale of
bricks.
19 And the officers of the children of Israel did
see *that* they *were* in evil *case*, after it was said, Ye
shall not minish *ought* from your bricks of your
daily task.
20 ¶ And they met Moses and Aaron, who stood
in the way, as they came forth from Pharaoh:
21 And they said unto them, The LORD look upon
you, and judge; because ye have made our savour
to be abhorred in the eyes of Pharaoh, and in the
eyes of his servants, to put a sword in their hand
to slay us.
22 And Moses returned unto the LORD, and said,
Lord, wherefore hast thou *so* evil entreated this
people? why *is* it *that* thou hast sent me?
23 For since I came to Pharaoh to speak in thy
name, he hath done evil to this people; neither
hast thou delivered thy people at all.

CHAPTER 6

THEN the LORD said unto Moses, Now shalt thou
see what I will do to Pharaoh: for with a strong
hand shall he let them go, and with a strong hand
shall he drive them out of his land.
2 And God spake unto Moses, and said unto him,
I *am* the LORD:
3 And I appeared unto Abraham, unto Isaac, and

5:13 *hasted*. Pressed, hurried.
5:14 *officers*. Officials. *Wherefore*. Why. *heretofore*. Before.
5:17 *ye are idle: therefore ye say, Let us go*. Pharaoh cleverly blamed his oppression on the words of God and the ministry of Moses and Aaron, turning the people against them.
5:18 *tale*. Number.
5:19 *in evil case*. In trouble. *not minish ought*. Not reduce any.
5:20 *stood in the way*. Stood or waited to meet them.
5:21 *the LORD look upon you, and judge*. They cursed Moses and Aaron for their trouble. *made our savour to be abhorred*. Or, made us "stink," that is, provoked and offended Pharaoh (Gen. 34:30). Moses was broken by the humiliation of apparent failure in God's service.
5:22 *wherefore hast thou so evil entreated*. Why have you done harm? Moses questioned God because the short-term results of his mission were disastrous. Remarkably, the Lord did not rebuke Moses but answered his doubts with promises (6:1–8).

Thoughts for Personal/Family Worship: Chapter 5

1. **Israel's salvation from Egypt is a type of salvation from sin. When the gospel of redemption comes to a sinner, he may experience the evil of his spiritual bondage even more than before he came under the preaching of the Word. Why? To prepare him to glorify God all the more when salvation comes, for he now knows that only a divine Savior can rescue him. How have you experienced the evil of your sin?**
2. **Servants of God should not assume that obedience will bring them a life of ease and quick success. The kingdom of darkness never rages so fiercely as when the Word invades the world. God's servants face stiff opposition from the enemy and sometimes from the visible church; they may even find their own hearts rising up against God. But Christ will build His church, and even the rage of Satan will result in His praise.**

Chapter 6: *The Lord promises to make Himself known by redeeming a people for Himself, and renews the calling of Moses and Aaron.*

6:1 *Now shalt thou see*. Now the stage was set for the Lord to display His glory by overcoming His enemy. *with a strong hand*. Not by Pharaoh's hand, but because of the Lord's power, represented as a finger, hand, or arm (3:20; 6:6; 7:5; 8:19; 9:15; 13:3,9,14,16; 15:6,12,16).
6:2–9 The repeated *I am*, *I have*, and *I will* stress that salvation is a work of sovereign grace. There is a mirror-image pattern in these verses, framed by divine revelation (vv. 2,9), *I am the LORD* (vv. 2,8), God's covenant with Abraham (vv. 3–5,8), and again, *I am the LORD*, the One who brings out His people (vv. 6–7). At the center of this covenant revelation are the promises (vv. 6–7) that structure Exodus: covenant redemption (chs. 1–18) and covenant relationship (chs. 19–40). See the fourth major theme in the Introduction: Synopsis.
6:2 *I am the LORD*. God designed salvation to make known His lordship. See the first major theme of the Synopsis in the Introduction.
6:3 *appeared*. See Gen. 12:7; 26:2; 35:1. *JEHOVAH*. The divine name of four Hebrew letters (*YHWH*), normally translated as "LORD." See note at 3:14 and comments in the Worship Section for ch. 3. *not known to them*. The patriarchs knew God's name (Gen. 12:8; 14:22; 15:2), but only in redemption does God

unto Jacob, by *the name of* God Almighty, but by
my name JEHOVAH was I not known to them.
4 And I have also established my covenant with
them, to give them the land of Canaan, the land
of their pilgrimage, wherein they were strangers.
5 And I have also heard the groaning of the
children of Israel, whom the Egyptians keep in
bondage; and I have remembered my covenant.
6 Wherefore say unto the children of Israel, I *am*
the LORD, and I will bring you out from under
the burdens of the Egyptians, and I will rid you
out of their bondage, and I will redeem you with
a stretched out arm, and with great judgments:
7 And I will take you to me for a people, and I
will be to you a God: and ye shall know that I *am*
the LORD your God, which bringeth you out from
under the burdens of the Egyptians.
8 And I will bring you in unto the land, concern-
ing the which I did swear to give it to Abraham,
to Isaac, and to Jacob; and I will give it you for an
heritage: I *am* the LORD.
9 ¶ And Moses spake so unto the children of
Israel: but they hearkened not unto Moses for
anguish of spirit, and for cruel bondage.
10 And the LORD spake unto Moses, saying,
11 Go in, speak unto Pharaoh king of Egypt, that
he let the children of Israel go out of his land.
12 And Moses spake before the LORD, saying, Be-
hold, the children of Israel have not hearkened
unto me; how then shall Pharaoh hear me, who
am of uncircumcised lips?
13 And the LORD spake unto Moses and unto
Aaron, and gave them a charge unto the children
of Israel, and unto Pharaoh king of Egypt, to bring
the children of Israel out of the land of Egypt.
14 ¶ These *be* the heads of their fathers' houses:
The sons of Reuben the firstborn of Israel;
Hanoch, and Pallu, Hezron, and Carmi: these *be*
the families of Reuben.
15 And the sons of Simeon; Jemuel, and Jamin,
and Ohad, and Jachin, and Zohar, and Shaul
the son of a Canaanitish woman: these *are* the
families of Simeon.
16 ¶ And these *are* the names of the sons of Levi
according to their generations; Gershon, and
Kohath, and Merari: and the years of the life of
Levi *were* an hundred thirty and seven years.
17 The sons of Gershon; Libni, and Shimi,
according to their families.
18 And the sons of Kohath; Amram, and Izhar,
and Hebron, and Uzziel: and the years of the life
of Kohath *were* an hundred thirty and three years.
19 And the sons of Merari; Mahali and Mushi:
these *are* the families of Levi according to their
generations.
20 And Amram took him Jochebed his father's
sister to wife; and she bare him Aaron and Moses:
and the years of the life of Amram *were* an hun-
dred and thirty and seven years.
21 ¶ And the sons of Izhar; Korah, and Nepheg,
and Zichri.
22 And the sons of Uzziel; Mishael, and Elzaphan,
and Zithri.
23 And Aaron took him Elisheba, daughter of
Amminadab, sister of Naashon, to wife; and she
bare him Nadab, and Abihu, Eleazar, and Ithamar.
24 And the sons of Korah; Assir, and Elkanah, and
Abiasaph: these *are* the families of the Korhites.
25 And Eleazar Aaron's son took him *one* of the
daughters of Putiel to wife; and she bare him
Phinehas: these *are* the heads of the fathers of the
Levites according to their families.

---

fully and experientially make Himself known. God's revelation climaxed in the coming of His Son, our Redeemer (Heb. 1:1–3).

6:4 *to give them the land.* After four hundred years, God still remembered His promises (Gen. 12:1,7; 13:15; 15:7–21; 17:8; 26:3; 28:13; 35:12; 50:24). God revealed Himself as faithful to keep His covenant. *pilgrimage.* Dwelling away from home as foreigners (*strangers*).

6:5 See notes at 2:23 and 2:24–25. God revealed Himself as compassionate and loving.

6:6–7 God's words, *I am the LORD, and I will bring you out*, echo His words to Abraham (Gen. 15:7), as does His promise to take them as His *people* and to be their *God* (Gen. 17:7–8).

6:8 God blesses His people with an inheritance (*heritage*) where they will enjoy His love forever, of which the *land* was a type (Heb. 11:16; 12:22).

6:9 *hearkened.* Listened. Their faith (4:31) quickly evaporated under trouble and persecution, showing that the Word had no root in them (Mark 4:17).

6:10–13 *Go in, speak.* After revealing His name and promises, the Lord renewed Moses' calling as God's prophet despite the opposition of the king. *uncircumcised lips.* Lips unfit to serve a holy, covenant God (v. 30; Isa. 6:5). *charge.* Command.

6:14–25 The genealogy links Israel's salvation to the promises of Abraham's blessed Seed (see note at 1:1). It focuses on the line of the priests (*Aaron, Nadab, Abihu, Eleazar, Ithamar*, and *Phineas*), while also highlighting persons noted elsewhere for their great sins (*Reuben*, Gen. 35:22; *Levi*, Gen. 34; *Moses*, Ex. 2:12; *Aaron*, Ex. 32; *Nadab* and *Abihu*, Lev. 10; *Korah*, Num. 16).

6:20 *to wife.* As a wife (vv. 23,25).

6:27 The repetition of *king* (vv. 11,13,29) hints that for Moses and Aaron to *bring out the children of Israel from Egypt*, they must have the power of the King of kings.

6:28–30 God renewed Moses' call as a prophet; the same event is described in vv. 10–13. Despite human weakness, the Lord insisted on saving through a man, a foreshadowing of the incarnation.

Thoughts for Personal/Family Worship: Chapter 6

1. The Lord revealed Himself through redemption to create a relationship with His covenant people. Thus Exodus foreshadows the work of Christ. The Lord Jesus gave Himself to redeem a people who would know Him, zealously serve Him, and hope in the coming of His glory (Titus 2:13–14). His redemption brings sinners into a relationship of being children of the living God (Gal. 4:4–7). Do you know this Lord? Is He your covenant God, and are you

26 These *are* that Aaron and Moses, to whom the
LORD said, Bring out the children of Israel from
the land of Egypt according to their armies.
27 These *are* they which spake to Pharaoh king
of Egypt, to bring out the children of Israel from
Egypt: these *are* that Moses and Aaron.
28 ¶ And it came to pass on the day *when* the
LORD spake unto Moses in the land of Egypt,
29 That the LORD spake unto Moses, saying, I *am*
the LORD: speak thou unto Pharaoh king of Egypt
all that I say unto thee.
30 And Moses said before the LORD, Behold, I
am of uncircumcised lips, and how shall Pharaoh
hearken unto me?

CHAPTER 7

AND the LORD said unto Moses, See, I have made
thee a god to Pharaoh: and Aaron thy brother
shall be thy prophet.
2 Thou shalt speak all that I command thee: and
Aaron thy brother shall speak unto Pharaoh, that
he send the children of Israel out of his land.
3 And I will harden Pharaoh's heart, and multiply
my signs and my wonders in the land of Egypt.
4 But Pharaoh shall not hearken unto you, that
I may lay my hand upon Egypt, and bring forth
mine armies, *and* my people the children of Israel,
out of the land of Egypt by great judgments.
5 And the Egyptians shall know that I *am* the
LORD, when I stretch forth mine hand upon
Egypt, and bring out the children of Israel from
among them.
6 And Moses and Aaron did as the LORD com-
manded them, so did they.
7 And Moses *was* fourscore years old, and Aaron
fourscore and three years old, when they spake
unto Pharaoh.
8 ¶ And the LORD spake unto Moses and unto
Aaron, saying,
9 When Pharaoh shall speak unto you, saying,
Shew a miracle for you: then thou shalt say unto
Aaron, Take thy rod, and cast *it* before Pharaoh,
and it shall become a serpent.
10 ¶ And Moses and Aaron went in unto Pharaoh,
and they did so as the LORD had commanded: and
Aaron cast down his rod before Pharaoh, and be-
fore his servants, and it became a serpent.
11 Then Pharaoh also called the wise men and
the sorcerers: now the magicians of Egypt, they
also did in like manner with their enchantments.
12 For they cast down every man his rod, and
they became serpents: but Aaron's rod swallowed
up their rods.
13 And he hardened Pharaoh's heart, that he
hearkened not unto them; as the LORD had said.
14 ¶ And the LORD said unto Moses, Pharaoh's
heart *is* hardened, he refuseth to let the people go.
15 Get thee unto Pharaoh in the morning; lo, he
goeth out unto the water; and thou shalt stand
by the river's brink against he come; and the rod
which was turned to a serpent shalt thou take in
thine hand.
16 And thou shalt say unto him, The LORD God
of the Hebrews hath sent me unto thee, saying,
Let my people go, that they may serve me in the

in relationship with Him as one of His covenant people?

2. Redemption requires a faithful prophet to speak God's words, a righteous priest to sacrifice and intercede, and a powerful king to deliver the enslaved. Moses, Aaron, and their family were inadequate to truly redeem God's people, for they were stained by sin. Though mere men are instruments of God's blessings, Christ is the only Mediator of the covenant of grace—the sufficient Prophet, Priest, and King. (See the fifth major theme in the Introduction: Synopsis.) Trust Him for salvation, and trust Him alone.

Chapter 7: *Moses and Aaron confront Pharaoh with the power of the Lord, showing signs and working the first plague on the Nile.*

7:1 God used Moses and Aaron to illustrate the office of a *prophet* speaking for God (4:15–16).

7:2 *children of Israel.* Adults and children descended from Jacob.

7:3 *harden.* Make stiff or stubborn. See the third major theme in the Introduction: Synopsis. *my signs and my wonders.* Amazing acts of power that demonstrate God's sovereignty.

7:4–5 *hearken.* Listen. *the Egyptians shall know.* God planned redemption not only to take a people (6:6–7) but also to glorify Himself as *the LORD* in the presence of His enemies.

7:7 *fourscore.* Eighty. Forty years had passed since Moses departed Egypt.

The Lord against the Gods of Egypt (7:8—15:21)

Confrontation of the Serpents (7:8–13)

7:8–13 This power encounter sets a pattern followed in each of the first three plagues: the Lord's command, His servants' obedience working a sign with the rod, the sorcerers' imitation by magic, and the hardening of Pharaoh's heart. This pattern reinforces the sense that everything was taking place according to God's words (*as the LORD had commanded* and *as the LORD had said*).

7:10 *serpent.* A direct challenge to the power and gods of Pharaoh. See note at 4:3 and the second major theme in the Introduction: Synopsis.

7:11 *magicians.* Sorcerer-priests who manipulated spirits for power or wisdom. Satan works deceptive wonders (Matt. 24:24; 2 Thess. 2:9; 2 Tim. 3:8; Rev. 13:13–15).

7:12 *swallowed up their rods.* Just as the Lord would "swallow" the power of Egypt (15:12), destroying its army by the *rod* of God at the Red Sea (14:16–17,26).

7:13 *hearkened.* Listened.

Plagues 1–3: No One Like the Lord (7:14—8:19)

The plagues come in three cycles of three, followed by the final plague. In the first plague of each cycle, Moses went in the morning to speak to Pharaoh (v. 15; 8:20; 9:13). The last plague of each cycle lacks any warning to Pharaoh and is more briefly reported (8:16; 9:8; 10:21). In the first cycle, each of the three plagues frames a declaration of God's supremacy (7:17; 8:10,19).

wilderness: and, behold, hitherto thou wouldest
not hear.
17 Thus saith the LORD, In this thou shalt know
that I *am* the LORD: behold, I will smite with the
rod that *is* in mine hand upon the waters which
are in the river, and they shall be turned to blood.
18 And the fish that *is* in the river shall die, and
the river shall stink; and the Egyptians shall lothe
to drink of the water of the river.
19 ¶ And the LORD spake unto Moses, Say unto
Aaron, Take thy rod, and stretch out thine hand
upon the waters of Egypt, upon their streams,
upon their rivers, and upon their ponds, and upon
all their pools of water, that they may become
blood; and *that* there may be blood throughout
all the land of Egypt, both in *vessels of* wood, and
in *vessels of* stone.
20 And Moses and Aaron did so, as the LORD com-
manded; and he lifted up the rod, and smote the
waters that *were* in the river, in the sight of Pha-
raoh, and in the sight of his servants; and all the
waters that *were* in the river were turned to blood.
21 And the fish that *was* in the river died; and the
river stank, and the Egyptians could not drink
of the water of the river; and there was blood
throughout all the land of Egypt.
22 And the magicians of Egypt did so with their
enchantments: and Pharaoh's heart was hard-
ened, neither did he hearken unto them; as the
LORD had said.
23 And Pharaoh turned and went into his house,
neither did he set his heart to this also.
24 And all the Egyptians digged round about the
river for water to drink; for they could not drink
of the water of the river.
25 And seven days were fulfilled, after that the
LORD had smitten the river.

CHAPTER 8

AND the LORD spake unto Moses, Go unto Pha-
raoh, and say unto him, Thus saith the LORD, Let
my people go, that they may serve me.
2 And if thou refuse to let *them* go, behold, I will
smite all thy borders with frogs:
3 And the river shall bring forth frogs abundantly,
which shall go up and come into thine house, and
into thy bedchamber, and upon thy bed, and into
the house of thy servants, and upon thy people, and
into thine ovens, and into thy kneadingtroughs:
4 And the frogs shall come up both on thee, and
upon thy people, and upon all thy servants.
5 ¶ And the LORD spake unto Moses, Say unto
Aaron, Stretch forth thine hand with thy rod over
the streams, over the rivers, and over the ponds,
and cause frogs to come up upon the land of Egypt.
6 And Aaron stretched out his hand over the
waters of Egypt; and the frogs came up, and
covered the land of Egypt.
7 And the magicians did so with their enchant-
ments, and brought up frogs upon the land of
Egypt.
8 ¶ Then Pharaoh called for Moses and Aaron,
and said, Intreat the LORD, that he may take away
the frogs from me, and from my people; and I will
let the people go, that they may do sacrifice unto
the LORD.
9 And Moses said unto Pharaoh, Glory over me:
when shall I intreat for thee, and for thy servants,
and for thy people, to destroy the frogs from thee

7:16 *hitherto.* Until now. *wouldest not.* Did not.
7:17 *In this thou shalt know that I am the LORD.* The plagues demonstrate that the God of Israel is faithful and sovereign. *smite.* Strike. Giving Egypt *blood* to drink was just punishment after it killed babies in the Nile (1:22; Rev. 15:3–7).
7:18 *lothe.* They were disgusted at the river that they once worshiped.
7:20 *as the LORD commanded.* The power of the Lord came through the obedience of His servants (vv. 6,10).
7:21–22 The great Nile is 2–5 miles wide and discharges an average of 100,000 cubic feet of water per second. Its water, fish, and agricultural fertility were central to Egypt's economy and religion; they believed that the blessings of the Nile came from their gods. The God of the Hebrews turned "all the waters" (v. 20) of the river into *blood*! The *magicians of Egypt* turned some water into blood, or made it appear so, but they could not cleanse the bloody Nile. In one stroke, God showed that He alone is God of gods and Lord of lords (Deut. 10:17).

Thoughts for Personal/Family Worship: Chapter 7

God alone is Lord. Physical goods are blessings, but men turn them into gods. Even in a secular culture, people worship money and the pleasures it can buy. They depend upon the experts to manipulate the world and give them happiness. But the Lord wages war against the idols to show that He alone is sovereign. His war will climax in the coming of Christ. Before it is too late, let us turn from idols to serve the living God and hope in His Son, the Savior. What idols tempt you? What does it mean to turn from them to the Lord?

Chapter 8: *The Lord works the second (frogs), third (biting insects), and fourth (swarms) plagues through Moses and Aaron.*

8:2 *frogs.* A judgment against the goddess of fertility and childbirth, symbolized by a frog. God's complete control of the animals shows that He is their Creator and Master.
8:3 *bedchamber.* Bedroom. *kneadingtroughs.* Bowls for preparing bread dough.
8:7 Satan can imitate God's judgments, but cannot save from them.
8:8 *Intreat.* Pray. Moses served as an intercessor for the Lord's mercy (v. 28; 9:28; 10:17).
8:9 *Glory over me.* I give you the honor of picking the time—mocking Pharaoh's sovereignty. The removal of the frogs from the land (but not the river, v. 11) whenever Pharaoh requested it showed it did not arise from natural causes, but from the Lord.
8:10 *that thou mayest know that there is none like unto the*

and thy houses, *that* they may remain in the river
only?
10 And he said, To morrow. And he said, *Be it*
according to thy word: that thou mayest know
that *there is* none like unto the LORD our God.
11 And the frogs shall depart from thee, and from
thy houses, and from thy servants, and from thy
people; they shall remain in the river only.
12 And Moses and Aaron went out from Pha-
raoh: and Moses cried unto the LORD because of
the frogs which he had brought against Pharaoh.
13 And the LORD did according to the word of
Moses; and the frogs died out of the houses, out
of the villages, and out of the fields.
14 And they gathered them together upon heaps:
and the land stank.
15 But when Pharaoh saw that there was respite,
he hardened his heart, and hearkened not unto
them; as the LORD had said.
16 ¶ And the LORD said unto Moses, Say unto
Aaron, Stretch out thy rod, and smite the dust of
the land, that it may become lice throughout all
the land of Egypt.
17 And they did so; for Aaron stretched out his
hand with his rod, and smote the dust of the
earth, and it became lice in man, and in beast; all
the dust of the land became lice throughout all
the land of Egypt.
18 And the magicians did so with their enchant-
ments to bring forth lice, but they could not: so
there were lice upon man, and upon beast.
19 Then the magicians said unto Pharaoh, This *is*
the finger of God: and Pharaoh's heart was hard-
ened, and he hearkened not unto them; as the
LORD had said.
20 ¶ And the LORD said unto Moses, Rise up early
in the morning, and stand before Pharaoh; lo,
he cometh forth to the water; and say unto him,
Thus saith the LORD, Let my people go, that they
may serve me.
21 Else, if thou wilt not let my people go, behold,
I will send swarms *of flies* upon thee, and upon
thy servants, and upon thy people, and into thy
houses: and the houses of the Egyptians shall
be full of swarms *of flies*, and also the ground
whereon they *are*.
22 And I will sever in that day the land of Goshen,
in which my people dwell, that no swarms *of flies*
shall be there; to the end thou mayest know that I
am the LORD in the midst of the earth.
23 And I will put a division between my people
and thy people: to morrow shall this sign be.
24 And the LORD did so; and there came a griev-
ous swarm *of flies* into the house of Pharaoh, and
into his servants' houses, and into all the land of
Egypt: the land was corrupted by reason of the
swarm *of flies*.
25 ¶ And Pharaoh called for Moses and for Aaron,
and said, Go ye, sacrifice to your God in the land.
26 And Moses said, It is not meet so to do; for we
shall sacrifice the abomination of the Egyptians
to the LORD our God: lo, shall we sacrifice the
abomination of the Egyptians before their eyes,
and will they not stone us?
27 We will go three days' journey into the wil-
derness, and sacrifice to the LORD our God, as he
shall command us.
28 And Pharaoh said, I will let you go, that ye may
sacrifice to the LORD your God in the wilderness;
only ye shall not go very far away: intreat for me.
29 And Moses said, Behold, I go out from thee,
and I will intreat the LORD that the swarms *of flies*
may depart from Pharaoh, from his servants, and
from his people, to morrow: but let not Pharaoh
deal deceitfully any more in not letting the people
go to sacrifice to the LORD.

LORD our God. The plagues showed God to be beyond all comparison or competitors (15:11; Deut. 33:26; 1 Sam. 2:2; 1 Kings 8:23; Isa. 40:18,25; 46:5; Jer. 10:6).

8:13 *the LORD did according to the word of Moses*. The intercession of the mediator is effective (v. 31).

8:14 *the land stank*. More disgusting humiliation for the proud idolaters (7:18,21).

8:15 *respite*. Relief. *hardened his heart*. Literally, "made it heavy," an expression in Egyptian literature for damnable guilt on judgment day. Pharaoh was responsible for his hard heart, for he abused God's mercy to avoid repentance (9:34).

8:16 *lice*. Some kind of biting insect, perhaps lice or mosquitoes. God uses weak, little things to overcome the strong.

8:19 The sorcerers were forced to confess that they had met a power greater than magic can conjure. The power of the Lord's kingdom (*finger*, 31:18) defeats the forces of the Devil and human idolatry and sorcery (Luke 11:20). No power is like the Lord.

Plagues 4–6: The Lord Sets Apart His People (8:20—9:12)

The second cycle of plagues reveals how the Lord distinguishes between His people and His enemies in His judgments (v. 22; 9:4,11). Plagues 1–3 and 6 were done through Moses and Aaron (7:19–20; 8:5–6,16–17; 9:8), but plagues 4–5 come directly from God (8:24; 9:6), for this was not sorcery but the Lord working through human instruments.

8:21 *swarms of flies*. Literally, "the swarm"; the kind of swarming creature is not specified.

8:22 *sever*. Distinguish, set apart. The Lord had chosen Israel for mercy, not judgment. The purpose is that *thou mayest know that I am the LORD in the midst of the earth*. God is present to judge and save according to His will even in the territory of His enemies.

8:23 *division*. Literally, "redemption" (Ps. 111:9; 130:7). The root means to pay the price to set free (13:13,15; 21:8), and is used of the Lord's redemption of Israel from Egypt (Deut. 7:8). Here redemption delivers not just from man's slavery but from God's wrath, like the Passover lamb (see note at 12:12–13).

8:26 *meet*. Fitting. *abomination*. Egyptians considered certain animals to be sacred, and so the sacrifices would offend.

8:28 *intreat*. Pray. Requests for prayer do not necessarily indicate saving faith (Acts 8:24).

30 And Moses went out from Pharaoh, and
intreated the LORD.
31 And the LORD did according to the word of
Moses; and he removed the swarms *of flies* from
Pharaoh, from his servants, and from his people;
there remained not one.
32 And Pharaoh hardened his heart at this time
also, neither would he let the people go.

CHAPTER 9

THEN the LORD said unto Moses, Go in unto Pha-
raoh, and tell him, Thus saith the LORD God of
the Hebrews, Let my people go, that they may
serve me.
2 For if thou refuse to let *them* go, and wilt hold
them still,
3 Behold, the hand of the LORD is upon thy cattle
which *is* in the field, upon the horses, upon the
asses, upon the camels, upon the oxen, and upon
the sheep: *there shall be* a very grievous murrain.
4 And the LORD shall sever between the cattle
of Israel and the cattle of Egypt: and there shall
nothing die of all *that is* the children's of Israel.
5 And the LORD appointed a set time, saying, To
morrow the LORD shall do this thing in the land.
6 And the LORD did that thing on the morrow,
and all the cattle of Egypt died: but of the cattle of
the children of Israel died not one.
7 And Pharaoh sent, and, behold, there was not
one of the cattle of the Israelites dead. And the
heart of Pharaoh was hardened, and he did not
let the people go.
8 ¶ And the LORD said unto Moses and unto
Aaron, Take to you handfuls of ashes of the fur-
nace, and let Moses sprinkle it toward the heaven
in the sight of Pharaoh.
9 And it shall become small dust in all the land
of Egypt, and shall be a boil breaking forth *with*
blains upon man, and upon beast, throughout all
the land of Egypt.
10 And they took ashes of the furnace, and stood
before Pharaoh; and Moses sprinkled it up toward
heaven; and it became a boil breaking forth *with*
blains upon man, and upon beast.
11 And the magicians could not stand before
Moses because of the boils; for the boil was upon
the magicians, and upon all the Egyptians.
12 And the LORD hardened the heart of Pharaoh,
and he hearkened not unto them; as the LORD had
spoken unto Moses.
13 ¶ And the LORD said unto Moses, Rise up early
in the morning, and stand before Pharaoh, and
say unto him, Thus saith the LORD God of the He-
brews, Let my people go, that they may serve me.
14 For I will at this time send all my plagues upon
thine heart, and upon thy servants, and upon thy
people; that thou mayest know that *there is* none
like me in all the earth.
15 For now I will stretch out my hand, that I may
smite thee and thy people with pestilence; and
thou shalt be cut off from the earth.

8:31 *there remained not one*. God rules over every little creature (10:19; Matt. 10:29).

Thoughts for Personal/Family Worship: Chapter 8

1. **When Christ confronts Satan's power, victory is sure. Sometimes God's people suffer great injustice; sometimes they fall into idolatry. But Christ will prevail, and the church of His elect and called will overcome (Rev. 17:14). There is no one like the Lord. How can this encourage believers in their sufferings and temptations?**
2. **In the darkest places on earth, Christ is still able to judge His enemies and save His people. Therefore, even if we are in the shadow of Satan's throne, let us hold fast to the Lord, not deny the faith, and bear witness even to death (Rev. 2:13). Christ will destroy our enemies, and His redemption will deliver us from His wrath.**

Chapter 9: ***The Lord sends the fifth (livestock), sixth (boils), and seventh (hail) plagues upon Egypt, while shielding Israel from His judgments.***

9:3 *grievous murrain*. Severe disease; same word as "pestilence" (v. 15; 5:3).

9:4 *sever*. Distinguish, set apart.

9:6 *all the cattle of Egypt died*. An insult to the Egyptian god and goddess depicted with bull or cow imagery. *All* means "many" or "all sorts," not necessarily every single one (Gen. 24:10; 1 Tim. 6:10), for a number of cattle and horses remained (v. 19; 11:5; 14:6).

9:7 *not one of the cattle of the Israelites*. God's mercy completely shielded His people from His judgment against His enemies (see notes at 8:22–23).

9:8 Hebrew slaves baked bricks in a kiln (*furnace*), so God used it to punish their masters.

9:9 *blains*. Sores. The Egyptians worshiped a goddess of war and healing, but she could not help them against the Lord, the true Warrior and Healer (15:3,26).

9:11 *magicians could not stand before Moses*. The boils particularly inflamed the knees and legs (Deut. 28:27,35). The gods of Egypt had utterly failed to defend their servants. God punishes His enemies with pain and humiliation but honors His servants.

Plagues 7–9: Devastation from the Lord (9:13—10:29)

The third cycle of plagues, like the first two, reveals God's supremacy (vv. 14,29; 10:2) and His selective judgments (9:26; 10:23). This cycle adds the theme of total disaster like nothing seen before (9:18,24; 10:6,14,22–23). The Lord worked plagues 7–9 through Moses alone (9:22–23; 10:12–13,21–22), highlighting Moses' growth into the role of God's prophet.

9:14 *all my plagues*. The Lord will no longer restrain His wrath but send complete destruction (Rev. 15:1). *upon thine heart*. God struck Pharaoh with the inward plagues of conviction of sin and horror (v. 27; 10:16–17), and still more hardness of heart (10:1,20,27). *none like me in all the earth*. God did all this to show His unique glory (see note at 8:10).

9:16 *have I raised thee up*. The Lord controlled Pharaoh's survival and stubbornness so that by the prolonged battle God could make known His glory (*name*) throughout *all the earth* (15:14–16; 18:8–12; Josh. 2:10–11).

16 And in very deed for this *cause* have I raised thee up, for to shew *in* thee my power; and that my name may be declared throughout all the earth.

17 As yet exaltest thou thyself against my people, that thou wilt not let them go?

18 Behold, to morrow about this time I will cause it to rain a very grievous hail, such as hath not been in Egypt since the foundation thereof even until now.

19 Send therefore now, *and* gather thy cattle, and all that thou hast in the field; *for upon* every man and beast which shall be found in the field, and shall not be brought home, the hail shall come down upon them, and they shall die.

20 He that feared the word of the LORD among the servants of Pharaoh made his servants and his cattle flee into the houses:

21 And he that regarded not the word of the LORD left his servants and his cattle in the field.

22 ¶ And the LORD said unto Moses, Stretch forth thine hand toward heaven, that there may be hail in all the land of Egypt, upon man, and upon beast, and upon every herb of the field, throughout the land of Egypt.

23 And Moses stretched forth his rod toward heaven: and the LORD sent thunder and hail, and the fire ran along upon the ground; and the LORD rained hail upon the land of Egypt.

24 So there was hail, and fire mingled with the hail, very grievous, such as there was none like it in all the land of Egypt since it became a nation.

25 And the hail smote throughout all the land of Egypt all that *was* in the field, both man and beast; and the hail smote every herb of the field, and brake every tree of the field.

26 Only in the land of Goshen, where the children of Israel *were*, was there no hail.

27 ¶ And Pharaoh sent, and called for Moses and Aaron, and said unto them, I have sinned this time: the LORD *is* righteous, and I and my people *are* wicked.

28 Intreat the LORD (for *it is* enough) that there be no *more* mighty thunderings and hail; and I will let you go, and ye shall stay no longer.

29 And Moses said unto him, As soon as I am gone out of the city, I will spread abroad my hands unto the LORD; *and* the thunder shall cease, neither shall there be any more hail; that thou mayest know how that the earth *is* the LORD's.

30 But as for thee and thy servants, I know that ye will not yet fear the LORD God.

31 And the flax and the barley was smitten: for the barley *was* in the ear, and the flax *was* bolled.

32 But the wheat and the rie were not smitten: for they *were* not grown up.

33 And Moses went out of the city from Pharaoh, and spread abroad his hands unto the LORD: and the thunders and hail ceased, and the rain was not poured upon the earth.

34 And when Pharaoh saw that the rain and the hail and the thunders were ceased, he sinned yet more, and hardened his heart, he and his servants.

35 And the heart of Pharaoh was hardened, neither would he let the children of Israel go; as the LORD had spoken by Moses.

CHAPTER 10

AND the LORD said unto Moses, Go in unto Pharaoh: for I have hardened his heart, and the heart of his servants, that I might shew these my signs before him:

2 And that thou mayest tell in the ears of thy son, and of thy son's son, what things I have wrought

---

9:18 *grievous*. Heavy or severe. *such as hath not been in Egypt*. The unique severity of the storm showed that we should fear God above all (v. 20).

9:20 *feared the word of the LORD*. God shows mercy to those who fear Him (1:17; Ps. 33:18; 103:11,17).

9:23 *fire ran along upon the ground*. Lightning flashed down to the ground.

9:25 *smote every herb*. Struck down every plant.

9:26 *Only in the land of Goshen*. Again, God shielded His people (8:22–23; 9:4,7).

9:27 God's judgments forced the king to confess that he had *sinned* and *the LORD is righteous*, but compelled confessions are not repentance (v. 34).

9:28 *Intreat*. Pray (see note at 8:8). *mighty thunderings*. Literally, "thunder of God."

9:31–32 *smitten*. Struck. *in the ear*. Produced grain. *bolled*. Budded. *rie*. Spelt, a kind of wheat. Egypt harvested *flax* and *barley* in February and March, *wheat* and *rie* a month later.

Thoughts for Personal/Family Worship: Chapter 9

1. **God will punish His enemies with pain, conviction of sin, and horror at His wrath. All these will fall upon the wicked on judgment day (Rev. 6:12–17; 20:11–15). Even today, the Lord may visit the wicked with these judgments. However, convictions and confessions are not repentance; at times they are accompanied by hardness of heart. Do not rest in them, but strive after the Lord with earnest prayer until you truly turn from sin to God. What is the difference between mere conviction of sin and repentance unto life?**
2. **Pharaoh's hardening reminds us that the Lord is free to save or to harden sinners as He wills, for He made us all and has the right to glorify Himself by wrath or mercy (Rom. 9:16–23). Therefore, let us fear the Lord and not tremble before the wicked, no matter how stubborn and arrogant they are. God will get glory through them one way or the other.**

Chapter 10: *The Lord hardens Pharaoh's heart again and strikes Egypt with the eighth (locusts) and ninth (darkness) plagues.*

10:1–2 Though Pharaoh sinned by hardening his heart (9:34), the Lord revealed that He ruled over sin for His holy purpose to cause many generations to know that *I am the LORD*.

in Egypt, and my signs which I have done among
them; that ye may know how that I *am* the LORD.
3 And Moses and Aaron came in unto Pharaoh,
and said unto him, Thus saith the LORD God of
the Hebrews, How long wilt thou refuse to hum-
ble thyself before me? let my people go, that they
may serve me.
4 Else, if thou refuse to let my people go, behold,
to morrow will I bring the locusts into thy coast:
5 And they shall cover the face of the earth, that
one cannot be able to see the earth: and they shall
eat the residue of that which is escaped, which
remaineth unto you from the hail, and shall eat
every tree which groweth for you out of the field:
6 And they shall fill thy houses, and the houses
of all thy servants, and the houses of all the Egyp-
tians; which neither thy fathers, nor thy fathers'
fathers have seen, since the day that they were
upon the earth unto this day. And he turned him-
self, and went out from Pharaoh.
7 And Pharaoh's servants said unto him, How
long shall this man be a snare unto us? let the
men go, that they may serve the LORD their God:
knowest thou not yet that Egypt is destroyed?
8 And Moses and Aaron were brought again unto
Pharaoh: and he said unto them, Go, serve the
LORD your God: *but* who *are* they that shall go?
9 And Moses said, We will go with our young and
with our old, with our sons and with our daugh-
ters, with our flocks and with our herds will we
go; for we *must hold* a feast unto the LORD.
10 And he said unto them, Let the LORD be so
with you, as I will let you go, and your little ones:
look *to it*; for evil *is* before you.
11 Not so: go now ye *that are* men, and serve the
LORD; for that ye did desire. And they were driven
out from Pharaoh's presence.
12 ¶ And the LORD said unto Moses, Stretch out
thine hand over the land of Egypt for the locusts,
that they may come up upon the land of Egypt,
and eat every herb of the land, *even* all that the
hail hath left.
13 And Moses stretched forth his rod over the
land of Egypt, and the LORD brought an east wind
upon the land all that day, and all *that* night; *and*
when it was morning, the east wind brought the
locusts.
14 And the locusts went up over all the land of
Egypt, and rested in all the coasts of Egypt: very
grievous *were they*; before them there were no
such locusts as they, neither after them shall be
such.
15 For they covered the face of the whole earth,
so that the land was darkened; and they did eat
every herb of the land, and all the fruit of the trees
which the hail had left: and there remained not
any green thing in the trees, or in the herbs of the
field, through all the land of Egypt.
16 ¶ Then Pharaoh called for Moses and Aaron in
haste; and he said, I have sinned against the LORD
your God, and against you.
17 Now therefore forgive, I pray thee, my sin only
this once, and intreat the LORD your God, that he
may take away from me this death only.
18 And he went out from Pharaoh, and intreated
the LORD.
19 And the LORD turned a mighty strong west
wind, which took away the locusts, and cast them
into the Red sea; there remained not one locust in
all the coasts of Egypt.
20 But the LORD hardened Pharaoh's heart, so
that he would not let the children of Israel go.
21 ¶ And the LORD said unto Moses, Stretch out
thine hand toward heaven, that there may be
darkness over the land of Egypt, even darkness
which may be felt.
22 And Moses stretched forth his hand toward
heaven; and there was a thick darkness in all the
land of Egypt three days:
23 They saw not one another, neither rose any

God's people have a duty to *tell* their children and grandchildren the mighty works of God (13:14–15).

10:3 *How long wilt thou refuse to humble thyself.* God's sovereignty does not take away in the least man's responsibility. *let my people go, that they may serve me.* The seventh and final time the Lord gave this command to Pharaoh (5:1–3; 7:16; 8:1,20; 9:1,13). See note at 5:1.

10:4 *coast.* Territory.

10:5 *residue of that which is escaped.* The agricultural produce not yet destroyed.

10:6 *which neither thy fathers, nor thy fathers' fathers have seen.* This unprecedented disaster (v. 14), like the hail (9:18,24), showed that God's wrath is more terrible than anything on earth.

10:7 *snare.* Trap.

10:10 *Let the LORD be so with you.* Sarcasm. He either threatened or accused them of *evil*.

10:14 *coasts.* Territories. *grievous.* Heavy or severe.

10:15 *herb.* Plant. God gives all men food and He can take it away (Ps. 104:14–15; Acts 14:17).

10:17 *I pray thee.* Please. *intreat.* Pray.

10:19 *Red sea.* Body of water on eastern border of Egypt. *not one locust.* See note at 8:31. *coasts.* Territories.

10:21–23 The day of the Lord's wrath is a day of *darkness* (Joel 2:1–2; Zeph. 1:15). This *thick darkness* might have been a massive dust storm (which can cause total darkness and zero visibility) or an entirely supernatural phenomenon. In any case, it paralyzed *all the land of Egypt* except Goshen for *three days.* The Egyptians viewed the Pharaoh as the son of the sun god, but the God of Israel made a mockery of Pharaoh and showed that He is the only Lord of light (Gen. 1:3).

10:24 *only let your flocks and your herds.* Pharaoh's offer to release Israel if their livestock remained (*be stayed*) was his last attempt to make Moses compromise God's clear call (v. 8; 8:25,28).

10:26 *not an hoof be left behind.* God's servants must not compromise their obedience to God's Word in the least. *thither.* To there.

from his place for three days: but all the children
of Israel had light in their dwellings.
24 ¶ And Pharaoh called unto Moses, and said,
Go ye, serve the LORD; only let your flocks and
your herds be stayed: let your little ones also go
with you.
25 And Moses said, Thou must give us also
sacrifices and burnt offerings, that we may
sacrifice unto the LORD our God.
26 Our cattle also shall go with us; there shall
not an hoof be left behind; for thereof must we
take to serve the LORD our God; and we know not
with what we must serve the LORD, until we come
thither.
27 ¶ But the LORD hardened Pharaoh's heart, and
he would not let them go.
28 And Pharaoh said unto him, Get thee from
me, take heed to thyself, see my face no more; for
in *that* day thou seest my face thou shalt die.
29 And Moses said, Thou hast spoken well, I will
see thy face again no more.

CHAPTER 11

AND the LORD said unto Moses, Yet will I bring
one plague *more* upon Pharaoh, and upon Egypt;
afterwards he will let you go hence: when he shall
let *you* go, he shall surely thrust you out hence
altogether.
2 Speak now in the ears of the people, and let
every man borrow of his neighbour, and every
woman of her neighbour, jewels of silver, and
jewels of gold.
3 And the LORD gave the people favour in the
sight of the Egyptians. Moreover the man Moses
was very great in the land of Egypt, in the sight of
Pharaoh's servants, and in the sight of the people.
4 And Moses said, Thus saith the LORD, About
midnight will I go out into the midst of Egypt:
5 And all the firstborn in the land of Egypt shall
die, from the firstborn of Pharaoh that sitteth
upon his throne, even unto the firstborn of the
maidservant that *is* behind the mill; and all the
firstborn of beasts.
6 And there shall be a great cry throughout all the
land of Egypt, such as there was none like it, nor
shall be like it any more.
7 But against any of the children of Israel shall
not a dog move his tongue, against man or beast:
that ye may know how that the LORD doth put a
difference between the Egyptians and Israel.
8 And all these thy servants shall come down
unto me, and bow down themselves unto me, say-
ing, Get thee out, and all the people that follow
thee: and after that I will go out. And he went out
from Pharaoh in a great anger.
9 And the LORD said unto Moses, Pharaoh shall
not hearken unto you; that my wonders may be
multiplied in the land of Egypt.
10 And Moses and Aaron did all these wonders

10:27 *he would not*. Literally, "he was not willing." God's hardening did not destroy Pharaoh's will but gave his will over to sin so that he was not willing to repent and obey.
10:28 *Get thee from me . . . thou shalt die*. With this death threat, Pharaoh cut off all further face-to-face conversation with Moses and shut the door against mercy.

Thoughts for Personal/Family Worship: Chapter 10

1. **Let us bow before God as Lord of all our nation's resources. He gives food and famine as He wills. He can shut down our country's industries and businesses whenever He pleases. It is the height of foolishness to turn away from the Lord and trust in ourselves or our possessions. God can make us helpless in an instant.**
2. **The Bible reveals both God's total sovereignty over all things and man's real responsibility for his willful choices. If we accept sovereignty but deny responsibility, we fall into fatalism, mysticism, and sin. If we accept responsibility but deny sovereignty, we fall into legalism, self-reliance, and pride. Even if we do not understand how these fit together, we must believe them both. How do both glorify God?**

Plague 10: Passover and Exodus from Egypt (11:1—13:22)
Chapter 11: *The Lord declares the final plague, the death of the firstborn.*

11:1 *Yet . . . one plague more*. Everything happened according to God's plan. *hence*. From here. It may be that the content of vv. 1–3 took place before Moses' last meeting with Pharaoh, and is inserted here as an explanation.
11:2 *borrow . . . jewels*. As the Lord had said before the plagues began (see note at 3:22).
11:3 Once despised and rejected, the Lord's servant had become *very great* in the esteem of the people, even the enemies of God. God honors those who honor Him (1 Sam. 2:30).
11:4 This verse resumes the narrative of Moses' last encounter with Pharaoh (10:24–29), until Moses left Pharaoh's presence (v. 8).
11:5 *firstborn*. See note at 4:22–23. Note that this was not limited to children but included the firstborn throughout the population regardless of age. The Egyptians regarded *Pharaoh* as the keeper of cosmic order and defender against chaos. For the Lord to strike all the firstborn with death shattered Egypt's sense of order and safety under their king. For death to fall upon the son of a female slave (*maidservant*) showed that all had sinned (Gen. 8:21; Ps. 51:5; 53:1–3; 58:3). Even livestock (*beasts*) must suffer, for the Egyptians had turned them into idols (see note at 9:6).
11:6 *none like it*. See note at 10:6.
11:7 *shall not a dog move his tongue*. Even the most despised animal (1 Sam. 24:14) could do no harm (Josh. 10:21)—God would shield Israel from the coming death. *the LORD doth put a difference between the Egyptians and Israel*. He has set apart His people for grace (8:22–23; 9:4,11; 10:23; 33:16; Ps. 4:3).
11:9–10 A summary of chs. 7–11. Compare 7:3–6.

Thoughts for Personal/Family Worship: Chapter 11

1. **The word of the Lord proves true. God told Moses what would happen beforehand (3:19–22; 4:21–23; 11:1)—and it did. God's great message to us in the plagues**

before Pharaoh: and the LORD hardened Pha-
raoh's heart, so that he would not let the children
of Israel go out of his land.

CHAPTER 12

AND the LORD spake unto Moses and Aaron in the
land of Egypt, saying,
2 This month *shall be* unto you the beginning of
months: it *shall be* the first month of the year to
you.
3 ¶ Speak ye unto all the congregation of Israel,
saying, In the tenth *day* of this month they shall
take to them every man a lamb, according to the
house of *their* fathers, a lamb for an house:
4 And if the household be too little for the lamb,
let him and his neighbour next unto his house
take *it* according to the number of the souls;
every man according to his eating shall make your
count for the lamb.
5 Your lamb shall be without blemish, a male of
the first year: ye shall take *it* out from the sheep,
or from the goats:
6 And ye shall keep it up until the fourteenth day
of the same month: and the whole assembly of the
congregation of Israel shall kill it in the evening.
7 And they shall take of the blood, and strike *it* on
the two side posts and on the upper door post of
the houses, wherein they shall eat it.
8 And they shall eat the flesh in that night, roast
with fire, and unleavened bread; *and* with bitter
herbs they shall eat it.
9 Eat not of it raw, nor sodden at all with water,
but roast *with* fire; his head with his legs, and with
the purtenance thereof.
10 And ye shall let nothing of it remain until the
morning; and that which remaineth of it until the
morning ye shall burn with fire.
11 ¶ And thus shall ye eat it; *with* your loins
girded, your shoes on your feet, and your staff
in your hand; and ye shall eat it in haste: it *is* the
LORD's passover.
12 For I will pass through the land of Egypt this
night, and will smite all the firstborn in the land of
Egypt, both man and beast; and against all the gods
of Egypt I will execute judgment: I *am* the LORD.
13 And the blood shall be to you for a token upon
the houses where ye *are*: and when I see the blood,
I will pass over you, and the plague shall not be
upon you to destroy *you*, when I smite the land
of Egypt.
14 And this day shall be unto you for a memorial;
and ye shall keep it a feast to the LORD through-
out your generations; ye shall keep it a feast by an
ordinance for ever.
15 Seven days shall ye eat unleavened bread; even
the first day ye shall put away leaven out of your
houses: for whosoever eateth leavened bread from
the first day until the seventh day, that soul shall
be cut off from Israel.
16 And in the first day *there shall be* an holy con-
vocation, and in the seventh day there shall be an
holy convocation to you; no manner of work shall
be done in them, save *that* which every man must
eat, that only may be done of you.
17 And ye shall observe *the feast of* unleavened

---

and Pharaoh's responses is, "I am the LORD." Therefore, let every knee bow and every tongue confess that He is Lord. One word from God outweighs all the wisdom of mankind.

2. Nothing on earth is more precious to us than our children. Yet even here the Lord reigns. When Job heard that his children had all died, he said, "The LORD gave, and the LORD hath taken away; blessed be the name of the LORD" (Job 1:21). Let us pray for grace to learn this submission so that if we lose a child, we can worship God like David (2 Sam. 12:20).

Chapter 12: *Moses receives instructions for the Passover, and God brings the people of Israel out of Egypt in triumph by the blood of the lamb.*

12:2 *This month.* March–April, called "Abib" (13:4; Deut. 16:1), or "Nisan" (Neh. 2:1).

12:3 *lamb.* Young sheep or goat.

12:4 *souls.* Persons.

12:5 *without blemish.* Perfection was required for sacrifices (v. 27) to be acceptable to God (Lev. 1:3; 1 Peter 1:19).

12:7 *strike.* Put. The manipulations of the *blood* were also done with sin offerings (Lev. 4:1–7).

12:8 *unleavened.* Flat bread made without yeast. The lamb must be roasted *with fire* (an emblem of divine wrath, 15:7; Deut. 32:22). It all must be eaten or burnt (v. 10), like the peace offerings (Lev. 7:15–17), a holy meal of fellowship shared between God and His people (24:11).

12:9 *sodden.* Boiled. *purtenance.* Middle part.

12:11 *loins girded.* Robe tied up for quick movement. *passover.* So called because the Lord passed over the homes of Israel when He came to destroy the firstborn of Egypt (vv. 13,23,27). The Passover is a type of Christ (1 Cor. 5:7).

12:12 *smite.* Strike, kill. *firstborn.* God struck down Egypt's pride and joy. See notes at 4:22–23; 11:5. Salvation came through *judgment*, redeeming God's people by God's just wrath falling upon the wicked (6:6; Ps. 78:49). *against all the gods of Egypt.* The Lord humiliated their gods by their inability to protect their worshipers from His wrath or to prevent His beloved from going free (Ps. 97:3,7; 136:10). Israel had worshiped Egypt's idols (Josh. 24:14; Ezek. 20:5–9; 23:3), but through this judgment God caused all to know that *I am the LORD* (6:7).

12:13 *token.* Sign for the Lord to *see* so that He did not *destroy* the firstborn of Israel. The lamb must die so that they would live—salvation by substitution of a sacrifice (v. 27; Gen. 22:8,13). God's loving election of Israel did not by itself protect them from death; His grace must provide redemption through *blood*, by which sin is atoned (Lev. 17:11).

12:14 *memorial.* Time for remembering.

12:15 See note at 13:7.

12:16 *convocation.* Assembly. *save.* Except.

12:17 *selfsame day.* Same day.

bread; for in this selfsame day have I brought your
armies out of the land of Egypt: therefore shall ye
observe this day in your generations by an ordinance for ever.
18 ¶ In the first *month*, on the fourteenth day of
the month at even, ye shall eat unleavened bread,
until the one and twentieth day of the month at
even.
19 Seven days shall there be no leaven found in
your houses: for whosoever eateth that which is
leavened, even that soul shall be cut off from the
congregation of Israel, whether he be a stranger,
or born in the land.
20 Ye shall eat nothing leavened; in all your habitations shall ye eat unleavened bread.
21 ¶ Then Moses called for all the elders of Israel,
and said unto them, Draw out and take you a
lamb according to your families, and kill the
passover.
22 And ye shall take a bunch of hyssop, and dip
it in the blood that *is* in the bason, and strike the
lintel and the two side posts with the blood that *is*
in the bason; and none of you shall go out at the
door of his house until the morning.
23 For the LORD will pass through to smite the
Egyptians; and when he seeth the blood upon
the lintel, and on the two side posts, the LORD
will pass over the door, and will not suffer the destroyer to come in unto your houses to smite *you*.
24 And ye shall observe this thing for an ordinance to thee and to thy sons for ever.
25 And it shall come to pass, when ye be come
to the land which the LORD will give you, according as he hath promised, that ye shall keep this
service.
26 And it shall come to pass, when your children
shall say unto you, What mean ye by this service?
27 That ye shall say, It *is* the sacrifice of the
LORD's passover, who passed over the houses of
the children of Israel in Egypt, when he smote
the Egyptians, and delivered our houses. And the
people bowed the head and worshipped.
28 And the children of Israel went away, and did
as the LORD had commanded Moses and Aaron,
so did they.
29 ¶ And it came to pass, that at midnight the
LORD smote all the firstborn in the land of Egypt,
from the firstborn of Pharaoh that sat on his
throne unto the firstborn of the captive that *was*
in the dungeon; and all the firstborn of cattle.
30 And Pharaoh rose up in the night, he, and all
his servants, and all the Egyptians; and there was a
great cry in Egypt; for *there was* not a house where
there was not one dead.
31 ¶ And he called for Moses and Aaron by night,
and said, Rise up, *and* get you forth from among
my people, both ye and the children of Israel; and
go, serve the LORD, as ye have said.
32 Also take your flocks and your herds, as ye
have said, and be gone; and bless me also.
33 And the Egyptians were urgent upon the
people, that they might send them out of the land
in haste; for they said, We *be* all dead *men*.
34 And the people took their dough before it was
leavened, their kneadingtroughs being bound up
in their clothes upon their shoulders.
35 And the children of Israel did according to
the word of Moses; and they borrowed of the
Egyptians jewels of silver, and jewels of gold, and
raiment:
36 And the LORD gave the people favour in the
sight of the Egyptians, so that they lent unto them
such things as they required. And they spoiled the
Egyptians.
37 ¶ And the children of Israel journeyed from
Rameses to Succoth, about six hundred thousand
on foot *that were* men, beside children.
38 And a mixed multitude went up also with
them; and flocks, and herds, *even* very much
cattle.
39 And they baked unleavened cakes of the
dough which they brought forth out of Egypt, for
it was not leavened; because they were thrust out
of Egypt, and could not tarry, neither had they
prepared for themselves any victual.
40 ¶ Now the sojourning of the children of Israel,

12:19 *stranger*. Foreigner.
12:20 *habitations*. Homes.
12:21 *Moses* kept the Passover by faith in the mere promise of God's salvation (Heb. 11:28).
12:22 *hyssop*. Perhaps Syrian oregano (za'atar), an aromatic herb about 2–4 feet tall. It was used for ritual cleansing (Lev. 14:4,6,49–52; Num. 19:6,18), a symbol of spiritual cleansing (Ps. 51:7). *bason*. basin or bowl. *lintel . . . side posts*. Frame around a door.
12:23 *smite*. Strike, kill.
12:25 Israel's first public *service* of worship as a congregation (v. 16).
12:26 *your children*. See 13:8.
12:31 *called for Moses and Aaron by night, and said*. Pharaoh did not personally meet them (10:29), but sent a proclamation by messengers (11:8).
12:34 *kneadingtroughs*. Bowls for preparing dough.
12:35 *borrowed*. Asked. *raiment*. Clothing. Redemption makes former slaves rich.
12:36 *lent*. Gave. *required*. Asked. *spoiled*. Plundered.
12:37 *Rameses*. Or Raamses (see notes at 1:11; Gen. 47:11). *Succoth*. East of the Nile delta. As He promised Abraham, God had multiplied the family of seventy that went down to Egypt into *six hundred thousand* fighting *men*, plus others (see note at 1:7). The word *thousand* can mean 1,000 individuals (18:21) or a clan or military unit of indefinite number (Judg. 6:15). In this case, the 100-plus talents of silver collected in the census apparently requires the term to be taken as a thousand people (see note at 38:25–26).
12:38 *mixed multitude*. People from other ethnic groups (Num. 11:4).
12:39 *tarry*. Wait. *victual*. Food.

who dwelt in Egypt, *was* four hundred and thirty
years.
41 And it came to pass at the end of the four hun-
dred and thirty years, even the selfsame day it
came to pass, that all the hosts of the LORD went
out from the land of Egypt.
42 It *is* a night to be much observed unto the LORD
for bringing them out from the land of Egypt: this
is that night of the LORD to be observed of all the
children of Israel in their generations.
43 ¶ And the LORD said unto Moses and Aaron,
This *is* the ordinance of the passover: There shall
no stranger eat thereof:
44 But every man's servant that is bought for
money, when thou hast circumcised him, then
shall he eat thereof.
45 A foreigner and an hired servant shall not eat
thereof.
46 In one house shall it be eaten; thou shalt not
carry forth ought of the flesh abroad out of the
house; neither shall ye break a bone thereof.
47 All the congregation of Israel shall keep it.
48 And when a stranger shall sojourn with thee,
and will keep the passover to the LORD, let all his
males be circumcised, and then let him come near
and keep it; and he shall be as one that is born in
the land: for no uncircumcised person shall eat
thereof.
49 One law shall be to him that is homeborn, and
unto the stranger that sojourneth among you.
50 Thus did all the children of Israel; as the LORD
commanded Moses and Aaron, so did they.
51 And it came to pass the selfsame day, *that* the
LORD did bring the children of Israel out of the
land of Egypt by their armies.

CHAPTER 13

AND the LORD spake unto Moses, saying,
2 Sanctify unto me all the firstborn, whatsoever
openeth the womb among the children of Israel,
both of man and of beast: it *is* mine.
3 ¶ And Moses said unto the people, Remember
this day, in which ye came out from Egypt, out of
the house of bondage; for by strength of hand the
LORD brought you out from this *place*: there shall
no leavened bread be eaten.
4 This day came ye out in the month Abib.
5 ¶ And it shall be when the LORD shall bring
thee into the land of the Canaanites, and the Hit-
tites, and the Amorites, and the Hivites, and the
Jebusites, which he sware unto thy fathers to give
thee, a land flowing with milk and honey, that
thou shalt keep this service in this month.
6 Seven days thou shalt eat unleavened bread,
and in the seventh day *shall be* a feast to the LORD.
7 Unleavened bread shall be eaten seven days;
and there shall no leavened bread be seen with
thee, neither shall there be leaven seen with thee
in all thy quarters.
8 ¶ And thou shalt shew thy son in that day, say-
ing, *This is done* because of that *which* the LORD
did unto me when I came forth out of Egypt.
9 And it shall be for a sign unto thee upon thine
hand, and for a memorial between thine eyes, that
the LORD's law may be in thy mouth: for with a

12:40 *sojourning.* Dwelling as foreigners. *four hundred and thirty years.* The time since Jacob went to Egypt, when the last covenant promise was given to the patriarchs (Gen. 46:3–4; Gal. 3:16–17).
12:41 *selfsame day.* Same day. God fulfilled His promise that their enslavement would last four centuries (Gen. 15:13; Acts 7:6). *hosts.* Armies.
12:43 *stranger.* Foreigner.
12:46 *neither shall ye break a bone thereof.* Fulfilled in Christ's crucifixion (John 19:31–37).
12:47–49 *sojourn.* Dwell as a foreigner. *All the congregation* but only the *circumcised* ate the Passover; it was a covenant meal requiring the sign of the covenant (Gen. 17:11).
12:50 *as the LORD commanded.* Worship must be done in obedience to the Word (v. 28; 39:1).
12:51 *selfsame day.* Same day.

Thoughts for Personal/Family Worship: Chapter 12

1. **Christ's work of salvation upon the cross was also a work of judgment against Satan and this world for the sake of the glory of God (John 12:27–33; Col. 2:15; Heb. 2:14). Christ is the Lamb that bought people from all nations for God, redeeming them from God's wrath with His blood (John 1:29; Eph. 1:7; Rev. 5:9) and setting them free from sin (1 Peter 1:18–19). He ultimately will save His people by pouring out judgment upon this world (2 Thess. 1:8; Rev. 19:1–3).**
2. **We must remember His sacrifice by preaching the gospel in public worship, celebrating the Lord's Supper, and catechizing our children. Why is it so important for each generation to train the children in the knowledge of God's saving ways?**

Chapter 13: *The Lord gives further instructions for the firstborn and feast of unleavened bread and leads Israel out by the fiery cloud of His presence.*

13:2 *Sanctify.* Set apart as holy. *mine.* When God's judgment fell on the oldest sons of Egypt but Israel was spared by the blood of the lamb, Israel's oldest sons became God's possession (Num. 3:13; 8:17). The *firstborn* were an example of what was true of all Israel, God's *firstborn* son (4:22), and His holy people and special possession (19:5–6; Deut. 7:6). Christ is the supreme *firstborn*, holy to the Lord (Luke 1:35; 2:23).
13:3 *by strength of hand the LORD brought you out.* This repeated phrase (vv. 9,14,16) calls God's people to never forget their salvation from slavery by the power of grace alone.
13:5 *milk and honey.* See note at 3:8.
13:7 *Unleavened bread* was a reminder of their sudden removal from Egypt (12:39; Deut. 16:3). As the feasts reminded Israel, so the Lord's Supper proclaims the Lord's death until He comes (1 Cor. 11:26). *leaven.* Yeast, a symbol of impurity (23:18; 34:25; Luke 12:1). God's people must worship God in purity (1 Cor. 5:6–8). *quarters.* Territories.
13:9 *memorial.* Reminder.

strong hand hath the LORD brought thee out of Egypt.

10 Thou shalt therefore keep this ordinance in his season from year to year.

11 ¶ And it shall be when the LORD shall bring thee into the land of the Canaanites, as he sware unto thee and to thy fathers, and shall give it thee,

12 That thou shalt set apart unto the LORD all that openeth the matrix, and every firstling that cometh of a beast which thou hast; the males *shall be* the LORD's.

13 And every firstling of an ass thou shalt redeem with a lamb; and if thou wilt not redeem it, then thou shalt break his neck: and all the firstborn of man among thy children shalt thou redeem.

14 ¶ And it shall be when thy son asketh thee in time to come, saying, What *is* this? that thou shalt say unto him, By strength of hand the LORD brought us out from Egypt, from the house of bondage:

15 And it came to pass, when Pharaoh would hardly let us go, that the LORD slew all the firstborn in the land of Egypt, both the firstborn of man, and the firstborn of beast: therefore I sacrifice to the LORD all that openeth the matrix, being males; but all the firstborn of my children I redeem.

16 And it shall be for a token upon thine hand, and for frontlets between thine eyes: for by strength of hand the LORD brought us forth out of Egypt.

17 ¶ And it came to pass, when Pharaoh had let the people go, that God led them not *through* the way of the land of the Philistines, although that *was* near; for God said, Lest peradventure the people repent when they see war, and they return to Egypt:

18 But God led the people about, *through* the way of the wilderness of the Red sea: and the children of Israel went up harnessed out of the land of Egypt.

19 And Moses took the bones of Joseph with him: for he had straitly sworn the children of Israel, saying, God will surely visit you; and ye shall carry up my bones away hence with you.

20 ¶ And they took their journey from Succoth, and encamped in Etham, in the edge of the wilderness.

21 And the LORD went before them by day in a pillar of a cloud, to lead them the way; and by night in a pillar of fire, to give them light; to go by day and night:

22 He took not away the pillar of the cloud by day, nor the pillar of fire by night, *from* before the people.

CHAPTER 14

AND the LORD spake unto Moses, saying,

2 Speak unto the children of Israel, that they turn and encamp before Pi-hahiroth, between Migdol and the sea, over against Baal-zephon: before it shall ye encamp by the sea.

13:12 *matrix.* Womb. *firstling.* First offspring.

13:14 *when thy son asketh thee.* Parents must teach children of God's great works (Ps. 78:4). Discussion with children in the form of questions and answers is a good method for family worship.

13:15 *hardly.* Stubbornly refused to. *matrix.* Womb.

13:16 *frontlets.* Some Jews have applied this command by tying small boxes (phylacteries) containing Scriptures to the head and arm (Matt. 23:5). But *it shall be* refers to the practice of redeeming the firstborn, an activity of remembrance compared to a reminder tied to the body.

13:17 *Lest.* Unless. *peradventure.* Perhaps (not in Hebrew text). The road northeast toward *the Philistines* was guarded by Egyptian fortresses and blocked by a wide canal. Though the Lord could easily overcome these obstacles, He anticipated the retreat they could provoke.

13:18 *Red sea.* From the Greek; the Hebrew phrase may be translated "sea of reeds" or "sea of the end." The phrase does not refer to a marshy lake, which would not be deep enough to drown the Egyptian army (15:5), but to the Red Sea and its arms, the Gulf of Suez and the Gulf of Aqaba (Num. 33:10–11; Deut. 2:1). *harnessed.* Armed and ready for battle.

13:19 *straitly sworn the children of Israel.* Placed the descendants of Israel under a solemn vow. God was fulfilling purposes revealed centuries earlier to the patriarchs (Gen. 50:24–25).

13:20 *Etham.* Location uncertain. *wilderness.* Sparsely populated, rocky desert of Sinai.

13:21–22 The *pillar* of *cloud* and *fire* assured Israel that God was with them, directed them in the way they should go, and filled them with awe at His holy majesty. From it God spoke His word to Moses (33:9–11), and its movements are called the "commandment" (Hebrew, "mouth") of the Lord to direct their journeys (17:1; Num. 9:17–18).

Thoughts for Personal/Family Worship: Chapter 13

1. **If Christ bought us with His blood, then we no longer belong to ourselves but to Him and must live for His glory (1 Cor. 6:19–20). Redeeming love produces personal dedication and holiness, a willing giving of ourselves to the One who saved us (Rom. 12:1; Titus 2:14). Christians, let us live under the banner, "He died for me; I'll live for Him."**
2. **The Lord is with His people. The cloud of glory was a public revelation to the whole people of God's presence and will, similar to the public revelation of the Scriptures given to the church, in which believers see the glory of Christ (2 Cor. 4:6). Christ assures believers that God is with them, directs them, and fills them with awe at His glory. How can Christians seek a deeper experience of Christ through the Word?**

Salvation to the Glory of God (14:1—15:21)

Chapter 14: ***The Lord hardened Pharaoh's heart to stage total victory for His glory in the parting of the Red Sea.***

14:2 *Pi-hahiroth.* Mouth of the canal. *Migdol.* Egyptian fortress. *the sea.* The Red Sea. *Baal-zephon.* Shrine to a major Canaanite god. The precise locations of these sites are uncertain.

3 For Pharaoh will say of the children of Israel,
They *are* entangled in the land, the wilderness
hath shut them in.
4 And I will harden Pharaoh's heart, that he shall
follow after them; and I will be honoured upon
Pharaoh, and upon all his host; that the Egyptians
may know that I *am* the LORD. And they did so.
5 ¶ And it was told the king of Egypt that the
people fled: and the heart of Pharaoh and of his
servants was turned against the people, and they
said, Why have we done this, that we have let
Israel go from serving us?
6 And he made ready his chariot, and took his
people with him:
7 And he took six hundred chosen chariots, and
all the chariots of Egypt, and captains over every
one of them.
8 And the LORD hardened the heart of Pharaoh
king of Egypt, and he pursued after the children
of Israel: and the children of Israel went out with
an high hand.
9 But the Egyptians pursued after them, all the
horses *and* chariots of Pharaoh, and his horsemen,
and his army, and overtook them encamping by
the sea, beside Pi-hahiroth, before Baal-zephon.
10 ¶ And when Pharaoh drew nigh, the chil-
dren of Israel lifted up their eyes, and, behold, the
Egyptians marched after them; and they were sore
afraid: and the children of Israel cried out unto
the LORD.
11 And they said unto Moses, Because *there were*
no graves in Egypt, hast thou taken us away to die
in the wilderness? wherefore hast thou dealt thus
with us, to carry us forth out of Egypt?
12 *Is* not this the word that we did tell thee in
Egypt, saying, Let us alone, that we may serve the
Egyptians? For *it had been* better for us to serve
the Egyptians, than that we should die in the
wilderness.
13 ¶ And Moses said unto the people, Fear ye
not, stand still, and see the salvation of the LORD,
which he will shew to you to day: for the Egyptians
whom ye have seen to day, ye shall see them again
no more for ever.
14 The LORD shall fight for you, and ye shall hold
your peace.
15 ¶ And the LORD said unto Moses, Wherefore
criest thou unto me? speak unto the children of
Israel, that they go forward:
16 But lift thou up thy rod, and stretch out thine
hand over the sea, and divide it: and the children
of Israel shall go on dry *ground* through the midst
of the sea.
17 And I, behold, I will harden the hearts of the
Egyptians, and they shall follow them: and I will
get me honour upon Pharaoh, and upon all his
host, upon his chariots, and upon his horsemen.
18 And the Egyptians shall know that I *am* the
LORD, when I have gotten me honour upon Pha-
raoh, upon his chariots, and upon his horsemen.
19 ¶ And the angel of God, which went before the
camp of Israel, removed and went behind them;
and the pillar of the cloud went from before their
face, and stood behind them:
20 And it came between the camp of the Egyp-
tians and the camp of Israel; and it was a cloud
and darkness *to them*, but it gave light by night *to*
these: so that the one came not near the other all
the night.
21 And Moses stretched out his hand over the
sea; and the LORD caused the sea to go *back* by a
strong east wind all that night, and made the sea
dry *land*, and the waters were divided.
22 And the children of Israel went into the midst
of the sea upon the dry *ground*: and the waters
were a wall unto them on their right hand, and
on their left.
23 ¶ And the Egyptians pursued, and went in

14:3 *entangled.* Confused. Obedience to God may appear foolish to human nature.
14:4 *honoured upon.* Glorified over (vv. 17–18). *host.* Army. God uses His sovereign control over good and evil to stage the battle so that people will *know that I am the LORD*.
14:5 *Why have we done this.* The wicked quickly forget the mighty works of the Lord.
14:6–7 *chariot.* Open, two-wheeled, horse-drawn carriage for driver and archer. Swift, agile, and thunderous, the hundreds of chariots of Egypt understandably terrified their former slaves.
14:10 *nigh.* Near. *sore.* Very.
14:11 *wherefore.* Why. Despite all the displays of the Lord's power against Egypt, Israel quickly fell into despair and accusations against Moses (and, by implication, the Lord).
14:13 The *salvation of the LORD* rescues from destruction and overcomes enemies. Manpower and technology are nothing compared to God (Ps. 20:7; Isa. 31:1–3).
14:14 *The LORD shall fight for you.* Salvation is by grace alone. *hold your peace.* Be quiet. Though God often works through means, He can also work without our help.
14:16 *thy rod.* Symbolic instrument of God's power (4:2,17; 7:9,15). On the third day, the Creator divided the *sea* and made *dry* ground (Gen. 1:9–10). *through the midst of the sea.* Probably the northern part of the Gulf of Suez. See note at 13:18.
14:17 *get me honour upon.* Glorify myself over.
14:19 *angel of God.* The angel of the Lord, who is the Lord (3:2–4; 13:21), a Christophany or preincarnate appearance of Christ. *removed.* Moved. God is the shield of His people (Ps. 3:3; 27:5; 91:4; Isa. 4:5–6).
14:22 *waters were a wall.* Supernatural display of the awesome power of the Creator (Ps. 33:6–9). Moses led them into the divided sea by faith (Heb. 11:29).
14:24 *morning watch.* Early morning hours before dawn. *looked unto.* Perhaps showed His glory in a thunderstorm (Ps. 77:16–20). *troubled.* Frightened and confused.
14:25 *took off.* Turned aside. *drave them heavily.* Drove them with difficulty.
14:27 *to his strength.* To its ordinary appearance and depth.
14:28–29 *there remained not so much as one of them.*

after them to the midst of the sea, *even* all Pharaoh's horses, his chariots, and his horsemen.
24 And it came to pass, that in the morning watch the LORD looked unto the host of the Egyptians through the pillar of fire and of the cloud, and troubled the host of the Egyptians,
25 And took off their chariot wheels, that they drave them heavily: so that the Egyptians said, Let us flee from the face of Israel; for the LORD fighteth for them against the Egyptians.
26 ¶ And the LORD said unto Moses, Stretch out thine hand over the sea, that the waters may come again upon the Egyptians, upon their chariots, and upon their horsemen.
27 And Moses stretched forth his hand over the sea, and the sea returned to his strength when the morning appeared; and the Egyptians fled against it; and the LORD overthrew the Egyptians in the midst of the sea.
28 And the waters returned, and covered the chariots, and the horsemen, *and* all the host of Pharaoh that came into the sea after them; there remained not so much as one of them.
29 But the children of Israel walked upon dry *land* in the midst of the sea; and the waters *were* a wall unto them on their right hand, and on their left.
30 Thus the LORD saved Israel that day out of the hand of the Egyptians; and Israel saw the Egyptians dead upon the sea shore.
31 And Israel saw that great work which the LORD did upon the Egyptians: and the people feared the LORD, and believed the LORD, and his servant Moses.

CHAPTER 15

THEN sang Moses and the children of Israel this song unto the LORD, and spake, saying, I will sing unto the LORD, for he hath triumphed gloriously: the horse and his rider hath he thrown into the sea.
2 The LORD *is* my strength and song, and he is become my salvation: he *is* my God, and I will prepare him an habitation; my father's God, and I will exalt him.
3 The LORD *is* a man of war: the LORD *is* his name.
4 Pharaoh's chariots and his host hath he cast into the sea: his chosen captains also are drowned in the Red sea.
5 The depths have covered them: they sank into the bottom as a stone.
6 Thy right hand, O LORD, is become glorious in power: thy right hand, O LORD, hath dashed in pieces the enemy.
7 And in the greatness of thine excellency thou hast overthrown them that rose up against thee: thou sentest forth thy wrath, *which* consumed them as stubble.
8 And with the blast of thy nostrils the waters were gathered together, the floods stood upright as an heap, *and* the depths were congealed in the heart of the sea.
9 The enemy said, I will pursue, I will overtake, I will divide the spoil; my lust shall be satisfied upon them; I will draw my sword, my hand shall destroy them.
10 Thou didst blow with thy wind, the sea covered them: they sank as lead in the mighty waters.
11 Who *is* like unto thee, O LORD, among the

Another sign of total sovereignty (8:31; 10:19). The same *sea* was destruction for one people and salvation for another, for God distinguished between Egypt and *Israel* (8:22; 9:4,11,26; 10:23; 11:7).

14:30–31 God's *great work* when He *saved Israel* moved them to belief and fear toward the Lord and belief in His prophet—sadly, however, not with true conversion.

Thoughts for Personal/Family Worship: Chapter 14

1. **God's ways can seem foolish, but the Lord designs them so that He is glorified in our weakness. God finds us in hopeless situations of spiritual death, only to raise us to life by grace alone for His glory alone (Eph. 2:1–10). Christians continue to experience this as they fight sin, Satan, and the world. We must move forward in obedience to God when all means fail us, waiting upon the Creator and Redeemer (2 Chron. 20:1–30; Ps. 27:14; 130:5; Isa. 30:15). What spiritual challenge or crisis are you facing?**
2. **Passing through the sea marked a decisive break from Israel's former subjection to Pharaoh, just as baptism is a sign of breaking from sin's mastery and beginning to live to God (Rom. 6:3–4,11). But fear and faith can be superficial and temporary, especially when based on outward signs (John 2:23—3:3; 1 Cor. 10:1–11). Do not rely on outward signs and seals, but rest your hope upon Christ and a living union with Him.**

Chapter 15: ***Moses and Israel sang the praises of their Savior, and experienced the grace of His provision in the wilderness.***

15:1 *I will sing*. Songs of praise are a fitting response to salvation (14:30; Rev. 15:3). *triumphed gloriously*. Literally, "rose up to rise up," was super exalted; same root as "excellency" (v. 7).

15:2 *my strength and song … my salvation*. See Ps. 118:14; Isa. 12:2. *I will prepare him an habitation*. Or, "I will praise Him." *my father's God*. Collective reference to godly ancestors back to Abraham (3:6,13–16). *exalt*. Lift up in honor.

15:3 *man of war*. Soldier, warrior.

15:4 *host*. Army.

15:5–10 Pharaoh's army *rose up against* the Lord, but He threw them down and they *sank as lead* into the *depths* and *bottom*, and He rose up in victory (v. 1) to be praised (v. 2).

15:6 *is become*. Is.

15:7 *excellency*. Majesty. *consumed them as stubble*. Metaphor of God's wrath as fire (Lev. 9:24—10:3), expressing His holiness (3:2,5)

15:8 *blast of thy nostrils*. Figure of speech for God's powerful anger. *congealed*. Thickened, as when water stood up like a solid wall (14:22).

15:9–10 *lust*. Desire, literally, "soul." The repeated *I will* highlights the pride of the enemy, suddenly silenced by the single *Thou didst* of the Lord's judgment.

15:11 God's works produce fear (*fearful*) and awe (*wonders*)

gods? who *is* like thee, glorious in holiness, fearful
in praises, doing wonders?
12 Thou stretchedst out thy right hand, the earth
swallowed them.
13 Thou in thy mercy hast led forth the people
which thou hast redeemed: thou hast guided *them*
in thy strength unto thy holy habitation.
14 The people shall hear, *and* be afraid: sorrow
shall take hold on the inhabitants of Palestina.
15 Then the dukes of Edom shall be amazed; the
mighty men of Moab, trembling shall take hold
upon them; all the inhabitants of Canaan shall
melt away.
16 Fear and dread shall fall upon them; by the
greatness of thine arm they shall be *as* still as a
stone; till thy people pass over, O LORD, till the
people pass over, *which* thou hast purchased.
17 Thou shalt bring them in, and plant them in
the mountain of thine inheritance, *in* the place, O
LORD, *which* thou hast made for thee to dwell in,
in the Sanctuary, O Lord, *which* thy hands have
established.
18 The LORD shall reign for ever and ever.
19 For the horse of Pharaoh went in with his
chariots and with his horsemen into the sea, and
the LORD brought again the waters of the sea
upon them; but the children of Israel went on dry
land in the midst of the sea.
20 ¶ And Miriam the prophetess, the sister of
Aaron, took a timbrel in her hand; and all the
women went out after her with timbrels and with
dances.
21 And Miriam answered them, Sing ye to the
LORD, for he hath triumphed gloriously; the
horse and his rider hath he thrown into the sea.
22 So Moses brought Israel from the Red sea, and
they went out into the wilderness of Shur; and
they went three days in the wilderness, and found
no water.
23 ¶ And when they came to Marah, they could
not drink of the waters of Marah, for they *were*
bitter: therefore the name of it was called Marah.
24 And the people murmured against Moses, say-
ing, What shall we drink?
25 And he cried unto the LORD; and the LORD
shewed him a tree, *which* when he had cast into
the waters, the waters were made sweet: there he
made for them a statute and an ordinance, and
there he proved them,
26 And said, If thou wilt diligently hearken to the
voice of the LORD thy God, and wilt do that which
is right in his sight, and wilt give ear to his com-
mandments, and keep all his statutes, I will put
none of these diseases upon thee, which I have
brought upon the Egyptians: for I *am* the LORD
that healeth thee.
27 ¶ And they came to Elim, where *were* twelve
wells of water, and threescore and ten palm trees:
and they encamped there by the waters.

CHAPTER 16

AND they took their journey from Elim, and all
the congregation of the children of Israel came
unto the wilderness of Sin, which *is* between
Elim and Sinai, on the fifteenth day of the second

---

at His *holiness*, which is not only moral perfection, but incomparable excellence in every way (1 Sam. 2:2; Isa. 6:1–3; 40:25).
15:13 *mercy*. Faithful love (34:6–7). *led . . . guided*. Like a shepherd (Ps. 78:52; Isa. 63:11). *redeemed*. Rescued from slavery and purchased for Himself (v. 16; 6:6–7). *habitation*. Home; see note at v. 17.
15:14 *Palestina*. Philistia.
15:15 *dukes*. See note at Gen. 36:15.
15:16 The news of how God caused the Egyptians to sink "as a stone" (v. 5) will paralyze the peoples of Canaan with fear so they are *as still as a stone* (Josh. 2:9–11; 9:9; cf. 1 Chron. 14:17).
15:17 *mountain of thine inheritance*. The singular *mountain* refers to Canaan as a hilly region (Num. 13:17), the holy land (*Sanctuary*) of the Lord (Ps. 78:54–55; Zech. 2:12).
15:18 *reign for ever*. Salvation reveals God's sovereignty as grace breaks in to conquer, rescue, and establish God's kingdom (Isa. 52:7; Rev. 11:15; 19:6).
15:20 *timbrel*. Tambourine.

Israel in the Wilderness with God (15:22—18:27)

Tests and Crises of Faith (15:22—17:16)

15:22 *wilderness of Shur*. Desert east of Egypt in northern Sinai peninsula. *three days . . . no water*. They were in danger of dying of thirst.
15:24 *murmured*. A tragic failure of their faith so soon after God's miracles (Ps. 106:12–13).
15:25–26 The Lord used trials to test (*proved*) whether they would hear (*hearken*) and obey *his commandments* or fall under God's judgments like the *Egyptians*. *I am the LORD that healeth thee*. He rules over sickness and health (Deut. 32:39; Job 5:18; Ps. 103:3; 107:17–22).
15:27 Israel traveled south through the coastal area of the Sinai peninsula, for the next stop after *Elim* was by the Red Sea (Num. 33:10). *threescore and ten*. Seventy. *encamped*. Set up camp.

Thoughts for Personal/Family Worship: Chapter 15

1. **Sing to the Lord! He is the strength and salvation of His people; He must also be our song. Much worship today revolves around our feelings, but biblical worship revolves around who God is and what He does for His people. The song of Moses teaches Christians to praise Him for His works in Christ, for they reveal His glory.**
2. **When we go from worship on the Lord's Day to the painful trials of the week, let us be careful not to fall into murmuring. Difficult providences prove our obedience and draw us to depend on the Mediator daily for His sweet grace. How are you being tested? How can you respond in a way that honors God?**

Chapter 16: *Israel grumbles bitterly again, and the Lord provides meat and manna, training them to trust Him and keep the Sabbath.*

16:1 *Sin*. Not related to the English word "sin."

month after their departing out of the land of
Egypt.
2 And the whole congregation of the children of
Israel murmured against Moses and Aaron in the
wilderness:
3 And the children of Israel said unto them,
Would to God we had died by the hand of the
LORD in the land of Egypt, when we sat by the
flesh pots, *and* when we did eat bread to the full;
for ye have brought us forth into this wilderness,
to kill this whole assembly with hunger.
4 ¶ Then said the LORD unto Moses, Behold, I
will rain bread from heaven for you; and the peo-
ple shall go out and gather a certain rate every day,
that I may prove them, whether they will walk in
my law, or no.
5 And it shall come to pass, that on the sixth day
they shall prepare *that* which they bring in; and it
shall be twice as much as they gather daily.
6 And Moses and Aaron said unto all the children
of Israel, At even, then ye shall know that the LORD
hath brought you out from the land of Egypt:
7 And in the morning, then ye shall see the glory
of the LORD; for that he heareth your murmur-
ings against the LORD: and what *are* we, that ye
murmur against us?
8 And Moses said, *This shall be*, when the LORD
shall give you in the evening flesh to eat, and in
the morning bread to the full; for that the LORD
heareth your murmurings which ye murmur
against him: and what *are* we? your murmurings
are not against us, but against the LORD.
9 ¶ And Moses spake unto Aaron, Say unto all
the congregation of the children of Israel, Come
near before the LORD: for he hath heard your
murmurings.
10 And it came to pass, as Aaron spake unto the
whole congregation of the children of Israel, that
they looked toward the wilderness, and, behold,
the glory of the LORD appeared in the cloud.
11 ¶ And the LORD spake unto Moses, saying,
12 I have heard the murmurings of the children
of Israel: speak unto them, saying, At even ye shall
eat flesh, and in the morning ye shall be filled with
bread; and ye shall know that I *am* the LORD your
God.
13 And it came to pass, that at even the quails
came up, and covered the camp: and in the morn-
ing the dew lay round about the host.
14 And when the dew that lay was gone up,
behold, upon the face of the wilderness *there lay*
a small round thing, *as* small as the hoar frost on
the ground.
15 And when the children of Israel saw *it*, they
said one to another, It *is* manna: for they wist not
what it *was*. And Moses said unto them, This *is*
the bread which the LORD hath given you to eat.
16 ¶ This *is* the thing which the LORD hath com-
manded, Gather of it every man according to his
eating, an omer for every man, *according to* the
number of your persons; take ye every man for
them which *are* in his tents.
17 And the children of Israel did so, and gathered,
some more, some less.
18 And when they did mete *it* with an omer, he
that gathered much had nothing over, and he that
gathered little had no lack; they gathered every
man according to his eating.
19 And Moses said, Let no man leave of it till the
morning.
20 Notwithstanding they hearkened not unto
Moses; but some of them left of it until the morn-
ing, and it bred worms, and stank: and Moses was
wroth with them.
21 And they gathered it every morning, every
man according to his eating: and when the sun
waxed hot, it melted.
22 ¶ And it came to pass, *that* on the sixth day
they gathered twice as much bread, two omers for
one *man*: and all the rulers of the congregation
came and told Moses.
23 And he said unto them, This *is that* which the

16:3 *Would to God*. If only. *flesh pots*. Containers of meat. Unbelief causes men to forget the oppression of sin, to idealize its pleasures, and to accuse God of hatred.

16:4 *I will rain*. The word used of the plague of hail (9:18). God might have rightly destroyed such grumblers with a plague, but He rained down mercy. *certain rate*. Daily portion. *prove*. Test. The Lord used hunger and manna to train Israel to obey Him by faith, relying humbly on whatever He decrees (Deut. 8:2–3). Obedience to God's *law* did not begin at Mt. Sinai; Abraham kept it (Gen. 17:1; 18:19; 26:5), and God expected it of Israel (15:26; 18:16).

16:5 *sixth day . . . twice*. Provision for the Sabbath rest (vv. 22–30).

16:6–12 God's name (*the LORD*) appears ten times here, twice in the phrase *the glory of the LORD* (vv. 7,10), framed by the phrase *ye shall know* (vv. 6,12). The Redeemer abides with Israel to give them life so that they will know His glory, (see the first major theme in the Introduction: Synopsis). The repeated pairing of *evening* (or *even*) and *morning* (vv. 6–8, 12–13) echoes the creation week (Gen. 1:1–2:3), reminding us of God's power, goodness, and Sabbath. Christ is the Creator, the bread of life, and the glory of God (John 1:3,14; 6:30–58).

16:13 *quails*. Small, round, migratory birds used for meat. *host*. Camp.

16:15 *manna*. Meaning, "What is it?" *wist*. Know. Manna was produced by a supernatural work of God, so it is called bread from heaven (v. 4; Neh. 9:15; Ps. 78:24–25; 105:40; John 6:31).

16:16 *omer*. A tenth of an ephah (v. 36); two to four quarts.

16:18 *mete*. Measure. *no lack*. God provided day by day as they gathered and shared.

16:20 *hearkened not*. Did not listen. They refused to trust God for tomorrow (Matt. 6:34). *stank*. Relying on God's gifts instead of God can turn gifts into plagues (7:18,21; 8:14). *wroth*. Angry.

16:21 *waxed hot*. Grew hot.

16:22–30 The Lord instituted the law of the *sabbath* as a day of holy rest at creation (Gen. 2:1–3), renewed it here (vv. 23,30),

LORD hath said, To morrow *is* the rest of the holy
sabbath unto the LORD: bake *that* which ye will
bake *to day*, and seethe that ye will seethe; and
that which remaineth over lay up for you to be
kept until the morning.
24 And they laid it up till the morning, as Moses
bade: and it did not stink, neither was there any
worm therein.
25 And Moses said, Eat that to day; for to day *is*
a sabbath unto the LORD: to day ye shall not find
it in the field.
26 Six days ye shall gather it; but on the seventh
day, *which is* the sabbath, in it there shall be none.
27 ¶ And it came to pass, *that* there went out *some*
of the people on the seventh day for to gather, and
they found none.
28 And the LORD said unto Moses, How long re-
fuse ye to keep my commandments and my laws?
29 See, for that the LORD hath given you the sab-
bath, therefore he giveth you on the sixth day the
bread of two days; abide ye every man in his place,
let no man go out of his place on the seventh day.
30 So the people rested on the seventh day.
31 And the house of Israel called the name thereof
Manna: and it *was* like coriander seed, white; and
the taste of it *was* like wafers *made* with honey.
32 ¶ And Moses said, This *is* the thing which the
LORD commandeth, Fill an omer of it to be kept
for your generations; that they may see the bread
wherewith I have fed you in the wilderness, when
I brought you forth from the land of Egypt.
33 And Moses said unto Aaron, Take a pot, and
put an omer full of manna therein, and lay it up
before the LORD, to be kept for your generations.
34 As the LORD commanded Moses, so Aaron laid
it up before the Testimony, to be kept.
35 And the children of Israel did eat manna forty
years, until they came to a land inhabited; they
did eat manna, until they came unto the borders
of the land of Canaan.
36 Now an omer *is* the tenth *part* of an ephah.

CHAPTER 17

AND all the congregation of the children of Israel
journeyed from the wilderness of Sin, after their
journeys, according to the commandment of the
LORD, and pitched in Rephidim: and *there was* no
water for the people to drink.
2 Wherefore the people did chide with Moses,
and said, Give us water that we may drink. And
Moses said unto them, Why chide ye with me?
wherefore do ye tempt the LORD?
3 And the people thirsted there for water; and
the people murmured against Moses, and said,
Wherefore *is* this *that* thou hast brought us up
out of Egypt, to kill us and our children and our
cattle with thirst?
4 And Moses cried unto the LORD, saying, What
shall I do unto this people? they be almost ready
to stone me.
5 And the LORD said unto Moses, Go on before
the people, and take with thee of the elders of
Israel; and thy rod, wherewith thou smotest the
river, take in thine hand, and go.
6 Behold, I will stand before thee there upon the
rock in Horeb; and thou shalt smite the rock, and
there shall come water out of it, that the people
may drink. And Moses did so in the sight of the
elders of Israel.
7 And he called the name of the place Mas-
sah, and Meribah, because of the chiding of the

and repeated it in the Ten Commandments (20:8–11).
16:23 *seethe*. Boil.
16:24 *bade*. Commanded.
16:31 The *coriander seed* is round, *white*, and about one-eighth of an inch in diameter. Manna came in flakes or sheets like "frost" (v. 14). Its sweetness like *honey* (Ps. 119:103) was a foretaste of their inheritance in the land (3:8,17).
16:32 *wherewith*. With which.
16:34 *Testimony*. The Ten Commandments, kept in the ark of the covenant (25:16; 31:18).

Thoughts for Personal/Family Worship: Chapter 16

1. **The Lord can work miracles. Naturalistic explanations of manna from insects or trees fail to account for how it came with the dew, melted in the sun, quickly decomposed, and sustained a hungry people for forty years. God is teaching us to rely on His power. We exercise such faith by observing the holy Sabbath rest, and by sharing what we have (v. 18; 2 Cor. 8:13–15). How do you need to trust God's provision right now?**
2. **Christ is the true manna (John 6:32,35), the daily bread of His people's spiritual lives. By faith in Him, we enjoy a sweet foretaste of our heavenly inheritance in the graces of the Holy Spirit (Eph. 1:13–14; Rom. 8:23). Daily nourishment for our souls comes by meditation on the promises and faith that receives Christ as a hungry mouth takes food.**

Chapter 17: ***Israel encounters the trials of thirst and war, and the Lord gives water and victory through the hands of Moses.***

17:1 *journeys*. See Num. 33. *commandment of the LORD*. Literally, "mouth of the Lord"—His will revealed by the movements of the cloud (see note at 13:21–22). *pitched*. Camped.
17:2 *chide*. Argue, as in a legal dispute. *Wherefore*. Why. *tempt*. Test. Testing the Lord showed the hardness of their hearts and provoked God's wrath (Deut. 9:22; Ps. 95:8–9; Heb. 3:8).
17:4 *stone*. Capital punishment by breaking the body with rocks (Lev. 24:23; 1 Kings 21:13).
17:5 *elders*. Leaders, here functioning as legal witnesses (Ruth 4:2). *smotest*. Struck. Taking the rod of the plagues into this legal setting implies that judgment was coming.
17:6 *I will stand*. The cloud of glory came down on a cliff (*rock*). *Horeb*. Mt. Sinai. *smite*. Strike. Shockingly, God instructed Moses to strike not at the grumblers but at the Lord, symbolized in the *rock* (Deut. 32:4; Ps. 78:15,20,35; 1 Cor. 10:4). *water*. Rivers (Ps. 78:16; 105:41). *in the sight of the elders*. A judicial setting (Deut. 25:9).

children of Israel, and because they tempted the
LORD, saying, Is the LORD among us, or not?
8 ¶ Then came Amalek, and fought with Israel in
Rephidim.
9 And Moses said unto Joshua, Choose us out
men, and go out, fight with Amalek: to morrow
I will stand on the top of the hill with the rod of
God in mine hand.
10 So Joshua did as Moses had said to him, and
fought with Amalek: and Moses, Aaron, and Hur
went up to the top of the hill.
11 And it came to pass, when Moses held up his
hand, that Israel prevailed: and when he let down
his hand, Amalek prevailed.
12 But Moses' hands *were* heavy; and they took a
stone, and put *it* under him, and he sat thereon;
and Aaron and Hur stayed up his hands, the one
on the one side, and the other on the other side;
and his hands were steady until the going down
of the sun.
13 And Joshua discomfited Amalek and his peo-
ple with the edge of the sword.
14 And the LORD said unto Moses, Write this *for* a
memorial in a book, and rehearse *it* in the ears of
Joshua: for I will utterly put out the remembrance
of Amalek from under heaven.
15 And Moses built an altar, and called the name
of it Jehovah-nissi:
16 For he said, Because the LORD hath sworn *that*
the LORD *will have* war with Amalek from genera-
tion to generation.

CHAPTER 18

WHEN Jethro, the priest of Midian, Moses' father
in law, heard of all that God had done for Moses,
and for Israel his people, *and* that the LORD had
brought Israel out of Egypt;
2 Then Jethro, Moses' father in law, took Zippo-
rah, Moses' wife, after he had sent her back,
3 And her two sons; of which the name of the one
was Gershom; for he said, I have been an alien in
a strange land:
4 And the name of the other *was* Eliezer; for the
God of my father, *said he, was* mine help, and
delivered me from the sword of Pharaoh:
5 And Jethro, Moses' father in law, came with his
sons and his wife unto Moses into the wilderness,
where he encamped at the mount of God:
6 And he said unto Moses, I thy father in law
Jethro am come unto thee, and thy wife, and her
two sons with her.
7 ¶ And Moses went out to meet his father in law,
and did obeisance, and kissed him; and they asked
each other of *their* welfare; and they came into the
tent.
8 And Moses told his father in law all that the
LORD had done unto Pharaoh and to the Egyptians

17:7 *chiding . . . tempted.* See note at v. 2.
17:8 *Amalek.* Descendants of Esau (Gen. 36:12). They cruelly attacked the weak stragglers behind Israel's armies (Deut. 25:17–18) in the first battle of the redeemed slaves.
17:9 *Joshua.* A military commander from Ephraim who personally assisted Moses (24:13; 33:11), helped to scout out the land (Num. 13:8; 14:6), and succeeded Moses as the leader of Israel (Num. 27:18). *rod of God.* Moses' staff, which God used to work miracles (v. 5).
17:11 *held up his hand.* As he did at the Red Sea (14:16). *prevailed.* The Amalekites were the superior force, but Israel gained divine power to overcome them through the combined efforts of those on the hill and those in the valley, each fulfilling their appointed tasks.
17:12 *thereon.* On it. *Hur.* An assistant of Aaron from Judah and grandfather of Bezalel, who built the tabernacle (24:14; 31:2). *stayed.* Held. Moses, the instrument of God's power, was himself weak.
17:13 *discomfited.* Weakened, disabled.
17:14 *Write this.* Evidence that Moses wrote the Pentateuch (24:4; 34:27). *memorial.* Reminder.
17:15 *Jehovah-nissi.* "The Lord my banner." The Lord is like the flag or standard on a pole that rallies, encourages, and leads His army to victory (Isa. 11:10).
17:16 *war with Amalek.* See Deut. 25:17–19; 1 Sam. 15:1–33; 27:8; 30:1–18; 1 Chron. 4:43.

Thoughts for Personal/Family Worship: Chapter 17

1. **When judgment fell from the Lord through the rod of Moses, rivers of water streamed out to give life to sinners. When God's wrath fell upon Christ through the cross, rivers of the Holy Spirit flowed from heaven to give life to sinners (John 7:37–39; Gal. 3:13–14). Let us marvel at God's grace and drink deeply of the streams of life He bought with blood. Why did judgment have to fall on Christ for the Spirit to give life to men?**
2. **We face a cruel and powerful enemy in Satan, but we can overcome him while our Mediator stretches out His hands in heaven. Trust not in your own strength, or the Devil will prevail. How can looking to Him who was stretched out on Calvary's hill and who even now intercedes at God's right hand help us overcome evil?**

Chapter 18: *Moses' father-in-law visits, worships the Lord as the only God because of His great works for Israel, and advises Moses on delegating authority.*

Jethro's Worship and Wisdom (18:1–27)

18:1 *priest of Midian.* An idolatrous nation (Num. 25:1–3). *all that God had done.* The news of Israel's complete redemption was glorifying God among the nations, as He intended (9:16; 1 Kings 10:1; Ps. 22:27; 96:3; Isa. 2:2).
18:2 *after he had sent her back.* Sometime after Moses went back to Egypt (4:20,25–26).
18:3 *alien . . . strange.* Foreigner . . . foreign.
18:5 *encamped.* Camped. *mount of God.* Mt. Sinai, where God appeared (3:1).
18:7 *went out to meet.* Ordinary hospitality to one arriving after a journey (Gen. 14:17; Num. 22:36; 31:13). *obesiance.* Bowed to honor him. *kissed.* A normal greeting (4:27).
18:8–11 *travail.* Trouble. The repetition of *all* (four times in vv. 1,8–9) emphasizes the complete salvation and rich *goodness* of the Lord for Israel. This good news won the heart (*rejoiced*) and worship (*Blessed*) of this former pagan. God kept

for Israel's sake, *and* all the travail that had come
upon them by the way, and *how* the LORD deliv-
ered them.
9 And Jethro rejoiced for all the goodness which
the LORD had done to Israel, whom he had deliv-
ered out of the hand of the Egyptians.
10 And Jethro said, Blessed *be* the LORD, who hath
delivered you out of the hand of the Egyptians, and
out of the hand of Pharaoh, who hath delivered
the people from under the hand of the Egyptians.
11 Now I know that the LORD *is* greater than all
gods: for in the thing wherein they dealt proudly
he was above them.
12 And Jethro, Moses' father in law, took a burnt
offering and sacrifices for God: and Aaron came,
and all the elders of Israel, to eat bread with
Moses' father in law before God.
13 ¶ And it came to pass on the morrow, that Mo-
ses sat to judge the people: and the people stood
by Moses from the morning unto the evening.
14 And when Moses' father in law saw all that he
did to the people, he said, What *is* this thing that
thou doest to the people? why sittest thou thy-
self alone, and all the people stand by thee from
morning unto even?
15 And Moses said unto his father in law, Because
the people come unto me to enquire of God:
16 When they have a matter, they come unto me;
and I judge between one and another, and I do
make *them* know the statutes of God, and his laws.
17 And Moses' father in law said unto him, The
thing that thou doest *is* not good.
18 Thou wilt surely wear away, both thou, and this
people that *is* with thee: for this thing *is* too heavy
for thee; thou art not able to perform it thyself alone.
19 Hearken now unto my voice, I will give thee
counsel, and God shall be with thee: Be thou for
the people to God-ward, that thou mayest bring
the causes unto God:
20 And thou shalt teach them ordinances and
laws, and shalt shew them the way wherein they
must walk, and the work that they must do.
21 Moreover thou shalt provide out of all the
people able men, such as fear God, men of truth,
hating covetousness; and place *such* over them, *to
be* rulers of thousands, *and* rulers of hundreds,
rulers of fifties, and rulers of tens:
22 And let them judge the people at all seasons:
and it shall be, *that* every great matter they shall
bring unto thee, but every small matter they shall
judge: so shall it be easier for thyself, and they
shall bear *the burden* with thee.
23 If thou shalt do this thing, and God command
thee *so*, then thou shalt be able to endure, and all
this people shall also go to their place in peace.
24 So Moses hearkened to the voice of his father
in law, and did all that he had said.
25 And Moses chose able men out of all Israel,
and made them heads over the people, rulers of
thousands, rulers of hundreds, rulers of fifties,
and rulers of tens.
26 And they judged the people at all seasons: the
hard causes they brought unto Moses, but every
small matter they judged themselves.
27 ¶ And Moses let his father in law depart; and
he went his way into his own land.

CHAPTER 19

IN the third month, when the children of Israel
were gone forth out of the land of Egypt, the same
day came they *into* the wilderness of Sinai.

His promise to bless all nations (Gen. 12:3) with the knowledge that He is the Lord, *greater than all gods* (7:5; 15:11–16; 2 Kings 5:15).

18:12 *took.* Brought. Jethro's sacrificial meal with *all the elders of Israel* showed the spiritual unity between people of different nations who worship the true God. Jethro's descendants later settled among the people of Judah (Judg. 1:16).

18:13 *morrow.* Morning.

18:14 *all that he did to the people.* Echoes earlier statements about "all" that the Lord did for Israel (vv. 1,8–9), suggesting Moses had taken on too much. *even.* Evening.

18:15 *enquire.* Seek, consult.

18:17 *not good.* Even prophets made mistakes when God had not spoken on a particular matter (2 Kings 4:29–31).

18:18 *wear away.* Wear out. Too much work and responsibility exhausts leaders.

18:19 *Hearken.* Listen. *for the people to God-ward.* Stand for the people in God's presence. Moses had a unique role in Israel as its prophet (19:3; 24:15–18; 33:7–11). *causes.* Legal cases.

18:21–22 Large organizations need a multilayer administration of *men* with competence and character, entrusted with varying degrees of responsibility (Deut. 1:9–18).

18:23 *If . . . God command thee.* Human counsel is subject to God's Word.

18:24 *hearkened.* Listened. Great leaders listen to sound advice and correction.

18:26 *hard causes.* Difficult legal cases.

Thoughts for Personal/Family Worship: Chapter 18

1. **God's saving work aims at His glory among all nations. He must be praised by all; He must become the joy of all the earth. This is why we must declare His glory among the nations and the gospel of His great works in Christ to all peoples. How will you use your abilities and resources to help your church to make disciples of all nations?**
2. **Leaders need help or they burn out. For this reason, God gives His churches elders and deacons for the ministry of the Word and the ministry of physical needs (Acts 6:1–7). Paul appointed more than one elder in each church (Acts 14:23). Every Christian should serve as a member in the body of Christ as he is able—all are needed (1 Cor. 12:21).**

THE LORD TAKES ISRAEL FOR HIS PEOPLE (19:1—40:38)

God's Gracious Covenant of Law (19:1—24:18)

Chapter 19: *The Lord proposes the covenant to Israel, and His holy presence comes down*

2 For they were departed from Rephidim, and
were come *to* the desert of Sinai, and had pitched
in the wilderness; and there Israel camped before
the mount.
3 And Moses went up unto God, and the LORD
called unto him out of the mountain, saying,
Thus shalt thou say to the house of Jacob, and tell
the children of Israel;
4 Ye have seen what I did unto the Egyptians, and
how I bare you on eagles' wings, and brought you
unto myself.
5 Now therefore, if ye will obey my voice indeed,
and keep my covenant, then ye shall be a pecu-
liar treasure unto me above all people: for all the
earth *is* mine:
6 And ye shall be unto me a kingdom of priests,
and an holy nation. These *are* the words which
thou shalt speak unto the children of Israel.
7 ¶ And Moses came and called for the elders of
the people, and laid before their faces all these
words which the LORD commanded him.
8 And all the people answered together, and said,
All that the LORD hath spoken we will do. And Mo-
ses returned the words of the people unto the LORD.
9 And the LORD said unto Moses, Lo, I come unto
thee in a thick cloud, that the people may hear when
I speak with thee, and believe thee for ever. And
Moses told the words of the people unto the LORD.
10 ¶ And the LORD said unto Moses, Go unto the
people, and sanctify them to day and to morrow,
and let them wash their clothes,
11 And be ready against the third day: for the
third day the LORD will come down in the sight of
all the people upon mount Sinai.
12 And thou shalt set bounds unto the people
round about, saying, Take heed to yourselves, *that*
ye go *not* up into the mount, or touch the bor-
der of it: whosoever toucheth the mount shall be
surely put to death:
13 There shall not an hand touch it, but he shall
surely be stoned, or shot through; whether *it be*
beast or man, it shall not live: when the trumpet
soundeth long, they shall come up to the mount.
14 ¶ And Moses went down from the mount
unto the people, and sanctified the people; and
they washed their clothes.
15 And he said unto the people, Be ready against
the third day: come not at *your* wives.
16 ¶ And it came to pass on the third day in the
morning, that there were thunders and light-
nings, and a thick cloud upon the mount, and the
voice of the trumpet exceeding loud; so that all
the people that *was* in the camp trembled.
17 And Moses brought forth the people out of
the camp to meet with God; and they stood at the
nether part of the mount.
18 And mount Sinai was altogether on a smoke,
because the LORD descended upon it in fire: and
the smoke thereof ascended as the smoke of a fur-
nace, and the whole mount quaked greatly.
19 And when the voice of the trumpet sounded
long, and waxed louder and louder, Moses spake,
and God answered him by a voice.
20 And the LORD came down upon mount Sinai,
on the top of the mount: and the LORD called Mo-
ses *up* to the top of the mount; and Moses went up.
21 And the LORD said unto Moses, Go down,
charge the people, lest they break through unto
the LORD to gaze, and many of them perish.
22 And let the priests also, which come near to

on Mt. Sinai in fire and a thunderstorm.

The Fearsome Majesty of the Lord (19:1–25)

19:1 *third month.* Late May to early June.

19:2 *pitched.* Set up camp. Israel arrived at the mountain (*mount*) where the Lord had appeared to Moses, as promised (3:12). They remained there almost a year (v. 1; Num. 10:11–12).

19:3 *Thus shalt thou say.* God's relationship with His people is through His Word. *house of Jacob.* Family or descendants of Jacob, with whom God made His covenant (2:24).

19:4 *bare.* Carried. *on eagles' wings.* Image of God's power (Isa. 40:31) and love for His children (Deut. 32:11). *unto myself.* The goal of redemption is God (6:7; 1 Peter 3:18).

19:5 *if ye will obey.* The Lord redeemed them out of His free grace promised to Abraham (v. 4; 6:6–8; 20:2), but the enjoyment of the blessings depended on the obedience of the nation (note plural *ye*). Only those who *keep my covenant* experience the covenant relationship (Gen. 17:9,14; Ps. 103:17–18). *peculiar treasure.* God's precious and beloved possession (Deut. 7:6; 14:2; 26:18; Ps. 135:4; Mal. 3:17); term used of a king's gold and silver (1 Chron. 29:3; Eccl. 2:8).

19:6 God defined His covenant relationship with Israel as the gift of His royal reign (*kingdom . . . nation*) and sacred presence (*priests . . . holy*). His reign came through the law (chs. 20–23), and His presence appears in the tabernacle (chs. 25–40).

19:7–8 *Moses came . . . Moses returned.* He acted as a mediator, a communications link between the Holy One and the people. *All that the LORD hath spoken we will do.* The right response to God's law (Deut. 5:29), but one impossible without saving grace (Deut. 29:4; 30:6).

19:9 The experience of God's glory drives people to trust in a mediator.

19:10 *sanctify.* Consecrate or set apart as holy (v. 23).

19:12 *Take heed.* Watch. The old covenant did not allow full access to God's holy presence.

19:15 *come not at your wives.* Abstain from sexual relations, which made a person ritually unclean though marital sex is not sin (Lev. 15:16–18; 1 Cor. 7:2–4).

19:16 The appearance of the Lord *on the third day* with *lightnings*, an earthquake (v. 18), and angels (Ps. 68:17) foreshadowed Christ's resurrection (Matt. 16:21; 28:2–4). With the *cloud* and *trumpet*, it also points to Christ's coming in glory (Matt. 13:41–43; 24:7,31; 26:64).

19:17 *nether.* Lower.

19:18 *altogether on a smoke.* Entirely engulfed in smoke. In Christ, we may approach God without facing the terrifying wrath of His fiery holiness (Heb. 12:18–24,29).

19:19 *waxed.* Grew.

19:21 *charge.* Warn.

the LORD, sanctify themselves, lest the LORD break
forth upon them.
23 And Moses said unto the LORD, The people
cannot come up to mount Sinai: for thou
chargedst us, saying, Set bounds about the mount,
and sanctify it.
24 And the LORD said unto him, Away, get thee
down, and thou shalt come up, thou, and Aaron
with thee: but let not the priests and the people
break through to come up unto the LORD, lest he
break forth upon them.
25 So Moses went down unto the people, and
spake unto them.

CHAPTER 20

AND God spake all these words, saying,
2 I *am* the LORD thy God, which have brought
thee out of the land of Egypt, out of the house
of bondage.
3 Thou shalt have no other gods before me.
4 Thou shalt not make unto thee any graven im-
age, or any likeness *of any thing* that *is* in heaven
above, or that *is* in the earth beneath, or that *is* in
the water under the earth:
5 Thou shalt not bow down thyself to them, nor
serve them: for I the LORD thy God *am* a jealous
God, visiting the iniquity of the fathers upon the
children unto the third and fourth *generation* of
them that hate me;
6 And shewing mercy unto thousands of them
that love me, and keep my commandments.
7 Thou shalt not take the name of the LORD thy
God in vain; for the LORD will not hold him guilt-
less that taketh his name in vain.
8 Remember the sabbath day, to keep it holy.
9 Six days shalt thou labour, and do all thy work:
10 But the seventh day *is* the sabbath of the LORD
thy God: *in it* thou shalt not do any work, thou,
nor thy son, nor thy daughter, thy manservant, nor
thy maidservant, nor thy cattle, nor thy stranger
that *is* within thy gates:

19:22 *priests.* Probably chief men who performed some priestlike functions before Aaron and his sons were ordained to the priesthood (chs. 28–29; Lev. 8–9).
19:23 *sanctify it.* Treat it as holy because of God's presence (3:5).
19:24 *Away.* Go.

Thoughts for Personal/Family Worship: Chapter 19

1. **God stands at an infinite distance above fallen mankind in His majesty and holiness. In this day of casual worship and irreverent prayer, let us never forget that He is the holy King. We may draw near to Him only through the blood and righteousness of Christ. How should our worship of God show our reverence for His holiness and majesty?**
2. **It was marvelous grace that the Lord, who can claim "all the earth is mine," took a small, enslaved people as His treasure. Israel broke the old covenant by disobedience to the law (v. 5), but the Lord accomplished His larger purposes in the new covenant, which promises inward grace to produce obedience for both Jews and Gentiles (Jer. 31:31–34). The church drawn from Jews and Gentiles is now called God's "peculiar" treasure, the kingdom of priests and a holy nation by Christ's blood (Titus 2:14; 1 Peter 2:4–5,9; Rev. 1:5–6; 5:9–10).**

Chapter 20: *The Lord speaks the moral law to Israel from the cloud of glory on Mt. Sinai, and they respond by fearfully looking to Moses to mediate God's Word.*

The Ten Commandments (20:1–21)

20:1–17 The Ten Commandments. The King establishes His constitution for His people as a holy nation. The Lord exalted the Ten Commandments—literally, "ten words" (Decalogue)—above the other laws given to Moses in a number of ways: (1) He spoke them directly to Israel out of the cloud; (2) He wrote them by His power on tablets of stone; (3) He commanded that they be placed in the ark of the covenant; (4) they are called "the covenant," the heart of Israel's obligation to God; (5) Moses repeated them in Deut. 5 before Israel entered the land, and (6) after repeating them, Moses commented, "These words the LORD spake unto all your assembly . . . and he added no more" (Deut. 5:22; see also Ex. 34:28; Deut. 4:12–14; 5:1–22; 9:9,11,15; 10:1–5). The Ten Commandments are a summary of God's moral law, rooted in God's nature, man's nature in the image of God, and the order of creation (Gen. 1:1—2:3). Christ and the apostles taught and applied them in the New Testament (Matt. 5:21,27; 12:1–13; 15:4; 19:18–19; Rom. 7:7; 13:9; Eph. 6:2–3; James 2:11; Rev. 1:10). You will find a detailed, helpful exposition of the law in the Westminster Larger Catechism (Q. 91–153).
20:2 Preface to the Ten Commandments. *bondage.* Slavery. God motivates obedience by His nature and covenant (*the LORD thy God*) and His sweet grace to His people (*brought thee out*).
20:3 First Commandment. *before me.* In His presence, for He sees all things. There is only one God; all else was created by Him (Gen. 1:1). He proved His supremacy by judging Pharaoh and the gods of Egypt (9:14; 12:12; 15:11). Therefore, our first obligation is to give our worship, absolute obedience, and supreme love to Him alone (Deut. 6:4–5; 10:12—11:1).
20:4–6 Second Commandment. *graven image.* Idol; visible representation of a divine being. God is the Creator of *heaven, earth,* and the *water,* and must not be confused with His creations (Rom. 1:19–23). In the plagues, He demonstrated His mastery over the created world and humiliated the idols of Egypt. Therefore, though God blesses some visual arts (31:1–11), we must never make an image of God (including any person of the Trinity) or worship with a man-made image of anything before us. For He is *a jealous God,* not in a petty or unjust sense, but with a holy zeal for His glory (34:14). *upon the children.* Insofar as they also *hate* God (34:7).
20:7 Third Commandment. *name.* How He makes His glory known and feared (Deut. 28:58). The revelation of God's name is central to the book of Exodus (3:13–15). *in vain.* For nothing. *not hold him guiltless.* Will punish him. We must never speak of God without reverence (Lev. 24:16), especially in prayer, worship, or a vow. Pharaoh despised God's name with defiance (5:2) and hypocritical confessions (9:27,30), but God teaches men to fear Him, for "I am the LORD" (20:2).
20:8–11 Fourth Commandment. *Remember.* Plan and do. *sabbath day.* Day to stop and rest. *manservant . . . maidservant.* Male and female servants. *stranger that is within thy gates.*

11 For *in* six days the LORD made heaven and
earth, the sea, and all that in them *is*, and rested
the seventh day: wherefore the LORD blessed the
sabbath day, and hallowed it.
12 ¶ Honour thy father and thy mother: that thy
days may be long upon the land which the LORD
thy God giveth thee.
13 Thou shalt not kill.
14 Thou shalt not commit adultery.
15 Thou shalt not steal.
16 Thou shalt not bear false witness against thy
neighbour.
17 Thou shalt not covet thy neighbour's house,
thou shalt not covet thy neighbour's wife, nor his
manservant, nor his maidservant, nor his ox, nor
his ass, nor any thing that *is* thy neighbour's.
18 ¶ And all the people saw the thunderings, and
the lightnings, and the noise of the trumpet, and
the mountain smoking: and when the people saw
it, they removed, and stood afar off.
19 And they said unto Moses, Speak thou with us,
and we will hear: but let not God speak with us,
lest we die.
20 And Moses said unto the people, Fear not: for
God is come to prove you, and that his fear may
be before your faces, that ye sin not.
21 And the people stood afar off, and Moses drew
near unto the thick darkness where God *was*.
22 ¶ And the LORD said unto Moses, Thus thou
shalt say unto the children of Israel, Ye have seen
that I have talked with you from heaven.
23 Ye shall not make with me gods of silver, nei-
ther shall ye make unto you gods of gold.
24 ¶ An altar of earth thou shalt make unto me,
and shalt sacrifice thereon thy burnt offerings,
and thy peace offerings, thy sheep, and thine oxen:
in all places where I record my name I will come
unto thee, and I will bless thee.
25 And if thou wilt make me an altar of stone,
thou shalt not build it of hewn stone: for if thou
lift up thy tool upon it, thou hast polluted it.
26 Neither shalt thou go up by steps unto mine

Foreigner living with the Israelites. *wherefore*. Therefore. *hallowed*. Set apart the entire day as holy. By His own example in the creation week, God instituted a pattern of *six days* of work and *the seventh day* for rest from ordinary labor and for holy assembly for worship (Gen. 2:1–3; Lev. 23:3). Christ affirmed this law by declaring Himself Lord of the Sabbath (Mark 2:27), which is now called the Lord's Day (Rev. 1:10), the first day of the week when Christ rose (Matt. 28:1).

20:12 Fifth Commandment. God created the family (Gen. 1:27–28). He is the Father of His people, and they must serve Him like a son (4:22–23). Therefore, glorifying God requires honoring *thy father and thy mother*, including other authorities that are like fathers (2 Kings 5:13; 1 Thess. 2:11).

20:13 Sixth Commandment. Human life is sacred above all animals, for God created us in the image of God (Gen. 1:26; 9:6). Therefore we should not desire harm or speak evil against another person (Matt. 5:21–22). This verb *kill* is used of murder and manslaughter, but never of war; God gave government the authority to use deadly force (Rom. 13:4).

20:14 Seventh Commandment. God is the author of marriage between one man and one woman (Gen. 2:18–25), and demands that we honor its commitments (Heb. 13:4). Christ explained that intentional sexual lust is adultery in the heart, a sin worthy of the fire of hell (Matt. 5:27–30).

20:15 Eighth Commandment. God gave man dominion of the earth (Gen. 1:26), and thus the right to personal property. We must respect and protect each other's property. We should not only cease stealing, but also work hard to give to those in need (Eph. 4:28).

20:16 Ninth Commandment. *witness*. Testimony with respect to law or covenant (23:1; Gen. 31:44; Deut. 19:15–20; 31:26). God speaks, and His words define reality and deserve trust (Gen. 1:3; 2:16–17; 3:1–5). We, created in His image, must speak only the truth (Lev. 19:11).

20:17 Tenth Commandment. *covet*. Desire. God's law regulates even the longing and contentment of the heart. He provides for His people, both in the garden (Gen. 2:8–15) and in the wilderness (15:23—17:7). Therefore we must be thankful, not covetous (Eph. 5:3–5).

20:18 *removed*. Shook.

20:19 *Speak thou . . . let not God speak*. This was God's intent: to push them to rely on His prophetic mediator (19:9; Deut. 5:23–31).

20:20 *prove*. Test.

The Book of the Covenant (20:22—23:33)

After speaking the Ten Commandments directly to Israel, the Lord gave Moses instructions for him to write for Israel in the book of the covenant (24:7). These are a mixture of moral, ceremonial, and judicial laws that reveal Christ and His will but bind us only insofar as they express the moral principles summarized in the Ten Commandments, since the ceremonial laws find fulfillment in Christ and the civil laws find fulfillment in Israel's theocracy.

20:24 *thereon*. On it. *record*. Cause to be "remembered," as in faith, prayer, and worship (Deut. 8:18–19; Josh. 23:7; Ps. 20:7; 45:17; 119:54–55; Isa. 12:4; 26:13; 48:1).

20:25 *hewn*. Cut. *polluted*. Failed to treat the holy as sacred. Shaping the stones of the altar could result in making it into an idol (v. 4).

20:26 *discovered*. Uncovered.

Thoughts for Personal/Family Worship: Chapter 20

1. Eight of the Ten Commandments are negative, "Thou shalt not," implying that God gave the law to convict fallen man of sin (Rom. 3:20; 1 Tim. 1:8–11). Conviction is painful and sinners hate the light of God's truth (John 3:19–20), but conviction of sin is a gift of the Holy Spirit (John 16:8) by which the law drives sinners to Christ (Gal. 3:22,24). How do you respond when God's Word makes you feel guilty? How should you respond?

2. The church's status as God's treasured possession is not based on its obedience to the law, but on the death of Christ (Titus 2:14). Significantly, God gave the law after the exodus and not before. Law followed grace, defining how the redeemed people were to live before God. You become part of God's people by faith in Christ alone. Yet obedience to God's Word is still a vital part of the covenant relationship (John 14:23; 15:5), for the law continues on as a rule of life for believers to which they respond with gratitude (Jer. 31:33; 32:40; Ezek. 36:27). So pursue holiness, but never try to keep God's covenant

altar, that thy nakedness be not discovered thereon.

CHAPTER 21

NOW these *are* the judgments which thou shalt set before them.
2 If thou buy an Hebrew servant, six years he shall serve: and in the seventh he shall go out free for nothing.
3 If he came in by himself, he shall go out by himself: if he were married, then his wife shall go out with him.
4 If his master have given him a wife, and she have born him sons or daughters; the wife and her children shall be her master's, and he shall go out by himself.
5 And if the servant shall plainly say, I love my master, my wife, and my children; I will not go out free:
6 Then his master shall bring him unto the judges; he shall also bring him to the door, or unto the door post; and his master shall bore his ear through with an aul; and he shall serve him for ever.
7 ¶ And if a man sell his daughter to be a maidservant, she shall not go out as the menservants do.
8 If she please not her master, who hath betrothed her to himself, then shall he let her be redeemed: to sell her unto a strange nation he shall have no power, seeing he hath dealt deceitfully with her.
9 And if he have betrothed her unto his son, he shall deal with her after the manner of daughters.
10 If he take him another *wife*; her food, her raiment, and her duty of marriage, shall he not diminish.
11 And if he do not these three unto her, then shall she go out free without money.
12 ¶ He that smiteth a man, so that he die, shall be surely put to death.
13 And if a man lie not in wait, but God deliver *him* into his hand; then I will appoint thee a place whither he shall flee.
14 But if a man come presumptuously upon his neighbour, to slay him with guile; thou shalt take him from mine altar, that he may die.
15 ¶ And he that smiteth his father, or his mother, shall be surely put to death.
16 ¶ And he that stealeth a man, and selleth him, or if he be found in his hand, he shall surely be put to death.
17 ¶ And he that curseth his father, or his mother, shall surely be put to death.
18 ¶ And if men strive together, and one smite another with a stone, or with *his* fist, and he die not, but keepeth *his* bed:
19 If he rise again, and walk abroad upon his staff, then shall he that smote *him* be quit: only he shall pay *for* the loss of his time, and shall cause *him* to be thoroughly healed.
20 ¶ And if a man smite his servant, or his maid, with a rod, and he die under his hand; he shall be surely punished.
21 Notwithstanding, if he continue a day or two, he shall not be punished: for he *is* his money.
22 ¶ If men strive, and hurt a woman with child, so that her fruit depart *from her*, and yet no mischief follow: he shall be surely punished, according as the woman's husband will lay upon him; and he shall pay as the judges *determine*.
23 And if *any* mischief follow, then thou shalt give life for life,
24 Eye for eye, tooth for tooth, hand for hand, foot for foot,

by your own strength. Rely on the work of Christ and God's grace will enable you to live in holiness.

Chapter 21: ***The Lord gives Moses laws about servants, murder, and personal injury, and liability for harm done by dangerous livestock.***

21:1 *judgments*. Laws of justice.

21:2–11 Laws concerning the rights of Hebrew servants. God's redeemed people were never to suffer the degradations of slavery again (Lev. 25:42–43). God's laws protect them from long-term enslavement (Jer. 34:13–14) and sexual trafficking.

21:6 *judges*. Literally, "God" or "gods" (perhaps referring to powerful men, Ps. 82:6). *bore*. Pierce. *aul*. Sharp tool. See Deut. 15:17. A picture of Christ's submission (Ps. 40:6–8).

21:7 *maidservant . . . menservants*. Female servants and male servants.

21:8 *betrothed*. Made a legal commitment leading to marriage. *strange*. Foreign.

21:10 *raiment*. Clothing. *duty of marriage*. Sexual intercourse.

21:12–27 Laws concerning murder and personal injury. All human beings are precious, including the servant (v. 20) and unborn child (vv. 22–23).

21:12–14 *smiteth*. Strikes. *lie not in wait*. Does not hunt or pursue. Murder involves the intent to harm. *God deliver*. If God causes it to happen. God is in control of human accidents and tragedies. *whither*. Where, to which place. *presumptuously*. Proudly. *guile*. Cunning. *from mine altar*. Seeking refuge from punishment (1 Kings 1:50; 2:28).

21:16 This law condemns the forcible enslavement of innocents (22:3; Deut. 24:7).

21:17 The penalty of *death* highlights the great obligation to honor our parents (Mark 7:10).

21:18 *keepeth his bed*. Is bedridden.

21:19 *quit*. Legally acquitted of the charge of murder.

21:20–21 While corporal punishment was permitted, killing one's servant was murder. However, a master who causes his servant to lose time at work has punished himself, forfeiting *his money*.

21:22–23 *her fruit*. Her children. If harm (*mischief*) comes to the woman or her children, then the offender must be punished because women and unborn children are human beings (Ps. 139:13).

25 Burning for burning, wound for wound, stripe
for stripe.
26 ¶ And if a man smite the eye of his servant, or
the eye of his maid, that it perish; he shall let him
go free for his eye's sake.
27 And if he smite out his manservant's tooth, or
his maidservant's tooth; he shall let him go free
for his tooth's sake.
28 ¶ If an ox gore a man or a woman, that they
die: then the ox shall be surely stoned, and his
flesh shall not be eaten; but the owner of the ox
shall be quit.
29 But if the ox were wont to push with his
horn in time past, and it hath been testified to
his owner, and he hath not kept him in, but that
he hath killed a man or a woman; the ox shall be
stoned, and his owner also shall be put to death.
30 If there be laid on him a sum of money, then
he shall give for the ransom of his life whatsoever
is laid upon him.
31 Whether he have gored a son, or have gored a
daughter, according to this judgment shall it be
done unto him.
32 If the ox shall push a manservant or a maid-
servant; he shall give unto their master thirty
shekels of silver, and the ox shall be stoned.
33 ¶ And if a man shall open a pit, or if a man
shall dig a pit, and not cover it, and an ox or an
ass fall therein;
34 The owner of the pit shall make *it* good, *and*
give money unto the owner of them; and the dead
beast shall be his.
35 ¶ And if one man's ox hurt another's, that he
die; then they shall sell the live ox, and divide the
money of it; and the dead *ox* also they shall divide.
36 Or if it be known that the ox hath used to push
in time past, and his owner hath not kept him in;
he shall surely pay ox for ox; and the dead shall
be his own.

CHAPTER 22

IF a man shall steal an ox, or a sheep, and kill it, or
sell it; he shall restore five oxen for an ox, and four
sheep for a sheep.
2 ¶ If a thief be found breaking up, and be smit-
ten that he die, *there shall* no blood *be shed* for
him.
3 If the sun be risen upon him, *there shall be*
blood *shed* for him; *for* he should make full res-
titution; if he have nothing, then he shall be sold
for his theft.
4 If the theft be certainly found in his hand alive,
whether it be ox, or ass, or sheep; he shall restore
double.
5 ¶ If a man shall cause a field or vineyard to be
eaten, and shall put in his beast, and shall feed in
another man's field; of the best of his own field,
and of the best of his own vineyard, shall he make
restitution.
6 ¶ If fire break out, and catch in thorns, so that
the stacks of corn, or the standing corn, or the
field, be consumed *therewith*; he that kindled the
fire shall surely make restitution.
7 ¶ If a man shall deliver unto his neighbour
money or stuff to keep, and it be stolen out of
the man's house; if the thief be found, let him pay
double.
8 If the thief be not found, then the master of
the house shall be brought unto the judges, *to
see* whether he have put his hand unto his neigh-
bour's goods.
9 For all manner of trespass, *whether it be* for ox,
for ass, for sheep, for raiment, *or* for any manner

21:24 *Eye for eye.* Not a justification for personal revenge (Matt. 5:38–39) or for mutilation of the violent (vv. 26–27), but a principle that punishment must be proportionate to the crime.
21:26–27 *maid.* Female servant. God did not demand a literal "eye for eye" or "tooth for tooth" (v. 24), but the liberation of the servant. This law protects servants from severe mistreatment.
21:28–36 Laws concerning liability for harm done by dangerous property, here an ox or pit. God holds us responsible for the effects of our property, requiring safety measures (22:5–6).
21:28 *quit.* Legally acquitted of the charge of murder.
21:29 *wont to.* Accustomed to.

Thoughts for Personal/Family Worship: Chapter 21

1. **While the judicial laws of the old covenant do not bind us today, they contain many moral principles. For instance, punishments should fit the crime; murder is not the same as accidentally killing someone. Another principle in this chapter is that all human beings, including women, servants, and unborn children, are precious persons, not mere property, and they should be protected from injury and death.**
2. **God's law held people accountable not only for their acts, but for harm done by their property, whether it is an ox, pit, or some modern equivalent. What do you own that could cause harm to others? What reasonable safeguards have you put in place?**

Chapter 22: ***The Lord instructs Moses in laws concerning property loss, social injustice, and various sins.***

22:1–15 Laws concerning stolen and damaged property. Not only does God condemn theft, but He demands *restitution* of the lost goods plus more (Luke 19:8). Ordinarily, restitution adds a fifth to their value (Lev. 6:4–5; Num. 5:7), but livestock are repaid four to five times as much, for these are the life of an agricultural people, especially the *oxen* that worked the land.
22:2 *breaking up.* Breaking into a home. *smitten.* Struck. *no blood.* No punishment against the homeowner. Self-defense is just, though only within reasonable limits.
22:6 *corn.* Grain. Men are accountable for negligence that destroys property (21:28–36).
22:8 *judges.* See note at 21:6.
22:9 *trespass.* Sin.

of lost thing, which *another* challengeth to be his,
the cause of both parties shall come before the
judges; *and* whom the judges shall condemn, he
shall pay double unto his neighbour.
10 If a man deliver unto his neighbour an ass, or
an ox, or a sheep, or any beast, to keep; and it die,
or be hurt, or driven away, no man seeing *it*:
11 *Then* shall an oath of the LORD be between
them both, that he hath not put his hand unto
his neighbour's goods; and the owner of it shall
accept *thereof*, and he shall not make *it* good.
12 And if it be stolen from him, he shall make
restitution unto the owner thereof.
13 If it be torn in pieces, *then* let him bring it *for*
witness, *and* he shall not make good that which
was torn.
14 ¶ And if a man borrow *ought* of his neighbour,
and it be hurt, or die, the owner thereof *being* not
with it, he shall surely make *it* good.
15 *But* if the owner thereof *be* with it, he shall not
make *it* good: if it *be* an hired *thing*, it came for
his hire.
16 ¶ And if a man entice a maid that is not be-
trothed, and lie with her, he shall surely endow
her to be his wife.
17 If her father utterly refuse to give her unto
him, he shall pay money according to the dowry
of virgins.
18 ¶ Thou shalt not suffer a witch to live.
19 ¶ Whosoever lieth with a beast shall surely be
put to death.
20 ¶ He that sacrificeth unto *any* god, save unto
the LORD only, he shall be utterly destroyed.
21 ¶ Thou shalt neither vex a stranger, nor
oppress him: for ye were strangers in the land of
Egypt.
22 ¶ Ye shall not afflict any widow, or fatherless
child.
23 If thou afflict them in any wise, and they cry at
all unto me, I will surely hear their cry;
24 And my wrath shall wax hot, and I will kill you
with the sword; and your wives shall be widows,
and your children fatherless.
25 ¶ If thou lend money to *any of* my people *that
is* poor by thee, thou shalt not be to him as an
usurer, neither shalt thou lay upon him usury.
26 If thou at all take thy neighbour's raiment to
pledge, thou shalt deliver it unto him by that the
sun goeth down:
27 For that *is* his covering only, it *is* his raiment
for his skin: wherein shall he sleep? and it shall
come to pass, when he crieth unto me, that I will
hear; for I *am* gracious.
28 ¶ Thou shalt not revile the gods, nor curse the
ruler of thy people.
29 ¶ Thou shalt not delay *to offer* the first of thy
ripe fruits, and of thy liquors: the firstborn of thy
sons shalt thou give unto me.
30 Likewise shalt thou do with thine oxen, *and*
with thy sheep: seven days it shall be with his
dam; on the eighth day thou shalt give it me.
31 ¶ And ye shall be holy men unto me: neither

22:11 *accept thereof.* Accept the oath and demand no restitution (Heb. 6:16).
22:14 *ought.* Anything. *thereof.* Of it.
22:16–20 Laws concerning sexuality, sorcery, and idolatry. Idolatry is linked to magic and immorality (Num. 25:1–9; 1 Sam. 15:23).
22:16 *entice.* Seduce sexually. *maid.* Virgin girl of marriageable age. *betrothed.* Legally committed to marry someone else. Immorality with a betrothed woman was adultery and punishable by death (Deut. 22:22–27). *endow.* Pay the dowry for a wife. Sex before marriage ("fornication" or "whoremongering") is condemned by God (1 Cor. 6:9; Heb. 13:4).
22:18 *suffer.* Allow. *witch.* Sorceress, a woman who manipulates powers through rituals (Deut. 18:9–14).
22:19 Canaanites engaged in this horrible impurity and believed that their gods did so.
22:20 *save.* Except.
22:21–28 Laws concerning social injustice. The Lord is *gracious* (v. 27) and looks with mercy on the poor but with *wrath* (v. 24) upon those who oppress the weak. His law demands mercy and justice to the foreigner, widow, and fatherless (23:9; Lev. 19:33–34; Deut. 10:18–19; 24:17–18; 27:19).
22:21 *vex.* Mistreat. *stranger.* Foreigner.
22:23 *any wise.* Any way.
22:24 *wax hot.* Grow warm, burn.
22:25 *usurer . . . usury.* One who lends money and charges interest of fellow Israelites—a crime under the law (Lev. 25:35–38; Deut. 23:19–20).
22:26 *raiment.* Clothing. *pledge.* Security or collateral on a loan. *by that.* Before.
22:28 *revile.* Insult. *gods.* "God" or "judges" (see note at 21:6). We must speak respectfully of authorities (Acts 23:5).
22:29–31 Laws concerning worship. As God's *holy* people, Israel must bring its offerings and *firstborn* (13:2,11–16), and avoid uncleanness by not eating animals that suffer natural death (Lev. 22:8).
22:29 *liquors.* Juice.
22:30 *dam.* Mother animal.

Thoughts for Personal/Family Worship: Chapter 22

1. **God's law requires justice in relationships and society. Not only is theft a crime, but God requires restitution for possessions stolen or destroyed. The Lord especially hates injustice against those who are weak. Human justice systems may fail, but God's wrath will inevitably strike the unrepentant sinner. In the fear of God, can you honestly say that you have not stolen from others, harmed their property, or oppressed the weak? If you have wronged someone, what must you do to make it right with God and man?**
2. **The strictly judicial laws like the death penalty for witches were abolished in Christ. He ended the earthly theocracy of Israel, ascending to a heavenly throne and bringing the kingdom of God through the means of the Word and the Spirit (John 18:33–37; Acts 2:33–26). However, these judicial laws point ahead to the coming of His kingdom in glory. Sin deserves death (Rom. 6:23). When Christ returns to judge the world, the wicked, including sorcerers, will be cast into hell (Rev. 21:8).**

shall ye eat *any* flesh *that is* torn of beasts in the
field; ye shall cast it to the dogs.

CHAPTER 23

THOU shalt not raise a false report: put not thine
hand with the wicked to be an unrighteous
witness.
2 ¶ Thou shalt not follow a multitude to *do* evil;
neither shalt thou speak in a cause to decline after
many to wrest *judgment*:
3 ¶ Neither shalt thou countenance a poor man
in his cause.
4 ¶ If thou meet thine enemy's ox or his ass go-
ing astray, thou shalt surely bring it back to him
again.
5 If thou see the ass of him that hateth thee lying
under his burden, and wouldest forbear to help
him, thou shalt surely help with him.
6 Thou shalt not wrest the judgment of thy poor
in his cause.
7 Keep thee far from a false matter; and the in-
nocent and righteous slay thou not: for I will not
justify the wicked.
8 ¶ And thou shalt take no gift: for the gift blind-
eth the wise, and perverteth the words of the
righteous.
9 ¶ Also thou shalt not oppress a stranger: for
ye know the heart of a stranger, seeing ye were
strangers in the land of Egypt.
10 And six years thou shalt sow thy land, and
shalt gather in the fruits thereof:
11 But the seventh *year* thou shalt let it rest and
lie still; that the poor of thy people may eat: and
what they leave the beasts of the field shall eat.
In like manner thou shalt deal with thy vine-
yard, *and* with thy oliveyard.
12 Six days thou shalt do thy work, and on the
seventh day thou shalt rest: that thine ox and
thine ass may rest, and the son of thy handmaid,
and the stranger, may be refreshed.
13 And in all *things* that I have said unto you be
circumspect: and make no mention of the name
of other gods, neither let it be heard out of thy
mouth.
14 ¶ Three times thou shalt keep a feast unto me
in the year.
15 Thou shalt keep the feast of unleavened bread:
(thou shalt eat unleavened bread seven days, as
I commanded thee, in the time appointed of
the month Abib; for in it thou camest out from
Egypt: and none shall appear before me empty:)
16 And the feast of harvest, the firstfruits of thy
labours, which thou hast sown in the field: and
the feast of ingathering, *which is* in the end of the
year, when thou hast gathered in thy labours out
of the field.
17 Three times in the year all thy males shall
appear before the Lord GOD.
18 Thou shalt not offer the blood of my sacrifice
with leavened bread; neither shall the fat of my
sacrifice remain until the morning.
19 The first of the firstfruits of thy land thou shalt
bring into the house of the LORD thy God. Thou
shalt not seethe a kid in his mother's milk.
20 ¶ Behold, I send an Angel before thee, to keep
thee in the way, and to bring thee into the place
which I have prepared.
21 Beware of him, and obey his voice, provoke
him not; for he will not pardon your transgres-
sions: for my name *is* in him.
22 But if thou shalt indeed obey his voice, and do

Chapter 23: *The Lord gives laws about justice, kindness, Sabbaths, and feasts and closes the book of the covenant with a call to covenant faithfulness.*

23:1–9 Laws concerning justice and love.

23:1 *put not thine hand.* Do not join or help.

23:2 *multitude.* Crowd. *cause.* Legal case. *decline after many to wrest judgment.* Join the majority in doing injustice.

23:3 *countenance.* Show favoritism.

23:4–5 *wouldest forbear to help him.* You shall not allow yourself to leave it. God's law requires us to love even the enemy who *hateth* us, just as Christ explained (Matt. 5:43–44).

23:6 *wrest the judgment of.* Distort justice for. *cause.* Legal case.

23:7 *I will not justify the wicked.* Justification does not change someone's character, but declares him righteous legally. The righteous God cannot justify sinners on their own merits (34:7; Prov. 17:15), but justifies sinners joined to Christ and His righteousness (Rom. 4:5; 2 Cor. 5:21).

23:8 *gift.* Bribe.

23:9 *stranger.* Foreigner.

23:10–19 Laws concerning Sabbath and feasts. In the book of the covenant, the moral law of the weekly holy day of rest (20:8–11; Gen. 2:1–3) was expanded in various regulations (31:13–14; 35:2–3; Lev. 23) that no longer bind us after the death of Christ (Col. 2:16).

23:12 *handmaid.* Female servant.

23:13 *be circumspect.* Guard yourself, be watchful. *make no mention.* Literally, "do not remember," call upon them in worship (see note at 20:24).

23:15 *feast of unleavened bread.* See 12:15–20; 13:3–10; 34:18; Lev. 23:6–8. *appear before me empty.* Fail to bring an offering (Deut. 16:16–17).

23:16 *feast of harvest . . . feast of ingathering.* Also known as Pentecost and the Feast of Tabernacles or Booths (34:22–23; Lev. 23:16–21,33–43).

23:19 *seethe a kid.* Boil a young goat. This ceremonial law (34:26; Deut. 14:21) is the basis for the separation of meat from dairy products in Judaism. The law most likely prohibits a magical ritual practiced in Canaanite worship though some relate it to laws of compassion for animals (Lev. 22:28; Deut. 22:6).

23:20–33 Promise to lead Israel into the land, and a call to covenant faithfulness.

23:20–23 *I send an Angel . . . my name is in him.* The angel of the Lord, a Christophany, was both sent by God and yet possessed God's own nature and glory (*name*). This was God the Son, sent as the Mediator to fulfill the covenant even before His incarnation (3:1–6; see note at Gen. 16:7). *Beware.* Pay attention.

all that I speak; then I will be an enemy unto thine
enemies, and an adversary unto thine adversaries.
23 For mine Angel shall go before thee, and bring
thee in unto the Amorites, and the Hittites, and
the Perizzites, and the Canaanites, the Hivites,
and the Jebusites: and I will cut them off.
24 Thou shalt not bow down to their gods, nor
serve them, nor do after their works: but thou
shalt utterly overthrow them, and quite break
down their images.
25 And ye shall serve the LORD your God, and he
shall bless thy bread, and thy water; and I will take
sickness away from the midst of thee.
26 ¶ There shall nothing cast their young, nor be
barren, in thy land: the number of thy days I will
fulfil.
27 I will send my fear before thee, and will de-
stroy all the people to whom thou shalt come,
and I will make all thine enemies turn their backs
unto thee.
28 And I will send hornets before thee, which
shall drive out the Hivite, the Canaanite, and the
Hittite, from before thee.
29 I will not drive them out from before thee in
one year; lest the land become desolate, and the
beast of the field multiply against thee.
30 By little and little I will drive them out from
before thee, until thou be increased, and inherit
the land.
31 And I will set thy bounds from the Red sea
even unto the sea of the Philistines, and from the
desert unto the river: for I will deliver the inhab-
itants of the land into your hand; and thou shalt
drive them out before thee.
32 Thou shalt make no covenant with them, nor
with their gods.
33 They shall not dwell in thy land, lest they make
thee sin against me: for if thou serve their gods, it
will surely be a snare unto thee.

CHAPTER 24

AND he said unto Moses, Come up unto the LORD,
thou, and Aaron, Nadab, and Abihu, and seventy
of the elders of Israel; and worship ye afar off.
2 And Moses alone shall come near the LORD: but
they shall not come nigh; neither shall the people
go up with him.
3 ¶ And Moses came and told the people all the
words of the LORD, and all the judgments: and all
the people answered with one voice, and said, All
the words which the LORD hath said will we do.
4 And Moses wrote all the words of the LORD,
and rose up early in the morning, and builded an
altar under the hill, and twelve pillars, according
to the twelve tribes of Israel.
5 And he sent young men of the children of Is-
rael, which offered burnt offerings, and sacrificed
peace offerings of oxen unto the LORD.
6 And Moses took half of the blood, and put *it*
in basons; and half of the blood he sprinkled on
the altar.
7 And he took the book of the covenant, and read
in the audience of the people: and they said, All

23:24 *quite break.* Completely shatter.
23:26 *nothing cast.* No animal miscarry. *fulfil.* Make full—give long life.
23:28 *hornets.* Stinging wasps—apparently a metaphor for God's power to drive out Israel's enemies (Deut. 7:20; Josh. 24:12), perhaps through fear (v. 27; Deut. 2:25; see note at Ex. 15:16).
23:31 *sea of the Philistines.* Mediterranean Sea. *the river.* Euphrates River.
23:33 *snare.* Trap.

Thoughts for Personal/Family Worship: Chapter 23

1. **Sinful men promote their party, but the Lord delights in truth and justice regardless of whether a person is rich or poor, in the majority or the minority. Why is it so easy to side with the majority or your particular group instead of standing for truth and justice?**
2. **God sent His Son, the Angel of the covenant (Mal. 3:1). The King and Captain of His people (Josh. 5:14) came to fulfill His covenant and destroy their enemies (Gen. 12:3). Drawing near to man in Immanuel, the angel of God's presence (Isa. 63:9), God increases our obligation to pay attention to Him, obey Him, and reject all other gods (Judg. 2:1–2; Heb. 2:1–4). We must give our devotion to Christ alone.**

Chapter 24: *God formally makes the covenant with Israel through the blood of sacrifices, and the priests and elders enjoy a meal of fellowship in God's presence.*

The Cutting of the Covenant (24:1–18)

24:1 *Nadab, and Abihu.* Aaron's oldest sons (6:23). *worship.* As promised (3:12).
24:2 *Moses alone.* The prophet here acts like a priestly mediator, foreshadowing Christ. *nigh.* Near. Access to the Holy was not yet opened (19:12; Heb. 9:8).
24:3 God's *words* (20:1) and regulations (*judgments*, 21:1) are central to the covenant; man's participation is always a response to the Word. The covenant required obedience to *all the words* spoken by God (vv. 4,7–8). The Lord made the covenant with Israel as a nation, *all the people* responding as *one.* The people's commitment (*All . . . will we do*) was a noble declaration of love (20:6), but most of them lacked the heart to carry it out (32:8–9; Ps. 95:10).
24:4 *Moses wrote all the words of the LORD.* See note at 17:14. The *altar* represented the holy Lord and the *twelve pillars* the *tribes of Israel* as the two parties in the covenant.
24:5 *Burnt offerings* atone for sin and please God (Lev. 1:3–9); the participants ate a portion of the *peace offerings* as a sacred meal shared with the Lord (vv. 9–11; Lev. 7:11,15–21).
24:6 *basons.* Basins. *sprinkled on the altar.* Presenting the atoning blood to God to satisfy His wrath against sin so that God considers His people clean (Lev. 16:11,14–16,19,30).
24:7 *book of the covenant.* Laws and promises revealed to Moses on Mt. Sinai (20:22—23:33). *audience.* Ears, hearing. *All . . . will we do.* The covenant is a bond of loyalty (see note at v. 3).

that the LORD hath said will we do, and be obedient.
8 And Moses took the blood, and sprinkled *it*
on the people, and said, Behold the blood of the
covenant, which the LORD hath made with you
concerning all these words.
9 ¶ Then went up Moses, and Aaron, Nadab, and
Abihu, and seventy of the elders of Israel:
10 And they saw the God of Israel: and *there was*
under his feet as it were a paved work of a sap-
phire stone, and as it were the body of heaven in
his clearness.
11 And upon the nobles of the children of Israel
he laid not his hand: also they saw God, and did
eat and drink.
12 ¶ And the LORD said unto Moses, Come up to
me into the mount, and be there: and I will give
thee tables of stone, and a law, and commandments
which I have written; that thou mayest teach them.
13 And Moses rose up, and his minister Joshua:
and Moses went up into the mount of God.
14 And he said unto the elders, Tarry ye here for
us, until we come again unto you: and, behold,
Aaron and Hur *are* with you: if any man have any
matters to do, let him come unto them.
15 And Moses went up into the mount, and a
cloud covered the mount.
16 And the glory of the LORD abode upon mount
Sinai, and the cloud covered it six days: and the
seventh day he called unto Moses out of the midst
of the cloud.
17 And the sight of the glory of the LORD *was* like
devouring fire on the top of the mount in the eyes
of the children of Israel.
18 And Moses went into the midst of the cloud,
and gat him up into the mount: and Moses was in
the mount forty days and forty nights.

CHAPTER 25

AND the LORD spake unto Moses, saying,
2 Speak unto the children of Israel, that they
bring me an offering: of every man that giveth it
willingly with his heart ye shall take my offering.
3 And this *is* the offering which ye shall take of
them; gold, and silver, and brass,
4 And blue, and purple, and scarlet, and fine
linen, and goats' *hair*,
5 And rams' skins dyed red, and badgers' skins,
and shittim wood,
6 Oil for the light, spices for anointing oil, and for
sweet incense,
7 Onyx stones, and stones to be set in the ephod,
and in the breastplate.
8 And let them make me a sanctuary; that I may
dwell among them.
9 According to all that I shew thee, *after* the pat-
tern of the tabernacle, and the pattern of all the
instruments thereof, even so shall ye make *it*.
10 ¶ And they shall make an ark *of* shittim wood:
two cubits and a half *shall be* the length thereof,

24:8 *sprinkled it on the people.* The sacrifice must be applied to the people to sanctify them as a holy priesthood (19:6; 29:19–21). *blood of the covenant.* The covenant between God and man is a bond of redeeming blood (Zech. 9:11). *which the LORD hath made.* Literally, "that the Lord has cut," a reference to the cutting apart of the sacrifices (Gen. 15:9–11,17–18; Jer. 34:18–20).
24:10 *they saw the God of Israel.* Not the divine essence, which is invisible (Col. 1:15), but a sign of His covenantal presence with His people, a foretaste of the incarnation. The fruit of the covenant is communion with God. *sapphire . . . body of heaven in his clearness.* Like a clear, blue sky (Ezek. 1:26). The covenant is a bond that joins heaven and earth (Gen. 28:12,17).
24:11 *nobles.* Leaders. *he laid not his hand.* He did not harm them, though no man may see God's unmediated glory and live (33:20), for the covenant opens the way for friendly fellowship between God and man, celebrated joyfully in a shared meal (*eat and drink*).
24:12 *tables.* Tablets. See 31:18; 2 Cor. 3:3.
24:13 *minister.* Servant.
24:14 *Tarry.* Wait.
24:17 *glory of the LORD . . . devouring fire.* The covenant does not change God's nature as a glorious flame of absolute holiness, so Christians must worship with reverence (Heb. 12:28–29).
24:18 *gat him.* Went up.

Thoughts for Personal/Family Worship: Chapter 24

1. **The old covenant came with external ceremonies and the blood of animals, none of which can save (Heb. 10:1,4). These pointed to Christ's blood of the covenant (1 Cor. 11:25; Heb. 12:24; 13:20), for the promised inheritance came only through the redeeming death of Christ, the Mediator (Heb. 9:15–21). The believing remnant in Israel clung by faith to the promise of the coming Redeemer (Gen. 3:15; 49:10). We too must cling by faith to Christ, who has established the new covenant in His blood.**
2. **Even in covenant mercies, God remains God and we must obey Him. This requires more than a verbal commitment; Israel pledged obedience but had no heart to perform it. We need the Spirit of God to sanctify our hearts by faith so that we experience Christ's blood applied to our guilt and obey God (1 Peter 1:2). Do you have this living hope that produces holiness? Or are you like most of Israel—all words but no reality?**

God's Holy Presence in the Tabernacle (25:1—40:38)
The Design of the Tabernacle (25:1—31:18)

Chapter 25: ***Moses receives the instructions for the materials of the tabernacle and the pattern of its ark, table, and lampstand.***

25:3 *brass.* Alloy of copper, either brass or bronze.
25:4 *linen.* Cloth made of flax fibers.
25:5 *badgers' skins.* Leather made of hides of unknown animal. *shittim.* Acacia, a dark, hard wood avoided by wood-eating insects.
25:7 *ephod.* Sleeveless outer garment of priests (28:4,6).
25:8 *sanctuary.* Holy place.
25:9 *tabernacle.* Literally, "a home" (Num. 16:24).
25:10 *ark.* Chest, not the same word as Noah's ark. *cubit.* Eighteen inches. *thereof.* Of it.

and a cubit and a half the breadth thereof, and a
cubit and a half the height thereof.
11 And thou shalt overlay it with pure gold,
within and without shalt thou overlay it, and shalt
make upon it a crown of gold round about.
12 And thou shalt cast four rings of gold for it,
and put *them* in the four corners thereof; and two
rings *shall be* in the one side of it, and two rings in
the other side of it.
13 And thou shalt make staves *of* shittim wood,
and overlay them with gold.
14 And thou shalt put the staves into the rings
by the sides of the ark, that the ark may be borne
with them.
15 The staves shall be in the rings of the ark: they
shall not be taken from it.
16 And thou shalt put into the ark the testimony
which I shall give thee.
17 And thou shalt make a mercy seat *of* pure gold:
two cubits and a half *shall be* the length thereof,
and a cubit and a half the breadth thereof.
18 And thou shalt make two cherubims *of* gold,
of beaten work shalt thou make them, in the two
ends of the mercy seat.
19 And make one cherub on the one end, and the
other cherub on the other end: *even* of the mercy
seat shall ye make the cherubims on the two ends
thereof.
20 And the cherubims shall stretch forth *their*
wings on high, covering the mercy seat with their
wings, and their faces *shall look* one to another;
toward the mercy seat shall the faces of the cheru-
bims be.
21 And thou shalt put the mercy seat above upon
the ark; and in the ark thou shalt put the testi-
mony that I shall give thee.
22 And there I will meet with thee, and I will com-
mune with thee from above the mercy seat, from
between the two cherubims which *are* upon the
ark of the testimony, of all *things* which I will give
thee in commandment unto the children of Israel.
23 ¶ Thou shalt also make a table *of* shittim
wood: two cubits *shall be* the length thereof, and
a cubit the breadth thereof, and a cubit and a half
the height thereof.
24 And thou shalt overlay it with pure gold, and
make thereto a crown of gold round about.
25 And thou shalt make unto it a border of an
hand breadth round about, and thou shalt make a
golden crown to the border thereof round about.
26 And thou shalt make for it four rings of gold,
and put the rings in the four corners that *are* on
the four feet thereof.
27 Over against the border shall the rings be for
places of the staves to bear the table.
28 And thou shalt make the staves *of* shittim
wood, and overlay them with gold, that the table
may be borne with them.
29 And thou shalt make the dishes thereof, and
spoons thereof, and covers thereof, and bowls
thereof, to cover withal: *of* pure gold shalt thou
make them.
30 And thou shalt set upon the table shewbread
before me alway.
31 ¶ And thou shalt make a candlestick *of* pure
gold: *of* beaten work shall the candlestick be
made: his shaft, and his branches, his bowls, his
knops, and his flowers, shall be of the same.
32 And six branches shall come out of the sides of
it; three branches of the candlestick out of the one
side, and three branches of the candlestick out of
the other side:
33 Three bowls made like unto almonds, *with* a
knop and a flower in one branch; and three bowls
made like almonds in the other branch, *with* a
knop and a flower: so in the six branches that
come out of the candlestick.
34 And in the candlestick *shall be* four bowls
made like unto almonds, *with* their knops and
their flowers.
35 And *there shall be* a knop under two branches
of the same, and a knop under two branches of

25:11 *crown*. Formed trim or moulding.
25:13–14 *staves*. Poles. *borne*. Carried. The Lord travels with His people.
25:16–17 *testimony*. The Ten Commandments, as a prophetic witness to the covenant (31:18). *mercy seat*. Place of turning away wrath and finding forgiveness. There the high priest made propitiation for Israel's sins (Lev. 16:14–16). These types show that God is with His people both in forgiveness and obedience to the law, the double grace of justification and sanctification.
25:18 *cherubims* (plural of cherub). Heavenly spirits present at the garden of Eden (Gen. 3:24; Ezek. 28:13–14), depicted as huge, winged creatures (1 Kings 6:23; Ezek. 1:5–14; 10:1), usually the guardians or proclaimers of God's holiness.
25:19 *thereof*. Of it.
25:22 *commune*. Speak. The King of heaven is present to *meet with* His people in the Word.
25:23 *shittim*. Acacia.
25:24 *crown*. Formed trim or moulding.
25:25 *hand breadth*. Three inches.
25:29 *covers*. Jars. *to cover withal*. With which to pour.
25:30 *shewbread*. Bread of the presence (Lev. 24:5–9).
25:31 *candlestick*. Lampstand for burning olive oil (27:20), not candles. *knops*. Buds from which *flowers* grow.
25:38 *snuffdishes*. Pans for holding hot coals.
25:39 *talent*. Unit of weight, about 75 lbs.
25:40 *look that thou make them*. God's worship must follow God's Word, neither adding nor subtracting (Deut. 12:32). *pattern*. A type of heavenly realities (Heb. 8:5).

Thoughts for Personal/Family Worship: Chapter 25

1. The ark of the covenant (vv. 10–22) symbolized God's chariot-throne carried by the spirits of heaven (Ps. 18:1; 99:1,5), a sign that the King of heaven lived with Israel. Yet there was no image for God Himself (20:4–6) for He is holy, more glorious than all idols (15:11). Christ is the heavenly King who lives with His people

the same, and a knop under two branches of the
same, according to the six branches that proceed
out of the candlestick.
36 Their knops and their branches shall be of the
same: all it *shall be* one beaten work *of* pure gold.
37 And thou shalt make the seven lamps thereof:
and they shall light the lamps thereof, that they
may give light over against it.
38 And the tongs thereof, and the snuffdishes
thereof, *shall be of* pure gold.
39 *Of* a talent of pure gold shall he make it, with
all these vessels.
40 And look that thou make *them* after their
pattern, which was shewed thee in the mount.

CHAPTER 26

MOREOVER thou shalt make the tabernacle *with*
ten curtains *of* fine twined linen, and blue, and
purple, and scarlet: *with* cherubims of cunning
work shalt thou make them.
2 The length of one curtain *shall be* eight and
twenty cubits, and the breadth of one curtain four
cubits: and every one of the curtains shall have
one measure.
3 The five curtains shall be coupled together one
to another; and *other* five curtains *shall be* cou-
pled one to another.
4 And thou shalt make loops of blue upon the
edge of the one curtain from the selvedge in the
coupling; and likewise shalt thou make in the ut-
termost edge of *another* curtain, in the coupling
of the second.
5 Fifty loops shalt thou make in the one curtain,
and fifty loops shalt thou make in the edge of the
curtain that *is* in the coupling of the second; that
the loops may take hold one of another.
6 And thou shalt make fifty taches of gold, and
couple the curtains together with the taches: and
it shall be one tabernacle.
7 ¶ And thou shalt make curtains *of* goats' *hair* to
be a covering upon the tabernacle: eleven curtains
shalt thou make.
8 The length of one curtain *shall be* thirty cubits,
and the breadth of one curtain four cubits: and
the eleven curtains *shall be all* of one measure.
9 And thou shalt couple five curtains by them-
selves, and six curtains by themselves, and shalt
double the sixth curtain in the forefront of the
tabernacle.
10 And thou shalt make fifty loops on the edge of
the one curtain *that is* outmost in the coupling,
and fifty loops in the edge of the curtain which
coupleth the second.
11 And thou shalt make fifty taches of brass, and
put the taches into the loops, and couple the tent
together, that it may be one.
12 And the remnant that remaineth of the cur-
tains of the tent, the half curtain that remaineth,
shall hang over the backside of the tabernacle.
13 And a cubit on the one side, and a cubit on the
other side of that which remaineth in the length
of the curtains of the tent, it shall hang over the
sides of the tabernacle on this side and on that
side, to cover it.
14 And thou shalt make a covering for the tent
of rams' skins dyed red, and a covering above *of*
badgers' skins.
15 ¶ And thou shalt make boards for the taber-
nacle *of* shittim wood standing up.
16 Ten cubits *shall be* the length of a board, and a
cubit and a half *shall be* the breadth of one board.
17 Two tenons *shall there be* in one board, set in
order one against another: thus shalt thou make
for all the boards of the tabernacle.
18 And thou shalt make the boards for the taber-
nacle, twenty boards on the south side southward.
19 And thou shalt make forty sockets of silver
under the twenty boards; two sockets under one
board for his two tenons, and two sockets under
another board for his two tenons.
20 And for the second side of the tabernacle on
the north side *there shall be* twenty boards:
21 And their forty sockets *of* silver; two sockets
under one board, and two sockets under another
board.

(Matt. 28:18,20). He is also our mercy seat, the propitiation of all the sins of believers (Rom. 3:24–25).

2. **The table of shewbread (vv. 23–30) represented God's fellowship with His people and pleasure in them (Ps. 149:4; Isa. 62:4–5). The golden lampstand (vv. 31–39), formed in the shape of a flowering tree, was a type of the light and life our Priest gives to His people (Num. 6:24–26; Ps. 36:9; John 1:4; Rev. 1:13; 2:1) through the Holy Spirit (Zech. 4:2,6). How do God's people experience communion with Christ today?**

Chapter 26: *Moses is taught the design of the holy tent where God dwells.*

26:1 *tabernacle.* See note at 25:9. *fine twined linen.* White cloth of very thin flax fibers carefully woven together. The colors (*blue, and purple,* and *scarlet*) are appropriate for wealth and royalty (Judg. 8:26; 2 Sam. 1:24; Est. 8:15). The combination of *blue* and *cherubims* also suggest heaven (see notes at 24:10; 25:18). This was the palace of the King of heaven. *cunning.* Skillful.

26:2 *cubits.* About eighteen inches each.

26:4 *selvedge.* Edge.

26:6 *taches.* Clasps or hooks.

26:9 *forefront.* Front.

26:14 *rams' skins dyed red.* Both the animal and the color are reminders of blood sacrifices. *badgers' skins.* See note at 25:5.

26:15–29 The tent frame supported the curtains, creating a rectangular tent 15 ft. wide, 15 ft. high, and 45 ft. long.

26:15 *shittim.* See note at 25:5.

26:17 *tenons.* Literally, "hands," projections that fit pieces together.

26:19 *sockets.* Bases.

22 And for the sides of the tabernacle westward
thou shalt make six boards.
23 And two boards shalt thou make for the
corners of the tabernacle in the two sides.
24 And they shall be coupled together beneath,
and they shall be coupled together above the head
of it unto one ring: thus shall it be for them both;
they shall be for the two corners.
25 And they shall be eight boards, and their sock-
ets *of* silver, sixteen sockets; two sockets under one
board, and two sockets under another board.
26 ¶ And thou shalt make bars *of* shittim wood;
five for the boards of the one side of the tabernacle,
27 And five bars for the boards of the other side of
the tabernacle, and five bars for the boards of the
side of the tabernacle, for the two sides westward.
28 And the middle bar in the midst of the boards
shall reach from end to end.
29 And thou shalt overlay the boards with gold,
and make their rings *of* gold *for* places for the
bars: and thou shalt overlay the bars with gold.
30 And thou shalt rear up the tabernacle accord-
ing to the fashion thereof which was shewed thee
in the mount.
31 ¶ And thou shalt make a vail *of* blue, and
purple, and scarlet, and fine twined linen of
cunning work: with cherubims shall it be made:
32 And thou shalt hang it upon four pillars of
shittim *wood* overlaid with gold: their hooks *shall
be of* gold, upon the four sockets of silver.
33 ¶ And thou shalt hang up the vail under the
taches, that thou mayest bring in thither within the
vail the ark of the testimony: and the vail shall divide
unto you between the holy *place* and the most holy.
34 And thou shalt put the mercy seat upon the
ark of the testimony in the most holy *place*.
35 And thou shalt set the table without the vail,
and the candlestick over against the table on the
side of the tabernacle toward the south: and thou
shalt put the table on the north side.
36 And thou shalt make an hanging for the door
of the tent, *of* blue, and purple, and scarlet, and
fine twined linen, wrought with needlework.
37 And thou shalt make for the hanging five
pillars *of* shittim *wood*, and overlay them with
gold, *and* their hooks *shall be of* gold: and thou
shalt cast five sockets of brass for them.

CHAPTER 27

AND thou shalt make an altar *of* shittim wood,
five cubits long, and five cubits broad; the altar
shall be foursquare: and the height thereof *shall
be* three cubits.
2 And thou shalt make the horns of it upon the
four corners thereof: his horns shall be of the
same: and thou shalt overlay it with brass.
3 And thou shalt make his pans to receive his
ashes, and his shovels, and his basons, and his
fleshhooks, and his firepans: all the vessels thereof
thou shalt make *of* brass.
4 And thou shalt make for it a grate of network
of brass; and upon the net shalt thou make four
brasen rings in the four corners thereof.
5 And thou shalt put it under the compass of
the altar beneath, that the net may be even to the
midst of the altar.
6 And thou shalt make staves for the altar, staves

26:30 *rear up*. Set up. *according to the fashion*. Literally, "according to its judgment/rule," following the laws revealed by God (25:40).
26:31 *vail*. Veil or curtain. Abolished in Christ's death (Luke 23:45).
26:33 *thither*. There, to that place. *the most holy*. In the temple this was a perfect cube (1 Kings 6:20), which suggests that here it was a 15 ft. cube, the back third of the tabernacle.
26:35 *without*. Outside. *candlestick*. See note at 25:31.
26:36 *wrought with needlework*. Made by embroidery.
26:37 *sockets*. Bases.

Thoughts for Personal/Family Worship: Chapter 26

1. **In the tabernacle, God's glory was both present and hidden. The tent curtains (vv. 1–14) in four layers hid its contents well. Outside it looked quite ordinary; inside were royal colors and sparkling gold. However, even the priests in the holy place faced the veil separating them from the most holy place. God's holiness separates Him from sinners (Isa. 59:2). Only Christ can open the way to God by His death and intercession (Heb. 9:6–8; 10:19–21). The divine glory comes to us hidden in humble, crucified flesh (John 1:14; 1 Cor. 1:23–24). His glorious presence with His people is seen only by faith and enjoyed by those who are humble and contrite over sin (Isa. 66:2; Phil. 3:3,8–10).**
2. **The abundance of gold inside the tabernacle, the lampstand shaped like a tree (v. 35), and cherubims (vv. 1,31) point back to the garden of Eden (Gen. 2:9,11–12; 3:24). God's presence with His people is a return to Paradise with all its sweet fruit (Rev. 2:7; 22:1–5). How does God give His children foretastes of the heavenly paradise even now?**

Chapter 27: *Moses receives instructions for the altar of burnt offerings, the court of the tabernacle, and the tending of the lamps.*

27:1 *altar*. The large altar of burnt offering (30:28; 40:29), where priests offered the burnt offerings to make propitiation for Israel's sin (29:38–42; Lev. 1:4). *shittim*. Acacia. *cubits*. Eighteen inches each. *foursquare*. Four-sided. *thereof*. Of it.
27:2 *horns*. Projections to which the sacrifice was tied (Ps. 118:27) and on which its blood was put to atone for sin (29:12; Lev. 16:18). Like animal horns, they were symbols of God's power to save (Ps. 18:2), in which repentant sinners find refuge (1 Kings 1:50–53).
27:3 *basons*. Basins or bowls. *fleshhooks*. Forks to pull out meat.
27:4 *grate of network*. Grill. *brasen*. Unlike the golden furniture inside the tabernacle, furniture outside was made of copper alloy, either bronze or brass.
27:5 *compass*. Rim, holding the grill at half the height of the altar.
27:6 *staves*. Poles.

of shittim wood, and overlay them with brass.
7 And the staves shall be put into the rings, and
the staves shall be upon the two sides of the altar,
to bear it.
8 Hollow with boards shalt thou make it: as it was
shewed thee in the mount, so shall they make *it*.
9 ¶ And thou shalt make the court of the tabernacle: for the south side southward *there shall be*
hangings for the court *of* fine twined linen of an
hundred cubits long for one side:
10 And the twenty pillars thereof and their
twenty sockets *shall be of* brass; the hooks of the
pillars and their fillets *shall be of* silver.
11 And likewise for the north side in length *there*
shall be hangings of an hundred *cubits* long, and
his twenty pillars and their twenty sockets *of* brass;
the hooks of the pillars and their fillets *of* silver.
12 ¶ And *for* the breadth of the court on the west
side *shall be* hangings of fifty cubits: their pillars
ten, and their sockets ten.
13 And the breadth of the court on the east side
eastward *shall be* fifty cubits.
14 The hangings of one side *of the gate shall be*
fifteen cubits: their pillars three, and their sockets three.
15 And on the other side *shall be* hangings fifteen
cubits: their pillars three, and their sockets three.
16 ¶ And for the gate of the court *shall be* an
hanging of twenty cubits, *of* blue, and purple,
and scarlet, and fine twined linen, wrought with
needlework: *and* their pillars *shall be* four, and
their sockets four.
17 All the pillars round about the court *shall be*
filleted with silver; their hooks *shall be of* silver,
and their sockets *of* brass.
18 ¶ The length of the court *shall be* an hundred
cubits, and the breadth fifty every where, and the
height five cubits *of* fine twined linen, and their
sockets *of* brass.
19 All the vessels of the tabernacle in all the
service thereof, and all the pins thereof, and all
the pins of the court, *shall be of* brass.
20 ¶ And thou shalt command the children of
Israel, that they bring thee pure oil olive beaten
for the light, to cause the lamp to burn always.
21 In the tabernacle of the congregation without
the vail, which *is* before the testimony, Aaron and
his sons shall order it from evening to morning before the LORD: *it shall be* a statute for ever unto their
generations on the behalf of the children of Israel.

CHAPTER 28

AND take thou unto thee Aaron thy brother, and
his sons with him, from among the children of
Israel, that he may minister unto me in the priest's
office, *even* Aaron, Nadab and Abihu, Eleazar and
Ithamar, Aaron's sons.
2 And thou shalt make holy garments for Aaron
thy brother for glory and for beauty.
3 And thou shalt speak unto all *that are* wise
hearted, whom I have filled with the spirit of
wisdom, that they may make Aaron's garments to
consecrate him, that he may minister unto me in
the priest's office.
4 And these *are* the garments which they shall
make; a breastplate, and an ephod, and a robe, and
a broidered coat, a mitre, and a girdle: and they
shall make holy garments for Aaron thy brother,
and his sons, that he may minister unto me in the
priest's office.
5 And they shall take gold, and blue, and purple,
and scarlet, and fine linen.
6 ¶ And they shall make the ephod *of* gold, *of*

27:8 *as it was shewed thee in the mount*. See 25:40; 26:30.
27:9–19 *court of the tabernacle*. Yard around the Lord's tent, measuring 150 ft. by 75 ft., fenced off by 7.5-ft.-high curtains hung from pillars to separate the holy places from ritual uncleanness (Lev. 15:31; Num. 5:3; 19:13,20). *sockets*. Bases. *fillets*. Bands. *pins*. Pegs or stakes.
27:21 *tabernacle of the congregation*. Tent of meeting, using a different word for *tabernacle* (see note at 25:9). *without the vail*. Outside the veil. *order*. Arrange.

Thoughts for Personal/Family Worship: Chapter 27

1. **The only way to draw near to God is through the altar. There the priests killed a sin offering and took its blood into the tabernacle. The Lord Jesus offered Himself once and for all and then brought His human nature into heaven itself to appear on behalf of His people (Heb. 9:11–14,24,28). Christians thus have a greater altar—not a physical object, but Christ Himself who strengthens our hearts with grace (Heb. 13:9–10). Let us pray for grace to be quick to use this altar for all our sins and all our needs.**
2. **Though outside the tabernacle, the court was still a holy place (Lev. 6:16,26). Here the worshipers would bring their sacrifices to the priests and sing God's praises (Ps. 96:8; 100:4; Isa. 1:11–12). How much more is the church a holy assembly when it gathers to worship on the Lord's Day? Indeed, through faith in Christ, we enter the most holy place and worship before God with the heavenly assembly of saints and angels (Heb. 10:19–22; 12:22–24). How could believing this transform our attitude toward church?**

Chapter 28: *God calls Aaron and his sons into the priesthood and reveals the sacred garments that the priests must wear for glory and beauty.*

28:1 *minister unto me in the priest's office*. Literally, "serve Me as a priest." The priest is called by God, and his work is primarily toward God (*unto me*) as the representative of the people (Heb. 5:1,4).
28:3 *wise hearted . . . spirit of wisdom*. The Holy Spirit is the source of all human ability (Job 32:8), including artistry and craftsmanship (31:3–5; 35:31–35). *consecrate*. Set apart as holy.
28:4 *ephod*. Sleeveless vest or apron worn over the robe. *broidered*. Woven in a checkered pattern. *mitre*. Turban. *girdle*. Belt or sash.
28:5 The priests were clothed in the colors and materials of

blue, and *of* purple, *of* scarlet, and fine twined
linen, with cunning work.
7 It shall have the two shoulderpieces thereof
joined at the two edges thereof; and *so* it shall be
joined together.
8 And the curious girdle of the ephod, which *is*
upon it, shall be of the same, according to the
work thereof; *even of* gold, *of* blue, and purple,
and scarlet, and fine twined linen.
9 And thou shalt take two onyx stones, and grave
on them the names of the children of Israel:
10 Six of their names on one stone, and *the other*
six names of the rest on the other stone, accord-
ing to their birth.
11 With the work of an engraver in stone, *like* the
engravings of a signet, shalt thou engrave the two
stones with the names of the children of Israel:
thou shalt make them to be set in ouches of gold.
12 And thou shalt put the two stones upon the
shoulders of the ephod *for* stones of memorial
unto the children of Israel: and Aaron shall bear
their names before the LORD upon his two shoul-
ders for a memorial.
13 ¶ And thou shalt make ouches *of* gold;
14 And two chains *of* pure gold at the ends; *of*
wreathen work shalt thou make them, and fasten
the wreathen chains to the ouches.
15 ¶ And thou shalt make the breastplate of judg-
ment with cunning work; after the work of the
ephod thou shalt make it; *of* gold, *of* blue, and *of*
purple, and *of* scarlet, and *of* fine twined linen,
shalt thou make it.
16 Foursquare it shall be *being* doubled; a span
shall be the length thereof, and a span *shall be* the
breadth thereof.
17 And thou shalt set in it settings of stones, *even*
four rows of stones: *the first* row *shall be* a sardius,
a topaz, and a carbuncle: *this shall be* the first row.
18 And the second row *shall be* an emerald, a sap-
phire, and a diamond.
19 And the third row a ligure, an agate, and an
amethyst.
20 And the fourth row a beryl, and an onyx, and a
jasper: they shall be set in gold in their inclosings.
21 And the stones shall be with the names of
the children of Israel, twelve, according to their
names, *like* the engravings of a signet; every one
with his name shall they be according to the
twelve tribes.
22 ¶ And thou shalt make upon the breastplate
chains at the ends *of* wreathen work *of* pure gold.
23 And thou shalt make upon the breastplate two
rings of gold, and shalt put the two rings on the
two ends of the breastplate.
24 And thou shalt put the two wreathen *chains* of
gold in the two rings *which are* on the ends of the
breastplate.
25 And *the other* two ends of the two wreathen
chains thou shalt fasten in the two ouches, and put
them on the shoulderpieces of the ephod before it.
26 ¶ And thou shalt make two rings of gold, and
thou shalt put them upon the two ends of the
breastplate in the border thereof, which *is* in the
side of the ephod inward.
27 And two *other* rings of gold thou shalt make,
and shalt put them on the two sides of the ephod
underneath, toward the forepart thereof, over
against the *other* coupling thereof, above the curi-
ous girdle of the ephod.
28 And they shall bind the breastplate by the
rings thereof unto the rings of the ephod with a
lace of blue, that *it* may be above the curious gir-
dle of the ephod, and that the breastplate be not
loosed from the ephod.
29 And Aaron shall bear the names of the chil-
dren of Israel in the breastplate of judgment upon
his heart, when he goeth in unto the holy *place*,
for a memorial before the LORD continually.
30 ¶ And thou shalt put in the breastplate of
judgment the Urim and the Thummim; and they

---

the tabernacle, representing holiness (*gold*) and royalty (see note at 26:1).

28:6–29 *cunning*. Skillfully woven. *thereof*. Of it. *curious*. Artistic. *grave*. Engrave. *signet*. Ring or other object with a seal. *ouches*. Wires, prongs, or pouches to hold gems. *memorial*. Remembrance. *wreathen*. Twisted like cord. *doubled*. Folded. *foursquare*. Four-sided. *span*. Nine inches.

28:17–20 Some of these twelve *stones* cannot be precisely identified.

28:30 *the Urim and the Thummim*. Used to receive direction (*judgment*) from God (Num. 27:21; 1 Sam. 14:41; 28:6; Ezra 2:63). The high priest was a prophet (John 11:51).

28:32 *habergeon*. Armored shirt; Hebrew uncertain. *rent*. Torn.

28:33–35 *pomegranates*. Round, edible fruit, two to five inches in size, found in the land of Canaan (Num. 13:23; Deut. 8:8). *bells*. The priest must walk with the sounds of holiness (*gold*) to avoid offending the Lord (*that he die not*).

28:36 *plate*. Literally, "shining thing" or "flower." Also called the "holy crown" (29:6).

28:37 *mitre*. Turban.

28:38 *hallow*. Set apart as holy. The golden head plate showed that the priest must *bear* the responsibility to be holy, clean, and obedient in order that the sacrifices (*holy gifts*) may *be accepted before the LORD* (Lev. 22:1–9).

28:40 *girdles*. Belts or sashes. *bonnets*. Caps.

28:41 *anoint... consecrate*. Explained in ch. 29. *minister*. See note at v. 1.

28:42 *breeches*. Underpants. *loins*. Pelvic area. The need to cover their *nakedness* points back to the fall of man into sin and misery (Gen. 3:7).

28:43 *bear not iniquity*. Do not become guilty of sin. *seed*. Offspring.

Thoughts for Personal/Family Worship: Chapter 28

1. How glorious and beautiful is our High Priest in the sight of God (Heb. 7:26)—holy, harmless, undefiled, separate from sinners, and made higher than the heavens! Surely the Father is delighted to hear His intercession. Are you

shall be upon Aaron's heart, when he goeth in be-
fore the LORD: and Aaron shall bear the judgment
of the children of Israel upon his heart before the
LORD continually.
31 ¶ And thou shalt make the robe of the ephod
all *of* blue.
32 And there shall be an hole in the top of it, in
the midst thereof: it shall have a binding of woven
work round about the hole of it, as it were the
hole of an habergeon, that it be not rent.
33 ¶ And *beneath* upon the hem of it thou shalt
make pomegranates *of* blue, and *of* purple, and *of*
scarlet, round about the hem thereof; and bells of
gold between them round about:
34 A golden bell and a pomegranate, a golden bell
and a pomegranate, upon the hem of the robe
round about.
35 And it shall be upon Aaron to minister: and
his sound shall be heard when he goeth in unto
the holy *place* before the LORD, and when he com-
eth out, that he die not.
36 ¶ And thou shalt make a plate *of* pure gold,
and grave upon it, *like* the engravings of a signet,
HOLINESS TO THE LORD.
37 And thou shalt put it on a blue lace, that it
may be upon the mitre; upon the forefront of the
mitre it shall be.
38 And it shall be upon Aaron's forehead, that
Aaron may bear the iniquity of the holy things,
which the children of Israel shall hallow in all
their holy gifts; and it shall be always upon his
forehead, that they may be accepted before the
LORD.
39 ¶ And thou shalt embroider the coat of fine
linen, and thou shalt make the mitre *of* fine linen,
and thou shalt make the girdle *of* needlework.
40 ¶ And for Aaron's sons thou shalt make coats,
and thou shalt make for them girdles, and bon-
nets shalt thou make for them, for glory and for
beauty.
41 And thou shalt put them upon Aaron thy
brother, and his sons with him; and shalt anoint
them, and consecrate them, and sanctify them, that
they may minister unto me in the priest's office.
42 And thou shalt make them linen breeches to
cover their nakedness; from the loins even unto
the thighs they shall reach:
43 And they shall be upon Aaron, and upon his
sons, when they come in unto the tabernacle of
the congregation, or when they come near unto
the altar to minister in the holy *place*; that they
bear not iniquity, and die: *it shall be* a statute for
ever unto him and his seed after him.

CHAPTER 29

AND this *is* the thing that thou shalt do unto them
to hallow them, to minister unto me in the priest's
office: Take one young bullock, and two rams
without blemish,
2 And unleavened bread, and cakes unleavened
tempered with oil, and wafers unleavened anointed
with oil: *of* wheaten flour shalt thou make them.
3 And thou shalt put them into one basket, and
bring them in the basket, with the bullock and the
two rams.
4 And Aaron and his sons thou shalt bring unto
the door of the tabernacle of the congregation,
and shalt wash them with water.
5 And thou shalt take the garments, and put
upon Aaron the coat, and the robe of the ephod,
and the ephod, and the breastplate, and gird him
with the curious girdle of the ephod:
6 And thou shalt put the mitre upon his head,
and put the holy crown upon the mitre.
7 Then shalt thou take the anointing oil, and
pour *it* upon his head, and anoint him.
8 And thou shalt bring his sons, and put coats
upon them.
9 And thou shalt gird them with girdles, Aaron
and his sons, and put the bonnets on them: and the
priest's office shall be theirs for a perpetual statute:
and thou shalt consecrate Aaron and his sons.
10 And thou shalt cause a bullock to be brought
before the tabernacle of the congregation: and
Aaron and his sons shall put their hands upon the
head of the bullock.
11 And thou shalt kill the bullock before the LORD,

---

relying upon this perfect Priest? Have you become experientially acquainted with the value of His constant intercessions (Rom. 8:34; Heb. 7:25)?

2. The presence of our High Priest before the Lord is a constant appeal for God to remember His covenant and show mercy to His people despite their sins (2:24; 6:5; 32:13; Lev. 26:44–45). Their names were on His shoulders (v. 12) as a sign that Christ took responsibility for them as their Surety, and upon His heart (v. 29) because He loves them. What does it mean to you that Christ has His people on what Thomas Goodwin called His "beautiful heart"?

Chapter 29: ***God reveals the ordination procedure for the priesthood of Aaron and the daily duty of the priests for His purpose of dwelling with Israel.***

29:1–2 *hallow*. Set apart as holy. *minister*. See note at 28:1. *bullock*. Bull. *rams*. Male sheep. *tempered*. Mixed. *wheaten*. Of wheat. The lack of *blemish* or leaven symbolized moral purity.

29:4 *tabernacle of the congregation*. See note at 27:21.

29:5–6 On these garments, see ch. 28. *gird*. Tie a belt or sash.

29:7 *anoint*. Put fragrant olive oil (30:22–33) on the head, a sign of the Holy Spirit's sanctification and power for the office of prophet, priest, or king (1 Sam. 16:13; Isa. 61:1).

29:9 *priest's office*. Priesthood. *consecrate*. Ordinarily translates the verb "make holy," but in 28:41 and this chapter it is another verb—literally, "fill the hand," meaning to "ordain."

by the door of the tabernacle of the congregation.
12 And thou shalt take of the blood of the
bullock, and put *it* upon the horns of the altar
with thy finger, and pour all the blood beside the
bottom of the altar.
13 And thou shalt take all the fat that covereth the
inwards, and the caul *that is* above the liver, and
the two kidneys, and the fat that *is* upon them,
and burn *them* upon the altar.
14 But the flesh of the bullock, and his skin, and
his dung, shalt thou burn with fire without the
camp: it *is* a sin offering.
15 ¶ Thou shalt also take one ram; and Aaron and
his sons shall put their hands upon the head of
the ram.
16 And thou shalt slay the ram, and thou shalt take
his blood, and sprinkle *it* round about upon the
altar.
17 And thou shalt cut the ram in pieces, and wash
the inwards of him, and his legs, and put *them*
unto his pieces, and unto his head.
18 And thou shalt burn the whole ram upon the
altar: it *is* a burnt offering unto the LORD: it *is* a
sweet savour, an offering made by fire unto the
LORD.
19 ¶ And thou shalt take the other ram; and Aaron
and his sons shall put their hands upon the head
of the ram.
20 Then shalt thou kill the ram, and take of his
blood, and put *it* upon the tip of the right ear of
Aaron, and upon the tip of the right ear of his
sons, and upon the thumb of their right hand,
and upon the great toe of their right foot, and
sprinkle the blood upon the altar round about.
21 And thou shalt take of the blood that *is* upon
the altar, and of the anointing oil, and sprinkle *it*
upon Aaron, and upon his garments, and upon
his sons, and upon the garments of his sons with
him: and he shall be hallowed, and his garments,
and his sons, and his sons' garments with him.
22 Also thou shalt take of the ram the fat and the
rump, and the fat that covereth the inwards, and
the caul *above* the liver, and the two kidneys, and
the fat that *is* upon them, and the right shoulder;
for it *is* a ram of consecration:
23 And one loaf of bread, and one cake of oiled
bread, and one wafer out of the basket of the un-
leavened bread that *is* before the LORD:
24 And thou shalt put all in the hands of Aaron,
and in the hands of his sons; and shalt wave them
for a wave offering before the LORD.
25 And thou shalt receive them of their hands,
and burn *them* upon the altar for a burnt offer-
ing, for a sweet savour before the LORD: it *is* an
offering made by fire unto the LORD.
26 And thou shalt take the breast of the ram of
Aaron's consecration, and wave it *for* a wave of-
fering before the LORD: and it shall be thy part.
27 And thou shalt sanctify the breast of the wave
offering, and the shoulder of the heave offering,
which is waved, and which is heaved up, of the
ram of the consecration, *even* of *that* which *is* for
Aaron, and of *that* which is for his sons:
28 And it shall be Aaron's and his sons' by a statute
for ever from the children of Israel: for it *is* an heave
offering: and it shall be an heave offering from the
children of Israel of the sacrifice of their peace
offerings, *even* their heave offering unto the LORD.
29 ¶ And the holy garments of Aaron shall be his
sons' after him, to be anointed therein, and to be
consecrated in them.
30 *And* that son that is priest in his stead shall
put them on seven days, when he cometh into the
tabernacle of the congregation to minister in the
holy *place*.
31 ¶ And thou shalt take the ram of the consecra-
tion, and seethe his flesh in the holy place.
32 And Aaron and his sons shall eat the flesh of
the ram, and the bread that *is* in the basket, *by* the
door of the tabernacle of the congregation.
33 And they shall eat those things wherewith
the atonement was made, to consecrate *and* to
sanctify them: but a stranger shall not eat *thereof*,
because they *are* holy.
34 And if ought of the flesh of the consecrations,
or of the bread, remain unto the morning, then

29:13 *inwards*. Inner organs.
29:14 *without*. Outside.
29:18 *sweet savour*. Pleasing aroma (Eph. 5:2; Phil. 4:18).
29:21 *hallowed*. Set apart as holy.
29:22 *consecration*. Literally, "filling" (see note at v. 9).
29:30 *stead*. Place.
29:31 *seethe*. Boil.
29:33 *wherewith*. With which. *stranger*. Outsider.
29:34 *ought*. Anything. *flesh of the consecrations*. Meat of the ram for ordination ("filling," see note at v. 9).
29:40 *deal*. Measure. *hin*. Four quarts.
29:41 *sweet savour*. Pleasing aroma.
29:43 *sanctified*. Set apart as holy.
29:45–46 The covenantal knowledge of God and enjoyment of His holy presence is the great purpose of redemption from Egypt—and of the church's redemption from sin by Christ.

Thoughts for Personal/Family Worship: Chapter 29

1. How does God make sinners like us into priests? Priests must be washed, clothed, and anointed (vv. 4–7). These three ideas appear in three sacrifices. The bull of sin offering (vv. 10–14) took the sinner's guilt and punishment so that he would be forgiven (Lev. 4). The ram of burnt offering (vv. 15–18), while making propitiation, also presented God with total self-dedication so that God would be pleased with the sinner (Lev. 1). The blood of the ram of consecration (vv. 19–34) was put on the ear, thumb, and toe like the cleansing of the healed leper (Lev. 14:7,14,25), and its meat was eaten like a peace offering as a sign of fellowship with God (Lev. 7:11,15–21). Therefore, God makes sinners into priests by washing away their guilt, clothing them with imputed righteousness,

thou shalt burn the remainder with fire: it shall
not be eaten, because it *is* holy.
35 And thus shalt thou do unto Aaron, and to his
sons, according to all *things* which I have commanded thee: seven days shalt thou consecrate
them.
36 And thou shalt offer every day a bullock *for* a
sin offering for atonement: and thou shalt cleanse
the altar, when thou hast made an atonement for
it, and thou shalt anoint it, to sanctify it.
37 Seven days thou shalt make an atonement for
the altar, and sanctify it; and it shall be an altar
most holy: whatsoever toucheth the altar shall be
holy.
38 ¶ Now this *is that* which thou shalt offer upon
the altar; two lambs of the first year day by day
continually.
39 The one lamb thou shalt offer in the morning;
and the other lamb thou shalt offer at even:
40 And with the one lamb a tenth deal of flour
mingled with the fourth part of an hin of beaten
oil; and the fourth part of an hin of wine *for* a
drink offering.
41 And the other lamb thou shalt offer at even,
and shalt do thereto according to the meat offering of the morning, and according to the drink
offering thereof, for a sweet savour, an offering
made by fire unto the LORD.
42 *This shall be* a continual burnt offering
throughout your generations *at* the door of the
tabernacle of the congregation before the LORD:
where I will meet you, to speak there unto thee.
43 And there I will meet with the children of
Israel, and *the tabernacle* shall be sanctified by my
glory.
44 And I will sanctify the tabernacle of the congregation, and the altar: I will sanctify also both
Aaron and his sons, to minister to me in the
priest's office.
45 ¶ And I will dwell among the children of Israel, and will be their God.
46 And they shall know that I *am* the LORD their
God, that brought them forth out of the land of
Egypt, that I may dwell among them: I *am* the
LORD their God.

CHAPTER 30

AND thou shalt make an altar to burn incense
upon: *of* shittim wood shalt thou make it.
2 A cubit *shall be* the length thereof, and a cubit
the breadth thereof; foursquare shall it be: and
two cubits *shall be* the height thereof: the horns
thereof *shall be* of the same.
3 And thou shalt overlay it with pure gold, the
top thereof, and the sides thereof round about,
and the horns thereof; and thou shalt make unto
it a crown of gold round about.
4 And two golden rings shalt thou make to it
under the crown of it, by the two corners thereof,
upon the two sides of it shalt thou make *it*; and
they shall be for places for the staves to bear it
withal.
5 And thou shalt make the staves *of* shittim wood,
and overlay them with gold.
6 And thou shalt put it before the vail that *is* by
the ark of the testimony, before the mercy seat
that *is* over the testimony, where I will meet with
thee.
7 And Aaron shall burn thereon sweet incense
every morning: when he dresseth the lamps, he
shall burn incense upon it.
8 And when Aaron lighteth the lamps at even, he
shall burn incense upon it, a perpetual incense
before the LORD throughout your generations.
9 Ye shall offer no strange incense thereon, nor
burnt sacrifice, nor meat offering; neither shall ye
pour drink offering thereon.
10 And Aaron shall make an atonement upon the
horns of it once in a year with the blood of the
sin offering of atonements: once in the year shall
he make atonement upon it throughout your
generations: it *is* most holy unto the LORD.
11 ¶ And the LORD spake unto Moses, saying,
12 When thou takest the sum of the children of
Israel after their number, then shall they give every man a ransom for his soul unto the LORD,
when thou numberest them; that there be no
plague among them, when *thou* numberest them.
13 This they shall give, every one that passeth
among them that are numbered, half a shekel after the shekel of the sanctuary: (a shekel *is* twenty

---

and anointing them for holy fellowship with Him—all by sacrifice.

2. How do Christians act as priests? By faith in Christ (1 Peter 2:4–6), they offer to God spiritual sacrifices—themselves, their praise and thanksgiving, and their financial gifts and intercessory prayers (Rom. 12:1; Heb. 13:15–16). How can you offer spiritual sacrifices to God?

Chapter 30: ***God shows Moses the design of the altar of incense, the requirement of ransom money, the design of the basin for washing, and the formula of the holy incense.***

30:1 *shittim.* Acacia.

30:2 *cubit.* Eighteen inches. *thereof.* Of it. *foursquare.* Four-sided.

30:3 *crown.* Trim.

30:4 *staves.* Poles. *withal.* With.

30:6 *vail.* Veil.

30:7 *thereon.* On it. *dresseth.* Cleans and maintains.

30:8 *even.* Evening.

30:9 *strange.* Not commanded.

30:10 *once in a year.* See Lev. 16.

30:12 *ransom.* Price paid to release a sinner from punishment (21:30); same root as "atonement" (v. 15). God satisfied His justice against sin by the payment of a price (Matt. 20:28; 26:28).

30:13 *shekel.* Two-fifths of an ounce.

gerahs:) an half shekel *shall be* the offering of
the LORD.
14 Every one that passeth among them that are
numbered, from twenty years old and above, shall
give an offering unto the LORD.
15 The rich shall not give more, and the poor
shall not give less than half a shekel, when *they*
give an offering unto the LORD, to make an atone-
ment for your souls.
16 And thou shalt take the atonement money of the
children of Israel, and shalt appoint it for the service
of the tabernacle of the congregation; that it may be
a memorial unto the children of Israel before the
LORD, to make an atonement for your souls.
17 ¶ And the LORD spake unto Moses, saying,
18 Thou shalt also make a laver *of* brass, and his
foot *also of* brass, to wash *withal*: and thou shalt
put it between the tabernacle of the congregation
and the altar, and thou shalt put water therein.
19 For Aaron and his sons shall wash their hands
and their feet thereat:
20 When they go into the tabernacle of the con-
gregation, they shall wash with water, that they die
not; or when they come near to the altar to minis-
ter, to burn offering made by fire unto the LORD:
21 So they shall wash their hands and their feet,
that they die not: and it shall be a statute for ever
to them, *even* to him and to his seed throughout
their generations.
22 ¶ Moreover the LORD spake unto Moses,
saying,
23 Take thou also unto thee principal spices, of
pure myrrh five hundred *shekels*, and of sweet
cinnamon half so much, *even* two hundred and
fifty *shekels*, and of sweet calamus two hundred
and fifty *shekels*,
24 And of cassia five hundred *shekels*, after the
shekel of the sanctuary, and of oil olive an hin:
25 And thou shalt make it an oil of holy oint-
ment, an ointment compound after the art of the
apothecary: it shall be an holy anointing oil.
26 And thou shalt anoint the tabernacle of the
congregation therewith, and the ark of the testimony,
27 And the table and all his vessels, and the can-
dlestick and his vessels, and the altar of incense,
28 And the altar of burnt offering with all his
vessels, and the laver and his foot.
29 And thou shalt sanctify them, that they may be
most holy: whatsoever toucheth them shall be holy.
30 And thou shalt anoint Aaron and his sons, and
consecrate them, that *they* may minister unto me
in the priest's office.
31 And thou shalt speak unto the children of
Israel, saying, This shall be an holy anointing oil
unto me throughout your generations.
32 Upon man's flesh shall it not be poured, neither
shall ye make *any other* like it, after the composi-
tion of it: it *is* holy, *and* it shall be holy unto you.
33 Whosoever compoundeth *any* like it, or who-
soever putteth *any* of it upon a stranger, shall even
be cut off from his people.
34 ¶ And the LORD said unto Moses, Take unto
thee sweet spices, stacte, and onycha, and galba-
num; *these* sweet spices with pure frankincense:
of each shall there be a like *weight*:
35 And thou shalt make it a perfume, a confection
after the art of the apothecary, tempered together,
pure *and* holy:
36 And thou shalt beat *some* of it very small, and
put of it before the testimony in the tabernacle of
the congregation, where I will meet with thee: it
shall be unto you most holy.
37 And *as for* the perfume which thou shalt make,
ye shall not make to yourselves according to the
composition thereof: it shall be unto thee holy for
the LORD.
38 Whosoever shall make like unto that, to smell
thereto, shall even be cut off from his people.

30:16 *memorial*. Reminder.
30:18 *laver*. Large basin for cleansing the priests and sacrifices (29:4,17; 40:30–32). *foot*. Stand. *withal*. With. *tabernacle of the congregation*. See note at 27:21. On the laver, see comments in the Worship Section for ch. 38.
30:19 *thereat*. At it.
30:20 *minister*. Serve.
30:21 *seed*. Offspring.
30:23 *principal*. High quality. *myrrh*. Somewhat bitter, earthy-smelling resin from a commiphora tree. *calamus*. Sweet-smelling plant.
30:24 *cassia*. Bark from plants in the cinnamon family. *hin*. Four quarts.
30:25 *compound after the art of the apothecary*. Blended with the work of a perfumer.
30:26 *therewith*. With it.
30:27 *candlestick*. Lampstand.
30:33 *compoundeth*. Makes a perfume.
30:34 *stacte*. Resin from a tree. *onycha*. Uncertain. *galbanum*. Resin from ferula plants with a musky odor. *frankincense*. Resin of boswellia tree with a sweet smell reminiscent of pine trees with lemon.
30:35 *confection*. Perfume. *apothecary*. Perfume or spice maker. *tempered*. Salted.
30:38 *whosoever shall make like unto that, to smell thereto*. Whoever makes anything that smells like this incense.

Thoughts for Personal/Family Worship: Chapter 30

1. The burning of fragrant spices on the golden altar of incense (vv. 1–10) was a symbol of prayer (Ps. 141:2; Luke 1:10; Rev. 5:8; 8:3–4). Christ's priestly intercession is based on His sacrificial blood (v. 10), and He intercedes morning and evening (vv. 7–8) to shield sinners from God's wrath (Lev. 16:12–13; Num. 16:46–48; Rom. 8:34). How can Christ's priestly intercession encourage us in our prayers to God?

2. The fragrances of the incense were a sign of God's delightful presence meeting with His people (25:22; 29:42–43; 30:6,36). Limiting this fragrance to the holy things showed that one can enjoy God's presence only through a mediator and the means He appointed. To unbelievers,

CHAPTER 31

AND the LORD spake unto Moses, saying,
2 See, I have called by name Bezaleel the son of
Uri, the son of Hur, of the tribe of Judah:
3 And I have filled him with the spirit of God,
in wisdom, and in understanding, and in knowl-
edge, and in all manner of workmanship,
4 To devise cunning works, to work in gold, and
in silver, and in brass,
5 And in cutting of stones, to set *them*, and
in carving of timber, to work in all manner of
workmanship.
6 And I, behold, I have given with him Aholiab,
the son of Ahisamach, of the tribe of Dan: and in
the hearts of all that are wise hearted I have put
wisdom, that they may make all that I have com-
manded thee;
7 The tabernacle of the congregation, and the ark
of the testimony, and the mercy seat that *is* there-
upon, and all the furniture of the tabernacle,
8 And the table and his furniture, and the pure
candlestick with all his furniture, and the altar of
incense,
9 And the altar of burnt offering with all his fur-
niture, and the laver and his foot,
10 And the cloths of service, and the holy gar-
ments for Aaron the priest, and the garments of
his sons, to minister in the priest's office,
11 And the anointing oil, and sweet incense for
the holy *place*: according to all that I have com-
manded thee shall they do.
12 ¶ And the LORD spake unto Moses, saying,
13 Speak thou also unto the children of Israel,
saying, Verily my sabbaths ye shall keep: for it *is* a
sign between me and you throughout your gener-
ations; that *ye* may know that I *am* the LORD that
doth sanctify you.
14 Ye shall keep the sabbath therefore; for it *is* holy
unto you: every one that defileth it shall surely be
put to death: for whosoever doeth *any* work therein,
that soul shall be cut off from among his people.
15 Six days may work be done; but in the seventh
is the sabbath of rest, holy to the LORD: whosoever
doeth *any* work in the sabbath day, he shall surely
be put to death.
16 Wherefore the children of Israel shall keep the
sabbath, to observe the sabbath throughout their
generations, *for* a perpetual covenant.
17 It *is* a sign between me and the children of
Israel for ever: for *in* six days the LORD made
heaven and earth, and on the seventh day he
rested, and was refreshed.
18 ¶ And he gave unto Moses, when he had made
an end of communing with him upon mount
Sinai, two tables of testimony, tables of stone,
written with the finger of God.

CHAPTER 32

AND when the people saw that Moses delayed to
come down out of the mount, the people gath-
ered themselves together unto Aaron, and said

the gospel is only the stench of death in its revelations of divine justice, but to believers it is the fragrance of life in Jesus Christ (2 Cor. 2:15–16).

Chapter 31: ***God calls workers and fills them with the wisdom of the Holy Spirit to build the tabernacle, reaffirms the Sabbath, and gives Moses the two tablets of the moral law.***

31:1 *the LORD spake unto Moses.* God spoke seven times in revealing the tabernacle (25:1; 30:11,17,22,34; 31:1,12), an allusion to the week of creation (see notes at 1:7; 2:2; 16:6–12, 22–30; 20:4–6,8–11). This is the sixth time He spoke, calling men to build His tabernacle just as on the sixth day God created man to rule the world (Gen. 1:26).
31:3 *spirit of God.* The Holy Spirit (28:3; 35:31).
31:4 *cunning.* Artistic.
31:6 *wisdom.* Here referring to craftsmanship. The list of objects opens and closes by stating that God's Word (*all that I have commanded*) must rule His worship (see notes at 12:50; 25:40).
31:7 *thereupon.* On it.
31:8–9 *furniture.* Utensils and vessels.
31:10 *cloths.* Clothing.
31:12 *the LORD spake unto Moses.* The seventh divine speech in the tabernacle instructions is the regulation of the Sabbath, the seventh day of creation (see note at 31:1). The tabernacle was a kind of new creation, a return to paradise to dwell with God in holy rest.
31:13 *Verily.* Surely. *sanctify.* Make holy.
31:14 *holy.* Set apart for the public and private worship of God. *defileth.* Treats a holy thing as ordinary. *whosoever.* Whoever. *cut off.* Shut out of the covenant people (Gen. 17:14) under the old covenant judicial system by the *death* penalty (Num. 15:30–36).
31:18 *communing.* Talking. *tables.* Tablets. *testimony.* Ten Commandments. *finger.* Power.

Thoughts for Personal/Family Worship: Chapter 31

1. **The Spirit of God created the whole world, including us (Gen. 1:2; Job 33:4). All life comes from Him (Ps. 104:30), as does all skill and wisdom. What abilities has He given you? Are you grateful for these gifts and do you rely on His help to use them for His glory?**
2. **The Sabbath was a sign of the covenant (vv. 13,16), just as the rainbow was for Noah and circumcision for Abraham (Gen. 9:12–13; 17:11). However, the Sabbath was not just a sign of the old covenant with Israel, but a sign of God's created order (Ex. 20:11; 31:17). Therefore, while Christians are not under the ceremonial and judicial system of Israel, they still have an obligation to keep the Sabbath as a day set apart to worship God. It is good to remember that "sabbath" does not mean seventh but rest or cessation. It is a day that is to be different from all other days; thus, it legitimately designates the first day of the week. How is keeping the Sabbath a sign of a covenant relationship with Christ and a foretaste of resting with Christ in the heavenly paradise?**

The Problem of God's Presence with Idolaters (32:1—34:35)

Chapter 32: ***Israel quickly turns to idols and breaks***

unto him, Up, make us gods, which shall go be-
fore us; for *as for* this Moses, the man that brought
us up out of the land of Egypt, we wot not what is
become of him.
2 And Aaron said unto them, Break off the golden
earrings, which *are* in the ears of your wives, of
your sons, and of your daughters, and bring *them*
unto me.
3 And all the people brake off the golden earrings
which *were* in their ears, and brought *them* unto
Aaron.
4 And he received *them* at their hand, and fash-
ioned it with a graving tool, after he had made it
a molten calf: and they said, These *be* thy gods, O
Israel, which brought thee up out of the land of
Egypt.
5 And when Aaron saw *it*, he built an altar before
it; and Aaron made proclamation, and said, To
morrow *is* a feast to the LORD.
6 And they rose up early on the morrow, and
offered burnt offerings, and brought peace
offerings; and the people sat down to eat and to
drink, and rose up to play.
7 ¶ And the LORD said unto Moses, Go, get thee
down; for thy people, which thou broughtest out
of the land of Egypt, have corrupted *themselves*:
8 They have turned aside quickly out of the way
which I commanded them: they have made them
a molten calf, and have worshipped it, and have
sacrificed thereunto, and said, These *be* thy gods,
O Israel, which have brought thee up out of the
land of Egypt.
9 And the LORD said unto Moses, I have seen this
people, and, behold, it *is* a stiffnecked people:
10 Now therefore let me alone, that my wrath
may wax hot against them, and that I may con-
sume them: and I will make of thee a great nation.
11 And Moses besought the LORD his God, and
said, LORD, why doth thy wrath wax hot against
thy people, which thou hast brought forth out of
the land of Egypt with great power, and with a
mighty hand?
12 Wherefore should the Egyptians speak, and
say, For mischief did he bring them out, to slay
them in the mountains, and to consume them
from the face of the earth? Turn from thy fierce
wrath, and repent of this evil against thy people.
13 Remember Abraham, Isaac, and Israel, thy
servants, to whom thou swarest by thine own self,
and saidst unto them, I will multiply your seed as
the stars of heaven, and all this land that I have
spoken of will I give unto your seed, and they
shall inherit *it* for ever.
14 And the LORD repented of the evil which he
thought to do unto his people.
15 ¶ And Moses turned, and went down from the
mount, and the two tables of the testimony *were*
in his hand: the tables *were* written on both their
sides; on the one side and on the other *were* they
written.
16 And the tables *were* the work of God, and the
writing *was* the writing of God, graven upon the
tables.
17 And when Joshua heard the noise of the peo-
ple as they shouted, he said unto Moses, *There is* a
noise of war in the camp.
18 And he said, *It is* not the voice of *them that*
shout for mastery, neither *is it* the voice of *them*
that cry for being overcome: *but* the noise of *them*
that sing do I hear.
19 ¶ And it came to pass, as soon as he came
nigh unto the camp, that he saw the calf, and the
dancing: and Moses' anger waxed hot, and he
cast the tables out of his hands, and brake them
beneath the mount.
20 And he took the calf which they had made, and
burnt *it* in the fire, and ground *it* to powder, and
strawed *it* upon the water, and made the children
of Israel drink *of it*.
21 And Moses said unto Aaron, What did this

the covenant so that Moses must intercede for God's mercy lest His wrath destroys the people.

32:1 *mount*. Mountain. *wot*. Know.

32:4 *graving tool*. Stylus or chisel. *molten*. Cast metal.

32:5 *feast to the LORD*. They mingled idols with the worship of the true God.

32:6 *morrow*. Morning. *play*. Possibly sexual play (Gen. 26:8). Though they experienced God's miracles and mercies, they proved to be idolaters—a warning to the church (1 Cor. 10:1–11).

32:7 *thy people, which thou broughtest*. A threat that the people are in danger of being disowned by God (not "My people"), and a call for Moses to take responsibility for interceding for them.

32:8 *thereunto*. To it.

32:9 *stiffnecked*. Stubbornly rebellious (Acts 7:51).

32:10 *let me alone*. If Moses did not intercede, God's wrath would destroy them, but Moses was chosen by God for this very task (Deut. 9:19; Ps. 106:23). *wax hot*. Grow warm, burn. *I will make of thee a great nation*. A test of Moses' humility and love for Israel.

32:11–13 *besought*. Prayed to. *mischief*. Evil. *repent of this evil*. Turn away from doing them harm. *swarest*. Swore an oath. *seed*. Offspring. Effective prayer appeals to God on the basis of His redemption, glory, and covenant.

32:14 *he thought*. Literally, "He said." *the LORD repented*. God's relationships change, as when He forgives sin and turns away His wrath (Jonah 3:10; 4:2). However, God does not change in His nature or His plans, for He decreed all things (Num. 23:19; Ps. 33:11; Isa. 46:10; Mal. 3:6).

32:15–16 *tables*. Tablets. *testimony*. Ten Commandments. *graven*. Engraved.

32:18 *mastery*. Great deeds. *overcome*. Defeated. *sing*. They rejoiced in idolatry (Acts 7:41).

32:19 *nigh*. Near. *waxed hot*. Burned. *brake them*. Not a temper tantrum, but a symbol of Israel breaking the covenant (Lev. 26:15; Deut. 31:16; Jer. 31:32).

32:20 *strawed*. Scattered.

people unto thee, that thou hast brought so great
a sin upon them?
22 And Aaron said, Let not the anger of my lord
wax hot: thou knowest the people, that they *are*
set on mischief.
23 For they said unto me, Make us gods, which
shall go before us: for *as for* this Moses, the man
that brought us up out of the land of Egypt, we
wot not what is become of him.
24 And I said unto them, Whosoever hath any
gold, let them break *it* off. So they gave *it* me: then
I cast it into the fire, and there came out this calf.
25 ¶ And when Moses saw that the people *were*
naked; (for Aaron had made them naked unto
their shame among their enemies:)
26 Then Moses stood in the gate of the camp, and
said, Who *is* on the LORD's side? *let him come* unto
me. And all the sons of Levi gathered themselves
together unto him.
27 And he said unto them, Thus saith the LORD
God of Israel, Put every man his sword by his side,
and go in and out from gate to gate throughout
the camp, and slay every man his brother, and
every man his companion, and every man his
neighbour.
28 And the children of Levi did according to the
word of Moses: and there fell of the people that
day about three thousand men.
29 For Moses had said, Consecrate yourselves to
day to the LORD, even every man upon his son,
and upon his brother; that he may bestow upon
you a blessing this day.
30 ¶ And it came to pass on the morrow, that Mo-
ses said unto the people, Ye have sinned a great
sin: and now I will go up unto the LORD; perad-
venture I shall make an atonement for your sin.
31 And Moses returned unto the LORD, and said,
Oh, this people have sinned a great sin, and have
made them gods of gold.
32 Yet now, if thou wilt forgive their sin—; and if
not, blot me, I pray thee, out of thy book which
thou hast written.
33 And the LORD said unto Moses, Whosoever
hath sinned against me, him will I blot out of my
book.
34 Therefore now go, lead the people unto *the*
place of which I have spoken unto thee: behold,
mine Angel shall go before thee: nevertheless in
the day when I visit I will visit their sin upon them.
35 And the LORD plagued the people, because
they made the calf, which Aaron made.

CHAPTER 33

AND the LORD said unto Moses, Depart, *and* go
up hence, thou and the people which thou hast
brought up out of the land of Egypt, unto the
land which I sware unto Abraham, to Isaac, and
to Jacob, saying, Unto thy seed will I give it:
2 And I will send an angel before thee; and I will
drive out the Canaanite, the Amorite, and the Hit-
tite, and the Perizzite, the Hivite, and the Jebusite:
3 Unto a land flowing with milk and honey: for I
will not go up in the midst of thee; for thou *art* a
stiffnecked people: lest I consume thee in the way.
4 ¶ And when the people heard these evil tidings,

32:22 *mischief.* Evil.
32:23 *wot.* Know.
32:24 *there came out this calf.* Minimizing your part in a sin is not true confession.
32:25 *naked.* Let loose, without restraint.
32:29 *Consecrate.* Not, "set apart as holy," but literally, "fill the hand," ordain for special ministry (see note at 29:9). *upon his brother.* Against his brother. It pleased God that they loved His honor more than their own families (Deut. 33:9; Matt. 10:37). *bestow.* Give. The Lord called the Levites to be the assistants of the priests at the tabernacle (38:21; Num. 1:47–53; 8:5–26).
32:30–32 *on the morrow.* In the morning. *peradventure.* Perhaps. *blot me . . . out of thy book.* Kill me like a condemned criminal (Ps. 69:28): *atonement* by substitution of a willing sacrifice.
32:33 *Whosoever.* Whoever. Only the one guilty of sin can be punished for sin (34:7; Ezek. 18:4). Substitution is only possible when the guilt can be transferred from the sinner and imputed to the substitute because of a legal union between them (2 Cor. 5:21; Phil. 3:9).
32:34 *mine Angel.* See 23:20–23. *visit their sin upon them.* Punish them for their sin.
32:35 *plagued.* Struck.

Thoughts for Personal/Family Worship: Chapter 32

1. **Israel's idolatry shows us the corruption of the human heart. They had God's prophet, miracles, and laws; they stood at the foot of Mt. Sinai with God's glory visibly shining over them. Yet they quickly turned aside to idols. Their sin was engraved on their hearts as with a diamond-tipped pen of iron (Jer. 17:1). Unless God gives grace in the heart, there is no hope for fallen man (Titus 3:3–5). What then should we ask for in prayer?**
2. **Moses here again is a type of Christ. The Lord Jesus is the Prophet preaching against idols, the King bringing the sword of discipline, and the Priest who offered Himself as the substitute for His people and intercedes for them. But where Moses could only bring truth and temporal deliverance, Christ can save from blindness, guilt, and sin.**

Chapter 33: *Moses prays for God to continue to grant His presence to His people despite their sin and asks for God to show him His glory.*

33:1 *hence.* From here. *seed.* Offspring.
33:3 *I will not go up . . . lest I consume thee.* God's holiness cannot tolerate sin (Hab. 1:13). Though He would still go before them to conquer their enemies (v. 2), He threatened to cancel the tabernacle and remove His presence among them because of their idolatry (Ezek. 8:1–18; 11:22–23). *stiffnecked.* The word "stiff" is of the same root used for Pharaoh's "hardness" (7:3; 13:15). Israel has the same stubborn, idol-worshiping heart as Pharaoh himself.
33:4 *tidings.* News. *ornaments.* Beautiful things.
33:7 *tabernacle.* Not the holy place, but a temporary tent to

they mourned: and no man did put on him his
ornaments.
5 For the LORD had said unto Moses, Say unto
the children of Israel, Ye *are* a stiffnecked people: I
will come up into the midst of thee in a moment,
and consume thee: therefore now put off thy
ornaments from thee, that I may know what to
do unto thee.
6 And the children of Israel stripped themselves
of their ornaments by the mount Horeb.
7 And Moses took the tabernacle, and pitched it
without the camp, afar off from the camp, and
called it the Tabernacle of the congregation. And
it came to pass, *that* every one which sought the
LORD went out unto the tabernacle of the congre-
gation, which *was* without the camp.
8 And it came to pass, when Moses went out
unto the tabernacle, *that* all the people rose up,
and stood every man *at* his tent door, and looked
after Moses, until he was gone into the tabernacle.
9 And it came to pass, as Moses entered into the
tabernacle, the cloudy pillar descended, and stood
at the door of the tabernacle, and *the LORD* talked
with Moses.
10 And all the people saw the cloudy pillar stand
at the tabernacle door: and all the people rose up
and worshipped, every man *in* his tent door.
11 And the LORD spake unto Moses face to face,
as a man speaketh unto his friend. And he turned
again into the camp: but his servant Joshua, the
son of Nun, a young man, departed not out of the
tabernacle.
12 ¶ And Moses said unto the LORD, See, thou
sayest unto me, Bring up this people: and thou
hast not let me know whom thou wilt send with
me. Yet thou hast said, I know thee by name, and
thou hast also found grace in my sight.
13 Now therefore, I pray thee, if I have found
grace in thy sight, shew me now thy way, that I
may know thee, that I may find grace in thy sight:
and consider that this nation *is* thy people.
14 And he said, My presence shall go *with thee*,
and I will give thee rest.
15 And he said unto him, If thy presence go not
with me, carry us not up hence.
16 For wherein shall it be known here that I and
thy people have found grace in thy sight? *is it* not
in that thou goest with us? so shall we be separated,
I and thy people, from all the people that *are* upon
the face of the earth.
17 And the LORD said unto Moses, I will do this
thing also that thou hast spoken: for thou hast
found grace in my sight, and I know thee by name.
18 And he said, I beseech thee, shew me thy glory.
19 And he said, I will make all my goodness pass
before thee, and I will proclaim the name of the
LORD before thee; and will be gracious to whom I
will be gracious, and will shew mercy on whom I
will shew mercy.
20 And he said, Thou canst not see my face: for
there shall no man see me, and live.
21 And the LORD said, Behold, *there is* a place by
me, and thou shalt stand upon a rock:
22 And it shall come to pass, while my glory pass-
eth by, that I will put thee in a clift of the rock, and
will cover thee with my hand while I pass by:

meet God. *without*. Outside. When God meets with Moses *afar off from* the people it implies His presence with them was not yet secure.

33:11–12 *face to face . . . I know thee by name*. Moses' astonishing intimacy with God (Num. 12:8; Deut. 34:10) qualifies him to intercede for God to dwell with His people—a foreshadowing of the true Mediator (John 1:14,18).

33:15 *hence*. From here.

33:16 *wherein*. How. *separated*. Distinguished. God's presence with His people is the soul of the covenant (29:46; Gen. 26:3,24; 28:15). *I and thy people*. God's people receive His *grace* through His relationship with the Mediator. We are blessed in union with Christ (Eph. 1:3).

33:18 *I beseech thee*. Plead.

33:19 *my goodness*. Through the intercession of Moses, the Lord's wrath against Israel became the occasion for an unprecedented display of His love to them. *I . . . will be gracious to whom I will be gracious*. God promised to reveal His glory (*name*) to Moses, but asserted His freedom to give the knowledge of Himself as He pleases (Matt. 11:25–27). Just as God had the right to harden Pharaoh for His glory (9:16; 14:4), so He has the right to show mercy not on the basis of human will or effort, but to whomever He wills (Rom. 9:14–18).

33:20 *there shall no man see me*. Literally, "no man shall see Me." God's open glory would destroy sinners, for He dwells in unapproachable light (1 Tim. 6:16). He gently conceals Himself even in His revelations.

33:21 *rock*. Stone cliff (17:6; Deut. 8:15). The Lord is our rock (Deut. 32:4; 1 Cor. 10:4).

33:22 *clift*. Opening, fissure, hiding place.

33:23 *back parts*. Not the literal back as of a man, but a figure of speech for an indirect revelation of God's nature.

Thoughts for Personal/Family Worship: Chapter 33

1. **The coming of the covenant God did not stop Israel from sinning. On the contrary, they plunged into sin before the face of God. The law does not conquer sin, but only expresses it to show that it abounds within us, for we are no better than Pharaoh. Therefore, let us humble ourselves and grieve over our sins. Our sin spits in the face of God's glory and reacts to His law with more rebellion. God would be right to abandon us forever, sentencing every one of us to "depart from me, ye cursed, into everlasting fire" (Matt. 25:41).**
2. **But where sin abounded, grace abounded all the more (Rom. 5:20). God used Israel's idolatry as an opportunity to display His goodness. He is sovereign and free to be gracious when He wills to be gracious, which means we must bow before His sovereign right to damn sinners or to save them. But it also means we can hope in His sovereign love. No matter how bad our sin is, God is still sovereign and free to save. Yet He always saves through the Mediator because God delights in Him. What strong reasons do we have to hope in Christ and Him alone?**

23 And I will take away mine hand, and thou shalt
see my back parts: but my face shall not be seen.

CHAPTER 34

AND the LORD said unto Moses, Hew thee two
tables of stone like unto the first: and I will write
upon *these* tables the words that were in the first
tables, which thou brakest.
2 And be ready in the morning, and come up in
the morning unto mount Sinai, and present thy-
self there to me in the top of the mount.
3 And no man shall come up with thee, neither
let any man be seen throughout all the mount;
neither let the flocks nor herds feed before that
mount.
4 ¶ And he hewed two tables of stone like unto
the first; and Moses rose up early in the morning,
and went up unto mount Sinai, as the LORD had
commanded him, and took in his hand the two
tables of stone.
5 And the LORD descended in the cloud, and
stood with him there, and proclaimed the name
of the LORD.
6 And the LORD passed by before him, and pro-
claimed, The LORD, The LORD God, merciful and
gracious, longsuffering, and abundant in good-
ness and truth,
7 Keeping mercy for thousands, forgiving
iniquity and transgression and sin, and that will
by no means clear *the guilty*; visiting the iniquity
of the fathers upon the children, and upon the
children's children, unto the third and to the
fourth *generation*.
8 And Moses made haste, and bowed his head
toward the earth, and worshipped.
9 And he said, If now I have found grace in thy
sight, O Lord, let my Lord, I pray thee, go among us;
for it *is* a stiffnecked people; and pardon our iniq-
uity and our sin, and take us for thine inheritance.
10 ¶ And he said, Behold, I make a covenant:
before all thy people I will do marvels, such as
have not been done in all the earth, nor in any
nation: and all the people among which thou *art*
shall see the work of the LORD: for it *is* a terrible
thing that I will do with thee.
11 Observe thou that which I command thee this
day: behold, I drive out before thee the Amorite,
and the Canaanite, and the Hittite, and the Per-
izzite, and the Hivite, and the Jebusite.
12 Take heed to thyself, lest thou make a covenant
with the inhabitants of the land whither thou
goest, lest it be for a snare in the midst of thee:
13 But ye shall destroy their altars, break their im-
ages, and cut down their groves:
14 For thou shalt worship no other god: for the
LORD, whose name *is* Jealous, *is* a jealous God:
15 Lest thou make a covenant with the inhabi-
tants of the land, and they go a whoring after their
gods, and do sacrifice unto their gods, and *one* call
thee, and thou eat of his sacrifice;
16 And thou take of their daughters unto thy sons,
and their daughters go a whoring after their gods,
and make thy sons go a whoring after their gods.
17 Thou shalt make thee no molten gods.
18 ¶ The feast of unleavened bread shalt thou
keep. Seven days thou shalt eat unleavened bread,
as I commanded thee, in the time of the month
Abib: for in the month Abib thou camest out
from Egypt.
19 All that openeth the matrix *is* mine; and every
firstling among thy cattle, *whether* ox or sheep,
that is male.
20 But the firstling of an ass thou shalt redeem
with a lamb: and if thou redeem *him* not, then
shalt thou break his neck. All the firstborn of thy
sons thou shalt redeem. And none shall appear
before me empty.

Chapter 34: *The Lord reveals His name and renews His covenant with Israel.*

34:1 *Hew*. Cut. *tables*. Tablets.

34:5 The remarkable revelation of God's nature (*name*) in vv. 6–7 became like a creed for Israel, parts of which are repeated through Scripture (Num. 14:18; 2 Sam. 2:6; 15:20; 2 Chron. 30:9; Neh. 9:17,31; Ps. 25:10; 40:10–11; 57:3,10; 61:7; 85:10; 86:15; 89:14; 103:8; 111:4; 117:2; 145:8; Joel 2:13; Jonah 4:2; Nah. 1:3; James 5:11).

34:6 *The LORD, The LORD God*. The God of absolute freedom and sovereignty who reveals Himself in His mighty works of redemption (see notes at 3:14; 6:3). *merciful*. Having the compassion of a father or mother to a dear child (Ps. 103:13, Jer. 31:20). *gracious*. Giving kindness to the poor and hearing the prayer of the needy (22:26–27; Ps. 4:1). *longsuffering*. God is angry against sin, but is patient and slow to act in anger (Nah. 1:3; Rom. 2:4–5). *goodness*. Loyalty and love, often stated in the refrain, "his mercy [loyal love] endureth forever" (Ps. 100:5; 136:1–26). *truth*. Faithfulness and trustworthiness (Gen. 24:27; Ps. 31:5; 132:11).

34:7 *mercy*. Same word as "goodness" (v. 6). *keeping mercy*. Keeping His covenant promises of faithful love. *thousands*. Thousands of generations (Deut. 7:9). *forgiving iniquity*. Releasing sinners and traitors from their guilt and punishment (Neh. 9:16–17; Ps. 103:12). *by no means clear the guilty*. God's justice requires that sin receive its due penalty (see note at 23:7). *upon the children's children*. See comments in the Worship Section below.

34:8 *made haste*. Hurried.

34:9 *I pray thee*. Please.

34:10 *I make*. Literally, "I am cutting" (see note at 24:8), renewing the *covenant* which Israel broke (see note at 32:19). *marvels*. Amazing works. *terrible*. Inspiring the fear of God.

34:12 *Take heed*. Guard.

34:13 *groves*. Asherah pillars (idols).

34:14–15 *Jealous*. Righteous, burning zeal for His honor, worship, and kingdom (Deut. 4:24; 5:9; Isa. 9:7), like a husband who passionately cares about his marriage (Song 8:6). *whoring*. Worshiping other gods is like a wife acting as a prostitute with other men.

34:17 *molten*. Made of cast metal.

21 ¶ Six days thou shalt work, but on the seventh
day thou shalt rest: in earing time and in harvest
thou shalt rest.
22 ¶ And thou shalt observe the feast of weeks, of
the firstfruits of wheat harvest, and the feast of in-
gathering at the year's end.
23 ¶ Thrice in the year shall all your men chil-
dren appear before the Lord GOD, the God of
Israel.
24 For I will cast out the nations before thee, and
enlarge thy borders: neither shall any man desire
thy land, when thou shalt go up to appear before
the LORD thy God thrice in the year.
25 Thou shalt not offer the blood of my sacrifice
with leaven; neither shall the sacrifice of the feast
of the passover be left unto the morning.
26 The first of the firstfruits of thy land thou shalt
bring unto the house of the LORD thy God. Thou
shalt not seethe a kid in his mother's milk.
27 And the LORD said unto Moses, Write thou
these words: for after the tenor of these words I
have made a covenant with thee and with Israel.
28 And he was there with the LORD forty days and
forty nights; he did neither eat bread, nor drink
water. And he wrote upon the tables the words of
the covenant, the ten commandments.
29 ¶ And it came to pass, when Moses came
down from mount Sinai with the two tables of
testimony in Moses' hand, when he came down
from the mount, that Moses wist not that the skin
of his face shone while he talked with him.
30 And when Aaron and all the children of Israel
saw Moses, behold, the skin of his face shone; and
they were afraid to come nigh him.
31 And Moses called unto them; and Aaron and
all the rulers of the congregation returned unto
him: and Moses talked with them.
32 And afterward all the children of Israel came
nigh: and he gave them in commandment all that
the LORD had spoken with him in mount Sinai.
33 And *till* Moses had done speaking with them,
he put a vail on his face.
34 But when Moses went in before the LORD
to speak with him, he took the vail off, until he
came out. And he came out, and spake unto the
children of Israel *that* which he was commanded.
35 And the children of Israel saw the face of
Moses, that the skin of Moses' face shone: and
Moses put the vail upon his face again, until he
went in to speak with him.

CHAPTER 35

AND Moses gathered all the congregation of the
children of Israel together, and said unto them,
These *are* the words which the LORD hath com-
manded, that *ye* should do them.
2 Six days shall work be done, but on the seventh
day there shall be to you an holy day, a sabbath of
rest to the LORD: whosoever doeth work therein
shall be put to death.
3 Ye shall kindle no fire throughout your habita-
tions upon the sabbath day.
4 ¶ And Moses spake unto all the congregation
of the children of Israel, saying, This *is* the thing
which the LORD commanded, saying,
5 Take ye from among you an offering unto the
LORD: whosoever *is* of a willing heart, let him
bring it, an offering of the LORD; gold, and silver,
and brass,
6 And blue, and purple, and scarlet, and fine
linen, and goats' *hair*,
7 And rams' skins dyed red, and badgers' skins,
and shittim wood,

34:19 *matrix.* Womb. *firstling.* Firstborn.
34:21 *earing.* Plowing.
34:24 *neither shall any man desire thy land.* God restrains sin in the world to protect His people (Gen. 20:6).
34:26 *seethe.* Boil. See note at 23:19.
34:27 *Write thou these words.* See 17:14; 24:4. *after the tenor.* Literally, "according to the mouth," that is, as God had spoken. *made a covenant.* Literally, "cut a covenant" (see note at v. 10).
34:28 *forty days and forty nights.* See Matt. 4:2. *ten commandments.* See notes at 20:1–17.
34:29 *wist not.* Did not know. *skin of his face shown.* A foretaste of the saints' glorification by seeing God's glory (Matt. 13:43; 2 Cor. 3:7,18; 1 John 3:2).
34:33 *vail.* A sign of the blindness of unbelievers to God's glory (2 Cor. 3:12–16; 4:4).

Thoughts for Personal/Family Worship: Chapter 34

1. **The Psalms are full of praise to God for the divine attributes outlined above (vv. 6–7). Moses is a model of how to respond to God's attributes with humble adoration (v. 8). Let us therefore fill our mouths with praises and focus our minds in worship not upon ourselves and our experiences, but upon who God is. What are some of your favorite psalms, hymns, and spiritual songs? How do they declare the attributes of God?**
2. **God does not punish anyone for the sins of his parents (Deut. 24:16; Ezek. 18:20; John 9:1–3), except for the sins of our covenant head, Adam (Rom. 5:12,18). However, children imitate their parents, and those who hate God often raise children who hate God and fall under the same punishment (Ex. 20:5; 34:7). We need not fear our past if we are in Christ. The blood of Christ redeems us from the futile ways of wicked ancestors (1 Peter 1:18–19), blessing our offspring to thousands of generations (Deut. 7:9). Does this strongly motivate you to follow Christ for the sake of future generations?**

The Construction and Filling of the Tabernacle (35:1—40:38)

Chapter 35: ***Moses directed the people to begin building the tabernacle, and they willingly gave the precious materials for God's holy tent.***

35:2–3 *sabbath of rest.* See 16:22–30; 20:7–11; 31:12–17. *habitations.* Homes.
35:5 *whosoever.* Whoever.
35:5–19 These items are discussed in chs. 25–30.

GOD'S LOVE AND JUSTICE

The love of God is the peculiar benevolence He possesses as the loving God Himself (1 John 4:8). His intra-trinitarian love is the delight that God has toward Himself (cf. John 5:20). This is the basis for the love God expresses toward His creatures, which can be classified as either *general* or *special*. The former relates to God's desire to bless all His creatures (Ps. 145:9), while the latter has the elect particularly as its object (John 3:16; Eph. 5:25). This is God's special fatherly delight in His elect as He views them through the lens of Christ Himself (John 16:27; Col. 2:10). This love causes the elect to be accepted for the sake of God's beloved Son (Eph. 1:4–6). Redemption appointed, redemption accomplished, and redemption applied all flow from this steadfast, ceaseless love of the triune God (Lam. 3:22; cf. Rom. 5:8; 1 John 4:10).

The justice or righteousness of God is His continual perfection according to the standard of what is pure and right—which is Himself. Exercised toward His creatures, the justice of God consists in the execution of judgment, either by reward or punishment, according to what is deserved, as determined by the standard of His holy law. All His works are just (Gen. 18:25; Ps. 7:9).

God's justice is wholly retributive, whether in His rewarding or in His punishing. This is opposed to justice by way of mutual exchange or *remunerative* justice. Since men's works are vile and filthy (Isa. 59:2–12; Rom. 3:10–18), there can be no proportionate relationship between man's work and God's remuneration. God is never constrained by or indebted to anyone; rather, He executes His justice according to His perfect standard.

Furthermore, because He acts not in response to man but according to His own way, God is just both in damning some (Pss. 51:4; 119:137; Nah. 1:2–3; Rom. 2:5–6) and delivering others (Rom. 3:21–22). "His work is perfect: for all his ways are judgment" (Deut. 32:4).

The love and justice of God are not incompatible; both are natural to Him to the superlative degree. God's love is always exercised within the bounds of justice, and He always enforces His justice in a loving manner. His love is wholly just, and His justice is entirely loving—this is the nature of God.

This means that, on the one hand, while He is loving God will not suffer men to trample on His holy law. For Him to allow the propagation of sin to continue would not be love. He must and will punish sin to the fullest degree. This should engender fear of sinning against a righteous God who "hatest all workers of iniquity" (Ps. 5:5–6). Noting God's justice, men must fear and tremble, allowing the terror of the Lord to move them to seek remission for their great sins through the blood of Christ.

On the other hand, this means that God, within His justice, exercises His wondrous love through His Son, Jesus Christ. We see the love of the Father in sending the Son; the love of the Son in bearing His people's sin; and the love of the Spirit in applying the benefits of salvation. All three Persons exercise the depths of eternal, sovereign, infinite, immutable love. No man, when gazing on this fountain, can help but stand captivated in amazement at the majestic love of the holy God.

The love and justice of God are understood best by observing the contours of the gospel. Therein God displayed publicly His righteousness (Rom. 3:21–26) and demonstrated His love (Rom. 5:8). Calvary's cross is where God's love and justice meet (Ps. 85:10). Within Christ, God's justice is not *against* but *for* His people. Christ's people are so fully united to Him that God's justice will not permit them to receive anything but that which is Christ's wage: eternal life in glory. Additionally, within Christ, God's love is unrestrained in bestowing His gifts (Zeph. 3:17; James 1:17). The exercising of His justice and His love come together in the gospel, both for God's glory and for His people's good.

—adapted from Wilhelmus à Brakel, *The Christian's Reasonable Service*, vol. 1, ch. 3

8 And oil for the light, and spices for anointing
oil, and for the sweet incense,
9 And onyx stones, and stones to be set for the
ephod, and for the breastplate.
10 And every wise hearted among you shall come,
and make all that the LORD hath commanded;
11 The tabernacle, his tent, and his covering, his
taches, and his boards, his bars, his pillars, and his
sockets,
12 The ark, and the staves thereof, *with* the mercy
seat, and the vail of the covering,
13 The table, and his staves, and all his vessels,
and the shewbread,
14 The candlestick also for the light, and his
furniture, and his lamps, with the oil for the light,
15 And the incense altar, and his staves, and the
anointing oil, and the sweet incense, and the hang-
ing for the door at the entering in of the tabernacle,
16 The altar of burnt offering, with his brasen
grate, his staves, and all his vessels, the laver and
his foot,
17 The hangings of the court, his pillars, and their
sockets, and the hanging for the door of the court,
18 The pins of the tabernacle, and the pins of the
court, and their cords,
19 The cloths of service, to do service in the holy
place, the holy garments for Aaron the priest, and
the garments of his sons, to minister in the priest's
office.
20 ¶ And all the congregation of the children of
Israel departed from the presence of Moses.
21 And they came, every one whose heart stirred
him up, and every one whom his spirit made will-
ing, *and* they brought the LORD's offering to the
work of the tabernacle of the congregation, and
for all his service, and for the holy garments.
22 And they came, both men and women, as
many as were willing hearted, *and* brought
bracelets, and earrings, and rings, and tablets, all
jewels of gold: and every man that offered *offered*
an offering of gold unto the LORD.
23 And every man, with whom was found blue,
and purple, and scarlet, and fine linen, and goats'
hair, and red skins of rams, and badgers' skins,
brought *them*.
24 Every one that did offer an offering of silver
and brass brought the LORD's offering: and every
man, with whom was found shittim wood for any
work of the service, brought *it*.
25 And all the women that were wise hearted did
spin with their hands, and brought that which
they had spun, *both* of blue, and of purple, *and* of
scarlet, and of fine linen.
26 And all the women whose heart stirred them
up in wisdom spun goats' *hair*.
27 And the rulers brought onyx stones, and stones
to be set, for the ephod, and for the breastplate;
28 And spice, and oil for the light, and for the
anointing oil, and for the sweet incense.
29 The children of Israel brought a willing offer-
ing unto the LORD, every man and woman, whose
heart made them willing to bring for all manner
of work, which the LORD had commanded to be
made by the hand of Moses.
30 ¶ And Moses said unto the children of Israel,
See, the LORD hath called by name Bezaleel the
son of Uri, the son of Hur, of the tribe of Judah;
31 And he hath filled him with the spirit of God,
in wisdom, in understanding, and in knowledge,
and in all manner of workmanship;
32 And to devise curious works, to work in gold,
and in silver, and in brass,
33 And in the cutting of stones, to set *them*,
and in carving of wood, to make any manner of
cunning work.
34 And he hath put in his heart that he may teach,
both he, and Aholiab, the son of Ahisamach, of
the tribe of Dan.
35 Them hath he filled with wisdom of heart, to
work all manner of work, of the engraver, and of
the cunning workman, and of the embroiderer, in
blue, and in purple, in scarlet, and in fine linen,
and of the weaver, *even* of them that do any work,
and of those that devise cunning work.

CHAPTER 36

THEN wrought Bezaleel and Aholiab, and every
wise hearted man, in whom the LORD put wis-
dom and understanding to know how to work all
manner of work for the service of the sanctuary,
according to all that the LORD had commanded.

35:12 *staves thereof.* Its poles. *vail.* Veil.
35:14 *furniture.* Utensils and vessels.
35:22 *tablets.* Jewelry.
35:30–35 See notes at 31:1–11.

Thoughts for Personal/Family Worship: Chapter 35

1. **The resources to build God's dwelling place came from redemption. Slaves do not usually own much gold, but when God redeemed Israel out of slavery, He caused the Egyptians to give them silver and gold (11:2; 12:35–36). Redemption made them rich and provided the resources to build God's tabernacle. Likewise, Christ's redemption won the riches of grace that we need to build the body of Christ (Eph. 4:7–16). Therefore, the only way to build the church is by faith in Christ, obtaining from Him everything His church needs.**
2. **The motivation to build God's dwelling place comes from a willing heart (v. 29). The church is built through cheerful giving and voluntary service of the people. The best of pastors can do little without a people willing to serve the Lord (Rom. 12:11). How are you using your abilities to serve in the church? What motivates you and how motivated are you?**

Chapter 36: *Bezaleel and Aholiab oversee the construction of the tent of God's dwelling.*

2 And Moses called Bezaleel and Aholiab, and ev-
ery wise hearted man, in whose heart the LORD
had put wisdom, *even* every one whose heart
stirred him up to come unto the work to do it:
3 And they received of Moses all the offering,
which the children of Israel had brought for the
work of the service of the sanctuary, to make it
withal. And they brought yet unto him free offer-
ings every morning.
4 And all the wise men, that wrought all the work
of the sanctuary, came every man from his work
which they made;
5 ¶ And they spake unto Moses, saying, The peo-
ple bring much more than enough for the service
of the work, which the LORD commanded to make.
6 And Moses gave commandment, and they
caused it to be proclaimed throughout the camp,
saying, Let neither man nor woman make any
more work for the offering of the sanctuary. So
the people were restrained from bringing.
7 For the stuff they had was sufficient for all the
work to make it, and too much.
8 ¶ And every wise hearted man among them
that wrought the work of the tabernacle made ten
curtains *of* fine twined linen, and blue, and pur-
ple, and scarlet: *with* cherubims of cunning work
made he them.
9 The length of one curtain *was* twenty and eight
cubits, and the breadth of one curtain four cubits:
the curtains *were* all of one size.
10 And he coupled the five curtains one unto an-
other: and *the other* five curtains he coupled one
unto another.
11 And he made loops of blue on the edge of one
curtain from the selvedge in the coupling: like-
wise he made in the uttermost side of *another*
curtain, in the coupling of the second.
12 Fifty loops made he in one curtain, and fifty
loops made he in the edge of the curtain which
was in the coupling of the second: the loops held
one *curtain* to another.
13 And he made fifty taches of gold, and coupled
the curtains one unto another with the taches: so
it became one tabernacle.
14 ¶ And he made curtains *of* goats' *hair* for the tent
over the tabernacle: eleven curtains he made them.
15 The length of one curtain *was* thirty cubits,
and four cubits *was* the breadth of one curtain:
the eleven curtains *were* of one size.
16 And he coupled five curtains by themselves,
and six curtains by themselves.
17 And he made fifty loops upon the uttermost
edge of the curtain in the coupling, and fifty loops
made he upon the edge of the curtain which cou-
pleth the second.
18 And he made fifty taches *of* brass to couple the
tent together, that it might be one.
19 And he made a covering for the tent *of* rams'
skins dyed red, and a covering *of* badgers' skins
above *that*.
20 ¶ And he made boards for the tabernacle *of*
shittim wood, standing up.
21 The length of a board *was* ten cubits, and the
breadth of a board one cubit and a half.
22 One board had two tenons, equally distant one
from another: thus did he make for all the boards
of the tabernacle.
23 And he made boards for the tabernacle; twenty
boards for the south side southward:
24 And forty sockets of silver he made under the
twenty boards; two sockets under one board for
his two tenons, and two sockets under another
board for his two tenons.
25 And for the other side of the tabernacle, *which*
is toward the north corner, he made twenty
boards,
26 And their forty sockets of silver; two sockets
under one board, and two sockets under another
board.
27 And for the sides of the tabernacle westward
he made six boards.
28 And two boards made he for the corners of the
tabernacle in the two sides.
29 And they were coupled beneath, and coupled
together at the head thereof, to one ring: thus he
did to both of them in both the corners.
30 And there were eight boards; and their sockets
were sixteen sockets of silver, under every board
two sockets.
31 ¶ And he made bars of shittim wood; five for
the boards of the one side of the tabernacle,
32 And five bars for the boards of the other side
of the tabernacle, and five bars for the boards of
the tabernacle for the sides westward.
33 And he made the middle bar to shoot through
the boards from the one end to the other.
34 And he overlaid the boards with gold, and
made their rings *of* gold *to be* places for the bars,
and overlaid the bars with gold.
35 ¶ And he made a vail *of* blue, and purple, and
scarlet, and fine twined linen: *with* cherubims
made he it of cunning work.
36 And he made thereunto four pillars *of* shittim
wood, and overlaid them with gold: their hooks

On the design and materials of the tent, see notes at ch. 26.
36:3 *withal.* With.
36:38 *chapiters.* Heads or capitals of the pillars. *fillets.* Bands.

Thoughts for Personal/Family Worship: Chapter 36

The people's generosity is commendable in itself, for they gave more than enough (v. 5). It is a model to us of cheerful giving. However, their faith in the Lord and obedience to His moral laws were sadly lacking (chs. 14–16; 32; Num. 11; 14). We dare not rest our confidence in external duties such as giving money to church or attending public worship, for these can be done for

were of gold; and he cast for them four sockets of
silver.
37 ¶ And he made an hanging for the taberna-
cle door *of* blue, and purple, and scarlet, and fine
twined linen, of needlework;
38 And the five pillars of it with their hooks: and
he overlaid their chapiters and their fillets with
gold: but their five sockets *were of* brass.

CHAPTER 37

AND Bezaleel made the ark *of* shittim wood: two
cubits and a half *was* the length of it, and a cubit
and a half the breadth of it, and a cubit and a half
the height of it:
2 And he overlaid it with pure gold within and
without, and made a crown of gold to it round
about.
3 And he cast for it four rings of gold, *to be set* by
the four corners of it; even two rings upon the one
side of it, and two rings upon the other side of it.
4 And he made staves *of* shittim wood, and over-
laid them with gold.
5 And he put the staves into the rings by the sides
of the ark, to bear the ark.
6 ¶ And he made the mercy seat *of* pure gold: two
cubits and a half *was* the length thereof, and one
cubit and a half the breadth thereof.
7 And he made two cherubims *of* gold, beaten
out of one piece made he them, on the two ends
of the mercy seat;
8 One cherub on the end on this side, and an-
other cherub on the *other* end on that side: out of
the mercy seat made he the cherubims on the two
ends thereof.
9 And the cherubims spread out *their* wings
on high, *and* covered with their wings over the
mercy seat, with their faces one to another;
even to the mercy seatward were the faces of the
cherubims.
10 ¶ And he made the table *of* shittim wood: two
cubits *was* the length thereof, and a cubit the
breadth thereof, and a cubit and a half the height
thereof:
11 And he overlaid it with pure gold, and made
thereunto a crown of gold round about.
12 Also he made thereunto a border of an hand-
breadth round about; and made a crown of gold
for the border thereof round about.
13 And he cast for it four rings of gold, and put
the rings upon the four corners that *were* in the
four feet thereof.
14 Over against the border were the rings, the
places for the staves to bear the table.
15 And he made the staves *of* shittim wood, and
overlaid them with gold, to bear the table.
16 And he made the vessels which *were* upon the
table, his dishes, and his spoons, and his bowls,
and his covers to cover withal, *of* pure gold.
17 ¶ And he made the candlestick *of* pure gold:
of beaten work made he the candlestick; his shaft,
and his branch, his bowls, his knops, and his flow-
ers, were of the same:
18 And six branches going out of the sides
thereof; three branches of the candlestick out of
the one side thereof, and three branches of the
candlestick out of the other side thereof:
19 Three bowls made after the fashion of al-
monds in one branch, a knop and a flower;
and three bowls made like almonds in another
branch, a knop and a flower: so throughout the
six branches going out of the candlestick.
20 And in the candlestick *were* four bowls made
like almonds, his knops, and his flowers:
21 And a knop under two branches of the same,
and a knop under two branches of the same, and
a knop under two branches of the same, accord-
ing to the six branches going out of it.
22 Their knops and their branches were of the
same: all of it *was* one beaten work *of* pure gold.
23 And he made his seven lamps, and his snuffers,
and his snuffdishes, *of* pure gold.
24 *Of* a talent of pure gold made he it, and all the
vessels thereof.
25 ¶ And he made the incense altar *of* shittim
wood: the length of it *was* a cubit, and the breadth
of it a cubit; *it was* foursquare; and two cubits
was the height of it; the horns thereof were of the
same.
26 And he overlaid it with pure gold, *both* the top
of it, and the sides thereof round about, and the
horns of it: also he made unto it a crown of gold
round about.
27 And he made two rings of gold for it under
the crown thereof, by the two corners of it, upon
the two sides thereof, to be places for the staves to
bear it withal.
28 And he made the staves *of* shittim wood, and
overlaid them with gold.
29 ¶ And he made the holy anointing oil, and

hypocritical reasons (Matt. 6:1; 23:23; Acts 5:1–11). It is easier to give money than to do justice, love mercy, and walk humbly with God (Mic. 6:8). How can we be zealous in outward things but also avoid hypocrisy?

Chapter 37: ***Bezaleel makes the ark, table, lampstand, altar of incense, anointing oil, and incense for the tabernacle.***

37:1–9 On the *ark*, see notes at 25:10–22.
37:2 *without*. Outside.
37:9 *to the mercy seatward*. Toward the mercy seat.
37:10–16 On the *table*, see notes at 25:23–30.
37:17–24 On the *candlestick*, see notes at 25:31–39.
37:23 *snuffers*. Tongs. *snuffdishes*. Pans for hot coals.
37:25–28 On the *incense altar*, see notes at 30:1–10.
37:29 On the *anointing oil* and *incense*, see notes at 30:22–38.

the pure incense of sweet spices, according to the work of the apothecary.

CHAPTER 38

AND he made the altar of burnt offering *of* shittim wood: five cubits *was* the length thereof, and five cubits the breadth thereof; *it was* foursquare; and three cubits the height thereof.

2 And he made the horns thereof on the four corners of it; the horns thereof were of the same: and he overlaid it with brass.

3 And he made all the vessels of the altar, the pots, and the shovels, and the basons, *and* the fleshhooks, and the firepans: all the vessels thereof made he *of* brass.

4 And he made for the altar a brasen grate of network under the compass thereof beneath unto the midst of it.

5 And he cast four rings for the four ends of the grate of brass, *to be* places for the staves.

6 And he made the staves *of* shittim wood, and overlaid them with brass.

7 And he put the staves into the rings on the sides of the altar, to bear it withal; he made the altar hollow with boards.

8 ¶ And he made the laver *of* brass, and the foot of it *of* brass, of the lookingglasses of *the women* assembling, which assembled *at* the door of the tabernacle of the congregation.

9 ¶ And he made the court: on the south side southward the hangings of the court *were of* fine twined linen, an hundred cubits:

10 Their pillars *were* twenty, and their brasen sockets twenty; the hooks of the pillars and their fillets *were of* silver.

11 And for the north side *the hangings were* an hundred cubits, their pillars *were* twenty, and their sockets of brass twenty; the hooks of the pillars and their fillets *of* silver.

12 And for the west side *were* hangings of fifty cubits, their pillars ten, and their sockets ten; the hooks of the pillars and their fillets *of* silver.

13 And for the east side eastward fifty cubits.

14 The hangings of the one side *of the gate were* fifteen cubits; their pillars three, and their sockets three.

15 And for the other side of the court gate, on this hand and that hand, *were* hangings of fifteen cubits; their pillars three, and their sockets three.

16 All the hangings of the court round about *were* of fine twined linen.

17 And the sockets for the pillars *were of* brass; the hooks of the pillars and their fillets *of* silver; and the overlaying of their chapiters *of* silver; and all the pillars of the court *were* filleted with silver.

18 And the hanging for the gate of the court *was* needlework, *of* blue, and purple, and scarlet, and fine twined linen: and twenty cubits *was* the length, and the height in the breadth *was* five cubits, answerable to the hangings of the court.

19 And their pillars *were* four, and their sockets *of* brass four; their hooks *of* silver, and the overlaying of their chapiters and their fillets *of* silver.

20 And all the pins of the tabernacle, and of the court round about, *were of* brass.

21 ¶ This is the sum of the tabernacle, *even* of the tabernacle of testimony, as it was counted, according to the commandment of Moses, *for* the service of the Levites, by the hand of Ithamar, son to Aaron the priest.

22 And Bezaleel the son of Uri, the son of Hur, of the tribe of Judah, made all that the LORD commanded Moses.

23 And with him *was* Aholiab, son of Ahisamach, of the tribe of Dan, an engraver, and a cunning workman, and an embroiderer in blue, and in purple, and in scarlet, and fine linen.

24 All the gold that was occupied for the work in all the work of the holy *place*, even the gold of the offering, was twenty and nine talents, and seven hundred and thirty shekels, after the shekel of the sanctuary.

Thoughts for Personal/Family Worship: Chapter 37

The word "gold" appears no less than twenty times in this chapter. Bronze was used in outside furniture, but gold in the holy places as a sign of God's holiness—not merely His moral purity, but His excellence above all other beings in every way (see note at 15:11). The enormous amount of pure gold used in the holy furniture (38:24) displayed the beauty and precious value of His holiness (28:36; 39:30). This King's wealth reflects Himself. Let us treasure Him above all and cast away everything in order to gain Him (Matt. 13:44; Phil. 3:7–8). Do you view God as your supreme treasure? How do true Christians show they view God as their supreme treasure?

Chapter 38: ***Bezaleel makes the altar of burnt offering, the laver, and the courtyard, and counts the total gold and silver used.***

38:1–7 On the *altar of burnt offering*, see notes at 27:1–8.

38:4 *compass thereof.* Its rim.

38:8 On the *laver*, see note at 30:18 and comments in the Worship Section below. *lookingglasses*. Mirrors of polished metal. *women assembling*. Women organized to help the priests, perhaps in preparing and washing various articles (1 Sam. 2:22).

38:9–20 On the *court* of the tabernacle, see notes at 27:9–19.

38:17 *chapiters*. Heads or capitals on the pillars. *filleted*. Banded.

38:25–26 *talents*. 75 pounds. *a thousand seven hundred and threescore and fifteen*. 1,775. *shekels*. 0.4 oz. *bekah*. 0.2 oz. The calculation is thus 603,550 men x 0.2 oz./man x 1 lb./16 oz. = 7,544.375 lbs. or 100 talents + 1,775 shekels.

Thoughts for Personal/Family Worship: Chapter 38

Those consecrated to serve the Lord by the blood of sacrifices still needed regular washing at the laver (30:18–20;

25 And the silver of them that were numbered of
the congregation *was* an hundred talents, and a
thousand seven hundred and threescore and fif-
teen shekels, after the shekel of the sanctuary:
26 A bekah for every man, *that is*, half a shekel,
after the shekel of the sanctuary, for every one
that went to be numbered, from twenty years old
and upward, for six hundred thousand and three
thousand and five hundred and fifty *men*.
27 And of the hundred talents of silver were cast
the sockets of the sanctuary, and the sockets of the
vail; an hundred sockets of the hundred talents, a
talent for a socket.
28 And of the thousand seven hundred seventy
and five *shekels* he made hooks for the pillars, and
overlaid their chapiters, and filleted them.
29 And the brass of the offering *was* seventy tal-
ents, and two thousand and four hundred shekels.
30 And therewith he made the sockets to the door
of the tabernacle of the congregation, and the
brasen altar, and the brasen grate for it, and all the
vessels of the altar,
31 And the sockets of the court round about, and
the sockets of the court gate, and all the pins of
the tabernacle, and all the pins of the court round
about.

CHAPTER 39

AND of the blue, and purple, and scarlet, they
made cloths of service, to do service in the holy
place, and made the holy garments for Aaron; as
the LORD commanded Moses.
2 And he made the ephod *of* gold, blue, and pur-
ple, and scarlet, and fine twined linen.
3 And they did beat the gold into thin plates, and
cut *it into* wires, to work *it* in the blue, and in the
purple, and in the scarlet, and in the fine linen,
with cunning work.
4 They made shoulderpieces for it, to couple *it*
together: by the two edges was it coupled together.
5 And the curious girdle of his ephod, that *was*
upon it, *was* of the same, according to the work
thereof; *of* gold, blue, and purple, and scarlet,
and fine twined linen; as the LORD commanded
Moses.
6 ¶ And they wrought onyx stones inclosed in
ouches of gold, graven, as signets are graven, with
the names of the children of Israel.
7 And he put them on the shoulders of the ephod,
that they should be stones for a memorial to the
children of Israel; as the LORD commanded Moses.
8 ¶ And he made the breastplate *of* cunning
work, like the work of the ephod; *of* gold, blue,
and purple, and scarlet, and fine twined linen.
9 It was foursquare; they made the breastplate
double: a span *was* the length thereof, and a span
the breadth thereof, *being* doubled.
10 And they set in it four rows of stones: *the first*
row *was* a sardius, a topaz, and a carbuncle: this
was the first row.
11 And the second row, an emerald, a sapphire,
and a diamond.
12 And the third row, a ligure, an agate, and an
amethyst.
13 And the fourth row, a beryl, an onyx, and a jas-
per: *they were* inclosed in ouches of gold in their
inclosings.
14 And the stones *were* according to the names of
the children of Israel, twelve, according to their
names, *like* the engravings of a signet, every one
with his name, according to the twelve tribes.
15 And they made upon the breastplate chains at
the ends, *of* wreathen work *of* pure gold.
16 And they made two ouches *of* gold, and two
gold rings; and put the two rings in the two ends
of the breastplate.
17 And they put the two wreathen chains of gold
in the two rings on the ends of the breastplate.
18 And the two ends of the two wreathen chains
they fastened in the two ouches, and put them on
the shoulderpieces of the ephod, before it.
19 And they made two rings of gold, and put
them on the two ends of the breastplate, upon the
border of it, which *was* on the side of the ephod
inward.
20 And they made two *other* golden rings, and
put them on the two sides of the ephod under-
neath, toward the forepart of it, over against the
other coupling thereof, above the curious girdle
of the ephod.
21 And they did bind the breastplate by his rings
unto the rings of the ephod with a lace of blue,
that it might be above the curious girdle of the
ephod, and that the breastplate might not be
loosed from the ephod; as the LORD commanded
Moses.
22 ¶ And he made the robe of the ephod *of* woven
work, all *of* blue.
23 And *there was* an hole in the midst of the robe,

38:8). Jesus taught us the same lesson when He washed the disciples' feet (John 13:1–11). As Christians, we must regularly confess our sins to the Lord so that our conscience can be freshly washed by the blood of Christ (1 John 1:7–10; Heb. 10:22). Confession costs us something. Just as the women gave up their mirrors to make the laver for washing (Ex. 38:8), so we must give up our pride and self-righteousness to find cleansing. Are you able to boldly draw near to God with a cleansed conscience? Why or why not?

Chapter 39: *The people make the sacred garments for the priest to wear.*

39:1 *cloths of service*. Priestly clothing.

39:2–21 On the *ephod*, see notes at 28:6–30.

as the hole of an habergeon, *with* a band round
about the hole, that it should not rend.
24 And they made upon the hems of the robe
pomegranates *of* blue, and purple, and scarlet,
and twined *linen*.
25 And they made bells *of* pure gold, and put the
bells between the pomegranates upon the hem of
the robe, round about between the pomegranates;
26 A bell and a pomegranate, a bell and a
pomegranate, round about the hem of the robe
to minister *in*; as the LORD commanded Moses.
27 ¶ And they made coats *of* fine linen *of* woven
work for Aaron, and for his sons,
28 And a mitre *of* fine linen, and goodly bonnets
of fine linen, and linen breeches *of* fine twined
linen,
29 And a girdle *of* fine twined linen, and blue, and
purple, and scarlet, *of* needlework; as the LORD
commanded Moses.
30 ¶ And they made the plate of the holy crown
of pure gold, and wrote upon it a writing, *like to*
the engravings of a signet, HOLINESS TO THE
LORD.
31 And they tied unto it a lace of blue, to fasten *it*
on high upon the mitre; as the LORD commanded
Moses.
32 ¶ Thus was all the work of the tabernacle of
the tent of the congregation finished: and the
children of Israel did according to all that the
LORD commanded Moses, so did they.
33 ¶ And they brought the tabernacle unto Mo-
ses, the tent, and all his furniture, his taches, his
boards, his bars, and his pillars, and his sockets,
34 And the covering of rams' skins dyed red, and
the covering of badgers' skins, and the vail of the
covering,
35 The ark of the testimony, and the staves there-
of, and the mercy seat,
36 The table, *and* all the vessels thereof, and the
shewbread,
37 The pure candlestick, *with* the lamps thereof,
even with the lamps to be set in order, and all the
vessels thereof, and the oil for light,
38 And the golden altar, and the anointing oil,
and the sweet incense, and the hanging for the
tabernacle door,
39 The brasen altar, and his grate of brass, his
staves, and all his vessels, the laver and his foot,
40 The hangings of the court, his pillars, and
his sockets, and the hanging for the court gate,
his cords, and his pins, and all the vessels of
the service of the tabernacle, for the tent of the
congregation,
41 The cloths of service to do service in the holy
place, and the holy garments for Aaron the priest,
and his sons' garments, to minister in the priest's
office.
42 According to all that the LORD commanded
Moses, so the children of Israel made all the work.
43 And Moses did look upon all the work, and,
behold, they had done it as the LORD had com-
manded, even so had they done it: and Moses
blessed them.

CHAPTER 40

AND the LORD spake unto Moses, saying,
2 On the first day of the first month shalt thou set
up the tabernacle of the tent of the congregation.
3 And thou shalt put therein the ark of the testi-
mony, and cover the ark with the vail.
4 And thou shalt bring in the table, and set in or-
der the things that are to be set in order upon it;
and thou shalt bring in the candlestick, and light
the lamps thereof.
5 And thou shalt set the altar of gold for the in-
cense before the ark of the testimony, and put the
hanging of the door to the tabernacle.
6 And thou shalt set the altar of the burnt offer-
ing before the door of the tabernacle of the tent of
the congregation.
7 And thou shalt set the laver between the tent
of the congregation and the altar, and shalt put
water therein.
8 And thou shalt set up the court round about,
and hang up the hanging at the court gate.
9 And thou shalt take the anointing oil, and
anoint the tabernacle, and all that *is* therein, and

39:22–26 On the *robe*, see notes at 28:31–35.
39:27–31 On these articles of clothing, see notes at 28:36–43.
39:33–41 An inventory comparable to 35:11–19.
39:42–43 *as the LORD had commanded*. Ten times this chapter states that Israel built the parts of the tabernacle according to God's directions (vv. 1,5,7,21,26,29,31–32,42–43).

Thoughts for Personal/Family Worship: Chapter 39

God's church must be built "as the LORD commanded." Whether we are considering the officers who govern the church, the church's worship, its evangelism, or any other aspect of church life, we must order the church according to the will of its King, Jesus Christ. Scripture warns against "will worship," forms of religion and spirituality invented by men according to their wisdom, but powerless to please God or conquer sin (Col. 2:20–23). The Bible is sufficient in every way to guide God's ministers to order the house of God (1 Tim. 3:15; 2 Tim. 3:16–17). What sad consequences result from adding to or subtracting from God's will for His church?

Chapter 40: *Moses assembles the tabernacle and God fills it with His glory.*

40:2 *first day of the first month*. A new beginning, like a new creation. *the tabernacle of the tent of the congregation*. Literally, "the home of the tent of meeting."
40:2–15 *thou*. God's commands were masculine singular,

shalt hallow it, and all the vessels thereof: and it
shall be holy.
10 And thou shalt anoint the altar of the burnt
offering, and all his vessels, and sanctify the altar:
and it shall be an altar most holy.
11 And thou shalt anoint the laver and his foot,
and sanctify it.
12 And thou shalt bring Aaron and his sons unto
the door of the tabernacle of the congregation,
and wash them with water.
13 And thou shalt put upon Aaron the holy gar-
ments, and anoint him, and sanctify him; that he
may minister unto me in the priest's office.
14 And thou shalt bring his sons, and clothe them
with coats:
15 And thou shalt anoint them, as thou didst
anoint their father, that they may minister unto
me in the priest's office: for their anointing shall
surely be an everlasting priesthood throughout
their generations.
16 Thus did Moses: according to all that the LORD
commanded him, so did he.
17 ¶ And it came to pass in the first month in the
second year, on the first *day* of the month, *that* the
tabernacle was reared up.
18 And Moses reared up the tabernacle, and fas-
tened his sockets, and set up the boards thereof, and
put in the bars thereof, and reared up his pillars.
19 And he spread abroad the tent over the taber-
nacle, and put the covering of the tent above upon
it; as the LORD commanded Moses.
20 ¶ And he took and put the testimony into the
ark, and set the staves on the ark, and put the
mercy seat above upon the ark:
21 And he brought the ark into the tabernacle,
and set up the vail of the covering, and covered
the ark of the testimony; as the LORD commanded
Moses.
22 ¶ And he put the table in the tent of the con-
gregation, upon the side of the tabernacle north-
ward, without the vail.
23 And he set the bread in order upon it before
the LORD; as the LORD had commanded Moses.
24 ¶ And he put the candlestick in the tent of the
congregation, over against the table, on the side of
the tabernacle southward.
25 And he lighted the lamps before the LORD; as
the LORD commanded Moses.
26 ¶ And he put the golden altar in the tent of the
congregation before the vail:
27 And he burnt sweet incense thereon; as the
LORD commanded Moses.
28 ¶ And he set up the hanging *at* the door of the
tabernacle.
29 And he put the altar of burnt offering *by* the
door of the tabernacle of the tent of the congre-
gation, and offered upon it the burnt offering
and the meat offering; as the LORD commanded
Moses.
30 ¶ And he set the laver between the tent of the
congregation and the altar, and put water there,
to wash *withal*.
31 And Moses and Aaron and his sons washed
their hands and their feet thereat:
32 When they went into the tent of the congrega-
tion, and when they came near unto the altar, they
washed; as the LORD commanded Moses.
33 And he reared up the court round about the
tabernacle and the altar, and set up the hanging of
the court gate. So Moses finished the work.
34 ¶ Then a cloud covered the tent of the con-
gregation, and the glory of the LORD filled the
tabernacle.
35 And Moses was not able to enter into the tent
of the congregation, because the cloud abode
thereon, and the glory of the LORD filled the
tabernacle.
36 And when the cloud was taken up from over
the tabernacle, the children of Israel went onward
in all their journeys:
37 But if the cloud were not taken up, then they
journeyed not till the day that it was taken up.
38 For the cloud of the LORD *was* upon the tab-
ernacle by day, and fire was on it by night, in the
sight of all the house of Israel, throughout all
their journeys.

---

addressed to Moses. This type teaches us that the Mediator, and He alone, can build God's dwelling place.

40:16–33 Eight times the text says that Moses constructed the tabernacle as God commanded him (vv. 16,19,21,23,25,27, 29,32). God's home is built on the Mediator's obedience.

40:34 *glory of the LORD filled the tabernacle.* A foreshadowing of Christ's personal glory and the glory of heaven (1 Kings 8:10–12; Isa. 4:5; Hag. 2:7; Zech. 2:5; John 1:14; Rev. 15:8; 21:23).

40:35 *abode thereon.* Rested on it.

40:38 *throughout all their journeys.* The Lord is with His people by the Word and Spirit as they travel like pilgrims to their inheritance and ultimate home.

Thoughts for Personal/Family Worship: Chapter 40

God's purpose is to fill His people and the new creation with His glory (Eph. 3:19–21; 4:10; Rev. 21:3). Christ has purchased our enjoyment of the fullness of God by His obedience, and is building God's dwelling now of godly people. The church should be filled with the Holy Spirit (Eph. 5:18), but the riches of spiritual experiences are a mere foretaste of glory (Rom. 8:23). One day Christians will enjoy the glory of God in a way that would kill us now. Our hope is to see His glory and be filled with Him (John 17:24; Rom. 5:2; Col. 1:27). How can we cultivate that hope in our hearts so that it controls our lives?

GOD'S DWELLING WITH MAN

God created man in His own image, as a being fitted to be the dwelling place of the triune God and capable of enjoying fellowship with Him. By our fall into sin we forfeited this indescribably wonderful privilege, however, and now, by nature, we find ourselves alienated from the life of God and walking in darkness (Isa. 9:2; Eph. 4:18; 1 John 1:6). Because God is infinitely and inflexibly holy, He can no longer dwell with man unless sin is put away (Pss. 5:4; 15:1–2; 101:7; 2 Cor. 6:16–18). In His infinite love and grace God therefore designed successive sanctuaries to serve as pictures of His saving presence in the world and of the way in which He could dwell and have fellowship with men in a manner consistent with His holy character.

In the Old Testament one such sanctuary was the tabernacle. The tabernacle served as a meeting place between God and sinful men, forming God's ordained point of contact between heaven and earth. There, in that tent pitched in Israel's camp, God took up His abode and indicated His desire to dwell in the midst of His people (Ex. 25:8,22; 29:42–46). The tabernacle also functioned as a place of revelation, proclaiming the holiness and majesty of God and acting as a tangible reminder of the fact that sin brings separation from God and of the need for an atoning sacrifice to make reconciliation (Lev. 16; Isa. 59:2; Rom. 3:25). God cannot be approached on our terms but only on the basis of His revealed will (Ex. 25:40).

God gave the tabernacle a more established form when He commissioned the son of David to build the temple in Jerusalem (1 Kings 6–8). God's covenant with David linked God's dwelling among the Israelites with the royal offspring of David such that God's "house" or temple became inseparable from David's "house" or dynasty (2 Sam. 7:4–17). God's abiding presence with His people depended upon the faithfulness of the son of David to the Lord (1 Kings 9:1–9).

The tabernacle/temple, with the ordinances belonging to it, was thus a type or picture of our Lord Jesus Christ, in whom God would become incarnate as the obedient son of David, and dwell—literally, "tabernacle"—with His people (John 1:14; 2:19–21). On account of the gracious provision of God in the person and work of His beloved Son, Christ Jesus is the only meeting place between the holy God and sinful man (John 14:6). In Christ we have redemption through His blood and the forgiveness of sins, according to the riches of His grace (Eph. 1:7). He is the One who spans the gulf between deity and humanity, so that through His blood we who were at one time far off might be brought near and enjoy fellowship with Him (Eph. 2:13,18; 1 Peter 3:18).

The tabernacle/temple of the Old Testament is also a type of the church built by Christ (Matt. 16:18). In the New Testament God no longer dwells in buildings made with hands (1 Kings 8:27; Acts 7:48–50) but in His people as "God's building" (1 Cor. 3:9,16–17). The church is "the house of God" or the "habitation of God through the Spirit" where believers "offer up spiritual sacrifices" (Eph. 2:21–22; 1 Tim. 3:15; 1 Peter 2: 5). As the tabernacle was consecrated by the glory of God and set apart as a holy place for the service of God, so believers in the New Testament, who are not their own but have been bought with a price, are to be consecrated and set apart for His use (Rom. 6:13; 1 Cor. 6:19–20).

The return of Christ will bring God's ideal for the tabernacle/temple to its ultimate fulfillment (Rev. 7:15). God will dwell with His redeemed people in the open glory of the Lamb of God, and they will see His face (Rev. 21:3–4,22–23; 22:3–5). Let us therefore seek and desire above all else that we may dwell in the house of the Lord forever, where we shall behold His beauty and be satisfied with His goodness (Pss. 23:6; 27:4; 65:4).

INTRODUCTION TO THE BOOK OF LEVITICUS

Authorship: Liberal scholarship has denied the Mosaic authorship of Leviticus, but conservatives identify Moses as the author and maintain the unity of the book as a unit as well as an integral part of the Pentateuch. Both external and internal evidence support Mosaic authorship.

Externally, more than two thousand years of tradition has accredited authorship with Moses. This has been maintained for a variety of reasons. *First*, Christ confirmed Moses as the author or originator of the "Law" (Luke 24:44). The Law (Hebrew, *torah*) was known to be the collection of Genesis, Exodus, Leviticus, Numbers, and Deuteronomy. Moreover, the New Testament refers to the laws in Leviticus as given to Moses (Matt. 8:4, referring to Lev. 14:2–3; Luke 2:22–24, citing Lev. 12:8; John 7:22–23, referring to Lev. 12:3).

Second, there is a strong literary and theological connection between Exodus and Leviticus. Exodus ends with the building of the tabernacle and the glory of God coming to settle into the Holy of Holies. From a literary perspective, it appears consistent that Leviticus would pick up with the regulations of worship within the tabernacle and the ordinances to be observed by Israel. There is good internal evidence for Mosaic authorship of Exodus (cf. Ex. 24:4), and given the close connection, most likely Moses simply picks up where he left off, continuing the statues and commandments of the Lord for His people.

Third, Moses (and Aaron) is certainly the dominant mediator between God and Israel. We read 39 times that the Lord spoke to Moses (cf. 1:1; 4:1; 5:14; etc.). Similarly, there are other forms of dictation between God and Moses. Because much of this book is composed of what God said to Moses and what he was commanded to reveal to the people of Israel, it is likely that the primary author of Leviticus was Moses. (For more information on authorship, see Introduction to the Pentateuch.)

Date: The date is inseparably linked to the date of the exodus. The biblical evidence from 1 Kings 6:1 and Judg. 11:26 (and others) points to the mid-fifteenth century BC. Exodus 40:17 indicates that the tabernacle was erected in the first month of the second year after the exodus. Leviticus 1:1 indicates the tabernacle was standing and Num. 1:1 indicates that Israel planned to leave Sinai on the first day of the second month of the second year after leaving Egypt. All this suggests the date then of 1445 BC for the composition of Leviticus.

Theme: Holiness resulting from atonement is essential to fellowship with God.

Purpose: God teaches His people how they can have fellowship with Him. Leviticus opens with the Lord calling to Moses out of the tabernacle of the congregation. In Exodus He was on Mount Sinai and none dared approach Him (Ex. 19:21). Now however, He dwells in the midst of His people for their sake. And this is possible through the messianic sacrifices with which the book opens. By these He can receive them graciously, both in their wilderness journeys and in the land of Canaan.

Synopsis: *The Contribution of Leviticus to Redemptive Revelation*

The Jews called the book simply by its opening phrase, "And called" (1:1). The word has the idea of crying out or preaching to someone. God captures Moses' attention and gives to him the laws and ceremonies of this book. The title "Leviticus" has come from the Septuagint, and means "relating to the Levites." This title is appropriate because the Levitical priests are central to the book. The Lord through Moses entrusts the laws and ceremonies to the Levitical priests (and the Levites, their helpers) to administer, and He instructs the people to observe the principles of true worship.

Exodus shows God bringing forth a redeemed people. Leviticus shows Him making a holy people. Two great themes dominate the book: atonement (mentioned 43 times) and holiness (77 times). These cannot be separated. In atonement, our guilt is covered and wiped clean; with holiness, we are separated to God and made clean. Atonement is made by offering sacrifices and the intercession of priests, both of which point to the Messiah to come. Holiness is effected by our contact with God, the work of His Spirit within, and our walk in light of His laws—this makes us consecrated to God (Ps. 4:3).

These themes can be seen in Leviticus through the use of types. Our word "types" means "example," "pattern," or "figure" (1 Cor. 10:6,11). That is, the laws and ceremonies are picture prophecies finding fulfillment in Christ and the gospel. God was teaching His people through these visual aids, but the reality would be when Jesus Christ came in the fullness of time. The gospel then was the same as now; the means of declaring the gospel was different—then in the visible pictures along with Moses' explanations, now in the preaching of completed revelation of God in the Scripture. Those who saw Christ in the sacrifices were saved and blessed on the same ground as we are—His finished work. The cross looks back through the ages, because Christ was the Lamb slain from the foundation of the world (Rev. 13:8).

Leviticus is also set forth as "shadows," as in Heb. 10:1, "a shadow of good things to come" (Hebrews is the New Testament counterpart of Leviticus). Shadow means "an image cast by an object which represents its form." Imagine someone coming toward you on a sunny day. The sun is behind him, and his shadow reaches you first. His shadow is a rough shape or outline of his person and substance. So it is on the pages of the Old Testament, including Leviticus. Our Lord and His gospel, with heavenly light behind, cast shadows as the fullness of time approaches. These tell us about His person and work. Leviticus gives the "good things to come" their outline and shape. And their blessings were for those who, through them, looked to the promised Redeemer.

Outline:

I. The Offerings (1:1–7:38)
   - A. The Burnt Offering (1:1–17)
   - B. The Meat Offering (2:1–16)
   - C. The Peace Offering (3:1–17)
   - D. The Sin Offerings (4:1—5:13)
   - E. The Trespass Offerings (5:14—6:7)
   - F. Instructions to Priests Concerning the Offerings (6:8—7:38)

II. Institution of the Aaronic Priesthood (8:1—10:20)
   - A. Priestly Consecration (8:1–36)
   - B. The Priests' Entrance into Office (9:1–24)
   - C. Nadab and Abihu's Sin (10:1–20)

III. Laws Relating to Ritual Uncleanness (11:1—15:33)
   - A. Uncleanness Due to Contact with Animals (11:1–47)
   - B. Uncleanness Due to Childbirth (12:1–8)
   - C. Uncleanness Due to Skin Diseases (13:1—14:57)
   - D. Uncleanness Due to Bodily Discharges (15:1–33)

IV. The Day of Atonement (16:1–34)

V. The Holiness God Requires of His People (17:1—22:33)
   - A. Holiness in Eating Food (17:1–16)
   - B. Holiness in the Marriage Relationship (18:1–30)
   - C. Holiness in Justice and Love toward God and Man (19:1–37)
   - D. Various Sins: Their Prohibition and Punishment (20:1–27)
   - E. Holiness of Priests, Gifts, and Sacrifices (21:1—22:33)

VI. The Sabbath and the Sacred Calendar (23:1–44)
   - A. The Sabbath (23:1–3)
   - B. The Passover and Unleavened Bread (23:4–8)
   - C. The Firstfruits (23:9–14)
   - D. The Feast of Weeks or Pentecost (23:15–22)
   - E. The Blowing of Trumpets (23:23–25)
   - F. The Day of Atonement (23:26–32)
   - G. The Feast of Tabernacles or Booths (23:33–44)

VII. Some Remaining Matters (24:1—27:34)
   - A. The Holy Lamps and Shewbread (24:1–9)
   - B. The Punishment of a Blasphemer (24:10–23)
   - C. The Sabbatical and Jubilee Years (25:1–55)
   - D. Promises and Warnings (26:1–46)
   - E. Directions Concerning Vows (27:1–34)

FOR I AM

THE LORD

Your God

YE SHALL THEREFORE

SANCTIFY

yourselves

AND YE SHALL

BE HOLY

FOR

I am holy

LEVITICUS 11:44

THE THIRD BOOK OF MOSES CALLED

LEVITICUS

CHAPTER 1

AND the LORD called unto Moses, and spake unto
him out of the tabernacle of the congregation,
saying,
2 Speak unto the children of Israel, and say unto
them, If any man of you bring an offering unto
the LORD, ye shall bring your offering of the cattle,
even of the herd, and of the flock.
3 If his offering *be* a burnt sacrifice of the herd,
let him offer a male without blemish: he shall of-
fer it of his own voluntary will at the door of the
tabernacle of the congregation before the LORD.
4 And he shall put his hand upon the head of the
burnt offering; and it shall be accepted for him to
make atonement for him.
5 And he shall kill the bullock before the LORD:
and the priests, Aaron's sons, shall bring the
blood, and sprinkle the blood round about upon
the altar that *is by* the door of the tabernacle of
the congregation.
6 And he shall flay the burnt offering, and cut it
into his pieces.
7 And the sons of Aaron the priest shall put fire
upon the altar, and lay the wood in order upon
the fire:
8 And the priests, Aaron's sons, shall lay the parts,
the head, and the fat, in order upon the wood that
is on the fire which *is* upon the altar:
9 But his inwards and his legs shall he wash in
water: and the priest shall burn all on the altar, *to*
be a burnt sacrifice, an offering made by fire, of a
sweet savour unto the LORD.
10 ¶ And if his offering *be* of the flocks, *namely*,
of the sheep, or of the goats, for a burnt sacrifice;
he shall bring it a male without blemish.
11 And he shall kill it on the side of the altar
northward before the LORD: and the priests, Aar-
on's sons, shall sprinkle his blood round about
upon the altar.
12 And he shall cut it into his pieces, with his
head and his fat: and the priest shall lay them
in order on the wood that *is* on the fire which *is*
upon the altar:
13 But he shall wash the inwards and the legs with
water: and the priest shall bring *it* all, and burn *it*
upon the altar: it *is* a burnt sacrifice, an offering
made by fire, of a sweet savour unto the LORD.
14 ¶ And if the burnt sacrifice for his offering to
the LORD *be* of fowls, then he shall bring his offer-
ing of turtledoves, or of young pigeons.
15 And the priest shall bring it unto the altar, and
wring off his head, and burn *it* on the altar; and
the blood thereof shall be wrung out at the side
of the altar:
16 And he shall pluck away his crop with his
feathers, and cast it beside the altar on the east
part, by the place of the ashes:
17 And he shall cleave it with the wings thereof,
but shall not divide *it* asunder: and the priest
shall burn it upon the altar, upon the wood that

THE OFFERINGS (1:1—7:38)

Chapter 1: *The Lord gives laws concerning the burnt offering taken from the herd, flocks, or birds.*

The Burnt Offering (1:1–17)

1:3 *male without blemish.* The selection of an animal without defect taught that salvation had to come from outside of oneself by a pure and innocent substitute and pointed to the perfect and pure Christ, the reality casting the shadow (1 Peter 1:19). *voluntary will.* Literally, "for his acceptance."

1:4 *put his hand.* A symbolic act of transferring one's guilt to the animal. *make atonement.* God's wrath is turned aside and the sin is covered.

1:5 *he shall kill the bullock.* The act of the offerer killing the bull symbolizes the personal responsibility for the death of the innocent substitute who took sin's penalty. Hence, believers acknowledge that it was for their own sin that Christ died. *sprinkle the blood.* This act symbolizes that atonement requires more than just death but the presentation and application of blood as well. It is not just the fact of Christ's death that saves but the application of His blood.

1:6 *flay.* Skin the animal. The hide was not burnt but kept by the priest to be used or sold (7:8).

1:9 *altar.* Altar in the court of the tabernacle. *burnt sacrifice.* The whole sacrifice is consumed by fire. The offerer is yielding up everything to God. *a sweet savour.* Denotes a quieting or peaceful fragrance, a smell of appeasement. Symbolic of God's anger turning to favor.

1:10 Slight details change if the animal is a *sheep* or another animal.

1:16 *crop.* The alimentary canal, the whole inner passage through which food passes.

is upon the fire: it *is* a burnt sacrifice, an offering
made by fire, of a sweet savour unto the LORD.

CHAPTER 2

AND when any will offer a meat offering unto
the LORD, his offering shall be *of* fine flour; and
he shall pour oil upon it, and put frankincense
thereon:
2 And he shall bring it to Aaron's sons the priests:
and he shall take thereout his handful of the
flour thereof, and of the oil thereof, with all the
frankincense thereof; and the priest shall burn the
memorial of it upon the altar, *to be* an offering
made by fire, of a sweet savour unto the LORD:
3 And the remnant of the meat offering *shall be*
Aaron's and his sons': *it is* a thing most holy of the
offerings of the LORD made by fire.
4 ¶ And if thou bring an oblation of a meat
offering baken in the oven, *it shall be* unleavened
cakes of fine flour mingled with oil, or unleavened
wafers anointed with oil.
5 ¶ And if thy oblation *be* a meat offering *baken*
in a pan, it shall be *of* fine flour unleavened,
mingled with oil.
6 Thou shalt part it in pieces, and pour oil
thereon: it *is* a meat offering.
7 ¶ And if thy oblation *be* a meat offering *baken*
in the fryingpan, it shall be made *of* fine flour
with oil.
8 And thou shalt bring the meat offering that is
made of these things unto the LORD: and when it
is presented unto the priest, he shall bring it unto
the altar.
9 And the priest shall take from the meat offering
a memorial thereof, and shall burn *it* upon the al-
tar: *it is* an offering made by fire, of a sweet savour
unto the LORD.
10 And that which is left of the meat offering *shall*
be Aaron's and his sons': *it is* a thing most holy of
the offerings of the LORD made by fire.
11 No meat offering, which ye shall bring unto
the LORD, shall be made with leaven: for ye shall
burn no leaven, nor any honey, in any offering of
the LORD made by fire.
12 ¶ As for the oblation of the firstfruits, ye shall
offer them unto the LORD: but they shall not be
burnt on the altar for a sweet savour.
13 And every oblation of thy meat offering shalt
thou season with salt; neither shalt thou suffer the
salt of the covenant of thy God to be lacking from
thy meat offering: with all thine offerings thou
shalt offer salt.
14 And if thou offer a meat offering of thy first-
fruits unto the LORD, thou shalt offer for the meat
offering of thy firstfruits green ears of corn dried

Thoughts for Personal/Family Worship: Chapter 1

1. **The burnt offering, along with all the other types of sacrifice, was a clear yet imperfect picture of the once-for-all sacrifice of Jesus Christ, the Lamb slain from the foundation of the world (Rev. 13:8). Animal sacrifices could never and were never intended to take away sin (Heb. 10:1–4). Only the sacrifice of Christ could do that (Heb. 10:12). But they were graphic sermons of the necessity of a perfect substitute, of death as sin's penalty, of blood shedding as the means of forgiveness, of reconciliation and consecration. Although it would be a sin against Christ to repeat the animal sacrifices, what aspects of their message preach about Him?**
2. **The peculiarity of the burnt offering was that the entire animal was placed on the altar. It pictures full and complete consecration; everything is given to the Lord with nothing being held back. It testifies of both the total dedication of Christ who gave Himself as a sweet savor (Eph. 5:2) and the consecration of the believer to the Lord of his life in view of gospel grace (Rom. 12:1–2). The burning of all on the altar would not have been a pleasant aroma to us, but it pleased the Lord. So putting ourselves on the altar of consecration may at times be unpleasant to self, but it is pleasing unto the Lord. In view of Christ's sacrifice, how are you offering yourself as a living sacrifice to God?**

Chapter 2: *The Lord instructs Moses concerning the meat or food offering of grain.*

The Meat Offering (2:1–16)

2:1 *meat.* The Hebrew simply means "gift" or "present" but often refers to a grain offering, the only offering without blood. In the early modern English of the KJV, "meat" meant "food" in general. The *meat offering* usually accompanied the burnt and peace offerings, one of the bloody sacrifices. *fine flour.* Finely ground flour.

2:2 *the memorial of it.* Refers to a portion of the offering that was burned as a token or sign.

2:3 *remnant.* What was left over.

2:4 *oblation.* The most general word for "offering" (throughout the book). It is the word "corban" that Christ refers to in Mark 7:11. *baken in the oven . . . unleavened.* Baked into bread cakes. *wafers.* A thin unleavened cake of bread. *anointed with oil.* Literally, "smeared with oil." The references to oil throughout symbolize the presence and work of the Holy Spirit in the activity of worship.

2:11 *No meat offering . . . with leaven . . . honey.* Likely because the yeast and honey can ferment which signifies corruption.

2:12 *oblation of the firstfruits.* The first sheaf of the harvest, offered to God to confess that all comes from Him.

2:13 *salt.* A preserving agent used as a symbol of God's covenant.

Thoughts for Personal/Family Worship: Chapter 2

1. **The meat or grain offering was an expression of the worshiper's confession that his daily bread was from above. With that recognition, the worshiper offered a token in consecration and dedication to the Lord. Similarly, we are to be thankful for outward and temporal benefits! The offering also points to the Lord Jesus who perfectly and completely lived in dedication to His Father. How can you express your dependence on God and your thankfulness for the daily bread He supplies?**
2. **Significantly, this sacrifice without blood was never offered independently; it was always in connection with**

by the fire, *even* corn beaten out of full ears.
15 And thou shalt put oil upon it, and lay frankincense thereon: it *is* a meat offering.
16 And the priest shall burn the memorial of it, *part* of the beaten corn thereof, and *part* of the oil thereof, with all the frankincense thereof: *it is* an offering made by fire unto the LORD.

CHAPTER 3

AND if his oblation *be* a sacrifice of peace offering, if he offer *it* of the herd; whether *it be* a male or female, he shall offer it without blemish before the LORD.
2 And he shall lay his hand upon the head of his offering, and kill it *at* the door of the tabernacle of the congregation: and Aaron's sons the priests shall sprinkle the blood upon the altar round about.
3 And he shall offer of the sacrifice of the peace offering an offering made by fire unto the LORD; the fat that covereth the inwards, and all the fat that *is* upon the inwards,
4 And the two kidneys, and the fat that *is* on them, which *is* by the flanks, and the caul above the liver, with the kidneys, it shall he take away.
5 And Aaron's sons shall burn it on the altar upon the burnt sacrifice, which *is* upon the wood that *is* on the fire: *it is* an offering made by fire, of a sweet savour unto the LORD.
6 ¶ And if his offering for a sacrifice of peace offering unto the LORD *be* of the flock; male or female, he shall offer it without blemish.
7 If he offer a lamb for his offering, then shall he offer it before the LORD.
8 And he shall lay his hand upon the head of his offering, and kill it before the tabernacle of the congregation: and Aaron's sons shall sprinkle the blood thereof round about upon the altar.
9 And he shall offer of the sacrifice of the peace offering an offering made by fire unto the LORD; the fat thereof, *and* the whole rump, it shall he take off hard by the backbone; and the fat that covereth the inwards, and all the fat that *is* upon the inwards,
10 And the two kidneys, and the fat that *is* upon them, which *is* by the flanks, and the caul above the liver, with the kidneys, it shall he take away.
11 And the priest shall burn it upon the altar: *it is* the food of the offering made by fire unto the LORD.
12 ¶ And if his offering *be* a goat, then he shall offer it before the LORD.
13 And he shall lay his hand upon the head of it, and kill it before the tabernacle of the congregation: and the sons of Aaron shall sprinkle the blood thereof upon the altar round about.
14 And he shall offer thereof his offering, *even* an offering made by fire unto the LORD; the fat that covereth the inwards, and all the fat that *is* upon the inwards,
15 And the two kidneys, and the fat that *is* upon them, which *is* by the flanks, and the caul above the liver, with the kidneys, it shall he take away.
16 And the priest shall burn them upon the altar: *it is* the food of the offering made by fire for a sweet savour: all the fat *is* the LORD's.
17 *It shall be* a perpetual statute for your generations throughout all your dwellings, that ye eat neither fat nor blood.

---

one of the bloody sacrifices. To offer the work of our hands to the Lord apart from the blood of Christ is to repeat the sin of Cain who assumed his works would be acceptable on their own merit. It is only through the blood of Christ's sacrifice that anything we offer to the Lord, even in thanksgiving, will be acceptable. How can we keep in mind that all our worship can only be offered with His blood?

Chapter 3: *The Lord gives instructions about the peace or fellowship offering taken from the herd or flock.*

The Peace Offering (3:1–17)

3:1 *peace offering.* See also 7:11–34; 19:5–8; 22:21–25. *male or female.* A female can also be used here, not typical of the previous offerings. The initial steps of the peace offering is the same as other bloody offerings (see notes at the burnt offering, ch. 1).
3:2 *door of the tabernacle.* The other three bloody offerings (burnt, sin, trespass) were killed on the north side of the altar.
3:3 It was common in the sacrificial laws to separate the *fat* surrounding the *inwards* parts and to burn them on the altar (vv. 9–10,14–15). Fat is considered the best and choicest part of the animal and therefore God's rightful portion. The burning of the viscera, representing the seat of emotions, also symbolized the surrender of self to the Lord.
3:4 *flanks.* Loins. *caul.* Fatty lobe above the liver (throughout the chapter).
3:5 *upon the burnt sacrifice.* In connection with the burnt offering. *sweet savour.* See note at 1:9.
3:11 *food of the offering.* The peace offering involved a sacrificial meal. Chapter 7 reveals that portions were for God, the priests, and the offerer. Sharing a meal pictured reconciliation.
3:17 *perpetual statue.* Everlasting commandment. *eat neither fat nor blood.* Because the fat, representing the best, belonged to God (v. 16) and the blood, the symbol of life, was offered to God in sacrifice for the remission of sin.

Thoughts for Personal/Family Worship: Chapter 3

1. **The peace offering was a shared meal in which the offerer celebrated the benefits of a peaceful relationship with God, a reconciliation accomplished by the shed blood. In this meal, God, the priest, and the offerer all received a portion, symbolizing that all the parties were satisfied with the atonement. The features of the peace offering draw a straight line to the blessings and benefits Christians know and enjoy in the new covenant. Our peace with God flows from Christ's atonement. God is satisfied with Christ's sacrifice; Christ is satisfied with those He purchased; and we are satisfied with peace with God through Him. How does the gospel bring satisfaction to the soul?**
2. **There are significant parallels between the peace offering and the communal meal that believers can**

CHAPTER 4

AND the LORD spake unto Moses, saying,

2 Speak unto the children of Israel, saying, If a soul shall sin through ignorance against any of the commandments of the LORD *concerning things* which ought not to be done, and shall do against any of them:

3 If the priest that is anointed do sin according to the sin of the people; then let him bring for his sin, which he hath sinned, a young bullock without blemish unto the LORD for a sin offering.

4 And he shall bring the bullock unto the door of the tabernacle of the congregation before the LORD; and shall lay his hand upon the bullock's head, and kill the bullock before the LORD.

5 And the priest that is anointed shall take of the bullock's blood, and bring it to the tabernacle of the congregation:

6 And the priest shall dip his finger in the blood, and sprinkle of the blood seven times before the LORD, before the vail of the sanctuary.

7 And the priest shall put *some* of the blood upon the horns of the altar of sweet incense before the LORD, which *is* in the tabernacle of the congregation; and shall pour all the blood of the bullock at the bottom of the altar of the burnt offering, which *is at* the door of the tabernacle of the congregation.

8 And he shall take off from it all the fat of the bullock for the sin offering; the fat that covereth the inwards, and all the fat that *is* upon the inwards,

9 And the two kidneys, and the fat that *is* upon them, which *is* by the flanks, and the caul above the liver, with the kidneys, it shall he take away,

10 As it was taken off from the bullock of the sacrifice of peace offerings: and the priest shall burn them upon the altar of the burnt offering.

11 And the skin of the bullock, and all his flesh, with his head, and with his legs, and his inwards, and his dung,

12 Even the whole bullock shall he carry forth without the camp unto a clean place, where the ashes are poured out, and burn him on the wood with fire: where the ashes are poured out shall he be burnt.

13 ¶ And if the whole congregation of Israel sin through ignorance, and the thing be hid from the eyes of the assembly, and they have done *somewhat against* any of the commandments of the LORD *concerning things* which should not be done, and are guilty;

14 When the sin, which they have sinned against it, is known, then the congregation shall offer a young bullock for the sin, and bring him before the tabernacle of the congregation.

15 And the elders of the congregation shall lay their hands upon the head of the bullock before the LORD: and the bullock shall be killed before the LORD.

16 And the priest that is anointed shall bring of the bullock's blood to the tabernacle of the congregation:

17 And the priest shall dip his finger *in some* of the blood, and sprinkle *it* seven times before the LORD, *even* before the vail.

18 And he shall put *some* of the blood upon the horns of the altar which *is* before the LORD, that *is* in the tabernacle of the congregation, and shall pour out all the blood at the bottom of the altar of the burnt offering, which *is at* the door of the tabernacle of the congregation.

19 And he shall take all his fat from him, and burn *it* upon the altar.

20 And he shall do with the bullock as he did with the bullock for a sin offering, so shall he do with this: and the priest shall make an atonement for them, and it shall be forgiven them.

21 And he shall carry forth the bullock without the camp, and burn him as he burned the first bullock: it *is* a sin offering for the congregation.

22 ¶ When a ruler hath sinned, and done

---

experience at the Lord's Table. The table is not a sacrifice but it declares the fact of the sacrifice Christ offered that removed every barrier, obstacle, and impediment to our fellowship with God as believers; it declares that we have peace with God through our Lord Jesus Christ. Rejoice in the One who accomplished this on your behalf!

The Sin Offerings (4:1—5:13)

Chapter 4: *The Lord directs the priests concerning the sin offering for various kinds of people.*

4:2 *soul.* Person. *through ignorance.* Inadvertently or unintentionally.

4:3 *If the priest . . . sin.* Priests were not exempt from sin, unlike Christ, the ideal Priest, who offered Himself without spot (Heb. 9:14).

4:4–7 *the door of the tabernacle.* The priest brought the blood into the tabernacle and sprinkled some on the incense altar located just in front of the veil, separating the holy place from the holiest place. In contrast, Christ offered His sacrifice behind the veil in the immediate presence of God (Heb. 6:19–20; 9:12).

4:9 *flanks . . . caul.* See note at 3:4.

4:12 *burn.* A burning to consume or destroy in contrast to the burning of the burnt offering, meaning to offer up in smoke (1:9).

4:13–21 *whole congregation of Israel sin.* For national sins, the elders (representing all the people) must place their hands on the head of the sin offering (v. 15). Corporate sins have consequences.

Thoughts for Personal/Family Worship: Chapter 4

1. Sin is the transgression of the law, and ignorance of the law is no excuse. God is so holy and His law is so inflexible that as fallen mankind we cannot help but offend God. The heart is "deceitful" and "desperately wicked" (Jer. 17:9). Sin is instinctive, and we can commit it carelessly, thoughtlessly, or unintentionally. We can be guilty of such sins more than we know, imagining all is well. But God has devised the means to deal with sin;

somewhat through ignorance *against* any of the
commandments of the LORD his God *concerning*
things which should not be done, and is guilty;
23 Or if his sin, wherein he hath sinned, come to
his knowledge; he shall bring his offering, a kid of
the goats, a male without blemish:
24 And he shall lay his hand upon the head of the
goat, and kill it in the place where they kill the
burnt offering before the LORD: it *is* a sin offering.
25 And the priest shall take of the blood of the sin
offering with his finger, and put *it* upon the horns
of the altar of burnt offering, and shall pour out his
blood at the bottom of the altar of burnt offering.
26 And he shall burn all his fat upon the altar, as
the fat of the sacrifice of peace offerings: and the
priest shall make an atonement for him as concerning his sin, and it shall be forgiven him.
27 ¶ And if any one of the common people sin
through ignorance, while he doeth *somewhat*
against any of the commandments of the LORD
concerning things which ought not to be done,
and be guilty;
28 Or if his sin, which he hath sinned, come to his
knowledge: then he shall bring his offering, a kid
of the goats, a female without blemish, for his sin
which he hath sinned.
29 And he shall lay his hand upon the head of the
sin offering, and slay the sin offering in the place
of the burnt offering.
30 And the priest shall take of the blood thereof
with his finger, and put *it* upon the horns of the
altar of burnt offering, and shall pour out all the
blood thereof at the bottom of the altar.
31 And he shall take away all the fat thereof, as the
fat is taken away from off the sacrifice of peace offerings; and the priest shall burn *it* upon the altar
for a sweet savour unto the LORD; and the priest
shall make an atonement for him, and it shall be
forgiven him.
32 And if he bring a lamb for a sin offering, he
shall bring it a female without blemish.
33 And he shall lay his hand upon the head of the
sin offering, and slay it for a sin offering in the
place where they kill the burnt offering.
34 And the priest shall take of the blood of the sin
offering with his finger, and put *it* upon the horns
of the altar of burnt offering, and shall pour out
all the blood thereof at the bottom of the altar:
35 And he shall take away all the fat thereof, as the
fat of the lamb is taken away from the sacrifice of
the peace offerings; and the priest shall burn them
upon the altar, according to the offerings made
by fire unto the LORD: and the priest shall make
an atonement for his sin that he hath committed,
and it shall be forgiven him.

CHAPTER 5

AND if a soul sin, and hear the voice of swearing,
and *is* a witness, whether he hath seen or known
of it; if he do not utter *it*, then he shall bear his
iniquity.
2 Or if a soul touch any unclean thing, whether
it be a carcase of an unclean beast, or a carcase of
unclean cattle, or the carcase of unclean creeping
things, and *if* it be hidden from him; he also shall
be unclean, and guilty.
3 Or if he touch the uncleanness of man, whatsoever uncleanness *it be* that a man shall be defiled
withal, and it be hid from him; when he knoweth
of it, then he shall be guilty.
4 Or if a soul swear, pronouncing with *his* lips to
do evil, or to do good, whatsoever *it be* that a man
shall pronounce with an oath, and it be hid from
him; when he knoweth *of it*, then he shall be guilty
in one of these.
5 And it shall be, when he shall be guilty in one
of these *things*, that he shall confess that he hath
sinned in that *thing*:
6 And he shall bring his trespass offering unto the
LORD for his sin which he hath sinned, a female
from the flock, a lamb or a kid of the goats, for a
sin offering; and the priest shall make an atonement for him concerning his sin.
7 And if he be not able to bring a lamb, then he
shall bring for his trespass, which he hath com-

---

there is a sacrifice for sins of ignorance. And when we realize and confess them, they are covered by the atonement of Christ. Let us pray with David, "Cleanse thou me from secret faults" (Ps. 19:12). How can you develop a habit of keeping short accounts with God?

2. The chapter ends with a glorious statement that links atonement with forgiveness (v. 35). Since the sacrifice appeases God's wrath and satisfies His justice for the sinner, forgiveness is the wonderful consequence. All those who truly trust Christ alone for salvation are covered by His precious blood and exempt from any personal experience of God's wrath. Christ took the wrath in our place, and God is, therefore, faithful and just to forgive us our sins (1 John 1:9). How would you counsel a person who sincerely trusts in the Lord Jesus Christ, but still feels guilty and afraid of God's wrath?

Chapter 5: *God gives more instructions for the sin offering and the trespass offering.*

5:1–13 Interpreters differ about whether the sin offering or the trespass offering is in view here. Although different, there are similarities.

5:1 *hear the voice of swearing.* An oath, referring to someone who withholds evidence in court when charged to tell the truth (1 Kings 22:16; Matt. 26:63).

5:2–3 *touch any unclean thing.* Contact with anything that is ceremonially unclean renders one unclean. Ignorance does not exempt from guilt.

5:6 *bring his trespass offering . . . for a sin offering.* The distinction between these two sacrifices are not yet defined; perhaps no distinction in view here.

5:7 *for his trespass.* Here referring to the actual guilt of the

mitted, two turtledoves, or two young pigeons,
unto the LORD; one for a sin offering, and the
other for a burnt offering.
8 And he shall bring them unto the priest, who
shall offer *that* which *is* for the sin offering first,
and wring off his head from his neck, but shall
not divide *it* asunder:
9 And he shall sprinkle of the blood of the sin of-
fering upon the side of the altar; and the rest of
the blood shall be wrung out at the bottom of the
altar: it *is* a sin offering.
10 And he shall offer the second *for* a burnt offer-
ing, according to the manner: and the priest shall
make an atonement for him for his sin which he
hath sinned, and it shall be forgiven him.
11 ¶ But if he be not able to bring two turtle-
doves, or two young pigeons, then he that sinned
shall bring for his offering the tenth part of an
ephah of fine flour for a sin offering; he shall put
no oil upon it, neither shall he put *any* frankin-
cense thereon: for it *is* a sin offering.
12 Then shall he bring it to the priest, and the
priest shall take his handful of it, *even* a memo-
rial thereof, and burn *it* on the altar, according to
the offerings made by fire unto the LORD: it *is* a
sin offering.
13 And the priest shall make an atonement for
him as touching his sin that he hath sinned in
one of these, and it shall be forgiven him: and the
remnant shall be the priest's, as a meat offering.
14 ¶ And the LORD spake unto Moses, saying,
15 If a soul commit a trespass, and sin through
ignorance, in the holy things of the LORD; then he
shall bring for his trespass unto the LORD a ram
without blemish out of the flocks, with thy esti-
mation by shekels of silver, after the shekel of the
sanctuary, for a trespass offering:
16 And he shall make amends for the harm that
he hath done in the holy thing, and shall add the
fifth part thereto, and give it unto the priest: and
the priest shall make an atonement for him with
the ram of the trespass offering, and it shall be
forgiven him.
17 ¶ And if a soul sin, and commit any of these
things which are forbidden to be done by the
commandments of the LORD; though he wist *it*
not, yet is he guilty, and shall bear his iniquity.
18 And he shall bring a ram without blemish out
of the flock, with thy estimation, for a trespass of-
fering, unto the priest: and the priest shall make
an atonement for him concerning his ignorance
wherein he erred and wist *it* not, and it shall be
forgiven him.
19 It *is* a trespass offering: he hath certainly tres-
passed against the LORD.

CHAPTER 6

AND the LORD spake unto Moses, saying,
2 If a soul sin, and commit a trespass against the
LORD, and lie unto his neighbour in that which
was delivered him to keep, or in fellowship, or in
a thing taken away by violence, or hath deceived
his neighbour;
3 Or have found that which was lost, and lieth
concerning it, and sweareth falsely; in any of all
these that a man doeth, sinning therein:
4 Then it shall be, because he hath sinned, and is
guilty, that he shall restore that which he took vio-
lently away, or the thing which he hath deceitfully
gotten, or that which was delivered him to keep,
or the lost thing which he found,

---

wrong done not the sacrifice. *two turtledoves, or two young pigeons.* The law allowed for lesser animals depending on one's economic status, suggesting the importance of heart over form or ritual (v. 11).

5:8 *divide it asunder.* Divide it into parts.

The Trespass Offerings (5:14—6:7)

5:15 *commit a trespass.* Literally, "act treacherously a treacherous act." *the shekel of the sanctuary.* The standard weight of measurement kept in the sanctuary.

5:16 *amends.* Restitution. The key distinction between the sin and trespass offering involved the reparation to the wronged party. Significantly, this is the particular sacrifice Isaiah used to designate the Suffering Servant (Isa. 53:10). *fifth part thereto.* What was withheld must be paid back plus twenty percent.

5:17 *wist.* Knew (v. 18).

Thoughts for Personal/Family Worship: Chapter 5

1. **How wonderful is God's grace! If people could not afford to offer the lamb or kid, just some flour would be acceptable. This is important evidence that there was nothing in the animal blood that had the power to deal with sin. God is always more concerned about the condition of the heart than conformity to ritual. Faith could see beyond whatever the sacrifice was to the reality casting the shadow—Jesus Christ. When our Lord fulfilled all these offerings, our forgiveness cost Him everything and cost us nothing (Rom. 6:23). What is the condition of your heart in light of Christ's sacrifice?**
2. **The trespass offering sees sin as debt to God: compensation must be paid to Him. Thus Christ taught us to pray, "And forgive us our debts" (Matt. 6:12). What we owed, Jesus paid. He made satisfaction to God. His passive obedience paid the Law's penalty; His active obedience paid the debt to the Law's precepts. These comprise His justifying righteousness. With our debts paid, what should be our focus? (See John 14:23–24.)**

Chapter 6: ***The Lord concludes the directions for the trespass offering, and gives further ordinances about the burnt offering, meat offering, priestly consecration, and sin offering.***

6:1–7 This passage is actually 5:20–26 in the Hebrew Bible.

6:2 *against the LORD.* Significantly, sins against men are ultimately against God. *in fellowship.* Literally, "in security of a hand," referring to property that had been entrusted.

6:4–5 *restore.* Restitution is required for these trespasses.

5 Or all that about which he hath sworn falsely;
he shall even restore it in the principal, and shall
add the fifth part more thereto, *and* give it unto
him to whom it appertaineth, in the day of his
trespass offering.
6 And he shall bring his trespass offering unto
the LORD, a ram without blemish out of the flock,
with thy estimation, for a trespass offering, unto
the priest:
7 And the priest shall make an atonement for
him before the LORD: and it shall be forgiven him
for any thing of all that he hath done in trespass-
ing therein.
8 ¶ And the LORD spake unto Moses, saying,
9 Command Aaron and his sons, saying, This *is*
the law of the burnt offering: It *is* the burnt of-
fering, because of the burning upon the altar all
night unto the morning, and the fire of the altar
shall be burning in it.
10 And the priest shall put on his linen garment,
and his linen breeches shall he put upon his flesh,
and take up the ashes which the fire hath con-
sumed with the burnt offering on the altar, and
he shall put them beside the altar.
11 And he shall put off his garments, and put on
other garments, and carry forth the ashes without
the camp unto a clean place.
12 And the fire upon the altar shall be burning in
it; it shall not be put out: and the priest shall burn
wood on it every morning, and lay the burnt of-
fering in order upon it; and he shall burn thereon
the fat of the peace offerings.
13 The fire shall ever be burning upon the altar; it
shall never go out.
14 ¶ And this *is* the law of the meat offering: the
sons of Aaron shall offer it before the LORD, be-
fore the altar.
15 And he shall take of it his handful, of the flour
of the meat offering, and of the oil thereof, and all
the frankincense which *is* upon the meat offering,
and shall burn *it* upon the altar *for* a sweet savour,
even the memorial of it, unto the LORD.
16 And the remainder thereof shall Aaron and his
sons eat: with unleavened bread shall it be eaten
in the holy place; in the court of the tabernacle of
the congregation they shall eat it.
17 It shall not be baken with leaven. I have given it
unto them for their portion of my offerings made
by fire; it *is* most holy, as *is* the sin offering, and as
the trespass offering.
18 All the males among the children of Aaron shall
eat of it. *It shall be* a statute for ever in your genera-
tions concerning the offerings of the LORD made
by fire: every one that toucheth them shall be holy.
19 ¶ And the LORD spake unto Moses, saying,
20 This *is* the offering of Aaron and of his sons,
which they shall offer unto the LORD in the day
when he is anointed; the tenth part of an ephah of
fine flour for a meat offering perpetual, half of it
in the morning, and half thereof at night.
21 In a pan it shall be made with oil; *and when*
it is baken, thou shalt bring it in: *and* the baken
pieces of the meat offering shalt thou offer *for* a
sweet savour unto the LORD.
22 And the priest of his sons that is anointed in
his stead shall offer it: *it is* a statute for ever unto
the LORD; it shall be wholly burnt.
23 For every meat offering for the priest shall be
wholly burnt: it shall not be eaten.
24 ¶ And the LORD spake unto Moses, saying,
25 Speak unto Aaron and to his sons, saying, This
is the law of the sin offering: In the place where
the burnt offering is killed shall the sin offering be
killed before the LORD: it *is* most holy.
26 The priest that offereth it for sin shall eat it: in
the holy place shall it be eaten, in the court of the
tabernacle of the congregation.
27 Whatsoever shall touch the flesh thereof shall
be holy: and when there is sprinkled of the blood
thereof upon any garment, thou shalt wash that
whereon it was sprinkled in the holy place.
28 But the earthen vessel wherein it is sodden
shall be broken: and if it be sodden in a brasen
pot, it shall be both scoured, and rinsed in water.

6:6 *estimation.* The value required for reparation, an essential component of the trespass offering as evidence of genuine repentance.

Instructions to Priests Concerning the Offerings (6:8—7:38)

6:10–11 *linen garment.* The priests must wear two sets of garments, one for clearing away the ashes and one for removing them from the camp.

6:14 *the meat offering.* This is the offering without blood but made up of grain products.

6:15 *sweet savour.* See note at 1:9. *memorial of it.* A token or memorial offering.

6:17 *leaven.* Yeast.

6:20 *a meat offering perpetual.* A complete grain offering.

6:27 *shall be holy.* Such objects must not be put to common use afterward.

6:28 *sodden.* Boiled. Unlike the metal vessel, the earthen vessel could not be thoroughly cleansed and therefore was to be broken.

Thoughts for Personal/Family Worship: Chapter 6

1. **Wrong done to others is wrong done to God. Verse 2 says, "a trespass against the LORD, and lie unto his neighbour." Sin breaks both tables of the law (James 2:10). Psalm 51 is a classic example of this principle. David's sin was against several people; yet he confessed that he had sinned only against God (Ps. 51:4). Why does God see our sins against others as being foremost against Him?**
2. **Scooping up ashes and removing them from the camp is humble, yet sacred service for priests. So with us who are priests (1 Peter 2:5,9). Not only worship but also practical service can be done as unto the Lord (Col. 3:17,22–23). Nothing is mundane or secular for us. What**

29 All the males among the priests shall eat
thereof: it *is* most holy.
30 And no sin offering, whereof *any* of the blood
is brought into the tabernacle of the congregation
to reconcile *withal* in the holy *place*, shall be eaten:
it shall be burnt in the fire.

CHAPTER 7

LIKEWISE this *is* the law of the trespass offering:
it *is* most holy.
2 In the place where they kill the burnt offering
shall they kill the trespass offering: and the blood
thereof shall he sprinkle round about upon the
altar.
3 And he shall offer of it all the fat thereof; the
rump, and the fat that covereth the inwards,
4 And the two kidneys, and the fat that *is* on them,
which *is* by the flanks, and the caul *that is* above
the liver, with the kidneys, it shall he take away:
5 And the priest shall burn them upon the altar
for an offering made by fire unto the LORD: it *is* a
trespass offering.
6 Every male among the priests shall eat thereof:
it shall be eaten in the holy place: it *is* most holy.
7 As the sin offering *is*, so *is* the trespass offering:
there is one law for them: the priest that maketh
atonement therewith shall have *it*.
8 And the priest that offereth any man's burnt
offering, *even* the priest shall have to himself the
skin of the burnt offering which he hath offered.
9 And all the meat offering that is baken in the
oven, and all that is dressed in the fryingpan, and
in the pan, shall be the priest's that offereth it.
10 And every meat offering, mingled with oil,
and dry, shall all the sons of Aaron have, one *as
much* as another.
11 And this *is* the law of the sacrifice of peace of-
ferings, which he shall offer unto the LORD.
12 If he offer it for a thanksgiving, then he shall
offer with the sacrifice of thanksgiving unleav-
ened cakes mingled with oil, and unleavened wa-
fers anointed with oil, and cakes mingled with oil,
of fine flour, fried.
13 Besides the cakes, he shall offer *for* his offering
leavened bread with the sacrifice of thanksgiving
of his peace offerings.
14 And of it he shall offer one out of the whole
oblation *for* an heave offering unto the LORD, *and*
it shall be the priest's that sprinkleth the blood of
the peace offerings.
15 And the flesh of the sacrifice of his peace offer-
ings for thanksgiving shall be eaten the same day
that it is offered; he shall not leave any of it until
the morning.
16 But if the sacrifice of his offering *be* a vow, or a
voluntary offering, it shall be eaten the same day
that he offereth his sacrifice: and on the morrow
also the remainder of it shall be eaten:
17 But the remainder of the flesh of the sacrifice
on the third day shall be burnt with fire.
18 And if *any* of the flesh of the sacrifice of his
peace offerings be eaten at all on the third day, it
shall not be accepted, neither shall it be imputed
unto him that offereth it: it shall be an abomina-
tion, and the soul that eateth of it shall bear his
iniquity.
19 And the flesh that toucheth any unclean *thing*
shall not be eaten; it shall be burnt with fire: and
as for the flesh, all that be clean shall eat thereof.
20 But the soul that eateth *of* the flesh of the sacri-
fice of peace offerings, that *pertain* unto the LORD,
having his uncleanness upon him, even that soul
shall be cut off from his people.
21 Moreover the soul that shall touch any un-
clean *thing, as* the uncleanness of man, or *any* un-
clean beast, or any abominable unclean *thing*, and
eat of the flesh of the sacrifice of peace offerings,
which *pertain* unto the LORD, even that soul shall
be cut off from his people.
22 ¶ And the LORD spake unto Moses, saying,
23 Speak unto the children of Israel, saying, Ye
shall eat no manner of fat, of ox, or of sheep, or
of goat.
24 And the fat of the beast that dieth of itself, and
the fat of that which is torn with beasts, may be used
in any other use: but ye shall in no wise eat of it.
25 For whosoever eateth the fat of the beast, of
which men offer an offering made by fire unto the
LORD, even the soul that eateth *it* shall be cut off
from his people.
26 Moreover ye shall eat no manner of blood,
whether it be of fowl or of beast, in any of your
dwellings.

little things are you able to do for the Lord that cause divine rejoicing? (See Zech. 4:10.)

3. The perpetual fire in part symbolizes the Holy Spirit (Isa. 4:4; Acts 2:3). His influences are enlightening, warming, comforting, and corrective. He also consumes our sin and purifies our hearts. Just as the priests ensured the continuous burning, how can we be sure to not quench the Spirit (1 Thess. 5:19)?

Chapter 7: *The Lord gives further ordinances about the trespass offering and peace offering.*

7:4 *the flanks, and the caul.* See note at 3:4.
7:9 *all that is dressed.* Literally, "all which is made or done."
7:12 *thanksgiving.* Spontaneous show of gratitude (cf. 19:5).
7:14 *oblation.* See note at 2:4. *heave offering.* That which is lifted up or dedicated in tribute.
7:16 *on the morrow.* On the next day.
7:18 *imputed.* Accounted. *an abomination.* Refuse or something foul.
7:20 *cut off from his people.* Some form of excommunication from the covenant privileges of God's people. A common discipline noted throughout Leviticus.

27 Whatsoever soul *it be* that eateth any manner
of blood, even that soul shall be cut off from his
people.
28 ¶ And the LORD spake unto Moses, saying,
29 Speak unto the children of Israel, saying, He
that offereth the sacrifice of his peace offerings
unto the LORD shall bring his oblation unto the
LORD of the sacrifice of his peace offerings.
30 His own hands shall bring the offerings of the
LORD made by fire, the fat with the breast, it shall
he bring, that the breast may be waved *for* a wave
offering before the LORD.
31 And the priest shall burn the fat upon the
altar: but the breast shall be Aaron's and his sons'.
32 And the right shoulder shall ye give unto the
priest *for* an heave offering of the sacrifices of
your peace offerings.
33 He among the sons of Aaron, that offereth
the blood of the peace offerings, and the fat, shall
have the right shoulder for *his* part.
34 For the wave breast and the heave shoulder
have I taken of the children of Israel from off the
sacrifices of their peace offerings, and have given
them unto Aaron the priest and unto his sons by a
statute for ever from among the children of Israel.
35 ¶ This *is the portion* of the anointing of
Aaron, and of the anointing of his sons, out of
the offerings of the LORD made by fire, in the day
when he presented them to minister unto the
LORD in the priest's office;
36 Which the LORD commanded to be given
them of the children of Israel, in the day that he
anointed them, *by* a statute for ever throughout
their generations.
37 This *is* the law of the burnt offering, of the
meat offering, and of the sin offering, and of the
trespass offering, and of the consecrations, and of
the sacrifice of the peace offerings;
38 Which the LORD commanded Moses in mount
Sinai, in the day that he commanded the children
of Israel to offer their oblations unto the LORD, in
the wilderness of Sinai.

CHAPTER 8

AND the LORD spake unto Moses, saying,
2 Take Aaron and his sons with him, and the
garments, and the anointing oil, and a bullock
for the sin offering, and two rams, and a basket of
unleavened bread;
3 And gather thou all the congregation together
unto the door of the tabernacle of the congregation.
4 And Moses did as the LORD commanded him;
and the assembly was gathered together unto the
door of the tabernacle of the congregation.
5 And Moses said unto the congregation, This *is*
the thing which the LORD commanded to be done.
6 And Moses brought Aaron and his sons, and
washed them with water.
7 And he put upon him the coat, and girded him
with the girdle, and clothed him with the robe,
and put the ephod upon him, and he girded him
with the curious girdle of the ephod, and bound
it unto him therewith.
8 And he put the breastplate upon him: also he put
in the breastplate the Urim and the Thummim.
9 And he put the mitre upon his head; also upon
the mitre, *even* upon his forefront, did he put the
golden plate, the holy crown; as the LORD com-
manded Moses.

7:34 *wave breast . . . heave shoulder.* Refers to the gestures of moving backward and forward and lifting up to symbolize dedication and presentation to the Lord (23:11; Ex. 29:24–27).

Thoughts for Personal/Family Worship: Chapter 7

Eating together was a symbol of fellowship and friendship. That the priests shared in some of the offerings and even the people in the peace offering was a beautiful picture of the reconciliation between God and the sinner. Even when the meal was limited to the priests, it points to what Christians enjoy, for we are kings and priests (Rev. 1:6). Rejoice in the fellowship we have with Christ in His love and strength, for He carries us in His bosom (Isa. 40:11; cf. John 13:25) and strengthens us (Phil. 4:13).

INSTITUTION OF THE AARONIC PRIESTHOOD (8:1—10:20)

Chapter 8: *Moses clothes and consecrates Aaron and his sons for the priesthood.*

Priestly Consecration (8:1–36)

8:1 *Moses.* Functioning as prophet (God's representative to man), he appoints Aaron and his sons to be priests (Ex. 29). On the garments and consecration of the priests, see notes at Ex. 28–29.

8:2 *garments.* All the priests had splendid garments (Ex. 28:40), but Aaron's were unique, "for glory and for beauty" (Ex. 28:2). *anointing oil.* For its composition, see Ex. 30:22–33. *bullock for the sin offering, and two rams, and a basket of unleavened bread.* Before the priests could minister for others, their own sins had to be addressed—unlike the ideal Priest, Christ, who had no sin of His own.

8:3 *all the congregation.* Most likely, the appointed representatives and elders.

8:5 Obedient response to the Lord's commands regarding worship is a key theme throughout Leviticus. Man can approach God only in the way He prescribes.

8:6 *washed them.* For ceremonial cleansing (Ex. 29:4; 30:17–21), a picture of spiritual cleansing (Pss. 24:4; 73:13; Isa. 1:16).

8:7 Aaron is first clothed with his garments, his symbolic dignity (Ex. 28). *coat.* Undergarment of fine linen. *girded him with the girdle.* Wrapped him with a sash. *ephod.* The priestly vest or apron hanging from the shoulders with pouches holding stones engraved with the tribal names. *curious girdle.* Embroidered cape or sash.

8:8 *breastplate.* Held the Urim and Thummim which were stones used to discern the Lord's will in addition to the twelve stones bearing the tribal names. This ephod highlights Aaron as the representative of the people before God.

8:9 *mitre.* A turban.

10 And Moses took the anointing oil, and
anointed the tabernacle and all that *was* therein,
and sanctified them.
11 And he sprinkled thereof upon the altar seven
times, and anointed the altar and all his vessels,
both the laver and his foot, to sanctify them.
12 And he poured of the anointing oil upon
Aaron's head, and anointed him, to sanctify him.
13 And Moses brought Aaron's sons, and put
coats upon them, and girded them with girdles,
and put bonnets upon them; as the LORD com-
manded Moses.
14 And he brought the bullock for the sin offer-
ing: and Aaron and his sons laid their hands upon
the head of the bullock for the sin offering.
15 And he slew *it*; and Moses took the blood, and
put *it* upon the horns of the altar round about
with his finger, and purified the altar, and poured
the blood at the bottom of the altar, and sancti-
fied it, to make reconciliation upon it.
16 And he took all the fat that *was* upon the in-
wards, and the caul *above* the liver, and the two
kidneys, and their fat, and Moses burned *it* upon
the altar.
17 But the bullock, and his hide, his flesh, and his
dung, he burnt with fire without the camp; as the
LORD commanded Moses.
18 ¶ And he brought the ram for the burnt offer-
ing: and Aaron and his sons laid their hands upon
the head of the ram.
19 And he killed *it*; and Moses sprinkled the
blood upon the altar round about.
20 And he cut the ram into pieces; and Moses
burnt the head, and the pieces, and the fat.
21 And he washed the inwards and the legs in
water; and Moses burnt the whole ram upon the
altar: it *was* a burnt sacrifice for a sweet savour,
and an offering made by fire unto the LORD; as the
LORD commanded Moses.
22 ¶ And he brought the other ram, the ram of
consecration: and Aaron and his sons laid their
hands upon the head of the ram.
23 And he slew *it*; and Moses took of the blood of
it, and put *it* upon the tip of Aaron's right ear, and
upon the thumb of his right hand, and upon the
great toe of his right foot.
24 And he brought Aaron's sons, and Moses put
of the blood upon the tip of their right ear, and
upon the thumbs of their right hands, and upon
the great toes of their right feet: and Moses sprin-
kled the blood upon the altar round about.
25 And he took the fat, and the rump, and all the
fat that *was* upon the inwards, and the caul *above*
the liver, and the two kidneys, and their fat, and
the right shoulder:
26 And out of the basket of unleavened bread,
that *was* before the LORD, he took one unleavened
cake, and a cake of oiled bread, and one wafer, and
put *them* on the fat, and upon the right shoulder:
27 And he put all upon Aaron's hands, and upon
his sons' hands, and waved them *for* a wave offer-
ing before the LORD.
28 And Moses took them from off their hands,
and burnt *them* on the altar upon the burnt offer-
ing: they *were* consecrations for a sweet savour: it
is an offering made by fire unto the LORD.
29 And Moses took the breast, and waved it *for* a
wave offering before the LORD: *for* of the ram of
consecration it was Moses' part; as the LORD com-
manded Moses.
30 And Moses took of the anointing oil, and of
the blood which *was* upon the altar, and sprinkled
it upon Aaron, *and* upon his garments, and upon
his sons, and upon his sons' garments with him;
and sanctified Aaron, *and* his garments, and his
sons, and his sons' garments with him.
31 ¶ And Moses said unto Aaron and to his sons,
Boil the flesh *at* the door of the tabernacle of the
congregation: and there eat it with the bread that
is in the basket of consecrations, as I commanded,
saying, Aaron and his sons shall eat it.
32 And that which remaineth of the flesh and of
the bread shall ye burn with fire.
33 And ye shall not go out of the door of the tab-
ernacle of the congregation *in* seven days, until
the days of your consecration be at an end: for

8:10 *anointing oil.* The anointing includes the tabernacle and culminates with Aaron. (See Ex. 40:15 for the anointing of all the priests.) *sanctified.* Set apart or consecrated (throughout the chapter for both people and things).

8:11 *laver and his foot.* Basin and its pedestal.

8:13 *put bonnets upon them.* Wrap a headband or turban on them.

8:15 *horns of the altar.* Refers to protrusions on the corners of the brazen altar in the tabernacle court resembling horns. An imperfect priesthood defiled the altar itself, hence the need for atonement (cf. Heb. 7:19).

8:16 *caul.* Fatty portion or membrane around the organ (v. 25).

8:18–21 *And he brought the ram for the burnt offering.* See Ex. 29:15–18.

8:23 *Aaron's right ear . . . thumb . . . toe.* This symbolizes that they were entirely set apart for God's service.

8:27 *wave offering.* See note at 7:34.

8:30 *the anointing oil, and of the blood.* This signified acceptance with God and consecration for service.

8:31–32 *Boil the flesh at the door of the tabernacle.* By this meal, God counts Aaron and his sons His friends. It pictures reconciliation.

Thoughts for Personal/Family Worship: Chapter 8

1. God swears no oath when consecrating the Levitical priests because they were to be only temporary pictures of the perfect Priest to come. However, God consecrates His Son as Priest with an oath to an everlasting priesthood after the order of Melchizedek, a more complete type of Christ (Ps. 110:4; Heb. 7:20–21). The most outstanding fact demonstrating Aaron's necessary obsolescence as a priest was his own sin that

seven days shall he consecrate you.
34 As he hath done this day, *so* the LORD hath
commanded to do, to make an atonement for you.
35 Therefore shall ye abide *at* the door of the tab-
ernacle of the congregation day and night seven
days, and keep the charge of the LORD, that ye die
not: for so I am commanded.
36 So Aaron and his sons did all things which the
LORD commanded by the hand of Moses.

CHAPTER 9

AND it came to pass on the eighth day, *that* Moses
called Aaron and his sons, and the elders of Israel;
2 And he said unto Aaron, Take thee a young calf
for a sin offering, and a ram for a burnt offering,
without blemish, and offer *them* before the LORD.
3 And unto the children of Israel thou shalt
speak, saying, Take ye a kid of the goats for a sin
offering; and a calf and a lamb, *both* of the first
year, without blemish, for a burnt offering;
4 Also a bullock and a ram for peace offerings,
to sacrifice before the LORD; and a meat offering
mingled with oil: for to day the LORD will appear
unto you.
5 ¶ And they brought *that* which Moses com-
manded before the tabernacle of the congrega-
tion: and all the congregation drew near and
stood before the LORD.
6 And Moses said, This *is* the thing which the
LORD commanded that ye should do: and the
glory of the LORD shall appear unto you.
7 And Moses said unto Aaron, Go unto the al-
tar, and offer thy sin offering, and thy burnt offer-
ing, and make an atonement for thyself, and for
the people: and offer the offering of the people,
and make an atonement for them; as the LORD
commanded.
8 ¶ Aaron therefore went unto the altar, and slew
the calf of the sin offering, which *was* for himself.
9 And the sons of Aaron brought the blood unto
him: and he dipped his finger in the blood, and
put *it* upon the horns of the altar, and poured out
the blood at the bottom of the altar:
10 But the fat, and the kidneys, and the caul
above the liver of the sin offering, he burnt upon
the altar; as the LORD commanded Moses.
11 And the flesh and the hide he burnt with fire
without the camp.
12 And he slew the burnt offering; and Aaron's
sons presented unto him the blood, which he
sprinkled round about upon the altar.
13 And they presented the burnt offering unto
him, with the pieces thereof, and the head: and he
burnt *them* upon the altar.
14 And he did wash the inwards and the legs, and
burnt *them* upon the burnt offering on the altar.
15 ¶ And he brought the people's offering, and
took the goat, which *was* the sin offering for the
people, and slew it, and offered it for sin, as the first.
16 And he brought the burnt offering, and of-
fered it according to the manner.
17 And he brought the meat offering, and took an
handful thereof, and burnt *it* upon the altar, be-
side the burnt sacrifice of the morning.
18 He slew also the bullock and the ram *for* a sac-
rifice of peace offerings, which *was* for the people:
and Aaron's sons presented unto him the blood,
which he sprinkled upon the altar round about,
19 And the fat of the bullock and of the ram, the
rump, and that which covereth *the inwards*, and
the kidneys, and the caul *above* the liver:
20 And they put the fat upon the breasts, and he
burnt the fat upon the altar:
21 And the breasts and the right shoulder Aaron
waved *for* a wave offering before the LORD; as
Moses commanded.
22 And Aaron lifted up his hand toward the
people, and blessed them, and came down from
offering of the sin offering, and the burnt offering,
and peace offerings.
23 And Moses and Aaron went into the tabernacle
of the congregation, and came out, and blessed
the people: and the glory of the LORD appeared

---

had to be addressed before he could serve others. Christ was perfect and undefiled with no sins of His own to limit the power of His service and sacrifice. How does Christ's sinless perfection help us to trust Him to make satisfaction to God for our sins?

2. **Oil upon Aaron is a symbol of the Holy Spirit equipping him for service. Israel's kings were anointed (1 Sam. 10:1) as were their prophets (Ps. 105:15; Isa. 61:1). Our Lord, by His anointing (Ps. 45:7) is the Prophet, Priest, and King of His elect people. He lovingly teaches them, saves them, and governs them. Pray that God would help you hear Him, rely on His mediation, and obey His gracious will. In Ps. 133:2 the anointing flows down to Christ's members, His church. Believers are all anointed ones, "Christ-ians" (1 John 2:20). How does Christ's anointing upon all believers affect your life choices?**

Chapter 9: *Moses completes the ordination of the priests, they offer their first sacrifices, and God shows His pleasure with holy fire.*

The Priests' Entrance into Office (9:1–24)

9:1 *eighth day.* The first day of work after their solemn consecration for seven days. On the sacrifices for the consecration of the priest, see notes at Ex. 29.

9:4 *meat offering.* The grain offering is always offered with a bloody sacrifice.

9:8 *for himself.* This fuels the anticipation for the ideal Priest who would not have to sacrifice for Himself.

9:9 *horns.* See note at 8:15.

9:10 *caul.* See notes at 8:16; 9:19.

9:16 *manner.* The Hebrew word refers to specifications. Everything was being done in accord with the commands.

9:22 *blessed them.* Perhaps, as recorded in Num. 6:24–26.

unto all the people.
24 And there came a fire out from before the
LORD, and consumed upon the altar the burnt
offering and the fat: *which* when all the people
saw, they shouted, and fell on their faces.

CHAPTER 10

AND Nadab and Abihu, the sons of Aaron, took
either of them his censer, and put fire therein, and
put incense thereon, and offered strange fire be-
fore the LORD, which he commanded them not.
2 And there went out fire from the LORD, and de-
voured them, and they died before the LORD.
3 Then Moses said unto Aaron, This *is it* that the
LORD spake, saying, I will be sanctified in them
that come nigh me, and before all the people I will
be glorified. And Aaron held his peace.
4 And Moses called Mishael and Elzaphan, the
sons of Uzziel the uncle of Aaron, and said unto
them, Come near, carry your brethren from
before the sanctuary out of the camp.
5 So they went near, and carried them in their
coats out of the camp; as Moses had said.
6 And Moses said unto Aaron, and unto Eleazar
and unto Ithamar, his sons, Uncover not your
heads, neither rend your clothes; lest ye die, and
lest wrath come upon all the people: but let your
brethren, the whole house of Israel, bewail the
burning which the LORD hath kindled.
7 And ye shall not go out from the door of the
tabernacle of the congregation, lest ye die: for the
anointing oil of the LORD *is* upon you. And they
did according to the word of Moses.
8 ¶ And the LORD spake unto Aaron, saying,
9 Do not drink wine nor strong drink, thou, nor
thy sons with thee, when ye go into the tabernacle
of the congregation, lest ye die: *it shall be* a statute
for ever throughout your generations:
10 And that ye may put difference between holy
and unholy, and between unclean and clean;
11 And that ye may teach the children of Israel
all the statutes which the LORD hath spoken unto
them by the hand of Moses.
12 ¶ And Moses spake unto Aaron, and unto
Eleazar and unto Ithamar, his sons that were
left, Take the meat offering that remaineth of
the offerings of the LORD made by fire, and eat it
without leaven beside the altar: for it *is* most holy:
13 And ye shall eat it in the holy place, because it
is thy due, and thy sons' due, of the sacrifices of
the LORD made by fire: for so I am commanded.
14 And the wave breast and heave shoulder shall
ye eat in a clean place; thou, and thy sons, and thy
daughters with thee: for *they be* thy due, and thy
sons' due, *which* are given out of the sacrifices of
peace offerings of the children of Israel.
15 The heave shoulder and the wave breast shall
they bring with the offerings made by fire of the
fat, to wave *it for* a wave offering before the LORD;
and it shall be thine, and thy sons' with thee, by
a statute for ever; as the LORD hath commanded.
16 ¶ And Moses diligently sought the goat of the
sin offering, and, behold, it was burnt: and he

9:23 *glory of the LORD appeared.* This is in fulfillment of v. 6.
9:24 *a fire.* Jehovah's benediction, showing His pleasure in the ceremonies inducting the priests into their office (cf. Judg. 13:20; 2 Chron. 7:1; 1 Kings 18:38).

Thoughts for Personal/Family Worship: Chapter 9

1. **The outstanding moment of Aaron's first day of work was the fire of blessing that came out from the Lord (v. 24). The fire that consumed the sacrifice symbolized God's acceptance and pleasure. Three things stand out as points to ponder. First, the fire was preceded by obedience. Throughout the chapter, Aaron did as the Lord commanded (v. 6). Second, the fire revealed the divine glory. Third, the fire was received with reverence as the people enthusiastically shouted for joy and fell in worship. This is a genuine encounter with God. The whole narrative pictures the grace of the gospel. How does the church encounter God and experience His acceptance today?**
2. **After Aaron offered the sacrifice to the Lord, he lifted up his hand toward the people, and blessed them (v. 22). We are reminded of when our Lord "came out" from death and the grave having finished His work. As He ascended to heaven, "he lifted up his hands, and blessed them" (Luke 24:50). How is the blessing of Christ better than that of Aaron?**

Chapter 10: ***Aaron's older sons offer incense not commanded by God, and God responds with death and further laws.***

Nadab and Abihu's Sin (10:1–20)

10:1 *strange fire.* Refers to illegitimate fire (Ex. 30:9), most likely taking firepans with burning coals and igniting sweet incense. *commanded them not.* These priests sought to worship God in a way He had not prescribed. God has a zeal for His own worship.
10:2 The fire that signified acceptance (9:24) now slays them in judgment.
10:3 *I will be sanctified.* An illustration of God's holiness (Ex. 19:22) and the need of approaching God in His appointed way. *held his peace.* Literally, "kept silent."
10:4–7 Being removed like this would warn others not to trifle with God's ordinances (Acts 5:1–11).
10:5 *carried . . . in their coats.* Perhaps to avoid direct contact since priests were forbidden to touch dead bodies (21:1,11).
10:6 *Uncover not your heads.* You are forbidden to mourn.
10:9–10 *Do not drink wine.* It may be that wine caused Nadab and Abihu to be careless in holy duty. *strong drink.* Normally a grain product in contrast to wine from the grape vine. *difference between holy and unholy.* Priests must abstain from alcohol (Ezek. 44:21) because they need clear minds to lead worship and judge soundly (Prov. 20:1).
10:12–15 These directions reiterate what had been said concerning the meat and peace offerings. See notes at chs. 2–3.
10:16 *the goat of the sin offering.* His concern is that this

was angry with Eleazar and Ithamar, the sons of
Aaron *which were* left *alive*, saying,
17 Wherefore have ye not eaten the sin offering in
the holy place, seeing it *is* most holy, and *God* hath
given it you to bear the iniquity of the congrega-
tion, to make atonement for them before the LORD?
18 Behold, the blood of it was not brought in
within the holy *place*: ye should indeed have eaten
it in the holy *place*, as I commanded.
19 And Aaron said unto Moses, Behold, this day
have they offered their sin offering and their
burnt offering before the LORD; and such things
have befallen me: and *if* I had eaten the sin of-
fering to day, should it have been accepted in the
sight of the LORD?
20 And when Moses heard *that*, he was content.

CHAPTER 11

AND the LORD spake unto Moses and to Aaron,
saying unto them,
2 Speak unto the children of Israel, saying, These
are the beasts which ye shall eat among all the
beasts that *are* on the earth.
3 Whatsoever parteth the hoof, and is cloven-
footed, *and* cheweth the cud, among the beasts,
that shall ye eat.
4 Nevertheless these shall ye not eat of them that
chew the cud, or of them that divide the hoof: *as*
the camel, because he cheweth the cud, but divid-
eth not the hoof; he *is* unclean unto you.
5 And the coney, because he cheweth the cud, but
divideth not the hoof; he *is* unclean unto you.
6 And the hare, because he cheweth the cud, but
divideth not the hoof; he *is* unclean unto you.
7 And the swine, though he divide the hoof, and
be clovenfooted, yet he cheweth not the cud; he *is*
unclean to you.
8 Of their flesh shall ye not eat, and their carcase
shall ye not touch; they *are* unclean to you.
9 ¶ These shall ye eat of all that *are* in the waters:
whatsoever hath fins and scales in the waters, in
the seas, and in the rivers, them shall ye eat.
10 And all that have not fins and scales in the seas,
and in the rivers, of all that move in the waters,
and of any living thing which *is* in the waters, they
shall be an abomination unto you:
11 They shall be even an abomination unto you;
ye shall not eat of their flesh, but ye shall have
their carcases in abomination.
12 Whatsoever hath no fins nor scales in the
waters, that *shall be* an abomination unto you.
13 ¶ And these *are they which* ye shall have in
abomination among the fowls; they shall not be
eaten, they *are* an abomination: the eagle, and the
ossifrage, and the ospray,
14 And the vulture, and the kite after his kind;
15 Every raven after his kind;
16 And the owl, and the night hawk, and the
cuckow, and the hawk after his kind,

should have been eaten by the priests in holy celebration, not burnt (6:24–29).

10:19 *Aaron said unto Moses.* Aaron justifies their action by the chastisement that fell on him. It may also be that they burnt it because part of it had been offered by Nadab and Abihu, and God's displeasure against them would extend to His displeasure against their sacrifice. Their motive is clearly worthy, and the action can be deemed variation not rebellion.

10:20 *he was content.* Literally, "it was good in his eyes." He agreed with the explanation.

Thoughts for Personal/Family Worship: Chapter 10

1. **Nadab and Abihu's sin concerned God's worship. Serious consequences followed because they departed from God's Word. There must be no "will worship" (Col. 2:23) such as worshiping as man wants and not as God commands. Divine worship is not a secondary issue. God is jealous for pure worship because it belongs to His glory. The contrast between the fire of blessing in ch. 9 and the fire of wrath here is instructive. Blessing was preceded by obedience; wrath was preceded by disobedience. Both revealed God's glory, and both were received with reverent fear. What principles must direct the church's worship if it is to obey God and honor His holiness?**
2. **Aaron's silence at the loss of his sons is impressive. Are you able to acknowledge the Lord in His chastisements (Heb. 12:5–6)? When we submit to God, we accept His discipline, then He sanctifies it to our good and His glory.**
3. **Fleshly and intoxicating worship is an abomination to God. This is why strong drink was forbidden to the priests (1 Tim. 3:8). Today, fleshly excesses mark worship styles in many churches. Use of worldly music and bodily movement appeal to the flesh instead of the understanding (Ps. 47:7), violate Scripture (Isa. 66:2; John 4:24), and resemble the worship of the heathen (Ex. 32:6–8). How can we ensure that we worship God in a reverent and glorifying way as He fills our praises (Ps. 22:3)?**

LAWS RELATING TO RITUAL UNCLEANNESS (11:1—15:33)

Chapter 11: ***The Lord teaches Moses and Aaron how to instruct Israel in avoiding uncleanness due to eating or touching certain animals.***

Uncleanness Due to Contact with Animals (11:1–47)

11:2 *the beasts which ye shall eat.* Opinions differ as to the categories of clean and unclean ranging from health issues to separation issues between Jews and Gentiles. At the very least, God is teaching His people the necessity of discernment, a key theme throughout Leviticus.

11:3 *clovenfooted.* Parted or divided hoof (vv. 7,26).

11:5 *coney.* Perhaps a rock badger or hyrax.

11:8 *their carcase shall ye not touch.* Not only was their meat forbidden, but also contact with their dead bodies.

11:10 *an abomination.* Something detestable, usually in a ceremonial or religious context.

11:13–23 Flying creatures are named according to their appearance and habits.

11:13 *eagle . . . ossifrage . . . ospray.* All these are in the vulture family.

11:14 *kite.* A falcon or hawk.

11:16 *cuckow.* A gull.

17 And the little owl, and the cormorant, and the
great owl,
18 And the swan, and the pelican, and the gier
eagle,
19 And the stork, the heron after her kind, and
the lapwing, and the bat.
20 All fowls that creep, going upon *all* four, *shall*
be an abomination unto you.
21 Yet these may ye eat of every flying creeping
thing that goeth upon *all* four, which have legs
above their feet, to leap withal upon the earth;
22 *Even* these of them ye may eat; the locust after
his kind, and the bald locust after his kind, and
the beetle after his kind, and the grasshopper af-
ter his kind.
23 But all *other* flying creeping things, which have
four feet, *shall be* an abomination unto you.
24 And for these ye shall be unclean: whosoever
toucheth the carcase of them shall be unclean un-
til the even.
25 And whosoever beareth *ought* of the carcase of
them shall wash his clothes, and be unclean until
the even.
26 *The carcases* of every beast which divideth
the hoof, and *is* not clovenfooted, nor cheweth
the cud, *are* unclean unto you: every one that
toucheth them shall be unclean.
27 And whatsoever goeth upon his paws, among
all manner of beasts that go on *all* four, those *are*
unclean unto you: whoso toucheth their carcase
shall be unclean until the even.
28 And he that beareth the carcase of them shall
wash his clothes, and be unclean until the even:
they *are* unclean unto you.
29 ¶ These also *shall be* unclean unto you among
the creeping things that creep upon the earth; the
weasel, and the mouse, and the tortoise after his
kind,
30 And the ferret, and the chameleon, and the liz-
ard, and the snail, and the mole.
31 These *are* unclean to you among all that creep:
whosoever doth touch them, when they be dead,
shall be unclean until the even.
32 And upon whatsoever *any* of them, when they
are dead, doth fall, it shall be unclean; whether *it*
be any vessel of wood, or raiment, or skin, or sack,
whatsoever vessel *it be*, wherein *any* work is done,
it must be put into water, and it shall be unclean
until the even; so it shall be cleansed.
33 And every earthen vessel, whereinto *any* of
them falleth, whatsoever *is* in it shall be unclean;
and ye shall break it.
34 Of all meat which may be eaten, *that* on which
such water cometh shall be unclean: and all drink
that may be drunk in every *such* vessel shall be
unclean.
35 And every *thing* whereupon *any part* of their
carcase falleth shall be unclean; *whether it be* oven,
or ranges for pots, they shall be broken down: *for*
they *are* unclean, and shall be unclean unto you.
36 Nevertheless a fountain or pit, *wherein there*
is plenty of water, shall be clean: but that which
toucheth their carcase shall be unclean.
37 And if *any part* of their carcase fall upon any
sowing seed which is to be sown, it *shall be* clean.
38 But if *any* water be put upon the seed, and *any*
part of their carcase fall thereon, it *shall be* un-
clean unto you.
39 And if any beast, of which ye may eat, die; he
that toucheth the carcase thereof shall be unclean
until the even.
40 And he that eateth of the carcase of it shall
wash his clothes, and be unclean until the even:
he also that beareth the carcase of it shall wash his
clothes, and be unclean until the even.
41 And every creeping thing that creepeth upon
the earth *shall be* an abomination; it shall not be
eaten.
42 Whatsoever goeth upon the belly, and what-
soever goeth upon *all* four, or whatsoever hath
more feet among all creeping things that creep
upon the earth, them ye shall not eat; for they *are*
an abomination.
43 Ye shall not make yourselves abominable with
any creeping thing that creepeth, neither shall
ye make yourselves unclean with them, that ye
should be defiled thereby.
44 For I *am* the LORD your God: ye shall there-
fore sanctify yourselves, and ye shall be holy; for
I *am* holy: neither shall ye defile yourselves with
any manner of creeping thing that creepeth upon
the earth.
45 For I *am* the LORD that bringeth you up out of
the land of Egypt, to be your God: ye shall there-
fore be holy, for I *am* holy.
46 This *is* the law of the beasts, and of the fowl,

11:17 *cormorant.* A pelican.
11:18 *gier eagle.* Carrion vulture.
11:20 *All fowls that creep.* Refers to anything that flies or swarms, including insects.
11:24–40 The prohibition covers people (vv. 24–31), articles (vv. 32–35), some exceptions (vv. 36–38), and carcasses of clean animals (vv. 39–40).
11:25 *even.* Evening time when the sun goes down.
11:35 *ranges for pots.* Refers to a cooking furnace, a small stove.
11:44–47 *I am the LORD your God.* Gratitude for redemption is the mainspring of obedience.

Thoughts for Personal/Family Worship: Chapter 11

1. **The laws of cleanness and uncleanness were designed to teach the meaning of the holiness required if man were to fellowship with God. Things unclean are to be avoided—a stigma is upon them. They are typical of sin, which is spiritual and moral uncleanness (Isa. 6:5). Nothing is literally unclean now under the gospel (Acts**

GOD'S HOLINESS AND OURS

Holiness, in both scriptural languages, carries the definite idea of *separation*. Both testaments consistently emphasize the idea of being set apart, yet there is often a distinction in their emphases. The Old Testament often identifies holiness in a physical sense, denoting cleanliness of an outward sort (Lev. 11:44–47). The New Testament stresses holiness in the spiritual sense, indicating purity of heart and hands (Rom. 12:1; 1 Peter 2:5).

Throughout the whole of Scripture there occurs a clear command to the believer: "Be ye holy; for I am holy" (Lev. 19:2; 1 Peter 1:16). As children resemble their father, so believers must look like their God (Eph. 4:24; 5:1; Phil. 2:15; 1 John 5:18).

God's Holiness

There is no adjective prefixed to God's name more often than *holy*. The book of Isaiah, laden with proclamations of holiness, serves as an example of how Scripture expounds the riches of God's holiness: God is the "Holy One" (occurring twenty-six times), and angels cry thrice "Holy!" (Isa. 6:3; cf. Rev. 4:8). God's holiness is said to be the very essence of His being (Isa. 57:15). How majestic—how glorious—is His holiness (Ex. 15:11)!

First, God is holy in His separation from all creation. He is wholly other—that is, entirely distinct and detached from all else: "To whom then will ye liken me, or shall I be equal? saith the Holy One" (Isa. 40:25). "There is none holy as the LORD" (1 Sam. 2:2; also Rev. 15:4).

Second, God is holy specifically in His separation from sin. This is expressed both *negatively* and *positively*: He is separated *from* sin and *unto* righteousness. Negatively, God is absolutely unpolluted by evil. Indeed, He cannot behold iniquity (Hab. 1:13), His loathing of wickedness is infinite (Amos 5:21), and His hatred is toward those who are workers of iniquity (Ps. 5:5). Woe unto him who approaches this Holy One without the holy robes of Christ!

Positively, God is separated unto righteousness (Ps. 145:17), which He loves (Ps. 11:7; Heb. 1:9). Thus, God gives honor to His law, for such is the substance of His holiness (Isa. 42:21). This holiness causes all else to dim in its brilliant light (Job 4:18). His holiness is His matchless beauty (2 Chron. 20:21; Ps. 29:2). Further, the holiness of God is so great that, rather than accept a sinner, He has seen fit to slay His very Son.

Our Holiness

Though containing no light of its own, a mirror overpowers the eyes when it reflects the sun. As believers we are called to shine with God's holiness to a greater degree than we will be able during this life (1 John 1:10). We must be *filled up* with holiness inwardly, within our hearts and minds; and we must *overflow* with holiness outwardly, touching all of life. Holiness is thus a comprehensive, whole-life commitment to live "Godward" (2 Cor. 3:4). Leviticus 20:26 makes plain that God's holiness calls us to be holy: "And ye shall be holy unto me: for I the LORD am holy." We are called to strive for holy lives (Heb. 12:14), as holiness must, and will, follow regeneration (Eph. 1:4; Phil. 3:12). Holiness is our joyous duty unto God as obedient children (Neh. 8:10; 1 Peter 1:14).

Describing the holiness of believers, Stephen Charnock identifies the Father as the fountain, the Son as the pattern, and the Spirit as the imprinter of holiness. The Father is the spring of holiness that sanctifies us (John 17:11,17). To cleanse our filth the Father sends Christ to remove the guilt of sin and His Spirit to remove its stain (Eph. 1:4; Col. 1:22; 2 Tim. 1:9). The Son is the model for our holiness, for it is to His image that we are conformed (Phil. 2:5–8). Even as Christ is pure, so are those who hope in Him (1 John 3:3). The Spirit is the One who stamps us with the holiness of God. He makes sinners holy, bringing us into submission to His mind (1 Cor. 2) and sanctifying us to pursue the things of the Spirit (Rom. 8:5).

God calls each of us to walk in His holiness: "My son, give me thine heart" (Prov. 23:26). May we strive after Him with all holiness of life (1 Peter 1:13–23).

and of every living creature that moveth in the
waters, and of every creature that creepeth upon
the earth:
47 To make a difference between the unclean
and the clean, and between the beast that may be
eaten and the beast that may not be eaten.

CHAPTER 12

AND the LORD spake unto Moses, saying,
2 Speak unto the children of Israel, saying, If a
woman have conceived seed, and born a man
child: then she shall be unclean seven days; ac-
cording to the days of the separation for her infir-
mity shall she be unclean.
3 And in the eighth day the flesh of his foreskin
shall be circumcised.
4 And she shall then continue in the blood of her
purifying three and thirty days; she shall touch
no hallowed thing, nor come into the sanctuary,
until the days of her purifying be fulfilled.
5 But if she bear a maid child, then she shall be
unclean two weeks, as in her separation: and she
shall continue in the blood of her purifying three-
score and six days.
6 And when the days of her purifying are ful-
filled, for a son, or for a daughter, she shall bring
a lamb of the first year for a burnt offering, and a
young pigeon, or a turtledove, for a sin offering,
unto the door of the tabernacle of the congrega-
tion, unto the priest:
7 Who shall offer it before the LORD, and make an
atonement for her; and she shall be cleansed from
the issue of her blood. This *is* the law for her that
hath born a male or a female.
8 And if she be not able to bring a lamb, then she
shall bring two turtles, or two young pigeons; the
one for the burnt offering, and the other for a sin
offering: and the priest shall make an atonement
for her, and she shall be clean.

CHAPTER 13

AND the LORD spake unto Moses and Aaron,
saying,
2 When a man shall have in the skin of his flesh a
rising, a scab, or bright spot, and it be in the skin
of his flesh *like* the plague of leprosy; then he shall
be brought unto Aaron the priest, or unto one of
his sons the priests:
3 And the priest shall look on the plague in the
skin of the flesh: and *when* the hair in the plague

10:13–15), but the principle applies that sin must be branded, repented of, and avoided (Prov. 4:14–15; 2 Cor. 6:17; 7:1). Significantly, the ultimate reason for keeping the laws was redemption. "For I am the LORD that bringeth you up out of the land of Egypt, to be your God: ye shall therefore be holy, for I am holy" (Lev. 11:45). What can we as the redeemed do to be more conformed to the image of our Redeemer (1 Peter 1:13–17)?

2. Some of the restrictions are very specific, naming the things to avoid; some are general, simply identifying characteristics such as fins and scales for water creatures. Even though a catfish is not specifically named, the absence of scales meant it was unclean. God expected His people to think. This parallels the call to walk in holiness in the world. The Bible does not identify every conceivable sin, but the principles of God's Word are clear enough to know what sin looks like. God expects us to think as well. Why is it necessary to cultivate discernment and careful thinking in order to be holy?

Chapter 12: *God instructs Moses about the purification and offerings required of a mother after giving birth to a boy or a girl.*

Uncleanness Due to Childbirth (12:1–8)

12:2 *unclean seven days.* The uncleanness is ceremonial, restricting outward behavior and associations; it does not describe the state of the heart before God. *days of the separation.* Like her monthly menstruation, two weeks (15:19–24).
12:3 *circumcised.* The mark of the covenant (Gen. 17:9–14).
12:4 *three and thirty days.* More than a month longer is needed to complete this ritual cleansing.
12:5 *maid child.* Girl. The purification is twice as long, for unknown reasons.
12:8 *turtles.* Turtledoves.

Thoughts for Personal/Family Worship: Chapter 12

1. The ceremonial uncleanness associated with childbirth is a vivid picture sermon of the inherent depravity of mankind from the inception of life. Circumcision, while it is a sign of the covenant, also declares by the removing of the flesh from the infant that sin is a problem from the beginning of life before any conscious transgression occurs. Here is the transmission of sin. The mother is classed as ceremonially unclean because she bears another sinner in Adam—a humbling reminder that "in sin did my mother conceive me" (Ps. 51:5). We need to guard against what is outside us and inside us. What are evidences that sin is in our hearts from our youth?
2. Although childbearing rendered mothers unclean because the children were born sinners, there were sacrifices in place to deal with sin and restore the mother to the place of fellowship. How wonderfully this anticipates the birth of One who would be without sin and would offer Himself as the sacrifice to restore sinners to an offended God. Rejoice that Christ came made of a woman and under the Law so that He could save sinners like us from our sin—actual and original.

Chapter 13: *The Lord guides the priests in detecting and identifying leprosy in human skin diseases.*

Uncleanness Due to Skin Diseases (13:1—14:57)

13:2 *a rising.* Refers to a swelling or an eruption of some sort in the skin (vv. 10,19,28,43). *plague of leprosy.* Literally, "contagion of a skin disease" (throughout chapter), a general designation for skin disorders and diseases perhaps, though disputed, including the leprosy known today as Hansen's disease with its disfiguring symptoms.
13:3 *look on the plague.* Observe the outbreak to determine if

is turned white, and the plague in sight *be* deeper
than the skin of his flesh, it *is* a plague of leprosy:
and the priest shall look on him, and pronounce
him unclean.
4 If the bright spot *be* white in the skin of his flesh,
and in sight *be* not deeper than the skin, and the
hair thereof be not turned white; then the priest
shall shut up *him that hath* the plague seven days:
5 And the priest shall look on him the seventh
day: and, behold, *if* the plague in his sight be at a
stay, *and* the plague spread not in the skin; then
the priest shall shut him up seven days more:
6 And the priest shall look on him again the sev-
enth day: and, behold, *if* the plague *be* somewhat
dark, *and* the plague spread not in the skin, the
priest shall pronounce him clean: it *is but* a scab:
and he shall wash his clothes, and be clean.
7 But if the scab spread much abroad in the skin,
after that he hath been seen of the priest for his
cleansing, he shall be seen of the priest again:
8 And *if* the priest see that, behold, the scab
spreadeth in the skin, then the priest shall pro-
nounce him unclean: it *is* a leprosy.
9 ¶ When the plague of leprosy is in a man, then
he shall be brought unto the priest;
10 And the priest shall see *him*: and, behold, *if* the
rising *be* white in the skin, and it have turned the
hair white, and *there be* quick raw flesh in the rising;
11 It *is* an old leprosy in the skin of his flesh, and
the priest shall pronounce him unclean, and shall
not shut him up: for he *is* unclean.
12 And if a leprosy break out abroad in the skin,
and the leprosy cover all the skin of *him that hath*
the plague from his head even to his foot, where-
soever the priest looketh;
13 Then the priest shall consider: and, behold,
if the leprosy have covered all his flesh, he shall
pronounce *him* clean *that hath* the plague: it is all
turned white: he *is* clean.
14 But when raw flesh appeareth in him, he shall
be unclean.
15 And the priest shall see the raw flesh, and pro-
nounce him to be unclean: *for* the raw flesh *is* un-
clean: it *is* a leprosy.
16 Or if the raw flesh turn again, and be changed
unto white, he shall come unto the priest;
17 And the priest shall see him: and, behold, *if* the
plague be turned into white; then the priest shall
pronounce *him* clean *that hath* the plague: he *is*
clean.
18 ¶ The flesh also, in which, *even* in the skin
thereof, was a boil, and is healed,
19 And in the place of the boil there be a white
rising, or a bright spot, white, and somewhat
reddish, and it be shewed to the priest;
20 And if, when the priest seeth it, behold, it *be* in
sight lower than the skin, and the hair thereof be
turned white; the priest shall pronounce him un-
clean: it *is* a plague of leprosy broken out of the boil.
21 But if the priest look on it, and, behold, *there*
be no white hairs therein, and *if* it *be* not lower
than the skin, but *be* somewhat dark; then the
priest shall shut him up seven days:
22 And if it spread much abroad in the skin, then
the priest shall pronounce him unclean: it *is* a
plague.
23 But if the bright spot stay in his place, *and*
spread not, it *is* a burning boil; and the priest shall
pronounce him clean.
24 ¶ Or if there be *any* flesh, in the skin whereof
there is a hot burning, and the quick *flesh* that
burneth have a white bright spot, somewhat
reddish, or white;
25 Then the priest shall look upon it: and, behold,
if the hair in the bright spot be turned white, and it
be in sight deeper than the skin; it *is* a leprosy bro-
ken out of the burning: wherefore the priest shall
pronounce him unclean: it *is* the plague of leprosy.
26 But if the priest look on it, and, behold, *there*
be no white hair in the bright spot, and it *be* no
lower than the *other* skin, but *be* somewhat dark;
then the priest shall shut him up seven days:
27 And the priest shall look upon him the seventh
day: *and* if it be spread much abroad in the skin,
then the priest shall pronounce him unclean: it *is*
the plague of leprosy.
28 And if the bright spot stay in his place, *and*
spread not in the skin, but it *be* somewhat dark;
it *is* a rising of the burning, and the priest shall
pronounce him clean: for it *is* an inflammation
of the burning.
29 ¶ If a man or woman have a plague upon the
head or the beard;
30 Then the priest shall see the plague: and,

indeed it is a contagious disease or something harmless.
13:5 *if the plague . . . be at a stay*. Literally, "if the outbreak stood," an idiom for stopping. *seven days more.* Another week of quarantine to make sure it is not contagious.
13:6 *he shall wash his clothes.* Although pronounced clean and not contagious, there was still need for cleansing. Even the appearance of sin is to be avoided.
13:7–8 The spreading of the sore indicated it was malignant and infectious.
13:10 *quick raw flesh*. Literally, "formation of new flesh of living flesh," most likely referring to an oozing sore.
13:11 *old leprosy.* It has flared up again and cannot be cured.
13:13 *covered all his flesh.* The whiteness over the body probably shows that the contagious period is over and he can be pronounced clean.
13:14 *raw flesh appeareth*. See note at v. 10. The sign of a leprous condition.
13:16–17 *Or if the raw . . . be changed unto white.* If it has healed and is therefore now ritually clean.
13:23 *burning boil.* Perhaps a scar or scab.
13:24 *hot burning*. Literally, "burn of fire," probably referring to an accidental burn that has not healed but turned septic.

behold, if it *be* in sight deeper than the skin; *and*
there be in it a yellow thin hair; then the priest
shall pronounce him unclean: it *is* a dry scall, *even*
a leprosy upon the head or beard.
31 And if the priest look on the plague of the
scall, and, behold, it *be* not in sight deeper than
the skin, and *that there is* no black hair in it; then
the priest shall shut up *him that hath* the plague
of the scall seven days:
32 And in the seventh day the priest shall look
on the plague: and, behold, *if* the scall spread not,
and there be in it no yellow hair, and the scall *be*
not in sight deeper than the skin;
33 He shall be shaven, but the scall shall he not
shave; and the priest shall shut up *him that hath*
the scall seven days more:
34 And in the seventh day the priest shall look
on the scall: and, behold, *if* the scall be not spread
in the skin, nor *be* in sight deeper than the skin;
then the priest shall pronounce him clean: and he
shall wash his clothes, and be clean.
35 But if the scall spread much in the skin after
his cleansing;
36 Then the priest shall look on him: and, behold,
if the scall be spread in the skin, the priest shall
not seek for yellow hair; he *is* unclean.
37 But if the scall be in his sight at a stay, and *that*
there is black hair grown up therein; the scall is
healed, he *is* clean: and the priest shall pronounce
him clean.
38 ¶ If a man also or a woman have in the skin of
their flesh bright spots, *even* white bright spots;
39 Then the priest shall look: and, behold, *if* the
bright spots in the skin of their flesh *be* darkish
white; it *is* a freckled spot *that* groweth in the skin;
he *is* clean.
40 And the man whose hair is fallen off his head,
he *is* bald; *yet is* he clean.
41 And he that hath his hair fallen off from the
part of his head toward his face, he *is* forehead
bald: *yet is* he clean.
42 And if there be in the bald head, or bald fore-
head, a white reddish sore; it *is* a leprosy sprung
up in his bald head, or his bald forehead.
43 Then the priest shall look upon it: and, behold,
if the rising of the sore *be* white reddish in his bald
head, or in his bald forehead, as the leprosy ap-
peareth in the skin of the flesh;
44 He is a leprous man, he *is* unclean: the priest
shall pronounce him utterly unclean; his plague
is in his head.
45 And the leper in whom the plague *is*, his
clothes shall be rent, and his head bare, and he
shall put a covering upon his upper lip, and shall
cry, Unclean, unclean.
46 All the days wherein the plague *shall be* in him
he shall be defiled; he *is* unclean: he shall dwell
alone; without the camp *shall* his habitation *be*.
47 ¶ The garment also that the plague of leprosy
is in, *whether it be* a woollen garment, or a linen
garment;
48 Whether *it be* in the warp, or woof; of linen,
or of woollen; whether in a skin, or in any thing
made of skin;
49 And if the plague be greenish or reddish in the
garment, or in the skin, either in the warp, or in
the woof, or in any thing of skin; it *is* a plague of
leprosy, and shall be shewed unto the priest:
50 And the priest shall look upon the plague, and
shut up *it that hath* the plague seven days:
51 And he shall look on the plague on the seventh
day: if the plague be spread in the garment, either
in the warp, or in the woof, or in a skin, *or* in any
work that is made of skin; the plague *is* a fretting
leprosy; it *is* unclean.
52 He shall therefore burn that garment, whether
warp or woof, in woollen or in linen, or any thing
of skin, wherein the plague is: for it *is* a fretting
leprosy; it shall be burnt in the fire.
53 And if the priest shall look, and, behold, the
plague be not spread in the garment, either in the
warp, or in the woof, or in any thing of skin;
54 Then the priest shall command that they wash
the thing wherein the plague *is*, and he shall shut
it up seven days more:
55 And the priest shall look on the plague, after
that it is washed: and, behold, *if* the plague have
not changed his colour, and the plague be not
spread; it *is* unclean; thou shalt burn it in the fire; it
is fret inward, *whether* it *be* bare within or without.

13:29 *upon the head or the beard.* Where hair can hide the disease.
13:30 *scall.* A mark of skin disease (also through v. 37).
13:37 *be in his sight at a stay.* Is determined to have stopped spreading (literally, "stood").
13:40–41 *hair is fallen off his head.* Baldness in this case is harmless, although sometimes a reproach (2 Kings 2:23).
13:42–44 *a white reddish sore.* Leprosy on the head.
13:45–46 *covering upon his upper lip.* This is a sign of mourning (Mic. 3:7). The cry of *unclean* warns others of ritual infection, also a sanitary precaution. *without the camp.* Outside the camp of the Israelites (cf. 2 Kings 7:3).
13:47–59 This section covers cases of damage to material due to fungoid infections. Not only the person but his clothing is affected by the disease. It too can carry infection and render the person ceremonially unclean. When so, it must be burned (vv. 52–57). When not, it must be washed (v. 58).
13:48 *warp, or woof.* The horizontal and vertical threads in a garment (vv. 49,51–53,57–59).
13:51 *fretting.* Malignant or painful (v. 52).
13:55 *it is fret inward . . . without.* The Hebrew is difficult, involving rare words. The idea seems to be referring to the rotten place being on either side of the garment.

Thoughts for Personal/Family Worship: Chapter 13

1. **Many of the details of this chapter are obscure and difficult to understand. Yet the message is remarkably sobering and clear. These leprous skin conditions picture**

56 And if the priest look, and, behold, the plague
be somewhat dark after the washing of it; then he
shall rend it out of the garment, or out of the skin,
or out of the warp, or out of the woof:
57 And if it appear still in the garment, either
in the warp, or in the woof, or in any thing of
skin; it *is* a spreading *plague*: thou shalt burn that
wherein the plague *is* with fire.
58 And the garment, either warp, or woof, or
whatsoever thing of skin *it be*, which thou shalt
wash, if the plague be departed from them, then
it shall be washed the second time, and shall be
clean.
59 This *is* the law of the plague of leprosy in a gar-
ment of woollen or linen, either in the warp, or
woof, or any thing of skins, to pronounce it clean,
or to pronounce it unclean.

CHAPTER 14

AND the LORD spake unto Moses, saying,
2 This shall be the law of the leper in the day of
his cleansing: He shall be brought unto the priest:
3 And the priest shall go forth out of the camp;
and the priest shall look, and, behold, *if* the plague
of leprosy be healed in the leper;
4 Then shall the priest command to take for him
that is to be cleansed two birds alive *and* clean,
and cedar wood, and scarlet, and hyssop:
5 And the priest shall command that one of the
birds be killed in an earthen vessel over running
water:
6 As for the living bird, he shall take it, and the
cedar wood, and the scarlet, and the hyssop, and
shall dip them and the living bird in the blood of
the bird *that was* killed over the running water:
7 And he shall sprinkle upon him that is to be
cleansed from the leprosy seven times, and shall
pronounce him clean, and shall let the living bird
loose into the open field.
8 And he that is to be cleansed shall wash his
clothes, and shave off all his hair, and wash him-
self in water, that he may be clean: and after that
he shall come into the camp, and shall tarry
abroad out of his tent seven days.
9 But it shall be on the seventh day, that he shall
shave all his hair off his head and his beard and
his eyebrows, even all his hair he shall shave off:
and he shall wash his clothes, also he shall wash
his flesh in water, and he shall be clean.
10 And on the eighth day he shall take two he
lambs without blemish, and one ewe lamb of the
first year without blemish, and three tenth deals
of fine flour *for* a meat offering, mingled with oil,
and one log of oil.
11 And the priest that maketh *him* clean shall
present the man that is to be made clean, and
those things, before the LORD, *at* the door of the
tabernacle of the congregation:
12 And the priest shall take one he lamb, and
offer him for a trespass offering, and the log of
oil, and wave them *for* a wave offering before the
LORD:
13 And he shall slay the lamb in the place where
he shall kill the sin offering and the burnt offer-
ing, in the holy place: for as the sin offering *is* the
priest's, *so is* the trespass offering: it *is* most holy:
14 And the priest shall take *some* of the blood of
the trespass offering, and the priest shall put *it*
upon the tip of the right ear of him that is to be
cleansed, and upon the thumb of his right hand,
and upon the great toe of his right foot:
15 And the priest shall take *some* of the log of oil,
and pour *it* into the palm of his own left hand:
16 And the priest shall dip his right finger in the
oil that *is* in his left hand, and shall sprinkle of the
oil with his finger seven times before the LORD:
17 And of the rest of the oil that *is* in his hand

sin and its effect on the whole man. They vividly picture sin as defiling, ugly, loathsome, and disfiguring. The skin sores also show that God is concerned for purity. He cannot have fellowship with iniquity (Hab. 1:13). The leper must dwell alone, outside the camp. Nothing spoils fellowship with God like sin (Isa. 59:2). Ironically and beautifully, lepers also point to Jesus Christ who alone could touch the leper without becoming defiled and who could so graciously provide healing. What more can we do to avoid sin? When we defile ourselves, what should we immediately do to receive the cleansing provided for us in Christ (1 John 1:7,9)?

2. The priests had the responsibility to discern the status of the potential leper, taking time and precautions to make their judgments. They had to patiently examine, wait, and come to conclusions based on evidence. This is a good rule for us when seeing faults in others. "Charity . . . thinketh no evil" (1 Cor. 13:4–7; cf. Zech. 7:10)—always think the best of a person until you are compelled to think otherwise. Why is it important for the church, especially its elders, to discern evil and exclude unrepentant sin from the church?

Chapter 14: *The Lord explains to Moses the ritual cleansing of people and houses purified from their leprosy.*

14:4 *cedar wood . . . scarlet . . . hyssop.* The scarlet yarn would be used to tie the hyssop to the stick for the sprinkling of the blood (v. 7; cf. Ps. 51:7).

14:5–7 The sacrificed bird pictured the atonement necessary for cleansing (vv. 51–53). The freed bird may picture the resurrection or newness of life as the consequence of atonement or the removal of guilt by placing it on a substitute (16:21–22).

14:7 *And he shall sprinkle* the blood and water *upon him . . . seven times*, the number of completeness (2 Kings 5:10).

14:8 *wash his clothes, and shave off all his hair.* To ensure eradication of the disease. *shall tarry abroad out of his tent.* Literally, "will live outside of his tent."

14:10 *Three tenth deals of fine flour.* Literally, "three-tenths of fine flour." The exact measurement is implied, most likely equivalent to three omers or about fourteen pounds dry weight. *log.* A measurement of oil; about a pint (throughout the chapter).

14:11 *maketh him clean.* Pronounces or declares him clean.

shall the priest put upon the tip of the right ear of
him that is to be cleansed, and upon the thumb of
his right hand, and upon the great toe of his right
foot, upon the blood of the trespass offering:
18 And the remnant of the oil that *is* in the priest's
hand he shall pour upon the head of him that is
to be cleansed: and the priest shall make an atone-
ment for him before the LORD.
19 And the priest shall offer the sin offering, and
make an atonement for him that is to be cleansed
from his uncleanness; and afterward he shall kill
the burnt offering:
20 And the priest shall offer the burnt offering
and the meat offering upon the altar: and the
priest shall make an atonement for him, and he
shall be clean.
21 And if he *be* poor, and cannot get so much;
then he shall take one lamb *for* a trespass offering
to be waved, to make an atonement for him, and
one tenth deal of fine flour mingled with oil for a
meat offering, and a log of oil;
22 And two turtledoves, or two young pigeons,
such as he is able to get; and the one shall be a sin
offering, and the other a burnt offering.
23 And he shall bring them on the eighth day for
his cleansing unto the priest, unto the door of the
tabernacle of the congregation, before the LORD.
24 And the priest shall take the lamb of the tres-
pass offering, and the log of oil, and the priest
shall wave them *for* a wave offering before the
LORD:
25 And he shall kill the lamb of the trespass of-
fering, and the priest shall take *some* of the blood
of the trespass offering, and put *it* upon the tip
of the right ear of him that is to be cleansed, and
upon the thumb of his right hand, and upon the
great toe of his right foot:
26 And the priest shall pour of the oil into the
palm of his own left hand:
27 And the priest shall sprinkle with his right fin-
ger *some* of the oil that *is* in his left hand seven
times before the LORD:
28 And the priest shall put of the oil that *is* in
his hand upon the tip of the right ear of him
that is to be cleansed, and upon the thumb of his
right hand, and upon the great toe of his right
foot, upon the place of the blood of the trespass
offering:
29 And the rest of the oil that *is* in the priest's
hand he shall put upon the head of him that is to
be cleansed, to make an atonement for him before
the LORD.
30 And he shall offer the one of the turtledoves,
or of the young pigeons, such as he can get;
31 *Even* such as he is able to get, the one *for* a sin
offering, and the other *for* a burnt offering, with
the meat offering: and the priest shall make an
atonement for him that is to be cleansed before
the LORD.
32 This *is* the law *of him* in whom *is* the plague of
leprosy, whose hand is not able to get *that which
pertaineth* to his cleansing.
33 ¶ And the LORD spake unto Moses and unto
Aaron, saying,
34 When ye be come into the land of Canaan,
which I give to you for a possession, and I put the
plague of leprosy in a house of the land of your
possession;
35 And he that owneth the house shall come and
tell the priest, saying, It seemeth to me *there is* as
it were a plague in the house:
36 Then the priest shall command that they
empty the house, before the priest go *into it* to
see the plague, that all that *is* in the house be not
made unclean: and afterward the priest shall go in
to see the house:
37 And he shall look on the plague, and, behold,
if the plague *be* in the walls of the house with hol-
low strakes, greenish or reddish, which in sight
are lower than the wall;
38 Then the priest shall go out of the house to the
door of the house, and shut up the house seven
days:
39 And the priest shall come again the seventh
day, and shall look: and, behold, *if* the plague be
spread in the walls of the house;
40 Then the priest shall command that they take
away the stones in which the plague *is*, and they
shall cast them into an unclean place without the
city:
41 And he shall cause the house to be scraped
within round about, and they shall pour out the
dust that they scrape off without the city into an
unclean place:
42 And they shall take other stones, and put *them*
in the place of those stones; and he shall take
other morter, and shall plaister the house.
43 And if the plague come again, and break out
in the house, after that he hath taken away the
stones, and after he hath scraped the house, and
after it is plaistered;
44 Then the priest shall come and look, and, be-
hold, *if* the plague be spread in the house, it *is* a
fretting leprosy in the house: it *is* unclean.
45 And he shall break down the house, the stones
of it, and the timber thereof, and all the morter of

14:12 *wave offering.* See note at 7:34 (v. 24).
14:14 *the blood . . . upon the tip of the right ear . . . thumb . . . toe.* Like the consecration of the high priest (v. 17; 8:23–24).
14:21 *tenth deal.* A tenth part or tithe.
14:34 *leprosy in a house.* In the form of mildew or mold.
14:37 *hollow strakes . . . lower than the wall.* Greenish or reddish streaks in depressions in the wall's surface.
14:44 *fretting.* Malignant.
14:45 *break down the house.* It is infected; the only course is destruction and disposal in a safe place.

the house; and he shall carry *them* forth out of the city into an unclean place.
46 Moreover he that goeth into the house all the while that it is shut up shall be unclean until the even.
47 And he that lieth in the house shall wash his clothes; and he that eateth in the house shall wash his clothes.
48 And if the priest shall come in, and look *upon it*, and, behold, the plague hath not spread in the house, after the house was plaistered: then the priest shall pronounce the house clean, because the plague is healed.
49 And he shall take to cleanse the house two birds, and cedar wood, and scarlet, and hyssop:
50 And he shall kill the one of the birds in an earthen vessel over running water:
51 And he shall take the cedar wood, and the hyssop, and the scarlet, and the living bird, and dip them in the blood of the slain bird, and in the running water, and sprinkle the house seven times:
52 And he shall cleanse the house with the blood of the bird, and with the running water, and with the living bird, and with the cedar wood, and with the hyssop, and with the scarlet:
53 But he shall let go the living bird out of the city into the open fields, and make an atonement for the house: and it shall be clean.
54 This *is* the law for all manner of plague of leprosy, and scall,
55 And for the leprosy of a garment, and of a house,
56 And for a rising, and for a scab, and for a bright spot:
57 To teach when *it is* unclean, and when *it is* clean: this *is* the law of leprosy.

CHAPTER 15

AND the LORD spake unto Moses and to Aaron, saying,
2 Speak unto the children of Israel, and say unto them, When any man hath a running issue out of his flesh, *because of* his issue he *is* unclean.
3 And this shall be his uncleanness in his issue: whether his flesh run with his issue, or his flesh be stopped from his issue, it *is* his uncleanness.
4 Every bed, whereon he lieth that hath the issue, is unclean: and every thing, whereon he sitteth, shall be unclean.
5 And whosoever toucheth his bed shall wash his clothes, and bathe *himself* in water, and be unclean until the even.
6 And he that sitteth on *any* thing whereon he sat that hath the issue shall wash his clothes, and bathe *himself* in water, and be unclean until the even.
7 And he that toucheth the flesh of him that hath the issue shall wash his clothes, and bathe *himself* in water, and be unclean until the even.
8 And if he that hath the issue spit upon him that is clean; then he shall wash his clothes, and bathe *himself* in water, and be unclean until the even.
9 And what saddle soever he rideth upon that hath the issue shall be unclean.
10 And whosoever toucheth any thing that was under him shall be unclean until the even: and he that beareth *any of* those things shall wash his clothes, and bathe *himself* in water, and be unclean until the even.
11 And whomsoever he toucheth that hath the issue, and hath not rinsed his hands in water, he shall wash his clothes, and bathe *himself* in water, and be unclean until the even.
12 And the vessel of earth, that he toucheth which hath the issue, shall be broken: and every vessel of wood shall be rinsed in water.
13 And when he that hath an issue is cleansed of his issue; then he shall number to himself seven days for his cleansing, and wash his clothes, and bathe his flesh in running water, and shall be clean.
14 And on the eighth day he shall take to him two turtledoves, or two young pigeons, and come before the LORD unto the door of the tabernacle of

Thoughts for Personal/Family Worship: Chapter 14

1. **The bleakness of ch. 13 gives way to the hope and rejoicing of ch. 14. The healed sufferer can return to the camp. Leprosy could be cured (Num. 12). Regardless of how terrible the sin and its consequences, there is an appropriate sacrifice to provide its remedy. All of this points wonderfully to the Lord Jesus both in His willingness and ability to heal lepers of His day, but also in His provision of the only sacrifice sufficient to deal with the root cause which is sin. Spend time in worship of Him!**
2. **All the sacrifices picture some aspect of Christ's atoning work, but the two birds together illustrate the two essential components of the gospel message. The slain bird along with its blood typifies the atoning death of Jesus; the living one that is let loose points to His resurrection (cf. Rom. 4:25; 1 Cor. 15:3–4). At the same time, the pair illustrates something of the nature of the atonement itself that involves both propitiation (the satisfaction of God's wrath) and expiation (the removal of sin and guilt, Ps. 103:12). What blessings are you reminded of as you imagine that bird flying away?**

Chapter 15: *The Lord instructs Moses and Aaron concerning uncleanness related to the sexual organs.*

Uncleanness Due to Bodily Discharges (15:1–33)

15:2 *running issue.* A genital discharge due to a health disorder.

15:3 *flesh be stopped from his issue.* Refers to some obstruction to the flow or discharge.

15:5–12 Everything in contact with the man becomes contaminated: a vivid picture of the power of the unclean to affect the clean.

15:13 *cleansed of his issue.* Healed of his disorder. *Seven days* probation is to make sure.

the congregation, and give them unto the priest:
15 And the priest shall offer them, the one *for* a
sin offering, and the other *for* a burnt offering;
and the priest shall make an atonement for him
before the LORD for his issue.
16 And if any man's seed of copulation go out
from him, then he shall wash all his flesh in water,
and be unclean until the even.
17 And every garment, and every skin, whereon
is the seed of copulation, shall be washed with
water, and be unclean until the even.
18 The woman also with whom man shall lie *with*
seed of copulation, they shall *both* bathe *them-
selves* in water, and be unclean until the even.
19 ¶ And if a woman have an issue, *and* her
issue in her flesh be blood, she shall be put apart
seven days: and whosoever toucheth her shall be
unclean until the even.
20 And every thing that she lieth upon in her sep-
aration shall be unclean: every thing also that she
sitteth upon shall be unclean.
21 And whosoever toucheth her bed shall wash
his clothes, and bathe *himself* in water, and be
unclean until the even.
22 And whosoever toucheth any thing that she sat
upon shall wash his clothes, and bathe *himself* in
water, and be unclean until the even.
23 And if it *be* on *her* bed, or on any thing
whereon she sitteth, when he toucheth it, he shall
be unclean until the even.
24 And if any man lie with her at all, and her flow-
ers be upon him, he shall be unclean seven days;
and all the bed whereon he lieth shall be unclean.
25 And if a woman have an issue of her blood
many days out of the time of her separation, or
if it run beyond the time of her separation; all the
days of the issue of her uncleanness shall be as the
days of her separation: she *shall be* unclean.
26 Every bed whereon she lieth all the days
of her issue shall be unto her as the bed of her
separation: and whatsoever she sitteth upon shall
be unclean, as the uncleanness of her separation.
27 And whosoever toucheth those things shall
be unclean, and shall wash his clothes, and bathe
himself in water, and be unclean until the even.
28 But if she be cleansed of her issue, then she
shall number to herself seven days, and after that
she shall be clean.
29 And on the eighth day she shall take unto
her two turtles, or two young pigeons, and bring
them unto the priest, to the door of the tabernacle
of the congregation.
30 And the priest shall offer the one *for* a sin
offering, and the other *for* a burnt offering; and
the priest shall make an atonement for her before
the LORD for the issue of her uncleanness.
31 Thus shall ye separate the children of Israel
from their uncleanness; that they die not in their
uncleanness, when they defile my tabernacle that
is among them.
32 This *is* the law of him that hath an issue, and
of him whose seed goeth from him, and is defiled
therewith;
33 And of her that is sick of her flowers, and of him
that hath an issue, of the man, and of the wom-
an, and of him that lieth with her that is unclean.

CHAPTER 16

AND the LORD spake unto Moses after the death
of the two sons of Aaron, when they offered be-
fore the LORD, and died;
2 And the LORD said unto Moses, Speak unto
Aaron thy brother, that he come not at all times

15:15 *make an atonement.* For the removal of the ceremonial defilement; the Lord graciously provides the means of restoration.

15:16 *seed of copulation.* Perhaps referring specifically to a nocturnal emission (Deut. 23:10).

15:19–23 A woman's menstruation renders her ceremonially unclean and defiles everything.

15:24 *flowers.* Refers to the menstrual blood (v. 33).

15:25–30 *out of the time of her separation.* A blood issue that is not related to her menstrual cycle (cf. Mark 5:25).

15:28 *cleansed.* Healed. The usual seven days were needed to confirm the cure.

15:30 Compare with v. 15.

15:31 These laws taught the Israelites that only ritually clean people may worship in God's holy place.

Thoughts for Personal/Family Worship: Chapter 15

1. **The bodily emissions addressed are part of the normal course of life and are not statements of the individual's personal relationship or standing with God. Inwardly one could be right with God and still be outwardly ceremonially unclean, thus prohibited from the public rituals of worship. These were graphic object lessons of spiritual truth. Discharge from the organs of procreation reminds us of our fall in our first parents and the transmission of sin to us and to our descendants. Sin is internal and oozes from within us, from our nature (Ps. 51:5). It is often secret (Pss. 19:12; 90:8). But what does God deem as essential (Matt 5:8)?**
2. **This chapter provides an outstanding lesson regarding the contaminating power of the unclean thing. Everything and anyone that had contact with the unclean became unclean. Sin is an impurity that not only defiles us but others (1 Cor. 15:33). It is a warning for every believer to walk through this world circumspectly to avoid anything that would rob us of our fellowship with God. What are some things around you that could contaminate you? How can you avoid their defilement?**

THE DAY OF ATONEMENT (16:1–34)

Chapter 16: *The Lord instructs Moses about the annual entrance of the high priest into the most holy place to cleanse Israel on the Day of Atonement.*

16:2 *not at all times into the holy place.* Access to the innermost sanctuary, behind the second veil was limited to once a

into the holy *place* within the vail before the
mercy seat, which *is* upon the ark; that he die not:
for I will appear in the cloud upon the mercy seat.
3 Thus shall Aaron come into the holy *place*: with
a young bullock for a sin offering, and a ram for
a burnt offering.
4 He shall put on the holy linen coat, and he shall
have the linen breeches upon his flesh, and shall be
girded with a linen girdle, and with the linen mitre
shall he be attired: these *are* holy garments; therefore
shall he wash his flesh in water, and *so* put them on.
5 And he shall take of the congregation of the
children of Israel two kids of the goats for a sin
offering, and one ram for a burnt offering.
6 And Aaron shall offer his bullock of the sin
offering, which *is* for himself, and make an
atonement for himself, and for his house.
7 And he shall take the two goats, and present
them before the LORD *at* the door of the tabernacle of the congregation.
8 And Aaron shall cast lots upon the two goats; one
lot for the LORD, and the other lot for the scapegoat.
9 And Aaron shall bring the goat upon which the
LORD's lot fell, and offer him *for* a sin offering.
10 But the goat, on which the lot fell to be the
scapegoat, shall be presented alive before the
LORD, to make an atonement with him, *and* to let
him go for a scapegoat into the wilderness.
11 And Aaron shall bring the bullock of the sin
offering, which *is* for himself, and shall make an
atonement for himself, and for his house, and
shall kill the bullock of the sin offering which *is* for
himself:
12 And he shall take a censer full of burning coals
of fire from off the altar before the LORD, and
his hands full of sweet incense beaten small, and
bring *it* within the vail:
13 And he shall put the incense upon the fire before the LORD, that the cloud of the incense may
cover the mercy seat that *is* upon the testimony,
that he die not:
14 And he shall take of the blood of the bullock,
and sprinkle *it* with his finger upon the mercy
seat eastward; and before the mercy seat shall he
sprinkle of the blood with his finger seven times.
15 ¶ Then shall he kill the goat of the sin offering,
that *is* for the people, and bring his blood within
the vail, and do with that blood as he did with
the blood of the bullock, and sprinkle it upon the
mercy seat, and before the mercy seat:
16 And he shall make an atonement for the holy
place, because of the uncleanness of the children
of Israel, and because of their transgressions in all
their sins: and so shall he do for the tabernacle of
the congregation, that remaineth among them in
the midst of their uncleanness.
17 And there shall be no man in the tabernacle
of the congregation when he goeth in to make an
atonement in the holy *place*, until he come out, and
have made an atonement for himself, and for his
household, and for all the congregation of Israel.
18 And he shall go out unto the altar that *is* before
the LORD, and make an atonement for it; and shall
take of the blood of the bullock, and of the blood
of the goat, and put *it* upon the horns of the altar
round about.
19 And he shall sprinkle of the blood upon it with
his finger seven times, and cleanse it, and hallow
it from the uncleanness of the children of Israel.
20 ¶ And when he hath made an end of reconciling the holy *place*, and the tabernacle of the congregation, and the altar, he shall bring the live goat:
21 And Aaron shall lay both his hands upon the
head of the live goat, and confess over him all the
iniquities of the children of Israel, and all their
transgressions in all their sins, putting them upon

year. In the Old Testament, the way to God was open but restricted, anticipating the perfect sacrifice to come.

16:4 *holy linen coat.* Instead of his splendid garments worn at other times. This simpler garb befits his penitence and offering of sacrifice for his sins and points to the humiliation of Christ who set aside the evidences of His eternal glory to be clothed in human flesh. *breeches.* Leggings or trousers. *girdle.* Sash or wrap around. *mitre.* A turban-like headband.

16:5 *two kids.* Although two, they formed one sin offering. *for a burnt offering.* To give thanks when the atonement was made.

16:7–8 *cast lots.* Not chance, but expecting the Lord would direct the outcome (Prov. 16:33). *scapegoat.* The Hebrew has been disputed. Either a proper name referring to where the goat was sent or more likely a compound word meaning "goat of disappearing."

16:9–10 The two goats picture the two aspects of atonement: propitiation and expiation. God is satisfied and sin is removed.

16:12 *within the vail.* The second curtain behind which was the ark of the covenant, the climactic symbol of God's presence.

16:13 *cloud of the incense.* Incense on the coals (from the altar of sacrifice) produces fragrant smoke, signifying God's acceptance of Aaron's sin offering. Unlike Christ, he had to offer sacrifice for his own sins.

16:14 *blood of the bullock.* He brought atoning blood into God's presence and it secured mercy (Heb. 9:7)—picturing propitiation.

16:15 Aaron must sacrifice the goat and repeat the process this time for the people.

16:16 *atonement for the holy place.* The defiling of the sanctuary underscored the power of sin and the need for a sinless Mediator.

16:17 *no man in the tabernacle.* Israel could see that atonement depended upon the representative God had chosen and pointed to the ideal Mediator to come (Acts 4:12).

16:18 *the altar.* The altar of incense in front of the second curtain. *horns.* Each corner had a protruding horn.

16:19 *hallow.* Consecrate or declare to be holy. Even the incense altar becomes defiled and must be sanctified.

16:20 *reconciling.* Making atonement, appeasing, or propitiating. Through the sprinkled blood, God's wrath is quieted into peace.

16:21 *lay both his hands.* More specifically, "lean his hands," symbolizing sin being transferred to the animal as a substitute.

the head of the goat, and shall send *him* away by
the hand of a fit man into the wilderness:
22 And the goat shall bear upon him all their
iniquities unto a land not inhabited: and he shall
let go the goat in the wilderness.
23 And Aaron shall come into the tabernacle
of the congregation, and shall put off the linen
garments, which he put on when he went into the
holy *place*, and shall leave them there:
24 And he shall wash his flesh with water in the
holy place, and put on his garments, and come
forth, and offer his burnt offering, and the burnt
offering of the people, and make an atonement
for himself, and for the people.
25 And the fat of the sin offering shall he burn
upon the altar.
26 And he that let go the goat for the scapegoat
shall wash his clothes, and bathe his flesh in water,
and afterward come into the camp.
27 And the bullock *for* the sin offering, and the goat
for the sin offering, whose blood was brought in to
make atonement in the holy *place*, shall *one* carry
forth without the camp; and they shall burn in the
fire their skins, and their flesh, and their dung.
28 And he that burneth them shall wash his
clothes, and bathe his flesh in water, and after-
ward he shall come into the camp.
29 ¶ And *this* shall be a statute for ever unto you:
that in the seventh month, on the tenth *day* of the
month, ye shall afflict your souls, and do no work
at all, *whether it be* one of your own country, or a
stranger that sojourneth among you:
30 For on that day shall *the priest* make an atone-
ment for you, to cleanse you, *that* ye may be clean
from all your sins before the LORD.
31 It *shall be* a sabbath of rest unto you, and ye
shall afflict your souls, by a statute for ever.
32 And the priest, whom he shall anoint, and
whom he shall consecrate to minister in the
priest's office in his father's stead, shall make the
atonement, and shall put on the linen clothes,
even the holy garments:
33 And he shall make an atonement for the holy
sanctuary, and he shall make an atonement for
the tabernacle of the congregation, and for the
altar, and he shall make an atonement for the
priests, and for all the people of the congregation.
34 And this shall be an everlasting statute unto
you, to make an atonement for the children of
Israel for all their sins once a year. And he did as
the LORD commanded Moses.

CHAPTER 17

AND the LORD spake unto Moses, saying,
2 Speak unto Aaron, and unto his sons, and unto
all the children of Israel, and say unto them; This
is the thing which the LORD hath commanded,
saying,
3 What man soever *there be* of the house of Israel,
that killeth an ox, or lamb, or goat, in the camp, or
that killeth *it* out of the camp,
4 And bringeth it not unto the door of the tab-
ernacle of the congregation, to offer an offering

16:22 *let go the goat in the wilderness.* A symbolic display of the expiation or the removal of the people's sins.
16:23 *Aaron . . . shall put off the linen garments.* Now the work of expiation was done, after washing, he could wear his splendid garments. Humiliation gave way to exaltation as in the ministry of Christ. Death gave way to resurrection.
16:29 *in the seventh month.* September/October, or Hebrew, *Tishri. afflict your souls.* Humble yourselves, an idiom for fasting. The Day of Atonement was the only fast day ordered by God in Israel's religious calendar (v. 31).
16:31 *sabbath of rest.* Literally, "a sabbath of special sabbath." This was observed once each year, by a holy rest, holy mourning for sin, and comprehensive pardon. *for ever.* The Hebrew can refer simply to a long time. As an aspect of ceremonial law, Christ fulfilled it and made it obsolete (Col. 2:16–17).

Thoughts for Personal/Family Worship: Chapter 16

1. **One of the most striking events of the Day of Atonement concerned the two goats, which together picture the effects of the one sacrifice for sin offered by Christ. The slain goat pictures the godward effect of the atonement to propitiate or satisfy God's wrath against sin. The sprinkling of the blood on the mercy seat that covered the righteous demands of the law satisfied the broken law. The scapegoat bearing the sins of the people away pictures expiation, the necessary consequence of propitiation. The guilt of sin was removed never again to appear; the goat did not wander back into camp. All the sins of the people were upon it and away into the wilderness it went forever (Ps. 103:12). The two are inseparably linked: if there is propitiation there must be expiation. Christ did not die in vain. How does this double sacrifice picture the assurance of the believer that God is pleased with him?**
2. **Aaron's role on the Day of Atonement dramatically portrayed the work of the ideal High Priest to come. When Aaron stripped himself of the royal garments of his office to do the work in the sanctuary, it pictured Christ's work of humiliation whereby He became obedient unto death. When Aaron entered behind the veil, it pictured the death of Christ whereby He presented the evidence of His sacrifice to the Father. But when Aaron exited the veil and put on his royal robes again, it pictured the resurrection of Christ and His earned exaltation. He entered with the blood of sacrifice; he exited as evidence of the accepted sacrifice. As dramatic as the events were, Aaron's sacrifice for himself was a clear indication that One greater than Aaron was necessary and was certain to come. Pray for grace to rejoice in the Savior, the fulfillment of these shadows!**

THE HOLINESS GOD REQUIRES OF HIS PEOPLE (17:1—22:33)

Chapter 17: ***The Lord commands that all blood and sacrifices must be offered at His tabernacle, and no blood or animal that dies naturally may be eaten.***

Holiness in Eating Food (17:1–16)

17:3–4 Centralized worship was a safeguard against imitating the heathen practices (2 Kings 16:4) as well as

unto the LORD before the tabernacle of the LORD;
blood shall be imputed unto that man; he hath
shed blood; and that man shall be cut off from
among his people:
5 To the end that the children of Israel may
bring their sacrifices, which they offer in the
open field, even that they may bring them unto
the LORD, unto the door of the tabernacle of the
congregation, unto the priest, and offer them *for*
peace offerings unto the LORD.
6 And the priest shall sprinkle the blood upon the
altar of the LORD *at* the door of the tabernacle of
the congregation, and burn the fat for a sweet savour unto the LORD.
7 And they shall no more offer their sacrifices
unto devils, after whom they have gone a whoring. This shall be a statute for ever unto them
throughout their generations.
8 ¶ And thou shalt say unto them, Whatsoever
man *there be* of the house of Israel, or of the
strangers which sojourn among you, that offereth
a burnt offering or sacrifice,
9 And bringeth it not unto the door of the tabernacle of the congregation, to offer it unto the
LORD; even that man shall be cut off from among
his people.
10 ¶ And whatsoever man *there be* of the house of
Israel, or of the strangers that sojourn among you,
that eateth any manner of blood; I will even set
my face against that soul that eateth blood, and
will cut him off from among his people.
11 For the life of the flesh *is* in the blood: and I
have given it to you upon the altar to make an
atonement for your souls: for it *is* the blood *that*
maketh an atonement for the soul.
12 Therefore I said unto the children of Israel,
No soul of you shall eat blood, neither shall any
stranger that sojourneth among you eat blood.
13 And whatsoever man *there be* of the children
of Israel, or of the strangers that sojourn among
you, which hunteth and catcheth any beast or
fowl that may be eaten; he shall even pour out the
blood thereof, and cover it with dust.
14 For *it is* the life of all flesh; the blood of it *is* for
the life thereof: therefore I said unto the children
of Israel, Ye shall eat the blood of no manner of
flesh: for the life of all flesh *is* the blood thereof:
whosoever eateth it shall be cut off.
15 And every soul that eateth that which died *of
itself*, or that which was torn *with beasts, whether
it be* one of your own country, or a stranger, he
shall both wash his clothes, and bathe *himself* in
water, and be unclean until the even: then shall
he be clean.
16 But if he wash *them* not, nor bathe his flesh;
then he shall bear his iniquity.

CHAPTER 18

AND the LORD spake unto Moses, saying,
2 Speak unto the children of Israel, and say unto
them, I am the LORD your God.
3 After the doings of the land of Egypt, wherein
ye dwelt, shall ye not do: and after the doings of
the land of Canaan, whither I bring you, shall ye
not do: neither shall ye walk in their ordinances.
4 Ye shall do my judgments, and keep mine ordinances, to walk therein: I *am* the LORD your God.
5 Ye shall therefore keep my statutes, and my
judgments: which if a man do, he shall live in
them: I *am* the LORD.
6 ¶ None of you shall approach to any that is

circumventing the chosen mediator. *blood shall be imputed.* An idiom for guilt being charged to him. *cut off.* Excluded from the worshiping community, excommunicated. Worshiping outside God's prescription was a serious offense (vv. 9–10,14).
17:7 *devils.* Suggesting they had already done this, perhaps with the golden calf (Ex. 32). Idolatry is devil worship (1 Cor. 10:20). *whoring.* Idolatry is a form of spiritual adultery.
17:11 *in the blood.* "Lifeblood" is from God and is to be reverenced (Gen. 9:6). *an atonement.* An offering of life through death (the pouring out of the life).
17:12 *eat blood.* Given the divine definition of blood, this would be sacrilege. *sojourneth.* Lives as an alien resident (v. 13).
17:13 *cover it with dust.* Honor it and keep it from wrong use.
17:15 *stranger.* Resident alien.
17:16 *iniquity.* Guilt.

Thoughts for Personal/Family Worship: Chapter 17

1. **We must have no do-it-yourself worship. Only what God has prescribed is acceptable and glorifying to Him. To worship otherwise is to serve the Devil (v. 7; 1 Cor. 10:20–21). How are modern Christians tempted to worship God in ways outside His commandments and thus unacceptable to Him?**
2. **The definition of the blood puts the atonement in view. Blood stands for life. Blood is a vital liquid circulating in our bodies conveying nutrients and oxygen. When blood is shed, life is taken. Sin's penalty is death. "The soul that sinneth, it shall die" (Ezek. 18:4). "The wages of sin is death" (Rom. 6:23). Our Lord shed His blood. This culminated in John 19:34 when one of the soldiers with a spear pierced His side, and blood and water came out. The One who is the Prince of life was sacrificed to the justice of a sin-hating God, which appeased His anger. On the cross Christ poured out His life. Take time to glory in the cross, the heart of the gospel.**

Chapter 18: *Unlike the surrounding pagans, Israel was to maintain pure sexual relations and family life.*

Holiness in the Marriage Relationship (18:1–30)

18:2 *I am the LORD your God.* The context of holiness is the covenant.
18:3 *doings of . . . Egypt . . . Canaan.* Holiness is contrary to the world.
18:5 *live in them.* Or by them. God's restraining and directing law is the only standard for life with Him.

near of kin to him, to uncover *their* nakedness: I
am the LORD.
7 The nakedness of thy father, or the nakedness
of thy mother, shalt thou not uncover: she *is* thy
mother; thou shalt not uncover her nakedness.
8 The nakedness of thy father's wife shalt thou
not uncover: it *is* thy father's nakedness.
9 The nakedness of thy sister, the daughter of thy
father, or daughter of thy mother, *whether she be*
born at home, or born abroad, *even* their naked-
ness thou shalt not uncover.
10 The nakedness of thy son's daughter, or of
thy daughter's daughter, *even* their nakedness
thou shalt not uncover: for theirs *is* thine own
nakedness.
11 The nakedness of thy father's wife's daughter,
begotten of thy father, she *is* thy sister, thou shalt
not uncover her nakedness.
12 Thou shalt not uncover the nakedness of thy
father's sister: she *is* thy father's near kinswoman.
13 Thou shalt not uncover the nakedness of
thy mother's sister: for she *is* thy mother's near
kinswoman.
14 Thou shalt not uncover the nakedness of thy
father's brother, thou shalt not approach to his
wife: she *is* thine aunt.
15 Thou shalt not uncover the nakedness of thy
daughter in law: she *is* thy son's wife; thou shalt
not uncover her nakedness.
16 Thou shalt not uncover the nakedness of thy
brother's wife: it *is* thy brother's nakedness.
17 Thou shalt not uncover the nakedness of a
woman and her daughter, neither shalt thou take
her son's daughter, or her daughter's daughter, to
uncover her nakedness; *for* they *are* her near kins-
women: it *is* wickedness.
18 Neither shalt thou take a wife to her sister,
to vex *her*, to uncover her nakedness, beside the
other in her life *time*.
19 Also thou shalt not approach unto a woman to
uncover her nakedness, as long as she is put apart
for her uncleanness.
20 Moreover thou shalt not lie carnally with thy
neighbour's wife, to defile thyself with her.
21 And thou shalt not let any of thy seed pass
through *the fire* to Molech, neither shalt thou pro-
fane the name of thy God: I *am* the LORD.
22 Thou shalt not lie with mankind, as with
womankind: it *is* abomination.
23 Neither shalt thou lie with any beast to defile
thyself therewith: neither shall any woman stand
before a beast to lie down thereto: it *is* confusion.
24 Defile not ye yourselves in any of these things:
for in all these the nations are defiled which I cast
out before you:
25 And the land is defiled: therefore I do visit the
iniquity thereof upon it, and the land itself vom-
iteth out her inhabitants.
26 Ye shall therefore keep my statutes and my
judgments, and shall not commit *any* of these
abominations; *neither* any of your own nation,
nor any stranger that sojourneth among you:
27 (For all these abominations have the men of
the land done, which *were* before you, and the
land is defiled;)
28 That the land spue not you out also, when
ye defile it, as it spued out the nations that *were*
before you.
29 For whosoever shall commit any of these
abominations, even the souls that commit *them*
shall be cut off from among their people.
30 Therefore shall ye keep mine ordinance, that

18:6 *near of kin.* Literally, "a flesh relation of his flesh," referring to a close relative.
18:7 *uncover her nakedness.* Euphemism for sexual intercourse.
18:9 *thy sister.* See the curse pronounced in Deut. 27:22. *Born abroad* means not in her father's house.
18:10 *thine own nakedness.* Grandchildren seen as part of grandparents' bodies (Gen. 31:43).
18:11–12 *father's wife's daughter . . . father's sister.* Prohibition of marriage relations because of blood relation to the father.
18:18 *take a wife to her sister, to vex her.* Literally, "woman to her sister you must not take to make her a rival wife."
18:19 *uncleanness.* Her monthly menstruation.
18:20 *lie carnally.* Commit an act of adultery (Ex. 20:14,17).
18:21 *Molech.* The Ammonites' god to whom infants were sacrificed by fire (20:2–5; 1 Kings 11:7). *profane.* Bring down to the level of the common or ordinary.
18:22 *lie with mankind, as with womankind.* Homosexuality is unequivocally forbidden.
18:23 *lie with any beast.* Practice bestiality. *confusion.* Perversion.
18:24 *Defile not ye yourselves.* Not only ceremonially, but spiritually and morally also.
18:25 Evidence from the Ancient Near East shows that these sexual perversions were not only practiced but even regulated by civil law.
18:26 *sojourneth among you.* Dwells for a time as a resident alien.
18:29 *cut off.* Excommunicated from the people of God.

Thoughts for Personal/Family Worship: Chapter 18

1. **Incest, voyeurism, adultery, homosexuality, and bestiality characterize a degenerate society. They show the unrenewed and unrestrained heart (Jer. 17:9). These perversions were rife in ancient Egypt and throughout Canaan. So perverse was the pagan society that even some Hittite laws identified what kind of animals were permitted for bestiality. Under God's judgment, those civilizations decayed and were destroyed. It is a solemn warning to Western nations with their liberal and relativistic outlook. Have God's standards of holiness changed (see James 1:17)?**
2. **God takes sexual sin very seriously. In v. 22 abomination means "disgusting," "hated," "abhorrent." For such perverted behavior the Canaanites were ejected from their land (vv. 25,28) as Israel was from that same land afterward (Ps. 106:40). Because sin is an outbreak, it needs**

ye commit not *any one* of these abominable
customs, which were committed before you, and
that ye defile not yourselves therein: I *am* the
LORD your God.

CHAPTER 19

AND the LORD spake unto Moses, saying,
2 Speak unto all the congregation of the children
of Israel, and say unto them, Ye shall be holy: for I
the LORD your God *am* holy.
3 ¶ Ye shall fear every man his mother, and his
father, and keep my sabbaths: I *am* the LORD your
God.
4 ¶ Turn ye not unto idols, nor make to your-
selves molten gods: I *am* the LORD your God.
5 ¶ And if ye offer a sacrifice of peace offerings
unto the LORD, ye shall offer it at your own will.
6 It shall be eaten the same day ye offer it, and on
the morrow: and if ought remain until the third
day, it shall be burnt in the fire.
7 And if it be eaten at all on the third day, it *is*
abominable; it shall not be accepted.
8 Therefore *every one* that eateth it shall bear his
iniquity, because he hath profaned the hallowed
thing of the LORD: and that soul shall be cut off
from among his people.
9 ¶ And when ye reap the harvest of your land,
thou shalt not wholly reap the corners of thy
field, neither shalt thou gather the gleanings of
thy harvest.
10 And thou shalt not glean thy vineyard, neither
shalt thou gather *every* grape of thy vineyard;
thou shalt leave them for the poor and stranger: I
am the LORD your God.
11 ¶ Ye shall not steal, neither deal falsely, neither
lie one to another.
12 ¶ And ye shall not swear by my name falsely,
neither shalt thou profane the name of thy God:
I *am* the LORD.
13 ¶ Thou shalt not defraud thy neighbour, nei-
ther rob *him*: the wages of him that is hired shall
not abide with thee all night until the morning.
14 ¶ Thou shalt not curse the deaf, nor put a
stumblingblock before the blind, but shalt fear
thy God: I *am* the LORD.
15 ¶ Ye shall do no unrighteousness in judgment:
thou shalt not respect the person of the poor, nor
honour the person of the mighty: *but* in righ-
teousness shalt thou judge thy neighbour.
16 ¶ Thou shalt not go up and down *as* a tale-
bearer among thy people: neither shalt thou
stand against the blood of thy neighbour: I *am*
the LORD.
17 ¶ Thou shalt not hate thy brother in thine
heart: thou shalt in any wise rebuke thy neigh-
bour, and not suffer sin upon him.
18 ¶ Thou shalt not avenge, nor bear any grudge
against the children of thy people, but thou shalt
love thy neighbour as thyself: I *am* the LORD.
19 ¶ Ye shall keep my statutes. Thou shalt not let
thy cattle gender with a diverse kind: thou shalt
not sow thy field with mingled seed: neither shall
a garment mingled of linen and woollen come
upon thee.
20 ¶ And whosoever lieth carnally with a woman,
that *is* a bondmaid, betrothed to an husband, and
not at all redeemed, nor freedom given her; she
shall be scourged; they shall not be put to death,
because she was not free.
21 And he shall bring his trespass offering unto
the LORD, unto the door of the tabernacle of the
congregation, *even* a ram for a trespass offering.
22 And the priest shall make an atonement for
him with the ram of the trespass offering before
the LORD for his sin which he hath done: and the

the bounds and reins of God's laws to keep it in check. Pray to be kept from such sins. How can God's Word help you (Ps. 119:9–10)?

Chapter 19: *The Lord calls Israel to be holy as He is holy, especially by loving their neighbors as themselves.*

Holiness in Justice and Love toward God and Man (19:1–37)

19:2 *Ye shall be holy.* These laws guard the sanctity of God's people.

19:3 *Ye shall fear every man his mother, and his father, and keep my sabbaths.* Reference to the fifth and fourth commandments.

19:4 *Turn ye not unto idols.* Idols were worthless and inept to help the people of God. This is a reference to the first commandment.

19:5–8 *your own will.* A voluntary sacrifice. To be eaten within two days to preserve spontaneity and prevent hoarding.

19:9–10 *not wholly reap.* Divine mercy for the poor and outcasts of society. This behavior imitates the Lord (Deut. 10:18–19). It is loving one's neighbor as self, the second greatest commandment.

19:11 *Ye shall not steal, neither deal falsely, neither lie one to another.* By the latter two, truth is stolen. Reference to eighth and ninth commandments.

19:12–13 *ye shall not swear by my name falsely . . . Thou shalt not defraud thy neighbour.* These breaches of the law link the first and second tables.

19:15 *respect.* Show partiality for. *in righteousness.* The way of dealing with one's neighbor ought not to be conditioned on economic status but on justice.

19:16 *talebearer.* Slanderer. *stand against.* The idea conveyed here is remaining idle while the life of one's neighbor is at stake.

19:18 *thou shalt love thy neighbour as thyself.* Jesus and Paul quote this as summarizing the second table of the law (Matt. 22:39; Rom. 13:9). This is one of the most quoted Old Testament passages in the New Testament.

19:19 *gender with a diverse kind.* Reproduce with a different breed. *mingled seed . . . garment mingled.* These object lessons of separation taught them to avoid mixture in worship and friendships (2 Cor. 6:14–18).

19:20–22 *bondmaid.* Her punishment was mitigated due to her inferior position as a slave. Normally the penalty was

sin which he hath done shall be forgiven him.
23 ¶ And when ye shall come into the land, and
shall have planted all manner of trees for food,
then ye shall count the fruit thereof as uncir-
cumcised: three years shall it be as uncircumcised
unto you: it shall not be eaten of.
24 But in the fourth year all the fruit thereof shall
be holy to praise the LORD *withal.*
25 And in the fifth year shall ye eat of the fruit
thereof, that it may yield unto you the increase
thereof: I *am* the LORD your God.
26 ¶ Ye shall not eat *any thing* with the blood:
neither shall ye use enchantment, nor observe
times.
27 Ye shall not round the corners of your heads,
neither shalt thou mar the corners of thy beard.
28 Ye shall not make any cuttings in your flesh for
the dead, nor print any marks upon you: I *am* the
LORD.
29 ¶ Do not prostitute thy daughter, to cause her
to be a whore; lest the land fall to whoredom, and
the land become full of wickedness.
30 ¶ Ye shall keep my sabbaths, and reverence my
sanctuary: I *am* the LORD.
31 ¶ Regard not them that have familiar spirits,
neither seek after wizards, to be defiled by them: I
am the LORD your God.
32 ¶ Thou shalt rise up before the hoary head,
and honour the face of the old man, and fear thy
God: I *am* the LORD.
33 ¶ And if a stranger sojourn with thee in your
land, ye shall not vex him.
34 *But* the stranger that dwelleth with you shall
be unto you as one born among you, and thou
shalt love him as thyself; for ye were strangers in
the land of Egypt: I *am* the LORD your God.
35 ¶ Ye shall do no unrighteousness in judgment,
in meteyard, in weight, or in measure.
36 Just balances, just weights, a just ephah, and a
just hin, shall ye have: I *am* the LORD your God,
which brought you out of the land of Egypt.
37 Therefore shall ye observe all my statutes, and
all my judgments, and do them: I *am* the LORD.

CHAPTER 20

AND the LORD spake unto Moses, saying,
2 Again, thou shalt say to the children of Israel,
Whosoever *he be* of the children of Israel, or of
the strangers that sojourn in Israel, that giveth
any of his seed unto Molech; he shall surely be
put to death: the people of the land shall stone
him with stones.
3 And I will set my face against that man, and will
cut him off from among his people; because he
hath given of his seed unto Molech, to defile my
sanctuary, and to profane my holy name.
4 And if the people of the land do any ways hide
their eyes from the man, when he giveth of his
seed unto Molech, and kill him not:
5 Then I will set my face against that man, and
against his family, and will cut him off, and all
that go a whoring after him, to commit whore-
dom with Molech, from among their people.
6 ¶ And the soul that turneth after such as have
familiar spirits, and after wizards, to go a whoring

death (Deut. 22:22). This protects the rights of slaves.

19:23–25 *uncircumcised.* Left unharvested.

19:26 *use enchantment.* Resort to occult and superstitious practices.

19:28 *cuttings in your flesh . . . marks.* Body piercing, self-mutilation, and tattoos can be expressions of worship (1 Kings 18:28; Jer. 41:5) or mourning *for the dead* (Deut. 14:1; Jer. 16:6–7; 48:37). God forbids degrading the human body, for He created man in His image.

19:29 *Prostitute* can mean "profane" and may refer to copying the cult prostitution of the Canaanites.

19:31 *familiar spirits.* Necromancers who seek to communicate with spirits of the dead. *wizards.* Soothsayers who seek knowledge through spirits.

19:32–34 Respect for the elderly and for the immigrant is enjoined here. *hoary head.* The gray hair of an old man. *stranger.* A resident alien. *vex.* Oppress or mistreat. The commandment to love one's neighbor includes people of other nations and cultures (Luke 10:25–37).

19:35–37 *no unrighteousness in judgment.* Honesty in judicial and business matters.

19:35 *meteyard.* Either the instrument used or the act of measuring. *in measure.* Usually, in reference to liquids.

Thoughts for Personal/Family Worship: Chapter 19

1. Many of these laws apply to inward feelings and are based on the fact that the Lord is our God. If there were no other reasons for obedience than to acknowledge the Lord and the relationship we have with Him, that would be enough. This is where obedience must begin (Ps. 51:6; Eph. 6:6). According to Rom. 8:13 and Col. 3:5, why must sin be put to death?

2. Leaving some of the corn and grape harvest behind for the poor shows that God is kind, and we also should be kind to those less favored. Even though we may not have fields or vineyards, it is still possible to keep the spirit of the law. However it is manifested, we are to love our neighbors as we love ourselves. It may look different for us than for historic Israel, but what might it look like for you?

3. God prohibited Israel from cutting or permanently marking their bodies as the pagans did (v. 28). Christians should not mar their bodies, for they are God's temple (1 Cor. 6:19–20). They also should not participate in customs that identify them with paganism. What does this imply about tattoos and body piercing?

Chapter 20: *Israel is instructed to not follow the sins of Canaanite paganism or sexual immorality.*

Various Sins: Their Prohibition and Punishment (20:1–27)

20:2–5 *sojourn.* Live as resident aliens. *Molech.* The Ammonite god worshiped by burning infants alive in the hollow belly of its idol. Those who looked the other way were equally guilty.

20:6 *familiar spirits . . . wizards.* See note at 19:31. The apostate King Saul is an example (1 Sam. 28).

after them, I will even set my face against that
soul, and will cut him off from among his people.
7 ¶ Sanctify yourselves therefore, and be ye holy:
for I *am* the LORD your God.
8 And ye shall keep my statutes, and do them: I
am the LORD which sanctify you.
9 ¶ For every one that curseth his father or his
mother shall be surely put to death: he hath
cursed his father or his mother; his blood *shall be*
upon him.
10 ¶ And the man that committeth adultery with
another man's wife, *even he* that committeth adul-
tery with his neighbour's wife, the adulterer and
the adulteress shall surely be put to death.
11 And the man that lieth with his father's wife
hath uncovered his father's nakedness: both of
them shall surely be put to death; their blood *shall
be* upon them.
12 And if a man lie with his daughter in law, both
of them shall surely be put to death: they have
wrought confusion; their blood *shall be* upon
them.
13 If a man also lie with mankind, as he lieth
with a woman, both of them have committed an
abomination: they shall surely be put to death;
their blood *shall be* upon them.
14 And if a man take a wife and her mother, it *is*
wickedness: they shall be burnt with fire, both he
and they; that there be no wickedness among you.
15 And if a man lie with a beast, he shall surely be
put to death: and ye shall slay the beast.
16 And if a woman approach unto any beast, and
lie down thereto, thou shalt kill the woman, and
the beast: they shall surely be put to death; their
blood *shall be* upon them.
17 And if a man shall take his sister, his father's
daughter, or his mother's daughter, and see her
nakedness, and she see his nakedness; it *is* a
wicked thing; and they shall be cut off in the sight
of their people: he hath uncovered his sister's
nakedness; he shall bear his iniquity.
18 And if a man shall lie with a woman having
her sickness, and shall uncover her nakedness; he
hath discovered her fountain, and she hath un-
covered the fountain of her blood: and both of
them shall be cut off from among their people.
19 And thou shalt not uncover the nakedness of
thy mother's sister, nor of thy father's sister: for
he uncovereth his near kin: they shall bear their
iniquity.
20 And if a man shall lie with his uncle's wife, he
hath uncovered his uncle's nakedness: they shall
bear their sin; they shall die childless.
21 And if a man shall take his brother's wife, it *is*
an unclean thing: he hath uncovered his brother's
nakedness; they shall be childless.
22 ¶ Ye shall therefore keep all my statutes, and all
my judgments, and do them: that the land, whither
I bring you to dwell therein, spue you not out.
23 And ye shall not walk in the manners of the
nation, which I cast out before you: for they com-
mitted all these things, and therefore I abhorred
them.
24 But I have said unto you, Ye shall inherit their
land, and I will give it unto you to possess it, a
land that floweth with milk and honey: I *am* the
LORD your God, which have separated you from
other people.
25 Ye shall therefore put difference between
clean beasts and unclean, and between unclean
fowls and clean: and ye shall not make your souls
abominable by beast, or by fowl, or by any man-
ner of living thing that creepeth on the ground,
which I have separated from you as unclean.
26 And ye shall be holy unto me: for I the LORD
am holy, and have severed you from *other* people,
that ye should be mine.
27 ¶ A man also or woman that hath a familiar

20:7–8 *Sanctify yourselves.* Holiness comes through obedience to God's Word (John 17:17; Eph. 5:26).

20:9 *curseth his father or his mother.* The death penalty was the punishment for this because parents are God's representatives in the home.

20:10 *committeth adultery.* The death penalty was also invoked for this to protect the sanctity of marriage.

20:12–15 *with his daughter in law . . . with mankind, as he lieth with a woman . . . a wife and her mother . . . with a beast.* Further cases of a man engaging in unnatural sexual relations.

20:12 *confusion.* That which is disgraceful and contrary to nature and the divine order.

20:14 *burnt with fire.* Perhaps after being stoned (Josh. 7:25).

20:16 *lie down thereto.* In order to solicit sex (18:23). All these gross perversions were practiced and even regulated in Egypt and Canaan (v. 23).

20:17 *nakedness.* Mutual exposure or sexual intercourse.

20:18 *her sickness . . . her fountain.* Relations with a woman who is menstruating.

20:19–21 Further examples of unlawful relationships. *they shall be childless.* A great affliction in those times.

20:22 *spue.* Vomit. A graphic image of the perversions making the land sick.

20:26 *be holy unto me: for I the LORD am holy.* The logic of holiness (1 Peter 1:16).

20:27 See note at 19:31.

Thoughts for Personal/Family Worship: Chapter 20

1. **A beautiful contrast to horrendous Molech is our Lord Jesus. He took infants in His arms and blessed them! Thank God for revealed religion: we are not left in heathen darkness and barbarity. How can we stand for the children today, both born and unborn, against those who would sacrifice them to the gods of pleasure, money, and selfish ambition?**
2. **The Lord who calls for holiness also works it in His people. Verses 7–8 say, "Sanctify yourselves . . . I am the LORD which sanctify you" (cf. v. 26). His will is that we be holy, and His power will make believers holy (1 Thess. 4:3; 5:23–24). This does not excuse laziness, but on the contrary it encourages and empowers our utmost effort, knowing all our efforts to become holy are from Him and**

spirit, or that is a wizard, shall surely be put to death: they shall stone them with stones: their blood *shall be* upon them.

CHAPTER 21

AND the LORD said unto Moses, Speak unto the priests the sons of Aaron, and say unto them, There shall none be defiled for the dead among his people:
2 But for his kin, that is near unto him, *that is*, for his mother, and for his father, and for his son, and for his daughter, and for his brother,
3 And for his sister a virgin, that is nigh unto him, which hath had no husband; for her may he be defiled.
4 *But* he shall not defile himself, *being* a chief man among his people, to profane himself.
5 They shall not make baldness upon their head, neither shall they shave off the corner of their beard, nor make any cuttings in their flesh.
6 They shall be holy unto their God, and not profane the name of their God: for the offerings of the LORD made by fire, *and* the bread of their God, they do offer: therefore they shall be holy.
7 They shall not take a wife *that is* a whore, or profane; neither shall they take a woman put away from her husband: for he *is* holy unto his God.
8 Thou shalt sanctify him therefore; for he offereth the bread of thy God: he shall be holy unto thee: for I the LORD, which sanctify you, *am* holy.
9 ¶ And the daughter of any priest, if she profane herself by playing the whore, she profaneth her father: she shall be burnt with fire.
10 And *he that is* the high priest among his brethren, upon whose head the anointing oil was poured, and that is consecrated to put on the garments, shall not uncover his head, nor rend his clothes;
11 Neither shall he go in to any dead body, nor defile himself for his father, or for his mother;
12 Neither shall he go out of the sanctuary, nor profane the sanctuary of his God; for the crown of the anointing oil of his God *is* upon him: I *am* the LORD.
13 And he shall take a wife in her virginity.
14 A widow, or a divorced woman, or profane, *or* an harlot, these shall he not take: but he shall take a virgin of his own people to wife.
15 Neither shall he profane his seed among his people: for I the LORD do sanctify him.
16 ¶ And the LORD spake unto Moses, saying,
17 Speak unto Aaron, saying, Whosoever *he be* of thy seed in their generations that hath *any* blemish, let him not approach to offer the bread of his God.
18 For whatsoever man *he be* that hath a blemish, he shall not approach: a blind man, or a lame, or he that hath a flat nose, or any thing superfluous,
19 Or a man that is brokenfooted, or brokenhanded,
20 Or crookbackt, or a dwarf, or that hath a blemish in his eye, or be scurvy, or scabbed, or hath his stones broken;
21 No man that hath a blemish of the seed of Aaron the priest shall come nigh to offer the offerings of the LORD made by fire: he hath a blemish; he shall not come nigh to offer the bread of his God.
22 He shall eat the bread of his God, *both* of the most holy, and of the holy.
23 Only he shall not go in unto the vail, nor come

---

through Him (Phil. 2:12–13). How does it encourage you knowing that God makes His children holy?

3. **Some of the sexual sins prohibited defy imagination, but they were common practices in the world into which God's people were going to live. Some ancient cultures even had laws to regulate the circumstances in which some of these horrendous acts were permissible. They testify to the depravity that is in man's heart. These perversions were also rife in Paul's day (Rom. 1:24–28) and are becoming so in our day (2 Tim. 3:1–3). We cannot be the friend of this corrupt world (James 4:4). True religion, based on God's law, lifts society's morals; when our true religion declines, so does our society. Remember to pray for those in authority and those who make our laws, so many of which, like Canaan of old, regulate rather than prohibit sin.**

Holiness of Priests, Gifts, and Sacrifices (21:1—22:33)

Chapter 21: *The Lord instructs Moses that the priests must excel in ritual holiness.*

21:1 *defiled.* Made ceremonially unclean by excessive mourning for the dead (vv. 10–11).
21:2–3 *for his kin.* Certain exceptions: parents, children, brother, unmarried sister; but the mourning rendered them unclean and temporarily disqualified them from their priestly duties.
21:5 Signs of grieving like the heathen did.
21:6 *profane.* Make common or bring down (the holy to the ordinary). To profane themselves was to profane the Lord.
21:7 *a wife.* Priests' wives must be blameless too (vv. 13–15).
21:9 *daughter of any priest.* She also must be blameless. If the priest tolerates this in his daughter, how can he expect otherwise from his people? The New Testament also places expectations on the conduct of the children of elders (1 Tim. 3:4).
21:12 *the crown of the anointing oil.* Literally, "the consecration of the anointing oil."
21:17 *any blemish.* Physical defect, a picture of moral blemish. This pointed to the beauty and perfection of Christ, whom they typified.
21:18 *any thing superfluous.* Some part too large or out of proportion, disfiguration.
21:20 *crookbackt.* Hunchbacked. *dwarf.* Someone overly thin or withered. *stones broken.* Testicles damaged.

Thoughts for Personal/Family Worship: Chapter 21

1. **The priests were man's representatives before God, and each one foreshadowed the coming of the ideal and**

nigh unto the altar, because he hath a blemish;
that he profane not my sanctuaries: for I the LORD
do sanctify them.
24 And Moses told *it* unto Aaron, and to his sons,
and unto all the children of Israel.

CHAPTER 22

AND the LORD spake unto Moses, saying,
2 Speak unto Aaron and to his sons, that they
separate themselves from the holy things of the
children of Israel, and that they profane not my
holy name *in those things* which they hallow unto
me: I *am* the LORD.
3 Say unto them, Whosoever *he be* of all your seed
among your generations, that goeth unto the holy
things, which the children of Israel hallow unto the
LORD, having his uncleanness upon him, that soul
shall be cut off from my presence: I *am* the LORD.
4 What man soever of the seed of Aaron *is* a leper,
or hath a running issue; he shall not eat of the holy
things, until he be clean. And whoso toucheth any
thing *that is* unclean *by* the dead, or a man whose
seed goeth from him;
5 Or whosoever toucheth any creeping thing,
whereby he may be made unclean, or a man of
whom he may take uncleanness, whatsoever un-
cleanness he hath;
6 The soul which hath touched any such shall be
unclean until even, and shall not eat of the holy
things, unless he wash his flesh with water.
7 And when the sun is down, he shall be clean,
and shall afterward eat of the holy things; because
it *is* his food.
8 That which dieth of itself, or is torn *with beasts*,
he shall not eat to defile himself therewith: I *am*
the LORD.
9 They shall therefore keep mine ordinance, lest
they bear sin for it, and die therefore, if they pro-
fane it: I the LORD do sanctify them.
10 There shall no stranger eat *of* the holy thing: a
sojourner of the priest, or an hired servant, shall
not eat *of* the holy thing.
11 But if the priest buy *any* soul with his money,
he shall eat of it, and he that is born in his house:
they shall eat of his meat.
12 If the priest's daughter also be *married* unto
a stranger, she may not eat of an offering of the
holy things.
13 But if the priest's daughter be a widow, or
divorced, and have no child, and is returned unto
her father's house, as in her youth, she shall eat
of her father's meat: but there shall no stranger
eat thereof.
14 ¶ And if a man eat *of* the holy thing unwittingly,
then he shall put the fifth *part* thereof unto it, and
shall give *it* unto the priest with the holy thing.
15 And they shall not profane the holy things of
the children of Israel, which they offer unto the
LORD;
16 Or suffer them to bear the iniquity of trespass,
when they eat their holy things: for I the LORD do
sanctify them.
17 ¶ And the LORD spake unto Moses, saying,
18 Speak unto Aaron, and to his sons, and unto
all the children of Israel, and say unto them,
Whatsoever *he be* of the house of Israel, or of
the strangers in Israel, that will offer his oblation
for all his vows, and for all his freewill offerings,
which they will offer unto the LORD for a burnt
offering;
19 *Ye shall offer* at your own will a male without
blemish, of the beeves, of the sheep, or of the goats.
20 *But* whatsoever hath a blemish, *that* shall ye
not offer: for it shall not be acceptable for you.
21 And whosoever offereth a sacrifice of peace
offerings unto the LORD to accomplish *his* vow,
or a freewill offering in beeves or sheep, it shall be
perfect to be accepted; there shall be no blemish
therein.

---

perfect Priest, the Lord Jesus Christ. Christ alone was free from blemish without any spot of imperfection, so all of these personal restrictions on the Old Testament imperfect priesthood were means of showing the absolute necessity of the Priest to come. Worship the perfect High Priest (Heb. 3:1–6)!

2. Although they were imperfect, the priests had to guard themselves so as not to distort any more the One they served and represented. So modern-day ministers, elders, and deacons must live beyond reproach so as not to obscure the One they serve and represent (1 Tim. 3). The example of God's servants is important. As chief men among His people (Lev. 21:4), people will look to them. How can you better reflect the image of Christ to those around you?

Chapter 22: ***The Lord commands Moses that the priests must honor His holiness by rightly handling the holy things of the tabernacle.***

22:2 *separate.* Deal respectfully or treat with awe. *profane.* Treat as common or ordinary. *hallow.* Consecrate or set apart as holy.

22:3 *uncleanness upon him.* State of ceremonial uncleanness, disqualifying him from priestly duty.

22:4 *leper.* Person suffering from some kind of skin disorder. *running issue.* Some kind of discharge.

22:6 *soul.* Person (v. 11).

22:10 *stranger.* Unauthorized person, perhaps a foreigner (v. 25). *sojourner.* Resident alien. Food allotted to the priests is only for his and his family's use.

22:14 *unwittingly.* Unknowingly; the Hebrew refers to an unintentional mistake. Restitution is to be made by an ordinary Israelite who eats consecrated food.

22:15 *profane.* Treat the holy as common or ordinary.

22:16 *suffer them to bear the iniquity of trespass.* Literally, "cause them to bear or endure the guilt or punishment of the trespass."

22:19 *beeves.* Cattle.

22:21–30 *perfect to be accepted.* Sacrifices for God must be without defects, not from a wrong source, nor of the wrong

22 Blind, or broken, or maimed, or having a wen,
or scurvy, or scabbed, ye shall not offer these unto
the LORD, nor make an offering by fire of them
upon the altar unto the LORD.
23 Either a bullock or a lamb that hath any thing
superfluous or lacking in his parts, that mayest
thou offer *for* a freewill offering; but for a vow it
shall not be accepted.
24 Ye shall not offer unto the LORD that which
is bruised, or crushed, or broken, or cut; neither
shall ye make *any offering thereof* in your land.
25 Neither from a stranger's hand shall ye offer
the bread of your God of any of these; because
their corruption *is* in them, *and* blemishes *be* in
them: they shall not be accepted for you.
26 ¶ And the LORD spake unto Moses, saying,
27 When a bullock, or a sheep, or a goat, is
brought forth, then it shall be seven days under
the dam; and from the eighth day and thenceforth
it shall be accepted for an offering made by fire
unto the LORD.
28 And *whether it be* cow or ewe, ye shall not kill
it and her young both in one day.
29 And when ye will offer a sacrifice of thanks-
giving unto the LORD, offer *it* at your own will.
30 On the same day it shall be eaten up; ye shall
leave none of it until the morrow: I *am* the LORD.
31 Therefore shall ye keep my commandments,
and do them: I *am* the LORD.
32 Neither shall ye profane my holy name; but I
will be hallowed among the children of Israel: I
am the LORD which hallow you,
33 That brought you out of the land of Egypt, to
be your God: I *am* the LORD.

CHAPTER 23

AND the LORD spake unto Moses, saying,
2 Speak unto the children of Israel, and say unto
them, *Concerning* the feasts of the LORD, which ye
shall proclaim *to be* holy convocations, *even* these
are my feasts.
3 Six days shall work be done: but the seventh day
is the sabbath of rest, an holy convocation; ye shall
do no work *therein*: it *is* the sabbath of the LORD
in all your dwellings.
4 ¶ These *are* the feasts of the LORD, *even* holy con-
vocations, which ye shall proclaim in their seasons.
5 In the fourteenth *day* of the first month at even
is the LORD'S passover.
6 And on the fifteenth day of the same month
is the feast of unleavened bread unto the LORD:
seven days ye must eat unleavened bread.
7 In the first day ye shall have an holy convoca-
tion: ye shall do no servile work therein.
8 But ye shall offer an offering made by fire unto
the LORD seven days: in the seventh day *is* an holy
convocation: ye shall do no servile work *therein*.
9 ¶ And the LORD spake unto Moses, saying,
10 Speak unto the children of Israel, and say unto
them, When ye be come into the land which I
give unto you, and shall reap the harvest thereof,
then ye shall bring a sheaf of the firstfruits of your
harvest unto the priest:
11 And he shall wave the sheaf before the LORD,
to be accepted for you: on the morrow after the
sabbath the priest shall wave it.
12 And ye shall offer that day when ye wave the
sheaf an he lamb without blemish of the first year
for a burnt offering unto the LORD.

kind, and must be offered in the right way.

22:22 *wen.* Malignant sore.

22:27 *dam.* Literally, "mother."

22:32 *profane.* Pollute or defile by treating as common. These regulations are to prevent the ultimate dishonor to God. *hallowed.* Set apart, regarded as distinct from the ordinary or mundane.

22:33 Redemption is the basis for holiness.

Thoughts for Personal/Family Worship: Chapter 22

1. **All believers are priests in Christ (1 Peter 2:5,9). They owe it to their God to be clean and abstain from all appearance of evil (1 Thess. 5:22). Those that belong to the Lord in this special relationship have a responsibility to behave differently and separately from the norms of the world. They must only offer their best to God—their wholehearted devotion. How should the knowledge that he or she is a priest shape a Christian's life?**
2. **That the Old Testament priests had to be free from outward blemish (v. 21) points to and anticipates the ideal Priest, our Lord Jesus, who alone is free from any inner or moral defect, and whose sacrifice, being perfect, perfects us (Heb. 10:14). When you see your spiritual blemishes, how can you look to Him, who is the righteousness of God for sinners?**

THE SABBATH AND THE SACRED CALENDAR (23:1–44)

Chapter 23: *The Lord gives Moses instructions about the feasts of Israel.*

The Sabbath (23:1–3)

23:2 *holy convocations.* Sacred assemblies to which all Israel was summoned (the word occurs throughout the chapter). This encourages unity.

23:3 *the sabbath of rest.* Literally, "a sabbath of sabbath observance," referring to the weekly Sabbath (the fourth commandment). The Hebrew term *sabbath* means, "cessation." From creation to the resurrection of Christ, the weekly Sabbath was the seventh day in imitation of God ceasing His creative work. From the resurrection, the weekly Sabbath is the first day celebrating Christ's finished work and the new creation. See Isa. 58:13 for guidelines of observance.

The Passover and Unleavened Bread (23:4–8)

23:5 *the first month.* This was Nisan, in the spring, commemorating the exodus of God's people from Egypt.

23:6 *feast of unleavened bread.* Commemorating leaving Egypt when the people did not have time to make their bread rise because of their hasty exit from Egypt.

23:7 *servile work.* Routine labors of life (throughout the chapter).

The Firstfruits (23:9–14)

23:10–11 *the sheaf.* A bundle of sheaves or small heap of cut grain representing all the harvest. It was waved and dedicated to God, to show He had given it all to them.

13 And the meat offering thereof *shall be* two
tenth deals of fine flour mingled with oil, an
offering made by fire unto the LORD *for* a sweet
savour: and the drink offering thereof *shall be* of
wine, the fourth *part* of an hin.
14 And ye shall eat neither bread, nor parched
corn, nor green ears, until the selfsame day that ye
have brought an offering unto your God: *it shall
be* a statute for ever throughout your generations
in all your dwellings.
15 ¶ And ye shall count unto you from the
morrow after the sabbath, from the day that ye
brought the sheaf of the wave offering; seven
sabbaths shall be complete:
16 Even unto the morrow after the seventh
sabbath shall ye number fifty days; and ye shall
offer a new meat offering unto the LORD.
17 Ye shall bring out of your habitations two
wave loaves of two tenth deals: they shall be of
fine flour; they shall be baken with leaven; *they are*
the firstfruits unto the LORD.
18 And ye shall offer with the bread seven lambs
without blemish of the first year, and one young
bullock, and two rams: they shall be *for* a burnt
offering unto the LORD, with their meat offering,
and their drink offerings, *even* an offering made
by fire, of sweet savour unto the LORD.
19 Then ye shall sacrifice one kid of the goats for
a sin offering, and two lambs of the first year for a
sacrifice of peace offerings.
20 And the priest shall wave them with the bread
of the firstfruits *for* a wave offering before the
LORD, with the two lambs: they shall be holy to
the LORD for the priest.
21 And ye shall proclaim on the selfsame day, *that*
it may be an holy convocation unto you: ye shall
do no servile work *therein: it shall be* a statute
for ever in all your dwellings throughout your
generations.
22 ¶ And when ye reap the harvest of your land,
thou shalt not make clean riddance of the corners
of thy field when thou reapest, neither shalt thou
gather any gleaning of thy harvest: thou shalt
leave them unto the poor, and to the stranger: I
am the LORD your God.
23 ¶ And the LORD spake unto Moses, saying,
24 Speak unto the children of Israel, saying, In
the seventh month, in the first *day* of the month,
shall ye have a sabbath, a memorial of blowing of
trumpets, an holy convocation.
25 Ye shall do no servile work *therein*: but ye shall
offer an offering made by fire unto the LORD.
26 ¶ And the LORD spake unto Moses, saying,
27 Also on the tenth *day* of this seventh month
there shall be a day of atonement: it shall be an
holy convocation unto you; and ye shall afflict
your souls, and offer an offering made by fire
unto the LORD.
28 And ye shall do no work in that same day: for
it *is* a day of atonement, to make an atonement for
you before the LORD your God.
29 For whatsoever soul *it be* that shall not be
afflicted in that same day, he shall be cut off from
among his people.
30 And whatsoever soul *it be* that doeth any work
in that same day, the same soul will I destroy from
among his people.
31 Ye shall do no manner of work: *it shall be* a
statute for ever throughout your generations in
all your dwellings.
32 It *shall be* unto you a sabbath of rest, and ye
shall afflict your souls: in the ninth *day* of the
month at even, from even unto even, shall ye
celebrate your sabbath.
33 ¶ And the LORD spake unto Moses, saying,
34 Speak unto the children of Israel, saying, The
fifteenth day of this seventh month *shall be* the
feast of tabernacles *for* seven days unto the LORD.
35 On the first day *shall be* an holy convocation:
ye shall do no servile work *therein*.
36 Seven days ye shall offer an offering made by
fire unto the LORD: on the eighth day shall be an
holy convocation unto you; and ye shall offer an
offering made by fire unto the LORD: it *is* a solemn
assembly; *and* ye shall do no servile work *therein*.
37 These *are* the feasts of the LORD, which ye shall
proclaim *to be* holy convocations, to offer an of-
fering made by fire unto the LORD, a burnt of-
fering, and a meat offering, a sacrifice, and drink
offerings, every thing upon his day:
38 Beside the sabbaths of the LORD, and beside
your gifts, and beside all your vows, and beside all
your freewill offerings, which ye give unto the LORD.
39 Also in the fifteenth day of the seventh month,

23:13 *deals.* Parts. *hin.* Approximately one and a half gallons.
23:14 *And ye shall eat neither.* None for themselves until God had His firstfruits, in recognition that God is the source of daily sustenance. He supplies the daily bread.

The Feast of Weeks or Pentecost (23:15–22)

23:15–16 *count unto you from the morrow after the sabbath ... fifty days.* The Feast of Weeks at harvest end, when the crops were gathered in. This is Pentecost, from the Greek word for "fifty."
23:22 *clean riddance.* A complete harvest or gathering in.

The Blowing of Trumpets (23:23–25)

23:24 *blowing of trumpets.* A series of blasts on ram's horns, to call the people together for sacred assembly and rest.

The Day of Atonement (23:26–32)

23:27 *day of atonement.* The greatest of all the annual feasts (ch. 16). *afflict your souls.* An idiom for fasting.
23:32 *sabbath of rest.* That this occurred yearly from evening to evening on the ninth to tenth day of the month illustrates that sabbath does not necessarily refer to the seventh day (v. 39). The day of the week would vary from year to year.

when ye have gathered in the fruit of the land, ye
shall keep a feast unto the LORD seven days: on the
first day *shall be* a sabbath, and on the eighth day
shall be a sabbath.
40 And ye shall take you on the first day the
boughs of goodly trees, branches of palm trees,
and the boughs of thick trees, and willows of the
brook; and ye shall rejoice before the LORD your
God seven days.
41 And ye shall keep it a feast unto the LORD
seven days in the year. *It shall be* a statute for ever
in your generations: ye shall celebrate it in the
seventh month.
42 Ye shall dwell in booths seven days; all that are
Israelites born shall dwell in booths:
43 That your generations may know that I made
the children of Israel to dwell in booths, when I
brought them out of the land of Egypt: I *am* the
LORD your God.
44 And Moses declared unto the children of Israel
the feasts of the LORD.

CHAPTER 24

AND the LORD spake unto Moses, saying,
2 Command the children of Israel, that they
bring unto thee pure oil olive beaten for the light,
to cause the lamps to burn continually.
3 Without the vail of the testimony, in the tab-
ernacle of the congregation, shall Aaron order it
from the evening unto the morning before the
LORD continually: *it shall be* a statute for ever in
your generations.
4 He shall order the lamps upon the pure candle-
stick before the LORD continually.
5 ¶ And thou shalt take fine flour, and bake twelve
cakes thereof: two tenth deals shall be in one cake.
6 And thou shalt set them in two rows, six on a
row, upon the pure table before the LORD.
7 And thou shalt put pure frankincense upon
each row, that it may be on the bread for a memo-
rial, *even* an offering made by fire unto the LORD.
8 Every sabbath he shall set it in order before the
LORD continually, *being taken* from the children
of Israel by an everlasting covenant.
9 And it shall be Aaron's and his sons'; and they
shall eat it in the holy place: for it *is* most holy unto
him of the offerings of the LORD made by fire by a
perpetual statute.
10 ¶ And the son of an Israelitish woman, whose
father *was* an Egyptian, went out among the chil-
dren of Israel: and this son of the Israelitish *woman*
and a man of Israel strove together in the camp;
11 And the Israelitish woman's son blasphemed the
name *of the LORD*, and cursed. And they brought
him unto Moses: (and his mother's name *was* She-
lomith, the daughter of Dibri, of the tribe of Dan:)
12 And they put him in ward, that the mind of
the LORD might be shewed them.
13 And the LORD spake unto Moses, saying,
14 Bring forth him that hath cursed without the
camp; and let all that heard *him* lay their hands

The Feast of Tabernacles or Booths (23:33–44)

23:40 *boughs*. Literally, "fruit."
23:43 *booths*. Tents. Commemorating their life in the wilderness when they lived in tents before inheriting Canaan and settled dwellings.

Thoughts for Personal/Family Worship: Chapter 23

1. **Whereas the weekly Sabbath belongs to the moral law and is thus timelessly relevant, the feasts are part of the ceremonial law and thus are temporary pictures or object lessons of some aspect of gospel truth, all of which are things to think about when keeping the weekly Sabbath. Notice in v. 3 "in all your dwellings"—we must observe the Sabbath at home as well as in the assembly. How do we keep it as "the sabbath of rest"? How do we keep it as "the sabbath of the LORD"?**
2. **Worship the Lord as you consider the ways He fulfilled the feasts. The Passover is fulfilled in the Lord's Supper (1 Cor. 5:7), that we might not forget the grace that redeemed us, by an infinitely greater Lamb without blemish (1 Cor. 11:24–25). The firstfruits of the harvest was for God, then the rest for His people. A type of resurrection—Christ first, afterward we all shall follow (1 Cor. 15:20). That this occurred the day following the Sabbath points to the day of Christ's resurrection. The Feast of Weeks is the New Testament day of Pentecost. Similarly, fifty days from the day after the Sabbath means Pentecost lands on the first day of the week—the new day for the Sabbath (Matt. 28:1–6). Thus, the day of Pentecost in Acts 2 fell on the Lord's Day. What more appropriate day for the giving of the Spirit (Acts 2:33; Rev. 1:10)? The blowing of trumpets is a type of gospel preaching which is always music to the convicted sinner's ears (Ps. 89:15). It calls us to rest in Christ (Matt. 11:28–30) and assemble with His people (Gen. 49:10; Acts 2:41–42).**

SOME REMAINING MATTERS (24:1—27:34)

Chapter 24: *God's gives additional instructions about proper worship and administering His justice.*

The Holy Lamps and Shewbread (24:1–9)

24:2 *pure oil olive beaten*. The olives were pounded, not pressed to produce the best oil.
24:3–4 *order it from the evening unto the morning*. Preparations were made to ensure continuous burning.
24:5 *twelve cakes*. Ring-shaped bread to be placed on the table. It was called "shewbread," literally, the "bread of presence" (Ex. 25:30). *two tenth deals*. Two-tenth parts.
24:7 *pure frankincense*. An aromatic gum resin that burned as a fragrant incense to signify that God accepted it.
24:9 *And it shall be Aaron's and his sons*. To eat when replaced by fresh loaves each Sabbath.

The Punishment of a Blasphemer (24:10–23)

24:11 *blasphemed*. Slandered or uttered a curse against.
24:12 *in ward*. In a guardhouse under custody. *that the mind of the LORD might be shewed them*. Literally, "to declare to them distinctly the mouth (word) of the Lord."
24:14–15 *stone him*. God clarifies the situation, producing a

upon his head, and let all the congregation stone him.
15 And thou shalt speak unto the children of Israel, saying, Whosoever curseth his God shall bear his sin.
16 And he that blasphemeth the name of the LORD, he shall surely be put to death, *and* all the congregation shall certainly stone him: as well the stranger, as he that is born in the land, when he blasphemeth the name *of the LORD*, shall be put to death.
17 ¶ And he that killeth any man shall surely be put to death.
18 And he that killeth a beast shall make it good; beast for beast.
19 And if a man cause a blemish in his neighbour; as he hath done, so shall it be done to him;
20 Breach for breach, eye for eye, tooth for tooth: as he hath caused a blemish in a man, so shall it be done to him *again*.
21 And he that killeth a beast, he shall restore it: and he that killeth a man, he shall be put to death.
22 Ye shall have one manner of law, as well for the stranger, as for one of your own country: for I *am* the LORD your God.
23 ¶ And Moses spake to the children of Israel, that they should bring forth him that had cursed out of the camp, and stone him with stones. And the children of Israel did as the LORD commanded Moses.

CHAPTER 25

AND the LORD spake unto Moses in mount Sinai, saying,
2 Speak unto the children of Israel, and say unto them, When ye come into the land which I give you, then shall the land keep a sabbath unto the LORD.
3 Six years thou shalt sow thy field, and six years thou shalt prune thy vineyard, and gather in the fruit thereof;
4 But in the seventh year shall be a sabbath of rest unto the land, a sabbath for the LORD: thou shalt neither sow thy field, nor prune thy vineyard.
5 That which groweth of its own accord of thy harvest thou shalt not reap, neither gather the grapes of thy vine undressed: *for* it is a year of rest unto the land.
6 And the sabbath of the land shall be meat for you; for thee, and for thy servant, and for thy maid, and for thy hired servant, and for thy stranger that sojourneth with thee,
7 And for thy cattle, and for the beast that *are* in thy land, shall all the increase thereof be meat.
8 ¶ And thou shalt number seven sabbaths of years unto thee, seven times seven years; and the space of the seven sabbaths of years shall be unto thee forty and nine years.
9 Then shalt thou cause the trumpet of the jubile to sound on the tenth *day* of the seventh month, in the day of atonement shall ye make the trumpet sound throughout all your land.
10 And ye shall hallow the fiftieth year, and proclaim liberty throughout *all* the land unto all the inhabitants thereof: it shall be a jubile unto you; and ye shall return every man unto his possession, and ye shall return every man unto his family.

---

case law for the future (v. 22). This illustrates the universal applicability of the moral law, for his father was an Egyptian. *bear his sin*. Bear the guilt and punishment due the sin.

24:17 *surely be put to death*. Murder demands a just punishment (Gen. 9:6; Ex. 21:12,23).

24:18–20 The principle of *lex talionis*, the law of retaliation, is seen here. The penalty fits the crime. For lesser offenses, a just and equitable penalty was exacted. This principle was to guide civil authorities in executing justice; it was not intended for personal vendettas. Christ corrects the abuse of this principle (Matt. 5:38–42).

24:19 *blemish*. Injury.

24:20 *breach*. Fracture.

Thoughts for Personal/Family Worship: Chapter 24

1. **Attention to two features of the tabernacle suggest aspects of worship. The candlestick represents Christ, who is our Light (Luke 2:32). It also represents His churches in a dark world (Phil. 2:15; Rev. 1:13,20). Some friends asked Robert Murray M'Cheyne about preparing sermons. He said, "Beaten oil—beaten oil for the lamps of the sanctuary" (cf. Ex. 27:20; Lev. 24:2). Diligent and thorough preparation, under God, will produce enlightening sermons. The loaves symbolized the Lord's presence with His people, and His provision for them. He is our "staff of life," who always satisfies our needs. Worship our Lord as the Light of the World and the Bread of Life.**
2. **The fact that the half-Israelite was subject to the Ten Commandments indicates their application to *all* men. The moral law summarized in the Ten Commandments is universal, timeless, and inflexible. The particular penalties for breaking the law were part of the civil laws given as specific applications of the moral law suited for that society. Whereas the moral law that defines God's unchanging standards retain their relevance, the applications vary. God has ordained governments for the administration of His justice (Rom. 13). Pray for those in authority over you (1 Tim. 2:1–3).**

Chapter 25: *The Lord gives instructions to Moses about the Sabbath year and the year of Jubilee.*

The Sabbatical and Jubilee Years (25:1–55)

25:2 *land keep a sabbath*. No sowing or harvesting during this year-long rest for the land. Even servants and cattle rest.

25:5 *own accord*. What has seeded itself and needs harvesting. *undressed*. Untrimmed with a free-growing crop. All labor is suspended.

25:6–7 *meat*. Food of any kind. Meaning, what is spontaneously produced can be eaten by people and livestock.

25:8 *forty and nine years*. The fiftieth year is a sabbath. It immediately follows the land's seventh cycle of sabbatical years.

25:9 *jubile*. Literally, "blast" and is translated the "joyful sound" (Ps. 89:15).

25:10 *liberty throughout all the land*. Mortgaged property

11 A jubile shall that fiftieth year be unto you: ye
shall not sow, neither reap that which groweth of
itself in it, nor gather *the grapes* in it of thy vine
undressed.
12 For it *is* the jubile; it shall be holy unto you: ye
shall eat the increase thereof out of the field.
13 In the year of this jubile ye shall return every
man unto his possession.
14 And if thou sell ought unto thy neighbour, or
buyest *ought* of thy neighbour's hand, ye shall not
oppress one another:
15 According to the number of years after the ju-
bile thou shalt buy of thy neighbour, *and* accord-
ing unto the number of years of the fruits he shall
sell unto thee:
16 According to the multitude of years thou shalt
increase the price thereof, and according to the
fewness of years thou shalt diminish the price of
it: for *according* to the number *of the years* of the
fruits doth he sell unto thee.
17 Ye shall not therefore oppress one another; but
thou shalt fear thy God: for I *am* the LORD your
God.
18 ¶ Wherefore ye shall do my statutes, and keep
my judgments, and do them; and ye shall dwell in
the land in safety.
19 And the land shall yield her fruit, and ye shall
eat your fill, and dwell therein in safety.
20 And if ye shall say, What shall we eat the sev-
enth year? behold, we shall not sow, nor gather in
our increase:
21 Then I will command my blessing upon you
in the sixth year, and it shall bring forth fruit for
three years.
22 And ye shall sow the eighth year, and eat *yet* of
old fruit until the ninth year; until her fruits come
in ye shall eat *of* the old *store*.
23 ¶ The land shall not be sold for ever: for the
land *is* mine; for ye *are* strangers and sojourners
with me.
24 And in all the land of your possession ye shall
grant a redemption for the land.
25 ¶ If thy brother be waxen poor, and hath sold
away *some* of his possession, and if any of his
kin come to redeem it, then shall he redeem that
which his brother sold.
26 And if the man have none to redeem it, and
himself be able to redeem it;
27 Then let him count the years of the sale thereof,
and restore the overplus unto the man to whom
he sold it; that he may return unto his possession.
28 But if he be not able to restore *it* to him, then
that which is sold shall remain in the hand of him
that hath bought it until the year of jubile: and in
the jubile it shall go out, and he shall return unto
his possession.
29 And if a man sell a dwelling house in a walled
city, then he may redeem it within a whole year
after it is sold; *within* a full year may he redeem it.
30 And if it be not redeemed within the space of
a full year, then the house that *is* in the walled city
shall be established for ever to him that bought it
throughout his generations: it shall not go out in
the jubile.
31 But the houses of the villages which have no
wall round about them shall be counted as the
fields of the country: they may be redeemed, and
they shall go out in the jubile.
32 Notwithstanding the cities of the Levites, *and*
the houses of the cities of their possession, may
the Levites redeem at any time.
33 And if a man purchase of the Levites, then the
house that was sold, and the city of his possession,
shall go out in *the year of* jubile: for the houses
of the cities of the Levites *are* their possession
among the children of Israel.
34 But the field of the suburbs of their cities may
not be sold; for it *is* their perpetual possession.
35 ¶ And if thy brother be waxen poor, and fallen
in decay with thee; then thou shalt relieve him:
yea, though he be a stranger, or a sojourner; that
he may live with thee.
36 Take thou no usury of him, or increase: but
fear thy God; that thy brother may live with thee.

---

were to be restored. Men who sold themselves to servitude because of poverty were to be freed. *jubile.* Remission or release announced with the blowing of a ram's horn. A different word from v. 9 (occurs throughout the chapter).

25:11–12 *ye shall not sow, neither reap.* The land was to enjoy a release from yielding produce for another year in addition to the sabbath year.

25:14 *not oppress one another.* The Hebrew means "to mistreat" (v. 17). The full value of anything sold was to be given back again.

25:15–16 *according unto the number of years of the fruits.* When land is sold and returned. The nearness of the Jubilee year would affect the amount of crops it could yield. To treat others fairly, its value must be estimated accordingly.

25:20–22 *What shall we eat?* Obedience means God will miraculously provide over three years.

25:25 *waxen poor.* Impoverished (vv. 35,39). *kin.* The near kinsman or kinsman-redeemer who was obligated to act for his relative.

25:26–27 *able to redeem it.* Because his finances have changed for the better. An evenhanded settlement must be made.

25:28 *not able to restore it.* In this case, the Jubilee would ensure it returns to him.

25:29–30 *sell a dwelling house in a walled city.* A special case; city dwellings were not subject to the same law.

25:32–34 *the cities of the Levites.* The exception because they had scattered towns as their possession, to perform their duties throughout the land.

25:34 *suburbs.* Pastureland or a strip of land outside a city's walls under the jurisdiction of the city.

25:35 *fallen in decay.* Literally, "his hand is shaky," an idiom for being in economic stress.

25:36 *usury.* Interest.

37 Thou shalt not give him thy money upon
usury, nor lend him thy victuals for increase.
38 I *am* the LORD your God, which brought you
forth out of the land of Egypt, to give you the land
of Canaan, *and* to be your God.
39 ¶ And if thy brother *that dwelleth* by thee be
waxen poor, and be sold unto thee; thou shalt not
compel him to serve as a bondservant:
40 *But* as an hired servant, *and* as a sojourner, he
shall be with thee, *and* shall serve thee unto the
year of jubile:
41 And *then* shall he depart from thee, *both* he
and his children with him, and shall return unto
his own family, and unto the possession of his
fathers shall he return.
42 For they *are* my servants, which I brought
forth out of the land of Egypt: they shall not be
sold as bondmen.
43 Thou shalt not rule over him with rigour; but
shalt fear thy God.
44 Both thy bondmen, and thy bondmaids,
which thou shalt have, *shall be* of the heathen that
are round about you; of them shall ye buy bond-
men and bondmaids.
45 Moreover of the children of the strangers that
do sojourn among you, of them shall ye buy, and
of their families that *are* with you, which they be-
gat in your land: and they shall be your possession.
46 And ye shall take them as an inheritance for
your children after you, to inherit *them for* a pos-
session; they shall be your bondmen for ever: but
over your brethren the children of Israel, ye shall
not rule one over another with rigour.
47 ¶ And if a sojourner or stranger wax rich by thee,
and thy brother *that dwelleth* by him wax poor, and
sell himself unto the stranger *or* sojourner by thee,
or to the stock of the stranger's family:
48 After that he is sold he may be redeemed again;
one of his brethren may redeem him:
49 Either his uncle, or his uncle's son, may re-
deem him, or *any* that is nigh of kin unto him of
his family may redeem him; or if he be able, he
may redeem himself.
50 And he shall reckon with him that bought him
from the year that he was sold to him unto the
year of jubile: and the price of his sale shall be ac-
cording unto the number of years, according to
the time of an hired servant shall it be with him.
51 If *there be* yet many years *behind*, according
unto them he shall give again the price of his re-
demption out of the money that he was bought for.
52 And if there remain but few years unto the
year of jubile, then he shall count with him, *and*
according unto his years shall he give him again
the price of his redemption.
53 *And* as a yearly hired servant shall he be with
him: *and the other* shall not rule with rigour over
him in thy sight.
54 And if he be not redeemed in these *years*, then
he shall go out in the year of jubile, *both* he, and
his children with him.
55 For unto me the children of Israel *are* servants;
they *are* my servants whom I brought forth out of
the land of Egypt: I *am* the LORD your God.

CHAPTER 26

YE shall make you no idols nor graven image,
neither rear you up a standing image, neither
shall ye set up *any* image of stone in your land, to
bow down unto it: for I *am* the LORD your God.
2 ¶ Ye shall keep my sabbaths, and reverence my
sanctuary: I *am* the LORD.
3 ¶ If ye walk in my statutes, and keep my com-
mandments, and do them;
4 Then I will give you rain in due season, and the
land shall yield her increase, and the trees of the
field shall yield their fruit.
5 And your threshing shall reach unto the vin-
tage, and the vintage shall reach unto the sowing

25:37 *victuals.* Food.

25:38 Redemption from Egypt is the grateful motive for kindness and fairness to others.

25:47–55 *if a sojourner or stranger wax rich by thee.* If a Hebrew has indentured himself to a non-Hebrew in Canaan. The Hebrew still retains his right of redemption. And the last resort is the Jubilee when he can go out free.

Thoughts for Personal/Family Worship: Chapter 25

1. **The land lying fallow each seventh year helps it to replenish and produce more the following year. The Lord's commands are wise and beneficial (Rom. 12:2). Also, if God gives the land a sabbath, He owns it, not the Israelites. All we have is entrusted to us as stewards. How should it change our attitude and use of our possessions when we know that God is the Owner, and we are just servants managing His property?**
2. **The year of Jubilee foreshadows the blessings of the gospel. Its trumpet was sounded immediately after the Day of Atonement. When sin is put away, God's favor makes joyful blessings abound toward us (Ps. 103:1–5; Isa. 61:1–3). How should we respond (Isa. 61:3)?**
3. **Throughout the chapter, the responsibility of the near kinsman to act in behalf of his needy relative is in focus. In the most sublime sense, the Lord Jesus is our kinsman-redeemer, who does for us what needs to be done for our welfare. He has the relational right, for through the covenant and incarnation he calls us brothers (Heb. 2:11–14). He has the resources and the love to release us and make us His own (Eph. 3:8; 5:25). According to these same verses, what responsibilities do we have as His redeemed?**

Chapter 26: *God declares blessings for obedience and curses for disobedience.*

Promises and Warnings (26:1–46)

26:4 *rain in due season.* The early and latter rain, autumn and spring. Essential for good harvests.

time: and ye shall eat your bread to the full, and
dwell in your land safely.
6 And I will give peace in the land, and ye shall lie
down, and none shall make *you* afraid: and I will
rid evil beasts out of the land, neither shall the
sword go through your land.
7 And ye shall chase your enemies, and they shall
fall before you by the sword.
8 And five of you shall chase an hundred, and an
hundred of you shall put ten thousand to flight:
and your enemies shall fall before you by the sword.
9 For I will have respect unto you, and make you
fruitful, and multiply you, and establish my cov-
enant with you.
10 And ye shall eat old store, and bring forth the
old because of the new.
11 And I will set my tabernacle among you: and
my soul shall not abhor you.
12 And I will walk among you, and will be your
God, and ye shall be my people.
13 I *am* the LORD your God, which brought you
forth out of the land of Egypt, that ye should not
be their bondmen; and I have broken the bands of
your yoke, and made you go upright.
14 ¶ But if ye will not hearken unto me, and will
not do all these commandments;
15 And if ye shall despise my statutes, or if your
soul abhor my judgments, so that ye will not do
all my commandments, *but* that ye break my
covenant:
16 I also will do this unto you; I will even appoint
over you terror, consumption, and the burning
ague, that shall consume the eyes, and cause sor-
row of heart: and ye shall sow your seed in vain,
for your enemies shall eat it.
17 And I will set my face against you, and ye shall
be slain before your enemies: they that hate you
shall reign over you; and ye shall flee when none
pursueth you.
18 And if ye will not yet for all this hearken unto
me, then I will punish you seven times more for
your sins.
19 And I will break the pride of your power; and
I will make your heaven as iron, and your earth
as brass:
20 And your strength shall be spent in vain: for
your land shall not yield her increase, neither
shall the trees of the land yield their fruits.
21 ¶ And if ye walk contrary unto me, and will
not hearken unto me; I will bring seven times
more plagues upon you according to your sins.
22 I will also send wild beasts among you, which
shall rob you of your children, and destroy your
cattle, and make you few in number; and your
high ways shall be desolate.
23 And if ye will not be reformed by me by these
things, but will walk contrary unto me;
24 Then will I also walk contrary unto you, and
will punish you yet seven times for your sins.
25 And I will bring a sword upon you, that shall
avenge the quarrel of *my* covenant: and when ye
are gathered together within your cities, I will
send the pestilence among you; and ye shall be
delivered into the hand of the enemy.
26 *And* when I have broken the staff of your
bread, ten women shall bake your bread in one
oven, and they shall deliver *you* your bread again
by weight: and ye shall eat, and not be satisfied.
27 And if ye will not for all this hearken unto me,
but walk contrary unto me;
28 Then I will walk contrary unto you also in
fury; and I, even I, will chastise you seven times
for your sins.
29 And ye shall eat the flesh of your sons, and the
flesh of your daughters shall ye eat.
30 And I will destroy your high places, and cut
down your images, and cast your carcases upon the
carcases of your idols, and my soul shall abhor you.
31 And I will make your cities waste, and bring
your sanctuaries unto desolation, and I will not
smell the savour of your sweet odours.
32 And I will bring the land into desolation: and
your enemies which dwell therein shall be aston-
ished at it.

26:5 *vintage.* Grape harvest. *dwell in your land safely.* God would be their security against enemy nations round them (cf. 1 Kings 4:25).
26:6 *evil beasts.* Dangerous wild animals or beasts of prey.
26:9 *I will have respect unto you.* Literally, "I will turn toward you or face you." *make you fruitful, and multiply.* The original blessing of creation (Gen. 1:28).
26:10 *old store.* Food from the previous harvest.
26:11 *my tabernacle.* Refers generally to the fact that God dwelt with His people, rather than specifically to the place where worship was conducted. *my soul.* An expression designating God's person, equivalent to the pronoun "I."
26:13 *upright.* Walk in an upright position in contrast to having been bowed down in bondage. This verse is a statement of liberation.
26:16 *I also will do this unto you.* As blessings accompanied obedience, so certainly curses accompanied disobedience. *consumption.* A wasting disease. *burning ague.* Fever.
26:17 *set my face against you.* The greatest calamity (in contrast with Num. 6:22–27).
26:18 *I will punish you seven times.* Figure of speech to denote the complete and appropriate chastisement (vv. 21, 24,28).
26:19 *pride of your power.* Your presumption of strength. *heaven as iron, . . . earth as brass.* No rain and no produce will grow (1 Kings 17:1).
26:23 *reformed.* Chastened or disciplined.
26:25 *quarrel.* Literally, "vengeance."
26:26 *the staff of your bread.* Refers to a device for stacking bread to keep it away from mice.
26:29 *eat the flesh of your sons.* While besieged by enemies, cities face starvation and it can result in atrocities as in Jehoram's time (2 Kings 6:28–29).
26:30 *my soul.* Equivalent to the personal pronoun "I."

33 And I will scatter you among the heathen, and
will draw out a sword after you: and your land
shall be desolate, and your cities waste.
34 Then shall the land enjoy her sabbaths, as long
as it lieth desolate, and ye *be* in your enemies'
land; *even* then shall the land rest, and enjoy her
sabbaths.
35 As long as it lieth desolate it shall rest; because it
did not rest in your sabbaths, when ye dwelt upon it.
36 And upon them that are left *alive* of you I will
send a faintness into their hearts in the lands of
their enemies; and the sound of a shaken leaf shall
chase them; and they shall flee, as fleeing from a
sword; and they shall fall when none pursueth.
37 And they shall fall one upon another, as it were
before a sword, when none pursueth: and ye shall
have no power to stand before your enemies.
38 And ye shall perish among the heathen, and
the land of your enemies shall eat you up.
39 And they that are left of you shall pine away in
their iniquity in your enemies' lands; and also in
the iniquities of their fathers shall they pine away
with them.
40 If they shall confess their iniquity, and the
iniquity of their fathers, with their trespass which
they trespassed against me, and that also they
have walked contrary unto me;
41 And *that* I also have walked contrary unto
them, and have brought them into the land of
their enemies; if then their uncircumcised hearts
be humbled, and they then accept of the punishment of their iniquity:
42 Then will I remember my covenant with
Jacob, and also my covenant with Isaac, and also
my covenant with Abraham will I remember; and
I will remember the land.
43 The land also shall be left of them, and shall
enjoy her sabbaths, while she lieth desolate without them: and they shall accept of the punishment of their iniquity: because, even because they
despised my judgments, and because their soul
abhorred my statutes.
44 And yet for all that, when they be in the land
of their enemies, I will not cast them away, neither
will I abhor them, to destroy them utterly, and to
break my covenant with them: for I *am* the LORD
their God.
45 But I will for their sakes remember the covenant of their ancestors, whom I brought forth
out of the land of Egypt in the sight of the
heathen, that I might be their God: I *am* the LORD.
46 These *are* the statutes and judgments and laws,
which the LORD made between him and the children of Israel in mount Sinai by the hand of Moses.

CHAPTER 27

AND the LORD spake unto Moses, saying,
2 Speak unto the children of Israel, and say unto
them, When a man shall make a singular vow, the
persons *shall be* for the LORD by thy estimation.
3 And thy estimation shall be of the male from
twenty years old even unto sixty years old, even
thy estimation shall be fifty shekels of silver, after
the shekel of the sanctuary.
4 And if it *be* a female, then thy estimation shall
be thirty shekels.
5 And if *it be* from five years old even unto twenty
years old, then thy estimation shall be of the male
twenty shekels, and for the female ten shekels.
6 And if *it be* from a month old even unto five
years old, then thy estimation shall be of the male

26:33 *scatter you among the heathen.* Fulfilled in the Assyrian and Babylonian captivities.
26:34 *the land enjoy her sabbaths.* The land did have seventy sabbatical years while Judah was in the Babylonian captivity (2 Chron. 36:21).
26:41 *uncircumcised hearts.* Inner man (will, emotions, mind) with its old nature opposed to God.
26:44–45 *I will for their sakes remember the covenant.* Though Israel's enjoyment of God's blessing in the land was conditional upon their obedience (18:5; Ex. 19:5), their sin could not ultimately cause God to break His covenant oath with Abraham and his offspring (v. 42; Rom. 11:28–29). Grace prevails over sin.

Thoughts for Personal/Family Worship: Chapter 26

1. **The blessings and curses of the law remind us that God is a righteous Judge who rewards obedience and punishes disobedience. The law threatens sinners with horrifying divine wrath, so that they might flee to the gospel of Christ crucified. Christ won the blessing by His perfect obedience and carried the curse in His death in the place of sinners (Gal. 3:13–14). If you have turned from your sin and trusted in Christ, rejoice that God's blessings are on you and that He will never curse you in His wrath because of what Christ has done (Isa. 54:9–10).**
2. **The warnings of God's law and the afflictions of His providence should motivate us to repentance, turning us away from sin and back to the Lord. If you are not converted, God is using these things to call you to repent and be saved. If you are converted, then God may still discipline you as a Father lovingly disciplines His erring child to bring him back to Himself. This chapter highlights key elements in true repentance: (1) grieving over sin (v. 39); (2) confession of sin (v. 40); (3) humiliation for it (v. 41); (4) acceptance of God's chastening (v. 41); and (5) divine mercy (v. 42). Do you know the reality of this repentance in your experience?**

Chapter 27: *The Lord gives Moses instructions regarding vows.*

Directions Concerning Vows (27:1–34)

27:2 *singular vow.* An exceptional and voluntary one. Perhaps an individual devoting himself to work at the tabernacle or donating some property to the Lord.
27:3 *thy estimation.* A table of penalties if such pledges to God are canceled.
27:5–7 *from five years old.* The amounts charged to redeem the pledges vary according to the relative ability and usefulness of the individuals in the workplace, not their inherent worth.

five shekels of silver, and for the female thy estimation *shall be* three shekels of silver.
7 And if *it be* from sixty years old and above; if *it be* a male, then thy estimation shall be fifteen shekels, and for the female ten shekels.
8 But if he be poorer than thy estimation, then he shall present himself before the priest, and the priest shall value him; according to his ability that vowed shall the priest value him.
9 And if *it be* a beast, whereof men bring an offering unto the LORD, all that *any man* giveth of such unto the LORD shall be holy.
10 He shall not alter it, nor change it, a good for a bad, or a bad for a good: and if he shall at all change beast for beast, then it and the exchange thereof shall be holy.
11 And if *it be* any unclean beast, of which they do not offer a sacrifice unto the LORD, then he shall present the beast before the priest:
12 And the priest shall value it, whether it be good or bad: as thou valuest it, *who art* the priest, so shall it be.
13 But if he will at all redeem it, then he shall add a fifth *part* thereof unto thy estimation.
14 ¶ And when a man shall sanctify his house *to be* holy unto the LORD, then the priest shall estimate it, whether it be good or bad: as the priest shall estimate it, so shall it stand.
15 And if he that sanctified it will redeem his house, then he shall add the fifth *part* of the money of thy estimation unto it, and it shall be his.
16 And if a man shall sanctify unto the LORD *some part* of a field of his possession, then thy estimation shall be according to the seed thereof: an homer of barley seed *shall be valued* at fifty shekels of silver.
17 If he sanctify his field from the year of jubile, according to thy estimation it shall stand.
18 But if he sanctify his field after the jubile, then the priest shall reckon unto him the money according to the years that remain, even unto the year of the jubile, and it shall be abated from thy estimation.
19 And if he that sanctified the field will in any wise redeem it, then he shall add the fifth *part* of the money of thy estimation unto it, and it shall be assured to him.
20 And if he will not redeem the field, or if he have sold the field to another man, it shall not be redeemed any more.
21 But the field, when it goeth out in the jubile, shall be holy unto the LORD, as a field devoted; the possession thereof shall be the priest's.
22 And if *a man* sanctify unto the LORD a field which he hath bought, which *is* not of the fields of his possession;
23 Then the priest shall reckon unto him the worth of thy estimation, *even* unto the year of the jubile: and he shall give thine estimation in that day, *as* a holy thing unto the LORD.
24 In the year of the jubile the field shall return unto him of whom it was bought, *even* to him to whom the possession of the land *did belong*.
25 And all thy estimations shall be according to the shekel of the sanctuary: twenty gerahs shall be the shekel.
26 ¶ Only the firstling of the beasts, which should be the LORD's firstling, no man shall sanctify it; whether *it be* ox, or sheep: it *is* the LORD's.
27 And if *it be* of an unclean beast, then he shall redeem *it* according to thine estimation, and shall add a fifth *part* of it thereto: or if it be not redeemed, then it shall be sold according to thy estimation.
28 Notwithstanding no devoted thing, that a man shall devote unto the LORD of all that he hath, *both* of man and beast, and of the field of his possession, shall be sold or redeemed: every devoted thing *is* most holy unto the LORD.
29 None devoted, which shall be devoted of men, shall be redeemed; *but* shall surely be put to death.
30 And all the tithe of the land, *whether* of the seed of the land, *or* of the fruit of the tree, *is* the LORD's: *it is* holy unto the LORD.
31 And if a man will at all redeem *ought* of his tithes, he shall add thereto the fifth *part* thereof.
32 And concerning the tithe of the herd, or of the flock, *even* of whatsoever passeth under the rod, the tenth shall be holy unto the LORD.
33 He shall not search whether it be good or bad, neither shall he change it: and if he change it at all, then both it and the change thereof shall be holy; it shall not be redeemed.
34 These *are* the commandments, which the LORD commanded Moses for the children of Israel in mount Sinai.

27:9–13 *a beast.* An animal donated. If a lesser beast were substituted, both it and the original animal are forfeited. An unclean animal could be recovered for its value plus 20 percent surcharge.
27:14 *sanctify.* Set apart.
27:16 *homer.* A dry measure equivalent to about nine and a half bushels.
27:26 *the firstling.* This cannot be included because it was set apart for the Lord in the first place (Ex. 13:2).
27:28–29 *devoted.* Dedicated to the Lord for His sovereign use, given to the Lord by a vow that made it irreversibly the Lord's.
27:32 *the rod.* The shepherd's crook by which the flock are numbered (Ps. 23:4; Ezek. 20:37).

Thoughts for Personal/Family Worship: Chapter 27

Beware of rashness in God's service. These people meant well when they vowed but they changed their minds and wanted to redeem their pledges. Much better to consider beforehand, and then follow through with whatever we promise to God (Eccl. 5:2,4). It is easy to act on impulse under pressure. Vows are not a means of bargaining with God. These penalties deter us from doing this. God wants us to be wise as well as zealous. The key point is that God takes vows seriously.

THE LORD
Bless Thee
AND KEEP THEE
THE LORD
MAKE HIS FACE
SHINE
upon thee
AND BE
GRACIOUS UNTO THEE
THE LORD
LIFT UP HIS
Countenance
UPON THEE
&
GIVE THEE
peace

NUMBERS 6:24-26

INTRODUCTION TO THE BOOK OF NUMBERS

Authorship: In Hebrew this book is called, "And He spoke," or, "In the wilderness" (both taken from its first verse). The Greek Septuagint gave it the name "Numbers" due to the focus on the issue of numbering that the book contains. Like the other four books of the Pentateuch, the Mosaic authorship of Numbers has always been unanimously ascribed by the ancient Jews, the custodians of the Old Testament Scriptures. In various Scriptures the term "the law of Moses" is employed, obviously referring to a body of literature that he wrote. An example is 2 Chron. 23:18 where reference is made to the presentation of burnt offerings "as it is written in the law of Moses." Numbers 28 contains much detail about the burnt offering, so we may legitimately conclude that Numbers belongs to "the law of Moses." Furthermore, Christ testifies in John 5:46, "Moses . . . wrote of me," and in v. 47 refers to "his writings." Thus the Savior verifies that Moses was an authentic person; that he was a writer with a plurality of writings ascribed to him; that his writings were extant in New Testament times; that the Jews had access to them; and that He, Christ, was the theme of them. In the light of these examples, we may deduce that Moses wrote Numbers.

Date: The events of Numbers begin in the second month of the second year after the exodus (1:1) and conclude when the nation is opposite Jericho at the end of their wanderings (35:1; 36:13). This would date Numbers between 1445 and 1405 BC. For further discussion of authorship and date, see Introduction to the Pentateuch.

Theme: Divine discipline, direction, and provision for God's people.

Purpose: To trace the transition from the old generation, who refused to enter Canaan, to the new generation, who would inherit the Promised Land, and to show the necessity of faith for following the Lord (ch. 14).

Synopsis: *The Contribution of Numbers to Redemptive Revelation*

Paul's assessment of Hebrew history was that "these things were our examples" and that they "happened unto them for ensamples: and they are written for our admonition, upon whom the ends of the world are come" (1 Cor. 10:6,11). Significantly, most of the events that Paul highlights occurred during the wilderness wanderings recorded in the book of Numbers. Therefore, the relevance of Numbers for the Christian is fixed with apostolic authority. It is an inspired history that teaches more than simple facts; it is replete with spiritual lessons and applications.

The book begins with a record of the Lord's detailed instructions of how the nation was to march into the Promised Land. He set the order of march; He provided the means for sanctified worship; and He promised His presence in the form of the cloud to lead them every step of the way. All they had to do was follow in faith and obedience, but that is exactly what they did not do. The New Testament sums it up this way: "The word preached did not profit them, not being mixed with faith in them that heard it" (Heb. 4:2). They were brought to the very border of blessing but refused to enter because of unbelief (Num. 14). That is a key gospel lesson underscored over and over again in Numbers, that without faith God will not be pleased (Heb. 11:6). The old generation stood as a warning to every other to trust the Lord (Ps. 95:8–11).

Although the wilderness wanderings were disciplinary, they were also gospel sermons. Since saving faith is always objectively placed in Christ, the book of Numbers sets forth the Messiah in many ways. Indeed, Numbers is full of Christ. The tabernacle worship and sacrifices that were offered regularly were picture prophecies of the Lamb without spot and blemish that would take away sin. But in addition there were other vivid pictures. Jesus Himself compared Moses' lifting up of the bronze serpent to His being lifted up on the cross (Num. 21:4–9; John 3:14). The one reversed the curse of the fiery serpent; the other the curse of sin itself. Similarly, the rock from which the water of life flowed is a type of Christ, who was the Rock (1 Cor. 10:4); the daily manna pointed to Christ as the Bread come down from heaven (John 6:31–33). Hebrews 9:13–14 compares the ashes of the red heifer (Num. 19) with the cleansing obtained through Christ's blood. The cities of refuge picture the safety to be found in Christ. Even the forced prophecies of Balaam look to the coming of Christ, the Star and Scepter, who will subdue every nation under His authority. On the one hand, Numbers chronicles a period when Israel was stalled in the desert. But on the other hand, Numbers records great strides in the progression of redemptive revelation.

Outline:

I. Israel at Sinai (1:1—10:10)
  A. Census and Organization of Israel (1:1—4:49)
    1. Numbering of Warriors (1:1–54)
    2. Arrangement of Tribes (2:1–34)
    3. Numbering and Duties of Levites (3:1—4:49)
  B. Various Laws and Events (5:1—9:14)
    1. Uncleanness, Restitution, and a Test for Adultery (5:1–31)
    2. Nazarites and the Priestly Blessing (6:1–27)
    3. Gifts for the Tabernacle (7:1–89)
    4. Consecration of the Levites (8:1–26)
    5. Celebration of Passover (9:1–14)
  C. Instructions for Moving the Camp (9:15—10:10)
    1. Cloud (9:15–23)
    2. Trumpets (10:1–10)

II. Journey from Sinai to Kadesh-Barnea (10:11—14:45)
  A. Procedures for Departure from Sinai (10:11–36)
  B. Provision of Quail and the Seventy Elders (11:1–35)
  C. Complaint of Miriam and Aaron against Moses (12:1–16)
  D. Mission and Report of the Spies (13:1–33)
  E. Failure of the People to Enter Canaan (14:1–45)

III. Period of Wilderness Wandering (15:1—21:35)
  A. Sacrifices, Sabbath Breakers, and Tassels (15:1–41)
  B. Rebellion against and Confirmation of Aaron's Priesthood (16:1—17:13)
  C. Instructions regarding the Levites (18:1–32)
  D. Purification Rites and the Red Heifer (19:1–22)
  E. Disobedience at Meribah, Deaths of Miriam and Aaron, and Conflict with Edom (20:1–29)
  F. Fiery Serpents and Defeat of Various Enemies (21:1–35)

IV. Story of Balaam (22:1—24:25)
  A. Balaam's Resistance to God's Will (22:1–41)
  B. Balaam's First Two Prophecies (23:1–30)
  C. Balaam's Third and Fourth Oracles (24:1–25)

V. Israel on the Plains of Moab (25:1—36:13)
  A. Sin of Baal-Peor (25:1–18)
  B. Second Census (26:1–65)
  C. Daughters of Zelophehad and Selection of Joshua to Follow Moses (27:1–23)
  D. Various Regulations (28:1—30:16)
    1. Regular Offerings (28:1–15)
    2. Festival Offerings (28:16—29:40)
    3. Vows (30:1–16)
  E. War against Midianites (31:1–54)
  F. Inheritance of Transjordan Tribes (32:1–42)
  G. Various Lists (33:1—35:34)
    1. Instructions for Encampment (33:1–56)
    2. Borders of Canaan and Procedures for Its Division (34:1–29)
    3. Levitical Cities and Cities of Refuge (35:1–34)
  H. Regulations Insuring Inheritances (36:1–13)

THE FOURTH BOOK OF MOSES CALLED

NUMBERS

CHAPTER 1

AND the LORD spake unto Moses in the wilderness of Sinai, in the tabernacle of the congregation, on the first *day* of the second month, in the second year after they were come out of the land of Egypt, saying,

2 Take ye the sum of all the congregation of the children of Israel, after their families, by the house of their fathers, with the number of *their* names, every male by their polls;

3 From twenty years old and upward, all that are able to go forth to war in Israel: thou and Aaron shall number them by their armies.

4 And with you there shall be a man of every tribe; every one head of the house of his fathers.

5 ¶ And these *are* the names of the men that shall stand with you: of *the tribe of* Reuben; Elizur the son of Shedeur.

6 Of Simeon; Shelumiel the son of Zurishaddai.

7 Of Judah; Nahshon the son of Amminadab.

8 Of Issachar; Nethaneel the son of Zuar.

9 Of Zebulun; Eliab the son of Helon.

10 Of the children of Joseph: of Ephraim; Elishama the son of Ammihud: of Manasseh; Gamaliel the son of Pedahzur.

11 Of Benjamin; Abidan the son of Gideoni.

12 Of Dan; Ahiezer the son of Ammishaddai.

13 Of Asher; Pagiel the son of Ocran.

14 Of Gad; Eliasaph the son of Deuel.

15 Of Naphtali; Ahira the son of Enan.

16 These *were* the renowned of the congregation, princes of the tribes of their fathers, heads of thousands in Israel.

17 ¶ And Moses and Aaron took these men which are expressed by *their* names:

18 And they assembled all the congregation together on the first *day* of the second month, and they declared their pedigrees after their families, by the house of their fathers, according to the number of the names, from twenty years old and upward, by their polls.

19 As the LORD commanded Moses, so he numbered them in the wilderness of Sinai.

20 And the children of Reuben, Israel's eldest son, by their generations, after their families, by the house of their fathers, according to the number of the names, by their polls, every male from twenty years old and upward, all that were able to go forth to war;

21 Those that were numbered of them, *even* of the tribe of Reuben, *were* forty and six thousand and five hundred.

22 ¶ Of the children of Simeon, by their generations, after their families, by the house of their fathers, those that were numbered of them, according to the number of the names, by their polls, every male from twenty years old and upward, all that were able to go forth to war;

23 Those that were numbered of them, *even* of the tribe of Simeon, *were* fifty and nine thousand and three hundred.

24 ¶ Of the children of Gad, by their generations, after their families, by the house of their fathers, according to the number of the names, from twenty years old and upward, all that were able to go forth to war;

25 Those that were numbered of them, *even* of the tribe of Gad, *were* forty and five thousand six hundred and fifty.

26 ¶ Of the children of Judah, by their generations,

ISRAEL AT SINAI (1:1—10:10)

Census and Organization of Israel (1:1—4:49)

Chapter 1: *Moses is commissioned by the Lord to take the sum of the tribes still assembled at Mt. Sinai.*

Numbering of Warriors (1:1–54)

1:1 *the tabernacle of the congregation.* Literally, "the tent of meeting."

1:2 *polls.* Heads, to take an individual "head count" (throughout the chapter).

1:4 *with you . . . a man of every tribe.* Twelve men to assist Moses and Aaron in the numbering of the men fit for war.

1:16 *renowned.* Literally, "the called ones," referring to those who were famous with a good reputation. *princes.* Exalted ones, referring to leaders in general, not sons of royalty (v. 44).

1:18 *declared their pedigrees.* Literally, "to be entered in a family registry," so as to have one's descent acknowledged.

1:20 *by their generations.* Their genealogical divisions (throughout the chapter).

after their families, by the house of their fathers,
according to the number of the names, from
twenty years old and upward, all that were able to
go forth to war;
27 Those that were numbered of them, *even* of
the tribe of Judah, *were* threescore and fourteen
thousand and six hundred.
28 ¶ Of the children of Issachar, by their gener-
ations, after their families, by the house of their
fathers, according to the number of the names,
from twenty years old and upward, all that were
able to go forth to war;
29 Those that were numbered of them, *even* of
the tribe of Issachar, *were* fifty and four thousand
and four hundred.
30 ¶ Of the children of Zebulun, by their gener-
ations, after their families, by the house of their
fathers, according to the number of the names,
from twenty years old and upward, all that were
able to go forth to war;
31 Those that were numbered of them, *even* of
the tribe of Zebulun, *were* fifty and seven thou-
sand and four hundred.
32 ¶ Of the children of Joseph, *namely*, of the chil-
dren of Ephraim, by their generations, after their
families, by the house of their fathers, according to
the number of the names, from twenty years old
and upward, all that were able to go forth to war;
33 Those that were numbered of them, *even* of
the tribe of Ephraim, *were* forty thousand and five
hundred.
34 ¶ Of the children of Manasseh, by their gen-
erations, after their families, by the house of their
fathers, according to the number of the names,
from twenty years old and upward, all that were
able to go forth to war;
35 Those that were numbered of them, *even* of
the tribe of Manasseh, *were* thirty and two thou-
sand and two hundred.
36 ¶ Of the children of Benjamin, by their gen-
erations, after their families, by the house of their
fathers, according to the number of the names,
from twenty years old and upward, all that were
able to go forth to war;
37 Those that were numbered of them, *even* of
the tribe of Benjamin, *were* thirty and five thou-
sand and four hundred.
38 ¶ Of the children of Dan, by their generations,
after their families, by the house of their fathers,
according to the number of the names, from
twenty years old and upward, all that were able to
go forth to war;
39 Those that were numbered of them, *even* of
the tribe of Dan, *were* threescore and two thou-
sand and seven hundred.
40 ¶ Of the children of Asher, by their genera-
tions, after their families, by the house of their
fathers, according to the number of the names,
from twenty years old and upward, all that were
able to go forth to war;
41 Those that were numbered of them, *even* of
the tribe of Asher, *were* forty and one thousand
and five hundred.
42 ¶ Of the children of Naphtali, throughout
their generations, after their families, by the house
of their fathers, according to the number of the
names, from twenty years old and upward, all that
were able to go forth to war;
43 Those that were numbered of them, *even* of
the tribe of Naphtali, *were* fifty and three thou-
sand and four hundred.
44 These *are* those that were numbered, which
Moses and Aaron numbered, and the princes of
Israel, *being* twelve men: each one was for the
house of his fathers.
45 So were all those that were numbered of the
children of Israel, by the house of their fathers,
from twenty years old and upward, all that were
able to go forth to war in Israel;
46 Even all they that were numbered were six
hundred thousand and three thousand and five
hundred and fifty.
47 ¶ But the Levites after the tribe of their fathers
were not numbered among them.
48 For the LORD had spoken unto Moses, saying,
49 Only thou shalt not number the tribe of Levi,
neither take the sum of them among the children
of Israel:
50 But thou shalt appoint the Levites over the
tabernacle of testimony, and over all the ves-
sels thereof, and over all things that *belong* to it:
they shall bear the tabernacle, and all the vessels
thereof; and they shall minister unto it, and shall
encamp round about the tabernacle.
51 And when the tabernacle setteth forward, the
Levites shall take it down: and when the taber-
nacle is to be pitched, the Levites shall set it up:
and the stranger that cometh nigh shall be put to
death.
52 And the children of Israel shall pitch their
tents, every man by his own camp, and every man
by his own standard, throughout their hosts.
53 But the Levites shall pitch round about the
tabernacle of testimony, that there be no wrath

1:44–46 *These are those that were numbered.* Precisely the same number as in Ex. 38:26 for the atonement money (Ex. 30:11–17; Num. 2:32).

1:47 *But the Levites . . . were not numbered.* Not numbered among the other tribes, but separate in order to serve in the tabernacle as the Lord had directed through Moses (vv. 48–54; see also 2:33).

1:50 *bear.* Carry. *minister.* Serve, referring specifically to liturgical service.

1:51 *setteth forward.* Breaks camp, pull up stakes. *stranger.* Any unauthorized person.

1:52 *standard.* A flag or banner to identify where each tribe was to camp.

upon the congregation of the children of Israel:
and the Levites shall keep the charge of the tabernacle of testimony.
54 And the children of Israel did according to all
that the LORD commanded Moses, so did they.

CHAPTER 2

AND the LORD spake unto Moses and unto Aaron,
saying,
2 Every man of the children of Israel shall pitch
by his own standard, with the ensign of their
father's house: far off about the tabernacle of the
congregation shall they pitch.
3 And on the east side toward the rising of the sun
shall they of the standard of the camp of Judah
pitch throughout their armies: and Nahshon
the son of Amminadab *shall be* captain of the
children of Judah.
4 And his host, and those that were numbered of
them, *were* threescore and fourteen thousand and
six hundred.
5 And those that do pitch next unto him *shall be*
the tribe of Issachar: and Nethaneel the son of
Zuar *shall be* captain of the children of Issachar.
6 And his host, and those that were numbered
thereof, *were* fifty and four thousand and four
hundred.
7 *Then* the tribe of Zebulun: and Eliab the son of
Helon *shall be* captain of the children of Zebulun.
8 And his host, and those that were numbered
thereof, *were* fifty and seven thousand and four
hundred.
9 All that were numbered in the camp of Judah
were an hundred thousand and fourscore
thousand and six thousand and four hundred,
throughout their armies. These shall first set forth.
10 ¶ On the south side *shall be* the standard of
the camp of Reuben according to their armies:
and the captain of the children of Reuben *shall be*
Elizur the son of Shedeur.
11 And his host, and those that were numbered
thereof, *were* forty and six thousand and five
hundred.
12 And those which pitch by him *shall be* the tribe
of Simeon: and the captain of the children of
Simeon *shall be* Shelumiel the son of Zurishaddai.
13 And his host, and those that were numbered
of them, *were* fifty and nine thousand and three
hundred.
14 Then the tribe of Gad: and the captain of the
sons of Gad *shall be* Eliasaph the son of Reuel.
15 And his host, and those that were numbered of
them, *were* forty and five thousand and six hundred and fifty.
16 All that were numbered in the camp of Reuben
were an hundred thousand and fifty and one thousand and four hundred and fifty, throughout their
armies. And they shall set forth in the second rank.
17 ¶ Then the tabernacle of the congregation
shall set forward with the camp of the Levites in
the midst of the camp: as they encamp, so shall
they set forward, every man in his place by their
standards.
18 ¶ On the west side *shall be* the standard of the
camp of Ephraim according to their armies: and

1:53 *keep the charge.* To observe or keep the service or ceremonial functions.

Thoughts for Personal/Family Worship: Chapter 1

1. **The numbering of the tribes of Israel reminds us that the Lord "knoweth them that are his" (2 Tim. 2:19). By this count an exact figure was revealed (Num. 1:46). Likewise, as God gathers a people from all nations, He knows their number, and He will keep each one. How does this truth bring comfort to your soul?**
2. **God revealed through Moses that every man numbered had to give "a ransom for his soul" (Ex. 30:12). God's numbered people are a ransomed people. No one can be in their ranks except on the basis of a price paid, and that price is the precious blood of Christ. Sinner, have you sought a place in the company of the saints through faith in Jesus' blood and righteousness?**
3. **Those numbered were to be "able to go forth to war." God's people are by nature and calling soldiers of the cross, for they are in warfare with sin, Satan, the flesh, and the world. Many would desire to be counted among the ranks of the redeemed, but they are not prepared to engage in the spiritual conflict that comes to the believer. We must enter the kingdom of heaven through much tribulation. In what ways is the church of Jesus Christ like an army at war? How is this spiritual warfare different from earthly wars?**

Chapter 2: *The Lord orders the arrangement of the tribes around the tabernacle for encampment and for marching.*

Arrangement of Tribes (2:1–34)

2:2 *pitch.* "Encamp" (v. 17), signifying tent dwellers, a nomadic culture. *by his own standard, with the ensign of their father's house.* Each tribe had a banner and every family in each tribe had its own sign flag. *far off about.* Literally, "from before surrounding," the idea being that tribes were camped facing and surrounding the tabernacle (throughout the chapter).
2:3 *And on the east side . . . Judah.* Judah was appointed to be the leading tribe, Messiah's tribe (1 Chron. 5:2). *captain.* An exalted one functioning as a leader (throughout the chapter).
2:4 *host.* Army (throughout the chapter).
2:10–11 *On the south side . . . Reuben.* Though the firstborn, Reuben, due to his immorality, forfeited the place of leadership (Gen. 49:3–4; 1 Chron. 5:1).
2:12,14 *those which pitch by him shall be . . . Simeon . . . Then the tribe of Gad.* Simeon by birth was next to Reuben and so occupies the second place on the south side. Gad, son of Zilpah, Leah's maid, is suitably placed with Reuben and Simeon.
2:17 *shall set forward.* Break camp, pull up stakes (v. 34). *the Levites in the midst of the camp.* Since they had charge of the service or the tabernacle, including its transport. *as they encamp, so shall they set forward.* Their marching sequence corresponded to the camp arrangement.
2:18–22 *On the west side shall be . . . Ephraim . . . Manasseh*

the captain of the sons of Ephraim *shall be* Elish-
ama the son of Ammihud.
19 And his host, and those that were numbered
of them, *were* forty thousand and five hundred.
20 And by him *shall be* the tribe of Manasseh: and
the captain of the children of Manasseh *shall be*
Gamaliel the son of Pedahzur.
21 And his host, and those that were numbered
of them, *were* thirty and two thousand and two
hundred.
22 Then the tribe of Benjamin: and the captain
of the sons of Benjamin *shall be* Abidan the son
of Gideoni.
23 And his host, and those that were numbered
of them, *were* thirty and five thousand and four
hundred.
24 All that were numbered of the camp of
Ephraim *were* an hundred thousand and eight
thousand and an hundred, throughout their
armies. And they shall go forward in the third
rank.
25 ¶ The standard of the camp of Dan *shall be*
on the north side by their armies: and the captain
of the children of Dan *shall be* Ahiezer the son of
Ammishaddai.
26 And his host, and those that were numbered
of them, *were* threescore and two thousand and
seven hundred.
27 And those that encamp by him *shall be* the
tribe of Asher: and the captain of the children of
Asher *shall be* Pagiel the son of Ocran.
28 And his host, and those that were numbered
of them, *were* forty and one thousand and five
hundred.
29 ¶ Then the tribe of Naphtali: and the captain
of the children of Naphtali *shall be* Ahira the son
of Enan.
30 And his host, and those that were numbered
of them, *were* fifty and three thousand and four
hundred.
31 All they that were numbered in the camp of
Dan *were* an hundred thousand and fifty and
seven thousand and six hundred. They shall go
hindmost with their standards.
32 ¶ These *are* those which were numbered of the
children of Israel by the house of their fathers: all
those that were numbered of the camps through-
out their hosts *were* six hundred thousand and
three thousand and five hundred and fifty.
33 But the Levites were not numbered among the
children of Israel; as the LORD commanded Moses.
34 And the children of Israel did according to all
that the LORD commanded Moses: so they pitched
by their standards, and so they set forward, every
one after their families, according to the house of
their fathers.

CHAPTER 3

THESE also *are* the generations of Aaron and
Moses in the day *that* the LORD spake with Moses
in mount Sinai.
2 And these *are* the names of the sons of Aaron;
Nadab the firstborn, and Abihu, Eleazar, and
Ithamar.
3 These *are* the names of the sons of Aaron, the
priests which were anointed, whom he conse-
crated to minister in the priest's office.
4 And Nadab and Abihu died before the LORD,
when they offered strange fire before the LORD, in

... *Benjamin.* The first two were the sons of Joseph, who along with Benjamin are sons of Rachel. In keeping with his grandfather Jacob's blessing, Ephraim is the leading tribe in this arrangement on the west side (Gen. 48:15–20; 1 Chron. 5:1–2).
2:25–31 *the north side . . . They shall go hindmost.* After Judah's encampment this was the most numerous; thus it was placed at the rear to provide greater security.

Thoughts for Personal/Family Worship: Chapter 2

1. **In the human heart there is the tendency to do that which is right in one's own eyes. But the arrangement of the tribes reminds us that God is the God of order not confusion (1 Cor. 14:33). Every tribe had to be in its own place contributing to a smoother passage through the wilderness. Our steps must be ordered according to His Word so that our walk to the heavenly Canaan will be less complicated with self-imposed difficulties. In the arrangement of the tribes the command was, "every man shall pitch by his own standard." In this way the entire company kept rank, providing for the unity and cohesion of the congregation. God's people need to know where they belong in the spiritual life of Christ's church and seek to remain there faithfully. How can this strengthen the whole life of Christ's church?**
2. **The tribes were all ranged around the tabernacle, on which the cloud of glory descended, the assurance of God's presence in the wilderness sojourning. Psalm 46 reminds us that "God is in the midst of her." To be in the center is the Lord's place alone and must be guarded against all usurpers. To have Him in the midst is a comforting truth. In the midst, He goes with us, secures us from all danger, and will bring us safely to our haven of eternal rest. How does the church know and experience that God is in its midst?**

Numbering and Duties of Levites (3:1—4:49)

Chapter 3: *The Levites are numbered.*

3:1 *the generations.* An account of men and their descendants.
3:2–3 *the names of the sons of Aaron, the priests.* The focus in this chapter is on Aaron and his descendants, to whom the priesthood was specifically entrusted. Moses and his branch of the Levitical family did not possess entitlement to the priesthood and are only obscurely in view in this chapter (v. 29; Ex. 6:18–20). *anointed.* To be spread over with a liquid, the verbal root for the noun, "Messiah." The priesthood, along with kings and prophets, constituted messianic offices and thus served as types or picture prophecies of the ideal Messiah, who was Prophet, Priest, and King in one person. *consecrated.* Literally, "to fill the hand" in the sense of being given a ministry.
3:4 *Nadab and Abihu died.* See Lev. 10:1–4; 16:1. *strange fire.*

the wilderness of Sinai, and they had no children:
and Eleazar and Ithamar ministered in the priest's
office in the sight of Aaron their father.
5 ¶ And the LORD spake unto Moses, saying,
6 Bring the tribe of Levi near, and present them
before Aaron the priest, that they may minister
unto him.
7 And they shall keep his charge, and the charge of
the whole congregation before the tabernacle of the
congregation, to do the service of the tabernacle.
8 And they shall keep all the instruments of the
tabernacle of the congregation, and the charge
of the children of Israel, to do the service of the
tabernacle.
9 And thou shalt give the Levites unto Aaron and
to his sons: they *are* wholly given unto him out of
the children of Israel.
10 And thou shalt appoint Aaron and his sons,
and they shall wait on their priest's office: and the
stranger that cometh nigh shall be put to death.
11 And the LORD spake unto Moses, saying,
12 And I, behold, I have taken the Levites from
among the children of Israel instead of all the
firstborn that openeth the matrix among the chil-
dren of Israel: therefore the Levites shall be mine;
13 Because all the firstborn *are* mine; *for* on the day
that I smote all the firstborn in the land of Egypt I
hallowed unto me all the firstborn in Israel, both
man and beast: mine shall they be: I *am* the LORD.
14 ¶ And the LORD spake unto Moses in the wil-
derness of Sinai, saying,
15 Number the children of Levi after the house of
their fathers, by their families: every male from a
month old and upward shalt thou number them.
16 And Moses numbered them according to the
word of the LORD, as he was commanded.
17 And these were the sons of Levi by their
names; Gershon, and Kohath, and Merari.
18 And these *are* the names of the sons of Ger-
shon by their families; Libni, and Shimei.
19 And the sons of Kohath by their families;
Amram, and Izehar, Hebron, and Uzziel.
20 And the sons of Merari by their families;
Mahli, and Mushi. These *are* the families of the
Levites according to the house of their fathers.
21 Of Gershon *was* the family of the Libnites, and
the family of the Shimites: these *are* the families
of the Gershonites.
22 Those that were numbered of them, according
to the number of all the males, from a month old
and upward, *even* those that were numbered of
them *were* seven thousand and five hundred.
23 The families of the Gershonites shall pitch
behind the tabernacle westward.
24 And the chief of the house of the father of the
Gershonites *shall be* Eliasaph the son of Lael.
25 And the charge of the sons of Gershon in the
tabernacle of the congregation *shall be* the tab-
ernacle, and the tent, the covering thereof, and
the hanging for the door of the tabernacle of the
congregation,
26 And the hangings of the court, and the curtain
for the door of the court, which *is* by the taber-
nacle, and by the altar round about, and the cords
of it for all the service thereof.
27 ¶ And of Kohath *was* the family of the Am-
ramites, and the family of the Izeharites, and the
family of the Hebronites, and the family of the
Uzzielites: these *are* the families of the Kohathites.
28 In the number of all the males, from a month
old and upward, *were* eight thousand and six
hundred, keeping the charge of the sanctuary.
29 The families of the sons of Kohath shall pitch
on the side of the tabernacle southward.
30 And the chief of the house of the father of the
families of the Kohathites *shall be* Elizaphan the
son of Uzziel.
31 And their charge *shall be* the ark, and the table,
and the candlestick, and the altars, and the vessels
of the sanctuary wherewith they minister, and the
hanging, and all the service thereof.
32 And Eleazar the son of Aaron the priest *shall
be* chief over the chief of the Levites, *and have*
the oversight of them that keep the charge of the
sanctuary.
33 ¶ Of Merari *was* the family of the Mahlites,
and the family of the Mushites: these *are* the
families of Merari.
34 And those that were numbered of them, ac-
cording to the number of all the males, from a

Alien or prohibited, fire that was foreign to the mind of the Lord, not being by His appointment.

3:6 *that they may minister unto him.* To be an attendant or engaged in liturgical service; the Levites specifically were given to Aaron and the priesthood to serve him in the tabernacle (v. 9). All priests were Levites, but not all Levites were priests.

3:7 *charge.* That which is to be watched. *before the tabernacle.* The Levites served outside the tabernacle itself, the priests alone being permitted to enter.

3:10 *they shall wait.* Literally, "they will carefully attend to." *the stranger.* Any unauthorized person (v. 38).

3:12–13 *matrix.* Womb. *hallowed.* Set apart (Ex. 13:12). The firstborn were the Lord's by right of redemption, but in this new arrangement the Levites take the place of the firstborn, thus the Levite is a reminder of what the believer is to be to the Lord—a redeemed workman.

3:15 *from a month old.* The age when the firstborn was offered to God (18:15–16).

3:16–20 *Gershon, and Kohath, and Merari.* The sons of Levi, whose descendants were numbered and assigned specific tasks in the service of the Lord. Note the summary of duties: Gershon (vv. 25–26; 4:24–28), Kohath (3:30–31; 4:4–15), and Merari (3:35–37; 4:29–33).

Family	Camp Location	Task
Gershon	West side of tabernacle	To carry its curtains
Kohath	South side of tabernacle	To carry its furniture
Merari	North side of tabernacle	To carry its pillars and framework

month old and upward, *were* six thousand and
two hundred.
35 And the chief of the house of the father of
the families of Merari *was* Zuriel the son of Abi-
hail: *these* shall pitch on the side of the tabernacle
northward.
36 And *under* the custody and charge of the sons
of Merari *shall be* the boards of the tabernacle,
and the bars thereof, and the pillars thereof, and
the sockets thereof, and all the vessels thereof, and
all that serveth thereto,
37 And the pillars of the court round about, and
their sockets, and their pins, and their cords.
38 ¶ But those that encamp before the tabernacle
toward the east, *even* before the tabernacle of the
congregation eastward, *shall be* Moses, and Aaron
and his sons, keeping the charge of the sanctuary
for the charge of the children of Israel; and the
stranger that cometh nigh shall be put to death.
39 All that were numbered of the Levites, which
Moses and Aaron numbered at the command-
ment of the LORD, throughout their families, all
the males from a month old and upward, *were*
twenty and two thousand.
40 ¶ And the LORD said unto Moses, Number all
the firstborn of the males of the children of Israel
from a month old and upward, and take the num-
ber of their names.
41 And thou shalt take the Levites for me (I *am*
the LORD) instead of all the firstborn among the
children of Israel; and the cattle of the Levites
instead of all the firstlings among the cattle of the
children of Israel.
42 And Moses numbered, as the LORD com-
manded him, all the firstborn among the children
of Israel.
43 And all the firstborn males by the number of
names, from a month old and upward, of those
that were numbered of them, were twenty and
two thousand two hundred and threescore and
thirteen.
44 ¶ And the LORD spake unto Moses, saying,
45 Take the Levites instead of all the firstborn
among the children of Israel, and the cattle of the
Levites instead of their cattle; and the Levites shall
be mine: I *am* the LORD.
46 And for those that are to be redeemed of the
two hundred and threescore and thirteen of the
firstborn of the children of Israel, which are more
than the Levites;
47 Thou shalt even take five shekels apiece by the
poll, after the shekel of the sanctuary shalt thou
take *them*: (the shekel *is* twenty gerahs:)
48 And thou shalt give the money, wherewith
the odd number of them is to be redeemed, unto
Aaron and to his sons.
49 And Moses took the redemption money of
them that were over and above them that were re-
deemed by the Levites:
50 Of the firstborn of the children of Israel took
he the money; a thousand three hundred and
threescore and five *shekels*, after the shekel of the
sanctuary:
51 And Moses gave the money of them that were
redeemed unto Aaron and to his sons, according
to the word of the LORD, as the LORD commanded
Moses.

CHAPTER 4

AND the LORD spake unto Moses and unto Aaron,
saying,
2 Take the sum of the sons of Kohath from
among the sons of Levi, after their families, by the
house of their fathers,
3 From thirty years old and upward even until
fifty years old, all that enter into the host, to do
the work in the tabernacle of the congregation.

3:38 *those that encamp before the tabernacle toward the east.* The eastward side was essentially the front and was occupied by Moses, Aaron, and his sons—the priests.
3:47 *five shekels apiece by the poll.* Literally, "five five shekels for the head." The Hebrew uses repetition for a distributive idea. *shekel.* A weight of about one-half ounce. *gerahs.* Each a twentieth of a shekel weight.
3:48 *the odd number of them is to be redeemed.* Literally, "the redemption of the excess or surplus."

Thoughts for Personal/Family Worship: Chapter 3

1. **The Levites were given to Aaron to keep his charge, and to keep the charge of the whole congregation. They remind us of the ministers of Christ and the charge given them, which is to keep the holy things that belong to the great High Priest, things centered on His sacrifice for sin. They are also to be faithful to the souls charged to them, being instant in season and out of season too (2 Tim. 4:2). Negligence is forbidden. How often do you pray for your pastors, that they would be faithful?**
2. **"The Levites shall be mine; because all the firstborn are mine" (vv. 12–13). The Lord laid claim to the Levites on the ground of redemption. The Levites stood in the place of the firstborn of the Israelites, and the firstborn child was redeemed (Ex. 13:13). God's claim to His people is based on Christ's redemptive work by which they are rescued from the stroke of death and become the Lord's. To be regarded as the firstborn is to enjoy privilege and honor. How can we more consciously claim this wonderful allotment as believers and the ownership of our Redeemer over us?**

Chapter 4: ***The Lord gives more specific instructions concerning the Levitical duties.***

4:2 *Take the sum of the sons of Kohath.* Kohath, the second son, has the place of preeminence in this numbering because the Kohathites were charged to carry the most holy things of the tabernacle. Sadly, these with the most honor later rebelled because they wanted more (16:1–11).
4:3 *From thirty years old . . . until fifty.* Their ministry did not

4 This *shall be* the service of the sons of Kohath
in the tabernacle of the congregation, *about* the
most holy things:
5 ¶ And when the camp setteth forward, Aaron
shall come, and his sons, and they shall take down
the covering vail, and cover the ark of testimony
with it:
6 And shall put thereon the covering of badgers'
skins, and shall spread over *it* a cloth wholly of
blue, and shall put in the staves thereof.
7 And upon the table of shewbread they shall
spread a cloth of blue, and put thereon the dishes,
and the spoons, and the bowls, and covers to cover
withal: and the continual bread shall be thereon:
8 And they shall spread upon them a cloth of
scarlet, and cover the same with a covering of
badgers' skins, and shall put in the staves thereof.
9 And they shall take a cloth of blue, and cover
the candlestick of the light, and his lamps, and his
tongs, and his snuffdishes, and all the oil vessels
thereof, wherewith they minister unto it:
10 And they shall put it and all the vessels thereof
within a covering of badgers' skins, and shall put
it upon a bar.
11 And upon the golden altar they shall spread a
cloth of blue, and cover it with a covering of bad-
gers' skins, and shall put to the staves thereof:
12 And they shall take all the instruments of min-
istry, wherewith they minister in the sanctuary,
and put *them* in a cloth of blue, and cover them
with a covering of badgers' skins, and shall put
them on a bar:
13 And they shall take away the ashes from the
altar, and spread a purple cloth thereon:
14 And they shall put upon it all the vessels
thereof, wherewith they minister about it, *even*
the censers, the fleshhooks, and the shovels, and
the basons, all the vessels of the altar; and they
shall spread upon it a covering of badgers' skins,
and put to the staves of it.
15 And when Aaron and his sons have made an
end of covering the sanctuary, and all the vessels
of the sanctuary, as the camp is to set forward;
after that, the sons of Kohath shall come to bear
it: but they shall not touch *any* holy thing, lest
they die. These *things are* the burden of the sons
of Kohath in the tabernacle of the congregation.
16 ¶ And to the office of Eleazar the son of Aaron
the priest *pertaineth* the oil for the light, and the
sweet incense, and the daily meat offering, and
the anointing oil, *and* the oversight of all the tab-
ernacle, and of all that therein *is*, in the sanctuary,
and in the vessels thereof.
17 ¶ And the LORD spake unto Moses and unto
Aaron, saying,
18 Cut ye not off the tribe of the families of the
Kohathites from among the Levites:
19 But thus do unto them, that they may live, and
not die, when they approach unto the most holy
things: Aaron and his sons shall go in, and appoint
them every one to his service and to his burden:
20 But they shall not go in to see when the holy
things are covered, lest they die.
21 ¶ And the LORD spake unto Moses, saying,
22 Take also the sum of the sons of Gershon,
throughout the houses of their fathers, by their
families;
23 From thirty years old and upward until fifty
years old shalt thou number them; all that enter
in to perform the service, to do the work in the
tabernacle of the congregation.
24 This *is* the service of the families of the
Gershonites, to serve, and for burdens:
25 And they shall bear the curtains of the taber-
nacle, and the tabernacle of the congregation, his
covering, and the covering of the badgers' skins
that *is* above upon it, and the hanging for the
door of the tabernacle of the congregation,
26 And the hangings of the court, and the hanging
for the door of the gate of the court, which *is* by the
tabernacle and by the altar round about, and their
cords, and all the instruments of their service, and
all that is made for them: so shall they serve.
27 At the appointment of Aaron and his sons shall
be all the service of the sons of the Gershonites, in
all their burdens, and in all their service: and ye
shall appoint unto them in charge all their burdens.
28 This *is* the service of the families of the sons
of Gershon in the tabernacle of the congrega-
tion: and their charge *shall be* under the hand of
Ithamar the son of Aaron the priest.
29 ¶ As for the sons of Merari, thou shalt number
them after their families, by the house of their
fathers;
30 From thirty years old and upward even unto
fifty years old shalt thou number them, every one

begin until in the prime of life, not as novices (1 Tim. 3:6). *host.* Army or warfare, underlining that God's work is a holy war.

4:5 *setteth forward.* Breaks camp, pulls up stakes. *Aaron shall come, and his sons.* The priests were the dismantlers of the tabernacle; the Kohathites were the transporters (v. 15).

4:6 *staves.* Poles or staffs (vv. 8,11,14).

4:7 *continual bread.* "The bread of continuance," referring to the regular shewbread.

4:10 *upon a bar.* On a frame for carrying.

4:14 *fleshhooks.* Forks to retrieve meat from a pot. *basons.* Bowls.

4:15 *bear.* Carry (v. 25). *the burden.* The load to be carried (throughout the chapter).

4:16 *the office of Eleazar.* See 3:32.

4:17–19 *And the LORD spake unto Moses and unto Aaron . . . Cut ye not off . . . the Kohathites.* Moses and Aaron were not to be guilty of carelessness in their oversight of the Kohathites. Making clear their job description was a means of preserving them.

4:23 *to perform the service.* Literally, "to war the warfare" or to be on duty in the war (see note at v. 3).

4:30 *service.* Warfare.

that entereth into the service, to do the work of
the tabernacle of the congregation.
31 And this *is* the charge of their burden,
according to all their service in the tabernacle of
the congregation; the boards of the tabernacle,
and the bars thereof, and the pillars thereof, and
sockets thereof,
32 And the pillars of the court round about, and
their sockets, and their pins, and their cords, with
all their instruments, and with all their service:
and by name ye shall reckon the instruments of
the charge of their burden.
33 This *is* the service of the families of the sons of
Merari, according to all their service, in the tab-
ernacle of the congregation, under the hand of
Ithamar the son of Aaron the priest.
34 ¶ And Moses and Aaron and the chief of the
congregation numbered the sons of the Kohathites
after their families, and after the house of their
fathers,
35 From thirty years old and upward even unto
fifty years old, every one that entereth into the
service, for the work in the tabernacle of the
congregation:
36 And those that were numbered of them by
their families were two thousand seven hundred
and fifty.
37 These *were* they that were numbered of the
families of the Kohathites, all that might do ser-
vice in the tabernacle of the congregation, which
Moses and Aaron did number according to the
commandment of the LORD by the hand of Moses.
38 And those that were numbered of the sons of
Gershon, throughout their families, and by the
house of their fathers,
39 From thirty years old and upward even unto
fifty years old, every one that entereth into the
service, for the work in the tabernacle of the
congregation,
40 Even those that were numbered of them,
throughout their families, by the house of their
fathers, were two thousand and six hundred and
thirty.
41 These *are* they that were numbered of the
families of the sons of Gershon, of all that might
do service in the tabernacle of the congregation,
whom Moses and Aaron did number according to
the commandment of the LORD.
42 ¶ And those that were numbered of the
families of the sons of Merari, throughout their
families, by the house of their fathers,
43 From thirty years old and upward even unto
fifty years old, every one that entereth into the
service, for the work in the tabernacle of the
congregation,
44 Even those that were numbered of them after
their families, were three thousand and two
hundred.
45 These *be* those that were numbered of the
families of the sons of Merari, whom Moses and
Aaron numbered according to the word of the
LORD by the hand of Moses.
46 All those that were numbered of the Levites,
whom Moses and Aaron and the chief of Israel
numbered, after their families, and after the house
of their fathers,
47 From thirty years old and upward even unto
fifty years old, every one that came to do the ser-
vice of the ministry, and the service of the burden
in the tabernacle of the congregation,
48 Even those that were numbered of them, were
eight thousand and five hundred and fourscore.
49 According to the commandment of the LORD
they were numbered by the hand of Moses, every
one according to his service, and according to his
burden: thus were they numbered of him, as the
LORD commanded Moses.

CHAPTER 5

AND the LORD spake unto Moses, saying,
2 Command the children of Israel, that they put

Thoughts for Personal/Family Worship: Chapter 4

1. **In their enlistment for service the Levites were said "to perform the service," or "war the warfare" (v. 23). Serving the Lord brings the believer into a spiritual battle, for the enemy is opposed to the things of Christ. From this conflict there is no escape. He who is a servant of Christ is a soldier of Christ too. Read Eph. 6:10–18 and consider how to prepare for our battle.**
2. **The Levites did not commence their actual service until the age of thirty, after they had passed through a probationary period of five years (8:24). The principle is clear—the servants of Christ must not be novices. Tried and proven men are needed to serve the Lord and then He will be well served. Who can help to mentor you as you prepare?**
3. **"So shall they serve"—these words spoken of the Gershonites' service are striking. Their sentiment was true for all the Levites: their service was to be rendered according to the revealed will of God. Scripture directs the believer to serve within the framework of the divine will. Not all have the same abilities and gifts, and some are more in the public eye than others. But God distributes His gifts according to His sovereign purpose, and as each member of the body functions according to its place and purpose all goes well. There is harmony when each part functions with a view to the whole, and there is discord when any one part becomes too concerned with self. Pray that God would help you to be satisfied with the calling He has given you and to serve Him with all your heart.**

Various Laws and Events (5:1—9:14)

Chapter 5: *The Lord gives instructions for maintaining purity in the camp.*

Uncleanness, Restitution, and a Test for Adultery (5:1–31)

out of the camp every leper, and every one that
hath an issue, and whosoever is defiled by the dead:
3 Both male and female shall ye put out, without
the camp shall ye put them; that they defile not
their camps, in the midst whereof I dwell.
4 And the children of Israel did so, and put them
out without the camp: as the LORD spake unto
Moses, so did the children of Israel.
5 ¶ And the LORD spake unto Moses, saying,
6 Speak unto the children of Israel, When a man
or woman shall commit any sin that men com-
mit, to do a trespass against the LORD, and that
person be guilty;
7 Then they shall confess their sin which they
have done: and he shall recompense his trespass
with the principal thereof, and add unto it the
fifth *part* thereof, and give *it* unto *him* against
whom he hath trespassed.
8 But if the man have no kinsman to recompense
the trespass unto, let the trespass be recompensed
unto the LORD, *even* to the priest; beside the ram
of the atonement, whereby an atonement shall be
made for him.
9 And every offering of all the holy things of
the children of Israel, which they bring unto the
priest, shall be his.
10 And every man's hallowed things shall be his:
whatsoever any man giveth the priest, it shall be
his.
11 ¶ And the LORD spake unto Moses, saying,
12 Speak unto the children of Israel, and say unto
them, If any man's wife go aside, and commit a
trespass against him,
13 And a man lie with her carnally, and it be hid
from the eyes of her husband, and be kept close,
and she be defiled, and *there be* no witness against
her, neither she be taken *with the manner*;
14 And the spirit of jealousy come upon him, and
he be jealous of his wife, and she be defiled: or if
the spirit of jealousy come upon him, and he be
jealous of his wife, and she be not defiled:
15 Then shall the man bring his wife unto the
priest, and he shall bring her offering for her, the
tenth *part* of an ephah of barley meal; he shall
pour no oil upon it, nor put frankincense thereon;
for it *is* an offering of jealousy, an offering of me-
morial, bringing iniquity to remembrance.
16 And the priest shall bring her near, and set her
before the LORD:
17 And the priest shall take holy water in an
earthen vessel; and of the dust that is in the floor
of the tabernacle the priest shall take, and put *it*
into the water:
18 And the priest shall set the woman before the
LORD, and uncover the woman's head, and put
the offering of memorial in her hands, which *is*
the jealousy offering: and the priest shall have in
his hand the bitter water that causeth the curse:
19 And the priest shall charge her by an oath, and
say unto the woman, If no man have lain with
thee, and if thou hast not gone aside to unclean-
ness *with another* instead of thy husband, be thou
free from this bitter water that causeth the curse:
20 But if thou hast gone aside *to another* instead
of thy husband, and if thou be defiled, and some
man have lain with thee beside thine husband:
21 Then the priest shall charge the woman with
an oath of cursing, and the priest shall say unto
the woman, The LORD make thee a curse and
an oath among thy people, when the LORD doth
make thy thigh to rot, and thy belly to swell;
22 And this water that causeth the curse shall go
into thy bowels, to make *thy* belly to swell, and
thy thigh to rot: And the woman shall say, Amen,
amen.
23 And the priest shall write these curses in a
book, and he shall blot *them* out with the bitter
water:

5:2 See Lev. 13–15 for specific details. All of these matters rendered a person ceremonially unclean, and therefore, excluded from community and worship rituals.

5:3 *without the camp*. Outside the boundary of the camp (v. 4). *defile*. To render unclean. *whereof I dwell*. God's presence was the reason for safeguarding the purity of the camp. Approaching God requires clean hands and pure hearts (Ps. 24:3–4).

5:7 *with the principal . . . add*. This offering required restitution of what was taken plus interest to the offended party.

5:8 *kinsman*. The near relative who stands legally in the place of his relative, when the relative is incapable of fulfilling his own responsibilities. He is responsible for doing whatever is necessary. *atonement*. A covering, to appease the Lord.

5:10 *hallowed things*. The things set apart.

5:12 *go aside*. In this case, to commit adultery.

5:13 *lie with her carnally*. The physical act of adultery. *be kept close*. To be hidden. *she be defiled*. Made unclean in a moral sense. *neither she be taken*. She is not caught.

5:14 The husband is suspicious regardless of the facts of the matter.

5:15 *ephah*. A dry measure of about a bushel. *offering of jealousy*. Offering brought because of jealousy. *offering of memorial*. Offering intended to bring something to mind, an appeal to the Lord's omniscience to reveal the facts. *bringing iniquity to remembrance*. Making iniquity known (vv. 18,26).

5:17 *holy water*. Water set apart for a sacred use.

5:18 *uncover the woman's head*. Or unbind the hair, allowing it to hang loosely.

5:19 *And the priest shall charge her by an oath*. Make her swear, solemnly adjuring her to tell the truth. *uncleanness*. Referring here to adultery. *be thou free*. Her innocence would be proved by the curse not coming upon her in its physical manifestation.

5:21 *charge . . . with an oath of cursing*. Make her swear an oath of the curse, in the sense of agreement with the curse or oath. *thigh to rot*. A thigh that falls or gives way (vv. 22,27).

5:22 *Amen, amen*. Hebrew words, meaning "truly, truly," expressing her agreement with the transaction.

24 And he shall cause the woman to drink the bitter water that causeth the curse: and the water that causeth the curse shall enter into her, *and become* bitter.

25 Then the priest shall take the jealousy offering out of the woman's hand, and shall wave the offering before the LORD, and offer it upon the altar:

26 And the priest shall take an handful of the offering, *even* the memorial thereof, and burn *it* upon the altar, and afterward shall cause the woman to drink the water.

27 And when he hath made her to drink the water, then it shall come to pass, *that*, if she be defiled, and have done trespass against her husband, that the water that causeth the curse shall enter into her, *and become* bitter, and her belly shall swell, and her thigh shall rot: and the woman shall be a curse among her people.

28 And if the woman be not defiled, but be clean; then she shall be free, and shall conceive seed.

29 This *is* the law of jealousies, when a wife goeth aside *to another* instead of her husband, and is defiled;

30 Or when the spirit of jealousy cometh upon him, and he be jealous over his wife, and shall set the woman before the LORD, and the priest shall execute upon her all this law.

31 Then shall the man be guiltless from iniquity, and this woman shall bear her iniquity.

CHAPTER 6

AND the LORD spake unto Moses, saying,

2 Speak unto the children of Israel, and say unto them, When either man or woman shall separate *themselves* to vow a vow of a Nazarite, to separate *themselves* unto the LORD:

3 He shall separate *himself* from wine and strong drink, and shall drink no vinegar of wine, or vinegar of strong drink, neither shall he drink any liquor of grapes, nor eat moist grapes, or dried.

4 All the days of his separation shall he eat nothing that is made of the vine tree, from the kernels even to the husk.

5 All the days of the vow of his separation there shall no razor come upon his head: until the days be fulfilled, in the which he separateth *himself* unto the LORD, he shall be holy, *and* shall let the locks of the hair of his head grow.

6 All the days that he separateth *himself* unto the LORD he shall come at no dead body.

7 He shall not make himself unclean for his father, or for his mother, for his brother, or for his sister, when they die: because the consecration of his God *is* upon his head.

8 All the days of his separation he *is* holy unto the LORD.

9 And if any man die very suddenly by him, and he hath defiled the head of his consecration; then he shall shave his head in the day of his cleansing, on the seventh day shall he shave it.

10 And on the eighth day he shall bring two turtles, or two young pigeons, to the priest, to the door of the tabernacle of the congregation:

11 And the priest shall offer the one for a sin offering, and the other for a burnt offering, and make an atonement for him, for that he sinned by the dead, and shall hallow his head that same day.

12 And he shall consecrate unto the LORD the days of his separation, and shall bring a lamb of

---

5:25 *wave the offering*. Hold it up in presentation.
5:29 *This is the law*. Or instruction to follow regarding suspicious jealousy. The ritual described and the consequences incurred remain obscure. But the point is clear: God was obviously in control of the whole matter to ensure the proper verdict. He would expose the guilty or exonerate the innocent according to His omniscience.

Thoughts for Personal/Family Worship: Chapter 5

1. **The expulsion of people from Israel's camp for ceremonial uncleanness reminds us that "the ungodly shall not stand in the judgment, nor sinners in the congregation of the righteous" (Ps. 1:5). What a solemn matter! Have you been to Jesus for the cleansing from sin found only in His blood? If we are in Christ then we know that we have been made fit to approach the Lord and we can enjoy fellowship with Him.**
2. **As odd as the trial of jealousy seems to us, it teaches vital spiritual lessons. Sins hidden will eventually be revealed. Sometimes the discovery of the concealed iniquity will be made in this life, like it would have been for the adulterous woman. But, if not, it most certainly will be at the coming of the Lord. "Some men's sins are open beforehand, going before to judgment; and some men they follow after" (1 Tim. 5:24). Then Christ the Judge of all "will bring to light the hidden things of darkness" (1 Cor. 4:5). Do not cover your sin; you will not prosper. Confess and forsake them and you will have mercy.**

Chapter 6: *The Lord gives the law for the Nazarites and the Aaronic blessing.*

Nazarites and the Priestly Blessing (6:1–27)

6:2 *Nazarite*. One who is devoted or consecrated to the Lord.
6:3–4 *wine*. The product of the vine. *strong drink*. The product of grain. *liquor of grapes*. Liquid or juice. *moist grapes, or dried*. Fresh grapes or raisins. *separation*. His special consecration. The Nazarite was forbidden to partake of any fruit of the vine (Luke 1:15). Given the prominence of grape products in that culture, this was a major restriction of the daily diet.
6:5 The uncut hair would be the visible sign of Nazariteship, making a public testimony of the consecration to God (Judg. 13:5; 16:17).
6:8 *holy unto the LORD*. Separated or set apart to the Lord.
6:10 *turtles*. Turtledoves.
6:11 *he sinned by the dead*. Unavoidable contact with the dead caused him to fall short of or miss the standard of his vow. *hallow his head*. Consecrate his head, a commitment to renew the vow.
6:12 *the days that were before shall be lost*. They will fall,

the first year for a trespass offering: but the days
that were before shall be lost, because his separa-
tion was defiled.
13 ¶ And this *is* the law of the Nazarite, when
the days of his separation are fulfilled: he shall be
brought unto the door of the tabernacle of the
congregation:
14 And he shall offer his offering unto the LORD,
one he lamb of the first year without blemish for a
burnt offering, and one ewe lamb of the first year
without blemish for a sin offering, and one ram
without blemish for peace offerings,
15 And a basket of unleavened bread, cakes of fine
flour mingled with oil, and wafers of unleavened
bread anointed with oil, and their meat offering,
and their drink offerings.
16 And the priest shall bring *them* before the
LORD, and shall offer his sin offering, and his
burnt offering:
17 And he shall offer the ram *for* a sacrifice of
peace offerings unto the LORD, with the basket
of unleavened bread: the priest shall offer also his
meat offering, and his drink offering.
18 And the Nazarite shall shave the head of his
separation *at* the door of the tabernacle of the
congregation, and shall take the hair of the head
of his separation, and put *it* in the fire which *is*
under the sacrifice of the peace offerings.
19 And the priest shall take the sodden shoulder
of the ram, and one unleavened cake out of the
basket, and one unleavened wafer, and shall put
them upon the hands of the Nazarite, after *the
hair of* his separation is shaven:
20 And the priest shall wave them *for* a wave
offering before the LORD: this *is* holy for the
priest, with the wave breast and heave shoulder:
and after that the Nazarite may drink wine.
21 This *is* the law of the Nazarite who hath vowed,
and of his offering unto the LORD for his separa-
tion, beside *that* that his hand shall get: according
to the vow which he vowed, so he must do after
the law of his separation.
22 ¶ And the LORD spake unto Moses, saying,
23 Speak unto Aaron and unto his sons, saying,
On this wise ye shall bless the children of Israel,
saying unto them,
24 The LORD bless thee, and keep thee:
25 The LORD make his face shine upon thee, and
be gracious unto thee:
26 The LORD lift up his countenance upon thee,
and give thee peace.
27 And they shall put my name upon the children
of Israel; and I will bless them.

CHAPTER 7

AND it came to pass on the day that Moses had
fully set up the tabernacle, and had anointed it,
and sanctified it, and all the instruments thereof,
both the altar and all the vessels thereof, and had

---

signifying forfeiture. He would have had to start again to keep his vow.

6:13 *law.* Instruction.

6:14–17 *And he shall offer his offering.* As strict as his vow was, it was not kept sinlessly; sacrifices were necessary.

6:18 *shall take the hair . . . and put it in the fire.* The symbol of his separation was burned *under the sacrifice* to signify that consecration is an offering to God, yet is only acceptable through the blood of a sacrifice.

6:19 *sodden.* Cooked or boiled.

6:20 *wave.* Lift back and forth before the altar, symbolic gesture of presenting the offering to the Lord.

6:23 *ye shall bless.* Declare blessed (vv. 24,27).

6:24–26 *keep.* Watch over. *make his face shine . . . lift up his countenance* [his face]. Show evidences of divine favor (Pss. 4:6; 31:16; 44:3; 67:1; 80:3,7,19; 89:15; 119:135; Dan. 9:17; 2 Cor. 4:6); an anthropomorphic expression as God "smiles" and rejoices over His people (cf. Job 29:24; Prov. 16:14–15; Eccl. 8:1). *peace.* A state of well-being, harmony, health, and prosperity.

6:27 *they shall put my name upon the children of Israel.* Signifies being identified with the Lord and being owned by Him (15:40–41).

Thoughts for Personal/Family Worship: Chapter 6

1. **Christ was not a Nazarite, yet in Him there converged all that the Nazarite vow signified. As the God-man He is the personification of all purity. He who could not sin was holy, harmless, undefiled, and separate from sinners. Spend time worshiping Christ as the Savior of sinners, who offered Himself without spot to God, to procure redemption for men and to save them from their sins.**
2. **To mark the close of the time of his vow the Nazarite brought an offering to the Lord. Though he had been specially set apart to the Lord he was not without sin. Even among the holiest of the saints, none is pure before a holy God. Thankfully, we are accepted in the Beloved (Eph. 1:6). Because God is pleased with Christ, He is pleased with those in Him. It is union with Christ and the power of His cleansing blood that makes any of our service to the Lord acceptable. For the remaining sin that taints the very best of our service, flee to Christ's merits and atonement.**
3. **Aaron pronounced blessing on Israel. Likewise, Christ our High Priest was sent into the world to bless sinners by turning them from their sins (Acts 3:26). At His ascension, Christ's final act was to bless His disciples with His uplifted hands (Luke 24:50–51). On those hands were the marks of His suffering—suffering that bought all spiritual blessings for us. The Aaronic blessing should be wonderfully directed to the living church through Christ's merits. Do you believe that, in Christ, God's face is shining upon you with grace and peace? Why or why not?**

Chapter 7: *Each of the tribes brings its contributions for the service of the tabernacle.*

Gifts for the Tabernacle (7:1–89)

7:1 *anointed it, and sanctified it.* The anointing was the ritual; being set apart was the consequence. The verb "anoint" is the root word for "Messiah" (the Anointed One.)

anointed them, and sanctified them;
2 That the princes of Israel, heads of the house of
their fathers, who *were* the princes of the tribes,
and were over them that were numbered, offered:
3 And they brought their offering before the
LORD, six covered wagons, and twelve oxen; a
wagon for two of the princes, and for each one an
ox: and they brought them before the tabernacle.
4 And the LORD spake unto Moses, saying,
5 Take *it* of them, that they may be to do the ser-
vice of the tabernacle of the congregation; and
thou shalt give them unto the Levites, to every
man according to his service.
6 And Moses took the wagons and the oxen, and
gave them unto the Levites.
7 Two wagons and four oxen he gave unto the
sons of Gershon, according to their service:
8 And four wagons and eight oxen he gave unto
the sons of Merari, according unto their service,
under the hand of Ithamar the son of Aaron the
priest.
9 But unto the sons of Kohath he gave none:
because the service of the sanctuary belonging
unto them *was that* they should bear upon their
shoulders.
10 ¶ And the princes offered for dedicating of
the altar in the day that it was anointed, even the
princes offered their offering before the altar.
11 And the LORD said unto Moses, They shall
offer their offering, each prince on his day, for the
dedicating of the altar.
12 ¶ And he that offered his offering the first day
was Nahshon the son of Amminadab, of the tribe
of Judah:
13 And his offering *was* one silver charger, the
weight thereof *was* an hundred and thirty *shekels*,
one silver bowl of seventy shekels, after the shekel
of the sanctuary; both of them *were* full of fine
flour mingled with oil for a meat offering:
14 One spoon of ten *shekels* of gold, full of in-
cense:
15 One young bullock, one ram, one lamb of the
first year, for a burnt offering:
16 One kid of the goats for a sin offering:
17 And for a sacrifice of peace offerings, two
oxen, five rams, five he goats, five lambs of the
first year: this *was* the offering of Nahshon the son
of Amminadab.
18 ¶ On the second day Nethaneel the son of
Zuar, prince of Issachar, did offer:
19 He offered *for* his offering one silver charger,
the weight whereof *was* an hundred and thirty
shekels, one silver bowl of seventy shekels, after
the shekel of the sanctuary; both of them full of
fine flour mingled with oil for a meat offering:
20 One spoon of gold of ten *shekels*, full of in-
cense:
21 One young bullock, one ram, one lamb of the
first year, for a burnt offering:
22 One kid of the goats for a sin offering:
23 And for a sacrifice of peace offerings, two
oxen, five rams, five he goats, five lambs of the
first year: this *was* the offering of Nethaneel the
son of Zuar.
24 ¶ On the third day Eliab the son of Helon,
prince of the children of Zebulun, *did offer*:
25 His offering *was* one silver charger, the weight
whereof *was* an hundred and thirty *shekels*, one
silver bowl of seventy shekels, after the shekel of
the sanctuary; both of them full of fine flour min-
gled with oil for a meat offering:
26 One golden spoon of ten *shekels*, full of in-
cense:
27 One young bullock, one ram, one lamb of the
first year, for a burnt offering:
28 One kid of the goats for a sin offering:
29 And for a sacrifice of peace offerings, two oxen,
five rams, five he goats, five lambs of the first year:
this *was* the offering of Eliab the son of Helon.
30 ¶ On the fourth day Elizur the son of Shedeur,
prince of the children of Reuben, *did offer*:
31 His offering *was* one silver charger of the
weight of an hundred and thirty *shekels*, one sil-
ver bowl of seventy shekels, after the shekel of the
sanctuary; both of them full of fine flour mingled
with oil for a meat offering:
32 One golden spoon of ten *shekels*, full of in-
cense:
33 One young bullock, one ram, one lamb of the
first year, for a burnt offering:
34 One kid of the goats for a sin offering:
35 And for a sacrifice of peace offerings, two oxen,
five rams, five he goats, five lambs of the first year:
this *was* the offering of Elizur the son of Shedeur.
36 ¶ On the fifth day Shelumiel the son of Zuri-
shaddai, prince of the children of Simeon, *did
offer*:
37 His offering *was* one silver charger, the weight
whereof *was* an hundred and thirty *shekels*, one
silver bowl of seventy shekels, after the shekel of
the sanctuary; both of them full of fine flour min-
gled with oil for a meat offering:

7:2 *the princes.* The exalted ones, the tribal leaders (throughout the chapter).

7:5 *give them unto the Levites, to every man according to his service.* The wagons and oxen were delegated to the Levites for their work, particularly in transporting the tabernacle.

7:8 Twice the number of oxen and wagons in comparison with the Gershonites (v. 7) because the Merarites had more to transport (4:31–32).

7:10–83 *And the princes offered.* Each prince brought exactly the same offering, and the complete list is repeated twelve times. See comments in the Worship Section below for the significance of the repetition.

7:13 *charger.* Dish or platter. *shekel of the sanctuary.* Weight of about one-half ounce.

38 One golden spoon of ten *shekels*, full of in-
cense:
39 One young bullock, one ram, one lamb of the
first year, for a burnt offering:
40 One kid of the goats for a sin offering:
41 And for a sacrifice of peace offerings, two oxen,
five rams, five he goats, five lambs of the first year:
this *was* the offering of Shelumiel the son of
Zurishaddai.
42 ¶ On the sixth day Eliasaph the son of Deuel,
prince of the children of Gad, *offered*:
43 His offering *was* one silver charger of the
weight of an hundred and thirty *shekels*, a silver
bowl of seventy shekels, after the shekel of the
sanctuary; both of them full of fine flour mingled
with oil for a meat offering:
44 One golden spoon of ten *shekels*, full of in-
cense:
45 One young bullock, one ram, one lamb of the
first year, for a burnt offering:
46 One kid of the goats for a sin offering:
47 And for a sacrifice of peace offerings, two oxen,
five rams, five he goats, five lambs of the first year:
this *was* the offering of Eliasaph the son of Deuel.
48 ¶ On the seventh day Elishama the son of Am-
mihud, prince of the children of Ephraim, *offered*:
49 His offering *was* one silver charger, the weight
whereof *was* an hundred and thirty *shekels*, one
silver bowl of seventy shekels, after the shekel
of the sanctuary; both of them full of fine flour
mingled with oil for a meat offering:
50 One golden spoon of ten *shekels*, full of in-
cense:
51 One young bullock, one ram, one lamb of the
first year, for a burnt offering:
52 One kid of the goats for a sin offering:
53 And for a sacrifice of peace offerings, two
oxen, five rams, five he goats, five lambs of the
first year: this *was* the offering of Elishama the
son of Ammihud.
54 ¶ On the eighth day *offered* Gamaliel the son
of Pedahzur, prince of the children of Manasseh:
55 His offering *was* one silver charger of the
weight of an hundred and thirty *shekels*, one silver
bowl of seventy shekels, after the shekel of the
sanctuary; both of them full of fine flour mingled
with oil for a meat offering:
56 One golden spoon of ten *shekels*, full of in-
cense:
57 One young bullock, one ram, one lamb of the
first year, for a burnt offering:
58 One kid of the goats for a sin offering:
59 And for a sacrifice of peace offerings, two
oxen, five rams, five he goats, five lambs of the
first year: this *was* the offering of Gamaliel the
son of Pedahzur.
60 ¶ On the ninth day Abidan the son of Gideoni,
prince of the children of Benjamin, *offered*:
61 His offering *was* one silver charger, the weight
whereof *was* an hundred and thirty *shekels*, one
silver bowl of seventy shekels, after the shekel
of the sanctuary; both of them full of fine flour
mingled with oil for a meat offering:
62 One golden spoon of ten *shekels*, full of in-
cense:
63 One young bullock, one ram, one lamb of the
first year, for a burnt offering:
64 One kid of the goats for a sin offering:
65 And for a sacrifice of peace offerings, two oxen,
five rams, five he goats, five lambs of the first year:
this *was* the offering of Abidan the son of Gideoni.
66 ¶ On the tenth day Ahiezer the son of Ammi-
shaddai, prince of the children of Dan, *offered*:
67 His offering *was* one silver charger, the weight
whereof *was* an hundred and thirty *shekels*, one
silver bowl of seventy shekels, after the shekel
of the sanctuary; both of them full of fine flour
mingled with oil for a meat offering:
68 One golden spoon of ten *shekels*, full of in-
cense:
69 One young bullock, one ram, one lamb of the
first year, for a burnt offering:
70 One kid of the goats for a sin offering:
71 And for a sacrifice of peace offerings, two
oxen, five rams, five he goats, five lambs of the
first year: this *was* the offering of Ahiezer the son
of Ammishaddai.
72 ¶ On the eleventh day Pagiel the son of Ocran,
prince of the children of Asher, *offered*:
73 His offering *was* one silver charger, the weight
whereof *was* an hundred and thirty *shekels*, one
silver bowl of seventy shekels, after the shekel
of the sanctuary; both of them full of fine flour
mingled with oil for a meat offering:
74 One golden spoon of ten *shekels*, full of in-
cense:
75 One young bullock, one ram, one lamb of the
first year, for a burnt offering:
76 One kid of the goats for a sin offering:
77 And for a sacrifice of peace offerings, two oxen,
five rams, five he goats, five lambs of the first year:
this *was* the offering of Pagiel the son of Ocran.
78 ¶ On the twelfth day Ahira the son of Enan,
prince of the children of Naphtali, *offered*:
79 His offering *was* one silver charger, the weight
whereof *was* an hundred and thirty *shekels*, one
silver bowl of seventy shekels, after the shekel
of the sanctuary; both of them full of fine flour
mingled with oil for a meat offering:
80 One golden spoon of ten *shekels*, full of in-
cense:
81 One young bullock, one ram, one lamb of the
first year, for a burnt offering:
82 One kid of the goats for a sin offering:
83 And for a sacrifice of peace offerings, two oxen,
five rams, five he goats, five lambs of the first year:

this *was* the offering of Ahira the son of Enan.
84 This *was* the dedication of the altar, in the day
when it was anointed, by the princes of Israel:
twelve chargers of silver, twelve silver bowls,
twelve spoons of gold:
85 Each charger of silver *weighing* an hundred
and thirty *shekels*, each bowl seventy: all the silver
vessels *weighed* two thousand and four hundred
shekels, after the shekel of the sanctuary:
86 The golden spoons *were* twelve, full of incense,
weighing ten *shekels* apiece, after the shekel of the
sanctuary: all the gold of the spoons *was* an hundred and twenty *shekels*.
87 All the oxen for the burnt offering *were* twelve
bullocks, the rams twelve, the lambs of the first
year twelve, with their meat offering: and the kids
of the goats for sin offering twelve.
88 And all the oxen for the sacrifice of the peace
offerings *were* twenty and four bullocks, the rams
sixty, the he goats sixty, the lambs of the first year
sixty. This *was* the dedication of the altar, after
that it was anointed.
89 And when Moses was gone into the tabernacle
of the congregation to speak with him, then he
heard the voice of one speaking unto him from
off the mercy seat that *was* upon the ark of testimony, from between the two cherubims: and he
spake unto him.

CHAPTER 8

AND the LORD spake unto Moses, saying,
2 Speak unto Aaron, and say unto him, When
thou lightest the lamps, the seven lamps shall give
light over against the candlestick.
3 And Aaron did so; he lighted the lamps thereof
over against the candlestick, as the LORD commanded Moses.
4 And this work of the candlestick *was of* beaten
gold, unto the shaft thereof, unto the flowers
thereof, *was* beaten work: according unto the pattern which the LORD had shewed Moses, so he
made the candlestick.
5 ¶ And the LORD spake unto Moses, saying,
6 Take the Levites from among the children of
Israel, and cleanse them.
7 And thus shalt thou do unto them, to cleanse
them: Sprinkle water of purifying upon them,
and let them shave all their flesh, and let them
wash their clothes, and *so* make themselves clean.
8 Then let them take a young bullock with his
meat offering, *even* fine flour mingled with oil,
and another young bullock shalt thou take for a
sin offering.
9 And thou shalt bring the Levites before the
tabernacle of the congregation: and thou shalt
gather the whole assembly of the children of
Israel together:
10 And thou shalt bring the Levites before the
LORD: and the children of Israel shall put their
hands upon the Levites:
11 And Aaron shall offer the Levites before the
LORD *for* an offering of the children of Israel, that
they may execute the service of the LORD.
12 And the Levites shall lay their hands upon the
heads of the bullocks: and thou shalt offer the one

7:84–88 A sum of the princes' offerings.

Thoughts for Personal/Family Worship: Chapter 7

1. **The twelve-fold repetition of the gifts offered to the Lord, on the surface, appears redundant, but it teaches a wonderful lesson. We should remember that what is offered to the Lord is not to enrich Him but to praise Him. The principle is that God does not tire of the sincere offerings of His people even when they are all the same. Some Christians get discouraged because they think they have no special talents and cannot really do anything special for the Lord. The Lord knows the heart and that is what He desires more than "stuff." Take to heart that the Lord "is not unrighteous to forget your work and labour of love, which ye have shewed toward his name" (Heb. 6:10). How can this encourage the Lord's people?**
2. **The offerings of the princes were for the dedicating of the altar, where the offerings for sin were made. Such liberal giving in relation to this altar of sacrifice underlines that the preaching of the cross must be richly supported (1 Cor. 9:13–14; Phil. 4:14–19). The message of Christ and Him crucified deserves the willing, liberal, and cheerful giving of God's people. How are you giving to this great cause?**
3. **To the sons of Kohath no wagons or oxen were given, for in their service they were to "bear upon their shoulders." They carried the most sacred things that especially pointed to Christ, a great privilege but one that brought a weighty burden. They needed to be strong men, just as gospel ministers must, to lift up Christ in this world. Pray that such men will be strengthened in the inward man by the Spirit of God.**

Chapter 8: *Aaron is instructed regarding the lighting of the lamps and the Levites are consecrated for service.*

Consecration of the Levites (8:1–26)

8:2–3 *over against the candlestick.* In front of the lampstand.
8:4 *beaten.* Hammered work, signifying the shaping of the lampstand from one piece of gold (Ex. 25:31).
8:6 *cleanse them.* To pronounce ceremonially clean and fit for their tabernacle service.
8:7 *Sprinkle.* Common practice for rites of purification, symbolic of the ultimate spiritual sprinkling accomplished by Christ (Isa. 52:15). *water of purifying.* See 19:9,17.
8:10 *the children of Israel shall put their hands upon the Levites.* Most likely, leaders from each tribe, to signify the Levites' representation of all the people before the Lord as living offerings to the Lord (cf. v. 12).
8:11 *offer . . . an offering.* Specifically, "wave the wave offering." Obviously not literal, but the Levites realized what the wave offering symbolized; they were presented to the Lord for His use (vv. 13,15,21).
8:12 *upon the heads of the bullocks.* The action signifies the imputation of sin to the substitute. God's true servants rest in the atonement.

for a sin offering, and the other *for* a burnt offer-
ing, unto the LORD, to make an atonement for the
Levites.
13 And thou shalt set the Levites before Aaron,
and before his sons, and offer them *for* an offering
unto the LORD.
14 Thus shalt thou separate the Levites from
among the children of Israel: and the Levites shall
be mine.
15 And after that shall the Levites go in to do the
service of the tabernacle of the congregation: and
thou shalt cleanse them, and offer them *for* an
offering.
16 For they *are* wholly given unto me from among
the children of Israel; instead of such as open
every womb, *even instead of* the firstborn of all the
children of Israel, have I taken them unto me.
17 For all the firstborn of the children of Israel
are mine, *both* man and beast: on the day that I
smote every firstborn in the land of Egypt I sanc-
tified them for myself.
18 And I have taken the Levites for all the first-
born of the children of Israel.
19 And I have given the Levites *as* a gift to Aaron
and to his sons from among the children of Israel,
to do the service of the children of Israel in the
tabernacle of the congregation, and to make an
atonement for the children of Israel: that there be
no plague among the children of Israel, when the
children of Israel come nigh unto the sanctuary.
20 And Moses, and Aaron, and all the congrega-
tion of the children of Israel, did to the Levites
according unto all that the LORD commanded
Moses concerning the Levites, so did the children
of Israel unto them.
21 And the Levites were purified, and they
washed their clothes; and Aaron offered them *as*
an offering before the LORD; and Aaron made an
atonement for them to cleanse them.
22 And after that went the Levites in to do their
service in the tabernacle of the congregation
before Aaron, and before his sons: as the LORD
had commanded Moses concerning the Levites,
so did they unto them.
23 ¶ And the LORD spake unto Moses, saying,
24 This *is it* that *belongeth* unto the Levites: from
twenty and five years old and upward they shall
go in to wait upon the service of the tabernacle of
the congregation:
25 And from the age of fifty years they shall cease
waiting upon the service *thereof*, and shall serve
no more:
26 But shall minister with their brethren in
the tabernacle of the congregation, to keep the
charge, and shall do no service. Thus shalt thou
do unto the Levites touching their charge.

CHAPTER 9

AND the LORD spake unto Moses in the wilderness
of Sinai, in the first month of the second year after
they were come out of the land of Egypt, saying,
2 Let the children of Israel also keep the passover
at his appointed season.
3 In the fourteenth day of this month, at even, ye
shall keep it in his appointed season: according to
all the rites of it, and according to all the ceremo-
nies thereof, shall ye keep it.
4 And Moses spake unto the children of Israel,
that they should keep the passover.
5 And they kept the passover on the fourteenth
day of the first month at even in the wilderness of
Sinai: according to all that the LORD commanded
Moses, so did the children of Israel.

8:16 *they are wholly given.* Literally, "ones being given, ones being given are they." The Hebrew uses repetition to express a superlative idea.
8:19 *no plague.* No affliction of any kind.
8:24 *to wait upon the service.* Literally, "to war the warfare" (4:23).
8:25 *from the age of fifty.* Perhaps because so much of the Levitical service involved heavy labor, the work was restricted to those in the prime of strength. *cease waiting.* To return from the warfare.
8:26 *shall minister . . . to keep the charge.* Released from Levitical service but not from the responsibility of oversight.

Thoughts for Personal/Family Worship: Chapter 8

1. **The Levites were set apart to serve by the laying on of hands, signifying their presentation to the Lord as a sacrifice (vv. 10–11). In that manner they were truly "living sacrifice[s]" just as the believer is to be (Rom. 12:1–2). The Christian is the New Testament Levite (Jer. 33:19–22). In light of Christ's atonement and the benefits enjoyed from it, serving the Lord is our reasonable service. Let us be careful that everything about us in body and soul is the Lord's and is spent in unceasing labor for Him, His glory, and His kingdom. If you are a Christian, what does it mean, practically speaking, for you to offer yourself to God as a living sacrifice today?**
2. **When the Levites officially retired from their set period of service, they did not cease from all work for the Lord (vv. 23–26). By ministering "with their brethren in the tabernacle," they brought their years of experience to good profit. Long after the earlier and more active years have passed, the child of God has much to contribute to Christ's cause, still bringing forth fruit in old age (Ps. 92:13–14). There is a wonderful sense in which servants of the Lord never retire. How can we honor this principle today?**

Chapter 9: *The Lord gives instructions concerning the celebration of the Passover.*

Celebration of Passover (9:1–14)

9:2 *appointed season.* See Ex. 12:2,14,25,43–49.
9:3 *at even.* Literally, "between the evenings." *according to all the rites.* God's worship is regulated by His Word (v. 5).
9:5 *in the wilderness.* The remote place was no barrier to the worship of God (Ps. 63:1–2).

6 ¶ And there were certain men, who were defiled
by the dead body of a man, that they could not
keep the passover on that day: and they came
before Moses and before Aaron on that day:
7 And those men said unto him, We *are* defiled
by the dead body of a man: wherefore are we kept
back, that we may not offer an offering of the
LORD in his appointed season among the children
of Israel?
8 And Moses said unto them, Stand still, and I
will hear what the LORD will command concerning you.
9 ¶ And the LORD spake unto Moses, saying,
10 Speak unto the children of Israel, saying, If any
man of you or of your posterity shall be unclean
by reason of a dead body, or *be* in a journey afar
off, yet he shall keep the passover unto the LORD.
11 The fourteenth day of the second month at
even they shall keep it, *and* eat it with unleavened
bread and bitter *herbs*.
12 They shall leave none of it unto the morning,
nor break any bone of it: according to all the ordinances of the passover they shall keep it.
13 But the man that *is* clean, and is not in a journey, and forbeareth to keep the passover, even the
same soul shall be cut off from among his people:
because he brought not the offering of the LORD in
his appointed season, that man shall bear his sin.
14 And if a stranger shall sojourn among you, and
will keep the passover unto the LORD; according
to the ordinance of the passover, and according to
the manner thereof, so shall he do: ye shall have
one ordinance, both for the stranger, and for him
that was born in the land.
15 ¶ And on the day that the tabernacle was reared
up the cloud covered the tabernacle, *namely*, the
tent of the testimony: and at even there was upon
the tabernacle as it were the appearance of fire,
until the morning.
16 So it was alway: the cloud covered it *by day*,
and the appearance of fire by night.
17 And when the cloud was taken up from the
tabernacle, then after that the children of Israel
journeyed: and in the place where the cloud abode,
there the children of Israel pitched their tents.
18 At the commandment of the LORD the children of Israel journeyed, and at the commandment of the LORD they pitched: as long as the
cloud abode upon the tabernacle they rested in
their tents.
19 And when the cloud tarried long upon the
tabernacle many days, then the children of Israel
kept the charge of the LORD, and journeyed not.
20 And *so* it was, when the cloud was a few days
upon the tabernacle; according to the commandment of the LORD they abode in their tents, and
according to the commandment of the LORD they
journeyed.
21 And *so* it was, when the cloud abode from
even unto the morning, and *that* the cloud was
taken up in the morning, then they journeyed:
whether *it was* by day or by night that the cloud

9:6 *defiled by the dead body of a man*. Contact with death rendered one ceremonially unclean and prohibited participation in the rituals of worship.

9:7 *kept back*. Restrained. The laws of cleanness and uncleanness were object lessons teaching that God requires sanctified worship, but the laws did not always correspond to the reality of the heart. A person could be ceremonially unclean but in a right relationship to the Lord as suggested by those men who had a desire to keep the Passover but could not.

9:10–12 The Lord knows the heart and makes provision for those who desired to worship but were providentially hindered (2 Chron. 30:13–20). *nor break any bone*. A type fulfilled in Christ's death (John 19:36).

9:13 The converse is true as well; a person could be ceremonially *clean* but not in a right relationship with God. *forbeareth*. To refrain from. *the same soul*. That person. *be cut off*. Excommunicated, placed outside the covenant community. There is no excuse for willful negligence of worship.

9:14 *a stranger*. A resident alien, who lives as a citizen in the land. Whether Jew or Gentile the regulations are the same; there is one way of approach to God.

Instructions for Moving the Camp (9:15—10:10)

Cloud (9:15–23)

9:15–16 *the cloud … fire*. Theophany, an appearance of God's presence that was visible day and night.

9:17–23 The moving or the resting of the cloud were the signs for the nation to travel or to camp.

9:18 *commandment of the LORD*. Literally, "mouth of the Lord" (Ex. 17:1). The motion of the cloud was God's visible Word publicly revealing His will, as the Scriptures do today.

9:19 *kept the charge*. Observed the injunction (v. 23).

Thoughts for Personal/Family Worship: Chapter 9

1. **The purpose of the Passover was much like the purpose of the Lord's Supper: an occasion for remembering God's gracious redemption through the sacrificed Lamb. Just as Moses reminded Israel of certain regulations about the Passover, so Paul reiterates to the Christian church the Lord's will concerning the communion feast (1 Cor. 11). God's people are forgetful. Often our minds grow so dull that it becomes essential to be taught again "the first principles of the oracles of God" (Heb. 5:12). But, knowing our infirmities, the Lord graciously repeats His truth in both the written and visible Word. Do not resent it when a preacher repeats truth you already know, but pray for grace to hear and see with profit.**
2. **That the Lord made provision for those who were providentially hindered from keeping the Passover at the designated time reminds us that God is more concerned about the heart than mere external performances of religion. Though unavoidably defiled by a dead body the Israelite was not permitted to keep the Passover. It is good when the Lord's people are so anxious for fellowship that they mourn when unable to partake of the means of grace. We need more of the spirit of the psalmist when, in his exile, he was jealous of the sparrow and the swallow enjoying their access to God's house (Ps. 84:3). But at the same time, it warns us that some can go through the**

was taken up, they journeyed.
22 Or *whether it were* two days, or a month, or a
year, that the cloud tarried upon the tabernacle,
remaining thereon, the children of Israel abode
in their tents, and journeyed not: but when it was
taken up, they journeyed.
23 At the commandment of the LORD they rested
in the tents, and at the commandment of the LORD
they journeyed: they kept the charge of the LORD,
at the commandment of the LORD by the hand of
Moses.

CHAPTER 10

AND the LORD spake unto Moses, saying,
2 Make thee two trumpets of silver; of a whole
piece shalt thou make them: that thou mayest use
them for the calling of the assembly, and for the
journeying of the camps.
3 And when they shall blow with them, all the
assembly shall assemble themselves to thee at the
door of the tabernacle of the congregation.
4 And if they blow *but* with one *trumpet*, then
the princes, *which are* heads of the thousands of
Israel, shall gather themselves unto thee.
5 When ye blow an alarm, then the camps that lie
on the east parts shall go forward.
6 When ye blow an alarm the second time, then
the camps that lie on the south side shall take their
journey: they shall blow an alarm for their journeys.
7 But when the congregation is to be gathered
together, ye shall blow, but ye shall not sound an
alarm.
8 And the sons of Aaron, the priests, shall blow
with the trumpets; and they shall be to you for an
ordinance for ever throughout your generations.
9 And if ye go to war in your land against the
enemy that oppresseth you, then ye shall blow
an alarm with the trumpets; and ye shall be
remembered before the LORD your God, and ye
shall be saved from your enemies.
10 Also in the day of your gladness, and in your
solemn days, and in the beginnings of your
months, ye shall blow with the trumpets over
your burnt offerings, and over the sacrifices of
your peace offerings; that they may be to you for
a memorial before your God: I *am* the LORD your
God.
11 ¶ And it came to pass on the twentieth *day* of
the second month, in the second year, that the
cloud was taken up from off the tabernacle of the
testimony.
12 And the children of Israel took their jour-
neys out of the wilderness of Sinai; and the cloud
rested in the wilderness of Paran.
13 And they first took their journey according to
the commandment of the LORD by the hand of
Moses.
14 ¶ In the first *place* went the standard of the
camp of the children of Judah according to their
armies: and over his host *was* Nahshon the son of
Amminadab.
15 And over the host of the tribe of the children
of Issachar *was* Nethaneel the son of Zuar.
16 And over the host of the tribe of the children
of Zebulun *was* Eliab the son of Helon.
17 And the tabernacle was taken down; and the
sons of Gershon and the sons of Merari set for-
ward, bearing the tabernacle.
18 ¶ And the standard of the camp of Reuben set

---

motions of religion without any real heart of worship for the Lord. In our sin, we can turn the very best of religious means into empty acts that mean nothing to God. How can we, as Paul admonished, "keep the feast . . . with the unleavened bread of sincerity and truth" (1 Cor. 5:8)?

3. The cloud and the fiery pillar, representing the presence of God, made it clear to Israel that wherever they were they were in God's presence. It was not for them to speculate or wonder where they might be next, but just to enjoy where they were and to serve the Lord in the place He had put them. The equivalent for Christians today is the Word of God illuminated by the Spirit of God. Too often, we tend to fixate on where the Lord will lead us next rather than serving Him to our fullest in the place He has put us now. How can we balance contentment with where we are, experiencing God's presence in the Spirit, and at the same time, sensitivity to obey the commands of God's Word, following His directions promptly and eagerly?

Chapter 10: ***The Lord gives instructions concerning the silver trumpets, and Israel begins their journey from Sinai.***

Trumpets (10:1–10)

10:2–3 *of a whole piece.* Hammered work, the trumpets being fashioned from one piece of silver to give a good sound. *for the calling.* For summons, to alert the people to assemble at the tabernacle, the place of worship and revelation. The word *silver* may link the trumpets to redemption (3:49–51; 18:16; Lev. 25:48–51; 27:15; Isa. 52:3, where *silver* is translated "money" as the price of redemption).

10:4–10 The trumpet sounds varied depending on the intended message. It was important for the people to listen carefully to discern the proper action to take.

10:4 *princes.* The exalted ones, specifically the tribal leaders.

10:5 *alarm.* Signal blast.

10:7 *sound an alarm.* Produce a sustained note as a signal for war or march.

10:9 *the enemy that oppresseth.* The adversary that attacks or harasses. *ye shall be remembered before the LORD.* At the sound of the trumpets by the priests (v. 8), the Lord would take note of their danger and bring deliverance (*be saved*).

10:10 As a reminder to heaven that their worship was offered on the basis of redemption.

JOURNEY FROM SINAI TO KADESH-BARNEA (10:11—14:45)

Procedures for Departure from Sinai (10:11–36)

10:14 *standard.* Flag or banner (throughout the chapter).

10:17 *set forward.* Break camp, pull up stakes (throughout the chapter).

forward according to their armies: and over his
host *was* Elizur the son of Shedeur.
19 And over the host of the tribe of the children
of Simeon *was* Shelumiel the son of Zurishaddai.
20 And over the host of the tribe of the children
of Gad *was* Eliasaph the son of Deuel.
21 And the Kohathites set forward, bearing the
sanctuary: and *the other* did set up the tabernacle
against they came.
22 ¶ And the standard of the camp of the chil-
dren of Ephraim set forward according to their
armies: and over his host *was* Elishama the son
of Ammihud.
23 And over the host of the tribe of the children
of Manasseh *was* Gamaliel the son of Pedahzur.
24 And over the host of the tribe of the children
of Benjamin *was* Abidan the son of Gideoni.
25 ¶ And the standard of the camp of the chil-
dren of Dan set forward, *which was* the rereward
of all the camps throughout their hosts: and over
his host *was* Ahiezer the son of Ammishaddai.
26 And over the host of the tribe of the children
of Asher *was* Pagiel the son of Ocran.
27 And over the host of the tribe of the children
of Naphtali *was* Ahira the son of Enan.
28 Thus *were* the journeyings of the children of
Israel according to their armies, when they set
forward.
29 ¶ And Moses said unto Hobab, the son of
Raguel the Midianite, Moses' father in law, We
are journeying unto the place of which the LORD
said, I will give it you: come thou with us, and we
will do thee good: for the LORD hath spoken good
concerning Israel.
30 And he said unto him, I will not go; but I will
depart to mine own land, and to my kindred.
31 And he said, Leave us not, I pray thee; forasmuch
as thou knowest how we are to encamp in the wil-
derness, and thou mayest be to us instead of eyes.
32 And it shall be, if thou go with us, yea, it shall
be, that what goodness the LORD shall do unto us,
the same will we do unto thee.
33 ¶ And they departed from the mount of the
LORD three days' journey: and the ark of the cov-
enant of the LORD went before them in the three
days' journey, to search out a resting place for
them.
34 And the cloud of the LORD *was* upon them by
day, when they went out of the camp.
35 And it came to pass, when the ark set forward,
that Moses said, Rise up, LORD, and let thine
enemies be scattered; and let them that hate thee
flee before thee.
36 And when it rested, he said, Return, O LORD,
unto the many thousands of Israel.

CHAPTER 11

AND *when* the people complained, it displeased
the LORD: and the LORD heard *it*; and his an-
ger was kindled; and the fire of the LORD burnt
among them, and consumed *them that were* in the
uttermost parts of the camp.
2 And the people cried unto Moses; and when Mo-
ses prayed unto the LORD, the fire was quenched.
3 And he called the name of the place Taberah:
because the fire of the LORD burnt among them.
4 ¶ And the mixt multitude that *was* among them

10:21 *and the other did set up the tabernacle against they came.* The sons of Gershon and Merari set up the tabernacle structure until or before the sons of Korah came with the furniture.

10:29 *Moses' father in law.* See Ex. 2:18; 18:1–27; Judg. 4:11.

10:35 *Rise up, LORD, and let thine enemies be scattered.* See Ps. 68:1.

Thoughts for Personal/Family Worship: Chapter 10

1. **The preaching of God's Word is symbolized by the blowing of the trumpet. The silver trumpets were blown for various purposes but obviously in such a manner that all were sure of the meaning of the sounds heard. How can we ensure that the Lord's message goes out with a clear sound that men will know the mind of the Lord (1 Cor. 14:8)?**
2. **The Levites remind us of the need to labor together in harmony. The Gershonites and the Merarites went first in the marching order to set up the tabernacle to receive the sacred furniture carried by the Kohathites. God has set each member of Christ's church to function in a certain way for the good of the whole body. Are you a member of a church? What is your place in the body? How has God equipped and called you to serve? Are you serving there in harmony with the other church members?**
3. **Just as Moses pled with Hobab to go with Israel to Canaan, so the child of God longs to take every family member to glory. To take loved ones to heaven with us is all we can take. All earthly things will be left behind, for they are temporal. But the souls of family and friends are eternal and will live forever in heaven or hell. What more can you be doing to plead with them, to win them, and to bring them to the better country?**

Chapter 11: *Israel complains, provoking the Lord to anger, and seventy elders are appointed to aid Moses.*

Provision of Quail and the Seventy Elders (11:1–35)

11:1 *the people complained.* Murmured. The first of several murmurings in Numbers, each provoking the Lord with significant consequence (14:1–4; 16:3,41; 20:2–3; 21:5). *it displeased the LORD.* Literally, "it was evil in the ears of the Lord." *the fire of the LORD burnt among them.* Complaining is a sin of the tongue and is likened to a fire (James 3:5–6), which here kindles divine fire.

11:2 *Moses prayed.* His intercession for the people was frequent and effective, one of the greatest ways Moses typifies Christ, the great Intercessor. *the fire was quenched.* It died or sunk down.

11:3 *Taberah.* Transliteration of, "a burning."

11:4 *the mixt multitude.* A bunch of vagabonds or rabble.

fell a lusting: and the children of Israel also wept again, and said, Who shall give us flesh to eat?

5 We remember the fish, which we did eat in Egypt freely; the cucumbers, and the melons, and the leeks, and the onions, and the garlick:

6 But now our soul *is* dried away: *there is* nothing at all, beside this manna, *before* our eyes.

7 And the manna *was* as coriander seed, and the colour thereof as the colour of bdellium.

8 *And* the people went about, and gathered *it*, and ground *it* in mills, or beat *it* in a mortar, and baked *it* in pans, and made cakes of it: and the taste of it was as the taste of fresh oil.

9 And when the dew fell upon the camp in the night, the manna fell upon it.

10 ¶ Then Moses heard the people weep throughout their families, every man in the door of his tent: and the anger of the LORD was kindled greatly; Moses also was displeased.

11 And Moses said unto the LORD, Wherefore hast thou afflicted thy servant? and wherefore have I not found favour in thy sight, that thou layest the burden of all this people upon me?

12 Have I conceived all this people? have I begotten them, that thou shouldest say unto me, Carry them in thy bosom, as a nursing father beareth the sucking child, unto the land which thou swarest unto their fathers?

13 Whence should I have flesh to give unto all this people? for they weep unto me, saying, Give us flesh, that we may eat.

14 I am not able to bear all this people alone, because *it is* too heavy for me.

15 And if thou deal thus with me, kill me, I pray thee, out of hand, if I have found favour in thy sight; and let me not see my wretchedness.

16 ¶ And the LORD said unto Moses, Gather unto me seventy men of the elders of Israel, whom thou knowest to be the elders of the people, and officers over them; and bring them unto the tabernacle of the congregation, that they may stand there with thee.

17 And I will come down and talk with thee there: and I will take of the spirit which *is* upon thee, and will put *it* upon them; and they shall bear the burden of the people with thee, that thou bear *it* not thyself alone.

18 And say thou unto the people, Sanctify yourselves against to morrow, and ye shall eat flesh: for ye have wept in the ears of the LORD, saying, Who shall give us flesh to eat? for *it was* well with us in Egypt: therefore the LORD will give you flesh, and ye shall eat.

19 Ye shall not eat one day, nor two days, nor five days, neither ten days, nor twenty days;

20 *But* even a whole month, until it come out at your nostrils, and it be loathsome unto you: because that ye have despised the LORD which *is* among you, and have wept before him, saying, Why came we forth out of Egypt?

21 And Moses said, The people, among whom I *am*, *are* six hundred thousand footmen; and thou hast said, I will give them flesh, that they may eat a whole month.

22 Shall the flocks and the herds be slain for them, to suffice them? or shall all the fish of the sea be gathered together for them, to suffice them?

23 And the LORD said unto Moses, Is the LORD's hand waxed short? thou shalt see now whether my word shall come to pass unto thee or not.

24 ¶ And Moses went out, and told the people the words of the LORD, and gathered the seventy men of the elders of the people, and set them round about the tabernacle.

25 And the LORD came down in a cloud, and spake unto him, and took of the spirit that *was* upon him, and gave *it* unto the seventy elders: and it came to pass, *that*, when the spirit rested upon them, they prophesied, and did not cease.

26 But there remained two *of the* men in the camp, the name of the one *was* Eldad, and the name of the other Medad: and the spirit rested upon them; and they *were* of them that were written, but went not out unto the tabernacle: and

---

Perhaps including non-Israelites, but most likely not exclusively so. *fell a lusting.* Literally, "they lusted a lust" or "craved a craving," signifying intense covetousness or greed (1 Cor. 10:6). *the children of Israel.* Complaining is infectious and spread throughout the nation. *Who shall give.* A Hebrew idiom expressing desire, "O that we had flesh to eat."

11:6 *our soul.* Equates to "we." *this manna.* Unusual food that God had given in grace as His daily provision (Ex. 16) and typical of Christ (John 6:48–51).

11:7 *coriander seed.* Small, round, spicy seeds.

11:10 *Moses also was displeased.* Literally, "it was evil in the eyes of Moses," a response mirroring the Lord (v. 1).

11:11 *Wherefore hast thou afflicted.* Literally, "Why have you hurt." *burden.* Load, a heavy responsibility.

11:12 *nursing father.* Guardian, a keeper of children.

11:15 *kill me . . . out of hand.* Literally, "kill me . . . a killing," expressing Moses' desire for immediate execution. *my wretchedness.* My evil or hurtful situation. Moses expresses his frustration, desiring death over the prospect of constantly dealing with the rebellious people.

11:17 *the spirit which is upon thee.* The empowering by the Holy Spirit to enable ministry (24:2; 27:18; Ex. 28:3; 31:3–5; 35:31–35; Deut. 34:9).

11:18 *Sanctify yourselves.* In the sense of getting ready. The Lord was going to give them what they wanted (Ps. 78:26–31; 106:14–15).

11:21 *six hundred thousand footmen.* An indication of the immensity of the congregation of Israel, thus Moses' incredulity at the thought of the amount of food required to feed them.

11:23 *Is the LORD's hand waxed short?* Has the Lord's hand become too short (ineffective or powerless)?

11:25 *prophesied.* Evidence of the Spirit's empowering (1 Sam. 10:5–6; 19:23–24). Prophesying includes Spirit-inspired praise and thanksgiving (1 Chron. 25:1–3).

they prophesied in the camp.
27 And there ran a young man, and told Moses,
and said, Eldad and Medad do prophesy in the
camp.
28 And Joshua the son of Nun, the servant of
Moses, *one* of his young men, answered and said,
My lord Moses, forbid them.
29 And Moses said unto him, Enviest thou for my
sake? would God that all the LORD's people were
prophets, *and* that the LORD would put his spirit
upon them!
30 And Moses gat him into the camp, he and the
elders of Israel.
31 ¶ And there went forth a wind from the LORD,
and brought quails from the sea, and let *them* fall
by the camp, as it were a day's journey on this side,
and as it were a day's journey on the other side,
round about the camp, and as it were two cubits
high upon the face of the earth.
32 And the people stood up all that day, and all
that night, and all the next day, and they gath-
ered the quails: he that gathered least gathered
ten homers: and they spread *them* all abroad for
themselves round about the camp.
33 And while the flesh *was* yet between their
teeth, ere it was chewed, the wrath of the LORD
was kindled against the people, and the LORD
smote the people with a very great plague.
34 And he called the name of that place Kibroth-
hattaavah: because there they buried the people
that lusted.
35 *And* the people journeyed from Kibroth-
hattaavah unto Hazeroth; and abode at Hazeroth.

CHAPTER 12

AND Miriam and Aaron spake against Moses
because of the Ethiopian woman whom he had
married: for he had married an Ethiopian woman.
2 And they said, Hath the LORD indeed spoken
only by Moses? hath he not spoken also by us?
And the LORD heard *it*.
3 (Now the man Moses *was* very meek, above all
the men which *were* upon the face of the earth.)
4 And the LORD spake suddenly unto Moses, and
unto Aaron, and unto Miriam, Come out ye three
unto the tabernacle of the congregation. And they
three came out.
5 And the LORD came down in the pillar of the
cloud, and stood *in* the door of the tabernacle,
and called Aaron and Miriam: and they both
came forth.
6 And he said, Hear now my words: If there be a
prophet among you, *I* the LORD will make myself
known unto him in a vision, *and* will speak unto
him in a dream.
7 My servant Moses *is* not so, who *is* faithful in
all mine house.
8 With him will I speak mouth to mouth, even
apparently, and not in dark speeches; and the
similitude of the LORD shall he behold: wherefore
then were ye not afraid to speak against my
servant Moses?
9 And the anger of the LORD was kindled against
them; and he departed.
10 And the cloud departed from off the taberna-
cle; and, behold, Miriam *became* leprous, *white* as
snow: and Aaron looked upon Miriam, and, be-
hold, *she was* leprous.
11 And Aaron said unto Moses, Alas, my lord, I
beseech thee, lay not the sin upon us, wherein we
have done foolishly, and wherein we have sinned.
12 Let her not be as one dead, of whom the flesh
is half consumed when he cometh out of his
mother's womb.
13 And Moses cried unto the LORD, saying, Heal

11:29 Moses' desire that all the Lord's people would be empowered by the Spirit anticipated Pentecost (Joel 2:28; Acts 2:4,16–21).
11:30 *gat him into the camp*. They gathered in the camp.
11:31 *cubits*. About 18 inches.
11:32 *homers*. Each about 9.5 bushels.
11:33 *plague*. A blow, strike, or defeat.
11:34 *Kibroth-hattaavah*. Transliteration of, "the graves of lust."

Thoughts for Personal/Family Worship: Chapter 11

1. **Complaining is a prevalent sin among those who profess to be the Lord's. It is easy to become discontent with whatever the situation of life may be. The first instance of murmuring in this chapter gives no reason, and that in itself is instructive. Complaining is never justified. It seems clear too, that this complaining was in secret. Moses appears to have known nothing of it, but the Lord heard it. How foolish to conclude that complaining can be concealed from an omniscient God. Why is complaining such a great sin and offense to God?**
2. **It was "the mixt multitude" who "fell a lusting" (v. 4). These rabble-rousers had no heart for the Lord, but instead yearned for Egypt. Their complaining spread like wildfire throughout the entire camp. They had a leavening influence and the lusting spread among the Lord's people, quickly developing into contempt for the manna, that wonderful reminder of God's provision. The church should guard from impurity and purge the leaven whenever it is known. The protection of the body as a whole requires sometimes the discipline and expulsion of the few. Pray for your church, that it would be spared division, but that it would be preserved in faithfulness if some members desire to return to worldliness.**

Chapter 12: *The Lord defends Moses against charges by Aaron and Miriam.*

Complaint of Miriam and Aaron against Moses (12:1–16)

12:1–2 *Ethiopian woman*. Cushite woman. Apparently jealous of Moses' unique ministry, they found no other point of criticism.
12:3 *meek*. Humble before God and gentle with men.
12:4 *spake suddenly*. Or spoke surprisingly.

her now, O God, I beseech thee.
14 ¶ And the LORD said unto Moses, If her father
had but spit in her face, should she not be ashamed
seven days? let her be shut out from the camp seven
days, and after that let her be received in *again*.
15 And Miriam was shut out from the camp
seven days: and the people journeyed not till
Miriam was brought in *again*.
16 And afterward the people removed from Ha-
zeroth, and pitched in the wilderness of Paran.

CHAPTER 13

AND the LORD spake unto Moses, saying,
2 Send thou men, that they may search the land
of Canaan, which I give unto the children of
Israel: of every tribe of their fathers shall ye send a
man, every one a ruler among them.
3 And Moses by the commandment of the LORD
sent them from the wilderness of Paran: all those
men *were* heads of the children of Israel.
4 And these *were* their names: of the tribe of
Reuben, Shammua the son of Zaccur.
5 Of the tribe of Simeon, Shaphat the son of Hori.
6 Of the tribe of Judah, Caleb the son of Jephun-
neh.
7 Of the tribe of Issachar, Igal the son of Joseph.
8 Of the tribe of Ephraim, Oshea the son of Nun.
9 Of the tribe of Benjamin, Palti the son of
Raphu.
10 Of the tribe of Zebulun, Gaddiel the son of
Sodi.
11 Of the tribe of Joseph, *namely*, of the tribe of
Manasseh, Gaddi the son of Susi.
12 Of the tribe of Dan, Ammiel the son of
Gemalli.
13 Of the tribe of Asher, Sethur the son of Michael.
14 Of the tribe of Naphtali, Nahbi the son of
Vophsi.
15 Of the tribe of Gad, Geuel the son of Machi.
16 These *are* the names of the men which Moses
sent to spy out the land. And Moses called Oshea
the son of Nun Jehoshua.
17 ¶ And Moses sent them to spy out the land of
Canaan, and said unto them, Get you up this *way*
southward, and go up into the mountain:
18 And see the land, what it *is*; and the people that
dwelleth therein, whether they *be* strong or weak,
few or many;
19 And what the land *is* that they dwell in, whether
it *be* good or bad; and what cities *they be* that they
dwell in, whether in tents, or in strong holds;
20 And what the land *is*, whether it *be* fat or lean,
whether there be wood therein, or not. And be
ye of good courage, and bring of the fruit of the
land. Now the time *was* the time of the firstripe
grapes.
21 ¶ So they went up, and searched the land from
the wilderness of Zin unto Rehob, as men come
to Hamath.
22 And they ascended by the south, and came
unto Hebron; where Ahiman, Sheshai, and Tal-
mai, the children of Anak, *were*. (Now Hebron
was built seven years before Zoan in Egypt.)
23 And they came unto the brook of Eshcol, and
cut down from thence a branch with one cluster
of grapes, and they bare it between two upon a
staff; and *they brought* of the pomegranates, and
of the figs.
24 The place was called the brook Eshcol, because
of the cluster of grapes which the children of Is-
rael cut down from thence.

12:6 *in a vision . . . in a dream*. Common modes of divine revelation (Heb. 1:1).
12:7 As great as Moses was, Christ is greater (Heb. 3:1–6).
12:8 *mouth to mouth*. Direct, face-to-face communication. *dark speeches*. Riddles, words not easily understood. *similitude of the LORD*. A visible appearance of the Lord's presence.
12:10 *Aaron looked upon Miriam*. It was Aaron's responsibility as priest to judge in cases of leprosy (Lev. 13:2–3).
12:13 Again Moses was the intercessor, even when personally wronged.
12:14 Exclusion for *seven days* was standard procedure for lepers (Lev. 13:50–51; 14:8).

Thoughts for Personal/Family Worship: Chapter 12

1. **The meekness of Moses was unparalleled in the Old Testament. He did not retaliate when Aaron and Miriam spoke against him. The natural response against criticism is to respond in kind, to answer fire with fire. Meekness or godly humility stops us from leaping to our own defense and is content to leave all injustices with the Lord, believing that He will defend and vindicate us as He sees fit. In this way, Moses is a good example for us all—and an image of Christ (1 Peter 2:21–23). How do you respond to criticism? How can you grow more like Christ in this?**
2. **How Moses responded to Aaron's request to him in behalf of Miriam is also a good pattern. Immediately, Moses interceded in her behalf to the Lord. It would have been so easy to rejoice in her affliction. But that kind of bitterness is never right, and Moses held no bitterness against Miriam though she led the rebellion against him. Nor did he find pleasure in her chastisement. Instead he prayed for her healing. Here also is a likeness to Christ who prayed for His crucifiers, who acted out of ignorance, to be forgiven (Luke 23:34). It is good to follow the example of Moses, but far better to follow the example of Christ, whom Moses had in view from the beginning (Heb. 11:26). For whom should you be praying, instead of stewing in bitterness?**

Chapter 13: *Moses sends spies into Canaan who return confirming the land to be all God had promised.*

Mission and Report of the Spies (13:1–33)

13:16 *Oshea*. The same name as the prophet Hosea, meaning "salvation," whereas *Jehoshua* means "Jehovah is salvation."
13:20 *fat or lean*. Fertile or barren.
13:21 *from . . . Zin unto Rehob*. From south to north.
13:23 *brook of Eshcol*. Valley of Eshcol, meaning "cluster."

25 And they returned from searching of the land
after forty days.
26 ¶ And they went and came to Moses, and to
Aaron, and to all the congregation of the children
of Israel, unto the wilderness of Paran, to Kadesh;
and brought back word unto them, and unto all
the congregation, and shewed them the fruit of
the land.
27 And they told him, and said, We came unto the
land whither thou sentest us, and surely it floweth
with milk and honey; and this *is* the fruit of it.
28 Nevertheless the people *be* strong that dwell in
the land, and the cities *are* walled, *and* very great:
and moreover we saw the children of Anak there.
29 The Amalekites dwell in the land of the south:
and the Hittites, and the Jebusites, and the Amor-
ites, dwell in the mountains: and the Canaanites
dwell by the sea, and by the coast of Jordan.
30 And Caleb stilled the people before Moses, and
said, Let us go up at once, and possess it; for we
are well able to overcome it.
31 But the men that went up with him said, We be
not able to go up against the people; for they *are*
stronger than we.
32 And they brought up an evil report of the
land which they had searched unto the children
of Israel, saying, The land, through which we
have gone to search it, *is* a land that eateth up the
inhabitants thereof; and all the people that we saw
in it *are* men of a great stature.
33 And there we saw the giants, the sons of Anak,
which come of the giants: and we were in our own
sight as grasshoppers, and so we were in their
sight.

CHAPTER 14

AND all the congregation lifted up their voice, and
cried; and the people wept that night.
2 And all the children of Israel murmured against
Moses and against Aaron: and the whole congre-
gation said unto them, Would God that we had
died in the land of Egypt! or would God we had
died in this wilderness!
3 And wherefore hath the LORD brought us unto
this land, to fall by the sword, that our wives and
our children should be a prey? were it not better
for us to return into Egypt?
4 And they said one to another, Let us make a
captain, and let us return into Egypt.
5 Then Moses and Aaron fell on their faces be-
fore all the assembly of the congregation of the
children of Israel.
6 ¶ And Joshua the son of Nun, and Caleb the son
of Jephunneh, *which were* of them that searched
the land, rent their clothes:
7 And they spake unto all the company of the
children of Israel, saying, The land, which we
passed through to search it, *is* an exceeding good
land.
8 If the LORD delight in us, then he will bring us
into this land, and give it us; a land which floweth
with milk and honey.
9 Only rebel not ye against the LORD, neither fear
ye the people of the land; for they *are* bread for
us: their defence is departed from them, and the
LORD *is* with us: fear them not.
10 But all the congregation bade stone them with
stones. And the glory of the LORD appeared in
the tabernacle of the congregation before all the
children of Israel.

13:27 *surely it floweth with milk and honey.* An expression of prosperity, and a reminder of God's promise (14:8; Ex. 3:8,17).
13:32 *evil report.* Bad report.

Thoughts for Personal/Family Worship: Chapter 13

The nation had reached the southern frontier of Canaan, the Promised Land. They were right on the border of blessing, but faced another crisis of faith. The spies returned from the land with vivid proof that the land was all God promised it would be. The evidence of blessing was unmistakable, but ten spies also reported a serious risk in claiming the promises. The grapes testified to incomparable blessing, but the giants threatened immense opposition, particularly when they saw themselves as grasshoppers in comparison. They were not adequate to face the risk. So they admired the blessing but failed to possess it. Many professing Christians tend to live on the border of blessing as well. It is one thing to consider all that we have in Christ, to theorize about it from every theological angle. We know it is good and we want it but for whatever reasons we stay on the fringes and do not lay claim by faith to all the promises we have in Christ which are yea and amen. God is greater than all the giants and can enable the grasshoppers to conquer. Caleb understood that and so should we. How can we overcome fear and unbelief in our hearts?

Chapter 14: *The people concur with the majority report, and the Lord sentences the nation to forty years in the wilderness.*

Failure of the People to Enter Canaan (14:1–45)

14:2–3 Ironically, they desired death in bondage to Egypt or in the waste of the wilderness but hesitated at the prospect of death by the sword. They failed to believe the promise that God would give them the land. *prey.* Plunder or spoil (v. 31).

14:4 *make a captain.* Appoint a head or leader. *return into Egypt.* Unbelief causes the world to become attractive by causing forgetfulness of its bondage (Acts 7:39).

14:5 *fell on their faces.* Gesture expressing their horror at the attack against God's holiness and Word.

14:6 *rent their clothes.* Gesture expressing contrition and grief.

14:9 *they are bread for us.* We will utterly consume them. *defence.* Shadow, figurative for protection. *the LORD is with us: fear them not.* The Lord's presence, which is invisible, dispels the fear of the enemy, who is visible. This is walking by faith and not by sight.

14:10 *bade.* Said.

11 ¶ And the LORD said unto Moses, How long
will this people provoke me? and how long will
it be ere they believe me, for all the signs which I
have shewed among them?
12 I will smite them with the pestilence, and
disinherit them, and will make of thee a greater
nation and mightier than they.
13 ¶ And Moses said unto the LORD, Then the
Egyptians shall hear *it*, (for thou broughtest up
this people in thy might from among them;)
14 And they will tell *it* to the inhabitants of this
land: *for* they have heard that thou LORD *art*
among this people, that thou LORD art seen face
to face, and *that* thy cloud standeth over them,
and *that* thou goest before them, by day time in
a pillar of a cloud, and in a pillar of fire by night.
15 ¶ Now *if* thou shalt kill *all* this people as one
man, then the nations which have heard the fame
of thee will speak, saying,
16 Because the LORD was not able to bring this
people into the land which he sware unto them,
therefore he hath slain them in the wilderness.
17 And now, I beseech thee, let the power of my
Lord be great, according as thou hast spoken,
saying,
18 The LORD *is* longsuffering, and of great mercy,
forgiving iniquity and transgression, and by no
means clearing *the guilty*, visiting the iniquity of
the fathers upon the children unto the third and
fourth *generation*.
19 Pardon, I beseech thee, the iniquity of this
people according unto the greatness of thy mercy,
and as thou hast forgiven this people, from Egypt
even until now.
20 And the LORD said, I have pardoned according
to thy word:
21 But *as* truly *as* I live, all the earth shall be filled
with the glory of the LORD.
22 Because all those men which have seen my
glory, and my miracles, which I did in Egypt and
in the wilderness, and have tempted me now these
ten times, and have not hearkened to my voice;
23 Surely they shall not see the land which I sware
unto their fathers, neither shall any of them that
provoked me see it:
24 But my servant Caleb, because he had another
spirit with him, and hath followed me fully, him
will I bring into the land whereinto he went; and
his seed shall possess it.
25 (Now the Amalekites and the Canaanites
dwelt in the valley.) To morrow turn you, and get
you into the wilderness by the way of the Red sea.
26 ¶ And the LORD spake unto Moses and unto
Aaron, saying,
27 How long *shall I bear with* this evil congrega-
tion, which murmur against me? I have heard the
murmurings of the children of Israel, which they
murmur against me.
28 Say unto them, *As truly as* I live, saith the
LORD, as ye have spoken in mine ears, so will I do
to you:
29 Your carcases shall fall in this wilderness; and
all that were numbered of you, according to your
whole number, from twenty years old and up-
ward, which have murmured against me,
30 Doubtless ye shall not come into the land, *con-
cerning* which I sware to make you dwell therein,
save Caleb the son of Jephunneh, and Joshua the
son of Nun.
31 But your little ones, which ye said should be a
prey, them will I bring in, and they shall know the
land which ye have despised.
32 But *as for* you, your carcases, they shall fall in
this wilderness.
33 And your children shall wander in the wilder-
ness forty years, and bear your whoredoms, until
your carcases be wasted in the wilderness.
34 After the number of the days in which ye

14:12 *disinherit them . . . make of thee a greater nation.* Cut this generation off from being the Lord's people and start over with Moses. This would have delayed the Abrahamic promise but would not have reversed it since Moses was of Abraham's seed.

14:13–16 The logic of Moses' intercession was based on jealousy for God's glory.

14:17 *according as thou hast spoken.* He pleads God's Word in prayer, a good pattern to emulate.

14:18 Moses quoted the Lord's revelation of His character (see notes at Ex. 34:6 and 7), again appealed to Him on the basis of His Word and nature.

14:19–20 *Pardon . . . I have pardoned.* How remarkably, specifically, and graciously the Lord answers prayer!

14:21 *all the earth shall be filled with the glory of the LORD.* God's great purpose in Christ (Ps. 72:19; Isa. 11:9; Hab. 2:14; Eph. 4:10).

14:22 *these ten times.* Trace their failures at (1) the Red Sea (Ex. 14:11–12); (2) Marah (Ex. 15:24); (3) the wilderness of Sin (Ex. 16:3); (4) hoarding manna (Ex. 16:20); (5) violating the Sabbath (Ex. 16:27–29); (6) Rephidim (Ex. 17:2–3); (7) the golden calf (Ex. 32); (8) Taberah (Num. 11:1); (9) more complaining about food (11:4); and (10) their refusal to enter Canaan (14:1–4).

14:24 *Caleb . . . followed me fully.* Literally, "he made it full or complete after me," a repeated commendation of Caleb (32:11–12; Deut. 1:36; Josh. 14:8–9,14) that means his heart was not divided but wholly given to pursuing God (1 Sam. 12:20; 1 Kings 11:4–6).

14:29 *Your carcases shall fall.* All that generation of men, except Caleb and Joshua, would die *in this wilderness* for their unbelief, a warning to all that hear the Word that they not harden their hearts (Ps. 95:10–11; Heb. 3:7—4:13).

14:31 *despised.* Rejected.

14:33 *bear your whoredoms.* Endure your unfaithfulness. Although the next generation was not responsible for the wanderings, they endured them. What was punishment for one generation became a means of testing and growth for the next. This highlights one of the themes of Numbers: out with the old, in with new.

searched the land, *even* forty days, each day for a
year, shall ye bear your iniquities, *even* forty years,
and ye shall know my breach of promise.
35 I the LORD have said, I will surely do it unto all
this evil congregation, that are gathered together
against me: in this wilderness they shall be
consumed, and there they shall die.
36 And the men, which Moses sent to search the
land, who returned, and made all the congrega-
tion to murmur against him, by bringing up a
slander upon the land,
37 Even those men that did bring up the evil re-
port upon the land, died by the plague before the
LORD.
38 But Joshua the son of Nun, and Caleb the son
of Jephunneh, *which were* of the men that went to
search the land, lived *still*.
39 And Moses told these sayings unto all the chil-
dren of Israel: and the people mourned greatly.
40 ¶ And they rose up early in the morning, and
gat them up into the top of the mountain, saying,
Lo, we *be here*, and will go up unto the place which
the LORD hath promised: for we have sinned.
41 And Moses said, Wherefore now do ye trans-
gress the commandment of the LORD? but it shall
not prosper.
42 Go not up, for the LORD *is* not among you;
that ye be not smitten before your enemies.
43 For the Amalekites and the Canaanites *are*
there before you, and ye shall fall by the sword:
because ye are turned away from the LORD, there-
fore the LORD will not be with you.
44 But they presumed to go up unto the hill top:
nevertheless the ark of the covenant of the LORD,
and Moses, departed not out of the camp.
45 Then the Amalekites came down, and the
Canaanites which dwelt in that hill, and smote
them, and discomfited them, *even* unto Hormah.

CHAPTER 15

AND the LORD spake unto Moses, saying,
2 Speak unto the children of Israel, and say unto
them, When ye be come into the land of your
habitations, which I give unto you,
3 And will make an offering by fire unto the LORD,
a burnt offering, or a sacrifice in performing a
vow, or in a freewill offering, or in your solemn
feasts, to make a sweet savour unto the LORD, of
the herd, or of the flock:
4 Then shall he that offereth his offering unto the
LORD bring a meat offering of a tenth deal of flour
mingled with the fourth *part* of an hin of oil.
5 And the fourth *part* of an hin of wine for a
drink offering shalt thou prepare with the burnt
offering or sacrifice, for one lamb.
6 Or for a ram, thou shalt prepare *for* a meat of-
fering two tenth deals of flour mingled with the
third *part* of an hin of oil.
7 And for a drink offering thou shalt offer the
third *part* of an hin of wine, *for* a sweet savour
unto the LORD.

14:34 *my breach of promise.* Literally, "my opposition or displeasure." God never breaks a promise (23:19).
14:36 *slander.* Unfavorable report.
14:37 *died by the plague before the LORD.* A sudden judgment for their sin, and thus a warning and precursor of what was ahead.
14:40 *gat them up.* They went up.
14:45 *discomfited them.* Defeated them. Going without the Lord's presence was certain defeat and disaster.

Thoughts for Personal/Family Worship: Chapter 14

1. **In the midst of all the unbelief and doubt, Joshua and Caleb sought to counter the report of their colleagues by drawing attention away from the greatness of the dangers to the greatness of God. They highlighted the invincible power of God, who could remove every defense of the enemy (v. 9); the immutable purpose of God, who, based on His sovereign good pleasure, would give them the land (v. 8); and the immediate presence of God, who would dispel every reason for being afraid (v. 9). The truths about God that should have encouraged ancient Israel to trust the Lord should encourage us today. The God of then is the God of now. How can these truths help you to follow the Lord fully, just as Caleb and Joshua did?**
2. **Apart from Jesus Christ, none was a more fervent intercessor than Moses. His intercessory prayer in this chapter is a great example not only of what prayer should look like but of his noble character. God had offered to make him the father of a nation, a prospect that most would have taken. But instead, he put thoughts of his glory aside and argued for God's reputation. His burden was that if the Lord destroyed Israel, then the enemy would mock the Lord and allege that He was not able to bring His people into the land as He had sworn to do. Prayer that is jealous for the Lord's name and glory will prevail. He prayed that God would pardon and He did. As remarkable as Moses' prayers are, they should point us to the One at God's right hand who ever lives to make intercession for us—One whose prayers are always answered. What encouragement do you find in that today?**

PERIOD OF WILDERNESS WANDERING (15:1—21:35)

Chapter 15: *The Lord repeats instructions concerning sacrifices, punishes the sin of presumption, and gives instruction concerning the ribbon of blue on the garment.*

Sacrifices, Sabbath Breakers, and Tassels (15:1–41)

15:2 *When ye be come into the land.* A gracious reassurance after being sentenced to forty years in the wilderness that they would inhabit the land (v. 18).
15:3 Right after the dark events of the preceding chapter, the Lord points to the sacrifices that pictured Christ's atoning work as the assurance that there is forgiveness with Him.
15:4–12 See Lev. 1–6 for detailed explanations of the various offerings. This repetition of details underlines that there is to be no divergence from God's way of redemption.
15:4 *a tenth deal.* A tenth part. *hin.* Approximately 1.5 gallons (throughout the chapter).

8 And when thou preparest a bullock *for* a burnt
offering, or *for* a sacrifice in performing a vow, or
peace offerings unto the LORD:
9 Then shall he bring with a bullock a meat offer-
ing of three tenth deals of flour mingled with half
an hin of oil.
10 And thou shalt bring for a drink offering half
an hin of wine, *for* an offering made by fire, of a
sweet savour unto the LORD.
11 Thus shall it be done for one bullock, or for
one ram, or for a lamb, or a kid.
12 According to the number that ye shall prepare,
so shall ye do to every one according to their
number.
13 All that are born of the country shall do these
things after this manner, in offering an offering
made by fire, of a sweet savour unto the LORD.
14 And if a stranger sojourn with you, or whoso-
ever *be* among you in your generations, and will
offer an offering made by fire, of a sweet savour
unto the LORD; as ye do, so he shall do.
15 One ordinance *shall be both* for you of the
congregation, and also for the stranger that
sojourneth *with you*, an ordinance for ever in
your generations: as ye *are*, so shall the stranger
be before the LORD.
16 One law and one manner shall be for you, and
for the stranger that sojourneth with you.
17 ¶ And the LORD spake unto Moses, saying,
18 Speak unto the children of Israel, and say
unto them, When ye come into the land whither
I bring you,
19 Then it shall be, that, when ye eat of the bread
of the land, ye shall offer up an heave offering
unto the LORD.
20 Ye shall offer up a cake of the first of your
dough *for* an heave offering: as *ye do* the heave of-
fering of the threshingfloor, so shall ye heave it.
21 Of the first of your dough ye shall give unto
the LORD an heave offering in your generations.
22 ¶ And if ye have erred, and not observed all
these commandments, which the LORD hath
spoken unto Moses,
23 *Even* all that the LORD hath commanded you
by the hand of Moses, from the day that the LORD
commanded *Moses*, and henceforward among
your generations;
24 Then it shall be, if *ought* be committed
by ignorance without the knowledge of the
congregation, that all the congregation shall offer
one young bullock for a burnt offering, for a sweet
savour unto the LORD, with his meat offering, and
his drink offering, according to the manner, and
one kid of the goats for a sin offering.
25 And the priest shall make an atonement for
all the congregation of the children of Israel, and
it shall be forgiven them; for it *is* ignorance: and
they shall bring their offering, a sacrifice made by
fire unto the LORD, and their sin offering before
the LORD, for their ignorance:
26 And it shall be forgiven all the congregation
of the children of Israel, and the stranger that so-
journeth among them; seeing all the people *were*
in ignorance.
27 ¶ And if any soul sin through ignorance, then
he shall bring a she goat of the first year for a sin
offering.
28 And the priest shall make an atonement for
the soul that sinneth ignorantly, when he sinneth
by ignorance before the LORD, to make an atone-
ment for him; and it shall be forgiven him.
29 Ye shall have one law for him that sinneth
through ignorance, *both for* him that is born
among the children of Israel, and for the stranger
that sojourneth among them.
30 ¶ But the soul that doeth *ought* presumptu-
ously, *whether he be* born in the land, or a stranger,
the same reproacheth the LORD; and that soul
shall be cut off from among his people.
31 Because he hath despised the word of the
LORD, and hath broken his commandment, that
soul shall utterly be cut off; his iniquity *shall be*
upon him.
32 ¶ And while the children of Israel were in the
wilderness, they found a man that gathered sticks
upon the sabbath day.
33 And they that found him gathering sticks
brought him unto Moses and Aaron, and unto all
the congregation.
34 And they put him in ward, because it was not

15:13–16 The requirements and procedures are the same for either a native Israelite or one who resides as a resident alien (v. 30). God is no respecter of persons. There is but one way: Jesus, whom all the sacrifices picture (John 14:6).

15:19 *bread.* Food in general. *heave offering.* The contribution which is lifted up (vv. 20–21).

15:20 *cake of the first of your dough.* Literally, "firstfruit or choicest portion of your whole-grain flour or dough [made into] a ring-shaped bread."

15:22 *have erred.* Have done wrong carelessly or ignorantly without evil intention.

15:24 *if ought be committed by ignorance.* Literally, "if from the eyes of the congregation it is done by unintentional sin."

15:25 *ignorance.* Careless or unintentional sin (vv. 26–29). Careless sins are still transgressions of God's law and require sacrifice.

15:30 *presumptuously.* Literally, "with a high hand." *reproacheth the LORD.* Blasphemes the Lord. *that soul.* That person (v. 31).

15:31 *despised.* Regarded with contempt. *shall utterly be cut off; his iniquity shall be upon him.* The one guilty of the sin of high hand was without hope under the rigor of the law.

15:32 *they found a man that gathered sticks upon the sabbath day.* An example of presumptuous sin: it was done directly against the fourth commandment and God's specific instructions (Ex. 16:23).

15:34 *in ward.* Under custody, in a guardhouse. *it was not declared.* It had not been explained.

declared what should be done to him.
35 And the LORD said unto Moses, The man shall
be surely put to death: all the congregation shall
stone him with stones without the camp.
36 And all the congregation brought him with-
out the camp, and stoned him with stones, and he
died; as the LORD commanded Moses.
37 ¶ And the LORD spake unto Moses, saying,
38 Speak unto the children of Israel, and bid
them that they make them fringes in the borders
of their garments throughout their generations,
and that they put upon the fringe of the borders
a ribband of blue:
39 And it shall be unto you for a fringe, that ye
may look upon it, and remember all the com-
mandments of the LORD, and do them; and that
ye seek not after your own heart and your own
eyes, after which ye use to go a whoring:
40 That ye may remember, and do all my com-
mandments, and be holy unto your God.
41 I *am* the LORD your God, which brought you
out of the land of Egypt, to be your God: I *am* the
LORD your God.

CHAPTER 16

NOW Korah, the son of Izhar, the son of Kohath,
the son of Levi, and Dathan and Abiram, the sons
of Eliab, and On, the son of Peleth, sons of Reu-
ben, took *men*:
2 And they rose up before Moses, with certain
of the children of Israel, two hundred and fifty
princes of the assembly, famous in the congrega-
tion, men of renown:
3 And they gathered themselves together against
Moses and against Aaron, and said unto them, *Ye
take* too much upon you, seeing all the congrega-
tion *are* holy, every one of them, and the LORD *is*
among them: wherefore then lift ye up yourselves
above the congregation of the LORD?
4 And when Moses heard *it*, he fell upon his face:
5 And he spake unto Korah and unto all his com-
pany, saying, Even to morrow the LORD will shew
who *are* his, and *who is* holy; and will cause *him*
to come near unto him: even *him* whom he hath
chosen will he cause to come near unto him.
6 This do; Take you censers, Korah, and all his
company;

15:35 The severity of the penalty indicates this was an intentional transgression, an affront against God's law.
15:38 *fringes*. Tassels. *borders*. Hems. *ribband*. Ribbon. *blue*. The color of the wrapping of the ark, the symbol of God's throne (4:5–6), the curtains of the tabernacle as the palace of the King (Ex. 26:1), and the uniform of the High Priest (Ex. 28:6), reminding them that they were a kingdom of priests and a holy nation (Ex. 19:6). What God intended as a humbling reminder some would take as an occasion for proud hypocrisy (Matt. 23:5).
15:39 *remember*. Think about intentionally.

Thoughts for Personal/Family Worship: Chapter 15

1. **"Sin is the transgression of the law" (1 John 3:4). God's moral law is inflexible, timeless, universal, and unchangeable. Any violation of it constitutes sin and is subject to penalty, even those violations that are unintentional or accidental. Ignorance of the law is no excuse. God in His mercy and grace has made provision by which sins may be forgiven, and we should make use of that cleansing in Jesus Christ. But it is a reminder that we should also walk carefully lest even by carelessness we offend the Lord. In what ways might you be tempted to live carelessly?**
2. **The tassels on the hems of the garments were visible reminders to the people of the special relationship they had with the Lord. Every step they took reminded them of a relationship with the Lord their God that was based on His grace and redemption. The tassels also declared to others that they belonged to the Lord, and must live as God's holy people. We no longer wear tassels but the Lord has given to us something to look at to remind us of redemption and our obligation as the redeemed to be marked as different from the world. The Lord's Supper is a visible Word to declare these truths. How can observing the Lord's Supper help us to remember what Christ has done and who we are in Him?**
3. **God's sacrificial ordinances had a place for the Gentile. Those foreigners who embraced Israel's God on the grounds of the shed blood were as fully accepted as those of Israel. The Lord testified, "as ye are, so shall the stranger be before the Lord" (v. 15)—that is both the believing Jew and Gentile are children of God by faith in Christ Jesus (Gal. 3:28–29). Rejoice in the Lord's lack of favoritism!**
4. **The man gathering sticks on the Sabbath day was stoned to death. The ungodly object at the severity of the penalty, yet in this manner the Lord teaches that "the soul that sinneth, it shall die" (Ezek. 18:4). God's law demands perfect obedience and disobedience will bring the wrath of God. Thank God for the perfect obedience of Christ for therein lies our shelter from the terrible stroke of judgment.**

Rebellion against and Confirmation of Aaron's Priesthood (16:1—17:13)

Chapter 16: *The Lord judges Korah for his rebellion along with those who followed and sympathized with him.*

16:1–2 *Korah*. A son of Kohath, the most prominent of the Levites responsible for the sacred furniture, but not a priest. *Dathan and Abiram . . . sons of Reuben*. From the tribe that had been stripped of the place of preeminence because of Reuben's sin (Gen. 49:3–4). *princes*. Exalted ones or leaders. *famous in the congregation, men of renown*. Literally, "called ones of the assembly, men of name." They were well-known and important.
16:3 *Ye take too much upon you*. They alleged that Moses and Aaron had arrogated to themselves their leadership roles. False teachers in the church act similarly (Jude 11). *all the congregation are holy*. Any of the nation were equally qualified.
16:5 *the LORD will shew who are his*. The Greek Septuagint translation of this text, "the Lord knoweth them that are his," is quoted by Paul (2 Tim. 2:19).
16:6 *censers*. Small pans with burning coals from the altar of sacrifice.
16:9–10 They were dissatisfied with their position and

7 And put fire therein, and put incense in them
before the LORD to morrow: and it shall be *that*
the man whom the LORD doth choose, he *shall be*
holy: *ye take* too much upon you, ye sons of Levi.
8 And Moses said unto Korah, Hear, I pray you,
ye sons of Levi:
9 *Seemeth it but* a small thing unto you, that the
God of Israel hath separated you from the con-
gregation of Israel, to bring you near to himself
to do the service of the tabernacle of the LORD,
and to stand before the congregation to minister
unto them?
10 And he hath brought thee near *to him*, and all
thy brethren the sons of Levi with thee: and seek
ye the priesthood also?
11 For which cause *both* thou and all thy com-
pany *are* gathered together against the LORD: and
what *is* Aaron, that ye murmur against him?
12 ¶ And Moses sent to call Dathan and Abiram,
the sons of Eliab: which said, We will not come
up:
13 *Is it* a small thing that thou hast brought us up
out of a land that floweth with milk and honey, to
kill us in the wilderness, except thou make thyself
altogether a prince over us?
14 Moreover thou hast not brought us into a
land that floweth with milk and honey, or given
us inheritance of fields and vineyards: wilt thou
put out the eyes of these men? we will not come
up.
15 And Moses was very wroth, and said unto the
LORD, Respect not thou their offering: I have not
taken one ass from them, neither have I hurt one
of them.
16 And Moses said unto Korah, Be thou and all
thy company before the LORD, thou, and they, and
Aaron, to morrow:
17 And take every man his censer, and put incense
in them, and bring ye before the LORD every man
his censer, two hundred and fifty censers; thou
also, and Aaron, each *of you* his censer.
18 And they took every man his censer, and put
fire in them, and laid incense thereon, and stood
in the door of the tabernacle of the congregation
with Moses and Aaron.
19 And Korah gathered all the congregation
against them unto the door of the tabernacle
of the congregation: and the glory of the LORD
appeared unto all the congregation.
20 And the LORD spake unto Moses and unto
Aaron, saying,
21 Separate yourselves from among this congre-
gation, that I may consume them in a moment.
22 And they fell upon their faces, and said, O
God, the God of the spirits of all flesh, shall one
man sin, and wilt thou be wroth with all the
congregation?
23 ¶ And the LORD spake unto Moses, saying,
24 Speak unto the congregation, saying, Get you
up from about the tabernacle of Korah, Dathan,
and Abiram.
25 And Moses rose up and went unto Dathan and
Abiram; and the elders of Israel followed him.
26 And he spake unto the congregation, saying,
Depart, I pray you, from the tents of these wicked
men, and touch nothing of theirs, lest ye be
consumed in all their sins.
27 So they gat up from the tabernacle of Korah,
Dathan, and Abiram, on every side: and Dathan
and Abiram came out, and stood in the door of
their tents, and their wives, and their sons, and
their little children.
28 And Moses said, Hereby ye shall know that
the LORD hath sent me to do all these works; for *I
have* not *done them* of mine own mind.
29 If these men die the common death of all men,
or if they be visited after the visitation of all men;
then the LORD hath not sent me.
30 But if the LORD make a new thing, and the
earth open her mouth, and swallow them up,
with all that *appertain* unto them, and they go
down quick into the pit; then ye shall understand
that these men have provoked the LORD.
31 ¶ And it came to pass, as he had made an end
of speaking all these words, that the ground clave
asunder that *was* under them:
32 And the earth opened her mouth, and swal-
lowed them up, and their houses, and all the men
that *appertained* unto Korah, and all *their* goods.
33 They, and all that *appertained* to them, went
down alive into the pit, and the earth closed
upon them: and they perished from among the
congregation.
34 And all Israel that *were* round about them fled

desired to be priests. They rejected the way of mediation God had set up and assumed they could get to God on their own, a fatal assumption.

16:15 *very wroth.* Extremely hot with anger.

16:21 *Separate yourselves.* An urgent command to take sides either with Korah or Aaron.

16:22 *God of the spirits of all flesh.* Life-giver who sustains all creatures (27:16; Job 12:10; Ps. 104:29–30; Dan. 5:23; Acts 17:25). *wroth.* Furious, a different word than in v. 15.

16:24 *tabernacle of Korah.* His tent or dwelling place.

16:27 *gat up.* Went up.

16:29 *If these men die the common death of all men.* Literally, "if as all men die these die." *visited after the visitation of all men.* Punished with the punishment of all men.

16:30 *make a new thing.* Literally, "create a creation," do something unique. *quick.* Alive. *pit.* In Hebrew, *sheol,* which can refer to death, the grave, or the abode of departed wicked spirits. Since Moses is speaking of the manner of death, the idea would be to be buried alive (v. 32).

16:31 *clave asunder.* Split apart.

16:32 *all the men.* This is later qualified to indicate that some of Korah's family survived (26:11).

at the cry of them: for they said, Lest the earth
swallow us up *also*.
35 And there came out a fire from the LORD, and
consumed the two hundred and fifty men that
offered incense.
36 ¶ And the LORD spake unto Moses, saying,
37 Speak unto Eleazar the son of Aaron the priest,
that he take up the censers out of the burning, and
scatter thou the fire yonder; for they are hallowed.
38 The censers of these sinners against their own
souls, let them make them broad plates *for* a cov-
ering of the altar: for they offered them before the
LORD, therefore they are hallowed: and they shall
be a sign unto the children of Israel.
39 And Eleazar the priest took the brasen censers,
wherewith they that were burnt had offered; and
they were made broad *plates for* a covering of the
altar:
40 *To be* a memorial unto the children of Israel,
that no stranger, which *is* not of the seed of Aaron,
come near to offer incense before the LORD; that
he be not as Korah, and as his company: as the
LORD said to him by the hand of Moses.
41 ¶ But on the morrow all the congregation of
the children of Israel murmured against Moses
and against Aaron, saying, Ye have killed the
people of the LORD.
42 And it came to pass, when the congregation
was gathered against Moses and against Aaron,
that they looked toward the tabernacle of the con-
gregation: and, behold, the cloud covered it, and
the glory of the LORD appeared.
43 And Moses and Aaron came before the taber-
nacle of the congregation.
44 ¶ And the LORD spake unto Moses, saying,
45 Get you up from among this congregation,
that I may consume them as in a moment. And
they fell upon their faces.
46 ¶ And Moses said unto Aaron, Take a censer,
and put fire therein from off the altar, and put on
incense, and go quickly unto the congregation, and
make an atonement for them: for there is wrath
gone out from the LORD; the plague is begun.
47 And Aaron took as Moses commanded, and ran
into the midst of the congregation; and, behold, the
plague was begun among the people: and he put
on incense, and made an atonement for the people.
48 And he stood between the dead and the living;
and the plague was stayed.
49 Now they that died in the plague were four-
teen thousand and seven hundred, beside them
that died about the matter of Korah.
50 And Aaron returned unto Moses unto the
door of the tabernacle of the congregation: and
the plague was stayed.

CHAPTER 17

AND the LORD spake unto Moses, saying,
2 Speak unto the children of Israel, and take of
every one of them a rod according to the house
of *their* fathers, of all their princes according to
the house of their fathers twelve rods: write thou
every man's name upon his rod.
3 And thou shalt write Aaron's name upon the
rod of Levi: for one rod *shall be* for the head of the
house of their fathers.
4 And thou shalt lay them up in the tabernacle
of the congregation before the testimony, where I
will meet with you.
5 And it shall come to pass, *that* the man's rod,
whom I shall choose, shall blossom: and I will make

16:37 *hallowed.* Holy, set apart (v. 38).
16:40 *stranger.* Any unauthorized person.
16:46 *the plague.* The blow or affliction.
16:48 *he stood between the dead and the living.* Where the plague had struck, to prevent it from proceeding any farther. *was stayed.* Was restrained or brought to a halt (v. 50).

Thoughts for Personal/Family Worship: Chapter 16

1. **Korah's rebellion teaches the necessity of the divinely chosen Mediator. Trying to get to God otherwise is fatal. The rebellion of Korah, Dathan, and Abiram was an attempt to usurp the divinely appointed priesthood. Consequently, the attempt was answered with holy wrath. Aaron's priesthood typified Christ's. The lessons are clear. Man cannot approach God on his own because his sin is too great and God's holiness is too glorious. The punishment for standing alone before God is eternally severe. Korah's death was unusual and inescapable, teaching us to fear the Lord. According to Matt. 10:28, what other reasons are we given for fearing God?**
2. **The plague that occurred after Korah's destruction teaches the effectiveness of the divinely chosen Mediator. After the drama of the burial and charred remains of the rebels, many accused God of not being fair because they had a faulty understanding of how holy God is and how sinful man is. So God's glory again was revealed in judgment. But Moses rushed to grace and instructed Aaron to stand between the living and the dead. The plague could not get past the priest. Here is the gospel lesson. God's wrath against sin is just, but God in grace sent His Son, the Mediator, to make atonement. Christ and the power of His sacrifice stands between the sinner and God's justice, and God's wrath cannot get past our great High Priest. Christ's sacrifice was successful. So this is our only hope: to have Christ stand between us and God. Are you trusting arrogantly in yourself or trusting dependently on the Mediator?**

Chapter 17: ***Aaron's rod buds to confirm him as the divinely chosen priest.***

17:2 *every one of them a rod.* Literally, "a rod a rod from the house of a father" (or a staff). The Hebrew uses repetition to express a distributive idea. *the princes.* The exalted ones or leaders (v. 6).
17:4 *before the testimony.* Before the ark that contained the stone tables on which were written the Ten Commandments (Ex. 25:16; 31:18; Heb. 9:4).
17:5 *the man's rod, whom I shall choose, shall blossom.* An event supernatural in nature as divine confirmation. Some in-

to cease from me the murmurings of the children of Israel, whereby they murmur against you.

6 ¶ And Moses spake unto the children of Israel, and every one of their princes gave him a rod apiece, for each prince one, according to their fathers' houses, *even* twelve rods: and the rod of Aaron *was* among their rods.

7 And Moses laid up the rods before the LORD in the tabernacle of witness.

8 And it came to pass, that on the morrow Moses went into the tabernacle of witness; and, behold, the rod of Aaron for the house of Levi was budded, and brought forth buds, and bloomed blossoms, and yielded almonds.

9 And Moses brought out all the rods from before the LORD unto all the children of Israel: and they looked, and took every man his rod.

10 ¶ And the LORD said unto Moses, Bring Aaron's rod again before the testimony, to be kept for a token against the rebels; and thou shalt quite take away their murmurings from me, that they die not.

11 And Moses did *so*: as the LORD commanded him, so did he.

12 And the children of Israel spake unto Moses, saying, Behold, we die, we perish, we all perish.

13 Whosoever cometh any thing near unto the tabernacle of the LORD shall die: shall we be consumed with dying?

CHAPTER 18

AND the LORD said unto Aaron, Thou and thy sons and thy father's house with thee shall bear the iniquity of the sanctuary: and thou and thy sons with thee shall bear the iniquity of your priesthood.

2 And thy brethren also of the tribe of Levi, the tribe of thy father, bring thou with thee, that they may be joined unto thee, and minister unto thee: but thou and thy sons with thee *shall minister* before the tabernacle of witness.

3 And they shall keep thy charge, and the charge of all the tabernacle: only they shall not come nigh the vessels of the sanctuary and the altar, that neither they, nor ye also, die.

4 And they shall be joined unto thee, and keep the charge of the tabernacle of the congregation, for all the service of the tabernacle: and a stranger shall not come nigh unto you.

5 And ye shall keep the charge of the sanctuary, and the charge of the altar: that there be no wrath any more upon the children of Israel.

6 And I, behold, I have taken your brethren the Levites from among the children of Israel: to you *they are* given *as* a gift for the LORD, to do the service of the tabernacle of the congregation.

7 Therefore thou and thy sons with thee shall keep your priest's office for every thing of the altar, and within the vail; and ye shall serve: I have given your priest's office *unto you as* a service of gift: and the stranger that cometh nigh shall be put to death.

8 ¶ And the LORD spake unto Aaron, Behold, I also have given thee the charge of mine heave offerings of all the hallowed things of the children of Israel; unto thee have I given them by reason of the anointing, and to thy sons, by an ordinance for ever.

9 This shall be thine of the most holy things,

---

terpreters see the budding rod as a picture of resurrection, life coming to the lifeless. Although that may be involved, the primary intent is to show that God has chosen the only Mediator.

17:10 *to be kept for a token*. To be held in trust as a sign or memorial. *quite take away*. Exhaust or bring to an end.

17:12 *we die, we perish*. The people realized that unless they approached God in His appointed way through His appointed priest, His holiness would destroy them (1 Sam. 6:19–20).

17:13 A key lesson learned: approaching God on one's own apart from His chosen priest is fatal.

Thoughts for Personal/Family Worship: Chapter 17

1. **Aaron's rod that budded teaches the uniqueness of the divinely chosen Mediator. It confirmed God's choice of Aaron and his line to be the priestly line in the old covenant, and it was to be kept as a reminder of that uniqueness. This all points to Christ, the eternal Priest (Ps. 110:4; Heb. 5). It underscores the vital truth that Christ is the only Mediator between God and men (1 Tim. 2:5), the only way by which man can be saved (John 14:6). Praise Him for His provision!**
2. **The rod was kept inside the ark (Heb. 9:4), where only God could see, for it declares that the covenant Mediator is always before Him. The central work of the High Priest is toward God, appearing in His presence for the sake of the people (Heb. 9:24). God sees His Son and the glorified scars of His atonement and remembers the covenant. What assurance does this give to those of us who are united with God's Son about our relationship with the Father?**
3. **For the sake of review put chs. 16–17 together for important lessons regarding the mediation of Christ. From the pit, we learn the necessity of the Mediator. From the plague, we learn the effectiveness of the Mediator. From the budding rod, we learn the uniqueness of the Mediator. Looking at John 14:6, how do these all come together in the person of Christ?**

Chapter 18: *The Lord gives further instructions concerning the priests and Levites.*

Instructions regarding the Levites (18:1–32)

18:1 *bear the iniquity of the sanctuary*. Be responsible for all profaning of the holy area under their charge. *bear the iniquity of your priesthood*. Bear the blame for sins committed in relation to their ministry.

18:3 *charge*. Service or function.

18:4 *stranger*. Any unauthorized person (v. 7).

18:7 *within the vail*. The curtain that divided the tabernacle from the outer court.

18:8 *heave offerings*. General term for the contributions offered. *hallowed things*. Consecrated or set apart things. *the anointing*. The portion.

reserved from the fire: every oblation of theirs, every meat offering of theirs, and every sin offering of theirs, and every trespass offering of theirs, which they shall render unto me, *shall be* most holy for thee and for thy sons.

10 In the most holy *place* shalt thou eat it; every male shall eat it: it shall be holy unto thee.

11 And this *is* thine; the heave offering of their gift, with all the wave offerings of the children of Israel: I have given them unto thee, and to thy sons and to thy daughters with thee, by a statute for ever: every one that is clean in thy house shall eat of it.

12 All the best of the oil, and all the best of the wine, and of the wheat, the firstfruits of them which they shall offer unto the LORD, them have I given thee.

13 *And* whatsoever is first ripe in the land, which they shall bring unto the LORD, shall be thine; every one that is clean in thine house shall eat *of* it.

14 Every thing devoted in Israel shall be thine.

15 Every thing that openeth the matrix in all flesh, which they bring unto the LORD, *whether it be* of men or beasts, shall be thine: nevertheless the firstborn of man shalt thou surely redeem, and the firstling of unclean beasts shalt thou redeem.

16 And those that are to be redeemed from a month old shalt thou redeem, according to thine estimation, for the money of five shekels, after the shekel of the sanctuary, which *is* twenty gerahs.

17 But the firstling of a cow, or the firstling of a sheep, or the firstling of a goat, thou shalt not redeem; they *are* holy: thou shalt sprinkle their blood upon the altar, and shalt burn their fat *for* an offering made by fire, for a sweet savour unto the LORD.

18 And the flesh of them shall be thine, as the wave breast and as the right shoulder are thine.

19 All the heave offerings of the holy things, which the children of Israel offer unto the LORD, have I given thee, and thy sons and thy daughters with thee, by a statute for ever: it *is* a covenant of salt for ever before the LORD unto thee and to thy seed with thee.

20 ¶ And the LORD spake unto Aaron, Thou shalt have no inheritance in their land, neither shalt thou have any part among them: I *am* thy part and thine inheritance among the children of Israel.

21 And, behold, I have given the children of Levi all the tenth in Israel for an inheritance, for their service which they serve, *even* the service of the tabernacle of the congregation.

22 Neither must the children of Israel henceforth come nigh the tabernacle of the congregation, lest they bear sin, and die.

23 But the Levites shall do the service of the tabernacle of the congregation, and they shall bear their iniquity: *it shall be* a statute for ever throughout your generations, that among the children of Israel they have no inheritance.

24 But the tithes of the children of Israel, which they offer *as* an heave offering unto the LORD, I have given to the Levites to inherit: therefore I have said unto them, Among the children of Israel they shall have no inheritance.

25 ¶ And the LORD spake unto Moses, saying,

26 Thus speak unto the Levites, and say unto them, When ye take of the children of Israel the tithes which I have given you from them for your inheritance, then ye shall offer up an heave offering of it for the LORD, *even* a tenth *part* of the tithe.

27 And *this* your heave offering shall be reckoned unto you, as though *it were* the corn of the threshingfloor, and as the fulness of the winepress.

28 Thus ye also shall offer an heave offering unto the LORD of all your tithes, which ye receive of the children of Israel; and ye shall give thereof the LORD's heave offering to Aaron the priest.

29 Out of all your gifts ye shall offer every heave offering of the LORD, of all the best thereof, *even* the hallowed part thereof out of it.

30 Therefore thou shalt say unto them, When ye have heaved the best thereof from it, then it shall be counted unto the Levites as the increase of the threshingfloor, and as the increase of the winepress.

31 And ye shall eat it in every place, ye and your households: for it *is* your reward for your service in the tabernacle of the congregation.

32 And ye shall bear no sin by reason of it, when ye have heaved from it the best of it: neither shall ye pollute the holy things of the children of Israel, lest ye die.

18:9 *oblation.* Offering or sacrifice.
18:11 *clean.* In regard to ceremonial participation.
18:14 *devoted.* What is dedicated exclusively to the Lord.
18:15 *matrix.* Womb.
18:16 *estimation.* Calculation of value. *shekel of the sanctuary.* Approximately one-half ounce. *gerahs.* Each a twentieth of a shekel.
18:19 *covenant of salt.* See Lev. 2:13.
18:22 *lest they bear sin, and die.* See 17:12–13.
18:23 *iniquity.* The guilt of sin.
18:26 The Levites had to tithe their portion of the *tithe* received from the people.
18:29 *hallowed part.* The sacred offering.
18:32 *pollute.* Treat as common or ordinary.

Thoughts for Personal/Family Worship: Chapter 18

1. His office having been vindicated, Aaron, along with his sons and the Levites, is now solemnly charged with preserving the sanctity of the tabernacle. Those whom God honors with office in His church He solemnly

CHAPTER 19

AND the LORD spake unto Moses and unto Aaron,
saying,
2 This *is* the ordinance of the law which the
LORD hath commanded, saying, Speak unto the
children of Israel, that they bring thee a red heifer
without spot, wherein *is* no blemish, *and* upon
which never came yoke:
3 And ye shall give her unto Eleazar the priest,
that he may bring her forth without the camp,
and *one* shall slay her before his face:
4 And Eleazar the priest shall take of her blood
with his finger, and sprinkle of her blood directly
before the tabernacle of the congregation seven
times:
5 And *one* shall burn the heifer in his sight; her
skin, and her flesh, and her blood, with her dung,
shall he burn:
6 And the priest shall take cedar wood, and
hyssop, and scarlet, and cast *it* into the midst of
the burning of the heifer.
7 Then the priest shall wash his clothes, and he
shall bathe his flesh in water, and afterward he
shall come into the camp, and the priest shall be
unclean until the even.
8 And he that burneth her shall wash his clothes
in water, and bathe his flesh in water, and shall be
unclean until the even.
9 And a man *that is* clean shall gather up the
ashes of the heifer, and lay *them* up without the
camp in a clean place, and it shall be kept for the
congregation of the children of Israel for a water
of separation: it *is* a purification for sin.
10 And he that gathereth the ashes of the heifer
shall wash his clothes, and be unclean until the
even: and it shall be unto the children of Israel,
and unto the stranger that sojourneth among
them, for a statute for ever.
11 ¶ He that toucheth the dead body of any man
shall be unclean seven days.
12 He shall purify himself with it on the third day,
and on the seventh day he shall be clean: but if he
purify not himself the third day, then the seventh
day he shall not be clean.
13 Whosoever toucheth the dead body of any
man that is dead, and purifieth not himself, de-
fileth the tabernacle of the LORD; and that soul
shall be cut off from Israel: because the water of
separation was not sprinkled upon him, he shall
be unclean; his uncleanness *is* yet upon him.
14 This *is* the law, when a man dieth in a tent: all
that come into the tent, and all that *is* in the tent,
shall be unclean seven days.
15 And every open vessel, which hath no covering
bound upon it, *is* unclean.
16 And whosoever toucheth one that is slain with
a sword in the open fields, or a dead body, or a
bone of a man, or a grave, shall be unclean seven
days.
17 And for an unclean *person* they shall take of the
ashes of the burnt heifer of purification for sin,
and running water shall be put thereto in a vessel:
18 And a clean person shall take hyssop, and dip
it in the water, and sprinkle *it* upon the tent, and
upon all the vessels, and upon the persons that
were there, and upon him that touched a bone, or
one slain, or one dead, or a grave:
19 And the clean *person* shall sprinkle upon the
unclean on the third day, and on the seventh day:
and on the seventh day he shall purify himself, and
wash his clothes, and bathe himself in water, and
shall be clean at even.
20 But the man that shall be unclean, and shall
not purify himself, that soul shall be cut off from
among the congregation, because he hath defiled
the sanctuary of the LORD: the water of separation
hath not been sprinkled upon him; he *is* unclean.
21 And it shall be a perpetual statute unto them,
that he that sprinkleth the water of separation
shall wash his clothes; and he that toucheth the
water of separation shall be unclean until even.
22 And whatsoever the unclean *person* toucheth
shall be unclean; and the soul that toucheth *it*
shall be unclean until even.

charges to preserve the holiness of His cause. Those who fail will "bear the iniquity of the sanctuary." They will be held accountable if they do not strive against sin. The ministry is a sacred task with extreme responsibility and accountability (James 3:1). Pray for your ministers that they may remain faithful to the charge to which God has called them.

2. The Levitical family was allowed a portion of the offerings of the people. Paul alludes to this provision and applies it to the support of God's servants in the New Testament church (1 Cor. 9:13–14). Let none who are taught in the Word fail to provide for those who teach (Gal. 6:6). What can you do to show gratitude for the blessing of having a faithful minister?

Chapter 19: ***The Lord gives instruction concerning rites of purification.***

Purification Rites and the Red Heifer (19:1–22)

19:2 *upon which never came yoke.* Had never been used in any form of agricultural work.

19:3 *without the camp.* Outside the camp (v. 9).

19:9 *a man that is clean.* A man ceremonially clean. *water of separation.* Water of impurity. *purification for sin.* Elsewhere the "sin offering." Thus this water typified the purification for sin that Christ obtained by His death.

19:10 *stranger that sojourneth.* One who lives as a resident alien.

19:11 Contact with death caused ceremonial uncleanness since death was the very curse of sin.

19:12 *with it.* With the water of separation or impurity (v. 9).

19:14 *the law.* The revealed instruction.

19:17 *running water.* Literally, "living waters."

19:20 *that soul.* That person (v. 22).

19:22 Uncleanness is contagious (Hag. 2:13).

CHAPTER 20

THEN came the children of Israel, *even* the whole
congregation, into the desert of Zin in the first
month: and the people abode in Kadesh; and
Miriam died there, and was buried there.
2 And there was no water for the congregation:
and they gathered themselves together against
Moses and against Aaron.
3 And the people chode with Moses, and spake,
saying, Would God that we had died when our
brethren died before the LORD!
4 And why have ye brought up the congregation
of the LORD into this wilderness, that we and our
cattle should die there?
5 And wherefore have ye made us to come up
out of Egypt, to bring us in unto this evil place?
it *is* no place of seed, or of figs, or of vines, or of
pomegranates; neither *is* there any water to drink.
6 And Moses and Aaron went from the presence
of the assembly unto the door of the tabernacle of
the congregation, and they fell upon their faces:
and the glory of the LORD appeared unto them.
7 ¶ And the LORD spake unto Moses, saying,
8 Take the rod, and gather thou the assembly
together, thou, and Aaron thy brother, and speak
ye unto the rock before their eyes; and it shall
give forth his water, and thou shalt bring forth to
them water out of the rock: so thou shalt give the
congregation and their beasts drink.
9 And Moses took the rod from before the LORD,
as he commanded him.
10 And Moses and Aaron gathered the congre-
gation together before the rock, and he said unto
them, Hear now, ye rebels; must we fetch you wa-
ter out of this rock?
11 And Moses lifted up his hand, and with his
rod he smote the rock twice: and the water came
out abundantly, and the congregation drank, and
their beasts *also*.
12 ¶ And the LORD spake unto Moses and Aaron,
Because ye believed me not, to sanctify me in the
eyes of the children of Israel, therefore ye shall not
bring this congregation into the land which I have
given them.
13 This *is* the water of Meribah; because the chil-
dren of Israel strove with the LORD, and he was
sanctified in them.
14 ¶ And Moses sent messengers from Kadesh
unto the king of Edom, Thus saith thy brother
Israel, Thou knowest all the travail that hath
befallen us:
15 How our fathers went down into Egypt, and
we have dwelt in Egypt a long time; and the Egyp-
tians vexed us, and our fathers:
16 And when we cried unto the LORD, he heard
our voice, and sent an angel, and hath brought us
forth out of Egypt: and, behold, we *are* in Kadesh,
a city in the uttermost of thy border:
17 Let us pass, I pray thee, through thy country:
we will not pass through the fields, or through the
vineyards, neither will we drink *of* the water of the
wells: we will go by the king's *high* way, we will
not turn to the right hand nor to the left, until we
have passed thy borders.
18 And Edom said unto him, Thou shalt not pass
by me, lest I come out against thee with the sword.
19 And the children of Israel said unto him, We
will go by the high way: and if I and my cattle drink
of thy water, then I will pay for it: I will only, with-
out *doing* any thing *else*, go through on my feet.
20 And he said, Thou shalt not go through. And
Edom came out against him with much people,
and with a strong hand.
21 Thus Edom refused to give Israel passage

Thoughts for Personal/Family Worship: Chapter 19

Death is the ultimate evidence of the curse of sin, and its effects are pervasive. But the beauty of the gospel is that God has devised the means to reverse the curse. The ashes of the red heifer and the water to be used for the ceremonial cleansings were shadows pointing to the real curse-reverser, the Lord Jesus. The red heifer was only a type, and the water of purification could only provide a symbolic cleansing. "The ashes of an heifer sprinkling the unclean, sanctifieth to the purifying of the flesh," but "the blood of Christ" can "purge your conscience from dead works to serve the living God" (Heb. 9:13–14). The red heifer was slain outside the camp, the place of the curse. This is a picture of Christ who "suffered without the gate" (Heb. 13:12). He was made a curse for us to give us a place in the camp of God. How can we find cleansing in Jesus Christ? How should a Christian wash his conscience daily?

Chapter 20: ***Miriam and Aaron die, and Moses smites the rock to supply water for the murmuring people.***

Disobedience at Meribah, Deaths of Miriam and Aaron, and Conflict with Edom (20:1–29)

20:1 *the first month.* The first month of the fortieth year from the exodus (33:38). The wanderings were coming to an end.
20:2 *the congregation.* The new generation with the same tendencies of the old.
20:3 *chode.* Quarreled or strived in a legal controversy.
20:5 *this evil place.* A bad or troublesome place.
20:10 *must we fetch you water out.* Cause to come out, bring out. Part of Moses' sin was that he was provoked to anger and spoke rashly (Ps. 106:32–33).
20:11 *smote.* Struck.
20:12 *ye believed me not, to sanctify me.* He was not living by faith in the Lord so as to honor His holiness (Lev. 10:3). Any sin can be described in terms of unbelief.
20:13 *Meribah.* Translated, "strife." See where this place is also named Meribah-Kadesh (Deut. 32:51) to distinguish it from the other Meribah they visited earlier (Ex. 17:7).
20:14 *Edom.* The nation descending from Esau. *the travail that hath befallen us.* The hardship which we have found.
20:15 *vexed.* Treated badly, inflicted injury.
20:16 *sent an angel.* Most likely referring to the Angel of the

through his border: wherefore Israel turned away
from him.
22 ¶ And the children of Israel, *even* the whole
congregation, journeyed from Kadesh, and came
unto mount Hor.
23 And the LORD spake unto Moses and Aaron
in mount Hor, by the coast of the land of Edom,
saying,
24 Aaron shall be gathered unto his people: for
he shall not enter into the land which I have given
unto the children of Israel, because ye rebelled
against my word at the water of Meribah.
25 Take Aaron and Eleazar his son, and bring
them up unto mount Hor:
26 And strip Aaron of his garments, and put them
upon Eleazar his son: and Aaron shall be gathered
unto his people, and shall die there.
27 And Moses did as the LORD commanded: and
they went up into mount Hor in the sight of all
the congregation.
28 And Moses stripped Aaron of his garments,
and put them upon Eleazar his son; and Aaron
died there in the top of the mount: and Moses
and Eleazar came down from the mount.
29 And when all the congregation saw that Aaron
was dead, they mourned for Aaron thirty days,
even all the house of Israel.

CHAPTER 21

AND *when* king Arad the Canaanite, which dwelt
in the south, heard tell that Israel came by the way
of the spies; then he fought against Israel, and
took *some* of them prisoners.
2 And Israel vowed a vow unto the LORD, and
said, If thou wilt indeed deliver this people into
my hand, then I will utterly destroy their cities.
3 And the LORD hearkened to the voice of Israel,
and delivered up the Canaanites; and they utterly
destroyed them and their cities: and he called the
name of the place Hormah.
4 ¶ And they journeyed from mount Hor by the
way of the Red sea, to compass the land of Edom:
and the soul of the people was much discouraged
because of the way.
5 And the people spake against God, and against
Moses, Wherefore have ye brought us up out of
Egypt to die in the wilderness? for *there is* no
bread, neither *is there any* water; and our soul
loatheth this light bread.
6 And the LORD sent fiery serpents among the
people, and they bit the people; and much people
of Israel died.
7 ¶ Therefore the people came to Moses, and
said, We have sinned, for we have spoken against
the LORD, and against thee; pray unto the LORD,
that he take away the serpents from us. And Mo-
ses prayed for the people.
8 And the LORD said unto Moses, Make thee a fi-
ery serpent, and set it upon a pole: and it shall
come to pass, that every one that is bitten, when
he looketh upon it, shall live.
9 And Moses made a serpent of brass, and put it
upon a pole, and it came to pass, that if a serpent
had bitten any man, when he beheld the serpent
of brass, he lived.

Lord, a Christophany or a preincarnate appearance of Christ (Ex. 23:20; Isa. 63:9). *uttermost.* Edge.
20:23 *coast.* Border.
20:26 *strip Aaron of his garments.* The holy garments of his high priesthood (Ex. 28; Lev. 8:6–9).

Thoughts for Personal/Family Worship: Chapter 20

1. **Because of his disobedience, Moses would not enter the Promised Land. God ordered him clearly to speak to the rock, yet Moses twice struck the rock (which symbolized Christ, 1 Cor. 10:4). The essence of Moses' sin was not how he handled the rod but how he spoke to the people (Num. 20:10; Ps. 106:32), driven by a heart that failed to trust and honor God. The penalty seemed harsh, but his position of leadership increased his accountability. It is a reminder to us all how important it is to obey God completely so that all glory is His. Though the water was given when Moses smote the rock, yet it would have been a greater miracle and more glorifying to the Lord had the water been obtained as a result of simply speaking. Let us seek to do His will without fail for then the Lord will make known that He is the glorious and holy God. What are some ways that you have a responsibility to obey God exactly as He commands?**
2. **One of the great tragedies in this episode is that it was the new generation that grumbled and complained against Moses. The wilderness wanderings were about to end; the old generation was out and the new was in. This generation had seen over and over again the complaining of their parents and how God had disciplined them. But they had failed to learn the lessons. Proverbs 19:25 says, "Smite a scorner, and the simple will beware." The simple refer to those who should be easily influenced and taught. How have you learned from the sins and punishments of others?**

Chapter 21: ***Israel defeats Arad, suffers from the fiery serpents, and gains victories over Sihon and Og.***

Fiery Serpents and Defeat of Various Enemies (21:1–35)

21:1 *way of the spies.* Or road of Atharim, a location.
21:3 *Hormah.* Transliteration of, "utter destruction," named to commemorate the victory.
21:4 *compass.* Make a circuit around, bypass. *was much discouraged.* Literally, "became impatient."
21:5 *our soul loatheth this light bread.* Literally, "we hate the wretched bread," a reference to manna, the bread from heaven (Ex. 16).
21:6 *fiery serpents.* Thus described either because of the bright appearance or the burning pain of the venom, which was a deadly poison.
21:8 *pole.* Flag or a standard.
21:9 *brass.* Bronze. *put it upon a pole.* Christ compared the lifting up of the serpent and looking to it for healing with His crucifixion and faith in Him (John 3:14–15; cf. John 12:32–33).

10 ¶ And the children of Israel set forward, and
pitched in Oboth.
11 And they journeyed from Oboth, and pitched
at Ije-abarim, in the wilderness which *is* before
Moab, toward the sunrising.
12 ¶ From thence they removed, and pitched in
the valley of Zared.
13 From thence they removed, and pitched on
the other side of Arnon, which *is* in the wilderness
that cometh out of the coasts of the Amorites: for
Arnon *is* the border of Moab, between Moab and
the Amorites.
14 Wherefore it is said in the book of the wars of
the LORD, What he did in the Red sea, and in the
brooks of Arnon,
15 And at the stream of the brooks that goeth
down to the dwelling of Ar, and lieth upon the
border of Moab.
16 And from thence *they went* to Beer: that *is* the
well whereof the LORD spake unto Moses, Gather
the people together, and I will give them water.
17 ¶ Then Israel sang this song, Spring up, O well;
sing ye unto it:
18 The princes digged the well, the nobles of the
people digged it, by *the direction of* the lawgiver,
with their staves. And from the wilderness *they
went* to Mattanah:
19 And from Mattanah to Nahaliel: and from
Nahaliel to Bamoth:
20 And from Bamoth *in* the valley, that *is* in the
country of Moab, to the top of Pisgah, which look-
eth toward Jeshimon.
21 ¶ And Israel sent messengers unto Sihon king
of the Amorites, saying,
22 Let me pass through thy land: we will not
turn into the fields, or into the vineyards; we will
not drink *of* the waters of the well: *but* we will go
along by the king's *high* way, until we be past thy
borders.
23 And Sihon would not suffer Israel to pass
through his border: but Sihon gathered all his
people together, and went out against Israel into
the wilderness: and he came to Jahaz, and fought
against Israel.
24 And Israel smote him with the edge of the
sword, and possessed his land from Arnon unto
Jabbok, even unto the children of Ammon: for the
border of the children of Ammon *was* strong.
25 And Israel took all these cities: and Israel
dwelt in all the cities of the Amorites, in Heshbon,
and in all the villages thereof.
26 For Heshbon *was* the city of Sihon the king of
the Amorites, who had fought against the former
king of Moab, and taken all his land out of his
hand, even unto Arnon.
27 Wherefore they that speak in proverbs say,
Come into Heshbon, let the city of Sihon be built
and prepared:
28 For there is a fire gone out of Heshbon, a
flame from the city of Sihon: it hath consumed
Ar of Moab, *and* the lords of the high places of
Arnon.
29 Woe to thee, Moab! thou art undone, O people
of Chemosh: he hath given his sons that escaped,
and his daughters, into captivity unto Sihon king
of the Amorites.
30 We have shot at them; Heshbon is perished
even unto Dibon, and we have laid them waste
even unto Nophah, which *reacheth* unto Medeba.
31 ¶ Thus Israel dwelt in the land of the Amorites.
32 And Moses sent to spy out Jaazer, and they
took the villages thereof, and drove out the Amor-
ites that *were* there.
33 ¶ And they turned and went up by the way
of Bashan: and Og the king of Bashan went out
against them, he, and all his people, to the battle
at Edrei.
34 And the LORD said unto Moses, Fear him not:
for I have delivered him into thy hand, and all his
people, and his land; and thou shalt do to him
as thou didst unto Sihon king of the Amorites,
which dwelt at Heshbon.

21:11 *sunrising.* East.
21:13 *coasts.* Borders or regions.
21:14 *book of the wars of the LORD.* An uninspired record of events that has not been preserved.
21:18 *lawgiver.* Moses. *staves.* Staffs.
21:21 *Amorites.* General term referring to Canaanites.
21:23 *suffer.* Allow.
21:25 *in Heshbon, and in all the villages thereof.* The territories east of the Jordan River that ultimately became the possession of Reuben, Gad, and the half tribe of Manasseh.
21:29 *Chemosh.* The Baal (master god) of Moab.

Thoughts for Personal/Family Worship: Chapter 21

1. **Meditating on Christ's comparison of Himself to the bronze serpent (John 3:15) teaches important lessons about sin (Num. 21:5). The people accused God of being evil, not good, in His ways toward them. They refused to be content with God's good provision of food and turned from it in disgust and ingratitude. The penalty was severe; the fiery serpents brought death. This is essentially what happened in the fall of man when he was tempted by another serpent: he rejected God's goodness and provision in the garden and so broke His law (Gen. 3:1–6). We, the fallen children of Adam, validate this hatred of God every time we turn discontentedly from God's will and choose to sin. According to Rev. 21:8, what penalty do we face if we do not look to Christ for salvation?**
2. **Christ's analogy also teaches us lessons about salvation. Provision for dying sinners was made in the bronze serpent on the pole. The symbolic curse-reverser took the shape of the curse. So God sent His Son in the likeness of sinful flesh to deal with sin (Rom. 8:3). He had to be lifted up on the cross becoming the curse (Gal. 3:13). Appropriation of salvation was by gazing at the serpent. Simply having the serpent on the pole was not**

35 So they smote him, and his sons, and all his
people, until there was none left him alive: and
they possessed his land.

CHAPTER 22

AND the children of Israel set forward, and
pitched in the plains of Moab on this side Jordan
by Jericho.
2 ¶ And Balak the son of Zippor saw all that Israel
had done to the Amorites.
3 And Moab was sore afraid of the people, be-
cause they *were* many: and Moab was distressed
because of the children of Israel.
4 And Moab said unto the elders of Midian, Now
shall this company lick up all *that are* round about
us, as the ox licketh up the grass of the field. And
Balak the son of Zippor *was* king of the Moabites
at that time.
5 He sent messengers therefore unto Balaam the
son of Beor to Pethor, which *is* by the river of the
land of the children of his people, to call him,
saying, Behold, there is a people come out from
Egypt: behold, they cover the face of the earth,
and they abide over against me:
6 Come now therefore, I pray thee, curse me this
people; for they *are* too mighty for me: perad-
venture I shall prevail, *that* we may smite them,
and *that* I may drive them out of the land: for I
wot that he whom thou blessest *is* blessed, and he
whom thou cursest is cursed.
7 And the elders of Moab and the elders of Mid-
ian departed with the rewards of divination in
their hand; and they came unto Balaam, and
spake unto him the words of Balak.
8 And he said unto them, Lodge here this night,
and I will bring you word again, as the LORD shall
speak unto me: and the princes of Moab abode
with Balaam.
9 And God came unto Balaam, and said, What
men *are* these with thee?
10 And Balaam said unto God, Balak the son of
Zippor, king of Moab, hath sent unto me, *saying*,
11 Behold, *there is* a people come out of Egypt,
which covereth the face of the earth: come now,
curse me them; peradventure I shall be able to
overcome them, and drive them out.
12 And God said unto Balaam, Thou shalt not go
with them; thou shalt not curse the people: for
they *are* blessed.
13 And Balaam rose up in the morning, and said
unto the princes of Balak, Get you into your land:
for the LORD refuseth to give me leave to go with
you.
14 And the princes of Moab rose up, and they
went unto Balak, and said, Balaam refuseth to
come with us.
15 ¶ And Balak sent yet again princes, more, and
more honourable than they.
16 And they came to Balaam, and said to him,
Thus saith Balak the son of Zippor, Let nothing,
I pray thee, hinder thee from coming unto me:
17 For I will promote thee unto very great hon-
our, and I will do whatsoever thou sayest unto me:
come therefore, I pray thee, curse me this people.
18 And Balaam answered and said unto the ser-
vants of Balak, If Balak would give me his house
full of silver and gold, I cannot go beyond the
word of the LORD my God, to do less or more.
19 Now therefore, I pray you, tarry ye also here
this night, that I may know what the LORD will
say unto me more.
20 And God came unto Balaam at night, and said
unto him, If the men come to call thee, rise up,
and go with them; but yet the word which I shall
say unto thee, that shalt thou do.
21 And Balaam rose up in the morning, and sad-
dled his ass, and went with the princes of Moab.
22 ¶ And God's anger was kindled because he
went: and the angel of the LORD stood in the way
for an adversary against him. Now he was riding
upon his ass, and his two servants *were* with him.
23 And the ass saw the angel of the LORD stand-
ing in the way, and his sword drawn in his hand:

---

enough; there had to be the look of faith. How does this help you understand your need for trust and faith in Christ alone for eternal life (John 3:15–16)?

STORY OF BALAAM (22:1—24:25)

Chapter 22: ***Balak, king of Moab, fears Israel and sends for Balaam to curse them.***

Balaam's Resistance to God's Will (22:1–41)

22:1 *set forward.* Broke camp, pulled up stakes. *pitched.* Set up camp.
22:3 *sore afraid.* Very afraid, but without cause since it was not the Lord's intention to give their land to Israel (Deut. 2:9).
22:4 *Midian.* A neighboring people to the Moabites.
22:5 *Balaam.* A prophet for hire, a pagan diviner not related to the true God but used by Him (2 Peter 2:15–16; Jude 11).
22:6 *peradventure.* Perhaps (v. 11). *I wot.* I know. *he whom thou blessest is blessed, and he whom thou cursest is cursed.* Balaam had a reputation as being a powerful sorcerer.
22:7 *rewards of divination.* The fees for divination; there would be a cost for his services (according to 2 Peter 2:15, "the wages of unrighteousness").
22:12 *thou shalt not curse the people: for they are blessed.* God's covenant blessing is irreversible (23:19–20; Rom. 11:27–29).
22:20 God permitted Balaam to go but held him under divine restraint to only speak the words revealed to Him.
22:22 *God's anger was kindled because he went.* God's permission for Balaam to go did not diminish His displeasure at his evil motives. *the angel of the LORD.* The Angel who is Jehovah, most likely a Christophany, a preincarnate appearance of Christ.
22:23 *the ass saw the angel.* Ironically, the dumb donkey was able to see what Balaam, the professional seer, could not.

and the ass turned aside out of the way, and went
into the field: and Balaam smote the ass, to turn
her into the way.
24 But the angel of the LORD stood in a path of
the vineyards, a wall *being* on this side, and a wall
on that side.
25 And when the ass saw the angel of the LORD,
she thrust herself unto the wall, and crushed
Balaam's foot against the wall: and he smote her
again.
26 And the angel of the LORD went further, and
stood in a narrow place, where *was* no way to turn
either to the right hand or to the left.
27 And when the ass saw the angel of the LORD,
she fell down under Balaam: and Balaam's anger
was kindled, and he smote the ass with a staff.
28 And the LORD opened the mouth of the ass,
and she said unto Balaam, What have I done unto
thee, that thou hast smitten me these three times?
29 And Balaam said unto the ass, Because thou
hast mocked me: I would there were a sword in
mine hand, for now would I kill thee.
30 And the ass said unto Balaam, *Am* not I thine
ass, upon which thou hast ridden ever since *I was*
thine unto this day? was I ever wont to do so unto
thee? And he said, Nay.
31 Then the LORD opened the eyes of Balaam,
and he saw the angel of the LORD standing in the
way, and his sword drawn in his hand: and he
bowed down his head, and fell flat on his face.
32 And the angel of the LORD said unto him,
Wherefore hast thou smitten thine ass these three
times? behold, I went out to withstand thee, be-
cause *thy* way is perverse before me:
33 And the ass saw me, and turned from me
these three times: unless she had turned from
me, surely now also I had slain thee, and saved
her alive.
34 And Balaam said unto the angel of the LORD, I
have sinned; for I knew not that thou stoodest in
the way against me: now therefore, if it displease
thee, I will get me back again.
35 And the angel of the LORD said unto Balaam,
Go with the men: but only the word that I shall
speak unto thee, that thou shalt speak. So Balaam
went with the princes of Balak.
36 ¶ And when Balak heard that Balaam was
come, he went out to meet him unto a city of
Moab, which *is* in the border of Arnon, which *is*
in the utmost coast.
37 And Balak said unto Balaam, Did I not
earnestly send unto thee to call thee? wherefore
camest thou not unto me? am I not able indeed to
promote thee to honour?
38 And Balaam said unto Balak, Lo, I am come
unto thee: have I now any power at all to say any
thing? the word that God putteth in my mouth,
that shall I speak.
39 And Balaam went with Balak, and they came
unto Kirjath-huzoth.
40 And Balak offered oxen and sheep, and sent to
Balaam, and to the princes that *were* with him.
41 And it came to pass on the morrow, that Balak
took Balaam, and brought him up into the high
places of Baal, that thence he might see the ut-
most *part* of the people.

CHAPTER 23

AND Balaam said unto Balak, Build me here seven
altars, and prepare me here seven oxen and seven
rams.
2 And Balak did as Balaam had spoken; and
Balak and Balaam offered on *every* altar a bullock
and a ram.
3 And Balaam said unto Balak, Stand by thy burnt
offering, and I will go: peradventure the LORD will
come to meet me: and whatsoever he sheweth me
I will tell thee. And he went to an high place.
4 And God met Balaam: and he said unto him,

22:28 *the LORD opened the mouth of the ass.* A demonstration of sovereign power over all His creation. Ironically, whereas Moses communicated with God "mouth to mouth" (12:8), Balaam received God's rebuke from the mouth of a donkey (2 Peter 2:16).
22:30 *was I ever wont to do?* Have I been in the habit of doing?
22:31 *fell flat on his face.* Literally, "he bowed down to his nose," not in worship but in fearful subjection (Phil. 2:10).
22:36 *utmost coast.* Edge of the border.
22:41 *uttermost part.* Edge or extremity.

Thoughts for Personal/Family Worship: Chapter 22

1. **All of these events were happening behind Israel's back. They had no knowledge of the conspiracy that was being schemed against them. But what was unknown to Israel was openly known to God. It is a wonderful blessing to know that God is with us when we are in the midst of difficulties and dangers. Here we learn that God's protection extends to unknown dangers as well. The extent to which God has kept us from danger is something we may never know (Ps. 139:5–6). Take time to rejoice and be thankful for these truths.**
2. **God is not fickle; unlike a sorcerer-for-hire, He cannot be paid off to change His ways. God's blessing is irreversible. No one can curse what God has blessed (v. 12). The unchanging and constant truth for everyone united to Christ is "if God be for us, who can be against us?" (Rom. 8:31). How can these truths help us when it seems that everything is against us and when the enemy gloats over our failures and desires our demise?**

Chapter 23: *Balaam's attempts to curse Israel are frustrated.*

Balaam's First Two Prophecies (23:1–30)

23:3 *peradventure.* Perhaps (v. 27). *high place.* Bare place or mountain.
23:5 *the LORD put a word in Balaam's mouth.* God uses His

I have prepared seven altars, and I have offered
upon *every* altar a bullock and a ram.
5 And the LORD put a word in Balaam's mouth,
and said, Return unto Balak, and thus thou shalt
speak.
6 And he returned unto him, and, lo, he stood
by his burnt sacrifice, he, and all the princes of
Moab.
7 And he took up his parable, and said, Balak the
king of Moab hath brought me from Aram, out of
the mountains of the east, *saying*, Come, curse me
Jacob, and come, defy Israel.
8 How shall I curse, whom God hath not cursed?
or how shall I defy, *whom* the LORD hath not
defied?
9 For from the top of the rocks I see him, and
from the hills I behold him: lo, the people shall
dwell alone, and shall not be reckoned among the
nations.
10 Who can count the dust of Jacob, and the
number of the fourth *part* of Israel? Let me die
the death of the righteous, and let my last end be
like his!
11 And Balak said unto Balaam, What hast thou
done unto me? I took thee to curse mine enemies,
and, behold, thou hast blessed *them* altogether.
12 And he answered and said, Must I not take
heed to speak that which the LORD hath put in
my mouth?
13 And Balak said unto him, Come, I pray thee,
with me unto another place, from whence thou
mayest see them: thou shalt see but the utmost
part of them, and shalt not see them all: and curse
me them from thence.
14 ¶ And he brought him into the field of Zo-
phim, to the top of Pisgah, and built seven altars,
and offered a bullock and a ram on *every* altar.
15 And he said unto Balak, Stand here by thy
burnt offering, while I meet *the LORD* yonder.
16 And the LORD met Balaam, and put a word in
his mouth, and said, Go again unto Balak, and say
thus.
17 And when he came to him, behold, he stood
by his burnt offering, and the princes of Moab
with him. And Balak said unto him, What hath
the LORD spoken?
18 And he took up his parable, and said, Rise up,
Balak, and hear; hearken unto me, thou son of
Zippor:
19 God *is* not a man, that he should lie; neither
the son of man, that he should repent: hath he
said, and shall he not do *it*? or hath he spoken,
and shall he not make it good?
20 Behold, I have received *commandment* to
bless: and he hath blessed; and I cannot reverse it.
21 He hath not beheld iniquity in Jacob, neither
hath he seen perverseness in Israel: the LORD his
God *is* with him, and the shout of a king *is* among
them.
22 God brought them out of Egypt; he hath as it
were the strength of an unicorn.
23 Surely *there is* no enchantment against Jacob,
neither *is there* any divination against Israel:
according to this time it shall be said of Jacob and
of Israel, What hath God wrought!
24 Behold, the people shall rise up as a great lion,
and lift up himself as a young lion: he shall not lie
down until he eat *of* the prey, and drink the blood
of the slain.
25 ¶ And Balak said unto Balaam, Neither curse
them at all, nor bless them at all.
26 But Balaam answered and said unto Balak,
Told not I thee, saying, All that the LORD speak-
eth, that I must do?
27 ¶ And Balak said unto Balaam, Come, I pray
thee, I will bring thee unto another place; perad-
venture it will please God that thou mayest curse
me them from thence.

---

sovereign control over men, even wicked men, so that the words of the prophets are exactly what He gave them to say (vv. 12,16,26; 24:2,4,13,16).

23:6 *lo, he stood.* Referring to Balak.

23:7 *parable.* A prophetic discourse in figurative language. *defy.* Denounce or express indignation in speech (v. 8).

23:9 *the people shall dwell alone.* Distinct and separate from all other peoples.

23:10 *Who can count the dust of Jacob, and the number of the fourth part of Israel?* An innumerable people (Gen. 13:16; 28:14). *Let me die the death of the righteous, and let my last end be like his!* An admission that those who are the Lord's will never come under the curse.

23:13 *utmost part.* Edge or extremity.

23:19 Unlike *man*, God is unable to *lie* (full of integrity, cf. Titus 1:2; Heb. 6:18), and He is unchanging (immutable, cf. Mal. 3:6; James 1:17). *not . . . repent.* Scripture speaks of God "repenting" when His relationships or ways with people change (Gen. 6:6–7; Ex. 32:12,14; Judg. 2:18; 1 Sam. 15:11,35; 2 Sam. 24:16), but God cannot "repent" in the sense of changing His nature or plans (see notes at 1 Sam. 15:11 and 29).

23:20 The key truth of the narrative is the irreversibility of God's blessing—the heart of His covenant oath (Gen. 12:2; 22:16–17; Ps. 89:33–37; Heb. 6:13–14).

23:21 *iniquity.* Not the usual word for iniquity; this word most often refers to "trouble" or "harm." *perverseness.* Distress or disaster. Balaam observed the special protection Israel experienced because *his God is with him* as a great *king* sounding the battle cry (*shout*) against His enemies.

23:22 *unicorn.* Wild bull or ox, a symbol of power (Ps. 92:10).

23:23 *enchantment.* Magic curse. *divination.* Prediction by magic or supernatural means. Both are associated with pagan practices, most likely involving demonic activity. *wrought.* Done.

23:27 *please.* Literally, "be right in the eyes of."

Thoughts for Personal/Family Worship: Chapter 23

1. **Balaam's efforts to curse Israel highlight some amazing realities about God's blessings on His covenant people. (1) God's people are special: they dwell alone (v. 9). All the earth is the Lord's but His people are unique; there is no people like God's people. (2) God's people are saved, redeemed from bondage by power, by blood, and by**

GOD'S IMMUTABILITY

In the final section of the epistle to the Hebrews, where the author delineates the implications of our having received "a kingdom which cannot be moved," we are told that Jesus Christ is "the same yesterday, and today, and forever" (Heb. 13:8). The character of Jesus as we find it depicted in the Gospels—loving and kind toward sinners, holy and utterly free from sin—has not changed one iota, even though He is now seated at the right hand of God and is the Sustainer of all that exists. Christ *is* eternal, holy love. If He were mutable, He simply would not be God. So the same has to be true of His Father (Ex. 34:6–7). God the Father also is immutable, and like His Son—and, we should add, the Holy Spirit—He is holy love.

God's moral character is the same now as it was when He created the universe, when He called Abram to faith in Himself and when He led Israel out of bondage to the Promised Land. He has always hated sin and always loved righteousness—God never acts in ways that are contrary to His character (James 1:17). Therefore, God's Word does not change: "For ever, O LORD, thy word is settled in heaven" (Ps. 119:89); it is "true from the beginning," and every one of God's "righteous judgments endureth for ever" (Ps. 119:160).

Neither do God's plans and purposes change: God's "counsel . . . standeth for ever, the thoughts of his heart to all generations" (Ps. 33:11). God never has to reevaluate his plans, for they are based on His absolutely exhaustive knowledge of all things past, present, and future. Men, on the other hand, even the best of them, are inconstant, for their knowledge is incomplete and they frequently have to make alternative plans. They are unable to prevent emergencies that alter the landscape of their lives entirely and force change upon them. Thus, God says of Himself by way of contrast with men: "the Strength of Israel will not lie nor repent: for he is not a man, that he should repent" (1 Sam. 15:29). Humanity, and indeed all of creation, is in this present time in the process of becoming. But not God.

Because God does not change, His people have hope: "I am the LORD, I change not; therefore ye sons of Jacob are not consumed" (Mal. 3:6). It is for this reason, Herman Bavinck observed, that God is so frequently called "the Rock" in Scripture (e.g., Deut. 32:4,15,18,30–31; 1 Sam. 2:2; 2 Sam. 22:32; Pss. 19:14; 31:3; 62:2,7). In Bavinck's words, "We humans can rely on him; he does not change in his being, knowing, or willing."

Yes, there are passages in Holy Scripture that speak of God repenting (Gen. 6:6; 1 Sam. 15:11; Amos 7:3,6; Jonah 3:9–10; 4:2). How are we to understand such texts? Some contain what theologians call anthropomorphisms, that is, descriptions of God in human terms. Also, some of these texts involve changes in man's relationship with God and thus depict changes in orientation on the part of God. So when the inhabitants of Nineveh repented God did not punish them. There was no alteration in God's plan. He had intended to punish the city if its occupants did not repent of their sin. They changed and so were spared; thus, it was the people of Nineveh who changed, not God.

Therefore, those who argue today that God, like the rest of reality, is in the process of becoming (the advocates of so-called open theism and those who adhere to process theology) have no biblical justification. In the minds of these thinkers, God is learning and developing, ever changing into a more perfect being. This perspective not only flounders because of philosophical problems but also flies in the face of the clear biblical evidence noted above and in many other passages of Scripture.

28 And Balak brought Balaam unto the top of
Peor, that looketh toward Jeshimon.
29 And Balaam said unto Balak, Build me here
seven altars, and prepare me here seven bullocks
and seven rams.
30 And Balak did as Balaam had said, and offered
a bullock and a ram on *every* altar.

CHAPTER 24

AND when Balaam saw that it pleased the LORD to
bless Israel, he went not, as at other times, to seek
for enchantments, but he set his face toward the
wilderness.
2 And Balaam lifted up his eyes, and he saw Israel
abiding *in his tents* according to their tribes; and
the spirit of God came upon him.
3 And he took up his parable, and said, Balaam
the son of Beor hath said, and the man whose eyes
are open hath said:
4 He hath said, which heard the words of God,
which saw the vision of the Almighty, falling *into
a trance*, but having his eyes open:
5 How goodly are thy tents, O Jacob, *and* thy tab-
ernacles, O Israel!
6 As the valleys are they spread forth, as gardens
by the river's side, as the trees of lign aloes which
the LORD hath planted, *and* as cedar trees beside
the waters.
7 He shall pour the water out of his buckets, and
his seed *shall be* in many waters, and his king shall
be higher than Agag, and his kingdom shall be
exalted.
8 God brought him forth out of Egypt; he hath
as it were the strength of an unicorn: he shall eat
up the nations his enemies, and shall break their
bones, and pierce *them* through with his arrows.
9 He couched, he lay down as a lion, and as a
great lion: who shall stir him up? Blessed *is* he that
blesseth thee, and cursed *is* he that curseth thee.
10 ¶ And Balak's anger was kindled against
Balaam, and he smote his hands together: and
Balak said unto Balaam, I called thee to curse
mine enemies, and, behold, thou hast altogether
blessed *them* these three times.
11 Therefore now flee thou to thy place: I thought
to promote thee unto great honour; but, lo, the
LORD hath kept thee back from honour.
12 And Balaam said unto Balak, Spake I not also
to thy messengers which thou sentest unto me,
saying,
13 If Balak would give me his house full of silver
and gold, I cannot go beyond the commandment
of the LORD, to do *either* good or bad of mine own
mind; *but* what the LORD saith, that will I speak?
14 And now, behold, I go unto my people: come
therefore, and I will advertise thee what this peo-
ple shall do to thy people in the latter days.
15 ¶ And he took up his parable, and said, Balaam
the son of Beor hath said, and the man whose eyes
are open hath said:
16 He hath said, which heard the words of God,
and knew the knowledge of the most High, *which*
saw the vision of the Almighty, falling *into a
trance*, but having his eyes open:
17 I shall see him, but not now: I shall behold
him, but not nigh: there shall come a Star out of
Jacob, and a Sceptre shall rise out of Israel, and

grace (v. 22). (3) God's people are strong (v. 24), like a strong beast, powerful and relentless in the pursuit of prey. Grace has made the believer capable of doing all things through Christ, more than conquerors through Him. (4) God's people are serene (v. 10). There is a peace for believers in death that the wicked can only envy. (5) God's people are secure (vv. 21,23). Those whom God has blessed cannot be cursed now; they will be free from the curse forever (Rom. 8:31–39). Balaam confessed "he hath blessed; and I cannot reverse it" (Num. 23:20). This was really Satan's admission of defeat. Believer, how can you keep the knowledge of the irreversible blessing that you have in Christ before you every day?

2. The exclamation, "What hath God wrought!" (v. 23) stands over the whole chapter. It was because God is who He is that Israel was protected from Balaam's efforts to curse. The whole episode highlights three truths about God worthy of meditation. (1) He is sovereign, a king in the midst (v. 21). His sovereignty is evident in His choice of Israel (no inherent worth), His use of Balaam (contrary to his will and efforts), His use of a donkey (contrary to nature), and His dominion over nations then and nations to come. (2) He is immutable (v. 19). It is because He does not change that Jacob is not consumed (Mal. 3:6). (3) He is active (Num. 23:23). God is not a spectator rooting for His people; He is actively engaged in their behalf. His activity covers the past (v. 22), the present (v. 21), and the future (24:8). Rejoice that Israel's God is our God and He neither slumbers nor sleeps (Ps. 121:3–4).

Chapter 24: ***God sovereignly uses Balaam to utter remarkable prophecies of sure blessings to come.***

Balaam's Third and Fourth Oracles (24:1–25)

24:1 *it pleased the LORD.* It was good in the eyes of the Lord. *seek for enchantments.* Resort to omens or sorcery. *toward the wilderness.* Toward the camp of Israel assembled in the wilderness.

24:2 *the spirit of God came upon him.* The Holy Spirit gave him unusual ability to serve (11:25; Judg. 3:10; 11:29; 1 Sam. 19:23; 2 Chron. 15:1; 20:14), here through prophecy. Such spiritual gifts do not imply that a person is godly (Matt. 7:22–23).

24:3 *the man whose eyes are open.* Literally, "a strong man whose eyes had been shut," implying that now they are open (v. 4).

24:5 *tabernacles.* Dwelling places.

24:6 *trees of lign aloes.* Sweet smelling trees (Prov. 7:17; John 19:39).

24:8 *unicorn.* Wild bull or ox, proverbial symbol of power.

24:9 *Blessed is he that blesseth thee.* The promise of God to Abram (Gen. 12:3).

24:14 *advertise.* Tell.

24:17–18 *Star out of Jacob.* A prophecy of Christ, the great

shall smite the corners of Moab, and destroy all
the children of Sheth.
18 And Edom shall be a possession, Seir also shall
be a possession for his enemies; and Israel shall
do valiantly.
19 Out of Jacob shall come he that shall have
dominion, and shall destroy him that remaineth
of the city.
20 ¶ And when he looked on Amalek, he took up
his parable, and said, Amalek *was* the first of the
nations; but his latter end *shall be* that he perish
for ever.
21 And he looked on the Kenites, and took up his
parable, and said, Strong is thy dwellingplace, and
thou puttest thy nest in a rock.
22 Nevertheless the Kenite shall be wasted, until
Asshur shall carry thee away captive.
23 And he took up his parable, and said, Alas,
who shall live when God doeth this!
24 And ships *shall come* from the coast of Chit-
tim, and shall afflict Asshur, and shall afflict Eber,
and he also shall perish for ever.
25 And Balaam rose up, and went and returned to
his place: and Balak also went his way.

CHAPTER 25

AND Israel abode in Shittim, and the people
began to commit whoredom with the daughters
of Moab.
2 And they called the people unto the sacrifices
of their gods: and the people did eat, and bowed
down to their gods.
3 And Israel joined himself unto Baal-peor: and
the anger of the LORD was kindled against Israel.
4 And the LORD said unto Moses, Take all the
heads of the people, and hang them up before
the LORD against the sun, that the fierce anger of
the LORD may be turned away from Israel.
5 And Moses said unto the judges of Israel, Slay ye
every one his men that were joined unto Baal-peor.
6 ¶ And, behold, one of the children of Israel
came and brought unto his brethren a Midianit-
ish woman in the sight of Moses, and in the sight
of all the congregation of the children of Israel,
who *were* weeping *before* the door of the taber-
nacle of the congregation.
7 And when Phinehas, the son of Eleazar, the son
of Aaron the priest, saw *it*, he rose up from among
the congregation, and took a javelin in his hand;
8 And he went after the man of Israel into the
tent, and thrust both of them through, the man
of Israel, and the woman through her belly. So the
plague was stayed from the children of Israel.
9 And those that died in the plague were twenty
and four thousand.
10 ¶ And the LORD spake unto Moses, saying,
11 Phinehas, the son of Eleazar, the son of Aaron
the priest, hath turned my wrath away from
the children of Israel, while he was zealous for
my sake among them, that I consumed not the
children of Israel in my jealousy.
12 Wherefore say, Behold, I give unto him my
covenant of peace:
13 And he shall have it, and his seed after him,
even the covenant of an everlasting priesthood;
because he was zealous for his God, and made an
atonement for the children of Israel.

Seed of Abraham and true Israel (Gen. 15:5; 22:17; 26:4; Ex. 32:13; Deut. 1:10; 10:22; 28:62). He will be the promised King (*Scepter*, Gen. 49:10) and Light of the World (Isa. 9:2–7; 42:6; 49:6; 60:1–3; Eph. 5:14; Rev. 22:16; cf. Matt. 2:2). *Moab* and *Edom* are symbolic of all those hostile to God (Isa. 25:10; 63:1).

24:20 *Amalek was the first of the nations.* The first to enter into conflict with Israel (Ex. 17:14).

Thoughts for Personal/Family Worship: Chapter 24

Balaam tried his best to curse Israel, but God used him to utter grand prophecies concerning His unfailing promise of Christ (vv. 17–19). Under the forced influence of God's Spirit, Balaam declared that all the promises of God are yea and amen in Christ. The welfare of Israel by covenant was linked to Christ, and so it is for every true believer. He declared two particular truths about the coming Messiah. The "Star" title declares the glory of Christ. All the radiant glory of God is in the face of Jesus Christ. The "Scepter" declares the might of Christ, His royal authority. This is a fuller development of Jacob's prophecy of the scepter or kingship being in Judah (Gen. 49:10). He will crush every enemy from then until the distant future. This victory is not just by the coming judgment, but is evidenced every time a sinner surrenders to King Jesus, being conquered by His grace. In a sense every conversion marks a fulfillment of Balaam's prophecy. Christ links Jacob's and Balaam's prophecies when He says, "I am the root and the offspring of David, and the bright and morning star" (Rev. 22:16). Is Christ shining in your heart? Is He ruling as your King?

ISRAEL ON THE PLAINS OF MOAB (25:1—36:13)

Chapter 25: *Israel commits fornication at Baal-peor, and the Lord commends Phinehas for his zeal in slaying the guilty.*

Sin of Baal-Peor (25:1–18)

25:1 *whoredom.* Fornication, sexual immorality.

25:3 *Baal-peor.* A Moabite god. On Baal worship, see notes at 1 Kings 16:31–32; 17:1. *the anger of the LORD.* Balaam could not manipulate God into anger (chs. 22–24), but he did teach the Moabites how to entice Israel into sin that provoked God's anger (31:16).

25:4 *heads of the people.* The ringleaders in this sin. *against the sun.* To the east.

25:8 *tent.* The word occurs only here and refers to the women's quarters. *stayed.* Restrained.

25:11 *zealous for my sake.* Literally, "zealous with my zeal."

25:12 *my covenant of peace.* See Ps. 106:28–31; Mal. 2:4–7.

25:13 *everlasting.* A long time, sometimes for an age but not necessarily eternal. The old covenant priesthood lasted a long time, but only until the Christ came, the ideal Priest.

14 Now the name of the Israelite that was slain,
even that was slain with the Midianitish woman,
was Zimri, the son of Salu, a prince of a chief
house among the Simeonites.
15 And the name of the Midianitish woman that
was slain *was* Cozbi, the daughter of Zur; he *was*
head over a people, *and* of a chief house in Midian.
16 ¶ And the LORD spake unto Moses, saying,
17 Vex the Midianites, and smite them:
18 For they vex you with their wiles, wherewith
they have beguiled you in the matter of Peor, and
in the matter of Cozbi, the daughter of a prince of
Midian, their sister, which was slain in the day of
the plague for Peor's sake.

CHAPTER 26

AND it came to pass after the plague, that the
LORD spake unto Moses and unto Eleazar the son
of Aaron the priest, saying,
2 Take the sum of all the congregation of the chil-
dren of Israel, from twenty years old and upward,
throughout their fathers' house, all that are able to
go to war in Israel.
3 And Moses and Eleazar the priest spake with
them in the plains of Moab by Jordan *near*
Jericho, saying,
4 *Take the sum of the people*, from twenty years
old and upward; as the LORD commanded Moses
and the children of Israel, which went forth out of
the land of Egypt.
5 ¶ Reuben, the eldest son of Israel: the children
of Reuben; Hanoch, *of whom cometh* the family of
the Hanochites: of Pallu, the family of the Palluites:
6 Of Hezron, the family of the Hezronites: of
Carmi, the family of the Carmites.
7 These *are* the families of the Reubenites: and
they that were numbered of them were forty and
three thousand and seven hundred and thirty.
8 And the sons of Pallu; Eliab.
9 And the sons of Eliab; Nemuel, and Dathan, and
Abiram. This *is that* Dathan and Abiram, *which*
were famous in the congregation, who strove
against Moses and against Aaron in the company
of Korah, when they strove against the LORD:
10 And the earth opened her mouth, and swal-
lowed them up together with Korah, when that
company died, what time the fire devoured two
hundred and fifty men: and they became a sign.
11 Notwithstanding the children of Korah died
not.
12 ¶ The sons of Simeon after their families: of
Nemuel, the family of the Nemuelites: of Jamin,
the family of the Jaminites: of Jachin, the family
of the Jachinites:
13 Of Zerah, the family of the Zarhites: of Shaul,
the family of the Shaulites.
14 These *are* the families of the Simeonites,
twenty and two thousand and two hundred.
15 ¶ The children of Gad after their families: of
Zephon, the family of the Zephonites: of Haggi,
the family of the Haggites: of Shuni, the family of
the Shunites:
16 Of Ozni, the family of the Oznites: of Eri, the
family of the Erites:
17 Of Arod, the family of the Arodites: of Areli,
the family of the Arelites.
18 These *are* the families of the children of Gad
according to those that were numbered of them,
forty thousand and five hundred.
19 ¶ The sons of Judah *were* Er and Onan: and Er
and Onan died in the land of Canaan.
20 And the sons of Judah after their families were;
of Shelah, the family of the Shelanites: of Pharez,
the family of the Pharzites: of Zerah, the family of
the Zarhites.

25:14 *prince of a chief house*. Literally, "exalted one of a house of a father" (v. 15).
25:17 *Vex*. Treat with hostility or enmity; attack or harass (v. 18).
25:18 *wiles*. Deception.

Thoughts for Personal/Family Worship: Chapter 25

1. **The fornication committed by Israel with the daughters of Moab was followed by idolatry. One sin leads to another. When the visible church gives way to the fleshly allurements of a corrupt world, it will not be long until she entertains and joins with its false religion. Purity of life and purity in worship go hand in hand. How are you guarding the purity of yourself, your family, and your church?**
2. **Phinehas was not deterred by the failure of others. The judge of this tribe of Simeon failed to carry out the command, thus Phinehas acted. What a dreadful day when there is no man to stand in the gap to deal with sin (Ezek. 22:30–31)! But the Lord had His Phinehas. Pray for Christlike men to stand and deal with sin and turn away the judgments of God.**
3. **Phinehas's zeal was like his God's, for literally the Lord said he was "zealous with my zeal" (v. 11). He had imbibed the nature of his God, who is a jealous God. Indeed this is one of His names (Ex. 34:14). He is jealous for His own holiness, and Phinehas had the same holy jealousy in his soul. What does God's holy jealousy desire for the people of God today? (See 2 Cor. 11:2.)**

Chapter 26: *The Lord orders a new census to be taken of Israel.*

Second Census (26:1–65)

26:4 This second numbering followed the same regulations as the first. The second census noted that four of the tribes were reduced in number and seven were higher.
26:11 *the children of Korah died not*. Some of Korah's family survived God's judgment (1 Chron. 26:1–9), probably because they listened to God's call to separate from their father so as to avoid sharing in his doom (16:23–27). Children who repent of the sinful ways of their fathers escape the punishment that falls on their fathers (Ezek. 18). Some of the descendants of Korah later became leaders in Israel's worship (1 Chron. 9:19; Pss. 42:1; 44:1; etc.).

21 And the sons of Pharez were; of Hezron, the
family of the Hezronites: of Hamul, the family of
the Hamulites.
22 These *are* the families of Judah according to
those that were numbered of them, threescore
and sixteen thousand and five hundred.
23 ¶ *Of* the sons of Issachar after their families: *of*
Tola, the family of the Tolaites: of Pua, the family
of the Punites:
24 Of Jashub, the family of the Jashubites: of
Shimron, the family of the Shimronites.
25 These *are* the families of Issachar according
to those that were numbered of them, threescore
and four thousand and three hundred.
26 ¶ *Of* the sons of Zebulun after their families:
of Sered, the family of the Sardites: of Elon, the
family of the Elonites: of Jahleel, the family of the
Jahleelites.
27 These *are* the families of the Zebulunites
according to those that were numbered of them,
threescore thousand and five hundred.
28 ¶ The sons of Joseph after their families *were*
Manasseh and Ephraim.
29 Of the sons of Manasseh: of Machir, the fam-
ily of the Machirites: and Machir begat Gilead: of
Gilead *come* the family of the Gileadites.
30 These *are* the sons of Gilead: *of* Jeezer, the fam-
ily of the Jeezerites: of Helek, the family of the
Helekites:
31 And *of* Asriel, the family of the Asrielites: and
of Shechem, the family of the Shechemites:
32 And *of* Shemida, the family of the Shemidaites:
and *of* Hepher, the family of the Hepherites.
33 ¶ And Zelophehad the son of Hepher had
no sons, but daughters: and the names of the
daughters of Zelophehad *were* Mahlah, and
Noah, Hoglah, Milcah, and Tirzah.
34 These *are* the families of Manasseh, and those
that were numbered of them, fifty and two thou-
sand and seven hundred.
35 ¶ These *are* the sons of Ephraim after their
families: of Shuthelah, the family of the Shuthal-
hites: of Becher, the family of the Bachrites: of Ta-
han, the family of the Tahanites.
36 And these *are* the sons of Shuthelah: of Eran,
the family of the Eranites.
37 These *are* the families of the sons of Ephraim
according to those that were numbered of them,
thirty and two thousand and five hundred. These
are the sons of Joseph after their families.
38 ¶ The sons of Benjamin after their families:
of Bela, the family of the Belaites: of Ashbel, the
family of the Ashbelites: of Ahiram, the family of
the Ahiramites:
39 Of Shupham, the family of the Shuphamites:
of Hupham, the family of the Huphamites.
40 And the sons of Bela were Ard and Naaman: *of*
Ard, the family of the Ardites: *and* of Naaman, the
family of the Naamites.
41 These *are* the sons of Benjamin after their
families: and they that were numbered of them
were forty and five thousand and six hundred.
42 ¶ These *are* the sons of Dan after their fami-
lies: of Shuham, the family of the Shuhamites.
These *are* the families of Dan after their families.
43 All the families of the Shuhamites, according
to those that were numbered of them, *were* three-
score and four thousand and four hundred.
44 ¶ *Of* the children of Asher after their families:
of Jimna, the family of the Jimnites: of Jesui, the
family of the Jesuites: of Beriah, the family of the
Beriites.
45 Of the sons of Beriah: of Heber, the family
of the Heberites: of Malchiel, the family of the
Malchielites.
46 And the name of the daughter of Asher *was*
Sarah.
47 These *are* the families of the sons of Asher ac-
cording to those that were numbered of them; *who*
were fifty and three thousand and four hundred.
48 ¶ *Of* the sons of Naphtali after their families:
of Jahzeel, the family of the Jahzeelites: of Guni,
the family of the Gunites:
49 Of Jezer, the family of the Jezerites: of Shillem,
the family of the Shillemites.
50 These *are* the families of Naphtali according
to their families: and they that were numbered
of them *were* forty and five thousand and four
hundred.
51 These *were* the numbered of the children of
Israel, six hundred thousand and a thousand
seven hundred and thirty.
52 ¶ And the LORD spake unto Moses, saying,
53 Unto these the land shall be divided for an

26:61 *strange fire.* Unauthorized or illegitimate fire (Lev. 10:1–3).

26:64–65 *not a man.* The old generation perished in the wilderness according to the divine sentence, except (*save*) faithful *Caleb* and *Joshua* (14:28–29,38).

Thoughts for Personal/Family Worship: Chapter 26

1. Those who died in the rebellion incited by Korah "became a sign" (v. 10). They were monuments of justice and served as an example both then and now (see comments in the Worship Sections for chs. 16–17). That the children of Korah did not die in the overthrow (26:11) stand out as a monument of divine mercy. Obviously they had not partaken of their father's sin and so did not die as God's law stipulated (Deut. 24:16). Every man will be judged for his own sin. Neither the sins of your parents nor their godliness will determine your eternal destiny. What will determine whether or not you escape the wrath that swallows up the ungodly and disobedient? (See Titus 3.)
2. In this second numbering there was not one of those adult men who had been numbered at Sinai, except for

inheritance according to the number of names.
54 To many thou shalt give the more inheritance,
and to few thou shalt give the less inheritance: to
every one shall his inheritance be given according
to those that were numbered of him.
55 Notwithstanding the land shall be divided by
lot: according to the names of the tribes of their
fathers they shall inherit.
56 According to the lot shall the possession
thereof be divided between many and few.
57 ¶ And these *are* they that were numbered of the
Levites after their families: of Gershon, the fam-
ily of the Gershonites: of Kohath, the family of the
Kohathites: of Merari, the family of the Merarites.
58 These *are* the families of the Levites: the family
of the Libnites, the family of the Hebronites, the
family of the Mahlites, the family of the Mushites,
the family of the Korathites. And Kohath begat
Amram.
59 And the name of Amram's wife *was* Jochebed,
the daughter of Levi, whom *her mother* bare to
Levi in Egypt: and she bare unto Amram Aaron
and Moses, and Miriam their sister.
60 And unto Aaron was born Nadab, and Abihu,
Eleazar, and Ithamar.
61 And Nadab and Abihu died, when they offered
strange fire before the LORD.
62 And those that were numbered of them
were twenty and three thousand, all males from
a month old and upward: for they were not
numbered among the children of Israel, because
there was no inheritance given them among the
children of Israel.
63 ¶ These *are* they that were numbered by
Moses and Eleazar the priest, who numbered the
children of Israel in the plains of Moab by Jordan
near Jericho.
64 But among these there was not a man of them
whom Moses and Aaron the priest numbered,
when they numbered the children of Israel in the
wilderness of Sinai.
65 For the LORD had said of them, They shall
surely die in the wilderness. And there was not left
a man of them, save Caleb the son of Jephunneh,
and Joshua the son of Nun.

CHAPTER 27

THEN came the daughters of Zelophehad, the son
of Hepher, the son of Gilead, the son of Machir,
the son of Manasseh, of the families of Manasseh
the son of Joseph: and these *are* the names of
his daughters; Mahlah, Noah, and Hoglah, and
Milcah, and Tirzah.
2 And they stood before Moses, and before Elea-
zar the priest, and before the princes and all the
congregation, *by* the door of the tabernacle of the
congregation, saying,
3 Our father died in the wilderness, and he was
not in the company of them that gathered them-
selves together against the LORD in the company
of Korah; but died in his own sin, and had no sons.
4 Why should the name of our father be done
away from among his family, because he hath no
son? Give unto us *therefore* a possession among
the brethren of our father.
5 And Moses brought their cause before the
LORD.
6 ¶ And the LORD spake unto Moses, saying,
7 The daughters of Zelophehad speak right: thou
shalt surely give them a possession of an inheri-
tance among their father's brethren; and thou
shalt cause the inheritance of their father to pass
unto them.
8 And thou shalt speak unto the children of Israel,
saying, If a man die, and have no son, then ye shall
cause his inheritance to pass unto his daughter.
9 And if he have no daughter, then ye shall give
his inheritance unto his brethren.
10 And if he have no brethren, then ye shall give
his inheritance unto his father's brethren.
11 And if his father have no brethren, then ye

Caleb and Joshua. God had sworn that they would surely die and so it came to pass (vv. 64–65). The divine Word that threatens judgment for sin will certainly be executed. Do not cling to the empty notion that you will escape the due reward of your evil deeds if you do not repent. It took almost forty years for the completion of the divine sentence, but it was completed. Judgment delayed is not judgment denied. Why must unrepentant sinners certainly be punished?

Chapter 27: ***The daughters of Zelophehad obtain their inheritance, Moses is informed of his impending death, and Joshua is appointed to be Moses' successor.***

Daughters of Zelophehad and Selection of Joshua to Follow Moses (27:1–23)

27:2 *princes.* Exalted ones, perhaps the seventy appointed to help Moses (11:16). It required considerable courage for these fatherless women to stand before such leaders and publicly make their request.

27:3 *not in the company . . . of Korah.* The rebels (ch. 16) lost their inheritance in the land for their sin (cf. 1 Kings 21:3,10–16).

27:4 *name of our father be done away.* A father with no sons could pass on his name or lineage through a daughter when she married and had a son (1 Chron. 2:34–35; Neh. 7:63), but his name would have no value if it did not include an inheritance (*possession*) in the land. Therefore, daughters of Zelophehad requested that their dead father's name be included in the distribution of the inheritance when Israel took the land, so their children might receive it.

27:7 *The daughters of Zelophehad speak right.* The Lord honored these women and granted their request (Josh. 17:3–4), establishing it as a principle of justice with further instructions (vv. 8–11). On an important qualification to their liberty regarding this principle, see ch. 36.

shall give his inheritance unto his kinsman that
is next to him of his family, and he shall possess
it: and it shall be unto the children of Israel a stat-
ute of judgment, as the LORD commanded Moses.
12 ¶ And the LORD said unto Moses, Get thee up
into this mount Abarim, and see the land which I
have given unto the children of Israel.
13 And when thou hast seen it, thou also shalt be
gathered unto thy people, as Aaron thy brother
was gathered.
14 For ye rebelled against my commandment in
the desert of Zin, in the strife of the congregation,
to sanctify me at the water before their eyes: that
is the water of Meribah in Kadesh in the wilder-
ness of Zin.
15 ¶ And Moses spake unto the LORD, saying,
16 Let the LORD, the God of the spirits of all flesh,
set a man over the congregation,
17 Which may go out before them, and which
may go in before them, and which may lead them
out, and which may bring them in; that the con-
gregation of the LORD be not as sheep which have
no shepherd.
18 ¶ And the LORD said unto Moses, Take thee
Joshua the son of Nun, a man in whom *is* the
spirit, and lay thine hand upon him;
19 And set him before Eleazar the priest, and
before all the congregation; and give him a charge
in their sight.
20 And thou shalt put *some* of thine honour
upon him, that all the congregation of the chil-
dren of Israel may be obedient.
21 And he shall stand before Eleazar the priest,
who shall ask *counsel* for him after the judgment
of Urim before the LORD: at his word shall they go
out, and at his word they shall come in, *both* he,
and all the children of Israel with him, even all the
congregation.
22 And Moses did as the LORD commanded him:
and he took Joshua, and set him before Eleazar
the priest, and before all the congregation:
23 And he laid his hands upon him, and gave him
a charge, as the LORD commanded by the hand
of Moses.

CHAPTER 28

AND the LORD spake unto Moses, saying,
2 Command the children of Israel, and say unto
them, My offering, *and* my bread for my sacrifices
made by fire, *for* a sweet savour unto me, shall ye
observe to offer unto me in their due season.
3 And thou shalt say unto them, This *is* the
offering made by fire which ye shall offer unto the
LORD; two lambs of the first year without spot day
by day, *for* a continual burnt offering.
4 The one lamb shalt thou offer in the morning,
and the other lamb shalt thou offer at even;
5 And a tenth *part* of an ephah of flour for a meat
offering, mingled with the fourth *part* of an hin
of beaten oil.
6 *It is* a continual burnt offering, which was
ordained in mount Sinai for a sweet savour, a
sacrifice made by fire unto the LORD.
7 And the drink offering thereof *shall be* the
fourth *part* of an hin for the one lamb: in the
holy *place* shalt thou cause the strong wine to be
poured unto the LORD *for* a drink offering.
8 And the other lamb shalt thou offer at even:
as the meat offering of the morning, and as the

27:13 *shalt be gathered unto thy people.* Will die (Gen. 25:8).
27:14 *sanctify me.* Set the Lord apart as being the Holy One that He is.
27:17 *sheep which have no shepherd.* Lacking a ruler's direction (1 Kings 22:17; Matt. 9:36).
27:18 *in whom is the spirit.* The Holy Spirit (11:25,29; 24:2). *lay thine hand upon him.* Symbolic of setting him aside to office (v. 23; Deut. 34:9).
27:19 *charge.* Command (v. 23).
27:20 *honour.* Dignity and authority.
27:21 *Urim.* An object in the priest's ephod by which they could inquire of God's will (Ex. 28:30; 1 Sam. 28:6; Ezra 2:63; cf. 1 Sam. 22:10; 30:7–8).

Thoughts for Personal/Family Worship: Chapter 27

1. **Zelophehad's daughters wanted a place for their father's name to continue in the Promised Land. He was a sinner, but had not forfeited his familial inheritance. However, they needed a mediator to bring their case to the Lord. So Moses brought their cause before the Lord, and they received their portion. This illustrates the need of sinners who on their own have no inheritance in heaven with the saints. They too need a mediator, and the only Mediator is the Lord Jesus Christ. According to 2 Cor. 5:20, what part can you play in bringing others to understand the work of Christ on their behalf?**
2. **Moses was a most selfless man. When the Lord reminded him that he was not permitted to enter Canaan, his only concern was that there would be a man to bring Israel into their possession. He did not want the Lord's people to be "as sheep which have no shepherd" (v. 17).This is the compassionate spirit of Christ (Matt. 9:36–38). The Lord indicated to Moses that Joshua was the man qualified to lead Israel. But the only quality He underlined was that Joshua had the Spirit in him (Num. 27:18). When a man has the Spirit of God filling him he will have everything required to minister. Spirit-filled men are always the need of the hour (Acts 6:3). Are you prepared to serve?**

Various Regulations (28:1—30:16)

Chapter 28: ***The Lord gives instructions concerning various sacrifices and feast days.***

Regular Offerings (28:1–15)

28:2 *a sweet savour.* Literally, "an aroma of my rest or pleasure," signifying God's satisfaction or appeasement through the *sacrifices*.
28:3 *day by day.* In a day, thus two lambs daily.
28:5 *ephah.* Approximately a bushel. *hin.* Approximately, a gallon and a half (throughout the chapter).
28:7 *strong wine.* The product of grain rather than the vine.

drink offering thereof, thou shalt offer *it*, a sacri-
fice made by fire, of a sweet savour unto the LORD.
9 ¶ And on the sabbath day two lambs of the first
year without spot, and two tenth deals of flour *for*
a meat offering, mingled with oil, and the drink
offering thereof:
10 *This is* the burnt offering of every sabbath,
beside the continual burnt offering, and his drink
offering.
11 ¶ And in the beginnings of your months ye
shall offer a burnt offering unto the LORD; two
young bullocks, and one ram, seven lambs of the
first year without spot;
12 And three tenth deals of flour *for* a meat of-
fering, mingled with oil, for one bullock; and two
tenth deals of flour *for* a meat offering, mingled
with oil, for one ram;
13 And a several tenth deal of flour mingled with
oil *for* a meat offering unto one lamb; *for* a burnt
offering of a sweet savour, a sacrifice made by fire
unto the LORD.
14 And their drink offerings shall be half an hin
of wine unto a bullock, and the third *part* of an
hin unto a ram, and a fourth *part* of an hin unto
a lamb: this *is* the burnt offering of every month
throughout the months of the year.
15 And one kid of the goats for a sin offering unto
the LORD shall be offered, beside the continual
burnt offering, and his drink offering.
16 And in the fourteenth day of the first month *is*
the passover of the LORD.
17 And in the fifteenth day of this month *is* the
feast: seven days shall unleavened bread be eaten.
18 In the first day *shall be* an holy convocation; ye
shall do no manner of servile work *therein*:
19 But ye shall offer a sacrifice made by fire *for*
a burnt offering unto the LORD; two young bull-
ocks, and one ram, and seven lambs of the first
year: they shall be unto you without blemish:
20 And their meat offering *shall be of* flour
mingled with oil: three tenth deals shall ye offer
for a bullock, and two tenth deals for a ram;
21 A several tenth deal shalt thou offer for every
lamb, throughout the seven lambs:
22 And one goat *for* a sin offering, to make an
atonement for you.
23 Ye shall offer these beside the burnt offering
in the morning, which *is* for a continual burnt
offering.
24 After this manner ye shall offer daily, through-
out the seven days, the meat of the sacrifice made
by fire, of a sweet savour unto the LORD: it shall be
offered beside the continual burnt offering, and
his drink offering.
25 And on the seventh day ye shall have an holy
convocation; ye shall do no servile work.
26 ¶ Also in the day of the firstfruits, when ye
bring a new meat offering unto the LORD, after
your weeks *be out*, ye shall have an holy convoca-
tion; ye shall do no servile work:
27 But ye shall offer the burnt offering for a sweet
savour unto the LORD; two young bullocks, one
ram, seven lambs of the first year;
28 And their meat offering of flour mingled with
oil, three tenth deals unto one bullock, two tenth
deals unto one ram,
29 A several tenth deal unto one lamb, through-
out the seven lambs;
30 *And* one kid of the goats, to make an atone-
ment for you.
31 Ye shall offer *them* beside the continual burnt
offering, and his meat offering, (they shall be unto
you without blemish) and their drink offerings.

CHAPTER 29

AND in the seventh month, on the first *day* of
the month, ye shall have an holy convocation; ye

28:9 *two tenth deals*. Two-tenth parts (throughout the chapter).
28:10 Offerings on the *sabbath* day were doubled. The Sabbath was a day of worship and rest in the experience of God's presence. It was not a day of idleness. The priests, whose ministry was worship, had double the labor in their service (Matt. 12:5). So the minister of the gospel labors on the Christian Sabbath as he leads others in the worship of God.

Festival Offerings (28:16—29:40)

28:18 *convocation*. Literally, "a calling together." *servile*. The work of employment or occupation (vv. 25–26).

Thoughts for Personal/Family Worship: Chapter 28

1. **The constant repetition of the sacrifices in the old dispensation was evidence of their inherent ineffectiveness to address the sin problem and pointed to the need for the once and for all sacrifice of Jesus Christ (Heb. 10:1–4). This is a key argument in the book of Hebrews to show the superiority of Christ and His sacrifice over the priests and sacrifices in the old order. Yet they were graphic pictures of the necessity of blood shedding if man were to be accepted before the Lord (Heb. 9:22). From the old we can learn the necessity of atonement by the death of a substitute. Rejoice that Christ, the spotless Lamb of God, has offered Himself as the only atonement that directly and finally satisfies God for sins.**
2. **On the "day of the firstfruits" (v. 26) a new meat offering was brought to the Lord, an offering of thankfulness. The feast in view is the Feast of Pentecost when the Holy Spirit was poured out and a great harvest of sinners was gathered to the Lord by the apostles. Those converted were the firstfruits of a great harvest still to come, a harvest that continues to be gathered and is presented to Christ continually. Read Eph. 1:15–16 and then offer your own offering of thanks for those in your life who have been converted.**

Chapter 29: *The Lord gives further instructions concerning offerings and feast days.*

29:1 *convocation*. Literally, "a calling together." *servile work*.

shall do no servile work: it is a day of blowing the
trumpets unto you.
2 And ye shall offer a burnt offering for a sweet
savour unto the LORD; one young bullock, one
ram, *and* seven lambs of the first year without
blemish:
3 And their meat offering *shall be of* flour min-
gled with oil, three tenth deals for a bullock, *and*
two tenth deals for a ram,
4 And one tenth deal for one lamb, throughout
the seven lambs:
5 And one kid of the goats *for* a sin offering, to
make an atonement for you:
6 Beside the burnt offering of the month, and his
meat offering, and the daily burnt offering, and
his meat offering, and their drink offerings, ac-
cording unto their manner, for a sweet savour, a
sacrifice made by fire unto the LORD.
7 ¶ And ye shall have on the tenth *day* of this sev-
enth month an holy convocation; and ye shall af-
flict your souls: ye shall not do any work *therein*:
8 But ye shall offer a burnt offering unto the
LORD *for* a sweet savour; one young bullock, one
ram, *and* seven lambs of the first year; they shall
be unto you without blemish:
9 And their meat offering *shall be of* flour min-
gled with oil, three tenth deals to a bullock, *and*
two tenth deals to one ram,
10 A several tenth deal for one lamb, throughout
the seven lambs:
11 One kid of the goats *for* a sin offering; beside
the sin offering of atonement, and the continual
burnt offering, and the meat offering of it, and
their drink offerings.
12 ¶ And on the fifteenth day of the seventh
month ye shall have an holy convocation; ye shall
do no servile work, and ye shall keep a feast unto
the LORD seven days:
13 And ye shall offer a burnt offering, a sacrifice
made by fire, of a sweet savour unto the LORD; thir-
teen young bullocks, two rams, *and* fourteen lambs
of the first year; they shall be without blemish:
14 And their meat offering *shall be of* flour
mingled with oil, three tenth deals unto every
bullock of the thirteen bullocks, two tenth deals
to each ram of the two rams,
15 And a several tenth deal to each lamb of the
fourteen lambs:
16 And one kid of the goats *for* a sin offering;
beside the continual burnt offering, his meat
offering, and his drink offering.
17 ¶ And on the second day *ye shall offer* twelve
young bullocks, two rams, fourteen lambs of the
first year without spot:
18 And their meat offering and their drink of-
ferings for the bullocks, for the rams, and for the
lambs, *shall be* according to their number, after
the manner:
19 And one kid of the goats *for* a sin offering;
beside the continual burnt offering, and the meat
offering thereof, and their drink offerings.
20 ¶ And on the third day eleven bullocks, two
rams, fourteen lambs of the first year without
blemish;
21 And their meat offering and their drink of-
ferings for the bullocks, for the rams, and for the
lambs, *shall be* according to their number, after
the manner:
22 And one goat *for* a sin offering; beside the
continual burnt offering, and his meat offering,
and his drink offering.
23 ¶ And on the fourth day ten bullocks, two
rams, *and* fourteen lambs of the first year with-
out blemish:
24 Their meat offering and their drink offerings
for the bullocks, for the rams, and for the lambs,
shall be according to their number, after the
manner:
25 And one kid of the goats *for* a sin offering;
beside the continual burnt offering, his meat
offering, and his drink offering.
26 ¶ And on the fifth day nine bullocks, two
rams, *and* fourteen lambs of the first year with-
out spot:
27 And their meat offering and their drink
offerings for the bullocks, for the rams, and for
the lambs, *shall be* according to their number,
after the manner:
28 And one goat *for* a sin offering; beside the
continual burnt offering, and his meat offering,
and his drink offering.
29 ¶ And on the sixth day eight bullocks, two
rams, *and* fourteen lambs of the first year with-
out blemish:
30 And their meat offering and their drink of-
ferings for the bullocks, for the rams, and for the

Work of employment or occupation (vv. 12,35).

29:3 *tenth deals.* Tenth parts (throughout the chapter).

29:7 *afflict your souls.* Fast. This is the spiritual discipline of setting aside normal meals to feed the body to devote oneself to feeding the inner man in a posture of humility and need before the Lord.

Thoughts for Personal/Family Worship: Chapter 29

1. The blowing of the trumpets that called the congregation together suggests a couple of important principles of worship. First, corporate worship is important. When the trumpets sounded the people gathered together. Likewise, we are not to forsake the assembling together (Heb. 10:25). The mutual exhortation and edification is important. Second, worship requires a frame of mind that is free from the distractions of life. Hence, they were to refrain from their normal occupations to have the time and mindset to worship. Thus observing the Sabbath is a key component of worship. How can you free yourself from the normal routines of life so that you

lambs, *shall be* according to their number, after the manner:

31 And one goat *for* a sin offering; beside the continual burnt offering, his meat offering, and his drink offering.

32 ¶ And on the seventh day seven bullocks, two rams, *and* fourteen lambs of the first year without blemish:

33 And their meat offering and their drink offerings for the bullocks, for the rams, and for the lambs, *shall be* according to their number, after the manner:

34 And one goat *for* a sin offering; beside the continual burnt offering, his meat offering, and his drink offering.

35 ¶ On the eighth day ye shall have a solemn assembly: ye shall do no servile work *therein*:

36 But ye shall offer a burnt offering, a sacrifice made by fire, of a sweet savour unto the LORD: one bullock, one ram, seven lambs of the first year without blemish:

37 Their meat offering and their drink offerings for the bullock, for the ram, and for the lambs, *shall be* according to their number, after the manner:

38 And one goat *for* a sin offering; beside the continual burnt offering, and his meat offering, and his drink offering.

39 These *things* ye shall do unto the LORD in your set feasts, beside your vows, and your freewill offerings, for your burnt offerings, and for your meat offerings, and for your drink offerings, and for your peace offerings.

40 And Moses told the children of Israel according to all that the LORD commanded Moses.

CHAPTER 30

AND Moses spake unto the heads of the tribes concerning the children of Israel, saying, This *is* the thing which the LORD hath commanded.

2 If a man vow a vow unto the LORD, or swear an oath to bind his soul with a bond; he shall not break his word, he shall do according to all that proceedeth out of his mouth.

3 If a woman also vow a vow unto the LORD, and bind *herself* by a bond, *being* in her father's house in her youth;

4 And her father hear her vow, and her bond wherewith she hath bound her soul, and her father shall hold his peace at her: then all her vows shall stand, and every bond wherewith she hath bound her soul shall stand.

5 But if her father disallow her in the day that he heareth; not any of her vows, or of her bonds wherewith she hath bound her soul, shall stand: and the LORD shall forgive her, because her father disallowed her.

6 And if she had at all an husband, when she vowed, or uttered ought out of her lips, wherewith she bound her soul;

7 And her husband heard *it*, and held his peace at her in the day that he heard *it*: then her vows shall stand, and her bonds wherewith she bound her soul shall stand.

8 But if her husband disallowed her on the day that he heard *it*; then he shall make her vow which she vowed, and that which she uttered with her lips, wherewith she bound her soul, of none effect: and the LORD shall forgive her.

9 But every vow of a widow, and of her that is divorced, wherewith they have bound their souls, shall stand against her.

10 And if she vowed in her husband's house, or bound her soul by a bond with an oath;

11 And her husband heard *it*, and held his peace at her, *and* disallowed her not: then all her vows shall stand, and every bond wherewith she bound her soul shall stand.

12 But if her husband hath utterly made them void on the day he heard *them; then* whatsoever proceeded out of her lips concerning her vows, or concerning the bond of her soul, shall not stand: her husband hath made them void; and the LORD shall forgive her.

13 Every vow, and every binding oath to afflict the soul, her husband may establish it, or her husband may make it void.

14 But if her husband altogether hold his peace

are able to think about spiritual matters with undivided attention in your weekly worship services?

2. The repetition of the details for the various offerings and particularly the eight days of the Feast of Tabernacles teach the vital lesson that we must worship the Lord according to His revealed will. The fallen fleshly mind cannot be trusted, so the Lord leaves no room for figuring out on our own how to worship Him. We are too susceptible to deception and to deviation from the Lord's mind. While we can thank God that new covenant worship does not have such complicated ceremonies to follow, we should also thank God that still today the church has clear instructions in the Scriptures about how God commands us to worship. How are we tempted to add to them or subtract from them?

Chapter 30: *The Lord gives instructions concerning vows.*

Vows (30:1–16)

30:2 *his soul.* Himself. *break.* Profane or make invalid. Vows are binding (Eccl. 5:4–5). Every word of the believer should be his bond (Matt. 5:33–37).

30:4 *hold his peace.* Remain silent (vv. 7,11,14). *stand.* Stand firm in the sense of being unbreakable. *her soul.* Herself (throughout the chapter).

30:5 *disallow.* Express disapproval, restrain, or forbid (vv. 8,11).

30:8 *make . . . of none effect.* Break or make void.

30:12 *made them void.* Same word as "make of none effect" (vv. 8,15).

at her from day to day; then he establisheth all her vows, or all her bonds, which *are* upon her: he confirmeth them, because he held his peace at her in the day that he heard *them*.
15 But if he shall any ways make them void after that he hath heard *them*; then he shall bear her iniquity.
16 These *are* the statutes, which the LORD commanded Moses, between a man and his wife, between the father and his daughter, *being yet* in her youth in her father's house.

CHAPTER 31

AND the LORD spake unto Moses, saying,
2 Avenge the children of Israel of the Midianites: afterward shalt thou be gathered unto thy people.
3 And Moses spake unto the people, saying, Arm some of yourselves unto the war, and let them go against the Midianites, and avenge the LORD of Midian.
4 Of every tribe a thousand, throughout all the tribes of Israel, shall ye send to the war.
5 So there were delivered out of the thousands of Israel, a thousand of *every* tribe, twelve thousand armed for war.
6 And Moses sent them to the war, a thousand of *every* tribe, them and Phinehas the son of Eleazar the priest, to the war, with the holy instruments, and the trumpets to blow in his hand.
7 And they warred against the Midianites, as the LORD commanded Moses; and they slew all the males.
8 And they slew the kings of Midian, beside the rest of them that were slain; *namely*, Evi, and Rekem, and Zur, and Hur, and Reba, five kings of Midian: Balaam also the son of Beor they slew with the sword.
9 And the children of Israel took *all* the women of Midian captives, and their little ones, and took the spoil of all their cattle, and all their flocks, and all their goods.
10 And they burnt all their cities wherein they dwelt, and all their goodly castles, with fire.
11 And they took all the spoil, and all the prey, *both* of men and of beasts.
12 And they brought the captives, and the prey, and the spoil, unto Moses, and Eleazar the priest, and unto the congregation of the children of Israel, unto the camp at the plains of Moab, which *are* by Jordan *near* Jericho.
13 ¶ And Moses, and Eleazar the priest, and all the princes of the congregation, went forth to meet them without the camp.
14 And Moses was wroth with the officers of the host, *with* the captains over thousands, and captains over hundreds, which came from the battle.
15 And Moses said unto them, Have ye saved all the women alive?
16 Behold, these caused the children of Israel, through the counsel of Balaam, to commit trespass against the LORD in the matter of Peor, and there was a plague among the congregation of the LORD.
17 Now therefore kill every male among the little ones, and kill every woman that hath known man by lying with him.
18 But all the women children, that have not known a man by lying with him, keep alive for yourselves.
19 And do ye abide without the camp seven days: whosoever hath killed any person, and whosoever hath touched any slain, purify *both* yourselves and

30:15 *iniquity*. Guilt.
30:16 *youth*. When she is single and not married.

Thoughts for Personal/Family Worship: Chapter 30

1. **The solemn comment about the one who made a vow was, "He shall not break his word" (v. 2). In the life of the believer his word should be his oath. A Christian essentially is one who claims to have bound himself to be the Lord's, so he must be careful not to violate that claim. "He shall do according to all that proceedeth out of his mouth" (v. 2) is a striking reminder of the Lord, who keeps His Word and will never alter it (Ps. 89:34). Let us be conformed to His image in everything (Rom. 8:29), including the words of our mouths. In what ways are you tempted to fail to live consistently with what you have said?**
2. **In the making of vows, daughters were under the jurisdiction of fathers, and wives under husbands. In this manner it was shown that the man is to be the head of his house and is to guide prudently and properly (1 Cor. 11:3; Eph. 5:23). It is not a position of dictatorship, but it is a position of authority that demands spiritual perception and maturity. To be responsible for others in leading them in the proper path is daunting and one that requires dependence on the Lord. Pray that God will help you to fulfill your role in a way that honors Him.**

Chapter 31: ***The Lord instructs Moses to war against the Midianites.***

War against Midianites (31:1–54)

31:2 *shalt thou be gathered unto thy people*. You will die.
31:10 *goodly castles*. Literally, "their encampments."
31:11–12 *prey*. Plunder or booty from the war (vv. 26–27,32).
31:14 *wroth*. Angry or furious.
31:16 *counsel of Balaam*. Literally, "word of Balaam." Ironically, the man whom God constrained to speak His divine Word (22:20,35), proved himself an enemy of Israel when allowed to speak his own words, perhaps to win honor and reward from Balak despite his noble prophecies (24:10–13). *matter of Peor*. Immorality and idolatry with Moab. There is no hint in the previous account of this event (ch. 25) that Balaam instigated it.
31:19 *abide without the camp*. Literally, "camp outside the encampment."
31:22 *brass*. Bronze.
31:23 *abide*. Endure. *water of separation*. Water for purifying the ceremonial unclean (ch. 19).

your captives on the third day, and on the seventh
day.
20 And purify all *your* raiment, and all that is
made of skins, and all work of goats' *hair*, and all
things made of wood.
21 ¶ And Eleazar the priest said unto the men
of war which went to the battle, This *is* the or-
dinance of the law which the LORD commanded
Moses;
22 Only the gold, and the silver, the brass, the
iron, the tin, and the lead,
23 Every thing that may abide the fire, ye shall
make *it* go through the fire, and it shall be clean:
nevertheless it shall be purified with the water
of separation: and all that abideth not the fire ye
shall make go through the water.
24 And ye shall wash your clothes on the seventh
day, and ye shall be clean, and afterward ye shall
come into the camp.
25 ¶ And the LORD spake unto Moses, saying,
26 Take the sum of the prey that was taken, *both*
of man and of beast, thou, and Eleazar the priest,
and the chief fathers of the congregation:
27 And divide the prey into two parts; between
them that took the war upon them, who went out
to battle, and between all the congregation:
28 And levy a tribute unto the LORD of the men
of war which went out to battle: one soul of five
hundred, *both* of the persons, and of the beeves,
and of the asses, and of the sheep:
29 Take *it* of their half, and give it unto Eleazar
the priest, *for* an heave offering of the LORD.
30 And of the children of Israel's half, thou shalt
take one portion of fifty, of the persons, of the
beeves, of the asses, and of the flocks, of all man-
ner of beasts, and give them unto the Levites,
which keep the charge of the tabernacle of the
LORD.
31 And Moses and Eleazar the priest did as the
LORD commanded Moses.
32 And the booty, *being* the rest of the prey which
the men of war had caught, was six hundred
thousand and seventy thousand and five thou-
sand sheep,
33 And threescore and twelve thousand beeves,
34 And threescore and one thousand asses,
35 And thirty and two thousand persons in all,
of women that had not known man by lying with
him.
36 And the half, *which was* the portion of them
that went out to war, was in number three hun-
dred thousand and seven and thirty thousand
and five hundred sheep:
37 And the LORD's tribute of the sheep was six
hundred and threescore and fifteen.
38 And the beeves *were* thirty and six thousand;
of which the LORD's tribute *was* threescore and
twelve.
39 And the asses *were* thirty thousand and five
hundred; of which the LORD's tribute *was* three-
score and one.
40 And the persons *were* sixteen thousand; of
which the LORD's tribute *was* thirty and two
persons.
41 And Moses gave the tribute, *which was* the
LORD's heave offering, unto Eleazar the priest, as
the LORD commanded Moses.
42 And of the children of Israel's half, which
Moses divided from the men that warred,
43 (Now the half *that pertained unto* the congre-
gation was three hundred thousand and thirty
thousand *and* seven thousand and five hundred
sheep,
44 And thirty and six thousand beeves,
45 And thirty thousand asses and five hundred,
46 And sixteen thousand persons;)
47 Even of the children of Israel's half, Moses
took one portion of fifty, *both* of man and of
beast, and gave them unto the Levites, which kept
the charge of the tabernacle of the LORD; as the
LORD commanded Moses.
48 ¶ And the officers which *were* over thousands
of the host, the captains of thousands, and cap-
tains of hundreds, came near unto Moses:
49 And they said unto Moses, Thy servants have
taken the sum of the men of war which *are* under
our charge, and there lacketh not one man of us.
50 We have therefore brought an oblation for the
LORD, what every man hath gotten, of jewels of
gold, chains, and bracelets, rings, earrings, and
tablets, to make an atonement for our souls be-
fore the LORD.
51 And Moses and Eleazar the priest took the
gold of them, *even* all wrought jewels.
52 And all the gold of the offering that they of-
fered up to the LORD, of the captains of thou-
sands, and of the captains of hundreds, was
sixteen thousand seven hundred and fifty shekels.
53 (*For* the men of war had taken spoil, every
man for himself.)
54 And Moses and Eleazar the priest took
the gold of the captains of thousands and of

31:28 *levy a tribute*. Lift up a tax. *beeves*. Herds, cattle (vv. 30, 33,38,44).
31:32 *booty*. "Prey," but a different word than the one for *prey* in the same verse.
31:50 *oblation*. Literally, "a thing brought near," referring to the offering. *gotten*. Obtained. *tablets*. Necklaces.
31:52 *shekels*. Each approximately one-half ounce.

Thoughts for Personal/Family Worship: Chapter 31

1. God gave the command for Israel to take just vengeance on the Midianites because vengeance belongs to Him (Deut. 32:35). By the deceptions of the Midianite women the men of Israel had been seduced into immorality and idol worship. Now the divine dictate came for divine

hundreds, and brought it into the tabernacle of the congregation, *for* a memorial for the children of Israel before the LORD.

CHAPTER 32

NOW the children of Reuben and the children of Gad had a very great multitude of cattle: and when they saw the land of Jazer, and the land of Gilead, that, behold, the place *was* a place for cattle;
2 The children of Gad and the children of Reuben came and spake unto Moses, and to Eleazar the priest, and unto the princes of the congregation, saying,
3 Ataroth, and Dibon, and Jazer, and Nimrah, and Heshbon, and Elealeh, and Shebam, and Nebo, and Beon,
4 *Even* the country which the LORD smote before the congregation of Israel, *is* a land for cattle, and thy servants have cattle:
5 Wherefore, said they, if we have found grace in thy sight, let this land be given unto thy servants for a possession, *and* bring us not over Jordan.
6 ¶ And Moses said unto the children of Gad and to the children of Reuben, Shall your brethren go to war, and shall ye sit here?
7 And wherefore discourage ye the heart of the children of Israel from going over into the land which the LORD hath given them?
8 Thus did your fathers, when I sent them from Kadesh-barnea to see the land.
9 For when they went up unto the valley of Eshcol, and saw the land, they discouraged the heart of the children of Israel, that they should not go into the land which the LORD had given them.
10 And the LORD's anger was kindled the same time, and he sware, saying,
11 Surely none of the men that came up out of Egypt, from twenty years old and upward, shall see the land which I sware unto Abraham, unto Isaac, and unto Jacob; because they have not wholly followed me:
12 Save Caleb the son of Jephunneh the Kenezite, and Joshua the son of Nun: for they have wholly followed the LORD.
13 And the LORD's anger was kindled against Israel, and he made them wander in the wilderness forty years, until all the generation, that had done evil in the sight of the LORD, was consumed.
14 And, behold, ye are risen up in your fathers' stead, an increase of sinful men, to augment yet the fierce anger of the LORD toward Israel.
15 For if ye turn away from after him, he will yet again leave them in the wilderness; and ye shall destroy all this people.
16 ¶ And they came near unto him, and said, We will build sheepfolds here for our cattle, and cities for our little ones:
17 But we ourselves will go ready armed before the children of Israel, until we have brought them unto their place: and our little ones shall dwell in the fenced cities because of the inhabitants of the land.
18 We will not return unto our houses, until the children of Israel have inherited every man his inheritance.
19 For we will not inherit with them on yonder side Jordan, or forward; because our inheritance is fallen to us on this side Jordan eastward.
20 ¶ And Moses said unto them, If ye will do this thing, if ye will go armed before the LORD to war,
21 And will go all of you armed over Jordan before the LORD, until he hath driven out his enemies from before him,
22 And the land be subdued before the LORD: then afterward ye shall return, and be guiltless before the LORD, and before Israel; and this land shall be your possession before the LORD.
23 But if ye will not do so, behold, ye have sinned

vengeance. Sinner, remember that "God is not mocked: for whatsoever a man soweth, that shall he also reap" (Gal. 6:7). How have you seen this principle at work in your own life or the lives of those around you?

2. **This battle also marked God's vengeance against Balaam. He expressed his desire earlier that he would die the death of the righteous (23:10). But tragically, what a sad end he met! He had sold himself to do evil. Even when God frustrated him from pronouncing a curse on Israel, he schemed against them. He forsook the right way and went astray (2 Peter 2:15), and eventually his sin found him out. Hypocrisy can only have one of two ends: true repentance or total destruction. How do hypocrites fool themselves into thinking they will escape judgment? Why are they fools to think so?**
3. **Of all those who went to war against Midian, not one was lost (v. 49). Consequently the officers of Israel's army brought an offering of thanks to the Lord for their preservation in the battle. They were fighting the Lord's battle, and the Lord preserved them. Engagement in warfare for the Lord does not necessarily guarantee exemption from casualties, but it does ensure victory for all those enlisted in the Lord's army. How can this serve to encourage you as you fight the good fight?**

Chapter 32: ***Reuben, Gad, and the half tribe of Manasseh receive their inheritance on the east side of Jordan along with some strict warnings from Moses.***

Inheritance of Transjordan Tribes (32:1–42)

32:2 *princes of the congregation.* Exalted ones, most likely the seventy appointed to help Moses.

32:6 *sit.* Dwell.

32:14 *in your fathers' stead.* Instead of or in the place of your fathers.

32:19 *forward.* Beyond.

32:33 *coasts.* Borders or circuits.

against the LORD: and be sure your sin will find
you out.
24 Build you cities for your little ones, and folds
for your sheep; and do that which hath proceeded
out of your mouth.
25 And the children of Gad and the children of
Reuben spake unto Moses, saying, Thy servants
will do as my lord commandeth.
26 Our little ones, our wives, our flocks, and all
our cattle, shall be there in the cities of Gilead:
27 But thy servants will pass over, every man
armed for war, before the LORD to battle, as my
lord saith.
28 So concerning them Moses commanded Eleazar the priest, and Joshua the son of Nun, and the
chief fathers of the tribes of the children of Israel:
29 And Moses said unto them, If the children of
Gad and the children of Reuben will pass with
you over Jordan, every man armed to battle, before the LORD, and the land shall be subdued
before you; then ye shall give them the land of
Gilead for a possession:
30 But if they will not pass over with you armed,
they shall have possessions among you in the land
of Canaan.
31 And the children of Gad and the children of
Reuben answered, saying, As the LORD hath said
unto thy servants, so will we do.
32 We will pass over armed before the LORD into
the land of Canaan, that the possession of our
inheritance on this side Jordan *may be* ours.
33 And Moses gave unto them, *even* to the
children of Gad, and to the children of Reuben,
and unto half the tribe of Manasseh the son of
Joseph, the kingdom of Sihon king of the Amorites, and the kingdom of Og king of Bashan, the
land, with the cities thereof in the coasts, *even*
the cities of the country round about.
34 ¶ And the children of Gad built Dibon, and
Ataroth, and Aroer,
35 And Atroth, Shophan, and Jaazer, and Jogbehah,
36 And Beth-nimrah, and Beth-haran, fenced
cities: and folds for sheep.
37 And the children of Reuben built Heshbon,
and Elealeh, and Kirjathaim,
38 And Nebo, and Baal-meon, (their names being
changed,) and Shibmah: and gave other names
unto the cities which they builded.
39 And the children of Machir the son of
Manasseh went to Gilead, and took it, and dispossessed the Amorite which *was* in it.
40 And Moses gave Gilead unto Machir the son
of Manasseh; and he dwelt therein.
41 And Jair the son of Manasseh went and
took the small towns thereof, and called them
Havoth-jair.
42 And Nobah went and took Kenath, and the
villages thereof, and called it Nobah, after his own
name.

CHAPTER 33

THESE *are* the journeys of the children of Israel,
which went forth out of the land of Egypt with
their armies under the hand of Moses and Aaron.
2 And Moses wrote their goings out according to
their journeys by the commandment of the LORD:
and these *are* their journeys according to their
goings out.
3 And they departed from Rameses in the first
month, on the fifteenth day of the first month;
on the morrow after the passover the children of
Israel went out with an high hand in the sight of
all the Egyptians.
4 For the Egyptians buried all *their* firstborn,
which the LORD had smitten among them: upon
their gods also the LORD executed judgments.
5 And the children of Israel removed from Rameses, and pitched in Succoth.

Thoughts for Personal/Family Worship: Chapter 32

1. **Moses put a very relevant question to Reuben, Gad, and the half tribe of Manasseh who had gained their inheritance easily on the east of Jordan: "Shall your brethren go to war, and shall ye sit here?" (v. 6). Christ's body is one, thus none can be at ease when other members are facing the conflict. We are to bear one another's burdens. We are to remember those in bonds as bound with them. There is a unity in the body of Christ that cannot be overlooked and should be cherished. How are you fighting alongside other Christians to support them in their spiritual battles?**
2. **"Be sure your sin will find you out" (v. 23) is a classic text with a sobering message. The consequences of sin will catch up to the sinner eventually. Some men's sins are openly found out in this life. But the sins of all who die impenitent will be found out at the great day of judgment. Then the Lord will bring to light the hidden things of darkness and will judge the secrets of men by Jesus Christ. Cover your sins and you will not prosper. Read Ps. 51, then spend some time confessing and forsaking your sins and resting in God's great mercy.**

Various Lists (33:1—35:34)

Chapter 33: *Moses reviewed the trek of the wilderness wanderings and warned that Canaanites must be destroyed.*

Instructions for Encampment (33:1–56)

33:2 *Moses wrote.* More evidence that Moses wrote the first five books of the Bible, being authorized *by the commandment of the LORD* (Ex. 17:14; 24:4). See the Introduction to the Pentateuch: Authorship.

33:3 *departed.* Broke camp and marched on (throughout the chapter). *with an high hand.* Expressing the victory of the exodus.

33:5 *pitched.* Encamped (throughout the chapter).

6 And they departed from Succoth, and pitched
in Etham, which *is* in the edge of the wilderness.
7 And they removed from Etham, and turned
again unto Pi-hahiroth, which *is* before Baal-
zephon: and they pitched before Migdol.
8 And they departed from before Pi-hahiroth,
and passed through the midst of the sea into the
wilderness, and went three days' journey in the
wilderness of Etham, and pitched in Marah.
9 And they removed from Marah, and came
unto Elim: and in Elim *were* twelve fountains of
water, and threescore and ten palm trees; and they
pitched there.
10 And they removed from Elim, and encamped
by the Red sea.
11 And they removed from the Red sea, and
encamped in the wilderness of Sin.
12 And they took their journey out of the wilder-
ness of Sin, and encamped in Dophkah.
13 And they departed from Dophkah, and en-
camped in Alush.
14 And they removed from Alush, and encamped
at Rephidim, where was no water for the people
to drink.
15 And they departed from Rephidim, and
pitched in the wilderness of Sinai.
16 And they removed from the desert of Sinai,
and pitched at Kibroth-hattaavah.
17 And they departed from Kibroth-hattaavah,
and encamped at Hazeroth.
18 And they departed from Hazeroth, and
pitched in Rithmah.
19 And they departed from Rithmah, and pitched
at Rimmon-parez.
20 And they departed from Rimmon-parez, and
pitched in Libnah.
21 And they removed from Libnah, and pitched
at Rissah.
22 And they journeyed from Rissah, and pitched
in Kehelathah.
23 And they went from Kehelathah, and pitched
in mount Shapher.
24 And they removed from mount Shapher, and
encamped in Haradah.
25 And they removed from Haradah, and pitched
in Makheloth.
26 And they removed from Makheloth, and en-
camped at Tahath.
27 And they departed from Tahath, and pitched
at Tarah.
28 And they removed from Tarah, and pitched in
Mithcah.
29 And they went from Mithcah, and pitched in
Hashmonah.
30 And they departed from Hashmonah, and
encamped at Moseroth.
31 And they departed from Moseroth, and
pitched in Bene-jaakan.
32 And they removed from Bene-jaakan, and
encamped at Hor-hagidgad.
33 And they went from Hor-hagidgad, and
pitched in Jotbathah.
34 And they removed from Jotbathah, and en-
camped at Ebronah.
35 And they departed from Ebronah, and en-
camped at Ezion-gaber.
36 And they removed from Ezion-gaber, and
pitched in the wilderness of Zin, which *is* Kadesh.
37 And they removed from Kadesh, and pitched
in mount Hor, in the edge of the land of Edom.
38 And Aaron the priest went up into mount
Hor at the commandment of the LORD, and died
there, in the fortieth year after the children of Is-
rael were come out of the land of Egypt, in the
first *day* of the fifth month.
39 And Aaron *was* an hundred and twenty and
three years old when he died in mount Hor.
40 And king Arad the Canaanite, which dwelt
in the south in the land of Canaan, heard of the
coming of the children of Israel.
41 And they departed from mount Hor, and
pitched in Zalmonah.
42 And they departed from Zalmonah, and
pitched in Punon.
43 And they departed from Punon, and pitched
in Oboth.
44 And they departed from Oboth, and pitched
in Ije-abarim, in the border of Moab.
45 And they departed from Iim, and pitched in
Dibon-gad.
46 And they removed from Dibon-gad, and en-
camped in Almon-diblathaim.
47 And they removed from Almon-diblathaim,
and pitched in the mountains of Abarim, before
Nebo.
48 And they departed from the mountains of
Abarim, and pitched in the plains of Moab by
Jordan *near* Jericho.
49 And they pitched by Jordan, from Beth-jesi-
moth *even* unto Abel-shittim in the plains of Moab.

33:8 *the sea.* The Red Sea.
33:52 *pictures.* Idols in the form of sculptures or carved figures. *quite pluck down.* Exterminate or destroy.
33:55 *pricks.* Thorns. *vex.* Treat with hostility, harass.

Thoughts for Personal/Family Worship: Chapter 33

1. The Lord commanded the record of the journeys of Israel from Egypt to Canaan. God's people are to keep in mind all the ways in which the Lord leads them, both as individuals yet especially through the history of His people. God led them out of Egypt through every turn and circle through the wilderness. There were times when Israel thought that they were lost; where they were did not make any sense. But Moses makes it clear that God had led all the way. Even though the trek goes through the wilderness of trouble, looking back makes it clear that

50 ¶ And the LORD spake unto Moses in the
plains of Moab by Jordan *near* Jericho, saying,
51 Speak unto the children of Israel, and say unto
them, When ye are passed over Jordan into the
land of Canaan;
52 Then ye shall drive out all the inhabitants of
the land from before you, and destroy all their
pictures, and destroy all their molten images, and
quite pluck down all their high places:
53 And ye shall dispossess *the inhabitants of* the
land, and dwell therein: for I have given you the
land to possess it.
54 And ye shall divide the land by lot for an inheritance among your families: *and* to the more
ye shall give the more inheritance, and to the
fewer ye shall give the less inheritance: every
man's *inheritance* shall be in the place where his
lot falleth; according to the tribes of your fathers
ye shall inherit.
55 But if ye will not drive out the inhabitants of
the land from before you; then it shall come to
pass, that those which ye let remain of them *shall
be* pricks in your eyes, and thorns in your sides,
and shall vex you in the land wherein ye dwell.
56 Moreover it shall come to pass, *that* I shall do
unto you, as I thought to do unto them.

CHAPTER 34

AND the LORD spake unto Moses, saying,
2 Command the children of Israel, and say unto
them, When ye come into the land of Canaan;
(this *is* the land that shall fall unto you for an inheritance, *even* the land of Canaan with the coasts
thereof:)
3 Then your south quarter shall be from the
wilderness of Zin along by the coast of Edom, and
your south border shall be the outmost coast of
the salt sea eastward:
4 And your border shall turn from the south to
the ascent of Akrabbim, and pass on to Zin: and
the going forth thereof shall be from the south to
Kadesh-barnea, and shall go on to Hazar-addar,
and pass on to Azmon:
5 And the border shall fetch a compass from
Azmon unto the river of Egypt, and the goings
out of it shall be at the sea.
6 And *as for* the western border, ye shall even have
the great sea for a border: this shall be your west
border.
7 And this shall be your north border: from the
great sea ye shall point out for you mount Hor:
8 From mount Hor ye shall point out *your border* unto the entrance of Hamath; and the goings
forth of the border shall be to Zedad:
9 ¶ And the border shall go on to Ziphron, and
the goings out of it shall be at Hazar-enan: this
shall be your north border.
10 And ye shall point out your east border from
Hazar-enan to Shepham:
11 And the coast shall go down from Shepham
to Riblah, on the east side of Ain; and the border
shall descend, and shall reach unto the side of the
sea of Chinnereth eastward:
12 And the border shall go down to Jordan, and
the goings out of it shall be at the salt sea: this shall
be your land with the coasts thereof round about.
13 And Moses commanded the children of Israel,
saying, This *is* the land which ye shall inherit by
lot, which the LORD commanded to give unto the
nine tribes, and to the half tribe:
14 For the tribe of the children of Reuben according to the house of their fathers, and the tribe
of the children of Gad according to the house of
their fathers, have received *their inheritance*; and
half the tribe of Manasseh have received their
inheritance:
15 The two tribes and the half tribe have received
their inheritance on this side Jordan *near* Jericho
eastward, toward the sunrising.
16 And the LORD spake unto Moses, saying,
17 These *are* the names of the men which shall
divide the land unto you: Eleazar the priest, and
Joshua the son of Nun.
18 And ye shall take one prince of every tribe, to
divide the land by inheritance.
19 And the names of the men *are* these: Of the
tribe of Judah, Caleb the son of Jephunneh.
20 And of the tribe of the children of Simeon,
Shemuel the son of Ammihud.

---

goodness and mercy followed them all the days of their lives. How does this encourage you as you move ahead?

2. Once they entered the land, Israel was to drive out the inhabitants of Canaan and destroy the relics of their idolatry. Toleration of their enemies would place God's people in jeopardy. Likewise, sin must be put to death in the lives of the saints. If not it will vex the soul and rob of the Lord's blessing. Every true Christian has crucified the flesh with its affections and lusts and labors to progressively kill remaining sin in his life. What sins and inward idols do you regularly confront that you must destroy?

Chapter 34: ***Moses outlines the borders of the land and identifies the men responsible for the divisions.***

Borders of Canaan and Procedures for Its Division (34:1–29)

34:2 *coasts.* Borders or circuits (v. 12).
34:3 *coast of Edom.* Literally, "hands of Edom," referring to the borders. *outmost coast.* End or extremity. *salt sea.* Dead Sea.
34:4 *the ascent.* The rising or the climb.
34:5 *fetch a compass.* Go round about, encircle, or surround.
34:6 *great sea.* Mediterranean Sea.
34:11 *sea of Chinnereth.* Sea of Galilee.
34:15 *The two tribes and the half tribe.* Reuben, Gad, and the half tribe of Manasseh.
34:18 *prince.* Exalted one, a leader, not a son of royalty (throughout the chapter).

21 Of the tribe of Benjamin, Elidad the son of
Chislon.
22 And the prince of the tribe of the children of
Dan, Bukki the son of Jogli.
23 The prince of the children of Joseph, for the
tribe of the children of Manasseh, Hanniel the
son of Ephod.
24 And the prince of the tribe of the children of
Ephraim, Kemuel the son of Shiphtan.
25 And the prince of the tribe of the children of
Zebulun, Elizaphan the son of Parnach.
26 And the prince of the tribe of the children of
Issachar, Paltiel the son of Azzan.
27 And the prince of the tribe of the children of
Asher, Ahihud the son of Shelomi.
28 And the prince of the tribe of the children of
Naphtali, Pedahel the son of Ammihud.
29 These *are they* whom the LORD commanded to
divide the inheritance unto the children of Israel
in the land of Canaan.

CHAPTER 35

AND the LORD spake unto Moses in the plains of
Moab by Jordan *near* Jericho, saying,
2 Command the children of Israel, that they
give unto the Levites of the inheritance of their
possession, cities to dwell in; and ye shall give
also unto the Levites suburbs for the cities round
about them.
3 And the cities shall they have to dwell in; and
the suburbs of them shall be for their cattle, and
for their goods, and for all their beasts.
4 And the suburbs of the cities, which ye shall
give unto the Levites, *shall reach* from the wall
of the city and outward a thousand cubits round
about.
5 And ye shall measure from without the city on
the east side two thousand cubits, and on the south
side two thousand cubits, and on the west side two
thousand cubits, and on the north side two thousand cubits; and the city *shall be* in the midst: this
shall be to them the suburbs of the cities.
6 And among the cities which ye shall give unto
the Levites *there shall be* six cities for refuge,
which ye shall appoint for the manslayer, that he
may flee thither: and to them ye shall add forty
and two cities.
7 *So* all the cities which ye shall give to the Levites
shall be forty and eight cities: them *shall ye give*
with their suburbs.
8 And the cities which ye shall give *shall be* of the
possession of the children of Israel: from *them
that have* many ye shall give many; but from *them
that have* few ye shall give few: every one shall give
of his cities unto the Levites according to his inheritance which he inheriteth.
9 ¶ And the LORD spake unto Moses, saying,
10 Speak unto the children of Israel, and say unto
them, When ye be come over Jordan into the land
of Canaan;
11 Then ye shall appoint you cities to be cities
of refuge for you; that the slayer may flee thither,
which killeth any person at unawares.
12 And they shall be unto you cities for refuge
from the avenger; that the manslayer die not, until he stand before the congregation in judgment.
13 And of these cities which ye shall give six cities
shall ye have for refuge.
14 Ye shall give three cities on this side Jordan,

Thoughts for Personal/Family Worship: Chapter 34

1. **The Lord set Israel's borders. The Lord appoints the bounds of our earthly existence, in space, time, and influence (Job 14:5; Ps. 31:15; Dan. 4:25,35; Acts 17:26). There is a border to life in this world that cannot be passed for "it is appointed unto men once to die" (Heb. 9:27). As you recognize the limits within which God has placed you, are you able to live with contentment within them and know that all is well with your soul?**
2. **The delineation of Israel's border began and ended at "the salt sea" (the Dead Sea, vv. 3,12). The salt sea was an enduring monument of the destruction of Sodom and Gomorrah (Gen. 19; Deut. 29:23). In this manner Israel had at their border a reminder not to cross the boundaries of God's law, a warning of the destruction that sin brings. How has God given you reminders of the consequences of sin? How can you use them like boundaries that hold you from evil?**
3. **The land of Canaan was comparatively small, nothing like the great empires that rose and fell in the Ancient Near East. Its smallness reminds the saints that, though they may possess little in this world, they are to be content. How can they do that? They must stay focused on the "better country, that is, an heavenly" inheritance, just as the patriarchs did (Heb. 11:16). Great lands and wealth will slip from the rich man's fingers at death, but the Christian will receive, "an inheritance incorruptible, and undefiled, and that fadeth not away, reserved in heaven for you" (1 Peter 1:4). How should this help you live in contentment?**

Chapter 35: *The Levites are allotted their cities, including the cities of refuge.*

Levitical Cities and Cities of Refuge (35:1–34)

35:2 *suburbs.* The area outside the city limits but under the jurisdiction of the city (throughout the chapter).
35:6 *manslayer.* Killer, same word as "murderer" (vv. 16–19, etc.), and as that used in the sixth commandment (Ex. 20:13).
35:7–8 The *Levites* were to settle in cities distributed proportionately throughout the land (Josh. 21:1–42), perhaps so that every area would have access to their spiritual guidance (cf. 2 Chron. 17:8–9; 30:22; 35:3; Neh. 8:9). Every locality needs a gospel preacher.
35:11 *at unawares.* By error, thus not premeditated murder (v. 15).
35:12 *avenger.* Near kinsman (Deut. 19:6,12), same root word as "redeem" (Ex. 6:6; 15:13), indicating the responsibility of a kinsman-redeemer to protect the family (Lev. 25:25–33,48–54).

and three cities shall ye give in the land of Canaan,
which shall be cities of refuge.
15 These six cities shall be a refuge, *both* for the
children of Israel, and for the stranger, and for the
sojourner among them: that every one that killeth
any person unawares may flee thither.
16 And if he smite him with an instrument of
iron, so that he die, he *is* a murderer: the mur-
derer shall surely be put to death.
17 And if he smite him with throwing a stone,
wherewith he may die, and he die, he *is* a mur-
derer: the murderer shall surely be put to death.
18 Or *if* he smite him with an hand weapon of
wood, wherewith he may die, and he die, he *is* a
murderer: the murderer shall surely be put to death.
19 The revenger of blood himself shall slay the
murderer: when he meeteth him, he shall slay him.
20 But if he thrust him of hatred, or hurl at him
by laying of wait, that he die;
21 Or in enmity smite him with his hand, that he
die: he that smote *him* shall surely be put to death;
for he *is* a murderer: the revenger of blood shall
slay the murderer, when he meeteth him.
22 But if he thrust him suddenly without enmity,
or have cast upon him any thing without laying
of wait,
23 Or with any stone, wherewith a man may die,
seeing *him* not, and cast *it* upon him, that he die,
and *was* not his enemy, neither sought his harm:
24 Then the congregation shall judge between
the slayer and the revenger of blood according to
these judgments:
25 And the congregation shall deliver the slayer
out of the hand of the revenger of blood, and the
congregation shall restore him to the city of his
refuge, whither he was fled: and he shall abide in
it unto the death of the high priest, which was
anointed with the holy oil.
26 But if the slayer shall at any time come with-
out the border of the city of his refuge, whither
he was fled;
27 And the revenger of blood find him without
the borders of the city of his refuge, and the re-
venger of blood kill the slayer; he shall not be
guilty of blood:
28 Because he should have remained in the city
of his refuge until the death of the high priest: but
after the death of the high priest the slayer shall
return into the land of his possession.
29 So these *things* shall be for a statute of judg-
ment unto you throughout your generations in
all your dwellings.
30 Whoso killeth any person, the murderer shall
be put to death by the mouth of witnesses: but
one witness shall not testify against any person *to
cause him* to die.
31 Moreover ye shall take no satisfaction for the
life of a murderer, which *is* guilty of death: but he
shall be surely put to death.
32 And ye shall take no satisfaction for him that is
fled to the city of his refuge, that he should come
again to dwell in the land, until the death of the
priest.
33 So ye shall not pollute the land wherein ye *are*:
for blood it defileth the land: and the land cannot
be cleansed of the blood that is shed therein, but
by the blood of him that shed it.
34 Defile not therefore the land which ye shall
inhabit, wherein I dwell: for I the LORD dwell
among the children of Israel.

CHAPTER 36

AND the chief fathers of the families of the children
of Gilead, the son of Machir, the son of Man-
asseh, of the families of the sons of Joseph, came
near, and spake before Moses, and before the
princes, the chief fathers of the children of Israel:

35:15 *stranger . . . sojourner.* A resident alien.
35:19 *revenger.* Same word as "avenger" (v. 12; throughout the chapter).
35:20–29 These caveats indicate that the real issue was a matter of the heart not just the act. This parallels Christ's exposition of the spiritual aspect of the law of murder (Matt. 5:21–22).
35:31 *satisfaction.* Ransom price (Ex. 30:12; Ps. 49:7), same root as "atonement" (v. 32).
35:32 *death of the priest.* The high priest (vv. 25,28). The priestly family settled in Hebron, one of the cities of refuge (Josh. 21:13; 1 Chron. 6:57). Just as the Levites acted as living sacrifices (ch. 8), so the death of the high priest functioned like an atoning sacrifice releasing the manslayer from his exile to return home.

Thoughts for Personal/Family Worship: Chapter 35

1. **Israel was commanded to provide cities as dwelling places for the Levites, the ministers of God. Thus, God clearly reveals that His servants are to be supported by His people. They that preach the gospel should live by the gospel—this the Lord has ordained (1 Cor. 9:13–14). How well does your church provide for its pastor?**
2. **Christ is the sinner's city of refuge. Every sinner desperately needs to flee for refuge to lay hold on the hope set before men in Jesus Christ, the great High Priest (Heb. 6:18–20). His death releases sinners from the danger of divine vengeance so that they may return from their exile back to God. Even if you have not physically murdered anyone, your heart contains the inner murder of hatred and sinful anger (Matt. 5:21–22; 1 John 3:15). Go to Christ at once and find refuge for your soul.**
3. **The city of refuge was not only for the Israelite but for the stranger and sojourner (v. 15), revealing the glorious truth that the gospel is for the Gentile as well as the Jew. Irrespective of the differences that exist among men, all who enter into Christ are one and enjoy the same privileges. In Christ there is no difference. How should that affect the way Christians evangelize and welcome people of other nations and ethnicities?**

2 And they said, The LORD commanded my lord
to give the land for an inheritance by lot to the
children of Israel: and my lord was commanded
by the LORD to give the inheritance of Zelophehad
our brother unto his daughters.
3 And if they be married to any of the sons of
the *other* tribes of the children of Israel, then shall
their inheritance be taken from the inheritance of
our fathers, and shall be put to the inheritance of
the tribe whereunto they are received: so shall it
be taken from the lot of our inheritance.
4 And when the jubile of the children of Israel
shall be, then shall their inheritance be put unto
the inheritance of the tribe whereunto they are
received: so shall their inheritance be taken away
from the inheritance of the tribe of our fathers.
5 And Moses commanded the children of Israel
according to the word of the LORD, saying, The
tribe of the sons of Joseph hath said well.
6 This *is* the thing which the LORD doth com-
mand concerning the daughters of Zelophehad,
saying, Let them marry to whom they think best;
only to the family of the tribe of their father shall
they marry.
7 So shall not the inheritance of the children of
Israel remove from tribe to tribe: for every one
of the children of Israel shall keep himself to the
inheritance of the tribe of his fathers.
8 And every daughter, that possesseth an inheri-
tance in any tribe of the children of Israel, shall
be wife unto one of the family of the tribe of her
father, that the children of Israel may enjoy every
man the inheritance of his fathers.
9 Neither shall the inheritance remove from *one*
tribe to another tribe; but every one of the tribes
of the children of Israel shall keep himself to his
own inheritance.
10 Even as the LORD commanded Moses, so did
the daughters of Zelophehad:
11 For Mahlah, Tirzah, and Hoglah, and Milcah,
and Noah, the daughters of Zelophehad, were
married unto their father's brothers' sons:
12 *And* they were married into the families of the
sons of Manasseh the son of Joseph, and their
inheritance remained in the tribe of the family of
their father.
13 These *are* the commandments and the judg-
ments, which the LORD commanded by the hand
of Moses unto the children of Israel in the plains
of Moab by Jordan *near* Jericho.

Chapter 36: *Moses gives further instructions concerning the inheritance of daughters.*

Regulations Insuring Inheritances (36:1–13)

36:3–9 Regulations are given to ensure that allotted land stayed within the jurisdiction of the *tribe* in which the lands was located. The Lord had assigned the land, and it was not to be passed *from tribe to tribe* (1 Kings 21:3).

36:4 *jubile.* Jubilee, the year of release (Lev. 25:10).

36:7 *keep himself to the inheritance.* Cleave or cling to the inheritance.

Thoughts for Personal/Family Worship: Chapter 36

1. **If the daughters of Zelophehad married into other tribes that part of the inheritance of Manasseh would have been lost. The leaders of God's work should be watchful lest any part of what the Lord has given His people should be forfeited. Our spiritual inheritance has been dearly won. Let us seek by wisdom and prudence to retain and enjoy it. This issue pertaining to Zelophehad's daughters resulted in an injunction for every Israelite. Each man was to cleave or cling intensely and faithfully to "the inheritance of the tribe of his fathers" (v. 7). How can we cleave to the Lord's inheritance and preserve God's work as a whole?**
2. **The daughters of Zelophehad were to marry within their own tribe, as the Lord commanded. Personal choices must be governed by more than personal desires; we must take into consideration the needs of others, especially our families and churches. This is especially true of whom we marry. This principle illustrates the point that God's people are to marry only those who are their people in the spiritual sense. They are to marry in the Lord and not be yoked together with unbelievers (1 Cor. 7:39; 2 Cor. 6:14). Disobedience in this matter will usually bring sorrow to the entire family.**

INTRODUCTION TO THE BOOK OF

DEUTERONOMY

Authorship: In the early 1800s, liberal scholars proposed that Deuteronomy was written by King Josiah and the high priest Hilkiah (2 Kings 22) to concentrate political unity and finances in Jerusalem. They argued that Josiah and Hilkiah conspired to produce a document that would eliminate worship outside of Jerusalem, ensuring that offerings would be brought to the temple and national unity cultivated. They invoked Moses as its author, staged its discovery, and with great drama proclaimed it as God's Word in a large, formal assembly.

Such an approach necessitated a compositional date of 621 BC, the date of Josiah's reformation. Whereas Christians throughout history have accepted Deuteronomy upon its own claims of Mosaic authorship some 800 years earlier, liberal scholars *en masse* opted for the later date. Since that time multiple theories, revisions, reversals, and contradictions have marked the stream of thinking regarding the date of Deuteronomy. Conservative scholars, though a minority, have consistently reaffirmed the claims of the book: "And it came to pass in the fortieth year, in the eleventh month, on the first day of the month, that Moses spake unto the children of Israel" (1:3).

Deuteronomy is divine revelation, and consequently reliable when it states that Moses is the author. Several considerations verify the conservative reading. Deuteronomy is written in the form of treaties dating from the second millennium BC—the time Moses lived—not in the form used in Josiah's day. Treaties from the second millennium included a review of history (chs. 1–4), stipulations of the treaty (chs. 5–26), and consequences of heeding or violating the treaty's terms (chs. 27–32). Treaties from Josiah's era generally include neither history nor consequences. Moreover, the treaty format indicates a single author, which militates against notions that Deuteronomy was compiled by multiple scribes.

In addition, the writer of Deuteronomy does not write like one living in Jerusalem in 621 BC, but like someone with Egyptian experience who is also very familiar with wilderness living. Animals named are native to the Sinai and Upper Egypt, not Palestine (14:5). The same is true of the acacia wood (10:3) and the sanitary instructions (23:12–14), which are clearly for a nomadic, desert existence, not for settled communities such as existed in Josiah's time. The author writes as an outsider to Canaan, as one would expect Moses to write.

Moreover, Deuteronomy claims Mosaic authorship (1:3; 31:9), and other biblical writers affirm the same. Second Chronicles 25:4, reporting events more than 200 years prior to Josiah, cites Deut. 24:16 and calls it "the book of Moses." Nehemiah refers to Deut. 23:3 as "the book of Moses" (Neh. 13:1). The Jewish leaders of Christ's day, like those since Christ, knew that Moses wrote Deuteronomy, and Christ confirmed their understanding (Matt. 19:7–8 citing Deut. 24:1–4; Matt. 22:24 citing Deut. 25:5). The New Testament quotes from Deuteronomy more than eighty times—this ought to be conclusive confirmation of the conservative position.

This has led a majority of Jewish and Christian scholars and writings to accept the opening words of Deuteronomy: "These be the words which Moses spake unto all Israel" (1:1). This and more than twenty other similar statements settle the question of authorship. Deuteronomy was written by Moses. (See also Introduction to the Pentateuch.)

Date: Trusting the authorship of Moses and the reliability of the historicity of Deuteronomy, we know that Moses received these words "in the fortieth year, in the eleventh month, on the first day of the month, that Moses spake unto the children of Israel" (1:3) and wrote them down shortly thereafter. This places the date of authorship near the end of Israel's wilderness wandering, forty years after the exodus and just prior to the entrance into Canaan, approximately 1406 BC.

Theme: Covenantal love between God and His people.

Purpose: To remind Israel of God's covenant as they prepare to enter into Canaan.

Synopsis: *The Contribution of Deuteronomy to Redemptive Revelation*

The title "Deuteronomy" means "second lawgiving" and is the Greek title found in the Greek Septuagint (LXX). Compare the statement that the future king shall write for himself "a copy of this law [Greek *deuteronomion*]" (17:18, LXX). Since the lawgiving on Sinai, Israel's adult population had died. The new generation had not heard Sinai's trumpets; they needed to hear from Moses what God had commanded.

A record of legal infractions, applications, and interpretations had been established during four decades in the wilderness. The relevance of the law could now be recognized in ways that it had not been earlier. Moses articulates the law again in a recitation that reflects Israel's temperament and four decades of experience in the wilderness.

He affirms again the precepts of Jehovah for the conduct of His chosen people. They were people of the divine covenant. The blessings of that covenant were sustained by their adherence to its terms.

Soon Israel would cross the Jordan River and enter the land covenanted to Abraham, a land inhabited by idolatrous nations. Israel's propensity toward idolatry was evident in the golden calf incident at Sinai (Ex. 32–34) and in the fact that the first prohibitions of God's law forbade other gods and graven images. In the land of promise Israel would face serious temptation in an area of great vulnerability. It was of primary urgency, therefore, that the law of God be repeated to Israel as a prelude to entering Canaan and to a new era of her history.

Moses would soon be dead. In a sense, he had been the embodiment of the law to Israel, for his very presence affirmed God's law. As if determined to make one last, memorable affirmation of the law, Moses speaks Deuteronomy, the "second lawgiving," at the border of Canaan.

Deuteronomy affirms God's love for His people and expounds the love they must have for Him. One of the most significant verses of all of Deuteronomy is "Hear, O Israel: The Lord our God is one Lord: and thou shalt love the Lord thy God with all thine heart, and with all thy soul, and with all thy might" (Deut. 6:4–5).

Israel's privileged position came from God's unconditional election of them (7:7–8). Just as divine love was demonstrated when God chose Abraham, Isaac, and Jacob he now shows this love by preserving their descendants throughout the Egyptian sojourn. Their deliverance and Pharaoh's destruction at the Red Sea exhibited God's unique love for His people.

God's love was further exhibited at Sinai, where Moses received the law. No other people received this manifestation of divine love. Israel's responding love was to be exhibited in obedience to the terms of the covenant.

Deuteronomy codifies the love covenant. Written in the form of a vassal-treaty, its affirmation of love includes instructions for respondent love exhibited in submission. Israel's obedience to the terms of that treaty would confirm to them the continuation of favors such as no other people would receive, repeatedly reinforcing that love.

A parent's love for offspring is demonstrated in careful guidance and discipline. God's love for His people is expressed in the precepts and promises of Deuteronomy. God loves His people and will therefore care for them, eliminating their enemies and giving them the land promised to Abraham. But to ensure these favors they must acknowledge His lordship through obedience to His law. As a people chosen for His special possession, they must be holy as He is holy.

Outline:

I. Introduction (1:1–5)

II. Preparatory Address (1:6—4:43)

- A. From Horeb to Kadesh (1:6–46)
- B. From Kadesh to Conquest (2:1—3:29)
- C. Exhortation to Heed God's Law (4:1–40)
- D. Cities of Refuge East of Jordan (4:41–43)

III. Expounding God's Law (4:44—26:19)

- A. Introductory Explanation (4:44–49)
- B. Commandments and Related Exhortations (5:1—11:32)
  1. The Ten Commandments (5:1–33)
  2. Love God and Remember His Commandments (6:1–25)
  3. Separation from Idolaters, God's Blessing (7:1–26)
  4. Exhortations, Blessings, and Curses (8:1—11:32)
- C. Statues and Judgments (12:1—26:15)
  1. God's Sanctuary (12:1–32)
  2. Deceivers and Idolaters (13:1–18)
  3. Customs: Mourning, Diet, and Levite's Care (14:1–29)
  4. Sabbath Release (15:1–23)
  5. Religious Feasts (16:1–22)
  6. Sacrifices, Idolaters, Adjudication, and Kings (17:1–20)
  7. Care of Priests, Idolaters, the Great Prophet (18:1–22)
  8. Cities of Refuge, False Witnesses (19:1–21)
  9. Regulations for Warfare (20:1–20)
  10. Unsolved Murder, War Captives, and Rebellious Sons (21:1–23)
  11. Civility, Distinctiveness, and Purity (22:1–30)
  12. Ethical and Moral Stipulations (23:1—25:19)
  13. Canaan's Firstfruits (26:1–15)
- D. Concluding Reminder and Exhortation (26:16–19)

IV. Blessing and Curses (27:1—28:68)
- A. Prescribed Ceremony at Ebal and Gerizim (27:1–26)
- B. Blessings and Curses (28:1–68)

V. Concluding Instruction (29:1—33:29)
- A. Past Blessing (29:1–29)
- B. Reaffirmed Covenant (30:1–20)
- C. Moses' Farewell (31:1–13)
- D. Jehovah's Warning (31:14–30)
- E. Song of Moses (32:1–52)
- F. Blessing the Tribes (33:1–29)

VI. Conclusion: Moses' Death and Joshua's Succession (34:1–12)

THE FIFTH BOOK OF MOSES CALLED

DEUTERONOMY

CHAPTER 1

THESE *be* the words which Moses spake unto all
Israel on this side Jordan in the wilderness, in the
plain over against the Red *sea*, between Paran, and
Tophel, and Laban, and Hazeroth, and Dizahab.
2 (*There are* eleven days' *journey* from Horeb by
the way of mount Seir unto Kadesh-barnea.)
3 And it came to pass in the fortieth year, in the
eleventh month, on the first *day* of the month,
that Moses spake unto the children of Israel,
according unto all that the LORD had given him in
commandment unto them;
4 After he had slain Sihon the king of the Amori-
tes, which dwelt in Heshbon, and Og the king of
Bashan, which dwelt at Astaroth in Edrei:
5 On this side Jordan, in the land of Moab, began
Moses to declare this law, saying,
6 The LORD our God spake unto us in Horeb,
saying, Ye have dwelt long enough in this mount:
7 Turn you, and take your journey, and go to the
mount of the Amorites, and unto all *the places*
nigh thereunto, in the plain, in the hills, and in the
vale, and in the south, and by the sea side, to the
land of the Canaanites, and unto Lebanon, unto
the great river, the river Euphrates.
8 Behold, I have set the land before you: go in and
possess the land which the LORD sware unto your
fathers, Abraham, Isaac, and Jacob, to give unto
them and to their seed after them.
9 ¶ And I spake unto you at that time, saying, I
am not able to bear you myself alone:
10 The LORD your God hath multiplied you, and,
behold, ye *are* this day as the stars of heaven for
multitude.
11 (The LORD God of your fathers make you a
thousand times so many more as ye *are*, and bless
you, as he hath promised you!)
12 How can I myself alone bear your cumbrance,
and your burden, and your strife?
13 Take you wise men, and understanding, and
known among your tribes, and I will make them
rulers over you.
14 And ye answered me, and said, The thing
which thou hast spoken *is* good *for us* to do.

Chapter 1: *Moses recounts God's guidance and Israel's rebellion and defeat when they were first to have entered Canaan.*

INTRODUCTION (1:1–5)

1:1 *All Israel* appears fourteen times in Deuteronomy, signifying Israel's unity. *on this side of Jordan.* East side, used seven times. *the plain over against the Red sea.* The Syrian-African Rift, a 4,500-mile geologic fault, stretches from the Lebanon Mountains into southeast Africa. It cradles the Sea of Galilee, Jordan River, Dead Sea, Gulf of Aqaba, and "way of the Red sea" (v. 40). This desert route connected sea and gulf. Israel followed it from Aqaba (Red Sea) to the northeast quadrant of the Dead Sea, encamping in Moab, named for Lot's descendants (Gen. 19:37). *Paran, and Tophel, and Laban, and Hazeroth.* The exact location of these places is unknown.
1:2 *Horeb.* Sinai. From Horeb to Kadesh-barnea was *eleven days' journey,* possibly a mode of expressing distance rather than actual time. *The way of mount Seir* was an ancient travel route, roughly 175 miles.
1:3 *fortieth year.* Following the exodus, likely 1406 BC. Deuteronomy is written as the Israelites prepare to enter into the Promised Land.
1:4 *Heshbon* is a city less than twenty miles northeast of the Dead Sea. *Bashan* is north of Heshbon, east and south of the Sea of Galilee. Victory over these kings was an oft-repeated reminder of God's care (2:24—3:11; 3:1–13; Josh. 2:10; 9:10; Pss. 135–136).
1:5 *declare.* Elucidate or expound. This was Moses' final sermon.

PREPARATORY ADDRESS (1:6—4:43)

From Horeb to Kadesh (1:6–46)

1:6 Biblical writers, conscious of divine inspiration, affirm that they spoke God's Word (cf. 2 Peter 1:21).
1:7 *nigh.* Near. *vale.* Valley.
1:8 *Behold.* Look! *I have set the land before you*. A challenge to catch the vision (v. 21). This is not merely national expansion but divine action in accordance with God's covenant to Abraham and his descendants.
1:9–18 Enlarged population necessitated multi-level government, which Moses established on the counsel of Jethro, his father-in-law (Ex. 18:24–26).
1:9 *bear.* Literally, "to lift" or "to carry." Moses was unable to care for the people by himself.
1:10 *as the stars of heaven for multitude.* A great multitude as God had promised (Gen. 15:5; 22:17).
1:12 *cumbrance.* Burden or cares.
1:16 *causes.* The Hebrew and context likely means "the conflicts" or "issues" between brothers. *judge righteously.*

15 So I took the chief of your tribes, wise men, and known, and made them heads over you, captains over thousands, and captains over hundreds, and captains over fifties, and captains over tens, and officers among your tribes.

16 And I charged your judges at that time, saying, Hear *the causes* between your brethren, and judge righteously between *every* man and his brother, and the stranger *that is* with him.

17 Ye shall not respect persons in judgment; *but* ye shall hear the small as well as the great; ye shall not be afraid of the face of man; for the judgment *is* God's: and the cause that is too hard for you, bring *it* unto me, and I will hear it.

18 And I commanded you at that time all the things which ye should do.

19 ¶ And when we departed from Horeb, we went through all that great and terrible wilderness, which ye saw by the way of the mountain of the Amorites, as the LORD our God commanded us; and we came to Kadesh-barnea.

20 And I said unto you, Ye are come unto the mountain of the Amorites, which the LORD our God doth give unto us.

21 Behold, the LORD thy God hath set the land before thee: go up *and* possess *it*, as the LORD God of thy fathers hath said unto thee; fear not, neither be discouraged.

22 ¶ And ye came near unto me every one of you, and said, We will send men before us, and they shall search us out the land, and bring us word again by what way we must go up, and into what cities we shall come.

23 And the saying pleased me well: and I took twelve men of you, one of a tribe:

24 And they turned and went up into the mountain, and came unto the valley of Eshcol, and searched it out.

25 And they took of the fruit of the land in their hands, and brought *it* down unto us, and brought us word again, and said, *It is* a good land which the LORD our God doth give us.

26 Notwithstanding ye would not go up, but rebelled against the commandment of the LORD your God:

27 And ye murmured in your tents, and said, Because the LORD hated us, he hath brought us forth out of the land of Egypt, to deliver us into the hand of the Amorites, to destroy us.

28 Whither shall we go up? our brethren have discouraged our heart, saying, The people *is* greater and taller than we; the cities *are* great and walled up to heaven; and moreover we have seen the sons of the Anakims there.

29 Then I said unto you, Dread not, neither be afraid of them.

30 The LORD your God which goeth before you, he shall fight for you, according to all that he did for you in Egypt before your eyes;

31 And in the wilderness, where thou hast seen how that the LORD thy God bare thee, as a man doth bear his son, in all the way that ye went, until ye came into this place.

32 Yet in this thing ye did not believe the LORD your God,

33 Who went in the way before you, to search you out a place to pitch your tents *in*, in fire by night, to shew you by what way ye should go, and in a cloud by day.

34 And the LORD heard the voice of your words, and was wroth, and sware, saying,

35 Surely there shall not one of these men of this evil generation see that good land, which I sware to give unto your fathers,

36 Save Caleb the son of Jephunneh; he shall see it, and to him will I give the land that he hath trodden upon, and to his children, because he hath wholly followed the LORD.

37 Also the LORD was angry with me for your sakes, saying, Thou also shalt not go in thither.

38 *But* Joshua the son of Nun, which standeth before thee, he shall go in thither: encourage him: for he shall cause Israel to inherit it.

39 Moreover your little ones, which ye said should be a prey, and your children, which in that day had no knowledge between good and evil, they shall go in thither, and unto them will I give it, and they shall possess it.

40 But *as for* you, turn you, and take your journey into the wilderness by the way of the Red sea.

Judges must be objective, resisting convenience, self-gain, and impulse. *the stranger.* A foreigner.

1:17 *respect.* Literally, "to regard faces." Not referring to honor but to unjust discrimination. *small as well as the great.* Rich and poor were to be treated equally. There was to be no favoritism. *be afraid of the face of man.* An idiom meaning "to fear the thoughts or attitudes of men." *judgment is God's.* Justice originates and is sustained only by His sovereign rule (Ps. 98:8–9).

1:19 *great and terrible wilderness.* A 100-mile, waterless plateau through which Israel passed. *Kadesh-barnea.* An oasis with many springs sixty miles southwest of the Dead Sea.

1:20–21 God gave the land, yet Israel had to take possession. Divine sovereignty does not diminish human responsibility.

1:25–27 Note the contradiction of human wisdom. Israel acknowledged it as the *land which the LORD our God doth give us* but *would not go up.* Murmuring and rebellion often accompany one another. Israel viewed blessings (i.e., deliverance from Egypt) as divine disfavor—*the LORD hated us.*

1:28 *Whither.* Where.

1:34 *wroth.* Angry.

1:38 *Joshua* is repeatedly mentioned by Moses, who is passing the baton to his successor (3:21,28; 31:3,7,14,23; 34:9).

1:39 Unbelief says our *little ones . . . should be a prey* (spoil or booty). God says, *they shall go in thither, and unto them will I give it, and they shall possess it.*

1:40 *The way of the Red sea* is the Reed Sea Road, east of

41 Then ye answered and said unto me, We have
sinned against the LORD, we will go up and fight,
according to all that the LORD our God commanded
us. And when ye had girded on every man his
weapons of war, ye were ready to go up into the hill.
42 And the LORD said unto me, Say unto them,
Go not up, neither fight; for I *am* not among you;
lest ye be smitten before your enemies.
43 So I spake unto you; and ye would not hear,
but rebelled against the commandment of the
LORD, and went presumptuously up into the hill.
44 And the Amorites, which dwelt in that moun-
tain, came out against you, and chased you, as bees
do, and destroyed you in Seir, *even* unto Hormah.
45 And ye returned and wept before the LORD;
but the LORD would not hearken to your voice,
nor give ear unto you.
46 So ye abode in Kadesh many days, according
unto the days that ye abode *there*.

CHAPTER 2

THEN we turned, and took our journey into the
wilderness by the way of the Red sea, as the LORD
spake unto me: and we compassed mount Seir
many days.
2 And the LORD spake unto me, saying,
3 Ye have compassed this mountain long enough:
turn you northward.
4 And command thou the people, saying, Ye *are*
to pass through the coast of your brethren the
children of Esau, which dwell in Seir; and they
shall be afraid of you: take ye good heed unto
yourselves therefore:
5 Meddle not with them; for I will not give you
of their land, no, not so much as a foot breadth;
because I have given mount Seir unto Esau *for* a
possession.
6 Ye shall buy meat of them for money, that ye
may eat; and ye shall also buy water of them for
money, that ye may drink.
7 For the LORD thy God hath blessed thee in all
the works of thy hand: he knoweth thy walking
through this great wilderness: these forty years
the LORD thy God *hath been* with thee; thou hast
lacked nothing.
8 And when we passed by from our brethren the
children of Esau, which dwelt in Seir, through
the way of the plain from Elath, and from Ezion-
gaber, we turned and passed by the way of the
wilderness of Moab.
9 And the LORD said unto me, Distress not the
Moabites, neither contend with them in battle:
for I will not give thee of their land *for* a posses-
sion; because I have given Ar unto the children of
Lot *for* a possession.
10 The Emims dwelt therein in times past, a
people great, and many, and tall, as the Anakims;
11 Which also were accounted giants, as the Ana-
kims; but the Moabites call them Emims.
12 The Horims also dwelt in Seir beforetime; but
the children of Esau succeeded them, when they
had destroyed them from before them, and dwelt
in their stead; as Israel did unto the land of his
possession, which the LORD gave unto them.
13 Now rise up, *said I*, and get you over the brook
Zered. And we went over the brook Zered.
14 And the space in which we came from Kadesh-
barnea, until we were come over the brook Zered,
was thirty and eight years; until all the generation

Kadesh-barnea connecting north Aqaba Gulf and the Dead Sea.

1:41 *girded.* Put on or fastened.

1:42 *I am not among you.* Israel's first priority was to be the divine presence (Judg. 16:20). They were not to presume upon God's presence. *smitten.* Killed or destroyed by the enemies.

1:45 *hearken.* Listen to.

Thoughts for Personal/Family Worship: Chapter 1

1. **God led Israel "as a man doth bare [carry] his son" (v. 31). This picture of God's loving care should inspire love and trust for Him. "He shall feed his flock like a shepherd: he shall gather the lambs with his arm, and carry them in his bosom, and shall gently lead those that are with young" (Isa. 40:11). Our Good Shepherd seeks the lost sheep, "and when he hath found it, he layeth it on his shoulders, rejoicing" (Luke 15:4–6).**
2. **God set the land before Israel and instructed her to take it (1:21), but Israel hesitated, yielded to human wisdom (v. 22), then succumbed to human fear (vv. 26,27) and unbelief (v. 32), resulting in loss of blessing (vv. 34–39), rebellion (vv. 26,40–43), defeat (v. 44), and alienation from God (v. 45). God's people must take Him at His Word (Prov. 3:5). Caleb "wholly followed the LORD" (Deut. 1:36). He and Joshua, a tiny minority, entered Canaan.**

Obedience may be a lonely, bumpy road, but its travelers always reach their destination. Why is it necessary to trust in God's wisdom if we will obey Him over the long term?

From Kadesh to Conquest (2:1—3:29)

Chapter 2: *Moses recounts Israel's journey in the wilderness, the peoples they encountered, and their responses.*

2:1–8 From Kadesh-barnea God led Israel southeast, away from Canaan, toward the Gulf of Aqaba, then northward through Mt. Seir, a mountain range southeast of the Dead Sea (v. 5). God gave this to Edom, Esau's descendants (Gen. 36:1–8), exhibiting divine sovereignty over lands and peoples.

2:1,3 *compassed.* Surrounded.

2:5 *Meddle.* Provoke or stir up strife.

2:8 *Elath* and *Ezion-gaber* were at the northern tip of Aqaba Gulf. Israel departed northward, following the Way of the Wilderness of Moab along the eastern flank of Edom.

2:9–13 Moab and *Ar* were descendants of Lot (Gen. 19:33–38). God gave them land east of the Dead Sea, where they displaced the *Emims*, just as Esau's descendants had displaced the *Horims*. Emims were compared to the *Anakims*, considered to be giants by Israel (Num. 13:28–33).

of the men of war were wasted out from among the host, as the LORD sware unto them.

15 For indeed the hand of the LORD was against them, to destroy them from among the host, until they were consumed.

16 ¶ So it came to pass, when all the men of war were consumed and dead from among the people,

17 That the LORD spake unto me, saying,

18 Thou art to pass over through Ar, the coast of Moab, this day:

19 And *when* thou comest nigh over against the children of Ammon, distress them not, nor meddle with them: for I will not give thee of the land of the children of Ammon *any* possession; because I have given it unto the children of Lot *for* a possession.

20 (That also was accounted a land of giants: giants dwelt therein in old time; and the Ammonites call them Zamzummims;

21 A people great, and many, and tall, as the Anakims; but the LORD destroyed them before them; and they succeeded them, and dwelt in their stead:

22 As he did to the children of Esau, which dwelt in Seir, when he destroyed the Horims from before them; and they succeeded them, and dwelt in their stead even unto this day:

23 And the Avims which dwelt in Hazerim, *even* unto Azzah, the Caphtorims, which came forth out of Caphtor, destroyed them, and dwelt in their stead.)

24 ¶ Rise ye up, take your journey, and pass over the river Arnon: behold, I have given into thine hand Sihon the Amorite, king of Heshbon, and his land: begin to possess *it*, and contend with him in battle.

25 This day will I begin to put the dread of thee and the fear of thee upon the nations *that are* under the whole heaven, who shall hear report of thee, and shall tremble, and be in anguish because of thee.

26 ¶ And I sent messengers out of the wilderness of Kedemoth unto Sihon king of Heshbon with words of peace, saying,

27 Let me pass through thy land: I will go along by the high way, I will neither turn unto the right hand nor to the left.

28 Thou shalt sell me meat for money, that I may eat; and give me water for money, that I may drink: only I will pass through on my feet;

29 (As the children of Esau which dwell in Seir, and the Moabites which dwell in Ar, did unto me;) until I shall pass over Jordan into the land which the LORD our God giveth us.

30 But Sihon king of Heshbon would not let us pass by him: for the LORD thy God hardened his spirit, and made his heart obstinate, that he might deliver him into thy hand, as *appeareth* this day.

31 And the LORD said unto me, Behold, I have begun to give Sihon and his land before thee: begin to possess, that thou mayest inherit his land.

32 Then Sihon came out against us, he and all his people, to fight at Jahaz.

33 And the LORD our God delivered him before us; and we smote him, and his sons, and all his people.

34 And we took all his cities at that time, and utterly destroyed the men, and the women, and the little ones, of every city, we left none to remain:

35 Only the cattle we took for a prey unto ourselves, and the spoil of the cities which we took.

36 From Aroer, which *is* by the brink of the river of Arnon, and *from* the city that *is* by the river, even unto Gilead, there was not one city too strong for us: the LORD our God delivered all unto us:

37 Only unto the land of the children of Ammon thou camest not, *nor* unto any place of the river Jabbok, nor unto the cities in the mountains, nor unto whatsoever the LORD our God forbad us.

CHAPTER 3

THEN we turned, and went up the way to Bashan: and Og the king of Bashan came out against us,

2:9 *Distress.* Harass. *contend.* Provoke (cf. v. 5).
2:12 *succeeded.* Dispossessed or conquered. *stead.* In place of.
2:14–18 Zered's location is unknown, but it appears to have flowed westward into the southern tip of the Dead Sea and comprised the southern boundary of Moab. After thirty-eight years, most who sinned at Kadesh-barnea were dead. They are called *men of war,* probably sarcastically. God led Israel across Zered and into Moab, where Deuteronomy was given.
2:19–23 *the children of Ammon.* Lot's descendants (Gen. 19:33–38). God gave them land occupied by the giant *Anakims* whom He destroyed, just as He destroyed the *Horims* so that Esau's descendants could possess their land (vv. 21–22).
2:24–37 *River Arnon,* located at the eastern midpoint of the Dead Sea, marked the entrance into Ammonite territory. God made surrounding nations fear Israel by rousing King *Sihon* of Heshbon against Israel and defeating him. This conquest continued northward to Gilead, southeast of the Sea of Galilee, where Israel subdued every city except those of the Ammonites.
2:35 *prey.* Plunder.

Thoughts for Personal/Family Worship: Chapter 2

1. **Moses told Israel that God "knoweth thy walking through this great wilderness" (v. 7). God knew their experience, for He was with them in the cloud and fire (Ex. 40:34–38). It is comforting to know that "the Word was made flesh, and dwelt among us" (John 1:14); that Christ was made like His people (Rom. 8:3; Heb. 2:17) to experience the believer's plight in this sin-cursed wilderness. "For in that he himself hath suffered being tempted, he is able to succour them that are tempted" (Heb. 2:18). Christian, how can this comfort you, to know that the Lord understands your experience and has suffered Himself?**
2. **"For indeed the hand of the LORD was against them, to destroy them from among the host, until they were consumed" (2:15). Disobedience wreaks horrible consequences. Even among God's people, those who rebelled made themselves God's enemies. They became the focus of God's progressive elimination, until all were gone.**

he and all his people, to battle at Edrei.
2 And the LORD said unto me, Fear him not: for
I will deliver him, and all his people, and his land,
into thy hand; and thou shalt do unto him as thou
didst unto Sihon king of the Amorites, which
dwelt at Heshbon.
3 So the LORD our God delivered into our hands
Og also, the king of Bashan, and all his people:
and we smote him until none was left to him
remaining.
4 And we took all his cities at that time, there was
not a city which we took not from them, three-
score cities, all the region of Argob, the kingdom
of Og in Bashan.
5 All these cities *were* fenced with high walls,
gates, and bars; beside unwalled towns a great
many.
6 And we utterly destroyed them, as we did unto
Sihon king of Heshbon, utterly destroying the
men, women, and children, of every city.
7 But all the cattle, and the spoil of the cities, we
took for a prey to ourselves.
8 And we took at that time out of the hand of
the two kings of the Amorites the land that *was*
on this side Jordan, from the river of Arnon unto
mount Hermon;
9 (*Which* Hermon the Sidonians call Sirion; and
the Amorites call it Shenir;)
10 All the cities of the plain, and all Gilead, and
all Bashan, unto Salchah and Edrei, cities of the
kingdom of Og in Bashan.
11 For only Og king of Bashan remained of the
remnant of giants; behold, his bedstead *was* a
bedstead of iron; *is* it not in Rabbath of the chil-
dren of Ammon? nine cubits *was* the length
thereof, and four cubits the breadth of it, after the
cubit of a man.
12 And this land, *which* we possessed at that time,
from Aroer, which *is* by the river Arnon, and half
mount Gilead, and the cities thereof, gave I unto
the Reubenites and to the Gadites.
13 And the rest of Gilead, and all Bashan, *be-
ing* the kingdom of Og, gave I unto the half tribe
of Manasseh; all the region of Argob, with all
Bashan, which was called the land of giants.
14 Jair the son of Manasseh took all the country of
Argob unto the coasts of Geshuri and Maachathi;
and called them after his own name, Bashan-
havoth-jair, unto this day.
15 And I gave Gilead unto Machir.
16 And unto the Reubenites and unto the Gadites
I gave from Gilead even unto the river Arnon
half the valley, and the border even unto the river
Jabbok, *which is* the border of the children of
Ammon;
17 The plain also, and Jordan, and the coast
thereof, from Chinnereth even unto the sea of
the plain, *even* the salt sea, under Ashdoth-pisgah
eastward.
18 ¶ And I commanded you at that time, saying,
The LORD your God hath given you this land to
possess it: ye shall pass over armed before your
brethren the children of Israel, all *that are* meet
for the war.
19 But your wives, and your little ones, and your
cattle, (*for* I know that ye have much cattle,) shall
abide in your cities which I have given you;
20 Until the LORD have given rest unto your
brethren, as well as unto you, and *until* they also
possess the land which the LORD your God hath
given them beyond Jordan: and *then* shall ye
return every man unto his possession, which I
have given you.
21 ¶ And I commanded Joshua at that time, say-
ing, Thine eyes have seen all that the LORD your
God hath done unto these two kings: so shall
the LORD do unto all the kingdoms whither thou
passest.
22 Ye shall not fear them: for the LORD your God
he shall fight for you.
23 And I besought the LORD at that time, saying,
24 O Lord GOD, thou hast begun to shew thy ser-

Chapter 3: *Moses recounts Israel's progress toward possessing Canaan, and conquest of land east of the Jordan River.*

3:1 *Bashan* was an area southeast of the Sea of Galilee, north of the point where Israel would cross the Jordan into Canaan.

3:4 *Argob* was a region within Bashan (1 Kings 4:13) and may refer to a confederation of cities. The region appears to have been fertile, more populated than it is today, and prosperous, for sixty (*threescore*) cities were captured by Israel (Amos 4:1).

3:5 *fenced.* Literally, "inaccessible" or "unassailable."

3:9 Mt. *Hermon* is a group of mountains with three summits, the highest measuring 9,232 feet, northeast of the Sea of Galilee and forming natural boundaries between nations, each of which called it a different name (4:48).

3:10 *Edrei* was Og's home (1:4; 3:10).

3:11 *bedstead.* Couch or sarcophagus. Its length (thirteen feet) suggests Og's immense stature. *Rabbath* (modern Amman, Jordan) was inhabited by descendants of Lot's son Ben-ammi (Gen. 19:38), from which Amman gets its name.

3:12–20 Land east of the Jordan River was divided among Reuben, Gad, and Manasseh. Their separation from other tribes by the Jordan resulted in misunderstandings later on (Josh. 1:10–16; 22:1–34). Moses commanded them to assist those tribes in possessing lands west of the Jordan (Deut. 3:20).

3:14 *coasts.* Regions. *Bashan-havoth-jair.* Literally, "Bashan the villages of Jair," who was likely a son of Manasseh.

3:18 *meet for the war.* Literally, "all sons of army," referring to those prepared to fight.

3:19 *much cattle.* Reuben, Gad, and Manasseh were prosperous. In a nomadic, noncommercial society, livestock constitute wealth. Moses includes this reminder of God's blessing, as he does when describing Israel's conquests (2:35; 3:7).

3:23 *besought.* Pleaded.

3:27 *Pisgah.* Slope where plateau gives way to mountain. Some scholars believe it is a mountain range of which Nebo

vant thy greatness, and thy mighty hand: for what
God *is there* in heaven or in earth, that can do ac-
cording to thy works, and according to thy might?
25 I pray thee, let me go over, and see the good
land that *is* beyond Jordan, that goodly mountain,
and Lebanon.
26 But the LORD was wroth with me for your
sakes, and would not hear me: and the LORD said
unto me, Let it suffice thee; speak no more unto
me of this matter.
27 Get thee up into the top of Pisgah, and lift up
thine eyes westward, and northward, and south-
ward, and eastward, and behold *it* with thine eyes:
for thou shalt not go over this Jordan.
28 But charge Joshua, and encourage him, and
strengthen him: for he shall go over before this
people, and he shall cause them to inherit the
land which thou shalt see.
29 So we abode in the valley over against
Beth-peor.

CHAPTER 4

NOW therefore hearken, O Israel, unto the statutes
and unto the judgments, which I teach you, for to
do *them*, that ye may live, and go in and possess
the land which the LORD God of your fathers
giveth you.
2 Ye shall not add unto the word which I com-
mand you, neither shall ye diminish *ought* from it,
that ye may keep the commandments of the LORD
your God which I command you.
3 Your eyes have seen what the LORD did because
of Baal-peor: for all the men that followed Baal-
peor, the LORD thy God hath destroyed them
from among you.
4 But ye that did cleave unto the LORD your God
are alive every one of you this day.
5 Behold, I have taught you statutes and judg-
ments, even as the LORD my God commanded
me, that ye should do so in the land whither ye
go to possess it.
6 Keep therefore and do *them*; for this *is* your
wisdom and your understanding in the sight of
the nations, which shall hear all these statutes,
and say, Surely this great nation *is* a wise and
understanding people.
7 For what nation *is there so* great, who *hath* God
so nigh unto them, as the LORD our God *is* in all
things that we call upon him *for*?
8 And what nation *is there so* great, that hath
statutes and judgments *so* righteous as all this law,
which I set before you this day?
9 Only take heed to thyself, and keep thy soul
diligently, lest thou forget the things which thine
eyes have seen, and lest they depart from thy heart
all the days of thy life: but teach them thy sons,
and thy sons' sons;
10 *Specially* the day that thou stoodest before the
LORD thy God in Horeb, when the LORD said unto
me, Gather me the people together, and I will
make them hear my words, that they may learn
to fear me all the days that they shall live upon
the earth, and *that* they may teach their children.
11 And ye came near and stood under the
mountain; and the mountain burned with fire
unto the midst of heaven, with darkness, clouds,
and thick darkness.
12 And the LORD spake unto you out of the midst
of the fire: ye heard the voice of the words, but
saw no similitude; only *ye heard* a voice.
13 And he declared unto you his covenant, which

---

is the summit. From Nebo Moses viewed the Promised Land, then died (32:49–51; 34:1–6).
3:29 *abode.* Dwelt.

Thoughts for Personal/Family Worship: Chapter 3

1. **God gave to Israel "all Bashan, which was called the land of giants" (v. 13). God would have His people remember the magnitude of His power to save. They went against giants and prevailed. Though God may lead His people into circumstances that appear insurmountable, they are attainable when undertaken with God's help (Eph. 6:12–17).**
2. **For forty years Moses led Israel through desolate wilderness, bringing them to the edge of Canaan. But one reason Moses himself could not enter was because the people had rebelled in unbelief at Kadesh-barnea (v. 26). Although Moses speaks to the children of those who rebelled, he reminds them of the price he is paying for their parents' sin. He speaks as if they and their parents are one, stressing again the unity of Israel. It is important to remember that our unbelief and rebellion affect others (1:37; 4:21). How have your sins hurt others?**

Chapter 4: *Moses exhorts Israel to heed God's law, warns against disobedience, promises restoration upon repentance, and recalls God's greatness and love evidenced in the cities of refuge and lands given to Israel.*

Exhortation to Heed God's Law (4:1–40)

4:2 Moses equated *the word which I command you* with *the commandments of the LORD your God* and affirmed its sufficiency. *Ye shall not add unto the word.* Biblical writers were conscious of its inspiration (2 Tim. 3:16; 2 Peter 1:21). The sufficiency of Scripture for our spiritual instruction is its final affirmation and warning (Rev. 22:18–19). *diminish ought.* Take away.
4:3 *Baal-peor* was a horrible memory. Israel's immoral, idolatrous unions with Moabites resulted in judgment and 24,000 deaths (Num. 24).
4:4 *cleave.* Hold fast.
4:6–8 Obedience to God's law *is your wisdom and your understanding.* Fear of the Lord is the beginning of wisdom and of understanding (Ps. 111:10; Prov. 1:7; 9:10; 15:33).
4:9 *keep thy soul.* Guard yourself. *thy sons, and thy sons' sons.* Great emphasis is placed upon multi-generational biblical instruction (6:7; 11:19).
4:12 *similitude.* Likeness or form.
4:13 *ten commandments*. Literally, "ten words," hence, the designation "Decalogue."

he commanded you to perform, *even* ten com-
mandments; and he wrote them upon two tables
of stone.
14 ¶ And the LORD commanded me at that time
to teach you statutes and judgments, that ye
might do them in the land whither ye go over to
possess it.
15 Take ye therefore good heed unto yourselves;
for ye saw no manner of similitude on the day
that the LORD spake unto you in Horeb out of the
midst of the fire:
16 Lest ye corrupt *yourselves*, and make you a
graven image, the similitude of any figure, the
likeness of male or female,
17 The likeness of any beast that *is* on the earth,
the likeness of any winged fowl that flieth in the air,
18 The likeness of any thing that creepeth on
the ground, the likeness of any fish that *is* in the
waters beneath the earth:
19 And lest thou lift up thine eyes unto heaven,
and when thou seest the sun, and the moon, and
the stars, *even* all the host of heaven, shouldest be
driven to worship them, and serve them, which
the LORD thy God hath divided unto all nations
under the whole heaven.
20 But the LORD hath taken you, and brought you
forth out of the iron furnace, *even* out of Egypt,
to be unto him a people of inheritance, as *ye are*
this day.
21 Furthermore the LORD was angry with me for
your sakes, and sware that I should not go over
Jordan, and that I should not go in unto that good
land, which the LORD thy God giveth thee *for* an
inheritance:
22 But I must die in this land, I must not go over
Jordan: but ye shall go over, and possess that good
land.
23 Take heed unto yourselves, lest ye forget the
covenant of the LORD your God, which he made
with you, and make you a graven image, *or* the
likeness of any *thing*, which the LORD thy God
hath forbidden thee.
24 For the LORD thy God *is* a consuming fire, *even*
a jealous God.
25 ¶ When thou shalt beget children, and chil-
dren's children, and ye shall have remained long
in the land, and shall corrupt *yourselves*, and make
a graven image, *or* the likeness of any *thing*, and
shall do evil in the sight of the LORD thy God, to
provoke him to anger:
26 I call heaven and earth to witness against you
this day, that ye shall soon utterly perish from off
the land whereunto ye go over Jordan to possess
it; ye shall not prolong *your* days upon it, but shall
utterly be destroyed.
27 And the LORD shall scatter you among the na-
tions, and ye shall be left few in number among
the heathen, whither the LORD shall lead you.
28 And there ye shall serve gods, the work of
men's hands, wood and stone, which neither see,
nor hear, nor eat, nor smell.
29 But if from thence thou shalt seek the LORD
thy God, thou shalt find *him*, if thou seek him
with all thy heart and with all thy soul.
30 When thou art in tribulation, and all these
things are come upon thee, *even* in the latter days,
if thou turn to the LORD thy God, and shalt be
obedient unto his voice;
31 (For the LORD thy God *is* a merciful God;) he
will not forsake thee, neither destroy thee, nor
forget the covenant of thy fathers which he sware
unto them.
32 For ask now of the days that are past, which
were before thee, since the day that God created
man upon the earth, and *ask* from the one side of
heaven unto the other, whether there hath been
any such thing as this great thing *is*, or hath been
heard like it?
33 Did *ever* people hear the voice of God speaking
out of the midst of the fire, as thou hast heard,
and live?
34 Or hath God assayed to go *and* take him a na-
tion from the midst of *another* nation, by tempta-
tions, by signs, and by wonders, and by war, and
by a mighty hand, and by a stretched out arm, and
by great terrors, according to all that the LORD
your God did for you in Egypt before your eyes?
35 Unto thee it was shewed, that thou mightest
know that the LORD he *is* God; *there is* none else
beside him.

4:15–19 Graven images are prohibited because *ye saw no manner of similitude on the day that the LORD spake unto you.* Depiction of the invisible God (Col. 1:15; 1 Tim. 1:17) is a contradiction, prohibited as the very core of idolatry (John 4:24).
4:15 *heed.* Carefully keep watch over.
4:16 *likeness.* The form.
4:17 *winged fowl.* Birds.
4:20,24 *The iron furnace* represented the hottest fire and described Israel's suffering in Egypt. Yet it had not consumed Israel. God *is a consuming fire, a jealous God* (5:9; 6:15; 29:20; 32:16,21). A husband is jealous for his wife; so God's love for His people exhibits in His zeal to possess them exclusively.
4:22 *I must die.* For Moses' sin of striking the rock he was barred from entering into the Promised Land (Num. 20).
4:23 *graven image.* Idol.
4:27 *scatter you.* Living in the land was conditioned on obedience and covenant faithfulness since rest in the land was symbolic of enjoying God's presence. *heathen.* Literally, "nations."
4:34 *hath God.* The KJV translates the Hebrew here as referring to Israel's God, which shows that the Lord is unlike any other god. Some translations take *God* here as a reference to the pagan gods (cf. v. 28) and their non-covenantal nature. *assayed.* Tested, tried, or proved.
4:35 True religion is monotheistic: there is only one God (6:4; Mark 12:32).
4:37–38 God's love for Israel was exclusive and effectual,

36 Out of heaven he made thee to hear his voice,
that he might instruct thee: and upon earth he
shewed thee his great fire; and thou heardest his
words out of the midst of the fire.
37 And because he loved thy fathers, therefore he
chose their seed after them, and brought thee out
in his sight with his mighty power out of Egypt;
38 To drive out nations from before thee greater
and mightier than thou *art*, to bring thee in, to give
thee their land *for* an inheritance, as *it is* this day.
39 Know therefore this day, and consider *it* in thine
heart, that the LORD he *is* God in heaven above, and
upon the earth beneath: *there is* none else.
40 Thou shalt keep therefore his statutes, and
his commandments, which I command thee this
day, that it may go well with thee, and with thy
children after thee, and that thou mayest prolong
thy days upon the earth, which the LORD thy God
giveth thee, for ever.
41 ¶ Then Moses severed three cities on this side
Jordan toward the sunrising;
42 That the slayer might flee thither, which
should kill his neighbour unawares, and hated
him not in times past; and that fleeing unto one
of these cities he might live:
43 *Namely*, Bezer in the wilderness, in the plain
country, of the Reubenites; and Ramoth in
Gilead, of the Gadites; and Golan in Bashan, of
the Manassites.
44 ¶ And this *is* the law which Moses set before
the children of Israel:
45 These *are* the testimonies, and the statutes, and
the judgments, which Moses spake unto the chil-
dren of Israel, after they came forth out of Egypt,
46 On this side Jordan, in the valley over against
Beth-peor, in the land of Sihon king of the
Amorites, who dwelt at Heshbon, whom Moses
and the children of Israel smote, after they were
come forth out of Egypt:
47 And they possessed his land, and the land of Og
king of Bashan, two kings of the Amorites, which
were on this side Jordan toward the sunrising;
48 From Aroer, which *is* by the bank of the river
Arnon, even unto mount Sion, which *is* Hermon,
49 And all the plain on this side Jordan eastward,
even unto the sea of the plain, under the springs
of Pisgah.

CHAPTER 5

AND Moses called all Israel, and said unto them,
Hear, O Israel, the statutes and judgments which
I speak in your ears this day, that ye may learn
them, and keep, and do them.
2 The LORD our God made a covenant with us
in Horeb.
3 The LORD made not this covenant with our
fathers, but with us, *even* us, who *are* all of us here
alive this day.
4 The LORD talked with you face to face in the
mount out of the midst of the fire,
5 (I stood between the LORD and you at that time,
to shew you the word of the LORD: for ye were
afraid by reason of the fire, and went not up into
the mount;) saying,
6 ¶ I *am* the LORD thy God, which brought
thee out of the land of Egypt, from the house of
bondage.

---

exhibited in her deliverance from Egypt and entrance into Canaan (6:10–11).

Cities of Refuge East of Jordan (4:41–43)

4:41–43 Cities of refuge (Num. 35; Deut. 19:1–13).
4:41 *severed.* Separated or divided. *sunrising.* To the east.
4:42 *unawares.* In ignorance or unknowingly.

EXPOUNDING GOD'S LAW (4:44—26:19)
Introductory Explanation (4:44–49)

4:44–45 *this is the law . . . These are the testimonies.* This introduces the restatement and exposition of the law that will continue through ch. 26.

Thoughts for Personal/Family Worship: Chapter 4

1. **God's love is inseparable from His omnipotence. It is therefore effective in all of His purposes. His love for Abraham, Isaac, and Jacob (Mal. 1:1–4; Rom. 9:10–13) brought Israel into Canaan (Deut. 4:37) and will bring all of His elect to glorification. Believers are sons of God because the Father bestowed His love upon them (1 John 3:1–2). He has loved believers with an everlasting love (Jer. 31:3). Why are both God's love and His power necessary for the hope of believers to be secure?**
2. **If a stranger who never saw your father purported to draw a picture of him, you might be offended. Should not this be our response when imagination produces drawings of unseen persons of the godhead? Such misrepresentation of God was a reason graven images were prohibited. Revelation, not imagination, is the only legitimate portrait of God. Ultimately, the only legitimate image or manifestation of God is Jesus Christ, the eternal Son of God (Heb. 1:3).**

Commandments and Related Exhortations (5:1—11:32)

Chapter 5: *God's law is a necessary foundation to taking possession of Canaan*
The Ten Commandments (5:1–33)

5:3 *our fathers.* The patriarchs, the preceding generations. *but with us.* Many hearing this were not at Sinai but are one with their fathers who were.
5:4 *Face to face* is not to be taken literally (4:12; cf. John 1:18; 1 John 4:12) but is a Hebrew idiom meaning "personally" or "directly."
5:5 *stood between.* Moses interceded for the people.
5:6–21 See the Ten Commandments notes at Ex. 20:1–17; Rom. 13:9.
5:6 God redeemed Israel from Pharaoh's *bondage* that He might rule them in love. His deliverance is foundational to His rule. God's law expressed how they were to live within a covenant relationship. Its obligations, unlike Pharaoh's, were for

7 Thou shalt have none other gods before me.
8 Thou shalt not make thee *any* graven image, *or*
any likeness *of any thing* that *is* in heaven above, or
that *is* in the earth beneath, or that *is* in the waters
beneath the earth:
9 Thou shalt not bow down thyself unto them,
nor serve them: for I the LORD thy God *am* a jeal-
ous God, visiting the iniquity of the fathers upon
the children unto the third and fourth *generation*
of them that hate me,
10 And shewing mercy unto thousands of them
that love me and keep my commandments.
11 Thou shalt not take the name of the LORD thy
God in vain: for the LORD will not hold *him* guilt-
less that taketh his name in vain.
12 Keep the sabbath day to sanctify it, as the LORD
thy God hath commanded thee.
13 Six days thou shalt labour, and do all thy work:
14 But the seventh day *is* the sabbath of the LORD
thy God: *in it* thou shalt not do any work, thou,
nor thy son, nor thy daughter, nor thy manservant,
nor thy maidservant, nor thine ox, nor thine
ass, nor any of thy cattle, nor thy stranger that
is within thy gates; that thy manservant and thy
maidservant may rest as well as thou.
15 And remember that thou wast a servant in the
land of Egypt, and *that* the LORD thy God brought
thee out thence through a mighty hand and by
a stretched out arm: therefore the LORD thy God
commanded thee to keep the sabbath day.
16 ¶ Honour thy father and thy mother, as the
LORD thy God hath commanded thee; that thy
days may be prolonged, and that it may go well
with thee, in the land which the LORD thy God
giveth thee.
17 Thou shalt not kill.
18 Neither shalt thou commit adultery.
19 Neither shalt thou steal.
20 Neither shalt thou bear false witness against
thy neighbour.
21 Neither shalt thou desire thy neighbour's wife,
neither shalt thou covet thy neighbour's house, his
field, or his manservant, or his maidservant, his
ox, or his ass, or any *thing* that *is* thy neighbour's.
22 ¶ These words the LORD spake unto all your
assembly in the mount out of the midst of the
fire, of the cloud, and of the thick darkness, with a
great voice: and he added no more. And he wrote
them in two tables of stone, and delivered them
unto me.
23 And it came to pass, when ye heard the voice
out of the midst of the darkness, (for the moun-
tain did burn with fire,) that ye came near unto
me, *even* all the heads of your tribes, and your
elders;
24 And ye said, Behold, the LORD our God hath
shewed us his glory and his greatness, and we
have heard his voice out of the midst of the fire:
we have seen this day that God doth talk with
man, and he liveth.
25 Now therefore why should we die? for this
great fire will consume us: if we hear the voice of
the LORD our God any more, then we shall die.
26 For who *is there of* all flesh, that hath heard the
voice of the living God speaking out of the midst
of the fire, as we *have*, and lived?
27 Go thou near, and hear all that the LORD our
God shall say: and speak thou unto us all that the
LORD our God shall speak unto thee; and we will
hear *it*, and do *it*.
28 And the LORD heard the voice of your words,
when ye spake unto me; and the LORD said unto
me, I have heard the voice of the words of this
people, which they have spoken unto thee: they
have well said all that they have spoken.
29 O that there were such an heart in them, that
they would fear me, and keep all my command-
ments always, that it might be well with them, and
with their children for ever!
30 Go say to them, Get you into your tents again.
31 But as for thee, stand thou here by me, and I
will speak unto thee all the commandments, and
the statutes, and the judgments, which thou shalt
teach them, that they may do *them* in the land
which I give them to possess it.
32 Ye shall observe to do therefore as the LORD

---

their good (vv. 16,29,33). Significantly, the commandments were not in order for redemption but because of redemption.

5:7 *before me.* The sin of having any other god. God demands total allegiance.

5:8 God is to be represented in word only; thus the preeminence of God's Word must be embraced (4:15–19).

5:9–10 Sin affects generations yet unborn. *Visiting* has the idea of inspecting. God will examine future generations regarding the sins of past generations. Conversely, obedience reaps multi-generational covenantal mercy.

5:11 God's name, an expression of His nature, is not to be used carelessly (*in vain*). God will not be manipulated by invoking His name for useless and selfish purposes.

5:12–15 On the seventh day God rested (Gen. 2:1–3). Man, made in God's image, was to rest (Mark 2:27). Whereas in Ex. 20, keeping the Sabbath was an imitation of God, Moses here connects it to the remembrance of redemption. Rest and worship go together.

5:12 *sanctify.* To set apart. The Sabbath was to be distinct from other days.

5:15 *servant.* Slave.

5:16 Children who dishonor parents transgress the principles of their preservation (v. 9) and would thus be short-lived in the land of promise (Matt. 15:4; Eph. 6:1–3).

5:17 On murder, see Gen. 9:6; Matt. 5:21–26; 1 John 3:15.

5:18 On adultery, see Gen. 2:24; Matt. 5:27–32.

5:20 *false witness.* Lie.

5:22 *assembly.* Congregation or localized gathering.

5:27 God's august majesty calls for obedience, though the people were terrified to hear God's voice.

5:32 *right hand or to the left.* Denotes a close watching with no slight straying.

THE USES OF THE MORAL LAW

The law is God's revealed will for the life of angels in heaven and humans on earth. As such, it is called the moral law. Three great summaries of the moral law have been given in history. *First*, God charged Adam and Eve: "Be fruitful and multiply, and replenish the earth and subdue it," adding that, "Of every tree of the garden thou mayest freely eat: but of the tree of the knowledge of good and evil, thou shalt not eat of it: for in the day thou eatest thereof thou shalt surely die" (Gen. 1:28; 2:16,17).

God gave the *second* summary to Moses at Sinai in the Ten Commandments, writing it with His own finger on stone tablets (Ex. 31:18; 32:16). This summary is reported in Exodus 20 and Deuteronomy 5. The whole body of Mosaic legislation, including the directory for worship known as the ceremonial law and the various civil laws given to Israel "as a body politic" (Westminster Confession of Faith, 19.3–4), is only the outworking of these "ten words," as they are called in Hebrew.

Finally, the Lord Jesus Christ, challenged to identify the great commandment of the law, reduced all to just two commandments: "Thou shalt love the Lord thy God with all thy heart, with all thy soul, and with all thy mind. This is the first and great commandment. And the second is like unto it, Thou shalt love thy neighbour as thyself. On these two commandments hang all the law and the prophets" (Matt. 22:36–40).

Under the gospel, the ceremonial law has been abrogated and the civil law has expired. But the moral law—written on the human heart at creation, ratified as the covenant of works, and confirmed by Christ—continues to bind all human beings to obey it. Of what use is the law to mankind in general? Before the fall, the law directed Adam to a blessed way of life. Since the fall, it can only serve to restrain sin, expose human sinfulness, condemn every sinner, and show how much we need Christ as the only Savior. Paul writes, "By the law is the knowledge of sin" (Rom. 3:20); "I had not known sin, but by the law" (Rom. 7:7).

So the moral law teaches us the reality of sin. Fallen, sinful human beings remain moral agents by nature, accountable to their Maker. Their conduct must be judged by His law. "Sin is any want of conformity unto, or transgression of the law of God" (Westminster Shorter Catechism, Q. 14). This definition frees us from slavish conformity to the laws and commandments of men, but it brings us face to face with the righteous demands of a holy God.

Because Christ blotted out "the handwriting of ordinances that was against us . . . and took it out of the way, nailing it to his cross" (Col. 2:14), some have taught that the moral law is no longer binding on Christians as "justified persons." But this "handwriting" was the law's sentence of condemnation on all who disobey. Christ died to atone for our sins, thus voiding that sentence of condemnation.

But the law is still of great use to the Christian. It teaches him to know his own sinful nature, to be earnest in seeking forgiveness of sin and righteousness in Christ, to hate all sin, and to delight in all righteousness. It is a mark of grace to love God's law as a rule of life (Ps. 119:97). The child of God wants to please his heavenly Father by doing His will on earth. Faith moves him, grace enables him, love constrains him, and the law of God directs him in the new life of obedience in Christ.

your God hath commanded you: ye shall not turn
aside to the right hand or to the left.
33 Ye shall walk in all the ways which the LORD
your God hath commanded you, that ye may
live, and *that it may be* well with you, and *that* ye
may prolong *your* days in the land which ye shall
possess.

CHAPTER 6

NOW these *are* the commandments, the statutes,
and the judgments, which the LORD your God
commanded to teach you, that ye might do *them*
in the land whither ye go to possess it:
2 That thou mightest fear the LORD thy God,
to keep all his statutes and his commandments,
which I command thee, thou, and thy son, and
thy son's son, all the days of thy life; and that thy
days may be prolonged.
3 ¶ Hear therefore, O Israel, and observe to do *it*;
that it may be well with thee, and that ye may in-
crease mightily, as the LORD God of thy fathers
hath promised thee, in the land that floweth with
milk and honey.
4 Hear, O Israel: The LORD our God *is* one LORD:
5 And thou shalt love the LORD thy God with all
thine heart, and with all thy soul, and with all thy
might.
6 And these words, which I command thee this
day, shall be in thine heart:
7 And thou shalt teach them diligently unto thy
children, and shalt talk of them when thou sittest in
thine house, and when thou walkest by the way, and
when thou liest down, and when thou risest up.
8 And thou shalt bind them for a sign upon thine
hand, and they shall be as frontlets between thine
eyes.
9 And thou shalt write them upon the posts of
thy house, and on thy gates.
10 And it shall be, when the LORD thy God shall
have brought thee into the land which he sware
unto thy fathers, to Abraham, to Isaac, and to Ja-
cob, to give thee great and goodly cities, which
thou buildedst not,
11 And houses full of all good *things*, which thou
filledst not, and wells digged, which thou diggedst
not, vineyards and olive trees, which thou plant-
edst not; when thou shalt have eaten and be full;
12 *Then* beware lest thou forget the LORD, which
brought thee forth out of the land of Egypt, from
the house of bondage.
13 Thou shalt fear the LORD thy God, and serve
him, and shalt swear by his name.
14 Ye shall not go after other gods, of the gods of
the people which *are* round about you;
15 (For the LORD thy God *is* a jealous God among
you) lest the anger of the LORD thy God be kin-
dled against thee, and destroy thee from off the
face of the earth.
16 ¶ Ye shall not tempt the LORD your God, as ye
tempted *him* in Massah.
17 Ye shall diligently keep the commandments of
the LORD your God, and his testimonies, and his
statutes, which he hath commanded thee.
18 And thou shalt do *that which is* right and good
in the sight of the LORD: that it may be well with
thee, and that thou mayest go in and possess the
good land which the LORD sware unto thy fathers,
19 To cast out all thine enemies from before thee,
as the LORD hath spoken.

Thoughts for Personal/Family Worship: Chapter 5

1. **At Mt. Sinai the people could not bear the terrifying manifestation of God. They needed a mediator. God provided in Moses a foreshadowing of Christ, who was given to be the one Mediator between God and men (1 Tim. 2:5). He is our only access unto God (John 14:6), by whom we come to God with confidence (Heb. 4:14–16).**
2. **Israel was awestruck in God's presence. So are the seraphim and inspired prophets (Isa. 6:1–5). Worship should manifest this sense of wonder and awe. It is not a venue for entertainment or novelties, but a time when the realization of our inadequacy compels us to desire the one Mediator, Jesus Christ, and to offer Him humble adoration.**
3. **God's law is given to aid, not to burden. Man's religion lays burdens upon people, but God's laws, given by grace, are given "that it may be well with you" (v. 33). What are some ways that keeping the Ten Commandments brings blessing to a person's life?**

Chapter 6: ***Moses proclaims the "great commandment" and affirms the need to teach future generations to keep God's law continually in view and to remember the deliverance represented by the law of God.***

Love God and Remember His Commandments (6:1–25)

6:1 *The commandments* (Hebrew is singular) is the whole law. *The statutes and the judgments* are specific elements.
6:2 Prolonged days suggests long life and long occupancy in the land.
6:3 *mightily.* Greatly.
6:4–5 The *Shema* (from the Hebrew word for *hear*) is the confession of monotheism affirmed by Christ as the greatest commandment (Matt. 22:36–40), showing that love is the heart of the law. This declares the foundation of true religion.
6:7–9 The law was acknowledged in every facet of life, promoting continual meditation (Ps. 1:2) and God-consciousness.
6:8 *sign . . . frontlets.* These later became little leather boxes tied to both the forearm and forehead. They were called "tefillin" or "phylacteries" and held sections of the law (Ex. 13:1–16). Sadly, they were reduced to outward gestures devoid of spiritual experience. Wearing the letter of law replaced living in the spirit of law.
6:13 To *swear by his name* makes God the guarantor of our truthfulness. It is not taking His name in vain (5:11) unless one's words are false or meaningless, which Christ rebuked (Matt. 5:34–36; 23:16–22). *serve him.* Worship Him alone (Matt. 4:10).
6:16 *not tempt the LORD.* Test Him by demanding that He do your will (Matt. 4:7). *Massah* means "testing" and is the place where Israel murmured for water (Ex. 17:1–7).
6:17 Diligence is commanded in spiritual matters (Ex. 15:26;

20 *And* when thy son asketh thee in time to come,
saying, What *mean* the testimonies, and the stat-
utes, and the judgments, which the LORD our God
hath commanded you?
21 Then thou shalt say unto thy son, We were
Pharaoh's bondmen in Egypt; and the LORD
brought us out of Egypt with a mighty hand:
22 And the LORD shewed signs and wonders,
great and sore, upon Egypt, upon Pharaoh, and
upon all his household, before our eyes:
23 And he brought us out from thence, that he
might bring us in, to give us the land which he
sware unto our fathers.
24 And the LORD commanded us to do all these
statutes, to fear the LORD our God, for our good
always, that he might preserve us alive, as *it is* at
this day.
25 And it shall be our righteousness, if we observe
to do all these commandments before the LORD
our God, as he hath commanded us.

CHAPTER 7

WHEN the LORD thy God shall bring thee into the
land whither thou goest to possess it, and hath cast
out many nations before thee, the Hittites, and the
Girgashites, and the Amorites, and the Canaanites,
and the Perizzites, and the Hivites, and the Jebu-
sites, seven nations greater and mightier than thou;
2 And when the LORD thy God shall deliver them
before thee; thou shalt smite them, *and* utterly
destroy them; thou shalt make no covenant with
them, nor shew mercy unto them:
3 Neither shalt thou make marriages with them;
thy daughter thou shalt not give unto his son, nor
his daughter shalt thou take unto thy son.
4 For they will turn away thy son from following
me, that they may serve other gods: so will the
anger of the LORD be kindled against you, and
destroy thee suddenly.
5 But thus shall ye deal with them; ye shall de-
stroy their altars, and break down their images,
and cut down their groves, and burn their graven
images with fire.
6 For thou *art* an holy people unto the LORD thy
God: the LORD thy God hath chosen thee to be a
special people unto himself, above all people that
are upon the face of the earth.
7 The LORD did not set his love upon you, nor
choose you, because ye were more in number than
any people; for ye *were* the fewest of all people:
8 But because the LORD loved you, and because
he would keep the oath which he had sworn unto
your fathers, hath the LORD brought you out with
a mighty hand, and redeemed you out of the
house of bondmen, from the hand of Pharaoh
king of Egypt.
9 Know therefore that the LORD thy God, he *is*
God, the faithful God, which keepeth covenant
and mercy with them that love him and keep his
commandments to a thousand generations;
10 And repayeth them that hate him to their face,
to destroy them: he will not be slack to him that
hateth him, he will repay him to his face.
11 Thou shalt therefore keep the command-
ments, and the statutes, and the judgments, which

Deut. 4:9; 6:5,7,17; Heb. 11:6; 2 Peter 1:5–10).

6:20–25 God's liberating law replaced Pharaoh's enslavement and would make Israel unique among nations.

6:22 *sore.* Very severe.

6:25 *our righteousness.* An approximate righteousness that relates to a man's attitude toward God's law. This does not suggest that justification is by keeping the law; rather, it simply says that obeying God is the right thing to do.

Thoughts for Personal/Family Worship: Chapter 6

1. **We need continual God-consciousness. Israel was commanded to talk of God's laws, to bind them to their hands and to write them upon their houses (Ex. 13:9, 16; Deut. 6:7–10; 11:18–21). In Christ's day this was observed, yet without conscience toward God (Matt. 23:1–5). Righteous people meditate on God's law day and night (Ps. 1:2; 119:97–99). They "pray without ceasing" (1 Thess. 5:17). Their life is a growing exercise in God-consciousness.**
2. **God's law is never a burden but a delight for those who love God (Pss. 1:2; 119:70; 1 John 5:3). This was Christ's testimony through the psalmist (Ps. 40:8; Heb. 10:5–7), when He was made "under the law" (Gal. 4:4–5) and did only those things that pleased the Father (John 8:29). He came to fulfill it (Matt. 5:17) because it was delightful to Him. How can God's people cultivate their delight in the written Word and communion with the living Word, Jesus Christ?**
3. **This chapter is a great summary of the theme of total devotion to God. The imperative of devotion is to love God completely (v. 5). The logic of devotion is based on who God is (the one true God, v. 4) and what God has done in redeeming His people (vv. 12,20–23). The performance of devotion includes fearing God (vv. 2,13,24), serving Him (v. 13), obeying Him (vv. 6,17,25), and remembering Him (vv. 7–9,12).**

Chapter 7: *God's love is exhibited in His giving the land to His people, who were to abhor sin and love Him exclusively.*

Separation from Idolators, God's Blessing (7:1–26)

7:1 *nations.* Canaan consisted of independent city states. Each nation typically included a fortified city and its surrounding area. Combined, they were larger and stronger than Israel, but would be given by God to her (Gen. 15:20; Ex. 3:8).

7:2–6 Destruction of these nations would protect Israel from idolatry. Commingling and marriage often lead one to idolatry. See Solomon's tragic example (1 Kings 11:1–8).

7:5 *groves.* Poles erected in worship of Asherah, a Canaanite goddess (12:3; Judg. 6:25).

7:6–11 God's sovereign electing love makes a holy people (Jer. 31:3; Rom. 5:7; Eph. 1:4). The wonders wrought for Israel exhibit the extremes by which God powerfully works in His love (Rom. 8:28–39).

7:8–13 See Gen. 15:1.

I command thee this day, to do them.
12 ¶ Wherefore it shall come to pass, if ye hearken
to these judgments, and keep, and do them, that the
LORD thy God shall keep unto thee the covenant
and the mercy which he sware unto thy fathers:
13 And he will love thee, and bless thee, and mul-
tiply thee: he will also bless the fruit of thy womb,
and the fruit of thy land, thy corn, and thy wine,
and thine oil, the increase of thy kine, and the
flocks of thy sheep, in the land which he sware
unto thy fathers to give thee.
14 Thou shalt be blessed above all people: there
shall not be male or female barren among you, or
among your cattle.
15 And the LORD will take away from thee all
sickness, and will put none of the evil diseases of
Egypt, which thou knowest, upon thee; but will
lay them upon all *them* that hate thee.
16 And thou shalt consume all the people which
the LORD thy God shall deliver thee; thine eye
shall have no pity upon them: neither shalt thou
serve their gods; for that *will be* a snare unto thee.
17 If thou shalt say in thine heart, These nations
are more than I; how can I dispossess them?
18 Thou shalt not be afraid of them: *but* shalt
well remember what the LORD thy God did unto
Pharaoh, and unto all Egypt;
19 The great temptations which thine eyes saw,
and the signs, and the wonders, and the mighty
hand, and the stretched out arm, whereby the
LORD thy God brought thee out: so shall the LORD
thy God do unto all the people of whom thou art
afraid.
20 Moreover the LORD thy God will send the
hornet among them, until they that are left, and
hide themselves from thee, be destroyed.
21 Thou shalt not be affrighted at them: for the
LORD thy God *is* among you, a mighty God and
terrible.
22 And the LORD thy God will put out those na-
tions before thee by little and little: thou mayest
not consume them at once, lest the beasts of the
field increase upon thee.
23 But the LORD thy God shall deliver them unto
thee, and shall destroy them with a mighty de-
struction, until they be destroyed.
24 And he shall deliver their kings into thine
hand, and thou shalt destroy their name from
under heaven: there shall no man be able to stand
before thee, until thou have destroyed them.
25 The graven images of their gods shall ye burn
with fire: thou shalt not desire the silver or gold
that is on them, nor take *it* unto thee, lest thou
be snared therein: for it *is* an abomination to the
LORD thy God.
26 Neither shalt thou bring an abomination into
thine house, lest thou be a cursed thing like it: *but*
thou shalt utterly detest it, and thou shalt utterly
abhor it; for it *is* a cursed thing.

CHAPTER 8

ALL the commandments which I command thee
this day shall ye observe to do, that ye may live,
and multiply, and go in and possess the land
which the LORD sware unto your fathers.
2 And thou shalt remember all the way which
the LORD thy God led thee these forty years in
the wilderness, to humble thee, *and* to prove thee,
to know what *was* in thine heart, whether thou
wouldest keep his commandments, or no.
3 And he humbled thee, and suffered thee to
hunger, and fed thee with manna, which thou
knewest not, neither did thy fathers know; that he

7:12 *keep unto thee.* God will be faithful.
7:13 *kine.* Cattle.
7:15 *evil diseases.* Perhaps referring to elephantiasis and boils. Israel would be spared, but not her enemies (28:27,60).
7:16 *shalt consume.* See Num. 14:9.
7:19 *temptations.* The Hebrew literally means "trials" (6:16).
7:20 *hornet.* Interpreters differ as to whether this refers to a literal hornet or is a figurative designation of some menace that will be used to rout the enemy.
7:25 No reminder of idols was to be kept; they were to be wholly separated (1 John 2:15–16).

Thoughts for Personal/Family Worship: Chapter 7

1. **God's zeal for holiness compels us to forsake the ways of wicked people. We are not to be fascinated by their gods. Israel was to destroy images, not to keep gold or silver parts of an idol. These would have been valuable in Israel's economy, but their association with idols was repugnant to God, so they were to be destroyed. We must recognize God's abhorrence of things that seduce man's devotion, and hate the things God hates.**
2. **God's delivering over the Canaanites and Israel's smiting the Canaanites (v. 2; 9:3) illustrate what happens in sanctification. God assured the victory, but Israel had to fight. Similarly, on the one hand, sin has been thoroughly defeated by Christ, who crushed the serpent's head. By faith we live in the reality of Christ's victory by not allowing sin to have dominion over us (Rom. 6:1–14). What sins do you need to conquer? How must you look to Christ for victory? How must you fight?**
3. **God's sovereign dominion extends to every creature. Even insects serve His kingdom. It is edifying to contemplate those instances where He utilized animals for His purposes (Ex. 8; 10; Num. 21:5–9; 22:21–31; 1 Sam. 6:7–14; 1 Kings 17:2–7; Dan. 6:16–24; Jonah 1–2; Luke 5:1–11; John 21:5–11).**

Exhortations, Blessings, and Curses (8:1—11:32)

Chapter 8: ***God tested Israel in the wilderness to reveal the thoughts and intents of their hearts.***

8:1–5 The title *LORD thy God* occurs ten times in this chapter (including *your God*, v. 20). God's personal nature and covenantal relationship with His people are emphasized.
8:3 *suffered thee to hunger.* God let them be hungry. *not live by bread alone.* Trusting and obeying God are more important

might make thee know that man doth not live by bread only, but by every *word* that proceedeth out of the mouth of the LORD doth man live.

4 Thy raiment waxed not old upon thee, neither did thy foot swell, these forty years.

5 Thou shalt also consider in thine heart, that, as a man chasteneth his son, *so* the LORD thy God chasteneth thee.

6 Therefore thou shalt keep the commandments of the LORD thy God, to walk in his ways, and to fear him.

7 For the LORD thy God bringeth thee into a good land, a land of brooks of water, of fountains and depths that spring out of valleys and hills;

8 A land of wheat, and barley, and vines, and fig trees, and pomegranates; a land of oil olive, and honey;

9 A land wherein thou shalt eat bread without scarceness, thou shalt not lack any *thing* in it; a land whose stones *are* iron, and out of whose hills thou mayest dig brass.

10 When thou hast eaten and art full, then thou shalt bless the LORD thy God for the good land which he hath given thee.

11 Beware that thou forget not the LORD thy God, in not keeping his commandments, and his judgments, and his statutes, which I command thee this day:

12 Lest *when* thou hast eaten and art full, and hast built goodly houses, and dwelt *therein*;

13 And *when* thy herds and thy flocks multiply, and thy silver and thy gold is multiplied, and all that thou hast is multiplied;

14 Then thine heart be lifted up, and thou forget the LORD thy God, which brought thee forth out of the land of Egypt, from the house of bondage;

15 Who led thee through that great and terrible wilderness, *wherein were* fiery serpents, and scorpions, and drought, where *there was* no water; who brought thee forth water out of the rock of flint;

16 Who fed thee in the wilderness with manna, which thy fathers knew not, that he might humble thee, and that he might prove thee, to do thee good at thy latter end;

17 And thou say in thine heart, My power and the might of *mine* hand hath gotten me this wealth.

18 But thou shalt remember the LORD thy God: for *it is* he that giveth thee power to get wealth, that he may establish his covenant which he sware unto thy fathers, as *it is* this day.

19 And it shall be, if thou do at all forget the LORD thy God, and walk after other gods, and serve them, and worship them, I testify against you this day that ye shall surely perish.

20 As the nations which the LORD destroyeth before your face, so shall ye perish; because ye would not be obedient unto the voice of the LORD your God.

CHAPTER 9

HEAR, O Israel: Thou *art* to pass over Jordan this day, to go in to possess nations greater and mightier than thyself, cities great and fenced up to heaven,

2 A people great and tall, the children of the Anakims, whom thou knowest, and *of whom* thou hast heard *say*, Who can stand before the children of Anak!

3 Understand therefore this day, that the LORD thy God *is* he which goeth over before thee; *as* a consuming fire he shall destroy them, and he shall bring them down before thy face: so shalt thou drive them out, and destroy them quickly, as the LORD hath said unto thee.

4 Speak not thou in thine heart, after that the LORD thy God hath cast them out from before thee, saying, For my righteousness the LORD hath brought me in to possess this land: but for the wickedness of these nations the LORD doth drive them out from before thee.

5 Not for thy righteousness, or for the uprightness of thine heart, dost thou go to possess their land: but for the wickedness of these nations the LORD thy God doth drive them out from before thee, and that he may perform the word which the LORD sware unto thy fathers, Abraham, Isaac, and Jacob.

---

than food (Matt. 4:4; John 4:34).

8:4 *waxed.* Became.

8:5 *chasteneth.* Instructs, warns, or disciplines.

8:6 Because God delivered them and preserved them, they must keep His commandments.

8:14 Prosperity often leads to neglecting God.

8:19 Continuation of blessing depends on obedience.

Thoughts for Personal/Family Worship: Chapter 8

1. **"They that will be rich fall into temptation and a snare, and into many foolish and hurtful lusts" (1 Tim. 6:9). God's goodness to Israel included abundance (Deut. 8:7–10). But blessings can be perverted in curses by forgetting that they are God-given (v. 17). Thus, the church of Laodicea said, "I am rich," ignorant that it was "wretched, and miserable, and poor, and blind, and naked" (Rev. 3:17). How can you guard your heart from this?**
2. **God does not always take His people on an easy path. He led Israel through the wilderness. Serpents and scorpions assaulted; drought and hunger oppressed. But trials were for their good, to humble them and to expose what was in their hearts. God purposes all things to conform His people to the image of His Son (Rom. 8:28–29). Christ Himself faced the most severe trials of all, and overcame them (Matt. 4:1–11; Heb. 5:7–9).**

Chapter 9: ***Moses encourages, warns, and recites the record of Israel's wickedness and his intercession.***

9:4–5 The destruction of Israel's enemies was not arbitrary injustice.

6 Understand therefore, that the LORD thy God
giveth thee not this good land to possess it for thy
righteousness; for thou *art* a stiffnecked people.
7 ¶ Remember, *and* forget not, how thou
provokedst the LORD thy God to wrath in the
wilderness: from the day that thou didst depart
out of the land of Egypt, until ye came unto this
place, ye have been rebellious against the LORD.
8 Also in Horeb ye provoked the LORD to wrath,
so that the LORD was angry with you to have
destroyed you.
9 When I was gone up into the mount to receive
the tables of stone, *even* the tables of the covenant
which the LORD made with you, then I abode in
the mount forty days and forty nights, I neither
did eat bread nor drink water:
10 And the LORD delivered unto me two tables of
stone written with the finger of God; and on them
was written according to all the words, which the
LORD spake with you in the mount out of the
midst of the fire in the day of the assembly.
11 And it came to pass at the end of forty days
and forty nights, *that* the LORD gave me the two
tables of stone, *even* the tables of the covenant.
12 And the LORD said unto me, Arise, get thee
down quickly from hence; for thy people which
thou hast brought forth out of Egypt have cor-
rupted *themselves*; they are quickly turned aside
out of the way which I commanded them; they
have made them a molten image.
13 Furthermore the LORD spake unto me, saying,
I have seen this people, and, behold, it *is* a stiff-
necked people:
14 Let me alone, that I may destroy them, and blot
out their name from under heaven: and I will make
of thee a nation mightier and greater than they.
15 So I turned and came down from the mount,
and the mount burned with fire: and the two
tables of the covenant *were* in my two hands.
16 And I looked, and, behold, ye had sinned
against the LORD your God, *and* had made you a
molten calf: ye had turned aside quickly out of the
way which the LORD had commanded you.
17 And I took the two tables, and cast them out of
my two hands, and brake them before your eyes.
18 And I fell down before the LORD, as at the
first, forty days and forty nights: I did neither eat
bread, nor drink water, because of all your sins
which ye sinned, in doing wickedly in the sight of
the LORD, to provoke him to anger.
19 For I was afraid of the anger and hot displea-
sure, wherewith the LORD was wroth against you
to destroy you. But the LORD hearkened unto me
at that time also.
20 And the LORD was very angry with Aaron to
have destroyed him: and I prayed for Aaron also
the same time.
21 And I took your sin, the calf which ye had
made, and burnt it with fire, and stamped it, *and*
ground *it* very small, *even* until it was as small as
dust: and I cast the dust thereof into the brook
that descended out of the mount.
22 And at Taberah, and at Massah, and at
Kibroth-hattaavah, ye provoked the LORD to
wrath.
23 Likewise when the LORD sent you from
Kadesh-barnea, saying, Go up and possess the
land which I have given you; then ye rebelled
against the commandment of the LORD your
God, and ye believed him not, nor hearkened to
his voice.
24 Ye have been rebellious against the LORD from
the day that I knew you.
25 Thus I fell down before the LORD forty days
and forty nights, as I fell down *at the first*; because
the LORD had said he would destroy you.
26 I prayed therefore unto the LORD, and said,
O Lord GOD, destroy not thy people and thine
inheritance, which thou hast redeemed through
thy greatness, which thou hast brought forth out
of Egypt with a mighty hand.
27 Remember thy servants, Abraham, Isaac, and
Jacob; look not unto the stubbornness of this
people, nor to their wickedness, nor to their sin:
28 Lest the land whence thou broughtest us
out say, Because the LORD was not able to bring
them into the land which he promised them, and
because he hated them, he hath brought them out
to slay them in the wilderness.
29 Yet they *are* thy people and thine inheritance,

9:6 *stiffnecked.* Stubborn, disobedient (Prov. 29:1).
9:9,18,25 Repeatedly. Moses spent forty days and forty nights in communion with God.
9:9 *abode.* Dwelt or remained.
9:10 *finger of God.* Revelation immediately from God (Dan. 5:5; John 8:8).
9:14 See Num. 12:3.
9:19 *wroth.* Angry.
9:22–23 *Taberah* relates to the burning of God's wrath (Num. 11:1–3). *Massah.* See 6:16; Ex. 17:7. *Kibroth-hattaavah.* Literally, "graves of lust," a place where many died from a plague after grumbling for meat (Num. 11:31–35). *Kadesh-barnea.* Where Israel refused to enter Canaan (Num. 13–14).
9:26–28 Moses' prayer focused upon God's works recounted throughout this section. He expresses his primary concern for God's glory and God's reputation among the heathen.

Thoughts for Personal/Family Worship: Chapter 9

1. **Israel "turned aside quickly out of the way" (v. 16). How quickly we are ensnared in sin! Our lusts war against our souls (1 Peter 2:11), and we remain one thought away from yielding. Satan is swift like a lion, so we must be sober and vigilant (1 Peter 5:8). "Wherefore let him that thinketh he standeth take heed lest he fall" (1 Cor. 10:12). How can we strive to be humble and watchful against sin?**
2. **Great men will be great in prayer. When God offered to make Moses the father of a greater nation, replacing**

which thou broughtest out by thy mighty power
and by thy stretched out arm.

CHAPTER 10

AT that time the LORD said unto me, Hew thee
two tables of stone like unto the first, and come
up unto me into the mount, and make thee an
ark of wood.
2 And I will write on the tables the words that
were in the first tables which thou brakest, and
thou shalt put them in the ark.
3 And I made an ark *of* shittim wood, and hewed
two tables of stone like unto the first, and went
up into the mount, having the two tables in mine
hand.
4 And he wrote on the tables, according to the first
writing, the ten commandments, which the LORD
spake unto you in the mount out of the midst of
the fire in the day of the assembly: and the LORD
gave them unto me.
5 And I turned myself and came down from the
mount, and put the tables in the ark which I had
made; and there they be, as the LORD commanded
me.
6 ¶ And the children of Israel took their journey
from Beeroth of the children of Jaakan to Mosera:
there Aaron died, and there he was buried; and
Eleazar his son ministered in the priest's office in
his stead.
7 From thence they journeyed unto Gudgodah;
and from Gudgodah to Jotbath, a land of rivers
of waters.
8 ¶ At that time the LORD separated the tribe of
Levi, to bear the ark of the covenant of the LORD,
to stand before the LORD to minister unto him,
and to bless in his name, unto this day.
9 Wherefore Levi hath no part nor inheritance
with his brethren; the LORD *is* his inheritance,
according as the LORD thy God promised him.
10 And I stayed in the mount, according to the
first time, forty days and forty nights; and the
LORD hearkened unto me at that time also, *and*
the LORD would not destroy thee.
11 And the LORD said unto me, Arise, take *thy*
journey before the people, that they may go in
and possess the land, which I sware unto their fa-
thers to give unto them.
12 ¶ And now, Israel, what doth the LORD thy
God require of thee, but to fear the LORD thy God,
to walk in all his ways, and to love him, and to
serve the LORD thy God with all thy heart and
with all thy soul,
13 To keep the commandments of the LORD, and
his statutes, which I command thee this day for
thy good?
14 Behold, the heaven and the heaven of heavens
is the LORD's thy God, the earth *also*, with all that
therein *is*.
15 Only the LORD had a delight in thy fathers to
love them, and he chose their seed after them,
even you above all people, as *it is* this day.
16 Circumcise therefore the foreskin of your
heart, and be no more stiffnecked.
17 For the LORD your God *is* God of gods, and
Lord of lords, a great God, a mighty, and a terrible,
which regardeth not persons, nor taketh reward:
18 He doth execute the judgment of the fatherless
and widow, and loveth the stranger, in giving him
food and raiment.
19 Love ye therefore the stranger: for ye were
strangers in the land of Egypt.
20 Thou shalt fear the LORD thy God; him shalt
thou serve, and to him shalt thou cleave, and
swear by his name.
21 He *is* thy praise, and he *is* thy God, that hath
done for thee these great and terrible things,
which thine eyes have seen.

Israel, he prayed for Israel's preservation. His praying was self-denying. He prayed persistently (forty days with fasting), and powerfully: "the LORD hearkened unto me" (v. 19). The intercessory prayer of Moses points to the even greater intercession of Christ in behalf of His people. In a sense, Israel owed their existence to the intercession of Moses. Believers owe all to Christ, who ever lives to make intercession for us.

Chapter 10: *God's law is reissued and encased in the ark, Levi is chosen for sacred service, and the people are instructed regarding their conduct and heart.*

10:1 at *that time.* After Moses' intercession (9:18–29). *Hew.* Form by cutting.

10:3 *shittim.* Acacia, a common timber tree in Sinai.

10:4 *ten commandments.* Literally, "ten words."

10:6–7 The location of these places is uncertain (Num. 33:31–33). Aaron's death confirms that Moses' intercession was effectual (9:19–20).

10:12–13 Compare the condensed summary of divine requirements in Mic. 6:8.

10:13 God's commands are *for thy good* (1 John 5:3).

10:14–15 *above all people.* Electing love favored Israel's fathers and their descendants.

10:16 *Circumcise . . . your heart.* A metaphor for removing worldly affections (see note at 30:6), an image of regeneration, receiving a new heart. Significantly, Moses was more concerned about the heart than the flesh, even though fleshly circumcision had not been practiced during the wilderness experience. The condition of the heart is always more important than that of the flesh.

10:17–19 *God of gods and Lord of lords.* God as absolute King is unimpressed with human genius, wealth, or power (Ps. 136:2–3; 1 Tim. 6:15; Rev. 17:14; 19:16). Yet He is tender toward the oppressed, as His people must be (Ex. 22:22–24; Matt. 11:28–30).

10:18 *raiment.* Clothes.

10:20 *cleave.* Cling to.

10:21–22 God's care for the oppressed is evident in Israel's experience of redemption. God had multiplied seventy people (*threescore and ten*) to become as numerous as the stars (Gen. 15:5; 22:17; 26:4).

22 Thy fathers went down into Egypt with three-
score and ten persons; and now the LORD thy God
hath made thee as the stars of heaven for multitude.

CHAPTER 11

THEREFORE thou shalt love the LORD thy God,
and keep his charge, and his statutes, and his
judgments, and his commandments, alway.
2 And know ye this day: for *I speak* not with your
children which have not known, and which have
not seen the chastisement of the LORD your God,
his greatness, his mighty hand, and his stretched
out arm,
3 And his miracles, and his acts, which he did
in the midst of Egypt unto Pharaoh the king of
Egypt, and unto all his land;
4 And what he did unto the army of Egypt, unto
their horses, and to their chariots; how he made
the water of the Red sea to overflow them as they
pursued after you, and *how* the LORD hath de-
stroyed them unto this day;
5 And what he did unto you in the wilderness,
until ye came into this place;
6 And what he did unto Dathan and Abiram, the
sons of Eliab, the son of Reuben: how the earth
opened her mouth, and swallowed them up, and
their households, and their tents, and all the sub-
stance that *was* in their possession, in the midst
of all Israel:
7 But your eyes have seen all the great acts of the
LORD which he did.
8 Therefore shall ye keep all the commandments
which I command you this day, that ye may be
strong, and go in and possess the land, whither ye
go to possess it;
9 And that ye may prolong *your* days in the land,
which the LORD sware unto your fathers to give
unto them and to their seed, a land that floweth
with milk and honey.
10 ¶ For the land, whither thou goest in to possess
it, *is* not as the land of Egypt, from whence ye
came out, where thou sowedst thy seed, and
wateredst *it* with thy foot, as a garden of herbs:
11 But the land, whither ye go to possess it, *is* a
land of hills and valleys, *and* drinketh water of the
rain of heaven:
12 A land which the LORD thy God careth for: the
eyes of the LORD thy God *are* always upon it, from
the beginning of the year even unto the end of
the year.
13 ¶ And it shall come to pass, if ye shall hearken
diligently unto my commandments which I
command you this day, to love the LORD your
God, and to serve him with all your heart and
with all your soul,
14 That I will give *you* the rain of your land in his
due season, the first rain and the latter rain, that
thou mayest gather in thy corn, and thy wine, and
thine oil.
15 And I will send grass in thy fields for thy cattle,
that thou mayest eat and be full.
16 Take heed to yourselves, that your heart be not
deceived, and ye turn aside, and serve other gods,
and worship them;
17 And *then* the LORD's wrath be kindled against
you, and he shut up the heaven, that there be no
rain, and that the land yield not her fruit; and *lest*
ye perish quickly from off the good land which
the LORD giveth you.
18 ¶ Therefore shall ye lay up these my words in
your heart and in your soul, and bind them for a
sign upon your hand, that they may be as frontlets
between your eyes.
19 And ye shall teach them your children, speak-
ing of them when thou sittest in thine house, and
when thou walkest by the way, when thou liest
down, and when thou risest up.
20 And thou shalt write them upon the door
posts of thine house, and upon thy gates:
21 That your days may be multiplied, and the
days of your children, in the land which the LORD
sware unto your fathers to give them, as the days
of heaven upon the earth.

Thoughts for Personal/Family Worship: Chapter 10

1. **"Fear the LORD thy God" (vv. 12,20). Reverent awe of our Creator will result in obedience, love, and service for God. The fear of the Lord is the beginning of wisdom and knowledge (Ps. 111:10; Prov. 1:7; 9:10). It hates evil (Prov. 8:13), prolongs life (Prov. 10:27), and brings prosperity (Prov. 14:26–27; 16:6; 19:23; 22:4). The Spirit of Christ is the Spirit of the fear of the Lord (Isa. 11:2). Why is the fear of God right for those in Christ?**
2. **"What doth the LORD thy God require of thee?" (v. 12). This question must penetrate the conscience. Nothing else matters. God is worthy of wholehearted devotion, "with all thy heart and with all thy soul" (v. 12). Significantly, right in the middle of the five things God requires is to love Him, the greatest of all the commandments. "Thou shalt love the Lord thy God with all thy heart, and with all thy soul, and with all thy mind, and with all thy strength: this is the first commandment" (Mark 12:30).**

Chapter 11: *Remembering God's dealing with rebels, Israel must obey and teach their children obedience.*

11:1 *love.* Prominent theme. God's love is expressed in covenant (4:37). Israel must love God (6:5) and exhibit that love by obedience (11:13,22). *alway.* Literally, "all the days."

11:6 See Num. 16.

11:10 *wateredst it with thy foot.* An idiom referring to an irrigation system.

11:14 *first rain . . . latter rain.* Around October to April. Marked the start and end of the rainy season. The appropriate amount and timing of rain were symbolic of God's blessing and favor.

11:16 *heed.* Watch over.

11:17 Obedience is essential.

11:18–21 God's law was acknowledged in every facet of

22 ¶ For if ye shall diligently keep all these commandments which I command you, to do them, to love the LORD your God, to walk in all his ways, and to cleave unto him;
23 Then will the LORD drive out all these nations from before you, and ye shall possess greater nations and mightier than yourselves.
24 Every place whereon the soles of your feet shall tread shall be yours: from the wilderness and Lebanon, from the river, the river Euphrates, even unto the uttermost sea shall your coast be.
25 There shall no man be able to stand before you: *for* the LORD your God shall lay the fear of you and the dread of you upon all the land that ye shall tread upon, as he hath said unto you.
26 ¶ Behold, I set before you this day a blessing and a curse;
27 A blessing, if ye obey the commandments of the LORD your God, which I command you this day:
28 And a curse, if ye will not obey the commandments of the LORD your God, but turn aside out of the way which I command you this day, to go after other gods, which ye have not known.
29 And it shall come to pass, when the LORD thy God hath brought thee in unto the land whither thou goest to possess it, that thou shalt put the blessing upon mount Gerizim, and the curse upon mount Ebal.
30 *Are* they not on the other side Jordan, by the way where the sun goeth down, in the land of the Canaanites, which dwell in the champaign over against Gilgal, beside the plains of Moreh?
31 For ye shall pass over Jordan to go in to possess the land which the LORD your God giveth you, and ye shall possess it, and dwell therein.
32 And ye shall observe to do all the statutes and judgments which I set before you this day.

CHAPTER 12

THESE *are* the statutes and judgments, which ye shall observe to do in the land, which the LORD God of thy fathers giveth thee to possess it, all the days that ye live upon the earth.
2 Ye shall utterly destroy all the places, wherein the nations which ye shall possess served their gods, upon the high mountains, and upon the hills, and under every green tree:
3 And ye shall overthrow their altars, and break their pillars, and burn their groves with fire; and ye shall hew down the graven images of their gods, and destroy the names of them out of that place.
4 Ye shall not do so unto the LORD your God.
5 But unto the place which the LORD your God shall choose out of all your tribes to put his name there, *even* unto his habitation shall ye seek, and thither thou shalt come:
6 And thither ye shall bring your burnt offerings, and your sacrifices, and your tithes, and heave offerings of your hand, and your vows, and your freewill offerings, and the firstlings of your herds and of your flocks:
7 And there ye shall eat before the LORD your God, and ye shall rejoice in all that ye put your hand unto, ye and your households, wherein the LORD thy God hath blessed thee.
8 Ye shall not do after all *the things* that we do here this day, every man whatsoever *is* right in his own eyes.
9 For ye are not as yet come to the rest and to the inheritance, which the LORD your God giveth you.
10 But *when* ye go over Jordan, and dwell in the land which the LORD your God giveth you to inherit, and *when* he giveth you rest from all your enemies round about, so that ye dwell in safety;
11 Then there shall be a place which the LORD

daily existence, fostering multi-generational prosperity.

11:18 *frontlets*. Some sort of headband.

11:26–32 Moses prescribes a ceremony, which is further expounded in chs. 27–28 and which Joshua celebrated in Canaan (Josh. 8:30–35).

11:30 *champaign*. A desert plain.

Thoughts for Personal/Family Worship: Chapter 11

1. **That God gives rain in recognition of Israel's obedience demonstrates His sovereign power and authority. God is the author of both biblical law and natural law. Thus, they harmonize, and obedience to the former will usually be in sync with the latter, producing blessing. Psalm 1 illustrates the principle: attention to God's Word results in divine blessing, here symbolized by the appropriate and timely rain.**
2. **Although possessing Canaan would involve military conflict, Israel's preparation to enter Canaan did not involve basic training in combat, but was rather to focus on spiritual readiness. God would deliver Canaan to Israel, and they were simply to follow Him to victory. He must therefore be the highest priority, demonstrated by obeying His commandments. Israel's strength was in obedience (v. 8). The strength of Christ's church is not in human schemes and methods, but by wholehearted adherence to God's Word.**

Statutes and Judgments (12:1—26:15)

Chapter 12: ***Israel is to destroy places of pagan idolatry and worship God in the place He has chosen and according to His instructions.***

God's Sanctuary (12:1–32)

12:3 *groves*. The wooden poles erected in worship of Asherah, a Canaanite goddess. *hew*. Chop.

12:5 *the place*. Thirteen times Deuteronomy states that God will reveal one place for sacrifice. These instructions are referred to as the laws of the central sanctuary, fulfilled by the tabernacle/temple (Gen. 22:2–3,9,14; 2 Sam. 24:10–25; 1 Chron. 21:18, 22:1; 2 Chron. 3:1–2). *habitation*. Dwelling place.

12:7 *eat before the LORD*. Sacrifices eaten at the tabernacle/temple signified the spiritual partaking of Christ's sacrifice by those for whom it was offered (John 6:32–25,53–58). Family, servants, and *Levite*[s] partook with joy (vv. 7,12,18).

12:8 See Judg. 21:25.

your God shall choose to cause his name to dwell
there; thither shall ye bring all that I command
you; your burnt offerings, and your sacrifices,
your tithes, and the heave offering of your hand,
and all your choice vows which ye vow unto the
LORD:
12 And ye shall rejoice before the LORD your God,
ye, and your sons, and your daughters, and your
menservants, and your maidservants, and the
Levite that *is* within your gates; forasmuch as he
hath no part nor inheritance with you.
13 Take heed to thyself that thou offer not thy
burnt offerings in every place that thou seest:
14 But in the place which the LORD shall choose
in one of thy tribes, there thou shalt offer thy
burnt offerings, and there thou shalt do all that I
command thee.
15 Notwithstanding thou mayest kill and eat
flesh in all thy gates, whatsoever thy soul lusteth
after, according to the blessing of the LORD thy
God which he hath given thee: the unclean and
the clean may eat thereof, as of the roebuck, and
as of the hart.
16 Only ye shall not eat the blood; ye shall pour it
upon the earth as water.
17 ¶ Thou mayest not eat within thy gates the
tithe of thy corn, or of thy wine, or of thy oil, or
the firstlings of thy herds or of thy flock, nor any
of thy vows which thou vowest, nor thy freewill
offerings, or heave offering of thine hand:
18 But thou must eat them before the LORD thy
God in the place which the LORD thy God shall
choose, thou, and thy son, and thy daughter, and
thy manservant, and thy maidservant, and the
Levite that *is* within thy gates: and thou shalt re-
joice before the LORD thy God in all that thou
puttest thine hands unto.
19 Take heed to thyself that thou forsake not the
Levite as long as thou livest upon the earth.
20 ¶ When the LORD thy God shall enlarge thy
border, as he hath promised thee, and thou shalt
say, I will eat flesh, because thy soul longeth to eat
flesh; thou mayest eat flesh, whatsoever thy soul
lusteth after.
21 If the place which the LORD thy God hath cho-
sen to put his name there be too far from thee,
then thou shalt kill of thy herd and of thy flock,
which the LORD hath given thee, as I have com-
manded thee, and thou shalt eat in thy gates
whatsoever thy soul lusteth after.
22 Even as the roebuck and the hart is eaten, so
thou shalt eat them: the unclean and the clean
shall eat *of* them alike.
23 Only be sure that thou eat not the blood: for
the blood *is* the life; and thou mayest not eat the
life with the flesh.
24 Thou shalt not eat it; thou shalt pour it upon
the earth as water.
25 Thou shalt not eat it; that it may go well with
thee, and with thy children after thee, when thou
shalt do *that which is* right in the sight of the
LORD.
26 Only thy holy things which thou hast, and thy
vows, thou shalt take, and go unto the place which
the LORD shall choose:
27 And thou shalt offer thy burnt offerings, the
flesh and the blood, upon the altar of the LORD
thy God: and the blood of thy sacrifices shall be
poured out upon the altar of the LORD thy God,
and thou shalt eat the flesh.
28 Observe and hear all these words which I com-
mand thee, that it may go well with thee, and with
thy children after thee for ever, when thou doest
that which is good and right in the sight of the
LORD thy God.
29 ¶ When the LORD thy God shall cut off the
nations from before thee, whither thou goest to
possess them, and thou succeedest them, and
dwellest in their land;
30 Take heed to thyself that thou be not snared by
following them, after that they be destroyed from
before thee; and that thou enquire not after their
gods, saying, How did these nations serve their
gods? even so will I do likewise.
31 Thou shalt not do so unto the LORD thy God:
for every abomination to the LORD, which he
hateth, have they done unto their gods; for even
their sons and their daughters they have burnt in
the fire to their gods.
32 What thing soever I command you, observe
to do it: thou shalt not add thereto, nor dimin-
ish from it.

12:12 *nor inheritance.* Levites belonged to the Lord.
12:15 *lusteth.* Not a negative term, "desires" (v. 21). *roebuck.* Gazelle. *hart.* Deer. Neither were sacrificial animals (v. 22).
12:17 *not eat . . . the tithe.* The tithe was God's, and was to be eaten only at the God-selected place of sacrifice. All other foods could be eaten at home (v. 15). *firstlings.* Firstborn.
12:30 *enquire.* Seek after.
12:32 *diminish.* Take away. See 4:2.

Thoughts for Personal/Family Worship: Chapter 12

1. **Israel was not to ask, "How did these nations serve their gods?" (v. 30). God's people must never pattern their worship after unregenerate men. True worship is done according to the directives of God's law—the Scriptures. Worship is defined and designed by God, not by man (v. 32). When seeking a church in which to worship, many look for one that pleases them. But we should ask, "Does it please God? Does it worship by the Word?"**
2. **Israel was to destroy every place where idolatry was practiced, to leave nothing of ungodly religious activity. So we must "have no fellowship with the unfruitful works of darkness, but rather reprove them" (Eph. 5:11). We must separate ourselves from the idolatry and uncleanness of this world (2 Cor. 6:16–17). What idols does your nation worship? How must you separate yourself from this idolatry?**

CHAPTER 13

IF there arise among you a prophet, or a dreamer
of dreams, and giveth thee a sign or a wonder,
2 And the sign or the wonder come to pass,
whereof he spake unto thee, saying, Let us go after
other gods, which thou hast not known, and let us
serve them;
3 Thou shalt not hearken unto the words of that
prophet, or that dreamer of dreams: for the LORD
your God proveth you, to know whether ye love
the LORD your God with all your heart and with
all your soul.
4 Ye shall walk after the LORD your God, and fear
him, and keep his commandments, and obey his
voice, and ye shall serve him, and cleave unto him.
5 And that prophet, or that dreamer of dreams,
shall be put to death; because he hath spoken to
turn *you* away from the LORD your God, which
brought you out of the land of Egypt, and re-
deemed you out of the house of bondage, to
thrust thee out of the way which the LORD thy
God commanded thee to walk in. So shalt thou
put the evil away from the midst of thee.
6 ¶ If thy brother, the son of thy mother, or thy
son, or thy daughter, or the wife of thy bosom, or
thy friend, which *is* as thine own soul, entice thee
secretly, saying, Let us go and serve other gods,
which thou hast not known, thou, nor thy fathers;
7 *Namely*, of the gods of the people which *are*
round about you, nigh unto thee, or far off from
thee, from the *one* end of the earth even unto the
other end of the earth;
8 Thou shalt not consent unto him, nor hearken
unto him; neither shall thine eye pity him, neither
shalt thou spare, neither shalt thou conceal him:
9 But thou shalt surely kill him; thine hand shall
be first upon him to put him to death, and after-
wards the hand of all the people.
10 And thou shalt stone him with stones, that he
die; because he hath sought to thrust thee away
from the LORD thy God, which brought thee out
of the land of Egypt, from the house of bondage.
11 And all Israel shall hear, and fear, and shall do
no more any such wickedness as this is among
you.
12 ¶ If thou shalt hear *say* in one of thy cities,
which the LORD thy God hath given thee to dwell
there, saying,
13 *Certain* men, the children of Belial, are gone
out from among you, and have withdrawn the
inhabitants of their city, saying, Let us go and
serve other gods, which ye have not known;
14 Then shalt thou enquire, and make search, and
ask diligently; and, behold, *if it be* truth, *and* the
thing certain, *that* such abomination is wrought
among you;
15 Thou shalt surely smite the inhabitants of
that city with the edge of the sword, destroying
it utterly, and all that *is* therein, and the cattle
thereof, with the edge of the sword.
16 And thou shalt gather all the spoil of it into the
midst of the street thereof, and shalt burn with
fire the city, and all the spoil thereof every whit,
for the LORD thy God: and it shall be an heap for
ever; it shall not be built again.
17 And there shall cleave nought of the cursed
thing to thine hand: that the LORD may turn from
the fierceness of his anger, and shew thee mercy,
and have compassion upon thee, and multiply
thee, as he hath sworn unto thy fathers;
18 When thou shalt hearken to the voice of the
LORD thy God, to keep all his commandments

Chapter 13: *God prescribes drastic measures to guard against apostasy from worshiping the one true God.*

Deceivers and Idolaters (13:1–18)

13:1–18 Here are three transgressions: the prophet who speaks falsely, the family member who seduces unto idolatry, and the community that has succumbed to idolatry (Ezek. 13:1–8; Zech. 10:2; Matt. 7:15; Gal. 1:8–9). In each case, the guilty parties are to be put to death, a severe punishment.

13:1–3 Conformity to truth is the criterion for acceptable ministry. False teachers may arise in order to test the allegiance of God's people.

13:3 *hearken.* Listen. *proveth.* Tests or tries. Significantly, the heart is more important than the head in discerning false teaching.

13:5 *thrust.* Drive away by force.

13:6 Enticement to depart from truth may come from our dearest friends.

13:12–15 Truth is known by Scripture. The entire community might be misled (v. 13), but we must not succumb to popular opinion or peer pressure.

13:13 *Belial.* Sons of worthlessness (2 Cor. 6:15).

13:16–17 An apostate community was to be utterly destroyed. God's people must not memorialize anything associated with ungodliness.

13:16 *whit.* The whole of it.

Thoughts for Personal/Family Worship: Chapter 13

1. **Satan will employ our dearest friends to distract us from God: "thy brother . . . or thy son, or thy daughter, or the wife of they bosom, or thy friend, which is as thine own soul" (v. 6). Judas was one of Christ's disciples. Jesus warned, "If any man come to me, and hate not his father, and mother, and wife, and children, and brethren, and sisters, yea, and his own life also, he cannot be my disciple" (Luke 14:26). Nadab and Abihu, Aaron's sons, were destroyed for their godless action, and God forbade Aaron to mourn (Lev. 10:1–6). Allegiance to Christ must supersede all other relationships (Luke 9:59–62). How can you prepare your heart now to follow Christ above all others when temptation comes?**
2. **False teachers do not announce that they are deceivers. Rather, they come with an "improvement" to the gospel message, with a "truth" everyone else has missed. Jesus said, "Beware of false prophets, which come to you in sheep's clothing, but inwardly they are ravening wolves" (Matt. 7:15). Like Paul, Christians must recognize and**

which I command thee this day, to do *that which*
is right in the eyes of the LORD thy God.

CHAPTER 14

YE *are* the children of the LORD your God: ye shall
not cut yourselves, nor make any baldness be-
tween your eyes for the dead.
2 For thou *art* an holy people unto the LORD thy
God, and the LORD hath chosen thee to be a pecu-
liar people unto himself, above all the nations that
are upon the earth.
3 ¶ Thou shalt not eat any abominable thing.
4 These *are* the beasts which ye shall eat: the ox,
the sheep, and the goat,
5 The hart, and the roebuck, and the fallow deer,
and the wild goat, and the pygarg, and the wild
ox, and the chamois.
6 And every beast that parteth the hoof, and
cleaveth the cleft into two claws, *and* cheweth the
cud among the beasts, that ye shall eat.
7 Nevertheless these ye shall not eat of them that
chew the cud, or of them that divide the cloven
hoof; *as* the camel, and the hare, and the coney:
for they chew the cud, but divide not the hoof;
therefore they *are* unclean unto you.
8 And the swine, because it divideth the hoof, yet
cheweth not the cud, it *is* unclean unto you: ye shall
not eat of their flesh, nor touch their dead carcase.
9 ¶ These ye shall eat of all that *are* in the waters:
all that have fins and scales shall ye eat:
10 And whatsoever hath not fins and scales ye
may not eat; it *is* unclean unto you.
11 ¶ *Of* all clean birds ye shall eat.
12 But these *are they* of which ye shall not eat: the
eagle, and the ossifrage, and the ospray,
13 And the glede, and the kite, and the vulture
after his kind,
14 And every raven after his kind,
15 And the owl, and the night hawk, and the
cuckow, and the hawk after his kind,
16 The little owl, and the great owl, and the swan,
17 And the pelican, and the gier eagle, and the
cormorant,
18 And the stork, and the heron after her kind,
and the lapwing, and the bat.
19 And every creeping thing that flieth *is* unclean
unto you: they shall not be eaten.
20 *But of* all clean fowls ye may eat.
21 ¶ Ye shall not eat *of* any thing that dieth of
itself: thou shalt give it unto the stranger that *is*
in thy gates, that he may eat it; or thou mayest sell
it unto an alien: for thou *art* an holy people unto
the LORD thy God. Thou shalt not seethe a kid in
his mother's milk.
22 Thou shalt truly tithe all the increase of thy
seed, that the field bringeth forth year by year.
23 And thou shalt eat before the LORD thy God, in
the place which he shall choose to place his name
there, the tithe of thy corn, of thy wine, and of
thine oil, and the firstlings of thy herds and of thy
flocks; that thou mayest learn to fear the LORD thy
God always.
24 And if the way be too long for thee, so that
thou art not able to carry it; *or* if the place be
too far from thee, which the LORD thy God shall
choose to set his name there, when the LORD thy
God hath blessed thee:
25 Then shalt thou turn *it* into money, and bind
up the money in thine hand, and shalt go unto the
place which the LORD thy God shall choose:
26 And thou shalt bestow that money for whatso-
ever thy soul lusteth after, for oxen, or for sheep,
or for wine, or for strong drink, or for whatsoever
thy soul desireth: and thou shalt eat there before
the LORD thy God, and thou shalt rejoice, thou,
and thine household,
27 And the Levite that *is* within thy gates; thou
shalt not forsake him; for he hath no part nor
inheritance with thee.

---

reject false teachers, for they are under the curse of God (Gal. 1:8; 2:1–5).

Chapter 14: *God's people must be distinctive in their customs, their diet, and their tithe.*

Customs: Mourning, Diet, and Levite's Care (14:1–29)

14:1 *not cut yourselves.* Laceration was part of pagan worship (1 Kings 18:25–28). *make any baldness.* Probably a pagan mourning ritual (Lev. 19:27–28).

14:2 *peculiar people.* The Hebrew refers to "a prized possession, a treasure" (translated "jewels" in Mal. 3:17). Everything belongs to the Lord, but His people are special to Him.

14:3–22 Israel's dietary code made God's people distinctive, separate unto Him. Some suggest that unclean animals posed health risks, others that they were associated with pagan worship and thus an *abominable thing* (v. 4; 7:25; 12:31). The modern inability to identify all the specific creatures is irrelevant to the spiritual truth that God has a right to restrict His people's behavior. A holy people are a different people.

14:5 *pygarg.* Antelope (1 Sam. 24:2). *chamois.* Mountain sheep.

14:6 *parteth the hoof.* Split hooves.

14:7 *hare.* Rabbit. *coney.* Rock badger.

14:12–20 Twenty birds, one flying mammal, and flying insects were unclean. Identity of these is not always clear.

14:12 *ossifrage.* Vulture. *ospray.* A bird of prey.

14:15 *cuckow.* Seagull.

14:18 *lapwing.* Hoopoe.

14:21 *dieth of itself.* Likely because death from natural causes would not bleed the animal (12:16,23–25,27). *seethe a kid.* Boil a young one; a Canaanite ritual.

14:22 *tithe.* One tenth. These verses speak of the harvest tithe brought to the place God chose for worship (12:5–6).

14:24–26 God makes concession for those who live far away. See the perversion in Christ's time (Matt. 21:12–13; John 2:13–17).

14:26 *bestow.* Give.

28 ¶ At the end of three years thou shalt bring
forth all the tithe of thine increase the same year,
and shalt lay *it* up within thy gates:
29 And the Levite, (because he hath no part nor
inheritance with thee,) and the stranger, and the
fatherless, and the widow, which *are* within thy
gates, shall come, and shall eat and be satisfied;
that the LORD thy God may bless thee in all the
work of thine hand which thou doest.

CHAPTER 15

AT the end of *every* seven years thou shalt make
a release.
2 And this *is* the manner of the release: Every
creditor that lendeth *ought* unto his neighbour
shall release *it*; he shall not exact *it* of his neigh-
bour, or of his brother; because it is called the
LORD's release.
3 Of a foreigner thou mayest exact *it again*: but
that which is thine with thy brother thine hand
shall release;
4 Save when there shall be no poor among you;
for the LORD shall greatly bless thee in the land
which the LORD thy God giveth thee *for* an inheri-
tance to possess it:
5 Only if thou carefully hearken unto the voice
of the LORD thy God, to observe to do all these
commandments which I command thee this day.
6 For the LORD thy God blesseth thee, as he
promised thee: and thou shalt lend unto many
nations, but thou shalt not borrow; and thou
shalt reign over many nations, but they shall not
reign over thee.
7 ¶ If there be among you a poor man of one of
thy brethren within any of thy gates in thy land
which the LORD thy God giveth thee, thou shalt
not harden thine heart, nor shut thine hand from
thy poor brother:
8 But thou shalt open thine hand wide unto him,
and shalt surely lend him sufficient for his need,
in that which he wanteth.
9 Beware that there be not a thought in thy wicked
heart, saying, The seventh year, the year of release,
is at hand; and thine eye be evil against thy poor
brother, and thou givest him nought; and he cry
unto the LORD against thee, and it be sin unto thee.
10 Thou shalt surely give him, and thine heart
shall not be grieved when thou givest unto him:
because that for this thing the LORD thy God shall
bless thee in all thy works, and in all that thou
puttest thine hand unto.
11 For the poor shall never cease out of the land:
therefore I command thee, saying, Thou shalt
open thine hand wide unto thy brother, to thy
poor, and to thy needy, in thy land.
12 ¶ *And* if thy brother, an Hebrew man, or an
Hebrew woman, be sold unto thee, and serve thee
six years; then in the seventh year thou shalt let
him go free from thee.
13 And when thou sendest him out free from
thee, thou shalt not let him go away empty:
14 Thou shalt furnish him liberally out of thy
flock, and out of thy floor, and out of thy wine-
press: *of that* wherewith the LORD thy God hath
blessed thee thou shalt give unto him.
15 And thou shalt remember that thou wast a
bondman in the land of Egypt, and the LORD thy
God redeemed thee: therefore I command thee
this thing to day.

14:28–29 Every third year the tithe was given locally for needs within the community: Levites, widows, orphans, and aliens who had no land for agriculture production. God shows special care for the needy (Lev. 19:9–10; 23:22; Deut. 24:21).

Thoughts for Personal/Family Worship: Chapter 14

1. **God's people must be separated unto Him. This was prescribed in Israel's customs of mourning (v. 1), their diet (vv. 2–21), and their tithes (vv. 22–29). We are not to be poured into the world's mold: "be not conformed to this world: but be ye transformed by the renewing of your mind" (Rom. 12:2). We are not to love this world system or its traditions and fads, which consist of "the lust of the flesh, and the lust of the eyes, and the pride of life" (1 John 2:16). As Israel was a holy people unto the Lord, chosen to be a peculiar people (Deut. 14:2), God's people in every age are "an holy nation, a peculiar people; that ye should shew forth the praises of him who hath called you out of darkness into his marvelous light" (1 Peter 2:9). Christians must be different, as pilgrims in this world.**
2. **God's goodness is evident in His care for the needy (Matt. 6:25–34). He designated that every third year the tithe be used for widows, orphans, and aliens who had no land on which to cultivate food (Deut. 14:28–29). He instructed that grain in the corners of fields be left for the needy to glean (Lev. 19:9–10; 23:22). Believers should honor this principle. They must "remember the poor" (Gal. 2:10), and "visit the fatherless and widows in their affliction" (James 1:27). Whereas this is not the gospel, it is an important part of Christian living. How are you caring for the poor and needy?**

Chapter 15: *Moses gives instructions regarding the year of release.*

Sabbath Release (15:1–23)

15:1–23 In this God-ordered economy every seventh year required indebtedness to be forgiven, indentured servants to be released (vv. 1–15), and land to be given rest (Lev. 25:1–7). This is not man's way to prosper. It teaches that prosperity is a divine gift, not ambition's reward (vv. 4–6,10–18).

15:1 *release.* A remitting of obligations.

15:2–3 *exact.* Demand precise payment.

15:5 *hearken.* Listen.

15:9 *nought.* Nothing.

15:14 *furnish . . . liberally.* Give freely.

15:15 Amid prosperity, Israel must remember its former state, and live compassionately.

16 And it shall be, if he say unto thee, I will not go
away from thee; because he loveth thee and thine
house, because he is well with thee;
17 Then thou shalt take an aul, and thrust *it*
through his ear unto the door, and he shall be thy
servant for ever. And also unto thy maidservant
thou shalt do likewise.
18 It shall not seem hard unto thee, when thou
sendest him away free from thee; for he hath been
worth a double hired servant *to thee*, in serving
thee six years: and the LORD thy God shall bless
thee in all that thou doest.
19 ¶ All the firstling males that come of thy herd
and of thy flock thou shalt sanctify unto the LORD
thy God: thou shalt do no work with the firstling
of thy bullock, nor shear the firstling of thy sheep.
20 Thou shalt eat *it* before the LORD thy God year
by year in the place which the LORD shall choose,
thou and thy household.
21 And if there be *any* blemish therein, *as if it be*
lame, or blind, *or have* any ill blemish, thou shalt
not sacrifice it unto the LORD thy God.
22 Thou shalt eat it within thy gates: the unclean
and the clean *person shall eat it* alike, as the roe-
buck, and as the hart.
23 Only thou shalt not eat the blood thereof;
thou shalt pour it upon the ground as water.

CHAPTER 16

OBSERVE the month of Abib, and keep the pass-
over unto the LORD thy God: for in the month of
Abib the LORD thy God brought thee forth out of
Egypt by night.
2 Thou shalt therefore sacrifice the passover unto
the LORD thy God, of the flock and the herd, in
the place which the LORD shall choose to place his
name there.
3 Thou shalt eat no leavened bread with it; seven
days shalt thou eat unleavened bread therewith,
even the bread of affliction; for thou camest forth
out of the land of Egypt in haste: that thou mayest
remember the day when thou camest forth out of
the land of Egypt all the days of thy life.
4 And there shall be no leavened bread seen with
thee in all thy coast seven days; neither shall there
any thing of the flesh, which thou sacrificedst
the first day at even, remain all night until the
morning.
5 Thou mayest not sacrifice the passover within
any of thy gates, which the LORD thy God giveth
thee:
6 But at the place which the LORD thy God shall
choose to place his name in, there thou shalt
sacrifice the passover at even, at the going down
of the sun, at the season that thou camest forth
out of Egypt.
7 And thou shalt roast and eat *it* in the place
which the LORD thy God shall choose: and thou
shalt turn in the morning, and go unto thy tents.
8 Six days thou shalt eat unleavened bread: and
on the seventh day *shall be* a solemn assembly to
the LORD thy God: thou shalt do no work *therein*.
9 ¶ Seven weeks shalt thou number unto thee:
begin to number the seven weeks from *such time*
as thou beginnest *to put* the sickle to the corn.
10 And thou shalt keep the feast of weeks unto
the LORD thy God with a tribute of a freewill

15:16–18 *aul.* An awl or a pointed tool. Pierced, the slave was marked for life (Ex. 21:6). This love bond of servant for master foreshadowed the submission of Christ to God (Ps. 40:6; Isa. 50:5). Christ's servants desire His mark upon their lives (Gal. 6:17).
15:19 *firstling.* Firstborn. *bullock.* Ox. *shear.* To cut or trim the hair.
15:20 See note at 12:7.
15:22 *roebuck.* Gazelle.

Thoughts for Personal/Family Worship: Chapter 15

1. **Christ came "not to be ministered unto, but to minister, and to give his life a ransom for many" (Matt. 20:28). This spirit should thrive within God's people. The law required creditors to forgive debtors (Deut. 15:1–2), avoid greed (vv. 7–11), show compassion toward the poor, release bond slaves, and supply them with life's necessities (vv. 12–14). From their herds and flocks they gave their first and best unto God. All of these requirements were fulfilled to the fullest by Christ. Therefore, strive to be conformed to the image of God's Son (Rom. 8:29).**
2. **When servants were released, the master shared his bounty with them: "wherewith the LORD thy God hath blessed thee thou shalt give unto him" (v. 14). This demonstrated that possessions come from God, that "the earth is the LORD's, and the fulness thereof" (Ps. 24:1), and that man is but a steward of God's possessions. We are to treat everything within our sphere of influence as the Lord's, not our own. How will this change the way we use our money and possessions?**

Chapter 16: *Moses prescribes the solemn feasts, provides for just judgments, and prohibits idolatry.*

Religious Feasts (16:1–22)

16:1–8 Passover was the fourteenth day of *Abib* (March/April), the date of the exodus (Ex. 12; Lev. 23:5–8; Num. 28:16–25) and of Christ's death (Matt. 26:17). It foreshadowed Christ's sacrifice for His people (1 Cor. 5:7).
16:2 Both feast and lamb are called the *passover*.
16:3 *leavened bread.* Bread containing yeast. *in haste.* Quickly. The events of the exodus did not allow time for the normal preparation of bread.
16:4 *coast.* Border.
16:6 *at the place.* God set both the location and the time for observing the feast. This became one of the pilgrimage feasts requiring journey to the central sanctuary (v. 16). *even.* Evening. *season.* Appointed time.
16:8 *thou shalt do no work.* The Passover had Sabbath status.
16:9–12 *seven weeks.* Fifty days after Passover, the Feast of Weeks celebrated the God-given harvest (Ex. 23:16; Num. 28:26). Later called "Pentecost," meaning "fifty," it foreshadowed

offering of thine hand, which thou shalt give *unto*
the LORD *thy God*, according as the LORD thy God
hath blessed thee:
11 And thou shalt rejoice before the LORD thy
God, thou, and thy son, and thy daughter, and thy
manservant, and thy maidservant, and the Levite
that *is* within thy gates, and the stranger, and the
fatherless, and the widow, that *are* among you, in
the place which the LORD thy God hath chosen to
place his name there.
12 And thou shalt remember that thou wast a
bondman in Egypt: and thou shalt observe and
do these statutes.
13 ¶ Thou shalt observe the feast of tabernacles
seven days, after that thou hast gathered in thy
corn and thy wine:
14 And thou shalt rejoice in thy feast, thou, and
thy son, and thy daughter, and thy manservant,
and thy maidservant, and the Levite, the stranger,
and the fatherless, and the widow, that *are* within
thy gates.
15 Seven days shalt thou keep a solemn feast unto
the LORD thy God in the place which the LORD
shall choose: because the LORD thy God shall bless
thee in all thine increase, and in all the works of
thine hands, therefore thou shalt surely rejoice.
16 ¶ Three times in a year shall all thy males
appear before the LORD thy God in the place
which he shall choose; in the feast of unleavened
bread, and in the feast of weeks, and in the feast of
tabernacles: and they shall not appear before the
LORD empty:
17 Every man *shall give* as he is able, according to
the blessing of the LORD thy God which he hath
given thee.
18 ¶ Judges and officers shalt thou make thee in
all thy gates, which the LORD thy God giveth thee,
throughout thy tribes: and they shall judge the
people with just judgment.
19 Thou shalt not wrest judgment; thou shalt not
respect persons, neither take a gift: for a gift doth
blind the eyes of the wise, and pervert the words
of the righteous.
20 That which is altogether just shalt thou follow,
that thou mayest live, and inherit the land which
the LORD thy God giveth thee.
21 ¶ Thou shalt not plant thee a grove of any trees
near unto the altar of the LORD thy God, which
thou shalt make thee.
22 Neither shalt thou set thee up *any* image;
which the LORD thy God hateth.

CHAPTER 17

THOU shalt not sacrifice unto the LORD thy God
any bullock, or sheep, wherein is blemish, *or* any
evilfavouredness: for that *is* an abomination unto
the LORD thy God.
2 ¶ If there be found among you, within any of
thy gates which the LORD thy God giveth thee,
man or woman, that hath wrought wickedness in
the sight of the LORD thy God, in transgressing
his covenant,
3 And hath gone and served other gods, and wor-
shipped them, either the sun, or moon, or any of
the host of heaven, which I have not commanded;
4 And it be told thee, and thou hast heard *of it*,
and enquired diligently, and, behold, *it be* true,
and the thing certain, *that* such abomination is
wrought in Israel:
5 Then shalt thou bring forth that man or that
woman, which have committed that wicked thing,
unto thy gates, *even* that man or that woman, and
shalt stone them with stones, till they die.

the coming of the Holy Spirit (Acts 2).

16:12 *wast.* Was.

16:13–15 Feast of Tabernacles, or booths, marked the end of harvest (Ex. 23:16; 34:22). People lived in temporary huts for seven days, commemorating their homeless days in the wilderness (Lev. 23:42–43), during which they daily depended on God for all their sustenance.

16:15 *increase.* Harvest.

16:18–20 God establishes justice and requires undistracted, exclusive worship. Bribes pervert judges and *wrest judgment* (i.e., distort justice).

16:21–22 Idolatry perverts truth and violates the first commandment. Moses directly prohibited the erecting of any kind of wooden pole (*grove*) alongside an altar to God. God demands exclusive worship and prohibits mixing worldly religious practices with true worship. The *grove* or wooden pole was a central piece in Canaanite rituals.

Thoughts for Personal/Family Worship: Chapter 16

1. **God instructed men of Israel to assemble three times annually for feasts: Passover, Weeks, and Tabernacles (v. 16; Ex. 34:23–24). One reason for this was to maintain national and spiritual unity among Israel. It is important for God's people to assemble, and He commands this. Attendance at public worship should be a priority with every believer, just as it is with God. How is our public worship like a feast?**
2. **God also established the feasts to memorialize His works for Israel. God desires that we remember His works. "Bless the LORD, O my soul, and forget not all his benefits" (Ps. 103:2). "I meditate on all thy works" (Ps. 143:5). Remembering God's works reminded Israel to remember His law (Deut. 8:11). God would have us remember His great work when Christ fulfilled the law through His sacrifice at Calvary. God has given us two (and only two) visible means of remembering Christ's work: baptism and the Lord's Supper.**

Sacrifices, Idolaters, Adjudication, and Kings (17:1–20)

Chapter 17: ***Moses gives instructions regarding the execution of justice and the duties of future kings.***

17:1 *evilfavouredness.* Literally, "any bad thing." In this case, an animal with a defect.

17:2–3 God hates idolatry, shown in His demand to stone idolaters (v. 5), thus eliminating idolatrous influence.

6 At the mouth of two witnesses, or three wit-
nesses, shall he that is worthy of death be put to
death; *but* at the mouth of one witness he shall
not be put to death.
7 The hands of the witnesses shall be first upon
him to put him to death, and afterward the hands
of all the people. So thou shalt put the evil away
from among you.
8 ¶ If there arise a matter too hard for thee in
judgment, between blood and blood, between
plea and plea, and between stroke and stroke,
being matters of controversy within thy gates:
then shalt thou arise, and get thee up into the
place which the LORD thy God shall choose;
9 And thou shalt come unto the priests the Le-
vites, and unto the judge that shall be in those
days, and enquire; and they shall shew thee the
sentence of judgment:
10 And thou shalt do according to the sentence,
which they of that place which the LORD shall
choose shall shew thee; and thou shalt observe to
do according to all that they inform thee:
11 According to the sentence of the law which
they shall teach thee, and according to the judg-
ment which they shall tell thee, thou shalt do:
thou shalt not decline from the sentence which
they shall shew thee, *to* the right hand, nor *to* the
left.
12 And the man that will do presumptuously, and
will not hearken unto the priest that standeth to
minister there before the LORD thy God, or unto
the judge, even that man shall die: and thou shalt
put away the evil from Israel.
13 And all the people shall hear, and fear, and do
no more presumptuously.
14 ¶ When thou art come unto the land which the
LORD thy God giveth thee, and shalt possess it, and
shalt dwell therein, and shalt say, I will set a king
over me, like as all the nations that *are* about me;
15 Thou shalt in any wise set *him* king over thee,
whom the LORD thy God shall choose: *one* from
among thy brethren shalt thou set king over thee:
thou mayest not set a stranger over thee, which *is*
not thy brother.
16 But he shall not multiply horses to himself,
nor cause the people to return to Egypt, to the
end that he should multiply horses: forasmuch as
the LORD hath said unto you, Ye shall henceforth
return no more that way.
17 Neither shall he multiply wives to himself, that
his heart turn not away: neither shall he greatly
multiply to himself silver and gold.
18 And it shall be, when he sitteth upon the
throne of his kingdom, that he shall write him
a copy of this law in a book out of *that which is*
before the priests the Levites:
19 And it shall be with him, and he shall read
therein all the days of his life: that he may learn to
fear the LORD his God, to keep all the words of this
law and these statutes, to do them:
20 That his heart be not lifted up above his breth-
ren, and that he turn not aside from the com-
mandment, *to* the right hand, or *to* the left: to the
end that he may prolong *his* days in his kingdom,
he, and his children, in the midst of Israel.

CHAPTER 18

THE priests the Levites, *and* all the tribe of Levi,
shall have no part nor inheritance with Israel:

17:6–7 God guarded against false accusation by requiring two or more eyewitnesses (19:15–20; Matt. 18:16; 2 Cor. 13:1; 1 Tim. 5:19). Accusers' integrity was checked by requiring them to initiate capital penalty (John 8:7). If later evidence vindicated the one they stoned, they would be judged. *The hands of all the people* implied that the idolater sinned against countrymen also, inasmuch as idolatry brought national judgment.
17:6 *At the mouth.* By the testimony.
17:8–9 Complex cases required the sophisticated discernment of priests. *blood and blood.* Cases involving bloodshed. *plea and plea.* An offense or legal claim. *stroke and stroke.* An assault or an accidental injury (19:4–6). Judgment at *the place which the LORD thy God shall choose,* administered by priests and Levites, signified that God is the source of justice.
17:10–13 Refusal of priestly judgment was rejection of divine rule, punishable by death.
17:11 *decline from the sentence.* To turn aside from by refusing to carry out the punishment.
17:12 *presumptuously.* To act proudly.
17:14–20 A monarchy was not opposed to God's will; indeed, it was central to God's redemptive purpose and promise (Gen. 49:10).
17:15 *any wise.* Literally, "you will certainly set over you." *brother.* A fellow Israelite.
17:16 *multiply horses.* Perhaps referring to building up the military, which would foster self-confidence rather than divine dependence.
17:17 *that his heart not turn away.* Precisely what happened with Solomon (1 Kings 11:1–4).
17:20 *lifted up.* Prided himself above others.

Thoughts for Personal/Family Worship: Chapter 17

1. **God's instruction to kings pertained to personal discipline and obeying God's law, not to skill in governing. "When the righteous are in authority, the people rejoice: but when the wicked beareth rule, the people mourn" (Prov. 29:2; cf. 2 Sam. 23:3). The ideal of a perfectly righteous king points to King Jesus, who alone fulfilled all the requirements of God's expectation. What does Deut. 17:16–20 teach us about the kingdom of Christ?**
2. **Two or more accusers were necessary to convict a man of a crime. This protected the innocent who might be accused and also restrained the schemer who might bear false witness out of jealousy or hatred. It also shows the high value God places upon truth. He is truth. God and truth are inseparable, thus truth will always stand.**

Chapter 18: ***Moses explains the rights of the Levites, exhorts against false worship, and expounds the function***

they shall eat the offerings of the LORD made by
fire, and his inheritance.
2 Therefore shall they have no inheritance among
their brethren: the LORD *is* their inheritance, as he
hath said unto them.
3 ¶ And this shall be the priest's due from the
people, from them that offer a sacrifice, whether *it*
be ox or sheep; and they shall give unto the priest
the shoulder, and the two cheeks, and the maw.
4 The firstfruit *also* of thy corn, of thy wine, and
of thine oil, and the first of the fleece of thy sheep,
shalt thou give him.
5 For the LORD thy God hath chosen him out of
all thy tribes, to stand to minister in the name of
the LORD, him and his sons for ever.
6 ¶ And if a Levite come from any of thy gates out
of all Israel, where he sojourned, and come with
all the desire of his mind unto the place which the
LORD shall choose;
7 Then he shall minister in the name of the LORD
his God, as all his brethren the Levites *do*, which
stand there before the LORD.
8 They shall have like portions to eat, beside that
which cometh of the sale of his patrimony.
9 ¶ When thou art come into the land which the
LORD thy God giveth thee, thou shalt not learn to
do after the abominations of those nations.
10 There shall not be found among you *any*
one that maketh his son or his daughter to pass
through the fire, *or* that useth divination, *or* an
observer of times, or an enchanter, or a witch,
11 Or a charmer, or a consulter with familiar
spirits, or a wizard, or a necromancer.
12 For all that do these things *are* an abomination
unto the LORD: and because of these abominations
the LORD thy God doth drive them out from
before thee.
13 Thou shalt be perfect with the LORD thy God.
14 For these nations, which thou shalt possess,
hearkened unto observers of times, and unto di-
viners: but as for thee, the LORD thy God hath not
suffered thee so *to do*.
15 ¶ The LORD thy God will raise up unto thee a
Prophet from the midst of thee, of thy brethren,
like unto me; unto him ye shall hearken;
16 According to all that thou desiredst of the
LORD thy God in Horeb in the day of the assem-
bly, saying, Let me not hear again the voice of the
LORD my God, neither let me see this great fire
any more, that I die not.
17 And the LORD said unto me, They have well
spoken that which they have spoken.
18 I will raise them up a Prophet from among
their brethren, like unto thee, and will put my
words in his mouth; and he shall speak unto them
all that I shall command him.
19 And it shall come to pass, *that* whosoever will
not hearken unto my words which he shall speak
in my name, I will require *it* of him.
20 But the prophet, which shall presume to speak
a word in my name, which I have not commanded
him to speak, or that shall speak in the name of
other gods, even that prophet shall die.
21 And if thou say in thine heart, How shall we
know the word which the LORD hath not spoken?
22 When a prophet speaketh in the name of the

of the prophetic office, pointing to the ideal Prophet.

Care of Priests, Idolaters, the Great Prophet (18:1–22)

18:1–8 Levites had no land (10:9; Num. 18:20; 26:62), and thus no livelihood except the offerings of the people. They shared also in the joys of the people (12:12,18; 16:11,14; 26:11), who were to give them the same care as widows and orphans (14:29; 26:12–13), making them dependent upon God through His people. Without inheritance, they were scattered throughout the tribes in forty-two cities (Num. 35:1–6; fulfilling the patriarchal declaration of Gen. 49:7) and thus representative of God among His people.
18:3 *maw.* Stomach.
18:8 *patrimony.* Inheritance.
18:9–14 Idolatry, human sacrifice, and forms of witchcraft are named together as abominations for which nations were driven from the land God gave to Israel.
18:10 *pass through the fire.* Child sacrifice. *divination.* Using magic. *observer of times.* One who tells the future.
18:11 *charmer.* Spell caster. *familiar spirits . . . necromancer.* One who uses rituals attempting to contact the dead.
18:13 *perfect.* Upright, sincere, having integrity.
18:14 *suffered.* Permitted.
18:15 *Prophet.* Ultimately, a reference to Christ (John 6:14; Acts 3:22–23). God promised Israel a revelation of Himself. The Prophet is God's representative to man, fulfilled completely in Christ (Heb. 1:3).
18:18 The Prophet's authority consisted in his declaring what God had declared to him. The Prophet was the messenger of the Lord (Hag. 1:13).
18:19 *require it of him.* Avenge or demand; hold him accountable.
18:22 The fulfillment of predictions, as well as conformity to revealed truth (13:1–3), were the two principal tests of the true prophet. Significantly, Christ Himself was subject to these tests. His own resurrection was the confirming prediction (John 2:19–22), and He defined His words as being in accordance with the Father's (John 8:14–18).

Thoughts for Personal/Family Worship: Chapter 18

1. **False prophets "presume to speak a word in my name" (v. 20). Christ warned that there will be many of these (Matt. 7:22–23). The test of their legitimacy is whether they do "the will of my Father which is in heaven" (Matt. 7:21). The will of God is revealed in Scripture; thus, teachers must be measured by its truth. It is imperative that we know what God says in His Word in order to guard against the false teaching that is more and more rampant as time progresses (1 Tim. 4:1; 1 John 4:1–2).**
2. **Priests and Levites were sustained by the offerings brought to God. This should have been a guard against greed, of which ministers are warned (1 Tim. 6:6–11). However, the Old Testament records violations of the principle (1 Sam. 2:12–17). Although the mechanics of application are different today, this remains the pattern**

LORD, if the thing follow not, nor come to pass,
that *is* the thing which the LORD hath not spoken,
but the prophet hath spoken it presumptuously:
thou shalt not be afraid of him.

CHAPTER 19

WHEN the LORD thy God hath cut off the nations,
whose land the LORD thy God giveth thee, and
thou succeedest them, and dwellest in their cities,
and in their houses;
2 Thou shalt separate three cities for thee in the
midst of thy land, which the LORD thy God giveth
thee to possess it.
3 Thou shalt prepare thee a way, and divide the
coasts of thy land, which the LORD thy God giveth
thee to inherit, into three parts, that every slayer
may flee thither.
4 ¶ And this *is* the case of the slayer, which shall
flee thither, that he may live: Whoso killeth his
neighbour ignorantly, whom he hated not in time
past;
5 As when a man goeth into the wood with his
neighbour to hew wood, and his hand fetcheth a
stroke with the axe to cut down the tree, and the
head slippeth from the helve, and lighteth upon
his neighbour, that he die; he shall flee unto one
of those cities, and live:
6 Lest the avenger of the blood pursue the slayer,
while his heart is hot, and overtake him, because
the way is long, and slay him; whereas he *was* not
worthy of death, inasmuch as he hated him not
in time past.
7 Wherefore I command thee, saying, Thou shalt
separate three cities for thee.
8 And if the LORD thy God enlarge thy coast, as he
hath sworn unto thy fathers, and give thee all the
land which he promised to give unto thy fathers;
9 If thou shalt keep all these commandments to
do them, which I command thee this day, to love
the LORD thy God, and to walk ever in his ways;
then shalt thou add three cities more for thee,
beside these three:
10 That innocent blood be not shed in thy land,
which the LORD thy God giveth thee *for* an inheri-
tance, and *so* blood be upon thee.
11 ¶ But if any man hate his neighbour, and lie in
wait for him, and rise up against him, and smite
him mortally that he die, and fleeth into one of
these cities:
12 Then the elders of his city shall send and fetch
him thence, and deliver him into the hand of the
avenger of blood, that he may die.
13 Thine eye shall not pity him, but thou shalt
put away *the guilt of* innocent blood from Israel,
that it may go well with thee.
14 ¶ Thou shalt not remove thy neighbour's
landmark, which they of old time have set in thine
inheritance, which thou shalt inherit in the land
that the LORD thy God giveth thee to possess it.
15 ¶ One witness shall not rise up against a man
for any iniquity, or for any sin, in any sin that
he sinneth: at the mouth of two witnesses, or at
the mouth of three witnesses, shall the matter be
established.
16 ¶ If a false witness rise up against any man to
testify against him *that which is* wrong;
17 Then both the men, between whom the con-
troversy *is*, shall stand before the LORD, before
the priests and the judges, which shall be in those
days;
18 And the judges shall make diligent inquisition:
and, behold, *if* the witness *be* a false witness, *and*
hath testified falsely against his brother;
19 Then shall ye do unto him, as he had thought
to have done unto his brother: so shalt thou put
the evil away from among you.
20 And those which remain shall hear, and fear,
and shall henceforth commit no more any such
evil among you.

---

of sustaining ministers (Matt. 10:9–10; Gal. 6:6; 1 Thess. 5:13; 1 Tim. 5:17–18). Will the Lord commend your church on judgment day for how it paid its pastor? Why or why not?

Chapter 19: *The Lord's concern for justice provides protection for the innocent and assures punishment for the guilty.*

Cities of Refuge, False Witnesses (19:1–21)

19:1–13 Six cities, three on each side of the Jordan River, were cities of refuge (4:41–49; Ex. 21:13; Num. 35; Josh. 20). The cities of refuge typify Christ. All who come to Him find refuge from the curse and judgment against sinners (Rom. 8:1,28–39; Heb. 6:16–20).

19:1 *succeedest.* Inherits.

19:3 *coasts.* Borders or territories (v. 8).

19:4 *ignorantly.* Literally, "without knowledge," referring to killing by accident or without premeditation.

19:5 *fetcheth.* Goes to make a cut. *head slippeth from the helve.* Axehead slips off. A clear illustration of accidental and unintentional killing.

19:6 *the avenger.* The near kinsman or kinsman-redeemer. *heart is hot.* Is angry.

19:12 Cities of refuge were not meant to circumvent justice. The real crime was in the heart, not in the act (Matt. 5:22).

19:13 *pity.* Feel remorse for. *from Israel.* Individual sins brought national guilt.

19:14 *landmark.* Property marker. Removal of a *neighbour's landmark* transgressed the One who established personal ownership and divided the land (27:17; Job 24:2; Prov. 22:28). This may refer to rich landowners pressuring the poor to sell their land (Prov. 23:10–11). Consider Ahab and Naboth (1 Kings 21).

19:15–21 Perjury is condemned (Ex. 20:16; see note at Deut. 17:6–7).

19:18 *make diligent inquisition.* Search out carefully.

19:20 The execution of justice serves in part to be a deterrent.

21 And thine eye shall not pity; *but* life *shall go* for
life, eye for eye, tooth for tooth, hand for hand,
foot for foot.

CHAPTER 20

WHEN thou goest out to battle against thine
enemies, and seest horses, and chariots, *and* a
people more than thou, be not afraid of them:
for the LORD thy God *is* with thee, which brought
thee up out of the land of Egypt.
2 And it shall be, when ye are come nigh unto the
battle, that the priest shall approach and speak
unto the people,
3 And shall say unto them, Hear, O Israel, ye ap-
proach this day unto battle against your enemies:
let not your hearts faint, fear not, and do not
tremble, neither be ye terrified because of them;
4 For the LORD your God *is* he that goeth with
you, to fight for you against your enemies, to save
you.
5 ¶ And the officers shall speak unto the people,
saying, What man *is there* that hath built a new
house, and hath not dedicated it? let him go and
return to his house, lest he die in the battle, and
another man dedicate it.
6 And what man *is he* that hath planted a vine-
yard, and hath not *yet* eaten of it? let him *also* go
and return unto his house, lest he die in the battle,
and another man eat of it.
7 And what man *is there* that hath betrothed
a wife, and hath not taken her? let him go and
return unto his house, lest he die in the battle, and
another man take her.
8 And the officers shall speak further unto the
people, and they shall say, What man *is there that
is* fearful and fainthearted? let him go and return
unto his house, lest his brethren's heart faint as
well as his heart.
9 And it shall be, when the officers have made an
end of speaking unto the people, that they shall
make captains of the armies to lead the people.
10 ¶ When thou comest nigh unto a city to fight
against it, then proclaim peace unto it.
11 And it shall be, if it make thee answer of peace,
and open unto thee, then it shall be, *that* all the
people *that is* found therein shall be tributaries
unto thee, and they shall serve thee.
12 And if it will make no peace with thee, but will
make war against thee, then thou shalt besiege it:
13 And when the LORD thy God hath delivered
it into thine hands, thou shalt smite every male
thereof with the edge of the sword:
14 But the women, and the little ones, and the
cattle, and all that is in the city, *even* all the spoil
thereof, shalt thou take unto thyself; and thou
shalt eat the spoil of thine enemies, which the
LORD thy God hath given thee.
15 Thus shalt thou do unto all the cities *which are*
very far off from thee, which *are* not of the cities
of these nations.
16 But of the cities of these people, which the
LORD thy God doth give thee *for* an inheritance,
thou shalt save alive nothing that breatheth:
17 But thou shalt utterly destroy them; *namely*,
the Hittites, and the Amorites, the Canaanites,
and the Perizzites, the Hivites, and the Jebusites;
as the LORD thy God hath commanded thee:
18 That they teach you not to do after all their
abominations, which they have done unto their
gods; so should ye sin against the LORD your God.
19 ¶ When thou shalt besiege a city a long time,
in making war against it to take it, thou shalt not
destroy the trees thereof by forcing an axe against

19:21 *eye for eye, tooth for tooth.* This is the principle of *lex talionis*, the law of retaliation. The penalty was to fit the crime. This protected the offender from punishment exceeding his offense (Ex. 21:23–25; Lev. 24:17–20).

Thoughts for Personal/Family Worship: Chapter 19

1. **God authored Israel's judicial plan and specified who its judges should be (16:18). God also prescribed the penalty for one who defended a false claim before those judges (19:16–19). To appear before the judges was to appear in God's court. An intentional misrepresentation there exhibited unbelief and contempt toward God Himself. Ultimately, deceit assaults God, the author of justice. God is truth, and every lie is against Him. Are you lying about something? What will repentance involve?**
2. **Without uttering a word, you can tell a lie: removing an established landmark (v. 14), misrepresented property boundaries. As long as that misrepresentation stood, the perpetrator lived a lie without speaking a word. Often people have misrepresented truth by various means of fraud and deception. But ultimately, the Lord is a God of truth (32:4), so the truth will prevail.**

Chapter 20: *Instructions for Israel's warfare exhibit absolute divine sovereignty and the absolute favor of God toward His chosen people.*

Regulations for Warfare (20:1–20)

20:2–4 The priest was the spokesman going into battle, implying that Israel's warfare was ultimately spiritual. God fought for them (vv. 1,4), destroying enemies as a defense against idolatry (vv. 17–18). Israel's deliverance preserved God's law and ultimately brought God's Son since there had to be an Israel if Christ was going to come (Rom 9:5).

20:5 *dedicate.* Consecrate or formally dedicate.

20:7 *betrothed.* Legally bound by a formal agreement of marriage. *not taken her.* Not entered into the consummation of marriage.

20:10–15 Israel's conquest sequence was peace first (v. 10) but, if unattainable, destruction of males (v. 13), thus ending future threats, and the assimilation of survivors and possessions into Israel's life (v. 14).

20:11 *tributaries.* Forced laborers.

20:12 *besiege.* To surround or encompass for the purpose of attack.

20:17 To these six peoples, the Septuagint (the Greek Old

them: for thou mayest eat of them, and thou shalt
not cut them down (for the tree of the field *is*
man's *life*) to employ *them* in the siege:
20 Only the trees which thou knowest that they
be not trees for meat, thou shalt destroy and
cut them down; and thou shalt build bulwarks
against the city that maketh war with thee, until
it be subdued.

CHAPTER 21

If *one* be found slain in the land which the LORD
thy God giveth thee to possess it, lying in the field,
and it be not known who hath slain him:
2 Then thy elders and thy judges shall come forth,
and they shall measure unto the cities which *are*
round about him that is slain:
3 And it shall be, *that* the city *which is* next unto
the slain man, even the elders of that city shall
take an heifer, which hath not been wrought with,
and which hath not drawn in the yoke;
4 And the elders of that city shall bring down the
heifer unto a rough valley, which is neither eared
nor sown, and shall strike off the heifer's neck
there in the valley:
5 And the priests the sons of Levi shall come
near; for them the LORD thy God hath chosen to
minister unto him, and to bless in the name of the
LORD; and by their word shall every controversy
and every stroke be *tried:*
6 And all the elders of that city, *that are* next unto
the slain *man*, shall wash their hands over the
heifer that is beheaded in the valley:
7 And they shall answer and say, Our hands have
not shed this blood, neither have our eyes seen *it.*
8 Be merciful, O LORD, unto thy people Israel,
whom thou hast redeemed, and lay not innocent
blood unto thy people of Israel's charge. And the
blood shall be forgiven them.
9 So shalt thou put away the *guilt of* innocent
blood from among you, when thou shalt do *that*
which is right in the sight of the LORD.
10 ¶ When thou goest forth to war against thine
enemies, and the LORD thy God hath delivered
them into thine hands, and thou hast taken them
captive,
11 And seest among the captives a beautiful
woman, and hast a desire unto her, that thou
wouldest have her to thy wife;
12 Then thou shalt bring her home to thine house;
and she shall shave her head, and pare her nails;
13 And she shall put the raiment of her captivity
from off her, and shall remain in thine house, and
bewail her father and her mother a full month:
and after that thou shalt go in unto her, and be
her husband, and she shall be thy wife.
14 And it shall be, if thou have no delight in her,
then thou shalt let her go whither she will; but
thou shalt not sell her at all for money, thou shalt
not make merchandise of her, because thou hast
humbled her.
15 ¶ If a man have two wives, one beloved, and

Testament) adds "Girgashites," which is consistent with 7:1.

20:19–20 In the long siege of a walled city, trees would be cut and utilized in battle strategies. Care was to be taken to preserve fruit-bearing trees as a food source.

20:20 *meat.* Food. *bulwarks.* Either trenches or siege works.

Thoughts for Personal/Family Worship: Chapter 20

1. **God ordered utter destruction of Canaanite peoples, "that they teach you not to do after all their abominations" (v. 18). Idolatry was Israel's greatest threat and had to be eliminated, whether idol, shrine, or idolater. God is zealous for His undivided honor and for the purity of His people. That zeal instructs us, "Love not the world, neither the things that are in the world. If any man love the world, the love of the Father is not in him" (1 John 2:15). The church does not kill sinners by the sword, but it must kill its sin by the Word.**
2. **The end of all war will come from the Prince of Peace, and Israel was the conduit through which He would come to mankind. Israel's advantage of having divine counsel in war ensured that end. It secured Christ's coming by annihilating peoples who would annihilate Israel via war or idolatry. Therefore foreign threats were subjugated (vv. 10–11), enemies rendered powerless (vv. 12–15), and idolatrous occupants of Canaan destroyed (vv. 16–18).**

Unsolved Murder, War Captives, and Rebellious Sons (21:1–23)

Chapter 21: ***Moses addresses miscellaneous things necessary to save the land from defilement.***

21:1–9 Life is precious, so murder by an unidentified assailant must be avenged. An innocent substitute—a heifer, never yoked or mated, killed in a fruitless ravine with a spring-fed stream—represents unfulfilled, innocent life. Over its dead body elders wash their hands, representing the people as being cleansed from bloodshed by the substitute's death (vv. 7–9).

21:1 *the land.* The land was holy and necessitated avenging of innocent bloodshed.

21:2 *measure unto.* Measure the distance to the closest city.

21:3 *not been wrought with.* A heifer that has not been worked. *not drawn in the yoke.* A heifer that has not pulled equipment.

21:4 *rough valley.* Literally, "valley of running water." *neither eared nor sown.* Unworked land. *strike off the heifer's neck.* Break the neck.

21:5 *every controversy and every stroke.* Every judicial case and crime.

21:8 *blood shall be forgiven.* Represents the guilt resulting from the crime.

21:10–14 God ensured rights to captive women: a home, identity, time to mourn, and protection from enslavement, brutality, and abandonment. War deaths diminished the male/female ratio (20:13), and a woman had no rights apart from a husband.

21:12 *pare.* To cut or trim the nails; literally, "she will make her nails."

21:13 *raiment.* Clothes. *bewail.* Weep or mourn.

21:15-17 This does not sanction polygamy; rather, it protects the innocent parties from abuse and injustice. Thus, it demonstrates an inherent evil in the plural marriage.

another hated, and they have born him children,
both the beloved and the hated; and *if* the first-
born son be hers that was hated:
16 Then it shall be, when he maketh his sons to
inherit *that* which he hath, *that* he may not make
the son of the beloved firstborn before the son of
the hated, *which is indeed* the firstborn:
17 But he shall acknowledge the son of the hated
for the firstborn, by giving him a double portion
of all that he hath: for he *is* the beginning of his
strength; the right of the firstborn *is* his.
18 ¶ If a man have a stubborn and rebellious son,
which will not obey the voice of his father, or the
voice of his mother, and *that*, when they have
chastened him, will not hearken unto them:
19 Then shall his father and his mother lay hold
on him, and bring him out unto the elders of his
city, and unto the gate of his place;
20 And they shall say unto the elders of his city,
This our son *is* stubborn and rebellious, he will
not obey our voice; *he is* a glutton, and a drunkard.
21 And all the men of his city shall stone him with
stones, that he die: so shalt thou put evil away
from among you; and all Israel shall hear, and fear.
22 ¶ And if a man have committed a sin worthy
of death, and he be to be put to death, and thou
hang him on a tree:
23 His body shall not remain all night upon the
tree, but thou shalt in any wise bury him that day;
(for he that is hanged *is* accursed of God;) that
thy land be not defiled, which the LORD thy God
giveth thee *for* an inheritance.

CHAPTER 22

THOU shalt not see thy brother's ox or his sheep
go astray, and hide thyself from them: thou shalt
in any case bring them again unto thy brother.
2 And if thy brother *be* not nigh unto thee, or if
thou know him not, then thou shalt bring it unto
thine own house, and it shall be with thee until
thy brother seek after it, and thou shalt restore it
to him again.
3 In like manner shalt thou do with his ass; and
so shalt thou do with his raiment; and with all
lost thing of thy brother's, which he hath lost,
and thou hast found, shalt thou do likewise: thou
mayest not hide thyself.
4 ¶ Thou shalt not see thy brother's ass or his ox
fall down by the way, and hide thyself from them:
thou shalt surely help him to lift *them* up again.
5 ¶ The woman shall not wear that which per-
taineth unto a man, neither shall a man put on a
woman's garment: for all that do so *are* abomina-
tion unto the LORD thy God.
6 ¶ If a bird's nest chance to be before thee in the
way in any tree, or on the ground, *whether they be*
young ones, or eggs, and the dam sitting upon the
young, or upon the eggs, thou shalt not take the
dam with the young:
7 *But* thou shalt in any wise let the dam go, and
take the young to thee; that it may be well with
thee, and *that* thou mayest prolong *thy* days.
8 ¶ When thou buildest a new house, then thou
shalt make a battlement for thy roof, that thou
bring not blood upon thine house, if any man fall
from thence.
9 ¶ Thou shalt not sow thy vineyard with divers
seeds: lest the fruit of thy seed which thou hast
sown, and the fruit of thy vineyard, be defiled.
10 ¶ Thou shalt not plow with an ox and an ass
together.
11 ¶ Thou shalt not wear a garment of divers
sorts, *as* of woollen and linen together.

21:17 *double portion.* The greater inheritance. *beginning of his strength.* His firstborn child.
21:20 *glutton.* The Hebrew refers to one who is thoughtless or rash.
21:23 See John 19:31; Gal. 3:13.

Thoughts for Personal/Family Worship: Chapter 21

1. **The regulations for treating a captive or hated wife demonstrate the importance of kindness and equity to all. These women were in circumstances beyond their control and for which they were not responsible. To add to their misery by unfair and cruel acts violated the second greatest commandment of loving your neighbor as yourself. God is concerned with protecting innocent victims of injustice, and we should follow His example. How are women mistreated today? What would God have us do?**
2. **Disobeying parents equates to disobeying God: "Honour thy father and thy mother: that thy days may be long upon the land" (Ex. 20:12). When respect for parents is gone, the root of respect in society has perished, jeopardizing all. Consequently, in Israel's theocracy, the rebellious son was a menace to civilization and was to be put to death by the society he threatened. Disruption in the family is no longer a capital offense, but it remains a serious threat to the welfare of society. Family structure and harmony should be a high priority in every Christian home.**

Chapter 22: *Moses gives various laws demonstrating that holiness touches every sphere of life.*

Civility, Distinctiveness, and Purity (22:1–30)

22:5 Transvestitism was common in many of the pagan religious rituals and thus was strictly forbidden. The distinction of genders was established at creation and is to be maintained in all spheres.
22:6–7 *dam.* Mother bird. The mother bird can survive without the eggs but not vice versa.
22:8 Man is duty-bound to his fellowman to minimize risks and threats. *battlement.* Parapet or fence along the roof. This is an application of the sixth commandment that includes the preserving of life.
22:9–11 *divers.* Diverse or different. Reasons for these restrictions are not known, but they set Israel apart from other nations, creating a distinctive people and serving as object lessons of separation.

12 ¶ Thou shalt make thee fringes upon the four
quarters of thy vesture, wherewith thou coverest
thyself.
13 ¶ If any man take a wife, and go in unto her,
and hate her,
14 And give occasions of speech against her, and
bring up an evil name upon her, and say, I took
this woman, and when I came to her, I found her
not a maid:
15 Then shall the father of the damsel, and her
mother, take and bring forth *the tokens of* the dam-
sel's virginity unto the elders of the city in the gate:
16 And the damsel's father shall say unto the
elders, I gave my daughter unto this man to wife,
and he hateth her;
17 And, lo, he hath given occasions of speech
against her, saying, I found not thy daughter a
maid; and yet these *are the tokens of* my daughter's
virginity. And they shall spread the cloth before
the elders of the city.
18 And the elders of that city shall take that man
and chastise him;
19 And they shall amerce him in an hundred
shekels of silver, and give *them* unto the father of
the damsel, because he hath brought up an evil
name upon a virgin of Israel: and she shall be his
wife; he may not put her away all his days.
20 But if this thing be true, *and the tokens of*
virginity be not found for the damsel:
21 Then they shall bring out the damsel to the
door of her father's house, and the men of her city
shall stone her with stones that she die: because
she hath wrought folly in Israel, to play the whore
in her father's house: so shalt thou put evil away
from among you.
22 ¶ If a man be found lying with a woman mar-
ried to an husband, then they shall both of them
die, *both* the man that lay with the woman, and the
woman: so shalt thou put away evil from Israel.
23 ¶ If a damsel *that is* a virgin be betrothed unto
an husband, and a man find her in the city, and
lie with her;
24 Then ye shall bring them both out unto the
gate of that city, and ye shall stone them with
stones that they die; the damsel, because she cried
not, *being* in the city; and the man, because he
hath humbled his neighbour's wife: so thou shalt
put away evil from among you.
25 ¶ But if a man find a betrothed damsel in the
field, and the man force her, and lie with her: then
the man only that lay with her shall die:
26 But unto the damsel thou shalt do nothing;
there is in the damsel no sin *worthy* of death: for
as when a man riseth against his neighbour, and
slayeth him, even so *is* this matter:
27 For he found her in the field, *and* the betrothed
damsel cried, and *there was* none to save her.
28 ¶ If a man find a damsel *that is* a virgin, which
is not betrothed, and lay hold on her, and lie with
her, and they be found;
29 Then the man that lay with her shall give unto
the damsel's father fifty *shekels* of silver, and she
shall be his wife; because he hath humbled her, he
may not put her away all his days.
30 ¶ A man shall not take his father's wife, nor
discover his father's skirt.

CHAPTER 23

HE that is wounded in the stones, or hath his
privy member cut off, shall not enter into the
congregation of the LORD.

22:12 *Fringes* were reminders to keep God's commandments (Num. 15:38–41).
22:13–21 These laws protected a virgin from scandalous lies and her family from shame, and they ensured her security (she could not be divorced).
22:14 *occasions of speech.* Slander; accusations of impropriety. *maid.* Virgin.
22:15 *damsel.* Girl or young woman.
22:17 *tokens.* Cloths spread on marriage beds to determine purity.
22:19 *amerce.* To fine or impose a penalty.
22:21 *folly.* Willful sin or disgrace.
22:23 *betrothed.* Legally bound in relationship prior to the actual marriage.
22:24 *cried not.* A victim had the responsibility to cry for help. *humbled.* Humiliated.
22:26 *for as.* Rape is likened to murder.
22:30 *discover his father's skirt.* What the skirt or wing covered was the object of protection and ownership. Here an idiom referring to the wife.

Thoughts for Personal/Family Worship: Chapter 22

1. **We have a community responsibility for others' possessions (vv. 1–4). God instructed Israel to be attentive to the welfare of straying livestock or overly burdened beasts. Cain's question, "Am I my brother's keeper" (Gen. 4:9), is hereby answered. It was disobedience to ignore the straying beast. If care must be taken for an animal, how much more is it to be taken for a human (Luke 14:1–6)? Why is sharing responsibility to care for each others' lives and property foundational for society?**
2. **Sexual purity is very important. Violators suffered severe penalties, and lies against an innocent person were punished. The matter of immorality was serious. Nations surrounding Israel were grossly immoral, and their idolatrous practices often included perverse actions as worship. The value God placed upon sexual purity cannot be overstated, and the warnings of the law are reiterated in the New Testament (1 Cor. 6:9–10,15–18). Marriage is a holy union of man and woman, and only within that union are sexual relations sanctified.**

Ethical and Moral Stipulations (23:1—25:19)

Chapter 23: ***Moses gives various laws demonstrating that holiness touches every sphere of life.***

23:1–2 Probably refers to cultic sexual perversions such as emasculation and children of a prostitute. *stones . . . privy*

2 A bastard shall not enter into the congregation
of the LORD; even to his tenth generation shall he
not enter into the congregation of the LORD.
3 An Ammonite or Moabite shall not enter
into the congregation of the LORD; even to their
tenth generation shall they not enter into the
congregation of the LORD for ever:
4 Because they met you not with bread and
with water in the way, when ye came forth out
of Egypt; and because they hired against thee
Balaam the son of Beor of Pethor of Mesopota-
mia, to curse thee.
5 Nevertheless the LORD thy God would not
hearken unto Balaam; but the LORD thy God
turned the curse into a blessing unto thee, because
the LORD thy God loved thee.
6 Thou shalt not seek their peace nor their
prosperity all thy days for ever.
7 ¶ Thou shalt not abhor an Edomite; for he *is* thy
brother: thou shalt not abhor an Egyptian; because
thou wast a stranger in his land.
8 The children that are begotten of them shall
enter into the congregation of the LORD in their
third generation.
9 ¶ When the host goeth forth against thine
enemies, then keep thee from every wicked thing.
10 ¶ If there be among you any man, that is not
clean by reason of uncleanness that chanceth him
by night, then shall he go abroad out of the camp,
he shall not come within the camp:
11 But it shall be, when evening cometh on, he
shall wash *himself* with water: and when the sun is
down, he shall come into the camp *again*.
12 ¶ Thou shalt have a place also without the
camp, whither thou shalt go forth abroad:
13 And thou shalt have a paddle upon thy
weapon; and it shall be, when thou wilt ease thy-
self abroad, thou shalt dig therewith, and shalt
turn back and cover that which cometh from thee:
14 For the LORD thy God walketh in the midst
of thy camp, to deliver thee, and to give up thine
enemies before thee; therefore shall thy camp be
holy: that he see no unclean thing in thee, and turn
away from thee.
15 ¶ Thou shalt not deliver unto his master the
servant which is escaped from his master unto thee:
16 He shall dwell with thee, *even* among you, in
that place which he shall choose in one of thy
gates, where it liketh him best: thou shalt not
oppress him.
17 ¶ There shall be no whore of the daughters of
Israel, nor a sodomite of the sons of Israel.
18 Thou shalt not bring the hire of a whore, or the
price of a dog, into the house of the LORD thy God
for any vow: for even both these *are* abomination
unto the LORD thy God.
19 ¶ Thou shalt not lend upon usury to thy
brother; usury of money, usury of victuals, usury
of any thing that is lent upon usury:
20 Unto a stranger thou mayest lend upon usury;
but unto thy brother thou shalt not lend upon
usury: that the LORD thy God may bless thee in all
that thou settest thine hand to in the land whither
thou goest to possess it.
21 ¶ When thou shalt vow a vow unto the LORD
thy God, thou shalt not slack to pay it: for the
LORD thy God will surely require it of thee; and it
would be sin in thee.
22 But if thou shalt forbear to vow, it shall be no
sin in thee.
23 That which is gone out of thy lips thou shalt
keep and perform; *even* a freewill offering, ac-
cording as thou hast vowed unto the LORD thy
God, which thou hast promised with thy mouth.
24 ¶ When thou comest into thy neighbour's
vineyard, then thou mayest eat grapes thy fill at
thine own pleasure; but thou shalt not put *any* in
thy vessel.
25 When thou comest into the standing corn of
thy neighbour, then thou mayest pluck the ears

---

member. Male organ. *bastard.* A child born from an illegitimate union, most likely incest.
23:3–4 See Gen. 19:33–38; Num. 22; Neh. 13:1–2. *met you not.* Did not provide food and water.
23:5 See Num. 22–24 for the whole Balaam narrative.
23:7 *abhor.* Hate or disdain. *Edomite.* Esau's descendant (Gen. 25:24–26; 36:1–19). *wast.* Was. This prohibition was in spite of Edom's hatred toward Israel (see Obad.).
23:9 *host.* Camp or army. *wicked thing.* Ceremonial iniquity or uncleanliness.
23:10 *uncleanness that chanceth him.* Likely a nocturnal emission (Lev. 15:2). *abroad.* Outside the camp.
23:12–13 Likely referring to a public place to be used as a latrine and the process of covering up excrement and waste. *paddle.* A type of spade. *ease thyself.* Relieve oneself.
23:14 *no unclean thing.* The Hebrew refers to anything unseemly or unbecoming. God's presence required both ceremonial cleanness and sanitary conditions.
23:15–16 Speaks of foreign slaves seeking asylum in Israel. Prohibited from covenants with nations, Israel had no extradition treaties.
23:17–18 *sodomite.* Male homosexual prostitute. *hire.* Prostitute earnings. *price of a dog.* An intentionally derogatory expression to underscore God's disgust regarding this male prostitution. Israel would later violate this (1 Kings 14:24; 15:12; 22:46; 2 Kings 23:7).
23:19–20 *usury.* Interest. *victuals.* Food. Loans were not commercial but for poverty relief. Creditors must not create poverty by charging an Israelite interest but could do so to foreigners (Gal. 6:10).
23:21 *slack.* Delay in paying.
23:22 *forbear.* Refrain. Vows were not required. See Eccl. 5:4–5.
23:25 *standing corn.* Ripened harvest.

Thoughts for Personal/Family Worship: Chapter 23

1. God is concerned for the purity of His congregation (vv. 1–6,17–18). Consequently, groups of people were excluded from the congregation of Israel. A church must

with thine hand; but thou shalt not move a sickle
unto thy neighbour's standing corn.

CHAPTER 24

WHEN a man hath taken a wife, and married her,
and it come to pass that she find no favour in his
eyes, because he hath found some uncleanness in
her: then let him write her a bill of divorcement,
and give *it* in her hand, and send her out of his
house.
2 And when she is departed out of his house, she
may go and be another man's *wife*.
3 And *if* the latter husband hate her, and write her
a bill of divorcement, and giveth *it* in her hand,
and sendeth her out of his house; or if the latter
husband die, which took her *to be* his wife;
4 Her former husband, which sent her away, may
not take her again to be his wife, after that she is
defiled; for that *is* abomination before the LORD:
and thou shalt not cause the land to sin, which
the LORD thy God giveth thee *for* an inheritance.
5 ¶ When a man hath taken a new wife, he shall
not go out to war, neither shall he be charged with
any business: *but* he shall be free at home one year,
and shall cheer up his wife which he hath taken.
6 ¶ No man shall take the nether or the upper mill-
stone to pledge: for he taketh *a man's* life to pledge.
7 ¶ If a man be found stealing any of his brethren
of the children of Israel, and maketh merchandise
of him, or selleth him; then that thief shall die;
and thou shalt put evil away from among you.
8 ¶ Take heed in the plague of leprosy, that thou
observe diligently, and do according to all that
the priests the Levites shall teach you: as I com-
manded them, *so* ye shall observe to do.
9 Remember what the LORD thy God did unto
Miriam by the way, after that ye were come forth
out of Egypt.
10 ¶ When thou dost lend thy brother any thing,
thou shalt not go into his house to fetch his
pledge.
11 Thou shalt stand abroad, and the man to
whom thou dost lend shall bring out the pledge
abroad unto thee.
12 And if the man *be* poor, thou shalt not sleep
with his pledge:
13 In any case thou shalt deliver him the pledge
again when the sun goeth down, that he may sleep
in his own raiment, and bless thee: and it shall be
righteousness unto thee before the LORD thy God.
14 ¶ Thou shalt not oppress an hired servant *that*
is poor and needy, *whether he be* of thy brethren,
or of thy strangers that *are* in thy land within thy
gates:
15 At his day thou shalt give *him* his hire, neither
shall the sun go down upon it; for he *is* poor, and
setteth his heart upon it: lest he cry against thee
unto the LORD, and it be sin unto thee.
16 The fathers shall not be put to death for the
children, neither shall the children be put to death
for the fathers: every man shall be put to death for
his own sin.
17 ¶ Thou shalt not pervert the judgment of the
stranger, *nor* of the fatherless; nor take a widow's
raiment to pledge:
18 But thou shalt remember that thou wast a
bondman in Egypt, and the LORD thy God re-
deemed thee thence: therefore I command thee
to do this thing.
19 ¶ When thou cuttest down thine harvest in
thy field, and hast forgot a sheaf in the field, thou
shalt not go again to fetch it: it shall be for the
stranger, for the fatherless, and for the widow:
that the LORD thy God may bless thee in all the
work of thine hands.
20 When thou beatest thine olive tree, thou shalt
not go over the boughs again: it shall be for the
stranger, for the fatherless, and for the widow.
21 When thou gatherest the grapes of thy vine-

---

not purpose to have a large congregation so much as a pure one. Purity must be of highest concern for all of God's people. Since a little leaven leavens the whole lump, the church must discipline and ultimately expel the unrepentant sinner (1 Cor. 5:6).

2. **God warns against stinginess and opportunism (vv. 24–25). Crops could be eaten by one passing by, helping travelers and widows, but only for immediate necessity; no supply could be taken. This implies that we are to be charitable in giving, but not selfish with others' charity. This illustrates the second greatest commandment to love our neighbor as ourselves. How are you sharing a portion of what God gives you with those in need?**

Chapter 24: ***Moses details regulations addressing marital relations and divorce, treatment of the poor, and leprosy.***

24:1–4 *no favour . . . uncleanness.* Some form of sexual impropriety being found. *bill of divorcement.* Not establishing divorce, but limiting a custom already known (Mark 10:4–9) and prohibiting additional adultery. See Mal. 2:16 for God's attitude. The legislation is not to sanction but to protect the innocent victims.

24:6 *nether.* Lower. The millstones were used to earn one's living. There were restrictions on what could be taken as collateral. Dignity of person is divinely established and to be honored.

24:7 *stealing.* Kidnapping or forced slavery. *maketh merchandise.* The Hebrew designates tyrannical or brutal treatment.

24:9 See Num. 12.

24:10 *pledge.* Object used for security of loan.

24:11 *abroad.* Outside.

24:12–13 *not sleep with his pledge.* If the man has given his garments (*raiment*) as collateral (23:19–20; 24:6; Ex. 22:25–26; Lev. 25:35–37).

24:15 *setteth his heart upon it.* Literally, "lifts up his soul unto it," an idiom expressing dependence on something.

24:19–22 Provision for the less fortunate was founded in the fact of redemption. Remembering grace should generate

yard, thou shalt not glean *it* afterward: it shall
be for the stranger, for the fatherless, and for the
widow.
22 And thou shalt remember that thou wast a
bondman in the land of Egypt: therefore I command thee to do this thing.

CHAPTER 25

IF there be a controversy between men, and they
come unto judgment, that *the judges* may judge
them; then they shall justify the righteous, and
condemn the wicked.
2 And it shall be, if the wicked man *be* worthy
to be beaten, that the judge shall cause him to lie
down, and to be beaten before his face, according
to his fault, by a certain number.
3 Forty stripes he may give him, *and* not exceed:
lest, *if* he should exceed, and beat him above these
with many stripes, then thy brother should seem
vile unto thee.
4 ¶ Thou shalt not muzzle the ox when he
treadeth out *the corn*.
5 ¶ If brethren dwell together, and one of them
die, and have no child, the wife of the dead shall
not marry without unto a stranger: her husband's
brother shall go in unto her, and take her to him
to wife, and perform the duty of an husband's
brother unto her.
6 And it shall be, *that* the firstborn which she
beareth shall succeed in the name of his brother
which is dead, that his name be not put out of
Israel.
7 And if the man like not to take his brother's wife,
then let his brother's wife go up to the gate unto
the elders, and say, My husband's brother refuseth
to raise up unto his brother a name in Israel, he
will not perform the duty of my husband's brother.
8 Then the elders of his city shall call him, and
speak unto him: and *if* he stand *to it*, and say, I like
not to take her;
9 Then shall his brother's wife come unto him in
the presence of the elders, and loose his shoe from
off his foot, and spit in his face, and shall answer
and say, So shall it be done unto that man that will
not build up his brother's house.
10 And his name shall be called in Israel, The
house of him that hath his shoe loosed.
11 ¶ When men strive together one with another,
and the wife of the one draweth near for to deliver
her husband out of the hand of him that smiteth
him, and putteth forth her hand, and taketh him
by the secrets:
12 Then thou shalt cut off her hand, thine eye
shall not pity *her*.
13 ¶ Thou shalt not have in thy bag divers
weights, a great and a small.
14 Thou shalt not have in thine house divers
measures, a great and a small.
15 *But* thou shalt have a perfect and just weight,
a perfect and just measure shalt thou have: that
thy days may be lengthened in the land which the
LORD thy God giveth thee.
16 For all that do such things, *and* all that do unrighteously, *are* an abomination unto the LORD
thy God.
17 ¶ Remember what Amalek did unto thee by
the way, when ye were come forth out of Egypt;
18 How he met thee by the way, and smote the
hindmost of thee, *even* all *that were* feeble behind
thee, when thou *wast* faint and weary; and he
feared not God.
19 Therefore it shall be, when the LORD thy God
hath given thee rest from all thine enemies round

---

gracious behavior to others. Christ taught this principle in the parable of the unmerciful servant (Matt. 18:23–34).

Thoughts for Personal/Family Worship: Chapter 24

1. **Powerless people are often abused, but God condemns the abuser. We are to help the powerless in their distress, never adding to their burden. Throughout Christ's ministry He helped and healed beggars and the afflicted, people who were at the bottom of the economic hierarchy. Deacons were appointed to address these needs (Acts 6), and the apostles were mindful of this duty (Gal. 2:10; James 2:1–9; 5:1–5). How does your church meet these needs today?**
2. **Farmers were to leave crops in the field for the poor to glean (vv. 19–22). This concept reappears in Scripture as an admonition to compassion and a warning against greed (Lev. 19:9–10; Ps. 41:1; Prov. 19:17; Luke 12:16–21). This principle is not limited to farmers. How we demonstrate concern for others will vary, but it is imperative that we show kindness to others, especially in light of what God has done for us.**

Chapter 25: *Moses gives assorted regulations ranging from humane punishments to just commerce to vengeance on the Amalekites.*

25:2 *certain number.* The punishment fits the crime.
25:3 *vile.* Degraded or of little value.
25:4 The working beast was nourished by the harvest it produced. Scripture applies this principle to compensating preachers (Matt. 10:10; Luke 10:7; 1 Cor. 9:7–14; 1 Tim. 5:17–18).
25:5–10 Laws regarding levirate (*brother*) marriages. See Gen. 38 for the violations of this custom.
25:6 *shall succeed.* Assume his family name.
25:8 *stand to it.* Persist in his refusal.
25:10 *The house of him that hath his shoe loosed.* Literally, "the family of the unsandaled."
25:11 *secrets.* Male organ.
25:13–16 Differing weights and measures, used for defrauding, were condemned. God requires equity, honesty, and fairness. These accompany blessing upon a land.
25:17–19 Esau's descendants (Gen. 36:12) extended his ill will against Jacob, attacking Israel (Ex. 17:8–16).
25:18 *hindmost.* The rear guard, likely in a position of weakness.
25:19 Moses reminds Israel of God's decree to destroy

about, in the land which the LORD thy God giveth thee *for* an inheritance to possess it, *that* thou shalt blot out the remembrance of Amalek from under heaven; thou shalt not forget *it*.

CHAPTER 26

AND it shall be, when thou *art* come in unto the land which the LORD thy God giveth thee *for* an inheritance, and possessest it, and dwellest therein;

2 That thou shalt take of the first of all the fruit of the earth, which thou shalt bring of thy land that the LORD thy God giveth thee, and shalt put *it* in a basket, and shalt go unto the place which the LORD thy God shall choose to place his name there.

3 And thou shalt go unto the priest that shall be in those days, and say unto him, I profess this day unto the LORD thy God, that I am come unto the country which the LORD sware unto our fathers for to give us.

4 And the priest shall take the basket out of thine hand, and set it down before the altar of the LORD thy God.

5 And thou shalt speak and say before the LORD thy God, A Syrian ready to perish *was* my father, and he went down into Egypt, and sojourned there with a few, and became there a nation, great, mighty, and populous:

6 And the Egyptians evil entreated us, and afflicted us, and laid upon us hard bondage:

7 And when we cried unto the LORD God of our fathers, the LORD heard our voice, and looked on our affliction, and our labour, and our oppression:

8 And the LORD brought us forth out of Egypt with a mighty hand, and with an outstretched arm, and with great terribleness, and with signs, and with wonders:

9 And he hath brought us into this place, and hath given us this land, *even* a land that floweth with milk and honey.

10 And now, behold, I have brought the firstfruits of the land, which thou, O LORD, hast given me. And thou shalt set it before the LORD thy God, and worship before the LORD thy God:

11 And thou shalt rejoice in every good *thing* which the LORD thy God hath given unto thee, and unto thine house, thou, and the Levite, and the stranger that *is* among you.

12 ¶ When thou hast made an end of tithing all the tithes of thine increase the third year, *which is* the year of tithing, and hast given *it* unto the Levite, the stranger, the fatherless, and the widow, that they may eat within thy gates, and be filled;

13 Then thou shalt say before the LORD thy God, I have brought away the hallowed things out of *mine* house, and also have given them unto the Levite, and unto the stranger, to the fatherless, and to the widow, according to all thy commandments which thou hast commanded me: I have not transgressed thy commandments, neither have I forgotten *them*:

14 I have not eaten thereof in my mourning, neither have I taken away *ought* thereof for *any* unclean *use*, nor given *ought* thereof for the dead: *but* I have hearkened to the voice of the LORD my God, *and* have done according to all that thou hast commanded me.

15 Look down from thy holy habitation, from heaven, and bless thy people Israel, and the land which thou hast given us, as thou swarest unto our fathers, a land that floweth with milk and honey.

16 ¶ This day the LORD thy God hath commanded thee to do these statutes and judgments: thou shalt therefore keep and do them with all thine heart, and with all thy soul.

Amalek. God rejected Saul for his failure to annihilate the Amalekites (1 Sam. 15:2–29).

Thoughts for Personal/Family Worship: Chapter 25

1. **Esau's animosity toward his younger brother, Jacob, was kept alive by his descendant Amalek (vv. 17–19). This is one example of a pattern traceable throughout Scripture, in which an older sibling is unwilling to accept God's blessing upon a younger. Consider Cain and Abel (Gen. 4); Ishmael and Isaac (Gen. 21:9); Esau and Jacob (Gen. 24:41); Joseph's brothers (Gen. 37:18–27); Miriam, Aaron, and Moses (Num. 12:1–2); Eliab and David (1 Sam. 17:28); and the elder brother and the prodigal (Luke 15:15–29). In blessed contrast, Christ, the elder brother of all the elect, "is not ashamed to call them brethren" (Heb. 2:11). Are you envious of those with greater privileges, or are you Christlike toward them?**
2. **Israel's practice of taking a brother's widow as wife (vv. 5–10) ensured the continuation of family lineage, clans, tribes, and the nation. This proved to be critical in the fulfillment of God's purpose to send Christ our Savior. Although the details differ, Boaz's marriage to Ruth approximates the principle and was a means of continuing the messianic line (Ruth 4:1–11,17–22; Matt. 1:1–17; 22:24).**

Chapter 26: *Moses gives instructions regarding the firstfruits and tithes to be offered in Canaan and reminds Israel of God's covenant with them.*

Canaan's Firstfruits (26:1–15)

26:2–11 The first harvest in Canaan signified the end of an exile that began with Jacob's migration to Egypt and extended through years of bondage and wandering. The offering of the *firstfruits* to God acknowledged His providence that turned a single family into a great nation.

26:12–15 Every *third year,* ten percent of the harvest was to be given to the Levites and needy persons (14:28–29), a continual reminder that the harvest was God's bounty.

26:13 *hallowed.* Sanctified or set apart.

17 Thou hast avouched the LORD this day to be
thy God, and to walk in his ways, and to keep
his statutes, and his commandments, and his
judgments, and to hearken unto his voice:
18 And the LORD hath avouched thee this day to
be his peculiar people, as he hath promised thee,
and that *thou* shouldest keep all his commandments;
19 And to make thee high above all nations which
he hath made, in praise, and in name, and in
honour; and that thou mayest be an holy people
unto the LORD thy God, as he hath spoken.

CHAPTER 27

AND Moses with the elders of Israel commanded
the people, saying, Keep all the commandments
which I command you this day.
2 And it shall be on the day when ye shall pass
over Jordan unto the land which the LORD thy
God giveth thee, that thou shalt set thee up great
stones, and plaister them with plaister:
3 And thou shalt write upon them all the words
of this law, when thou art passed over, that thou
mayest go in unto the land which the LORD thy
God giveth thee, a land that floweth with milk
and honey; as the LORD God of thy fathers hath
promised thee.
4 Therefore it shall be when ye be gone over
Jordan, *that* ye shall set up these stones, which I
command you this day, in mount Ebal, and thou
shalt plaister them with plaister.
5 And there shalt thou build an altar unto the
LORD thy God, an altar of stones: thou shalt not
lift up *any* iron *tool* upon them.
6 Thou shalt build the altar of the LORD thy
God of whole stones: and thou shalt offer burnt
offerings thereon unto the LORD thy God:
7 And thou shalt offer peace offerings, and shalt
eat there, and rejoice before the LORD thy God.
8 And thou shalt write upon the stones all the
words of this law very plainly.
9 ¶ And Moses and the priests the Levites spake
unto all Israel, saying, Take heed, and hearken, O
Israel; this day thou art become the people of the
LORD thy God.
10 Thou shalt therefore obey the voice of the
LORD thy God, and do his commandments and
his statutes, which I command thee this day.
11 ¶ And Moses charged the people the same day,
saying,
12 These shall stand upon mount Gerizim to
bless the people, when ye are come over Jordan;
Simeon, and Levi, and Judah, and Issachar, and
Joseph, and Benjamin:
13 And these shall stand upon mount Ebal to
curse; Reuben, Gad, and Asher, and Zebulun,
Dan, and Naphtali.
14 ¶ And the Levites shall speak, and say unto all
the men of Israel with a loud voice,
15 Cursed *be* the man that maketh *any* graven or
molten image, an abomination unto the LORD,
the work of the hands of the craftsman, and
putteth *it* in *a* secret *place*. And all the people shall
answer and say, Amen.
16 Cursed *be* he that setteth light by his father or
his mother. And all the people shall say, Amen.
17 Cursed *be* he that removeth his neighbour's
landmark. And all the people shall say, Amen.
18 Cursed *be* he that maketh the blind to wander

Concluding Reminder and Exhortation (26:16–19)

26:17 *avouched.* Declared.

26:18 *peculiar people.* Treasured possession.

Thoughts for Personal/Family Worship: Chapter 26

1. **Israel was to remember that Canaan was given to them by God by tithing the harvest. No less than Israel, all people should recognize that the land they inhabit is God's. The crops they harvest and consume are produced by His power and goodness. We are all indebted to Him for our very lives. All that we are, own, and enjoy is the Lord's (Ps. 24:1).**
2. **God's people are "his peculiar people" (v. 18). God sets them apart to Himself and regards them as special. They must remember and reflect this in obedience to His commandments, resisting the evil passions of this present world (1 John 2:15). They are "a chosen generation, a royal priesthood, an holy nation, a peculiar people; that ye should shew forth the praises of him who hath called you" (1 Peter 2:9). Which commandments especially make obedient Christians different from other people in your culture? Why?**

BLESSINGS AND CURSES (27:1—28:68)

Chapter 27: ***A ceremony reaffirming God's law was to be enacted as the formal inauguration into Canaan.***

Prescribed Ceremony at Ebal and Gerizim (27:1–26)

27:2 *pass over* [the] *Jordan.* This ceremony reaffirmed God's law visibly, audibly, and solemnly after Israel entered Canaan (Josh. 8:30–35). *plaister.* Whitewash, cover with plaster.

27:4 *Ebal* and "Gerizim" (v. 12) were roughly forty miles north of Jerusalem at Shechem, where an ancient trade route passed between the mountains, and where the law written on stones upon the mountains would be visible. These mountains were significant (Gen. 12:6–7; 33:18–20; Josh. 24:32).

27:5–6 The altar was from natural stone, uncut by iron tools (Ex. 20:24–25), perhaps because of Israel's dependence upon heathen nations for iron or exclusion of human instrumentality.

27:8 *very plainly.* Easily seen and read. Precision and exactness must characterize matters relating to God's Word.

27:9 *this day.* Refers not to its beginning but to the conscious renewal of the covenant.

27:15 *secret.* Most of the sins named are secret, yet cursed by God. Nothing is hidden from Him. All sin must be judged (Heb. 4:13). *Amen.* A word of solemn agreement.

27:16 *setteth light.* Dishonors or disrespects.

27:17 An Israelite equivalent to the Mesopotamian *kudurru* stone may be in view here—not just a boundary marker but a

out of the way. And all the people shall say, Amen.
19 Cursed *be* he that perverteth the judgment of
the stranger, fatherless, and widow. And all the
people shall say, Amen.
20 Cursed *be* he that lieth with his father's wife;
because he uncovereth his father's skirt. And all
the people shall say, Amen.
21 Cursed *be* he that lieth with any manner of
beast. And all the people shall say, Amen.
22 Cursed *be* he that lieth with his sister, the
daughter of his father, or the daughter of his
mother. And all the people shall say, Amen.
23 Cursed *be* he that lieth with his mother in law.
And all the people shall say, Amen.
24 Cursed *be* he that smiteth his neighbour
secretly. And all the people shall say, Amen.
25 Cursed *be* he that taketh reward to slay an in-
nocent person. And all the people shall say, Amen.
26 Cursed *be* he that confirmeth not *all* the words
of this law to do them. And all the people shall
say, Amen.

CHAPTER 28

AND it shall come to pass, if thou shalt hearken
diligently unto the voice of the LORD thy God, to
observe *and* to do all his commandments which
I command thee this day, that the LORD thy God
will set thee on high above all nations of the earth:
2 And all these blessings shall come on thee, and
overtake thee, if thou shalt hearken unto the voice
of the LORD thy God.
3 Blessed *shalt* thou *be* in the city, and blessed
shalt thou *be* in the field.
4 Blessed *shall be* the fruit of thy body, and the
fruit of thy ground, and the fruit of thy cattle, the
increase of thy kine, and the flocks of thy sheep.
5 Blessed *shall be* thy basket and thy store.
6 Blessed *shalt* thou *be* when thou comest in, and
blessed *shalt* thou *be* when thou goest out.
7 The LORD shall cause thine enemies that rise
up against thee to be smitten before thy face:
they shall come out against thee one way, and flee
before thee seven ways.
8 The LORD shall command the blessing upon
thee in thy storehouses, and in all that thou settest
thine hand unto; and he shall bless thee in the
land which the LORD thy God giveth thee.
9 The LORD shall establish thee an holy people
unto himself, as he hath sworn unto thee, if thou
shalt keep the commandments of the LORD thy
God, and walk in his ways.
10 And all people of the earth shall see that thou
art called by the name of the LORD; and they shall
be afraid of thee.
11 And the LORD shall make thee plenteous in
goods, in the fruit of thy body, and in the fruit of
thy cattle, and in the fruit of thy ground, in the
land which the LORD sware unto thy fathers to
give thee.
12 The LORD shall open unto thee his good trea-
sure, the heaven to give the rain unto thy land in
his season, and to bless all the work of thine hand:
and thou shalt lend unto many nations, and thou
shalt not borrow.
13 And the LORD shall make thee the head, and
not the tail; and thou shalt be above only, and
thou shalt not be beneath; if that thou hearken
unto the commandments of the LORD thy God,
which I command thee this day, to observe and
to do *them*:
14 And thou shalt not go aside from any of the
words which I command thee this day, *to* the right
hand, or *to* the left, to go after other gods to serve
them.
15 ¶ But it shall come to pass, if thou wilt not
hearken unto the voice of the LORD thy God, to
observe to do all his commandments and his stat-
utes which I command thee this day; that all these
curses shall come upon thee, and overtake thee:

---

stone engraved with property details and rights, the taking of which amounted to theft of property (19:14).

27:18–19 Taking advantage of the helpless was cursed behavior. This was one indictment of Pharisees in Jesus' day (Matt. 23:14).

27:20 *uncovereth his father's skirt.* Dishonors his father. See note at 22:30.

27:26 *confirmeth not.* Rejects.

Thoughts for Personal/Family Worship: Chapter 27

1. **Moses instructed Israel to "obey the voice of the LORD thy God, and to do his commandments and his statutes" (v. 10), because they were "the people of the LORD thy God" (v. 9). God's grace establishes one's relationship as a member of God's people, and obedience to His Word evidences that grace. Some confuse church membership or theological persuasion with citizenship among God's elect. But the primary mark that God observes and demands is obedience to His Word (1 John 2:3–5).**
2. **The ceremony at Ebal and Gerizim included all Israel affirming the curses proclaimed by saying "Amen," which means "may it be so." God expected the entire congregation of Israel to affirm His Word. In some congregations "Amen" is said audibly within the assembly. However, all Christians should affirm the Word in their hearts. At the essence of faith is saying "Amen" to God's promises in Christ Jesus (2 Cor. 1:20).**

Blessings and Curses (28:1–68)

Chapter 28: *Moses delineates the consequences of obedience and disobedience.*

28:1 *set thee on high.* Exalt you among the nations.

28:4 *fruit of thy body.* Children. *kine.* Cattle (vv. 18,51)

28:5 *store.* Kneading troughs.

28:6 *comest in . . . goest out.* An idiom referring to all of life (v. 19).

28:7 *seven ways.* An idiom referring to every direction (v. 25).

16 Cursed *shalt* thou *be* in the city, and cursed
shalt thou *be* in the field.
17 Cursed *shall be* thy basket and thy store.
18 Cursed *shall be* the fruit of thy body, and the
fruit of thy land, the increase of thy kine, and the
flocks of thy sheep.
19 Cursed *shalt* thou *be* when thou comest in,
and cursed *shalt* thou *be* when thou goest out.
20 The LORD shall send upon thee cursing, vexa-
tion, and rebuke, in all that thou settest thine hand
unto for to do, until thou be destroyed, and until
thou perish quickly; because of the wickedness of
thy doings, whereby thou hast forsaken me.
21 The LORD shall make the pestilence cleave
unto thee, until he have consumed thee from off
the land, whither thou goest to possess it.
22 The LORD shall smite thee with a consumption,
and with a fever, and with an inflammation, and
with an extreme burning, and with the sword,
and with blasting, and with mildew; and they
shall pursue thee until thou perish.
23 And thy heaven that *is* over thy head shall be
brass, and the earth that is under thee *shall be* iron.
24 The LORD shall make the rain of thy land
powder and dust: from heaven shall it come down
upon thee, until thou be destroyed.
25 The LORD shall cause thee to be smitten before
thine enemies: thou shalt go out one way against
them, and flee seven ways before them: and shalt
be removed into all the kingdoms of the earth.
26 And thy carcase shall be meat unto all fowls of
the air, and unto the beasts of the earth, and no
man shall fray *them* away.
27 The LORD will smite thee with the botch of
Egypt, and with the emerods, and with the scab,
and with the itch, whereof thou canst not be healed.
28 The LORD shall smite thee with madness, and
blindness, and astonishment of heart:
29 And thou shalt grope at noonday, as the blind
gropeth in darkness, and thou shalt not prosper
in thy ways: and thou shalt be only oppressed and
spoiled evermore, and no man shall save *thee*.
30 Thou shalt betroth a wife, and another man
shall lie with her: thou shalt build an house, and
thou shalt not dwell therein: thou shalt plant a
vineyard, and shalt not gather the grapes thereof.
31 Thine ox *shall be* slain before thine eyes,
and thou shalt not eat thereof: thine ass *shall be*
violently taken away from before thy face, and
shall not be restored to thee: thy sheep *shall be*
given unto thine enemies, and thou shalt have
none to rescue *them*.
32 Thy sons and thy daughters *shall be* given unto
another people, and thine eyes shall look, and fail
with longing for them all the day long: and *there*
shall be no might in thine hand.
33 The fruit of thy land, and all thy labours, shall
a nation which thou knowest not eat up; and thou
shalt be only oppressed and crushed alway:
34 So that thou shalt be mad for the sight of thine
eyes which thou shalt see.
35 The LORD shall smite thee in the knees, and in
the legs, with a sore botch that cannot be healed,
from the sole of thy foot unto the top of thy head.
36 The LORD shall bring thee, and thy king which
thou shalt set over thee, unto a nation which nei-
ther thou nor thy fathers have known; and there
shalt thou serve other gods, wood and stone.
37 And thou shalt become an astonishment, a
proverb, and a byword, among all nations whither
the LORD shall lead thee.
38 Thou shalt carry much seed out into the field,
and shalt gather *but* little in; for the locust shall
consume it.
39 Thou shalt plant vineyards, and dress *them*,
but shalt neither drink *of* the wine, nor gather *the*
grapes; for the worms shall eat them.
40 Thou shalt have olive trees throughout all thy
coasts, but thou shalt not anoint *thyself* with the
oil; for thine olive shall cast *his fruit*.
41 Thou shalt beget sons and daughters, but
thou shalt not enjoy them; for they shall go into
captivity.
42 All thy trees and fruit of thy land shall the
locust consume.
43 The stranger that *is* within thee shall get up
above thee very high; and thou shalt come down
very low.
44 He shall lend to thee, and thou shalt not lend
to him: he shall be the head, and thou shalt be
the tail.
45 Moreover all these curses shall come upon
thee, and shall pursue thee, and overtake thee,
till thou be destroyed; because thou hearkenedst
not unto the voice of the LORD thy God, to keep
his commandments and his statutes which he
commanded thee:
46 And they shall be upon thee for a sign and for
a wonder, and upon thy seed for ever.
47 Because thou servedst not the LORD thy God

28:20 *vexation.* Confusion.
28:22 *consumption.* Refers to a weakening of the physical body and may be pulmonary tuberculosis, which is accompanied by the *fever, inflammation,* and *extreme burning.* Tubercular decay has been found in Egyptian mummies. Judgment would include Egyptian diseases (vv. 27, 60; see note at 7:12). *blasting.* Blight.
28:23 *brass . . . iron.* Metaphors for producing neither rain nor vegetation.
28:26 *fray.* Make afraid, or chase off.
28:27 *botch.* Perhaps Egyptian boils (v. 35; Ex. 9:9–12). *emerods.* Perhaps hemorrhoids or tumors.
28:28 *astonishment of heart.* Confusion of mind.
28:29 *grope.* Feel one's way around.
28:37 *byword.* Taunt or proverb. A sign signifying the Lord's wrath.
28:40 *coasts.* Borders or regions.

with joyfulness, and with gladness of heart, for
the abundance of all *things*;
48 Therefore shalt thou serve thine enemies
which the LORD shall send against thee, in hunger,
and in thirst, and in nakedness, and in want of all
things: and he shall put a yoke of iron upon thy
neck, until he have destroyed thee.
49 The LORD shall bring a nation against thee
from far, from the end of the earth, *as swift* as the
eagle flieth; a nation whose tongue thou shalt not
understand;
50 A nation of fierce countenance, which shall
not regard the person of the old, nor shew favour
to the young:
51 And he shall eat the fruit of thy cattle, and the
fruit of thy land, until thou be destroyed: which
also shall not leave thee *either* corn, wine, or oil,
or the increase of thy kine, or flocks of thy sheep,
until he have destroyed thee.
52 And he shall besiege thee in all thy gates, until
thy high and fenced walls come down, wherein
thou trustedst, throughout all thy land: and he
shall besiege thee in all thy gates throughout all
thy land, which the LORD thy God hath given thee.
53 And thou shalt eat the fruit of thine own body,
the flesh of thy sons and of thy daughters, which
the LORD thy God hath given thee, in the siege,
and in the straitness, wherewith thine enemies
shall distress thee:
54 *So that* the man *that is* tender among you,
and very delicate, his eye shall be evil toward his
brother, and toward the wife of his bosom, and
toward the remnant of his children which he shall
leave:
55 So that he will not give to any of them of the
flesh of his children whom he shall eat: because
he hath nothing left him in the siege, and in the
straitness, wherewith thine enemies shall distress
thee in all thy gates.
56 The tender and delicate woman among you,
which would not adventure to set the sole of her
foot upon the ground for delicateness and tender-
ness, her eye shall be evil toward the husband of
her bosom, and toward her son, and toward her
daughter,
57 And toward her young one that cometh out
from between her feet, and toward her children
which she shall bear: for she shall eat them
for want of all *things* secretly in the siege and
straitness, wherewith thine enemy shall distress
thee in thy gates.
58 If thou wilt not observe to do all the words of
this law that are written in this book, that thou
mayest fear this glorious and fearful name, THE
LORD THY GOD;
59 Then the LORD will make thy plagues
wonderful, and the plagues of thy seed, *even*
great plagues, and of long continuance, and sore
sicknesses, and of long continuance.
60 Moreover he will bring upon thee all the dis-
eases of Egypt, which thou wast afraid of; and
they shall cleave unto thee.
61 Also every sickness, and every plague, which *is*
not written in the book of this law, them will the
LORD bring upon thee, until thou be destroyed.
62 And ye shall be left few in number, whereas ye
were as the stars of heaven for multitude; because
thou wouldest not obey the voice of the LORD thy
God.
63 And it shall come to pass, *that* as the LORD
rejoiced over you to do you good, and to multiply
you; so the LORD will rejoice over you to destroy
you, and to bring you to nought; and ye shall be
plucked from off the land whither thou goest to
possess it.
64 And the LORD shall scatter thee among all
people, from the one end of the earth even unto
the other; and there thou shalt serve other gods,
which neither thou nor thy fathers have known,
even wood and stone.
65 And among these nations shalt thou find no
ease, neither shall the sole of thy foot have rest:
but the LORD shall give thee there a trembling
heart, and failing of eyes, and sorrow of mind:
66 And thy life shall hang in doubt before thee;
and thou shalt fear day and night, and shalt have
none assurance of thy life:
67 In the morning thou shalt say, Would God
it were even! and at even thou shalt say, Would
God it were morning! for the fear of thine heart

28:53–57 See 2 Kings 6:24–29.
28:53,55,57 *straitness.* Distress.
28:54 The tenderhearted man would be callous and fierce.
28:56 *adventure.* To attempt.
28:59 *wonderful.* Refers to that which is extraordinary. *sore.* Severe.

Thoughts for Personal/Family Worship: Chapter 28

1. **"Among these nations shalt thou find no ease . . . but the LORD shall give thee there a trembling heart" (v. 65). Fear is a result of sin (Gen. 3:10); thus Israel's sin would beget fear. "The wicked flee when no man pursueth: but the righteous are bold as a lion" (Prov. 28:1). The godly have nothing to fear, for they rest in the sovereign rule of God, who is good. The ungodly have every reason to fear. "The wicked are like the troubled sea, when it cannot rest, those waters cast up mire and dirt. There is no peace, saith my God, to the wicked" (Isa. 57:20–21).**
2. **God warned Israel that He would judge her sin by sending her into idolatry (v. 64). Sin becomes its own punishment. Divine wrath delivers the disobedient unto uncleanness, vile affections, and reprobate minds (Rom. 1:18–32), giving rebels over unto greater sin, corruption, and contamination. They sin without conscience. This counsels everyone to immediate repentance before they become past feeling toward sin in the blindness of the heart (Eph. 4:18–19). Of what sins do you need to repent right now?**

wherewith thou shalt fear, and for the sight of
thine eyes which thou shalt see.
68 And the LORD shall bring thee into Egypt
again with ships, by the way whereof I spake unto
thee, Thou shalt see it no more again: and there ye
shall be sold unto your enemies for bondmen and
bondwomen, and no man shall buy *you*.

CHAPTER 29

THESE *are* the words of the covenant, which the
LORD commanded Moses to make with the
children of Israel in the land of Moab, beside the
covenant which he made with them in Horeb.
2 ¶ And Moses called unto all Israel, and said
unto them, Ye have seen all that the LORD did be-
fore your eyes in the land of Egypt unto Pharaoh,
and unto all his servants, and unto all his land;
3 The great temptations which thine eyes have
seen, the signs, and those great miracles:
4 Yet the LORD hath not given you an heart to per-
ceive, and eyes to see, and ears to hear, unto this day.
5 And I have led you forty years in the wilderness:
your clothes are not waxen old upon you, and thy
shoe is not waxen old upon thy foot.
6 Ye have not eaten bread, neither have ye drunk
wine or strong drink: that ye might know that I
am the LORD your God.
7 And when ye came unto this place, Sihon the
king of Heshbon, and Og the king of Bashan, came
out against us unto battle, and we smote them:
8 And we took their land, and gave it for an in-
heritance unto the Reubenites, and to the Gadites,
and to the half tribe of Manasseh.
9 Keep therefore the words of this covenant, and
do them, that ye may prosper in all that ye do.
10 ¶ Ye stand this day all of you before the LORD
your God; your captains of your tribes, your
elders, and your officers, *with* all the men of Israel,
11 Your little ones, your wives, and thy stranger
that *is* in thy camp, from the hewer of thy wood
unto the drawer of thy water:
12 That thou shouldest enter into covenant with
the LORD thy God, and into his oath, which the
LORD thy God maketh with thee this day:
13 That he may establish thee to day for a people
unto himself, and *that* he may be unto thee a God,
as he hath said unto thee, and as he hath sworn
unto thy fathers, to Abraham, to Isaac, and to Jacob.
14 Neither with you only do I make this covenant
and this oath;
15 But with *him* that standeth here with us this
day before the LORD our God, and also with *him*
that *is* not here with us this day:
16 (For ye know how we have dwelt in the land
of Egypt; and how we came through the nations
which ye passed by;
17 And ye have seen their abominations, and
their idols, wood and stone, silver and gold, which
were among them:)
18 Lest there should be among you man, or
woman, or family, or tribe, whose heart turn-
eth away this day from the LORD our God, to go
and serve the gods of these nations; lest there
should be among you a root that beareth gall and
wormwood;
19 And it come to pass, when he heareth the
words of this curse, that he bless himself in his
heart, saying, I shall have peace, though I walk in
the imagination of mine heart, to add drunken-
ness to thirst:
20 The LORD will not spare him, but then the
anger of the LORD and his jealousy shall smoke
against that man, and all the curses that are
written in this book shall lie upon him, and the
LORD shall blot out his name from under heaven.
21 And the LORD shall separate him unto evil
out of all the tribes of Israel, according to all the
curses of the covenant that are written in this
book of the law:
22 So that the generation to come of your children
that shall rise up after you, and the stranger that
shall come from a far land, shall say, when they see
the plagues of that land, and the sicknesses which
the LORD hath laid upon it;
23 *And that* the whole land thereof *is* brimstone,

CONCLUDING INSTRUCTION (29:1—30:20)

Chapter 29: *The past reviews God's care of Israel, the present exhorts unto faithfulness, and the future expounds results of unfaithfulness.*

Past Blessing (29:1–29)

29:1 *beside the covenant.* Likely a renewal of the covenant (5:2,3).
29:3 *temptations.* Trials.
29:4 Idolatrous nations saw their gods but saw none of their works. Israel did not see God but beheld His works—yet they could not recognize His glory in His works without the work of the Spirit to give them spiritual sight and hearing (1 Cor. 2:9–14).
29:5 *are not waxen old.* Have not worn out.
29:11 *hewer of thy wood . . . drawer of thy water.* Resident non-Israelites who gathered Israel's wood and carried her water (Josh. 9:21–27).
29:18 *root.* Metaphor for wayward people. *gall.* Bitterness or poison. *wormwood.* Figurative for bitterness.
29:19 *in his heart.* Sin originates in the heart (Mark 7:15–23; James 1:14–15). *imagination.* Stubbornness. *add drunkenness to thirst.* An uncertain Hebrew metaphor, most likely referring to delusion.
29:23 *brimstone.* Sulfur. *Sodom and Gomorrah,* often used as an example of judgment (Gen. 19; Isa. 1:10; Luke 17:28–35; 2 Peter 2:6).

Thoughts for Personal/Family Worship: Chapter 29

1. Warning against departure from God's law, Moses equated cursed actions with one who says, "I walk in the imagination of mine heart" (v. 19). Thereby he identifies

and salt, *and* burning, *that* it is not sown, nor
beareth, nor any grass groweth therein, like the
overthrow of Sodom, and Gomorrah, Admah,
and Zeboim, which the LORD overthrew in his
anger, and in his wrath:
24 Even all nations shall say, Wherefore hath the
LORD done thus unto this land? what *meaneth* the
heat of this great anger?
25 Then men shall say, Because they have forsaken
the covenant of the LORD God of their fathers,
which he made with them when he brought them
forth out of the land of Egypt:
26 For they went and served other gods, and wor-
shipped them, gods whom they knew not, and
whom he had not given unto them:
27 And the anger of the LORD was kindled against
this land, to bring upon it all the curses that are
written in this book:
28 And the LORD rooted them out of their land in
anger, and in wrath, and in great indignation, and
cast them into another land, as *it is* this day.
29 The secret *things belong* unto the LORD our
God: but those *things which are* revealed *belong*
unto us and to our children for ever, that *we* may
do all the words of this law.

CHAPTER 30

AND it shall come to pass, when all these things
are come upon thee, the blessing and the curse,
which I have set before thee, and thou shalt call
them to mind among all the nations, whither the
LORD thy God hath driven thee,
2 And shalt return unto the LORD thy God, and
shalt obey his voice according to all that I com-
mand thee this day, thou and thy children, with
all thine heart, and with all thy soul;
3 That then the LORD thy God will turn thy
captivity, and have compassion upon thee, and
will return and gather thee from all the nations,
whither the LORD thy God hath scattered thee.
4 If *any* of thine be driven out unto the outmost
parts of heaven, from thence will the LORD thy God
gather thee, and from thence will he fetch thee:
5 And the LORD thy God will bring thee into the
land which thy fathers possessed, and thou shalt
possess it; and he will do thee good, and multiply
thee above thy fathers.
6 And the LORD thy God will circumcise thine
heart, and the heart of thy seed, to love the LORD
thy God with all thine heart, and with all thy soul,
that thou mayest live.
7 And the LORD thy God will put all these curses
upon thine enemies, and on them that hate thee,
which persecuted thee.
8 And thou shalt return and obey the voice of
the LORD, and do all his commandments which I
command thee this day.
9 And the LORD thy God will make thee plente-
ous in every work of thine hand, in the fruit of thy
body, and in the fruit of thy cattle, and in the fruit
of thy land, for good: for the LORD will again rejoice
over thee for good, as he rejoiced over thy fathers:
10 If thou shalt hearken unto the voice of the
LORD thy God, to keep his commandments and
his statutes which are written in this book of the
law, *and* if thou turn unto the LORD thy God with
all thine heart, and with all thy soul.
11 ¶ For this commandment which I command
thee this day, it *is* not hidden from thee, neither
is it far off.
12 It *is* not in heaven, that thou shouldest say,
Who shall go up for us to heaven, and bring it
unto us, that we may hear it, and do it?
13 Neither *is* it beyond the sea, that thou should-
est say, Who shall go over the sea for us, and bring
it unto us, that we may hear it, and do it?
14 But the word *is* very nigh unto thee, in thy
mouth, and in thy heart, that thou mayest do it.
15 ¶ See, I have set before thee this day life and
good, and death and evil;
16 In that I command thee this day to love the

the root of sin: the hardness of the heart. The heart is deceitful above all things, and desperately wicked: who can know it and its secrets (Ps. 19:12; Jer. 17:9)? Those who follow their own hearts ignore God's law, resulting in sin (Prov. 3:1–8, Mark 7:15–23, Rom. 1:20–21). The heart departs from the Lord (Jer. 17:5). How can we overcome our own hearts?

2. Scripture provides information to satisfy faith, but not curiosity. God reveals and God conceals, thus "the secret things belong unto the LORD our God" (v. 29). Prophets did not understand all of the things they wrote (1 Peter 1:10–12), and Paul confessed "now we know in part" (1 Cor. 13:12). This should promote diligence in searching out what God has revealed and humility in our limited understanding. Even the God-inspired, inerrant writers possessed partial knowledge. God has not chosen to reveal everything concerning Himself, and it is not wise to speculate beyond what the Bible reveals.

Chapter 30: *Moses assures God's mercy to the penitent and issues the final warning to heed God's covenant.*

Reaffirmed Covenant (3:1–20)

30:3 *turn thy captivity.* Change the course of His judgments.
30:4 *fetch.* Gather together.
30:6 Circumcision distinguished Israel from the nations (Gen. 17:9–14). It symbolized putting off worldly cravings and pride from the *heart* (Lev. 26:41; Jer. 9:26; Ezek. 44:7, 9; Acts 7:51) and putting on *love* for God in personal conversion (Deut. 10:16; Jer. 4:4), something worked ultimately by God (Deut. 29:4) through Christ and His Spirit (Rom. 2:29; Col. 2:10–15).
30:12–14 Paul cites this promise in Rom. 10:6–8. The message of the gospel is comprehensible; it is gracious revelation.
30:15–20 *life and good, and death and evil* (vv. 15,19). Responsibility for obedience rested upon Israel. Divine sovereignty does not diminish human responsibility.

LORD thy God, to walk in his ways, and to keep
his commandments and his statutes and his
judgments, that thou mayest live and multiply:
and the LORD thy God shall bless thee in the land
whither thou goest to possess it.
17 But if thine heart turn away, so that thou wilt
not hear, but shalt be drawn away, and worship
other gods, and serve them;
18 I denounce unto you this day, that ye shall
surely perish, *and that* ye shall not prolong *your*
days upon the land, whither thou passest over
Jordan to go to possess it.
19 I call heaven and earth to record this day
against you, *that* I have set before you life and
death, blessing and cursing: therefore choose life,
that both thou and thy seed may live:
20 That thou mayest love the LORD thy God, *and*
that thou mayest obey his voice, and that thou
mayest cleave unto him: for he *is* thy life, and the
length of thy days: that thou mayest dwell in the
land which the LORD sware unto thy fathers, to
Abraham, to Isaac, and to Jacob, to give them.

CHAPTER 31

AND Moses went and spake these words unto all
Israel.
2 And he said unto them, I *am* an hundred and
twenty years old this day; I can no more go out
and come in: also the LORD hath said unto me,
Thou shalt not go over this Jordan.
3 The LORD thy God, he will go over before thee,
and he will destroy these nations from before
thee, and thou shalt possess them: *and* Joshua, he
shall go over before thee, as the LORD hath said.
4 And the LORD shall do unto them as he did to
Sihon and to Og, kings of the Amorites, and unto
the land of them, whom he destroyed.
5 And the LORD shall give them up before your
face, that ye may do unto them according unto all
the commandments which I have commanded you.
6 Be strong and of a good courage, fear not, nor
be afraid of them: for the LORD thy God, he *it is*
that doth go with thee; he will not fail thee, nor
forsake thee.
7 ¶ And Moses called unto Joshua, and said unto
him in the sight of all Israel, Be strong and of a
good courage: for thou must go with this people
unto the land which the LORD hath sworn unto
their fathers to give them; and thou shalt cause
them to inherit it.
8 And the LORD, he *it is* that doth go before thee;
he will be with thee, he will not fail thee, neither
forsake thee: fear not, neither be dismayed.
9 ¶ And Moses wrote this law, and delivered it
unto the priests the sons of Levi, which bare the
ark of the covenant of the LORD, and unto all the
elders of Israel.
10 And Moses commanded them, saying, At the
end of *every* seven years, in the solemnity of the
year of release, in the feast of tabernacles,
11 When all Israel is come to appear before the
LORD thy God in the place which he shall choose,
thou shalt read this law before all Israel in their
hearing.
12 Gather the people together, men, and women,
and children, and thy stranger that *is* within thy
gates, that they may hear, and that they may learn,
and fear the LORD your God, and observe to do all
the words of this law:
13 And *that* their children, which have not known
any thing, may hear, and learn to fear the LORD
your God, as long as ye live in the land whither ye
go over Jordan to possess it.
14 ¶ And the LORD said unto Moses, Behold, thy
days approach that thou must die: call Joshua,
and present yourselves in the tabernacle of the
congregation, that I may give him a charge. And

30:18 *denounce.* To prophesy or declare.
30:19 *record.* To testify.

Thoughts for Personal/Family Worship: Chapter 30

1. **God foreknew that despite His mercies Israel would rebel against Him and suffer the curses of the law. However, He had already planned long beforehand that He would restore His exiled people. Even more, He planned to restore them to repentance and supreme love for Him by the inward work of His grace. God is not trying to catch up with our sins and figure out how to patch up the mess we have made. God planned it all, and His sovereign grace will transform His elect at the time He has decreed in Christ.**
2. **The Lord has linked together love for Him, obedience to His commands, and experiencing His blessings (v. 16). We should see these three as inseparably one. Let us never divide what God has joined. Love and law are not opposites, but one. To love the Lord is to obey His laws. To walk in His ways is to be blessed by God. It is not merely the way to happiness, but it is our happiness to love Him and do His will. How would seeing love, obedience, and joy as one change the way people think about religion?**

Chapter 31: ***Moses commissions Joshua and laments that Israel will ultimately break the covenant.***
Moses' Farewell (31:1–13)

31:2 See Num. 20:12.
31:6 The Lord repeated these words in Josh. 1:6–9.
31:9 *Moses wrote this law.* Moses is the author of Deuteronomy and the books preceding it (vv. 19,22,24; Ex. 17:14; 24:4; 34:27; Num. 33:2).
31:11–13 Without mass printing, there were few written copies of the Law (Pentateuch); thus public reading was important. The public reading was evidence of Scripture's canonical authority as the rule of faith and obedience for God's people. Other biblical exhortations call for audible reading of Scripture (Neh. 8:4–8; 9:3; Luke 4:16–21; 1 Tim. 4:13; Rev. 1:3). This ensures that every generation would hear the Word of the Lord.

Moses and Joshua went, and presented themselves in the tabernacle of the congregation.
15 And the LORD appeared in the tabernacle in a pillar of a cloud: and the pillar of the cloud stood over the door of the tabernacle.
16 ¶ And the LORD said unto Moses, Behold, thou shalt sleep with thy fathers; and this people will rise up, and go a whoring after the gods of the strangers of the land, whither they go *to be* among them, and will forsake me, and break my covenant which I have made with them.
17 Then my anger shall be kindled against them in that day, and I will forsake them, and I will hide my face from them, and they shall be devoured, and many evils and troubles shall befall them; so that they will say in that day, Are not these evils come upon us, because our God *is* not among us?
18 And I will surely hide my face in that day for all the evils which they shall have wrought, in that they are turned unto other gods.
19 Now therefore write ye this song for you, and teach it the children of Israel: put it in their mouths, that this song may be a witness for me against the children of Israel.
20 For when I shall have brought them into the land which I sware unto their fathers, that floweth with milk and honey; and they shall have eaten and filled themselves, and waxen fat; then will they turn unto other gods, and serve them, and provoke me, and break my covenant.
21 And it shall come to pass, when many evils and troubles are befallen them, that this song shall testify against them as a witness; for it shall not be forgotten out of the mouths of their seed: for I know their imagination which they go about, even now, before I have brought them into the land which I sware.
22 ¶ Moses therefore wrote this song the same day, and taught it the children of Israel.
23 And he gave Joshua the son of Nun a charge, and said, Be strong and of a good courage: for thou shalt bring the children of Israel into the land which I sware unto them: and I will be with thee.
24 ¶ And it came to pass, when Moses had made an end of writing the words of this law in a book, until they were finished,
25 That Moses commanded the Levites, which bare the ark of the covenant of the LORD, saying,
26 Take this book of the law, and put it in the side of the ark of the covenant of the LORD your God, that it may be there for a witness against thee.
27 For I know thy rebellion, and thy stiff neck: behold, while I am yet alive with you this day, ye have been rebellious against the LORD; and how much more after my death?
28 ¶ Gather unto me all the elders of your tribes, and your officers, that I may speak these words in their ears, and call heaven and earth to record against them.
29 For I know that after my death ye will utterly corrupt *yourselves*, and turn aside from the way which I have commanded you; and evil will befall you in the latter days; because ye will do evil in the sight of the LORD, to provoke him to anger through the work of your hands.
30 And Moses spake in the ears of all the congregation of Israel the words of this song, until they were ended.

CHAPTER 32

GIVE ear, O ye heavens, and I will speak; and hear, O earth, the words of my mouth.
2 My doctrine shall drop as the rain, my speech shall distil as the dew, as the small rain upon the tender herb, and as the showers upon the grass:
3 Because I will publish the name of the LORD: ascribe ye greatness unto our God.

Jehovah's Warning (31:14–30)

31:16 *shalt sleep.* Die. *go a whoring.* A common image for falling away from the true God and committing spiritual adultery with other gods (Ex. 34:15–16; Lev. 17:7; 20:5–6; Num. 15:39). God foretold the failure of Israel to keep the covenant.
31:20 *waxen fat.* To become fat.
31:21 *shall testify.* The songs of God's praise served an important function in the religious life of Israel.
31:26 *put it in the side of the ark.* Depositing the book was also evidence of its canonical authority.

Thoughts for Personal/Family Worship: Chapter 31

1. **Chapter 31 is a study in divine mercy. God knew that Israel would depart from Him. Yet He loved Israel and remained faithful. He provided the song of ch. 32 to remind and to reprimand Israel when they turned away. Anticipating our sinfulness, God calls us to repentance and promises grace before we even know we need it, grace to forgive and grace to change the heart, both through Jesus Christ (Acts 5:30–31).**
2. **One might imagine Joshua's burden as he contemplated leading Israel to claim the Canaanite homeland. This anxiety was addressed by Moses: "Be strong and of good courage, fear not . . . nor forsake thee" (31:6,23). God assured Joshua, "Thou shalt bring the children of Israel into the land," and promised, "I will be with thee" (v. 23). God ensures the completion of His call and purpose. What God has instructed us to do, He enables us to do.**

Chapter 32: *Moses' sermon-song extols the Lord and rebukes the wayward.*

Song of Moses (32:1–52)

32:1–44 In cultures lacking print media, songs play an important role in transmitting knowledge to future generations. God employed this technique to give Israel an understanding of her history and of the *Rock* from whom her blessings, both past and future, came. These truths committed to song would pass from generation to generation, like the recurring yearly rains that refresh the earth (v. 2; cf. Ps. 78).
32:2 *distil.* Flow. *small rain.* Gentle rain.

4 *He is* the Rock, his work *is* perfect: for all his
ways *are* judgment: a God of truth and without
iniquity, just and right *is* he.
5 They have corrupted themselves, their spot *is*
not *the spot* of his children: *they are* a perverse and
crooked generation.
6 Do ye thus requite the LORD, O foolish people
and unwise? *is* not he thy father *that* hath bought
thee? hath he not made thee, and established thee?
7 ¶ Remember the days of old, consider the years
of many generations: ask thy father, and he will
shew thee; thy elders, and they will tell thee.
8 When the most High divided to the nations
their inheritance, when he separated the sons of
Adam, he set the bounds of the people according
to the number of the children of Israel.
9 For the LORD's portion *is* his people; Jacob *is* the
lot of his inheritance.
10 He found him in a desert land, and in the
waste howling wilderness; he led him about, he
instructed him, he kept him as the apple of his eye.
11 As an eagle stirreth up her nest, fluttereth over
her young, spreadeth abroad her wings, taketh
them, beareth them on her wings:
12 *So* the LORD alone did lead him, and *there was*
no strange god with him.
13 He made him ride on the high places of the
earth, that he might eat the increase of the fields;
and he made him to suck honey out of the rock,
and oil out of the flinty rock;
14 Butter of kine, and milk of sheep, with fat
of lambs, and rams of the breed of Bashan, and
goats, with the fat of kidneys of wheat; and thou
didst drink the pure blood of the grape.
15 ¶ But Jeshurun waxed fat, and kicked: thou art
waxen fat, thou art grown thick, thou art covered
with fatness; then he forsook God *which* made him,
and lightly esteemed the Rock of his salvation.
16 They provoked him to jealousy with strange
gods, with abominations provoked they him to
anger.
17 They sacrificed unto devils, not to God; to
gods whom they knew not, to new *gods that* came
newly up, whom your fathers feared not.
18 Of the Rock *that* begat thee thou art unmind-
ful, and hast forgotten God that formed thee.
19 And when the LORD saw *it*, he abhorred *them*,
because of the provoking of his sons, and of his
daughters.
20 And he said, I will hide my face from them, I
will see what their end *shall be*: for they *are* a very
froward generation, children in whom *is* no faith.
21 They have moved me to jealousy with *that*
which is not God; they have provoked me to
anger with their vanities: and I will move them to
jealousy with *those which are* not a people; I will
provoke them to anger with a foolish nation.
22 For a fire is kindled in mine anger, and shall
burn unto the lowest hell, and shall consume the
earth with her increase, and set on fire the foun-
dations of the mountains.
23 I will heap mischiefs upon them; I will spend
mine arrows upon them.
24 *They shall be* burnt with hunger, and devoured
with burning heat, and with bitter destruction: I
will also send the teeth of beasts upon them, with
the poison of serpents of the dust.
25 The sword without, and terror within, shall
destroy both the young man and the virgin, the
suckling *also* with the man of gray hairs.
26 I said, I would scatter them into corners, I
would make the remembrance of them to cease
from among men:
27 Were it not that I feared the wrath of the en-
emy, lest their adversaries should behave them-
selves strangely, *and* lest they should say, Our
hand *is* high, and the LORD hath not done all this.
28 For they *are* a nation void of counsel, neither *is*
there any understanding in them.
29 O that they were wise, *that* they understood
this, *that* they would consider their latter end!
30 How should one chase a thousand, and two
put ten thousand to flight, except their Rock had
sold them, and the LORD had shut them up?
31 For their rock *is* not as our Rock, even our
enemies themselves *being* judges.

32:3 *publish.* Proclaim.

32:4 *He is the Rock.* Five times God is called the *Rock.* This word refers to a huge, unmovable boulder. This imagery, realized in Christ (1 Cor. 10:4), is also used in other Old Testament songs. See 2 Sam. 22; Pss. 18; 28; 31; 42; 62; 71; 89. *judgment.* Justice. God's massive, solid, unchangeable glory is particularly highlighted with respect to His righteousness and faithfulness.

32:5 *corrupted themselves.* In stark contrast to the righteous Rock (v. 4), Israel is ruined by its sin. *spot is not the spot.* The people are blemished and not as His children should be.

32:6 *requite.* Repay or reward.

32:8 See Gen. 11.

32:10 *apple of his eye.* The pupil of the eye, which is sensitive and thus the object of protection.

32:12 *strange god.* God of a foreign country (v. 16).

32:14 *kine.* Cattle. *kidneys of wheat.* Finest part of the wheat. *pure blood of the grape.* The best juice from the grape.

32:15 *Jeshurun.* A name of endearment for Israel, meaning "upright" (33:5,26; Isa. 44:2). Here used ironically since they were not behaving uprightly. *waxed fat.* Became fat, an image of becoming insensitive. *lightly esteemed the Rock of his salvation.* Despised their glorious Savior.

32:17 *sacrificed unto devils.* Idolatry is devil worship (Lev. 17:7; 1 Cor. 10:20).

32:20 *froward.* Perverse.

32:21 *vanities.* Worthless idols.

32:22 *lowest hell.* Hebrew, *sheol.*

32:23 *mischiefs.* Calamities.

32:24 *burnt with hunger.* Suffered severe hunger.

32:25 *suckling.* Literally, a "tender plant," referring to a nursing child.

32 For their vine *is* of the vine of Sodom, and of
the fields of Gomorrah: their grapes *are* grapes of
gall, their clusters *are* bitter:
33 Their wine *is* the poison of dragons, and the
cruel venom of asps.
34 *Is* not this laid up in store with me, *and* sealed
up among my treasures?
35 To me *belongeth* vengeance, and recompence;
their foot shall slide in *due* time: for the day of
their calamity *is* at hand, and the things that shall
come upon them make haste.
36 For the LORD shall judge his people, and repent
himself for his servants, when he seeth that *their*
power is gone, and *there is* none shut up, or left.
37 And he shall say, Where *are* their gods, *their*
rock in whom they trusted,
38 Which did eat the fat of their sacrifices, *and*
drank the wine of their drink offerings? let them
rise up and help you, *and* be your protection.
39 See now that I, *even* I, *am* he, and *there is* no
god with me: I kill, and I make alive; I wound, and
I heal: neither *is there any* that can deliver out of
my hand.
40 For I lift up my hand to heaven, and say, I live
for ever.
41 If I whet my glittering sword, and mine hand
take hold on judgment; I will render vengeance to
mine enemies, and will reward them that hate me.
42 I will make mine arrows drunk with blood,
and my sword shall devour flesh; *and that* with
the blood of the slain and of the captives, from the
beginning of revenges upon the enemy.
43 Rejoice, O ye nations, *with* his people: for he
will avenge the blood of his servants, and will
render vengeance to his adversaries, and will be
merciful unto his land, *and* to his people.
44 ¶ And Moses came and spake all the words of
this song in the ears of the people, he, and Hoshea
the son of Nun.
45 And Moses made an end of speaking all these
words to all Israel:
46 And he said unto them, Set your hearts unto
all the words which I testify among you this day,
which ye shall command your children to observe
to do, all the words of this law.
47 For it *is* not a vain thing for you; because it *is*
your life: and through this thing ye shall prolong
your days in the land, whither ye go over Jordan
to possess it.
48 And the LORD spake unto Moses that selfsame
day, saying,
49 Get thee up into this mountain Abarim, *unto*
mount Nebo, which *is* in the land of Moab, that
is over against Jericho; and behold the land of
Canaan, which I give unto the children of Israel
for a possession:
50 And die in the mount whither thou goest up,
and be gathered unto thy people; as Aaron thy
brother died in mount Hor, and was gathered
unto his people:
51 Because ye trespassed against me among
the children of Israel at the waters of Meribah-
Kadesh, in the wilderness of Zin; because ye sanc-
tified me not in the midst of the children of Israel.
52 Yet thou shalt see the land before *thee*; but
thou shalt not go thither unto the land which I
give the children of Israel.

CHAPTER 33

AND this *is* the blessing, wherewith Moses the
man of God blessed the children of Israel before
his death.
2 And he said, The LORD came from Sinai, and
rose up from Seir unto them; he shined forth
from mount Paran, and he came with ten thou-
sands of saints: from his right hand *went* a fiery
law for them.
3 Yea, he loved the people; all his saints *are* in thy
hand: and they sat down at thy feet; *every one* shall
receive of thy words.
4 Moses commanded us a law, *even* the inheri-
tance of the congregation of Jacob.
5 And he was king in Jeshurun, when the heads

32:33 *dragons.* Serpents.
32:36 *repent himself.* An expression meaning to show compassion.
32:41 *whet.* Sharpen.
32:44 *Hoshea.* Joshua.
32:51 See Num. 20:11–13; 21:14.

Thoughts for Personal/Family Worship: Chapter 32

1. **"Bless the LORD, O my soul, and forget not all his benefits" (Ps. 103:2). Moses' song reviews God's blessings and warnings. Israel would thus review God's goodness and cautions whenever the song was sung. God's works should be remembered by frequent recitation, and His words should be quoted as the key to understanding life's events.**
2. **We see in this chapter a sobering contrast between the Lord and humanity. God is the "Rock," righteous and true, powerful and unchangeable. However, despite all that the Lord did in choosing, redeeming, and caring for Israel, the people despised Him and provoked His holy vengeance. Centuries later, those returning from exile would remember their national history and confess to the Lord, "thou has done right, but we have done wickedly" (Neh. 9:33). Therefore, let us humble ourselves, for we are no better than they, but let us worship the Lord, for He is the Rock of salvation.**

Chapter 33: *Moses blesses each of the tribes of Israel.*
Blessing the Tribes (33:1–29)

33:1 Blessings before death were common (Gen. 49).
33:2 *ten thousands of saints.* Holy ones, here angels (Acts 7:53; Gal. 3:19; Heb. 2:2).
33:5 *Jeshurun.* See note at 32:15. *tribes.* All but Simeon are mentioned.

of the people *and* the tribes of Israel were gathered together.
6 ¶ Let Reuben live, and not die; and let *not* his men be few.
7 ¶ And this *is the blessing* of Judah: and he said, Hear, LORD, the voice of Judah, and bring him unto his people: let his hands be sufficient for him; and be thou an help *to him* from his enemies.
8 ¶ And of Levi he said, *Let* thy Thummim and thy Urim *be* with thy holy one, whom thou didst prove at Massah, *and with* whom thou didst strive at the waters of Meribah;
9 Who said unto his father and to his mother, I have not seen him; neither did he acknowledge his brethren, nor knew his own children: for they have observed thy word, and kept thy covenant.
10 They shall teach Jacob thy judgments, and Israel thy law: they shall put incense before thee, and whole burnt sacrifice upon thine altar.
11 Bless, LORD, his substance, and accept the work of his hands: smite through the loins of them that rise against him, and of them that hate him, that they rise not again.
12 ¶ *And* of Benjamin he said, The beloved of the LORD shall dwell in safety by him; *and the LORD* shall cover him all the day long, and he shall dwell between his shoulders.
13 ¶ And of Joseph he said, Blessed of the LORD *be* his land, for the precious things of heaven, for the dew, and for the deep that coucheth beneath,
14 And for the precious fruits *brought forth* by the sun, and for the precious things put forth by the moon,
15 And for the chief things of the ancient mountains, and for the precious things of the lasting hills,
16 And for the precious things of the earth and fulness thereof, and *for* the good will of him that dwelt in the bush: let *the blessing* come upon the head of Joseph, and upon the top of the head of him *that was* separated from his brethren.
17 His glory *is like* the firstling of his bullock, and his horns *are like* the horns of unicorns: with them he shall push the people together to the ends of the earth: and they *are* the ten thousands of Ephraim, and they *are* the thousands of Manasseh.
18 ¶ And of Zebulun he said, Rejoice, Zebulun, in thy going out; and, Issachar, in thy tents.
19 They shall call the people unto the mountain; there they shall offer sacrifices of righteousness: for they shall suck *of* the abundance of the seas, and *of* treasures hid in the sand.
20 ¶ And of Gad he said, Blessed *be* he that enlargeth Gad: he dwelleth as a lion, and teareth the arm with the crown of the head.
21 And he provided the first part for himself, because there, *in* a portion of the lawgiver, *was he* seated; and he came with the heads of the people, he executed the justice of the LORD, and his judgments with Israel.
22 ¶ And of Dan he said, Dan *is* a lion's whelp: he shall leap from Bashan.
23 ¶ And of Naphtali he said, O Naphtali, satisfied with favour, and full with the blessing of the LORD: possess thou the west and the south.
24 ¶ And of Asher he said, *Let* Asher *be* blessed with children; let him be acceptable to his brethren, and let him dip his foot in oil.
25 Thy shoes *shall be* iron and brass; and as thy days, *so shall* thy strength *be*.
26 ¶ *There is* none like unto the God of Jeshurun, *who* rideth upon the heaven in thy help, and in his excellency on the sky.
27 The eternal God *is thy* refuge, and underneath *are* the everlasting arms: and he shall thrust out the enemy from before thee; and shall say, Destroy *them*.
28 Israel then shall dwell in safety alone: the fountain of Jacob *shall be* upon a land of corn and wine; also his heavens shall drop down dew.
29 Happy *art* thou, O Israel: who *is* like unto thee, O people saved by the LORD, the shield of thy help, and who *is* the sword of thy excellency! and thine enemies shall be found liars unto thee; and thou shalt tread upon their high places.

33:8 *Thummim and . . . Urim.* See Ex. 28:30. *prove.* To try or test (Ex. 17).
33:9 *not seen him.* Perhaps referring to the Levites' destruction of their brothers after the golden calf (Ex. 32:25–29).
33:11 *loins.* Considered the center of one's strength.
33:12 *between his shoulders.* Chest.
33:13 *coucheth.* Lies down.
33:16 *bush.* See Ex. 3:2–6.
33:17 *bullock.* Ox. *unicorns.* Wild oxen.
33:19 *suck.* Or to soak up, denoting great prosperity.
33:22 *whelp.* Cub.
33:24 *dip his foot in oil.* A sign of prosperity.

Thoughts for Personal/Family Worship: Chapter 33

1. **A leader's proper role is to selflessly bless his followers. Moses chose "to suffer affliction with the people of God" and esteemed "the reproach of Christ greater riches than the treasures in Egypt" (Heb. 11:25–26), so that he might bring Israel into the blessings promised to them centuries earlier. Fathers and leaders are to be "used up" for the good of those placed under their authority. Jesus Christ is the premier example of this.**
2. **"Happy art thou, O Israel: who is like unto thee, O people saved by the LORD" (v. 29). No other nation has experienced such blessing as Israel. This signified that God had set Israel apart unto Himself. What national Israel experienced is ultimately true of the church. Christ's people are set apart unto Him and blessed. There are no peoples comparable to Christ's true church. "Behold, what manner of love the Father hath bestowed upon us, that we should be called the sons of God" (1 John 3:1). It is good to ponder this truth and then to offer praise to God for all the benefits of His saving grace.**

CHAPTER 34

AND Moses went up from the plains of Moab
unto the mountain of Nebo, to the top of Pisgah,
that *is* over against Jericho. And the LORD shewed
him all the land of Gilead, unto Dan,
2 And all Naphtali, and the land of Ephraim, and
Manasseh, and all the land of Judah, unto the
utmost sea,
3 And the south, and the plain of the valley of
Jericho, the city of palm trees, unto Zoar.
4 And the LORD said unto him, This *is* the land
which I sware unto Abraham, unto Isaac, and
unto Jacob, saying, I will give it unto thy seed: I
have caused thee to see *it* with thine eyes, but thou
shalt not go over thither.
5 ¶ So Moses the servant of the LORD died there
in the land of Moab, according to the word of the
LORD.
6 And he buried him in a valley in the land of
Moab, over against Beth-peor: but no man
knoweth of his sepulchre unto this day.
7 ¶ And Moses *was* an hundred and twenty years
old when he died: his eye was not dim, nor his
natural force abated.
8 ¶ And the children of Israel wept for Moses in
the plains of Moab thirty days: so the days of weep-
ing *and* mourning for Moses were ended.
9 ¶ And Joshua the son of Nun was full of the
spirit of wisdom; for Moses had laid his hands
upon him: and the children of Israel hearkened
unto him, and did as the LORD commanded Moses.
10 ¶ And there arose not a prophet since in Israel
like unto Moses, whom the LORD knew face to
face,
11 In all the signs and the wonders, which the
LORD sent him to do in the land of Egypt to Pha-
raoh, and to all his servants, and to all his land,
12 And in all that mighty hand, and in all the
great terror which Moses shewed in the sight of
all Israel.

Chapter 34: *Moses views the Promised Land and dies.*

CONCLUSION: MOSES' DEATH AND JOSHUA'S SUCCESSION (34:1–12)

34:1–4 Moses viewed the Promised Land from northernmost *Dan* to its southernmost region.

34:5–9 The report of Moses' death in a book which he authored is not problematic. Moses had many "assistants" (Ex. 18:13–24), an absolute necessity for a man handling his responsibilities. Surely scribes were among them, who recorded "the words which Moses spake unto all Israel" (1:1). It is reasonable that they would conclude their record by reporting Moses' death, burial, the mourning that ensued (v. 8), and the transfer of authority to Joshua (v. 9). Divine inspiration guaranteed canonicity and preservation.

34:6 *sepulchre.* Grave. See Jude 9.

34:10 *face to face.* Intimately (Num. 12:8; Deut. 18:15–18).

Thoughts for Personal/Family Worship: Chapter 34

1. **Moses led the nation out of Egypt and through the wilderness, but the privilege of leading Israel into Canaan was reserved for Joshua. Piece by piece, portions of God's work are done by servants of His choosing. Each should recognize that he is a small piece of a larger work that God is doing. We work earnestly in the progress of God's kingdom, yet it may be God's wisdom to allow others to take the prize we sought. In God's plan, there is always a Joshua to replace a Moses, and in the end all is of the Lord.**
2. **Moses, whom the Lord knew "face to face" (v. 10), experienced divine intimacy unknown to any other leader except Christ (18:18; John 1:17–18; Acts 3:20–23; Heb. 3:4–6). Yet the Son of God reveals the Father to whomever He pleases (Matt. 11:27). He enables us to know the true God, and such knowledge gives eternal life (John 17:3,6; 1 John 5:20). One day, believers in Christ will also know God face-to-face (1 Cor. 13:12; Rev. 22:4), and intimacy with Him will be their eternal joy. How does that give us hope?**

Introduction to the Historical Books

The Historical Books constitute a large segment of the Old Testament. In the English Bible, these books are sequential beginning with Joshua and ending with Esther. The Hebrew Bible is divided into three sections: the Law, the Prophets and the Writings. The books of history are in the second and third divisions: Except for Ruth, Joshua through 2 Kings are part of the Prophets, usually referred to as the Former Prophets, whereas Ruth, Esther, Ezra, Nehemiah and 1, 2 Chronicles are in the Writings. The books are the same; the order is different.

That so much of the Old Testament is history is significant. On one hand, it marks biblical religion as different from other religions in the Ancient Near East, whether Egyptian, Canaanite, or Mesopotamian. Virtually all the religious literature from Israel's neighbors was in the form of myths that describe the adventures of humanly conceived deities that were often humanized with more vices than virtues. But in the religion of Scripture, the one true and living God, who eternally exists independently of man's conceptions, actually reveals Himself to people in real time and space. Biblical religion rests on a historical foundation. Biblical religion, Christianity, is fact not fiction or make-believe.

On another hand, the Historical books are essential for tracing God's redemptive plan and purpose that reaches its climax in the fullness of time when Christ would come. The Historical Books flesh out the Seed promise revealed in the Pentateuch. The seed of the woman would come through the seed of Abraham through the seed of Isaac through the seed of Jacob/Israel. There had to be an Israel if there was going to be Christ (Rom. 9:4-5). Consequently, the whole checkered history of Israel contributes directly to the revelation of God's redemptive message. There were times when it appeared the serpent's seed would gain the advantage and thwart the progress, but over and again, whether the opposition came from outside the nation or as so frequently from inside, God's purpose in preparing the way for Christ to come directly into time and space to deal with sin could not be frustrated.

The unfolding of God's redemptive plan recorded in the record of Hebrew history includes many salient spiritual lessons along the way. There is more to history than just facts about people, event or dates. Significantly, the Psalmist, before surveying Israel's history, said that he would open his "mouth in a parable" (Ps. 78:2). In other words, the facts of history were like something else, something in the spiritual sphere (see 1 Cor. 10:6,11). Biblical history teaches lessons in morality and ethics, the consequences of sin, and the blessings of obedience and faithfulness to God's gracious covenant.

Biblical history's connection to the progression of redemption with all of redemption's implications and applications makes it unique among historical records. That uniqueness sometimes puts Old Testament history at odds with secular accounts that recorded the same event. Not surprisingly, rationalistic critics of the Scripture cite these points of disagreement as evidence of mistakes in the Bible. Rather, the points of contradiction evidence error in the secular accounts. Understanding something of the nature of writing history helps to confirm this conclusion. Writing history requires two things: knowledge of the past and a point of view that determines what is significant from the past. Every secular history suffers on both accounts. No human author knows all the past, and every human author has a point of view that reflects a particular agenda. Every secular history, therefore, is limited and biased. Particularly in the ancient world, most historical documents were official state records designed to create and preserve a legacy for the king; they were intentionally biased and based on incomplete knowledge of facts. To write a truly significant history requires omniscience and a pure motive or agenda. Only God knows everything and has the infinitely holy perspective to select from all the past what is really important. In a very real sense, the Bible is the only truly significant and infallibly accurate history ever written. So of all the things that happened in the world from the fourteenth to the fifth centuries BC, the Historical Books record the most important things to know and to believe.

The centuries of Hebrew history covered by the Historical Books logically fall into six divisions: Conquest (1406-1380 BC), Judges (1380-1050 BC), Monarchy (1050-931 BC), Divided Monarchy (931-586 BC), Exile (586-539 BC), and Post-Exile (539-424 BC). Each of these periods in some way relates to promises and warnings of the Pentateuch, particularly Deuteronomy. One of the great themes of Deuteronomy concerned God's promise of land, the possession of which was conditioned by faith and obedience to the demands of the covenant. The land referred to literal territory, but more significantly, God used the land as an object lesson to represent the fullness of spiritual blessing. Rest in the land was associated with the experience and enjoyment of God's presence. Moses made it clear that both entrance and continuance in the land required faith. Three parts of the land contract are evident in the Historical Books. *First*, if they kept the commandments, the Lord would bless them in the land (Deut. 28:1-2, 8-13). *Second*, if they violated the commandments, particularly by going after other gods, the Lord would curse them (Deut. 28:14-15) primarily by plucking them up from the land and scattering them among the nations (Deut. 28:63-64). *Third*, if they returned to the Lord, He would be gracious and gather them back to the land (Deut. 30:2-3). The checkered history of Israel mirrors each of these contractual points.

The Lord's behind-the-scene manipulation of nations was His primary method of executing the components of the land contract. In the conquest, sovereignty over the various Canaanite nations was obvious as the Lord fought for Israel. During the judges, the Lord used some of those same Canaanites as the instrument of His chastening of His people. This means of accomplishing His will was most obvious when the time came for Israel and then for Judah to be expelled from the land. Regarding Israel, the Lord used the Assyrians as His weapon. Militarily and politically, Assyria had become the most powerful nation in the world of the Near East, and they forged a plan of deportation to control their vast territories. It is notable that this seems to be the first time in the history of ancient warfare that this tactic was employed, at the very time when God exiled Israel (722 BC). The Assyrians were powerful enough to conquer Judah as well, but God prevented them from doing so until Judah's sin was ripe for judgment. That day came, and God then used the Babylonians to accomplish His purpose. In three stages (605, 597, 586 BC), the Babylonians under God's servant Nebuchadnezzar exiled Judah from the land. But the day came when God purposed to bring the people back. When that time came, God raised Cyrus, the Persian King. Whereas the Babylonians continued Assyria's practice of deportation, Cyrus changed policies by allowing previously exiled people to return to their native lands, including Judah. Although Cyrus and the Assyrian and Babylonian kings before him were ignorant of their manipulation by God and their role in divine providence, they were nonetheless His subjects and accountable to Him.

The message of the Historical Books is clear that God controls time, circumstance, individuals and kingdoms to accomplish His purpose. As you read through all the narratives, pay attention and learn the immediate lessons that will direct behavior. But as you read all the details and learn all the specific lessons, do so with the eye open to where the history is leading. Christ is coming.

INTRODUCTION TO THE BOOK OF JOSHUA

Authorship: Most conservatives, as well as Jewish tradition, attribute the book to Joshua, the successor of Moses. Joshua 24:26 states explicitly, "Joshua wrote these words in the book of the law of God." Even if this refers specifically to his farewell address, the first person references and personal biographical insights throughout the book point to his authorship of the whole. The reference to his death and burial (24:29–30) could be an addition by another inspired prophet, just as Joshua himself may have appended the reference to Moses' death to Deuteronomy (34:5–8). Joshua's name means either "Jehovah saves" or "Jehovah is salvation." It is the Hebrew equivalent to the Greek "Jesus." In Heb. 4:8, "Jesus" is clearly the Old Testament "Joshua." According to Num. 13:8,16 his name was originally Hosea, meaning "salvation" ("Oshea" in the KJV), but Moses lengthened it to Joshua ("Jehoshua" in the KJV) when he chose him to be one of the twelve spies. The name change puts in focus the truth that although "Hosea" was the human leader, it was in fact Jehovah who led and delivered the nation into the Promised Land. By his name and his work, Joshua points to his ideal namesake, the Lord Jesus Christ.

Date: 1406–1386 BC. It is generally assumed that the events of Joshua cover approximately twenty years. Dating the conquest is inseparably linked to the exodus. These dates follow from the traditionally conservative dating of the exodus to the mid-fifteenth century about 1446 BC (based on calculations from 1 Kings 6:1). The year 1406 would mark the end of the wilderness experience, and 1386 would coincide with the death of Joshua at 110 years old (24:29). Although subject to interpretation, significant archaeological evidence exists to support the biblical evidence of the conquest, including the date. This would include site excavations and especially the Tell el-Amarna letters (correspondence between Canaanite cities and Egypt) that very likely describe the conquest from the Canaanite perspective.

Theme: Conquest and Inheritance: God fulfills His promise to give Israel the land of Canaan. Several subthemes interweave to develop the principal theme, such as the presence of the Lord (particularly in the symbolism of the ark), the power of the Lord (demonstrated in supernatural acts), and the judgment of the Lord (evidenced in the divine sentence against the Canaanites). Joshua 21:45 sums up the principal theme: "There failed not ought of any good thing which the Lord had spoken."

Purpose: To show God's fidelity to His covenant promises and the necessity of living by faith by relying on and acting on the reality of the promises.

Synopsis: *The Contribution of Joshua to Redemptive Revelation*

Joshua, by recording the historical facts of the conquest and allotment of Canaan, interprets and illustrates the message of redemption along several lines—not the least of which is that Joshua was a type or a prophetic figure pointing to the greater Joshua (Jesus) to come. His encounter with "the captain of the Lord's host"—a Christophany or preincarnate appearance of Jesus—at the beginning of his career (5:13–15) suggests that there was a leader of the people greater than he. Joshua, leading Israel into their inheritance, is a picture-prophecy of Jesus, leading His church to glory (see Heb. 2:10, where Christ is specifically identified as the "captain of their salvation"). The Promised Land symbolizes the inheritance and spiritual rest that belongs to God's people in the experience and enjoyment of His presence (Heb. 4:8–11).

That Israel conquered the land in increments vividly pictures the progressive nature of sanctification. God dispossessed the Canaanites and gave the land to Israel as their possession. Nonetheless, Israel had to fight to expel the Canaanites. So spiritually, Christ has conquered sin so that it no longer has dominion over us (Rom. 6:14), yet we must actively be engaged in fighting against sin (Rom. 6:12–13). Victory over one city led to another city to conquer. So we must die more and more to sin and live more and more to righteousness. Sanctification progresses until glorification.

Joshua also shows the need for the gospel by underscoring the terrible consequences of sin. The divine sentence against the Canaanites testifies to the certain execution of divine justice. Similarly, the episode with Achan (ch. 7) illustrates the power of sin to affect others and the impossibility of hiding sin from God. Joshua shows that there is more to biblical history than just facts.

Outline:

I. The Entrance into Canaan (1:1—5:15)
  A. Personal Instructions for Joshua (1:1–9)
  B. Preparations for Crossing the Jordan (1:10—2:24)
  C. Crossing the Jordan (3:1—4:24)
  D. Renewal of Circumcision (5:1–15)

II. The Conquest of Canaan (6:1—12:24)
  A. The Central Campaign (6:1—9:27)
    1. Victory at Jericho (6:1–27)
    2. Defeat and Victory at Ai (7:1—8:29)
    3. Reading of the Law (8:30–35)
    4. Alliance with Gibeon (9:1–27)
  B. The Southern Campaign (10:1–43)
  C. The Northern Campaign (11:1–15)
  D. An Overview of the Conquest (11:16—12:24)

III. The Division of the Land (13:1—21:45)
  A. The Procedure for Allotment (13:1–7)
  B. The Inheritance for the Eastern Tribes (13:8–33)
  C. The Inheritance for the Western Tribes (14:1—19:51)
  D. The Designation of Special Cities (20:1—21:45)
    1. Cities of Refuge (20:1–9)
    2. Cities for the Levites (21:1–45)

IV. The Maintenance of the Land (22:1—24:33)
  A. Warnings for the Transjordan Tribes (22:1–34)
  B. Admonitions from Joshua (23:1—24:33)

THE BOOK OF JOSHUA

CHAPTER 1

NOW after the death of Moses the servant of the
LORD it came to pass, that the LORD spake unto
Joshua the son of Nun, Moses' minister, saying,
2 Moses my servant is dead; now therefore arise,
go over this Jordan, thou, and all this people,
unto the land which I do give to them, *even* to the
children of Israel.
3 Every place that the sole of your foot shall tread
upon, that have I given unto you, as I said unto
Moses.
4 From the wilderness and this Lebanon even
unto the great river, the river Euphrates, all the
land of the Hittites, and unto the great sea toward
the going down of the sun, shall be your coast.
5 There shall not any man be able to stand before
thee all the days of thy life: as I was with Moses,
so I will be with thee: I will not fail thee, nor for-
sake thee.
6 Be strong and of a good courage: for unto
this people shalt thou divide for an inheritance
the land, which I sware unto their fathers to give
them.
7 Only be thou strong and very courageous, that
thou mayest observe to do according to all the law,
which Moses my servant commanded thee: turn
not from it *to* the right hand or *to* the left, that
thou mayest prosper whithersoever thou goest.
8 This book of the law shall not depart out of thy
mouth; but thou shalt meditate therein day and
night, that thou mayest observe to do according
to all that is written therein: for then thou shalt
make thy way prosperous, and then thou shalt
have good success.
9 Have not I commanded thee? Be strong and
of a good courage; be not afraid, neither be thou
dismayed: for the LORD thy God *is* with thee
whithersoever thou goest.
10 ¶ Then Joshua commanded the officers of the
people, saying,
11 Pass through the host, and command the
people, saying, Prepare you victuals; for within
three days ye shall pass over this Jordan, to go in
to possess the land, which the LORD your God
giveth you to possess it.
12 ¶ And to the Reubenites, and to the Gadites,
and to half the tribe of Manasseh, spake Joshua,
saying,
13 Remember the word which Moses the servant
of the LORD commanded you, saying, The LORD

THE ENTRANCE INTO CANAAN (1:1—5:15)

Chapter 1: ***God gives specific orders to Joshua about the conquest assuring him of His abiding presence and unchanging promise, and Joshua then orders the people to prepare for the crossing of the Jordan.***

Personal Instructions for Joshua (1:1–9)

1:1 *after the death of Moses . . . the LORD spake unto Joshua.* God often uses human mediation to do His work on the earth, but no man is indispensable. As great as Moses was (he is designated as the servant of the Lord fourteen times in this book), there was a Joshua to carry on and do what he could not do.
1:2 *I do give.* The verb form indicates that the Lord is in the process of giving them the land.
1:3 *have I given.* The verb form indicates the certain fact of God's gift of the land.
1:4 *the great sea . . . going down of the sun.* The Mediterranean Sea to the west.
1:5 *able to stand.* Resist or hold one's ground. *as I was with Moses . . . with thee.* The "Immanuel" principle (God with us) was the experience of Old Testament saints but reaches its climax in the incarnation. *I will not fail thee.* Literally, "to abandon" or "to leave in the lurch."
1:6 *be . . . of a good courage.* Literally, "be bold" or "courageous."
1:7 *prosper.* Achieve success. The reference is specifically to the conquest of the land, not financial gain.
1:8 *This book of the law.* The "Torah" which designates the five books of Moses, at that time the whole Bible. *day and night.* An idiom for doing something constantly, throughout the day. *observe to do.* Be careful or diligent to do.

Preparations for Crossing the Jordan (1:10—2:24)

1:10 *Then Joshua commanded.* This introduces the common pattern of God first speaking to the chosen leader who in turn passes on divine commands to the people.
1:11 *victuals.* Provisions, food for the journey.
1:12 *Reubenites.* The two and a half tribes that received their inheritance in the Transjordan region (the east side of the river, see v. 5, "the sunrising").
1:13 *rest.* A symbolic reference to the land of promise (Ps. 95:11). The rest is associated with the enjoyment of both a cessation of hostility and the presence of God. That is one key reason the nation could not possess the land in unbelief.

your God hath given you rest, and hath given you
this land.
14 Your wives, your little ones, and your cattle,
shall remain in the land which Moses gave you
on this side Jordan; but ye shall pass before your
brethren armed, all the mighty men of valour,
and help them;
15 Until the LORD have given your brethren rest,
as *he hath given* you, and they also have possessed
the land which the LORD your God giveth them:
then ye shall return unto the land of your posses-
sion, and enjoy it, which Moses the LORD's servant
gave you on this side Jordan toward the sunrising.
16 ¶ And they answered Joshua, saying, All that
thou commandest us we will do, and whithersoever
ever thou sendest us, we will go.
17 According as we hearkened unto Moses in
all things, so will we hearken unto thee: only the
LORD thy God be with thee, as he was with Moses.
18 Whosoever *he be* that doth rebel against thy
commandment, and will not hearken unto thy
words in all that thou commandest him, he shall be
put to death: only be strong and of a good courage.

CHAPTER 2

AND Joshua the son of Nun sent out of Shittim
two men to spy secretly, saying, Go view the land,
even Jericho. And they went, and came into an
harlot's house, named Rahab, and lodged there.
2 And it was told the king of Jericho, saying,
Behold, there came men in hither to night of the
children of Israel to search out the country.
3 And the king of Jericho sent unto Rahab, saying,
Bring forth the men that are come to thee, which
are entered into thine house: for they be come to
search out all the country.
4 And the woman took the two men, and hid
them, and said thus, There came men unto me,
but I wist not whence they *were*:
5 And it came to pass *about the time* of shutting
of the gate, when it was dark, that the men went
out: whither the men went I wot not: pursue after
them quickly; for ye shall overtake them.
6 But she had brought them up to the roof of the
house, and hid them with the stalks of flax, which
she had laid in order upon the roof.
7 And the men pursued after them the way to Jor-
dan unto the fords: and as soon as they which pur-
sued after them were gone out, they shut the gate.
8 ¶ And before they were laid down, she came up
unto them upon the roof;
9 And she said unto the men, I know that the
LORD hath given you the land, and that your terror
is fallen upon us, and that all the inhabitants of
the land faint because of you.
10 For we have heard how the LORD dried up the
water of the Red sea for you, when ye came out
of Egypt; and what ye did unto the two kings of
the Amorites, that *were* on the other side Jordan,
Sihon and Og, whom ye utterly destroyed.
11 And as soon as we had heard *these things*, our
hearts did melt, neither did there remain any
more courage in any man, because of you: for the

Thoughts for Personal/Family Worship: Chapter 1

1. **Moses was dead, but the work of God was continuing without him because it was the work of God and not of Moses (1:1–2). Notwithstanding how great Moses was and how many extraordinary things he did, he was not indispensable. Joshua was there with the same promises God had given Moses to carry on the work. There was a work for Joshua to do that Moses could not do. This transition from Moses to Joshua stands as a warning to not put hope in man. Too often in Christendom today men try to build empires around themselves, and their work ultimately falls because it was centered in a personality. On the other hand, church history is full of outstandingly great men who served the Lord in their generation only to be replaced by others who served the same Lord in another generation. Thank God that He gives these leaders as His gifts for the good of the church (Eph. 4:11–13).**
2. **The book of Joshua illustrates how God uses men as His ordained ministers or servants to lead His people. The recurring pattern is that God speaks to the leader who in turn speaks to the people (vv. 9–10). It is imperative, then, that ministers know God's Word so that they can effectively communicate that Word to the people. However, the instructions for Joshua to meditate on and obey God's Word constantly as the means for successful living is a paradigm that should be followed by all of God's people. How can you follow Joshua's example in his attitude toward God's Word?**

Chapter 2: ***Rahab conceals the two men sent to spy out Jericho, and they in turn repay her with the promise of deliverance from the city's destruction.***

2:1 *Shittim.* The last encampment before crossing the Jordan, located almost directly east of *Jericho*, which was on the west side of Jordan.

2:2 *king of Jericho.* An appropriate title, since Canaan was comprised of multiple city-states, all of which were independent of each other.

2:3 *be come.* Have come.

2:4–5 *I wist not whence they were.* I did not know from where they were. *whither the men went I wot not.* I do not know where the men went. The sin of Rahab's lie does not negate the reality of her faith, for she received the spies of Israel and sent them out another way because she believed in the Lord (Heb. 11:31; James 2:25). She sided with God's people and sought to share in their inheritance. However, her lie does remind us that believers still sin.

2:9–13 Rahab's confession and appeal for clemency. She acknowledges the Lord's might displayed in what He had done for Israel (vv. 9–11), recognizes His majesty as God of heaven and earth (v. 11), and pleads for mercy (vv. 12–13). She pleads for *kindness* in reciprocation of the *kindness* she had shown the spies. This word designates covenant loyalty and expects mutuality between the parties. *token.* A sign or distinguishing

LORD your God, he *is* God in heaven above, and
in earth beneath.
12 Now therefore, I pray you, swear unto me by
the LORD, since I have shewed you kindness, that
ye will also shew kindness unto my father's house,
and give me a true token:
13 And *that* ye will save alive my father, and my
mother, and my brethren, and my sisters, and all
that they have, and deliver our lives from death.
14 And the men answered her, Our life for yours,
if ye utter not this our business. And it shall be,
when the LORD hath given us the land, that we
will deal kindly and truly with thee.
15 Then she let them down by a cord through the
window: for her house *was* upon the town wall,
and she dwelt upon the wall.
16 And she said unto them, Get you to the
mountain, lest the pursuers meet you; and hide
yourselves there three days, until the pursuers be
returned: and afterward may ye go your way.
17 And the men said unto her, We *will be*
blameless of this thine oath which thou hast
made us swear.
18 Behold, *when* we come into the land, thou
shalt bind this line of scarlet thread in the window
which thou didst let us down by: and thou shalt
bring thy father, and thy mother, and thy brethren,
and all thy father's household, home unto thee.
19 And it shall be, *that* whosoever shall go out of
the doors of thy house into the street, his blood
shall be upon his head, and we *will be* guiltless:
and whosoever shall be with thee in the house, his
blood *shall be* on our head, if *any* hand be upon
him.
20 And if thou utter this our business, then we
will be quit of thine oath which thou hast made
us to swear.
21 And she said, According unto your words, so
be it. And she sent them away, and they departed:
and she bound the scarlet line in the window.
22 And they went, and came unto the mountain,
and abode there three days, until the pursuers
were returned: and the pursuers sought *them*
throughout all the way, but found *them* not.
23 ¶ So the two men returned, and descended
from the mountain, and passed over, and came
to Joshua the son of Nun, and told him all *things*
that befell them:
24 And they said unto Joshua, Truly the LORD
hath delivered into our hands all the land; for
even all the inhabitants of the country do faint
because of us.

CHAPTER 3

AND Joshua rose early in the morning; and they
removed from Shittim, and came to Jordan, he
and all the children of Israel, and lodged there
before they passed over.
2 And it came to pass after three days, that the
officers went through the host;
3 And they commanded the people, saying,
When ye see the ark of the covenant of the LORD
your God, and the priests the Levites bearing it,

mark, something that would assure her of their loyalty to her.
2:14 *deal kindly*. The same expression as v. 12—to demonstrate covenant loyalty.
2:17–21 The spies set the terms by which Rahab and her family will be delivered from destruction. If the terms are not met, the spies will be *blameless* (v. 17) and *quit* (v. 20) of the oath. Both translate the same Hebrew word, meaning "free" or "exempt from obligation." *thread*. Since this was the rope used to lower the spies, it was more than just a strand. It was large enough and bright enough (scarlet) to easily identify Rahab's residence during the siege. She agreed to the terms.
2:23 *all things that befell them*. All the things that happened to them.
2:24 *faint*. Despair or melt away.

Thoughts for Personal/Family Worship: Chapter 2

1. **Rahab is a wonderful example of the power and sovereignty of grace. She appears to be an unlikely candidate for grace, but that is the point. She is a vivid picture of all who are dead in sin and who are made alive by the greater Joshua, the Lord Jesus Christ. The depths of her sin magnify the beauty of grace. From every appearance Rahab was without hope, a citizen of a doomed city, alienated from the commonwealth of Israel, a stranger to the covenant promise. But God sovereignly directed the spies to her house. Indeed, God had put the "scarlet cord" there in eternity long before the spies arrived. Although Joshua sent the men to spy the land, they had a commission from God to preach to Rahab. Significantly, James refers to them not as spies but as messengers (James 2:25). They had a word for Rahab. Faith comes by hearing the Word of God and that hearing comes through preachers (Rom. 10:13–14). How has God's sovereign hand reached out to you?**
2. **Not only does grace find the sinner, it awakens the sinner. Rahab believed (Heb. 11:31), and she made a confession of her faith. She acknowledged God's mighty and fear-producing power that had saved Israel (Josh. 2:9–10). She knew that it would be a fearful thing to fall into the hands of such a God (Heb. 10:31). She expressed the sure conviction that Jehovah was the one true and living God in heaven and earth (Josh. 2:11). According to Paul, no one can make such a genuine heart confession except by the Holy Spirit (1 Cor. 12:3). By pleading for mercy (Josh. 2:12–13), she recognized that God was her only hope, her only place of refuge. Reflect on these components of her confession since the object and nature of saving faith is the same now as then.**

Crossing the Jordan (3:1—4:24)

Chapter 3: *The priests, carrying the ark of the covenant, lead the people across the Jordan on dry land into the Promised Land.*

3:1 *Shittim*. See note at 2:1.
3:2 *the host*. Literally, "the midst of the camp."
3:3 *ark of the covenant*. The preeminent piece of tabernacle

then ye shall remove from your place, and go after
it.
4 Yet there shall be a space between you and it,
about two thousand cubits by measure: come not
near unto it, that ye may know the way by which ye
must go: for ye have not passed *this* way heretofore.
5 And Joshua said unto the people, Sanctify
yourselves: for to morrow the LORD will do
wonders among you.
6 And Joshua spake unto the priests, saying,
Take up the ark of the covenant, and pass over
before the people. And they took up the ark of the
covenant, and went before the people.
7 ¶ And the LORD said unto Joshua, This day will I
begin to magnify thee in the sight of all Israel, that
they may know that, as I was with Moses, *so* I will
be with thee.
8 And thou shalt command the priests that bear
the ark of the covenant, saying, When ye are come
to the brink of the water of Jordan, ye shall stand
still in Jordan.
9 ¶ And Joshua said unto the children of Israel,
Come hither, and hear the words of the LORD
your God.
10 And Joshua said, Hereby ye shall know that the
living God *is* among you, and *that* he will without
fail drive out from before you the Canaanites, and
the Hittites, and the Hivites, and the Perizzites, and
the Girgashites, and the Amorites, and the Jebusites.
11 Behold, the ark of the covenant of the Lord of
all the earth passeth over before you into Jordan.
12 Now therefore take you twelve men out of the
tribes of Israel, out of every tribe a man.
13 And it shall come to pass, as soon as the soles
of the feet of the priests that bear the ark of the
LORD, the Lord of all the earth, shall rest in the
waters of Jordan, *that* the waters of Jordan shall
be cut off *from* the waters that come down from
above; and they shall stand upon an heap.
14 ¶ And it came to pass, when the people
removed from their tents, to pass over Jordan, and
the priests bearing the ark of the covenant before
the people;
15 And as they that bare the ark were come unto
Jordan, and the feet of the priests that bare the ark
were dipped in the brim of the water, (for Jordan
overfloweth all his banks all the time of harvest,)
16 That the waters which came down from above
stood *and* rose up upon an heap very far from the
city Adam, that *is* beside Zaretan: and those that
came down toward the sea of the plain, *even* the
salt sea, failed, *and* were cut off: and the people
passed over right against Jericho.
17 And the priests that bare the ark of the cov-
enant of the LORD stood firm on dry ground in the
midst of Jordan, and all the Israelites passed over
on dry ground, until all the people were passed
clean over Jordan.

CHAPTER 4

AND it came to pass, when all the people were
clean passed over Jordan, that the LORD spake
unto Joshua, saying,

---

furniture, symbolizing the presence of the Lord. As the priests carried it in the sight of the people, it was a visible object lesson assuring them that the Lord was with them and going before them into the Promised Land.

3:4 *two thousand cubits*. A cubit was about eighteen inches, so this would be a distance of about three thousand feet.

3:5 *wonders*. The Hebrew word refers to extraordinary and uniquely divine acts, the miraculous or supernatural.

3:7 *to magnify*. To make great. The Lord would use the supernatural crossing of the Jordan to confirm Joshua's leadership as being equal to that of Moses.

3:8 *brink*. Edge.

3:10 *the Canaanites . . . .* The same seven nations that Moses said were greater and mightier than Israel (Deut. 7:1). Moses predicted their destruction by divine intervention (Deut. 7:2), and the prophecy was about to be fulfilled under Joshua's leadership.

3:13 *cut off . . . from above . . . an heap*. The upstream flow of the Jordan would be stopped like a dam.

3:15 *brim*. Edge, same word as v. 8. *overfloweth*. The Jordan was in the flood stage, so the current would have been swift and the waters high. This magnifies the greatness of the miracle.

3:16 *Adam . . . salt sea*. This would be just less than twenty-five miles of dry land miraculously provided for the people to cross.

3:17 *all the people were passed clean over Jordan*. All the nation finished passing over the Jordan.

Thoughts for Personal/Family Worship: Chapter 3

1. **The statement, "For ye have not passed this way heretofore" (3:4), certainly describes the new venture that Israel was about to experience. But in reality, it is the headline over every day of life for all of us. Every day brings new experiences, situations, and so many uncertainties. It had to be an encouraging comfort and source of confidence for Israel to know that the ark, the visible token of God's presence, was leading them. As believers today, we do not have a visible object to assure us of God's presence, but we have His word that He will not leave nor forsake us. We have the abiding presence of the indwelling Holy Spirit as our comforter and guide. Spend time praising God that even though every step of life is new, we can confidently walk through even the darkest shadows knowing that He is with us (Ps. 23:4).**
2. **Joshua 3:10 is a wonderful reminder that even though ministers change, God's Word remains constant. The word that Joshua gives to the people on the eve of their crossing the Jordan is the same that Moses had given them earlier (Deut. 7:1–2). Nothing had changed except the mouthpiece. God's Word is forever settled in heaven (Ps. 119:89), and the authority is in the Word and not in the spokesman. How have you seen this to be true in your own life?**

Chapter 4: *Twelve stones are taken from the Jordan to erect a memorial for following generations to be reminded of the Lord's mighty act in behalf of His people.*

2 Take you twelve men out of the people, out of
every tribe a man,
3 And command ye them, saying, Take you hence
out of the midst of Jordan, out of the place where
the priests' feet stood firm, twelve stones, and ye
shall carry them over with you, and leave them in
the lodging place, where ye shall lodge this night.
4 Then Joshua called the twelve men, whom
he had prepared of the children of Israel, out of
every tribe a man:
5 And Joshua said unto them, Pass over before
the ark of the LORD your God into the midst of
Jordan, and take ye up every man of you a stone
upon his shoulder, according unto the number of
the tribes of the children of Israel:
6 That this may be a sign among you, *that* when
your children ask *their fathers* in time to come,
saying, What *mean* ye by these stones?
7 Then ye shall answer them, That the waters of
Jordan were cut off before the ark of the covenant
of the LORD; when it passed over Jordan, the
waters of Jordan were cut off: and these stones
shall be for a memorial unto the children of Israel
for ever.
8 And the children of Israel did so as Joshua
commanded, and took up twelve stones out
of the midst of Jordan, as the LORD spake unto
Joshua, according to the number of the tribes of
the children of Israel, and carried them over with
them unto the place where they lodged, and laid
them down there.
9 And Joshua set up twelve stones in the midst of
Jordan, in the place where the feet of the priests
which bare the ark of the covenant stood: and
they are there unto this day.
10 ¶ For the priests which bare the ark stood in
the midst of Jordan, until every thing was fin-
ished that the LORD commanded Joshua to speak
unto the people, according to all that Moses
commanded Joshua: and the people hasted and
passed over.
11 And it came to pass, when all the people were
clean passed over, that the ark of the LORD passed
over, and the priests, in the presence of the people.
12 And the children of Reuben, and the children
of Gad, and half the tribe of Manasseh, passed
over armed before the children of Israel, as Moses
spake unto them:
13 About forty thousand prepared for war passed
over before the LORD unto battle, to the plains of
Jericho.
14 ¶ On that day the LORD magnified Joshua in
the sight of all Israel; and they feared him, as they
feared Moses, all the days of his life.
15 And the LORD spake unto Joshua, saying,
16 Command the priests that bear the ark of the
testimony, that they come up out of Jordan.
17 Joshua therefore commanded the priests,
saying, Come ye up out of Jordan.
18 And it came to pass, when the priests that bare
the ark of the covenant of the LORD were come
up out of the midst of Jordan, *and* the soles of the
priests' feet were lifted up unto the dry land, that
the waters of Jordan returned unto their place,
and flowed over all his banks, as *they did* before.
19 ¶ And the people came up out of Jordan on
the tenth *day* of the first month, and encamped in
Gilgal, in the east border of Jericho.
20 And those twelve stones, which they took out
of Jordan, did Joshua pitch in Gilgal.
21 And he spake unto the children of Israel, say-
ing, When your children shall ask their fathers in
time to come, saying, What *mean* these stones?
22 Then ye shall let your children know, saying,
Israel came over this Jordan on dry land.
23 For the LORD your God dried up the waters of
Jordan from before you, until ye were passed over,
as the LORD your God did to the Red sea, which he
dried up from before us, until we were gone over:
24 That all the people of the earth might know
the hand of the LORD, that it *is* mighty: that ye
might fear the LORD your God for ever.

4:6 *sign.* Token or memorial.

4:9 *in the midst of the Jordan.* The place from where the stones were taken, not where the monument was raised.

4:11 *were clean passed over.* Finished passing over (see the same expression in 3:17).

4:14 *magnified.* Made great. *they feared.* Fear has the sense of respect and includes the corollary component of obeying. They submitted to Joshua's leadership as they did to Moses'.

4:24 *fear the LORD.* Fearing God also includes both ideas of respect and obedience (Eccl. 12:13). It directs both worship and behavior.

Thoughts for Personal/Family Worship: Chapter 4

1. **Raising the monument to commemorate the crossing of the Jordan illustrates the responsibility one generation has to the next to teach about the Lord and His mighty acts. The memorial became the occasion for children to ask fathers, "What mean these stones?" (4:21). It provided fathers the opportunity to direct their children to the knowledge of God. So, Christian parents must erect the "family altar of witness" in the home as a means of fostering a spiritual curiosity among their children and of teaching them to fear God and obey Him, which ultimately and primarily involves obeying the gospel in repenting of their sins and believing in Jesus Christ. God has set the home as a principal place of religious training, both by precept and example. What can you be doing to pass on your faith stories?**
2. **Joshua 4:24 suggests that the memorial witness to God's covenant faithfulness and mighty power would serve as a means of evangelism to the world as well as to the family. For the world to see the effects of gospel grace in the lives of His people gives effective witness to the power of grace. Living in the fear of God is then a private matter, speaking to the family, and a public matter, speaking to strangers. Fearing God affects all of life.**

CHAPTER 5

AND it came to pass, when all the kings of the
Amorites, which *were* on the side of Jordan
westward, and all the kings of the Canaanites,
which *were* by the sea, heard that the LORD had
dried up the waters of Jordan from before the
children of Israel, until we were passed over, that
their heart melted, neither was there spirit in
them any more, because of the children of Israel.
2 ¶ At that time the LORD said unto Joshua, Make
thee sharp knives, and circumcise again the chil-
dren of Israel the second time.
3 And Joshua made him sharp knives, and
circumcised the children of Israel at the hill of the
foreskins.
4 And this *is* the cause why Joshua did circumcise:
All the people that came out of Egypt, *that were*
males, *even* all the men of war, died in the wilder-
ness by the way, after they came out of Egypt.
5 Now all the people that came out were
circumcised: but all the people *that were* born in
the wilderness by the way as they came forth out
of Egypt, *them* they had not circumcised.
6 For the children of Israel walked forty years in
the wilderness, till all the people *that were* men of
war, which came out of Egypt, were consumed,
because they obeyed not the voice of the LORD:
unto whom the LORD sware that he would not
shew them the land, which the LORD sware unto
their fathers that he would give us, a land that
floweth with milk and honey.
7 And their children, *whom* he raised up in their
stead, them Joshua circumcised: for they were
uncircumcised, because they had not circumcised
them by the way.
8 And it came to pass, when they had done
circumcising all the people, that they abode in
their places in the camp, till they were whole.
9 And the LORD said unto Joshua, This day have
I rolled away the reproach of Egypt from off you.
Wherefore the name of the place is called Gilgal
unto this day.
10 ¶ And the children of Israel encamped in
Gilgal, and kept the passover on the fourteenth
day of the month at even in the plains of Jericho.
11 And they did eat of the old corn of the land on
the morrow after the passover, unleavened cakes,
and parched *corn* in the selfsame day.
12 ¶ And the manna ceased on the morrow after
they had eaten of the old corn of the land; neither
had the children of Israel manna any more; but
they did eat of the fruit of the land of Canaan that
year.
13 ¶ And it came to pass, when Joshua was by
Jericho, that he lifted up his eyes and looked, and,
behold, there stood a man over against him with
his sword drawn in his hand: and Joshua went
unto him, and said unto him, *Art* thou for us, or
for our adversaries?
14 And he said, Nay; but *as* captain of the host of
the LORD am I now come. And Joshua fell on his
face to the earth, and did worship, and said unto
him, What saith my lord unto his servant?
15 And the captain of the LORD's host said unto

How are you able to make God's work of grace in your life public to unbelievers around you?

Chapter 5: *Circumcision is renewed, the Passover is celebrated, the manna ceases, and Joshua encounters the captain of the Lord's host.*

Renewal of Circumcision (5:1–15)

5:1 *Amorites . . . Canaanites.* Palestine was inhabited by a number of independent nations, seven of which were specified in 3:10. These two are generic designations referring to the whole population, and the word *and* does not add, it explains: the Amorites "even" the Canaanites.

5:2 *circumcise.* Circumcision was the sign of the covenant with Abraham (Gen. 17:9–14), identifying the individual as a member of the covenant community. It was a prerequisite for participating in the Passover (Ex. 12:48). As important as circumcision of the flesh was, the Old Testament emphasizes more the spiritual circumcision of the heart (Deut. 10:16; Jer. 4:4). *the second time.* Individual circumcision was a one-time ritual; this refers to the renewal of the rite for the wilderness generation (vv. 5,7).

5:8 *till they were whole.* Literally, "until they were revived or had gotten well."

5:9 *I rolled away . . . Gilgal unto this day.* The circumcision marked their separation from Egypt, and the rolling away of the *reproach* or shameful disgrace associated with that old life. The name "Gilgal" means "the rolling away place." The place received this name because of the circumcision event; thus the mention of Gilgal in 4:20 was in anticipation of what it would be called. Joshua obviously wrote the narrative after the events had transpired.

5:10 *kept the passover.* Having been circumcised (identification with the covenant community), they were now qualified for the Passover (celebration of redemption). Significantly, these two principal Old Testament sacraments parallel the New Testament's baptism and Lord's Supper. *on the fourteenth day.* According to Ex. 12:6, this was the day for sacrificing the Passover lambs, which had been selected from the flock on the tenth day of the first month (Ex. 12:3). Israel crossed the Jordan on the tenth day of the first month (4:19), giving them time to follow the Passover liturgy.

5:11–12 *the old corn.* The produce. *the morrow.* The next day. *unleavened cakes.* Unleavened bread. *fruit.* Produce. The ordinary provisions of the land replace the extraordinary provision of the manna. Whether through natural means or supernatural, God supplies our daily bread.

5:14 *captain of the host of the LORD.* The chief leader or commander of the army of the Lord. *Joshua . . . did worship.* Since God is the only legitimate object of worship, Joshua's response is irrefutable evidence of the deity of this Chief Commander. This is a Christophany, a preincarnate appearance of the second person of the Trinity. *my lord.* Not a title of deity specifically, but it does express Joshua's recognition of one who is his superior.

5:15 *Loose thy shoe.* This parallels Moses at the burning bush (Ex. 3:5–6) and is another evidence of the Commander's deity.

Joshua, Loose thy shoe from off thy foot; for the
place whereon thou standest *is* holy. And Joshua
did so.

CHAPTER 6

NOW Jericho was straitly shut up because of the
children of Israel: none went out, and none came in.
2 And the LORD said unto Joshua, See, I have
given into thine hand Jericho, and the king
thereof, *and* the mighty men of valour.
3 And ye shall compass the city, all *ye* men of war,
and go round about the city once. Thus shalt thou
do six days.
4 And seven priests shall bear before the ark
seven trumpets of rams' horns: and the seventh
day ye shall compass the city seven times, and the
priests shall blow with the trumpets.
5 And it shall come to pass, that when they make
a long *blast* with the ram's horn, *and* when ye hear
the sound of the trumpet, all the people shall
shout with a great shout; and the wall of the city
shall fall down flat, and the people shall ascend up
every man straight before him.
6 ¶ And Joshua the son of Nun called the priests,
and said unto them, Take up the ark of the cov-
enant, and let seven priests bear seven trumpets
of rams' horns before the ark of the LORD.
7 And he said unto the people, Pass on, and
compass the city, and let him that is armed pass
on before the ark of the LORD.
8 ¶ And it came to pass, when Joshua had spoken
unto the people, that the seven priests bearing the
seven trumpets of rams' horns passed on before
the LORD, and blew with the trumpets: and the
ark of the covenant of the LORD followed them.
9 ¶ And the armed men went before the priests
that blew with the trumpets, and the rereward
came after the ark, *the priests* going on, and
blowing with the trumpets.
10 And Joshua had commanded the people,
saying, Ye shall not shout, nor make any noise
with your voice, neither shall *any* word proceed
out of your mouth, until the day I bid you shout;
then shall ye shout.
11 So the ark of the LORD compassed the city,
going about *it* once: and they came into the camp,
and lodged in the camp.
12 ¶ And Joshua rose early in the morning, and
the priests took up the ark of the LORD.
13 And seven priests bearing seven trumpets of
rams' horns before the ark of the LORD went on
continually, and blew with the trumpets: and the
armed men went before them; but the rereward
came after the ark of the LORD, *the priests* going
on, and blowing with the trumpets.
14 And the second day they compassed the city
once, and returned into the camp: so they did six
days.
15 And it came to pass on the seventh day, that
they rose early about the dawning of the day, and
compassed the city after the same manner seven
times: only on that day they compassed the city
seven times.
16 And it came to pass at the seventh time, when
the priests blew with the trumpets, Joshua said
unto the people, Shout; for the LORD hath given
you the city.

Thoughts for Personal/Family Worship: Chapter 5

1. **Gilgal was Israel's first claim in the Promised Land; it anticipated future blessings as well as being a reminder to future generations of past blessings. It is where the strategy for the conquest was set in place and suggests a strategy for all believers as they seek to advance in their spiritual lives. First, circumcision shows the importance of dealing with the flesh. Circumcision is important on many levels, but certainly the removal of the flesh pictures the cleansing from sin and the necessity of separation from the old life (Egypt). Every Christian must experience what it means for old things to pass away and all things to become new. How have you experienced this in your life?**
2. **Second, the Passover celebration shows the importance of remembering the redemption we have through the sacrifice of Christ in our behalf. The Passover teaches lessons about grace, about the power of God, the necessity of blood atonement, the objectivity of faith, and spiritual sustenance as we feast on the Lamb. How have you been able to celebrate Christ's sacrifice lately?**
3. **Third, the Christophany underscores the importance of meeting with Christ Himself. The sacraments serve as helpful visible signs of spiritual truths, but there is no substitute for experiencing and enjoying a personal relationship with Jesus Christ, to worship Him and to listen to His Word. "What saith my lord unto his servant" (v. 14) ought to be the sincere question of every believer every time he opens the Scripture. The bottom line is that we all need a place we call Gilgal. What can you do to help develop a daily habit of meeting with your Lord?**

THE CONQUEST OF CANAAN (6:1—12:24)

The Central Campaign (6:1—9:27)

Chapter 6: *Jericho is destroyed with all its inhabitants except Rahab and her family.*

Victory at Jericho (6:1–27)

6:1 *Jericho was straitly shut up*. Jericho was closed and staying closed. It was in lockdown. Jericho—ironically known as the city of palms—was under a sentence of destruction.

6:3 *compass*. Encircle or surround, a synonym of *go round about*.

6:4 *trumpets of rams' horns*. Literally, just "horns of rams," that would function as trumpets (vv. 6,8,13).

6:5 *shall fall down flat*. Literally, the wall "will fall under itself." A portion of the wall would sink down allowing the army to go straight into the gap in the wall, the rest of which stood entrapping the inhabitants. There was no escape. Obviously, Rahab's house was on a portion of the wall that remained.

6:7 *let him that is armed*. Equipped and ready for fighting.

6:9,13 *the rereward*. Those forming a rear guard.

17 ¶ And the city shall be accursed, *even* it, and all
that *are* therein, to the LORD: only Rahab the harlot
shall live, she and all that *are* with her in the house,
because she hid the messengers that we sent.
18 And ye, in any wise keep *yourselves* from the
accursed thing, lest ye make *yourselves* accursed,
when ye take of the accursed thing, and make the
camp of Israel a curse, and trouble it.
19 But all the silver, and gold, and vessels of brass
and iron, *are* consecrated unto the LORD: they
shall come into the treasury of the LORD.
20 So the people shouted when *the priests* blew
with the trumpets: and it came to pass, when the
people heard the sound of the trumpet, and the
people shouted with a great shout, that the wall
fell down flat, so that the people went up into the
city, every man straight before him, and they took
the city.
21 And they utterly destroyed all that *was* in the
city, both man and woman, young and old, and
ox, and sheep, and ass, with the edge of the sword.
22 But Joshua had said unto the two men that
had spied out the country, Go into the harlot's
house, and bring out thence the woman, and all
that she hath, as ye sware unto her.
23 And the young men that were spies went in,
and brought out Rahab, and her father, and her
mother, and her brethren, and all that she had;
and they brought out all her kindred, and left
them without the camp of Israel.
24 And they burnt the city with fire, and all that
was therein: only the silver, and the gold, and
the vessels of brass and of iron, they put into the
treasury of the house of the LORD.
25 And Joshua saved Rahab the harlot alive, and
her father's household, and all that she had; and
she dwelleth in Israel *even* unto this day; because
she hid the messengers, which Joshua sent to spy
out Jericho.
26 ¶ And Joshua adjured *them* at that time,
saying, Cursed *be* the man before the LORD, that
riseth up and buildeth this city Jericho: he shall
lay the foundation thereof in his firstborn, and in
his youngest *son* shall he set up the gates of it.
27 So the LORD was with Joshua; and his fame
was *noised* throughout all the country.

6:17 *the city shall be accursed.* The city will be under a ban, meaning that it was devoted to the Lord exclusively to His use. Here the city was divinely dedicated to destruction, and its spoil or booty were off-limits (see Lev. 27:28, "every devoted thing is most holy unto the LORD"). Its New Testament counterpart is "anathema" (1 Cor. 16:22; Gal. 1:8). Only Rahab was spared because of her faith and faithful act in hiding the *messengers* (spies of the city but the bearers of "good news" to Rahab).
6:18 *in any wise keep yourselves.* Literally, "only you yourselves guard or be careful about." Joshua's instructions specify clearly the implications of the city being under the ban. To take for one's own use what God had reserved uniquely to Himself had serious consequence. *trouble it.* Bring disaster, ruin, or throw into confusion.
6:19 *consecrated unto the LORD.* Holy to the Lord. It is distinct, set apart for the Lord. *treasury of the LORD.* The storehouse connected to the tabernacle service. It was not for personal use.
6:20 Jericho's fall was supernatural. Ultimately, it was the Lord and not Joshua that fought the battle of Jericho. As the Lord had said would happen (v. 5), a portion of the wall sunk under itself creating a breach allowing the army to march straight into the city. Picture a horseshoe to visualize how the walls appeared.
6:21 *they utterly destroyed.* This is the verbal form of the word for a devoted thing or a ban that the KJV has commonly translated "accursed." The total destruction illustrates the fearful truth that whatever or whoever is under the ban is beyond redemption (Lev. 27:29).
6:26 *Joshua adjured.* He urged with an oath. *in his firstborn . . . in his youngest.* The Hebrew preposition "in" can express price or value. The idea would be that whoever rebuilds the city would do so at the expense of his children.
6:27 *his fame.* The news about him.

Thoughts for Personal/Family Worship: Chapter 6

1. **Jericho is a real example of Bunyan's City of Destruction. Its destruction puts in bold the severity of divine justice. Three thoughts particularly are in focus. First, divine justice is patient. Jericho was one of the world's oldest cities. Archaeological evidence indicates a level of occupation predating Abraham by hundreds of years. We know that the sins of the Canaanites were not yet full in his day (Gen. 15:16), but now they were. The city had been given years of time and opportunity to repent but it did not. Now the day of judgment had arrived. We should not presume on God's longsuffering but repent without delay. Second, divine justice is irresistible. The city was securely shut, and the inhabitants trusted the security of walls that appeared to be impenetrable. But without a hand, God took away their security. Jericho prefigures a judgment ahead in which more than walls will fall (Heb. 12:26). Sinners will not be able to stand in that day (Nah. 1:6). Third, divine justice is not capricious. Both the Old Testament and secular historic records show the extent of the wickedness of Canaan: Jericho got what it deserved. That none were spared shows that justice is without discrimination: All souls belong to the Lord and the soul that sins will die (Ezek. 18:4). Jericho is a lesson in how God deals with sin. Spend time praising God for His patience, His justice, and His mercy.**
2. **Jericho is also a pattern for sanctification. As Jericho stood in the way of Israel's possession of the land, so sin looms large as the obstacle every believer must encounter. God promised that Jericho would fall, and so He has promised us that sin will no longer have dominion over us (Rom. 6:14). The power to overcome Jericho was the Lord's. Note how the divine plan to defeat Jericho focused on the ark, the symbol of God's presence, and the atonement (Josh. 6:4,6–9,11–13). This points directly to Christ, His atonement, and our union with Him that is the ultimate power for victory (Col. 2:14–15; Heb. 2:14–15). Although the victory was God's, Israel had to march and stick close to the ark. According to Heb. 11:30 they did so in faith. So in sanctification by faith we know what we have in Christ, we reckon it to be personally true and we behave accordingly (see logic of Rom. 6). Ask God to give you victory through grace and the will to live by faithful obedience.**

CHAPTER 7

BUT the children of Israel committed a trespass in
the accursed thing: for Achan, the son of Carmi,
the son of Zabdi, the son of Zerah, of the tribe of
Judah, took of the accursed thing: and the anger
of the LORD was kindled against the children of
Israel.
2 And Joshua sent men from Jericho to Ai, which
is beside Beth-aven, on the east side of Beth-el,
and spake unto them, saying, Go up and view the
country. And the men went up and viewed Ai.
3 And they returned to Joshua, and said unto
him, Let not all the people go up; but let about
two or three thousand men go up and smite Ai;
and make not all the people to labour thither; for
they *are but* few.
4 So there went up thither of the people about
three thousand men: and they fled before the men
of Ai.
5 And the men of Ai smote of them about thirty
and six men: for they chased them *from* before the
gate *even* unto Shebarim, and smote them in the
going down: wherefore the hearts of the people
melted, and became as water.
6 ¶ And Joshua rent his clothes, and fell to the
earth upon his face before the ark of the LORD
until the eventide, he and the elders of Israel, and
put dust upon their heads.
7 And Joshua said, Alas, O Lord GOD, wherefore
hast thou at all brought this people over Jordan,
to deliver us into the hand of the Amorites, to de-
stroy us? would to God we had been content, and
dwelt on the other side Jordan!
8 O Lord, what shall I say, when Israel turneth
their backs before their enemies!
9 For the Canaanites and all the inhabitants
of the land shall hear *of it*, and shall environ us
round, and cut off our name from the earth: and
what wilt thou do unto thy great name?
10 ¶ And the LORD said unto Joshua, Get thee up;
wherefore liest thou thus upon thy face?
11 Israel hath sinned, and they have also trans-
gressed my covenant which I commanded them:
for they have even taken of the accursed thing,
and have also stolen, and dissembled also, and
they have put *it* even among their own stuff.
12 Therefore the children of Israel could not
stand before their enemies, *but* turned *their* backs
before their enemies, because they were accursed:
neither will I be with you any more, except ye
destroy the accursed from among you.
13 Up, sanctify the people, and say, Sanctify
yourselves against to morrow: for thus saith the
LORD God of Israel, *There is* an accursed thing in
the midst of thee, O Israel: thou canst not stand
before thine enemies, until ye take away the
accursed thing from among you.
14 In the morning therefore ye shall be brought
according to your tribes: and it shall be, *that* the
tribe which the LORD taketh shall come according
to the families *thereof*; and the family which the
LORD shall take shall come by households; and the
household which the LORD shall take shall come
man by man.
15 And it shall be, *that* he that is taken with the
accursed thing shall be burnt with fire, he and
all that he hath: because he hath transgressed
the covenant of the LORD, and because he hath
wrought folly in Israel.
16 ¶ So Joshua rose up early in the morning, and
brought Israel by their tribes; and the tribe of
Judah was taken:
17 And he brought the family of Judah; and he
took the family of the Zarhites: and he brought
the family of the Zarhites man by man; and Zabdi
was taken:
18 And he brought his household man by man;
and Achan, the son of Carmi, the son of Zabdi,
the son of Zerah, of the tribe of Judah, was taken.
19 And Joshua said unto Achan, My son, give, I
pray thee, glory to the LORD God of Israel, and
make confession unto him; and tell me now what
thou hast done; hide *it* not from me.
20 And Achan answered Joshua, and said, Indeed

Defeat and Victory at Ai (7:1—8:29)

Chapter 7: *Israel suffered defeat at Ai because of Achan's secret sin that was discovered and punished with death.*

7:1 *committed a trespass.* Literally, they "acted unfaithfully an unfaithful act." The verb and noun of the same root involve the violation of legal obligations. The words often describe infidelity. *in the accursed thing.* The violation was taking what God had put off limits. Significantly, one man sinned, but God charged the whole nation with the guilt. Ultimately, no sin is private.
7:2 *view . . . viewed.* Spy out.
7:3 *make not all the people to labour thither.* Do not trouble all the people there.
7:5 *in the going down.* A reference to a mountainside or slope.
7:6 Rending clothes and putting dust on the head were common gestures of grief or mourning.
7:7 Joshua expresses the conflict between the knowledge of God's promise of victory and the experience of defeat. This is a common conflict in believers when experience seems to counter creed. *Amorites.* Refers to Canaanites without specifying the particular nation.
7:9 *environ us round.* Surround us.
7:11 *the accursed thing.* The ban, that which was devoted to the Lord. *dissembled.* Concealed deceptively.
7:13 *sanctify.* Set apart, consecrate.
7:15 *wrought folly.* Do "stupidity" or "sacrilege."
7:16 *rose up early.* Not particularly a reference to time, but an idiom for doing something first thing, making it a matter of urgent priority.
7:19 *confession.* The Hebrew word also means "praise" or "thanksgiving."
7:20 *thus and thus.* The narrator's summary of Achan's detailed confession.

I have sinned against the LORD God of Israel, and
thus and thus have I done:
21 When I saw among the spoils a goodly Bab-
ylonish garment, and two hundred shekels of
silver, and a wedge of gold of fifty shekels weight,
then I coveted them, and took them; and, behold,
they *are* hid in the earth in the midst of my tent,
and the silver under it.
22 ¶ So Joshua sent messengers, and they ran
unto the tent; and, behold, *it was* hid in his tent,
and the silver under it.
23 And they took them out of the midst of the
tent, and brought them unto Joshua, and unto all
the children of Israel, and laid them out before
the LORD.
24 And Joshua, and all Israel with him, took
Achan the son of Zerah, and the silver, and the
garment, and the wedge of gold, and his sons, and
his daughters, and his oxen, and his asses, and his
sheep, and his tent, and all that he had: and they
brought them unto the valley of Achor.
25 And Joshua said, Why hast thou troubled us?
the LORD shall trouble thee this day. And all Israel
stoned him with stones, and burned them with
fire, after they had stoned them with stones.
26 And they raised over him a great heap of
stones unto this day. So the LORD turned from the
fierceness of his anger. Wherefore the name of that
place was called, The valley of Achor, unto this day.

CHAPTER 8

AND the LORD said unto Joshua, Fear not, neither
be thou dismayed: take all the people of war with
thee, and arise, go up to Ai: see, I have given into
thy hand the king of Ai, and his people, and his
city, and his land:
2 And thou shalt do to Ai and her king as thou
didst unto Jericho and her king: only the spoil
thereof, and the cattle thereof, shall ye take for a
prey unto yourselves: lay thee an ambush for the
city behind it.
3 ¶ So Joshua arose, and all the people of war,
to go up against Ai: and Joshua chose out thirty
thousand mighty men of valour, and sent them
away by night.
4 And he commanded them, saying, Behold, ye
shall lie in wait against the city, *even* behind the
city: go not very far from the city, but be ye all
ready:
5 And I, and all the people that *are* with me, will
approach unto the city: and it shall come to pass,
when they come out against us, as at the first, that
we will flee before them,
6 (For they will come out after us) till we have
drawn them from the city; for they will say, They
flee before us, as at the first: therefore we will flee
before them.
7 Then ye shall rise up from the ambush, and
seize upon the city: for the LORD your God will
deliver it into your hand.
8 And it shall be, when ye have taken the city,
that ye shall set the city on fire: according to the
commandment of the LORD shall ye do. See, I
have commanded you.
9 ¶ Joshua therefore sent them forth: and they
went to lie in ambush, and abode between Beth-el
and Ai, on the west side of Ai: but Joshua lodged

7:24–25 *Achor . . . troubled us . . . trouble thee.* All from the same Hebrew root meaning "to make something taboo" (untouchable) or "to disturb." Illustrates the *lex talionis* principle of eye for eye. As Achan had done, the Lord would do to him. It is always a fearful thing to get from God what is deserved. *him . . . them.* He sinned alone but all his family suffered the consequence. The effects of sin are pervasive and tragic.

Thoughts for Personal/Family Worship: Chapter 7

1. **There is always an Ai to follow Jericho. Jericho was an amazing victory and remarkable start to the conquest of Canaan. But the rest of the Canaanites did not automatically surrender; they were going to defend their territory. The battles were going to continue, and Israel could not rest in past victory. The parallels to the Christian life with its struggles against sin and striving for holiness are noteworthy. Because of the ultimate victory Christ won on the cross, sin no longer has dominion over the believer. But just like the Canaanites, sin is going to defend its territory in the heart and not surrender easily. We must fight against sin and temptation and experience the victory by faith and obedience. It is imperative to remember that getting the victory over one temptation does not prevent the next one from coming. Sanctification is a lifelong process. What can you do to keep this important perspective in mind?**
2. **The connection between Achan's sin and Israel's defeat at Ai teaches important and sobering lessons. The disobedience of one culprit caused defeat for the entire nation and ended with the punishment of his entire family. Although he sinned in secret, his sin was detected and the consequences were public. In a very real sense, there is no such thing as a private sin. Either by results (the loss of thirty-six lives in battle) or by imitation (apparently the case with his family who became privy to his crime), sin affects others. The narrative also underscores the fact that secret sins are openly known by God, and in His time all sin will be detected and dealt with. Paul said, "Some men's sins are open beforehand, going before to judgment; and some men they follow after" (1 Tim. 5:24). One way or another and sooner or later, all sin is exposed and its penalty executed. How can knowing this help you in your own battle for sanctification?**

Chapter 8: *Following the Lord's instructions, Joshua reveals and executes the strategy leading to Ai's destruction after which he erected an altar for sacrifice and read all the law of Moses to the nation.*

8:1 After the sin issue was resolved, the path to victory was open. *neither be thou dismayed.* Do not be filled with terror.
8:2–8 Although the strategy for defeating Ai did not entail

that night among the people.
10 And Joshua rose up early in the morning, and
numbered the people, and went up, he and the
elders of Israel, before the people to Ai.
11 And all the people, *even the people* of war that
were with him, went up, and drew nigh, and came
before the city, and pitched on the north side of
Ai: now *there was* a valley between them and Ai.
12 And he took about five thousand men, and set
them to lie in ambush between Beth-el and Ai, on
the west side of the city.
13 And when they had set the people, *even* all the
host that *was* on the north of the city, and their
liers in wait on the west of the city, Joshua went
that night into the midst of the valley.
14 ¶ And it came to pass, when the king of Ai
saw *it*, that they hasted and rose up early, and the
men of the city went out against Israel to battle,
he and all his people, at a time appointed, before
the plain; but he wist not that *there were* liers in
ambush against him behind the city.
15 And Joshua and all Israel made as if they were
beaten before them, and fled by the way of the
wilderness.
16 And all the people that *were* in Ai were called
together to pursue after them: and they pursued
after Joshua, and were drawn away from the city.
17 And there was not a man left in Ai or Beth-el,
that went not out after Israel: and they left the city
open, and pursued after Israel.
18 And the LORD said unto Joshua, Stretch out
the spear that *is* in thy hand toward Ai; for I will
give it into thine hand. And Joshua stretched out
the spear that *he had* in his hand toward the city.
19 And the ambush arose quickly out of their
place, and they ran as soon as he had stretched
out his hand: and they entered into the city, and
took it, and hasted and set the city on fire.
20 And when the men of Ai looked behind them,
they saw, and, behold, the smoke of the city as-
cended up to heaven, and they had no power to
flee this way or that way: and the people that fled
to the wilderness turned back upon the pursuers.
21 And when Joshua and all Israel saw that the
ambush had taken the city, and that the smoke
of the city ascended, then they turned again, and
slew the men of Ai.
22 And the other issued out of the city against
them; so they were in the midst of Israel, some on
this side, and some on that side: and they smote
them, so that they let none of them remain or
escape.
23 And the king of Ai they took alive, and brought
him to Joshua.
24 And it came to pass, when Israel had made an
end of slaying all the inhabitants of Ai in the field,
in the wilderness wherein they chased them, and
when they were all fallen on the edge of the sword,
until they were consumed, that all the Israelites
returned unto Ai, and smote it with the edge of
the sword.
25 And *so* it was, *that* all that fell that day, both of
men and women, *were* twelve thousand, *even* all
the men of Ai.
26 For Joshua drew not his hand back, wherewith
he stretched out the spear, until he had utterly
destroyed all the inhabitants of Ai.
27 Only the cattle and the spoil of that city Israel
took for a prey unto themselves, according unto the
word of the LORD which he commanded Joshua.
28 And Joshua burnt Ai, and made it an heap for
ever, *even* a desolation unto this day.
29 And the king of Ai he hanged on a tree until
eventide: and as soon as the sun was down, Joshua
commanded that they should take his carcase
down from the tree, and cast it at the entering of
the gate of the city, and raise thereon a great heap
of stones, *that remaineth* unto this day.
30 ¶ Then Joshua built an altar unto the LORD
God of Israel in mount Ebal,
31 As Moses the servant of the LORD commanded
the children of Israel, as it is written in the book
of the law of Moses, an altar of whole stones, over
which no man hath lift up *any* iron: and they
offered thereon burnt offerings unto the LORD,
and sacrificed peace offerings.
32 ¶ And he wrote there upon the stones a copy
of the law of Moses, which he wrote in the pres-
ence of the children of Israel.
33 And all Israel, and their elders, and officers,
and their judges, stood on this side the ark and
on that side before the priests the Levites, which
bare the ark of the covenant of the LORD, as well
the stranger, as he that was born among them;
half of them over against mount Gerizim, and
half of them over against mount Ebal; as Moses

---

the same supernatural intervention as Jericho, it was nonetheless the divine plan. Unlike Jericho, the contents of Ai were not under the ban; they were the spoil for the people. This casts a shadow of irony over Achan's sin; in due time, the bounty he sinned to obtain could have been his by divine sanction.

8:10 *rose up early*. See note at 7:16.

8:14 *he wist not*. He did not know.

8:18 *spear*. Traditionally, a javelin. Some contemporary evidence suggests a short, perhaps curved sword used for cutting or thrusting. God often instructed Moses to stretch out his rod as a visible token of His powerful word and work, so here He uses Joshua's spear.

8:20 *they had no power*. Literally, "a pair of hands was not in them."

8:22 *issued out*. Went out.

8:26 Compare Joshua stretching out his spear with Moses holding up the rod against the Amalekites (Ex. 17:8–16).

8:28 *an heap*. In Hebrew, a *tel*, a mound of ruins. Ironically, this root relates to the city "Ai" meaning heap. The word *tel* is used today to designate the location of ancient buried cities.

the servant of the LORD had commanded before,
that they should bless the people of Israel.
34 And afterward he read all the words of the law,
the blessings and cursings, according to all that is
written in the book of the law.
35 There was not a word of all that Moses com-
manded, which Joshua read not before all the
congregation of Israel, with the women, and the
little ones, and the strangers that were conversant
among them.

CHAPTER 9

AND it came to pass, when all the kings which
were on this side Jordan, in the hills, and in the
valleys, and in all the coasts of the great sea over
against Lebanon, the Hittite, and the Amorite,
the Canaanite, the Perizzite, the Hivite, and the
Jebusite, heard *thereof*;
2 That they gathered themselves together, to fight
with Joshua and with Israel, with one accord.
3 ¶ And when the inhabitants of Gibeon heard
what Joshua had done unto Jericho and to Ai,
4 They did work wilily, and went and made as if
they had been ambassadors, and took old sacks
upon their asses, and wine bottles, old, and rent,
and bound up;
5 And old shoes and clouted upon their feet, and
old garments upon them; and all the bread of
their provision was dry *and* mouldy.
6 And they went to Joshua unto the camp at
Gilgal, and said unto him, and to the men of
Israel, We be come from a far country: now
therefore make ye a league with us.
7 And the men of Israel said unto the Hivites,
Peradventure ye dwell among us; and how shall
we make a league with you?
8 And they said unto Joshua, We *are* thy servants.
And Joshua said unto them, Who *are* ye? and
from whence come ye?
9 And they said unto him, From a very far coun-
try thy servants are come because of the name of
the LORD thy God: for we have heard the fame of
him, and all that he did in Egypt,
10 And all that he did to the two kings of the
Amorites, that *were* beyond Jordan, to Sihon king
of Heshbon, and to Og king of Bashan, which *was*
at Ashtaroth.
11 Wherefore our elders and all the inhabitants of
our country spake to us, saying, Take victuals with
you for the journey, and go to meet them, and say
unto them, We *are* your servants: therefore now
make ye a league with us.
12 This our bread we took hot *for* our provision

Reading of the Law (8:30–35)

8:30–35 *As Moses . . . commanded.* See Deut. 27:4–8.
8:35 *the strangers that were conversant among them.* The alien who was walking or traveling in their midst.

Thoughts for Personal/Family Worship: Chapter 8

1. **Achan's sin and the nation's presumption (7:3) resulted in tragic loss at the first encounter with Ai. But defeat was not the end of the story. After they dealt with the sin and renewed their dependence on the Lord's Word, victory was assured. This is a wonderful message of hope for every believer who has failed the Lord. Defeated believers often convince themselves that there is no hope of ever enjoying spiritual victory again. But Israel's second encounter with Ai suggests otherwise. If we confess our sins, He will forgive (1 John 1:9), and if we will hear and obey His instructions, the way to victory over sin is set before us. That Ai is a heap and desolation to this day (Josh. 8:28) testifies to how God gives His people yet another chance to experience victory and to enjoy the inheritance He has given. How have you witnessed the place of defeat become the place of victory in your own life or the life of another believer?**
2. **The reading of the Law (at that time the totality of inspired Scripture) to all the population is a reminder of the importance of the Bible for the life and welfare of every believer. As the leader of the people, Joshua was to devote himself to the Word of God (1:8). But it was just as important for the people to listen firsthand to what God had to say. Similarly, it is not just the obligation of the minister to read and obey the Scripture, but every believer should read it thoroughly and regularly. How can you give God's Word a more prominent place in your life?**

Chapter 9: *The Gibeonites deceptively seek peace with Israel, resulting in a covenant that spares them from destruction but places them under servitude.*

Alliance with Gibeon (9:1–27)

9:1–2 *with one accord.* Literally, "one mouth," an idiom expressing unanimity. This Canaanite coalition was most unusual in that these kingdoms were rivals but regarded Israel to be a common enemy. The fall of Jericho and Ai demonstrated that their walled cities, the chief means of defense, were not obstacles to Joshua's army. So they allied themselves to fight collectively, not the normal military strategy. This posed an apparent threat to Israel, but it was all part of the divine strategy. Providence is often mysterious but always the evidence of divine wisdom. See comments in the Worship Section below.
9:3 The Gibeonites heard the same report but rather than allying with the enemies of God's people, they devised a scheme to sue for peace with Israel. Being at peace with God and His people is far better than being at war.
9:4 *wilily.* Cunningly. The Hebrew word includes the ideas of shrewdness, cleverness, or craftiness.
9:5 *old shoes . . . clouted upon their feet.* Patched up or worn sandals on their feet. *mouldy.* Dry or crumbling bread (v. 12).
9:6 *make ye a league with us.* Literally, "cut for us a covenant." This is the common formula for initiating a covenant or mutually binding agreement (vv. 9:7,11).
9:7 *Peradventure.* In Hebrew, a particle used to express an element of either fear or hope. Here it expresses their fear of entering an inappropriate alliance.
9:9 *fame of him.* Report about him.
9:11,14 *victuals.* Provisions, including food.
9:14 Failure to seek the Lord had serious and long-lasting consequences, extending as far as Israel's early monarchy (v. 20; 2 Sam. 21).

out of our houses on the day we came forth to
go unto you; but now, behold, it is dry, and it is
mouldy:
13 And these bottles of wine, which we filled,
were new; and, behold, they be rent: and these our
garments and our shoes are become old by reason
of the very long journey.
14 And the men took of their victuals, and asked
not *counsel* at the mouth of the LORD.
15 And Joshua made peace with them, and made
a league with them, to let them live: and the
princes of the congregation sware unto them.
16 ¶ And it came to pass at the end of three days
after they had made a league with them, that they
heard that they *were* their neighbours, and *that*
they dwelt among them.
17 And the children of Israel journeyed, and
came unto their cities on the third day. Now their
cities *were* Gibeon, and Chephirah, and Beeroth,
and Kirjath-jearim.
18 And the children of Israel smote them not, be-
cause the princes of the congregation had sworn
unto them by the LORD God of Israel. And all the
congregation murmured against the princes.
19 But all the princes said unto all the congrega-
tion, We have sworn unto them by the LORD God
of Israel: now therefore we may not touch them.
20 This we will do to them; we will even let them
live, lest wrath be upon us, because of the oath
which we sware unto them.
21 And the princes said unto them, Let them live;
but let them be hewers of wood and drawers of
water unto all the congregation; as the princes
had promised them.
22 ¶ And Joshua called for them, and he spake
unto them, saying, Wherefore have ye beguiled us,
saying, We *are* very far from you; when ye dwell
among us?
23 Now therefore ye *are* cursed, and there shall
none of you be freed from being bondmen, and
hewers of wood and drawers of water for the
house of my God.
24 And they answered Joshua, and said, Because it
was certainly told thy servants, how that the LORD
thy God commanded his servant Moses to give
you all the land, and to destroy all the inhabitants
of the land from before you, therefore we were
sore afraid of our lives because of you, and have
done this thing.
25 And now, behold, we *are* in thine hand: as it
seemeth good and right unto thee to do unto us,
do.
26 And so did he unto them, and delivered them
out of the hand of the children of Israel, that they
slew them not.
27 And Joshua made them that day hewers of
wood and drawers of water for the congregation,
and for the altar of the LORD, even unto this day,
in the place which he should choose.

CHAPTER 10

NOW it came to pass, when Adoni-zedek king of
Jerusalem had heard how Joshua had taken Ai,
and had utterly destroyed it; as he had done to
Jericho and her king, so he had done to Ai and
her king; and how the inhabitants of Gibeon had
made peace with Israel, and were among them;
2 That they feared greatly, because Gibeon *was* a
great city, as one of the royal cities, and because it

9:15 *the princes.* Not a reference to royalty but to the leaders (vv. 18–19,21). *sware.* Refers to the oath, which was a critical component of a covenant agreement.
9:16 *neighbours.* Literally, "near ones."
9:19 *touch.* Hurt.
9:21 *hewers of wood.* Those that gather wood (vv. 23,27).
9:22 *beguiled.* Deceived.
9:23 *for the house of my God.* Equates to the congregation. See also Num. 12:7 where the Lord's house refers to His people. Similarly, the church is the temple or dwelling place of God.
9:24 How the word was reported to them is not known, except the Lord had told Moses that He would send an angel or messenger before them to drive out the Canaanites (Ex. 33:2). That the Gibeonites heeded the report and other nations did not illustrates the gospel being a savor of death or of life (2 Cor. 2:16).

Thoughts for Personal/Family Worship: Chapter 9

1. **Notwithstanding the intrigue and deception employed by the Gibeonites, their pursuit of peace with Joshua illustrates gospel truths. They recognized that unless they entered into covenant with Joshua they would be doomed. Only identification with Israel would save them. The way they sought for mercy was flawed and far from perfect but the fact of the matter is they recognized their need for mercy. Similarly, there has never been a sinner who has come to Christ with perfect faith or repentance, but the gospel promise is that Christ will not cast out those who come to Him (John 6:37). It is only as sinners sue for peace with the greater Joshua through the blood of His cross that they can be delivered from death. The key difference between the lesser and the greater Joshua is that the lesser was duped into showing mercy whereas the greater Joshua knows every sinner who comes to Him for what he really is and receives him nonetheless. His grace is greater than our sin. Praise Jesus for His grace and mercy!**
2. **Joshua 9:25 expresses the proper sentiment of all who have been delivered from the sentence and bondage of death: surrendering to the will and good pleasure of the new master. The Gibeonites gladly became servants to those who by covenant oath had spared them. So Christians, who by a greater covenant and oath have been delivered, ought gladly to surrender themselves to the service of Jesus, the new Lord and Master. In the light of grace, how can you find joy in serving Jesus?**

Chapter 10: ***With the help of divinely supernatural intervention, Joshua defeats a coalition of nations***

was greater than Ai, and all the men thereof *were*
mighty.
3 Wherefore Adoni-zedek king of Jerusalem sent
unto Hoham king of Hebron, and unto Piram
king of Jarmuth, and unto Japhia king of Lachish,
and unto Debir king of Eglon, saying,
4 Come up unto me, and help me, that we may
smite Gibeon: for it hath made peace with Joshua
and with the children of Israel.
5 Therefore the five kings of the Amorites, the
king of Jerusalem, the king of Hebron, the king of
Jarmuth, the king of Lachish, the king of Eglon,
gathered themselves together, and went up, they
and all their hosts, and encamped before Gibeon,
and made war against it.
6 ¶ And the men of Gibeon sent unto Joshua to
the camp to Gilgal, saying, Slack not thy hand
from thy servants; come up to us quickly, and save
us, and help us: for all the kings of the Amorites
that dwell in the mountains are gathered together
against us.
7 So Joshua ascended from Gilgal, he, and all the
people of war with him, and all the mighty men
of valour.
8 ¶ And the LORD said unto Joshua, Fear them
not: for I have delivered them into thine hand;
there shall not a man of them stand before thee.
9 Joshua therefore came unto them suddenly,
and went up from Gilgal all night.
10 And the LORD discomfited them before Israel,
and slew them with a great slaughter at Gibeon,
and chased them along the way that goeth up to
Beth-horon, and smote them to Azekah, and unto
Makkedah.
11 And it came to pass, as they fled from before
Israel, *and* were in the going down to Beth-horon,
that the LORD cast down great stones from heaven
upon them unto Azekah, and they died: *they were*
more which died with hailstones than *they* whom
the children of Israel slew with the sword.
12 ¶ Then spake Joshua to the LORD in the day
when the LORD delivered up the Amorites before
the children of Israel, and he said in the sight of
Israel, Sun, stand thou still upon Gibeon; and
thou, Moon, in the valley of Ajalon.
13 And the sun stood still, and the moon stayed,
until the people had avenged themselves upon
their enemies. *Is* not this written in the book
of Jasher? So the sun stood still in the midst of
heaven, and hasted not to go down about a whole
day.
14 And there was no day like that before it or after
it, that the LORD hearkened unto the voice of a
man: for the LORD fought for Israel.
15 ¶ And Joshua returned, and all Israel with
him, unto the camp to Gilgal.
16 But these five kings fled, and hid themselves in
a cave at Makkedah.
17 And it was told Joshua, saying, The five kings
are found hid in a cave at Makkedah.
18 And Joshua said, Roll great stones upon the
mouth of the cave, and set men by it for to keep
them:
19 And stay ye not, *but* pursue after your enemies,
and smite the hindmost of them; suffer them not
to enter into their cities: for the LORD your God
hath delivered them into your hand.
20 And it came to pass, when Joshua and the
children of Israel had made an end of slaying
them with a very great slaughter, till they were
consumed, that the rest *which* remained of them
entered into fenced cities.

in a single day and then in a succession of battles conquers the southern region of Palestine.

The Southern Campaign (10:1–43)

10:3 See note at 9:1–2.

10:4–5 Although Joshua was the principal threat, the allied armies (*hosts*) planned to attack the Gibeonites, who had made peace and sided with Joshua. This is the common strategy of the world and Satan, who being incapable of mounting a direct assault against Christ, attack those who have made peace with Him. The church corporately and believers individually are the battlegrounds of spiritual warfare.

10:6–7 *slack not thy hand.* Dropping the hands is an image for losing courage: "do not stop helping." *Amorites.* A general term designating the inhabitants of Canaan. On the grounds of the covenant, they appeal for help; on the grounds of the covenant, Joshua arises to help.

10:8 *Fear them not.* An unnatural response given the circumstance, but faith in God's promise is contrary to natural behavior. The enemy that was seen was intimidating, but the God that is unseen is the supreme and ultimate reality. This illustrates walking by faith rather than sight.

10:9 *suddenly.* Or surprisingly.

10:10 *discomfited them.* Brought them into confusion. Significantly, Joshua and his army went against the foe, but it was the Lord who discomfited, slew, and chased. Christians fight, but the battle is the Lord's.

10:12–14 Various explanations exist regarding "Joshua's Long Day," including the slowing of the earth's rotation, an out-of-schedule solar eclipse, etc. The unmistakable point is that whatever happened was an extraordinary and supernatural event that God performed in behalf of His people. To explain the miraculous is to eliminate the miraculous. Something happened that was absolutely contrary to nature.

10:13 *the sun stood still.* It was motionless. *the moon stayed.* The moon stood. *the book of Jasher.* Literally, "the book of the upright." Since it has not been preserved, it was an uninspired record of the historical events. Inspiration guarantees preservation. *about a whole day.* A complete or regular day. Underscores the irregular and supernatural nature of the event.

10:14 *that the LORD hearkened.* As extraordinary as the day was, the unique (*no day like that*) feature is that it happened as the Lord heard the voice of man. This points to the second and greater Joshua who, as the perfect Son of Man, often showed His dominion over the things of nature.

10:18 *set men . . . to keep them.* Appoint men over them to guard them.

10:19 *smite the hindmost of them.* Seize or destroy the rear

21 And all the people returned to the camp to
Joshua at Makkedah in peace: none moved his
tongue against any of the children of Israel.
22 Then said Joshua, Open the mouth of the cave,
and bring out those five kings unto me out of the
cave.
23 And they did so, and brought forth those five
kings unto him out of the cave, the king of Jerusa-
lem, the king of Hebron, the king of Jarmuth, the
king of Lachish, *and* the king of Eglon.
24 And it came to pass, when they brought out
those kings unto Joshua, that Joshua called for all
the men of Israel, and said unto the captains of
the men of war which went with him, Come near,
put your feet upon the necks of these kings. And
they came near, and put their feet upon the necks
of them.
25 And Joshua said unto them, Fear not, nor be
dismayed, be strong and of good courage: for
thus shall the LORD do to all your enemies against
whom ye fight.
26 And afterward Joshua smote them, and slew
them, and hanged them on five trees: and they
were hanging upon the trees until the evening.
27 And it came to pass at the time of the going
down of the sun, *that* Joshua commanded, and
they took them down off the trees, and cast them
into the cave wherein they had been hid, and laid
great stones in the cave's mouth, *which remain*
until this very day.
28 ¶ And that day Joshua took Makkedah, and
smote it with the edge of the sword, and the king
thereof he utterly destroyed, them, and all the
souls that *were* therein; he let none remain: and
he did to the king of Makkedah as he did unto the
king of Jericho.
29 Then Joshua passed from Makkedah, and all
Israel with him, unto Libnah, and fought against
Libnah:
30 And the LORD delivered it also, and the king
thereof, into the hand of Israel; and he smote it
with the edge of the sword, and all the souls that
were therein; he let none remain in it; but did unto
the king thereof as he did unto the king of Jericho.
31 ¶ And Joshua passed from Libnah, and all
Israel with him, unto Lachish, and encamped
against it, and fought against it:
32 And the LORD delivered Lachish into the hand
of Israel, which took it on the second day, and
smote it with the edge of the sword, and all the
souls that *were* therein, according to all that he
had done to Libnah.
33 ¶ Then Horam king of Gezer came up to help
Lachish; and Joshua smote him and his people,
until he had left him none remaining.
34 ¶ And from Lachish Joshua passed unto Eglon,
and all Israel with him; and they encamped
against it, and fought against it:
35 And they took it on that day, and smote it with
the edge of the sword, and all the souls that *were*
therein he utterly destroyed that day, according to
all that he had done to Lachish.
36 And Joshua went up from Eglon, and all Israel
with him, unto Hebron; and they fought against it:
37 And they took it, and smote it with the edge of
the sword, and the king thereof, and all the cities
thereof, and all the souls that *were* therein; he left
none remaining, according to all that he had done
to Eglon; but destroyed it utterly, and all the souls
that *were* therein.
38 ¶ And Joshua returned, and all Israel with
him, to Debir; and fought against it:
39 And he took it, and the king thereof, and all
the cities thereof; and they smote them with the
edge of the sword, and utterly destroyed all the
souls that *were* therein; he left none remaining: as
he had done to Hebron, so he did to Debir, and to
the king thereof; as he had done also to Libnah,
and to her king.
40 ¶ So Joshua smote all the country of the
hills, and of the south, and of the vale, and of
the springs, and all their kings: he left none
remaining, but utterly destroyed all that breathed,
as the LORD God of Israel commanded.
41 And Joshua smote them from Kadesh-barnea
even unto Gaza, and all the country of Goshen,
even unto Gibeon.
42 And all these kings and their land did Joshua
take at one time, because the LORD God of Israel
fought for Israel.

guard. *suffer them not.* Do not allow them.
10:20 *fenced cities.* Cities which were heavily fortified.
10:21 *none moved his tongue.* Pointing the tongue was a threatening gesture. The inhabitants of the land recognized that Israel was a force not to be taken lightly.
10:24–25 *put your feet upon the necks.* A gesture both to humiliate the defeated kings and to symbolize for the people the certainty of the divinely promised victories to follow.
10:26 *hanged them.* A vivid symbol of being cursed by God (Deut. 21:23).
10:28–39 *souls.* A designation of the whole person not the immaterial part of man's being.
10:42 *at one time.* The normal strategy for conquering these cities would involve one siege after another, which would require considerable time. God had moved the Canaanites out of their fortified cities so that they could be defeated far more quickly.

Thoughts for Personal/Family Worship: Chapter 10

1. God's providence is often mysterious but always wise and always leads to His glory and His people's good. At first glance, the Canaanite coalition would be a fearful thing: multiple enemies ganging up against a people inexperienced in warfare. They had only engaged in two battles, the first of which (Jericho) did not even put them in harm's way. But God was fighting for them, and this alliance was a means of bringing the enemies out from the fortifications into the open so that they could

43 And Joshua returned, and all Israel with him,
unto the camp to Gilgal.

CHAPTER 11

AND it came to pass, when Jabin king of Hazor
had heard *those things*, that he sent to Jobab king
of Madon, and to the king of Shimron, and to the
king of Achshaph,
2 And to the kings that *were* on the north of
the mountains, and of the plains south of Chin-
neroth, and in the valley, and in the borders of
Dor on the west,
3 *And to* the Canaanite on the east and on the
west, and *to* the Amorite, and the Hittite, and
the Perizzite, and the Jebusite in the mountains,
and *to* the Hivite under Hermon in the land of
Mizpeh.
4 And they went out, they and all their hosts with
them, much people, even as the sand that *is* upon
the sea shore in multitude, with horses and chari-
ots very many.
5 And when all these kings were met together,
they came and pitched together at the waters of
Merom, to fight against Israel.
6 ¶ And the LORD said unto Joshua, Be not afraid
because of them: for to morrow about this time
will I deliver them up all slain before Israel: thou
shalt hough their horses, and burn their chariots
with fire.
7 So Joshua came, and all the people of war
with him, against them by the waters of Merom
suddenly; and they fell upon them.
8 And the LORD delivered them into the hand of
Israel, who smote them, and chased them unto
great Zidon, and unto Misrephoth-maim, and
unto the valley of Mizpeh eastward; and they
smote them, until they left them none remaining.
9 And Joshua did unto them as the LORD bade
him: he houghed their horses, and burnt their
chariots with fire.
10 ¶ And Joshua at that time turned back, and
took Hazor, and smote the king thereof with the
sword: for Hazor beforetime was the head of all
those kingdoms.
11 And they smote all the souls that *were* therein
with the edge of the sword, utterly destroying
them: there was not any left to breathe: and he
burnt Hazor with fire.
12 And all the cities of those kings, and all the
kings of them, did Joshua take, and smote them
with the edge of the sword, *and* he utterly de-
stroyed them, as Moses the servant of the LORD
commanded.
13 But *as for* the cities that stood still in their
strength, Israel burned none of them, save Hazor
only; *that* did Joshua burn.
14 And all the spoil of these cities, and the
cattle, the children of Israel took for a prey unto
themselves; but every man they smote with the
edge of the sword, until they had destroyed them,
neither left they any to breathe.
15 ¶ As the LORD commanded Moses his ser-
vant, so did Moses command Joshua, and so did
Joshua; he left nothing undone of all that the
LORD commanded Moses.
16 So Joshua took all that land, the hills, and all
the south country, and all the land of Goshen,

---

be defeated all at once. What would normally have required years to achieve was accomplished in essentially one battle. It involved a supernatural occurrence (the "long day"), which provided obvious evidence of the battle being the Lord's. In the moment, we sometimes question why God's providence does what it does—seeing only the moment can be deceiving. God knows the end from the beginning, and His wise providence employs the best means to accomplish His intended purpose. So it is important to trust Him, walking by faith and not sight. Even if the immediate circumstance appears to be against us, it cannot be, because if God is for us none can successfully be against us. How have you seen God work in overwhelming circumstances to bring about His glory and our good?

2. Joshua, coming to Gibeon's defense, illustrates a beautiful gospel truth. They were being threatened because of their covenant relationship with Joshua. The enemy could not get to Joshua, so they came against those who had made peace with Joshua. Because of the covenant, Joshua was obligated to their protection. Undoubtedly, the world hates Christ but because it cannot get to Him it takes out its hatred against those with whom Christ has a relationship, His church. We are not to marvel if the world hates us (1 John 3:13) because it hated Him first. Pray for God to give you confidence to live boldly, knowing that Christ is our guaranteed Protector and in union with Him we are secure (Rom. 8:31–39). "If God be for us, who can be against us?" (v.31).

Chapter 11: ***Joshua conquers the northern regions of Canaan bringing to a close the conquest of all the lands God had promised Moses.***

The Northern Campaign (11:1–15)

11:1–5 Another coalition of independent city-states brings the Canaanites out of their fortifications into the open fields of battle. This was a strategic blunder by the Canaanites that was orchestrated by God (v. 20) to reduce years of siege work to a single battle.

11:2 *Chinneroth.* What the New Testament refers to as the Sea of Galilee.

11:6 *Be not afraid.* God assures Joshua of victory notwithstanding the sight of the huge army. Not fearing was an act of faith in God's promise. *hough.* Hamstring or cripple (v. 9).

11:11 *souls.* Persons.

11:13 *in their strength.* Literally, "on their mounds." Many Canaanite cities were built on top of the ruins of earlier cities, creating the appearance of a hill or mound. The burning of Hazor is apparent by archaeological evidence from the site that shows a burn level dating to the time of Joshua's conquest.

and the valley, and the plain, and the mountain of
Israel, and the valley of the same;
17 *Even* from the mount Halak, that goeth up to
Seir, even unto Baal-gad in the valley of Lebanon
under mount Hermon: and all their kings he
took, and smote them, and slew them.
18 Joshua made war a long time with all those
kings.
19 There was not a city that made peace with the
children of Israel, save the Hivites the inhabitants
of Gibeon: all *other* they took in battle.
20 For it was of the LORD to harden their hearts,
that they should come against Israel in battle,
that he might destroy them utterly, *and* that they
might have no favour, but that he might destroy
them, as the LORD commanded Moses.
21 ¶ And at that time came Joshua, and cut
off the Anakims from the mountains, from
Hebron, from Debir, from Anab, and from all the
mountains of Judah, and from all the mountains
of Israel: Joshua destroyed them utterly with their
cities.
22 There was none of the Anakims left in the land
of the children of Israel: only in Gaza, in Gath,
and in Ashdod, there remained.
23 So Joshua took the whole land, according to all
that the LORD said unto Moses; and Joshua gave
it for an inheritance unto Israel according to their
divisions by their tribes. And the land rested from
war.

CHAPTER 12

NOW these *are* the kings of the land, which the
children of Israel smote, and possessed their land
on the other side Jordan toward the rising of the
sun, from the river Arnon unto mount Hermon,
and all the plain on the east:
2 Sihon king of the Amorites, who dwelt in
Heshbon, *and* ruled from Aroer, which *is* upon
the bank of the river Arnon, and from the middle
of the river, and from half Gilead, even unto the
river Jabbok, *which is* the border of the children
of Ammon;
3 And from the plain to the sea of Chinneroth on
the east, and unto the sea of the plain, *even* the salt
sea on the east, the way to Beth-jeshimoth; and
from the south, under Ashdoth-pisgah:
4 ¶ And the coast of Og king of Bashan, *which
was* of the remnant of the giants, that dwelt at
Ashtaroth and at Edrei,
5 And reigned in mount Hermon, and in Salcah,
and in all Bashan, unto the border of the Geshu-
rites and the Maachathites, and half Gilead, the
border of Sihon king of Heshbon.
6 Them did Moses the servant of the LORD
and the children of Israel smite: and Moses the
servant of the LORD gave it *for* a possession unto
the Reubenites, and the Gadites, and the half tribe
of Manasseh.
7 ¶ And these *are* the kings of the country which
Joshua and the children of Israel smote on this
side Jordan on the west, from Baal-gad in the
valley of Lebanon even unto the mount Halak,
that goeth up to Seir; which Joshua gave unto the
tribes of Israel *for* a possession according to their
divisions;
8 In the mountains, and in the valleys, and in
the plains, and in the springs, and in the wilder-
ness, and in the south country; the Hittites, the

An Overview of the Conquest (11:16—12:24)

11:18 *a long time.* Literally, "many days."

11:20 *to harden their hearts.* To strengthen or arouse their thoughts. This illustrates Prov. 21:1, "The king's heart is in the hand of the LORD." They thought that their strategy would succeed against Israel, but God caused them to devise a plan that would end in their own destruction.

11:23 *took the whole land.* This appears to contradict 13:1, "yet very much land to be possessed." Rather than being a contradiction, it points to the fact that the land represented more than just geographical territory. Each generation, and indeed each individual, must engage in experiencing God's blessing for themselves. *rested from war.* Was at peace from war.

Thoughts for Personal/Family Worship: Chapter 11

1. **God's good providence is often contrary to expectation. The gathering of a huge army against Israel would have been a terrifying scene. It would have given the appearance of the enemy getting the upper hand; defeat would have seemed certain in light of all the chariots and horses. Humanly speaking, Israel was outarmed. Yet appearance and reality were far different. God had Himself mustered the army as a means of bringing them out into the open and away from their fortified cities to hasten their utter destruction. It did not look like victory at first, but God was working all out for the good of His people. So often, it is only as we look back on the events of providence that we recognize the good. Have you learned to walk by faith and not by sight even when what you see contradicts what you think to be good? How have you seen that God's ways are always best?**
2. **Over and again, the chapter declares that what Joshua accomplished is what the Lord had commanded Moses ("he left nothing undone of all that the LORD commanded Moses" [v. 15]). It provides a wonderful reminder of God's faithfulness in keeping His promises. Recall other ways that God has kept His promises.**

Chapter 12: *The details of the conquest are listed.*

12:1–6 The details of the Transjordan conquest (east of Jordan regions) under the leadership of Moses. This became the inheritance of the tribes of Reuben, Gad, and half of Manasseh.

12:7–24 A summary of Joshua's conquest on the west side of Jordan, including a list of the individual kings.

Thoughts of Personal/Family Worship: Chapter 12

The detailed summary of the conquest, and particularly the list of the conquered kings by name one by one, provides an important lesson for praise and thanksgiving. It is an example of naming our blessings one by one in

CANAAN AND THE INHERITANCE

By our sin we departed from God and lost the inheritance that was ours in the garden of Eden. The Lord did not leave fallen humanity without a promise, which included victory for the seed of the woman (Gen. 3:15). In the call of Abraham, however, the Lord gave a new shape and direction to that promise. The possession of an inheritance was one of the things most distinctly promised in the Abrahamic covenant (Gen 12:1–7). Canaan was therefore an inheritance, a place of rest and blessing for the seed of Abraham, though still only a temporary inheritance. It was a type and pledge of the spiritual blessings the believer obtains and enjoys in and by Christ (Eph. 1:18) and of the final rest that remains for the people of God in heaven (Heb. 4:8–9).

The family of Abraham had no natural right to the inheritance of Canaan. Canaan, as an inheritance, was bestowed upon the seed of Abraham by promise, as the free gift of God's love (Gal. 3:18). Abraham's descendants didn't win the land as the spoils of battle or purchase it as in a business transaction. Their ownership of the land was purely a gracious act of God. He was faithful to give Israel the land (Josh. 21:43).

In like manner, a spiritual inheritance is bestowed upon God's people on the ground of God's eternal promise by virtue of His divine election (Luke 1:68–72; Heb. 13:20–21). It is promised to them in Christ (Titus 1:2), in whom all believers are one, being heirs of God and joint heirs with Christ (Rom. 8:16–18; Gal. 3:26–29; 4:4–7). The believer therefore has obtained an inheritance in Christ, according to the good pleasure of God, "being predestined according to the purpose of him who worketh all things after the counsel of his own will" (Eph. 1:11–12).

While Canaan was bestowed as the free gift of God on the seed of Abraham, the possession and enjoyment of the land were not easy. It had to be taken by faith in submission and obedience to the Lord (Lev. 26; Deut. 27–30). The way to victory was through the battlefield of warfare. The end of that war was never in doubt, however (Josh. 1:5); the Lord gave the victory (Josh. 10:30,32,42; 11:6,8). The same holds true today for the children of God who want to enjoy the spiritual inheritance bequeathed to them in Christ. Though their citizenship is in heaven (Phil. 3:20), "it is through much tribulation that we must enter the kingdom of God" (Acts 14:22). The Christian is to "fight the good fight of faith" and "lay hold of eternal life" by faith (1 Tim. 6:12). The outcome of the Christian's warfare, however, is never in doubt, just as the conquest of Canaan was never in doubt.

The distribution of Canaan was by lot and entirely by divine determination. In like manner, the Christian has a portion allotted to him by the Lord (Ps. 16:5). The Lord "shall choose our inheritance for us, the excellency of Jacob whom he loved" (Ps. 47:4). The allotment of Israel's inheritance was conveyed through the exercise of the priest's office (Josh. 14:11). In like manner, it is through Christ, our Great High Priest of good things to come, that we receive the promise of eternal inheritance (Heb. 9:11–15).

The land of Canaan was described as abundant and far reaching, a land in which the inhabitants would find all they needed in every area of life: "a land flowing with milk and honey" (Ex. 3:8). Far greater is the inheritance of the Christian. God will supply all our needs according to His riches in glory by Christ Jesus (Phil. 4:19). His riches are unsearchable (Eph. 3:8), and thus Paul prayed that the eyes of the understanding of the Ephesians might be enlightened, that they might "know what is the hope of his calling, and what the riches of the glory of his inheritance in the saints" (Eph. 1:18). In heaven all of the redeemed will be entirely content and perfectly happy (Ps. 16:11). All will be fully satisfied (Ps. 17:15); nothing there can or will disappoint (Rev. 7:16–17).

Amorites, and the Canaanites, the Perizzites, the
Hivites, and the Jebusites:
9 ¶ The king of Jericho, one; the king of Ai, which
is beside Beth-el, one;
10 The king of Jerusalem, one; the king of
Hebron, one;
11 The king of Jarmuth, one; the king of Lachish,
one;
12 The king of Eglon, one; the king of Gezer, one;
13 The king of Debir, one; the king of Geder, one;
14 The king of Hormah, one; the king of Arad,
one;
15 The king of Libnah, one; the king of Adullam,
one;
16 The king of Makkedah, one; the king of Beth-
el, one;
17 The king of Tappuah, one; the king of Hepher,
one;
18 The king of Aphek, one; the king of Lasharon,
one;
19 The king of Madon, one; the king of Hazor,
one;
20 The king of Shimron-meron, one; the king of
Achshaph, one;
21 The king of Taanach, one; the king of Megiddo,
one;
22 The king of Kedesh, one; the king of Jokneam
of Carmel, one;
23 The king of Dor in the coast of Dor, one; the
king of the nations of Gilgal, one;
24 The king of Tirzah, one: all the kings thirty
and one.

CHAPTER 13

NOW Joshua was old *and* stricken in years; and the
LORD said unto him, Thou art old *and* stricken in
years, and there remaineth yet very much land to
be possessed.
2 This *is* the land that yet remaineth: all the
borders of the Philistines, and all Geshuri,
3 From Sihor, which *is* before Egypt, even unto
the borders of Ekron northward, *which* is counted
to the Canaanite: five lords of the Philistines; the
Gazathites, and the Ashdothites, the Eshkalonites,
the Gittites, and the Ekronites; also the Avites:
4 From the south, all the land of the Canaanites,
and Mearah that *is* beside the Sidonians, unto
Aphek, to the borders of the Amorites:
5 And the land of the Giblites, and all Lebanon,
toward the sunrising, from Baal-gad under
mount Hermon unto the entering into Hamath.
6 All the inhabitants of the hill country from
Lebanon unto Misrephoth-maim, *and* all the
Sidonians, them will I drive out from before
the children of Israel: only divide thou it by lot
unto the Israelites for an inheritance, as I have
commanded thee.
7 Now therefore divide this land for an inheri-
tance unto the nine tribes, and the half tribe of
Manasseh,
8 With whom the Reubenites and the Gadites
have received their inheritance, which Moses gave
them, beyond Jordan eastward, *even* as Moses the
servant of the LORD gave them;
9 From Aroer, that *is* upon the bank of the river
Arnon, and the city that *is* in the midst of the
river, and all the plain of Medeba unto Dibon;
10 And all the cities of Sihon king of the Amori-
tes, which reigned in Heshbon, unto the border of
the children of Ammon;
11 And Gilead, and the border of the Geshurites
and Maachathites, and all mount Hermon, and all
Bashan unto Salcah;
12 All the kingdom of Og in Bashan, which
reigned in Ashtaroth and in Edrei, who remained
of the remnant of the giants: for these did Moses
smite, and cast them out.
13 Nevertheless the children of Israel expelled
not the Geshurites, nor the Maachathites: but the
Geshurites and the Maachathites dwell among
the Israelites until this day.
14 Only unto the tribe of Levi he gave none
inheritance; the sacrifices of the LORD God of

---

conscious recognition of what God has done in fulfilling His promises and keeping His word. Too often our thanksgiving to God is expressed in sweeping statements. Be specific in giving thanks for each and every benefit that He has provided for you.

THE DIVISION OF THE LAND (13:1—21:45)

Chapter 13: *Even though the conquest of the land was incomplete, the allotment of the land begins with the tribes on the east of Jordan.*

The Procedure for Allotment (13:1–7)

13:1 *stricken in years*. Literally, "going in the days," an idiom for growing old.

13:2 See note at 11:23.

13:3 *lords*. Princes.

13:6–7 *divide . . . by lot*. Literally, "cause it to fall." Numbers 36:2 indicates the use of lots in the distribution. But even so, the inheritance was not distributed by random chance; rather, it fell to each tribe according to God's command and will (Prov. 16:33). Even though the land was not entirely in Israel's possession, God's promise was so certain that it was to be divided among the *nine tribes*, those who would settle on the west side of Jordan.

The Inheritance for the Eastern Tribes (13:8–33)

13:8–32 Significantly, the distribution begins with the two and a half tribes that settled east of Jordan to show the unity of the people on both sides of Jordan and to demonstrate that Joshua's work was a continuation of that of Moses. These verses are a synopsis of the conquest of the Transjordan under the leadership of Moses, most of the details of which are in the book of Numbers.

Israel made by fire *are* their inheritance, as he
said unto them.
15 ¶ And Moses gave unto the tribe of the chil-
dren of Reuben *inheritance* according to their
families.
16 And their coast was from Aroer, that *is* on the
bank of the river Arnon, and the city that *is* in the
midst of the river, and all the plain by Medeba;
17 Heshbon, and all her cities that *are* in the plain;
Dibon, and Bamoth-baal, and Beth-baal-meon,
18 And Jahazah, and Kedemoth, and Mephaath,
19 And Kirjathaim, and Sibmah, and Zareth-
shahar in the mount of the valley,
20 And Beth-peor, and Ashdoth-pisgah, and
Beth-jeshimoth,
21 And all the cities of the plain, and all the
kingdom of Sihon king of the Amorites, which
reigned in Heshbon, whom Moses smote with
the princes of Midian, Evi, and Rekem, and Zur,
and Hur, and Reba, *which were* dukes of Sihon,
dwelling in the country.
22 ¶ Balaam also the son of Beor, the soothsayer,
did the children of Israel slay with the sword
among them that were slain by them.
23 And the border of the children of Reuben was
Jordan, and the border *thereof*. This *was* the in-
heritance of the children of Reuben after their
families, the cities and the villages thereof.
24 And Moses gave *inheritance* unto the tribe of
Gad, *even* unto the children of Gad according to
their families.
25 And their coast was Jazer, and all the cities
of Gilead, and half the land of the children of
Ammon, unto Aroer that *is* before Rabbah;
26 And from Heshbon unto Ramath-mizpeh,
and Betonim; and from Mahanaim unto the
border of Debir;
27 And in the valley, Beth-aram, and Beth-nimrah,
and Succoth, and Zaphon, the rest of the kingdom
of Sihon king of Heshbon, Jordan and *his* border,
even unto the edge of the sea of Chinnereth on the
other side Jordan eastward.
28 This *is* the inheritance of the children of Gad
after their families, the cities, and their villages.
29 ¶ And Moses gave *inheritance* unto the half
tribe of Manasseh: and *this* was *the possession* of
the half tribe of the children of Manasseh by their
families.
30 And their coast was from Mahanaim, all
Bashan, all the kingdom of Og king of Bashan,
and all the towns of Jair, which *are* in Bashan,
threescore cities:
31 And half Gilead, and Ashtaroth, and Edrei,
cities of the kingdom of Og in Bashan, *were
pertaining* unto the children of Machir the son of
Manasseh, *even* to the one half of the children of
Machir by their families.
32 These *are the countries* which Moses did
distribute for inheritance in the plains of Moab,
on the other side Jordan, by Jericho, eastward.
33 But unto the tribe of Levi Moses gave not *any*
inheritance: the LORD God of Israel *was* their
inheritance, as he said unto them.

CHAPTER 14

AND these *are the countries* which the children of
Israel inherited in the land of Canaan, which El-
eazar the priest, and Joshua the son of Nun, and
the heads of the fathers of the tribes of the chil-
dren of Israel, distributed for inheritance to them.
2 By lot *was* their inheritance, as the LORD
commanded by the hand of Moses, for the nine
tribes, and *for* the half tribe.
3 For Moses had given the inheritance of two
tribes and an half tribe on the other side Jordan:

13:14,33 *Levi* was scattered throughout the land with no inheritance apart from their service unto the Lord (14:3–4; 18:7; Deut. 18:1–8). This fulfilled the patriarchal prophecy that the Lord would "divide them in Jacob, and scatter them in Israel" (Gen. 49:7).

13:27 *sea of Chinnereth*. The Old Testament name for the Sea of Galilee.

Thoughts for Personal/Family Worship: Chapter 13

1. **The distribution of the land among the tribes gives material substance to God's promise and testifies to His faithfulness to fulfill His promises. As far back as Abraham God had promised that His covenant people would possess this land. That promise was repeated by Moses and claimed by Joshua as he led the nation into conquest. And now as the tribes received their "titles" of possession, they experienced the tangible evidence of God's fidelity. This provides a wonderful example for all believers that regardless of how far off God's promises may appear to be, He is faithful to fulfill His Word. It is never a vain thing to wait upon the Lord, for those who wait will never be disappointed. Let us take every token of blessing as tangible evidence that all the promises of God are yea and amen in our greater Joshua, Jesus Christ (2 Cor. 1:20). How have you seen God's faithfulness to those who wait upon Him?**
2. **The contradiction between Josh. 11:23 and 13:1–2 is only apparent and reflects a significant truth that every Christian knows in experience: the tension between the "already" and the "not yet." Every believer is complete in Christ (Col. 2:10) and is blessed with "all spiritual blessings in heavenly places in Christ" (Eph. 1:3). The wonder of this is beyond comprehension. Yet as amazing as this is, we have now the Holy Spirit who promises even more, for He is "the earnest of our inheritance until the redemption of the purchased possession" (Eph. 1:14). Already it is good, but the best is yet to be (1 John 3:2).**

The Inheritance for the Western Tribes (14:1—19:51)

Chapter 14: ***Before the land is distributed among the tribes, Caleb chooses and receives his own inheritance because he had faithfully followed the Lord.***

14:2 *the half tribe*. Manasseh was allotted land on both sides of Jordan.

but unto the Levites he gave none inheritance
among them.
4 For the children of Joseph were two tribes,
Manasseh and Ephraim: therefore they gave no
part unto the Levites in the land, save cities to
dwell *in*, with their suburbs for their cattle and
for their substance.
5 As the LORD commanded Moses, so the chil-
dren of Israel did, and they divided the land.
6 ¶ Then the children of Judah came unto Joshua
in Gilgal: and Caleb the son of Jephunneh the
Kenezite said unto him, Thou knowest the thing
that the LORD said unto Moses the man of God
concerning me and thee in Kadesh-barnea.
7 Forty years old *was* I when Moses the servant
of the LORD sent me from Kadesh-barnea to espy
out the land; and I brought him word again as *it*
was in mine heart.
8 Nevertheless my brethren that went up with me
made the heart of the people melt: but I wholly
followed the LORD my God.
9 And Moses sware on that day, saying, Surely the
land whereon thy feet have trodden shall be thine
inheritance, and thy children's for ever, because
thou hast wholly followed the LORD my God.
10 And now, behold, the LORD hath kept me alive,
as he said, these forty and five years, even since
the LORD spake this word unto Moses, while *the*
children of Israel wandered in the wilderness: and
now, lo, I *am* this day fourscore and five years old.
11 As yet I *am as* strong this day as *I was* in the day
that Moses sent me: as my strength *was* then, even
so *is* my strength now, for war, both to go out, and
to come in.
12 Now therefore give me this mountain, whereof
the LORD spake in that day; for thou heardest in
that day how the Anakims *were* there, and *that* the
cities *were* great *and* fenced: if so be the LORD *will*
be with me, then I shall be able to drive them out,
as the LORD said.
13 And Joshua blessed him, and gave unto Caleb
the son of Jephunneh Hebron for an inheritance.
14 Hebron therefore became the inheritance of
Caleb the son of Jephunneh the Kenezite unto
this day, because that he wholly followed the
LORD God of Israel.
15 And the name of Hebron before *was* Kirjath-
arba; *which Arba was* a great man among the
Anakims. And the land had rest from war.

CHAPTER 15

THIS then was the lot of the tribe of the children
of Judah by their families; *even* to the border of
Edom the wilderness of Zin southward *was* the
uttermost part of the south coast.
2 And their south border was from the shore of
the salt sea, from the bay that looketh southward:
3 And it went out to the south side to Maaleh-
acrabbim, and passed along to Zin, and ascended
up on the south side unto Kadesh-barnea, and
passed along to Hezron, and went up to Adar, and
fetched a compass to Karkaa:
4 *From thence* it passed toward Azmon, and went
out unto the river of Egypt; and the goings out of
that coast were at the sea: this shall be your south
coast.
5 And the east border *was* the salt sea, *even*

14:4 *suburbs.* Pastureland just outside the city limits but under the jurisdiction of the city. *substance.* Personal property including but not limited to cattle or flocks. The Levites were not allotted land like the other tribes but were assigned cities throughout all the nation (see note at 13:14).
14:6 *Thou knowest.* See Num. 14:24,30,38. Moses declared that from their generation only Caleb and Joshua would survive the wilderness and be allowed to enter Canaan.
14:8 *heart . . . melt.* An idiom for losing heart or morale. *I wholly followed.* Literally, "I filled after," an idiom for remaining loyal. Also v. 14.
14:10 *fourscore and five.* Eighty-five.
14:12 *Anakims.* See Num. 13:33, the same people the fearful spies had described as giants. *fenced.* Barricaded or enclosed. *if so be.* An expression of hope or entreaty.
14:15 *had rest from war.* Had peace.

Thoughts for Personal/Family Worship: Chapter 14

1. **Caleb and Joshua were the only two of the twelve spies that recommended to Israel that they should enter and possess Canaan (Num. 13–14). Consequently, they were the only ones preserved through the wilderness and allowed to enter the land of promise. Although Caleb was just as faithful as Joshua, the Lord had commissioned Joshua as the successor to Moses, and Caleb was in the background. Nonetheless, he remained loyal to the Lord even though Joshua was in the spotlight. What attitudes can we foster that will not allow any place for competition or envy in the work of the Lord?**
2. **Only Caleb and Joshua (19:50) were allowed to choose the place of their inheritance in the Promised Land. Although Caleb was advanced in years, he claimed that his strength had not abated. He could have chosen wherever he wanted, but he laid claim to what potentially was the most difficult and dangerous to possess. He chose the place where the Anakims were. Ironically, it was the sight of the Anakims, the giants, that caused the fear and convinced the nation that they could not possess the land. Not only had Caleb's strength not abated, neither had his faith. Before the wilderness, he believed God would deliver the giants into the hands of His people, and nothing had changed. Believers often hesitate to ask of God the big things. Caleb is a wonderful example of asking God for big things because nothing is impossible for Him. What big things should you be asking and trusting God for?**

Chapters 15–19: ***Joshua records the specific details of the distribution of territory to the tribes on the west side of Jordan beginning with Judah and ending with Dan.***

15:3 *fetched a compass.* Turned its boundary toward.
15:4,7,11; 16:3,8 *goings out.* Boundaries.

unto the end of Jordan. And *their* border in the
north quarter *was* from the bay of the sea at the
uttermost part of Jordan:
6 And the border went up to Beth-hogla, and
passed along by the north of Beth-arabah; and
the border went up to the stone of Bohan the son
of Reuben:
7 And the border went up toward Debir from the
valley of Achor, and so northward, looking toward
Gilgal, that *is* before the going up to Adummim,
which *is* on the south side of the river: and the
border passed toward the waters of En-shemesh,
and the goings out thereof were at En-rogel:
8 And the border went up by the valley of the son
of Hinnom unto the south side of the Jebusite;
the same *is* Jerusalem: and the border went up
to the top of the mountain that *lieth* before the
valley of Hinnom westward, which *is* at the end
of the valley of the giants northward:
9 And the border was drawn from the top of
the hill unto the fountain of the water of Neph-
toah, and went out to the cities of mount Ephron;
and the border was drawn to Baalah, which *is*
Kirjath-jearim:
10 And the border compassed from Baalah
westward unto mount Seir, and passed along unto
the side of mount Jearim, which *is* Chesalon, on
the north side, and went down to Beth-shemesh,
and passed on to Timnah:
11 And the border went out unto the side of
Ekron northward: and the border was drawn to
Shicron, and passed along to mount Baalah, and
went out unto Jabneel; and the goings out of the
border were at the sea.
12 And the west border *was* to the great sea, and
the coast *thereof*. This *is* the coast of the children
of Judah round about according to their families.
13 ¶ And unto Caleb the son of Jephunneh
he gave a part among the children of Judah,
according to the commandment of the LORD to
Joshua, *even* the city of Arba the father of Anak,
which *city is* Hebron.
14 And Caleb drove thence the three sons of
Anak, Sheshai, and Ahiman, and Talmai, the
children of Anak.
15 And he went up thence to the inhabitants
of Debir: and the name of Debir before *was*
Kirjath-sepher.
16 ¶ And Caleb said, He that smiteth Kirjath-sep-
her, and taketh it, to him will I give Achsah my
daughter to wife.
17 And Othniel the son of Kenaz, the brother
of Caleb, took it: and he gave him Achsah his
daughter to wife.
18 And it came to pass, as she came *unto him*, that
she moved him to ask of her father a field: and she
lighted off *her* ass; and Caleb said unto her, What
wouldest thou?
19 Who answered, Give me a blessing; for thou
hast given me a south land; give me also springs
of water. And he gave her the upper springs, and
the nether springs.
20 This *is* the inheritance of the tribe of the
children of Judah according to their families.
21 And the uttermost cities of the tribe of the
children of Judah toward the coast of Edom
southward were Kabzeel, and Eder, and Jagur,
22 And Kinah, and Dimonah, and Adadah,
23 And Kedesh, and Hazor, and Ithnan,
24 Ziph, and Telem, and Bealoth,
25 And Hazor, Hadattah, and Kerioth, *and*
Hezron, which *is* Hazor,
26 Amam, and Shema, and Moladah,
27 And Hazar-gaddah, and Heshmon, and
Beth-palet,
28 And Hazar-shual, and Beer-sheba, and
Bizjothjah,
29 Baalah, and Iim, and Azem,
30 And Eltolad, and Chesil, and Hormah,
31 And Ziklag, and Madmannah, and Sansannah,
32 And Lebaoth, and Shilhim, and Ain, and
Rimmon: all the cities *are* twenty and nine, with
their villages:
33 *And* in the valley, Eshtaol, and Zoreah, and
Ashnah,
34 And Zanoah, and En-gannim, Tappuah, and
Enam,
35 Jarmuth, and Adullam, Socoh, and Azekah,
36 And Sharaim, and Adithaim, and Gederah, and
Gederothaim; fourteen cities with their villages:
37 Zenan, and Hadashah, and Migdal-gad,
38 And Dilean, and Mizpeh, and Joktheel,
39 Lachish, and Bozkath, and Eglon,
40 And Cabbon, and Lahmam, and Kithlish,
41 And Gederoth, Beth-dagon, and Naamah, and
Makkedah; sixteen cities with their villages:
42 Libnah, and Ether, and Ashan,
43 And Jiphtah, and Ashnah, and Nezib,
44 And Keilah, and Achzib, and Mareshah; nine
cities with their villages:
45 Ekron, with her towns and her villages:
46 From Ekron even unto the sea, all that *lay* near
Ashdod, with their villages:
47 Ashdod with her towns and her villages, Gaza
with her towns and her villages, unto the river of
Egypt, and the great sea, and the border *thereof*:
48 ¶ And in the mountains, Shamir, and Jattir,
and Socoh,
49 And Dannah, and Kirjath-sannah, which *is*
Debir,

15:14 *Sheshai, and Ahiman, and Talmai* may be designations of family units.

15:18 *she lighted off her ass*. She got off her donkey.

15:19 *nether springs*. Lower springs.

50 And Anab, and Eshtemoh, and Anim,
51 And Goshen, and Holon, and Giloh; eleven
cities with their villages:
52 Arab, and Dumah, and Eshean,
53 And Janum, and Beth-tappuah, and Aphekah,
54 And Humtah, and Kirjath-arba, which *is*
Hebron, and Zior; nine cities with their villages:
55 Maon, Carmel, and Ziph, and Juttah,
56 And Jezreel, and Jokdeam, and Zanoah,
57 Cain, Gibeah, and Timnah; ten cities with
their villages:
58 Halhul, Beth-zur, and Gedor,
59 And Maarath, and Beth-anoth, and Eltekon;
six cities with their villages:
60 Kirjath-baal, which *is* Kirjath-jearim, and
Rabbah; two cities with their villages:
61 In the wilderness, Beth-arabah, Middin, and
Secacah,
62 And Nibshan, and the city of Salt, and En-
gedi; six cities with their villages.
63 ¶ As for the Jebusites the inhabitants of
Jerusalem, the children of Judah could not drive
them out: but the Jebusites dwell with the children
of Judah at Jerusalem unto this day.

CHAPTER 16

AND the lot of the children of Joseph fell from
Jordan by Jericho, unto the water of Jericho on
the east, to the wilderness that goeth up from
Jericho throughout mount Beth-el,
2 And goeth out from Beth-el to Luz, and passeth
along unto the borders of Archi to Ataroth,
3 And goeth down westward to the coast of Japh-
leti, unto the coast of Beth-horon the nether, and
to Gezer: and the goings out thereof are at the sea.
4 So the children of Joseph, Manasseh and
Ephraim, took their inheritance.
5 ¶ And the border of the children of Ephraim
according to their families was *thus*: even the
border of their inheritance on the east side was
Ataroth-addar, unto Beth-horon the upper;
6 And the border went out toward the sea to Mich-
methah on the north side; and the border went
about eastward unto Taanath-shiloh, and passed
by it on the east to Janohah;
7 And it went down from Janohah to Ataroth,
and to Naarath, and came to Jericho, and went
out at Jordan.
8 The border went out from Tappuah westward
unto the river Kanah; and the goings out thereof
were at the sea. This *is* the inheritance of the tribe
of the children of Ephraim by their families.
9 And the separate cities for the children of
Ephraim *were* among the inheritance of the chil-
dren of Manasseh, all the cities with their villages.
10 And they drave not out the Canaanites that
dwelt in Gezer: but the Canaanites dwell among
the Ephraimites unto this day, and serve under
tribute.

CHAPTER 17

THERE was also a lot for the tribe of Manasseh; for
he *was* the firstborn of Joseph; *to wit*, for Machir
the firstborn of Manasseh, the father of Gilead:
because he was a man of war, therefore he had
Gilead and Bashan.
2 There was also *a lot* for the rest of the children of
Manasseh by their families; for the children of Abi-
ezer, and for the children of Helek, and for the
children of Asriel, and for the children of Shechem,
and for the children of Hepher, and for the
children of Shemida: these *were* the male children

15:63 The *Jebusites* controlled Jerusalem until the time of David (2 Sam. 5:6).

16:3 *the nether*. Beneath or lower.

16:9 *separate cities*. Selected cities.

16:10 *under tribute*. Compulsory labor.

Thoughts for Personal/Family Worship: Chapter 15

1. It is astonishing at times how God uses His people to do great exploits for His glory in fulfilling His own promises when they trust solely in Him. Israel was condemned to wander in the wilderness for forty years because the nation as a whole refused to embrace God's promises, fearing that they could not defeat the giants of Canaan, particularly the sons of Anak (Num. 13:28,33). After forty years, Caleb, who followed God fully all those years, goes into Canaan, and with his sons, singlehandedly "drives thence" those giants. What areas of your life are you holding back from acting on by faith out of fear that God will not fulfil His promises?
2. Caleb is much more than an exemplar of faith. The story of Caleb is ultimately about the historical progress of God's redemption. For those who truly trust in Christ alone for salvation, this history will find its ultimate fulfilment in the inheritance of salvation in Christ (Matt. 25:34; Col. 3:24; Heb. 9:15). What comfort should believers draw from this for their daily life?

Thoughts for Personal/Family Worship: Chapter 16

The details in chs. 16–19 are significant. Together they show how minutely God fulfills His promises. For years He had promised that the covenant people would inherit this land so often described as flowing with milk and honey. It seemed to be a broad and general promise of good things to come. But as the promise comes to fact, the point-by-point distribution of districts, towns, and villages to every tribe shows how specifically, definitely, and tangibly God keeps His Word. Every part of the nation received their portion; none were left out. Often Christians regard God's promise of a glorious future in eternity in happy but general terms that things will someday be better. But the day will come when every promise will be experienced as fact in real and tangible ways that we cannot imagine. And so it will be that everyone of God's chosen people will receive his inheritance; none will be left out. How does it encourage you now to know that we will never tire of enjoying all the details of God's blessings?

of Manasseh the son of Joseph by their families.
3 ¶ But Zelophehad, the son of Hepher, the son
of Gilead, the son of Machir, the son of Manasseh,
had no sons, but daughters: and these *are* the
names of his daughters, Mahlah, and Noah,
Hoglah, Milcah, and Tirzah.
4 And they came near before Eleazar the priest,
and before Joshua the son of Nun, and before the
princes, saying, The LORD commanded Moses
to give us an inheritance among our brethren.
Therefore according to the commandment of
the LORD he gave them an inheritance among the
brethren of their father.
5 And there fell ten portions to Manasseh, beside
the land of Gilead and Bashan, which *were* on the
other side Jordan;
6 Because the daughters of Manasseh had an
inheritance among his sons: and the rest of
Manasseh's sons had the land of Gilead.
7 ¶ And the coast of Manasseh was from Asher
to Michmethah, that *lieth* before Shechem; and
the border went along on the right hand unto the
inhabitants of En-tappuah.
8 *Now* Manasseh had the land of Tappuah: but
Tappuah on the border of Manasseh *belonged* to
the children of Ephraim;
9 And the coast descended unto the river Kanah,
southward of the river: these cities of Ephraim
are among the cities of Manasseh: the coast of
Manasseh also *was* on the north side of the river,
and the outgoings of it were at the sea:
10 Southward *it was* Ephraim's, and northward
it was Manasseh's, and the sea is his border; and
they met together in Asher on the north, and in
Issachar on the east.
11 And Manasseh had in Issachar and in Asher
Beth-shean and her towns, and Ibleam and her
towns, and the inhabitants of Dor and her towns,
and the inhabitants of En-dor and her towns, and
the inhabitants of Taanach and her towns, and the
inhabitants of Megiddo and her towns, *even* three
countries.
12 Yet the children of Manasseh could not drive
out *the inhabitants of* those cities; but the Canaan-
ites would dwell in that land.
13 Yet it came to pass, when the children of Israel
were waxen strong, that they put the Canaanites
to tribute; but did not utterly drive them out.
14 And the children of Joseph spake unto Joshua,
saying, Why hast thou given me *but* one lot and
one portion to inherit, seeing I *am* a great people,
forasmuch as the LORD hath blessed me hitherto?
15 And Joshua answered them, If thou *be* a great
people, *then* get thee up to the wood *country*,
and cut down for thyself there in the land of the
Perizzites and of the giants, if mount Ephraim be
too narrow for thee.
16 And the children of Joseph said, The hill is not
enough for us: and all the Canaanites that dwell
in the land of the valley have chariots of iron, *both*
they who *are* of Beth-shean and her towns, and
they who *are* of the valley of Jezreel.
17 And Joshua spake unto the house of Joseph,
even to Ephraim and to Manasseh, saying, Thou
art a great people, and hast great power: thou
shalt not have one lot *only*:
18 But the mountain shall be thine; for it *is* a
wood, and thou shalt cut it down: and the out-
goings of it shall be thine: for thou shalt drive out
the Canaanites, though they have iron chariots,
and though they *be* strong.

CHAPTER 18

AND the whole congregation of the children of
Israel assembled together at Shiloh, and set up
the tabernacle of the congregation there. And the
land was subdued before them.
2 And there remained among the children of
Israel seven tribes, which had not yet received
their inheritance.
3 And Joshua said unto the children of Israel,
How long *are* ye slack to go to possess the land,
which the LORD God of your fathers hath given
you?
4 Give out from among you three men for *each*
tribe: and I will send them, and they shall rise, and
go through the land, and describe it according
to the inheritance of them; and they shall come
again to me.
5 And they shall divide it into seven parts: Judah
shall abide in their coast on the south, and the
house of Joseph shall abide in their coasts on the
north.

17:9,18 *the outgoings.* The boundaries. See also 18:19; 19:14, 22,29,33
17:13 *were waxen.* Had become. *tribute.* Compulsory labor.

Thoughts for Personal/Family Worship: Chapter 17

God had commanded Israel to destroy the Canaanites completely. These nations that represented the world and sin were not to coexist with God's people. The failure to drive them out completely was incomplete obedience, and the attempt to subdue them to compulsory labor was folly (vv. 12–13). This illustrates an important lesson that we must learn regarding sin. When they felt strong, they thought they could use the Canaanites to their advantage as their servants. But it was not long before they lost control, as the book of Judges records. We cannot control sin in our own strength. It will not be long before the sin we think we can manage overcomes us. It is only as we rest by faith in the victory over sin won by Christ that we can be freed from sin's dominion (Rom. 6). Will power by itself is never powerful enough. According to Rom. 6, how can we live out this truth in our daily lives?

6 Ye shall therefore describe the land *into* seven
parts, and bring *the description* hither to me, that I
may cast lots for you here before the LORD our God.
7 But the Levites have no part among you; for the
priesthood of the LORD *is* their inheritance: and
Gad, and Reuben, and half the tribe of Manasseh,
have received their inheritance beyond Jordan
on the east, which Moses the servant of the LORD
gave them.
8 ¶ And the men arose, and went away: and
Joshua charged them that went to describe the
land, saying, Go and walk through the land, and
describe it, and come again to me, that I may here
cast lots for you before the LORD in Shiloh.
9 And the men went and passed through the
land, and described it by cities into seven parts
in a book, and came *again* to Joshua to the host
at Shiloh.
10 ¶ And Joshua cast lots for them in Shiloh
before the LORD: and there Joshua divided the
land unto the children of Israel according to their
divisions.
11 ¶ And the lot of the tribe of the children of
Benjamin came up according to their families:
and the coast of their lot came forth between the
children of Judah and the children of Joseph.
12 And their border on the north side was from
Jordan; and the border went up to the side of
Jericho on the north side, and went up through
the mountains westward; and the goings out
thereof were at the wilderness of Beth-aven.
13 And the border went over from thence toward
Luz, to the side of Luz, which *is* Beth-el, south-
ward; and the border descended to Ataroth-adar,
near the hill that *lieth* on the south side of the
nether Beth-horon.
14 And the border was drawn *thence*, and com-
passed the corner of the sea southward, from the
hill that *lieth* before Beth-horon southward; and
the goings out thereof were at Kirjath-baal, which
is Kirjath-jearim, a city of the children of Judah:
this *was* the west quarter.
15 And the south quarter *was* from the end
of Kirjath-jearim, and the border went out on
the west, and went out to the well of waters of
Nephtoah:
16 And the border came down to the end of
the mountain that *lieth* before the valley of the
son of Hinnom, *and* which *is* in the valley of the
giants on the north, and descended to the valley
of Hinnom, to the side of Jebusi on the south, and
descended to En-rogel,
17 And was drawn from the north, and went
forth to En-shemesh, and went forth toward
Geliloth, which *is* over against the going up of
Adummim, and descended to the stone of Bohan
the son of Reuben,
18 And passed along toward the side over against
Arabah northward, and went down unto Arabah:
19 And the border passed along to the side of
Beth-hoglah northward: and the outgoings of the
border were at the north bay of the salt sea at the
south end of Jordan: this *was* the south coast.
20 And Jordan was the border of it on the east
side. This *was* the inheritance of the children of
Benjamin, by the coasts thereof round about,
according to their families.
21 Now the cities of the tribe of the children of
Benjamin according to their families were Jericho,
and Beth-hoglah, and the valley of Keziz,
22 And Beth-arabah, and Zemaraim, and Beth-el,
23 And Avim, and Parah, and Ophrah,
24 And Chephar-haammonai, and Ophni, and
Gaba; twelve cities with their villages:
25 Gibeon, and Ramah, and Beeroth,
26 And Mizpeh, and Chephirah, and Mozah,
27 And Rekem, and Irpeel, and Taralah,
28 And Zelah, Eleph, and Jebusi, which *is*
Jerusalem, Gibeath, *and* Kirjath; fourteen cities
with their villages. This *is* the inheritance of the
children of Benjamin according to their families.

CHAPTER 19

AND the second lot came forth to Simeon, *even*
for the tribe of the children of Simeon according
to their families: and their inheritance was within
the inheritance of the children of Judah.
2 And they had in their inheritance Beer-sheba,
or Sheba, and Moladah,
3 And Hazar-shual, and Balah, and Azem,
4 And Eltolad, and Bethul, and Hormah,
5 And Ziklag, and Beth-marcaboth, and Hazar-
susah,
6 And Beth-lebaoth, and Sharuhen; thirteen
cities and their villages:
7 Ain, Remmon, and Ether, and Ashan; four cities
and their villages:
8 And all the villages that *were* round about these
cities to Baalath-beer, Ramath of the south. This

18:7 See note at 13:14.
18:9 *host*. Camp.
18:12 *goings out*. Boundaries.

Thoughts for Personal/Family Worship: Chapter 18

Israel's taking possession of the land of Canaan was an act of faith. Not to take possession of that land, therefore, or to be slow to do it, as was the case of the seven tribes (vv. 2–3), was an act of unbelief. Accordingly, Joshua admonishes the people in these tribes for their slackness (v. 3). It is fascinating that he does not just admonish them, however; he also provides them with a plan of action (vv. 4–7), which God blesses to stir the men up to act (v. 8). What can we learn from Joshua's leadership, counsel, and call to action in this chapter that can assist us in guiding those who struggle with unbelief and indecisiveness?

is the inheritance of the tribe of the children of
Simeon according to their families.
9 Out of the portion of the children of Judah *was*
the inheritance of the children of Simeon: for the
part of the children of Judah was too much for
them: therefore the children of Simeon had their
inheritance within the inheritance of them.
10 ¶ And the third lot came up for the children
of Zebulun according to their families: and the
border of their inheritance was unto Sarid:
11 And their border went up toward the sea,
and Maralah, and reached to Dabbasheth, and
reached to the river that *is* before Jokneam;
12 And turned from Sarid eastward toward the
sunrising unto the border of Chisloth-tabor,
and then goeth out to Daberath, and goeth up to
Japhia,
13 And from thence passeth on along on the east
to Gittah-hepher, to Ittah-kazin, and goeth out to
Remmon-methoar to Neah;
14 And the border compasseth it on the north
side to Hannathon: and the outgoings thereof are
in the valley of Jiphthah-el:
15 And Kattath, and Nahallal, and Shimron, and
Idalah, and Beth-lehem: twelve cities with their
villages.
16 This *is* the inheritance of the children of Zeb-
ulun according to their families, these cities with
their villages.
17 ¶ *And* the fourth lot came out to Issachar, for
the children of Issachar according to their families.
18 And their border was toward Jezreel, and
Chesulloth, and Shunem,
19 And Hapharaim, and Shion, and Anaharath,
20 And Rabbith, and Kishion, and Abez,
21 And Remeth, and En-gannim, and En-haddah,
and Beth-pazzez;
22 And the coast reacheth to Tabor, and Shahaz-
imah, and Beth-shemesh; and the outgoings of
their border were at Jordan: sixteen cities with
their villages.
23 This *is* the inheritance of the tribe of the
children of Issachar according to their families,
the cities and their villages.
24 ¶ And the fifth lot came out for the tribe of the
children of Asher according to their families.
25 And their border was Helkath, and Hali, and
Beten, and Achshaph,
26 And Alammelech, and Amad, and Misheal;
and reacheth to Carmel westward, and to Shihor-
libnath;
27 And turneth toward the sunrising to Beth-
dagon, and reacheth to Zebulun, and to the valley
of Jiphthah-el toward the north side of Beth-
emek, and Neiel, and goeth out to Cabul on the
left hand,
28 And Hebron, and Rehob, and Hammon, and
Kanah, *even* unto great Zidon;
29 And *then* the coast turneth to Ramah, and
to the strong city Tyre; and the coast turneth to
Hosah; and the outgoings thereof are at the sea
from the coast to Achzib:
30 Ummah also, and Aphek, and Rehob: twenty
and two cities with their villages.
31 This *is* the inheritance of the tribe of the
children of Asher according to their families,
these cities with their villages.
32 ¶ The sixth lot came out to the children of
Naphtali, *even* for the children of Naphtali ac-
cording to their families.
33 And their coast was from Heleph, from Allon to
Zaanannim, and Adami, Nekeb, and Jabneel, unto
Lakum; and the outgoings thereof were at Jordan:
34 And *then* the coast turneth westward to
Aznoth-tabor, and goeth out from thence to
Hukkok, and reacheth to Zebulun on the south
side, and reacheth to Asher on the west side, and
to Judah upon Jordan toward the sunrising.
35 And the fenced cities *are* Ziddim, Zer, and
Hammath, Rakkath, and Chinnereth,
36 And Adamah, and Ramah, and Hazor,
37 And Kedesh, and Edrei, and En-hazor,
38 And Iron, and Migdal-el, Horem, and Beth-
anath, and Beth-shemesh; nineteen cities with
their villages.
39 This *is* the inheritance of the tribe of the chil-
dren of Naphtali according to their families, the
cities and their villages.
40 ¶ *And* the seventh lot came out for the tribe of
the children of Dan according to their families.
41 And the coast of their inheritance was Zorah,
and Eshtaol, and Ir-shemesh,
42 And Shaalabbin, and Ajalon, and Jethlah,
43 And Elon, and Thimnathah, and Ekron,
44 And Eltekeh, and Gibbethon, and Baalath,
45 And Jehud, and Bene-berak, and Gath-rimmon,
46 And Me-jarkon, and Rakkon, with the border
before Japho.
47 And the coast of the children of Dan went out
too little for them: therefore the children of Dan
went up to fight against Leshem, and took it, and
smote it with the edge of the sword, and possessed

19:9 Simeon received its inheritance within Judah and was essentially assimilated, at times losing its identity. This is the consequence of the same patriarchal prophecy regarding Levi (Gen. 49:7) but fulfilled in a completely different manner. Levi's scattering involved honor; Simeon's did not.

19:49–50 Only Joshua and his fellow spy Caleb received their inheritances by request.

Thoughts for Personal/Family Worship: Chapter 19

It is fascinating that at the end of this long, detailed list of how Israel's tribes received their allotted territory in Canaan, that Joshua also received an allotment (v. 49). Thus, both of Israel's heroes of faith, Joshua and Caleb, received an inheritance—Caleb at the beginning of the allotment

it, and dwelt therein, and called Leshem, Dan,
after the name of Dan their father.
48 This *is* the inheritance of the tribe of the
children of Dan according to their families, these
cities with their villages.
49 ¶ When they had made an end of dividing the
land for inheritance by their coasts, the children
of Israel gave an inheritance to Joshua the son of
Nun among them:
50 According to the word of the LORD they gave
him the city which he asked, *even* Timnath-serah
in mount Ephraim: and he built the city, and
dwelt therein.
51 These *are* the inheritances, which Eleazar the
priest, and Joshua the son of Nun, and the heads
of the fathers of the tribes of the children of Israel,
divided for an inheritance by lot in Shiloh before
the LORD, at the door of the tabernacle of the
congregation. So they made an end of dividing
the country.

CHAPTER 20

THE LORD also spake unto Joshua, saying,
2 Speak to the children of Israel, saying, Appoint
out for you cities of refuge, whereof I spake unto
you by the hand of Moses:
3 That the slayer that killeth *any* person unawares
and unwittingly may flee thither: and they shall
be your refuge from the avenger of blood.
4 And when he that doth flee unto one of those
cities shall stand at the entering of the gate of the
city, and shall declare his cause in the ears of the
elders of that city, they shall take him into the city
unto them, and give him a place, that he may dwell
among them.
5 And if the avenger of blood pursue after
him, then they shall not deliver the slayer up
into his hand; because he smote his neighbour
unwittingly, and hated him not beforetime.
6 And he shall dwell in that city, until he stand
before the congregation for judgment, *and* until
the death of the high priest that shall be in those
days: then shall the slayer return, and come unto
his own city, and unto his own house, unto the
city from whence he fled.
7 ¶ And they appointed Kedesh in Galilee in
mount Naphtali, and Shechem in mount Ephra-
im, and Kirjath-arba, which *is* Hebron, in the
mountain of Judah.
8 And on the other side Jordan by Jericho
eastward, they assigned Bezer in the wilderness
upon the plain out of the tribe of Reuben, and
Ramoth in Gilead out of the tribe of Gad, and
Golan in Bashan out of the tribe of Manasseh.
9 These were the cities appointed for all the chil-
dren of Israel, and for the stranger that sojourn-
eth among them, that whosoever killeth *any*

chapters (14:6–15) and Joshua at the end. In this way, the book of Joshua, which is "the book of the land," continues to teach us that both the history of progressive redemption and our ultimate journey to the heavenly Canaan, must always be placed in the framework of faith. Joshua and Caleb, who had risked their lives to live by faith and had remained steadfast for forty years in the midst of murmuring Israelites while in the wilderness, are now rewarded. We again learn that faith will always be more than amply rewarded by God's grace. What additional lessons does this history teach us about the importance of living and persevering consistently by saving faith?

The Designation of Special Cities (20:1—21:45)

Chapter 20: *Joshua designates six cities of refuge, three on each side of Jordan.*

Cities of Refuge (20:1–9)

20:2 *refuge.* Asylum. *Moses.* See Num. 35:6,11–15; Deut. 19:2–6. This is another evidence of Joshua carrying on the ministry of Moses.

20:3 *slayer.* This is the word used in the sixth commandment and always involves the taking of human life. *unawares.* Accidentally, not on purpose. *unwittingly.* Without knowledge. *avenger.* The word designates the kinsman-redeemer, who because of the family relationship assumes the responsibility to act in behalf of his kinsman—here to avenge murder.

20:4–5 *they shall take him into the city.* The elders judge and determine whether to give asylum. This implies that the cities of refuge provided no safety for those guilty of intentional murder.

20:6 Those given asylum stand trial before an assembly and if proven innocent remain in the city for the duration of the life of the high priest, after which there is no jeopardy.

20:9 *the stranger that sojourneth.* The foreigner who has taken up alien residence. *unawares . . . avenger.* See v. 3.

Thoughts for Personal/Family Worship: Chapter 20

1. **The cities of refuge indicate that the spirituality of the law that Jesus underscored in His Sermon on the Mount (Matt. 5) was true in the Old Testament as well. Christ made it clear that those who hated were guilty of murder even if they did not actually take a life. The cities of refuge show the other side by revealing that those who inadvertently took a life without malice or forethought are not held guilty of murder and thus not liable to its consequence. The heart is the key. It does not remove the tragedy of the loss of human life but it does focus on the spiritual significance of God's law. The fact that those guilty of intentional murder receive no asylum teaches the same. Take this opportunity to apply this principle to all the Ten Commandments and remember that the heart, although unseen to man, is known by God. Motives matter.**
2. **The avenger is the kinsman-redeemer whose responsibility it was to help his family in whatever way was necessary. Sometimes, it involved purchasing property to keep it within the family like Boaz the near kinsman did for Ruth. Here in this context the act involved the execution of justice. The main point is that the kinsman does whatever must be done for the welfare of family. Significantly, the term is used of God (Ps. 19:14). The wonderful truth is that because of His covenant relationship with His people, the Lord will do for them whatever**

person at unawares might flee thither, and not
die by the hand of the avenger of blood, until he
stood before the congregation.

CHAPTER 21

THEN came near the heads of the fathers of the
Levites unto Eleazar the priest, and unto Joshua
the son of Nun, and unto the heads of the fathers
of the tribes of the children of Israel;
2 And they spake unto them at Shiloh in the land
of Canaan, saying, The LORD commanded by the
hand of Moses to give us cities to dwell in, with
the suburbs thereof for our cattle.
3 And the children of Israel gave unto the Levites
out of their inheritance, at the commandment of
the LORD, these cities and their suburbs.
4 And the lot came out for the families of the
Kohathites: and the children of Aaron the priest,
which were of the Levites, had by lot out of the
tribe of Judah, and out of the tribe of Simeon, and
out of the tribe of Benjamin, thirteen cities.
5 And the rest of the children of Kohath *had* by
lot out of the families of the tribe of Ephraim, and
out of the tribe of Dan, and out of the half tribe of
Manasseh, ten cities.
6 And the children of Gershon *had* by lot out of
the families of the tribe of Issachar, and out of the
tribe of Asher, and out of the tribe of Naphtali,
and out of the half tribe of Manasseh in Bashan,
thirteen cities.
7 The children of Merari by their families *had*
out of the tribe of Reuben, and out of the tribe of
Gad, and out of the tribe of Zebulun, twelve cities.
8 And the children of Israel gave by lot unto the
Levites these cities with their suburbs, as the LORD
commanded by the hand of Moses.
9 ¶ And they gave out of the tribe of the children
of Judah, and out of the tribe of the children of
Simeon, these cities which are *here* mentioned by
name,
10 Which the children of Aaron, *being* of the
families of the Kohathites, *who were* of the
children of Levi, had: for theirs was the first lot.
11 And they gave them the city of Arba the father
of Anak, which *city is* Hebron, in the hill *country*
of Judah, with the suburbs thereof round about it.
12 But the fields of the city, and the villages
thereof, gave they to Caleb the son of Jephunneh
for his possession.
13 ¶ Thus they gave to the children of Aaron the
priest Hebron with her suburbs, *to be* a city of
refuge for the slayer; and Libnah with her suburbs,
14 And Jattir with her suburbs, and Eshtemoa
with her suburbs,
15 And Holon with her suburbs, and Debir with
her suburbs,
16 And Ain with her suburbs, and Juttah with her
suburbs, *and* Beth-shemesh with her suburbs;
nine cities out of those two tribes.
17 And out of the tribe of Benjamin, Gibeon with
her suburbs, Geba with her suburbs,
18 Anathoth with her suburbs, and Almon with
her suburbs; four cities.
19 All the cities of the children of Aaron, the
priests, *were* thirteen cities with their suburbs.
20 ¶ And the families of the children of Kohath,
the Levites which remained of the children of
Kohath, even they had the cities of their lot out of
the tribe of Ephraim.
21 For they gave them Shechem with her suburbs
in mount Ephraim, *to be* a city of refuge for the
slayer; and Gezer with her suburbs,
22 And Kibzaim with her suburbs, and Beth-ho-
ron with her suburbs; four cities.
23 And out of the tribe of Dan, Eltekeh with her
suburbs, Gibbethon with her suburbs,
24 Aijalon with her suburbs, Gath-rimmon with
her suburbs; four cities.
25 And out of the half tribe of Manasseh, Tanach
with her suburbs, and Gath-rimmon with her
suburbs; two cities.
26 All the cities *were* ten with their suburbs for the
families of the children of Kohath that remained.

needs to be done for their welfare. Ultimately, it points to Christ who as our kinsman-redeemer has delivered us from death and has provided for us an inheritance of spiritual blessing. We can count on Him to act in our behalf in whatever way is needful for us. Spend some time exalting Christ as our kinsman-redeemer!

Chapter 21: *Joshua allots forty-eight cities to the tribe of Levi in the midst of the other tribal territories.*

Cities for the Levites (21:1–45)

21:1 *Levites.* See notes at 13:14 and 14:4. *fathers.* Used here as an honorific title of the leaders of the tribes.

21:2 *suburbs.* Pasturelands outside the city limits but under the jurisdiction of the city.

21:43–45 Sums up the end of the conquest and land allotment. *gave them rest.* Enabled them to settle down. *there failed not ought.* Literally, "a word did not fall from any good word." God always keeps His word.

Thoughts for Personal/Family Worship: Chapter 21

1. The tribe of Levi was divinely chosen to be the special servants of the Lord for the ministry of tabernacle. Not all were priests, but all in some capacity enjoyed the unique privilege of being employed in sacred service. The Lord Himself was their ultimate inheritance, and so they did not inherit land as the other tribes. But as the servants of God, He had a place for them to serve for the welfare and advantage of the entire nation. He scattered them in such a way that their influence and ministry could be experienced throughout the nation. They were God's gift to the nation. Similarly, God has called men to sacred ministry and given them to local and specific congregations for the edification and spiritual welfare of

27 ¶ And unto the children of Gershon, of the families of the Levites, out of the *other* half tribe of Manasseh *they gave* Golan in Bashan with her suburbs, *to be* a city of refuge for the slayer; and Beesh-terah with her suburbs; two cities.

28 And out of the tribe of Issachar, Kishon with her suburbs, Dabareh with her suburbs,

29 Jarmuth with her suburbs, En-gannim with her suburbs; four cities.

30 And out of the tribe of Asher, Mishal with her suburbs, Abdon with her suburbs,

31 Helkath with her suburbs, and Rehob with her suburbs; four cities.

32 And out of the tribe of Naphtali, Kedesh in Galilee with her suburbs, *to be* a city of refuge for the slayer; and Hammoth-dor with her suburbs, and Kartan with her suburbs; three cities.

33 All the cities of the Gershonites according to their families *were* thirteen cities with their suburbs.

34 ¶ And unto the families of the children of Merari, the rest of the Levites, out of the tribe of Zebulun, Jokneam with her suburbs, and Kartah with her suburbs,

35 Dimnah with her suburbs, Nahalal with her suburbs; four cities.

36 And out of the tribe of Reuben, Bezer with her suburbs, and Jahazah with her suburbs,

37 Kedemoth with her suburbs, and Mephaath with her suburbs; four cities.

38 And out of the tribe of Gad, Ramoth in Gilead with her suburbs, *to be* a city of refuge for the slayer; and Mahanaim with her suburbs,

39 Heshbon with her suburbs, Jazer with her suburbs; four cities in all.

40 So all the cities for the children of Merari by their families, which were remaining of the families of the Levites, were *by* their lot twelve cities.

41 All the cities of the Levites within the possession of the children of Israel *were* forty and eight cities with their suburbs.

42 These cities were every one with their suburbs round about them: thus *were* all these cities.

43 ¶ And the LORD gave unto Israel all the land which he sware to give unto their fathers; and they possessed it, and dwelt therein.

44 And the LORD gave them rest round about, according to all that he sware unto their fathers: and there stood not a man of all their enemies before them; the LORD delivered all their enemies into their hand.

45 There failed not ought of any good thing which the LORD had spoken unto the house of Israel; all came to pass.

CHAPTER 22

THEN Joshua called the Reubenites, and the Gadites, and the half tribe of Manasseh,

2 And said unto them, Ye have kept all that Moses the servant of the LORD commanded you, and have obeyed my voice in all that I commanded you:

3 Ye have not left your brethren these many days unto this day, but have kept the charge of the commandment of the LORD your God.

4 And now the LORD your God hath given rest unto your brethren, as he promised them: therefore now return ye, and get you unto your tents, *and* unto the land of your possession, which Moses the servant of the LORD gave you on the other side Jordan.

5 But take diligent heed to do the commandment and the law, which Moses the servant of the LORD charged you, to love the LORD your God, and to walk in all his ways, and to keep his commandments, and to cleave unto him, and to serve him with all your heart and with all your soul.

6 So Joshua blessed them, and sent them away: and they went unto their tents.

7 ¶ Now to the *one* half of the tribe of Manasseh Moses had given *possession* in Bashan: but unto the *other* half thereof gave Joshua among their brethren on this side Jordan westward. And when Joshua sent them away also unto their tents, then he blessed them,

8 And he spake unto them, saying, Return with

---

believers (Eph. 4:11–12). How can you show honor and appreciation for these men?

2. Joshua 21:43–45 declares the fulfillment of God's promise of land in absolute terms, yet Judges reveals that not all the land was actually conquered, and yet another rest was to come in the time of David (2 Sam. 7:1,11). The focus of the promise included something beyond just a geographical component. Ultimately, this rest involved the enjoyment of God's presence and was the experience of faith. Under Joshua, this generation had conquered the enemies before them and entered into their inheritance. The fact that there was more to come did not distract from the fullness of their enjoyment of what God had promised. This illustrates once again the "already-not yet" principle that characterizes the Christian experience. How does it encourage you today to know that in Christ, we are blessed with all the spiritual blessings in the heavenly places, but the best is yet to be (Eph. 1)?

THE MAINTENANCE OF THE LAND (22:1—24:33)

Chapter 22: ***The two and a half tribes return to their inheritance on the east of the Jordan, but a controversy arises over an altar of witness that jeopardizes the unity of the nation.***

Warnings for the Transjordan Tribes (22:1–34)

22:1–5 The two and a half tribes had faithfully discharged their duty in fighting the battles to aid their countrymen even though their own inheritance had already been secured (Num. 32:20–22; Deut. 3:18–20; Josh. 1:12–15). *take diligent heed to do.* Be very careful to do. The five infinitives define the

much riches unto your tents, and with very much
cattle, with silver, and with gold, and with brass,
and with iron, and with very much raiment: di-
vide the spoil of your enemies with your brethren.
9 ¶ And the children of Reuben and the children
of Gad and the half tribe of Manasseh returned,
and departed from the children of Israel out of
Shiloh, which *is* in the land of Canaan, to go unto
the country of Gilead, to the land of their posses-
sion, whereof they were possessed, according to
the word of the LORD by the hand of Moses.
10 ¶ And when they came unto the borders
of Jordan, that *are* in the land of Canaan, the
children of Reuben and the children of Gad and
the half tribe of Manasseh built there an altar by
Jordan, a great altar to see to.
11 ¶ And the children of Israel heard say, Behold,
the children of Reuben and the children of Gad
and the half tribe of Manasseh have built an altar
over against the land of Canaan, in the borders
of Jordan, at the passage of the children of Israel.
12 And when the children of Israel heard *of it*,
the whole congregation of the children of Israel
gathered themselves together at Shiloh, to go up
to war against them.
13 And the children of Israel sent unto the
children of Reuben, and to the children of Gad,
and to the half tribe of Manasseh, into the land
of Gilead, Phinehas the son of Eleazar the priest,
14 And with him ten princes, of each chief house
a prince throughout all the tribes of Israel; and
each one *was* an head of the house of their fathers
among the thousands of Israel.
15 ¶ And they came unto the children of Reuben,
and to the children of Gad, and to the half tribe
of Manasseh, unto the land of Gilead, and they
spake with them, saying,
16 Thus saith the whole congregation of the
LORD, What trespass *is* this that ye have committed
against the God of Israel, to turn away this day
from following the LORD, in that ye have builded
you an altar, that ye might rebel this day against
the LORD?
17 *Is* the iniquity of Peor too little for us, from
which we are not cleansed until this day, although
there was a plague in the congregation of the LORD,
18 But that ye must turn away this day from
following the LORD? and it will be, *seeing* ye rebel
to day against the LORD, that to morrow he will be
wroth with the whole congregation of Israel.
19 Notwithstanding, if the land of your posses-
sion *be* unclean, *then* pass ye over unto the land
of the possession of the LORD, wherein the LORD's
tabernacle dwelleth, and take possession among
us: but rebel not against the LORD, nor rebel
against us, in building you an altar beside the
altar of the LORD our God.
20 Did not Achan the son of Zerah commit a
trespass in the accursed thing, and wrath fell
on all the congregation of Israel? and that man
perished not alone in his iniquity.
21 ¶ Then the children of Reuben and the chil-
dren of Gad and the half tribe of Manasseh an-
swered, and said unto the heads of the thousands
of Israel,
22 The LORD God of gods, the LORD God of gods,
he knoweth, and Israel he shall know; if *it be* in
rebellion, or if in transgression against the LORD,
(save us not this day,)
23 That we have built us an altar to turn from
following the LORD, or if to offer thereon burnt
offering or meat offering, or if to offer peace
offerings thereon, let the LORD himself require *it*;
24 And if we have not *rather* done it for fear of
this thing, saying, In time to come your children
might speak unto our children, saying, What have
ye to do with the LORD God of Israel?
25 For the LORD hath made Jordan a border
between us and you, ye children of Reuben and
children of Gad; ye have no part in the LORD: so
shall your children make our children cease from
fearing the LORD.
26 Therefore we said, Let us now prepare to
build us an altar, not for burnt offering, nor for
sacrifice:
27 But *that* it *may be* a witness between us, and

---

essence of obedience to the commandments. Compare with Deut. 10:12–13. *with all your heart and with all your soul.* The *heart* includes the entire inner man—mind, affections, and will. *Soul* designates the whole person. Together they express the idea of total devotion. No part of life is unaffected by one's relationship to God.

22:10 *great altar to see to.* Great altar in regard to appearance.

22:12 *Shiloh* was the location of the tabernacle, the only legitimate place for sacrifice. The western tribes assumed that the altar erected was going to violate the law of the central sanctuary (Deut. 12).

22:14 *prince(s).* An exalted leader but not royalty.

22:16 *What trespass . . . have committed.* The noun and verb are the same root and refer to acts of unfaithfulness directed against God. *rebel.* Implies the rejection of God's authority.

22:17 *iniquity.* Pictures sin as twisted and perverted behavior. See Num. 23:28 for the historical occasion of *Peor. plague.* Can refer to either a stumbling or an affliction.

22:18 *turn away.* The common word for repentance, picturing a reversal of direction. *wroth.* Angry.

22:20 *accursed thing.* That which God had devoted to Himself for destruction.

22:22 *God of gods.* The Hebrew way to express a superlative; hence, the supreme God.

22:24 *for fear.* This word for *fear* has the idea of anxious worry or dread.

22:25 *fearing the LORD.* This word for fear expresses the essence of true religion and piety.

22:26–29 The eastern tribes pledge their allegiance to the Lord and His requirements, explaining that the altar is a monument to remind future generations of that commitment. *God forbid.* Literally, "far be it from us," may it never

you, and our generations after us, that we might
do the service of the LORD before him with our
burnt offerings, and with our sacrifices, and with
our peace offerings; that your children may not
say to our children in time to come, Ye have no
part in the LORD.
28 Therefore said we, that it shall be, when they
should *so* say to us or to our generations in time to
come, that we may say *again*, Behold the pattern
of the altar of the LORD, which our fathers made,
not for burnt offerings, nor for sacrifices; but it *is*
a witness between us and you.
29 God forbid that we should rebel against the
LORD, and turn this day from following the LORD,
to build an altar for burnt offerings, for meat
offerings, or for sacrifices, beside the altar of the
LORD our God that *is* before his tabernacle.
30 ¶ And when Phinehas the priest, and the
princes of the congregation and heads of the
thousands of Israel which *were* with him, heard
the words that the children of Reuben and the
children of Gad and the children of Manasseh
spake, it pleased them.
31 And Phinehas the son of Eleazar the priest said
unto the children of Reuben, and to the children
of Gad, and to the children of Manasseh, This day
we perceive that the LORD *is* among us, because
ye have not committed this trespass against the
LORD: now ye have delivered the children of Israel
out of the hand of the LORD.
32 ¶ And Phinehas the son of Eleazar the priest,
and the princes, returned from the children of
Reuben, and from the children of Gad, out of the
land of Gilead, unto the land of Canaan, to the
children of Israel, and brought them word again.
33 And the thing pleased the children of Israel;
and the children of Israel blessed God, and did
not intend to go up against them in battle, to de-
stroy the land wherein the children of Reuben
and Gad dwelt.
34 And the children of Reuben and the children
of Gad called the altar *Ed*: for it *shall be* a witness
between us that the LORD *is* God.

CHAPTER 23

AND it came to pass a long time after that the
LORD had given rest unto Israel from all their en-
emies round about, that Joshua waxed old *and*
stricken in age.
2 And Joshua called for all Israel, *and* for their
elders, and for their heads, and for their judges,
and for their officers, and said unto them, I am
old *and* stricken in age:
3 And ye have seen all that the LORD your God
hath done unto all these nations because of you;
for the LORD your God *is* he that hath fought for
you.
4 Behold, I have divided unto you by lot these
nations that remain, to be an inheritance for your
tribes, from Jordan, with all the nations that I
have cut off, even unto the great sea westward.
5 And the LORD your God, he shall expel them
from before you, and drive them from out of your
sight; and ye shall possess their land, as the LORD
your God hath promised unto you.
6 Be ye therefore very courageous to keep and
to do all that is written in the book of the law of
Moses, that ye turn not aside therefrom *to* the
right hand or *to* the left;

---

happen that we would rebel.

22:30 *it pleased them*. Literally, "it was good in their eyes." They were satisfied with the explanation. See also v. 33.

22:34 *Ed*. The translators simply transliterated the Hebrew word for "witness."

Thoughts for Personal/Family Worship: Chapter 22

1. **This episode illustrates the unity of God's people and the pervasive consequences of sin that can affect the whole body. The nation remembered the terrible consequences of the sin of many at Baal Peor and the sin of one at Jericho (Achan) that caused the shameful defeat at Ai. They learned the lesson and did not want to repeat it. So if the eastern tribes were guilty of violating God's commandment, they were ready to deal with it immediately lest the whole nation would suffer. They knew that a little leaven leavens the whole lump and therefore they had to purge out the old (1 Cor. 5:6–7). We must remember how powerful sin is, and that by either example or consequence the most private of sins have the potential of affecting others. For the sake of the body, it is imperative for the church to exercise discipline when aware of sin in others. How can we, for the sake of ourselves and of the body, strive for victory over every sin?**
2. **The manner in which the western tribes handled the issue with their eastern brothers is exemplary. There was no rush to judgment. Inquiry was made before action was taken, and they gave them the benefit of the doubt. Too often, some Christians think the worst and condemn fellow believers on the basis of suspicion rather than fact. Here is an Old Testament example of the procedure Christ outlines in Matt. 18 for dealing with offending brothers. When they talked together and the facts were known, the result was peace and not war. Since it is good to preserve the unity of the brothers rather than incite unnecessary division, what wise practices should you establish?**

Admonitions from Joshua (23:1—24:33)

Chapter 23: ***Joshua exhorts the nation in the light of his impending death.***

23:1–2 *Joshua waxed old and stricken in age*. Joshua was old and, literally, "going in the days."

23:4–5 Joshua assured them that even the territories allotted to them that had not yet been conquered would become their possession. The Lord had won the victory but the possession was gradual. Spiritually, this parallels progressive sanctification.

23:6 *Be . . . very courageous*. Literally, "be exceedingly strong." *written in the book of the law of Moses*. A reference to the whole

7 That ye come not among these nations, these
that remain among you; neither make mention
of the name of their gods, nor cause to swear *by
them*, neither serve them, nor bow yourselves
unto them:
8 But cleave unto the LORD your God, as ye have
done unto this day.
9 For the LORD hath driven out from before you
great nations and strong: but *as for* you, no man
hath been able to stand before you unto this day.
10 One man of you shall chase a thousand: for
the LORD your God, he *it is* that fighteth for you,
as he hath promised you.
11 Take good heed therefore unto yourselves, that
ye love the LORD your God.
12 Else if ye do in any wise go back, and cleave
unto the remnant of these nations, *even* these that
remain among you, and shall make marriages
with them, and go in unto them, and they to you:
13 Know for a certainty that the LORD your God
will no more drive out *any of* these nations from
before you; but they shall be snares and traps unto
you, and scourges in your sides, and thorns in
your eyes, until ye perish from off this good land
which the LORD your God hath given you.
14 And, behold, this day I *am* going the way of all
the earth: and ye know in all your hearts and in
all your souls, that not one thing hath failed of all
the good things which the LORD your God spake
concerning you; all are come to pass unto you,
and not one thing hath failed thereof.
15 Therefore it shall come to pass, *that* as all good
things are come upon you, which the LORD your
God promised you; so shall the LORD bring upon
you all evil things, until he have destroyed you
from off this good land which the LORD your God
hath given you.
16 When ye have transgressed the covenant of
the LORD your God, which he commanded you,
and have gone and served other gods, and bowed
yourselves to them; then shall the anger of the
LORD be kindled against you, and ye shall perish quickly from off the good land which he hath
given unto you.

CHAPTER 24

AND Joshua gathered all the tribes of Israel to
Shechem, and called for the elders of Israel, and for
their heads, and for their judges, and for their officers; and they presented themselves before God.
2 And Joshua said unto all the people, Thus saith
the LORD God of Israel, Your fathers dwelt on the
other side of the flood in old time, *even* Terah, the
father of Abraham, and the father of Nachor: and
they served other gods.
3 And I took your father Abraham from the other
side of the flood, and led him throughout all the
land of Canaan, and multiplied his seed, and gave
him Isaac.
4 And I gave unto Isaac Jacob and Esau: and
I gave unto Esau mount Seir, to possess it; but
Jacob and his children went down into Egypt.
5 I sent Moses also and Aaron, and I plagued
Egypt, according to that which I did among them:
and afterward I brought you out.
6 And I brought your fathers out of Egypt: and
ye came unto the sea; and the Egyptians pursued
after your fathers with chariots and horsemen
unto the Red sea.
7 And when they cried unto the LORD, he put
darkness between you and the Egyptians, and
brought the sea upon them, and covered them;
and your eyes have seen what I have done in Egypt:

Pentateuch, which was written by inspiration and preserved by providence for their instruction.

23:7 *mention . . . swear . . . serve . . . bow*. In reference to these actions, the Hebrew uses the emphatic prohibition: "You must not."

23:11 *Take good heed*. The Hebrew uses the emphatic command: "You must guard yourselves exceedingly."

23:12 *Else if ye do in any wise go back*. If indeed you certainly return.

23:15–16 *evil things*. Not in the sense of moral evil but disasters or harmful things. All this is in keeping with Moses (Deut. 28:63). Possession of the land was always conditioned by faith and obedience.

Thoughts for Personal/Family Worship: Chapter 23

1. **Israel's possession of the Promised Land was rooted in God's fulfillment of His promise and experienced in terms of their faithful obedience. God promised victory and fought for them, but they had to love and obey Him in order to experience the blessing. This parallels spiritually the procedure for our sanctification. Christ has conquered our spiritual enemies so that sin no longer has dominion over us. In the light of that victory and promise, we must die to sin and live to righteousness. Our sanctification is progressive and involves cooperation between what God has done in Christ and what we must do in Christ to experience victory. Ponder or discuss Paul's logic in Rom. 6.**
2. **Loving God and loving the world are mutually exclusive. As evidence of their obedience and love for God, Israel was to have no alliance with the worldly and pagan inhabitants of the land. Those nations were cut off by God and destined to destruction. So we as Christians, who love God, are not to love the things of this world, which are opposed to God and destined to pass away (1 John 2:15–17). How can we keep our hearts from the love of the world?**

Chapter 24: *Joshua reviews Israel's history as the basis for renewing the covenant with the nation prior to his death.*

24:2–3 *flood*. River, a specific reference to the Euphrates. *they served other gods*. Prior to his call and conversion, Abraham was a pagan idolater. This highlights the grace of God in bringing him out of Ur. The following review of history is a pattern of grace.

and ye dwelt in the wilderness a long season.
8 And I brought you into the land of the
Amorites, which dwelt on the other side Jordan;
and they fought with you: and I gave them into
your hand, that ye might possess their land; and I
destroyed them from before you.
9 Then Balak the son of Zippor, king of Moab,
arose and warred against Israel, and sent and
called Balaam the son of Beor to curse you:
10 But I would not hearken unto Balaam; there-
fore he blessed you still: so I delivered you out of
his hand.
11 And ye went over Jordan, and came unto
Jericho: and the men of Jericho fought against
you, the Amorites, and the Perizzites, and the
Canaanites, and the Hittites, and the Girgashites,
the Hivites, and the Jebusites; and I delivered
them into your hand.
12 And I sent the hornet before you, which drave
them out from before you, *even* the two kings of
the Amorites; *but* not with thy sword, nor with
thy bow.
13 And I have given you a land for which ye did
not labour, and cities which ye built not, and ye
dwell in them; of the vineyards and oliveyards
which ye planted not do ye eat.
14 ¶ Now therefore fear the LORD, and serve him
in sincerity and in truth: and put away the gods
which your fathers served on the other side of the
flood, and in Egypt; and serve ye the LORD.
15 And if it seem evil unto you to serve the LORD,
choose you this day whom ye will serve; whether
the gods which your fathers served that *were* on
the other side of the flood, or the gods of the
Amorites, in whose land ye dwell: but as for me
and my house, we will serve the LORD.
16 And the people answered and said, God forbid
that we should forsake the LORD, to serve other
gods;
17 For the LORD our God, he *it is* that brought
us up and our fathers out of the land of Egypt,
from the house of bondage, and which did those
great signs in our sight, and preserved us in all the
way wherein we went, and among all the people
through whom we passed:
18 And the LORD drave out from before us all
the people, even the Amorites which dwelt in the
land: *therefore* will we also serve the LORD; for he
is our God.
19 And Joshua said unto the people, Ye cannot
serve the LORD: for he *is* an holy God; he *is* a jeal-
ous God; he will not forgive your transgressions
nor your sins.
20 If ye forsake the LORD, and serve strange gods,
then he will turn and do you hurt, and consume
you, after that he hath done you good.
21 And the people said unto Joshua, Nay; but we
will serve the LORD.
22 And Joshua said unto the people, Ye *are*
witnesses against yourselves that ye have chosen
you the LORD, to serve him. And they said, *We are*
witnesses.
23 Now therefore put away, *said he*, the strange
gods which *are* among you, and incline your heart
unto the LORD God of Israel.
24 And the people said unto Joshua, The LORD
our God will we serve, and his voice will we obey.
25 So Joshua made a covenant with the people
that day, and set them a statute and an ordinance
in Shechem.
26 ¶ And Joshua wrote these words in the book
of the law of God, and took a great stone, and set
it up there under an oak, that *was* by the sanctu-
ary of the LORD.
27 And Joshua said unto all the people, Behold,
this stone shall be a witness unto us; for it hath
heard all the words of the LORD which he spake
unto us: it shall be therefore a witness unto you,
lest ye deny your God.
28 So Joshua let the people depart, every man
unto his inheritance.
29 ¶ And it came to pass after these things, that
Joshua the son of Nun, the servant of the LORD,
died, *being* an hundred and ten years old.

24:8 *the Amorites.* A general term referring to all Canaanite peoples. *the other side Jordan.* Here referring to Transjordan or eastern side.
24:12 *the hornet.* See Deut. 7:20. Interpreters differ regarding the meaning of this word. It could refer to an actual hornet, the abstract idea of discouragement, or an angel (Ex. 23:28).
24:14 *in sincerity.* Completely or totally. *flood.* The Euphrates, also v. 15. *in Egypt.* Israel practiced idolatry while in bondage; they were not suffering in slavery as persecuted saints. This highlights the grace of God in delivering them in the exodus.
24:15 *evil.* a hard or harmful thing. *choose you this day.* True religion is exclusive. God does not tolerate shared allegiance (see the first commandment in Ex. 20:3).
24:16 *God forbid.* Literally, "far be it from us."
24:18 *drave out.* Banished.
24:19 Joshua used hyperbolic language to underscore the importance of the decision to follow the Lord. Man must not trifle with God; He takes confessions of commitment seriously. The Bible is clear that God does forgive sins upon confession, but this makes it clear that there is no forgiveness for those who reject Him. *holy.* Distinct and separate. *jealous.* God is zealous for His own name, His Word, and His people.
24:20 *strange gods.* The gods of a foreign land (v. 23). *do you hurt.* Punish you. *consume.* Destroy or exterminate.
24:27 *it hath heard.* A figure of speech in which an inanimate object (the stone) is attributed with human activity.
24:29–33 These verses are most likely post-Joshua. See Introduction: Authorship.
24:32 See Ex. 13:19.

Thoughts for Personal/Family Worship: Chapter 24

1. **Joshua's final charge outlines a formula for keeping and enjoying God's blessing. First, remember that sovereign**

30 And they buried him in the border of his
inheritance in Timnath-serah, which *is* in mount
Ephraim, on the north side of the hill of Gaash.
31 And Israel served the LORD all the days of
Joshua, and all the days of the elders that over-
lived Joshua, and which had known all the works
of the LORD, that he had done for Israel.
32 ¶ And the bones of Joseph, which the children
of Israel brought up out of Egypt, buried they
in Shechem, in a parcel of ground which Jacob
bought of the sons of Hamor the father of
Shechem for an hundred pieces of silver: and it
became the inheritance of the children of Joseph.
33 And Eleazar the son of Aaron died; and they
buried him in a hill *that pertained to* Phinehas his
son, which was given him in mount Ephraim.

grace is the cause of blessing. Abraham was as guilty of idolatry as any one else in Ur, but God graciously entered into covenant with him. Israel was as guilty as the Egyptians that held them in bondage but God graciously redeemed them with His power and the blood of the sacrifice. So it is that we are not saved by any self-merit or effort but purely by grace which is so undeserved. Spend time praising God for His gifts of grace.

2. **Second, remember that divine faithfulness is the guarantee of blessing. Joshua's review of history cited instance after instance of God's faithfulness in keeping His word, defeating every enemy they confronted. They inherited the land because God's promise was certain. And so we should remember that all of God's promises are yea and amen in Jesus Christ. God was faithful to every covenant promise to send His Son to be the Redeemer of His people, and Christ faithfully fulfilled His commission to redeem them. What future promises can we then cling to with great hope?**
3. **Third, acknowledge that personal commitment is the condition for blessing. In the light of God's grace and faithfulness, Israel was to fear Him and serve Him in sincerity and truth. Joshua flatly said they could not do this on their own. That commitment was the evidence of grace received. This parallels what Christ expects of His disciples. In Luke 14, the greater Joshua said three times that one cannot be His disciple unless he regards Christ above others (v. 26), above self (vv. 26–27), and above everything (v. 33). Pray for God's continued gift of grace that makes this kind of commitment possible.**

INTRODUCTION TO THE BOOK OF JUDGES

JGS RTH SAM

Authorship: Although the book is anonymous, tradition has identified Samuel or one of his contemporaries as the likely author. The book certainly reflects the prophetic spirit.

Date: The date of composition is uncertain but is suggested by internal evidence. Many interpreters identify the reference to the "captivity of the land" in 18:30 to equate to the captivity of the ark mentioned in 1 Sam. 4:11. This occurred approximately 1090 BC. The reference to the Jebusite occupation of Jerusalem in Judg. 1:21 points to a time before David took possession of the city recorded in 2 Sam. 5. This occurred approximately 1003 BC. This evidence would put the composition sometime between 1090 and 1003 BC. If the book was written toward the beginning of this period, it is well within the lifetime of Samuel.

Theme: The faithfulness of a covenant-keeping God to deliver His people from their oppressors.

Purpose: To set the stage for the coming of Christ as the Savior of His sin-troubled people by showing how God delights to intervene in mercy.

Synopsis: *The Contribution of Judges to Redemptive Revelation*

Judges covers approximately 350 years of Israel's history from the death of Joshua to the ministry of Samuel. The recorded years of oppression and rest give a much higher number but most of the oppressions were geographically localized and temporally overlapping. It warns against compromising with the ungodly and their idolatrous ways. Israel's compromises are all the more glaring in light of God's carefully stated instructions to utterly destroy the heathen nations (Deut. 12:2; 17:2; 20:17). There was divine justice behind the command to eradicate these nations (Deut. 18:9–13). However, Israel failed by allowing the heathen to dwell in the land, making alliances with them, and encouraging intermarriage. This inevitably led Israel to idolatrous worship. Time and again the children of Israel sinned against the Lord, and each and every time they cried for deliverance God answered in grace by raising up a judge.

There is a remarkable yet pathetic pattern of rebellion, retribution, repentance, and restoration listing twelve judges. Six stand out preeminently as deliverers—Othniel, Shamgar, Deborah (with Barak), Gideon, Jephthah, and Samson (3:7,12; 4:1; 6:1; 10:6; 13:1). Man's hopeless condition is highlighted by the failure of one generation being repeated by the next generation (2:10). The apostasy of God's people was swift and its idolatry spread through the nation like a disease. With each cycle of apostasy the nation plummeted to greater depths. Israel became incorrigible in their pursuit of evil: "every man did that which was right in his own eyes" (17:6; 18:1; 19:1; 21:25). The message of Judges is clear. When sin is not thoroughly slain it will rise up to trouble us, but when sin is confessed and mercy is sought God will rise up to save us.

Each history of deliverance is different. From Jael with the nail, to Gideon with his trumpets and pitchers, to Samson pulling down the house of Dagon upon the Philistines, God shows His ability to give His people the victory, and each judge reveals some aspect of the power and grace of our Lord Jesus as Savior. Through this history of deliverances God was preparing His people to expect the Son of God to come as the Savior of the world. Every deliverer raised the anticipation for the ideal Deliverer who would come in the fullness of time.

Outline:

- I. Israel's Failure and Folly through Compromise with the Ungodly (1:1—3:7)
  - A. Driving Out the Other Nations (1:1–36)
  - B. Israel's Cycles of Apostasy (2:1—3:7)
- II. Cycles of Evil, Oppression, and Deliverance by Divinely Appointed Judges (3:8—16:31)
  - A. God's Fury and Faithfulness (3:8–31)
  - B. Deborah and Barak (4:1—5:31)
    1. Deborah's Judgeship and Sisera's Death (4:1–24)
    2. The Freedom Fighter's Song (5:1–31)
  - C. Gideon (6:1—9:57)
    1. Gideon Is God's Man to Save Israel from the Midianites (6:1–40)
    2. The Sword of the Lord and of Gideon (7:1–25)
    3. Gideon Fully and Finally Destroys the Midianites (8:1–35)
    4. The Enemies of the House of Gideon Self-Destruct (9:1–57)
  - D. Further Apostasy after Tola and Jair (10:1–18)
  - E. Jephthah (11:1—12:7)
    1. Jephthah: A Mighty Man of Valor (11:1–40)
    2. Ephraim's Defeat in Battle and Denial of Escape (12:1–7)
  - F. Ibzan, Elon, Abdon (12:8–15)
  - G. Samson (13:1—16:31)
    1. The Lord Announces Samson's Birth (13:1–25)
    2. Samson's Wife Turns Traitor (14:1–20)
    3. Samson Retaliates against the Philistines (15:1–20)
    4. Samson Is Bound and Blinded, Then Dies with the Philistines (16:1–31)
- III. Israel's Tragic Days with No King, No Law, and No Shame (17:1—21:25)
  - A. Micah Rejoices in His Silver Image and Hired Priest (17:1–13)
  - B. Dan Becomes a Center of False Worship (18:1–31)
  - C. The Benjamites Stoop to Sodomy (19:1–30)
  - D. Benjamin Is Nearly Exterminated (20:1–48)
  - E. Israel Finds Wives for Benjamin (21:1–25)

THE BOOK OF

JUDGES

CHAPTER 1

NOW after the death of Joshua it came to pass, that
the children of Israel asked the LORD, saying, Who
shall go up for us against the Canaanites first, to
fight against them?
2 And the LORD said, Judah shall go up: behold, I
have delivered the land into his hand.
3 And Judah said unto Simeon his brother, Come
up with me into my lot, that we may fight against
the Canaanites; and I likewise will go with thee
into thy lot. So Simeon went with him.
4 And Judah went up; and the LORD delivered the
Canaanites and the Perizzites into their hand: and
they slew of them in Bezek ten thousand men.
5 And they found Adoni-bezek in Bezek: and
they fought against him, and they slew the Ca-
naanites and the Perizzites.
6 But Adoni-bezek fled; and they pursued after
him, and caught him, and cut off his thumbs and
his great toes.
7 And Adoni-bezek said, Threescore and ten
kings, having their thumbs and their great toes
cut off, gathered *their meat* under my table: as I
have done, so God hath requited me. And they
brought him to Jerusalem, and there he died.
8 Now the children of Judah had fought against
Jerusalem, and had taken it, and smitten it with
the edge of the sword, and set the city on fire.
9 ¶ And afterward the children of Judah went
down to fight against the Canaanites, that dwelt
in the mountain, and in the south, and in the
valley.
10 And Judah went against the Canaanites that
dwelt in Hebron: (now the name of Hebron be-
fore *was* Kirjath-arba:) and they slew Sheshai, and
Ahiman, and Talmai.
11 And from thence he went against the inhabi-
tants of Debir: and the name of Debir before *was*
Kirjath-sepher:
12 And Caleb said, He that smiteth Kirjath-se-
pher, and taketh it, to him will I give Achsah my
daughter to wife.
13 And Othniel the son of Kenaz, Caleb's younger
brother, took it: and he gave him Achsah his
daughter to wife.
14 And it came to pass, when she came *to him*,
that she moved him to ask of her father a field:
and she lighted from off *her* ass; and Caleb said
unto her, What wilt thou?
15 And she said unto him, Give me a blessing:
for thou hast given me a south land; give me also
springs of water. And Caleb gave her the upper
springs and the nether springs.
16 ¶ And the children of the Kenite, Moses' father
in law, went up out of the city of palm trees with
the children of Judah into the wilderness of
Judah, which *lieth* in the south of Arad; and they
went and dwelt among the people.
17 And Judah went with Simeon his brother, and
they slew the Canaanites that inhabited Zephath,
and utterly destroyed it. And the name of the city
was called Hormah.
18 Also Judah took Gaza with the coast thereof,
and Askelon with the coast thereof, and Ekron
with the coast thereof.
19 And the LORD was with Judah; and he drave

ISRAEL'S FAILURE AND FOLLY THROUGH COMPROMISE WITH THE UNGODLY (1:1—3:7)

Chapter 1: *After the death of Joshua, Israel battles again to drive out the nations.*

Driving Out the Nations (1:1–36)

1:1 *Now after the death of Joshua.* Judges records the second wave of battles to possess the land.
1:2 *Judah shall go up.* Judah should have the preeminence (Gen. 49:8).
1:3 *lot.* Property or land.
1:5 *Adoni-bezek.* Lord of Bezek, a Canaanite king.
1:7 *meat.* Food. *requited.* Repaid. This is Bezek's confession that God's justice found him out.
1:12 See Josh. 15:13–19.
1:14 *lighted from off her ass.* Dismounted her donkey.
1:15 *give me also springs of water.* Without water the field would be of little use. *nether springs.* The lower springs.
1:16 *city of palm trees.* Jericho.
1:17 *utterly destroyed.* The Hebrew word means "to put under the ban," used frequently in the context of the conquest for complete destruction.
1:18 *coast.* Border (v. 36).
1:19 *drave out.* Drove out or dispossessed. *chariots of iron.*

out *the inhabitants of* the mountain; but could
not drive out the inhabitants of the valley, because
they had chariots of iron.
20 And they gave Hebron unto Caleb, as Moses
said: and he expelled thence the three sons of
Anak.
21 And the children of Benjamin did not drive
out the Jebusites that inhabited Jerusalem; but the
Jebusites dwell with the children of Benjamin in
Jerusalem unto this day.
22 ¶ And the house of Joseph, they also went up
against Beth-el: and the LORD *was* with them.
23 And the house of Joseph sent to descry Beth-el.
(Now the name of the city before *was* Luz.)
24 And the spies saw a man come forth out of
the city, and they said unto him, Shew us, we pray
thee, the entrance into the city, and we will shew
thee mercy.
25 And when he shewed them the entrance into
the city, they smote the city with the edge of the
sword; but they let go the man and all his family.
26 And the man went into the land of the Hittites,
and built a city, and called the name thereof Luz:
which *is* the name thereof unto this day.
27 ¶ Neither did Manasseh drive out *the inhab-
itants of* Beth-shean and her towns, nor Taanach
and her towns, nor the inhabitants of Dor and
her towns, nor the inhabitants of Ibleam and her
towns, nor the inhabitants of Megiddo and her
towns: but the Canaanites would dwell in that land.
28 And it came to pass, when Israel was strong,
that they put the Canaanites to tribute, and did
not utterly drive them out.
29 ¶ Neither did Ephraim drive out the Canaan-
ites that dwelt in Gezer; but the Canaanites dwelt
in Gezer among them.
30 ¶ Neither did Zebulun drive out the inhabi-
tants of Kitron, nor the inhabitants of Nahalol;
but the Canaanites dwelt among them, and
became tributaries.
31 ¶ Neither did Asher drive out the inhabi-
tants of Accho, nor the inhabitants of Zidon, nor
of Ahlab, nor of Achzib, nor of Helbah, nor of
Aphik, nor of Rehob:
32 But the Asherites dwelt among the Canaanites,
the inhabitants of the land: for they did not drive
them out.
33 ¶ Neither did Naphtali drive out the
inhabitants of Beth-shemesh, nor the inhabitants
of Beth-anath; but he dwelt among the Canaanites,
the inhabitants of the land: nevertheless the
inhabitants of Beth-shemesh and of Beth-anath
became tributaries unto them.
34 And the Amorites forced the children of Dan
into the mountain: for they would not suffer
them to come down to the valley:
35 But the Amorites would dwell in mount Heres
in Aijalon, and in Shaalbim: yet the hand of the
house of Joseph prevailed, so that they became
tributaries.
36 And the coast of the Amorites *was* from the go-
ing up to Akrabbim, from the rock, and upward.

CHAPTER 2

AND an angel of the LORD came up from Gilgal
to Bochim, and said, I made you to go up out of
Egypt, and have brought you unto the land which
I sware unto your fathers; and I said, I will never
break my covenant with you.
2 And ye shall make no league with the
inhabitants of this land; ye shall throw down their
altars: but ye have not obeyed my voice: why have
ye done this?
3 Wherefore I also said, I will not drive them out
from before you; but they shall be *as thorns* in your

Formidable war machines pulled by horses, possibly with knives attached to their wheels. These should not have been a deterrent to victory (Josh. 17:18).

1:21 *Benjamin did not drive out the Jebusites.* Jerusalem remained unconquered until the reign of David (2 Sam. 5:7).

1:23 *descry.* Explore or spy.

1:27–33 *Neither did.* Stated five times in these verses to show Israel's failure and to show the stubbornness of the Canaanites.

1:28 *to tribute.* Forced labor (vv. 30,33,35). Israel erred in thinking they could control the enemy to their advantage.

1:34 *forced the children of Dan.* This shows their complete failure and the consequence of thinking it possible to control the enemy. So those who think to control sin end up being controlled.

Thoughts for Personal/Family Worship: Chapter 1

1. **Living under the threat of the ungodly we must pray for God's help to remain separate unto Him and the gospel. We constantly need spiritual victory to drive the spirit of the world out of our hearts. What are some specific forms of worldliness calling you and your friends to compromise?**
2. **What Judah and Simeon accomplished together with the Lord's help is a model for us. We need fellowship for our spiritual growth, we need the prayers of God's people, and we need the means of grace ordained by the Lord through the ministry of His church. No one can live the Christian life alone.**
3. **As Achsah realized the importance of a water supply in the dry southern land, we should recognize the need of God's grace for our souls in this barren world. God has promised the supply of His Spirit to meet the need of our fainting hearts (Phil. 1:19).**

Israel's Cycles of Apostasy (2:1—3:7)

Chapter 2: *Cycles of rebellion, retribution, repentance, and restoration mark Israel's history.*

2:1 *angel of the LORD.* "The messenger who is the Lord." A Christophany, a preincarnate appearance of Christ (see note at Gen. 16:7). As evidence of the angel's deity, note what He

sides, and their gods shall be a snare unto you.
4 And it came to pass, when the angel of the LORD
spake these words unto all the children of Israel,
that the people lifted up their voice, and wept.
5 And they called the name of that place Bochim:
and they sacrificed there unto the LORD.
6 ¶ And when Joshua had let the people go, the
children of Israel went every man unto his inheri-
tance to possess the land.
7 And the people served the LORD all the days of
Joshua, and all the days of the elders that outlived
Joshua, who had seen all the great works of the
LORD, that he did for Israel.
8 And Joshua the son of Nun, the servant of the
LORD, died, *being* an hundred and ten years old.
9 And they buried him in the border of his
inheritance in Timnath-heres, in the mount of
Ephraim, on the north side of the hill Gaash.
10 And also all that generation were gathered
unto their fathers: and there arose another
generation after them, which knew not the LORD,
nor yet the works which he had done for Israel.
11 ¶ And the children of Israel did evil in the
sight of the LORD, and served Baalim:
12 And they forsook the LORD God of their
fathers, which brought them out of the land of
Egypt, and followed other gods, of the gods of the
people that *were* round about them, and bowed
themselves unto them, and provoked the LORD to
anger.
13 And they forsook the LORD, and served Baal
and Ashtaroth.
14 ¶ And the anger of the LORD was hot against Is-
rael, and he delivered them into the hands of spoil-
ers that spoiled them, and he sold them into the
hands of their enemies round about, so that they
could not any longer stand before their enemies.
15 Whithersoever they went out, the hand of the
LORD was against them for evil, as the LORD had
said, and as the LORD had sworn unto them: and
they were greatly distressed.
16 ¶ Nevertheless the LORD raised up judges,
which delivered them out of the hand of those
that spoiled them.
17 And yet they would not hearken unto their
judges, but they went a whoring after other gods,
and bowed themselves unto them: they turned
quickly out of the way which their fathers walked
in, obeying the commandments of the LORD; *but*
they did not so.
18 And when the LORD raised them up judges,
then the LORD was with the judge, and delivered
them out of the hand of their enemies all the days
of the judge: for it repented the LORD because of
their groanings by reason of them that oppressed
them and vexed them.
19 And it came to pass, when the judge was dead,
that they returned, and corrupted *themselves*
more than their fathers, in following other gods
to serve them, and to bow down unto them; they
ceased not from their own doings, nor from their
stubborn way.
20 ¶ And the anger of the LORD was hot against
Israel; and he said, Because that this people hath
transgressed my covenant which I commanded
their fathers, and have not hearkened unto my
voice;
21 I also will not henceforth drive out any from
before them of the nations which Joshua left
when he died:
22 That through them I may prove Israel, whether
they will keep the way of the LORD to walk therein,
as their fathers did keep *it*, or not.
23 Therefore the LORD left those nations, without
driving them out hastily; neither delivered he
them into the hand of Joshua.

---

speaks elsewhere is attributed to the Lord (cf. Josh. 5:13–15).
2:2 *league.* Covenant.
2:4–5 *Bochim.* Here the people *wept* over their sin; however, it was short-lived (v. 17).
2:6 *inheritance.* Land allotment.
2:11 *Baalim.* The plural of "Baal" (v. 13), meaning "lord" or "master." Often each city had its own patron "Baal."
2:13 *Ashtaroth.* A Canaanite female deity, often the consort of *Baal*.
2:14 *spoilers that spoiled.* Plunderers who plundered. *he sold them.* The language of the slave market.
2:15 *for evil.* For harm or calamity, a reference to God's chastisement.
2:16 Just as God raised up enemies, He also raised up *judges*, or rulers, to deliver them.
2:17 *whoring.* Idolatry is spiritual adultery.
2:18 *repented the LORD.* The Lord grieved. *vexed.* To oppress or maltreat.
2:19 *when the judge was dead.* Their repentance endured only until each judge died.
2:22 *prove.* To test or try.

Thoughts for Personal/Family Worship: Chapter 2

1. Godly leaders are God's instruments for blessing. Each judge raised up by the Lord was used to lead the people away from sin and unto godliness. Hence, it is important to pray for the leaders that God raises up that they might be instruments of peace (1 Tim. 2:2). In addition every godly man or woman will be God's instrument to influence others for good. Particularly parents are to direct their family in the paths of blessing. Ask the Lord to use your example to bless others.
2. When God allows oppressors against us, He is drawing us to seek His plan of mercy. Adversity often increases our sense of dependence on God (Eccl. 7:14). By this means God will work true repentance in our hearts for sin and true faith toward our Savior. Why do we often need to suffer in order to seek God?
3. Generation degeneration set in as "there arose another generation after them, which knew not the LORD" (2:10). The spirituality of the next generation is always a pressing concern for the church. Parents must fulfill their

CHAPTER 3

NOW these *are* the nations which the LORD left, to
prove Israel by them, *even* as many *of Israel* as had
not known all the wars of Canaan;
2 Only that the generations of the children of
Israel might know, to teach them war, at the least
such as before knew nothing thereof;
3 *Namely*, five lords of the Philistines, and all the
Canaanites, and the Sidonians, and the Hivites
that dwelt in mount Lebanon, from mount Baal-
hermon unto the entering in of Hamath.
4 And they were to prove Israel by them, to know
whether they would hearken unto the command-
ments of the LORD, which he commanded their
fathers by the hand of Moses.
5 ¶ And the children of Israel dwelt among the
Canaanites, Hittites, and Amorites, and Perizzites,
and Hivites, and Jebusites:
6 And they took their daughters to be their wives,
and gave their daughters to their sons, and served
their gods.
7 And the children of Israel did evil in the sight
of the LORD, and forgat the LORD their God, and
served Baalim and the groves.
8 ¶ Therefore the anger of the LORD was hot
against Israel, and he sold them into the hand of
Chushan-rishathaim king of Mesopotamia: and
the children of Israel served Chushan-rishathaim
eight years.
9 And when the children of Israel cried unto
the LORD, the LORD raised up a deliverer to the
children of Israel, who delivered them, *even*
Othniel the son of Kenaz, Caleb's younger brother.
10 And the Spirit of the LORD came upon him,
and he judged Israel, and went out to war: and
the LORD delivered Chushan-rishathaim king
of Mesopotamia into his hand; and his hand
prevailed against Chushan-rishathaim.
11 And the land had rest forty years. And Othniel
the son of Kenaz died.
12 ¶ And the children of Israel did evil again in
the sight of the LORD: and the LORD strengthened
Eglon the king of Moab against Israel, because
they had done evil in the sight of the LORD.
13 And he gathered unto him the children of
Ammon and Amalek, and went and smote Israel,
and possessed the city of palm trees.
14 So the children of Israel served Eglon the king
of Moab eighteen years.
15 But when the children of Israel cried unto the
LORD, the LORD raised them up a deliverer, Ehud
the son of Gera, a Benjamite, a man lefthanded:
and by him the children of Israel sent a present
unto Eglon the king of Moab.
16 But Ehud made him a dagger which had two
edges, of a cubit length; and he did gird it under
his raiment upon his right thigh.
17 And he brought the present unto Eglon king
of Moab: and Eglon *was* a very fat man.
18 And when he had made an end to offer the
present, he sent away the people that bare the
present.
19 But he himself turned again from the quarries
that *were* by Gilgal, and said, I have a secret errand
unto thee, O king: who said, Keep silence. And all
that stood by him went out from him.
20 And Ehud came unto him; and he was sitting
in a summer parlour, which he had for himself
alone. And Ehud said, I have a message from God
unto thee. And he arose out of *his* seat.
21 And Ehud put forth his left hand, and took the
dagger from his right thigh, and thrust it into his
belly:
22 And the haft also went in after the blade; and the
fat closed upon the blade, so that he could not draw
the dagger out of his belly; and the dirt came out.

God-given responsibility to train up their children in the way they should go (Prov. 22:6). Every family needs a daily devotional time with solid Bible teaching.

Chapter 3: ***In spite of His fury, God raises up three judges to deliver Israel.***

3:1 *prove.* See 2:22 and 3:4.

3:2 *to teach them war.* The people were inexperienced, and God's people cannot settle in peace among the ungodly.

3:3 *lords.* Governors.

3:4 *hearken.* Obey. God was looking for obedience.

3:7 *Israel did evil in the sight of the LORD.* This statement is repeated through six cycles of apostasy (vv. 7,12; 4:1; 6:1; 10:6; 13:1). *groves.* The reference may be to wooden poles that were erected as part of the pagan rituals worshiping Asherah, one of the Canaanite goddesses.

CYCLES OF EVIL, OPPRESSION, AND DELIVERANCE BY DIVINELY APPOINTED JUDGES (3:8—16:31)

God's Fury and Faithfulness (3:8–31)

3:9 *Othniel.* Means "lion of God," significantly, from the tribe of Judah (Gen. 49:9). He fought to claim Achsah for his wife (1:12–13).

3:10 *Spirit of the LORD.* Whom God appointed He anointed and empowered to accomplish his commissioned service. Since Pentecost, every Christian can know some degree of divine empowering for service (Acts 2).

3:12 *did evil again.* The cycle continues.

3:13 Moab and Ammon, descendants of Lot's incest, were joined by the Amalekites, all traditional enemies of Israel.

3:15 *Ehud.* He was of the tribe of Benjamin, which excelled in training left-handed warriors (20:16). Ironically, "Benjamin" means "son of my right hand."

3:16 *cubit.* Approximately eighteen inches. *gird it under his raiment.* Secured it with a belt under his garment.

3:19 *quarries.* Refers to idols, particularly to a place where idols were carved, sufficiently known to become a landmark (v. 26).

3:20 *a summer parlour.* Literally, "the coolness of the upper room," perhaps a roof chamber (vv. 23–25).

3:22 *haft.* The grip or handle. *the dirt came out.* The Hebrew is ambiguous and means "hole," referring either to what came

23 Then Ehud went forth through the porch,
and shut the doors of the parlour upon him, and
locked them.
24 When he was gone out, his servants came;
and when they saw that, behold, the doors of the
parlour *were* locked, they said, Surely he covereth
his feet in his summer chamber.
25 And they tarried till they were ashamed: and,
behold, he opened not the doors of the parlour;
therefore they took a key, and opened *them*: and,
behold, their lord *was* fallen down dead on the
earth.
26 And Ehud escaped while they tarried, and
passed beyond the quarries, and escaped unto
Seirath.
27 And it came to pass, when he was come, that
he blew a trumpet in the mountain of Ephraim,
and the children of Israel went down with him
from the mount, and he before them.
28 And he said unto them, Follow after me:
for the LORD hath delivered your enemies the
Moabites into your hand. And they went down
after him, and took the fords of Jordan toward
Moab, and suffered not a man to pass over.
29 And they slew of Moab at that time about ten
thousand men, all lusty, and all men of valour;
and there escaped not a man.
30 So Moab was subdued that day under the hand
of Israel. And the land had rest fourscore years.
31 ¶ And after him was Shamgar the son of
Anath, which slew of the Philistines six hundred
men with an ox goad: and he also delivered Israel.

CHAPTER 4

AND the children of Israel again did evil in the
sight of the LORD, when Ehud was dead.
2 And the LORD sold them into the hand of
Jabin king of Canaan, that reigned in Hazor; the
captain of whose host *was* Sisera, which dwelt in
Harosheth of the Gentiles.
3 And the children of Israel cried unto the LORD:
for he had nine hundred chariots of iron; and
twenty years he mightily oppressed the children
of Israel.
4 ¶ And Deborah, a prophetess, the wife of
Lapidoth, she judged Israel at that time.
5 And she dwelt under the palm tree of Deborah
between Ramah and Beth-el in mount Ephraim:
and the children of Israel came up to her for
judgment.
6 And she sent and called Barak the son of Abin-
oam out of Kedesh-naphtali, and said unto him,
Hath not the LORD God of Israel commanded,
saying, Go and draw toward mount Tabor, and
take with thee ten thousand men of the children
of Naphtali and of the children of Zebulun?
7 And I will draw unto thee to the river Kishon
Sisera, the captain of Jabin's army, with his
chariots and his multitude; and I will deliver him
into thine hand.
8 And Barak said unto her, If thou wilt go with
me, then I will go: but if thou wilt not go with me,
then I will not go.
9 And she said, I will surely go with thee: not-
withstanding the journey that thou takest shall
not be for thine honour; for the LORD shall sell

out of the hole caused by the stab wound or a hole through which Ehud escaped.

3:24 *covereth his feet.* A euphemism for using the toilet; the eastern gown literally, "covered their feet." Hence, the delay to check on their king.

3:29 *lusty.* Robust. *men of valour.* Refers to men of the army, those experienced at warfare.

3:31 The *Philistines*, a coastal people, with interactions with God's people from the days of Abraham. *an ox goad.* A long pole with a flat end to scrape the plowshare and a pointed end to goad or prod the ox.

Thoughts for Personal/Family Worship: Chapter 3

1. **The Spirit's coming upon Othniel sets a pattern for the book of Judges and provides a good lesson for believers regarding the Spirit's ministry. The Spirit empowered the judge, enabling him to accomplish the work of the Lord. The Spirit's empowerment is usually for service in the work of God's kingdom. Whereas in the Old Testament era, that kind of empowering was often limited to Israel's leadership, at Pentecost the Spirit came down upon all flesh (Joel 2:28) enabling every believer to serve the Lord with that special divine energy and power. Judges will illustrate over and again what man can do when God gives the power. That same power is available for every Christian. How can we seek it and take hold of it?**
2. **God's indignation was rightly directed against those who paraded their sins "in the sight of the LORD" (v. 7). Every sin is an affront against God and committed directly in His face. God's wrath and punishment against sin, evidenced when he sold them into the hands of Chushan-rishathaim, is well justified. Israel's bad example should be a warning to live in the reality of God's presence and avoid offending Him. As well, we should remember that the rod of chastisement is God's way of bringing His erring people to a renewed repentance and happy service under His loving hand (Heb. 12:6–7).**

Deborah and Barak (4:1—5:31)

Chapter 4: *Sisera is defeated by Deborah and Barak and is killed by Jael with the nail.*

Deborah's Judgeship and Sisera's Death (4:1–24)

4:3 *chariots of iron.* These were terrifying war machines but should not have terrified the people given God's promise (Josh. 17:18).

4:6 *she . . . called Barak.* She recognized her place and did not usurp authority to command the army on her own. *draw.* Here, "march."

4:7 *draw.* Here, "to drag." God would drag Sisera to the place of battle. This was Deborah's cue to send Barak into battle (v. 14).

4:9 *the hand of a woman.* A reproof to Barak for his faithless and cowardly response.

Sisera into the hand of a woman. And Deborah
arose, and went with Barak to Kedesh.
10 ¶ And Barak called Zebulun and Naphtali to
Kedesh; and he went up with ten thousand men at
his feet: and Deborah went up with him.
11 Now Heber the Kenite, *which was* of the chil-
dren of Hobab the father in law of Moses, had
severed himself from the Kenites, and pitched
his tent unto the plain of Zaanaim, which *is* by
Kedesh.
12 And they shewed Sisera that Barak the son of
Abinoam was gone up to mount Tabor.
13 And Sisera gathered together all his chariots,
even nine hundred chariots of iron, and all the
people that *were* with him, from Harosheth of the
Gentiles unto the river of Kishon.
14 And Deborah said unto Barak, Up; for this *is*
the day in which the LORD hath delivered Sisera
into thine hand: is not the LORD gone out before
thee? So Barak went down from mount Tabor,
and ten thousand men after him.
15 And the LORD discomfited Sisera, and all *his*
chariots, and all *his* host, with the edge of the
sword before Barak; so that Sisera lighted down
off *his* chariot, and fled away on his feet.
16 But Barak pursued after the chariots, and after
the host, unto Harosheth of the Gentiles: and all
the host of Sisera fell upon the edge of the sword;
and there was not a man left.
17 Howbeit Sisera fled away on his feet to the tent
of Jael the wife of Heber the Kenite: for *there was*
peace between Jabin the king of Hazor and the
house of Heber the Kenite.
18 ¶ And Jael went out to meet Sisera, and said
unto him, Turn in, my lord, turn in to me; fear
not. And when he had turned in unto her into the
tent, she covered him with a mantle.
19 And he said unto her, Give me, I pray thee,
a little water to drink; for I am thirsty. And she
opened a bottle of milk, and gave him drink, and
covered him.
20 Again he said unto her, Stand in the door of
the tent, and it shall be, when any man doth come
and enquire of thee, and say, Is there any man
here? that thou shalt say, No.
21 Then Jael Heber's wife took a nail of the tent,
and took an hammer in her hand, and went softly
unto him, and smote the nail into his temples,
and fastened it into the ground: for he was fast
asleep and weary. So he died.
22 And, behold, as Barak pursued Sisera, Jael
came out to meet him, and said unto him, Come,
and I will shew thee the man whom thou seekest.
And when he came into her *tent*, behold, Sisera
lay dead, and the nail *was* in his temples.
23 So God subdued on that day Jabin the king of
Canaan before the children of Israel.
24 And the hand of the children of Israel pros-
pered, and prevailed against Jabin the king of
Canaan, until they had destroyed Jabin king of
Canaan.

CHAPTER 5

THEN sang Deborah and Barak the son of Abin-
oam on that day, saying,
2 Praise ye the LORD for the avenging of Israel,
when the people willingly offered themselves.
3 Hear, O ye kings; give ear, O ye princes; I, *even*
I, will sing unto the LORD; I will sing *praise* to the
LORD God of Israel.
4 LORD, when thou wentest out of Seir, when
thou marchedst out of the field of Edom, the
earth trembled, and the heavens dropped, the
clouds also dropped water.
5 The mountains melted from before the LORD,

4:13 *Sisera gathered.* See v. 7. Unwittingly, he "followed" the Lord to his destruction.
4:15 *discomfited.* Confusion (5:4,20–21). *lighted down.* Dismounted.
4:17 *for there was peace.* Deceived by peaceful relations with the Kenites, Sisera assumed he could safely take refuge in Jael's tent.
4:18 *mantle.* A covering, like a rug or blanket.
4:23 *God subdued.* Notwithstanding all the human agents, the battle was the Lord's as well as the victory.

Thoughts for Personal/Family Worship: Chapter 4

1. **"Hath not the LORD God of Israel commanded" (4:6)? Knowing that God has spoken and revealed His will generates confidence and assurance for doing His will. Even though militarily, the odds were against Israel, God's word assured the victory. Often times doing God's will seems to go against what appears to be the logical course of action, but when we have the Lord's Word to direct us in God's service we must rise up in faith to obey His commands and plead His power. It is imperative to trust His Word and then to go.**
2. **It is God's pattern to choose "weak things of the world to confound the things that are mighty" (1 Cor. 1:27). No one is too weak to be used by the Lord. Deborah was a woman, but God used her. Jael was a woman with only a nail, but God used her. Barak had no weapons equal to Sisera's iron chariots, but God used him. As Christians, we should be encouraged that God demonstrates His strength through our weakness (2 Cor. 12:9). How do you feel weak when facing your spiritual enemies? How does this principle encourage you?**

Chapter 5: *Deborah & Barak sing of their triumph over Sisera and Jabin.*

The Freedom Fighter's Song (5:1–31)

5:3–5 Deborah's praise includes review of God's past dealings with His people as evidence of His power and faithfulness. There is more to biblical history than facts; it reveals God's redemptive purpose (Deut. 4:11; 33:2; Ps. 78; Isa. 64:3; Hab. 3:3,10).

even that Sinai from before the LORD God of Israel.
6 In the days of Shamgar the son of Anath, in the
days of Jael, the highways were unoccupied, and
the travellers walked through byways.
7 *The inhabitants of* the villages ceased, they
ceased in Israel, until that I Deborah arose, that I
arose a mother in Israel.
8 They chose new gods; then *was* war in the gates:
was there a shield or spear seen among forty
thousand in Israel?
9 My heart *is* toward the governors of Israel, that
offered themselves willingly among the people.
Bless ye the LORD.
10 Speak, ye that ride on white asses, ye that sit in
judgment, and walk by the way.
11 *They that are delivered* from the noise of
archers in the places of drawing water, there shall
they rehearse the righteous acts of the LORD, *even*
the righteous acts *toward the inhabitants* of his
villages in Israel: then shall the people of the LORD
go down to the gates.
12 Awake, awake, Deborah: awake, awake, utter a
song: arise, Barak, and lead thy captivity captive,
thou son of Abinoam.
13 Then he made him that remaineth have do-
minion over the nobles among the people: the
LORD made me have dominion over the mighty.
14 Out of Ephraim *was there* a root of them
against Amalek; after thee, Benjamin, among thy
people; out of Machir came down governors, and
out of Zebulun they that handle the pen of the
writer.
15 And the princes of Issachar *were* with Deborah;
even Issachar, and also Barak: he was sent on foot
into the valley. For the divisions of Reuben *there
were* great thoughts of heart.
16 Why abodest thou among the sheepfolds, to
hear the bleatings of the flocks? For the divisions
of Reuben *there were* great searchings of heart.
17 Gilead abode beyond Jordan: and why did
Dan remain in ships? Asher continued on the sea
shore, and abode in his breaches.
18 Zebulun and Naphtali *were* a people *that*
jeoparded their lives unto the death in the high
places of the field.
19 The kings came *and* fought, then fought the
kings of Canaan in Taanach by the waters of
Megiddo; they took no gain of money.
20 They fought from heaven; the stars in their
courses fought against Sisera.
21 The river of Kishon swept them away, that
ancient river, the river Kishon. O my soul, thou
hast trodden down strength.
22 Then were the horsehoofs broken by the
means of the pransings, the pransings of their
mighty ones.
23 Curse ye Meroz, said the angel of the LORD,
curse ye bitterly the inhabitants thereof; because
they came not to the help of the LORD, to the help
of the LORD against the mighty.
24 Blessed above women shall Jael the wife of
Heber the Kenite be, blessed shall she be above
women in the tent.
25 He asked water, *and* she gave *him* milk; she
brought forth butter in a lordly dish.
26 She put her hand to the nail, and her right
hand to the workmen's hammer; and with the
hammer she smote Sisera, she smote off his head,
when she had pierced and stricken through his
temples.
27 At her feet he bowed, he fell, he lay down: at
her feet he bowed, he fell: where he bowed, there
he fell down dead.
28 The mother of Sisera looked out at a window,
and cried through the lattice, Why is his chariot
so long in coming? why tarry the wheels of his
chariots?
29 Her wise ladies answered her, yea, she returned
answer to herself,
30 Have they not sped? have they *not* divided the
prey; to every man a damsel *or* two; to Sisera a prey
of divers colours, a prey of divers colours of nee-
dlework, of divers colours of needlework on both
sides, *meet* for the necks of *them that take* the spoil?
31 So let all thine enemies perish, O LORD: but *let*
them that love him *be* as the sun when he goeth

5:6 *the highways . . . byways.* The roadways were so dangerous the people used lesser-known paths.
5:7 *The inhabitants of the villages ceased.* Isolated villages were emptied. *mother in Israel.* A title designating her leadership role in the capacity God called her to serve.
5:8 *then was war in the gates.* Their idolatry brought God's swift punishment. *a shield or spear.* Defensive and offensive weapons. They could neither protect themselves nor mount any resistance against an enemy.
5:9 *offered themselves willingly.* These governors followed Deborah's lead.
5:11 *rehearse.* To recount. *the righteous acts of the LORD.* God's acts of judgment are righteous, in perfect conformity to His divine perfections. *to the gates.* The public places of commerce and city life, showing normal activities were returning.
5:15–16 *For the divisions of Reuben . . . great thoughts.* Parts of Reuben resolved to join with Deborah, others had significant questions and did not commit.
5:17 *breaches.* Refers to a mooring point or landing place; they stayed where they were and did not join the battle.
5:18 *jeoparded their lives.* They risked their lives, regarding the cause greater than themselves.
5:25 *lordly dish.* A magnificent meal.
5:30 *prey.* The booty or spoil of conquest. *divers.* Diverse.
5:31 Deborah's conclusion parallels the thought of Ps. 2:12 that those who do not submit to the Lord will perish and those who do submit will be blessed.

Thoughts for Personal/Family Worship: Chapter 5

1. The Song of Deborah provides a pattern for worship with its focus on praise. Much of our time in public and private worship should be in the attitude of praise unto

forth in his might. And the land had rest forty
years.

CHAPTER 6

AND the children of Israel did evil in the sight of
the LORD: and the LORD delivered them into the
hand of Midian seven years.
2 And the hand of Midian prevailed against
Israel: *and* because of the Midianites the children
of Israel made them the dens which *are* in the
mountains, and caves, and strong holds.
3 And *so* it was, when Israel had sown, that the
Midianites came up, and the Amalekites, and the
children of the east, even they came up against
them;
4 And they encamped against them, and
destroyed the increase of the earth, till thou come
unto Gaza, and left no sustenance for Israel,
neither sheep, nor ox, nor ass.
5 For they came up with their cattle and their tents,
and they came as grasshoppers for multitude; *for*
both they and their camels were without number:
and they entered into the land to destroy it.
6 And Israel was greatly impoverished because
of the Midianites; and the children of Israel cried
unto the LORD.
7 ¶ And it came to pass, when the children of Is-
rael cried unto the LORD because of the Midianites,
8 That the LORD sent a prophet unto the chil-
dren of Israel, which said unto them, Thus saith
the LORD God of Israel, I brought you up from
Egypt, and brought you forth out of the house of
bondage;
9 And I delivered you out of the hand of the
Egyptians, and out of the hand of all that
oppressed you, and drave them out from before
you, and gave you their land;
10 And I said unto you, I *am* the LORD your God;
fear not the gods of the Amorites, in whose land
ye dwell: but ye have not obeyed my voice.
11 ¶ And there came an angel of the LORD, and
sat under an oak which *was* in Ophrah, that
pertained unto Joash the Abi-ezrite: and his son
Gideon threshed wheat by the winepress, to hide
it from the Midianites.
12 And the angel of the LORD appeared unto him,
and said unto him, The LORD *is* with thee, thou
mighty man of valour.
13 And Gideon said unto him, Oh my Lord, if
the LORD be with us, why then is all this
befallen us? and where *be* all his miracles which our
fathers told us of, saying, Did not the LORD bring
us up from Egypt? but now the LORD hath for-
saken us, and delivered us into the hands of the
Midianites.
14 And the LORD looked upon him, and said, Go
in this thy might, and thou shalt save Israel from
the hand of the Midianites: have not I sent thee?
15 And he said unto him, Oh my Lord, where-
with shall I save Israel? behold, my family *is* poor
in Manasseh, and I *am* the least in my father's
house.
16 And the LORD said unto him, Surely I will be

---

the Lord as the giver of every blessing (James 1:17). Singing is a key means by which we can render our praise unto the Lord. A well-used hymnal in the home will glorify the Lord. A Spirit-filled people who know the victory of Christ in their lives will feel compelled to sing. When are you singing His praise?

2. Tragically, there were some in Deborah's day that refused to join in the Lord's battle, and sadly, the case is the same today. Let our names be among the worthies who rise up for the cause of Christ. When the battle for Christ is on let there be no sitting on the fence as Reuben, standing on the sidelines as Dan, or remaining careless as Asher.

Gideon (6:1—9:57)

Chapter 6: ***God hears His people's cries of despair because of the Midianites and gives Gideon a clear call to deliver Israel.***

Gideon Is God's Man to Save Israel from the Midianites (6:1–40)

6:1 *Midian.* Descendants from Abraham and Keturah (Gen. 25:2). Also referred to as Ishmaelites; suggests some link to Abraham (Judg. 8:24). A nomadic people (6:5) dwelling in the Transjordan (east of Jordan). They allied themselves with other Transjordan peoples against Israel (v. 3).

6:2 *And the hand of Midian prevailed.* Ironically, Israel vacated their rich lands for nomadic mountain life while the Midianite nomads took over the abandoned cities.

6:3 *sown.* The Midianites allowed Israel to sow in peace but always arrived for harvest.

6:4 *sustenance.* Food.

6:6 *greatly impoverished.* Brought exceedingly low.

6:8 *sent a prophet.* God always has a word for His people in times of crisis.

6:9 *drave.* Drove.

6:10 *I am the LORD.* Israel's first responsibility was to obey the one true God with whom they were in covenant. *fear not the gods.* A prohibition against worshiping the false gods. *Amorites.* While it can refer to a specific people, it occurs as a general designation for all the inhabitants of Canaan.

6:11 *an angel of the LORD.* "The Messenger who is the Lord," as Gideon recognizes (vv. 14,16,22). A Christophany, the pre-incarnate Son of God. *Gideon.* Means "warrior." *threshed wheat by the winepress.* A covert act to evade Midianite oppressors.

6:12 *thou mighty man of valour.* Some take this assessment as sarcasm, given Gideon's secret threshing; others as divine acknowledgement of Gideon's capacity for leadership.

6:13 *why then . . . ?* Gideon's question was justifiable given the circumstances, but it was all wrong in terms of God's covenant with His people. *forsaken us.* What appeared to be God's casting them off was in reality God's means of restoring them.

6:15 Acknowledgment of personal insignificance is a key qualification for being used by God.

6:16 *as one man.* Easily, as if a small task; the Lord's presence was the key.

6:17 *grace.* Favor and acceptance with God. *a sign.* A confir-

with thee, and thou shalt smite the Midianites as one man.

17 And he said unto him, If now I have found grace in thy sight, then shew me a sign that thou talkest with me.

18 Depart not hence, I pray thee, until I come unto thee, and bring forth my present, and set *it* before thee. And he said, I will tarry until thou come again.

19 ¶ And Gideon went in, and made ready a kid, and unleavened cakes of an ephah of flour: the flesh he put in a basket, and he put the broth in a pot, and brought *it* out unto him under the oak, and presented *it*.

20 And the angel of God said unto him, Take the flesh and the unleavened cakes, and lay *them* upon this rock, and pour out the broth. And he did so.

21 ¶ Then the angel of the LORD put forth the end of the staff that *was* in his hand, and touched the flesh and the unleavened cakes; and there rose up fire out of the rock, and consumed the flesh and the unleavened cakes. Then the angel of the LORD departed out of his sight.

22 And when Gideon perceived that he *was* an angel of the LORD, Gideon said, Alas, O Lord GOD! for because I have seen an angel of the LORD face to face.

23 And the LORD said unto him, Peace *be* unto thee; fear not: thou shalt not die.

24 Then Gideon built an altar there unto the LORD, and called it Jehovah-shalom: unto this day it *is* yet in Ophrah of the Abi-ezrites.

25 ¶ And it came to pass the same night, that the LORD said unto him, Take thy father's young bullock, even the second bullock of seven years old, and throw down the altar of Baal that thy father hath, and cut down the grove that *is* by it:

26 And build an altar unto the LORD thy God upon the top of this rock, in the ordered place, and take the second bullock, and offer a burnt sacrifice with the wood of the grove which thou shalt cut down.

27 Then Gideon took ten men of his servants, and did as the LORD had said unto him: and *so* it was, because he feared his father's household, and the men of the city, that he could not do *it* by day, that he did *it* by night.

28 ¶ And when the men of the city arose early in the morning, behold, the altar of Baal was cast down, and the grove was cut down that *was* by it, and the second bullock was offered upon the altar *that was* built.

29 And they said one to another, Who hath done this thing? And when they enquired and asked, they said, Gideon the son of Joash hath done this thing.

30 Then the men of the city said unto Joash, Bring out thy son, that he may die: because he hath cast down the altar of Baal, and because he hath cut down the grove that *was* by it.

31 And Joash said unto all that stood against him, Will ye plead for Baal? will ye save him? he that will plead for him, let him be put to death whilst *it is yet* morning: if he *be* a god, let him plead for himself, because *one* hath cast down his altar.

32 Therefore on that day he called him Jerubbaal, saying, Let Baal plead against him, because he hath thrown down his altar.

33 ¶ Then all the Midianites and the Amalekites and the children of the east were gathered together, and went over, and pitched in the valley of Jezreel.

34 But the Spirit of the LORD came upon Gideon, and he blew a trumpet; and Abi-ezer was gathered after him.

35 And he sent messengers throughout all Manasseh; who also was gathered after him: and he sent

---

mation, not necessarily miraculous.

6:18 *present.* Most likely the sacrificial offering since Gideon knew he was communing with the Lord. *tarry.* Remain.

6:19 *ephah.* A dry measure approximately a bushel.

6:24 *Jehovah-shalom.* The Lord is peace. *unto this day.* Until the writing of the book in Samuel's time.

6:25 *bullock.* Bull. *grove.* A wooden pole erected as part of pagan worship (vv. 26,28,30).

6:27 Significantly, his first act of judging was not against Midian but his kin. Judgment begins at the house of God.

6:31 *if he be a god, let him plead for himself.* Joash's wise words won the day; the inability to speak was evidence that Baal was not god (Isa. 41:22–29).

6:32 *Jerubbaal.* Literally, *"Let Baal plead,"* the name given to Gideon as a testimony to Baal's impotence.

6:33–40 God confirms Gideon's call by dew on a fleece.

6:36–38 *If thou wilt save Israel.* Although God's word was clear, Gideon sought further evidence expressing doubt and weakness in faith, but God graciously gave the signs. Gideon then rose up in full confidence to fight the Midianites (7:1).

Thoughts for Personal/Family Worship: Chapter 6

1. **The tension between faith and experience is common among believers. We cannot determine God's blessing by circumstances alone. God stated categorically "The LORD is with thee" (v. 12), but Gideon felt compelled to ask, "If the LORD be with us, why then is all this befallen us?" (6:13). It was hard to see what was happening as evidence of God's presence and blessing. We need to read our circumstances in the light of God's revealed Word. His promise, "I will never leave thee, nor forsake thee" (Heb. 13:5) is every bit as true during the Christian's worst day on earth as on his best day. Faith must interpret sight in the light of God's Word. What promise do you need to cling to by faith today?**
2. **When determining God's will, first impressions are to be checked by earnest prayer but always with our wills submitted to His. God will call us in His time and in His way. God finds His man when busy at his common work (v. 11), confirms His will through His Word (v. 16), and**

messengers unto Asher, and unto Zebulun, and
unto Naphtali; and they came up to meet them.
36 ¶ And Gideon said unto God, If thou wilt save
Israel by mine hand, as thou hast said,
37 Behold, I will put a fleece of wool in the floor;
and if the dew be on the fleece only, and *it be* dry
upon all the earth *beside*, then shall I know that
thou wilt save Israel by mine hand, as thou hast said.
38 And it was so: for he rose up early on the mor-
row, and thrust the fleece together, and wringed
the dew out of the fleece, a bowl full of water.
39 And Gideon said unto God, Let not thine
anger be hot against me, and I will speak but this
once: let me prove, I pray thee, but this once with
the fleece; let it now be dry only upon the fleece,
and upon all the ground let there be dew.
40 And God did so that night: for it was dry
upon the fleece only, and there was dew on all the
ground.

CHAPTER 7

THEN Jerubbaal, who *is* Gideon, and all the people
that *were* with him, rose up early, and pitched
beside the well of Harod: so that the host of the
Midianites were on the north side of them, by the
hill of Moreh, in the valley.
2 And the LORD said unto Gideon, The people
that *are* with thee *are* too many for me to give
the Midianites into their hands, lest Israel vaunt
themselves against me, saying, Mine own hand
hath saved me.
3 Now therefore go to, proclaim in the ears of the
people, saying, Whosoever *is* fearful and afraid, let
him return and depart early from mount Gilead.
And there returned of the people twenty and two
thousand; and there remained ten thousand.
4 And the LORD said unto Gideon, The people *are*
yet *too* many; bring them down unto the water,
and I will try them for thee there: and it shall be,
that of whom I say unto thee, This shall go with
thee, the same shall go with thee; and of whom-
soever I say unto thee, This shall not go with thee,
the same shall not go.
5 So he brought down the people unto the water:
and the LORD said unto Gideon, Every one that
lappeth of the water with his tongue, as a dog lap-
peth, him shalt thou set by himself; likewise every
one that boweth down upon his knees to drink.
6 And the number of them that lapped, *putting*
their hand to their mouth, were three hundred
men: but all the rest of the people bowed down
upon their knees to drink water.
7 And the LORD said unto Gideon, By the three
hundred men that lapped will I save you, and
deliver the Midianites into thine hand: and let all
the *other* people go every man unto his place.
8 So the people took victuals in their hand, and
their trumpets: and he sent all *the rest of* Israel
every man unto his tent, and retained those
three hundred men: and the host of Midian was
beneath him in the valley.
9 ¶ And it came to pass the same night, that the
LORD said unto him, Arise, get thee down unto
the host; for I have delivered it into thine hand.
10 But if thou fear to go down, go thou with
Phurah thy servant down to the host:
11 And thou shalt hear what they say; and
afterward shall thine hands be strengthened to
go down unto the host. Then went he down with
Phurah his servant unto the outside of the armed
men that *were* in the host.
12 And the Midianites and the Amalekites and all
the children of the east lay along in the valley

---

equips him by His Spirit (v. 34). But Gideon's reaction to second guess God's word and look for more confirmation is a common experience. God takes our frailty into account and may give further confirmations, but the time must come when we submit to and rest in His Word without doubt or fear.

Chapter 7: *God reduces Gideon's army and scatters the Midianites.*

The Sword of the Lord and of Gideon (7:1–25)

7:1 *all the people that were with him.* Thiry-two thousand men (v. 3). A small number compared to the Midianite army which numbered as grasshoppers (v. 12), yet too many for God's purposes. *rose up early.* Gideon wasted no time when he was sure of God's will. *the well of Harod.* Means "fountain of trembling."

7:2 *vaunt.* To boast in themselves. God knew the people's tendency to boast in themselves and take credit for victory. God shares His glory with none.

7:4 *I will try them.* Often used in Scripture to test metal. God had a way of seeking out the best men for the task.

7:6 *hand to their mouth.* Indication of vigilance, a necessary quality of disciplined soldiers.

7:8 *victuals.* Provisions or food. *host.* Army (vv. 9–10,14–15, 21–22).

7:9 *Arise, get thee down unto the host.* God directed Gideon and his servant Phurah to eavesdrop on the enemy at the edge of their camp to give him yet another confirmation. Gideon seemed fearful at every step.

7:13–15 Hearing the dream and interpretation convinced Gideon. Full of faith he called for battle.

7:16 He planned to shock and awe the enemy by blasts of trumpets and with sudden illumination by fire. *pitchers.* Clay vessels. *lamps.* Fiery torches.

7:18 *The sword of the LORD, and of Gideon.* The name Jehovah would be a terror to His enemies, while Gideon's name was already feared in Midian (9:14).

7:19 *the middle watch.* Between 10:00 p.m. and 2:00 a.m. Gideon chose the dead of night at the changing of the guard to attack when the Midianites were most vulnerable.

7:21–22 God caused panic and confusion thus moving His enemies to work His own will, causing the Midianites to slay one another.

7:23 *pursued after the Midianites.* No escape was permitted nor terms of peace offered.

like grasshoppers for multitude; and their camels
were without number, as the sand by the sea side
for multitude.
13 And when Gideon was come, behold, *there*
was a man that told a dream unto his fellow, and
said, Behold, I dreamed a dream, and, lo, a cake
of barley bread tumbled into the host of Midian,
and came unto a tent, and smote it that it fell, and
overturned it, that the tent lay along.
14 And his fellow answered and said, This *is*
nothing else save the sword of Gideon the son of
Joash, a man of Israel: *for* into his hand hath God
delivered Midian, and all the host.
15 ¶ And it was *so*, when Gideon heard the telling
of the dream, and the interpretation thereof, that
he worshipped, and returned into the host of
Israel, and said, Arise; for the LORD hath delivered
into your hand the host of Midian.
16 And he divided the three hundred men *into*
three companies, and he put a trumpet in every
man's hand, with empty pitchers, and lamps
within the pitchers.
17 And he said unto them, Look on me, and do
likewise: and, behold, when I come to the outside
of the camp, it shall be *that*, as I do, so shall ye do.
18 When I blow with a trumpet, I and all that *are*
with me, then blow ye the trumpets also on every
side of all the camp, and say, *The sword* of the
LORD, and of Gideon.
19 ¶ So Gideon, and the hundred men that *were*
with him, came unto the outside of the camp in the
beginning of the middle watch; and they had but
newly set the watch: and they blew the trumpets,
and brake the pitchers that *were* in their hands.
20 And the three companies blew the trumpets,
and brake the pitchers, and held the lamps in
their left hands, and the trumpets in their right
hands to blow *withal*: and they cried, The sword
of the LORD, and of Gideon.
21 And they stood every man in his place round
about the camp: and all the host ran, and cried,
and fled.
22 And the three hundred blew the trumpets, and
the LORD set every man's sword against his fellow,
even throughout all the host: and the host fled
to Beth-shittah in Zererath, *and* to the border of
Abel-meholah, unto Tabbath.
23 And the men of Israel gathered themselves to-
gether out of Naphtali, and out of Asher, and out
of all Manasseh, and pursued after the Midianites.
24 ¶ And Gideon sent messengers throughout
all mount Ephraim, saying, Come down against
the Midianites, and take before them the waters
unto Beth-barah and Jordan. Then all the men of
Ephraim gathered themselves together, and took
the waters unto Beth-barah and Jordan.
25 And they took two princes of the Midianites,
Oreb and Zeeb; and they slew Oreb upon the
rock Oreb, and Zeeb they slew at the winepress
of Zeeb, and pursued Midian, and brought the
heads of Oreb and Zeeb to Gideon on the other
side Jordan.

CHAPTER 8

AND the men of Ephraim said unto him, Why
hast thou served us thus, that thou calledst us not,
when thou wentest to fight with the Midianites?
And they did chide with him sharply.
2 And he said unto them, What have I done now
in comparison of you? *Is* not the gleaning of the
grapes of Ephraim better than the vintage of
Abi-ezer?
3 God hath delivered into your hands the princes
of Midian, Oreb and Zeeb: and what was I able to
do in comparison of you? Then their anger was
abated toward him, when he had said that.
4 ¶ And Gideon came to Jordan, *and* passed over,
he, and the three hundred men that *were* with
him, faint, yet pursuing *them*.
5 And he said unto the men of Succoth, Give, I
pray you, loaves of bread unto the people that
follow me; for they *be* faint, and I am pursuing
after Zebah and Zalmunna, kings of Midian.

Thoughts for Personal/Family Worship: Chapter 7

1. **The reduction of the army illustrates that God's work is not accomplished by might or power but by His Spirit (Zech. 4:6). God works in ways to show His own glory. While praying, preaching, or evangelizing we are all too quick to take honor to ourselves. We need to humble ourselves in submission to the cross of Christ. The cross is God's instrument to slay our fleshly pride. When we boast in Christ's cross we give our Lord Jesus all the glory for the victory He won for His people (Gal. 6:14).**
2. **On the other hand, God does use human means to do His work. The army was small, but it was an army. It should be our desire and prayer to be used as God's instrument to carry out His purposes. God does not use angels to preach the gospel, but He does use redeemed sinners. To be useful to God we need to obey His call and the commands of His Word. What are some ways God is using obedient people in your family or church to accomplish His work?**

Chapter 8: ***While victorious over the Midianites, Gideon refuses to reign over Israel and leaves a confusing legacy of good and evil.***

Gideon Fully and Finally Destroys the Midianites (8:1–35)

8:1 *served us thus.* Treated in this manner. *chide.* Contend. An emphatic expression of anger or disappointment.
8:2–3 *Is not the gleaning of the grapes . . . better.* Gideon commended the work of Ephraim for slaying two Midianitish princes, Oreb and Zeeb. Gideon's soft words turned away Ephraim's wrath (Prov. 15:1). *abated.* Calmed.
8:4 *the three hundred men.* Not one of Gideon's men was lost

6 ¶ And the princes of Succoth said, *Are* the hands of Zebah and Zalmunna now in thine hand, that we should give bread unto thine army?

7 And Gideon said, Therefore when the LORD hath delivered Zebah and Zalmunna into mine hand, then I will tear your flesh with the thorns of the wilderness and with briers.

8 ¶ And he went up thence to Penuel, and spake unto them likewise: and the men of Penuel answered him as the men of Succoth had answered *him*.

9 And he spake also unto the men of Penuel, saying, When I come again in peace, I will break down this tower.

10 ¶ Now Zebah and Zalmunna *were* in Karkor, and their hosts with them, about fifteen thousand *men*, all that were left of all the hosts of the children of the east: for there fell an hundred and twenty thousand men that drew sword.

11 ¶ And Gideon went up by the way of them that dwelt in tents on the east of Nobah and Jogbehah, and smote the host: for the host was secure.

12 And when Zebah and Zalmunna fled, he pursued after them, and took the two kings of Midian, Zebah and Zalmunna, and discomfited all the host.

13 ¶ And Gideon the son of Joash returned from battle before the sun *was up*,

14 And caught a young man of the men of Succoth, and enquired of him: and he described unto him the princes of Succoth, and the elders thereof, *even* threescore and seventeen men.

15 And he came unto the men of Succoth, and said, Behold Zebah and Zalmunna, with whom ye did upbraid me, saying, *Are* the hands of Zebah and Zalmunna now in thine hand, that we should give bread unto thy men *that are* weary?

16 And he took the elders of the city, and thorns of the wilderness and briers, and with them he taught the men of Succoth.

17 And he beat down the tower of Penuel, and slew the men of the city.

18 ¶ Then said he unto Zebah and Zalmunna, What manner of men *were they* whom ye slew at Tabor? And they answered, As thou *art*, so *were* they; each one resembled the children of a king.

19 And he said, They *were* my brethren, *even* the sons of my mother: *as* the LORD liveth, if ye had saved them alive, I would not slay you.

20 And he said unto Jether his firstborn, Up, *and* slay them. But the youth drew not his sword: for he feared, because he *was* yet a youth.

21 Then Zebah and Zalmunna said, Rise thou, and fall upon us: for as the man *is, so is* his strength. And Gideon arose, and slew Zebah and Zalmunna, and took away the ornaments that *were* on their camels' necks.

22 ¶ Then the men of Israel said unto Gideon, Rule thou over us, both thou, and thy son, and thy son's son also: for thou hast delivered us from the hand of Midian.

23 And Gideon said unto them, I will not rule over you, neither shall my son rule over you: the LORD shall rule over you.

24 ¶ And Gideon said unto them, I would desire a request of you, that ye would give me every man the earrings of his prey. (For they had golden earrings, because they *were* Ishmaelites.)

25 And they answered, We will willingly give *them*. And they spread a garment, and did cast therein every man the earrings of his prey.

26 And the weight of the golden earrings that he requested was a thousand and seven hundred *shekels* of gold; beside ornaments, and collars, and purple raiment that *was* on the kings of Midian, and beside the chains that *were* about their camels' necks.

---

in battle. Compare the huge number of slain Midianites (v. 10).

8:6–9 The princes of Succoth and Penuel were pessimistic about siding with Gideon too soon. Gideon threatens severe retaliation.

8:11 *for the host was secure.* The Midianites thought they were safe, so they left the camp undefended.

8:12 *discomfited.* Cast into panic.

8:14 *described.* Wrote.

8:15 *Behold Zeba and Zalmunna.* Gideon presented the two Midianite warriors to the men of Succoth to prove their error in judgment. *upbraid.* Insult or reproach.

8:16 *taught the men.* He punished them severely.

8:18 *As thou art, so were they.* The Midianite leaders incriminated themselves, expressing pride rather than regret.

8:19 *the sons of my mother.* Those slain at Tabor were Gideon's half brothers. *as the LORD liveth.* A common oath formula.

8:22 *Rule thou over us.* It was honorable of the men of Israel to offer king-like leadership to Gideon and it was admirable of Gideon to turn it down.

8:24 *prey.* The spoil or booty taken in conquest.

8:26 *collars.* Likely referring to pendants.

8:27 *And Gideon made an ephod thereof.* An ephod was for priestly work, therefore to create such a new golden ephod for private worship was idolatrous. *whoring.* Alludes to Israel as the Lord's spouse, and indicates that idolatry was spiritual adultery and fornication.

8:30–31 *he had many wives . . . concubine.* Contrary to God's law (Deut. 17:17).

8:33 *as soon as Gideon was dead.* It was a mercy that this developed after Gideon was dead, but his own example was greatly to blame. *Baal-berith.* Means, "Baal, lord of the covenant."

Thoughts for Personal/Family Worship: Chapter 8

1. The men of Succoth and the men of Penuel were deficient in faith and thereby lacking in courage. They were opportunists without principles, fearful of taking the right stand just in case things did not turn out. They failed in the day of opportunity to help those whom God raised up to help them. Let this be a check to us. It is

27 And Gideon made an ephod thereof, and put
it in his city, *even* in Ophrah: and all Israel went
thither a whoring after it: which thing became a
snare unto Gideon, and to his house.
28 ¶ Thus was Midian subdued before the chil-
dren of Israel, so that they lifted up their heads
no more. And the country was in quietness forty
years in the days of Gideon.
29 ¶ And Jerubbaal the son of Joash went and
dwelt in his own house.
30 And Gideon had threescore and ten sons of his
body begotten: for he had many wives.
31 And his concubine that *was* in Shechem,
she also bare him a son, whose name he called
Abimelech.
32 ¶ And Gideon the son of Joash died in a good
old age, and was buried in the sepulchre of Joash
his father, in Ophrah of the Abi-ezrites.
33 And it came to pass, as soon as Gideon was
dead, that the children of Israel turned again,
and went a whoring after Baalim, and made Baal-
berith their god.
34 And the children of Israel remembered not the
LORD their God, who had delivered them out of
the hands of all their enemies on every side:
35 Neither shewed they kindness to the house of
Jerubbaal, *namely*, Gideon, according to all the
goodness which he had shewed unto Israel.

CHAPTER 9

AND Abimelech the son of Jerubbaal went
to Shechem unto his mother's brethren, and
communed with them, and with all the family of
the house of his mother's father, saying,
2 Speak, I pray you, in the ears of all the men of
Shechem, Whether *is* better for you, either that all
the sons of Jerubbaal, *which are* threescore and
ten persons, reign over you, or that one reign over
you? remember also that I *am* your bone and your
flesh.
3 And his mother's brethren spake of him in the
ears of all the men of Shechem all these words:
and their hearts inclined to follow Abimelech; for
they said, He *is* our brother.
4 And they gave him threescore and ten *pieces* of
silver out of the house of Baal-berith, wherewith
Abimelech hired vain and light persons, which
followed him.
5 And he went unto his father's house at Ophrah,
and slew his brethren the sons of Jerubbaal, *being*
threescore and ten persons, upon one stone:
notwithstanding yet Jotham the youngest son of
Jerubbaal was left; for he hid himself.
6 And all the men of Shechem gathered together,
and all the house of Millo, and went, and made
Abimelech king, by the plain of the pillar that *was*
in Shechem.
7 ¶ And when they told *it* to Jotham, he went and
stood in the top of mount Gerizim, and lifted up
his voice, and cried, and said unto them, Hearken
unto me, ye men of Shechem, that God may
hearken unto you.
8 The trees went forth *on a time* to anoint a king
over them; and they said unto the olive tree, Reign
thou over us.
9 But the olive tree said unto them, Should I leave
my fatness, wherewith by me they honour God
and man, and go to be promoted over the trees?
10 And the trees said to the fig tree, Come thou,
and reign over us.
11 But the fig tree said unto them, Should I
forsake my sweetness, and my good fruit, and go
to be promoted over the trees?
12 Then said the trees unto the vine, Come thou,
and reign over us.

---

better to be fellow helpers to the truth (3 John 8) than to waste God-given opportunities. Living by the principles of God's Word rather than by sight of circumstances is the essence of walking by faith. What opportunities do you have to stand?

2. Gideon's fall into idolatry did great harm. Even the best of men have the potential of failure and disappointment. Gideon's failure increases the anticipation for the One who will neither fail nor disappoint. Flaws in the best of men must not keep us from following our Lord Jesus who was perfect in all His ways. He alone is worthy of our worship and our praises. He will never disappoint us, nor lead us in a wrong path. Therefore, let us keep "looking unto Jesus the author and finisher of our faith" (Heb. 12:2).

Chapter 9: *God sends judgment from within Israel fulfilling the curse of Jotham's parable.*

The Enemies of the House of Gideon Self-Destruct (9:1–57)

9:1 *Abimelech*. Ironically, his name means "my father is king." *communed*. Spoke.

9:2–3 *the men of Shechem*. Literally, "baals," referring to the leaders (v. 26). *your bone and your flesh*. He plays on the spirit of nepotism; his mother's family became his best supporters.

9:4 *vain and light persons*. Empty and worthless persons became his mercenaries.

9:5 *slew his brethren the sons of Jerubbaal*. Such murderous deeds were common in eastern dynasties to control power within families. This was Gideon's evil legacy of polygamy and concubinage, not unlike the consequences in David's family years later.

9:6 *the plain of the pillar*. Literally, "the oak which was set up," a pagan place of worship.

9:7 *mount Gerizim*. Ironically, the mountain of blessing (Deut. 11:29) becomes the place of solemn pronouncement which was effectively a curse upon them if they did not listen.

9:8–14 *the olive tree . . . fig . . . vine . . . bramble*. The most useful and constant of all trees in Israel in contrast to the most useless. The thrust of this parable is that the most unworthy and incapable assumes the place of authority.

9:11 *sweetness*. Sweet figs.

13 And the vine said unto them, Should I leave
my wine, which cheereth God and man, and go to
be promoted over the trees?
14 Then said all the trees unto the bramble, Come
thou, *and* reign over us.
15 And the bramble said unto the trees, If in
truth ye anoint me king over you, *then* come *and*
put your trust in my shadow: and if not, let fire
come out of the bramble, and devour the cedars
of Lebanon.
16 Now therefore, if ye have done truly and
sincerely, in that ye have made Abimelech king,
and if ye have dealt well with Jerubbaal and his
house, and have done unto him according to the
deserving of his hands;
17 (For my father fought for you, and adventured
his life far, and delivered you out of the hand of
Midian:
18 And ye are risen up against my father's house
this day, and have slain his sons, threescore and ten
persons, upon one stone, and have made Abim-
elech, the son of his maidservant, king over the
men of Shechem, because he *is* your brother;)
19 If ye then have dealt truly and sincerely with
Jerubbaal and with his house this day, *then* rejoice
ye in Abimelech, and let him also rejoice in you:
20 But if not, let fire come out from Abimelech,
and devour the men of Shechem, and the house
of Millo; and let fire come out from the men
of Shechem, and from the house of Millo, and
devour Abimelech.
21 And Jotham ran away, and fled, and went to
Beer, and dwelt there, for fear of Abimelech his
brother.
22 ¶ When Abimelech had reigned three years
over Israel,
23 Then God sent an evil spirit between Abim-
elech and the men of Shechem; and the men of
Shechem dealt treacherously with Abimelech:
24 That the cruelty *done* to the threescore and
ten sons of Jerubbaal might come, and their
blood be laid upon Abimelech their brother,
which slew them; and upon the men of Shechem,
which aided him in the killing of his brethren.
25 And the men of Shechem set liers in wait for
him in the top of the mountains, and they robbed
all that came along that way by them: and it was
told Abimelech.
26 And Gaal the son of Ebed came with his
brethren, and went over to Shechem: and the men
of Shechem put their confidence in him.
27 And they went out into the fields, and gathered
their vineyards, and trode *the grapes*, and made
merry, and went into the house of their god, and
did eat and drink, and cursed Abimelech.
28 And Gaal the son of Ebed said, Who *is* Abim-
elech, and who *is* Shechem, that we should serve
him? *is* not *he* the son of Jerubbaal? and Zebul
his officer? serve the men of Hamor the father of
Shechem: for why should we serve him?
29 And would to God this people were under my
hand! then would I remove Abimelech. And he
said to Abimelech, Increase thine army, and come
out.
30 ¶ And when Zebul the ruler of the city heard
the words of Gaal the son of Ebed, his anger was
kindled.
31 And he sent messengers unto Abimelech
privily, saying, Behold, Gaal the son of Ebed and
his brethren be come to Shechem; and, behold,
they fortify the city against thee.
32 Now therefore up by night, thou and the
people that *is* with thee, and lie in wait in the field:
33 And it shall be, *that* in the morning, as soon as
the sun is up, thou shalt rise early, and set upon
the city: and, behold, *when* he and the people that
is with him come out against thee, then mayest
thou do to them as thou shalt find occasion.
34 ¶ And Abimelech rose up, and all the people
that *were* with him, by night, and they laid wait
against Shechem in four companies.
35 And Gaal the son of Ebed went out, and stood
in the entering of the gate of the city: and Abime-
lech rose up, and the people that *were* with him,
from lying in wait.
36 And when Gaal saw the people, he said to Zebul,

9:15 *If in truth ye anoint me king over you.* There is no hesitation with the bramble. It is ready to take on the task of reigning over trees that are altogether superior. *trust in my shadow.* Common expression for a place of protection or safety.
9:16 *if ye have done truly and sincerely.* He appeals to what is according to truth and uprightness. *deserving of his hands.* Crowning Abimelech was not honoring to the accomplishments of Gideon.
9:17 *adventured his life far.* Risked his life in front of them.
9:20 *let fire come out.* God's curse on the guilty parties. It was fulfilled in an ugly round of revenge until all were destroyed (vv. 25–55).
9:23 *God sent an evil spirit.* A demonstration of God's absolute sovereignty, even using satanic powers to accomplish His purpose against the evildoers (1 Kings 22:19–23).
9:24 *the cruelty done.* The justice principle of "eye for eye," *lex talionis*, the law of retaliation (v. 53). *threescore and ten.* Seventy.
9:25 *liers.* Men prepared for ambush.
9:29 *under my hand.* Under his command.
9:31 *privily.* Secretly or craftily.
9:45 *sowed it with salt.* Most likely, a gesture symbolizing the permanence of the destruction.
9:46 *the god Berith.* See 8:33.
9:48 *gat him up.* Went up.
9:53 *a piece of a millstone.* Ironically, as Abimelech slew seventy men upon one stone (v. 5), he would perish by a single piece of millstone.

Thoughts for Personal/Family Worship: Chapter 9

1. From Jotham's parable we learn that good men are reluctant to promote themselves while useless men

Behold, there come people down from the top of the
mountains. And Zebul said unto him, Thou seest
the shadow of the mountains as *if they were* men.
37 And Gaal spake again and said, See there
come people down by the middle of the land,
and another company come along by the plain of
Meonenim.
38 Then said Zebul unto him, Where *is* now thy
mouth, wherewith thou saidst, Who *is* Abimelech,
that we should serve him? *is* not this the people
that thou hast despised? go out, I pray now, and
fight with them.
39 And Gaal went out before the men of Shechem,
and fought with Abimelech.
40 And Abimelech chased him, and he fled before
him, and many were overthrown *and* wounded,
even unto the entering of the gate.
41 And Abimelech dwelt at Arumah: and Zebul
thrust out Gaal and his brethren, that they should
not dwell in Shechem.
42 And it came to pass on the morrow, that the
people went out into the field; and they told
Abimelech.
43 And he took the people, and divided them into
three companies, and laid wait in the field, and
looked, and, behold, the people *were* come forth
out of the city; and he rose up against them, and
smote them.
44 And Abimelech, and the company that *was*
with him, rushed forward, and stood in the en-
tering of the gate of the city: and the two *other*
companies ran upon all *the people* that *were* in the
fields, and slew them.
45 And Abimelech fought against the city all that
day; and he took the city, and slew the people that
was therein, and beat down the city, and sowed it
with salt.
46 ¶ And when all the men of the tower of
Shechem heard *that*, they entered into an hold of
the house of the god Berith.
47 And it was told Abimelech, that all the men of
the tower of Shechem were gathered together.
48 And Abimelech gat him up to mount Zalmon,
he and all the people that *were* with him; and
Abimelech took an axe in his hand, and cut down
a bough from the trees, and took it, and laid *it* on
his shoulder, and said unto the people that *were*
with him, What ye have seen me do, make haste,
and do as I *have done*.
49 And all the people likewise cut down every
man his bough, and followed Abimelech, and put
them to the hold, and set the hold on fire upon
them; so that all the men of the tower of Shechem
died also, about a thousand men and women.
50 ¶ Then went Abimelech to Thebez, and en-
camped against Thebez, and took it.
51 But there was a strong tower within the city,
and thither fled all the men and women, and all
they of the city, and shut *it* to them, and gat them
up to the top of the tower.
52 And Abimelech came unto the tower, and
fought against it, and went hard unto the door of
the tower to burn it with fire.
53 And a certain woman cast a piece of a millstone
upon Abimelech's head, and all to brake his skull.
54 Then he called hastily unto the young man
his armourbearer, and said unto him, Draw thy
sword, and slay me, that men say not of me, A
woman slew him. And his young man thrust him
through, and he died.
55 And when the men of Israel saw that Abimelech
was dead, they departed every man unto his place.
56 ¶ Thus God rendered the wickedness of
Abimelech, which he did unto his father, in slaying
his seventy brethren:
57 And all the evil of the men of Shechem did
God render upon their heads: and upon them
came the curse of Jotham the son of Jerubbaal.

CHAPTER 10

AND after Abimelech there arose to defend Israel
Tola the son of Puah, the son of Dodo, a man
of Issachar; and he dwelt in Shamir in mount
Ephraim.
2 And he judged Israel twenty and three years,
and died, and was buried in Shamir.
3 ¶ And after him arose Jair, a Gileadite, and
judged Israel twenty and two years.
4 And he had thirty sons that rode on thirty ass

---

tend to consider themselves suited to any task. Great harm can come when the wrong man is in leadership. The best person for God's work will be the one found busy in his own sphere of service. Let us beware of the man who promotes himself over his fellow men, for such men as Abimelech who offer their services at will, may have nothing of worth to offer.

2. The whole chapter illustrates principles of divine judgment. God's use of the evil spirit shows His absolute authority over every realm. He may well bring judgment upon His enemies by allowing Satan to work his wicked will in evil hearts. The spirit of treachery is self-destructive, and part of divine judgment is to abandon the wicked to their own devices. The principle of poetic justice ("eye for eye," [Ex. 21:24]) is also evident. There is nothing more fearful than to get from God's justice what is deserved. God's justice is on the side of those who obey His Word and do the right, but they who do evil shall be judged according to their works. How does this teach us to fear the Lord and turn from evil?

Chapter 10: ***After the judgeships of Tola and Jair, Israel sins again resulting in the Philistine and Ammonite oppressions.***

Further Apostasy after Tola and Jair (10:1–18)

10:3 *after him.* Jair rose up without any reference to the cycle of apostasy.

colts, and they had thirty cities, which are called
Havoth-jair unto this day, which *are* in the land
of Gilead.
5 And Jair died, and was buried in Camon.
6 ¶ And the children of Israel did evil again in
the sight of the LORD, and served Baalim, and
Ashtaroth, and the gods of Syria, and the gods of
Zidon, and the gods of Moab, and the gods of the
children of Ammon, and the gods of the Philis-
tines, and forsook the LORD, and served not him.
7 And the anger of the LORD was hot against
Israel, and he sold them into the hands of the
Philistines, and into the hands of the children of
Ammon.
8 And that year they vexed and oppressed the
children of Israel: eighteen years, all the children
of Israel that *were* on the other side Jordan in the
land of the Amorites, which *is* in Gilead.
9 Moreover the children of Ammon passed over
Jordan to fight also against Judah, and against
Benjamin, and against the house of Ephraim; so
that Israel was sore distressed.
10 ¶ And the children of Israel cried unto the
LORD, saying, We have sinned against thee, both
because we have forsaken our God, and also served
Baalim.
11 And the LORD said unto the children of Israel,
Did not *I deliver you* from the Egyptians, and
from the Amorites, from the children of Ammon,
and from the Philistines?
12 The Zidonians also, and the Amalekites, and
the Maonites, did oppress you; and ye cried to me,
and I delivered you out of their hand.
13 Yet ye have forsaken me, and served other
gods: wherefore I will deliver you no more.
14 Go and cry unto the gods which ye have
chosen; let them deliver you in the time of your
tribulation.
15 ¶ And the children of Israel said unto the LORD,
We have sinned: do thou unto us whatsoever
seemeth good unto thee; deliver us only, we pray
thee, this day.
16 And they put away the strange gods from
among them, and served the LORD: and his soul
was grieved for the misery of Israel.
17 Then the children of Ammon were gathered
together, and encamped in Gilead. And the chil-
dren of Israel assembled themselves together, and
encamped in Mizpeh.
18 And the people *and* princes of Gilead said one
to another, What man *is he* that will begin to fight
against the children of Ammon? he shall be head
over all the inhabitants of Gilead.

CHAPTER 11

NOW Jephthah the Gileadite was a mighty man
of valour, and he *was* the son of an harlot: and
Gilead begat Jephthah.
2 And Gilead's wife bare him sons; and his wife's
sons grew up, and they thrust out Jephthah, and
said unto him, Thou shalt not inherit in our
father's house; for thou *art* the son of a strange
woman.
3 Then Jephthah fled from his brethren, and
dwelt in the land of Tob: and there were gathered
vain men to Jephthah, and went out with him.
4 ¶ And it came to pass in process of time, that
the children of Ammon made war against Israel.
5 And it was so, that when the children of Am-
mon made war against Israel, the elders of Gilead
went to fetch Jephthah out of the land of Tob:

10:6 The list of false gods showed a total abandonment to any god who served their depraved purposes. *forsook the LORD.* Idolatry and the worship of Jehovah are mutually exclusive. There can be no compromise in the breach of the first commandment (Ex. 20:1–3).
10:7 *hot against Israel.* God is zealous for the glory of His own name. *the Philistines, and into the hands of the children of Ammon.* Israel was sandwiched between the encroachments of the Philistines from the west and the Ammonites from the east (vv. 8–9).
10:8 *that year.* The sentence was as sudden as it was serious. *vexed and oppressed.* Literally, "they shattered and grievously crushed."
10:9 *sore distressed.* Coming from two sides, this cycle of oppression appeared to be more extensive than others that were more localized.
10:13 *will deliver you no more.* This is the first refusal of mercy from the Lord. Their call for help was presumptuous without sincerity.
10:14 *cry unto the gods which ye have chosen.* This underscores the folly of choosing gods incapable of doing anything.
10:15 *do thou unto us whatsoever seemeth good unto thee.* Now they cast themselves on God's mercy alone, submitting to Him.
10:16 *and they put away the strange gods from among them.* They displayed their brokenness of heart by breaking off from their strange gods. *and his soul was grieved.* A Hebrew way of saying "the Lord Himself was troubled."
10:18 *What man is he that will begin to fight against the children of Ammon?* The hope for the next judge builds the expectation for the coming of the Messiah.

Thoughts for Personal/Family Worship: Chapter 10

1. **God will not be manipulated, and certainly not by superficial prayers. God is not an instrument to be used just to rescue from trouble (v. 13). If we understand the holiness of God, we cannot make a game out of our Christianity and still expect God's blessing. We must not develop a cheap "bunker theology," thinking that we can sow to the flesh and still have God by our side in any time of crisis. God wants our first love and full loyalty, not sham cries from unrepentant hearts. What is the difference between using God and crying out to Him in true faith?**
2. **If we are true believers, our God is a true Father to pity us in our sufferings (v. 16). Isaiah wrote of God's tenderness toward His suffering people, "In all their affliction he was afflicted, and the angel of his presence saved them: in his love and in his pity he redeemed them; and**

6 And they said unto Jephthah, Come, and be
our captain, that we may fight with the children
of Ammon.
7 And Jephthah said unto the elders of Gilead,
Did not ye hate me, and expel me out of my fa-
ther's house? and why are ye come unto me now
when ye are in distress?
8 And the elders of Gilead said unto Jephthah,
Therefore we turn again to thee now, that thou
mayest go with us, and fight against the children
of Ammon, and be our head over all the inhabi-
tants of Gilead.
9 And Jephthah said unto the elders of Gilead,
If ye bring me home again to fight against the
children of Ammon, and the LORD deliver them
before me, shall I be your head?
10 And the elders of Gilead said unto Jephthah,
The LORD be witness between us, if we do not so
according to thy words.
11 Then Jephthah went with the elders of Gilead,
and the people made him head and captain over
them: and Jephthah uttered all his words before
the LORD in Mizpeh.
12 ¶ And Jephthah sent messengers unto the king
of the children of Ammon, saying, What hast
thou to do with me, that thou art come against
me to fight in my land?
13 And the king of the children of Ammon
answered unto the messengers of Jephthah,
Because Israel took away my land, when they
came up out of Egypt, from Arnon even unto
Jabbok, and unto Jordan: now therefore restore
those *lands* again peaceably.
14 And Jephthah sent messengers again unto the
king of the children of Ammon:
15 And said unto him, Thus saith Jephthah, Israel
took not away the land of Moab, nor the land of
the children of Ammon:
16 But when Israel came up from Egypt, and
walked through the wilderness unto the Red sea,
and came to Kadesh;
17 Then Israel sent messengers unto the king of
Edom, saying, Let me, I pray thee, pass through
thy land: but the king of Edom would not hearken
thereto. And in like manner they sent unto the
king of Moab: but he would not *consent*: and
Israel abode in Kadesh.
18 Then they went along through the wilderness,
and compassed the land of Edom, and the land
of Moab, and came by the east side of the land of
Moab, and pitched on the other side of Arnon,
but came not within the border of Moab: for
Arnon *was* the border of Moab.
19 And Israel sent messengers unto Sihon king of
the Amorites, the king of Heshbon; and Israel said
unto him, Let us pass, we pray thee, through thy
land into my place.
20 But Sihon trusted not Israel to pass through his
coast: but Sihon gathered all his people together,
and pitched in Jahaz, and fought against Israel.
21 And the LORD God of Israel delivered Sihon
and all his people into the hand of Israel, and they
smote them: so Israel possessed all the land of the
Amorites, the inhabitants of that country.
22 And they possessed all the coasts of the
Amorites, from Arnon even unto Jabbok, and
from the wilderness even unto Jordan.
23 So now the LORD God of Israel hath dispos-
sessed the Amorites from before his people Israel,
and shouldest thou possess it?
24 Wilt not thou possess that which Chemosh
thy god giveth thee to possess? So whomsoever
the LORD our God shall drive out from before us,
them will we possess.
25 And now *art* thou any thing better than Balak
the son of Zippor, king of Moab? did he ever strive
against Israel, or did he ever fight against them,
26 While Israel dwelt in Heshbon and her towns,
and in Aroer and her towns, and in all the cities
that *be* along by the coasts of Arnon, three hun-
dred years? why therefore did ye not recover *them*
within that time?
27 Wherefore I have not sinned against thee, but
thou doest me wrong to war against me: the LORD

he bare them, and carried them all the days of old" (Isa. 63:9). God takes no delight in our self-destruction, but is moved by divine pity at our cries for mercy. When overwhelmed by life's struggles be sure to cry to your heavenly Father for deliverance. God knows the difference between sincere cries of repentance and superficial cries for temporal relief.

Jephthah (11:1—12:7)

Chapter 11: ***Jephthah is called to fight the Ammonites and by a serious vow obligates himself to offer up his daughter.***

Jephthah: A Mighty Man of Valour (11:1–40)

11:1 *mighty man of valour.* Renowned in Israel for leadership and courage (Heb. 11:32). *the son of an harlot.* A child of his times; his honor did not come from his heritage.

11:2 *strange woman.* A foreigner.

11:3 *vain men.* Unprincipled or worthless men.

11:6 *captain.* Leader or commander.

11:9 *the LORD deliver.* The elders looked to Jephthah for leadership, but Jephthah acknowledged any victory was due to the Lord and not his skill.

11:20 *coast.* Borders (v. 22).

11:22 *Amorites.* A general term for Canaanites.

11:24 *Chemosh.* The chief god of both the Moabites and Ammonites. *whomsoever the LORD our God shall drive out.* If the Ammonites claimed their land in the name of Chemosh, then Israel could do the same in the name of Jehovah.

11:26 *three hundred years.* A crucial number for Jephthah's argument. This would date the exodus to the fifteenth century BC.

the Judge be judge this day between the children
of Israel and the children of Ammon.
28 Howbeit the king of the children of Ammon
hearkened not unto the words of Jephthah which
he sent him.
29 ¶ Then the Spirit of the LORD came upon Jephthah, and he passed over Gilead, and Manasseh,
and passed over Mizpeh of Gilead, and from
Mizpeh of Gilead he passed over *unto* the children
of Ammon.
30 And Jephthah vowed a vow unto the LORD,
and said, If thou shalt without fail deliver the
children of Ammon into mine hands,
31 Then it shall be, that whatsoever cometh forth
of the doors of my house to meet me, when I
return in peace from the children of Ammon,
shall surely be the LORD's, and I will offer it up for
a burnt offering.
32 ¶ So Jephthah passed over unto the children
of Ammon to fight against them; and the LORD
delivered them into his hands.
33 And he smote them from Aroer, even till thou
come to Minnith, *even* twenty cities, and unto the
plain of the vineyards, with a very great slaughter.
Thus the children of Ammon were subdued
before the children of Israel.
34 ¶ And Jephthah came to Mizpeh unto his
house, and, behold, his daughter came out to
meet him with timbrels and with dances: and she
was his only child; beside her he had neither son
nor daughter.
35 And it came to pass, when he saw her, that he
rent his clothes, and said, Alas, my daughter! thou
hast brought me very low, and thou art one of
them that trouble me: for I have opened my mouth
unto the LORD, and I cannot go back.
36 And she said unto him, My father, *if* thou
hast opened thy mouth unto the LORD, do to me
according to that which hath proceeded out of
thy mouth; forasmuch as the LORD hath taken
vengeance for thee of thine enemies, *even* of the
children of Ammon.
37 And she said unto her father, Let this thing be
done for me: let me alone two months, that I may
go up and down upon the mountains, and bewail
my virginity, I and my fellows.
38 And he said, Go. And he sent her away *for* two
months: and she went with her companions, and
bewailed her virginity upon the mountains.
39 And it came to pass at the end of two months,
that she returned unto her father, who did with
her *according* to his vow which he had vowed: and
she knew no man. And it was a custom in Israel,
40 *That* the daughters of Israel went yearly to
lament the daughter of Jephthah the Gileadite
four days in a year.

CHAPTER 12

AND the men of Ephraim gathered themselves
together, and went northward, and said unto
Jephthah, Wherefore passedst thou over to fight

11:29 *the Spirit of the LORD came upon Jephthah.* A proof of God's call. This is God empowering him for service.
11:30 *vowed a vow unto the LORD.* Significantly, the vow was the first act after the Spirit's empowerment. Rather than being rash, it expressed Jepthah's sense of dependence on God.
11:31 *whatsoever cometh forth of the doors of my house to meet me.* He knew this would be a person and would mean great personal cost. A vow requires something of personal value. *burnt offering.* The sacrifice symbolizing complete and total dedication or consecration.
11:34 *timbrels.* Some kind of hand drum or tambourine used in the victory celebration. *beside her.* She was his only child. Keeping his vow would mean an end to his family line.
11:35 *trouble me.* To throw into confusion. The prospect of keeping his vow was most disturbing. *I cannot go back.* In spite of the heartbreaking personal cost to fulfill his vow, Jephthah fulfilled his promise to God (Eccl. 5:4–5).
11:39 *who did with her according to his vow.* The arguments that Jephthah's vow referred to giving his daughter over to perpetual virginity seem to outweigh the arguments that Jephthah offered her up as a human sacrifice. God never required His people to offer human sacrifices. He forbade them. In the case of Abraham offering Isaac, God intended it for a test and intervened to prevent it (Gen. 22). *and she knew no man.* This meant she was to remain unmarried and childless all her days. It seems to be the final word on the meaning of Jephthah's vow.
11:40 *to lament.* The Hebrew means "to recount," suggesting a yearly conversation with Jephthah's daughter.

Thoughts for Personal/Family Worship: Chapter 11

1. **Though Jephthah was of questionable heritage and rejected by his fellows, God took him up to deliver Israel. He was despised but rose up to be the deliverer of his people. In this way, his ministry draws a straight line to Christ. The Lord Jesus was also despised of men (Isa. 53:3; John 1:11) but He was the instrument of God's mighty power to redeem His people from the bondage of sin. This is a reminder as we read Judges that every deliverer God raised up anticipates and points to the ultimate and only Redeemer, the Lord Jesus Christ, who in no way fails His mission or disappoints His people.**
2. **Regarding vows, we must take Jephthah's position, "I cannot go back" (v. 35). There is wisdom for us in Eccl. 5:5: "Better is it that thou shouldest not vow, than that thou shouldest vow and not pay." Vows are not to be put off, but to be paid immediately. However, a rash vow that proves to be unlawful to God should be repented of and not carried out. If the vow was wrong in the first place it would be wrong to fulfill it when we know better. Though vows should never be made casually or lightly, they are permissible when they are based in truth and intended for greater dedication to God's service. What vows have you taken over the course of your life? What does fulfilling them mean now?**

Chapter 12: ***Civil war breaks out between Ephraim and the men of Gilead, after which Jephthah dies***

against the children of Ammon, and didst not call
us to go with thee? we will burn thine house upon
thee with fire.
2 And Jephthah said unto them, I and my people
were at great strife with the children of Ammon;
and when I called you, ye delivered me not out of
their hands.
3 And when I saw that ye delivered *me* not, I
put my life in my hands, and passed over against
the children of Ammon, and the LORD delivered
them into my hand: wherefore then are ye come
up unto me this day, to fight against me?
4 Then Jephthah gathered together all the men
of Gilead, and fought with Ephraim: and the men
of Gilead smote Ephraim, because they said, Ye
Gileadites *are* fugitives of Ephraim among the
Ephraimites, *and* among the Manassites.
5 And the Gileadites took the passages of Jordan
before the Ephraimites: and it was *so*, that when
those Ephraimites which were escaped said, Let
me go over; that the men of Gilead said unto him,
Art thou an Ephraimite? If he said, Nay;
6 Then said they unto him, Say now Shibboleth:
and he said Sibboleth: for he could not frame to
pronounce *it* right. Then they took him, and slew
him at the passages of Jordan: and there fell at that
time of the Ephraimites forty and two thousand.
7 And Jephthah judged Israel six years. Then died
Jephthah the Gileadite, and was buried in *one of*
the cities of Gilead.
8 ¶ And after him Ibzan of Beth-lehem judged
Israel.
9 And he had thirty sons, and thirty daughters,
whom he sent abroad, and took in thirty daughters
from abroad for his sons. And he judged Israel
seven years.
10 Then died Ibzan, and was buried at Beth-lehem.
11 ¶ And after him Elon, a Zebulonite, judged
Israel; and he judged Israel ten years.
12 And Elon the Zebulonite died, and was buried
in Aijalon in the country of Zebulun.
13 ¶ And after him Abdon the son of Hillel, a Pir-
athonite, judged Israel.
14 And he had forty sons and thirty nephews,
that rode on threescore and ten ass colts: and he
judged Israel eight years.
15 And Abdon the son of Hillel the Pirathonite
died, and was buried in Pirathon in the land of
Ephraim, in the mount of the Amalekites.

CHAPTER 13

AND the children of Israel did evil again in the
sight of the LORD; and the LORD delivered them
into the hand of the Philistines forty years.
2 ¶ And there was a certain man of Zorah, of the
family of the Danites, whose name *was* Manoah;
and his wife *was* barren, and bare not.
3 And the angel of the LORD appeared unto the
woman, and said unto her, Behold now, thou *art*
barren, and bearest not: but thou shalt conceive,
and bear a son.
4 Now therefore beware, I pray thee, and drink
not wine nor strong drink, and eat not any un-
clean *thing*:
5 For, lo, thou shalt conceive, and bear a son; and

and is followed by Ibzan, Elon, and Abdon.

Ephraim's Defeat in Battle and Denial of Escape (12:1–7)

12:1 *and didst not call us to go with thee?* See the similar complaint of Ephraim to Gideon (8:1).

12:2 *and when I called you.* Jephthah claims that he did call on Ephraim for help, but they refused.

12:3 It was Jephthah and the men of Gilead who bore the dangers of war with Ammon. Jephthah gives honor to the Lord.

12:4 *Gileadites.* The *Gileadites*, like Ephraim and Manasseh, were descendants from Joseph (Num. 26:28–29). They belittled Jephthah as an outcast with no part in their heritage.

12:5 *passages of Jordan.* Crossing places. By control of these places, retreat was made impossible for Ephraim (3:27–30; 7:24–25).

12:6 *Shibboleth . . . Sibboleth.* The words mean "ear of corn," and became a password based on a dialectical difference between those east and west of the Jordan.

Ibzan, Elon, Abdon (12:8–15)

12:8–15 Three minor judges deliver Israel for twenty-five years. The large families and multiple animals suggest years of prosperity.

Thoughts for Personal/Family Worship: Chapter 12

1. The Gileadites were a small insignificant component of Joseph's descendants, who had settled east of Jordan. They were despised and ridiculed by Ephraim, their more significant "cousins." Ephraim's pride got the best of them when they saw the accomplishments of little Gilead. Pride is a tinderbox that only needs the match of envy to start fires of conflict. Pride is at the root of wars and world conflicts, strife in local politics, misery in homes, and trouble in the Lord's church. Pride must be rooted out of our hearts by much prayer. It can be broken by the power of Christ's cross. How has pride shown itself in your life? How are you fighting it?

2. While God raises up key men for mighty acts in His service there is a lot of ordinary work to be done. Not every servant of God will leave a legacy of memorable accomplishments. But every servant must serve the Lord in the venue and with the influence He orders. History knows nothing of the accomplishments of Ibzan, Elon, or Abdon, but God raised them to serve their generation. We may never be famous but it is important that we be found faithful in our sphere of service.

Samson (13:1—16:31)

Chapter 13: *The Angel of the Lord appears to Samson's parents, announcing his birth and his appointment to deliver Israel from the Philistines.*

The Lord Announces Samson's Birth (13:1–25)

13:1 *forty years.* Samson judged Israel for twenty of those years (16:31).

13:3 *the angel of the LORD.* See note at 2:1.

13:5 *Nazarite unto God.* Samson was consecrated to God from

no razor shall come on his head: for the child shall
be a Nazarite unto God from the womb: and he
shall begin to deliver Israel out of the hand of the
Philistines.
6 ¶ Then the woman came and told her husband,
saying, A man of God came unto me, and his
countenance *was* like the countenance of an angel
of God, very terrible: but I asked him not whence
he *was*, neither told he me his name:
7 But he said unto me, Behold, thou shalt conceive,
and bear a son; and now drink no wine
nor strong drink, neither eat any unclean *thing*:
for the child shall be a Nazarite to God from the
womb to the day of his death.
8 ¶ Then Manoah intreated the LORD, and said,
O my Lord, let the man of God which thou didst
send come again unto us, and teach us what we
shall do unto the child that shall be born.
9 And God hearkened to the voice of Manoah;
and the angel of God came again unto the woman
as she sat in the field: but Manoah her husband
was not with her.
10 And the woman made haste, and ran, and
shewed her husband, and said unto him, Behold,
the man hath appeared unto me, that came unto
me the *other* day.
11 And Manoah arose, and went after his wife,
and came to the man, and said unto him, *Art*
thou the man that spakest unto the woman? And
he said, I *am*.
12 And Manoah said, Now let thy words come to
pass. How shall we order the child, and *how* shall
we do unto him?
13 And the angel of the LORD said unto Manoah,
Of all that I said unto the woman let her beware.
14 She may not eat of any *thing* that cometh of
the vine, neither let her drink wine or strong
drink, nor eat any unclean *thing*: all that I commanded
her let her observe.
15 ¶ And Manoah said unto the angel of the
LORD, I pray thee, let us detain thee, until we shall
have made ready a kid for thee.
16 And the angel of the LORD said unto Manoah,
Though thou detain me, I will not eat of thy
bread: and if thou wilt offer a burnt offering, thou
must offer it unto the LORD. For Manoah knew
not that he *was* an angel of the LORD.
17 And Manoah said unto the angel of the LORD,
What *is* thy name, that when thy sayings come to
pass we may do thee honour?
18 And the angel of the LORD said unto him, Why
askest thou thus after my name, seeing it *is* secret?
19 So Manoah took a kid with a meat offering,
and offered *it* upon a rock unto the LORD: and *the
angel* did wondrously; and Manoah and his wife
looked on.
20 For it came to pass, when the flame went up
toward heaven from off the altar, that the angel
of the LORD ascended in the flame of the altar.
And Manoah and his wife looked on *it*, and fell
on their faces to the ground.
21 But the angel of the LORD did no more appear
to Manoah and to his wife. Then Manoah knew
that he *was* an angel of the LORD.
22 And Manoah said unto his wife, We shall
surely die, because we have seen God.
23 But his wife said unto him, If the LORD were
pleased to kill us, he would not have received a
burnt offering and a meat offering at our hands,
neither would he have shewed us all these *things*,
nor would as at this time have told us *such things*
as these.
24 ¶ And the woman bare a son, and called his
name Samson: and the child grew, and the LORD
blessed him.
25 And the Spirit of the LORD began to move him
at times in the camp of Dan between Zorah and
Eshtaol.

the womb. The Nazarite vow was taken by those who separated themselves for God's service (Num. 6). *begin to deliver Israel.* Samson's divine appointment from birth. It expresses hope but also foreboding in that he would only begin the deliverance. The Philistine nemesis remained long after Samson.
13:6 *countenance.* Appearance. *very terrible.* Extremely frightening. She recognized something supernatural about the angel, something so awesome that she was dumbfounded, asking no questions about His identity.
13:8 *intreated.* To plead or pray earnestly.
13:10 *shewed.* To report or tell.
13:12 *How shall we order the child, and how shall we do unto him.* "What will be the custom or mode of life of the child and his work?"
13:15 *made ready a kid.* A reference to slaying, dressing, and cooking a goat.
13:18 *secret?* That which is wonderful and incomprehensible. This was a revelation of the angel's deity.
13:19 *wondrously.* Did that which was miraculous, another evidence of His being supernatural.
13:21–22 *Manoah* made the correct deductions for the evidence, ascribing full deity to the angel. *We shall surely die.* They would not die because they saw God through His Son, the only way man can see God and live.

Thoughts for Personal/Family Worship: Chapter 13

1. **God planned to deliver His people from the Philistines before they cried out for help. When we are believers, this parallels also the order in our salvation. Before we were born or ever knew our need to be saved God had prepared the way for His Son to suffer and die for us. From all eternity Christ's redeeming work was laid out. Let us lift up our praises to the Lord in the same thankful submission as the apostle John, "We love him, because he first loved us" (1 John 4:19).**
2. **The Lord is not only omnipotent to deliver us from our enemies, He is also immanent to be with us in our struggles of life. At a moment of crisis, the preincarnate Christ appeared to give a message of hope and encouragement. Can we doubt our Emmanuel when He took our very nature to dwell among us? The Lord will not fail us for He has promised, "I will not leave you comfortless:**

THE ANGEL OF THE LORD

As the eternal Word and the express image of the invisible God, Jesus Christ is the usual way God speaks and appears to humanity. This is self-evident in the New Testament, but the Old Testament contains abundant witness of this truth as well. Throughout the Old Testament the Angel of the Lord is one way in which the eternal Son of God speaks and appears to men. The Son of God comes in human form as the Angel of the Lord prior to His coming in human flesh as Jesus Christ.

The term *angel of the Lord* appears more than fifty times in the Old Testament, and the similar phrase *angel of God* occurs nine times (cf. Judg. 6:20–21 and 13:3,9, where the phrases are used synonymously). While some of these references speak of ordinary angels (Gen. 28:12; 32:1), many refer to a special Angel. It is helpful to note that the Hebrew word translated "angel" is not limited in scope as is the English word—that is, it does not always refer strictly to a created spirit sent from heaven. The word often means simply "a messenger," as when Jesus Christ is called "the messenger of the covenant" who will come later into His temple (Mal. 3:1).

The Old Testament portrays this special Angel as *divine*—that is, He is the Lord—and yet *distinct*—that is, He is unique from the Lord. These two points concord with the understanding of the Trinity: one Lord in three distinct Persons. The Old Testament demonstrates these two truths about the Angel of the Lord in five ways:

1. *The Angel of the Lord claims divine authority*. He speaks as God and swears by Himself to fulfill His covenant (Gen. 16:10; 22:15–16).
2. *The Angel of the Lord exhibits divine attributes and performs divine actions*. He has knowledge that only God possesses (Gen. 16:7–8,11,13). He judges and redeems as God (Gen. 48:15–16; Judg. 5:23; 2 Sam. 24:14–17; 2 Kings 19:35).
3. *The Angel of the Lord receives divine worship*. He is treated as God Himself, receiving sacrifices and homage paid to His Person (Ex. 23:20–21; Judg. 6:20–21,24). No ordinary angel would accept man's worship (Rev. 19:10).
4. *The Angel of the Lord is identified explicitly as God*. He is distinctly said to be the Lord (Gen. 16:13; 22:12,15–18; 31:11–13; 48:15–16; Ex. 14:19; 23:21; Judg. 6:11–23; 13:19–22; cf. Isa. 42:8).
5. *The Angel of the Lord is a distinct divine Person*. He is evidently divine and yet carefully distinguished from the Lord (Gen. 24:7,40; 32:24–30; Ex. 3:4–5; 23:20; Num. 20:16; Josh. 5:14–15; Judg. 2:1; 6:11–24; 13:2–24; 2 Sam. 24:16; Isa. 63:9; Zech. 1:12–13).

Consequently, the Old Testament portrays this Angel as one of the Persons of the Godhead. The Angel of the Lord should be identified as the second Person of the Trinity because He is the sent One who appears bodily. He cannot be the Father, who is the Sender. He cannot be the Spirit, who has no form. Further, the divine Angel of the Lord no longer appeared after the Son of God came in flesh at His incarnation. New Testament writings reveal continuity between the activity of the Son of God as the Angel of the Lord and His work as the incarnate Jesus Christ. In both His form and His flesh, the Son of God performs a redemptive messianic work.

The presence of the Angel of the Lord in the Old Testament communicates two important truths. *First*, the appearances of the Angel of the Lord prepared the church for her Christ. The temporary form of the Angel aroused a deep love and longing within the people of God for the coming of Jesus Christ in the flesh. The church in the Old Testament searched earnestly for her Beloved to bound over the hills and dwell with her (Song 2:8). *Second*, the appearances of the Angel of the Lord prepared Christ for His church. His ministry in alleviating His people's misery throughout the Old Testament was a foretaste of His messianic mission. The Son of God's appearances can be seen as expressions of holy impatience for the erupting of His presence on earth, when He took up His threefold role as Prophet, Priest, and King of His people.

CHAPTER 14

AND Samson went down to Timnath, and saw
a woman in Timnath of the daughters of the
Philistines.
2 And he came up, and told his father and his
mother, and said, I have seen a woman in Timnath
of the daughters of the Philistines: now therefore
get her for me to wife.
3 Then his father and his mother said unto him,
Is there never a woman among the daughters
of thy brethren, or among all my people, that
thou goest to take a wife of the uncircumcised
Philistines? And Samson said unto his father, Get
her for me; for she pleaseth me well.
4 But his father and his mother knew not that
it *was* of the LORD, that he sought an occasion
against the Philistines: for at that time the Philis-
tines had dominion over Israel.
5 ¶ Then went Samson down, and his father and
his mother, to Timnath, and came to the vine-
yards of Timnath: and, behold, a young lion
roared against him.
6 And the Spirit of the LORD came mightily upon
him, and he rent him as he would have rent a kid,
and *he had* nothing in his hand: but he told not
his father or his mother what he had done.
7 And he went down, and talked with the woman;
and she pleased Samson well.
8 ¶ And after a time he returned to take her, and
he turned aside to see the carcase of the lion: and,
behold, *there was* a swarm of bees and honey in
the carcase of the lion.
9 And he took thereof in his hands, and went on
eating, and came to his father and mother, and he
gave them, and they did eat: but he told not them
that he had taken the honey out of the carcase of
the lion.
10 ¶ So his father went down unto the woman:
and Samson made there a feast; for so used the
young men to do.
11 And it came to pass, when they saw him, that
they brought thirty companions to be with him.
12 ¶ And Samson said unto them, I will now put
forth a riddle unto you: if ye can certainly declare
it me within the seven days of the feast, and find
it out, then I will give you thirty sheets and thirty
change of garments:
13 But if ye cannot declare *it* me, then shall ye give
me thirty sheets and thirty change of garments.
And they said unto him, Put forth thy riddle, that
we may hear it.
14 And he said unto them, Out of the eater came
forth meat, and out of the strong came forth
sweetness. And they could not in three days ex-
pound the riddle.
15 And it came to pass on the seventh day, that
they said unto Samson's wife, Entice thy husband,
that he may declare unto us the riddle, lest we
burn thee and thy father's house with fire: have ye
called us to take that we have? *is it* not *so*?
16 And Samson's wife wept before him, and said,
Thou dost but hate me, and lovest me not: thou
hast put forth a riddle unto the children of my
people, and hast not told *it* me. And he said unto
her, Behold, I have not told *it* my father nor my
mother, and shall I tell *it* thee?
17 And she wept before him the seven days,
while their feast lasted: and it came to pass on the
seventh day, that he told her, because she lay sore
upon him: and she told the riddle to the children
of her people.
18 And the men of the city said unto him on the
seventh day before the sun went down, What *is*
sweeter than honey? and what *is* stronger than a
lion? And he said unto them, If ye had not plowed
with my heifer, ye had not found out my riddle.

I will come to you" (John 14:18). The angel of the Lord who announced the birth of Samson is our Lord Jesus Christ, "the same yesterday, and to day, and for ever" (Heb. 13:8).

Chapter 14: *Samson's marriage to a Philistine leads to his first conflict with the Philistines.*

Samson's Wife Turns Traitor (14:1–20)

14:1–4 Samson seeks a wife from among the Philistines contrary to God's Word (Deut. 7:2–4).

14:3 *she pleaseth me well.* Literally, "right in my eyes" (v. 7). Samson followed the custom of the day (17:6; 21:25). Disregarding God's standards leads to no standards other than self.

14:4 *he sought an occasion.* The sovereign God uses, without condoning, the folly and sin of men to accomplish His purpose (Josh. 11:20; 2 Chron. 10:15; 22:7; 25:20; Ps. 115:3).

14:6 *the Spirit of the LORD came mightily upon him.* Even this constituted a component of Samson's kingdom work, so God empowered him for his work, literally, "rushing upon him" (v. 19). *rent a kid.* Tear in pieces a baby goat.

14:8 *to take her.* Refers to marriage.

14:9 To take and eat from the unclean violated his Nazarite vow (Num. 6:6–7). Seeing, taking, eating, and sharing with others parallels the pattern of the first sin recorded in Gen. 3.

14:12 *riddle.* Dark saying, enigma, or perplexing question (1 Kings 10:1). *sheets…garments.* Inner shirts and outer gowns (v. 13).

14:14 *meat.* Food or general nourishment.

14:15 *Entice.* Persuade, using whatever means. *to take that we have.* To impoverish.

14:17 *she lay sore upon him.* Literally, "she drove him into a corner."

14:18 *plowed with my heifer.* Idiomatic for consulting with my wife (Amos 4:1).

14:19 *spoil.* Refers to the equipment that is stripped from slain men, here their garments specifically. *expounded.* To declare or make known.

Thoughts for Personal/Family Worship: Chapter 14

1. **God's purpose cannot be frustrated regardless of the opposition of the enemy or even the folly of His servants. The Philistines were among Israel's most powerful enemies, but they would not ultimately prevail against**

19 ¶ And the Spirit of the LORD came upon him,
and he went down to Ashkelon, and slew thirty
men of them, and took their spoil, and gave
change of garments unto them which expounded
the riddle. And his anger was kindled, and he
went up to his father's house.
20 But Samson's wife was *given* to his companion,
whom he had used as his friend.

CHAPTER 15

BUT it came to pass within a while after, in the
time of wheat harvest, that Samson visited his
wife with a kid; and he said, I will go in to my wife
into the chamber. But her father would not suffer
him to go in.
2 And her father said, I verily thought that thou
hadst utterly hated her; therefore I gave her to thy
companion: *is* not her younger sister fairer than
she? take her, I pray thee, instead of her.
3 ¶ And Samson said concerning them, Now shall
I be more blameless than the Philistines, though I
do them a displeasure.
4 And Samson went and caught three hundred
foxes, and took firebrands, and turned tail to tail,
and put a firebrand in the midst between two tails.
5 And when he had set the brands on fire, he let
them go into the standing corn of the Philistines,
and burnt up both the shocks, and also the stand-
ing corn, with the vineyards *and* olives.
6 ¶ Then the Philistines said, Who hath done
this? And they answered, Samson, the son in law
of the Timnite, because he had taken his wife, and
given her to his companion. And the Philistines
came up, and burnt her and her father with fire.
7 ¶ And Samson said unto them, Though ye have
done this, yet will I be avenged of you, and after
that I will cease.
8 And he smote them hip and thigh with a great
slaughter: and he went down and dwelt in the top
of the rock Etam.
9 ¶ Then the Philistines went up, and pitched in
Judah, and spread themselves in Lehi.
10 And the men of Judah said, Why are ye come
up against us? And they answered, To bind
Samson are we come up, to do to him as he hath
done to us.
11 Then three thousand men of Judah went to
the top of the rock Etam, and said to Samson,
Knowest thou not that the Philistines *are* rulers
over us? what *is* this *that* thou hast done unto us?
And he said unto them, As they did unto me, so
have I done unto them.
12 And they said unto him, We are come down
to bind thee, that we may deliver thee into the
hand of the Philistines. And Samson said unto
them, Swear unto me, that ye will not fall upon
me yourselves.
13 And they spake unto him, saying, No; but we
will bind thee fast, and deliver thee into their
hand: but surely we will not kill thee. And they
bound him with two new cords, and brought him
up from the rock.
14 ¶ *And* when he came unto Lehi, the Philistines
shouted against him: and the Spirit of the LORD
came mightily upon him, and the cords that *were*
upon his arms became as flax that was burnt with
fire, and his bands loosed from off his hands.

God's kingdom. Although Samson violated God's law and was not a clean vessel to be used, God nonetheless used him and manipulated circumstances in such a way that Samson would begin a deliverance from the Philistines that ultimately climaxed with David. We can rest knowing that God brings good out of evil and even though there appears to be no deliverer, everything is on track for David's greater Son to achieve the ultimate and final victory.

2. **Whereas Samson was the strongest of men physically, in the face of temptation he was the weakest of men. No matter how strong we think we are, we must all beware lest we fall through the lust of the flesh. Entrust the care of your soul to the Lord only, for the arm of flesh will fail you. In what areas of your life do you especially need to watch and pray against temptation?**

Chapter 15: *Samson retaliates against the Philistines for wrongs done against him.*

Samson Retaliates against the Philistines (15:1–20)

15:1 *a kid.* He took a young goat, probably to continue the wedding festival that had been interrupted. *not suffer.* Not permit to enter.
15:2 *verily thought.* Or, "certainly said." *fairer than she.* Better.
15:3 Although doing the work of the Lord and claiming innocence (*blameless*), Samson's motive is personal revenge. *displeasure.* The Hebrew word usually translated "evil" referring to a calamity or disaster.
15:4–5 Samson burned the fields of the Philistines, who retaliated with a burning of their own. *firebrands . . . brands.* Torches with open flame. *standing corn.* Grain still growing on the stalk. *shocks.* Stacks of harvested sheaves. Being fully ripe the fields were in their most flammable condition.
15:6 *burnt her and her father.* It is unclear whether the reference is to them personally or their property. Ironically, it is what she tried to avoid in betraying Samson (14:15).
15:7 *after that I will cease.* The idea is that he will not cease until the vengeance is complete.
15:8 *hip and thigh.* An idiom or figure of speech signifying to defeat utterly.
15:9–14 The Philistines in turn seek vengeance on Samson.
15:9 *Lehi.* Means "jawbone." Here the city is so named anachronistically reflecting its name received after Samson's slaughter (v. 17).
15:10 *to do to him.* Reflects the back and forth between the Philistines and Samson. Were it not so tragic, it is almost childlike behavior.
15:12–13 Judah, unaware that Samson was their divinely chosen deliverer, bound him and delivered him to the enemy.
15:14 *Spirit of the LORD.* See comments at 14:6. *flax.* Used for making linen and the least fire would turn it to ash. *loosed*

15 And he found a new jawbone of an ass, and put
forth his hand, and took it, and slew a thousand
men therewith.
16 And Samson said, With the jawbone of an ass,
heaps upon heaps, with the jaw of an ass have I
slain a thousand men.
17 And it came to pass, when he had made an end
of speaking, that he cast away the jawbone out of
his hand, and called that place Ramath-lehi.
18 ¶ And he was sore athirst, and called on the
LORD, and said, Thou hast given this great deliverance
into the hand of thy servant: and now
shall I die for thirst, and fall into the hand of the
uncircumcised?
19 But God clave an hollow place that *was* in the
jaw, and there came water thereout; and when he
had drunk, his spirit came again, and he revived:
wherefore he called the name thereof En-hakkore,
which *is* in Lehi unto this day.
20 And he judged Israel in the days of the
Philistines twenty years.

CHAPTER 16

THEN went Samson to Gaza, and saw there an
harlot, and went in unto her.
2 *And it was told* the Gazites, saying, Samson is
come hither. And they compassed *him* in, and laid
wait for him all night in the gate of the city, and
were quiet all the night, saying, In the morning,
when it is day, we shall kill him.
3 And Samson lay till midnight, and arose at midnight,
and took the doors of the gate of the city, and
the two posts, and went away with them, bar and
all, and put *them* upon his shoulders, and carried
them up to the top of an hill that *is* before Hebron.
4 ¶ And it came to pass afterward, that he loved
a woman in the valley of Sorek, whose name *was*
Delilah.
5 And the lords of the Philistines came up unto
her, and said unto her, Entice him, and see wherein
his great strength *lieth*, and by what *means* we
may prevail against him, that we may bind him to
afflict him: and we will give thee every one of us
eleven hundred *pieces* of silver.
6 ¶ And Delilah said to Samson, Tell me, I pray
thee, wherein thy great strength *lieth*, and wherewith
thou mightest be bound to afflict thee.
7 And Samson said unto her, If they bind me
with seven green withs that were never dried, then
shall I be weak, and be as another man.
8 Then the lords of the Philistines brought up to
her seven green withs which had not been dried,
and she bound him with them.
9 Now *there were* men lying in wait, abiding with
her in the chamber. And she said unto him, The
Philistines *be* upon thee, Samson. And he brake
the withs, as a thread of tow is broken when it
toucheth the fire. So his strength was not known.
10 And Delilah said unto Samson, Behold, thou
hast mocked me, and told me lies: now tell me,
I pray thee, wherewith thou mightest be bound.
11 And he said unto her, If they bind me fast with
new ropes that never were occupied, then shall I
be weak, and be as another man.
12 Delilah therefore took new ropes, and bound

---

from off his hands. Bonds fell from him.
15:15 *a new jawbone of an ass.* A cheekbone of a donkey that was fresh and moist.
15:17 *Ramath-lehi.* Literally, "the casting away of the jawbone," the full name of the city that was shortened to "Lehi."
15:18 *sore athirst.* Extremely thirsty. *the uncircumcised.* A common designation for the heathen who were not in covenant with God. His fear of death after victory parallels the experience of Elijah after his victory on Carmel (1 Kings 19:1–3).
15:19 *God clave an hollow place.* God made a hole resembling what would remain after the extraction of a tooth. *in the jaw.* Not the donkey jaw but Lehi, the placed named "Jaw" to commemorate the event. *his spirit came again.* His vitality returned. *En-hakkore* means "fountain of the praying one."

Thoughts for Personal/Family Worship: Chapter 15

1. **Israel binding Samson and handing him over to the Philistines parallels the betrayal of the Lord Jesus by the Jews when they handed Him over to the Romans. God sent His Son to be their Savior but they cried out, "Away with him, crucify him" (John 19:15). Sin is so severe that man cannot recognize the Savior without divine aid. We learn that God is the author of salvation, not man. He first loved us and sent His Son to save us. Only when we are brought to behold the glory and saving power of Christ are we made to comprehend the love of God for our souls (Rom. 5:8). Do you believe that apart from God's grace you would hand over Christ to death? Why?**
2. **Samson, the weakest of men in temptation, became the strongest of men when "the Spirit of the LORD came mightily upon him" (v. 14). Being a God-appointed judge or deliverer of Israel, he was given the power to fulfill his work. Every servant of God needs the Spirit of the Lord for power in God's service. Remember to pray for the power of God to fall on your minister to do his work. Remember those on the mission field who are facing the forces of evil and the enemies of the Lord every day. Pray for God's power to come upon them.**

Chapter 16: *Samson reveals the source of his strength to Delilah who betrays him to the Philistines and after recovering his strength executes his final act of vengeance.*

Samson Is Bound and Blinded, Then Dies with the Philistines (16:1–31)

16:2 *compassed.* Surrounded.
16:3 *bar and all.* The crossbar, referring to the lock system.
16:4 *in the valley.* Rather a stream or small river.
16:5 *afflict him.* To humble or overpower (v. 6).
16:7 *green withs.* Moist cords; being undried gave them more strength (vv. 8–9). *as another man.* As one man (v. 11).
16:9 *as a thread of tow.* A single strand made of flax, with little resistance to fire.
16:11 *that never were occupied.* With which work was not done.

him therewith, and said unto him, The Philistines *be* upon thee, Samson. And *there were* liers in wait abiding in the chamber. And he brake them from off his arms like a thread.

13 And Delilah said unto Samson, Hitherto thou hast mocked me, and told me lies: tell me wherewith thou mightest be bound. And he said unto her, If thou weavest the seven locks of my head with the web.

14 And she fastened *it* with the pin, and said unto him, The Philistines *be* upon thee, Samson. And he awaked out of his sleep, and went away with the pin of the beam, and with the web.

15 ¶ And she said unto him, How canst thou say, I love thee, when thine heart *is* not with me? thou hast mocked me these three times, and hast not told me wherein thy great strength *lieth*.

16 And it came to pass, when she pressed him daily with her words, and urged him, *so* that his soul was vexed unto death;

17 That he told her all his heart, and said unto her, There hath not come a razor upon mine head; for I *have been* a Nazarite unto God from my mother's womb: if I be shaven, then my strength will go from me, and I shall become weak, and be like any *other* man.

18 And when Delilah saw that he had told her all his heart, she sent and called for the lords of the Philistines, saying, Come up this once, for he hath shewed me all his heart. Then the lords of the Philistines came up unto her, and brought money in their hand.

19 And she made him sleep upon her knees; and she called for a man, and she caused him to shave off the seven locks of his head; and she began to afflict him, and his strength went from him.

20 And she said, The Philistines *be* upon thee, Samson. And he awoke out of his sleep, and said, I will go out as at other times before, and shake myself. And he wist not that the LORD was departed from him.

21 ¶ But the Philistines took him, and put out his eyes, and brought him down to Gaza, and bound him with fetters of brass; and he did grind in the prison house.

22 Howbeit the hair of his head began to grow again after he was shaven.

23 Then the lords of the Philistines gathered them together for to offer a great sacrifice unto Dagon their god, and to rejoice: for they said, Our god hath delivered Samson our enemy into our hand.

24 And when the people saw him, they praised their god: for they said, Our god hath delivered into our hands our enemy, and the destroyer of our country, which slew many of us.

25 And it came to pass, when their hearts were merry, that they said, Call for Samson, that he may make us sport. And they called for Samson out of the prison house; and he made them sport: and they set him between the pillars.

26 And Samson said unto the lad that held him by the hand, Suffer me that I may feel the pillars whereupon the house standeth, that I may lean upon them.

27 Now the house was full of men and women; and all the lords of the Philistines *were* there; and *there were* upon the roof about three thousand men and women, that beheld while Samson made sport.

28 And Samson called unto the LORD, and said, O Lord GOD, remember me, I pray thee, and strengthen me, I pray thee, only this once, O God, that I may be at once avenged of the Philistines for my two eyes.

29 And Samson took hold of the two middle pillars upon which the house stood, and on which it was borne up, of the one with his right hand, and of the other with his left.

30 And Samson said, Let me die with the Philistines. And he bowed himself with *all his* might; and the house fell upon the lords, and upon all

16:13 *seven locks.* Refers to his whole head of hair (v. 19). *the web.* Perhaps refers to a tool used for weaving.
16:14 *the pin of the beam.* The frame of a weaving loom.
16:16 *vexed unto death.* An idiom referring to impatience and annoyance.
16:20 *And he wist not.* He did not know.
16:21 *put out his eyes.* Gouge or bore out. *fetters of brass.* Shackles or metal bands.
16:23 *Dagon their god.* Their patron god, referring either to a fish god or grain god.
16:25 *and he made them sport.* They laughed in his face.
16:26 *Suffer me.* Allow me.
16:27 *made sport.* To amuse or serve as a joker.
16:30 *upon the lords.* With one great calamity the Philistines were left leaderless.

Thoughts for Personal/Family Worship: Chapter 16

1. Contrary to expectation, Hebrews names Samson among those "who through faith subdued kingdoms" (Heb. 11:32–33). There was apparently more to Samson's ministry than is recorded in the book of Judges. He judged Israel for twenty years (Judg. 16:31); yet the narrative isolates just a few incidents in his career, none of which were high-water marks of spirituality or which covered significant periods of time. In those low points, he achieved great things for the cause of God's kingdom in the power of God's Spirit but without much faithfulness. But the Holy Spirit records that he subdued kingdoms through faith. None of God's servants are perfect, and all are prone to failure. But Hebrews would suggest that between those low points Samson was not always doing that which was right in his own eyes. Judges does not put him in a great light, but the last word about him marks his faith. Better is the end of a matter.

2. Certainly not by virtue of his person but by virtue of his office, Samson (like all the judges) pointed to Christ,

the people that *were* therein. So the dead which
he slew at his death were more than *they* which he
slew in his life.
31 Then his brethren and all the house of his
father came down, and took him, and brought
him up, and buried him between Zorah and
Eshtaol in the buryingplace of Manoah his father.
And he judged Israel twenty years.

CHAPTER 17

AND there was a man of mount Ephraim, whose
name *was* Micah.
2 And he said unto his mother, The eleven
hundred *shekels* of silver that were taken from
thee, about which thou cursedst, and spakest of
also in mine ears, behold, the silver *is* with me; I
took it. And his mother said, Blessed *be thou* of
the LORD, my son.
3 And when he had restored the eleven hundred
shekels of silver to his mother, his mother said, I
had wholly dedicated the silver unto the LORD
from my hand for my son, to make a graven
image and a molten image: now therefore I will
restore it unto thee.
4 Yet he restored the money unto his mother; and
his mother took two hundred *shekels* of silver, and
gave them to the founder, who made thereof a
graven image and a molten image: and they were
in the house of Micah.
5 And the man Micah had an house of gods, and
made an ephod, and teraphim, and consecrated
one of his sons, who became his priest.
6 In those days *there was* no king in Israel, *but* ev-
ery man did *that which was* right in his own eyes.
7 ¶ And there was a young man out of Beth-
lehem-judah of the family of Judah, who *was* a
Levite, and he sojourned there.
8 And the man departed out of the city from
Beth-lehem-judah to sojourn where he could find
a place: and he came to mount Ephraim to the
house of Micah, as he journeyed.
9 And Micah said unto him, Whence comest
thou? And he said unto him, I *am* a Levite of
Beth-lehem-judah, and I go to sojourn where I
may find *a place*.
10 And Micah said unto him, Dwell with me, and
be unto me a father and a priest, and I will give
thee ten *shekels* of silver by the year, and a suit of
apparel, and thy victuals. So the Levite went in.
11 And the Levite was content to dwell with the
man; and the young man was unto him as one
of his sons.
12 And Micah consecrated the Levite; and the
young man became his priest, and was in the
house of Micah.
13 Then said Micah, Now know I that the LORD
will do me good, seeing I have a Levite to *my* priest.

CHAPTER 18

IN those days *there was* no king in Israel: and in
those days the tribe of the Danites sought them
an inheritance to dwell in; for unto that day *all*

---

the ultimate Savior. There are lines in Samson's life that parallel the life of Christ. Like our Lord, Samson was a specially announced son; and like our Lord, he was despised by his own people as a deliverer in Israel. As Samson brought down the house of Dagon, destroying Israel's enemies, so our Lord Jesus conquered all His and our enemies at the cross. While we see a mixture of failure and hope in Samson's life we see only perfection in our Lord Jesus. Let us go to Him with confidence that He is an all-sufficient Savior.

ISRAEL'S TRAGIC DAYS WITH NO KING, NO LAW, AND NO SHAME (17:1—21:25)

Chapter 17: *Micah restores stolen silver to his mother and hires a Levite to be his family priest.*

Micah Rejoices in His Silver Image and Hired Priest (17:1–13)

17:1 *there was a man.* Judges shifts attention to specific instances to highlight how the nation's sin permeated the entire society.

17:3 *I had wholly dedicated.* Previously set apart unto the Lord. *to make a graven image.* A carved image. *molten image.* Made by pouring liquid metal over a mold (v. 4).

17:4 *founder.* One who molds metal.

17:5 *ephod.* An apron or embroidered cape worn by a priest. *teraphim.* Images. *consecrated.* Filled the hand or the payment of wages.

17:7 *sojourned.* To take up residence as an alien.

17:10 *a father and a priest.* The role of advisor and intercessor. *a suit of apparel, and thy victuals.* A supply of clothing and food.

17:12 *consecrated the Levite.* Literally, he "filled the hand of the Levite," meaning he contracted the position with material rewards.

Thoughts for Personal/Family Worship: Chapter 17

1. **The second commandment is absolute: "Thou shalt not make unto thee any graven image, or any likeness of any thing that is in heaven above, or that is in the earth beneath, or that is in the water under the earth: thou shalt not bow down thyself to them, nor serve them" (Ex. 20:4–5). Breaking this commandment leads to the greatest of perversions. Any sort of idolatry is an abomination to the Lord. Our God is a jealous God who will not share His glory with another. What are the popular forms of idolatry in your culture?**
2. **The Levite was a religious mercenary who abandoned the God-given ministry that was his heritage to serve man-made gods for personal gain. Micah was so blinded by his idolatry that he presumed that his hireling was evidence of God's favor. Herein is a danger. Too many charlatan preachers have controlled and convinced people that adhering to them and their teaching will bring them divine blessing. It is imperative to worship God in spirit and truth and to test the legitimacy of any minister in the clear light of God's Word. Everything in this chapter is a violation of God's law.**

their inheritance had not fallen unto them among
the tribes of Israel.
2 And the children of Dan sent of their family
five men from their coasts, men of valour, from
Zorah, and from Eshtaol, to spy out the land, and
to search it; and they said unto them, Go, search
the land: who when they came to mount Ephraim,
to the house of Micah, they lodged there.
3 When they *were* by the house of Micah, they
knew the voice of the young man the Levite: and
they turned in thither, and said unto him, Who
brought thee hither? and what makest thou in this
place? and what hast thou here?
4 And he said unto them, Thus and thus dealeth
Micah with me, and hath hired me, and I am his
priest.
5 And they said unto him, Ask counsel, we pray
thee, of God, that we may know whether our way
which we go shall be prosperous.
6 And the priest said unto them, Go in peace:
before the LORD *is* your way wherein ye go.
7 ¶ Then the five men departed, and came to
Laish, and saw the people that *were* therein,
how they dwelt careless, after the manner of the
Zidonians, quiet and secure; and *there was* no
magistrate in the land, that might put *them* to
shame in *any* thing; and they *were* far from the
Zidonians, and had no business with *any* man.
8 And they came unto their brethren to Zorah
and Eshtaol: and their brethren said unto them,
What *say* ye?
9 And they said, Arise, that we may go up against
them: for we have seen the land, and, behold, it *is*
very good: and *are* ye still? be not slothful to go,
and to enter to possess the land.
10 When ye go, ye shall come unto a people
secure, and to a large land: for God hath given it
into your hands; a place where *there is* no want of
any thing that *is* in the earth.
11 ¶ And there went from thence of the family of
the Danites, out of Zorah and out of Eshtaol, six
hundred men appointed with weapons of war.
12 And they went up, and pitched in Kirjath-
jearim, in Judah: wherefore they called that place
Mahaneh-dan unto this day: behold, *it is* behind
Kirjath-jearim.
13 And they passed thence unto mount Ephraim,
and came unto the house of Micah.
14 ¶ Then answered the five men that went to
spy out the country of Laish, and said unto their
brethren, Do ye know that there is in these houses
an ephod, and teraphim, and a graven image, and
a molten image? now therefore consider what ye
have to do.
15 And they turned thitherward, and came to the
house of the young man the Levite, *even* unto the
house of Micah, and saluted him.
16 And the six hundred men appointed with
their weapons of war, which *were* of the children
of Dan, stood by the entering of the gate.
17 And the five men that went to spy out the land
went up, *and* came in thither, *and* took the graven
image, and the ephod, and the teraphim, and the
molten image: and the priest stood in the enter-
ing of the gate with the six hundred men *that were*
appointed with weapons of war.
18 And these went into Micah's house, and
fetched the carved image, the ephod, and the tera-
phim, and the molten image. Then said the priest
unto them, What do ye?
19 And they said unto him, Hold thy peace, lay
thine hand upon thy mouth, and go with us, and
be to us a father and a priest: *is it* better for thee
to be a priest unto the house of one man, or that
thou be a priest unto a tribe and a family in Israel?
20 And the priest's heart was glad, and he took
the ephod, and the teraphim, and the graven
image, and went in the midst of the people.
21 So they turned and departed, and put the little
ones and the cattle and the carriage before them.
22 ¶ *And* when they were a good way from the
house of Micah, the men that *were* in the houses
near to Micah's house were gathered together, and
overtook the children of Dan.
23 And they cried unto the children of Dan. And
they turned their faces, and said unto Micah, What
aileth thee, that thou comest with such a company?
24 And he said, Ye have taken away my gods
which I made, and the priest, and ye are gone
away: and what have I more? and what *is* this *that*
ye say unto me, What aileth thee?
25 And the children of Dan said unto him, Let
not thy voice be heard among us, lest angry
fellows run upon thee, and thou lose thy life, with
the lives of thy household.
26 And the children of Dan went their way: and
when Micah saw that they *were* too strong for
him, he turned and went back unto his house.

Chapter 18: *The Danites establish the city of Dan and make it a center of idolatry.*

Dan Becomes a Center of False Worship (18:1–31)

18:1 *inheritance.* Lot or portion.
18:2 *men of valour.* Refers to their strength or courage.
18:6 *before the LORD is your way.* You will have God's favor.
18:7 *dwelt careless.* The Hebrew refers to dwelling securely. *after the manner of the Zidonians.* The Sidonians did not build fortifications. *no magistrate.* An absence of any oppressor.
18:11 *appointed with.* Girded with (vv. 16–17).
18:12 *Mahaneh-dan.* Camp of Dan.
18:14 *ephod.* Embroidered cape or apron worn by priests. *teraphim.* Images, using household gods (vv. 17–18,20).
18:15 *saluted him.* Asked of his welfare.
18:21 *carriage.* Baggage—including the idols from Micah's house collection.
18:23 *What aileth thee.* What troubles you.

27 And they took *the things* which Micah had
made, and the priest which he had, and came
unto Laish, unto a people *that were* at quiet and
secure: and they smote them with the edge of the
sword, and burnt the city with fire.
28 And *there was* no deliverer, because it *was* far
from Zidon, and they had no business with *any*
man; and it was in the valley that *lieth* by Beth-
rehob. And they built a city, and dwelt therein.
29 And they called the name of the city Dan, after
the name of Dan their father, who was born unto
Israel: howbeit the name of the city *was* Laish at
the first.
30 ¶ And the children of Dan set up the graven im-
age: and Jonathan, the son of Gershom, the son of
Manasseh, he and his sons were priests to the tribe
of Dan until the day of the captivity of the land.
31 And they set them up Micah's graven image,
which he made, all the time that the house of God
was in Shiloh.

CHAPTER 19

AND it came to pass in those days, when *there was*
no king in Israel, that there was a certain Levite so-
journing on the side of mount Ephraim, who took
to him a concubine out of Beth-lehem-judah.
2 And his concubine played the whore against
him, and went away from him unto her father's
house to Beth-lehem-judah, and was there four
whole months.
3 And her husband arose, and went after her, to
speak friendly unto her, *and* to bring her again,
having his servant with him, and a couple of asses:
and she brought him into her father's house:
and when the father of the damsel saw him, he
rejoiced to meet him.
4 And his father in law, the damsel's father,
retained him; and he abode with him three days:
so they did eat and drink, and lodged there.
5 ¶ And it came to pass on the fourth day, when
they arose early in the morning, that he rose up
to depart: and the damsel's father said unto his
son in law, Comfort thine heart with a morsel of
bread, and afterward go your way.
6 And they sat down, and did eat and drink both
of them together: for the damsel's father had said
unto the man, Be content, I pray thee, and tarry
all night, and let thine heart be merry.
7 And when the man rose up to depart, his father
in law urged him: therefore he lodged there again.
8 And he arose early in the morning on the
fifth day to depart: and the damsel's father said,
Comfort thine heart, I pray thee. And they tarried
until afternoon, and they did eat both of them.
9 And when the man rose up to depart, he, and
his concubine, and his servant, his father in law,
the damsel's father, said unto him, Behold, now
the day draweth toward evening, I pray you tarry
all night: behold, the day groweth to an end,
lodge here, that thine heart may be merry; and
to morrow get you early on your way, that thou
mayest go home.
10 But the man would not tarry that night, but he
rose up and departed, and came over against Jebus,
which *is* Jerusalem; and *there were* with him two
asses saddled, his concubine also *was* with him.
11 *And* when they *were* by Jebus, the day was
far spent; and the servant said unto his master,
Come, I pray thee, and let us turn in into this city
of the Jebusites, and lodge in it.
12 And his master said unto him, We will not
turn aside hither into the city of a stranger, that
is not of the children of Israel; we will pass over
to Gibeah.
13 And he said unto his servant, Come, and let us
draw near to one of these places to lodge all night,
in Gibeah, or in Ramah.

18:30 *Manasseh.* Probably rather a reference to Moses. This reflects an ancient Jewish tradition where they added the letter "n" above the line to preserve Moses' reputation by altering the name to Manasseh.
18:31 *all the time that the house of God was in Shiloh.* The tabernacle remained in Shiloh until the days of Samuel. Dan became a competing center of worship.

Thoughts for Personal/Family Worship: Chapter 18

1. **The Levite again shows himself to be a religious mercenary for hire to the highest bidder. He had no convictions or concerns apart from himself. It will be terror on judgment day for false prophets who enrich themselves on religion. True worship and true Christian service demand loyalty to God and His Word. We must be willing to pay the price of faithful discipleship that we may receive the "well done, good and faithful servant" (Matt. 25:23).**
2. **Micah thought the presence of his idols in his shrine would be his safety (17:13). But there is no security in apostate religion, and his gods were easily stolen by others. The Lord alone is the protector of His people. The Christian who trusts in the Lord Jesus as Savior has found a true refuge. "For this God is our God for ever and ever: he will be our guide even unto death" (Ps. 48:14). In what ways do you tend to trust in idols instead of the Lord?**

Chapter 19: ***A Levite is reunited to his wayward concubine only to have her brutalized to death by vile men in Gibeah, after which he distributes her dismembered body throughout Israel.***

The Benjamites Stoop to Sodomy (19:1–30)

19:1 *concubine.* A secondary wife of lower social standing.
19:2 *played the whore.* The Hebrew word means "feeling repugnance toward" or "having a dislike of."
19:3 *damsel.* A young woman.
19:5 *Comfort.* Strengthen.
19:12 *stranger.* Foreigner. *Gibeah.* A town three miles north of Jerusalem.
19:13 *Ramah.* A town about six miles north of Jerusalem.

14 And they passed on and went their way; and
the sun went down upon them *when they were* by
Gibeah, which *belongeth* to Benjamin.
15 And they turned aside thither, to go in *and* to
lodge in Gibeah: and when he went in, he sat him
down in a street of the city: for *there was* no man
that took them into his house to lodging.
16 ¶ And, behold, there came an old man from
his work out of the field at even, which *was* also of
mount Ephraim; and he sojourned in Gibeah: but
the men of the place *were* Benjamites.
17 And when he had lifted up his eyes, he saw a
wayfaring man in the street of the city: and the
old man said, Whither goest thou? and whence
comest thou?
18 And he said unto him, We *are* passing from
Beth-lehem-judah toward the side of mount
Ephraim; from thence *am* I: and I went to Beth-
lehem-judah, but I *am now* going to the house of
the LORD; and there *is* no man that receiveth me
to house.
19 Yet there is both straw and provender for our
asses; and there is bread and wine also for me, and
for thy handmaid, and for the young man *which
is* with thy servants: *there is* no want of any thing.
20 And the old man said, Peace *be* with thee;
howsoever *let* all thy wants *lie* upon me; only
lodge not in the street.
21 So he brought him into his house, and gave
provender unto the asses: and they washed their
feet, and did eat and drink.
22 ¶ *Now* as they were making their hearts merry,
behold, the men of the city, certain sons of Belial,
beset the house round about, *and* beat at the door,
and spake to the master of the house, the old man,
saying, Bring forth the man that came into thine
house, that we may know him.
23 And the man, the master of the house, went
out unto them, and said unto them, Nay, my
brethren, *nay*, I pray you, do not *so* wickedly; see-
ing that this man is come into mine house, do not
this folly.
24 Behold, *here is* my daughter a maiden, and
his concubine; them I will bring out now, and
humble ye them, and do with them what seemeth
good unto you: but unto this man do not so vile
a thing.
25 But the men would not hearken to him: so the
man took his concubine, and brought her forth
unto them; and they knew her, and abused her
all the night until the morning: and when the day
began to spring, they let her go.
26 Then came the woman in the dawning of the
day, and fell down at the door of the man's house
where her lord *was*, till it was light.
27 And her lord rose up in the morning, and
opened the doors of the house, and went out to go
his way: and, behold, the woman his concubine
was fallen down *at* the door of the house, and her
hands *were* upon the threshold.
28 And he said unto her, Up, and let us be going.
But none answered. Then the man took her *up*
upon an ass, and the man rose up, and gat him
unto his place.
29 ¶ And when he was come into his house, he
took a knife, and laid hold on his concubine, and
divided her, *together* with her bones, into twelve
pieces, and sent her into all the coasts of Israel.
30 And it was so, that all that saw it said, There
was no such deed done nor seen from the day that
the children of Israel came up out of the land of
Egypt unto this day: consider of it, take advice,
and speak *your minds*.

CHAPTER 20

THEN all the children of Israel went out, and the
congregation was gathered together as one man,
from Dan even to Beer-sheba, with the land of
Gilead, unto the LORD in Mizpeh.

19:16 *sojourned.* Resident alien.
19:17 *wayfaring man.* Traveling man.
19:19 *provender.* Fodder (v. 21).
19:20 *let all thy wants lie upon me.* The old man assumed the full responsibility of a host to provide and protect. This explains his actions in vv. 23–24.
19:22. *Sons of Belial.* Men of wickedness, who are worthless. *beset . . . round about.* Surrounded. *that we may know him.* To have illegitimate sexual relations with him.
19:24 *and humble ye them.* To force and defile.
19:25 *hearken.* Listen. *to spring.* To dawn.
19:27 *lord.* Ruler or master.
19:28 *gat him unto his place.* He went to his place.

Thoughts for Personal/Family Worship: Chapter 19

1. **This chapter describes the tragedy of how far sin will go when there is no thought of God. Although there was no king in Israel (v. 1), there was a God in heaven who observed all the perverse behavior and would in due course punish accordingly. The chapter's closing admonition to consider and make plans to avoid the same tragedy remains valid. We should tremble for any people who are given over to practice vile sins. Judgment is not far away from those who stoop to these practices and we must remember that on the eternal day there awaits "the lake which burneth with fire and brimstone" (Rev. 21:8) for the unbelieving and the abominable in God's sight. These are warnings for us to flee from all forms of sin.**
2. **The master-secondary wife relationship between the Levite and his concubine is contrary to God's design for marriage. The whole episode betrays an unscriptural union and portrays a denigrating view of women. We should be thankful for the Christian gospel that has lifted societies out of such depths. Christianity has restored a nobility to manhood and womanhood, for in the power of the gospel "there is neither male nor female: for ye are all one in Christ Jesus" (Gal. 3:28). Let**

2 And the chief of all the people, *even* of all the tribes of Israel, presented themselves in the assembly of the people of God, four hundred thousand footmen that drew sword.
3 (Now the children of Benjamin heard that the children of Israel were gone up to Mizpeh.) Then said the children of Israel, Tell *us*, how was this wickedness?
4 And the Levite, the husband of the woman that was slain, answered and said, I came into Gibeah that *belongeth* to Benjamin, I and my concubine, to lodge.
5 And the men of Gibeah rose against me, and beset the house round about upon me by night, *and* thought to have slain me: and my concubine have they forced, that she is dead.
6 And I took my concubine, and cut her in pieces, and sent her throughout all the country of the inheritance of Israel: for they have committed lewdness and folly in Israel.
7 Behold, ye *are* all children of Israel; give here your advice and counsel.
8 ¶ And all the people arose as one man, saying, We will not any *of us* go to his tent, neither will we any *of us* turn into his house.
9 But now this *shall be* the thing which we will do to Gibeah; *we will go up* by lot against it;
10 And we will take ten men of an hundred throughout all the tribes of Israel, and an hundred of a thousand, and a thousand out of ten thousand, to fetch victual for the people, that they may do, when they come to Gibeah of Benjamin, according to all the folly that they have wrought in Israel.
11 So all the men of Israel were gathered against the city, knit together as one man.
12 ¶ And the tribes of Israel sent men through all the tribe of Benjamin, saying, What wickedness *is* this that is done among you?
13 Now therefore deliver *us* the men, the children of Belial, which *are* in Gibeah, that we may put them to death, and put away evil from Israel. But the children of Benjamin would not hearken to the voice of their brethren the children of Israel:
14 But the children of Benjamin gathered themselves together out of the cities unto Gibeah, to go out to battle against the children of Israel.
15 And the children of Benjamin were numbered at that time out of the cities twenty and six thousand men that drew sword, beside the inhabitants of Gibeah, which were numbered seven hundred chosen men.
16 Among all this people *there were* seven hundred chosen men lefthanded; every one could sling stones at an hair *breadth*, and not miss.
17 And the men of Israel, beside Benjamin, were numbered four hundred thousand men that drew sword: all these *were* men of war.
18 ¶ And the children of Israel arose, and went up to the house of God, and asked counsel of God, and said, Which of us shall go up first to the battle against the children of Benjamin? And the LORD said, Judah *shall go up* first.
19 And the children of Israel rose up in the morning, and encamped against Gibeah.
20 And the men of Israel went out to battle against Benjamin; and the men of Israel put themselves in array to fight against them at Gibeah.
21 And the children of Benjamin came forth out of Gibeah, and destroyed down to the ground of the Israelites that day twenty and two thousand men.
22 And the people the men of Israel encouraged themselves, and set their battle again in array in the place where they put themselves in array the first day.
23 (And the children of Israel went up and wept before the LORD until even, and asked counsel of the LORD, saying, Shall I go up again to battle against the children of Benjamin my brother? And the LORD said, Go up against him.)
24 And the children of Israel came near against the children of Benjamin the second day.
25 And Benjamin went forth against them out of Gibeah the second day, and destroyed down to the ground of the children of Israel again eighteen thousand men; all these drew the sword.
26 ¶ Then all the children of Israel, and all the people, went up, and came unto the house of God, and wept, and sat there before the LORD, and

---

us thank the Lord for the new minds, new hearts, and new lives the gospel has given to us and let us pray for gospel power to evangelize the nations that are headed for terrible judgment.

Chapter 20: *The tribes of Israel go to war against Benjamin because of the sins of Gibeah.*

Benjamin Is Nearly Exterminated (20:1–48)

20:1 *from Dan even to Beer-sheba. Dan* was the most northerly city in Israel; *Beer-sheba* was furthest to the south. This was a way of referring to the whole country.

20:5 *beset the house round about.* surrounded the house. *they forced.* They did violence against her.

20:6 *lewdness.* Refers to infamous, shameful, wicked behavior.

20:9 *by lot.* The use of a small stone by which decisions were made.

20:10 *to fetch victual.* To bring back supplies of food.

20:16 *not miss.* Often translated "to sin" and thus illustrates the definition of sin as "missing the mark."

20:18 *asked counsel of God.* Requested earnestly (vv. 23,27).

20:20 *put themselves in array to fight.* Put themselves in battle formation (v. 22).

20:21 *destroyed down to the ground.* To cut down and leave dead on the ground (v. 25).

20:29 *liers in wait.* To set an ambush.

fasted that day until even, and offered burnt offerings and peace offerings before the LORD.
27 And the children of Israel enquired of the
LORD, (for the ark of the covenant of God *was*
there in those days,
28 And Phinehas, the son of Eleazar, the son of
Aaron, stood before it in those days,) saying, Shall
I yet again go out to battle against the children
of Benjamin my brother, or shall I cease? And the
LORD said, Go up; for to morrow I will deliver
them into thine hand.
29 And Israel set liers in wait round about Gibeah.
30 And the children of Israel went up against the
children of Benjamin on the third day, and put
themselves in array against Gibeah, as at other
times.
31 And the children of Benjamin went out against
the people, *and* were drawn away from the city;
and they began to smite of the people, *and* kill,
as at other times, in the highways, of which one
goeth up to the house of God, and the other to
Gibeah in the field, about thirty men of Israel.
32 And the children of Benjamin said, They *are*
smitten down before us, as at the first. But the
children of Israel said, Let us flee, and draw them
from the city unto the highways.
33 And all the men of Israel rose up out of their
place, and put themselves in array at Baal-tamar:
and the liers in wait of Israel came forth out of
their places, *even* out of the meadows of Gibeah.
34 And there came against Gibeah ten thousand
chosen men out of all Israel, and the battle was
sore: but they knew not that evil *was* near them.
35 And the LORD smote Benjamin before Israel:
and the children of Israel destroyed of the Benjamites that day twenty and five thousand and an
hundred men: all these drew the sword.
36 So the children of Benjamin saw that they
were smitten: for the men of Israel gave place to
the Benjamites, because they trusted unto the
liers in wait which they had set beside Gibeah.
37 And the liers in wait hasted, and rushed upon
Gibeah; and the liers in wait drew *themselves*
along, and smote all the city with the edge of the
sword.
38 Now there was an appointed sign between
the men of Israel and the liers in wait, that they
should make a great flame with smoke rise up out
of the city.
39 And when the men of Israel retired in the
battle, Benjamin began to smite *and* kill of the
men of Israel about thirty persons: for they said,
Surely they are smitten down before us, as *in* the
first battle.
40 But when the flame began to arise up out of
the city with a pillar of smoke, the Benjamites
looked behind them, and, behold, the flame of
the city ascended up to heaven.
41 And when the men of Israel turned again, the
men of Benjamin were amazed: for they saw that
evil was come upon them.
42 Therefore they turned *their backs* before the
men of Israel unto the way of the wilderness; but
the battle overtook them; and them which *came*
out of the cities they destroyed in the midst of them.
43 *Thus* they inclosed the Benjamites round
about, *and* chased them, *and* trode them down
with ease over against Gibeah toward the
sunrising.
44 And there fell of Benjamin eighteen thousand
men; all these *were* men of valour.
45 And they turned and fled toward the wilderness unto the rock of Rimmon: and they gleaned
of them in the highways five thousand men; and
pursued hard after them unto Gidom, and slew
two thousand men of them.
46 So that all which fell that day of Benjamin
were twenty and five thousand men that drew the
sword; all these *were* men of valour.
47 But six hundred men turned and fled to the

20:31 *house of God.* Most likely referring to Beth-el.
20:34 *the battle was sore.* Heavy fighting. *evil.* Here referring to calamity (v. 41).
20:37 *drew themselves along.* They marched on.
20:38 *sign.* Time. *great flame.* A great elevation.
20:39 *retired.* Literally, "turned back."
20:41 *amazed.* Overwhelmed with surprise; terrified.
20:45 *gleaned.* To hunt down after the main battle was over.

Thoughts for Personal/Family Worship: Chapter 20

1. By sending a piece of his wife's body to each of the tribes of Israel, the Levite created a remarkable unity of purpose to punish the tribe of Benjamin. If only Israel had been so united in the cause of the Lord in past times they would have known many victories. When Christians stand together, pray together, and show forth the love of Christ with one accord, evil and wickedness can be put to flight. Solomon's maxim holds true, "A threefold cord is not quickly broken" (Eccl. 4:12).

2. The consequences of Gibeah's sins were certain and severe. "Be sure your sin will find you out" (Num. 32:23). God's righteous character demands that sin be punished in full. The just punishment leveled against Gibeah points to just execution of God's wrath against Christ. The whole gospel stands upon God's demand to judge sin to the full. As believers, we confess that on that awful day at Calvary the full weight of divine justice fell on our Lord Jesus when He suffered in our place as our substitute. The gospel is not a cover up of sin, for in Christ's redeeming work justice was fully and legally settled. Justice being settled, it now stands guard for our salvation, for "Payment God cannot twice demand— / First at my bleeding Surety's hand, / And then again at mine," as hymnwriter Augustus Toplady expressed it. Because of Christ's sacrifice at Calvary there is a sure hope for every soul who trusts in Him for salvation. How does it stir your soul to consider that God's wrath fell on Christ instead of sinners?

wilderness unto the rock Rimmon, and abode in
the rock Rimmon four months.
48 And the men of Israel turned again upon the
children of Benjamin, and smote them with the
edge of the sword, as well the men of *every* city, as
the beast, and all that came to hand: also they set
on fire all the cities that they came to.

CHAPTER 21

NOW the men of Israel had sworn in Mizpeh, say-
ing, There shall not any of us give his daughter
unto Benjamin to wife.
2 And the people came to the house of God, and
abode there till even before God, and lifted up
their voices, and wept sore;
3 And said, O LORD God of Israel, why is this
come to pass in Israel, that there should be to day
one tribe lacking in Israel?
4 And it came to pass on the morrow, that the
people rose early, and built there an altar, and
offered burnt offerings and peace offerings.
5 And the children of Israel said, Who *is there*
among all the tribes of Israel that came not up
with the congregation unto the LORD? For they
had made a great oath concerning him that came
not up to the LORD to Mizpeh, saying, He shall
surely be put to death.
6 And the children of Israel repented them for
Benjamin their brother, and said, There is one
tribe cut off from Israel this day.
7 How shall we do for wives for them that remain,
seeing we have sworn by the LORD that we will not
give them of our daughters to wives?
8 ¶ And they said, What one *is there* of the tribes
of Israel that came not up to Mizpeh to the LORD?
And, behold, there came none to the camp from
Jabesh-gilead to the assembly.
9 For the people were numbered, and, behold,
there were none of the inhabitants of Jabesh-gilead
there.
10 And the congregation sent thither twelve
thousand men of the valiantest, and commanded
them, saying, Go and smite the inhabitants of
Jabesh-gilead with the edge of the sword, with the
women and the children.
11 And this *is* the thing that ye shall do, Ye shall
utterly destroy every male, and every woman that
hath lain by man.
12 And they found among the inhabitants of
Jabesh-gilead four hundred young virgins, that
had known no man by lying with any male: and
they brought them unto the camp to Shiloh,
which *is* in the land of Canaan.
13 And the whole congregation sent *some* to
speak to the children of Benjamin that *were* in the
rock Rimmon, and to call peaceably unto them.
14 And Benjamin came again at that time; and
they gave them wives which they had saved alive
of the women of Jabesh-gilead: and yet so they
sufficed them not.
15 And the people repented them for Benjamin,
because that the LORD had made a breach in the
tribes of Israel.
16 ¶ Then the elders of the congregation said,
How shall we do for wives for them that remain,
seeing the women are destroyed out of Benjamin?
17 And they said, *There must be* an inheritance
for them that be escaped of Benjamin, that a tribe
be not destroyed out of Israel.
18 Howbeit we may not give them wives of
our daughters: for the children of Israel have
sworn, saying, Cursed *be* he that giveth a wife to
Benjamin.
19 Then they said, Behold, *there is* a feast of the
LORD in Shiloh yearly *in a place* which *is* on the
north side of Beth-el, on the east side of the high-
way that goeth up from Beth-el to Shechem, and
on the south of Lebonah.
20 Therefore they commanded the children
of Benjamin, saying, Go and lie in wait in the
vineyards;
21 And see, and, behold, if the daughters of
Shiloh come out to dance in dances, then come
ye out of the vineyards, and catch you every man
his wife of the daughters of Shiloh, and go to the
land of Benjamin.
22 And it shall be, when their fathers or their
brethren come unto us to complain, that we will
say unto them, Be favourable unto them for our
sakes: because we reserved not to each man his
wife in the war: for ye did not give unto them at
this time, *that* ye should be guilty.
23 And the children of Benjamin did so, and

Chapter 21: ***The Israelites vow not to allow their daughters to marry into Benjamin and then devise a plan to provide wives for them.***

Israel Finds Wives for Benjamin (21:1–25)

21:2 *wept sore.* Wept greatly.
21:3 *one tribe lacking.* Missing or cut off.
21:6 *one tribe cut off from Israel.* Without wives their tribe was in danger of extinction.
21:7 They took their vow seriously but evidenced a lack of true spirituality in the plan devised to circumvent the vow.
21:10 *men of the valiantest.* Literally, "sons of strength."
21:12 *Shiloh.* The place where the tabernacle stood with the ark of the covenant.
21:14 *sufficed them not.* There was not enough to meet the demands.
21:21 *catch you every man his wife.* This scheme implied that while the men of Israel would be under a curse for agreeing to give their daughters to the men of Benjamin, they would be free from such an oath if their daughters were violently abducted (v. 22), yet did not give unto them. This was a scheme hatched in expediency without living up to the spirit of their oath.

took *them* wives, according to their number, of
them that danced, whom they caught: and they
went and returned unto their inheritance, and
repaired the cities, and dwelt in them.
24 And the children of Israel departed thence at
that time, every man to his tribe and to his family,
and they went out from thence every man to his
inheritance.
25 In those days *there was* no king in Israel: every
man did *that which was* right in his own eyes.

21:25 *no king in Israel.* The thrust of the book of Judges falls on this final point (17:6; 18:1; 19:1), that God's people need a righteous and powerful king to turn them from doing their will to obey the revealed will of God (Isa. 9:7; Jer. 23:5; Acts 3:26; 5:31).

Thoughts for Personal/Family Worship: Chapter 21

1. **This caveat at the close of the book (v. 25) is a reminder that these were days of deep apostasy. The dark and distressing days of the judges provide warnings that man's heart is evil and that without restraint that evil progresses to unimaginable depths. Should we try to follow our own imaginations we will depart from God and stoop to heathen practices; we are not exempt. Grace and God's law must rule our hearts.**
2. **The book of Judges serves redemptive history by intensifying the desire and expectation for the perfect and final deliverer to come. Let us rejoice in the wonderful Savior God has given to deliver us from our sin. As the Savior of sinners our Lord Jesus is the great Judge. He is given by the Father to declare us righteous according to the law and to empower us to live godly in fellowship with Him. When we are born from above, we will seek those things which are above. When we are raised up with Christ by His resurrection power, we will reign with Him as sons of God. Heaven, the city of the great King, will be all the brighter when compared with the darkness of this rebellious world, where there is no king, no law, and no shame.**

FOR WHITHER

Thou Goest

I WILL GO

AND WHERE

Thou Lodgest

I WILL LODGE

Thy People

SHALL

BE MY PEOPLE

AND

Thy God

MY GOD

RUTH 1:16

INTRODUCTION TO THE BOOK OF RUTH

Authorship and Date: The Bible does not indicate the author of this book. Jewish tradition attributes it to Samuel (see the Babylonian Talmud, *Baba Bathra* 14b). The genealogy at the very end of the book implies that the author wrote after David (c. 1040–970 BC) became a significant figure in Israel. Samuel did not live to see David enthroned (1 Sam. 25:1; 2 Sam. 5:4), though it is possible that the prophet wrote this in anticipation that the man he had anointed would become a great king (1 Sam. 16:1,13). However, the expression "in former time in Israel" (Ruth 4:7) suggests that the book was written some generations after its events took place.

Theme: Redeeming love.

Purpose: To encourage believers to persevere in faithful love toward one another despite dark times, trusting that God's providence is working redemption for Israel in and through the Greater Boaz, Jesus Christ.

Synopsis: *The Contribution of Ruth to Redemptive Revelation*

In the book of Ruth, the Holy Spirit gives us a skillfully told and captivating account of historical events involving two poor widows and a kind Judean man. Their actions present valuable lessons about faithful love in bitter times. Ruth is a marvelous example of a committed friend (1:17) who works hard to support her family (2:2,7,17) and displays humility and respect for authority (vv. 5–6). Naomi is slow to emerge from bitterness (1:20), but as she experiences the Lord's grace, she begins to give Ruth motherly guidance to obtain lasting peace for herself and their posterity (3:1–2). Boaz shines as a model of true manhood (see note at 2:1), providing, protecting, and redeeming the poor through faith and love (chs. 3–4).

However, the moral examples of this book's characters do not exhaust its full meaning. Though at first glance it may appear to be nothing more than a delightful love story, it is in fact rich with theological truth and pictures of the gospel of Christ.

The theological truth of the book centers on the doctrine of *providence*. In some respects, God seems strangely absent from this story. While its characters speak sometimes of "God" (1:16; 2:12) and often of "the Lord" (1:8–9,13,17,21; 2:4,12,20; 3:10,13; 4:11–12,14), the book holds no prophecies or divine appearances, no miracles or wonders—a marked contrast to Genesis through Judges. Yet the book of Ruth pulsates with God's secret providence as tragedy, personal choices, and seemingly random events (2:3; 4:1) lead to a surprising conclusion involving a future king of Israel (4:22). God works all things to build His kingdom. His providence rules all things. He controls the weather and food supplies (1:6); He gives husbands to women (vv. 8–9). Behind tragedy and sorrow is "the hand of the Lord," the Judge of all the earth (vv. 13,21). He is present to bless men as they work in the fields (2:4). He rewards those who trust Him and love people (vv. 11–12). He forms children in the womb to build families (4:11–13).

The book of Ruth especially shows that God works through the faithful love of ordinary people. Ruth, Boaz, and over time even Naomi all gave themselves to serve others. Ruth sought refuge under God's "wings" (2:12), and God gave her that refuge under the "wings" of Boaz's kindness (see note at 3:9). Boaz cared for Naomi and Ruth, and Naomi gave glory to the Lord (2:20). Their human love was an instrument of God's love.

Boaz was a redeemer. The word "redeemer" (often translated "kinsman") and terms related to it appear twenty-three times in the book (2:20; 3:9,12 [2 times], 13 [4 times]; 4:1,3–4, [5 times],

6 [5 times],7–8,14). A kinsman-redeemer was a member of the extended family who at his own expense restored or avenged the family when it suffered loss (Lev. 25:23–33,48–49; Num. 5:8; "avenger" or "revenger" in Num. 35:9–28; Deut. 19:6,12). The word "redeem" has a rich theological meaning, for the Lord worked redemption when He brought Israel out of slavery in Egypt (Ex. 6:6; 15:13). Later, Isaiah proclaimed the good news of Israel's salvation by declaring God to be the Redeemer of His people (Isa. 43:1; 44:6; 49:7; 52:9; 54:8). Redemption would be a central idea in the New Testament gospel of Christ (Mark 10:45; Gal. 3:13; 4:5; Titus 2:14; 1 Peter 1:18; Rev. 5:9). The redemption of Naomi's family included the elements of cost (Ruth 4:6), legal commitment (vv. 2,7,9), and inheritance (vv. 5,10)—all of which correspond to aspects of redemption by Christ's blood.

Therefore, Boaz was a type of Christ. Types are people, institutions, and events designed by God's providence to be imperfect pictures of who Christ is and what He would do to save His people. Not only does Boaz's life shed light on redemption, but in him we can see a prototype of the King of grace, Jesus Christ. Boaz was a mighty man of valor (see notes at 2:1), and he used his power and wealth to welcome the outsider, protect the endangered, and provide for the needy (ch. 2). He is compared to the Lord as one who covers the needy with his "wings" of grace (2:12; 3:9). He was an ancestor of King David, himself a type of Christ (4:18–22).

As they studied Boaz in ancient times, the people of Israel could grow in their hope in the coming Redeemer-King. As we study Boaz today, we can grow in our faith, love, and imitation of the Savior who has already come as our Lord Jesus Christ.

Outline:

I. Providence Veiled: Disaster Strikes (1:1–5)
II. Returning Home to the Lord (1:6–22)
III. Finding Shelter under the Redeemer's Wings (2:1–23)
IV. Seeking Union with the Redeemer (3:1–18)
V. Accomplishing Redemption (4:1–17)
VI. Providence Unveiled: A King Is Born (4:18–22)

THE BOOK OF RUTH

CHAPTER 1

NOW it came to pass in the days when the judges
ruled, that there was a famine in the land. And
a certain man of Beth-lehem-judah went to
sojourn in the country of Moab, he, and his wife,
and his two sons.
2 And the name of the man *was* Elimelech, and
the name of his wife Naomi, and the name of his
two sons Mahlon and Chilion, Ephrathites of
Beth-lehem-judah. And they came into the coun-
try of Moab, and continued there.
3 And Elimelech Naomi's husband died; and she
was left, and her two sons.
4 And they took them wives of the women of
Moab; the name of the one *was* Orpah, and the
name of the other Ruth: and they dwelled there
about ten years.
5 And Mahlon and Chilion died also both of
them; and the woman was left of her two sons
and her husband.
6 ¶ Then she arose with her daughters in law, that
she might return from the country of Moab: for
she had heard in the country of Moab how that
the LORD had visited his people in giving them
bread.
7 Wherefore she went forth out of the place
where she was, and her two daughters in law with
her; and they went on the way to return unto the
land of Judah.
8 And Naomi said unto her two daughters in law,
Go, return each to her mother's house: the LORD
deal kindly with you, as ye have dealt with the
dead, and with me.
9 The LORD grant you that ye may find rest, each
of you in the house of her husband. Then she
kissed them; and they lifted up their voice, and
wept.
10 And they said unto her, Surely we will return
with thee unto thy people.
11 And Naomi said, Turn again, my daughters:
why will ye go with me? *are* there yet *any more* sons
in my womb, that they may be your husbands?
12 Turn again, my daughters, go *your way*; for I
am too old to have an husband. If I should say,
I have hope, *if* I should have an husband also to
night, and should also bear sons;
13 Would ye tarry for them till they were grown?
would ye stay for them from having husbands?
nay, my daughters; for it grieveth me much for
your sakes that the hand of the LORD is gone out
against me.
14 And they lifted up their voice, and wept again:
and Orpah kissed her mother in law; but Ruth
clave unto her.

Chapter 1: *Naomi moves to Moab where her husband and sons die, and then returns to Beth-lehem-judah with no one but her daughter-in-law, Ruth.*

PROVIDENCE VEILED: DISASTER STRIKES (1:1–5)

1:1 *when the judges ruled.* A time of national spiritual decline into idolatry and immorality in the eleventh to fourteenth centuries BC. *famine.* God's discipline upon Israel for breaking the covenant (Deut. 28:17–18,23–24). *sojourn.* Live for a time in a foreign land. *Moab.* A nation dwelling sixty-five miles away from Bethlehem, descending from Lot's son Moab and known for seducing the Israelites into sin (Num. 25:1–3).

1:4 *took them wives of the women of Moab.* Despising the law that excluded descendants of the Moabites from joining the church (Deut. 23:3–6). *Ruth.* Probably means "friend" or "companion."

1:5 *the woman was left.* Alone and old in the ancient world without a husband or son to support and protect her, Naomi was in a desperate condition, a widow indeed.

RETURNING HOME TO THE LORD (1:6–22)

1:6 *return.* This verb, the main Hebrew verb for "repentance," appears twelve times in ch. 1. Naomi and Ruth's return to Judah signified their turning to the Lord.

1:7 *Wherefore.* Therefore.

1:8 *deal kindly.* Naomi still believed in God's faithful love. *dealt with the dead.* The women had been good wives to her sons, and Naomi prayed that God would give them husbands again (v. 9).

1:9 *rest.* Security with a new husband. *lifted up their voice.* Wailed.

1:11 *more sons.* In levirate marriage, if a man dies childless, his brother or near relative married the widow to raise up children for the deceased (Gen. 38:8–11; Deut. 25:5–10).

1:13 *tarry.* Wait. *stay.* Restrain yourselves, here from marrying someone else. *nay.* No. *hand of the LORD.* God's power controls life and death (1 Sam. 2:6). Despite her belief in God's sovereignty, Naomi had little hope for her own future (v. 12).

1:14 *clave.* Clung in love and stubborn commitment.

15 And she said, Behold, thy sister in law is gone
back unto her people, and unto her gods: return
thou after thy sister in law.
16 And Ruth said, Intreat me not to leave thee, *or*
to return from following after thee: for whither
thou goest, I will go; and where thou lodgest, I
will lodge: thy people *shall be* my people, and thy
God my God:
17 Where thou diest, will I die, and there will I be
buried: the LORD do so to me, and more also, *if*
ought but death part thee and me.
18 When she saw that she was stedfastly minded
to go with her, then she left speaking unto her.
19 ¶ So they two went until they came to Beth-
lehem. And it came to pass, when they were come
to Beth-lehem, that all the city was moved about
them, and they said, *Is* this Naomi?
20 And she said unto them, Call me not Naomi,
call me Mara: for the Almighty hath dealt very
bitterly with me.
21 I went out full, and the LORD hath brought me
home again empty: why *then* call ye me Naomi,
seeing the LORD hath testified against me, and the
Almighty hath afflicted me?
22 So Naomi returned, and Ruth the Moabitess,
her daughter in law, with her, which returned out
of the country of Moab: and they came to Beth-
lehem in the beginning of barley harvest.

CHAPTER 2

AND Naomi had a kinsman of her husband's, a
mighty man of wealth, of the family of Elimelech;
and his name *was* Boaz.
2 And Ruth the Moabitess said unto Naomi, Let
me now go to the field, and glean ears of corn
after *him* in whose sight I shall find grace. And
she said unto her, Go, my daughter.
3 And she went, and came, and gleaned in the
field after the reapers: and her hap was to light on
a part of the field *belonging* unto Boaz, who *was* of
the kindred of Elimelech.
4 ¶ And, behold, Boaz came from Beth-lehem,
and said unto the reapers, The LORD *be* with you.
And they answered him, The LORD bless thee.
5 Then said Boaz unto his servant that was set
over the reapers, Whose damsel *is* this?
6 And the servant that was set over the reapers an-
swered and said, It *is* the Moabitish damsel that
came back with Naomi out of the country of Moab:
7 And she said, I pray you, let me glean and
gather after the reapers among the sheaves: so she
came, and hath continued even from the morn-
ing until now, that she tarried a little in the house.
8 Then said Boaz unto Ruth, Hearest thou not,
my daughter? Go not to glean in another field,
neither go from hence, but abide here fast by my
maidens:

1:16 *Intreat me not*. Do not press me. *whither*. Where. Ruth committed herself to be her mother-in-law's lifelong companion, and embraced Israel as *my people* and the Lord as *my God*. Her words echo the promise of the covenant of grace that the Lord will be our God and we will be His people (Gen. 17:7–8; Ex. 6:7; Lev. 26:12,44–45; Jer. 31:33; 2 Cor. 6:16; Heb. 8:10; Rev. 21:3). She had been converted to true religion and by faith entered the covenant of grace.
1:17 *the LORD do so to me*. An oath. Sworn in His name, it confirmed her allegiance to the Lord as her God. *if ought*. If anything.
1:18 *stedfastly minded*. Determined. *left speaking*. Stopped talking about it.
1:19 *moved*. Stirred up, disturbed.
1:20–21 *Almighty*. Hebrew, *Shaddai*, a title of God's all-sufficient power (Job 37:23) to bless and judge (Gen. 17:1–2; Ps. 91:1; Isa. 13:6). Naomi spoke of changing her name from "Pleasant" to "Bitter" because she believed God had judged her for her sins (*testified against me*).
1:22 Though Naomi saw nothing but bitterness and emptiness, the Lord had blessed her with two great gifts: her faithful *daughter in law*, and food from the *barley harvest* in late April.

Thoughts for Personal/Family Worship: Chapter 1

1. **God's people can experience times of great darkness. Their nation may fall away from true religion into idolatry and immoral living; their family may face devastating consequences of poor decisions. In such times, all can seem like bitterness and emptiness, but it is essential that we cling to each other with faithful, committed love. To have a true companion like Ruth means the world to someone in pain. Be a true friend.**
2. **God converts pagan outsiders into believers who love the church. In His free grace, He may do so even when the church flounders in sin and misery. Like Ruth, true converts embrace the Lord and His people and hold on with holy stubbornness. The promises of the covenant of grace are written on their hearts and confessed by their mouths—God is their God. Are you experientially acquainted with Ruth's remarkable confession in vv. 16–17?**

Chapter 2: ***Ruth faithfully labors to support her mother-in-law, and God's providence brings the two widows under the kindness of a local farmer.***

FINDING SHELTER UNDER THE REDEEMER'S WINGS (2:1–23)

2:1 *kinsman*. Relative. *mighty man of wealth*. Mighty man of valor; strong person of excellence. Boaz was not only wealthy but possessed the inward power of faith and love.
2:2 *glean*. The law gave the poor the right to gather what remained on the ground and edges of the field after the reapers had cut and bundled the stalks of grain (Lev. 19:9–10; 23:22). *corn*. Any grain; in this case, barley (1:22). *grace*. Favor or kindness toward someone in need.
2:3 *her hap was to light*. She happened to come. *kindred*. Extended family. Seemingly chance events serve God's purposes, for He rules over them all (Prov.16:33; Matt. 10:29).
2:4 Boaz's greetings resemble the blessing of Aaron (Num. 6:22–27). Boaz was like a priest in his home, a spiritual father even to his workers.
2:5 *damsel*. Young woman. Ruth probably was in her twenties (1:4).
2:7 *I pray you*. Please. *sheaves*. Bundles of stalks of grain. *tarried*. Rested.
2:8 *Hearest thou not*. Listen. *hence*. From here. *abide here fast*.

9 *Let* thine eyes *be* on the field that they do reap,
and go thou after them: have I not charged the
young men that they shall not touch thee? and
when thou art athirst, go unto the vessels, and
drink of *that* which the young men have drawn.
10 Then she fell on her face, and bowed herself
to the ground, and said unto him, Why have I
found grace in thine eyes, that thou shouldest
take knowledge of me, seeing I *am* a stranger?
11 And Boaz answered and said unto her, It hath
fully been shewed me, all that thou hast done unto
thy mother in law since the death of thine hus-
band: and *how* thou hast left thy father and thy
mother, and the land of thy nativity, and art come
unto a people which thou knewest not heretofore.
12 The LORD recompense thy work, and a full
reward be given thee of the LORD God of Israel,
under whose wings thou art come to trust.
13 Then she said, Let me find favour in thy sight,
my lord; for that thou hast comforted me, and
for that thou hast spoken friendly unto thine
handmaid, though I be not like unto one of thine
handmaidens.
14 And Boaz said unto her, At mealtime come
thou hither, and eat of the bread, and dip thy
morsel in the vinegar. And she sat beside the
reapers: and he reached her parched *corn*, and she
did eat, and was sufficed, and left.
15 And when she was risen up to glean, Boaz
commanded his young men, saying, Let her glean
even among the sheaves, and reproach her not:
16 And let fall also *some* of the handfuls of pur-
pose for her, and leave *them*, that she may glean
them, and rebuke her not.
17 So she gleaned in the field until even, and beat
out that she had gleaned: and it was about an
ephah of barley.
18 ¶ And she took *it* up, and went into the city:
and her mother in law saw what she had gleaned:
and she brought forth, and gave to her that she
had reserved after she was sufficed.
19 And her mother in law said unto her, Where
hast thou gleaned to day? and where wrought-
est thou? blessed be he that did take knowledge
of thee. And she shewed her mother in law with
whom she had wrought, and said, The man's
name with whom I wrought to day *is* Boaz.
20 And Naomi said unto her daughter in law,
Blessed *be* he of the LORD, who hath not left off
his kindness to the living and to the dead. And
Naomi said unto her, The man *is* near of kin unto
us, one of our next kinsmen.
21 And Ruth the Moabitess said, He said unto me
also, Thou shalt keep fast by my young men, until
they have ended all my harvest.
22 And Naomi said unto Ruth her daughter in
law, *It is* good, my daughter, that thou go out with
his maidens, that they meet thee not in any other
field.
23 So she kept fast by the maidens of Boaz to
glean unto the end of barley harvest and of wheat
harvest; and dwelt with her mother in law.

CHAPTER 3

THEN Naomi her mother in law said unto her, My
daughter, shall I not seek rest for thee, that it may
be well with thee?

Stay close. *maidens.* Young women, here female servants.
2:9 *touch.* Boaz protected her from sexual assault in the lawless times of the judges (1:1). *art athirst.* Are thirsty.
2:10 *shouldest take knowledge.* Notice. *stranger.* Foreigner. Ruth was humble, honoring Boaz as her superior, and grateful, recognizing his *grace* to a poor woman from another nation.
2:11 *shewed.* Shown. *nativity.* Birth. *art come.* Have come. *heretofore.* Before. Boaz compared Ruth to Abraham, who left his home to go to an unknown land by faith in God (Gen. 12:1).
2:12 *recompense.* Or, "bring to completion, wholeness, and peace," filling her up in the emptiness of her widowhood and poverty. Hiding under God's *wings* like a chick with a hen is a picture of trusting in God's grace for salvation (Ps. 57:1; 91:4). Though Ruth was a Moabite, Boaz accepted her as a believer in covenant with the Lord.
2:13 *handmaid.* Female servant.
2:14 *hither.* To here. *morsel.* Piece of bread. *reached.* Handed. *sufficed.* Satisfied. Boaz welcomed Ruth as if she were a member of his household ("my daughter," v. 8).
2:15 *glean.* See note at v. 2.
2:17 *even.* Evening. *beat out.* Threshed, striking the harvested plants to separate out the grain. Estimates of an *ephah* vary from six to ten gallons (thirty to fifty pounds of barley), far more than the small amount normally obtained by gleaning (Isa. 17:5–6).
2:18 *reserved after she was sufficed.* Set aside after she was satisfied (at the meal, v. 14).
2:19 *where wroughtest thou?* Where did you work? *take knowledge.* Notice. *shewed.* Told.
2:20 *hath not left off his kindness.* Has not stopped showing His loyal affection and reliable love (1:8; Gen. 24:27; Ezra 9:9; Neh. 9:17). Naomi's faith in God's enduring love was rekindled by the kindness of Boaz. *kinsman.* This is the first appearance in Ruth of the word for redeemer (see Introduction: Synopsis).
2:21 *keep fast.* Stay close.
2:22 *maidens.* Young women, here servants. *meet thee not.* Or, "not fall upon you," so that Ruth would not be assaulted.
2:23 Ruth gleaned barley and *wheat* for about seven weeks from late April to early June (Deut. 16:9). *dwelt with her mother in law.* Ruth faithfully loved Naomi as she promised (1:16).

Thoughts for Personal/Family Worship: Chapter 2

1. **Ruth served her family, honored her mother-in-law, and demonstrated humility, respect, and gratitude. Boaz led his household to worship God in everyday life, protected and provided for the needy, spoke blessing on the faithful, and loved the foreigner and outsider. They are models worthy of our imitation.**
2. **The fatherly love of Boaz points us to Christ. Christ is full of strength and compassion as our mighty God and everlasting Father (Isa. 9:6). He protects and provides for all who hide under His wings. He reaches out to all**

2 And now *is* not Boaz of our kindred, with
whose maidens thou wast? Behold, he winnoweth
barley to night in the threshingfloor.
3 Wash thyself therefore, and anoint thee, and put
thy raiment upon thee, and get thee down to the
floor: *but* make not thyself known unto the man,
until he shall have done eating and drinking.
4 And it shall be, when he lieth down, that thou
shalt mark the place where he shall lie, and thou
shalt go in, and uncover his feet, and lay thee
down; and he will tell thee what thou shalt do.
5 And she said unto her, All that thou sayest unto
me I will do.
6 ¶ And she went down unto the floor, and did
according to all that her mother in law bade her.
7 And when Boaz had eaten and drunk, and his
heart was merry, he went to lie down at the end of
the heap of corn: and she came softly, and uncov-
ered his feet, and laid her down.
8 ¶ And it came to pass at midnight, that the man
was afraid, and turned himself: and, behold, a
woman lay at his feet.
9 And he said, Who *art* thou? And she answered,
I *am* Ruth thine handmaid: spread therefore thy
skirt over thine handmaid; for thou *art* a near
kinsman.
10 And he said, Blessed *be* thou of the LORD, my
daughter: *for* thou hast shewed more kindness in
the latter end than at the beginning, inasmuch as
thou followedst not young men, whether poor or
rich.
11 And now, my daughter, fear not; I will do to
thee all that thou requirest: for all the city of my
people doth know that thou *art* a virtuous woman.
12 And now it is true that I *am thy* near kinsman:
howbeit there is a kinsman nearer than I.
13 Tarry this night, and it shall be in the morning,
that if he will perform unto thee the part of a
kinsman, well; let him do the kinsman's part: but
if he will not do the part of a kinsman to thee,
then will I do the part of a kinsman to thee, *as* the
LORD liveth: lie down until the morning.
14 ¶ And she lay at his feet until the morning: and
she rose up before one could know another. And
he said, Let it not be known that a woman came
into the floor.
15 Also he said, Bring the vail that *thou hast*
upon thee, and hold it. And when she held it, he
measured six *measures* of barley, and laid *it* on
her: and she went into the city.
16 And when she came to her mother in law, she
said, Who *art* thou, my daughter? And she told
her all that the man had done to her.
17 And she said, These six *measures* of barley gave
he me; for he said to me, Go not empty unto thy
mother in law.
18 Then said she, Sit still, my daughter, until
thou know how the matter will fall: for the man

nations. How beautiful is Christ, our Boaz! Love Him, adore Him, and trust in His mercy.

Chapter 3: *Naomi sends Ruth to propose marriage in the middle of the night, and Boaz is surprised but commits himself to redeem them if possible.*

SEEKING UNION WITH THE REDEEMER (3:1–18)

3:1 *rest for thee.* Security of a husband (1:9). Restored hope (2:20) moved Naomi from bitterness (1:20) and passivity (2:2) to seeking the good of her family.

3:2 *kindred.* Family. *maidens.* Young women or servants. *wast.* Were. In ancient agriculture, people would lay stalks and ears of grain on a *threshingfloor* of stone or hard earth, and drive livestock and farm implements over them to break them up. Then the farmer tossed (*winnoweth*) the threshed plants with a pitchfork so that the wind carried the light chaff away but the heavier grain fell down. He gathered the grain into a pile and guarded it at night (v. 7).

3:3 *anoint.* Put on fragrant oil or lotion. *raiment.* Clothing.

3:4 *mark.* Know. Ruth could privately discuss the delicate subject of marriage with her social superior when his uncovered feet got chilly and he awoke.

3:5–6 Though Naomi's scheme involved considerable risks of shame and rejection, Ruth submitted to her and obediently did *all that her mother in law bade* (told) *her.*

3:7 *merry.* Happy. *corn.* Grain, here barley or wheat. *softly.* Quietly.

3:8 *lay at his feet.* The expression does not refer to an embrace or sexual activity.

3:9 *handmaid.* Female servant. By *skirt* Ruth was not talking about clothing, but the covenant of marriage (Ezek. 16:8). She did not wait for Boaz to tell her what to do but made it clear that she sought a husband. She had taken refuge under the Lord's "wings" (2:12; same word as *skirt*). Now she boldly asked if Boaz would be the instrument of God's redeeming love by marrying her. Similarly, needy sinners who fly to Christ, the Greater Boaz, seek to be united with Him in spiritual marriage.

3:10 *kindness.* Faithful love, same word used of God's love and mercy (1:8; 2:20; Ex. 34:6). Ruth prized godliness and loyalty above lust and greed. *inasmuch.* In that. *followedst.* Literally, "walked," here in the sense of pursued.

3:11 *requirest.* Ask. *virtuous.* Valor or excellence, same word used of Boaz (2:2). Ruth is of more value to Naomi than seven sons (4:15).

3:12 *kinsman nearer than I.* He had the right to redeem them before Boaz did.

3:13 *Tarry.* Stay. He swore an oath (*as the LORD liveth*) to redeem them if he could.

3:14 *lay at his feet until morning.* They were near each other all night but did not engage in sex. *Let it not be known.* He was concerned to protect their reputation.

3:15 *vail.* Cloak. *six measures of barley.* Twice as much as an ephah, so sixty to a hundred pounds (2:17). It was a down payment of sorts to assure them that he would keep his pledge.

3:16 *Who art thou.* Naomi knew it was her *daughter*; the question may be understood as implying, "Are you now the betrothed of Boaz, engaged to marry him?"

Thoughts for Personal/Family Worship: Chapter 3

1. **Faith energizes love, submission, and self-denial. Naomi's renewed hope led her to take positive steps for the future of her family. Ruth's faith in the Lord made her**

will not be in rest, until he have finished the thing
this day.

CHAPTER 4

THEN went Boaz up to the gate, and sat him down
there: and, behold, the kinsman of whom Boaz
spake came by; unto whom he said, Ho, such a
one! turn aside, sit down here. And he turned
aside, and sat down.
2 And he took ten men of the elders of the city,
and said, Sit ye down here. And they sat down.
3 And he said unto the kinsman, Naomi, that is
come again out of the country of Moab, selleth a
parcel of land, which *was* our brother Elimelech's:
4 And I thought to advertise thee, saying, Buy *it*
before the inhabitants, and before the elders of
my people. If thou wilt redeem *it*, redeem *it*: but
if thou wilt not redeem *it*, *then* tell me, that I may
know: for *there is* none to redeem *it* beside thee;
and I *am* after thee. And he said, I will redeem *it*.
5 Then said Boaz, What day thou buyest the field
of the hand of Naomi, thou must buy *it* also of
Ruth the Moabitess, the wife of the dead, to raise
up the name of the dead upon his inheritance.
6 ¶ And the kinsman said, I cannot redeem *it* for
myself, lest I mar mine own inheritance: redeem
thou my right to thyself; for I cannot redeem *it*.
7 Now this *was the manner* in former time in
Israel concerning redeeming and concerning
changing, for to confirm all things; a man plucked
off his shoe, and gave *it* to his neighbour: and this
was a testimony in Israel.
8 Therefore the kinsman said unto Boaz, Buy *it*
for thee. So he drew off his shoe.
9 ¶ And Boaz said unto the elders, and *unto* all
the people, Ye *are* witnesses this day, that I have
bought all that *was* Elimelech's, and all that *was*
Chilion's and Mahlon's, of the hand of Naomi.
10 Moreover Ruth the Moabitess, the wife of
Mahlon, have I purchased to be my wife, to raise
up the name of the dead upon his inheritance,
that the name of the dead be not cut off from
among his brethren, and from the gate of his
place: ye *are* witnesses this day.
11 And all the people that *were* in the gate, and the
elders, said, *We are* witnesses. The LORD make the
woman that is come into thine house like Rachel
and like Leah, which two did build the house of
Israel: and do thou worthily in Ephratah, and be
famous in Beth-lehem:
12 And let thy house be like the house of Pharez,
whom Tamar bare unto Judah, of the seed which
the LORD shall give thee of this young woman.
13 ¶ So Boaz took Ruth, and she was his wife:
and when he went in unto her, the LORD gave her
conception, and she bare a son.
14 And the women said unto Naomi, Blessed *be*
the LORD, which hath not left thee this day with-
out a kinsman, that his name may be famous in
Israel.
15 And he shall be unto thee a restorer of *thy* life,
and a nourisher of thine old age: for thy daughter
in law, which loveth thee, which is better to thee
than seven sons, hath born him.
16 And Naomi took the child, and laid it in her
bosom, and became nurse unto it.
17 And the women her neighbours gave it a
name, saying, There is a son born to Naomi; and
they called his name Obed: he *is* the father of

---

a woman of excellence, who honored her mother and sought a godly husband. What fine examples they are of the impact godly women can have on their families!

2. The Lord has given His pledge to His waiting bride, the church. God gives His oath to anchor our covenant hope in Christ (Heb. 6:17–18), for He cannot lie, and He gives His Spirit as the seal of our assurance and down payment on our inheritance in Christ (Eph. 1:13–14). Let us therefore have hope, for Christ will come for poor sinners who cast all their hope on Him.

Chapter 4: *Boaz redeems Naomi and Ruth and marries Ruth, and they become the great-grandparents of King David.*

ACCOMPLISHING REDEMPTION (4:1–17)

4:1 *gate.* See note at Gen. 22:16–17. *kinsman.* Redeemer. Verses 1–6 contain the highest concentration of redemption language in the Old Testament. *such a one.* So-and-so, i.e., a nameless relative of Elimelech.

4:2 *elders.* Men of wisdom and authority who governed the city (Deut. 19:12; 21:19; 22:15). Boaz acted publicly to redeem them according to their laws.

4:3 *parcel.* Piece.

4:4 *advertise.* Make it known. *Buy.* This verb appears six times here (vv. 4–5,8–10). Redemption required paying the price to buy people and inheritance out of poverty and bondage. Christ's redemption required giving His life as the purchase price for sinners (Matt. 20:28).

4:5 *to raise up the name of the dead.* To produce children to carry on the family line of Mahlon, Ruth's deceased husband (v. 4:10; see note at 1:11).

4:6 *lest I mar.* So that I will not ruin. He would have to invest his resources into redeeming the family property and raising her children, only to have her son inherit that property in the name of the deceased Mahlon. Levirate marriage was costly and required self-sacrifice.

4:7 *changing.* Exchanging or barter. *plucked.* Pulled.

4:9 *Ye are witnesses.* Boaz made a public, legally binding commitment to Ruth and Naomi.

4:10 *name of the dead.* See note at v. 5.

4:11 The phrase *do thou worthily* (same verb used in 2:11; 3:11) can mean "to conquer enemies" (Num. 24:18; Ps. 60:12), "to live in excellence" (Prov. 31:29), or "to get wealth" (Deut. 8:17–18).

4:15 *restorer of thy life.* These words are also used of Elijah raising the dead (1 Kings 17:21–22).

4:16 *bosom . . . nurse.* Not breast-feeding, for neither the words nor Naomi's age permit this meaning, but caring for the child with tender love.

Jesse, the father of David.
18 ¶ Now these *are* the generations of Pharez:
Pharez begat Hezron,
19 And Hezron begat Ram, and Ram begat
Amminadab,
20 And Amminadab begat Nahshon, and Nah-
shon begat Salmon,
21 And Salmon begat Boaz, and Boaz begat
Obed,
22 And Obed begat Jesse, and Jesse begat David.

4:17 *Obed.* His name means "one who serves," the character of his parents.

PROVIDENCE UNVEILED: A KING IS BORN (4:18–22)

4:18 *these are the generations.* Common phrase in Genesis; links David's line back to the patriarchs (see notes at Gen. 25:12,19). *Pharez.* Son of Judah and Tamar (Gen. 38:29; 46:12). *begat.* Became the father of a child.

4:20 *Nahshon.* Commander of the armies of Judah in the days of Moses (Num. 1:7; 2:3; 7:12,17; 10:14). *Salmon.* Also called "Salma" (1 Chron. 2:11).

4:22 *Jesse.* See 1 Sam. 16:1; 17:12. *David.* Spirit-anointed psalmist, king of Israel, and father of the line of Christ (1 Sam. 16:1,13; 2 Sam. 5:1–3; 23:1–5; Matt. 1:1). In the lawless time of the judges (1:1), God used a widow, an immigrant, and a farmer to bring the king that Israel desperately needed (Judg. 21:25).

Thoughts for Personal/Family Worship: Chapter 4

1. **Christ redeemed His people; He paid their ransom price at His own expense. He took the outsider as His bride. He made a public and binding commitment. He did it all, so that poor outsiders might rejoice in His love and give glory to God. If you are a believer, never lose sight of the wonder of your redemption. It should always put a song in your heart. If you have not been brought into spiritual union with Christ Jesus, consider seriously that you are lacking the greatest joy in life. Do not rest until you too can say, by God's amazing grace, that Christ is your perfect Bridegroom.**
2. **God uses ordinary people to build the reputation and kingdom of His Son; this is the great aim of providence. Jonathan Edwards wrote, "God hath had it much on his heart, from all eternity, to glorify his dear and only-begotten Son." This kingdom is built of faithful love—the love of God and the love of believers being blessed by God. Therefore, do not grow weary in doing good, especially to the family of God. If you are faithful to serve where God put you, it will impact generations to come.**

INTRODUCTION TO THE BOOKS OF 1ST AND 2ND
SAMUEL

Authorship: First and Second Samuel is one book but was divided into two with the writing of the Septuagint (Greek translation of the Old Testament) in the second century BC. The Septuagint designates the two books as "1 and 2 Kingdoms," and what we call 1 and 2 Kings as 3 and 4 Kingdoms. Although the book of Samuel does not identify its author, Scripture reveals that the prophets Samuel, Nathan, and Gad recorded the acts of David (1 Chron. 29:29). As early as the Babylonian Talmud (*Baba Bathra*, 15a), the first part of the book was attributed to Samuel (1 Sam. 10:25), and later portions to Nathan (2 Sam. 7:2; 12:1) and Gad (24:11). However, the book stands as a unified whole and should be interpreted as such. Though Samuel dies partway through this book (1 Sam. 25:1), it fittingly bears his name because he served as the last of the judges (7:15) and anointed both of the first two kings of Israel (10:1; 16:13)—thus forming a bridge from the time of the judges to the monarchy.

Date: The books of Samuel were composed between 1050 BC (the time when Samuel began to write) and 970 BC (the end of David's reign).

Theme: The sovereignty of God in humbling and exalting leaders according to His judgment of their heart, in order to prepare the way for the coming Messiah.

Purpose: To promote humility before the Lord as the true King of kings, and to encourage hope in the coming King of whom David was a type and shadow.

Synopsis: *The Contribution of 1 and 2 Samuel to Redemptive Revelation*
The Lord summed up the course of redemptive history when He said that two seeds would be in conflict, with the seed of the woman triumphing over the seed of the serpent (Gen. 3:15). Biblical history records the epochs of that conflict, giving the assurance that regardless of the intensity of the opposition to the coming Savior, God's purpose of grace was unfailing. First Samuel advances the promise specifically through the unveiling of God's appointed king. The Lord had revealed centuries earlier to Abraham that from his blessed offspring ("seed") with Sarah God would raise up kings (17:6,16). God repeated this promise to Jacob (35:11), who prophesied that the kingdom would particularly belong to the tribe of Judah (49:10). Moses later revealed the pattern for the ideal king: a descendant of Jacob who did not multiply his power, pleasures, or treasures but who humbly devoted himself to knowing and doing the law of the Lord (Deut. 17:14–20).

Hundreds of years passed without a hint how the promise would be fulfilled since Israel had no king at all. However, with the birth of Samuel the Lord revealed more of His purposes through the song of Samuel's mother, Hannah (1 Sam. 2:1–10). Hannah's song in many ways encapsulates the message of the book of Samuel. The Lord is incomparably holy (v. 2; cf. 6:20), the sovereign King over all things (2:6–7). His salvation for His people (v. 1) appears in surprising reversals, overturning human expectations: he devastates the proud and mighty but blesses and honors the humble, godly ones (vv. 3–5,8–10). Thus even apparent disasters such as the capture of the ark of the covenant take a surprising turn to glorify the Lord as the holy and sovereign King (chs. 4–6). He will accomplish His salvation and judgment for His glory by raising up His anointed king (2:10). The Hebrew word translated "anointed" is the basis for the word "*Messiah*," or in Greek, "Christ."

The book of Samuel reveals the process by which the line of this king was established. Just as the ancient promise of the two seeds foretold, it takes place through conflict and suffering.

Samuel features two kings. The first, Saul, was appointed by God (9:15–16; 10:1) but proved to be a traitor who rejected the word of the Lord (15:23,26). Saul's sin provoked him to persecute God's servant out of envy (18:6–29; 19:9–10), just as the first seed of Adam and Eve, Cain, murdered his godly brother (Gen. 4) and the Jewish religious leaders persecuted Christ out of envy (Matt. 27:18).

The second king, David, is both the forefather of Christ and a type (picture prophecy) of Christ's office as King, one of the essential functions of the Mediator. David, though deeply flawed, was still a man after God's own heart, committed to doing God's will as He commanded (1 Sam. 13:13–14; Acts 13:22). David was a humble man without outward majesty, and yet the Spirit of the Lord anointed Him to save Israel (1 Sam. 16–17). Before being enthroned as king, he had to suffer intense persecution from the wicked authorities, even as they nominally professed allegiance to the Lord (chs. 18–31), until finally God exalted him as king, first over Judah and then over all Israel (2 Sam. 2:4,11; 5:3). His kingdom was one of righteousness and justice (8:15; cf. 1 Kings 10:9).

Unlike the short-lived kingship of Saul, David received from God the covenant that his seed would reign forever (2 Sam. 7:12–16; cf. 22:51; 23:3–5). This is a high-water text in the Old Testament for its development of the promise of the coming seed (Gen. 3:15), specifically identifying the conquering Savior with the seed of David. In the covenant with David, the Lord also revealed that David's son would build a house for the Lord, the temple that would give a more established place for God's holy presence with Israel than the tent of the tabernacle. These promises find their initial fulfillment in Solomon and the temple in Jerusalem (1 Kings 8:15–21), but look yet further. The book of Samuel takes a major step toward the fullness of time when God would send forth His Son (Gal. 4:4) to reign as the Son of David (Matt. 1:1; Luke 1:32–33) and establish God's presence with His church in the Spirit (Eph. 2:20–22; 1 Peter 2:4–6).

The further revelation of Christ's kingdom in Samuel is interwoven with a call to subjection to the King of kings. The book provides many ethical and moral lessons giving direction as to how the godly are to live in a world of hypocrisy and hostility to grace. Through vivid sketches of persons such as Hannah, Eli, Samuel, Saul, Jonathan, Goliath, David, Abigail, Joab, Uriah, Bathsheba, Amnon, and Absalom, the book illustrates the contrast between godliness and rebellion, confirming that the Lord knows the way of the righteous but that the way of the wicked will perish (Ps. 1).

The kingdom of God is a kingdom of grace to sinners, and Samuel is a book of grace. It highlights the mercies of God against the dark backdrop of the depravity of fallen man exhibited in the horrible sins of David (2 Sam. 11–12). His crimes brought great sorrow to his later years and threatened to destroy his family and kingdom (chs. 13–20). However, God gave David the graces of repentance and forgiveness of sins (12:13; Pss. 25; 32; 51), free gifts that would be paid for by Christ (Luke 24:46–47; Acts 5:30–31). God's fatherly love was bound to David's line in the covenant, and though sin could bring discipline it could not break God's faithfulness (2 Sam. 7:14–15; 22:51). David's experiences of God's grace to sinners found expression in the Psalms, which serve as experiential models of true prayer, piety, and praise for the people of God in all ages.

Outline:

I. The Birth and Early Ministry of Samuel (1 Sam. 1:1—7:17)
- A. Hannah's Prayer and Samuel's Birth (1 Sam. 1:1—2:11)
- B. The Lord's Judgment upon Eli's Household (1 Sam. 2:12–36)
- C. The Call of Samuel to Prophetic Ministry (1 Sam. 3:1—4:1)
- D. The Departure and Return of the Glory (1 Sam. 4:1—7:1)
- E. Israel's Return to the Lord through Samuel (1 Sam. 7:2–17)

II. The Rise and Rejection of King Saul (1 Sam. 8:1—15:35)
- A. Israel's Rejection of the Lord as King (1 Sam. 8:1–22)
- B. God's Sovereign Selection of a King (1 Sam. 9:1—10:27)
- C. Saul's Promising Start (1 Sam. 11:1–15)
- D. Samuel's Integrity and Exhortation to Israel (1 Sam. 12:1–25)
- E. Saul's Rebellion and Jonathan's Faith (1 Sam. 13:1—15:35)

III. The Victories and Persecution of David (1 Sam. 16:1—26:25)
- A. David's Anointing as King and Enlisting to Serve Saul (1 Sam. 16:1–23)
- B. Saul's Failure and David's Victory by Faith (1 Sam. 17:1–54)

- C. Saul's Jealousy and Jonathan's Loyalty to David (1 Sam. 17:55—20:42)
- D. David's Flight from Saul into the Wilderness (1 Sam. 21:1—26:25)

IV. The End of Saul and Rise of King David (1 Sam. 27:1—2 Sam. 4:12)
- A. David's Deceptive Sojourn with Achish (1 Sam. 27:1—28:2)
- B. Saul's Terror and Consulting a Witch (1 Sam. 28:3–25)
- C. David's Release from Achish and War with Amalek (1 Sam. 29:1—30:31)
- D. The Deaths of Saul and His Sons (1 Sam. 31:1–13)
- E. David's Lamentation over Saul and Jonathan (2 Sam. 1:1–27)
- F. David, King of Judah, against Ish-bosheth, King of Israel (2 Sam. 2:1—4:12)

V. The Triumphant Reign of David over All Israel (2 Sam. 5:1—10:19)
- A. The Establishment of David's Kingdom (2 Sam. 5:1–25)
- B. The Bringing of the Ark of the Covenant to Jerusalem (2 Sam. 6:1–23)
- C. The Lord's Covenant with David (2 Sam. 7:1–29)
- D. The Power, Justice, and Mercy of King David (2 Sam. 8:1—10:19)

VI. The Crimes and Troubles of David and His Household (2 Sam. 11:1—20:26)
- A. David's Adultery, Murder, and Repentance (2 Sam. 11:1—12:31)
- B. Amnon's Incest and Absalom's Revenge (2 Sam. 13:1—14:33)
- C. Absalom's Rebellion against David (2 Sam. 15:1—17:29)
- D. Absalom's Death and David's Restoration (2 Sam. 18:1—19:40)
- E. The Rebellion of Sheba against David (2 Sam. 19:41—20:26)

VII. The Conclusion of David's Reign (2 Sam. 21:1—24:25)
- A. Vengeance for the Gibeonites on Saul's Family (2 Sam. 21:1–14)
- B. War between the Philistines and an Aging David (2 Sam. 21:15–22)
- C. The Song of David to the Lord (2 Sam. 22:1–51)
- D. David's Last Words (2 Sam. 23:1–7)
- E. David's Mighty Men (2 Sam. 23:8–39)
- F. The Tragic Census of Israel (2 Sam. 24:1–25)

THE FIRST BOOK OF

SAMUEL

CHAPTER 1

NOW there was a certain man of Ramathaim-
zophim, of mount Ephraim, and his name *was*
Elkanah, the son of Jeroham, the son of Elihu, the
son of Tohu, the son of Zuph, an Ephrathite:
2 And he had two wives; the name of the one *was*
Hannah, and the name of the other Peninnah:
and Peninnah had children, but Hannah had no
children.
3 And this man went up out of his city yearly to
worship and to sacrifice unto the LORD of hosts
in Shiloh. And the two sons of Eli, Hophni and
Phinehas, the priests of the LORD, *were* there.
4 ¶ And when the time was that Elkanah offered,
he gave to Peninnah his wife, and to all her sons
and her daughters, portions:
5 But unto Hannah he gave a worthy portion; for
he loved Hannah: but the LORD had shut up her
womb.
6 And her adversary also provoked her sore, for
to make her fret, because the LORD had shut up
her womb.
7 And *as* he did so year by year, when she went
up to the house of the LORD, so she provoked her;
therefore she wept, and did not eat.
8 Then said Elkanah her husband to her, Hannah,
why weepest thou? and why eatest thou not? and
why is thy heart grieved? *am* not I better to thee
than ten sons?
9 ¶ So Hannah rose up after they had eaten in
Shiloh, and after they had drunk. Now Eli the
priest sat upon a seat by a post of the temple of
the LORD.
10 And she *was* in bitterness of soul, and prayed
unto the LORD, and wept sore.
11 And she vowed a vow, and said, O LORD of
hosts, if thou wilt indeed look on the affliction
of thine handmaid, and remember me, and not
forget thine handmaid, but wilt give unto thine
handmaid a man child, then I will give him unto
the LORD all the days of his life, and there shall no
razor come upon his head.
12 And it came to pass, as she continued praying
before the LORD, that Eli marked her mouth.
13 Now Hannah, she spake in her heart; only her
lips moved, but her voice was not heard: therefore
Eli thought she had been drunken.
14 And Eli said unto her, How long wilt thou be
drunken? put away thy wine from thee.
15 And Hannah answered and said, No, my lord,

THE BIRTH AND EARLY MINISTRY OF SAMUEL (1 SAM. 1–7)

Hannah's Prayer and Samuel's Birth (1 Sam. 1:1—2:11)

Chapter 1: *Hannah pours out her heart to the Lord for a son and promises that if He would grant her request, she would give that child to the Lord for His service.*

1:1 *Ramathaim-zophim*. Elsewhere, "Ramah" (v. 19; 2:11). *Ephrathite*. Ordinarily one belonging to the tribe of Ephraim. Yet Elkanah and Samuel were of the tribe of Levi (1 Chron. 6:16–28), which was necessary for his priestly apprenticeship. The Levites were scattered throughout the country, so *Ephrathite* refers to the place of residence, not tribal identity.

1:2 *two wives*. Polygamy is not in accordance with God's ordinance (Gen. 2:24). Although the law of Moses does not expressly forbid it, it does not endorse it, and in every instance the Scripture puts in bold the conflicts it causes. *no children*. Considered a reproach from the Lord (30:1–2,23).

1:3 the *LORD of hosts*. The Supreme Commander of all spiritual and physical forces.

1:5 *worthy portion*. A double portion, expressing favor. *the LORD had shut up her womb*. Both conception and barrenness are subject to God's sovereign purpose (Ps. 127:3).

1:6 *her adversary*. The Hebrew term occurs only here and refers to the rival wife. *provoked her sore*. Literally, "grieved her a grief," an idiom expressing intense grief. *for to make her fret*. Literally, "in order to irritate or humiliate her."

1:10 *bitterness of soul*. Deep distress. *wept sore*. Wept intensely.

1:11 *handmaid*. Female slave. *no razor come upon his head*. He would be a Nazarite (see Num. 6:5).

1:12 *marked her mouth*. Observed her mouth.

1:13 *spake in her heart*. Her prayer was not audible as was common practice, a good reminder that true prayer is directed to God and is not to impress men.

1:16 *daughter of Belial*. Worthless or wicked person (2:12; 10:27; 25:17,25; 30:22; 2 Sam. 16:7; 20:1; 22:5; 23:6); *Belial* would later be used as a name for Satan (2 Cor. 6:15). *complaint*. Trouble or anxiety. *hithero*. Until now.

1:20 *Samuel*. The name seems to mean "his name is God," in recognition of God, who gave Hannah a son in answer to prayer.

1:24 *weaned*. Samuel was probably three years old. *three bullocks*. Required for the burnt offering, the thank-offering,

I *am* a woman of a sorrowful spirit: I have drunk
neither wine nor strong drink, but have poured
out my soul before the LORD.
16 Count not thine handmaid for a daughter of
Belial: for out of the abundance of my complaint
and grief have I spoken hitherto.
17 Then Eli answered and said, Go in peace: and
the God of Israel grant *thee* thy petition that thou
hast asked of him.
18 And she said, Let thine handmaid find grace
in thy sight. So the woman went her way, and did
eat, and her countenance was no more *sad*.
19 ¶ And they rose up in the morning early, and
worshipped before the LORD, and returned, and
came to their house to Ramah: and Elkanah knew
Hannah his wife; and the LORD remembered her.
20 Wherefore it came to pass, when the time was
come about after Hannah had conceived, that she
bare a son, and called his name Samuel, *saying*,
Because I have asked him of the LORD.
21 And the man Elkanah, and all his house, went
up to offer unto the LORD the yearly sacrifice, and
his vow.
22 But Hannah went not up; for she said unto
her husband, *I will not go up* until the child be
weaned, and *then* I will bring him, that he may
appear before the LORD, and there abide for ever.
23 And Elkanah her husband said unto her, Do
what seemeth thee good; tarry until thou have
weaned him; only the LORD establish his word. So
the woman abode, and gave her son suck until she
weaned him.
24 ¶ And when she had weaned him, she took
him up with her, with three bullocks, and one
ephah of flour, and a bottle of wine, and brought
him unto the house of the LORD in Shiloh: and
the child *was* young.
25 And they slew a bullock, and brought the child
to Eli.
26 And she said, Oh my lord, *as* thy soul liveth,
my lord, I *am* the woman that stood by thee here,
praying unto the LORD.
27 For this child I prayed; and the LORD hath
given me my petition which I asked of him:
28 Therefore also I have lent him to the LORD; as
long as he liveth he shall be lent to the LORD. And
he worshipped the LORD there.

CHAPTER 2

AND Hannah prayed, and said, My heart rejoiceth
in the LORD, mine horn is exalted in the LORD: my
mouth is enlarged over mine enemies; because I
rejoice in thy salvation.
2 *There is* none holy as the LORD: for *there is* none
beside thee: neither *is there* any rock like our God.
3 Talk no more so exceeding proudly; let *not* ar-
rogancy come out of your mouth: for the LORD
is a God of knowledge, and by him actions are
weighed.
4 The bows of the mighty men *are* broken, and
they that stumbled are girded with strength.
5 *They that were* full have hired out themselves
for bread; and *they that were* hungry ceased: so
that the barren hath born seven; and she that hath
many children is waxed feeble.
6 The LORD killeth, and maketh alive: he bringeth
down to the grave, and bringeth up.
7 The LORD maketh poor, and maketh rich: he
bringeth low, and lifteth up.
8 He raiseth up the poor out of the dust, *and*
lifteth up the beggar from the dunghill, to set
them among princes, and to make them inherit
the throne of glory: for the pillars of the earth *are*

---

and most likely a special offering to mark the consecration of Samuel into the Lord's work.

1:25 *slew a bullock.* Most likely referring specifically to the sacrifice for consecration.

1:28 *lent.* The Hebrew has the idea of letting someone have what was asked for. Ironically, the Lord had given Hannah her petition, which she now returns in keeping with her vow.

Thoughts for Personal/Family Worship: Chapter 1

1. **This chapter teaches us so much about effectual, fervent prayer. Hannah is in complete submission to the will of the Lord, confessing that she is His "handmaid" (v. 11). She is dependent upon God; therefore she prays with real purpose and desires that her request will be to the glory of God. Her prayer is earnest; she "wept sore" (v. 10), and like the widow in the parable of the unjust judge (Luke 18:1–8) she persevered until her request was answered. How can we pray like Hannah?**
2. **Hannah's taking Samuel to the tabernacle and dedicating him to the service of the Lord demonstrates the importance of keeping vows made to the Lord. Humanly speaking, this had to have been an emotional trauma, but Hannah was not deterred from keeping her promise. Her vow was not rash. Vows are not "bargaining chips" to be used in prayer to get God to answer us according to our own will or desires. God takes vows seriously and expects us to keep our word (Eccl. 5:2–7).**

Chapter 2: *Hannah's prayer of thanksgiving stands in contrast to the wickedness of Eli's sons.*

2:1 *Hannah prayed.* She rejoiced in the Lord and in His salvation. This is a psalm of thankfulness and of prophecy. *horn.* Symbol of strength and power (v. 10). *enlarged.* Opened wide. Note the parallels between Hannah's prayer ending with the prospect of Messiah (v. 10) and Mary's prayer in response to the conception of Messiah in her womb (Luke 1:46–55).

2:2 *rock.* A huge, immovable boulder, indicating the certainty and sureness of the Lord's protection.

2:3 *weighed.* Measured, or examined as to whether they are just.

2:4 *girded.* Encircled or secured with a belt.

2:8 *the pillars of the earth.* Referring to the Lord's creative work, which highlights His unique power and authority to humble the high and exalt the low.

2:10 *exalt the horn.* See note at v. 1 and parallel in Luke 1:69.

the LORD's, and he hath set the world upon them.
9 He will keep the feet of his saints, and the
wicked shall be silent in darkness; for by strength
shall no man prevail.
10 The adversaries of the LORD shall be broken to
pieces; out of heaven shall he thunder upon them:
the LORD shall judge the ends of the earth; and
he shall give strength unto his king, and exalt the
horn of his anointed.
11 And Elkanah went to Ramah to his house. And
the child did minister unto the LORD before Eli
the priest.
12 ¶ Now the sons of Eli *were* sons of Belial; they
knew not the LORD.
13 And the priests' custom with the people *was,*
that, when any man offered sacrifice, the priest's
servant came, while the flesh was in seething, with
a fleshhook of three teeth in his hand;
14 And he struck *it* into the pan, or kettle, or
caldron, or pot; all that the fleshhook brought up
the priest took for himself. So they did in Shiloh
unto all the Israelites that came thither.
15 Also before they burnt the fat, the priest's
servant came, and said to the man that sacrificed,
Give flesh to roast for the priest; for he will not
have sodden flesh of thee, but raw.
16 And *if* any man said unto him, Let them not
fail to burn the fat presently, and *then* take *as*
much as thy soul desireth; then he would answer
him, *Nay*; but thou shalt give *it me* now: and if
not, I will take *it* by force.
17 Wherefore the sin of the young men was very
great before the LORD: for men abhorred the of-
fering of the LORD.
18 ¶ But Samuel ministered before the LORD,
being a child, girded with a linen ephod.
19 Moreover his mother made him a little coat,
and brought *it* to him from year to year, when
she came up with her husband to offer the yearly
sacrifice.
20 ¶ And Eli blessed Elkanah and his wife, and
said, The LORD give thee seed of this woman for
the loan which is lent to the LORD. And they went
unto their own home.
21 And the LORD visited Hannah, so that she con-
ceived, and bare three sons and two daughters.
And the child Samuel grew before the LORD.
22 ¶ Now Eli was very old, and heard all that his
sons did unto all Israel; and how they lay with the
women that assembled *at* the door of the taber-
nacle of the congregation.
23 And he said unto them, Why do ye such
things? for I hear of your evil dealings by all this
people.
24 Nay, my sons; for *it is* no good report that I
hear: ye make the LORD's people to transgress.
25 If one man sin against another, the judge shall
judge him: but if a man sin against the LORD,
who shall intreat for him? Notwithstanding they
hearkened not unto the voice of their father,
because the LORD would slay them.
26 And the child Samuel grew on, and was in
favour both with the LORD, and also with men.
27 ¶ And there came a man of God unto Eli, and
said unto him, Thus saith the LORD, Did I plainly
appear unto the house of thy father, when they
were in Egypt in Pharaoh's house?
28 And did I choose him out of all the tribes of
Israel *to be* my priest, to offer upon mine altar,
to burn incense, to wear an ephod before me?
and did I give unto the house of thy father all the
offerings made by fire of the children of Israel?
29 Wherefore kick ye at my sacrifice and at
mine offering, which I have commanded *in my*

---

his king . . . his anointed. Since there was no king in Israel at this point, this is an expression of Hannah's faith in the coming Messiah and Christ (Hebrew and Greek words for *anointed*). The king was anointed with oil (1 Sam. 9:16; 10:1; 12:3,5; 15:1,17; 16:3,8,12–13; 24:6,10; 26:9,11,16,23; 2 Sam. 1:14,16,21; 2:4,7; 3:39; 5:3,17; 12:7) as a sign of the empowerment of the Holy Spirit for his office (1 Sam. 10:6,10; 11:6; 16:13; 2 Sam. 23:2; cf. Isa. 61:1).

The Lord's Judgment upon Eli's Household (1 Sam. 2:12–36)

2:12 *sons of Belial.* Worthless people characterized by wickedness.

2:13 *seething.* Boiling. *fleshhook of three teeth.* A three-pronged fork for retrieving meat from the cooking pot (v. 14).

2:14 *the priest took for himself.* Through greed, Hophni and Phinehas robbed those bringing offerings to the Lord by taking the giver's portion of the offering as well as their own entitlement (Lev. 7:30–34).

2:15 *fat.* The part to be offered to the Lord (Lev. 3:16; 7:23). *sodden.* Boiled. These wicked priests demanded their portion before the Lord was given His, evidence of their contempt toward God.

2:16 *presently.* Literally, "as the day," an idiom meaning soon or quickly.

2:18 *girded.* Encircled with a band or belt. *ephod.* Embroidered cape worn by priests.

2:19 *little coat.* A sleeveless, cloak-like outer garment.

2:20–21 *loan which is lent.* Literally, "the request which he asked." The faithfulness of Elkanah and Hannah results in further blessing from God—*three sons and two daughters.* The Lord is no man's debtor.

2:22 *women that assembled at the door.* Perhaps women who served the tabernacle in mending its fabric or furniture (Ex. 35:25; 38:8) or women devoted to prayer and worship (Luke 2:36–37). They were targets of sexual abuse. *lay.* Had sexual relations.

2:25 *they hearkened not . . . because the LORD would slay them.* God, in His righteous wrath against their sin, gave them over to hardness of heart because He had decided to destroy them for their sins (Josh. 11:20). This is the sobering doctrine of reprobation (Rom. 9:17–22).

2:26 The language is similar to that which describes the child Jesus (Luke 2:52).

2:27 *man of God.* One of the Old Testament designations for a prophet. *house of thy father.* Aaron, the first high priest.

2:28 *choose.* Only God could choose the priests, whether

habitation; and honourest thy sons above me, to
make yourselves fat with the chiefest of all the
offerings of Israel my people?
30 Wherefore the LORD God of Israel saith, I said
indeed *that* thy house, and the house of thy father,
should walk before me for ever: but now the LORD
saith, Be it far from me; for them that honour me
I will honour, and they that despise me shall be
lightly esteemed.
31 Behold, the days come, that I will cut off thine
arm, and the arm of thy father's house, that there
shall not be an old man in thine house.
32 And thou shalt see an enemy *in my* habitation,
in all *the wealth* which *God* shall give Israel: and
there shall not be an old man in thine house for
ever.
33 And the man of thine, *whom* I shall not cut off
from mine altar, *shall be* to consume thine eyes,
and to grieve thine heart: and all the increase of
thine house shall die in the flower of their age.
34 And this *shall be* a sign unto thee, that shall
come upon thy two sons, on Hophni and Phine-
has; in one day they shall die both of them.
35 And I will raise me up a faithful priest, *that*
shall do according to *that* which *is* in mine heart
and in my mind: and I will build him a sure house;
and he shall walk before mine anointed for ever.
36 And it shall come to pass, *that* every one that
is left in thine house shall come *and* crouch to
him for a piece of silver and a morsel of bread,
and shall say, Put me, I pray thee, into one of the
priests' offices, that I may eat a piece of bread.

CHAPTER 3

AND the child Samuel ministered unto the LORD
before Eli. And the word of the LORD was precious
in those days; *there was* no open vision.
2 And it came to pass at that time, when Eli *was*
laid down in his place, and his eyes began to wax
dim, *that* he could not see;
3 And ere the lamp of God went out in the
temple of the LORD, where the ark of God *was*,
and Samuel was laid down *to sleep*;
4 That the LORD called Samuel: and he answered,
Here *am* I.
5 And he ran unto Eli, and said, Here *am* I; for
thou calledst me. And he said, I called not; lie
down again. And he went and lay down.
6 And the LORD called yet again, Samuel. And
Samuel arose and went to Eli, and said, Here *am* I;
for thou didst call me. And he answered, I called
not, my son; lie down again.
7 Now Samuel did not yet know the LORD, nei-
ther was the word of the LORD yet revealed unto
him.
8 And the LORD called Samuel again the third
time. And he arose and went to Eli, and said, Here
am I; for thou didst call me. And Eli perceived
that the LORD had called the child.

---

those of the Levitical priesthood or Jesus Christ (Heb. 5:1,4–5).
2:29 *Wherefore kick ye at my sacrifice?* Why do you scorn my sacrifice? *make yourselves fat.* Though Eli was literally, "a heavy man" (4:18), this is most likely an idiom for prosperity.
2:31 *cut off thine arm.* Take away the strength and influence of your family.
2:35 Abiathar, the last of Eli's descendants, was replaced by Zadok as high priest (1 Kings 1:7–8; 2:27,35; Ezek. 44:15). Ultimately God abolished the entire Aaronic priesthood and anointed the only perfectly *faithful priest*, the Lord Jesus Christ (Heb. 2:17; 7:11–17). *according to that which is in my heart.* One who will do God's will (see note at 1 Sam. 13:14). *he shall walk before mine anointed for ever.* The Hebrew verb could take as its subject either "priest" or "house." It could be understood either as the priest serving in the presence of God's king or, more likely, as the people of Christ (His *house*, Heb. 3:6) living in the presence of their *anointed* Priest. Both priests and kings were anointed (Ex. 28:41; 29:7; see note at 1 Sam. 2:10), and this text suggests the merging of the two offices in the ideal Priest-King (Ps. 110:1,4).

Thoughts for Personal/Family Worship: Chapter 2

1. **Hannah sets a wonderful example. When God answered her heartfelt prayer she was quick to acknowledge His goodness and to rejoice in Him. If we would desire the Lord to answer our prayers, let us be sure to give Him our thanks and praise for those petitions already granted. "It is a good thing to give thanks unto the LORD, and to sing praises unto thy name, O most High" (Ps. 92:1). We should always rejoice in the Lord for His saving us through the work of His anointed, Jesus Christ. How have God's acts in your life revealed His glorious attributes in Jesus Christ? How are you praising Him for this?**
2. **There is a stark contrast between the wickedness of Eli's sons and the righteousness of Samuel. Both had the advantage of having godly parents; yet how differently they turned out. Despite the immense privilege of being born into a family of high spiritual standing, Hophni and Phinehas turned their backs upon the Lord and spurned His ways, seeking rather to exploit the people for personal gain. By way of contrast, Samuel was growing "in favour both with the LORD, and also with men" (v. 26). You who are the parents of young children, pray not only that the Lord would have mercy and save your offspring, but also seek by God's grace to correct any wayward behavior in them. Do not wait too long, as Eli did. Let us remember that the Lord says "them that honour me I will honour" (v. 30).**

The Call of Samuel to Prophetic Ministry (1 Sam. 3:1—4:1)
Chapter 3: *The Lord calls Samuel and instructs him to reveal to Eli the end of his house.*

3:1 *precious.* Scarce or rare. *no open vision.* Literally, "there was no vision being spread abroad." This refers to the rarity of prophetic activity.
3:2 *eyes began to wax dim.* His eyesight was failing.
3:3 *ere.* before. *the lamp of God.* The seven-branched lampstand, or "candlestick," situated in the holy place.
3:7 *did not yet know the LORD.* Either was not yet converted to a living faith (2:12; but see 2:26), or was inexperienced in receiving revelation from God as a prophet.

9 Therefore Eli said unto Samuel, Go, lie down:
and it shall be, if he call thee, that thou shalt say,
Speak, LORD; for thy servant heareth. So Samuel
went and lay down in his place.
10 And the LORD came, and stood, and called
as at other times, Samuel, Samuel. Then Samuel
answered, Speak; for thy servant heareth.
11 ¶ And the LORD said to Samuel, Behold, I will
do a thing in Israel, at which both the ears of
every one that heareth it shall tingle.
12 In that day I will perform against Eli all *things*
which I have spoken concerning his house: when
I begin, I will also make an end.
13 For I have told him that I will judge his house
for ever for the iniquity which he knoweth;
because his sons made themselves vile, and he
restrained them not.
14 And therefore I have sworn unto the house
of Eli, that the iniquity of Eli's house shall not be
purged with sacrifice nor offering for ever.
15 ¶ And Samuel lay until the morning, and
opened the doors of the house of the LORD. And
Samuel feared to shew Eli the vision.
16 Then Eli called Samuel, and said, Samuel, my
son. And he answered, Here *am* I.
17 And he said, What *is* the thing that *the LORD*
hath said unto thee? I pray thee hide *it* not from
me: God do so to thee, and more also, if thou hide
any thing from me of all the things that he said
unto thee.
18 And Samuel told him every whit, and hid
nothing from him. And he said, It *is* the LORD: let
him do what seemeth him good.
19 ¶ And Samuel grew, and the LORD was with
him, and did let none of his words fall to the
ground.
20 And all Israel from Dan even to Beer-sheba
knew that Samuel *was* established *to be* a prophet
of the LORD.
21 And the LORD appeared again in Shiloh: for
the LORD revealed himself to Samuel in Shiloh by
the word of the LORD.

CHAPTER 4

AND the word of Samuel came to all Israel. Now
Israel went out against the Philistines to battle,
and pitched beside Eben-ezer: and the Philistines
pitched in Aphek.
2 And the Philistines put themselves in array
against Israel: and when they joined battle, Israel
was smitten before the Philistines: and they slew
of the army in the field about four thousand men.
3 ¶ And when the people were come into the
camp, the elders of Israel said, Wherefore hath the
LORD smitten us to day before the Philistines? Let
us fetch the ark of the covenant of the LORD out
of Shiloh unto us, that, when it cometh among
us, it may save us out of the hand of our enemies.
4 So the people sent to Shiloh, that they might

3:10 *the LORD came and stood.* Samuel not only hears the voice of the Lord, but here he also sees a vision of the Lord's presence.
3:11 *The ears of every one that heareth it shall tingle* indicates the horror of hearing about the destruction of Shiloh (Jer. 7:12–14; 26:6–9).
3:12 *when I begin, I will also make an end.* Literally, "a beginning and ending." The Lord will not stop until all threats are fulfilled.
3:13 *his sons made themselves vile.* One of eighteen corrections of the scribes (*tiqqune sopherim*), where scribes ensured that the text did not jeopardize God's dignity. Some ancient traditions, for instance the Septuagint, charge the sons with cursing God. Such behavior would certainly have brought a curse upon them. *he restrained them not.* He did not rebuke them.
3:14 The iniquity of Eli's house was so great that no amount of *sacrifice* or *offering* would appease the Lord's wrath.
3:18 *every whit.* Everything; the Hebrew is "all the words." *It is the LORD.* Submission to, and acceptance of, the Lord's will is the only way to handle His judgment.
3:19 *let none of his words fall to the ground.* The Lord is with His messenger (Hag. 1:13), so that the prophet's words are God's Word, and not one of God's words can fail (1 Kings 8:56; 2 Kings 10:10).
3:20 *Dan even to Beer-sheba.* Refers to Israel's northern and southern extremes, thus designating the entire nation.

Thoughts for Personal/Family Worship: Chapter 3

When the Lord called young Samuel, Samuel imagined it was Eli who spoke; yet his response provides a model of how we should perform our duties. No doubt Samuel's training for the Lord's service was demanding, with many chores. He probably looked forward to a good night's rest. Having "laid down to sleep" (v. 3), Samuel heard a voice calling him. He did not lie in bed or pretend to be asleep; he did not get up begrudging this interruption to his rest; instead he "ran unto Eli" (v. 5). There was a willingness to serve. Three times he got up and went to Eli without complaint or bitterness. It was only after this that he came to understand that it was the Lord who was calling him. Could there be times when we miss what the Lord is saying to us through His Word because we are overwhelmed by circumstances of life? Let us be sensitive to God's Word and not miss the blessings by failing to answer the Lord's calling us. What does it mean to pray "Speak, LORD; for thy servant heareth"?

The Departure and Return of the Glory (1 Sam. 4:1—7:1)

Chapter 4: *Israel's sin leads to utter defeat by the Philistines, the capture of the ark, and the deaths of Eli and his sons.*

4:1 *the word of Samuel came to all Israel.* God blessed his prophetic preaching, and it reached the whole nation (3:19–21).
4:2 *put themselves in array.* Lined up to fight.
4:3 *Let us fetch the ark.* They regarded the ark as a talisman, a magic charm. Man is capable of transforming things with spiritual significance to external trinkets of idolatry (Jer. 7:4). The box represented God's presence, but God was not in the box.

bring from thence the ark of the covenant of
the LORD of hosts, which dwelleth *between* the
cherubims: and the two sons of Eli, Hophni and
Phinehas, *were* there with the ark of the covenant
of God.
5 And when the ark of the covenant of the LORD
came into the camp, all Israel shouted with a great
shout, so that the earth rang again.
6 And when the Philistines heard the noise of the
shout, they said, What *meaneth* the noise of this
great shout in the camp of the Hebrews? And they
understood that the ark of the LORD was come
into the camp.
7 And the Philistines were afraid, for they said,
God is come into the camp. And they said, Woe
unto us! for there hath not been such a thing
heretofore.
8 Woe unto us! who shall deliver us out of the
hand of these mighty Gods? these *are* the Gods
that smote the Egyptians with all the plagues in
the wilderness.
9 Be strong, and quit yourselves like men, O ye
Philistines, that ye be not servants unto the He-
brews, as they have been to you: quit yourselves
like men, and fight.
10 ¶ And the Philistines fought, and Israel was
smitten, and they fled every man into his tent:
and there was a very great slaughter; for there fell
of Israel thirty thousand footmen.
11 And the ark of God was taken; and the two
sons of Eli, Hophni and Phinehas, were slain.
12 ¶ And there ran a man of Benjamin out of the
army, and came to Shiloh the same day with his
clothes rent, and with earth upon his head.
13 And when he came, lo, Eli sat upon a seat by
the wayside watching: for his heart trembled for
the ark of God. And when the man came into the
city, and told *it*, all the city cried out.
14 And when Eli heard the noise of the crying, he
said, What *meaneth* the noise of this tumult? And
the man came in hastily, and told Eli.
15 Now Eli was ninety and eight years old; and
his eyes were dim, that he could not see.
16 And the man said unto Eli, I *am* he that came
out of the army, and I fled to day out of the army.
And he said, What is there done, my son?
17 And the messenger answered and said, Israel
is fled before the Philistines, and there hath been
also a great slaughter among the people, and thy
two sons also, Hophni and Phinehas, are dead,
and the ark of God is taken.
18 And it came to pass, when he made mention
of the ark of God, that he fell from off the seat
backward by the side of the gate, and his neck
brake, and he died: for he was an old man, and
heavy. And he had judged Israel forty years.
19 ¶ And his daughter in law, Phinehas' wife, was
with child, *near* to be delivered: and when she
heard the tidings that the ark of God was taken,
and that her father in law and her husband were
dead, she bowed herself and travailed; for her
pains came upon her.
20 And about the time of her death the women
that stood by her said unto her, Fear not; for thou
hast born a son. But she answered not, neither did
she regard *it*.
21 And she named the child Ichabod, saying, The
glory is departed from Israel: because the ark of
God was taken, and because of her father in law
and her husband.
22 And she said, The glory is departed from
Israel: for the ark of God is taken.

4:5 *the earth rang again.* The earth reechoed with the noise.
4:7 *heretofore.* Previously.
4:9 *quit yourselves like men.* Literally, "become men," with the sense of acting like men.
4:12 *his clothes rent, and with earth upon his head.* Signs of mourning and humiliation.
4:13 *his heart trembled.* He was anxious, an indication of his concern for the safety of the ark.
4:14 *tumult.* Commotion.
4:19 *travailed.* Went into labor to give birth.
4:21 *Ichabod.* The Hebrew means either "no glory" or "Where is glory?" God withdraws His glory from an apostate people (Ezek. 11:23).

Thoughts for Personal/Family Worship: Chapter 4

1. **The defeat of Israel (v. 2) clearly revealed that the Lord was not among them. This defeat should have humbled them to seek the Lord, as Joshua did after Israel's defeat at Ai (Josh. 7:6–13). However, neither Hophni and Phinehas nor the people humbled themselves and prayed. Instead, they foolishly thought they could force God's hand to defend them by unlawfully bringing the ark onto the battlefield. They imagined that God would never allow the ark to fall into enemy hands. After all, the ark had been central in so many miracles and victories in the past (e.g., crossing the Jordan, Josh. 3, and the fall of Jericho, Josh. 6) that they viewed this sacred item as a mere good luck charm. The result was catastrophic for Israel. Religion is not a means of manipulating God for personal advantage. God will not be used. If we want to enjoy the blessings of His presence, we must obey His commands (Josh. 1:8–9). God hides His face from the wicked (Deut. 31:17). What religious objects or rituals do people trust in today?**
2. **The name "Ichabod" represents a tragedy for the Lord's people. The glory of the Lord departed from Israel because of their sins, and likewise we find it gone in many churches today. Some churches may appear to be lively and well attended. Some individuals may put on an outward, public show of humility and faith. But appearance does not equate to reality. The accusation of Christ is this: "I know thy works, that thou hast a name that thou livest, and art dead" (Rev. 3:1). What about you? What does the Lord Jesus say of you? O how we need, by God's grace, to hide His Word in our hearts that we do not sin against Him (cf. Ps. 119:11). Whenever we do sin let us ensure that we make all haste to truly repent and wait upon the Lord.**

CHAPTER 5

AND the Philistines took the ark of God, and brought it from Eben-ezer unto Ashdod.

2 When the Philistines took the ark of God, they brought it into the house of Dagon, and set it by Dagon.

3 ¶ And when they of Ashdod arose early on the morrow, behold, Dagon *was* fallen upon his face to the earth before the ark of the LORD. And they took Dagon, and set him in his place again.

4 And when they arose early on the morrow morning, behold, Dagon *was* fallen upon his face to the ground before the ark of the LORD; and the head of Dagon and both the palms of his hands *were* cut off upon the threshold; only *the stump of* Dagon was left to him.

5 Therefore neither the priests of Dagon, nor any that come into Dagon's house, tread on the threshold of Dagon in Ashdod unto this day.

6 But the hand of the LORD was heavy upon them of Ashdod, and he destroyed them, and smote them with emerods, *even* Ashdod and the coasts thereof.

7 And when the men of Ashdod saw that *it was* so, they said, The ark of the God of Israel shall not abide with us: for his hand is sore upon us, and upon Dagon our god.

8 They sent therefore and gathered all the lords of the Philistines unto them, and said, What shall we do with the ark of the God of Israel? And they answered, Let the ark of the God of Israel be carried about unto Gath. And they carried the ark of the God of Israel about *thither*.

9 And it was *so*, that, after they had carried it about, the hand of the LORD was against the city with a very great destruction: and he smote the men of the city, both small and great, and they had emerods in their secret parts.

10 ¶ Therefore they sent the ark of God to Ekron. And it came to pass, as the ark of God came to Ekron, that the Ekronites cried out, saying, They have brought about the ark of the God of Israel to us, to slay us and our people.

11 So they sent and gathered together all the lords of the Philistines, and said, Send away the ark of the God of Israel, and let it go again to his own place, that it slay us not, and our people: for there was a deadly destruction throughout all the city; the hand of God was very heavy there.

12 And the men that died not were smitten with the emerods: and the cry of the city went up to heaven.

CHAPTER 6

AND the ark of the LORD was in the country of the Philistines seven months.

2 And the Philistines called for the priests and the diviners, saying, What shall we do to the ark of the LORD? tell us wherewith we shall send it to his place.

3 And they said, If ye send away the ark of the God of Israel, send it not empty; but in any wise return him a trespass offering: then ye shall be healed, and it shall be known to you why his hand is not removed from you.

4 Then said they, What *shall be* the trespass offering which we shall return to him? They answered, Five golden emerods, and five golden mice, *according to* the number of the lords of the Philistines: for one plague *was* on you all, and on your lords.

5 Wherefore ye shall make images of your emerods, and images of your mice that mar the land; and ye shall give glory unto the God of Israel: per-

Chapter 5: *The Philistines place the ark of the Lord in the temple of Dagon, resulting in the destruction of Dagon's image and the infliction of the Philistines with a painful plague.*

5:1 *Ashdod.* One of the five principal cities of the Philistines.
5:2 *Dagon.* Opinions differ as to whether *Dagon* was the god of grain, as identified in Canaanite literature, or a fish god. Regardless, *Dagon* was the chief god or Baal of the Philistines.
5:6 *emerods.* Some sort of swelling, an ulcer or hemorrhoid (vv. 9,12). *coasts.* Borders or regions.
5:7 *his hand is sore upon us.* Literally, "his hand is heavy upon us."
5:8–10 *Gath* and *Ekron* were also among the five principal cities of the Philistines.
5:11 *deadly destruction.* Literally, "the panic of death."

Thoughts for Personal/Family Worship: Chapter 5

1. **Although the ark was not the reality of God's person, it was symbolic of His presence, and the Philistines were aware of its significance. For the sake of His own glory, God would not allow the heathen, who in their ignorance equated the box with Jehovah, to elevate their idol above Himself. Without human aid, He demonstrated that Dagon was nothing, a figment of their imagination without life or power. We learn an important lesson here: that while God is often pleased to use human instrumentality in His service, He needs no one to rescue Him or help Him. Therefore we must always ensure that our work for Him is carried out in reverent humility, for the Lord is not dependent upon anyone. His power and might are beyond human comprehension.**
2. **The Philistines acted ignorantly but were nonetheless held accountable for their blasphemy and violation of the first commandment. God's law is absolute, and ignorance of it is no excuse. What are the implications of this for missions?**

Chapter 6: *The Philistines send the ark back to Israel, and many in Israel are slain for looking into the ark.*

6:2 *diviners.* Fortune-tellers or those who make predictions with magic.
6:3 *trespass offering.* Not according to Mosaic definition, but a compensation offered in hope of pacifying Israel's God and diverting His plague against them.
6:4–5 *Five* represents the five Philistine lords and their five principal cities. *golden emerods.* See notes at 5:6. The five

adventure he will lighten his hand from off you,
and from off your gods, and from off your land.
6 Wherefore then do ye harden your hearts, as the
Egyptians and Pharaoh hardened their hearts?
when he had wrought wonderfully among them,
did they not let the people go, and they departed?
7 Now therefore make a new cart, and take two
milch kine, on which there hath come no yoke,
and tie the kine to the cart, and bring their calves
home from them:
8 And take the ark of the LORD, and lay it upon
the cart; and put the jewels of gold, which ye
return him *for* a trespass offering, in a coffer by
the side thereof; and send it away, that it may go.
9 And see, if it goeth up by the way of his own
coast to Beth-shemesh, *then* he hath done us this
great evil: but if not, then we shall know that *it is*
not his hand *that* smote us: it *was* a chance *that*
happened to us.
10 ¶ And the men did so; and took two milch
kine, and tied them to the cart, and shut up their
calves at home:
11 And they laid the ark of the LORD upon the
cart, and the coffer with the mice of gold and the
images of their emerods.
12 And the kine took the straight way to the way of
Beth-shemesh, *and* went along the highway, low-
ing as they went, and turned not aside *to* the right
hand or *to* the left; and the lords of the Philistines
went after them unto the border of Beth-shemesh.
13 And *they of* Beth-shemesh *were* reaping their
wheat harvest in the valley: and they lifted up
their eyes, and saw the ark, and rejoiced to see *it*.
14 And the cart came into the field of Joshua, a
Beth-shemite, and stood there, where *there was* a
great stone: and they clave the wood of the cart, and
offered the kine a burnt offering unto the LORD.
15 And the Levites took down the ark of the LORD,
and the coffer that *was* with it, wherein the jewels
of gold *were*, and put *them* on the great stone: and
the men of Beth-shemesh offered burnt offerings
and sacrificed sacrifices the same day unto the
LORD.
16 And when the five lords of the Philistines had
seen *it*, they returned to Ekron the same day.
17 And these *are* the golden emerods which the
Philistines returned *for* a trespass offering unto
the LORD; for Ashdod one, for Gaza one, for
Askelon one, for Gath one, for Ekron one;
18 And the golden mice, *according to* the number
of all the cities of the Philistines *belonging* to the
five lords, *both* of fenced cities, and of country
villages, even unto the great *stone of* Abel, whereon
they set down the ark of the LORD: *which stone
remaineth* unto this day in the field of Joshua, the
Beth-shemite.
19 ¶ And he smote the men of Beth-shemesh, be-
cause they had looked into the ark of the LORD,
even he smote of the people fifty thousand and
threescore and ten men: and the people lamented,
because the LORD had smitten *many* of the people
with a great slaughter.
20 And the men of Beth-shemesh said, Who is
able to stand before this holy LORD God? and to
whom shall he go up from us?
21 ¶ And they sent messengers to the inhabitants
of Kirjath-jearim, saying, The Philistines have
brought again the ark of the LORD; come ye down,
and fetch it up to you.

CHAPTER 7

AND the men of Kirjath-jearim came, and fetched
up the ark of the LORD, and brought it into the
house of Abinadab in the hill, and sanctified
Eleazar his son to keep the ark of the LORD.

golden mice represent the mice that *mar* or destroy the land (vv. 17–18). This rodent devastation of crops is evidence that Dagon was the god of grain. This was his domain, but he was powerless against the true God. *peradventure*. Perhaps.
6:6 *he had wrought wonderfully*. The Hebrew carries the idea of making a fool of someone, playing a dirty trick, or dealing ruthlessly. The Philistines were aware of the exodus but failed to understand its spiritual significance.
6:7 *milch kine*. Milk cows (vv. 10,12,14).
6:8 *coffer*. Box (vv. 11,15).
6:9 *coast*. Border or territory. *Beth-shemesh*. Literally, "house of the sun," one of the Levitical cities (Josh. 21:16). *evil*. calamity.
6:14 *clave*. Split.
6:19 *fifty thousand and three score and ten men*. 50,070 men. By means of a disjunctive marking, the Hebrew separates the 70 from the 50,000. This may suggest that the large number is divided between the two groups who died in this whole narrative, both among the Philistines (most likely, the 50,000) and the men of Beth-shemesh (most likely, the 70).

Thoughts for Personal/Family Worship: Chapter 6

1. **That the Philistines kept the ark for seven months (v. 1) testifies to the nature of spiritual deadness and insensitivity. Notwithstanding the irrefutable evidence of God's power and the excruciating pain of the plague, they refused to acknowledge God and the consequences of their sin. Why did they wait so long before returning the ark? This is reminiscent of Pharaoh's putting off Moses' offer to rid the land of frogs (Ex. 8:10). But it is the nature of sin to be blind to sin's solution. It ought to be our desire to remain sensitive to sin and to be quick in dealing with it before the Lord.**
2. **"Who is able to stand before this holy LORD God?" (v. 20) is an important question. The Philistines could not, nor could the men of Beth-shemesh. Whether by the heathen or religious, trying to access God in a way that He has not prescribed is fatal. The question points to the ultimate answer that the only way man can stand before the Lord and live is through the only Mediator, the Lord Jesus (Heb. 10:19–22).**

Chapter 7: ***Israel's repentance leads to God's intervention in subduing the Philistines.***

2 And it came to pass, while the ark abode in
Kirjath-jearim, that the time was long; for it was
twenty years: and all the house of Israel lamented
after the LORD.
3 ¶ And Samuel spake unto all the house of Israel,
saying, If ye do return unto the LORD with all
your hearts, *then* put away the strange gods and
Ashtaroth from among you, and prepare your
hearts unto the LORD, and serve him only: and he
will deliver you out of the hand of the Philistines.
4 Then the children of Israel did put away Baalim
and Ashtaroth, and served the LORD only.
5 And Samuel said, Gather all Israel to Mizpeh,
and I will pray for you unto the LORD.
6 And they gathered together to Mizpeh, and
drew water, and poured *it* out before the LORD,
and fasted on that day, and said there, We have
sinned against the LORD. And Samuel judged the
children of Israel in Mizpeh.
7 And when the Philistines heard that the children
of Israel were gathered together to Mizpeh, the
lords of the Philistines went up against Israel. And
when the children of Israel heard *it*, they were
afraid of the Philistines.
8 And the children of Israel said to Samuel, Cease
not to cry unto the LORD our God for us, that he
will save us out of the hand of the Philistines.
9 ¶ And Samuel took a sucking lamb, and offered
it for a burnt offering wholly unto the LORD: and
Samuel cried unto the LORD for Israel; and the
LORD heard him.
10 And as Samuel was offering up the burnt offering, the Philistines drew near to battle against
Israel: but the LORD thundered with a great thunder on that day upon the Philistines, and discomfited them; and they were smitten before Israel.
11 And the men of Israel went out of Mizpeh, and
pursued the Philistines, and smote them, until
they came under Beth-car.
12 Then Samuel took a stone, and set *it* between
Mizpeh and Shen, and called the name of it Ebenezer, saying, Hitherto hath the LORD helped us.
13 ¶ So the Philistines were subdued, and they
came no more into the coast of Israel: and the
hand of the LORD was against the Philistines all
the days of Samuel.
14 And the cities which the Philistines had taken
from Israel were restored to Israel, from Ekron
even unto Gath; and the coasts thereof did Israel
deliver out of the hands of the Philistines. And
there was peace between Israel and the Amorites.
15 And Samuel judged Israel all the days of his
life.
16 And he went from year to year in circuit to
Beth-el, and Gilgal, and Mizpeh, and judged
Israel in all those places.
17 And his return *was* to Ramah; for there *was* his
house; and there he judged Israel; and there he
built an altar unto the LORD.

CHAPTER 8

AND it came to pass, when Samuel was old, that
he made his sons judges over Israel.

7:1 *fetched up.* Brought up. *sanctified.* Set apart for sacred service.

Israel's Return to the Lord through Samuel (1 Sam. 7:2–17)

7:2–3 *lamented.* Groaned. A continuation of the pattern of the judges era: after Israel grieves over its sins, God raises up a judge, in this instance Samuel. *strange gods.* Foreign gods. *Ashtaroth.* The plural form of the Canaanite goddess, perhaps referring to the wooden poles erected as part of her worship ritual.

7:4 *Baalim.* The plural of "Baal," meaning "master" or "lord," a title to designate the chief deity of any location. Dagon was the Baal of Philistia. The plural suggests that Israel had incorporated numerous pagan deities into their worship.

7:8 *Cease not to cry.* Literally, "keep not silence from us, from crying" (see Ps. 28:1).

7:10–11 *discomfited.* Defeated, confused, or routed. It appears that the Philistines were routed by divine intervention, allowing Israel to chase them down and smite them without resistance.

7:12 *Eben-ezer.* Literally, "stone of help." *Hitherto.* Until now.

7:13 *coast.* Territory or region (v. 14). *all the days of Samuel.* Since Saul later engaged the Philistines, the reference is to the tenure of Samuel's judgeship before the monarchy.

Thoughts for Personal/Family Worship: Chapter 7

1. **Samuel served as a prophet, a judge, and a priest. This chapter illustrates two connected functions of the priest, both of which point to work of the ideal Priest, the Lord Jesus: he offered sacrifices and then interceded for the people (vv. 8–9). Likewise, our Savior's intercession for His people is on the grounds of His supreme sacrifice for sin, which is pleasing unto the Father (1 John 2:1–2). The Lord heard and answered Samuel (Ps. 99:6), and we can have even more confidence and assurance of faith that God will never turn away from the intercessions of His Son. Israel owed deliverance from the Philistines to Samuel's intercession; we owe everything to Christ's intercession for us. How does this encourage you to call upon Jesus Christ in prayer for your spiritual needs?**
2. **It is a blessed and comforting thought to know that God is faithful in all of His dealings with His people. He has promised to always be with those who are called by His grace. Surely every true child of God can say with Samuel, "Hitherto hath the LORD helped us" (v. 12). He has walked with us in our trials. He has comforted us in our grief. He has protected us from our foes and been to us an ever-present help in trouble. Christ says, "I am with you alway, even unto the end of the world" (Matt. 28:20). Let us therefore raise our Ebenezer of praise and rejoice in the Lord's goodness.**

THE RISE AND REJECTION OF KING SAUL (1 SAM. 8:1—15:35)

Chapter 8: ***Israel desires to be like the surrounding nations by having an earthly king.***

Israel's Rejection of the Lord as King (1 Sam. 8:1–22)

8:1 *made his sons judges.* Judges ruled by divine calling and

2 Now the name of his firstborn was Joel; and
the name of his second, Abiah: *they were* judges
in Beer-sheba.
3 And his sons walked not in his ways, but turned
aside after lucre, and took bribes, and perverted
judgment.
4 Then all the elders of Israel gathered themselves
together, and came to Samuel unto Ramah,
5 And said unto him, Behold, thou art old, and
thy sons walk not in thy ways: now make us a king
to judge us like all the nations.
6 ¶ But the thing displeased Samuel, when they
said, Give us a king to judge us. And Samuel
prayed unto the LORD.
7 And the LORD said unto Samuel, Hearken unto
the voice of the people in all that they say unto
thee: for they have not rejected thee, but they have
rejected me, that I should not reign over them.
8 According to all the works which they have
done since the day that I brought them up out
of Egypt even unto this day, wherewith they have
forsaken me, and served other gods, so do they
also unto thee.
9 Now therefore hearken unto their voice: how-
beit yet protest solemnly unto them, and shew
them the manner of the king that shall reign over
them.
10 ¶ And Samuel told all the words of the LORD
unto the people that asked of him a king.
11 And he said, This will be the manner of the
king that shall reign over you: He will take your
sons, and appoint *them* for himself, for his
chariots, and *to be* his horsemen; and *some* shall
run before his chariots.
12 And he will appoint him captains over thou-
sands, and captains over fifties; and *will set them*
to ear his ground, and to reap his harvest, and to
make his instruments of war, and instruments of
his chariots.
13 And he will take your daughters *to be* confec-
tionaries, and *to be* cooks, and *to be* bakers.
14 And he will take your fields, and your
vineyards, and your oliveyards, *even* the best *of*
them, and give *them* to his servants.
15 And he will take the tenth of your seed, and
of your vineyards, and give to his officers, and to
his servants.
16 And he will take your menservants, and your
maidservants, and your goodliest young men,
and your asses, and put *them* to his work.
17 He will take the tenth of your sheep: and ye
shall be his servants.
18 And ye shall cry out in that day because of
your king which ye shall have chosen you; and the
LORD will not hear you in that day.
19 ¶ Nevertheless the people refused to obey the
voice of Samuel; and they said, Nay; but we will
have a king over us;
20 That we also may be like all the nations; and
that our king may judge us, and go out before us,
and fight our battles.
21 And Samuel heard all the words of the people,
and he rehearsed them in the ears of the LORD.
22 And the LORD said to Samuel, Hearken unto
their voice, and make them a king. And Samuel
said unto the men of Israel, Go ye every man unto
his city.

CHAPTER 9

NOW there was a man of Benjamin, whose name
was Kish, the son of Abiel, the son of Zeror, the

commission (Judg. 2:16); Samuel had overstepped his authority. Nepotism is a temptation even to the most spiritual.

8:3 *lucre.* Ill-gotten or unlawful gain. Samuel was seemingly oblivious to his sons' faults, a sad repetition of the sin of Eli.

8:5 *make us a king . . . like all the nations.* Moses anticipated this request (Deut. 17:14–20).

8:6 *displeased Samuel.* Literally, "the matter was evil in the eyes of Samuel."

8:9 *hearken unto their voice.* Literally, "obey their voice." *howbeit yet protest solemnly.* Literally, "however, you should earnestly warn."

8:11–17 The predominant verb in Samuel's warning is *take* (vv. 11,13–17). Having a king will be costly.

8:12 *to ear his ground.* Literally, "to plow his plowing,"

8:13 *confectionaries.* Ointment makers or perfumers.

8:21 *he rehearsed.* Literally, "he spoke them."

Thoughts for Personal/Family Worship: Chapter 8

1. **Dissatisfaction with government is common, regardless of what form it takes. Israel was discontent with judges and assumed that a monarchy would solve their problems. Samuel rightly predicted that the day would come when monarchy would disappoint as well (v. 18). It is imperative to remember that all government is ordained by God (Rom. 13), and it should be our prayer that God would favor us with a government that is wise and righteous (2 Sam. 23:3; Prov. 8:12–16; 1 Tim. 2:1–2). But let us never forget that government cannot be our God, for it consists of fallen human beings. How can we honor civil leaders and honor God above all?**
2. **Kingship in Israel was part of God's purpose for His people and had notable messianic significance (Gen. 49:10). Israel's request for a king was a great disappointment to Samuel because it was motivated by selfish interests (1 Sam. 8:20) rather than concern for God's glory and the progression of His redemptive purpose. He also took it personally, as a rejection of his ministry. But at this critical point, Samuel provides the pattern of how we should respond to displeasing news: "Samuel prayed unto the LORD" (v. 6). Our very first thought should be to take it to the Lord. Praying for God's will to be done and for His kingdom to come focuses the heart where it needs to be.**

God's Sovereign Selection of a King (1 Sam. 9:1—10:27)

Chapter 9: ***The Lord providentially directs events leading Samuel to Saul, revealing to him that Saul will be king.***

son of Bechorath, the son of Aphiah, a Benjamite,
a mighty man of power.
2 And he had a son, whose name *was* Saul, a
choice young man, and a goodly: and *there was*
not among the children of Israel a goodlier
person than he: from his shoulders and upward
he was higher than any of the people.
3 And the asses of Kish Saul's father were lost.
And Kish said to Saul his son, Take now one of
the servants with thee, and arise, go seek the asses.
4 And he passed through mount Ephraim, and
passed through the land of Shalisha, but they
found *them* not: then they passed through the
land of Shalim, and *there they were* not: and he
passed through the land of the Benjamites, but
they found *them* not.
5 *And* when they were come to the land of Zuph,
Saul said to his servant that *was* with him, Come,
and let us return; lest my father leave *caring* for
the asses, and take thought for us.
6 And he said unto him, Behold now, *there is* in
this city a man of God, and *he is* an honourable
man; all that he saith cometh surely to pass: now
let us go thither; peradventure he can shew us our
way that we should go.
7 Then said Saul to his servant, But, behold, *if* we
go, what shall we bring the man? for the bread is
spent in our vessels, and *there is* not a present to
bring to the man of God: what have we?
8 And the servant answered Saul again, and said,
Behold, I have here at hand the fourth part of a
shekel of silver: *that* will I give to the man of God,
to tell us our way.
9 (Beforetime in Israel, when a man went to en-
quire of God, thus he spake, Come, and let us go
to the seer: for *he that is* now *called* a Prophet was
beforetime called a Seer.)
10 Then said Saul to his servant, Well said; come,
let us go. So they went unto the city where the
man of God *was*.
11 ¶ *And* as they went up the hill to the city, they
found young maidens going out to draw water,
and said unto them, Is the seer here?
12 And they answered them, and said, He is; be-
hold, *he is* before you: make haste now, for he
came to day to the city; for *there is* a sacrifice of
the people to day in the high place:
13 As soon as ye be come into the city, ye shall
straightway find him, before he go up to the high
place to eat: for the people will not eat until he
come, because he doth bless the sacrifice; *and*
afterwards they eat that be bidden. Now therefore
get you up; for about this time ye shall find him.
14 And they went up into the city: *and* when they
were come into the city, behold, Samuel came out
against them, for to go up to the high place.
15 ¶ Now the LORD had told Samuel in his ear a
day before Saul came, saying,
16 To morrow about this time I will send thee a
man out of the land of Benjamin, and thou shalt
anoint him *to be* captain over my people Israel,
that he may save my people out of the hand of
the Philistines: for I have looked upon my people,
because their cry is come unto me.
17 And when Samuel saw Saul, the LORD said
unto him, Behold the man whom I spake to thee
of! this same shall reign over my people.
18 Then Saul drew near to Samuel in the gate,
and said, Tell me, I pray thee, where the seer's
house *is*.
19 And Samuel answered Saul, and said, I *am* the
seer: go up before me unto the high place; for ye
shall eat with me to day, and to morrow I will let
thee go, and will tell thee all that *is* in thine heart.
20 And as for thine asses that were lost three days
ago, set not thy mind on them; for they are found.

9:2 *choice young man*. The Hebrew refers to a young, fully-grown, vigorous, unmarried man. *goodly*. Good, most likely referring to his appearance, not his character. Saul, with his good looks and great height, exemplifies a man whose appearance impresses the world.
9:5 *take thought for us*. Become anxious or concerned about us.
9:6 *man of God*. Prophet or seer (vv. 9–10). *peradventure*. Perhaps.
9:7 *spent*. Used up, gone.
9:9 *Prophet . . . Seer*. Both terms refer to the reception of the message from God. The prophet is one to whom God speaks; the seer is one to whom God gives visions. Their authority comes not from self but from divine revelation.
9:12 *high place*. Probably the highest point of the city that had been consecrated as a place of sacrifice; Jerusalem had not yet been appointed by God.
9:13 *straightway*. The Hebrew means "thus."
9:15 *told Samuel in his ear*. Literally, "uncovered the ear of Samuel," an idiom expressing communication.
9:16 *captain*. Leader or ruler.
9:22 *parlour*. Hall or room. *chiefest place*. Literally, "the place in the head," the place of honor.
9:25 *upon the top of the house*. Most likely a house constructed with a flat roof.
9:26 *spring of the day*. Start of the day, as dawn was breaking.
9:27 *shew thee the word of God*. Literally, "cause you to hear the word of God."

Thoughts for Personal/Family Worship: Chapter 9

1. **The circumstances leading to Samuel's meeting with Saul illustrate the remarkable providence of God that directs all the affairs of life, including human choices and seemingly random events, to accomplish His ultimate purpose (Gen. 50:20; Prov. 16:33). The search for lost donkeys appeared to be an exercise in futility and failure, but it was the means of bringing Saul to a critical moment that defined his life from that day forward. Little did he know when leaving home on the donkey hunt that he would return as the "king elect" of the nation. This is a reminder that we do not know what a day will bring forth and that it is good to know that our times are in the hands of God.**
2. **The occurrence of the titles "man of God," "Prophet," and**

And on whom *is* all the desire of Israel? *Is it* not
on thee, and on all thy father's house?
21 And Saul answered and said, *Am* not I a Ben-
jamite, of the smallest of the tribes of Israel? and
my family the least of all the families of the tribe of
Benjamin? wherefore then speakest thou so to me?
22 And Samuel took Saul and his servant, and
brought them into the parlour, and made them
sit in the chiefest place among them that were
bidden, which *were* about thirty persons.
23 And Samuel said unto the cook, Bring the
portion which I gave thee, of which I said unto
thee, Set it by thee.
24 And the cook took up the shoulder, and *that*
which *was* upon it, and set *it* before Saul. And
Samuel said, Behold that which is left! set *it* before
thee, *and* eat: for unto this time hath it been kept
for thee since I said, I have invited the people. So
Saul did eat with Samuel that day.
25 ¶ And when they were come down from the
high place into the city, *Samuel* communed with
Saul upon the top of the house.
26 And they arose early: and it came to pass about
the spring of the day, that Samuel called Saul to
the top of the house, saying, Up, that I may send
thee away. And Saul arose, and they went out both
of them, he and Samuel, abroad.
27 *And* as they were going down to the end of the
city, Samuel said to Saul, Bid the servant pass on
before us, (and he passed on,) but stand thou still
a while, that I may shew thee the word of God.

CHAPTER 10

THEN Samuel took a vial of oil, and poured *it*
upon his head, and kissed him, and said, *Is it* not
because the LORD hath anointed thee *to be* captain
over his inheritance?
2 When thou art departed from me to day, then
thou shalt find two men by Rachel's sepulchre in
the border of Benjamin at Zelzah; and they will
say unto thee, The asses which thou wentest to
seek are found: and, lo, thy father hath left the
care of the asses, and sorroweth for you, saying,
What shall I do for my son?
3 Then shalt thou go on forward from thence,
and thou shalt come to the plain of Tabor, and
there shall meet thee three men going up to God
to Beth-el, one carrying three kids, and another
carrying three loaves of bread, and another carry-
ing a bottle of wine:
4 And they will salute thee, and give thee two
loaves of bread; which thou shalt receive of their
hands.
5 After that thou shalt come to the hill of God,
where *is* the garrison of the Philistines: and it shall
come to pass, when thou art come thither to the
city, that thou shalt meet a company of prophets
coming down from the high place with a psaltery,
and a tabret, and a pipe, and a harp, before them;
and they shall prophesy:
6 And the Spirit of the LORD will come upon thee,
and thou shalt prophesy with them, and shalt be
turned into another man.
7 And let it be, when these signs are come unto
thee, *that* thou do as occasion serve thee; for God
is with thee.
8 And thou shalt go down before me to Gilgal;
and, behold, I will come down unto thee, to offer
burnt offerings, *and* to sacrifice sacrifices of peace
offerings: seven days shalt thou tarry, till I come to
thee, and shew thee what thou shalt do.
9 ¶ And it was *so*, that when he had turned his
back to go from Samuel, God gave him another
heart: and all those signs came to pass that day.
10 And when they came thither to the hill,

"Seer" in this chapter reminds us both of the necessary character and of the authority of the one God called to declare His word to others. The prophet's character is to be godly, and his message is never self-generated. The prophet is to speak only what has been spoken to him, and the seer is to reveal only what has been revealed to him. The principle applies to modern ministry as well, as preachers are to be examples of godliness and have the authority to preach only God's Word (2 Tim. 4:1–2).

Chapter 10: *Saul is symbolically anointed by Samuel, actually anointed by the Holy Spirit, and publicly presented as king.*

10:1 *vial.* Flask or small jug. *poured.* Symbolic of the Spirit's anointing. This anointing marked kingship as one of the messianic (meaning *anointed*) offices. *captain.* See note at 9:16. *inheritance.* A designation for God's people as God's beloved treasure (Deut. 4:20; 9:26,29; 32:9; 1 Kings 8:51; Ps. 28:9; 33:12; 94:5).

10:2 *the care of the asses.* The affair or matter of the asses. *sorroweth for you.* Is anxious or concerned about you.

10:4 *they will salute you.* The Hebrew means "they will ask about your welfare."

10:5 *psaltery.* Stringed instrument. *tabret.* Small drum. *pipe.* A flute-like instrument. *harp.* A zither or lyre. *they shall prophesy.* See 2 Chron. 25:1–3. Prophecy includes giving thanks and praising God (see vv. 10–11,13).

10:6 *the Spirit of the LORD will come upon thee.* A particular reference to Saul's being empowered to fulfill his God-given ministry. God's Spirit is the source of all life, power, and wisdom (Job 32:8; 33:4; Ps. 104:30) and can give unusual or even supernatural strength, skill, or knowledge as He wills to men (Ex. 31:3; 35:31; Num. 11:17,24–29; 27:18; Deut. 34:9; Judg. 3:10; 6:34; 11:29; 13:25; 14:6,19; 15:14; 1 Sam. 11:6; 16:13; 19:20,23; 2 Sam. 23:2), including at times the wicked (Num. 24:2; cf. Matt. 7:21–23). This spiritual gift for leadership was later withdrawn when God rejected Saul from being king (1 Sam. 16:1,14).

10:7 *do as occasion serve thee.* Literally, "do for yourself that which your hand finds."

10:9 *God gave him another heart.* Perhaps a reference to the Spirit's common work rather than to regeneration, or to the gift of boldness to speak and lead (Acts 4:31).

behold, a company of prophets met him; and the
Spirit of God came upon him, and he prophesied
among them.
11 And it came to pass, when all that knew him
beforetime saw that, behold, he prophesied
among the prophets, then the people said one to
another, What *is* this *that* is come unto the son of
Kish? *Is* Saul also among the prophets?
12 And one of the same place answered and said,
But who *is* their father? Therefore it became a
proverb, *Is* Saul also among the prophets?
13 And when he had made an end of prophesy-
ing, he came to the high place.
14 ¶ And Saul's uncle said unto him and to his
servant, Whither went ye? And he said, To seek
the asses: and when we saw that *they were* no
where, we came to Samuel.
15 And Saul's uncle said, Tell me, I pray thee,
what Samuel said unto you.
16 And Saul said unto his uncle, He told us
plainly that the asses were found. But of the
matter of the kingdom, whereof Samuel spake, he
told him not.
17 ¶ And Samuel called the people together unto
the LORD to Mizpeh;
18 And said unto the children of Israel, Thus saith
the LORD God of Israel, I brought up Israel out of
Egypt, and delivered you out of the hand of the
Egyptians, and out of the hand of all kingdoms,
and of them that oppressed you:
19 And ye have this day rejected your God, who
himself saved you out of all your adversities and
your tribulations; and ye have said unto him,
Nay, but set a king over us. Now therefore present
yourselves before the LORD by your tribes, and by
your thousands.
20 And when Samuel had caused all the tribes
of Israel to come near, the tribe of Benjamin was
taken.
21 When he had caused the tribe of Benjamin to
come near by their families, the family of Matri
was taken, and Saul the son of Kish was taken: and
when they sought him, he could not be found.
22 Therefore they enquired of the LORD further,
if the man should yet come thither. And the LORD
answered, Behold, he hath hid himself among the
stuff.
23 And they ran and fetched him thence: and
when he stood among the people, he was higher
than any of the people from his shoulders and
upward.
24 And Samuel said to all the people, See ye him
whom the LORD hath chosen, that *there is* none
like him among all the people? And all the people
shouted, and said, God save the king.
25 Then Samuel told the people the manner of
the kingdom, and wrote *it* in a book, and laid *it* up
before the LORD. And Samuel sent all the people
away, every man to his house.
26 ¶ And Saul also went home to Gibeah; and
there went with him a band of men, whose hearts
God had touched.
27 But the children of Belial said, How shall this
man save us? And they despised him, and brought
him no presents. But he held his peace.

CHAPTER 11

THEN Nahash the Ammonite came up, and en-
camped against Jabesh-gilead: and all the men of
Jabesh said unto Nahash, Make a covenant with
us, and we will serve thee.
2 And Nahash the Ammonite answered them,
On this *condition* will I make *a covenant* with you,
that I may thrust out all your right eyes, and lay it
for a reproach upon all Israel.
3 And the elders of Jabesh said unto him, Give us
seven days' respite, that we may send messengers
unto all the coasts of Israel: and then, if *there be*
no man to save us, we will come out to thee.

10:10 *thither.* There or thence.
10:11 *beforetime.* Previously.
10:14 *Whither went ye?* Where did you go?
10:17 *Mizpeh.* Where Samuel frequently assembled the people for public announcements (7:5). Near the stone erected as a monument to the Lord's help (7:12).
10:22 *stuff.* Equipment.
10:24 *God save the king.* Literally, "may the king live."
10:26 *whose hearts God had touched.* Refers to those the Lord had made supportive of Saul.
10:27 *children of Belial.* Those who are wicked or useless (see note at 1:16).

Thoughts for Personal/Family Worship: Chapter 10

Opinions differ on exactly what Saul's "another heart" means. Regardless, the narrative of Saul's anointing illustrates a vital truth: God is able to transform people. Notwithstanding Saul's physical stature, he lacked self-confidence and evidenced no particular skills of leadership. But God equipped him for his ordained office, and his transformation was evident to those who knew him before and after his anointing. The Holy Spirit is able to equip people with spiritual gifts (v. 6; 1 Cor. 12:4–7). Only by His power can we serve God's kingdom effectively. However, the greatest gift is the transformation of the new birth. Let us never rest in gifts and abilities, but earnestly seek assurance that we are true children born of God (John 1:12–13).

Chapter 11: *Saul's leadership against the Ammonite threat becomes the occasion for confirming his kingship over Israel.*

Saul's Promising Start (1 Sam. 11:1–15)

11:1 *Make a covenant.* Literally, "cut a covenant," here a treaty of some sort.
11:3 *Give us . . . respite.* Literally, "leave us alone." *Coasts.* Borders or regions (v. 7).

4 ¶ Then came the messengers to Gibeah of Saul,
and told the tidings in the ears of the people: and
all the people lifted up their voices, and wept.
5 And, behold, Saul came after the herd out of the
field; and Saul said, What *aileth* the people that
they weep? And they told him the tidings of the
men of Jabesh.
6 And the Spirit of God came upon Saul when
he heard those tidings, and his anger was kindled
greatly.
7 And he took a yoke of oxen, and hewed them in
pieces, and sent *them* throughout all the coasts of
Israel by the hands of messengers, saying, Whoso-
ever cometh not forth after Saul and after Samuel,
so shall it be done unto his oxen. And the fear of
the LORD fell on the people, and they came out
with one consent.
8 And when he numbered them in Bezek, the
children of Israel were three hundred thousand,
and the men of Judah thirty thousand.
9 And they said unto the messengers that came,
Thus shall ye say unto the men of Jabesh-gilead,
To morrow, by *that time* the sun be hot, ye shall
have help. And the messengers came and shewed
it to the men of Jabesh; and they were glad.
10 Therefore the men of Jabesh said, To morrow
we will come out unto you, and ye shall do with
us all that seemeth good unto you.
11 And it was *so* on the morrow, that Saul put
the people in three companies; and they came
into the midst of the host in the morning watch,
and slew the Ammonites until the heat of the day:
and it came to pass, that they which remained
were scattered, so that two of them were not left
together.
12 ¶ And the people said unto Samuel, Who *is* he
that said, Shall Saul reign over us? bring the men,
that we may put them to death.
13 And Saul said, There shall not a man be put to
death this day: for to day the LORD hath wrought
salvation in Israel.
14 Then said Samuel to the people, Come, and let
us go to Gilgal, and renew the kingdom there.
15 And all the people went to Gilgal; and there
they made Saul king before the LORD in Gilgal;
and there they sacrificed sacrifices of peace offer-
ings before the LORD; and there Saul and all the
men of Israel rejoiced greatly.

CHAPTER 12

AND Samuel said unto all Israel, Behold, I have
hearkened unto your voice in all that ye said unto
me, and have made a king over you.
2 And now, behold, the king walketh before you:
and I am old and grayheaded; and, behold, my
sons *are* with you: and I have walked before you
from my childhood unto this day.
3 Behold, here I *am*: witness against me before
the LORD, and before his anointed: whose ox have
I taken? or whose ass have I taken? or whom have
I defrauded? whom have I oppressed? or of whose
hand have I received *any* bribe to blind mine eyes
therewith? and I will restore it you.
4 And they said, Thou hast not defrauded us, nor
oppressed us, neither hast thou taken ought of
any man's hand.
5 And he said unto them, The LORD *is* witness
against you, and his anointed *is* witness this day,
that ye have not found ought in my hand. And
they answered, *He is* witness.
6 ¶ And Samuel said unto the people, *It is* the
LORD that advanced Moses and Aaron, and that
brought your fathers up out of the land of Egypt.
7 Now therefore stand still, that I may reason
with you before the LORD of all the righteous
acts of the LORD, which he did to you and to your
fathers.

11:6 *the Spirit of God came upon Saul.* See note at 10:6.
11:7 *yoke of oxen.* Two oxen. *hewed.* Cut in pieces. *with one consent.* Literally, "as one man."
11:11 *on the morrow.* The following day. *morning watch.* Between 2:00 a.m. and 6:00 a.m.

Thoughts for Personal/Family Worship: Chapter 11

1. **When Israel gained victory, Saul reminded the people that their triumph did not come because they had an earthly king but because "the LORD hath wrought salvation in Israel" (v. 13). This is a principle that we also must remember: whenever we obtain a victory, it is solely the result of God's power. As Christ reminds us, "without me ye can do nothing" (John 15:5).**
2. **It is significant that when Samuel confirmed Saul as king, he did so by calling the people to gather at Gilgal (v. 14). This was the place where Israel first set up camp when entering the Promised Land (Josh. 4:19). It was the place where Joshua instructed Israel to take twelve stones from the midst of the Jordan "for a memorial unto the children of Israel for ever" (Josh. 4:7). In coming to this place, the people were surely reminded of the Lord's past help. When looking to the future, it is a good thing for us to consider the past. Such reminders of His goodness will be of great benefit to our souls, especially when the future looks uncertain.**

Chapter 12: ***Samuel defends his ministry and exhorts the nation to learn the lessons from the past and to fear the Lord, lest they suffer judgment.***

Samuel's Integrity and Exhortation to Israel (1 Sam. 12:1–25)

12:3 *before his anointed.* Most likely referring to Saul, the anointed king, whose office points to the ideal yet to come (v. 5). *to blind mine eyes therewith.* To avert my eyes, or look the other way. Contrast Samuel's not taking with the much taking of kings (8:11–17).
12:4 *taken ought.* Taken anything.
12:5 *not found ought.* Found nothing.
12:6 *advanced.* Literally, "made," in the sense that they were appointed to their roles by God.

8 When Jacob was come into Egypt, and your fa-
thers cried unto the LORD, then the LORD sent Mo-
ses and Aaron, which brought forth your fathers
out of Egypt, and made them dwell in this place.
9 And when they forgat the LORD their God, he
sold them into the hand of Sisera, captain of the
host of Hazor, and into the hand of the Philistines,
and into the hand of the king of Moab, and they
fought against them.
10 And they cried unto the LORD, and said, We
have sinned, because we have forsaken the LORD,
and have served Baalim and Ashtaroth: but now
deliver us out of the hand of our enemies, and we
will serve thee.
11 And the LORD sent Jerubbaal, and Bedan, and
Jephthah, and Samuel, and delivered you out of
the hand of your enemies on every side, and ye
dwelled safe.
12 And when ye saw that Nahash the king of the
children of Ammon came against you, ye said
unto me, Nay; but a king shall reign over us: when
the LORD your God *was* your king.
13 Now therefore behold the king whom ye have
chosen, *and* whom ye have desired! and, behold,
the LORD hath set a king over you.
14 If ye will fear the LORD, and serve him,
and obey his voice, and not rebel against the
commandment of the LORD, then shall both ye
and also the king that reigneth over you continue
following the LORD your God:
15 But if ye will not obey the voice of the LORD,
but rebel against the commandment of the LORD,
then shall the hand of the LORD be against you, as
it was against your fathers.
16 ¶ Now therefore stand and see this great thing,
which the LORD will do before your eyes.
17 *Is it* not wheat harvest to day? I will call unto
the LORD, and he shall send thunder and rain; that
ye may perceive and see that your wickedness *is*
great, which ye have done in the sight of the LORD,
in asking you a king.
18 So Samuel called unto the LORD; and the LORD
sent thunder and rain that day: and all the people
greatly feared the LORD and Samuel.
19 And all the people said unto Samuel, Pray for
thy servants unto the LORD thy God, that we die
not: for we have added unto all our sins *this* evil,
to ask us a king.
20 ¶ And Samuel said unto the people, Fear not:
ye have done all this wickedness: yet turn not aside
from following the LORD, but serve the LORD with
all your heart;
21 And turn ye not aside: for *then should ye go*
after vain *things*, which cannot profit nor deliver;
for they *are* vain.
22 For the LORD will not forsake his people for
his great name's sake: because it hath pleased the
LORD to make you his people.
23 Moreover as for me, God forbid that I should
sin against the LORD in ceasing to pray for you:
but I will teach you the good and the right way:
24 Only fear the LORD, and serve him in truth
with all your heart: for consider how great *things*
he hath done for you.
25 But if ye shall still do wickedly, ye shall be
consumed, both ye and your king.

CHAPTER 13

SAUL reigned one year; and when he had reigned
two years over Israel,
2 Saul chose him three thousand *men* of Israel;
whereof two thousand were with Saul in Mich-
mash and in mount Beth-el, and a thousand were
with Jonathan in Gibeah of Benjamin: and the
rest of the people he sent every man to his tent.

12:10 *Baalim and Ashtaroth.* The plurals of the Canaanite gods Baal (the supreme male deity) and Ashtoreth (the chief female deity). See note at 7:4.
12:11 *Bedan.* An alternate designation for Barak (Judg. 4–5).
12:14–15 Samuel echoes the warning of Moses (Lev. 26:1–13; Deut. 28:1–14).
12:17 *wheat harvest.* This usually took place in the very dry months, but the Lord would send thunder and rain now when it was least expected.
12:18 *feared the LORD and Samuel.* See the similar response in Ex. 14:31.
12:21 *vain.* Futile.
12:23 *God forbid.* Literally, "far be it from me."

Thoughts for Personal/Family Worship: Chapter 12

1. **Samuel declares to the people that he would not hold their sin against them, he would not cease to pray for them, and he would teach them the good way (vv. 20,23). In considering this, do we not see a far greater One than Samuel who intercedes on our behalf? What a blessing it is to know that though we have sinned against Christ, He never ceases to remember us in mercy, He pleads with the Father on our behalf, and He teaches us the good way through His Word and by His Spirit. How are you consciously exercising faith in Christ in all of these?**
2. **It is a sad failing in many of us that there are times when we are prone to dwell upon the disappointments and miseries of life rather than upon the many blessings that we receive from the Lord's merciful hand. Samuel could have wallowed in self-pity at the passing of his judgeship and the failure of his sons, but instead he said, "Consider how great things he [the Lord] hath done for you" (v. 24). The greatest thing is that Christ suffered and died that we might be redeemed through the shedding of His precious blood. Let us consider this and give Him all the glory, that our hearts may rejoice even in tribulation.**

Saul's Rebellion and Jonathan's Faith (1 Sam. 13:1—15:35)

Chapter 13: ***Saul enters into conflict with the Philistines, impatiently offers sacrifices, and suffers rebuke from Samuel, who declares the demise of his kingdom.***

3 And Jonathan smote the garrison of the Philis-
tines that *was* in Geba, and the Philistines heard *of*
it. And Saul blew the trumpet throughout all the
land, saying, Let the Hebrews hear.
4 And all Israel heard say *that* Saul had smitten a
garrison of the Philistines, and *that* Israel also was
had in abomination with the Philistines. And the
people were called together after Saul to Gilgal.
5 ¶ And the Philistines gathered themselves
together to fight with Israel, thirty thousand
chariots, and six thousand horsemen, and people
as the sand which *is* on the sea shore in multitude:
and they came up, and pitched in Michmash,
eastward from Beth-aven.
6 When the men of Israel saw that they were in
a strait, (for the people were distressed,) then the
people did hide themselves in caves, and in thick-
ets, and in rocks, and in high places, and in pits.
7 And *some of* the Hebrews went over Jordan to
the land of Gad and Gilead. As for Saul, he *was*
yet in Gilgal, and all the people followed him
trembling.
8 ¶ And he tarried seven days, according to the
set time that Samuel *had appointed*: but Samuel
came not to Gilgal; and the people were scattered
from him.
9 And Saul said, Bring hither a burnt offering to
me, and peace offerings. And he offered the burnt
offering.
10 And it came to pass, that as soon as he had
made an end of offering the burnt offering, be-
hold, Samuel came; and Saul went out to meet
him, that he might salute him.
11 ¶ And Samuel said, What hast thou done?
And Saul said, Because I saw that the people were
scattered from me, and *that* thou camest not
within the days appointed, and *that* the Philistines
gathered themselves together at Michmash;
12 Therefore said I, The Philistines will come
down now upon me to Gilgal, and I have not
made supplication unto the LORD: I forced myself
therefore, and offered a burnt offering.
13 And Samuel said to Saul, Thou hast done
foolishly: thou hast not kept the commandment
of the LORD thy God, which he commanded thee:
for now would the LORD have established thy
kingdom upon Israel for ever.
14 But now thy kingdom shall not continue: the
LORD hath sought him a man after his own heart,
and the LORD hath commanded him *to be* captain
over his people, because thou hast not kept *that*
which the LORD commanded thee.
15 And Samuel arose, and gat him up from Gilgal
unto Gibeah of Benjamin. And Saul numbered
the people *that were* present with him, about six
hundred men.
16 And Saul, and Jonathan his son, and the people
that were present with them, abode in Gibeah
of Benjamin: but the Philistines encamped in
Michmash.
17 ¶ And the spoilers came out of the camp of
the Philistines in three companies: one company
turned unto the way *that leadeth to* Ophrah, unto
the land of Shual:
18 And another company turned the way *to* Beth-
horon: and another company turned *to* the way
of the border that looketh to the valley of Zeboim
toward the wilderness.
19 ¶ Now there was no smith found throughout
all the land of Israel: for the Philistines said, Lest
the Hebrews make *them* swords or spears:
20 But all the Israelites went down to the Phi-
listines, to sharpen every man his share, and his
coulter, and his axe, and his mattock.
21 Yet they had a file for the mattocks, and for the
coulters, and for the forks, and for the axes, and to
sharpen the goads.
22 So it came to pass in the day of battle, that
there was neither sword nor spear found in the
hand of any of the people that *were* with Saul and
Jonathan: but with Saul and with Jonathan his
son was there found.
23 And the garrison of the Philistines went out to
the passage of Michmash.

13:1 *Saul reigned one year.* Literally, "Saul was a son of a year in his reigning." Although this is often an idiom to designate age, the reference here is to the duration of his kingship prior to his conflict with the Philistines.
13:4 *was had in abomination.* Literally, "had made themselves to stink or be offensive."
13:6 *they were in a strait.* Literally, "it was hard pressed for them," meaning that they were cramped in, a cause for panic.
13:9–10 Saul takes matters into his own hands and offers a burnt offering. This task was uniquely reserved for the priestly office. *salute.* Hebrew, "to bless" him, an expression of greeting.
13:14 *thy kingdom shall not continue.* Saul's obedience could have secured a dynasty, but he forfeited that prospect by disobedience. *man after his own heart.* A person submitted to the Lord to do God's will (cf. 14:7; Acts 13:22), in contrast to Saul, who did not do what God *commanded* him. Obedience to God's law is central to kingship (Deut. 17:18–20), for the king sits as God's representative, mediating His authority, not exercising any of his own.
13:15 *gat him up.* He went up.
13:17 *spoilers.* Those who destroy or ruin.
13:19 *smith.* Craftsman.
13:20 *share . . . coulter . . . mattock.* Digging tools of a farmer, such as a hoe or the blade of a plough (v. 21).
13:21 *they had a file.* The Hebrew could read "there was a charge of a pim," about two-thirds of a shekel. *goads.* Cattle prods.
13:23 *passage.* Mountain pass or gorge.

Thoughts for Personal/Family Worship: Chapter 13

Waiting is often one of the most difficult tests of faith. Impatience can result in rash acts that dishonor the Lord. From impatience came the golden calf (Ex. 32:1). Here it was Saul's impatience in waiting for Samuel that

CHAPTER 14

NOW it came to pass upon a day, that Jonathan
the son of Saul said unto the young man that
bare his armour, Come, and let us go over to the
Philistines' garrison, that *is* on the other side. But
he told not his father.
2 And Saul tarried in the uttermost part of Gib-
eah under a pomegranate tree which *is* in Migron:
and the people that *were* with him *were* about six
hundred men;
3 And Ahiah, the son of Ahitub, I-chabod's
brother, the son of Phinehas, the son of Eli, the
LORD's priest in Shiloh, wearing an ephod. And
the people knew not that Jonathan was gone.
4 ¶ And between the passages, by which Jonathan
sought to go over unto the Philistines' garrison,
there was a sharp rock on the one side, and a sharp
rock on the other side: and the name of the one
was Bozez, and the name of the other Seneh.
5 The forefront of the one *was* situate northward
over against Michmash, and the other southward
over against Gibeah.
6 And Jonathan said to the young man that bare
his armour, Come, and let us go over unto the
garrison of these uncircumcised: it may be that
the LORD will work for us: for *there is* no restraint
to the LORD to save by many or by few.
7 And his armourbearer said unto him, Do all
that *is* in thine heart: turn thee; behold, I *am* with
thee according to thy heart.
8 Then said Jonathan, Behold, we will pass over
unto *these* men, and we will discover ourselves
unto them.
9 If they say thus unto us, Tarry until we come to
you; then we will stand still in our place, and will
not go up unto them.
10 But if they say thus, Come up unto us; then we
will go up: for the LORD hath delivered them into
our hand: and this *shall be* a sign unto us.
11 And both of them discovered themselves unto
the garrison of the Philistines: and the Philistines
said, Behold, the Hebrews come forth out of the
holes where they had hid themselves.
12 And the men of the garrison answered Jonathan
and his armourbearer, and said, Come up to us,
and we will shew you a thing. And Jonathan said
unto his armourbearer, Come up after me: for the
LORD hath delivered them into the hand of Israel.
13 And Jonathan climbed up upon his hands
and upon his feet, and his armourbearer after
him: and they fell before Jonathan; and his
armourbearer slew after him.
14 And that first slaughter, which Jonathan and
his armourbearer made, was about twenty men,
within as it were an half acre of land, *which* a yoke
of oxen might plow.
15 And there was trembling in the host, in the
field, and among all the people: the garrison, and
the spoilers, they also trembled, and the earth
quaked: so it was a very great trembling.
16 And the watchmen of Saul in Gibeah of Ben-
jamin looked; and, behold, the multitude melted
away, and they went on beating down *one another*.
17 Then said Saul unto the people that *were* with
him, Number now, and see who is gone from us.
And when they had numbered, behold, Jonathan
and his armourbearer *were* not *there*.
18 And Saul said unto Ahiah, Bring hither the ark
of God. For the ark of God was at that time with
the children of Israel.
19 ¶ And it came to pass, while Saul talked unto
the priest, that the noise that *was* in the host of the
Philistines went on and increased: and Saul said
unto the priest, Withdraw thine hand.
20 And Saul and all the people that *were* with
him assembled themselves, and they came to the

led to his infringing on the priestly office, a most serious offense for kings (2 Chron. 26:16–21). In Christ these functions would merge. Saul's impatience warranted severe consequences: only two years into his reign and the prospect of a dynasty was gone. Waiting time is never wasted time, as it increases our sense of dependence on the Lord. Those who wait on the Lord will never be disappointed with the Lord and His timing (Ps. 37:7–11; Isa. 40:31). Let us learn from Israel's and Saul's impatience that God's timing is best and that we can trust Him completely.

Chapter 14: *Jonathan infiltrates the Philistine camp, unknowingly violates Saul's prohibition against eating, and is spared death by the intervention of the people.*

14:2 *tarried.* Stayed; literally, "sat."

14:3 *Ahiah . . . the son of Eli.* Ironically, the rejected line of priests (2:31–35) is with Saul, who had just been denied a dynasty (13:14). *ephod.* A priestly garment, an embroidered cape worn over the shoulders (Ex. 28).

14:4 *passages.* Mountain passes, gorges, or ravines.

14:5 *forefront.* The Hebrew word is "tooth," referring to a crag.

14:6 *these uncircumcised.* A common designation for the Philistines, identifying them as outside God's covenant. *it may be.* The Hebrew means "perhaps," expressing faith without presumption. *there is no restraint.* Literally, "nonexistence of an impediment or limitation." Nothing can hinder God from doing what He chooses to do (Gen. 18:14; Jer. 32:17).

14:8 *discover ourselves.* Reveal or disclose ourselves (v. 11).

14:12 *shew you a thing.* Literally, "make you know something." A cocky statement like, "We will teach you a lesson you won't soon forget."

14:15 *trembling.* Panic. *very great trembling.* Literally, "quaking of God." The Lord's intervention by sending an earthquake contributed directly to Jonathan's victory.

14:16 *the multitude melted . . . beating down.* Literally, "the multitude moved back and forth and they went even hither," a picture of total confusion as in the panic they did not know where to go.

14:20 *discomfiture.* Consternation and panic, as the Philistines were fighting one another.

battle: and, behold, every man's sword was against
his fellow, *and there was* a very great discomfiture.
21 Moreover the Hebrews *that* were with the
Philistines before that time, which went up with
them into the camp *from the country* round about,
even they also *turned* to be with the Israelites that
were with Saul and Jonathan.
22 Likewise all the men of Israel which had hid
themselves in mount Ephraim, *when* they heard
that the Philistines fled, even they also followed
hard after them in the battle.
23 So the LORD saved Israel that day: and the
battle passed over unto Beth-aven.
24 ¶ And the men of Israel were distressed that
day: for Saul had adjured the people, saying,
Cursed *be* the man that eateth *any* food until
evening, that I may be avenged on mine enemies.
So none of the people tasted *any* food.
25 And all *they of* the land came to a wood; and
there was honey upon the ground.
26 And when the people were come into the
wood, behold, the honey dropped; but no man
put his hand to his mouth: for the people feared
the oath.
27 But Jonathan heard not when his father
charged the people with the oath: wherefore he
put forth the end of the rod that *was* in his hand,
and dipped it in an honeycomb, and put his hand
to his mouth; and his eyes were enlightened.
28 Then answered one of the people, and said,
Thy father straitly charged the people with an
oath, saying, Cursed *be* the man that eateth *any*
food this day. And the people were faint.
29 Then said Jonathan, My father hath troubled
the land: see, I pray you, how mine eyes have been
enlightened, because I tasted a little of this honey.
30 How much more, if haply the people had
eaten freely to day of the spoil of their enemies
which they found? for had there not been now a
much greater slaughter among the Philistines?
31 And they smote the Philistines that day from
Michmash to Aijalon: and the people were very
faint.
32 And the people flew upon the spoil, and took
sheep, and oxen, and calves, and slew *them* on
the ground: and the people did eat *them* with the
blood.
33 ¶ Then they told Saul, saying, Behold, the
people sin against the LORD, in that they eat with
the blood. And he said, Ye have transgressed: roll
a great stone unto me this day.
34 And Saul said, Disperse yourselves among
the people, and say unto them, Bring me hither
every man his ox, and every man his sheep, and
slay *them* here, and eat; and sin not against the
LORD in eating with the blood. And all the people
brought every man his ox with him that night,
and slew *them* there.
35 And Saul built an altar unto the LORD: the same
was the first altar that he built unto the LORD.
36 ¶ And Saul said, Let us go down after the
Philistines by night, and spoil them until the
morning light, and let us not leave a man of them.
And they said, Do whatsoever seemeth good unto
thee. Then said the priest, Let us draw near hither
unto God.
37 And Saul asked counsel of God, Shall I go
down after the Philistines? wilt thou deliver them
into the hand of Israel? But he answered him not
that day.
38 And Saul said, Draw ye near hither, all the
chief of the people: and know and see wherein
this sin hath been this day.
39 For, *as* the LORD liveth, which saveth Israel,
though it be in Jonathan my son, he shall surely
die. But *there was* not a man among all the people
that answered him.
40 Then said he unto all Israel, Be ye on one side,
and I and Jonathan my son will be on the other
side. And the people said unto Saul, Do what seem-
eth good unto thee.
41 Therefore Saul said unto the LORD God of
Israel, Give a perfect *lot*. And Saul and Jonathan
were taken: but the people escaped.
42 And Saul said, Cast *lots* between me and Jona-
than my son. And Jonathan was taken.
43 Then Saul said to Jonathan, Tell me what thou
hast done. And Jonathan told him, and said, I did
but taste a little honey with the end of the rod that
was in mine hand, *and*, lo, I must die.
44 And Saul answered, God do so and more also:
for thou shalt surely die, Jonathan.
45 And the people said unto Saul, Shall Jonathan
die, who hath wrought this great salvation in

14:21 *Hebrews . . . Israelites.* In the Old Testament the terms are not identical. Abraham was called a Hebrew long before there was Israel (Gen. 14:13). Here, some of the *Hebrews* changed sides from the Philistines to the Israelites; they were apparently transients with no national loyalty who served as mercenaries. In time, the terms overlapped (Phil. 3:5).
14:24 *adjured.* Put under oath.
14:25 *wood.* Thicket or forest.
14:27 *his eyes were enlightened.* An idiom meaning that he was refreshed or rejuvenated (v. 29).
14:28 *straitly charged . . . with an oath.* He certainly made the people swear. *faint.* Became tired (v. 31).
14:30 Literally, "Surely indeed, would that the people had certainly eaten today."
14:32 *flew.* Literally, "darted greedily or swooped down with a shriek." A vivid image depicting desperation, as evidenced in the people's violation of Levitical law by eating *the blood* (Lev. 19:26).
14:33–34 *great stone.* Place to slay the animals so the blood could properly drain.
14:41 *Give a perfect lot.* Literally, "give a correct, completely clear answer."

Israel? God forbid: *as* the LORD liveth, there shall
not one hair of his head fall to the ground; for he
hath wrought with God this day. So the people
rescued Jonathan, that he died not.
46 Then Saul went up from following the Philis-
tines: and the Philistines went to their own place.
47 ¶ So Saul took the kingdom over Israel,
and fought against all his enemies on every
side, against Moab, and against the children of
Ammon, and against Edom, and against the
kings of Zobah, and against the Philistines: and
whithersoever he turned himself, he vexed *them*.
48 And he gathered an host, and smote the Ama-
lekites, and delivered Israel out of the hands of
them that spoiled them.
49 Now the sons of Saul were Jonathan, and
Ishui, and Melchi-shua: and the names of his two
daughters *were these*; the name of the firstborn
Merab, and the name of the younger Michal:
50 And the name of Saul's wife *was* Ahinoam, the
daughter of Ahimaaz: and the name of the cap-
tain of his host *was* Abner, the son of Ner, Saul's
uncle.
51 And Kish *was* the father of Saul; and Ner the
father of Abner *was* the son of Abiel.
52 And there was sore war against the Philistines
all the days of Saul: and when Saul saw any strong
man, or any valiant man, he took him unto him.

CHAPTER 15

SAMUEL also said unto Saul, The LORD sent me to
anoint thee *to be* king over his people, over Israel:
now therefore hearken thou unto the voice of the
words of the LORD.
2 Thus saith the LORD of hosts, I remember *that*
which Amalek did to Israel, how he laid *wait* for
him in the way, when he came up from Egypt.
3 Now go and smite Amalek, and utterly destroy
all that they have, and spare them not; but slay
both man and woman, infant and suckling, ox
and sheep, camel and ass.
4 And Saul gathered the people together, and
numbered them in Telaim, two hundred thou-
sand footmen, and ten thousand men of Judah.
5 And Saul came to a city of Amalek, and laid
wait in the valley.
6 ¶ And Saul said unto the Kenites, Go, depart,
get you down from among the Amalekites, lest I
destroy you with them: for ye shewed kindness to
all the children of Israel, when they came up out
of Egypt. So the Kenites departed from among the
Amalekites.
7 And Saul smote the Amalekites from Havilah
until thou comest to Shur, that *is* over against
Egypt.
8 And he took Agag the king of the Amalekites
alive, and utterly destroyed all the people with the
edge of the sword.
9 But Saul and the people spared Agag, and the
best of the sheep, and of the oxen, and of the
fatlings, and the lambs, and all *that was* good,
and would not utterly destroy them: but every
thing *that was* vile and refuse, that they destroyed
utterly.
10 ¶ Then came the word of the LORD unto
Samuel, saying,
11 It repenteth me that I have set up Saul *to be*
king: for he is turned back from following me,
and hath not performed my commandments.
And it grieved Samuel; and he cried unto the
LORD all night.

14:45 *wrought*. Done or accomplished. *God forbid*. Literally, "far from it" or "far be it."
14:47 *vexed*. The Hebrew word means "to declare guilty" and has the sense here of inflicting punishment.
14:48 *spoiled them*. Plundered them.
14:52 *sore*. Severe or hot.

Thoughts for Personal/Family Worship: Chapter 14

1. **The situation looked hopeless for Israel, but Jonathan looked beyond the circumstances to the Lord. Like Caleb, his confidence was in God (Num. 13:30; 14:6–9). He knew the Lord could "save by many or by few" (1 Sam. 14:6). What an encouragement Jonathan ought to be to us in our service to the Lord. His faith and love raised him above any anxious cares. His first concern was for the honor of the Lord. By God's grace, let us strive to uphold this same principle, by "looking unto Jesus the author and finisher of our faith" (Heb. 12:2). How can we grow in such a faith?**
2. **Saul issued a very foolish command that his army should not eat until the Philistines were defeated. It was a command that God had not required, and it nearly cost Jonathan his life because he was unaware of the oath (v. 27). It is of vital importance that Christians never seek to impose upon the Lord's people those things that God has not insisted upon. Too many in the professing church seek to turn their own ideas into biblical commands. Let us never make a personal preference into a precept.**

Chapter 15: *Saul's incomplete obedience regarding the slaughter of the Amalekites seals his rejection as king.*

15:1–3 *I remember that which Amalek did to Israel*. See Ex. 17:8–16; Deut. 25:17–19. God's delay in the execution of justice does not diminish its certainty.
15:3 *utterly destroy*. To put under a ban, to devote to the Lord for His disposal—the root "accursed" used regarding Jericho (Josh. 6:17,21). Saul was to be the instrument of execution, but God was the judge.
15:6 *Kenites*. See Ex. 18:9,10,19; Num. 10:29,31–32; Judg. 1:16; 4:11.
15:9 *fatlings*. The young rams fattened for slaughter. *vile and refuse*. Despised and weak. They devoted to the Lord what they regarded as worthless and kept the best for themselves.
15:11 *It repenteth me*. The Hebrew word can mean repenting of one's own sins (impossible for God); finding comfort (inappropriate in this context); or here, God feeling sorrow

12 And when Samuel rose early to meet Saul in
the morning, it was told Samuel, saying, Saul
came to Carmel, and, behold, he set him up a
place, and is gone about, and passed on, and gone
down to Gilgal.
13 And Samuel came to Saul: and Saul said unto
him, Blessed *be* thou of the LORD: I have per-
formed the commandment of the LORD.
14 And Samuel said, What *meaneth* then this
bleating of the sheep in mine ears, and the lowing
of the oxen which I hear?
15 And Saul said, They have brought them from
the Amalekites: for the people spared the best
of the sheep and of the oxen, to sacrifice unto
the LORD thy God; and the rest we have utterly
destroyed.
16 Then Samuel said unto Saul, Stay, and I will
tell thee what the LORD hath said to me this night.
And he said unto him, Say on.
17 And Samuel said, When thou *wast* little in
thine own sight, *wast* thou not *made* the head of
the tribes of Israel, and the LORD anointed thee
king over Israel?
18 And the LORD sent thee on a journey, and said,
Go and utterly destroy the sinners the Amalekites,
and fight against them until they be consumed.
19 Wherefore then didst thou not obey the voice
of the LORD, but didst fly upon the spoil, and
didst evil in the sight of the LORD?
20 And Saul said unto Samuel, Yea, I have obeyed
the voice of the LORD, and have gone the way
which the LORD sent me, and have brought Agag
the king of Amalek, and have utterly destroyed
the Amalekites.
21 But the people took of the spoil, sheep and
oxen, the chief of the things which should have
been utterly destroyed, to sacrifice unto the LORD
thy God in Gilgal.
22 And Samuel said, Hath the LORD *as great* de-
light in burnt offerings and sacrifices, as in obey-
ing the voice of the LORD? Behold, to obey *is* better
than sacrifice, *and* to hearken than the fat of rams.
23 For rebellion *is as* the sin of witchcraft, and
stubbornness *is as* iniquity and idolatry. Because
thou hast rejected the word of the LORD, he hath
also rejected thee from *being* king.
24 ¶ And Saul said unto Samuel, I have sinned:
for I have transgressed the commandment of the
LORD, and thy words: because I feared the people,
and obeyed their voice.
25 Now therefore, I pray thee, pardon my sin, and
turn again with me, that I may worship the LORD.
26 And Samuel said unto Saul, I will not return
with thee: for thou hast rejected the word of the
LORD, and the LORD hath rejected thee from be-
ing king over Israel.
27 And as Samuel turned about to go away, he
laid hold upon the skirt of his mantle, and it rent.
28 And Samuel said unto him, The LORD hath
rent the kingdom of Israel from thee this day, and
hath given it to a neighbour of thine, *that is* better
than thou.
29 And also the Strength of Israel will not lie nor
repent: for he *is* not a man, that he should repent.
30 Then he said, I have sinned: *yet* honour me
now, I pray thee, before the elders of my people,
and before Israel, and turn again with me, that I
may worship the LORD thy God.
31 So Samuel turned again after Saul; and Saul
worshipped the LORD.
32 ¶ Then said Samuel, Bring ye hither to me
Agag the king of the Amalekites. And Agag came
unto him delicately. And Agag said, Surely the
bitterness of death is past.
33 And Samuel said, As thy sword hath made
women childless, so shall thy mother be childless
among women. And Samuel hewed Agag in pieces
before the LORD in Gilgal.
34 ¶ Then Samuel went to Ramah; and Saul went
up to his house to Gibeah of Saul.
35 And Samuel came no more to see Saul until
the day of his death: nevertheless Samuel

---

over man's sins (Isa. 63:10) and reversing His former course of action (2 Sam. 24:16; Jonah 4:2) in appointing Saul as king, just as He had grieved over the sin of mankind and reversed His act of creating them by destroying them with the flood (Gen. 6:5–7). *it grieved.* Literally "it was hot to," an idiom designating anger. God's displeasure at the treason of His king was humanly imaged by Samuel's anger and sadness (1 Sam. 15:35). This is anthropopathism, human emotion figuratively applied to God to help us understand His infinite wrath against sin.

15:19 *fly.* Dart greedily or swoop down with a shriek.

15:22 External religious rituals cannot substitute for trust and obedience (Hos. 6:6; Mic. 6:7–8; Mark 12:33).

15:23 *witchcraft.* Divination.

15:27 *skirt of his mantle.* Hem of his sleeveless cloak or cape.

15:29 *repent.* The same word as in vv. 11,35. By saying that God both repents and cannot repent, the text is making a subtle but important distinction about God and change. God's relationships change and His course of action changes because His creatures change over time (see note at v. 11). However, God's nature and plans never change, *for he is not a man* but God (Num. 23:19; Ps. 33:10–11; James 1:17). Even the fall of Saul was in His plan, for He had ordained beforehand that kingship would belong to the tribe of Judah (Gen. 49:10). Therefore, his rejection of wicked Saul as king was final. God's unchanging nature and plan are the reason He is the *Strength of Israel,* the eternal victory of His covenant people (Mal. 3:6).

15:32 *delicately.* The Hebrew term is uncertain, having either the idea of coming in fetters with trembling or coming calmly. However he came, his assessment that the threat of death was gone was ill founded.

15:33 *hewed.* Chopped.

Thoughts for Personal/Family Worship: Chapter 15

1. God's dealing with the Amalekites illustrates how slow God is to express His anger, and yet how certain it is that His judgment will fall on the wicked (Nah. 1:3). God

OBEDIENCE TO GOD'S WILL

Obedience to God's will summarizes the duty of Christian religion (Deut. 10:20; 1 Sam. 12:24; Eccl. 12:13). We can identify four areas related to this reasonable service (Rom. 12:1): its foundation or basis, its form or essence, its regulating principle, and its practical manifestation.

First, the foundation for this obedience is the character of God. God possesses within Himself all glory and worthiness to be served (Ps. 119:90–91; Jer. 10:7). His being demands man's subjection to honor and serve Him truly, to devote his entire existence to God. God's character as the foundation does not exclude entirely the works He exercises toward men; rather, it recognizes that the basis for man's obedience is first God's glorious nature that He possesses within Himself, even if there were nothing else. This obligation to obey God's will is effected by God's majesty. Therein lies the basis for man's duty of service to God, for living in dedication to his Maker.

Second, the form or essence of this obedience consists of man's knowledge, recognition, and heartfelt endorsement of this binding obligation: living wholly for God at all times and in all things. This affirmation is best understood as the internal resolve for a life of glorifying God, both by understanding intellectually what is required and by deciding volitionally to live according to the duties demanded by God. With sincere resolution, the believer willingly sacrifices himself to the service of God, proclaiming, "O LORD, truly I am thy servant; I am thy servant" (Ps. 116:16; cf. Isa. 44:5). Further, underlying this commitment is the believer's continual plea to God to "create in me a clean heart, and renew a right spirit within me" (Ps. 51:10). The believer's desire is for all that is void of godliness to be thrown off and all that is suffused with holiness to be taken on.

Third, the regulating principle for obedience to God's will is the revelation of the content of His will in Scripture. It has not been left to man to determine the duties he owes to God (cf. Matt. 15:9); rather, they have been fixed, both positively and negatively. The latter consists of the prohibition of all that lacks conformity to God's standard of holiness. The former refers not only to the letter of the moral law, as expressed in the Ten Commandments and its exposition, but also to its spirit: "Thou shalt love the Lord thy God with all thy heart, and with all thy soul, and with all thy strength, and with all thy mind; and thy neighbour as thyself" (Luke 10:27; cf. Gal. 5:14). Therein lies what is the "good, and acceptable, and perfect, will of God" (Rom. 12:2). Thus, God's will holds demands for the whole of man. This complete standard for obedience has been fleshed out in perfection for imitation—observe the obedient Christ (Heb. 5:8; cf. 1 Cor. 11:1; Eph. 5:1–2; Phil. 2:5–8).

Fourth, the practical manifestation of obedience is both an active agreement with and an execution of the will of God (cf. James 1:22; 2:24). The former denominates the internal act of obedience, for obedience is that which proceeds from a heart offered sincerely to God. The believer continually recalls Christ's words to him: "If ye love me, keep my commandments" (John 14:15; cf. Matt. 7:21; Luke 6:46; John 14:21). Therefore, all that God wills the believer wills, because the will of God is the object of his heart's desire and delight. The believer performs the will of God earnestly from his heart (Eph. 6:6), with joyfulness (Ps. 100:2).

The execution of the will of God describes the outward acts of the believer: an obedience extending to all matters of daily living. This obedience is most commonly known as good works, which God has revealed to us that we may be careful to do them (Deut. 29:29b). Thus, for the believer, pure and undefiled religion can be reduced to its simplest form: "to visit the fatherless and widows in their affliction, and to keep himself unspotted from the world" (James 1:27).

—adapted from Wilhelmus à Brakel, *The Christian's Reasonable Service*, vol. 1, ch. 1

mourned for Saul: and the LORD repented that he
had made Saul king over Israel.

CHAPTER 16

AND the LORD said unto Samuel, How long wilt
thou mourn for Saul, seeing I have rejected him
from reigning over Israel? fill thine horn with oil,
and go, I will send thee to Jesse the Beth-lehemite:
for I have provided me a king among his sons.
2 And Samuel said, How can I go? if Saul hear *it*,
he will kill me. And the LORD said, Take an heifer
with thee, and say, I am come to sacrifice to the
LORD.
3 And call Jesse to the sacrifice, and I will shew
thee what thou shalt do: and thou shalt anoint
unto me *him* whom I name unto thee.
4 And Samuel did that which the LORD spake,
and came to Beth-lehem. And the elders of the
town trembled at his coming, and said, Comest
thou peaceably?
5 And he said, Peaceably: I am come to sacrifice
unto the LORD: sanctify yourselves, and come
with me to the sacrifice. And he sanctified Jesse
and his sons, and called them to the sacrifice.
6 ¶ And it came to pass, when they were come,
that he looked on Eliab, and said, Surely the
LORD's anointed *is* before him.
7 But the LORD said unto Samuel, Look not on
his countenance, or on the height of his stature;
because I have refused him: for *the LORD seeth* not
as man seeth; for man looketh on the outward
appearance, but the LORD looketh on the heart.
8 Then Jesse called Abinadab, and made him
pass before Samuel. And he said, Neither hath the
LORD chosen this.
9 Then Jesse made Shammah to pass by. And he
said, Neither hath the LORD chosen this.
10 Again, Jesse made seven of his sons to pass
before Samuel. And Samuel said unto Jesse, The
LORD hath not chosen these.
11 And Samuel said unto Jesse, Are here all *thy*
children? And he said, There remaineth yet the
youngest, and, behold, he keepeth the sheep. And
Samuel said unto Jesse, Send and fetch him: for
we will not sit down till he come hither.
12 And he sent, and brought him in. Now he *was*
ruddy, *and* withal of a beautiful countenance,
and goodly to look to. And the LORD said, Arise,
anoint him: for this *is* he.
13 Then Samuel took the horn of oil, and
anointed him in the midst of his brethren: and the
Spirit of the LORD came upon David from that day
forward. So Samuel rose up, and went to Ramah.
14 ¶ But the Spirit of the LORD departed from
Saul, and an evil spirit from the LORD troubled
him.
15 And Saul's servants said unto him, Behold
now, an evil spirit from God troubleth thee.
16 Let our lord now command thy servants, *which*
are before thee, to seek out a man, *who is* a cunning
player on an harp: and it shall come to pass, when

---

had announced in Ex. 17:14 that He would destroy the Amalekites because of their wicked attack upon Israel as they traveled through the wilderness. Many years had passed, evidencing the patience of God. But God had not forgotten, and the sin of Amalek had now come to full fruition; their judgment was impending. Sinners often interpret the delay of justice as evidence of God's inability to judge (Ps. 94:5–11; Ezek. 12:21–25; 2 Peter 3:4–7). Rather, the patient goodness of God is designed to lead to repentance (Rom. 2:3–4). How has God been patient with you? How should you repent thoroughly of your sins?

2. **The mere outward expression of worship, without the engaging of the heart, means nothing to God. Saul had disobeyed the Lord and had tried to appease Him through the sacrifice. The Lord requires and delights in the submission of the human will to His Word: "Behold, to obey is better than sacrifice" (v. 22). Obedience demonstrates our love for God (Ex. 20:6; John 14:21). Through His obedience our Lord Jesus Christ saved sinners and brought them to eternal joy in God (Ps. 40:6–8; Matt. 26:42; John 4:34; 6:38–40; 17:4; Rom. 5:19; Phil. 2:8). Therefore, love obedience, delight in obedience, treasure obedience, and pursue full obedience by the grace of Christ.**

THE VICTORIES AND PERSECUTION OF DAVID (1 SAM. 16:1—26:25)

Chapter 16: ***The Lord directs Samuel to Bethlehem to anoint David as king, after which David providentially is brought into Saul's special service.***

David's Anointing as King and Enlisting to Serve Saul (1 Sam. 16:1–23)

16:1 *horn.* Animal horn, used to store liquids (v. 13). *I have provided me a king.* Literally, "I have seen for myself a king," in the sense of giving attention to fulfilling His purposes (Gen. 22:8,14).

16:2 This is not a lie; God is incapable of lying (15:29). However, honesty does not require telling everything we know or intend, especially to dangerous enemies.

16:7 *countenance.* Appearance. *the outward appearance.* Literally, "the eyes," referring to what can be seen.

16:11 *we will not sit down.* Literally, "we will not encircle," referring to sitting around the table to dine.

16:12 *ruddy.* A reddish complexion evidencing health. *withal of a beautiful countenance.* Literally, "as well as fairness of eyes." *goodly to look to.* Literally, "good of appearance."

16:13 The oil was symbolic of the Holy Spirit, who empowered David for his service (see note at 10:6). *The Spirit of the LORD came upon David.* The Hebrew has the idea of rushing upon.

16:14–15 *The Spirit of the LORD departed from Saul.* He was no longer divinely empowered to function in his anointed role as king. *evil spirit from the LORD.* Either Saul's own spirit (inner being), which tormented him for his sins, or a demonic spirit that God sent as punishment upon the wicked king (cf. Judg. 9:23–24; 2 Kings 22:19–23).

16:16 *cunning player.* Skilled player (v. 18). That music could soothe suggests that the *evil spirit* was Saul's own troubled inner self.

the evil spirit from God is upon thee, that he shall
play with his hand, and thou shalt be well.
17 And Saul said unto his servants, Provide me
now a man that can play well, and bring *him* to me.
18 Then answered one of the servants, and
said, Behold, I have seen a son of Jesse the Beth-
lehemite, *that is* cunning in playing, and a mighty
valiant man, and a man of war, and prudent in
matters, and a comely person, and the LORD *is*
with him.
19 ¶ Wherefore Saul sent messengers unto Jesse,
and said, Send me David thy son, which *is* with
the sheep.
20 And Jesse took an ass *laden* with bread, and a
bottle of wine, and a kid, and sent *them* by David
his son unto Saul.
21 And David came to Saul, and stood before
him: and he loved him greatly; and he became his
armourbearer.
22 And Saul sent to Jesse, saying, Let David, I pray
thee, stand before me; for he hath found favour
in my sight.
23 And it came to pass, when the *evil* spirit from
God was upon Saul, that David took an harp, and
played with his hand: so Saul was refreshed, and
was well, and the evil spirit departed from him.

CHAPTER 17

Now the Philistines gathered together their armies
to battle, and were gathered together at Shochoh,
which *belongeth* to Judah, and pitched between
Shochoh and Azekah, in Ephes-dammim.
2 And Saul and the men of Israel were gathered
together, and pitched by the valley of Elah, and set
the battle in array against the Philistines.
3 And the Philistines stood on a mountain on the
one side, and Israel stood on a mountain on the
other side: and *there was* a valley between them.
4 ¶ And there went out a champion out of the
camp of the Philistines, named Goliath, of Gath,
whose height *was* six cubits and a span.
5 And *he had* an helmet of brass upon his head,
and he *was* armed with a coat of mail; and the
weight of the coat *was* five thousand shekels of
brass.
6 And *he had* greaves of brass upon his legs, and a
target of brass between his shoulders.
7 And the staff of his spear *was* like a weaver's
beam; and his spear's head *weighed* six hundred
shekels of iron: and one bearing a shield went
before him.
8 And he stood and cried unto the armies of
Israel, and said unto them, Why are ye come out
to set *your* battle in array? *am* not I a Philistine,
and ye servants to Saul? choose you a man for
you, and let him come down to me.
9 If he be able to fight with me, and to kill me,
then will we be your servants: but if I prevail
against him, and kill him, then shall ye be our
servants, and serve us.
10 And the Philistine said, I defy the armies of
Israel this day; give me a man, that we may fight
together.
11 When Saul and all Israel heard those words
of the Philistine, they were dismayed, and greatly
afraid.
12 ¶ Now David *was* the son of that Ephrathite of
Beth-lehem-judah, whose name *was* Jesse; and he
had eight sons: and the man went among men *for*
an old man in the days of Saul.
13 And the three eldest sons of Jesse went *and*
followed Saul to the battle: and the names of his
three sons that went to the battle *were* Eliab the

16:18 *prudent in matters.* Skillful with words or speech.
16:23 *so Saul was refreshed.* Literally, "it became wide for Saul," meaning that he was relieved from the weight that had been pressing in on him.

Thoughts for Personal/Family Worship: Chapter 16

1. **Man looks on the outside, but God looks on the inside (v. 7). This should produce sobriety and the fear of the Lord (Prov. 15:11; 16:2; Heb. 4:13). It ought to be our constant desire and prayer that as the Lord looks at us He will see nothing that displeases Him (Pss. 17:3; 139:23–24). But man's looking on the outside ought to be a motive for proper living as well, since trees are known by their fruit (Matt. 7:16–20). As Christians we should strive to live before men bearing fruit in such a way that evidences that we are united to Christ, the vine (John 15:5).**
2. **That Saul's troubled soul could be soothed by David's harp suggests something about the inherent power of music to affect the person even apart from its words. Music is often the instrument of Satan to arouse passions and behaviors that are destructive to self and society. On the other hand, music is a means of praising and worshiping God and can direct our hearts heavenward. Let us be careful therefore not to listen to music that incites the works of the flesh, like sensuality and anger, but instead to listen to music that helps us to think, feel, and act for the glory of God.**

Chapter 17: *David accepts Goliath's defiant challenge and slays the giant, resulting in Israel's routing of the Philistines.*

Saul's Failure and David's Victory by Faith (1 Sam. 17:1–54)

17:2 *set the battle in array.* Line up for battle (vv. 8,21).
17:4 *six cubits and a span.* Over nine feet tall.
17:5 *brass.* Bronze. *coat of mail.* Literally, "a body armor of scales," because its construction resembled fish scales. *five thousand shekels of brass.* About 110 pounds of bronze.
17:6 *greaves.* Shin protectors, probably made of metal or hardened leather. *target . . . between his shoulders.* A dagger or javelin slung over the shoulders.
17:7 *six hundred shekels.* About thirteen pounds.
17:8 *servants to Saul.* Goliath implicitly challenges Saul, himself a tall man (9:2), but the king of Israel failed to lead Israel by faith (17:11).
17:12–18 David appears as an insignificant figure, a young

firstborn, and next unto him Abinadab, and the
third Shammah.
14 And David *was* the youngest: and the three
eldest followed Saul.
15 But David went and returned from Saul to
feed his father's sheep at Beth-lehem.
16 And the Philistine drew near morning and
evening, and presented himself forty days.
17 And Jesse said unto David his son, Take now
for thy brethren an ephah of this parched *corn*,
and these ten loaves, and run to the camp to thy
brethren;
18 And carry these ten cheeses unto the captain
of *their* thousand, and look how thy brethren fare,
and take their pledge.
19 Now Saul, and they, and all the men of Israel,
were in the valley of Elah, fighting with the
Philistines.
20 ¶ And David rose up early in the morning, and
left the sheep with a keeper, and took, and went,
as Jesse had commanded him; and he came to the
trench, as the host was going forth to the fight,
and shouted for the battle.
21 For Israel and the Philistines had put the battle
in array, army against army.
22 And David left his carriage in the hand of the
keeper of the carriage, and ran into the army, and
came and saluted his brethren.
23 And as he talked with them, behold, there
came up the champion, the Philistine of Gath,
Goliath by name, out of the armies of the Philis-
tines, and spake according to the same words: and
David heard *them*.
24 And all the men of Israel, when they saw the
man, fled from him, and were sore afraid.
25 And the men of Israel said, Have ye seen this
man that is come up? surely to defy Israel is he
come up: and it shall be, *that* the man who killeth
him, the king will enrich him with great riches,
and will give him his daughter, and make his
father's house free in Israel.
26 And David spake to the men that stood by
him, saying, What shall be done to the man that
killeth this Philistine, and taketh away the re-
proach from Israel? for who *is* this uncircumcised
Philistine, that he should defy the armies of the
living God?
27 And the people answered him after this
manner, saying, So shall it be done to the man
that killeth him.
28 ¶ And Eliab his eldest brother heard when he
spake unto the men; and Eliab's anger was kindled
against David, and he said, Why camest thou
down hither? and with whom hast thou left those
few sheep in the wilderness? I know thy pride, and
the naughtiness of thine heart; for thou art come
down that thou mightest see the battle.
29 And David said, What have I now done? *Is
there* not a cause?
30 ¶ And he turned from him toward another,
and spake after the same manner: and the people
answered him again after the former manner.
31 And when the words were heard which David
spake, they rehearsed *them* before Saul: and he
sent for him.
32 ¶ And David said to Saul, Let no man's heart
fail because of him; thy servant will go and fight
with this Philistine.
33 And Saul said to David, Thou art not able to
go against this Philistine to fight with him: for
thou *art but* a youth, and he a man of war from
his youth.
34 And David said unto Saul, Thy servant kept
his father's sheep, and there came a lion, and a
bear, and took a lamb out of the flock:
35 And I went out after him, and smote him, and
delivered *it* out of his mouth: and when he arose
against me, I caught *him* by his beard, and smote
him, and slew him.
36 Thy servant slew both the lion and the bear:
and this uncircumcised Philistine shall be as one
of them, seeing he hath defied the armies of the
living God.
37 David said moreover, The LORD that delivered
me out of the paw of the lion, and out of the paw
of the bear, he will deliver me out of the hand of
this Philistine. And Saul said unto David, Go, and
the LORD be with thee.
38 ¶ And Saul armed David with his armour, and
he put an helmet of brass upon his head; also he

shepherd sent on an errand to his brothers. But God saw his heart and had anointed him with the Spirit to lead Israel (16:7,12–13). Christ also came humbly, but anointed with the Spirit (Isa. 42:1).

17:17 *ephah.* Dry measure almost equivalent to a bushel.

17:20 *trench.* The entrenchment or perhaps a ring of wagons.

17:22 *carriage.* Vessels or equipment. *saluted.* Asked regarding one's welfare.

17:24 *sore.* Very.

17:26 *defy the armies of the living God.* Other men saw Goliath as an invincible warrior defying Israel (vv. 10,25), but by faith David saw him as a man outside of God's covenant blessing (*uncircumcised*), mocking the true and sovereign Lord (vv. 36,45).

17:28 *kindled.* Burned. *naughtiness.* Wickedness. David's family did not celebrate his faith but despised him, just as Christ would be despised and rejected by men (Isa. 49:7; 53:3).

17:29 *Is there not a cause?* Literally, "Is it not a word?" David defends himself against Eliab's accusation by saying, "I'm only asking a question."

17:31 *rehearsed.* Told.

17:34 David was a shepherd who risked his life to fight for the sheep, an image of what a king should be (Ps. 78:70–72) and a type of Christ (John 10:11–14).

17:35 *beard.* Could refer to the side whiskers or lower jaw.

17:38 *helmet of brass . . . coat of mail.* Same words used of Goliath's armor (v. 5). Saul was like Goliath in that he relied on human resources.

armed him with a coat of mail.
39 And David girded his sword upon his armour,
and he assayed to go; for he had not proved *it*.
And David said unto Saul, I cannot go with these;
for I have not proved *them*. And David put them
off him.
40 And he took his staff in his hand, and chose
him five smooth stones out of the brook, and put
them in a shepherd's bag which he had, even in a
scrip; and his sling *was* in his hand: and he drew
near to the Philistine.
41 And the Philistine came on and drew near
unto David; and the man that bare the shield *went*
before him.
42 And when the Philistine looked about, and
saw David, he disdained him: for he was *but* a
youth, and ruddy, and of a fair countenance.
43 And the Philistine said unto David, *Am* I a
dog, that thou comest to me with staves? And the
Philistine cursed David by his gods.
44 And the Philistine said to David, Come to me,
and I will give thy flesh unto the fowls of the air,
and to the beasts of the field.
45 Then said David to the Philistine, Thou
comest to me with a sword, and with a spear, and
with a shield: but I come to thee in the name of
the LORD of hosts, the God of the armies of Israel,
whom thou hast defied.
46 This day will the LORD deliver thee into mine
hand; and I will smite thee, and take thine head
from thee; and I will give the carcases of the host
of the Philistines this day unto the fowls of the
air, and to the wild beasts of the earth; that all the
earth may know that there is a God in Israel.
47 And all this assembly shall know that the LORD
saveth not with sword and spear: for the battle *is*
the LORD's, and he will give you into our hands.
48 And it came to pass, when the Philistine arose,
and came and drew nigh to meet David, that
David hasted, and ran toward the army to meet
the Philistine.
49 And David put his hand in his bag, and took
thence a stone, and slang *it*, and smote the Phi-
listine in his forehead, that the stone sunk into his
forehead; and he fell upon his face to the earth.
50 So David prevailed over the Philistine with a
sling and with a stone, and smote the Philistine,
and slew him; but *there was* no sword in the hand
of David.
51 Therefore David ran, and stood upon the
Philistine, and took his sword, and drew it out
of the sheath thereof, and slew him, and cut off
his head therewith. And when the Philistines saw
their champion was dead, they fled.
52 And the men of Israel and of Judah arose, and
shouted, and pursued the Philistines, until thou
come to the valley, and to the gates of Ekron. And
the wounded of the Philistines fell down by the
way to Shaaraim, even unto Gath, and unto Ekron.
53 And the children of Israel returned from
chasing after the Philistines, and they spoiled
their tents.
54 And David took the head of the Philistine, and
brought it to Jerusalem; but he put his armour in
his tent.
55 ¶ And when Saul saw David go forth against
the Philistine, he said unto Abner, the captain of
the host, Abner, whose son *is* this youth? And Ab-
ner said, *As* thy soul liveth, O king, I cannot tell.
56 And the king said, Enquire thou whose son the
stripling *is*.
57 And as David returned from the slaughter of
the Philistine, Abner took him, and brought him
before Saul with the head of the Philistine in his
hand.
58 And Saul said to him, Whose son *art* thou,
thou young man? And David answered, I *am* the
son of thy servant Jesse the Beth-lehemite.

17:39 *girded*. Secured with a belt or band, encircled. *assayed to go*. Attempted to walk. *not proved*. Not tried or tested.

17:40 *scrip*. Pouch. *sling*. Weapon that hurled stones with great force (Judg. 20:16; 1 Chron. 12:2).

17:43 *staves*. Staffs.

17:45–47 David's faith was not in weapons but in the greatness (*name*) of the Lord. The anointed king fought by God's grace and for His glory, *that all the earth may know that there is a God in Israel* (Ex. 9:16; Josh. 4:24; 1 Kings 8:43; 18:36; 2 Kings 19:19).

17:48 *hasted, and ran*. Ran quickly.

17:49–51 *he fell upon his face to the earth. . . . cut off his head.* David did to Goliath what the ark of the Lord had done to the Philistine god, Dagon (5:1–5). The king's victory was not merely over wicked men but over the evil spiritual powers behind them (17:43; cf. Col. 2:15).

17:53 *spoiled*. Plundered. The victory of God's anointed is the victory of all His people.

Saul's Jealousy and Jonathan's Loyalty to David (1 Sam. 17:55—20:42)

17:55–58 There is some tension between Saul's ignorance about David's family here and the earlier account of David's entrance into Saul's service as a musician and armor-bearer (16:18–23). It is possible that the earlier account overlaps the events of ch. 17 to some extent, summarizing events that took place before or after the defeat of Goliath. However, two factors also make Saul's questions understandable even if David already served in his court. First, Saul did not ask for David's name but his father's name; as king he may not have remembered all the family connections of his court servants. Second, Saul's mind had been afflicted by the "evil spirit from the Lord" (16:14), and he would act increasingly irrational as time progressed. Thus his thinking and memory may have been muddled.

17:55 *whose son is this youth?* The question is important because Saul had promised that the father's household of whoever defeated Goliath would be free from taxation (v. 25).

17:56 *stripling*. Youth.

17:58 *son of thy servant*. Though the triumphant hero of Israel, David answered the king humbly and respectfully.

CHAPTER 18

AND it came to pass, when he had made an end of
speaking unto Saul, that the soul of Jonathan was
knit with the soul of David, and Jonathan loved
him as his own soul.
2 And Saul took him that day, and would let him
go no more home to his father's house.
3 Then Jonathan and David made a covenant,
because he loved him as his own soul.
4 And Jonathan stripped himself of the robe
that *was* upon him, and gave it to David, and his
garments, even to his sword, and to his bow, and
to his girdle.
5 ¶ And David went out whithersoever Saul sent
him, *and* behaved himself wisely: and Saul set
him over the men of war, and he was accepted in
the sight of all the people, and also in the sight of
Saul's servants.
6 And it came to pass as they came, when David
was returned from the slaughter of the Philistine,
that the women came out of all cities of Israel,
singing and dancing, to meet king Saul, with tab-
rets, with joy, and with instruments of musick.
7 And the women answered *one another* as they
played, and said, Saul hath slain his thousands,
and David his ten thousands.
8 And Saul was very wroth, and the saying
displeased him; and he said, They have ascribed
unto David ten thousands, and to me they have
ascribed *but* thousands: and *what* can he have
more but the kingdom?
9 And Saul eyed David from that day and
forward.
10 ¶ And it came to pass on the morrow, that
the evil spirit from God came upon Saul, and he
prophesied in the midst of the house: and David
played with his hand, as at other times: and *there
was* a javelin in Saul's hand.
11 And Saul cast the javelin; for he said, I will
smite David even to the wall *with it*. And David
avoided out of his presence twice.
12 ¶ And Saul was afraid of David, because the
LORD was with him, and was departed from Saul.
13 Therefore Saul removed him from him, and
made him his captain over a thousand; and he
went out and came in before the people.
14 And David behaved himself wisely in all his
ways; and the LORD *was* with him.
15 Wherefore when Saul saw that he behaved
himself very wisely, he was afraid of him.
16 But all Israel and Judah loved David, because
he went out and came in before them.
17 ¶ And Saul said to David, Behold my elder
daughter Merab, her will I give thee to wife:
only be thou valiant for me, and fight the LORD's
battles. For Saul said, Let not mine hand be upon
him, but let the hand of the Philistines be upon
him.
18 And David said unto Saul, Who *am* I? and
what *is* my life, *or* my father's family in Israel, that
I should be son in law to the king?
19 But it came to pass at the time when Merab
Saul's daughter should have been given to David,
that she was given unto Adriel the Meholathite to
wife.
20 And Michal Saul's daughter loved David: and
they told Saul, and the thing pleased him.
21 And Saul said, I will give him her, that she

Thoughts for Personal/Family Worship: Chapter 17

1. **The conflict between David and Goliath is a microcosm of the conflict between the two seeds, the seed of the woman, Christ, and the seed of the serpent (Gen. 3:15). Since David was in the line of Christ, his death at this time would have put the messianic promise in jeopardy. But against all odds, for Goliath had every natural advantage, God gave David the victory and advanced the promise leading to the fullness of time when Christ came. The hostility continues, and it often seems as though the advantage belongs to the serpent. But God's redemptive purpose in Christ is certain, and Christ's church and kingdom will advance regardless of the opposition. The King greater than David will keep on slaying the enemies greater than Goliath until every enemy is placed under His feet (Ps. 110:1–2). How do you need to look to Christ for victory over sin and Satan today?**
2. **Reflecting on past victories from the Lord fuels faith for the next battle, which will certainly come. God enabled David to slay the lion and the bear, and he believed that God would likewise enable him to slay the giant. The God of the past is the God of the present. How much easier our own trials would be if we would remember this principle! Were there not many times in the past when God delivered you from situations that would otherwise have defeated you and brought you down? Then why will He not do the same in your present difficulties? Christian, remember and take hold of this thought: "The LORD is my light and my salvation; whom shall I fear? The LORD is the strength of my life; of whom shall I be afraid?" (Ps. 27:1).**

Chapter 18: ***Jealousy over David's popularity causes Saul to plot against his life.***

18:1 *knit.* The Hebrew means "to bind oneself," in the sense of committing oneself, as himself (v. 3).
18:3 *made a covenant.* Literally, "cut a covenant," the common expression for initiating a covenant, a mutually binding agreement, here between equal parties.
18:4 *stripped himself of the robe.* Jonathan's giving David his royal robe and weapons indicates his acknowledgment that David will be king. *girdle.* Belt.
18:5 *whithersoever.* Wherever. *behaved himself wisely.* Literally, "achieved success" or "prospered" (vv. 14,30).
18:6 *tabrets.* Small drums or tambourines.
18:8 *wroth.* Angry.
18:9 *eyed.* The Hebrew means "treated with suspicion."
18:10 *morrow.* The following day. *evil spirit from God.* See note at 16:14–15. *David played with his hand.* Played the harp with his hands.
18:11 *avoided out of his presence.* Literally, David "turned in a circle from him," evading the attack.

may be a snare to him, and that the hand of the
Philistines may be against him. Wherefore Saul
said to David, Thou shalt this day be my son in
law in *the one of* the twain.
22 ¶ And Saul commanded his servants, *saying*,
Commune with David secretly, and say, Behold,
the king hath delight in thee, and all his servants
love thee: now therefore be the king's son in law.
23 And Saul's servants spake those words in the
ears of David. And David said, Seemeth it to you
a light *thing* to be a king's son in law, seeing that I
am a poor man, and lightly esteemed?
24 And the servants of Saul told him, saying, On
this manner spake David.
25 And Saul said, Thus shall ye say to David, The
king desireth not any dowry, but an hundred
foreskins of the Philistines, to be avenged of the
king's enemies. But Saul thought to make David
fall by the hand of the Philistines.
26 And when his servants told David these words,
it pleased David well to be the king's son in law:
and the days were not expired.
27 Wherefore David arose and went, he and his
men, and slew of the Philistines two hundred
men; and David brought their foreskins, and they
gave them in full tale to the king, that he might be
the king's son in law. And Saul gave him Michal
his daughter to wife.
28 ¶ And Saul saw and knew that the LORD *was*
with David, and *that* Michal Saul's daughter loved
him.
29 And Saul was yet the more afraid of David;
and Saul became David's enemy continually.
30 Then the princes of the Philistines went forth:
and it came to pass, after they went forth, *that*
David behaved himself more wisely than all the
servants of Saul; so that his name was much set by.

CHAPTER 19

AND Saul spake to Jonathan his son, and to all his
servants, that they should kill David.
2 But Jonathan Saul's son delighted much in
David: and Jonathan told David, saying, Saul my
father seeketh to kill thee: now therefore, I pray
thee, take heed to thyself until the morning, and
abide in a secret *place*, and hide thyself:
3 And I will go out and stand beside my father
in the field where thou *art*, and I will commune
with my father of thee; and what I see, that I will
tell thee.
4 ¶ And Jonathan spake good of David unto Saul
his father, and said unto him, Let not the king
sin against his servant, against David; because
he hath not sinned against thee, and because his
works *have been* to thee-ward very good:
5 For he did put his life in his hand, and slew the
Philistine, and the LORD wrought a great salva-
tion for all Israel: thou sawest *it*, and didst rejoice:
wherefore then wilt thou sin against innocent
blood, to slay David without a cause?
6 And Saul hearkened unto the voice of Jonathan:
and Saul sware, *As* the LORD liveth, he shall not be
slain.
7 And Jonathan called David, and Jonathan
shewed him all those things. And Jonathan
brought David to Saul, and he was in his presence,
as in times past.
8 ¶ And there was war again: and David went out,
and fought with the Philistines, and slew them
with a great slaughter; and they fled from him.
9 And the evil spirit from the LORD was upon
Saul, as he sat in his house with his javelin in his
hand: and David played with *his* hand.
10 And Saul sought to smite David even to the
wall with the javelin; but he slipped away out of

18:21 *Saul said to David . . . in the one of the twain.* Literally, "Saul said to David the second time."
18:24 *On this manner.* Literally, "according to these words."
18:26 *the days were not expired.* Perhaps referring to "this day" of v. 21. David did not delay in fulfilling Saul's dowry demands.
18:27 *they gave them in full tale.* Literally, "they completed them," presenting the total amount.
18:30 *his name was much set by.* He was highly esteemed.

Thoughts for Personal/Family Worship: Chapter 18

1. **David and Jonathan exemplify the beauty of friendship (Prov. 17:17; 18:24). They enjoyed a bond of love and loyalty that transcended even blood relation. This was evidenced throughout their lives and by David even after Jonathan's death (2 Sam. 9:1). The bond subdued envy and endured even at personal risk. Today the idea of friendship has been reduced to refer to mere acquaintances who share little in common. Christians should seek out good friends for mutual accountability and edification. We should, likewise, rejoice that in the ideal sense we have the Friend who by virtue of His covenant is closer to us than anyone else could be.**
2. **Desire for self-glory rather than God's glory is always disastrous. Saul and David fought a common enemy in the Philistines; they were both engaged in advancing the kingdom. But because David received accolades for slaying more than he did (v. 7), Saul became envious, bitter, and obsessive against David. All too often in the work of God there is the temptation to look at what others are doing in the church and become envious of their ministries. Those in "small ministries" may turn their attacks against those in "larger ministries" rather than battling the common enemy. As Paul said, some plant and some water, but the increase is God's (1 Cor. 3:6–9). We should learn to be faithful in the service God has given us and rejoice at every advance of the kingdom, even when God places someone besides ourselves in the spotlight.**

Chapter 19: ***David escapes various attempts by Saul to kill him.***

19:4 *thee-ward.* To you.
19:5 *he did put his life in his hand.* An idiom for risking life.
19:9 *the evil spirit.* See notes at 16:14. *played with his hand.* Played the harp with his hands.

Saul's presence, and he smote the javelin into the
wall: and David fled, and escaped that night.
11 Saul also sent messengers unto David's house,
to watch him, and to slay him in the morning:
and Michal David's wife told him, saying, If thou
save not thy life to night, to morrow thou shalt
be slain.
12 ¶ So Michal let David down through a window: and he went, and fled, and escaped.
13 And Michal took an image, and laid *it* in the
bed, and put a pillow of goats' *hair* for his bolster,
and covered *it* with a cloth.
14 And when Saul sent messengers to take David,
she said, He *is* sick.
15 And Saul sent the messengers *again* to see
David, saying, Bring him up to me in the bed, that
I may slay him.
16 And when the messengers were come in,
behold, *there was* an image in the bed, with a
pillow of goats' *hair* for his bolster.
17 And Saul said unto Michal, Why hast thou
deceived me so, and sent away mine enemy, that
he is escaped? And Michal answered Saul, He said
unto me, Let me go; why should I kill thee?
18 ¶ So David fled, and escaped, and came to
Samuel to Ramah, and told him all that Saul had
done to him. And he and Samuel went and dwelt
in Naioth.
19 And it was told Saul, saying, Behold, David *is*
at Naioth in Ramah.
20 And Saul sent messengers to take David: and
when they saw the company of the prophets
prophesying, and Samuel standing *as* appointed
over them, the Spirit of God was upon the
messengers of Saul, and they also prophesied.
21 And when it was told Saul, he sent other
messengers, and they prophesied likewise. And
Saul sent messengers again the third time, and
they prophesied also.
22 Then went he also to Ramah, and came to a
great well that *is* in Sechu: and he asked and said,
Where *are* Samuel and David? And *one* said,
Behold, *they be* at Naioth in Ramah.
23 And he went thither to Naioth in Ramah: and
the Spirit of God was upon him also, and he went
on, and prophesied, until he came to Naioth in
Ramah.
24 And he stripped off his clothes also, and
prophesied before Samuel in like manner, and lay
down naked all that day and all that night. Wherefore they say, *Is* Saul also among the prophets?

CHAPTER 20

AND David fled from Naioth in Ramah, and came
and said before Jonathan, What have I done? what
is mine iniquity? and what *is* my sin before thy
father, that he seeketh my life?
2 And he said unto him, God forbid; thou shalt
not die: behold, my father will do nothing either
great or small, but that he will shew it me: and
why should my father hide this thing from me?
it *is* not *so*.
3 And David sware moreover, and said, Thy father certainly knoweth that I have found grace in
thine eyes; and he saith, Let not Jonathan know
this, lest he be grieved: but truly *as* the LORD
liveth, and *as* thy soul liveth, *there is* but a step
between me and death.
4 Then said Jonathan unto David, Whatsoever
thy soul desireth, I will even do *it* for thee.
5 And David said unto Jonathan, Behold, to morrow *is* the new moon, and I should not fail to sit
with the king at meat: but let me go, that I may
hide myself in the field unto the third *day* at even.
6 If thy father at all miss me, then say, David
earnestly asked *leave* of me that he might run to
Beth-lehem his city: for *there is* a yearly sacrifice
there for all the family.
7 If he say thus, *It is* well; thy servant shall have

19:13 *image*. The word normally refers to a household idol, but here most likely to collections of rags formed to represent a person. *for his bolster*. The Hebrew refers to the place at the head (v. 16).
19:21–24 *prophesied*. Most likely in the sense of praising and giving thanks (1 Chron. 25:3).
19:24 *naked*. The Hebrew term does not demand total nakedness; he removed his outer garments.

Thoughts for Personal/Family Worship: Chapter 19

1. **That "there was war again" (v. 8) sums up much of the Christian life. No matter how many times David killed some Philistines, they kept showing up as a renewed threat. David could rejoice in past victories, but he could not rest in them. So it is in the battle against self, sin, and Satan. The enemy of holiness is relentless, and we must be on constant guard. We can rejoice that God has given victory over temptations in the past, but we cannot assume that past victory guarantees the next. Such is the nature of sin and our weakness that the same temptations show up over and over. But new victories are possible every time as we rely upon the provision we have in Christ.**
2. **Although various people came to David's rescue, God was the ultimate deliverer (vv. 20–24). The Spirit of God intervened, turning every threat—even Saul himself—into an instrument of praise. The power of God's Spirit is irresistible (Zech. 4:6–7). So as we fight against sin's dominion, we should do so through the Holy Spirit (Rom. 8:13).**

Chapter 20: *David and Jonathan devise a plan to discover Saul's intentions regarding David.*

20:2 *God forbid*. Literally, "far from it."
20:5 *at meat*. Eating food of any sort, but here a reference to mealtime (vv. 24,27,34). *the third day at even*. Evening of the third day.
20:7 *wroth*. Angry. *evil*. Harm (vv. 9,13).

peace: but if he be very wroth, *then* be sure that
evil is determined by him.
8 Therefore thou shalt deal kindly with thy
servant; for thou hast brought thy servant into a
covenant of the LORD with thee: notwithstanding,
if there be in me iniquity, slay me thyself; for why
shouldest thou bring me to thy father?
9 And Jonathan said, Far be it from thee: for if I
knew certainly that evil were determined by my
father to come upon thee, then would not I tell
it thee?
10 Then said David to Jonathan, Who shall tell
me? or what *if* thy father answer thee roughly?
11 ¶ And Jonathan said unto David, Come, and
let us go out into the field. And they went out
both of them into the field.
12 And Jonathan said unto David, O LORD God
of Israel, when I have sounded my father about to
morrow any time, *or* the third *day*, and, behold, *if*
there be good toward David, and I then send not
unto thee, and shew it thee;
13 The LORD do so and much more to Jonathan:
but if it please my father *to do* thee evil, then I will
shew it thee, and send thee away, that thou mayest
go in peace: and the LORD be with thee, as he hath
been with my father.
14 And thou shalt not only while yet I live shew
me the kindness of the LORD, that I die not:
15 But *also* thou shalt not cut off thy kindness
from my house for ever: no, not when the LORD
hath cut off the enemies of David every one from
the face of the earth.
16 So Jonathan made *a covenant* with the house
of David, *saying*, Let the LORD even require *it* at
the hand of David's enemies.
17 And Jonathan caused David to swear again,
because he loved him: for he loved him as he
loved his own soul.
18 Then Jonathan said to David, To morrow *is*
the new moon: and thou shalt be missed, because
thy seat will be empty.
19 And *when* thou hast stayed three days, *then*
thou shalt go down quickly, and come to the place
where thou didst hide thyself when the business
was *in hand*, and shalt remain by the stone Ezel.
20 And I will shoot three arrows on the side
thereof, as though I shot at a mark.
21 And, behold, I will send a lad, *saying*, Go, find
out the arrows. If I expressly say unto the lad,
Behold, the arrows *are* on this side of thee, take
them; then come thou: for *there is* peace to thee,
and no hurt; *as* the LORD liveth.
22 But if I say thus unto the young man, Behold,
the arrows *are* beyond thee; go thy way: for the
LORD hath sent thee away.
23 And *as touching* the matter which thou and I
have spoken of, behold, the LORD *be* between thee
and me for ever.
24 ¶ So David hid himself in the field: and when
the new moon was come, the king sat him down
to eat meat.
25 And the king sat upon his seat, as at other
times, *even* upon a seat by the wall: and Jonathan
arose, and Abner sat by Saul's side, and David's
place was empty.
26 Nevertheless Saul spake not any thing that
day: for he thought, Something hath befallen him,
he *is* not clean; surely he *is* not clean.
27 And it came to pass on the morrow, *which was*
the second *day* of the month, that David's place
was empty: and Saul said unto Jonathan his son,
Wherefore cometh not the son of Jesse to meat,
neither yesterday, nor to day?
28 And Jonathan answered Saul, David earnestly
asked *leave* of me *to go* to Beth-lehem:
29 And he said, Let me go, I pray thee; for our
family hath a sacrifice in the city; and my brother,
he hath commanded me *to be there*: and now, if I
have found favour in thine eyes, let me get away,
I pray thee, and see my brethren. Therefore he
cometh not unto the king's table.
30 Then Saul's anger was kindled against
Jonathan, and he said unto him, Thou son of
the perverse rebellious *woman*, do not I know
that thou hast chosen the son of Jesse to thine
own confusion, and unto the confusion of thy
mother's nakedness?
31 For as long as the son of Jesse liveth upon the
ground, thou shalt not be established, nor thy
kingdom. Wherefore now send and fetch him

20:8 *thou shalt deal kindly.* Literally, "you will do lovingkindness." Such was required by the covenant between them; this refers to covenant loyalty (as well as "kindness," vv. 14–15).
20:10 *roughly.* Harshly or severely.
20:12 *sounded.* Searched or questioned.
20:30 *kindled.* Inflamed or burned. *confusion.* Shame or disgrace.
20:40 *artillery.* Weapons.
20:41 *David exceeded.* Literally, "David made great," indicating that he wept more.

Thoughts for Personal/Family Worship: Chapter 20

1. David's difficulties teach us that God's love and favor do not shield us from the trials and bitter experiences of life. Indeed, God's blessings often promote hostility from the world and enmity from those who are mere professors of Christianity. David's trials were particularly hard to bear because he had been Saul's faithful servant. Yet he could say "weeping may endure for a night, but joy cometh in the morning" (Ps. 30:5). It is at these very times of trial that we need to rest upon the promises of God. How can trusting that trials are ordained for our good (Rom. 8:28) enable you to rejoice even now in the sorrows you are facing?
2. David's lament "there is but a step between me and death" (v. 3) had pointed bearing on the issues David was facing. Yet it is a statement with universal and timeless

unto me, for he shall surely die.
32 And Jonathan answered Saul his father, and
said unto him, Wherefore shall he be slain? what
hath he done?
33 And Saul cast a javelin at him to smite him:
whereby Jonathan knew that it was determined of
his father to slay David.
34 So Jonathan arose from the table in fierce
anger, and did eat no meat the second day of the
month: for he was grieved for David, because his
father had done him shame.
35 ¶ And it came to pass in the morning, that
Jonathan went out into the field at the time ap-
pointed with David, and a little lad with him.
36 And he said unto his lad, Run, find out now
the arrows which I shoot. *And* as the lad ran, he
shot an arrow beyond him.
37 And when the lad was come to the place of the
arrow which Jonathan had shot, Jonathan cried
after the lad, and said, *Is* not the arrow beyond
thee?
38 And Jonathan cried after the lad, Make speed,
haste, stay not. And Jonathan's lad gathered up
the arrows, and came to his master.
39 But the lad knew not any thing: only Jonathan
and David knew the matter.
40 And Jonathan gave his artillery unto his lad,
and said unto him, Go, carry *them* to the city.
41 ¶ *And* as soon as the lad was gone, David arose
out of *a place* toward the south, and fell on his
face to the ground, and bowed himself three
times: and they kissed one another, and wept one
with another, until David exceeded.
42 And Jonathan said to David, Go in peace,
forasmuch as we have sworn both of us in the
name of the LORD, saying, The LORD be between
me and thee, and between my seed and thy seed
for ever. And he arose and departed: and Jonathan
went into the city.

CHAPTER 21

THEN came David to Nob to Ahimelech the
priest: and Ahimelech was afraid at the meeting
of David, and said unto him, Why *art* thou alone,
and no man with thee?
2 And David said unto Ahimelech the priest, The
king hath commanded me a business, and hath
said unto me, Let no man know any thing of
the business whereabout I send thee, and what I
have commanded thee: and I have appointed *my*
servants to such and such a place.
3 Now therefore what is under thine hand? give
me five *loaves of* bread in mine hand, or what
there is present.
4 And the priest answered David, and said, *There*
is no common bread under mine hand, but there
is hallowed bread; if the young men have kept
themselves at least from women.
5 And David answered the priest, and said unto
him, Of a truth women *have been* kept from us
about these three days, since I came out, and the
vessels of the young men are holy, and *the bread is*
in a manner common, yea, though it were sancti-
fied this day in the vessel.
6 So the priest gave him hallowed *bread*: for there
was no bread there but the shewbread, that was
taken from before the LORD, to put hot bread in
the day when it was taken away.
7 Now a certain man of the servants of Saul *was*
there that day, detained before the LORD; and his
name *was* Doeg, an Edomite, the chiefest of the
herdmen that *belonged* to Saul.
8 ¶ And David said unto Ahimelech, And is there
not here under thine hand spear or sword? for I
have neither brought my sword nor my weap-
ons with me, because the king's business required
haste.
9 And the priest said, The sword of Goliath the
Philistine, whom thou slewest in the valley of
Elah, behold, it *is here* wrapped in a cloth behind
the ephod: if thou wilt take that, take *it*: for *there*
is no other save that here. And David said, *There is*
none like that; give it me.
10 ¶ And David arose, and fled that day for fear of
Saul, and went to Achish the king of Gath.
11 And the servants of Achish said unto him,
Is not this David the king of the land? did they
not sing one to another of him in dances, saying,
Saul hath slain his thousands, and David his ten
thousands?
12 And David laid up these words in his heart,

relevance. The preacher said, "For man also knoweth not his time . . . when it falleth suddenly upon them" (Eccl. 9:12). The time of death is uncertain, but the fact of it is unavoidable (Heb. 9:27). We are not to morbidly wonder about the day of death, but we are to live in its certainty, knowing that it is only during life that we can get ready for eternity. Awareness of being only a step away, indeed a heartbeat away, from death should generate an urgency in every heart that today is the day of salvation (2 Cor. 6:2).

David's Flight from Saul into the Wilderness (1 Sam. 21:1—26:25)

Chapter 21: ***Fearful of Saul's determination to kill him, David flees to Ahimelech the priest and then to Achish the Philistine king.***

21:2 David tells a lie, the result of being overcome with fear.
21:3 *what is under thine hand.* What is under your control or supervision (vv. 4,8). *what there is present.* What is found.
21:4 *common bread.* Bread for ordinary use. *hallowed bread.* The holy bread that had been consecrated for the shewbread in the tabernacle (Ex. 25:30), reserved for priestly consumption (Lev. 24:5–9).
21:9 *ephod.* An embroidered cape hanging from the shoulders and worn by priests. *save.* Except.

and was sore afraid of Achish the king of Gath.
13 And he changed his behaviour before them,
and feigned himself mad in their hands, and
scrabbled on the doors of the gate, and let his
spittle fall down upon his beard.
14 Then said Achish unto his servants, Lo, ye see
the man is mad: wherefore *then* have ye brought
him to me?
15 Have I need of mad men, that ye have brought
this *fellow* to play the mad man in my presence?
shall this *fellow* come into my house?

CHAPTER 22

DAVID therefore departed thence, and escaped to
the cave Adullam: and when his brethren and all
his father's house heard *it*, they went down thither
to him.
2 And every one *that was* in distress, and every
one that *was* in debt, and every one *that was* dis-
contented, gathered themselves unto him; and he
became a captain over them: and there were with
him about four hundred men.
3 ¶ And David went thence to Mizpeh of Moab:
and he said unto the king of Moab, Let my father
and my mother, I pray thee, come forth, *and be*
with you, till I know what God will do for me.
4 And he brought them before the king of Moab:
and they dwelt with him all the while that David
was in the hold.
5 ¶ And the prophet Gad said unto David, Abide
not in the hold; depart, and get thee into the land
of Judah. Then David departed, and came into
the forest of Hareth.
6 ¶ When Saul heard that David was discovered,
and the men that *were* with him, (now Saul abode
in Gibeah under a tree in Ramah, having his spear
in his hand, and all his servants *were* standing
about him;)
7 Then Saul said unto his servants that stood
about him, Hear now, ye Benjamites; will the son
of Jesse give every one of you fields and vineyards,
and make you all captains of thousands, and
captains of hundreds;
8 That all of you have conspired against me, and
there is none that sheweth me that my son hath
made a league with the son of Jesse, and *there is*
none of you that is sorry for me, or sheweth unto
me that my son hath stirred up my servant against
me, to lie in wait, as at this day?
9 ¶ Then answered Doeg the Edomite, which was
set over the servants of Saul, and said, I saw the
son of Jesse coming to Nob, to Ahimelech the son
of Ahitub.
10 And he enquired of the LORD for him, and gave
him victuals, and gave him the sword of Goliath
the Philistine.
11 Then the king sent to call Ahimelech the priest,
the son of Ahitub, and all his father's house, the
priests that *were* in Nob: and they came all of
them to the king.
12 And Saul said, Hear now, thou son of Ahitub.
And he answered, Here I *am*, my lord.
13 And Saul said unto him, Why have ye con-
spired against me, thou and the son of Jesse, in
that thou hast given him bread, and a sword, and
hast enquired of God for him, that he should rise
against me, to lie in wait, as at this day?
14 Then Ahimelech answered the king, and said,
And who *is so* faithful among all thy servants as
David, which is the king's son in law, and goeth
at thy bidding, and is honourable in thine house?
15 Did I then begin to enquire of God for him? be
it far from me: let not the king impute *any* thing
unto his servant, *nor* to all the house of my father:
for thy servant knew nothing of all this, less or
more.
16 And the king said, Thou shalt surely die,

21:12 *sore.* Greatly.
21:13 *feigned himself mad.* Pretended to act like a madman. *scrabbled.* Scribbled or made marks. *spittle.* Saliva.

Thoughts for Personal/Family Worship: Chapter 21

1. **The Lord Jesus appeals to the episode with the priests' bread to refute and rebuke the Pharisees for their legalism regarding the Sabbath. Christ taught that works of necessity, such as eating, do not violate the spiritual precept of the law (Mark 2:25). David's eating the consecrated bread was out of the norm but necessary. The Lord reminds us that God looks on the heart, which is more important than rigid and heartless conformity to form. It is possible to do things right on the outside, like the Pharisees, without a heart toward the Lord. How can we avoid this?**
2. **Proverbs 29:25 says that fearing man brings a snare. This episode in David's career illustrates this truth; he feared Saul and Achish (1 Sam. 21:10,12). That fear led to foolish and sinful behavior, including a lie to the priest and trying to find safety with the enemy. Given the circumstances, David's fear was understandable, for his life was indeed under threat, but his actions were inexcusable. Proverbs 29:25 also says that the one who trusts the Lord will be safe. There were times and there would be times in the future when David's trust and fear of the Lord, instead of his circumstances, overwhelmed him (Ps. 31:13–16; 112:7). David learned his lesson even in this particular situation (see Ps. 34:4 and its superscription). We all should follow his counsel and "fear the LORD . . . for there is no want to them that fear him" (Ps. 34:8,9).**

Chapter 22: ***David escapes to the wilderness, but his lie to Ahimelech results in the massacre of eighty-five priests.***

22:4 *the hold.* A mountain stronghold or fortress (v. 5).
22:8 *hath made a league.* Literally, "has cut," an abbreviated idiom for making a covenant. *there is none . . . that is sorry for me.* None feels my pain. Saul was feeling sorry for himself and wanted sympathy from others.
22:10 *victuals.* Food, specifically provisions for a journey.

Ahimelech, thou, and all thy father's house.
17 ¶ And the king said unto the footmen that
stood about him, Turn, and slay the priests of
the LORD; because their hand also *is* with David,
and because they knew when he fled, and did not
shew it to me. But the servants of the king would
not put forth their hand to fall upon the priests
of the LORD.
18 And the king said to Doeg, Turn thou, and fall
upon the priests. And Doeg the Edomite turned,
and he fell upon the priests, and slew on that day
fourscore and five persons that did wear a linen
ephod.
19 And Nob, the city of the priests, smote he with
the edge of the sword, both men and women,
children and sucklings, and oxen, and asses, and
sheep, with the edge of the sword.
20 ¶ And one of the sons of Ahimelech the son of
Ahitub, named Abiathar, escaped, and fled after
David.
21 And Abiathar shewed David that Saul had
slain the LORD's priests.
22 And David said unto Abiathar, I knew *it* that
day, when Doeg the Edomite *was* there, that he
would surely tell Saul: I have occasioned *the death*
of all the persons of thy father's house.
23 Abide thou with me, fear not: for he that
seeketh my life seeketh thy life: but with me thou
shalt be in safeguard.

CHAPTER 23

THEN they told David, saying, Behold, the Phi-
listines fight against Keilah, and they rob the
threshingfloors.
2 Therefore David enquired of the LORD, saying,
Shall I go and smite these Philistines? And the
LORD said unto David, Go, and smite the Philis-
tines, and save Keilah.
3 And David's men said unto him, Behold, we
be afraid here in Judah: how much more then
if we come to Keilah against the armies of the
Philistines?
4 Then David enquired of the LORD yet again.
And the LORD answered him and said, Arise, go
down to Keilah; for I will deliver the Philistines
into thine hand.
5 So David and his men went to Keilah, and
fought with the Philistines, and brought away
their cattle, and smote them with a great slaugh-
ter. So David saved the inhabitants of Keilah.
6 And it came to pass, when Abiathar the son of
Ahimelech fled to David to Keilah, *that* he came
down *with* an ephod in his hand.
7 ¶ And it was told Saul that David was come to
Keilah. And Saul said, God hath delivered him
into mine hand; for he is shut in, by entering into
a town that hath gates and bars.
8 And Saul called all the people together to war, to
go down to Keilah, to besiege David and his men.
9 ¶ And David knew that Saul secretly practised
mischief against him; and he said to Abiathar the
priest, Bring hither the ephod.
10 Then said David, O LORD God of Israel, thy
servant hath certainly heard that Saul seeketh to
come to Keilah, to destroy the city for my sake.
11 Will the men of Keilah deliver me up into his
hand? will Saul come down, as thy servant hath
heard? O LORD God of Israel, I beseech thee, tell thy
servant. And the LORD said, He will come down.
12 Then said David, Will the men of Keilah de-
liver me and my men into the hand of Saul? And
the LORD said, They will deliver *thee* up.
13 ¶ Then David and his men, *which were* about
six hundred, arose and departed out of Keilah,
and went whithersoever they could go. And it was
told Saul that David was escaped from Keilah; and
he forbare to go forth.
14 And David abode in the wilderness in strong
holds, and remained in a mountain in the

22:18 *fourscore and five.* Eighty-five. *ephod.* Embroidered cape of the priests.
22:19 *sucklings.* Infants.
22:23 *in safeguard.* Kept safe.

Thoughts for Personal/Family Worship: Chapter 22

1. **Some things are hard to understand, especially when evil runs riot and innocent blood is shed. Yet even in this God is working out His purposes; even the "wrath of man" will praise the Lord (Ps. 76:10). The slaughter of the priests was a fulfillment of God's word of judgment against them (1 Sam. 2:31–33).**
2. **The death of the priests also puts in bold the truth that sin has consequences that go beyond the sinner himself. David's lie to Ahimelech may have seemed trivial. At the time, he may well have justified it as a "harmless" sin to help him escape from Saul, yet what terrible consequences resulted. There is actually no such thing as a private sin. Either by consequence or example sin affects others. How have you justified "little" sins in your life? What is the right way to deal with them?**

Chapter 23: ***Regardless of David's defense of Keilah, the Lord reveals that the people of Keilah will betray him to Saul, causing David to flee again to the wilderness.***

23:1 *rob the threshing floors.* Steal the harvested grain.
23:6 *ephod.* An embroidered priestly garment worn on the shoulders that carried the Urim and Thummin, objects used to determine the will of God (v. 9; Ex. 28:30; Num. 27:21).
23:7 *gates and bars.* Indicating an enclosed city, the bars referring to the beams used to secure the gates. Saul thought David was trapped.
23:9 *Saul secretly practised mischief.* Literally, "Saul was plotting or fabricating harm."
23:12 *They will deliver thee up.* God knows all things possible as well as actual. The Lord is "a God of knowledge" (2:3); His knowledge is infinite (Ps. 147:5; Isa. 40:28).
23:13 *forebare to go forth.* Refrained from going out.

wilderness of Ziph. And Saul sought him every
day, but God delivered him not into his hand.
15 And David saw that Saul was come out to seek
his life: and David *was* in the wilderness of Ziph
in a wood.
16 ¶ And Jonathan Saul's son arose, and went to
David into the wood, and strengthened his hand
in God.
17 And he said unto him, Fear not: for the hand
of Saul my father shall not find thee; and thou
shalt be king over Israel, and I shall be next unto
thee; and that also Saul my father knoweth.
18 And they two made a covenant before the
LORD: and David abode in the wood, and Jonathan went to his house.
19 ¶ Then came up the Ziphites to Saul to Gibeah,
saying, Doth not David hide himself with us in
strong holds in the wood, in the hill of Hachilah,
which *is* on the south of Jeshimon?
20 Now therefore, O king, come down according
to all the desire of thy soul to come down; and our
part *shall be* to deliver him into the king's hand.
21 And Saul said, Blessed *be* ye of the LORD; for ye
have compassion on me.
22 Go, I pray you, prepare yet, and know and see
his place where his haunt is, *and* who hath seen
him there: for it is told me *that* he dealeth very
subtilly.
23 See therefore, and take knowledge of all the
lurking places where he hideth himself, and come
ye again to me with the certainty, and I will go
with you: and it shall come to pass, if he be in the
land, that I will search him out throughout all the
thousands of Judah.
24 And they arose, and went to Ziph before Saul:
but David and his men *were* in the wilderness of
Maon, in the plain on the south of Jeshimon.
25 Saul also and his men went to seek *him*. And
they told David: wherefore he came down into a
rock, and abode in the wilderness of Maon. And
when Saul heard *that*, he pursued after David in
the wilderness of Maon.
26 And Saul went on this side of the mountain,
and David and his men on that side of the mountain: and David made haste to get away for fear of
Saul; for Saul and his men compassed David and
his men round about to take them.
27 ¶ But there came a messenger unto Saul,
saying, Haste thee, and come; for the Philistines
have invaded the land.
28 Wherefore Saul returned from pursuing after
David, and went against the Philistines: therefore
they called that place Sela-hammahlekoth.
29 ¶ And David went up from thence, and dwelt
in strong holds at En-gedi.

CHAPTER 24

AND it came to pass, when Saul was returned from
following the Philistines, that it was told him, saying, Behold, David *is* in the wilderness of En-gedi.
2 Then Saul took three thousand chosen men out
of all Israel, and went to seek David and his men
upon the rocks of the wild goats.
3 And he came to the sheepcotes by the way,
where *was* a cave; and Saul went in to cover his
feet: and David and his men remained in the sides
of the cave.
4 And the men of David said unto him, Behold
the day of which the LORD said unto thee, Behold,
I will deliver thine enemy into thine hand, that
thou mayest do to him as it shall seem good unto
thee. Then David arose, and cut off the skirt of
Saul's robe privily.

23:18 *made a covenant.* The common idiom is literally, "cut a covenant," a mutually binding agreement.
23:19 *on the south of Jeshimon.* Literally, "from the right of the desert or wilderness," reflecting the ancient map orientation with east at the top and south being on the right side (v. 24).
23:22 *where his haunt is.* Literally, "where his foot is." *he dealeth very subtilly.* Literally, "he behaves shrewdly."
23:26 *compassed.* Surrounded.
23:28 *Sela-hammahlekoth.* Translated, "the rock of divisions."

Thoughts for Personal/Family Worship: Chapter 23

1. **David's dealings with Keilah show the importance of discerning and doing the Lord's will in making decisions. David inquired of the Lord through prayer and through the priest who apparently employed the Urim and Thummim, the means God had ordained for discovering His will. He used the means of grace. How important it is to commit matters to the Lord before embarking on any venture, even when we think we know what we should do (Josh. 9:14). The Christian is not an independent agent but rather the servant of Christ. There should be no place for rash action or even calculated reasoning apart from the Lord (Prov. 3:5–6). We should take everything to the Lord, seeking Him in prayer and searching His Word for direction.**
2. **How wonderful the providences of God are! David and his men were completely surrounded by Saul's forces. He was between the rock and the hard place, with seemingly no way of escape. But at the critical moment the Philistines invaded the land, diverting Saul from his pursuit of David. Ironically, the Philistines David defeated at the beginning of the chapter unknowingly come to his rescue at the end. This intervention gave David the opportunity to escape. Let us therefore take heart when things seem hopeless, "For with God nothing shall be impossible" (Luke 1:37). What situations seem impossible to you now? Take them to the Lord in prayer.**

Chapter 24: *Saul resumes his pursuit of David, who spares his life as evidence that Saul's suspicions about David are ill founded.*

24:3 *sheepcotes.* Shelters for sheep. *cover his feet.* An idiom for relieving oneself.
24:4 *skirt.* The edge or hem of the robe (vv. 5,11). *privily.* Secretly.

5 And it came to pass afterward, that David's heart
smote him, because he had cut off Saul's skirt.
6 And he said unto his men, The LORD forbid that
I should do this thing unto my master, the LORD's
anointed, to stretch forth mine hand against him,
seeing he *is* the anointed of the LORD.
7 So David stayed his servants with these words,
and suffered them not to rise against Saul. But
Saul rose up out of the cave, and went on *his* way.
8 David also arose afterward, and went out of the
cave, and cried after Saul, saying, My lord the king.
And when Saul looked behind him, David stooped
with his face to the earth, and bowed himself.
9 ¶ And David said to Saul, Wherefore hearest
thou men's words, saying, Behold, David seeketh
thy hurt?
10 Behold, this day thine eyes have seen how that
the LORD had delivered thee to day into mine
hand in the cave: and *some* bade *me* kill thee: but
mine eye spared thee; and I said, I will not put
forth mine hand against my lord; for he *is* the
LORD's anointed.
11 Moreover, my father, see, yea, see the skirt of
thy robe in my hand: for in that I cut off the skirt
of thy robe, and killed thee not, know thou and
see that *there is* neither evil nor transgression in
mine hand, and I have not sinned against thee; yet
thou huntest my soul to take it.
12 The LORD judge between me and thee, and the
LORD avenge me of thee: but mine hand shall not
be upon thee.
13 As saith the proverb of the ancients, Wicked-
ness proceedeth from the wicked: but mine hand
shall not be upon thee.
14 After whom is the king of Israel come out? after
whom dost thou pursue? after a dead dog, after a
flea.
15 The LORD therefore be judge, and judge be-
tween me and thee, and see, and plead my cause,
and deliver me out of thine hand.
16 ¶ And it came to pass, when David had made
an end of speaking these words unto Saul, that
Saul said, *Is* this thy voice, my son David? And
Saul lifted up his voice, and wept.
17 And he said to David, Thou *art* more righteous
than I: for thou hast rewarded me good, whereas
I have rewarded thee evil.
18 And thou hast shewed this day how that thou
hast dealt well with me: forasmuch as when the
LORD had delivered me into thine hand, thou
killedst me not.
19 For if a man find his enemy, will he let him go
well away? wherefore the LORD reward thee good
for that thou hast done unto me this day.
20 And now, behold, I know well that thou shalt
surely be king, and that the kingdom of Israel
shall be established in thine hand.
21 Swear now therefore unto me by the LORD,
that thou wilt not cut off my seed after me, and
that thou wilt not destroy my name out of my
father's house.
22 And David sware unto Saul. And Saul went
home; but David and his men gat them up unto
the hold.

CHAPTER 25

AND Samuel died; and all the Israelites were
gathered together, and lamented him, and buried
him in his house at Ramah. And David arose, and
went down to the wilderness of Paran.
2 And *there was* a man in Maon, whose posses-
sions *were* in Carmel; and the man *was* very great,
and he had three thousand sheep, and a thousand
goats: and he was shearing his sheep in Carmel.
3 Now the name of the man *was* Nabal; and the
name of his wife Abigail: and *she was* a woman
of good understanding, and of a beautiful

24:5 *David's heart smote him.* His conscience disturbed him.
24:7 *David stayed.* Literally, "David sharply reprimanded or restrained the enthusiasm of." *suffered them not.* Did not allow them.
24:10 *some bade me.* Literally, "one said."
24:17 *rewarded.* The Hebrew means "to deal out." *evil.* Hurt or harm.
24:22 *gat them up unto the hold.* Literally, they "went up to the mountain stronghold."

Thoughts for Personal/Family Worship: Chapter 24

1. **David's sparing Saul illustrates two important principles: respect for office and reliance on divine justice. Saul had abused the office and on the personal level deserved no respect or honor. But David recognized that Saul was the Lord's anointed. Heads of government often fail to govern justly, but God's command is that we are to fear Him and honor the king (1 Peter 2:17). David also shows a willingness to wait upon the Lord rather than take action himself to improve his status or remove the threat to his own life. Vengeance belongs to the Lord (Heb. 10:30), and He will execute justice (Rom. 12:19). The temptation when justice is delayed is to take matters into our own hands, but those who fear God know that ultimately justice prevails (Eccl. 8:11–13). How can you apply this lesson to your life?**
2. **Saul's reaction to David's sparing his life is emotional and seemingly sincere, but only temporary. Saul's tears were no doubt real. His conscience was sufficiently moved to feel some remorse for his vindictive behavior toward David, yet his sorrow is not that of one who is truly penitent. There is more to true repentance than just being sorry for a particular deed. There is turning from sin to God.**

Chapter 25: *After the death of Samuel, David encounters Nabal, whose foolish behavior is countered by the wisdom of his wife, who marries David after Nabal's death.*

25:1 *And Samuel died.* Samuel's life marked the transition

countenance: but the man *was* churlish and evil
in his doings; and he *was* of the house of Caleb.
4 ¶ And David heard in the wilderness that Nabal
did shear his sheep.
5 And David sent out ten young men, and David
said unto the young men, Get you up to Carmel,
and go to Nabal, and greet him in my name:
6 And thus shall ye say to him that liveth *in*
prosperity, Peace *be* both to thee, and peace *be* to
thine house, and peace *be* unto all that thou hast.
7 And now I have heard that thou hast shearers:
now thy shepherds which were with us, we hurt
them not, neither was there ought missing unto
them, all the while they were in Carmel.
8 Ask thy young men, and they will shew thee.
Wherefore let the young men find favour in thine
eyes: for we come in a good day: give, I pray thee,
whatsoever cometh to thine hand unto thy ser-
vants, and to thy son David.
9 And when David's young men came, they spake
to Nabal according to all those words in the name
of David, and ceased.
10 ¶ And Nabal answered David's servants, and
said, Who *is* David? and who *is* the son of Jesse?
there be many servants now a days that break
away every man from his master.
11 Shall I then take my bread, and my water, and
my flesh that I have killed for my shearers, and give
it unto men, whom I know not whence they *be*?
12 So David's young men turned their way, and
went again, and came and told him all those
sayings.
13 And David said unto his men, Gird ye on every
man his sword. And they girded on every man his
sword; and David also girded on his sword: and
there went up after David about four hundred
men; and two hundred abode by the stuff.
14 ¶ But one of the young men told Abigail,
Nabal's wife, saying, Behold, David sent messen-
gers out of the wilderness to salute our master;
and he railed on them.
15 But the men *were* very good unto us, and we
were not hurt, neither missed we any thing, as
long as we were conversant with them, when we
were in the fields:
16 They were a wall unto us both by night and
day, all the while we were with them keeping the
sheep.
17 Now therefore know and consider what thou
wilt do; for evil is determined against our master,
and against all his household: for he *is such* a son
of Belial, that *a man* cannot speak to him.
18 ¶ Then Abigail made haste, and took two
hundred loaves, and two bottles of wine, and five
sheep ready dressed, and five measures of parched
corn, and an hundred clusters of raisins, and two
hundred cakes of figs, and laid *them* on asses.
19 And she said unto her servants, Go on before
me; behold, I come after you. But she told not her
husband Nabal.
20 And it was *so*, *as* she rode on the ass, that she
came down by the covert of the hill, and, behold,
David and his men came down against her; and
she met them.
21 Now David had said, Surely in vain have I kept
all that this *fellow* hath in the wilderness, so that
nothing was missed of all that *pertained* unto
him: and he hath requited me evil for good.
22 So and more also do God unto the enemies of
David, if I leave of all that *pertain* to him by the
morning light any that pisseth against the wall.
23 And when Abigail saw David, she hasted, and
lighted off the ass, and fell before David on her
face, and bowed herself to the ground,
24 And fell at his feet, and said, Upon me, my
lord, *upon* me *let this* iniquity *be*: and let thine
handmaid, I pray thee, speak in thine audience,
and hear the words of thine handmaid.
25 Let not my lord, I pray thee, regard this man
of Belial, *even* Nabal: for as his name *is*, so *is* he;
Nabal *is* his name, and folly *is* with him: but I
thine handmaid saw not the young men of my
lord, whom thou didst send.
26 Now therefore, my lord, *as* the LORD liveth,
and *as* thy soul liveth, seeing the LORD hath
withholden thee from coming to *shed* blood, and

from the formal theocracy to the monarchy; his death marked the end of an era.

25:3 *churlish.* Rough or rude.

25:10 *Who is David?* The question is dismissive of David (similar to "Who does David think he is?").

25:13 *Gird.* To encircle or secure with a belt. *stuff.* Equipment.

25:14 *to salute.* The Hebrew is "to bless." *railed.* Shouted or screamed angrily.

25:15 *as long as . . . conversant with them.* Literally, "all the days we walked around with them."

25:16 *wall.* Image of protection, guardianship.

25:17 *evil is determined.* Harm or calamity has been determined. *Belial.* See note at 1:16.

25:18 *sheep ready dressed.* Literally, "sheep which have been done," which have been to some degree prepared for consumption. *parched corn.* Roasted grain.

25:20 *covert of the hill.* Referring to the shelter provided by the hill.

25:21 *requited.* Returned.

25:22 *any that pisseth against the wall.* Any males (v. 34).

25:24 *thine audience.* Literally, "your ear."

25:25 *Nabal* means "fool," and he acts according to his name.

25:26 *evil.* Harm or hurt.

25:28 *a sure house.* A confirmed, enduring dynasty (2 Sam. 7:11–12,27).

25:37 *his heart died within him.* Perhaps a heart attack caused by the shocking report.

25:43 *both of them his wives.* See note at 1:2.

Thoughts for Personal/Family Worship: Chapter 25

1. It is significant to note the emphasis that Nabal places

from avenging thyself with thine own hand, now let thine enemies, and they that seek evil to my lord, be as Nabal.

27 And now this blessing which thine handmaid hath brought unto my lord, let it even be given unto the young men that follow my lord.

28 I pray thee, forgive the trespass of thine handmaid: for the LORD will certainly make my lord a sure house; because my lord fighteth the battles of the LORD, and evil hath not been found in thee *all* thy days.

29 Yet a man is risen to pursue thee, and to seek thy soul: but the soul of my lord shall be bound in the bundle of life with the LORD thy God; and the souls of thine enemies, them shall he sling out, *as out* of the middle of a sling.

30 And it shall come to pass, when the LORD shall have done to my lord according to all the good that he hath spoken concerning thee, and shall have appointed thee ruler over Israel;

31 That this shall be no grief unto thee, nor offence of heart unto my lord, either that thou hast shed blood causeless, or that my lord hath avenged himself: but when the LORD shall have dealt well with my lord, then remember thine handmaid.

32 ¶ And David said to Abigail, Blessed *be* the LORD God of Israel, which sent thee this day to meet me:

33 And blessed *be* thy advice, and blessed *be* thou, which hast kept me this day from coming to *shed* blood, and from avenging myself with mine own hand.

34 For in very deed, *as* the LORD God of Israel liveth, which hath kept me back from hurting thee, except thou hadst hasted and come to meet me, surely there had not been left unto Nabal by the morning light any that pisseth against the wall.

35 So David received of her hand *that* which she had brought him, and said unto her, Go up in peace to thine house; see, I have hearkened to thy voice, and have accepted thy person.

36 ¶ And Abigail came to Nabal; and, behold, he held a feast in his house, like the feast of a king; and Nabal's heart *was* merry within him, for he *was* very drunken: wherefore she told him nothing, less or more, until the morning light.

37 But it came to pass in the morning, when the wine was gone out of Nabal, and his wife had told him these things, that his heart died within him, and he became *as* a stone.

38 And it came to pass about ten days *after*, that the LORD smote Nabal, that he died.

39 ¶ And when David heard that Nabal was dead, he said, Blessed *be* the LORD, that hath pleaded the cause of my reproach from the hand of Nabal, and hath kept his servant from evil: for the LORD hath returned the wickedness of Nabal upon his own head. And David sent and communed with Abigail, to take her to him to wife.

40 And when the servants of David were come to Abigail to Carmel, they spake unto her, saying, David sent us unto thee, to take thee to him to wife.

41 And she arose, and bowed herself on *her* face to the earth, and said, Behold, *let* thine handmaid *be* a servant to wash the feet of the servants of my lord.

42 And Abigail hasted, and arose, and rode upon an ass, with five damsels of hers that went after her; and she went after the messengers of David, and became his wife.

43 David also took Ahinoam of Jezreel; and they were also both of them his wives.

44 ¶ But Saul had given Michal his daughter, David's wife, to Phalti the son of Laish, which *was* of Gallim.

CHAPTER 26

AND the Ziphites came unto Saul to Gibeah, saying, Doth not David hide himself in the hill of Hachilah, *which is* before Jeshimon?

2 Then Saul arose, and went down to the wilderness of Ziph, having three thousand chosen men of Israel with him, to seek David in the wilderness of Ziph.

3 And Saul pitched in the hill of Hachilah, which *is* before Jeshimon, by the way. But David abode in the wilderness, and he saw that Saul came after him into the wilderness.

4 David therefore sent out spies, and understood that Saul was come in very deed.

---

on his possessions: he says "*my* bread, and *my* water, and *my* flesh that I have killed" (v. 11, emphasis added). This proud boast of his possessions is similar to the parable Jesus tells where the farmer says "*my* barns . . . *my* fruits and *my* goods" (Luke 12:18, emphasis added). In response to this boasting, we read, "But God said unto him, Thou fool, this night thy soul shall be required of thee: then whose shall those things be, which thou hast provided?" (v. 20). Let us never boast of the possessions that God has given us or selfishly keep all for ourselves, but rather let us use such gifts in the Lord's service, as He directs. Nabal was a fool by name and a fool by nature, and the Lord smote him (1 Sam. 25:38). How can we avoid such foolishness in our own lives?

2. In stark contrast to Nabal, what wonderful spiritual qualities we see in Abigail. She typifies the virtuous woman whose "price is far above rubies" (Prov. 31:10), and she uses her God-given gifts to turn David's heart from revenge against her husband and all in his household. She displays wisdom and grace. David came to understand that the hand of God was upon Abigail, and he said, "Blessed be the LORD God of Israel, which sent thee this day to meet me" (1 Sam. 25:32). Let us pray that such spiritual qualities might be seen in us, and let us be quick to rejoice when we find them in others.

Chapter 26: ***Once again David has opportunity to slay Saul but refrains.***

5 ¶ And David arose, and came to the place
where Saul had pitched: and David beheld the
place where Saul lay, and Abner the son of Ner,
the captain of his host: and Saul lay in the trench,
and the people pitched round about him.
6 Then answered David and said to Ahimelech
the Hittite, and to Abishai the son of Zeruiah,
brother to Joab, saying, Who will go down with
me to Saul to the camp? And Abishai said, I will
go down with thee.
7 So David and Abishai came to the people by
night: and, behold, Saul lay sleeping within the
trench, and his spear stuck in the ground at his
bolster: but Abner and the people lay round about
him.
8 Then said Abishai to David, God hath delivered
thine enemy into thine hand this day: now there-
fore let me smite him, I pray thee, with the spear
even to the earth at once, and I will not *smite* him
the second time.
9 And David said to Abishai, Destroy him not: for
who can stretch forth his hand against the LORD's
anointed, and be guiltless?
10 David said furthermore, *As* the LORD liveth,
the LORD shall smite him; or his day shall come
to die; or he shall descend into battle, and perish.
11 The LORD forbid that I should stretch forth
mine hand against the LORD's anointed: but, I
pray thee, take thou now the spear that *is* at his
bolster, and the cruse of water, and let us go.
12 So David took the spear and the cruse of water
from Saul's bolster; and they gat them away, and
no man saw *it*, nor knew *it*, neither awaked: for
they *were* all asleep; because a deep sleep from the
LORD was fallen upon them.
13 ¶ Then David went over to the other side, and
stood on the top of an hill afar off; a great space
being between them:
14 And David cried to the people, and to Abner
the son of Ner, saying, Answerest thou not,
Abner? Then Abner answered and said, Who *art*
thou *that* criest to the king?
15 And David said to Abner, *Art* not thou a *valiant*
man? and who *is* like to thee in Israel? wherefore
then hast thou not kept thy lord the king? for
there came one of the people in to destroy the
king thy lord.
16 This thing *is* not good that thou hast done. *As*
the LORD liveth, ye *are* worthy to die, because ye
have not kept your master, the LORD's anointed.
And now see where the king's spear *is*, and the
cruse of water that *was* at his bolster.
17 And Saul knew David's voice, and said, *Is* this
thy voice, my son David? And David said, *It is* my
voice, my lord, O king.
18 And he said, Wherefore doth my lord thus
pursue after his servant? for what have I done? or
what evil *is* in mine hand?
19 Now therefore, I pray thee, let my lord the king
hear the words of his servant. If the LORD have
stirred thee up against me, let him accept an of-
fering: but if *they be* the children of men, cursed
be they before the LORD; for they have driven me
out this day from abiding in the inheritance of the
LORD, saying, Go, serve other gods.
20 Now therefore, let not my blood fall to the
earth before the face of the LORD: for the king of
Israel is come out to seek a flea, as when one doth
hunt a partridge in the mountains.
21 ¶ Then said Saul, I have sinned: return, my
son David: for I will no more do thee harm,
because my soul was precious in thine eyes this
day: behold, I have played the fool, and have erred
exceedingly.
22 And David answered and said, Behold the
king's spear! and let one of the young men come
over and fetch it.
23 The LORD render to every man his righteous-
ness and his faithfulness: for the LORD delivered
thee into *my* hand to day, but I would not stretch
forth mine hand against the LORD's anointed.
24 And, behold, as thy life was much set by this
day in mine eyes, so let my life be much set by in
the eyes of the LORD, and let him deliver me out
of all tribulation.
25 Then Saul said to David, Blessed *be* thou, my

26:5 *trench*. An entrenchment, perhaps a ring of wagons as a makeshift fortress.
26:7 *bolster*. The Hebrew is "at the head" or "the head-place" (vv. 26:11–12,16).
26:8 *I will not smite him the second time*. Repeating the blow will not be necessary.
26:11–12 *cruse*. Jug (v. 16). *they gat them away*. They went from them.
26:24 *much set by*. Hebrew, "to be great."

Thoughts for Personal/Family Worship: Chapter 26

1. **Once again Saul is delivered into David's hands, yet once again David is convicted by the Spirit of God not to take Saul's life. Scripture repeats the lesson of 24:1–22 that we might learn from David's example. We must never take matters into our own hands; instead we must wait upon the Lord to vindicate us. Those who wait on the Lord will never be ashamed, for they follow in the footsteps of Christ, who patiently endured suffering while entrusting Himself to a faithful and just Judge (1 Peter 2:19–23; 4:12–19). In what ways are you tempted to take revenge? How can you resist this urge?**
2. **Toward the end of his life, Saul makes a very sad confession: "I have played the fool, and have erred exceedingly" (v. 21). Tragically, there are many who, like Saul, looking back on their lives must also confess to having played the fool. What a multitude of missed opportunities and failures there can be for such people! What a blessing therefore at the end of our lives if we can say with the Saul (Paul) of the New Testament, "I have fought a good fight, I have finished my course, I have kept the faith" (2 Tim. 4:7). May God help us to be like**

son David: thou shalt both do great *things*, and also shalt still prevail. So David went on his way, and Saul returned to his place.

CHAPTER 27

AND David said in his heart, I shall now perish one day by the hand of Saul: *there is* nothing better for me than that I should speedily escape into the land of the Philistines; and Saul shall despair of me, to seek me any more in any coast of Israel: so shall I escape out of his hand.
2 And David arose, and he passed over with the six hundred men that *were* with him unto Achish, the son of Maoch, king of Gath.
3 And David dwelt with Achish at Gath, he and his men, every man with his household, *even* David with his two wives, Ahinoam the Jezreelitess, and Abigail the Carmelitess, Nabal's wife.
4 And it was told Saul that David was fled to Gath: and he sought no more again for him.
5 ¶ And David said unto Achish, If I have now found grace in thine eyes, let them give me a place in some town in the country, that I may dwell there: for why should thy servant dwell in the royal city with thee?
6 Then Achish gave him Ziklag that day: wherefore Ziklag pertaineth unto the kings of Judah unto this day.
7 And the time that David dwelt in the country of the Philistines was a full year and four months.
8 ¶ And David and his men went up, and invaded the Geshurites, and the Gezrites, and the Amalekites: for those *nations were* of old the inhabitants of the land, as thou goest to Shur, even unto the land of Egypt.
9 And David smote the land, and left neither man nor woman alive, and took away the sheep, and the oxen, and the asses, and the camels, and the apparel, and returned, and came to Achish.
10 And Achish said, Whither have ye made a road to day? And David said, Against the south of Judah, and against the south of the Jerahmeelites, and against the south of the Kenites.
11 And David saved neither man nor woman alive, to bring *tidings* to Gath, saying, Lest they should tell on us, saying, So did David, and so *will be* his manner all the while he dwelleth in the country of the Philistines.
12 And Achish believed David, saying, He hath made his people Israel utterly to abhor him; therefore he shall be my servant for ever.

CHAPTER 28

AND it came to pass in those days, that the Philistines gathered their armies together for warfare, to fight with Israel. And Achish said unto David, Know thou assuredly, that thou shalt go out with me to battle, thou and thy men.
2 And David said to Achish, Surely thou shalt know what thy servant can do. And Achish said to David, Therefore will I make thee keeper of mine head for ever.
3 ¶ Now Samuel was dead, and all Israel had lamented him, and buried him in Ramah, even

Paul and make an exclamation of triumph rather than a confession of tragedy as King Saul was forced to utter.

THE END OF SAUL AND RISE OF KING DAVID (1 SAM. 27:1—2 SAM. 4:12)
David's Deceptive Sojourn with Achish (1 Sam. 27:1—28:2)

Chapter 27: *Convinced that Saul will kill him, David finds refuge with the Philistines.*

27:1 *David said in his heart.* At Keilah David inquired of the Lord (23:1–28); now he talks to himself with disastrous consequences, for the heart is deceitful (Jer. 17:9). *coast.* Border, or possibly territory.
27:4 David's decision brought the desired result: Saul *sought no more.* David's plan appeared to be successful, but appearance was not reality.
27:6 *pertaineth unto.* Belongs to.
27:8–9 *the Geshurites, and the Gezrites, and the Amalekites.* He fought Israel's historic enemies (Ex. 17:8; Josh. 12:5; 13:2; 16:3) with the zeal of Joshua. Engagement in "the Lord's work" was another apparent justification of his decision. However, the Amalekites would later bring David great trouble (1 Sam. 30:1–31).
27:10 *made a road.* The Hebrew has the idea of stretching or making a dash toward the plunder. *Judah.* David's pretending to attack his fellow Israelites dishonored the God of Israel.

Thoughts for Personal/Family Worship: Chapter 27

1. **Failures of faith often come immediately after victories of faith. David's refusal to take personal vengeance on Saul was a high water mark of faith (26:1–25); his consulting with himself and fleeing to Achish was a low point. Notwithstanding the number of times God had preserved him, David convinced himself that sooner or later Saul would succeed. He thought about negative possibilities rather than the certain promises of God. We must never let down our guard and must remember that we are often most susceptible to falling immediately after times of blessing and spiritual victories.**
2. **In the spiritual realm, appearance and reality are seldom the same. David made a carnal decision, and it appeared from circumstances to be the right move. Saul no longer pursued him, and he was able to engage in kingdom work by fighting against the enemies of God's people. But these ends did not justify the means. Just because something seems to work does not mean it is God's will. It must always be God's Word, rather than circumstances, that governs. We are to walk by faith, not sight.**

Chapter 28: *The Philistines plan an attack against Israel, and Saul in desperation goes to the witch at En-dor.*

28:1 David finds himself in a dilemma as Achish expects him to fight against Israel—the consequence of his bad decision.
28:2 *keeper of mine head.* Most likely, David's becoming the personal bodyguard.

in his own city. And Saul had put away those that
had familiar spirits, and the wizards, out of the
land.
4 And the Philistines gathered themselves to-
gether, and came and pitched in Shunem: and
Saul gathered all Israel together, and they pitched
in Gilboa.
5 And when Saul saw the host of the Philistines,
he was afraid, and his heart greatly trembled.
6 And when Saul enquired of the LORD, the LORD
answered him not, neither by dreams, nor by
Urim, nor by prophets.
7 ¶ Then said Saul unto his servants, Seek me a
woman that hath a familiar spirit, that I may go
to her, and enquire of her. And his servants said to
him, Behold, *there is* a woman that hath a familiar
spirit at En-dor.
8 And Saul disguised himself, and put on other
raiment, and he went, and two men with him, and
they came to the woman by night: and he said, I
pray thee, divine unto me by the familiar spirit, and
bring me *him* up, whom I shall name unto thee.
9 And the woman said unto him, Behold, thou
knowest what Saul hath done, how he hath cut off
those that have familiar spirits, and the wizards,
out of the land: wherefore then layest thou a snare
for my life, to cause me to die?
10 And Saul sware to her by the LORD, saying,
As the LORD liveth, there shall no punishment
happen to thee for this thing.
11 Then said the woman, Whom shall I bring up
unto thee? And he said, Bring me up Samuel.
12 And when the woman saw Samuel, she cried
with a loud voice: and the woman spake to Saul,
saying, Why hast thou deceived me? for thou *art*
Saul.
13 And the king said unto her, Be not afraid: for
what sawest thou? And the woman said unto Saul,
I saw gods ascending out of the earth.
14 And he said unto her, What form *is* he of?
And she said, An old man cometh up; and he *is*
covered with a mantle. And Saul perceived that it
was Samuel, and he stooped with *his* face to the
ground, and bowed himself.
15 ¶ And Samuel said to Saul, Why hast thou dis-
quieted me, to bring me up? And Saul answered,
I am sore distressed; for the Philistines make war
against me, and God is departed from me, and
answereth me no more, neither by prophets, nor
by dreams: therefore I have called thee, that thou
mayest make known unto me what I shall do.
16 Then said Samuel, Wherefore then dost thou
ask of me, seeing the LORD is departed from thee,
and is become thine enemy?
17 And the LORD hath done to him, as he spake
by me: for the LORD hath rent the kingdom out
of thine hand, and given it to thy neighbour, *even*
to David:
18 Because thou obeyedst not the voice of the
LORD, nor executedst his fierce wrath upon
Amalek, therefore hath the LORD done this thing
unto thee this day.
19 Moreover the LORD will also deliver Israel
with thee into the hand of the Philistines: and to
morrow *shalt* thou and thy sons *be* with me: the
LORD also shall deliver the host of Israel into the
hand of the Philistines.
20 Then Saul fell straightway all along on the
earth, and was sore afraid, because of the words
of Samuel: and there was no strength in him; for
he had eaten no bread all the day, nor all the night.
21 ¶ And the woman came unto Saul, and saw
that he was sore troubled, and said unto him, Be-
hold, thine handmaid hath obeyed thy voice, and
I have put my life in my hand, and have hearkened
unto thy words which thou spakest unto me.
22 Now therefore, I pray thee, hearken thou also
unto the voice of thine handmaid, and let me set
a morsel of bread before thee; and eat, that thou
mayest have strength, when thou goest on thy way.
23 But he refused, and said, I will not eat. But his
servants, together with the woman, compelled

Saul's Terror and Consulting a Witch (1 Sam. 28:3–25)

28:3 *those that had familiar spirits.* Those that sought to contact spirits of the dead (vv. 7,9). *wizards.* Those who sought knowledge of the future through magic. The law of Moses required the punishment of these sins (Lev. 19:31; 20:6,27; Deut. 18:9–14).

28:6 *dreams . . . prophets.* A typical means by which God revealed His word in the Old Testament era (Heb. 1:1). Using the means of grace, such as prayer (*enquired of the LORD*), is worthless if one persists in lack of repentance and in unbelief (Prov. 15:8,29).

28:8 *raiment.* Clothing.

28:12 *when the woman saw Samuel.* The Lord intervened on this occasion and allowed this, for the woman herself could never have done such a thing.

28:15 *Why hast thou disquieted me?* Why have you disturbed me? *I am sore distressed.* Literally, "it is exceedingly cramped for me," in the sense that he is in difficult straits and hard pressed.

28:19 *tomorrow shalt thou and thy sons be with me.* Saul and his sons would die the next day.

28:20 *sore afraid.* Feared exceedingly.

28:21 *sore troubled.* The Hebrew has the idea of being greatly horrified, out of one's senses.

Thoughts for Personal/Family Worship: Chapter 28

This chapter illustrates the tragic consequences of sin. Saul's public sin started with incomplete obedience to God's command (v. 18) and ended with his blatant violations of God's command. Sin indeed is a slippery slope that leads to a very deep bottom. Saul was pressed down from the outside in and felt the desperation that God had departed from him. He could get no word from the Lord. What a warning this is to listen to God's Word and to keep our accounts with the Lord short so that we can have access to His Word. Child of God, is it not the

him; and he hearkened unto their voice. So he
arose from the earth, and sat upon the bed.
24 And the woman had a fat calf in the house;
and she hasted, and killed it, and took flour,
and kneaded *it*, and did bake unleavened bread
thereof:
25 And she brought *it* before Saul, and before his
servants; and they did eat. Then they rose up, and
went away that night.

CHAPTER 29

NOW the Philistines gathered together all their
armies to Aphek: and the Israelites pitched by a
fountain which *is* in Jezreel.
2 And the lords of the Philistines passed on by
hundreds, and by thousands: but David and his
men passed on in the rereward with Achish.
3 Then said the princes of the Philistines, What
do these Hebrews *here*? And Achish said unto
the princes of the Philistines, *Is* not this David,
the servant of Saul the king of Israel, which hath
been with me these days, or these years, and I have
found no fault in him since he fell *unto me* unto
this day?
4 And the princes of the Philistines were wroth
with him; and the princes of the Philistines said
unto him, Make this fellow return, that he may go
again to his place which thou hast appointed him,
and let him not go down with us to battle, lest
in the battle he be an adversary to us: for where-
with should he reconcile himself unto his master?
should it not *be* with the heads of these men?
5 *Is* not this David, of whom they sang one to an-
other in dances, saying, Saul slew his thousands,
and David his ten thousands?
6 ¶ Then Achish called David, and said unto him,
Surely, *as* the LORD liveth, thou hast been upright,
and thy going out and thy coming in with me in the
host *is* good in my sight: for I have not found evil in
thee since the day of thy coming unto me unto this
day: nevertheless the lords favour thee not.
7 Wherefore now return, and go in peace, that
thou displease not the lords of the Philistines.
8 ¶ And David said unto Achish, But what have I
done? and what hast thou found in thy servant so
long as I have been with thee unto this day, that I
may not go fight against the enemies of my lord
the king?
9 And Achish answered and said to David, I
know that thou *art* good in my sight, as an angel
of God: notwithstanding the princes of the Phi-
listines have said, He shall not go up with us to
the battle.
10 Wherefore now rise up early in the morning
with thy master's servants that are come with
thee: and as soon as ye be up early in the morning,
and have light, depart.
11 So David and his men rose up early to depart
in the morning, to return into the land of the Phi-
listines. And the Philistines went up to Jezreel.

CHAPTER 30

AND it came to pass, when David and his men
were come to Ziklag on the third day, that the

most wonderful blessing that you were made to hear His voice? How you ought to praise the Lord that He has not left you! Ironically, the chapter begins with David in a most compromising situation. Will David descend the slippery slope? Will you?

David's Release from Achish and War with Amalek (1 Sam. 29:1—30:31)

Chapter 29: *God providentially intervenes to prevent David from going to war against his own nation.*

29:2 *rereward.* Literally, "at the last," referring to the rear guard.
29:3 *What do these Hebrews here?* See note at 14:21. They feared that the same thing would happen again (v. 4).
29:4 *princes.* Leaders. *wroth.* Furious.
29:6 *the lords favour thee not.* Literally, "in the eyes of the governors you are not good."
29:7 *that thou displease not.* Literally, "that you do not do something bad in the eyes of the governors."
29:8 *But what have I done?* It appears that David had determined to fight against his own people, the unforeseen consequence of his faithless decision (27:1–2).
29:9 *good . . . as an angel of God.* These words should have pierced David's conscience, given his lies to Achish.

Thoughts for Personal/Family Worship: Chapter 29

1. **Fearing the threats of Saul and failing to fully trust the Lord, David and his men sought shelter with the Philistines, Israel's enemy. This led to a very difficult situation. They found themselves united with Achish, who would do harm to the Lord's people. Mercifully, providence intervened, and God used the ungodly as His agents to keep David from further sin. They said, "What do these Hebrews here?" (v. 3). A similar question might be asked of those professing Christians who side with the world. Are we not commanded, "Be ye not unequally yoked together with unbelievers" (2 Cor. 6:14)? Christian, where are you standing at present? Let us ensure that we are always on the Lord's side, and with the Lord's people.**
2. **This chapter wonderfully illustrates the principle set out in 1 Cor. 10:13: "There hath no temptation taken you but such as is common to man: but God is faithful, who will not suffer you to be tempted above that ye are able; but will with the temptation also make a way to escape, that ye may be able to bear it." Perhaps to David's eyes there was no way to extricate himself from the mess he had gotten himself into, but God delivered him. Let us take comfort in this when we find ourselves in wrong situations of our own making, and let us confidently call on the Lord to deliver us.**

Chapter 30: *David returns to Ziklag to find it burned and plundered by the Amalekites, and then by the help of God recovers the losses.*

Amalekites had invaded the south, and Ziklag,
and smitten Ziklag, and burned it with fire;
2 And had taken the women captives, that *were*
therein: they slew not any, either great or small,
but carried *them* away, and went on their way.
3 ¶ So David and his men came to the city, and,
behold, *it was* burned with fire; and their wives,
and their sons, and their daughters, were taken
captives.
4 Then David and the people that *were* with him
lifted up their voice and wept, until they had no
more power to weep.
5 And David's two wives were taken captives,
Ahinoam the Jezreelitess, and Abigail the wife of
Nabal the Carmelite.
6 And David was greatly distressed; for the people
spake of stoning him, because the soul of all the
people was grieved, every man for his sons and
for his daughters: but David encouraged himself
in the LORD his God.
7 And David said to Abiathar the priest, Ahime-
lech's son, I pray thee, bring me hither the ephod.
And Abiathar brought thither the ephod to David.
8 And David enquired at the LORD, saying, Shall
I pursue after this troop? shall I overtake them?
And he answered him, Pursue: for thou shalt
surely overtake *them*, and without fail recover *all*.
9 So David went, he and the six hundred men
that *were* with him, and came to the brook Besor,
where those that were left behind stayed.
10 But David pursued, he and four hundred
men: for two hundred abode behind, which were
so faint that they could not go over the brook
Besor.
11 ¶ And they found an Egyptian in the field, and
brought him to David, and gave him bread, and
he did eat; and they made him drink water;
12 And they gave him a piece of a cake of figs,
and two clusters of raisins: and when he had
eaten, his spirit came again to him: for he had
eaten no bread, nor drunk *any* water, three days
and three nights.
13 And David said unto him, To whom *belongest*
thou? and whence *art* thou? And he said, I *am* a
young man of Egypt, servant to an Amalekite;
and my master left me, because three days agone
I fell sick.
14 We made an invasion *upon* the south of the
Cherethites, and upon *the coast* which *belongeth*
to Judah, and upon the south of Caleb; and we
burned Ziklag with fire.
15 And David said to him, Canst thou bring me
down to this company? And he said, Swear unto
me by God, that thou wilt neither kill me, nor
deliver me into the hands of my master, and I will
bring thee down to this company.
16 ¶ And when he had brought him down, be-
hold, *they were* spread abroad upon all the earth,
eating and drinking, and dancing, because of all
the great spoil that they had taken out of the land
of the Philistines, and out of the land of Judah.
17 And David smote them from the twilight
even unto the evening of the next day: and there
escaped not a man of them, save four hundred
young men, which rode upon camels, and fled.
18 And David recovered all that the Amalekites
had carried away: and David rescued his two
wives.
19 And there was nothing lacking to them, nei-
ther small nor great, neither sons nor daughters,
neither spoil, nor any *thing* that they had taken to
them: David recovered all.
20 And David took all the flocks and the herds,
which they drave before those *other* cattle, and
said, This *is* David's spoil.
21 ¶ And David came to the two hundred men,
which were so faint that they could not follow
David, whom they had made also to abide at the

30:1 *smitten.* Struck.

30:2 David had killed all the men and women when he raided Amalekite towns (27:8–11), but, surprisingly, the Amalekites killed not one of David's people. This ironically illustrates that sometimes unbelievers can act with more justice and kindness than believers. It also points to the sovereign mercy of God in sparing David even as He disciplined him.

30:3–4 David's seeming wisdom in pretending to serve the Philistines has led to disaster.

30:6 *encouraged himself.* Literally, "strengthened himself." When our sins bring down horrible consequences, and our friends turn against us, we may still find strength in the Lord by turning to Him in repentance and faith.

30:7 *ephod.* See notes at 23:6.

30:8 *enquired at the LORD.* Having experienced the disastrous results of following his own wisdom in unbelief (27:1), David returned to his former practice of seeking the Lord's wisdom through the means of grace (23:2,4,9–12).

30:10 *faint.* Exhausted.

30:11 *found an Egyptian.* This "chance" event proved to be a gift of God's all-ruling providence to guide them to their enemies.

30:13 *three days agone.* Three days ago.

30:14 *coast.* Border.

30:17 *save.* Except.

30:18–19 God's mercy was great in allowing David to recover *all* the people and goods taken from Ziglag, including his wives.

30:20 *drave.* Drove.

30:21 *he saluted them.* Literally, "he asked them concerning their welfare."

30:22 *Belial.* See note at 1:16.

30:24 *stuff.* Equipment.

30:31 *where . . . wont to haunt.* Literally, "where David and his men walked around," referring to where they were accustomed to staying.

Thoughts for Personal/Family Worship: Chapter 30

1. **It is very often in times of distress and adversity that we most acknowledge our dependence on God. So it was**

brook Besor: and they went forth to meet David, and to meet the people that *were* with him: and when David came near to the people, he saluted them.
22 Then answered all the wicked men and *men*
of Belial, of those that went with David, and said, Because they went not with us, we will not give them *ought* of the spoil that we have recovered, save to every man his wife and his children, that they may lead *them* away, and depart.
23 Then said David, Ye shall not do so, my
brethren, with that which the LORD hath given us, who hath preserved us, and delivered the company that came against us into our hand.
24 For who will hearken unto you in this matter?
but as his part *is* that goeth down to the battle, so *shall* his part *be* that tarrieth by the stuff: they shall part alike.
25 And it was *so* from that day forward, that he
made it a statute and an ordinance for Israel unto this day.
26 ¶ And when David came to Ziklag, he sent
of the spoil unto the elders of Judah, *even* to his friends, saying, Behold a present for you of the spoil of the enemies of the LORD;
27 To *them* which *were* in Beth-el, and to *them*
which *were* in south Ramoth, and to *them* which *were* in Jattir,
28 And to *them* which *were* in Aroer, and to *them*
which *were* in Siphmoth, and to *them* which *were* in Eshtemoa,
29 And to *them* which *were* in Rachal, and to
them which *were* in the cities of the Jerahmeelites, and to *them* which *were* in the cities of the Kenites,
30 And to *them* which *were* in Hormah, and
to *them* which *were* in Chorashan, and to *them* which *were* in Athach,
31 And to *them* which *were* in Hebron, and to all
the places where David himself and his men were wont to haunt.

CHAPTER 31

NOW the Philistines fought against Israel: and the men of Israel fled from before the Philistines, and fell down slain in mount Gilboa.
2 And the Philistines followed hard upon Saul
and upon his sons; and the Philistines slew Jonathan, and Abinadab, and Malchi-shua, Saul's sons.
3 And the battle went sore against Saul, and the
archers hit him; and he was sore wounded of the archers.
4 Then said Saul unto his armourbearer, Draw
thy sword, and thrust me through therewith; lest these uncircumcised come and thrust me through, and abuse me. But his armourbearer would not; for he was sore afraid. Therefore Saul took a sword, and fell upon it.
5 And when his armourbearer saw that Saul was
dead, he fell likewise upon his sword, and died with him.
6 So Saul died, and his three sons, and his ar-
mourbearer, and all his men, that same day together.
7 ¶ And when the men of Israel that *were* on the
other side of the valley, and *they* that *were* on the other side Jordan, saw that the men of Israel fled, and that Saul and his sons were dead, they forsook the cities, and fled; and the Philistines came and dwelt in them.
8 And it came to pass on the morrow, when the
Philistines came to strip the slain, that they found Saul and his three sons fallen in mount Gilboa.
9 And they cut off his head, and stripped off his
armour, and sent into the land of the Philistines round about, to publish *it in* the house of their idols, and among the people.

---

with David. At Ziklag, God brought him to the end of himself; he lost everything. However, it is here that David shows himself a true man of God: "David encouraged himself in the LORD his God" (v. 6). What an example David is to us here. When terrible catastrophes come upon us, how easy it is to become overwhelmed with sorrow and grief. Yet if we would know true deliverance and desire spiritual benefit, there can be no better way than to look to the Lord and encourage ourselves in Him. He has promised "I am with you alway, even unto the end of the world" (Matt. 28:20) and assured us of "an inheritance incorruptible, and undefiled, and that fadeth not away" (1 Peter 1:4). Let us, then, look to these promises and encourage ourselves in the Lord; then we shall grow in grace and be better fitted for the Master's service.

2. **The two words "recover all" (vv. 8,18–19) constitute a statement of hope. Everything that David lost because of his sin and God's chastening hand was recovered when he strengthened himself in the Lord and sought to do God's will. There is hope for the backslider that God will restore him to fellowship and usefulness upon returning to Him. David's recovering all parallels the equally encouraging promise that God later gives through Joel after the devastation of the locust plague: "and I will restore to you the years that the locust hath eaten" (Joel 2:25). Let us never fail to seek the Lord because He will draw near to those who draw near to Him (James 4:8).**

Chapter 31: *The Philistines defeat Israel at Gilboa, resulting in the deaths of Saul and his sons.*

The Deaths of Saul and His Sons (1 Sam. 31:1–13)

31:2 *followed hard.* Hebrew means "to pursue closely, to overtake."

31:3 *the battle went sore.* Literally, "the battle was heavy." *sore wounded.* In severe agony.

31:4 *sore.* Greatly. *Saul took a sword, and fell upon it.* The Lord disciplined David unto repentance and renewal of his faith (30:1–31), but Saul died in despair.

31:8 *morrow.* The following day.

31:9 *publish.* Announce good news.

10 And they put his armour in the house of
Ashtaroth: and they fastened his body to the wall
of Beth-shan.
11 ¶ And when the inhabitants of Jabesh-gilead
heard of that which the Philistines had done to
Saul;
12 All the valiant men arose, and went all night,
and took the body of Saul and the bodies of his
sons from the wall of Beth-shan, and came to
Jabesh, and burnt them there.
13 And they took their bones, and buried *them*
under a tree at Jabesh, and fasted seven days.

31:10 *Ashtaroth.* Female deity (see 7:3).

Thoughts for Personal/Family Worship: Chapter 31

1. **The narrative of Saul ends tragically with a shameful death in defeat. His life seemed so promising and full of potential but took a disastrous turn with his disobedience. From that moment on it was filled with misery and envy, and his death came in excruciating agony. People debate whether Saul was an unbelieving hypocrite or a backslidden believer, but it is clear that he descended into great depths of spiritual darkness. His life is a sober warning that sin leads to great sorrow, and repentance can never come too soon.**
2. **On the same day and in the same battle as Saul died, Jonathan also died. His righteous behavior and loyalty to David as God's anointed did not spare him. Thus, the book ends with a sober reminder that it is appointed unto all men to die and after that the judgment (Heb. 9:27). Death comes to the wise and foolish alike (Ps. 49:10). It is imperative and urgent in the life that remains to be ready for the judgment to come. If you knew you would soon die, what you would do differently? Why not seek God's grace to change today?**

INTRODUCTION TO THE BOOK OF
2 SAMUEL

Authorship, Date, Theme, Purpose, and Synopsis:

First and Second Samuel are one book, and therefore are treated together in the Introduction to 1 and 2 Samuel located before 1 Samuel.

Outline: Second Samuel begins partway through the section dealing with a battle with the Philistines, the death of Saul, and increasing power of David (1 Sam. 27:1—2 Sam. 4:12).

I. The Birth and Early Ministry of Samuel (1 Sam. 1:1—7:17)
   A. Hannah's Prayer and Samuel's Birth (1 Sam. 1:1—2:11)
   B. The Lord's Judgment upon Eli's Household (1 Sam. 2:12–36)
   C. The Call of Samuel to Prophetic Ministry (1 Sam. 3:1—4:1)
   D. The Departure and Return of the Glory (1 Sam. 4:1—7:1)
   E. Israel's Return to the Lord through Samuel (1 Sam. 7:2–17)
II. The Rise and Rejection of King Saul (1 Sam. 8:1—15:35)
   A. Israel's Rejection of the Lord as King (1 Sam. 8:1–22)
   B. God's Sovereign Selection of a King (1 Sam. 9:1—10:27)
   C. Saul's Promising Start (1 Sam. 11:1–15)
   D. Samuel's Integrity and Exhortation to Israel (1 Sam. 12:1–25)
   E. Saul's Rebellion and Jonathan's Faith (1 Sam. 13:1—15:35)
III. The Victories and Persecution of David (1 Sam. 16:1—26:25)
   A. David's Anointing as King and Enlisting to Serve Saul (1 Sam. 16:1–23)
   B. Saul's Failure and David's Victory by Faith (1 Sam. 17:1–54)
   C. Saul's Jealousy and Jonathan's Loyalty to David (1 Sam. 17:55—20:42)
   D. David's Flight from Saul into the Wilderness (1 Sam. 21:1—26:25)
IV. The End of Saul and Rise of King David (1 Sam. 27:1—2 Sam. 4:12)
   A. David's Deceptive Sojourn with Achish (1 Sam. 27:1—28:2)
   B. Saul's Terror and Consulting a Witch (1 Sam. 28:3–25)
   C. David's Release from Achish and War with Amalek (1 Sam. 29:1—30:31)
   D. The Deaths of Saul and His Sons (1 Sam. 31:1–13)
   E. David's Lamentation over Saul and Jonathan (2 Sam. 1:1–27)
   F. David, King of Judah, against Ish-bosheth, King of Israel (2 Sam. 2:1—4:12)
V. The Triumphant Reign of David over All Israel (2 Sam. 5:1—10:19)
   A. The Establishment of David's Kingdom (2 Sam. 5:1–25)
   B. The Bringing of the Ark of the Covenant to Jerusalem (2 Sam. 6:1–23)
   C. The Lord's Covenant with David (2 Sam. 7:1–29)
   D. The Power, Justice, and Mercy of King David (2 Sam. 8:1—10:19)
VI. The Crimes and Troubles of David and His Household (2 Sam. 11:1—20:26)
   A. David's Adultery, Murder, and Repentance (2 Sam. 11:1—12:31)
   B. Amnon's Incest and Absalom's Revenge (2 Sam. 13:1—14:33)
   C. Absalom's Rebellion against David (2 Sam. 15:1—17:29)
   D. Absalom's Death and David's Restoration (2 Sam. 18:1—19:40)
   E. The Rebellion of Sheba against David (2 Sam. 19:41—20:26)

VII. The Conclusion of David's Reign (2 Sam. 21:1—24:25)
   A. Vengeance for the Gibeonites on Saul's Family (2 Sam. 21:1–14)
   B. War between the Philistines and an Aging David (2 Sam. 21:15–22)
   C. The Song of David to the Lord (2 Sam. 22:1–51)
   D. David's Last Words (2 Sam. 23:1–7)
   E. David's Mighty Men (2 Sam. 23:8–39)
   F. The Tragic Census of Israel (2 Sam. 24:1–25)

THE SECOND BOOK OF

SAMUEL

CHAPTER 1

NOW it came to pass after the death of Saul, when
David was returned from the slaughter of the
Amalekites, and David had abode two days in
Ziklag;
2 It came even to pass on the third day, that,
behold, a man came out of the camp from Saul
with his clothes rent, and earth upon his head:
and *so* it was, when he came to David, that he fell
to the earth, and did obeisance.
3 And David said unto him, From whence comest
thou? And he said unto him, Out of the camp of
Israel am I escaped.
4 And David said unto him, How went the mat-
ter? I pray thee, tell me. And he answered, That
the people are fled from the battle, and many of
the people also are fallen and dead; and Saul and
Jonathan his son are dead also.
5 And David said unto the young man that told
him, How knowest thou that Saul and Jonathan
his son be dead?
6 And the young man that told him said, As I
happened by chance upon mount Gilboa, behold,
Saul leaned upon his spear; and, lo, the chariots
and horsemen followed hard after him.
7 And when he looked behind him, he saw me,
and called unto me. And I answered, Here *am* I.
8 And he said unto me, Who *art* thou? And I
answered him, I *am* an Amalekite.
9 He said unto me again, Stand, I pray thee, upon
me, and slay me: for anguish is come upon me,
because my life *is* yet whole in me.
10 So I stood upon him, and slew him, because
I was sure that he could not live after that he was
fallen: and I took the crown that *was* upon his
head, and the bracelet that *was* on his arm, and
have brought them hither unto my lord.
11 Then David took hold on his clothes, and rent
them; and likewise all the men that *were* with him:
12 And they mourned, and wept, and fasted
until even, for Saul, and for Jonathan his son, and
for the people of the LORD, and for the house of
Israel; because they were fallen by the sword.
13 ¶ And David said unto the young man that
told him, Whence *art* thou? And he answered, I
am the son of a stranger, an Amalekite.
14 And David said unto him, How wast thou not
afraid to stretch forth thine hand to destroy the
LORD's anointed?
15 And David called one of the young men, and
said, Go near, *and* fall upon him. And he smote
him that he died.
16 And David said unto him, Thy blood *be* upon
thy head; for thy mouth hath testified against
thee, saying, I have slain the LORD's anointed.
17 ¶ And David lamented with this lamentation
over Saul and over Jonathan his son:
18 (Also he bade them teach the children of
Judah *the use of* the bow: behold, *it is* written in
the book of Jasher.)
19 The beauty of Israel is slain upon thy high
places: how are the mighty fallen!
20 Tell *it* not in Gath, publish *it* not in the streets
of Askelon; lest the daughters of the Philistines

THE END OF SAUL AND RISE OF KING DAVID (1 SAM. 27:1—2 SAM. 4:12)

Chapter 1: *David laments the deaths of Saul and Jonathan.*

David's Lamentation over Saul and Jonathan (2 Sam. 1:1–27)

1:2 *did obeisance.* Bowed down as a gesture of respect and submission.

1:9 *anguish is come upon me.* Literally, "trembling or weakness has seized me."

1:11 *rent.* Tore, a common gesture expressing grief.

1:13 *the son of a stranger.* A resident alien living as a protected citizen.

1:18 *bade them teach.* Literally, "said to teach." *the book of Jasher.* Translated, "the book of the upright," an uninspired book, now lost, that recorded significant events regarding national Israel (Josh. 10:13).

1:19–27 Some of the most touching and poetic words ever recorded in the Word of God. This was intended to be a testimony to Saul, the Lord's anointed. His bravery and military might are celebrated, and his faults are set aside. There was more to Saul than met the eye.

1:19 *The beauty of Israel.* Saul and Jonathan were the ornaments of the nation, cut down *upon thy high places* (Mount Gilboa).

1:20 *Gath . . . Askelon.* Two principal cities in Philistia, here representing the whole nation.

rejoice, lest the daughters of the uncircumcised
triumph.
21 Ye mountains of Gilboa, *let there be* no dew,
neither *let there be* rain, upon you, nor fields of of-
ferings: for there the shield of the mighty is vilely
cast away, the shield of Saul, *as though he had* not
been anointed with oil.
22 From the blood of the slain, from the fat of the
mighty, the bow of Jonathan turned not back, and
the sword of Saul returned not empty.
23 Saul and Jonathan *were* lovely and pleasant in
their lives, and in their death they were not di-
vided: they were swifter than eagles, they were
stronger than lions.
24 Ye daughters of Israel, weep over Saul, who
clothed you in scarlet, with *other* delights, who
put on ornaments of gold upon your apparel.
25 How are the mighty fallen in the midst of the
battle! O Jonathan, *thou wast* slain in thine high
places.
26 I am distressed for thee, my brother Jonathan:
very pleasant hast thou been unto me: thy love
to me was wonderful, passing the love of women.
27 How are the mighty fallen, and the weapons
of war perished!

CHAPTER 2

AND it came to pass after this, that David enquired
of the LORD, saying, Shall I go up into any of the
cities of Judah? And the LORD said unto him, Go
up. And David said, Whither shall I go up? And he
said, Unto Hebron.
2 So David went up thither, and his two wives
also, Ahinoam the Jezreelitess, and Abigail Nabal's
wife the Carmelite.
3 And his men that *were* with him did David
bring up, every man with his household: and they
dwelt in the cities of Hebron.
4 And the men of Judah came, and there they
anointed David king over the house of Judah.
And they told David, saying, *That* the men of
Jabesh-gilead *were they* that buried Saul.
5 ¶ And David sent messengers unto the men of
Jabesh-gilead, and said unto them, Blessed *be* ye of
the LORD, that ye have shewed this kindness unto
your lord, *even* unto Saul, and have buried him.
6 And now the LORD shew kindness and truth
unto you: and I also will requite you this kind-
ness, because ye have done this thing.
7 Therefore now let your hands be strengthened,
and be ye valiant: for your master Saul is dead,
and also the house of Judah have anointed me
king over them.
8 ¶ But Abner the son of Ner, captain of Saul's
host, took Ish-bosheth the son of Saul, and
brought him over to Mahanaim;
9 And made him king over Gilead, and over the
Ashurites, and over Jezreel, and over Ephraim,
and over Benjamin, and over all Israel.

1:21 *let there be no dew, neither let there be rain.* This would be abnormal in a place as lush and green as Gilboa. Here poetic language is employed to express the grief of the heart. *vilely cast away*. Hebrew, "to be defiled."
1:22 *the fat of the mighty*. Referring to that which covers the inner body. Together with *blood*, refers to the relentless prowess of Jonathan's and Saul's military skills. They went for the kill.
1:23 *lovely*. The Hebrew form means "worthy of love." *pleasant*. Delightful or lovely, a word that elsewhere describes God's name (Ps. 135:3).
1:24 *delights*. Luxurious things.
1:26 *very pleasant hast thou been*. The Hebrew suggests "you have been a dear friend." *wonderful.* Extraordinary. In Jonathan, David had a friend closer than a brother (Prov. 18:24). That is rare; hence, the statement that it surpassed *the love of women*, which is far more common.
1:27 *How are the mighty fallen*. Three times these words occur, making up the chorus of this epic poem and establishing its theme.

Thoughts for Personal/Family Worship: Chapter 1

1. **The Amalekite lied, assuming the deception would earn him a reward. Almost every lie is motivated by self-preservation or self-advancement. Very often lies are discovered and consequences must be faced. Here the Amalekite's lie is not discovered, but he suffers the consequence of being believed. The bottom line is that one way or another and sooner or later our words will betray us. We can be sure that our sins will find us out. There is no covering ourselves or escaping the One who sees all, no matter how well we plan or how detailed our lie. In this life or the next, sin will be punished unless Christ has borne the penalty. Why must we be totally honest to the Lord when confessing our sins?**
2. **David's anguish over Jonathan is intense. How tender the son of Jesse's love is for his friend! But as close knit as the friendship of David and Jonathan was, it pales in comparison to Christ's friendship with His people. "I have called you friends," He says to His disciples, who were at the point of either denying or abandoning Him (John 15:15). We see here why David is the prophetic image of Christ, who, "having loved his own which were in the world, he loved them unto the end" (John 13:1).**

David, King of Judah, against Ish-bosheth, King of Israel (2 Sam. 2:1–4:12)

Chapter 2: *David is anointed king over Judah, but Ish-bosheth, the son of Saul, over Israel, resulting in a power struggle between the two houses.*

2:1 *enquired of the LORD*. Having learned his lesson at Ziklag (1 Sam. 30), David wisely seeks the Lord's will.
2:3 *cities of Hebron*. Plural because it includes the surrounding villages.
2:4 *they anointed David*. David had been privately anointed by Samuel (1 Sam. 16:13), and now publicly. The delay between the initial promise and its fulfillment did not jeopardize the promise. God's timing is always best, and it is always best to wait on Him.
2:5 *ye have shewed this kindness*. This was an act of loyalty based on their relationship with Saul.
2:6 *the LORD shew kindness and truth*. Expressions of loyalty

10 Ish-bosheth Saul's son *was* forty years old
when he began to reign over Israel, and reigned
two years. But the house of Judah followed David.
11 And the time that David was king in Hebron
over the house of Judah was seven years and six
months.
12 ¶ And Abner the son of Ner, and the servants
of Ish-bosheth the son of Saul, went out from
Mahanaim to Gibeon.
13 And Joab the son of Zeruiah, and the servants
of David, went out, and met together by the pool
of Gibeon: and they sat down, the one on the one
side of the pool, and the other on the other side
of the pool.
14 And Abner said to Joab, Let the young men
now arise, and play before us. And Joab said, Let
them arise.
15 Then there arose and went over by number
twelve of Benjamin, which *pertained* to Ish-
bosheth the son of Saul, and twelve of the servants
of David.
16 And they caught every one his fellow by the
head, and *thrust* his sword in his fellow's side; so
they fell down together: wherefore that place was
called Helkath-hazzurim, which *is* in Gibeon.
17 And there was a very sore battle that day; and
Abner was beaten, and the men of Israel, before
the servants of David.
18 ¶ And there were three sons of Zeruiah there,
Joab, and Abishai, and Asahel: and Asahel *was as*
light of foot as a wild roe.
19 And Asahel pursued after Abner; and in going
he turned not to the right hand nor to the left
from following Abner.
20 Then Abner looked behind him, and said, *Art*
thou Asahel? And he answered, I *am*.
21 And Abner said to him, Turn thee aside to thy
right hand or to thy left, and lay thee hold on one
of the young men, and take thee his armour. But
Asahel would not turn aside from following of
him.
22 And Abner said again to Asahel, Turn thee
aside from following me: wherefore should I
smite thee to the ground? how then should I hold
up my face to Joab thy brother?
23 Howbeit he refused to turn aside: wherefore
Abner with the hinder end of the spear smote him
under the fifth *rib*, that the spear came out behind
him; and he fell down there, and died in the same
place: and it came to pass, *that* as many as came to
the place where Asahel fell down and died stood
still.
24 Joab also and Abishai pursued after Abner:
and the sun went down when they were come to
the hill of Ammah, that *lieth* before Giah by the
way of the wilderness of Gibeon.
25 ¶ And the children of Benjamin gathered
themselves together after Abner, and became one
troop, and stood on the top of an hill.
26 Then Abner called to Joab, and said, Shall the
sword devour for ever? knowest thou not that it
will be bitterness in the latter end? how long shall
it be then, ere thou bid the people return from
following their brethren?
27 And Joab said, *As* God liveth, unless thou
hadst spoken, surely then in the morning the
people had gone up every one from following his
brother.
28 So Joab blew a trumpet, and all the people
stood still, and pursued after Israel no more,
neither fought they any more.
29 And Abner and his men walked all that night
through the plain, and passed over Jordan, and
went through all Bithron, and they came to
Mahanaim.
30 And Joab returned from following Abner: and
when he had gathered all the people together,
there lacked of David's servants nineteen men
and Asahel.
31 But the servants of David had smitten of Ben-
jamin, and of Abner's men, *so that* three hundred
and threescore men died.

---

are mutual and often linked with *truth* to stress steadfast fidelity; the *kindness* is certain. *I also will requite.* Literally, "I will do with you this good thing."

2:8 *Abner the son of Ner.* Saul's cousin and captain of his armies. *Ish-bosheth.* Translated, "man of shame." His real name was Esh-baal, translated, "man of Baal" (1 Chron. 8:33). However, to avoid any reference to a false god, Baal was replaced with *bosheth*, meaning "shame."

2:13 *pool of Gibeon.* Bubbling springs flowing from limestone rock.

2:14 *play before us.* The Hebrew means "to struggle or fight."

2:16 *Helkath-hazzurim.* Translated, "the field or plot of the ones pressing hard," where each of the combatants perished.

2:17 *a very sore battle.* An extremely severe battle involving the opposing sides followed the contest of the twenty-four.

2:18 *Zeruiah.* David's sister (1 Chron. 2:16). *light of foot.* Nimble or quick on his feet. *wild roe.* Gazelle.

2:21 *Take thee his armor.* As a trophy.

2:23 *the hinder end of the spear.* The back or butt end of the spear. *under the fifth rib.* Specifically refers to the abdomen. *came out behind him.* So fierce was the blow that even the butt end pierced him through.

2:31 *three hundred and threescore.* 360.

Thoughts for Personal/Family Worship: Chapter 2

1. **Although David had been promised the kingdom years earlier (1 Sam. 16), he did not try to establish it on his own. He refused to kill Saul even though he had multiple chances, and now he is still patient. He was willing to be guided by the Lord's will as to both time and manner of his promotion. This reminds us that "He that believeth shall not make haste" (Isa. 28:16). By David's example we are reminded that in all of life's dealings, hopes, and fears, we must seek the will of God by faith and prayer. "In all thy ways acknowledge him, and he shall direct thy paths" (Prov. 3:6). David's example also reminds us not**

32 ¶ And they took up Asahel, and buried him
in the sepulchre of his father, which *was in* Beth-lehem. And Joab and his men went all night, and
they came to Hebron at break of day.

CHAPTER 3

Now there was long war between the house of Saul and the house of David: but David waxed stronger and stronger, and the house of Saul waxed weaker and weaker.
2 ¶ And unto David were sons born in Hebron:
and his firstborn was Amnon, of Ahinoam the
Jezreelitess;
3 And his second, Chileab, of Abigail the wife of
Nabal the Carmelite; and the third, Absalom the
son of Maacah the daughter of Talmai king of
Geshur;
4 And the fourth, Adonijah the son of Haggith;
and the fifth, Shephatiah the son of Abital;
5 And the sixth, Ithream, by Eglah David's wife.
These were born to David in Hebron.
6 ¶ And it came to pass, while there was war be-
tween the house of Saul and the house of David,
that Abner made himself strong for the house of
Saul.
7 And Saul had a concubine, whose name *was*
Rizpah, the daughter of Aiah: and *Ish-bosheth* said
to Abner, Wherefore hast thou gone in unto my
father's concubine?
8 Then was Abner very wroth for the words of
Ish-bosheth, and said, *Am* I a dog's head, which
against Judah do shew kindness this day unto the
house of Saul thy father, to his brethren, and to his
friends, and have not delivered thee into the hand
of David, that thou chargest me to day with a fault
concerning this woman?
9 So do God to Abner, and more also, except, as
the LORD hath sworn to David, even so I do to him;
10 To translate the kingdom from the house of
Saul, and to set up the throne of David over Israel
and over Judah, from Dan even to Beer-sheba.
11 And he could not answer Abner a word again,
because he feared him.
12 ¶ And Abner sent messengers to David on
his behalf, saying, Whose *is* the land? saying *also*,
Make thy league with me, and, behold, my hand
shall be with thee, to bring about all Israel unto
thee.
13 ¶ And he said, Well; I will make a league with
thee: but one thing I require of thee, that is, Thou
shalt not see my face, except thou first bring
Michal Saul's daughter, when thou comest to see
my face.
14 And David sent messengers to Ish-bosheth
Saul's son, saying, Deliver *me* my wife Michal,
which I espoused to me for an hundred foreskins
of the Philistines.
15 And Ish-bosheth sent, and took her from *her*
husband, *even* from Phaltiel the son of Laish.
16 And her husband went with her along weep-
ing behind her to Bahurim. Then said Abner unto
him, Go, return. And he returned.
17 ¶ And Abner had communication with the
elders of Israel, saying, Ye sought for David in
times past *to be* king over you:
18 Now then do *it*: for the LORD hath spoken of
David, saying, By the hand of my servant David
I will save my people Israel out of the hand of
the Philistines, and out of the hand of all their
enemies.
19 And Abner also spake in the ears of Benjamin:
and Abner went also to speak in the ears of David
in Hebron all that seemed good to Israel, and that
seemed good to the whole house of Benjamin.
20 So Abner came to David to Hebron, and
twenty men with him. And David made Abner
and the men that *were* with him a feast.
21 And Abner said unto David, I will arise and
go, and will gather all Israel unto my lord the

---

to give up on God's promises. Delay of promise is not denial of promise. We must learn to wait on the Lord with the confidence that He will accomplish His word in His way and in His time. How does waiting on God increase your faith and dependence on Him?

2. **Resorting to violence to resolve differences, even at the national level, should be the last resort. It was God's will that David rule in Saul's place (1 Sam. 13:13–14; 15:28). Had Israel sought the Lord, David's kingdom could have been established without bloodshed. Discerning God's will ought always to be a priority for God's people. But instead, the narrative records the brutality of the battle. If we love our neighbors as ourselves, let us use the best means possible to advance the principle of peace with all men and look to that perfect day when "they shall beat their swords into plowshares, and their spears into pruning-hooks" (Isa. 2:4).**

Chapter 3: *David grows stronger against the house of Saul, leading to Abner's defection to David and then his vengeful death by Joab.*

3:1 *waxed stronger . . . waxed weaker.* Literally, David "was walking and strong," and the house of Saul "was walking and powerless," a Hebrew idiom meaning "increasing in strength," on the one side, and increasing in weakness on the other.

3:8 *very wroth.* Exceedingly angry.

3:10 *To translate.* Literally, "to cause to pass over" or "to transfer." *from Dan even to Beer-sheba.* The extreme northern city and the extreme southern city are a means of designating the entire country.

3:12 *Make thy league with me.* Literally, "cut your covenant with me," referring to a mutually binding agreement between them (vv. 13,21).

3:13 *require.* Literally, "ask."

3:20 *twenty men.* Most likely representatives of all Israel. *a feast.* Most likely connected to the sealing of the covenant between them, an evidence of reconciliation between the

king, that they may make a league with thee, and that thou mayest reign over all that thine heart desireth. And David sent Abner away; and he went in peace.
22 ¶ And, behold, the servants of David and Joab came from *pursuing* a troop, and brought in a great spoil with them: but Abner *was* not with David in Hebron; for he had sent him away, and he was gone in peace.
23 When Joab and all the host that *was* with him were come, they told Joab, saying, Abner the son of Ner came to the king, and he hath sent him away, and he is gone in peace.
24 Then Joab came to the king, and said, What hast thou done? behold, Abner came unto thee; why *is* it *that* thou hast sent him away, and he is quite gone?
25 Thou knowest Abner the son of Ner, that he came to deceive thee, and to know thy going out and thy coming in, and to know all that thou doest.
26 And when Joab was come out from David, he sent messengers after Abner, which brought him again from the well of Sirah: but David knew *it* not.
27 And when Abner was returned to Hebron, Joab took him aside in the gate to speak with him quietly, and smote him there under the fifth *rib*, that he died, for the blood of Asahel his brother.
28 ¶ And afterward when David heard *it*, he said, I and my kingdom *are* guiltless before the LORD for ever from the blood of Abner the son of Ner:
29 Let it rest on the head of Joab, and on all his father's house; and let there not fail from the house of Joab one that hath an issue, or that is a leper, or that leaneth on a staff, or that falleth on the sword, or that lacketh bread.
30 So Joab and Abishai his brother slew Abner, because he had slain their brother Asahel at Gibeon in the battle.
31 ¶ And David said to Joab, and to all the people that *were* with him, Rend your clothes, and gird you with sackcloth, and mourn before Abner. And king David *himself* followed the bier.
32 And they buried Abner in Hebron: and the king lifted up his voice, and wept at the grave of Abner; and all the people wept.
33 And the king lamented over Abner, and said, Died Abner as a fool dieth?
34 Thy hands *were* not bound, nor thy feet put into fetters: as a man falleth before wicked men, *so* fellest thou. And all the people wept again over him.
35 And when all the people came to cause David to eat meat while it was yet day, David sware, saying, So do God to me, and more also, if I taste bread, or ought else, till the sun be down.
36 And all the people took notice *of it*, and it pleased them: as whatsoever the king did pleased all the people.
37 For all the people and all Israel understood that day that it was not of the king to slay Abner the son of Ner.
38 And the king said unto his servants, Know ye not that there is a prince and a great man fallen this day in Israel?
39 And I *am* this day weak, though anointed king; and these men the sons of Zeruiah *be* too

previously hostile parties (Gen. 26:30; 31:54; Ps. 41:9).

3:24 *is quite gone.* Literally, "went walking," suggesting that he kept on walking further and further away.

3:26 *the well of Sirah.* Josephus locates this about two and a half miles from Hebron; Abner had not gone as far as Joab thought.

3:27 *quietly.* In tranquility or peaceably. *under the fifth rib.* In the abdomen.

3:28 *the blood.* The Hebrew is plural, referring to blood shedding or blood guiltiness.

3:29 *hath an issue.* Refers to some sort of bodily discharge. *leper.* Refers to some sort of skin disorder or disease. *leaneth on a staff.* Literally, "takes hold of a spindle-whorl," regarded as the work of a woman (Prov. 31:19), hence perhaps referring to a weak or effeminate person.

3:31 *Rend . . . gird.* Tearing clothes and putting on sackcloth were common gestures associated with grief. *bier.* A portable framework holding a coffin; the Hebrew is simply "bed" or "couch."

3:34 *Thy hands were not bound.* He was unsuspecting and taken off guard.

3:35 *meat.* Food of any kind.

3:38 *prince.* A leader, but not necessarily royalty.

3:39 *Weak.* Tender or sensitive.

Thoughts for Personal/Family Worship: Chapter 3

1. It was God's purpose for David to reign over Israel. Divine providence assured that the divine will would happen. As God is able to turn the heart of kings (Prov. 21:1), so He turned the heart of Abner, the chief leader in Saul's house, to become a principal agent in uniting the nation under David. Regardless of Abner's motives, selfish or otherwise, God used him to accomplish the divine will. We can be confident that God's power to control circumstances and people has never diminished. Thus, as we pray for God's will to be done and for His kingdom to come, we can be sure that nothing can ultimately prevent either from occurring.

2. Vengeance belongs to the Lord (Heb. 10:30). To presume to take upon oneself a work that belongs to God is always going to have serious consequences. Joab's treacherous murder of Abner is a tragic illustration. Abner had indeed killed Joab's brother, but it was in battle and not a surprising casualty of war. Joab's murder was calculated, hateful, and under the guise of peace. David recognized the cold-blooded nature of the crime and pronounced a curse on Joab and his family. In all likelihood there are going to be times when we will be wronged by others, and our natural impulse will be to get even. We should learn to leave with the Lord what belongs to Him and not take matters into our own hands. Indeed, Christ teaches us that when we suffer personal wrong we are to turn the other cheek (Matt. 5:39).

hard for me: the LORD shall reward the doer of
evil according to his wickedness.

CHAPTER 4

AND when Saul's son heard that Abner was dead
in Hebron, his hands were feeble, and all the Isra-
elites were troubled.
2 And Saul's son had two men *that were* captains
of bands: the name of the one *was* Baanah, and the
name of the other Rechab, the sons of Rimmon
a Beerothite, of the children of Benjamin: (for
Beeroth also was reckoned to Benjamin:
3 And the Beerothites fled to Gittaim, and were
sojourners there until this day.)
4 And Jonathan, Saul's son, had a son *that was*
lame of *his* feet. He was five years old when the
tidings came of Saul and Jonathan out of Jezreel,
and his nurse took him up, and fled: and it came
to pass, as she made haste to flee, that he fell, and
became lame. And his name *was* Mephibosheth.
5 And the sons of Rimmon the Beerothite,
Rechab and Baanah, went, and came about the
heat of the day to the house of Ish-bosheth, who
lay on a bed at noon.
6 And they came thither into the midst of the
house, *as though* they would have fetched wheat;
and they smote him under the fifth *rib*: and
Rechab and Baanah his brother escaped.
7 For when they came into the house, he lay on
his bed in his bedchamber, and they smote him,
and slew him, and beheaded him, and took his
head, and gat them away through the plain all
night.
8 And they brought the head of Ish-bosheth unto
David to Hebron, and said to the king, Behold the
head of Ish-bosheth the son of Saul thine enemy,
which sought thy life; and the LORD hath avenged
my lord the king this day of Saul, and of his seed.
9 ¶ And David answered Rechab and Baanah
his brother, the sons of Rimmon the Beerothite,
and said unto them, *As* the LORD liveth, who hath
redeemed my soul out of all adversity,
10 When one told me, saying, Behold, Saul is
dead, thinking to have brought good tidings, I
took hold of him, and slew him in Ziklag, who
thought that I would have given him a reward for
his tidings:
11 How much more, when wicked men have slain
a righteous person in his own house upon his
bed? shall I not therefore now require his blood
of your hand, and take you away from the earth?
12 And David commanded his young men, and
they slew them, and cut off their hands and their
feet, and hanged *them* up over the pool in He-
bron. But they took the head of Ish-bosheth, and
buried *it* in the sepulchre of Abner in Hebron.

CHAPTER 5

THEN came all the tribes of Israel to David unto
Hebron, and spake, saying, Behold, we *are* thy
bone and thy flesh.
2 Also in time past, when Saul was king over us,
thou wast he that leddest out and broughtest in
Israel: and the LORD said to thee, Thou shalt feed
my people Israel, and thou shalt be a captain over
Israel.
3 So all the elders of Israel came to the king to
Hebron; and king David made a league with them
in Hebron before the LORD: and they anointed
David king over Israel.

Chapter 4: *Ish-bosheth is murdered, and David executes justice on his assassins.*

4:4 *Mephibosheth*. Also called Merib-baal (1 Chron. 8:34), meaning "antagonist of Baal," similar to Gideon's being called Jerubbaal (Judg. 6:32) because he contended against Baal (on the substitution of *bosheth* for *baal*, see note at 2 Sam. 2:8). This was Jonathan's son, soon to be the last survivor of Saul's house.

4:6 *under the fifth rib*. In the stomach.

4:7 *gat them away through the plain*. Literally, "went the way of the desert plain."

4:10 *When one told me*. See 1:2.

4:11 *take you away from the earth*. A phrase used of removing the guilt of murder from the land (Deut. 19:13,19). The guilt of murder contaminated the whole land until removed by the execution of the murderer (Num. 35:33).

4:12 *cut off their hands and their feet*. Popular custom of warning others by exposing the heads and limbs of traitors on the gates of the city.

Thoughts for Personal/Family Worship: Chapter 4

Ish-bosheth was sleeping when he should have been vigilant and on guard. While he slumbered, the enemy came in unawares, and he was slain in his sleep. It is only common sense to stay awake and watchful in the face of danger. But this is an important strategy for spiritual life as well. First Peter 5:8 says, "Be sober, be vigilant; because your adversary the devil, as a roaring lion, walketh about, seeking whom he may devour." Christ's words to His sleepy disciples are also to the point: "Watch and pray, that ye enter not into temptation: the spirit indeed is willing, but the flesh is weak" (Matt. 26:41). How can Christians stay vigilant in the spiritual battle?

THE TRIUMPHANT REIGN OF DAVID OVER ALL ISRAEL (2 SAM. 5:1—10:19)

Chapter 5: *David is anointed king over Israel, establishes Jerusalem as the capital, and engages the Philistines in battle.*

The Establishment of David's Kingdom (2 Sam. 5:1–25)

5:2 *feed*. Shepherd. The king as shepherd was a common image of sovereign rule throughout the Old Testament, as well as in the ancient near-eastern world (7:7; Num. 27:17; 1 Kings 22:17; Ps. 78:71–72; Isa. 44:28; 56:11; Jer. 2:8; 23:1–6; Ezek. 34), and thus also a title for the Lord (Gen. 48:15; 49:24; Pss. 23:1; 28:9; 80:1; Eccl. 12:11; Isa. 40:11; Ezek. 34:15; Mic. 5:4; John 10).

5:3 *all the elders of Israel*. The representative delegates from every tribe. *made a league*. Literally, "cut a covenant," the

4 ¶ David *was* thirty years old when he began to reign, *and* he reigned forty years.

5 In Hebron he reigned over Judah seven years and six months: and in Jerusalem he reigned thirty and three years over all Israel and Judah.

6 ¶ And the king and his men went to Jerusalem unto the Jebusites, the inhabitants of the land: which spake unto David, saying, Except thou take away the blind and the lame, thou shalt not come in hither: thinking, David cannot come in hither.

7 Nevertheless David took the strong hold of Zion: the same *is* the city of David.

8 And David said on that day, Whosoever getteth up to the gutter, and smiteth the Jebusites, and the lame and the blind, *that are* hated of David's soul, *he shall be chief and captain.* Wherefore they said, The blind and the lame shall not come into the house.

9 So David dwelt in the fort, and called it the city of David. And David built round about from Millo and inward.

10 And David went on, and grew great, and the LORD God of hosts *was* with him.

11 ¶ And Hiram king of Tyre sent messengers to David, and cedar trees, and carpenters, and masons: and they built David an house.

12 And David perceived that the LORD had established him king over Israel, and that he had exalted his kingdom for his people Israel's sake.

13 ¶ And David took *him* more concubines and wives out of Jerusalem, after he was come from Hebron: and there were yet sons and daughters born to David.

14 And these *be* the names of those that were born unto him in Jerusalem; Shammua, and Shobab, and Nathan, and Solomon,

15 Ibhar also, and Elishua, and Nepheg, and Japhia,

16 And Elishama, and Eliada, and Eliphalet.

17 ¶ But when the Philistines heard that they had anointed David king over Israel, all the Philistines came up to seek David; and David heard *of it*, and went down to the hold.

18 The Philistines also came and spread themselves in the valley of Rephaim.

19 And David enquired of the LORD, saying, Shall I go up to the Philistines? wilt thou deliver them into mine hand? And the LORD said unto David, Go up: for I will doubtless deliver the Philistines into thine hand.

20 And David came to Baal-perazim, and David smote them there, and said, The LORD hath broken forth upon mine enemies before me, as the breach of waters. Therefore he called the name of that place Baal-perazim.

21 And there they left their images, and David and his men burned them.

22 ¶ And the Philistines came up yet again, and spread themselves in the valley of Rephaim.

23 And when David enquired of the LORD, he said, Thou shalt not go up; *but* fetch a compass behind them, and come upon them over against the mulberry trees.

24 And let it be, when thou hearest the sound of a going in the tops of the mulberry trees, that then thou shalt bestir thyself: for then shall the LORD go out before thee, to smite the host of the Philistines.

25 And David did so, as the LORD had commanded him; and smote the Philistines from Geba until thou come to Gazer.

CHAPTER 6

AGAIN, David gathered together all *the* chosen *men* of Israel, thirty thousand.

2 And David arose, and went with all the people

common idiom for ratifying the covenant terms.

5:8 *gutter.* The Hebrew is uncertain; some sort of a canal, conduit, pipe, or spout.

5:9 *fort.* Mountain stronghold. *Millo.* Literally, a "filling," a terrace-like structure.

5:11 *Hiram.* Later, Solomon's ally (1 Kings 5:15; 2 Chron. 2:2).

5:14 *Shammua.* A summary but not chronological statement since there is reference to the sons born to Bath-sheba (chronologically after ch. 12). See also 1 Chron. 3:5.

5:17 *to the hold.* A fortified rallying point or stronghold.

5:20 *Baal-perazim.* Translated "possessor of breaches," probably between two strongholds.

5:21 *And there they left their images.* History tells us that these were turtle-like idols that were taken into battle with the army.

5:23 *fetch a compass.* Get behind the enemy.

5:24 *bestir thyself.* The Hebrew means "to pay attention" or "to act decisively."

Thoughts for Personal/Family Worship: Chapter 5

1. **One of the most important statements in this chapter is verse 19, "And David enquired of the LORD." He was the king of a great realm, but David felt that even on a throne he needed the Lord's counsel. David was not satisfied without something higher and greater than himself. There is no status in life beyond the necessity of prayer. The day will come when prayer gives way to only praise. But in this world no one can rise above their circumstances. No one can escape the many needs to be filled, sins to be forgiven, and tears to be wiped away. We need to inquire of the Lord. There is nothing so small that He does not know, care for, and control. Do you inquire of the Lord as you should? How can you grow in your prayer life?**
2. **God leads His people in different ways, and we must learn to be sensitive and open to Him. It was just the sound of rustling leaves that was David's sign to move against the enemy—something very ordinary and very subtle. Yet having prayed for God to lead, he was paying attention to the divine instruction. Too often in seeking God's will we try to set the terms or devise scenarios in which we challenge the Lord to act in the most obvious of ways (fleece after fleece). Sometimes He does. But more often it is just the "whisper" of His Spirit through**

that *were* with him from Baale of Judah, to bring
up from thence the ark of God, whose name
is called by the name of the LORD of hosts that
dwelleth *between* the cherubims.
3 And they set the ark of God upon a new cart,
and brought it out of the house of Abinadab that
was in Gibeah: and Uzzah and Ahio, the sons of
Abinadab, drave the new cart.
4 And they brought it out of the house of Abin-
adab which *was* at Gibeah, accompanying the ark
of God: and Ahio went before the ark.
5 And David and all the house of Israel played
before the LORD on all manner of *instruments*
made of fir wood, even on harps, and on psalteries,
and on timbrels, and on cornets, and on cymbals.
6 ¶ And when they came to Nachon's threshing-
floor, Uzzah put forth *his hand* to the ark of God,
and took hold of it; for the oxen shook *it*.
7 And the anger of the LORD was kindled against
Uzzah; and God smote him there for *his* error;
and there he died by the ark of God.
8 And David was displeased, because the LORD
had made a breach upon Uzzah: and he called the
name of the place Perez-uzzah to this day.
9 And David was afraid of the LORD that day, and
said, How shall the ark of the LORD come to me?
10 So David would not remove the ark of the
LORD unto him into the city of David: but David
carried it aside into the house of Obed-edom the
Gittite.
11 And the ark of the LORD continued in the
house of Obed-edom the Gittite three months:
and the LORD blessed Obed-edom, and all his
household.
12 ¶ And it was told king David, saying, The
LORD hath blessed the house of Obed-edom, and
all that *pertaineth* unto him, because of the ark of
God. So David went and brought up the ark of
God from the house of Obed-edom into the city
of David with gladness.
13 And it was *so*, that when they that bare the ark
of the LORD had gone six paces, he sacrificed oxen
and fatlings.
14 And David danced before the LORD with all
his might; and David *was* girded with a linen
ephod.
15 So David and all the house of Israel brought
up the ark of the LORD with shouting, and with
the sound of the trumpet.
16 And as the ark of the LORD came into the city
of David, Michal Saul's daughter looked through
a window, and saw king David leaping and
dancing before the LORD; and she despised him
in her heart.
17 ¶ And they brought in the ark of the LORD, and
set it in his place, in the midst of the tabernacle
that David had pitched for it: and David offered
burnt offerings and peace offerings before the
LORD.
18 And as soon as David had made an end of
offering burnt offerings and peace offerings, he
blessed the people in the name of the LORD of
hosts.
19 And he dealt among all the people, *even*

His Word that gives the answer we need. The key is to fear Him so that He gives us His counsel (Ps. 25:14).

Chapter 6: *Transporting the ark contrary to God's prescription leads to tragedy, but doing so according to God's way leads to rejoicing.*

The Bringing of the Ark of the Covenant to Jerusalem (2 Sam. 6:1–23)

6:2 *Baale.* More commonly, Kirjath-jearim, meaning "city of woods" (Josh. 15:9; 1 Sam. 7:1; also Ps. 132:6, where the statement "fields of the wood" suggests the same location). *the LORD of hosts. Jehovah* of armies, declaring God's power and authority; the Commander-in-Chief. *between the cherubims.* See Ex. 25:22; Ps. 80:1. The cherubim are very often associated with God's presence as the guardians of His holiness (see the living creatures of Ezek. 1).

6:3 *they set the ark.* Literally, "they loaded the ark or made it ride." *drave.* Drove. Transporting the ark in this way violated God's directive (Ex. 25:12–14; Num. 4:4–15), which threatened the death penalty for touching any holy thing.

6:5 *played.* Their jubilant celebration before the Lord. That v. 21 and 1 Chron. 15:29 use the same word to describe David's behavior when the ark was retrieved properly suggests that no carelessness or irreverence was intended. Their celebration was sincere and genuine but biblically unfounded. *harps . . . cymbals.* Different sorts of instruments, the first two being some sort of stringed instruments and the last three some sort of percussion instruments.

6:6 *the oxen shook it.* The Hebrew term means "to let fall" or "to drop," referring either to the oxen stumbling (causing the ark to totter) or perhaps to becoming loose from their yoke (leaving the ark on a runaway wagon). Something happened to cause Uzzah to attempt to stabilize the ark.

6:7 *his error.* The Hebrew occurs only here and has the idea of irreverence. No one was to even look at the ark without punishment, let alone touch it (Num. 4:15,16,20).

6:8 *And David was displeased.* Literally, "it was hot to David." The same word used for the Lord's anger (v. 7). *made a breach.* Literally, "made an outburst or broke out violently." *Perez-uzzah* means "the outburst of Uzzah."

6:10 *Obed-edom.* A Levite (1 Chron. 15:17–18; 26:4–8). *the Gittite.* A reference to where he was from.

6:12 *gladness.* Jubilation and joy.

6:13 *sacrificed.* Offered in thanksgiving and praise. Six steps were sufficient to convince David that God was pleased when worship conformed to His word.

6:14 *David danced.* This was a ceremonial dancing and not to be equated with the recreational dancing in our modern times. *girded with a linen ephod.* He buckled a cape over his shoulders.

6:17 *tabernacle.* Not the official tabernacle, but a temporary tent structure erected to house the ark. *David offered burnt offerings.* This does not imply that David himself offered the sacrifices; rather, as the king he ordered the priests to do so.

6:19 *dealt.* Divided or allotted. *flagon of wine.* The Hebrew refers to "a raisin cake."

among the whole multitude of Israel, as well to
the women as men, to every one a cake of bread,
and a good piece *of flesh*, and a flagon *of wine*. So
all the people departed every one to his house.
20 ¶ Then David returned to bless his house-
hold. And Michal the daughter of Saul came out
to meet David, and said, How glorious was the
king of Israel to day, who uncovered himself to
day in the eyes of the handmaids of his servants,
as one of the vain fellows shamelessly uncovereth
himself!
21 And David said unto Michal, *It was* before
the LORD, which chose me before thy father, and
before all his house, to appoint me ruler over the
people of the LORD, over Israel: therefore will I
play before the LORD.
22 And I will yet be more vile than thus, and will
be base in mine own sight: and of the maidser-
vants which thou hast spoken of, of them shall I
be had in honour.
23 Therefore Michal the daughter of Saul had no
child unto the day of her death.

CHAPTER 7

AND it came to pass, when the king sat in his
house, and the LORD had given him rest round
about from all his enemies;
2 That the king said unto Nathan the prophet,
See now, I dwell in an house of cedar, but the ark
of God dwelleth within curtains.
3 And Nathan said to the king, Go, do all that *is* in
thine heart; for the LORD *is* with thee.
4 ¶ And it came to pass that night, that the word
of the LORD came unto Nathan, saying,
5 Go and tell my servant David, Thus saith the
LORD, Shalt thou build me an house for me to
dwell in?
6 Whereas I have not dwelt in *any* house since the
time that I brought up the children of Israel out
of Egypt, even to this day, but have walked in a
tent and in a tabernacle.
7 In all *the places* wherein I have walked with all
the children of Israel spake I a word with any of
the tribes of Israel, whom I commanded to feed
my people Israel, saying, Why build ye not me an
house of cedar?
8 Now therefore so shalt thou say unto my
servant David, Thus saith the LORD of hosts, I
took thee from the sheepcote, from following the
sheep, to be ruler over my people, over Israel:
9 And I was with thee whithersoever thou went-
est, and have cut off all thine enemies out of thy
sight, and have made thee a great name, like unto
the name of the great *men* that *are* in the earth.
10 Moreover I will appoint a place for my people
Israel, and will plant them, that they may dwell in
a place of their own, and move no more; neither
shall the children of wickedness afflict them any
more, as beforetime,
11 And as since the time that I commanded
judges *to be* over my people Israel, and have

6:20 *uncovered himself to day.* In the sense of removing the royal garments, making him appear as a commoner. *vain fellows.* Worthless ones, the rabble.
6:22 *will yet be more vile.* Demean myself even more or be more lightly esteemed. *base.* Of little value or of low standing. David was gladly humbled before the Lord in order to magnify God and the goodness of His grace.

Thoughts for Personal/Family Worship: Chapter 6

1. **David's desire for the ark expressed his desire for the manifest presence of God. This man after God's own heart purposed to put the ark of the Lord in the place of preeminence it deserved. He had nothing but the glory of the Lord in mind. But tragically, he was taken away with the fervency of his zeal. His desire was good and his motives pure, but he displeased the Lord he sought to honor. It is not sufficient to claim a worthy purpose without conforming as well to the clear mandates of God's Word. He adopted the practice of the pagans in transporting the ark (1 Sam. 6) in violation of the precise method that God had prescribed. Methods of worship do matter, and we must avoid adopting or adapting the practices of the world for use in sacred worship. There are many Christians who desire the right things but are lax in the mode of practice. Not only is God the sole object of worship, but He has revealed the acceptable way of worshiping.**
2. **The ark was the ultimate symbol in the Old Testament for God's presence. This narrative highlights four important lessons about experiencing God's presence. First, it is something to be understood. The ark declares God's sovereignty, holiness, righteousness, grace, and mercy, all of which are realized in Christ (see notes at Ex. 25:10–22). Second, it is something to be desired. David's desire was intensified by the ark's long absence (1 Sam. 7:1–2). The absence of God's presence should be intolerable to us. Third, it is something to be feared. This was learned the hard way in the death of Uzzah. Not even the most godly dare become familiar with holy things by treating them as common. Fourth, it is something to be enjoyed. The house of Obed-edom experienced real and obvious blessing, which motivated David to enjoy the blessing for himself. Enjoying God is worth doing things the right way. When David brought up the ark according to God's way, he was overwhelmed with joy and humble worship. How should these principles shape the way that we approach God in worship?**

Chapter 7: *The Lord rejects David's plan to build a house for the ark and gives a solemn promise to build a house for David.*

The Lord's Covenant with David (2 Sam. 7:1–29)

7:1 *rest.* Cessation of hostility, an experience of peace and quiet.
7:2 *within curtains.* In the middle of the tent.
7:3 A prophet never has authority to speak without a word from the Lord.
7:8 *sheepcote.* Grazing place or pen for sheep.
7:11 *house.* Dynasty.

caused thee to rest from all thine enemies. Also the LORD telleth thee that he will make thee an house.

12 ¶ And when thy days be fulfilled, and thou shalt sleep with thy fathers, I will set up thy seed after thee, which shall proceed out of thy bowels, and I will establish his kingdom.

13 He shall build an house for my name, and I will stablish the throne of his kingdom for ever.

14 I will be his father, and he shall be my son. If he commit iniquity, I will chasten him with the rod of men, and with the stripes of the children of men:

15 But my mercy shall not depart away from him, as I took *it* from Saul, whom I put away before thee.

16 And thine house and thy kingdom shall be established for ever before thee: thy throne shall be established for ever.

17 According to all these words, and according to all this vision, so did Nathan speak unto David.

18 ¶ Then went king David in, and sat before the LORD, and he said, Who *am* I, O Lord GOD? and what *is* my house, that thou hast brought me hitherto?

19 And this was yet a small thing in thy sight, O Lord GOD; but thou hast spoken also of thy servant's house for a great while to come. And *is* this the manner of man, O Lord GOD?

20 And what can David say more unto thee? for thou, Lord GOD, knowest thy servant.

21 For thy word's sake, and according to thine own heart, hast thou done all these great things, to make thy servant know *them*.

22 Wherefore thou art great, O LORD God: for *there is* none like thee, neither *is there any* God beside thee, according to all that we have heard with our ears.

23 And what one nation in the earth *is* like thy people, *even* like Israel, whom God went to redeem for a people to himself, and to make him a name, and to do for you great things and terrible, for thy land, before thy people, which thou redeemedst to thee from Egypt, *from* the nations and their gods?

24 For thou hast confirmed to thyself thy people Israel *to be* a people unto thee for ever: and thou, LORD, art become their God.

25 And now, O LORD God, the word that thou hast spoken concerning thy servant, and concerning his house, establish *it* for ever, and do as thou hast said.

26 And let thy name be magnified for ever, saying, The LORD of hosts *is* the God over Israel: and let the house of thy servant David be established before thee.

27 For thou, O LORD of hosts, God of Israel, hast revealed to thy servant, saying, I will build thee an house: therefore hath thy servant found in his heart to pray this prayer unto thee.

28 And now, O Lord GOD, thou *art* that God, and thy words be true, and thou hast promised this goodness unto thy servant:

7:12–17 The Davidic covenant was a major advance in God's redemptive message regarding the Messiah (Gen. 49:10). Note the divine initiative (repeated *I will*), the unique relationship (*father* and *son*), the everlasting *throne* and *kingdom*, and the unconditional guarantee unlike that given to Saul (Ps. 89:29–37).

7:13 *He shall build an house for my name.* Solomon's temple was the first stage of this house, but the promise was ultimately fulfilled in Christ, in whom the fullness of deity dwells bodily (John 2:19–22; Col. 2:9) and in His church in union with Him (1 Cor. 3:16; Eph. 2:21–22). *and I will stablish the throne of his kingdom for ever.* Uniquely applies to Christ (Isa. 9:7; Luke 1:31–32).

7:14 *I will be his father, and he shall be my son.* A legal relationship applicable to every Davidic king but uniquely descriptive of Christ, both as the eternal Son of God and the appointed Son of Man. *If he commit iniquity, I will chasten.* Literally, "when he goes astray, I will correct or rebuke." David's lesser sons will certainly sin, indeed in far worse ways than Saul, and they will be held accountable.

7:15 *my mercy shall not depart.* My covenant loyalty will not turn aside. The sins of the lesser sons could not jeopardize the coming of David's greater son. The covenant promise is unconditional because the ideal seed or offspring of David is Christ.

7:18–19 David realized that God had a greater purpose beyond his family and time. *manner of man.* Literally, "instruction or revelation for mankind." Part of a declarative statement revealing David's understanding of the worldwide implications of the messianic promise.

7:20 *thy servant.* The Lord had addressed King David as "my servant" (v. 8), and David repeatedly echoes these words (ten times in vv. 19–29) to express his humble commitment to do God's will for His glory.

7:22 *neither is there any God beside thee.* God's covenant and messianic kingdom reveal His unique greatness, moving people to praise Him.

7:23 *thy people.* God's covenant with David advances the fulfillment of His covenant with *Israel* through Moses. *terrible.* Fearful or awe-inspiring.

7:25 *And now, O LORD God.* Having learned God's will, he prays for God's will to be done. God's Word and prayer are always linked.

Thoughts for Personal/Family Worship: Chapter 7

1. **Although God's covenant promise to David narrowed the identity of the Messiah to the family of David, David realized that the significance of the promise went far beyond the concerns of his family and little kingdom. He made a profound statement reflecting his faith and insight into worldwide significance: "this is the revelation for humanity." David saw that his Seed was going to be a source of blessing for the world, just as in the promise to Abraham hundreds of years earlier (Gen. 12:3; 22:18). How does the gospel make the covenant with David good news for us today?**
2. **David's prayer following the promise provides a wonderful pattern for us as we pray. As you work through the prayer, note the recognition of God's free grace (v. 21), greatness (v. 22), goodness (v. 23), and gracious covenant (v. 24). Our prayers likewise should be full of praises for these things. Note also the desire for God's**

THE SON OF DAVID

Both the Old and New Testaments frequently refer to the Son of David (see 2 Sam. 7:12; Matt. 22:41–46; Mark 10:47). Of course, David had many sons, but only one of them, Solomon, succeeded him on the throne (1 Kings 1:32–34). Yet when the Bible speaks of "the son of David" it often means someone far greater than Solomon or any other mere human descendant of David. Simply put, the term "Son of David" became a term for the Messiah, who has other titles as well, such as Son of God, Servant of the Lord, and Anointed One. We know from the New Testament that Christ is the true Son of David (Matt. 1:1; Rev. 22:16).

What is the significance of Christ being the Son of David? *First*, this means that God is faithful to His promises. God promised that David's seed, that is, his dynasty, "would be established forever before thee; thy throne shall be established for ever" (2 Sam. 7:16). Though many of David's descendants, such as Rehoboam, Asa, Hezekiah, and Josiah, sat on the throne of Judah, after the exile into Babylon none of David's physical descendants reigned. Yet in Jesus Christ God was faithful to this promise to David. God told Mary, the mother of Jesus, regarding the Son who would be born to her, "He shall be great, and shall be called the Son of the Highest: and the Lord God shall give unto him the throne of his father David: and he shall reign over the house of Jacob for ever; and of his kingdom there shall be no end" (Luke 1:33).

Second, it means that Christ took upon Himself a human nature through the line of David. Paul makes this point in Romans 1:3: "Concerning his Son Jesus Christ our Lord, which was made of the seed of David according to the flesh." Christ did not come just as true God but also as true man. He was content to take upon Himself a human nature, and specifically one from the line of David.

Third, it means that Christ was like David in many ways, though unlike him in other ways. Sons are often like their fathers, and David's life and work prefigured Christ's life and ministry in some ways. Both were hounded by their enemies. Both gave themselves to the service of God. Both were known for their kindness to people such as Mephibosheth (2 Sam. 9), Bartimaeus (Mark 10:48), and the Canaanite woman (Matt. 15:22,28). Of course, Christ was unlike David in many other ways. He was without sin. He was permitted to build the temple of the Lord. His kingship is everlasting. And His death was meritorious.

Fourth, this means that Christ was greater than David. According to Psalm 110:1, David called His own Son "Lord" (cf. Matt. 22:45). He did this because His Son was actually at the same time the Son of God.

Fifth, it means that those engrafted into Christ can be called children of God. If Christ had not become the Son of David, sinners could not have been saved, and neither could they have received the privilege of calling God "Father" and be heirs of God together with Christ, the great Son of David. Psalm 89:26–36 gives the right and privilege of adoption to all those who belong to David's Son. This is confirmed repeatedly in the New Testament (Rom. 8:15–17; Gal. 4:6; 1 John 3:1–3).

Finally, it means that Christ is the great Bridegroom of His church and people. The Song of Solomon speaks of the relationship between Christ and His church under the names of Solomon, the son of David, and the Shulamite. Christ was the ultimate Son of David who wins a bride for Himself, cares for her, nourishes and sustains her, and shows her His beauty and grace forever.

29 Therefore now let it please thee to bless the
house of thy servant, that it may continue for ever
before thee: for thou, O Lord GOD, hast spoken *it*:
and with thy blessing let the house of thy servant
be blessed for ever.

CHAPTER 8

AND after this it came to pass, that David smote
the Philistines, and subdued them: and David
took Metheg-ammah out of the hand of the
Philistines.
2 And he smote Moab, and measured them with a
line, casting them down to the ground; even with
two lines measured he to put to death, and with
one full line to keep alive. And *so* the Moabites
became David's servants, *and* brought gifts.
3 ¶ David smote also Hadadezer, the son of
Rehob, king of Zobah, as he went to recover his
border at the river Euphrates.
4 And David took from him a thousand *chariots*,
and seven hundred horsemen, and twenty
thousand footmen: and David houghed all
the chariot *horses*, but reserved of them *for* an
hundred chariots.
5 And when the Syrians of Damascus came to
succour Hadadezer king of Zobah, David slew of
the Syrians two and twenty thousand men.
6 Then David put garrisons in Syria of Damas-
cus: and the Syrians became servants to David,
and brought gifts. And the LORD preserved David
whithersoever he went.
7 And David took the shields of gold that were
on the servants of Hadadezer, and brought them
to Jerusalem.
8 And from Betah, and from Berothai, cities of
Hadadezer, king David took exceeding much
brass.
9 ¶ When Toi king of Hamath heard that David
had smitten all the host of Hadadezer,
10 Then Toi sent Joram his son unto king David,
to salute him, and to bless him, because he had
fought against Hadadezer, and smitten him: for
Hadadezer had wars with Toi. And *Joram* brought
with him vessels of silver, and vessels of gold, and
vessels of brass:
11 Which also king David did dedicate unto the
LORD, with the silver and gold that he had dedi-
cated of all nations which he subdued;
12 Of Syria, and of Moab, and of the children of
Ammon, and of the Philistines, and of Amalek,
and of the spoil of Hadadezer, son of Rehob, king
of Zobah.
13 And David gat *him* a name when he returned
from smiting of the Syrians in the valley of salt,
being eighteen thousand *men*.
14 ¶ And he put garrisons in Edom; throughout
all Edom put he garrisons, and all they of Edom
became David's servants. And the LORD preserved
David whithersoever he went.
15 And David reigned over all Israel; and David
executed judgment and justice unto all his people.
16 And Joab the son of Zeruiah *was* over the host;
and Jehoshaphat the son of Ahilud *was* recorder;

---

glory (v. 26) and the plea for God's revealed will to be done (vv. 28–29). In the same way we should seek God's honor in all our prayers and turn God's promises into petitions that He would do what He has said.

The Power, Justice, and Mercy of King David (2 Sam. 8:1—10:19)

Chapter 8: *David defeats a host of Israel's enemies and reigns over Israel with justice.*

8:2 *and measured them with a line.* A rope was used to divide the prisoners of war into two groups, one sentenced to death and the other spared. The criterion for the allotment is not specified. *casting them down.* Making them lie down. *brought gifts.* In the sense of tribute payments, a common practice for a vassal state (v. 6).

8:3 *to recover his border.* Literally, "to restore his hand," in the sense of reclaiming possessions.

8:4 *houghed.* Cut the hamstring, making the horses unusable.

8:5 *succour.* Help or assist.

8:8 *brass.* See 1 Chron. 18:8.

8:10 *salute him.* Send greetings by asking about his welfare. *bless him.* In the sense of praising or congratulating him on his victory.

8:11 *dedicate unto the LORD.* He set aside or consecrated the spoils of war for the building of the temple. He did not keep it for himself.

8:13 *gat him a name.* Became famous in the land.

8:15 *David executed judgment and justice.* He demonstrated righteousness and justice in all of his legal decisions and administration—key qualities of a godly king (1 Kings 10:9; Ps. 72:1; Prov. 8:15–20; Isa. 9:7; Jer. 22:15; 23:5; Ezek. 45:9), for they reflect the character of God (Job 37:23; Pss. 33:5; 36:6; 89:14; 99:4; 103:6; Isa. 5:16).

8:16 *recorder.* Secretary, chronicling David's memorial accomplishments (a form of the word "to remember").

8:17 *scribe.* Secretary of state.

8:18 *chief rulers.* The Hebrew calls them priests, for which office *David's sons* would not have qualified. The word can have the sense of chieftain (1 Chron. 18:17).

Thoughts for Personal/Family Worship: Chapter 8

1. **David's subduing one enemy after another is a wonderful picture pointing to the One greater than David, the Lord Jesus. He is the messianic and mediatorial King of His people, who conquers all of His and our enemies. He conquers His people by grace, making them willing in the day of His power (Ps. 110:3). He conquers His enemies with the rod of His strength (110:2). But whether by grace or by rod, He conquers. Those of us who are willing subjects should be careful to pledge to Him our allegiance and to praise Him for His benefits to us. Those who remain rebels should obey the call of the Spirit to honor the Son before it is too late (2:12).**
2. **David's just rule of his people is another pointer to the ideal King. God's decree regarding Messiah's kingdom**

17 And Zadok the son of Ahitub, and Ahimelech
the son of Abiathar, *were* the priests; and Seraiah
was the scribe;
18 And Benaiah the son of Jehoiada *was over* both
the Cherethites and the Pelethites; and David's
sons were chief rulers.

CHAPTER 9

AND David said, Is there yet any that is left of the
house of Saul, that I may shew him kindness for
Jonathan's sake?
2 And *there was* of the house of Saul a servant
whose name *was* Ziba. And when they had called
him unto David, the king said unto him, *Art* thou
Ziba? And he said, Thy servant *is he*.
3 And the king said, *Is* there not yet any of the
house of Saul, that I may shew the kindness of
God unto him? And Ziba said unto the king,
Jonathan hath yet a son, *which is* lame on *his* feet.
4 And the king said unto him, Where *is* he? And
Ziba said unto the king, Behold, he *is* in the house
of Machir, the son of Ammiel, in Lo-debar.
5 ¶ Then king David sent, and fetched him out
of the house of Machir, the son of Ammiel, from
Lo-debar.
6 Now when Mephibosheth, the son of Jonathan,
the son of Saul, was come unto David, he fell on
his face, and did reverence. And David said, Me-
phibosheth. And he answered, Behold thy servant!
7 ¶ And David said unto him, Fear not: for I
will surely shew thee kindness for Jonathan thy
father's sake, and will restore thee all the land of
Saul thy father; and thou shalt eat bread at my
table continually.
8 And he bowed himself, and said, What *is* thy
servant, that thou shouldest look upon such a
dead dog as I *am*?
9 ¶ Then the king called to Ziba, Saul's servant,
and said unto him, I have given unto thy master's
son all that pertained to Saul and to all his house.
10 Thou therefore, and thy sons, and thy servants,
shall till the land for him, and thou shalt bring
in *the fruits*, that thy master's son may have food
to eat: but Mephibosheth thy master's son shall
eat bread alway at my table. Now Ziba had fifteen
sons and twenty servants.
11 Then said Ziba unto the king, According to all
that my lord the king hath commanded his ser-
vant, so shall thy servant do. As for Mephibosheth,
said the king, he shall eat at my table, as one of the
king's sons.
12 And Mephibosheth had a young son, whose
name *was* Micha. And all that dwelt in the house
of Ziba *were* servants unto Mephibosheth.
13 So Mephibosheth dwelt in Jerusalem: for he
did eat continually at the king's table; and was
lame on both his feet.

CHAPTER 10

AND it came to pass after this, that the king of
the children of Ammon died, and Hanun his son
reigned in his stead.

---

was "to order it, and to establish it with judgment and with justice" forever (Isa. 9:7). Similarly, Ps. 72 details Messiah's execution of righteous judgments; His rule is ideal (45:6–7; Isa. 11:1–5). None other than Jesus satisfies the inspired job description of kings: "He that ruleth over men must be just, ruling in the fear of God" (2 Sam. 23:3). This should be great comfort to believers. So often it appears that wickedness reigns supreme and that life is filled with inequities. But the King and Judge of all the earth does only right, and justice will prevail (Eccl. 8:12–13). How can this truth strengthen Christians?

Chapter 9: *In keeping covenant with Jonathan, David shows kindness to Mephibosheth, Jonathan's son.*

9:1 *shew him kindness*. Literally, "do with him covenant loyalty" (v. 7). David was moved both by love and by covenant obligation (1 Sam. 20:14–17).
9:3 *lame on his feet*. His nurse had dropped him when he was a child (4:4).
9:6 *Mephibosheth*. On his name, see note at 4:4.
9:10 *till the land . . . at my table*. David made provision for daily sustenance from Mephibosheth's land but reserved a place for him at the royal table at times of special feasting.

Thoughts for Personal/Family Worship: Chapter 9

1. **This narrative is rich in parallels to the gospel that deserve meditation. We are reminded of the love of Jesus, who seeks out, saves, loves, and dwells with poor, ruined, worthless sinners and lays on them great and lasting mercy. David is a picture of the Savior who graciously and mercifully seeks those whom He will save. Mephibosheth is a picture of the sinner. His being lame and living in Lo-debar (no pasture) illustrate the sinner who has no power or resources of his own to remedy his dreadful state of misery. The bountiful provisions picture salvation itself. Being regarded and treated as the king's son and feasting at the royal banquets point to the believer's adoption into God's family and the enjoyment of all the benefits of grace as He brings poor, vile sinners into His house of wine (Song 2:4).**
2. **The episode also teaches very practical lessons. As David remembered his promise to Jonathan, so the child of God should always keep his word to others. Let it never be said that the men of this world keep their word better than the believer. The example of David here is worthy of imitation. The kindness that David showed to Mephibosheth also teaches us to show kindness to those who are in need. All true kindness shown by a child of God is Christlike. "Let us do good unto all men, but especially unto them who are of the household of faith" (Gal. 6:10).**

Chapter 10: *David triumphs over more enemies and executes vengeance against those who had humiliated his servants.*

10:1 *king of the children of Ammon*. Nahash (v. 2).

2 Then said David, I will shew kindness unto
Hanun the son of Nahash, as his father shewed
kindness unto me. And David sent to comfort
him by the hand of his servants for his father.
And David's servants came into the land of the
children of Ammon.
3 And the princes of the children of Ammon said
unto Hanun their lord, Thinkest thou that David
doth honour thy father, that he hath sent com-
forters unto thee? hath not David *rather* sent his
servants unto thee, to search the city, and to spy it
out, and to overthrow it?
4 Wherefore Hanun took David's servants, and
shaved off the one half of their beards, and cut
off their garments in the middle, *even* to their
buttocks, and sent them away.
5 When they told *it* unto David, he sent to meet
them, because the men were greatly ashamed: and
the king said, Tarry at Jericho until your beards be
grown, and *then* return.
6 ¶ And when the children of Ammon saw that
they stank before David, the children of Ammon
sent and hired the Syrians of Beth-rehob, and the
Syrians of Zoba, twenty thousand footmen, and
of king Maacah a thousand men, and of Ish-tob
twelve thousand men.
7 And when David heard of *it*, he sent Joab, and
all the host of the mighty men.
8 And the children of Ammon came out, and put
the battle in array at the entering in of the gate:
and the Syrians of Zoba, and of Rehob, and Ish-
tob, and Maacah, *were* by themselves in the field.
9 When Joab saw that the front of the battle was
against him before and behind, he chose of all
the choice *men* of Israel, and put *them* in array
against the Syrians:
10 And the rest of the people he delivered into
the hand of Abishai his brother, that he might put
them in array against the children of Ammon.
11 And he said, If the Syrians be too strong for
me, then thou shalt help me: but if the children of
Ammon be too strong for thee, then I will come
and help thee.
12 Be of good courage, and let us play the men for
our people, and for the cities of our God: and the
LORD do that which seemeth him good.
13 And Joab drew nigh, and the people that *were*
with him, unto the battle against the Syrians: and
they fled before him.
14 And when the children of Ammon saw that
the Syrians were fled, then fled they also before
Abishai, and entered into the city. So Joab
returned from the children of Ammon, and came
to Jerusalem.
15 ¶ And when the Syrians saw that they were
smitten before Israel, they gathered themselves
together.
16 And Hadarezer sent, and brought out the Syr-
ians that *were* beyond the river: and they came to
Helam; and Shobach the captain of the host of
Hadarezer *went* before them.
17 And when it was told David, he gathered all
Israel together, and passed over Jordan, and came
to Helam. And the Syrians set themselves in array
against David, and fought with him.
18 And the Syrians fled before Israel; and Da-
vid slew *the men of* seven hundred chariots of the
Syrians, and forty thousand horsemen, and smote
Shobach the captain of their host, who died there.
19 And when all the kings *that were* servants
to Hadarezer saw that they were smitten before
Israel, they made peace with Israel, and served

10:2 *shew kindness unto Hanun . . . as his father shewed kindness unto me.* Illustrates the reciprocal nature of covenant loyalty. Most likely *Nahash* had protected David when fleeing from Saul.
10:4 *shaved off the one half of their beards.* Obvious acts of disrespect and humiliation.
10:6 *they stank.* They were hated, or became odious (1 Chron. 19:6). *hired the Syrians.* They were mercenary soldiers, 33,000 in total.
10:8 *put the battle in array.* Lined up in preparation for battle (vv. 10,17).
10:9 *the front of the battle . . . before and behind.* The attack or assault was coming from two directions; there were two front lines.
10:12 *Be of good courage, and let us play the men.* Literally, "be strong and show yourself to be strong." *the LORD do . . . good.* Strong human effort and activity are perfectly compatible with faith in God's sovereignty over the results.
10:13 *drew nigh.* Came near.
10:16 *the river.* The Euphrates.

Thoughts for Personal/Family Worship: Chapter 10

1. **Hanun's rejection of David's kindness is analogous to the way sinners reject the mercy of God in the gospel. So many benefits were offered, but he was blinded to them by his own mind and by those who advised him. In this regard, he is much like the cursed man described in Jer. 17, who listens to his own deceitful heart leading him to depart from God (vv. 5,9) and is like the desert shrub that is insensitive to the good (v. 6). It is the deadness of the heart and the blindness of the eyes caused by sin that keeps man from seeing the beauty and wonder of the gospel. Hanun's repudiation of David's mercy was foolish and resulted in devastating consequences. But even more foolish and more severe are the consequences of rejecting the gospel.**
2. **Although Hanun rejected David, he showed his rejection by humiliating David's servants. Hanun could not get to David, so he took things out on those who represented him. This parallels the treatment believers often receive in this world, which is so hostile to God and grace. It is impossible for the world to get to God, so it demonstrates hatred of God by persecuting the church. But this should not be surprising. We should not marvel if the world hates us (1 John 3:13) because Christ said "if the world hate you, ye know that it hated me before it hated you" (John 15:18). In the end, the son of David will repay the humiliation heaped on his people from the impenitent, unbelieving, and disobedient world.**

them. So the Syrians feared to help the children
of Ammon any more.

CHAPTER 11

AND it came to pass, after the year was expired,
at the time when kings go forth *to battle*, that
David sent Joab, and his servants with him, and
all Israel; and they destroyed the children of
Ammon, and besieged Rabbah. But David tarried
still at Jerusalem.
2 ¶ And it came to pass in an eveningtide, that
David arose from off his bed, and walked upon
the roof of the king's house: and from the roof
he saw a woman washing herself; and the woman
was very beautiful to look upon.
3 And David sent and enquired after the woman.
And *one* said, *Is* not this Bath-sheba, the daughter
of Eliam, the wife of Uriah the Hittite?
4 And David sent messengers, and took her; and
she came in unto him, and he lay with her; for
she was purified from her uncleanness: and she
returned unto her house.
5 And the woman conceived, and sent and told
David, and said, I *am* with child.
6 ¶ And David sent to Joab, *saying*, Send me
Uriah the Hittite. And Joab sent Uriah to David.
7 And when Uriah was come unto him, David
demanded *of him* how Joab did, and how the
people did, and how the war prospered.
8 And David said to Uriah, Go down to thy
house, and wash thy feet. And Uriah departed out
of the king's house, and there followed him a mess
of meat from the king.
9 But Uriah slept at the door of the king's house
with all the servants of his lord, and went not
down to his house.
10 And when they had told David, saying, Uriah
went not down unto his house, David said unto
Uriah, Camest thou not from *thy* journey? why
then didst thou not go down unto thine house?
11 And Uriah said unto David, The ark, and Is-
rael, and Judah, abide in tents; and my lord Joab,
and the servants of my lord, are encamped in the
open fields; shall I then go into mine house, to eat
and to drink, and to lie with my wife? *as* thou liv-
est, and *as* thy soul liveth, I will not do this thing.
12 And David said to Uriah, Tarry here to day
also, and to morrow I will let thee depart. So Uriah
abode in Jerusalem that day, and the morrow.
13 And when David had called him, he did eat
and drink before him; and he made him drunk:
and at even he went out to lie on his bed with the
servants of his lord, but went not down to his
house.
14 ¶ And it came to pass in the morning, that
David wrote a letter to Joab, and sent *it* by the
hand of Uriah.
15 And he wrote in the letter, saying, Set ye Uriah
in the forefront of the hottest battle, and retire ye
from him, that he may be smitten, and die.
16 And it came to pass, when Joab observed the
city, that he assigned Uriah unto a place where he
knew that valiant men *were*.
17 And the men of the city went out, and fought
with Joab: and there fell *some* of the people of the
servants of David; and Uriah the Hittite died also.
18 ¶ Then Joab sent and told David all the things
concerning the war;
19 And charged the messenger, saying, When
thou hast made an end of telling the matters of
the war unto the king,
20 And if so be that the king's wrath arise, and he
say unto thee, Wherefore approached ye so nigh
unto the city when ye did fight? knew ye not that
they would shoot from the wall?
21 Who smote Abimelech the son of Jerub-
besheth? did not a woman cast a piece of a mill-
stone upon him from the wall, that he died in
Thebez? why went ye nigh the wall? then say thou,
Thy servant Uriah the Hittite is dead also.
22 ¶ So the messenger went, and came and
shewed David all that Joab had sent him for.
23 And the messenger said unto David, Surely the
men prevailed against us, and came out unto us
into the field, and we were upon them even unto
the entering of the gate.
24 And the shooters shot from off the wall upon
thy servants; and *some* of the king's servants be
dead, and thy servant Uriah the Hittite is dead also.
25 Then David said unto the messenger, Thus
shalt thou say unto Joab, Let not this thing dis-
please thee, for the sword devoureth one as well as
another: make thy battle more strong against the

"Vengeance is mine; I will repay, saith the Lord" (Rom. 12:19). How have you suffered humiliation for Christ?

THE CRIMES AND TROUBLES OF DAVID AND HIS HOUSEHOLD (2 SAM. 11:1—20:26)

David's Adultery, Murder, and Repentance (2 Sam. 11:1—12:31)

Chapter 11: *David commits adultery and attempts to cover up his sin with deception and ultimately with murder.*

11:2 *in an eveningtide.* Toward evening. *upon the roof.* In the architecture of that day, the flat-style roof was the place of entertainment and relaxation.

11:3 *Uriah the Hittite.* One of David's mighty men (23:39).

11:4 *was purified from her uncleanness.* See Lev. 15:18.

11:7 *demanded.* Literally, "asked concerning the welfare of."

11:8 *mess of meat from the king.* Literally, "the portion of the king."

11:11 *shall I then go into mine house.* Uriah's self-control and loyalty are in sharp contrast to David's lust and deception.

11:17 *there fell some of the people.* In trying to kill Uriah, David became a mass murderer.

city, and overthrow it: and encourage thou him.
26 ¶ And when the wife of Uriah heard that
Uriah her husband was dead, she mourned for
her husband.
27 And when the mourning was past, David sent
and fetched her to his house, and she became his
wife, and bare him a son. But the thing that David
had done displeased the LORD.

CHAPTER 12

AND the LORD sent Nathan unto David. And he
came unto him, and said unto him, There were two
men in one city; the one rich, and the other poor.
2 The rich *man* had exceeding many flocks and
herds:
3 But the poor *man* had nothing, save one little
ewe lamb, which he had bought and nourished
up: and it grew up together with him, and with
his children; it did eat of his own meat, and drank
of his own cup, and lay in his bosom, and was
unto him as a daughter.
4 And there came a traveller unto the rich man,
and he spared to take of his own flock and of his
own herd, to dress for the wayfaring man that was
come unto him; but took the poor man's lamb,
and dressed it for the man that was come to him.
5 And David's anger was greatly kindled against
the man; and he said to Nathan, *As* the LORD
liveth, the man that hath done this *thing* shall
surely die:
6 And he shall restore the lamb fourfold, because
he did this thing, and because he had no pity.
7 ¶ And Nathan said to David, Thou *art* the man.
Thus saith the LORD God of Israel, I anointed thee
king over Israel, and I delivered thee out of the
hand of Saul;
8 And I gave thee thy master's house, and thy
master's wives into thy bosom, and gave thee the
house of Israel and of Judah; and if *that had been*
too little, I would moreover have given unto thee
such and such things.
9 Wherefore hast thou despised the command-
ment of the LORD, to do evil in his sight? thou
hast killed Uriah the Hittite with the sword, and
hast taken his wife *to be* thy wife, and hast slain
him with the sword of the children of Ammon.
10 Now therefore the sword shall never depart
from thine house; because thou hast despised me,
and hast taken the wife of Uriah the Hittite to be
thy wife.
11 Thus saith the LORD, Behold, I will raise up
evil against thee out of thine own house, and I
will take thy wives before thine eyes, and give
them unto thy neighbour, and he shall lie with thy
wives in the sight of this sun.
12 For thou didst *it* secretly: but I will do this
thing before all Israel, and before the sun.
13 And David said unto Nathan, I have sinned
against the LORD. And Nathan said unto David,
The LORD also hath put away thy sin; thou shalt
not die.
14 Howbeit, because by this deed thou hast given
great occasion to the enemies of the LORD to blas-
pheme, the child also *that is* born unto thee shall
surely die.
15 ¶ And Nathan departed unto his house. And
the LORD struck the child that Uriah's wife bare

11:27 *displeased the LORD.* Literally, "was evil in the eyes of the Lord."

Thoughts for Personal/Family Worship: Chapter 11

1. Here we see sin in its progression from lust to act. In this case it arose from a casual glance at a beautiful woman. This shows how Eye-Gate, as John Bunyan calls it, is an entrance for sin into Man-Soul. We have a great need to do what Job did, to make a covenant with our eyes (Job 31:1). The eyes are not only a window to the soul but the inlet to many sins. Here we also see sin in its growth. A look led to lusting, lusting to adultery, adultery to lying, and lying to the murder of a valiant soldier. A conscience that is hardening to sin is a dangerous thing. The lusts of the flesh are powerful and deceitful. When we are out of God's plan we cannot expect His protection. If our eyes wander from Him, our hearts and feet will soon follow. Check your armor. Hold tight the sword of the Spirit, waging war against your own flesh. Never stop praying, "And lead us not into temptation, but deliver us from evil" (Matt. 6:13).
2. David created this temptation by neglecting his duty as the Lord's king. As is true of so many other occasions in life, David should have been leading the battle, not relaxing at home. Thomas Watson said, "An idle person is the devil's tennis ball, which he bandies up and down with temptation till at last the ball goes out of play." In many ways the whole Christian life is the time for battle, and there is no discharge in this conflict. The enemy of the soul is constantly on the prowl, looking for places to attack. It is imperative that we do not neglect our duty to be on guard, to be equipped with the armor and arsenal God has provided, and to fight the good fight.

Chapter 12: ***David repents of his sin in response to the prophet, accepts as God's will the death of his child, is comforted by the birth of Solomon, and returns to the place of battle.***

12:3 *meat.* Any kind of food.
12:4 *dress.* Prepare food for eating.
12:11 *evil.* Trouble or calamity. *neighbour.* Companion, comrade, or friend. *in the sight of this sun.* Private sins bring public consequences, either now or on judgment day.
12:13 *I have sinned.* The prophetic word brought David to confession. His conscience had kept him in misery, but confessing sin brought freedom (Ps. 32:1–5). Sin is always a hostile presence in a believer.
12:14 *occasion to the enemies of the LORD to blaspheme.* The sins of believers publically dishonor God in the eyes of the world (Rom. 2:24; Titus 2:5,8,10).
12:16 *besought God.* Sought or pleaded in prayer. *fasted.* David refrained from eating in order to devote himself to uninterrupted prayer.

unto David, and it was very sick.
16 David therefore besought God for the child;
and David fasted, and went in, and lay all night
upon the earth.
17 And the elders of his house arose, *and went* to
him, to raise him up from the earth: but he would
not, neither did he eat bread with them.
18 And it came to pass on the seventh day, that
the child died. And the servants of David feared
to tell him that the child was dead: for they said,
Behold, while the child was yet alive, we spake
unto him, and he would not hearken unto our
voice: how will he then vex himself, if we tell him
that the child is dead?
19 But when David saw that his servants whis-
pered, David perceived that the child was dead:
therefore David said unto his servants, Is the child
dead? And they said, He is dead.
20 Then David arose from the earth, and washed,
and anointed *himself*, and changed his apparel,
and came into the house of the LORD, and wor-
shipped: then he came to his own house; and
when he required, they set bread before him, and
he did eat.
21 Then said his servants unto him, What thing *is*
this that thou hast done? thou didst fast and weep
for the child, *while it was* alive; but when the child
was dead, thou didst rise and eat bread.
22 And he said, While the child was yet alive, I
fasted and wept: for I said, Who can tell *whether*
GOD will be gracious to me, that the child may live?
23 But now he is dead, wherefore should I fast?
can I bring him back again? I shall go to him, but
he shall not return to me.
24 ¶ And David comforted Bath-sheba his wife,
and went in unto her, and lay with her: and she
bare a son, and he called his name Solomon: and
the LORD loved him.
25 And he sent by the hand of Nathan the
prophet; and he called his name Jedidiah, because
of the LORD.
26 ¶ And Joab fought against Rabbah of the
children of Ammon, and took the royal city.
27 And Joab sent messengers to David, and said,
I have fought against Rabbah, and have taken the
city of waters.
28 Now therefore gather the rest of the people to-
gether, and encamp against the city, and take it:
lest I take the city, and it be called after my name.
29 And David gathered all the people together,
and went to Rabbah, and fought against it, and
took it.
30 And he took their king's crown from off his
head, the weight whereof *was* a talent of gold
with the precious stones: and it was *set* on David's
head. And he brought forth the spoil of the city in
great abundance.
31 And he brought forth the people that *were*
therein, and put *them* under saws, and under har-
rows of iron, and under axes of iron, and made
them pass through the brickkiln: and thus did he
unto all the cities of the children of Ammon. So
David and all the people returned unto Jerusalem.

CHAPTER 13

AND it came to pass after this, that Absalom the
son of David had a fair sister, whose name *was*

12:18 *vex himself.* Literally, "do a harmful thing."
12:20 *came into the house of the LORD, and worshipped.* He acknowledged the justice of God, being at peace with God's will as evidence of a restored relationship with God. *required.* Asked.
12:23 *I shall go to him, but he shall not return to me.* At the very least, David's acknowledgment that he, too, would go to the grave. But David's peaceful reaction to the death of this child, in contrast to his exceeding grief over Absalom's death (18:33), suggests his hope regarding covenant children dying in infancy.
12:24 *Solomon.* The name (Hebrew, *Shelomoh*) is related to the word "peace" (*shalom*).
12:25 *Jedidiah.* Means "beloved of the Lord" (v. 24). The Lord revealed that Solomon would be the heir of David's throne, rule the kingdom in peace, and build the temple (1 Chron. 22:9–10), as promised in the covenant with David (2 Sam. 7:12–17).
12:29 *David gathered all the people together.* Having learned his lesson, he went to battle instead of staying at home.
12:30 *talent.* A weight between sixty-five and seventy pounds.
12:31 *put them under.* Appointed them to various spheres of forced labor. *harrows.* Some sort of pick or sharp instrument. *pass through the brickkiln.* Work at or bring what they had cut to an oven that baked and hardened bricks.

Thoughts for Personal/Family Worship: Chapter 12

1. David had persisted in unconfessed sin for some time, though as far as anyone else could tell all was well. But according to Pss. 32 and 51 a battle was raging within David: his sin was ever before him, as two armies lining up for war (51:3; also the turmoil described in 32:3–5). David was miserable in his sin, yet he made no confession to the Lord. God graciously sent the prophet with a word, not to remind David of his sin but to bring David to his spiritual senses to appeal to God for mercy. Although God is plenteous in mercy and ready to pardon (Neh. 9:17), believers are often slow to confess and enjoy restoration to the place of fellowship with God. It is wise to keep our accounts short before the Lord, confessing our sins immediately, lest the sense of guilt rob us of all spiritual joy. First John 1:9 should be the Nathan-like word for sinning Christians: "If we confess our sins, he is faithful and just to forgive us our sins."
2. The death of the child indicates that consequences for sin are necessary parts of God's discipline (Ps. 94:12; Prov. 3:11–12; Heb. 12:5–11; Rev. 3:19). Even sorrow over sin and the resolution to turn from it do not exempt us from all its consequences. Sometimes erring children assume that simply telling their parents they are sorry for a bad behavior will excuse them from any disciplinary action. But learning that sin has consequences and then experiencing those consequences is itself a sanctifying process (Prov. 20:30). The best way to avoid sin's

Tamar; and Amnon the son of David loved her.
2 And Amnon was so vexed, that he fell sick for
his sister Tamar; for she *was* a virgin; and Amnon
thought it hard for him to do any thing to her.
3 But Amnon had a friend, whose name *was*
Jonadab, the son of Shimeah David's brother: and
Jonadab *was* a very subtil man.
4 And he said unto him, Why *art* thou, *being* the
king's son, lean from day to day? wilt thou not tell
me? And Amnon said unto him, I love Tamar, my
brother Absalom's sister.
5 And Jonadab said unto him, Lay thee down
on thy bed, and make thyself sick: and when thy
father cometh to see thee, say unto him, I pray
thee, let my sister Tamar come, and give me meat,
and dress the meat in my sight, that I may see *it*,
and eat *it* at her hand.
6 ¶ So Amnon lay down, and made himself sick:
and when the king was come to see him, Amnon
said unto the king, I pray thee, let Tamar my sister
come, and make me a couple of cakes in my sight,
that I may eat at her hand.
7 Then David sent home to Tamar, saying, Go now
to thy brother Amnon's house, and dress him meat.
8 So Tamar went to her brother Amnon's house;
and he was laid down. And she took flour, and
kneaded *it*, and made cakes in his sight, and did
bake the cakes.
9 And she took a pan, and poured *them* out
before him; but he refused to eat. And Amnon
said, Have out all men from me. And they went
out every man from him.
10 And Amnon said unto Tamar, Bring the meat
into the chamber, that I may eat of thine hand.
And Tamar took the cakes which she had made,
and brought *them* into the chamber to Amnon
her brother.
11 And when she had brought *them* unto him to
eat, he took hold of her, and said unto her, Come
lie with me, my sister.
12 And she answered him, Nay, my brother, do
not force me; for no such thing ought to be done
in Israel: do not thou this folly.
13 And I, whither shall I cause my shame to go?
and as for thee, thou shalt be as one of the fools in
Israel. Now therefore, I pray thee, speak unto the
king; for he will not withhold me from thee.
14 Howbeit he would not hearken unto her voice:
but, being stronger than she, forced her, and lay
with her.
15 ¶ Then Amnon hated her exceedingly; so that
the hatred wherewith he hated her *was* greater
than the love wherewith he had loved her. And
Amnon said unto her, Arise, be gone.
16 And she said unto him, *There is* no cause: this
evil in sending me away *is* greater than the other
that thou didst unto me. But he would not hearken
unto her.
17 Then he called his servant that ministered
unto him, and said, Put now this *woman* out from
me, and bolt the door after her.
18 And *she had* a garment of divers colours upon
her: for with such robes were the king's daugh-
ters *that were* virgins apparelled. Then his servant
brought her out, and bolted the door after her.
19 ¶ And Tamar put ashes on her head, and rent
her garment of divers colours that *was* on her, and
laid her hand on her head, and went on crying.
20 And Absalom her brother said unto her, Hath
Amnon thy brother been with thee? but hold now
thy peace, my sister: he *is* thy brother; regard not
this thing. So Tamar remained desolate in her
brother Absalom's house.
21 ¶ But when king David heard of all these
things, he was very wroth.
22 And Absalom spake unto his brother Amnon
neither good nor bad: for Absalom hated Amnon,
because he had forced his sister Tamar.
23 ¶ And it came to pass after two full years, that
Absalom had sheepshearers in Baal-hazor, which
is beside Ephraim: and Absalom invited all the
king's sons.
24 And Absalom came to the king, and said,
Behold now, thy servant hath sheepshearers; let the
king, I beseech thee, and his servants go with thy
servant.

consequences is to avoid sin. Why is it a mercy that God disciplines His people?

Amnon's Incest and Absalom's Revenge (2 Sam. 13:1—14:33)

Chapter 13: *Amnon commits incest with his half sister and then is murdered by Absalom.*

13:1 *fair.* Beautiful.

13:2 *vexed.* Depressed. *Amnon thought it hard.* Literally, "it was difficult in the eyes of Amnon."

13:3 *subtil.* Skillful in the sense of being cunning.

13:4 *lean.* As well as "thin," the Hebrew can mean "downcast" or "sullen."

13:5 *dress the meat.* Administer a patient's or sick person's diet of food (also vv. 7,10).

13:6 *cakes.* Most likely some sort of pancake (v. 8).

13:11 *Come lie with me, my sister.* A forbidden act in the law of God (Lev. 18:9; 20:17).

13:12 *do not force me.* The Hebrew means "do not do violence to me" or "humble me" (vv. 14,22).

13:14 *Howbeit he would not hearken.* But he would not listen.

13:18–19 *garment of divers colours.* A tunic of multi-colored material (Gen. 37:3). *put ashes . . . rent.* Common gestures of grief and mourning.

13:21 *wroth.* Angry.

13:25 *lest we be chargeable unto thee.* Literally, "lest we be heavy upon you," in the sense of being a burden. *pressed.* Urged (v. 27).

13:29 *gat him up upon his mule.* Literally, "rode upon his mule."

13:31 *tare his garments.* Tore his clothes, a gesture expressing grief or mourning.

25 And the king said to Absalom, Nay, my son, let
us not all now go, lest we be chargeable unto thee.
And he pressed him: howbeit he would not go, but
blessed him.
26 Then said Absalom, If not, I pray thee, let my
brother Amnon go with us. And the king said
unto him, Why should he go with thee?
27 But Absalom pressed him, that he let Amnon
and all the king's sons go with him.
28 ¶ Now Absalom had commanded his servants,
saying, Mark ye now when Amnon's heart is
merry with wine, and when I say unto you, Smite
Amnon; then kill him, fear not: have not I com-
manded you? be courageous, and be valiant.
29 And the servants of Absalom did unto Amnon
as Absalom had commanded. Then all the king's
sons arose, and every man gat him up upon his
mule, and fled.
30 ¶ And it came to pass, while they were in the
way, that tidings came to David, saying, Absalom
hath slain all the king's sons, and there is not one
of them left.
31 Then the king arose, and tare his garments,
and lay on the earth; and all his servants stood by
with their clothes rent.
32 And Jonadab, the son of Shimeah David's
brother, answered and said, Let not my lord sup-
pose *that* they have slain all the young men the
king's sons; for Amnon only is dead: for by the ap-
pointment of Absalom this hath been determined
from the day that he forced his sister Tamar.
33 Now therefore let not my lord the king take the
thing to his heart, to think that all the king's sons
are dead: for Amnon only is dead.
34 But Absalom fled. And the young man that
kept the watch lifted up his eyes, and looked, and,
behold, there came much people by the way of the
hill side behind him.
35 And Jonadab said unto the king, Behold, the
king's sons come: as thy servant said, so it is.
36 And it came to pass, as soon as he had made
an end of speaking, that, behold, the king's sons
came, and lifted up their voice and wept: and the
king also and all his servants wept very sore.
37 ¶ But Absalom fled, and went to Talmai, the
son of Ammihud, king of Geshur. And *David*
mourned for his son every day.
38 So Absalom fled, and went to Geshur, and was
there three years.
39 And *the soul of* king David longed to go forth
unto Absalom: for he was comforted concerning
Amnon, seeing he was dead.

CHAPTER 14

Now Joab the son of Zeruiah perceived that the
king's heart *was* toward Absalom.
2 And Joab sent to Tekoah, and fetched thence a
wise woman, and said unto her, I pray thee, feign
thyself to be a mourner, and put on now mourn-
ing apparel, and anoint not thyself with oil, but be
as a woman that had a long time mourned for the
dead:
3 And come to the king, and speak on this man-
ner unto him. So Joab put the words in her mouth.
4 ¶ And when the woman of Tekoah spake to the
king, she fell on her face to the ground, and did
obeisance, and said, Help, O king.
5 And the king said unto her, What aileth thee?
And she answered, I *am* indeed a widow woman,
and mine husband is dead.
6 And thy handmaid had two sons, and they two
strove together in the field, and *there was* none to
part them, but the one smote the other, and slew
him.
7 And, behold, the whole family is risen against
thine handmaid, and they said, Deliver him that
smote his brother, that we may kill him, for the
life of his brother whom he slew; and we will de-
stroy the heir also: and so they shall quench my

13:36 *very sore.* Greatly. Already the sword was coming down upon David's household for his sins (12:10).
13:37 *Talmai . . . king of Geshur.* Absalom fled to his maternal grandfather (1 Chron. 3:2).

Thoughts for Personal/Family Worship: Chapter 13

1. **The friendship between Amnon and Jonadab is a warning about having the right kind of friends. Godly friends can be effective in providing accountability and preventing behavior that is displeasing to God. But Jonadab was just the opposite. Instead of trying to quench the lusts that burned in the heart of Amnon, he advised him how he might satisfy his lust. Christian parents should always keep before their children the directive of Prov. 1:10, "My son, if sinners entice thee, consent thou not." We all should avoid the kind of friendships that corrupt and foster those that aid for godliness.**
2. **Amnon was a fornicator before he forced Tamar (Matt. 5:28). Similarly, Absalom was a murderer long before he plotted Amnon's death, for he hated him (v. 22; see Matt. 5:22; 1 John 3:15). Both testify to what happens when lust is not subdued. Sin begins in the head and heart before it shows itself in action. This is why it is so vital to think proper and godly thoughts. Had the minds of Amnon and Absalom been filled with the thoughts expressed in Phil. 4:8, the tragedy of this narrative could have been avoided. Let us learn from their tragedy to keep our minds and hearts fixed on spiritual matters. Right thinking produces right living.**

Chapter 14: ***Joab schemes for Absalom's return, and Absalom pressures Joab to gain an audience with the king.***

14:1 *the king's heart was toward Absalom.* David's heart longed to be reunited with his son (13:39).
14:2 *feign thyself to be a mourner.* Literally, "observe mourning rites" or "play the mourner."
14:4 *did obeisance.* Bowed down.

coal which is left, and shall not leave to my hus-
band *neither* name nor remainder upon the earth.
8 And the king said unto the woman, Go to thine
house, and I will give charge concerning thee.
9 And the woman of Tekoah said unto the king,
My lord, O king, the iniquity *be* on me, and on
my father's house: and the king and his throne *be*
guiltless.
10 And the king said, Whosoever saith *ought* unto
thee, bring him to me, and he shall not touch thee
any more.
11 Then said she, I pray thee, let the king
remember the LORD thy God, that thou wouldest
not suffer the revengers of blood to destroy any
more, lest they destroy my son. And he said, *As*
the LORD liveth, there shall not one hair of thy son
fall to the earth.
12 Then the woman said, Let thine handmaid, I
pray thee, speak *one* word unto my lord the king.
And he said, Say on.
13 And the woman said, Wherefore then hast
thou thought such a thing against the people of
God? for the king doth speak this thing as one
which is faulty, in that the king doth not fetch
home again his banished.
14 For we must needs die, and *are* as water spilt
on the ground, which cannot be gathered up
again; neither doth God respect *any* person: yet
doth he devise means, that his banished be not
expelled from him.
15 Now therefore that I am come to speak of this
thing unto my lord the king, *it is* because the peo-
ple have made me afraid: and thy handmaid said,
I will now speak unto the king; it may be that the
king will perform the request of his handmaid.
16 For the king will hear, to deliver his handmaid
out of the hand of the man *that would* destroy
me and my son together out of the inheritance
of God.
17 Then thine handmaid said, The word of my
lord the king shall now be comfortable: for as an
angel of God, so *is* my lord the king to discern
good and bad: therefore the LORD thy God will
be with thee.
18 Then the king answered and said unto the
woman, Hide not from me, I pray thee, the thing
that I shall ask thee. And the woman said, Let my
lord the king now speak.
19 And the king said, *Is not* the hand of Joab with
thee in all this? And the woman answered and
said, *As* thy soul liveth, my lord the king, none can
turn to the right hand or to the left from ought
that my lord the king hath spoken: for thy servant
Joab, he bade me, and he put all these words in the
mouth of thine handmaid:
20 To fetch about this form of speech hath thy
servant Joab done this thing: and my lord *is* wise,
according to the wisdom of an angel of God, to
know all *things* that *are* in the earth.
21 ¶ And the king said unto Joab, Behold now,
I have done this thing: go therefore, bring the
young man Absalom again.
22 And Joab fell to the ground on his face, and
bowed himself, and thanked the king: and Joab
said, To day thy servant knoweth that I have
found grace in thy sight, my lord, O king, in that
the king hath fulfilled the request of his servant.
23 So Joab arose and went to Geshur, and brought
Absalom to Jerusalem.
24 And the king said, Let him turn to his own
house, and let him not see my face. So Absalom
returned to his own house, and saw not the king's
face.
25 ¶ But in all Israel there was none to be so much
praised as Absalom for his beauty: from the sole
of his foot even to the crown of his head there was
no blemish in him.
26 And when he polled his head, (for it was at
every year's end that he polled *it*: because *the
hair* was heavy on him, therefore he polled it:)
he weighed the hair of his head at two hundred
shekels after the king's weight.
27 And unto Absalom there were born three sons,
and one daughter, whose name *was* Tamar: she
was a woman of a fair countenance.
28 ¶ So Absalom dwelt two full years in Jerusa-
lem, and saw not the king's face.
29 Therefore Absalom sent for Joab, to have sent
him to the king; but he would not come to him:
and when he sent again the second time, he would
not come.
30 Therefore he said unto his servants, See, Joab's
field is near mine, and he hath barley there; go
and set it on fire. And Absalom's servants set the
field on fire.
31 Then Joab arose, and came to Absalom unto

14:8 *give charge*. Command.
14:11 *suffer*. Allow.
14:13 *faulty*. Guilty.
14:17 *angel of God*. Messenger of or from God (v. 20).
14:19 *bade*. Hebrew, "commanded."
14:25 *his beauty*. Ironically, one so handsome on the outside was so ugly within.
14:26 *polled*. Cut or shaved. *two hundred shekels*. Approximately five-and-a-half pounds.
14:27 *fair countenance*. Literally, "beautiful of appearance."

Thoughts for Personal/Family Worship: Chapter 14

1. In her story to David, the woman of Tekoa makes a remarkable statement deserving of pause and meditation (v. 14). The first part reminds us of the certainty of death: "we must needs die" (cf. Pss. 49:7–12,17,20; 89:47–48; Heb. 9:27). Acknowledging the certainty of death is not to generate morbid thoughts, but it should be a motive to take full advantage of the time that God allots us to be ready for eternity by trusting in Christ and serving

his house, and said unto him, Wherefore have thy
servants set my field on fire?
32 And Absalom answered Joab, Behold, I sent
unto thee, saying, Come hither, that I may send
thee to the king, to say, Wherefore am I come
from Geshur? *it had been* good for me *to have*
been there still: now therefore let me see the king's
face; and if there be *any* iniquity in me, let him
kill me.
33 So Joab came to the king, and told him: and
when he had called for Absalom, he came to the
king, and bowed himself on his face to the ground
before the king: and the king kissed Absalom.

CHAPTER 15

AND it came to pass after this, that Absalom prepared him chariots and horses, and fifty men to
run before him.
2 And Absalom rose up early, and stood beside
the way of the gate: and it was *so*, that when any
man that had a controversy came to the king for
judgment, then Absalom called unto him, and
said, Of what city *art* thou? And he said, Thy
servant *is* of one of the tribes of Israel.
3 And Absalom said unto him, See, thy matters
are good and right; but *there is* no man *deputed* of
the king to hear thee.
4 Absalom said moreover, Oh that I were made
judge in the land, that every man which hath any
suit or cause might come unto me, and I would
do him justice!
5 And it was *so*, that when any man came nigh *to*
him to do him obeisance, he put forth his hand,
and took him, and kissed him.
6 And on this manner did Absalom to all Israel
that came to the king for judgment: so Absalom
stole the hearts of the men of Israel.
7 ¶ And it came to pass after forty years, that
Absalom said unto the king, I pray thee, let me
go and pay my vow, which I have vowed unto the
LORD, in Hebron.
8 For thy servant vowed a vow while I abode at
Geshur in Syria, saying, If the LORD shall bring me
again indeed to Jerusalem, then I will serve the
LORD.
9 And the king said unto him, Go in peace. So he
arose, and went to Hebron.
10 ¶ But Absalom sent spies throughout all the
tribes of Israel, saying, As soon as ye hear the
sound of the trumpet, then ye shall say, Absalom
reigneth in Hebron.
11 And with Absalom went two hundred men
out of Jerusalem, *that were* called; and they went
in their simplicity, and they knew not any thing.
12 And Absalom sent for Ahithophel the Gilonite,
David's counsellor, from his city, *even* from Giloh,
while he offered sacrifices. And the conspiracy
was strong; for the people increased continually
with Absalom.
13 ¶ And there came a messenger to David,
saying, The hearts of the men of Israel are after
Absalom.
14 And David said unto all his servants that *were*
with him at Jerusalem, Arise, and let us flee; for
we shall not *else* escape from Absalom: make
speed to depart, lest he overtake us suddenly, and
bring evil upon us, and smite the city with the
edge of the sword.
15 And the king's servants said unto the king,
Behold, thy servants *are ready to do* whatsoever
my lord the king shall appoint.
16 And the king went forth, and all his household
after him. And the king left ten women, *which*
were concubines, to keep the house.
17 And the king went forth, and all the people
after him, and tarried in a place that was far off.
18 And all his servants passed on beside him; and
all the Cherethites, and all the Pelethites, and all
the Gittites, six hundred men which came after
him from Gath, passed on before the king.
19 ¶ Then said the king to Ittai the Gittite,
Wherefore goest thou also with us? return to
thy place, and abide with the king: for thou *art* a
stranger, and also an exile.
20 Whereas thou camest *but* yesterday, should I

Him wholeheartedly, since death marks the end of earthly opportunity (like water that is spilled, v.14).

2. The second part of verse 14 draws a straight and bold line to the gospel: God devises "means, that his banished be not expelled from him." In Adam, all humanity was banished from Paradise (Gen. 3:24). But God in His grace devised a plan whereby sinners, outcasts from His presence, might be reconciled to Him. The promised Seed of the Woman, the Seed of Abraham and David, would come in the fullness of time to redeem those who were under the curse. Because of the work of Jesus Christ, the way of access has been opened to the very presence of God for all those who trust in Him as the only way, truth, and life. The first Adam lost the earthly Paradise; the second Adam regains the heavenly paradise for His people.

Absalom's Rebellion against David (2 Sam. 15:1—17:29)

Chapter 15: *Absalom schemes to usurp the throne, and David flees for safety.*

15:5 *do him obeisance.* Bow down to him. By turning the people's submissive gestures to expressions of approachability and warmth, Absalom flattered them and won their hearts.
15:7 *Hebron.* Both the place of his birth and the place of David's initial coronation.
15:8 *I will serve the LORD.* Seemingly without conscience, he uses religion to mask his treachery and treason.
15:11 *their simplicity.* Their innocence; they were not part of the conspiracy.
15:14 *bring evil upon us.* Hebrew, "thrust calamity on us."
15:15 *appoint.* Hebrew, "choose."
15:19 *stranger.* Foreigner.

this day make thee go up and down with us? see-
ing I go whither I may, return thou, and take back
thy brethren: mercy and truth *be* with thee.
21 And Ittai answered the king, and said, *As* the
LORD liveth, and *as* my lord the king liveth, surely
in what place my lord the king shall be, whether
in death or life, even there also will thy servant be.
22 And David said to Ittai, Go and pass over. And
Ittai the Gittite passed over, and all his men, and
all the little ones that *were* with him.
23 And all the country wept with a loud voice, and
all the people passed over: the king also himself
passed over the brook Kidron, and all the people
passed over, toward the way of the wilderness.
24 ¶ And lo Zadok also, and all the Levites *were*
with him, bearing the ark of the covenant of God:
and they set down the ark of God; and Abiathar
went up, until all the people had done passing out
of the city.
25 And the king said unto Zadok, Carry back the
ark of God into the city: if I shall find favour in
the eyes of the LORD, he will bring me again, and
shew me *both* it, and his habitation:
26 But if he thus say, I have no delight in thee; be-
hold, *here am* I, let him do to me as seemeth good
unto him.
27 The king said also unto Zadok the priest, *Art
not* thou a seer? return into the city in peace, and
your two sons with you, Ahimaaz thy son, and
Jonathan the son of Abiathar.
28 See, I will tarry in the plain of the wilderness,
until there come word from you to certify me.
29 Zadok therefore and Abiathar carried the ark
of God again to Jerusalem: and they tarried there.
30 ¶ And David went up by the ascent of *mount*
Olivet, and wept as he went up, and had his head
covered, and he went barefoot: and all the people
that *was* with him covered every man his head,
and they went up, weeping as they went up.
31 ¶ And *one* told David, saying, Ahithophel
is among the conspirators with Absalom. And
David said, O LORD, I pray thee, turn the counsel
of Ahithophel into foolishness.
32 ¶ And it came to pass, that *when* David was
come to the top *of the mount*, where he wor-
shipped God, behold, Hushai the Archite came to
meet him with his coat rent, and earth upon his
head:
33 Unto whom David said, If thou passest on
with me, then thou shalt be a burden unto me:
34 But if thou return to the city, and say unto Ab-
salom, I will be thy servant, O king; *as* I *have been*
thy father's servant hitherto, so *will* I now also *be*
thy servant: then mayest thou for me defeat the
counsel of Ahithophel.
35 And *hast thou* not there with thee Zadok and
Abiathar the priests? therefore it shall be, *that*
what thing soever thou shalt hear out of the king's
house, thou shalt tell *it* to Zadok and Abiathar the
priests.
36 Behold, *they have* there with them their
two sons, Ahimaaz Zadok's *son*, and Jonathan
Abiathar's *son*; and by them ye shall send unto me
every thing that ye can hear.
37 So Hushai David's friend came into the city,
and Absalom came into Jerusalem.

CHAPTER 16

AND when David was a little past the top *of the
hill*, behold, Ziba the servant of Mephibosheth
met him, with a couple of asses saddled, and
upon them two hundred *loaves* of bread, and an
hundred bunches of raisins, and an hundred of
summer fruits, and a bottle of wine.
2 And the king said unto Ziba, What meanest

15:27 *seer.* Prophet.
15:31 *O LORD, I pray thee.* David's prayer for the frustration of Ahithophel's *counsel* showed his continuing dependence on God, and God's answer would prove decisive in the conflict (17:14).
15:32 *his coat rent, and earth upon his head.* Gestures of grief and mourning.

Thoughts for Personal/Family Worship: Chapter 15

1. **In many ways, David's family trouble is his reaping what he has sown. On the one hand, David is reaping the sad consequences of the complex home situation of having multiple wives with competing children. Marriage outside God's revealed standard is always an open door to trouble. But most to the point is that this rebellion by Absalom is the consequence of David's sin with Bathsheba: "the sword shall never depart from thine house" (12:10). His sin was forgiven, and even some good things followed from this union, including the coming Christ (Matt. 1:6). Nonetheless, there are unavoidable consequences of sin; hence the warning of Gal. 6:7: what you sow you will reap.**
2. **Although Absalom's rebellion was a component in David's predicted family trouble, Absalom was not exempt from personal responsibility and guilt for his actions. He was deceitful, treacherous, and disloyal to his father, whom he should have honored (fifth commandment). His charisma and bold promises appealed to the temporal needs of those he seduced from David's kingdom. He had ambition, but ambition in fools is a dangerous thing. He thought more highly of himself than he ought and sought a position for himself that was not ordained by God. His folly stands as a warning against all selfish ambition. We must remember that God makes men what they are, and the child of God should always be submissive to the place to which he is called (1 Cor. 7:20). Are you envious of others or content to serve the Lord where He has placed you?**

Chapter 16: ***David is deceived by Ziba and cursed by Shimei, and Absalom enters Jerusalem and follows the advice of Ahithophel.***

thou by these? And Ziba said, The asses *be* for the
king's household to ride on; and the bread and
summer fruit for the young men to eat; and the
wine, that such as be faint in the wilderness may
drink.
3 And the king said, And where *is* thy master's
son? And Ziba said unto the king, Behold, he
abideth at Jerusalem: for he said, To day shall the
house of Israel restore me the kingdom of my
father.
4 Then said the king to Ziba, Behold, thine *are* all
that *pertained* unto Mephibosheth. And Ziba said,
I humbly beseech thee *that* I may find grace in thy
sight, my lord, O king.
5 ¶ And when king David came to Bahurim, be-
hold, thence came out a man of the family of the
house of Saul, whose name *was* Shimei, the son of
Gera: he came forth, and cursed still as he came.
6 And he cast stones at David, and at all the
servants of king David: and all the people and all
the mighty men *were* on his right hand and on
his left.
7 And thus said Shimei when he cursed, Come
out, come out, thou bloody man, and thou man
of Belial:
8 The LORD hath returned upon thee all the
blood of the house of Saul, in whose stead thou
hast reigned; and the LORD hath delivered the
kingdom into the hand of Absalom thy son: and,
behold, thou *art taken* in thy mischief, because
thou *art* a bloody man.
9 ¶ Then said Abishai the son of Zeruiah unto the
king, Why should this dead dog curse my lord the
king? let me go over, I pray thee, and take off his
head.
10 And the king said, What have I to do with you,
ye sons of Zeruiah? so let him curse, because the
LORD hath said unto him, Curse David. Who shall
then say, Wherefore hast thou done so?
11 And David said to Abishai, and to all his
servants, Behold, my son, which came forth of my
bowels, seeketh my life: how much more now *may
this* Benjamite *do it*? let him alone, and let him
curse; for the LORD hath bidden him.
12 It may be that the LORD will look on mine af-
fliction, and that the LORD will requite me good
for his cursing this day.
13 And as David and his men went by the way,
Shimei went along on the hill's side over against
him, and cursed as he went, and threw stones at
him, and cast dust.
14 And the king, and all the people that *were* with
him, came weary, and refreshed themselves there.
15 ¶ And Absalom, and all the people the men of
Israel, came to Jerusalem, and Ahithophel with
him.
16 And it came to pass, when Hushai the Archite,
David's friend, was come unto Absalom, that
Hushai said unto Absalom, God save the king,
God save the king.
17 And Absalom said to Hushai, *Is* this thy kind-
ness to thy friend? why wentest thou not with thy
friend?
18 And Hushai said unto Absalom, Nay; but
whom the LORD, and this people, and all the men
of Israel, choose, his will I be, and with him will
I abide.
19 And again, whom should I serve? *should I* not
serve in the presence of his son? as I have served in
thy father's presence, so will I be in thy presence.
20 ¶ Then said Absalom to Ahithophel, Give
counsel among you what we shall do.
21 And Ahithophel said unto Absalom, Go in
unto thy father's concubines, which he hath left to
keep the house; and all Israel shall hear that thou
art abhorred of thy father: then shall the hands of
all that *are* with thee be strong.
22 So they spread Absalom a tent upon the top of
the house; and Absalom went in unto his father's
concubines in the sight of all Israel.

16:3 *where is thy master's son?* Saul was the master (9:2) and Mephibosheth the son, Saul's grandson. *for he said.* Mephibosheth denies this (19:24–34). David was deceived.

16:4 *thine are all that pertained unto Mephibosheth.* David makes a hasty decision without consulting Mephibosheth. Ziba took advantage of David in a time of trouble.

16:5 *he came forth, and cursed still as he came.* Literally, "one going out was going out and [he was] one cursing"; he was railing and declaring a curse on David with every step.

16:7 *bloody man.* Literally, "man of bloods," referring to blood shedding or blood guiltiness (v. 8). *man of Belial.* One who is a useless, worthless good-for-nothing (see note at 1 Sam. 1:16).

16:8 *the blood of the house of Saul.* In Hebrew, "blood" is plural, here referring to blood that has been shed. *behold, thou art taken in thy mischief.* Literally, "behold you, in your evil," the idea being "here you are in your trouble," getting what you deserve.

16:11 *the LORD hath bidden him.* God commanded him, not in the sense of speaking a word for Shimei to obey but in secretly decreeing all that comes to pass (Lam. 3:37–38). David's faith in God's providence preserved him from seeking personal revenge.

16:12 *mine affliction.* Literally, "my eyes," perhaps referring to his tears. *requite.* The Hebrew is "to return."

16:13 *cursed as he went.* Literally, "walking and he cursed," an idiom meaning that he cursed continually.

16:15 *Ahithophel.* Previously part of David's inner circle (15:12; 1 Chron. 27:33).

16:16 *God save the king.* Literally, "may the king live." Hushai was David's agent to defeat Ahithophel's counsel (15:32–37).

16:17 *kindness to thy friend.* Loyalty to David. Absalom expressed suspicion regarding Hushai.

16:18–19 Reassuring words to Absalom to ensure the success of his mission against David.

16:22 *Absalom went in unto his father's concubines in the sight of all Israel.* The public violation of David's concubines was a despicable crime by Absalom, and yet this was also God's just judgment against the house of David for his sins (12:11–12).

23 And the counsel of Ahithophel, which he
counselled in those days, *was* as if a man had
enquired at the oracle of God: so *was* all the
counsel of Ahithophel both with David and with
Absalom.

CHAPTER 17

MOREOVER Ahithophel said unto Absalom, Let
me now choose out twelve thousand men, and I
will arise and pursue after David this night:
2 And I will come upon him while he *is* weary
and weak handed, and will make him afraid: and
all the people that *are* with him shall flee; and I
will smite the king only:
3 And I will bring back all the people unto thee:
the man whom thou seekest *is* as if all returned: *so*
all the people shall be in peace.
4 And the saying pleased Absalom well, and all
the elders of Israel.
5 Then said Absalom, Call now Hushai the
Archite also, and let us hear likewise what he saith.
6 And when Hushai was come to Absalom,
Absalom spake unto him, saying, Ahithophel
hath spoken after this manner: shall we do *after*
his saying? if not; speak thou.
7 And Hushai said unto Absalom, The counsel
that Ahithophel hath given *is* not good at this time.
8 For, said Hushai, thou knowest thy father and
his men, that they *be* mighty men, and they *be*
chafed in their minds, as a bear robbed of her
whelps in the field: and thy father *is* a man of war,
and will not lodge with the people.
9 Behold, he is hid now in some pit, or in some
other place: and it will come to pass, when some
of them be overthrown at the first, that whoso-
ever heareth it will say, There is a slaughter among
the people that follow Absalom.
10 And he also *that is* valiant, whose heart *is* as
the heart of a lion, shall utterly melt: for all Israel
knoweth that thy father *is* a mighty man, and *they*
which *be* with him *are* valiant men.
11 Therefore I counsel that all Israel be generally
gathered unto thee, from Dan even to Beer-sheba,
as the sand that *is* by the sea for multitude; and
that thou go to battle in thine own person.
12 So shall we come upon him in some place
where he shall be found, and we will light upon
him as the dew falleth on the ground: and of him
and of all the men that *are* with him there shall
not be left so much as one.
13 Moreover, if he be gotten into a city, then shall
all Israel bring ropes to that city, and we will draw
it into the river, until there be not one small stone
found there.
14 And Absalom and all the men of Israel said,
The counsel of Hushai the Archite *is* better
than the counsel of Ahithophel. For the LORD
had appointed to defeat the good counsel of
Ahithophel, to the intent that the LORD might
bring evil upon Absalom.
15 ¶ Then said Hushai unto Zadok and to Abi-
athar the priests, Thus and thus did Ahithophel
counsel Absalom and the elders of Israel; and thus
and thus have I counselled.
16 Now therefore send quickly, and tell David,
saying, Lodge not this night in the plains of the
wilderness, but speedily pass over; lest the king be
swallowed up, and all the people that *are* with him.
17 Now Jonathan and Ahimaaz stayed by En-
rogel; for they might not be seen to come into the
city: and a wench went and told them; and they
went and told king David.
18 Nevertheless a lad saw them, and told Absa-

Thoughts for Personal/Family Worship: Chapter 16

1. **Proverbs 18:17 says, "He that is first in his own cause seemeth just." This is why it is always wise to hear both sides of a matter before rushing to judgment. The interchange between Ziba and David is a case in point. Ziba sought to gain favor with David by misrepresenting Mephibosheth, and David took Ziba at his word without consulting with Mephibosheth to get his side of the story, which later exposed Ziba's deception (2 Sam 19:24–30). Ziba's actions were contemptible, and David's were rash and unfounded. Too often we rush to judgment without knowing all the facts and do harm to our fellow believers. Before believing every accusation or rumor, let us learn all the facts and give priority to meeting directly with the other person (Matt. 18:15).**
2. **David once again expresses his confidence in God's justice. Rather than taking personal vengeance on Shimei, which he had the opportunity to do, he left the matter with the Lord (v. 12). This relative of Saul (v. 5) experienced the same mercy from David that Saul himself had experienced when David passed up opportunities to take revenge. It is always easiest to fight fire with fire, but allowing oneself to be abused and then showing mercy is often a more powerful weapon (Prov. 25:21–22).**

Chapter 17: *Hushai overturns Ahithophel's counsel, causing him to hang himself.*

17:3 *I will bring back.* The Hebrew is not a prediction but a statement of resolve: "I am determined to bring back." He is certain that killing David will solidify the kingdom for Absalom.

17:8 *chafed in their minds.* Literally, "bitter or fierce ones of soul."

17:13 *if he be gotten into a city.* Literally, "if to a city he is gathered."

17:14 *had appointed to defeat.* Literally, "had commanded to foil or make ineffectual." *bring evil.* Cause calamity or disaster. In answer to David's prayer (15:31), God exercised His sovereignty over the minds of Absalom and his men to blind them to Ahithophel's *good counsel.*

17:17 *Jonathan and Ahimaaz.* Those sent by the priests to warn David (15:27–28). *wench.* Slave-girl.

17:20 *the woman said unto them.* Truth is ultimately fidelity

lom: but they went both of them away quickly,
and came to a man's house in Bahurim, which
had a well in his court; whither they went down.
19 And the woman took and spread a covering
over the well's mouth, and spread ground corn
thereon; and the thing was not known.
20 And when Absalom's servants came to the
woman to the house, they said, Where *is* Ahimaaz
and Jonathan? And the woman said unto them,
They be gone over the brook of water. And when
they had sought and could not find *them*, they
returned to Jerusalem.
21 And it came to pass, after they were departed,
that they came up out of the well, and went and
told king David, and said unto David, Arise,
and pass quickly over the water: for thus hath
Ahithophel counselled against you.
22 Then David arose, and all the people that *were*
with him, and they passed over Jordan: by the
morning light there lacked not one of them that
was not gone over Jordan.
23 ¶ And when Ahithophel saw that his counsel
was not followed, he saddled *his* ass, and arose,
and gat him home to his house, to his city, and
put his household in order, and hanged himself,
and died, and was buried in the sepulchre of his
father.
24 Then David came to Mahanaim. And Absalom
passed over Jordan, he and all the men of Israel
with him.
25 ¶ And Absalom made Amasa captain of the
host instead of Joab: which Amasa *was* a man's
son, whose name *was* Ithra an Israelite, that went
in to Abigail the daughter of Nahash, sister to Zer-
uiah Joab's mother.
26 So Israel and Absalom pitched in the land of
Gilead.
27 ¶ And it came to pass, when David was come
to Mahanaim, that Shobi the son of Nahash of
Rabbah of the children of Ammon, and Machir
the son of Ammiel of Lo-debar, and Barzillai the
Gileadite of Rogelim,
28 Brought beds, and basons, and earthen vessels,
and wheat, and barley, and flour, and parched
corn, and beans, and lentiles, and parched *pulse*,
29 And honey, and butter, and sheep, and cheese
of kine, for David, and for the people that *were*
with him, to eat: for they said, The people *is*
hungry, and weary, and thirsty, in the wilderness.

CHAPTER 18

AND David numbered the people that *were* with
him, and set captains of thousands and captains
of hundreds over them.
2 And David sent forth a third part of the people
under the hand of Joab, and a third part under
the hand of Abishai the son of Zeruiah, Joab's
brother, and a third part under the hand of Ittai
the Gittite. And the king said unto the people, I
will surely go forth with you myself also.
3 But the people answered, Thou shalt not go
forth: for if we flee away, they will not care for us;
neither if half of us die, will they care for us: but
now *thou art* worth ten thousand of us: therefore
now *it is* better that thou succour us out of the
city.
4 And the king said unto them, What seemeth
you best I will do. And the king stood by the gate
side, and all the people came out by hundreds and
by thousands.
5 And the king commanded Joab and Abishai
and Ittai, saying, *Deal* gently for my sake with
the young man, *even* with Absalom. And all the
people heard when the king gave all the captains
charge concerning Absalom.
6 ¶ So the people went out into the field against
Israel: and the battle was in the wood of Ephraim;
7 Where the people of Israel were slain before
the servants of David, and there was there a great
slaughter that day of twenty thousand *men*.
8 For the battle was there scattered over the face
of all the country: and the wood devoured more
people that day than the sword devoured.

---

to God and His cause.

17:23 *gat him home to his house.* Literally, "went to his house."

17:26 *Gilead,* the mountain range east of the Jordan.

17:27 *Shobi the son of Nahash.* Ironically, it was his brother Hanun who had treated David's servants with contempt (10:1–4).

17:28 *basons.* Cups or bowls. *parched.* Roasted.

17:29 *kine.* Cows.

Thoughts for Personal/Family Worship: Chapter 17

Verse 14 is the key thought in the chapter. The scene is filled with intrigue, political maneuvering, daring courage, and humanitarian relief, but behind the scene is the throne of God. The Lord decreed and orchestrated every detail to bring down Absalom in order to preserve David and his throne (Ps. 33:9–11). As events unfolded, there were moments when it seemed that Absalom would prevail, but God ordained his failure, and David's safety was never in real jeopardy. This should be a comforting thought for all of God's people. It is easy to become distracted and discouraged by the things we see happening, but we should always remember that God is in heaven and that He does what pleases Him (Ps. 135:5–6). No power in hell or on earth can stop Christ (Rom. 8:38–39). How do you need to rely upon Him today?

Absalom's Death and David's Restoration (2 Sam. 18:1—19:40)

Chapter 18: ***David's forces defeat their enemies and kill Absalom, bringing great grief to David.***

18:3 *better that thou succour us out of the city.* Literally, it is "good that you should be for us to help from the city."

18:8 *the wood devoured more . . . than the sword devoured.*

9 ¶ And Absalom met the servants of David. And
Absalom rode upon a mule, and the mule went
under the thick boughs of a great oak, and his
head caught hold of the oak, and he was taken up
between the heaven and the earth; and the mule
that *was* under him went away.
10 And a certain man saw *it*, and told Joab, and
said, Behold, I saw Absalom hanged in an oak.
11 And Joab said unto the man that told him,
And, behold, thou sawest *him*, and why didst thou
not smite him there to the ground? and I would
have given thee ten *shekels* of silver, and a girdle.
12 And the man said unto Joab, Though I should
receive a thousand *shekels* of silver in mine hand,
yet would I not put forth mine hand against the
king's son: for in our hearing the king charged
thee and Abishai and Ittai, saying, Beware that
none *touch* the young man Absalom.
13 Otherwise I should have wrought falsehood
against mine own life: for there is no matter hid
from the king, and thou thyself wouldest have set
thyself against *me*.
14 Then said Joab, I may not tarry thus with thee.
And he took three darts in his hand, and thrust
them through the heart of Absalom, while he *was*
yet alive in the midst of the oak.
15 And ten young men that bare Joab's armour
compassed about and smote Absalom, and slew
him.
16 And Joab blew the trumpet, and the people
returned from pursuing after Israel: for Joab held
back the people.
17 And they took Absalom, and cast him into a
great pit in the wood, and laid a very great heap
of stones upon him: and all Israel fled every one
to his tent.
18 ¶ Now Absalom in his lifetime had taken and
reared up for himself a pillar, which *is* in the king's
dale: for he said, I have no son to keep my name
in remembrance: and he called the pillar after his
own name: and it is called unto this day, Absa-
lom's place.
19 ¶ Then said Ahimaaz the son of Zadok, Let me
now run, and bear the king tidings, how that the
LORD hath avenged him of his enemies.
20 And Joab said unto him, Thou shalt not
bear tidings this day, but thou shalt bear tidings
another day: but this day thou shalt bear no
tidings, because the king's son is dead.
21 Then said Joab to Cushi, Go tell the king what
thou hast seen. And Cushi bowed himself unto
Joab, and ran.
22 Then said Ahimaaz the son of Zadok yet again
to Joab, But howsoever, let me, I pray thee, also
run after Cushi. And Joab said, Wherefore wilt
thou run, my son, seeing that thou hast no tidings
ready?
23 But howsoever, *said he*, let me run. And he said
unto him, Run. Then Ahimaaz ran by the way of
the plain, and overran Cushi.
24 And David sat between the two gates: and the
watchman went up to the roof over the gate unto
the wall, and lifted up his eyes, and looked, and
behold a man running alone.
25 And the watchman cried, and told the king.
And the king said, If he *be* alone, *there is* tidings
in his mouth. And he came apace, and drew near.
26 And the watchman saw another man running:
and the watchman called unto the porter, and
said, Behold *another* man running alone. And the
king said, He also bringeth tidings.
27 And the watchman said, Me thinketh the
running of the foremost is like the running of
Ahimaaz the son of Zadok. And the king said, He
is a good man, and cometh with good tidings.
28 And Ahimaaz called, and said unto the king,
All is well. And he fell down to the earth upon
his face before the king, and said, Blessed *be* the
LORD thy God, which hath delivered up the men
that lifted up their hand against my lord the king.
29 And the king said, Is the young man Absalom
safe? And Ahimaaz answered, When Joab sent the
king's servant, and *me* thy servant, I saw a great
tumult, but I knew not what *it was*.
30 And the king said *unto him*, Turn aside, *and*
stand here. And he turned aside, and stood still.
31 And, behold, Cushi came; and Cushi said, Ti-
dings, my lord the king: for the LORD hath avenged
thee this day of all them that rose up against thee.
32 And the king said unto Cushi, Is the young
man Absalom safe? And Cushi answered, The en-
emies of my lord the king, and all that rise against
thee to do *thee* hurt, be as *that* young man *is*.
33 ¶ And the king was much moved, and went

Most of Absalom's losses took place due to his getting caught in dense brush (v. 9) or to wild animals or other dangers in the forest.

18:9 *his head caught hold of the oak.* Providentially, one of the casualties of the woods.

18:11 *a girdle.* A belt, perhaps signifying some sort of promotion in military rank.

18:12 *Beware.* Hebrew, "be on guard or watch carefully."

18:13 *wrought falsehood.* The Hebrew can mean "to do what is wrong."

18:14 *darts.* Rods used as weapons, perhaps iron with spikes.

18:15 *compassed about.* Surrounded.

18:18 *king's dale.* Valley of the king.

18:25 *came apace, and drew near.* Literally, "came walking and approaching," an idiom for coming closer and closer.

18:27 *Me thinketh the running.* Literally, "I see the running style of."

18:31 *Tidings, my lord.* Literally, "may the lord receive good news."

18:32 *be as that young man is.* That is, dead like his son Absalom.

18:33 *the king was much moved.* He trembled, being greatly

up to the chamber over the gate, and wept: and as
he went, thus he said, O my son Absalom, my son,
my son Absalom! would God I had died for thee,
O Absalom, my son, my son!

CHAPTER 19

AND it was told Joab, Behold, the king weepeth
and mourneth for Absalom.
2 And the victory that day was *turned* into mourn-
ing unto all the people: for the people heard say
that day how the king was grieved for his son.
3 And the people gat them by stealth that day into
the city, as people being ashamed steal away when
they flee in battle.
4 But the king covered his face, and the king cried
with a loud voice, O my son Absalom, O Absalom,
my son, my son!
5 And Joab came into the house to the king, and
said, Thou hast shamed this day the faces of all thy
servants, which this day have saved thy life, and
the lives of thy sons and of thy daughters, and the
lives of thy wives, and the lives of thy concubines;
6 In that thou lovest thine enemies, and hatest thy
friends. For thou hast declared this day, that thou
regardest neither princes nor servants: for this day
I perceive, that if Absalom had lived, and all we
had died this day, then it had pleased thee well.
7 Now therefore arise, go forth, and speak com-
fortably unto thy servants: for I swear by the
LORD, if thou go not forth, there will not tarry
one with thee this night: and that will be worse
unto thee than all the evil that befell thee from thy
youth until now.
8 Then the king arose, and sat in the gate. And
they told unto all the people, saying, Behold, the
king doth sit in the gate. And all the people came
before the king: for Israel had fled every man to
his tent.
9 ¶ And all the people were at strife throughout
all the tribes of Israel, saying, The king saved us
out of the hand of our enemies, and he delivered
us out of the hand of the Philistines; and now he
is fled out of the land for Absalom.
10 And Absalom, whom we anointed over us, is
dead in battle. Now therefore why speak ye not a
word of bringing the king back?
11 ¶ And king David sent to Zadok and to
Abiathar the priests, saying, Speak unto the elders
of Judah, saying, Why are ye the last to bring the
king back to his house? seeing the speech of all
Israel is come to the king, *even* to his house.
12 Ye *are* my brethren, ye *are* my bones and my
flesh: wherefore then are ye the last to bring back
the king?
13 And say ye to Amasa, *Art* thou not of my bone,
and of my flesh? God do so to me, and more
also, if thou be not captain of the host before me
continually in the room of Joab.
14 And he bowed the heart of all the men of
Judah, even as *the heart of* one man; so that they
sent *this word* unto the king, Return thou, and all
thy servants.
15 So the king returned, and came to Jordan. And
Judah came to Gilgal, to go to meet the king, to
conduct the king over Jordan.
16 ¶ And Shimei the son of Gera, a Benjamite,
which *was* of Bahurim, hasted and came down
with the men of Judah to meet king David.
17 And *there were* a thousand men of Benjamin
with him, and Ziba the servant of the house of Saul,
and his fifteen sons and his twenty servants with
him; and they went over Jordan before the king.
18 And there went over a ferry boat to carry over
the king's household, and to do what he thought
good. And Shimei the son of Gera fell down
before the king, as he was come over Jordan;
19 And said unto the king, Let not my lord im-
pute iniquity unto me, neither do thou remember
that which thy servant did perversely the day that

troubled. *would God I had died for thee.* An idiom expressing desire; literally, "who would give my death, I instead of you."

Thoughts for Personal/Family Worship: Chapter 18

1. **Absalom has been justly denounced as "the first of traitors and the worst of sons." We see in this chapter that the end of the rebellious is destruction. Absalom, who aspired to the crown, found a grave instead. Ironically, He had set up a monument to his own name and was buried beneath a heap of stones. He had hoped to make his name famous, similar to Shebna, who made a conspicuous grave for himself, only to be cast out in shame (Isa. 22:15–19). Pride comes before destruction. We should all learn that there is a watchful eye of justice for rebellion and disobedience against authority.**
2. **We see the pain of heart in a good father. The sins of children are always a grief to Christian parents, and tragically so when rebellious children persist in their sins to the end without repentance. David was overwhelmed with grief when he heard of his son's tragic end, for he knew that his son had died without hope in the world. Like Paul, who wished himself accursed from Christ if it meant the salvation of his kinsmen (Rom. 9:3–4), David wished that he could have died if it had meant sparing his son from condemnation. Children should always remember how much their salvation means to their believing parents and follow their parental instruction to submit to the Lord.**

Chapter 19: *David is restored to the throne and deals kindly and justly with both his antagonists and loyalists.*

19:3 *gat them by stealth.* Entered stealthily. They had been victorious, but they acted as though they had been defeated.
19:4 *covered his face.* A gesture of mourning.
19:7 *speak comfortably.* Literally, "speak to the heart." *evil.* Trouble.
19:13 *in the room of.* Instead of.

my lord the king went out of Jerusalem, that the
king should take it to his heart.
20 For thy servant doth know that I have sinned:
therefore, behold, I am come the first this day of
all the house of Joseph to go down to meet my
lord the king.
21 But Abishai the son of Zeruiah answered and
said, Shall not Shimei be put to death for this,
because he cursed the LORD's anointed?
22 And David said, What have I to do with you,
ye sons of Zeruiah, that ye should this day be
adversaries unto me? shall there any man be put
to death this day in Israel? for do not I know that
I *am* this day king over Israel?
23 Therefore the king said unto Shimei, Thou
shalt not die. And the king sware unto him.
24 ¶ And Mephibosheth the son of Saul came
down to meet the king, and had neither dressed
his feet, nor trimmed his beard, nor washed his
clothes, from the day the king departed until the
day he came *again* in peace.
25 And it came to pass, when he was come to
Jerusalem to meet the king, that the king said
unto him, Wherefore wentest not thou with me,
Mephibosheth?
26 And he answered, My lord, O king, my servant
deceived me: for thy servant said, I will saddle me
an ass, that I may ride thereon, and go to the king;
because thy servant *is* lame.
27 And he hath slandered thy servant unto my
lord the king; but my lord the king *is* as an angel
of God: do therefore *what is* good in thine eyes.
28 For all *of* my father's house were but dead
men before my lord the king: yet didst thou set
thy servant among them that did eat at thine own
table. What right therefore have I yet to cry any
more unto the king?
29 And the king said unto him, Why speakest
thou any more of thy matters? I have said, Thou
and Ziba divide the land.
30 And Mephibosheth said unto the king, Yea,
let him take all, forasmuch as my lord the king is
come again in peace unto his own house.
31 ¶ And Barzillai the Gileadite came down from
Rogelim, and went over Jordan with the king, to
conduct him over Jordan.
32 Now Barzillai was a very aged man, *even* four-
score years old: and he had provided the king of
sustenance while he lay at Mahanaim; for he *was*
a very great man.
33 And the king said unto Barzillai, Come thou
over with me, and I will feed thee with me in
Jerusalem.
34 And Barzillai said unto the king, How long
have I to live, that I should go up with the king
unto Jerusalem?
35 I *am* this day fourscore years old: *and* can I
discern between good and evil? can thy servant
taste what I eat or what I drink? can I hear any
more the voice of singing men and singing
women? wherefore then should thy servant be yet
a burden unto my lord the king?
36 Thy servant will go a little way over Jordan
with the king: and why should the king recom-
pense it me with such a reward?
37 Let thy servant, I pray thee, turn back again,
that I may die in mine own city, *and be buried* by
the grave of my father and of my mother. But be-
hold thy servant Chimham; let him go over with
my lord the king; and do to him what shall seem
good unto thee.
38 And the king answered, Chimham shall go
over with me, and I will do to him that which
shall seem good unto thee: and whatsoever thou
shalt require of me, *that* will I do for thee.
39 And all the people went over Jordan. And
when the king was come over, the king kissed
Barzillai, and blessed him; and he returned unto
his own place.
40 Then the king went on to Gilgal, and
Chimham went on with him: and all the people
of Judah conducted the king, and also half the
people of Israel.
41 ¶ And, behold, all the men of Israel came to
the king, and said unto the king, Why have our
brethren the men of Judah stolen thee away, and
have brought the king, and his household, and all
David's men with him, over Jordan?

19:25 *Wherefore wentest not thou.* Why did you not go . . . ?
19:27 *angel of God.* Messenger of God.
19:28–30 Mephibosheth demonstrated great humility, gratitude, and love for David despite the injustice done to him. His greatest joy was seeing David return *in peace*, not recovering property. In this Mephibosheth showed himself a true son of Jonathan (1 Sam. 18:1–4; 20:16–17).
19:32 *fourscore.* Eighty.
19:35 *can I discern between good and evil?* Barzillai's ability to reason rightly was departing with age.
19:38 *require of me.* The Hebrew is "to choose."

The Rebellion of Sheba against David (2 Sam. 19:41—20:26)

19:41–43 Although it was a united monarchy, there was always a tension between *Judah* and the other tribes of *Israel* (1 Sam. 11:8; 17:52; 18:16; 2 Sam. 2:8–10; 20:2) that would intensify in time.

Thoughts for Personal/Family Worship: Chapter 19

David's treatment of Shimei illustrates how to deal with those who have wronged us and points to the even greater mercy shown by Christ, David's greater son. David never looked more Christlike than when he pardoned Shimei. Shimei's sins were great, making David's forgiveness that much greater. This reminds us of the great work of Christ, that "God commendeth his love toward us, in that, while we were yet sinners, Christ died for us" (Rom. 5:8). As Matthew Henry says, "They that are forgiven, must forgive."

42 And all the men of Judah answered the men of
Israel, Because the king *is* near of kin to us: wherefore then be ye angry for this matter? have we eaten at all of the king's *cost*? or hath he given us any gift?
43 And the men of Israel answered the men of
Judah, and said, We have ten parts in the king, and we have also more *right* in David than ye: why then did ye despise us, that our advice should not be first had in bringing back our king? And the words of the men of Judah were fiercer than the words of the men of Israel.

CHAPTER 20

AND there happened to be there a man of Belial, whose name *was* Sheba, the son of Bichri, a Benjamite: and he blew a trumpet, and said, We have no part in David, neither have we inheritance in the son of Jesse: every man to his tents, O Israel.
2 So every man of Israel went up from after
David, *and* followed Sheba the son of Bichri: but the men of Judah clave unto their king, from Jordan even to Jerusalem.
3 ¶ And David came to his house at Jerusalem;
and the king took the ten women *his* concubines, whom he had left to keep the house, and put them in ward, and fed them, but went not in unto them. So they were shut up unto the day of their death, living in widowhood.
4 ¶ Then said the king to Amasa, Assemble me
the men of Judah within three days, and be thou here present.
5 So Amasa went to assemble *the men of* Judah:
but he tarried longer than the set time which he had appointed him.
6 And David said to Abishai, Now shall Sheba the
son of Bichri do us more harm than *did* Absalom: take thou thy lord's servants, and pursue after him, lest he get him fenced cities, and escape us.
7 And there went out after him Joab's men, and
the Cherethites, and the Pelethites, and all the mighty men: and they went out of Jerusalem, to pursue after Sheba the son of Bichri.
8 When they *were* at the great stone which *is* in
Gibeon, Amasa went before them. And Joab's garment that he had put on was girded unto him, and upon it a girdle *with* a sword fastened upon his loins in the sheath thereof; and as he went forth it fell out.
9 And Joab said to Amasa, *Art* thou in health, my
brother? And Joab took Amasa by the beard with the right hand to kiss him.
10 But Amasa took no heed to the sword that *was*
in Joab's hand: so he smote him therewith in the fifth *rib*, and shed out his bowels to the ground, and struck him not again; and he died. So Joab and Abishai his brother pursued after Sheba the son of Bichri.
11 And one of Joab's men stood by him, and said,
He that favoureth Joab, and he that *is* for David, *let him go* after Joab.
12 And Amasa wallowed in blood in the midst of
the highway. And when the man saw that all the people stood still, he removed Amasa out of the highway into the field, and cast a cloth upon him, when he saw that every one that came by him stood still.
13 When he was removed out of the highway,
all the people went on after Joab, to pursue after Sheba the son of Bichri.
14 ¶ And he went through all the tribes of Israel
unto Abel, and to Beth-maachah, and all the Berites: and they were gathered together, and went also after him.
15 And they came and besieged him in Abel of
Beth-maachah, and they cast up a bank against the city, and it stood in the trench: and all the people that *were* with Joab battered the wall, to throw it down.
16 ¶ Then cried a wise woman out of the city,
Hear, hear; say, I pray you, unto Joab, Come near hither, that I may speak with thee.
17 And when he was come near unto her, the
woman said, *Art* thou Joab? And he answered, I *am he*. Then she said unto him, Hear the words of thine handmaid. And he answered, I do hear.
18 Then she spake, saying, They were wont to
speak in old time, saying, They shall surely ask

Chapter 20: *Sheba's revolt is subdued, assuring the restoration of David, and Joab murders Amasa, securing his command of Israel's army.*

20:1 *man of Belial.* See note at 16:7.
20:2 *clave.* Clung; the men of Judah stuck with David. Here is evidence of the tension between Judah and the other tribes.
20:3 *in ward.* Under guard. *shut up.* Locked in. No reason is given, but perhaps because of the affair involving Absalom (16:20–22).
20:4 *Amasa.* Commissioned by David to replace Joab (19:13).
20:5 *he tarried longer than the set time.* Perhaps delayed by the people's suspicion of him since he had served under Absalom (17:25).
20:7 *the Cherethites, and the Pelethites.* Mercenaries who had helped David before (8:18; 15:18).
20:8 *girded unto him.* Secured with a belt. *girdle.* Band or belt for carrying the sword. *upon his loins.* Around his hips.
20:9 *Art thou in health.* Literally, "Are you [in] peace?" a common greeting like "How are you?"
20:10 *the fifth rib.* The Hebrew designates the abdomen. *bowels.* Entrails or intestines. *struck him not again.* Literally, "did not repeat," so severe and on target was the first thrust that death was certain even if not immediate.
20:12 *the man.* A man; the Hebrew often uses the article "the" in a generic or indefinite sense.
20:15 *a bank.* A mound or assault ramp to scale the city wall. *it stood in the trench.* Literally, "it stood [was placed] against the outer rampart."
20:18 *were wont to speak in old time.* Were accustomed to

counsel at Abel: and so they ended *the matter*.
19 I *am one of them that are* peaceable *and* faith-
ful in Israel: thou seekest to destroy a city and a
mother in Israel: why wilt thou swallow up the
inheritance of the LORD?
20 And Joab answered and said, Far be it, far be
it from me, that I should swallow up or destroy.
21 The matter *is* not so: but a man of mount
Ephraim, Sheba the son of Bichri by name, hath
lifted up his hand against the king, *even* against
David: deliver him only, and I will depart from
the city. And the woman said unto Joab, Behold,
his head shall be thrown to thee over the wall.
22 Then the woman went unto all the people in
her wisdom. And they cut off the head of Sheba
the son of Bichri, and cast *it* out to Joab. And
he blew a trumpet, and they retired from the
city, every man to his tent. And Joab returned to
Jerusalem unto the king.
23 ¶ Now Joab *was* over all the host of Israel:
and Benaiah the son of Jehoiada *was* over the
Cherethites and over the Pelethites:
24 And Adoram *was* over the tribute: and Je-
hoshaphat the son of Ahilud *was* recorder:
25 And Sheva *was* scribe: and Zadok and Abia-
thar *were* the priests:
26 And Ira also the Jairite was a chief ruler about
David.

CHAPTER 21

THEN there was a famine in the days of David
three years, year after year; and David enquired
of the LORD. And the LORD answered, *It is* for
Saul, and for *his* bloody house, because he slew
the Gibeonites.
2 And the king called the Gibeonites, and said
unto them; (now the Gibeonites *were* not of
the children of Israel, but of the remnant of the
Amorites; and the children of Israel had sworn
unto them: and Saul sought to slay them in his
zeal to the children of Israel and Judah.)
3 Wherefore David said unto the Gibeonites,
What shall I do for you? and wherewith shall I
make the atonement, that ye may bless the inheri-
tance of the LORD?
4 And the Gibeonites said unto him, We will have
no silver nor gold of Saul, nor of his house; nei-
ther for us shalt thou kill any man in Israel. And
he said, What ye shall say, *that* will I do for you.
5 And they answered the king, The man that
consumed us, and that devised against us *that* we
should be destroyed from remaining in any of the
coasts of Israel,
6 Let seven men of his sons be delivered unto us,
and we will hang them up unto the LORD in Gib-
eah of Saul, *whom* the LORD did choose. And the
king said, I will give *them*.
7 But the king spared Mephibosheth, the son of
Jonathan the son of Saul, because of the LORD's
oath that *was* between them, between David and
Jonathan the son of Saul.
8 But the king took the two sons of Rizpah the
daughter of Aiah, whom she bare unto Saul,
Armoni and Mephibosheth; and the five sons of
Michal the daughter of Saul, whom she brought
up for Adriel the son of Barzillai the Meholathite:
9 And he delivered them into the hands of the
Gibeonites, and they hanged them in the hill
before the LORD: and they fell *all* seven together,
and were put to death in the days of harvest, in
the first *days*, in the beginning of barley harvest.

speak; literally, "certainly spoke in former time."
20:22 *retired.* Dispersed.

Thoughts for Personal/Family Worship: Chapter 20

1. **Joab's treacherous murder of Amasa shows the depths to which envy and selfish ambition can plunge. Because of Amasa's promotion, Joab no longer enjoyed the rank and privilege that once had been his, and he was willing and capable of doing anything to regain it, including murder. Discontent with one's position and envy over another's may not lead to the same horrific crime, but those attitudes are always violations of the tenth commandment not to covet what belongs to another. It is a noble Christian virtue to be able to rejoice with others (Rom. 12:15) without yielding to the temptation to envy. Sadly, the church of Christ is not immune to this creeping sin. The Lord's own disciples were guilty of it. We must pray against the spirit that asks, "Who is the greatest in the kingdom of heaven?" (Matt. 18:1). The only remedy is to be like Christ, who humbled himself (Phil. 2:5).**
2. **The wise woman of Abel mirrors the poor wise man who by his wisdom delivered a city (Eccl. 8:14–15). Without her actions, a whole city of innocent people would have been destroyed because of the rebellion of one man. Should not the believer follow her example and strive, even if the task is hard, to calm the storm of contending parties? "Blessed are the peacemakers" (Matt. 5:9). Do you know people in conflict? How might you speak a word of peace?**

THE CONCLUSION OF DAVID'S REIGN (2 SAM. 21:1—24:25)

Chapter 21: *David allows the Gibeonites to avenge themselves for Saul's breaking an ancient covenant, and war erupts with the Philistines.*

Vengeance for the Gibeonites on Saul's Family (21:1–14)

21:1 *enquired of the LORD.* Literally, "sought the face of the Lord."
21:2 See Josh. 9:3–17 for Israel's covenant with the Gibeonites, which Saul violated.
21:3 *wherewith shall I make the atonement.* What can I do to appease or make amends?
21:6 *Let seven men of his sons be delivered.* Most likely these sons were complicit in the attack on the Gibeonites.
21:7 *But the king spared Mephibosheth.* David's covenant with Jonathan guaranteed Mephibosheth's safety (1 Sam. 18:3; 20:8, 42; 23:18).

10 ¶ And Rizpah the daughter of Aiah took sack-
cloth, and spread it for her upon the rock, from
the beginning of harvest until water dropped
upon them out of heaven, and suffered neither
the birds of the air to rest on them by day, nor the
beasts of the field by night.
11 And it was told David what Rizpah the daugh-
ter of Aiah, the concubine of Saul, had done.
12 ¶ And David went and took the bones of Saul
and the bones of Jonathan his son from the men
of Jabesh-gilead, which had stolen them from
the street of Beth-shan, where the Philistines had
hanged them, when the Philistines had slain Saul
in Gilboa:
13 And he brought up from thence the bones of
Saul and the bones of Jonathan his son; and they
gathered the bones of them that were hanged.
14 And the bones of Saul and Jonathan his son
buried they in the country of Benjamin in Zelah,
in the sepulchre of Kish his father: and they
performed all that the king commanded. And
after that God was intreated for the land.
15 ¶ Moreover the Philistines had yet war again
with Israel; and David went down, and his ser-
vants with him, and fought against the Philistines:
and David waxed faint.
16 And Ishbi-benob, which *was* of the sons of
the giant, the weight of whose spear *weighed*
three hundred *shekels* of brass in weight, he being
girded with a new *sword*, thought to have slain
David.
17 But Abishai the son of Zeruiah succoured him,
and smote the Philistine, and killed him. Then
the men of David sware unto him, saying, Thou
shalt go no more out with us to battle, that thou
quench not the light of Israel.
18 And it came to pass after this, that there was
again a battle with the Philistines at Gob: then
Sibbechai the Hushathite slew Saph, which *was* of
the sons of the giant.
19 And there was again a battle in Gob with
the Philistines, where Elhanan the son of Jaare-
oregim, a Beth-lehemite, slew *the brother of*
Goliath the Gittite, the staff of whose spear *was*
like a weaver's beam.
20 And there was yet a battle in Gath, where was
a man of *great* stature, that had on every hand
six fingers, and on every foot six toes, four and
twenty in number; and he also was born to the
giant.
21 And when he defied Israel, Jonathan the son of
Shimea the brother of David slew him.
22 These four were born to the giant in Gath, and
fell by the hand of David, and by the hand of his
servants.

CHAPTER 22

AND David spake unto the LORD the words of this
song in the day *that* the LORD had delivered him
out of the hand of all his enemies, and out of the
hand of Saul:
2 And he said, The LORD *is* my rock, and my
fortress, and my deliverer;
3 The God of my rock; in him will I trust: *he is*
my shield, and the horn of my salvation, my high
tower, and my refuge, my saviour; thou savest me
from violence.
4 I will call on the LORD, *who is* worthy to be
praised: so shall I be saved from mine enemies.
5 When the waves of death compassed me, the
floods of ungodly men made me afraid;

21:10 *took sackcloth.* A sign of mourning.

War between the Philistines and an Aging David (21:15–22)

21:15 *waxed faint.* Became tired.
21:16 *three hundred shekels.* Approximately eight and a quarter pounds. *girded.* Secured with a belt.
21:17 *succoured.* Helped. *that thou quench not the light.* Literally, "lest you extinguish the lamp." David's death in battle would bring chaos, like floundering in the dark. His dynasty was later compared to a lamp kept shining in Jerusalem by God's mercy (1 Kings 11:36; 15:4; 2 Kings 8:19). David was *the light of Israel*, but his descendant Jesus Christ is the "light of the world" (John 8:12).

Thoughts for Personal/Family Worship: Chapter 21

1. **Covenant promises are binding, and breaking them has serious consequences. Joshua made a covenant with the Gibeonites to let them live (Josh. 9:15). Years later, Saul broke that covenant by slaying the Gibeonites (2 Sam. 21:1). Years after that Israel suffers a famine, and it is not until David seeks the reason from the Lord that he learns that it is because of Saul's covenant transgression. Saul did not make the covenant, but he was liable to it. David had not violated the covenant, but he was liable for it. Could it be that troubles and trials that seem to come without reason can be traced to vows made long ago that have been forgotten? We may forget, but God does not. Vows, if made, must be kept (Eccl. 5:4–6). God takes them seriously.**
2. **That the nation suffered because of Saul's sin is a vivid reminder of the powerful influence of sin. In one sense, there is no such thing as private sin. Either by example or by consequence, sin affects others. This is magnified when leaders sin because the sphere of their influence is so great. It is particularly important for those in authority, whether civil, religious, or in the home, to live in such a way as to influence positively those under their authority. It is important to pray for those in authority that they might rule well for our own benefit (1 Tim. 2:2).**

Chapter 22: *Recognizing God as the source of every deliverance and blessing, David offers his praise and thanksgiving.*

The Song of David to the Lord (2 Sam. 22:1–51)

22:1 *in the day.* A Hebrew idiom meaning "when."
22:2 With only minor variations, this psalm of thanksgiving is the same as Ps. 18 (see the notes there).
22:3 *horn.* A common image for strength or power.

6 The sorrows of hell compassed me about; the
snares of death prevented me;
7 In my distress I called upon the LORD, and cried
to my God: and he did hear my voice out of his
temple, and my cry *did enter* into his ears.
8 Then the earth shook and trembled; the foun-
dations of heaven moved and shook, because he
was wroth.
9 There went up a smoke out of his nostrils,
and fire out of his mouth devoured: coals were
kindled by it.
10 He bowed the heavens also, and came down;
and darkness *was* under his feet.
11 And he rode upon a cherub, and did fly: and
he was seen upon the wings of the wind.
12 And he made darkness pavilions round about
him, dark waters, *and* thick clouds of the skies.
13 Through the brightness before him were coals
of fire kindled.
14 The LORD thundered from heaven, and the
most High uttered his voice.
15 And he sent out arrows, and scattered them;
lightning, and discomfited them.
16 And the channels of the sea appeared, the
foundations of the world were discovered, at the
rebuking of the LORD, at the blast of the breath of
his nostrils.
17 He sent from above, he took me; he drew me
out of many waters;
18 He delivered me from my strong enemy, *and*
from them that hated me: for they were too
strong for me.
19 They prevented me in the day of my calamity:
but the LORD was my stay.
20 He brought me forth also into a large place: he
delivered me, because he delighted in me.
21 The LORD rewarded me according to my righ-
teousness: according to the cleanness of my hands
hath he recompensed me.
22 For I have kept the ways of the LORD, and have
not wickedly departed from my God.
23 For all his judgments *were* before me: and *as
for* his statutes, I did not depart from them.
24 I was also upright before him, and have kept
myself from mine iniquity.
25 Therefore the LORD hath recompensed me
according to my righteousness; according to my
cleanness in his eye sight.
26 With the merciful thou wilt shew thyself
merciful, *and* with the upright man thou wilt
shew thyself upright.
27 With the pure thou wilt shew thyself pure;
and with the froward thou wilt shew thyself
unsavoury.
28 And the afflicted people thou wilt save: but
thine eyes *are* upon the haughty, *that* thou mayest
bring *them* down.
29 For thou *art* my lamp, O LORD: and the LORD
will lighten my darkness.
30 For by thee I have run through a troop: by my
God have I leaped over a wall.
31 *As for* God, his way *is* perfect; the word of the
LORD *is* tried: he *is* a buckler to all them that trust
in him.
32 For who *is* God, save the LORD? and who *is* a
rock, save our God?
33 God *is* my strength *and* power: and he maketh
my way perfect.
34 He maketh my feet like hinds' *feet*: and setteth
me upon my high places.
35 He teacheth my hands to war; so that a bow of
steel is broken by mine arms.
36 Thou hast also given me the shield of thy sal-
vation: and thy gentleness hath made me great.
37 Thou hast enlarged my steps under me; so that
my feet did not slip.
38 I have pursued mine enemies, and destroyed
them; and turned not again until I had consumed
them.
39 And I have consumed them, and wounded
them, that they could not arise: yea, they are fallen
under my feet.
40 For thou hast girded me with strength to
battle: them that rose up against me hast thou
subdued under me.
41 Thou hast also given me the necks of mine
enemies, that I might destroy them that hate me.
42 They looked, but *there was* none to save; *even*
unto the LORD, but he answered them not.
43 Then did I beat them as small as the dust of
the earth, I did stamp them as the mire of the
street, *and* did spread them abroad.
44 Thou also hast delivered me from the striv-
ings of my people, thou hast kept me *to be* head
of the heathen: a people *which* I knew not shall
serve me.
45 Strangers shall submit themselves unto me: as
soon as they hear, they shall be obedient unto me.

22:6 *hell*. The Hebrew, *sheol*, can refer to death, the grave, or the abode of departed wicked spirits. The parallelism here would suggest that it refers to death.
22:8 *wroth*. Angry.
22:12 *pavilions*. Booths or tents.
22:15 *discomfited*. Confused.
22:16 *discovered*. Uncovered or exposed.
22:19 *prevented*. The Hebrew is "confronted." *stay*. Support or staff.
22:27 *froward*. Twisted or perverted. *shew thyself unsavoury*. Hebrew, "prove oneself tortuous."
22:30 *run through a troop . . . leaped over a wall*. The image of bursting through a marauding band, the enemy lines, and jumping over their defenses.
22:31 *tried*. Refined and therefore pure. *buckler*. Shield.
22:32 *save*. Except.
22:34 *hinds' feet*. Feet of does of fallow deer.
22:40 *girded*. Surrounded.

46 Strangers shall fade away, and they shall be
afraid out of their close places.
47 The LORD liveth; and blessed *be* my rock; and
exalted be the God of the rock of my salvation.
48 It *is* God that avengeth me, and that bringeth
down the people under me,
49 And that bringeth me forth from mine enemies: thou also hast lifted me up on high above
them that rose up against me: thou hast delivered
me from the violent man.
50 Therefore I will give thanks unto thee, O
LORD, among the heathen, and I will sing praises
unto thy name.
51 *He is* the tower of salvation for his king: and
sheweth mercy to his anointed, unto David, and
to his seed for evermore.

CHAPTER 23

1 NOW these *be* the last words of David. David the
son of Jesse said, and the man *who was* raised up
on high, the anointed of the God of Jacob, and the
sweet psalmist of Israel, said,
2 The Spirit of the LORD spake by me, and his
word *was* in my tongue.
3 The God of Israel said, the Rock of Israel spake
to me, He that ruleth over men *must be* just, ruling in the fear of God.
4 And *he shall be* as the light of the morning, *when*
the sun riseth, *even* a morning without clouds; *as*
the tender grass *springing* out of the earth by clear
shining after rain.
5 Although my house *be* not so with God; yet
he hath made with me an everlasting covenant,
ordered in all *things*, and sure: for *this is* all my
salvation, and all *my* desire, although he make *it*
not to grow.
6 ¶ But *the sons* of Belial *shall be* all of them as
thorns thrust away, because they cannot be taken
with hands:
7 But the man *that* shall touch them must be
fenced with iron and the staff of a spear; and they
shall be utterly burned with fire in the *same* place.
8 ¶ These *be* the names of the mighty men whom
David had: The Tachmonite that sat in the seat,
chief among the captains; the same *was* Adino the
Eznite: *he lift up his spear* against eight hundred,
whom he slew at one time.
9 And after him *was* Eleazar the son of Dodo the
Ahohite, *one* of the three mighty men with David,
when they defied the Philistines *that* were there
gathered together to battle, and the men of Israel
were gone away:
10 He arose, and smote the Philistines until his
hand was weary, and his hand clave unto the
sword: and the LORD wrought a great victory that
day; and the people returned after him only to
spoil.
11 And after him *was* Shammah the son of Agee
the Hararite. And the Philistines were gathered
together into a troop, where was a piece of
ground full of lentiles: and the people fled from
the Philistines.
12 But he stood in the midst of the ground, and
defended it, and slew the Philistines: and the
LORD wrought a great victory.
13 And three of the thirty chief went down, and
came to David in the harvest time unto the cave of
Adullam: and the troop of the Philistines pitched
in the valley of Rephaim.
14 And David *was* then in an hold, and the garrison of the Philistines *was* then *in* Beth-lehem.
15 And David longed, and said, Oh that one
would give me drink of the water of the well of
Beth-lehem, which *is* by the gate!
16 And the three mighty men brake through

22:45–46 *Strangers.* Foreigners.

Thoughts for Personal/Family Worship: Chapter 22

This song of David testifies to his recognition that he owes everything to the Lord's mercy, covenant faithfulness, and timely providences. He is careful to give the Lord the thanks and praise He deserves. Similarly, we should be conscious of and sensitive to all that God does for us in preserving, protecting, and providentially meeting our every need. Like David, we should lift our hearts and voices in praise and thanksgiving. God does not grow weary of the praise of His people, even when they are praising Him for the same things over and again. That David's song in this chapter is virtually the same as Ps. 18 directs us never to forget the Lord's benefits to us and never to cease praising Him for them. It is quite acceptable to repeat; God is not looking for originality so much as He desires genuineness and sincerity.

Chapter 23: ***David speaks his last words and recounts the mighty men of valor.***

David's Last Words (2 Sam. 23:1–7)

23:1 *anointed.* The Hebrew is transliterated into English as "Messiah" and was translated into Greek as "Christ." David, one of the lesser "messiahs," prefigured and pointed to the ideal Messiah or Anointed One to come.

23:2 *The Spirit of the LORD spake by me.* David was aware that his words came by divine inspiration of the Spirit.

23:5 This statement is a high water mark of David's faith, expressing his understanding that even though his house would fail and falter, the *covenant* was *sure* because it would find unconditional fulfillment in the Christ, his salvation and all his desire (7:12–16; Ps. 89:19–37).

23:6 *Belial.* See note at 16:7.

23:7 *fenced with iron.* Hebrew, "filled with iron."

David's Mighty Men (23:8–39)

23:10 *clave.* To cling or to remain stuck. His grip became frozen because he had been holding it so long.

23:11 *troop.* Army.

23:13 *pitched.* Encamped.

23:14 *an hold.* A mountain fortress or stronghold.

the host of the Philistines, and drew water out of
the well of Beth-lehem, that *was* by the gate, and
took *it*, and brought *it* to David: nevertheless he
would not drink thereof, but poured it out unto
the LORD.
17 And he said, Be it far from me, O LORD, that
I should do this: *is not this* the blood of the men
that went in jeopardy of their lives? therefore he
would not drink it. These things did these three
mighty men.
18 And Abishai, the brother of Joab, the son of
Zeruiah, was chief among three. And he lifted up
his spear against three hundred, *and* slew *them*,
and had the name among three.
19 Was he not most honourable of three? there-
fore he was their captain: howbeit he attained not
unto the *first* three.
20 And Benaiah the son of Jehoiada, the son of
a valiant man, of Kabzeel, who had done many
acts, he slew two lionlike men of Moab: he went
down also and slew a lion in the midst of a pit in
time of snow:
21 And he slew an Egyptian, a goodly man: and
the Egyptian had a spear in his hand; but he went
down to him with a staff, and plucked the spear
out of the Egyptian's hand, and slew him with his
own spear.
22 These *things* did Benaiah the son of Jehoiada,
and had the name among three mighty men.
23 He was more honourable than the thirty, but
he attained not to the *first* three. And David set
him over his guard.
24 Asahel the brother of Joab *was* one of the
thirty; Elhanan the son of Dodo of Beth-lehem,
25 Shammah the Harodite, Elika the Harodite,
26 Helez the Paltite, Ira the son of Ikkesh the
Tekoite,
27 Abi-ezer the Anethothite, Mebunnai the Hu-
shathite,
28 Zalmon the Ahohite, Maharai the Netopha-
thite,
29 Heleb the son of Baanah, a Netophathite, Ittai
the son of Ribai out of Gibeah of the children of
Benjamin,
30 Benaiah the Pirathonite, Hiddai of the brooks
of Gaash,
31 Abi-albon the Arbathite, Azmaveth the Barhu-
mite,
32 Eliahba the Shaalbonite, of the sons of Jashen,
Jonathan,
33 Shammah the Hararite, Ahiam the son of
Sharar the Hararite,
34 Eliphelet the son of Ahasbai, the son of the Ma-
achathite, Eliam the son of Ahithophel the Gilonite,
35 Hezrai the Carmelite, Paarai the Arbite,
36 Igal the son of Nathan of Zobah, Bani the
Gadite,
37 Zelek the Ammonite, Naharai the Beerothite,
armourbearer to Joab the son of Zeruiah,
38 Ira an Ithrite, Gareb an Ithrite,
39 Uriah the Hittite: thirty and seven in all.

CHAPTER 24

AND again the anger of the LORD was kindled
against Israel, and he moved David against them
to say, Go, number Israel and Judah.
2 For the king said to Joab the captain of the
host, which *was* with him, Go now through all the
tribes of Israel, from Dan even to Beer-sheba, and

23:16 *poured it out unto the LORD.* As an offering to him and a display of his dedication.
23:18 *had the name among three.* The most famous of the three.
23:21 *a goodly man.* Literally, "a man of appearance." See 1 Chron. 11:23, where he is called a "man of measure" or great stature.
23:23 *He was more honourable than the thirty . . . attained not to the first three.* His reputation was greater than that of most, but not the best.
23:24 *Asahel . . . was one of the thirty.* More properly, "over the thirty."
23:39 *Uriah the Hittite.* David now comes full circle to all his troubles, giving honor to the man who died for his lust.

Thoughts for Personal/Family Worship: Chapter 23

1. **David's description of the ideal ruler (vv. 3–4) points directly to the one and only King who meets the requirements, the Lord Jesus. David rejoiced at the prospect of the coming of Messiah, the ultimate fulfillment of the covenant promise. He acknowledged Christ as his salvation and the totality of his desire. David looked to Christ's coming; we rejoice in the fact that He has come and indeed is coming again. Christ is the salvation of His people. Let it be true that He is all our hearts' desire as well.**
2. **The exploits of David's mighty men are noteworthy. Each of these men was completely devoted and loyal to David to the extent that they risked their own lives for the welfare of their king. They were courageous and determined in serving their king. If they were willing to expend themselves in such ways in the service of an earthly king, how much more should the servants of Christ, the heavenly King, not give themselves in total devotion and selfless service to Him and the advancing of His kingdom? He has given us the equipment we need to fight our battles (Eph. 6:10–18), so let us abandon ourselves to His service. In your particular calling and place in life, how can you strive to be a mighty man or woman for the Lord?**

Chapter 24: ***David numbers the people, bringing a plague upon them that stops after David's repentance.***

The Tragic Census of Israel (2 Sam. 24:1–25)

24:1 *he moved David.* Here the Lord incites David, whereas 1 Chron. 21:1 attributes the action to Satan. There is no contradiction nor any suggestion that God tempts to sin, something He does not do (James 1:13–14). What God uses as a test Satan turns into a temptation to sin.
24:2 *that I may know.* Numbering the people would have

number ye the people, that I may know the number of the people.
3 And Joab said unto the king, Now the LORD thy
God add unto the people, how many soever they be, an hundredfold, and that the eyes of my lord the king may see *it*: but why doth my lord the king delight in this thing?
4 Notwithstanding the king's word prevailed
against Joab, and against the captains of the host. And Joab and the captains of the host went out from the presence of the king, to number the people of Israel.
5 ¶ And they passed over Jordan, and pitched in
Aroer, on the right side of the city that *lieth* in the midst of the river of Gad, and toward Jazer:
6 Then they came to Gilead, and to the land of
Tahtim-hodshi; and they came to Dan-jaan, and about to Zidon,
7 And came to the strong hold of Tyre, and to all
the cities of the Hivites, and of the Canaanites: and they went out to the south of Judah, *even* to Beer-sheba.
8 So when they had gone through all the land,
they came to Jerusalem at the end of nine months and twenty days.
9 And Joab gave up the sum of the number of
the people unto the king: and there were in Israel eight hundred thousand valiant men that drew the sword; and the men of Judah *were* five hundred thousand men.
10 ¶ And David's heart smote him after that he
had numbered the people. And David said unto the LORD, I have sinned greatly in that I have done: and now, I beseech thee, O LORD, take away the iniquity of thy servant; for I have done very foolishly.
11 For when David was up in the morning, the
word of the LORD came unto the prophet Gad, David's seer, saying,
12 Go and say unto David, Thus saith the LORD,
I offer thee three *things*; choose thee one of them, that I may *do it* unto thee.
13 So Gad came to David, and told him, and said
unto him, Shall seven years of famine come unto thee in thy land? or wilt thou flee three months before thine enemies, while they pursue thee? or that there be three days' pestilence in thy land? now advise, and see what answer I shall return to him that sent me.
14 And David said unto Gad, I am in a great
strait: let us fall now into the hand of the LORD; for his mercies *are* great: and let me not fall into the hand of man.
15 ¶ So the LORD sent a pestilence upon Israel
from the morning even to the time appointed: and there died of the people from Dan even to Beer-sheba seventy thousand men.
16 And when the angel stretched out his hand
upon Jerusalem to destroy it, the LORD repented him of the evil, and said to the angel that destroyed the people, It is enough: stay now thine hand. And the angel of the LORD was by the threshingplace of Araunah the Jebusite.
17 And David spake unto the LORD when he saw
the angel that smote the people, and said, Lo, I have sinned, and I have done wickedly: but these sheep, what have they done? let thine hand, I pray thee, be against me, and against my father's house.
18 ¶ And Gad came that day to David, and said
unto him, Go up, rear an altar unto the LORD in the threshingfloor of Araunah the Jebusite.
19 And David, according to the saying of Gad,
went up as the LORD commanded.
20 And Araunah looked, and saw the king and
his servants coming on toward him: and Araunah went out, and bowed himself before the king on his face upon the ground.
21 And Araunah said, Wherefore is my lord the
king come to his servant? And David said, To buy the threshingfloor of thee, to build an altar unto the LORD, that the plague may be stayed from the people.
22 And Araunah said unto David, Let my lord the
king take and offer up what *seemeth* good unto him: behold, *here be* oxen for burnt sacrifice, and threshing instruments and *other* instruments of the oxen for wood.
23 All these *things* did Araunah, *as* a king, give

been an expression of pride rather than humble acknowledgement of the Lord as the builder of the kingdom.

24:5 *the river of Gad.* A small river or wadi (a stream-bed that flows during rainy seasons).

24:10 *And David's heart smote him after.* A stricken conscience regarding sin is an evidence of grace since sin is always a hostile presence in a believer (1 Sam. 24:5). *iniquity.* The principal word in the Old Testament for guilt. David's sense of guilt leads to immediate confession, unlike his wallowing in guilt when he sinned with Bath-sheba (chs. 11–12).

24:11 *seer.* Prophet.

24:13 *pestilence.* Plague (v. 15).

24:14 *strait.* Distress. *mercies.* Acts of compassion from seeing the misery of another.

24:16 *repented him of the evil.* Relented regarding the disaster (here the plague). On divine repentance and unchangeableness, see notes at 1 Sam. 15:11,29. *stay now thine hand.* Let the hand drop that was stretched out to execute the plague.

24:18 *rear.* Erect.

24:21 *stayed.* Restrained or brought to a halt (v. 25).

24:23 *accept thee.* Take pleasure or be favorable to you.

24:24 *fifty shekels.* Whereas 1 Chron. 21:25 says David paid 600 shekels. Rather than being a contradiction, what was purchased accounts for the discrepancy: 50 shekels for the threshing floor and oxen and 600 shekels for the whole piece of property that ultimately became the site of the temple (2 Chron. 3:1).

Thoughts for Personal/Family Worship: Chapter 24

1. Nebuchadnezzar boasted, "Is not this great Babylon,

unto the king. And Araunah said unto the king,
The LORD thy God accept thee.
24 And the king said unto Araunah, Nay; but I
will surely buy *it* of thee at a price: neither will
I offer burnt offerings unto the LORD my God
of that which doth cost me nothing. So David
bought the threshingfloor and the oxen for fifty
shekels of silver.
25 And David built there an altar unto the LORD,
and offered burnt offerings and peace offerings.
So the LORD was intreated for the land, and the
plague was stayed from Israel.

that I have built . . . ?" (Dan. 4:30). In many ways that boast is an echo of David at the close of his reign. David's numbering the people expressed his pride and sense of self-achievement. Throughout David's career, the evidence was unmistakable that it was God who built David's house, his kingdom (2 Sam. 7:8–16). During his reign, David himself confessed that even though some trusted in chariots and horses, he would acknowledge God (Ps. 20:7). Sadly, at the end his focus at least momentarily is on self. What appeared to be an innocent act had tragic consequences, touching the object of his pride. Let us be warned and let us walk humbly before God in all things, to His glory, not our own.

2. That David confessed immediately when his heart struck him (v. 10) is one of the most encouraging statements in the narrative. The Spirit dwelling in the believer reveals sin to the conscience and leads him to repentance. David did not delay; as soon as his conscience smote him he appealed to the Lord for mercy. That is the pattern to follow: deal with sin immediately. Sacrifices (v. 25) point to Christ's sacrifice that keeps on cleansing from sin (1 John 1:7). Significantly, David offers the burnt offering, which in part pictures complete consecration (everything on the altar), and the peace offering, which pictures the fellowship between God and the repentant sinner. When we receive forgiveness from God (1 John 1:9) we ought to dedicate ourselves anew to Him in thanksgiving (that's our reasonable service, Rom. 12:1). That the burnt offering particularly pictures consecration of self explains why David refused to offer to the Lord something that cost him nothing (2 Sam. 24:24). Christ's sacrifice cost Him everything upon the cross. While you cannot pay for your sins, following Christ will be costly. What has it cost you to be a Christian? Is there any area of repentance that you are avoiding because of the cost?

INTRODUCTION TO THE BOOKS OF 1ST AND 2ND KINGS

Authorship: First and Second Kings constitute a single book, just as 1 and 2 Samuel are a single unit. Their division into four books traces back to the translation of Hebrew Scriptures into Greek in the Septuagint, which designated the books as the four books of Kingdoms. The currently accepted designations are attributed to Daniel Bomberg's printed edition of the Hebrew Scriptures in 1518. The different titles used to designate the books have no bearing on the content. But since 1 and 2 Kings are a single unit, their introductory matters are treated together.

The author of Kings was a prophet from the kingdom of Judah who lived through the first part of the Babylonian exile. His historical narrative ends with the lifting up of Jehoiachin from the Babylonian prison at the beginning of the reign of King Evil-merodach, Nebuchadnezzar's successor. The book is anonymous, but both the Jewish and Christian traditions identify Jeremiah as the author. Nothing in the book would prevent Jeremiah's authorship, and it would be fitting for this prophet, whose ministry focused on the events and causes leading to the Babylonian exile, to have been the inspired chronicler.

Date: The composition of 1 and 2 Kings would have been between 586 BC and 561 BC. These dates mark the destruction of Jerusalem and the death of Nebuchadnezzar, who was succeeded by Evil-merodach. These dates do not preclude Jeremiah's authorship, since he records the same events in his prophecy (Jer. 52:31).

The books' canonical context (the time of their composition) dates to the sixth century BC, but the historical context (the events detailed) is more extensive. There are inherent difficulties in determining an absolute chronology because of different ways of reckoning the reigns of kings, as well as periods of co-regencies, but the following provides a general chronology of key events and a chart with pertinent data for each king.

Dates (BC)	Key Events
1050–1010	Reign of King Saul
1010–970	Reign of King David
970–931	Reign of King Solomon
931	Division of the Kingdom between Rehoboam and Jeroboam
722	Israel's Exile by Assyria
606	Judah's First Partial Exile by Babylon
597	Judah's Second Partial Exile by Babylon
586	Jerusalem's Destruction and Judah's Exile by Babylon

THE KINGS OF ISRAEL

King	Dates (BC)	Years	Scripture	Prophets
Jeroboam I	931–910	22	1 Kings 12:25—14:20	Ahijah
Nadab	910–909	2	15:25–32	
Baasha	909–886	24	15:33—16:7	Jehu
Elah	886–885	2	16:8–14	
Zimri	885	7 days	16:15–20	
Omri	885–874	12	16:21–28	
Ahab	874–853	22	16:29—22:40	Elijah, Micaiah

KGS
CHR
EZR

THE KINGS OF ISRAEL (CONTINUED)

King	Dates (BC)	Years	Scripture	Prophets
Ahaziah	853–852	2	1 Kings 22:51—2 Kings 1:18	Elijah
Jehoram	852–841	12	2 Kings 3:1—9:24	Elijah, Elisha
Jehu	842–814	28	9:1—10:36	Elisha
Jehoahaz	814–798	17	13:1–9	Elisha
Jehoash	798–782	16	13:10–25	Elisha
Jeroboam II	793–753	41	14:23–29	Jonah, Hosea, Amos
Zechariah	753–752	6 months	15:8–12	Hosea
Shallum	752	1 month	15:13–16	Hosea
Menahem	752–742	10	15:17–22	Hosea
Pekahiah	742–740	2	15:23–26	Hosea
Pekah	752–732	20	15:27–31	Hosea, Oded
Hoshea	732–722	9	17:1–6	Hosea

THE KINGS OF JUDAH

King (Queen)	Dates (BC)	Years	Scripture	Prophets
Rehoboam	931–913	17	1 Kings 14:21–31	Shemiah
Abijam	913–911	3	15:1–8	
Asa	911–870	41	15:9–24	Azariah
Jehoshaphat	873–848	25	1 Kings 22:41–50; 2 Kings 3	Jehu, Jehaziel, Eliezer
Jehoram	848–841	8	2 Kings 8:16–24	Elijah
Ahaziah	841	1	8:25–29	
(Athaliah)	841–835	6	11:1–21	
Jehoash	835–796	40	12:1–21	Zechariah
Amaziah	796–767	29	14:1–22	
Azariah	791–740	52	15:1–7	Zechariah, Isaiah
Jotham	750–734	16	15:32–38	Isaiah, Micah
Ahaz	734–716	16	16:1–20	Isaiah, Micah
Hezekiah	716–687	29	18:1—20:21	Isaiah, Micah
Manasseh	696–642	55	21:1–18	
Amon	642–640	2	21:19–26	
Josiah	640–609	31	22:1—23:30	Huldah, Jeremiah
Jehoahaz	609	3 months	23:31–34	Jeremiah
Jehoiakim	609–598	11	23:25—24:7	Jeremiah
Jehoiachin	598–597	3 months	24:8–16	Jeremiah
Zedekiah	597–586	11	24:17–20	Jeremiah

Theme: The development, disruption, division, decline, and dispersion of the kingdom of God through the sons of David.

Purpose: To demonstrate that apostasy leads to judgment even as God remains faithful to His covenant promises.

Synopsis: *The Contribution of 1 and 2 Kings to Redemptive Revelation*

The book is in part a theodicy, a defense of divine justice. The nation had done that which was evil in the sight of the Lord, and in anger the Lord cast them out from His presence (2 Kings 24:19–20). The exile of Israel and later of Judah was not evidence of God's inability or failure to protect His covenant people, but rather the means He used to progress the promise and keep His covenant word. The purpose of the book is directly linked to the theology of Deuteronomy and its covenant warnings that possession of the land depended on covenant obedience (Deut. 27–28). By focusing on the religious history more than the civil, the book of Kings makes it undeniably clear that the Lord cast the people out from His presence because of their sins against Him. The Assyrians and Babylonians were the weapons in God's hand to accomplish His covenant purpose. God's faithfulness to the covenant promise to David is also in focus as David's dynasty continues, even though many of the kings failed terribly. But even the failure of Judah's kings served the purpose of increasing the desire and expectation of David's greater son, Jesus Christ, who would establish a perfect kingdom of righteousness and peace.

First Kings overviews Israel's history from David's death to Ahab's death, a period of approximately 120 years. This period was marked by God's continuing and unfailing covenant faithfulness, in contrast to the nation's checkered history of covenant obedience and covenant transgression. Kings were evaluated not according to their military or civil feats but on how they conformed to God's law, with Deuteronomy in the background. The focus on sins and failures serves an important redemptive function by highlighting the human condition that has no remedy apart from the King who was coming in fulfillment of God's covenant promise. The worst of kings, whether from Judah or from Israel, contributed to messianic theology and expectation. Understanding the need for Christ is a crucial component of understanding the gospel.

There were, as well, some high points that in a positive way pointed to the Messiah. The early days of Solomon highlighting his wisdom, his wealth, and his works are certainly typical (as in representative) of Christ, though they pale before Jesus, who said of Himself, "behold, a greater than Solomon is here" (Matt. 12:42). Likewise, the construction of the temple with all of its ornate beauty and ceremonial rituals points directly to Jesus, who said, "in this place is one greater than the temple" (Matt. 12:6).

Second Kings overviews the history of the divided monarchy from the reign of the northern king Ahaziah, Ahab's successor, to the favorable treatment of the southern king Jehoichin while he was a captive in Babylon, a period of approximately 290 years. This period was marked by spiritual darkness and decline in both kingdoms, apart from glimmers of light coming from the south (Judah), particularly during the reigns of Hezekiah and Josiah.

The special attention of Kings to the prophetic word also has redemptive significance since faith comes by hearing the Word of God. The kings of Judah and Israel were subject to the prophetic office. God sent His prophets to bring His authoritative Word, threatening these kings with punishment, calling them to repentance, and announcing deliverance. Most significant were Elijah and Elisha, whom God raised up at a crucial moment when the existence of true religion was under threat. Due to their preaching and miracles, the uniqueness of the one true and living God became indisputable. No matter how dark the day, God has a word that sheds light on the darkness.

Although not all of the writing prophets are mentioned in Kings, the fact that all of them (except the postexilic prophets Haggai, Zechariah, and Malachi) ministered and wrote during the timeframe of 2 Kings testifies to God's grace in sending preachers to warn of judgment, to command repentance, and to announce the gospel of the Messiah as the only hope for sinners. The intensity of prophetic activity during this period, categorically rejected as it was by most who heard, heightens the sense of human depravity that makes the gospel so necessary. Even sin contributes to the redemptive message; apart from sin the need for the gospel would not exist.

God's covenant faithfulness in ensuring the coming of Christ is most vividly displayed in the treason of the wicked queen Athaliah (2 Kings 11), a seed of the serpent (Gen. 3:15). Had she succeeded in destroying the royal house, which was her intention, the promise of Messiah as the son of David would have been nullified. But God providentially secured Joash from her scheme, thus guaranteeing the line of David into which Christ would come. Nothing can frustrate God's unfailing redemptive purpose to send His Son as the Redeemer. As the book of Kings testifies, the rise and fall of various human kingdoms is all under the sovereign control of the one divine King, and He will establish the kingdom of His Son without fail.

Outline: Rather than repeating the list of kings presented earlier in this Introduction, the following outline will be briefer and more thematic.

I. The Development and Decline of the Kingdom under Solomon (1 Kings 1:1—11:43)
   A. Solomon's Coronation and Consolidation of the Kingdom (1 Kings 1:1—4:34)
   B. Solomon's Construction of the Temple by God's Covenant (1 Kings 5:1—9:9)
   C. Solomon's Wisdom and Wealth from the Lord (1 Kings 9:10—10:29)
   D. Solomon's Breaking the Covenant (1 Kings 11:1–43)
II. The Disruption and Division of the Kingdom (1 Kings 12:1–16:28)
   A. The Splitting of the Kingdom (1 Kings 12:1–24)

- B. The Apostasy of Israel and Discipline of Judah (1 Kings 12:25—14:31)
- C. Two Kingdoms in Conflict (1 Kings 15:1—16:28)

III. The Dispute of Elijah and Elisha for the Lord (1 Kings 16:29—2 Kings 13:25)

- A. The Ministry of Elijah against Ahab's House (1 Kings 16:29—2 Kings 1:18)
- B. The Glorification of Elijah and Empowerment of Elisha (2 Kings 2:1–25)
- C. The Ministry of Elisha against Ahab's House (2 Kings 3:1—10:36)
- D. The Deliverance of the Line of David in Judah (2 Kings 11:1—12:21)
- E. God's Patient Mercies toward Israel (2 Kings 13:1–25)

IV. The Dispersion of the Kingdom (2 Kings 14:1—25:30)

- A. The Downward Spiral of Israel and Judah (2 Kings 14:1—16:20)
- B. The Destruction of Israel by Assyria (2 Kings 17:1–41)
- C. The Spiritual Revival of Judah under Hezekiah (2 Kings 18:1—20:21)
- D. The Spiritual Ruin of Judah by Manasseh and Amon (2 Kings 21:1–26)
- E. Another Revival of Judah under Josiah (2 Kings 22:1—23:30)
- F. The End of the Kingdom of Judah (2 Kings 23:31—25:30)

THE FIRST BOOK OF

KINGS

CHAPTER 1

NOW king David was old *and* stricken in years; and they covered him with clothes, but he gat no heat.

2 Wherefore his servants said unto him, Let there be sought for my lord the king a young virgin: and let her stand before the king, and let her cherish him, and let her lie in thy bosom, that my lord the king may get heat.

3 So they sought for a fair damsel throughout all the coasts of Israel, and found Abishag a Shunammite, and brought her to the king.

4 And the damsel *was* very fair, and cherished the king, and ministered to him: but the king knew her not.

5 ¶ Then Adonijah the son of Haggith exalted himself, saying, I will be king: and he prepared him chariots and horsemen, and fifty men to run before him.

6 And his father had not displeased him at any time in saying, Why hast thou done so? and he also *was a* very goodly *man*; and *his mother* bare him after Absalom.

7 And he conferred with Joab the son of Zeruiah, and with Abiathar the priest: and they following Adonijah helped *him*.

8 But Zadok the priest, and Benaiah the son of Jehoiada, and Nathan the prophet, and Shimei, and Rei, and the mighty men which *belonged* to David, were not with Adonijah.

9 And Adonijah slew sheep and oxen and fat cattle by the stone of Zoheleth, which *is* by En-rogel, and called all his brethren the king's sons, and all the men of Judah the king's servants:

10 But Nathan the prophet, and Benaiah, and the mighty men, and Solomon his brother, he called not.

11 ¶ Wherefore Nathan spake unto Bath-sheba the mother of Solomon, saying, Hast thou not heard that Adonijah the son of Haggith doth reign, and David our lord knoweth *it* not?

12 Now therefore come, let me, I pray thee, give thee counsel, that thou mayest save thine own life, and the life of thy son Solomon.

13 Go and get thee in unto king David, and say unto him, Didst not thou, my lord, O king, swear unto thine handmaid, saying, Assuredly Solomon thy son shall reign after me, and he shall sit upon my throne? why then doth Adonijah reign?

14 Behold, while thou yet talkest there with the king, I also will come in after thee, and confirm thy words.

15 ¶ And Bath-sheba went in unto the king into the chamber: and the king was very old; and Abishag the Shunammite ministered unto the king.

16 And Bath-sheba bowed, and did obeisance unto the king. And the king said, What wouldest thou?

17 And she said unto him, My lord, thou swarest by the LORD thy God unto thine handmaid, *saying*, Assuredly Solomon thy son shall reign after me, and he shall sit upon my throne.

18 And now, behold, Adonijah reigneth; and now, my lord the king, thou knowest *it* not:

THE DEVELOPMENT AND DECLINE OF THE KINGDOM UNDER SOLOMON (1 KINGS 1:1—11:43)

Solomon's Coronation and Consolidation of the Kingdom (1 Kings 1:1—4:34)

Chapter 1: ***Before David dies, he declares that Solomon will be his successor to the throne.***

1:1 *stricken in years.* Literally, "one who enters into the days," an idiom for growing old. David is now seventy years old, having begun to reign at the age of thirty (2 Sam. 5:4) and reigning for a total of forty years (1 Kings 2:11). *gat no heat.* Literally, "it did not feel warm to him."

1:2 *let her cherish him.* The Hebrew indicates that she will be a nurse for him (v. 4).

1:3 *damsel.* Young woman (v. 4). *coasts.* Borders or regions.

1:5 *Adonijah.* The oldest surviving son of David. *prepared chariots.* His forming a royal procession to gain status among the people mirrors Absalom's action (2 Sam. 15:1).

1:6 *had not displeased.* David had not admonished or rebuked Adonijah. *very goodly man.* A reference to his appearance, not his character. *his mother bare him after Absalom.* Adonijah was born after Absalom but to a different mother (2 Sam. 3:4; 1 Chron. 3:2).

1:16 *bowed and, did obeisance.* Kneeled down in respect or submission.

1:17 *thou swarest.* The Lord had revealed to David that Solomon would be the heir to his throne (2 Sam. 7:13; 12:24–25; 1 Chron. 22:9–10; 28:5–6).

19 And he hath slain oxen and fat cattle and
sheep in abundance, and hath called all the sons
of the king, and Abiathar the priest, and Joab the
captain of the host: but Solomon thy servant hath
he not called.
20 And thou, my lord, O king, the eyes of all Israel
are upon thee, that thou shouldest tell them who
shall sit on the throne of my lord the king after
him.
21 Otherwise it shall come to pass, when my lord
the king shall sleep with his fathers, that I and my
son Solomon shall be counted offenders.
22 ¶ And, lo, while she yet talked with the king,
Nathan the prophet also came in.
23 And they told the king, saying, Behold Nathan
the prophet. And when he was come in before the
king, he bowed himself before the king with his
face to the ground.
24 And Nathan said, My lord, O king, hast thou
said, Adonijah shall reign after me, and he shall sit
upon my throne?
25 For he is gone down this day, and hath slain
oxen and fat cattle and sheep in abundance, and
hath called all the king's sons, and the captains
of the host, and Abiathar the priest; and, behold,
they eat and drink before him, and say, God save
king Adonijah.
26 But me, *even* me thy servant, and Zadok the
priest, and Benaiah the son of Jehoiada, and thy
servant Solomon, hath he not called.
27 Is this thing done by my lord the king, and thou
hast not shewed *it* unto thy servant, who should sit
on the throne of my lord the king after him?
28 ¶ Then king David answered and said, Call
me Bath-sheba. And she came into the king's
presence, and stood before the king.
29 And the king sware, and said, *As* the LORD liv-
eth, that hath redeemed my soul out of all distress,
30 Even as I sware unto thee by the LORD God of
Israel, saying, Assuredly Solomon thy son shall
reign after me, and he shall sit upon my throne in
my stead; even so will I certainly do this day.
31 Then Bath-sheba bowed with *her* face to the
earth, and did reverence to the king, and said, Let
my lord king David live for ever.
32 ¶ And king David said, Call me Zadok the
priest, and Nathan the prophet, and Benaiah the
son of Jehoiada. And they came before the king.
33 The king also said unto them, Take with you
the servants of your lord, and cause Solomon my
son to ride upon mine own mule, and bring him
down to Gihon:
34 And let Zadok the priest and Nathan the
prophet anoint him there king over Israel: and
blow ye with the trumpet, and say, God save king
Solomon.
35 Then ye shall come up after him, that he may
come and sit upon my throne; for he shall be king
in my stead: and I have appointed him to be ruler
over Israel and over Judah.
36 And Benaiah the son of Jehoiada answered the
king, and said, Amen: the LORD God of my lord
the king say so *too*.
37 As the LORD hath been with my lord the king,
even so be he with Solomon, and make his throne
greater than the throne of my lord king David.
38 So Zadok the priest, and Nathan the prophet,
and Benaiah the son of Jehoiada, and the Cher-
ethites, and the Pelethites, went down, and caused
Solomon to ride upon king David's mule, and
brought him to Gihon.
39 And Zadok the priest took an horn of oil out
of the tabernacle, and anointed Solomon. And
they blew the trumpet; and all the people said,
God save king Solomon.
40 And all the people came up after him, and the
people piped with pipes, and rejoiced with great
joy, so that the earth rent with the sound of them.
41 ¶ And Adonijah and all the guests that *were*
with him heard *it* as they had made an end of
eating. And when Joab heard the sound of the
trumpet, he said, Wherefore *is this* noise of the
city being in an uproar?
42 And while he yet spake, behold, Jonathan the
son of Abiathar the priest came: and Adonijah
said unto him, Come in; for thou *art* a valiant
man, and bringest good tidings.
43 And Jonathan answered and said to Adonijah,
Verily our lord king David hath made Solomon
king.
44 And the king hath sent with him Zadok the
priest, and Nathan the prophet, and Benaiah the

1:21 *sleep with his fathers.* Hebrew, "lie down" with his fathers, a euphemism for death that anticipates an awakening. Life after death and the hope of resurrection were integral to Old Testament theology (see Job 19:25–27; Ps. 49:15; Eccl. 12:7; Isa. 26:19; Dan. 12:2).

1:25 *God save king Adonijah.* Literally, "May the king Adonijah live."

1:30 See comments at v. 17.

1:33 *the servants of your lord.* Most likely David's personal bodyguards. David's assigning them to Solomon would have been a token of royal honor, a public proclamation of him as king over Israel.

1:34 *God save king Solomon.* Literally, "may the king Solomon live" (v. 39).

1:36 *Amen.* Translated, "surely" or "truly."

1:37 Despite all sinful human ambition, the Lord will establish His chosen king of the line of David (Isa. 9:7).

1:39 *anointed.* This symbolized the Spirit's empowering for the kingly office (1 Sam. 16:13). Kings, prophets, and priests were anointed for their respective ministries as representatives of the coming Messiah, who would unite the three offices in Himself as the ideal Mediator.

1:40 *piped with pipes.* Played some sort of flutelike instrument. *rent.* Split, an obvious hyperbole to describe the magnitude of the loud exaltation.

1:43 *Verily.* Surely or indeed.

son of Jehoiada, and the Cherethites, and the
Pelethites, and they have caused him to ride upon
the king's mule:
45 And Zadok the priest and Nathan the prophet
have anointed him king in Gihon: and they are
come up from thence rejoicing, so that the city
rang again. This *is* the noise that ye have heard.
46 And also Solomon sitteth on the throne of the
kingdom.
47 And moreover the king's servants came to
bless our lord king David, saying, God make the
name of Solomon better than thy name, and
make his throne greater than thy throne. And the
king bowed himself upon the bed.
48 And also thus said the king, Blessed *be* the
LORD God of Israel, which hath given *one* to sit
on my throne this day, mine eyes even seeing *it*.
49 And all the guests that *were* with Adonijah were
afraid, and rose up, and went every man his way.
50 ¶ And Adonijah feared because of Solomon,
and arose, and went, and caught hold on the
horns of the altar.
51 And it was told Solomon, saying, Behold,
Adonijah feareth king Solomon: for, lo, he hath
caught hold on the horns of the altar, saying, Let
king Solomon swear unto me to day that he will
not slay his servant with the sword.
52 And Solomon said, If he will shew himself a
worthy man, there shall not an hair of him fall to
the earth: but if wickedness shall be found in him,
he shall die.
53 So king Solomon sent, and they brought him
down from the altar. And he came and bowed
himself to king Solomon: and Solomon said unto
him, Go to thine house.

CHAPTER 2

NOW the days of David drew nigh that he should
die; and he charged Solomon his son, saying,
2 I go the way of all the earth: be thou strong
therefore, and shew thyself a man;
3 And keep the charge of the LORD thy God, to
walk in his ways, to keep his statutes, and his
commandments, and his judgments, and his
testimonies, as it is written in the law of Moses,
that thou mayest prosper in all that thou doest,
and whithersoever thou turnest thyself:
4 That the LORD may continue his word which he
spake concerning me, saying, If thy children take
heed to their way, to walk before me in truth with
all their heart and with all their soul, there shall not
fail thee (said he) a man on the throne of Israel.
5 Moreover thou knowest also what Joab the son
of Zeruiah did to me, *and* what he did to the two
captains of the hosts of Israel, unto Abner the son
of Ner, and unto Amasa the son of Jether, whom he
slew, and shed the blood of war in peace, and put
the blood of war upon his girdle that *was* about his
loins, and in his shoes that *were* on his feet.
6 Do therefore according to thy wisdom, and let
not his hoar head go down to the grave in peace.
7 But shew kindness unto the sons of Barzillai
the Gileadite, and let them be of those that eat

1:47 *bowed.* The usual Hebrew word for "worship."
1:50–53 *caught hold on the horns of the altar.* This was an ancient custom in Israel to allow those who were guilty of a crime to plead for mercy and escape capital punishment by holding on to one of the four horns of the burnt offering altar. This gesture was no protection for the blatantly guilty (2:28; Ex. 21:14). Solomon gave him the benefit of the doubt.

Thoughts for Personal/Family Worship: Chapter 1

1. **Adonijah shared with Absalom, his elder half brother, not only good looks but also a selfish, unharnessed ambition for power. Proverbs teaches that the judgment that falls on the mocker should be a warning to others not to follow the same course (Prov. 19:25; 21:11). Unfortunately, Adonijah failed to learn from Absalom's rebellion and demise that elevating self above and against God's will is foolishness with devastating consequences. Adonijah knew that Solomon had been designated as the successor to the royal throne, and yet he opposed this. Opposing God's will always leads to misery. Man needs to be on guard for pride and rash presumption that will motivate self-promotion. To defer to another with regard to some promotion when we think we possess all the necessary qualifications is an unnatural response that requires the kind of humility exemplified by the Savior. This was Paul's directive against the strife in the church: to have the mind of Christ (Phil. 2:1–5). What can you do when you are tempted to be like Adonijah?**
2. **Although Adonijah's motives are suspect, his taking hold of the horns of the altar suggests a beautiful gospel picture. The altar was the place of sacrifice, reconciliation, and deliverance. Solomon, the peace giver, spared Adonijah even though he was deserving of death. This is a symbol of a sinner taking hold of Christ Jesus, who is greater than both Solomon and the temple with all of its furniture and rituals. It is only when the sinner lays hold of Christ that he is delivered from death to life.**

Chapter 2: ***David gives Solomon instructions concerning the administration of the kingdom, including the purging of those who were disloyal to his administration.***

2:1 *he charged.* Literally, "he commanded."
2:3 These obligations correspond to God's initial instructions regarding kings (Deut. 17:19–20). *that thou mayest prosper.* That you may achieve success.
2:4 David reiterates God's covenant promise to him (2 Sam. 7:12–13), the ultimate fulfillment being the coming of Christ, who will reign forever.
2:5 *shed the blood of war in peace.* What is legitimate in time of war is murder in time of peace. Joab was guilty of murder (2 Sam 20:9–10). *girdle . . . loins.* The belt around his waist or hips. A gruesome picture of his being splattered with the blood of his victims.
2:6 *hoar head.* Gray hair (v. 9).
2:7 *shew kindness.* Practice covenant loyalty, involving mutual reciprocation.

at thy table: for so they came to me when I fled
because of Absalom thy brother.
8 And, behold, *thou hast* with thee Shimei the son
of Gera, a Benjamite of Bahurim, which cursed
me with a grievous curse in the day when I went
to Mahanaim: but he came down to meet me at
Jordan, and I sware to him by the LORD, saying, I
will not put thee to death with the sword.
9 Now therefore hold him not guiltless: for thou
art a wise man, and knowest what thou ought-
est to do unto him; but his hoar head bring thou
down to the grave with blood.
10 So David slept with his fathers, and was buried
in the city of David.
11 And the days that David reigned over Israel
were forty years: seven years reigned he in
Hebron, and thirty and three years reigned he in
Jerusalem.
12 ¶ Then sat Solomon upon the throne of David
his father; and his kingdom was established
greatly.
13 ¶ And Adonijah the son of Haggith came to
Bath-sheba the mother of Solomon. And she said,
Comest thou peaceably? And he said, Peaceably.
14 He said moreover, I have somewhat to say
unto thee. And she said, Say on.
15 And he said, Thou knowest that the kingdom
was mine, and *that* all Israel set their faces on
me, that I should reign: howbeit the kingdom is
turned about, and is become my brother's: for it
was his from the LORD.
16 And now I ask one petition of thee, deny me
not. And she said unto him, Say on.
17 And he said, Speak, I pray thee, unto Solomon
the king, (for he will not say thee nay,) that he give
me Abishag the Shunammite to wife.
18 And Bath-sheba said, Well; I will speak for thee
unto the king.
19 ¶ Bath-sheba therefore went unto king Solo-
mon, to speak unto him for Adonijah. And the
king rose up to meet her, and bowed himself unto
her, and sat down on his throne, and caused a seat
to be set for the king's mother; and she sat on his
right hand.
20 Then she said, I desire one small petition of
thee; *I pray thee*, say me not nay. And the king said
unto her, Ask on, my mother: for I will not say
thee nay.
21 And she said, Let Abishag the Shunammite be
given to Adonijah thy brother to wife.
22 And king Solomon answered and said unto his
mother, And why dost thou ask Abishag the Shu-
nammite for Adonijah? ask for him the kingdom
also; for he *is* mine elder brother; even for him,
and for Abiathar the priest, and for Joab the son
of Zeruiah.
23 Then king Solomon sware by the LORD, say-
ing, God do so to me, and more also, if Adonijah
have not spoken this word against his own life.
24 Now therefore, *as* the LORD liveth, which hath
established me, and set me on the throne of David
my father, and who hath made me an house, as he
promised, Adonijah shall be put to death this day.
25 And king Solomon sent by the hand of
Benaiah the son of Jehoiada; and he fell upon him
that he died.
26 ¶ And unto Abiathar the priest said the king,
Get thee to Anathoth, unto thine own fields; for
thou *art* worthy of death: but I will not at this
time put thee to death, because thou barest the
ark of the Lord GOD before David my father, and
because thou hast been afflicted in all wherein my
father was afflicted.
27 So Solomon thrust out Abiathar from being
priest unto the LORD; that he might fulfil the word
of the LORD, which he spake concerning the house
of Eli in Shiloh.
28 ¶ Then tidings came to Joab: for Joab had
turned after Adonijah, though he turned not after
Absalom. And Joab fled unto the tabernacle of the
LORD, and caught hold on the horns of the altar.
29 And it was told king Solomon that Joab was
fled unto the tabernacle of the LORD; and, behold,
he is by the altar. Then Solomon sent Benaiah the
son of Jehoiada, saying, Go, fall upon him.
30 And Benaiah came to the tabernacle of the
LORD, and said unto him, Thus saith the king,
Come forth. And he said, Nay; but I will die here.

2:8 *cursed me with a grievous curse.* Literally, "cursed me a curse," an idiom expressing intensity. He cursed greatly.
2:10 *David slept.* See note at 1:21.
2:12 *his kingdom was established.* Four times this chapter says that the Lord established the kingdom (vv. 12,24,45–46). The kingdom was moving into a new phase of peace and glory (5:3–4). This may explain why sinners who had been patiently tolerated in David's reign were now punished.
2:27 *fulfil the word of the LORD.* See notes at 1 Sam. 2:31,35. The rejection of *Abiathar* is a key step in showing the obsolescence of the Aaronic priesthood in anticipation of the ideal Priest to come.
2:28–29 *the horns of the altar.* See note at 1:50–53. There is no safety in religious ritual without a genuine heart of repentance.
2:32 *to wit.* That is.
2:36 *any wither.* Anywhere (v. 42).
2:44 *thine heart is privy to.* Literally, "your heart has known."

Thoughts for Personal/Family Worship: Chapter 2

1. God often delays the execution of His justice, but He never sets it aside. Joab had sinned greatly, seemingly with impunity. But "though a sinner do evil an hundred times, and his days be prolonged . . . it shall not be well with the wicked . . . because he feareth not before God" (Eccl. 8:12–13). The goodness and longsuffering of God should lead to repentance (Rom. 2:4), but the impenitent persist in wickedness, eventually getting from God what they deserve. Joab had shed man's blood, and by man his blood was to be shed. In the same way sinners

And Benaiah brought the king word again, say-
ing, Thus said Joab, and thus he answered me.
31 And the king said unto him, Do as he hath
said, and fall upon him, and bury him; that thou
mayest take away the innocent blood, which Joab
shed, from me, and from the house of my father.
32 And the LORD shall return his blood upon
his own head, who fell upon two men more
righteous and better than he, and slew them with
the sword, my father David not knowing *thereof,*
to wit, Abner the son of Ner, captain of the host of
Israel, and Amasa the son of Jether, captain of the
host of Judah.
33 Their blood shall therefore return upon the
head of Joab, and upon the head of his seed for
ever: but upon David, and upon his seed, and
upon his house, and upon his throne, shall there
be peace for ever from the LORD.
34 So Benaiah the son of Jehoiada went up, and
fell upon him, and slew him: and he was buried in
his own house in the wilderness.
35 ¶ And the king put Benaiah the son of Je-
hoiada in his room over the host: and Zadok the
priest did the king put in the room of Abiathar.
36 ¶ And the king sent and called for Shimei,
and said unto him, Build thee an house in Jeru-
salem, and dwell there, and go not forth thence
any whither.
37 For it shall be, *that* on the day thou goest out,
and passest over the brook Kidron, thou shalt
know for certain that thou shalt surely die: thy
blood shall be upon thine own head.
38 And Shimei said unto the king, The saying *is*
good: as my lord the king hath said, so will thy
servant do. And Shimei dwelt in Jerusalem many
days.
39 And it came to pass at the end of three years,
that two of the servants of Shimei ran away unto
Achish son of Maachah king of Gath. And they
told Shimei, saying, Behold, thy servants *be* in
Gath.
40 And Shimei arose, and saddled his ass, and
went to Gath to Achish to seek his servants: and
Shimei went, and brought his servants from Gath.
41 And it was told Solomon that Shimei had gone
from Jerusalem to Gath, and was come again.
42 And the king sent and called for Shimei, and
said unto him, Did I not make thee to swear by
the LORD, and protested unto thee, saying, Know
for a certain, on the day thou goest out, and
walkest abroad any whither, that thou shalt surely
die? and thou saidst unto me, The word *that* I
have heard *is* good.
43 Why then hast thou not kept the oath of the
LORD, and the commandment that I have charged
thee with?
44 The king said moreover to Shimei, Thou
knowest all the wickedness which thine heart
is privy to, that thou didst to David my father:
therefore the LORD shall return thy wickedness
upon thine own head;
45 And king Solomon *shall be* blessed, and the
throne of David shall be established before the
LORD for ever.
46 So the king commanded Benaiah the son of
Jehoiada; which went out, and fell upon him, that
he died. And the kingdom was established in the
hand of Solomon.

CHAPTER 3

AND Solomon made affinity with Pharaoh king of
Egypt, and took Pharaoh's daughter, and brought
her into the city of David, until he had made an
end of building his own house, and the house of
the LORD, and the wall of Jerusalem round about.
2 Only the people sacrificed in high places, be-
cause there was no house built unto the name of
the LORD, until those days.
3 And Solomon loved the LORD, walking in the
statutes of David his father: only he sacrificed and
burnt incense in high places.
4 And the king went to Gibeon to sacrifice there;
for that *was* the great high place: a thousand
burnt offerings did Solomon offer upon that altar.
5 ¶ In Gibeon the LORD appeared to Solomon in

---

today should not interpret "life as usual" to be evidence of God's inactivity or His ignoring of justice. God will repay the sinner for the evil he has done. The Lord remembers the evil deeds of the wicked, and sooner or later He will execute His punishments upon them. The only remedy for us is to flee to the Lord Jesus Christ and be washed from all our sins in His blood by true, saving faith alone.

2. Joab's vainly hanging on to the horns of the altar provides a sobering lesson in the ineffectiveness of trusting in religious routines, rituals, or traditions for salvation. Religion without Christ and a saving dependence on Him is worthless. Yet so many convince themselves that just going to church or performing some other religious acts will be good enough. Going to the tabernacle was not enough to save Joab, and simply going to church is not enough to save anyone. What must we do in order to be forgiven of our sins?

Chapter 3: ***The Lord grants Solomon's request for wisdom, which Solomon displays in judging between two women, leaving a profound impression upon the whole nation.***

3:1 *made affinity*. Hebrew, "to become a son-in-law."

3:2 *sacrificed in high places*. A violation of the law of the central sanctuary (Lev. 17:3–5; Deut. 12:5–7). Circumstances sometimes prevented this during the tabernacle era (for instance, when the ark was captured and then secluded). Yet even when the temple was erected, eliminating the high places proved difficult even for the best of kings (1 Kings 15:14).

3:4 *Gibeon . . . the great high place*. The tabernacle had been

a dream by night: and God said, Ask what I shall
give thee.
6 And Solomon said, Thou hast shewed unto thy
servant David my father great mercy, according as
he walked before thee in truth, and in righteous-
ness, and in uprightness of heart with thee; and
thou hast kept for him this great kindness, that
thou hast given him a son to sit on his throne, as
it is this day.
7 And now, O LORD my God, thou hast made
thy servant king instead of David my father: and
I *am but* a little child: I know not *how* to go out
or come in.
8 And thy servant *is* in the midst of thy people
which thou hast chosen, a great people, that
cannot be numbered nor counted for multitude.
9 Give therefore thy servant an understanding
heart to judge thy people, that I may discern be-
tween good and bad: for who is able to judge this
thy so great a people?
10 And the speech pleased the Lord, that Solo-
mon had asked this thing.
11 And God said unto him, Because thou hast
asked this thing, and hast not asked for thyself
long life; neither hast asked riches for thyself, nor
hast asked the life of thine enemies; but hast asked
for thyself understanding to discern judgment;
12 Behold, I have done according to thy words:
lo, I have given thee a wise and an understanding
heart; so that there was none like thee before thee,
neither after thee shall any arise like unto thee.
13 And I have also given thee that which thou
hast not asked, both riches, and honour: so that
there shall not be any among the kings like unto
thee all thy days.
14 And if thou wilt walk in my ways, to keep my
statutes and my commandments, as thy father
David did walk, then I will lengthen thy days.
15 And Solomon awoke; and, behold, *it was* a
dream. And he came to Jerusalem, and stood
before the ark of the covenant of the LORD, and
offered up burnt offerings, and offered peace
offerings, and made a feast to all his servants.
16 ¶ Then came there two women, *that were*
harlots, unto the king, and stood before him.
17 And the one woman said, O my lord, I and this
woman dwell in one house; and I was delivered of
a child with her in the house.
18 And it came to pass the third day after that I
was delivered, that this woman was delivered also:
and we *were* together; *there was* no stranger with
us in the house, save we two in the house.
19 And this woman's child died in the night; be-
cause she overlaid it.
20 And she arose at midnight, and took my son
from beside me, while thine handmaid slept, and
laid it in her bosom, and laid her dead child in
my bosom.
21 And when I rose in the morning to give my
child suck, behold, it was dead: but when I had
considered it in the morning, behold, it was not
my son, which I did bear.
22 And the other woman said, Nay; but the living
is my son, and the dead *is* thy son. And this said,
No; but the dead *is* thy son, and the living *is* my
son. Thus they spake before the king.
23 Then said the king, The one saith, This *is* my
son that liveth, and thy son *is* the dead: and the
other saith, Nay; but thy son *is* the dead, and my
son *is* the living.
24 And the king said, Bring me a sword. And they
brought a sword before the king.
25 And the king said, Divide the living child in
two, and give half to the one, and half to the other.
26 Then spake the woman whose the living child
was unto the king, for her bowels yearned upon
her son, and she said, O my lord, give her the
living child, and in no wise slay it. But the other
said, Let it be neither mine nor thine, *but* divide *it*.
27 Then the king answered and said, Give her

set up here with the altar for burnt offering (2 Chron. 1:3–5) while the ark had been transported to Jerusalem by David and placed in a tent (2 Sam. 6:17).

3:5 *in a dream.* Dreams were a frequent means of divine revelation in the Old Testament, one of the diverse manners of God's speaking (Heb. 1:1).

3:6 *mercy . . . kindness.* Both translate the same Hebrew word for covenant faithfulness and loyalty.

3:7 *I am but a little child.* Not a reference to size or age but to lack of experience.

3:9 *an understanding heart.* Literally, "a hearing heart." The ability to listen well is an essential component in fair and just discernment.

3:12 *wise.* The Hebrew root for "wise" or "wisdom" has the essential idea of "skill" or "ability." The Lord gave Solomon the wisdom, skill, and ability to know what to do in ruling and to understand the best means to achieve the best end.

3:15 *offered up burnt offerings . . . peace offerings.* This is an expression of Solomon's personal dedication and deep gratitude for God's covenant mercies.

3:18 *no stranger.* Literally, "nonexistence of another"; no one else was there except (*save*) the two of them.

3:19 *overlaid it.* Lay upon it.

3:26 *her bowels yearned.* Literally, "her compassion" or "her feelings of love" . . . "grew excited" or "warm and tender."

3:28 *wisdom of God.* Wisdom from God. *judgment.* Justice. In Solomon we see a type of the divine wisdom given by God to Christ so that He reigns in justice (Isa. 11:1–5).

Thoughts for Personal/Family Worship: Chapter 3

1. The Lord granted Solomon's unselfish request for wisdom, as well as giving him things he did not ask for (vv. 12–13). This testifies to God's amazing goodness and grace; in Paul's inspired words, he "is able to do exceeding abundantly above all that we ask or think" (Eph. 3:20). We should learn from this that prayer is not just a list of wants in order to enrich ourselves but a means of seeking the Lord for His will to be done. We

the living child, and in no wise slay it: she *is* the
mother thereof.
28 And all Israel heard of the judgment which
the king had judged; and they feared the king: for
they saw that the wisdom of God *was* in him, to
do judgment.

CHAPTER 4

So king Solomon was king over all Israel.
2 And these *were* the princes which he had;
Azariah the son of Zadok the priest,
3 Elihoreph and Ahiah, the sons of Shisha, scribes;
Jehoshaphat the son of Ahilud, the recorder.
4 And Benaiah the son of Jehoiada *was* over the
host: and Zadok and Abiathar *were* the priests:
5 And Azariah the son of Nathan *was* over the of-
ficers: and Zabud the son of Nathan *was* principal
officer, *and* the king's friend:
6 And Ahishar *was* over the household: and
Adoniram the son of Abda *was* over the tribute.
7 ¶ And Solomon had twelve officers over all
Israel, which provided victuals for the king and
his household: each man his month in a year
made provision.
8 And these *are* their names: The son of Hur, in
mount Ephraim:
9 The son of Dekar, in Makaz, and in Shaalbim,
and Beth-shemesh, and Elon-beth-hanan:
10 The son of Hesed, in Aruboth; to him *per-
tained* Sochoh, and all the land of Hepher:
11 The son of Abinadab, in all the region of Dor;
which had Taphath the daughter of Solomon to
wife:
12 Baana the son of Ahilud; *to him pertained*
Taanach and Megiddo, and all Beth-shean, which
is by Zartanah beneath Jezreel, from Beth-shean
to Abel-meholah, *even* unto *the place that is*
beyond Jokneam:
13 The son of Geber, in Ramoth-gilead; to him
pertained the towns of Jair the son of Manasseh,
which *are* in Gilead; to him *also pertained* the
region of Argob, which *is* in Bashan, threescore
great cities with walls and brasen bars:
14 Ahinadab the son of Iddo *had* Mahanaim:
15 Ahimaaz *was* in Naphtali; he also took Bas-
math the daughter of Solomon to wife:
16 Baanah the son of Hushai *was* in Asher and
in Aloth:
17 Jehoshaphat the son of Paruah, in Issachar:
18 Shimei the son of Elah, in Benjamin:
19 Geber the son of Uri *was* in the country
of Gilead, *in* the country of Sihon king of the
Amorites, and of Og king of Bashan; and *he was*
the only officer which *was* in the land.
20 ¶ Judah and Israel *were* many, as the sand
which *is* by the sea in multitude, eating and drink-
ing, and making merry.
21 And Solomon reigned over all kingdoms from
the river unto the land of the Philistines, and unto
the border of Egypt: they brought presents, and
served Solomon all the days of his life.
22 ¶ And Solomon's provision for one day was
thirty measures of fine flour, and threescore
measures of meal,
23 Ten fat oxen, and twenty oxen out of the pas-
tures, and an hundred sheep, beside harts, and
roebucks, and fallowdeer, and fatted fowl.
24 For he had dominion over all *the region* on
this side the river, from Tiphsah even to Azzah,
over all the kings on this side the river: and he had
peace on all sides round about him.
25 And Judah and Israel dwelt safely, every man
under his vine and under his fig tree, from Dan
even to Beer-sheba, all the days of Solomon.
26 ¶ And Solomon had forty thousand stalls
of horses for his chariots, and twelve thousand
horsemen.
27 And those officers provided victual for
king Solomon, and for all that came unto king

need to pray that God will grant us the wisdom or skill to fulfill well whatever calling and tasks He has for us. What wisdom do you need from the Lord today?

2. **Christ the King has received the Spirit in His fullness to reign in perfect wisdom and justice. His Word and Spirit are the source of all the church's wisdom (Eph. 1:17; Col. 3:16). It is not enough to pray for wisdom and then to consult this world for guidance. We must look to Christ in faith and depend upon the Holy Scriptures as the Word of our King. Then we show Christ the reverence He deserves (1 Kings 3:28).**

Chapter 4: *Solomon reigns over a glorious and vast kingdom and gains a worldwide reputation for his wisdom.*

4:2 *priest.* The Hebrew word can also designate a political rather than a religious official. See v. 5, where the word is translated "principal officer."

4:3 *scribes.* Secretaries to the king. *recorder.* One who chronicles the royal career.

4:6 *tribute.* Annual income and revenues of the king.

4:7 *provided victuals for the king.* Provided food; literally, "nourished the king" (v. 27).

4:20 *as the sand which is by the sea in multitude.* God was fulfilling His covenant with Abraham (Gen. 22:17; 32:12) through the wisdom of the royal son of David (1 Kings 4:29). *making merry.* Joyful in the sense of being satisfied or content. These are components of the ideal life (Eccl. 2:24; 3:22). Life was good in Solomon's kingdom.

4:21 *reigned over all kingdoms.* Compare the borders with the divine promises given to Abraham (Gen. 15:18), Moses (Ex. 23:31), and Joshua (Josh. 1:4).

4:25 *under his vine and under his fig tree.* An expression denoting peace and prosperity, not only in material matters but also spiritually (Mic. 4:4; Zech. 3:10).

4:26 This contradicted the divine mandate against kings multiplying horses (Deut. 17:16)—a military buildup that

Solomon's table, every man in his month: they
lacked nothing.
28 Barley also and straw for the horses and drom-
edaries brought they unto the place where *the offi-
cers* were, every man according to his charge.
29 ¶ And God gave Solomon wisdom and under-
standing exceeding much, and largeness of heart,
even as the sand that *is* on the sea shore.
30 And Solomon's wisdom excelled the wisdom
of all the children of the east country, and all the
wisdom of Egypt.
31 For he was wiser than all men; than Ethan the
Ezrahite, and Heman, and Chalcol, and Darda,
the sons of Mahol: and his fame was in all nations
round about.
32 And he spake three thousand proverbs: and
his songs were a thousand and five.
33 And he spake of trees, from the cedar tree that
is in Lebanon even unto the hyssop that spring-
eth out of the wall: he spake also of beasts, and of
fowl, and of creeping things, and of fishes.
34 And there came of all people to hear the
wisdom of Solomon, from all kings of the earth,
which had heard of his wisdom.

CHAPTER 5

AND Hiram king of Tyre sent his servants unto
Solomon; for he had heard that they had anointed
him king in the room of his father: for Hiram was
ever a lover of David.
2 And Solomon sent to Hiram, saying,
3 Thou knowest how that David my father could
not build an house unto the name of the LORD his
God for the wars which were about him on every
side, until the LORD put them under the soles of
his feet.
4 But now the LORD my God hath given me rest
on every side, *so that there is* neither adversary nor
evil occurrent.
5 And, behold, I purpose to build an house unto
the name of the LORD my God, as the LORD spake
unto David my father, saying, Thy son, whom
I will set upon thy throne in thy room, he shall
build an house unto my name.
6 Now therefore command thou that they hew
me cedar trees out of Lebanon; and my servants
shall be with thy servants: and unto thee will
I give hire for thy servants according to all that
thou shalt appoint: for thou knowest that *there is*
not among us any that can skill to hew timber like
unto the Sidonians.
7 ¶ And it came to pass, when Hiram heard the
words of Solomon, that he rejoiced greatly, and
said, Blessed *be* the LORD this day, which hath
given unto David a wise son over this great people.
8 And Hiram sent to Solomon, saying, I have
considered the things which thou sentest to me
for: *and* I will do all thy desire concerning timber
of cedar, and concerning timber of fir.
9 My servants shall bring *them* down from Leba-
non unto the sea: and I will convey them by sea in

---

potentially became a source of confidence, as opposed to trusting God (Ps 20:7; Isa. 31:1,3).

4:28 *dromedaries*. Camels, but the Hebrew refers to teams of horses used to carry loads.

4:29 *heart*. The inner man, including the mind, emotions, and will. Here *largeness* most likely refers to the greatness of mental power rather than to compassion.

4:32 *proverbs...songs*. Many of these were divinely inspired and thus preserved in the Bible in Proverbs, Ecclesiastes, and the Song of Solomon.

4:34 *all people...all kings*. God used the *wisdom* of Solomon to bless many nations, another fulfillment of the covenant with Abraham (Gen. 12:3; 22:18). This too is fulfilled in Christ (Isa. 2:3; 42:4).

Thoughts for Personal/Family Worship: Chapter 4

1. **The glories and expanse of Solomon's kingdom serve as a beautiful picture or type of Christ and His kingdom. As great as Solomon was, he pales before Christ, who is greater (Matt. 12:42). Solomon received wisdom from God, but Christ is Himself the Wisdom of God (Prov. 8:12–35; 1 Cor. 1:30). The borders of Israel were expansive under Solomon's administration, but the kingdom of Christ is without borders, including subjects from every nation and people on the planet (Ps. 2:8). Solomon had to build up a military, but Christ rules with an irresistible rod of iron against all His enemies and has people who are irresistibly made willing in the day of His power (110:2–3). Solomon ruled over a kingdom at peace in which all his subjects had what was necessary for a contented life (1 Kings 4:20). How much more do those citizens in Christ's kingdom enjoy a peace that surpasses all understanding!**
2. **Solomon displayed profound wisdom, not only in human affairs and in politics but also regarding the matters of nature and biology. All of creation testifies to God's glory and reveals something of His great person and work. Christian faith encourages learning. Many universities were started at the initiative of godly men who desired an institution of sanctified learning. True godliness promotes scholarship, and true science is in strict adherence to the Word of God. "The fear of the LORD is the beginning of wisdom" (Ps. 111:10). How can researchers and scientists glorify God?**

Solomon's Construction of the Temple by God's Covenant (1 Kings 5:1—9:9)

Chapter 5: *Solomon makes preparations for building the temple.*

5:1 *Tyre*. A wealthy Phoenician city of commerce, located on an island in the Mediterranean Sea just off the coast of Phoenicia.

5:3–5 *under the soles of his feet*. An image of bringing enemies into subjugation. *nor evil occurrent*. Literally, "nonexistence of a harmful occurrence." Nothing bad was happening to hinder the work. The kingdom had transitioned from a time of war to a time of *rest*, opening the door for the building of the temple for God's glory (*name*, Deut. 12:9–11).

floats unto the place that thou shalt appoint me,
and will cause them to be discharged there, and
thou shalt receive *them*: and thou shalt accom-
plish my desire, in giving food for my household.
10 So Hiram gave Solomon cedar trees and fir
trees *according to* all his desire.
11 And Solomon gave Hiram twenty thousand
measures of wheat *for* food to his household, and
twenty measures of pure oil: thus gave Solomon
to Hiram year by year.
12 And the LORD gave Solomon wisdom, as he
promised him: and there was peace between
Hiram and Solomon; and they two made a league
together.
13 ¶ And king Solomon raised a levy out of all
Israel; and the levy was thirty thousand men.
14 And he sent them to Lebanon, ten thousand a
month by courses: a month they were in Lebanon,
and two months at home: and Adoniram *was* over
the levy.
15 And Solomon had threescore and ten thou-
sand that bare burdens, and fourscore thousand
hewers in the mountains;
16 Beside the chief of Solomon's officers which
were over the work, three thousand and three
hundred, which ruled over the people that
wrought in the work.
17 And the king commanded, and they brought
great stones, costly stones, *and* hewed stones, to
lay the foundation of the house.
18 And Solomon's builders and Hiram's builders
did hew *them*, and the stonesquarers: so they
prepared timber and stones to build the house.

CHAPTER 6

AND it came to pass in the four hundred and
eightieth year after the children of Israel were
come out of the land of Egypt, in the fourth year
of Solomon's reign over Israel, in the month Zif,
which *is* the second month, that he began to build
the house of the LORD.
2 And the house which king Solomon built
for the LORD, the length thereof *was* threescore
cubits, and the breadth thereof twenty *cubits*, and
the height thereof thirty cubits.
3 And the porch before the temple of the house,
twenty cubits *was* the length thereof, according to
the breadth of the house; *and* ten cubits *was* the
breadth thereof before the house.
4 And for the house he made windows of narrow
lights.
5 ¶ And against the wall of the house he built
chambers round about, *against* the walls of the
house round about, *both* of the temple and of the
oracle: and he made chambers round about:
6 The nethermost chamber *was* five cubits broad,
and the middle *was* six cubits broad, and the third
was seven cubits broad: for without *in the wall* of
the house he made narrowed rests round about,
that *the beams* should not be fastened in the walls
of the house.

5:6 *that can skill to hew timber*. Literally, "that knows how to cut wood."
5:7 Solomon's wisdom was crucial for obtaining the materials from surrounding nations to build the temple (v. 12).
5:9 *floats*. Rafts constructed of logs bound together. *in giving food*. Tyre had little agricultural land and depended on food imports, primarily from the land of Israel (Acts 12:20).
5:12 *made a league*. Cut a covenant, here referring to a mutually accepted and binding business contract.
5:13 *levy*. This is not a monetary taxation but a draft of forced laborers. Samuel had predicted that kings would do this (1 Sam. 8:11–16).

Thoughts for Personal/Family Worship: Chapter 5

1. **When Christ ascended into heaven, His earthly warfare had come to an end and He entered His rest. However, Solomon's kingdom reminds us that our own day is not a time of inactivity for our King but the era during which He is using His wisdom to enlist people from the nations to build His living temple, the church. One day the whole church will enter its rest; then the glory of God will dwell with man so that no temple will be needed.**
2. **One lesson from this chapter is the importance of preparing for the tasks before you. Wise Solomon put it this way: "If the iron be blunt, and he do not whet the edge, then must he put to more strength: but wisdom is profitable to direct" (Eccl. 10:10). Getting the tools ready before using them only makes sense. Solomon demonstrated his wisdom by making due preparations for the construction of the temple. This was a matter of common sense, but a lack of common sense can dishonor the Lord, as with a half-built construction project by a church. Christ applied this principle to spiritual life (Luke 14:25–33). Following the Lord Jesus incurs a cost—hardships and even suffering. To follow Him to the end you must look ahead, count the cost, and prepare yourself.**

Chapter 6: *Solomon builds the temple of the Lord.*
6:1 *in the four hundred and eightieth year*. This is a crucial point of data for dating the exodus. Virtually all agree that Solomon's fourth year was 966 BC. If we assume that the 480 years are to be taken literally (and there is no contextual warrant to assume otherwise), adding 480 years gives the date 1446 BC for the exodus. Other references, such as Judg. 11:26, also point to a mid-fifteenth-century BC date.
6:2 *house*. The house of the Lord was comparable to the tabernacle, although the temple was twice as large. Each consisted of three sections: the front or outer court, the sanctuary (the holy place), and the inner sanctuary (the Holy of Holies), where the ark of the covenant was situated.
6:4 *windows of narrow lights*. The Hebrew is uncertain but seems to describe windows that were wide on the inside but narrow on the outside, allowing light to enter but preventing the elements from entering.
6:5 *of the temple*. Most likely referring specifically to the holy place. *the oracle*. Most likely referring specifically to the most holy place (vv. 19–20).
6:6 *nethermost*. Lowest. The storied chambers of increasing size were rooms for storage.

7 And the house, when it was in building, was built of stone made ready before it was brought thither: so that there was neither hammer nor axe *nor* any tool of iron heard in the house, while it was in building.

8 The door for the middle chamber *was* in the right side of the house: and they went up with winding stairs into the middle *chamber*, and out of the middle into the third.

9 So he built the house, and finished it; and covered the house with beams and boards of cedar.

10 And *then* he built chambers against all the house, five cubits high: and they rested on the house with timber of cedar.

11 ¶ And the word of the LORD came to Solomon, saying,

12 *Concerning* this house which thou art in building, if thou wilt walk in my statutes, and execute my judgments, and keep all my commandments to walk in them; then will I perform my word with thee, which I spake unto David thy father:

13 And I will dwell among the children of Israel, and will not forsake my people Israel.

14 So Solomon built the house, and finished it.

15 And he built the walls of the house within with boards of cedar, both the floor of the house, and the walls of the cieling: *and* he covered *them* on the inside with wood, and covered the floor of the house with planks of fir.

16 And he built twenty cubits on the sides of the house, both the floor and the walls with boards of cedar: he even built *them* for it within, *even* for the oracle, *even* for the most holy *place*.

17 And the house, that *is*, the temple before it, was forty cubits *long*.

18 And the cedar of the house within *was* carved with knops and open flowers: all *was* cedar; there was no stone seen.

19 And the oracle he prepared in the house within, to set there the ark of the covenant of the LORD.

20 And the oracle in the forepart *was* twenty cubits in length, and twenty cubits in breadth, and twenty cubits in the height thereof: and he overlaid it with pure gold; and *so* covered the altar *which was of* cedar.

21 So Solomon overlaid the house within with pure gold: and he made a partition by the chains of gold before the oracle; and he overlaid it with gold.

22 And the whole house he overlaid with gold, until he had finished all the house: also the whole altar that *was* by the oracle he overlaid with gold.

23 ¶ And within the oracle he made two cherubims *of* olive tree, *each* ten cubits high.

24 And five cubits *was* the one wing of the cherub, and five cubits the other wing of the cherub: from the uttermost part of the one wing unto the uttermost part of the other *were* ten cubits.

25 And the other cherub *was* ten cubits: both the cherubims *were* of one measure and one size.

26 The height of the one cherub *was* ten cubits, and so *was it* of the other cherub.

27 And he set the cherubims within the inner house: and they stretched forth the wings of the cherubims, so that the wing of the one touched the *one* wall, and the wing of the other cherub touched the other wall; and their wings touched one another in the midst of the house.

28 And he overlaid the cherubims with gold.

29 And he carved all the walls of the house round about with carved figures of cherubims and palm trees and open flowers, within and without.

30 And the floor of the house he overlaid with gold, within and without.

31 ¶ And for the entering of the oracle he made doors *of* olive tree: the lintel *and* side posts *were* a fifth part *of the wall*.

32 The two doors also *were of* olive tree; and he carved upon them carvings of cherubims and palm trees and open flowers, and overlaid *them* with gold, and spread gold upon the cherubims, and upon the palm trees.

33 So also made he for the door of the temple posts *of* olive tree, a fourth part *of the wall*.

34 And the two doors *were of* fir tree: the two leaves of the one door *were* folding, and the two leaves of the other door *were* folding.

35 And he carved *thereon* cherubims and palm trees and open flowers: and covered *them* with gold fitted upon the carved work.

36 ¶ And he built the inner court with three rows of hewed stone, and a row of cedar beams.

37 ¶ In the fourth year was the foundation of the

6:12–13 *if thou wilt walk . . . then will I.* God's blessing on the kingdom and His dwelling in the temple depended upon the obedience of the king to the law of God (9:4).

6:18 *knops.* Ornaments in the shape of gourds.

6:21 *made a partition.* Literally, "drew across it," most likely referring to the thick curtain separating the holy place from the most holy place (Ex. 26:31–33).

6:22 *altar.* The golden incense altar, situated in the sanctuary in front of the curtain of the inner sanctuary.

6:23 *olive tree.* Literally, "wood of oil," referring either to the oily kind of wood of the olive tree or perhaps to a fir tree. The same expression (vv. 31–32) is defined more specifically in v. 34 as a fir tree.

6:29–30 The *cherubims, trees, flowers,* and *gold* in the temple's artwork suggest that it was like the garden of Eden (Gen. 2:8–9,12; 3:24). The Lord restores His people from the fall and returns them to His presence, as in Paradise (Isa. 51:3; Rev. 22:1–5). *within and without.* Inside and outside, probably meaning in both the most holy place and the holy place.

6:31 These *doors* separated the sanctuary from the outer court (v. 33).

Thoughts for Personal/Family Worship: Chapter 6

1. **We read that there was "neither hammer nor axe nor any tool of iron heard in the house, while it was in building" (v. 7). The temple was built in relative silence. Since the**

house of the LORD laid, in the month Zif:
38 And in the eleventh year, in the month Bul,
which *is* the eighth month, was the house finished
throughout all the parts thereof, and according
to all the fashion of it. So was he seven years in
building it.

CHAPTER 7

BUT Solomon was building his own house
thirteen years, and he finished all his house.
2 ¶ He built also the house of the forest of
Lebanon; the length thereof *was* an hundred
cubits, and the breadth thereof fifty cubits, and
the height thereof thirty cubits, upon four rows of
cedar pillars, with cedar beams upon the pillars.
3 And *it was* covered with cedar above upon the
beams, that *lay* on forty five pillars, fifteen *in* a row.
4 And *there were* windows *in* three rows, and light
was against light *in* three ranks.
5 And all the doors and posts *were* square, with
the windows: and light *was* against light *in* three
ranks.
6 ¶ And he made a porch of pillars; the length
thereof *was* fifty cubits, and the breadth thereof
thirty cubits: and the porch *was* before them: and
the *other* pillars and the thick beam *were* before
them.
7 ¶ Then he made a porch for the throne where
he might judge, *even* the porch of judgment: and
it was covered with cedar from one side of the
floor to the other.
8 ¶ And his house where he dwelt *had* another
court within the porch, *which* was of the like
work. Solomon made also an house for Pharaoh's
daughter, whom he had taken *to wife*, like unto
this porch.
9 All these *were of* costly stones, according to the
measures of hewed stones, sawed with saws, within
and without, even from the foundation unto the
coping, and *so* on the outside toward the great
court.
10 And the foundation *was of* costly stones, even
great stones, stones of ten cubits, and stones of
eight cubits.
11 And above *were* costly stones, after the mea-
sures of hewed stones, and cedars.
12 And the great court round about *was* with
three rows of hewed stones, and a row of cedar
beams, both for the inner court of the house of
the LORD, and for the porch of the house.
13 ¶ And king Solomon sent and fetched Hiram
out of Tyre.
14 He *was* a widow's son of the tribe of Naphtali,
and his father *was* a man of Tyre, a worker in brass:
and he was filled with wisdom, and understand-
ing, and cunning to work all works in brass. And he
came to king Solomon, and wrought all his work.
15 For he cast two pillars of brass, of eighteen
cubits high apiece: and a line of twelve cubits did
compass either of them about.
16 And he made two chapiters *of* molten brass, to
set upon the tops of the pillars: the height of the
one chapiter *was* five cubits, and the height of the
other chapiter *was* five cubits:
17 *And* nets of checker work, and wreaths of
chain work, for the chapiters which *were* upon the
top of the pillars; seven for the one chapiter, and
seven for the other chapiter.
18 And he made the pillars, and two rows round
about upon the one network, to cover the chapi-
ters that *were* upon the top, with pomegranates:
and so did he for the other chapiter.
19 And the chapiters that *were* upon the top of the
pillars *were* of lily work in the porch, four cubits.
20 And the chapiters upon the two pillars *had*

New Testament identifies believers, both individually and corporately, as the temple of God, this is suggestive or characteristic of the manner in which the Lord builds His church. Without much public show or loud proclamation the Lord converts sinners and expands His church. He performs His work in the private lives of people and causes them to be His witnesses in this world, but without ostentatious display or fanfare.

2. The temple, like the tabernacle before it, symbolized God's dwelling with His people. The temple was beautiful and ornate, a most special place filled with pointers to the One coming who was greater than the temple (Matt. 12:6). In the person of Christ, God came to dwell directly with man and revealed His glory, full of grace and truth (John 1:14). Solomon's temple was glorious, but nowhere does the glory of God shine more brightly than in the face of Jesus Christ (2 Cor. 4:6). An even greater wonder is that Christ dwells now in a most special and intimate way in the hearts of His people (Col. 1:27). However, God's dwelling with Christians does not depend upon the obedience of a fallen, sinful man like Solomon but upon the perfect righteousness of the God-man (Heb. 7:26). Therefore, believers in Christ will enjoy God's presence forever.

Chapter 7: *Solomon completes various building projects, including items and utensils for the temple.*

7:1 *thirteen years.* It took Solomon nearly twice as long to build the royal palace as the temple (6:38), implying that his priorities were right.

7:9 *coping.* The eaves or top part of the wall.

7:13–14 *Hiram.* Not to be confused with Hiram, the king of Tyre (5:1). *filled with wisdom.* Had skill and ability, specifically as an artisan with bronze. *cunning to work.* Had the skill or "know-how" to work with bronze.

7:15 *cast.* Formed or fashioned. *a line . . . did compass.* A thread or cord of some sort surrounded (v. 23).

7:16 *chapiters.* The capitals of a column or pillar. Here referring to some ornamentations placed at the top (vv. 17–20,31, 41–42).

7:17 *nets of checker work.* Some sort of lattice or trellis work, an ornamental grating.

7:20 *belly.* Bulging section or rounded projection.

pomegranates also above, over against the belly
which *was* by the network: and the pomegranates
were two hundred in rows round about upon the
other chapiter.
21 And he set up the pillars in the porch of the
temple: and he set up the right pillar, and called
the name thereof Jachin: and he set up the left
pillar, and called the name thereof Boaz.
22 And upon the top of the pillars *was* lily work:
so was the work of the pillars finished.
23 ¶ And he made a molten sea, ten cubits from
the one brim to the other: *it was* round all about,
and his height *was* five cubits: and a line of thirty
cubits did compass it round about.
24 And under the brim of it round about *there*
were knops compassing it, ten in a cubit, com-
passing the sea round about: the knops *were* cast
in two rows, when it was cast.
25 It stood upon twelve oxen, three looking
toward the north, and three looking toward the
west, and three looking toward the south, and
three looking toward the east: and the sea *was set*
above upon them, and all their hinder parts *were*
inward.
26 And it *was* an hand breadth thick, and the
brim thereof was wrought like the brim of a cup,
with flowers of lilies: it contained two thousand
baths.
27 ¶ And he made ten bases of brass; four cubits
was the length of one base, and four cubits the
breadth thereof, and three cubits the height of it.
28 And the work of the bases *was* on this *manner*:
they had borders, and the borders *were* between
the ledges:
29 And on the borders that *were* between the
ledges *were* lions, oxen, and cherubims: and upon
the ledges *there was* a base above: and beneath
the lions and oxen *were* certain additions made
of thin work.
30 And every base had four brasen wheels, and
plates of brass: and the four corners thereof had
undersetters: under the laver *were* undersetters
molten, at the side of every addition.
31 And the mouth of it within the chapiter and
above *was* a cubit: but the mouth thereof *was*
round *after* the work of the base, a cubit and an
half: and also upon the mouth of it *were* gravings
with their borders, foursquare, not round.
32 And under the borders *were* four wheels; and
the axletrees of the wheels *were joined* to the base:
and the height of a wheel *was* a cubit and half a
cubit.
33 And the work of the wheels *was* like the work
of a chariot wheel: their axletrees, and their naves,
and their felloes, and their spokes, *were* all molten.
34 And *there were* four undersetters to the four
corners of one base: *and* the undersetters *were* of
the very base itself.
35 And in the top of the base *was there* a round
compass of half a cubit high: and on the top of the
base the ledges thereof and the borders thereof
were of the same.
36 For on the plates of the ledges thereof, and on
the borders thereof, he graved cherubims, lions,
and palm trees, according to the proportion of
every one, and additions round about.
37 After this *manner* he made the ten bases: all of
them had one casting, one measure, *and* one size.
38 ¶ Then made he ten lavers of brass: one laver
contained forty baths: *and* every laver was four
cubits: *and* upon every one of the ten bases one
laver.
39 And he put five bases on the right side of the
house, and five on the left side of the house: and
he set the sea on the right side of the house east-
ward over against the south.
40 ¶ And Hiram made the lavers, and the shovels,
and the basons. So Hiram made an end of doing
all the work that he made king Solomon for the
house of the LORD:
41 The two pillars, and the *two* bowls of the chap-
iters that *were* on the top of the two pillars; and
the two networks, to cover the two bowls of the
chapiters which *were* upon the top of the pillars;
42 And four hundred pomegranates for the two
networks, *even* two rows of pomegranates for one
network, to cover the two bowls of the chapiters
that *were* upon the pillars;
43 And the ten bases, and ten lavers on the bases;
44 And one sea, and twelve oxen under the sea;

7:21 *Jachin.* Translated, "he shall establish." *Boaz.* Translated, "in Him is strength." A symbolic depiction of the spiritual reality that the church of Christ, the spiritual temple of the Lord, is established by the almighty power of God and rests in His strength.
7:23 *molten sea.* The sea of cast metal, referring to a large basin containing an abundance of water to be used by the priests and Levites for their ceremonial washings (Ex. 30:18–21). *compass.* Surround.
7:24 *knops.* See note at 6:18.
7:25 *their hinder parts were inward.* The molten sea, the laver, stood upon a base of twelve oxen that were all facing outward. The back parts of these oxen could not be seen from the outside.
7:26 *two thousand baths.* One bath is around nine gallons (also v. 38).
7:30,34 *undersetters.* Supports or bases.
7:31 *gravings.* Engravings.
7:32–33 *axletrees.* Axles, bars connecting the wheels. *naves.* Rims. *felloes.* Spokes. *spokes.* Hubs.
7:50 *to wit.* That is.

Thoughts for Personal/Family Worship: Chapter 7

1. **Solomon's priority in finishing the temple before finishing his own palace (6:38; 7:1) stands in stark contrast to the rebuilding of the temple after the Babylonian exile. Haggai lamented that those who returned to the land were comfortable in their finished houses while the temple was still in ruins (Hag. 1:4). They put their own**

45 And the pots, and the shovels, and the basons:
and all these vessels, which Hiram made to king
Solomon for the house of the LORD, *were of* bright
brass.
46 In the plain of Jordan did the king cast them,
in the clay ground between Succoth and Zarthan.
47 And Solomon left all the vessels *unweighed*,
because they were exceeding many: neither was
the weight of the brass found out.
48 And Solomon made all the vessels that
pertained unto the house of the LORD: the altar
of gold, and the table of gold, whereupon the
shewbread *was*,
49 And the candlesticks of pure gold, five on the
right *side*, and five on the left, before the oracle,
with the flowers, and the lamps, and the tongs *of*
gold,
50 And the bowls, and the snuffers, and the basons, and the spoons, and the censers *of* pure
gold; and the hinges *of* gold, *both* for the doors of
the inner house, the most holy *place, and* for the
doors of the house, *to wit,* of the temple.
51 So was ended all the work that king Solomon
made for the house of the LORD. And Solomon
brought in the things which David his father had
dedicated; *even* the silver, and the gold, and the
vessels, did he put among the treasures of the
house of the LORD.

CHAPTER 8

THEN Solomon assembled the elders of Israel,
and all the heads of the tribes, the chief of the fathers of the children of Israel, unto king Solomon
in Jerusalem, that they might bring up the ark of
the covenant of the LORD out of the city of David,
which *is* Zion.
2 And all the men of Israel assembled themselves
unto king Solomon at the feast in the month
Ethanim, which *is* the seventh month.
3 And all the elders of Israel came, and the priests
took up the ark.
4 And they brought up the ark of the LORD, and
the tabernacle of the congregation, and all the
holy vessels that *were* in the tabernacle, even those
did the priests and the Levites bring up.
5 And king Solomon, and all the congregation
of Israel, that were assembled unto him, *were*
with him before the ark, sacrificing sheep and
oxen, that could not be told nor numbered for
multitude.
6 And the priests brought in the ark of the covenant of the LORD unto his place, into the oracle of
the house, to the most holy *place, even* under the
wings of the cherubims.
7 For the cherubims spread forth *their* two wings
over the place of the ark, and the cherubims
covered the ark and the staves thereof above.
8 And they drew out the staves, that the ends of
the staves were seen out in the holy *place* before
the oracle, and they were not seen without: and
there they are unto this day.
9 *There was* nothing in the ark save the two tables
of stone, which Moses put there at Horeb, when
the LORD made *a covenant* with the children of
Israel, when they came out of the land of Egypt.
10 And it came to pass, when the priests were
come out of the holy *place*, that the cloud filled
the house of the LORD,
11 So that the priests could not stand to minister
because of the cloud: for the glory of the LORD
had filled the house of the LORD.
12 ¶ Then spake Solomon, The LORD said that he
would dwell in the thick darkness.

---

interests ahead of God, and the work of God suffered. Solomon's example charts the proper course. Putting God and His kingdom work first puts everything else in its proper place. Significantly, Solomon's personal interests did not suffer, and the construction projects in his kingdom were magnificent. God is no man's debtor; He will take care of His people. He will honor those who honor Him.

2. **Every component of the temple has significance in what it reveals about God and how to worship Him. Special attention in this chapter is given to the molten sea (v. 23), the washbasin in the outer court just beyond the altar of sacrifice. The whole tripartite design of the tabernacle/temple, with its corresponding furniture, teaches how to approach God. The altar is first because approaching God cannot begin apart from the blood sacrifice. Then, before entering the holy place, the priests had to wash at the laver, illustrating Ps. 24:3–4, "Who shall stand in his holy place? He that hath clean hands, and a pure heart." What the priests pictured remains the requirement for Christians today. Fellowship with God requires pardon and purity, both walking in the light and being cleansed with Christ's blood (1 John 1:7).**

Chapter 8: ***Solomon dedicates the temple, after which the Lord manifests His glory and Solomon offers a prayer of praise and intercession.***

8:2 *the feast in the month Ethanim.* Most likely the Feast of Tabernacles (Lev. 23:24; Deut. 16:13), commemorating the wilderness wanderings and the nation's total dependence upon God.

8:4 *brought up the ark.* From the special place David had made when he retrieved it from Kirjath-jearim (2 Sam. 6:17; 2 Chron. 1:4). *tabernacle of the congregation.* From Gibeon (v. 3).

8:6 *oracle of the house.* The most holy place behind the veil.

8:7 *staves.* Poles used to transport the ark.

8:8 *in the holy place. Place* is not in the Hebrew text; the *holy* thing was the ark itself (2 Chron. 5:9). Thus, the staves were removed but remained with the ark in the most holy place and could not be seen from the outside (*without*).

8:9 *There was nothing in the ark save the two tables of stone.* A pot of manna and Aaron's rod had been kept either with or inside the ark (Ex. 16:33–34; Num. 17:10; Heb. 9:4). These items had disappeared by the time of the temple, perhaps during the ark's Philistine captivity (1 Sam. 4–6).

8:10 *cloud.* An appearance of God's glory (theophany) and

13 I have surely built thee an house to dwell in, a settled place for thee to abide in for ever.

14 And the king turned his face about, and blessed all the congregation of Israel: (and all the congregation of Israel stood;)

15 And he said, Blessed *be* the LORD God of Israel, which spake with his mouth unto David my father, and hath with his hand fulfilled *it*, saying,

16 Since the day that I brought forth my people Israel out of Egypt, I chose no city out of all the tribes of Israel to build an house, that my name might be therein; but I chose David to be over my people Israel.

17 And it was in the heart of David my father to build an house for the name of the LORD God of Israel.

18 And the LORD said unto David my father, Whereas it was in thine heart to build an house unto my name, thou didst well that it was in thine heart.

19 Nevertheless thou shalt not build the house; but thy son that shall come forth out of thy loins, he shall build the house unto my name.

20 And the LORD hath performed his word that he spake, and I am risen up in the room of David my father, and sit on the throne of Israel, as the LORD promised, and have built an house for the name of the LORD God of Israel.

21 And I have set there a place for the ark, wherein *is* the covenant of the LORD, which he made with our fathers, when he brought them out of the land of Egypt.

22 ¶ And Solomon stood before the altar of the LORD in the presence of all the congregation of Israel, and spread forth his hands toward heaven:

23 And he said, LORD God of Israel, *there is* no God like thee, in heaven above, or on earth beneath, who keepest covenant and mercy with thy servants that walk before thee with all their heart:

24 Who hast kept with thy servant David my father that thou promisedst him: thou spakest also with thy mouth, and hast fulfilled *it* with thine hand, as *it is* this day.

25 Therefore now, LORD God of Israel, keep with thy servant David my father that thou promisedst him, saying, There shall not fail thee a man in my sight to sit on the throne of Israel; so that thy children take heed to their way, that they walk before me as thou hast walked before me.

26 And now, O God of Israel, let thy word, I pray thee, be verified, which thou spakest unto thy servant David my father.

27 But will God indeed dwell on the earth? behold, the heaven and heaven of heavens cannot contain thee; how much less this house that I have builded?

28 Yet have thou respect unto the prayer of thy servant, and to his supplication, O LORD my God, to hearken unto the cry and to the prayer, which thy servant prayeth before thee to day:

29 That thine eyes may be open toward this house night and day, *even* toward the place of which thou hast said, My name shall be there: that thou mayest hearken unto the prayer which thy servant shall make toward this place.

30 And hearken thou to the supplication of thy servant, and of thy people Israel, when they shall pray toward this place: and hear thou in heaven thy dwelling place: and when thou hearest, forgive.

31 ¶ If any man trespass against his neighbour, and an oath be laid upon him to cause him to swear, and the oath come before thine altar in this house:

32 Then hear thou in heaven, and do, and judge thy servants, condemning the wicked, to bring his way upon his head; and justifying the righteous, to give him according to his righteousness.

33 ¶ When thy people Israel be smitten down before the enemy, because they have sinned against thee, and shall turn again to thee, and confess thy name, and pray, and make supplication unto thee in this house:

34 Then hear thou in heaven, and forgive the sin of thy people Israel, and bring them again unto the land which thou gavest unto their fathers.

35 ¶ When heaven is shut up, and there is no rain, because they have sinned against thee; if they pray toward this place, and confess thy name, and turn from their sin, when thou afflictest them:

36 Then hear thou in heaven, and forgive the sin

---

sign of His presence (Ex. 40:34).

8:12 *thick darkness.* A sign of God's infinite holiness and inaccessibility to human sight (Pss. 18:11–12; 97:2). Ironically, even His dwelling in light has the same consequence (1 Tim. 6:16). This highlights the grace of God in allowing Himself to be approached through the gospel, which is pictured in the temple (His dwelling place). God would live with His people by means of His Word and the visible signs of His grace.

8:13 *I have surely built thee an house to dwell in.* God works through the mediation of His king to establish His gracious presence with His people (Matt. 16:18; 18:20; 28:18,20).

8:15 *which spake with his mouth . . . and hath with his hand fulfilled it.* God's dwelling with His people is His fulfillment of the promise of all His covenants, including those with *Israel* and *David* (vv. 16–17,20–21,23–24; Gen. 26:3; Ex. 29:45–46; 2 Sam. 7:13; 2 Cor. 6:16; Rev. 21:3,7).

8:16 *my name might be therein.* This marks the climax to the law of central sanctuary (Deut. 12:5).

8:20 *in the room of.* In the place of or instead of.

8:21 *the covenant of the LORD.* The Ten Commandments in the *ark*, detailing the people's obligations to God's covenant of grace.

8:22 *spread forth his hands.* A common prayer gesture (Pss. 134:2; 141:2).

8:23 *mercy.* Covenant love and loyalty.

8:26 *be verified.* Prove to be firm and reliable. The Hebrew word is the basis of "Amen."

8:27 *heaven of heavens cannot contain thee.* God is both in

of thy servants, and of thy people Israel, that thou
teach them the good way wherein they should
walk, and give rain upon thy land, which thou
hast given to thy people for an inheritance.
37 ¶ If there be in the land famine, if there be
pestilence, blasting, mildew, locust, *or* if there be
caterpiller; if their enemy besiege them in the land
of their cities; whatsoever plague, whatsoever
sickness *there be*;
38 What prayer and supplication soever be *made*
by any man, *or* by all thy people Israel, which shall
know every man the plague of his own heart, and
spread forth his hands toward this house:
39 Then hear thou in heaven thy dwelling place,
and forgive, and do, and give to every man according to his ways, whose heart thou knowest;
(for thou, *even* thou only, knowest the hearts of
all the children of men;)
40 That they may fear thee all the days that
they live in the land which thou gavest unto our
fathers.
41 Moreover concerning a stranger, that *is* not of
thy people Israel, but cometh out of a far country
for thy name's sake;
42 (For they shall hear of thy great name, and of
thy strong hand, and of thy stretched out arm;)
when he shall come and pray toward this house;
43 Hear thou in heaven thy dwelling place, and
do according to all that the stranger calleth to
thee for: that all people of the earth may know
thy name, to fear thee, as *do* thy people Israel; and
that they may know that this house, which I have
builded, is called by thy name.
44 ¶ If thy people go out to battle against their
enemy, whithersoever thou shalt send them, and
shall pray unto the LORD toward the city which
thou hast chosen, and *toward* the house that I
have built for thy name:
45 Then hear thou in heaven their prayer and
their supplication, and maintain their cause.
46 If they sin against thee, (for *there is* no man
that sinneth not,) and thou be angry with them,
and deliver them to the enemy, so that they carry
them away captives unto the land of the enemy,
far or near;
47 *Yet* if they shall bethink themselves in the land
whither they were carried captives, and repent,
and make supplication unto thee in the land
of them that carried them captives, saying, We
have sinned, and have done perversely, we have
committed wickedness;
48 And *so* return unto thee with all their heart,
and with all their soul, in the land of their enemies,
which led them away captive, and pray unto thee
toward their land, which thou gavest unto their
fathers, the city which thou hast chosen, and the
house which I have built for thy name:
49 Then hear thou their prayer and their supplication in heaven thy dwelling place, and maintain
their cause,
50 And forgive thy people that have sinned
against thee, and all their transgressions wherein
they have transgressed against thee, and give
them compassion before them who carried them
captive, that they may have compassion on them:
51 For they *be* thy people, and thine inheritance,
which thou broughtest forth out of Egypt, from
the midst of the furnace of iron:
52 That thine eyes may be open unto the supplication of thy servant, and unto the supplication
of thy people Israel, to hearken unto them in all
that they call for unto thee.
53 For thou didst separate them from among all
the people of the earth, *to be* thine inheritance, as
thou spakest by the hand of Moses thy servant,
when thou broughtest our fathers out of Egypt,
O Lord GOD.
54 And it was *so*, that when Solomon had made
an end of praying all this prayer and supplication
unto the LORD, he arose from before the altar of
the LORD, from kneeling on his knees with his
hands spread up to heaven.
55 And he stood, and blessed all the congregation
of Israel with a loud voice, saying,
56 Blessed *be* the LORD, that hath given rest
unto his people Israel, according to all that he
promised: there hath not failed one word of all
his good promise, which he promised by the hand
of Moses his servant.
57 The LORD our God be with us, as he was with

---

all places (omnipresent) and beyond all places—infinite with regard to space (Ps. 139:7–10; Isa. 66:1; Jer. 23:23–24). This makes it all the more remarkable that He would manifest His presence in the temple.

8:30 *hear thou in heaven.* A central function of the temple was to offer access to God through prayer (vv. 32,34,36,39,43,45). God's house is a house of prayer (Isa. 56:7). Access to the Father comes through Christ by a Spirit-worked faith (Eph. 2:18; 3:12).

8:31 *neighbour.* Fellow man, not the resident next door.

8:33 *smitten down.* Defeated.

8:35 See Deut. 11:17; 28:11–12,23.

8:37 *blasting.* Blight or scourging, generally affecting foliage (Joel 1).

8:39 *thou only, knowest.* See Jer. 17:10.

8:40 *That they may fear thee.* Fearing God is living in conscious awareness of God, resulting in worship and godly behavior.

8:41–42 *stranger.* Foreigner. *thy great name.* God's temple was to attract people from all nations to recognize the glory of the Lord and seek Him (Isa. 2:3). The church should do the same today.

8:47 *bethink themselves.* Literally, "return to their heart," with the sense of having a change of heart or coming back to their senses spiritually.

8:51 *furnace of iron.* The Hebrew word signifies a pot in which metal alloys are molten, symbolizing the severity of the sufferings in Egypt.

8:54 *kneeling on his knees.* Gesture of humility and unworthiness before the Lord.

our fathers: let him not leave us, nor forsake us:
58 That he may incline our hearts unto him, to
walk in all his ways, and to keep his command-
ments, and his statutes, and his judgments, which
he commanded our fathers.
59 And let these my words, wherewith I have
made supplication before the LORD, be nigh unto
the LORD our God day and night, that he main-
tain the cause of his servant, and the cause of
his people Israel at all times, as the matter shall
require:
60 That all the people of the earth may know that
the LORD *is* God, *and that there is* none else.
61 Let your heart therefore be perfect with the
LORD our God, to walk in his statutes, and to keep
his commandments, as at this day.
62 ¶ And the king, and all Israel with him, offered
sacrifice before the LORD.
63 And Solomon offered a sacrifice of peace of-
ferings, which he offered unto the LORD, two
and twenty thousand oxen, and an hundred and
twenty thousand sheep. So the king and all the
children of Israel dedicated the house of the LORD.
64 The same day did the king hallow the middle
of the court that *was* before the house of the
LORD: for there he offered burnt offerings, and
meat offerings, and the fat of the peace offerings:
because the brasen altar that *was* before the LORD
was too little to receive the burnt offerings, and
meat offerings, and the fat of the peace offerings.
65 And at that time Solomon held a feast, and all
Israel with him, a great congregation, from the
entering in of Hamath unto the river of Egypt,
before the LORD our God, seven days and seven
days, *even* fourteen days.
66 On the eighth day he sent the people away:
and they blessed the king, and went unto their
tents joyful and glad of heart for all the goodness
that the LORD had done for David his servant, and
for Israel his people.

CHAPTER 9

AND it came to pass, when Solomon had finished
the building of the house of the LORD, and the
king's house, and all Solomon's desire which he
was pleased to do,
2 That the LORD appeared to Solomon the second
time, as he had appeared unto him at Gibeon.
3 And the LORD said unto him, I have heard thy
prayer and thy supplication, that thou hast made
before me: I have hallowed this house, which
thou hast built, to put my name there for ever;
and mine eyes and mine heart shall be there
perpetually.
4 And if thou wilt walk before me, as David
thy father walked, in integrity of heart, and in
uprightness, to do according to all that I have
commanded thee, *and* wilt keep my statutes and
my judgments:
5 Then I will establish the throne of thy kingdom
upon Israel for ever, as I promised to David thy
father, saying, There shall not fail thee a man
upon the throne of Israel.
6 *But* if ye shall at all turn from following me,
ye or your children, and will not keep my com-
mandments *and* my statutes which I have set
before you, but go and serve other gods, and wor-
ship them:
7 Then will I cut off Israel out of the land which
I have given them; and this house, which I have
hallowed for my name, will I cast out of my sight;
and Israel shall be a proverb and a byword among
all people:

8:61 *be perfect.* Have whole and undivided determination and resolve to do something.
8:64 *hallow.* Dedicate or consecrate. *meat offerings.* Grain offerings that were always in connection with a bloody sacrifice.
8:65 *feast.* Feast of Tabernacles, lasting seven days (Lev. 23:34).
8:65 *Hamath unto the river of Egypt.* Northern and southern extremes of the kingdom.

Thoughts for Personal/Family Worship: Chapter 8

1. **As beautiful and glorious as the temple was, it was nothing but a building until the Lord filled it with His glorious presence (vv. 10–11). It is the Lord's presence that makes a house to be God's house. How much more is that true today, when God has no holy buildings, but His temple is the people of the church (1 Cor. 3:16)? Beautiful architecture and impressive gatherings of people are no substitute for the presence of the living God. Let us beware of the error of Laodicea, thinking that our church is rich while Christ is outside knocking to enter (Rev. 3:17,20). Praying for God's special presence ought to be a regular routine in our preparations for worship.**
2. **We can learn to pray from the prayers recorded for us in Scripture. Solomon's prayer offers a pattern to follow. His prayer involves praise and worship, confession, intercessions, and supplications. He often appeals to God's words and promises. It would be a good spiritual exercise to work through the prayer, praying with Solomon and addressing your own personal needs and issues. Prayer always is evidence of our sense of dependence upon God. The more conscious we are of needing the Lord, the more often and effectively we will pray.**

Chapter 9: *The Lord repeats the covenant to Solomon, and Solomon continues to build up the kingdom.*

9:3 *hallowed.* Consecrated or set aside (v. 7). *mine eyes and mine heart.* He will ever be present to receive the prayers of His people (8:29).
9:4 *integrity of heart.* To serve the Lord with one's whole heart, in simplicity and sincerity. Though the covenant with David committed the Lord unconditionally to David's line (2 Sam. 7:13–15; Ps. 89:34–37), the enjoyment of covenant blessings upon the kingdom and the temple depended on the sincere obedience of each reigning son of David (1 Kings 6:12–13; 11:11).
9:7 *proverb and a byword.* A sharp word or taunt directed toward an object of scorn or derision.

8 And at this house, *which* is high, every one that
passeth by it shall be astonished, and shall hiss;
and they shall say, Why hath the LORD done thus
unto this land, and to this house?
9 And they shall answer, Because they forsook the
LORD their God, who brought forth their fathers
out of the land of Egypt, and have taken hold
upon other gods, and have worshipped them, and
served them: therefore hath the LORD brought
upon them all this evil.
10 ¶ And it came to pass at the end of twenty
years, when Solomon had built the two houses,
the house of the LORD, and the king's house,
11 (*Now* Hiram the king of Tyre had furnished
Solomon with cedar trees and fir trees, and with
gold, according to all his desire,) that then king
Solomon gave Hiram twenty cities in the land of
Galilee.
12 And Hiram came out from Tyre to see the
cities which Solomon had given him; and they
pleased him not.
13 And he said, What cities *are* these which thou
hast given me, my brother? And he called them
the land of Cabul unto this day.
14 And Hiram sent to the king sixscore talents of
gold.
15 ¶ And this *is* the reason of the levy which king
Solomon raised; for to build the house of the
LORD, and his own house, and Millo, and the wall
of Jerusalem, and Hazor, and Megiddo, and Gezer.
16 *For* Pharaoh king of Egypt had gone up, and
taken Gezer, and burnt it with fire, and slain the
Canaanites that dwelt in the city, and given it *for* a
present unto his daughter, Solomon's wife.
17 And Solomon built Gezer, and Beth-horon the
nether,
18 And Baalath, and Tadmor in the wilderness,
in the land,
19 And all the cities of store that Solomon had,
and cities for his chariots, and cities for his horse-
men, and that which Solomon desired to build in
Jerusalem, and in Lebanon, and in all the land of
his dominion.
20 *And* all the people *that were* left of the Amor-
ites, Hittites, Perizzites, Hivites, and Jebusites,
which *were* not of the children of Israel,
21 Their children that were left after them in the
land, whom the children of Israel also were not
able utterly to destroy, upon those did Solomon
levy a tribute of bondservice unto this day.
22 But of the children of Israel did Solomon
make no bondmen: but they *were* men of war,
and his servants, and his princes, and his captains,
and rulers of his chariots, and his horsemen.
23 These *were* the chief of the officers that *were*
over Solomon's work, five hundred and fifty,
which bare rule over the people that wrought in
the work.
24 ¶ But Pharaoh's daughter came up out of the
city of David unto her house which *Solomon* had
built for her: then did he build Millo.
25 ¶ And three times in a year did Solomon of-
fer burnt offerings and peace offerings upon the
altar which he built unto the LORD, and he burnt
incense upon the altar that *was* before the LORD.
So he finished the house.
26 ¶ And king Solomon made a navy of ships in
Ezion-geber, which *is* beside Eloth, on the shore
of the Red sea, in the land of Edom.
27 And Hiram sent in the navy his servants,
shipmen that had knowledge of the sea, with the
servants of Solomon.
28 And they came to Ophir, and fetched from
thence gold, four hundred and twenty talents, and
brought *it* to king Solomon.

CHAPTER 10

AND when the queen of Sheba heard of the fame
of Solomon concerning the name of the LORD,
she came to prove him with hard questions.
2 And she came to Jerusalem with a very great

9:8–9 *hiss.* Or to whistle as an expression of mockery. These verses echo the warning of covenant curses in the law of Moses (Deut. 29:24–27).

Solomon's Wisdom and Wealth from the Lord (1 Kings 9:10—10:29)

9:13 *Cabul.* Worthless, displeasing, or dirty (2 Chron. 8:2).
9:14 *sixscore talents.* 120 talents or almost 8,000 pounds, a talent being about 66 pounds (v. 28).
9:15 *levy.* Not taxes but the drafting of a labor force. *Millo.* Probably the name of a large building in the proximity of the king's palace where visitors to the king were received and the king's personal bodyguards were stationed. *Hazor, and Megiddo, and Gezer.* Three strategically important cities.
9:17 *nether.* Lower or lowest.
9:24 *Millo.* Some sort of terraced structure.
9:25 *three times in a year.* The pilgrimages for the Feasts of Unleavened Bread, Tabernacles, and Weeks or Pentecost (2 Chron. 8:13).
9:26 *Red sea.* Ancient name given to the Gulf of Suez and the Gulf of Aqaba.

Thoughts for Personal/Family Worship: Chapter 9

1. **The Lord appeared to King Solomon to reiterate the covenant promise given to David and to warn him against forsaking the covenant obligations (vv. 1–9). As king of Israel, he represented the nation before God in the covenant. His obedience would establish God's kingdom and presence among them, whereas his disobedience would lead the nation into apostasy and judgment. How precious then is the promise of a King of perfect righteousness, even divine righteousness (Jer. 23:5–6)! Christ's perfect obedience has secured God's kingdom and presence forever for those united to Him. In Christ they are counted righteous before God, and by Christ's Spirit they too walk in sincere obedience.**
2. **The Lord explains what the cost would be if Israel were**

train, with camels that bare spices, and very much
gold, and precious stones: and when she was
come to Solomon, she communed with him of all
that was in her heart.
3 And Solomon told her all her questions: there
was not *any* thing hid from the king, which he
told her not.
4 And when the queen of Sheba had seen all Sol-
omon's wisdom, and the house that he had built,
5 And the meat of his table, and the sitting of his
servants, and the attendance of his ministers, and
their apparel, and his cupbearers, and his ascent
by which he went up unto the house of the LORD;
there was no more spirit in her.
6 And she said to the king, It was a true report
that I heard in mine own land of thy acts and of
thy wisdom.
7 Howbeit I believed not the words, until I came,
and mine eyes had seen *it*: and, behold, the half
was not told me: thy wisdom and prosperity
exceedeth the fame which I heard.
8 Happy *are* thy men, happy *are* these thy ser-
vants, which stand continually before thee, *and*
that hear thy wisdom.
9 Blessed be the LORD thy God, which delighted
in thee, to set thee on the throne of Israel: because
the LORD loved Israel for ever, therefore made he
thee king, to do judgment and justice.
10 And she gave the king an hundred and twenty
talents of gold, and of spices very great store,
and precious stones: there came no more such
abundance of spices as these which the queen of
Sheba gave to king Solomon.
11 And the navy also of Hiram, that brought gold
from Ophir, brought in from Ophir great plenty
of almug trees, and precious stones.
12 And the king made of the almug trees pillars
for the house of the LORD, and for the king's
house, harps also and psalteries for singers: there
came no such almug trees, nor were seen unto
this day.
13 And king Solomon gave unto the queen of
Sheba all her desire, whatsoever she asked, beside
that which Solomon gave her of his royal bounty.
So she turned and went to her own country, she
and her servants.
14 ¶ Now the weight of gold that came to Solo-
mon in one year was six hundred threescore and
six talents of gold,
15 Beside *that he had* of the merchantmen, and
of the traffick of the spice merchants, and of all
the kings of Arabia, and of the governors of the
country.
16 ¶ And king Solomon made two hundred
targets *of* beaten gold: six hundred *shekels* of gold
went to one target.
17 And *he made* three hundred shields *of* beaten
gold; three pound of gold went to one shield: and
the king put them in the house of the forest of
Lebanon.
18 ¶ Moreover the king made a great throne of
ivory, and overlaid it with the best gold.
19 The throne had six steps, and the top of the
throne *was* round behind: and *there were* stays on
either side on the place of the seat, and two lions
stood beside the stays.
20 And twelve lions stood there on the one side
and on the other upon the six steps: there was not
the like made in any kingdom.
21 ¶ And all king Solomon's drinking vessels
were of gold, and all the vessels of the house of the
forest of Lebanon *were of* pure gold; none *were of*

---

to forsake His commandments and embrace false gods (v. 9). The Lord would forsake His temple and give up the people of Israel to discipline and misery. Enjoying fellowship with God required purity of life and the forsaking of sin (2 Cor. 6:17–18; 1 John 1:5–10). Today there are many temptations alluring churches away from the truth of God's Word. The stakes for such apostasy are high: the Lord withdraws Himself. When Christians start backsliding, let them be quick to confess their sins and seek forgiveness and restoration by the blood of Christ.

Chapter 10: *The Queen of Sheba visits Solomon and is astounded by his wisdom and wealth, which is described in detail.*

10:1 *Sheba.* Located in the southwest of the Arabian Peninsula, approximately 1,000 miles from Jerusalem. This indicates how extensive Solomon's reputation was. *prove him with hard questions.* Test him with riddles or perplexing questions.
10:2 *a very great train.* Elsewhere refers to a numerous army (2 Kings 6:14), here most likely to the queen's entourage of guards.
10:5 *meat.* Food of any kind. *the sitting.* The assembly.
10:8 *Happy.* Often translated, "blessed" (Ps. 1:1), describing the benefits that belong to someone.
10:9 *Blessed.* Synonymous with a different Hebrew word translated, "happy" (v. 8); designates the ascription of praise when applied to God. *because the LORD loved Israel.* The king is God's love gift to His people (Isa. 9:6). *judgment and justice.* Justice and righteousness (Ps. 72:1–2).
10:10 *talents.* Each approximately 66 pounds (v. 14).
10:12 *pillars.* Handrails used for support between the king's palace and the temple. *harps . . . psalteries.* Stringed instruments of some sort.
10:15 *merchantmen.* Traders or traveling merchants. *traffick of the spice merchants.* Merchandise of the vendors.
10:16 *targets.* Round shields.
10:17 *pound.* About 6.5 pounds.
10:19 *stays.* Literally, "hands," referring to armrests *on either side* of the throne's seat.
10:22 *Tharshish.* Or Tarshish (22:48; 2 Chron. 9:21).
10:24 *sought to Solomon.* Literally, "were seeking the face of Solomon," wanting to be in his presence.
10:26 *in the cities.* Most likely Gezer, Megiddo, and Hazor (see note at 9:15).
10:28 *linen yarn.* Most likely a proper name, "Kue," referring to a town in Asia Minor, present day Turkey. *the king's merchants received the linen yarn at a price.* Literally, "the traders of the

silver: it was nothing accounted of in the days of
Solomon.
22 For the king had at sea a navy of Tharshish
with the navy of Hiram: once in three years came
the navy of Tharshish, bringing gold, and silver,
ivory, and apes, and peacocks.
23 So king Solomon exceeded all the kings of the
earth for riches and for wisdom.
24 ¶ And all the earth sought to Solomon, to hear
his wisdom, which God had put in his heart.
25 And they brought every man his present,
vessels of silver, and vessels of gold, and garments,
and armour, and spices, horses, and mules, a rate
year by year.
26 ¶ And Solomon gathered together chariots
and horsemen: and he had a thousand and four
hundred chariots, and twelve thousand horse-
men, whom he bestowed in the cities for chariots,
and with the king at Jerusalem.
27 And the king made silver *to be* in Jerusalem as
stones, and cedars made he *to be* as the sycomore
trees that *are* in the vale, for abundance.
28 ¶ And Solomon had horses brought out of
Egypt, and linen yarn: the king's merchants re-
ceived the linen yarn at a price.
29 And a chariot came up and went out of Egypt
for six hundred *shekels* of silver, and an horse for
an hundred and fifty: and so for all the kings of
the Hittites, and for the kings of Syria, did they
bring *them* out by their means.

CHAPTER 11

BUT king Solomon loved many strange women,
together with the daughter of Pharaoh, women of
the Moabites, Ammonites, Edomites, Zidonians,
and Hittites;
2 Of the nations *concerning* which the LORD said
unto the children of Israel, Ye shall not go in to
them, neither shall they come in unto you: *for*
surely they will turn away your heart after their
gods: Solomon clave unto these in love.
3 And he had seven hundred wives, princesses,
and three hundred concubines: and his wives
turned away his heart.
4 For it came to pass, when Solomon was old,
that his wives turned away his heart after other
gods: and his heart was not perfect with the LORD
his God, as *was* the heart of David his father.
5 For Solomon went after Ashtoreth the goddess
of the Zidonians, and after Milcom the abomina-
tion of the Ammonites.
6 And Solomon did evil in the sight of the LORD,
and went not fully after the LORD, as *did* David
his father.
7 Then did Solomon build an high place for
Chemosh, the abomination of Moab, in the hill
that *is* before Jerusalem, and for Molech, the
abomination of the children of Ammon.
8 And likewise did he for all his strange wives,
which burnt incense and sacrificed unto their
gods.
9 ¶ And the LORD was angry with Solomon,
because his heart was turned from the LORD God
of Israel, which had appeared unto him twice,
10 And had commanded him concerning this
thing, that he should not go after other gods: but
he kept not that which the LORD commanded.
11 Wherefore the LORD said unto Solomon, For-
asmuch as this is done of thee, and thou hast not

---

king acquired from Kue at the purchase price."

Thoughts for Personal/Family Worship: Chapter 10

1. **The glorious reign of King Solomon is a reflection of the glorious kingdom of Christ, the One greater than Solomon. The wisdom, prosperity, abundance, wealth, and glory are but a weak resemblance of the eternal glory of the reign of Christ, whose kingdom shall endure forever in blessing and peace (Ps. 72; Eph. 1:3). The Queen of Sheba saw all the glory of Solomon and declared that the half of Solomon's glory had not been revealed to her. When God's people enter heaven and see the glories of His kingdom and the blessedness of His people, they will also be, so to speak, breathless, and each one of them will have to say that the half of the glories of Christ had not been told to them. Just as King Solomon gave regal gifts to the Queen of Sheba, so Christ shares with His people from the abundance of His riches the very fullness of God (1 Kings 10:16–19).**
2. **Solomon's gathering of many horses (vv. 26–29) casts a shadow across his kingdom, for this defied the Lord's command and suggests a worldly glorying in earthly strength (see note at 4:26). The temptations of affliction are hard, but the temptations of prosperity may be much worse. The king was ever to be a servant of the Lord. Let us all beware of glorying in our strengths and resources and always live as humble servants, even if God blesses us with success.**

Chapter 11: ***Solomon sins against the Lord, disrupting the peace of the kingdom and setting the course for the kingdom's division.***

Solomon's Breaking the Covenant (1 Kings 11:1–43)

11:1–2 *strange*. Foreign (v. 8). *clave unto these*. Clung to them. Marrying foreign women violated God's law (Ex. 34:16; Deut. 7:3), not because of race but because being unequally yoked with unbelievers has serious consequences (2 Cor. 6:14).
11:3 *seven hundred wives*. A violation of Deut. 17:17. *concubines*. Of a lower status than wives but kept in a harem as a status symbol. Most likely many of these relationships were politically arranged. It was not uncommon in treaties for one king to give another his daughter in marriage as a means of solidifying political or commercial contracts. *his wives turned away his heart*. The predicted outcome (Deut. 7:4). Solomon ignored his own advice (Eccl. 7:26).
11:4 *not perfect*. Undivided or not whole.
11:5 *Milcom*. Molech (v. 7; Lev. 18:21).
11:7 *an high place*. See 2 Kings 23:13, where this is referred to as the "mount of corruption."

kept my covenant and my statutes, which I have
commanded thee, I will surely rend the kingdom
from thee, and will give it to thy servant.
12 Notwithstanding in thy days I will not do it for
David thy father's sake: *but* I will rend it out of the
hand of thy son.
13 Howbeit I will not rend away all the kingdom;
but will give one tribe to thy son for David my
servant's sake, and for Jerusalem's sake which I
have chosen.
14 ¶ And the LORD stirred up an adversary unto
Solomon, Hadad the Edomite: he *was* of the
king's seed in Edom.
15 For it came to pass, when David was in Edom,
and Joab the captain of the host was gone up to
bury the slain, after he had smitten every male in
Edom;
16 (For six months did Joab remain there with all
Israel, until he had cut off every male in Edom:)
17 That Hadad fled, he and certain Edomites of
his father's servants with him, to go into Egypt;
Hadad *being* yet a little child.
18 And they arose out of Midian, and came
to Paran: and they took men with them out of
Paran, and they came to Egypt, unto Pharaoh
king of Egypt; which gave him an house, and appointed him victuals, and gave him land.
19 And Hadad found great favour in the sight of
Pharaoh, so that he gave him to wife the sister of
his own wife, the sister of Tahpenes the queen.
20 And the sister of Tahpenes bare him Genubath
his son, whom Tahpenes weaned in Pharaoh's
house: and Genubath was in Pharaoh's household
among the sons of Pharaoh.
21 And when Hadad heard in Egypt that David
slept with his fathers, and that Joab the captain of
the host was dead, Hadad said to Pharaoh, Let me
depart, that I may go to mine own country.
22 Then Pharaoh said unto him, But what hast
thou lacked with me, that, behold, thou seekest
to go to thine own country? And he answered,
Nothing: howbeit let me go in any wise.
23 ¶ And God stirred him up *another* adversary,
Rezon the son of Eliadah, which fled from his lord
Hadadezer king of Zobah:
24 And he gathered men unto him, and became
captain over a band, when David slew them *of
Zobah*: and they went to Damascus, and dwelt
therein, and reigned in Damascus.
25 And he was an adversary to Israel all the days
of Solomon, beside the mischief that Hadad *did*:
and he abhorred Israel, and reigned over Syria.
26 ¶ And Jeroboam the son of Nebat, an Ephrathite of Zereda, Solomon's servant, whose mother's
name *was* Zeruah, a widow woman, even he lifted
up *his* hand against the king.
27 And this *was* the cause that he lifted up *his*
hand against the king: Solomon built Millo, *and*
repaired the breaches of the city of David his
father.
28 And the man Jeroboam *was* a mighty man of
valour: and Solomon seeing the young man that
he was industrious, he made him ruler over all the
charge of the house of Joseph.
29 And it came to pass at that time when Jeroboam went out of Jerusalem, that the prophet
Ahijah the Shilonite found him in the way; and
he had clad himself with a new garment; and they
two *were* alone in the field:
30 And Ahijah caught the new garment that *was*
on him, and rent it *in* twelve pieces:
31 And he said to Jeroboam, Take thee ten pieces:
for thus saith the LORD, the God of Israel, Behold,
I will rend the kingdom out of the hand of
Solomon, and will give ten tribes to thee:
32 (But he shall have one tribe for my servant
David's sake, and for Jerusalem's sake, the city
which I have chosen out of all the tribes of Israel:)
33 Because that they have forsaken me, and have
worshipped Ashtoreth the goddess of the Zidonians, Chemosh the god of the Moabites, and
Milcom the god of the children of Ammon, and
have not walked in my ways, to do *that which is*
right in mine eyes, and *to keep* my statutes and my
judgments, as *did* David his father.
34 Howbeit I will not take the whole kingdom
out of his hand: but I will make him prince all the
days of his life for David my servant's sake, whom
I chose, because he kept my commandments and
my statutes:
35 But I will take the kingdom out of his son's
hand, and will give it unto thee, *even* ten tribes.

11:11 *rend.* Tear.
11:13 *one tribe.* The Lord kept His promise (Gen. 49:10; 2 Sam. 7:14–15) by preserving David's throne in the tribe of Judah (1 Kings 12:20). The tribe of Benjamin, located around Jerusalem, joined Judah (vv. 21,23), as did Simeon, whose lands were enclosed by Judah (2 Chron. 15:9), and the Levites and godly people from all Israel (1 Kings 11:13–17).
11:14 *stirred up an adversary.* As He had stated in the covenant, the Lord disciplined the disobedient son of David with the opposition of men (2 Sam. 7:14).
11:18 *victuals.* Food, including provisions in general.
11:23 See 2 Sam. 8:2–3.
11:27 *Millo.* See note at 9:15.
11:28 *ruler over all the charge of the house of Joseph.* Overseer or foreman over all the forced labor from the descendants of Joseph, the combined tribes of Ephraim and Manasseh.
11:31 *Take thee ten pieces.* This symbolizes that Jeroboam would be king over ten tribes of Israel (see v. 35).
11:32 *one tribe.* See note at v. 13. *which I have chosen.* God's election of David to be His *servant*-king and Jerusalem to be His dwelling place preserved the kingdom even after Solomon's great sins (vv. 13,34,36).
11:34 *prince.* Literally, "one who is lifted up or exalted," referring to a leader but generally not to the son of a king.

36 And unto his son will I give one tribe, that
David my servant may have a light alway before
me in Jerusalem, the city which I have chosen me
to put my name there.
37 And I will take thee, and thou shalt reign according to all that thy soul desireth, and shalt be
king over Israel.
38 And it shall be, if thou wilt hearken unto all
that I command thee, and wilt walk in my ways,
and do *that is* right in my sight, to keep my
statutes and my commandments, as David my
servant did; that I will be with thee, and build thee
a sure house, as I built for David, and will give
Israel unto thee.
39 And I will for this afflict the seed of David, but
not for ever.
40 Solomon sought therefore to kill Jeroboam.
And Jeroboam arose, and fled into Egypt, unto
Shishak king of Egypt, and was in Egypt until the
death of Solomon.
41 ¶ And the rest of the acts of Solomon, and all
that he did, and his wisdom, *are* they not written
in the book of the acts of Solomon?
42 And the time that Solomon reigned in Jerusalem over all Israel *was* forty years.
43 And Solomon slept with his fathers, and was
buried in the city of David his father: and Rehoboam his son reigned in his stead.

CHAPTER 12

AND Rehoboam went to Shechem: for all Israel
were come to Shechem to make him king.
2 And it came to pass, when Jeroboam the son of
Nebat, who was yet in Egypt, heard *of it*, (for he
was fled from the presence of king Solomon, and
Jeroboam dwelt in Egypt;)
3 That they sent and called him. And Jeroboam
and all the congregation of Israel came, and spake
unto Rehoboam, saying,
4 Thy father made our yoke grievous: now therefore make thou the grievous service of thy father,
and his heavy yoke which he put upon us, lighter,
and we will serve thee.
5 And he said unto them, Depart yet *for* three
days, then come again to me. And the people
departed.
6 ¶ And king Rehoboam consulted with the old
men, that stood before Solomon his father while
he yet lived, and said, How do ye advise that I may
answer this people?
7 And they spake unto him, saying, If thou wilt
be a servant unto this people this day, and wilt
serve them, and answer them, and speak good
words to them, then they will be thy servants for
ever.
8 But he forsook the counsel of the old men,
which they had given him, and consulted with
the young men that were grown up with him, *and*
which stood before him:
9 And he said unto them, What counsel give ye
that we may answer this people, who have spoken
to me, saying, Make the yoke which thy father did
put upon us lighter?
10 And the young men that were grown up with
him spake unto him, saying, Thus shalt thou

11:36 *have a light alway*. David was the light of Israel, and the Lord was his light (2 Sam. 21:17; 22:29). The unconditional and unfailing promise to David found fulfillment in Christ (1 Kings 11:39; Ps. 132:17; 2 Chron. 21:7; Isa. 9:1–2; Luke 1:33), who is the light of the world (John 1:7–9).
11:38 *a sure house*. An established dynasty, though conditioned on obedience (*if thou wilt hearken*), whereas the promise to David was unconditional.
11:41 *the book of the acts of Solomon*. Keeping such a record was common practice among kings. This record was not inspired and has not been preserved.

Thoughts for Personal/Family Worship: Chapter 11

1. **When Solomon was old his wives turned his heart away from God (v. 4). Solomon's downfall was gradual. At the beginning of his reign he married Pharaoh's daughter (3:1). Although that violated God's stipulation not to intermarry with pagans, apparently Solomon was able to hold in check its consequences, as the first part of his reign was marked by his service to the Lord. But this led Solomon to more sin. Let us be warned that, apart from repentance, sin will only grow and take us further from the Lord. It is imperative that we address sin immediately, confessing it and seeking the Lord's forgiveness and help to resist temptation.**
2. **Solomon's downfall is a reminder of what he himself summarized: "Better is the end of a thing than the beginning thereof" (Eccl. 7:8). Solomon had an exemplary beginning as he acknowledged his utter dependence on the Lord by seeking wisdom and dedicating himself wholeheartedly to the work of temple. But, sadly, Solomon is often remembered as much for his folly as for his wisdom. Church history, ancient and modern, is filled with tragic examples of those who started well but ruined their testimonies by some sin after years of God-honoring service. We should devote ourselves to constant prayer and vigilance that we will remain faithful until the end.**

THE DISRUPTION AND DIVISION OF THE KINGDOM (1 KINGS 12:1—16:28)

Chapter 12: *The northern tribes, led by Jeroboam, revolt against Judah and Rehoboam, resulting in the division of the kingdom.*

The Splitting of the Kingdom (1 Kings 12:1–24)

12:1 *Shechem*. Located about 35 miles north of Jerusalem, historically associated with covenant commitment (Josh. 24). Perhaps selected as the coronation site to foster allegiance from the northern tribes. Tension between the north and the south was never far beneath the surface.
12:4 The *yoke*, used to restrict oxen for work, symbolizes the forced labor and other burdens imposed on the people by Solomon. *heavy*. Burdensome or oppressive.
12:7 A wise ruler wins the loyalty of his people by being

speak unto this people that spake unto thee, say-
ing, Thy father made our yoke heavy, but make
thou *it* lighter unto us; thus shalt thou say unto
them, My little *finger* shall be thicker than my
father's loins.
11 And now whereas my father did lade you with
a heavy yoke, I will add to your yoke: my father
hath chastised you with whips, but I will chastise
you with scorpions.
12 ¶ So Jeroboam and all the people came to Re-
hoboam the third day, as the king had appointed,
saying, Come to me again the third day.
13 And the king answered the people roughly,
and forsook the old men's counsel that they gave
him;
14 And spake to them after the counsel of the
young men, saying, My father made your yoke
heavy, and I will add to your yoke: my father *also*
chastised you with whips, but I will chastise you
with scorpions.
15 Wherefore the king hearkened not unto the
people; for the cause was from the LORD, that he
might perform his saying, which the LORD spake
by Ahijah the Shilonite unto Jeroboam the son of
Nebat.
16 ¶ So when all Israel saw that the king heark-
ened not unto them, the people answered the
king, saying, What portion have we in David?
neither *have we* inheritance in the son of Jesse: to
your tents, O Israel: now see to thine own house,
David. So Israel departed unto their tents.
17 But *as for* the children of Israel which dwelt in
the cities of Judah, Rehoboam reigned over them.
18 Then king Rehoboam sent Adoram, who *was*
over the tribute; and all Israel stoned him with
stones, that he died. Therefore king Rehoboam
made speed to get him up to his chariot, to flee
to Jerusalem.
19 So Israel rebelled against the house of David
unto this day.
20 And it came to pass, when all Israel heard that
Jeroboam was come again, that they sent and
called him unto the congregation, and made him
king over all Israel: there was none that followed
the house of David, but the tribe of Judah only.
21 ¶ And when Rehoboam was come to Jerusa-
lem, he assembled all the house of Judah, with
the tribe of Benjamin, an hundred and fourscore
thousand chosen men, which were warriors, to
fight against the house of Israel, to bring the king-
dom again to Rehoboam the son of Solomon.
22 But the word of God came unto Shemaiah the
man of God, saying,
23 Speak unto Rehoboam, the son of Solomon,
king of Judah, and unto all the house of Judah
and Benjamin, and to the remnant of the people,
saying,
24 Thus saith the LORD, Ye shall not go up, nor
fight against your brethren the children of Israel:
return every man to his house; for this thing is
from me. They hearkened therefore to the word
of the LORD, and returned to depart, according to
the word of the LORD.
25 ¶ Then Jeroboam built Shechem in mount
Ephraim, and dwelt therein; and went out from
thence, and built Penuel.
26 And Jeroboam said in his heart, Now shall the
kingdom return to the house of David:
27 If this people go up to do sacrifice in the house
of the LORD at Jerusalem, then shall the heart of
this people turn again unto their lord, *even* unto
Rehoboam king of Judah, and they shall kill me,
and go again to Rehoboam king of Judah.
28 Whereupon the king took counsel, and made
two calves *of* gold, and said unto them, It is too
much for you to go up to Jerusalem: behold thy
gods, O Israel, which brought thee up out of the
land of Egypt.
29 And he set the one in Beth-el, and the other
put he in Dan.
30 And this thing became a sin: for the people
went *to worship* before the one, *even* unto Dan.

---

their *servant* in response to their legitimate desires (Mark 10:42–44).

12:10 *My little finger shall be thicker than my father's loins.* He would increase the demands upon the people instead of lightning them.

12:11 *lade.* Imposed on. *chastise you with scorpions.* Refers to an especially painful scourge, another figure of speech to express increased burdens (v. 14).

12:13 *roughly.* Harshly or severely.

12:15 *for the cause was from the LORD.* The turn of events was under God's direction. God fulfills His Word (*which the LORD spake*) through His providence over historical events (Isa. 46:11; Ezek. 22:14). Here He gave a sinner over to His own pride and foolishness (2 Sam. 17:14).

12:16 *What portion.* What interest or share?

12:18 *over the tribute.* Over the forced labor or labor gangs. *made speed to get him up to his chariot.* Hurried to mount his war chariot.

12:22 *Shemaiah.* See 2 Chron. 11:2; 12:5.

12:24 *this thing is from me.* The Lord has decreed both the good and the bad (v. 15).

The Apostasy of Israel and Discipline of Judah (1 Kings 12:25—14:31)

12:25 *Shechem.* The first capital of the Northern Kingdom. *Penuel.* Straight east of Shechem on the east side of the Jordan, a strategic city of defense.

12:27–28 Erecting the *two calves* was a brilliant move both strategically and politically, since he surmised that a people that "pray together will stay together." False religion often serves as a tool for political unity and power (Rev. 13:11–15). Religiously, it was a tragic move that became the sin for which every other king of Israel was to be judged (1 Kings 13:34; 15:26). *behold thy gods . . . which brought thee up out of the land of Egypt.* He does not introduce a newly named deity but identifies the calves as representing *Jehovah,* the God of

31 And he made an house of high places, and
made priests of the lowest of the people, which
were not of the sons of Levi.
32 And Jeroboam ordained a feast in the eighth
month, on the fifteenth day of the month, like
unto the feast that *is* in Judah, and he offered
upon the altar. So did he in Beth-el, sacrificing
unto the calves that he had made: and he placed
in Beth-el the priests of the high places which he
had made.
33 So he offered upon the altar which he had
made in Beth-el the fifteenth day of the eighth
month, *even* in the month which he had devised
of his own heart; and ordained a feast unto the
children of Israel: and he offered upon the altar,
and burnt incense.

CHAPTER 13

AND, behold, there came a man of God out of
Judah by the word of the LORD unto Beth-el: and
Jeroboam stood by the altar to burn incense.
2 And he cried against the altar in the word of the
LORD, and said, O altar, altar, thus saith the LORD;
Behold, a child shall be born unto the house of
David, Josiah by name; and upon thee shall he of-
fer the priests of the high places that burn incense
upon thee, and men's bones shall be burnt upon
thee.
3 And he gave a sign the same day, saying, This *is*
the sign which the LORD hath spoken; Behold, the
altar shall be rent, and the ashes that *are* upon it
shall be poured out.
4 And it came to pass, when king Jeroboam heard
the saying of the man of God, which had cried
against the altar in Beth-el, that he put forth his
hand from the altar, saying, Lay hold on him. And
his hand, which he put forth against him, dried
up, so that he could not pull it in again to him.
5 The altar also was rent, and the ashes poured
out from the altar, according to the sign which the
man of God had given by the word of the LORD.
6 And the king answered and said unto the man
of God, Intreat now the face of the LORD thy
God, and pray for me, that my hand may be re-
stored me again. And the man of God besought
the LORD, and the king's hand was restored him
again, and became as *it was* before.
7 And the king said unto the man of God, Come
home with me, and refresh thyself, and I will give
thee a reward.
8 And the man of God said unto the king, If thou
wilt give me half thine house, I will not go in with
thee, neither will I eat bread nor drink water in
this place:
9 For so was it charged me by the word of the
LORD, saying, Eat no bread, nor drink water, nor
turn again by the same way that thou camest.
10 So he went another way, and returned not by
the way that he came to Beth-el.
11 ¶ Now there dwelt an old prophet in Beth-el;
and his sons came and told him all the works that

---

the exodus—a direct violation of the second commandment that prohibits any kind of image of the true God (Ex. 20:4–6; 32:4–8).

12:29 *Beth-el . . . Dan.* Located in the southern and northern borders of the kingdom. This was an effort to make false religion more convenient than traveling to the central sanctuary.

12:31 *house of high places.* Temple built on an elevation, where the Israelites committed idolatry.

12:31 *the lowest of the people.* Literally, "the extremities of the people," meaning that anyone qualified regardless of tribal identity or character. The legitimate priesthood was restricted to the sons of Aaron from tribe of *Levi*.

12:32 *ordained a feast.* Approximated and replaced the divinely ordained feast, probably here the Feast of Tabernacles.

12:33 *he had devised of his own heart.* Jeroboam had invented all these rituals and ceremonies of worship without any divine guidance, a vivid example of what Paul calls "will worship" (Col. 2:23).

Thoughts for Personal/Family Worship: Chapter 12

1. **Rehoboam is a classic example of the folly of bowing to peer pressure. From the divine perspective, all this was orchestrated to accomplish the divine purpose. Yet from the human perspective, had he listened to the counsel of his elders, with their wisdom and experience, he could have avoided the calamity of losing the majority of his kingdom. This should be a warning to all, and particularly to young people. Listen to what Solomon, in all likelihood, told Rehoboam directly, as well as ourselves: "My son, if sinners entice thee, consent thou not" (Prov. 1:10). Rather, "My son, hear the instruction of thy father, and forsake not the law of thy mother" (v. 8). Why is it hard at times to listen to our elders?**
2. **Rehoboam listened to foolish friends, but Jeroboam listened to himself, which is even more dangerous. He devised a course of action in his own heart (v. 33) that put the newly formed kingdom on the downward slope from its inauguration. The heart is deceitful above all things, leading us to depart from the Lord (Jer. 17:5,9). The plan he devised was logical in its policy and apparently successful in its effect, but it was neither right nor wise. God had given him the condition for establishing the kingdom: obedience (1 Kings 11:38). Following God's ways may seem to jeopardize our future, but it actually secures it.**

Chapter 13: ***An unnamed prophet from Judah obeys God by boldly rebuking Jeroboam and then is slain for his disobedience.***

13:1 *man of God.* A common designation for a prophet.

13:2 *O altar, altar.* A rhetorical devise called apostrophe in which an inanimate object is addressed like a person. The message is ultimately for Jeroboam. *Josiah.* The Lord knew his name and what he would do hundreds of years before he appeared on the scene (2 Kings 23:14–17).

13:3 *sign.* A wonder or token, frequently in connection with a prophetic word to confirm reliability. *rent.* Torn in pieces (v. 5).

13:4 *dried up.* Withered.

GOD'S FOREKNOWLEDGE

Knowledge of all things is properly attributed to God (2 Cor. 12:2–3; cf. Acts 2:23; Rom. 8:29; 11:2; 1 Peter 1:2). The idea of foreknowledge can be used in two ways: as an expression of knowledge of all things, even prior to their happening in time, and as an act of choice or ordaining. The former is the subject for consideration here; the latter is treated briefly in the article on election.

The idea of foreknowledge relates to the things known by God and the order in which they stand to each other as they are, whether they be to us past, present, or future. All of these things God knows equally from eternity. Things that to us are yet future have been known by God from eternity; His knowledge of the future is so real that when events become "past" to us (based on their actual occurrence in time), God knows them in the same way He did before. Nothing is altered in His knowledge by the passage of time; His understanding is infinite and unchanging.

Some have objected to the premise of God's perfect and complete knowledge of all things prior to their occurrence. Such challengers point to passages in Scripture that appear to suggest God's lack of knowledge: God's fearing or being afraid (Gen. 3:22–23; Ex. 13:17; Deut. 32:26–27); His repentance (1 Sam. 15:10–11); a change or alteration of His mind (Num. 14:27, 30; 1 Sam. 2:30); or His testing of men's hearts to discover their contents (Judg. 3:1,4; 2 Chron. 32:31; Dan. 12:10).

However, each of these passages speaks of God in a figurative fashion, or *anthropomorphically*. Thus these passages do not describe the nature of God as He is. Rather, God condescends to speak at our level, to express reality in human terms. This idea could be likened to a father's talking to a newborn. The father babbles in "baby talk" to accommodate himself to the baby's level.

In other places of Scripture God is directly said *not* to do these things, for He is *not a man* (1 Sam. 15:29). Such traits would destroy God's immutability. How, for example, could God in His omnipotence and true nature properly be termed *afraid* in the sense that we ourselves experience fear? Furthermore, the abundance of scriptural evidence in favor of God's knowledge overwhelmingly demonstrates the verity of the doctrine of His foreknowledge.

Scripture attests that God knows all things in all details, whether past, present, or future. He understands all the ways and actions of men, even before their occurrence (1 Sam. 2:3; Pss. 139:2–4; 147:5; Isa. 40:13–14,28; Acts 15:18; Rom. 11:36; Heb. 4:13; 1 John 3:20). The countless miraculous predictions in Scripture necessitate a detailed knowledge of all things. By His holy prophets God foretold the free actions of men, what they would do and what they should do, long before they were born (cf. Gen. 15:13–14; 18:18–19; Deut. 31:16–18; 1 Kings 13:2; 22:28; Matt. 24:5; Mark 13:6; 14:30; Acts 20:29; 2 Thess. 2:3,4; 1 Tim. 4:1; 2 Tim. 3:1; 2 Peter 2:1). Thus God perfectly knew from eternity all of the free actions of men before they performed them. This knowledge extends even to those things that deal with the secrets of men's hearts (Deut. 31:21; 1 Sam. 16:7; 23:12; 1 Kings 8:39; 2 Kings 8:12–13; Job 31:4; Pss. 38:9; 94:11; Prov. 15:11; Isa. 48:4; Jer. 17:9–10; Ezek. 11:5; Matt. 6:4,6,8; Luke 16:15; Acts 1:24; Rev. 3:15).

Some wrongly view God's foreknowledge of all men's actions as the logical, *a priori* cause of His predetermining all things. God's knowledge, they incorrectly assume, caused Him to shape His plan for eternity. However, while both God's foreknowledge and His predeterminate counsel occur from eternity (temporally considered), God's foreknowledge must be viewed as coming after His predetermination (logically considered). God's knowledge of all men's future free actions did not cause Him to adapt His workings accordingly—for this would have placed God below man, as One reactive and subject rather than determinate and sovereign. Surely, what is not pre-decreed cannot be certain and therefore cannot be known. Yet upon the determination of God's sovereign counsel out of eternity, His foreknowledge extends to a grasp of all things—also from eternity.

—adapted from John Owen, *Vindiciae Evangelicae*, ch. 5

the man of God had done that day in Beth-el: the
words which he had spoken unto the king, them
they told also to their father.
12 And their father said unto them, What way
went he? For his sons had seen what way the man
of God went, which came from Judah.
13 And he said unto his sons, Saddle me the ass.
So they saddled him the ass: and he rode thereon,
14 And went after the man of God, and found
him sitting under an oak: and he said unto him,
Art thou the man of God that camest from Judah?
And he said, I *am*.
15 Then he said unto him, Come home with me,
and eat bread.
16 And he said, I may not return with thee, nor
go in with thee: neither will I eat bread nor drink
water with thee in this place:
17 For it was said to me by the word of the LORD,
Thou shalt eat no bread nor drink water there,
nor turn again to go by the way that thou camest.
18 He said unto him, I *am* a prophet also as thou
art; and an angel spake unto me by the word of
the LORD, saying, Bring him back with thee into
thine house, that he may eat bread and drink
water. *But* he lied unto him.
19 So he went back with him, and did eat bread in
his house, and drank water.
20 ¶ And it came to pass, as they sat at the table,
that the word of the LORD came unto the prophet
that brought him back:
21 And he cried unto the man of God that came
from Judah, saying, Thus saith the LORD, Foras-
much as thou hast disobeyed the mouth of the
LORD, and hast not kept the commandment
which the LORD thy God commanded thee,
22 But camest back, and hast eaten bread and
drunk water in the place, of the which *the LORD*
did say to thee, Eat no bread, and drink no water;
thy carcase shall not come unto the sepulchre of
thy fathers.
23 ¶ And it came to pass, after he had eaten bread,
and after he had drunk, that he saddled for him
the ass, *to wit*, for the prophet whom he had
brought back.
24 And when he was gone, a lion met him by the
way, and slew him: and his carcase was cast in the
way, and the ass stood by it, the lion also stood by
the carcase.
25 And, behold, men passed by, and saw the car-
case cast in the way, and the lion standing by the
carcase: and they came and told *it* in the city
where the old prophet dwelt.
26 And when the prophet that brought him back
from the way heard *thereof*, he said, It *is* the man
of God, who was disobedient unto the word of
the LORD: therefore the LORD hath delivered him
unto the lion, which hath torn him, and slain
him, according to the word of the LORD, which he
spake unto him.
27 And he spake to his sons, saying, Saddle me
the ass. And they saddled *him*.
28 And he went and found his carcase cast in the
way, and the ass and the lion standing by the car-
case: the lion had not eaten the carcase, nor torn
the ass.
29 And the prophet took up the carcase of the
man of God, and laid it upon the ass, and brought
it back: and the old prophet came to the city, to
mourn and to bury him.
30 And he laid his carcase in his own grave; and
they mourned over him, *saying*, Alas, my brother!
31 And it came to pass, after he had buried him,
that he spake to his sons, saying, When I am dead,
then bury me in the sepulchre wherein the man
of God *is* buried; lay my bones beside his bones:
32 For the saying which he cried by the word of
the LORD against the altar in Beth-el, and against
all the houses of the high places which *are* in the
cities of Samaria, shall surely come to pass.
33 ¶ After this thing Jeroboam returned not

13:19 *he went back with him.* He was duped because he failed to discern the spirit of prophecy. One of the key tests to identify a true prophet was whether or not his word conformed to what God had already revealed (Deut. 13:1–3; 1 Cor. 14:32). God never contradicts Himself.

13:21 *he cried.* The Lord still used this old prophet as a means to convey His Word, in spite of his sins and deceit. Spiritual gifts are not the same as godliness (Matt. 7:21–23).

13:23 *to wit.* That is.

13:24 *the lion also stood.* The lion stood there not as an animal of prey but as the agent of God's providence.

13:33 *the lowest of the people.* See note at 12:31.

Thoughts for Personal/Family Worship: Chapter 13

1. **The unnamed prophet is a lesson in contrast. On the one hand he is to be imitated. The Lord commissioned him with a dangerous task, but without hesitation he obeyed God, entering hostile territory with a fearless message to the hostile king. In the same way we all should have the courage to witness for God and Christ in the midst of a hostile world.**
2. **On the other hand, the prophet stands as a stark warning against disobeying God. He trusted an older prophet who appeared to have more experience but who contradicted God's Word rather than trusting in the clear, unmistakable commands that God had given. He paid the consequence for his disobedience, and justly so. We should always be careful to discern the spirits. We are not to obey our own reasoning, nor are we to follow the words of others, but to abide with the clear directions of God's Word.**
3. **The prophecy about Josiah (v. 2) illustrates the amazing accuracy of God's prophetic word (2 Kings 23:14–17). The events of fulfillment occurred over 300 years later and yet were accurate to every detail of the prediction. God knows and has decreed the end from the beginning, so predicting the future is not difficult for Him; it is evidence of His deity (Isa. 46:9–10). Seeing how accurately**

from his evil way, but made again of the lowest of
the people priests of the high places: whosoever
would, he consecrated him, and he became *one* of
the priests of the high places.
34 And this thing became sin unto the house of
Jeroboam, even to cut *it* off, and to destroy *it* from
off the face of the earth.

CHAPTER 14

AT that time Abijah the son of Jeroboam fell sick.
2 And Jeroboam said to his wife, Arise, I pray
thee, and disguise thyself, that thou be not known
to be the wife of Jeroboam; and get thee to Shiloh:
behold, there *is* Ahijah the prophet, which told
me that *I should be* king over this people.
3 And take with thee ten loaves, and cracknels,
and a cruse of honey, and go to him: he shall tell
thee what shall become of the child.
4 And Jeroboam's wife did so, and arose, and
went to Shiloh, and came to the house of Ahijah.
But Ahijah could not see; for his eyes were set by
reason of his age.
5 ¶ And the LORD said unto Ahijah, Behold, the
wife of Jeroboam cometh to ask a thing of thee
for her son; for he *is* sick: thus and thus shalt thou
say unto her: for it shall be, when she cometh in,
that she shall feign herself *to be* another *woman*.
6 And it was *so*, when Ahijah heard the sound of
her feet, as she came in at the door, that he said,
Come in, thou wife of Jeroboam; why feignest
thou thyself *to be* another? for I *am* sent to thee
with heavy *tidings*.
7 Go, tell Jeroboam, Thus saith the LORD God of
Israel, Forasmuch as I exalted thee from among
the people, and made thee prince over my people
Israel,
8 And rent the kingdom away from the house of
David, and gave it thee: and *yet* thou hast not been
as my servant David, who kept my command-
ments, and who followed me with all his heart, to
do *that* only *which was* right in mine eyes;
9 But hast done evil above all that were before
thee: for thou hast gone and made thee other
gods, and molten images, to provoke me to anger,
and hast cast me behind thy back:
10 Therefore, behold, I will bring evil upon the
house of Jeroboam, and will cut off from Jer-
oboam him that pisseth against the wall, *and* him
that is shut up and left in Israel, and will take away
the remnant of the house of Jeroboam, as a man
taketh away dung, till it be all gone.
11 Him that dieth of Jeroboam in the city shall the
dogs eat; and him that dieth in the field shall the
fowls of the air eat: for the LORD hath spoken *it*.
12 Arise thou therefore, get thee to thine own
house: *and* when thy feet enter into the city, the
child shall die.
13 And all Israel shall mourn for him, and bury
him: for he only of Jeroboam shall come to the
grave, because in him there is found *some* good
thing toward the LORD God of Israel in the house
of Jeroboam.
14 Moreover the LORD shall raise him up a king
over Israel, who shall cut off the house of Jero-
boam that day: but what? even now.
15 For the LORD shall smite Israel, as a reed is
shaken in the water, and he shall root up Israel out
of this good land, which he gave to their fathers,
and shall scatter them beyond the river, because
they have made their groves, provoking the LORD
to anger.
16 And he shall give Israel up because of the sins
of Jeroboam, who did sin, and who made Israel
to sin.
17 ¶ And Jeroboam's wife arose, and departed,

---

prophecy has been fulfilled should encourage us that what God has predicted is as certain as though it has already happened.

Chapter 14: *The Lord punishes both Jeroboam and Rehoboam for their persistent sins.*

14:2 *Shiloh.* A city located in the tribe of Ephraim, the previous site of the tabernacle (Josh. 18:1; Ps. 78:60; Jer. 7:12,14).

14:3 *cracknels.* Small pastries or cakes. *cruse.* Bottle or jar. *child.* The term is not age specific, ranging from infant to young adult.

14:4 *his eyes were set by reason of his age.* Literally, "his eyes arose because of his gray-headedness," an idiom describing his inability to focus because of his age.

14:5 *feign.* Pretend; she will try to make herself unrecognizable.

14:6 *heavy tidings.* Severe words.

14:7 *prince.* A leader or ruler who was not the son of royalty.

14:9 *cast me behind thy back.* An expression designating complete rejection, putting God out of one's sight.

14:10 *him that pisseth against the wall.* A Hebrew idiom designating a male, without any vulgar connotation. Every male was going to be put to death; no hiding place (*shut up*) would provide escape (15:29).

14:11 *shall the dogs eat.* Referring to stray and wild dogs, not pets. Being eaten by scavengers, instead of receiving a decent burial, pictures a disgraceful death under the covenant curse of God (Deut. 28:15,26; Jer. 16:4; 34:18–20).

14:13 Although Abijah's death was part of Jeroboam's chastisement, the fact that he died a natural death and was buried was a mercy of God, who *found some good thing* in him.

14:14 *but what? even now.* From now on.

14:15 *as a reed is shaken.* A picture of instability. *beyond the river.* The Euphrates, referring to the Assyrian exile (2 Kings 17:6). *groves.* Asherah, the cultic poles erected near an altar used for pagan rituals. Israel was guilty of the sins that excluded them from living in the Promised Land (Lev. 26:15–39).

14:16 *because of the sins of Jeroboam.* Jeroboam's guilt and lingering influence by establishing idolatry as the state religion of Israel doomed the nation to spiritual decline and divine judgment. *made Israel to sin.* The tragic epitaph by which Jeroboam was remembered (15:26,30,34; 16:26; 2 Kings 3:3; 10:29,31; 13:2,11; 14:24; 15:9,18,24; 23:15).

and came to Tirzah: *and* when she came to the
threshold of the door, the child died;
18 And they buried him; and all Israel mourned
for him, according to the word of the LORD,
which he spake by the hand of his servant Ahijah
the prophet.
19 And the rest of the acts of Jeroboam, how he
warred, and how he reigned, behold, they *are*
written in the book of the chronicles of the kings
of Israel.
20 And the days which Jeroboam reigned *were*
two and twenty years: and he slept with his
fathers, and Nadab his son reigned in his stead.
21 ¶ And Rehoboam the son of Solomon reigned
in Judah. Rehoboam *was* forty and one years old
when he began to reign, and he reigned seven-
teen years in Jerusalem, the city which the LORD
did choose out of all the tribes of Israel, to put his
name there. And his mother's name *was* Naamah
an Ammonitess.
22 And Judah did evil in the sight of the LORD,
and they provoked him to jealousy with their sins
which they had committed, above all that their
fathers had done.
23 For they also built them high places, and
images, and groves, on every high hill, and under
every green tree.
24 And there were also sodomites in the land: *and*
they did according to all the abominations of the
nations which the LORD cast out before the chil-
dren of Israel.
25 ¶ And it came to pass in the fifth year of king
Rehoboam, *that* Shishak king of Egypt came up
against Jerusalem:
26 And he took away the treasures of the house
of the LORD, and the treasures of the king's house;
he even took away all: and he took away all the
shields of gold which Solomon had made.
27 And king Rehoboam made in their stead
brasen shields, and committed *them* unto the
hands of the chief of the guard, which kept the
door of the king's house.
28 And it was *so*, when the king went into the
house of the LORD, that the guard bare them, and
brought them back into the guard chamber.
29 ¶ Now the rest of the acts of Rehoboam, and
all that he did, *are* they not written in the book of
the chronicles of the kings of Judah?
30 And there was war between Rehoboam and
Jeroboam all *their* days.
31 And Rehoboam slept with his fathers, and was
buried with his fathers in the city of David. And
his mother's name *was* Naamah an Ammonitess.
And Abijam his son reigned in his stead.

CHAPTER 15

NOW in the eighteenth year of king Jeroboam the
son of Nebat reigned Abijam over Judah.
2 Three years reigned he in Jerusalem. And his
mother's name *was* Maachah, the daughter of
Abishalom.
3 And he walked in all the sins of his father, which
he had done before him: and his heart was not
perfect with the LORD his God, as the heart of
David his father.
4 Nevertheless for David's sake did the LORD his
God give him a lamp in Jerusalem, to set up his

14:17 *Tirzah.* A city of Manasseh, the first capital of the Northern Kingdom.

14:19 *in the book of the chronicles.* Literally, "in the book of the words of the days," an uninspired record of the king's career that has not been preserved (v. 29). The canonical books of Chronicles had not yet been composed.

14:22 *Judah did evil.* In the first three years of Rehoboam's reign they walked in the ways of the Lord (2 Chron. 11:17). The transition to evil was perhaps due to his Ammonite mother's influence (1 Kings 14:21), another bitter fruit of Solomon's infidelity.

14:23 *groves.* See note at v. 15.

14:24 *sodomites.* Homosexual male prostitutes (15:12; 22:46; 2 Kings 23:7), forbidden by the law of God (Deut. 23:7).

14:27 *brasen shields.* Shields made of copper or bronze (copper alloyed with tin).

Thoughts for Personal/Family Worship: Chapter 14

1. **God remembers mercy in His wrath (Hab. 3:2). God pronounced His just wrath and punishment on Jeroboam because of his sin. The fatal illness of his son Abijah was a component of that wrath, but it is here that God shows His mercy. This child would be spared the disgraceful death to be suffered by all his male relatives, as God mercifully brought him to death through natural causes. We know virtually nothing about this child, neither his age nor anything regarding his behavior, but God saw in Abijah something that pleased Him. The Lord takes no pleasure in the death of the wicked (Ezek. 18:32), yet the deaths of saints is precious to Him (Ps. 116:15).**
2. **Jeroboam owns the most dreadful legacy in the entire history of the Northern Kingdom: the one who made Israel sin. Any and every sin is a terrible offense against God, but the Lord Jesus said that leading others into sin deserves special punishment (Mark 9:42). What a tragedy it would be to be remembered for sin rather than for piety. "A good name is better than precious ointment" (Eccl. 7:1). Having a good reputation and godly testimony should be a concern for every believer. None of us will be remembered for very long (Eccl. 1:11), but as short-lived as our legacy may be, let it be that we feared God and influenced others for righteousness (Dan. 12:3).**

Two Kingdoms in Conflict (1 Kings 15:1—16:28)

Chapter 15: ***Conflicts continue between Israel and Judah, and God consistently judges the wicked rulers of both kingdoms, while preserving Judah for David's sake.***

15:3 *not perfect.* Not completely undivided; no wholehearted consecration to the Lord.

15:4–5 *lamp in Jerusalem.* See note at 11:36. Neither David's sin nor that of his sons threatened God's unfailing promise to

son after him, and to establish Jerusalem:
5 Because David did *that which was* right in the
eyes of the LORD, and turned not aside from any
thing that he commanded him all the days of his
life, save only in the matter of Uriah the Hittite.
6 And there was war between Rehoboam and
Jeroboam all the days of his life.
7 Now the rest of the acts of Abijam, and all that
he did, *are* they not written in the book of the
chronicles of the kings of Judah? And there was
war between Abijam and Jeroboam.
8 And Abijam slept with his fathers; and they
buried him in the city of David: and Asa his son
reigned in his stead.
9 ¶ And in the twentieth year of Jeroboam king
of Israel reigned Asa over Judah.
10 And forty and one years reigned he in Jerusalem.
And his mother's name *was* Maachah, the
daughter of Abishalom.
11 And Asa did *that which was* right in the eyes of
the LORD, as *did* David his father.
12 And he took away the sodomites out of the
land, and removed all the idols that his fathers
had made.
13 And also Maachah his mother, even her he
removed from *being* queen, because she had
made an idol in a grove; and Asa destroyed her
idol, and burnt *it* by the brook Kidron.
14 But the high places were not removed: nevertheless
Asa's heart was perfect with the LORD all
his days.
15 And he brought in the things which his father
had dedicated, and the things which himself had
dedicated, into the house of the LORD, silver, and
gold, and vessels.
16 ¶ And there was war between Asa and Baasha
king of Israel all their days.
17 And Baasha king of Israel went up against
Judah, and built Ramah, that he might not suffer
any to go out or come in to Asa king of Judah.
18 Then Asa took all the silver and the gold *that*
were left in the treasures of the house of the
LORD, and the treasures of the king's house, and
delivered them into the hand of his servants:
and king Asa sent them to Ben-hadad, the son of
Tabrimon, the son of Hezion, king of Syria, that
dwelt at Damascus, saying,
19 *There is* a league between me and thee, *and*
between my father and thy father: behold, I have
sent unto thee a present of silver and gold; come
and break thy league with Baasha king of Israel,
that he may depart from me.
20 So Ben-hadad hearkened unto king Asa, and
sent the captains of the hosts which he had against
the cities of Israel, and smote Ijon, and Dan, and
Abel-beth-maachah, and all Cinneroth, with all
the land of Naphtali.
21 And it came to pass, when Baasha heard
thereof, that he left off building of Ramah, and
dwelt in Tirzah.
22 Then king Asa made a proclamation throughout
all Judah; none *was* exempted: and they took
away the stones of Ramah, and the timber thereof,
wherewith Baasha had builded; and king Asa built
with them Geba of Benjamin, and Mizpah.
23 The rest of all the acts of Asa, and all his might,
and all that he did, and the cities which he built,
are they not written in the book of the chronicles
of the kings of Judah? Nevertheless in the time of
his old age he was diseased in his feet.
24 And Asa slept with his fathers, and was buried
with his fathers in the city of David his father: and
Jehoshaphat his son reigned in his stead.
25 ¶ And Nadab the son of Jeroboam began to
reign over Israel in the second year of Asa king of
Judah, and reigned over Israel two years.
26 And he did evil in the sight of the LORD, and
walked in the way of his father, and in his sin
wherewith he made Israel to sin.
27 ¶ And Baasha the son of Ahijah, of the house
of Issachar, conspired against him; and Baasha
smote him at Gibbethon, which *belonged* to the
Philistines; for Nadab and all Israel laid siege to
Gibbethon.
28 Even in the third year of Asa king of Judah did
Baasha slay him, and reigned in his stead.
29 And it came to pass, when he reigned, *that* he
smote all the house of Jeroboam; he left not to Jer-

---

bless the line of David and bring through it His Son (2 Sam. 7:14–16).

15:7 *the chronicles*. See note 14:19.

15:10 *his mother's name was Maachah*. Actually, his grandmother's (v. 2), likely mentioned because she led the people into idolatry (v. 13). It was customary to refer to any ancestor as father or mother.

15:12 *sodomites*. See note at 14:24. *his fathers had made*. Referring to his father, Abijam, his grandfather, Rehoboam, and his great-grandfather, Solomon.

15:13 *an idol in a grove*. See note at 14:15.

15:14 *heart was perfect*. Allegiance to the Lord was undivided.

15:17 *suffer*. Allow. Baasha blockaded the way to Jerusalem lest those going to worship the true God (2 Chron. 15:9) would transfer their allegiance to Asa, the thing Jeroboam had tried to prevent with his two calves.

15:18 *the silver and the gold that were left*. After Shishak ransacked the temple (14:26).

15:19 *league*. Covenant or treaty. Asa sent a bribe to Syria to break alliance with Israel. Since Syria was directly north of Israel, this would divert Israel's attention away from Judah. The plan worked (17:21).

15:29 *according unto the saying of the LORD*. See 14:10,14.

Thoughts for Personal/Family Worship: Chapter 15

"Asa did that which was right in the eyes of the LORD" (v. 11), and his "heart was perfect with the LORD all his days" (v. 14). Yet notwithstanding his overall devotion and uncompromising loyalty to the Lord, he did things

oboam any that breathed, until he had destroyed
him, according unto the saying of the LORD, which
he spake by his servant Ahijah the Shilonite:
30 Because of the sins of Jeroboam which he
sinned, and which he made Israel sin, by his
provocation wherewith he provoked the LORD
God of Israel to anger.
31 ¶ Now the rest of the acts of Nadab, and all
that he did, *are* they not written in the book of the
chronicles of the kings of Israel?
32 And there was war between Asa and Baasha
king of Israel all their days.
33 In the third year of Asa king of Judah began
Baasha the son of Ahijah to reign over all Israel in
Tirzah, twenty and four years.
34 And he did evil in the sight of the LORD, and
walked in the way of Jeroboam, and in his sin
wherewith he made Israel to sin.

CHAPTER 16

THEN the word of the LORD came to Jehu the son
of Hanani against Baasha, saying,
2 Forasmuch as I exalted thee out of the dust, and
made thee prince over my people Israel; and thou
hast walked in the way of Jeroboam, and hast
made my people Israel to sin, to provoke me to
anger with their sins;
3 Behold, I will take away the posterity of Baa-
sha, and the posterity of his house; and will make
thy house like the house of Jeroboam the son of
Nebat.
4 Him that dieth of Baasha in the city shall the
dogs eat; and him that dieth of his in the fields
shall the fowls of the air eat.
5 Now the rest of the acts of Baasha, and what
he did, and his might, *are* they not written in the
book of the chronicles of the kings of Israel?
6 So Baasha slept with his fathers, and was buried
in Tirzah: and Elah his son reigned in his stead.
7 And also by the hand of the prophet Jehu the
son of Hanani came the word of the LORD against
Baasha, and against his house, even for all the evil
that he did in the sight of the LORD, in provoking
him to anger with the work of his hands, in be-
ing like the house of Jeroboam; and because he
killed him.
8 ¶ In the twenty and sixth year of Asa king of
Judah began Elah the son of Baasha to reign over
Israel in Tirzah, two years.
9 And his servant Zimri, captain of half *his*
chariots, conspired against him, as he was in
Tirzah, drinking himself drunk in the house of
Arza steward of *his* house in Tirzah.
10 And Zimri went in and smote him, and killed
him, in the twenty and seventh year of Asa king of
Judah, and reigned in his stead.
11 ¶ And it came to pass, when he began to reign,
as soon as he sat on his throne, *that* he slew all the
house of Baasha: he left him not one that pisseth
against a wall, neither of his kinsfolks, nor of his
friends.
12 Thus did Zimri destroy all the house of Baa-
sha, according to the word of the LORD, which he
spake against Baasha by Jehu the prophet,
13 For all the sins of Baasha, and the sins of Elah
his son, by which they sinned, and by which they
made Israel to sin, in provoking the LORD God of
Israel to anger with their vanities.
14 Now the rest of the acts of Elah, and all that he
did, *are* they not written in the book of the chron-
icles of the kings of Israel?
15 ¶ In the twenty and seventh year of Asa king of
Judah did Zimri reign seven days in Tirzah. And
the people *were* encamped against Gibbethon,
which *belonged* to the Philistines.
16 And the people *that were* encamped heard
say, Zimri hath conspired, and hath also slain the
king: wherefore all Israel made Omri, the captain
of the host, king over Israel that day in the camp.
17 And Omri went up from Gibbethon, and all
Israel with him, and they besieged Tirzah.
18 And it came to pass, when Zimri saw that the
city was taken, that he went into the palace of the
king's house, and burnt the king's house over him
with fire, and died,

---

that evidenced a lack of faith, a fearing of man more than God. Asa used temple money to bribe Ben-hadad to deliver him from Baasha. Instead of trusting a heathen king, he should have sought deliverance from the Lord. The Lord was not pleased and sent a prophet to rebuke Asa for his folly (2 Chron. 16). The danger was real, but he allowed the fear of what he saw to cloud his faith. Walking by sight instead of by faith is always easier, but we are to fear God above all and to trust Him to direct our paths in every circumstance of life (Prov. 3:6).

Chapter 16: ***A succession of wicked kings rules over the kingdom of Israel.***

16:2 *out of the dust.* God is sovereign over mankind, appointing whomever he pleases to rule (1 Sam. 2:8) *prince.* Ruler or leader, but not a royal son. *walked in the way of Jeroboam.* Continued to lead Israel in idol worship (1 Kings 15:34).

16:4 *shall the dogs eat.* See note at 14:11.

16:5 *chronicles.* See note at 14:19 (16:14,20).

16:7 *because he killed him.* Baasha's killing the descendants of Jeroboam (15:29) fulfilled God's word of judgment on the wicked (14:10–11), but God held him accountable for his idolatry (16:2–3) and his sin in murdering Jeroboam's house (15:27–29). That his house would receive the same fate (16:4) illustrates *lex talionis* (the law of retaliation, Ex. 21:24).

16:11 *pisseth against a wall.* See note at 14:10.

16:12 *according to the word of the LORD.* God's threat of judgment would be fulfilled (v. 34; 14:18). Turning from sin to God is the only course of wisdom.

16:13 *vanities.* Idols, as worthless things without real existence (v. 26).

16:18 *burnt the king's house over him.* A destructive suicide.

19 For his sins which he sinned in doing evil in
the sight of the LORD, in walking in the way of
Jeroboam, and in his sin which he did, to make
Israel to sin.
20 Now the rest of the acts of Zimri, and his
treason that he wrought, *are* they not written in
the book of the chronicles of the kings of Israel?
21 ¶ Then were the people of Israel divided
into two parts: half of the people followed Tibni
the son of Ginath, to make him king; and half
followed Omri.
22 But the people that followed Omri prevailed
against the people that followed Tibni the son of
Ginath: so Tibni died, and Omri reigned.
23 ¶ In the thirty and first year of Asa king of
Judah began Omri to reign over Israel, twelve
years: six years reigned he in Tirzah.
24 And he bought the hill Samaria of Shemer
for two talents of silver, and built on the hill, and
called the name of the city which he built, after
the name of Shemer, owner of the hill, Samaria.
25 ¶ But Omri wrought evil in the eyes of the
LORD, and did worse than all that *were* before him.
26 For he walked in all the way of Jeroboam the
son of Nebat, and in his sin wherewith he made
Israel to sin, to provoke the LORD God of Israel to
anger with their vanities.
27 Now the rest of the acts of Omri which he
did, and his might that he shewed, *are* they not
written in the book of the chronicles of the kings
of Israel?
28 So Omri slept with his fathers, and was buried
in Samaria: and Ahab his son reigned in his stead.
29 ¶ And in the thirty and eighth year of Asa king
of Judah began Ahab the son of Omri to reign
over Israel: and Ahab the son of Omri reigned
over Israel in Samaria twenty and two years.
30 And Ahab the son of Omri did evil in the sight
of the LORD above all that *were* before him.
31 And it came to pass, as if it had been a light
thing for him to walk in the sins of Jeroboam
the son of Nebat, that he took to wife Jezebel the
daughter of Ethbaal king of the Zidonians, and
went and served Baal, and worshipped him.
32 And he reared up an altar for Baal in the house
of Baal, which he had built in Samaria.
33 And Ahab made a grove; and Ahab did more
to provoke the LORD God of Israel to anger than
all the kings of Israel that were before him.
34 ¶ In his days did Hiel the Beth-elite build Jer-
icho: he laid the foundation thereof in Abiram
his firstborn, and set up the gates thereof in his
youngest *son* Segub, according to the word of the
LORD, which he spake by Joshua the son of Nun.

CHAPTER 17

AND Elijah the Tishbite, *who was* of the inhabi-
tants of Gilead, said unto Ahab, *As* the LORD God
of Israel liveth, before whom I stand, there shall
not be dew nor rain these years, but according to
my word.
2 And the word of the LORD came unto him,
saying,

16:23 *Omri* is the first king of Israel mentioned in an extant non-biblical record (the Mesha inscription or Moabite Stone), particularly for his conquest of the Moabites. The Assyrians referred to the king of Israel as the "son of Omri" and called Israel "Omri-land" even after his dynasty ended.

16:24 *talents*. Each approximately 66 pounds. *Samaria*. The new capital of the Northern Kingdom.

THE DISPUTE OF ELIJAH AND ELISHA FOR THE LORD (1 KINGS 16:29—2 KINGS 13:25)

The Ministry of Elijah against Ahab's House (1 Kings 16:29—2 Kings 1:18)

16:31–32 In addition to Jeroboam's state religion that continued, Ahab introduced the worship of pagan gods as an officially recognized religion. *Baal*. Title meaning "lord" or "master." The name depended on the particular location (Hadad for Phoenicia, Chemosh for Moab, etc.), but the rituals connected with each were similar. Baal worship was a fertility cult connected with the agricultural cycle, seeking to manipulate the gods by perverse rituals to obtain a good harvest. Archaeology has provided much information about Baal worship, particularly from a place called Ras Shamra, ancient Ugarit, not far from Jezebel's home.

16:33 *grove*. See note at 14:15.

16:34 Centuries later, *the word of the LORD* through *Joshua* came true (Josh. 6:26).

Thoughts for Personal/Family Worship: Chapter 16

Comparing the biblical assessment of Omri with that of the secular historian illustrates how differently God sees things and what is truly significant. In terms of statesmanship, this king accomplished much. He conquered the Moabites and forged trade treaties with the Phoenicians, marrying his son Ahab to one of their princesses. He founded a dynasty of kings in Israel and built a brand new capital city, controlling the trade routes and securing income for his kingdom. Yet none of his accomplishments is even mentioned in Scripture. What is recorded is that he did not fear the Lord but did more wickedly than all who had reigned before him. This shows us that the important matter in life is not what we accomplish in terms of prestige or income but whether we fear and love the Lord. That will bring eternal blessings, but all the accomplishments in this life will soon wither and come to nothing. Of your life's efforts, which will last for eternity?

Chapter 17: ***Elijah confronts Ahab and begins to show the absurdity of Baal worship.***

17:1 *Elijah the Tishbite*. Nothing is known about the prophet other than his name and home, but his name, "My God is Jehovah," sums up his ministry as a defender of true religion, particularly against Baal. Tishbe was on the east side of Jordan in Gilead, part of the Northern Kingdom. *not be dew nor rain*. Divine judgment for breaking the covenant (Deut. 28:23–24) and a direct attack against Baal (particularly Baal-Hadad of Jezebel's homeland), supposedly the god of thunder and rain. *Jehovah*, not Baal, controlled the rains.

3 Get thee hence, and turn thee eastward, and
hide thyself by the brook Cherith, that *is* before
Jordan.
4 And it shall be, *that* thou shalt drink of the
brook; and I have commanded the ravens to feed
thee there.
5 So he went and did according unto the word
of the LORD: for he went and dwelt by the brook
Cherith, that *is* before Jordan.
6 And the ravens brought him bread and flesh in
the morning, and bread and flesh in the evening;
and he drank of the brook.
7 And it came to pass after a while, that the brook
dried up, because there had been no rain in the
land.
8 ¶ And the word of the LORD came unto him,
saying,
9 Arise, get thee to Zarephath, which *belongeth*
to Zidon, and dwell there: behold, I have com-
manded a widow woman there to sustain thee.
10 So he arose and went to Zarephath. And
when he came to the gate of the city, behold, the
widow woman *was* there gathering of sticks: and
he called to her, and said, Fetch me, I pray thee, a
little water in a vessel, that I may drink.
11 And as she was going to fetch *it*, he called to
her, and said, Bring me, I pray thee, a morsel of
bread in thine hand.
12 And she said, *As* the LORD thy God liveth, I
have not a cake, but an handful of meal in a bar-
rel, and a little oil in a cruse: and, behold, I *am*
gathering two sticks, that I may go in and dress
it for me and my son, that we may eat it, and die.
13 And Elijah said unto her, Fear not; go *and* do
as thou hast said: but make me thereof a little cake
first, and bring *it* unto me, and after make for thee
and for thy son.
14 For thus saith the LORD God of Israel, The bar-
rel of meal shall not waste, neither shall the cruse
of oil fail, until the day *that* the LORD sendeth rain
upon the earth.
15 And she went and did according to the saying
of Elijah: and she, and he, and her house, did eat
many days.
16 *And* the barrel of meal wasted not, neither did
the cruse of oil fail, according to the word of the
LORD, which he spake by Elijah.
17 ¶ And it came to pass after these things, *that*
the son of the woman, the mistress of the house,
fell sick; and his sickness was so sore, that there
was no breath left in him.
18 And she said unto Elijah, What have I to do
with thee, O thou man of God? art thou come
unto me to call my sin to remembrance, and to
slay my son?
19 And he said unto her, Give me thy son. And
he took him out of her bosom, and carried him
up into a loft, where he abode, and laid him upon
his own bed.
20 And he cried unto the LORD, and said, O LORD
my God, hast thou also brought evil upon the
widow with whom I sojourn, by slaying her son?
21 And he stretched himself upon the child three
times, and cried unto the LORD, and said, O LORD
my God, I pray thee, let this child's soul come into
him again.
22 And the LORD heard the voice of Elijah; and
the soul of the child came into him again, and he
revived.
23 And Elijah took the child, and brought him
down out of the chamber into the house, and
delivered him unto his mother: and Elijah said,
See, thy son liveth.
24 ¶ And the woman said to Elijah, Now by this

17:3 *Get thee hence.* Go from this place. *Cherith.* A tributary brook leading to the Jordan River.
17:9 *get thee.* Go. *Zarephath.* A city in Phoenicia, in the middle of Baal territory. *I have commanded a widow.* Not in the sense of speaking a message for her to obey, but in that God had decreed that she would care for the prophet (see note at 2 Kings 24:3). God's decree determines all events, including the actions of animals (1 Kings 17:4) and the choices of human beings (see notes at 12:15,24).
17:11 *morsel.* Scrap or fragment. He did not ask for much.
17:12 *cake.* Loaf. *but an handful.* Ironically, Baal had no power in the heart of his own territory to prevent famine. *meal.* Flour (vv. 14,16). *cruse.* Bottle or jar (vv. 14,16). *dress.* Make or prepare.
17:14 *shall not waste.* The supply will not finish or run out (v. 16). *until the day that the LORD sendeth rain.* Jehovah, not Baal, controlled the weather (Hos. 2:8).
17:17 *mistress.* The female owner or master; the Hebrew is the feminine form of "baal." *sore.* Severe. *no breath left in him.* Literally, "breath did not remain in him," referring to his death.
17:18 *What have I to do with thee.* Literally, "what to me and to you?" expressing wonder or bewilderment. *man of God.* Prophet (12:22; 13:1).
17:20 *evil.* Not referring to sin but to something hurtful, a calamity.
17:21 *stretched himself upon the child.* Dead bodies were unclean, but Elijah lay down in the uncleanness and death of the child of a sinner (v. 18) to raise him to life, just as Christ would embrace the uncleanness and death of sinners to raise them to life (Eph. 2:4–5). *soul.* Here referring to the principle of life.
17:22 *he revived.* This miracle was another attack against Baal. Baal's chief enemy was Mot, the god of death, whom he defeated in regular cycles. By raising the boy from the dead in a stronghold of Baal, Elijah declared that only *Jehovah* is the giver of life and the victor over death.
17:24 *by this I know.* Miracles confirmed that the message of the prophet was truly a new revelation from God. *the word of the LORD in thy mouth is truth.* Divine inspiration extends not merely to the ideas in the prophet's mind but also to the specific words he spoke and wrote, so that every word is true (Prov. 30:5; Matt. 5:18; John 10:35).

Thoughts for Personal/Family Worship: Chapter 17

1. The ministry of Elijah introduces a period of miracles. Christians rightly see God's providence in all events, but miracles in the strictest sense are extraordinary works

I know that thou *art* a man of God, *and* that the
word of the LORD in thy mouth *is* truth.

CHAPTER 18

AND it came to pass *after* many days, that the
word of the LORD came to Elijah in the third year,
saying, Go, shew thyself unto Ahab; and I will
send rain upon the earth.
2 And Elijah went to shew himself unto Ahab.
And *there was* a sore famine in Samaria.
3 And Ahab called Obadiah, which *was* the
governor of *his* house. (Now Obadiah feared the
LORD greatly:
4 For it was *so*, when Jezebel cut off the proph-
ets of the LORD, that Obadiah took an hundred
prophets, and hid them by fifty in a cave, and fed
them with bread and water.)
5 And Ahab said unto Obadiah, Go into the land,
unto all fountains of water, and unto all brooks:
peradventure we may find grass to save the horses
and mules alive, that we lose not all the beasts.
6 So they divided the land between them to pass
throughout it: Ahab went one way by himself, and
Obadiah went another way by himself.
7 ¶ And as Obadiah was in the way, behold, Elijah
met him: and he knew him, and fell on his face,
and said, *Art* thou that my lord Elijah?
8 And he answered him, I *am*: go, tell thy lord,
Behold, Elijah *is here*.
9 And he said, What have I sinned, that thou
wouldest deliver thy servant into the hand of
Ahab, to slay me?
10 *As* the LORD thy God liveth, there is no nation
or kingdom, whither my lord hath not sent to
seek thee: and when they said, *He is* not *there*;
he took an oath of the kingdom and nation, that
they found thee not.
11 And now thou sayest, Go, tell thy lord, Behold,
Elijah *is here*.
12 And it shall come to pass, *as soon as* I am gone
from thee, that the Spirit of the LORD shall carry
thee whither I know not; and *so* when I come
and tell Ahab, and he cannot find thee, he shall
slay me: but I thy servant fear the LORD from my
youth.
13 Was it not told my lord what I did when Jeze-
bel slew the prophets of the LORD, how I hid an
hundred men of the LORD's prophets by fifty in a
cave, and fed them with bread and water?
14 And now thou sayest, Go, tell thy lord, Behold,
Elijah *is here*: and he shall slay me.
15 And Elijah said, *As* the LORD of hosts liveth,
before whom I stand, I will surely shew myself
unto him to day.
16 So Obadiah went to meet Ahab, and told him:
and Ahab went to meet Elijah.
17 ¶ And it came to pass, when Ahab saw Elijah,
that Ahab said unto him, *Art* thou he that trou-
bleth Israel?
18 And he answered, I have not troubled Israel;
but thou, and thy father's house, in that ye have
forsaken the commandments of the LORD, and
thou hast followed Baalim.
19 Now therefore send, *and* gather to me all Israel
unto mount Carmel, and the prophets of Baal
four hundred and fifty, and the prophets of the
groves four hundred, which eat at Jezebel's table.
20 So Ahab sent unto all the children of Israel,
and gathered the prophets together unto mount
Carmel.
21 And Elijah came unto all the people, and said,
How long halt ye between two opinions? if the
LORD *be* God, follow him: but if Baal, *then* follow
him. And the people answered him not a word.
22 Then said Elijah unto the people, I, *even* I

of God's supernatural power that occurred at crucial moments in redemptive history to testify to His unique glory. For example, the Bible speaks of the miracles done through Moses to glorify the Lord above the gods of Egypt, those done through Elijah and Elisha to declare God's supremacy against Baal worship, and those done in the days of the Lord Jesus and His apostles to bear witness to Christ's coming and accomplishment of redemption. Though such miracles are rare, they teach us that God's power has no limits. Therefore, just as Elijah called down the covenant curses of the Law upon Israel through His prayers, so we can pray God's promises with great faith (James 5:16–18), since He is able to do more than we can ask or think (Eph. 3:20).

2. The miracles performed by Elijah (and later Elisha) stand by themselves as testimonies to God's power, but it is clear from the ancient literature that virtually every miracle was directed at some pagan belief about Baal. Point by point the prophets proved that the powers associated with Baal in truth belonged to Jehovah alone. It seems as though they knew what the worshipers of Baal believed. This is a good lesson in apologetics, the discipline of defending the Scriptures against those who attack them. The aim of apologetics is to display the emptiness and futility of the idolatrous beliefs of this world and to demonstrate that power, wisdom, and goodness belong to the Lord alone.

Chapter 18: ***Elijah meets with Ahab and challenges the prophets of Baal to a contest to prove whether Baal or Jehovah is the true God.***

18:1 *many days.* Three years and six months (Luke 4:25; James 5:17). *I will send rain.* Elijah had said that there would be no rain "but according to my word" (1 Kings 17:1); the prophetic word equates to the word of the Lord Himself.

18:2 *sore.* Severe.

18:17 *troubleth.* Puts into disorder, brings disaster, or throws into confusion (v. 18).

18:19 *groves.* See note at 14:15.

18:21 *How long halt ye between two opinions?* The Hebrew could be either "how long do you limp on two wooden crutches?" or "how long do you limp on two divided (thoughts)?" Either way they were unstable and uncommitted.

only, remain a prophet of the LORD; but Baal's prophets *are* four hundred and fifty men.

23 Let them therefore give us two bullocks; and let them choose one bullock for themselves, and cut it in pieces, and lay *it* on wood, and put no fire *under*: and I will dress the other bullock, and lay *it* on wood, and put no fire *under*:

24 And call ye on the name of your gods, and I will call on the name of the LORD: and the God that answereth by fire, let him be God. And all the people answered and said, It is well spoken.

25 And Elijah said unto the prophets of Baal, Choose you one bullock for yourselves, and dress *it* first; for ye *are* many; and call on the name of your gods, but put no fire *under*.

26 And they took the bullock which was given them, and they dressed *it*, and called on the name of Baal from morning even until noon, saying, O Baal, hear us. But *there was* no voice, nor any that answered. And they leaped upon the altar which was made.

27 And it came to pass at noon, that Elijah mocked them, and said, Cry aloud: for he *is* a god; either he is talking, or he is pursuing, or he is in a journey, *or* peradventure he sleepeth, and must be awaked.

28 And they cried aloud, and cut themselves after their manner with knives and lancets, till the blood gushed out upon them.

29 And it came to pass, when midday was past, and they prophesied until the *time* of the offering of the *evening* sacrifice, that *there was* neither voice, nor any to answer, nor any that regarded.

30 And Elijah said unto all the people, Come near unto me. And all the people came near unto him. And he repaired the altar of the LORD *that was* broken down.

31 And Elijah took twelve stones, according to the number of the tribes of the sons of Jacob, unto whom the word of the LORD came, saying, Israel shall be thy name:

32 And with the stones he built an altar in the name of the LORD: and he made a trench about the altar, as great as would contain two measures of seed.

33 And he put the wood in order, and cut the bullock in pieces, and laid *him* on the wood, and said, Fill four barrels with water, and pour *it* on the burnt sacrifice, and on the wood.

34 And he said, Do *it* the second time. And they did *it* the second time. And he said, Do *it* the third time. And they did *it* the third time.

35 And the water ran round about the altar; and he filled the trench also with water.

36 And it came to pass at *the time of* the offering of the *evening* sacrifice, that Elijah the prophet came near, and said, LORD God of Abraham, Isaac, and of Israel, let it be known this day that thou *art* God in Israel, and *that* I *am* thy servant, and *that* I have done all these things at thy word.

37 Hear me, O LORD, hear me, that this people may know that thou *art* the LORD God, and *that* thou hast turned their heart back again.

38 Then the fire of the LORD fell, and consumed the burnt sacrifice, and the wood, and the stones, and the dust, and licked up the water that *was* in the trench.

39 And when all the people saw *it*, they fell on their faces: and they said, The LORD, he *is* the God; the LORD, he *is* the God.

40 And Elijah said unto them, Take the prophets of Baal; let not one of them escape. And they took them: and Elijah brought them down to the brook Kishon, and slew them there.

41 ¶ And Elijah said unto Ahab, Get thee up, eat and drink; for *there is* a sound of abundance of rain.

42 So Ahab went up to eat and to drink. And Elijah went up to the top of Carmel; and he cast himself down upon the earth, and put his face between his knees,

43 And said to his servant, Go up now, look toward the sea. And he went up, and looked, and said, *There is* nothing. And he said, Go again seven times.

44 And it came to pass at the seventh time, that he said, Behold, there ariseth a little cloud out of the sea, like a man's hand. And he said, Go up, say unto Ahab, Prepare *thy chariot*, and get thee down, that the rain stop thee not.

18:23 *I will dress*. I will prepare; the Hebrew is simply "make" (v. 26).

18:24 *the God that answereth by fire, let him be God*. A contest of sovereignty between the Lord and the demonic gods of the world, similar to the way the Lord humiliated the gods of Egypt in the plagues and exodus of Israel (Ex. 7–12).

18:26 *they leaped upon the altar*. Some sort of cultic dance.

18:27 *mocked*. Elijah employed a bit of sanctified sarcasm. Each of these taunts alludes to some act associated with Baal referred to in the Canaanite literature. *peradventure*. Perhaps.

18:28 *knives and lancets*. Swords and spears.

18:29 *prophesied*. Ecstatic, self-induced frenzy. *nor any that regarded*. Literally, "nonexistence of attentiveness."

18:36 *God of Abraham, Isaac, and of Israel*. The faithful God who keeps His covenant promises. *let it be known this day that thou art God*. God always aims to glorify Himself as the only Lord (Ex. 6:7; 7:5; 9:16; Isa. 48:11).

18:38 *the fire of the LORD fell*. Another point against Baal, since he was the god of thunder and lightning. Icons of Baal often portray him with a lightning bolt as his scepter.

18:40 *slew them*. As commanded in the Law (Deut. 13:1–5; 18:20).

18:42 *put his face between his knees*. Knowing that God's will is to send rain, Elijah prays for God to do so. A key petition in prayer is "Thy will be done" (Matt. 6:10).

18:43 *seven times*. Sometimes God answers prayer immediately, as in the sending of fire (v. 38). At other times He delays, as in the sending of the rain. His timing is always best.

45 And it came to pass in the mean while, that
the heaven was black with clouds and wind, and
there was a great rain. And Ahab rode, and went
to Jezreel.
46 And the hand of the LORD was on Elijah; and
he girded up his loins, and ran before Ahab to the
entrance of Jezreel.

CHAPTER 19

AND Ahab told Jezebel all that Elijah had done,
and withal how he had slain all the prophets with
the sword.
2 Then Jezebel sent a messenger unto Elijah,
saying, So let the gods do *to me*, and more also, if
I make not thy life as the life of one of them by to
morrow about this time.
3 And when he saw *that*, he arose, and went for
his life, and came to Beer-sheba, which *belongeth*
to Judah, and left his servant there.
4 ¶ But he himself went a day's journey into the
wilderness, and came and sat down under a ju-
niper tree: and he requested for himself that he
might die; and said, It is enough; now, O LORD,
take away my life; for I *am* not better than my
fathers.
5 And as he lay and slept under a juniper tree,
behold, then an angel touched him, and said unto
him, Arise *and* eat.
6 And he looked, and, behold, *there was* a cake
baken on the coals, and a cruse of water at his
head. And he did eat and drink, and laid him
down again.
7 And the angel of the LORD came again the
second time, and touched him, and said, Arise
and eat; because the journey *is* too great for thee.
8 And he arose, and did eat and drink, and went
in the strength of that meat forty days and forty
nights unto Horeb the mount of God.
9 ¶ And he came thither unto a cave, and lodged
there; and, behold, the word of the LORD *came* to
him, and he said unto him, What doest thou here,
Elijah?
10 And he said, I have been very jealous for the
LORD God of hosts: for the children of Israel have
forsaken thy covenant, thrown down thine al-
tars, and slain thy prophets with the sword; and
I, *even* I only, am left; and they seek my life, to
take it away.
11 And he said, Go forth, and stand upon the
mount before the LORD. And, behold, the LORD
passed by, and a great and strong wind rent the
mountains, and brake in pieces the rocks before
the LORD; *but* the LORD *was* not in the wind: and
after the wind an earthquake; *but* the LORD *was*
not in the earthquake:
12 And after the earthquake a fire; *but* the LORD
was not in the fire: and after the fire a still small
voice.
13 And it was *so*, when Elijah heard *it*, that he
wrapped his face in his mantle, and went out, and
stood in the entering in of the cave. And, behold,

18:45 *great rain.* The acknowledgment of the Lord by the people turned back the covenant curse of famine and restored the covenant blessing of rain (Deut. 28:12,23–24; see note at 1 Kings 17:1).

Thoughts for Personal/Family Worship: Chapter 18

1. **The Lord works to make Himself known as the only true God. Idols always challenge His sovereignty over some area of life. Christ's death on the cross, like Elijah's sacrifice at Carmel, decisively defeated the powers of this world (Col. 2:15). Now, through the proclamation of the cross and the power of the risen Savior, the Lord is causing all peoples to know that He is the Lord God, and that there is no other (1 Kings 8:60; Deut. 4:35). This is a key component of our witness: telling people that the Lord alone is God (Isa. 43:10–13) and calling all peoples to turn to Him as the only Savior (45:21–22).**
2. **James says that Elijah was "a man subject to like passions as we are, and he prayed earnestly" (James 5:17–18). When we consider the boldness of Elijah in confronting Ahab and the prophets of Baal, or the power of Elijah in performing so many miracles, it is hard to see any similarities at all between him and ourselves. Yet he provides for us an example, particularly in the practice of prayer. He prayed *humbly*, with his face to the ground; *specifically*, for the need of the people; *persistently*, despite six prayers without an answer; and *effectively*. Elijah was able to do what he did because he knew God's Word and trusted God to accomplish His Word. How does Elijah's example challenge you to grow in prayer?**

Chapter 19: *Fearing Jezebel, Elijah flees to the wilderness, where the Lord provides for him and gives him various instructions, including the anointing of his successor.*

19:1 *withal.* Also.

19:2 *So let the gods do to me.* An oath formula by which Jezebel swears to kill Elijah.

19:3 *Beer-sheba.* In the south of Judah. The whole of the Southern Kingdom became a buffer zone between him and Jezebel.

19:4 *into the wilderness.* Most likely desiring solitude; he would have been safe enough in Beer-sheba. *juniper tree.* A kind of broom-shrub, a source of shade (v. 5). *he requested for himself that he might die.* Literally, "he asked his soul (himself) to die." Fatigue and emotion overcame him and skewed his thinking, so that he ran for his life and now desired death.

19:6 *baken.* Baked. *cruse.* Bottle or jar.

19:8 *meat.* Food of any kind. *forty days and forty nights.* A duration often linked to testing (Ex. 24:18; 34:28; Matt. 4:2). *Horeb.* Where the Lord had appeared to Moses and Israel (Ex. 3:1; 19:18).

19:10 *very jealous.* Fervently zealous (v. 14). *I only, am left.* Loneliness in his calling overwhelmed him (18:22).

19:11–12 The Lord demonstrated His power in the *strong wind*, the *earthquake* and the *fire*—signs of His holiness and wrath against sin (Ex. 19:18; Isa. 29:6; Nah. 1:5–6). But the Lord revealed Himself in a soft breeze (*still small voice*). He met His depressed servant with gentleness and grace and is often working quietly when not blatantly visible (1 Kings 19:18).

there came a voice unto him, and said, What doest
thou here, Elijah?
14 And he said, I have been very jealous for the
LORD God of hosts: because the children of Israel
have forsaken thy covenant, thrown down thine
altars, and slain thy prophets with the sword; and
I, *even* I only, am left; and they seek my life, to
take it away.
15 And the LORD said unto him, Go, return on
thy way to the wilderness of Damascus: and when
thou comest, anoint Hazael *to be* king over Syria:
16 And Jehu the son of Nimshi shalt thou anoint
to be king over Israel: and Elisha the son of
Shaphat of Abel-meholah shalt thou anoint *to be*
prophet in thy room.
17 And it shall come to pass, *that* him that esca-
peth the sword of Hazael shall Jehu slay: and him
that escapeth from the sword of Jehu shall Elisha
slay.
18 Yet I have left *me* seven thousand in Israel, all
the knees which have not bowed unto Baal, and
every mouth which hath not kissed him.
19 ¶ So he departed thence, and found Elisha
the son of Shaphat, who *was* plowing *with* twelve
yoke *of oxen* before him, and he with the twelfth:
and Elijah passed by him, and cast his mantle
upon him.
20 And he left the oxen, and ran after Elijah, and
said, Let me, I pray thee, kiss my father and my
mother, and *then* I will follow thee. And he said
unto him, Go back again: for what have I done
to thee?
21 And he returned back from him, and took
a yoke of oxen, and slew them, and boiled their
flesh with the instruments of the oxen, and gave
unto the people, and they did eat. Then he arose,
and went after Elijah, and ministered unto him.

CHAPTER 20

AND Ben-hadad the king of Syria gathered all his
host together: and *there were* thirty and two kings
with him, and horses, and chariots: and he went
up and besieged Samaria, and warred against it.
2 And he sent messengers to Ahab king of Is-
rael into the city, and said unto him, Thus saith
Ben-hadad,
3 Thy silver and thy gold *is* mine; thy wives also
and thy children, *even* the goodliest, *are* mine.
4 And the king of Israel answered and said, My
lord, O king, according to thy saying, I *am* thine,
and all that I have.
5 And the messengers came again, and said, Thus
speaketh Ben-hadad, saying, Although I have sent
unto thee, saying, Thou shalt deliver me thy silver,
and thy gold, and thy wives, and thy children;
6 Yet I will send my servants unto thee to morrow
about this time, and they shall search thine house,
and the houses of thy servants; and it shall be, *that*
whatsoever is pleasant in thine eyes, they shall put
it in their hand, and take *it* away.
7 Then the king of Israel called all the elders of
the land, and said, Mark, I pray you, and see how
this *man* seeketh mischief: for he sent unto me for

19:13 *mantle.* Cloak or cape (v. 19).
19:15–16 *anoint Hazael . . . Jehu.* These directions were not carried out by Elijah but left to *Elisha* (2 Kings 8:13; 9:1–3), whose name means "My God delivers" and who would serve instead of his master (*in thy room*).
19:17 The Lord will use these agents to destroy the house of Ahab.
19:18 *Yet I have left.* The Hebrew expresses the idea that God had been in the process of leaving. All the time Elijah thought he was alone, the Lord was gathering His people, preserving a remnant by His grace (Rom. 11:2–6). The Lord's working is not limited by our sight.
19:21 Elisha showed that he had forsaken his former occupation and would now be devoted to Elijah and the Lord; he left all behind him to obey the Lord's calling.

Thoughts for Personal/Family Worship: Chapter 19

1. **All too often low points in our spiritual lives immediately follow the high points. On the top of Mt. Carmel Elijah performed bold exploits for God and prayed exemplary prayers. Yet immediately after the extraordinary victories, he became overcome with fear, fled for his life, and thought irrationally. Elijah was "subject to like passions as we are" (James 5:17)—and we can relate to him. Most likely he was physically exhausted, which contributed to his depression. There is a connection between the physical and the spiritual that cannot be ignored. Significantly, before the Lord said anything to him, He allowed Elijah to sleep and then provided necessary nourishment. The Lord knows the frailty of His people, and He gave no rebuke to Elijah. But this should be a warning to us to be on special guard after spiritual victories and to give attention to our physical as well as spiritual needs.**
2. **Elisha's response to his commission to be a prophet is exemplary for all who would be followers of Christ. He left his oxen behind, unlike those who refused to follow Christ because of their new oxen (Luke 14:19). But as the disciples left their nets and followed the Lord Jesus (Mark 1:18), so Elisha left his life of farming to do the will of God. Christ said, "whosoever he be of you that forsaketh not all that he hath, he cannot be my disciple" (Luke 14:33). The Lord calls for total commitment to Himself. He first gave Himself on the cross, and now He calls us to take up our cross (v. 27). Whatever the cost to follow Christ, it is worth it. What will it mean for you to take up your cross?**

Chapter 20: *Wars between Israel and Syria rage, and Ahab is rebuked for entering a covenant with Ben-hadad.*

20:1 *Ben-hadad.* Translated, "the son of Hadad," not the name of his father but the principal deity or Baal of that region. *besieged Samaria.* The Syrian army with a large coalition encircled the capital city. Israel was outnumbered, and Ahab acquiesced to the demands (v. 4).
20:6 *whatsoever is pleasant.* Literally, "all the desire of your eyes." They would plunder whatever they determined to be Ahab's prized possessions. Ben-hadad increased the demands.

my wives, and for my children, and for my silver,
and for my gold; and I denied him not.
8 And all the elders and all the people said unto
him, Hearken not *unto him*, nor consent.
9 Wherefore he said unto the messengers of
Ben-hadad, Tell my lord the king, All that thou
didst send for to thy servant at the first I will do:
but this thing I may not do. And the messengers
departed, and brought him word again.
10 And Ben-hadad sent unto him, and said, The
gods do so unto me, and more also, if the dust of
Samaria shall suffice for handfuls for all the peo-
ple that follow me.
11 And the king of Israel answered and said, Tell
him, Let not him that girdeth on *his harness* boast
himself as he that putteth it off.
12 And it came to pass, when *Ben-hadad* heard
this message, as he *was* drinking, he and the kings
in the pavilions, that he said unto his servants,
Set *yourselves in array*. And they set *themselves in
array* against the city.
13 ¶ And, behold, there came a prophet unto
Ahab king of Israel, saying, Thus saith the LORD,
Hast thou seen all this great multitude? behold, I
will deliver it into thine hand this day; and thou
shalt know that I *am* the LORD.
14 And Ahab said, By whom? And he said, Thus
saith the LORD, *Even* by the young men of the
princes of the provinces. Then he said, Who shall
order the battle? And he answered, Thou.
15 Then he numbered the young men of the
princes of the provinces, and they were two hun-
dred and thirty two: and after them he numbered
all the people, *even* all the children of Israel, *being*
seven thousand.
16 And they went out at noon. But Ben-hadad
was drinking himself drunk in the pavilions,
he and the kings, the thirty and two kings that
helped him.
17 And the young men of the princes of the
provinces went out first; and Ben-hadad sent out,
and they told him, saying, There are men come
out of Samaria.
18 And he said, Whether they be come out for
peace, take them alive; or whether they be come
out for war, take them alive.
19 So these young men of the princes of the prov-
inces came out of the city, and the army which
followed them.
20 And they slew every one his man: and the
Syrians fled; and Israel pursued them: and Ben-
hadad the king of Syria escaped on an horse with
the horsemen.
21 And the king of Israel went out, and smote the
horses and chariots, and slew the Syrians with a
great slaughter.
22 ¶ And the prophet came to the king of Israel,
and said unto him, Go, strengthen thyself, and
mark, and see what thou doest: for at the return
of the year the king of Syria will come up against
thee.
23 And the servants of the king of Syria said unto
him, Their gods *are* gods of the hills; therefore
they were stronger than we; but let us fight against
them in the plain, and surely we shall be stronger
than they.
24 And do this thing, Take the kings away, every
man out of his place, and put captains in their
rooms:
25 And number thee an army, like the army that
thou hast lost, horse for horse, and chariot for
chariot: and we will fight against them in the
plain, *and* surely we shall be stronger than they.
And he hearkened unto their voice, and did so.
26 And it came to pass at the return of the year,
that Ben-hadad numbered the Syrians, and went
up to Aphek, to fight against Israel.
27 And the children of Israel were numbered,
and were all present, and went against them: and
the children of Israel pitched before them like
two little flocks of kids; but the Syrians filled the
country.
28 ¶ And there came a man of God, and spake
unto the king of Israel, and said, Thus saith the
LORD, Because the Syrians have said, The LORD *is*
God of the hills, but he *is* not God of the valleys,
therefore will I deliver all this great multitude into
thine hand, and ye shall know that I *am* the LORD.
29 And they pitched one over against the other
seven days. And *so* it was, that in the seventh day

20:7 *Mark.* Hebrew, "know." *mischief.* Harm, calamity, something hurtful.
20:10 *The gods do so.* An oath formula whereby Ben-hadad swears what he will do. *if the dust . . . for handfuls for all the people.* Total devastation.
20:11 *girdeth on his harness.* Puts on his armor. *let not him . . . boast himself.* A warning against bragging of victory before the battle.
20:12 *pavilions.* Huts or some sort of temporary structures like tents (v. 16). *Set yourselves in array.* Prepare or line up for battle.
20:13 *know that I am the LORD.* See note at 18:36.
20:14 *young men of the princes.* Most likely an appositional statement: the young men were the leaders in their respective districts. They would serve as a special force under Ahab's command.
20:22 *mark.* Know.
20:24 *in their rooms.* In their places, instead of them.
20:27 *like two little flocks of kids.* Israel was vastly outnumbered.
20:28 *man of God.* Prophet. *God of the hills . . . not God of the valleys.* Idolatry divides sovereignty over different spheres of the world among various gods, just as today secularism claims that God is irrelevant or inappropriate to certain areas of life, especially in the public arena. This is a great offense to the Lord.
20:29 *the battle was joined.* Literally, "the battle drew near."

the battle was joined: and the children of Israel
slew of the Syrians an hundred thousand foot-
men in one day.
30 But the rest fled to Aphek, into the city; and
there a wall fell upon twenty and seven thousand
of the men *that were* left. And Ben-hadad fled,
and came into the city, into an inner chamber.
31 ¶ And his servants said unto him, Behold now,
we have heard that the kings of the house of Israel
are merciful kings: let us, I pray thee, put sack-
cloth on our loins, and ropes upon our heads, and
go out to the king of Israel: peradventure he will
save thy life.
32 So they girded sackcloth on their loins, and
put ropes on their heads, and came to the king
of Israel, and said, Thy servant Ben-hadad saith, I
pray thee, let me live. And he said, *Is* he yet alive?
he *is* my brother.
33 Now the men did diligently observe whether
any thing would come from him, and did hastily
catch *it*: and they said, Thy brother Ben-hadad.
Then he said, Go ye, bring him. Then Ben-hadad
came forth to him; and he caused him to come up
into the chariot.
34 And *Ben-hadad* said unto him, The cities,
which my father took from thy father, I will re-
store; and thou shalt make streets for thee in Da-
mascus, as my father made in Samaria. Then *said*
Ahab, I will send thee away with this covenant. So
he made a covenant with him, and sent him away.
35 ¶ And a certain man of the sons of the
prophets said unto his neighbour in the word
of the LORD, Smite me, I pray thee. And the man
refused to smite him.
36 Then said he unto him, Because thou hast not
obeyed the voice of the LORD, behold, as soon as
thou art departed from me, a lion shall slay thee.
And as soon as he was departed from him, a lion
found him, and slew him.
37 Then he found another man, and said, Smite
me, I pray thee. And the man smote him, so that
in smiting he wounded *him*.
38 So the prophet departed, and waited for the
king by the way, and disguised himself with ashes
upon his face.
39 And as the king passed by, he cried unto the
king: and he said, Thy servant went out into the
midst of the battle; and, behold, a man turned
aside, and brought a man unto me, and said, Keep
this man: if by any means he be missing, then
shall thy life be for his life, or else thou shalt pay a
talent of silver.
40 And as thy servant was busy here and there, he
was gone. And the king of Israel said unto him,
So *shall* thy judgment *be*; thyself hast decided *it*.
41 And he hasted, and took the ashes away from
his face; and the king of Israel discerned him that
he *was* of the prophets.
42 And he said unto him, Thus saith the LORD,
Because thou hast let go out of *thy* hand a man
whom I appointed to utter destruction, therefore
thy life shall go for his life, and thy people for his
people.
43 And the king of Israel went to his house heavy
and displeased, and came to Samaria.

CHAPTER 21

AND it came to pass after these things, *that* Naboth
the Jezreelite had a vineyard, which *was* in Jezreel,
hard by the palace of Ahab king of Samaria.
2 And Ahab spake unto Naboth, saying, Give me

20:31 *merciful kings*. Kings of covenant loyalty. The plan was to sign a treaty with Israel, being confident that Israel would honor the terms. *put sackcloth on*. A gesture of contrition, submission, and surrender. *peradventure*. Perhaps.

20:33 *the men did diligently observe*. Literally, "the men divined"; they took as an omen or sign. *did hastily catch it*. They caught the significance of Ahab's referring to Ben-hadad as a brother.

20:34 *The cities which my father took*. See 15:20. Ben-hadad made significant concessions, which Ahab accepted, entering *a covenant with him* (a mutually binding agreement, a peace treaty).

20:35 *sons of the prophets*. Prophets, not children of prophets or prophets-in-training. The Hebrew uses the word "son" to designate class or category. *neighbour*. Fellow person, not the resident next door.

20:39 *pay a talent of silver*. Weigh out a talent, about 66 pounds, usually in the form of a disk.

20:40 The prophet's object lesson, whereby Ahab makes the judgment ultimately against himself, parallels Nathan's story to David, whereby he also condemned himself (2 Sam. 12:5–7).

20:43 *heavy and displeased*. Resentful (or impossible to satisfy) and furious.

Thoughts for Personal/Family Worship: Chapter 20

As wicked and undeserving as Ahab was, God gave him an opportunity to come to his spiritual senses. Although he was vastly outnumbered by the enemy and was willing to surrender, God sent a prophet promising victory so that Ahab would "know that I am the LORD" (vv. 13,28). Ahab received God's word and saw firsthand its truth, yet he did not repent of his sins and turn to the Lord with saving knowledge. It is easy to see Ahab among the fools who hated knowledge and did not choose the fear of God (Prov. 1:22–33). This is a warning to those who sit regularly under the teaching of God's Word and have opportunity after opportunity to submit in faith and repentance. Remember that the same message that can bring life can harden those who hear and reject. This is an opportunity to press this truth upon the children in every Christian home.

Chapter 21: ***Jezebel plots to acquire Naboth's vineyard for Ahab, and Elijah declares God's punishment on the house of Ahab.***

21:1 *hard by the palace*. Adjacent to Ahab's royal palace in Jezreel.

thy vineyard, that I may have it for a garden of
herbs, because it *is* near unto my house: and I will
give thee for it a better vineyard than it; *or*, if it
seem good to thee, I will give thee the worth of it
in money.
3 And Naboth said to Ahab, The LORD forbid
it me, that I should give the inheritance of my
fathers unto thee.
4 And Ahab came into his house heavy and dis-
pleased because of the word which Naboth the
Jezreelite had spoken to him: for he had said, I will
not give thee the inheritance of my fathers. And
he laid him down upon his bed, and turned away
his face, and would eat no bread.
5 ¶ But Jezebel his wife came to him, and said
unto him, Why is thy spirit so sad, that thou eatest
no bread?
6 And he said unto her, Because I spake unto
Naboth the Jezreelite, and said unto him, Give me
thy vineyard for money; or else, if it please thee,
I will give thee *another* vineyard for it: and he
answered, I will not give thee my vineyard.
7 And Jezebel his wife said unto him, Dost thou
now govern the kingdom of Israel? arise, *and* eat
bread, and let thine heart be merry: I will give
thee the vineyard of Naboth the Jezreelite.
8 So she wrote letters in Ahab's name, and sealed
them with his seal, and sent the letters unto the
elders and to the nobles that *were* in his city,
dwelling with Naboth.
9 And she wrote in the letters, saying, Proclaim a
fast, and set Naboth on high among the people:
10 And set two men, sons of Belial, before him, to
bear witness against him, saying, Thou didst blas-
pheme God and the king. And *then* carry him out,
and stone him, that he may die.
11 And the men of his city, *even* the elders and
the nobles who were the inhabitants in his city,
did as Jezebel had sent unto them, *and* as it *was*
written in the letters which she had sent unto
them.
12 They proclaimed a fast, and set Naboth on
high among the people.
13 And there came in two men, children of
Belial, and sat before him: and the men of Belial
witnessed against him, *even* against Naboth, in
the presence of the people, saying, Naboth did
blaspheme God and the king. Then they carried
him forth out of the city, and stoned him with
stones, that he died.
14 Then they sent to Jezebel, saying, Naboth is
stoned, and is dead.
15 ¶ And it came to pass, when Jezebel heard that
Naboth was stoned, and was dead, that Jezebel said
to Ahab, Arise, take possession of the vineyard of
Naboth the Jezreelite, which he refused to give
thee for money: for Naboth is not alive, but dead.
16 And it came to pass, when Ahab heard that
Naboth was dead, that Ahab rose up to go down
to the vineyard of Naboth the Jezreelite, to take
possession of it.
17 ¶ And the word of the LORD came to Elijah the
Tishbite, saying,
18 Arise, go down to meet Ahab king of Israel,
which *is* in Samaria: behold, *he is* in the vineyard
of Naboth, whither he is gone down to possess it.
19 And thou shalt speak unto him, saying, Thus
saith the LORD, Hast thou killed, and also taken
possession? And thou shalt speak unto him, say-
ing, Thus saith the LORD, In the place where dogs
licked the blood of Naboth shall dogs lick thy
blood, even thine.
20 And Ahab said to Elijah, Hast thou found me,
O mine enemy? And he answered, I have found
thee: because thou hast sold thyself to work evil in
the sight of the LORD.
21 Behold, I will bring evil upon thee, and will
take away thy posterity, and will cut off from
Ahab him that pisseth against the wall, and him
that is shut up and left in Israel,
22 And will make thine house like the house of
Jeroboam the son of Nebat, and like the house
of Baasha the son of Ahijah, for the provocation
wherewith thou hast provoked *me* to anger, and
made Israel to sin.
23 And of Jezebel also spake the LORD, saying,
The dogs shall eat Jezebel by the wall of Jezreel.
24 Him that dieth of Ahab in the city the dogs

21:3 *The LORD forbid it me.* Literally, "far be it for me from the Lord." Such a transaction was forbidden (Lev. 25:23; Num. 36:7).

21:4 *heavy and displeased.* See note at 20:43.

21:5 *sad.* Sullen, dejected, or unable to be satisfied. Same Hebrew word as "heavy" (v. 4).

21:9 *Proclaim a fast.* Fasts were often called to discover the cause of some perceived transgression. Here the occasion was to accuse *Naboth* of the false charges.

21:10–14 *sons of Belial.* Those who were worthless, wicked, good for nothing. They executed Jezebel's scheme.

21:19 *Hast thou killed.* Ahab's sins of killing Naboth and stealing his ancestral inheritance were exposed, and God's just punishment was pronounced against him.

21:19 *In the place where dogs licked the blood of Naboth.* Dogs licked Naboth's blood, and they would also lick Ahab's blood—a most shameful death. This sentence was fulfilled first when dogs licked Ahab's blood outside of Samaria (22:38) and, second, when Jehu had the body of Jehoram, Ahab's son, cast on the field of Naboth (2 Kings 9:25–26).

21:20 *sold thyself to work evil.* Gave himself up to the slavery of sin (2 Kings 17:17).

21:21 *evil.* Calamity, referring to the judgment to come. *him that pisseth against the wall.* A Hebrew idiom for males, without any vulgar connotation. *him that is shut up and left in Israel.* A proverb implying total destruction; there was no place to hide in order to escape (14:10).

21:22 *provocation.* Offensive irritation.

21:23 *The dogs shall eat Jezebel.* Fulfilled after Jehu killed her (2 Kings 9:35–36).

shall eat; and him that dieth in the field shall the
fowls of the air eat.
25 ¶ But there was none like unto Ahab, which
did sell himself to work wickedness in the sight of
the LORD, whom Jezebel his wife stirred up.
26 And he did very abominably in following idols,
according to all *things* as did the Amorites, whom
the LORD cast out before the children of Israel.
27 And it came to pass, when Ahab heard those
words, that he rent his clothes, and put sackcloth
upon his flesh, and fasted, and lay in sackcloth,
and went softly.
28 And the word of the LORD came to Elijah the
Tishbite, saying,
29 Seest thou how Ahab humbleth himself be-
fore me? because he humbleth himself before me,
I will not bring the evil in his days: *but* in his son's
days will I bring the evil upon his house.

CHAPTER 22

AND they continued three years without war
between Syria and Israel.
2 And it came to pass in the third year, that
Jehoshaphat the king of Judah came down to the
king of Israel.
3 And the king of Israel said unto his servants,
Know ye that Ramoth in Gilead *is* ours, and we
be still, *and* take it not out of the hand of the king
of Syria?
4 And he said unto Jehoshaphat, Wilt thou go
with me to battle to Ramoth-gilead? And Jehosh-
aphat said to the king of Israel, I *am* as thou *art*,
my people as thy people, my horses as thy horses.
5 And Jehoshaphat said unto the king of Israel,
Enquire, I pray thee, at the word of the LORD to day.
6 Then the king of Israel gathered the prophets
together, about four hundred men, and said unto
them, Shall I go against Ramoth-gilead to battle,
or shall I forbear? And they said, Go up; for the
Lord shall deliver *it* into the hand of the king.
7 And Jehoshaphat said, *Is there* not here a
prophet of the LORD besides, that we might en-
quire of him?
8 And the king of Israel said unto Jehoshaphat,
There is yet one man, Micaiah the son of Imlah,
by whom we may enquire of the LORD: but I hate
him; for he doth not prophesy good concerning
me, but evil. And Jehoshaphat said, Let not the
king say so.
9 Then the king of Israel called an officer, and
said, Hasten *hither* Micaiah the son of Imlah.
10 And the king of Israel and Jehoshaphat the
king of Judah sat each on his throne, having put
on their robes, in a void place in the entrance of
the gate of Samaria; and all the prophets proph-
esied before them.
11 And Zedekiah the son of Chenaanah made
him horns of iron: and he said, Thus saith the
LORD, With these shalt thou push the Syrians,
until thou have consumed them.
12 And all the prophets prophesied so, saying, Go
up to Ramoth-gilead, and prosper: for the LORD
shall deliver *it* into the king's hand.
13 And the messenger that was gone to call Mica-
iah spake unto him, saying, Behold now, the
words of the prophets *declare* good unto the king
with one mouth: let thy word, I pray thee, be like

21:24 See note at 14:11.
21:26 *idols*. The Hebrew root is similar to the word for "dung" to show how disgusting idols are in God's sight (Lev. 26:30). *Amorites*. General term for all the Canaanite nations.
21:27 *rent his clothes*. Gesture of sorrow and mourning. *went softly*. Walked around in a depressed or dejected mood.
21:29 *I will not bring the evil in his days*. The punishment will be delayed. The focus is on God's mercy, not on the genuineness of Ahab's repentance.

Thoughts for Personal/Family Worship: Chapter 21

1. **Ahab's behavior in response to Naboth's refusal to turn over his vineyard was like that of a selfish child who does not get his own way. He got mad and pouted (v. 4). Rather than being grateful for the many things he did have, he wanted what belonged to another. His breaking of the tenth commandment led to the breaking of commandments six and nine as well. Children should learn early to be content with what the Lord has given them, not to envy what belongs to another and not to pout when they don't get their own way. But, in reality, that is a lesson for all to learn, regardless of age.**
2. **Tragically, earthly tribunals do not always serve justice (Eccl. 3:16; 5:8). Jezebel's mock court appeared to follow the proper legal procedures. The law required two or three witnesses to condemn in the case of a capital offense (Deut. 17:6), and she arranged for the two witnesses to make the accusation. The just one was condemned, but God, who is higher than any earthly court, knows, and in the end justice prevails. The greatest miscarriage of justice the world has ever known was in the trials of the Lord Jesus, where He was falsely accused by the Jews, recognized as innocent by Pilate, but nonetheless condemned. Even though we stand aghast at the debacle that transpired at Christ's trial before wicked men, we must rejoice that His death sentence that led to Calvary was the execution of God's will for our salvation (Acts 2:23). God rules, even through human injustice. How can that comfort us when we face the injustice around us today?**

Chapter 22: ***In alliance with Jehoshaphat, Ahab goes to war against the Syrians and is mortally wounded in battle.***

22:3 *we be still, and take it not*. Literally, "we have been hesitating from taking it."
22:6–7 The identity of the prophets is uncertain, but Jehoshaphat is suspicious and so requests a prophet of the Lord.
22:10 *void place*. The Hebrew refers to a threshing floor.
22:11 *horns of iron*. Prophets frequently used props or object lessons to illustrate or symbolize their message (Jer. 27:2). Bullhorns symbolize power and here picture the easy defeat of the enemy.

the word of one of them, and speak *that which is*
good.
14 And Micaiah said, *As* the LORD liveth, what the
LORD saith unto me, that will I speak.
15 ¶ So he came to the king. And the king said
unto him, Micaiah, shall we go against Ramoth-
gilead to battle, or shall we forbear? And he
answered him, Go, and prosper: for the LORD
shall deliver *it* into the hand of the king.
16 And the king said unto him, How many times
shall I adjure thee that thou tell me nothing but
that which is true in the name of the LORD?
17 And he said, I saw all Israel scattered upon the
hills, as sheep that have not a shepherd: and the
LORD said, These have no master: let them return
every man to his house in peace.
18 And the king of Israel said unto Jehoshaphat,
Did I not tell thee that he would prophesy no
good concerning me, but evil?
19 And he said, Hear thou therefore the word of
the LORD: I saw the LORD sitting on his throne,
and all the host of heaven standing by him on his
right hand and on his left.
20 And the LORD said, Who shall persuade Ahab,
that he may go up and fall at Ramoth-gilead? And
one said on this manner, and another said on that
manner.
21 And there came forth a spirit, and stood before
the LORD, and said, I will persuade him.
22 And the LORD said unto him, Wherewith? And
he said, I will go forth, and I will be a lying spirit
in the mouth of all his prophets. And he said,
Thou shalt persuade *him*, and prevail also: go
forth, and do so.
23 Now therefore, behold, the LORD hath put a
lying spirit in the mouth of all these thy prophets,
and the LORD hath spoken evil concerning thee.
24 But Zedekiah the son of Chenaanah went near,
and smote Micaiah on the cheek, and said, Which
way went the Spirit of the LORD from me to speak
unto thee?
25 And Micaiah said, Behold, thou shalt see
in that day, when thou shalt go into an inner
chamber to hide thyself.
26 And the king of Israel said, Take Micaiah, and
carry him back unto Amon the governor of the
city, and to Joash the king's son;
27 And say, Thus saith the king, Put this *fellow* in
the prison, and feed him with bread of affliction
and with water of affliction, until I come in peace.
28 And Micaiah said, If thou return at all in
peace, the LORD hath not spoken by me. And he
said, Hearken, O people, every one of you.
29 So the king of Israel and Jehoshaphat the king
of Judah went up to Ramoth-gilead.
30 And the king of Israel said unto Jehoshaphat,
I will disguise myself, and enter into the battle;
but put thou on thy robes. And the king of Israel
disguised himself, and went into the battle.
31 But the king of Syria commanded his thirty
and two captains that had rule over his chariots,
saying, Fight neither with small nor great, save
only with the king of Israel.
32 And it came to pass, when the captains of the
chariots saw Jehoshaphat, that they said, Surely it
is the king of Israel. And they turned aside to fight
against him: and Jehoshaphat cried out.
33 And it came to pass, when the captains of
the chariots perceived that it *was* not the king of
Israel, that they turned back from pursuing him.
34 And a *certain* man drew a bow at a venture, and
smote the king of Israel between the joints of the
harness: wherefore he said unto the driver of his
chariot, Turn thine hand, and carry me out of the
host; for I am wounded.
35 And the battle increased that day: and the king
was stayed up in his chariot against the Syrians,
and died at even: and the blood ran out of the
wound into the midst of the chariot.
36 And there went a proclamation throughout
the host about the going down of the sun, saying,
Every man to his city, and every man to his own
country.
37 ¶ So the king died, and was brought to Sa-
maria; and they buried the king in Samaria.
38 And *one* washed the chariot in the pool of
Samaria; and the dogs licked up his blood; and
they washed his armour; according unto the word
of the LORD which he spake.
39 Now the rest of the acts of Ahab, and all that

22:15–16 *Go, and prosper.* Probably said in a mocking, sarcastic tone that Ahab easily discerned. *adjure.* To swear or urgently beg.

22:17 *as sheep that have not a shepherd.* The imagery of shepherdless sheep is graphically clear. In the Ancient Near East kings were often designated as shepherds (see note at 2 Sam. 5:2).

22:19 *I saw the LORD sitting on his throne.* Though men may sit on thrones (v. 10), the Lord is the true King (Isa. 6:1). *host of heaven.* Army of heaven, here referring to angels.

22:22 *I will be a lying spirit in the mouth of all his prophets.* Whether this is a demon of Satan (Job 1:6) or a personification of the spirit of false prophecy (Zech. 13:2; 1 John 4:6), the point is that God can use even false prophets to accomplish His purpose (Deut. 13:1–3; Ezek. 14:9; 2 Thess. 2:11).

22:23 *evil.* Calamity, referring to the sentence of judgment.

22:27 *bread of affliction.* Refers to a meager ration.

22:28 Fulfilled predictions were evidence of a true prophet (Deut. 18:20–22). Micaiah stakes his prophetic reputation on the certainty of Ahab's death.

22:34 *at a venture.* At random. The Hebrew has the idea of doing it in innocence or simplicity. *joints of the harness.* The scales of the body armor.

22:37 *was brought to Samaria.* They transported the dead body of Ahab to Samaria for burial.

22:38 *they washed.* More properly translated, "the harlots washed." This pool was the place where the temple prostitutes would wash themselves. Ironically, Ahab introduced temple

he did, and the ivory house which he made, and
all the cities that he built, *are* they not written in
the book of the chronicles of the kings of Israel?
40 So Ahab slept with his fathers; and Ahaziah his
son reigned in his stead.
41 ¶ And Jehoshaphat the son of Asa began to
reign over Judah in the fourth year of Ahab king
of Israel.
42 Jehoshaphat *was* thirty and five years old when
he began to reign; and he reigned twenty and five
years in Jerusalem. And his mother's name *was*
Azubah the daughter of Shilhi.
43 And he walked in all the ways of Asa his fa-
ther; he turned not aside from it, doing *that which*
was right in the eyes of the LORD: nevertheless the
high places were not taken away; *for* the people
offered and burnt incense yet in the high places.
44 And Jehoshaphat made peace with the king of
Israel.
45 Now the rest of the acts of Jehoshaphat, and
his might that he shewed, and how he warred, *are*
they not written in the book of the chronicles of
the kings of Judah?
46 And the remnant of the sodomites, which
remained in the days of his father Asa, he took
out of the land.
47 *There was* then no king in Edom: a deputy *was*
king.
48 Jehoshaphat made ships of Tharshish to go to
Ophir for gold: but they went not; for the ships
were broken at Ezion-geber.
49 Then said Ahaziah the son of Ahab unto Je-
hoshaphat, Let my servants go with thy servants
in the ships. But Jehoshaphat would not.
50 ¶ And Jehoshaphat slept with his fathers, and
was buried with his fathers in the city of David his
father: and Jehoram his son reigned in his stead.
51 ¶ Ahaziah the son of Ahab began to reign
over Israel in Samaria the seventeenth year of Je-
hoshaphat king of Judah, and reigned two years
over Israel.
52 And he did evil in the sight of the LORD, and
walked in the way of his father, and in the way of
his mother, and in the way of Jeroboam the son of
Nebat, who made Israel to sin:
53 For he served Baal, and worshipped him,
and provoked to anger the LORD God of Israel,
according to all that his father had done.

prostitution in Israel, and in death his sins followed him.

22:39 *chronicles.* Uninspired records of royal careers that have not been preserved (v. 45).

22:46 *sodomites.* See note at 14:24.

22:47 *deputy.* Overseer.

22:48–49 *made ships of Tharshish.* Like his forefather, Solomon (9:26,28; 10:22). The whole project failed because the ships were *broken* by the Lord, perhaps by a storm (Ps. 48:7), while still lying in harbor because they were intended for a joint venture with the *son of Ahab* (2 Chron. 20:36–37). *Jehoshaphat would not.* He had learned his lesson not to collaborate with the wicked in such an endeavor.

Thoughts for Personal/Family Worship: Chapter 22

1. **"And a certain man drew a bow at a venture" (v. 34). This is a simple yet profound illustration of the unfailing providence of God. Ahab was sentenced to death in the battle, and he did his best to hide from that judgment by disguising himself. An unnamed soldier shot his arrow, apparently aiming at nothing in particular, but God guided the flight of that arrow to the precise point it needed to go. We can learn from this that there is no escape from judgment by disguise, flight, or hiding (Amos 5:19). Instead of hiding ourselves and trying to escape, it is eternally better to surrender to Him whose eyes are a flame of fire (Rev. 1:14). Christ is the sovereign King over all mankind, even over kings (Matt. 28:18; Rev. 1:5). In what specific ways are you to honor Him with the power or authority He has given you?**
2. **"Jehoshaphat made peace with the king of Israel" (v. 44). This was an unlikely alliance between the worst of Israel's kings and a king of Judah who received the epitaph that he did "right in the eyes of the LORD" (v. 43), except for failing to remove the high places and for making peace with Ahab. God mercifully spared him from being killed in battle (vv. 32–33), but his own foolishness put him in danger. Second Chronicles 20:35–37 also records God's rebuke to Jehoshaphat for entering a commercial relationship with Ahab's son, who did wickedly. Paul warns that believers are not to be unequally yoked with unbelievers because light has nothing in common with darkness (2 Cor. 6:14–15).**

I HAVE HEARD

Thy

PRAYER

I HAVE SEEN

Thy Tears

BEHOLD

I WILL

Heal

THEE

2 KINGS 20:5

INTRODUCTION TO THE BOOK OF
2 KINGS

Authorship, Date, Theme, Purpose, and Synopsis:

First and Second Kings are one book, and therefore these matters are discussed just before 1 Kings in the Introduction to 1 and 2 Kings.

Outline: For the full outline and lists of the kings of Judah and Israel, see the Introduction to 1 and 2 Kings.

- I. The Development and Decline of the Kingdom under Solomon (1 Kings 1:1—11:43)
  - A. Solomon's Coronation and Consolidation of the Kingdom (1 Kings 1:1—4:34)
  - B. Solomon's Construction of the Temple by God's Covenant (1 Kings 5:1—9:9)
  - C. Solomon's Wisdom and Wealth from the Lord (1 Kings 9:10—10:29)
  - D. Solomon's Breaking the Covenant (1 Kings 11:1–43)
- II. The Disruption and Division of the Kingdom (1 Kings 12:1–16:28)
  - A. The Splitting of the Kingdom (1 Kings 12:1–24)
  - B. The Apostasy of Israel and Discipline of Judah (1 Kings 12:25—14:31)
  - C. Two Kingdoms in Conflict (1 Kings 15:1—16:28)
- III. The Dispute of Elijah and Elisha for the Lord (1 Kings 16:29—2 Kings 13:25)
  - A. The Ministry of Elijah against Ahab's House (1 Kings 16:29—2 Kings 1:18)
  - B. The Glorification of Elijah and Empowerment of Elisha (2 Kings 2:1–25)
  - C. The Ministry of Elisha against Ahab's House (2 Kings 3:1—10:36)
  - D. The Deliverance of the Line of David in Judah (2 Kings 11:1—12:21)
  - E. God's Patient Mercies toward Israel (2 Kings 13:1–25)
- IV. The Dispersion of the Kingdom (2 Kings 14:1—25:30)
  - A. The Downward Spiral of Israel and Judah (2 Kings 14:1—16:20)
  - B. The Destruction of Israel by Assyria (2 Kings 17:1–41)
  - C. The Spiritual Revival of Judah under Hezekiah (2 Kings 18:1—20:21)
  - D. The Spiritual Ruin of Judah by Manasseh and Amon (2 Kings 21:1–26)
  - E. Another Revival of Judah under Josiah (2 Kings 22:1—23:30)
  - F. The End of the Kingdom of Judah (2 Kings 23:31—25:30)

THE SECOND BOOK OF

KINGS

CHAPTER 1

THEN Moab rebelled against Israel after the death
of Ahab.
2 And Ahaziah fell down through a lattice in his
upper chamber that *was* in Samaria, and was sick:
and he sent messengers, and said unto them, Go,
enquire of Baal-zebub the god of Ekron whether I
shall recover of this disease.
3 But the angel of the LORD said to Elijah the
Tishbite, Arise, go up to meet the messengers of
the king of Samaria, and say unto them, *Is it* not
because *there is* not a God in Israel, *that* ye go to
enquire of Baal-zebub the god of Ekron?
4 Now therefore thus saith the LORD, Thou shalt
not come down from that bed on which thou art
gone up, but shalt surely die. And Elijah departed.
5 ¶ And when the messengers turned back unto
him, he said unto them, Why are ye now turned
back?
6 And they said unto him, There came a man up
to meet us, and said unto us, Go, turn again unto
the king that sent you, and say unto him, Thus
saith the LORD, *Is it* not because *there is* not a God
in Israel, *that* thou sendest to enquire of Baal-
zebub the god of Ekron? therefore thou shalt not
come down from that bed on which thou art gone
up, but shalt surely die.
7 And he said unto them, What manner of man
was he which came up to meet you, and told you
these words?
8 And they answered him, *He was* an hairy man,
and girt with a girdle of leather about his loins.
And he said, It *is* Elijah the Tishbite.
9 Then the king sent unto him a captain of fifty
with his fifty. And he went up to him: and, be-
hold, he sat on the top of an hill. And he spake
unto him, Thou man of God, the king hath said,
Come down.
10 And Elijah answered and said to the captain
of fifty, If I *be* a man of God, then let fire come
down from heaven, and consume thee and thy
fifty. And there came down fire from heaven, and
consumed him and his fifty.
11 Again also he sent unto him another captain
of fifty with his fifty. And he answered and said
unto him, O man of God, thus hath the king said,
Come down quickly.
12 And Elijah answered and said unto them, If I
be a man of God, let fire come down from heaven,
and consume thee and thy fifty. And the fire of
God came down from heaven, and consumed
him and his fifty.
13 ¶ And he sent again a captain of the third fifty
with his fifty. And the third captain of fifty went
up, and came and fell on his knees before Elijah,
and besought him, and said unto him, O man of
God, I pray thee, let my life, and the life of these
fifty thy servants, be precious in thy sight.
14 Behold, there came fire down from heaven,
and burnt up the two captains of the former fif-
ties with their fifties: therefore let my life now be
precious in thy sight.
15 And the angel of the LORD said unto Elijah,
Go down with him: be not afraid of him. And he
arose, and went down with him unto the king.
16 And he said unto him, Thus saith the LORD,

THE DISPUTE OF ELIJAH AND ELISHA FOR THE LORD (1 KINGS 16:29—2 KINGS 13:25)

The Ministry of Elijah against Ahab's House (1 Kings 16:29—2 Kings 1:18)

Chapter 1: *Elijah finishes his ministry by announcing the certain death of Ahaziah, Ahab's son.*

1:1 *Moab rebelled against Israel*. The Moabite Stone or Mesha inscription notes this rebellion (see note at 1 Kings 16:23).

1:2 *lattice*. Ornamental grating or railing. *Baal-zebub*. Literally, "the lord of flies," a contemptuous alteration of the Canaanite title Baal-zebul, meaning "the lord prince" (see note at 1 Kings 16:32). In New Testament times this became a designation for the Devil (Matt. 12:24; Mark 3:22).

1:8 *hairy man*. Literally, "a baal (owner) of hairiness." *girt with a girdle*. Waistcoat of skin or leather was wrapped around his hips.

1:9 *man of God*. Prophet.

1:10 *let fire come down*. Ironically, Elijah's call for fire, perhaps lightning, demonstrates *Jehovah*'s superiority over Baal (see note at 1 Kings 18:38).

1:15 *the angel of the LORD*. An expression that usually refers to a Christophany, a pre-incarnate appearance of the second person of the Trinity, the messenger who is *Jehovah* (Gen. 16:7;

Forasmuch as thou hast sent messengers to
enquire of Baal-zebub the god of Ekron, *is it* not
because *there is* no God in Israel to enquire of
his word? therefore thou shalt not come down
off that bed on which thou art gone up, but shalt
surely die.
17 ¶ So he died according to the word of the LORD
which Elijah had spoken. And Jehoram reigned in
his stead in the second year of Jehoram the son
of Jehoshaphat king of Judah; because he had no
son.
18 Now the rest of the acts of Ahaziah which he
did, *are* they not written in the book of the chron-
icles of the kings of Israel?

CHAPTER 2

AND it came to pass, when the LORD would take
up Elijah into heaven by a whirlwind, that Elijah
went with Elisha from Gilgal.
2 And Elijah said unto Elisha, Tarry here, I pray
thee; for the LORD hath sent me to Beth-el. And
Elisha said *unto him, As* the LORD liveth, and *as*
thy soul liveth, I will not leave thee. So they went
down to Beth-el.
3 And the sons of the prophets that *were* at
Beth-el came forth to Elisha, and said unto him,
Knowest thou that the LORD will take away thy
master from thy head to day? And he said, Yea, I
know *it*; hold ye your peace.
4 And Elijah said unto him, Elisha, tarry here, I
pray thee; for the LORD hath sent me to Jericho.
And he said, *As* the LORD liveth, and *as* thy soul
liveth, I will not leave thee. So they came to Jericho.
5 And the sons of the prophets that *were* at Jericho
came to Elisha, and said unto him, Knowest thou
that the LORD will take away thy master from thy
head to day? And he answered, Yea, I know *it*; hold
ye your peace.
6 And Elijah said unto him, Tarry, I pray thee,
here; for the LORD hath sent me to Jordan. And
he said, *As* the LORD liveth, and *as* thy soul liveth, I
will not leave thee. And they two went on.
7 And fifty men of the sons of the prophets went,
and stood to view afar off: and they two stood by
Jordan.
8 And Elijah took his mantle, and wrapped *it*
together, and smote the waters, and they were
divided hither and thither, so that they two went
over on dry ground.
9 ¶ And it came to pass, when they were gone
over, that Elijah said unto Elisha, Ask what I shall
do for thee, before I be taken away from thee. And
Elisha said, I pray thee, let a double portion of thy
spirit be upon me.
10 And he said, Thou hast asked a hard thing:
nevertheless, if thou see me *when I am* taken from
thee, it shall be so unto thee; but if not, it shall
not be *so*.
11 And it came to pass, as they still went on, and
talked, that, behold, *there appeared* a chariot of
fire, and horses of fire, and parted them both

Ex. 3:2; 23:20–23).

1:17 *Jehoram*. Ahaziah's brother, another son of Ahab (3:1).

1:18 *chronicles*. An uninspired record of the king's career that has not been preserved.

Thoughts for Personal/Family Worship: Chapter 1

1. **Calling down fire from heaven was an unmistakable sign of divine power. But even beyond the immediate consequence, it was another demonstration of Jehovah's superiority over Baal. We know from Canaanite literature that fire, and particularly lightning, was considered to be Baal's domain. One common image of Baal depicts him as holding a bolt of lightning as his scepter. Ironically, those going to seek Baal met the real God, who controlled every force of nature as the Creator. They were seeking help in the wrong place. It is only in the one true and living God that we can find the help we need, regardless of the need. We should never follow the ways of the world and its perceived notions. Our dependence is on the Lord.**
2. **The Lord will punish with fire those who seek to destroy His servants. This is not a justification for taking personal vengeance, nor a promise of immediate judgment on the wicked—now is the time of enduring affliction for the sake of the gospel (Luke 9:54–56). However, the time will come when the fire will fall, and those who have conspired to destroy the church will face the wrath of Christ (Rev. 20:9). How can this give hope to persecuted believers?**

Chapter 2: *Elijah ascends into heaven, and Elisha begins his ministry.*

The Glorification of Elijah and Empowerment of Elisha (2 Kings 2:1–25)

2:1 *whirlwind*. Gale or windstorm. Canaanite references to Baal depict him as riding the clouds. So, even in leaving this world Elijah demonstrates God's control over what was perceived to be Baal's domain.

2:3 *the sons of the prophets*. Those who occupied the prophetic office, not prophets-in-training (1 Kings 20:35). The Hebrew uses the word "son" to refer to a category or class of something.

2:3 *from thy head*. Elijah served as Elisha's mentor and held the predominant place.

2:8 *mantle*. Robe (v. 13). *waters . . . were divided*. Repetition of Joshua's crossing of the Jordan to lead Israel into the inheritance of Canaan (Josh. 3:15–17) and reminder of the salvation of Israel from the forces of Egypt at the Red Sea (Ex. 14:1–31). Even centuries later Israel could trust that their Redeemer remained the same.

2:9 *double portion*. Literally, "mouth of two," an idiom for two parts. Elisha recognized that without divine aid he could not conduct the ministry before him.

2:10–11 *taken from thee*. Same word used of God's taking Enoch to heaven (Gen. 5:24; cf. Heb. 11:5) and the psalmist's hope for God's receiving him into heavenly glory (Ps. 73:24). *chariot of fire*. Elijah was physically taken up into heaven by a heavenly chariot (2 Kings 6:17), evidence of the Old Testament hope of heaven. He and Enoch are the only two

asunder; and Elijah went up by a whirlwind into
heaven.
12 ¶ And Elisha saw *it*, and he cried, My father,
my father, the chariot of Israel, and the horse-
men thereof. And he saw him no more: and he
took hold of his own clothes, and rent them in
two pieces.
13 He took up also the mantle of Elijah that fell
from him, and went back, and stood by the bank
of Jordan;
14 And he took the mantle of Elijah that fell from
him, and smote the waters, and said, Where *is* the
LORD God of Elijah? and when he also had smit-
ten the waters, they parted hither and thither: and
Elisha went over.
15 And when the sons of the prophets which *were*
to view at Jericho saw him, they said, The spirit
of Elijah doth rest on Elisha. And they came to
meet him, and bowed themselves to the ground
before him.
16 ¶ And they said unto him, Behold now, there
be with thy servants fifty strong men; let them go,
we pray thee, and seek thy master: lest peradven-
ture the Spirit of the LORD hath taken him up,
and cast him upon some mountain, or into some
valley. And he said, Ye shall not send.
17 And when they urged him till he was ashamed,
he said, Send. They sent therefore fifty men; and
they sought three days, but found him not.
18 And when they came again to him, (for he
tarried at Jericho,) he said unto them, Did I not
say unto you, Go not?
19 ¶ And the men of the city said unto Elisha,
Behold, I pray thee, the situation of this city *is*
pleasant, as my lord seeth: but the water *is* naught,
and the ground barren.
20 And he said, Bring me a new cruse, and put
salt therein. And they brought *it* to him.
21 And he went forth unto the spring of the
waters, and cast the salt in there, and said, Thus
saith the LORD, I have healed these waters; there
shall not be from thence any more death or
barren *land*.
22 So the waters were healed unto this day, ac-
cording to the saying of Elisha which he spake.
23 ¶ And he went up from thence unto Beth-el:
and as he was going up by the way, there came
forth little children out of the city, and mocked
him, and said unto him, Go up, thou bald head;
go up, thou bald head.
24 And he turned back, and looked on them, and
cursed them in the name of the LORD. And there
came forth two she bears out of the wood, and
tare forty and two children of them.
25 And he went from thence to mount Carmel,
and from thence he returned to Samaria.

CHAPTER 3

NOW Jehoram the son of Ahab began to reign over
Israel in Samaria the eighteenth year of Jehosha-
phat king of Judah, and reigned twelve years.
2 And he wrought evil in the sight of the LORD;
but not like his father, and like his mother: for
he put away the image of Baal that his father had
made.

---

men mentioned in Scripture who ascended to heaven without seeing death. Heaven is a real place, where even people in physical bodies can exist.

2:12 *chariot of Israel, and the horsemen thereof.* Elijah symbolized the real strength of Israel, as his prayers and doctrine were more powerful than all its horses and chariots.

2:15 *bowed themselves.* A gesture of respect, not worship.

2:16 *peradventure.* Perhaps.

2:19 *the situation . . . is pleasant.* The location is good. *naught.* Bad. *the ground barren.* Literally, "the land is causing miscarriage," an idiom describing its failure to produce crops.

2:20 *cruse.* Bottle or jar.

2:23 *Beth-el.* Literally, "house of God," but referred to as Beth-aven, literally, "house of wickedness" (Hos. 4:15; 10:5). *little children.* The reference is not age specific but probably points to teens or young adults who were products of their environment, showing no respect for God or His prophet. *go up.* Perhaps a wish that he would leave the earth as his master had—an implicit threat (same verb as in 2 Kings 2:1,11). To mock the messenger is to mock the message along with the One who sent the messenger.

2:24 *cursed them.* Not from personal vindictiveness but because God's honor was at stake.

Thoughts for Personal/Family Worship: Chapter 2

1. **Elijah's ascent to heaven without dying was a final act of humiliating Baal and glorifying *Jehovah*, since Baal was the rider of clouds who supposedly had power over death. This is one of the principal passages in the Old Testament dealing with life after death, showing that the Old Testament saints had essentially the same hope as the New Testament saints. Absence from the body is presence with the Lord (2 Cor. 5:8). God will take all who are His into His very presence.**
2. **The ascension of Elijah foreshadowed the ascension of Jesus Christ, who also physically went up into heaven attended by angels (Acts 1:9–11). His mantle of spiritual power has fallen upon the church, filled with the Spirit of Christ to continue His mission (2:1–47). Christ will return, calling His people up to meet Him in the sky so that they will be with the Lord forever (1 Thess. 4:13–18).**
3. **In all likelihood the young people who mocked the prophet echoed what they had learned at home. Beth-el had earned the name Beth-aven, as God had been replaced with wickedness. Exposing children to vicious criticism of God's servants can have devastating effects. Christian parents should raise their children in the fear of the Lord, teaching them to honor God and those who preach the Word.**

The Ministry of Elisha against Ahab's House (2 Kings 3:1—10:36)

Chapter 3: ***With the help of God, a coalition among Israel, Judah, and Edom put down the Moabite rebellion.***

3:2 *the image of Baal that his father had made.* See 1 Kings 16:32.

3 Nevertheless he cleaved unto the sins of Jer-
oboam the son of Nebat, which made Israel to sin;
he departed not therefrom.
4 ¶ And Mesha king of Moab was a sheepmaster,
and rendered unto the king of Israel an hundred
thousand lambs, and an hundred thousand rams,
with the wool.
5 But it came to pass, when Ahab was dead, that
the king of Moab rebelled against the king of
Israel.
6 ¶ And king Jehoram went out of Samaria the
same time, and numbered all Israel.
7 And he went and sent to Jehoshaphat the king
of Judah, saying, The king of Moab hath rebelled
against me: wilt thou go with me against Moab
to battle? And he said, I will go up: I *am* as thou
art, my people as thy people, *and* my horses as thy
horses.
8 And he said, Which way shall we go up? And
he answered, The way through the wilderness of
Edom.
9 So the king of Israel went, and the king of
Judah, and the king of Edom: and they fetched a
compass of seven days' journey: and there was no
water for the host, and for the cattle that followed
them.
10 And the king of Israel said, Alas! that the LORD
hath called these three kings together, to deliver
them into the hand of Moab!
11 But Jehoshaphat said, *Is there* not here a
prophet of the LORD, that we may enquire of the
LORD by him? And one of the king of Israel's ser-
vants answered and said, Here *is* Elisha the son
of Shaphat, which poured water on the hands of
Elijah.
12 And Jehoshaphat said, The word of the LORD
is with him. So the king of Israel and Jehoshaphat
and the king of Edom went down to him.
13 And Elisha said unto the king of Israel, What
have I to do with thee? get thee to the prophets of
thy father, and to the prophets of thy mother. And
the king of Israel said unto him, Nay: for the LORD
hath called these three kings together, to deliver
them into the hand of Moab.
14 And Elisha said, *As* the LORD of hosts liveth,
before whom I stand, surely, were it not that I
regard the presence of Jehoshaphat the king of
Judah, I would not look toward thee, nor see thee.
15 But now bring me a minstrel. And it came to
pass, when the minstrel played, that the hand of
the LORD came upon him.
16 And he said, Thus saith the LORD, Make this
valley full of ditches.
17 For thus saith the LORD, Ye shall not see wind,
neither shall ye see rain; yet that valley shall be
filled with water, that ye may drink, both ye, and
your cattle, and your beasts.
18 And this is *but* a light thing in the sight of the
LORD: he will deliver the Moabites also into your
hand.
19 And ye shall smite every fenced city, and every
choice city, and shall fell every good tree, and stop
all wells of water, and mar every good piece of
land with stones.
20 And it came to pass in the morning, when
the meat offering was offered, that, behold, there
came water by the way of Edom, and the country
was filled with water.
21 ¶ And when all the Moabites heard that the
kings were come up to fight against them, they
gathered all that were able to put on armour, and
upward, and stood in the border.
22 And they rose up early in the morning, and the
sun shone upon the water, and the Moabites saw
the water on the other side *as* red as blood:
23 And they said, This *is* blood: the kings are
surely slain, and they have smitten one another:
now therefore, Moab, to the spoil.
24 And when they came to the camp of Israel,
the Israelites rose up and smote the Moabites, so
that they fled before them: but they went forward
smiting the Moabites, even in *their* country.

3:3 *cleaved unto the sins of Jeroboam.* Maintained the state religion instituted by Jeroboam (1 Kings 12:28).
3:4 *sheepmaster.* A breeder of sheep, one of the chief industries of Moab. This provided part of the tribute demanded by the house of Omri.
3:5 *Moab rebelled.* Delineates the details of the rebellion mentioned in 1:1.
3:7 Jehoshaphat continued the alliance with Israel that had begun with Ahab.
3:9 *king of Edom.* A governor who ruled over Edom on behalf of the king of Judah (1 Kings 22:47). *fetched a compass.* Literally, "encircled a way," marched around. *host.* Camp, referring to the army.
3:11 *Is there not here a prophet.* Jehoshaphat's question is the same one as when he had fought with Ahab (1 Kings 22:5,7). *poured water on the hands.* A gesture expressing service to someone.
3:13 *What have I to do with thee?* Elisha declares that there was no point of contact with the king of Israel, nothing in common. This should have been Jehoshaphat's attitude as well.
3:14 *regard the presence of Jehoshaphat.* Recognize the legitimacy of the Southern Kingdom, established by the covenant with David (2 Sam. 7). The presence of the son of David brings blessing.
3:15 *minstrel.* Musician (1 Sam. 16:16–18,23). Music was associated with prophetic activity (2 Kings 10:5).
3:16 *Make this valley full of ditches.* Dig cisterns in the wadi or dry river bed.
3:19 *fenced.* Fortified.
3:20 *there came water.* Flashfloods coming from the mountains of Edom filled the valley or river beds, providing abundance of water for the men and their animals.
3:21 *upward.* At a high vantage point.
3:22 *as red as blood.* The rising sun shone on the water, reflecting the red sandstone of Edom, which the Moabites mistook for blood.

25 And they beat down the cities, and on every
good piece of land cast every man his stone, and
filled it; and they stopped all the wells of water,
and felled all the good trees: only in Kir-haraseth
left they the stones thereof; howbeit the slingers
went about *it*, and smote it.
26 ¶ And when the king of Moab saw that the
battle was too sore for him, he took with him
seven hundred men that drew swords, to break
through *even* unto the king of Edom: but they
could not.
27 Then he took his eldest son that should have
reigned in his stead, and offered him *for* a burnt
offering upon the wall. And there was great in-
dignation against Israel: and they departed from
him, and returned to *their own* land.

CHAPTER 4

Now there cried a certain woman of the wives of
the sons of the prophets unto Elisha, saying, Thy
servant my husband is dead; and thou knowest
that thy servant did fear the LORD: and the
creditor is come to take unto him my two sons to
be bondmen.
2 And Elisha said unto her, What shall I do for
thee? tell me, what hast thou in the house? And
she said, Thine handmaid hath not any thing in
the house, save a pot of oil.
3 Then he said, Go, borrow thee vessels abroad
of all thy neighbours, *even* empty vessels; borrow
not a few.
4 And when thou art come in, thou shalt shut
the door upon thee and upon thy sons, and shalt
pour out into all those vessels, and thou shalt set
aside that which is full.
5 So she went from him, and shut the door upon
her and upon her sons, who brought *the vessels* to
her; and she poured out.
6 And it came to pass, when the vessels were full,
that she said unto her son, Bring me yet a vessel.
And he said unto her, *There is* not a vessel more.
And the oil stayed.
7 Then she came and told the man of God. And
he said, Go, sell the oil, and pay thy debt, and live
thou and thy children of the rest.
8 ¶ And it fell on a day, that Elisha passed to Shu-
nem, where *was* a great woman; and she con-
strained him to eat bread. And *so* it was, *that* as oft
as he passed by, he turned in thither to eat bread.
9 And she said unto her husband, Behold now,
I perceive that this *is* an holy man of God, which
passeth by us continually.
10 Let us make a little chamber, I pray thee, on
the wall; and let us set for him there a bed, and a
table, and a stool, and a candlestick: and it shall be,
when he cometh to us, that he shall turn in thither.
11 And it fell on a day, that he came thither, and
he turned into the chamber, and lay there.
12 And he said to Gehazi his servant, Call this
Shunammite. And when he had called her, she
stood before him.
13 And he said unto him, Say now unto her,
Behold, thou hast been careful for us with all this
care; what *is* to be done for thee? wouldest thou
be spoken for to the king, or to the captain of the

3:26 *sore.* Severe.
3:27 *offered him for a burnt offering.* Most likely to Chemosh, the national deity or Baal of Moab. Such was forbidden by God (Lev. 18:21; 20:2; Deut. 18:10). *great indignation against Israel.* The Moabites, stirred by their leader's horrible sacrifice, rallied against Israel and drove them back.

Thoughts for Personal/Family Worship: Chapter 3

1. **Though Jehoshaphat's alliance with Israel was questionable, it was his presence that caused the prophet to seek the Lord on behalf of the coalition. God's children should be a blessing for those around them. There is a principle that the presence of the remnant is a preserving influence. Isaiah said that were it not for the remnant the nation would have been like Sodom (Isa. 1:9). The Lord Jesus expressed this in terms of being salt (Luke 14:34). Salt is a preserving agent, but it is also a source for irritation and aggravation to a sore spot. We are in the world but cannot be of the world or like the world. We should strive to be the kind of influence in society that reflects well on the Lord. Before Jehoshaphat sought the Lord, he too shared in confusion; blessing came when he asked for God's guidance through the Word of the Lord. So it is with us.**
2. **The Lord's instruction to "make this valley full of ditches" (2 Kings 3:16) is suggestive. God was going to do the miraculous in defeating the Moabites, but He wanted the people to prepare for the blessing of deliverance. Digging the ditches beforehand was an expression of their confidence that God would work. The spiritual application is significant: we should make due preparation of our hearts in anticipation of the Lord's blessing. There is a sense in which before every Sabbath worship we should "dig some ditches" in preparation for and anticipation of being filled with all that the Lord has in store for us. God says, "Open thy mouth wide, and I will fill it" (Ps. 81:10).**

Chapter 4: ***Elisha performs miracles on behalf of two women and a group of fellow prophets.***

4:1 *woman of the wives of the sons of the prophets.* Her husband was a prophet. *sons to be bondmen.* This was prohibited by the law, which said that debtors could become indentured servants but could not be enslaved (Lev. 25:39–41).
4:2 *save.* Except.
4:6 *the oil stayed.* Literally, "the oil stood," meaning that it stopped flowing. Oil is sometimes a symbol of the Holy Spirit (1 Sam. 10:1,6; 16:13; Isa. 61:1,3; Zech. 4), and God has an inexhaustible supply of the Spirit to pour out through Christ to meet the needs of His people (John 3:34; 7:37–39; Eph. 3:16–17).
4:7 *man of God.* Prophet (vv. 9,21–22).
4:8 *Shunem.* Sixteen miles southwest of the Sea of Galilee, a central location for someone traveling in Israel.

host? And she answered, I dwell among mine own
people.
14 And he said, What then *is* to be done for her?
And Gehazi answered, Verily she hath no child,
and her husband is old.
15 And he said, Call her. And when he had called
her, she stood in the door.
16 And he said, About this season, according to
the time of life, thou shalt embrace a son. And she
said, Nay, my lord, *thou* man of God, do not lie
unto thine handmaid.
17 And the woman conceived, and bare a son at
that season that Elisha had said unto her, accord-
ing to the time of life.
18 ¶ And when the child was grown, it fell on a
day, that he went out to his father to the reapers.
19 And he said unto his father, My head, my head.
And he said to a lad, Carry him to his mother.
20 And when he had taken him, and brought him
to his mother, he sat on her knees till noon, and
then died.
21 And she went up, and laid him on the bed of
the man of God, and shut *the door* upon him, and
went out.
22 And she called unto her husband, and said,
Send me, I pray thee, one of the young men, and
one of the asses, that I may run to the man of
God, and come again.
23 And he said, Wherefore wilt thou go to him to
day? *it is* neither new moon, nor sabbath. And she
said, *It shall be* well.
24 Then she saddled an ass, and said to her ser-
vant, Drive, and go forward; slack not *thy* riding
for me, except I bid thee.
25 So she went and came unto the man of God
to mount Carmel. And it came to pass, when the
man of God saw her afar off, that he said to Gehazi
his servant, Behold, *yonder is* that Shunammite:
26 Run now, I pray thee, to meet her, and say unto
her, *Is it* well with thee? *is it* well with thy hus-
band? *is it* well with the child? And she answered,
It is well.
27 And when she came to the man of God to the
hill, she caught him by the feet: but Gehazi came
near to thrust her away. And the man of God said,
Let her alone; for her soul *is* vexed within her: and
the LORD hath hid *it* from me, and hath not told
me.
28 Then she said, Did I desire a son of my lord?
did I not say, Do not deceive me?
29 Then he said to Gehazi, Gird up thy loins, and
take my staff in thine hand, and go thy way: if
thou meet any man, salute him not; and if any
salute thee, answer him not again: and lay my staff
upon the face of the child.
30 And the mother of the child said, *As* the LORD
liveth, and *as* thy soul liveth, I will not leave thee.
And he arose, and followed her.
31 And Gehazi passed on before them, and laid
the staff upon the face of the child; but *there was*
neither voice, nor hearing. Wherefore he went
again to meet him, and told him, saying, The
child is not awaked.
32 And when Elisha was come into the house,
behold, the child was dead, *and* laid upon his bed.
33 He went in therefore, and shut the door upon
them twain, and prayed unto the LORD.
34 And he went up, and lay upon the child, and
put his mouth upon his mouth, and his eyes upon
his eyes, and his hands upon his hands: and he
stretched himself upon the child; and the flesh of
the child waxed warm.
35 Then he returned, and walked in the house to
and fro; and went up, and stretched himself upon
him: and the child sneezed seven times, and the
child opened his eyes.
36 And he called Gehazi, and said, Call this Shu-
nammite. So he called her. And when she was
come in unto him, he said, Take up thy son.
37 Then she went in, and fell at his feet, and
bowed herself to the ground, and took up her son,
and went out.
38 ¶ And Elisha came again to Gilgal: and *there
was* a dearth in the land; and the sons of the
prophets *were* sitting before him: and he said
unto his servant, Set on the great pot, and seethe

4:8 *great woman.* She was great in wealth, and reputation.
4:13 *careful . . . this care.* Literally, "you have trembled with all this trembling," expressing that she had gone to a lot of trouble and shown him great respect. *I dwell among mine own people.* An expression of contentment.
4:17 *bare a son.* The Lord often showed special mercy on barren women, such as Rebekah (Gen. 25:21), Hannah (1 Sam. 1:1–28), and the wife of Manoah (Judg. 13:1–25).
4:18 *fell on a day.* Happened one day.
4:23 *neither new moon, nor sabbath.* Expressing doubt that the prophet could be found, since it was not a religious day.
4:24 *slack not thy riding.* Do not check your riding; do not slow down on my account.
4:26 *It is well.* Showing astonishing submission in the midst of great need.
4:27 *caught him by the feet.* Detained him from a sense of urgency and need. *vexed.* Troubled.
4:29 *Gird up thy loins.* Put a belt around your waist to get ready for action. *staff.* A symbol of God's power; the Lord had worked many miracles through the staff of Moses (Ex. 4:2–4, 17,20; 7:1—10:29; 14:16; 17:5,9; Num. 20:8–11). *salute.* To bless, a term of greeting.
4:33 *them twain.* The two of them.
4:34 *lay upon the child.* As did Elijah in a similar case (1 Kings 17:21). Corpses were unclean, and touching one would have excluded a person from public worship (Num. 19:11–13). *waxed.* Became. The connection of mouth, eyes, and hands suggests a union or bond, as if the prophet shared his breath, sight, and strength with the child. This is a shadow of union with Christ in His resurrection power (Eph. 2:5–6).
4:35 *to and fro.* Back and forth.
4:38 *dearth.* Famine. *seethe pottage.* Boil food, like lentil soup.

pottage for the sons of the prophets.
39 And one went out into the field to gather herbs,
and found a wild vine, and gathered thereof wild
gourds his lap full, and came and shred *them* into
the pot of pottage: for they knew *them* not.
40 So they poured out for the men to eat. And it
came to pass, as they were eating of the pottage,
that they cried out, and said, O *thou* man of God,
there is death in the pot. And they could not eat
thereof.
41 But he said, Then bring meal. And he cast *it*
into the pot; and he said, Pour out for the people,
that they may eat. And there was no harm in the
pot.
42 ¶ And there came a man from Baal-shalisha,
and brought the man of God bread of the first-
fruits, twenty loaves of barley, and full ears of
corn in the husk thereof. And he said, Give unto
the people, that they may eat.
43 And his servitor said, What, should I set this
before an hundred men? He said again, Give the
people, that they may eat: for thus saith the LORD,
They shall eat, and shall leave *thereof*.
44 So he set *it* before them, and they did eat, and
left *thereof*, according to the word of the LORD.

CHAPTER 5

NOW Naaman, captain of the host of the king
of Syria, was a great man with his master, and
honourable, because by him the LORD had given
deliverance unto Syria: he was also a mighty man
in valour, *but he was* a leper.
2 And the Syrians had gone out by companies,
and had brought away captive out of the land of
Israel a little maid; and she waited on Naaman's
wife.
3 And she said unto her mistress, Would God my
lord *were* with the prophet that *is* in Samaria! for
he would recover him of his leprosy.
4 And *one* went in, and told his lord, saying, Thus
and thus said the maid that *is* of the land of Israel.
5 And the king of Syria said, Go to, go, and I will
send a letter unto the king of Israel. And he de-
parted, and took with him ten talents of silver,
and six thousand *pieces* of gold, and ten changes
of raiment.
6 And he brought the letter to the king of Israel,
saying, Now when this letter is come unto thee,
behold, I have *therewith* sent Naaman my ser-
vant to thee, that thou mayest recover him of his
leprosy.
7 And it came to pass, when the king of Israel had
read the letter, that he rent his clothes, and said,
Am I God, to kill and to make alive, that this man
doth send unto me to recover a man of his lep-
rosy? wherefore consider, I pray you, and see how
he seeketh a quarrel against me.
8 ¶ And it was *so*, when Elisha the man of God
had heard that the king of Israel had rent his

4:40 *death*. A figure of speech where the effect stands for the cause: there was something poisonous in the pot, causing death.
4:41 *meal*. Flour.
4:43 *servitor*. Attendant or waiter.
4:44 *did eat, and left thereof, according to the word of the LORD*. The Word of God has power to supply all our needs (Deut. 8:3). Christ also fed many with just a little food, and there were leftovers, showing that He is the all-sufficient Bread of Life (John 6:1–14,35).

Thoughts for Personal/Family Worship: Chapter 4

1. **In His providence God takes His people through hard times, but always ultimately for their good. The widow suffered bereavement, debt, and potential bondage, but the Lord had not forsaken her. He had brought her to this low position to make her like the empty vessels in her home so that He could fill her with His grace. Similarly, the Lord uses trials to empty His children of their self-sufficiency so that He can lovingly fill them with His Spirit. How has God been doing this for you through your afflictions?**
2. **God is no man's debtor. The Lord Jesus said, "But seek ye first the kingdom of God, and his righteousness; and all these things shall be added unto you" (Matt. 6:33). The widow had been the wife of a preacher, and after his death God was more than a husband to her, meeting all her financial needs. For her part, the Shunammite went out of her way to provide for the prophet, and God repaid her kindness with a son. The prophets were servants of the Lord, and He provided their food even during the famine. In one way or another God takes care of His own.**
3. **Elisha's strange method of raising the boy from the dead is a wonderful picture of the saving work of Jesus Christ. Christ embraced His people when they were spiritual corpses, taking the uncleanness of their sins upon Himself and so closely uniting them to Himself that when He rose they too rose from the dead. Look to Christ, and He will be your life, your sight, and your strength each day.**

Chapter 5: *Elisha prescribes the way for Naaman to be healed of his leprosy.*

5:1 *captain of the host*. Chief leader over the Syrian army. *The LORD had given deliverance*. The God of Israel gave Syria victory, a testimony to God's sovereignty and providence even over those who do not recognize Him as God. *leper*. Having a skin disease that in Israel would have excluded him from God's holy presence (Lev. 13:45–46; Num. 5:1–3). Leprosy was sometimes a sign of God's judgment (Num. 12:9–16; Deut. 24:8–9; 2 Sam. 3:29; 2 Kings 15:5; 2 Chron. 26:19–23).
5:2 *companies*. Marauding bands or raiders.
5:3 *Would*. Hebrew, "I wish," or "If only," an expression of desire.
5:5 *talents*. About 66 pounds (v. 22). *Ten talents of silver* is an enormous amount of money; King Omri had paid only two talents for the hill of Samaria (1 Kings 16:24).
5:7 *rent his clothes*. Gesture expressing grief or sorrow, here also anxiety. *seeketh a quarrel against me*. Literally, "is seeking an occasion or opportunity against me."
5:8 *man of God*. Prophet (vv. 15,20).

clothes, that he sent to the king, saying, Where-
fore hast thou rent thy clothes? let him come now
to me, and he shall know that there is a prophet
in Israel.
9 So Naaman came with his horses and with his
chariot, and stood at the door of the house of
Elisha.
10 And Elisha sent a messenger unto him, saying,
Go and wash in Jordan seven times, and thy flesh
shall come again to thee, and thou shalt be clean.
11 But Naaman was wroth, and went away, and
said, Behold, I thought, He will surely come out to
me, and stand, and call on the name of the LORD
his God, and strike his hand over the place, and
recover the leper.
12 *Are* not Abana and Pharpar, rivers of Damas-
cus, better than all the waters of Israel? may I not
wash in them, and be clean? So he turned and
went away in a rage.
13 And his servants came near, and spake unto
him, and said, My father, *if* the prophet had bid
thee *do some* great thing, wouldest thou not have
done *it*? how much rather then, when he saith to
thee, Wash, and be clean?
14 Then went he down, and dipped himself seven
times in Jordan, according to the saying of the
man of God: and his flesh came again like unto
the flesh of a little child, and he was clean.
15 ¶ And he returned to the man of God, he and
all his company, and came, and stood before him:
and he said, Behold, now I know that *there is* no
God in all the earth, but in Israel: now therefore, I
pray thee, take a blessing of thy servant.
16 But he said, *As* the LORD liveth, before whom
I stand, I will receive none. And he urged him to
take *it*; but he refused.
17 And Naaman said, Shall there not then, I pray
thee, be given to thy servant two mules' burden of
earth? for thy servant will henceforth offer neither
burnt offering nor sacrifice unto other gods, but
unto the LORD.
18 In this thing the LORD pardon thy servant, *that*
when my master goeth into the house of Rimmon
to worship there, and he leaneth on my hand, and
I bow myself in the house of Rimmon: when I
bow down myself in the house of Rimmon, the
LORD pardon thy servant in this thing.
19 And he said unto him, Go in peace. So he de-
parted from him a little way.
20 ¶ But Gehazi, the servant of Elisha the man of
God, said, Behold, my master hath spared Naa-
man this Syrian, in not receiving at his hands that
which he brought: but, *as* the LORD liveth, I will
run after him, and take somewhat of him.
21 So Gehazi followed after Naaman. And when
Naaman saw *him* running after him, he lighted
down from the chariot to meet him, and said, *Is*
all well?
22 And he said, All *is* well. My master hath sent
me, saying, Behold, even now there be come to
me from mount Ephraim two young men of the
sons of the prophets: give them, I pray thee, a
talent of silver, and two changes of garments.
23 And Naaman said, Be content, take two talents.
And he urged him, and bound two talents of
silver in two bags, with two changes of garments,
and laid *them* upon two of his servants; and they
bare *them* before him.
24 And when he came to the tower, he took *them*
from their hand, and bestowed *them* in the house:
and he let the men go, and they departed.
25 But he went in, and stood before his mas-
ter. And Elisha said unto him, Whence *comest*
thou, Gehazi? And he said, Thy servant went no
whither.
26 And he said unto him, Went not mine heart
with thee, when the man turned again from his
chariot to meet thee? *Is it* a time to receive money,
and to receive garments, and oliveyards, and
vineyards, and sheep, and oxen, and menservants,
and maidservants?
27 The leprosy therefore of Naaman shall cleave

5:11 *wroth.* Furious. *strike.* Wave.
5:14 *little child.* Same phrase used of the "little maid" from Israel who had told Naaman of Elisha (2 Kings 5). A picture of conversion: proud Naaman had become a new, humble, childlike, clean man (Matt. 18:3; Titus 3:5–7).
5:15 *blessing.* Gift.
5:16 *I will receive none.* Elisha swears by the Lord that he may not receive any payment, lest he be under God's punishment. God's gifts are the result of free grace.
5:17 *two mules' burden of earth.* A load that can be carried by a pair of mules. Although not perfect, this appears to have been a genuine conversion, pointing to and anticipating the inclusion of Gentiles in Christ's kingdom. Most Gentile conversions in the Old Testament required submission to all the legal and ceremonial demands.
5:18–19 *Rimmon.* National deity of Syria. *he leaneth on my hand.* An expression for Naaman's position as an important official in the king's service, his right-hand man (7:2,17). Elisha recognizes Naaman's dilemma, as well as his heart's desire, so sends him away in *peace,* implying that all will be well (1 Sam. 1:17; 20:42).
5:20 *this Syrian.* Words of contempt. The Lord's healing of a Syrian confronted Israel with its racial pride (Luke 4:27–28).
5:21 *lighted down.* Literally, "fell from the chariot," indicating that he got down quickly. *Is all well?* Literally, "Peace?"
5:24 *tower.* Fortified mound or hill within a city.
5:25 *no wither.* Nowhere; Hebrew, "neither here nor there."
5:26 *Went not mine heart with thee.* The prophet's supernatural knowledge shows that the Lord knows all things and sees through all the lies of hypocrites.

Thoughts for Personal/Family Worship: Chapter 5

1. Leprosy is a picture of sin and the uncleanness that prevents any relationship with God. When Naaman first learned the prescribed manner of cleansing, he rejected it as being too demeaning and too simple. He was ready

unto thee, and unto thy seed for ever. And he went
out from his presence a leper *as white* as snow.

CHAPTER 6

AND the sons of the prophets said unto Elisha,
Behold now, the place where we dwell with thee
is too strait for us.
2 Let us go, we pray thee, unto Jordan, and
take thence every man a beam, and let us make
us a place there, where we may dwell. And he
answered, Go ye.
3 And one said, Be content, I pray thee, and go
with thy servants. And he answered, I will go.
4 So he went with them. And when they came to
Jordan, they cut down wood.
5 But as one was felling a beam, the axe head fell
into the water: and he cried, and said, Alas, mas-
ter! for it was borrowed.
6 And the man of God said, Where fell it? And he
shewed him the place. And he cut down a stick,
and cast *it* in thither; and the iron did swim.
7 Therefore said he, Take *it* up to thee. And he put
out his hand, and took it.
8 ¶ Then the king of Syria warred against Israel,
and took counsel with his servants, saying, In
such and such a place *shall be* my camp.
9 And the man of God sent unto the king of
Israel, saying, Beware that thou pass not such a
place; for thither the Syrians are come down.
10 And the king of Israel sent to the place which
the man of God told him and warned him of, and
saved himself there, not once nor twice.
11 Therefore the heart of the king of Syria was
sore troubled for this thing; and he called his
servants, and said unto them, Will ye not shew
me which of us *is* for the king of Israel?
12 And one of his servants said, None, my lord, O
king: but Elisha, the prophet that *is* in Israel, tell-
eth the king of Israel the words that thou speakest
in thy bedchamber.
13 ¶ And he said, Go and spy where he *is*, that
I may send and fetch him. And it was told him,
saying, Behold, *he is* in Dothan.
14 Therefore sent he thither horses, and chari-
ots, and a great host: and they came by night, and
compassed the city about.
15 And when the servant of the man of God was
risen early, and gone forth, behold, an host com-
passed the city both with horses and chariots.
And his servant said unto him, Alas, my master!
how shall we do?
16 And he answered, Fear not: for they that *be*
with us *are* more than they that *be* with them.
17 And Elisha prayed, and said, LORD, I pray thee,
open his eyes, that he may see. And the LORD
opened the eyes of the young man; and he saw:
and, behold, the mountain *was* full of horses and
chariots of fire round about Elisha.
18 And when they came down to him, Elisha
prayed unto the LORD, and said, Smite this people,
I pray thee, with blindness. And he smote them
with blindness according to the word of Elisha.
19 ¶ And Elisha said unto them, This *is* not the
way, neither *is* this the city: follow me, and I will
bring you to the man whom ye seek. But he led
them to Samaria.
20 And it came to pass, when they were come into
Samaria, that Elisha said, LORD, open the eyes
of these *men*, that they may see. And the LORD

to do anything and pay any price (v. 13), but to humble himself by doing nothing other than obeying the prophet's word to wash in the Jordan repulsed him. That is so often the sinner's reaction to the gospel message. Sinners think they have to add something on their own. Indeed, they want to merit something. It is humbling to acknowledge that there is nothing one can add or contribute to salvation, which comes only from taking God at His word. But until a sinner so humbles himself he remains unchanged. Salvation is by grace, through faith, without works (Eph. 2:8–9).

2. Gehazi is a portrait of a hypocrite. Like Judas at the feet of Jesus, so Gehazi at the feet of Elisha did not take into his heart the benefits of the grace that surrounded him. Hypocrites are not what they appear to be. Gehazi lived in a good environment, knew the language of Zion, and had the respect of men. He fooled Naaman with his lies. However, a hypocrite cannot fool God. The eyes of the Lord see the evil and the good. God will judge hypocrites. In a great reversal, the outsider to Israel was healed, but the servant of the prophet was struck with leprosy. Remember that God knows us for what we really are; that ought to drive us to Christ as our only hope. There is hope for the hypocrite who repents and seeks the Lord with all his heart.

Chapter 6: *Elisha miraculously intervenes on behalf of his fellow prophets and becomes involved in the conflicts between Syria and Israel.*

6:1 *sons of the prophets.* Group of prophets. *strait.* Cramped or small.

6:2 *we pray thee.* The Hebrew is "please" or "now."

6:3 *Be content, I pray thee.* Literally, "be willing, please."

6:5 *the axe head.* Literally, "the iron," referring to the axe head. Iron was an expensive commodity, not easily replaced.

6:6 *man of God.* Prophet (vv. 9,15). *the iron did swim.* Literally, "he made the iron to float."

6:10 *not once nor twice.* Repeatedly on multiple occasions.

6:11 *sore troubled.* Enraged. *which of us is for the king of Israel?* He assumed that a traitor was among them.

6:13 *spy.* See. *fetch.* Take.

6:14 *great host.* Large army. *compassed.* Surrounded (v. 15).

6:15 *how shall we do?* What shall we do?—a question revealing his anxiety.

6:17 *he saw.* He was enabled to see the spiritual reality that had been present before he saw. *horses and chariots.* The angelic army assembled for their protection.

6:18 *blindness.* The Hebrew refers to "dazzling light," occurring only here and in Gen. 19:11. So bright was the light that they lost vision, resulting in confusion.

opened their eyes, and they saw; and, behold, *they*
were in the midst of Samaria.
21 And the king of Israel said unto Elisha, when
he saw them, My father, shall I smite *them*? shall
I smite *them*?
22 And he answered, Thou shalt not smite *them*:
wouldest thou smite those whom thou hast taken
captive with thy sword and with thy bow? set
bread and water before them, that they may eat
and drink, and go to their master.
23 And he prepared great provision for them: and
when they had eaten and drunk, he sent them
away, and they went to their master. So the bands
of Syria came no more into the land of Israel.
24 ¶ And it came to pass after this, that Ben-ha-
dad king of Syria gathered all his host, and went
up, and besieged Samaria.
25 And there was a great famine in Samaria: and,
behold, they besieged it, until an ass's head was
sold for fourscore *pieces* of silver, and the fourth
part of a cab of dove's dung for five *pieces* of silver.
26 And as the king of Israel was passing by upon
the wall, there cried a woman unto him, saying,
Help, my lord, O king.
27 And he said, If the LORD do not help thee,
whence shall I help thee? out of the barnfloor, or
out of the winepress?
28 And the king said unto her, What aileth thee?
And she answered, This woman said unto me,
Give thy son, that we may eat him to day, and we
will eat my son to morrow.
29 So we boiled my son, and did eat him: and I
said unto her on the next day, Give thy son, that
we may eat him: and she hath hid her son.
30 ¶ And it came to pass, when the king heard
the words of the woman, that he rent his clothes;
and he passed by upon the wall, and the people
looked, and, behold, *he had* sackcloth within
upon his flesh.
31 Then he said, God do so and more also to me,
if the head of Elisha the son of Shaphat shall stand
on him this day.
32 But Elisha sat in his house, and the elders sat
with him; and *the king* sent a man from before
him: but ere the messenger came to him, he said
to the elders, See ye how this son of a murderer
hath sent to take away mine head? look, when the
messenger cometh, shut the door, and hold him
fast at the door: *is* not the sound of his master's
feet behind him?
33 And while he yet talked with them, behold,
the messenger came down unto him: and he said,
Behold, this evil *is* of the LORD; what should I wait
for the LORD any longer?

CHAPTER 7

THEN Elisha said, Hear ye the word of the LORD;
Thus saith the LORD, To morrow about this time
shall a measure of fine flour *be sold* for a shekel,
and two measures of barley for a shekel, in the
gate of Samaria.

6:23 *the bands*. Specifically, marauding bands, not the Syrian army that would soon be mustered against Samaria (v. 24).
6:25 *cab*. Dry measure of about 3.5 pints.
6:29 *we boiled my son*. This gruesome cannibalism was predicted by the Lord as a punishment for forsaking His ways (Lev. 26:29; Deut. 28:53).
6:30 *he rent his clothes . . . sackcloth*. Expressions of grief and sorrow.
6:32 *ere*. Before.
6:32 *hold him fast at the door*. Elisha commands that they drive the messenger with force out of the door so that Elisha can continue his prophetic ministry. Elisha already heard *the sound of his master's feet behind him*, meaning that the king would soon follow this messenger and speak personally to Elisha.
6:33 *evil*. Calamity.

Thoughts for Personal/Family Worship: Chapter 6

1. **Elisha's ministry was marked by miracles. Some were big; others were small and personal. But all demonstrated the absolute ability of God and His supremacy over all His creation. The floating of the iron axe head was personal yet instructive, apart from the surface warning it provides against borrowing (Prov. 22:7). The prophets were engaged in the work of the kingdom. Then something happened that stopped progress: they lost the axe head. Today that seems to be such a small problem, as a new axe could be attained quite easily. But that was not the case then. They were doing their best, and now a situation had occurred that was beyond their ability to remedy; there seemed to be no hope for going forward. Something extraordinary had to happen. The lesson is that God is not hindered by obstacles—sinking iron was no problem for Him. He caused the iron to float, and the work continued. There may be times when the church today seems to have lost its axe, the power and means to do its work. The answer is prayer. How should you be praying that God will "float the ax" for your church?**
2. **Elisha's prayer for God to open the eyes of his servant to see the angelic army surrounding the enemy that was surrounding them should encourage all of God's people. The servant's eyes being opened did not bring the angelic army but rather revealed what was already there. Before his eyes were opened he saw only the danger. Physical sight sees only what appears; spiritual sight (faith) sees what really is. The angel of the Lord encamps around about those that fear Him (Ps. 34:7). Our inability to see him with the physical eye does not negate the fact that he is there. We are to walk by faith and not by sight. This is the way to peace and joy.**

Chapter 7: *Elisha's prediction of the end of the famine caused by the Syrian siege is precisely fulfilled.*

7:1 *shekel*. Weight just under one-half ounce. Most likely referring to a weight of silver. Food would be in such abundance that it would be sold for very low prices. Contrast this with the enormous prices for disgusting food (6:25).

2 Then a lord on whose hand the king leaned
answered the man of God, and said, Behold, *if* the
LORD would make windows in heaven, might this
thing be? And he said, Behold, thou shalt see *it*
with thine eyes, but shalt not eat thereof.
3 ¶ And there were four leprous men at the en-
tering in of the gate: and they said one to another,
Why sit we here until we die?
4 If we say, We will enter into the city, then the
famine *is* in the city, and we shall die there: and if
we sit still here, we die also. Now therefore come,
and let us fall unto the host of the Syrians: if they
save us alive, we shall live; and if they kill us, we
shall but die.
5 And they rose up in the twilight, to go unto the
camp of the Syrians: and when they were come to
the uttermost part of the camp of Syria, behold,
there was no man there.
6 For the Lord had made the host of the Syrians
to hear a noise of chariots, and a noise of horses,
even the noise of a great host: and they said one to
another, Lo, the king of Israel hath hired against
us the kings of the Hittites, and the kings of the
Egyptians, to come upon us.
7 Wherefore they arose and fled in the twilight,
and left their tents, and their horses, and their
asses, even the camp as it *was*, and fled for their life.
8 And when these lepers came to the uttermost
part of the camp, they went into one tent, and did
eat and drink, and carried thence silver, and gold,
and raiment, and went and hid *it*; and came again,
and entered into another tent, and carried thence
also, and went and hid *it*.
9 Then they said one to another, We do not well:
this day *is* a day of good tidings, and we hold our
peace: if we tarry till the morning light, some
mischief will come upon us: now therefore come,
that we may go and tell the king's household.
10 So they came and called unto the porter of the
city: and they told them, saying, We came to the
camp of the Syrians, and, behold, *there was* no
man there, neither voice of man, but horses tied,
and asses tied, and the tents as they *were*.
11 And he called the porters; and they told *it* to
the king's house within.
12 ¶ And the king arose in the night, and said
unto his servants, I will now shew you what the
Syrians have done to us. They know that we *be*
hungry; therefore are they gone out of the camp
to hide themselves in the field, saying, When they
come out of the city, we shall catch them alive,
and get into the city.
13 And one of his servants answered and said,
Let *some* take, I pray thee, five of the horses that
remain, which are left in the city, (behold, they
are as all the multitude of Israel that are left in it:
behold, *I say*, they *are* even as all the multitude of
the Israelites that are consumed:) and let us send
and see.
14 They took therefore two chariot horses; and
the king sent after the host of the Syrians, saying,
Go and see.
15 And they went after them unto Jordan: and, lo,
all the way *was* full of garments and vessels, which
the Syrians had cast away in their haste. And the
messengers returned, and told the king.
16 And the people went out, and spoiled the tents
of the Syrians. So a measure of fine flour was *sold*
for a shekel, and two measures of barley for a
shekel, according to the word of the LORD.
17 ¶ And the king appointed the lord on whose
hand he leaned to have the charge of the gate:

7:2 *lord.* Adjutant or officer assisting the king. *man of God.* Prophet.

7:3 *four leprous men.* Legally ostracized from the community (Lev. 13:46).

7:4 *let us fall unto the host of the Syrians.* They resolved to desert to or surrender themselves to the camp of the Syrians, seeing this as their only hope of survival.

7:6–7 Without human instrument, the Lord confused and scattered the Syrians, the first step in fulfilling Elisha's prediction.

7:9 *mischief.* The Hebrew word is "punishment." Only after they had eaten their fill and taken abundant spoil for themselves did it register with them to share, the second step in fulfilling Elisha's prediction.

7:10–11 *porter.* Gatekeeper.

7:16 The first prediction was fulfilled (v. 1). This confirmed the legitimacy of Elisha's ministry (Deut. 18:22).

7:17–20 The second prediction was fulfilled precisely.

Thoughts for Personal/Family Worship: Chapter 7

1. **This episode detailing the prophetic prediction, followed immediately by the details of the fulfillment, is instructive as to how we ought to understand those parts of God's Word that have yet to be fulfilled. A key purpose of predictive prophecy is to demonstrate the sovereignty of God over all time and circumstance. Declaring the end from the beginning is evidence of deity (Isa. 41:21–29). There can be no doubt from this chapter that every detail of the prophecy was specifically fulfilled. Yet Elisha did not reveal all the specific details in the prophecy as to how the fulfillment would take place. He made no reference to the Syrian retreat, the lepers' role, or the mocker's inability to control the crowd that led to his seeing the supply of cheap food without experiencing it. Enough details are given to affirm the certainty, but not so much as to replace faith by sight. Prophecy is not to produce fatalism but faith. So as we consider the great things about the future that God has revealed in His Word, we should have the confident assurance that everything God says will happen is going to happen. Even if we can't sort out all of the details of prophecy, let us learn to trust God now.**
2. **The initial behavior of the lepers was tragic in their selfish thoughtlessness for others. They gorged themselves with food and stashed away as much spoil as they could gather. Thankfully, they came to their senses. Even more tragic is how their behavior mirrors that of many Christians who enjoy the benefits and blessings of salvation**

and the people trode upon him in the gate, and
he died, as the man of God had said, who spake
when the king came down to him.
18 And it came to pass as the man of God had
spoken to the king, saying, Two measures of barley for a shekel, and a measure of fine flour for a
shekel, shall be to morrow about this time in the
gate of Samaria:
19 And that lord answered the man of God, and
said, Now, behold, *if* the LORD should make windows in heaven, might such a thing be? And he
said, Behold, thou shalt see it with thine eyes, but
shalt not eat thereof.
20 And so it fell out unto him: for the people
trode upon him in the gate, and he died.

CHAPTER 8

THEN spake Elisha unto the woman, whose son he
had restored to life, saying, Arise, and go thou and
thine household, and sojourn wheresoever thou
canst sojourn: for the LORD hath called for a famine; and it shall also come upon the land seven
years.
2 And the woman arose, and did after the saying
of the man of God: and she went with her household, and sojourned in the land of the Philistines
seven years.
3 And it came to pass at the seven years' end, that
the woman returned out of the land of the Philistines: and she went forth to cry unto the king for
her house and for her land.
4 And the king talked with Gehazi the servant of
the man of God, saying, Tell me, I pray thee, all
the great things that Elisha hath done.
5 And it came to pass, as he was telling the king
how he had restored a dead body to life, that,
behold, the woman, whose son he had restored
to life, cried to the king for her house and for her
land. And Gehazi said, My lord, O king, this *is* the
woman, and this *is* her son, whom Elisha restored
to life.
6 And when the king asked the woman, she told
him. So the king appointed unto her a certain
officer, saying, Restore all that *was* hers, and all
the fruits of the field since the day that she left the
land, even until now.
7 ¶ And Elisha came to Damascus; and Ben-hadad the king of Syria was sick; and it was told him,
saying, The man of God is come hither.
8 And the king said unto Hazael, Take a present
in thine hand, and go, meet the man of God, and
enquire of the LORD by him, saying, Shall I recover of this disease?
9 So Hazael went to meet him, and took a present
with him, even of every good thing of Damascus,
forty camels' burden, and came and stood before
him, and said, Thy son Ben-hadad king of Syria
hath sent me to thee, saying, Shall I recover of this
disease?
10 And Elisha said unto him, Go, say unto him,
Thou mayest certainly recover: howbeit the LORD
hath shewed me that he shall surely die.
11 And he settled his countenance stedfastly, until
he was ashamed: and the man of God wept.
12 And Hazael said, Why weepeth my lord? And
he answered, Because I know the evil that thou
wilt do unto the children of Israel: their strong
holds wilt thou set on fire, and their young men
wilt thou slay with the sword, and wilt dash their
children, and rip up their women with child.
13 And Hazael said, But what, *is* thy servant a dog,
that he should do this great thing? And Elisha
answered, The LORD hath shewed me that thou
shalt be king over Syria.
14 So he departed from Elisha, and came to his
master; who said to him, What said Elisha to thee?
And he answered, He told me *that* thou shouldest
surely recover.
15 And it came to pass on the morrow, that he
took a thick cloth, and dipped *it* in water, and
spread *it* on his face, so that he died: and Hazael
reigned in his stead.
16 ¶ And in the fifth year of Joram the son of
Ahab king of Israel, Jehoshaphat *being* then king
of Judah, Jehoram the son of Jehoshaphat king of
Judah began to reign.
17 Thirty and two years old was he when he began
to reign; and he reigned eight years in Jerusalem.
18 And he walked in the way of the kings of

---

but never share the good news of the gospel with those who are starving for truth all around them. May the Lord bring every believer to recognize the obligation to share the gospel with a lost and dying world. For whose salvation are you praying? With whom are you seeking to share the gospel?

Chapter 8: *Elisha intervenes on behalf of the woman whose son he has raised and then declares that Hazael will be king over Syria, after which attention is given to kings in Judah.*

8:1 *whose son he had restored to life.* See 4:34. *sojourn.* Dwell as a resident alien (8:2). The *famine* ended before Gehazi (v. 4) became a leper (5:1–27). The events of these chapters are not in chronological order.

8:7 *Elisha came to Damascus.* To fulfill the mission the Lord had given to Elijah (1 Kings 19:15–17). *man of God.* Prophet. *hither.* Here.

8:10 The king's sickness was not fatal, but his death was certain.

8:11 *settled his countenance stedfastly.* Literally, "caused his face to stand and put (it in place)," having the idea that he stared straight ahead.

8:12 *evil.* The harm that Hazael would do (10:32–33).

8:15 Hazael took matters into his own hands by murdering his master, thus demonstrating the ruthlessness Elisha lamented.

Israel, as did the house of Ahab: for the daughter
of Ahab was his wife: and he did evil in the sight
of the LORD.
19 Yet the LORD would not destroy Judah for
David his servant's sake, as he promised him to
give him alway a light, *and* to his children.
20 ¶ In his days Edom revolted from under the
hand of Judah, and made a king over themselves.
21 So Joram went over to Zair, and all the chari-
ots with him: and he rose by night, and smote the
Edomites which compassed him about, and the
captains of the chariots: and the people fled into
their tents.
22 Yet Edom revolted from under the hand of
Judah unto this day. Then Libnah revolted at the
same time.
23 And the rest of the acts of Joram, and all that
he did, *are* they not written in the book of the
chronicles of the kings of Judah?
24 And Joram slept with his fathers, and was
buried with his fathers in the city of David: and
Ahaziah his son reigned in his stead.
25 ¶ In the twelfth year of Joram the son of Ahab
king of Israel did Ahaziah the son of Jehoram
king of Judah begin to reign.
26 Two and twenty years old *was* Ahaziah when
he began to reign; and he reigned one year in
Jerusalem. And his mother's name *was* Athaliah,
the daughter of Omri king of Israel.
27 And he walked in the way of the house of
Ahab, and did evil in the sight of the LORD, as *did*
the house of Ahab: for he *was* the son in law of the
house of Ahab.
28 ¶ And he went with Joram the son of Ahab to
the war against Hazael king of Syria in Ramoth-
gilead; and the Syrians wounded Joram.
29 And king Joram went back to be healed in
Jezreel of the wounds which the Syrians had given
him at Ramah, when he fought against Hazael
king of Syria. And Ahaziah the son of Jehoram
king of Judah went down to see Joram the son of
Ahab in Jezreel, because he was sick.

CHAPTER 9

AND Elisha the prophet called one of the children
of the prophets, and said unto him, Gird up thy
loins, and take this box of oil in thine hand, and
go to Ramoth-gilead:
2 And when thou comest thither, look out there
Jehu the son of Jehoshaphat the son of Nimshi,
and go in, and make him arise up from among
his brethren, and carry him to an inner chamber;
3 Then take the box of oil, and pour *it* on his head,
and say, Thus saith the LORD, I have anointed thee
king over Israel. Then open the door, and flee, and
tarry not.
4 ¶ So the young man, *even* the young man the

8:18 *he walked in the way of the kings of Israel.* A tragic comparison for a king of Judah. His marriage to *the daughter of Ahab* was most likely a component of the alliance between his father and Ahab, a common practice in that ancient world. Jehoshaphat failed to see the far-reaching consequences of his association with Ahab. This daughter was Athaliah (v. 26), who not only influenced Jehoram for evil but was guilty of a treason that threatened to destroy the royal line (11:1–21).
8:19 *alway a light.* See note at 1 Kings 11:36.
8:21 *compassed him about.* Surrounded him.
8:22 *Libnah.* A Levitical city (Josh. 21:13).
8:23 *chronicles.* An uninspired record that has not been preserved.
8:26 *daughter of Omri.* In fact, the granddaughter of Omri. It is not uncommon in Hebrew statements of ancestry to skip a generation, here linking her to the founder of the dynasty (1 Kings 16:16–28).
8:27 The wickedness extended to yet another generation (see note at v. 18).

Thoughts for Personal/Family Worship: Chapter 8

1. **Jeremiah declared that the "heart is . . . desperately wicked," beyond comprehension (Jer. 17:9). It is rare that sinners recognize the depths of their sin nature and what they are capable of doing. When Elisha told Hazael the heinous things he was going to do, he immediately protested that he was incapable of such atrocities (2 Kings 8:12–13). Yet the very next day he committed coldblooded murder (v. 15). We must understand the wickedness of the human heart and admit that apart from the grace of God every man has within him the ability to commit the darkest of sins. Those who profess to have experienced God's grace must live daily in dependence on that grace, praying that the Lord will preserve them from evil.**
2. **Jehoshaphat in many ways was a good king, but his alliance with Ahab put in motion circumstances that threatened the continuation of the Davidic line. His son and grandson were so wicked that their careers were compared to that of Ahab, the worst of Israel's kings. Much of their sin is traced to the influence of Athaliah, the daughter of Ahab and Jezebel, the wife of Jehoram, and the mother of Ahaziah. This was a marriage fostered by Jehoshaphat's compromise with Ahab. Let us be warned, and let us be cautious regarding the unforeseen effects of sins. The best way to avoid the future consequences of sin is to resist the temptation to sin now.**

Chapter 9: ***Jehu is anointed as king in Israel and is commissioned to execute God's judgment against the house of Ahab.***

9:1 *children of the prophets.* Usually translated "sons of the prophets," referring to the order of prophets. This man is also designated simply as "the prophet" (v. 4). *Gird up thy loins.* Put a belt around your waist, an idiom for getting ready to do something. *box.* Small jug or flask (v. 3).
9:2 *son of Jehoshaphat.* Not the king of Judah.
9:3 *anointed.* This is the verbal root of the word "messiah," which means "one who has been anointed." Kings, prophets, and priests were anointed to their functions with oil, symbolizing empowerment by the Holy Spirit to fulfill their tasks (Ex. 28:41; 1 Sam. 16:13; 1 Kings 19:16). Every prophet, priest, and king was a lesser messiah who by virtue of their office pointed to the coming of the ideal Messiah, the One who in His single

prophet, went to Ramoth-gilead.
5 And when he came, behold, the captains of the
host *were* sitting; and he said, I have an errand to
thee, O captain. And Jehu said, Unto which of all
us? And he said, To thee, O captain.
6 And he arose, and went into the house; and
he poured the oil on his head, and said unto
him, Thus saith the LORD God of Israel, I have
anointed thee king over the people of the LORD,
even over Israel.
7 And thou shalt smite the house of Ahab thy
master, that I may avenge the blood of my servants
the prophets, and the blood of all the servants of
the LORD, at the hand of Jezebel.
8 For the whole house of Ahab shall perish: and
I will cut off from Ahab him that pisseth against
the wall, and him that is shut up and left in Israel:
9 And I will make the house of Ahab like the
house of Jeroboam the son of Nebat, and like the
house of Baasha the son of Ahijah:
10 And the dogs shall eat Jezebel in the portion of
Jezreel, and *there shall be* none to bury *her*. And he
opened the door, and fled.
11 ¶ Then Jehu came forth to the servants of his
lord: and *one* said unto him, *Is* all well? wherefore
came this mad *fellow* to thee? And he said unto
them, Ye know the man, and his communication.
12 And they said, *It is* false; tell us now. And he
said, Thus and thus spake he to me, saying, Thus
saith the LORD, I have anointed thee king over
Israel.
13 Then they hasted, and took every man his gar-
ment, and put *it* under him on the top of the stairs,
and blew with trumpets, saying, Jehu is king.
14 So Jehu the son of Jehoshaphat the son of
Nimshi conspired against Joram. (Now Joram
had kept Ramoth-gilead, he and all Israel, because
of Hazael king of Syria.
15 But king Joram was returned to be healed in
Jezreel of the wounds which the Syrians had given
him, when he fought with Hazael king of Syria.)
And Jehu said, If it be your minds, *then* let none
go forth *nor* escape out of the city to go to tell *it*
in Jezreel.
16 So Jehu rode in a chariot, and went to Jezreel;
for Joram lay there. And Ahaziah king of Judah
was come down to see Joram.
17 And there stood a watchman on the tower in
Jezreel, and he spied the company of Jehu as he
came, and said, I see a company. And Joram said,
Take an horseman, and send to meet them, and let
him say, *Is it* peace?
18 So there went one on horseback to meet him,
and said, Thus saith the king, *Is it* peace? And Jehu
said, What hast thou to do with peace? turn thee
behind me. And the watchman told, saying, The
messenger came to them, but he cometh not again.
19 Then he sent out a second on horseback, which
came to them, and said, Thus saith the king, *Is it*
peace? And Jehu answered, What hast thou to do
with peace? turn thee behind me.
20 And the watchman told, saying, He came even
unto them, and cometh not again: and the driving
is like the driving of Jehu the son of Nimshi; for
he driveth furiously.
21 And Joram said, Make ready. And his chariot
was made ready. And Joram king of Israel and
Ahaziah king of Judah went out, each in his char-
iot, and they went out against Jehu, and met him
in the portion of Naboth the Jezreelite.
22 And it came to pass, when Joram saw Jehu,
that he said, *Is it* peace, Jehu? And he answered,
What peace, so long as the whoredoms of thy
mother Jezebel and her witchcrafts *are so* many?
23 And Joram turned his hands, and fled, and
said to Ahaziah, *There is* treachery, O Ahaziah.
24 And Jehu drew a bow with his full strength,
and smote Jehoram between his arms, and the
arrow went out at his heart, and he sunk down
in his chariot.
25 Then said *Jehu* to Bidkar his captain, Take up,
and cast him in the portion of the field of Naboth
the Jezreelite: for remember how that, when I and
thou rode together after Ahab his father, the LORD
laid this burden upon him;
26 Surely I have seen yesterday the blood of Na-
both, and the blood of his sons, saith the LORD;
and I will requite thee in this plat, saith the LORD.
Now therefore take *and* cast him into the plat *of
ground*, according to the word of the LORD.

person was Prophet, Priest, and King.

9:5 *captains of the host*. Officers or leaders of the army.

9:7–10 The fulfillment of Elijah's earlier prophecy (1 Kings 21:17–24). *him that pisseth against the wall*. A reference to males, with no vulgar connotations. *him that is shut up and left*. Those who separated themselves from their relatives would still be killed. *like the house of Jeroboam*. The end of the dynasty. Significantly, the Northern Kingdom had few dynasties, none of which lasted long, in contrast to the Southern Kingdom with its continuing Davidic dynasty, in keeping with God's covenant promise (2 Sam. 7:1–29).

9:11 *this mad fellow*. A contemptuous designation for the prophet. It is not uncommon in any age for God's servants to be mocked by the world. *communication*. Literally, "gossip or prattle." Jehu attempted to conceal the message from his comrades by dismissing it as gibberish, but unconvincingly (v. 12).

9:13–14 *they hasted*. Such was the unrest in the kingdom that the army did not resist the coup, perhaps because of the ongoing conflict with Hazael. *took every man his garment, and put it under him*. Gesture expressing their submission (Luke 19:36).

9:17 *spied the company*. Saw a crowd or multitude.

9:23 *turned his hands*. Manipulated the reins on the horses to redirect the chariot and begin to retreat.

9:25 *field of Naboth*. This fulfills the oracle of the Lord (1 Kings 21:19). *laid this burden upon him*. Literally, "raised over him this pronouncement or utterance."

9:26 *plat*. Plot of ground.

27 ¶ But when Ahaziah the king of Judah saw *this*,
he fled by the way of the garden house. And Jehu
followed after him, and said, Smite him also in the
chariot. *And they did so* at the going up to Gur,
which *is* by Ibleam. And he fled to Megiddo, and
died there.
28 And his servants carried him in a chariot to
Jerusalem, and buried him in his sepulchre with
his fathers in the city of David.
29 And in the eleventh year of Joram the son of
Ahab began Ahaziah to reign over Judah.
30 ¶ And when Jehu was come to Jezreel, Jezebel
heard *of it*; and she painted her face, and tired her
head, and looked out at a window.
31 And as Jehu entered in at the gate, she said,
Had Zimri peace, who slew his master?
32 And he lifted up his face to the window, and
said, Who *is* on my side? who? And there looked
out to him two *or* three eunuchs.
33 And he said, Throw her down. So they threw
her down: and *some* of her blood was sprinkled
on the wall, and on the horses: and he trode her
under foot.
34 And when he was come in, he did eat and
drink, and said, Go, see now this cursed *woman*,
and bury her: for she *is* a king's daughter.
35 And they went to bury her: but they found no
more of her than the skull, and the feet, and the
palms of *her* hands.
36 Wherefore they came again, and told him. And
he said, This *is* the word of the LORD, which he
spake by his servant Elijah the Tishbite, saying, In
the portion of Jezreel shall dogs eat the flesh of
Jezebel:
37 And the carcase of Jezebel shall be as dung
upon the face of the field in the portion of Jezreel;
so that they shall not say, This *is* Jezebel.

CHAPTER 10

AND Ahab had seventy sons in Samaria. And Jehu
wrote letters, and sent to Samaria, unto the rulers
of Jezreel, to the elders, and to them that brought
up Ahab's *children*, saying,
2 Now as soon as this letter cometh to you, see-
ing your master's sons *are* with you, and *there are*
with you chariots and horses, a fenced city also,
and armour;
3 Look even out the best and meetest of your
master's sons, and set *him* on his father's throne,
and fight for your master's house.
4 But they were exceedingly afraid, and said, Be-
hold, two kings stood not before him: how then
shall we stand?
5 And he that *was* over the house, and he that
was over the city, the elders also, and the bringers
up *of the children*, sent to Jehu, saying, We *are* thy
servants, and will do all that thou shalt bid us;
we will not make any king: do thou *that which is*
good in thine eyes.

9:27 *garden house*. Translation of the city name "Beth-Haggan," located south of Jezreel.
9:28 *buried him . . . with his fathers*. An honor given him because he was the son of the godly King Jehoshaphat (2 Chron. 22:9).
9:30 *she painted her face, and tired her head*. Literally, "she put her eyes in black eye paint and made good her head," perhaps assuming that her appearance would dissuade Jehu.
9:31 *Had Zimri peace*. Zimri revolted against Elah and subsequently died a horrible death by suicide in a burning palace (1 Kings 16:9,18). She intimates that Jehu will suffer a similar fate if he harms her.
9:32 *eunuchs*. High court officials.
9:36 *shall dogs eat the flesh of Jezebel*. For the prediction, see 1 Kings 21:19,23.

Thoughts for Personal/Family Worship: Chapter 9

1. **Justice delayed is not justice denied. Perhaps as many as twenty years passed between the treachery of Ahab and Jezebel against Naboth and the execution of the judgment that Elijah had pronounced against them at that time. But God's justice is certain, and His timing is perfect, as Jehu is set apart to be the agent of God's wrath. Ruthlessly and relentlessly he executes the judgments of the Lord, precisely as Elijah had declared. From a purely human perspective, his actions seem to be harsh and without mercy, but to every detail the punishment fit the crime. So also the final judgment will come upon the world according to God's will and in His timing. That judgment will be terrifying, and yet heaven will ring in songs of praise because God is just and righteous in His judgments (Rev. 19:1–2). In view of that far greater judgment in which sinners will get what they deserve, there is a great urgency to be reconciled to God by the blood of Christ, the only way to escape judgment. Jezebel tried to escape Jehu by exhibiting her self-perceived beauty; it is the beauty of Christ's righteousness that will rescue His people.**
2. **Jezebel's horrific end is a vivid illustration of Ps. 49, which teaches that death is the great equalizer. She had used her wealth and power to get everything she had wanted during her life, but when it came to dying none of that availed. All she had possessed remained behind for others. The psalmist said concerning the rich and powerful that "when he dieth he shall carry nothing away: his glory shall not descend after him" (Ps. 49:17). So horrific was Jezebel's death that she did not even leave a body to take to the grave. Her life of luxury paled in comparison to the ignominy of her death and the terror of her eternal fate. Death indeed will come to all. Are you prepared for eternity? How can you live in such a way that you are prepared to die?**

Chapter 10: ***Jehu executes judgment against the house of Ahab and destroys the worshipers of Baal but continues to follow in the sin of Jeroboam.***

10:3 *meetest*. Most qualified. Jehu challenged the royal guardians to set one of Ahab's descendants on the throne.
10:4 *two kings stood not*. Referring to Jehu's slaying of Jehoram and Ahaziah (9:24,27).
10:6 *If ye be mine*. If you are for me or on my side.
10:10 *there shall fall unto the earth nothing of the word of the*

6 Then he wrote a letter the second time to them, saying, If ye *be* mine, and *if* ye will hearken unto my voice, take ye the heads of the men your master's sons, and come to me to Jezreel by to morrow this time. Now the king's sons, *being* seventy persons, *were* with the great men of the city, which brought them up.

7 And it came to pass, when the letter came to them, that they took the king's sons, and slew seventy persons, and put their heads in baskets, and sent him *them* to Jezreel.

8 ¶ And there came a messenger, and told him, saying, They have brought the heads of the king's sons. And he said, Lay ye them in two heaps at the entering in of the gate until the morning.

9 And it came to pass in the morning, that he went out, and stood, and said to all the people, Ye *be* righteous: behold, I conspired against my master, and slew him: but who slew all these?

10 Know now that there shall fall unto the earth nothing of the word of the LORD, which the LORD spake concerning the house of Ahab: for the LORD hath done *that* which he spake by his servant Elijah.

11 So Jehu slew all that remained of the house of Ahab in Jezreel, and all his great men, and his kinsfolks, and his priests, until he left him none remaining.

12 ¶ And he arose and departed, and came to Samaria. *And* as he *was* at the shearing house in the way,

13 Jehu met with the brethren of Ahaziah king of Judah, and said, Who *are* ye? And they answered, We *are* the brethren of Ahaziah; and we go down to salute the children of the king and the children of the queen.

14 And he said, Take them alive. And they took them alive, and slew them at the pit of the shearing house, *even* two and forty men; neither left he any of them.

15 ¶ And when he was departed thence, he lighted on Jehonadab the son of Rechab *coming* to meet him: and he saluted him, and said to him, Is thine heart right, as my heart *is* with thy heart? And Jehonadab answered, It is. If it be, give *me* thine hand. And he gave *him* his hand; and he took him up to him into the chariot.

16 And he said, Come with me, and see my zeal for the LORD. So they made him ride in his chariot.

17 And when he came to Samaria, he slew all that remained unto Ahab in Samaria, till he had destroyed him, according to the saying of the LORD, which he spake to Elijah.

18 ¶ And Jehu gathered all the people together, and said unto them, Ahab served Baal a little; *but* Jehu shall serve him much.

19 Now therefore call unto me all the prophets of Baal, all his servants, and all his priests; let none be wanting: for I have a great sacrifice *to do* to Baal; whosoever shall be wanting, he shall not live. But Jehu did *it* in subtilty, to the intent that he might destroy the worshippers of Baal.

20 And Jehu said, Proclaim a solemn assembly for Baal. And they proclaimed *it*.

21 And Jehu sent through all Israel: and all the worshippers of Baal came, so that there was not a man left that came not. And they came into the house of Baal; and the house of Baal was full from one end to another.

22 And he said unto him that *was* over the vestry, Bring forth vestments for all the worshippers of Baal. And he brought them forth vestments.

23 And Jehu went, and Jehonadab the son of Rechab, into the house of Baal, and said unto the worshippers of Baal, Search, and look that there be here with you none of the servants of the LORD, but the worshippers of Baal only.

24 And when they went in to offer sacrifices and burnt offerings, Jehu appointed fourscore men without, and said, *If* any of the men whom I have brought into your hands escape, *he that letteth him go*, his life *shall be* for the life of him.

25 And it came to pass, as soon as he had made an end of offering the burnt offering, that Jehu said to the guard and to the captains, Go in, *and* slay them; let none come forth. And they smote them with the edge of the sword; and the guard and the captains cast *them* out, and went to the city of the house of Baal.

26 And they brought forth the images out of the house of Baal, and burned them.

27 And they brake down the image of Baal, and brake down the house of Baal, and made it a draught house unto this day.

LORD. God fulfilled Elijah's prophesy (1 Kings 21:21–29), proving that His Word cannot fail (1 Sam. 3:19). *the LORD hath done that which he spake.* What God has decreed He will cause to take place. He is the supreme and sovereign King.
10:11 *his kinsfolks.* Literally, "those who were acquainted with him." Jehu extends the judgment on Ahab's house beyond just relatives to include associates, going beyond the divine mandate.
10:13 *to salute.* Literally, "to peace." They were going to see how they were.
10:14 *shearing house.* Translation of the city "Beth-eked," located almost halfway between Samaria and Megiddo.
10:15 *lighted on.* Literally, "found." *Jehonadab the son of Rechab.* From the descendants of Jethro, Moses' father-in-law. Rechab was the founder of the Rechabites, a nomadic people noted for their abstinence (1 Chron. 2:55; Jer. 35:6). *he saluted.* Literally, "he blessed," a term of greeting. *Is thine heart right.* Is your heart sincere? The issue is whether they were in agreement with each other.
10:19 *in subtilty.* With craftiness or cunning.
10:22 *vestry.* Wardrobe or closet. *vestments.* Garments.
10:27 *draught house.* Latrine or sewer.

28 Thus Jehu destroyed Baal out of Israel.
29 ¶ Howbeit *from* the sins of Jeroboam the son
of Nebat, who made Israel to sin, Jehu departed
not from after them, *to wit*, the golden calves that
were in Beth-el, and that *were* in Dan.
30 And the LORD said unto Jehu, Because thou
hast done well in executing *that which is* right
in mine eyes, *and* hast done unto the house of
Ahab according to all that *was* in mine heart, thy
children of the fourth *generation* shall sit on the
throne of Israel.
31 But Jehu took no heed to walk in the law of
the LORD God of Israel with all his heart: for he
departed not from the sins of Jeroboam, which
made Israel to sin.
32 ¶ In those days the LORD began to cut Israel
short: and Hazael smote them in all the coasts of
Israel;
33 From Jordan eastward, all the land of Gilead,
the Gadites, and the Reubenites, and the Manas-
sites, from Aroer, which *is* by the river Arnon,
even Gilead and Bashan.
34 Now the rest of the acts of Jehu, and all that he
did, and all his might, *are* they not written in the
book of the chronicles of the kings of Israel?
35 And Jehu slept with his fathers: and they bur-
ied him in Samaria. And Jehoahaz his son reigned
in his stead.
36 And the time that Jehu reigned over Israel in
Samaria *was* twenty and eight years.

CHAPTER 11

AND when Athaliah the mother of Ahaziah saw
that her son was dead, she arose and destroyed all
the seed royal.
2 But Jehosheba, the daughter of king Joram,
sister of Ahaziah, took Joash the son of Ahaziah,
and stole him from among the king's sons *which*
were slain; and they hid him, *even* him and his
nurse, in the bedchamber from Athaliah, so that
he was not slain.
3 And he was with her hid in the house of the LORD
six years. And Athaliah did reign over the land.
4 ¶ And the seventh year Jehoiada sent and
fetched the rulers over hundreds, with the cap-
tains and the guard, and brought them to him
into the house of the LORD, and made a covenant
with them, and took an oath of them in the house
of the LORD, and shewed them the king's son.
5 And he commanded them, saying, This *is* the
thing that ye shall do; A third part of you that
enter in on the sabbath shall even be keepers of
the watch of the king's house;
6 And a third part *shall be* at the gate of Sur; and
a third part at the gate behind the guard: so shall
ye keep the watch of the house, that it be not bro-
ken down.
7 And two parts of all you that go forth on the
sabbath, even they shall keep the watch of the
house of the LORD about the king.
8 And ye shall compass the king round about,
every man with his weapons in his hand: and he
that cometh within the ranges, let him be slain:
and be ye with the king as he goeth out and as he
cometh in.
9 And the captains over the hundreds did
according to all *things* that Jehoiada the priest
commanded: and they took every man his men
that were to come in on the sabbath, with them
that should go out on the sabbath, and came to
Jehoiada the priest.

10:29 *to wit*. That is.
10:30 *thy children of the fourth generation*. In commendation for executing justice on the house of Ahab, the Lord promised Jehu a dynasty of four generations (Jehoahaz, v. 35; Jehoash, 13:10; Jeroboam, 14:23; and Zachariah, 15:8). See also the note at Hos. 1:4.
10:32 *to cut Israel short*. Literally, "to break off piece by piece." *Hazael smote them*. See 8:12. *coasts*. Regions or borders.
10:34 *chronicles*. Uninspired records of the king's career that have not been preserved.

Thoughts for Personal/Family Worship: Chapter 10

The Lord commended Jehu for doing right in His eyes, according to all that was in His heart (v. 30). Jehu was the effective instrument in the Lord's hand to execute justice against the house of Ahab, precisely fulfilling Elijah's prophecy. However, he did not follow the law of the Lord with all his heart, for he retained the worship of Jeroboam's golden calves (v. 31). Even if keeping the official state religion was politically motivated to prevent any possible reunion with the south and not an expression of his own religious convictions, his actions were still offensive to God and contrary to His Word. Jehu was indeed "a double minded man" (James 1:8), who acted according to pragmatism rather than principle. How long would his dynasty have lasted had he devoted himself wholeheartedly to the Lord? Be sure to guard your own heart and keep your focus singularly on seeking to please the Lord in all that you do. In so doing, you follow Christ, who always rules His kingdom with righteousness (Isa. 9:7; Jer. 23:5).

The Deliverance of the Line of David in Judah (2 Kings 11:1—12:21)

Chapter 11: *Athaliah usurps the royal throne and rules for six years before being overthrown and replaced by Joash, the legitimate heir to the throne.*

11:1 *Athaliah*. The daughter of Ahab and Jezebel (see notes at 8:18,26). *the seed royal*. The seed of the kingdom, referring to the royal line.
11:2–3 *Jehosheba*. The wife of the high priest Jehoiada (2 Chron. 22:11), accounting for her residence *in the house of the LORD*. *Joash*. Also known as Jehoash (2 Kings 11:21). *stole him*. Took him by stealth. *his nurse*. This unnamed woman risked her life to save Joash and as a result was one of God's instruments to preserve the line of Christ.
11:8 *compass*. Surround. *within the ranges*. To the guards or ranks of foot soldiers.

10 And to the captains over hundreds did the
priest give king David's spears and shields, that
were in the temple of the LORD.
11 And the guard stood, every man with his
weapons in his hand, round about the king, from
the right corner of the temple to the left corner of
the temple, *along* by the altar and the temple.
12 And he brought forth the king's son, and put
the crown upon him, and *gave him* the testimony;
and they made him king, and anointed him; and
they clapped their hands, and said, God save the
king.
13 ¶ And when Athaliah heard the noise of the
guard *and* of the people, she came to the people
into the temple of the LORD.
14 And when she looked, behold, the king stood
by a pillar, as the manner *was*, and the princes and
the trumpeters by the king, and all the people of
the land rejoiced, and blew with trumpets: and
Athaliah rent her clothes, and cried, Treason,
Treason.
15 But Jehoiada the priest commanded the cap-
tains of the hundreds, the officers of the host,
and said unto them, Have her forth without the
ranges: and him that followeth her kill with the
sword. For the priest had said, Let her not be slain
in the house of the LORD.
16 And they laid hands on her; and she went by
the way by the which the horses came into the
king's house: and there was she slain.
17 ¶ And Jehoiada made a covenant between
the LORD and the king and the people, that they
should be the LORD's people; between the king
also and the people.
18 And all the people of the land went into the
house of Baal, and brake it down; his altars and
his images brake they in pieces thoroughly, and
slew Mattan the priest of Baal before the altars.
And the priest appointed officers over the house
of the LORD.
19 And he took the rulers over hundreds, and the
captains, and the guard, and all the people of
the land; and they brought down the king from
the house of the LORD, and came by the way of the
gate of the guard to the king's house. And he sat
on the throne of the kings.
20 And all the people of the land rejoiced, and the
city was in quiet: and they slew Athaliah with the
sword *beside* the king's house.
21 Seven years old *was* Jehoash when he began to
reign.

CHAPTER 12

IN the seventh year of Jehu Jehoash began to
reign; and forty years reigned he in Jerusalem.
And his mother's name *was* Zibiah of Beer-sheba.
2 And Jehoash did *that which was* right in the
sight of the LORD all his days wherein Jehoiada
the priest instructed him.
3 But the high places were not taken away: the
people still sacrificed and burnt incense in the
high places.
4 ¶ And Jehoash said to the priests, All the money

11:10 *king David's spears and shields.* Most likely those taken from his adversaries and dedicated to the sanctuary of the Lord, for instance Goliath's sword (1 Sam. 21:9) and the golden shields of Hadadezer (2 Sam. 8:7).
11:12 *the testimony.* The law of God. *God save the king.* Literally, "May the king live."
11:14 *by a pillar.* Most likely where the king would sit to worship in his official capacity as king (2 Chron. 6:13).
11:15 *Have her forth without the ranges.* Literally, "take her out from between the guards or ranks of foot soldiers."
11:17 *made a covenant.* Renewed the covenant, as delineated in Deuteronomy.
11:20 *in quiet.* At peace.
11:21 *Seven years old.* During the years of his minority Jehoash was under the direct tutelage of Jehoida, the high priest who orchestrated his ascension to the throne (12:2).

Thoughts for Personal/Family Worship: Chapter 11

1. **Athaliah's renegade rule over Judah after slaying all but one of the royal line of David underscores two significant lessons. First, it warns against the far-reaching and unpredictable consequences of sin. She was in a position to execute her dastardly deeds because of the unwise compromise of Jehoshaphat with Ahab that had brought her into Judah's royal family. Her godless influence affected her husband, infected her son, and brought Baal worship openly into Judah, just as Jezebel, her mother, had done in Israel. Her godless heart caused innocent blood to be shed as she usurped the very throne of David. We should never take sin lightly or dismiss it as simply being a private matter. As devastating as the effects of sin are to the guilty sinner, the potential of its poison spreading in one way or another should serve as an additional deterrent. Let us pray that God will stop us short of sin, and let us think of the implications of our behavior beyond ourselves.**
2. **A second lesson from Athaliah's rule is that it encourages us to have confidence in God's unfailing purposes. Although Athaliah's treachery was experienced by the royal seed, it was directed ultimately against God and Christ. Had she succeeded in destroying the royal family, God's promise to David would have become null and void. There had to be a line of David through which the Christ would come. Athaliah was just one more expression of the hostility of the serpent's seed (Gen. 3:15) that is always doomed to failure. God's Word is certain. Christ came. We can be certain that every other component of God's purpose and plan are just as sure, both in terms of the big picture and of our individuals lives, for our times are in His hand. This should give us great courage to serve Him in the face of terrible danger, as did Jehosheba, Jehoiada, and Joash's nurse.**

Chapter 12: *Jehoash provides for renovating the temple, avoids confrontation with Syria, and is assassinated by his servants.*

12:2 *all his days.* Sadly, after the death of Jehoida, Joash turned to idolatry and injustice (2 Chron. 24:17–22).

of the dedicated things that is brought into the
house of the LORD, *even* the money of every one
that passeth *the account*, the money that every man
is set at, *and* all the money that cometh into any
man's heart to bring into the house of the LORD,
5 Let the priests take *it* to them, every man of his
acquaintance: and let them repair the breaches of
the house, wheresoever any breach shall be found.
6 But it was *so, that* in the three and twentieth
year of king Jehoash the priests had not repaired
the breaches of the house.
7 Then king Jehoash called for Jehoiada the
priest, and the *other* priests, and said unto them,
Why repair ye not the breaches of the house? now
therefore receive no *more* money of your acquain-
tance, but deliver it for the breaches of the house.
8 And the priests consented to receive no *more*
money of the people, neither to repair the
breaches of the house.
9 But Jehoiada the priest took a chest, and bored
a hole in the lid of it, and set it beside the altar,
on the right side as one cometh into the house of
the LORD: and the priests that kept the door put
therein all the money *that was* brought into the
house of the LORD.
10 And it was *so*, when they saw that *there was*
much money in the chest, that the king's scribe
and the high priest came up, and they put up in
bags, and told the money that was found in the
house of the LORD.
11 And they gave the money, being told, into the
hands of them that did the work, that had the
oversight of the house of the LORD: and they laid
it out to the carpenters and builders, that wrought
upon the house of the LORD,
12 And to masons, and hewers of stone, and
to buy timber and hewed stone to repair the
breaches of the house of the LORD, and for all that
was laid out for the house to repair *it*.
13 Howbeit there were not made for the house of
the LORD bowls of silver, snuffers, basons, trum-
pets, any vessels of gold, or vessels of silver, of the
money *that was* brought into the house of the
LORD:
14 But they gave that to the workmen, and re-
paired therewith the house of the LORD.
15 Moreover they reckoned not with the men,
into whose hand they delivered the money to be
bestowed on workmen: for they dealt faithfully.
16 The trespass money and sin money was not
brought into the house of the LORD: it was the
priests'.
17 ¶ Then Hazael king of Syria went up, and
fought against Gath, and took it: and Hazael set
his face to go up to Jerusalem.
18 And Jehoash king of Judah took all the hal-
lowed things that Jehoshaphat, and Jehoram, and
Ahaziah, his fathers, kings of Judah, had dedicated,
and his own hallowed things, and all the gold *that*
was found in the treasures of the house of the
LORD, and in the king's house, and sent *it* to Hazael
king of Syria: and he went away from Jerusalem.
19 ¶ And the rest of the acts of Joash, and all that
he did, *are* they not written in the book of the
chronicles of the kings of Judah?
20 And his servants arose, and made a conspiracy,
and slew Joash in the house of Millo, which goeth
down to Silla.

12:4 *dedicated.* Holy. There were three sources of revenue: first, a levy on those coming of military age (*every one that passeth*, see Ex. 30:11–16); second, a levy on those making vows (*every man is set at*, literally, "the souls of his estimate value"; see Lev. 27:1–8); and third, free will offerings (*cometh into any man's heart*).
12:5 *acquaintance.* Most likely referring to the donors (v. 7).
12:10 *told.* Counted (v. 11).
12:11 *wrought.* Worked.
12:12 *hewers.* Cutters.
12:13 After all the renovations were finished they focused on the utensils (2 Chron. 24:14).
12:15 *they reckoned not.* They did not require an accounting because they were trustworthy.
12:16 *trespass money.* Paid to atone for violations against the holy things (Lev. 5:15).
12:17 *Gath.* A principal Philistine city, sometimes under the control of Judah (1 Chron. 18:1). *set his face.* An expression indicating determination. The Syrian invasion occurred after the death of Jehoida (2 Chron. 24:22–23).
12:19 *chronicles.* An uninspired record of the king's career that has not been preserved.
12:20 *house of Millo.* Probably a building or terrace-like structure constructed on the earthworks that Solomon had built in Jerusalem (1 Kings 9:15).
12:21 Because Joash had slain the sons of Jehoida, some of Joash's servants *made a conspiracy* and killed him. He was buried *in the city of David* but not in the royal cemetery (2 Chron. 24:25).

Thoughts for Personal/Family Worship: Chapter 12

The career of Joash illustrates the truth of Eccl. 7:8 that "better is the end of a thing than the beginning thereof." His first days as the boy-king of only seven years old were his best. Without doubt, it was the godly influence of Jehoida that directed his behavior and determined his policy. But being instructed in the ways of the Lord is not enough. Such instruction needs to be appropriated by God's Spirit in the heart, and that apparently did not take place. When the external pressure to do right was gone, there was no internal impulse to holiness. Second Chronicles 24 gives greater detail regarding how quickly and dramatically things deteriorated. Ironically, at the beginning of Joash's life he was spared from the hands of a wicked assassin, but his life ended at the hands of assassins who were avenging his wicked acts. This tragic story should be a warning to every young person under godly influence and direction in a Christian home. It is not enough just to hear and externally follow. There must be a personal appropriation by the Holy Spirit of all that is taught from the Scriptures. To rebel after a good beginning is tragic.

21 For Jozachar the son of Shimeath, and Jehoz-
abad the son of Shomer, his servants, smote him,
and he died; and they buried him with his fathers
in the city of David: and Amaziah his son reigned
in his stead.

CHAPTER 13

IN the three and twentieth year of Joash the son of
Ahaziah king of Judah Jehoahaz the son of Jehu
began to reign over Israel in Samaria, *and reigned*
seventeen years.
2 And he did *that which was* evil in the sight of
the LORD, and followed the sins of Jeroboam the
son of Nebat, which made Israel to sin; he de-
parted not therefrom.
3 ¶ And the anger of the LORD was kindled
against Israel, and he delivered them into the
hand of Hazael king of Syria, and into the hand
of Ben-hadad the son of Hazael, all *their* days.
4 And Jehoahaz besought the LORD, and the LORD
hearkened unto him: for he saw the oppression of
Israel, because the king of Syria oppressed them.
5 (And the LORD gave Israel a saviour, so that
they went out from under the hand of the Syrians:
and the children of Israel dwelt in their tents, as
beforetime.
6 Nevertheless they departed not from the sins of
the house of Jeroboam, who made Israel sin, *but*
walked therein: and there remained the grove also
in Samaria.)
7 Neither did he leave of the people to Jehoahaz
but fifty horsemen, and ten chariots, and ten
thousand footmen; for the king of Syria had de-
stroyed them, and had made them like the dust
by threshing.
8 ¶ Now the rest of the acts of Jehoahaz, and all
that he did, and his might, *are* they not written in
the book of the chronicles of the kings of Israel?
9 And Jehoahaz slept with his fathers; and they
buried him in Samaria: and Joash his son reigned
in his stead.
10 ¶ In the thirty and seventh year of Joash king of
Judah began Jehoash the son of Jehoahaz to reign
over Israel in Samaria, *and reigned* sixteen years.
11 And he did *that which was* evil in the sight of
the LORD; he departed not from all the sins of
Jeroboam the son of Nebat, who made Israel sin:
but he walked therein.
12 And the rest of the acts of Joash, and all that he
did, and his might wherewith he fought against
Amaziah king of Judah, *are* they not written in
the book of the chronicles of the kings of Israel?
13 And Joash slept with his fathers; and Jeroboam
sat upon his throne: and Joash was buried in
Samaria with the kings of Israel.
14 ¶ Now Elisha was fallen sick of his sickness
whereof he died. And Joash the king of Israel
came down unto him, and wept over his face, and
said, O my father, my father, the chariot of Israel,
and the horsemen thereof.
15 And Elisha said unto him, Take bow and ar-
rows. And he took unto him bow and arrows.
16 And he said to the king of Israel, Put thine
hand upon the bow. And he put his hand *upon it*:
and Elisha put his hands upon the king's hands.
17 And he said, Open the window eastward. And
he opened *it*. Then Elisha said, Shoot. And he
shot. And he said, The arrow of the LORD's deliv-
erance, and the arrow of deliverance from Syria:
for thou shalt smite the Syrians in Aphek, till thou
have consumed *them*.
18 And he said, Take the arrows. And he took
them. And he said unto the king of Israel, Smite
upon the ground. And he smote thrice, and stayed.
19 And the man of God was wroth with him,
and said, Thou shouldest have smitten five or
six times; then hadst thou smitten Syria till thou
hadst consumed *it*: whereas now thou shalt smite
Syria *but* thrice.
20 ¶ And Elisha died, and they buried him. And
the bands of the Moabites invaded the land at the
coming in of the year.
21 And it came to pass, as they were burying a
man, that, behold, they spied a band *of men*; and
they cast the man into the sepulchre of Elisha:

God's Patient Mercies toward Israel (2 Kings 13:1–25)

Chapter 13: *Wicked kings continue to rule in Israel, and Elisha becomes sick and dies.*

13:4 *besought the LORD*. The Hebrew has the idea of seeking to appease or mollify the Lord. This evidences his less than orthodox understanding of the Lord, his thinking that he could somehow soften Him up to provide deliverance. *the LORD hearkened*. Not because of the king's attempt to pacify Him but because of His mercy and compassion on the nation, and because of His promise to Jehoahaz's father, Jehu (10:30).

13:5 *saviour*. One who would deliver from the oppression (Judg. 2:16). *tents*. Homes.

13:6 *grove*. Asherah, the sacred pole typically erected near an altar.

13:8 *chronicles*. Uninspired records of the king's career that have not been preserved (v. 12).

13:14 *the chariot of Israel*. The same epitaph that Elisha ascribed to Elijah (2:12).

13:15–17 Elisha was going to give an object lesson, a common prophetic tactic to illustrate the message. This was the sign of victory over the Syrians.

13:19 *wroth*. Furious. *smite Syria but thrice*. The prophecy was exactly fulfilled (v. 25).

13:20 *the bands of the Moabites*. Marauding groups of men who conducted raids.

13:21 Baal claimed through his adherents to conquer death, but even a dead prophet of God had more power than all of the Baals around and in Israel. The miracle, of course, was the work of God. Just as the Lord had raised the dead to life by His prophet's embracing them (see notes at 1 Kings 17:21; 2 Kings 4:34), so the dead are raised to life by being buried with the

and when the man was let down, and touched the
bones of Elisha, he revived, and stood up on his
feet.
22 ¶ But Hazael king of Syria oppressed Israel all
the days of Jehoahaz.
23 And the LORD was gracious unto them, and
had compassion on them, and had respect unto
them, because of his covenant with Abraham,
Isaac, and Jacob, and would not destroy them,
neither cast he them from his presence as yet.
24 So Hazael king of Syria died; and Ben-hadad
his son reigned in his stead.
25 And Jehoash the son of Jehoahaz took again
out of the hand of Ben-hadad the son of Hazael
the cities, which he had taken out of the hand of
Jehoahaz his father by war. Three times did Joash
beat him, and recovered the cities of Israel.

CHAPTER 14

IN the second year of Joash son of Jehoahaz king
of Israel reigned Amaziah the son of Joash king
of Judah.
2 He was twenty and five years old when he be-
gan to reign, and reigned twenty and nine years in
Jerusalem. And his mother's name *was* Jehoaddan
of Jerusalem.
3 And he did *that which was* right in the sight
of the LORD, yet not like David his father: he did
according to all things as Joash his father did.
4 Howbeit the high places were not taken away:
as yet the people did sacrifice and burnt incense
on the high places.
5 ¶ And it came to pass, as soon as the kingdom
was confirmed in his hand, that he slew his
servants which had slain the king his father.
6 But the children of the murderers he slew not:
according unto that which is written in the book
of the law of Moses, wherein the LORD com-
manded, saying, The fathers shall not be put to
death for the children, nor the children be put to
death for the fathers; but every man shall be put
to death for his own sin.
7 He slew of Edom in the valley of salt ten thou-
sand, and took Selah by war, and called the name
of it Joktheel unto this day.
8 ¶ Then Amaziah sent messengers to Jehoash,
the son of Jehoahaz son of Jehu, king of Israel,
saying, Come, let us look one another in the face.
9 And Jehoash the king of Israel sent to Amaziah
king of Judah, saying, The thistle that *was* in
Lebanon sent to the cedar that *was* in Lebanon,
saying, Give thy daughter to my son to wife: and
there passed by a wild beast that *was* in Lebanon,
and trode down the thistle.
10 Thou hast indeed smitten Edom, and thine
heart hath lifted thee up: glory *of this*, and tarry at
home: for why shouldest thou meddle to *thy* hurt,
that thou shouldest fall, *even* thou, and Judah
with thee?
11 But Amaziah would not hear. Therefore
Jehoash king of Israel went up; and he and
Amaziah king of Judah looked one another in the
face at Beth-shemesh, which *belongeth* to Judah.
12 And Judah was put to the worse before Israel;
and they fled every man to their tents.
13 And Jehoash king of Israel took Amaziah king
of Judah, the son of Jehoash the son of Ahaziah,

---

prophet. This too is a shadow or representation of finding spiritual life by dying with Christ and being buried with Him (Rom. 6:1–4).

13:23 Though Israel had fallen far from keeping God's covenant, the Lord continued to remember *his covenant with Abraham, Isaac, and Jacob* (Lev. 26:42,44; Pss. 105:8; 106:45).

Thoughts for Personal/Family Worship: Chapter 13

1. **Do not assume that you are in right relationship with God just because He has answered some of your prayers. God is merciful, but His mercies are not tokens by which we can presume to belong to Him. Jehoahaz appealed to the Lord when he was in trouble (v. 4), but he continued in the sins of Jeroboam and even some Baal worship as well (v. 6). He did not display a heart of true repentance, yet the Lord mercifully helped him and Israel to get free from their oppressors. Perhaps you have experienced an answer to your prayers for temporal help. Thank God for it. However, do not make that an excuse for remaining in half-hearted religion. How should God's kindnesses move us to serve Him with all our hearts?**
2. **God's mercies to Israel even as they worshiped idols and false gods vividly illustrates the truth that God answers prayer because of His grace alone. He is full of mercy and compassion, and He remembers His covenant (vv. 4,23). Therefore, let us not think like Jehoahaz that we can manipulate God into hearing us. Even our most sincere prayers God does not answer for our sakes or because of our merit. Let us turn to him in humility, confessing our transgressions and asking Him for His undeserved mercy. Any mercy received is mercy undeserved.**

THE DISPERSION OF THE KINGDOM (2 KINGS 14:1—25:30)

The Downward Spiral of Israel and Judah (2 Kings 14:1—16:20)

Chapter 14: *Israel dominates in conflicts with Judah during the reign of Jehoash and experiences expansion during the reign of Jeroboam II.*

14:5 *servants which had slain the king his father.* See 12:20.

14:6 *that which is written.* Quoted from Deut. 24:16 (cf. Ezek. 18:4–20). This quotation from *the book of the law of Moses* is evidence that Deuteronomy was not written in the days of Josiah (2 Kings 22:1,8), as liberal scholars claim, but by Moses long before the monarchy (see Introduction to Deuteronomy).

14:7 On Amaziah's military exploits, see 2 Chron. 25:5–12.

14:9 *The thistle . . . sent to the cedar.* Jehoash used a parable to dissuade Amaziah from battle, insinuating that Amaziah did not stand a chance against him.

14:10 *why shouldest thou meddle.* Literally, "why should you engage in strife?"

14:12 *put to the worse.* Literally, "struck."

14:15 *chronicles.* Uninspired records of the king's career that

at Beth-shemesh, and came to Jerusalem, and
brake down the wall of Jerusalem from the gate
of Ephraim unto the corner gate, four hundred
cubits.
14 And he took all the gold and silver, and all the
vessels that were found in the house of the LORD,
and in the treasures of the king's house, and hos-
tages, and returned to Samaria.
15 ¶ Now the rest of the acts of Jehoash which
he did, and his might, and how he fought with
Amaziah king of Judah, *are* they not written in
the book of the chronicles of the kings of Israel?
16 And Jehoash slept with his fathers, and was
buried in Samaria with the kings of Israel; and
Jeroboam his son reigned in his stead.
17 ¶ And Amaziah the son of Joash king of Judah
lived after the death of Jehoash son of Jehoahaz
king of Israel fifteen years.
18 And the rest of the acts of Amaziah, *are* they
not written in the book of the chronicles of the
kings of Judah?
19 Now they made a conspiracy against him in
Jerusalem: and he fled to Lachish; but they sent
after him to Lachish, and slew him there.
20 And they brought him on horses: and he was
buried at Jerusalem with his fathers in the city of
David.
21 ¶ And all the people of Judah took Azariah,
which *was* sixteen years old, and made him king
instead of his father Amaziah.
22 He built Elath, and restored it to Judah, after
that the king slept with his fathers.
23 ¶ In the fifteenth year of Amaziah the son of
Joash king of Judah Jeroboam the son of Joash
king of Israel began to reign in Samaria, *and
reigned* forty and one years.
24 And he did *that which was* evil in the sight of
the LORD: he departed not from all the sins of Jer-
oboam the son of Nebat, who made Israel to sin.
25 He restored the coast of Israel from the enter-
ing of Hamath unto the sea of the plain, according
to the word of the LORD God of Israel, which he
spake by the hand of his servant Jonah, the son of
Amittai, the prophet, which *was* of Gath-hepher.
26 For the LORD saw the affliction of Israel, *that it
was* very bitter: for *there was* not any shut up, nor
any left, nor any helper for Israel.
27 And the LORD said not that he would blot out
the name of Israel from under heaven: but he
saved them by the hand of Jeroboam the son of
Joash.
28 ¶ Now the rest of the acts of Jeroboam, and all
that he did, and his might, how he warred, and
how he recovered Damascus, and Hamath, *which
belonged* to Judah, for Israel, are they not writ-
ten in the book of the chronicles of the kings of
Israel?
29 And Jeroboam slept with his fathers, *even* with
the kings of Israel; and Zachariah his son reigned
in his stead.

CHAPTER 15

IN the twenty and seventh year of Jeroboam king
of Israel began Azariah son of Amaziah king of
Judah to reign.
2 Sixteen years old was he when he began to
reign, and he reigned two and fifty years in Jeru-
salem. And his mother's name *was* Jecholiah of
Jerusalem.
3 And he did *that which was* right in the sight of
the LORD, according to all that his father Amaziah
had done;
4 Save that the high places were not removed: the
people sacrificed and burnt incense still on the
high places.
5 ¶ And the LORD smote the king, so that he was
a leper unto the day of his death, and dwelt in a

have not been preserved (vv. 18,28).

14:25 *coast.* Border. *Jonah, the son of Amittai.* See Jonah 1:1. The prophets Hosea and Amos also ministered during the reign of Jeroboam II.

14:26 *the LORD saw the affliction of Israel.* God had compassion on His suffering people.

14:28 In spite of the king's wickedness, the Lord still delivered Israel from its enemies and caused the reign of Jeroboam II to be very prosperous.

Thoughts for Personal/Family Worship: Chapter 14

1. **"Pride goeth before destruction, and an haughty spirit before a fall" (Prov. 16:18). This describes Amaziah. His victory over Edom led to his bravado to Israel, which led to his fall before one stronger than himself. He was warned about the certain outcome, but thinking more highly of himself that he ought he rushed to the battle and defeat. We must assess ourselves realistically (Rom. 12:3). Humility should mark every Christian, for it is being like Christ (Phil. 2:5).**
2. **The mercy and loving kindness of the Lord are beyond understanding. He delivered Israel from their oppressors, even though the nation was deserving of immediate judgment. The Lord's patience was very great during the administration of Jeroboam II. Read the prophets Hosea and Amos to see how entrenched the nation was in sin while they enjoyed significant economic and political prosperity. In due course the judgment came, but not before God had extended His patient calling for their repentance over and again. Even when we are least deserving of receiving mercy of the Lord, let us not despair of His goodness. The Lord receives sinners who repent. He is willing to grant deliverance and grace to us.**

Chapter 15: ***Judah enjoys the reign of good kings as Israel experiences one bad king after other, taking the nation ever closer to judgment.***

15:1 *Azariah.* Also known as Uzziah (v. 13).

15:5 *he was a leper.* Because he burned incense in the temple, a ministry reserved for the priesthood (2 Chron. 26:16–20).

several house. And Jotham the king's son *was* over
the house, judging the people of the land.
6 And the rest of the acts of Azariah, and all that
he did, *are* they not written in the book of the
chronicles of the kings of Judah?
7 So Azariah slept with his fathers; and they bur-
ied him with his fathers in the city of David: and
Jotham his son reigned in his stead.
8 ¶ In the thirty and eighth year of Azariah king
of Judah did Zachariah the son of Jeroboam reign
over Israel in Samaria six months.
9 And he did *that which was* evil in the sight of
the LORD, as his fathers had done: he departed not
from the sins of Jeroboam the son of Nebat, who
made Israel to sin.
10 And Shallum the son of Jabesh conspired
against him, and smote him before the people,
and slew him, and reigned in his stead.
11 And the rest of the acts of Zachariah, behold,
they *are* written in the book of the chronicles of
the kings of Israel.
12 This *was* the word of the LORD which he spake
unto Jehu, saying, Thy sons shall sit on the throne
of Israel unto the fourth *generation*. And so it
came to pass.
13 ¶ Shallum the son of Jabesh began to reign
in the nine and thirtieth year of Uzziah king of
Judah; and he reigned a full month in Samaria.
14 For Menahem the son of Gadi went up from
Tirzah, and came to Samaria, and smote Shallum
the son of Jabesh in Samaria, and slew him, and
reigned in his stead.
15 And the rest of the acts of Shallum, and his
conspiracy which he made, behold, they *are* writ-
ten in the book of the chronicles of the kings of
Israel.
16 ¶ Then Menahem smote Tiphsah, and all that
were therein, and the coasts thereof from Tirzah:
because they opened not *to him*, therefore he
smote *it; and* all the women therein that were
with child he ripped up.
17 In the nine and thirtieth year of Azariah king
of Judah began Menahem the son of Gadi to reign
over Israel, *and reigned* ten years in Samaria.
18 And he did *that which was* evil in the sight of
the LORD: he departed not all his days from the
sins of Jeroboam the son of Nebat, who made
Israel to sin.
19 *And* Pul the king of Assyria came against the
land: and Menahem gave Pul a thousand talents
of silver, that his hand might be with him to
confirm the kingdom in his hand.
20 And Menahem exacted the money of Israel,
even of all the mighty men of wealth, of each man
fifty shekels of silver, to give to the king of Assyria.
So the king of Assyria turned back, and stayed not
there in the land.
21 ¶ And the rest of the acts of Menahem, and all
that he did, *are* they not written in the book of the
chronicles of the kings of Israel?
22 And Menahem slept with his fathers; and
Pekahiah his son reigned in his stead.
23 ¶ In the fiftieth year of Azariah king of Judah
Pekahiah the son of Menahem began to reign
over Israel in Samaria, *and reigned* two years.
24 And he did *that which was* evil in the sight of
the LORD: he departed not from the sins of Jer-
oboam the son of Nebat, who made Israel to sin.
25 But Pekah the son of Remaliah, a captain of
his, conspired against him, and smote him in
Samaria, in the palace of the king's house, with
Argob and Arieh, and with him fifty men of the
Gileadites: and he killed him, and reigned in his
room.
26 And the rest of the acts of Pekahiah, and all
that he did, behold, they *are* written in the book
of the chronicles of the kings of Israel.
27 ¶ In the two and fiftieth year of Azariah king of
Judah Pekah the son of Remaliah began to reign
over Israel in Samaria, *and reigned* twenty years.
28 And he did *that which was* evil in the sight of
the LORD: he departed not from the sins of Jer-
oboam the son of Nebat, who made Israel to sin.
29 In the days of Pekah king of Israel came Tig-
lath-pileser king of Assyria, and took Ijon, and
Abel-beth-maachah, and Janoah, and Kedesh,
and Hazor, and Gilead, and Galilee, all the land
of Naphtali, and carried them captive to Assyria.
30 And Hoshea the son of Elah made a conspiracy
against Pekah the son of Remaliah, and smote
him, and slew him, and reigned in his stead, in
the twentieth year of Jotham the son of Uzziah.
31 And the rest of the acts of Pekah, and all that
he did, behold, they *are* written in the book of the
chronicles of the kings of Israel.
32 ¶ In the second year of Pekah the son of Rem-
aliah king of Israel began Jotham the son of
Uzziah king of Judah to reign.
33 Five and twenty years old was he when he
began to reign, and he reigned sixteen years in
Jerusalem. And his mother's name *was* Jerusha,
the daughter of Zadok.

It was imperative for the kingly and priestly functions to be distinct. Only in Jesus Christ, the ideal King and Priest, would the offices be united in a single person. *several house*. Literally, "the house of separation." Even a royal leper was unclean and had to be ostracized from the community (Lev. 13:46).

15:6 *chronicles*. Uninspired records of the king's career that have not been preserved (vv. 11,15,21,26,31,36).

15:10 *before the people*. Publicly.

15:12 *fourth generation*. Zachariah's death marked the end of Jehu's promised dynasty (see 10:30).

15:16 *coasts*. Regions.

15:19 *talents*. A talent is a weight of 66 pounds.

15:20 *shekel*. A weight of approximately one-half ounce.

15:25 *in his room*. In his place, instead of him.

34 And he did *that which was* right in the sight of
the LORD: he did according to all that his father
Uzziah had done.
35 ¶ Howbeit the high places were not removed:
the people sacrificed and burned incense still in
the high places. He built the higher gate of the
house of the LORD.
36 ¶ Now the rest of the acts of Jotham, and all
that he did, *are* they not written in the book of the
chronicles of the kings of Judah?
37 In those days the LORD began to send against
Judah Rezin the king of Syria, and Pekah the son
of Remaliah.
38 And Jotham slept with his fathers, and was
buried with his fathers in the city of David his fa-
ther: and Ahaz his son reigned in his stead.

CHAPTER 16

IN the seventeenth year of Pekah the son of Rema-
liah Ahaz the son of Jotham king of Judah began
to reign.
2 Twenty years old *was* Ahaz when he began to
reign, and reigned sixteen years in Jerusalem, and
did not *that which was* right in the sight of the
LORD his God, like David his father.
3 But he walked in the way of the kings of Israel,
yea, and made his son to pass through the fire,
according to the abominations of the heathen,
whom the LORD cast out from before the children
of Israel.
4 And he sacrificed and burnt incense in the high
places, and on the hills, and under every green
tree.
5 ¶ Then Rezin king of Syria and Pekah son of
Remaliah king of Israel came up to Jerusalem to
war: and they besieged Ahaz, but could not over-
come *him*.
6 At that time Rezin king of Syria recovered Elath
to Syria, and drave the Jews from Elath: and the
Syrians came to Elath, and dwelt there unto this
day.
7 So Ahaz sent messengers to Tiglath-pileser king
of Assyria, saying, I *am* thy servant and thy son:
come up, and save me out of the hand of the king
of Syria, and out of the hand of the king of Israel,
which rise up against me.
8 And Ahaz took the silver and gold that was
found in the house of the LORD, and in the trea-
sures of the king's house, and sent *it for* a present
to the king of Assyria.
9 And the king of Assyria hearkened unto him:
for the king of Assyria went up against Damascus,
and took it, and carried *the people of* it captive to
Kir, and slew Rezin.
10 ¶ And king Ahaz went to Damascus to meet
Tiglath-pileser king of Assyria, and saw an al-
tar that *was* at Damascus: and king Ahaz sent to
Urijah the priest the fashion of the altar, and the
pattern of it, according to all the workmanship
thereof.
11 And Urijah the priest built an altar according
to all that king Ahaz had sent from Damascus: so
Urijah the priest made *it* against king Ahaz came
from Damascus.
12 And when the king was come from Damascus,
the king saw the altar: and the king approached to
the altar, and offered thereon.
13 And he burnt his burnt offering and his meat
offering, and poured his drink offering, and
sprinkled the blood of his peace offerings, upon
the altar.
14 And he brought also the brasen altar, which
was before the LORD, from the forefront of the
house, from between the altar and the house of
the LORD, and put it on the north side of the altar.
15 And king Ahaz commanded Urijah the
priest, saying, Upon the great altar burn the
morning burnt offering, and the evening meat
offering, and the king's burnt sacrifice, and his

15:37 *In those days.* These are the events that led to Isaiah's prophecy of the virgin birth of Christ (Isa. 7:1,9,14,21).

Thoughts for Personal/Family Worship: Chapter 15

No less than four times are the careers of Israel's final kings compared to that of Jeroboam I, who provoked Israel to sin (vv. 9,18,24,28). What started as a single step on a slippery slope snowballed into an avalanche of wickedness that ended in disaster. The only northern king who escaped this evaluation was Shallum, and that was only because his reign was cut so short (one month, v. 13). After the relative stability of Jehu's dynasty, the kingdom was in chaos, resulting ultimately in captivity under the Assyrians as God used this wicked people as the instrument of His judgment (Isa. 10:5). The history of the Northern Kingdom illustrates the uncontrollable power of unchecked sin and its certain and terrible consequences. The kings of Israel all committed evil in the sight of the Lord. Sooner or later judgment comes. Do not think you will escape it just because it has not come yet. The only way to escape punishment from evil is to bow to the Lord Jesus Christ, believing in the gospel.

Chapter 16: *Ahaz seeks help from Assyria, erects a pagan altar, and desecrates parts of the temple.*

16:3 *made his son to pass through the fire.* He engaged in child sacrifice more than once (2 Chron. 28:3), a crime strictly forbidden by God (Lev. 18:21; Ps. 106:37–38).

16:4 *sacrificed . . . in the high places.* See Deut. 12:2.

16:6 *recovered Elath.* A long way from Syria, but a strategic city at the north of the Gulf of Aqaba, under Judah's control since the days of Azariah (14:22).

16:9 *Kir.* The exact location is uncertain, most likely a region in Mesopotamia (Isa. 15:1; 22:6; Amos 1:5).

16:10 Ahaz's desire for an altar that obviously had no power to help its worshipers in the defeated nation of Syria reveals his spiritual blindness.

16:11 *against king Ahaz came.* Literally, "until or before king Ahaz came."

meat offering, with the burnt offering of all the people of the land, and their meat offering, and their drink offerings; and sprinkle upon it all the blood of the burnt offering, and all the blood of the sacrifice: and the brasen altar shall be for me to enquire *by*.
16 Thus did Urijah the priest, according to all that king Ahaz commanded.
17 ¶ And king Ahaz cut off the borders of the bases, and removed the laver from off them; and took down the sea from off the brasen oxen that *were* under it, and put it upon a pavement of stones.
18 And the covert for the sabbath that they had built in the house, and the king's entry without, turned he from the house of the LORD for the king of Assyria.
19 ¶ Now the rest of the acts of Ahaz which he did, *are* they not written in the book of the chronicles of the kings of Judah?
20 And Ahaz slept with his fathers, and was buried with his fathers in the city of David: and Hezekiah his son reigned in his stead.

CHAPTER 17

IN the twelfth year of Ahaz king of Judah began Hoshea the son of Elah to reign in Samaria over Israel nine years.
2 And he did *that which was* evil in the sight of the LORD, but not as the kings of Israel that were before him.
3 ¶ Against him came up Shalmaneser king of Assyria; and Hoshea became his servant, and gave him presents.
4 And the king of Assyria found conspiracy in Hoshea: for he had sent messengers to So king of Egypt, and brought no present to the king of Assyria, as *he had done* year by year: therefore the king of Assyria shut him up, and bound him in prison.
5 ¶ Then the king of Assyria came up throughout all the land, and went up to Samaria, and besieged it three years.
6 ¶ In the ninth year of Hoshea the king of Assyria took Samaria, and carried Israel away into Assyria, and placed them in Halah and in Habor *by* the river of Gozan, and in the cities of the Medes.
7 For *so* it was, that the children of Israel had sinned against the LORD their God, which had brought them up out of the land of Egypt, from under the hand of Pharaoh king of Egypt, and had feared other gods,
8 And walked in the statutes of the heathen, whom the LORD cast out from before the children of Israel, and of the kings of Israel, which they had made.
9 And the children of Israel did secretly *those* things that *were* not right against the LORD their God, and they built them high places in all their

16:16 *Thus did Urijah the priest.* Contrast this with the priest who withstood Azariah (2 Chron. 26:17–18). It is a dark day when religious leaders bow to political pressures rather than defending the cause of true religion.
16:17 Ahaz closed the temple of the Lord and dismantled part of its furnishings (2 Chron. 28:24). So far had the son of David fallen that he had become an enemy of the very temple that his forefathers had built for God's name.
16:18 *covert.* Refers to some sort of a covered structure, perhaps for temple guards. *for the king of Assyria.* Literally, "because of the face of the king of Assyria," indicating that what he did was in order to appease the king of Assyria.
16:19 *chronicles.* Uninspired records of the king's career that have not been preserved.
16:20 *buried with his fathers.* But, like Joash, not buried in the royal tombs (2 Chron. 24:25; 28:27).

Thoughts for Personal/Family Worship: Chapter 16

1. **"Like father, like son" is not always true. Sometimes that is a bad thing and sometimes good. Ahaz was the son of Jotham, one of Judah's kings who "did that which was right in the sight of the LORD" (15:34). But Ahaz was nothing like his father, and he became the most wicked king in Judah's history up to this point. He was so wicked that his career is evaluated in terms of Israel's kings and his religious practices in terms of the heathen (16:3). He refused to trust the Lord for help (Isa. 7:1–25). He erected a pagan altar to replace what God had designed and desecrated the temple. However, his son Hezekiah thankfully was nothing like him. Ironically, Judah's worst king gave birth to one of Judah's best. Such is the grace of God. This is a reminder that environment is not what makes a sinner or a saint. Ahaz was in a good home with all of its blessing and benefits, but he rejected his father's God. Hezekiah likewise rejected his father's gods and came to genuine faith in the one true and living God. This should be a warning to everyone raised in a Christian home that you must individually come to a personal knowledge of the Lord, believing and obeying the Word of the Lord.**
2. **Ahaz's replacing God's altar with a pagan altar illustrates a fundamental error of all false religion: the assumption that God can be approached in a way other than what He has commanded. The brazen altar was the place for all of the sacrifices that represented the sacrifice of Christ, the Lamb slain from the foundation of the world. Replacing God's ordained worship with man-made worship ("will worship") ultimately leads to rejecting the gospel of Jesus Christ (Col. 2:19,23).**

The Destruction of Israel by Assyria (2 Kings 17:1–41)
Chapter 17: ***The Assyrians carry Israel captive and repopulate Samaria with those they have exiled from other nations.***

17:3 *presents.* Tribute money (v. 4).
17:6 Israel was deported to the regions of northern Mesopotamia.
17:7–23 The theological justification for and explanation of Israel's deportation. Militarily, Israel was no match against the Assyrians, but their defeat was the consequence of their sin against God, not of their military weakness.
17:7 *feared.* Worshiped.

cities, from the tower of the watchmen to the
fenced city.
10 And they set them up images and groves in
every high hill, and under every green tree:
11 And there they burnt incense in all the high
places, as *did* the heathen whom the LORD carried
away before them; and wrought wicked things to
provoke the LORD to anger:
12 For they served idols, whereof the LORD had
said unto them, Ye shall not do this thing.
13 Yet the LORD testified against Israel, and
against Judah, by all the prophets, *and by* all the
seers, saying, Turn ye from your evil ways, and
keep my commandments *and* my statutes, according to all the law which I commanded your
fathers, and which I sent to you by my servants
the prophets.
14 Notwithstanding they would not hear, but
hardened their necks, like to the neck of their fathers, that did not believe in the LORD their God.
15 And they rejected his statutes, and his covenant that he made with their fathers, and his
testimonies which he testified against them; and
they followed vanity, and became vain, and went
after the heathen that *were* round about them,
concerning whom the LORD had charged them,
that they should not do like them.
16 And they left all the commandments of the
LORD their God, and made them molten images,
even two calves, and made a grove, and worshipped all the host of heaven, and served Baal.
17 And they caused their sons and their daughters to pass through the fire, and used divination
and enchantments, and sold themselves to do evil
in the sight of the LORD, to provoke him to anger.
18 Therefore the LORD was very angry with Israel,
and removed them out of his sight: there was
none left but the tribe of Judah only.
19 Also Judah kept not the commandments of
the LORD their God, but walked in the statutes of
Israel which they made.
20 And the LORD rejected all the seed of Israel,
and afflicted them, and delivered them into the
hand of spoilers, until he had cast them out of his
sight.
21 For he rent Israel from the house of David;
and they made Jeroboam the son of Nebat king:
and Jeroboam drave Israel from following the
LORD, and made them sin a great sin.
22 For the children of Israel walked in all the sins
of Jeroboam which he did; they departed not
from them;
23 Until the LORD removed Israel out of his sight,
as he had said by all his servants the prophets. So
was Israel carried away out of their own land to
Assyria unto this day.
24 ¶ And the king of Assyria brought *men* from
Babylon, and from Cuthah, and from Ava, and
from Hamath, and from Sepharvaim, and placed
them in the cities of Samaria instead of the children of Israel: and they possessed Samaria, and
dwelt in the cities thereof.
25 And *so* it was at the beginning of their dwelling
there, *that* they feared not the LORD: therefore the
LORD sent lions among them, which slew *some* of
them.
26 Wherefore they spake to the king of Assyria,
saying, The nations which thou hast removed,
and placed in the cities of Samaria, know not the
manner of the God of the land: therefore he hath
sent lions among them, and, behold, they slay
them, because they know not the manner of the
God of the land.
27 Then the king of Assyria commanded, saying,
Carry thither one of the priests whom ye brought
from thence; and let them go and dwell there, and
let him teach them the manner of the God of the
land.
28 Then one of the priests whom they had carried
away from Samaria came and dwelt in Beth-el,
and taught them how they should fear the LORD.
29 Howbeit every nation made gods of their own,
and put *them* in the houses of the high places
which the Samaritans had made, every nation in
their cities wherein they dwelt.
30 And the men of Babylon made Succoth-benoth, and the men of Cuth made Nergal, and the
men of Hamath made Ashima,
31 And the Avites made Nibhaz and Tartak,
and the Sepharvites burnt their children in fire

17:9 *did secretly.* The word occurs only here and may refer either to behavior they attempted to cover up or to false accusations they made against the Lord.
17:10 *groves.* Asherah, wooden poles erected near an altar used in pagan rituals (v. 16).
17:13 *my servants the prophets.* The central function of the prophets was to be the voice of the Lord testifying to Israel of His covenant promises, laws, and threats (v. 15; Judg. 6:8–10; 2 Chron. 24:19–20; Neh. 9:26,30).
17:15 *vanity.* Worthless idols, in reality nonexistent or nothing.
17:16 *the host of heaven.* The sun, planets, and stars. Such worship was forbidden by the Lord (Deut. 4:19).
17:20 *spoilers.* Those who plundered.
17:23 *as he had said by all his servants the prophets.* The warnings of God's covenant witnesses against lawbreakers (v. 13) all came true, according to the curses for disobedience declared by Moses (Lev. 26; Deut. 28).
17:24 *the king of Assyria brought men from Babylon.* The beginning of the Samaritans (v. 29; John 4:9).
17:25 *feared not the LORD.* Did not worship the Lord according to the Mosaic laws.
17:26 *know not the manner of the God of the land.* Typical of pagans, they thought that different regions were governed by different deities (1 Kings 20:23), each requiring their own particular form of worship.
17:28 *how they should fear the LORD.* Here referring only to the rituals of worship.

to Adrammelech and Anammelech, the gods of
Sepharvaim.
32 So they feared the LORD, and made unto
themselves of the lowest of them priests of the
high places, which sacrificed for them in the
houses of the high places.
33 They feared the LORD, and served their own
gods, after the manner of the nations whom they
carried away from thence.
34 Unto this day they do after the former
manners: they fear not the LORD, neither do they
after their statutes, or after their ordinances, or
after the law and commandment which the LORD
commanded the children of Jacob, whom he
named Israel;
35 With whom the LORD had made a covenant,
and charged them, saying, Ye shall not fear other
gods, nor bow yourselves to them, nor serve them,
nor sacrifice to them:
36 But the LORD, who brought you up out of the
land of Egypt with great power and a stretched
out arm, him shall ye fear, and him shall ye wor-
ship, and to him shall ye do sacrifice.
37 And the statutes, and the ordinances, and the
law, and the commandment, which he wrote for
you, ye shall observe to do for evermore; and ye
shall not fear other gods.
38 And the covenant that I have made with you
ye shall not forget; neither shall ye fear other gods.
39 But the LORD your God ye shall fear; and
he shall deliver you out of the hand of all your
enemies.
40 Howbeit they did not hearken, but they did
after their former manner.
41 So these nations feared the LORD, and served
their graven images, both their children, and their
children's children: as did their fathers, so do they
unto this day.

CHAPTER 18

NOW it came to pass in the third year of Hoshea
son of Elah king of Israel, *that* Hezekiah the son
of Ahaz king of Judah began to reign.
2 Twenty and five years old was he when he began
to reign; and he reigned twenty and nine years in
Jerusalem. His mother's name also *was* Abi, the
daughter of Zachariah.
3 And he did *that which was* right in the sight of
the LORD, according to all that David his father
did.
4 ¶ He removed the high places, and brake the
images, and cut down the groves, and brake in
pieces the brasen serpent that Moses had made:
for unto those days the children of Israel did burn
incense to it: and he called it Nehushtan.
5 He trusted in the LORD God of Israel; so that
after him was none like him among all the kings
of Judah, nor *any* that were before him.
6 For he clave to the LORD, *and* departed not
from following him, but kept his command-
ments, which the LORD commanded Moses.
7 And the LORD was with him; *and* he prospered
whithersoever he went forth: and he rebelled
against the king of Assyria, and served him not.
8 He smote the Philistines, *even* unto Gaza, and
the borders thereof, from the tower of the watch-
men to the fenced city.
9 ¶ And it came to pass in the fourth year of king
Hezekiah, which *was* the seventh year of Hoshea

17:33–34 *They feared the LORD, and served their own gods.* The new inhabitants were syncretistic, thinking they could serve the Lord as well as their own false gods. But in reality *they fear[ed] not the LORD*, for the true fear of the Lord consists not merely of some outward forms of worship but in supreme and exclusive love, adoration, hope, and obedience in response to His Word (vv. 35–39; Deut. 6:13–14; 10:12).

Thoughts for Personal/Family Worship: Chapter 17

1. **Had there been newspapers or news blogs back when Israel fell to the Assyrians (722 BC), the reports would have been much the same as news reports today about the affairs of the state. There would have been headlines regarding Assyria's ruthless military machine and commentaries on their newly devised scheme of deportation and reassignment of populations in order to maintain control over their annexed territories. Although there were indeed military and political explanations for what happened to Israel, those were not the real story. The Scripture makes it clear that all of this happened because of Israel's sin and that godless and fierce Assyria was the weapon God used to accomplish His purpose of judgment (Isa. 8:7). God is still on His throne, governing all the events of this world with a view to His unfailing purpose. Let us place our trust in the Lord and not in men or governments.**
2. **The worship of the Samaritans resembles far too much of modern worship. They had a problem (lions), so they learned how to give to God what they thought He wanted in order to alleviate the trouble. Worship was not about God but about making life better. So today, many think that Jesus is a quick fix to their problems, whether financial, physical, relational, or whatever. Going to church or praying is just a means of giving to God what they think He wants in order to gain what they want. We must learn that God will not be manipulated or used as a means to an end.**

The Spiritual Revival of Judah under Hezekiah (2 Kings 18:1—20:21)

Chapter 18: *Hezekiah restores true worship and is threatened by the Assyrians.*

18:4 *groves*. See note at 17:10. *brake . . . the brasen serpent.* Israel had turned a wonderful symbol of God's grace into an object of idolatry. *Nehushtan*. Literally, "the bronze thing," indicating that it was just a piece of metal.
18:6 *clave*. Clung to. This is what God required (Deut. 10:20).
18:7 *rebelled against the king of Assyria*. Breaking the vassal agreement of his father, Ahaz (16:7).

son of Elah king of Israel, *that* Shalmaneser king of
Assyria came up against Samaria, and besieged it.
10 And at the end of three years they took it: *even*
in the sixth year of Hezekiah, that *is* the ninth year
of Hoshea king of Israel, Samaria was taken.
11 And the king of Assyria did carry away Israel
unto Assyria, and put them in Halah and in Ha-
bor *by* the river of Gozan, and in the cities of the
Medes:
12 Because they obeyed not the voice of the LORD
their God, but transgressed his covenant, *and* all
that Moses the servant of the LORD commanded,
and would not hear *them*, nor do *them*.
13 ¶ Now in the fourteenth year of king Hezekiah
did Sennacherib king of Assyria come up against
all the fenced cities of Judah, and took them.
14 And Hezekiah king of Judah sent to the king
of Assyria to Lachish, saying, I have offended; re-
turn from me: that which thou puttest on me will
I bear. And the king of Assyria appointed unto
Hezekiah king of Judah three hundred talents of
silver and thirty talents of gold.
15 And Hezekiah gave *him* all the silver that was
found in the house of the LORD, and in the trea-
sures of the king's house.
16 At that time did Hezekiah cut off *the gold from*
the doors of the temple of the LORD, and *from*
the pillars which Hezekiah king of Judah had
overlaid, and gave it to the king of Assyria.
17 ¶ And the king of Assyria sent Tartan and
Rab-saris and Rab-shakeh from Lachish to king
Hezekiah with a great host against Jerusalem.
And they went up and came to Jerusalem. And
when they were come up, they came and stood
by the conduit of the upper pool, which *is* in the
highway of the fuller's field.
18 And when they had called to the king, there
came out to them Eliakim the son of Hilkiah,
which *was* over the household, and Shebna the
scribe, and Joah the son of Asaph the recorder.
19 And Rab-shakeh said unto them, Speak ye
now to Hezekiah, Thus saith the great king, the
king of Assyria, What confidence *is* this wherein
thou trustest?
20 Thou sayest, (but *they are but* vain words,) *I
have* counsel and strength for the war. Now on
whom dost thou trust, that thou rebellest against
me?
21 Now, behold, thou trustest upon the staff of
this bruised reed, *even* upon Egypt, on which if
a man lean, it will go into his hand, and pierce
it: so *is* Pharaoh king of Egypt unto all that trust
on him.
22 But if ye say unto me, We trust in the LORD our
God: *is* not that he, whose high places and whose
altars Hezekiah hath taken away, and hath said to
Judah and Jerusalem, Ye shall worship before this
altar in Jerusalem?
23 Now therefore, I pray thee, give pledges to my
lord the king of Assyria, and I will deliver thee two
thousand horses, if thou be able on thy part to set
riders upon them.
24 How then wilt thou turn away the face of
one captain of the least of my master's servants,
and put thy trust on Egypt for chariots and for
horsemen?
25 Am I now come up without the LORD against
this place to destroy it? The LORD said to me, Go
up against this land, and destroy it.
26 Then said Eliakim the son of Hilkiah, and
Shebna, and Joah, unto Rab-shakeh, Speak, I pray
thee, to thy servants in the Syrian language; for
we understand *it*: and talk not with us in the Jews'
language in the ears of the people that *are* on the
wall.
27 But Rab-shakeh said unto them, Hath my
master sent me to thy master, and to thee, to
speak these words? *hath he* not *sent me* to the men
which sit on the wall, that they may eat their own
dung, and drink their own piss with you?
28 Then Rab-shakeh stood and cried with a
loud voice in the Jews' language, and spake, say-
ing, Hear the word of the great king, the king of
Assyria:
29 Thus saith the king, Let not Hezekiah deceive
you: for he shall not be able to deliver you out of
his hand:
30 Neither let Hezekiah make you trust in the
LORD, saying, The LORD will surely deliver us, and
this city shall not be delivered into the hand of the
king of Assyria.
31 Hearken not to Hezekiah: for thus saith the

18:14 *talents*. A talent is a weight of about 66 pounds.
18:17 *Tartan, Rab-saris, Rab-shakeh*. Not names but titles referring to military positions: "field-marshal," "high official," and "chief spokesman" or "chief of the officers," respectively. *host*. Army. *conduit*. Man-made aqueduct. *fuller*. One who washes garments.
18:20 *vain words*. Literally, "a word of lips," an expression indicating empty talk.
18:23 *give pledges*. Literally, "make a wager," the terms of which follow. The bet was that Hezekiah could not find enough men to mount the horses if Sennacherib supplied them.
18:25 *The LORD said to me*. A common ploy in ancient warfare; for instance, Cyrus would later claim that Marduk, the chief Babylonian god, had commissioned him to conquer Babylon (recorded on the Cyrus Cylinder).
18:26 *the Syrian language*. Aramaic, which would become the language of international communication. *Jews' language*. Hebrew, then the native language of Judah.
18:27 *their own piss*. Literally, "the water of their feet." The disgusting diet describes what would happen if the city were sieged, a most intimating and mocking threat.
18:31 *Make an agreement with me by a present*. Literally, "make with me a blessing," referring here to a surrender of capitulation.

king of Assyria, Make *an agreement* with me by
a present, and come out to me, and *then* eat ye
every man of his own vine, and every one of his
fig tree, and drink ye every one the waters of his
cistern:
32 Until I come and take you away to a land like
your own land, a land of corn and wine, a land
of bread and vineyards, a land of oil olive and of
honey, that ye may live, and not die: and hearken
not unto Hezekiah, when he persuadeth you,
saying, The LORD will deliver us.
33 Hath any of the gods of the nations delivered at all his land out of the hand of the king of
Assyria?
34 Where *are* the gods of Hamath, and of Arpad?
where *are* the gods of Sepharvaim, Hena, and
Ivah? have they delivered Samaria out of mine
hand?
35 Who *are* they among all the gods of the countries, that have delivered their country out of
mine hand, that the LORD should deliver Jerusalem out of mine hand?
36 But the people held their peace, and answered
him not a word: for the king's commandment
was, saying, Answer him not.
37 Then came Eliakim the son of Hilkiah, which
was over the household, and Shebna the scribe,
and Joah the son of Asaph the recorder, to Hezekiah with *their* clothes rent, and told him the
words of Rab-shakeh.

CHAPTER 19

AND it came to pass, when king Hezekiah heard *it*,
that he rent his clothes, and covered himself with
sackcloth, and went into the house of the LORD.
2 And he sent Eliakim, which *was* over the household, and Shebna the scribe, and the elders of
the priests, covered with sackcloth, to Isaiah the
prophet the son of Amoz.
3 And they said unto him, Thus saith Hezekiah,
This day *is* a day of trouble, and of rebuke, and
blasphemy: for the children are come to the birth,
and *there is* not strength to bring forth.
4 It may be the LORD thy God will hear all the
words of Rab-shakeh, whom the king of Assyria
his master hath sent to reproach the living God;
and will reprove the words which the LORD thy
God hath heard: wherefore lift up *thy* prayer for
the remnant that are left.
5 So the servants of king Hezekiah came to
Isaiah.
6 ¶ And Isaiah said unto them, Thus shall ye say
to your master, Thus saith the LORD, Be not afraid
of the words which thou hast heard, with which
the servants of the king of Assyria have blasphemed me.
7 Behold, I will send a blast upon him, and he
shall hear a rumour, and shall return to his own
land; and I will cause him to fall by the sword in
his own land.
8 ¶ So Rab-shakeh returned, and found the king
of Assyria warring against Libnah: for he had
heard that he was departed from Lachish.
9 And when he heard say of Tirhakah king of
Ethiopia, Behold, he is come out to fight against
thee: he sent messengers again unto Hezekiah,
saying,
10 Thus shall ye speak to Hezekiah king of Judah,
saying, Let not thy God in whom thou trustest

18:32 *persuadeth*. Hebrew, "misleads."
18:34 *Where are the gods of*. We have here a list of the cities the Assyrians had recently conquered. They boasted that the gods of these cities were unable to deliver their people and concluded that God would not be able to deliver Jerusalem either.
18:36 *the people held their peace*. The Assyrian attempt to instigate an uprising against Hezekiah was a complete failure. The people remained silent.
18:37 *with their clothes rent*. A gesture of great anxiety and sorrow.

Thoughts for Personal/Family Worship: Chapter 18

1. **God's people, even those who live exemplary lives, are not exempt from trouble. Hezekiah was a man who depended completely on the Lord. He trusted God, clung to Him, opposed false worship, and obeyed His commands (vv. 4–6). He demonstrated his dependence on the Lord by his boldness against enemies (vv. 7–8). Yet after fourteen years of consistently doing what was right, trouble came in the person of Sennacherib. A proper relationship with God does not eliminate threats and troubles. In fact, the closer to God one is, the greater the potential for hostility from the world, for it hates Christ (John 15:18; 1 John 3:13). So trouble is not necessarily God's chastening; it can be a means of testing and strengthening faith and dependence. Submit to God's tests, that they may do their good work.**
2. **Rab-shakeh represents the tactics Satan often uses to intimidate God's people, and we are not to be ignorant of his devices (2 Cor. 2:11). First, he accused Hezekiah of narrow-mindedness (2 Kings 18:22), deception (v. 29), and misguidance (v. 30), all attempts to get the people to turn against their king. Second, he tried to make surrendering to the enemy attractive, with the prospect of a stronger army (v. 23) and prosperity (vv. 31–32). Third, he cast doubt on God's goodness (v. 25) and power (vv. 32–35), a tactic that dates to the garden of Eden (Gen. 3:1–6). Similarly, Satan attempts to turn us against King Jesus, to woo our hearts with the supposed joys of sin, and to weaken our faith in God. How can Christians resist each one of these temptations?**

Chapter 19: ***Hezekiah sends for Isaiah and then prays for deliverance, which God gives in a miraculous way.***

19:1 *rent his clothes . . . sackcloth*. Gestures of mourning and sorrow.
19:2 *Isaiah*. Hezekiah's calling for the prophet expressed his

deceive thee, saying, Jerusalem shall not be
delivered into the hand of the king of Assyria.
11 Behold, thou hast heard what the kings of
Assyria have done to all lands, by destroying them
utterly: and shalt thou be delivered?
12 Have the gods of the nations delivered them
which my fathers have destroyed; *as* Gozan, and
Haran, and Rezeph, and the children of Eden
which *were* in Thelasar?
13 Where *is* the king of Hamath, and the king of
Arpad, and the king of the city of Sepharvaim, of
Hena, and Ivah?
14 ¶ And Hezekiah received the letter of the hand
of the messengers, and read it: and Hezekiah went
up into the house of the LORD, and spread it be-
fore the LORD.
15 And Hezekiah prayed before the LORD, and
said, O LORD God of Israel, which dwellest *be-*
tween the cherubims, thou art the God, *even* thou
alone, of all the kingdoms of the earth; thou hast
made heaven and earth.
16 LORD, bow down thine ear, and hear: open,
LORD, thine eyes, and see: and hear the words of
Sennacherib, which hath sent him to reproach the
living God.
17 Of a truth, LORD, the kings of Assyria have
destroyed the nations and their lands,
18 And have cast their gods into the fire: for they
were no gods, but the work of men's hands, wood
and stone: therefore they have destroyed them.
19 Now therefore, O LORD our God, I beseech
thee, save thou us out of his hand, that all the
kingdoms of the earth may know that thou *art*
the LORD God, *even* thou only.
20 ¶ Then Isaiah the son of Amoz sent to
Hezekiah, saying, Thus saith the LORD God of
Israel, *That* which thou hast prayed to me against
Sennacherib king of Assyria I have heard.
21 This *is* the word that the LORD hath spoken
concerning him; The virgin the daughter of Zion
hath despised thee, *and* laughed thee to scorn; the
daughter of Jerusalem hath shaken her head at
thee.
22 Whom hast thou reproached and blasphemed?
and against whom hast thou exalted *thy* voice,
and lifted up thine eyes on high? *even* against the
Holy *One* of Israel.
23 By thy messengers thou hast reproached the
Lord, and hast said, With the multitude of my
chariots I am come up to the height of the moun-
tains, to the sides of Lebanon, and will cut down
the tall cedar trees thereof, *and* the choice fir trees
thereof: and I will enter into the lodgings of his
borders, *and into* the forest of his Carmel.
24 I have digged and drunk strange waters, and
with the sole of my feet have I dried up all the
rivers of besieged places.
25 Hast thou not heard long ago *how* I have done
it, *and* of ancient times that I have formed it? now
have I brought it to pass, that thou shouldest be to
lay waste fenced cities *into* ruinous heaps.
26 Therefore their inhabitants were of small
power, they were dismayed and confounded; they
were *as* the grass of the field, and *as* the green
herb, *as* the grass on the housetops, and *as corn*
blasted before it be grown up.
27 But I know thy abode, and thy going out, and
thy coming in, and thy rage against me.
28 Because thy rage against me and thy tumult is
come up into mine ears, therefore I will put my
hook in thy nose, and my bridle in thy lips, and
I will turn thee back by the way by which thou
camest.
29 And this *shall be* a sign unto thee, Ye shall eat
this year such things as grow of themselves, and in
the second year that which springeth of the same;
and in the third year sow ye, and reap, and plant
vineyards, and eat the fruits thereof.
30 And the remnant that is escaped of the house
of Judah shall yet again take root downward, and
bear fruit upward.
31 For out of Jerusalem shall go forth a remnant,
and they that escape out of mount Zion: the zeal
of the LORD *of hosts* shall do this.
32 Therefore thus saith the LORD concerning the
king of Assyria, He shall not come into this city,

---

dependence on God's Word. The prophet would be to Hezekiah as the Bible is for us.

19:3 *blasphemy*. Hebrew, "humiliation or contempt."

19:4 *It may be the LORD thy God will hear*. An expression of faith without presumption as Hezekiah bows before the sovereignty of God. *the living God*. The God who works powerfully for those who call upon Him, in contrast to dead idols (vv. 16–18; Jer. 10:1–16; cf. Ps. 115).

19:7 *blast*. Wind or spirit. *rumour*. Report or news. *fall . . . in his own land*. He was killed by his sons in the temple of his own god (v. 37).

19:8 *Libnah*. A city of Judah located at the Philistine border.

19:14 *spread it before the LORD*. A gesture symbolic of casting all care upon the Lord.

19:15 *thou alone*. Hezekiah rejected the polytheism and pluralism of the nations and asserted the unique sovereignty of the Creator over all that He had made (v. 19; Deut. 4:35,39; Neh. 9:8).

19:21 *despised . . . laughed . . . shaken*. Showed the greatest disdain, disregard, and contempt.

19:22 *the Holy One of Israel*. One of Isaiah's common designations of the Lord in his prophecy, expressing God's supreme glory (Isa. 1:4; 6:1–4; 57:15) and yet His bond with and nearness to His people (12:6; 41:14).

19:25 *how I have done it*. The Lord proclaims that He has given the king of Assyria these victories of which he has boasted (vv. 23–24), for the Lord used Assyria to punish the nations (Isa. 10:5).

19:28 *hook . . . bridle*. God would turn upon the Assyrians the technique they commonly used in leading their captives.

19:31 *the zeal of the LORD*. The burning love of the Lord, combined with His power, shall work this deliverance of Jerusalem.

19:32 *cast a bank*. Construct a ramp to scale the city wall.

THE ONLY TRUE GOD

Within the borders of the universe that humanity inhabits, there are two types of beings. There are those beings that are dependent on another. This category encompasses everything from elephants to snails, from angels to demons, from human beings to viruses. Then there is that one being upon whom all of this depends. He alone is self-existent—the great Yahweh (Jehovah), who told Moses that His name is "I AM THAT I AM" (Ex. 3:14; see also Rev. 1:4). All other beings draw their sustenance and existence from Him. He is utterly unique in that He has no need of anything outside Himself. He alone possesses what students of theology call aseity, the attribute of self-existence (John 1:4; 5:26). Because He gives life to all of creation, from the greatest object to the smallest particle, He is to be confessed as the one and only Creator and God (1 Cor. 8:6).

The Bible's confession of God's uniqueness is also found in the statement that He is holy (Isa. 6:3; Rev. 4:8). The holiness of God means first that He is completely different from His creation. He is the Creator, unique and in total control of all that He has made. Human beings are limited in what we can do. Our knowledge is finite, never exhaustive. And our lives on this earth are relatively short in duration and often dogged by painful experiences—"nasty, brutish, and short," as the philosopher Thomas Hobbes once described them. Not so God. He is immortal, can do all that His good pleasure decides, and has absolutely no limitations. To say that God is holy, then, is to speak of His uniqueness, His otherness from His creation.

Men and women worship many gods. Being made in the image of the true God, human beings have an unquenchable desire to worship. But being fallen, they inevitably worship gods of their own making. John Calvin, the French Reformer, accurately pointed out that the human mind is "a perpetual factory of idols" (*Institutes of the Christian Religion,* 1.11.8; cf. Rom 1:18–25). The sole remedy is God's gift of spiritual sight, by which, when it is given like a ray of light from heaven, people are awakened to know the true God and know themselves as His creatures.

God is thus sovereign over His creation. He gives life and takes it away, raises up nations and mountains and casts them down, and brings suns to light and extinguishes them. And none can hinder Him. What He has decided will surely come to pass, and in this exercise of sovereignty is His glory.

Human beings have the privilege and responsibility of acknowledging this sovereignty of God. However, they can do so only when God so inclines their hearts. By nature they are rebels, despising His authority, with some going against what they instinctively know and claiming that God does not exist.

But He does exist! Of that fact the Christian is more certain than of anything else he or she knows. And it is the Christian's "sweet delight"—to borrow a phrase from Jonathan Edwards, the eighteenth-century gospel preacher—to submit to this great God, to acknowledge his utter dependence upon Him, and to live for Him and His glory. As such, Christian talk about God is far more than a philosophical discussion about His existence. It is joy itself, for the Christian has come to know the one and only true God, and in knowing Him has found meaning for life and, yes, also life eternal (1 John 5:20)—in which he will forever enjoy knowing, loving, and communing with the triune God, basking in His smile and feasting in His presence.

nor shoot an arrow there, nor come before it with
shield, nor cast a bank against it.
33 By the way that he came, by the same shall he
return, and shall not come into this city, saith the
LORD.
34 For I will defend this city, to save it, for mine
own sake, and for my servant David's sake.
35 ¶ And it came to pass that night, that the
angel of the LORD went out, and smote in the
camp of the Assyrians an hundred fourscore and
five thousand: and when they arose early in the
morning, behold, they *were* all dead corpses.
36 So Sennacherib king of Assyria departed, and
went and returned, and dwelt at Nineveh.
37 And it came to pass, as he was worshipping in
the house of Nisroch his god, that Adrammelech
and Sharezer his sons smote him with the sword:
and they escaped into the land of Armenia. And
Esar-haddon his son reigned in his stead.

CHAPTER 20

IN those days was Hezekiah sick unto death. And
the prophet Isaiah the son of Amoz came to him,
and said unto him, Thus saith the LORD, Set thine
house in order; for thou shalt die, and not live.
2 Then he turned his face to the wall, and prayed
unto the LORD, saying,
3 I beseech thee, O LORD, remember now how
I have walked before thee in truth and with a
perfect heart, and have done *that which is* good in
thy sight. And Hezekiah wept sore.
4 And it came to pass, afore Isaiah was gone out
into the middle court, that the word of the LORD
came to him, saying,
5 Turn again, and tell Hezekiah the captain of my
people, Thus saith the LORD, the God of David
thy father, I have heard thy prayer, I have seen thy
tears: behold, I will heal thee: on the third day
thou shalt go up unto the house of the LORD.
6 And I will add unto thy days fifteen years; and
I will deliver thee and this city out of the hand of
the king of Assyria; and I will defend this city for
mine own sake, and for my servant David's sake.
7 And Isaiah said, Take a lump of figs. And they
took and laid *it* on the boil, and he recovered.
8 ¶ And Hezekiah said unto Isaiah, What *shall
be* the sign that the LORD will heal me, and that I
shall go up into the house of the LORD the third
day?
9 And Isaiah said, This sign shalt thou have of the
LORD, that the LORD will do the thing that he hath
spoken: shall the shadow go forward ten degrees,
or go back ten degrees?
10 And Hezekiah answered, It is a light thing for
the shadow to go down ten degrees: nay, but let
the shadow return backward ten degrees.
11 And Isaiah the prophet cried unto the LORD:

19:35 *the angel of the LORD.* Often a designation of a Christophany, a pre-incarnate appearance of Christ, "the messenger who is Jehovah" (Gen. 16:7–14; Ex. 3:1–4). *smote.* Struck. *an hundred fourscore and five thousand.* 185,000. An extant Assyrian record called the Taylor Prism details Sennacherib's campaigns in Judah, saying that he caged up Hezekiah like a bird. In keeping with ancient Near Eastern chronicles, it makes no mention of the slaughter that caused him to retreat.
19:37 *his sons smote him with the sword.* Sennacherib's campaigns against Judah occurred in 701 BC, and his death in 680 BC. Twenty years passed, but God's word was precisely fulfilled (v. 7). The delay did not alter the certainty.

Thoughts for Personal/Family Worship: Chapter 19

1. **Hezekiah provides a wonderful example of how we are to bring all our needs before the Lord. Hezekiah was a man of prayer, and both his prayer and his preparations for prayer set a pattern to follow. Consider first his preparations. *He recognized his need* (v. 3). He was in deep distress, without any ability or power to find remedy without divine intervention. Prayer is always a mark of our sense of dependence upon God. *He was contrite* (v. 1). With humility and reverence and without presumption he entered the Lord's house. His attire spoke of his confession and repentance. *He depended on the Word of God* (v. 2). His calling for Isaiah was not just to gain a prayer partner but to get a fresh word from the Lord to take to prayer to plead before the Lord. He received the word of promise (vv. 6–7). Linking prayer to God's Word is a principle found throughout Scripture (Dan. 9:1–27). We should learn to go to the Lord with our Bibles open as we pray for His will to be done.**
2. **Consider the prayer itself (vv. 14–19). Spreading the letter symbolized what it is for us to cast all our cares and concerns before the throne of grace. First, note the *Person* addressed (v. 15). He appeals to *Jehovah*, the covenant-making and keeping God, who has entered into a living relationship with His people. Second, note the *praise*. He focuses on God's unique position as sovereign and His unique work as Creator. All power and authority are His. Third, note the *petitions*. He uses five imperatives, pleading with God to take note of his problem and be moved to act on his behalf. Prayer should be specific. Fourth, note the *purpose* of the prayer. Ultimately nothing matters but the glory of God (v. 19). He argues that God's name is at stake (v. 16). We can be certain that whatever God does to get glory to Himself will benefit His people.**

Chapter 20: *Hezekiah recovers from a fatal sickness and unwisely displays the riches of the kingdom to emissaries from Babylon.*
20:1 *Set thine house in order.* Literally, "command regarding your house," an expression referring to final preparations. See 2 Chron. 32:24; Isa. 38:1–8.
20:3 *perfect heart.* Whole-hearted consecration. *wept sore.* Literally, "wept a great weeping."
20:4 *afore.* Before.
20:7 *lump of figs.* Apparently there was medicinal strength in figs, yet the healing was of the Lord. God often uses secondary causes to accomplish His will. Taking medicine and trusting God are both wise. *boil.* Ulcer or inflamed spot of some sort.
20:8 *What shall be the sign?* The sign was a divine confirmation of the truth of the word, designed to strengthen faith.

and he brought the shadow ten degrees backward,
by which it had gone down in the dial of Ahaz.
12 ¶ At that time Berodach-baladan, the son
of Baladan, king of Babylon, sent letters and
a present unto Hezekiah: for he had heard that
Hezekiah had been sick.
13 And Hezekiah hearkened unto them, and
shewed them all the house of his precious things,
the silver, and the gold, and the spices, and the
precious ointment, and *all* the house of his ar-
mour, and all that was found in his treasures:
there was nothing in his house, nor in all his do-
minion, that Hezekiah shewed them not.
14 ¶ Then came Isaiah the prophet unto king
Hezekiah, and said unto him, What said these
men? and from whence came they unto thee? And
Hezekiah said, They are come from a far country,
even from Babylon.
15 And he said, What have they seen in thine
house? And Hezekiah answered, All *the things* that
are in mine house have they seen: there is nothing
among my treasures that I have not shewed them.
16 And Isaiah said unto Hezekiah, Hear the word
of the LORD.
17 Behold, the days come, that all that *is* in thine
house, and that which thy fathers have laid up in
store unto this day, shall be carried into Babylon:
nothing shall be left, saith the LORD.
18 And of thy sons that shall issue from thee,
which thou shalt beget, shall they take away; and
they shall be eunuchs in the palace of the king of
Babylon.
19 Then said Hezekiah unto Isaiah, Good *is* the
word of the LORD which thou hast spoken. And
he said, *Is it* not *good*, if peace and truth be in my
days?
20 ¶ And the rest of the acts of Hezekiah, and all
his might, and how he made a pool, and a con-
duit, and brought water into the city, *are* they not
written in the book of the chronicles of the kings
of Judah?
21 And Hezekiah slept with his fathers: and
Manasseh his son reigned in his stead.

CHAPTER 21

MANASSEH *was* twelve years old when he began
to reign, and reigned fifty and five years in Jeru-
salem. And his mother's name *was* Hephzi-bah.
2 And he did *that which was* evil in the sight of
the LORD, after the abominations of the heathen,
whom the LORD cast out before the children of
Israel.
3 For he built up again the high places which
Hezekiah his father had destroyed; and he reared
up altars for Baal, and made a grove, as did Ahab
king of Israel; and worshipped all the host of
heaven, and served them.

Although not always or necessarily, these signs were often supernatural.

20:11 *the dial.* Literally, "the steps or staircase." *degrees.* Steps (vv. 9–10). Sundials of this era were often designed as staircases, so constructed that the shadow would go up or down the steps. Reversing the direction required supernatural intervention.

20:13 Hezekiah did this in pride (2 Chron. 32:25–31; cf. Isa. 39:2). Note how often the word *his* appears here (and "mine" or "my" in 2 Kings 20:15) as he claimed the riches and glory of the kingdom, temporarily forgetting that it was all of God's grace (1 Cor. 4:7).

20:17 *shall be carried into Babylon.* This prophecy would be fulfilled in about 115 years.

20:18 *eunuchs.* Males employed as officers or high officials to the ruler.

20:19 *Good is the word of the LORD.* Hezekiah bowed to God's will. *Is it not good, if peace.* Rather, "will there surely be peace?" The question does not imply selfishness or personal relief but expresses gratitude and amazement for God's mercy in delaying the judgment.

20:20 *conduit.* A channel for carrying water. Hezekiah's water tunnel hewn in the rock underneath Jerusalem was a major accomplishment of engineering. This was especially important in days of war when the city was besieged. The famous Siloam inscription inside the tunnel marks the spot where the two teams of excavators, working in different directions, met to complete the project.

Thoughts for Personal/Family Worship: Chapter 20

1. **Hezekiah's sickness unto death became a most personal test of his faith. His first response was not panic but prayer. When the nation was confronted with certain defeat, he took the matter to the Lord. He did the same when the problem was uniquely his. He is an example of consistency. The fact that he had already demonstrated himself to be a man of prayer gives more credence to his behavior now. This was not desperation; it was normal procedure. We see God's mercy and goodness shining forth in the fact that He heard Hezekiah's cries. Let this be a major encouragement for us to pour out all our needs and cares before the Lord and to do so consistently. God loves to hear and answer prayer.**
2. **Even the best of men are only men and thus are subject to flaws. Hezekiah had demonstrated a humble spirit before God when seeking Him for deliverance. But it appears that some pride rose up within him after receiving that divine help. This is evidenced in the private tour he gave to the emissaries from Babylon, showing off "*his* precious things," "*his* armour," "*his* treasures," "*his* house," and "*his* dominion" (v. 13, emphasis added). In reality, all these things had come from God's goodness and grace to him. It is tragic when tokens of grace become objects of pride and boasting. It is good to remember that we have nothing apart from what God has given to us; we own nothing but owe Him all our thanks and praise. Being the recipients of God's goodness is never reason for arrogance.**

Chapter 21: ***Manasseh's wicked reign earns the sentence of divine judgment, and Amon follows in his ways.***

The Spiritual Ruin of Judah by Manasseh and Amon (2 Kings 21:1–26)

4 And he built altars in the house of the LORD,
of which the LORD said, In Jerusalem will I put
my name.
5 And he built altars for all the host of heaven in
the two courts of the house of the LORD.
6 And he made his son pass through the fire,
and observed times, and used enchantments,
and dealt with familiar spirits and wizards: he
wrought much wickedness in the sight of the
LORD, to provoke *him* to anger.
7 And he set a graven image of the grove that he
had made in the house, of which the LORD said to
David, and to Solomon his son, In this house, and
in Jerusalem, which I have chosen out of all tribes
of Israel, will I put my name for ever:
8 Neither will I make the feet of Israel move any
more out of the land which I gave their fathers;
only if they will observe to do according to all that
I have commanded them, and according to all the
law that my servant Moses commanded them.
9 But they hearkened not: and Manasseh seduced
them to do more evil than did the nations whom
the LORD destroyed before the children of Israel.
10 ¶ And the LORD spake by his servants the
prophets, saying,
11 Because Manasseh king of Judah hath done
these abominations, *and* hath done wickedly
above all that the Amorites did, which *were* be-
fore him, and hath made Judah also to sin with
his idols:
12 Therefore thus saith the LORD God of Israel,
Behold, I *am* bringing *such* evil upon Jerusalem
and Judah, that whosoever heareth of it, both his
ears shall tingle.
13 And I will stretch over Jerusalem the line of
Samaria, and the plummet of the house of Ahab:
and I will wipe Jerusalem as *a man* wipeth a dish,
wiping *it*, and turning *it* upside down.
14 And I will forsake the remnant of mine in-
heritance, and deliver them into the hand of their
enemies; and they shall become a prey and a spoil
to all their enemies;
15 Because they have done *that which was* evil in
my sight, and have provoked me to anger, since
the day their fathers came forth out of Egypt, even
unto this day.
16 Moreover Manasseh shed innocent blood very
much, till he had filled Jerusalem from one end to
another; beside his sin wherewith he made Judah
to sin, in doing *that which was* evil in the sight of
the LORD.
17 ¶ Now the rest of the acts of Manasseh, and
all that he did, and his sin that he sinned, *are* they
not written in the book of the chronicles of the
kings of Judah?
18 And Manasseh slept with his fathers, and was
buried in the garden of his own house, in the
garden of Uzza: and Amon his son reigned in his
stead.
19 ¶ Amon *was* twenty and two years old when he
began to reign, and he reigned two years in Jeru-
salem. And his mother's name *was* Meshullemeth,
the daughter of Haruz of Jotbah.
20 And he did *that which was* evil in the sight of
the LORD, as his father Manasseh did.
21 And he walked in all the way that his father
walked in, and served the idols that his father
served, and worshipped them:
22 And he forsook the LORD God of his fathers,
and walked not in the way of the LORD.

21:1 *reigned fifty and five years in Jerusalem.* See 2 Chron. 33 for the parallel account. The most wicked of Judah's kings has the longest reign.
21:3 Whereas Hezekiah had reversed the evil done by his father, his own son reversed the good that he had done. *grove.* An Asherah, a wooden pole erected near an altar, a key component in the Baal rituals (v. 7). *host of heaven.* Army of heaven, referring to the heavenly bodies (v. 5).
21:6 *observed times.* Interpreted signs to predict the future. *used enchantments.* Sought or gave omens, practicing divination.
21:8 *Neither will I make the feet of Israel move any more out of the land.* Literally, "I will not make them homeless again or cause them to wander." *only if.* Remaining in the land was conditioned upon their faithfulness (Deut. 4:25–28; 28:64).
21:9 *seduced.* Misled, caused to err, or tempted.
21:11 *Because Manasseh king of Judah hath done these abominations.* Manasseh's sin, both in its offense against God and its influence on the people, became the ruin of Judah and ultimately the end of the national monarchy (23:26; 24:3–4). *Amorites.* The term applies to the whole of the Canaanite nations.
21:12 *evil.* Calamity or disaster, referring to the judgment to come. *both his ears shall tingle.* What is heard is astonishing.
21:13 *the line of Samaria, and the plummet of the house of Ahab.* Masons use a plummet, a weight on a string to ensure that walls are built vertically straight. Now the Lord measures Judah and Jerusalem in the same way he did Israel and Samaria. This implies that Judah and Jerusalem would be struck with the same judgment and destruction (Isa. 28:17). *I will wipe Jerusalem as a man wipeth a dish.* The Lord will bring destruction and emptiness to the city for its uncleanness.
21:16 *his sin wherewith he made Judah to sin.* Idolatry.
21:17 *all that he did.* Later the Lord humbled Manasseh, and he turned away from his idolatry (2 Chron. 33:11–19). *chronicles.* Uninspired records of the king's career that have not been preserved (2 Kings 21:25).
21:18 *in his stead.* In place of him.
21:20–21 *his father.* Manasseh's son sadly imitated his father's sins, but not his repentance (2 Chron. 33:23).
21:22 *forsook the LORD.* To abandon the Lord as one's only God was to break His covenant and bring down its curses (Deut. 28:20; 29:25–27; 31:16).

Thoughts for Personal/Family Worship: Chapter 21

After the godly reign of Hezekiah, Manasseh departed from the ways of the Lord. The heart of man is inclined to all wickedness. Godliness is not automatically inherited. Every man must receive heart-renewing grace. This is a personal matter. Every generation must discover

23 ¶ And the servants of Amon conspired against
him, and slew the king in his own house.
24 And the people of the land slew all them that
had conspired against king Amon; and the people
of the land made Josiah his son king in his stead.
25 Now the rest of the acts of Amon which he did,
are they not written in the book of the chronicles
of the kings of Judah?
26 And he was buried in his sepulchre in the gar-
den of Uzza: and Josiah his son reigned in his
stead.

CHAPTER 22

JOSIAH *was* eight years old when he began to
reign, and he reigned thirty and one years in Je-
rusalem. And his mother's name *was* Jedidah, the
daughter of Adaiah of Boscath.
2 And he did *that which was* right in the sight of
the LORD, and walked in all the way of David his
father, and turned not aside to the right hand or
to the left.
3 ¶ And it came to pass in the eighteenth year of
king Josiah, *that* the king sent Shaphan the son of
Azaliah, the son of Meshullam, the scribe, to the
house of the LORD, saying,
4 Go up to Hilkiah the high priest, that he may
sum the silver which is brought into the house
of the LORD, which the keepers of the door have
gathered of the people:
5 And let them deliver it into the hand of the
doers of the work, that have the oversight of the
house of the LORD: and let them give it to the
doers of the work which *is* in the house of the
LORD, to repair the breaches of the house,
6 Unto carpenters, and builders, and masons,
and to buy timber and hewn stone to repair the
house.
7 Howbeit there was no reckoning made with
them of the money that was delivered into their
hand, because they dealt faithfully.
8 ¶ And Hilkiah the high priest said unto Sha-
phan the scribe, I have found the book of the law
in the house of the LORD. And Hilkiah gave the
book to Shaphan, and he read it.
9 And Shaphan the scribe came to the king,
and brought the king word again, and said, Thy
servants have gathered the money that was found
in the house, and have delivered it into the hand
of them that do the work, that have the oversight
of the house of the LORD.
10 And Shaphan the scribe shewed the king,
saying, Hilkiah the priest hath delivered me a
book. And Shaphan read it before the king.
11 And it came to pass, when the king had heard
the words of the book of the law, that he rent his
clothes.
12 And the king commanded Hilkiah the priest,
and Ahikam the son of Shaphan, and Achbor the
son of Michaiah, and Shaphan the scribe, and
Asahiah a servant of the king's, saying,
13 Go ye, enquire of the LORD for me, and for the
people, and for all Judah, concerning the words
of this book that is found: for great *is* the wrath of
the LORD that is kindled against us, because our
fathers have not hearkened unto the words of this
book, to do according unto all that which is writ-
ten concerning us.
14 So Hilkiah the priest, and Ahikam, and Achbor,
and Shaphan, and Asahiah, went unto Huldah the
prophetess, the wife of Shallum the son of Tikvah,
the son of Harhas, keeper of the wardrobe; (now
she dwelt in Jerusalem in the college;) and they
communed with her.
15 ¶ And she said unto them, Thus saith the
LORD God of Israel, Tell the man that sent you
to me,
16 Thus saith the LORD, Behold, I will bring evil
upon this place, and upon the inhabitants thereof,
even all the words of the book which the king of
Judah hath read:
17 Because they have forsaken me, and have
burned incense unto other gods, that they might
provoke me to anger with all the works of their

the blessing of fearing the Lord. By nature we all have a wicked heart. Therefore the Lord Jesus teaches us that we must be born again (John 3:3). Let us emphasize this necessity and pray for this grace, that our eyes may be opened, our hearts circumcised, and our lives renewed. Children, do not take for granted that because your parents are Christians you are a Christian. Conversion is personal.

Another Revival of Judah under Josiah (1 Kings 22:1—23:30)

Chapter 22: ***The book of the Law is discovered during temple renovations, and its reading convicts Josiah, leading him to seek the Lord.***

22:3 *in the eighteenth year.* By this time Josiah had already begun significant religious reforms to reverse the policies of his father and grandfather (2 Chron. 34:3–8).

22:4–5 *sum.* Count. The Hebrew has the idea of "doing something with the silver." Rather than hoarding the silver, he ordered that it be put to use in repairing the temple.

22:7 *dealt faithfully.* Worked in honesty, were trustworthy.

22:8 *the book of the law.* Perhaps the first five books of Moses, but most likely the book of Deuteronomy (quoted in 14:6; cf. 1 Kings 9:8–9), in which the Lord announces specific judgments upon transgressing His covenant (Deut. 4; 28).

22:9 *gathered the money.* Literally, "melted the silver," expressing the spending of the money.

22:11 *rent his clothes.* A gesture of mourning and sorrow, expressing his sense of conviction (v. 19).

22:14 *keeper of the wardrobe.* The one supervising the garments. The Hebrew is clear that this was Shallum's occupation, not Huldah's. *the college.* The second quarter or district.

22:16 *evil.* Calamity or disaster, referring to the divine judgment (v. 20).

hands; therefore my wrath shall be kindled
against this place, and shall not be quenched.
18 But to the king of Judah which sent you to en-
quire of the LORD, thus shall ye say to him, Thus
saith the LORD God of Israel, *As touching* the
words which thou hast heard;
19 Because thine heart was tender, and thou hast
humbled thyself before the LORD, when thou
heardest what I spake against this place, and
against the inhabitants thereof, that they should
become a desolation and a curse, and hast rent
thy clothes, and wept before me; I also have heard
thee, saith the LORD.
20 Behold therefore, I will gather thee unto thy
fathers, and thou shalt be gathered into thy grave
in peace; and thine eyes shall not see all the evil
which I will bring upon this place. And they
brought the king word again.

CHAPTER 23

AND the king sent, and they gathered unto him all
the elders of Judah and of Jerusalem.
2 And the king went up into the house of the
LORD, and all the men of Judah and all the inhab-
itants of Jerusalem with him, and the priests, and
the prophets, and all the people, both small and
great: and he read in their ears all the words of
the book of the covenant which was found in the
house of the LORD.
3 ¶ And the king stood by a pillar, and made
a covenant before the LORD, to walk after the
LORD, and to keep his commandments and his
testimonies and his statutes with all *their* heart
and all *their* soul, to perform the words of this
covenant that were written in this book. And all
the people stood to the covenant.
4 And the king commanded Hilkiah the high
priest, and the priests of the second order, and
the keepers of the door, to bring forth out of the
temple of the LORD all the vessels that were made
for Baal, and for the grove, and for all the host of
heaven: and he burned them without Jerusalem
in the fields of Kidron, and carried the ashes of
them unto Beth-el.
5 And he put down the idolatrous priests, whom
the kings of Judah had ordained to burn incense
in the high places in the cities of Judah, and in
the places round about Jerusalem; them also that
burned incense unto Baal, to the sun, and to the
moon, and to the planets, and to all the host of
heaven.
6 And he brought out the grove from the house
of the LORD, without Jerusalem, unto the brook
Kidron, and burned it at the brook Kidron, and
stamped *it* small to powder, and cast the powder
thereof upon the graves of the children of the
people.
7 And he brake down the houses of the sod-
omites, that *were* by the house of the LORD, where
the women wove hangings for the grove.
8 And he brought all the priests out of the cities
of Judah, and defiled the high places where the
priests had burned incense, from Geba to Beer-
sheba, and brake down the high places of the
gates that *were* in the entering in of the gate of
Joshua the governor of the city, which *were* on a
man's left hand at the gate of the city.
9 Nevertheless the priests of the high places came
not up to the altar of the LORD in Jerusalem, but
they did eat of the unleavened bread among their
brethren.

22:19 *heart was tender.* Softened and made penitent.
22:20 *grave in peace.* Josiah was killed in battle against the Egyptians (23:29) but was preserved from the horrors of the impending divine judgment against Judah.

Thoughts for Personal/Family Worship: Chapter 22

As soon as Josiah heard the law of God, he became a doer of the Word and not just a hearer (James 1:22). During his days the inspired Scriptures were still in the process of being revealed, and actual copies of Scripture were rare. It was a wonderful providence of God that led to the discovery of a portion of Scripture that had been hidden somewhere in the temple. Josiah heard it read only once, and it immediately changed him. Most of us have multiple copies of the whole Bible that we can access so easily. Tragically, many homes have Bibles that are hidden in plain sight, never being read. Some people read the Bible on a regular basis without being affected by its message. We should acknowledge the wonderful privilege that is ours in having ready access to the Scriptures and remember that increased privilege increases responsibility. How can we train ourselves to consciously approach the reading or preaching of the Bible with an eye on immediate obedience?

Chapter 23: ***Josiah enforces religious reforms throughout the land, but too late to avert ultimate judgment.***

23:2 *book of the covenant.* Most likely Deuteronomy (see note at 22:8).
23:3 *stood by a pillar.* See note at 11:14. *all the people stood to the covenant.* The people pledged to live according to the covenant of the Lord.
23:4 *grove.* The wooden pole erected near an altar that was integral to pagan rituals (vv. 6,14). *host of heaven.* The army of heaven, referring to the heavenly bodies that had become objects of worship (see vv. 5,11).
23:6 *children of the people.* Literally, "the sons of the people," not young children but a reference to the common people (Jer. 17:19; 26:23). In particular, it was the graves of those who had worshiped the idols (2 Chron. 34:4).
23:7 *sodomites.* Homosexual male prostitutes, strictly forbidden by the Lord (Deut. 23:17). *wove hangings.* Literally, "wove houses," referring to some sort of drapery for the *grove* or the wooden pole.
23:8 *from Geba to Beersheba.* Refers to the whole land, from north to south. *left hand.* Refers to the north, since ancient maps were oriented with east on top.

10 And he defiled Topheth, which *is* in the valley
of the children of Hinnom, that no man might
make his son or his daughter to pass through the
fire to Molech.
11 And he took away the horses that the kings
of Judah had given to the sun, at the entering
in of the house of the LORD, by the chamber of
Nathan-melech the chamberlain, which *was* in
the suburbs, and burned the chariots of the sun
with fire.
12 And the altars that *were* on the top of the
upper chamber of Ahaz, which the kings of Judah
had made, and the altars which Manasseh had
made in the two courts of the house of the LORD,
did the king beat down, and brake *them* down
from thence, and cast the dust of them into the
brook Kidron.
13 And the high places that *were* before Jerusa-
lem, which *were* on the right hand of the mount
of corruption, which Solomon the king of Israel
had builded for Ashtoreth the abomination of the
Zidonians, and for Chemosh the abomination of
the Moabites, and for Milcom the abomination of
the children of Ammon, did the king defile.
14 And he brake in pieces the images, and cut
down the groves, and filled their places with the
bones of men.
15 ¶ Moreover the altar that *was* at Beth-el, *and*
the high place which Jeroboam the son of Nebat,
who made Israel to sin, had made, both that altar
and the high place he brake down, and burned the
high place, *and* stamped *it* small to powder, and
burned the grove.
16 And as Josiah turned himself, he spied the
sepulchres that *were* there in the mount, and sent,
and took the bones out of the sepulchres, and
burned *them* upon the altar, and polluted it, ac-
cording to the word of the LORD which the man
of God proclaimed, who proclaimed these words.
17 Then he said, What title *is* that that I see? And
the men of the city told him, *It is* the sepulchre
of the man of God, which came from Judah,
and proclaimed these things that thou hast done
against the altar of Beth-el.
18 And he said, Let him alone; let no man move
his bones. So they let his bones alone, with the
bones of the prophet that came out of Samaria.
19 And all the houses also of the high places that
were in the cities of Samaria, which the kings of
Israel had made to provoke *the* LORD to anger,
Josiah took away, and did to them according to all
the acts that he had done in Beth-el.
20 And he slew all the priests of the high places
that *were* there upon the altars, and burned men's
bones upon them, and returned to Jerusalem.
21 ¶ And the king commanded all the people,
saying, Keep the passover unto the LORD your
God, as *it is* written in the book of this covenant.
22 Surely there was not holden such a passover
from the days of the judges that judged Israel, nor
in all the days of the kings of Israel, nor of the
kings of Judah;
23 But in the eighteenth year of king Josiah,
wherein this passover was holden to the LORD in
Jerusalem.
24 ¶ Moreover the *workers with* familiar spirits,
and the wizards, and the images, and the idols,
and all the abominations that were spied in the
land of Judah and in Jerusalem, did Josiah put
away, that he might perform the words of the law
which were written in the book that Hilkiah the
priest found in the house of the LORD.
25 And like unto him was there no king before
him, that turned to the LORD with all his heart,
and with all his soul, and with all his might, ac-
cording to all the law of Moses; neither after him
arose there *any* like him.
26 ¶ Notwithstanding the LORD turned not from
the fierceness of his great wrath, wherewith his
anger was kindled against Judah, because of all
the provocations that Manasseh had provoked
him withal.
27 And the LORD said, I will remove Judah also
out of my sight, as I have removed Israel, and will
cast off this city Jerusalem which I have chosen,
and the house of which I said, My name shall be
there.
28 Now the rest of the acts of Josiah, and all that

23:10 *Topheth*. A location in the vicinity of Jerusalem, a place associated with child sacrifice. *valley of . . . Hinnom*. See note at Jer. 19:6.
23:11 *chamberlain*. Officer. *suburbs*. Annexes on the western side of the temple.
23:13 *mount of corruption*. The Mount of Olives, where the Jews corrupted themselves because of the idolatry facilitated by Solomon (1 Kings 11:5,7).
23:16 *burned them upon the altar*. The Lord's prophet had declared this around 300 years earlier (1 Kings 13:2). The passing of time does not nullify the certainty of fulfillment.
23:19 *Samaria*. The capital city designates the entire country.
23:20 *he slew all the priests of the high places*. Josiah killed the priests who were still engaged in idolatry and in the worship of the golden calf. He slaughtered them upon their own altars. He burned human bones on these altars, rendering them permanently unusable for worship.
23:22 *there was not holden*. There was not done or kept a Passover like this one.
23:26 *the Lord turned not from the fierceness of his great wrath*. Although Manasseh was converted and forgiven by God (2 Chron. 33:12–13), his idolatry had so dishonored the Lord and corrupted Judah that the Lord had resolved to severely judge Jerusalem and the temple (v. 27; 21:11–16). Even Josiah's reforms did not change this, and the people continued down the path of idolatry (Jer. 3:1–2; 6:7–8; 7:8–10; 8:5–6; Ezek. 22).
23:27 *My name shall be there*. His glory was revealed in the temple (1 Kings 8:10–11,16–19,29; 9:3), and therefore to introduce idolatry there was a horrible offense (Ezek. 8).

he did, *are* they not written in the book of the
chronicles of the kings of Judah?
29 ¶ In his days Pharaoh-nechoh king of Egypt
went up against the king of Assyria to the river
Euphrates: and king Josiah went against him; and
he slew him at Megiddo, when he had seen him.
30 And his servants carried him in a chariot dead
from Megiddo, and brought him to Jerusalem,
and buried him in his own sepulchre. And the
people of the land took Jehoahaz the son of Jo-
siah, and anointed him, and made him king in his
father's stead.
31 ¶ Jehoahaz *was* twenty and three years old
when he began to reign; and he reigned three
months in Jerusalem. And his mother's name *was*
Hamutal, the daughter of Jeremiah of Libnah.
32 And he did *that which was* evil in the sight of
the LORD, according to all that his fathers had
done.
33 And Pharaoh-nechoh put him in bands at
Riblah in the land of Hamath, that he might not
reign in Jerusalem; and put the land to a tribute of
an hundred talents of silver, and a talent of gold.
34 And Pharaoh-nechoh made Eliakim the son
of Josiah king in the room of Josiah his father, and
turned his name to Jehoiakim, and took Jehoahaz
away: and he came to Egypt, and died there.
35 And Jehoiakim gave the silver and the gold to
Pharaoh; but he taxed the land to give the money
according to the commandment of Pharaoh: he
exacted the silver and the gold of the people of
the land, of every one according to his taxation,
to give *it* unto Pharaoh-nechoh.
36 ¶ Jehoiakim *was* twenty and five years old
when he began to reign; and he reigned eleven
years in Jerusalem. And his mother's name *was*
Zebudah, the daughter of Pedaiah of Rumah.
37 And he did *that which was* evil in the sight of
the LORD, according to all that his fathers had
done.

CHAPTER 24

IN his days Nebuchadnezzar king of Babylon
came up, and Jehoiakim became his servant three
years: then he turned and rebelled against him.
2 And the LORD sent against him bands of the
Chaldees, and bands of the Syrians, and bands
of the Moabites, and bands of the children of
Ammon, and sent them against Judah to destroy
it, according to the word of the LORD, which he
spake by his servants the prophets.
3 Surely at the commandment of the LORD came
this upon Judah, to remove *them* out of his sight,
for the sins of Manasseh, according to all that he
did;
4 And also for the innocent blood that he shed:
for he filled Jerusalem with innocent blood;
which the LORD would not pardon.
5 ¶ Now the rest of the acts of Jehoiakim, and all
that he did, *are* they not written in the book of the
chronicles of the kings of Judah?

23:28 *chronicles.* Uninspired records of the king's career that have not been preserved.
23:29 *king Josiah went against him.* Josiah unwisely interfered in the power struggle taking place with the Assyrians and the Egyptians against the Babylonians. This struggle ultimately climaxed at the Battle of Carchemish on the Euphrates (2 Chron. 35:20). Babylon's victory marked the beginning of the Neo-Babylonian Empire.

The End of the Kingdom of Judah (2 Kings 23:31—25:30)

23:31 *Jehoahaz.* Also known as Shallum (Jer. 22:11).
23:33 *put the land to a tribute.* Imposed a fine or penalty on the land. *talent.* Approximately 66 pounds.
23:34 *in the room of.* In the place of.

Thoughts for Personal/Family Worship: Chapter 23

1. **Civil authority is a blessing when it has the courage and convictions to address moral issues with wisdom from God (Prov. 8:12–16; Rom. 13:1–5). We should pray that our leaders will use their authority such that the godly may live in peace and the gospel may be freely proclaimed (1 Tim. 2:1–2) and not give legal sanction to immorality and injustice (Dan. 4:27). Righteousness brings honor to a nation, but sin brings disgrace to a society (Prov. 14:34). Do you regularly pray for the leaders in your national and local governments?**
2. **Josiah's life also demonstrated the inherent powerlessness of legislation to change the hearts of people. He was able to force outward conformity but unable to effect inward obedience. As soon as he died all of the pent-up wickedness had free reign once again. It is certainly better to legislate morality than immorality, but we must never lose sight of the real issue: the need for a new heart (Deut. 30:6; Ezek. 36:26). The principle is the same in our homes. We set and enforce rules for our children, but we cannot assume that outward obedience equates to inward conversion. As parents we must always press upon our children the necessity of a personal and inward relationship with Christ that will demonstrate itself in outward behavior as well. God desires "truth in the inward parts" (Ps. 51:6).**

Chapter 24: *Babylon's domination of Judah begins.*

24:1 *Nebuchadnezzar . . . came up.* Nebuchadnezzar was God's servant to accomplish His purpose of chastising Judah because of their sins (v. 2). The Babylonian exile occurred in three stages: first, in 605 BC, the beginning of the Neo-Babylonian Empire after the victory at Carchemish, when Nebuchadnezzar took various trophies and exiles back to Babylon, including Daniel (Dan. 1:1–2); second, in 598/597 BC, the exile of Jehoaichin and 10,000 others, including Ezekiel (2 Kings 24:14–15; Ezek. 1:1–2); and third, in 586 BC, the final destruction of the city (2 Kings 25:1–30).
24:3 *at the commandment of the LORD.* Not in God's revealed Word but in His sovereign decree (Lam. 3:37–38; see note at 1 Kings 17:9). *for the sins of Manasseh.* His idolatry and injustice, degrading Judah even lower than the Canaanites (2 Kings 21:9–16; 23:26–27).
24:5 *chronicles.* Uninspired records of the king's career that

6 So Jehoiakim slept with his fathers: and Jehoi-
achin his son reigned in his stead.
7 And the king of Egypt came not again any more
out of his land: for the king of Babylon had taken
from the river of Egypt unto the river Euphrates
all that pertained to the king of Egypt.
8 ¶ Jehoiachin *was* eighteen years old when he
began to reign, and he reigned in Jerusalem three
months. And his mother's name *was* Nehushta,
the daughter of Elnathan of Jerusalem.
9 And he did *that which was* evil in the sight of
the LORD, according to all that his father had
done.
10 ¶ At that time the servants of Nebuchadnezzar
king of Babylon came up against Jerusalem, and
the city was besieged.
11 And Nebuchadnezzar king of Babylon came
against the city, and his servants did besiege it.
12 And Jehoiachin the king of Judah went out to
the king of Babylon, he, and his mother, and his
servants, and his princes, and his officers: and the
king of Babylon took him in the eighth year of
his reign.
13 And he carried out thence all the treasures of
the house of the LORD, and the treasures of the
king's house, and cut in pieces all the vessels of
gold which Solomon king of Israel had made in
the temple of the LORD, as the LORD had said.
14 And he carried away all Jerusalem, and all the
princes, and all the mighty men of valour, *even*
ten thousand captives, and all the craftsmen and
smiths: none remained, save the poorest sort of
the people of the land.
15 And he carried away Jehoiachin to Babylon,
and the king's mother, and the king's wives, and
his officers, and the mighty of the land, *those* car-
ried he into captivity from Jerusalem to Babylon.
16 And all the men of might, *even* seven thou-
sand, and craftsmen and smiths a thousand, all
that were strong *and* apt for war, even them the
king of Babylon brought captive to Babylon.
17 ¶ And the king of Babylon made Mattaniah
his father's brother king in his stead, and changed
his name to Zedekiah.
18 Zedekiah *was* twenty and one years old when
he began to reign, and he reigned eleven years in
Jerusalem. And his mother's name *was* Hamutal,
the daughter of Jeremiah of Libnah.
19 And he did *that which was* evil in the sight of
the LORD, according to all that Jehoiakim had
done.
20 For through the anger of the LORD it came
to pass in Jerusalem and Judah, until he had cast
them out from his presence, that Zedekiah re-
belled against the king of Babylon.

CHAPTER 25

AND it came to pass in the ninth year of his reign,
in the tenth month, in the tenth *day* of the month,
that Nebuchadnezzar king of Babylon came, he,
and all his host, against Jerusalem, and pitched
against it; and they built forts against it round
about.
2 And the city was besieged unto the eleventh
year of king Zedekiah.
3 And on the ninth *day* of the *fourth* month the
famine prevailed in the city, and there was no
bread for the people of the land.
4 ¶ And the city was broken up, and all the men
of war *fled* by night by the way of the gate between
two walls, which *is* by the king's garden: (now the
Chaldees *were* against the city round about:) and
the king went the way toward the plain.
5 And the army of the Chaldees pursued after the
king, and overtook him in the plains of Jericho:
and all his army were scattered from him.
6 So they took the king, and brought him up to
the king of Babylon to Riblah; and they gave judg-
ment upon him.
7 And they slew the sons of Zedekiah before
his eyes, and put out the eyes of Zedekiah, and
bound him with fetters of brass, and carried him
to Babylon.

---

have not been preserved.

24:12 *Jehoiachin . . . went out to the king of Babylon.* Perhaps at the instruction of Jeremiah (Jer. 27:17). Surrendering was his only hope of survival.

Thoughts for Personal/Family Worship: Chapter 24

The sins of Judah had finally ripened, and the judgment began. God had warned of this day as far back as Moses (Deut. 28:1–68), and He had sent prophet after prophet to them, encouraging repentance so that this day could have been averted. But they persisted in their sins, rejected the prophets' preaching, and now had crossed the line. The exile was inevitable and inescapable. The nation's history testifies to both God's patience and His inflexible justice. But Judah's judgment pales before the final judgment to come. Throughout Scripture God has warned of its coming and has through His Word and servants offered hope and deliverance for all those who will repent and believe the gospel. That judgment finally came on Judah testifies that delay of judgment does not alter its certainty. It appears that, while life goes on with generations going and coming, the end remains certain. Interpret the delay as evidence of God's patience, and flee to Him through Christ, the only way to escape the otherwise inescapable.

Chapter 25: *Judah suffers its final devastating and destructive defeat by the Babylonians.*

25:1 *host.* Army. *forts.* Bulwarks or siege walls.

25:6 *Riblah.* A city in the north Lebanon Valley that functioned as the headquarters for Nebuchadnezzar during his siege against Jerusalem.

25:7 *fetters.* Shackles.

8 ¶ And in the fifth month, on the seventh *day* of
the month, which *is* the nineteenth year of king
Nebuchadnezzar king of Babylon, came Nebuzar-
adan, captain of the guard, a servant of the king of
Babylon, unto Jerusalem:
9 And he burnt the house of the LORD, and the
king's house, and all the houses of Jerusalem, and
every great *man's* house burnt he with fire.
10 And all the army of the Chaldees, that *were*
with the captain of the guard, brake down the
walls of Jerusalem round about.
11 Now the rest of the people *that were* left in the
city, and the fugitives that fell away to the king
of Babylon, with the remnant of the multitude,
did Nebuzar-adan the captain of the guard carry
away.
12 But the captain of the guard left of the poor
of the land *to be* vinedressers and husbandmen.
13 And the pillars of brass that *were* in the house
of the LORD, and the bases, and the brasen sea that
was in the house of the LORD, did the Chaldees
break in pieces, and carried the brass of them to
Babylon.
14 And the pots, and the shovels, and the snuffers,
and the spoons, and all the vessels of brass where-
with they ministered, took they away.
15 And the firepans, and the bowls, *and* such
things as *were* of gold, *in* gold, and of silver, *in*
silver, the captain of the guard took away.
16 The two pillars, one sea, and the bases which
Solomon had made for the house of the LORD; the
brass of all these vessels was without weight.
17 The height of the one pillar *was* eighteen cu-
bits, and the chapiter upon it *was* brass: and the
height of the chapiter three cubits; and the wreath-
en work, and pomegranates upon the chapiter
round about, all of brass: and like unto these had
the second pillar with wreathen work.
18 ¶ And the captain of the guard took Seraiah
the chief priest, and Zephaniah the second priest,
and the three keepers of the door:
19 And out of the city he took an officer that was
set over the men of war, and five men of them
that were in the king's presence, which were
found in the city, and the principal scribe of the
host, which mustered the people of the land, and
threescore men of the people of the land *that were*
found in the city:
20 And Nebuzar-adan captain of the guard took
these, and brought them to the king of Babylon
to Riblah:
21 And the king of Babylon smote them, and slew
them at Riblah in the land of Hamath. So Judah
was carried away out of their land.
22 ¶ And *as for* the people that remained in the
land of Judah, whom Nebuchadnezzar king of
Babylon had left, even over them he made Geda-
liah the son of Ahikam, the son of Shaphan, ruler.
23 And when all the captains of the armies, they
and their men, heard that the king of Babylon had
made Gedaliah governor, there came to Gedaliah
to Mizpah, even Ishmael the son of Nethaniah,
and Johanan the son of Careah, and Seraiah the
son of Tanhumeth the Netophathite, and Jaaza-
niah the son of a Maachathite, they and their men.
24 And Gedaliah sware to them, and to their men,
and said unto them, Fear not to be the servants of
the Chaldees: dwell in the land, and serve the king
of Babylon; and it shall be well with you.
25 But it came to pass in the seventh month,
that Ishmael the son of Nethaniah, the son of
Elishama, of the seed royal, came, and ten men
with him, and smote Gedaliah, that he died, and
the Jews and the Chaldees that were with him at
Mizpah.
26 And all the people, both small and great, and
the captains of the armies, arose, and came to
Egypt: for they were afraid of the Chaldees.
27 ¶ And it came to pass in the seven and
thirtieth year of the captivity of Jehoiachin king
of Judah, in the twelfth month, on the seven and
twentieth *day* of the month, *that* Evil-merodach
king of Babylon in the year that he began to
reign did lift up the head of Jehoiachin king of

25:9 In addition to destroying the temple, Babylon especially targeted the houses of the royalty and the wealthy. The poor were left in the land (v. 12).

25:12 *husbandmen*. Farmers.

25:13–17 The list of items taken from the temple emphasizes its complete destruction—a stunning horror to the Jews as God's glory disappeared from the Promised Land.

25:16 *without weight*. There was so much copper used in the temple of Solomon that it was not even weighed (1 Kings 7:47).

25:17 *chapiter*. Top of a column, usually with some ornamentation. *wreathen work*. Some sort of trellis or lattice work.

25:19 *host*. Army. *mustered the people*. Conscripted them for military service.

25:22 *Gedaliah*. See Jer. 40:5–7.

25:24 Submission to the Babylonians was not treason but obedience to the Lord's message through Jeremiah (Jer. 27:12, 17; 38:17,20; 40:9).

25:25–26 On the rebellion of *Ishmael* and the flight of the Jews to Egypt, see Jer. 40:13—43:7.

25:27–30 *Evil-merodach*. Translated, "the man of Marduk," indicating his devotion to Marduk, the patron deity of Babylon. The honoring of Jehoiachin was a hopeful sign that even in His wrath against Judah the Lord was remembering His covenant with David (see note at Jer. 52:32–33).

Thoughts for Personal/Family Worship: Chapter 25

The book of 2 Kings seems to end in dismal darkness and gloom. But in His wrath God remembers mercy (Hab. 3:2). Where sin abounds, grace super-abounds. The last verses point to the beginning of a new future. Although the royal throne of David had been cast down, God's promise that David would always have one of his sons on the throne remained true (2 Sam. 7:16). God

Judah out of prison;
28 And he spake kindly to him, and set his throne
above the throne of the kings that *were* with him
in Babylon;
29 And changed his prison garments: and he did
eat bread continually before him all the days of
his life.
30 And his allowance *was* a continual allowance
given him of the king, a daily rate for every day, all
the days of his life.

used the pagan king to ensure the continuation of His promise. Jehoiachin received royal treatment and bore sons (1 Chron. 3:17). One of these sons was Salathiel, who in turn bore Zerubbabel, who became governor of Judah when the exile ended. Although he did not sit on the throne, he was of the royal line and designated as God's signet, guaranteeing the Messiah to come (Hag. 2:23). Christ is the true and ideal son of David, and His kingdom shall never end (Luke 1:33). He is now enthroned at the right hand of God in glory (Acts 2:34), and unto Him is given all power in heaven and on earth (Matt. 28:18). The Lord still continues His plans, even if everything seems to fall apart. God's Word endures and will certainly be fulfilled.

INTRODUCTION TO THE BOOKS OF 1ST AND 2ND
CHRONICLES

Authorship: First and Second Chronicles are one book. It is uncertain who authored Chronicles. The traditional belief of rabbinical Judaism and medieval Christianity has been that Chronicles through Nehemiah were a single work written by Ezra the scribe. It is clear that the four books share many linguistic and theological concepts. Others have maintained that while Chronicles and Ezra/Nehemiah were written by one author, that author was not Ezra but another scribe. Still others maintain that Chronicles and Ezra/Nehemiah derived from different authors. Proponents of this position highlight the differences rather than similarities of literary and theological concepts. This view has become increasingly popular since the late nineteenth century among modern biblical scholars.

In favor of seeing one author behind these four books, whether Ezra or not, are the following arguments. *First*, the ending of Chronicles (2 Chron. 36:22–23) overlaps with the beginning of Ezra (Ezra 1:1–4), which was standard practice for books that were intended to build on each other. *Second*, despite some variety in literary and theological elements between Chronicles and Ezra/Nehemiah, there appears to be more continuity than discontinuity. *Third*, Chronicles and Ezra/Nehemiah both include many scriptural and historical documents and sources and they both quote from these often. The author frequently makes use of the historical, prophetic, and wisdom books of the Old Testament Scriptures. Certainly as a scribe, Ezra was well versed in such documents and writings and would be a likely candidate in utilizing them in his writings. *Fourth*, given Ezra's influence and the spiritual revival among those returning from exile, Ezra would have had a good incentive as a leader in the new community to produce these two combined works for the edification of the Jews.

In a final analysis, however, absolute certainty regarding who wrote Chronicles and/or Ezra/Nehemiah is not possible. Neither Scripture nor reason allows us to solve this tension beyond all dispute. And in reality, the importance of these works does not depend on identifying the human author but what they contain and communicate about God, His plan, and His purpose.

Date: Chronicles was written shortly before or during the ministry of Ezra in Judah. In 586 BC the Babylonian army conquered the land of Judah and sent the remaining tribes of Israel into exile (the northern tribes were exiled around 721 BC). The exile was God's judgment against His people for their failure to repent. God sent many prophets like Jeremiah and Ezekiel to condemn the people for their sins and call them to repentance. But Judah failed to listen to God's message and continued her path to ruin. The end result was complete and utter destruction. Jerusalem was destroyed. The temple was torn down. The people were cast into exile.

The exile of Judah continued for about seventy years. But Persia rose to power over Babylon in 539 BC. Around 538 BC Cyrus, king of Persia, issued a decree that the exiled people could return to their land to rebuild the temple and the walls of Jerusalem. There they waited for the final fulfillment of God's promises.

It is into this frame of reference that 1 and 2 Chronicles was written. The chronicler's view of history was meant to enliven, strengthen, and encourage the Lord's people—reminding them that God was not through working with them.

Considering the prophecy of Cyrus's edict at the end of 2 Chronicles, the earliest date Chronicles could have been composed would be about 538 BC. But given the internal evidence from the genealogies, Chronicles was most likely composed sometime between 450 and 425 BC. (For a chronology of the kings of Judah and Israel, see Introduction to 1 and 2 Kings: Date.)

Theme: God's acts in history from Adam through the son of David to build a kingdom of true worship from the heart.

Purpose: To call people to turn from idols and seek the Lord in holy worship, motivated by hope in God's covenant faithfulness to the son of David.

Synopsis: *The Contribution of Chronicles to Redemptive Revelation*

Chronicles records a worship-centered history of God's kingdom going back to the creation of the world. This focus has not always been properly recognized. The Septuagint (the Greek translation of the Old Testament) titles Chronicles, "things left out concerning the kings of Judah" (*paralipomena ton basileon Iouda*), which gives the impression that this volume is nothing more than historical leftovers concerning the history of Joshua through Kings. But those who see Chronicles as nothing more than historical leftovers miss the true significance of these books.

The Hebrew title of the work is "the matters of the days" (*dibre hayyamim*). Jerome titled these books "First and Second Chronicles" from the fourth century AD. This would carry the connotation that Chronicles was nothing more than short annals of the kings of Israel and Judah. However, Chronicles tends to give more extensive biographical information regarding kings, rulers, and individuals than typically found in extrabiblical chronicles.

In addition, Chronicles is selective when compared to the material in the books of Samuel and Kings. For example, it passes over Saul's kingship, David's adultery with Bath-sheba, and Absalom's rebellion against his father. It views Israel's history through the lens of a kingdom of priests (Ex. 19:6), giving particular attention to the tribe and kingdom of Judah, and the construction and use of the temple. Chronicles focuses upon the gift of God's presence.

This emphasis upon the presence of God with His people appears in the frequent references to seeking the Lord. To seek the Lord (sometimes translated "enquire" of Him) means to draw near to God in worship and prayer with desire for His presence ("face"), reliance upon Him for salvation, repentance of sins against Him, and submission to His laws (1 Chron. 13:3; 15:13; 21:30; 22:19; 28:8–9; 2 Chron. 7:14; 12:14; 14:4,7; 15:2,4,12–13,15; 16:12; 17:3–4; 18:4–7; 19:3; 20:3–4; 22:9; 25:15,20; 26:5; 30:19; 31:21; 34:3,21,26).

Though Chronicles centers its plot upon the temple in Jerusalem, it emphasizes the "heart" as the key to true godliness. Seeking God must engage the heart (1 Chron. 16:10; 22:19), for He sees the heart and desires righteousness in it (28:9; 29:17; 2 Chron. 6:30). People must serve the Lord with a "perfect" heart, that is, one that is not divided among many gods but entirely (though not sinlessly) devoted to Him (1 Chron. 28:9; 29:9,19; 2 Chron. 15:17; 16:9; 19:9; 25:2). They must seek Him with "all" their heart (6:14,38; 15:12,15; 22:9; 31:21; 34:31). Their hearts must be "tender" and humble, easily broken by God's words to sinners, and not "hardened" and stubborn (34:27; 36:13). Otherwise their hearts will be "lifted up" with pride (25:19; 26:16; 32:25–26). Therefore people of God must "prepare" their hearts, that is, intentionally direct their thoughts and affections toward the Lord as their only God (12:14; 19:3; 20:33; 30:19). This all must come of God's grace, who alone can give people a heart to keep His commandments (1 Chron. 29:18–19; 2 Chron. 30:11–12).

Seeking God results in experiencing His "rest" (2 Chron. 15:15). This term is linked to the golden years of Solomon's reign. It denotes both the peace of His salvation from their enemies and the joy of His presence with them in the temple (1 Chron. 22:8–10,17–19; 23:25; 28:2; 2 Chron. 14:6–7; 15:15; 20:30; cf. Pss. 95:11; 132:8,14; Heb. 3:7—4:13). Having set their hearts by His grace to seek Him, they will enjoy access to God's own heart in His temple (2 Chron. 7:16).

The concern for a godly heart in Chronicles comes to particular focus in its more than a dozen references to the spiritual condition of the heart of the king. God's blessing upon His people and temple depends upon the heart of the son of David toward God. David's preparations for the temple climax in his prayer, "And give unto Solomon my son a perfect heart, to keep thy commandments, thy testimonies, and thy statutes, and to do all these things, and to build the palace, for the which I have made provision" (1 Chron. 29:19).

Chronicles intertwines the Davidic monarchy with God's dwelling among His worshipers. Its plot rises to a peak in the covenant God made with David (1 Chron. 17), where He promised that David's seed or offspring would build God's house and would reign forever. God gloriously (though only partially) fulfilled that covenant when Solomon constructed the temple (2 Chron. 2–7). However, Chronicles concludes with the tragic history of how the sinful and hardened hearts of the seed of David provoked the Lord to end the monarchy and destroy the temple (2 Chron. 36). Yet hope remained, for the Lord restored His people from exile to rebuild God's house (v. 23). Therefore, Chronicles encouraged the postexilic remnant to hope in the coming, righteous son of David who would establish God's presence with them in a far more glorious and permanent manner.

Looking ahead and looking back in time, Chronicles indicates that the son of David is the climax of human history. That is the implicit point of the long section of genealogies on which the author spends almost a third of his first book. Beginning with Adam, these genealogies trace the development of God's purpose for mankind to the line of David. They testify to God's faithfulness in preserving the line of the promised Seed through whom God would restore His blessing to fallen man (Gen. 3:15; 22:18). The exile of Israel could not overthrow God's purposes of salvation any more than previous judgments such as the flood of Noah. Chronicles contributes to the redemptive message by showing that the progression toward the fullness of time was right on track. God's presence, lost in the garden, will be restored through the coming King. The temple, decorated with trees, fruit, gold, gems, and cherubim (2 Chron. 3) was a type of the return to dwell with God in paradise (Gen. 2; Rev. 22).

Chronicles is thus a bridge from creation to new creation and from the old covenant to the new. It is the last book in the order of the Hebrew Old Testament. The gospel of Matthew picks up where Chronicles stopped with another genealogy leading to Jesus, and the revelation that Christ is Immanuel, God dwelling with His people through the son of David. He is the hope of God's people.

Outline:

- I. Kingdom Promised (1 Chron. 1:1—9:44)
  - A. Adam to Abraham (1 Chron. 1:1–27)
  - B. Esau (1 Chron. 1:28–54)
  - C. Jacob to David (1 Chron. 2:1–55)
  - D. David (1 Chron. 3:1–24)
  - E. Twelve Tribes (1 Chron. 4:1—8:40)
  - F. Returning Exiles (1 Chron. 9:1–34)
  - G. Saul (1 Chron. 9:35–44)
- II. Kingdom Established (1 Chron. 10:1—2 Chron. 9:31)
  - A. Saul's Death (1 Chron. 10:1–14)
  - B. David's Rise to Power (1 Chron. 11:1—12:40)
    - 1. David's Pursuit of God's Presence (1 Chron. 13:1—17:27)
    - 2. David's Attempts to Bring the Ark to Jerusalem (1 Chron. 13:1—16:43)
    - 3. God's Promise to David: Covenant Made (1 Chron. 17:1–27)
  - C. David's Military Victories (1 Chron. 18:1—20:8)
    - 1. David's Wars with His Enemies (1 Chron. 18:1–13)
    - 2. David's Rule (1 Chron. 18:14–17)
    - 3. David and the Ammonites (1 Chron. 19:1–19)
    - 4. David's Other Battles (1 Chron. 20:1–8)
  - D. David's Preparations for the Temple (1 Chron. 21:1—26:32)
    - 1. David's Sinful Census and the Temple Site (1 Chron. 21:1—22:1)
    - 2. David's Preparations for the Construction of the Temple (1 Chron. 22:2–19)
    - 3. David's Organization of the Levites for the Temple (1 Chron. 23:1—26:32)
  - E. David's Administration of the Nation (1 Chron. 27:1–34)
  - F. David's Assembly for the Future Temple (1 Chron. 28:1—29:22)
  - G. David's Death and Solomon's Glory (1 Chron. 29:23—2 Chron. 1:17)
  - H. Solomon's Construction of the Temple: Covenant Partially Fulfilled (2 Chron. 2:1—7:22)
    - 1. Solomon's Arrangements for Materials and Workers (2 Chron. 2:1–18)
    - 2. Solomon's Construction of the Building and Furnishings (2 Chron. 3:1—4:22)
    - 3. Solomon's Assembly to Dedicate the Temple (2 Chron. 5:1—7:22)
  - I. Solomon's Works, Wisdom, and Death (2 Chron. 8:1—9:31)
- III. Kingdom Divided (2 Chron. 10:1—28:27)
  - A. King Rehoboam (2 Chron. 10:1—12:16)
  - B. King Abijah (2 Chron. 13:1–22)
  - C. King Asa (2 Chron. 14:1—16:14)

D. King Jehoshaphat (2 Chron. 17:1—20:37)
E. King Jehoram (2 Chron. 21:1–20)
F. King Ahaziah (2 Chron. 22:1–9)
G. Queen Athaliah (2 Chron. 22:10–12)
H. King Joash (2 Chron. 23:1—24:27)
I. King Amaziah (2 Chron. 25:1–28)
J. King Uzziah (2 Chron. 26:1–23)
K. King Jotham (2 Chron. 27:1–9)
L. King Ahaz (2 Chron. 28:1–27)

IV. Kingdom Reformed and Ruined (2 Chron. 29:1—35:27)
A. Hezekiah's Righteous Reign (2 Chron. 29:1—32:33)
B. Manasseh's Idolatry and Repentance (2 Chron. 33:1–20)
C. Amon's Idolatry (2 Chron. 33:21–25)
D. Josiah's Righteous Reign (2 Chron. 34:1—35:27)

V. Kingdom Destroyed (2 Chron. 36:1–23)
A. King Jehoahaz (2 Chron. 36:1–3)
B. King Jehoiakim (2 Chron. 36:4–8)
C. King Jehoiachin (2 Chron. 36:9–10)
D. King Zedekiah (2 Chron. 36:11–16)
E. Jerusalem Conquered (2 Chron. 36:17–21)
F. Cyrus's Proclamation (2 Chron. 36:22–23)

THE FIRST BOOK OF

CHRONICLES

CHAPTER 1

ADAM, Sheth, Enosh,
2 Kenan, Mahalaleel, Jered,
3 Henoch, Methuselah, Lamech,
4 Noah, Shem, Ham, and Japheth.
5 ¶ The sons of Japheth; Gomer, and Magog, and
Madai, and Javan, and Tubal, and Meshech, and
Tiras.
6 And the sons of Gomer; Ashchenaz, and
Riphath, and Togarmah.
7 And the sons of Javan; Elishah, and Tarshish,
Kittim, and Dodanim.
8 ¶ The sons of Ham; Cush, and Mizraim, Put,
and Canaan.
9 And the sons of Cush; Seba, and Havilah, and
Sabta, and Raamah, and Sabtecha. And the sons
of Raamah; Sheba, and Dedan.
10 And Cush begat Nimrod: he began to be
mighty upon the earth.
11 And Mizraim begat Ludim, and Anamim, and
Lehabim, and Naphtuhim,
12 And Pathrusim, and Casluhim, (of whom
came the Philistines,) and Caphthorim.
13 And Canaan begat Zidon his firstborn, and
Heth,
14 The Jebusite also, and the Amorite, and the
Girgashite,
15 And the Hivite, and the Arkite, and the Sinite,
16 And the Arvadite, and the Zemarite, and the
Hamathite.
17 ¶ The sons of Shem; Elam, and Asshur, and
Arphaxad, and Lud, and Aram, and Uz, and Hul,
and Gether, and Meshech.
18 And Arphaxad begat Shelah, and Shelah be-
gat Eber.
19 And unto Eber were born two sons: the name
of the one *was* Peleg; because in his days the earth
was divided: and his brother's name *was* Joktan.
20 And Joktan begat Almodad, and Sheleph, and
Hazarmaveth, and Jerah,
21 Hadoram also, and Uzal, and Diklah,
22 And Ebal, and Abimael, and Sheba,
23 And Ophir, and Havilah, and Jobab. All these
were the sons of Joktan.
24 ¶ Shem, Arphaxad, Shelah,
25 Eber, Peleg, Reu,
26 Serug, Nahor, Terah,
27 Abram; the same *is* Abraham.
28 The sons of Abraham; Isaac, and Ishmael.
29 ¶ These *are* their generations: The firstborn of
Ishmael, Nebaioth; then Kedar, and Adbeel, and
Mibsam,
30 Mishma, and Dumah, Massa, Hadad, and Tema,
31 Jetur, Naphish, and Kedemah. These are the
sons of Ishmael.
32 ¶ Now the sons of Keturah, Abraham's concu-
bine: she bare Zimran, and Jokshan, and Medan,
and Midian, and Ishbak, and Shuah. And the sons
of Jokshan; Sheba, and Dedan.
33 And the sons of Midian; Ephah, and Epher,
and Henoch, and Abida, and Eldaah. All these *are*
the sons of Keturah.

KINGDOM PROMISED (1 CHRON. 1:1—9:44)

Chapter 1: ***This chapter opens the genealogical record of Israel from Adam to Jacob, with a section on Esau's descendants.***

Adam to Abraham (1 Chron. 1:1–27)

1:1 The genealogy of Chronicles starts at the beginning of mankind with *Adam, Sheth, Enosh* (Gen. 5:1–11). Chronicles has a universal scope, emphasizing God's sovereign choice of Jacob among all nations, and grounding His purposes for Israel in creation. Adam was the first king in the world (Gen. 1:26–28), but like Saul he fell by disobedience to God (Gen. 3), so that God promised to raise up another, more righteous king—the seed of the woman (Gen. 3:15).

1:4 *Shem, Ham, and Japheth.* The sons of Noah. *Shem* was the line from which the promised seed of the woman would ultimately spring (Gen. 9:26–27; 11:10–26).

1:10 *Nimrod.* A powerful leader with a Mesopotamian kingdom (Gen. 10:8–12).

1:19 *Peleg; because in his days the earth was divided.* A reference to the nations being divided after the tower of Babel (Gen. 10:25; 11:1–9). Chronicles affirms the historical reality of Gen. 1–11.

1:27 *Abram . . . Abraham.* In the context of changing Abram's name, the Lord also revealed that kings would arise from his offspring (Gen. 17:5–6; cf. Gen. 17:16; 35:11).

Esau (1 Chron. 1:28–54)

1:28–34 The genealogy is also given in Gen. 25:1–4.

1:32 *Keturah.* A concubine of Abraham (Gen. 25:1,6).

34 And Abraham begat Isaac. The sons of Isaac; Esau and Israel.
35 ¶ The sons of Esau; Eliphaz, Reuel, and Jeush, and Jaalam, and Korah.
36 The sons of Eliphaz; Teman, and Omar, Zephi, and Gatam, Kenaz, and Timna, and Amalek.
37 The sons of Reuel; Nahath, Zerah, Shammah, and Mizzah.
38 And the sons of Seir; Lotan, and Shobal, and Zibeon, and Anah, and Dishon, and Ezer, and Dishan.
39 And the sons of Lotan; Hori, and Homam: and Timna *was* Lotan's sister.
40 The sons of Shobal; Alian, and Manahath, and Ebal, Shephi, and Onam. And the sons of Zibeon; Aiah, and Anah.
41 The sons of Anah; Dishon. And the sons of Dishon; Amram, and Eshban, and Ithran, and Cheran.
42 The sons of Ezer; Bilhan, and Zavan, *and* Jakan. The sons of Dishan; Uz, and Aran.
43 ¶ Now these *are* the kings that reigned in the land of Edom before *any* king reigned over the children of Israel; Bela the son of Beor: and the name of his city *was* Dinhabah.
44 And when Bela was dead, Jobab the son of Zerah of Bozrah reigned in his stead.
45 And when Jobab was dead, Husham of the land of the Temanites reigned in his stead.
46 And when Husham was dead, Hadad the son of Bedad, which smote Midian in the field of Moab, reigned in his stead: and the name of his city *was* Avith.
47 And when Hadad was dead, Samlah of Masrekah reigned in his stead.
48 And when Samlah was dead, Shaul of Rehoboth by the river reigned in his stead.
49 And when Shaul was dead, Baal-hanan the son of Achbor reigned in his stead.
50 And when Baal-hanan was dead, Hadad reigned in his stead: and the name of his city *was* Pai; and his wife's name *was* Mehetabel, the daughter of Matred, the daughter of Mezahab.
51 ¶ Hadad died also. And the dukes of Edom were; duke Timnah, duke Aliah, duke Jetheth,
52 Duke Aholibamah, duke Elah, duke Pinon,
53 Duke Kenaz, duke Teman, duke Mibzar,
54 Duke Magdiel, duke Iram. These *are* the dukes of Edom.

CHAPTER 2

THESE *are* the sons of Israel; Reuben, Simeon, Levi, and Judah, Issachar, and Zebulun,
2 Dan, Joseph, and Benjamin, Naphtali, Gad, and Asher.
3 ¶ The sons of Judah; Er, and Onan, and Shelah: *which* three were born unto him of the daughter of Shua the Canaanitess. And Er, the firstborn of Judah, was evil in the sight of the LORD; and he slew him.
4 And Tamar his daughter in law bare him Pharez and Zerah. All the sons of Judah *were* five.
5 The sons of Pharez; Hezron, and Hamul.
6 And the sons of Zerah; Zimri, and Ethan, and Heman, and Calcol, and Dara: five of them in all.
7 And the sons of Carmi; Achar, the troubler of Israel, who transgressed in the thing accursed.
8 And the sons of Ethan; Azariah.
9 The sons also of Hezron, that were born unto him; Jerahmeel, and Ram, and Chelubai.
10 And Ram begat Amminadab; and Amminadab begat Nahshon, prince of the children of Judah;

1:34 *Israel.* The author goes straight to Jacob's new name, Israel.
1:35 *The sons of Esau.* Listed in Gen. 36:10–43. These sons were later known as the Edomites, frequently enemies of the people of Israel.
1:44 *stead.* Place.
1:51 *dukes.* Chiefs.

Thoughts for Personal/Family Worship: Chapter 1

We have all descended from one man: Adam. The existence of Adam was as much history as the existence of David. In Adam, we were all made in God's image and likeness. God's purpose for His people therefore remains to fill the earth with His living image. In Adam, we all sinned and have fallen into spiritual corruption and enduring misery. We all share the same fallen nature as the Canaanites. We all die and face judgment, and human life is so transient that from God's perspective all the generations from Adam to Israel fit on a single page of history. God's people consequently must be redeemed by the Lord's grace if they will ever achieve their high calling and eternal life. Mankind needs a new Adam. How has God met that need in Christ?

Chapter 2: *This chapter contains the genealogy from the time of Jacob to David.*

Jacob to David (1 Chron. 2:1–55)

2:1 *sons of Israel.* Listed according to their mothers with the exception of Dan (Gen. 35:22–26). *Israel.* Chronicles is clearly concerned about showing the unity of the people, and hence he uses Jacob's second name, *Israel,* to include both the northern and southern kingdoms.
2:3—4:23 *Judah* appears first because to him was promised the scepter or rule over his brothers (Gen. 49:10). The lineage of David, founded in Judah, is of particular importance to Israel's history and the redemption of God.
2:3–4 The history of the tribe of Judah, on which Chronicles concentrates, begins in a rather sordid way (Gen. 38). This serves to glorify the sovereign grace of God, who included *Tamar* in the line of Jesus Christ (Matt. 1:3).
2:7 *troubler of Israel.* Achan (*Achar*) took things devoted to destruction and hid them, bringing God's judgment on the people (Josh. 7). Judah's lineage included the names of infamous sinners.
2:10 *Nahshon.* Brother of Aaron's wife, Elisheba (Ex. 6:23; Ruth 4:19–22).

11 And Nahshon begat Salma, and Salma begat Boaz,

12 And Boaz begat Obed, and Obed begat Jesse,

13 ¶ And Jesse begat his firstborn Eliab, and Abinadab the second, and Shimma the third,

14 Nethaneel the fourth, Raddai the fifth,

15 Ozem the sixth, David the seventh:

16 Whose sisters *were* Zeruiah, and Abigail. And the sons of Zeruiah; Abishai, and Joab, and Asahel, three.

17 And Abigail bare Amasa: and the father of Amasa *was* Jether the Ishmeelite.

18 ¶ And Caleb the son of Hezron begat *children* of Azubah *his* wife, and of Jerioth: her sons *are* these; Jesher, and Shobab, and Ardon.

19 And when Azubah was dead, Caleb took unto him Ephrath, which bare him Hur.

20 And Hur begat Uri, and Uri begat Bezaleel.

21 ¶ And afterward Hezron went in to the daughter of Machir the father of Gilead, whom he married when he *was* threescore years old; and she bare him Segub.

22 And Segub begat Jair, who had three and twenty cities in the land of Gilead.

23 And he took Geshur, and Aram, with the towns of Jair, from them, with Kenath, and the towns thereof, *even* threescore cities. All these *belonged to* the sons of Machir the father of Gilead.

24 And after that Hezron was dead in Calebephratah, then Abiah Hezron's wife bare him Ashur the father of Tekoa.

25 ¶ And the sons of Jerahmeel the firstborn of Hezron were, Ram the firstborn, and Bunah, and Oren, and Ozem, *and* Ahijah.

26 Jerahmeel had also another wife, whose name *was* Atarah; she *was* the mother of Onam.

27 And the sons of Ram the firstborn of Jerahmeel were, Maaz, and Jamin, and Eker.

28 And the sons of Onam were, Shammai, and Jada. And the sons of Shammai; Nadab, and Abishur.

29 And the name of the wife of Abishur *was* Abihail, and she bare him Ahban, and Molid.

30 And the sons of Nadab; Seled, and Appaim: but Seled died without children.

31 And the sons of Appaim; Ishi. And the sons of Ishi; Sheshan. And the children of Sheshan; Ahlai.

32 And the sons of Jada the brother of Shammai; Jether, and Jonathan: and Jether died without children.

33 And the sons of Jonathan; Peleth, and Zaza. These were the sons of Jerahmeel.

34 ¶ Now Sheshan had no sons, but daughters. And Sheshan had a servant, an Egyptian, whose name *was* Jarha.

35 And Sheshan gave his daughter to Jarha his servant to wife; and she bare him Attai.

36 And Attai begat Nathan, and Nathan begat Zabad,

37 And Zabad begat Ephlal, and Ephlal begat Obed,

38 And Obed begat Jehu, and Jehu begat Azariah,

39 And Azariah begat Helez, and Helez begat Eleasah,

40 And Eleasah begat Sisamai, and Sisamai begat Shallum,

41 And Shallum begat Jekamiah, and Jekamiah begat Elishama.

42 ¶ Now the sons of Caleb the brother of Jerahmeel *were*, Mesha his firstborn, which *was* the father of Ziph; and the sons of Mareshah the father of Hebron.

43 And the sons of Hebron; Korah, and Tappuah, and Rekem, and Shema.

44 And Shema begat Raham, the father of Jorkoam: and Rekem begat Shammai.

45 And the son of Shammai *was* Maon: and Maon *was* the father of Beth-zur.

46 And Ephah, Caleb's concubine, bare Haran, and Moza, and Gazez: and Haran begat Gazez.

47 And the sons of Jahdai; Regem, and Jotham, and Geshan, and Pelet, and Ephah, and Shaaph.

48 Maachah, Caleb's concubine, bare Sheber, and Tirhanah.

49 She bare also Shaaph the father of Madmannah, Sheva the father of Machbenah, and the father of Gibea: and the daughter of Caleb *was* Achsah.

50 ¶ These were the sons of Caleb the son of Hur, the firstborn of Ephratah; Shobal the father of Kirjath-jearim,

51 Salma the father of Beth-lehem, Hareph the father of Beth-gader.

52 And Shobal the father of Kirjath-jearim had

2:12 The reference to *Boaz* reminds us of the story of Ruth. The lead-up to David has a number of turns that illustrate the grace and providence of God.

2:15 *David the seventh.* David is recorded as the eighth son of Jesse (1 Sam. 17:12). Perhaps one of the others died young or did not have any sons, and therefore is not counted here.

2:18 *Caleb.* Not the same man who spied out the land with Joshua (4:15).

2:20 *Bezaleel.* The one known for building the tabernacle (Ex. 31:2).

2:25–33 These verses include the genealogy of the Jerahmeelites. Little is known of the men listed here other than they lived in the Negev, south of Judah (1 Sam. 27:10; 30:29).

2:34–35 Nothing more is known of *Sheshan* other than what is noted here.

Thoughts for Personal/Family Worship: Chapter 2

The history of God's people is full of examples of sin, such as sexual lust and selfishness (Judah, Onan, and Tamar, vv. 3–4), and greed and disobedience (Achan, v. 7). The Old Testament warns us not to follow in their footsteps, lest we suffer God's judgment. However, it

sons; Haroeh, *and* half of the Manahethites.
53 And the families of Kirjath-jearim; the Ithrites,
and the Puhites, and the Shumathites, and the
Mishraites; of them came the Zareathites, and the
Eshtaulites.
54 The sons of Salma; Beth-lehem, and the Ne-
tophathites, Ataroth, the house of Joab, and half
of the Manahethites, the Zorites.
55 And the families of the scribes which dwelt
at Jabez; the Tirathites, the Shimeathites, *and*
Suchathites. These *are* the Kenites that came of
Hemath, the father of the house of Rechab.

CHAPTER 3

Now these were the sons of David, which were
born unto him in Hebron; the firstborn Amnon,
of Ahinoam the Jezreelitess; the second Daniel, of
Abigail the Carmelitess:
2 The third, Absalom the son of Maachah the
daughter of Talmai king of Geshur: the fourth,
Adonijah the son of Haggith:
3 The fifth, Shephatiah of Abital: the sixth,
Ithream by Eglah his wife.
4 *These* six were born unto him in Hebron; and
there he reigned seven years and six months: and
in Jerusalem he reigned thirty and three years.
5 And these were born unto him in Jerusalem;
Shimea, and Shobab, and Nathan, and Solomon,
four, of Bath-shua the daughter of Ammiel:
6 Ibhar also, and Elishama, and Eliphelet,
7 And Nogah, and Nepheg, and Japhia,
8 And Elishama, and Eliada, and Eliphelet, nine.
9 *These were* all the sons of David, beside the sons
of the concubines, and Tamar their sister.
10 ¶ And Solomon's son *was* Rehoboam, Abia his
son, Asa his son, Jehoshaphat his son,
11 Joram his son, Ahaziah his son, Joash his son,
12 Amaziah his son, Azariah his son, Jotham his
son,
13 Ahaz his son, Hezekiah his son, Manasseh his
son,
14 Amon his son, Josiah his son.
15 And the sons of Josiah *were*, the firstborn Jo-
hanan, the second Jehoiakim, the third Zedekiah,
the fourth Shallum.
16 And the sons of Jehoiakim: Jeconiah his son,
Zedekiah his son.
17 ¶ And the sons of Jeconiah; Assir, Salathiel his
son,
18 Malchiram also, and Pedaiah, and Shenazar,
Jecamiah, Hoshama, and Nedabiah.
19 And the sons of Pedaiah *were*, Zerubbabel, and
Shimei: and the sons of Zerubbabel; Meshullam,
and Hananiah, and Shelomith their sister:
20 And Hashubah, and Ohel, and Berechiah, and
Hasadiah, Jushab-hesed, five.
21 And the sons of Hananiah; Pelatiah, and
Jesaiah: the sons of Rephaiah, the sons of Arnan,
the sons of Obadiah, the sons of Shechaniah.
22 And the sons of Shechaniah; Shemaiah: and
the sons of Shemaiah; Hattush, and Igeal, and
Bariah, and Neariah, and Shaphat, six.
23 And the sons of Neariah; Elioenai, and Heze-
kiah, and Azrikam, three.
24 And the sons of Elioenai *were*, Hodaiah, and
Eliashib, and Pelaiah, and Akkub, and Johanan,
and Dalaiah, and Anani, seven.

CHAPTER 4

THE sons of Judah; Pharez, Hezron, and Carmi,
and Hur, and Shobal.
2 And Reaiah the son of Shobal begat Jahath; and

---

also teaches us to trust in God's grace, for from such sinful families God brought the Savior. How do the examples of such people lead us to faith and repentance?

Chapter 3: ***Following the ancestors of David, this chapter focuses on the descendants of David including after the exile.***

David (1 Chron. 3:1–24)

3:1–3 The line of Judah picks back up here from 2:15–17. The following lists six children from six different wives, probably the firstborn son of each, to note the line of kingly succession.

3:4–5 *Hebron . . . Jerusalem.* David's kingship was marked by two distinctive time eras. He ruled over Judah from Hebron for seven years and then over all Israel from Jerusalem (2 Sam. 2:11; 5:4–5).

3:9 *all the sons of David.* All of David's legitimate sons are named where only the king's successors are mentioned in the remainder of the royal line.

3:16 *Zedekiah.* The temple and Jerusalem were destroyed in his days. He was a wicked king who did not heed the Lord's commands (2 Chron. 36:11–21).

3:17–24 The Davidic throne as a political force ended with the exile but the line of David continued through the duration of the exile. Though they did not occupy a throne, they continued David's line until Christ was born from the root of Jesse (Isa. 11:1).

Thoughts for Personal/Family Worship: Chapter 3

God's plan for a new Adam to undo the effects of the fall and restore man to His divine purpose focuses upon Israel (ch. 1), zooms in from all Israel to Judah (ch. 2), and comes to rest on David (ch. 3). David plays a very central role in the book of Chronicles. In a sense, all of Old Testament history leads up to David, and then follows upon David. The Savior declared to Adam (Gen. 3:15) would be a king of the line of David. Christ was born from the seed of David (Matt. 1:1; Rom. 1:3), and He is the promised Savior-King (Luke 1:31–33,69; 2:11). In turn, Christ has made all his people "kings," spiritually speaking (Rev. 1:6). They will sit with Him on His throne (Rev. 3:21). How can you know if you are part of His kingdom?

Twelve Tribes (1 Chron. 4:1—8:40)

This section of genealogies highlights Judah at the beginning (ch. 4), Levi at the center (ch. 6), and Benjamin at the end

Jahath begat Ahumai, and Lahad. These *are* the
families of the Zorathites.
3 And these *were of* the father of Etam; Jezreel,
and Ishma, and Idbash: and the name of their
sister *was* Hazelelponi:
4 And Penuel the father of Gedor, and Ezer the
father of Hushah. These *are* the sons of Hur, the
firstborn of Ephratah, the father of Beth-lehem.
5 ¶ And Ashur the father of Tekoa had two wives,
Helah and Naarah.
6 And Naarah bare him Ahuzam, and Hepher,
and Temeni, and Haahashtari. These *were* the
sons of Naarah.
7 And the sons of Helah *were*, Zereth, and Jezoar,
and Ethnan.
8 And Coz begat Anub, and Zobebah, and the
families of Aharhel the son of Harum.
9 ¶ And Jabez was more honourable than his
brethren: and his mother called his name Jabez,
saying, Because I bare him with sorrow.
10 And Jabez called on the God of Israel, saying,
Oh that thou wouldest bless me indeed, and en-
large my coast, and that thine hand might be with
me, and that thou wouldest keep *me* from evil,
that it may not grieve me! And God granted him
that which he requested.
11 ¶ And Chelub the brother of Shuah begat
Mehir, which *was* the father of Eshton.
12 And Eshton begat Beth-rapha, and Paseah,
and Tehinnah the father of Ir-nahash. These *are*
the men of Rechah.
13 And the sons of Kenaz; Othniel, and Seraiah:
and the sons of Othniel; Hathath.
14 And Meonothai begat Ophrah: and Seraiah
begat Joab, the father of the valley of Charashim;
for they were craftsmen.
15 And the sons of Caleb the son of Jephunneh;
Iru, Elah, and Naam: and the sons of Elah, even
Kenaz.
16 And the sons of Jehaleleel; Ziph, and Ziphah,
Tiria, and Asareel.
17 And the sons of Ezra *were*, Jether, and Mered,
and Epher, and Jalon: and she bare Miriam, and
Shammai, and Ishbah the father of Eshtemoa.
18 And his wife Jehudijah bare Jered the father
of Gedor, and Heber the father of Socho, and
Jekuthiel the father of Zanoah. And these *are* the
sons of Bithiah the daughter of Pharaoh, which
Mered took.
19 And the sons of *his* wife Hodiah the sister of
Naham, the father of Keilah the Garmite, and
Eshtemoa the Maachathite.
20 And the sons of Shimon *were*, Amnon, and
Rinnah, Ben-hanan, and Tilon. And the sons of
Ishi *were*, Zoheth, and Ben-zoheth.
21 ¶ The sons of Shelah the son of Judah *were*,
Er the father of Lecah, and Laadah the father of
Mareshah, and the families of the house of them
that wrought fine linen, of the house of Ashbea,
22 And Jokim, and the men of Chozeba, and Jo-
ash, and Saraph, who had the dominion in Moab,
and Jashubi-lehem. And *these are* ancient things.
23 These *were* the potters, and those that dwelt
among plants and hedges: there they dwelt with
the king for his work.
24 ¶ The sons of Simeon *were*, Nemuel, and
Jamin, Jarib, Zerah, *and* Shaul:
25 Shallum his son, Mibsam his son, Mishma his
son.
26 And the sons of Mishma; Hamuel his son,
Zacchur his son, Shimei his son.
27 And Shimei had sixteen sons and six daugh-
ters; but his brethren had not many children,
neither did all their family multiply, like to the
children of Judah.
28 And they dwelt at Beer-sheba, and Moladah,
and Hazar-shual,
29 And at Bilhah, and at Ezem, and at Tolad,
30 And at Bethuel, and at Hormah, and at Ziklag,
31 And at Beth-marcaboth, and Hazar-susim,
and at Beth-birei, and at Shaaraim. These *were*
their cities unto the reign of David.
32 And their villages *were*, Etam, and Ain,
Rimmon, and Tochen, and Ashan, five cities:
33 And all their villages that *were* round about
the same cities, unto Baal. These *were* their habi-
tations, and their genealogy.
34 And Meshobab, and Jamlech, and Joshah the
son of Amaziah,
35 And Joel, and Jehu the son of Josibiah, the son
of Seraiah, the son of Asiel,
36 And Elioenai, and Jaakobah, and Jeshohaiah,
and Asaiah, and Adiel, and Jesimiel, and Benaiah,
37 And Ziza the son of Shiphi, the son of Allon,
the son of Jedaiah, the son of Shimri, the son of
Shemaiah;
38 These mentioned by *their* names *were* princes
in their families: and the house of their fathers
increased greatly.
39 ¶ And they went to the entrance of Gedor,

(ch. 8), as these were the sources of Israel's kings and priests, and the most prominent tribes after the exile.

Chapter 4: ***This chapter traces the genealogies of the tribes completing Judah and then Simeon.***

4:1 *The sons of Judah.* Having traced the tribe of Judah through the line of Ram (chs. 2–3), Chronicles now completes his record of Judah with other Judahite families.

4:9–10 *Jabez.* Means "sorrowful." He was born in sorrow and yet prayed for God to bless him, reversing his sorrow to prosperity. *coast.* Region. This prayer was not motivated by selfish greed, but faith in God's covenant promises of an inheritance (Ex. 34:24; Deut. 12:20; 19:8).

4:13 *Othniel.* A Spirit-empowered judge over Israel whose father was the nephew of Caleb (Josh. 15:17; Judg. 1:13; 3:9–11).

even unto the east side of the valley, to seek pas-
ture for their flocks.
40 And they found fat pasture and good, and the
land *was* wide, and quiet, and peaceable; for *they*
of Ham had dwelt there of old.
41 And these written by name came in the days
of Hezekiah king of Judah, and smote their tents,
and the habitations that were found there, and
destroyed them utterly unto this day, and dwelt in
their rooms: because *there was* pasture there for
their flocks.
42 And *some* of them, *even* of the sons of Simeon,
five hundred men, went to mount Seir, having
for their captains Pelatiah, and Neariah, and
Rephaiah, and Uzziel, the sons of Ishi.
43 And they smote the rest of the Amalekites that
were escaped, and dwelt there unto this day.

CHAPTER 5

NOW the sons of Reuben the firstborn of Israel,
(for he *was* the firstborn; but, forasmuch as he de-
filed his father's bed, his birthright was given unto
the sons of Joseph the son of Israel: and the gene-
alogy is not to be reckoned after the birthright.
2 For Judah prevailed above his brethren, and of
him *came* the chief ruler; but the birthright *was*
Joseph's:)
3 The sons, *I say*, of Reuben the firstborn of Israel
were, Hanoch, and Pallu, Hezron, and Carmi.
4 The sons of Joel; Shemaiah his son, Gog his son,
Shimei his son,
5 Micah his son, Reaia his son, Baal his son,
6 Beerah his son, whom Tilgath-pilneser king of
Assyria carried away *captive*: he *was* prince of the
Reubenites.
7 And his brethren by their families, when the
genealogy of their generations was reckoned, *were*
the chief, Jeiel, and Zechariah,
8 And Bela the son of Azaz, the son of Shema, the
son of Joel, who dwelt in Aroer, even unto Nebo
and Baal-meon:
9 And eastward he inhabited unto the entering
in of the wilderness from the river Euphrates:
because their cattle were multiplied in the land of
Gilead.
10 And in the days of Saul they made war with
the Hagarites, who fell by their hand: and they
dwelt in their tents throughout all the east *land*
of Gilead.
11 ¶ And the children of Gad dwelt over against
them, in the land of Bashan unto Salchah:
12 Joel the chief, and Shapham the next, and Jaa-
nai, and Shaphat in Bashan.
13 And their brethren of the house of their fa-
thers *were*, Michael, and Meshullam, and Sheba,
and Jorai, and Jachan, and Zia, and Heber, seven.
14 These *are* the children of Abihail the son of
Huri, the son of Jaroah, the son of Gilead, the son
of Michael, the son of Jeshishai, the son of Jahdo,
the son of Buz;
15 Ahi the son of Abdiel, the son of Guni, chief of
the house of their fathers.
16 And they dwelt in Gilead in Bashan, and in
her towns, and in all the suburbs of Sharon, upon
their borders.
17 All these were reckoned by genealogies in the
days of Jotham king of Judah, and in the days of
Jeroboam king of Israel.
18 ¶ The sons of Reuben, and the Gadites, and
half the tribe of Manasseh, of valiant men, men
able to bear buckler and sword, and to shoot with
bow, and skilful in war, *were* four and forty thou-
sand seven hundred and threescore, that went out
to the war.
19 And they made war with the Hagarites, with
Jetur, and Nephish, and Nodab.
20 And they were helped against them, and the
Hagarites were delivered into their hand, and all
that *were* with them: for they cried to God in the

4:24–43 *Simeon.* By David's time much of this tribe had been absorbed into Judah as the land allotment originally given it was encapsulated in Judah (Gen. 49:5–7; Josh. 19:1).

4:41 *smote their tents.* Some from Simeon had made inroads among the Amalekites during the time of king *Hezekiah* (cf. 2 Chron. 29–32). *rooms.* Places.

Thoughts for Personal/Family Worship: Chapter 4

Jabez's prayer (vv. 9–10) should not simply be taken as a request for earthly or temporal blessings. He prayed by faith to the God of the covenant to prosper him in the promised inheritance. God's people today should plead God's promises, looking past their painful circumstances to the riches of Jesus Christ (Eph. 1:3). Presently this means praying for a deeper experience of the work of the Holy Spirit, who is the down payment of our inheritance (Eph. 1:13–14). Ultimately this is prayer driven by hope in Christ's coming with glory (Eph. 1:17–18). How does Jabez's example encourage you to pray today?

Chapter 5: *Chronicles continues the genealogical record of Israel with Reuben, Gad, and the half tribe of Manasseh, the tribes that settled east of the Jordan River.*

5:1–2 *forasmuch.* Because. The parenthetic statement shows why the birthright was taken from *Reuben* (Gen. 35:22; 49:3–4).

5:2 *Judah prevailed.* Before Jacob died, he blessed his sons, saying that Judah would be king among his brothers (Gen. 49:10). Though Judah received the right to rule, *Joseph*('s) inheritance was the double portion of a firstborn son's *birthright* from his father's fortune (Gen. 48:5).

5:6 *Tilgath-pilneser.* Otherwise known as Tiglath-Pileser III, or "Pul" (v. 26; also see 2 Kings 15:29; 16:7). The Assyrian Empire destroyed Samaria in 722/21 BC.

5:11–17 The genealogy of *Gad.*

5:18–22 A recounting of the war against the Hagarites, descendants of Hagar, Ishmaelites. The trust of these men in the Lord is underscored by their crying out to God in the battle (v. 20).

5:18 *buckler.* Small shield.

battle, and he was intreated of them; because they
put their trust in him.
21 And they took away their cattle; of their camels
fifty thousand, and of sheep two hundred and
fifty thousand, and of asses two thousand, and of
men an hundred thousand.
22 For there fell down many slain, because the
war *was* of God. And they dwelt in their steads
until the captivity.
23 ¶ And the children of the half tribe of
Manasseh dwelt in the land: they increased from
Bashan unto Baal-hermon and Senir, and unto
mount Hermon.
24 And these *were* the heads of the house of their
fathers, even Epher, and Ishi, and Eliel, and Azriel,
and Jeremiah, and Hodaviah, and Jahdiel, mighty
men of valour, famous men, *and* heads of the
house of their fathers.
25 ¶ And they transgressed against the God of
their fathers, and went a whoring after the gods
of the people of the land, whom God destroyed
before them.
26 And the God of Israel stirred up the spirit
of Pul king of Assyria, and the spirit of Tilgath-
pilneser king of Assyria, and he carried them
away, even the Reubenites, and the Gadites, and
the half tribe of Manasseh, and brought them
unto Halah, and Habor, and Hara, and to the river
Gozan, unto this day.

CHAPTER 6

THE sons of Levi; Gershon, Kohath, and Merari.
2 And the sons of Kohath; Amram, Izhar, and
Hebron, and Uzziel.
3 And the children of Amram; Aaron, and Moses,
and Miriam. The sons also of Aaron; Nadab, and
Abihu, Eleazar, and Ithamar.
4 ¶ Eleazar begat Phinehas, Phinehas begat
Abishua,
5 And Abishua begat Bukki, and Bukki begat
Uzzi,
6 And Uzzi begat Zerahiah, and Zerahiah begat
Meraioth,
7 Meraioth begat Amariah, and Amariah begat
Ahitub,
8 And Ahitub begat Zadok, and Zadok begat
Ahimaaz,
9 And Ahimaaz begat Azariah, and Azariah begat
Johanan,
10 And Johanan begat Azariah, (he *it is* that
executed the priest's office in the temple that
Solomon built in Jerusalem:)
11 And Azariah begat Amariah, and Amariah be-
gat Ahitub,
12 And Ahitub begat Zadok, and Zadok begat
Shallum,
13 And Shallum begat Hilkiah, and Hilkiah begat
Azariah,
14 And Azariah begat Seraiah, and Seraiah begat
Jehozadak,
15 And Jehozadak went *into captivity*, when the
LORD carried away Judah and Jerusalem by the
hand of Nebuchadnezzar.
16 ¶ The sons of Levi; Gershom, Kohath, and
Merari.
17 And these *be* the names of the sons of Ger-
shom; Libni, and Shimei.
18 And the sons of Kohath *were*, Amram, and
Izhar, and Hebron, and Uzziel.
19 The sons of Merari; Mahli, and Mushi. And
these *are* the families of the Levites according to
their fathers.
20 Of Gershom; Libni his son, Jahath his son,
Zimmah his son,
21 Joah his son, Iddo his son, Zerah his son, Jeat-
erai his son.
22 The sons of Kohath; Amminadab his son,
Korah his son, Assir his son,
23 Elkanah his son, and Ebiasaph his son, and
Assir his son,
24 Tahath his son, Uriel his son, Uzziah his son,
and Shaul his son.
25 And the sons of Elkanah; Amasai, and Ahimoth.

5:22 *captivity.* The exile.

5:25 *they transgressed.* The climax here is the exile of the tribes Chronicles has just recorded. There was faithfulness among the tribes, but they were largely marked by gross immorality and sin. *whoring.* Worshiping false gods through idols, often pictured as spiritual adultery (Ezek. 16; 23).

5:26 *God of Israel stirred up.* Though bound by covenant only to Israel, God's sovereignty is not limited, for He controls all people, even pagan kings (Prov. 21:1; Isa. 10:5–19). *Pul . . . Tilgath-pilneser.* See note at v. 6.

Thoughts for Personal/Family Worship: Chapter 5

As Reuben's adultery with his father's concubine cost him the right of the firstborn (vv. 1–2), so Israel's spiritual adultery with idols cost them their inheritance in the land (vv. 25–26). God is a jealous God. He rules as the Sovereign over all people and all events (v. 26). He demands our complete allegiance, and will bless those who seek Him as their only Lord, but will punish those who cherish idols in their hearts or worship them with their lives. What idols are popular in your nation? What idols tempt your own heart?

Chapter 6: ***This chapter details the genealogy of Levi, the priests of Israel and their assistants chosen by God to serve in the tabernacle and temple.***

6:1–15 *Kohath.* The line of Eleazar, the son of Aaron through the line of Kohath who was in the line of the high priest (Ex. 6:16–25). Again, Chronicles is selective, omitting several high priests from its genealogical record.

6:10 *Azariah.* First priest of the temple Solomon built, and so a prominent and well-remembered priest (1 Kings 4:2).

6:16–30 This section follows the three Levitical lines of *Gershom, Kohath, and Merari.*

26 *As for* Elkanah: the sons of Elkanah; Zophai his
son, and Nahath his son,
27 Eliab his son, Jeroham his son, Elkanah his
son.
28 And the sons of Samuel; the firstborn Vashni,
and Abiah.
29 The sons of Merari; Mahli, Libni his son,
Shimei his son, Uzza his son,
30 Shimea his son, Haggiah his son, Asaiah his son.
31 And these *are they* whom David set over the
service of song in the house of the LORD, after that
the ark had rest.
32 And they ministered before the dwelling place
of the tabernacle of the congregation with sing-
ing, until Solomon had built the house of the
LORD in Jerusalem: and *then* they waited on their
office according to their order.
33 And these *are* they that waited with their chil-
dren. Of the sons of the Kohathites: Heman a
singer, the son of Joel, the son of Shemuel,
34 The son of Elkanah, the son of Jeroham, the
son of Eliel, the son of Toah,
35 The son of Zuph, the son of Elkanah, the son
of Mahath, the son of Amasai,
36 The son of Elkanah, the son of Joel, the son of
Azariah, the son of Zephaniah,
37 The son of Tahath, the son of Assir, the son of
Ebiasaph, the son of Korah,
38 The son of Izhar, the son of Kohath, the son of
Levi, the son of Israel.
39 And his brother Asaph, who stood on his right
hand, *even* Asaph the son of Berachiah, the son
of Shimea,
40 The son of Michael, the son of Baaseiah, the
son of Malchiah,
41 The son of Ethni, the son of Zerah, the son of
Adaiah,
42 The son of Ethan, the son of Zimmah, the son
of Shimei,
43 The son of Jahath, the son of Gershom, the
son of Levi.
44 And their brethren the sons of Merari *stood* on
the left hand: Ethan the son of Kishi, the son of
Abdi, the son of Malluch,
45 The son of Hashabiah, the son of Amaziah, the
son of Hilkiah,
46 The son of Amzi, the son of Bani, the son of
Shamer,
47 The son of Mahli, the son of Mushi, the son of
Merari, the son of Levi.
48 Their brethren also the Levites *were* appointed
unto all manner of service of the tabernacle of the
house of God.
49 ¶ But Aaron and his sons offered upon the
altar of the burnt offering, and on the altar of
incense, *and were appointed* for all the work of the
place most holy, and to make an atonement for
Israel, according to all that Moses the servant of
God had commanded.
50 And these *are* the sons of Aaron; Eleazar his
son, Phinehas his son, Abishua his son,
51 Bukki his son, Uzzi his son, Zerahiah his son,
52 Meraioth his son, Amariah his son, Ahitub his
son,
53 Zadok his son, Ahimaaz his son.
54 ¶ Now these *are* their dwelling places through-
out their castles in their coasts, of the sons of
Aaron, of the families of the Kohathites: for theirs
was the lot.
55 And they gave them Hebron in the land of
Judah, and the suburbs thereof round about it.
56 But the fields of the city, and the villages
thereof, they gave to Caleb the son of Jephunneh.
57 And to the sons of Aaron they gave the cities
of Judah, *namely*, Hebron, *the city* of refuge, and
Libnah with her suburbs, and Jattir, and Eshte-
moa, with their suburbs,
58 And Hilen with her suburbs, Debir with her
suburbs,
59 And Ashan with her suburbs, and Beth-
shemesh with her suburbs:
60 And out of the tribe of Benjamin; Geba with

6:28 *Samuel.* The prophet who would later anoint both Saul and David as kings over Israel. There is some confusion over Samuel being named as a Levite because his father was a descendant of an Ephrathite (1 Sam. 1:1). But the latter refers to his homeland, not his tribal identity, since the Levites were scattered throughout the country.

6:31 Chronicles introduces the functions of the Levitical singers. They were designated to orchestrate the worship of the tabernacle and later the temple.

6:33–47 Chronicles traces the lines of three prominent singers, *Heman* (v. 33), *Asaph* (v. 39), and *Ethan* (v. 44), back to their father Levi (15:17,19).

6:48 *manner.* Kind.

6:49 The main ministry of the Aaronic priests was to *make an atonement for Israel* by blood sacrifice, a type of Christ's priestly work (Heb. 9:6–14).

6:54–56 The high priestly line from *Aaron* dwelt in *Hebron* in the inheritance of *Caleb*, the man who with Joshua followed the Lord fully (Num. 13–14; 32:12; Josh. 14:6–15; 21:10–12).

6:54 *their dwelling places.* The cities that the tribe of Levi received from the people for their residence. *coasts.* Regions (v. 66).

6:57–81 The remaining *sons of Aaron* and other Levites received cities among the other tribes (cf. Josh. 21).

Thoughts for Personal/Family Worship: Chapter 6

The prominence of the Levites in the genealogies reminds us that God's purpose required not just a king but also a priest. The primary function of the priesthood was to "make an atonement for Israel" (v. 49). Only by the forgiveness of sins could God dwell among His people as He once dwelt with Adam without violating His holiness. The sons of Aaron could only cleanse the flesh with outward rituals, but Christ alone cleanses the conscience with forgiveness (Heb. 9:13–14), for He "put away sin by the sacrifice of himself" (v. 26). It was a great

her suburbs, and Alemeth with her suburbs,
and Anathoth with her suburbs. All their cities
throughout their families *were* thirteen cities.
61 And unto the sons of Kohath, *which were* left
of the family of that tribe, *were cities given* out
of the half tribe, *namely, out of* the half *tribe* of
Manasseh, by lot, ten cities.
62 And to the sons of Gershom throughout their
families out of the tribe of Issachar, and out of
the tribe of Asher, and out of the tribe of Naph-
tali, and out of the tribe of Manasseh in Bashan,
thirteen cities.
63 Unto the sons of Merari *were given* by lot,
throughout their families, out of the tribe of
Reuben, and out of the tribe of Gad, and out of
the tribe of Zebulun, twelve cities.
64 And the children of Israel gave to the Levites
these cities with their suburbs.
65 And they gave by lot out of the tribe of the
children of Judah, and out of the tribe of the
children of Simeon, and out of the tribe of the
children of Benjamin, these cities, which are
called by *their* names.
66 And *the residue* of the families of the sons of
Kohath had cities of their coasts out of the tribe
of Ephraim.
67 And they gave unto them, *of* the cities of
refuge, Shechem in mount Ephraim with her
suburbs; *they gave* also Gezer with her suburbs,
68 And Jokmeam with her suburbs, and Beth-
horon with her suburbs,
69 And Aijalon with her suburbs, and Gath-rim-
mon with her suburbs:
70 And out of the half tribe of Manasseh; Aner
with her suburbs, and Bileam with her suburbs, for
the family of the remnant of the sons of Kohath.
71 Unto the sons of Gershom *were given* out of
the family of the half tribe of Manasseh, Golan
in Bashan with her suburbs, and Ashtaroth with
her suburbs:
72 And out of the tribe of Issachar; Kedesh with
her suburbs, Daberath with her suburbs,
73 And Ramoth with her suburbs, and Anem
with her suburbs:
74 And out of the tribe of Asher; Mashal with her
suburbs, and Abdon with her suburbs,
75 And Hukok with her suburbs, and Rehob with
her suburbs:
76 And out of the tribe of Naphtali; Kedesh in
Galilee with her suburbs, and Hammon with her
suburbs, and Kirjathaim with her suburbs.
77 Unto the rest of the children of Merari *were
given* out of the tribe of Zebulun, Rimmon with
her suburbs, Tabor with her suburbs:
78 And on the other side Jordan by Jericho, on
the east side of Jordan, *were given them* out of the
tribe of Reuben, Bezer in the wilderness with her
suburbs, and Jahzah with her suburbs,
79 Kedemoth also with her suburbs, and Meph-
aath with her suburbs:
80 And out of the tribe of Gad; Ramoth in
Gilead with her suburbs, and Mahanaim with her
suburbs,
81 And Heshbon with her suburbs, and Jazer
with her suburbs.

CHAPTER 7

NOW the sons of Issachar *were*, Tola, and Puah,
Jashub, and Shimron, four.
2 And the sons of Tola; Uzzi, and Rephaiah, and
Jeriel, and Jahmai, and Jibsam, and Shemuel,
heads of their father's house, *to wit*, of Tola: *they
were* valiant men of might in their generations;
whose number *was* in the days of David two and
twenty thousand and six hundred.
3 And the sons of Uzzi; Izrahiah: and the sons of
Izrahiah; Michael, and Obadiah, and Joel, Ishiah,
five: all of them chief men.
4 And with them, by their generations, after the
house of their fathers, *were* bands of soldiers for
war, six and thirty thousand *men*: for they had
many wives and sons.
5 And their brethren among all the families of
Issachar *were* valiant men of might, reckoned
in all by their genealogies fourscore and seven
thousand.
6 ¶ *The sons* of Benjamin; Bela, and Becher, and
Jediael, three.
7 And the sons of Bela; Ezbon, and Uzzi, and
Uzziel, and Jerimoth, and Iri, five; heads of the
house of *their* fathers, mighty men of valour; and
were reckoned by their genealogies twenty and
two thousand and thirty and four.
8 And the sons of Becher; Zemira, and Joash, and
Eliezer, and Elioenai, and Omri, and Jerimoth,

consolation to Israel that they had the high priest appointed by God living among them. To whom do you look to make atonement for your sins? Anyone besides Christ who claims to be a priest and offers you absolution for your sins is a pretender and an offense to God, for He said to His Son, "Thou art a priest for ever" (Ps. 110:4; Heb. 5:5–6).

Chapter 7: ***Chronicles continues tracing the genealogies of the sons of Jacob, focusing on Issachar, Benjamin, Naphtali, Manasseh, Ephraim, and Asher, but omitting Dan and Zebulun.***

7:1–5 The genealogical record now traces the line of *Issachar* (Gen. 46:13; Num. 26:23–25).

7:2 *to wit.* That is to say. *valiant men of might.* These men are remembered for their strength and bravery in the days of David.

7:6–12 The tribe of *Benjamin* (Gen. 46:21; Num. 26:38–39) will receive fuller treatment in the section leading up to its most famous member, King Saul (ch. 8). Perhaps one of the

and Abiah, and Anathoth, and Alameth. All these
are the sons of Becher.
9 And the number of them, after their genealogy
by their generations, heads of the house of their
fathers, mighty men of valour, *was* twenty thou-
sand and two hundred.
10 The sons also of Jediael; Bilhan: and the sons
of Bilhan; Jeush, and Benjamin, and Ehud, and
Chenaanah, and Zethan, and Tharshish, and
Ahishahar.
11 All these the sons of Jediael, by the heads of
their fathers, mighty men of valour, *were* seven-
teen thousand and two hundred *soldiers*, fit to go
out for war *and* battle.
12 Shuppim also, and Huppim, the children of Ir,
and Hushim, the sons of Aher.
13 ¶ The sons of Naphtali; Jahziel, and Guni, and
Jezer, and Shallum, the sons of Bilhah.
14 ¶ The sons of Manasseh; Ashriel, whom she
bare: (*but* his concubine the Aramitess bare
Machir the father of Gilead:
15 And Machir took to wife *the sister* of Huppim
and Shuppim, whose sister's name *was* Maachah;)
and the name of the second *was* Zelophehad: and
Zelophehad had daughters.
16 And Maachah the wife of Machir bare a son,
and she called his name Peresh; and the name of
his brother *was* Sheresh; and his sons *were* Ulam
and Rakem.
17 And the sons of Ulam; Bedan. These *were*
the sons of Gilead, the son of Machir, the son of
Manasseh.
18 And his sister Hammoleketh bare Ishod, and
Abi-ezer, and Mahalah.
19 And the sons of Shemida were, Ahian, and
Shechem, and Likhi, and Aniam.
20 ¶ And the sons of Ephraim; Shuthelah, and
Bered his son, and Tahath his son, and Eladah his
son, and Tahath his son,
21 ¶ And Zabad his son, and Shuthelah his son,
and Ezer, and Elead, whom the men of Gath *that*
were born in *that* land slew, because they came
down to take away their cattle.
22 And Ephraim their father mourned many
days, and his brethren came to comfort him.
23 ¶ And when he went in to his wife, she
conceived, and bare a son, and he called his name
Beriah, because it went evil with his house.
24 (And his daughter *was* Sherah, who built
Beth-horon the nether, and the upper, and
Uzzen-sherah.)
25 And Rephah *was* his son, also Resheph, and
Telah his son, and Tahan his son,
26 Laadan his son, Ammihud his son, Elishama
his son,
27 Non his son, Jehoshua his son.
28 ¶ And their possessions and habitations *were*,
Beth-el and the towns thereof, and eastward
Naaran, and westward Gezer, with the towns
thereof; Shechem also and the towns thereof,
unto Gaza and the towns thereof:
29 And by the borders of the children of
Manasseh, Beth-shean and her towns, Taanach
and her towns, Megiddo and her towns, Dor and
her towns. In these dwelt the children of Joseph
the son of Israel.
30 ¶ The sons of Asher; Imnah, and Isuah, and
Ishuai, and Beriah, and Serah their sister.
31 And the sons of Beriah; Heber, and Malchiel,
who *is* the father of Birzavith.
32 And Heber begat Japhlet, and Shomer, and
Hotham, and Shua their sister.
33 And the sons of Japhlet; Pasach, and Bimhal,
and Ashvath. These *are* the children of Japhlet.
34 And the sons of Shamer; Ahi, and Rohgah,
Jehubbah, and Aram.
35 And the sons of his brother Helem; Zophah,
and Imna, and Shelesh, and Amal.
36 The sons of Zophah; Suah, and Harnepher,
and Shual, and Beri, and Imrah,
37 Bezer, and Hod, and Shamma, and Shilshah,
and Ithran, and Beera.

reasons Benjamin is partly treated here is because it fits the theme on *mighty men of valour*, military men (vv. 2,4–5,7, 9,40).

7:13–19 The tribes of *Naphtali* and *Manasseh* (Gen. 46:24; Num. 26:29–33,48–49; Josh. 17:1–3). The author had already covered the half tribe of Manasseh east of the Jordan (5:23–24).

7:14 *she bare.* This must be the first wife, the nonconcubine. *Aramitess.* Aramean.

7:15 *Zelophehad had daughters.* See Num. 26:33; 27:1–11, which details this narrative.

7:20–29 The tribe of *Ephraim* was counted as one of the tribes of Israel because of the double portion Joseph received in his birthright (see note at 5:2).

7:21 *the men of Gath.* Philistines who caused trouble for the tribe of Ephraim, killing some of them.

7:22 This *Ephraim* cannot be the original father of the tribe, the son of Joseph, for he would have died in Egypt. It must be some descendant who took his name, not an unusual custom.

7:23 *Beriah* means "trouble," and is linguistically related to *went evil*, or "badly."

7:24 *Sherah.* This is an unusual note as it records a woman *who built* a town. *nether.* Lower.

7:27 *Jehoshua.* Joshua, the son of Nun (Num. 13:8).

7:30–40 The tribe of *Asher* (Gen. 46:17; Num. 26:44–46).

Thoughts for Personal/Family Worship: Chapter 7

This chapter contains a lot of disparate information. However, a common thread through it all is the bravery and strength of military men (vv. 2,4–5,7,9,40). It also speaks of those who died violently at the hands of enemies to the grief of their surviving family (vv. 21–23). It is very fitting that the most famous person in this chapter is Joshua, who led Israel to successful war in order to receive its inheritance in the land (v. 27). Far from being ashamed of military service, the Bible teaches us that God's people are a spiritual army (Eph. 6:10–18), and

38 And the sons of Jether; Jephunneh, and
Pispah, and Ara.
39 And the sons of Ulla; Arah, and Haniel, and
Rezia.
40 All these *were* the children of Asher, heads
of *their* father's house, choice *and* mighty men
of valour, chief of the princes. And the number
throughout the genealogy of them that were apt
to the war *and* to battle *was* twenty and six thou-
sand men.

CHAPTER 8

NOW Benjamin begat Bela his firstborn, Ashbel
the second, and Aharah the third,
2 Nohah the fourth, and Rapha the fifth.
3 And the sons of Bela were, Addar, and Gera,
and Abihud,
4 And Abishua, and Naaman, and Ahoah,
5 And Gera, and Shephuphan, and Huram.
6 And these *are* the sons of Ehud: these are the
heads of the fathers of the inhabitants of Geba,
and they removed them to Manahath:
7 And Naaman, and Ahiah, and Gera, he re-
moved them, and begat Uzza, and Ahihud.
8 And Shaharaim begat *children* in the country of
Moab, after he had sent them away; Hushim and
Baara *were* his wives.
9 And he begat of Hodesh his wife, Jobab, and
Zibia, and Mesha, and Malcham,
10 And Jeuz, and Shachia, and Mirma. These *were*
his sons, heads of the fathers.
11 And of Hushim he begat Abitub, and Elpaal.
12 The sons of Elpaal; Eber, and Misham, and
Shamed, who built Ono, and Lod, with the towns
thereof:
13 Beriah also, and Shema, who *were* heads of the
fathers of the inhabitants of Aijalon, who drove
away the inhabitants of Gath:
14 And Ahio, Shashak, and Jeremoth,
15 And Zebadiah, and Arad, and Ader,
16 And Michael, and Ispah, and Joha, the sons of
Beriah;
17 And Zebadiah, and Meshullam, and Hezeki,
and Heber,
18 Ishmerai also, and Jezliah, and Jobab, the sons
of Elpaal;
19 And Jakim, and Zichri, and Zabdi,
20 And Elienai, and Zilthai, and Eliel,
21 And Adaiah, and Beraiah, and Shimrath, the
sons of Shimhi;
22 And Ishpan, and Heber, and Eliel,
23 And Abdon, and Zichri, and Hanan,
24 And Hananiah, and Elam, and Antothijah,
25 And Iphedeiah, and Penuel, the sons of
Shashak;
26 And Shamsherai, and Shehariah, and Athaliah,
27 And Jaresiah, and Eliah, and Zichri, the sons
of Jeroham.
28 These *were* heads of the fathers, by their gen-
erations, chief *men*. These dwelt in Jerusalem.
29 And at Gibeon dwelt the father of Gibeon;
whose wife's name *was* Maachah:
30 And his firstborn son Abdon, and Zur, and
Kish, and Baal, and Nadab,
31 And Gedor, and Ahio, and Zacher.
32 And Mikloth begat Shimeah. And these also
dwelt with their brethren in Jerusalem, over
against them.
33 ¶ And Ner begat Kish, and Kish begat Saul,
and Saul begat Jonathan, and Malchi-shua, and
Abinadab, and Esh-baal.
34 And the son of Jonathan *was* Merib-baal; and
Merib-baal begat Micah.
35 And the sons of Micah *were*, Pithon, and
Melech, and Tarea, and Ahaz.
36 And Ahaz begat Jehoadah; and Jehoadah begat
Alemeth, and Azmaveth, and Zimri; and Zimri
begat Moza,
37 And Moza begat Binea: Rapha *was* his son,
Eleasah his son, Azel his son:
38 And Azel had six sons, whose names *are* these,
Azrikam, Bocheru, and Ishmael, and Sheariah,
and Obadiah, and Hanan. All these *were* the sons
of Azel.
39 And the sons of Eshek his brother *were*, Ulam
his firstborn, Jehush the second, and Eliphelet the
third.
40 And the sons of Ulam were mighty men of
valour, archers, and had many sons, and sons'

Jesus, our greater Joshua, is the Captain of our salvation (Heb. 2:10). How do we fight for Him?

Chapter 8: ***Chronicles gives a fuller genealogy of Benjamin, leading up to the record of Saul, the first king of Israel.***

8:1 This genealogy of the tribe of *Benjamin* is more detailed than the one that preceded (7:6–12) and closes the genealogies.
8:6 *Ehud.* The famous left-handed judge who killed the king of Moab (Judg. 3:12–30). *removed them to Manahath.* Not the Babylonian exile but a tribal exile (cf. 2 Sam. 4:2–3).
8:28 *dwelt in Jerusalem.* Jerusalem was originally allotted to the tribe of Benjamin, right on the border with Judah (Josh. 15:8; 18:28). David later defeated the Jebusites, giving the city to the people of Judah (2 Sam. 5:6–10).
8:29–40 These verses record the most famous lineage in Benjamin, the house of *Saul.* This prepares the way for the narrative of Saul's death (ch. 10) and the kingdom of David (chs. 11–29).
8:33 *Esh-baal.* Also known as Ish-bosheth (see note at 2 Sam. 2:8).
8:34 *Merib-baal.* Also known as Mephibosheth (2 Sam. 4:4; 9:6–13).

Thoughts for Personal/Family Worship: Chapter 8

Though Benjamin was the youngest of the sons of Jacob, his tribe was by no means the least significant. Jacob

sons, an hundred and fifty. All these *are* of the
sons of Benjamin.

CHAPTER 9

SO all Israel were reckoned by genealogies; and,
behold, they *were* written in the book of the kings
of Israel and Judah, *who* were carried away to
Babylon for their transgression.
2 ¶ Now the first inhabitants that *dwelt* in their
possessions in their cities *were*, the Israelites, the
priests, Levites, and the Nethinims.
3 And in Jerusalem dwelt of the children of
Judah, and of the children of Benjamin, and of
the children of Ephraim, and Manasseh;
4 Uthai the son of Ammihud, the son of Omri,
the son of Imri, the son of Bani, of the children of
Pharez the son of Judah.
5 And of the Shilonites; Asaiah the firstborn, and
his sons.
6 And of the sons of Zerah; Jeuel, and their
brethren, six hundred and ninety.
7 And of the sons of Benjamin; Sallu the son
of Meshullam, the son of Hodaviah, the son of
Hasenuah,
8 And Ibneiah the son of Jeroham, and Elah the
son of Uzzi, the son of Michri, and Meshullam
the son of Shephathiah, the son of Reuel, the son
of Ibnijah;
9 And their brethren, according to their gener-
ations, nine hundred and fifty and six. All these
men *were* chief of the fathers in the house of their
fathers.
10 ¶ And of the priests; Jedaiah, and Jehoiarib,
and Jachin,
11 And Azariah the son of Hilkiah, the son of
Meshullam, the son of Zadok, the son of Mera-
ioth, the son of Ahitub, the ruler of the house of
God;
12 And Adaiah the son of Jeroham, the son of
Pashur, the son of Malchijah, and Maasiai the son
of Adiel, the son of Jahzerah, the son of Meshul-
lam, the son of Meshillemith, the son of Immer;
13 And their brethren, heads of the house of
their fathers, a thousand and seven hundred and
threescore; very able men for the work of the
service of the house of God.
14 And of the Levites; Shemaiah the son of Has-
shub, the son of Azrikam, the son of Hashabiah,
of the sons of Merari;
15 And Bakbakkar, Heresh, and Galal, and
Mattaniah the son of Micah, the son of Zichri, the
son of Asaph;
16 And Obadiah the son of Shemaiah, the son of
Galal, the son of Jeduthun, and Berechiah the son
of Asa, the son of Elkanah, that dwelt in the vil-
lages of the Netophathites.
17 And the porters *were*, Shallum, and Akkub,
and Talmon, and Ahiman, and their brethren:
Shallum *was* the chief;
18 Who hitherto *waited* in the king's gate east-
ward: they *were* porters in the companies of the
children of Levi.
19 And Shallum the son of Kore, the son of
Ebiasaph, the son of Korah, and his brethren, of
the house of his father, the Korahites, *were* over
the work of the service, keepers of the gates of the
tabernacle: and their fathers, *being* over the host
of the LORD, *were* keepers of the entry.
20 And Phinehas the son of Eleazar was the ruler
over them in time past, *and* the LORD *was* with
him.
21 *And* Zechariah the son of Meshelemiah
was porter of the door of the tabernacle of the
congregation.
22 All these *which were* chosen to be porters in
the gates *were* two hundred and twelve. These
were reckoned by their genealogy in their villages,
whom David and Samuel the seer did ordain in
their set office.
23 So they and their children *had* the oversight
of the gates of the house of the LORD, *namely*, the
house of the tabernacle, by wards.
24 In four quarters were the porters, toward the
east, west, north, and south.
25 And their brethren, *which were* in their villages,

had prophesied that Benjamin would be like a wolf: "In the morning he shall devour the prey, and at night he shall divide the spoil" (Gen. 49:27). From Benjamin would come the important judge Ehud (1 Chron. 8:6), a clan of skillful archers (v. 40), and the first king of Israel, Saul (v. 33). The apostle Paul, known for his zealous work for the gospel, hailed from the tribe of Benjamin (Rom. 11:1; Phil. 3:5). This reminds us that God's purposes for His people are not reserved for the greatest leaders or those from the most prominent families. However, the reference to King Saul also reminds us that the crucial factor in a person's service to God is obedience (1 Chron. 10:13–14; 1 Sam. 15:13–23). Why is obedience to God so much more important than skill or family pedigree?

Chapter 9: ***Chronicles now segues into a genealogical record of those individuals who returned from the Babylonian exile under Cyrus's decree before repeating Saul's genealogy another time.***

Returning Exiles (1 Chron. 9:1–34)

9:1 *carried away to Babylon*. The narrative leaps forward in history to the exile (2 Chron. 36).

9:2 *first inhabitants that dwelt*. First people to return after the exile and dwell in their ancestral cities. *Nethinims*. See Ezra 2:43–58.

9:17–32 The vocation of *porters* had importance for Judah after the exile. They literally served as gatekeepers for the worship of the Lord, opening the doors of the temple every morning, shutting them every night, and guarding it from anyone who was ceremonially unclean (Ps. 84:10; Neh. 12:25,45).

9:18 *hitherto*. Before, prior to this time.

were to come after seven days from time to time
with them.
26 For these Levites, the four chief porters, were
in *their* set office, and were over the chambers and
treasuries of the house of God.
27 ¶ And they lodged round about the house of
God, because the charge *was* upon them, and
the opening thereof every morning *pertained* to
them.
28 And *certain* of them had the charge of the
ministering vessels, that they should bring them
in and out by tale.
29 *Some* of them also *were* appointed to oversee
the vessels, and all the instruments of the sanctu-
ary, and the fine flour, and the wine, and the oil,
and the frankincense, and the spices.
30 And *some* of the sons of the priests made the
ointment of the spices.
31 And Mattithiah, *one* of the Levites, who *was*
the firstborn of Shallum the Korahite, had the set
office over the things that were made in the pans.
32 And *other* of their brethren, of the sons of the
Kohathites, *were* over the shewbread, to prepare *it*
every sabbath.
33 And these *are* the singers, chief of the fathers
of the Levites, *who remaining* in the chambers
were free: for they were employed in *that* work
day and night.
34 These chief fathers of the Levites *were* chief
throughout their generations; these dwelt at
Jerusalem.
35 ¶ And in Gibeon dwelt the father of Gibeon,
Jehiel, whose wife's name *was* Maachah:
36 And his firstborn son Abdon, then Zur, and
Kish, and Baal, and Ner, and Nadab,
37 And Gedor, and Ahio, and Zechariah, and
Mikloth.
38 And Mikloth begat Shimeam. And they also
dwelt with their brethren at Jerusalem, over
against their brethren.
39 And Ner begat Kish; and Kish begat Saul; and
Saul begat Jonathan, and Malchi-shua, and Abin-
adab, and Esh-baal.
40 And the son of Jonathan *was* Merib-baal: and
Merib-baal begat Micah.
41 And the sons of Micah *were*, Pithon, and
Melech, and Tahrea, *and Ahaz*.
42 And Ahaz begat Jarah; and Jarah begat
Alemeth, and Azmaveth, and Zimri; and Zimri
begat Moza;
43 And Moza begat Binea; and Rephaiah his son,
Eleasah his son, Azel his son.
44 And Azel had six sons, whose names *are* these,
Azrikam, Bocheru, and Ishmael, and Sheariah,
and Obadiah, and Hanan: these *were* the sons
of Azel.

CHAPTER 10

NOW the Philistines fought against Israel; and the
men of Israel fled from before the Philistines, and
fell down slain in mount Gilboa.
2 And the Philistines followed hard after Saul,
and after his sons; and the Philistines slew Jona-
than, and Abinadab, and Malchi-shua, the sons of
Saul.
3 And the battle went sore against Saul, and
the archers hit him, and he was wounded of the
archers.
4 Then said Saul to his armourbearer, Draw thy
sword, and thrust me through therewith; lest
these uncircumcised come and abuse me. But his
armourbearer would not; for he was sore afraid.
So Saul took a sword, and fell upon it.
5 And when his armourbearer saw that Saul was
dead, he fell likewise on the sword, and died.

9:28 *tale.* Number.
9:29 *frankincense.* Fragrant incense.

Saul (1 Chron. 9:35–44)

9:35–44 The genealogy of *Saul* (v. 39) is traced out again (cf. 8:29–40) before Chronicles addresses his death (10:13) and how God handed the kingdom over to David (11:1–3). The genealogical section of Chronicles begins with Adam (1:1) and ends with Saul, both men to whom God gave dominion, both charged to obey His commandments, and both judged for their disobedience.

Thoughts for Personal/Family Worship: Chapter 9

Rather than just a boring list of names, Chronicles has thus far outlined the story of the whole Bible. These genealogies begin in the garden of Eden (1:1) and end with people worshiping God in His city, Jerusalem, after the exile (9:33–34). In between there is much sin and sorrow, but also God's grace in the raising up of kings and priests. Chronicles taught the returning exiles that they should hope in the Lord because, although man's sin abounds, God's grace will abound much more through His chosen and coming King. The gospel of Jesus Christ reveals this King, who is both Priest and sacrifice for His people, so that they will worship God in the new Jerusalem coming down from heaven (Rev. 21:2). How can this vision give us hope?

KINGDOM ESTABLISHED (1 CHRON. 10:1—2 CHRON. 9:31)

Chapter 10: *God delivers the kingdom to David after Saul's death.*

Saul's Death (1 Chron. 10:1–14)

10:1 *Philistines fought against Israel.* Chronicles opens by noting the defeat of the Israelites by the Philistines (1 Sam. 31). For the purposes of focusing on David, the author portrays Saul very briefly and negatively.
10:2 *slew . . . the sons of Saul.* The royal heirs to the throne are killed first. Saul's house and lineage are coming to an end—just as was prophesied by the prophet Samuel (1 Sam. 15:23).
10:4 *Saul* was afraid that the Philistines would capture him and *abuse* him. To avoid this, Saul impaled himself with his own *sword.*

6 So Saul died, and his three sons, and all his
house died together.
7 And when all the men of Israel that *were* in the
valley saw that they fled, and that Saul and his
sons were dead, then they forsook their cities, and
fled: and the Philistines came and dwelt in them.
8 ¶ And it came to pass on the morrow, when the
Philistines came to strip the slain, that they found
Saul and his sons fallen in mount Gilboa.
9 And when they had stripped him, they took his
head, and his armour, and sent into the land of
the Philistines round about, to carry tidings unto
their idols, and to the people.
10 And they put his armour in the house of their
gods, and fastened his head in the temple of
Dagon.
11 ¶ And when all Jabesh-gilead heard all that the
Philistines had done to Saul,
12 They arose, all the valiant men, and took away
the body of Saul, and the bodies of his sons, and
brought them to Jabesh, and buried their bones
under the oak in Jabesh, and fasted seven days.
13 ¶ So Saul died for his transgression which he
committed against the LORD, *even* against the
word of the LORD, which he kept not, and also for
asking *counsel* of *one that had* a familiar spirit, to
enquire *of it*;
14 And enquired not of the LORD: therefore he
slew him, and turned the kingdom unto David
the son of Jesse.

CHAPTER 11

THEN all Israel gathered themselves to David unto
Hebron, saying, Behold, we *are* thy bone and thy
flesh.
2 And moreover in time past, even when Saul was
king, thou *wast* he that leddest out and broughtest
in Israel: and the LORD thy God said unto thee,
Thou shalt feed my people Israel, and thou shalt
be ruler over my people Israel.
3 Therefore came all the elders of Israel to the
king to Hebron; and David made a covenant
with them in Hebron before the LORD; and they
anointed David king over Israel, according to the
word of the LORD by Samuel.
4 ¶ And David and all Israel went to Jerusalem,
which *is* Jebus; where the Jebusites *were*, the
inhabitants of the land.
5 And the inhabitants of Jebus said to David,
Thou shalt not come hither. Nevertheless David
took the castle of Zion, which *is* the city of David.
6 And David said, Whosoever smiteth the Jeb-
usites first shall be chief and captain. So Joab the
son of Zeruiah went first up, and was chief.
7 And David dwelt in the castle; therefore they
called it the city of David.
8 And he built the city round about, even from
Millo round about: and Joab repaired the rest of
the city.
9 So David waxed greater and greater: for the
LORD of hosts *was* with him.

10:6 *all his house died together.* In line with his purpose, the author passes over the slow or gradual decline of Saul's house under his son, Ish-bosheth (2 Sam. 2:8; 3:1; 4:8).
10:7 *and fled: and the Philistines came and dwelt in them.* At this point in the narrative, Israel was without a king, scattered like a scared flock from their cities and towns. The Philistines took possession of these towns as their own.
10:8 *morrow.* Next morning.
10:9 *carry tidings unto their idols.* The Philistines marked the defeat of Saul as a victory of their gods (cf. 1 Sam. 5:1–2). It is telling that the idols need to hear news (*tidings*), for they have no divine knowledge (Ps. 115:5). There is no victory here for the other gods, for God had punished Saul (v. 13).
10:11–12 The people of *Jabesh-gilead* show their allegiance to Saul by claiming his body, just as Saul had formerly rescued the people of *Jabesh-gilead* (1 Sam. 11:1–11).
10:13–14 *The LORD* took Saul's life because he did not obey God's Word and consulted a demonic *spirit* (1 Sam. 13:13–14; 15:13–23; 28:7). Disobedience and false worship prove fatal for Israel's kings and people.

Thoughts for Personal/Family Worship: Chapter 10

Saul's tragic rebellion and death stands as a solemn reminder that Israel's hope did not merely rest in restoring a king to its throne. The returned exiles must learn from history that kings are curses if they do not obey the Lord and give Him their undivided allegiance. Too often the kings reigning in Jerusalem had failed at precisely this point, and thus came the exile. In the same way, we all deserve eternal punishment from God because we have broken God's laws and given our hearts to false gods. The need of Israel and of all mankind is not just a king, but a king who is the obedient servant of the Lord. How does Jesus Christ perfectly meet this need?

David's Rise to Power (1 Chron. 11:1—12:40)

Chapter 11: *David becomes king, captures Jerusalem, and gathers all Israel around him, including many mighty men.*

11:1 *all Israel.* Just as all Israel fled from the Philistines (10:7), so now all Israel gathered together under David. *thy bone and thy flesh.* An idiomatic phrase relating the strong allegiance the people of Israel had to David, like husband and wife or close relatives (Gen. 2:23; 29:14; Judg. 9:2; 2 Sam. 19:12–13).
11:2 *thou wast he that leddest out and broughtest in.* Like a shepherd with his flock, David had led them into pastures by day and brought them into safety by night (cf. Ps. 78:71; Ezek. 37:24–28). The people of Israel confessed their allegiance to David, noting that he had been, in effect, their acting king since he defeated Goliath.
11:3 *David made a covenant with them.* The king and representatives of the people entered into a mutually binding promise to be loyal to each other (2 Sam. 3:21; 2 Chron. 16:3; 23:3), defining their responsibilities by God's Word (*according to the word of the LORD by Samuel*).
11:4 *all Israel.* Unity marked the initial days of the kingdom under David.
11:5 *hither.* Here, to this place. *castle of Zion.* Fortress built on a hill of Jerusalem, conquered by David's men (2 Sam. 5:6–9). Jerusalem plays a vital role in the message of Chronicles.
11:9 *waxed greater and greater.* Grew in his honor and power.

10 ¶ These also *are* the chief of the mighty men
whom David had, who strengthened themselves
with him in his kingdom, *and* with all Israel, to
make him king, according to the word of the
LORD concerning Israel.
11 And this *is* the number of the mighty men
whom David had; Jashobeam, an Hachmonite,
the chief of the captains: he lifted up his spear
against three hundred slain *by him* at one time.
12 And after him *was* Eleazar the son of Dodo,
the Ahohite, who *was one* of the three mighties.
13 He was with David at Pas-dammim, and there
the Philistines were gathered together to battle,
where was a parcel of ground full of barley; and
the people fled from before the Philistines.
14 And they set themselves in the midst of *that*
parcel, and delivered it, and slew the Philistines;
and the LORD saved *them* by a great deliverance.
15 ¶ Now three of the thirty captains went down
to the rock to David, into the cave of Adullam;
and the host of the Philistines encamped in the
valley of Rephaim.
16 And David *was* then in the hold, and the
Philistines' garrison *was* then at Beth-lehem.
17 And David longed, and said, Oh that one
would give me drink of the water of the well of
Beth-lehem, that *is* at the gate!
18 And the three brake through the host of the
Philistines, and drew water out of the well of
Beth-lehem, that *was* by the gate, and took *it*, and
brought *it* to David: but David would not drink *of*
it, but poured it out to the LORD,
19 And said, My God forbid it me, that I should
do this thing: shall I drink the blood of these men
that have put their lives in jeopardy? for with *the
jeopardy of* their lives they brought it. Therefore
he would not drink it. These things did these
three mightiest.
20 ¶ And Abishai the brother of Joab, he was chief
of the three: for lifting up his spear against three
hundred, he slew *them*, and had a name among
the three.
21 Of the three, he was more honourable than the
two; for he was their captain: howbeit he attained
not to the *first* three.
22 Benaiah the son of Jehoiada, the son of a val-
iant man of Kabzeel, who had done many acts;
he slew two lionlike men of Moab: also he went
down and slew a lion in a pit in a snowy day.
23 And he slew an Egyptian, a man of *great*
stature, five cubits high; and in the Egyptian's
hand *was* a spear like a weaver's beam; and he
went down to him with a staff, and plucked the
spear out of the Egyptian's hand, and slew him
with his own spear.
24 These *things* did Benaiah the son of Jehoiada,
and had the name among the three mighties.
25 Behold, he was honourable among the thirty,
but attained not to the *first* three: and David set
him over his guard.
26 ¶ Also the valiant men of the armies *were*,
Asahel the brother of Joab, Elhanan the son of
Dodo of Beth-lehem,
27 Shammoth the Harorite, Helez the Pelonite,
28 Ira the son of Ikkesh the Tekoite, Abi-ezer the
Antothite,
29 Sibbecai the Hushathite, Ilai the Ahohite,
30 Maharai the Netophathite, Heled the son of
Baanah the Netophathite,
31 Ithai the son of Ribai of Gibeah, *that per-
tained* to the children of Benjamin, Benaiah the
Pirathonite,
32 Hurai of the brooks of Gaash, Abiel the
Arbathite,
33 Azmaveth the Baharumite, Eliahba the Shaal-
bonite,
34 The sons of Hashem the Gizonite, Jonathan
the son of Shage the Hararite,

---

the LORD of hosts. This title is used to denote the Lord as the defender of His people by the armies (*hosts*) of beings He created and controls in heaven and earth (Isa. 45:12–13; Amos 4:13). He is the supreme King and Commander of all things (Isa. 6:1–3), including the armies of His angels (2 Chron. 18:18) and the armies of His people (12:22; Ex. 12:41; Josh. 5:14; cf. 1 Sam. 17:26,36; 2 Chron. 14:13). Before narrating David's mighty men, Chronicles shows us that the Lord is the power and salvation of His people (v. 14).

11:11–47 Chronicles records the names of David's mighty men at the outset of David's history. In the history of 1 and 2 Samuel, the account of David's mighty men is placed toward the end of David's ministry (2 Sam. 23).

11:11–12 *three mighties.* Three powerful men, apparently David's closest companions and best warriors: *Jashobeam*, *Eleazar*, and "Shammah," not mentioned here (2 Sam. 23:8–12). The author did not intend to have a complete listing, but more of a sampling.

11:13 *parcel.* Piece, portion.

11:14 *the LORD saved them.* Unlike the ungodly king Saul, in Chronicle's account, David is given victory over the Philistines by the power of the Lord.

11:17–19 There is a twofold significance to David pouring out the *water* gathered by his men at great risk to their lives. First, David shows a godward focus as was shown in sacrifice (Deut. 12:16). This water was as precious as blood since it had been in essence gathered at the risk of blood. Second, David realizes that what he is longing for deep down is much more than just water (Ps. 63:1–2).

11:20–47 After having dealt with the three most notable warriors of David, the author now turns to a sampling of the thirty in a second tier of David's warriors, headed by *Abishai* and *Benaiah*.

11:23 *slew an Egyptian.* There is a great similarity between this account and the account of David and Goliath, implying that no man wins victory by his own strength, but by the Lord (Ps. 33:16–18).

11:26—12:22 Chronicles briefly records the names of many of David's mighty men. It is worth noting that many of these individuals were not Israelites but come from different nations. David's kingship is not simply one for Israel alone, but is meant to extend as far as the whole world (Gen. 22:18; Ps. 2:8).

35 Ahiam the son of Sacar the Hararite, Eliphal
the son of Ur,
36 Hepher the Mecherathite, Ahijah the Pelonite,
37 Hezro the Carmelite, Naarai the son of Ezbai,
38 Joel the brother of Nathan, Mibhar the son of
Haggeri,
39 Zelek the Ammonite, Naharai the Berothite,
the armourbearer of Joab the son of Zeruiah,
40 Ira the Ithrite, Gareb the Ithrite,
41 Uriah the Hittite, Zabad the son of Ahlai,
42 Adina the son of Shiza the Reubenite, a captain
of the Reubenites, and thirty with him,
43 Hanan the son of Maachah, and Joshaphat the
Mithnite,
44 Uzzia the Ashterathite, Shama and Jehiel the
sons of Hothan the Aroerite,
45 Jediael the son of Shimri, and Joha his brother,
the Tizite,
46 Eliel the Mahavite, and Jeribai, and Joshaviah,
the sons of Elnaam, and Ithmah the Moabite,
47 Eliel, and Obed, and Jasiel the Mesobaite.

CHAPTER 12

NOW these *are* they that came to David to Ziklag,
while he yet kept himself close because of Saul
the son of Kish: and they *were* among the mighty
men, helpers of the war.
2 *They were* armed with bows, and could use
both the right hand and the left in *hurling* stones
and *shooting* arrows out of a bow, *even* of Saul's
brethren of Benjamin.
3 The chief *was* Ahiezer, then Joash, the sons of
Shemaah the Gibeathite; and Jeziel, and Pelet, the
sons of Azmaveth; and Berachah, and Jehu the
Antothite,
4 And Ismaiah the Gibeonite, a mighty man
among the thirty, and over the thirty; and Jeremiah,
and Jahaziel, and Johanan, and Josabad the
Gederathite,
5 Eluzai, and Jerimoth, and Bealiah, and Shemariah,
and Shephatiah the Haruphite,
6 Elkanah, and Jesiah, and Azareel, and Joezer,
and Jashobeam, the Korhites,
7 And Joelah, and Zebadiah, the sons of Jeroham
of Gedor.
8 And of the Gadites there separated themselves
unto David into the hold to the wilderness men
of might, *and* men of war *fit* for the battle, that
could handle shield and buckler, whose faces *were*
like the faces of lions, and *were* as swift as the roes
upon the mountains;
9 Ezer the first, Obadiah the second, Eliab the
third,
10 Mishmannah the fourth, Jeremiah the fifth,
11 Attai the sixth, Eliel the seventh,
12 Johanan the eighth, Elzabad the ninth,
13 Jeremiah the tenth, Machbanai the eleventh.
14 These *were* of the sons of Gad, captains of the
host: one of the least *was* over an hundred, and
the greatest over a thousand.
15 These *are* they that went over Jordan in the
first month, when it had overflown all his banks;
and they put to flight all *them* of the valleys, *both*
toward the east, and toward the west.
16 And there came of the children of Benjamin
and Judah to the hold unto David.
17 And David went out to meet them, and answered
and said unto them, If ye be come peaceably
unto me to help me, mine heart shall be knit
unto you: but if *ye be come* to betray me to mine
enemies, seeing *there is* no wrong in mine hands,
the God of our fathers look *thereon*, and rebuke *it*.
18 Then the spirit came upon Amasai, *who was*

11:41 *Uriah the Hittite.* The husband of Bath-sheba was one of David's mighty men. Thus David betrayed and murdered one of his most trusted and valuable aids.

Thoughts for Personal/Family Worship: Chapter 11

1. **Israel submitted to David's reign because they recognized their close bond with him ("thy bone and thy flesh") and his loving leadership of them like a shepherd (v. 1). How much more then should the church submit to Jesus Christ (Eph. 5:23)! He has taken on our flesh (John 1:14; Heb. 2:14). He loved the church supremely as its Shepherd by laying down His life for His sheep (John 10:14–15; Eph. 5:25). He has united us to Himself as His own body, His flesh and bone (Eph. 5:30). What would it look like for you to humbly give your allegiance and submission to King Jesus?**
2. **David's mighty men had developed their strength and skills to a high degree, and performed remarkable feats out of love for their king. Yet, every victory was from the Lord (v. 14). This teaches us to give all our heart and all our strength to perform our callings with excellence, and simultaneously to do all things in dependent prayer and give all the glory to the Lord. How can Christians strive to be mighty men and women for the Lord, and yet remain humble before Him?**

Chapter 12: ***This chapter backs up to before David's coronation as king over all Israel to when people came to him in Ziklag and Hebron.***

12:1 *Ziklag.* David was still wandering in the wilderness and Saul was persecuting him (1 Sam. 27:1–6).

12:2 *Saul's brethren of Benjamin.* The author underlines David's attractiveness by showing first how many Benjamites, Saul's own kin, deserted Saul, and came over to David. Others, however, stuck with Saul, as the author later notes (v. 29). The Benjamites were known for their ability with the *bow* (8:40).

12:8 *buckler.* Small shield.

12:15 *overflown all his banks.* This would have been a difficult water to ford (Josh. 3:15). David's mighty men are known for acts that require great strength.

12:17 *mine heart shall be knit unto you.* There is a strong sense of love and devotion between David and the house of Israel (11:1).

12:18 *the spirit came.* The Holy Spirit clothed him, equipping him to speak prophetically (2 Chron. 24:20). It is uncertain if

chief of the captains, *and he said*, Thine *are we*,
David, and on thy side, thou son of Jesse: peace,
peace *be* unto thee, and peace *be* to thine helpers;
for thy God helpeth thee. Then David received
them, and made them captains of the band.
19 And there fell *some* of Manasseh to David,
when he came with the Philistines against Saul to
battle: but they helped them not: for the lords of
the Philistines upon advisement sent him away,
saying, He will fall to his master Saul to *the jeopardy of* our heads.
20 As he went to Ziklag, there fell to him of
Manasseh, Adnah, and Jozabad, and Jediael, and
Michael, and Jozabad, and Elihu, and Zilthai,
captains of the thousands that *were* of Manasseh.
21 And they helped David against the band *of the rovers*: for they *were* all mighty men of valour, and
were captains in the host.
22 For at *that* time day by day there came to
David to help him, until *it was* a great host, like
the host of God.
23 ¶ And these *are* the numbers of the bands *that*
were ready armed to the war, *and* came to David
to Hebron, to turn the kingdom of Saul to him,
according to the word of the LORD.
24 The children of Judah that bare shield and
spear *were* six thousand and eight hundred, ready
armed to the war.
25 Of the children of Simeon, mighty men of
valour for the war, seven thousand and one
hundred.
26 Of the children of Levi four thousand and six
hundred.
27 And Jehoiada *was* the leader of the Aaronites, and with him *were* three thousand and seven
hundred;
28 And Zadok, a young man mighty of valour,
and of his father's house twenty and two captains.
29 And of the children of Benjamin, the kindred of
Saul, three thousand: for hitherto the greatest part
of them had kept the ward of the house of Saul.
30 And of the children of Ephraim twenty thousand and eight hundred, mighty men of valour,
famous throughout the house of their fathers.
31 And of the half tribe of Manasseh eighteen
thousand, which were expressed by name, to
come and make David king.
32 And of the children of Issachar, *which were*
men that had understanding of the times, to know
what Israel ought to do; the heads of them *were*
two hundred; and all their brethren *were* at their
commandment.
33 Of Zebulun, such as went forth to battle, expert in war, with all instruments of war, fifty
thousand, which could keep rank: *they were* not
of double heart.
34 And of Naphtali a thousand captains, and
with them with shield and spear thirty and seven
thousand.
35 And of the Danites expert in war twenty and
eight thousand and six hundred.
36 And of Asher, such as went forth to battle,
expert in war, forty thousand.
37 And on the other side of Jordan, of the Reubenites, and the Gadites, and of the half tribe of
Manasseh, with all manner of instruments of war
for the battle, an hundred and twenty thousand.
38 All these men of war, that could keep rank,
came with a perfect heart to Hebron, to make
David king over all Israel: and all the rest also of
Israel *were* of one heart to make David king.
39 And there they were with David three days,
eating and drinking: for their brethren had prepared for them.
40 Moreover they that were nigh them, *even* unto
Issachar and Zebulun and Naphtali, brought bread
on asses, and on camels, and on mules, and on
oxen, *and* meat, meal, cakes of figs, and bunches
of raisins, and wine, and oil, and oxen, and sheep
abundantly: for *there was* joy in Israel.

---

this *Amasai* is the Amasa who joined Absalom in his revolt against David, then briefly served David (2 Sam. 17:25; 19:13; 20:4–13; cf. 2:17; 1 Kings 2:5,32).

12:19 *advisement*. Consideration, taking advice.

12:22 *until it was a great host, like the host of God*. The description of David's kingdom opened by speaking of the Lord of hosts (11:9), and now this unit closes by speaking of the army as the host of God. David was doing more than raising a physical army, he was raising an army for the Lord to fight by faith in the promises of God (1 Sam. 17:45).

12:23–40 Chronicles records the men of Israel from the twelve tribes who supported and fought for David. Representatives from all Israel had come to the defense of David to rise up against the ungodly kingdom of Saul.

12:29 *hitherto*. Until now.

12:33 *not of double heart*. Not divided in allegiance (James 1:8), but steadfastly determined to *keep rank* and file in the fight against the house of Saul.

12:37 *manner*. Sort, kind.

12:38 *with a perfect heart to Hebron*. With immense devotion to David. These armies and men were of one mind with their king and sought his exaltation in everything they did and fought for.

12:40 *brought bread . . . sheep*. The people provided abundantly for the needs of David and his men. *joy in Israel*. The Lord was with David and the people of Israel.

Thoughts for Personal/Family Worship: Chapter 12

If the Spirit moved Amasai to declare Israel's allegiance to David and God's peace upon him (v. 18), then how much more does the Holy Spirit move people to declare the son of David, Jesus Christ, as Lord (1 Cor. 12:3)? The Lord's presence with David attracted many people from all walks of life to serve David, and in the same way the Spirit's anointing of Christ draws many different kinds of people to serve Him (Luke 15:1; 1 Cor. 1:27). Have you felt that spiritual attraction to Christ? Has the Spirit drawn you to serve Him as your King?

CHAPTER 13

AND David consulted with the captains of thou-
sands and hundreds, *and* with every leader.
2 And David said unto all the congregation of
Israel, If *it seem* good unto you, and *that it be* of
the LORD our God, let us send abroad unto our
brethren every where, *that are* left in all the land
of Israel, and with them *also* to the priests and
Levites *which are* in their cities *and* suburbs, that
they may gather themselves unto us:
3 And let us bring again the ark of our God to us:
for we enquired not at it in the days of Saul.
4 And all the congregation said that they would
do so: for the thing was right in the eyes of all the
people.
5 So David gathered all Israel together, from Shi-
hor of Egypt even unto the entering of Hemath,
to bring the ark of God from Kirjath-jearim.
6 And David went up, and all Israel, to Baalah,
that is, to Kirjath-jearim, which *belonged* to Judah,
to bring up thence the ark of God the LORD, that
dwelleth *between* the cherubims, whose name is
called *on it*.
7 And they carried the ark of God in a new cart
out of the house of Abinadab: and Uzza and Ahio
drave the cart.
8 And David and all Israel played before God
with all *their* might, and with singing, and with
harps, and with psalteries, and with timbrels, and
with cymbals, and with trumpets.
9 ¶ And when they came unto the threshingfloor
of Chidon, Uzza put forth his hand to hold the
ark; for the oxen stumbled.
10 And the anger of the LORD was kindled against
Uzza, and he smote him, because he put his hand
to the ark: and there he died before God.
11 And David was displeased, because the LORD
had made a breach upon Uzza: wherefore that
place is called Perez-uzza to this day.
12 And David was afraid of God that day, saying,
How shall I bring the ark of God *home* to me?
13 So David brought not the ark *home* to himself
to the city of David, but carried it aside into the
house of Obed-edom the Gittite.
14 And the ark of God remained with the family
of Obed-edom in his house three months. And
the LORD blessed the house of Obed-edom, and
all that he had.

CHAPTER 14

NOW Hiram king of Tyre sent messengers to
David, and timber of cedars, with masons and
carpenters, to build him an house.
2 And David perceived that the LORD had con-
firmed him king over Israel, for his kingdom was
lifted up on high, because of his people Israel.
3 ¶ And David took more wives at Jerusalem: and

David's Pursuit of God's Presence (1 Chron. 13:1—17:27)

David's Attempts to Bring the Ark to Jerusalem (1 Chron. 13:1—16:43)

Chapter 13: *David attempts to bring the ark of the Lord to Jerusalem, but Uzzah reaches out to touch it and is killed.*

13:3 *let us bring again the ark.* The ark represented God's presence with His people and David desired to see the true worship of God settled in Jerusalem (Ps. 132:1–5). *we enquired not at it in the days of Saul.* They did not seek God in public worship. Saul's kingship was marked by rebellion against the will of God (10:13–14).

13:5 *gathered all Israel together.* David succeeded in unifying all Israel. *Shihor of Egypt . . . Hemath.* David summoned the people of Israel together within these two geographical landmarks. This is Israel considered as broadly as possible.

13:7 *new cart.* David thought to provide a sturdy transportation for the ark. This, however, was not in obedience to God's law (15:2,13), which required that the priests cover the ark and the Levites carry it on its poles. No one other than the priests should see it or touch it lest they die (Ex. 25:12–15; Num. 3:31; 4:4–6,15,20; Deut. 10:8; 31:9,25; Josh. 3–4). *drave.* Drove.

13:8 *psalteries.* Stringed instruments perhaps like a lyre or guitar. *timbrels.* Tambourines.

13:9–10 *anger of the LORD.* God is to be worshiped as He has commanded, not after man's imagination or invention (Lev. 10:1–3; Deut. 12:30–32), no matter how sincere or noble (v. 8).

13:11 *David was displeased.* David was deeply troubled, which reflects well on how greatly he desired the sign of God's presence in Jerusalem (Ps. 27:4). *made a breach.* Burst out to destroy.

13:12 *David was afraid.* This is proper. God is to be feared among the assembly of His saints (Ps. 89:7).

Thoughts for Personal/Family Worship: Chapter 13

1. **Uzzah may have thought he had good motives in grasping the ark. However, he refused to recognize the holiness of God and his own sinfulness. He assumed his hand was cleaner than the dirt on which the ark would have fallen, if God did not sovereignly prevent it. The root of inventing our own worship instead of following God's Word is a disregard for God's holiness (Lev. 10:1–3; 1 Sam. 6:19–20). We should not presume to be able to approach or worship God according to our own imagination. How can we worship in the fear of the Lord and bow under the revelation of His will for worship?**
2. **We know that it was a great disappointment to David that the ark did not arrive in Jerusalem after this first attempt. We see how deeply David desired communion with God. "How shall I bring the ark of God home to me?" (v. 12). Do you desire communion with God? Do disappointments strengthen your desire for communion with God?**

Chapter 14: *David's kingdom grows and is established.*

14:1 *to build him an house.* For the construction of a palace for David, *Hiram king of Tyre* sent materials.

14:2 *David perceived.* The favorable providence working for David *confirmed* his calling and the establishment of *his kingdom. because of his people Israel.* God's purposes went beyond David; the king is God's servant for the good of His people (2 Chron. 9:8).

David begat more sons and daughters.
4 Now these *are* the names of *his* children which
he had in Jerusalem; Shammua, and Shobab,
Nathan, and Solomon,
5 And Ibhar, and Elishua, and Elpalet,
6 And Nogah, and Nepheg, and Japhia,
7 And Elishama, and Beeliada, and Eliphalet.
8 ¶ And when the Philistines heard that David
was anointed king over all Israel, all the Philistines
went up to seek David. And David heard *of it*, and
went out against them.
9 And the Philistines came and spread them-
selves in the valley of Rephaim.
10 And David enquired of God, saying, Shall I go
up against the Philistines? and wilt thou deliver
them into mine hand? And the LORD said unto
him, Go up; for I will deliver them into thine hand.
11 So they came up to Baal-perazim; and David
smote them there. Then David said, God hath
broken in upon mine enemies by mine hand like
the breaking forth of waters: therefore they called
the name of that place Baal-perazim.
12 And when they had left their gods there, David
gave a commandment, and they were burned
with fire.
13 And the Philistines yet again spread them-
selves abroad in the valley.
14 Therefore David enquired again of God; and
God said unto him, Go not up after them; turn
away from them, and come upon them over
against the mulberry trees.
15 And it shall be, when thou shalt hear a sound of
going in the tops of the mulberry trees, *that* then
thou shalt go out to battle: for God is gone forth
before thee to smite the host of the Philistines.
16 David therefore did as God commanded him:
and they smote the host of the Philistines from
Gibeon even to Gazer.
17 And the fame of David went out into all lands;
and the LORD brought the fear of him upon all
nations.

CHAPTER 15

AND *David* made him houses in the city of David,
and prepared a place for the ark of God, and
pitched for it a tent.
2 Then David said, None ought to carry the ark
of God but the Levites: for them hath the LORD
chosen to carry the ark of God, and to minister
unto him for ever.
3 And David gathered all Israel together to Jeru-
salem, to bring up the ark of the LORD unto his
place, which he had prepared for it.
4 And David assembled the children of Aaron,
and the Levites:
5 Of the sons of Kohath; Uriel the chief, and his
brethren an hundred and twenty:
6 Of the sons of Merari; Asaiah the chief, and his
brethren two hundred and twenty:
7 Of the sons of Gershom; Joel the chief, and his
brethren an hundred and thirty:
8 Of the sons of Elizaphan; Shemaiah the chief,
and his brethren two hundred:

14:8 *the Philistines went up to seek David.* This was a declaration of war.

14:10 *enquired of God.* Asked God for wisdom. David learned his dependence on God for everything, including defeating the Philistines.

14:11 *Baal-perazim.* Literally, "the Lord of breaking forth." *God hath broken in upon mine enemies.* God fought for Israel. This is the same Hebrew root used of God breaking in on Uzza (13:11; 15:13).

14:12 *left their gods there.* The idols were incompetent to save the Philistines. As a sign of their uselessness, they *were burned with fire* by David's armies (Deut. 7:5).

14:13 *yet again spread themselves abroad.* The Philistines sought again to destroy the Israelites.

14:14 *David enquired.* David approached God a second time, not assuming that the first victory guaranteed a second victory.

14:15 *sound of going.* A noise as if an army marched in the air above the *tops* of the *trees.* The Lord had commissioned His angelic army to fight for David (2 Kings 6:16–17).

14:17 *the LORD brought the fear of him upon all nations.* While Israel's heart was knit to David, the nations stood in fear of David because the Lord was with him (2 Chron. 14:14; 17:10; 20:29).

Thoughts for Personal/Family Worship: Chapter 14

Though God established a human king over His people, that king was not to reign by human power or wisdom. The Lord confirmed the kingdom (v. 2). The king sought and found his wisdom in God (vv. 10,14). God broke out to destroy the enemies of the king (v. 11). God's invisible armies fought for him (v. 15). The king obeyed God's Word (v. 16). The Lord caused the nations to fear the king (v. 17). In these ways David foreshadows Christ and His kingdom. Jesus was truly human, but He did not build His kingdom on human strength. His kingdom comes in the Holy Spirit. He sought His Father regularly in prayer. The angels gave Christ strength in His darkest moments. He obeyed God to the death, even death on the cross. And now, risen from the dead, Christ has received authority from the Father to make disciples among all nations. If this is true of Christ, who is both God and man, how much more is it true of Christians? What lessons can we learn from this chapter about how we should seek the kingdom of God?

Chapter 15: *This time, with the Levites carrying the ark, David successfully brings the ark to Jerusalem.*

15:1 *houses . . . tent.* David built multiple houses for himself and yet God's ark only dwelt in a tent.

15:2 God only authorized *the Levites* to carry the ark, and only the priests to have direct contact with it (v. 15; see note at 13:7).

15:3 *all Israel.* The author stresses the involvement of the whole nation.

15:5–10 David divided the sons of Aaron by their clans. The priests took a prominent role in the bringing up of the ark.

9 Of the sons of Hebron; Eliel the chief, and his
brethren fourscore:
10 Of the sons of Uzziel; Amminadab the chief,
and his brethren an hundred and twelve.
11 And David called for Zadok and Abiathar the
priests, and for the Levites, for Uriel, Asaiah, and
Joel, Shemaiah, and Eliel, and Amminadab,
12 And said unto them, Ye *are* the chief of the
fathers of the Levites: sanctify yourselves, *both* ye
and your brethren, that ye may bring up the ark of
the LORD God of Israel unto *the place that* I have
prepared for it.
13 For because ye *did it* not at the first, the LORD
our God made a breach upon us, for that we
sought him not after the due order.
14 So the priests and the Levites sanctified them-
selves to bring up the ark of the LORD God of
Israel.
15 And the children of the Levites bare the ark of
God upon their shoulders with the staves thereon,
as Moses commanded according to the word of
the LORD.
16 And David spake to the chief of the Levites
to appoint their brethren *to be* the singers with
instruments of musick, psalteries and harps and
cymbals, sounding, by lifting up the voice with
joy.
17 So the Levites appointed Heman the son
of Joel; and of his brethren, Asaph the son of
Berechiah; and of the sons of Merari their breth-
ren, Ethan the son of Kushaiah;
18 And with them their brethren of the second
degree, Zechariah, Ben, and Jaaziel, and Shemira-
moth, and Jehiel, and Unni, Eliab, and Benaiah,
and Maaseiah, and Mattithiah, and Elipheleh, and
Mikneiah, and Obed-edom, and Jeiel, the porters.
19 So the singers, Heman, Asaph, and Ethan, *were*
appointed to sound with cymbals of brass;
20 And Zechariah, and Aziel, and Shemiramoth,
and Jehiel, and Unni, and Eliab, and Maaseiah,
and Benaiah, with psalteries on Alamoth;
21 And Mattithiah, and Elipheleh, and Mikneiah,
and Obed-edom, and Jeiel, and Azaziah, with
harps on the Sheminith to excel.
22 And Chenaniah, chief of the Levites, *was* for
song: he instructed about the song, because he
was skilful.
23 And Berechiah and Elkanah *were* doorkeepers
for the ark.
24 And Shebaniah, and Jehoshaphat, and Nethan-
eel, and Amasai, and Zechariah, and Benaiah, and
Eliezer, the priests, did blow with the trumpets
before the ark of God: and Obed-edom and Jehiah
were doorkeepers for the ark.
25 ¶ So David, and the elders of Israel, and the
captains over thousands, went to bring up the ark
of the covenant of the LORD out of the house of
Obed-edom with joy.
26 And it came to pass, when God helped the
Levites that bare the ark of the covenant of the
LORD, that they offered seven bullocks and seven
rams.
27 And David *was* clothed with a robe of fine
linen, and all the Levites that bare the ark, and the
singers, and Chenaniah the master of the song
with the singers: David also *had* upon him an
ephod of linen.
28 Thus all Israel brought up the ark of the cov-
enant of the LORD with shouting, and with sound
of the cornet, and with trumpets, and with cym-
bals, making a noise with psalteries and harps.
29 ¶ And it came to pass, *as* the ark of the
covenant of the LORD came to the city of David,
that Michal the daughter of Saul looking out at a
window saw king David dancing and playing: and
she despised him in her heart.

15:12 *I have prepared for it.* This shows David's longing and zeal for the glory of the Lord with His people (Ps. 132:1–5).
15:13 *made a breach.* Broke out in judgment (13:11). *after the due order.* Literally, "according to the judgment" or "decree of God" (Ex. 26:30). The Lord desires men to seek and worship Him in the manner in which He has declared and has not left them to worship Him according to their imagination (cf. Ex. 20:4–6).
15:14 *sanctified themselves.* Set themselves apart for sacred ministry, per David's request.
15:16 *psalteries.* See note at 13:8. *with joy.* Worship is not a mere formality, but a celebration of God's glory and grace with great happiness (v. 25).
15:22 *skilful.* Levites were appointed to serve according to their ability.
15:24 *doorkeepers.* Same word as "porters" (see note at 9:17–32).
15:26 *God helped.* There was a clear sense of God's blessing over the occasion.
15:27 *ephod of linen.* Linen cape or sleeveless garment used by those officiating in the temple (1 Sam. 2:18).
15:29 *Michal . . . despised him.* She thought his joy and humble clothing in worship was unfitting for a king and suffered for her arrogance (2 Sam. 6:16,20–23).

Thoughts for Personal/Family Worship: Chapter 15

1. **When King David took care that the people follow God's commands in worship (vv. 13–15), God assisted their worship with His grace (v. 26) and the people worshiped with great humility and joy (vv. 27–28). In the same way, the Lord Jesus, the King of the church, has directed the church in the right way of worship. Why is it crucial that the church worship God according to the Word of Christ? What does this mean, practically speaking?**
2. **Ironically, precisely when King David worshiped God in obedience to His Word, his wife Michal despised him for rejoicing in great humility (v. 29). How should we respond when worldly people likewise despise Christ and us if we are following Him in biblical worship?**

Chapter 16: *David celebrates the arrival of the ark with thanksgiving and praise.*

16:1–3 Chronicles records the conclusion of the transfer of the ark and the celebration in Jerusalem.

WORSHIP BY THE WORD

What is worship? The earliest mention of public worship is found in Genesis 4:26, in the days of Seth and Enos: "Then began men to call upon the name of the LORD." Psalm 100:2 exhorts us to "serve the LORD with gladness, and come into his presence with thanksgiving." James urges us to "draw nigh to God, and he will draw nigh to you" (James 4:8). The apostle Paul also speaks of drawing near to God, by the "new and living way" consecrated for us in the person of Christ crucified, risen, and ascended into heaven as our High Priest (Heb. 10:19–22). Christ Himself said, "No man cometh unto the Father, but by me" (John 14:6).

What kind of worship is acceptable to God? This question lives throughout Scripture, beginning with the sacrifices of Cain and Abel (Gen. 4). One man's offering was accepted, while the other's was not. Why? Like all good works, true worship must proceed from faith and be performed according to God's law and to His glory. God is worshiped whenever and wherever His Word is believed, His commands are obeyed, and His glory is exalted by intelligent creatures in heaven and on earth.

The Old Testament church existed in a world rife with polytheism, idolatry, and manmade forms of worship that were abominations in God's sight. The first and second commandments (Ex. 20:3–6) address all three sins. They bind God's people to worship Him in no other way than as He commands in His Word, proclaiming the jealousy of God for His worship and His determination to punish all who depart from it, while showing mercy to those who love and obey Him. God inflicted fiery death on Nadab and Abihu for offering "strange fire before the LORD, which he commanded them not" (Lev. 10:1–2); Hophni and Phinehas were slain in battle (1 Sam. 5:11) after they corrupted the worship of God, exploiting it for their own purposes (1 Sam. 2:17); and later the Lord struck Uzzah dead for his error in touching the ark of the covenant (2 Sam. 6:7).

The last chapter of the Bible addresses the same concern. In Revelation 22 John records how, in a moment of carelessness, he fell down to worship at the feet of an angel. He was instantly rebuked: "See thou do it not: for I am thy fellow servant, and of thy brethren the prophets, and of them which keep the sayings of this book: worship God" (Rev. 22:9).

These examples have much to teach Christians today. Worship is not a matter of indifference, human tradition, or popular taste. Christ summarizes and confirms the teaching of the Old Testament, declaring that "God is a Spirit: and they that worship him must worship him in spirit and in truth" (John 4:24). We are still bound by the law of God to follow the acceptable way of worship He has instituted in His Word and regulated by His commandments.

Under the new covenant the ceremonies of the law have ceased and a simpler form of worship has been introduced by Christ and the apostles. Prayer with thanksgiving, the reading of Scripture, sound preaching and the faithful hearing of the Word, the singing of the Psalms, and the administration of the sacraments according to the command and example of Christ are all parts of the worship of God under the gospel.

History shows that the church under both testaments has been prone to corrupt the true worship of God with human innovations, to offer formal worship to God while withholding the love of the heart, or else to neglect true worship, turning aside to gods that are no gods or taking up practices that have no warrant in Scripture. Recent decades have seen the eruption of "worship wars" in many churches, pitting traditionalists against innovators. Many people feel free to do as they please. Errors and abuses will abound until we all agree to test all things by the Word of God (1 Thess. 5:21).

CHAPTER 16

So they brought the ark of God, and set it in the
midst of the tent that David had pitched for it:
and they offered burnt sacrifices and peace offer-
ings before God.
2 And when David had made an end of offering
the burnt offerings and the peace offerings, he
blessed the people in the name of the LORD.
3 And he dealt to every one of Israel, both man
and woman, to every one a loaf of bread, and a
good piece of flesh, and a flagon *of wine.*
4 ¶ And he appointed *certain* of the Levites to
minister before the ark of the LORD, and to record,
and to thank and praise the LORD God of Israel:
5 Asaph the chief, and next to him Zechariah,
Jeiel, and Shemiramoth, and Jehiel, and Matti-
thiah, and Eliab, and Benaiah, and Obed-edom:
and Jeiel with psalteries and with harps; but
Asaph made a sound with cymbals;
6 Benaiah also and Jahaziel the priests with trum-
pets continually before the ark of the covenant of
God.
7 ¶ Then on that day David delivered first *this
psalm* to thank the LORD into the hand of Asaph
and his brethren.
8 Give thanks unto the LORD, call upon his name,
make known his deeds among the people.
9 Sing unto him, sing psalms unto him, talk ye of
all his wondrous works.
10 Glory ye in his holy name: let the heart of
them rejoice that seek the LORD.
11 Seek the LORD and his strength, seek his face
continually.
12 Remember his marvellous works that he hath
done, his wonders, and the judgments of his
mouth;
13 O ye seed of Israel his servant, ye children of
Jacob, his chosen ones.
14 He *is* the LORD our God; his judgments *are* in
all the earth.
15 Be ye mindful always of his covenant; the word
which he commanded to a thousand generations;
16 *Even of the covenant* which he made with
Abraham, and of his oath unto Isaac;
17 And hath confirmed the same to Jacob for a
law, *and* to Israel *for* an everlasting covenant,
18 Saying, Unto thee will I give the land of
Canaan, the lot of your inheritance;
19 When ye were but few, even a few, and strang-
ers in it.
20 And *when* they went from nation to nation,
and from *one* kingdom to another people;
21 He suffered no man to do them wrong: yea, he
reproved kings for their sakes,
22 *Saying,* Touch not mine anointed, and do my
prophets no harm.
23 Sing unto the LORD, all the earth; shew forth
from day to day his salvation.
24 Declare his glory among the heathen; his
marvellous works among all nations.
25 For great *is* the LORD, and greatly to be praised:
he also *is* to be feared above all gods.
26 For all the gods of the people *are* idols: but the
LORD made the heavens.
27 Glory and honour *are* in his presence; strength
and gladness *are* in his place.
28 Give unto the LORD, ye kindreds of the people,
give unto the LORD glory and strength.
29 Give unto the LORD the glory *due* unto his
name: bring an offering, and come before him:
worship the LORD in the beauty of holiness.
30 Fear before him, all the earth: the world also
shall be stable, that it be not moved.
31 Let the heavens be glad, and let the earth re-
joice: and let *men* say among the nations, The
LORD reigneth.
32 Let the sea roar, and the fulness thereof: let the
fields rejoice, and all that *is* therein.
33 Then shall the trees of the wood sing out at
the presence of the LORD, because he cometh to
judge the earth.
34 O give thanks unto the LORD; for *he is* good;
for his mercy *endureth* for ever.
35 And say ye, Save us, O God of our salvation,
and gather us together, and deliver us from the
heathen, that we may give thanks to thy holy
name, *and* glory in thy praise.
36 Blessed *be* the LORD God of Israel for ever and
ever. And all the people said, Amen, and praised
the LORD.

16:4–6 David arranged the musical instruments for the service before the ark. The king *appointed* Levites to new functions because he was a prophet of the Lord, declaring God's will (28:12,19; 2 Chron. 8:14).

16:7 *this psalm.* With minor variations, vv. 8–22 correspond to Ps. 105:1–15, vv. 23–33 to Ps. 96:1–13, and vv. 34–36 to Ps. 106:1,47–48.

16:9 *Sing . . . talk.* Worship is a vocal act as much as it is an act of the heart.

16:10–11 *Glory ye in his holy name.* Boast in the qualities of the Lord that make Him and Him alone to be God. This psalm repeatedly celebrates God's greatness and calls men to fear and honor Him (vv. 24,27–29,35). *seek the LORD.* Pursue His special presence by submission to His Word; a major theme of Chronicles (see Introduction: Synopsis). David had sought God wrongly the first time he brought the ark up (15:13), but he now commanded Israel to seek the Lord according to His Word.

16:14 The covenant Lord of Israel (*our God*) is the Lord of *all the earth.*

16:18 *Canaan.* The Promised Land was Israel's by divine right.

16:21 World history is ultimately the history of God's redeeming work for His people. In this sense, David writes that God reproved the nations *for their sakes* (cf. Gen. 12:17).

16:36 *Amen.* A similar response was given when Moses renewed the covenant with the people of Israel before they entered the Promised Land (Deut. 27:15–26).

37 ¶ So he left there before the ark of the cov-
enant of the LORD Asaph and his brethren, to
minister before the ark continually, as every day's
work required:
38 And Obed-edom with their brethren, three-
score and eight; Obed-edom also the son of
Jeduthun and Hosah *to be* porters:
39 And Zadok the priest, and his brethren the
priests, before the tabernacle of the LORD in the
high place that *was* at Gibeon,
40 To offer burnt offerings unto the LORD
upon the altar of the burnt offering continually
morning and evening, and *to do* according to all
that is written in the law of the LORD, which he
commanded Israel;
41 And with them Heman and Jeduthun, and
the rest that were chosen, who were expressed
by name, to give thanks to the LORD, because his
mercy *endureth* for ever;
42 And with them Heman and Jeduthun with
trumpets and cymbals for those that should make
a sound, and with musical instruments of God.
And the sons of Jeduthun *were* porters.
43 And all the people departed every man to his
house: and David returned to bless his house.

CHAPTER 17

NOW it came to pass, as David sat in his house,
that David said to Nathan the prophet, Lo, I dwell
in an house of cedars, but the ark of the covenant
of the LORD *remaineth* under curtains.
2 Then Nathan said unto David, Do all that *is* in
thine heart; for God *is* with thee.
3 ¶ And it came to pass the same night, that the
word of God came to Nathan, saying,
4 Go and tell David my servant, Thus saith the
LORD, Thou shalt not build me an house to dwell in:
5 For I have not dwelt in an house since the day
that I brought up Israel unto this day; but have
gone from tent to tent, and from *one* tabernacle
to another.
6 Wheresoever I have walked with all Israel, spake
I a word to any of the judges of Israel, whom I
commanded to feed my people, saying, Why have
ye not built me an house of cedars?
7 Now therefore thus shalt thou say unto my
servant David, Thus saith the LORD of hosts, I
took thee from the sheepcote, *even* from following
the sheep, that thou shouldest be ruler over my
people Israel:
8 And I have been with thee whithersoever thou
hast walked, and have cut off all thine enemies
from before thee, and have made thee a name like
the name of the great men that *are* in the earth.
9 Also I will ordain a place for my people Israel,
and will plant them, and they shall dwell in their
place, and shall be moved no more; neither shall
the children of wickedness waste them any more,
as at the beginning,
10 And since the time that I commanded judges
to be over my people Israel. Moreover I will sub-
due all thine enemies. Furthermore I tell thee that
the LORD will build thee an house.
11 ¶ And it shall come to pass, when thy days be
expired that thou must go *to be* with thy fathers,
that I will raise up thy seed after thee, which shall
be of thy sons; and I will establish his kingdom.
12 He shall build me an house, and I will stablish
his throne for ever.
13 I will be his father, and he shall be my son: and
I will not take my mercy away from him, as I took

16:39 *Gibeon.* The altar of burnt offering was not yet moved to Jerusalem at this time (21:29).

Thoughts for Personal/Family Worship: Chapter 16

1. **At the heart of worship is seeking God (vv. 10–11). By nature we have lost God and have turned our backs to Him. Nevertheless, it is only in His presence that there is light and life. It is only through Jesus Christ that we can have fellowship with Him and taste of His goodness and grace. Through Christ, we can have access to the Father in the Holy Spirit. This was David's one passion: to seek God and enjoy His glory (Ps. 27:4,8). How can you kindle the same passion in your own heart?**
2. **Thanksgiving (v. 34) is the overflow in the heart of what God has done in His grace for undeserving sinners. It is the response of human love to the love of the Lord. It shows itself in our thoughts, words, and actions. David was overwhelmed that God would draw so near to him and his nation. He spent a lot of time and energy praising Him. How thankful are we? Why do we lack a thankful attitude many times?**

Chapter 17: ***God makes many great promises to David regarding His throne and seed—the pinnacle of Chronicles—to which David responds in worship.***

God's Promise to David: Covenant Made (1 Chron. 17:1–27)

17:1 *house of cedars . . . curtains.* David saw the paradox of his own honor and the lowliness of God's dwelling.

17:5 *one tabernacle to another.* One dwelling to another.

17:6 *Why have ye not built me an house.* Without condemning David's motives, the Lord reminded him that God is Lord of His worship, and the temple must come from His will, not man's.

17:7–9 *I took . . . I have been . . . cut off . . . made thee a name . . . I will ordain.* God recounted His covenant faithfulness to His people Israel, again emphasizing the sovereign initiative of His grace.

17:10 *build thee an house.* David sought to build God a physical house, but God promised to first build David a lasting household or lineage.

17:11 *thy seed.* David's offspring. The language of *seed* reaches through the covenants back to the first declaration of the Savior from sin (Gen. 3:15; 9:9; 17:7). Here God revealed the coming Savior in the everlasting *kingdom* of the son of David (Isa. 9:6–7; Luke 1:32–33).

17:13 *his father . . . my son.* The adoption given to Israel (Ex. 4:22) was focused on the line of David (Ps. 89:26–27) in a

it from *him* that was before thee:

14 But I will settle him in mine house and in my kingdom for ever: and his throne shall be established for evermore.

15 According to all these words, and according to all this vision, so did Nathan speak unto David.

16 ¶ And David the king came and sat before the LORD, and said, Who *am* I, O LORD God, and what *is* mine house, that thou hast brought me hitherto?

17 And *yet* this was a small thing in thine eyes, O God; for thou hast *also* spoken of thy servant's house for a great while to come, and hast regarded me according to the estate of a man of high degree, O LORD God.

18 What can David *speak* more to thee for the honour of thy servant? for thou knowest thy servant.

19 O LORD, for thy servant's sake, and according to thine own heart, hast thou done all this greatness, in making known all *these* great things.

20 O LORD, *there is* none like thee, neither *is there any* God beside thee, according to all that we have heard with our ears.

21 And what one nation in the earth *is* like thy people Israel, whom God went to redeem *to be* his own people, to make thee a name of greatness and terribleness, by driving out nations from before thy people, whom thou hast redeemed out of Egypt?

22 For thy people Israel didst thou make thine own people for ever; and thou, LORD, becamest their God.

23 Therefore now, LORD, let the thing that thou hast spoken concerning thy servant and concerning his house be established for ever, and do as thou hast said.

24 Let it even be established, that thy name may be magnified for ever, saying, The LORD of hosts *is* the God of Israel, *even* a God to Israel: and *let* the house of David thy servant *be* established before thee.

25 For thou, O my God, hast told thy servant that thou wilt build him an house: therefore thy servant hath found *in his heart* to pray before thee.

26 And now, LORD, thou art God, and hast promised this goodness unto thy servant:

27 Now therefore let it please thee to bless the house of thy servant, that it may be before thee for ever: for thou blessest, O LORD, and *it shall be* blessed for ever.

CHAPTER 18

NOW after this it came to pass, that David smote the Philistines, and subdued them, and took Gath and her towns out of the hand of the Philistines.

2 And he smote Moab; and the Moabites became David's servants, *and* brought gifts.

3 ¶ And David smote Hadarezer king of Zobah unto Hamath, as he went to stablish his dominion by the river Euphrates.

4 And David took from him a thousand chariots, and seven thousand horsemen, and twenty thousand footmen: David also houghed all the chariot *horses*, but reserved of them an hundred chariots.

5 And when the Syrians of Damascus came to

---

covenant of unbreakable *mercy* (Ps. 89:28–37). God fulfilled this covenant in His only begotten Son, in whom believers are also adopted by God (John 1:12,14,18; Gal. 4:4–7).

17:16–27 David's prayer is divided into three sections: a prayer for himself (vv. 16–20), a prayer for the nation (vv. 21–22), and a prayer for God to remember His covenant faithfulness (vv. 23–27). David repeatedly called himself *thy servant*, echoing God's own designation for him (vv. 4,7).

17:17 *a small thing in thine eyes.* Easy for God and not troublesome (Luke 1:46–55).

17:21–22 God's deliverance of Israel through their history was both to exalt Himself as *God* and to redeem a *people* in covenant with Himself.

17:23 *do as thou hast said.* David prayed God's promises back to God.

Thoughts for Personal/Family Worship: Chapter 17

1. **God promised that through David He would provide a king to rule His people in His presence forever. The good news of the New Testament is that this king has come, the very Son of God who has risen from the dead (Rom. 1:1–4). Jesus Christ presently reigns from heaven by His Spirit. If God kept His promise to David by bringing His Son to earth, how much more now that Christ has come can we trust God to keep His promise that His Son will return? How is the kingdom of Christ (both present and future) the hope and joy of His people?**
2. **David was overwhelmed by God's tender mercies not only in the present but also regarding the future. He was deeply humbled and exclaimed in amazement and wonder, "Who am I, O LORD God, and what is mine house, that thou hast brought me hitherto?" (v. 16). Whenever God manifests His grace, He brings an abiding sense of wonder, for we could never fathom any reason from our perspective that God would deal with us in such grace. Spend some time praising God for His mercy and grace.**

David's Military Victories (1 Chron. 18:1—20:8)

Chronicles now details the battles of David, skipping over many events in David's life and showing him to be the warrior-king of Israel. David's battles against the enemies of Israel will prepare for the peace of Israel, which will be followed by Solomon's construction of the temple.

Chapter 18: *David's kingdom expands beyond his existing territory.*

David's Wars with His Enemies (1 Chron. 18:1–13)

18:1–6 David has great military success over the *Philistines*, the *Moabites*, the Zobahites, and the *Syrians*. As far as his kingdom extended, David saw victory on every side.

18:1 *after this.* This phrase does not necessarily signify a chronological sequence following the events of ch. 17. It appears that *Gath* was later returned to the Philistines by the time Solomon came to power (1 Kings 2:39).

18:4 *houghed.* Cut the hamstring or hock.

help Hadarezer king of Zobah, David slew of the
Syrians two and twenty thousand men.
6 Then David put *garrisons* in Syria-damascus;
and the Syrians became David's servants, *and*
brought gifts. Thus the LORD preserved David
whithersoever he went.
7 And David took the shields of gold that were
on the servants of Hadarezer, and brought them
to Jerusalem.
8 Likewise from Tibhath, and from Chun, cities
of Hadarezer, brought David very much brass,
wherewith Solomon made the brasen sea, and the
pillars, and the vessels of brass.
9 ¶ Now when Tou king of Hamath heard how
David had smitten all the host of Hadarezer king
of Zobah;
10 He sent Hadoram his son to king David, to
enquire of his welfare, and to congratulate him,
because he had fought against Hadarezer, and
smitten him; (for Hadarezer had war with Tou;)
and *with him* all manner of vessels of gold and
silver and brass.
11 ¶ Them also king David dedicated unto the
LORD, with the silver and the gold that he brought
from all *these* nations; from Edom, and from
Moab, and from the children of Ammon, and
from the Philistines, and from Amalek.
12 Moreover Abishai the son of Zeruiah slew
of the Edomites in the valley of salt eighteen
thousand.
13 ¶ And he put garrisons in Edom; and all the
Edomites became David's servants. Thus the
LORD preserved David whithersoever he went.
14 ¶ So David reigned over all Israel, and exe-
cuted judgment and justice among all his people.
15 And Joab the son of Zeruiah *was* over the host;
and Jehoshaphat the son of Ahilud, recorder.
16 And Zadok the son of Ahitub, and Abimelech
the son of Abiathar, *were* the priests; and Shavsha
was scribe;
17 And Benaiah the son of Jehoiada *was* over the
Cherethites and the Pelethites; and the sons of
David *were* chief about the king.

CHAPTER 19

NOW it came to pass after this, that Nahash the
king of the children of Ammon died, and his son
reigned in his stead.
2 And David said, I will shew kindness unto Ha-
nun the son of Nahash, because his father shewed
kindness to me. And David sent messengers to
comfort him concerning his father. So the ser-
vants of David came into the land of the children
of Ammon to Hanun, to comfort him.
3 But the princes of the children of Ammon said
to Hanun, Thinkest thou that David doth honour
thy father, that he hath sent comforters unto thee?
are not his servants come unto thee for to search,
and to overthrow, and to spy out the land?
4 Wherefore Hanun took David's servants, and
shaved them, and cut off their garments in the
midst hard by their buttocks, and sent them away.
5 Then there went *certain*, and told David how
the men were served. And he sent to meet them:
for the men were greatly ashamed. And the king
said, Tarry at Jericho until your beards be grown,
and *then* return.
6 ¶ And when the children of Ammon saw
that they had made themselves odious to Da-
vid, Hanun and the children of Ammon sent a
thousand talents of silver to hire them chariots

18:6 *the LORD preserved David.* Literally, He "saved" him (v. 13; cf. 11:14; 16:35).
18:7–8 David used the plunder of his enemies for the worship of the Lord (v. 11; cf. Ex. 12:35–36; 25:1–3).
18:9–10 David did not engage in open battle with all surrounding nations. But as these verses indicate, *Hamath*, as it were, joined herself to Israel by bringing peace offerings to David. *manner.* Kind.
18:12–13 Joab saw success as he fought. His subjugation of the Edomites was a startling fulfillment of Gen. 25:23.

David's Rule (1 Chron. 18:14–17)

18:14 David's reign was marked by *judgment and justice among all his people*, the mark of a good and righteous king.
18:15–17 Scripture shows a very structured and organized chain of command under David's monarchy.

Thoughts for Personal/Family Worship: Chapter 18

1. **God prospered David so that the surrounding nations were either conquered by David or they came to serve him with gifts. Concerning Christ, the great son of David, the Bible says, "Be wise now therefore, O ye kings: be instructed, ye judges of the earth. Serve the LORD with fear, and rejoice with trembling. Kiss the Son, lest he be angry, and ye perish from the way" (Ps. 2:10–12). To kiss the Son is to give Him your sincere submission. How do you show your respect to our King?**
2. **David understood the need for structure and order in his administration, appointing qualified men to specific offices. Christ, the great son of David, has established a spiritual order for His kingdom with church officers with specified qualifications (1 Tim. 3). All the gatherings of the church should be well ordered, since God is not a God of confusion, but of peace (1 Cor. 14:33). Why are order and officers important for justice and righteousness?**

Chapter 19: *When Ammon seeks help from Syria, David's armies defeat the Syrians until they become David's servants.*

David and the Ammonites (1 Chron. 19:1–19)

19:1 *after this.* See note at 18:1. *stead.* Place.
19:2 *kindness.* Loyalty and faithfulness, sometimes in the context of a covenant or treaty (Gen. 21:22–23,32).
19:4 *shaved them, and cut off their garments.* This was an act of great humiliation.
19:5 *Tarry at Jericho.* Wait there until their hair had grown back.
19:6 *odious.* Offensive.
19:10 *the choice of Israel.* The best soldiers in the army.

and horsemen out of Mesopotamia, and out of
Syria-maachah, and out of Zobah.
7 So they hired thirty and two thousand chari-
ots, and the king of Maachah and his people; who
came and pitched before Medeba. And the chil-
dren of Ammon gathered themselves together
from their cities, and came to battle.
8 And when David heard *of it*, he sent Joab, and
all the host of the mighty men.
9 And the children of Ammon came out, and put
the battle in array before the gate of the city: and
the kings that were come *were* by themselves in the
field.
10 Now when Joab saw that the battle was set
against him before and behind, he chose out of all
the choice of Israel, and put *them* in array against
the Syrians.
11 And the rest of the people he delivered unto
the hand of Abishai his brother, and they set *them-*
selves in array against the children of Ammon.
12 And he said, If the Syrians be too strong for
me, then thou shalt help me: but if the children
of Ammon be too strong for thee, then I will help
thee.
13 Be of good courage, and let us behave our-
selves valiantly for our people, and for the cities of
our God: and let the LORD do *that which is* good
in his sight.
14 So Joab and the people that *were* with him
drew nigh before the Syrians unto the battle; and
they fled before him.
15 And when the children of Ammon saw that the
Syrians were fled, they likewise fled before Abishai
his brother, and entered into the city. Then Joab
came to Jerusalem.
16 ¶ And when the Syrians saw that they were
put to the worse before Israel, they sent messen-
gers, and drew forth the Syrians that *were* beyond
the river: and Shophach the captain of the host of
Hadarezer *went* before them.
17 And it was told David; and he gathered all
Israel, and passed over Jordan, and came upon
them, and set *the battle* in array against them. So
when David had put the battle in array against the
Syrians, they fought with him.
18 But the Syrians fled before Israel; and David
slew of the Syrians seven thousand *men which*
fought in chariots, and forty thousand footmen,
and killed Shophach the captain of the host.
19 And when the servants of Hadarezer saw that
they were put to the worse before Israel, they
made peace with David, and became his servants:
neither would the Syrians help the children of
Ammon any more.

CHAPTER 20

AND it came to pass, that after the year was ex-
pired, at the time that kings go out *to battle*, Joab
led forth the power of the army, and wasted the
country of the children of Ammon, and came and
besieged Rabbah. But David tarried at Jerusalem.
And Joab smote Rabbah, and destroyed it.
2 And David took the crown of their king from
off his head, and found it to weigh a talent of gold,
and *there were* precious stones in it; and it was set
upon David's head: and he brought also exceed-
ing much spoil out of the city.
3 And he brought out the people that *were* in it,
and cut *them* with saws, and with harrows of iron,
and with axes. Even so dealt David with all the
cities of the children of Ammon. And David and
all the people returned to Jerusalem.
4 ¶ And it came to pass after this, that there arose

19:13 *Be of good courage.* Reminiscent of Joshua's admonition to the people of Israel before taking the land of Canaan in their initial conquest (Josh. 1:6,9). *cities of our God.* This was more than a political conflict, but a battle for the land God had promised. Therefore, they could fight with all their might, trusting in the providence of God (*let the LORD do that which is good in his sight*).

19:16 *Hadarezer.* King of Zobah (18:3).

19:19 *put to the worse.* Defeated.

Thoughts for Personal/Family Worship: Chapter 19

1. **Like the servants of King David, the servants of Jesus Christ may experience times of humiliation (v. 4) and face overwhelming forces of opposition (vv. 6–7). Yet they should take heart, be courageous, and fight for the people of God, trusting that the Lord will do what is good (v. 13). In what ways do you need courage today? How can you find it in the Lord?**
2. **Just as the Ammonites distrusted David's heart of mercy and thus insulted him and his servants, so the wicked view Christ with unbelieving, suspicious eyes and greatly dishonor Him. How foolish it is to distrust and dishonor the Lord of love and kindness, especially in His gospel invitations. They greatly provoke His wrath. It was wise for the servants of Hadarezer to make peace with David when they saw his victory (v. 19); it is even wiser for sinners to find peace with God through repentance and faith in the gospel, for Jesus is Lord. Which group do you belong to? Who can you be praying for?**

Chapter 20: *David's territory increases further as he conquers his foes.*

David's Other Battles (1 Chron. 20:1–8)

20:1–3 *the time that kings go out to battle.* In ancient times, spring was the most practical and advantageous time to fight wars. David's men had victory over the people of *Ammon* and *Rabbah*. *tarried.* Stayed in the city, the sad occasion of his adultery (2 Sam. 11:1–5).

20:2 *crown . . . talent of gold.* This was no ordinary *crown*, weighing over sixty pounds.

20:3 *cut them with saws.* The word *them* is not in the Hebrew text, and thus should most likely be understood as "caused them to cut" or put them to work as forced laborers using these tools (22:2; Judg. 1:28; 2 Sam. 12:31; 1 Kings 9:20–21). *harrows.* Plow shears.

war at Gezer with the Philistines; at which time
Sibbechai the Hushathite slew Sippai, *that was* of
the children of the giant: and they were subdued.
5 And there was war again with the Philistines;
and Elhanan the son of Jair slew Lahmi the
brother of Goliath the Gittite, whose spear staff
was like a weaver's beam.
6 And yet again there was war at Gath, where was
a man of *great* stature, whose fingers and toes
were four and twenty, six *on each hand*, and six
on each foot: and he also was the son of the giant.
7 But when he defied Israel, Jonathan the son of
Shimea David's brother slew him.
8 These were born unto the giant in Gath; and
they fell by the hand of David, and by the hand
of his servants.

CHAPTER 21

AND Satan stood up against Israel, and provoked
David to number Israel.
2 And David said to Joab and to the rulers of the
people, Go, number Israel from Beer-sheba even
to Dan; and bring the number of them to me, that
I may know *it*.
3 And Joab answered, The LORD make his people
an hundred times so many more as they *be*: but,
my lord the king, *are* they not all my lord's ser-
vants? why then doth my lord require this thing?
why will he be a cause of trespass to Israel?
4 Nevertheless the king's word prevailed against
Joab. Wherefore Joab departed, and went
throughout all Israel, and came to Jerusalem.
5 ¶ And Joab gave the sum of the number of the
people unto David. And all *they of* Israel were a
thousand thousand and an hundred thousand
men that drew sword: and Judah *was* four hun-
dred threescore and ten thousand men that drew
sword.
6 But Levi and Benjamin counted he not among
them: for the king's word was abominable to Joab.
7 And God was displeased with this thing; there-
fore he smote Israel.
8 And David said unto God, I have sinned greatly,
because I have done this thing: but now, I beseech
thee, do away the iniquity of thy servant; for I
have done very foolishly.
9 ¶ And the LORD spake unto Gad, David's seer,
saying,
10 Go and tell David, saying, Thus saith the LORD,
I offer thee three *things*: choose thee one of them,
that I may do *it* unto thee.
11 So Gad came to David, and said unto him,
Thus saith the LORD, Choose thee
12 Either three years' famine; or three months to
be destroyed before thy foes, while that the sword
of thine enemies overtaketh *thee*; or else three
days the sword of the LORD, even the pestilence,
in the land, and the angel of the LORD destroying
throughout all the coasts of Israel. Now therefore
advise thyself what word I shall bring again to
him that sent me.
13 And David said unto Gad, I am in a great
strait: let me fall now into the hand of the LORD;
for very great *are* his mercies: but let me not fall
into the hand of man.

20:4–8 David's subjection of the *Philistines* came in three steps. These are the last recorded battles with the Philistines in Chronicles. *children of the giant.* Descendants of the Rephaim, a people known for their great height (Deut. 2:10–11,20–21; 3:11).
20:5 *Lahmi the brother of Goliath the Gittite.* See 2 Sam. 21:19.

Thoughts for Personal/Family Worship: Chapter 20
David's victory over Goliath by faith in the Lord (1 Sam. 17) evidently inspired his servants to take on similarly gigantic enemies and defeat them. The bravery and victory of one's king can strongly motivate his servants to attempt great feats as well. In the same way, Christ's victory over sin and Satan makes believers strong and courageous to fight their own personal spiritual battles and anticipate victory by faith in Him (John 16:33; Eph. 6:10; Col. 2:15; 1 John 5:4–5). What spiritual enemies seem gigantic to you right now? How can you look to Christ's victory?

David's Preparations for the Temple (1 Chron. 21:1—26:32)
David's Sinful Census and the Temple Site (1 Chron. 21:1—22:1)
Chapter 21: *David sinfully numbers Israel, and when the nation is punished by a plague, David makes atonement on the future site of the temple.*
21:1 *Satan.* Literally, "an adversary," sometimes a name for the Devil (Zech. 3:1–2). The Lord incited David to take the census (2 Sam. 24:1), using an adversary (whether a man or the Devil). Even the enemies of God's people are subject to God's sovereign will (1 Kings 11:14,23,25; Job 1:6–12; 2:1–7). *number Israel.* Take a census of the people.
21:3 *cause of trespass.* God sometimes commanded a census of the men of Israel (Num. 1:1–3), but David's census offended God (vv. 7–8), perhaps because it violated the law of Moses (Ex. 30:11–16), or was not divinely commanded, or was motivated by pride and trusting in man (Jer. 9:23; 17:5–6). First Chronicles later implies that censuses should be restrained by faith in God's promises (27:23–24).
21:5 *a thousand thousand and an hundred thousand.* 1,100,000. *four hundred threescore and ten thousand.* 470,000. The figures in 2 Sam. 24:9 are 800,000 and 500,000. The difference between these numbers should not be seen as contradictory, for Samuel might be leaving out some class of people, which Chronicles is including, such as the rotating military regiments from each tribe (27:1–15). *drew sword.* Were able to fight.
21:9 *seer.* Prophet.
21:12 *sword of the LORD.* In contrast to David's census of the men who could draw the "sword" (v. 5; cf. vv. 16,27,30). God reminded him not to trust in man's strength, but to fear the power of the Lord. *coasts.* Regions.
21:13 *in a great strait.* In severe distress. *hand of the LORD.* David chose to fall into the hand of the Lord, because he hoped that despite his sin and punishment, he might still find

14 ¶ So the LORD sent pestilence upon Israel: and
there fell of Israel seventy thousand men.
15 And God sent an angel unto Jerusalem to
destroy it: and as he was destroying, the LORD
beheld, and he repented him of the evil, and said
to the angel that destroyed, It is enough, stay now
thine hand. And the angel of the LORD stood by
the threshingfloor of Ornan the Jebusite.
16 And David lifted up his eyes, and saw the
angel of the LORD stand between the earth and
the heaven, having a drawn sword in his hand
stretched out over Jerusalem. Then David and the
elders *of Israel, who were* clothed in sackcloth, fell
upon their faces.
17 And David said unto God, *Is it* not I *that*
commanded the people to be numbered? even I
it is that have sinned and done evil indeed; but
as for these sheep, what have they done? let thine
hand, I pray thee, O LORD my God, be on me, and
on my father's house; but not on thy people, that
they should be plagued.
18 ¶ Then the angel of the LORD commanded
Gad to say to David, that David should go up, and
set up an altar unto the LORD in the threshing-
floor of Ornan the Jebusite.
19 And David went up at the saying of Gad,
which he spake in the name of the LORD.
20 And Ornan turned back, and saw the angel;
and his four sons with him hid themselves. Now
Ornan was threshing wheat.
21 And as David came to Ornan, Ornan looked
and saw David, and went out of the threshing-
floor, and bowed himself to David with *his* face
to the ground.
22 Then David said to Ornan, Grant me the place
of *this* threshingfloor, that I may build an altar
therein unto the LORD: thou shalt grant it me for
the full price: that the plague may be stayed from
the people.
23 And Ornan said unto David, Take *it* to thee,
and let my lord the king do *that which is* good in
his eyes: lo, I give *thee* the oxen *also* for burnt of-
ferings, and the threshing instruments for wood,
and the wheat for the meat offering; I give it all.
24 And king David said to Ornan, Nay; but I will
verily buy it for the full price: for I will not take
that which *is* thine for the LORD, nor offer burnt
offerings without cost.
25 So David gave to Ornan for the place six
hundred shekels of gold by weight.
26 And David built there an altar unto the LORD,
and offered burnt offerings and peace offerings,
and called upon the LORD; and he answered
him from heaven by fire upon the altar of burnt
offering.
27 And the LORD commanded the angel; and he
put up his sword again into the sheath thereof.
28 ¶ At that time when David saw that the LORD
had answered him in the threshingfloor of Ornan
the Jebusite, then he sacrificed there.
29 For the tabernacle of the LORD, which Moses
made in the wilderness, and the altar of the burnt
offering, *were* at that season in the high place at
Gibeon.

---

some mercy in the presence of God.

21:14 *pestilence upon Israel.* The king of Israel was especially responsible to obey God's laws as God's servant and representative (22:12–13; 28:9; 29:19; 2 Chron. 7:17; cf. Deut. 17:19–20). The king's obedience brought lasting blessing to Israel (1 Kings 15:3–5), but his sins brought terrible consequences upon the nation (2 Kings 24:3).

21:15 *he repented him of the evil.* He mercifully relented of the destruction He might have done. *stay.* Stop, hold back. *Ornan.* Same as Araunah (2 Sam. 24:16).

21:16 *stand between the earth and the heaven.* The angel stood in the sky as the agent of God's judgment (Ezek. 8:3; Zech. 5:9; cf. Rev. 10:1–7). *drawn sword in his hand.* As when the angel was sent against Balaam (Num. 22:23). *fell upon their faces.* David and the elders interceded for the people of Jerusalem.

21:17 *be on me.* David pled with God to take out His vindictive justice against him.

21:18 *threshingfloor of Ornan the Jebusite.* Located on Mt. Moriah, the same site as Abraham's near sacrifice of Isaac (Gen. 22:2; 2 Chron. 3:1).

21:24 *Nay; but I will verily buy it for the full price.* David refuses to accept the threshingfloor and the oxen without paying for it. David knew his responsibility in the plague and as the head of Israel and refused to bypass the personal cost that the sacrifice would cost him.

21:25 *six hundred shekels.* The price of the whole piece of property (see note at 2 Sam. 24:24).

21:26 *burnt offerings and peace offerings.* The same offerings made by Moses and Aaron at the dedication of the tabernacle (Num. 7:84–88), and later by Solomon at the dedication of the temple (2 Chron. 7:7), of which on both occasions the Lord showed His approval of the sacrifices by heavenly *fire* (Ex. 40:38; Lev. 9:24; 2 Chron. 7:1–3; cf. 1 Kings 18:38).

21:28 *sacrificed there.* David follows up his previous sacrifices with additional sacrifices to God.

21:29 *were at that season in the high place at Gibeon.* It should seem strange that David made a sacrifice when he was not at the tabernacle. But God had commanded, through Gad, for this to be the place of the altar (v. 18).

Thoughts for Personal/Family Worship: Chapter 21

1. **Even godly David fell into sin, a warning to us that the best of men is but a man. His sin brought deadly consequences upon the people because he was their king. The plague that came from David's sin is a small reminder of the death that has consumed billions of people because of Adam's sin (Rom. 5:12). How does God view sin, that it causes Him to pronounce such terrible judgments?**
2. **David took full, personal responsibility for this calamity, offering to bear the punishment himself (v. 17) and insisting on paying the price for atonement at his own expense (vv. 24–25). As a result, he obtained a lasting place for the temple where the people would find forgiveness of their sins (2 Chron. 6:21–39). Here we have a beautiful picture of Jesus Christ. Although He never**

30 But David could not go before it to enquire of
God: for he was afraid because of the sword of the
angel of the LORD.

CHAPTER 22

THEN David said, This *is* the house of the LORD
God, and this *is* the altar of the burnt offering for
Israel.
2 And David commanded to gather together the
strangers that *were* in the land of Israel; and he set
masons to hew wrought stones to build the house
of God.
3 And David prepared iron in abundance for
the nails for the doors of the gates, and for the
joinings; and brass in abundance without weight;
4 Also cedar trees in abundance: for the Zido-
nians and they of Tyre brought much cedar wood
to David.
5 And David said, Solomon my son *is* young and
tender, and the house *that is* to be builded for the
LORD *must be* exceeding magnifical, of fame and
of glory throughout all countries: I will *therefore*
now make preparation for it. So David prepared
abundantly before his death.
6 ¶ Then he called for Solomon his son, and
charged him to build an house for the LORD God
of Israel.
7 And David said to Solomon, My son, as for
me, it was in my mind to build an house unto the
name of the LORD my God:
8 But the word of the LORD came to me, saying,
Thou hast shed blood abundantly, and hast made
great wars: thou shalt not build an house unto my
name, because thou hast shed much blood upon
the earth in my sight.
9 Behold, a son shall be born to thee, who shall
be a man of rest; and I will give him rest from all
his enemies round about: for his name shall be
Solomon, and I will give peace and quietness unto
Israel in his days.
10 He shall build an house for my name; and he
shall be my son, and I *will be* his father; and I will
establish the throne of his kingdom over Israel for
ever.
11 Now, my son, the LORD be with thee; and
prosper thou, and build the house of the LORD
thy God, as he hath said of thee.
12 Only the LORD give thee wisdom and under-
standing, and give thee charge concerning Israel,
that thou mayest keep the law of the LORD thy God.
13 Then shalt thou prosper, if thou takest heed to
fulfil the statutes and judgments which the LORD
charged Moses with concerning Israel: be strong,
and of good courage; dread not, nor be dismayed.
14 Now, behold, in my trouble I have prepared
for the house of the LORD an hundred thousand
talents of gold, and a thousand thousand talents
of silver; and of brass and iron without weight;
for it is in abundance: timber also and stone have
I prepared; and thou mayest add thereto.
15 Moreover *there are* workmen with thee in
abundance, hewers and workers of stone and
timber, and all manner of cunning men for every
manner of work.
16 Of the gold, the silver, and the brass, and the
iron, *there is* no number. Arise *therefore*, and be
doing, and the LORD be with thee.
17 ¶ David also commanded all the princes of
Israel to help Solomon his son, *saying*,
18 *Is* not the LORD your God with you? and hath
he *not* given you rest on every side? for he hath

---

sinned, He took full responsibility for the sins of His people, personally paying the price for atonement by His own obedience and death, so that they may enjoy God's forgiveness forever. What does this teach us about the character of God?

Chapter 22: *David prepares for and gives the command to build the temple.*

22:1 *the house of the LORD God.* God's temple, where He would dwell. By the word of the prophet (21:18), David understood that this would be the location where God's temple should be built. The *house* belongs to God for His dwelling but the *altar* is for the people's sacrifices and worship.

David's Preparation for the Construction of the Temple (1 Chron. 22:2–19)

22:2 *strangers.* Foreigners. *hew.* Chop.
22:3 *joinings.* Clamps.
22:5 *tender.* Weak, inexperienced. *magnifical.* Magnificent. David made plans for the building of a large and beautiful temple, for God's glory throughout the whole earth (2 Chron. 6:32–33).
22:6–16 David commissioned Solomon to carry on the work of the temple, using language that echoed the covenant of the Lord (17:11–15).
22:8–9 *Thou hast shed blood.* God was not rebuking David for his wars, for God strongly supported him in his battles (14:8–17; 18:6,13; Ps. 18:34). David's wars subdued the nations around Israel, so that the nation enjoyed *rest* from its *enemies* (v. 18), a condition which God had decreed for the building of a place for His name (Deut. 12:9–11). Solomon's name (Hebrew, *Shelōmōh*) is from the same root as *peace* (*shalōm*). Solomon was God's man of peace, a type of Christ (Isa. 9:6).
22:10 *for ever.* As this book was written after the exile, this promise would have been an assurance and comfort to believers waiting for the Christ.
22:12 *wisdom and understanding.* The very things Solomon later asked of God (2 Chron. 1:10).
22:13 *takest heed to fulfil the statutes.* Pay careful attention to obey the laws. David's call for Solomon to obey God's law and to *be strong* and courageous because of God's presence with him (vv. 11,16) echoes the Lord's charge to Joshua after the death of Moses (Josh. 1:7–9).
22:15 *hewers.* Choppers. *manner.* Kind, sort. *cunning.* Skillful.
22:16 *Arise therefore, and be doing.* David solemnly charges Solomon to build the temple of God with the abundance of materials David has provided for the house.
22:17–19 David charged his administration to *help* Solomon.

given the inhabitants of the land into mine hand; and the land is subdued before the LORD, and before his people.
19 Now set your heart and your soul to seek the LORD your God; arise therefore, and build ye the sanctuary of the LORD God, to bring the ark of the covenant of the LORD, and the holy vessels of God, into the house that is to be built to the name of the LORD.

CHAPTER 23

SO when David was old and full of days, he made Solomon his son king over Israel.
2 ¶ And he gathered together all the princes of Israel, with the priests and the Levites.
3 Now the Levites were numbered from the age of thirty years and upward: and their number by their polls, man by man, was thirty and eight thousand.
4 Of which, twenty and four thousand *were* to set forward the work of the house of the LORD; and six thousand *were* officers and judges:
5 Moreover four thousand *were* porters; and four thousand praised the LORD with the instruments which I made, *said David*, to praise *therewith*.
6 And David divided them into courses among the sons of Levi, *namely*, Gershon, Kohath, and Merari.
7 ¶ Of the Gershonites *were*, Laadan, and Shimei.
8 The sons of Laadan; the chief *was* Jehiel, and Zetham, and Joel, three.
9 The sons of Shimei; Shelomith, and Haziel, and Haran, three. These *were* the chief of the fathers of Laadan.
10 And the sons of Shimei *were*, Jahath, Zina, and Jeush, and Beriah. These four *were* the sons of Shimei.
11 And Jahath was the chief, and Zizah the second: but Jeush and Beriah had not many sons; therefore they were in one reckoning, according to *their* father's house.
12 ¶ The sons of Kohath; Amram, Izhar, Hebron, and Uzziel, four.
13 The sons of Amram; Aaron and Moses: and Aaron was separated, that he should sanctify the most holy things, he and his sons for ever, to burn incense before the LORD, to minister unto him, and to bless in his name for ever.
14 Now *concerning* Moses the man of God, his sons were named of the tribe of Levi.
15 The sons of Moses *were*, Gershom, and Eliezer.
16 Of the sons of Gershom, Shebuel *was* the chief.
17 And the sons of Eliezer *were*, Rehabiah the chief. And Eliezer had none other sons; but the sons of Rehabiah were very many.
18 Of the sons of Izhar; Shelomith the chief.
19 Of the sons of Hebron; Jeriah the first, Amariah the second, Jahaziel the third, and Jekameam the fourth.
20 Of the sons of Uzziel; Michah the first, and Jesiah the second.
21 ¶ The sons of Merari; Mahli, and Mushi. The sons of Mahli; Eleazar, and Kish.
22 And Eleazar died, and had no sons, but

Thoughts for Personal/Family Worship: Chapter 22

1. **David was a type of Christ, who also went through a bloody conflict, but not in the killing of others. Christ's kingdom was not of this world (John 18:36), and He conquered not by killing but by submitting to a violent death (Rev. 5:5,9). Yet by His death on the cross He conquered the powers of hell (Col. 2:15). Solomon also was a type of Christ, but of Christ reigning in the peace He won by His blood (Eph. 2:14–17). Christ is building a new temple, not of stones and gold (Eph. 2:18–22). Of what is His new temple being built and with what and whom will it be filled?**
2. **David challenged Solomon not to take his privileges for granted. Faith, courage, and obedience must propel him to his work (vv. 11–13). He needed to be busy and active fulfilling the calling with which he had been charged, using the resources prepared by his father (vv. 14–16). What resources and calling has God entrusted to you? How are you busily serving the Lord?**

David's Organization of the Levites for the Temple (1 Chron. 23:1—26:32)

Chapter 23: ***David organizes the Levites into their several duties.***

23:1 *made Solomon his son king.* Perhaps a declaration of royal succession in view of David's *old* age, possibly linked to Adonijah's rebellion (1 Kings 1:1,32–40); the more formal coronation came later (1 Chron. 29:22–23). What follows in chs. 23–27 records the highly structured administration of worship and the kingdom.

23:3–5 *polls.* Heads. Of the 38,000 Levites eligible to serve, 24,000 helped to administer the work of the temple, 6,000 served as officers and judges, 4,000 were porters, and 4,000 were musicians.

23:3 *age of thirty years.* The Old Testament records the age necessary to serve as priesthood variously, at thirty (Num. 4:3,23,30), twenty-five (Num. 8:24), and twenty (v. 27; Ezra 3:8). The difference in accounting may be due to the number of available Levites to fulfill the ministry, or it might reflect a period of apprenticeship.

23:4 *set forward.* Oversee.

23:6 *courses.* Divisions, namely, the Gershonites (vv. 7–11), the Kohathites (vv. 12–20), and the Merarites (vv. 21–23).

23:13 *Aaron was separated.* The Lord set apart Aaron and his sons to serve as priests (Ex. 28:1). *holy things.* Objects dedicated to the Lord (Num. 4:4,19), including offerings (Num. 18:8–9; Deut. 12:26; 2 Chron. 31:14). *burn incense.* Literally, just "burn, cause to smoke" (*incense* is not in the Hebrew). The verb is used of burning both offerings and incense (Ex. 30:7–8; Lev. 1:9). *minister.* Serve. *bless in his name.* See Num. 6:22–27. Chronicles outlines three responsibilities of the Aaronic priests: to bring offerings and incense to the Lord, to serve Him in worship, and to declare His blessing on Israel.

23:15 *Gershom, and Eliezer.* See Ex. 18:3–4.

daughters: and their brethren the sons of Kish
took them.
23 The sons of Mushi; Mahli, and Eder, and Jer-
emoth, three.
24 ¶ These *were* the sons of Levi after the house
of their fathers; *even* the chief of the fathers, as
they were counted by number of names by their
polls, that did the work for the service of the
house of the LORD, from the age of twenty years
and upward.
25 For David said, The LORD God of Israel hath
given rest unto his people, that they may dwell in
Jerusalem for ever:
26 And also unto the Levites; they shall no *more*
carry the tabernacle, nor any vessels of it for the
service thereof.
27 For by the last words of David the Levites *were*
numbered from twenty years old and above:
28 Because their office *was* to wait on the sons of
Aaron for the service of the house of the LORD,
in the courts, and in the chambers, and in the
purifying of all holy things, and the work of the
service of the house of God;
29 Both for the shewbread, and for the fine flour
for meat offering, and for the unleavened cakes,
and for *that which is baked in* the pan, and for that
which is fried, and for all manner of measure and
size;
30 And to stand every morning to thank and
praise the LORD, and likewise at even;
31 And to offer all burnt sacrifices unto the LORD
in the sabbaths, in the new moons, and on the set
feasts, by number, according to the order com-
manded unto them, continually before the LORD:
32 And that they should keep the charge of the
tabernacle of the congregation, and the charge of
the holy *place*, and the charge of the sons of Aaron
their brethren, in the service of the house of the
LORD.

CHAPTER 24

NOW *these are* the divisions of the sons of Aaron.
The sons of Aaron; Nadab, and Abihu, Eleazar,
and Ithamar.
2 But Nadab and Abihu died before their fa-
ther, and had no children: therefore Eleazar and
Ithamar executed the priest's office.
3 And David distributed them, both Zadok of
the sons of Eleazar, and Ahimelech of the sons of
Ithamar, according to their offices in their service.
4 And there were more chief men found of the
sons of Eleazar than of the sons of Ithamar; and
thus were they divided. Among the sons of Eleazar
there were sixteen chief men of the house of *their*
fathers, and eight among the sons of Ithamar ac-
cording to the house of their fathers.
5 Thus were they divided by lot, one sort with
another; for the governors of the sanctuary, and
governors *of the house* of God, were of the sons of
Eleazar, and of the sons of Ithamar.
6 And Shemaiah the son of Nethaneel the scribe,
one of the Levites, wrote them before the king, and
the princes, and Zadok the priest, and Ahimelech
the son of Abiathar, and *before* the chief of the
fathers of the priests and Levites: one principal
household being taken for Eleazar, and *one* taken
for Ithamar.
7 Now the first lot came forth to Jehoiarib, the
second to Jedaiah,
8 The third to Harim, the fourth to Seorim,
9 The fifth to Malchijah, the sixth to Mijamin,
10 The seventh to Hakkoz, the eighth to Abijah,
11 The ninth to Jeshua, the tenth to Shecaniah,
12 The eleventh to Eliashib, the twelfth to Jakim,
13 The thirteenth to Huppah, the fourteenth to
Jeshebeab,
14 The fifteenth to Bilgah, the sixteenth to Immer,
15 The seventeenth to Hezir, the eighteenth to
Aphses,

23:26 As David was ushering the ark into its rest in the coming temple, the service of the Levites was changing from their previous responsibility to *carry the tabernacle* (Num. 3–4). They are given three principal duties: guarding the temple, assisting the priests, and singing (vv. 28–32).
23:27 *twenty years old and above.* Perhaps the Levites were counted when twenty but not put into service until thirty (v. 3).
23:29 *manner.* Kind, sort.
23:32 *keep the charge.* Guard, watch over, in the sense of protecting God's holiness from any dishonor (Num. 1:53; 3:7).

Thoughts for Personal/Family Worship: Chapter 23

David said, "The LORD God of Israel hath given rest unto his people, that they may dwell in Jerusalem for ever" (v. 25). Thus the Levites ceased to carry the tabernacle in its travels, but instead served God in the permanent home for His presence. In this way, the earthly Jerusalem foreshadowed the heavenly Jerusalem, which was to come. The heavenly Jerusalem will usher in the eternal rest for God's redeemed people forever. Presently, we travel as on a pilgrimage, and God assigns every Christian duties necessary for our pilgrim state. However, when Christ returns with His kingdom of glory and peace we will enter into our eternal worship and the permanent enjoyment of His glory. All God's people will serve as priests and reign as kings in His presence (Rev. 5:10; 22:4–5). How does that promise comfort you?

Chapter 24: *David specifies the orders and duties of the Levites.*
24:2 *Nadab and Abihu died.* God punished them for dishonoring His holiness by bringing worship He had not commanded (Lev. 10:1–3).
24:4 *sixteen . . . and eight.* David divided the priests into a rotation of twenty-four groups (Luke 1:5,8).
24:5 Two primary offices are distinguished for the divisions, that of the *governors of the sanctuary* (literally, "officers of holiness") and the *governors of the house of God* (literally, "officers of God").
24:7–19 Twenty four lots in all.

16 The nineteenth to Pethahiah, the twentieth to
Jehezekel,
17 The one and twentieth to Jachin, the two and
twentieth to Gamul,
18 The three and twentieth to Delaiah, the four
and twentieth to Maaziah.
19 These *were* the orderings of them in their
service to come into the house of the LORD, ac-
cording to their manner, under Aaron their father,
as the LORD God of Israel had commanded him.
20 ¶ And the rest of the sons of Levi *were these*:
Of the sons of Amram; Shubael: of the sons of
Shubael; Jehdeiah.
21 Concerning Rehabiah: of the sons of Reha-
biah, the first *was* Isshiah.
22 Of the Izharites; Shelomoth: of the sons of
Shelomoth; Jahath.
23 And the sons *of Hebron*; Jeriah *the first*, Ama-
riah the second, Jahaziel the third, Jekameam the
fourth.
24 *Of* the sons of Uzziel; Michah: of the sons of
Michah; Shamir.
25 The brother of Michah *was* Isshiah: of the sons
of Isshiah; Zechariah.
26 The sons of Merari *were* Mahli and Mushi: the
sons of Jaaziah; Beno.
27 ¶ The sons of Merari by Jaaziah; Beno, and
Shoham, and Zaccur, and Ibri.
28 Of Mahli *came* Eleazar, who had no sons.
29 Concerning Kish: the son of Kish *was* Jerah-
meel.
30 The sons also of Mushi; Mahli, and Eder, and
Jerimoth. These *were* the sons of the Levites after
the house of their fathers.
31 These likewise cast lots over against their
brethren the sons of Aaron in the presence of
David the king, and Zadok, and Ahimelech, and
the chief of the fathers of the priests and Levites,
even the principal fathers over against their
younger brethren.

CHAPTER 25

MOREOVER David and the captains of the host
separated to the service of the sons of Asaph, and
of Heman, and of Jeduthun, who should proph-
esy with harps, with psalteries, and with cymbals:
and the number of the workmen according to
their service was:
2 Of the sons of Asaph; Zaccur, and Joseph, and
Nethaniah, and Asarelah, the sons of Asaph under
the hands of Asaph, which prophesied according
to the order of the king.
3 Of Jeduthun: the sons of Jeduthun; Gedaliah,
and Zeri, and Jeshaiah, Hashabiah, and Matti-
thiah, six, under the hands of their father Jedu-
thun, who prophesied with a harp, to give thanks
and to praise the LORD.
4 Of Heman: the sons of Heman; Bukkiah, Mat-
taniah, Uzziel, Shebuel, and Jerimoth, Hananiah,
Hanani, Eliathah, Giddalti, and Romamti-ezer,
Joshbekashah, Mallothi, Hothir, *and* Mahazioth:
5 All these *were* the sons of Heman the king's seer
in the words of God, to lift up the horn. And God
gave to Heman fourteen sons and three daughters.
6 All these *were* under the hands of their father
for song *in* the house of the LORD, with cymbals,
psalteries, and harps, for the service of the house
of God, according to the king's order to Asaph,
Jeduthun, and Heman.
7 So the number of them, with their brethren
that were instructed in the songs of the LORD,
even all that were cunning, was two hundred
fourscore and eight.
8 ¶ And they cast lots, ward against *ward*, as well
the small as the great, the teacher as the scholar.

24:19 *manner*. Custom, habit.
24:20–30 Chronicles records the remainder of *the sons of Levi* who were not priests.
24:31 By using lots, it was ensured that there would be no favoritism or nepotism (26:14). They looked to God to guide the lot (Prov. 16:33).

Thoughts for Personal/Family Worship: Chapter 24

The service of God's worship requires plans, organization, and structure. Many people may be involved, and they need to have a clear knowledge of their responsibilities. It is often helpful to set up schedules of rotating duties among those qualified to perform them. Just as King David determined the distribution of the offices of the Levites (v. 3), so King Jesus determines the structure and officers of the church by the directions of His Word and gifts of His Spirit (1 Cor. 12:4–7; Eph. 4:7–8,11). However, some practical details about the church and its worship are not specified by the Scriptures, and therefore must be determined by other means. Why is it so important to the church to have well-organized structures and plans governed by the Word and Spirit of Christ?

Chapter 25: *David organizes the Levites who were to serve as musicians for the temple.*

25:1–7 David established the singers for the house of the Lord. *Asaph . . . Heman*. See note at 6:33–47. *Jeduthun*. A music leader among the Levites (vv. 3,6; 16:41–43; Pss. 39; 62; 77 titles). *psalteries*. Musical instruments (see note at 13:8).
25:1 *prophesy with harps*. Lest we think that the temple music was merely music, David made clear that it had a function in relationship to the revealed truths of the Word.
25:2 *under the hands*. Under the authority and direction (also vv. 3,6). *according to the order of the king*. Literally, "by the hands of the king." Both the music and prophesying of public worship were done in submission to God's anointed king and his appointed officials.
25:5 *Heman* had fourteen of the listed twenty four divisions. *to lift up the horn*. To play the horn.
25:7 *cunning*. Skillful.
25:8–31 *Lots* were cast for the divisions of the singers into a rotation of twenty-four groups (24:4,18).
25:8 *ward against ward*. Or, "for their duties." *teacher*. Instructor (v. 7). *scholar*. Pupil, student (v. 3).

9 Now the first lot came forth for Asaph to
Joseph: the second to Gedaliah, who with his
brethren and sons *were* twelve:
10 The third to Zaccur, *he*, his sons, and his
brethren, *were* twelve:
11 The fourth to Izri, *he*, his sons, and his
brethren, *were* twelve:
12 The fifth to Nethaniah, *he*, his sons, and his
brethren, *were* twelve:
13 The sixth to Bukkiah, *he*, his sons, and his
brethren, *were* twelve:
14 The seventh to Jesharelah, *he*, his sons, and his
brethren, *were* twelve:
15 The eighth to Jeshaiah, *he*, his sons, and his
brethren, *were* twelve:
16 The ninth to Mattaniah, *he*, his sons, and his
brethren, *were* twelve:
17 The tenth to Shimei, *he*, his sons, and his
brethren, *were* twelve:
18 The eleventh to Azareel, *he*, his sons, and his
brethren, *were* twelve:
19 The twelfth to Hashabiah, *he*, his sons, and his
brethren, *were* twelve:
20 The thirteenth to Shubael, *he*, his sons, and his
brethren, *were* twelve:
21 The fourteenth to Mattithiah, *he*, his sons, and
his brethren, *were* twelve:
22 The fifteenth to Jeremoth, *he*, his sons, and his
brethren, *were* twelve:
23 The sixteenth to Hananiah, *he*, his sons, and
his brethren, *were* twelve:
24 The seventeenth to Joshbekashah, *he*, his sons,
and his brethren, *were* twelve:
25 The eighteenth to Hanani, *he*, his sons, and his
brethren, *were* twelve:
26 The nineteenth to Mallothi, *he*, his sons, and
his brethren, *were* twelve:
27 The twentieth to Eliathah, *he*, his sons, and his
brethren, *were* twelve:
28 The one and twentieth to Hothir, *he*, his sons,
and his brethren, *were* twelve:
29 The two and twentieth to Giddalti, *he*, his
sons, and his brethren, *were* twelve:
30 The three and twentieth to Mahazioth, *he*, his
sons, and his brethren, *were* twelve:
31 The four and twentieth to Romamti-ezer, *he*,
his sons, and his brethren, *were* twelve.

CHAPTER 26

CONCERNING the divisions of the porters: Of the
Korhites *was* Meshelemiah the son of Kore, of the
sons of Asaph.
2 And the sons of Meshelemiah *were*, Zechariah
the firstborn, Jediael the second, Zebadiah the
third, Jathniel the fourth,
3 Elam the fifth, Jehohanan the sixth, Elioenai the
seventh.
4 Moreover the sons of Obed-edom *were*, She-
maiah the firstborn, Jehozabad the second, Joah
the third, and Sacar the fourth, and Nethaneel the
fifth,
5 Ammiel the sixth, Issachar the seventh, Peulthai
the eighth: for God blessed him.
6 Also unto Shemaiah his son were sons born,
that ruled throughout the house of their father:
for they *were* mighty men of valour.
7 The sons of Shemaiah; Othni, and Rephael, and
Obed, Elzabad, whose brethren *were* strong men,
Elihu, and Semachiah.
8 All these of the sons of Obed-edom: they
and their sons and their brethren, able men for
strength for the service, *were* threescore and two
of Obed-edom.
9 And Meshelemiah had sons and brethren,
strong men, eighteen.
10 Also Hosah, of the children of Merari, had
sons; Simri the chief, (for *though* he was not the
firstborn, yet his father made him the chief;)
11 Hilkiah the second, Tebaliah the third,
Zechariah the fourth: all the sons and brethren of
Hosah *were* thirteen.
12 Among these *were* the divisions of the por-
ters, *even* among the chief men, *having* wards one
against another, to minister in the house of the
LORD.

Thoughts for Personal/Family Worship: Chapter 25

David separated the musicians for the service of the temple and these men were to "prophesy with harps, with psalteries, and with cymbals" (v. 1). It is no accident that David was known as the sweet psalmist of Israel (2 Sam. 23:1). He loved music and loved singing to the Lord (Ps. 89:1; Ps. 101:1). He knew the power of music as it relates to shaping one's worldview. Above all, David realized that God inhabited the praises of His people (Ps. 22:3). Why is song so important and helpful for the worship of the church? Why must church music be done in submission to Christ and the officers He appoints in the church?

Chapter 26: ***This chapter records the divisions of the gatekeepers, treasurers, and other officials that served the temple.***

26:1–19 The first section of this chapter relates to the *porters* or gatekeepers and their organizations according to lots. This follows a similar pattern as noted in the previous chapters.

26:1–11 The families set charge over the gates were the families of *Meshelemiah* (vv. 1–3,9), *Obed-edom* (vv. 4–8), and *Hosah* (vv. 10–11).

26:1 *Meshelemiah.* Also known as Shallum (Ezra 2:42) and Meshullam (Neh. 12:25).

26:6 *mighty men of valour*. Men of great ability. The same Hebrew word as *valour* (vv. 30–32) is also translated "strong" (vv. 7,9) and "able" (v. 8).

26:10 *not the firstborn.* We do not know why Hosah made his second born son the chief; it is likely that the firstborn somehow forfeited his right for this position.

13 ¶ And they cast lots, as well the small as the
great, according to the house of their fathers, for
every gate.
14 And the lot eastward fell to Shelemiah. Then
for Zechariah his son, a wise counsellor, they cast
lots; and his lot came out northward.
15 To Obed-edom southward; and to his sons the
house of Asuppim.
16 To Shuppim and Hosah *the lot came forth*
westward, with the gate Shallecheth, by the cause-
way of the going up, ward against ward.
17 Eastward *were* six Levites, northward four a
day, southward four a day, and toward Asuppim
two *and* two.
18 At Parbar westward, four at the causeway, *and*
two at Parbar.
19 These *are* the divisions of the porters among
the sons of Kore, and among the sons of Merari.
20 ¶ And of the Levites, Ahijah *was* over the trea-
sures of the house of God, and over the treasures
of the dedicated things.
21 *As concerning* the sons of Laadan; the sons
of the Gershonite Laadan, chief fathers, *even* of
Laadan the Gershonite, *were* Jehieli.
22 The sons of Jehieli; Zetham, and Joel his
brother, *which were* over the treasures of the
house of the LORD.
23 Of the Amramites, *and* the Izharites, the He-
bronites, *and* the Uzzielites:
24 And Shebuel the son of Gershom, the son of
Moses, *was* ruler of the treasures.
25 And his brethren by Eliezer; Rehabiah his
son, and Jeshaiah his son, and Joram his son, and
Zichri his son, and Shelomith his son.
26 Which Shelomith and his brethren *were* over
all the treasures of the dedicated things, which
David the king, and the chief fathers, the captains
over thousands and hundreds, and the captains of
the host, had dedicated.
27 Out of the spoils won in battles did they
dedicate to maintain the house of the LORD.
28 And all that Samuel the seer, and Saul the son
of Kish, and Abner the son of Ner, and Joab the
son of Zeruiah, had dedicated; *and* whosoever
had dedicated *any thing, it was* under the hand of
Shelomith, and of his brethren.
29 ¶ Of the Izharites, Chenaniah and his sons
were for the outward business over Israel, for of-
ficers and judges.
30 *And* of the Hebronites, Hashabiah and his
brethren, men of valour, a thousand and seven
hundred, *were* officers among them of Israel on
this side Jordan westward in all the business of the
LORD, and in the service of the king.
31 Among the Hebronites *was* Jerijah the chief,
even among the Hebronites, according to the
generations of his fathers. In the fortieth year of
the reign of David they were sought for, and there
were found among them mighty men of valour at
Jazer of Gilead.
32 And his brethren, men of valour, *were* two
thousand and seven hundred chief fathers, whom
king David made rulers over the Reubenites, the
Gadites, and the half tribe of Manasseh, for every
matter pertaining to God, and affairs of the king.

CHAPTER 27

NOW the children of Israel after their number, *to
wit*, the chief fathers and captains of thousands
and hundreds, and their officers that served the
king in any matter of the courses, which came in
and went out month by month throughout all the
months of the year, of every course *were* twenty
and four thousand.
2 Over the first course for the first month *was*
Jashobeam the son of Zabdiel: and in his course
were twenty and four thousand.
3 Of the children of Perez *was* the chief of all the
captains of the host for the first month.
4 And over the course of the second month *was*
Dodai an Ahohite, and of his course *was* Mikloth
also the ruler: in his course likewise *were* twenty
and four thousand.
5 The third captain of the host for the third
month *was* Benaiah the son of Jehoiada, a chief

26:13–18 These verses record the specific work of each division in relation to the temple.
26:14 *wise counsellor.* Someone able to give insightful direction and advice. By using *lots*, it was ensured that there would be no favoritism or nepotism (see also 24:31).
26:16 *causeway.* Paved road.
26:20–32 The second division of this chapter deals with the treasurers, officers, and judges.

Thoughts for Personal/Family Worship: Chapter 26

God gives people different callings. We should not envy what God has asked others to do in His kingdom. In order for God's kingdom to function, we need people, all in their own stations of life, to do what God has called and gifted them to do. Hence, the Bible says: "Ye are the body of Christ, and members in particular" (1 Cor. 12:27). How precious it is to have people of ability and wisdom (1 Chron. 26:6–9,14,30–32)! Each member should realistically evaluate his abilities, strive to develop them, and seek to serve in the church accordingly (Rom. 12:3–8). What are some things that by God's grace you can do well? How are you using them in the church?

Chapter 27: *The military divisions and leaders of the twelve tribes are assigned.*

David's Administration of the Nation (1 Chron. 27:1–34)

27:1–15 A record of the captains and military divisions of the people of Israel. Each division would serve for one month out of the year and offer 24,000 men for service. This was not David's permanent army but rather his civilian militia. The men of Israel were expected to serve.
27:1 *to wit.* That is.

priest: and in his course *were* twenty and four
thousand.
6 This *is that* Benaiah, *who was* mighty *among* the
thirty, and above the thirty: and in his course *was*
Ammizabad his son.
7 The fourth *captain* for the fourth month *was*
Asahel the brother of Joab, and Zebadiah his son
after him: and in his course *were* twenty and four
thousand.
8 The fifth captain for the fifth month *was*
Shamhuth the Izrahite: and in his course *were*
twenty and four thousand.
9 The sixth *captain* for the sixth month *was* Ira
the son of Ikkesh the Tekoite: and in his course
were twenty and four thousand.
10 The seventh *captain* for the seventh month
was Helez the Pelonite, of the children of
Ephraim: and in his course *were* twenty and four
thousand.
11 The eighth *captain* for the eighth month *was*
Sibbecai the Hushathite, of the Zarhites: and in
his course *were* twenty and four thousand.
12 The ninth *captain* for the ninth month *was*
Abi-ezer the Anetothite, of the Benjamites: and in
his course *were* twenty and four thousand.
13 The tenth *captain* for the tenth month *was*
Maharai the Netophathite, of the Zarhites: and in
his course *were* twenty and four thousand.
14 The eleventh *captain* for the eleventh month
was Benaiah the Pirathonite, of the children of
Ephraim: and in his course *were* twenty and four
thousand.
15 The twelfth *captain* for the twelfth month *was*
Heldai the Netophathite, of Othniel: and in his
course *were* twenty and four thousand.
16 ¶ Furthermore over the tribes of Israel: the
ruler of the Reubenites *was* Eliezer the son of
Zichri: of the Simeonites, Shephatiah the son of
Maachah:
17 Of the Levites, Hashabiah the son of Kemuel:
of the Aaronites, Zadok:
18 Of Judah, Elihu, *one* of the brethren of David:
of Issachar, Omri the son of Michael:
19 Of Zebulun, Ishmaiah the son of Obadiah: of
Naphtali, Jerimoth the son of Azriel:
20 Of the children of Ephraim, Hoshea the son
of Azaziah: of the half tribe of Manasseh, Joel the
son of Pedaiah:
21 Of the half *tribe* of Manasseh in Gilead, Iddo
the son of Zechariah: of Benjamin, Jaasiel the son
of Abner:
22 Of Dan, Azareel the son of Jeroham. These
were the princes of the tribes of Israel.
23 ¶ But David took not the number of them
from twenty years old and under: because the
LORD had said he would increase Israel like to the
stars of the heavens.
24 Joab the son of Zeruiah began to number, but
he finished not, because there fell wrath for it
against Israel; neither was the number put in the
account of the chronicles of king David.
25 ¶ And over the king's treasures *was* Azmaveth
the son of Adiel: and over the storehouses in the
fields, in the cities, and in the villages, and in the
castles, *was* Jehonathan the son of Uzziah:
26 And over them that did the work of the field
for tillage of the ground *was* Ezri the son of
Chelub:
27 And over the vineyards *was* Shimei the Rama-
thite: over the increase of the vineyards for the
wine cellars *was* Zabdi the Shiphmite:
28 And over the olive trees and the sycomore
trees that *were* in the low plains *was* Baal-hanan
the Gederite: and over the cellars of oil *was* Joash:
29 And over the herds that fed in Sharon *was*
Shitrai the Sharonite: and over the herds *that were*
in the valleys *was* Shaphat the son of Adlai:
30 Over the camels also *was* Obil the Ishmaelite:
and over the asses *was* Jehdeiah the Meronothite:
31 And over the flocks *was* Jaziz the Hagerite. All
these *were* the rulers of the substance which *was*
king David's.
32 Also Jonathan David's uncle was a counsel-
lor, a wise man, and a scribe: and Jehiel the son of
Hachmoni *was* with the king's sons:
33 And Ahithophel *was* the king's counsellor: and
Hushai the Archite *was* the king's companion:
34 And after Ahithophel *was* Jehoiada the son
of Benaiah, and Abiathar: and the general of the
king's army *was* Joab.

27:16–22 A record of the officers overseeing each of the twelve tribes of Israel. Gad and Asher are missing from the accounting for some unknown reason.
27:23 *stars of the heavens.* See God's promises in Gen. 15:5; 22:17.
27:24 *he finished not.* It seems likely that the numbers in vv. 1–23 were not part of the fateful census taken earlier (ch. 21; 2 Sam. 24), but now that he has covered another census, he alludes back to the census that brought the plague.
27:25–31 A record of David's stewards who took care of *the king's treasures* or private property.
27:26 *tillage.* Cultivation.
27:32–34 A record of David's counselors. *Ahithophel* joined with Absalom in rebellion against David (2 Sam. 15:31).

Thoughts for Personal/Family Worship: Chapter 27

1. **By having a rotating force from the twelve tribes, David not only made the tribes share the burden of Israel's defense, but he trained the men so that they could be leaders in their own areas of labor and leadership. God's people have to stand ready for spiritual battle at any time (Eph. 6:10–18). If we are skilled in this battle this will help us greatly to be strong wherever God has placed us. How can we train for the battles we face?**
3. **Instead of constantly counting people and their resources to assess our strength, believers should be counting on the promises of God (v. 23). Why is it a trap for churches to measure themselves by attendance or**

CHAPTER 28

AND David assembled all the princes of Israel,
the princes of the tribes, and the captains of the
companies that ministered to the king by course,
and the captains over the thousands, and captains
over the hundreds, and the stewards over all the
substance and possession of the king, and of his
sons, with the officers, and with the mighty men,
and with all the valiant men, unto Jerusalem.
2 Then David the king stood up upon his feet,
and said, Hear me, my brethren, and my people:
As for me, I *had* in mine heart to build an house of
rest for the ark of the covenant of the LORD, and
for the footstool of our God, and had made ready
for the building:
3 But God said unto me, Thou shalt not build an
house for my name, because thou *hast been* a man
of war, and hast shed blood.
4 Howbeit the LORD God of Israel chose me
before all the house of my father to be king over
Israel for ever: for he hath chosen Judah *to be* the
ruler; and of the house of Judah, the house of my
father; and among the sons of my father he liked
me to make *me* king over all Israel:
5 And of all my sons, (for the LORD hath given me
many sons,) he hath chosen Solomon my son to
sit upon the throne of the kingdom of the LORD
over Israel.
6 And he said unto me, Solomon thy son, he shall
build my house and my courts: for I have chosen
him *to be* my son, and I will be his father.
7 Moreover I will establish his kingdom for ever,
if he be constant to do my commandments and
my judgments, as at this day.
8 Now therefore in the sight of all Israel the
congregation of the LORD, and in the audience of
our God, keep and seek for all the commandments
of the LORD your God: that ye may possess this
good land, and leave *it* for an inheritance for your
children after you for ever.
9 ¶ And thou, Solomon my son, know thou the
God of thy father, and serve him with a perfect
heart and with a willing mind: for the LORD
searcheth all hearts, and understandeth all the
imaginations of the thoughts: if thou seek him, he
will be found of thee; but if thou forsake him, he
will cast thee off for ever.
10 Take heed now; for the LORD hath chosen thee
to build an house for the sanctuary: be strong,
and do *it*.
11 ¶ Then David gave to Solomon his son the
pattern of the porch, and of the houses thereof,
and of the treasuries thereof, and of the upper
chambers thereof, and of the inner parlours
thereof, and of the place of the mercy seat,
12 And the pattern of all that he had by the spirit,
of the courts of the house of the LORD, and of
all the chambers round about, of the treasuries
of the house of God, and of the treasuries of the
dedicated things:
13 Also for the courses of the priests and the
Levites, and for all the work of the service of the
house of the LORD, and for all the vessels of ser-
vice in the house of the LORD.
14 *He gave* of gold by weight for *things* of gold,
for all instruments of all manner of service; *silver*
also for all instruments of silver by weight, for all
instruments of every kind of service:
15 Even the weight for the candlesticks of gold,
and for their lamps of gold, by weight for every
candlestick, and for the lamps thereof: and for the
candlesticks of silver by weight, *both* for the can-
dlestick, and *also* for the lamps thereof, according
to the use of every candlestick.

---

finances? How can we cultivate gospel optimism by learning to focus on the promises of the riches of glory in Christ?

David's Assembly for the Future Temple (1 Chron. 28:1—29:22)

Chapter 28: *David gives several final charges, both to Israel and to Solomon focused on the building of the temple.*

28:1 *David assembled* together all the prominent people of Israel in order to address them one last time before handing the kingdom over to his son Solomon.

28:2–7 *God said unto me.* David's last speech is cast within the mold of the covenant, restating God's promises to him (17:3–15) and applying them to *Solomon* as God had directed him (22:8–10).

28:2–3 *my brethren, and my people.* The king related to the people of God as his family, bound to him by covenant (11:1,3). *house of rest.* The home for God's glory when His people enjoyed their victory and peace in the Promised Land (Deut. 12:9–11). *ark of the covenant.* The symbol of the presence of the King of glory with Israel. *footstool.* The ark was like an extension of God's heavenly throne into the lower, earthly world (Pss. 99:5; 132:7; cf. Isa. 66:1). *shed blood.* Not a sin by David, but a stage in God's plan as He brought His people to *rest* in the Promised Land through the conflicts of their king (see note at 22:8–9).

28:4–5 *chose me . . . hath chosen Solomon.* Just as Israel was God's elect or chosen people (Deut. 7:6; 1 Chron. 16:13; Isa. 41:8–9), so the king of Israel was particularly God's elect man (Deut. 17:15; 1 Sam. 16:8–10; 2 Sam. 6:21; 1 Chron. 29:1; 2 Chron. 6:6; Pss. 78:70; 89:3). Thus Christ is especially God's chosen one (Isa. 42:1; 1 Peter 1:20; 2:4,6) and the King of His elect (Rev. 17:14).

28:6 *chosen him to be my son.* Election of sinners is unto adoption by God (Deut. 14:1–2; Eph. 1:4–5).

28:11–19 David gave the plans for the temple to Solomon so that he would build it. *candlesticks . . . tables of shewbread . . . altar of incense . . . ark.* On the spiritual significance of these holy objects, see notes at Ex. 25:10–40; 30:1–10.

28:11–12 *parlours.* Rooms. *by the spirit.* These plans were not of human invention, but revealed by God's Spirit to David (v. 19), just as God revealed the *pattern* for the tabernacle (same word as in Ex. 25:9,40).

28:14 *manner.* Kind, sort.

16 And by weight *he gave* gold for the tables of
shewbread, for every table; and *likewise* silver for
the tables of silver:
17 Also pure gold for the fleshhooks, and the
bowls, and the cups: and for the golden basons *he*
gave gold by weight for every bason; and *likewise*
silver by weight for every bason of silver:
18 And for the altar of incense refined gold by
weight; and gold for the pattern of the chariot of
the cherubims, that spread out *their wings*, and
covered the ark of the covenant of the LORD.
19 All *this, said David*, the LORD made me under-
stand in writing by *his* hand upon me, *even* all the
works of this pattern.
20 And David said to Solomon his son, Be strong
and of good courage, and do *it*: fear not, nor be
dismayed: for the LORD God, *even* my God, *will*
be with thee; he will not fail thee, nor forsake
thee, until thou hast finished all the work for the
service of the house of the LORD.
21 And, behold, the courses of the priests and
the Levites, *even they shall be with thee* for all the
service of the house of God: and *there shall be*
with thee for all manner of workmanship every
willing skilful man, for any manner of service:
also the princes and all the people *will be* wholly
at thy commandment.

CHAPTER 29

FURTHERMORE David the king said unto all the
congregation, Solomon my son, whom alone
God hath chosen, *is yet* young and tender, and the
work *is* great: for the palace *is* not for man, but for
the LORD God.
2 Now I have prepared with all my might for the
house of my God the gold for *things to be made*
of gold, and the silver for *things* of silver, and the
brass for *things* of brass, the iron for *things* of iron,
and wood for *things* of wood; onyx stones, and
stones to be set, glistering stones, and of divers
colours, and all manner of precious stones, and
marble stones in abundance.
3 Moreover, because I have set my affection to
the house of my God, I have of mine own proper
good, of gold and silver, *which* I have given to the
house of my God, over and above all that I have
prepared for the holy house,
4 *Even* three thousand talents of gold, of the gold
of Ophir, and seven thousand talents of refined
silver, to overlay the walls of the houses *withal*:
5 The gold for *things* of gold, and the silver for
things of silver, and for all manner of work *to be*
made by the hands of artificers. And who *then* is
willing to consecrate his service this day unto the
LORD?
6 ¶ Then the chief of the fathers and princes of
the tribes of Israel, and the captains of thousands
and of hundreds, with the rulers of the king's
work, offered willingly,
7 And gave for the service of the house of God
of gold five thousand talents and ten thousand
drams, and of silver ten thousand talents, and of
brass eighteen thousand talents, and one hundred
thousand talents of iron.
8 And they with whom *precious* stones were
found gave *them* to the treasure of the house of
the LORD, by the hand of Jehiel the Gershonite.
9 Then the people rejoiced, for that they offered
willingly, because with perfect heart they offered
willingly to the LORD: and David the king also
rejoiced with great joy.

28:18 *chariot of the cherubims.* The ark, a symbolic, mobile throne for the Lord (v. 2), was like a chariot on which God traveled with His people and fought for them while accompanied by His heavenly servants (Ps. 18:10; Ezek. 1).
28:20 *fear not, nor be dismayed.* Similar commission given to Joshua and Israel at the time of conquest (see notes at 19:13; 22:13). The king's work in building the temple fulfilled the purpose for which Joshua brought Israel into Canaan: to serve in the presence of the Lord as His covenant worshipers (Josh. 24:14–15).

Thoughts for Personal/Family Worship: Chapter 28

David's words at the close of his life reveal that the building of the temple was more than constructing an attractive building for worship. It was the culmination of God's purposes in old covenant history, and a type of Christ's work. Through God's chosen and Spirit-led King, the Lord is establishing His presence with His people. God will live among them as their King as He promised in His covenant. He will receive their obedient worship while they enjoy the peace He gives them. How does it affect your view of public worship to see it as drawing near to the King? How does it affect your view of heaven to see it as dwelling in God's presence?

Chapter 29: *David and Israel make offerings for the building of the temple, whereupon David dies and Solomon takes the throne.*
29:1 *tender.* Weak, inexperienced in ruling (1 Kings 3:7). *palace.* God's house is like the castle of a great king (Neh. 1:1; Est. 1:2).
29:2 *glistering.* Shining. *divers.* Diverse, various. *manner.* Kind, sort.
29:3 *set my affection to the house of my God.* The great desire and delight of the godly is to glorify and enjoy God (Pss. 42:2; 43:4–5; 63:1–2; 84:2). *proper good.* Personal wealth.
29:4 *withal.* With.
29:5–6 *consecrate.* Set apart for the service of *the LORD*. David gave all Israel and Judah the opportunity to join in building the temple. The response of the people was that they offered *willingly.*
29:5 *artificers.* Skilled craftsmen. *consecrate his service.* Literally, "fill his hand," an expression used of setting a person aside for ministry (see note at Ex. 29:9). David called the people to dedicate themselves and their possessions to serving the Lord.
29:7 *drams.* Measurement of bullion or the weight of precious metal.
29:9 *perfect heart they offered willingly.* Their generosity was

10 ¶ Wherefore David blessed the LORD before all
the congregation: and David said, Blessed *be* thou,
LORD God of Israel our father, for ever and ever.
11 Thine, O LORD, *is* the greatness, and the power,
and the glory, and the victory, and the majesty: for
all *that is* in the heaven and in the earth *is thine*;
thine *is* the kingdom, O LORD, and thou art exalted as head above all.
12 Both riches and honour *come* of thee, and
thou reignest over all; and in thine hand *is* power
and might; and in thine hand *it is* to make great,
and to give strength unto all.
13 Now therefore, our God, we thank thee, and
praise thy glorious name.
14 But who *am* I, and what *is* my people, that we
should be able to offer so willingly after this sort?
for all things *come* of thee, and of thine own have
we given thee.
15 For we *are* strangers before thee, and sojourners, as *were* all our fathers: our days on the earth
are as a shadow, and *there is* none abiding.
16 O LORD our God, all this store that we have
prepared to build thee an house for thine holy
name *cometh* of thine hand, and *is* all thine own.
17 I know also, my God, that thou triest the heart,
and hast pleasure in uprightness. As for me, in the
uprightness of mine heart I have willingly offered
all these things: and now have I seen with joy thy
people, which are present here, to offer willingly
unto thee.
18 O LORD God of Abraham, Isaac, and of Israel,
our fathers, keep this for ever in the imagination
of the thoughts of the heart of thy people, and
prepare their heart unto thee:
19 And give unto Solomon my son a perfect
heart, to keep thy commandments, thy testimonies, and thy statutes, and to do all *these things*,
and to build the palace, *for* the which I have made
provision.
20 ¶ And David said to all the congregation, Now
bless the LORD your God. And all the congregation blessed the LORD God of their fathers, and
bowed down their heads, and worshipped the
LORD, and the king.
21 And they sacrificed sacrifices unto the LORD,
and offered burnt offerings unto the LORD, on the
morrow after that day, *even* a thousand bullocks, a
thousand rams, *and* a thousand lambs, with their
drink offerings, and sacrifices in abundance for
all Israel:
22 And did eat and drink before the LORD on
that day with great gladness. And they made
Solomon the son of David king the second time,
and anointed *him* unto the LORD *to be* the chief
governor, and Zadok *to be* priest.
23 Then Solomon sat on the throne of the LORD
as king instead of David his father, and prospered;
and all Israel obeyed him.
24 And all the princes, and the mighty men, and
all the sons likewise of king David, submitted
themselves unto Solomon the king.
25 And the LORD magnified Solomon exceedingly
in the sight of all Israel, and bestowed upon him
such royal majesty as had not been on any king
before him in Israel.
26 ¶ Thus David the son of Jesse reigned over all
Israel.
27 And the time that he reigned over Israel *was*
forty years; seven years reigned he in Hebron, and
thirty and three *years* reigned he in Jerusalem.
28 And he died in a good old age, full of days,
riches, and honour: and Solomon his son reigned
in his stead.
29 Now the acts of David the king, first and last,

---

marked by wholehearted sincerity.

29:11–12 *Thine, O LORD.* These verses contain a marvelous declaration of God's sovereignty and sufficiency. Even while leading Israel to bring an enormous offering to God, David was not impressed with the gifts so much as with the infinite glory of God, who possesses all glory and power in Himself and gives to His creation any good that it has (Dan. 2:20–21; Acts 17:24–25; Rom. 11:33–36).

29:14 *who am I.* Since all things come from God, it is an undeserved privilege to bring Him our gifts with a willing heart. All our giving comes from His grace, and should humble us (17:16). *sort.* Manner.

29:17 *thou triest the heart.* God tests the inner thoughts and motives (28:9; 2 Chron. 6:30; Jer. 17:10), and delights not in outward things, no matter how impressive, but in righteousness, reverence, and love (1 Sam. 16:6–7; Ps. 147:10–11).

29:18 *imagination.* Purpose, design. *prepare their heart.* Direct or establish their souls in willing obedience. Inward righteousness is a gift of God's grace (Deut. 30:6; Ezek. 36:26–27).

29:19 *give unto Solomon . . . a perfect heart.* God did not fully answer this prayer in Solomon (1 Kings 11:4), but He did in David's greater *son*, the holy Son of God, Jesus Christ (Luke 1:32–35).

29:21 *morrow.* Morning.

David's Death and Solomon's Glory (1 Chron. 29:23—2 Chron. 1:17)

29:22 *the second time.* See 23:1. *chief governor.* Ruler.

29:23 *Solomon sat on the throne of the LORD.* The kingdom of David and Solomon was the kingdom of God (28:5), for the Lord reigned through His servant and the king established the temple of his God.

29:24 *submitted themselves.* The people acknowledged Solomon's reign much as they acknowledged David's reign.

29:25 *magnified . . . exceedingly.* Made him very great (2 Chron. 1:1).

29:28 *good old age.* Like Abraham (Gen. 15:15; 25:8). *stead.* Place.

Thoughts for Personal/Family Worship: Chapter 29

1. In all our giving to build the church, whether with our abilities, time, or money, we must recognize that God does not need us. He is all-sufficient in Himself to accomplish all His will. In fact, our ability to give, willingness to give, and actual giving are the gifts of His grace to us (2 Cor. 8:1–5; Phil. 2:12–13). The sovereignty of God's

behold, they *are* written in the book of Samuel
the seer, and in the book of Nathan the prophet,
and in the book of Gad the seer,
30 With all his reign and his might, and the times
that went over him, and over Israel, and over all
the kingdoms of the countries.

---

grace releases us to be cheerful givers, rejoicing in the infinite depths of God's indescribable grace even as we pour out our resources for Him (2 Cor. 9:7–8,15). Who can ever outgive a God like this?

2. Solomon's reign opened with unprecedented splendor and universal obedience among the people. Yet by its end it had fallen into the darkness of pride and idolatry. The kingdom of Solomon was but a small and passing shadow of Christ's eternal kingdom. Truly, Christ sits on the throne of the Lord, for He is the all-sufficient Lord. He has a perfect heart toward His Father. All of His redeemed people willingly submit to Him and serve Him. How should it affect our lives knowing that the son of David reigns now on the throne of heaven?

IF MY
PEOPLE
WHICH ARE CALLED
BY
My Name
SHALL
HUMBLE
THEMSELVES
&
PRAY
AND
SEEK
My Face
AND TURN FROM THEIR
WICKED
WAYS
THEN WILL I
Hear
FROM *Heaven*
AND WILL
FORGIVE
their sin
AND WILL
HEAL
THEIR LAND

2 CHRONICLES 7:14

INTRODUCTION TO THE BOOK OF
2 CHRONICLES

Authorship, Date, Theme, Purpose, Synopsis:

See the Introduction to 1 and 2 Chronicles, located before 1 Chronicles.

Outline: For the complete outline, see the Introduction to 1 and 2 Chronicles.

I. Kingdom Promised (1 Chron. 1:1—9:44)
II. Kingdom Established (1 Chron. 10:1—2 Chron. 9:31)
   A. Saul's Death (1 Chron. 10:1–14)
   B. David's Rise to Power (1 Chron. 11:1—12:40)
   C. David's Pursuit of God's Presence (1 Chron. 13:1—17:27)
   D. David's Military Victories (1 Chron. 18:1—20:8)
   E. David's Preparations for the Temple (1 Chron. 21:1—26:32)
   F. David's Administration of the Nation (1 Chron. 27:1–34)
   G. David's Assembly for the Future Temple (1 Chron. 28:1—29:22)
   H. David's Death and Solomon's Glory (1 Chron. 29:23—2 Chron. 1:17)
   I. Solomon's Construction of the Temple: Covenant Partially Fulfilled (2 Chron. 2:1—7:22)
      1. Solomon's Arrangements for Materials and Workers (2 Chron. 2:1–18)
      2. Solomon's Construction of the Building and Furnishings (2 Chron. 3:1—4:22)
      3. Solomon's Assembly to Dedicate the Temple (2 Chron. 5:1—7:22)
   J. Solomon's Works, Wisdom, and Death (2 Chron. 8:1—9:31)
III. Kingdom Divided (2 Chron. 10:1—28:27)
   A. King Rehoboam (2 Chron. 10:1—12:16)
   B. King Abijah (2 Chron. 13:1–22)
   C. King Asa (2 Chron. 14:1—16:14)
   D. King Jehoshaphat (2 Chron. 17:1—20:37)
   E. King Jehoram (2 Chron. 21:1–20)
   F. King Ahaziah (2 Chron. 22:1–9)
   G. Queen Athaliah (2 Chron. 22:10–12)
   H. King Joash (2 Chron. 23:1—24:27)
   I. King Amaziah (2 Chron. 25:1–28)
   J. King Uzziah (2 Chron. 26:1–23)
   K. King Jotham (2 Chron. 27:1–9)
   L. King Ahaz (2 Chron. 28:1–27)
IV. Kingdom Reformed and Ruined (2 Chron. 29:1—35:27)
   A. Hezekiah's Righteous Reign (2 Chron. 29:1—32:33)
   B. Manasseh's Idolatry and Repentance (2 Chron. 33:1–20)
   C. Amon's Idolatry (2 Chron. 33:21–25)
   D. Josiah's Righteous Reign (2 Chron. 34:1—35:27)
V. Kingdom Destroyed (2 Chron. 36:1–23)
   A. King Jehoahaz (2 Chron. 36:1–3)
   B. King Jehoiakim (2 Chron. 36:4–8)
   C. King Jehoiachin (2 Chron. 36:9–10)
   D. King Zedekiah (2 Chron. 36:11–16)
   E. Jerusalem Conquered (2 Chron. 36:17–21)
   F. Cyrus's Proclamation (2 Chron. 36:22–23)

THE SECOND BOOK OF

CHRONICLES

CHAPTER 1

AND Solomon the son of David was strengthened
in his kingdom, and the LORD his God *was* with
him, and magnified him exceedingly.
2 Then Solomon spake unto all Israel, to the cap-
tains of thousands and of hundreds, and to the
judges, and to every governor in all Israel, the
chief of the fathers.
3 So Solomon, and all the congregation with
him, went to the high place that *was* at Gibeon;
for there was the tabernacle of the congregation
of God, which Moses the servant of the LORD had
made in the wilderness.
4 But the ark of God had David brought up
from Kirjath-jearim to *the place which* David had
prepared for it: for he had pitched a tent for it at
Jerusalem.
5 Moreover the brasen altar, that Bezaleel the son
of Uri, the son of Hur, had made, he put before
the tabernacle of the LORD: and Solomon and the
congregation sought unto it.
6 And Solomon went up thither to the brasen
altar before the LORD, which *was* at the taberna-
cle of the congregation, and offered a thousand
burnt offerings upon it.
7 ¶ In that night did God appear unto Solomon,
and said unto him, Ask what I shall give thee.
8 And Solomon said unto God, Thou hast
shewed great mercy unto David my father, and
hast made me to reign in his stead.
9 Now, O LORD God, let thy promise unto David
my father be established: for thou hast made me
king over a people like the dust of the earth in
multitude.
10 Give me now wisdom and knowledge, that I
may go out and come in before this people: for
who can judge this thy people, *that is so* great?
11 And God said to Solomon, Because this was
in thine heart, and thou hast not asked riches,
wealth, or honour, nor the life of thine enemies,
neither yet hast asked long life; but hast asked
wisdom and knowledge for thyself, that thou
mayest judge my people, over whom I have made
thee king:
12 Wisdom and knowledge *is* granted unto
thee; and I will give thee riches, and wealth, and
honour, such as none of the kings have had that
have been before thee, neither shall there any after
thee have the like.
13 ¶ Then Solomon came *from his journey* to the
high place that *was* at Gibeon to Jerusalem, from
before the tabernacle of the congregation, and
reigned over Israel.
14 And Solomon gathered chariots and horse-
men: and he had a thousand and four hundred
chariots, and twelve thousand horsemen, which

KINGDOM ESTABLISHED (1 CHRON. 10:1—2 CHRON. 9:31)

David's Death and Solomon's Glory (1 Chron. 29:23—2 Chron. 1:17)

Chapter 1: *Solomon is established as king over Israel.*

1:1 *Solomon.* Means "peace," fitting the character of his reign (see note at 1 Chron. 22:8–9). *magnified . . . exceedingly.* Made very great. This verse continues the narrative of Solomon's reign begun in 1 Chron. 29:23.

1:2 *all Israel.* The kingdom was unified.

1:3 Solomon's first recorded act was to worship God at the *high place that was at Gibeon.* This was a legitimate place of worship (1 Chron. 16:39).

1:4 *ark . . . David brought up.* See 1 Chron. 15.

1:5 *brasen.* Bronze. *altar . . . the tabernacle.* See 1 Chron. 21:29.

1:8 *great mercy.* The covenant love of God shown to David and desired by Solomon. *stead.* Place.

1:9 *thy promise.* The covenant with David (1 Chron. 17). *like the dust of the earth in multitude.* As promised in the Abrahamic covenant (Gen. 13:16).

1:10–11 *go out and come in.* Lead them like a shepherd (1 Chron. 11:2). *thy people . . . my people.* Israel remained God's covenant possession, and the king was God's servant and steward.

1:13–17 Solomon's military and economic strength is depicted here (1 Kings 10:27–29). *horses brought out of Egypt.* In the law of Moses, the Lord specifically forbade the king from multiplying horses from Egypt (Deut. 17:16). This sets an ominous note early in Solomon's reign.

Thoughts for Personal/Family Worship: Chapter 1

Solomon's famous prayer for wisdom is a model for our prayers. He acknowledged God's faithful love and sovereignty over his life (v. 8). He took hold of God's promises and turned them into petitions, asking God to do what He had said (v. 9). He prayed for the ability and

he placed in the chariot cities, and with the king
at Jerusalem.
15 And the king made silver and gold at Jerusa-
lem *as plenteous* as stones, and cedar trees made
he as the sycomore trees that *are* in the vale for
abundance.
16 And Solomon had horses brought out of
Egypt, and linen yarn: the king's merchants re-
ceived the linen yarn at a price.
17 And they fetched up, and brought forth out of
Egypt a chariot for six hundred *shekels* of silver,
and an horse for an hundred and fifty: and so
brought they out *horses* for all the kings of the
Hittites, and for the kings of Syria, by their means.

CHAPTER 2

AND Solomon determined to build an house
for the name of the LORD, and an house for his
kingdom.
2 And Solomon told out threescore and ten
thousand men to bear burdens, and fourscore
thousand to hew in the mountain, and three
thousand and six hundred to oversee them.
3 ¶ And Solomon sent to Huram the king of Tyre,
saying, As thou didst deal with David my father,
and didst send him cedars to build him an house
to dwell therein, *even so deal with me.*
4 Behold, I build an house to the name of the
LORD my God, to dedicate *it* to him, *and* to burn
before him sweet incense, and for the continual
shewbread, and for the burnt offerings morning
and evening, on the sabbaths, and on the new
moons, and on the solemn feasts of the LORD our
God. This *is an ordinance* for ever to Israel.
5 And the house which I build *is* great: for great *is*
our God above all gods.
6 But who is able to build him an house, seeing
the heaven and heaven of heavens cannot contain
him? who *am* I then, that I should build him an
house, save only to burn sacrifice before him?
7 Send me now therefore a man cunning to work
in gold, and in silver, and in brass, and in iron,
and in purple, and crimson, and blue, and that
can skill to grave with the cunning men that *are*
with me in Judah and in Jerusalem, whom David
my father did provide.
8 Send me also cedar trees, fir trees, and algum
trees, out of Lebanon: for I know that thy servants
can skill to cut timber in Lebanon; and, behold,
my servants *shall be* with thy servants,
9 Even to prepare me timber in abundance: for
the house which I am about to build *shall be*
wonderful great.
10 And, behold, I will give to thy servants,
the hewers that cut timber, twenty thousand
measures of beaten wheat, and twenty thousand
measures of barley, and twenty thousand baths of
wine, and twenty thousand baths of oil.
11 ¶ Then Huram the king of Tyre answered in
writing, which he sent to Solomon, Because the
LORD hath loved his people, he hath made thee
king over them.
12 Huram said moreover, Blessed *be* the LORD
God of Israel, that made heaven and earth, who
hath given to David the king a wise son, endued
with prudence and understanding, that might
build an house for the LORD, and an house for his
kingdom.
13 And now I have sent a cunning man, endued
with understanding, of Huram my father's,
14 The son of a woman of the daughters of Dan,
and his father *was* a man of Tyre, skilful to work in
gold, and in silver, in brass, in iron, in stone, and

---

gifts to do what God had called him to do (v. 10). He did not pray out of worldly lusts for riches, honor, or revenge (v. 11). God answered his prayer by doing more than he asked (v. 12). Think of some concern weighing upon your heart. How does Solomon's example guide you in how to lift that concern up to the Lord in prayer?

Solomon's Construction of the Temple: Covenant Partially Fulfilled (2 Chron. 2:1—7:22)

Chapter 2: *Solomon makes preparations to begin building the temple.*

Solomon's Arrangements for Materials and Workers (2 Chron. 2:1–18)

2:1 *house for the name of the LORD.* A place where God would reveal the glory of His attributes through the sacrificial ministry of the priests (Deut. 12:5–28). The temple is central to Chronicles. *house for his kingdom.* Palace for the king (7:11; 8:1).

2:2 *threescore . . . fourscore.* Sixty . . . eighty (v. 18). A score is twenty. *hew.* Cut out or cleave.

2:3 *Huram.* Or Hiram (1 Chron. 14:1).

2:4 In the theocracy of Israel, the king actively supported religious worship.

2:5 *God above all gods.* Not that the Lord is the best among many gods, for there is only one God (Gen. 1:1; Deut. 4:35,39; 6:4), but that the Lord is sovereign over all things and other religions worship idols (1 Chron. 16:25–26).

2:6 *who is able to build him an house.* Unlike pagan worshippers, Israel must remember that its God is not limited to any place (1 Kings 20:23,28), but is infinite and everywhere present with His creation (6:18; Isa. 66:1–2; Acts 7:47–50; 17:24). *who am I.* Humility before God (1 Chron. 17:16; 29:14). *save.* Except. The temple served man's needs to draw near to God through *sacrifice*.

2:7 *cunning.* Skillful.

2:8 *algum.* Almug or sandlewood.

2:10 *hewers.* Choppers, cutters.

2:11–12 The Lord raised up a wise king to do good to Israel because He *loved his people*, moving people from other nations to praise Him (9:8).

2:12 *endued.* Endowed.

2:13 *cunning.* Skillful. *of Huram my father's.* It may mean something closer to "Master Huram," or be a compound name "Huram-abi."

2:14 *daughters of Dan.* This is reminiscent of the craftsman for the tabernacle, Aholiab, from the tribe of Dan (Ex. 31:6).

in timber, in purple, in blue, and in fine linen, and in crimson; also to grave any manner of graving, and to find out every device which shall be put to him, with thy cunning men, and with the cunning men of my lord David thy father.

15 Now therefore the wheat, and the barley, the oil, and the wine, which my lord hath spoken of, let him send unto his servants:

16 And we will cut wood out of Lebanon, as much as thou shalt need: and we will bring it to thee in floats by sea to Joppa; and thou shalt carry it up to Jerusalem.

17 ¶ And Solomon numbered all the strangers that *were* in the land of Israel, after the numbering wherewith David his father had numbered them; and they were found an hundred and fifty thousand and three thousand and six hundred.

18 And he set threescore and ten thousand of them *to be* bearers of burdens, and fourscore thousand *to be* hewers in the mountain, and three thousand and six hundred overseers to set the people a work.

CHAPTER 3

THEN Solomon began to build the house of the LORD at Jerusalem in mount Moriah, where *the LORD* appeared unto David his father, in the place that David had prepared in the threshingfloor of Ornan the Jebusite.

2 And he began to build in the second *day* of the second month, in the fourth year of his reign.

3 ¶ Now these *are the things wherein* Solomon was instructed for the building of the house of God. The length by cubits after the first measure *was* threescore cubits, and the breadth twenty cubits.

4 And the porch that *was* in the front *of the house*, the length *of it was* according to the breadth of the house, twenty cubits, and the height *was* an hundred and twenty: and he overlaid it within with pure gold.

5 And the greater house he cieled with fir tree, which he overlaid with fine gold, and set thereon palm trees and chains.

6 And he garnished the house with precious stones for beauty: and the gold *was* gold of Parvaim.

7 He overlaid also the house, the beams, the posts, and the walls thereof, and the doors thereof, with gold; and graved cherubims on the walls.

8 And he made the most holy house, the length whereof *was* according to the breadth of the house, twenty cubits, and the breadth thereof twenty cubits: and he overlaid it with fine gold, *amounting* to six hundred talents.

9 And the weight of the nails *was* fifty shekels of gold. And he overlaid the upper chambers with gold.

10 And in the most holy house he made two cherubims of image work, and overlaid them with gold.

11 ¶ And the wings of the cherubims *were* twenty cubits long: one wing *of the one cherub was* five cubits, reaching to the wall of the house: and the other wing *was likewise* five cubits, reaching to the wing of the other cherub.

12 And *one* wing of the other cherub *was* five cubits, reaching to the wall of the house: and the other wing *was* five cubits *also*, joining to the wing of the other cherub.

13 The wings of these cherubims spread themselves forth twenty cubits: and they stood on their feet, and their faces *were* inward.

---

grave. Engrave. *manner*. Kind, sort. *graving*. Engraving.
2:16 *floats.* Rafts to carry logs.
2:18 *bearers of burdens.* Heavy laborers. Indentured servitude was common. *hewers*. Choppers, cutters.

Thoughts for Personal/Family Worship: Chapter 2

The temple was "an house for the name of the LORD" (v. 1). God designed it so that people would know His glorious attributes. Yet it could not contain His glory, for God is infinite. Indeed, God's purposes could not be contained by Israel, for His temple would bring Him glory among the nations as the only true God. In the new covenant the Lord no longer links His presence to a special building, but Christ and His people are God's house (1 Peter 2:4–5). Yet God's nature and purposes remain the same. What then does this teach us about the church?

Solomon's Construction of the Building and Furnishings (2 Chron. 3:1—4:22)

Chapter 3: *Solomon begins the building of the temple.*

3:1 *began to build the house of the LORD.* Chronicles records the building of the temple beginning with the total dimensions of the building and then going from the holy place to the most holy place. Solomon's other projects are mentioned elsewhere (8:1–6). *mount Moriah.* Location where Abraham was to sacrifice Isaac (Gen. 22:2). *threshingfloor of Ornan.* Where David built an altar to turn away God's wrath by sacrifice (1 Chron. 21:18).
3:3 A cubit was about eighteen inches, so the *house of God* measured ninety feet long (*threescore* or sixty *cubits*) and thirty feet wide.
3:4 *porch.* Entrance to the holy place. *an hundred and twenty.* One hundred eighty feet.
3:5 *greater house.* The holy place where priests ministered. *cieled.* Covered, paneled. *palm trees*. Symbols of flourishing life in God's presence (Ps. 92:12–13; cf. Ex. 15:27), and perhaps an allusion to the garden of Eden (Gen. 2:8–9).
3:6–7 *garnished.* Decorated. *Parvaim.* A country perhaps located in Arabia. *cherubim.* Reminiscent of the entrance to the garden of Eden (Gen. 3:24), which was also associated with *gold* and *precious stones* (Gen. 2:11–12).
3:8 *most holy house.* Holy of Holies, where the ark rested. The most holy place was a cube, which signified perfection, and overlaid with the finest metal, *fine gold.*
3:10 *cherubims.* Freestanding statues of angelic beings in

14 ¶ And he made the vail *of* blue, and purple,
and crimson, and fine linen, and wrought cheru-
bims thereon.
15 Also he made before the house two pillars of
thirty and five cubits high, and the chapiter that
was on the top of each of them *was* five cubits.
16 And he made chains, *as* in the oracle, and
put *them* on the heads of the pillars; and made
an hundred pomegranates, and put *them* on the
chains.
17 And he reared up the pillars before the temple,
one on the right hand, and the other on the left;
and called the name of that on the right hand
Jachin, and the name of that on the left Boaz.

CHAPTER 4

MOREOVER he made an altar of brass, twenty cubits the length thereof, and twenty cubits the breadth thereof, and ten cubits the height thereof.
2 ¶ Also he made a molten sea of ten cubits from
brim to brim, round in compass, and five cubits
the height thereof; and a line of thirty cubits did
compass it round about.
3 And under it *was* the similitude of oxen, which
did compass it round about: ten in a cubit, com-
passing the sea round about. Two rows of oxen
were cast, when it was cast.
4 It stood upon twelve oxen, three looking to-
ward the north, and three looking toward the
west, and three looking toward the south, and
three looking toward the east: and the sea *was set*
above upon them, and all their hinder parts *were*
inward.
5 And the thickness of it *was* an handbreadth,
and the brim of it like the work of the brim of a
cup, with flowers of lilies; *and* it received and held
three thousand baths.
6 ¶ He made also ten lavers, and put five on the
right hand, and five on the left, to wash in them:
such things as they offered for the burnt offer-
ing they washed in them; but the sea *was* for the
priests to wash in.
7 And he made ten candlesticks of gold according
to their form, and set *them* in the temple, five on
the right hand, and five on the left.
8 He made also ten tables, and placed *them* in the
temple, five on the right side, and five on the left.
And he made an hundred basons of gold.
9 ¶ Furthermore he made the court of the priests,
and the great court, and doors for the court, and
overlaid the doors of them with brass.
10 And he set the sea on the right side of the east
end, over against the south.
11 And Huram made the pots, and the shovels,
and the basons. And Huram finished the work
that he was to make for king Solomon for the
house of God;

---

the *holy house*. God dwelt in the circle made by their arching wings.

3:14 *vail.* Curtain, which kept the priests from entering into full communion with God. This veil was torn in two at Christ's death (Matt. 27:51). *wrought cherubims.* Representations of cherubim were woven into it, to symbolize that sin's curse still kept man out of God's presence (Gen. 3:24).

3:15 *chapiter.* A piece that was placed at the top of the pillar, a capital.

3:16 *pomegranates.* Round, edible fruit found in the land of Canaan (Num. 13:23; Deut. 8:8).

3:17 *Jachin.* Literally, "he establishes." *Boaz.* Literally, "in him is strength." These pillars served to remind the people of the strength that God is for His people in His covenant.

Thoughts for Personal/Family Worship: Chapter 3

The gold and precious stones in God's holy house communicated the precious value of His holiness. The emblems of palm trees and pomegranates and the names of the pillars invited Israel to find abundant life and strength in God's presence, but the cherubim stood as a warning that man was still excluded from paradise for his sins. How can sinners be brought back to God and find life in Him? It was no accident that the temple was built on the very spot where a millennium earlier Isaac's life was spared through the sacrifice of the substitute ram (Gen. 22:13). Abraham prophesied that on that mountain the Lord would provide a lamb for sacrifice in the future (Gen. 22:8; cf. 22:14). The type of that sacrifice appeared in the sacrifices of the priests at Solomon's temple, and the reality appeared when the Lamb of God took away the sin of the world by dying upon the cross just outside the city. How can a sinner draw near to God through the blood of Christ?

Chapter 4: ***The temple is furnished with furniture and utensils.***

4:1 *altar of brass.* For making sacrifices, thus of special significance (see notes at Ex. 27:1—28:8). Exact placement is not known (Ex. 40:6).

4:2 *molten sea.* Fifteen-foot diameter, metal bowl for ritual cleansing before priests entered the temple, located in the southeast corner (cf. Ex. 30:18–20; 38:8). *compass.* Circumference. *did compass.* Surrounded.

4:4 *twelve oxen.* Representative of the twelve tribes. They faced outward in every direction.

4:5 *three thousand baths.* Chronicles and Kings give different numbers (1 Kings 7:26). Chronicles may be including the water held in reserve in smaller basins (vv. 6,14).

4:6 *lavers.* Basins.

4:7 *candlesticks.* Lampstands. The tabernacle had only one lampstand (Ex. 25:31–36). Each one had seven lamps, for a total of seventy.

4:8 *ten tables.* Reserved for the shewbread (v. 19; Ex. 25:30; Lev. 24:5–9), symbolizing God's provision for His people and their holy fellowship with Him.

4:9 *court of the priests.* Only priests were permitted in this court (Ex. 27:9–19).

4:11–22 The outer courts had bronze (*brass*) utensils, but as one progressed further into the temple, the utensils were made of *gold*, reflecting the heightened value of being nearer to the holy presence of God (see comments in the Worship Section for Ex. 37).

12 *To wit,* the two pillars, and the pommels, and
the chapiters *which were* on the top of the two pil-
lars, and the two wreaths to cover the two pommels
of the chapiters which *were* on the top of the pillars;
13 And four hundred pomegranates on the two
wreaths; two rows of pomegranates on each
wreath, to cover the two pommels of the chapi-
ters which *were* upon the pillars.
14 He made also bases, and lavers made he upon
the bases;
15 One sea, and twelve oxen under it.
16 The pots also, and the shovels, and the flesh-
hooks, and all their instruments, did Huram his
father make to king Solomon for the house of the
LORD of bright brass.
17 In the plain of Jordan did the king cast them, in
the clay ground between Succoth and Zeredathah.
18 Thus Solomon made all these vessels in great
abundance: for the weight of the brass could not
be found out.
19 ¶ And Solomon made all the vessels that *were*
for the house of God, the golden altar also, and the
tables whereon the shewbread *was set;*
20 Moreover the candlesticks with their lamps,
that they should burn after the manner before the
oracle, of pure gold;
21 And the flowers, and the lamps, and the tongs,
made he of gold, *and* that perfect gold;
22 And the snuffers, and the basons, and the
spoons, and the censers, *of* pure gold: and the
entry of the house, the inner doors thereof for the
most holy *place,* and the doors of the house of the
temple, *were of* gold.

CHAPTER 5

THUS all the work that Solomon made for the
house of the LORD was finished: and Solomon
brought in *all* the things that David his father had
dedicated; and the silver, and the gold, and all the
instruments, put he among the treasures of the
house of God.
2 ¶ Then Solomon assembled the elders of Israel,
and all the heads of the tribes, the chief of the
fathers of the children of Israel, unto Jerusalem,
to bring up the ark of the covenant of the LORD
out of the city of David, which *is* Zion.
3 Wherefore all the men of Israel assembled
themselves unto the king in the feast which *was* in
the seventh month.
4 And all the elders of Israel came; and the Levites
took up the ark.
5 And they brought up the ark, and the taberna-
cle of the congregation, and all the holy vessels
that *were* in the tabernacle, these did the priests
and the Levites bring up.
6 Also king Solomon, and all the congregation of
Israel that were assembled unto him before the
ark, sacrificed sheep and oxen, which could not
be told nor numbered for multitude.
7 And the priests brought in the ark of the cov-
enant of the LORD unto his place, to the oracle of
the house, into the most holy *place, even* under
the wings of the cherubims:
8 For the cherubims spread forth *their* wings over
the place of the ark, and the cherubims covered
the ark and the staves thereof above.
9 And they drew out the staves *of the ark,* that the
ends of the staves were seen from the ark before
the oracle; but they were not seen without. And
there it is unto this day.
10 *There was* nothing in the ark save the two
tables which Moses put *therein* at Horeb, when
the LORD made *a covenant* with the children of
Israel, when they came out of Egypt.
11 ¶ And it came to pass, when the priests were

4:12 *pommels.* Bowls. *chapiters.* Capitals.
4:14 *lavers.* Basins.
4:17 *Zeredathah.* Zarthan (1 Kings 7:46).
4:20 *manner.* Custom, habit. *the oracle.* The Holy of Holies.

Thoughts for Personal/Family Worship: Chapter 4

The temple had many of the things that we would have in our homes: wash basins, lights, tables, and so on, communicating that God really dwelt with His people. The brazen altar at the entrance was a visible message that blood needed to be shed for there to be communion between the holy God and unholy sinners. Notice that, unlike our homes, there were no chairs in the temple. The priests who labored in the temple never sat down. They only stood as servants ministering before their Master. The closest thing was a footstool, the ark (5:7). God alone could sit down, so to speak, between the cherubim (Ps. 80:1), as on His throne. Christ now sits on the throne of heaven (Heb. 1:3). How should it affect us to know that God really dwells with His people through the Christ, our Prophet, Priest, and King?

Solomon's Assembly to Dedicate the Temple (2 Chron. 5:1—7:22)

Chapter 5: ***The ark of the covenant, the most important piece of furniture in the temple, is brought into the temple, marking the completion of the temple building.***

5:1 *was finished.* A similar phrase is used of the tabernacle in Ex. 40:33. *brought in.* The instruments were built outside of the temple.
5:2 *elders.* Representatives and leaders of the people of Israel.
5:3 This was the *feast* of booths (Lev. 23:33–43). People lived in tents commemorating God's faithfulness during the wilderness wandering. *seventh month.* It took seven years to complete the temple (1 Kings 6:38).
5:4 *took up the ark.* The priests were consecrated to carry the ark.
5:8 *staves.* Poles to carry the ark.
5:9 *without.* Outside. *unto this day.* The author obviously was using an ancient source from before the exile.
5:10 *two tables.* Two tablets bearing the Ten Commandments, placed inside the ark (Ex. 25:16). In earlier days, Aaron's rod and

come out of the holy *place*: (for all the priests *that*
were present were sanctified, *and* did not *then*
wait by course:
12 Also the Levites *which were* the singers, all of
them of Asaph, of Heman, of Jeduthun, with their
sons and their brethren, *being* arrayed in white
linen, having cymbals and psalteries and harps,
stood at the east end of the altar, and with them
an hundred and twenty priests sounding with
trumpets:)
13 It came even to pass, as the trumpeters and
singers *were* as one, to make one sound to be
heard in praising and thanking the LORD; and
when they lifted up *their* voice with the trum-
pets and cymbals and instruments of musick, and
praised the LORD, *saying*, For *he is* good; for his
mercy *endureth* for ever: that *then* the house was
filled with a cloud, *even* the house of the LORD;
14 So that the priests could not stand to minister
by reason of the cloud: for the glory of the LORD
had filled the house of God.

CHAPTER 6

THEN said Solomon, The LORD hath said that he
would dwell in the thick darkness.
2 But I have built an house of habitation for thee,
and a place for thy dwelling for ever.
3 And the king turned his face, and blessed the
whole congregation of Israel: and all the congre-
gation of Israel stood.
4 And he said, Blessed *be* the LORD God of Israel,
who hath with his hands fulfilled *that* which he
spake with his mouth to my father David, saying,
5 Since the day that I brought forth my people
out of the land of Egypt I chose no city among all
the tribes of Israel to build an house in, that my
name might be there; neither chose I any man to
be a ruler over my people Israel:
6 But I have chosen Jerusalem, that my name
might be there; and have chosen David to be over
my people Israel.
7 Now it was in the heart of David my father to
build an house for the name of the LORD God of
Israel.
8 But the LORD said to David my father, Forasmuch
as it was in thine heart to build an house for my
name, thou didst well in that it was in thine heart:
9 Notwithstanding thou shalt not build the
house; but thy son which shall come forth out of
thy loins, he shall build the house for my name.
10 The LORD therefore hath performed his word
that he hath spoken: for I am risen up in the room
of David my father, and am set on the throne of
Israel, as the LORD promised, and have built the
house for the name of the LORD God of Israel.
11 And in it have I put the ark, wherein *is* the
covenant of the LORD, that he made with the
children of Israel.
12 ¶ And he stood before the altar of the LORD in
the presence of all the congregation of Israel, and
spread forth his hands:

---

a jar of manna were also kept with the ark (Ex. 16:33–34; Num. 17:10–11; Heb. 9:4).

5:13 *cloud.* God's glory filled the temple, a sign that God's presence had taken up residence with Israel in His house (6:1–2). The temple was not just a building but a home for God's glory cloud, which had followed the people of Israel from the land of Egypt (Ex. 13:21–22), traveled with them in the tabernacle (40:34–38), and now came to rest in the temple.

5:14 *priests could not stand.* The result of the overwhelming glory of God (Ex. 40:35).

Thoughts for Personal/Family Worship: Chapter 5

1. **The event of the ark coming to rest in this splendid sanctuary is given a good amount of space, showing its importance (vv. 1–10). The stability of rest that God had promised to give the Israelites when they departed from Egypt was finally realized (Ex. 15:17). With this event, God visibly took up His residence with His people in the temple, showing His permanence in the land and His abiding peace with His people. Today God dwells in His people by the Holy Spirit. How can you celebrate this important blessing God has given us today?**
2. **After the dedication of the temple and the praises of the people, the temple was filled with God's glory (v. 13). In Jewish history this would later be known as the Shekinah glory, based on the Hebrew word "dwell" (*shakan*, 6:1). In the fullness of time, God's glory would dwell among His people through His Son Jesus Christ, of whom John writes that He "dwelt among us, (and we beheld his glory)" (John 1:14). Through the Word and the Spirit of Christ, the glory of God shines in the heart of every believer (2 Cor. 3:17–18; 4:6). Why is it better for us to have the glory of God dwelling in us by the Spirit than to have it outside us in a visible cloud?**

Chapter 6: ***As king over Israel, Solomon now blesses the people and gives a prayer of dedication for the temple.***

6:1 *dwell in the thick darkness.* God reveals His glory in ways that hide His full glory (Lev. 16:2; Deut. 4:11; Pss. 18:11; 97:2; 104:3), for if He did not we would all perish in His brightness (5:14; 7:2; 1 Tim. 6:16).

6:3 *blessed the whole congregation.* The king called upon God to give grace and peace to the people after the nation had obediently built the temple, as Moses did earlier regarding the tabernacle (Ex. 39:43). Ordinarily, declaring God's blessing over Israel was the work of priests (Lev. 9:22–23; Num. 6:22–27; Deut. 10:8; 1 Chron. 23:13), but it could be done by others (Josh. 22:6–7; 1 Chron. 16:2).

6:4–11 Solomon recounted how the Lord made a covenant with his father, *David* (1 Chron. 17:3–15), giving God praise for doing *as the LORD promised.* The temple revealed the Lord's unique glory as the God who faithfully keeps His covenant (vv. 14–15).

6:10 *room.* Place.

6:11 *the covenant of the LORD.* The tablets of the Ten Commandments (5:10; Ex. 34:28). God's covenant engages people to obey His unchanging moral law, which would later stand as a testimony against the people of Israel when they were cast into exile because of their sin (cf. Deut. 31:19–27).

13 For Solomon had made a brasen scaffold, of
five cubits long, and five cubits broad, and three
cubits high, and had set it in the midst of the
court: and upon it he stood, and kneeled down
upon his knees before all the congregation of
Israel, and spread forth his hands toward heaven,
14 And said, O LORD God of Israel, *there is* no
God like thee in the heaven, nor in the earth;
which keepest covenant, and *shewest* mercy unto
thy servants, that walk before thee with all their
hearts:
15 Thou which hast kept with thy servant David
my father that which thou hast promised him;
and spakest with thy mouth, and hast fulfilled *it*
with thine hand, as *it is* this day.
16 Now therefore, O LORD God of Israel, keep
with thy servant David my father that which thou
hast promised him, saying, There shall not fail
thee a man in my sight to sit upon the throne of
Israel; yet so that thy children take heed to their
way to walk in my law, as thou hast walked be-
fore me.
17 Now then, O LORD God of Israel, let thy word
be verified, which thou hast spoken unto thy
servant David.
18 But will God in very deed dwell with men
on the earth? behold, heaven and the heaven of
heavens cannot contain thee; how much less this
house which I have built!
19 Have respect therefore to the prayer of thy
servant, and to his supplication, O LORD my God,
to hearken unto the cry and the prayer which thy
servant prayeth before thee:
20 That thine eyes may be open upon this house
day and night, upon the place whereof thou hast
said that thou wouldest put thy name there; to
hearken unto the prayer which thy servant pray-
eth toward this place.
21 Hearken therefore unto the supplications of
thy servant, and of thy people Israel, which they
shall make toward this place: hear thou from thy
dwelling place, *even* from heaven; and when thou
hearest, forgive.
22 ¶ If a man sin against his neighbour, and an
oath be laid upon him to make him swear, and the
oath come before thine altar in this house;
23 Then hear thou from heaven, and do, and
judge thy servants, by requiting the wicked, by
recompensing his way upon his own head; and by
justifying the righteous, by giving him according
to his righteousness.
24 ¶ And if thy people Israel be put to the worse
before the enemy, because they have sinned
against thee; and shall return and confess thy
name, and pray and make supplication before
thee in this house;
25 Then hear thou from the heavens, and forgive
the sin of thy people Israel, and bring them again
unto the land which thou gavest to them and to
their fathers.
26 ¶ When the heaven is shut up, and there is no
rain, because they have sinned against thee; *yet* if
they pray toward this place, and confess thy name,
and turn from their sin, when thou dost afflict
them;
27 Then hear thou from heaven, and forgive the
sin of thy servants, and of thy people Israel, when
thou hast taught them the good way, wherein they
should walk; and send rain upon thy land, which
thou hast given unto thy people for an inheritance.
28 ¶ If there be dearth in the land, if there be pes-
tilence, if there be blasting, or mildew, locusts, or
caterpillers; if their enemies besiege them in the
cities of their land; whatsoever sore or whatsoever
sickness *there be*:
29 *Then* what prayer *or* what supplication soever
shall be made of any man, or of all thy people
Israel, when every one shall know his own sore
and his own grief, and shall spread forth his
hands in this house:
30 Then hear thou from heaven thy dwelling
place, and forgive, and render unto every man
according unto all his ways, whose heart thou
knowest; (for thou only knowest the hearts of the
children of men:)
31 That they may fear thee, to walk in thy ways,
so long as they live in the land which thou gavest
unto our fathers.

6:13 Solomon interceded for the spiritual functions of the temple, a shadow of Christ interceding for the spiritual activity of His church (John 17; Rom. 8:34; Heb. 7:25).

6:16 *keep . . . that which thou hast promised.* Solomon prayed the promises of God.

6:18 *will God . . . dwell with men.* The immanence of God does not detract from His transcendence, and His special presence must not distract from His infinite presence throughout and beyond all places, for He remains the Holy One who inhabits heaven, earth, and eternity (Isa. 57:15; see note at 2:6). Men must not think they have captured God in the temple, but marvel at His grace to meet thus with them.

6:19–21 *hearken.* Listen. It is grace, not a debt, for God to answer prayers, even to the covenant people. *toward this place.* By faith in the promise of His presence. Christ, the fulfillment of the temple, commanded his disciples to make their prayers in His name (John 14:13).

6:22–39 Solomon recounted different scenarios where the people of Israel would pray to God, often in repentance of sins that bring down the curses of the old covenant (Lev. 26; Deut. 28). The repeated prayer for God to *forgive* (vv. 21,25,27,30,39) would give great hope to the people after the exile.

6:22–23 This section pertains to individuals. *requiting.* Returning the consequences of sin upon the sinner in justice. *recompensing.* Giving. *justifying.* Declaring innocent. *his righteousness.* Innocence of the particular crimes with which they had been charged (Ps. 43:1).

6:24–31 This section pertains to national repentance.

6:24 *put to the worse.* Defeated.

6:28 *dearth.* Hunger, famine.

32 ¶ Moreover concerning the stranger, which is
not of thy people Israel, but is come from a far
country for thy great name's sake, and thy mighty
hand, and thy stretched out arm; if they come and
pray in this house;
33 Then hear thou from the heavens, *even* from
thy dwelling place, and do according to all that the
stranger calleth to thee for; that all people of the
earth may know thy name, and fear thee, as *doth*
thy people Israel, and may know that this house
which I have built is called by thy name.
34 If thy people go out to war against their en-
emies by the way that thou shalt send them, and
they pray unto thee toward this city which thou
hast chosen, and the house which I have built for
thy name;
35 Then hear thou from the heavens their prayer
and their supplication, and maintain their cause.
36 If they sin against thee, (for *there is* no man
which sinneth not,) and thou be angry with them,
and deliver them over before *their* enemies, and
they carry them away captives unto a land far off
or near;
37 Yet *if* they bethink themselves in the land
whither they are carried captive, and turn and
pray unto thee in the land of their captivity, say-
ing, We have sinned, we have done amiss, and
have dealt wickedly;
38 If they return to thee with all their heart and
with all their soul in the land of their captivity,
whither they have carried them captives, and
pray toward their land, which thou gavest unto
their fathers, and *toward* the city which thou hast
chosen, and toward the house which I have built
for thy name:
39 Then hear thou from the heavens, *even* from
thy dwelling place, their prayer and their suppli-
cations, and maintain their cause, and forgive thy
people which have sinned against thee.
40 Now, my God, let, I beseech thee, thine eyes be
open, and *let* thine ears *be* attent unto the prayer
that is made in this place.
41 Now therefore arise, O LORD God, into thy
resting place, thou, and the ark of thy strength:
let thy priests, O LORD God, be clothed with
salvation, and let thy saints rejoice in goodness.
42 O LORD God, turn not away the face of thine
anointed: remember the mercies of David thy
servant.

CHAPTER 7

NOW when Solomon had made an end of praying,
the fire came down from heaven, and consumed
the burnt offering and the sacrifices; and the glory
of the LORD filled the house.
2 And the priests could not enter into the house
of the LORD, because the glory of the LORD had
filled the LORD's house.
3 And when all the children of Israel saw how the
fire came down, and the glory of the LORD upon
the house, they bowed themselves with their faces
to the ground upon the pavement, and wor-
shipped, and praised the LORD, *saying*, For *he is*
good; for his mercy *endureth* for ever.
4 ¶ Then the king and all the people offered sac-
rifices before the LORD.
5 And king Solomon offered a sacrifice of twenty
and two thousand oxen, and an hundred and
twenty thousand sheep: so the king and all the
people dedicated the house of God.
6 And the priests waited on their offices: the

6:32 *stranger.* Foreigner. Mercy is not restricted to the Israelites only. God's house was meant to be a house of prayer for all nations (Isa. 56:7). *for thy great name's sake, and thy mighty hand.* They heard of God's great acts, such as the exodus (Ex. 3:19–20; 9:16).

6:34–39 This section pertains to those at war. Many times prayer was a means of defeating one's enemies (13:14–15; 14:11; 32:20–22).

6:36 *no man which sinneth not.* Solomon understood the doctrine of the universal sinfulness of man (Prov. 20:9; Eccl. 7:20,29), and how it provokes the anger of God (Gen. 6:5–7; Ps. 5:4–6).

6:37 *bethink.* Come to think about and recognize their sin (Luke 15:17), a special encouragement after the exile (*carried captive*).

6:38 *land . . . city . . . house.* All three represent God's gracious presence and love for His people.

6:40 *attent.* Attentive.

6:41–42 Language similar to Ps. 132:8–10.

Thoughts for Personal/Family Worship: Chapter 6

1. **God's purposes for the temple revolved around five things highlighted here: humility in the presence of the infinite God, repentance of sin, prayer for forgiveness and restoration, confidence in God's faithfulness to keep His promises, and drawing the nations to seek God. In the new covenant there is no particular nation in covenant with God, and Christ has sent His people out to make disciples of all the nations. However, these remain His purposes for the church. Consider each of these five purposes. How does your church seek to fulfill them?**
2. **Solomon envisioned the temple as a place where sinners would come repenting and praying for grace. How do you come into God's presence? Does your church encourage turning from sin to God and praying for His forgiveness and restoration? Why or why not?**

Chapter 7: *God hears the prayer of Solomon, whereupon more sacrifices are made, and God appears to Solomon to set forth His covenant again.*

7:1 *fire came down from heaven.* A sign of divine presence and approval (see note at 1 Chron. 21:26).

7:2 *priests could not enter . . . glory of the LORD.* See notes at 5:13 and 14.

7:3 The people responded in humble worship with a common refrain from the Psalter (5:13; Ps. 136), celebrating God's loyal and endless love (*mercy*).

7:6 *waited on their offices.* Stood at their posts or assignments.

Levites also with instruments of musick of the
LORD, which David the king had made to praise
the LORD, because his mercy *endureth* for ever,
when David praised by their ministry; and the
priests sounded trumpets before them, and all
Israel stood.
7 Moreover Solomon hallowed the middle of the
court that *was* before the house of the LORD: for
there he offered burnt offerings, and the fat of the
peace offerings, because the brasen altar which
Solomon had made was not able to receive the
burnt offerings, and the meat offerings, and the
fat.
8 ¶ Also at the same time Solomon kept the feast
seven days, and all Israel with him, a very great
congregation, from the entering in of Hamath
unto the river of Egypt.
9 And in the eighth day they made a solemn as-
sembly: for they kept the dedication of the altar
seven days, and the feast seven days.
10 And on the three and twentieth day of the
seventh month he sent the people away into their
tents, glad and merry in heart for the goodness
that the LORD had shewed unto David, and to
Solomon, and to Israel his people.
11 Thus Solomon finished the house of the LORD,
and the king's house: and all that came into Sol-
omon's heart to make in the house of the LORD,
and in his own house, he prosperously effected.
12 ¶ And the LORD appeared to Solomon by
night, and said unto him, I have heard thy prayer,
and have chosen this place to myself for an house
of sacrifice.
13 If I shut up heaven that there be no rain, or if
I command the locusts to devour the land, or if I
send pestilence among my people;
14 If my people, which are called by my name,
shall humble themselves, and pray, and seek my
face, and turn from their wicked ways; then will I
hear from heaven, and will forgive their sin, and
will heal their land.
15 Now mine eyes shall be open, and mine ears
attent unto the prayer *that is made* in this place.
16 For now have I chosen and sanctified this
house, that my name may be there for ever:
and mine eyes and mine heart shall be there
perpetually.
17 And as for thee, if thou wilt walk before me, as
David thy father walked, and do according to all
that I have commanded thee, and shalt observe
my statutes and my judgments;
18 Then will I stablish the throne of thy kingdom,
according as I have covenanted with David thy
father, saying, There shall not fail thee a man *to
be* ruler in Israel.
19 But if ye turn away, and forsake my statutes
and my commandments, which I have set before
you, and shall go and serve other gods, and wor-
ship them;
20 Then will I pluck them up by the roots out of
my land which I have given them; and this house,
which I have sanctified for my name, will I cast
out of my sight, and will make it *to be* a proverb
and a byword among all nations.
21 And this house, which is high, shall be an as-
tonishment to every one that passeth by it; so that
he shall say, Why hath the LORD done thus unto
this land, and unto this house?
22 And it shall be answered, Because they forsook
the LORD God of their fathers, which brought
them forth out of the land of Egypt, and laid hold
on other gods, and worshipped them, and served
them: therefore hath he brought all this evil upon
them.

7:7 *hallowed.* Set apart as holy, consecrated for sacred use.
7:8 *Hamath unto the river of Egypt.* The extent of Solomon's kingdom.
7:9 *solemn assembly.* Religious gathering.
7:10 *merry in heart.* Great joy and gladness accompanied the dedication of the temple.
7:11 *he prosperously effected.* Solomon prospered in his work.
7:12 *appeared.* By deed and word, God confirmed the acceptance of Solomon and Israel. It is probable that this vision occurred thirteen years after the temple was dedicated (1 Kings 7:1; 9:1–2). *house of sacrifice.* This expression is only used here in the Bible and ties temple and sacrifice together.
7:14 *my people.* Israel was God's treasured, particular, and covenantal people among all nations. *heal their land.* Remove the curses and give the blessings according to the old covenant (Lev. 26; Deut. 28). Restoration can only come in the way of humiliation before God and putting sin to death.
7:15 *eyes . . . ears.* God takes notice (*attent*) of His people and their affairs.
7:17–22 *as for thee.* The singular (*thee, thou, thy*) refers to the king, and the plural (*ye, you, them, they*) to the nation. There is a close connection between the king and the nation, both in their obedience or disobedience, and in their blessing or curse from God. As goes the king, so goes the nation. Therefore, the future of God's *house* and Israel's inheritance in the *land* hinged upon the righteousness of the king.

Thoughts for Personal/Family Worship: Chapter 7

1. **Three great themes should direct our worship: adoration of God's glory, praise of God's faithful love, and repentance of our wicked ways (vv. 1–3,6,10,14). We should always come to worship with a sense that God is so glorious that we belong on our faces before Him. We should never approach the Lord without an inward brokenness and hatred of our sin against Him. Yet humility and contrition of sin should never take away our sense of joy in His goodness in Jesus Christ, the son of David (v. 10). Our constant refrain should be, "He is good; for his mercy endureth for ever" (v. 3). How can we cultivate in our worship a rich experience of God's love?**
2. **Israel's enjoyment of the temple and the land depended upon the obedience of their king, upon whom the Lord had focused the demands of His holy law. As the rest of Chronicles makes plain, no mere man could bear this burden; all sinned and sinned greatly. However, long after the covenant curses fell upon Israel, another Son of**

CHAPTER 8

AND it came to pass at the end of twenty years,
wherein Solomon had built the house of the
LORD, and his own house,
2 That the cities which Huram had restored to
Solomon, Solomon built them, and caused the
children of Israel to dwell there.
3 And Solomon went to Hamath-zobah, and
prevailed against it.
4 And he built Tadmor in the wilderness, and all
the store cities, which he built in Hamath.
5 Also he built Beth-horon the upper, and Beth-
horon the nether, fenced cities, with walls, gates,
and bars;
6 And Baalath, and all the store cities that Solo-
mon had, and all the chariot cities, and the cities
of the horsemen, and all that Solomon desired to
build in Jerusalem, and in Lebanon, and through-
out all the land of his dominion.
7 ¶ *As for* all the people *that were* left of the Hit-
tites, and the Amorites, and the Perizzites, and the
Hivites, and the Jebusites, which *were* not of Israel,
8 *But* of their children, who were left after them in
the land, whom the children of Israel consumed
not, them did Solomon make to pay tribute until
this day.
9 But of the children of Israel did Solomon make
no servants for his work; but they *were* men of
war, and chief of his captains, and captains of his
chariots and horsemen.
10 And these *were* the chief of king Solomon's
officers, *even* two hundred and fifty, that bare rule
over the people.
11 ¶ And Solomon brought up the daughter of
Pharaoh out of the city of David unto the house
that he had built for her: for he said, My wife shall
not dwell in the house of David king of Israel,
because *the places are* holy, whereunto the ark of
the LORD hath come.
12 ¶ Then Solomon offered burnt offerings unto
the LORD on the altar of the LORD, which he had
built before the porch,
13 Even after a certain rate every day, offering
according to the commandment of Moses, on
the sabbaths, and on the new moons, and on
the solemn feasts, three times in the year, *even* in
the feast of unleavened bread, and in the feast of
weeks, and in the feast of tabernacles.
14 ¶ And he appointed, according to the order
of David his father, the courses of the priests to
their service, and the Levites to their charges, to
praise and minister before the priests, as the duty
of every day required: the porters also by their
courses at every gate: for so had David the man of
God commanded.
15 And they departed not from the command-
ment of the king unto the priests and Levites con-
cerning any matter, or concerning the treasures.
16 Now all the work of Solomon was prepared
unto the day of the foundation of the house of
the LORD, and until it was finished. *So* the house
of the LORD was perfected.
17 ¶ Then went Solomon to Ezion-geber, and to
Eloth, at the sea side in the land of Edom.
18 And Huram sent him by the hands of his
servants ships, and servants that had knowledge
of the sea; and they went with the servants of
Solomon to Ophir, and took thence four hundred
and fifty talents of gold, and brought *them* to king
Solomon.

David came to the remnant. God sent His Son, born of a woman, born under the law, who fulfilled all righteousness. If we are in union with Him by a Spirit-worked faith, then we will enjoy God's presence forever in a better land than Canaan. Praise God for His faithfulness, that He has done it all in His Son.

Solomon's Works, Wisdom, and Death (2 Chron. 8:1—9:31)

Chapter 8: ***Solomon's other accomplishments are recorded after the completion of the temple and his own house. Solomon is greatly prospered by the hand of the Lord.***

8:1–6 Solomon worked to develop the *cities* of Israel.

8:2 *cities which Huram had restored to Solomon.* Solomon gave cities to Huram which did not please him (1 Kings 9:11–13). This might refer to another exchange of land, or to the return of those cities.

8:3–4 *Hamath-zobah.* A city about 120 miles north of Damascus. *Tadmor.* About 125 miles northeast of Damascus. These two cities formed the furthest boundaries of Solomon's kingdom and manifest the extent of Solomon's civil and economic rule over all Israel.

8:5 *Beth-horon the upper, and . . . the nether.* Upper and lower *Beth-horon* were northwest of Jerusalem above the Valley of Aijalon. The importance of these cities was their proximity to the international highway.

8:7–10 Solomon made the enemies of Israel into his forced laborers (*tribute*) to build and organize the cities of Israel.

8:13 *rate.* The number of offerings that the law of Moses prescribed for sacred times of worship.

8:14 *man of God.* Prophet (11:2; 25:7). David established a new order for the Levites based upon direct revelation from God (1 Chron. 28:12,19; Neh. 12:24). Solomon loved God and was careful in his early years to worship according to God's Word (1 Kings 3:3).

8:16 *perfected.* Completed.

8:18 *four hundred and fifty talents of gold.* With Solomon's kingdom established, Chronicles now begins to show the exceeding wealth of Solomon's kingdom.

Thoughts for Personal/Family Worship: Chapter 8

1. **Solomon's kingdom extended far to the north and south. Christ's kingdom is, however, all over this world. Since a sovereign's authority is limited to his borders, Christ's authority is absolute and universal. His kingdom has no borders. This gives Christians the right to preach the gospel and make disciples of Christ in all nations, regardless of whether the governments of those lands approve, for Christ is King of kings. How can you become involved in God's mission?**

CHAPTER 9

AND when the queen of Sheba heard of the fame
of Solomon, she came to prove Solomon with
hard questions at Jerusalem, with a very great
company, and camels that bare spices, and gold
in abundance, and precious stones: and when she
was come to Solomon, she communed with him
of all that was in her heart.
2 And Solomon told her all her questions: and
there was nothing hid from Solomon which he
told her not.
3 And when the queen of Sheba had seen the wis-
dom of Solomon, and the house that he had built,
4 And the meat of his table, and the sitting of his
servants, and the attendance of his ministers, and
their apparel; his cupbearers also, and their ap-
parel; and his ascent by which he went up into the
house of the LORD; there was no more spirit in her.
5 And she said to the king, *It was* a true report
which I heard in mine own land of thine acts, and
of thy wisdom:
6 Howbeit I believed not their words, until I
came, and mine eyes had seen *it*: and, behold, the
one half of the greatness of thy wisdom was not
told me: *for* thou exceedest the fame that I heard.
7 Happy *are* thy men, and happy *are* these thy
servants, which stand continually before thee, and
hear thy wisdom.
8 Blessed be the LORD thy God, which delighted
in thee to set thee on his throne, *to be* king for
the LORD thy God: because thy God loved Israel,
to establish them for ever, therefore made he thee
king over them, to do judgment and justice.
9 And she gave the king an hundred and twenty
talents of gold, and of spices great abundance,
and precious stones: neither was there any such
spice as the queen of Sheba gave king Solomon.
10 And the servants also of Huram, and the
servants of Solomon, which brought gold from
Ophir, brought algum trees and precious stones.
11 And the king made *of* the algum trees terraces
to the house of the LORD, and to the king's pal-
ace, and harps and psalteries for singers: and there
were none such seen before in the land of Judah.
12 And king Solomon gave to the queen of Sheba
all her desire, whatsoever she asked, beside *that*
which she had brought unto the king. So she
turned, and went away to her own land, she and
her servants.
13 ¶ Now the weight of gold that came to Solo-
mon in one year was six hundred and threescore
and six talents of gold;
14 Beside *that which* chapmen and merchants
brought. And all the kings of Arabia and gover-
nors of the country brought gold and silver to
Solomon.
15 ¶ And king Solomon made two hundred
targets *of* beaten gold: six hundred *shekels* of
beaten gold went to one target.
16 And three hundred shields *made he of* beaten
gold: three hundred *shekels* of gold went to one
shield. And the king put them in the house of the
forest of Lebanon.
17 Moreover the king made a great throne of
ivory, and overlaid it with pure gold.
18 And *there were* six steps to the throne, with
a footstool of gold, *which were* fastened to the
throne, and stays on each side of the sitting place,
and two lions standing by the stays:
19 And twelve lions stood there on the one side
and on the other upon the six steps. There was
not the like made in any kingdom.
20 ¶ And all the drinking vessels of king Solomon
were of gold, and all the vessels of the house of the
forest of Lebanon *were of* pure gold: none *were
of* silver; it was *not* any thing accounted of in the
days of Solomon.
21 For the king's ships went to Tarshish with the
servants of Huram: every three years once came
the ships of Tarshish bringing gold, and silver,
ivory, and apes, and peacocks.
22 And king Solomon passed all the kings of the
earth in riches and wisdom.
23 ¶ And all the kings of the earth sought the

2. From the Bible we know that Moses, David, and Solomon, all mentioned in this chapter, were preoccupied with the worship of God. Our lives will only be worthwhile to the extent that we are properly and biblically focused on the glory of God in all we say, do, or think. Let us not assume that we are living for God's glory, but search the Scriptures and worship by the Word. How can we bring more glory to God in our worship and in our lives?

Chapter 9: *These last recorded events of Solomon's life show his influence over the nations and his material prosperity.*

9:1 *Sheba.* Likely a place in Ethiopia. For this queen to come to Solomon shows that Solomon's fame had spread across the world. *communed.* Spoke.

9:4 *no more spirit.* We would say that it "took her breath away."

9:7–8 Solomon's wisdom was a gift of God's love for His people to establish His righteous kingdom (*judgment and justice*) among them—a type of Christ (Isa. 11:1–5).

9:8 *to be king for the LORD thy God.* God's kingdom comes to earth through David's throne.

9:9–12 An exchange of commodities was not uncommon, though Solomon used the gifts for the house of the Lord. *algum trees.* Sandalwood trees or junipers.

9:13–28 This is a record of the immense wealth and prosperity of Israel's golden years.

9:13 *six hundred and threescore and six.* 666.

9:14 *chapmen.* Explorers, those who traveled.

9:15 *targets.* Shields; larger than those of v. 16.

9:18 *stays.* Handrests.

9:22 *passed all the kings of the earth.* In fulfillment of God's promise to David and Solomon (1:12).

presence of Solomon, to hear his wisdom, that
God had put in his heart.
24 And they brought every man his present,
vessels of silver, and vessels of gold, and raiment,
harness, and spices, horses, and mules, a rate year
by year.
25 ¶ And Solomon had four thousand stalls for
horses and chariots, and twelve thousand horse-
men; whom he bestowed in the chariot cities, and
with the king at Jerusalem.
26 ¶ And he reigned over all the kings from the
river even unto the land of the Philistines, and to
the border of Egypt.
27 And the king made silver in Jerusalem as
stones, and cedar trees made he as the sycomore
trees that *are* in the low plains in abundance.
28 And they brought unto Solomon horses out of
Egypt, and out of all lands.
29 ¶ Now the rest of the acts of Solomon, first
and last, *are* they not written in the book of Na-
than the prophet, and in the prophecy of Ahijah
the Shilonite, and in the visions of Iddo the seer
against Jeroboam the son of Nebat?
30 And Solomon reigned in Jerusalem over all
Israel forty years.
31 And Solomon slept with his fathers, and he
was buried in the city of David his father: and
Rehoboam his son reigned in his stead.

CHAPTER 10

AND Rehoboam went to Shechem: for to Shechem
were all Israel come to make him king.
2 And it came to pass, when Jeroboam the son
of Nebat, who *was* in Egypt, whither he had fled
from the presence of Solomon the king, heard *it*,
that Jeroboam returned out of Egypt.
3 And they sent and called him. So Jeroboam and
all Israel came and spake to Rehoboam, saying,
4 Thy father made our yoke grievous: now there-
fore ease thou somewhat the grievous servitude
of thy father, and his heavy yoke that he put upon
us, and we will serve thee.
5 And he said unto them, Come again unto me
after three days. And the people departed.
6 ¶ And king Rehoboam took counsel with the
old men that had stood before Solomon his father
while he yet lived, saying, What counsel give ye *me*
to return answer to this people?
7 And they spake unto him, saying, If thou be
kind to this people, and please them, and speak
good words to them, they will be thy servants for
ever.
8 But he forsook the counsel which the old men
gave him, and took counsel with the young men
that were brought up with him, that stood before
him.
9 And he said unto them, What advice give ye
that we may return answer to this people, which
have spoken to me, saying, Ease somewhat the
yoke that thy father did put upon us?
10 And the young men that were brought up
with him spake unto him, saying, Thus shalt thou
answer the people that spake unto thee, saying,
Thy father made our yoke heavy, but make thou *it*
somewhat lighter for us; thus shalt thou say unto

9:23 *all the kings of the earth sought . . . Solomon.* Just as the temple served to draw the nations to pray to the Lord (6:32–33), so the wisdom of the king of Israel attracted the nations to praise *God* who gave it to him (v. 8).
9:24 *raiment.* Clothing, attire.
9:25 The multiplication of *horses* was forbidden to the king, especially horses from Egypt (v. 28, see note at 1:13–17).
9:29–30 *seer.* A designation for a prophet. The identity of *Iddo* is not known with certainty.

Thoughts for Personal/Family Worship: Chapter 9

The queen of Sheba marveled at the wisdom and wealth Solomon had from God. His wisdom attracted the attention of the world. Yet Solomon's kingdom pales in comparison to the kingdom of Christ, and it quickly faded after his death. How much more then should we marvel at the wisdom of Jesus Christ (Matt. 12:42; 13:54), who is anointed with the Spirit of wisdom (Isa. 11:2). In Christ are all the treasures of wisdom, and He is our wisdom if God has united us to Him (1 Cor. 1:30–31; Col. 2:3). Therefore, let us boast in Christ alone. The beauty of His wisdom will attract all nations to seek Him, so let us walk in His light, and make it shine to all the world (Isa. 2:1–5). Why is Christ's wisdom one of the greatest treasures of His kingdom? How can we showcase His wisdom in our families and church to win lost sinners?

KINGDOM DIVIDED (2 CHRON. 10:1—28:27)

King Rehoboam (2 Chron. 10:1—12:16)

Chapter 10: *Rehoboam follows the advice of his young counselors and as a result, the united kingdom of Israel becomes divided.*

10:1 *Shechem.* Rehoboam was crowned in *Shechem*, but David had been crowned in Hebron (1 Chron. 11:1). *all Israel.* Rehoboam's reign began on a positive note of unity, which shows all the more the seriousness of the division under his reign.
10:2 *fled from the presence of Solomon.* Chronicles has passed over Solomon's idolatry, the Lord's appointment of Jeroboam to take part of the kingdom, and Solomon's attempt to kill Jeroboam (1 Kings 11).
10:3 *all Israel.* The contrast to v. 1 is striking: for the most part, Israel united behind Jeroboam.
10:4 *made our yoke grievous.* Solomon placed heavy demands on the people to maintain his administration and projects. Israel was bartering the terms of kingship with Rehoboam.
10:6–7 *be kind.* Literally, "be for good." The *old* counselors advised the king to show his intent to lead the people for their good. Though rulers commonly use people for their own profit (1 Sam. 8:10–18), God intended that the rulers over His people be a blessing to them (2:11; 9:8; Mark 10:42–45).
10:8–11 *young men.* Rehoboam listened to his less mature counselors and boasted that his power would far exceed his father's kingdom (*little finger shall be thicker*).

them, My little *finger* shall be thicker than my
father's loins.
11 For whereas my father put a heavy yoke upon
you, I will put more to your yoke: my father chas-
tised you with whips, but I *will chastise you* with
scorpions.
12 So Jeroboam and all the people came to Re-
hoboam on the third day, as the king bade, saying,
Come again to me on the third day.
13 And the king answered them roughly; and
king Rehoboam forsook the counsel of the old
men,
14 And answered them after the advice of the
young men, saying, My father made your yoke
heavy, but I will add thereto: my father chas-
tised you with whips, but I *will chastise you* with
scorpions.
15 So the king hearkened not unto the people:
for the cause was of God, that the LORD might
perform his word, which he spake by the hand
of Ahijah the Shilonite to Jeroboam the son of
Nebat.
16 ¶ And when all Israel *saw* that the king would
not hearken unto them, the people answered the
king, saying, What portion have we in David? and
we have none inheritance in the son of Jesse: every
man to your tents, O Israel: *and* now, David, see to
thine own house. So all Israel went to their tents.
17 But *as for* the children of Israel that dwelt in
the cities of Judah, Rehoboam reigned over them.
18 Then king Rehoboam sent Hadoram that *was*
over the tribute; and the children of Israel stoned
him with stones, that he died. But king Rehoboam
made speed to get him up to *his* chariot, to flee to
Jerusalem.
19 And Israel rebelled against the house of David
unto this day.

CHAPTER 11

AND when Rehoboam was come to Jerusalem,
he gathered of the house of Judah and Benjamin
an hundred and fourscore thousand chosen *men*,
which were warriors, to fight against Israel, that
he might bring the kingdom again to Rehoboam.
2 But the word of the LORD came to Shemaiah
the man of God, saying,
3 Speak unto Rehoboam the son of Solomon,
king of Judah, and to all Israel in Judah and Ben-
jamin, saying,
4 Thus saith the LORD, Ye shall not go up, nor
fight against your brethren: return every man to
his house: for this thing is done of me. And they
obeyed the words of the LORD, and returned from
going against Jeroboam.
5 ¶ And Rehoboam dwelt in Jerusalem, and built
cities for defence in Judah.
6 He built even Beth-lehem, and Etam, and Tekoa,
7 And Beth-zur, and Shoco, and Adullam,
8 And Gath, and Mareshah, and Ziph,
9 And Adoraim, and Lachish, and Azekah,
10 And Zorah, and Aijalon, and Hebron, which
are in Judah and in Benjamin fenced cities.
11 And he fortified the strong holds, and put
captains in them, and store of victual, and of oil
and wine.

10:12 *bade.* Invited.
10:15 *hearkened.* Listened. *the cause was of God.* Though Rehoboam was responsible for his folly, God's sovereign hand directed it. Thus Scripture explains the division of Israel on two levels: the political cause from men, and the divine cause ruling over men.
10:16 *What portion have we in David?* The rejection of David's line was a sign of unbelief in the promise (13:5). *all Israel went to their tents.* Israel remained divided from Judah until the exile of the northern tribes (722 BC).
10:18 *tribute.* The forced laborers. Rehoboam appears not to understand the crisis until the death of his taskmaster.
10:19 *rebelled against the house of David.* The division was not merely political, but it was rebellion against the covenant God made with David, "The LORD will build thee an house" (1 Chron. 17:10).

Thoughts for Personal/Family Worship: Chapter 10

1. **It is remarkable that Rehoboam, the son of Solomon, threw away his father's wisdom: "A soft answer turneth away wrath: but grievous words stir up anger" (Prov. 15:1). We often confuse meekness with weakness. Moses was a great leader, but the meekest man on earth (Num. 12:3). It is far wiser for leaders to exercise their authority with love and humility, listening to legitimate complaints from people, than to try to rule by sheer force. On the other hand, the people took Rehoboam's pride as an occasion to throw away their inheritance in Christ. Beware of a spirit of rebellion against authority, for it often hides wicked unbelief toward God. Can you think of examples of both kinds of leadership in the people around you?**
2. **The Bible teaches us to view history and contemporary events through a double perspective. On the one hand, we see the human causes, and acknowledge the responsibility of each person for his own attitude and actions. On the other hand, the believer sees the divine cause ruling over all, using even sin to accomplish His righteous purposes. How does this teach us both to fear the Lord and to hope in His mercy?**

Chapter 11: *Rehoboam solidifies his kingdom and builds up Judah militarily, while the Levites resort to Judah as the religious center of Israel.*

11:1 *an hundred and fourscore thousand.* 180,000 (a score is twenty).
11:4 *this thing is done of me.* The Lord stopped Rehoboam's plan to reunite Judah and Israel by declaring His sovereign control over the division.
11:5–12 Rehoboam fortified and strengthened the cities for war, showing that Solomon's peace was shattered and Israel no longer enjoyed the promised rest (1 Chron. 22:8–9,18; 23:25).
11:10 *fenced cities.* Fortified cities or fortresses.
11:11 *store of victual.* Supplies of food.

12 And in every several city *he put* shields and
spears, and made them exceeding strong, having
Judah and Benjamin on his side.
13 ¶ And the priests and the Levites that *were* in
all Israel resorted to him out of all their coasts.
14 For the Levites left their suburbs and their
possession, and came to Judah and Jerusalem: for
Jeroboam and his sons had cast them off from
executing the priest's office unto the LORD:
15 And he ordained him priests for the high
places, and for the devils, and for the calves which
he had made.
16 And after them out of all the tribes of Israel
such as set their hearts to seek the LORD God of
Israel came to Jerusalem, to sacrifice unto the
LORD God of their fathers.
17 So they strengthened the kingdom of Judah,
and made Rehoboam the son of Solomon strong,
three years: for three years they walked in the way
of David and Solomon.
18 ¶ And Rehoboam took him Mahalath the
daughter of Jerimoth the son of David to wife,
and Abihail the daughter of Eliab the son of Jesse;
19 Which bare him children; Jeush, and Shama-
riah, and Zaham.
20 And after her he took Maachah the daughter
of Absalom; which bare him Abijah, and Attai,
and Ziza, and Shelomith.
21 And Rehoboam loved Maachah the daugh-
ter of Absalom above all his wives and his concu-
bines: (for he took eighteen wives, and threescore
concubines; and begat twenty and eight sons, and
threescore daughters.)
22 And Rehoboam made Abijah the son of
Maachah the chief, *to be* ruler among his brethren:
for *he thought* to make him king.
23 And he dealt wisely, and dispersed of all his
children throughout all the countries of Judah
and Benjamin, unto every fenced city: and he
gave them victual in abundance. And he desired
many wives.

CHAPTER 12

AND it came to pass, when Rehoboam had
established the kingdom, and had strengthened
himself, he forsook the law of the LORD, and all
Israel with him.
2 And it came to pass, *that* in the fifth year of
king Rehoboam Shishak king of Egypt came up
against Jerusalem, because they had transgressed
against the LORD,
3 With twelve hundred chariots, and threescore
thousand horsemen: and the people *were* without
number that came with him out of Egypt; the
Lubims, the Sukkiims, and the Ethiopians.
4 And he took the fenced cities which *pertained*
to Judah, and came to Jerusalem.
5 ¶ Then came Shemaiah the prophet to Re-
hoboam, and *to* the princes of Judah, that were
gathered together to Jerusalem because of
Shishak, and said unto them, Thus saith the LORD,
Ye have forsaken me, and therefore have I also left
you in the hand of Shishak.
6 Whereupon the princes of Israel and the king
humbled themselves; and they said, The LORD *is*
righteous.
7 And when the LORD saw that they humbled
themselves, the word of the LORD came to She-
maiah, saying, They have humbled themselves;
therefore I will not destroy them, but I will grant
them some deliverance; and my wrath shall not

11:13–17 The Levites' godliness contrasts with Jeroboam's idolatry and apostasy. The Levites strengthened the nation of Judah by joining themselves to them and carrying out the worship and temple service required of the faithful people.
11:13 *resorted to him*. Presented themselves to him. *coasts*. Regions.
11:15 *ordained him priests . . . for the calves*. Jeroboam enticed Israel to follow humanly invented worship and idols (1 Kings 12:26–33). This sin became the standard by which future kings of Israel would be evaluated. *devils*. Literally, "goats," perhaps a reference to idols or demons.
11:16 *such as set their hearts to seek the LORD*. Not all Israel followed in the idol worship, but some remained faithful to pursue God's presence through His priesthood and temple.
11:23 *he desired many wives*. Rehoboam was following in his father's tragic footsteps.

Thoughts for Personal/Family Worship: Chapter 11

Shortly after renouncing the house of David, the northern tribes turned to false worship and idolatry from which they never recovered. The path of apostasy is a dreadful slide to hell. Faithfulness to Christ as the king of the church is inseparable from faithfulness in worship to God. If we begin to replace the authority of the Word of Christ with human ideas, then we will soon replace God-glorifying worship with idols. Why is this so? How can we guard against it?

Chapter 12: *The rest and peace under Solomon further unravels as Rehoboam forsakes the Lord and finds Egypt plundering Jerusalem.*

12:1 *established . . . strengthened . . . forsook the law of the LORD*. Pride and self-sufficiency leads to disobedience to God (25:16; 26:16), including idolatry and sexual perversion (1 Kings 14:21–24).
12:2 *transgressed*. The Hebrew literally means "committed a breach of faith," the same word used for Saul's treachery against God (1 Chron. 10:13).
12:3 *without number*. So many, they could not be counted. This had been the promise to Abraham regarding his seed (Gen. 13:16); however, this reality now applied to the enemy.
12:4 *took the fenced cities*. Rehoboam's defensive measures (11:5–12) meant nothing when God brought judgment through Shishak.
12:6–7 *The LORD is righteous*. A fundamental part of humble confession and repentance, so that God turned back His *wrath*, an answer to Solomon's earlier intercession (6:24–31).

be poured out upon Jerusalem by the hand of
Shishak.
8 Nevertheless they shall be his servants; that
they may know my service, and the service of the
kingdoms of the countries.
9 So Shishak king of Egypt came up against
Jerusalem, and took away the treasures of the
house of the LORD, and the treasures of the king's
house; he took all: he carried away also the shields
of gold which Solomon had made.
10 Instead of which king Rehoboam made shields
of brass, and committed *them* to the hands of the
chief of the guard, that kept the entrance of the
king's house.
11 And when the king entered into the house of
the LORD, the guard came and fetched them, and
brought them again into the guard chamber.
12 And when he humbled himself, the wrath of
the LORD turned from him, that he would not
destroy *him* altogether: and also in Judah things
went well.
13 ¶ So king Rehoboam strengthened himself in
Jerusalem, and reigned: for Rehoboam *was* one
and forty years old when he began to reign, and
he reigned seventeen years in Jerusalem, the city
which the LORD had chosen out of all the tribes
of Israel, to put his name there. And his mother's
name *was* Naamah an Ammonitess.
14 And he did evil, because he prepared not his
heart to seek the LORD.
15 Now the acts of Rehoboam, first and last, *are*
they not written in the book of Shemaiah the
prophet, and of Iddo the seer concerning gene-
alogies? And *there were* wars between Rehoboam
and Jeroboam continually.
16 And Rehoboam slept with his fathers, and was
buried in the city of David: and Abijah his son
reigned in his stead.

CHAPTER 13

NOW in the eighteenth year of king Jeroboam
began Abijah to reign over Judah.
2 He reigned three years in Jerusalem. His
mother's name also *was* Michaiah the daughter
of Uriel of Gibeah. And there was war between
Abijah and Jeroboam.
3 And Abijah set the battle in array with an army
of valiant men of war, *even* four hundred thou-
sand chosen men: Jeroboam also set the battle in
array against him with eight hundred thousand
chosen men, *being* mighty men of valour.
4 ¶ And Abijah stood up upon mount Zemaraim,
which *is* in mount Ephraim, and said, Hear me,
thou Jeroboam, and all Israel;
5 Ought ye not to know that the LORD God of
Israel gave the kingdom over Israel to David for
ever, *even* to him and to his sons by a covenant
of salt?
6 Yet Jeroboam the son of Nebat, the servant of
Solomon the son of David, is risen up, and hath
rebelled against his lord.
7 And there are gathered unto him vain men, the
children of Belial, and have strengthened them-
selves against Rehoboam the son of Solomon,
when Rehoboam was young and tenderhearted,
and could not withstand them.
8 And now ye think to withstand the kingdom of
the LORD in the hand of the sons of David; and ye
be a great multitude, and *there are* with you golden
calves, which Jeroboam made you for gods.
9 Have ye not cast out the priests of the LORD,

12:9–10 *made shields of brass.* The degradation of the kingdom vividly appears in the replacement of Solomon's *shields of gold* (9:16) with Rehoboam's *shields of brass* or bronze. Since *gold* is closely associated with God's holiness in the temple (chs. 3–4), this also suggests a religious decline.

12:13 *his mother's name was Naamah an Ammonitess.* A reminder of how Solomon's marriages to wicked women harmed the kingdom for generations.

12:14 *he did evil.* Despite his repentance, Rehoboam's reign was summarized as one of wickedness. *prepared not his heart to seek the LORD.* He lacked the grace for which David prayed (1 Chron. 29:18).

12:16 *Abijah.* Or Abijam; not Rehoboam's firstborn, but his son by Maachah (11:18–20). *stead.* Place.

Thoughts for Personal/Family Worship: Chapter 12

God blesses those who humble themselves and repent of their sins, confessing that God is right in all the hardships He sent upon them. Whatever your sins may be, repentance is the only path of escape from God's wrath. Do not cling to your pride. When Rehoboam proudly turned away from serving the Lord, he found himself serving the wicked king of Egypt. We all serve someone, and rebellion against God only puts us under a far worse master. Do not trade your gold for bronze. The service of the Lord is the best service we could ever be in, for Christ's yoke is easy and his burden is light (Matt. 11:30). How does this chapter encourage you to repentance?

Chapter 13: ***Under Abijah, the south wins a major victory against the north, as the Lord hears the prayer of Judah for help.***

King Abijah (2 Chron. 13:1–22)

13:3 *war.* See 1 Kings 14:30; 15:6. Judah was outnumbered two to one.

13:5 *covenant of salt.* Likely meaning "an enduring covenant" (Num. 18:19), clearly a reference to God's promise to *David* and *his sons* (1 Chron. 17). War against the house of David was rebellion against God.

13:7 The author records the fight in terms of righteousness and wickedness. Though there was sin on both sides, God remembered His covenant with David. *children of Belial.* Wicked or worthless people. *tenderhearted.* Weak, inexperienced.

13:8 *kingdom of the LORD in the hand of the sons of David.* Judah's kingdom was God's kingdom, which He ruled through the Davidic king as His representative.

13:9 *manner.* Custom, habit. The people of Israel had dese-

the sons of Aaron, and the Levites, and have made
you priests after the manner of the nations of
other lands? so that whosoever cometh to consecrate himself with a young bullock and seven
rams, *the same* may be a priest of *them that are*
no gods.
10 But as for us, the LORD *is* our God, and we have
not forsaken him; and the priests, which minister unto the LORD, *are* the sons of Aaron, and the
Levites *wait* upon *their* business:
11 And they burn unto the LORD every morning
and every evening burnt sacrifices and sweet
incense: the shewbread also *set they in order* upon
the pure table; and the candlestick of gold with
the lamps thereof, to burn every evening: for we
keep the charge of the LORD our God; but ye have
forsaken him.
12 And, behold, God himself *is* with us for *our*
captain, and his priests with sounding trumpets
to cry alarm against you. O children of Israel,
fight ye not against the LORD God of your fathers;
for ye shall not prosper.
13 ¶ But Jeroboam caused an ambushment to
come about behind them: so they were before
Judah, and the ambushment *was* behind them.
14 And when Judah looked back, behold, the battle *was* before and behind: and they cried unto the
LORD, and the priests sounded with the trumpets.
15 Then the men of Judah gave a shout: and as
the men of Judah shouted, it came to pass, that
God smote Jeroboam and all Israel before Abijah
and Judah.
16 And the children of Israel fled before Judah:
and God delivered them into their hand.
17 And Abijah and his people slew them with a
great slaughter: so there fell down slain of Israel
five hundred thousand chosen men.
18 Thus the children of Israel were brought under
at that time, and the children of Judah prevailed,
because they relied upon the LORD God of their
fathers.
19 And Abijah pursued after Jeroboam, and took
cities from him, Beth-el with the towns thereof,
and Jeshanah with the towns thereof, and Ephrain
with the towns thereof.
20 Neither did Jeroboam recover strength again
in the days of Abijah: and the LORD struck him,
and he died.
21 ¶ But Abijah waxed mighty, and married fourteen wives, and begat twenty and two sons, and
sixteen daughters.
22 And the rest of the acts of Abijah, and his ways,
and his sayings, *are* written in the story of the
prophet Iddo.

CHAPTER 14

SO Abijah slept with his fathers, and they buried
him in the city of David: and Asa his son reigned
in his stead. In his days the land was quiet ten
years.
2 And Asa did *that which was* good and right in
the eyes of the LORD his God:
3 For he took away the altars of the strange *gods*,
and the high places, and brake down the images,
and cut down the groves:
4 And commanded Judah to seek the LORD
God of their fathers, and to do the law and the
commandment.
5 Also he took away out of all the cities of Judah
the high places and the images: and the kingdom
was quiet before him.
6 ¶ And he built fenced cities in Judah: for the
land had rest, and he had no war in those years;
because the LORD had given him rest.
7 Therefore he said unto Judah, Let us build

crated the priestly office instituted by the Lord and created their own priesthood, but the idols set up by Jeroboam were *no gods* (1 Cor. 8:4–6).

13:10 *we have not forsaken him.* Judah still lived under the divinely instituted worship of God with His *priests*, marks of the true people of God. However, Abijah overlooked the sins of Solomon and Rehoboam, not to mention himself (1 Kings 15:3).

13:13 *ambushment.* A cunning strategy of surrounding Judah's army by surprise.

13:14 *priests sounded with the trumpets.* A form of priestly intercession before the Lord so that He would save His people from their enemies (Num. 10:8–9). Holding to God's priests (v. 10) brought God's help.

13:18 *they relied upon the LORD God.* Literally, they "rested" or "leaned" on Him (14:11)—the essence of faith (Prov. 3:5). They did so by looking to God's covenant (v. 5) and crying out to God in earnest prayer (v. 14), and God saved them against the odds.

Thoughts for Personal/Family Worship: Chapter 13

1. **If we would count ourselves God's people and look for His help, we must hold to God's appointed king, the son of David, and cling to God's commanded form of worship through His appointed priest. The true church is defined by its submission to Jesus Christ as its head and by its worship of the true God through His righteousness (Eph. 5:23–24; Phil. 3:3; Heb. 13:15). Spend some time giving your "sacrifice of praise to God."**
2. **The key to experiencing God's salvation is relying upon the Lord (v. 18) through heartfelt prayer (v. 14). When we rely on God, no matter how weak we are, we are strong (2 Cor. 12:10). Therefore, the greatest danger we face is our own pride, for its leads to self-sufficiency. How can we develop a heart of humble reliance upon the Lord?**

King Asa (2 Chron. 14:1—16:14)

Chapter 14: ***Asa reigns and wins a surprising victory over the Ethiopians.***

14:1 *stead.* Place.

14:3 *strange gods.* Foreign gods. *groves.* The Hebrew is sometimes translated as "Asherim," wooden poles that represented Asherah, the Canaanite goddess associated with fertility. The people of Israel and Judah were often led astray worshiping

these cities, and make about *them* walls, and
towers, gates, and bars, *while* the land *is* yet before
us; because we have sought the LORD our God,
we have sought *him*, and he hath given us rest on
every side. So they built and prospered.
8 And Asa had an army *of men* that bare targets
and spears, out of Judah three hundred thousand;
and out of Benjamin, that bare shields and drew
bows, two hundred and fourscore thousand: all
these *were* mighty men of valour.
9 ¶ And there came out against them Zerah
the Ethiopian with an host of a thousand thou-
sand, and three hundred chariots; and came unto
Mareshah.
10 Then Asa went out against him, and they set
the battle in array in the valley of Zephathah at
Mareshah.
11 And Asa cried unto the LORD his God, and
said, LORD, *it is* nothing with thee to help, whether
with many, or with them that have no power: help
us, O LORD our God; for we rest on thee, and in
thy name we go against this multitude. O LORD,
thou *art* our God; let not man prevail against thee.
12 So the LORD smote the Ethiopians before Asa,
and before Judah; and the Ethiopians fled.
13 And Asa and the people that *were* with him
pursued them unto Gerar: and the Ethiopians
were overthrown, that they could not recover
themselves; for they were destroyed before the
LORD, and before his host; and they carried away
very much spoil.
14 And they smote all the cities round about
Gerar; for the fear of the LORD came upon them:
and they spoiled all the cities; for there was ex-
ceeding much spoil in them.
15 They smote also the tents of cattle, and
carried away sheep and camels in abundance, and
returned to Jerusalem.

CHAPTER 15

AND the Spirit of God came upon Azariah the son
of Oded:
2 And he went out to meet Asa, and said unto
him, Hear ye me, Asa, and all Judah and Benja-
min; The LORD *is* with you, while ye be with him;
and if ye seek him, he will be found of you; but if
ye forsake him, he will forsake you.
3 Now for a long season Israel *hath been* without
the true God, and without a teaching priest, and
without law.
4 But when they in their trouble did turn unto
the LORD God of Israel, and sought him, he was
found of them.
5 And in those times *there was* no peace to him
that went out, nor to him that came in, but great
vexations *were* upon all the inhabitants of the
countries.
6 And nation was destroyed of nation, and city of
city: for God did vex them with all adversity.
7 Be ye strong therefore, and let not your hands
be weak: for your work shall be rewarded.
8 And when Asa heard these words, and the
prophecy of Oded the prophet, he took courage,

these poles (15:16; 17:6; 19:3; 24:18).

14:7 *land is yet before us.* The Lord had not taken away the land because they *sought* Him in repentance from idolatry and obedience to His laws (vv. 3–4). *given us rest.* War had marred Judah's history since Rehoboam, but under Asa's reforms, the Lord had restored peace (see note at 11:5–12).

14:9 *Zerah the Ethiopian.* Otherwise unknown in biblical records. *thousand thousand.* One million troops. To put it mildly, this was an overwhelming force.

14:11 *it is nothing with thee to help.* With God's salvation it does not matter whether one has many resources or few (1 Sam. 14:6), for He is the all-sufficient *God*, and His enemies are mere *man* (Isa. 31:3). *we rest on thee.* Same verb as "relied" (13:18; 16:7).

14:13 *the LORD, and . . . his host.* The armies of the faithful son of David are the armies of God (see note at 1 Chron. 11:9), and God's terror and destroying power fall upon their enemies (vv. 12,14).

14:14 *the fear of the LORD.* Not the word typically used of godly reverence; here it refers to the dread and terror God places upon His enemies (Gen. 35:5; Ex. 15:16; Deut. 28:67; 1 Chron. 14:17; 2 Chron. 17:10; 19:7; 20:29). The Lord had promised to send this terror with Israel to ensure their victory over the nations (Deut. 2:25; 11:25; cf. Est. 8:17; 9:2–3; Pss. 14:5; 105:38).

Thoughts for Personal/Family Worship: Chapter 14

1. **Asa's religion was not just positive in the sense that he sought the Lord and encouraged others to seek the Lord. He also tore down institutions of false worship. This would have made some unhappy, but Asa had a comprehensive and thoroughgoing view of what God demands of us. Faithful service to the Lord requires us to oppose what is evil. How can we be this proactive in our culture? What obstacles do we face?**
2. **What seemed to be a terrifying threat turned into a remarkable blessing through the Lord's delivering hand. Powerless in himself, Asa entrusted himself to the powerful God. When our troubles stir anxiety in our hearts, let us bring our concerns to God with believing, thankful prayer, and His peace will guard us (Phil. 4:6–7). What concerns can you bring before the Lord today?**

Chapter 15: *Asa also made many religious reforms.*

15:1 *Spirit of God came upon.* The Holy Spirit empowered *Azariah* to speak God's Word as a prophet, not in predicting the future, but in pressing the claims and promises of God's covenant.

15:2 *if ye seek him.* The idea of seeking God appears throughout this chapter (vv. 4,12–13,15). To seek God is to draw near to Him in worship and prayer with desire, reliance, repentance, and submission (see Introduction to 1 and 2 Chronicles: Synopsis).

15:3 *a long season Israel hath been without . . . a teaching priest.* The days of the judges after Joshua and before Samuel, a period of spiritual ignorance and decline.

15:5 *vexations.* Troubles, afflictions.

15:6 *vex.* Trouble.

15:7–8 *Be ye strong . . . took courage.* Both translate the same Hebrew verb. This echoes David's charge to Solomon (1 Chron. 22:13; 28:10,20).

and put away the abominable idols out of all the
land of Judah and Benjamin, and out of the cities
which he had taken from mount Ephraim, and
renewed the altar of the LORD, that *was* before the
porch of the LORD.
9 And he gathered all Judah and Benjamin, and
the strangers with them out of Ephraim and
Manasseh, and out of Simeon: for they fell to him
out of Israel in abundance, when they saw that the
LORD his God *was* with him.
10 So they gathered themselves together at Jerusalem in the third month, in the fifteenth year of
the reign of Asa.
11 And they offered unto the LORD the same
time, of the spoil *which* they had brought, seven
hundred oxen and seven thousand sheep.
12 And they entered into a covenant to seek the
LORD God of their fathers with all their heart and
with all their soul;
13 That whosoever would not seek the LORD God
of Israel should be put to death, whether small or
great, whether man or woman.
14 And they sware unto the LORD with a loud
voice, and with shouting, and with trumpets, and
with cornets.
15 And all Judah rejoiced at the oath: for they had
sworn with all their heart, and sought him with
their whole desire; and he was found of them: and
the LORD gave them rest round about.
16 ¶ And also *concerning* Maachah the mother of
Asa the king, he removed her from *being* queen,
because she had made an idol in a grove: and Asa
cut down her idol, and stamped *it*, and burnt *it* at
the brook Kidron.
17 But the high places were not taken away out
of Israel: nevertheless the heart of Asa was perfect
all his days.
18 ¶ And he brought into the house of God the
things that his father had dedicated, and that he
himself had dedicated, silver, and gold, and vessels.
19 And there was no *more* war unto the five and
thirtieth year of the reign of Asa.

CHAPTER 16

IN the six and thirtieth year of the reign of Asa
Baasha king of Israel came up against Judah, and
built Ramah, to the intent that he might let none
go out or come in to Asa king of Judah.
2 Then Asa brought out silver and gold out of
the treasures of the house of the LORD and of the
king's house, and sent to Ben-hadad king of Syria,
that dwelt at Damascus, saying,
3 *There is* a league between me and thee, as *there*
was between my father and thy father: behold, I
have sent thee silver and gold; go, break thy league
with Baasha king of Israel, that he may depart
from me.
4 And Ben-hadad hearkened unto king Asa, and
sent the captains of his armies against the cities of
Israel; and they smote Ijon, and Dan, and Abel-maim, and all the store cities of Naphtali.
5 And it came to pass, when Baasha heard *it*, that
he left off building of Ramah, and let his work
cease.
6 Then Asa the king took all Judah; and they
carried away the stones of Ramah, and the timber
thereof, wherewith Baasha was building; and he
built therewith Geba and Mizpah.
7 ¶ And at that time Hanani the seer came to Asa
king of Judah, and said unto him, Because thou
hast relied on the king of Syria, and not relied on
the LORD thy God, therefore is the host of the king
of Syria escaped out of thine hand.

15:9 *they fell to him out of Israel in abundance.* God's presence with the godly king motivated many from the northern kingdom of Israel to defect to the Lord's kingdom in the south.
15:12 *entered into a covenant.* Not a new or man-made covenant, but a renewed and public commitment to keep the covenant the Lord already had made with *their fathers* (23:16; 29:10; 34:21).
15:15 *rest.* Salvation from enemies and enjoyment of God's presence, an allusion to the peace of Solomon (1 Chron. 22:8–10) and a shadow of the peace of Christ's kingdom.
15:16 *Maachah.* As queen mother, Maachah would normally have had significant influence. *brook Kidron.* The brook was outside Jerusalem and a common place for dumping refuse.
15:17 *heart of Asa was perfect.* His love and loyalty was not divided between the Lord and idols.

Thoughts for Personal/Family Worship: Chapter 15

1. **This chapter gives us a vivid picture of a major theme in Chronicles: seeking God. All people pursue something, and ours is meant to be the pursuit of God in Christ (Phil. 3:12–14). What does it mean to seek God? Asa's example shows that we seek God by finding strength and courage in God's promises, by removing idols from our lives and circles of influence, and by worshiping God with all our hearts in the ways He commands in His covenant. What would it mean in your life to seek the Lord with all your soul?**
2. **Asa showed remarkable consistency, removing his own mother from her royal position because she promoted idolatry (v. 16). Reformation must begin in the home before it can take root in the church or nation. This can be extremely costly, but Christ taught us that His disciples must hate their parents and families in comparison to their love for Him (Luke 14:26).**

Chapter 16: ***The events of the latter part of Asa's reign show a number of his faults.***

16:2 *brought out . . . of the treasures of the house of the LORD.* Asa will be reprimanded for failing to trust in God to deliver them (vv. 7–8). *Ben-hadad.* This name, meaning "son of Hadad," was likely a title for the *king of Syria.* Hadad was the Baal of the area.
16:3 *league.* Covenant, treaty.
16:7 *relied on the king of Syria.* Asa had wandered from his earlier trust in the Lord (14:11) and had esteemed the help of

8 Were not the Ethiopians and the Lubims a huge
host, with very many chariots and horsemen? yet,
because thou didst rely on the LORD, he delivered
them into thine hand.
9 For the eyes of the LORD run to and fro through-
out the whole earth, to shew himself strong in the
behalf of *them* whose heart *is* perfect toward him.
Herein thou hast done foolishly: therefore from
henceforth thou shalt have wars.
10 Then Asa was wroth with the seer, and put him
in a prison house; for *he was* in a rage with him
because of this *thing*. And Asa oppressed *some* of
the people the same time.
11 ¶ And, behold, the acts of Asa, first and last, lo,
they *are* written in the book of the kings of Judah
and Israel.
12 And Asa in the thirty and ninth year of his
reign was diseased in his feet, until his disease *was*
exceeding *great*: yet in his disease he sought not to
the LORD, but to the physicians.
13 ¶ And Asa slept with his fathers, and died in
the one and fortieth year of his reign.
14 And they buried him in his own sepulchres,
which he had made for himself in the city of
David, and laid him in the bed which was filled
with sweet odours and divers kinds *of spices*
prepared by the apothecaries' art: and they made
a very great burning for him.

CHAPTER 17

AND Jehoshaphat his son reigned in his stead, and
strengthened himself against Israel.
2 And he placed forces in all the fenced cities of
Judah, and set garrisons in the land of Judah, and
in the cities of Ephraim, which Asa his father had
taken.
3 And the LORD was with Jehoshaphat, because
he walked in the first ways of his father David, and
sought not unto Baalim;
4 But sought to the *LORD* God of his father, and
walked in his commandments, and not after the
doings of Israel.
5 Therefore the LORD stablished the kingdom in
his hand; and all Judah brought to Jehoshaphat
presents; and he had riches and honour in
abundance.
6 And his heart was lifted up in the ways of the
LORD: moreover he took away the high places and
groves out of Judah.
7 ¶ Also in the third year of his reign he sent to
his princes, *even* to Ben-hail, and to Obadiah, and
to Zechariah, and to Nethaneel, and to Michaiah,
to teach in the cities of Judah.
8 And with them *he sent* Levites, *even* Shemaiah,
and Nethaniah, and Zebadiah, and Asahel, and
Shemiramoth, and Jehonathan, and Adonijah,
and Tobijah, and Tob-adonijah, Levites; and with
them Elishama and Jehoram, priests.
9 And they taught in Judah, and *had* the book of
the law of the LORD with them, and went about
throughout all the cities of Judah, and taught the
people.
10 ¶ And the fear of the LORD fell upon all the
kingdoms of the lands that *were* round about Ju-
dah, so that they made no war against Jehoshaphat.
11 Also *some* of the Philistines brought Jehoshaphat
presents, and tribute silver; and the Arabians

Syria to be of greater value than the help of God.

16:9 *run to and fro throughout the whole earth.* God's knowledge (*eyes*) reaches all His creation, like travelers visiting every place in *the whole earth* to see what happens there (Zech. 4:10; Rev. 5:6), even the thoughts and motives of the *heart* (Jer. 17:10). *perfect.* Not sinless (6:36), but trusting in the Lord alone, and not men or their works. *thou shalt have wars.* God removed His gift of "rest" (15:15).

16:10 *wroth.* Angry. He added sin to his sin by condemning the *seer*, or prophet, to prison for his truthful words, and persecuting *some of the people* as well.

16:14 *divers.* Diverse, various. *apothecaries.* Embalmers, perfumers. *very great burning.* Perhaps a bonfire with fragrant spices to honor him and lament his death (21:19; Jer. 34:5).

Thoughts for Personal/Family Worship: Chapter 16

1. **Asa was not constant in his faithfulness. The backsliding of a godly man into inconsistency is perplexing to all who know him. Pride and unrepentance can turn a good leader into a stubborn oppressor. The end of a matter is more important than the beginning. We need God's grace to finish well. In particular, Asa's sins sprang from weakness of faith in God's promises, and resting his hope in man. How can we stay alert against such misplaced trust?**
2. **We have here a magnificent promise: "For the eyes of the LORD run to and fro throughout the whole earth, to shew himself strong in the behalf of them whose heart is perfect toward him" (v. 9). God engages His knowledge of all things and His infinite power to strongly support every man, woman, or child who trusts in Him alone. How does this promise show the foolishness and wickedness of trusting in man? How does it encourage us to look to the Lord?**

King Jehoshaphat (2 Chron. 17:1—20:37)

Chapter 17: *Jehoshaphat walks in the steps of his father David.*

17:3–17 This section outlines the religious, civil, economic, and militaristic prosperity of Jehoshaphat.

17:3–9 Jehoshaphat was a model king like *David* who *sought* the Lord and removed idols. *Baalim.* Plural of Baal, meaning lord or master, the chief god worshiped in a particular location.

17:6 *heart was lifted up.* An expression usually of pride (25:19; 26:16; 32:25), but here of courageous obedience to the Lord. *groves.* Asherah poles (see note at 14:3).

17:7–9 *third year.* Most agree that Jehoshaphat was a coregent with his father, Asa, for about three years. It is likely that while Asa was plagued with his foot disease (16:12), Jehoshaphat unofficially ruled in his place. Jehoshaphat sent both *princes* and *priests* to teach the people the *law* of God.

17:10 *fear of the LORD.* The dread of His power with His

brought him flocks, seven thousand and seven
hundred rams, and seven thousand and seven
hundred he goats.
12 ¶ And Jehoshaphat waxed great exceedingly;
and he built in Judah castles, and cities of store.
13 And he had much business in the cities of
Judah: and the men of war, mighty men of valour,
were in Jerusalem.
14 And these *are* the numbers of them according
to the house of their fathers: Of Judah, the captains of thousands; Adnah the chief, and with him
mighty men of valour three hundred thousand.
15 And next to him *was* Jehohanan the captain, and with him two hundred and fourscore
thousand.
16 And next him *was* Amasiah the son of Zichri,
who willingly offered himself unto the LORD; and
with him two hundred thousand mighty men of
valour.
17 And of Benjamin; Eliada a mighty man of
valour, and with him armed men with bow and
shield two hundred thousand.
18 And next him *was* Jehozabad, and with him an
hundred and fourscore thousand ready prepared
for the war.
19 These waited on the king, beside *those* whom
the king put in the fenced cities throughout all
Judah.

CHAPTER 18

NOW Jehoshaphat had riches and honour in
abundance, and joined affinity with Ahab.
2 And after *certain* years he went down to Ahab
to Samaria. And Ahab killed sheep and oxen for
him in abundance, and for the people that *he had*
with him, and persuaded him to go up *with him*
to Ramoth-gilead.
3 And Ahab king of Israel said unto Jehoshaphat
king of Judah, Wilt thou go with me to Ramoth-gilead? And he answered him, I *am* as thou *art*,
and my people as thy people; and *we will be* with
thee in the war.
4 ¶ And Jehoshaphat said unto the king of Israel,
Enquire, I pray thee, at the word of the LORD to day.
5 Therefore the king of Israel gathered together
of prophets four hundred men, and said unto
them, Shall we go to Ramoth-gilead to battle, or
shall I forbear? And they said, Go up; for God will
deliver *it* into the king's hand.
6 But Jehoshaphat said, *Is there* not here a prophet
of the LORD besides, that we might enquire of him?
7 And the king of Israel said unto Jehoshaphat,
There is yet one man, by whom we may enquire
of the LORD: but I hate him; for he never prophesied good unto me, but always evil: the same *is*
Micaiah the son of Imla. And Jehoshaphat said,
Let not the king say so.
8 And the king of Israel called for one *of his*
officers, and said, Fetch quickly Micaiah the son
of Imla.
9 And the king of Israel and Jehoshaphat king of
Judah sat either of them on his throne, clothed
in *their* robes, and they sat in a void place at the
entering in of the gate of Samaria; and all the
prophets prophesied before them.
10 And Zedekiah the son of Chenaanah had
made him horns of iron, and said, Thus saith the
LORD, With these thou shalt push Syria until they
be consumed.
11 And all the prophets prophesied so, saying, Go
up to Ramoth-gilead, and prosper: for the LORD

people (see note at 14:14).

17:12 *waxed.* Became.

17:13–18 Jehoshaphat had a group of great warriors (*mighty men of valour*) as David did (1 Chron. 11:10–47).

17:15 *two hundred and fourscore thousand.* 280,000. A score is twenty.

17:19 *waited.* Served. The total number of men the king had at his disposal was almost 1.2 million men. This is the largest army on record that Judah ever maintained.

Thoughts for Personal/Family Worship: Chapter 17

1. **Chronicles draws parallels between Jehoshaphat and David. Both sought the Lord in wholehearted devotion. Both kept God's commandments. Both enlisted the services of mighty men. Through these comparisons, Chronicles fostered hope in the people after the exile that God would raise up a new king, of whom David was only a shadow. How does this foster hope for us?**
2. **Jehoshaphat's reformation of the people of God had two sides: he destroyed the idols of Judah, and he sent out teachers to instruct Judah in God's Word. The reformation of the church always requires both. We saw this in the sixteenth century, when God used the Reformers to root out idolatry from the church's worship and to train men to teach the Bible to the people. Why does reformation require opposing idolatry? Why does it involve teaching the Word?**

Chapter 18: *Jehoshaphat allies himself with Ahab, who is killed in accordance with the word of the prophet Micaiah.*

18:1 *joined affinity.* Made a marriage alliance by joining his son, Jehoram, to Ahab's daughter, Athaliah (21:6; 22:2). As expected, this would prove to be a disastrous union (22:10).

18:2 *persuaded.* Incited to do someone's wishes. Ahab was an aggressive agitator slyly leading Jehoshaphat into battle.

18:3 *Ramoth-gilead.* Southeast of the Sea of Galilee. *I am as thou art, and my people as thy people.* Jehoshaphat expresses loyalty to his covenant with Ahab (Ruth 1:16).

18:4 *Enquire.* Literally, "seek."

18:5 *prophets.* False prophets.

18:6 *prophet of the LORD.* True prophets were not yes-men who sought to please kings, but messengers sent from God to rebuke sin and call men to faithfulness (2 Kings 17:13–15; Neh. 9:26; Jer. 25:4).

18:9 *void place.* Open area, threshingfloor.

18:10 *horns of iron.* Symbols of great strength and endurance, illustrating a prophecy of Ahab's glorious victory.

shall deliver *it* into the hand of the king.
12 And the messenger that went to call Micaiah
spake to him, saying, Behold, the words of the
prophets *declare* good to the king with one assent;
let thy word therefore, I pray thee, be like one of
theirs, and speak thou good.
13 And Micaiah said, *As* the LORD liveth, even
what my God saith, that will I speak.
14 And when he was come to the king, the king
said unto him, Micaiah, shall we go to Ramoth-
gilead to battle, or shall I forbear? And he said,
Go ye up, and prosper, and they shall be delivered
into your hand.
15 And the king said to him, How many times
shall I adjure thee that thou say nothing but the
truth to me in the name of the LORD?
16 Then he said, I did see all Israel scattered upon
the mountains, as sheep that have no shepherd:
and the LORD said, These have no master; let them
return *therefore* every man to his house in peace.
17 And the king of Israel said to Jehoshaphat, Did
I not tell thee *that* he would not prophesy good
unto me, but evil?
18 Again he said, Therefore hear the word of the
LORD; I saw the LORD sitting upon his throne, and
all the host of heaven standing on his right hand
and *on* his left.
19 And the LORD said, Who shall entice Ahab
king of Israel, that he may go up and fall at Ra-
moth-gilead? And one spake saying after this
manner, and another saying after that manner.
20 Then there came out a spirit, and stood before
the LORD, and said, I will entice him. And the
LORD said unto him, Wherewith?
21 And he said, I will go out, and be a lying spirit
in the mouth of all his prophets. And *the LORD*
said, Thou shalt entice *him*, and thou shalt also
prevail: go out, and do *even* so.
22 Now therefore, behold, the LORD hath put a
lying spirit in the mouth of these thy prophets,
and the LORD hath spoken evil against thee.
23 Then Zedekiah the son of Chenaanah came
near, and smote Micaiah upon the cheek, and
said, Which way went the Spirit of the LORD from
me to speak unto thee?
24 And Micaiah said, Behold, thou shalt see on
that day when thou shalt go into an inner cham-
ber to hide thyself.
25 Then the king of Israel said, Take ye Micaiah,
and carry him back to Amon the governor of the
city, and to Joash the king's son;
26 And say, Thus saith the king, Put this *fellow* in
the prison, and feed him with bread of affliction
and with water of affliction, until I return in peace.
27 And Micaiah said, If thou certainly return in
peace, *then* hath not the LORD spoken by me. And
he said, Hearken, all ye people.
28 So the king of Israel and Jehoshaphat the king
of Judah went up to Ramoth-gilead.
29 And the king of Israel said unto Jehoshaphat,
I will disguise myself, and will go to the battle;
but put thou on thy robes. So the king of Israel
disguised himself; and they went to the battle.
30 Now the king of Syria had commanded the
captains of the chariots that *were* with him,
saying, Fight ye not with small or great, save only
with the king of Israel.
31 And it came to pass, when the captains of the
chariots saw Jehoshaphat, that they said, It *is* the
king of Israel. Therefore they compassed about
him to fight: but Jehoshaphat cried out, and the
LORD helped him; and God moved them *to depart*
from him.
32 For it came to pass, that, when the captains of
the chariots perceived that it was not the king of
Israel, they turned back again from pursuing him.
33 And a *certain* man drew a bow at a venture,
and smote the king of Israel between the joints of
the harness: therefore he said to his chariot man,
Turn thine hand, that thou mayest carry me out
of the host; for I am wounded.
34 And the battle increased that day: howbeit

18:13 *As the LORD liveth.* An oath. *what my God saith, that will I speak.* Micaiah remained firm and declared that he could not prophesy anything God does not put into his mouth, a sign of a true prophet.
18:14–15 Micaiah's prophecy was likely expressed in an obviously sarcastic tone, spurring Ahab ironically to put him under oath (*adjure*) to speak the truth of God.
18:16 *shepherd.* Common metaphor for a king (1 Chron. 11:2; cf. Matt. 9:36).
18:18 *the LORD sitting upon his throne.* The real King, in contrast to merely human kings on their thrones (v. 9). *host of heaven.* Angelic armies. Ahab stood indicted by the heavenly court, and though he oppressed the faithful, God would hold him accountable.
18:20–21 *Wherewith?* By what means? *lying spirit.* Though God cannot lie (Num. 23:19), He controls all things, including deceitful demons and men (Job 12:16; 2 Thess. 2:11).
18:23 The false prophet *Zedekiah* claimed that he had *the Spirit of the LORD* but that Micaiah did not. *smote . . . upon the cheek.* Struck on the side of the face, a public insult (Job 16:10; Matt. 5:39).
18:27 *then hath not the LORD spoken by me.* A mark of true prophecy is that God's Word always proves true (Deut. 18:22). *Hearken.* Listen.
18:30 *save.* Except.
18:31 *compassed about.* Surrounded. *God moved them.* God's providence rescued Jehoshaphat.
18:33 *at a venture.* Literally, "in his simplicity" (2 Sam. 15:11), meaning that the man did not aim at Ahab. *harness.* The king's armor. The arrow struck precisely in a weak point in Ahab's armor. *Turn thine hand.* Turn around.

Thoughts for Personal/Family Worship: Chapter 18

1. Beware of binding yourself in agreements with the wicked as Jehoshaphat did with Ahab. Perhaps Jehoshaphat cherished hopes that Judah and Israel and Ahab

the king of Israel stayed *himself* up in *his* chariot
against the Syrians until the even: and about the
time of the sun going down he died.

CHAPTER 19

AND Jehoshaphat the king of Judah returned to
his house in peace to Jerusalem.
2 And Jehu the son of Hanani the seer went
out to meet him, and said to king Jehoshaphat,
Shouldest thou help the ungodly, and love them
that hate the LORD? therefore *is* wrath upon thee
from before the LORD.
3 Nevertheless there are good things found in
thee, in that thou hast taken away the groves out
of the land, and hast prepared thine heart to seek
God.
4 And Jehoshaphat dwelt at Jerusalem: and he
went out again through the people from Beer-
sheba to mount Ephraim, and brought them back
unto the LORD God of their fathers.
5 ¶ And he set judges in the land throughout all
the fenced cities of Judah, city by city,
6 And said to the judges, Take heed what ye do:
for ye judge not for man, but for the LORD, who *is*
with you in the judgment.
7 Wherefore now let the fear of the LORD be upon
you; take heed and do *it*: for *there is* no iniquity
with the LORD our God, nor respect of persons,
nor taking of gifts.
8 ¶ Moreover in Jerusalem did Jehoshaphat set
of the Levites, and *of* the priests, and of the chief
of the fathers of Israel, for the judgment of the
LORD, and for controversies, when they returned
to Jerusalem.
9 And he charged them, saying, Thus shall ye
do in the fear of the LORD, faithfully, and with a
perfect heart.
10 And what cause soever shall come to you of
your brethren that dwell in their cities, between
blood and blood, between law and command-
ment, statutes and judgments, ye shall even warn
them that they trespass not against the LORD, and
so wrath come upon you, and upon your breth-
ren: this do, and ye shall not trespass.
11 And, behold, Amariah the chief priest *is* over
you in all matters of the LORD; and Zebadiah the
son of Ishmael, the ruler of the house of Judah,
for all the king's matters: also the Levites *shall be*
officers before you. Deal courageously, and the
LORD shall be with the good.

CHAPTER 20

IT came to pass after this also, *that* the children
of Moab, and the children of Ammon, and with

would enter a new phase of cooperation; however, he barely escaped alive. While we are to love all people, we must separate ourselves from sin and therefore not yoke ourselves with unbelievers (2 Cor. 6:14). Do not say, "I am as thou art, and my people as thy people" (v. 3), unless you are one in Christ. Where do you see unhealthy alliances happening in our day?

2. **Treasure the Word of God in the fear of God. One man speaking God's truth is worth more than 400 men telling us what we want to hear. Thank God for faithful ministers who refuse to speak anything except God's Word. The Word of the Lord proves true because it is backed by the providence of God. When God threatens death on an unrepentant sinner, be sure it will come, even if by a random shot by an archer. How then should we respond when God's Word says hard things against us and our sin?**

Chapter 19: ***A prophet reproves Jehoshaphat, who enacts further religious reforms.***

19:2 *Jehu the son of Hanani.* A prophet who also served in the time of Baasha, king of Israel some years before Ahab (1 Kings 16:1–3). *love them that hate the LORD.* See 18:1–3.

19:3 *good things found in thee.* Jehoshaphat was not altogether wicked. *prepared thine heart to seek God.* Directed his thoughts and affections to pursue God (12:14; Col. 3:1–2), the gift of God's grace (30:12) for which David had prayed (1 Chron. 29:18–19).

19:4 *brought them back.* Chronicles again returns to the religious integrity of Jehoshaphat as he guided Judah in repentance, turning them from sin back to the Lord.

19:5–7 *the LORD . . . is with you.* God not only oversees religious ministers, but also the civil rulers such as *judges*, who must use their authority in *the fear of the LORD* (Deut. 1:16–17; 16:18–19; Ps. 82:1–8).

19:9 *perfect heart.* Fearing God far above all others and not with divided allegiance.

19:10 *cause.* Legal case or lawsuit. As experts in the *law* of God (Mal. 2:7), priests and Levites assisted the judges in making judgments (Deut. 17:8–9).

Thoughts for Personal/Family Worship: Chapter 19

1. **While we should love the wicked in the sense of having mercy on them even when they harm us (Matt. 5:45; Acts 7:60), we must not love them in the sense of joining ourselves to them or sharing in their wicked deeds (Eph. 5:7–14). Though we must live in the world, we must be wise not to compromise ourselves with the world. What can we do to pursue this wisdom that begins with the fear of the Lord in the heart, hates sin, and turns from it in disgust?**
2. **Spiritual reformation is not confined to the worship services of the church, any more than God's sovereignty is limited to the church building. Repentance must reach the people in their day-to-day lives (v. 4). The dread of God's judgment must penetrate into the halls of power and courts of justice (vv. 5–7). The fear of God must control the decisions of church elders (vv. 8–11). Just as King Jehoshaphat labored to bring reformation to every part of society, so the greater son of David works to save and sanctify all kinds of people, including kings (1 Tim. 2:1–7). Why does the fear of the Lord transform everything and not just part of human life?**

Chapter 20: ***Jehoshaphat seeks God in prayer, and God delivers the people of Judah again, this time against the Moabites and Ammonites.***

20:1 *It came to pass after this.* A chronological note that this

them *other* beside the Ammonites, came against
Jehoshaphat to battle.
2 Then there came some that told Jehoshaphat,
saying, There cometh a great multitude against
thee from beyond the sea on this side Syria;
and, behold, they *be* in Hazazon-tamar, which *is*
En-gedi.
3 And Jehoshaphat feared, and set himself to seek
the LORD, and proclaimed a fast throughout all
Judah.
4 And Judah gathered themselves together, to ask
help of the LORD: even out of all the cities of Judah
they came to seek the LORD.
5 ¶ And Jehoshaphat stood in the congregation
of Judah and Jerusalem, in the house of the LORD,
before the new court,
6 And said, O LORD God of our fathers, *art* not
thou God in heaven? and rulest *not* thou over all
the kingdoms of the heathen? and in thine hand
is there not power and might, so that none is able
to withstand thee?
7 *Art* not thou our God, *who* didst drive out the
inhabitants of this land before thy people Israel,
and gavest it to the seed of Abraham thy friend
for ever?
8 And they dwelt therein, and have built thee a
sanctuary therein for thy name, saying,
9 If, *when* evil cometh upon us, *as* the sword,
judgment, or pestilence, or famine, we stand be-
fore this house, and in thy presence, (for thy name
is in this house,) and cry unto thee in our afflic-
tion, then thou wilt hear and help.
10 And now, behold, the children of Ammon
and Moab and mount Seir, whom thou wouldest
not let Israel invade, when they came out of the
land of Egypt, but they turned from them, and
destroyed them not;
11 Behold, *I say, how* they reward us, to come to
cast us out of thy possession, which thou hast
given us to inherit.
12 O our God, wilt thou not judge them? for we
have no might against this great company that
cometh against us; neither know we what to do:
but our eyes *are* upon thee.
13 And all Judah stood before the LORD, with
their little ones, their wives, and their children.
14 ¶ Then upon Jahaziel the son of Zechariah,
the son of Benaiah, the son of Jeiel, the son
of Mattaniah, a Levite of the sons of Asaph,
came the Spirit of the LORD in the midst of the
congregation;
15 And he said, Hearken ye, all Judah, and
ye inhabitants of Jerusalem, and thou king
Jehoshaphat, Thus saith the LORD unto you, Be
not afraid nor dismayed by reason of this great
multitude; for the battle *is* not yours, but God's.
16 To morrow go ye down against them: behold,
they come up by the cliff of Ziz; and ye shall find
them at the end of the brook, before the wilder-
ness of Jeruel.
17 Ye shall not *need* to fight in this *battle*: set
yourselves, stand ye *still*, and see the salvation of
the LORD with you, O Judah and Jerusalem: fear
not, nor be dismayed; to morrow go out against
them: for the LORD *will be* with you.
18 And Jehoshaphat bowed his head with *his* face
to the ground: and all Judah and the inhabitants
of Jerusalem fell before the LORD, worshipping
the LORD.
19 And the Levites, of the children of the Kohath-
ites, and of the children of the Korhites, stood up
to praise the LORD God of Israel with a loud voice
on high.
20 ¶ And they rose early in the morning, and went
forth into the wilderness of Tekoa: and as they
went forth, Jehoshaphat stood and said, Hear me,
O Judah, and ye inhabitants of Jerusalem; Believe
in the LORD your God, so shall ye be established;
believe his prophets, so shall ye prosper.
21 And when he had consulted with the people,

occurred after Jehoshaphat's reforms. He was given a second opportunity to rely on the hand of God and not the arm of flesh.

20:4 *ask help of the LORD.* Literally, "seek from the Lord," the same verb as in *seek the LORD* in this verse (though not the same as "seek" in v. 3).

20:6–9 Jehoshaphat's prayer echoes elements of Solomon's prayer at the dedication of the temple (ch. 6), showing Jehoshaphat to be a faithful son of David fulfilling God's purposes.

20:6 *God of our fathers.* The faithful God of the covenant (6:14–15; Ex. 3:15). *rulest . . . over all the kingdoms.* Unlike the limited domains of pagan gods, the sovereignty of the Lord extended over all things (6:14,18; 1 Chron. 16:14,31; 29:11).

20:7 *Abraham thy friend.* A statement of God's remarkable grace and covenant with Israel (1 Chron. 16:16; Isa. 41:8).

20:9 *when evil cometh upon us.* Judgments for breaking the covenant (6:28–29). *for thy name.* Where His glory would dwell (6:20). *hear and help.* Literally, "hear and save" (Pss. 34:6; 145:19).

20:10 *And now.* Jehoshaphat's prayer turned from God's past faithfulness to the present. *Ammon . . . Moab . . . Seir.* The Lord did not allow Israel to invade these lands and destroy their peoples (Num. 20:14–21; Deut. 2:4–6,9,18–19).

20:11 *thy possession, which thou hast given us.* Jehoshaphat pleaded the promises of God.

20:14 *upon Jahaziel . . . came the Spirit of the LORD.* See note at 15:1.

20:15–17 *Hearken.* Listen. There are many similarities between this prophecy and Moses' charge as Israel faced the Egyptian army at the Red Sea (Ex. 14:13–14). *the battle is not yours, but God's.* The Lord determines the victor, not human ability (1 Sam. 17:47).

20:20 *Believe in the LORD . . . believe his prophets.* Trusting in God's Word is equivalent to trusting in God. *established.* The same verb as *believe*; the Hebrew root means "to make sure or firm." Trusting God's Word as something solid and established will make you solid and established (Isa. 7:9).

20:21–23 Jehoshaphat appointed Levitical singers and

he appointed singers unto the LORD, and that
should praise the beauty of holiness, as they went
out before the army, and to say, Praise the LORD;
for his mercy *endureth* for ever.
22 ¶ And when they began to sing and to praise,
the LORD set ambushments against the children
of Ammon, Moab, and mount Seir, which were
come against Judah; and they were smitten.
23 For the children of Ammon and Moab stood
up against the inhabitants of mount Seir, utterly
to slay and destroy *them*: and when they had
made an end of the inhabitants of Seir, every one
helped to destroy another.
24 And when Judah came toward the watch tower
in the wilderness, they looked unto the multitude,
and, behold, they *were* dead bodies fallen to the
earth, and none escaped.
25 And when Jehoshaphat and his people came
to take away the spoil of them, they found among
them in abundance both riches with the dead
bodies, and precious jewels, which they stripped
off for themselves, more than they could carry
away: and they were three days in gathering of the
spoil, it was so much.
26 ¶ And on the fourth day they assembled them-
selves in the valley of Berachah; for there they
blessed the LORD: therefore the name of the same
place was called, The valley of Berachah, unto this
day.
27 Then they returned, every man of Judah and
Jerusalem, and Jehoshaphat in the forefront of
them, to go again to Jerusalem with joy; for the
LORD had made them to rejoice over their enemies.
28 And they came to Jerusalem with psalteries and
harps and trumpets unto the house of the LORD.
29 And the fear of God was on all the kingdoms
of *those* countries, when they had heard that the
LORD fought against the enemies of Israel.
30 So the realm of Jehoshaphat was quiet: for his
God gave him rest round about.
31 ¶ And Jehoshaphat reigned over Judah: *he was*
thirty and five years old when he began to reign,
and he reigned twenty and five years in Jerusalem.
And his mother's name *was* Azubah the daughter
of Shilhi.
32 And he walked in the way of Asa his father, and
departed not from it, doing *that which was* right
in the sight of the LORD.
33 Howbeit the high places were not taken away:
for as yet the people had not prepared their hearts
unto the God of their fathers.
34 Now the rest of the acts of Jehoshaphat, first
and last, behold, they *are* written in the book of
Jehu the son of Hanani, who *is* mentioned in the
book of the kings of Israel.
35 ¶ And after this did Jehoshaphat king of Judah
join himself with Ahaziah king of Israel, who did
very wickedly:
36 And he joined himself with him to make ships
to go to Tarshish: and they made the ships in
Ezion-geber.
37 Then Eliezer the son of Dodavah of Mareshah
prophesied against Jehoshaphat, saying, Because
thou hast joined thyself with Ahaziah, the LORD
hath broken thy works. And the ships were
broken, that they were not able to go to Tarshish.

CHAPTER 21

NOW Jehoshaphat slept with his fathers, and was
buried with his fathers in the city of David. And
Jehoram his son reigned in his stead.
2 And he had brethren the sons of Jehoshaphat,
Azariah, and Jehiel, and Zechariah, and Azariah,
and Michael, and Shephatiah: all these *were* the
sons of Jehoshaphat king of Israel.
3 And their father gave them great gifts of silver,
and of gold, and of precious things, with fenced
cities in Judah: but the kingdom gave he to Je-
horam; because he *was* the firstborn.
4 Now when Jehoram was risen up to the king-
dom of his father, he strengthened himself, and

musicians to go ahead of the army. To *praise the LORD* before the battle was an act of faith in His promise. The Lord inhabits the praises of His people (Ps. 22:3). *ambushments.* Ambushes, hidden attackers (13:13). The Lord turned the Ammonites and Moabites against the Edomites so that they betrayed and slaughtered each other.

20:30 *rest.* A common trait for the faithful reigns of the kings of Judah (14:6–7; 15:15).

20:35–37 Another cooperative alliance between *Jehoshaphat* and a wicked king of Israel, resulting in discipline from God (*the LORD hath broken thy works*).

Thoughts for Personal/Family Worship: Chapter 20

God gave Jehoshaphat another opportunity to either trust in man's strength or God's infinite power, and this time the king sought the Lord (vv. 3–4). This time Jehoshaphat relied on divine omnipotence and sought the favor of the Lord. It must have been intensely difficult to wait upon God in such frightening circumstances, but the battle belongs to the Lord (v. 15). We need to trust in the Lord at all times, pouring out the concerns of our hearts in prayer (Ps. 62:8). With God is everlasting strength (Isa. 26:4), and if we will wait quietly upon Him then in His time the Lord alone will be exalted (Ps. 46:10). Then, like Jehoshaphat and Judah, we can bow down and worship the Lord (2 Chron. 20:18). It is good, however, to begin praising Him before His salvation comes (v. 21), so that by faith we may find strength (v. 20). How is your faith being tested even now?

Chapter 21: *Jehoram leads the people into all sorts of idolatry, harvesting sad political results and a dreadful death.*

King Jehoram (2 Chron. 21:1–20)

21:1 *stead.* Place.

slew all his brethren with the sword, and *divers*
also of the princes of Israel.
5 ¶ Jehoram *was* thirty and two years old when
he began to reign, and he reigned eight years in
Jerusalem.
6 And he walked in the way of the kings of Is-
rael, like as did the house of Ahab: for he had the
daughter of Ahab to wife: and he wrought *that*
which was evil in the eyes of the LORD.
7 Howbeit the LORD would not destroy the house
of David, because of the covenant that he had
made with David, and as he promised to give a
light to him and to his sons for ever.
8 ¶ In his days the Edomites revolted from under
the dominion of Judah, and made themselves a
king.
9 Then Jehoram went forth with his princes, and
all his chariots with him: and he rose up by night,
and smote the Edomites which compassed him
in, and the captains of the chariots.
10 So the Edomites revolted from under the hand
of Judah unto this day. The same time *also* did
Libnah revolt from under his hand; because he
had forsaken the LORD God of his fathers.
11 Moreover he made high places in the moun-
tains of Judah, and caused the inhabitants of Je-
rusalem to commit fornication, and compelled
Judah *thereto*.
12 ¶ And there came a writing to him from Elijah
the prophet, saying, Thus saith the LORD God of
David thy father, Because thou hast not walked
in the ways of Jehoshaphat thy father, nor in the
ways of Asa king of Judah,
13 But hast walked in the way of the kings of
Israel, and hast made Judah and the inhabitants
of Jerusalem to go a whoring, like to the whore-
doms of the house of Ahab, and also hast slain thy
brethren of thy father's house, *which were* better
than thyself:
14 Behold, with a great plague will the LORD
smite thy people, and thy children, and thy wives,
and all thy goods:
15 And thou *shalt have* great sickness by disease
of thy bowels, until thy bowels fall out by reason
of the sickness day by day.
16 ¶ Moreover the LORD stirred up against
Jehoram the spirit of the Philistines, and of the
Arabians, that *were* near the Ethiopians:
17 And they came up into Judah, and brake into
it, and carried away all the substance that was
found in the king's house, and his sons also, and
his wives; so that there was never a son left him,
save Jehoahaz, the youngest of his sons.
18 ¶ And after all this the LORD smote him in his
bowels with an incurable disease.
19 And it came to pass, that in process of time,
after the end of two years, his bowels fell out by
reason of his sickness: so he died of sore diseases.
And his people made no burning for him, like the
burning of his fathers.
20 Thirty and two years old was he when he
began to reign, and he reigned in Jerusalem
eight years, and departed without being desired.
Howbeit they buried him in the city of David, but
not in the sepulchres of the kings.

CHAPTER 22

AND the inhabitants of Jerusalem made Ahaziah
his youngest son king in his stead: for the band of

21:4 *slew all his brethren.* Jehoram *strengthened* his hand by killing potential rivals for the throne. *divers.* Diverse, various.

21:6 *walked in the way of the kings of Israel . . . house of Ahab.* Judah had descended into the same depths of sin as the northern kingdom, because its king had married the *daughter of Ahab* (18:1).

21:7 *the covenant . . . with David.* Even when Judah became as wicked as Israel, the Lord did not destroy it immediately because of His faithful love to David, having promised to preserve his line (1 Kings 11:13). *light.* Lamp (see note at 2 Sam. 21:17).

21:9 *compassed.* Surrounded.

21:10 *Edomites . . . Libnah.* Edom was located to the east and Libnah to the west.

21:11 *commit fornication.* Fertility prostitution in Canaanite worship. *compelled Judah thereto.* Not only permitted it but enforced it.

21:12 *Elijah the prophet* (1 Kings 17:1) sent a letter to Jehoram rebuking him for his sins. *God of David thy father.* A reminder of God's covenant with David (1 Chron. 17).

21:13 *whoredoms.* Acts of idolatry, like spiritual adultery against God. *Ahab.* The most wicked king in the land of Israel, a fearful point of comparison (1 Kings 16:30,33; 21:25).

21:15 *bowels.* Organs of the abdomen. Jehoram would die a slow, painful, and humiliating death for his disobedience (vv. 18–19).

21:16 *the LORD stirred up.* God in His sovereignty used men, even wicked men, to discipline the sons of David, as He said in the covenant (2 Sam. 7:14).

21:17 *save.* Except.

21:19 *sore.* Severe. *burning.* An honor in memory of the dead (see note at 16:14).

21:20 *without being desired.* Without being mourned.

Thoughts for Personal/Family Worship: Chapter 21

A godly father can still leave a bitter legacy if he does not separate himself from the wicked world, for his children may very well fully embrace the world. A horrible example of this principle appears in Lot's daughters (Gen. 19), and we see it again with Jehoram, son of Jehoshaphat. He not only sinned himself in dreadful ways, but he forced others to sin and died under God's judgment. Sin is like a cancer that spreads unless it is mortified by God's grace of repentance. Do not play with sin or with alliances with the world. If you continue in sin, you do so warned of the dreadful consequences. Heb. 12:1 says that sin can "easily beset us." What example did Christ leave us for resisting sin in our lives?

Chapter 22: *Ahaziah's reign continues the wickedness of Jehoram and ends with Athaliah destroying*

men that came with the Arabians to the camp had
slain all the eldest. So Ahaziah the son of Jehoram
king of Judah reigned.
2 Forty and two years old *was* Ahaziah when he
began to reign, and he reigned one year in Jeru-
salem. His mother's name also *was* Athaliah the
daughter of Omri.
3 He also walked in the ways of the house of
Ahab: for his mother was his counsellor to do
wickedly.
4 Wherefore he did evil in the sight of the LORD
like the house of Ahab: for they were his counsel-
lors after the death of his father to his destruction.
5 ¶ He walked also after their counsel, and went
with Jehoram the son of Ahab king of Israel to
war against Hazael king of Syria at Ramoth-gil-
ead: and the Syrians smote Joram.
6 And he returned to be healed in Jezreel because
of the wounds which were given him at Ramah,
when he fought with Hazael king of Syria. And
Azariah the son of Jehoram king of Judah went
down to see Jehoram the son of Ahab at Jezreel,
because he was sick.
7 And the destruction of Ahaziah was of God by
coming to Joram: for when he was come, he went
out with Jehoram against Jehu the son of Nim-
shi, whom the LORD had anointed to cut off the
house of Ahab.
8 And it came to pass, that, when Jehu was ex-
ecuting judgment upon the house of Ahab, and
found the princes of Judah, and the sons of the
brethren of Ahaziah, that ministered to Ahaziah,
he slew them.
9 And he sought Ahaziah: and they caught
him, (for he was hid in Samaria,) and brought
him to Jehu: and when they had slain him, they
buried him: Because, said they, he *is* the son of
Jehoshaphat, who sought the LORD with all his
heart. So the house of Ahaziah had no power to
keep still the kingdom.
10 ¶ But when Athaliah the mother of Ahaziah
saw that her son was dead, she arose and de-
stroyed all the seed royal of the house of Judah.
11 But Jehoshabeath, the daughter of the king,
took Joash the son of Ahaziah, and stole him
from among the king's sons that were slain, and
put him and his nurse in a bedchamber. So Je-
hoshabeath, the daughter of king Jehoram, the
wife of Jehoiada the priest, (for she was the sister
of Ahaziah,) hid him from Athaliah, so that she
slew him not.
12 And he was with them hid in the house of God
six years: and Athaliah reigned over the land.

CHAPTER 23

AND in the seventh year Jehoiada strengthened
himself, and took the captains of hundreds, Aza-
riah the son of Jeroham, and Ishmael the son of
Jehohanan, and Azariah the son of Obed, and

all the royal seed except for Joash, who is hidden in God's house.

King Ahaziah (2 Chron. 22:1–9)

22:1 *stead.* Place.
22:2 *Athaliah.* The granddaughter of Israel's wicked king *Omri* (1 Kings 16:16–28). The word *daughter* in Scripture can mean female descendant. She married Jehoram (21:6). Her reign was the only time in Judah's history that a descendant of David did not reign.
22:5 This military alliance is strongly condemned by Chronicles. *Jehoram . . . Joram.* The same person. He is not the same Jehoram as the son of Jehosphat (ch. 21), but a son of Ahab who reigned over Israel (2 Kings 1:17; 3:1).
22:7 *destruction . . . was of God.* God put Ahaziah to death in fulfillment of the prophecy spoken against *the house of Ahab* and fulfilled through *Jehu* (1 Kings 19:16–17; 21:21–22; 2 Kings 9).
22:8 Jehu defeated even the relatives (*sons of the brethren*) of Ahaziah.
22:9 *no power to keep still the kingdom.* Ahaziah's descendants were not able to retain the throne.

Queen Athaliah (2 Chron. 22:10–12)

22:10 *Athaliah* sought to destroy the house of David forever by mercilessly slaughtering any who might ascend to the throne (*all the seed royal*).
22:11 *Jehoshabeath.* She had connections with both the monarchy and the priesthood, as *the daughter of king Jehoram* and *the wife of Jehoiada the priest.*

Thoughts for Personal/Family Worship: Chapter 22

1. **Jehoshaphat's foolish alliance with the house of Ahab (18:1) reaped such a bitter harvest that it nearly destroyed the line of David. The promise of God's covenant seemed to hang by a thread (1 Chron. 17:11–12). Satan certainly would have been happy with Athaliah's design to kill "all the seed royal of the house of Judah" (2 Chron. 22:10). He has been set against the seed of the woman from the first promise of God (Gen. 3:15). Sometimes Satan works by drawing the church into compromise and entanglement with the world. Sometimes Satan uses violence, as when he killed all the children of Bethlehem. Whether he entices us to sin or threaten us with persecution, how can we be prepared to stand against him?**
2. **The bravery of two women saved the line of Christ from extinction. One was a daughter of a king, but the other an ordinary (and unnamed) servant. They risked their lives to preserve the house of David, and proved to be instruments in God's hand to fulfill His covenant. Never underestimate the significance of ordinary men and women who trust the Lord and do His will. God's sovereignty often works through human means, and the godly are His servants. How does the courage of Jehoshabeath and the nurse motivate you to serve God courageously?**

King Joash (2 Chron. 23:1—24:27)

Chapter 23: ***Joash is crowned king at age seven by Jehoiada, the priest, and Athaliah is killed.***

23:1–7 *Jehoiada* the priest (22:11) carefully prepared for the coup.

Maaseiah the son of Adaiah, and Elishaphat the
son of Zichri, into covenant with him.
2 And they went about in Judah, and gathered
the Levites out of all the cities of Judah, and the
chief of the fathers of Israel, and they came to
Jerusalem.
3 And all the congregation made a covenant with
the king in the house of God. And he said unto
them, Behold, the king's son shall reign, as the
LORD hath said of the sons of David.
4 This *is* the thing that ye shall do; A third part of
you entering on the sabbath, of the priests and of
the Levites, *shall be* porters of the doors;
5 And a third part *shall be* at the king's house; and
a third part at the gate of the foundation: and all
the people *shall be* in the courts of the house of
the LORD.
6 But let none come into the house of the LORD,
save the priests, and they that minister of the
Levites; they shall go in, for they *are* holy: but all
the people shall keep the watch of the LORD.
7 And the Levites shall compass the king round
about, every man with his weapons in his hand;
and whosoever *else* cometh into the house, he
shall be put to death: but be ye with the king when
he cometh in, and when he goeth out.
8 So the Levites and all Judah did according to all
things that Jehoiada the priest had commanded,
and took every man his men that were to come in
on the sabbath, with them that were to go *out* on
the sabbath: for Jehoiada the priest dismissed not
the courses.
9 Moreover Jehoiada the priest delivered to the
captains of hundreds spears, and bucklers, and
shields, that *had been* king David's, which *were* in
the house of God.
10 And he set all the people, every man having
his weapon in his hand, from the right side of the
temple to the left side of the temple, along by the
altar and the temple, by the king round about.
11 Then they brought out the king's son, and put
upon him the crown, and *gave him* the testimony,
and made him king. And Jehoiada and his sons
anointed him, and said, God save the king.
12 ¶ Now when Athaliah heard the noise of the
people running and praising the king, she came to
the people into the house of the LORD:
13 And she looked, and, behold, the king stood at
his pillar at the entering in, and the princes and
the trumpets by the king: and all the people of the
land rejoiced, and sounded with trumpets, also
the singers with instruments of musick, and such
as taught to sing praise. Then Athaliah rent her
clothes, and said, Treason, Treason.
14 Then Jehoiada the priest brought out the cap-
tains of hundreds that were set over the host, and
said unto them, Have her forth of the ranges:
and whoso followeth her, let him be slain with
the sword. For the priest said, Slay her not in the
house of the LORD.
15 So they laid hands on her; and when she was
come to the entering of the horse gate by the
king's house, they slew her there.
16 ¶ And Jehoiada made a covenant between
him, and between all the people, and between the
king, that they should be the LORD's people.
17 Then all the people went to the house of Baal,
and brake it down, and brake his altars and his
images in pieces, and slew Mattan the priest of
Baal before the altars.
18 Also Jehoiada appointed the offices of the house
of the LORD by the hand of the priests the Levites,
whom David had distributed in the house of the
LORD, to offer the burnt offerings of the LORD, as
it is written in the law of Moses, with rejoicing and
with singing, *as it was ordained* by David.
19 And he set the porters at the gates of the house
of the LORD, that none *which was* unclean in any
thing should enter in.
20 And he took the captains of hundreds, and
the nobles, and the governors of the people, and
all the people of the land, and brought down the
king from the house of the LORD: and they came
through the high gate into the king's house, and
set the king upon the throne of the kingdom.
21 And all the people of the land rejoiced: and the
city was quiet, after that they had slain Athaliah
with the sword.

23:3 *made a covenant with the king.* Rulers and people mutually bound themselves to each other in mutual loyalty based upon God's covenant (1 Chron. 11:3). *as the LORD hath said of the sons of David.* Jehoiada acted on the belief that God would keep His covenant with David (1 Chron. 17).

23:6 *save.* Except.

23:7 *compass.* The people were to surround the king for protection.

23:8 *courses.* A divided group of priests and Levites.

23:9 *bucklers.* Small shields.

23:11 *God save the king.* Literally, "May the king live" (1 Sam. 10:24; 2 Sam. 16:16; 1 Kings 1:25,31,34,39; Neh. 2:3).

23:13 *rent.* Tearing of the garments, a sign of mourning. *Treason, Treason.* An ironic cry, since she had murdered the sons of the king.

23:14 *ranges.* Ranks of soldiers. *Slay her not in the house of the LORD.* Despite the importance of the coup for preserving the monarchy, the sanctity of the temple must be preserved.

23:16 *Jehoiada* was not content simply to have Joash in the kingship, but urged *the people* to renew their commitment to the *covenant* as *the LORD's people* (see note at 15:12).

23:19 *porters.* Gatekeepers.

23:21 *Athaliah*'s reign was conceived in violence (22:10) and ended in a violent death (v. 15). Her burial is not recounted. Chronicles does not consider her to be a true ruler but one who had usurped the throne of David. Thus her death was a cause of joy and peace.

Thoughts for Personal/Family Worship: Chapter 23

1. Just as the courage of Jehoshabeath had saved the line

CHAPTER 24

JOASH *was* seven years old when he began to
reign, and he reigned forty years in Jerusalem. His
mother's name also *was* Zibiah of Beer-sheba.
2 And Joash did *that which was* right in the sight
of the LORD all the days of Jehoiada the priest.
3 And Jehoiada took for him two wives; and he
begat sons and daughters.
4 ¶ And it came to pass after this, *that* Joash was
minded to repair the house of the LORD.
5 And he gathered together the priests and the
Levites, and said to them, Go out unto the cities
of Judah, and gather of all Israel money to repair
the house of your God from year to year, and see
that ye hasten the matter. Howbeit the Levites
hastened *it* not.
6 And the king called for Jehoiada the chief, and
said unto him, Why hast thou not required of the
Levites to bring in out of Judah and out of Jerusa-
lem the collection, *according to the commandment*
of Moses the servant of the LORD, and of the con-
gregation of Israel, for the tabernacle of witness?
7 For the sons of Athaliah, that wicked woman,
had broken up the house of God; and also all the
dedicated things of the house of the LORD did
they bestow upon Baalim.
8 And at the king's commandment they made a
chest, and set it without at the gate of the house
of the LORD.
9 And they made a proclamation through
Judah and Jerusalem, to bring in to the LORD
the collection *that* Moses the servant of God *laid*
upon Israel in the wilderness.
10 And all the princes and all the people rejoiced,
and brought in, and cast into the chest, until they
had made an end.
11 Now it came to pass, that at what time the
chest was brought unto the king's office by the
hand of the Levites, and when they saw that *there
was* much money, the king's scribe and the high
priest's officer came and emptied the chest, and
took it, and carried it to his place again. Thus they
did day by day, and gathered money in abundance.
12 And the king and Jehoiada gave it to such as
did the work of the service of the house of the
LORD, and hired masons and carpenters to repair
the house of the LORD, and also such as wrought
iron and brass to mend the house of the LORD.
13 So the workmen wrought, and the work was
perfected by them, and they set the house of God
in his state, and strengthened it.
14 And when they had finished *it*, they brought
the rest of the money before the king and Je-
hoiada, whereof were made vessels for the house
of the LORD, *even* vessels to minister, and to offer
withal, and spoons, and vessels of gold and silver.
And they offered burnt offerings in the house of
the LORD continually all the days of Jehoiada.
15 ¶ But Jehoiada waxed old, and was full of days
when he died; an hundred and thirty years old
was he when he died.
16 And they buried him in the city of David
among the kings, because he had done good in
Israel, both toward God, and toward his house.
17 Now after the death of Jehoiada came the
princes of Judah, and made obeisance to the king.

of David from total destruction (22:11), so the patient and careful planning of her husband, Jehoiada, restored the son of David to the throne of Judah. The house of David appeared to be in ruin for over seven years, a terrible test for those who believed God's promise but knew nothing of Joash's preservation. However, by faith in that promise (23:3), the priest and Levites took their lives into their hands to crown the boy-king Joash. God had not abandoned His people. The gates of hell cannot prevail against His church. God will ever preserve His kingdom in this world through the living faith of His people. How is your faith producing patience in seemingly hopeless days, as well as wise and bold actions?

2. **The monarchy was lost because they abandoned God's covenant (22:4), and so the restoration of the kingdom must engage the people to keep covenant with the Lord as faithful worshipers. We cannot cry out to God, "Thy kingdom come" (Matt. 6:10), with true hearts unless we also turn from our disobedience and idolatry and renew our commitment to obedience and faithful worship. How then should we pray for revival in the church?**

Chapter 24: *Joash walked in the ways of God under the supervision of Jehoiada, but wandered from them after Jehoiada's death.*

24:1 *Joash.* Also called "Jehoash" (2 Kings 11:21; 12:1), not to be confused with a king of Israel of the same name (25:17; 2 Kings 13:10).

24:2 *all the days of Jehoiada.* The author hints at the coming unfaithfulness even before speaking of the good things Joash did. The priest took charge of Joash beyond the initial coronation.

24:4 *repair the house of the LORD.* Chronicles does not record the details of the damage to the temple due to Athaliah (v. 7), but it was extensive and required much wealth and time to repair.

24:5 *Levites hastened it not.* The Levites withstood Joash's command for twenty-three years (2 Kings 12:6).

24:6 *required.* Asked. *commandment of Moses.* This was a temple tax (Ex. 30:11–16). *tabernacle of witness.* The tabernacle built in the day of Moses.

24:8 *chest.* This was a compromise where the people could offer their finances and yet the Levites were not burdened to collect the finances year by year. *without.* Outside.

24:10 *rejoiced.* The collection was more than a dutiful tax, rather a heartfelt act of worship (1 Chron. 29:9).

24:14 *withal.* With them. *all the days of Jehoiada.* See note at v. 2.

24:15–16 *an hundred and thirty years old.* God gave Jehoiada long life and great influence over the people of Judah and the Davidic king. *buried him . . . among the kings.* He was given a respectful burial among the royal tombs, an honor later denied to Joash (v. 25).

24:17 *obeisance.* Bowing to show respect. *hearkened.* Listened. The text suggests that their flattery of the king swayed

Then the king hearkened unto them.
18 And they left the house of the LORD God of their fathers, and served groves and idols: and wrath came upon Judah and Jerusalem for this their trespass.
19 Yet he sent prophets to them, to bring them again unto the LORD; and they testified against them: but they would not give ear.
20 And the Spirit of God came upon Zechariah the son of Jehoiada the priest, which stood above the people, and said unto them, Thus saith God, Why transgress ye the commandments of the LORD, that ye cannot prosper? because ye have forsaken the LORD, he hath also forsaken you.
21 And they conspired against him, and stoned him with stones at the commandment of the king in the court of the house of the LORD.
22 Thus Joash the king remembered not the kindness which Jehoiada his father had done to him, but slew his son. And when he died, he said, The LORD look upon *it*, and require *it*.
23 ¶ And it came to pass at the end of the year, *that* the host of Syria came up against him: and they came to Judah and Jerusalem, and destroyed all the princes of the people from among the people, and sent all the spoil of them unto the king of Damascus.
24 For the army of the Syrians came with a small company of men, and the LORD delivered a very great host into their hand, because they had forsaken the LORD God of their fathers. So they executed judgment against Joash.
25 And when they were departed from him, (for they left him in great diseases,) his own servants conspired against him for the blood of the sons of Jehoiada the priest, and slew him on his bed, and he died: and they buried him in the city of David, but they buried him not in the sepulchres of the kings.
26 And these are they that conspired against him; Zabad the son of Shimeath an Ammonitess, and Jehozabad the son of Shimrith a Moabitess.
27 ¶ Now *concerning* his sons, and the greatness of the burdens *laid* upon him, and the repairing of the house of God, behold, they *are* written in the story of the book of the kings. And Amaziah his son reigned in his stead.

CHAPTER 25

AMAZIAH *was* twenty and five years old *when* he began to reign, and he reigned twenty and nine years in Jerusalem. And his mother's name *was* Jehoaddan of Jerusalem.
2 And he did *that which was* right in the sight of the LORD, but not with a perfect heart.
3 ¶ Now it came to pass, when the kingdom was established to him, that he slew his servants that had killed the king his father.
4 But he slew not their children, but *did* as *it is* written in the law in the book of Moses, where the LORD commanded, saying, The fathers shall not die for the children, neither shall the children die for the fathers, but every man shall die for his own sin.
5 ¶ Moreover Amaziah gathered Judah together,

---

him to follow them in sin.
24:18 *left the house.* Abandoned the worship of the Lord at the temple. *wrath.* God's anger for their sin.
24:20 *Spirit of God came upon.* Literally, the Spirit "clothed" him, a metaphor for equipping him with supernatural ability (Judg. 6:34; 1 Chron. 12:18), as the Spirit does all the prophets (v. 19).
24:22 *his father.* Not his biological father, but his spiritual father, emphasizing the evil of his sin against Jehoiada's son. *require it.* Avenge it. He committed his cause to God, and God heard him.
24:23 *end of the year.* Zechariah's vindication came, though it was delayed for a time.
24:25 *great diseases.* Serious wounds. *sons of Jehoiada.* Evidently he killed more than Zechariah. *buried him not.* Joash was not given a royal burial, but died in disgrace.
24:26 *Ammonitess . . . Moabitess.* Those who killed Joash were descendants of Lot's daughters (Gen. 19:34–38); a scathing rebuke and judgment against Joash.
24:27 *stead.* Place.

Thoughts for Personal/Family Worship: Chapter 24

1. **Joash was faithful as long as Jehoiada was alive (v. 2). The prayers, counsel, and presence of godly people make an incalculable difference for good. This is what Christ means when He speaks about His people as the salt of the earth and the light of the world (Matt. 5:13–14). When faithful Christians are gone, much often goes with them. Thank God for spiritual fathers and mothers who have influenced you. Yet ask yourself, if they were to die, would you continue to walk with God as faithfully as you do when they are here?**
2. **Zechariah was faithful unto death. Empowered by the Holy Spirit, he courageously stood against the king, princes, and people. He rebuked them of their sin and warned them of God's anger, but they would not hear God's message and killed the messenger. As Zechariah died, broken by the stones of the wicked, he entrusted his case to the righteous Judge. Pray for God to give to the church preachers like Zechariah, filled with the Spirit's boldness and humility.**

Chapter 25: ***Though the reign of Amaziah begins well, he ends his reign in idolatry and hardheartedness, and he dies as a result of a conspiracy.***

King Amaziah (2 Chron. 25:1–28)

25:1 *twenty and nine years in Jerusalem.* It may be that Amaziah's reign was a coregency with Uzziah for twenty-four years (2 Kings 14:2,23; 15:1).
25:2 *not with a perfect heart.* Not with wholehearted dedication and submission to God's Word, as the rest of this chapter shows.
25:4 *written in the law . . . of Moses.* In punishing the servants who killed his father, Amaziah followed the principles of

and made them captains over thousands, and
captains over hundreds, according to the houses
of *their* fathers, throughout all Judah and Benja-
min: and he numbered them from twenty years
old and above, and found them three hundred
thousand choice *men, able* to go forth to war, that
could handle spear and shield.
6 He hired also an hundred thousand mighty
men of valour out of Israel for an hundred tal-
ents of silver.
7 But there came a man of God to him, saying,
O king, let not the army of Israel go with thee;
for the LORD *is* not with Israel, *to wit, with* all the
children of Ephraim.
8 But if thou wilt go, do *it*, be strong for the
battle: God shall make thee fall before the enemy:
for God hath power to help, and to cast down.
9 And Amaziah said to the man of God, But what
shall we do for the hundred talents which I have
given to the army of Israel? And the man of God
answered, The LORD is able to give thee much
more than this.
10 Then Amaziah separated them, *to wit*, the
army that was come to him out of Ephraim, to
go home again: wherefore their anger was greatly
kindled against Judah, and they returned home
in great anger.
11 ¶ And Amaziah strengthened himself, and led
forth his people, and went to the valley of salt, and
smote of the children of Seir ten thousand.
12 And *other* ten thousand *left* alive did the chil-
dren of Judah carry away captive, and brought
them unto the top of the rock, and cast them
down from the top of the rock, that they all were
broken in pieces.
13 ¶ But the soldiers of the army which Amaziah
sent back, that they should not go with him to
battle, fell upon the cities of Judah, from Samaria
even unto Beth-horon, and smote three thousand
of them, and took much spoil.
14 ¶ Now it came to pass, after that Amaziah was
come from the slaughter of the Edomites, that he
brought the gods of the children of Seir, and set
them up *to be* his gods, and bowed down himself
before them, and burned incense unto them.
15 Wherefore the anger of the LORD was kindled
against Amaziah, and he sent unto him a prophet,
which said unto him, Why hast thou sought after
the gods of the people, which could not deliver
their own people out of thine hand?
16 And it came to pass, as he talked with him,
that *the king* said unto him, Art thou made of
the king's counsel? forbear; why shouldest thou
be smitten? Then the prophet forbare, and said, I
know that God hath determined to destroy thee,
because thou hast done this, and hast not heark-
ened unto my counsel.
17 ¶ Then Amaziah king of Judah took advice,
and sent to Joash, the son of Jehoahaz, the son of
Jehu, king of Israel, saying, Come, let us see one
another in the face.
18 And Joash king of Israel sent to Amaziah king
of Judah, saying, The thistle that *was* in Lebanon
sent to the cedar that *was* in Lebanon, saying, Give
thy daughter to my son to wife: and there passed
by a wild beast that *was* in Lebanon, and trode
down the thistle.
19 Thou sayest, Lo, thou hast smitten the
Edomites; and thine heart lifteth thee up to boast:
abide now at home; why shouldest thou meddle
to *thine* hurt, that thou shouldest fall, *even* thou,
and Judah with thee?
20 But Amaziah would not hear; for it *came* of
God, that he might deliver them into the hand *of
their enemies*, because they sought after the gods
of Edom.

---

justice in God's law (Deut. 24:16). *own sin.* Though God used the sin of the men who killed Joash (24:25), they were still held accountable for their actions.

25:5 The military census was likely in preparation for the attack against Seir or Edom (v. 11).

25:7 *man of God.* Prophet (11:2). *the LORD is not with Israel.* A remarkable statement about some of the descendants of Jacob. The northern kingdom had abandoned the Lord (13:8–11), indeed Israel hated God (19:2), so He had abandoned them (15:2). *to wit.* That is (v. 10).

25:8 *God hath power to help, and to cast down.* God controls every victory and every defeat (20:15), and therefore His servants must not rely on the power of mere men (16:7).

25:9 *The LORD is able to give thee much more.* We never ultimately lose out when we obey God (Matt. 19:29).

25:10 *great anger.* Either at being dishonored or at the loss of plunder of war they anticipated getting.

25:11–12 Amaziah's victory demonstrates that he did not need the assistance of wicked Israel, but the Lord alone gave salvation.

25:11 *Seir.* Edom.

25:13 *fell upon the cities of Judah.* Israel proved to be no ally to Judah, but treacherous, violent, and greedy, showing the foolishness of Amaziah's alliance (v. 6).

25:15 *which could not deliver their own people.* The stupidity of man's impulse to idolatry is well illustrated in Amaziah's embrace of the gods of the people he had just defeated in battle.

25:16 *Art thou made of the king's counsel?* Have you been asked to be the counselor of the king? *forbear.* Stop and be silent. *God hath determined.* Literally, "God has counseled," using the same Hebrew root as *counsel*. The king's refusal to hear the *counsel* or wise advice of God's Word shows that God had decreed his destruction in God's eternal *counsel* or wise plan.

25:17 *Joash.* The son of Jehoahaz, a king of the northern tribes. *see one another in the face.* Amaziah's request is not one of peace and friendship, but it is a challenge to Joash to come and fight him.

25:18 *thistle.* Judah. *cedar.* Edom. *wild beast.* Israel.

25:19 *thine heart lifteth thee up to boast.* A common expression for pride, an attitude which God hates and punishes (1 Sam. 2:3; Prov. 8:13; 16:5; Zeph. 2:10).

25:20 *would not hear . . . it came of God.* As in his response to the prophet (v. 16), Amaziah's stubborn refusal to listen to good advice was itself a judgment from God for his idolatry

21 So Joash the king of Israel went up; and they
saw one another in the face, *both* he and Amaziah
king of Judah, at Beth-shemesh, which *belongeth*
to Judah.
22 And Judah was put to the worse before Israel,
and they fled every man to his tent.
23 And Joash the king of Israel took Amaziah king
of Judah, the son of Joash, the son of Jehoahaz, at
Beth-shemesh, and brought him to Jerusalem, and
brake down the wall of Jerusalem from the gate of
Ephraim to the corner gate, four hundred cubits.
24 And *he took* all the gold and the silver, and all
the vessels that were found in the house of God
with Obed-edom, and the treasures of the king's
house, the hostages also, and returned to Samaria.
25 ¶ And Amaziah the son of Joash king of Judah
lived after the death of Joash son of Jehoahaz king
of Israel fifteen years.
26 Now the rest of the acts of Amaziah, first and
last, behold, *are* they not written in the book of
the kings of Judah and Israel?
27 ¶ Now after the time that Amaziah did turn
away from following the LORD they made a con-
spiracy against him in Jerusalem; and he fled to
Lachish: but they sent to Lachish after him, and
slew him there.
28 And they brought him upon horses, and
buried him with his fathers in the city of Judah.

CHAPTER 26

THEN all the people of Judah took Uzziah, who
was sixteen years old, and made him king in the
room of his father Amaziah.
2 He built Eloth, and restored it to Judah, after
that the king slept with his fathers.
3 Sixteen years old *was* Uzziah when he began
to reign, and he reigned fifty and two years in Je-
rusalem. His mother's name also *was* Jecoliah of
Jerusalem.
4 And he did *that which was* right in the sight of
the LORD, according to all that his father Amaziah
did.
5 And he sought God in the days of Zechariah,
who had understanding in the visions of God:
and as long as he sought the LORD, God made
him to prosper.
6 And he went forth and warred against the Phi-
listines, and brake down the wall of Gath, and the
wall of Jabneh, and the wall of Ashdod, and built
cities about Ashdod, and among the Philistines.
7 And God helped him against the Philistines,
and against the Arabians that dwelt in Gur-baal,
and the Mehunims.
8 And the Ammonites gave gifts to Uzziah: and
his name spread abroad *even* to the entering in
of Egypt; for he strengthened *himself* exceedingly.
9 Moreover Uzziah built towers in Jerusalem at
the corner gate, and at the valley gate, and at the
turning *of the wall*, and fortified them.
10 Also he built towers in the desert, and digged
many wells: for he had much cattle, both in the
low country, and in the plains: husbandmen *also*,
and vine dressers in the mountains, and in Car-
mel: for he loved husbandry.
11 Moreover Uzziah had an host of fighting men,
that went out to war by bands, according to the
number of their account by the hand of Jeiel the
scribe and Maaseiah the ruler, under the hand of
Hananiah, *one* of the king's captains.
12 The whole number of the chief of the fathers
of the mighty men of valour *were* two thousand
and six hundred.
13 And under their hand *was* an army, three
hundred thousand and seven thousand and five
hundred, that made war with mighty power, to
help the king against the enemy.
14 And Uzziah prepared for them throughout
all the host shields, and spears, and helmets, and
habergeons, and bows, and slings *to cast* stones.

---

with *the gods of Edom* (v. 14). God gives the proud and idolatrous over to blindness (Rom. 1:21–23,28; 11:8–10).
25:22 *put to the worse.* Defeated.
25:24 *the gold and the silver . . . in the house of God.* God judged Judah's temple because Judah had turned to idols.

Thoughts for Personal/Family Worship: Chapter 25

It is extremely dangerous to remain in a condition of halfhearted religion (v. 2). Though we may do some good things, like Amaziah we may also waste our resources pursuing the favor of the world (v. 6), make ourselves vulnerable to the wicked by our alliances with them (v. 13), be attracted to imitate the world in its corrupt forms of worship (v. 14), proudly take on projects beyond our means to our defeat and disgrace (v. 19), and alienate those around us (v. 27). It is far wiser to humble ourselves before the Lord, give Him our total devotion, and submit to all that His Word counsels us to do. What are the benefits of wholehearted religion?

Chapter 26: *Uzziah is noted as a king of great military prowess, who eventually presumed to act as a priest and who was punished with leprosy.*

King Uzziah (2 Chron. 26:1–23)

26:1 *Uzziah.* Also known as Azariah (2 Kings 15:1). *room.* Place.
26:2 *Eloth.* An important city in Edom, conquered by Solomon but later lost by Jehoram (21:8–10).
26:5 *sought God.* A summary statement of his godliness (see note at 15:2). *Zechariah.* The identity of this prophet is not known with certainty; he is not the author of the biblical book by that name, for it was written after the exile.
26:6–15 *Uzziah* had considerable military, civil, and economic success throughout his long, fifty-two-year reign.
26:12 *mighty men of valour.* Strong and capable soldiers.
26:14 *habergeons.* Armor.
26:15 *engines.* Machines to throw military projectiles. *cunning.* Skillful. *bulwarks.* Defensive walls. *withal.* With them. *marvellously helped.* God gave the king supernatural assis-

15 And he made in Jerusalem engines, invented
by cunning men, to be on the towers and upon
the bulwarks, to shoot arrows and great stones
withal. And his name spread far abroad; for he
was marvellously helped, till he was strong.
16 ¶ But when he was strong, his heart was lifted
up to *his* destruction: for he transgressed against
the LORD his God, and went into the temple of the
LORD to burn incense upon the altar of incense.
17 And Azariah the priest went in after him, and
with him fourscore priests of the LORD, *that were*
valiant men:
18 And they withstood Uzziah the king, and said
unto him, *It appertaineth* not unto thee, Uzziah,
to burn incense unto the LORD, but to the priests
the sons of Aaron, that are consecrated to burn
incense: go out of the sanctuary; for thou hast
trespassed; neither *shall it be* for thine honour
from the LORD God.
19 Then Uzziah was wroth, and *had* a censer in
his hand to burn incense: and while he was wroth
with the priests, the leprosy even rose up in his
forehead before the priests in the house of the
LORD, from beside the incense altar.
20 And Azariah the chief priest, and all the
priests, looked upon him, and, behold, he *was*
leprous in his forehead, and they thrust him out
from thence; yea, himself hasted also to go out,
because the LORD had smitten him.
21 And Uzziah the king was a leper unto the day
of his death, and dwelt in a several house, *being*
a leper; for he was cut off from the house of the
LORD: and Jotham his son *was* over the king's
house, judging the people of the land.
22 ¶ Now the rest of the acts of Uzziah, first and
last, did Isaiah the prophet, the son of Amoz, write.
23 So Uzziah slept with his fathers, and they bur-
ied him with his fathers in the field of the burial
which *belonged* to the kings; for they said, He *is*
a leper: and Jotham his son reigned in his stead.

CHAPTER 27

JOTHAM *was* twenty and five years old when he
began to reign, and he reigned sixteen years in Je-
rusalem. His mother's name also *was* Jerushah,
the daughter of Zadok.
2 And he did *that which was* right in the sight of
the LORD, according to all that his father Uzziah
did: howbeit he entered not into the temple of the
LORD. And the people did yet corruptly.
3 He built the high gate of the house of the LORD,
and on the wall of Ophel he built much.
4 Moreover he built cities in the mountains of Ju-
dah, and in the forests he built castles and towers.
5 ¶ He fought also with the king of the Am-
monites, and prevailed against them. And the
children of Ammon gave him the same year an
hundred talents of silver, and ten thousand mea-
sures of wheat, and ten thousand of barley. So
much did the children of Ammon pay unto him,
both the second year, and the third.
6 So Jotham became mighty, because he prepared
his ways before the LORD his God.
7 ¶ Now the rest of the acts of Jotham, and all his
wars, and his ways, lo, they *are* written in the book
of the kings of Israel and Judah.
8 He was five and twenty years old when he began
to reign, and reigned sixteen years in Jerusalem.
9 ¶ And Jotham slept with his fathers, and they
buried him in the city of David: and Ahaz his son
reigned in his stead.

tance (v. 7) that amazed people.

26:16 *his heart was lifted up.* He became proud. *burn incense upon the altar of incense.* Unlawful for anyone but a priest (Ex. 30:7; Num. 16:35; 18:7). Only Christ could unite the offices of priest and king in Israel (Heb. 7:1,17).

26:17 *fourscore.* Eighty.

26:19 *wroth.* Angry. *leprosy.* A disease that made a person severely unclean and required him to separate himself from the sacred congregation of worshipers (Lev. 13:45–46).

26:20 *thrust him out from thence.* Hurried him out of there. *hasted...to go out.* Quickly removed himself from the temple, recognizing God's judgment.

26:21 *several house.* Separate house.

26:23 *stead.* Place.

Thoughts for Personal/Family Worship: Chapter 26

1. **The Lord prospered Uzziah for much of the five decades that he reigned. Prosperity, however, is dangerous when we do not guard our hearts. We read, "But when he was strong, his heart was lifted up to his destruction" (v. 16). It is sad but far too common that when the Lord prospers us, we seize His gifts as an occasion for pride. How has the Lord blessed you? How can you make that an occasion for humility instead of pride?**
2. **Uzziah's pride particularly showed itself when he presumed to intrude into the worship God had reserved for the priests. He made himself spiritually unclean, and so God made him physically unclean with leprosy. Pride is often at the root of presumption in worship, whereas humility leads us to worship God in exactly the way He has commanded it. Christ alone is the Mediator between God and man, our great High Priest. Are you trusting in yourself or anyone or anything else to gain access to God?**

Chapter 27: *Jotham's reign is briefly recounted without major incidents.*

King Jotham (2 Chron. 27:1–9)

27:2 *howbeit.* However, except. *did yet corruptly.* Continued to act sinfully. Though we may lament the lack of Jotham's influence, his refusal to follow in his father's sins or to go with the crowd is exemplary.

27:6 *became mighty.* Jotham's reign is marked by building up the military prowess of Judah and Jerusalem and the tribute that Ammon paid to Judah. *prepared his ways before the LORD his God.* He lived as one in the presence of God, ordering his conduct according to the covenant (Gen. 17:1; Ps. 119:5).

27:9 *stead.* Place.

CHAPTER 28

AHAZ *was* twenty years old when he began to
reign, and he reigned sixteen years in Jerusalem:
but he did not *that which was* right in the sight of
the LORD, like David his father:
2 For he walked in the ways of the kings of Israel,
and made also molten images for Baalim.
3 Moreover he burnt incense in the valley of the
son of Hinnom, and burnt his children in the fire,
after the abominations of the heathen whom the
LORD had cast out before the children of Israel.
4 He sacrificed also and burnt incense in the high
places, and on the hills, and under every green tree.
5 Wherefore the LORD his God delivered him
into the hand of the king of Syria; and they smote
him, and carried away a great multitude of them
captives, and brought *them* to Damascus. And he
was also delivered into the hand of the king of
Israel, who smote him with a great slaughter.
6 ¶ For Pekah the son of Remaliah slew in Judah
an hundred and twenty thousand in one day,
which were all valiant men; because they had
forsaken the LORD God of their fathers.
7 And Zichri, a mighty man of Ephraim, slew
Maaseiah the king's son, and Azrikam the gover-
nor of the house, and Elkanah *that was* next to
the king.
8 And the children of Israel carried away captive
of their brethren two hundred thousand, women,
sons, and daughters, and took also away much
spoil from them, and brought the spoil to
Samaria.
9 But a prophet of the LORD was there, whose
name *was* Oded: and he went out before the
host that came to Samaria, and said unto them,
Behold, because the LORD God of your fathers
was wroth with Judah, he hath delivered them
into your hand, and ye have slain them in a rage
that reacheth up unto heaven.
10 And now ye purpose to keep under the chil-
dren of Judah and Jerusalem for bondmen and
bondwomen unto you: *but are there* not with you,
even with you, sins against the LORD your God?
11 Now hear me therefore, and deliver the
captives again, which ye have taken captive of
your brethren: for the fierce wrath of the LORD
is upon you.
12 Then certain of the heads of the children of
Ephraim, Azariah the son of Johanan, Berechiah
the son of Meshillemoth, and Jehizkiah the son of
Shallum, and Amasa the son of Hadlai, stood up
against them that came from the war,
13 And said unto them, Ye shall not bring in the
captives hither: for whereas we have offended
against the LORD *already*, ye intend to add *more*
to our sins and to our trespass: for our trespass is
great, and *there is* fierce wrath against Israel.
14 So the armed men left the captives and the
spoil before the princes and all the congregation.
15 And the men which were expressed by name
rose up, and took the captives, and with the spoil
clothed all that were naked among them, and
arrayed them, and shod them, and gave them to
eat and to drink, and anointed them, and carried
all the feeble of them upon asses, and brought
them to Jericho, the city of palm trees, to their
brethren: then they returned to Samaria.
16 ¶ At that time did king Ahaz send unto the
kings of Assyria to help him.
17 For again the Edomites had come and smitten
Judah, and carried away captives.
18 The Philistines also had invaded the cities
of the low country, and of the south of Judah,
and had taken Beth-shemesh, and Ajalon, and

Thoughts for Personal/Family Worship: Chapter 27

Jotham reigned successfully and admirably because "he prepared his ways before the LORD his God" (v. 6). This is a summary of true religion. First, it means that a godly person lives in the presence of God. He does not limit his religion to sacred places or times, but constantly walks with a sense that God is here to keep His promises. Second, it means that a godly person directs his life according to God's covenant. His authority is not mere tradition, for he knows that his fathers erred in some things. His guide is not popularity, for the majority can be wicked. He does not simply follow his impulses. He orders his ways before his covenant Lord according to His Word. What would that look like in your own life?

Chapter 28: *Under Ahaz, Judah suffers military defeat by Syria, and he leads the people into idolatry.*

King Ahaz (2 Chron. 28:1–27)

28:1 *Ahaz.* Ahaz experienced the curse of military defeat time and again.

28:3 *burnt his children in the fire.* Child sacrifice was a pagan notion of attempting to appease the gods and forbidden in Israel (Lev. 18:21; 20:2–4; Deut. 12:31).

28:4 *under every green tree.* Ahaz's idolatry was prolific and public.

28:5 *Syria . . . Israel.* At this time in Judah's history, both its northern neighbors were formidable forces. Syria took many from Judah into an exile to Damascus, their capital city.

28:6 *Pekah* became king over Israel in the last year of king Azariah's reign.

28:9 *Oded.* Nothing more is recorded of him. *wroth.* Angry. *rage.* Though Judah's defeat was predetermined by God, Israel committed the sin of killing the people of Judah with vengeance and *rage.*

28:10 *bondmen and bondwomen.* Slaves.

28:11 *fierce wrath.* During Ahaz's reign, Assyria would conquer and exile Israel (722 BC) as God's judgment for their persistent idolatry (2 Kings 17:5–23). Chronicles does not recount the history of Assyria's invasion, but assumes it (29:9; 30:6).

28:15 The Israelites show great kindness to the men of Judah in a manner that anticipates elements of the parable of the Good Samaritan (Luke 10:30–35).

28:16–21 Ahaz's fault was that he sought military aid from the pagan empire of Assyria. Assyria would exile Israel and

Gederoth, and Shocho with the villages thereof,
and Timnah with the villages thereof, Gimzo also
and the villages thereof: and they dwelt there.
19 For the LORD brought Judah low because of
Ahaz king of Israel; for he made Judah naked, and
transgressed sore against the LORD.
20 And Tilgath-pilneser king of Assyria came
unto him, and distressed him, but strengthened
him not.
21 For Ahaz took away a portion *out* of the house
of the LORD, and *out* of the house of the king,
and of the princes, and gave *it* unto the king of
Assyria: but he helped him not.
22 ¶ And in the time of his distress did he tres-
pass yet more against the LORD: this *is that* king
Ahaz.
23 For he sacrificed unto the gods of Damascus,
which smote him: and he said, Because the gods
of the kings of Syria help them, *therefore* will I
sacrifice to them, that they may help me. But they
were the ruin of him, and of all Israel.
24 And Ahaz gathered together the vessels of the
house of God, and cut in pieces the vessels of the
house of God, and shut up the doors of the house
of the LORD, and he made him altars in every
corner of Jerusalem.
25 And in every several city of Judah he made
high places to burn incense unto other gods, and
provoked to anger the LORD God of his fathers.
26 ¶ Now the rest of his acts and of all his ways,
first and last, behold, they *are* written in the book
of the kings of Judah and Israel.
27 And Ahaz slept with his fathers, and they bur-
ied him in the city, *even* in Jerusalem: but they
brought him not into the sepulchres of the kings
of Israel: and Hezekiah his son reigned in his stead.

CHAPTER 29

HEZEKIAH began to reign *when he was* five and
twenty years old, and he reigned nine and twenty
years in Jerusalem. And his mother's name *was*
Abijah, the daughter of Zechariah.
2 And he did *that which was* right in the sight of
the LORD, according to all that David his father
had done.
3 ¶ He in the first year of his reign, in the first
month, opened the doors of the house of the
LORD, and repaired them.
4 And he brought in the priests and the Levites,
and gathered them together into the east street,
5 And said unto them, Hear me, ye Levites,
sanctify now yourselves, and sanctify the house of
the LORD God of your fathers, and carry forth the
filthiness out of the holy *place*.
6 For our fathers have trespassed, and done *that
which was* evil in the eyes of the LORD our God,
and have forsaken him, and have turned away
their faces from the habitation of the LORD, and
turned *their* backs.
7 Also they have shut up the doors of the porch,
and put out the lamps, and have not burned
incense nor offered burnt offerings in the holy
place unto the God of Israel.
8 Wherefore the wrath of the LORD was upon
Judah and Jerusalem, and he hath delivered them

---

would pose a formidable threat to Judah until the days of Hezekiah.

28:19 *naked.* Exposed and humiliated. *sore.* Exceedingly.

28:20 Though Ahaz turned to receive help from *Tilgath-pilneser king of Assyria*, they did not help but instead *distressed* Judah.

28:23 *which smote him.* Ahaz failed to understand the judgment of God, assuming that the *gods of Damascus* had defeated him, and therefore he worshiped them instead of repenting.

28:24 *shut up the doors of the house of the LORD.* Though idols may initially creep in alongside the worship of God, ultimately they will displace God altogether unless removed.

28:27 *kings of Israel.* A reference to the kings of Judah. *stead.* Place.

Thoughts for Personal/Family Worship: Chapter 28

1. **In a way that seems insane, Ahaz threw himself and his nation into the worship of idols, even at the cost of sacrificing some of his children. When the Lord gave him over to the forces of Damascus as punishment, Ahaz added the idols of Damascus to his worship instead of turning back to the Lord. His mind was so ruled by idolatry that he assumed he was defeated by the power of a superior idol. People today run from idol to idol in their trials, but apart from God's grace, they will not turn to the Lord. How do you see this around you today?**
2. **After so many years of apostasy in the northern kingdom, it seemed like a hopeless case for the prophet Oded to call Israel to show mercy on the captives of Judah. However, when he faithfully preached God's Word, some leaders in Israel responded with a touching display of kindness to their defeated brothers. Let us never assume that it is worthless to speak God's Word to a group of sinners, no matter what their reputation. They may put us to shame with how they respond. Where are you tempted to think that it is not worth sharing God's Word?**

KINGDOM REFORMED AND RUINED (2 CHRON. 29:1—35:27)

Hezekiah's Righteous Reign (2 Chron. 29:1—32:33)

Chapter 29: *The reign of Hezekiah is marked by religious reforms that cleansed the temple and restored worship.*

29:1–2 *Hezekiah* was a bright spot in Judah's fading history, a brief return to the godly ways of *David his father* (11:17; 17:3; 28:1).

29:3 *first year . . . in the first month.* He quickly reinstituted the worship of God. *opened the doors.* The doors by which the priests would enter the holy place from the outer court (v. 7). Ahaz had shut the doors and essentially forbidden the worship of God (28:24).

29:4 *priests and the Levites.* The following monologue was addressed to those responsible to lead Judah in the worship of the Lord.

to trouble, to astonishment, and to hissing, as ye
see with your eyes.
9 For, lo, our fathers have fallen by the sword, and
our sons and our daughters and our wives *are* in
captivity for this.
10 Now *it is* in mine heart to make a covenant
with the LORD God of Israel, that his fierce wrath
may turn away from us.
11 My sons, be not now negligent: for the LORD
hath chosen you to stand before him, to serve
him, and that ye should minister unto him, and
burn incense.
12 ¶ Then the Levites arose, Mahath the son of
Amasai, and Joel the son of Azariah, of the sons
of the Kohathites: and of the sons of Merari, Kish
the son of Abdi, and Azariah the son of Jehalelel:
and of the Gershonites; Joah the son of Zimmah,
and Eden the son of Joah:
13 And of the sons of Elizaphan; Shimri, and
Jeiel: and of the sons of Asaph; Zechariah, and
Mattaniah:
14 And of the sons of Heman; Jehiel, and Shim-
ei: and of the sons of Jeduthun; Shemaiah, and
Uzziel.
15 And they gathered their brethren, and sanc-
tified themselves, and came, according to the
commandment of the king, by the words of the
LORD, to cleanse the house of the LORD.
16 And the priests went into the inner part of
the house of the LORD, to cleanse *it*, and brought
out all the uncleanness that they found in the
temple of the LORD into the court of the house of
the LORD. And the Levites took *it*, to carry *it* out
abroad into the brook Kidron.
17 Now they began on the first *day* of the first
month to sanctify, and on the eighth day of the
month came they to the porch of the LORD: so
they sanctified the house of the LORD in eight
days; and in the sixteenth day of the first month
they made an end.
18 Then they went in to Hezekiah the king, and
said, We have cleansed all the house of the LORD,
and the altar of burnt offering, with all the vessels
thereof, and the shewbread table, with all the
vessels thereof.
19 Moreover all the vessels, which king Ahaz in
his reign did cast away in his transgression, have
we prepared and sanctified, and, behold, they *are*
before the altar of the LORD.
20 ¶ Then Hezekiah the king rose early, and
gathered the rulers of the city, and went up to the
house of the LORD.
21 And they brought seven bullocks, and seven
rams, and seven lambs, and seven he goats, for a
sin offering for the kingdom, and for the sanctu-
ary, and for Judah. And he commanded the priests
the sons of Aaron to offer *them* on the altar of the
LORD.
22 So they killed the bullocks, and the priests re-
ceived the blood, and sprinkled *it* on the altar: like-
wise, when they had killed the rams, they sprinkled
the blood upon the altar: they killed also the lambs,
and they sprinkled the blood upon the altar.
23 And they brought forth the he goats *for* the
sin offering before the king and the congregation;
and they laid their hands upon them:
24 And the priests killed them, and they made
reconciliation with their blood upon the altar,
to make an atonement for all Israel: for the king
commanded *that* the burnt offering and the sin
offering *should be made* for all Israel.
25 And he set the Levites in the house of the LORD
with cymbals, with psalteries, and with harps,
according to the commandment of David, and
of Gad the king's seer, and Nathan the prophet:
for *so was* the commandment of the LORD by his
prophets.
26 And the Levites stood with the instruments of
David, and the priests with the trumpets.
27 And Hezekiah commanded to offer the burnt
offering upon the altar. And when the burnt
offering began, the song of the LORD began *also*
with the trumpets, and with the instruments
ordained by David king of Israel.
28 And all the congregation worshipped, and
the singers sang, and the trumpeters sounded:
and all *this continued* until the burnt offering was
finished.
29 And when they had made an end of offering,
the king and all that were present with him bowed
themselves, and worshipped.
30 Moreover Hezekiah the king and the princes
commanded the Levites to sing praise unto the
LORD with the words of David, and of Asaph the

29:10 *make a covenant.* See note at 15:12.
29:11 *My sons.* The king spoke to the priests and Levites as an affectionate father. *burn incense.* The word *incense* is not in the original Hebrew, and the verb *burn* can be used of either incense or offerings (1 Chron. 23:13).
29:16 *uncleanness.* Likely the idols in the temple. *abroad.* Away from the place. *brook Kidron.* A burial site outside Jerusalem that was used to dispose of such things.
29:18–19 *cleansed.* Removed all ceremonial uncleanness according to the law of Moses. *sanctified.* Made holy and thus ready for the worship of God.
29:21 *bullocks.* Bulls.
29:24 *all Israel* (repeated). Probably both kingdoms. Later, Hezekiah invited the northern tribes to come and celebrate the Passover with the tribes of Judah (30:1,5–6; 31:1).
29:25 *commandment of the LORD by his prophets.* Worship must be structured by the Word.
29:27 *when the burnt offering began, the song of the LORD began.* Musical worship in Israel was closely connected to temple sacrifice.
29:30 *with the words of David.* They sang the Psalms. The content of worship must come from the Word.

seer. And they sang praises with gladness, and
they bowed their heads and worshipped.
31 Then Hezekiah answered and said, Now ye
have consecrated yourselves unto the LORD, come
near and bring sacrifices and thank offerings into
the house of the LORD. And the congregation
brought in sacrifices and thank offerings; and as
many as were of a free heart burnt offerings.
32 And the number of the burnt offerings, which
the congregation brought, was threescore and
ten bullocks, an hundred rams, *and* two hundred
lambs: all these *were* for a burnt offering to the
LORD.
33 And the consecrated things *were* six hundred
oxen and three thousand sheep.
34 But the priests were too few, so that they could
not flay all the burnt offerings: wherefore their
brethren the Levites did help them, till the work
was ended, and until the *other* priests had sancti-
fied themselves: for the Levites *were* more upright
in heart to sanctify themselves than the priests.
35 And also the burnt offerings *were* in abun-
dance, with the fat of the peace offerings, and the
drink offerings for *every* burnt offering. So the
service of the house of the LORD was set in order.
36 And Hezekiah rejoiced, and all the people, that
God had prepared the people: for the thing was
done suddenly.

CHAPTER 30

AND Hezekiah sent to all Israel and Judah, and
wrote letters also to Ephraim and Manasseh,
that they should come to the house of the LORD
at Jerusalem, to keep the passover unto the LORD
God of Israel.
2 For the king had taken counsel, and his princes,
and all the congregation in Jerusalem, to keep the
passover in the second month.
3 For they could not keep it at that time, because
the priests had not sanctified themselves suffi-
ciently, neither had the people gathered them-
selves together to Jerusalem.
4 And the thing pleased the king and all the
congregation.
5 So they established a decree to make proclama-
tion throughout all Israel, from Beer-sheba even
to Dan, that they should come to keep the pass-
over unto the LORD God of Israel at Jerusalem: for
they had not done *it* of a long *time in such sort* as
it was written.
6 So the posts went with the letters from the king
and his princes throughout all Israel and Judah,
and according to the commandment of the king,
saying, Ye children of Israel, turn again unto the
LORD God of Abraham, Isaac, and Israel, and he
will return to the remnant of you, that are escaped
out of the hand of the kings of Assyria.
7 And be not ye like your fathers, and like your
brethren, which trespassed against the LORD God
of their fathers, *who* therefore gave them up to
desolation, as ye see.
8 Now be ye not stiffnecked, as your fathers *were*,
but yield yourselves unto the LORD, and enter into
his sanctuary, which he hath sanctified for ever:
and serve the LORD your God, that the fierceness
of his wrath may turn away from you.
9 For if ye turn again unto the LORD, your
brethren and your children *shall find* compassion
before them that lead them captive, so that they
shall come again into this land: for the LORD your
God *is* gracious and merciful, and will not turn
away *his* face from you, if ye return unto him.
10 So the posts passed from city to city through

29:31 *free heart.* Those who were generous.
29:34 *flay.* Remove the skin of the offering.
29:36 *God had prepared the people.* Their readiness to return to biblical worship was a gift of grace and an answer to David's prayer (1 Chron. 29:18).

Thoughts for Personal/Family Worship: Chapter 29

1. **Reformation centers upon worship, and nothing is more urgent than to begin to restore biblical worship after it has been corrupted or lost. Central to this work is the calling of the ministers who lead worship back to their holy duties. They must lead the church to cleanse away all that offends the Lord and to sanctify God's temple, which in Christ is the people themselves. They must take both the structure and content of worship from the Word of God. How can you pray for your leaders? And how can you use God's Word in your own private worship?**
2. **The only way that leaders can bring the people to willingly and gladly embrace reformation, especially in worship, is if God prepares the people. Apart from divine grace, people will resist godly leadership and reject godly example (27:2). However, when the Lord works in their hearts, they embrace reformation willingly and eagerly, to the joy of all involved (29:36). How should this motivate us to pray?**

Chapter 30: *The Passover is memorably observed under the reign of Hezekiah.*

30:1 *all Israel. Hezekiah* sought to bring in all the tribes to keep the feast. *Israel* had already been exiled by Assyria; the invitation went only to the remnant still living in the north (v. 6). *passover.* A feast instituted by God to commemorate Israel's deliverance from Egypt (Ex. 12:1–28).
30:2 *second month.* Passover was to be held in the first month, but the temple was not prepared (v. 3). The law of Moses allowed, under certain instances, for the people to celebrate it on the second month (Num. 9:10–11).
30:5 *as it was written.* As the law of God required. The king is God's servant to promote obedience to God's will.
30:6 *posts.* Runners (v. 10). *turn again . . . and he will return.* God promises that He will be with those who repent of sin and come back to Him (James 4:8), because He is compassionate (v. 9; Luke 15:11–32). *God of . . . Israel.* The God who is faithful to His covenant promises.
30:9 *gracious and merciful.* God's character that He revealed to Moses (Ex. 34:6).

the country of Ephraim and Manasseh even unto
Zebulun: but they laughed them to scorn, and
mocked them.
11 Nevertheless divers of Asher and Manasseh
and of Zebulun humbled themselves, and came
to Jerusalem.
12 Also in Judah the hand of God was to give
them one heart to do the commandment of the
king and of the princes, by the word of the LORD.
13 ¶ And there assembled at Jerusalem much
people to keep the feast of unleavened bread in
the second month, a very great congregation.
14 And they arose and took away the altars that
were in Jerusalem, and all the altars for incense
took they away, and cast *them* into the brook
Kidron.
15 Then they killed the passover on the four-
teenth *day* of the second month: and the priests
and the Levites were ashamed, and sanctified
themselves, and brought in the burnt offerings
into the house of the LORD.
16 And they stood in their place after their man-
ner, according to the law of Moses the man of
God: the priests sprinkled the blood, *which they*
received of the hand of the Levites.
17 For *there were* many in the congregation that
were not sanctified: therefore the Levites had the
charge of the killing of the passovers for every one
that was not clean, to sanctify *them* unto the LORD.
18 For a multitude of the people, *even* many of
Ephraim, and Manasseh, Issachar, and Zebulun,
had not cleansed themselves, yet did they eat
the passover otherwise than it was written. But
Hezekiah prayed for them, saying, The good LORD
pardon every one
19 *That* prepareth his heart to seek God, the LORD
God of his fathers, though *he be* not *cleansed*
according to the purification of the sanctuary.
20 And the LORD hearkened to Hezekiah, and
healed the people.
21 And the children of Israel that were present
at Jerusalem kept the feast of unleavened bread
seven days with great gladness: and the Levites
and the priests praised the LORD day by day,
singing with loud instruments unto the LORD.
22 And Hezekiah spake comfortably unto all
the Levites that taught the good knowledge of
the LORD: and they did eat throughout the feast
seven days, offering peace offerings, and making
confession to the LORD God of their fathers.
23 And the whole assembly took counsel to keep
other seven days: and they kept *other* seven days
with gladness.
24 For Hezekiah king of Judah did give to the con-
gregation a thousand bullocks and seven thousand
sheep; and the princes gave to the congregation a
thousand bullocks and ten thousand sheep: and a
great number of priests sanctified themselves.
25 And all the congregation of Judah, with the
priests and the Levites, and all the congregation
that came out of Israel, and the strangers that
came out of the land of Israel, and that dwelt in
Judah, rejoiced.
26 So there was great joy in Jerusalem: for since
the time of Solomon the son of David king of
Israel *there was* not the like in Jerusalem.
27 ¶ Then the priests the Levites arose and
blessed the people: and their voice was heard, and
their prayer came *up* to his holy dwelling place,
even unto heaven.

CHAPTER 31

NOW when all this was finished, all Israel that were
present went out to the cities of Judah, and brake
the images in pieces, and cut down the groves,

30:10 *laughed them to scorn, and mocked.* Even after the horrific judgment of their exile by Assyria, the majority of the people met the call to repentance with proud contempt.
30:11–12 *divers.* Various. Humility, desire to worship God, and submission to His Word produced spiritual unity (*one heart*) between Judah and some of the people from three of the northern tribes. They responded differently than the proud mockers only because of the power of God's sovereign grace (*the hand of God was to give them*, cf. Acts 11:18,21).
30:15 *passover.* The lamb *killed* in the feast. *were ashamed … sanctified themselves.* Probably a reference to those who did not prepare themselves earlier (29:34).
30:17–19 *Levites had the charge.* The people were supposed to slaughter the Passover lambs (Ex. 12:3–7; Deut. 16:5–6), but could not because they were not prepared according to the ceremonial law, which required that all participants in the feast be purified of uncleanness (Num. 9:6). Hezekiah understood that the purification of the *heart*, not merely ceremonial cleansing, is the root of true worship. Therefore, he prayed for God to *pardon* the transgression of the ceremonial law.
30:22 *comfortably.* Literally, "from the heart."
30:27 At the conclusion of the feast, the *priests* called upon God to bless the people, and God heard their *prayer* from heaven (*his holy dwelling place*), as Solomon had asked long before (6:21).

Thoughts for Personal/Family Worship: Chapter 30

1. **Just as King Hezekiah sent messengers throughout all Israel to call people to turn back to God, so the Lord Jesus, King of heaven and earth, sent messengers into all nations to call people to repent and become His disciples (Matt. 28:18–20; Luke 24:44–49). Hezekiah called them to celebrate the Passover, but Christ is our Passover, the Lamb of God whose blood saves sinners from the wrath to come (John 1:29; 1 Cor. 5:7). Missions and evangelism is a matter of obedience to our King. Let us therefore not be lacking in this great effort, nor let us be discouraged because many mock and scorn the message. Who can you be in fervent prayer for, that the hand of the Lord would be with them, and that by His grace many will turn to the Lord?**
2. **Just as Hezekiah asked God to overlook the ceremonial uncleanness of some of the people eating the Passover,**

and threw down the high places and the altars out of all Judah and Benjamin, in Ephraim also and Manasseh, until they had utterly destroyed them all. Then all the children of Israel returned, every man to his possession, into their own cities.
2 ¶ And Hezekiah appointed the courses of the priests and the Levites after their courses, every man according to his service, the priests and Levites for burnt offerings and for peace offerings, to minister, and to give thanks, and to praise in the gates of the tents of the LORD.
3 *He appointed* also the king's portion of his substance for the burnt offerings, *to wit*, for the morning and evening burnt offerings, and the burnt offerings for the sabbaths, and for the new moons, and for the set feasts, as *it is* written in the law of the LORD.
4 Moreover he commanded the people that dwelt in Jerusalem to give the portion of the priests and the Levites, that they might be encouraged in the law of the LORD.
5 ¶ And as soon as the commandment came abroad, the children of Israel brought in abundance the firstfruits of corn, wine, and oil, and honey, and of all the increase of the field; and the tithe of all *things* brought they in abundantly.
6 And *concerning* the children of Israel and Judah, that dwelt in the cities of Judah, they also brought in the tithe of oxen and sheep, and the tithe of holy things which were consecrated unto the LORD their God, and laid *them* by heaps.
7 In the third month they began to lay the foundation of the heaps, and finished *them* in the seventh month.
8 And when Hezekiah and the princes came and saw the heaps, they blessed the LORD, and his people Israel.
9 Then Hezekiah questioned with the priests and the Levites concerning the heaps.
10 And Azariah the chief priest of the house of Zadok answered him, and said, Since *the people* began to bring the offerings into the house of the LORD, we have had enough to eat, and have left plenty: for the LORD hath blessed his people; and that which is left *is* this great store.
11 ¶ Then Hezekiah commanded to prepare chambers in the house of the LORD; and they prepared *them*,
12 And brought in the offerings and the tithes and the dedicated *things* faithfully: over which Cononiah the Levite *was* ruler, and Shimei his brother *was* the next.
13 And Jehiel, and Azaziah, and Nahath, and Asahel, and Jerimoth, and Jozabad, and Eliel, and Ismachiah, and Mahath, and Benaiah, *were* overseers under the hand of Cononiah and Shimei his brother, at the commandment of Hezekiah the king, and Azariah the ruler of the house of God.
14 And Kore the son of Imnah the Levite, the porter toward the east, *was* over the freewill offerings of God, to distribute the oblations of the LORD, and the most holy things.
15 And next him *were* Eden, and Miniamin, and Jeshua, and Shemaiah, Amariah, and Shecaniah, in the cities of the priests, in *their* set office, to give to their brethren by courses, as well to the great as to the small:
16 Beside their genealogy of males, from three years old and upward, *even* unto every one that entereth into the house of the LORD, his daily portion for their service in their charges according to their courses;
17 Both to the genealogy of the priests by the house of their fathers, and the Levites from twenty years old and upward, in their charges by their courses;
18 And to the genealogy of all their little ones, their wives, and their sons, and their daughters, through all the congregation: for in their set office they sanctified themselves in holiness:
19 Also of the sons of Aaron the priests, *which were* in the fields of the suburbs of their cities, in every several city, the men that were expressed by name, to give portions to all the males among the priests, and to all that were reckoned by genealogies among the Levites.

---

so Christ intercedes for His people that God will pardon the sins that mar their sincere worship. Breaking the ceremonial law required God's forgiveness (v. 18), so how much more do we need His forgiveness for our violations of the moral law. However, the Lord is pleased to forgive such faults by the intercession of His Son if our hearts sincerely seek Him. How does this encourage the repentant sinner? How does it warn the hypocrite?

Chapter 31: *Hezekiah organizes the priests for religious worship in the temple.*

31:1 *all Israel.* Again emphasizing how Hezekiah's leadership reached beyond Judah (30:1,6). *groves.* Asherah poles (see note at 14:3). The renewal of worship in the Passover led to reformation throughout the land.

31:2 *courses.* Appointed times. Hezekiah was concerned with establishing a permanent pattern of temple worship, not just celebrating the Passover feast.

31:3 *king's portion.* The Mosaic law did not command kings to give of their own wealth, but Hezekiah was following in the steps of both David and Solomon who committed their wealth to the house of the Lord (1 Chron. 29:2–5). *to wit.* That is. *written in the law.* Obedience is crucial for God-pleasing worship.

31:4 *encouraged in the law.* The people were to give to help provide for the Levites, so that they might be freed to fulfill their calling to study the Law and teach it to the people (Mal. 2:7; 1 Cor. 9:13–14; Gal. 6:6).

31:5 *firstfruits.* As commanded in Num. 18:12–13. *tithe.* As commanded in Num. 18:21.

31:11–16 Hezekiah appointed priests to care for the continual offering of the sacrifices.

20 ¶ And thus did Hezekiah throughout all Judah,
and wrought *that which was* good and right and
truth before the LORD his God.
21 And in every work that he began in the service
of the house of God, and in the law, and in the
commandments, to seek his God, he did *it* with
all his heart, and prospered.

CHAPTER 32

AFTER these things, and the establishment thereof,
Sennacherib king of Assyria came, and entered
into Judah, and encamped against the fenced
cities, and thought to win them for himself.
2 And when Hezekiah saw that Sennacherib was
come, and that he was purposed to fight against
Jerusalem,
3 He took counsel with his princes and his mighty
men to stop the waters of the fountains which
were without the city: and they did help him.
4 So there was gathered much people together,
who stopped all the fountains, and the brook that
ran through the midst of the land, saying, Why
should the kings of Assyria come, and find much
water?
5 Also he strengthened himself, and built up all
the wall that was broken, and raised *it* up to the
towers, and another wall without, and repaired
Millo *in* the city of David, and made darts and
shields in abundance.
6 And he set captains of war over the people, and
gathered them together to him in the street of the
gate of the city, and spake comfortably to them,
saying,
7 Be strong and courageous, be not afraid nor
dismayed for the king of Assyria, nor for all the
multitude that *is* with him: for *there be* more with
us than with him:
8 With him *is* an arm of flesh; but with us *is* the
LORD our God to help us, and to fight our battles.
And the people rested themselves upon the words
of Hezekiah king of Judah.
9 ¶ After this did Sennacherib king of Assyria
send his servants to Jerusalem, (but he *himself
laid siege* against Lachish, and all his power with
him,) unto Hezekiah king of Judah, and unto all
Judah that *were* at Jerusalem, saying,
10 Thus saith Sennacherib king of Assyria,
Whereon do ye trust, that ye abide in the siege in
Jerusalem?
11 Doth not Hezekiah persuade you to give over
yourselves to die by famine and by thirst, say-
ing, The LORD our God shall deliver us out of the
hand of the king of Assyria?
12 Hath not the same Hezekiah taken away his
high places and his altars, and commanded Judah
and Jerusalem, saying, Ye shall worship before one
altar, and burn incense upon it?
13 Know ye not what I and my fathers have done
unto all the people of *other* lands? were the gods
of the nations of those lands any ways able to
deliver their lands out of mine hand?
14 Who *was there* among all the gods of those na-
tions that my fathers utterly destroyed, that could
deliver his people out of mine hand, that your
God should be able to deliver you out of mine
hand?
15 Now therefore let not Hezekiah deceive you,
nor persuade you on this manner, neither yet be-
lieve him: for no god of any nation or kingdom
was able to deliver his people out of mine hand,
and out of the hand of my fathers: how much
less shall your God deliver you out of mine hand?
16 And his servants spake yet *more* against the
LORD God, and against his servant Hezekiah.
17 He wrote also letters to rail on the LORD God
of Israel, and to speak against him, saying, As
the gods of the nations of *other* lands have not

31:20 *wrought.* Worked.
31:21 *to seek his God, he did it with all his heart, and prospered.* The wholehearted pursuit of God is the only path to blessing (Matt. 6:33).

Thoughts for Personal/Family Worship: Chapter 31

1. **The renewal of worship that God worked through Hezekiah was not just one big event, but a transformation that overthrew idolatry in the ordinary lives of the people and made them zealous to support true worship, to the joy of their leaders. Real revival is not just a big meeting with a lot of excitement, but a Spirit-worked transformation that touches the home life and finances. Pray for such revival in your nation and in every nation.**
2. **Hezekiah gave much attention to making sure the ministers of the temple were provided for and organized. Christ also has given instructions for the ministers of His church, so that they can be freed from the necessity of providing for their families to focus their time and energy on the work of the ministry. Why is it important for churches to care for the physical and financial needs of their pastors?**

Chapter 32: ***Sennacherib attacks Judah and blasphemes God, but God delivers Judah.***
32:1 *Sennacherib.* King of Assyria, known for great conquests of surrounding nations. *win them for himself.* The northern tribes were already exiled and there was an imminent threat to Judah as well.
32:3 *without.* Outside.
32:7 *Be strong and courageous.* Common charge to God's people (Josh. 1:6,9; 1 Chron. 19:13; 28:10,20).
32:8 *rested themselves.* Relied or leaned, an expression for faith in God's promises (for the same idea using a different Hebrew word, see 13:18; 14:11; 16:7–8).
32:9 *Lachish.* Important city of military strength (Mic. 1:13). A blow to Judah's confidence.
32:17 *wrote also letters.* This was a mounting verbal attack against God and an attempt to prevent Judah from relying on God. *rail.* Insult.

delivered their people out of mine hand, so shall
not the God of Hezekiah deliver his people out of
mine hand.
18 Then they cried with a loud voice in the Jews'
speech unto the people of Jerusalem that *were* on
the wall, to affright them, and to trouble them;
that they might take the city.
19 And they spake against the God of Jerusalem,
as against the gods of the people of the earth,
which were the work of the hands of man.
20 And for this *cause* Hezekiah the king, and the
prophet Isaiah the son of Amoz, prayed and cried
to heaven.
21 ¶ And the LORD sent an angel, which cut off
all the mighty men of valour, and the leaders and
captains in the camp of the king of Assyria. So he
returned with shame of face to his own land. And
when he was come into the house of his god, they
that came forth of his own bowels slew him there
with the sword.
22 Thus the LORD saved Hezekiah and the inhab-
itants of Jerusalem from the hand of Sennacherib
the king of Assyria, and from the hand of all *other*,
and guided them on every side.
23 And many brought gifts unto the LORD to
Jerusalem, and presents to Hezekiah king of
Judah: so that he was magnified in the sight of all
nations from thenceforth.
24 ¶ In those days Hezekiah was sick to the death,
and prayed unto the LORD: and he spake unto
him, and he gave him a sign.
25 But Hezekiah rendered not again according to
the benefit *done* unto him; for his heart was lifted
up: therefore there was wrath upon him, and
upon Judah and Jerusalem.
26 Notwithstanding Hezekiah humbled himself
for the pride of his heart, *both* he and the inhabi-
tants of Jerusalem, so that the wrath of the LORD
came not upon them in the days of Hezekiah.
27 ¶ And Hezekiah had exceeding much riches
and honour: and he made himself treasuries for
silver, and for gold, and for precious stones, and
for spices, and for shields, and for all manner of
pleasant jewels;
28 Storehouses also for the increase of corn, and
wine, and oil; and stalls for all manner of beasts,
and cotes for flocks.
29 Moreover he provided him cities, and posses-
sions of flocks and herds in abundance: for God
had given him substance very much.
30 This same Hezekiah also stopped the upper
watercourse of Gihon, and brought it straight
down to the west side of the city of David. And
Hezekiah prospered in all his works.
31 ¶ Howbeit in *the business of* the ambassadors
of the princes of Babylon, who sent unto him to
enquire of the wonder that was *done* in the land,
God left him, to try him, that he might know all
that was in his heart.
32 ¶ Now the rest of the acts of Hezekiah, and his
goodness, behold, they *are* written in the vision
of Isaiah the prophet, the son of Amoz, *and* in the
book of the kings of Judah and Israel.
33 And Hezekiah slept with his fathers, and they
buried him in the chiefest of the sepulchres of the
sons of David: and all Judah and the inhabitants
of Jerusalem did him honour at his death. And
Manasseh his son reigned in his stead.

32:18 *Jews' speech.* Spoken in their language, the terms of surrender were not directed to the leaders only but meant to terrify (*affright*) the whole city.
32:19 *work of the hands of man.* Assyrians said that God is nothing more than a man-made idol.
32:20 *Hezekiah . . . Isaiah.* The king and prophet are joined together in crying out to the Lord for deliverance. Trusting in the Lord (vv. 7–8) leads people to earnestly pray to God.
32:21–22 *sent an angel.* One mighty act of God laid waste to the Assyrians (2 Kings 19:35). *they . . . of his own bowels slew him.* His sons killed him (2 Kings 19:37). Sennacherib had insulted the Lord (vv. 16–17), but it was Sennacherib who was put to *shame* (Isa. 37:21–23). His murder in the temple of *his god* proves how powerless idols are to save their worshipers, but *the LORD saved* His people, for victory belongs to Him alone. *on every side.* From all their enemies.
32:23 *magnified.* God exalted His anointed king before all the peoples. Through humiliation comes exaltation.
32:25–26 *rendered not again according to the benefit.* He did not respond to God's mercy with humble gratitude (Ps. 116:12). *his heart was lifted up.* Prosperity led to Hezekiah's pride. *the wrath of the LORD.* The exile was imminent, but because of Hezekiah's repentance, it would not happen in his life.
32:27–30 The latter part of Hezekiah's reign was marked by prosperity, pride, and chastisement.
32:27 *manner.* Kind, sort.
32:28 *cotes.* Small shelters for birds or livestock.
32:31 *God left him, to try him.* God withdrew some of His grace from Hezekiah to test *his heart*. Left to himself, Hezekiah proudly boasted of his treasures to the *ambassadors* from *Babylon*, and the Lord revealed that his treasures and sons would be taken away to *Babylon* (2 Kings 20:12–18).
32:33 *stead.* Place.

Thoughts for Personal/Family Worship: Chapter 32

1. **The people "rested" upon the words of Hezekiah (v. 8). They leaned the weight of their fears and futures in the promises of God. What strength God's promises prove to be to those who lean the weight of their lives on them! Apart from His grace, we will quickly slip into pride and destruction (vv. 25,31). We must therefore earnestly seek His grace for everything and give Him thanks for every good gift, because apart from Christ we can do nothing, but in Him we can do many good things (John 15:5).**
2. **Sennacherib sent his servants to Judah to mock the God of Judah, but God will not be mocked (Gal. 6:7). God struck the king down by the hand of his own sons in the house of his own idol (2 Chron. 32:21), showing His sovereignty over everyone everywhere. How is this a warning to all who mock God and trust in the resources and idols of man?**

CHAPTER 33

MANASSEH *was* twelve years old when he began
to reign, and he reigned fifty and five years in
Jerusalem:
2 But did *that which was* evil in the sight of the
LORD, like unto the abominations of the heathen,
whom the LORD had cast out before the children
of Israel.
3 ¶ For he built again the high places which Hez-
ekiah his father had broken down, and he reared
up altars for Baalim, and made groves, and wor-
shipped all the host of heaven, and served them.
4 Also he built altars in the house of the LORD,
whereof the LORD had said, In Jerusalem shall my
name be for ever.
5 And he built altars for all the host of heaven in
the two courts of the house of the LORD.
6 And he caused his children to pass through
the fire in the valley of the son of Hinnom: also
he observed times, and used enchantments, and
used witchcraft, and dealt with a familiar spirit,
and with wizards: he wrought much evil in the
sight of the LORD, to provoke him to anger.
7 And he set a carved image, the idol which he had
made, in the house of God, of which God had said
to David and to Solomon his son, In this house,
and in Jerusalem, which I have chosen before all
the tribes of Israel, will I put my name for ever:
8 Neither will I any more remove the foot of Israel
from out of the land which I have appointed for
your fathers; so that they will take heed to do all
that I have commanded them, according to the
whole law and the statutes and the ordinances by
the hand of Moses.
9 So Manasseh made Judah and the inhabitants of
Jerusalem to err, *and* to do worse than the heathen,
whom the LORD had destroyed before the children
of Israel.
10 And the LORD spake to Manasseh, and to his
people: but they would not hearken.
11 ¶ Wherefore the LORD brought upon them the
captains of the host of the king of Assyria, which
took Manasseh among the thorns, and bound
him with fetters, and carried him to Babylon.
12 And when he was in affliction, he besought
the LORD his God, and humbled himself greatly
before the God of his fathers,
13 And prayed unto him: and he was intreated
of him, and heard his supplication, and brought
him again to Jerusalem into his kingdom. Then
Manasseh knew that the LORD he *was* God.
14 Now after this he built a wall without the city
of David, on the west side of Gihon, in the valley,
even to the entering in at the fish gate, and com-
passed about Ophel, and raised it up a very great
height, and put captains of war in all the fenced
cities of Judah.
15 And he took away the strange gods, and the
idol out of the house of the LORD, and all the
altars that he had built in the mount of the house
of the LORD, and in Jerusalem, and cast *them* out
of the city.
16 And he repaired the altar of the LORD, and
sacrificed thereon peace offerings and thank
offerings, and commanded Judah to serve the
LORD God of Israel.
17 Nevertheless the people did sacrifice still in the
high places, *yet* unto the LORD their God only.
18 ¶ Now the rest of the acts of Manasseh, and his
prayer unto his God, and the words of the seers
that spake to him in the name of the LORD God of
Israel, behold, they *are written* in the book of the
kings of Israel.
19 His prayer also, and *how God* was intreated
of him, and all his sin, and his trespass, and the
places wherein he built high places, and set up
groves and graven images, before he was hum-
bled: behold, they *are* written among the sayings
of the seers.
20 ¶ So Manasseh slept with his fathers, and they
buried him in his own house: and Amon his son
reigned in his stead.
21 ¶ Amon *was* two and twenty years old when
he began to reign, and reigned two years in
Jerusalem.
22 But he did *that which was* evil in the sight of

Chapter 33: *Manasseh's reign is divided into a time of wicked idolatry and a time of auspicious repentance.*

Manasseh's Idolatry and Repentance (2 Chron. 33:1–20)

33:1–5 Manasseh desecrated the worship of God and therefore did *evil in the sight of the LORD.*

33:6 *pass through the fire.* Child sacrifice was forbidden in the Mosaic law (see 28:3). *familiar spirit.* A medium, someone who consults a demonic spirit.

33:9 *made Judah . . . to err.* Manasseh's sin is the sin of the people and his apostasy the apostasy of the people. *worse than the heathen.* The king actually led Judah into greater depths of idolatry and depravity than the Canaanites whom God obliterated for their sins (Gen. 15:16; Deut. 9:5). The nation was ripe for judgment (Lev. 18:24–28; 20:22–23).

33:10 *hearken.* Listen.

33:11 *among the thorns.* With hooks, as captives were cruelly led (cf. Isa. 37:29). *fetters.* Chains.

33:12 *besought.* Prayed for mercy (2 Kings 13:4).

33:13 *knew that the LORD he was God.* The Lord's discipline and salvation of Manasseh brought him to an experiential knowledge of God's unique sovereignty.

33:14 *without.* Outside. *compassed about.* Surrounded.

33:15–17 *took away . . . cast them out . . . repaired . . . sacrificed . . . commanded.* Manasseh's repentance of mind was evidenced in a thorough change of action (Acts 26:20). *strange.* Foreign.

33:20 *stead.* Place.

Amon's Idolatry (2 Chron. 33:21–25)

33:21–25 A short summary of Amon's wicked reign.

33:22–23 Sadly, Amon followed his father's former idolatry

REPENTANCE

Repentance is a grace of God's Spirit whereby a sinner is inwardly humbled and visibly reformed. In Adam all suffered shipwreck; repentance is the only plank by which we may swim to heaven. It is a grace required under the gospel. The first sermon Christ preached—indeed, the very first word of His sermon—was "Repent" (Matt. 4:17). This was also His farewell message, which He commanded to be proclaimed in all the earth (Luke 24:47). Repentance was what the apostles went out to preach (Mark 6:12). God Himself commands all men everywhere to repent (Matt. 3:2; Acts 3:19; 8:22; 17:30; cf. Heb. 6:1).

Though faith is wrought first in the heart, doubtless repentance shows itself first in the Christian's life. Repentance is not a legal terror, for there may be terror of punishment without a change of heart. Further, repentance is not only resolution against sin (Jer. 2:20; cf. Rev. 6:8). True repentance for sin is present when the acts of sin cease because of the infusion of a principle of grace by the Spirit, just as the air ceases to be dark because of the infusion of light.

Repentance is a spiritual medicine composed of six ingredients. *First*, repentance involves a *sight of sin*, wherein a man comes to himself (Luke 15:17), recognizing what his sin is and what he himself is before a holy God. This causes him to cry with the prophet, "Woe is me! for I am undone" (Isa. 6:5).

Second, repentance consists of *sorrow for sin*. This is the embittering of the soul to the extent that it is crucified in sorrow (cf. Zech. 12:10; Luke 7:38). Such sorrow of the heart runs out of the eyes with bitter tears of holy agony (Ezra 9:3; Ps. 51:17; Isa. 22:12; Jer. 31:19; Joel 2:13; Luke 18:13). In such tears sin must drown or the soul will burn. Those who mourn after a godly manner are then comforted (Matt. 5:4; 2 Cor. 7:9).

Third, repentance includes *confession of sin* (Neh. 9:2; Hos. 5:15). This confession is self-accusing (2 Sam. 24:17; cf. Neh. 9:33), voluntary (Luke 15:18), with compunction (Ps. 38:4), and sincere (Luke 18:10–14) and includes a resolution not to act in sin again (Prov. 28:13; Isa. 1:16; Ezek. 18:21). This confession purges out sin and endears Christ to the soul (Rom. 7:25). Thereby is the way made clear for pardon (2 Sam. 12:13; 1 John 1:9).

Fourth, repentance includes *shame for sin* (Ezek. 43:10). When the heart has been made black by sin, grace makes the face red from blushing (Ezra 9:6; cf. Luke 15:21). This holy embarrassment is due to the recognition of sin's many distresses, among them its guiltiness, its abuse of Christ, and its corrupting power, its folly, and its extent.

Fifth, repentance necessitates a *hatred of sin* (Ezek. 36:31). A true penitent is a sin-loather (Zech. 3:4–5). Further, he hates not just one sin but all sin (Ps. 119:104); indeed, he spurns sin in any form. He hates sin not only *for* hell but *as* hell.

Sixth, repentance works a *turning from sin*. This turning is *from all sin* (Isa. 55:7) *fully unto God* (Acts 26:20). As a ship going east is turned west by the wind, a man who was bent hellward before the contrary wind of the Spirit began to blow on him turns his course in repentance and is caused to sail heavenward. This turning is called a forsaking of sin (Isa. 55:7), a putting of sin far away (Job 11:14), and a dying to sin (Rom. 6:2). This is a whole-souled turning: the eye turns from impure glances, the ear from hearing slanders, the tongue from abusive speech, the hands from all evil, the feet from the path of the prostitute, and the soul from the love of wickedness.

There is no rowing to paradise except upon this stream of repentant tears. How earnestly does God call upon men to turn to Him? He swears, "As I live . . . I have no pleasure in the death of the wicked . . . turn ye, turn ye from your evil ways" (Ezek. 33:11). God would rather have our repenting tears than our blood. If we turn to God, He will turn to us (Zech. 1:3); He will turn His anger from us and His face toward us. Then all things, both mercies and afflictions, will turn to our good; we will taste honey at the end of the rod.

—adapted from Thomas Watson, *The Doctrine of Repentance*

the LORD, as did Manasseh his father: for Amon
sacrificed unto all the carved images which
Manasseh his father had made, and served them;
23 And humbled not himself before the LORD, as
Manasseh his father had humbled himself; but
Amon trespassed more and more.
24 And his servants conspired against him, and
slew him in his own house.
25 ¶ But the people of the land slew all them that
had conspired against king Amon; and the people
of the land made Josiah his son king in his stead.

CHAPTER 34

JOSIAH *was* eight years old when he began to
reign, and he reigned in Jerusalem one and thirty
years.
2 And he did *that which was* right in the sight of
the LORD, and walked in the ways of David his
father, and declined *neither* to the right hand, nor
to the left.
3 ¶ For in the eighth year of his reign, while he
was yet young, he began to seek after the God of
David his father: and in the twelfth year he began
to purge Judah and Jerusalem from the high
places, and the groves, and the carved images, and
the molten images.
4 And they brake down the altars of Baalim in his
presence; and the images, that *were* on high above
them, he cut down; and the groves, and the carved
images, and the molten images, he brake in pieces,
and made dust *of them*, and strowed *it* upon the
graves of them that had sacrificed unto them.
5 And he burnt the bones of the priests upon
their altars, and cleansed Judah and Jerusalem.
6 And *so did he* in the cities of Manasseh, and
Ephraim, and Simeon, even unto Naphtali, with
their mattocks round about.
7 And when he had broken down the altars and
the groves, and had beaten the graven images into
powder, and cut down all the idols throughout all
the land of Israel, he returned to Jerusalem.
8 ¶ Now in the eighteenth year of his reign, when
he had purged the land, and the house, he sent
Shaphan the son of Azaliah, and Maaseiah the
governor of the city, and Joah the son of Joahaz
the recorder, to repair the house of the LORD his
God.
9 And when they came to Hilkiah the high priest,
they delivered the money that was brought into
the house of God, which the Levites that kept the
doors had gathered of the hand of Manasseh and
Ephraim, and of all the remnant of Israel, and
of all Judah and Benjamin; and they returned to
Jerusalem.
10 And they put *it* in the hand of the workmen
that had the oversight of the house of the LORD,
and they gave it to the workmen that wrought in
the house of the LORD, to repair and amend the
house:
11 Even to the artificers and builders gave they *it*,
to buy hewn stone, and timber for couplings, and
to floor the houses which the kings of Judah had
destroyed.
12 And the men did the work faithfully: and the
overseers of them *were* Jahath and Obadiah, the
Levites, of the sons of Merari; and Zechariah and
Meshullam, of the sons of the Kohathites, to set
it forward; and *other of* the Levites, all that could
skill of instruments of musick.
13 Also *they were* over the bearers of burdens, and
were overseers of all that wrought the work in any
manner of service: and of the Levites *there were*
scribes, and officers, and porters.
14 ¶ And when they brought out the money that
was brought into the house of the LORD, Hilkiah
the priest found a book of the law of the LORD
given by Moses.

---

but not his later humility. The sins of parents may have great consequences upon their family even after the parents repent, as the life of David shows.

33:24 *his servants conspired against him*. His assassination revealed the disloyalty and disunity that often characterizes an unjust regime (24:25; 25:27; 32:21).

33:25 *stead*. Place.

Thoughts for Personal/Family Worship: Chapter 33

Manasseh gives us a model of a sinner's repentance. Affliction often serves God's providence to bring down the proud (v. 11). The proper response to outward humiliation is inward humiliation with earnest prayer to God based upon His covenant promises (v. 12). God is amazingly patient and kind and willingly saves sinners who turn to Him in repentance, so that they know by experience that He is the Lord (v. 13). True repentance results in putting old patterns of sin to death (v. 15) and establishing new habits of obedience (v. 16), especially with regard to what one worships and serves. Reflect upon this model. How has God used affliction to bring you to an end of yourself? How have you responded to affliction and conviction of sin? Have you experienced the salvation and lordship of God? How has your lifestyle changed as a result?

Josiah's Righteous Reign (2 Chron. 34:1—35:27)

Chapter 34: *Josiah's reign is marked by a recovery of the law of Moses, a reading of the Law to the people, and a renewal of the covenant.*

34:2 *declined*. Turned aside, an idiomatic phrase showing Josiah's devotion to the Lord (Deut. 17:20; 28:14; Josh. 1:7).

34:3 *groves*. Asherah poles (see 14:3).

34:4–5 Josiah burnt the *images* to symbolize the absolute destruction of idolaters under God's wrath and burnt the *bones of the priests upon their altars* to make the places of pagan worship unclean. *strowed*. Sprinkled.

34:6 *mattocks*. Implements like axes or plough shears.

34:11 *artificers*. Craftsmen. *hewn*. Shaped by cutting.

34:12 *set it forward*. Oversee it. *all that could skill*. Everyone who had understanding or skill.

15 And Hilkiah answered and said to Shaphan the scribe, I have found the book of the law in the house of the LORD. And Hilkiah delivered the book to Shaphan.

16 And Shaphan carried the book to the king, and brought the king word back again, saying, All that was committed to thy servants, they do *it*.

17 And they have gathered together the money that was found in the house of the LORD, and have delivered it into the hand of the overseers, and to the hand of the workmen.

18 Then Shaphan the scribe told the king, saying, Hilkiah the priest hath given me a book. And Shaphan read it before the king.

19 And it came to pass, when the king had heard the words of the law, that he rent his clothes.

20 And the king commanded Hilkiah, and Ahikam the son of Shaphan, and Abdon the son of Micah, and Shaphan the scribe, and Asaiah a servant of the king's, saying,

21 Go, enquire of the LORD for me, and for them that are left in Israel and in Judah, concerning the words of the book that is found: for great *is* the wrath of the LORD that is poured out upon us, because our fathers have not kept the word of the LORD, to do after all that is written in this book.

22 And Hilkiah, and *they* that the king *had appointed*, went to Huldah the prophetess, the wife of Shallum the son of Tikvath, the son of Hasrah, keeper of the wardrobe; (now she dwelt in Jerusalem in the college:) and they spake to her to that *effect*.

23 ¶ And she answered them, Thus saith the LORD God of Israel, Tell ye the man that sent you to me,

24 Thus saith the LORD, Behold, I will bring evil upon this place, and upon the inhabitants thereof, *even* all the curses that are written in the book which they have read before the king of Judah:

25 Because they have forsaken me, and have burned incense unto other gods, that they might provoke me to anger with all the works of their hands; therefore my wrath shall be poured out upon this place, and shall not be quenched.

26 And as for the king of Judah, who sent you to enquire of the LORD, so shall ye say unto him, Thus saith the LORD God of Israel *concerning* the words which thou hast heard;

27 Because thine heart was tender, and thou didst humble thyself before God, when thou heardest his words against this place, and against the inhabitants thereof, and humbledst thyself before me, and didst rend thy clothes, and weep before me; I have even heard *thee* also, saith the LORD.

28 Behold, I will gather thee to thy fathers, and thou shalt be gathered to thy grave in peace, neither shall thine eyes see all the evil that I will bring upon this place, and upon the inhabitants of the same. So they brought the king word again.

29 ¶ Then the king sent and gathered together all the elders of Judah and Jerusalem.

30 And the king went up into the house of the LORD, and all the men of Judah, and the inhabitants of Jerusalem, and the priests, and the Levites, and all the people, great and small: and he read in their ears all the words of the book of the covenant that was found in the house of the LORD.

31 And the king stood in his place, and made a covenant before the LORD, to walk after the LORD, and to keep his commandments, and his testimonies, and his statutes, with all his heart, and with all his soul, to perform the words of the covenant which are written in this book.

32 And he caused all that were present in Jerusalem and Benjamin to stand *to it*. And the inhabitants of Jerusalem did according to the covenant of God, the God of their fathers.

33 And Josiah took away all the abominations out of all the countries that *pertained* to the children of Israel, and made all that were present in Israel to serve, *even* to serve the LORD their God. *And*

34:19 *rent his clothes.* Tore his clothes, a sign of mourning.
34:21 Israel and Judah were suffering the *wrath of the LORD* because they failed to keep the *word of the LORD*.
34:22 *Huldah the prophetess.* Nothing more is known of her other than what is written here. *college.* Literally, "second," probably the second quarter of *Jerusalem*.
34:23–25 The first oracle was one of judgment: *the curses . . . written in the book* (Deut. 28:15–68).
34:26–28 The second oracle was one of salvation. Josiah would die in peace before the judgment came because his *heart* was not hard (36:13) but soft (*tender*) to the Word of God and he humbled himself with grief over sin (Isa. 66:2; Ezek. 9:4).
34:30–31 *made a covenant.* Publically renewed his commitment to keep the covenant that the Lord had made and written in His *book* (see note at 15:12). *with all his heart, and with all his soul.* In complete love for the Lord, as His law commands (Deut. 4:29; 6:5; 10:12; 11:13; 26:16; 30:2,6,10).
34:32 *caused all . . . to stand to it.* Josiah led the people to commit themselves to the covenant.
34:33 *present.* Found.

Thoughts for Personal/Family Worship: Chapter 34

1. **Josiah did these things when he was very young (vv.1,3,8). God does not care whether you are young or old; the Lord looks at the heart. Do you have a heart like Josiah? His heart was soft to God's Word, so that he grieved deeply and humbled himself over his sins and the sins of his people (v. 27). His heart was also fully engaged to pursue the Lord and keep His commandments (v. 31). You may not be a king, but if you follow God with your whole heart, who can tell how God will use you for His glory?**
2. **Josiah had a burden that the whole nation would hear God's Word and walk in God's ways. It is a mark of God's work in our hearts when we want others to know God's truth and experience the grace He has shown to us. How big is your heart for others? How are you using the**

all his days they departed not from following the LORD, the God of their fathers.

CHAPTER 35

MOREOVER Josiah kept a passover unto the LORD in Jerusalem: and they killed the passover on the fourteenth *day* of the first month.

2 And he set the priests in their charges, and encouraged them to the service of the house of the LORD,

3 And said unto the Levites that taught all Israel, which were holy unto the LORD, Put the holy ark in the house which Solomon the son of David king of Israel did build; *it shall* not *be* a burden upon *your* shoulders: serve now the LORD your God, and his people Israel,

4 And prepare *yourselves* by the houses of your fathers, after your courses, according to the writing of David king of Israel, and according to the writing of Solomon his son.

5 And stand in the holy *place* according to the divisions of the families of the fathers of your brethren the people, and *after* the division of the families of the Levites.

6 So kill the passover, and sanctify yourselves, and prepare your brethren, that *they* may do according to the word of the LORD by the hand of Moses.

7 And Josiah gave to the people, of the flock, lambs and kids, all for the passover offerings, for all that were present, to the number of thirty thousand, and three thousand bullocks: these *were* of the king's substance.

8 And his princes gave willingly unto the people, to the priests, and to the Levites: Hilkiah and Zechariah and Jehiel, rulers of the house of God, gave unto the priests for the passover offerings two thousand and six hundred *small cattle*, and three hundred oxen.

9 Conaniah also, and Shemaiah and Nethaneel, his brethren, and Hashabiah and Jeiel and Jozabad, chief of the Levites, gave unto the Levites for passover offerings five thousand *small cattle*, and five hundred oxen.

10 So the service was prepared, and the priests stood in their place, and the Levites in their courses, according to the king's commandment.

11 And they killed the passover, and the priests sprinkled *the blood* from their hands, and the Levites flayed *them*.

12 And they removed the burnt offerings, that they might give according to the divisions of the families of the people, to offer unto the LORD, as *it is* written in the book of Moses. And so *did they* with the oxen.

13 And they roasted the passover with fire according to the ordinance: but the *other* holy *offerings* sod they in pots, and in caldrons, and in pans, and divided *them* speedily among all the people.

14 And afterward they made ready for themselves, and for the priests: because the priests the sons of Aaron *were busied* in offering of burnt offerings and the fat until night; therefore the Levites prepared for themselves, and for the priests the sons of Aaron.

15 And the singers the sons of Asaph *were* in their place, according to the commandment of David, and Asaph, and Heman, and Jeduthun the king's seer; and the porters *waited* at every gate; they might not depart from their service; for their brethren the Levites prepared for them.

16 So all the service of the LORD was prepared the same day, to keep the passover, and to offer burnt offerings upon the altar of the LORD, according to the commandment of king Josiah.

17 And the children of Israel that were present kept the passover at that time, and the feast of unleavened bread seven days.

18 And there was no passover like to that kept in Israel from the days of Samuel the prophet; neither did all the kings of Israel keep such a passover as Josiah kept, and the priests, and the Levites, and all Judah and Israel that were present, and the inhabitants of Jerusalem.

19 In the eighteenth year of the reign of Josiah was this passover kept.

20 ¶ After all this, when Josiah had prepared the temple, Necho king of Egypt came up to fight against Carchemish by Euphrates: and Josiah went out against him.

21 But he sent ambassadors to him, saying, What have I to do with thee, thou king of Judah? *I come* not against thee this day, but against the house wherewith I have war: for God commanded me

---

calling and influence God has given to you to engage other people for the kingdom of God?

Chapter 35: *Like Hezekiah, Josiah keeps the Passover, after which he dies an untimely death in a battle at Megiddo.*

35:1 Again, the keeping of the *passover* marked the devotion of a godly king (ch. 30).

35:2 *charges.* Priestly duties and responsibilities.

35:3 *Put the holy ark in the house.* There is no record that the ark was ever removed from the temple, but it is possible it was removed during the time of Manasseh or Amon (33:7). *not be a burden.* The priests no longer needed to carry the ark, for it rested in the temple (1 Chron. 28:2).

35:4 *courses.* Divisions. The priests were divided into different groups according to their ministries.

35:8 *willingly.* Not under compulsion.

35:11–19 Details on how the people kept the Passover.

35:11 *flayed.* Skinned.

35:13 *sod.* Boiled.

35:20 The Egyptian forces of *Necho* were going up to fight

to make haste: forbear thee from *meddling with*
God, who *is* with me, that he destroy thee not.
22 Nevertheless Josiah would not turn his face
from him, but disguised himself, that he might
fight with him, and hearkened not unto the words
of Necho from the mouth of God, and came to
fight in the valley of Megiddo.
23 And the archers shot at king Josiah; and the
king said to his servants, Have me away; for I am
sore wounded.
24 His servants therefore took him out of that
chariot, and put him in the second chariot that he
had; and they brought him to Jerusalem, and he
died, and was buried in *one of* the sepulchres of
his fathers. And all Judah and Jerusalem mourned
for Josiah.
25 ¶ And Jeremiah lamented for Josiah: and all
the singing men and the singing women spake of
Josiah in their lamentations to this day, and made
them an ordinance in Israel: and, behold, they *are*
written in the lamentations.
26 Now the rest of the acts of Josiah, and his
goodness, according to *that which was* written in
the law of the LORD,
27 And his deeds, first and last, behold, they *are*
written in the book of the kings of Israel and Judah.

CHAPTER 36

THEN the people of the land took Jehoahaz the
son of Josiah, and made him king in his father's
stead in Jerusalem.
2 Jehoahaz *was* twenty and three years old when
he began to reign, and he reigned three months
in Jerusalem.
3 And the king of Egypt put him down at Jerusa-
lem, and condemned the land in an hundred tal-
ents of silver and a talent of gold.
4 And the king of Egypt made Eliakim his brother
king over Judah and Jerusalem, and turned his
name to Jehoiakim. And Necho took Jehoahaz his
brother, and carried him to Egypt.
5 ¶ Jehoiakim *was* twenty and five years old when
he began to reign, and he reigned eleven years in
Jerusalem: and he did *that which was* evil in the
sight of the LORD his God.
6 Against him came up Nebuchadnezzar king of
Babylon, and bound him in fetters, to carry him
to Babylon.
7 Nebuchadnezzar also carried of the vessels of
the house of the LORD to Babylon, and put them
in his temple at Babylon.
8 Now the rest of the acts of Jehoiakim, and his
abominations which he did, and that which was
found in him, behold, they *are* written in the
book of the kings of Israel and Judah: and Jehoi-
achin his son reigned in his stead.
9 ¶ Jehoiachin *was* eight years old when he began
to reign, and he reigned three months and ten
days in Jerusalem: and he did *that which was* evil
in the sight of the LORD.
10 And when the year was expired, king Nebu-
chadnezzar sent, and brought him to Babylon,
with the goodly vessels of the house of the LORD,

---

against Babylon at *Carchemish* by the river *Euphrates* (2 Kings 23:29).

35:22 *disguised himself.* A similar tactic to that of Ahab, with similar results (18:29,33–34). *from the mouth of God.* Surprisingly, God spoke through the pagan king, but Josiah would not listen (*hearkened not*). Like Amaziah, he proudly engaged an enemy too great for him without due cause (25:17–24).

35:23 *sore.* Severely.

35:24 *he died.* Josiah was cut off in his prime, not yet being forty years old (34:1).

35:25 *Jeremiah.* The prophet (36:12; Jer. 1:2; 25:2–3).

35:26 *his goodness.* Literally, "his acts of faithful love."

Thoughts for Personal/Family Worship: Chapter 35

1. **Josiah led Judah to celebrate the Passover in a grand manner. It was a glorious remembrance of how God redeemed Israel through the blood of the lamb. Josiah directed them to keep it in accordance with the law of Moses (vv. 6,11) and the writings of David, Solomon, and the prophets (vv. 4,15). In a similar though far greater way, the Lord Jesus leads His people to remember His body and blood by which He redeemed them and to worship God according to the commands of the new covenant. Worshiping God and celebrating the Lord's Supper according to the principles of Scripture is obedience to our King. Why does Christ, as the king of His church, care so much about its worship?**
2. **Josiah came to a very untimely end. The godly among Judah were crushed to see this good king slain at an early age (vv. 24–25). After his death, the kingdom rapidly declined (ch. 36). How could this happen? On the divine level, God had ordained his death. However, on a human level, he died because he thrust himself into a battle that did not belong to him. Scripture warns that meddling in strife that does not belong to us can have tragic results (Prov. 26:17). How did Josiah make this mistake? How can we avoid it?**

Chapter 36: ***The final kings of Judah follow in rapid succession, giving way to the threatened exile, but God later restores the people to the land and temple through Cyrus.***

KINGDOM DESTROYED (2 CHRON. 36:1–23)

King Jehoahaz (2 Chron. 36:1–3)

36:1 *stead.* Place.

36:3 *condemned the land.* Egypt imposed a tribute on Judah which would later foster a rebellion.

King Jehoiakim (2 Chron. 36:4–8)

36:4 *Eliakim.* A vassal king under the command of the king of Egypt. Jehoahaz was taken into exile, perhaps for not submitting to Egypt's wishes.

36:6 *Nebuchadnezzar king of Babylon.* First mention of the man who took Judah into exile in stages. *fetters.* Chains.

36:7 *vessels.* Treasures of the temple.

36:8 *stead.* Place.

King Jehoiachin (2 Chron. 36:9–10)

and made Zedekiah his brother king over Judah
and Jerusalem.
11 ¶ Zedekiah *was* one and twenty years old
when he began to reign, and reigned eleven years
in Jerusalem.
12 And he did *that which was* evil in the sight
of the LORD his God, *and* humbled not himself
before Jeremiah the prophet *speaking* from the
mouth of the LORD.
13 And he also rebelled against king Nebuchad-
nezzar, who had made him swear by God: but he
stiffened his neck, and hardened his heart from
turning unto the LORD God of Israel.
14 ¶ Moreover all the chief of the priests, and
the people, transgressed very much after all the
abominations of the heathen; and polluted the
house of the LORD which he had hallowed in
Jerusalem.
15 And the LORD God of their fathers sent to
them by his messengers, rising up betimes, and
sending; because he had compassion on his peo-
ple, and on his dwelling place:
16 But they mocked the messengers of God, and
despised his words, and misused his prophets,
until the wrath of the LORD arose against his
people, till *there was* no remedy.
17 Therefore he brought upon them the king of
the Chaldees, who slew their young men with the
sword in the house of their sanctuary, and had
no compassion upon young man or maiden, old
man, or him that stooped for age: he gave *them* all
into his hand.
18 And all the vessels of the house of God, great
and small, and the treasures of the house of the
LORD, and the treasures of the king, and of his
princes; all *these* he brought to Babylon.
19 And they burnt the house of God, and brake
down the wall of Jerusalem, and burnt all the pal-
aces thereof with fire, and destroyed all the goodly
vessels thereof.
20 And them that had escaped from the sword
carried he away to Babylon; where they were
servants to him and his sons until the reign of the
kingdom of Persia:
21 To fulfil the word of the LORD by the mouth of
Jeremiah, until the land had enjoyed her sabbaths:
for as long as she lay desolate she kept sabbath, to
fulfil threescore and ten years.
22 ¶ Now in the first year of Cyrus king of Persia,
that the word of the LORD *spoken* by the mouth of
Jeremiah might be accomplished, the LORD stirred
up the spirit of Cyrus king of Persia, that he made
a proclamation throughout all his kingdom, and
put it also in writing, saying,

36:10 *Zedekiah his brother.* Another vassal king set up under Babylon's domain.

King Zedekiah (2 Chron. 36:11–16)

36:12 *Jeremiah.* The prophet (35:25) whose words to Zedekiah are written in the book named after him (Jer. 27:1–15).

36:13 *rebelled.* Perhaps for economic or political reasons, though God's sovereignty was at work to bring about Judah's exile. Babylon had no tolerance for unfaithful vassal kings. *stiffened his neck.* The king of Judah became stubborn and refused to listen; his hard heart contrasts with Josiah (34:27).

36:15 *betimes.* Literally, "early," an idiom for urgency and determination.

36:16 *no remedy.* No cure but exile. God in His compassion sent the exile in increments to allow for the preaching of repentance, but the people would not turn.

Jerusalem Conquered (2 Chron. 36:17–21)

36:17–20 Chronicles records the destruction of Jerusalem, the burning of the temple, and the exile of the people (586 BC). Those who were not killed by the assault were taken away as captives.

36:21 *by the mouth of Jeremiah.* The prophet had announced the length of exile beforehand (Jer. 25:11–12; 29:10). *kept sabbath.* The exile gave the land its neglected sabbatical rests that Israel should have observed every seven years (Lev. 25:1–7; 26:34–35). *threescore and ten.* Seventy.

Cyrus's Proclamation (2 Chron. 36:22–23)

36:22–23 *Cyrus king of Persia* conquered the Babylonian Empire and issued a decree to allow the people to return to the Promised Land. *build him an house.* The purpose of the return from exile focused on the rebuilding of the temple in Jerusalem. These two verses are repeated in Ezra 1:1–2, which takes up the history of the postexilic period.

Thoughts for Personal/Family Worship: Chapter 36

1. **The words, "they burnt the house of God" (v. 19) must have been like a flaming brand pressed into the hearts of God's people. It must have felt like God's promise to David was revoked forever (1 Chron. 17:12). However, God was keeping His Word, for He had told Solomon that if the king and the people turned away from the Lord to other gods, He would make His people into exiles and His house into a horror (2 Chron. 7:19–22). God's judgments prove His faithfulness and call us to hope in His promises of restoration, which He will fulfill in His timing by His sovereignty over all nations (36:21–23). Do you wholeheartedly believe in both God's promises of grace and His threats of wrath? How can you order your life accordingly?**
2. **The end of the monarchy must have raised questions in the minds of believers. How would God fulfill His covenant with David? Chronicles encourages us to hope in a righteous son of David. How could God keep His promises if the people were so guilty and hardened in sin? The Lord must provide satisfaction for sin and a transformed heart. How would the kingdom come if Israel lived under foreign domination? It must come first as a spiritual kingdom, not like the kingdoms of this world but composed of true worshipers. All these questions and answers point to Jesus Christ and His life, death, resurrection, ascension, and pouring out of the Spirit. Worship our Lord for His faithfulness to His promises!**
3. **The last verse of Chronicles must have greatly encouraged Israel after it returned from exile: "Who is there among you of all his people? The LORD his God be with him, and let him go up" (v. 23). God's people are not to brood passively over the sorrows of the past, but to press on in the building of God's temple for His glory.**

23 Thus saith Cyrus king of Persia, All the kingdoms of the earth hath the LORD God of heaven given me; and he hath charged me to build him an house in Jerusalem, which *is* in Judah. Who *is there* among you of all his people? The LORD his God *be* with him, and let him go up.

This is a call that rings down through the ages. God's judgments fall upon the nations, but the church continues its mission to build a living temple where God dwells by the Spirit, and Christ is with us to the end of the age. How can this encourage you as you seek to build the kingdom today? (See Phil. 3:13–14.)

Arise

BE OF GOOD

COURAGE

&

DO IT

EZRA 10:4

INTRODUCTION TO THE BOOK OF EZRA

Authorship: When considering the authorship of Ezra, it is necessary to examine the unity between Ezra, Nehemiah, and Chronicles. Ezra and Nehemiah cover an overlapping time frame, and Ezra, Nehemiah, and Chronicles have many similar themes. Understanding their relationship to each other helps to determine the original author or compiler of the books.

The closest relationship exists between Ezra and Nehemiah. Throughout much of history, these books were taken together and appear in some manuscripts as a single composition. Clearly, both books include memoirs of Ezra and Nehemiah respectively. However, at some early point, the books appeared together, and this continued into the early centuries when, for instance, Jerome made a formal distinction between them in his Latin translation of the Bible, the Vulgate. The first Hebrew manuscript to divide them is from AD 1448. What seems most likely is that Ezra and Nehemiah composed their own accounts of what they witnessed during their ministries. One of them or perhaps a third person put their records together filling out the history of the events after the exile.

Further, the authorship of Ezra/Nehemiah has been long attributed to the author of Chronicles. One notes that there is a strong historical continuity as Chronicles ends where Ezra begins. There are also strong linguistic and theological similarities between these books. The Talmud and the popular academic consensus is that Ezra was the author of 1 and 2 Chronicles and Ezra/Nehemiah. Other scholars argue that there is not necessarily a common author, but a common editor or compiler of the books, while some believe they were written and edited by different people.

It is worth observing that much of Ezra and Nehemiah are written in the first person. This means, by first glance, that it would appear likely that large sections of these books were written by the men whose names they bear. This does not exclude the idea of a common compiler, however, who may have had access to these personal memoirs.

Thus, we cannot discern whether the books had a single author despite all the connections. The best solution is that Ezra, one of his close affiliates, or a group of editors and compilers associated with Ezra and Nehemiah put these books together, organizing their material into a unified whole. There are certainly strong connections between Ezra/Nehemiah and Chronicles, but nothing substantial can be definitively ascertained.

Ezra's name likely means "God helps," and he was a priest and scribe (7:11). He was esteemed by Artaxerxes I and sent back to Jerusalem. Ezra, being a priest, and according to some Jewish sources a high priest, reintroduced the Torah to the postexilic people and sought to reform the religious worship of the Jews. Ezra "prepared his heart to seek the law of the LORD, and to do it, and to teach in Israel statutes and judgments" (v. 10).

Date: The books of Ezra and Nehemiah cover the years from 538 to 433 BC, and the material in them was written likely during this time or shortly afterward (538–400 BC). The broader historical setting of Ezra/Nehemiah is important. Cyrus II of Persia, commonly known as Cyrus the Great, founded the so-called Achaemenid Empire. After defeating the Median and Lydian Empires, Cyrus moved to take the neo-Babylonian Empire, which he did (539 BC). Persia reigned supreme for the next two centuries until Alexander the Great (356–323 BC) overthrew them after a series of battles—most notably the Battle of Issus (333 BC) and the Battle of Gaugamela (331 BC).

POSTEXILIC TIMELINE

Cyrus II (the Great) reigns over Persia	559–530
Cyrus captures Babylon	539
Cyrus issues his decree (1:1)	538
Jews return to Palestine under Sheshbazzar and Zerubbabel (2:1–70)	538/37
The altar of the temple is rebuilt (3:2)	538/37
The foundation of the temple is laid (3:8–10)	536
The Jews experience opposition in rebuilding (4:1–5,24)	536–520
Darius I reigns over Persia (4:1—6:22)	522–486
The temple is completed and dedicated (6:15; Hag. 1:14–15)	520–516
Ahasuerus reigns over Persia	486–465
Esther and Mordecai serve in the courts of Ahaseurus	484–465
Artaxerxes I reigns in Persia	465–424
Jews return to Jerusalem under Ezra (7:1,8)	458
Three month investigation (10:16–17)	458–457
Jews return to Jerusalem under Nehemiah (Neh. 2:1)	445
The walls of Jerusalem rebuilt (Neh. 6:15; 7:1)	445
Nehemiah goes to Babylon and returns to Jerusalem (Neh. 13:6–7)	433

Theme: God's faithfulness to His Word as shown in returning His people—physically to His land, ceremonially to His worship, and spiritually to His laws.

Purpose: The purpose of Ezra and Nehemiah is to exalt God over the nations as He providentially and sovereignly brings His people back from exile. As such, Ezra and Nehemiah show how God brings His people back to His covenant, gathers them around a rebuilt temple, and effects a heartfelt rededication to Him. Simultaneously, however, this book shows that the mere physical return was not sufficient as the people still needed the work of someone greater than Zerubbabel, Ezra, and Nehemiah, namely, Jesus Christ.

Synopsis: *The Contribution of Ezra to Redemptive Revelation*

The book of Ezra traces the rebuilding of the temple (chs. 1–6) and the initial ministry of Ezra (chs. 7–10). The book opens where 2 Chronicles ended with the decree of Cyrus, king of Persia, allowing Jewish exiles to return to Jerusalem after many decades of being in exile (1:1). The book moves through two main time periods. The first period is the time of Sheshbazzar and Zerubbabel when a small band of exiles returned from Babylon with them (chs. 1–2). These exiles returned to Judea living in their own towns (2:70).

When Zerubbabel and the exiles returned to Jerusalem, their first order of business was to construct the sacrificial altar (3:2) and to commence with the sacrifices that had been neglected after the destruction of the temple by the Babylonians. Following the building of the altar, there is a large building project undertaken by the Jews to rebuild the temple, starting first with laying down the foundation (v. 10).

After the building of the foundation, however, the people experience opposition from their adversaries who desired to prevent the building of the temple (4:4–6). Due to fallacious reports and scandalous reports by the adversaries, king Artaxerxes ordered that the building of the temple be ceased (v. 21). This law was in effect for nearly twenty years until the second year of king Darius of Persia, who permitted the exiles to finish building the temple (6:12).

Fast-forward to the second main time period about sixty years later when Ezra the son of Seraiah left Babylon with a large group of exiles for Jerusalem (7:1–6). As Ezra and the Jews made their way to Jerusalem, they were given the riches and wealth of the temple to bring back to Jerusalem. After some initial genealogies and lists, we find Ezra leading the people in repentance for the intermarriages. We see the people repenting of their sins and confessing their sins before the Lord (ch. 10).

Outline:

I. The Decree of Cyrus (1:1—2:70)
   A. The People Return to Jerusalem to Rebuild the Temple (1:1–11)
   B. List of Returnees (2:1–70)

II. Restoration of the Temple Begins (3:1–13)
   A. Preparations (3:1–7)
   B. The Work (3:8–13)

III. Resistance against the Temple (4:1–24)
   A. Adversaries Challenge the Builders (4:1–5)
   B. Letters to Ahasuerus and Artaxerxes I (4:6–16)
   C. The Command to Cease the Work (4:17–22)
   D. The Work of the Temple Ceases (4:23–24)

IV. The Temple Is Completed (5:1—6:22)
   A. Rebuilding Is Resumed (Second Year of Darius) (5:1–5)
   B. Letter Sent to Darius (5:6–17)
   C. Darius's Decree (6:1–12)
   D. The Temple Is Completed (Sixth Year of Darius) (6:13–18)
   E. Passover Is Celebrated (6:19–22)

V. Exiles Return with Ezra (7:1—8:36)
   A. Ezra Returns to Jerusalem (7:1–10)
   B. Artaxerxes I Writes to Ezra and Supplies Treasures for the Temple (7:11–28)
   C. List of Returnees (8:1–14)
   D. Exiles Reenter Jerusalem (8:15–36)

VI. Intermarriage Among the Exiles (9:1—10:44)
   A. The Problem of Intermarriage (9:1–2)
   B. Ezra's Prayer of Repentance (9:3–15)
   C. The People's Repentance and a Solemn Assembly (10:1–8)
   D. The People of Israel Are Purified (10:9–44)

THE BOOK OF
EZRA

CHAPTER 1

NOW in the first year of Cyrus king of Persia, that
the word of the LORD by the mouth of Jeremiah
might be fulfilled, the LORD stirred up the spirit
of Cyrus king of Persia, that he made a proclama-
tion throughout all his kingdom, and *put it* also
in writing, saying,
2 Thus saith Cyrus king of Persia, The LORD God
of heaven hath given me all the kingdoms of the
earth; and he hath charged me to build him an
house at Jerusalem, which *is* in Judah.
3 Who *is there* among you of all his people? his
God be with him, and let him go up to Jerusa-
lem, which *is* in Judah, and build the house of the
LORD God of Israel, (he *is* the God,) which *is* in
Jerusalem.
4 And whosoever remaineth in any place where
he sojourneth, let the men of his place help him
with silver, and with gold, and with goods, and
with beasts, beside the freewill offering for the
house of God that *is* in Jerusalem.
5 ¶ Then rose up the chief of the fathers of Judah
and Benjamin, and the priests, and the Levites,
with all *them* whose spirit God had raised, to go
up to build the house of the LORD which *is* in
Jerusalem.
6 And all they that *were* about them strengthened
their hands with vessels of silver, with gold, with
goods, and with beasts, and with precious things,
beside all *that* was willingly offered.
7 ¶ Also Cyrus the king brought forth the vessels
of the house of the LORD, which Nebuchadnezzar
had brought forth out of Jerusalem, and had put
them in the house of his gods;
8 Even those did Cyrus king of Persia bring forth
by the hand of Mithredath the treasurer, and
numbered them unto Sheshbazzar, the prince of
Judah.
9 And this *is* the number of them: thirty chargers
of gold, a thousand chargers of silver, nine and
twenty knives,
10 Thirty basons of gold, silver basons of a second
sort four hundred and ten, *and* other vessels a
thousand.
11 All the vessels of gold and of silver *were* five
thousand and four hundred. All *these* did Shesh-

THE DECREE OF CYRUS (1:1—2:70)

Chapter 1: *Cyrus issues a decree for the exiles of Judah to return to their land, and the first wave returns under the leadership of Sheshbazzar.*

The People Return to Jerusalem to Rebuild the Temple (1:1–11)

1:1 *first year of Cyrus king of Persia.* Cyrus conquered Babylon in October of 539 BC. His edict to allow exiles of Judah to return, from Cyrus's own standpoint, fits his foreign policy as we know from sources outside the Bible. But behind Cyrus's decisions was the providential hand of the Lord. *by the mouth of Jeremiah.* Years before Cyrus's birth, Jeremiah prophesied this event (29:10; cf. Jer. 51:1,11; Isa. 41:2,25; 44:28; 45:1,13; Jer. 25:11–12).
1:2 *The LORD God of heaven hath given me all the kingdoms of the earth.* This is not so much a testimony of Cyrus's faith, for in other writings outside of the Bible he gave allegiance to other gods. Nevertheless, from a biblical point of view, what Cyrus writes is truer than he intended it.
1:5 *all them whose spirit God had raised.* Again we see the sovereignty of God. He not only stirred up the spirit of Cyrus, but he also stirred up the heart of those who would return.
1:6 The exiles returning to Jerusalem brought many riches from the land of Babylon. In many ways, the return from exile was like a new exodus from captivity (Ex. 12:36).
1:8 *Sheshbazzar* was most likely a Jew with a Persian name. He led the first group of exiles back into Judah as the *prince* or chief of the returning men.
1:9–11 *chargers.* Dishes, large plates. Ezra records that all of the articles brought back were 5,400. This is not a discrepancy from the tally of the items mentioned, which is 2,499. It is likely that he lists only the more notable articles.

Thoughts for Personal/Family Worship: Chapter 1

1. **God never forgets His Word to fulfill it. This is true of what He threatens as well as promises. Though we forget God's Word, He does not, but He is faithful to it. Bring His own Word back to Him in prayer and plead that He would fulfill it in your life.**
2. **God is sovereign. He works on the level of nations and the heads of nations (v. 1). However, He also stirs up individual people to walk in His ways and seek His promised inheritance (v. 5). How does this encourage you to pray for nations? For individuals?**
3. **Cyrus had a unique role in God's plan and purpose (Isa. 44:28; 45:1). God used him to set His people free. Christ, however, would set His people free in ways that Cyrus never could. He would enter into death and pay**

bazzar bring up with *them of* the captivity that
were brought up from Babylon unto Jerusalem.

CHAPTER 2

NOW these *are* the children of the province that
went up out of the captivity, of those which had
been carried away, whom Nebuchadnezzar the
king of Babylon had carried away unto Babylon,
and came again unto Jerusalem and Judah, every
one unto his city;
2 Which came with Zerubbabel: Jeshua, Ne-
hemiah, Seraiah, Reelaiah, Mordecai, Bilshan,
Mispar, Bigvai, Rehum, Baanah. The number of
the men of the people of Israel:
3 The children of Parosh, two thousand an hun-
dred seventy and two.
4 The children of Shephatiah, three hundred
seventy and two.
5 The children of Arah, seven hundred seventy
and five.
6 The children of Pahath-moab, of the children
of Jeshua *and* Joab, two thousand eight hundred
and twelve.
7 The children of Elam, a thousand two hundred
fifty and four.
8 The children of Zattu, nine hundred forty and
five.
9 The children of Zaccai, seven hundred and
threescore.
10 The children of Bani, six hundred forty and
two.
11 The children of Bebai, six hundred twenty and
three.
12 The children of Azgad, a thousand two hun-
dred twenty and two.
13 The children of Adonikam, six hundred sixty
and six.
14 The children of Bigvai, two thousand fifty and
six.
15 The children of Adin, four hundred fifty and
four.
16 The children of Ater of Hezekiah, ninety and
eight.
17 The children of Bezai, three hundred twenty
and three.
18 The children of Jorah, an hundred and twelve.
19 The children of Hashum, two hundred twenty
and three.
20 The children of Gibbar, ninety and five.
21 The children of Beth-lehem, an hundred
twenty and three.
22 The men of Netophah, fifty and six.
23 The men of Anathoth, an hundred twenty and
eight.
24 The children of Azmaveth, forty and two.
25 The children of Kirjath-arim, Chephirah, and
Beeroth, seven hundred and forty and three.
26 The children of Ramah and Gaba, six hundred
twenty and one.
27 The men of Michmas, an hundred twenty and
two.
28 The men of Beth-el and Ai, two hundred
twenty and three.
29 The children of Nebo, fifty and two.
30 The children of Magbish, an hundred fifty and
six.
31 The children of the other Elam, a thousand
two hundred fifty and four.
32 The children of Harim, three hundred and
twenty.
33 The children of Lod, Hadid, and Ono, seven
hundred twenty and five.
34 The children of Jericho, three hundred forty
and five.
35 The children of Senaah, three thousand and
six hundred and thirty.
36 ¶ The priests: the children of Jedaiah, of the
house of Jeshua, nine hundred seventy and three.
37 The children of Immer, a thousand fifty and
two.
38 The children of Pashur, a thousand two hun-
dred forty and seven.
39 The children of Harim, a thousand and
seventeen.
40 ¶ The Levites: the children of Jeshua and Kad-
miel, of the children of Hodaviah, seventy and four.
41 ¶ The singers: the children of Asaph, an
hundred twenty and eight.
42 ¶ The children of the porters: the children
of Shallum, the children of Ater, the children of
Talmon, the children of Akkub, the children of
Hatita, the children of Shobai, *in* all an hundred
thirty and nine.

---

the penalty they deserved. Praise God for delivering us from the kingdom of darkness and translating us into the kingdom of light (Col. 1:13).

Chapter 2: *A list of those who returned to Judah after Cyrus gave his decree is recorded. Just over 40,000 individuals return to inhabit the territory of Judah.*

List of Returnees (2:1–70)

2:1–70 This list of people who returned from exile is repeated in large part in Neh. 7. Every name is proof that God was faithful to His promise, bringing back a remnant (Isa. 6:13).

2:1–2 The first group mentioned here are the leaders of Judah. *Zerubbabel*, a descendant of King David (see note at Jer. 52:32–33), and *Jeshua* (or Joshua), a priest, were prominent leaders of the returning exiles (Hag. 1:1).

2:3–20 The second named group are the names of different clans.

2:21–35 The third group is comprised of geographical names.

2:36–39 The fourth group concerns the priests.

2:40–42 The fifth group names the Levites, those descended from Levi but not Aaron.

43 ¶ The Nethinims: the children of Ziha, the
children of Hasupha, the children of Tabbaoth,
44 The children of Keros, the children of Siaha,
the children of Padon,
45 The children of Lebanah, the children of
Hagabah, the children of Akkub,
46 The children of Hagab, the children of Shal-
mai, the children of Hanan,
47 The children of Giddel, the children of Gahar,
the children of Reaiah,
48 The children of Rezin, the children of Nekoda,
the children of Gazzam,
49 The children of Uzza, the children of Paseah,
the children of Besai,
50 The children of Asnah, the children of Mehu-
nim, the children of Nephusim,
51 The children of Bakbuk, the children of
Hakupha, the children of Harhur,
52 The children of Bazluth, the children of
Mehida, the children of Harsha,
53 The children of Barkos, the children of Sisera,
the children of Thamah,
54 The children of Neziah, the children of
Hatipha.
55 ¶ The children of Solomon's servants: the
children of Sotai, the children of Sophereth, the
children of Peruda,
56 The children of Jaalah, the children of Darkon,
the children of Giddel,
57 The children of Shephatiah, the children of
Hattil, the children of Pochereth of Zebaim, the
children of Ami.
58 All the Nethinims, and the children of Solo-
mon's servants, *were* three hundred ninety and two.
59 And these *were* they which went up from Tel-
melah, Tel-harsa, Cherub, Addan, *and* Immer: but
they could not shew their father's house, and their
seed, whether they *were* of Israel:
60 The children of Delaiah, the children of To-
biah, the children of Nekoda, six hundred fifty
and two.
61 ¶ And of the children of the priests: the
children of Habaiah, the children of Koz, the
children of Barzillai; which took a wife of the
daughters of Barzillai the Gileadite, and was
called after their name:
62 These sought their register *among* those that
were reckoned by genealogy, but they were not
found: therefore were they, as polluted, put from
the priesthood.
63 And the Tirshatha said unto them, that they
should not eat of the most holy things, till there
stood up a priest with Urim and with Thummim.
64 ¶ The whole congregation together *was* forty
and two thousand three hundred *and* threescore,
65 Beside their servants and their maids, of
whom *there were* seven thousand three hundred
thirty and seven: and *there were* among them two
hundred singing men and singing women.
66 Their horses *were* seven hundred thirty and
six; their mules, two hundred forty and five;
67 Their camels, four hundred thirty and five;
their asses, six thousand seven hundred and
twenty.
68 ¶ And *some* of the chief of the fathers, when
they came to the house of the LORD which *is* at
Jerusalem, offered freely for the house of God to
set it up in his place:
69 They gave after their ability unto the treasure
of the work threescore and one thousand drams
of gold, and five thousand pound of silver, and
one hundred priests' garments.
70 So the priests, and the Levites, and *some* of the
people, and the singers, and the porters, and the
Nethinims, dwelt in their cities, and all Israel in
their cities.

2:43–54 The sixth group names the temple servants, the *Nethinims.* They are thought to be servants who helped the Levites, probably with menial tasks.
2:55–58 The seventh group numbered are the servants of Solomon, another group of priestly servants.
2:59–63 The final and eighth group is a miscellaneous group, some of whom lacked proper ancestral documentation.
2:63 *Tirshatha.* Persian title for governor, probably a reference to Sheshbazzar (1:8). *Urim and . . . Thummim.* Lots cast by the high priest to determine God's will (Num. 27:21; 1 Sam. 14:36–37). The priests who could not prove their lineage were restricted from eating the holy things. As the nation struggled to purify itself, the leaders took great care to follow the Lord's law (Num. 16:40).
2:65 The number of slaves indicates that those who were returning were prosperous.
2:69 *drams.* Here a measurement of precious metals.

Thoughts for Personal/Family Worship: Chapter 2

1. **Though Zerubbabel was not a king, he descended from the kingly line and was in the genealogy of the Lord Jesus (Matt. 1:12–13, "Zorobabel"). The exile would not prevent the coming of the Christ. The Lord saw to it that priests, prophets (5:1), and the line of David resettled the land. Christ would combine the three offices in Himself, as the Prophet, Priest, and King of His people. In that office, He draws people from darkness to light, and makes them citizens in His kingdom (Eph. 2:19). Despite the sins of man, encourage one another that Christ's kingdom will be established and prevail.**
2. **The Urim and Thummim (v. 63) refer to stones kept in the breastplate of judgment worn on Aaron's heart (Ex. 28:30). We know very little about how the Urim and Thummim functioned, but as they appear in Israel's history, we learn that they were used in discerning the will of God (Num. 27:21; Deut. 33:8; 1 Sam. 23:6–12; 28:6). Regardless of how they functioned, we know that they communicated to the Israelite community what God's will was for them. What has God given to His people today to lead us in the ways of truth (John 16:13)?**
3. **What a disappointment it must have been to those who could not show their proper credentials to work in the temple service (v. 59)! Do you have assurance to rejoice that your name is written in heaven (Luke 10:20)?**

CHAPTER 3

AND when the seventh month was come, and
the children of Israel *were* in the cities, the peo-
ple gathered themselves together as one man to
Jerusalem.
2 Then stood up Jeshua the son of Jozadak, and
his brethren the priests, and Zerubbabel the son
of Shealtiel, and his brethren, and builded the al-
tar of the God of Israel, to offer burnt offerings
thereon, as *it is* written in the law of Moses the
man of God.
3 And they set the altar upon his bases; for fear
was upon them because of the people of those
countries: and they offered burnt offerings
thereon unto the LORD, *even* burnt offerings
morning and evening.
4 They kept also the feast of tabernacles, as *it is*
written, and *offered* the daily burnt offerings by
number, according to the custom, as the duty of
every day required;
5 And afterward *offered* the continual burnt of-
fering, both of the new moons, and of all the set
feasts of the LORD that were consecrated, and of
every one that willingly offered a freewill offering
unto the LORD.
6 From the first day of the seventh month began
they to offer burnt offerings unto the LORD. But
the foundation of the temple of the LORD was not
yet laid.
7 They gave money also unto the masons, and to
the carpenters; and meat, and drink, and oil, unto
them of Zidon, and to them of Tyre, to bring cedar
trees from Lebanon to the sea of Joppa, according
to the grant that they had of Cyrus king of Persia.
8 ¶ Now in the second year of their coming unto
the house of God at Jerusalem, in the second
month, began Zerubbabel the son of Shealtiel,
and Jeshua the son of Jozadak, and the rem-
nant of their brethren the priests and the Levites,
and all they that were come out of the captivity
unto Jerusalem; and appointed the Levites, from
twenty years old and upward, to set forward the
work of the house of the LORD.
9 Then stood Jeshua *with* his sons and his
brethren, Kadmiel and his sons, the sons of Judah,
together, to set forward the workmen in the house
of God: the sons of Henadad, *with* their sons and
their brethren the Levites.
10 And when the builders laid the foundation
of the temple of the LORD, they set the priests in
their apparel with trumpets, and the Levites the
sons of Asaph with cymbals, to praise the LORD,
after the ordinance of David king of Israel.
11 And they sang together by course in prais-
ing and giving thanks unto the LORD; because *he
is* good, for his mercy *endureth* for ever toward
Israel. And all the people shouted with a great
shout, when they praised the LORD, because the
foundation of the house of the LORD was laid.
12 But many of the priests and Levites and chief
of the fathers, *who were* ancient men, that had
seen the first house, when the foundation of this
house was laid before their eyes, wept with a loud
voice; and many shouted aloud for joy:
13 So that the people could not discern the noise
of the shout of joy from the noise of the weeping
of the people: for the people shouted with a loud
shout, and the noise was heard afar off.

---

4. Note how the people gave to the work of the Lord. We are told that they "gave after their ability unto the treasure of the work" (v. 69). How beautiful it is to see many giving cheerfully to the work of the Lord (2 Cor. 9:7)! How are you offering yourself and your money to His work?

Chapter 3: ***The people begin to restore the temple and reconstitute the worship God had prescribed; the reconstruction, however, is greeted with jubilant shouts on the one hand and dreadful mourning on the other.***

RESTORATION OF THE TEMPLE BEGINS (3:1–13)

Preparations (3:1–7)

3:1 *seventh month.* The month of Tishri (September/October), the great month of feasts, including the Feast of Trumpets, the Day of Atonement, and the Feast of Tabernacles (Lev. 23:24–44; Num. 29).

3:2 *Jeshua.* Same as Joshua the high priest (Zech. 3:1; 6:11). *the law of Moses the man of God.* The returning exiles show their dedication to following the law of God from the start.

3:3 *burnt offerings.* The burnt offering declared total dedication (Num. 28:2,4).

3:4 The feasts and sacrifices of the Lord were also reinstated once the altar was set up (Lev. 23).

3:7 *meat.* Food of any kind.

The Work (3:8–13)

3:8 They restarted the work seven months after they had erected the altar (see v. 1). The *second month* is also the beginning of the dry season for Israel and thus serves as a good time to begin building.

3:9 *set forward.* Oversee.

3:10 *apparel.* Clothing.

3:11 *they sang together by course.* The content of their song was from Ps. 100:5. Jeremiah prophesied that this song would be sung with gladness after Jerusalem had been destroyed (Jer. 33:11).

3:12 Many of the older generation *wept* when they saw the foundation of this new temple, remembering the grandeur and beauty of Solomon's temple and comparing it with the smallness of their present efforts (Zech. 4:10).

3:13 The mixture of sorrow and joy serves as a reminder that there are greater things in store. As wonderful as it was that they had returned from exile, this would not be the climax of God's saving deeds.

Thoughts for Personal/Family Worship: Chapter 3

1. The people quickly worked to reinstitute the sacrifices. It is a good sign when we sense that we need to have our sins blotted out and we need to know God's favor

CHAPTER 4

NOW when the adversaries of Judah and Ben-
jamin heard that the children of the captivity
builded the temple unto the LORD God of Israel;
2 Then they came to Zerubbabel, and to the chief
of the fathers, and said unto them, Let us build
with you: for we seek your God, as ye *do*; and we
do sacrifice unto him since the days of Esarhad-
don king of Assur, which brought us up hither.
3 But Zerubbabel, and Jeshua, and the rest of the
chief of the fathers of Israel, said unto them, Ye
have nothing to do with us to build an house unto
our God; but we ourselves together will build
unto the LORD God of Israel, as king Cyrus the
king of Persia hath commanded us.
4 Then the people of the land weakened the
hands of the people of Judah, and troubled them
in building,
5 And hired counsellors against them, to frus-
trate their purpose, all the days of Cyrus king
of Persia, even until the reign of Darius king of
Persia.
6 And in the reign of Ahasuerus, in the beginning
of his reign, wrote they *unto him* an accusation
against the inhabitants of Judah and Jerusalem.
7 ¶ And in the days of Artaxerxes wrote Bishlam,
Mithredath, Tabeel, and the rest of their com-
panions, unto Artaxerxes king of Persia; and the
writing of the letter *was* written in the Syrian
tongue, and interpreted in the Syrian tongue.
8 Rehum the chancellor and Shimshai the scribe
wrote a letter against Jerusalem to Artaxerxes the
king in this sort:
9 Then *wrote* Rehum the chancellor, and Shim-
shai the scribe, and the rest of their companions;
the Dinaites, the Apharsathchites, the Tarpelites,
the Apharsites, the Archevites, the Babylonians, the
Susanchites, the Dehavites, *and* the Elamites,
10 And the rest of the nations whom the great
and noble Asnappar brought over, and set in the
cities of Samaria, and the rest *that are* on this side
the river, and at such a time.
11 ¶ This *is* the copy of the letter that they sent
unto him, *even* unto Artaxerxes the king; Thy
servants the men on this side the river, and at such
a time.
12 Be it known unto the king, that the Jews which
came up from thee to us are come unto Jerusa-
lem, building the rebellious and the bad city,
and have set up the walls *thereof*, and joined the
foundations.
13 Be it known now unto the king, that, if this
city be builded, and the walls set up *again, then*
will they not pay toll, tribute, and custom, and *so*
thou shalt endamage the revenue of the kings.
14 Now because we have maintenance from *the*
king's palace, and it was not meet for us to see
the king's dishonour, therefore have we sent and
certified the king;
15 That search may be made in the book of the
records of thy fathers: so shalt thou find in the
book of the records, and know that this city *is* a
rebellious city, and hurtful unto kings and prov-
inces, and that they have moved sedition within
the same of old time: for which cause was this city
destroyed.
16 We certify the king that, if this city be builded
again, and the walls thereof set up, by this means
thou shalt have no portion on this side the river.
17 ¶ *Then* sent the king an answer unto Rehum
the chancellor, and *to* Shimshai the scribe, and
to the rest of their companions that dwell in
Samaria, and *unto* the rest beyond the river, Peace,
and at such a time.
18 The letter which ye sent unto us hath been
plainly read before me.

---

through His appointed sacrifice, Christ Jesus, to whom all the sacrifices pointed (Heb. 7:27). How eager is your heart to run to Christ's sacrifice for forgiveness? How long do you linger in guilt before confessing your sin? Why?

2. **The joy of those who witnessed the foundation rising was mixed with weeping. Is it not true that often the Christian's joy is mixed with weeping? As long as believers dwell in flesh, we carry this tension of rejoicing and weeping with us (2 Cor. 6:10), until the day when every tear shall be wiped from our eyes (Rev. 21:4). Then joy will be unmixed, but, incidentally, there will be no temple (Rev. 21:22). Why is that? What do we know about that day?**

Chapter 4: *Adversaries oppose the rebuilding efforts.*

RESISTANCE AGAINST THE TEMPLE (4:1–24)

Adversaries Challenge the Builders (4:1–5)

4:1 *adversaries.* At first, they did not present themselves as adversaries, but they will prove to be adversaries.

4:3 *Ye have nothing to do with us.* This appears to be a harsh statement against those who appeared to want to help. However, we know that they were accustomed to worshiping other gods (2 Kings 17:33).

Letters to Ahasuerus and Artaxerxes I (4:6–16)

4:6–23 There is a break in the chronology of this book with this section. The letters that are copied here for us come from the respective reigns of Xerxes (Ahasuerus) (486–465 BC) and Artaxerxes I (465–424 BC). These letters reflect the recurring opposition the people of Judah faced from those around them.

4:7 *in the Syrian tongue.* What follows in 4:8—6:18 is in Aramaic, reflecting the language of official correspondence during these times.

4:8 *chancellor.* Chief governor or commander.

4:10 *Asnappar*, or Ashurbanipal, was an Assyrian king (669–663 BC). The Assyrians would have relocated exiled people groups into different regions, thus creating what was viewed as a mixed race and culture.

4:13 *custom.* Tribute, tax. *endamage.* Cause damage.

The Command to Cease the Work (4:17–22)

4:17 *chancellor.* Chief governor.

19 And I commanded, and search hath been
made, and it is found that this city of old time
hath made insurrection against kings, and *that*
rebellion and sedition have been made therein.
20 There have been mighty kings also over Jeru-
salem, which have ruled over all *countries* beyond
the river; and toll, tribute, and custom, was paid
unto them.
21 Give ye now commandment to cause these
men to cease, and that this city be not builded,
until *another* commandment shall be given from
me.
22 Take heed now that ye fail not to do this: why
should damage grow to the hurt of the kings?
23 ¶ Now when the copy of king Artaxerxes' letter
was read before Rehum, and Shimshai the scribe,
and their companions, they went up in haste to
Jerusalem unto the Jews, and made them to cease
by force and power.
24 Then ceased the work of the house of God
which *is* at Jerusalem. So it ceased unto the second
year of the reign of Darius king of Persia.

CHAPTER 5

THEN the prophets, Haggai the prophet, and
Zechariah the son of Iddo, prophesied unto the
Jews that *were* in Judah and Jerusalem in the
name of the God of Israel, *even* unto them.
2 Then rose up Zerubbabel the son of Shealtiel,
and Jeshua the son of Jozadak, and began to build
the house of God which *is* at Jerusalem: and with
them *were* the prophets of God helping them.
3 ¶ At the same time came to them Tatnai, gover-
nor on this side the river, and Shethar-boznai, and
their companions, and said thus unto them, Who
hath commanded you to build this house, and to
make up this wall?
4 Then said we unto them after this manner,
What are the names of the men that make this
building?
5 But the eye of their God was upon the elders of
the Jews, that they could not cause them to cease,
till the matter came to Darius: and then they
returned answer by letter concerning this *matter*.
6 ¶ The copy of the letter that Tatnai, governor
on this side the river, and Shethar-boznai, and his
companions the Apharsachites, which *were* on
this side the river, sent unto Darius the king:
7 They sent a letter unto him, wherein was
written thus; Unto Darius the king, all peace.
8 Be it known unto the king, that we went into
the province of Judea, to the house of the great
God, which is builded with great stones, and
timber is laid in the walls, and this work goeth fast
on, and prospereth in their hands.
9 Then asked we those elders, *and* said unto them
thus, Who commanded you to build this house,
and to make up these walls?
10 We asked their names also, to certify thee, that
we might write the names of the men that *were*
the chief of them.
11 And thus they returned us answer, saying, We
are the servants of the God of heaven and earth,
and build the house that was builded these many
years ago, which a great king of Israel builded and
set up.
12 But after that our fathers had provoked the
God of heaven unto wrath, he gave them into the
hand of Nebuchadnezzar the king of Babylon,
the Chaldean, who destroyed this house, and
carried the people away into Babylon.

4:21 Artaxerxes said that the building should stop *until another commandment shall be given,* indicating that it was not a closed case.

The Work of the Temple Ceases (4:23–24)

4:24 After the documents of vv. 8–23, the narrative picks up again. *Darius king of Persia* (522–486 BC) took over the Persian Empire after the death of Cambyses.

Thoughts for Personal/Family Worship: Chapter 4

1. **We might be tempted to shrink back from what seems to be a harsh response of Zerubbabel and Joshua and the other leaders (v. 3). But this is not just an Old Testament emphasis as can be seen from Heb. 13:10: "We have an altar, whereof they have no right to eat which serve the tabernacle." Spiritual fellowship and partnership can only be had with those who share the same Spirit, worship the same God, and glory only in Christ (Phil. 3:3). Pray for discernment, so as not to compromise.**
2. **Christ told His disciples that they should expect persecution (John 16:33). Some victories are not achieved within one generation, as the fight continues beyond our generation. We need to arm ourselves for a drawn-out battle against those who take aim at the cause of Christ (Eph. 6:10–13). What battles face the church today? How can the church prepare herself to fight these with endurance over the long term?**

THE TEMPLE IS COMPLETED (5:1—6:22)

Chapter 5: *Haggai and Zechariah stir up the people to begin rebuilding the temple.*

Rebuilding Is Resumed (Second Year of Darius) (5:1–5)

5:1 *Haggai* ministered between August and December of 520 BC. *Zechariah*['s] ministry began in October of 520 BC and lasted until February 519 BC. The temple construction was restarted in September of 520 BC. Both prophets commanded the people to continue to restore the temple. Apparently they had left off the building out of fear of their adversaries (3:3; 4:4–5). Whenever God begins a spiritual movement, He begins it by His Word.

5:2 Again there is a partnership between the descendant of David, Zerubbabel, and the high priest, Jeshua (3:2,8; 4:3).

5:4 The governing authorities appear to still be talking in this verse (cf. v. 10).

5:5 *eye of their God.* God's sovereignty over the affairs of His people (2 Chron. 6:40; 16:9).

Letter Sent to Darius (5:6–17)

13 But in the first year of Cyrus the king of Baby-
lon *the same* king Cyrus made a decree to build
this house of God.
14 And the vessels also of gold and silver of the
house of God, which Nebuchadnezzar took out
of the temple that *was* in Jerusalem, and brought
them into the temple of Babylon, those did Cyrus
the king take out of the temple of Babylon, and
they were delivered unto *one*, whose name *was*
Sheshbazzar, whom he had made governor;
15 And said unto him, Take these vessels, go,
carry them into the temple that *is* in Jerusalem,
and let the house of God be builded in his place.
16 Then came the same Sheshbazzar, *and* laid
the foundation of the house of God which *is* in
Jerusalem: and since that time even until now
hath it been in building, and *yet* it is not finished.
17 Now therefore, if *it seem* good to the king, let
there be search made in the king's treasure house,
which *is* there at Babylon, whether it be *so*, that a
decree was made of Cyrus the king to build this
house of God at Jerusalem, and let the king send
his pleasure to us concerning this matter.

CHAPTER 6

THEN Darius the king made a decree, and search
was made in the house of the rolls, where the trea-
sures were laid up in Babylon.
2 And there was found at Achmetha, in the palace
that *is* in the province of the Medes, a roll, and
therein *was* a record thus written:
3 In the first year of Cyrus the king *the same* Cyrus
the king made a decree *concerning* the house of
God at Jerusalem, Let the house be builded, the
place where they offered sacrifices, and let the
foundations thereof be strongly laid; the height
thereof threescore cubits, *and* the breadth thereof
threescore cubits;
4 *With* three rows of great stones, and a row of
new timber: and let the expenses be given out of
the king's house:
5 And also let the golden and silver vessels of
the house of God, which Nebuchadnezzar took
forth out of the temple which *is* at Jerusalem, and
brought unto Babylon, be restored, and brought
again unto the temple which *is* at Jerusalem, *every
one* to his place, and place *them* in the house of
God.
6 Now *therefore*, Tatnai, governor beyond the
river, Shethar-boznai, and your companions the
Apharsachites, which *are* beyond the river, be ye
far from thence:
7 Let the work of this house of God alone; let the
governor of the Jews and the elders of the Jews
build this house of God in his place.
8 Moreover I make a decree what ye shall do to
the elders of these Jews for the building of this
house of God: that of the king's goods, *even* of the
tribute beyond the river, forthwith expenses be
given unto these men, that they be not hindered.
9 And that which they have need of, both young
bullocks, and rams, and lambs, for the burnt of-
ferings of the God of heaven, wheat, salt, wine,
and oil, according to the appointment of the
priests which *are* at Jerusalem, let it be given them
day by day without fail:
10 That they may offer sacrifices of sweet savours
unto the God of heaven, and pray for the life of
the king, and of his sons.
11 Also I have made a decree, that whosoever
shall alter this word, let timber be pulled down
from his house, and being set up, let him be
hanged thereon; and let his house be made a
dunghill for this.
12 And the God that hath caused his name to
dwell there destroy all kings and people, that shall
put to their hand to alter *and* to destroy this house
of God which *is* at Jerusalem. I Darius have made
a decree; let it be done with speed.
13 ¶ Then Tatnai, governor on this side the river,
Shethar-boznai, and their companions, according
to that which Darius the king had sent, so they
did speedily.

5:13 The fact that Cyrus had issued a *decree* gave the people of Judah a legal backing.

Thoughts for Personal/Family Worship: Chapter 5

1. **God uses His Word to give life to His people. After twenty years, the preaching of Haggai and Zechariah was the catalyst for encouraging the Jews to finish building the temple. God used His Word to move His people to action. Therefore, let us strongly support the preaching of God's Word. How can we be doers of the Word, and not hearers only (James 1:22–27)?**
2. **This section is proof of the following truth: "The king's heart is in the hand of the LORD, as the rivers of water: he turneth it whithersoever he will" (Prov. 21:1). Behind the actions of princes and rulers, the hand of divine providence brings about His purposes for His people. How can this encourage Christians when government leaders seem to frustrate God's purposes?**
3. **Why did Judah face so much opposition? Could God not have made things much easier for them? Through trials, God strengthens His people. He teaches them patience. God is not just working around His people, but within them (Phil. 2:13).**

Chapter 6: ***Darius gives the decree for the temple to be finished, which takes place in the sixth year of his reign, and the people of Judah dedicate the temple and celebrate the Passover.***

Darius's Decree (6:1–12)

6:1 *the house of the rolls*. The archives.

6:2 *Achmetha*, also known as Ecbatana, was Cyrus's summer home located to the northwest of Babylon and north of Shushan, in present day Iran. *roll*. Scroll.

14 And the elders of the Jews builded, and they
prospered through the prophesying of Haggai the
prophet and Zechariah the son of Iddo. And they
builded, and finished *it*, according to the com-
mandment of the God of Israel, and according
to the commandment of Cyrus, and Darius, and
Artaxerxes king of Persia.
15 And this house was finished on the third day
of the month Adar, which was in the sixth year of
the reign of Darius the king.
16 ¶ And the children of Israel, the priests, and
the Levites, and the rest of the children of the
captivity, kept the dedication of this house of God
with joy,
17 And offered at the dedication of this house
of God an hundred bullocks, two hundred rams,
four hundred lambs; and for a sin offering for all
Israel, twelve he goats, according to the number of
the tribes of Israel.
18 And they set the priests in their divisions, and
the Levites in their courses, for the service of God,
which *is* at Jerusalem; as it is written in the book
of Moses.
19 And the children of the captivity kept the
passover upon the fourteenth *day* of the first
month.
20 For the priests and the Levites were purified
together, all of them *were* pure, and killed the
passover for all the children of the captivity, and
for their brethren the priests, and for themselves.
21 And the children of Israel, which were come
again out of captivity, and all such as had sepa-
rated themselves unto them from the filthiness of
the heathen of the land, to seek the LORD God of
Israel, did eat,
22 And kept the feast of unleavened bread seven
days with joy: for the LORD had made them joyful,
and turned the heart of the king of Assyria unto
them, to strengthen their hands in the work of the
house of God, the God of Israel.

CHAPTER 7

NOW after these things, in the reign of Artaxerxes
king of Persia, Ezra the son of Seraiah, the son of
Azariah, the son of Hilkiah,
2 The son of Shallum, the son of Zadok, the son
of Ahitub,
3 The son of Amariah, the son of Azariah, the son
of Meraioth,
4 The son of Zerahiah, the son of Uzzi, the son
of Bukki,
5 The son of Abishua, the son of Phinehas, the
son of Eleazar, the son of Aaron the chief priest:
6 This Ezra went up from Babylon; and he *was* a
ready scribe in the law of Moses, which the LORD

The Temple Is Completed (Sixth Year of Darius) (6:13–18)

6:14 First Haggai and Zechariah prophesied to the people to rebuild the temple. Then they helped them through their prophesying. Now the people prosper through the prophesying of the prophets. God's Word accompanied the people through every stage.

6:15 After beginning the rebuilding for a second time in 520 BC, the people of Judah finished the temple on March 12, 515 BC. This was 72 years after the temple had been destroyed by the Babylonians and corresponds closely to Jeremiah's rounded number of 70 years of captivity (Jer. 25:12–14; 29:10; Zech. 1:12–17).

6:17 *according to the number of the tribes of Israel.* Though most of the people at the dedication of the temple were from the tribes of Judah, Benjamin, or Levi, those in charge ensured that the dedication of the temple had all twelve tribes in view.

6:18 This is the last verse of the text written in Aramaic (4:8—6:18). The next verse begins again in Hebrew.

Passover Is Celebrated (6:19–22)

6:21 *all such as had separated.* There is more than simply an ethnic focus or allegiance. People understood their ceremonial uncleanness and separated themselves according to the dictates that God stipulated.

6:22 This is a summary statement of the book thus far. *the LORD had made them joyful.* The faithful God had exercised His sovereignty over men (*turned the heart*) so as to bring praise to His name. *king of Assyria*. Here the equivalent of Babylon, which inherited the kingdom of Assyria (Neh. 9:32).

Thoughts for Personal/Family Worship: Chapter 6

1. **The books of Moses continued to be the guide for these people (v. 18). Whenever there is a heaven-sent awakening or revival, people will go back to the Word of God (Neh. 8:1). There may be great emotional excitement, large crowds of people, or impressive acts of religious devotion, but if they are not driven by faith and love toward the Holy Scriptures, they are not of the Spirit of the Lord. Do you need to renew your commitment to God's Word?**
2. **Our chapter commemorates and celebrates a milestone. When God's people go through difficult or disciplinary times they must always remember that the end is better than the beginning (Eccl. 7:8) and that all things work together for their good (Rom. 8:28). Have you experienced seasons of celebration after times of great trials?**
3. **The Lord alone can work true joy in His people's hearts (v. 22). As the psalmist sings, "His anger endureth but a moment; in his favour is life: weeping may endure for a night, but joy cometh in the morning" (Ps. 30:5). If you are in a season of weeping, how can you find the strength to endure with hope?**

EXILES RETURN WITH EZRA (7:1—8:36)

Chapter 7: ***Ezra returns to Judah to teach the people the law, and being ensured of provisions by Artaxerxes, he thanks God for His mercy.***

Ezra Returns to Jerusalem (7:1–10)

7:1–5 This genealogy follows 1 Chron. 6:3–14 very closely. Ezra is a descendant of Aaron, and thus of priestly lineage.

7:1 The year is 458 BC. There is a 56-year span of time passed over in relative obscurity.

7:6 Many of the exiles lived around Babylon and had not journeyed back to Jerusalem in 538 BC. *a ready scribe in the law of Moses.* Clearly, the law of Moses has not only great

God of Israel had given: and the king granted him
all his request, according to the hand of the LORD
his God upon him.
7 And there went up *some* of the children of
Israel, and of the priests, and the Levites, and the
singers, and the porters, and the Nethinims, unto
Jerusalem, in the seventh year of Artaxerxes the
king.
8 And he came to Jerusalem in the fifth month,
which *was* in the seventh year of the king.
9 For upon the first *day* of the first month began
he to go up from Babylon, and on the first *day* of
the fifth month came he to Jerusalem, according
to the good hand of his God upon him.
10 For Ezra had prepared his heart to seek the law
of the LORD, and to do *it*, and to teach in Israel
statutes and judgments.
11 ¶ Now this *is* the copy of the letter that the
king Artaxerxes gave unto Ezra the priest, the
scribe, *even* a scribe of the words of the com-
mandments of the LORD, and of his statutes to
Israel.
12 Artaxerxes, king of kings, unto Ezra the priest,
a scribe of the law of the God of heaven, perfect
peace, and at such a time.
13 I make a decree, that all they of the people of
Israel, and *of* his priests and Levites, in my realm,
which are minded of their own freewill to go up
to Jerusalem, go with thee.
14 Forasmuch as thou art sent of the king, and
of his seven counsellors, to enquire concerning
Judah and Jerusalem, according to the law of thy
God which *is* in thine hand;
15 And to carry the silver and gold, which the
king and his counsellors have freely offered
unto the God of Israel, whose habitation *is* in
Jerusalem,
16 And all the silver and gold that thou canst find
in all the province of Babylon, with the freewill
offering of the people, and of the priests, offer-
ing willingly for the house of their God which *is*
in Jerusalem:
17 That thou mayest buy speedily with this
money bullocks, rams, lambs, with their meat
offerings and their drink offerings, and offer them
upon the altar of the house of your God which *is*
in Jerusalem.
18 And whatsoever shall seem good to thee, and
to thy brethren, to do with the rest of the silver
and the gold, that do after the will of your God.
19 The vessels also that are given thee for the
service of the house of thy God, *those* deliver thou
before the God of Jerusalem.
20 And whatsoever more shall be needful for the
house of thy God, which thou shalt have occa-
sion to bestow, bestow *it* out of the king's treasure
house.
21 And I, *even* I Artaxerxes the king, do make a
decree to all the treasurers which *are* beyond the
river, that whatsoever Ezra the priest, the scribe of
the law of the God of heaven, shall require of you,
it be done speedily,
22 Unto an hundred talents of silver, and to an
hundred measures of wheat, and to an hundred
baths of wine, and to an hundred baths of oil, and
salt without prescribing *how much*.
23 Whatsoever is commanded by the God of
heaven, let it be diligently done for the house of
the God of heaven: for why should there be wrath
against the realm of the king and his sons?
24 Also we certify you, that touching any of the
priests and Levites, singers, porters, Nethinims, or
ministers of this house of God, it shall not be law-
ful to impose toll, tribute, or custom, upon them.
25 And thou, Ezra, after the wisdom of thy God,
that *is* in thine hand, set magistrates and judges,
which may judge all the people that *are* beyond
the river, all such as know the laws of thy God;
and teach ye them that know *them* not.
26 And whosoever will not do the law of thy God,
and the law of the king, let judgment be executed
speedily upon him, whether *it be* unto death, or
to banishment, or to confiscation of goods, or to
imprisonment.
27 ¶ Blessed *be* the LORD God of our fathers,
which hath put *such a thing* as this in the king's

---

antiquity but also great authority. Ezra was likely appointed by the king to maintain a high office, a secretary of sorts, in Jerusalem. Ezra prospered in the presence of the king because the Lord's *hand* was upon him (vv. 9,28; 8:18,22,31).

7:7 *the children of Israel*. Most of those returning are from Judah and Benjamin. However, they see themselves as continuing the legacy of the nation of Israel. *Nethinims*. See note at 2:43–54.

7:10 This is a description of Ezra's focus as a scribe: study, practice, and teaching.

Artaxerxes I Writes to Ezra and Supplies Treasures for the Temple (7:11–28)

7:12–26 This section is again in Aramaic (as was 4:8—6:18; see note at 4:7).

7:14 *Forasmuch*. Since, because.

7:22 *baths*. Measurement for liquids. One bath was about 9 gallons or 34 liters.

7:24 *custom*. Tax.

7:25 The law of God is referred to as *the wisdom of thy God* (Deut. 4:5–6).

7:27 The Hebrew begins again here. *beautify*. Adorn, make lovely.

Thoughts for Personal/Family Worship: Chapter 7

1. **Every Christian can learn from Ezra. He prepared his heart to study God's Word, practice its teaching, and pass its teaching on to others (v. 10). This is the duty of everyone charged to teach the Word, whether heads of household in the family or pastors and teachers in the church. Even if we do not have official responsibilities to teach, we can still share the Word of God with others.**

heart, to beautify the house of the LORD which *is* in Jerusalem:
28 And hath extended mercy unto me before the
king, and his counsellors, and before all the king's
mighty princes. And I was strengthened as the
hand of the LORD my God *was* upon me, and I
gathered together out of Israel chief men to go up
with me.

CHAPTER 8

THESE *are* now the chief of their fathers, and *this*
is the genealogy of them that went up with me
from Babylon, in the reign of Artaxerxes the king.
2 Of the sons of Phinehas; Gershom: of the sons
of Ithamar; Daniel: of the sons of David; Hattush.
3 Of the sons of Shechaniah, of the sons of Pharosh;
Zechariah: and with him were reckoned by
genealogy of the males an hundred and fifty.
4 Of the sons of Pahath-moab; Elihoenai the son
of Zerahiah, and with him two hundred males.
5 Of the sons of Shechaniah; the son of Jahaziel,
and with him three hundred males.
6 Of the sons also of Adin; Ebed the son of Jonathan,
and with him fifty males.
7 And of the sons of Elam; Jeshaiah the son of
Athaliah, and with him seventy males.
8 And of the sons of Shephatiah; Zebadiah the
son of Michael, and with him fourscore males.
9 Of the sons of Joab; Obadiah the son of Jehiel,
and with him two hundred and eighteen males.
10 And of the sons of Shelomith; the son of Josiphiah,
and with him an hundred and threescore
males.
11 And of the sons of Bebai; Zechariah the son of
Bebai, and with him twenty and eight males.
12 And of the sons of Azgad; Johanan the son
of Hakkatan, and with him an hundred and ten
males.
13 And of the last sons of Adonikam, whose
names *are* these, Eliphelet, Jeiel, and Shemaiah,
and with them threescore males.
14 Of the sons also of Bigvai; Uthai, and Zabbud,
and with them seventy males.
15 ¶ And I gathered them together to the river
that runneth to Ahava; and there abode we in
tents three days: and I viewed the people, and the
priests, and found there none of the sons of Levi.
16 Then sent I for Eliezer, for Ariel, for Shemaiah,
and for Elnathan, and for Jarib, and for
Elnathan, and for Nathan, and for Zechariah, and
for Meshullam, chief men; also for Joiarib, and for
Elnathan, men of understanding.
17 And I sent them with commandment unto
Iddo the chief at the place Casiphia, and I told
them what they should say unto Iddo, *and* to his
brethren the Nethinims, at the place Casiphia,
that they should bring unto us ministers for the
house of our God.
18 And by the good hand of our God upon us
they brought us a man of understanding, of the
sons of Mahli, the son of Levi, the son of Israel;
and Sherebiah, with his sons and his brethren,
eighteen;
19 And Hashabiah, and with him Jeshaiah of
the sons of Merari, his brethren and their sons,
twenty;
20 Also of the Nethinims, whom David and the
princes had appointed for the service of the Levites,
two hundred and twenty Nethinims: all of
them were expressed by name.
21 ¶ Then I proclaimed a fast there, at the river of
Ahava, that we might afflict ourselves before our
God, to seek of him a right way for us, and for our
little ones, and for all our substance.
22 For I was ashamed to require of the king a band
of soldiers and horsemen to help us against the
enemy in the way: because we had spoken unto

Pray for parents, teachers, leaders in your church and yourself that all would have the heart of Ezra.

2. **Artaxerxes helped Ezra and thus also the cause of God. We can be thankful for how God used him. Nevertheless, Artaxerxes never had a heartfelt attachment to the Lord. Is it enough to simply advance the cause of God? Or like Ezra, have you learned to love God and His commandments more than gold (Ps. 119:127; Matt. 6:24; 22:37)?**
3. **Ezra recognized God's hand of mercy in his circumstances (v. 28). If we are the Lord's, our life is filled with tokens of God's mercy. Like Ezra, do you trace them and thank the Lord for them? How has God's hand of mercy appeared in your life recently?**

Chapter 8: *Ezra lists those who returned with him, refuses a military consort, and relies on the strength of the Lord to protect the people on the four-month journey.*

List of Returnees (8:1–14)

8:1 *chief of their fathers.* The structure of family leadership was in place, with fathers leading their children, and children following the guidance of their fathers.

8:2–14 There are differences between this list and that in ch. 2 and Neh. 7. Here the priestly families are mentioned first (v. 2), whereas in ch. 2 and Neh. 7, they are mentioned last.

8:2 *Hattush.* A descendant of Zerubbabel and thus from the royal family of David (1 Chron. 3:21–22).

Exiles Reenter Jerusalem (8:15–36)

8:15–20 Ezra notices that there are no Levites and so he sends a request to *Casiphia,* where Levitical families must have been known to live. *Sherebiah,* his brothers, and sons, are found willing to come along.

8:21 *fast.* Ezra prepared the people spiritually before entering Jerusalem.

8:22 Ezra was *ashamed* because if he had asked for military support, it would have reflected little trust in God. This is not a normative principle that we must all live by. Nehemiah accepted a military escort (Neh. 2:7–9) and Paul clearly relied on his Roman citizenship to avoid being unjustly flogged (Acts 22). *require.* Request.

the king, saying, The hand of our God *is* upon all
them for good that seek him; but his power and
his wrath *is* against all them that forsake him.
23 So we fasted and besought our God for this:
and he was intreated of us.
24 ¶ Then I separated twelve of the chief of the
priests, Sherebiah, Hashabiah, and ten of their
brethren with them,
25 And weighed unto them the silver, and the
gold, and the vessels, *even* the offering of the
house of our God, which the king, and his coun-
sellors, and his lords, and all Israel *there* present,
had offered:
26 I even weighed unto their hand six hundred
and fifty talents of silver, and silver vessels an
hundred talents, *and* of gold an hundred talents;
27 Also twenty basons of gold, of a thousand
drams; and two vessels of fine copper, precious as
gold.
28 And I said unto them, Ye *are* holy unto the
LORD; the vessels *are* holy also; and the silver and
the gold *are* a freewill offering unto the LORD God
of your fathers.
29 Watch ye, and keep *them*, until ye weigh *them*
before the chief of the priests and the Levites, and
chief of the fathers of Israel, at Jerusalem, in the
chambers of the house of the LORD.
30 So took the priests and the Levites the weight
of the silver, and the gold, and the vessels, to bring
them to Jerusalem unto the house of our God.
31 ¶ Then we departed from the river of Ahava
on the twelfth *day* of the first month, to go unto
Jerusalem: and the hand of our God was upon us,
and he delivered us from the hand of the enemy,
and of such as lay in wait by the way.
32 And we came to Jerusalem, and abode there
three days.
33 ¶ Now on the fourth day was the silver and the
gold and the vessels weighed in the house of our
God by the hand of Meremoth the son of Uriah
the priest; and with him *was* Eleazar the son of
Phinehas; and with them *was* Jozabad the son of
Jeshua, and Noadiah the son of Binnui, Levites;
34 By number *and* by weight of every one: and all
the weight was written at that time.
35 *Also* the children of those that had been carried
away, which were come out of the captivity, offered
burnt offerings unto the God of Israel, twelve bull-
ocks for all Israel, ninety and six rams, seventy and
seven lambs, twelve he goats *for* a sin offering: all
this was a burnt offering unto the LORD.
36 ¶ And they delivered the king's commissions
unto the king's lieutenants, and to the governors
on this side the river: and they furthered the
people, and the house of God.

CHAPTER 9

NOW when these things were done, the princes
came to me, saying, The people of Israel, and
the priests, and the Levites, have not separated
themselves from the people of the lands, *doing*
according to their abominations, *even* of the
Canaanites, the Hittites, the Perizzites, the
Jebusites, the Ammonites, the Moabites, the
Egyptians, and the Amorites.
2 For they have taken of their daughters for
themselves, and for their sons: so that the holy
seed have mingled themselves with the people of
those lands: yea, the hand of the princes and rulers
hath been chief in this trespass.
3 And when I heard this thing, I rent my garment
and my mantle, and plucked off the hair of my
head and of my beard, and sat down astonied.

8:23 Despite Ezra's confidence that God would protect his people on their journey, Ezra and the people sought the Lord's favor through prayer. God's sovereignty is not an excuse to neglect spiritual duties, but it should cause us to seek the Lord's favor.

8:27 *drams.* Measurement of precious metals.

8:31 The journey from Babylon to Jerusalem took four months and was over 900 miles. The road was not safe, especially in light of the 5,000 unarmed men and the massive amounts of riches. Ezra praised the Lord for His protection.

8:33–34 Babylonian and Persian law required careful documentation of transactions and funds. It is likely that Ezra had to report back to Artaxerxes the amount of treasures received. Ezra modeled good stewardship.

Thoughts for Personal/Family Worship: Chapter 8

1. **God's will was Ezra's chief concern (v. 21). Even to a man like Ezra, who relied on God, discerning God's will was not always easy. He went to great lengths to discern God's will, fasting and seeking the Lord. We too must invest time and energy into seeking God and His will when we face significant decisions. The very process honors Him. What major decisions do you face as an individual, family, church, or society? How are you seeking the Lord?**
2. **Ezra knew the power of seeking God. He also knew that those who forsake God are under His wrath (v. 22). Paul writes something similar: "Behold therefore the goodness and severity of God: on them which fell, severity; but toward thee, goodness, if thou continue in his goodness: otherwise thou also shalt be cut off" (Rom. 11:22).**

INTERMARRIAGE AMONG THE EXILES (9:1—10:44)

Chapter 9: ***Ezra mourns over the compromises of the people who joined in marriage with the surrounding people, and he confesses this sin.***

The Problem of Intermarriage (9:1–2)

9:1 Four months had passed since the end of ch. 8. Though there are instances of marriage with people from other nations in former times in Israel (Gen. 16:3; 41:45; Ex. 2:21; Num. 12:1; 2 Sam. 3:3), what is happening here involved widespread participation in *abominations*, idolatrous and immoral practices (Ex. 34:11–16).

9:2 *holy seed.* Offspring or descendants of Abraham, Isaac, and Jacob whom God set apart for His sacred purposes

4 Then were assembled unto me every one
that trembled at the words of the God of Israel,
because of the transgression of those that had
been carried away; and I sat astonied until the
evening sacrifice.
5 ¶ And at the evening sacrifice I arose up from
my heaviness; and having rent my garment and my
mantle, I fell upon my knees, and spread out my
hands unto the LORD my God,
6 And said, O my God, I am ashamed and blush
to lift up my face to thee, my God: for our iniqui-
ties are increased over *our* head, and our trespass
is grown up unto the heavens.
7 Since the days of our fathers *have* we *been* in a
great trespass unto this day; and for our iniquities
have we, our kings, *and* our priests, been
delivered into the hand of the kings of the lands,
to the sword, to captivity, and to a spoil, and to
confusion of face, as *it is* this day.
8 And now for a little space grace hath been
shewed from the LORD our God, to leave us a rem-
nant to escape, and to give us a nail in his holy
place, that our God may lighten our eyes, and give
us a little reviving in our bondage.
9 For we *were* bondmen; yet our God hath not
forsaken us in our bondage, but hath extended
mercy unto us in the sight of the kings of Persia,
to give us a reviving, to set up the house of our
God, and to repair the desolations thereof, and to
give us a wall in Judah and in Jerusalem.
10 And now, O our God, what shall we say after
this? for we have forsaken thy commandments,
11 Which thou hast commanded by thy servants
the prophets, saying, The land, unto which ye go
to possess it, is an unclean land with the filthiness
of the people of the lands, with their abomina-
tions, which have filled it from one end to another
with their uncleanness.
12 Now therefore give not your daughters unto
their sons, neither take their daughters unto your
sons, nor seek their peace or their wealth for
ever: that ye may be strong, and eat the good of
the land, and leave *it* for an inheritance to your
children for ever.
13 And after all that is come upon us for our evil
deeds, and for our great trespass, seeing that thou
our God hast punished us less than our iniquities
deserve, and hast given us *such* deliverance as this;
14 Should we again break thy commandments,
and join in affinity with the people of these abom-
inations? wouldest not thou be angry with us till
thou hadst consumed *us*, so that *there should be*
no remnant nor escaping?
15 O LORD God of Israel, thou *art* righteous: for
we remain yet escaped, as *it is* this day: behold, we
are before thee in our trespasses: for we cannot
stand before thee because of this.

CHAPTER 10

NOW when Ezra had prayed, and when he had
confessed, weeping and casting himself down
before the house of God, there assembled unto
him out of Israel a very great congregation of
men and women and children: for the people
wept very sore.
2 And Shechaniah the son of Jehiel, *one* of the
sons of Elam, answered and said unto Ezra, We

(Gen. 17:7,19; 28:4; Deut. 7:6–8; Isa. 6:13; Rom. 11:16,28). By virtue of God's covenant, those who descend from believing parents are considered set apart (1 Cor. 7:14). This does not refer to an internal holiness. The *princes and rulers* were leading the way in this sinful intermixing.

Ezra's Prayer of Repentance (9:3–15)

9:4 *trembled at the words of the God of Israel*. Feared God and desired to keep His commands (Isa. 66:2).

9:6 *our*. Ezra shows corporate solidarity in the guilt of the people (Dan. 9:5).

9:7–8 *a little space grace hath been shewed*. He is referring to God's grace in these initial returns from exile. *nail*. Peg, in the sense of security, stability.

9:9 *wall*. Literally, "a protective wall," as about a vineyard, used figuratively of the protection God had given those who had returned.

9:14 *affinity*. Relationship by marriage. *no remnant nor escaping*. Ezra knew that the Lord could wipe out everyone in Israel for their sins and still remain faithful in drawing back a second group of exiles. Ezra did not depend on Israel's status as the covenantal people, but on the mercy of God.

Thoughts for Personal/Family Worship: Chapter 9

1. **The inhabitants of Judah were at risk of being swallowed up by the nations around them and their idolatries. Still today, we are called to a life of separation from worldliness. Paul challenged the Corinthians, "For what fellowship hath righteousness with unrighteousness? and what communion hath light with darkness?" (2 Cor. 6:14). Why might a romantic relationship with an unbeliever attract a Christian? How can he or she resist this temptation?**
2. **Ezra readily confessed sin as sin. He knew that God had punished the nation far less than it had deserved (v. 13). If we know anything of our wicked hearts, we will find it difficult to complain that our circumstances are unfair. When we are tempted to question God's goodness, let us give consideration to our sinfulness, and what we deserve.**
3. **We can only fight sin by the grace of God. Ezra shows the right way by running to the Lord in prayer. How does God say He will help us in the midst of temptation (1 Cor. 10:13)?**

Chapter 10: ***The people confess their sin and deal with the issue of intermarriage.***

The People's Repentance and a Solemn Assembly (10:1–8)

10:1 *there assembled . . . a very great congregation*. Ezra's repentance is contagious. *sore*. Greatly.

10:2 *Shechaniah*. He spoke for many others. *strange*. Foreign.

have trespassed against our God, and have taken
strange wives of the people of the land: yet now
there is hope in Israel concerning this thing.
3 Now therefore let us make a covenant with
our God to put away all the wives, and such as
are born of them, according to the counsel of my
lord, and of those that tremble at the command-
ment of our God; and let it be done according to
the law.
4 Arise; for *this* matter *belongeth* unto thee: we also
will be with thee: be of good courage, and do *it*.
5 Then arose Ezra, and made the chief priests, the
Levites, and all Israel, to swear that they should do
according to this word. And they sware.
6 ¶ Then Ezra rose up from before the house of
God, and went into the chamber of Johanan the
son of Eliashib: and *when* he came thither, he did
eat no bread, nor drink water: for he mourned be-
cause of the transgression of them that had been
carried away.
7 And they made proclamation throughout
Judah and Jerusalem unto all the children of
the captivity, that they should gather themselves
together unto Jerusalem;
8 And that whosoever would not come within
three days, according to the counsel of the
princes and the elders, all his substance should
be forfeited, and himself separated from the
congregation of those that had been carried away.
9 ¶ Then all the men of Judah and Benjamin
gathered themselves together unto Jerusalem
within three days. It *was* the ninth month, on the
twentieth *day* of the month; and all the people
sat in the street of the house of God, trembling
because of *this* matter, and for the great rain.
10 And Ezra the priest stood up, and said unto
them, Ye have transgressed, and have taken
strange wives, to increase the trespass of Israel.
11 Now therefore make confession unto the LORD
God of your fathers, and do his pleasure: and
separate yourselves from the people of the land,
and from the strange wives.
12 Then all the congregation answered and said
with a loud voice, As thou hast said, so must we do.
13 But the people *are* many, and *it is* a time of
much rain, and we are not able to stand without,
neither *is this* a work of one day or two: for we are
many that have transgressed in this thing.
14 Let now our rulers of all the congregation
stand, and let all them which have taken strange
wives in our cities come at appointed times, and
with them the elders of every city, and the judges
thereof, until the fierce wrath of our God for this
matter be turned from us.
15 ¶ Only Jonathan the son of Asahel and Jaha-
ziah the son of Tikvah were employed about this
matter: and Meshullam and Shabbethai the Levite
helped them.
16 And the children of the captivity did so. And
Ezra the priest, *with* certain chief of the fathers,
after the house of their fathers, and all of them by
their names, were separated, and sat down in the
first day of the tenth month to examine the matter.
17 And they made an end with all the men that
had taken strange wives by the first day of the first
month.
18 ¶ And among the sons of the priests there
were found that had taken strange wives: *namely*,
of the sons of Jeshua the son of Jozadak, and his
brethren; Maaseiah, and Eliezer, and Jarib, and
Gedaliah.
19 And they gave their hands that they would put
away their wives; and *being* guilty, *they offered* a
ram of the flock for their trespass.
20 And of the sons of Immer; Hanani, and
Zebadiah.
21 And of the sons of Harim; Maaseiah, and
Elijah, and Shemaiah, and Jehiel, and Uzziah.
22 And of the sons of Pashur; Elioenai, Maaseiah,
Ishmael, Nethaneel, Jozabad, and Elasah.
23 Also of the Levites; Jozabad, and Shimei, and
Kelaiah, (the same *is* Kelita,) Pethahiah, Judah,
and Eliezer.
24 Of the singers also; Eliashib: and of the por-
ters; Shallum, and Telem, and Uri.
25 Moreover of Israel: of the sons of Parosh;

10:3 *tremble at the commandment*. See note at 9:4.

10:4 Shechaniah agreed to support Ezra, but he knew that *this matter belongeth* to Ezra, that is to say: the Lord raised Ezra up to lead this.

The People of Israel Are Purified (10:9–44)

10:12 *All* the people of Israel agreed to the oath Ezra laid before them.

10:13 *without*. Outside.

10:14–15 *employed about this matter*. The Hebrew carries the idea that these men opposed the suggestion of Ezra. What exactly they were opposing is not clear, whether it was their separation from the strange wives, or whether it was the delay of the inspection for those who had married foreigners.

10:17 *strange*. Foreign (v. 44). The text indicates by the following list that 111 persons were found guilty. Though this was a small number compared to the 30,000 who dwelt in the area, throughout the history of Israel the sins of one person or a few had a dramatic effect on the whole community.

10:19 *put away their wives*. Literally, "sent out their wives from among them." The Old Testament law regulated divorce but did not encourage it (Gen. 2:24; Deut. 24:1–4; Matt. 19:3–9). In considering Ezra's authorization of divorce, it is important to note that, first, these marriages were illegal, being contracted contrary to the law of Moses (Deut. 7:1–3); second, these men may have divorced their original Jewish wives in favor of a more cosmopolitan marriage (Mal. 2:11,15).

Thoughts for Personal/Family Worship: Chapter 10

1. If leaders in church, state, and family could, like Ezra, lead in repentance, who can tell what would happen?

Ramiah, and Jeziah, and Malchiah, and Miamin,
and Eleazar, and Malchijah, and Benaiah.
26 And of the sons of Elam; Mattaniah, Zecha-
riah, and Jehiel, and Abdi, and Jeremoth, and
Eliah.
27 And of the sons of Zattu; Elioenai, Eliashib,
Mattaniah, and Jeremoth, and Zabad, and Aziza.
28 Of the sons also of Bebai; Jehohanan, Hana-
niah, Zabbai, *and* Athlai.
29 And of the sons of Bani; Meshullam, Malluch,
and Adaiah, Jashub, and Sheal, and Ramoth.
30 And of the sons of Pahath-moab; Adna, and
Chelal, Benaiah, Maaseiah, Mattaniah, Bezaleel,
and Binnui, and Manasseh.
31 And *of* the sons of Harim; Eliezer, Ishijah,
Malchiah, Shemaiah, Shimeon,
32 Benjamin, Malluch, *and* Shemariah.
33 Of the sons of Hashum; Mattenai, Mattathah,
Zabad, Eliphelet, Jeremai, Manasseh, *and* Shimei.
34 Of the sons of Bani; Maadai, Amram, and Uel,
35 Benaiah, Bedeiah, Chelluh,
36 Vaniah, Meremoth, Eliashib,
37 Mattaniah, Mattenai, and Jaasau,
38 And Bani, and Binnui, Shimei,
39 And Shelemiah, and Nathan, and Adaiah,
40 Machnadebai, Shashai, Sharai,
41 Azareel, and Shelemiah, Shemariah,
42 Shallum, Amariah, *and* Joseph.
43 Of the sons of Nebo; Jeiel, Mattithiah, Zabad,
Zebina, Jadau, and Joel, Benaiah.
44 All these had taken strange wives: and *some* of
them had wives by whom they had children.

Of what major sins does your nation need to repent? Are there ways that your church or denomination needs to repent? Begin praying for God to give hearty repentance through Jesus Christ, beginning with the leadership—and with you.

2. Though true repentance begins with the mind, its essence is a change of heart that produces action, as we see with the people in this chapter. Paul gives us a picture of such repentance in 2 Cor. 7:10–11. Of what sins have you repented recently? How does your repentance match up with these biblical models? Where do you need to implement a more thorough repentance?

FOR
This Day
IS
HOLY
UNTO
our Lord
NEITHER BE YE SORRY
FOR
The Joy
OF
THE LORD
IS YOUR
Strength

NEHEMIAH 8:10

INTRODUCTION TO THE BOOK OF NEHEMIAH

Authorship and Date: See the Introduction to Ezra.

Theme: God's faithfulness in protecting and providing for His people through godly, prayerful, and proactive leadership.

Purpose: To encourage righteous leaders and those who follow them that God can restore His people against all human expectations, if His servants will faithfully keep His commands.

Synopsis: *The Contribution of Nehemiah to Redemptive Revelation*

Nehemiah stands in close relation to Ezra, tracing God's act behind the rebuilding of Jerusalem as well as spiritual reforms. Nehemiah received reports of the remnant of exiles who had returned to Jerusalem (1:2) and he heard of the affliction and reproach they were suffering because of the broken-down wall of Jerusalem (v. 3). Nehemiah was struck to the heart (v. 4) and prayed that God would provide a way to rebuild the walls and so take away the reproach of His covenantal people.

As the king's cupbearer, Nehemiah was given a providential opening to ask for permission to go and rebuild the walls of Jerusalem. Once in Jerusalem, Nehemiah made a night journey to survey the situation (ch. 2). The next chapters recount the efforts of the Jews in rebuilding the walls of Jerusalem, despite external opposition and internal strife (chs. 3–7). The second part of the book narrates the consecration to the Lord of the people along with the city (chs. 8–12), and some continued reforms that proved necessary (ch. 13).

Despite being known mostly as the builder of the wall, Nehemiah realized that Judah's biggest need was not physical walls, but spiritual dedication to God. A zeal for God's house and name motivated Nehemiah to do what he did. He pointed forward to the greater Rebuilder who will come and save His people from their sin and deliver them from their spiritual bondage and exile once and for all.

Nehemiah made a significant contribution to the advancement of the fullness of time when Christ would come. For Christ to fulfill all righteousness, certain things had to be in place. The Messiah was to be born into a Jewish community that observed the ceremonial laws (cf. Luke 2:21–22,27), for the Lord would appear suddenly in His temple (Mal. 3:1). There had to be a clear distinction between the Gentiles and Jews for a proper and unmistakable identification of the Messiah, for salvation comes from the Jews (John 4:22) in the person of the Seed of Abraham and David (Matt. 1:1; Rom. 1:2–3; Gal. 3:16). For that to happen there had to be a strong Jewish community with the mechanisms in place to exclude Gentile influence. To sum it up simply, there had to be an Israel if there was going to be a Christ. Nehemiah's work in building that city and his demand for purity of worship was a key component toward the coming of Christ.

Outline:

I. Report from Jerusalem and Nehemiah's Prayer (1:1–11)
   - A. Report Concerning the Condition of Jerusalem (1:1–3)
   - B. Nehemiah's Prayer of Repentance (1:4–11)

II. Nehemiah Petitions the King and Returns to Jerusalem (2:1–16)
   - A. Nehemiah Petitions the King (2:1–10)
   - B. Nehemiah Investigates the Walls (2:11–16)

III. The Gates of the City Are Rebuilt Despite Opposition (2:17—7:4)

   - A. Nehemiah Encourages the Jews to Rebuild the Walls (2:17–20)
   - B. The Gates of the City Are Repaired (3:1–32)
   - C. Opposition to Rebuilding the Walls (4:1–23)
   - D. Usury Condemned and Nehemiah Appointed Governor (5:1–19)
   - E. Nehemiah Opposed and Walls Finished (6:1—7:4)

IV. List of Exiles Living in Jerusalem (7:5–73)

V. Ezra Reads the Law and the Covenant Is Renewed (8:1—10:39)
   - A. Ezra Reads the Law and the Feast of Booths Is Kept (8:1–18)
   - B. The Law Read in the Presence of the People (9:1–3)
   - C. God's Faithfulness to Israel Recounted (9:4–31)
   - D. The Covenant Is Renewed (9:32—10:39)

VI. Division of the People, Priests, and Levites (11:1—12:47)
   - A. People of Judah (11:1–9)
   - B. Priests (11:10–36)
   - C. Levites (12:1–47)

VII. Abiding Problems in the Renewed Community (13:1–31)
   - A. Tobiah Defiles the Temple (13:1–9)
   - B. Levites Deprived of Offerings (13:10–14)
   - C. Sabbath Profaned (13:15–22)
   - D. Intermarriage (13:23–31)

THE BOOK OF NEHEMIAH

CHAPTER 1

THE words of Nehemiah the son of Hachaliah. And it came to pass in the month Chisleu, in the twentieth year, as I was in Shushan the palace,
2 That Hanani, one of my brethren, came, he and *certain* men of Judah; and I asked them concerning the Jews that had escaped, which were left of the captivity, and concerning Jerusalem.
3 And they said unto me, The remnant that are left of the captivity there in the province *are* in great affliction and reproach: the wall of Jerusalem also *is* broken down, and the gates thereof are burned with fire.
4 ¶ And it came to pass, when I heard these words, that I sat down and wept, and mourned *certain* days, and fasted, and prayed before the God of heaven,
5 And said, I beseech thee, O LORD God of heaven, the great and terrible God, that keepeth covenant and mercy for them that love him and observe his commandments:
6 Let thine ear now be attentive, and thine eyes open, that thou mayest hear the prayer of thy servant, which I pray before thee now, day and night, for the children of Israel thy servants, and confess the sins of the children of Israel, which we have sinned against thee: both I and my father's house have sinned.
7 We have dealt very corruptly against thee, and have not kept the commandments, nor the statutes, nor the judgments, which thou commandedst thy servant Moses.
8 Remember, I beseech thee, the word that thou commandedst thy servant Moses, saying, *If* ye transgress, I will scatter you abroad among the nations:
9 But *if* ye turn unto me, and keep my commandments, and do them; though there were of you cast out unto the uttermost part of the heaven, *yet* will I gather them from thence, and will bring them unto the place that I have chosen to set my name there.
10 Now these *are* thy servants and thy people, whom thou hast redeemed by thy great power, and by thy strong hand.
11 O Lord, I beseech thee, let now thine ear be

Chapter 1: *Nehemiah, hearing the report of Jerusalem's condition, repents before God and seeks for the pardon of his and the people's iniquities.*

REPORT FROM JERUSALEM AND NEHEMIAH'S PRAYER (1:1–11)

Report Concerning the Condition of Jerusalem (1:1–3)

1:1 *Nehemiah* means "The LORD comforts." In many ways, God comforts Nehemiah and His people throughout this book. *Chisleu.* Commonly reckoned as mid-November or December. *the twentieth year.* Thirteen years after Ezra traveled to Jerusalem, around 445 BC. *Shushan.* Also called Susa, the winter home of the Persian king (Est. 1:2; Dan. 8:2).

1:2 *Hanani.* Close kin of Nehemiah, perhaps his very brother (7:2). Knowing of the plots of the adversaries and the suffering of his people, Nehemiah was eager to hear a report of those *left of the captivity*, that is those who had returned to Judah.

1:3 *affliction and reproach.* Trouble and disgrace; not specifically identified, but likely the oppression detailed in Ezra 4:6–23. *broken down.* Likely the attempts by adversaries to break down their rebuild of the walls.

Nehemiah's Prayer of Repentance (1:4–11)

1:4 *prayed.* There are nine recorded prayers in Nehemiah. Here, he demonstrates a knowledge of God, Scripture, and what it means to be broken on account of sin. Some of Nehemiah's prayers are lengthy and others are spontaneous and short. *God of heaven.* Supreme Lord over all creation (Gen. 24:3,7; Ps. 136:1–2,26), a title frequently used of the Lord in communications from or to Gentiles (v. 5; 2:4,20; Ezra 1:2; 5:11–12; 6:9–10; 7:12,21–23; Dan. 2:37,44).

1:5 Nehemiah made his prayer on the basis of God's promises. *beseech.* To plead with. *terrible.* Not a negative description but one that evokes godly fear and respect. *keepeth covenant and mercy.* God is faithful to keep His promises and love His people (Deut. 7:9,12; 2 Chron. 6:14; Dan. 9:4).

1:8–9 The exile was a curse for turning away from the Lord. Nehemiah knew this from reading the Scriptures (Deut. 4:25–31; 28:36–58). Meanwhile, his hope of forgiveness rested on God's goodness and love. *Remember.* An appeal for God to act on His promises (Ex. 32:13; Deut. 9:27).

1:9 *uttermost.* Outermost. *unto the place I have chosen to set my name.* Jerusalem, home of God's glory in the temple (Deut. 12:5–6,11; 2 Chron. 6:5–6,34,38; 7:16; 12:13; 33:7).

1:10 Almost an exact quotation of Deut. 9:29, where Israel was threatened with extinction if it had not been for Moses' intercession. Similarly, Nehemiah interceded with God's promises.

1:11 *desire to fear thy name.* Delight to honor, worship, and

attentive to the prayer of thy servant, and to the
prayer of thy servants, who desire to fear thy
name: and prosper, I pray thee, thy servant this
day, and grant him mercy in the sight of this man.
For I was the king's cupbearer.

CHAPTER 2

AND it came to pass in the month Nisan, in the
twentieth year of Artaxerxes the king, *that* wine
was before him: and I took up the wine, and gave
it unto the king. Now I had not been *beforetime*
sad in his presence.
2 Wherefore the king said unto me, Why *is* thy
countenance sad, seeing thou *art* not sick? this *is*
nothing *else* but sorrow of heart. Then I was very
sore afraid,
3 And said unto the king, Let the king live for
ever: why should not my countenance be sad,
when the city, the place of my fathers' sepulchres,
lieth waste, and the gates thereof are consumed
with fire?
4 Then the king said unto me, For what dost thou
make request? So I prayed to the God of heaven.
5 And I said unto the king, If it please the king,
and if thy servant have found favour in thy sight,
that thou wouldest send me unto Judah, unto the
city of my fathers' sepulchres, that I may build it.
6 And the king said unto me, (the queen also
sitting by him,) For how long shall thy journey
be? and when wilt thou return? So it pleased the
king to send me; and I set him a time.
7 Moreover I said unto the king, If it please the
king, let letters be given me to the governors
beyond the river, that they may convey me over
till I come into Judah;
8 And a letter unto Asaph the keeper of the king's
forest, that he may give me timber to make beams
for the gates of the palace which *appertained* to
the house, and for the wall of the city, and for the
house that I shall enter into. And the king granted
me, according to the good hand of my God upon
me.
9 ¶ Then I came to the governors beyond the
river, and gave them the king's letters. Now the
king had sent captains of the army and horsemen
with me.
10 When Sanballat the Horonite, and Tobiah
the servant, the Ammonite, heard *of it*, it grieved
them exceedingly that there was come a man to
seek the welfare of the children of Israel.
11 So I came to Jerusalem, and was there three
days.
12 ¶ And I arose in the night, I and some few men
with me; neither told I *any* man what my God had
put in my heart to do at Jerusalem: neither *was*
there any beast with me, save the beast that I rode
upon.

---

obey God because of love for His glory (Deut. 10:12; Pss. 2:11; 112:1). The fear of God is a key motive in Nehemiah's leadership (5:9,15; 7:2). *prosper.* Cause to succeed in his endeavors. *this man.* King Artaxerxes. Nehemiah likely knew of the king's command (Ezra 4:21). *cupbearer.* A prestigious vocation in Persia, responsible to ensure that the king's cup was not poisoned. The Lord had sovereignly placed Nehemiah in this high position (Est. 4:14).

Thoughts for Personal/Family Worship: Chapter 1

1. **This affluent servant of the king was touched with the suffering and anguish of his fellow Jews. Far greater is Christ's love for His people. Though He dwelt in the greatest places of honor and glory (John 17:5), He came down to die for them (Matt. 1:20–21; 20:28), and being raised for their justification (Rom. 4:25), He now intercedes in heaven for them (Rom. 8:34). Just as it was a great comfort to the Jews that they had a Nehemiah, so it is an infinite comfort to Christians that they have a sympathetic Savior at God's right hand. Praise God for His love and intercession on our behalf!**
2. **As is clear from his prayer, Nehemiah knew and believed the truth of Scripture. How does knowing and believing God's Word help in prayer? Using Nehemiah as an example, how can we use God's attributes (v. 5) in prayer? How can we use His laws (v. 7)? His promises (vv. 8–9)? His great works of salvation (v. 10)?**

Chapter 2: ***Nehemiah receives permission from the king to go and rebuild the walls of Jerusalem and, upon his arrival, inspects the fallen walls of Jerusalem under the cover of dark.***

NEHEMIAH PETITIONS THE KING AND RETURNS TO JERUSALEM (2:1–16)

Nehemiah Petitions the King (2:1–10)

2:1 *Nisan.* March/April. Four months had passed since the initial report.
2:2 *sore afraid.* Greatly afraid. Nehemiah greatly feared presenting his request to the king. Under Persian law an individual could be killed at the whim of the king.
2:3 *sepulchres.* Graves or tombs. *consumed with fire.* Lie in ruins and destruction.
2:4 *prayed.* A brief, spontaneous prayer.
2:6 *queen.* We do not know if her presence helped influence the king, or if this denoted a less formal, more private occasion. *set him a time.* The time frame is not mentioned.
2:7 *letters.* Official notices from the king for safe conduct and proof of the authoritative mission (Ezra 4:7–9). Nehemiah anticipated difficulty. *convey.* Let him pass.
2:8 *timber.* It was common in the Ancient Near East to build city walls of wood. *according to the good hand of my God.* Nehemiah saw God's providential power and wisdom orchestrating the lavish kindness of Artaxerxes.
2:9 *captains . . . horsemen.* Nehemiah had a military escort whereas Ezra had refused one.
2:10 *Sanballat the Horonite.* Governor of Samaria. *Tobiah the servant, the Ammonite.* The chief official of Ammon, an enemy of Israel (2 Sam. 10). Both these men proved to be antagonists to the work of Nehemiah. *grieved them exceedingly.* The governors relished their efforts of opposing the Jews.

Nehemiah Investigates the Walls (2:11–16)

2:12 *in the night.* Nehemiah kept his mission secret from his enemies and the Jews (v. 16).

13 And I went out by night by the gate of the
valley, even before the dragon well, and to the
dung port, and viewed the walls of Jerusalem,
which were broken down, and the gates thereof
were consumed with fire.
14 Then I went on to the gate of the fountain, and
to the king's pool: but *there was* no place for the
beast *that was* under me to pass.
15 Then went I up in the night by the brook, and
viewed the wall, and turned back, and entered by
the gate of the valley, and *so* returned.
16 And the rulers knew not whither I went, or
what I did; neither had I as yet told *it* to the Jews,
nor to the priests, nor to the nobles, nor to the
rulers, nor to the rest that did the work.
17 ¶ Then said I unto them, Ye see the distress
that we *are* in, how Jerusalem *lieth* waste, and the
gates thereof are burned with fire: come, and let
us build up the wall of Jerusalem, that we be no
more a reproach.
18 Then I told them of the hand of my God which
was good upon me; as also the king's words that
he had spoken unto me. And they said, Let us rise
up and build. So they strengthened their hands
for *this* good *work*.
19 But when Sanballat the Horonite, and Tobiah
the servant, the Ammonite, and Geshem the
Arabian, heard *it*, they laughed us to scorn, and
despised us, and said, What *is* this thing that ye
do? will ye rebel against the king?
20 Then answered I them, and said unto them,
The God of heaven, he will prosper us; therefore
we his servants will arise and build: but ye have no
portion, nor right, nor memorial, in Jerusalem.

CHAPTER 3

THEN Eliashib the high priest rose up with his
brethren the priests, and they builded the sheep
gate; they sanctified it, and set up the doors of it;
even unto the tower of Meah they sanctified it,
unto the tower of Hananeel.
2 And next unto him builded the men of Jericho.
And next to them builded Zaccur the son of Imri.
3 But the fish gate did the sons of Hassenaah
build, who *also* laid the beams thereof, and set up
the doors thereof, the locks thereof, and the bars
thereof.
4 And next unto them repaired Meremoth the
son of Urijah, the son of Koz. And next unto them
repaired Meshullam the son of Berechiah, the son
of Meshezabeel. And next unto them repaired
Zadok the son of Baana.
5 And next unto them the Tekoites repaired; but

2:13–14 *gate of the valley.* Chief gate overlooking the Tyropoeon Valley on the southwestern side of the city. *dragon well.* Likely on the southwest side. *dung port.* Southern end of the city where the Tyropoeon and Hinnom Valleys meet. Sometimes referred to as the Potsherd Gate (Jer. 19:2), it opened to the city waste pile. *gate of the fountain.* East side near the south end of the city. *kings's pool.* Outside the wall; it served as an overflow pool for the Pool of Siloam. Nehemiah eventually built the city walls near the crest of the hill due to the large amount of debris from the destruction of the earlier walls. This resulted in a smaller city than before the exile.
2:15 *brook.* The Kidron Valley, which ran along the eastern side of the city.
2:16 *whither.* Where.

THE GATES OF THE CITY ARE REBUILT DESPITE OPPOSITION (2:17—7:4)

Nehemiah Encourages the Jews to Rebuild the Walls (2:17–20)

2:17 *reproach.* Disgrace, plainly visible in the dilapidated state of the city, which reflected the reality of exile and God's curse. Nehemiah sought a reversal of the reproach.
2:18 *hand of my God which was good upon.* God's power had worked favorably for Nehemiah and the Jews. *strengthened their hands.* They prepared themselves for the work.
2:19 *Geshem.* Powerful leader of Qedar, a collection of Arab tribes that included Edom and the southern part of Judah. *rebel.* Rebellion against the Persian kingdom was cause for death.
2:20 *ye have no . . . memorial.* Like Ezra, Nehemiah rejected the help of these wicked men because they had no inheritance from the Lord in the land (Ezra 4:3).

Thoughts for Personal/Family Worship: Chapter 2

1. Nehemiah was a man of prayer. Again and again we read of him praying before he does something (vv. 4,20; 1:11; etc.). Some prayers were long times of devotion; others very short but heartfelt cries to heaven. A man who realizes his dependence on God will be frequently directing prayer heavenward. How would you describe your prayer life?

2. Nehemiah did not rush into a plan without surveying the rubble firsthand. Once he was intimately acquainted with what was needed, he called others to rise up and build with him. He is a model of wisdom, especially wise leadership. Why is it important to carefully investigate and understand a situation before proposing action? See Prov. 18:17; 29:20; Luke 14:28–30.

3. The cause of God will be opposed by the world, yet the gates of hell cannot prevail against it (Matt. 16:18). God's servants should expect both opposition and victory, suffering and success, if they seek God's kingdom and righteousness. Reading through Heb. 11–12, what should be our sources of encouragement, endurance, and optimism?

Chapter 3: ***The people begin the rebuilding of the walls of Jerusalem.***

The Gates of the City Are Repaired (3:1–32)

3:1 The rebuilding began at the northern part of the city and worked counterclockwise around the city. Many of these places are either unknown or uncertain. Some archaeological finds show that the wall was more than eight feet thick. *sheep gate.* Gate that led to the temple and through which the sheep for the sacrifices passed. *sanctified.* Consecrated or set apart.
3:3 *fish gate.* Near the northwest corner and likely known as the Ephraim Gate and the Middle Gate.
3:5 Tekoa was in southeast Bethlehem, about twelve miles from Jerusalem, and was the city of the prophet Amos. *nobles.*

their nobles put not their necks to the work of
their Lord.
6 Moreover the old gate repaired Jehoiada the son
of Paseah, and Meshullam the son of Besodeiah;
they laid the beams thereof, and set up the doors
thereof, and the locks thereof, and the bars thereof.
7 And next unto them repaired Melatiah the
Gibeonite, and Jadon the Meronothite, the men
of Gibeon, and of Mizpah, unto the throne of the
governor on this side the river.
8 Next unto him repaired Uzziel the son of
Harhaiah, of the goldsmiths. Next unto him
also repaired Hananiah the son of *one of* the
apothecaries, and they fortified Jerusalem unto
the broad wall.
9 And next unto them repaired Rephaiah the son
of Hur, the ruler of the half part of Jerusalem.
10 And next unto them repaired Jedaiah the
son of Harumaph, even over against his house.
And next unto him repaired Hattush the son of
Hashabniah.
11 Malchijah the son of Harim, and Hashub the
son of Pahath-moab, repaired the other piece,
and the tower of the furnaces.
12 And next unto him repaired Shallum the son
of Halohesh, the ruler of the half part of Jerusa-
lem, he and his daughters.
13 The valley gate repaired Hanun, and the in-
habitants of Zanoah; they built it, and set up
the doors thereof, the locks thereof, and the bars
thereof, and a thousand cubits on the wall unto
the dung gate.
14 But the dung gate repaired Malchiah the son
of Rechab, the ruler of part of Beth-haccerem;
he built it, and set up the doors thereof, the locks
thereof, and the bars thereof.
15 But the gate of the fountain repaired Shallun
the son of Col-hozeh, the ruler of part of Mizpah;
he built it, and covered it, and set up the doors
thereof, the locks thereof, and the bars thereof,
and the wall of the pool of Siloah by the king's
garden, and unto the stairs that go down from the
city of David.
16 After him repaired Nehemiah the son of
Azbuk, the ruler of the half part of Beth-zur, unto
the place over against the sepulchres of David, and
to the pool that was made, and unto the house of
the mighty.
17 After him repaired the Levites, Rehum the son
of Bani. Next unto him repaired Hashabiah, the
ruler of the half part of Keilah, in his part.
18 After him repaired their brethren, Bavai the son
of Henadad, the ruler of the half part of Keilah.
19 And next to him repaired Ezer the son of
Jeshua, the ruler of Mizpah, another piece over
against the going up to the armoury at the turn-
ing *of the wall*.
20 After him Baruch the son of Zabbai earnestly
repaired the other piece, from the turning *of the
wall* unto the door of the house of Eliashib the
high priest.
21 After him repaired Meremoth the son of
Urijah the son of Koz another piece, from the
door of the house of Eliashib even to the end of
the house of Eliashib.
22 And after him repaired the priests, the men of
the plain.
23 After him repaired Benjamin and Hashub over
against their house. After him repaired Azariah
the son of Maaseiah the son of Ananiah by his
house.
24 After him repaired Binnui the son of Henadad
another piece, from the house of Azariah unto the
turning *of the wall*, even unto the corner.
25 Palal the son of Uzai, over against the turning
of the wall, and the tower which lieth out from
the king's high house, that *was* by the court of the
prison. After him Pedaiah the son of Parosh.
26 Moreover the Nethinims dwelt in Ophel, unto
the place over against the water gate toward the

Not everyone agreed with Nehemiah, and because of it missed out on doing *the work of their Lord. their necks.* The place of the yoke and thus a figure of speech for service and labor (Gen. 27:40; Deut. 28:48; Isa. 10:27; Jer. 27:8).

3:6 *Jehoiada.* Opens into the second district of Jerusalem on the western side of the city.

3:8 *apothecaries.* Ointment mixers.

3:9 *half part of Jerusalem.* Jerusalem was divided into several districts, even as the province was divided into six districts.

3:10 *over against his house.* Opposite his house. Assigning men to repair the wall by their own homes (vv. 23,28–30) no doubt motivated them to work hard to protect their families (4:14).

3:12 The mention that *daughters* helped to rebuild the wall, shows the great influence that Nehemiah had on the people and the unity and cooperation of many in Jerusalem.

3:13 *Zanoah.* Thirteen miles southwest of Jerusalem in the Shephelah.

3:16 *Beth-zur.* Thirteen miles south of Jerusalem. It marked the southern border of Judah.

3:22 *men of the plain.* A subdivision of priests likely from the surrounding area; perhaps the Jordan Valley around Jericho.

3:26,31 *Nethinims.* Temple assistants.

Thoughts for Personal/Family Worship: Chapter 3

1. **It is sad to see some who have no heart for the work of the Lord (v. 5). What a blessing they missed through failing to put their shoulders under the work! God has made sure their stubborn and selfish spirit was recorded for succeeding generations. Let this be a warning to us. How do you want to be remembered by generations to come?**
2. **It is stirring to see small and great doing their part to help protect the city of God. Though each built only a portion, God noticed the labors of everyone and honored them in Scripture. The church is a body and none can say he or she does not need another member (1 Cor. 12:21). Every Christian has a part to play in building the**

east, and the tower that lieth out.
27 After them the Tekoites repaired another
piece, over against the great tower that lieth out,
even unto the wall of Ophel.
28 From above the horse gate repaired the priests,
every one over against his house.
29 After them repaired Zadok the son of Immer
over against his house. After him repaired also
Shemaiah the son of Shechaniah, the keeper of
the east gate.
30 After him repaired Hananiah the son of
Shelemiah, and Hanun the sixth son of Zalaph,
another piece. After him repaired Meshullam the
son of Berechiah over against his chamber.
31 After him repaired Malchiah the goldsmith's
son unto the place of the Nethinims, and of the
merchants, over against the gate Miphkad, and to
the going up of the corner.
32 And between the going up of the corner unto
the sheep gate repaired the goldsmiths and the
merchants.

CHAPTER 4

BUT it came to pass, that when Sanballat heard
that we builded the wall, he was wroth, and took
great indignation, and mocked the Jews.
2 And he spake before his brethren and the army
of Samaria, and said, What do these feeble Jews?
will they fortify themselves? will they sacrifice?
will they make an end in a day? will they revive
the stones out of the heaps of the rubbish which
are burned?
3 Now Tobiah the Ammonite *was* by him, and he
said, Even that which they build, if a fox go up, he
shall even break down their stone wall.
4 Hear, O our God; for we are despised: and turn
their reproach upon their own head, and give
them for a prey in the land of captivity:
5 And cover not their iniquity, and let not their
sin be blotted out from before thee: for they have
provoked *thee* to anger before the builders.
6 So built we the wall; and all the wall was joined
together unto the half thereof: for the people had
a mind to work.
7 ¶ But it came to pass, *that* when Sanballat, and
Tobiah, and the Arabians, and the Ammonites,
and the Ashdodites, heard that the walls of Jeru-
salem were made up, *and* that the breaches began
to be stopped, then they were very wroth,
8 And conspired all of them together to come
and to fight against Jerusalem, and to hinder it.
9 Nevertheless we made our prayer unto our
God, and set a watch against them day and night,
because of them.
10 And Judah said, The strength of the bearers of
burdens is decayed, and *there is* much rubbish; so
that we are not able to build the wall.
11 And our adversaries said, They shall not know,
neither see, till we come in the midst among
them, and slay them, and cause the work to cease.
12 And it came to pass, that when the Jews which
dwelt by them came, they said unto us ten times,
From all places whence ye shall return unto us
they will be upon you.
13 ¶ Therefore set I in the lower places behind
the wall, *and* on the higher places, I even set the
people after their families with their swords, their
spears, and their bows.
14 And I looked, and rose up, and said unto the
nobles, and to the rulers, and to the rest of the
people, Be not ye afraid of them: remember the
Lord, *which is* great and terrible, and fight for your
brethren, your sons, and your daughters, your
wives, and your houses.
15 And it came to pass, when our enemies heard
that it was known unto us, and God had brought
their counsel to nought, that we returned all of us

---

church. Let us not be lazy, nor envy the gifts and position of another, but let each of us work hard to serve according to his gifts and calling. God will reward us. How are you helping to build the city of God?

Chapter 4: *Because of opposition to the building of the wall, Nehemiah prays, arms the builders, and sets a watch.*

Opposition to Rebuilding the Walls (4:1–23)

4:1 *wroth.* Greatly angered.

4:3 *if a fox go up.* Tobiah exaggerated. Archaeological remains have shown the wall was more than eight feet thick.

4:4–5 Nehemiah did not retaliate but he prayed fervently against his enemies (Rom. 12:19). *we.* The first person plural indicates Nehemiah's solidarity with God's people in their tribulations.

4:4 *prey in the land of captivity.* Nehemiah prayed that they would be judged according to what they sought for the Jews.

4:6 *half.* The wall's height was now *half* complete, and it was *joined together* all the way around.

4:7–8 Bare verbal attacks were insufficient to deter the Jews, so their enemies resorted to planning military violence against them.

4:7 Geographically, Jerusalem is surrounded by enemies.

4:8 *hinder.* Stop the rebuilding of the walls, which were not yet complete.

4:9 *prayer unto our God.* Nehemiah again showed his unswerving dedication to God. *a watch.* The people were prudent to protect themselves.

4:10 *decayed.* Their strength had left them.

4:11 *They shall not know.* The enemies were boasting of their sly stratagems.

4:12 *Jews.* Jews who heard these plans warned the people of the evil intentions.

4:13–15 Nehemiah's response was unhindered by the rumors. God showed Himself more powerful than the plans of man, though Nehemiah again took precautionary measures.

4:15 *nought.* Nothing. God's overriding sovereignty worked through means to deliver His people.

THIS EVIL WORLD

"This evil world" identifies the common commitment of worldly people in their carnal minds, evil desires, and depraved consciences. Evil lifestyles, conduct, and conversation—this is the "course of this world" (Eph. 2:2), that which is common among worldly people. The Christian who wants to practice godliness in all sincerity should be mindful of the existence of this undivided power of darkness. It opposes and besieges anyone who practices true godliness, and it seeks to obstruct and thwart everyone in his holy work (Matt. 12:26; Col. 1:13). The whole world, which lies in wickedness (1 John 5:19), is always seeking to defile the believer (James 1:27) and to lead him down the wrong path.

There are three specific horns by which the evil world mortally wounds many souls and completely overthrows godliness in many hearts when no appropriate action is taken against it. The first horn of the world is its *wrong traditions and customs.* These customs are entirely opposed to the right practice of true godliness that admonishes the believer, "[B]e not conformed to this world" (Rom. 12:2). On the contrary, such customs engender worldly conformity, calling the believer to the idolatrous, pagan, devilish practices common to the age. When the godly object to these practices the world labels them "legalists." Many sinful, capricious people challenge the church as a collection of extremists or narrow-minded souls. Therefore, the world often succeeds in enticing the careless children of men with the glitter of its outward appeal, though such things run contrary to the God of Jacob (Ps. 81:4).

The second horn of the world is *wrong, though celebrated and distinguished, role models.* These important and prominent people are lauded for their brazen activity. Their example is impressive enough for others to follow their lead (Ps. 106:35; John 7:48). The world exalts such people to a position of desirability and envy, identifying them as intelligent and respectable people who are to be admired, and uses such celebrity people to wound the soul and hinder godliness. The defense for a man's wickedness becomes the example of some celebrity who is highly regarded and popular and who has done—or neglected to do—the same things to which he himself aspires. Because of such celebrities, a man is able to justify his conduct by reminding himself, "Well, I am not the only one. Everyone else does it." This has resulted in untold harm to true godliness. Therefore, we must be on our guard against being gored by this horn.

The third horn of the world is its *erroneous and evil premise of reward and recompense.* Thus the world turns on its head the ordained justice of God—blessings for righteousness and cursings for wickedness—by making it difficult, and even punishable, for the godly to live holy lives. Further, the world lends its hand in aiding ungodliness, proclaiming it fashionable (Num. 22:7,16–41). Often the godly who resist such wickedness are branded as uncooperative, intolerant, bigoted, backward, and otherwise disagreeable to the modern age. By contrast, the world promises everything to those who conform and adapt to its ways. They are welcomed and loved by great and small alike.

The person who sincerely wants to practice godliness must arm himself thoroughly for defense against these three horns. The practice of godliness in this evil world is a strenuous undertaking that must undergird the whole of life, like a good yeast that must permeate every part of the loaf. This undertaking is not one that can be accomplished by the believer's own strength. It is necessary to earnestly warn against an antagonistic power—this evil world—that opposes those who walk in true godliness and works. However, it is just as necessary for the encouragement of godly people to point out that there is a divine power, the united kingdom of grace, that is on the side of all who sincerely surrender their hearts and souls to practice true godliness (2 Peter 1:3).

—adapted from Willem Teellinck, *The Path of True Godliness*, book 2

to the wall, every one unto his work.
16 And it came to pass from that time forth, *that*
the half of my servants wrought in the work, and
the other half of them held both the spears, the
shields, and the bows, and the habergeons; and
the rulers *were* behind all the house of Judah.
17 They which builded on the wall, and they that
bare burdens, with those that laded, *every one*
with one of his hands wrought in the work, and
with the other *hand* held a weapon.
18 For the builders, every one had his sword
girded by his side, and *so* builded. And he that
sounded the trumpet *was* by me.
19 ¶ And I said unto the nobles, and to the rulers,
and to the rest of the people, The work *is* great
and large, and we are separated upon the wall, one
far from another.
20 In what place *therefore* ye hear the sound of
the trumpet, resort ye thither unto us: our God
shall fight for us.
21 So we laboured in the work: and half of them
held the spears from the rising of the morning till
the stars appeared.
22 Likewise at the same time said I unto the
people, Let every one with his servant lodge
within Jerusalem, that in the night they may be a
guard to us, and labour on the day.
23 So neither I, nor my brethren, nor my servants,
nor the men of the guard which followed me,
none of us put off our clothes, *saving that* every
one put them off for washing.

CHAPTER 5

AND there was a great cry of the people and of
their wives against their brethren the Jews.
2 For there were that said, We, our sons, and our
daughters, *are* many: therefore we take up corn
for them, that we may eat, and live.
3 *Some* also there were that said, We have mort-
gaged our lands, vineyards, and houses, that we
might buy corn, because of the dearth.
4 There were also that said, We have borrowed
money for the king's tribute, *and that upon* our
lands and vineyards.
5 Yet now our flesh *is* as the flesh of our brethren,
our children as their children: and, lo, we bring
into bondage our sons and our daughters to be
servants, and *some* of our daughters are brought
unto bondage *already*: neither *is it* in our power
to redeem them; for other men have our lands and
vineyards.
6 ¶ And I was very angry when I heard their cry
and these words.
7 Then I consulted with myself, and I rebuked
the nobles, and the rulers, and said unto them, Ye
exact usury, every one of his brother. And I set a
great assembly against them.
8 And I said unto them, We after our ability have
redeemed our brethren the Jews, which were
sold unto the heathen; and will ye even sell your
brethren? or shall they be sold unto us? Then held
they their peace, and found nothing *to answer*.
9 Also I said, It *is* not good that ye do: ought ye

4:16 *wrought.* Worked, did, or made. *habergeons.* Armor.
4:17 *bare burdens.* Those who labored. *laded.* Loaded. The people worked holding their swords.
4:18 *girded.* Strapped onto or alongside.
4:19 *separated.* The people were divided because they were on different parts of the wall.
4:20 *trumpet.* To give a warning to the people should the need arise. *for us.* Before us or with us.
4:22 *within Jerusalem.* Jerusalem offered protection in the night.
4:23 *put them off for washing.* Clearly, the builders were militarily on high alert.

Thoughts for Personal/Family Worship: Chapter 4

1. **The adversaries of the Jews looked at their work and mocked it as feeble (v. 3). Often when the world looks at the church, it sees the imperfection, the faults, the sins, and its "rubble," but fails to see and understand that it is a work in progress (Phil. 1:6). One day, however, the church will be a pure and spotless bride to our heavenly Bridegroom (Eph. 5:25–27; Jude 24–25). How can this hope help you be diligent with the work at hand?**
2. **Nehemiah prayed and worked. Prayer should not be a substitute for exercising our responsibility. It is true that builders build in vain without the Lord's blessing (Ps. 127:1); however, having His blessing does not mean we do not have to build. God's servants must mix intense labor with devotion to prayer as they seek the kingdom of God. How might someone use prayer as an excuse not to work? How might he use work as an excuse not to pray? How do we exercise both prayer and work together?**

Chapter 5: *The Jews face internal challenges, and Nehemiah puts an end to the oppression and sets a good example as governor.*

Usury Condemned and Nehemiah Appointed Governor (5:1–19)

5:1 *great cry.* We do not know to what extent this problem had been going on before Nehemiah arrived in Judah. Likely, the desperate plight of the people was exacerbated during the wall-rebuilding efforts.
5:3–4 The Persian Empire made it difficult to keep property due to high taxes with high interest rates, especially during times with little yields. This led people to borrow against their possessions. Debt is a form of slavery (Prov. 22:7).
5:3 *dearth.* Hunger, perhaps because of a famine or a shortage of food.
5:5 Indentured servitude was not prohibited in the Mosaic law but it was to be carefully regulated (Ex. 21:1–11). *neither is it in our power to redeem.* Literally, "there is not power in our hand." The people were powerless to buy back their sons and daughters because their finances were not available.
5:7 *usury.* Lending money at exorbitant rates. Nehemiah condemns this because it is a means of exploitation. God's law requires the covenant community to live in unity and harmony with one another. *great assembly.* Nehemiah calls for a public assembly.
5:8 *held they their peace.* They were silent.

not to walk in the fear of our God because of the
reproach of the heathen our enemies?
10 I likewise, *and* my brethren, and my servants,
might exact of them money and corn: I pray you,
let us leave off this usury.
11 Restore, I pray you, to them, even this day,
their lands, their vineyards, their oliveyards,
and their houses, also the hundredth *part* of the
money, and of the corn, the wine, and the oil, that
ye exact of them.
12 Then said they, We will restore *them*, and will
require nothing of them; so will we do as thou
sayest. Then I called the priests, and took an oath
of them, that they should do according to this
promise.
13 Also I shook my lap, and said, So God shake
out every man from his house, and from his
labour, that performeth not this promise, even
thus be he shaken out, and emptied. And all the
congregation said, Amen, and praised the LORD.
And the people did according to this promise.
14 ¶ Moreover from the time that I was appointed
to be their governor in the land of Judah, from
the twentieth year even unto the two and thirtieth
year of Artaxerxes the king, *that is*, twelve years, I
and my brethren have not eaten the bread of the
governor.
15 But the former governors that *had been* be-
fore me were chargeable unto the people, and had
taken of them bread and wine, beside forty shekels
of silver; yea, even their servants bare rule over the
people: but so did not I, because of the fear of God.
16 Yea, also I continued in the work of this wall,
neither bought we any land: and all my servants
were gathered thither unto the work.
17 Moreover *there were* at my table an hundred
and fifty of the Jews and rulers, beside those that
came unto us from among the heathen that *are*
about us.
18 Now *that* which was prepared *for me* daily
was one ox *and* six choice sheep; also fowls were
prepared for me, and once in ten days store of all
sorts of wine: yet for all this required not I the
bread of the governor, because the bondage was
heavy upon this people.
19 Think upon me, my God, for good, *according*
to all that I have done for this people.

CHAPTER 6

NOW it came to pass, when Sanballat, and Tobiah,
and Geshem the Arabian, and the rest of our en-
emies, heard that I had builded the wall, and *that*
there was no breach left therein; (though at that
time I had not set up the doors upon the gates;)
2 That Sanballat and Geshem sent unto me,
saying, Come, let us meet together in *some one of*
the villages in the plain of Ono. But they thought
to do me mischief.
3 And I sent messengers unto them, saying, I *am*
doing a great work, so that I cannot come down:
why should the work cease, whilst I leave it, and
come down to you?
4 Yet they sent unto me four times after this sort;

5:10 Nehemiah knew his privileged position, but relinquished this liberty for the good of his brothers and the fear of God (vv. 9,14–15). He not only led with words, but by example.
5:11 *Restore.* Property and proceeds are to be returned to their original owners, though the extent of this giving back is ambiguous. Nehemiah calls the people to have mercy and grace toward their brothers at great personal sacrifice.
5:12 *require.* Seek.
5:13 *shook my lap.* Symbolic for the curse upon any who broke the agreement.
5:14 *governor.* When he was appointed is unknown though likely after the events of ch. 2. Nehemiah probably returned to Shushan after building the wall and was then appointed. *bread of the governor.* The governor was allowed by the Persians to receive taxes from the people to finance his own household (v. 10).
5:15 *shekels.* A standard of monetary measurement, at this time not a coin but a weight of precious metal. *bare rule.* Servants of officials ruled over and exacted income from the people as well. *fear of God.* Nehemiah's motivation was his faith in God, reverence for His majesty, and desire to please Him.
5:16 *thither.* To or toward a place.
5:17 *at my table.* Nehemiah helped many of the Jews, including those who were migrating back into Judah from surrounding Gentile nations (*the heathen*).
5:19 *Think upon me . . . all that I have done.* Nehemiah was not motivated by a works-righteousness mindset as if he could merit God's blessing (Ps. 143:2), but did have faith in the God of grace who rewards those who seek Him (13:14,22,29,31; Heb. 11:6).

Thoughts for Personal/Family Worship: Chapter 5

1. **As the Jewish community faced problems from without as well as within, so believers face a war with multiple fronts. Never be surprised when the church must face sin in its midst, but be prepared to deal with it with love and justice (Gal. 6:1–2). Our own hearts are our worst enemy in the spiritual battle, so beware first of the log in your own eye before criticizing another (Matt. 7:3). How can we stand for justice among Christians without becoming cynical or bitter?**
2. **Nehemiah led both by what he said and what he did. Leaders in home, church, and society have much they can learn from Nehemiah. Even then, Nehemiah was imperfect, like we all are. Only Christ led in a way that never had any stain. Take time to pray for those in leadership in your life.**

Nehemiah Opposed and Walls Finished (6:1—7:4)

Chapter 6: *Nehemiah's adversaries plot against him, but despite all the opposition the walls are finished.*

6:1 *breach.* A break or means of entering into the city.
6:2 *Geshem.* The same as Gashmu (v. 6). These are two different ways of transliterating the Hebrew. Little is known as to his exact identification or nationality. *Ono.* Extreme northwestern

and I answered them after the same manner.

5 Then sent Sanballat his servant unto me in like manner the fifth time with an open letter in his hand;

6 Wherein *was* written, It is reported among the heathen, and Gashmu saith *it, that* thou and the Jews think to rebel: for which cause thou buildest the wall, that thou mayest be their king, according to these words.

7 And thou hast also appointed prophets to preach of thee at Jerusalem, saying, *There is* a king in Judah: and now shall it be reported to the king according to these words. Come now therefore, and let us take counsel together.

8 Then I sent unto him, saying, There are no such things done as thou sayest, but thou feignest them out of thine own heart.

9 For they all made us afraid, saying, Their hands shall be weakened from the work, that it be not done. Now therefore, *O God*, strengthen my hands.

10 Afterward I came unto the house of Shemaiah the son of Delaiah the son of Mehetabeel, who *was* shut up; and he said, Let us meet together in the house of God, within the temple, and let us shut the doors of the temple: for they will come to slay thee; yea, in the night will they come to slay thee.

11 And I said, Should such a man as I flee? and who *is there*, that, *being* as I *am*, would go into the temple to save his life? I will not go in.

12 And, lo, I perceived that God had not sent him; but that he pronounced this prophecy against me: for Tobiah and Sanballat had hired him.

13 Therefore *was* he hired, that I should be afraid, and do so, and sin, and *that* they might have *matter* for an evil report, that they might reproach me.

14 My God, think thou upon Tobiah and Sanballat according to these their works, and on the prophetess Noadiah, and the rest of the prophets, that would have put me in fear.

15 ¶ So the wall was finished in the twenty and fifth *day* of *the month* Elul, in fifty and two days.

16 And it came to pass, that when all our enemies heard *thereof*, and all the heathen that *were* about us saw *these things*, they were much cast down in their own eyes: for they perceived that this work was wrought of our God.

17 ¶ Moreover in those days the nobles of Judah sent many letters unto Tobiah, and *the letters* of Tobiah came unto them.

18 For *there were* many in Judah sworn unto him, because he *was* the son in law of Shechaniah the son of Arah; and his son Johanan had taken the daughter of Meshullam the son of Berechiah.

---

area of Judah. Likely a strategic move to remove Nehemiah from the help he would have needed. *mischief.* Nehemiah understood their intentions to lure him away from God's work.

6:4 *sort.* Manner.

6:6 *heathen.* Literally, "the nations." *rebel.* This accusation was serious and if believed would result in death.

6:7 Sanballat's false accusations were meant to stir up trouble with the possibility of King Artaxerxes finding out. There are no records of the prophecies pointed to here, or the supposed prophets who proclaimed them.

6:8–9 Nehemiah dismissed the charges as false (*thou feignest them*), but the slanderous reports were still enough to cause the people to be afraid. Nehemiah's peace rested with God and he prayed that God would give him the courage and ability (*strengthen my hands*) to finish the project (Isa. 35:3–4).

6:10 *house of Shemaiah the son of Delaiah.* Shemaiah may have been a priest with special access to the temple (1 Chron. 24:18). It would not have been lawful for Nehemiah to enter the temple, and this may have been used as a ground to eliminate him. *shut up.* Confined or restricted (Jer. 36:5). There is ambiguity as to the exact meaning. Clearly, this is another attempt to get Nehemiah into a compromising situation, at a minimum, to besmirch his name.

6:11–13 *into the temple to save his life.* Nehemiah shows a good understanding of the law as he was likely forbidden from entering into the temple, and if he should so *sin*, his enemies would have justification for killing him. Shemaiah's words were weighed against the law of God.

6:14 *think thou upon Tobiah and Sanballat.* This prayer uses the same words as Nehemiah's prayer concerning himself (5:19), but with the opposite meaning. *rest of the prophets.* Shemaiah was not a lone prophetic voice in conjuring up this plan.

6:15 Despite the continual opposition, the walls of Jerusalem were *finished*. It took the Jews fifty-two days to complete. This shows the speed by which they worked. *Elul.* Sixth month, August/September.

6:16 *cast down in their own eyes.* Idiomatic phrase highlighting how the adversaries had been frustrated and humiliated. *wrought of our God.* Even the nations around them recognized the hand of the Lord in helping the Jews finish the wall.

6:17–18 *in those days.* Around this same time. *Meshullam.* He gave his daughter to Tobiah, but also helped to build the wall (3:4,30). Meshullam shows that people within the Jewish community were working against Nehemiah.

Thoughts for Personal/Family Worship: Chapter 6

1. **Though the Lord had called Nehemiah, He did not remove the challenges and make everything easy as we would like it. Often difficulties come to the situations and people that God is using for great good. We should not be discouraged when difficulty arises, but trust in God's providence and press on with great courage. Courage may be found by faith and prayer (v. 9). Pray that God would help you to continue steadfast through temptation and intimidation, to cry to God, rely on Him, and view your situation and challenges with much spiritual discernment (v. 12).**
2. **"This work was wrought of our God" (v. 16). God's cause is not in doubt. He is never without resources. He says, "My counsel shall stand, and I will do all my pleasure" (Isa. 46:10). He will keep His covenant (1:5). This is the foundation of our courage and the bedrock of our prayers. How can you build on this foundation and shore up your walls of defense?**

19 Also they reported his good deeds before me,
and uttered my words to him. *And* Tobiah sent
letters to put me in fear.

CHAPTER 7

NOW it came to pass, when the wall was built, and
I had set up the doors, and the porters and the
singers and the Levites were appointed,
2 That I gave my brother Hanani, and Hananiah
the ruler of the palace, charge over Jerusalem:
for he *was* a faithful man, and feared God above
many.
3 And I said unto them, Let not the gates of Jeru-
salem be opened until the sun be hot; and while
they stand by, let them shut the doors, and bar
them: and appoint watches of the inhabitants of
Jerusalem, every one in his watch, and every one
to be over against his house.
4 Now the city *was* large and great: but the people
were few therein, and the houses *were* not builded.
5 ¶ And my God put into mine heart to gather to-
gether the nobles, and the rulers, and the people,
that they might be reckoned by genealogy. And I
found a register of the genealogy of them which
came up at the first, and found written therein,
6 These *are* the children of the province, that
went up out of the captivity, of those that had
been carried away, whom Nebuchadnezzar the
king of Babylon had carried away, and came again
to Jerusalem and to Judah, every one unto his city;
7 Who came with Zerubbabel, Jeshua, Nehe-
miah, Azariah, Raamiah, Nahamani, Mordecai,
Bilshan, Mispereth, Bigvai, Nehum, Baanah. The
number, *I say*, of the men of the people of Israel
was this;
8 The children of Parosh, two thousand an
hundred seventy and two.
9 The children of Shephatiah, three hundred
seventy and two.
10 The children of Arah, six hundred fifty and
two.
11 The children of Pahath-moab, of the children
of Jeshua and Joab, two thousand and eight
hundred *and* eighteen.
12 The children of Elam, a thousand two hun-
dred fifty and four.
13 The children of Zattu, eight hundred forty and
five.
14 The children of Zaccai, seven hundred and
threescore.
15 The children of Binnui, six hundred forty and
eight.
16 The children of Bebai, six hundred twenty and
eight.
17 The children of Azgad, two thousand three
hundred twenty and two.
18 The children of Adonikam, six hundred three-
score and seven.
19 The children of Bigvai, two thousand three-
score and seven.
20 The children of Adin, six hundred fifty and
five.
21 The children of Ater of Hezekiah, ninety and
eight.
22 The children of Hashum, three hundred
twenty and eight.
23 The children of Bezai, three hundred twenty
and four.
24 The children of Hariph, an hundred and
twelve.
25 The children of Gibeon, ninety and five.
26 The men of Beth-lehem and Netophah, an
hundred fourscore and eight.
27 The men of Anathoth, an hundred twenty and
eight.
28 The men of Beth-azmaveth, forty and two.
29 The men of Kirjath-jearim, Chephirah, and
Beeroth, seven hundred forty and three.
30 The men of Ramah and Geba, six hundred
twenty and one.
31 The men of Michmas, an hundred and twenty
and two.
32 The men of Beth-el and Ai, an hundred twenty
and three.
33 The men of the other Nebo, fifty and two.
34 The children of the other Elam, a thousand
two hundred fifty and four.
35 The children of Harim, three hundred and
twenty.

Chapter 7: *Nehemiah puts Hanani in charge of the city and registers the people by their genealogy.*

7:1–2 Nehemiah's desire was to do more than rebuild the wall. The community needed to be well organized and suitable leaders needed to be put in places of responsibility. *porters.* Gatekeepers. Likely a type of guard or security. *singers and the Levites.* Mentioned here with porters because of the religious significance that the porters carried (12:25,45). *feared God above many.* He had an unusual reverence for God as Lord over all (1 Chron. 16:25; see note at 1:11) that made him trustworthy and reliable (*faithful*), an important quality in a public officer in state or church (Ex. 18:21; 2 Chron. 19:6–9).
7:3 *sun be hot.* The gates should not be opened in the early morning but later. *watches of the inhabitants.* Residents were responsible for keeping the watch of the walls.
7:4 *large and great.* Relatively speaking, compared to the people in it. *houses were not builded.* A massive building project was necessary.

LIST OF EXILES LIVING IN JERUSALEM (7:5–73)

7:5 *God put into mine heart.* Not a prophecy or direct revelation, but God's gifts of wisdom and holy resolution by the Spirit (2:12). *reckoned by genealogy.* A census to be taken.
7:6–73 This list of names is almost identical to that of Ezra 2.
7:6 Now the people have been reconstituted as the people of God coming *out of the captivity* to continue the heritage of their fathers.

36 The children of Jericho, three hundred forty and five.
37 The children of Lod, Hadid, and Ono, seven hundred twenty and one.
38 The children of Senaah, three thousand nine hundred and thirty.
39 ¶ The priests: the children of Jedaiah, of the house of Jeshua, nine hundred seventy and three.
40 The children of Immer, a thousand fifty and two.
41 The children of Pashur, a thousand two hundred forty and seven.
42 The children of Harim, a thousand and seventeen.
43 ¶ The Levites: the children of Jeshua, of Kadmiel, *and* of the children of Hodevah, seventy and four.
44 ¶ The singers: the children of Asaph, an hundred forty and eight.
45 ¶ The porters: the children of Shallum, the children of Ater, the children of Talmon, the children of Akkub, the children of Hatita, the children of Shobai, an hundred thirty and eight.
46 ¶ The Nethinims: the children of Ziha, the children of Hashupha, the children of Tabbaoth,
47 The children of Keros, the children of Sia, the children of Padon,
48 The children of Lebana, the children of Hagaba, the children of Shalmai,
49 The children of Hanan, the children of Giddel, the children of Gahar,
50 The children of Reaiah, the children of Rezin, the children of Nekoda,
51 The children of Gazzam, the children of Uzza, the children of Phaseah,
52 The children of Besai, the children of Meunim, the children of Nephishesim,
53 The children of Bakbuk, the children of Hakupha, the children of Harhur,
54 The children of Bazlith, the children of Mehida, the children of Harsha,
55 The children of Barkos, the children of Sisera, the children of Tamah,
56 The children of Neziah, the children of Hatipha.
57 ¶ The children of Solomon's servants: the children of Sotai, the children of Sophereth, the children of Perida,
58 The children of Jaala, the children of Darkon, the children of Giddel,
59 The children of Shephatiah, the children of Hattil, the children of Pochereth of Zebaim, the children of Amon.
60 All the Nethinims, and the children of Solomon's servants, *were* three hundred ninety and two.
61 And these *were* they which went up *also* from Tel-melah, Tel-haresha, Cherub, Addon, and Immer: but they could not shew their father's house, nor their seed, whether they *were* of Israel.
62 The children of Delaiah, the children of Tobiah, the children of Nekoda, six hundred forty and two.
63 ¶ And of the priests: the children of Habaiah, the children of Koz, the children of Barzillai, which took *one* of the daughters of Barzillai the Gileadite to wife, and was called after their name.
64 These sought their register *among* those that were reckoned by genealogy, but it was not found: therefore were they, as polluted, put from the priesthood.
65 And the Tirshatha said unto them, that they should not eat of the most holy things, till there stood *up* a priest with Urim and Thummim.
66 ¶ The whole congregation together *was* forty and two thousand three hundred and threescore,
67 Beside their manservants and their maidservants, of whom *there were* seven thousand three hundred thirty and seven: and they had two hundred forty and five singing men and singing women.
68 Their horses, seven hundred thirty and six: their mules, two hundred forty and five:
69 *Their* camels, four hundred thirty and five: six thousand seven hundred and twenty asses.
70 ¶ And some of the chief of the fathers gave unto the work. The Tirshatha gave to the treasure a thousand drams of gold, fifty basons, five hundred and thirty priests' garments.
71 And *some* of the chief of the fathers gave to the treasure of the work twenty thousand drams of gold, and two thousand and two hundred pound of silver.
72 And *that* which the rest of the people gave *was* twenty thousand drams of gold, and two thousand pound of silver, and threescore and seven priests' garments.
73 So the priests, and the Levites, and the porters, and the singers, and *some* of the people, and the Nethinims, and all Israel, dwelt in their cities; and

7:7 A list of twelve priests.
7:70–72 *drams.* A measurement of precious metals. *pound.* Literally, "minas," another measurement of precious metals.
7:73 A new narrative to the story is introduced, to be taken with the following narrative (ch. 8). *seventh month.* An important month on the Jewish calendar. The first of the month was the Feast of Trumpets. The tenth day was the Day of Atonement. The fifteenth was the Feast of Tabernacles. During the Feast of Tabernacles the law was to be read to every man, woman, and child.

Thoughts for Personal/Family Worship: Chapter 7

1. The fear of God is a necessary element of any good leader (v. 2). For that matter, it is a basic mark of true believers (Jer. 32:40). They fear God more than they fear people. To fear God means to reverence His majesty, love

when the seventh month came, the children of
Israel *were* in their cities.

CHAPTER 8

AND all the people gathered themselves together
as one man into the street that *was* before the
water gate; and they spake unto Ezra the scribe
to bring the book of the law of Moses, which the
LORD had commanded to Israel.
2 And Ezra the priest brought the law before the
congregation both of men and women, and all
that could hear with understanding, upon the
first day of the seventh month.
3 And he read therein before the street that *was*
before the water gate from the morning until
midday, before the men and the women, and
those that could understand; and the ears of all
the people *were attentive* unto the book of the law.
4 And Ezra the scribe stood upon a pulpit of
wood, which they had made for the purpose; and
beside him stood Mattithiah, and Shema, and
Anaiah, and Urijah, and Hilkiah, and Maaseiah,
on his right hand; and on his left hand, Pedaiah,
and Mishael, and Malchiah, and Hashum, and
Hashbadana, Zechariah, *and* Meshullam.
5 And Ezra opened the book in the sight of all
the people; (for he was above all the people;) and
when he opened it, all the people stood up:
6 And Ezra blessed the LORD, the great God. And
all the people answered, Amen, Amen, with lift-
ing up their hands: and they bowed their heads,
and worshipped the LORD with *their* faces to the
ground.
7 Also Jeshua, and Bani, and Sherebiah, Jamin,
Akkub, Shabbethai, Hodijah, Maaseiah, Kelita,
Azariah, Jozabad, Hanan, Pelaiah, and the Levites,
caused the people to understand the law: and the
people *stood* in their place.
8 So they read in the book in the law of God
distinctly, and gave the sense, and caused *them* to
understand the reading.
9 ¶ And Nehemiah, which *is* the Tirshatha, and
Ezra the priest the scribe, and the Levites that
taught the people, said unto all the people, This
day *is* holy unto the LORD your God; mourn not,
nor weep. For all the people wept, when they
heard the words of the law.
10 Then he said unto them, Go your way, eat the
fat, and drink the sweet, and send portions unto
them for whom nothing is prepared: for *this* day
is holy unto our Lord: neither be ye sorry; for the
joy of the LORD is your strength.
11 So the Levites stilled all the people, saying,
Hold your peace, for the day *is* holy; neither be
ye grieved.
12 And all the people went their way to eat, and
to drink, and to send portions, and to make great
mirth, because they had understood the words
that were declared unto them.
13 ¶ And on the second day were gathered to-
gether the chief of the fathers of all the people,
the priests, and the Levites, unto Ezra the scribe,
even to understand the words of the law.

His glory, obey His will as revealed in the Bible, be afraid to sin, and seek His grace and mercy. It directs both worship and behavior. What are signs in a person's life that he does or does not fear the Lord? Why is the fear of God so important in leadership?

2. "And my God put into mine heart" (v. 5). Nehemiah traced his good ideas and godly actions back to God (Phil. 2:13). Apart from God's grace, our good intentions, attitudes, and inventions will mean nothing. We need to be led by the Spirit of God (Rom. 8:14). How quick are you to give glory to God for any good in you, both with your lips and your heart? Do you secretly boast in yourself?

EZRA READS THE LAW AND THE COVENANT IS RENEWED (8:1—10:39)

Chapter 8: ***The people gather to hear the reading and receive the teaching of the law, after which they keep the Feast of Tabernacles.***

Ezra Reads the Law and the Feast of Booths Is Kept (8:1–18)

8:1 The first day of the seventh month was the Feast of Trumpets (Lev. 23:24), a Jewish festival involving a holy convocation. From Ezra's podium, God's Word certainly had the effect of a trumpet, as it rallied the people. *book of the law of Moses.* The reading of the law was in the street before the water gate, on the eastern side of the city, not in the temple court (Ezra 3).
8:2 The whole covenant community was present (Deut. 31:10–13; 2 Chron. 20:13). *first day.* A day of rest in the Jewish calendar.
8:3 *street.* The law is read in the center of city life (Prov. 1:20–21). *morning until midday.* A span of six hours.
8:5 *stood up.* Common show of respect in hearing God's law.
8:6 *Amen, Amen.* An expression of their agreement. There was unified worship among the Jews.
8:7 These men, unlike the men of v. 4, probably walked amongst the crowds teaching the people what the law meant and helping them to understand the Hebrew language (Deut. 33:10).
8:8 *the sense, and caused them to understand the reading.* An ambiguous clause in the Hebrew. It may mean they exposited the texts for the people to understand. But it can also mean they translated the text into Aramaic for those who were not familiar with the Hebrew language. According to rabbinic tradition, the first Targum (Aramaic paraphrase of the Old Testament) is presented here.
8:9 *Tirshatha.* A transliteration of the original word that means "governor." *mourn not, nor weep.* It was the Feast of Trumpets, a day of rejoicing (Lev. 23:23–25). Chapter 9 will show the proper place of contrition and mourning.
8:10 *sweet.* Something that tasted sweet. *the joy of the LORD is your strength.* The people are commanded to keep a festal worship of God (Num. 29:2–6; see also Deut. 12:12; 14:26; 2 Chron. 29:36). He is their strength and salvation, and therefore they sing His praises (Ex. 15:2; Ps. 28:7–9; Isa. 12:2–3). The word *joy* used here is uncommon in the Old Testament (1 Chron. 16:27).
8:11 *stilled.* They quieted the people.
8:12 *mirth.* Joy, different word than v. 10.

14 And they found written in the law which the
LORD had commanded by Moses, that the chil-
dren of Israel should dwell in booths in the feast
of the seventh month:
15 And that they should publish and proclaim in
all their cities, and in Jerusalem, saying, Go forth
unto the mount, and fetch olive branches, and
pine branches, and myrtle branches, and palm
branches, and branches of thick trees, to make
booths, as *it is* written.
16 ¶ So the people went forth, and brought *them*,
and made themselves booths, every one upon
the roof of his house, and in their courts, and in
the courts of the house of God, and in the street
of the water gate, and in the street of the gate of
Ephraim.
17 And all the congregation of them that were
come again out of the captivity made booths, and
sat under the booths: for since the days of Jeshua
the son of Nun unto that day had not the chil-
dren of Israel done so. And there was very great
gladness.
18 Also day by day, from the first day unto the last
day, he read in the book of the law of God. And
they kept the feast seven days; and on the eighth
day *was* a solemn assembly, according unto the
manner.

CHAPTER 9

NOW in the twenty and fourth day of this month
the children of Israel were assembled with fasting,
and with sackclothes, and earth upon them.
2 And the seed of Israel separated themselves
from all strangers, and stood and confessed their
sins, and the iniquities of their fathers.
3 And they stood up in their place, and read in the
book of the law of the LORD their God *one* fourth
part of the day; and *another* fourth part they
confessed, and worshipped the LORD their God.
4 ¶ Then stood up upon the stairs, of the Levites,
Jeshua, and Bani, Kadmiel, Shebaniah, Bunni,
Sherebiah, Bani, *and* Chenani, and cried with a
loud voice unto the LORD their God.
5 Then the Levites, Jeshua, and Kadmiel, Bani,
Hashabniah, Sherebiah, Hodijah, Shebaniah, *and*
Pethahiah, said, Stand up *and* bless the LORD your
God for ever and ever: and blessed be thy glori-
ous name, which is exalted above all blessing and
praise.
6 Thou, *even* thou, *art* LORD alone; thou hast
made heaven, the heaven of heavens, with all their
host, the earth, and all *things* that *are* therein, the
seas, and all that *is* therein, and thou preservest
them all; and the host of heaven worshippeth thee.
7 Thou *art* the LORD the God, who didst choose

8:14 *booths.* Tents or tabernacles, commemorating God's faithfulness during the wilderness wandering (Lev. 23:42–43).
8:15 Different branches likely used in the construction of the booths.
8:16 *upon the roof.* Houses in Israel during this time had flat roofs where the people would build their booths to honor the day they came out of Egypt.
8:17 There are passages indicating that the Feast of Booths was observed in the days of Solomon, Hezekiah, and Josiah. Most scholars believe that it is significant that the people neglected to observe this feast for many years. The Feast of Booths was both to recognize the wilderness wandering after the exile, but it was also to commemorate the harvest. It is suspected that this latter recognition is what the people focused on since the days of *Jeshua*, that is Joshua, the son of Nun. *great gladness.* A day of celebration and joy (Deut. 16:15).

Thoughts for Personal/Family Worship: Chapter 8

1. **Just like the walls of Jerusalem provided physical protection (chs. 1–6), so the precepts of God provide spiritual safety (Ps. 119:165). Rebuilding the walls without returning to the Word of God would be foolish. Why would this be foolish and how would it provoke the Lord to jealousy?**
2. **Ezra did not merely read the law in the presence of the people, but the Levites were assigned to teach and instruct the people in the will of God. Give thanks for godly ministers from the past as well as the present whom God has sent to explain and apply the truth of God in your life.**
3. **Has God's truth ever broken your heart so that you wept like these people here in v. 9? When God's Word takes hold of us, we can weep over our sins, which God's Word unmasks. We can weep because we long for (more) communion with God.**
4. **There is a time for mourning; but the other side of godly emotions should not be forgotten. Here, the Levites direct the people so that their sadness is turned to gladness (v. 10). Indeed, the joy of the Lord is a great defense, or shield, against undue sadness. How can the Christian learn to rejoice in the Lord always?**

Chapter 9: ***The people keep a solemn day of fasting and prayer, confessing their national sins in light of God's faithfulness.***

The Law Read in the Presence of the People (9:1–3)

9:1 *twenty and fourth day.* The people had listened to the Word on the twenty-first day. The chiefs of the families came to hear the law, again, on the twenty-second day. There was a day between the festivities and the solemn assembly recorded here in ch. 9. *fasting . . . sackclothes . . . earth.* All signs of contrition and humility.
9:2 *seed of Israel.* Israel, the seed or offspring of Abraham, was chosen as a holy nation unto the Lord (vv. 7–8; Ezra 9:2). *strangers.* Those who were not rightfully part of the Jewish community.
9:3 Half of the day, the people either listened to the Word or confessed their sins in light of the Word.

God's Faithfulness to Israel Recounted (9:4–31)

9:6 *thou hast made . . . and thou preservest them all.* God has universal claims over all things, not just over Israel, because He created all things and sustains them by His providence (Gen. 1; Ps. 104). The doctrine of creation is an important part of the faith, for it reveals God's absolute claim on our lives, and thus the horrible evil of our rebellion against His Lordship (*Thou . . . art LORD alone*).
9:7–31 They praised God for His covenant faithfulness throughout the history of Israel from the calling of Abram, and they confess their faithlessness.
9:7 *didst choose Abram . . . out of Ur.* God's calling of Abram

Abram, and broughtest him forth out of Ur of the
Chaldees, and gavest him the name of Abraham;
8 And foundest his heart faithful before thee, and
madest a covenant with him to give the land of
the Canaanites, the Hittites, the Amorites, and the
Perizzites, and the Jebusites, and the Girgashites,
to give *it, I say,* to his seed, and hast performed thy
words; for thou *art* righteous:
9 And didst see the affliction of our fathers in
Egypt, and heardest their cry by the Red sea;
10 And shewedst signs and wonders upon Pha-
raoh, and on all his servants, and on all the
people of his land: for thou knewest that they
dealt proudly against them. So didst thou get thee
a name, as *it is* this day.
11 And thou didst divide the sea before them, so
that they went through the midst of the sea on the
dry land; and their persecutors thou threwest into
the deeps, as a stone into the mighty waters.
12 Moreover thou leddest them in the day by a
cloudy pillar; and in the night by a pillar of fire, to
give them light in the way wherein they should go.
13 Thou camest down also upon mount Sinai,
and spakest with them from heaven, and gavest
them right judgments, and true laws, good stat-
utes and commandments:
14 And madest known unto them thy holy sab-
bath, and commandedst them precepts, statutes,
and laws, by the hand of Moses thy servant:
15 And gavest them bread from heaven for their
hunger, and broughtest forth water for them out
of the rock for their thirst, and promisedst them
that they should go in to possess the land which
thou hadst sworn to give them.
16 But they and our fathers dealt proudly, and
hardened their necks, and hearkened not to thy
commandments,
17 And refused to obey, neither were mindful
of thy wonders that thou didst among them;
but hardened their necks, and in their rebellion
appointed a captain to return to their bondage:
but thou *art* a God ready to pardon, gracious and
merciful, slow to anger, and of great kindness, and
forsookest them not.
18 Yea, when they had made them a molten calf,
and said, This *is* thy God that brought thee up out
of Egypt, and had wrought great provocations;
19 Yet thou in thy manifold mercies forsookest
them not in the wilderness: the pillar of the cloud
departed not from them by day, to lead them in
the way; neither the pillar of fire by night, to shew
them light, and the way wherein they should go.
20 Thou gavest also thy good spirit to instruct
them, and withheldest not thy manna from their
mouth, and gavest them water for their thirst.
21 Yea, forty years didst thou sustain them in
the wilderness, *so that* they lacked nothing; their
clothes waxed not old, and their feet swelled not.
22 Moreover thou gavest them kingdoms and
nations, and didst divide them into corners: so
they possessed the land of Sihon, and the land of
the king of Heshbon, and the land of Og king of
Bashan.
23 Their children also multipliedst thou as the
stars of heaven, and broughtest them into the
land, concerning which thou hadst promised to
their fathers, that they should go in to possess *it.*
24 So the children went in and possessed the land,
and thou subduedst before them the inhabitants
of the land, the Canaanites, and gavest them into
their hands, with their kings, and the people of the
land, that they might do with them as they would.
25 And they took strong cities, and a fat land, and
possessed houses full of all goods, wells digged,
vineyards, and oliveyards, and fruit trees in
abundance: so they did eat, and were filled, and
became fat, and delighted themselves in thy great
goodness.

---

out of an idolatrous nation (Gen. 11:31; 12:1; 15:7; Josh. 24:2–3; Acts 7:2–3) was an act of free and sovereign grace according to His election or choice (Deut. 4:37; 7:6–8; 10:14–15; 14:2; Pss. 33:12; 105:6; 135:4; Isa. 41:8–9). *gavest him the name of Abraham.* Meaning father of many/multitudes (Gen. 17:5). The path that Abram took in leaving Ur was the same path taken by the exiles returning from Babylon.

9:9 In the time of Moses and the exodus (Ex. 2:24; 3:7).

9:10 *signs and wonders.* The ten plagues that God worked through Moses' hand. *get thee a name.* God made Himself known among the Israelites and Egyptians (see the first key theme in the Introduction to Exodus: Synopsis).

9:11 The crossing of the Red Sea (Ex. 14–15).

9:12 *leddest.* Led.

9:13 These Jews understood that the law was graciously given to them by God. They confess the law to not be burdensome but *right* and *true* and *good* (Rom. 7:12).

9:15 *bread from heaven.* The manna (Ex. 16). *water . . . out of the rock.* The waters of Meribah (Ex. 17; Num. 20).

9:16 *proudly.* Same Hebrew word as in v. 10, referring to the Egyptians. The Israelites in the wilderness showed that they had the same heart as the Egyptians. *hearkened.* Listened.

9:17 *mindful.* Remembered. *God ready to pardon.* Literally, "God of forgivenesses," abundantly forgiving sinners. *gracious and merciful . . . kindness.* God's character revealed to Moses after Israel made the golden calf (Ex. 34:6)—the only hope of Israel (v. 31). *forsookest them not.* Did not abandon them (vv. 19,31; Deut. 31:6).

9:18 *molten calf.* The golden calf in the wilderness. *provocations.* Literally, "blasphemies." The people credited the golden calf with delivering them from Egypt.

9:20 *good spirit.* The Holy Spirit (Isa. 63:10–14), who throughout the Old Testament, taught the people through various individuals, including the teaching offices of prophet, priest, and kings.

9:21 *waxed.* Grew or became.

9:22 *corners.* The division of the land. Nehemiah transitioned into conquering the land.

9:23 *multipliedst . . . as the stars.* An allusion to the Abrahamic covenant (Gen. 15:5; 22:17; 26:4).

9:24 *thou subduedst.* God was the One fighting for His people.

9:26 *rebelled.* Same word used in the false accusations

26 Nevertheless they were disobedient, and
rebelled against thee, and cast thy law behind
their backs, and slew thy prophets which testified
against them to turn them to thee, and they
wrought great provocations.
27 Therefore thou deliveredst them into the hand
of their enemies, who vexed them: and in the time
of their trouble, when they cried unto thee, thou
heardest *them* from heaven; and according to thy
manifold mercies thou gavest them saviours, who
saved them out of the hand of their enemies.
28 But after they had rest, they did evil again
before thee: therefore leftest thou them in the
hand of their enemies, so that they had the
dominion over them: yet when they returned,
and cried unto thee, thou heardest *them* from
heaven; and many times didst thou deliver them
according to thy mercies;
29 And testifiedst against them, that thou might-
est bring them again unto thy law: yet they dealt
proudly, and hearkened not unto thy command-
ments, but sinned against thy judgments, (which
if a man do, he shall live in them;) and withdrew
the shoulder, and hardened their neck, and would
not hear.
30 Yet many years didst thou forbear them,
and testifiedst against them by thy spirit in thy
prophets: yet would they not give ear: therefore
gavest thou them into the hand of the people of
the lands.
31 Nevertheless for thy great mercies' sake thou
didst not utterly consume them, nor forsake
them; for thou *art* a gracious and merciful God.
32 Now therefore, our God, the great, the mighty,
and the terrible God, who keepest covenant and
mercy, let not all the trouble seem little before
thee, that hath come upon us, on our kings, on our
princes, and on our priests, and on our prophets,
and on our fathers, and on all thy people, since the
time of the kings of Assyria unto this day.
33 Howbeit thou *art* just in all that is brought
upon us; for thou hast done right, but we have
done wickedly:
34 Neither have our kings, our princes, our
priests, nor our fathers, kept thy law, nor heark-
ened unto thy commandments and thy testimo-
nies, wherewith thou didst testify against them.
35 For they have not served thee in their kingdom,
and in thy great goodness that thou gavest them,
and in the large and fat land which thou gavest
before them, neither turned they from their
wicked works.
36 Behold, we *are* servants this day, and *for* the
land that thou gavest unto our fathers to eat the
fruit thereof and the good thereof, behold, we *are*
servants in it:
37 And it yieldeth much increase unto the kings
whom thou hast set over us because of our sins:
also they have dominion over our bodies, and
over our cattle, at their pleasure, and we *are* in
great distress.
38 And because of all this we make a sure *cove-
nant*, and write *it*; and our princes, Levites, *and*
priests, seal *unto it*.

stating that Nehemiah was planning on rebelling against the king. Israel's problem did not lie in their rebellion against an earthly king, but against their heavenly King. *slew thy prophets.* Killed them (Matt. 23:34–36).

9:27 *vexed.* Literally, "bound" or "restricted." *trouble.* The time of the judges. *saviours.* Leaders who delivered Israel from its enemies (Judg. 2:16,18; 3:9,15). The Hebrew word is the root of the name "Joshua." The saviors of the Old Testament were shadows of Christ, the true Savior of God's people (Matt. 1:20–21).

9:28 *returned.* Repentance, turning to God and turning away from sin.

9:29 *testifiedst.* Bore witness against. *proudly.* See vv. 10,16. *withdrew the shoulder.* An idiom for being stubborn toward someone or something.

9:30 *forbear.* The idea of continuing or prolonging something. God bore with the sins of His people. *give ear.* Listen (Deut. 6:4).

9:31 *for thy great mercies' sake.* God's mercy is shown for His glory. *consume.* Destroy or eat up.

The Covenant Is Renewed (9:32—10:39)

9:32 *our God.* The people profess that God is their God and they are His people. *keepest covenant and mercy.* In spite of all their sin and corruption, they rest on the sure mercies of God (see note at 1:5). *terrible.* Not a negative connotation but one that evokes respect or reverent fear. *let not all the trouble seem little before thee.* Have compassion on us for our great troubles. *Assyria.* Israel was first exiled by the Assyrians before Judah was exiled by Babylon.

9:33 *right.* Acted in truth. No wrong can be charged against God.

9:35 *fat land.* Land rich or plentiful in good things.

9:37 *yieldeth.* Produces. The people lament that they are still in bondage. Their prayer of confession culminates in seeking deliverance from their oppressors.

9:38 *make a sure covenant.* Literally, "we are cutting an agreement," which carries the idea of covenant making.

Thoughts for Personal/Family Worship: Chapter 9

1. **For centuries, it was quite customary for governments and churches to call for days of fasting, humiliation, and prayer, especially during times of calamity, trouble, war, and so on. We ought to read God's providence with an eye to God's righteousness. Times of humbling ourselves, whether personal or public, are important to any close walk with God. How could you incorporate these habits into your walk with the Lord?**
2. **The memories of most of us are poor. For this reason, it is necessary that we continually hold before our mind's eye the great acts of redemption and salvation that God has wrought. Our children, grandchildren, and all around us need to hear of the great works that God has worked in and for us (Pss. 78:4; 96:3). Share with someone close to you how God has worked and is working in your life.**
3. **Reviewing the history of Israel from Abraham to the exile, one can sum up its lesson in these words: God is righteous and keeps His promises, but man is wicked**

CHAPTER 10

NOW those that sealed *were*, Nehemiah, the Tirshatha, the son of Hachaliah, and Zidkijah,
2 Seraiah, Azariah, Jeremiah,
3 Pashur, Amariah, Malchijah,
4 Hattush, Shebaniah, Malluch,
5 Harim, Meremoth, Obadiah,
6 Daniel, Ginnethon, Baruch,
7 Meshullam, Abijah, Mijamin,
8 Maaziah, Bilgai, Shemaiah: these *were* the priests.
9 And the Levites: both Jeshua the son of Azaniah, Binnui of the sons of Henadad, Kadmiel;
10 And their brethren, Shebaniah, Hodijah, Kelita, Pelaiah, Hanan,
11 Micha, Rehob, Hashabiah,
12 Zaccur, Sherebiah, Shebaniah,
13 Hodijah, Bani, Beninu.
14 The chief of the people; Parosh, Pahath-moab, Elam, Zatthu, Bani,
15 Bunni, Azgad, Bebai,
16 Adonijah, Bigvai, Adin,
17 Ater, Hizkijah, Azzur,
18 Hodijah, Hashum, Bezai,
19 Hariph, Anathoth, Nebai,
20 Magpiash, Meshullam, Hezir,
21 Meshezabeel, Zadok, Jaddua,
22 Pelatiah, Hanan, Anaiah,
23 Hoshea, Hananiah, Hashub,
24 Hallohesh, Pileha, Shobek,
25 Rehum, Hashabnah, Maaseiah,
26 And Ahijah, Hanan, Anan,
27 Malluch, Harim, Baanah.
28 ¶ And the rest of the people, the priests, the
Levites, the porters, the singers, the Nethinims,
and all they that had separated themselves from
the people of the lands unto the law of God, their
wives, their sons, and their daughters, every one
having knowledge, and having understanding;
29 They clave to their brethren, their nobles, and
entered into a curse, and into an oath, to walk in
God's law, which was given by Moses the servant
of God, and to observe and do all the commandments of the LORD our Lord, and his judgments
and his statutes;
30 And that we would not give our daughters
unto the people of the land, nor take their daughters for our sons:
31 And *if* the people of the land bring ware or any
victuals on the sabbath day to sell, *that* we would
not buy it of them on the sabbath, or on the holy
day: and *that* we would leave the seventh year, and
the exaction of every debt.
32 Also we made ordinances for us, to charge
ourselves yearly with the third part of a shekel for
the service of the house of our God;
33 For the shewbread, and for the continual meat
offering, and for the continual burnt offering, of
the sabbaths, of the new moons, for the set feasts,
and for the holy *things*, and for the sin offerings to
make an atonement for Israel, and *for* all the work
of the house of our God.
34 And we cast the lots among the priests, the
Levites, and the people, for the wood offering,
to bring *it* into the house of our God, after the
houses of our fathers, at times appointed year by
year, to burn upon the altar of the LORD our God,
as *it is* written in the law:
35 And to bring the firstfruits of our ground, and
the firstfruits of all fruit of all trees, year by year,
unto the house of the LORD:
36 Also the firstborn of our sons, and of our
cattle, as *it is* written in the law, and the firstlings
of our herds and of our flocks, to bring to the

and breaks God's laws. How then should we live? We must humble ourselves very low, recognizing that we and our families would have rebelled against God's laws as bad or worse than the Israelites, and rest our hope in the grace of God alone. Cry out for the grace of Jesus Christ even as we have seen in this chapter.

Chapter 10: *The people sign an agreement, binding themselves to God's precepts in general with a number of particular precepts emphasized.*

10:1–27 The men who entered into the covenant include *Nehemiah* and *Zidkijah* (Zedekiah), followed by twenty-one priests, seventeen Levites, and another forty-four others. A total of eighty-four signers are listed here.

10:1 *sealed.* Shows a firmness or resolve in making the covenant. The Hebrew word may be used to distinguish it from the covenant God made with His people.

10:28 *separated themselves.* The verb is used of distinguishing between the clean and the unclean, the holy and the common (Lev. 10:10; 11:47). God chose Israel to be a distinctly clean and holy people, separated from the pagan world (9:2; Lev. 20:24–26; 1 Kings 8:53; Ezra 6:21; 9:1–2) through their obedience to the *law of God.* Not only the wall bound these people together and shut out the intruder, but also the will of God as revealed in His law.

10:29 *clave.* Joined with their brothers. *curse.* A common part of covenant making. Covenant breakers justly endure the curse (Deut. 28:15).

10:30 The law against intermarriage is not about racial boundaries but religious ones. Those whom God had marked as the "holy seed" could not be contaminated with the "unholy seed."

10:31 *ware.* Goods such as agricultural produce. *victuals.* Harvest or grains. *exaction.* Literally, "usury," or interest payments.

10:32 *charge ourselves yearly.* This temple tax was not necessarily commanded in the law, though there was precedence for a similar tax (Ex. 30:11–16; 38:25–26).

10:33 *atonement.* To cover over.

10:34 *lots.* A way of deciding the Lord's will. *wood offering.* Not an offering specifically commanded in the law, but provision of fuel so that the fire on the altar would remain burning (Lev. 6:12–13). *written in the law.* They were dedicated to obeying the law.

10:35–39 The people provided for the needs of the Levites.

house of our God, unto the priests that minister
in the house of our God:
37 And *that* we should bring the firstfruits of
our dough, and our offerings, and the fruit of
all manner of trees, of wine and of oil, unto the
priests, to the chambers of the house of our God;
and the tithes of our ground unto the Levites, that
the same Levites might have the tithes in all the
cities of our tillage.
38 And the priest the son of Aaron shall be with
the Levites, when the Levites take tithes: and the
Levites shall bring up the tithe of the tithes unto
the house of our God, to the chambers, into the
treasure house.
39 For the children of Israel and the children of
Levi shall bring the offering of the corn, of the
new wine, and the oil, unto the chambers, where
are the vessels of the sanctuary, and the priests
that minister, and the porters, and the singers:
and we will not forsake the house of our God.

CHAPTER 11

AND the rulers of the people dwelt at Jerusalem:
the rest of the people also cast lots, to bring one
of ten to dwell in Jerusalem the holy city, and nine
parts *to dwell* in *other* cities.
2 And the people blessed all the men, that will-
ingly offered themselves to dwell at Jerusalem.
3 ¶ Now these *are* the chief of the province that
dwelt in Jerusalem: but in the cities of Judah dwelt
every one in his possession in their cities, *to wit*,
Israel, the priests, and the Levites, and the Nethi-
nims, and the children of Solomon's servants.
4 And at Jerusalem dwelt *certain* of the children
of Judah, and of the children of Benjamin. Of the
children of Judah; Athaiah the son of Uzziah, the
son of Zechariah, the son of Amariah, the son of
Shephatiah, the son of Mahalaleel, of the children
of Perez;
5 And Maaseiah the son of Baruch, the son of
Col-hozeh, the son of Hazaiah, the son of Adaiah,
the son of Joiarib, the son of Zechariah, the son
of Shiloni.
6 All the sons of Perez that dwelt at Jerusalem
were four hundred threescore and eight valiant
men.
7 And these *are* the sons of Benjamin; Sallu the
son of Meshullam, the son of Joed, the son of
Pedaiah, the son of Kolaiah, the son of Maaseiah,
the son of Ithiel, the son of Jesaiah.
8 And after him Gabbai, Sallai, nine hundred
twenty and eight.
9 And Joel the son of Zichri *was* their overseer:
and Judah the son of Senuah *was* second over the
city.
10 Of the priests: Jedaiah the son of Joiarib,
Jachin.
11 Seraiah the son of Hilkiah, the son of Meshul-
lam, the son of Zadok, the son of Meraioth, the
son of Ahitub, *was* the ruler of the house of God.
12 And their brethren that did the work of the
house *were* eight hundred twenty and two: and
Adaiah the son of Jeroham, the son of Pelaliah,
the son of Amzi, the son of Zechariah, the son of
Pashur, the son of Malchiah,
13 And his brethren, chief of the fathers, two
hundred forty and two: and Amashai the son of
Azareel, the son of Ahasai, the son of Meshille-
moth, the son of Immer,
14 And their brethren, mighty men of valour, an
hundred twenty and eight: and their overseer *was*
Zabdiel, the son of *one of* the great men.
15 Also of the Levites: Shemaiah the son of

Thoughts for Personal/Family Worship: Chapter 10

1. **These people are not reenacting what God had done through Moses at Sinai in making a covenant with Israel. That had happened and was still binding. These people are expressing the vow to keep these things God had ordered with an emphasis on specific things that thus far had slipped. It is very important for all believers, especially leaders, to discern in what areas our spiritual boundaries are under attack and vulnerable. Pray for wisdom to know what sins God is convicting you of by His Holy Spirit.**
2. **This agreement does not only emphasize negatives, but also positives, such as an offering to God and support for the Levites. Obedience to God is not only forsaking what is sinful, but doing that which is good. Read James 4:17. What "good" have you been neglecting?**
3. **Note the strong resolution at the close of this chapter, "We will not forsake the house of our God" (v. 39). Christ preeminently had a zeal for the house of the Lord (John 2:17). Can you put your amen to this? Are you zealous for the church of Christ and the worship of God? How are you showing your support and zeal?**

DIVISION OF THE PEOPLE, PRIESTS, AND LEVITES (11:1—12:47)

Chapter 11: *The leaders of Jerusalem are listed and the cities that lay outside of Jerusalem.*

People of Judah (11:1–9)

11:1 Now that the people had consecrated themselves to the Lord, they could take steps to have Jerusalem inhabited and maintained. The narrative picks up where it left off in 7:4–5. *holy city.* Jerusalem, home of God's holy presence in the temple (Isa. 48:2; 52:1; Dan. 9:24).

11:3–9 Various others from Judah and Benjamin, nonpriests, non-Levites.

11:4–24 There are many similarities between this list and the one found in 1 Chron. 9:2–17. It is likely that both Nehemiah and Chronicles depended on government archives to form their lists, while God's inspiration gave discernment and guaranteed the accuracy of what was used.

Priests (11:10–36)

11:10–14 The priests representing six different houses of the priests.

11:15–24 The Levites and porters.

Hashub, the son of Azrikam, the son of Hasha-
biah, the son of Bunni;
16 And Shabbethai and Jozabad, of the chief
of the Levites, *had* the oversight of the outward
business of the house of God.
17 And Mattaniah the son of Micha, the son of
Zabdi, the son of Asaph, *was* the principal to be-
gin the thanksgiving in prayer: and Bakbukiah the
second among his brethren, and Abda the son of
Shammua, the son of Galal, the son of Jeduthun.
18 All the Levites in the holy city *were* two hun-
dred fourscore and four.
19 Moreover the porters, Akkub, Talmon, and
their brethren that kept the gates, *were* an hundred
seventy and two.
20 ¶ And the residue of Israel, of the priests, *and*
the Levites, *were* in all the cities of Judah, every
one in his inheritance.
21 But the Nethinims dwelt in Ophel: and Ziha
and Gispa *were* over the Nethinims.
22 The overseer also of the Levites at Jerusalem
was Uzzi the son of Bani, the son of Hashabiah,
the son of Mattaniah, the son of Micha. Of the
sons of Asaph, the singers *were* over the business
of the house of God.
23 For *it was* the king's commandment concern-
ing them, that a certain portion should be for the
singers, due for every day.
24 And Pethahiah the son of Meshezabeel, of the
children of Zerah the son of Judah, *was* at the
king's hand in all matters concerning the people.
25 And for the villages, with their fields, *some*
of the children of Judah dwelt at Kirjath-arba,
and *in* the villages thereof, and at Dibon, and *in*
the villages thereof, and at Jekabzeel, and *in* the
villages thereof,
26 And at Jeshua, and at Moladah, and at Beth-
phelet,
27 And at Hazar-shual, and at Beer-sheba, and *in*
the villages thereof,
28 And at Ziklag, and at Mekonah, and in the
villages thereof,
29 And at En-rimmon, and at Zareah, and at
Jarmuth,
30 Zanoah, Adullam, and *in* their villages, at
Lachish, and the fields thereof, at Azekah, and *in*
the villages thereof. And they dwelt from Beer-
sheba unto the valley of Hinnom.
31 The children also of Benjamin from Geba
dwelt at Michmash, and Aija, and Beth-el, and *in*
their villages,
32 *And* at Anathoth, Nob, Ananiah,
33 Hazor, Ramah, Gittaim,
34 Hadid, Zeboim, Neballat,
35 Lod, and Ono, the valley of craftsmen.
36 And of the Levites *were* divisions *in* Judah, *and*
in Benjamin.

CHAPTER 12

Now these *are* the priests and the Levites that
went up with Zerubbabel the son of Shealtiel, and
Jeshua: Seraiah, Jeremiah, Ezra,
2 Amariah, Malluch, Hattush,
3 Shechaniah, Rehum, Meremoth,
4 Iddo, Ginnetho, Abijah,
5 Miamin, Maadiah, Bilgah,
6 Shemaiah, and Joiarib, Jedaiah,
7 Sallu, Amok, Hilkiah, Jedaiah. These *were* the
chief of the priests and of their brethren in the
days of Jeshua.
8 Moreover the Levites: Jeshua, Binnui, Kadmiel,
Sherebiah, Judah, *and* Mattaniah, *which was* over
the thanksgiving, he and his brethren.
9 Also Bakbukiah and Unni, their brethren, *were*
over against them in the watches.
10 ¶ And Jeshua begat Joiakim, Joiakim also be-
gat Eliashib, and Eliashib begat Joiada,
11 And Joiada begat Jonathan, and Jonathan
begat Jaddua.
12 And in the days of Joiakim were priests, the
chief of the fathers: of Seraiah, Meraiah; of
Jeremiah, Hananiah;
13 Of Ezra, Meshullam; of Amariah, Jehohanan;

11:16 *outward business.* Included the keeping of the building and property and the storing of provisions.
11:20 *residue.* Literally, "remnant." Not all the Levites lived in Jerusalem.
11:23 *king's commandment.* The king of Persia. The people of Judah settled south of Jerusalem.
11:31–36 The villages of Benjamin are to the north and west of Jerusalem.

Thoughts for Personal/Family Worship: Chapter 11

1. **Here one-tenth of the people of God lived in Jerusalem. This was a special "tithe," consecrated to the Lord to sustain His holy city. Through Zechariah, God envisioned a time when everywhere, not just one city, would be called holy (Zech. 14:20–21). This is true in Christ. There is no longer one city where God has His presence in a particular way (John 4:21–24). The "city of God" touches believers throughout this world, and is found in its glory in heaven (Heb. 12:22–24). Praise God for the hope we have of His glory to be revealed one day!**
2. **What a note of joy there is in this verse: "And the residue of Israel, of the priests, and the Levites, were in all the cities of Judah, every one in his inheritance" (v. 20). After a long time of exile, these prodigals were back, each in their own inheritance. Have you returned to the Lord and the heritage of Abraham, Isaac, and Jacob? This is a lifelong process, but it begins with turning to God and forsaking the world.**

Chapter 12: *The priests and Levites are listed along with their functions in the temple.*
Levites (12:1–47)

12:10–11 *Jeshua* was the high priest at the time of the exiles

14 Of Melicu, Jonathan; of Shebaniah, Joseph;
15 Of Harim, Adna; of Meraioth, Helkai;
16 Of Iddo, Zechariah; of Ginnethon, Meshul-
lam;
17 Of Abijah, Zichri; of Miniamin, of Moadiah,
Piltai;
18 Of Bilgah, Shammua; of Shemaiah, Jehona-
than;
19 And of Joiarib, Mattenai; of Jedaiah, Uzzi;
20 Of Sallai, Kallai; of Amok, Eber;
21 Of Hilkiah, Hashabiah; of Jedaiah, Nethaneel.
22 ¶ The Levites in the days of Eliashib, Joiada,
and Johanan, and Jaddua, *were* recorded chief of
the fathers: also the priests, to the reign of Darius
the Persian.
23 The sons of Levi, the chief of the fathers, *were*
written in the book of the chronicles, even until
the days of Johanan the son of Eliashib.
24 And the chief of the Levites: Hashabiah, Shere-
biah, and Jeshua the son of Kadmiel, with their
brethren over against them, to praise *and* to give
thanks, according to the commandment of David
the man of God, ward over against ward.
25 Mattaniah, and Bakbukiah, Obadiah, Meshul-
lam, Talmon, Akkub, *were* porters keeping the
ward at the thresholds of the gates.
26 These *were* in the days of Joiakim the son of
Jeshua, the son of Jozadak, and in the days of
Nehemiah the governor, and of Ezra the priest,
the scribe.
27 ¶ And at the dedication of the wall of Jerusa-
lem they sought the Levites out of all their places,
to bring them to Jerusalem, to keep the dedication
with gladness, both with thanksgivings, and with
singing, *with* cymbals, psalteries, and with harps.
28 And the sons of the singers gathered them-
selves together, both out of the plain country
round about Jerusalem, and from the villages of
Netophathi;
29 Also from the house of Gilgal, and out of the
fields of Geba and Azmaveth: for the singers had
builded them villages round about Jerusalem.
30 And the priests and the Levites purified them-
selves, and purified the people, and the gates, and
the wall.
31 Then I brought up the princes of Judah upon
the wall, and appointed two great *companies of
them that gave* thanks, *whereof one* went on the
right hand upon the wall toward the dung gate:
32 And after them went Hoshaiah, and half of the
princes of Judah,
33 And Azariah, Ezra, and Meshullam,
34 Judah, and Benjamin, and Shemaiah, and
Jeremiah,
35 And *certain* of the priests' sons with trumpets;
namely, Zechariah the son of Jonathan, the son
of Shemaiah, the son of Mattaniah, the son of
Michaiah, the son of Zaccur, the son of Asaph:
36 And his brethren, Shemaiah, and Azarael,
Milalai, Gilalai, Maai, Nethaneel, and Judah,
Hanani, with the musical instruments of David
the man of God, and Ezra the scribe before them.
37 And at the fountain gate, which was over
against them, they went up by the stairs of the
city of David, at the going up of the wall, above
the house of David, even unto the water gate
eastward.
38 And the other *company of them that gave*
thanks went over against *them*, and I after them,
and the half of the people upon the wall, from
beyond the tower of the furnaces even unto the
broad wall;
39 And from above the gate of Ephraim, and
above the old gate, and above the fish gate, and the
tower of Hananeel, and the tower of Meah, even
unto the sheep gate: and they stood still in the
prison gate.
40 So stood the two *companies of them that gave*

---

first return and in the time of Haggai and Zechariah. *Joiakim* was the high priest after this time—perhaps when Ezra returned to Jerusalem. There is uncertainty about the chronology of the other high priests.

12:22 *Darius the Persian.* A title to distinguish him from Darius the Mede (Dan. 5:31; 9:1).

12:23 *chronicles.* Not a reference to the biblical book.

12:24 *ward over against ward.* Watch by watch.

12:30 The purification indicated dedication and holiness to the Lord.

12:31–43 Two groups encircled the city by walking on top of the walls, one group clockwise, another group counterclockwise, meeting in the middle.

12:31 *Then I.* Nehemiah. The first person narrative continues again (7:5).

12:33 *Ezra.* Most probably, Ezra the scribe. He was involved in this as well.

12:36 *musical instruments of David.* The men were keen to show the connection between their day and the days of Israel's glory under David and Solomon, particularly in their obedience to the pattern of worship revealed by God under their reigns (vv. 24,37,45–46). *man of God.* Prophet, through whom God spoke His Word (2 Chron. 11:2).

Thoughts for Personal/Family Worship: Chapter 12

1. **The priests descended from Levi foreshadowed the greater Priest. Christ did not come from the line of Levi, but the line of Judah. Thus He could be a king. However, He is also a priest, but after a different order, the order of Melchizedek (Ps. 110:4; Heb. 7:14–16). The work of this greater Priest would be to forever rebuild and reestablish the spiritual house of God. Read Heb. 7:23–25 and then spend time worshiping our great Priest!**
2. **Chapter 12 includes one of the climactic moments in the books of Ezra and Nehemiah. After such a long time the walls and city of Jerusalem were dedicated (v. 27). When God does a work of revival like this, the refrain is: "God had made them rejoice with great joy" (v. 43). Revival brings life to bear on what was otherwise dull and dead. Joy is the only fitting response, so do not be ashamed**

thanks in the house of God, and I, and the half of
the rulers with me:
41 And the priests; Eliakim, Maaseiah, Miniamin,
Michaiah, Elioenai, Zechariah, *and* Hananiah,
with trumpets;
42 And Maaseiah, and Shemaiah, and Eleazar,
and Uzzi, and Jehohanan, and Malchijah, and
Elam, and Ezer. And the singers sang loud, with
Jezrahiah *their* overseer.
43 Also that day they offered great sacrifices, and
rejoiced: for God had made them rejoice with
great joy: the wives also and the children rejoiced:
so that the joy of Jerusalem was heard even afar off.
44 ¶ And at that time were some appointed over
the chambers for the treasures, for the offerings,
for the firstfruits, and for the tithes, to gather into
them out of the fields of the cities the portions
of the law for the priests and Levites: for Judah
rejoiced for the priests and for the Levites that
waited.
45 And both the singers and the porters kept the
ward of their God, and the ward of the purification, according to the commandment of David,
and of Solomon his son.
46 For in the days of David and Asaph of old *there*
were chief of the singers, and songs of praise and
thanksgiving unto God.
47 And all Israel in the days of Zerubbabel, and
in the days of Nehemiah, gave the portions of the
singers and the porters, every day his portion: and
they sanctified *holy things* unto the Levites; and
the Levites sanctified *them* unto the children of
Aaron.

CHAPTER 13

ON that day they read in the book of Moses in
the audience of the people; and therein was found
written, that the Ammonite and the Moabite
should not come into the congregation of God
for ever;
2 Because they met not the children of Israel with
bread and with water, but hired Balaam against
them, that he should curse them: howbeit our
God turned the curse into a blessing.
3 Now it came to pass, when they had heard the
law, that they separated from Israel all the mixed
multitude.
4 ¶ And before this, Eliashib the priest, having the
oversight of the chamber of the house of our God,
was allied unto Tobiah:
5 And he had prepared for him a great chamber,
where aforetime they laid the meat offerings, the
frankincense, and the vessels, and the tithes of the
corn, the new wine, and the oil, which was commanded *to be given* to the Levites, and the singers,
and the porters; and the offerings of the priests.
6 But in all this *time* was not I at Jerusalem: for
in the two and thirtieth year of Artaxerxes king of
Babylon came I unto the king, and after certain
days obtained I leave of the king:
7 And I came to Jerusalem, and understood of
the evil that Eliashib did for Tobiah, in preparing
him a chamber in the courts of the house of God.
8 And it grieved me sore: therefore I cast forth all
the household stuff of Tobiah out of the chamber.
9 Then I commanded, and they cleansed the
chambers: and thither brought I again the vessels
of the house of God, with the meat offering and
the frankincense.
10 ¶ And I perceived that the portions of the
Levites had not been given *them*: for the Levites
and the singers, that did the work, were fled every
one to his field.
11 Then contended I with the rulers, and said,
Why is the house of God forsaken? And I gathered them together, and set them in their place.
12 Then brought all Judah the tithe of the corn

to rejoice and celebrate over God's works. What inhibits joy in worship?

3. The Bible everywhere is concerned about purity of worship. This same concern appears here: they worshiped "according to the commandment of David" (vv. 24,45). Revival is not a time of innovation in doctrine or worship, but a time of returning to the old paths of God's Word. It is a pressing need today to see the worship of God regulated by the commandment of God. In what ways do you think your worship could follow more closely the purity found in God's Word?

Chapter 13: ***In the face of threats of compromise and the continuing need for reforms, Nehemiah carries out steps that make the community live up to its agreement.***

ABIDING PROBLEMS IN THE RENEWED COMMUNITY (13:1–31)

Tobiah Defiles the Temple (13:1–9)

13:1 *therein was found written.* This reading was from Deut. 23:3–6.

13:2 *hired Balaam.* See Num. 22–24.

13:3 *mixed multitude.* Mixed in national and thus religious backgrounds.

13:5 *great chamber.* Eliashib prepared a room, probably a storage chamber, for Tobiah, an Ammonite, thus giving him influence. By the law he should have been excluded. *aforetime.* Beforehand. *frankincense.* A fragrant incense.

13:6 It was during Nehemiah's time back in Persia that unlawful laxity overcame the people. We do not know how long he was gone and when exactly he returned. *king of Babylon.* Though Artaxerxes was technically king of the Persians, because the Persians conquered the Babylonians, this title was fitting, just as other kings took titles from the lands they conquered (Ezra 5:13; 6:22).

13:9 Nehemiah has the chambers ceremonially cleansed due to the defilement of Tobiah.

Levites Deprived of Offerings (13:10–14)

13:10 A second challenge to the reformation of the people, the Levites were not receiving their portion (Num. 18:21). This

and the new wine and the oil unto the treasuries.
13 And I made treasurers over the treasuries,
Shelemiah the priest, and Zadok the scribe, and of
the Levites, Pedaiah: and next to them *was* Hanan
the son of Zaccur, the son of Mattaniah: for they
were counted faithful, and their office *was* to
distribute unto their brethren.
14 Remember me, O my God, concerning this, and
wipe not out my good deeds that I have done for
the house of my God, and for the offices thereof.
15 ¶ In those days saw I in Judah *some* treading
wine presses on the sabbath, and bringing in
sheaves, and lading asses; as also wine, grapes,
and figs, and all *manner of* burdens, which they
brought into Jerusalem on the sabbath day: and I
testified *against them* in the day wherein they sold
victuals.
16 There dwelt men of Tyre also therein, which
brought fish, and all manner of ware, and sold
on the sabbath unto the children of Judah, and
in Jerusalem.
17 Then I contended with the nobles of Judah,
and said unto them, What evil thing *is* this that ye
do, and profane the sabbath day?
18 Did not your fathers thus, and did not our
God bring all this evil upon us, and upon this
city? yet ye bring more wrath upon Israel by pro-
faning the sabbath.
19 And it came to pass, that when the gates of
Jerusalem began to be dark before the sabbath,
I commanded that the gates should be shut, and
charged that they should not be opened till after
the sabbath: and *some* of my servants set I at the
gates, *that* there should no burden be brought in
on the sabbath day.
20 So the merchants and sellers of all kind of
ware lodged without Jerusalem once or twice.
21 Then I testified against them, and said unto
them, Why lodge ye about the wall? if ye do *so*
again, I will lay hands on you. From that time
forth came they no *more* on the sabbath.
22 And I commanded the Levites that they
should cleanse themselves, and *that* they should
come *and* keep the gates, to sanctify the sabbath
day. Remember me, O my God, *concerning* this
also, and spare me according to the greatness of
thy mercy.
23 ¶ In those days also saw I Jews *that* had married
wives of Ashdod, of Ammon, *and* of Moab:
24 And their children spake half in the speech
of Ashdod, and could not speak in the Jews' lan-
guage, but according to the language of each
people.
25 And I contended with them, and cursed them,
and smote certain of them, and plucked off their
hair, and made them swear by God, *saying*, Ye shall
not give your daughters unto their sons, nor take
their daughters unto your sons, or for yourselves.
26 Did not Solomon king of Israel sin by these
things? yet among many nations was there no
king like him, who was beloved of his God, and
God made him king over all Israel: nevertheless
even him did outlandish women cause to sin.
27 Shall we then hearken unto you to do all this
great evil, to transgress against our God in marry-
ing strange wives?
28 And *one* of the sons of Joiada, the son of
Eliashib the high priest, *was* son in law to Sanbal-
lat the Horonite: therefore I chased him from me.
29 Remember them, O my God, because they

---

is a contrast to 12:44 where the people gave the Levites their portion with joy.

13:14 *Remember me . . . my good deeds.* Nehemiah remained faithful and loyal to God's commandments and anticipated the rewards of grace (vv. 22,29,31; see note at 5:19). The word translated *good deeds* is the same word as God's "mercy" (v. 22), and refers to faithful love, especially covenant loyalty (1:5; 9:32). By grace, Nehemiah had kept the covenant of the Lord, and therefore believed God's promise that He would keep covenant with Nehemiah (Ps. 103:17–18).

Sabbath Profaned (13:15–22)

13:15 A third challenge was that of keeping the Sabbath. *lading.* Loading. The Sabbath was to be a time of rest from labor and commercial trade (10:31; Ex. 20:8–11).

13:20–21 The people resisted Nehemiah's attempt at reforms.

13:21 *lodge ye.* Some spent the Sabbath by the wall to assure a good place in the market the following morning.

Intermarriage (13:23–31)

13:23 A fourth challenge was intermarriage with unbelieving nations.

13:24 *speech of Ashdod.* A different dialect from that of the returned exiles.

13:25 *cursed.* Not a reference to inappropriate language, but invoking the curses of the covenant on lawbreakers if they did not repent. *smote.* Struck. As a civil official, Nehemiah had the authority to apply physical punishment to lawbreakers (Deut. 25:2–3; Prov. 10:13; 26:3; Rom. 13:4).

13:28 The religious laxity was even among the priests of Israel.

13:31 *Remember me, O my God, for good.* See note at v. 14.

Thoughts for Personal/Family Worship: Chapter 13

1. **There will always be forces for evil. The history of Balaam and Balak reminds us that people will try to work against the people of God and the purposes of God. However, God is such that He will turn "the curse into a blessing" (v. 2). How can we be on our guard that we do not fall on the side of the curse, but experience God's work unto blessing through Christ?**
2. **How is it possible that an arch-enemy of Israel got a great chamber in the house of our God? In many churches and seminaries in our day, enemies of the gospel have a lot of sway. We should pray and labor that this not happen on our watch.**
3. **Many have felt that Nehemiah's actions were too harsh (v. 25). Let us remember, however, the time when Christ made a whip to drive out the money changers from the**

have defiled the priesthood, and the covenant of
the priesthood, and of the Levites.
30 Thus cleansed I them from all strangers, and
appointed the wards of the priests and the Levites,
every one in his business;
31 And for the wood offering, at times appointed,
and for the firstfruits. Remember me, O my God,
for good.

temple (John 2:15–16). Certainly, no one can say that Nehemiah was without sin, but Christ was. And Nehemiah was a man who desired fervently and acted decisively for the honor of his God. We may not have the authority to use physical force, but how are we using the authority and influence we do have for the glory of God?

INTRODUCTION TO THE BOOK OF ESTHER

Authorship: There are varied opinions regarding who wrote the book of Esther. Augustine argued that Ezra wrote it. The Talmud states that men of the Great Synagogue penned Esther (*Baba Bathra*, 15a). Clement of Alexandria and many of the ancient Jewish and Christian sources maintain that Mordecai is the author. Finally, other sources believe that Esther was simply written by a scribe, perhaps one in the courts of the Persian king. Our lack of certainty as to who wrote Esther does not prevent us from seeing this book as canonical.

The historicity of Esther has often been questioned. There are a number of biblical scholars who believe that the whole story is fabricated and not grounded in any real events. Others have been avid defenders of its historicity. A large number of scholars have argued that Esther is perhaps a historical fiction—an embellished story containing true elements.

Usually, scholars who dispute the historicity of Esther, think that Esther does not fit what we know from other sources, such as the Greek historian Herodotus. However, the author's details of Persian affairs are consistent with contemporary research. More importantly, the book presents itself as history, and there is nothing in the book or elsewhere in the canon that suggests it is not what it presents itself to be. The genre of the book and our understanding of the Scriptures do not permit us to believe that it was intended to be anything but a historical narrative. Indeed, there is no history like biblical history, true both to fact and life.

Date: Esther begins by noting, "Now it came to pass in the days of Ahasuerus" (1:1). Ahasuerus is also known as King Xerxes, the king of Persia (486–465 BC). Though canonically Esther comes after Nehemiah, chronologically Esther takes place between the time after the completion of the temple under Zerubbabel, who rebuilt the temple in 516 BC under the reign of Darius I, and the return of more exiles under Ezra in 458 BC, under the reign of Artaxerxes I (Xerxes's son).

Darius I brought the Persian Empire to its greatest glory. Under Ahasuerus, his son, the empire saw tremendous success like the reconquering and subjection of Egypt and the suppression of a Babylonian rebellion. But he also suffered great loss, particularly in the Battle of Salamis against Greece (480 BC). We do have extrabiblical references to King Ahasuerus as recorded by the ancient historian Herodotus who characterized Ahasuerus as an ill-tempered and impatient king. This accords with the biblical testimony regarding him. Ahasuerus was killed in 465 BC and was succeeded by his son Artaxerxes I.

The date of composition has been largely debated in biblical scholarship. There are some who maintain that Esther was written at a late date during the Grecian or Maccabean period. But it is largely recognized that Esther was written before Alexander the Great Hellenized the world. Thus, it is dubious to think that Esther is a Jewish response to the Hellenizing of the world. The author was clearly familiar with Ahasuerus, Persian forms of execution, and the like. In light of all this, it is likely that Esther was written around 450 BC since the book refers to some things after the death of Xerxes (10:2).

Theme: God sovereignly ensures that those who seek to destroy His people will in turn be destroyed.

Purpose: To motivate God's people to serve submissively and yet with godly courage under wicked rulers through faith in God's hidden providence, by which He will bring the King of peace.

Synopsis: *The Contribution of Esther to Redemptive Revelation*

Esther explains the origin of the Jewish Feast of Purim, where the Jews celebrate their deliverance from the malevolent actions of Haman, an enemy of the Jews. This book serves to show how this feast originated and its importance. The word "Purim" is likely derived from the Akkadian word *Pur*, which relates to the lots cast by Haman to destroy the Jews. Though these lots initially meant the destruction of the Jews (3:7), it would later become the occasion of the Jews' celebration and joy (9:23–32).

Through the narrative of the beginnings of Purim, this book exalts God as the sovereign over all things from the casting of lots to major world events—though His name is never mentioned. The author of Esther does not recount the events of this narrative in a mundane fashion. Rather, Esther is a carefully crafted masterpiece of literature. The author uses many literary techniques, drawing the reader into the story. God's hand of providence shows itself in surprising turns of historical events.

Banquets and fasts frame the center of this drama. It is at a banquet that Vashti is rejected as a queen. At the banquet of Esther, Haman receives his death sentence. The Jews celebrate their deliverance with a feast called Purim. The details of Esther are just enough to carry us along without bogging us down in unnecessary facts. The author uses foreshadowing and surprise for rhetorical effect. Repetition is used in various spots to connect different elements of the story. The whole of Esther is a drama (not fictitious theater play, but an engaging narrative of real events) in which the reader is drawn and interested. The highly suspenseful story brings us to feel the relief and joy of the Jews as they overturn Haman's wicked decree.

The opening chapter does not include Esther as a character, but recounts the banquet where Ahasuerus called his wife, Vashti, to present herself before the assembly. Vashti refused and in a fit of rage, Ahasuerus banished her from being queen. This set the stage for Esther to come into the narrative.

Esther was one of the many women who were brought before King Ahasuerus, as he attempted to decide who he wanted to be his queen. Esther underwent a long process of preparation before she was escorted into the presence of the king for a night. After winning the favor of Ahasuerus, Esther was made queen, all the while concealing her lineage.

While all this was occurring, an evil leader among the Persians, Haman, was devising a plot to kill the Jews. The Jews and Agagites had a long history of animosity, and Haman used his privileged position to get the king to sign into law a day to kill the Jews. Mordecai, Esther's cousin, had foiled a plot to assassinate King Ahasuerus; however, because Mordecai failed to flatter Haman's ego, Haman targeted him, preparing gallows to see Mordecai hanged.

After making Esther aware of the plot against the Jews, Mordecai challenged her to use her influence. According to Persian law, however, once a law was signed into legislation, not even the king could revoke it. And approaching the king without his bidding could easily result in a death sentence.

Defying the seeming impossibilities, Esther approached the king and disclosed Haman's plot. The king ordered Haman's death, and in divine irony, Haman was hanged on the gallows he built for Mordecai. The king then issued a law that the Jews could defend themselves on the day of the great assault.

When the fateful date for the Jews arrived, they rose up against their persecutors, slaying many of them. To commemorate this day, the Feast of Purim recounts the way in which the Jews were delivered from the hands of their enemies.

But there is also a larger purpose that forms the background of this book. While the book does not explicitly mention God, it is apparent that the hand of God was moving the historical narrative of Esther forward. God is known by His acts as well as His words. Haman's wife issued an insightful commentary on Haman's action: "If Mordecai be of the seed of the Jews, before whom thou hast begun to fall, thou shalt not prevail against him, but shalt surely fall before him" (6:13). The real background to this tension between the Jews and those who wanted to kill them, is the struggle between the seed of the woman and the seed of the serpent (Gen. 3:15). Even while the people were in exile, God remained faithful to His covenant promises. God is the author and sovereign of all of history. Esther contributes to redemptive revelation by showing God's preservation of the nation of Israel, which was crucial for the coming of the Messiah in the fullness of time. Concerning the flesh, Christ came through Israel (Rom. 9:5). In God's redemptive plan there had to be an Israel for the Christ to come.

Outline:

I. King Ahasuerus Takes Esther as His Queen (1:1—2:23)
   A. Ahasuerus Sends Queen Vashti Away (1:1–22)
   B. Esther Wins the Approval of King Ahasuerus (2:1–20)
   C. Mordecai Uncovers a Plot to Kill Ahasuerus (2:21–23)

II. Haman's Plot to Kill the Jews (3:1—4:17)
   A. Haman Is Promoted (3:1–2)
   B. Haman's Hatred for the Jews Grows Because Mordecai Refuses to Bow (3:3–6)
   C. King Ahasuerus Issues a Decree to Kill the Jews (3:7–15)
   D. Mordecai Reveals the Plot to Esther (4:1–17)

III. Haman's Demise and Mordecai's Exaltation (5:1—8:2)
   A. Esther Pleases the King and Has a Banquet (5:1–8)
   B. Haman Plots Mordecai's Death (5:9–14)
   C. Haman Humiliated and Mordecai Exalted (6:1–14)
   D. The Death of Haman and Exaltation of Mordecai (7:1—8:2)

IV. The King's Second Decree (8:3—9:32)
   A. The King Issues a Second Decree to Save the Jews (8:3–17)
   B. The Jews Are Saved from Destruction (9:1–19)
   C. Purim Instituted (9:20–32)

V. Epilogue (10:1–3)

THE BOOK OF
ESTHER

CHAPTER 1

Now it came to pass in the days of Ahasuerus,
(this *is* Ahasuerus which reigned, from India even
unto Ethiopia, *over* an hundred and seven and
twenty provinces:)
2 *That* in those days, when the king Ahasuerus
sat on the throne of his kingdom, which *was* in
Shushan the palace,
3 In the third year of his reign, he made a feast
unto all his princes and his servants; the power of
Persia and Media, the nobles and princes of the
provinces, *being* before him:
4 When he shewed the riches of his glorious
kingdom and the honour of his excellent majesty
many days, *even* an hundred and fourscore days.
5 And when these days were expired, the king
made a feast unto all the people that were present in
Shushan the palace, both unto great and small, seven
days, in the court of the garden of the king's palace;
6 *Where were* white, green, and blue, *hangings*,
fastened with cords of fine linen and purple to sil-
ver rings and pillars of marble: the beds *were of*
gold and silver, upon a pavement of red, and blue,
and white, and black, marble.
7 And they gave *them* drink in vessels of gold,
(the vessels being diverse one from another,) and
royal wine in abundance, according to the state
of the king.
8 And the drinking *was* according to the law;
none did compel: for so the king had appointed
to all the officers of his house, that they should do
according to every man's pleasure.
9 Also Vashti the queen made a feast for the
women *in* the royal house which *belonged* to king
Ahasuerus.
10 ¶ On the seventh day, when the heart of the
king was merry with wine, he commanded Me-
human, Biztha, Harbona, Bigtha, and Abagtha,
Zethar, and Carcas, the seven chamberlains that
served in the presence of Ahasuerus the king,
11 To bring Vashti the queen before the king
with the crown royal, to shew the people and the
princes her beauty: for she *was* fair to look on.
12 But the queen Vashti refused to come at the
king's commandment by *his* chamberlains:
therefore was the king very wroth, and his anger
burned in him.
13 ¶ Then the king said to the wise men, which
knew the times, (for so *was* the king's manner
toward all that knew law and judgment:
14 And the next unto him *was* Carshena, Shethar,
Admatha, Tarshish, Meres, Marsena, *and* Memu-
can, the seven princes of Persia and Media, which
saw the king's face, *and* which sat the first in the
kingdom;)
15 What shall we do unto the queen Vashti ac-

KING AHASUERUS TAKES ESTHER AS HIS QUEEN (1:1—2:23)

Chapter 1: *Queen Vashti refuses to come to Ahasuerus's banquet, which prompts Ahasuerus to depose her from being queen.*

Ahasuerus Sends Queen Vashti Away (1:1–22)

1:1 *Ahasuerus*. Also known as Xerxes I (reigned 486–465 BC). *India*. Present day Pakistan. *Ethiopia*. Territory south of Egypt, modern Sudan.

1:2 *Shushan*. Location of the winter dwellings of the king of Persia.

1:3 *third year.* 483 BC. *feast.* Banquets were times when the king would display his greatness to everyone and seek the faithfulness of his subjects. *power.* Army.

1:4 *hundred and fourscore days.* The feast may have been shorter, but the display of the splendor of his kingdom lasted 180 days. Ahasuerus might have intended to soften the military commanders and his subjects for his proposal to invade Greece.

1:5 *expired.* Finished.

1:6 *beds.* Couches.

1:7 *state.* Literally, "hand."

1:9 *Vashti.* According to the Greek historian Herodotus, Ahasuerus's wife was named Amestris. Perhaps *Vashti* was another name or a second wife. Transliterating the name from Persian to Hebrew and Greek and then to English accounts for much of the problem.

1:10 *chamberlains.* Likely eunuchs.

1:11 *crown royal.* The crown of the kingdom. *fair to look on.* Good-looking, beautiful.

1:12 *wroth.* Enraged.

1:13 *knew the times.* Perhaps a reference to astrologers. *manner.* Custom or habit.

1:14 *sat the first.* In the highest or most honored position.

1:15 *What shall we do.* The powerlessness of this great king to deal with his own wife is a pointed reminder that the greatest of men are mere men.

cording to law, because she hath not performed
the commandment of the king Ahasuerus by the
chamberlains?
16 And Memucan answered before the king
and the princes, Vashti the queen hath not done
wrong to the king only, but also to all the princes,
and to all the people that *are* in all the provinces
of the king Ahasuerus.
17 For *this* deed of the queen shall come abroad
unto all women, so that they shall despise their
husbands in their eyes, when it shall be reported,
The king Ahasuerus commanded Vashti the queen
to be brought in before him, but she came not.
18 *Likewise* shall the ladies of Persia and Media
say this day unto all the king's princes, which have
heard of the deed of the queen. Thus *shall there*
arise too much contempt and wrath.
19 If it please the king, let there go a royal com-
mandment from him, and let it be written among
the laws of the Persians and the Medes, that it be
not altered, That Vashti come no more before
king Ahasuerus; and let the king give her royal es-
tate unto another that is better than she.
20 And when the king's decree which he shall
make shall be published throughout all his
empire, (for it is great,) all the wives shall give to
their husbands honour, both to great and small.
21 And the saying pleased the king and the
princes; and the king did according to the word
of Memucan:
22 For he sent letters into all the king's provinces,
into every province according to the writing
thereof, and to every people after their language,
that every man should bear rule in his own house,
and that *it* should be published according to the
language of every people.

CHAPTER 2

AFTER these things, when the wrath of king Ahas-
uerus was appeased, he remembered Vashti, and
what she had done, and what was decreed against
her.
2 Then said the king's servants that ministered
unto him, Let there be fair young virgins sought
for the king:
3 And let the king appoint officers in all the
provinces of his kingdom, that they may gather
together all the fair young virgins unto Shushan
the palace, to the house of the women, unto the
custody of Hege the king's chamberlain, keeper
of the women; and let their things for purification
be given *them*:
4 And let the maiden which pleaseth the king be
queen instead of Vashti. And the thing pleased the
king; and he did so.
5 ¶ *Now* in Shushan the palace there was a certain
Jew, whose name *was* Mordecai, the son of Jair,
the son of Shimei, the son of Kish, a Benjamite;
6 Who had been carried away from Jerusalem
with the captivity which had been carried away
with Jeconiah king of Judah, whom Nebuchad-
nezzar the king of Babylon had carried away.
7 And he brought up Hadassah, that *is*, Esther,
his uncle's daughter: for she had neither father
nor mother, and the maid *was* fair and beautiful;
whom Mordecai, when her father and mother
were dead, took for his own daughter.

1:17 *come abroad.* Become known throughout the land.
1:19 *written among the laws.* The laws of the Persians and the Medes were noted for their immutable character.
1:20 *published.* Proclaimed.
1:22 *letters.* We know from history that the communication system of Persia was remarkably advanced (3:14–15).

Thoughts for Personal/Family Worship: Chapter 1

1. **The world's ideas regarding marriage are warped. Still today, the marriages of famous people rarely speak well of the institution of marriage, but instead they reflect the sinful hearts of men and women by nature. Christ's glorious marriage to the church is the great model for marriage (Eph. 5:22–33). How can we as Christian husbands and wives follow Christ's model and display marriages that are nobler than kings' marriages?**
2. **We often wonder how God is working through our world and its leaders—corrupt, vain, and petty as they often are. Yet God's hand is in control, whether we recognize it or not. As Esther unfolds, we will see that God is working straight through the whims and follies of Ahasuerus and his officials. Pray that God will help you to trust that His hand is at work in our times as well.**
3. **God's law sets the rules for how men and women, parents and children, and superiors and subjects ought to relate. It is pitiful to see a king, who lacks all fear of God, try to gain by civil law the respect that he did not earn by his actions and personal dignity (v. 20). How can God's values help you to gain respect?**

Chapter 2: *King Ahasuerus ends up selecting Esther, a Jew, as the new queen, while Mordecai her cousin uncovers a plot to assassinate Ahasuerus.*

Esther Wins the Approval of King Ahasuerus (2:1–20)

2:1 *After.* Esther came before the king in his seventh year (v. 16). That would indicate a span of four years between chs. 1 and 2. It is likely that the Grecian campaign transpired during this time. *appeased.* Abated.
2:3 *king's chamberlain.* Official of the royal court. *things for purification.* There was an extended period of purification preparing the virgins to see the king.
2:4 *maiden.* Young woman (also translated, "maid").
2:5 *Benjamite.* Mordecai was from the tribe of Benjamin, the same tribe as Israel's first king, Saul, who slaughtered the Amalekites, the enemies of Israel, but preserved their king, Agag, until Samuel killed him (1 Sam. 15). Haman was an Agagite (3:1).
2:6 *captivity.* Babylonian exile.
2:7 *fair.* Lovely in form. *took for his own daughter.* Adoption within extended families was not unheard of in the Ancient Near East.

8 ¶ So it came to pass, when the king's commandment and his decree was heard, and when many
maidens were gathered together unto Shushan
the palace, to the custody of Hegai, that Esther
was brought also unto the king's house, to the
custody of Hegai, keeper of the women.
9 And the maiden pleased him, and she obtained
kindness of him; and he speedily gave her her
things for purification, with such things as belonged to her, and seven maidens, *which were*
meet to be given her, out of the king's house: and
he preferred her and her maids unto the best *place*
of the house of the women.
10 Esther had not shewed her people nor her
kindred: for Mordecai had charged her that she
should not shew *it*.
11 And Mordecai walked every day before the
court of the women's house, to know how Esther
did, and what should become of her.
12 ¶ Now when every maid's turn was come to
go in to king Ahasuerus, after that she had been
twelve months, according to the manner of the
women, (for so were the days of their purifications accomplished, *to wit*, six months with oil
of myrrh, and six months with sweet odours, and
with *other* things for the purifying of the women;)
13 Then thus came *every* maiden unto the king;
whatsoever she desired was given her to go with
her out of the house of the women unto the king's
house.
14 In the evening she went, and on the morrow
she returned into the second house of the women,
to the custody of Shaashgaz, the king's chamberlain, which kept the concubines: she came in unto
the king no more, except the king delighted in her,
and that she were called by name.
15 ¶ Now when the turn of Esther, the daughter
of Abihail the uncle of Mordecai, who had taken
her for his daughter, was come to go in unto the
king, she required nothing but what Hegai the
king's chamberlain, the keeper of the women,
appointed. And Esther obtained favour in the
sight of all them that looked upon her.
16 So Esther was taken unto king Ahasuerus into
his house royal in the tenth month, which *is* the
month Tebeth, in the seventh year of his reign.
17 And the king loved Esther above all the
women, and she obtained grace and favour in his
sight more than all the virgins; so that he set the
royal crown upon her head, and made her queen
instead of Vashti.
18 Then the king made a great feast unto all his
princes and his servants, *even* Esther's feast; and
he made a release to the provinces, and gave gifts,
according to the state of the king.
19 And when the virgins were gathered together
the second time, then Mordecai sat in the king's
gate.
20 Esther had not *yet* shewed her kindred nor her
people; as Mordecai had charged her: for Esther
did the commandment of Mordecai, like as when
she was brought up with him.
21 ¶ In those days, while Mordecai sat in the
king's gate, two of the king's chamberlains, Bigthan and Teresh, of those which kept the door,
were wroth, and sought to lay hand on the king
Ahasuerus.
22 And the thing was known to Mordecai, who
told *it* unto Esther the queen; and Esther certified
the king *thereof* in Mordecai's name.
23 And when inquisition was made of the matter,
it was found out; therefore they were both hanged
on a tree: and it was written in the book of the
chronicles before the king.

2:8 *women.* The royal harem.

2:9 *meet.* Suitable. *preferred.* Esther received much preference by the king's court and eventually by the king himself.

2:10 *kindred.* Race or lineage. We do not know why Mordecai charged her not to reveal her nationality.

2:12 *manner.* Custom or habit. *to wit.* That is.

2:14 *the morrow.* The next day.

2:15 *required.* Requested. *appointed.* Said. Esther showed wisdom and humility in not relying upon her own beauty, but in following the counsel of an official in the king's court (Prov. 12:15).

2:18 *made a release.* Proclaimed a holiday. *state.* Generosity.

2:19 *the second time.* This probably refers to the women being gathered after Esther had been made queen. *sat.* Held some official position. *the king's gate.* A place of legal importance in the city.

2:20 *Esther did the commandment of Mordecai.* Her submission and obedience to authority is a striking contrast to the disobedience of Vashti (1:12,16–17).

Mordecai Uncovers a Plot to Kill Ahasuerus (2:21–23)

2:21–23 This whole account proves to be no small event. Mordecai's discovery of this plot and faithfulness to report it to protect the king would change the course of his and Esther's life, along with the history of the Jewish people. One can see the invisible hand of God behind Mordecai's discovery.

2:21 *wroth.* Angry.

2:23 *inquisition.* Investigation.

Thoughts for Personal/Family Worship: Chapter 2

1. **The world prizes the outward appearance of people. The world, sadly, has no regard for the beauty of Christ (Isa. 53:2). The Bible prizes inward beauty, moral and spiritual beauty, particularly the beauty of a submissive spirit toward authority (1 Peter 3:3–6). This was a key character quality of Esther, who sought wise counsel and obeyed Mordecai (vv. 15,20). How can you be exercising and developing such humility? Do you follow the world's standards of beauty or God's?**
2. **Christ desires the beauty of His bride, as you can read in the messianic song, "So shall the king greatly desire thy beauty: for he is thy Lord; and worship thou him" (Ps. 45:11). Are you part of Christ's bride? Paul identified the bride of Christ by her submission to the Lord as her head (Eph. 5:23–24). Is your heart submitted to Jesus as Lord? How does that show in your actions?**

CHAPTER 3

AFTER these things did king Ahasuerus promote
Haman the son of Hammedatha the Agagite,
and advanced him, and set his seat above all the
princes that *were* with him.
2 And all the king's servants, that *were* in the
king's gate, bowed, and reverenced Haman: for
the king had so commanded concerning him. But
Mordecai bowed not, nor did *him* reverence.
3 Then the king's servants, which *were* in the
king's gate, said unto Mordecai, Why transgress-
est thou the king's commandment?
4 Now it came to pass, when they spake daily
unto him, and he hearkened not unto them,
that they told Haman, to see whether Mordecai's
matters would stand: for he had told them that
he *was* a Jew.
5 And when Haman saw that Mordecai bowed
not, nor did him reverence, then was Haman full
of wrath.
6 And he thought scorn to lay hands on Morde-
cai alone; for they had shewed him the people of
Mordecai: wherefore Haman sought to destroy all
the Jews that *were* throughout the whole kingdom
of Ahasuerus, *even* the people of Mordecai.
7 ¶ In the first month, that *is*, the month Nisan,
in the twelfth year of king Ahasuerus, they cast
Pur, that *is*, the lot, before Haman from day to day,
and from month to month, *to* the twelfth *month*,
that *is*, the month Adar.
8 ¶ And Haman said unto king Ahasuerus, There
is a certain people scattered abroad and dispersed
among the people in all the provinces of thy king-
dom; and their laws *are* diverse from all people;
neither keep they the king's laws: therefore it *is*
not for the king's profit to suffer them.
9 If it please the king, let it be written that they
may be destroyed: and I will pay ten thousand
talents of silver to the hands of those that have the
charge of the business, to bring *it* into the king's
treasuries.
10 And the king took his ring from his hand, and
gave it unto Haman the son of Hammedatha the
Agagite, the Jews' enemy.
11 And the king said unto Haman, The silver *is*
given to thee, the people also, to do with them as
it seemeth good to thee.
12 Then were the king's scribes called on the thir-
teenth day of the first month, and there was writ-
ten according to all that Haman had commanded
unto the king's lieutenants, and to the governors
that *were* over every province, and to the rulers of
every people of every province according to the
writing thereof, and *to* every people after their
language; in the name of king Ahasuerus was it
written, and sealed with the king's ring.
13 And the letters were sent by posts into all the
king's provinces, to destroy, to kill, and to cause to
perish, all Jews, both young and old, little children
and women, in one day, *even* upon the thirteenth
day of the twelfth month, which is the month
Adar, and *to take* the spoil of them for a prey.
14 The copy of the writing for a commandment to
be given in every province was published unto all
people, that they should be ready against that day.
15 The posts went out, being hastened by the

HAMAN'S PLOT TO KILL THE JEWS (3:1—4:17)

Chapter 3: ***Haman devises a devious plot to kill the Jews, which, once the king Ahasuerus makes it into an official law, cannot be broken.***

Haman Is Promoted (3:1–2)

3:1 *Haman . . . the Agagite.* Agag was the royal house of the Amalekites, a desert nation descending from Esau and one of Israel's ancient enemies and so cursed by God (Ex. 17:14; Num. 24:7; Deut. 25:17–19). *advanced him.* Promoted him. No reason is given why.

3:2 *did him reverence.* Honored him with a bow, either as an act of divine worship or mere respect for an authority (1 Sam. 24:8; 1 Kings 1:16,23). The combination of the verbs *bowed* and *reverenced* may imply that they honored *Haman* as a god (2 Chron. 7:3; 29:29; Pss. 22:29; 95:6). Alternatively, *Mordecai* may have refused to honor a man from a nation that God had cursed (v. 1).

Haman's Hatred for the Jews Grows Because Mordecai Refuses to Bow (3:3–6)

3:4 *matters.* Refusal to bow.

3:6 *scorn.* Haman despised the idea of killing only Mordecai. Such was his arrogance and malice that he would only be satisfied if Mordecai's people were destroyed.

King Ahasuerus Issues a Decree to Kill the Jews (3:7–15)

3:7 *twelfth year.* Five years have passed. This was about 64 years after the first exiles returned under Zerubbabel. *Pur.* Name for lots, which were cast to decide certain matters. Many in the Ancient Near East superstitiously sought to control events by casting small pebbles or dice in an attempt to evade fate, but the Lord controls *the lot* (Prov. 16:33). It is thought that the Persians cast lots in *the first month* of the year to determine when they should carry out important events.

3:8 *abroad.* Over a wide area. *neither keep they the king's laws.* Though believing Jews served a greater King than the Persian king, there is no evidence that they did not generally submit to the social order of Persia. Daniel's three friends disobeyed the king's edict (Dan. 3); however, many of the Jews also advised the kings and served them (e.g., Daniel and his friends, Ezra, Nehemiah). This is instead an early example of anti-Semitism. *to suffer.* Literally, "to rest," or to provide a safe haven for the Jews.

3:9 *ten thousand talents of silver.* This is a huge sum (Matt. 18:24). Haman probably anticipated paying for this bribe using the plunder of the Jews.

3:10 *ring.* The signet ring giving unlimited jurisdiction.

3:12 *lieutenants.* Provincial rulers.

3:13 *by posts.* By couriers. *prey.* Plunder.

3:14 *published.* Proclaimed or made known.

Thoughts for Personal/Family Worship: Chapter 3

1. **We do not know exactly what Mordecai's reason was for not bowing to Haman. However, we do know that the world wants us to submit to its schemes and often demands a public sign of submission (Dan. 3). When we**

king's commandment, and the decree was given in Shushan the palace. And the king and Haman sat down to drink; but the city Shushan was perplexed.

CHAPTER 4

WHEN Mordecai perceived all that was done,
Mordecai rent his clothes, and put on sackcloth
with ashes, and went out into the midst of the
city, and cried with a loud and a bitter cry;
2 And came even before the king's gate: for none
might enter into the king's gate clothed with
sackcloth.
3 And in every province, whithersoever the king's
commandment and his decree came, *there was*
great mourning among the Jews, and fasting, and
weeping, and wailing; and many lay in sackcloth
and ashes.
4 ¶ So Esther's maids and her chamberlains came
and told *it* her. Then was the queen exceedingly
grieved; and she sent raiment to clothe Mordecai,
and to take away his sackcloth from him: but he
received *it* not.
5 Then called Esther for Hatach, *one* of the king's
chamberlains, whom he had appointed to attend
upon her, and gave him a commandment to
Mordecai, to know what it *was*, and why it *was*.
6 So Hatach went forth to Mordecai unto the
street of the city, which *was* before the king's gate.
7 And Mordecai told him of all that had hap-
pened unto him, and of the sum of the money
that Haman had promised to pay to the king's
treasuries for the Jews, to destroy them.
8 Also he gave him the copy of the writing of the
decree that was given at Shushan to destroy them,
to shew *it* unto Esther, and to declare *it* unto her,
and to charge her that she should go in unto the
king, to make supplication unto him, and to make
request before him for her people.
9 And Hatach came and told Esther the words of
Mordecai.
10 ¶ Again Esther spake unto Hatach, and gave
him commandment unto Mordecai;
11 All the king's servants, and the people of
the king's provinces, do know, that whosoever,
whether man or woman, shall come unto the
king into the inner court, who is not called, *there
is* one law of his to put *him* to death, except such
to whom the king shall hold out the golden scep-
tre, that he may live: but I have not been called to
come in unto the king these thirty days.
12 And they told to Mordecai Esther's words.
13 Then Mordecai commanded to answer Esther,
Think not with thyself that thou shalt escape in
the king's house, more than all the Jews.
14 For if thou altogether holdest thy peace at this
time, *then* shall there enlargement and deliverance
arise to the Jews from another place; but thou and
thy father's house shall be destroyed: and who
knoweth whether thou art come to the kingdom
for *such* a time as this?
15 ¶ Then Esther bade *them* return Mordecai *this
answer*,
16 Go, gather together all the Jews that are present
in Shushan, and fast ye for me, and neither eat
nor drink three days, night or day: I also and my
maidens will fast likewise; and so will I go in unto
the king, which *is* not according to the law: and if
I perish, I perish.
17 So Mordecai went his way, and did according
to all that Esther had commanded him.

fail to fall into line, we face the consequences, which may include social isolation, insult, and incarceration—or worse. The great question is this: Will you bow to God alone with all your mind, heart, and strength?

2. **The way in which Haman schemed and bargained for the destruction of the Jews reminds us that the world hates God's people and delights in their destruction (John 15:18; Rev. 11:7–10; 20:7–9). Certainly the world showed its true colors when it tortured and murdered the Son of God on the cross. When you face persecutors, and rulers like Ahasuerus and Pontius Pilate, who permit such gross injustice, pray that as a Christian you will not respond in hatred but remember that you too were once full of hatred. Labor to be respectful and gentle to all men, hoping and praying that God will regenerate them by the Holy Spirit (Titus 3:1–8).**

Chapter 4: ***Mordecai urges Esther to consider seeing how her influence might be used for the good of her people.***

Mordecai Reveals the Plot to Esther (4:1–17)

4:1 *rent his clothes.* Tore them, a sign of grief, like wearing uncomfortable clothing (*sackcloth*) and *ashes* (Gen. 37:34; Jonah 3:5–6).

4:4 *her chamberlains.* Officials assigned to serve her. *raiment.* Garments.

4:5 *what it was, and why it was.* What was his present distress and the reason for it.

4:8 *make supplication.* Earnestly ask.

4:11 Esther ran the risk of losing her life if she approached in a way the king thought unfitting. Vashti's actions (ch. 1) made this a real possibility and hung as a cloud over this proposed course of action.

4:14 *holdest thy peace.* Remain silent. *enlargement.* Relief. If Esther refused to help, the Lord would preserve His people but judge her. *for such a time as this.* Mordecai encouraged Esther to see her rise to the position of queen as God's providence, positioning her to be His instrument to save His people.

4:15 *bade.* Asked.

4:16 *fast ye for me.* Abstaining from food is a means of humbling oneself, concentrating one's mind, and stirring one's heart for serious prayer (Ezra 8:23; Neh. 1:4). *not according to the law.* The immutable Persian *law* is a main focus of the book of Esther that drives the plot and anticipation of the whole book. Here Esther chooses to willingly disobey *the law* in hopes of saving her people. *if I perish, I perish.* Her spirit of submission to God's will and self-sacrifice is an image of Christ.

CHAPTER 5

NOW it came to pass on the third day, that Esther
put on *her* royal *apparel*, and stood in the inner
court of the king's house, over against the king's
house: and the king sat upon his royal throne in
the royal house, over against the gate of the house.
2 And it was so, when the king saw Esther the
queen standing in the court, *that* she obtained
favour in his sight: and the king held out to Esther
the golden sceptre that *was* in his hand. So Esther
drew near, and touched the top of the sceptre.
3 Then said the king unto her, What wilt thou,
queen Esther? and what *is* thy request? it shall be
even given thee to the half of the kingdom.
4 And Esther answered, If *it seem* good unto the
king, let the king and Haman come this day unto
the banquet that I have prepared for him.
5 Then the king said, Cause Haman to make
haste, that he may do as Esther hath said. So the
king and Haman came to the banquet that Esther
had prepared.
6 ¶ And the king said unto Esther at the banquet
of wine, What *is* thy petition? and it shall be
granted thee: and what *is* thy request? even to the
half of the kingdom it shall be performed.
7 Then answered Esther, and said, My petition
and my request *is;*
8 If I have found favour in the sight of the king,
and if it please the king to grant my petition, and
to perform my request, let the king and Haman
come to the banquet that I shall prepare for them,
and I will do to morrow as the king hath said.
9 ¶ Then went Haman forth that day joyful and
with a glad heart: but when Haman saw Morde-
cai in the king's gate, that he stood not up, nor
moved for him, he was full of indignation against
Mordecai.
10 Nevertheless Haman refrained himself: and
when he came home, he sent and called for his
friends, and Zeresh his wife.
11 And Haman told them of the glory of his
riches, and the multitude of his children, and all
the things wherein the king had promoted him,
and how he had advanced him above the princes
and servants of the king.
12 Haman said moreover, Yea, Esther the queen
did let no man come in with the king unto the
banquet that she had prepared but myself; and to
morrow am I invited unto her also with the king.
13 Yet all this availeth me nothing, so long as I see
Mordecai the Jew sitting at the king's gate.
14 ¶ Then said Zeresh his wife and all his friends
unto him, Let a gallows be made of fifty cubits
high, and to morrow speak thou unto the king
that Mordecai may be hanged thereon: then go
thou in merrily with the king unto the banquet.
And the thing pleased Haman; and he caused the
gallows to be made.

Thoughts for Personal/Family Worship: Chapter 4

1. **Though God's name does not appear in the book of Esther, Mordecai's conviction that deliverance will come to the Jews (v. 14) clearly suggests he has confidence in the fact that God would not forsake His people and promise. His confidence in God's providence did not make him passive however, but energized him to call Esther to act decisively for her people. Believing that God is in control never excuses us from using our position and abilities for the good of His people. Instead, it gives us hope that God has put us here for that very purpose, and will therefore give success to our efforts to serve His cause. How do God's promises energize you?**
2. **Esther listened to the counsel of Mordecai, evidently believed the promises of God about His people, and resolved to take action. And yet she needed discernment about her course of action and called for fasting (v. 16) and presumably prayer as well. Likewise with us, knowing the will of God requires listening to wise people whom God places in our lives (especially parents and pastors), knowing and believing His Word, resolving to obey Him at any cost, and praying for His wisdom while asking other Christians to pray too. What significant decisions are you facing or will you face soon? How can you use these same means to discern God's will?**

HAMAN'S DEMISE AND MORDECAI'S EXALTATION (5:1—8:2)

Chapter 5: ***Ahasuerus agrees to Esther's request for a banquet, while Haman prepares a gallows to execute Mordecai, infuriated by Mordecai's continued slights.***

Esther Pleases the King and Has a Banquet (5:1–8)

5:1 *apparel.* Clothing. *stood in the inner court.* Uninvited into Ahasuerus's presence, Esther has taken her life into her hands (4:11). Having put away Queen Vashti in his rashness, Ahasuerus may kill her. *over against.* Opposite of.
5:3 *What wilt thou?* What do you want? *half of the kingdom.* A grandiose exaggeration (Mark 6:23).
5:4 *banquet that I have prepared.* Esther again showed her wisdom by pleasing the king before making her request, using the very means to honor him by which Vashti dishonored and offended him, a feast (ch. 1). *Haman.* Perhaps invited so that he would not suspect anything.
5:6 *petition.* Request.
5:7–8 Whether Esther delayed her request because she lost courage, or to further win the king's heart, we do not know, but in God's providence this delay led to major developments in the situation (ch. 6).

Haman Plots Mordecai's Death (5:9–14)

5:9 *nor moved.* Did not tremble.
5:11 Haman gloated over his apparent good fortune with the king and queen. Pride comes before a fall (Prov. 16:18).
5:13 *availeth me nothing.* Is not enough. No measure of honor can satisfy the proud man; he always wants more.
5:14 *gallows.* Literally, "tree," used for a wooden pole or structure of wooden lumber (6:4; 7:9–10; 8:7; 9:13,25). *fifty cubits.* About 75 feet. *Haman* wanted to show everyone his triumph over his enemy.

Thoughts for Personal/Family Worship: Chapter 5

1. **What a difference there is between Ahasuerus's throne and the Lord's throne! Because of Christ, heaven's throne is called a throne of grace, which is always open**

CHAPTER 6

On that night could not the king sleep, and he
commanded to bring the book of records of the
chronicles; and they were read before the king.
2 And it was found written, that Mordecai had
told of Bigthana and Teresh, two of the king's
chamberlains, the keepers of the door, who
sought to lay hand on the king Ahasuerus.
3 And the king said, What honour and dignity
hath been done to Mordecai for this? Then said
the king's servants that ministered unto him,
There is nothing done for him.
4 ¶ And the king said, Who *is* in the court? Now
Haman was come into the outward court of the
king's house, to speak unto the king to hang Mor-
decai on the gallows that he had prepared for him.
5 And the king's servants said unto him, Behold,
Haman standeth in the court. And the king said,
Let him come in.
6 So Haman came in. And the king said unto
him, What shall be done unto the man whom the
king delighteth to honour? Now Haman thought
in his heart, To whom would the king delight to
do honour more than to myself?
7 And Haman answered the king, For the man
whom the king delighteth to honour,
8 Let the royal apparel be brought which the king
useth to wear, and the horse that the king rideth
upon, and the crown royal which is set upon his
head:
9 And let this apparel and horse be delivered to
the hand of one of the king's most noble princes,
that they may array the man *withal* whom the
king delighteth to honour, and bring him on
horseback through the street of the city, and
proclaim before him, Thus shall it be done to the
man whom the king delighteth to honour.
10 Then the king said to Haman, Make haste, *and*
take the apparel and the horse, as thou hast said,
and do even so to Mordecai the Jew, that sitteth
at the king's gate: let nothing fail of all that thou
hast spoken.
11 Then took Haman the apparel and the horse,
and arrayed Mordecai, and brought him on
horseback through the street of the city, and
proclaimed before him, Thus shall it be done unto
the man whom the king delighteth to honour.
12 ¶ And Mordecai came again to the king's gate.
But Haman hasted to his house mourning, and
having his head covered.
13 And Haman told Zeresh his wife and all his
friends every *thing* that had befallen him. Then
said his wise men and Zeresh his wife unto him, If
Mordecai *be* of the seed of the Jews, before whom
thou hast begun to fall, thou shalt not prevail
against him, but shalt surely fall before him.
14 And while they *were* yet talking with him,
came the king's chamberlains, and hasted to
bring Haman unto the banquet that Esther had
prepared.

---

for needy sinners to come to "obtain mercy, and find grace to help in time of need" (Heb. 4:16). As believers praise God that we can come before the Lord's throne with boldness (Heb. 10:19–22).

2. **When Esther fasted and sought God with God's people (4:16), it resulted in remarkable courage and wisdom. She risked her life to speak with the king in order to save Israel. Yet she did not rashly rush to him, demanding help, but thoughtfully and with apparent calmness, invited him to a feast. This is the power of God's grace obtained through fervent prayer. While this was brought about through a crisis, it was also the result of habits of humility developed over years (2:15,20). How can you grow in wisdom and peace like Esther, so that you can respond well to crises?**
3. **Haman's arrogance, we might say, was 75 feet high. The perceived insult of a single man outweighed all the honor and wealth he had received. As a result, he was provoked to murder a faithful servant in the king's administration. Which weighs most heavily upon your heart: gratitude for the honors and blessings you have undeservedly received or an insult? Beware, lest your pride drive you to hatred and perhaps even the harm of others.**

Chapter 6: *A sleepless night occasions a dramatic turn of events for Mordecai and Haman and anticipates Haman's ultimate downfall.*

Haman Humiliated and Mordecai Exalted (6:1–14)

6:1–2 *records of the chronicles.* All Persian kings kept *records* of their acts. *Mordecai had told.* See 2:21–23. *chamberlains.* Officials of the king's administration. The inability of the king to *sleep* and the circumstance of reading about the particular event where Mordecai protected the king are examples of God's secret providence directing human lives (1 Sam. 9:1–16; see note at James 4:15).

6:3 *honour and dignity.* The Persian kings prided themselves in rewarding handsomely those who helped them. Up until this point Mordecai had not been rewarded.

6:6 *To whom would the king delight to do honour more than to myself?* Again, Haman's pride is ridiculously puffed up and will prove to be the means of his own downfall (5:9–14).

6:8 *apparel . . . which the king useth to wear.* Clothing ordinarily worn by the king. The individual would be honored like a king among the people.

6:9 *array.* Clothe. *withal.* With it.

6:10 *Make haste.* Hurry, be quick.

6:12 *hasted.* Went quickly. *head covered.* A sign of humiliation or shame, and a foreshadowing of his doom (7:8).

6:13 *befallen him.* Happened to him. *seed of the Jews.* An allusion to God's covenant with Abraham (Gen. 17:7) and promise that the seed of the woman would *prevail* against the seed of the serpent (Gen. 3:15). Though *Haman* sought to crush *the Jews,* God would give victory to His people for there had to be an Israel for there to be the Christ (John 4:22; Rom. 9:4–5).

6:14 *hasted to bring.* Quickly or anxiously brought. Haman's time had come, and the Lord dealt with him quickly.

Thoughts for Personal/Family Worship: Chapter 6

1. **God's providence not only appears in mighty miracles, but in mundane events like a king who cannot sleep and so reads some boring government records. Billions of**

CHAPTER 7

So the king and Haman came to banquet with
Esther the queen.
2 And the king said again unto Esther on the
second day at the banquet of wine, What *is* thy
petition, queen Esther? and it shall be granted
thee: and what *is* thy request? and it shall be
performed, *even* to the half of the kingdom.
3 Then Esther the queen answered and said, If I
have found favour in thy sight, O king, and if it
please the king, let my life be given me at my peti-
tion, and my people at my request:
4 For we are sold, I and my people, to be destroyed,
to be slain, and to perish. But if we had been sold
for bondmen and bondwomen, I had held my
tongue, although the enemy could not countervail
the king's damage.
5 ¶ Then the king Ahasuerus answered and said
unto Esther the queen, Who is he, and where is he,
that durst presume in his heart to do so?
6 And Esther said, The adversary and enemy
is this wicked Haman. Then Haman was afraid
before the king and the queen.
7 ¶ And the king arising from the banquet of
wine in his wrath *went* into the palace garden:
and Haman stood up to make request for his life
to Esther the queen; for he saw that there was evil
determined against him by the king.
8 Then the king returned out of the palace
garden into the place of the banquet of wine; and
Haman was fallen upon the bed whereon Esther
was. Then said the king, Will he force the queen
also before me in the house? As the word went out
of the king's mouth, they covered Haman's face.
9 And Harbonah, one of the chamberlains, said
before the king, Behold also, the gallows fifty cubits
high, which Haman had made for Mordecai, who
had spoken good for the king, standeth in the
house of Haman. Then the king said, Hang him
thereon.
10 So they hanged Haman on the gallows that he
had prepared for Mordecai. Then was the king's
wrath pacified.

CHAPTER 8

On that day did the king Ahasuerus give the
house of Haman the Jews' enemy unto Esther the

such events take place every day, and we scarcely notice them, but the Lord directs every one of them according to His decree (Eph. 1:11). His timing is perfect, reminding the king of Mordecai's faithfulness just as Haman comes to have him hung. How can this give Christians hope to know that this God of providence is our Father?

2. **Haman was a high official in the mighty Persian Empire, but he could not destroy a conquered and dispersed people, for they were the people of the living God. On the contrary, his empty boasting and foolish pride only led him into shame and defeat. Let us not fear those who persecute the church, but rather pity them and pray for them.**

Chapter 7: ***At the second banquet, Esther reveals the plot of Haman to kill the Jews, and the king orders Haman to be killed on the gallows he built for Mordecai.***

The Death of Haman and Exaltation of Mordecai (7:1—8:2)

7:3 *my life . . . and my people.* Esther's plea was both wise and risky. It was wise because the king might be strongly motivated to save the Jews when he discovered they were the people of his beloved queen. Yet it was personally a great risk, for he could easily kill her with the Jews and find another queen.
7:4 *I and my people.* Again, Esther closely identified herself with them, tying their destiny together as one. *to be destroyed, to be slain, and to perish.* The words of the decree against the Jews (3:13; 8:11), implicitly identifying her people, though she did not explicitly name them yet. *bondmen and bondwomen.* Slaves. *countervail the king's damage.* Compensate for the loss of revenue to the king resulting from the death of the Jews.
7:5 *Who is he.* Ahasuerus did not yet grasp that she was a Jew. *durst.* Dared to.
7:7 *wrath.* Anger; because *Haman* sold the Jewish people and the king's wife to death.
7:8 *bed.* Couch. *force.* Molest. *word went out.* A phrase alluding to the king's sentence. *covered Haman's face.* To cover the head was a sign of mourning (6:12; 2 Sam. 15:30; Jer. 14:3–4); this was a sign of Haman's imminent death.
7:9–10 *gallows.* Literally, "tree" (see note at 5:14). In the law of Moses, hanging a person's body upon a tree or pole of wood was a sign of dying under God's curse (Deut. 21:22–23). *spoken good for the king.* In uncovering the plot to assassinate him (2:21–23; 6:2). *Hang him.* Haman's instrument to destroy Mordecai became the means of his own death. *wrath pacified.* Anger subsided.

Thoughts for Personal/Family Worship: Chapter 7

1. **Esther here is a picture of Christ. Just as Esther publicly identified herself with the Jewish nation so that the king would not destroy them, so Christ publicly identified with His people of all nations so that His Father would not destroy them. Esther risked her life by identifying with the Jews; Christ gave His life as the substitute and surety of His people, bearing the punishment for their sins. Esther pled for her nation, and Christ intercedes for each of His children from heaven. How does this picture help you appreciate the work of Christ on your behalf?**
2. **Haman's devices were all brought to light and punished. Many today walk in pride and seem to have everything going for them. God's Word reminds us that the day is coming when everything that has been done in secret will be brought into full light (1 Cor. 4:5). How does Haman's story motivate you to be humble and live in the fear of the Lord?**
3. **Haman's death illustrates the work of Christ, yet with great irony. Haman was destroyed by the gallows he constructed for Mordecai. Like Haman, Satan plotted Christ's destruction through the cross, only to have his power shattered by Christ's death (John 12:31–33; 13:2; 14:30; 16:11). However, though Haman was hung upon the gallows (Hebrew, "tree"), it was not Satan but Jesus Christ who was hung upon the cross ("tree," Acts 5:30; 10:39; 13:29) to pacify God's righteous wrath by bearing the curse of God against lawbreakers (Gal. 3:13). Oh, the**

queen. And Mordecai came before the king; for
Esther had told what he *was* unto her.
2 And the king took off his ring, which he had
taken from Haman, and gave it unto Mordecai.
And Esther set Mordecai over the house of Haman.
3 ¶ And Esther spake yet again before the king,
and fell down at his feet, and besought him
with tears to put away the mischief of Haman
the Agagite, and his device that he had devised
against the Jews.
4 Then the king held out the golden sceptre
toward Esther. So Esther arose, and stood before
the king,
5 And said, If it please the king, and if I have
found favour in his sight, and the thing *seem* right
before the king, and I *be* pleasing in his eyes, let it
be written to reverse the letters devised by Haman
the son of Hammedatha the Agagite, which he
wrote to destroy the Jews which *are* in all the
king's provinces:
6 For how can I endure to see the evil that shall
come unto my people? or how can I endure to see
the destruction of my kindred?
7 ¶ Then the king Ahasuerus said unto Esther the
queen and to Mordecai the Jew, Behold, I have
given Esther the house of Haman, and him they
have hanged upon the gallows, because he laid his
hand upon the Jews.
8 Write ye also for the Jews, as it liketh you, in the
king's name, and seal *it* with the king's ring: for
the writing which is written in the king's name,
and sealed with the king's ring, may no man
reverse.
9 Then were the king's scribes called at that time
in the third month, that *is*, the month Sivan, on
the three and twentieth *day* thereof; and it was
written according to all that Mordecai com-
manded unto the Jews, and to the lieutenants, and
the deputies and rulers of the provinces which *are*
from India unto Ethiopia, an hundred twenty and
seven provinces, unto every province according to
the writing thereof, and unto every people after
their language, and to the Jews according to their
writing, and according to their language.
10 And he wrote in the king Ahasuerus' name,
and sealed *it* with the king's ring, and sent letters
by posts on horseback, *and* riders on mules,
camels, *and* young dromedaries:
11 Wherein the king granted the Jews which *were*
in every city to gather themselves together, and to
stand for their life, to destroy, to slay, and to cause
to perish, all the power of the people and prov-
ince that would assault them, *both* little ones and
women, and *to take* the spoil of them for a prey,
12 Upon one day in all the provinces of king
Ahasuerus, *namely*, upon the thirteenth *day* of
the twelfth month, which *is* the month Adar.
13 The copy of the writing for a commandment to
be given in every province *was* published unto all
people, and that the Jews should be ready against
that day to avenge themselves on their enemies.
14 *So* the posts that rode upon mules *and* camels
went out, being hastened and pressed on by the
king's commandment. And the decree was given
at Shushan the palace.
15 ¶ And Mordecai went out from the presence
of the king in royal apparel of blue and white, and
with a great crown of gold, and with a garment
of fine linen and purple: and the city of Shushan
rejoiced and was glad.
16 The Jews had light, and gladness, and joy, and
honour.
17 And in every province, and in every city,
whithersoever the king's commandment and his
decree came, the Jews had joy and gladness, a
feast and a good day. And many of the people of
the land became Jews; for the fear of the Jews fell
upon them.

---

wonder of His love! Worship Christ in light of this strange victory: death for Him and salvation for sinners!

Chapter 8: *Though the former decree cannot be undone, another decree will permit the Jews to defend themselves.*

8:2 *his ring.* A sign of authority (3:10,12). *Mordecai* was promoted to Haman's old position. *over the house.* All of Haman's great wealth and possessions (5:11) becomes Mordecai's.

THE KING'S SECOND DECREE (8:3—9:32)

The King Issues a Second Decree to Save the Jews (8:3–17)

8:3 *besought him.* Asked for grace from him. With Haman himself out of the way, Esther approached the king again asking that he nullify the evil (*mischief*) of Haman's plan (*device*).

8:5 Even though Ahasuerus had been at least partially tricked into the previous decree, *to reverse* a royal order was another issue altogether.

8:8 The king helped Esther and Mordecai, directing them to write the appropriate law.

8:9 *the month Sivan, on the three and twentieth day.* Two months and ten days after Haman's decree. *lieutenants.* Provincial rulers.

8:10 *posts.* Couriers (v. 14).

8:11 *stand for their life.* Defend themselves.

8:15 *apparel.* Clothing. Mordecai was glorified with *royal* garments. The *blue* (or violet) and *purple* cloth and *gold* signified his authority in the kingdom of the Persian Empire (1:6–7); they were also associated with the tabernacle and priesthood (Ex. 25:3–4; 28:5–6,36–37).

8:16 *had light, and gladness, and joy, and honour.* A happy contrast to their response to the previous edict (4:3).

8:17 *became Jews.* When God performs great acts of deliverance, He draws people to Himself.

Thoughts for Personal/Family Worship: Chapter 8

1. Just as Ahasuerus gave Mordecai his signet ring and glorified him as a great prince in the Persian Empire in order to save the Jews from destruction, so God the Father has given Jesus Christ all authority in heaven and earth as our exalted Priest and King in order to save His people from eternal destruction (Matt. 28:18; John 17:2;

CHAPTER 9

NOW in the twelfth month, that *is*, the month
Adar, on the thirteenth day of the same, when the
king's commandment and his decree drew near to
be put in execution, in the day that the enemies of
the Jews hoped to have power over them, (though
it was turned to the contrary, that the Jews had
rule over them that hated them;)
2 The Jews gathered themselves together in their
cities throughout all the provinces of the king
Ahasuerus, to lay hand on such as sought their
hurt: and no man could withstand them; for the
fear of them fell upon all people.
3 And all the rulers of the provinces, and the lieu-
tenants, and the deputies, and officers of the king,
helped the Jews; because the fear of Mordecai fell
upon them.
4 For Mordecai *was* great in the king's house, and
his fame went out throughout all the provinces:
for this man Mordecai waxed greater and greater.
5 Thus the Jews smote all their enemies with the
stroke of the sword, and slaughter, and destruc-
tion, and did what they would unto those that
hated them.
6 And in Shushan the palace the Jews slew and
destroyed five hundred men.
7 And Parshandatha, and Dalphon, and Aspatha,
8 And Poratha, and Adalia, and Aridatha,
9 And Parmashta, and Arisai, and Aridai, and
Vajezatha,
10 The ten sons of Haman the son of Hammeda-
tha, the enemy of the Jews, slew they; but on the
spoil laid they not their hand.
11 On that day the number of those that were
slain in Shushan the palace was brought before
the king.
12 ¶ And the king said unto Esther the queen,
The Jews have slain and destroyed five hundred
men in Shushan the palace, and the ten sons of
Haman; what have they done in the rest of the
king's provinces? now what *is* thy petition? and
it shall be granted thee: or what *is* thy request
further? and it shall be done.
13 Then said Esther, If it please the king, let it be
granted to the Jews which *are* in Shushan to do to
morrow also according unto this day's decree, and
let Haman's ten sons be hanged upon the gallows.
14 And the king commanded it so to be done:
and the decree was given at Shushan; and they
hanged Haman's ten sons.
15 For the Jews that *were* in Shushan gathered
themselves together on the fourteenth day also of
the month Adar, and slew three hundred men at
Shushan; but on the prey they laid not their hand.
16 But the other Jews that *were* in the king's prov-
inces gathered themselves together, and stood for
their lives, and had rest from their enemies, and
slew of their foes seventy and five thousand, but
they laid not their hands on the prey,
17 On the thirteenth day of the month Adar; and
on the fourteenth day of the same rested they, and
made it a day of feasting and gladness.
18 But the Jews that *were* at Shushan assembled
together on the thirteenth *day* thereof, and on the
fourteenth thereof; and on the fifteenth *day* of the
same they rested, and made it a day of feasting
and gladness.
19 Therefore the Jews of the villages, that dwelt

Heb. 8:1). He is glorified at the Father's right hand with unspeakable beauty, joy, and riches. If we belong to Christ, what things are ours (1 Cor. 3:21–23) and how is God working on our behalf (Rom. 8:28,32)?

2. **Note the great joy of the Jews as the king grants Esther's petition to respond in like to their enemies (vv. 15–17). The Jews had essentially been brought back from a sentence of death. If the Jews' redemption from physical death caused such joy and elation, how much more should this be so of us, if we have been redeemed from a far greater death than physical death? Why then do Christians sometimes have so little joy? Look in Phil. 4:4 for the key. Just as the Jews rejoiced in the glory of Mordecai, so believers must focus their minds and engage their hearts to rejoice in the glory of Jesus Christ, our heavenly King.**

Chapter 9: ***On the day the Jews would have been destroyed, they instead defeat their enemies, and the celebration of Purim is instituted.***

The Jews Are Saved from Destruction (9:1–19)

9:1 *hoped to have power.* Despite the king's decree allowing the Jews to defend themselves, many still hoped to destroy them.

9:2 *no man could withstand them.* Despite the fact that the Jews were assailed, their enemies could not prevail. Like many times in the past, the Lord miraculously delivered His people from the hands of their enemies.

9:3 Mordecai's high position won the Jews the favor of the government officials, such as *lieutenants* or provincial rulers.

9:4 *waxed.* Became, grew.

9:10 *The ten sons of Haman.* The Jews destroyed the seed of *Haman*, fulfilling God's ancient curse upon the Amalekites (see note at 3:1). *on the spoil laid they not their hand.* Their property was untouched. Unlike King Saul, they were not motivated by mercenary gain and knew they should not take the plunder (1 Sam. 15:1–23).

9:13 *hanged upon the gallows.* A request to display the bodies of Haman's dead sons (v. 10), as a public warning to the enemies of the Jews.

9:15 *prey.* Booty or plunder.

9:16–18 *seventy and five thousand.* An indication of the powerful forces that would have slaughtered the Jews under Haman's decree. *had rest from their enemies . . . rested . . . rested.* The language here is similar to that of the defeat of the Canaanites in the Promised Land through Joshua and David (Deut. 12:10; 25:19; Josh. 1:13,15; 21:44; 22:4; 23:1; 1 Chron. 22:9,18; 23:25).

9:19 The Jews in Shushan celebrated the Feast of Purim on the fifteenth day because they had a second day of slaughtering their enemies. The Jews in the provinces celebrated it on

in the unwalled towns, made the fourteenth day
of the month Adar *a day of* gladness and feast-
ing, and a good day, and of sending portions one
to another.
20 ¶ And Mordecai wrote these things, and sent
letters unto all the Jews that *were* in all the prov-
inces of the king Ahasuerus, *both* nigh and far,
21 To stablish *this* among them, that they should
keep the fourteenth day of the month Adar, and
the fifteenth day of the same, yearly,
22 As the days wherein the Jews rested from their
enemies, and the month which was turned unto
them from sorrow to joy, and from mourning
into a good day: that they should make them days
of feasting and joy, and of sending portions one to
another, and gifts to the poor.
23 And the Jews undertook to do as they had
begun, and as Mordecai had written unto them;
24 Because Haman the son of Hammedatha, the
Agagite, the enemy of all the Jews, had devised
against the Jews to destroy them, and had cast
Pur, that *is*, the lot, to consume them, and to de-
stroy them;
25 But when *Esther* came before the king, he
commanded by letters that his wicked device,
which he devised against the Jews, should return
upon his own head, and that he and his sons
should be hanged on the gallows.
26 Wherefore they called these days Purim after
the name of Pur. Therefore for all the words of
this letter, and *of that* which they had seen con-
cerning this matter, and which had come unto
them,
27 The Jews ordained, and took upon them,
and upon their seed, and upon all such as joined
themselves unto them, so as it should not fail, that
they would keep these two days according to their
writing, and according to their *appointed* time
every year;
28 And *that* these days *should be* remembered
and kept throughout every generation, every
family, every province, and every city; and *that*
these days of Purim should not fail from among
the Jews, nor the memorial of them perish from
their seed.
29 Then Esther the queen, the daughter of
Abihail, and Mordecai the Jew, wrote with all
authority, to confirm this second letter of Purim.
30 And he sent the letters unto all the Jews, to the
hundred twenty and seven provinces of the king-
dom of Ahasuerus, *with* words of peace and truth,
31 To confirm these days of Purim in their times
appointed, according as Mordecai the Jew and
Esther the queen had enjoined them, and as they
had decreed for themselves and for their seed, the
matters of the fastings and their cry.
32 And the decree of Esther confirmed these
matters of Purim; and it was written in the book.

CHAPTER 10

AND the king Ahasuerus laid a tribute upon the
land, and *upon* the isles of the sea.
2 And all the acts of his power and of his might,
and the declaration of the greatness of Mordecai,
whereunto the king advanced him, *are* they not

---

the *fourteenth* day because they were done slaughtering their enemies on the thirteenth day.

Purim Instituted (9:20–32)

9:20 *nigh.* Near. This closing section of the chapter (vv. 20–32) summarizes the events that led to the celebration of Purim.

9:21 *stablish.* Literally, "cause to stand"; establish by power or legal authority (Ruth 4:7 [confirm]; 2 Chron. 7:18). The same word is translated "ordained" (v. 27), "confirm" (vv. 29,31–32), "enjoined" (v. 31), and "decreed" (v. 31). Its repetition emphasizes the importance and obligation to remember God's work of saving the Jews through Esther and Mordecai.

9:25 *device.* Plot.

9:26 *Purim.* Plural of the Hebrew word *Pur* or "lot" (v. 24).

9:32 *the decree of Esther confirmed these matters of Purim.* The Jews did not have the spiritual authority to invent a new element of public worship (Lev. 10:1–3; Deut. 12:32). The decree of Purim entailed no special ceremonies for the priests or temple service. However, God's people and civil rulers may set aside special days of thanksgiving for God's acts of mercy, and so they did.

Thoughts for Personal/Family Worship: Chapter 9

1. **In an amazing reversal, the destruction of the Jews was turned into their victory over their enemies. The seed of Israel went from the bottom to the top. Our God is a God of great reversals (1 Sam. 2:4–8; Luke 1:52–53), the greatest of which is the resurrection from the dead of Christ, who died the accursed death on the cross, and His exaltation to God's right hand. Christian, even if you are the lowest of the low in this world, take heart. Humble yourself right now before the Lord, and He will lift you up, even into the glory of Jesus Christ.**
2. **God's works deserve to be commemorated. Though all the shadows of the Old Testament, including the feasts, are fulfilled in Christ (Col. 2:16–17), Christians are called to lives of sacrifice to God for the redemption He has performed. We are also called weekly to commemorate the final victory of Christ over death in His resurrection (1 Cor. 16:1–2; Heb. 10:25). Christians should ever be characterized by giving thanks to God for His mercies to oneself, one's family, one's people, and the church throughout the world.**

Chapter 10: *Esther concludes with Mordecai's greatness being recounted.*

EPILOGUE (10:1–3)

10:1 *laid a tribute.* Imposed a tax or requirement of labor. *Ahasuerus* or Xerxes I, after failing in his military campaigns against Greece, completed massive building projects of roads, monuments, and his palace, the cost of which placed heavy demands on his subjects. *isles of the sea.* Coasts or islands, representing the farthest reaches of the empire.

10:2 *his might . . . the book of the chronicles of the kings.* The careers of Ahasuerus and Mordecai are summed up much as

written in the book of the chronicles of the kings of Media and Persia?
3 For Mordecai the Jew *was* next unto king Ahasuerus, and great among the Jews, and accepted of the multitude of his brethren, seeking the wealth of his people, and speaking peace to all his seed.

the kings of Israel and Judah (1 Kings 15:23; 16:5,27; 22:45; 2 Kings 10:34; 13:8,12; 14:15,28; 20:20). Though he was not of the line of David (2:5), Mordecai was a reminder that even under Persian domination the hope of the coming King remained alive.

10:3 *wealth*. Good. *speaking peace*. Mordecai became a symbol of God's purpose of peace with His people, and made it his habit to remind the Jews of it. *to all his seed*. Parallel to and explained by *his people*, that is, not just Mordecai's offspring but all the Jews (6:13). This language may allude to God's promises of blessed offspring to Abraham and David (Gen. 17:7,19; 2 Sam. 22:51; Neh. 9:8).

Thoughts for Personal/Family Worship: Chapter 10

This book concludes with a lovely image of Mordecai reigning as the king's right-hand man for the peace of the covenant seed. Christ is our peace through His blood, and the gospel is His proclamation of peace to those near and far, Jew and Gentile (Eph. 2:14–17). He reigns forever over heaven and earth and is enjoying the fulfillment of God's promise that He will see His spiritual seed and be satisfied with the fruit of His sorrows (Isa. 53:10). He is a far better king than any Persian emperor, for rather than using up His subjects' money and labor, He gives them all good gifts (Eph. 4:7–8). Are you part of Christ's spiritual family? Has He spoken peace to your soul through the gospel of His death for sinners? Does He reign over you as your Lord? Is He your hope for glory? If so, rejoice. If not, pray for grace to surrender to Christ today.

THY WORD IS *a Lamp* UNTO MY FEET AND *a Light* UNTO MY PATH

PSALM 119:105

INTRODUCTION TO THE BOOKS OF POETRY & WISDOM

Understanding Hebrew poetry helps in interpreting much of the Bible, since approximately one-third of the Old Testament is poetry, with portions in every major section of the Old Testament. Unlike English poetry that depends so much on sound effects of rhyme and meter, Hebrew poetry is based more on components of thought rather than sound. Although Hebrew at times plays on the sound, either by way of alliteration or assonance, it primarily rhymes the meaning rather than the sound. This repetition of thought is called parallelism. Consequently and almost uniquely, Hebrew poetry is translatable into other languages in ways that retain the poetic effect and beauty of the original. Furthermore, by repeating ideas often using vivid imagery, the message is imprinted on the memory through the stirring of the emotions.

There are five standard types of parallelism.

1. *Synonymous Parallelism:* In this pattern, the second line repeats the idea of the first by using synonymous expressions. Consider Ps. 49:1.

   Hear this all ye people;
   Give ear all ye inhabitants of the world.

   Or Ps. 103:14

   For he knoweth our frame;
   He remembereth that we are dust.

   This example illustrates how the parallelism aids in interpretation. Although the thought is the same, the second line is more specific identifying what God knows about our frame. Hebrew poetry often interprets itself. Psalm 16:10, for instance, is a classic example of the second line interpreting the first, making it clear that "hell" refers to the grave (the place of "corruption") just as the New Testament says (Acts 2:31; 13:35–37).

2. *Antithetic Parallelism:* In this pattern, the second line states the opposite idea or makes a contrast with the first. This type is especially common in Proverbs. Consider Prov. 15:1.

   A soft answer turneth away wrath;
   But grievous words stir up anger.

3. *Emblematic or Comparative Parallelism:* In this pattern, one line explains the other by using some analogy. Consider Ps. 42:1.

   As the hart panteth after the water brooks,
   So panteth my soul after thee, O God.

4. *Climactic or Stair-like Parallelism:* In this pattern, each line advances or builds on the thought of the preceding line creating a stair-like effect. Each line begins with the same word or expression with the following line adding new information. Consider Ps. 29:1–2.

   Give unto the LORD O ye mighty,
   Give unto the LORD glory and strength.
   Give unto the LORD the glory due unto his name.

5. *Synthetic Parallelism:* In this pattern, the second line progresses the thought of the first rather than repeating or contrasting it. The two lines together express one complete thought. Consider Ps. 2:6.

   Yet have I set my king
   Upon my holy hill of Zion.

   Or Prov. 15:16

   Better is little with the fear of the LORD
   Than great treasure and trouble therewith.

Another outstanding feature of poetry is the common use of figures of speech. Figures of speech can occur in prose as well, but they are far more prominent in poetry. Basically, by using figures of speech authors refer to their principal topic in terms of another topic because there is some point of analogy between the topic and the image. Figures of speech can compress ideas into a few words that otherwise may require full sentences to convey. Recognizing and interpreting them properly is a key concern when reading poetry. It is not possible here to list, define, and illustrate all of the categories of figures, but these are some of the most common that you are likely to encounter.

1. *Simile:* A comparison between the topic and the image that uses the word "like" or "as." Jeremiah 23:29 says, "Is not my word *like as a fire* . . . and *like a hammer* that breaketh the rock in pieces?"
2. *Metaphor:* A direct comparison between the topic and the image without using "like" or "as." Psalm 28:7 says, "The LORD is . . . my shield." The Lord is not a round disk, but He is protection for His people.
3. *Metonymy:* The use of one word for another based on some point of association between the two words or thoughts. Second Kings 4:40 says there was "death in the pot." This means that there was something poisonous in the pot causing death, so death (the effect or consequence) is used to refer to poison (the cause).
4. *Synecdoche:* This is a specific type of metonymy where the part is used for the whole or the whole for a part. Psalm 63:3 says, "my lips shall praise thee." The psalmist means that he will praise the Lord, not just his lips.
5. *Personification:* This is when something inanimate is described in personal or living terms. Psalm 114:3 says, "The sea saw it, and fled."
6. *Hyperbole:* This is a purposeful exaggeration to drive home a truth. Deuteronomy 1:28 mentions cities that were "walled up to heaven," not in actual fact but expressive of the intimidating appearance.

Wisdom is a special category of poetry that can be classified either formally according to literary style or thematically according to content. Many Psalms fall within the wisdom category (1; 8; 19; 29; 49; etc.) and even sections from prose narrative (e.g., Samson's riddles, Judg. 14; parables of Nathan, 2 Sam. 12; and the woman of Tekoa, 2 Sam. 14). But there are four books that are designated as the wisdom books: Job, Proverbs, Ecclesiastes, and Song of Solomon. Jeremiah 18:18 identifies three groups of men who proclaimed God's word in the Old Testament era: priests, prophets, and wise men. God used Solomon, the greatest of all the wise men, to write much of Old Testament wisdom.

The Hebrew word for wisdom has the basic meaning of "skill or ability" that is applied in many spheres of life (for instance, a wise or skillful soldier, Isa. 10:13; a wise or skillful craftsman, Ex. 28:3). When applied to the ethical and moral sphere, it is the art or skill of performing the biblical ethic. Job teaches the skill of suffering well, how to face the anomalies of life. Proverbs teaches the skill of behaving well in every circumstance of life, how to relate religion to the routines of life. Ecclesiastes teaches the skill of enjoying and using life as a gift from God. Song of Solomon teaches the skill of maintaining and enjoying the God-given sanctity, beauty, and purity of marriage, particularly as a gospel sermon directing attention to the ideal marriage bond between Christ and His bride, the church.

The Wisdom books fall into two categories: didactic and reflective. Proverbs is didactic as it is concerned with matters of practical morality and ethics. Its many terse, right-to-the-point maxims deal with proper conduct in virtually every context of life. It shows what sanctified living looks like on a daily basis. The other books are reflective as they address the problems and big issues of life and faith. Job and Ecclesiastes particularly deal with the tension between faith and experience—the big "whys" that so often test faith.

Most of the topics addressed in the Wisdom books fall into three broad focal points. *First*, special attention is directed *to the individual*. Wisdom allows no room or way to escape its message. *Second*, attention is directed *to common or mundane concerns*. Theology is brought to the level of daily conduct. Even matters of formal worship receive little attention since external rituals mean nothing unless a person lives properly outside of church. *Third*, attention is directed *to God's absolute sovereignty and providence*. Trusting God and fearing Him when everything in life seems to be contrary is essential. Wisdom teaches us to walk by faith and not by sight.

INTRODUCTION TO THE BOOK OF JOB

Authorship: The author of the book of Job is uncertain. Some believe that either Job or Elihu is the author. Others believe the book was written sometime after the events. Since the setting of the book is outside of Israel and the date is most likely in the patriarchal period, none of the book's characters are likely its authors since they would not have spoken Hebrew, the original language of its composition. From a literary perspective, it is a masterpiece of wisdom writing. In addition, the vast knowledge that is displayed in the book covering an array of wisdom subjects suggests that Solomon, the wisest of all the ancients, could be the author. The fact that the author cannot be positively identified indicates that God did not think it important to reveal the author of the book. That Job is not the actual author does bring into question his historicity. The Bible is clear that Job was a real person (Ezek. 14:14; James 5:11).

Date: The date of the historical setting of the book and the date of composition are very likely different. The book gives evidence of an ancient setting. The non-Israelite characters suggest a time before Abraham since after Abraham God limited special revelation to Israel, and there is no question that each of the characters had knowledge of the true God. That Job functioned as the priest of his own house suggests the patriarchal period. His long life and evaluation of wealth in terms of cattle are also features of this time period. The frequent use of the divine title God Almighty (*El Shaddai*) occurs more in the book of Job than anywhere else (Ex. 6:3 links this title to the patriarchal period). The internal evidence points to a historical context from approximately 2500 to 2000 BC.

Suggestions regarding the time of composition range from contemporary with the events all the way to the post-exilic period. Since it was during the Solomonic era that the production of wisdom writing reached its zenith, this may be the most credible of composition dates. If indeed Solomon himself was the inspired writer, the date of writing would be 970 to 930 BC, the dates of his reign. But regardless of the date, the truths contained in the book of Job are timeless and find application in every age.

Theme: The sovereignty and grace of God in the suffering of His servants.

Purpose: To encourage believers to humbly submit to God's hand in painful trials, hoping in His justice and His ultimate vindication of the godly.

Synopsis: *The Contribution of Job to Redemptive Revelation*

The book of Job is full of wisdom. In particular, it bears witness to the majesty of God, to the ancient faith in the message of the gospel, and to the mystery of the suffering of God's people. *First*, both the narratives and monologues of this book speak much of *the majesty of God*. The Lord is the King of heaven who summons all the spirits of the invisible world to give an account (1:6–7). When He protects a man, no one can touch him (v. 10). Even Satan, the great enemy of the righteous, can do nothing apart from His will (v. 12; 2:6). Job rightly attributed to God's providence every good gift and every painful loss, and he declared Him worthy of submission and praise, even in the most horrible tragedy (1:20–22; 2:9–10). The Lord reigns over all people and all events, both good and bad (3:18; 12:9–10,17–25). He created the earth, the seas, and the constellations of the stars (9:8–10; 26:7–13). Man is utterly dependent on the common gifts of God's Spirit for life and understanding (32:8; 33:4). God possesses wisdom and strength, and who can stop His will or successfully fight against Him (9:4–7; 12:13–16)? He is the judge of all men, and who will teach Him anything (21:19–22)? His perfections are infinite, higher than the heavens, deeper than the seas, and wider than the world (11:7–9). We know but the smallest part of His glory and do not begin to understand the thunder of His power (26:14). With God is terrifying majesty, glorious power, and abundant justice, and therefore men fear Him (37:22–24). In the concluding chapters of Job, God dwells long upon His unspeakable majesty as the Creator and King of a world full of mysteries, leaving Job silenced in his questions and profoundly humbled before the sovereign God (40:1–5; 42:1–6).

Therefore, Job teaches us that the essence of wisdom consists in fearing God (1:1,8; 2:3; 6:14). The wisdom of fallen man is foolishness, a trap in which God catches and punishes the wicked by their own foolishness (3:13; cited in 1 Cor. 3:19). Wisdom is only of the Lord. The book brings this message into focus in the literary artistry of its structure, using chiasm, a common technique in Hebrew writing and logic, like a series of concentric circles drawing attention to their center.

- **A** Prose Prologue (chs. 1–2)
  - **B** Job's Initial Statement of Lamentation (ch. 3)
    - **C** Three Cycles of Dialogue (chs. 4–14, 15–21, and 22–27)
      - **D** Poem on Wisdom (ch. 28)
    - **C′** Three Series of Monologues (chs. 29–31, 32–37, and 38–41)
  - **B′** Job's Final Statements: Confession (40:3–5; 42:1–6)
- **A′** Prose Epilogue (42:7–17)

The wisdom revealed in Job reaches its apex in ch. 28, which contrasts man's skill in mining precious materials from the depths of the earth with man's inability to find wisdom. True understanding belongs to God the Creator, and He alone reveals it to man. Thus, Job declares, "Behold, the fear of the Lord, that is wisdom; and to depart from evil is understanding" (28:28). This is the only proper response to the infinite majesty of God.

Second, these events, set in history around the time of the patriarchs of Israel, show the reader that believers in ancient times already understood much of *the message of the gospel*, both in terms of the problem it exposes and the solution it offers. The essence of sin is not just bad behavior but hostility to God deeply entrenched in the heart, even in the children of the godly (1:5). To be sure, sin expresses itself in outward acts such as dishonest commerce, adultery, refusal to care for the poor, social injustice, and the worship of creation (31:1). But its roots are inward uncleanness, such as sexual lust (vv. 1–40) or putting one's hope in material wealth (vv. 24–25). Man's corrupt heart moves him to drink up sin like water (15:16). Job showed greater understanding than the Pharisees who needed Christ to remind them that the law of God measures not just outward actions but the intents of the heart as well (Matt. 5:21–22,27–28). The need for salvation then becomes the problem of how to bring a clean thing out of an unclean thing (Job 14:4; cf. Matt. 15:18–19). This is humanly impossible, but unless the problem is solved mankind remains under a sentence of misery and death by the decree of God (Job 14:1–5). The great question is: How can a man be righteous before God (9:2)? Thus Job bears witness to the fallen condition of mankind as the basis for man's need of the gospel.

The book of Job also testifies of the gospel solution to this problem, albeit in shadows appropriate for the time before the coming of Christ. The fact that Job sacrificed burnt offerings to God for his children (1:5) demonstrates Job's knowledge of the necessity for substitution and satisfaction for sin (Lev. 1:4). Job functioned as a priest for his family, and in the end his priestly intercession with sacrifices saved his three friends from the burning wrath of God (Job 42:7–8). Yet Job was not the Mediator. He needed a mediator and longed for a "daysman" who would plead his case with God (9:33), a "surety" who would fulfill his obligations before God (17:3). He trusted in a mysterious heavenly "witness" who would "plead for a man with God" (16:19–21). He knew there is no such friend among mere men but hoped in the Kinsman-Redeemer who would come visibly to this world and raise His people from the dead (14:14; 19:25–27). Job had faith in Christ. Elihu also spoke of the unique Mediator who would teach righteousness and bring a ransom to God so that repentant sinners might be saved from death and rejuvenated in life (33:23–28). The pattern of Job's own life, like that of Joseph (Gen. 37–45), foreshadowed the coming Savior in that the righteous man was humiliated for a period of time when God seemed hidden but then was exalted to prosperity with an awesome display of God's glory—as in Christ's sufferings and glorification. Thus Job is a gospel book.

Third, the book of Job is best known for the way it addresses *the mystery of suffering*. Skeptics reason that an all-powerful and all-good God could not allow suffering in His creation. Believers may also doubt God's sovereignty or goodness when life seems cruel and meaningless. Job's experience was a case in point, for he was a man of integrity and righteousness (Job 1:1; 2:3) who nonetheless experienced horrible suffering. Why would God let one who feared Him and shunned evil suffer the way Job did? Job's friends pressed him with the doctrine that suffering comes from sin. In a sense they were right, because all suffering springs from the fall of man into disobedience to God (Gen. 3; Eccl. 7:29; Rom. 5:12). However, Job's specific sorrows fell upon him not because of any sin in his life but precisely because of His obedience to the Lord. Therefore, Job is an example of the suffering of the righteous people of God in a world dominated by Satan (Job 1:7; 2:2) and full of wicked men (1:15,17). This suffering climaxed in redemptive history in the crucifixion of the righteous Son of God, and the suffering of all the righteous must be seen in light of their union with Him in His death and resurrection (2 Cor. 1:3–5; Phil. 3:10).

There is a complexity to the way the book of Job addresses the mystery of suffering. In fact, the book addresses suffering from five perspectives.

1. The Inspired Narrator: Suffering is a spiritual battle for God's glory.
2. The Three Friends: Suffering is the consequence of man's sin.
3. Job: Suffering is an inexplicable and perplexing problem.
4. Elihu: Suffering is a purifying process from God.
5. God: Suffering is a call to trust and submission.

Each one of these perspectives contributes something to understanding the suffering of the righteous, although the three friends misapply a general truth by accusing Job of unrepentant sin.

The forty-two chapters of the book of Job draw the reader into the mystery of suffering, and through the great struggles of these five men to deal with this mystery, the book imparts greater wisdom than can be found in simplistic answers to the problem of evil. It does not analyze evil and suffering so much as call upon suffering believers to endure with hope. Job's pattern of life reflects not just the humiliation and exaltation of Christ (as noted above) but also the sorrows of God's people in a world where God seems hidden as they hope in the appearing of the glory of God for their final vindication and inheritance. Thus the New Testament holds up Job as a model of endurance in the hope of Christ's return: "Be patient therefore, brethren, unto the coming of the Lord . . . Behold, we count them happy which endure. Ye have heard of the patience of Job, and have seen the end of the Lord; that the Lord is very pitiful, and of tender mercy" (James 5:7,11).

As Job shows us, enduring hope is possible when we embrace a glorious vision of the majesty of God, the sovereign Lord who initiates, controls, and ends all our trials at His will, and when we trust in the gospel's promise of the Mediator whose sacrifice atones for the deepest blasphemies of the heart, whose intercession lays a hand on both God and redeemed sinners, and whose coming will resurrect to joyful life those who belong to Him so that they may be with Him and see His glory forever.

Outline:

- I. God's Controversy with Satan over Righteous Job (1:1—2:13)
- II. Job's Lamentation (3:1–26)
- III. Job's Debate with His Friends (4:1—27:23)
  - A. First Cycle of Dialogue (4:1—14:22)
    1. Eliphaz: You Strengthened Others but Now Are Fainting (4:1—5:27)
    2. Job: You Do Not Know the Weight of My Grief (6:1—7:21)
    3. Bildad: All Agree that God Is Just (8:1–22)
    4. Job: But How Can Man Be Just before God? (9:1—10:22)
    5. Zophar: Does Your Talk Justify You? (11:1–20)
    6. Job: I Know that I Shall Be Justified (12:1—14:22)
  - B. Second Cycle of Dialogue (15:1—21:34)
    1. Eliphaz: How Can He Who Is Born of a Woman Be Righteous? (15:1–35)
    2. Job: You Are All Miserable Comforters (16:1—17:16)
    3. Bildad: God Judges the Wicked (18:1–21)
    4. Job: But I Know that My Redeemer Lives (19:1–29)

5. Zophar: The Triumph of the Wicked Is Short (20:1–29)
6. Job: But the Wicked Live Long and Prosper (21:1–34)

C. Third Cycle of Dialogue (22:1—27:23)

1. Eliphaz: Is It Gain to God that You Make Your Way Perfect? (22:1–30)
2. Job: I Shall Come Forth as Gold (23:1—24:25)
3. Bildad: But How Can Man Be Justified with God? (25:1–6)
4. Job: How Have You Helped Him Who Has No Power? (26:1—27:23)

IV. Wisdom Is the Fear of the Lord (28:1–28)

V. Three Monologues (29:1—41:34)

A. Job's Remembrance of His Prosperity and Righteousness (29:1—31:40)

B. Elihu's Speech for God (32:1—37:24)

1. Elihu's Rebuke of Job (32:1—35:16)
2. Elihu's Proclamation of God (36:1—37:24)

C. The Lord's Interrogation of Job (38:1—41:34)

1. The Lord's Questions about Creation (38:1—39:30)
2. The Lord's Challenge regarding the Great Beasts (40:1—41:34)

VI. Job's Confession (42:1–6)

VII. God's Restoration of Job (42:7–17)

THE BOOK OF

JOB

CHAPTER 1

THERE was a man in the land of Uz, whose name
was Job; and that man was perfect and upright,
and one that feared God, and eschewed evil.
2 And there were born unto him seven sons and
three daughters.
3 His substance also was seven thousand sheep,
and three thousand camels, and five hundred
yoke of oxen, and five hundred she asses, and a
very great household; so that this man was the
greatest of all the men of the east.
4 And his sons went and feasted *in their* houses,
every one his day; and sent and called for their
three sisters to eat and to drink with them.
5 And it was so, when the days of *their* feasting
were gone about, that Job sent and sanctified
them, and rose up early in the morning, and of-
fered burnt offerings *according* to the number of
them all: for Job said, It may be that my sons have
sinned, and cursed God in their hearts. Thus did
Job continually.
6 ¶ Now there was a day when the sons of God
came to present themselves before the LORD, and
Satan came also among them.
7 And the LORD said unto Satan, Whence comest
thou? Then Satan answered the LORD, and said,
From going to and fro in the earth, and from
walking up and down in it.
8 And the LORD said unto Satan, Hast thou
considered my servant Job, that *there is* none like
him in the earth, a perfect and an upright man,
one that feareth God, and escheweth evil?
9 Then Satan answered the LORD, and said, Doth
Job fear God for nought?
10 Hast not thou made an hedge about him,
and about his house, and about all that he hath
on every side? thou hast blessed the work of his
hands, and his substance is increased in the land.
11 But put forth thine hand now, and touch all
that he hath, and he will curse thee to thy face.
12 And the LORD said unto Satan, Behold, all that
he hath *is* in thy power; only upon himself put not
forth thine hand. So Satan went forth from the
presence of the LORD.
13 ¶ And there was a day when his sons and his
daughters *were* eating and drinking wine in their
eldest brother's house:
14 And there came a messenger unto Job, and
said, The oxen were plowing, and the asses feed-
ing beside them:
15 And the Sabeans fell *upon them,* and took
them away; yea, they have slain the servants with
the edge of the sword; and I only am escaped
alone to tell thee.
16 While he *was* yet speaking, there came also
another, and said, The fire of God is fallen from

GOD'S CONTROVERSY WITH SATAN OVER RIGHTEOUS JOB (1:1—2:13)

Chapter 1: *God brings Job to the attention of Satan and allows him to strike Job's household.*

1:1 *the land of Uz.* Located to the east of Palestine, Uz is mentioned in only two other places in the Bible (Jer. 25:20; Lam. 4:21). *a man . . . whose name was Job.* Job was a real, historical person. *perfect.* Genuine or sincere in integrity (v. 8). *eschewed evil.* Turned away from evil.

1:3 *the east.* East of Palestine.

1:5 *sanctified them.* Dedicated them to the Lord. The fact that Job, who was not of the tribe of Levi, offered burnt offerings indicates that this was before the time of the Levitical priesthood (Lev. 17:1–5).

1:6 *the sons of God.* A phrase sometimes used of angels (38:7). *present themselves.* Perhaps like servants called to hear their Lord's will (Zech. 6:5). *Satan.* Literally, "accuser" or "adversary" (Zech. 3:1). The Devil was brought to account before God and is here clearly under the Lord's sovereignty.

1:7 *From going to and fro in the earth.* Satan is not omnipresent but is constantly active, ruling over fallen mankind (Rev. 12:9) and seeking to devour the godly (1 Peter 5:8).

1:8 *the LORD said unto Satan.* The Lord first mentioned Job to Satan; his trial was of divine origin and design, arising from God's challenge to the Devil. This testifies to Job's character in that God singled him out as an example of godliness.

1:10–11 *substance.* Property, livestock. *touch.* Strike. *he will curse thee.* Satan's accusation of Job is that Job does not worship God for who God is but only for the blessings God gives.

1:12 Satan can afflict only by God's will and within God's limits (2:6). Yet he is able to exercise surprising power (vv. 16,19) and to move wicked men to execute his evil plans (vv. 15,17).

1:15 *Sabeans.* People of Sheba, probably Ethiopia. *fell upon.* Attacked.

1:16 *fire of God.* Perhaps lightning, igniting a wildfire.

heaven, and hath burned up the sheep, and the
servants, and consumed them; and I only am es-
caped alone to tell thee.
17 While he *was* yet speaking, there came also
another, and said, The Chaldeans made out three
bands, and fell upon the camels, and have carried
them away, yea, and slain the servants with the
edge of the sword; and I only am escaped alone
to tell thee.
18 While he *was* yet speaking, there came also
another, and said, Thy sons and thy daughters
were eating and drinking wine in their eldest
brother's house:
19 And, behold, there came a great wind from
the wilderness, and smote the four corners of the
house, and it fell upon the young men, and they
are dead; and I only am escaped alone to tell thee.
20 Then Job arose, and rent his mantle, and
shaved his head, and fell down upon the ground,
and worshipped,
21 And said, Naked came I out of my mother's
womb, and naked shall I return thither: the LORD
gave, and the LORD hath taken away; blessed be
the name of the LORD.
22 In all this Job sinned not, nor charged God
foolishly.

CHAPTER 2

AGAIN there was a day when the sons of God
came to present themselves before the LORD, and
Satan came also among them to present himself
before the LORD.
2 And the LORD said unto Satan, From whence
comest thou? And Satan answered the LORD, and
said, From going to and fro in the earth, and from
walking up and down in it.
3 And the LORD said unto Satan, Hast thou con-
sidered my servant Job, that *there is* none like him
in the earth, a perfect and an upright man, one
that feareth God, and escheweth evil? and still he
holdeth fast his integrity, although thou movedst
me against him, to destroy him without cause.
4 And Satan answered the LORD, and said, Skin
for skin, yea, all that a man hath will he give for
his life.
5 But put forth thine hand now, and touch his
bone and his flesh, and he will curse thee to thy
face.
6 And the LORD said unto Satan, Behold, he *is* in
thine hand; but save his life.
7 ¶ So went Satan forth from the presence of the
LORD, and smote Job with sore boils from the sole
of his foot unto his crown.
8 And he took him a potsherd to scrape himself
withal; and he sat down among the ashes.
9 ¶ Then said his wife unto him, Dost thou still
retain thine integrity? curse God, and die.
10 But he said unto her, Thou speakest as one of
the foolish women speaketh. What? shall we re-
ceive good at the hand of God, and shall we not
receive evil? In all this did not Job sin with his lips.

1:17 *Chaldeans*. People from Mesopotamia. *fell upon*. Plundered.
1:20 *rent his mantle*. Tore his robe; that and shaving the head were signs of grief. *fell down . . . and worshipped*. Acts of reverent submission. Submitting to God's sovereignty does not diminish personal sorrow over loss. Indeed, not to weep in tragedy ignores God's sovereignly ordained times (Eccl. 3:1,4,11).
1:21 *Naked came I*. A statement of humility and dependence upon God for all things (1 Cor. 4:7). *naked shall I return*. Death separates us from all our possessions (Ps. 49:17; Eccl. 5:15; 1 Tim. 6:7). *the LORD gave, and the LORD hath taken away*. God controls both every blessing and every loss (1 Sam. 2:6–7; Isa. 45:7; James 1:17). *blessed be the name of the LORD*. Contrary to Satan's prediction, Job did not curse God but continued to worship Him even in grief, proving the genuineness of his fear of the Lord (vv. 9–11).
1:22 *Job sinned not*. It was right for Job to ascribe to God total sovereignty over all things and to worship Him even in the midst of shattering loss.

Thoughts for Personal/Family Worship: Chapter 1

1. **Job loved his family and understood his responsibility to pray for his children (v. 5). His offering finds its application today in parents pleading the substitutionary atonement of Christ for the salvation and sanctification of their children. Perhaps the most impressive aspect of Job's devotion is that it was demonstrated before his trial began. How often times of prosperity become times of spiritual carelessness. How can you imitate Job's example of family devotion?**
2. **The first chapter in Job lays the foundation for the rest of the book by taking the reader behind the scenes, enabling him to see that Job had the blessing of God's commendation. The test to the Christian's faith comes when circumstances around him are shouting at him that God must have condemned him. When friends and even loved ones lend their voices to such a chorus, it becomes a daunting challenge for faith to continue to affirm the favor of God. The key is for the Christian to see that the burnt offering points to Christ and that so long as God is pleased with Christ, God will be pleased with the Christian that is joined to Christ, circumstances notwithstanding.**

Chapter 2: ***God allows Job's trial to continue after Satan, unimpressed with the integrity of Job, challenges God again.***

2:1–2 *sons of God . . . Satan*. See notes at 1:6 and 7.
2:3 *perfect . . . escheweth evil*. See note at 1:1. Even in his mourning Job received the commendation of God (1:22). *destroy*. Hebrew, "swallow up." *without cause*. Undeservedly.
2:4 *Skin for skin*. A proverbial expression meaning that a man will be willing to sacrifice anything in order to live.
2:6 *but save his life*. Another example that demonstrates the limits God places upon Satan's activities.
2:7 *sore boils*. Possibly a form of leprosy or elephantiasis.
2:8 *potsherd*. A piece of a broken vessel used for scratching and scraping the ooze of his sores. The fact that Job was sitting *among the ashes* may indicate that he had separated himself

11 ¶ Now when Job's three friends heard of all
this evil that was come upon him, they came ev-
ery one from his own place; Eliphaz the Temanite,
and Bildad the Shuhite, and Zophar the Naama-
thite: for they had made an appointment together
to come to mourn with him and to comfort him.
12 And when they lifted up their eyes afar off, and
knew him not, they lifted up their voice, and wept;
and they rent every one his mantle, and sprinkled
dust upon their heads toward heaven.
13 So they sat down with him upon the ground
seven days and seven nights, and none spake a
word unto him: for they saw that *his* grief was
very great.

CHAPTER 3

AFTER this opened Job his mouth, and cursed his
day.
2 And Job spake, and said,
3 Let the day perish wherein I was born, and the
night *in which* it was said, There is a man child
conceived.
4 Let that day be darkness; let not God regard it
from above, neither let the light shine upon it.
5 Let darkness and the shadow of death stain it;
let a cloud dwell upon it; let the blackness of the
day terrify it.
6 *As for* that night, let darkness seize upon it; let
it not be joined unto the days of the year, let it not
come into the number of the months.
7 Lo, let that night be solitary, let no joyful voice
come therein.
8 Let them curse it that curse the day, who are
ready to raise up their mourning.
9 Let the stars of the twilight thereof be dark; let
it look for light, but *have* none; neither let it see
the dawning of the day:
10 Because it shut not up the doors of my *moth-
er's* womb, nor hid sorrow from mine eyes.
11 Why died I not from the womb? *why* did I *not*
give up the ghost when I came out of the belly?
12 Why did the knees prevent me? or why the
breasts that I should suck?
13 For now should I have lain still and been quiet,
I should have slept: then had I been at rest,
14 With kings and counsellors of the earth, which
built desolate places for themselves;
15 Or with princes that had gold, who filled their
houses with silver:
16 Or as an hidden untimely birth I had not been;
as infants *which* never saw light.
17 There the wicked cease *from* troubling; and
there the weary be at rest.
18 *There* the prisoners rest together; they hear
not the voice of the oppressor.
19 The small and great are there; and the servant
is free from his master.
20 Wherefore is light given to him that is in
misery, and life unto the bitter *in* soul;
21 Which long for death, but it *cometh* not; and
dig for it more than for hid treasures;

---

from his home and taken his place in the community ash heap, a shameful place.

2:9 *curse God, and die.* Job's wife told him to do exactly what Satan desired (v. 5); yet we must also remember how much she too had lost.

2:10 *shall we receive good . . . not receive evil.* Again, Job rightly honored God as sovereign over happiness and sorrow and submitted himself to God's will in both (1:21; Heb. 12:5–11).

2:11 *Job's three friends* displayed compassion initially by taking the time to sit with Job to comfort him. *Temanite.* Possibly a descendant of Teman, and so of Esau (Gen. 36:10–11). *Shuhite.* Perhaps a descendant of Shuah, one of Abraham's sons by Keturah (Gen. 25:1–2).

2:12 *knew him not.* His case was worse than they thought. *lifted up their voice.* It was the ancient custom in the East to give full expression to grief and sorrow. *rent . . . his mantle.* See note at 1:20.

2:13 *seven days and seven nights.* This is the most definite time reference found in the book of Job. Job's trial undoubtedly began several weeks, and perhaps months, earlier.

Thoughts for Personal/Family Worship: Chapter 2

1. **Job's submission to God's will was remarkable. He lost his wealth, his children, the favor of his wife, and his own health, and yet he honored God humbly. He was no superman, and we will see his struggle with doubt and questions. However, he fundamentally honored God (42:7). Why does bitterness so quickly rise up in our hearts when suffering comes? How can we become more like Job?**
2. **Because of the ineffective way Job's friends would minister to him it becomes easy to overlook the fact that they were acting as true friends by setting out to comfort him. We too must bear each other's burdens and so fulfill the law of Christ (Gal. 6:2). Real love means laying down our lives for others and grieving with them (Rom. 12:15; 1 John 3:16). Job's friends were at their best through their ministry of silent empathy (Prov.10:19). Often the best comfort that can be given to those who suffer is just to be present with them.**

Chapter 3: *Job breaks the silence with curses and "why" questions.*

JOB'S LAMENTATION (3:1–26)

3:1–10 The Devil had pledged that he could get Job to curse God to his face. While not cursing God directly, Job questioned the purpose of his own existence.

3:1 *his day.* A reference to his life.

3:4–8 *Let that day be darkness . . . Let them curse it that curse the day.* Expressions of the depth of his despair as the physical suffering and mental anguish cloud Job's thinking. But the darkness Job felt paled in comparison to a day of darkness that would come upon Christ (Matt. 27:45) as He became a curse (Gal. 3:13).

3:11 *give up the ghost.* Literally, "pass away" or "expire."

3:12 *prevent.* Literally, "meet" or "receive," referring to the birthing process.

3:13–19 Death is the great equalizer; in the grave all are the same, free from the problems of this life.

SATAN

Satan's existence is attested in nine Old Testament books and by every New Testament writer. In the Old Testament the word *Satan*, meaning "adversary or accuser," occurs nineteen times. The word appears to be employed both as a title (*the Accuser*; Zech. 3:1–2) and as a personal name (*Satan*; 1 Chron. 21:1; Ps. 109:6). Many of the usages occur in Job 1 and 2.

In the New Testament Satan is denominated most often as *the devil* (*diabolos*; occurring sixty times, forty times in the Gospels alone). This is a term that means "traducer or slanderer." The word *Satan* itself occurs thirty-four times, half in the Gospels and Acts and half in the epistles and Revelation. Additionally, there are other New Testament names and titles for Satan: the accuser (Rev. 12:10), the adversary (1 Peter 5:8), Apollyon (Rev. 9:11), Beelzebub (Matt. 12:24), Belial (2 Cor. 6:15), the dragon (Rev. 12:7), the god of this world (2 Cor. 4:4), the prince of the air (Eph. 2:2), the prince of this world (John 12:31), the serpent (Rev. 20:2), the tempter (Matt. 4:3), and a roaring lion (1 Peter 5:8).

Satan is not an impersonal force but the chief fallen angel who rebelled against God (Isa. 14:12–15). He has all the traits of personality, such as intellect (2 Cor. 11:3), emotion (Rev. 12:17), and will (2 Tim. 2:26). Furthermore, personal pronouns are ascribed to him (Matt. 4:1–12).

From his very first success in tempting Adam and Eve to sin, Satan is seen as warring against mankind in general and believers in particular. In opposition to all the world, Satan blinds, deceives, and rules over men in wickedness (2 Cor. 4:3–4; Eph. 2:2; Col. 1:13; Rev. 20:7–8). In hostility to all believers, Satan roams "as a roaring lion, seeking whom he may devour" (1 Peter 5:8). Satan incited David to sin (1 Chron. 21:1), accused Job and Joshua the high priest (Job 1–2; Zech. 3:1), corrupted Peter's thinking (Matt. 16:23), and inflicted a thorn in Paul's side (2 Cor. 12:7). Satan seeks to accuse all believers before God and opposes them with all his might (Rev. 12:10). He is aptly described as wily (Eph. 6:11), necessitating that the believer don armor for both offense and defense against him (Eph. 6).

Satan can be seen as executing four strategies against the believer. *First*, Satan leads the believer off the path, enticing him with sinful fruit tailored to his taste. Satan knows the individual believer's weaknesses and quickly capitalizes on them. Each believer must be wary of his areas of weakness and make fortifications against Satan in those places.

Second, Satan places mountainous obstacles along the way of spiritual discipline, making headway tedious and demanding. He confronts the believer with apparent impasses, many of which are common, such as busyness, loneliness, and weariness. With these and numerous others strategies, Satan attempts to discourage and overcome the believer. The believer must flee to the Lord as his strength and rock (Pss. 18:2; 28:7), employ the means of grace, and fellowship regularly with other Christians.

Third, Satan lays pitfalls for the believer by deceiving him about God and His truth. From the beginning (Gen. 3:4–5) Satan has corrupted the truth in immeasurable ways. The believer must bathe in the truth of the Word. He must ensure that scriptural truth is being set before his eyes, is ringing in his ears, and is dwelling within his heart and mind (Deut. 6:7–9; Josh. 1:8; Ps. 119:11).

Fourth, Satan continually opposes each step of sanctification. Because the believer's progress is the Devil's regress, Satan relentlessly impedes obedience. Christ is the remedy. When Satan throws snares to topple him, the believer must beseech Christ, who is his first love (Rev. 2:4–5). When Satan builds walls to bar him, the believer must look to Christ, who breaks blockades (Mic. 2:13). When Satan forges chains to bind him, the believer must implore Christ, who liberates captives (Luke 4:18).

Comfort is to be had, however, for Satan has already been defeated by the death and resurrection of Christ (Gen. 3:15; Rev. 20). His destruction is sure in the end. Until then the believer must recognize that his "sufficiency is of God" to triumph against Satan (2 Cor. 3:5).

22 Which rejoice exceedingly, *and* are glad, when
they can find the grave?
23 *Why is light given* to a man whose way is hid,
and whom God hath hedged in?
24 For my sighing cometh before I eat, and my
roarings are poured out like the waters.
25 For the thing which I greatly feared is come
upon me, and that which I was afraid of is come
unto me.
26 I was not in safety, neither had I rest, neither
was I quiet; yet trouble came.

CHAPTER 4

THEN Eliphaz the Temanite answered and said,
2 *If* we assay to commune with thee, wilt thou
be grieved? but who can withhold himself from
speaking?
3 Behold, thou hast instructed many, and thou
hast strengthened the weak hands.
4 Thy words have upholden him that was falling,
and thou hast strengthened the feeble knees.
5 But now it is come upon thee, and thou faint-
est; it toucheth thee, and thou art troubled.
6 *Is* not *this* thy fear, thy confidence, thy hope,
and the uprightness of thy ways?
7 Remember, I pray thee, who *ever* perished, be-
ing innocent? or where were the righteous cut off?
8 Even as I have seen, they that plow iniquity, and
sow wickedness, reap the same.
9 By the blast of God they perish, and by the
breath of his nostrils are they consumed.
10 The roaring of the lion, and the voice of the
fierce lion, and the teeth of the young lions, are
broken.
11 The old lion perisheth for lack of prey, and the
stout lion's whelps are scattered abroad.
12 Now a thing was secretly brought to me, and
mine ear received a little thereof.
13 In thoughts from the visions of the night,
when deep sleep falleth on men,
14 Fear came upon me, and trembling, which
made all my bones to shake.
15 Then a spirit passed before my face; the hair of
my flesh stood up:
16 It stood still, but I could not discern the form
thereof: an image *was* before mine eyes, *there was*
silence, and I heard a voice, *saying,*
17 Shall mortal man be more just than God? shall
a man be more pure than his maker?

3:25 *the thing which I greatly feared is come.* Possibly a reference to Job's relationship to God, though not the same word used of Job's fear of God (1:1,8; 2:3); possibly Job's natural concerns that harm might come to his person and household, which had come true.

Thoughts for Personal/Family Worship: Chapter 3

1. **The contrast between Job in ch. 3, as over against chs. 1 and 2, is great. The only difference in the settings is time ("after this," v. 1). Suffering and sorrow become overwhelming when they persist without an end in sight. Even a righteous man who fears God and turns from evil (2:3) still possesses sin. He is capable of misunderstanding and of questioning what God is doing. The tension between faith and experience is real. One of the purposes that trials serve is to make the believer face the reality of his inherent weakness and the truth that he must walk by faith, regardless of the perceptions of his sight. Without painful trials the believer is vulnerable to pride. Trials help the believer bridge the gap between belief and experience by a deeper trust in God.**
2. **We find Job in this chapter sinking to the depths of despair, and the question that naturally arises is, "Why?" The answer is not so mysterious as a believer might think when he remembers Christ. Christians tend to think of conformity to Christ in terms of the radiant splendor that was displayed by Christ on the Mount of Transfiguration (Matt. 17:1–2). However, as Paul makes plain to the Philippians, conformity to Christ also means conformity to his death (Phil. 3:10). The suffering Christian is not only learning through his trials to die more and more to sin and live more and more to righteousness, but he is learning to identify more closely with the One who loved him and gave Himself for him.**

JOB'S DEBATE WITH HIS FRIENDS (4:1—27:23)

First Cycle of Dialogue (4:1—14:22)

Eliphaz: You Strengthened Others but Now Are Fainting (4:1—5:27)

Chapter 4: ***Job's friends are appalled at the way Job would question God's dealings with him; therefore Eliphaz feels compelled to defend God's honor.***

4:1–11 Eliphaz accused Job of not applying the counsel to himself that he had given to others. His words bring the purpose of suffering into focus (2 Cor. 1:4).
4:2 *assay to commune.* Literally, "venture a word."
4:3–4 *strengthened the weak hands . . . the feeble knees.* Figures of speech for how Job's wise counsel had encouraged people to persevere in hope and righteousness (Isa. 35:3; Heb. 12:12).
4:7 *Remember, I pray thee, who ever perished, being innocent?* Eliphaz considered Job's troubles to be the result of serious personal sin in his life.
4:8 *sow . . . reap.* See Gal. 6:7–8 for the same principle.
4:9 *blast.* Breath.
4:11 *lion's whelps are scattered.* Literally, "the sons of a lioness become separated from one another."
4:13 *In thoughts from the visions.* Eliphaz claimed divine revelation (7:14; see note at 33:15–16).
4:15 *spirit.* An angel or demon (v. 18; 1:6).
4:17 *shall a man be more pure than his maker?* Or possibly, "be pure before his Maker"; a key question in the debate between Job and his friends (9:2; 15:14; 25:4).

Thoughts for Personal/Family Worship: Chapter 4

1. **We should not be impatient with believers when great suffering throws them into doubts and confusion. Just because someone like Job possesses much wisdom (v. 3) does not mean that he is above questioning God when tragedy strikes. This is not necessarily a sign of hypocrisy, but of the weakness of our humanity. How might Eliphaz have responded better to Job's lamentation?**
2. **The most important question in all the world for a man**

18 Behold, he put no trust in his servants; and his angels he charged with folly:

19 How much less *in* them that dwell in houses of clay, whose foundation *is* in the dust, *which* are crushed before the moth?

20 They are destroyed from morning to evening: they perish for ever without any regarding *it*.

21 Doth not their excellency *which is* in them go away? they die, even without wisdom.

CHAPTER 5

CALL now, if there be any that will answer thee; and to which of the saints wilt thou turn?

2 For wrath killeth the foolish man, and envy slayeth the silly one.

3 I have seen the foolish taking root: but suddenly I cursed his habitation.

4 His children are far from safety, and they are crushed in the gate, neither *is there* any to deliver *them*.

5 Whose harvest the hungry eateth up, and taketh it even out of the thorns, and the robber swalloweth up their substance.

6 Although affliction cometh not forth of the dust, neither doth trouble spring out of the ground;

7 Yet man is born unto trouble, as the sparks fly upward.

8 I would seek unto God, and unto God would I commit my cause:

9 Which doeth great things and unsearchable; marvellous things without number:

10 Who giveth rain upon the earth, and sendeth waters upon the fields:

11 To set up on high those that be low; that those which mourn may be exalted to safety.

12 He disappointeth the devices of the crafty, so that their hands cannot perform *their* enterprise.

13 He taketh the wise in their own craftiness: and the counsel of the froward is carried headlong.

14 They meet with darkness in the daytime, and grope in the noonday as in the night.

15 But he saveth the poor from the sword, from their mouth, and from the hand of the mighty.

16 So the poor hath hope, and iniquity stoppeth her mouth.

17 Behold, happy *is* the man whom God correcteth: therefore despise not thou the chastening of the Almighty:

18 For he maketh sore, and bindeth up: he woundeth, and his hands make whole.

19 He shall deliver thee in six troubles: yea, in seven there shall no evil touch thee.

20 In famine he shall redeem thee from death: and in war from the power of the sword.

21 Thou shalt be hid from the scourge of the tongue: neither shalt thou be afraid of destruction when it cometh.

22 At destruction and famine thou shalt laugh: neither shalt thou be afraid of the beasts of the earth.

23 For thou shalt be in league with the stones of the field: and the beasts of the field shall be at peace with thee.

24 And thou shalt know that thy tabernacle *shall be* in peace; and thou shalt visit thy habitation, and shalt not sin.

25 Thou shalt know also that thy seed *shall be* great, and thine offspring as the grass of the earth.

26 Thou shalt come to *thy* grave in a full age, like as a shock of corn cometh in in his season.

27 Lo this, we have searched it, so it *is*; hear it, and know thou *it* for thy good.

---

to consider is, How can a man be right with God (v. 17)? This is a question with eternal ramifications because the answer to it impacts the destiny of a man's soul in heaven or hell forever. The book of Job, as well as the entire Bible, is devoted to answering the question of a man's standing before God. Time spent in God's Word, therefore, becomes an investment in eternity.

Chapter 5: *Eliphaz continues his speech and insists that Job should repent of his sin that he may know the Lord's blessing again.*

5:2 *envy slayeth the silly one*. Literally, "anger kills one who is gullible or simpleminded."

5:3 *cursed his habitation*. Witnessed his habitation being cursed.

5:4 *His children are far from safety . . . crushed*. Shows insensitivity to the loss of Job's children.

5:6 *Affliction* and *trouble* are not random circumstances but are ordained by God (1 Peter 1:6).

5:7 *man is born unto trouble*. A picturesque illustration of the inevitability of trouble.

5:8–27 Eliphaz advised Job as to what he would do if he were in Job's place.

5:8 *I would seek unto God*. The implication is not only that Job had not been seeking God but that anybody suffering such afflictions must have stopped seeking God.

5:12 *perform their enterprise*. Accomplish a good result or have abiding success.

5:13 *taketh the wise in their own craftiness*. Quoted by Paul (1 Cor. 3:19), evidence that in some respects the three friends of Job spoke truth. *the counsel of the froward is carried headlong*. The counsel of the twisted or subtle one acts rashly or is hurried to destruction.

5:17 *happy is the man whom God correcteth*. Divine discipline is a mark of God's fatherly love for His children (Prov. 3:11–12; Heb. 12:5–7), particularly when it bears the fruit of repentance and obedience to God's law (Ps. 94:12; Rev. 3:19). *the Almighty*. Frequent title for God in Job (see note at 37:23).

5:19 *six . . . seven*. An idiom expressing completeness; thus, regardless of the trouble, God will deliver him. *evil*. Harm or hurt.

5:24 *tabernacle*. Tent or dwelling place.

5:26 *a shock of corn*. A heap of cut stalks of harvested grain.

5:27 *we have searched it*. Eliphaz believed that he completely understood Job's case; if he just followed Eliphaz's advice to repent, all would be *good*.

CHAPTER 6

BUT Job answered and said,
2 Oh that my grief were throughly weighed, and
my calamity laid in the balances together!
3 For now it would be heavier than the sand of
the sea: therefore my words are swallowed up.
4 For the arrows of the Almighty *are* within me,
the poison whereof drinketh up my spirit: the ter-
rors of God do set themselves in array against me.
5 Doth the wild ass bray when he hath grass? or
loweth the ox over his fodder?
6 Can that which is unsavoury be eaten without
salt? or is there *any* taste in the white of an egg?
7 The things *that* my soul refused to touch *are* as
my sorrowful meat.
8 Oh that I might have my request; and that God
would grant *me* the thing that I long for!
9 Even that it would please God to destroy me;
that he would let loose his hand, and cut me off!
10 Then should I yet have comfort; yea, I would
harden myself in sorrow: let him not spare; for I
have not concealed the words of the Holy One.
11 What *is* my strength, that I should hope? and
what *is* mine end, that I should prolong my life?
12 *Is* my strength the strength of stones? or *is* my
flesh of brass?
13 *Is* not my help in me? and is wisdom driven
quite from me?
14 To him that is afflicted pity *should be shewed*
from his friend; but he forsaketh the fear of the
Almighty.
15 My brethren have dealt deceitfully as a brook,
and as the stream of brooks they pass away;
16 Which are blackish by reason of the ice, *and*
wherein the snow is hid:
17 What time they wax warm, they vanish: when
it is hot, they are consumed out of their place.
18 The paths of their way are turned aside; they
go to nothing, and perish.
19 The troops of Tema looked, the companies of
Sheba waited for them.
20 They were confounded because they had
hoped; they came thither, and were ashamed.
21 For now ye are nothing; ye see *my* casting
down, and are afraid.
22 Did I say, Bring unto me? or, Give a reward for
me of your substance?
23 Or, Deliver me from the enemy's hand? or, Re-
deem me from the hand of the mighty?
24 Teach me, and I will hold my tongue: and
cause me to understand wherein I have erred.
25 How forcible are right words! but what doth
your arguing reprove?
26 Do ye imagine to reprove words, and the
speeches of one that is desperate, *which are* as
wind?
27 Yea, ye overwhelm the fatherless, and ye dig *a*
pit for your friend.
28 Now therefore be content, look upon me; for *it*
is evident unto you if I lie.
29 Return, I pray you, let it not be iniquity; yea,
return again, my righteousness *is* in it.
30 Is there iniquity in my tongue? cannot my
taste discern perverse things?

Thoughts for Personal/Family Worship: Chapter 5

"Happy is the man whom God correcteth" (v. 17). No experience of correction or discipline is pleasant, but it brings great benefits. It purifies believers from sin and strengthens them in faith. Rather than a sign of God's anger against His children, chastening is evidence of His love. We should be sensitive to God's Word that exposes our sin and dependent upon the Holy Spirit to lead us by that Word to behavior that is pleasing to our heavenly Father. We should not rebel under God's chastening hand but quickly submit to it. The believer desires correction because he has been given a new heart that loves the law of God (Ps. 119:97). He who hates correction is a fool. How can we learn to love correction and even discipline from God?

Job: You Do Not Know the Weight of My Grief (6:1—7:21)
Chapter 6: *Job rejects Eliphaz's counsel as counter-productive and only making matters worse.*

6:3 *my words are swallowed up.* Literally, "my words speak incoherently or wildly." His torment is so great that he cannot speak in a comprehensible way, which may account for Eliphaz's failure to grasp the real issue.
6:4 *arrows of the Almighty.* Job attributed his sufferings to God, as to a warrior (Pss. 7:11–13; 38:2). *set themselves in array against me.* Military imagery: God's *terrors* line up for battle against him.
6:5–6 All these questions expect a negative answer, implying that Job has just cause for his complaints.
6:7 *sorrowful meat.* Loathsome food.
6:8–9 Job's desire was that God would end his suffering by taking his life (3:1–26).
6:10 *would harden myself in sorrow.* Literally, "will jump in pain," as an indication of his joyous relief if God would take his life.
6:11–12 Job believed that his trial was more than he could bear. God, however, does not see as man sees (1 Cor. 10:13).
6:13 *Is not my help in me?* There is no hope in me, and deliverance is driven away from me.
6:14 Job advised his comforters as to how they should be consoling him, namely with *pity*; literally, "faithful love."
6:24 *Teach me.* Job pledged to submit himself to the teaching of his friends if they could present a case that would win his conscience.
6:26 *speeches of one that is desperate.* Job insisted that his words were but expressions of a man in despair, not those of a man who had given up on God.
6:27 *ye dig a pit for your friend.* Eliphaz's arguments made Job's suffering worse.
6:30 *cannot my taste discern.* Spiritual maturity gives discernment (34:3; Heb. 5:14). Job confessed that he knew what sin is and would admit it if sin were the cause of his suffering.

Thoughts for Personal/Family Worship: Chapter 6

1. **We should show faithful love to suffering friends (v. 14). As well intentioned as Job's friends were, they actually made his situation worse (v. 27). Parents can fail in the same way if they fail to take into account the weight**

CHAPTER 7

Is there not an appointed time to man upon earth?
are not his days also like the days of an hireling?
2 As a servant earnestly desireth the shadow, and
as an hireling looketh for *the reward of* his work:
3 So am I made to possess months of vanity, and
wearisome nights are appointed to me.
4 When I lie down, I say, When shall I arise, and
the night be gone? and I am full of tossings to and
fro unto the dawning of the day.
5 My flesh is clothed with worms and clods of
dust; my skin is broken, and become loathsome.
6 My days are swifter than a weaver's shuttle, and
are spent without hope.
7 O remember that my life *is* wind: mine eye shall
no more see good.
8 The eye of him that hath seen me shall see me
no *more*: thine eyes *are* upon me, and I *am* not.
9 *As* the cloud is consumed and vanisheth away:
so he that goeth down to the grave shall come up
no *more*.
10 He shall return no more to his house, neither
shall his place know him any more.
11 Therefore I will not refrain my mouth; I will
speak in the anguish of my spirit; I will complain
in the bitterness of my soul.
12 *Am* I a sea, or a whale, that thou settest a watch
over me?
13 When I say, My bed shall comfort me, my
couch shall ease my complaint;
14 Then thou scarest me with dreams, and terrifi-
est me through visions:
15 So that my soul chooseth strangling, *and* death
rather than my life.
16 I loathe *it*; I would not live alway: let me alone;
for my days *are* vanity.
17 What *is* man, that thou shouldest magnify
him? and that thou shouldest set thine heart upon
him?
18 And *that* thou shouldest visit him every
morning, *and* try him every moment?
19 How long wilt thou not depart from me, nor
let me alone till I swallow down my spittle?
20 I have sinned; what shall I do unto thee, O thou
preserver of men? why hast thou set me as a mark
against thee, so that I am a burden to myself?
21 And why dost thou not pardon my transgres-
sion, and take away mine iniquity? for now shall

---

with which matters may be pressing their children. It is easy to dismiss the burdens of our children as being insignificant or due entirely to their sin. Beware of the danger of digging pits for your children. How can you respond more compassionately to the burdens of other people, whether children or adults?

2. **There comes a time in every Christian's life when he will be called upon to encourage a friend whose trial may run deeper and be more prolonged than anything he himself has ever experienced. In such circumstances that Christian does well not to pretend he understands something he does not but instead to point his friend to someone who does. Christ was "in all points tempted like as we are, yet without sin" (Heb. 4:15). In all of Job's sufferings he would never suffer more than his Savior would eventually suffer. The Christian's ability to minister encouragement, therefore, does not depend on similar experiences so much as it does on his ability to point a tried and afflicted friend to Christ.**

Chapter 7: ***Job turns from Eliphaz and addresses his complaint directly to God.***

7:1 *appointed time*. The Hebrew word is "army," referring to the warfare of life. *like the days of an hireling*. The day-laborer looks forward to rest at the end of the day.

7:2 *earnestly desireth the shadow*. Pants after shade from the sun, looking for some temporary relief. *hireling looketh*. The day-laborer looks forward eagerly to his wage, the reason he toils.

7:3 In contrast, Job has nothing (*vanity*) but trouble without the prospect of relief or reason.

7:6 *weaver's shuttle*. Wooden tool used to pass thread back and forth in a loom for weaving; an image of Job's life quickly passing away.

7:10 Death is final (Pss. 37:10; 103:16).

7:11 *Therefore*. Job built an argument from the extremity of his circumstances (v. 5) and the brevity of life (vv. 6–8) to justify his complaint to God.

7:12 *whale*. Huge sea creature of some sort (Gen. 1:21); sometimes translated "serpent" or "dragon" (Ps. 148:7; Isa. 27:1). In comparison, Job is so small, raising his question as to why God has set a guard (*watch*) over him.

7:14 *visions*. See 4:12–21.

7:16 *vanity*. A breath, something insubstantial (Pss. 62:9; 144:4).

7:17–18 *What is man*. David asked the question out of awe that God would care so much about man, who is such a small part of the vast creation (Ps. 8:4). Job asked in bewilderment, desiring God to pay attention to or scrutinize (*visit*) bigger things and leave him alone.

7:20 *I have sinned*. Job does not claim sinlessness but only that his conscience is clear concerning any sin that warrants his calamity. *mark*. Target.

Thoughts for Personal/Family Worship: Chapter 7

1. **Life is short (vv. 6,16). The Bible is filled with symbols that emphasize that truth: "a tale that is told" (Ps. 90:9) and "a vapour, that appeareth for a little time, and then vanisheth away" (James 4:14). Job's afflictions taught him the brevity of life not just in theory but experientially. During times of prosperity, the brevity of life becomes easy to forget. Like the foolish rich man (Luke 12:18), it is easy to grow comfortable, thinking that life will go on indefinitely. Afflictions preach to us that we should use our time wisely in light of death and eternity (Ps. 90:12).**
2. **Job demonstrates the believer's freedom to go to God even with his complaints (Pss. 73; 77; 88). The Christian should ever keep in mind that God invites him to come boldly before the throne of grace (Heb. 4:16). Job laid his heart bare before the Lord and expressed his concerns forthrightly. Too often even though God knows the thoughts of our heart, we are reluctant to speak to Him candidly and honestly. This does not mean that the Christian approaches God irreverently, but it does mean that he is free to bring to God the burdens of his heart even when those burdens pertain to how we perceive**

I sleep in the dust; and thou shalt seek me in the
morning, but I *shall* not *be*.

CHAPTER 8

THEN answered Bildad the Shuhite, and said,
2 How long wilt thou speak these *things*? and *how*
long shall the words of thy mouth *be like* a strong
wind?
3 Doth God pervert judgment? or doth the Al-
mighty pervert justice?
4 If thy children have sinned against him, and he
have cast them away for their transgression;
5 If thou wouldest seek unto God betimes, and
make thy supplication to the Almighty;
6 If thou *wert* pure and upright; surely now he
would awake for thee, and make the habitation of
thy righteousness prosperous.
7 Though thy beginning was small, yet thy latter
end should greatly increase.
8 For enquire, I pray thee, of the former age, and
prepare thyself to the search of their fathers:
9 (For we *are but of* yesterday, and know nothing,
because our days upon earth *are* a shadow:)
10 Shall not they teach thee, *and* tell thee, and
utter words out of their heart?
11 Can the rush grow up without mire? can the
flag grow without water?
12 Whilst it *is* yet in his greenness, *and* not cut
down, it withereth before any *other* herb.
13 So *are* the paths of all that forget God; and the
hypocrite's hope shall perish:
14 Whose hope shall be cut off, and whose trust
shall be a spider's web.
15 He shall lean upon his house, but it shall not
stand: he shall hold it fast, but it shall not endure.
16 He *is* green before the sun, and his branch
shooteth forth in his garden.
17 His roots are wrapped about the heap, *and*
seeth the place of stones.
18 If he destroy him from his place, then *it* shall
deny him, *saying*, I have not seen thee.
19 Behold, this *is* the joy of his way, and out of the
earth shall others grow.
20 Behold, God will not cast away a perfect *man*,
neither will he help the evil doers:
21 Till he fill thy mouth with laughing, and thy
lips with rejoicing.
22 They that hate thee shall be clothed with
shame; and the dwelling place of the wicked shall
come to nought.

CHAPTER 9

THEN Job answered and said,
2 I know *it is* so of a truth: but how should man
be just with God?
3 If he will contend with him, he cannot answer
him one of a thousand.
4 *He is* wise in heart, and mighty in strength:

God's dealings with us. What burdens do you need to honestly take to Him today?

Chapter 8: *Astonished that Job would think that God perverts justice, Bildad proceeds to set forth some basic truths about the righteousness of God.*

Bildad: All Agree that God Is Just (8:1–22)

8:3 *pervert.* To bend or twist. *judgment.* Justice. *justice.* Righteousness. God is righteous in all his ways (34:10–12).

8:4 *If thy children have sinned.* Again, the assumption is that sorrow and death imply personal sin.

8:5 *betimes.* Early and earnestly.

8:6 *the habitation of thy righteousness prosperous.* Your righteous home to be safe.

8:8–10 *fathers.* Whereas Eliphaz appealed to revelation (4:13), Bildad appealed to history and tradition, arguing that all the sources of antiquity vindicate his opinion.

8:11–13 *rush . . . flag.* Two papyrus-like plants that grew in wet ground. Bildad drew an illustration from nature to say that Job could not flourish because he had forgotten God. *hypocrite.* Godless or profane one.

8:14 *spider's web.* Literally, "the house of a spider," parallel with "his house" (v. 15). The *trust* or confidence of the wicked is flimsy and cannot support him, like a house without a foundation.

8:20 *God will not cast away.* Bildad was judging Job's character based on Job's circumstances. He reasoned that had Job been godly God would never have allowed such calamities to afflict him. *perfect.* Having integrity, or sincere godliness.

Thoughts for Personal/Family Worship: Chapter 8

1. **Though Bildad's argument was misapplied, he did nevertheless recognize that God will do justice (v. 3); His relationship with the Christian stands upon His righteousness. Moses said, "He is the Rock, his work is perfect: for all his ways are judgment: a God of truth and without iniquity, just and right is he" (Deut. 32:4). Justice is not compromised in salvation but rather is satisfied in Christ's atoning death. To enjoy God's peace we must understand not only God's mercy and grace in salvation but God's righteousness also (Rom. 3:21–26). Only when we realize that God does not set aside justice but fulfills it in Christ can we trust Him. Why is it dangerous when we focus so much on God's love that we neglect His justice and righteousness?**
2. **Bildad's appeal to the teachings of the "fathers" (v. 8) reminds us to be careful when citing tradition to support our point of view. To be sure, much biblical truth is contained in the traditions of the church, but the teachings of the fathers lack divine authority in themselves and often err and contradict each other. They may also fail to reflect biblical balance by so emphasizing one truth that they virtually contradict another.**

Job: But How Can Man Be Just before God? (9:1—10:22)

Chapter 9: *After conceding that there is truth in Bildad's speech, Job describes the transcendence of God and laments that there is no daysman who could function as a mediator.*

9:3 *contend.* Make a legal argument against one's opponent in a lawsuit.

9:4 *wise in heart, and mighty in strength.* God is infinitely greater than anyone else in wisdom and power (12:13,16; 36:5; Jer. 10:12; Dan. 2:20). *hath hardened . . . prospered.*

who hath hardened *himself* against him, and hath
prospered?
5 Which removeth the mountains, and they
know not: which overturneth them in his anger.
6 Which shaketh the earth out of her place, and
the pillars thereof tremble.
7 Which commandeth the sun, and it riseth not;
and sealeth up the stars.
8 Which alone spreadeth out the heavens, and
treadeth upon the waves of the sea.
9 Which maketh Arcturus, Orion, and Pleiades,
and the chambers of the south.
10 Which doeth great things past finding out; yea,
and wonders without number.
11 Lo, he goeth by me, and I see *him* not: he
passeth on also, but I perceive him not.
12 Behold, he taketh away, who can hinder him?
who will say unto him, What doest thou?
13 *If* God will not withdraw his anger, the proud
helpers do stoop under him.
14 How much less shall I answer him, *and* choose
out my words *to reason* with him?
15 Whom, though I were righteous, *yet* would I
not answer, *but* I would make supplication to my
judge.
16 If I had called, and he had answered me; *yet*
would I not believe that he had hearkened unto
my voice.
17 For he breaketh me with a tempest, and multi-
plieth my wounds without cause.
18 He will not suffer me to take my breath, but
filleth me with bitterness.
19 If *I speak* of strength, lo, *he is* strong: and if of
judgment, who shall set me a time *to plead*?
20 If I justify myself, mine own mouth shall
condemn me: *if I say*, I *am* perfect, it shall also
prove me perverse.
21 *Though* I *were* perfect, *yet* would I not know
my soul: I would despise my life.
22 This *is* one *thing*, therefore I said *it*, He de-
stroyeth the perfect and the wicked.
23 If the scourge slay suddenly, he will laugh at
the trial of the innocent.
24 The earth is given into the hand of the wicked:
he covereth the faces of the judges thereof; if not,
where, *and* who *is* he?
25 Now my days are swifter than a post: they flee
away, they see no good.
26 They are passed away as the swift ships: as the
eagle *that* hasteth to the prey.
27 If I say, I will forget my complaint, I will leave
off my heaviness, and comfort *myself*:
28 I am afraid of all my sorrows, I know that thou
wilt not hold me innocent.
29 *If* I be wicked, why then labour I in vain?
30 If I wash myself with snow water, and make
my hands never so clean;
31 Yet shalt thou plunge me in the ditch, and
mine own clothes shall abhor me.
32 For *he is* not a man, as I *am*, *that* I should
answer him, *and* we should come together in
judgment.
33 Neither is there any daysman betwixt us, *that*
might lay his hand upon us both.
34 Let him take his rod away from me, and let not
his fear terrify me:

Literally, "has shown stubbornness to him and stayed uninjured or at peace."

9:9 *Arcturus, Orion, and Pleiades.* Constellations (*chambers*) of stars recognized since days of antiquity (38:31–32; Isa. 13:10; Amos 5:8). People have often worshiped the stars or believed they held power over our lives, but God created them and rules them (Gen. 1:16; Deut. 4:19; Ps. 147:4).

9:11–16 Job was frustrated by the invisibility and transcendence of God: He cannot be seen or stopped.

9:13 *proud helpers do stoop.* Possibly, "helpers of Rahab bow down." The mythical Rahab was seen as a great serpent of the sea, a symbol of the power of evil (Ps. 89:9–10).

9:15 *make supplication to my judge.* Pray to God, the Judge, for grace.

9:18 *suffer.* Allow.

9:23 *scourge.* Whip.

9:25 *post.* Runner or courier.

9:33 *daysman.* Arbiter, umpire, or mediator; same word as "plead" (16:21). *betwixt.* Between. Job recognized the need for a mediator between himself and God and thus anticipated the Messiah, realizing that no mere man can take up his own cause.

Thoughts for Personal/Family Worship: Chapter 9

1. **God is "wise in heart, and mighty in strength" (v. 4). He is beyond man's comprehension (vv. 5–11). The world in its wisdom cannot know God (1 Cor. 1:21). Despite all our technological achievements, man cannot discover God. If we arrogantly insist that we cannot believe in what we cannot understand, then we logically exclude believing in a God who is so much greater than ourselves. The only way to know Him is to humble ourselves and quietly listen to His Word. The greatest wonders of the Bible, such as God's having created the world in six days, are completely believable if we start from the premise, expressed as a rhetorical question, "Is anything too hard for the Lord?" The Christian must ever keep this in mind in a world of arrogant skepticism and foolish unbelief. He must especially remember that he cannot comprehend God when God's ways with us are hard. Let us remember that it was precisely when Christ's disciples could not trace God's purpose that He was accomplishing our salvation by the crucifixion of His Son. Much of life is beyond our understanding, but nothing is without purpose.**
2. **Job saw himself in the court of the almighty Judge (vv. 3,15–16; cf. 10:2,14,17), unable to speak for himself yet in need of vindication before the Lord. No one on earth could be the mediator to lay a hand on both God and man and to plead for men (v. 33). However, his longing was perfectly fulfilled by the One who would come to earth, Jesus Christ. Do you see yourself as one who stands in the courtroom of God, the glorious Judge? How will you be counted righteous before Him? There is no other way than by the heavenly Mediator, the righteous Son of God (1 John 2:1).**

35 *Then* would I speak, and not fear him; but *it is*
not so with me.

CHAPTER 10

MY soul is weary of my life; I will leave my com-
plaint upon myself; I will speak in the bitterness
of my soul.
2 I will say unto God, Do not condemn me; shew
me wherefore thou contendest with me.
3 *Is it* good unto thee that thou shouldest op-
press, that thou shouldest despise the work of
thine hands, and shine upon the counsel of the
wicked?
4 Hast thou eyes of flesh? or seest thou as man
seeth?
5 *Are* thy days as the days of man? *are* thy years
as man's days,
6 That thou enquirest after mine iniquity, and
searchest after my sin?
7 Thou knowest that I am not wicked; and *there
is* none that can deliver out of thine hand.
8 Thine hands have made me and fashioned me
together round about; yet thou dost destroy me.
9 Remember, I beseech thee, that thou hast made
me as the clay; and wilt thou bring me into dust
again?
10 Hast thou not poured me out as milk, and
curdled me like cheese?
11 Thou hast clothed me with skin and flesh, and
hast fenced me with bones and sinews.
12 Thou hast granted me life and favour, and thy
visitation hath preserved my spirit.
13 And these *things* hast thou hid in thine heart: I
know that this *is* with thee.
14 If I sin, then thou markest me, and thou wilt
not acquit me from mine iniquity.
15 If I be wicked, woe unto me; and *if* I be righ-
teous, *yet* will I not lift up my head. *I am* full of
confusion; therefore see thou mine affliction;
16 For it increaseth. Thou huntest me as a fierce
lion: and again thou shewest thyself marvellous
upon me.
17 Thou renewest thy witnesses against me, and
increasest thine indignation upon me; changes
and war *are* against me.
18 Wherefore then hast thou brought me forth
out of the womb? Oh that I had given up the
ghost, and no eye had seen me!
19 I should have been as though I had not been;
I should have been carried from the womb to the
grave.
20 *Are* not my days few? cease *then, and* let me
alone, that I may take comfort a little,
21 Before I go *whence* I shall not return, *even* to
the land of darkness and the shadow of death;
22 A land of darkness, as darkness *itself; and*
of the shadow of death, without any order, and
where the light *is* as darkness.

CHAPTER 11

THEN answered Zophar the Naamathite, and said,
2 Should not the multitude of words be answered?

Chapter 10: *Job complains that God does not understand him because God is not a man.*

10:1 In *bitterness* of soul even a man like Job may speak in an ill-advised manner.
10:2 *contendest.* See note at 9:3.
10:3 *shine upon the counsel of the wicked.* Give success to the plans of sinners.
10:4–7 Job asked a series of rhetorical questions to press home the point that God is not a man limited by human senses and investigation, and therefore he concluded, *Thou knowest that I am not wicked.* God's omniscience (perfect knowledge of all things) made the suffering of the righteous all the more perplexing to Job.
10:8 It seems absurd that the God who *made* man would *destroy* him for no apparent reason.
10:9 *bring me into dust again.* Literally, "to dust return me," using the same words that God spoke to the fallen Adam (Gen. 3:19; cf. Job 34:15; Eccl. 3:20).
10:10 *milk . . . cheese.* Figures of speech for God's formation of a child in the womb (Ps. 139:13–16).
10:11 *fenced me.* Hebrew, "to intertwine or weave," suggesting the intricacy of his created body.
10:12 *thy visitation.* The Hebrew word has the idea of giving special attention.
10:15 *confusion.* Shame.
10:16 *shewest thyself marvellous.* The root of this verb means to do something amazing; in this form it means that God proves Himself to be beyond man's comprehension.
10:18 *given up the ghost.* Literally, "expired or passed away."
10:21 *land of darkness.* The grave, where his body, though not his spirit, will lie senseless.

Thoughts for Personal/Family Worship: Chapter 10

God's sovereignty implies that He is intimately involved in our lives. He forms us in the womb (vv. 10–11), knows us completely and perfectly (vv. 4–7), and sustains our lives (v. 12). When one is convinced of God's love and grace, these truths are a great comfort (Ps. 139). However, the sovereignty of God can become an offense when someone feels trapped in a living hell of bitterness and weariness under a sense of God's condemnation (Job 10:1–2). When we meet a godly Christian in such a sad condition, it may not help him simply to tell him that God is in control. This book reminds such a sufferer that he is not alone or unique but stands in solidarity with people like Job, and especially with the Lord Jesus Christ, who cried out on the cross, "My God, my God, why hast thou forsaken me?" (Mark 15:34). Christ alone could say to God, "Thou knowest that I am not wicked" (Job 10:7). He suffered for sinners. On the basis of His agony, whatever taste of hell the believer may endure on earth will never become the eternal hell. What a Savior!

Chapter 11: *Zophar presses the argument with even greater fervor that Job is a sinner who needs to repent.*

Zophar: Does Your Talk Justify You? (11:1–20)

11:1 Zophar, the least sympathetic of the three friends,

and should a man full of talk be justified?
3 Should thy lies make men hold their peace?
and when thou mockest, shall no man make thee
ashamed?
4 For thou hast said, My doctrine *is* pure, and I
am clean in thine eyes.
5 But oh that God would speak, and open his lips
against thee;
6 And that he would shew thee the secrets of
wisdom, that *they are* double to that which is!
Know therefore that God exacteth of thee *less*
than thine iniquity *deserveth*.
7 Canst thou by searching find out God? canst
thou find out the Almighty unto perfection?
8 *It is* as high as heaven; what canst thou do?
deeper than hell; what canst thou know?
9 The measure thereof *is* longer than the earth,
and broader than the sea.
10 If he cut off, and shut up, or gather together,
then who can hinder him?
11 For he knoweth vain men: he seeth wickedness
also; will he not then consider *it*?
12 For vain man would be wise, though man be
born *like* a wild ass's colt.
13 If thou prepare thine heart, and stretch out
thine hands toward him;
14 If iniquity *be* in thine hand, put it far away, and
let not wickedness dwell in thy tabernacles.
15 For then shalt thou lift up thy face without
spot; yea, thou shalt be stedfast, and shalt not fear:
16 Because thou shalt forget *thy* misery, *and*
remember *it* as waters *that* pass away:
17 And *thine* age shall be clearer than the noon-
day; thou shalt shine forth, thou shalt be as the
morning.
18 And thou shalt be secure, because there is
hope; yea, thou shalt dig *about thee, and* thou
shalt take thy rest in safety.
19 Also thou shalt lie down, and none shall make
thee afraid; yea, many shall make suit unto thee.
20 But the eyes of the wicked shall fail, and they
shall not escape, and their hope *shall be as* the
giving up of the ghost.

CHAPTER 12

AND Job answered and said,
2 No doubt but ye *are* the people, and wisdom
shall die with you.
3 But I have understanding as well as you; I *am*
not inferior to you: yea, who knoweth not such
things as these?
4 I am *as* one mocked of his neighbour, who call-
eth upon God, and he answereth him: the just
upright *man is* laughed to scorn.
5 He that is ready to slip with *his* feet *is as* a lamp
despised in the thought of him that is at ease.
6 The tabernacles of robbers prosper, and they

---

claims that Job is suffering less than he deserves (v. 6).

11:3 *Should thy lies make men hold their peace?* Literally, "should your loose talk reduce men to silence?"

11:6 *God exacteth of thee less . . . deserveth.* Literally, "God has allowed to be forgotten for you part of your iniquity."

11:7–9 *high as heaven . . . deeper than hell.* The extremes of height and depth, expressing the idea that God is infinite (without limitation, Ps. 145:3; Eph. 3:8,18) and incomprehensible (beyond our full understanding, Job 5:9; 9:10; Isa. 55:9). Zophar's theology is sound but his application skewed.

11:11 *vain.* False, lying, or worthless. Zophar's harshness toward Job is evident here.

11:12 *vain.* Hollow-minded; a different word from that used in v. 11.

11:14 *tabernacles.* Tents or dwelling places.

11:17 *thine age shall be clearer than the noonday.* Literally, "[your] lifespan shall arise higher than noon," an image expressing an appearance of vigor and vitality.

11:19 *shall make suit unto thee.* Literally, "will ask for your favor."

11:20 *giving up of the ghost.* Literally, "expiring of soul."

Thoughts for Personal/Family Worship: Chapter 11

1. **Zophar exemplifies something every Christian should want, as well as something he should avoid. He demonstrates a jealousy for the honor of God. This jealousy is something that is too rare in times when ungodliness permeates the world. Blasphemy and the profaning of God's name become so commonplace that the Christian too often accepts them and becomes desensitized to them. To the degree that Zophar was jealous for God's honor, he is commendable. Unfortunately, Zophar lacked proper humility. It never crossed his mind that he could be wrong, and so with unrelenting dogmatism he condemned Job as though speaking for God. His theology was sound, but his spirit and applications were wrong. May the Lord grant a proper jealousy for his honor, accompanied by the proper humility. There is hardly a worse manifestation of pride than the assurance of always being right.**
2. **This chapter presents one of the most sublime statements about the transcendence of God (vv. 7–9). The Christian need never fear overestimating the greatness of God. There is a constant danger, on the other hand, of underestimating His greatness. Beware of limiting the Holy One of Israel (Ps. 78:41). Meditate frequently on how small you are compared to Him, both in mind and in strength. What are some ways you have recently been reminded that God is far beyond your understanding?**

Job: I Know that I Shall Be Justified (12:1—14:22)

Chapter 12: ***Job senses that his friends feel superior to him and resists their efforts to treat him as inferior.***

12:2 *No doubt but ye are the people.* By his sarcasm Job scorned the arrogance of his comforters.

12:3 *who knoweth not such things as these?* Their assessment of Job reflected common knowledge but failed to address the real issue. Job did not deny the content of what they said, only its relevance to him.

12:4 *neighbour.* His fellow man in general, not the resident next door.

12:5 Those who are *at ease* are prone to judge with contempt those whose feet *slip*.

12:6 *The tabernacles of robbers prosper.* The dwelling places

that provoke God are secure; into whose hand
God bringeth *abundantly*.
7 But ask now the beasts, and they shall teach
thee; and the fowls of the air, and they shall tell
thee:
8 Or speak to the earth, and it shall teach thee:
and the fishes of the sea shall declare unto thee.
9 Who knoweth not in all these that the hand of
the LORD hath wrought this?
10 In whose hand *is* the soul of every living thing,
and the breath of all mankind.
11 Doth not the ear try words? and the mouth
taste his meat?
12 With the ancient *is* wisdom; and in length of
days understanding.
13 With him *is* wisdom and strength, he hath
counsel and understanding.
14 Behold, he breaketh down, and it cannot be
built again: he shutteth up a man, and there can
be no opening.
15 Behold, he withholdeth the waters, and they
dry up: also he sendeth them out, and they over-
turn the earth.
16 With him *is* strength and wisdom: the de-
ceived and the deceiver *are* his.
17 He leadeth counsellors away spoiled, and
maketh the judges fools.
18 He looseth the bond of kings, and girdeth
their loins with a girdle.
19 He leadeth princes away spoiled, and over-
throweth the mighty.
20 He removeth away the speech of the trusty,
and taketh away the understanding of the aged.
21 He poureth contempt upon princes, and
weakeneth the strength of the mighty.
22 He discovereth deep things out of darkness,
and bringeth out to light the shadow of death.
23 He increaseth the nations, and destroyeth
them: he enlargeth the nations, and straiteneth
them *again*.
24 He taketh away the heart of the chief of the
people of the earth, and causeth them to wander
in a wilderness *where there is* no way.
25 They grope in the dark without light, and he
maketh them to stagger like *a* drunken *man*.

CHAPTER 13

LO, mine eye hath seen all *this*, mine ear hath
heard and understood it.
2 What ye know, *the same* do I know also: I *am*
not inferior unto you.
3 Surely I would speak to the Almighty, and I de-
sire to reason with God.
4 But ye *are* forgers of lies, ye *are* all physicians
of no value.
5 O that ye would altogether hold your peace!
and it should be your wisdom.

---

of those who destroy are at ease. Some wicked men seem to have every temporal advantage (21:7–15). This is a common problem for faith (Pss. 37; 49; 73).

12:9 *the hand of the LORD hath wrought this*. God has done it by His power.

12:10 *soul*. Life. *mankind*. Literally, "all flesh of man." All living things, including people, depend upon God for life and breath (34:14–15; Ps. 104:29–30; Isa. 42:5; Acts 17:25).

12:11 *meat*. Any kind of food.

12:12 *the ancient*. Old men.

12:13–25 Job declared that the God rules over all events and all kinds of people, being the source of all *wisdom* and *strength* (vv. 13,16; cf. 9:4), and therefore controlling every gain or loss of either.

12:16 *deceived and the deceiver*. Though God cannot lie (Num. 23:19), He rules over liars and determines the degree of their success (2 Thess. 2:11).

12:17 *spoiled*. As captives, stripped of everything.

12:18 *girdeth their loins with a girdle*. Literally, "secures a waistcloth around their hips with a belt."

12:19 *spoiled*. The Hebrew has the idea of being barefoot, a sign of humiliation.

12:20 *trusty*. Those trusted for their wisdom.

12:23 *enlargeth . . . straiteneth*. Scatters abroad and leads in.

Thoughts for Personal/Family Worship: Chapter 12

1. **Job said, "I am not inferior to you" (v. 3, cf. 13:2). One of the Devil's tactics for keeping a Christian in despair is to make him feel inferior to his critics. Job's antidote to inferiority, however, was not self-esteem but the knowledge of his God (Jer. 9:23–24). Understanding God's sovereignty both shielded him from their false arguments and made all men look very small and insignificant. When you are despised because of your suffering or weakness by those at ease, do not respond with hatred and vengeance but by looking to the greatness of your God. He will be your wisdom and your strength. If the Christian can lay hold of the most basic of all truths, that God rules over all, he will not be crushed to despair by what he perceives to be his shortcomings, sins, or failures. He does not need to be a god, for he has God.**
2. **"Who knoweth not in all these that the hand of the LORD hath wrought this?" (v. 9). Nothing escapes the sovereign rule of God. Not even a sparrow can fall to the ground apart from God's rule. The Christian may not understand why God is dealing the way He does. Job did not understand. Yet all the Christian's seasons of adversity are known to God and in a mysterious way directed by God. The affirmation of the simple and sublime truth of God's sovereign dominion over every realm of life will instill in the Christian hope that his trial will not only pass but will have a sanctifying effect on his life, preparing him for service here and for future service in the glories to come. How has God's sovereignty comforted you in your trials?**

Chapter 13: *Job pleads with his friends to keep silence and expresses his confidence that he will be vindicated and that his friends will be reproved.*

13:3 *reason*. Go to court; Job desires to argue his case before the Lord.

13:4 *forgers of lies*. Those who smear or plaster with falsehoods.

13:5 *hold your peace*. Literally, "keep silent," just as they had at the beginning (2:13).

GOD'S WISDOM

The wisdom of God is one of His infinite, eternal, and unchangeable attributes (Westminster Shorter Catechism, Q. 4). God's wisdom is not only one of His divine perfections, but it designates the very Person of God, specifically the Second Person of the Trinity.

Essential to understanding the significance of wisdom, both as a divine perfection and as a Person, is understanding the meaning of the word *wisdom*, which simply refers to skill or ability. The sphere of application of that skill or ability is defined by the context in which the word occurs. In Old Testament times whatever someone was good at was considered his wisdom.

Wisdom, as a divine perfection, highlights God's infinite ability to do whatever is appropriate for God to do. It is related to His infinite knowledge, His omniscience, in that He knows all things. It is also related to His infinite power, His omnipotence, in that He can do all things. In His infinite wisdom God uses the best possible means to achieve the best possible ends. His comprehensive knowledge of everything is coupled with His ability to execute His purposes. He is all-wise; therefore, God is infinitely good in everything He does.

The operations of God's wisdom occur principally in His works of creation and providence. Creation is a uniquely divine activity, giving evidence of God's infinite power to bring His purpose and plan into fruition: "The LORD by wisdom hath founded the earth" (Prov. 3:19). With infinite skill and ability He spoke the world into existence. Providence is the ongoing work of God's infinite wisdom whereby He preserves and governs His creation to the end that He has purposed for His own glory. This wise providence extends to the natural order, as He sets the course for the oceans, wind, weather, and animal migrations (Job 28:26; 37:1–24; 38:10–11; 39:26; Eccl. 1:6–7). It also includes the moral order, extending to every way and motive of man (Prov. 15:11; 16:2). The Lord's challenge to Job to sit upon the throne and govern testifies to His absolute control (Job 40:8–14). The workings of providence are often mysterious: "Whence then cometh wisdom . . . it is hid from the eyes of all living" (Job 28:20–21). But even when the circumstances of life seem to be out of control, we can rest assured that God, according to His wisdom, is working all things together for good (Rom. 8:28). He knows what He is doing, and He is doing it in the best possible way to accomplish the best possible end. Trust His wisdom.

Wisdom, as a divine Person, is a title of Christ. Chapters 1, 8, and 9 of Proverbs employ the word *Wisdom* to refer to the person of the Messiah, not just to personify a divine perfection. That Proverbs calls the Messiah "Wisdom" is not much different from Isaiah's calling God "the Holy One of Israel." Both titles use one of the Lord's perfections to designate Him. The New Testament sanctions the messianic interpretation. Consider these New Testament texts that identify Christ as Wisdom: Matthew 11:19,25–30; 23:34; Luke 11:49; 1 Corinthians 1:24,30; and Colossians 2:3.

Proverbs 8 is perhaps the most detailed description of Wisdom; it sets forth three strands of evidence that point to the messianic identification. *First*, Wisdom is God. Wisdom is distinct from God, speaking of God in the third person (vv. 27–30), yet He makes statements demanding deity. This reflects the trinitarian relationship between Father and Son. For instance, there are at least ten statements suggesting that Wisdom was present prior to creation (vv. 22–30) and involved in the creative work (v. 30, see explanation in Proverbs notes). Compare this with John 1:1,3; the only difference is that John calls Christ "the Word" and Solomon calls Him "Wisdom." *Second*, Wisdom is the Messiah. He does what elsewhere in Scripture the Messiah does. This is particularly true in Proverbs 8:1–21. As Prophet He speaks God's Word (vv. 6–8). As King He exercises absolute rule over lesser sovereigns (v. 16). What Isaiah says about the Messiah in his prophecy (Isa. 11:2) parallels what Solomon says in Proverbs 8:12–14. *Third*, Wisdom is the object of saving faith (v. 17; cf. John 6:37). Saving faith always and only has Christ as its object.

6 Hear now my reasoning, and hearken to the
pleadings of my lips.
7 Will ye speak wickedly for God? and talk deceit-
fully for him?
8 Will ye accept his person? will ye contend for
God?
9 Is it good that he should search you out? or as
one man mocketh another, do ye *so* mock him?
10 He will surely reprove you, if ye do secretly
accept persons.
11 Shall not his excellency make you afraid? and
his dread fall upon you?
12 Your remembrances *are* like unto ashes, your
bodies to bodies of clay.
13 Hold your peace, let me alone, that I may
speak, and let come on me what *will*.
14 Wherefore do I take my flesh in my teeth, and
put my life in mine hand?
15 Though he slay me, yet will I trust in him: but I
will maintain mine own ways before him.
16 He also *shall be* my salvation: for an hypocrite
shall not come before him.
17 Hear diligently my speech, and my declaration
with your ears.
18 Behold now, I have ordered *my* cause; I know
that I shall be justified.
19 Who *is* he *that* will plead with me? for now, if I
hold my tongue, I shall give up the ghost.
20 Only do not two *things* unto me: then will I
not hide myself from thee.
21 Withdraw thine hand far from me: and let not
thy dread make me afraid.
22 Then call thou, and I will answer: or let me
speak, and answer thou me.
23 How many *are* mine iniquities and sins? make
me to know my transgression and my sin.
24 Wherefore hidest thou thy face, and holdest
me for thine enemy?
25 Wilt thou break a leaf driven to and fro? and
wilt thou pursue the dry stubble?
26 For thou writest bitter things against me, and
makest me to possess the iniquities of my youth.
27 Thou puttest my feet also in the stocks, and
lookest narrowly unto all my paths; thou settest a
print upon the heels of my feet.
28 And he, as a rotten thing, consumeth, as a
garment that is moth eaten.

CHAPTER 14

MAN *that is* born of a woman *is* of few days, and
full of trouble.
2 He cometh forth like a flower, and is cut down:
he fleeth also as a shadow, and continueth not.
3 And dost thou open thine eyes upon such an
one, and bringest me into judgment with thee?
4 Who can bring a clean *thing* out of an unclean?
not one.
5 Seeing his days *are* determined, the number of
his months *are* with thee, thou hast appointed his
bounds that he cannot pass;
6 Turn from him, that he may rest, till he shall
accomplish, as an hireling, his day.
7 For there is hope of a tree, if it be cut down, that
it will sprout again, and that the tender branch
thereof will not cease.

13:6 *reasoning . . . pleadings.* Legal arguments.
13:7 *speak wickedly for God.* As typical in theological controversy, all involved claim that God is on their side, even if they speak wrongly about Him (42:7).
13:10 *accept persons.* Literally, "lift up faces," an idiom expressing favoritism.
13:12 *Your remembrances are like unto ashes.* Literally, "your memorial words are proverbs of dust or ashes."
13:13 *Hold your peace.* Be quiet.
13:15 *Though.* The Hebrew word is used as an interjection and is best expressed with an exclamation mark: "He may kill me; I will hope in Him!"—an expression of great faith. *I will maintain mine own ways before him.* I will argue my case in His presence, an attitude for which the Lord would rebuke Job (40:2).
13:16 *He also shall be my salvation.* An expression of Job's confidence in the Lord (Ex. 15:2; Ps. 18:46). *hypocrite.* A godless or profane person.
13:18 *I shall be justified.* God, the Judge, would declare him righteous.
13:19 *hold my tongue.* Literally, "am silent." *shall give up the ghost.* Literally, "will expire."
13:27 *Thou . . . lookest narrowly unto all my paths.* As a guard who keeps watch over a prisoner.

Thoughts for Personal/Family Worship: Chapter 13

1. **"Though he slay me, yet will I trust in him" (v. 15). At times Job's faith seemed to waiver, but he never gave up trusting God. Trials test the quality of the Christian's faith. There is such a thing as temporary faith (Matt. 13:20–21) or vain faith (1 Cor. 15:2), but saving faith perseveres when life seems dark and God's dealings do not seem right. God is pleased to subject Christians to trials so that they may perceive the quality of their own faith (1 Peter 1:6–7). For Job to affirm that he would continue to trust God even if God were to slay him means that Job saw beyond this present life (1 Cor. 15:19). Does your faith see beyond this world?**
2. **"But I will maintain mine own ways before him" (v. 15). It's amazing that such a statement could follow Job's strong affirmation of faith. The first part of the verse brings Job's faith into view. But the second part brings the corruption of Job's flesh into view. Trials work to strengthen faith by highlighting and exposing the weakness of our faith and the reality of our sin. Apart from such fiery trials, it becomes easy to become self-righteous or self-sufficient.**

Chapter 14: ***Job recognizes the brevity and troubles of life and anticipates the change that is coming.***

14:4 *Who can bring a clean thing out of an unclean?* Fallen human nature cannot produce a life that will please the holy God (Rom. 8:7–8). This is why the new birth is necessary (John 3:3–7).
14:7 *it will sprout again.* There is hope of life after death (see note at v. 14).

8 Though the root thereof wax old in the earth,
and the stock thereof die in the ground;
9 *Yet* through the scent of water it will bud, and
bring forth boughs like a plant.
10 But man dieth, and wasteth away: yea, man
giveth up the ghost, and where *is* he?
11 *As* the waters fail from the sea, and the flood
decayeth and drieth up:
12 So man lieth down, and riseth not: till the
heavens *be* no more, they shall not awake, nor be
raised out of their sleep.
13 O that thou wouldest hide me in the grave,
that thou wouldest keep me secret, until thy
wrath be past, that thou wouldest appoint me a
set time, and remember me!
14 If a man die, shall he live *again*? all the days
of my appointed time will I wait, till my change
come.
15 Thou shalt call, and I will answer thee: thou
wilt have a desire to the work of thine hands.
16 For now thou numberest my steps: dost thou
not watch over my sin?
17 My transgression *is* sealed up in a bag, and
thou sewest up mine iniquity.
18 And surely the mountain falling cometh to
nought, and the rock is removed out of his place.
19 The waters wear the stones: thou washest away
the things which grow *out* of the dust of the earth;
and thou destroyest the hope of man.
20 Thou prevailest for ever against him, and he
passeth: thou changest his countenance, and
sendest him away.
21 His sons come to honour, and he knoweth *it*
not; and they are brought low, but he perceiveth
it not of them.
22 But his flesh upon him shall have pain, and his
soul within him shall mourn.

CHAPTER 15

THEN answered Eliphaz the Temanite, and said,
2 Should a wise man utter vain knowledge, and
fill his belly with the east wind?
3 Should he reason with unprofitable talk? or
with speeches wherewith he can do no good?
4 Yea, thou castest off fear, and restrainest prayer
before God.
5 For thy mouth uttereth thine iniquity, and thou
choosest the tongue of the crafty.
6 Thine own mouth condemneth thee, and not I:
yea, thine own lips testify against thee.
7 *Art* thou the first man *that* was born? or wast
thou made before the hills?
8 Hast thou heard the secret of God? and dost
thou restrain wisdom to thyself?
9 What knowest thou, that we know not? *what*
understandest thou, which *is* not in us?
10 With us *are* both the grayheaded and very
aged men, much elder than thy father.
11 *Are* the consolations of God small with thee? is
there any secret thing with thee?
12 Why doth thine heart carry thee away? and
what do thy eyes wink at,
13 That thou turnest thy spirit against God, and
lettest *such* words go out of thy mouth?
14 What *is* man, that he should be clean? and

14:8 *wax.* To grow. *stock.* Stump.

14:9 The tree appeared to be dead but gave evidence of new life.

14:10 *wasteth.* Dwindles, describing the decay of the body in the grave. *giveth up the ghost.* Expires, and that appears to be the end.

14:12 *riseth not: till the heavens be no more.* Death will not be overcome until God creates a new heavens and a new earth (Rev. 21:1–4).

14:13 Job still longed for physical death as his only hope of physical relief.

14:14 *my appointed time.* The warfare or hard service of his earthly life (7:1). Job was placing his hope in life after death. *my change.* His bodily resurrection; same root word as "sprout," used of the stump of a tree in v. 7. As a tree stump may sprout again, so believers cut off by death will be called out of the grave by the Lord (v. 15; 1 Thess. 4:13–16).

14:16 *For now.* Hope for the future gives way to despair in the present.

Thoughts for Personal/Family Worship: Chapter 14

1. **"Who can bring a clean thing out of an unclean? Not one" (v. 4). Man must be born again (John 3:3), as he is helpless to wash away his defilement (Jer. 2:22). However, what is impossible for man is possible for God (Matt. 19:26). God cleansed sinners by sending His Son to shed His blood for their sins (1 John 1:7). Today it can be said of the Christian that he is completely clean in his position before God (John 13:10). The Christian also needs practical cleansing each day by confessing his sins and calling upon Christ (1 John 1:9).**
2. **"All the days of my appointed time will I wait, till my change come" (v. 14). Job demonstrates in this saying the kind of groaning that characterizes every true child of God (Rom. 8:23). As long as the Christian lives in a world that is marked by sin, he will experience dissatisfaction. But like Job he can anticipate a coming change: we "look for new heavens and a new earth, wherein dwelleth righteousness" (2 Peter 3:13). What a change will be marked by the second coming of Christ! That change will also come to the Christian himself: "when he shall appear, we shall be like him; for we shall see him as he is" (1 John 3:2). How can this hope give a Christian patience in suffering?**

Second Cycle of Dialogue (15:1—21:34)

Chapter 15: *Eliphaz intensifies his reproof of Job.*

Eliphaz: How Can He Who Is Born of a Woman Be Righteous? (15:1–35)

15:2 *vain knowledge.* Literally, "knowledge of wind."

15:4 *thou castest off fear.* You destroy the fear of God.

15:10 *very aged men.* Another appeal to the tradition of the fathers (8:8).

15:14 *clean . . . righteous.* Eliphaz here expressed a true view

he which is born of a woman, that he should be
righteous?
15 Behold, he putteth no trust in his saints; yea,
the heavens are not clean in his sight.
16 How much more abominable and filthy *is*
man, which drinketh iniquity like water?
17 I will shew thee, hear me; and that *which* I have
seen I will declare;
18 Which wise men have told from their fathers,
and have not hid *it*:
19 Unto whom alone the earth was given, and no
stranger passed among them.
20 The wicked man travaileth with pain all *his*
days, and the number of years is hidden to the
oppressor.
21 A dreadful sound *is* in his ears: in prosperity
the destroyer shall come upon him.
22 He believeth not that he shall return out of
darkness, and he is waited for of the sword.
23 He wandereth abroad for bread, *saying*, Where
is it? he knoweth that the day of darkness is ready
at his hand.
24 Trouble and anguish shall make him afraid;
they shall prevail against him, as a king ready to
the battle.
25 For he stretcheth out his hand against God,
and strengtheneth himself against the Almighty.
26 He runneth upon him, *even* on *his* neck, upon
the thick bosses of his bucklers:
27 Because he covereth his face with his fatness,
and maketh collops of fat on *his* flanks.
28 And he dwelleth in desolate cities, *and* in
houses which no man inhabiteth, which are ready
to become heaps.
29 He shall not be rich, neither shall his substance
continue, neither shall he prolong the perfection
thereof upon the earth.
30 He shall not depart out of darkness; the flame
shall dry up his branches, and by the breath of his
mouth shall he go away.
31 Let not him that is deceived trust in vanity: for
vanity shall be his recompence.
32 It shall be accomplished before his time, and
his branch shall not be green.
33 He shall shake off his unripe grape as the vine,
and shall cast off his flower as the olive.
34 For the congregation of hypocrites *shall be*
desolate, and fire shall consume the tabernacles
of bribery.
35 They conceive mischief, and bring forth
vanity, and their belly prepareth deceit.

CHAPTER 16

THEN Job answered and said,
2 I have heard many such things: miserable
comforters *are* ye all.
3 Shall vain words have an end? or what embold-
eneth thee that thou answerest?
4 I also could speak as ye *do*: if your soul were
in my soul's stead, I could heap up words against
you, and shake mine head at you.
5 *But* I would strengthen you with my mouth, and
the moving of my lips should asswage *your grief*.
6 Though I speak, my grief is not asswaged: and
though I forbear, what am I eased?
7 But now he hath made me weary: thou hast
made desolate all my company.

of man's sinfulness (14:4) but applied it wrongly to Job's situation. It is tragically possible to deduce error from truth.

15:15 *no trust in his saints . . . heavens are not clean*. Eliphaz returned to the message he had received from the vision of the spirit (4:15–18).

15:16 *drinketh iniquity like water*. Fallen man desires and delights in sin as if it were his very life, even while it kills him (Prov. 4:16–17; 9:17; 15:14; 19:28; Isa. 44:20).

15:19 *stranger*. Foreigner.

15:20 *the number of years is hidden*. Most likely that his years were numbered by God but unknown to him, a cause for fear.

15:22 *is waited for of*. Literally, "is destined to."

15:26 *thick bosses of his bucklers*. The thick knobs of his shields, referring to the strength of the shields.

15:27 *maketh collops of fat on his flanks*. Makes his waist area bulge with a superabundance of fat.

15:31 *vanity*. Nothingness.

15:34 *hypocrites*. Godless or profane people; not the same idea as hypocrites who play parts like actors in religion (Matt. 6:1–2; 23:25). *tabernacles*. Tents or dwelling places.

15:35 *mischief*. The Hebrew, "trouble." *vanity*. Misery, a different word from that in v. 31.

Thoughts for Personal/Family Worship: Chapter 15

1. **Eliphaz was under the mistaken impression that Job was treating God lightly so that He would not be feared (v. 4). If this were true, as a result sin would not be hated, for "the fear of the LORD is to hate evil" (Prov. 8:13). Though falsely applied to Job, this was a very serious charge. We should be careful, whether in suffering or in prosperity, never to say or do anything that would diminish the awe and respect people have toward God or to encourage a light view of sin.**
2. **Sin is not only engaging in bad behavior or making poor choices but is an inward love for what is bad that deeply motivates mankind to pursue evil (v. 16). The heart itself is corrupt, and this corrupts everything in human life (Gen. 6:5; Prov. 4:23; Mark 7:21–23; Rom. 3:9–18). Our problem is who we are and what we love (1 John 2:15–16). How should this truth affect how we view ourselves? How should it affect our sense of need for Christ?**

Job: You Are All Miserable Comforters (16:1—17:16)

Chapter 16: ***Job rebukes his friends, describes his misery, and appeals to God.***

16:2 *miserable comforters*. Literally, "comforters of trouble."

16:3 *vain*. Literally, "of air or wind," expressing that these words are without substance. *emboldeneth thee*. Provokes you.

16:5 *asswage*. Relieve (v. 6).

16:7–17 What Job felt, Christ experienced to the full. The language itself draws a line to Christ.

8 And thou hast filled me with wrinkles, *which* is
a witness *against me*: and my leanness rising up in
me beareth witness to my face.
9 He teareth *me* in his wrath, who hateth me: he
gnasheth upon me with his teeth; mine enemy
sharpeneth his eyes upon me.
10 They have gaped upon me with their mouth;
they have smitten me upon the cheek reproachfully;
they have gathered themselves together against me.
11 God hath delivered me to the ungodly, and
turned me over into the hands of the wicked.
12 I was at ease, but he hath broken me asunder:
he hath also taken *me* by my neck, and shaken me
to pieces, and set me up for his mark.
13 His archers compass me round about, he
cleaveth my reins asunder, and doth not spare; he
poureth out my gall upon the ground.
14 He breaketh me with breach upon breach, he
runneth upon me like a giant.
15 I have sewed sackcloth upon my skin, and
defiled my horn in the dust.
16 My face is foul with weeping, and on my eye-
lids *is* the shadow of death;
17 Not for *any* injustice in mine hands: also my
prayer *is* pure.
18 O earth, cover not thou my blood, and let my
cry have no place.
19 Also now, behold, my witness *is* in heaven, and
my record *is* on high.
20 My friends scorn me: *but* mine eye poureth
out *tears* unto God.
21 O that one might plead for a man with God, as
a man *pleadeth* for his neighbour!
22 When a few years are come, then I shall go the
way *whence* I shall not return.

CHAPTER 17

My breath is corrupt, my days are extinct, the
graves *are ready* for me.
2 *Are there* not mockers with me? and doth not
mine eye continue in their provocation?
3 Lay down now, put me in a surety with thee;
who *is* he *that* will strike hands with me?
4 For thou hast hid their heart from understand-
ing: therefore shalt thou not exalt *them*.
5 He that speaketh flattery to *his* friends, even the
eyes of his children shall fail.
6 He hath made me also a byword of the people;
and aforetime I was as a tabret.
7 Mine eye also is dim by reason of sorrow, and
all my members *are* as a shadow.
8 Upright *men* shall be astonied at this, and the in-
nocent shall stir up himself against the hypocrite.
9 The righteous also shall hold on his way, and
he that hath clean hands shall be stronger and
stronger.
10 But as for you all, do ye return, and come now:

16:10 *gaped.* Opened against me.
16:12 *broken me asunder.* Shattered me into pieces.
16:13 *compass.* Surround. *cleaveth.* Slices open or pierces. *reins.* Kidneys, referring generally to the innards. *gall.* Bile, representative of bodily fluids.
16:14 *breach.* Break. *giant.* A mighty man, a warrior.
16:15 *horn.* Symbol for power or strength.
16:18 *earth, cover not thou my blood.* An appeal for divine justice against those who mistreat him (Gen. 4:10–11; Isa. 26:21).
16:19 *my witness . . . record.* The words are synonyms, both referring to a person who testifies in a legal case. The mediator whom Job could not find on earth (9:33) he now affirms that he has *in heaven*. Christ, the only Mediator, already interceded for His people in heaven before His incarnation (Zech. 3:1–5).
16:21 *plead.* Same word as that translated "daysman" (9:33). *neighbour.* Or friend (same word as in v. 20). Job's friends had failed to comfort him, but he sought comfort from a heavenly Advocate.

Thoughts for Personal/Family Worship: Chapter 16

1. **"Miserable comforters are ye all" (v. 2). Counsel that is void of Christ is also void of comfort. There is a place for the Christian to come under a sense of sin, but if all a counselor manages to do is to keep his focus on sin, real or imagined, then his counsel will accomplish no more than that of Job's friends. Job recognized that true encouragement will strengthen the weak and relieve the grieving (v. 5). Whether it is a pastor speaking to a church member, a parent dealing with a child, or a person coming alongside a suffering friend, let us seek by God's grace not to degenerate into "miserable comforters" who only dwell on sin and fail to make much of Christ.**
2. **Job desired a sympathetic high priest (v. 21). The function of the priest was to plead for the people he represented. And in order to plead effectively, that priest had to have some idea of the struggles that were being experienced by the people he represented. Christ is such a High Priest for his people (Heb. 2:17–18; 4:14–16). As He is a man, Christ can sympathize with men. As One without sin He can offer a perfect plea for the men He represents. When your friends fail you, Jesus Christ is a friend who can both comfort you and obtain grace and mercy for you from God.**

Chapter 17: ***Job seems to give up, believing his only hope is death.***

17:1 *breath is corrupt.* Literally, "spirit is broken," expressing that Job could not take any more.
17:3 *put me in a surety.* Pledge to fulfill my obligations. *strike hands.* An idiom for confirming a contract, similar to our shaking hands. The picture here is of a person who puts himself under binding obligation to pay another's debt (Prov. 6:1; 17:18; 22:26).
17:5 Job is evidently quoting a proverb from his day. His friends were flattering him with vain hopes of restored prosperity, contingent on his repentance.
17:6 *byword.* Object of scorn or derision. *aforetime.* Before or previously. *tabret.* The English word means "a small drum," but the Hebrew term refers to spittle.
17:8 *astonied.* Astonished. *hypocrite.* A godless or profane person.
17:16 *bars of the pit.* Entrance to *sheol* or the grave.

for I cannot find *one* wise *man* among you.
11 My days are past, my purposes are broken off,
even the thoughts of my heart.
12 They change the night into day: the light *is*
short because of darkness.
13 If I wait, the grave *is* mine house: I have made
my bed in the darkness.
14 I have said to corruption, Thou *art* my father:
to the worm, *Thou art* my mother, and my sister.
15 And where *is* now my hope? as for my hope,
who shall see it?
16 They shall go down to the bars of the pit, when
our rest together *is* in the dust.

CHAPTER 18

THEN answered Bildad the Shuhite, and said,
2 How long *will it be ere* ye make an end of words?
mark, and afterwards we will speak.
3 Wherefore are we counted as beasts, *and*
reputed vile in your sight?
4 He teareth himself in his anger: shall the earth
be forsaken for thee? and shall the rock be re-
moved out of his place?
5 Yea, the light of the wicked shall be put out, and
the spark of his fire shall not shine.
6 The light shall be dark in his tabernacle, and his
candle shall be put out with him.
7 The steps of his strength shall be straitened, and
his own counsel shall cast him down.
8 For he is cast into a net by his own feet, and he
walketh upon a snare.
9 The gin shall take *him* by the heel, *and* the
robber shall prevail against him.
10 The snare *is* laid for him in the ground, and a
trap for him in the way.
11 Terrors shall make him afraid on every side,
and shall drive him to his feet.
12 His strength shall be hungerbitten, and de-
struction *shall be* ready at his side.
13 It shall devour the strength of his skin: *even*
the firstborn of death shall devour his strength.
14 His confidence shall be rooted out of his
tabernacle, and it shall bring him to the king of
terrors.
15 It shall dwell in his tabernacle, because *it is*
none of his: brimstone shall be scattered upon his
habitation.
16 His roots shall be dried up beneath, and above
shall his branch be cut off.
17 His remembrance shall perish from the earth,
and he shall have no name in the street.
18 He shall be driven from light into darkness,
and chased out of the world.
19 He shall neither have son nor nephew among
his people, nor any remaining in his dwellings.
20 They that come after *him* shall be astonied at
his day, as they that went before were affrighted.
21 Surely such *are* the dwellings of the wicked,
and this *is* the place *of him that* knoweth not God.

CHAPTER 19

THEN Job answered and said,

Thoughts for Personal/Family Worship: Chapter 17

The striking of hands was the customary form for entering into a contract (v. 3). Just as Job had expressed his hope in a mediator, he now expressed his desire for an advocate or guarantor (surety). We are at once reminded that Christ serves both functions as the Priest of His people. He is their advocate (Heb. 7:25; 1 John 2:1) and their surety by the oath of the Lord (Heb. 7:21–22). Outward circumstances may seem to convey a different message, but when the Christian sees Christ as his advocate and surety, he can affirm like Paul that nothing can separate him from the love of God (Rom. 8:38–39). Yet he may also feel like a sheep destined for slaughter and have little expectation of deliverance in this life (Rom. 8:36). How can a believer simultaneously have such a strong hope and yet experience such darkness?

Chapter 18: ***Bildad elaborates on the judgment that awaits those who do not know God.***

Bildad: God Judges the Wicked (18:1–21)

18:2 *mark*. Understand.
18:3 *reputed vile*. Regarded as unclean.
18:6 *tabernacle*. Tent or dwelling place (vv. 14–15). *candle*. Lamp.
18:7 *straitened*. Restricted or hampered.
18:9 *gin*. Trap or snare. *robber*. Or a trapping device.
18:10 *laid*. Concealed or fixed secretly.
18:12 *hungerbitten*. Hungry or starved.
18:15 *brimstone*. Sulfur.
18:19 *nephew*. Refers to any descendent or posterity.
18:20 *astonied*. Astonished. *affrighted*. Frightened or afraid.

Thoughts for Personal/Family Worship: Chapter 18

1. **Bildad's description of death as the "king of terrors" (v. 14) is a reminder of the power of the gospel that can "deliver them who through fear of death were all their lifetime subject to bondage" (Heb. 2:15). The fear of death can be alleviated for the Christian because Christ has removed its sting (1 Cor. 15:55) by His victorious resurrection, and God delivers all His people from the power of death and the grave (Ps. 49:15). Life after death is certain, and even entering into the valley of death's shadow God's people have no reason for fear because the Lord, our Shepherd, has promised His presence (Ps. 23:4).**
2. **The wicked do not know God (v. 21)—the most profound ignorance possible. God's purpose in creating man was that he might know God. It was man's highest privilege before the fall to enjoy the presence of God, to walk with Him and talk with Him (Gen. 2:15–25; 3:8). When Adam plunged the human race into sin, this privilege was lost. But through the gospel, knowledge lost is knowledge restored so that the Christian can know God anew (Col. 3:10). The Christian should ever keep in mind the difference between knowing God and knowing about God, striving to know Him better whom to know is life eternal (John 17:3).**

2 How long will ye vex my soul, and break me in pieces with words?
3 These ten times have ye reproached me: ye are not ashamed *that* ye make yourselves strange to me.
4 And be it indeed *that* I have erred, mine error remaineth with myself.
5 If indeed ye will magnify *yourselves* against me, and plead against me my reproach:
6 Know now that God hath overthrown me, and hath compassed me with his net.
7 Behold, I cry out of wrong, but I am not heard: I cry aloud, but *there is* no judgment.
8 He hath fenced up my way that I cannot pass, and he hath set darkness in my paths.
9 He hath stripped me of my glory, and taken the crown *from* my head.
10 He hath destroyed me on every side, and I am gone: and mine hope hath he removed like a tree.
11 He hath also kindled his wrath against me, and he counteth me unto him as *one of* his enemies.
12 His troops come together, and raise up their way against me, and encamp round about my tabernacle.
13 He hath put my brethren far from me, and mine acquaintance are verily estranged from me.
14 My kinsfolk have failed, and my familiar friends have forgotten me.
15 They that dwell in mine house, and my maids, count me for a stranger: I am an alien in their sight.
16 I called my servant, and he gave *me* no answer; I intreated him with my mouth.
17 My breath is strange to my wife, though I intreated for the children's *sake* of mine own body.
18 Yea, young children despised me; I arose, and they spake against me.
19 All my inward friends abhorred me: and they whom I loved are turned against me.
20 My bone cleaveth to my skin and to my flesh, and I am escaped with the skin of my teeth.
21 Have pity upon me, have pity upon me, O ye my friends; for the hand of God hath touched me.
22 Why do ye persecute me as God, and are not satisfied with my flesh?
23 Oh that my words were now written! oh that they were printed in a book!
24 That they were graven with an iron pen and lead in the rock for ever!
25 For I know *that* my redeemer liveth, and *that* he shall stand at the latter *day* upon the earth:
26 And *though* after my skin *worms* destroy this *body*, yet in my flesh shall I see God:
27 Whom I shall see for myself, and mine eyes shall behold, and not another; *though* my reins be consumed within me.
28 But ye should say, Why persecute we him, seeing the root of the matter is found in me?
29 Be ye afraid of the sword: for wrath *bringeth* the punishments of the sword, that ye may know *there is* a judgment.

Chapter 19: *In the midst of suffering, Job nevertheless affirms his faith in Christ as his Redeemer.*

Job: But I Know that My Redeemer Lives (19:1–29)

19:2 *vex my soul.* Torment or grieve me.
19:3 *ten times.* Symbolic of many times (Gen. 31:7; Rev. 2:10). *make yourselves strange to me.* Attack me vigorously.
19:6 *compassed.* Surrounded.
19:7 *wrong.* Violence. *judgment.* Justice.
19:12 *tabernacle.* Tent or dwelling place.
19:13 *verily.* Truly.
19:17 *strange.* Loathsome or disgusting.
19:21 *Have pity . . . have pity.* Literally, "give me grace," the need of the suffering from their *friends*.
19:23 *printed.* Inscribed or recorded.
19:25 *redeemer.* A near kinsman who was obligated to defend his family and rescue its members and their inheritance at his own expense (Lev. 25:25,47–49; Ruth 4:1–12). *liveth.* Already in Job's day the Redeemer, the living God, was alive (v. 26; Deut. 5:26; Ps. 42:2). *shall stand.* Will stand up to vindicate. *at the latter day.* Simply means, "later"; no specific day or end-times chronology is in view. *earth.* Literally, "dust," most likely the grave (7:21; 10:9; 17:16).
19:26 The words *though, worms,* and *body* (italicized in the KJV) are not in the Hebrew text, but can be simply rendered, "After my skin has then been destroyed, yet in my flesh I will see God." *In my flesh* after death implies the raising of the body to life again. The word *skin* may also be translated, "I awake," implying resurrection after the sleep of death (14:12). God will raise believers physically from the dead (Isa. 26:19; Dan. 12:2), and they will see His glory in Christ (Ps. 17:15; John 17:24; Rev. 22:4).
19:27 *reins.* Inward organs that will be *consumed* in the grave. The dissolution of the body cannot prevent believers from seeing the Lord, either at death or at the resurrection.

Thoughts for Personal/Family Worship: Chapter 19

1. Job exclaimed, "Oh that my words were now written! Oh that they were printed in a book!" (v. 23). God answered Job's desire in the very book we now read. God had a purpose in Job's sufferings that would benefit future generations of Christians throughout the history of redemption. Who of us has not found comfort for his own sufferings by seeing a purpose of grace behind Job's sufferings? Christians should consider during their seasons of suffering that the purpose in their affliction is not just for their good and God's glory but also for the good of others (2 Cor. 1:6), including generations to come. How might that help those who are suffering?

2. "I know that my redeemer liveth" (v. 25). This statement shows the indestructible nature of true, saving faith. In the midst of circumstances that Job did not understand, he nevertheless fell back on the most basic truth of the gospel—his Redeemer lives! When the storms of life are intense and there does not seem to be any end in sight, the Christian must affirm that Christ is his Redeemer. Redemption brings to mind the glorious truth that the Christian is owned by God, purchased with His own blood (Acts 20:28; 1 Cor. 6:20; Eph. 1:14). And he must make such an affirmation on a personal level. Can you say, "I know that my Redeemer lives"? Is He yours?

CHAPTER 20

THEN answered Zophar the Naamathite, and said,
2 Therefore do my thoughts cause me to answer, and for *this* I make haste.
3 I have heard the check of my reproach, and the spirit of my understanding causeth me to answer.
4 Knowest thou *not* this of old, since man was placed upon earth,
5 That the triumphing of the wicked *is* short, and the joy of the hypocrite *but* for a moment?
6 Though his excellency mount up to the heavens, and his head reach unto the clouds;
7 *Yet* he shall perish for ever like his own dung: they which have seen him shall say, Where *is* he?
8 He shall fly away as a dream, and shall not be found: yea, he shall be chased away as a vision of the night.
9 The eye also *which* saw him shall *see him* no more; neither shall his place any more behold him.
10 His children shall seek to please the poor, and his hands shall restore their goods.
11 His bones are full *of the sin* of his youth, which shall lie down with him in the dust.
12 Though wickedness be sweet in his mouth, *though* he hide it under his tongue;
13 *Though* he spare it, and forsake it not; but keep it still within his mouth:
14 *Yet* his meat in his bowels is turned, *it is* the gall of asps within him.
15 He hath swallowed down riches, and he shall vomit them up again: God shall cast them out of his belly.
16 He shall suck the poison of asps: the viper's tongue shall slay him.
17 He shall not see the rivers, the floods, the brooks of honey and butter.
18 That which he laboured for shall he restore, and shall not swallow *it* down: according to *his* substance *shall* the restitution *be*, and he shall not rejoice *therein*.
19 Because he hath oppressed *and* hath forsaken the poor; *because* he hath violently taken away an house which he builded not;
20 Surely he shall not feel quietness in his belly, he shall not save of that which he desired.
21 There shall none of his meat be left; therefore shall no man look for his goods.
22 In the fulness of his sufficiency he shall be in straits: every hand of the wicked shall come upon him.
23 *When* he is about to fill his belly, *God* shall cast the fury of his wrath upon him, and shall rain *it* upon him while he is eating.
24 He shall flee from the iron weapon, *and* the bow of steel shall strike him through.
25 It is drawn, and cometh out of the body; yea, the glittering sword cometh out of his gall: terrors *are* upon him.
26 All darkness *shall be* hid in his secret places: a fire not blown shall consume him; it shall go ill with him that is left in his tabernacle.
27 The heaven shall reveal his iniquity; and the earth shall rise up against him.
28 The increase of his house shall depart, *and his goods* shall flow away in the day of his wrath.
29 This *is* the portion of a wicked man from God, and the heritage appointed unto him by God.

CHAPTER 21

BUT Job answered and said,
2 Hear diligently my speech, and let this be your consolations.

Chapter 20: *Zophar vents his anger against Job and reminds him that the triumph of the wicked is short but that their judgment is great.*

Zophar: The Triumph of the Wicked Is Short (20:1–29)

20:3 *check of my reproach.* Literally, "exhortation of my insult," meaning the exhortation that has insulted him. Feeling insulted, he became defensive.
20:5 *hypocrite.* A godless or profane person.
20:6 *excellency.* Pride.
20:10 *please.* Entreat or seek favor.
20:14 *meat.* Food of any kind (v. 21). *gall of asps.* Poison of venomous serpents (v. 16, though using a different word for poison).
20:22 *straights.* Trouble.
20:24 *steel.* Bronze.
20:25 *gall.* Gallbladder.
20:26 *tabernacle.* Tent or dwelling place.

Thoughts for Personal/Family Worship: Chapter 20

1. **"The triumphing of the wicked is short" (vv. 4–5). Although his assessment of Job was wrong, Zophar's theology was right on this point. The Christian is tempted at times to believe that the triumphing of the wicked is long-lasting. It seems that wicked men rule in high places and that men who make dishonest gain are the ones who get ahead, while the Lord's people are plagued and chastened. So bothered was the psalmist by this phenomenon that he concluded it was vain to serve the Lord (Ps. 73:13–14). When the Christian's heart becomes so overwhelmed by the inequalities of the world, he needs to put things in proper perspective (Ps. 73:16–17). Eternity is the best interpreter of time.**
2. **Zophar described the portion of the wicked man that awaits him in eternity: "he shall perish for ever" (v. 7); "God shall cast the fury of his wrath upon him" (v. 23); "the heaven shall reveal his iniquity" (v. 27). This life is the best it will ever be for the wicked, unless they repent. Here is cause for Christians to thank God, for apart from Christ the portion of the wicked would also be their portion.**

Chapter 21: *Job notes that the wicked often prosper for long periods of time and feel no need or desire*

3 Suffer me that I may speak; and after that I have
spoken, mock on.
4 As for me, *is* my complaint to man? and if *it*
were so, why should not my spirit be troubled?
5 Mark me, and be astonished, and lay *your* hand
upon *your* mouth.
6 Even when I remember I am afraid, and trem-
bling taketh hold on my flesh.
7 Wherefore do the wicked live, become old, yea,
are mighty in power?
8 Their seed is established in their sight with
them, and their offspring before their eyes.
9 Their houses *are* safe from fear, neither *is* the
rod of God upon them.
10 Their bull gendereth, and faileth not; their cow
calveth, and casteth not her calf.
11 They send forth their little ones like a flock,
and their children dance.
12 They take the timbrel and harp, and rejoice at
the sound of the organ.
13 They spend their days in wealth, and in a
moment go down to the grave.
14 Therefore they say unto God, Depart from us;
for we desire not the knowledge of thy ways.
15 What *is* the Almighty, that we should serve
him? and what profit should we have, if we pray
unto him?
16 Lo, their good *is* not in their hand: the counsel
of the wicked is far from me.
17 How oft is the candle of the wicked put out!
and *how oft* cometh their destruction upon them!
God distributeth sorrows in his anger.
18 They are as stubble before the wind, and as
chaff that the storm carrieth away.
19 God layeth up his iniquity for his children: he
rewardeth him, and he shall know *it*.
20 His eyes shall see his destruction, and he shall
drink of the wrath of the Almighty.
21 For what pleasure *hath* he in his house after
him, when the number of his months is cut off
in the midst?
22 Shall *any* teach God knowledge? seeing he
judgeth those that are high.
23 One dieth in his full strength, being wholly at
ease and quiet.
24 His breasts are full of milk, and his bones are
moistened with marrow.
25 And another dieth in the bitterness of his soul,
and never eateth with pleasure.
26 They shall lie down alike in the dust, and the
worms shall cover them.
27 Behold, I know your thoughts, and the devices
which ye wrongfully imagine against me.
28 For ye say, Where *is* the house of the prince?
and where *are* the dwelling places of the wicked?
29 Have ye not asked them that go by the way?
and do ye not know their tokens,
30 That the wicked is reserved to the day of de-
struction? they shall be brought forth to the day
of wrath.
31 Who shall declare his way to his face? and who
shall repay him *what* he hath done?
32 Yet shall he be brought to the grave, and shall
remain in the tomb.

for God, though in the end all die alike.

Job: But the Wicked Live Long and Prosper (21:1–34)

21:3 *Suffer me*. The Hebrew, "lift me up"; the idea being to bear with him or endure him as he speaks. *mock on*. Job anticipated that his discourse would not alter his friend's opinions.
21:5 *Mark me*. "Face to me," meaning to pay attention. *lay your hand upon your mouth*. A gesture of astonishment or speechlessness.
21:7–13 The prosperity of the wicked may be short in terms of eternity, but from the perspective of time it seems to endure. Therefore, one cannot judge character by prosperity.
21:10 *gendereth*. Breeds. *casteth not*. Does not miscarry.
21:12 *timbrel*. Hand-drum or tambourine. *harp*. Stringed instrument, such as a lyre. *organ*. Musical instrument, perhaps a long flute.
21:13 *in wealth*. Literally, "in the good of their days."
21:15 *What is the Almighty?* Those who prosper often see no need of God.
21:17 *candle*. Lamp or light.
21:19 *iniquity*. Trouble or looming disaster.
21:24 *His breasts*. The Hebrew occurs only here, and the meaning is uncertain, perhaps "his pails are full of milk" or "his thighs are full of fat." Either translation pictures one who dies in opulence.
21:26 *alike in the dust*. Death is the great equalizer; there are no distinctions in the grave.
21:27 *devices*. Plots or schemes.
21:29 *them that go by the way*. Travelers. *Tokens*. Signs, referring to their testimony or witness.
21:30 *wrath*. Plural in Hebrew, adding intensity.
21:34 *in vain*. Without purpose. *falsehood*. Fraud or faithlessness.

Thoughts for Personal/Family Worship: Chapter 21

1. **Job's friends had come to him to comfort and console him in his sufferings. They proved, however, that good intentions do not always lead to good results. Far from meeting Job in the depth of his need, their counsel became a mockery (v. 3). In order to enter into the ministry of encouragement, we must be able to meet a person in his need or be honest enough to confess that our friend's distress is beyond our comprehension. Either way, we must point the sufferer to the Lord's compassion. How much more is this our duty after the Lord has taken on our own flesh and suffered with us? There is no depth to our distress that Christ does not know.**
2. **We must face the reality that sometimes the wicked enjoy long and prosperous lives. They may boast in their self-sufficiency and mock at God without immediate consequences. At the same time believers may be suffering horribly, even at the hands of these boasters. However, Christians can endure by embracing three principles. First, we are to reject "the counsel of the wicked"; to refuse to see life through their twisted perspective (v. 16). Second, we are to rest in the judgment to come on the sinner, for "he shall drink of the wrath of the Almighty" (v. 20). Third, we are to remember that our mind cannot**

33 The clods of the valley shall be sweet unto
him, and every man shall draw after him, as *there*
are innumerable before him.
34 How then comfort ye me in vain, seeing in
your answers there remaineth falsehood?

CHAPTER 22

THEN Eliphaz the Temanite answered and said,
2 Can a man be profitable unto God, as he that is
wise may be profitable unto himself?
3 *Is it* any pleasure to the Almighty, that thou art
righteous? or *is it* gain *to him*, that thou makest
thy ways perfect?
4 Will he reprove thee for fear of thee? will he
enter with thee into judgment?
5 *Is* not thy wickedness great? and thine iniqui-
ties infinite?
6 For thou hast taken a pledge from thy brother for
nought, and stripped the naked of their clothing.
7 Thou hast not given water to the weary to
drink, and thou hast withholden bread from the
hungry.
8 But *as for* the mighty man, he had the earth;
and the honourable man dwelt in it.
9 Thou hast sent widows away empty, and the
arms of the fatherless have been broken.
10 Therefore snares *are* round about thee, and
sudden fear troubleth thee;
11 Or darkness, *that* thou canst not see; and
abundance of waters cover thee.
12 *Is* not God in the height of heaven? and behold
the height of the stars, how high they are!
13 And thou sayest, How doth God know? can he
judge through the dark cloud?
14 Thick clouds *are* a covering to him, that he
seeth not; and he walketh in the circuit of heaven.
15 Hast thou marked the old way which wicked
men have trodden?
16 Which were cut down out of time, whose
foundation was overflown with a flood:
17 Which said unto God, Depart from us: and
what can the Almighty do for them?
18 Yet he filled their houses with good *things*: but
the counsel of the wicked is far from me.
19 The righteous see *it*, and are glad: and the
innocent laugh them to scorn.
20 Whereas our substance is not cut down, but
the remnant of them the fire consumeth.
21 Acquaint now thyself with him, and be at
peace: thereby good shall come unto thee.
22 Receive, I pray thee, the law from his mouth,
and lay up his words in thine heart.
23 If thou return to the Almighty, thou shalt be
built up, thou shalt put away iniquity far from thy
tabernacles.
24 Then shalt thou lay up gold as dust, and the
gold of Ophir as the stones of the brooks.
25 Yea, the Almighty shall be thy defence, and
thou shalt have plenty of silver.
26 For then shalt thou have thy delight in the
Almighty, and shalt lift up thy face unto God.
27 Thou shalt make thy prayer unto him, and he
shall hear thee, and thou shalt pay thy vows.
28 Thou shalt also decree a thing, and it shall be
established unto thee: and the light shall shine
upon thy ways.
29 When *men* are cast down, then thou shalt say,
There is lifting up; and he shall save the humble
person.
30 He shall deliver the island of the innocent: and
it is delivered by the pureness of thine hands.

fully comprehend God's ways, much less correct Him: "Shall any teach God knowledge?" (v. 22).

Third Cycle of Dialogue (22:1—27:23)

Chapter 22: *Eliphaz continues to accuse Job of sin, and this time he names specific sins.*

Eliphaz: Is It Gain to God that You Make Your Way Perfect? (22:1–30)

22:2–3 *be profitable*. Benefit God. Humanity adds nothing to God, for He is all-sufficient in Himself (35:7; 1 Chron. 29:11–14; Acts 17:25; Rom. 11:33–36). *perfect*. Blameless.
22:5 *infinite*. Literally, "nonexistence of an end."
22:6–9 In exasperation with Job's insistence on maintaining his integrity, Eliphaz seemingly made up a list of sins of which he assumed Job must be guilty.
22:10 *snares*. Net or traps.
22:12–14 *can he judge . . . he seeth not*. This expresses the attitude of the wicked (Pss. 73:11; 94:7).
22:15–16 *overflown with a flood*. Possibly an allusion to the flood of Noah's day (Gen. 6–9).
22:21 *Acquaint now thyself with him, and be at peace*. Be reconciled with God.
22:22 *law*. Hebrew, *torah*, referring to the whole of God's instruction.
22:23 *tabernacles*. Tents or dwelling places.
22:25 *defence*. Gold. *plenty of silver*. Literally, "silver of massive heaps." The Lord Himself is the treasure of those who repent, as well as their joy (v. 26; Ps. 73:25–26).
22:28 *decree a thing*. Literally, "decide something or plan."
22:30 *the island of the innocent: and it is delivered*. Could also be translated "the one not innocent: and he is delivered."

Thoughts for Personal/Family Worship: Chapter 22

1. **God owes men nothing (v. 3). God is not indebted to men, but men are indebted to God. The Christian's understanding of this truth will enable him to magnify God's grace all the more, for in the covenant of grace God obligated Himself to accomplish and apply salvation to the elect. He did so not because He needed them or they deserved it, but because He is love. Be sure to magnify God's grace today!**
2. **Eliphaz gave good advice to those who have strayed from God: "Acquaint now thyself with him, and be at peace . . . Receive, I pray thee, the law from his mouth, and lay up his words in thine heart . . . Return to the Almighty (vv. 21–23). The Christian life may be described**

CHAPTER 23

THEN Job answered and said,
2 Even to day *is* my complaint bitter: my stroke is
heavier than my groaning.
3 Oh that I knew where I might find him! *that* I
might come *even* to his seat!
4 I would order *my* cause before him, and fill my
mouth with arguments.
5 I would know the words *which* he would answer
me, and understand what he would say unto me.
6 Will he plead against me with *his* great power?
No; but he would put *strength* in me.
7 There the righteous might dispute with him; so
should I be delivered for ever from my judge.
8 Behold, I go forward, but he *is* not *there*; and
backward, but I cannot perceive him:
9 On the left hand, where he doth work, but I
cannot behold *him*: he hideth himself on the right
hand, that I cannot see *him*:
10 But he knoweth the way that I take: *when* he
hath tried me, I shall come forth as gold.
11 My foot hath held his steps, his way have I
kept, and not declined.
12 Neither have I gone back from the command-
ment of his lips; I have esteemed the words of his
mouth more than my necessary *food*.
13 But he *is* in one *mind*, and who can turn him?
and *what* his soul desireth, even *that* he doeth.
14 For he performeth *the thing that is* appointed
for me: and many such *things are* with him.
15 Therefore am I troubled at his presence: when
I consider, I am afraid of him.
16 For God maketh my heart soft, and the
Almighty troubleth me:
17 Because I was not cut off before the darkness,
neither hath he covered the darkness from my face.

CHAPTER 24

WHY, seeing times are not hidden from the
Almighty, do they that know him not see his days?
2 *Some* remove the landmarks; they violently take
away flocks, and feed *thereof*.
3 They drive away the ass of the fatherless, they
take the widow's ox for a pledge.
4 They turn the needy out of the way: the poor of
the earth hide themselves together.
5 Behold, *as* wild asses in the desert, go they
forth to their work; rising betimes for a prey: the
wilderness *yieldeth* food for them *and* for *their*
children.
6 They reap *every one* his corn in the field: and
they gather the vintage of the wicked.
7 They cause the naked to lodge without cloth-
ing, that *they have* no covering in the cold.
8 They are wet with the showers of the moun-
tains, and embrace the rock for want of a shelter.
9 They pluck the fatherless from the breast, and
take a pledge of the poor.
10 They cause *him* to go naked without clothing,
and they take away the sheaf *from* the hungry;
11 *Which* make oil within their walls, *and* tread
their winepresses, and suffer thirst.
12 Men groan from out of the city, and the soul

---

as a life of constantly returning to God. So long as sin remains in his heart, the Christian will always have a propensity to drift from God, but on account of Christ's atoning death the way is always open for him to return to the God who loves him. Have you drifted from God? How? Your peace can be restored to you by returning to Him through Christ.

Job: I Shall Come Forth as Gold (23:1—24:25)

Chapter 23: ***Job expresses his longing to dispute his case with God and his confidence that he will come forth as gold.***

23:2 *bitter*. Or obstinate. *stroke*. Literally, "hand."
23:3 *seat*. Fixed place.
23:6–7 God does not bully people *with his great power* but is truly concerned with justice for *the righteous* (Gen. 18:25).
23:10 *when he hath tried me, I shall come forth as gold.* Through they are suffering, God tests the faith of believers to prove its genuineness and great value (Ps. 66:10; Zech. 13:9; 1 Peter 1:7).
23:11 *not declined.* Did not turn aside. Job had his fears, troubles, and misunderstandings, but he never abandoned the Lord. That is the mark of a true and persevering faith.
23:16 *soft*. Tender.

Thoughts for Personal/Family Worship: Chapter 23

1. **There are times in the Christian's life when God seems far from him and his prayers (v. 3). The psalmists complained of feeling forsaken by God (Pss. 13:1; 77:7–9; 89:46). This was Job's worst affliction, more terrible than losing his possessions, worse even than losing his health and his family. This was also the crowning affliction of Christ as he died under the punishment for man's sins (Matt. 27:46). God designs times of divine withdrawal to increase the Christian's sense of dependence upon God, to whet his appetite for closer fellowship, and to focus his hope on the vindication of judgment day. Do you groan in the hope of the glory of God?**
2. **"He knoweth the way that I take: when he hath tried me, I shall come forth as gold" (v. 10). When Christians experience painful seasons or when God seems far away, God knows precisely where we are and the way that we take (v. 10). He has not abandoned us. Even though the trial may be long and hard, there is a gracious purpose behind it that will lead to our coming forth as gold. Thank God today that the trial of your faith will lead to praise and honor and glory at the appearing of Christ.**

Chapter 24: ***Job again argues that the wicked often go unpunished in life.***

24:1 The godly, like Job, often wonder why they do not see the *days* of judgment from *the Almighty* against sin and injustice.
24:2–4 Job described the dishonesty, cruelty, and violence of the wicked.
24:5 *rising betimes for a prey*. Seeking eagerly for food.
24:6 *corn*. Fodder. *they gather the vintage of the wicked.*

of the wounded crieth out: yet God layeth not
folly *to them.*
13 They are of those that rebel against the light;
they know not the ways thereof, nor abide in the
paths thereof.
14 The murderer rising with the light killeth the
poor and needy, and in the night is as a thief.
15 The eye also of the adulterer waiteth for the
twilight, saying, No eye shall see me: and disguis-
eth *his* face.
16 In the dark they dig through houses, *which*
they had marked for themselves in the daytime:
they know not the light.
17 For the morning *is* to them even as the shadow
of death: if *one* know *them, they are in* the terrors
of the shadow of death.
18 He *is* swift as the waters; their portion is
cursed in the earth: he beholdeth not the way of
the vineyards.
19 Drought and heat consume the snow waters:
so doth the grave *those which* have sinned.
20 The womb shall forget him; the worm shall
feed sweetly on him; he shall be no more remem-
bered; and wickedness shall be broken as a tree.
21 He evil entreateth the barren *that* beareth not:
and doeth not good to the widow.
22 He draweth also the mighty with his power: he
riseth up, and no *man* is sure of life.
23 *Though* it be given him *to be* in safety, whereon
he resteth; yet his eyes *are* upon their ways.
24 They are exalted for a little while, but are gone
and brought low; they are taken out of the way as
all *other*, and cut off as the tops of the ears of corn.
25 And if *it be* not *so* now, who will make me a
liar, and make my speech nothing worth?

CHAPTER 25

THEN answered Bildad the Shuhite, and said,
2 Dominion and fear *are* with him, he maketh
peace in his high places.
3 Is there any number of his armies? and upon
whom doth not his light arise?
4 How then can man be justified with God? or
how can he be clean *that is* born of a woman?
5 Behold even to the moon, and it shineth not;
yea, the stars are not pure in his sight.
6 How much less man, *that is* a worm? and the
son of man, *which is* a worm?

CHAPTER 26

BUT Job answered and said,
2 How hast thou helped *him that is* without

Literally, "the wicked grab [the] vineyard."

24:12 *layeth not folly.* God does not charge them with wrong (1:22) and punish them.

24:13 *rebel against the light.* Sinners hate the light of God's truth (John 3:19–20).

24:14–16 Men use the darkness of *night* as a cover for sin, as though God cannot see them. Night becomes a metaphor for the spiritual blindness of sinners to the coming judgment (Rom. 13:11–14; 1 Thess. 5:1–7).

24:21 *entreateth the barren.* Feeds on the infertile, taking advantage of them.

Thoughts for Personal/Family Worship: Chapter 24

1. **Those who know God do not always see His judgment upon the wicked (v. 1). Yet justice will be executed. Regardless of how long the wicked seem to get a away with their wickedness, death comes (v. 24) and after that the judgment (21:20; Heb. 9:27). The Christian should not judge before that time but look ahead to the time when Christ will return to set things right. Does the wickedness of the day cause you to groan for Christ's return? Be encouraged. His cause will prevail in the end.**
2. **The heinousness of sin is magnified all the more when those engaged in sin know better (v. 13). Sinning in the light increases responsibility and accountability. To those who receive much, from them much will be required. When a nation has received much truth from God, its sins are all the more offensive to God, whether that nation is Israel or a modern land that has received the gospel of Jesus Christ. What does this imply about your nation? How should you respond?**

Chapter 25: ***Bildad raises the question of how man in his sin can be justified before a holy God.***

Bildad: But How Can Man Be Justified with God? (25:1–6)

25:4 *How then can man be justified with God?* This question is at the heart of the debate (4:17; 9:2; 15:14). Given his description of God's transcendence and power (vv. 2–3), it is clear that Bildad held out no prospect for man's justification.

25:5 *the stars are not pure.* Bildad picked up Eliphaz's theme, derived from his vision (4:15–18; 15:15).

25:6 *worm . . . worm.* Maggot and grub, both pictures of man's lowliness and total helplessness (Ps. 22:6; Isa. 41:14).

Thoughts for Personal/Family Worship: Chapter 25

"How then can man be justified with God?" (v. 4) The placement of this question in Bildad's argument sets in bold the tension that can only be resolved in the gospel. He begins with a lofty description of God's sovereignty, power, and authority and ends with a vivid, if disgusting, image of the depths of man's condition (maggots and grubs). The distance between the two is infinite, and there is nothing a worm can do to elevate itself from the dirt. So the question is raised, and the answer, though not given here, is man's only hope. The infinite God in the second person of the holy Trinity became man, indeed a worm (Ps. 22:6). The God-man did everything necessary in His living to earn life for His people and everything necessary in His dying to pay the penalty for His people's sins. Because of Christ God remains just but can also be the justifier of those who believe (Rom. 3:26). The gospel answers Bildad's question. Have you experienced that answer by finding peace with God through our Lord Jesus Christ?

Job: How Have You Helped Him Who Has No Power? (26:1—27:23)

Chapter 26: ***Job recognizes God's greatness and power.***

power? *how* savest thou the arm *that hath* no
strength?
3 How hast thou counselled *him that hath* no
wisdom? and *how* hast thou plentifully declared
the thing as it is?
4 To whom hast thou uttered words? and whose
spirit came from thee?
5 Dead *things* are formed from under the waters,
and the inhabitants thereof.
6 Hell *is* naked before him, and destruction hath
no covering.
7 He stretcheth out the north over the empty
place, *and* hangeth the earth upon nothing.
8 He bindeth up the waters in his thick clouds;
and the cloud is not rent under them.
9 He holdeth back the face of his throne, *and*
spreadeth his cloud upon it.
10 He hath compassed the waters with bounds,
until the day and night come to an end.
11 The pillars of heaven tremble and are aston-
ished at his reproof.
12 He divideth the sea with his power, and by his
understanding he smiteth through the proud.
13 By his spirit he hath garnished the heavens; his
hand hath formed the crooked serpent.
14 Lo, these *are* parts of his ways: but how little
a portion is heard of him? but the thunder of his
power who can understand?

CHAPTER 27

MOREOVER Job continued his parable, and said,
2 *As* God liveth, *who* hath taken away my judg-
ment; and the Almighty, *who* hath vexed my soul;
3 All the while my breath *is* in me, and the spirit
of God *is* in my nostrils;
4 My lips shall not speak wickedness, nor my
tongue utter deceit.
5 God forbid that I should justify you: till I die I
will not remove mine integrity from me.
6 My righteousness I hold fast, and will not let it
go: my heart shall not reproach *me* so long as I live.
7 Let mine enemy be as the wicked, and he that
riseth up against me as the unrighteous.
8 For what *is* the hope of the hypocrite, though
he hath gained, when God taketh away his soul?
9 Will God hear his cry when trouble cometh
upon him?
10 Will he delight himself in the Almighty? will
he always call upon God?
11 I will teach you by the hand of God: *that* which
is with the Almighty will I not conceal.
12 Behold, all ye yourselves have seen *it*; why then
are ye thus altogether vain?
13 This *is* the portion of a wicked man with God,
and the heritage of oppressors, *which* they shall
receive of the Almighty.
14 If his children be multiplied, *it is* for the sword:

26:2 Job agreed with Bildad's theology but first reproved his failure to apply the truth in a helpful way.

26:5 *Dead things are formed.* Literally, "the spirits of the dead are made to tremble," evidence of existence after death even for the wicked.

26:6 *Hell.* The Hebrew, *sheol*, can refer to death, the grave, or the place of punishment for departed wicked spirits, the last most likely in this context (v. 5). God sees even into the depths of hell, and so He certainly sees our inward thoughts and motives (Prov. 15:11).

26:8 *is not rent.* Does not burst open.

26:9 *holdeth back.* Covers or encloses. What we see of God's glory is "the hiding of his power" (Hab. 3:4; see Ex. 33:20; Ps. 97:2; 1 Tim. 6:16). The totality of His power and glory is incomprehensible.

26:10 *He hath compassed the waters with bounds.* Literally, "a boundary He has drawn as circle over the face of [the] water." *until the day and night come to an end.* Literally, "unto the boundary of light with darkness," where day transitions into night.

26:13 *By his spirit he had garnished the heavens.* Literally, "with His wind He stirs up heavens," referring to the storms moving through the sky. *crooked serpent.* Or fleeing serpent (Ps. 74:13–14; Isa. 27:1), often a symbolic title of Satan.

26:14 *Lo, these are parts of his ways.* Even the most eloquent and lofty description of the majesty and power of God does not come close to comprehending His fullness (v. 9).

Thoughts for Personal/Family Worship: Chapter 26

1. **Orthodox theology is important, and it must be guarded, but orthodoxy in the head without its proper application to the heart does little good (v. 1). Job in no way disputed Bildad's theology, and he indeed even expanded on it. God is infinitely great. Yet Bildad failed to apply the truth to Job in a way that helped him. We must learn to receive and apply biblical truth with faithful love and grace so that we might find and share true spiritual comfort (6:14; 19:21).**
2. **True knowledge of God must also be held with a profound awareness that we know only a small portion of God's greatness: "but the thunder of his power who can understand?" (v. 14). While we should trust all that Scripture tells us about God, we are at best stammering children in the things of God. Why is this so important to remember when we stand up for the truths of the Bible?**

Chapter 27: *Job reiterates his innocence with the knowledge that the godless have no hope.*

27:1 *parable.* Wisdom discourse.

27:2 *hath taken away my judgment.* Refuses to vindicate me from the accusations of my friends. *vexed my soul.* Caused me grief.

27:3 *the spirit of God . . . in my nostrils.* The *breath* that God gives him (12:10; 32:8; Gen. 2:7).

27:6 *My righteousness.* His innocence regarding any sin that has caused his calamity. *my heart shall not reproach.* He makes the claim with a clear conscience that does not taunt or annoy him.

27:8 *hypocrite.* A godless or profane person. *soul.* Life.

27:12 *why then are ye thus altogether vain?* Job asked why they talked about total nothingness in view of what they themselves had seen.

27:13 *the portion of a wicked man.* Job agreed with his friends that God will certainly punish the wicked with death, loss, and disgrace (vv. 14–23).

27:22 *fain flee.* Hebrew, "certainly flee"; "fain" means gladly.

and his offspring shall not be satisfied with bread.
15 Those that remain of him shall be buried in
death: and his widows shall not weep.
16 Though he heap up silver as the dust, and
prepare raiment as the clay;
17 He may prepare *it*, but the just shall put *it* on,
and the innocent shall divide the silver.
18 He buildeth his house as a moth, and as a
booth *that* the keeper maketh.
19 The rich man shall lie down, but he shall not
be gathered: he openeth his eyes, and he *is* not.
20 Terrors take hold on him as waters, a tempest
stealeth him away in the night.
21 The east wind carrieth him away, and he de-
parteth: and as a storm hurleth him out of his
place.
22 For *God* shall cast upon him, and not spare: he
would fain flee out of his hand.
23 *Men* shall clap their hands at him, and shall
hiss him out of his place.

CHAPTER 28

SURELY there is a vein for the silver, and a place for
gold *where* they fine *it*.
2 Iron is taken out of the earth, and brass *is*
molten *out of* the stone.
3 He setteth an end to darkness, and searcheth
out all perfection: the stones of darkness, and the
shadow of death.
4 The flood breaketh out from the inhabitant;
even the waters forgotten of the foot: they are
dried up, they are gone away from men.
5 *As for* the earth, out of it cometh bread: and
under it is turned up as it were fire.
6 The stones of it *are* the place of sapphires: and
it hath dust of gold.
7 *There is* a path which no fowl knoweth, and
which the vulture's eye hath not seen:
8 The lion's whelps have not trodden it, nor the
fierce lion passed by it.
9 He putteth forth his hand upon the rock; he
overturneth the mountains by the roots.
10 He cutteth out rivers among the rocks; and his
eye seeth every precious thing.
11 He bindeth the floods from overflowing; and
the thing that is hid bringeth he forth to light.
12 But where shall wisdom be found? and where
is the place of understanding?
13 Man knoweth not the price thereof; neither is
it found in the land of the living.
14 The depth saith, It *is* not in me: and the sea
saith, *It is* not with me.
15 It cannot be gotten for gold, neither shall silver
be weighed *for* the price thereof.
16 It cannot be valued with the gold of Ophir,
with the precious onyx, or the sapphire.
17 The gold and the crystal cannot equal it: and
the exchange of it *shall not be for* jewels of fine
gold.
18 No mention shall be made of coral, or of
pearls: for the price of wisdom *is* above rubies.
19 The topaz of Ethiopia shall not equal it, nei-
ther shall it be valued with pure gold.
20 Whence then cometh wisdom? and where *is*
the place of understanding?
21 Seeing it is hid from the eyes of all living, and
kept close from the fowls of the air.
22 Destruction and death say, We have heard the
fame thereof with our ears.

27:23 *clap . . . hiss.* Gestures of mockery, shock, or disdain.

Thoughts for Personal/Family Worship: Chapter 27

1. **Job's integrity (v. 5) was the focal point of his spiritual warfare (2:3). A Christian's integrity consists of a loving life, heartfelt pursuit of purity, good conscience, and sincere faith (Ps. 26:1–5; 1 Tim. 1:5; 2 Tim. 2:22). Had Job yielded to the arguments of his friends, he would have denied his integrity. If the Devil cannot lead us into unrepentant sin, he will attempt to destroy our assurance, unjustly inflame our conscience, and cripple our faith with hard thoughts of God. How can the Christian resist the Devil and hold on to his integrity?**
2. **The mystery surrounding the suffering of the righteous should never hinder us from clearly seeing that God will punish the wicked (vv. 13–23). Job believed this even in the midst of his questions about God's justice (v. 2). Do not be deceived by temporary circumstances or the lies of Satan. Sinners will face the wrath of God (Eph. 5:6). Therefore, do not envy them, but repent.**

Chapter 28: *Wisdom is found only in God.*

WISDOM IS THE FEAR OF THE LORD (28:1–28)

28:1–28 Interpreters differ as to whether this poem continues Job's discourse or presents a separate unit by the inspired narrator. The openings of chs. 27 and 29 are the same, which may suggest that ch. 28 should be taken as a separate unit. See Introduction: Synopsis for a proposed chiastic pattern in the book, centering on this chapter.

28:1 *vein.* Mine. *fine.* Refine or purify. The poem opens with a celebration of man's ancient skill in mining precious metals and stones (vv. 1–11; cf. Gen. 4:22).

28:2 *molten.* Melted.

28:3 *shadow of death.* Used figuratively to refer to deep and total darkness.

28:7 *vultures.* Falcon or hawk, a bird with remarkable eyesight.

28:12 *where shall wisdom be found?* This question is the focal point of the chapter. Despite man's technological skill to mine the earth, mankind cannot penetrate into true wisdom but can only receive it reverently from God (vv. 23,28; Prov. 2:1–6).

28:13–19 Job compares wisdom with the precious metals of the earth and states that the value of wisdom is greater than the riches of the earth (Prov. 2:3–4; 3:13–14; 8:10,19; 16:16; 20:15; 25:11–12).

28:15 *It cannot be gotten for gold.* Literally, "fine gold cannot be given instead of it."

28:21 *kept close from the fowls.* Concealed from the birds.

28:22 *Destruction.* Hebrew, *Abaddon*, referring to the underworld. *fame.* News or report.

23 God understandeth the way thereof, and he
knoweth the place thereof.
24 For he looketh to the ends of the earth, *and*
seeth under the whole heaven;
25 To make the weight for the winds; and he
weigheth the waters by measure.
26 When he made a decree for the rain, and a way
for the lightning of the thunder:
27 Then did he see it, and declare it; he prepared
it, yea, and searched it out.
28 And unto man he said, Behold, the fear of the
Lord, that *is* wisdom; and to depart from evil *is*
understanding.

CHAPTER 29

MOREOVER Job continued his parable, and said,
2 Oh that I were as *in* months past, as *in* the days
when God preserved me;
3 When his candle shined upon my head, *and*
when by his light I walked *through* darkness;
4 As I was in the days of my youth, when the
secret of God *was* upon my tabernacle;
5 When the Almighty *was* yet with me, *when* my
children *were* about me;
6 When I washed my steps with butter, and the
rock poured me out rivers of oil;
7 When I went out to the gate through the city,
when I prepared my seat in the street!
8 The young men saw me, and hid themselves:
and the aged arose, *and* stood up.
9 The princes refrained talking, and laid *their*
hand on their mouth.
10 The nobles held their peace, and their tongue
cleaved to the roof of their mouth.
11 When the ear heard *me*, then it blessed me;
and when the eye saw *me*, it gave witness to me:
12 Because I delivered the poor that cried, and
the fatherless, and *him that had* none to help him.
13 The blessing of him that was ready to perish
came upon me: and I caused the widow's heart
to sing for joy.
14 I put on righteousness, and it clothed me: my
judgment *was* as a robe and a diadem.
15 I was eyes to the blind, and feet *was* I to the
lame.
16 I *was* a father to the poor: and the cause *which*
I knew not I searched out.
17 And I brake the jaws of the wicked, and
plucked the spoil out of his teeth.
18 Then I said, I shall die in my nest, and I shall
multiply *my* days as the sand.
19 My root *was* spread out by the waters, and the
dew lay all night upon my branch.

28:28 *fear of the Lord.* A comprehensive expression that sums up true religion (Eccl. 12:13; Rev. 14:7). The fear of God is a mindset of *wisdom*, an awareness of the reality and holiness of God (Gen. 28:16–17; Prov. 9:10) that produces awe, love, worship, and obedience (Deut. 10:12; Rev. 15:4). *to depart from evil.* Practical results of the fear of God are repentance and hatred of sin (1:1,8; 2:3; Prov. 3:7; 14:16; 16:6).

Thoughts for Personal/Family Worship: Chapter 28

1. The Hebrew word for "wisdom" has the basic idea of skill or ability (Ex. 31:3–6). With respect to God, it refers to His infinite skill to accomplish all His purposes in the best possible ways. With respect to believers, it refers to the skill to live well in God's world. This is why the starting place and the essence of wisdom is the fear of God (v. 28). Only as the reality of God in all His perfection governs the conscience and consciousness will we be rightly motivated to worship God as He is and to avoid doing things that displease Him. Likewise, fearing God means trusting His wisdom that all the circumstances He brings into our lives are according to a perfect plan He is executing in the best possible way. That is the lesson Job had to learn in the throes of his troubles, and indeed the lesson he would learn.

2. Christ is our wisdom (1 Cor. 1:30). Wisdom is the ability to please God—something we can never achieve by ourselves. It cannot be found by man's technological skill (vv. 1–14) or procured with gold because its value exceeds that of all gold (vv. 15–17). Christ is for His people what they cannot be for themselves. The pursuit of wisdom, therefore, is nothing short of the pursuit of Christ (Col. 2:2–3; 3:16). How can we pursue wisdom in Jesus Christ?

THREE MONOLOGUES (29:1—41:34)

Job's Remembrance of His Prosperity and Righteousness (29:1—31:40)

Chapter 29: *Job reflects on the days of prosperity before his trial.*

29:1 *parable.* Wisdom discourse.

29:2 *Oh that I were as in months past.* These chapters (29–31) contain more biographical information about Job than any others, contrasting Job's past blessings (ch. 29) and righteousness (ch. 31) with his present afflictions (ch. 30).

29:3 *candle.* Lamp. God's *light* shining upon a person consists of His blessing and favor (Num. 6:24–26). *by his light I walked through darkness.* Job had known trials in the past but had also known the light of God's presence in those trials (Ps. 27:1).

29:4 *secret.* Intimate and confidential communication between friends (Ps. 25:14). Job remembered God dwelling in his tent or home (*tabernacle*) and their communing together in close fellowship.

29:6 *washed my steps with butter.* An image of bounty and prosperity.

29:7 *gate.* The place of business, judgment, and social activity. *seat in the street.* The plaza or broad place in the gate area where Job sat, exercising some degree of authority.

29:8–11 Gestures of respect from all ages and ranks.

29:11 *blessed me.* Recognized all the benefits and blessings he enjoyed.

29:12–16 Job had a testimony of compassion. He had done what Eliphaz accused him of not doing (22:6–9).

29:14 *put on righteousness.* Embraced obedience to God's commands like one's daily clothing by faith in the Lord (Rom. 13:12–14; Eph. 4:22–25; Col. 3:8–12). *judgment.* Justice, particularly in caring for and protecting the poor (vv. 12–13,15–17). *diadem.* A turban-like headdress.

20 My glory *was* fresh in me, and my bow was
renewed in my hand.
21 Unto me *men* gave ear, and waited, and kept
silence at my counsel.
22 After my words they spake not again; and my
speech dropped upon them.
23 And they waited for me as for the rain; and
they opened their mouth wide *as* for the latter
rain.
24 *If* I laughed on them, they believed *it* not; and
the light of my countenance they cast not down.
25 I chose out their way, and sat chief, and dwelt
as a king in the army, as one *that* comforteth the
mourners.

CHAPTER 30

BUT now *they that are* younger than I have me in
derision, whose fathers I would have disdained to
have set with the dogs of my flock.
2 Yea, whereto *might* the strength of their hands
profit me, in whom old age was perished?
3 For want and famine *they were* solitary; fleeing
into the wilderness in former time desolate and
waste.
4 Who cut up mallows by the bushes, and juniper
roots *for* their meat.
5 They were driven forth from among *men*, (they
cried after them as *after* a thief;)
6 To dwell in the clifts of the valleys, *in* caves of
the earth, and *in* the rocks.
7 Among the bushes they brayed; under the net-
tles they were gathered together.
8 *They were* children of fools, yea, children of
base men: they were viler than the earth.
9 And now am I their song, yea, I am their
byword.
10 They abhor me, they flee far from me, and
spare not to spit in my face.
11 Because he hath loosed my cord, and afflicted
me, they have also let loose the bridle before me.
12 Upon *my* right *hand* rise the youth; they push
away my feet, and they raise up against me the
ways of their destruction.
13 They mar my path, they set forward my ca-
lamity, they have no helper.
14 They came *upon me* as a wide breaking in *of*
waters: in the desolation they rolled themselves
upon me.
15 Terrors are turned upon me: they pursue my
soul as the wind: and my welfare passeth away as
a cloud.
16 And now my soul is poured out upon me; the
days of affliction have taken hold upon me.
17 My bones are pierced in me in the night sea-
son: and my sinews take no rest.
18 By the great force *of my disease* is my garment
changed: it bindeth me about as the collar of my
coat.
19 He hath cast me into the mire, and I am
become like dust and ashes.
20 I cry unto thee, and thou dost not hear me: I
stand up, and thou regardest me *not*.
21 Thou art become cruel to me: with thy strong
hand thou opposest thyself against me.
22 Thou liftest me up to the wind; thou causest

29:18 *I shall die in my nest.* An image of prosperity and comfort continuing to the end of his days, which would be many (*as the sand*).
29:19 *waters . . . dew.* Images of bountiful supply for every need.
29:23 *waited for me.* Job alluded to how much better his counsel was to others than the counsel he had been receiving from his friends.
29:24 *If I laughed on them, they believed it not.* Because of Job's sincerity, those around him did not know how to understand his playful joking.

Thoughts for Personal/Family Worship: Chapter 29

1. **We learn much about Job in this chapter through his personal testimony. He walked in the light of God (v. 3), fellowshipped with God as with a friend (v. 4), and knew the presence of God (v. 5). Job's self-assessment agreed with God's testimony about him (1:1; 2:3). This is the mark of a true Christian. He had been born again and through the new birth had tasted the goodness of God (Ps. 34:8), not just God's blessings but God Himself. How does your own testimony compare with Job's? Have you experienced God's spiritual grace?**
2. **Job had a reputation for compassion (vv. 12–17). We cannot know the love of Christ without being moved to demonstrate that love to others. Christ says that everything hangs on two great commandments: to love God completely and to love one's neighbor as oneself (Matt. 22:37–39). James describes pure and undefiled religion as visiting the fatherless and widows in their affliction and keeping one's self unspotted by the world (James 1:27). By God's definition, Job's religion was pure religion. Can it be said of you that you are generous, compassionate, and separated from the contamination of the world? Why or why not?**

Chapter 30: *Job laments how drastically his situation has changed from prosperity to distress, from being respected to being disdained.*
30:4 *mallows . . . juniper roots.* Herbs of some sort and roots from the broom tree that were used for food (*meat*) by those who were poor.
30:7 *brayed.* Cried out.
30:8 *fools.* People who are good for nothing. *base men.* Literally, those "without a name" having no reputation. *viler than the earth.* Literally, "they were cast out of the earth," expressing their lowliness.
30:9 *song.* Specifically, a mocking song. *byword.* An object of scorn.
30:11 *he hath loosed my cord.* God had made Job like a warrior with an unstrung bow, unable to defend himself. *let loose the bridle.* Threw off any restraint.
30:13 *set forward my calamity.* Promote my destruction.
30:15 *soul.* Literally, "dignity or honor." *welfare.* Prosperity.

me to ride *upon it*, and dissolvest my substance.
23 For I know *that* thou wilt bring me *to* death,
and *to* the house appointed for all living.
24 Howbeit he will not stretch out *his* hand to the
grave, though they cry in his destruction.
25 Did not I weep for him that was in trouble?
was *not* my soul grieved for the poor?
26 When I looked for good, then evil came *unto*
me: and when I waited for light, there came
darkness.
27 My bowels boiled, and rested not: the days of
affliction prevented me.
28 I went mourning without the sun: I stood up,
and I cried in the congregation.
29 I am a brother to dragons, and a companion
to owls.
30 My skin is black upon me, and my bones are
burned with heat.
31 My harp also is *turned* to mourning, and my
organ into the voice of them that weep.

CHAPTER 31

I MADE a covenant with mine eyes; why then
should I think upon a maid?
2 For what portion of God *is there* from above?
and *what* inheritance of the Almighty from on
high?
3 *Is* not destruction to the wicked? and a strange
punishment to the workers of iniquity?
4 Doth not he see my ways, and count all my steps?
5 If I have walked with vanity, or if my foot hath
hasted to deceit;
6 Let me be weighed in an even balance, that God
may know mine integrity.
7 If my step hath turned out of the way, and mine
heart walked after mine eyes, and if any blot hath
cleaved to mine hands;
8 *Then* let me sow, and let another eat; yea, let my
offspring be rooted out.
9 If mine heart have been deceived by a woman,
or *if* I have laid wait at my neighbour's door;
10 *Then* let my wife grind unto another, and let
others bow down upon her.
11 For this *is* an heinous crime; yea, it *is* an iniq-
uity *to be punished by* the judges.
12 For it *is* a fire *that* consumeth to destruction,
and would root out all mine increase.
13 If I did despise the cause of my manservant
or of my maidservant, when they contended with
me;
14 What then shall I do when God riseth up? and
when he visiteth, what shall I answer him?
15 Did not he that made me in the womb make
him? and did not one fashion us in the womb?
16 If I have withheld the poor from *their* desire,
or have caused the eyes of the widow to fail;
17 Or have eaten my morsel myself alone, and the
fatherless hath not eaten thereof;
18 (For from my youth he was brought up with

30:22 *substance.* Or wisdom.
30:23 *house.* The place of the dead (17:13; Eccl. 12:5).
30:24 Cries for help from *the grave* will be of no avail (Luke 16:22–26).
30:27 *bowels boiled.* An image of inner turmoil of heart. *prevented.* Confronted.
30:29 *dragons.* Most likely jackals. *owls.* Or ostriches.
30:31 *harp.* A zither or some other sort of stringed instrument. *organ.* A flute-like instrument.

Thoughts for Personal/Family Worship: Chapter 30

1. **Job laments that he had become a reproach to his neighbors (vv. 9–10). Suffering contempt or insults from our neighbors is not unusual for Christians. To this we are called, for Christ suffered as an example that we should follow in His steps (1 Peter 2:21–23). The challenge Christians face when it comes to bearing reproach is to make sure the reproach is not on account of their sins but on account of Christ (1 Peter 2:20).**
2. **Comparing ch. 29 with ch. 30, the reader can perceive how Job had gone from the mountaintops of spiritual bliss to the deepest valleys of humiliation. The providence of God leads Christians through both the mountaintop of blessing and the valley of humiliation as parts of His work of making them holy. When Paul wrote that "all things work together for good to them that love God" (Rom. 8:28), he was not limiting "all things" to the mountaintop experiences of God. How have you seen God's wisdom and goodness in both the peaks and valleys of your life or that of others? How can that give you patience today?**

Chapter 31: *Job professes both his innocence and his willingness to suffer the consequences if he is not innocent.*

31:1 *maid.* Virgin, young woman.
31:3 *strange punishment.* A feeling of strangeness or calamity.
31:4 *see my ways.* God is omniscient, knowing all things (Pss. 33:13–15; 139:1–4; Prov. 15:3; John 21:17; Heb. 4:13).
31:5 *If.* Throughout this chapter Job called on God to scrutinize his integrity and judge him accordingly. *vanity.* Deceitfulness.
31:7 *blot.* Blemish or defect.
31:8 *offspring.* What emerges from sowing. The reference is not to Job's children, as they had already died (1:18–19), but to whatever Job had sown.
31:9 Job understood that adultery begins in the *heart* (Prov. 6:25; 7:25; Matt. 5:28).
31:10 *grind.* At a millstone, here representing slavery.
31:11 *heinous crime.* Specifically, the sin of adultery (v. 9), good evidence that the moral law was known before the revelation of the Ten Commandments at Mt. Sinai (Ex. 20:14).
31:14 *when he visiteth.* When God investigates and brings into account.
31:15 *make him.* The recognition that all people have one Maker, the Lord God, gives us a foundation for opposing all social oppression and racism (34:19; Prov. 14:31; 22:2; Mal. 2:10; Acts 17:26).
31:16–23 Job declared the importance of loving one's neighbor and saw a lack of compassion as being a serious sin.
31:18 *her.* The widow (v. 16).

me, as *with* a father, and I have guided her from
my mother's womb;)
19 If I have seen any perish for want of clothing,
or any poor without covering;
20 If his loins have not blessed me, and *if* he were
not warmed with the fleece of my sheep;
21 If I have lifted up my hand against the father-
less, when I saw my help in the gate:
22 *Then* let mine arm fall from my shoulder
blade, and mine arm be broken from the bone.
23 For destruction *from* God *was* a terror to me,
and by reason of his highness I could not endure.
24 If I have made gold my hope, or have said to
the fine gold, *Thou art* my confidence;
25 If I rejoiced because my wealth *was* great, and
because mine hand had gotten much;
26 If I beheld the sun when it shined, or the moon
walking *in* brightness;
27 And my heart hath been secretly enticed, or
my mouth hath kissed my hand:
28 This also *were* an iniquity *to be punished by* the
judge: for I should have denied the God *that is*
above.
29 If I rejoiced at the destruction of him that
hated me, or lifted up myself when evil found him:
30 Neither have I suffered my mouth to sin by
wishing a curse to his soul.
31 If the men of my tabernacle said not, Oh that
we had of his flesh! we cannot be satisfied.
32 The stranger did not lodge in the street: *but* I
opened my doors to the traveller.
33 If I covered my transgressions as Adam, by
hiding mine iniquity in my bosom:
34 Did I fear a great multitude, or did the con-
tempt of families terrify me, that I kept silence,
and went not out of the door?
35 Oh that one would hear me! behold, my desire
is, that the Almighty would answer me, and *that*
mine adversary had written a book.
36 Surely I would take it upon my shoulder, *and*
bind it *as* a crown to me.
37 I would declare unto him the number of my
steps; as a prince would I go near unto him.
38 If my land cry against me, or that the furrows
likewise thereof complain;
39 If I have eaten the fruits thereof without
money, or have caused the owners thereof to lose
their life:
40 Let thistles grow instead of wheat, and cockle
instead of barley. The words of Job are ended.

CHAPTER 32

So these three men ceased to answer Job, because
he *was* righteous in his own eyes.
2 Then was kindled the wrath of Elihu the son
of Barachel the Buzite, of the kindred of Ram:
against Job was his wrath kindled, because he
justified himself rather than God.
3 Also against his three friends was his wrath
kindled, because they had found no answer, and
yet had condemned Job.
4 Now Elihu had waited till Job had spoken,
because they *were* elder than he.

31:20 *blessed me*. By expressing thanks.
31:24 *made gold my hope*. See 1 Tim. 6:10,17. All *confidence* except that placed in the Lord will prove unable to support us (8:14).
31:25 *gotten*. Obtained; Hebrew, "found."
31:26–27 *beheld the sun . . . kissed my hand*. Evidently the worship of the heavenly bodies (Deut. 4:19; 17:3; 2 Kings 17:16; Jer. 8:2).
31:29 *rejoiced at the destruction*. Job understood that he should love his enemies (Ex. 23:4–5; Prov. 17:5; 24:17; Matt. 5:44–45).
31:31 *tabernacle*. Tent or dwelling place.
31:32 *stranger*. A temporary dweller or newcomer.
31:33 *Adam*. The first man, a real, historical person (Gen. 1–3; Hos. 6:7). Alludes to Adam's trying to hide from God after the first sin (Gen. 3:8–9).
31:40 *cockle*. Bramble or briar. *words of Job are ended*. This speech (29:1—31:40) completed Job's case for his righteousness, and his three friends ceased debating with him (32:1).

Thoughts for Personal/Family Worship: Chapter 31

1. **In this climactic finish to his speech, Job forcefully declared his righteousness. Since God commended Job as a model of righteousness, we should carefully observe and follow his example. Job made a covenant with his eyes (v. 1). He was careful about his conduct (v. 5). He resisted sins within his heart (v. 9). He showed consideration toward those who were under his authority (v. 13). He had compassion for the poor (v. 16). He was careful not to put his hope in the riches of this world (v. 24). While not a complete picture of righteousness, this chapter is a beautiful example of the obedience produced by a living faith in the Lord. When you reach the end of your life, will you be able to say such things? How can you prepare now?**
2. **Job recognized the essential equality of men as God's creations, as well as the implications of this reality for how to treat one another (v. 15). People under his authority and below his social rank still shared with him a common humanity. In this statement Job set forth the foundation for compassion and justice that ought to characterize every Christian. In what ways do people in your circles commonly treat others as less important or less valuable than themselves? How should you be different?**

Elihu's Speech for God (32:1—37:24)

Elihu's Rebuke of Job (32:1—35:16)

Chapter 32: ***Elihu expresses his anger regarding the friends' counsel and Job's self-defense, claiming to have the answer.***

32:2 Of all the characters in the book, *Elihu* is the most enigmatic. Some regard Elihu as God's representative, as Elihu claimed himself to be (33:6). Others see him as a proud young man. Some Jewish traditions say that he was Balaam (Jerusalem Talmud) or that he had the spirit of Satan (*Testament of Job*). It is best to see Elihu in much the same way as we view

5 When Elihu saw that *there was* no answer in
the mouth of *these* three men, then his wrath was
kindled.
6 And Elihu the son of Barachel the Buzite answered and said, I *am* young, and ye *are* very old;
wherefore I was afraid, and durst not shew you
mine opinion.
7 I said, Days should speak, and multitude of
years should teach wisdom.
8 But *there is* a spirit in man: and the inspiration
of the Almighty giveth them understanding.
9 Great men are not *always* wise: neither do the
aged understand judgment.
10 Therefore I said, Hearken to me; I also will
shew mine opinion.
11 Behold, I waited for your words; I gave ear to
your reasons, whilst ye searched out what to say.
12 Yea, I attended unto you, and, behold, *there
was* none of you that convinced Job, *or* that answered his words:
13 Lest ye should say, We have found out wisdom:
God thrusteth him down, not man.
14 Now he hath not directed *his* words against
me: neither will I answer him with your speeches.
15 They were amazed, they answered no more:
they left off speaking.
16 When I had waited, (for they spake not, but
stood still, *and* answered no more;)
17 *I said*, I will answer also my part, I also will
shew mine opinion.
18 For I am full of matter, the spirit within me
constraineth me.
19 Behold, my belly *is* as wine *which* hath no vent;
it is ready to burst like new bottles.
20 I will speak, that I may be refreshed: I will
open my lips and answer.
21 Let me not, I pray you, accept any man's person, neither let me give flattering titles unto man.
22 For I know not to give flattering titles; *in so
doing* my maker would soon take me away.

CHAPTER 33

WHEREFORE, Job, I pray thee, hear my speeches,
and hearken to all my words.
2 Behold, now I have opened my mouth, my
tongue hath spoken in my mouth.
3 My words *shall be of* the uprightness of my
heart: and my lips shall utter knowledge clearly.
4 The Spirit of God hath made me, and the
breath of the Almighty hath given me life.
5 If thou canst answer me, set *thy words* in order
before me, stand up.
6 Behold, I *am* according to thy wish in God's
stead: I also am formed out of the clay.
7 Behold, my terror shall not make thee afraid,
neither shall my hand be heavy upon thee.
8 Surely thou hast spoken in mine hearing, and I
have heard the voice of *thy* words, *saying*,
9 I am clean without transgression, I *am* innocent; neither *is there* iniquity in me.
10 Behold, he findeth occasions against me, he
counteth me for his enemy,
11 He putteth my feet in the stocks, he marketh
all my paths.
12 Behold, *in* this thou art not just: I will answer
thee, that God is greater than man.
13 Why dost thou strive against him? for he
giveth not account of any of his matters.
14 For God speaketh once, yea twice, *yet man*
perceiveth it not.
15 In a dream, in a vision of the night, when deep

Job's other three friends—as speaking some truths but not always assessing Job accurately.

32:6 *durst not shew*. Feared to make known.

32:8 *inspiration*. Breath (27:3).

32:15 *amazed*. Hebrew, "to be terrified or dismayed."

32:17 *I will answer*. Notwithstanding his somewhat arrogant claim, Elihu does not add much insight to the issue. He still associates Job's situation with his sin, perhaps focusing more on his present than his past sins.

32:18 *matter*. Words.

32:19 *no vent*. Has not been opened. *burst like new bottles*. See Luke 5:37.

32:21 *accept any man's person*. Hebrew, "to lift up the face of man," an idiom expressing favoritism.

Thoughts for Personal/Family Worship: Chapter 32

1. **On the one hand, Elihu showed some humility, so he is a good example to all, and particularly to youth. Despite his desire to enter the conversation, he respected his elders and allowed them to speak until they were finished. This conforms to the principle of the fifth commandment to honor one's parents, including all others of higher rank. Failure to honor others contributes to the breakdown of society and introduces all manner of sin and misery. So young people should learn to respect their elders, even those who are not their parents.**
2. **On the other hand, Elihu demonstrated that youthful zeal can be quick to recognize problems without offering any real solutions. His claim to have the answer was idealistic and expressed with a degree of pride. Christ said, "Wisdom is justified of her children" (Matt. 11:19). In other words, wisdom is vindicated by what it produces. Before we start talking about our wisdom, we should invest time in practicing wisdom so that it bears good fruit in our lives (James 3:13–18).**

Chapter 33: *Elihu claims to speak in God's place, desiring to vindicate Job.*

33:6 *thy wish in God's stead*. Literally, "your mouth for God." Elihu professed to be the mediator Job desired (9:32–35). Many false prophets have made the same claim (see 1 Kings 13:17; Jer. 28:1–2). On assessing Elihu, see note at 32:2.

33:9 *I am clean without transgression*. A misrepresentation, for Job never claimed to be without sin (13:23,26; 14:4,16). He claimed only that sin was not the cause of his calamity, for he had walked in integrity, and in this he was right (1:1—2:13).

33:13 *he giveth not account*. God's ways are indeed inexplicable, and no one has the right to judge Him (9:12; Isa. 45:9;

sleep falleth upon men, in slumberings upon the
bed;
16 Then he openeth the ears of men, and sealeth
their instruction,
17 That he may withdraw man *from his* purpose,
and hide pride from man.
18 He keepeth back his soul from the pit, and his
life from perishing by the sword.
19 He is chastened also with pain upon his bed,
and the multitude of his bones with strong *pain*:
20 So that his life abhorreth bread, and his soul
dainty meat.
21 His flesh is consumed away, that it cannot be
seen; and his bones *that* were not seen stick out.
22 Yea, his soul draweth near unto the grave, and
his life to the destroyers.
23 If there be a messenger with him, an inter-
preter, one among a thousand, to shew unto man
his uprightness:
24 Then he is gracious unto him, and saith,
Deliver him from going down to the pit: I have
found a ransom.
25 His flesh shall be fresher than a child's: he shall
return to the days of his youth:
26 He shall pray unto God, and he will be favour-
able unto him: and he shall see his face with joy:
for he will render unto man his righteousness.
27 He looketh upon men, and *if any* say, I have
sinned, and perverted *that which was* right, and it
profited me not;
28 He will deliver his soul from going into the pit,
and his life shall see the light.
29 Lo, all these *things* worketh God oftentimes
with man,
30 To bring back his soul from the pit, to be
enlightened with the light of the living.
31 Mark well, O Job, hearken unto me: hold thy
peace, and I will speak.
32 If thou hast any thing to say, answer me: speak,
for I desire to justify thee.
33 If not, hearken unto me: hold thy peace, and I
shall teach thee wisdom.

CHAPTER 34

FURTHERMORE Elihu answered and said,
2 Hear my words, O ye wise *men*; and give ear
unto me, ye that have knowledge.
3 For the ear trieth words, as the mouth tasteth
meat.

Dan. 4:35; Rom. 9:20). God confirmed that these words are true (38:1—42:6).

33:15–16 A *dream* and *vision* were ways by which God revealed truth (4:13; Gen. 15:1; 20:3; 28:12; 31:10–11,24; 37:5,9; 40:5; 41:1; 46:2) before the coming of His Son completed divine revelation (Heb. 1:1–2).

33:19 God's discipline purifies and protects (so Eliphaz, 5:17, and Job, 23:10).

33:20 *dainty meat.* Tasty and pleasant food.

33:23–28 In this remarkable section, Elihu recognized the need for a gracious mediator to represent God to men and men to God, a role fulfilled only by Jesus Christ.

33:23 *messenger.* Word alternatively translated as "angel" (4:18); here one sent by God as a teacher of *uprightness* (Mal. 2:7; 3:1). *interpreter.* One who speaks for another, like a translator or ambassador (Gen. 42:23; 2 Chron. 32:31; Isa. 43:27). *one among a thousand.* A figure of speech similar to "one in a million"—one who is extraordinary, preeminent, or without equal.

33:24 *ransom.* Atonement, or price to satisfy justice so that the lawbreaker goes free (Ex. 21:30; 30:12; Prov. 6:35). This Mediator not only teaches the way of righteousness (v. 23) but also presents to God a ransom necessary to save the sinner from the *pit* or death (vv. 18,22 ["grave"],28,30).

33:25 *flesh . . . a child's.* This promise goes beyond healing Job's sores (2:7) to a miraculous restoration from the effects of aging (2 Kings 5:14). The forgiveness of sins, deliverance from death, and restoration to youth correspond to the complete salvation of body and soul (Ps. 103:3–5).

33:26 *he will render unto man his righteousness.* The Lord will reward each person according to his faithfulness (34:10–11; 1 Sam. 26:23; Prov. 12:14), not because his works merit blessing but because God will receive His Mediator's ransom (v. 24) and have mercy upon every person who will *pray* for grace and repent of sin (v. 27) in response to the Mediator's teaching (v. 23).

33:31 *Mark well.* Pay close attention. *hold thy peace.* Be silent (v. 33).

Thoughts for Personal/Family Worship: Chapter 33

1. **God is absolutely independent and not accountable to any creature (v. 13). What He does, He does according to His pleasure (Ps. 115:3). We are not to presume to know why God acts as He does. The lesson is plain, therefore, that when the Christian does not understand God's dealings he must realize that God's thoughts and ways are beyond him, but also that God is righteous and always does the right thing (Gen.18:25). It is the Christian's duty, therefore, to submit to God rather than expect God to submit to him. The cross of Christ is sufficient to demonstrate that every dealing of God with His people has a purpose of grace behind it (Rom. 8:32).**
2. **Elihu's statement points directly to the Lord Jesus Christ (vv. 23–28). Christ is the messenger of the covenant, the divine ambassador who spoke the final Word from God (Heb. 1:1–2). He is truly one of a kind, the only Mediator between God and man (1 Tim. 2:5). When He humbly laid down His life, He presented Himself to God as the ransom, as the substitute for many sinners (Mark 10:45). His death redeems His people from the hellish curse of God's law and wrath (Rom. 3:19–26; Gal. 3:13), and His resurrection will restore them to immortality (1 Cor. 15:20–23,53). Whenever the Holy Spirit works prayerful faith and sorrowful repentance for sin, the saving power of Christ has taken hold of a lost soul. Has He taken hold of you? How do you know?**

Chapter 34: *Elihu defends God's justice and blames Job for his unwise remarks.*

34:3 *as the mouth tasteth meat.* Spiritual discernment is like the physical sense of taste by which one distinguishes good from bad (6:30; Pss. 34:8; 119:103).

4 Let us choose to us judgment: let us know
among ourselves what *is* good.
5 For Job hath said, I am righteous: and God hath
taken away my judgment.
6 Should I lie against my right? my wound *is*
incurable without transgression.
7 What man *is* like Job, *who* drinketh up scorn-
ing like water?
8 Which goeth in company with the workers of
iniquity, and walketh with wicked men.
9 For he hath said, It profiteth a man nothing
that he should delight himself with God.
10 Therefore hearken unto me, ye men of un-
derstanding: far be it from God, *that he should do*
wickedness; and *from* the Almighty, *that he should*
commit iniquity.
11 For the work of a man shall he render unto
him, and cause every man to find according to *his*
ways.
12 Yea, surely God will not do wickedly, neither
will the Almighty pervert judgment.
13 Who hath given him a charge over the earth?
or who hath disposed the whole world?
14 If he set his heart upon man, *if* he gather unto
himself his spirit and his breath;
15 All flesh shall perish together, and man shall
turn again unto dust.
16 If now *thou hast* understanding, hear this:
hearken to the voice of my words.
17 Shall even he that hateth right govern? and
wilt thou condemn him that is most just?
18 *Is it fit* to say to a king, *Thou art* wicked? *and* to
princes, *Ye are* ungodly?
19 *How much less to him* that accepteth not the
persons of princes, nor regardeth the rich more
than the poor? for they all *are* the work of his
hands.
20 In a moment shall they die, and the people
shall be troubled at midnight, and pass away: and
the mighty shall be taken away without hand.
21 For his eyes *are* upon the ways of man, and he
seeth all his goings.
22 *There is* no darkness, nor shadow of death,
where the workers of iniquity may hide themselves.
23 For he will not lay upon man more *than right*;
that he should enter into judgment with God.
24 He shall break in pieces mighty men without
number, and set others in their stead.
25 Therefore he knoweth their works, and he
overturneth *them* in the night, so that they are
destroyed.
26 He striketh them as wicked men in the open
sight of others;
27 Because they turned back from him, and
would not consider any of his ways:
28 So that they cause the cry of the poor to come
unto him, and he heareth the cry of the afflicted.
29 When he giveth quietness, who then can make
trouble? and when he hideth *his* face, who then
can behold him? whether *it be done* against a na-
tion, or against a man only:
30 That the hypocrite reign not, lest the people
be ensnared.
31 Surely it is meet to be said unto God, I have
borne *chastisement*, I will not offend *any more*:
32 *That which* I see not teach thou me: if I have
done iniquity, I will do no more.
33 *Should it be* according to thy mind? he will
recompense it, whether thou refuse, or whether
thou choose; and not I: therefore speak what thou
knowest.
34 Let men of understanding tell me, and let a
wise man hearken unto me.
35 Job hath spoken without knowledge, and his
words *were* without wisdom.
36 My desire *is that* Job may be tried unto the end
because of *his* answers for wicked men.
37 For he addeth rebellion unto his sin, he clap-
peth *his hands* among us, and multiplieth his
words against God.

34:5 *Job hath said.* Throughout this discourse Elihu singled out some of Job's extreme statements that were wrong and rebuked him accordingly. He failed to recognize that extreme suffering can lead righteous men to make imbalanced statements, and that Job also confessed faith in the Lord.
34:10 *far be it from God, that he should do wickedness; and from the Almighty, that he should commit iniquity.* God cannot sin or commit injustice (8:3; 23:6; 36:23; Gen. 18:25; Deut. 32:4; 1 John 1:5).
34:14–15 Mankind's very life is evidence of God's common grace; otherwise none could survive (12:10; 27:3).
34:23 *he will not lay upon man more.* God never gives a greater trial than man can endure, if man will depend upon the power of God's grace (1 Cor. 10:13; 2 Cor. 12:9).
34:24 *in their stead.* In their place, instead of them.
34:30 *hypocrite.* A godless or profane person.
34:31 *meet.* Fitting. Literally the first part of this verse reads, "Indeed to God it is said."
34:36 *My desire.* In Hebrew, this word is either an interjection ("O that") or the word for "my father." The KJV takes it as the interjection; literally, "O that Job were tested until the end." Alternatively, some take it as a prayer: "My Father, let Job be tested until the end." Either way, Elihu believed that Job had not yet learned his lesson and that the trial should continue.
34:37 *clappeth his hands among us.* A gesture of disgust, expressing frustration with all of the counsel given.

Thoughts for Personal/Family Worship: Chapter 34

God will never do wrong (v. 10). Elihu, as every character in the book, knew some good theology. It is an absolute truth that "the righteous LORD loveth righteousness" (Ps. 11:7). This statement provides a basic and necessary principle for the Christian when it comes to interpreting the difficulties of life. Whatever the Christian understands or does not understand about God's dealings with him, and whether he agrees or disagrees with those dealings, he can mark this as being absolutely certain: God is righteous in all his dealings and does

CHAPTER 35

ELIHU spake moreover, and said,
2 Thinkest thou this to be right, *that* thou saidst,
My righteousness *is* more than God's?
3 For thou saidst, What advantage will it be unto
thee? *and,* What profit shall I have, *if I be cleansed*
from my sin?
4 I will answer thee, and thy companions with
thee.
5 Look unto the heavens, and see; and behold the
clouds *which* are higher than thou.
6 If thou sinnest, what doest thou against him?
or *if* thy transgressions be multiplied, what doest
thou unto him?
7 If thou be righteous, what givest thou him? or
what receiveth he of thine hand?
8 Thy wickedness *may hurt* a man as thou *art;*
and thy righteousness *may profit* the son of man.
9 By reason of the multitude of oppressions they
make *the oppressed* to cry: they cry out by reason
of the arm of the mighty.
10 But none saith, Where *is* God my maker, who
giveth songs in the night;
11 Who teacheth us more than the beasts of the
earth, and maketh us wiser than the fowls of
heaven?
12 There they cry, but none giveth answer, be-
cause of the pride of evil men.
13 Surely God will not hear vanity, neither will
the Almighty regard it.
14 Although thou sayest thou shalt not see him,
yet judgment *is* before him; therefore trust thou
in him.
15 But now, because *it is* not *so,* he hath visited in
his anger; yet he knoweth *it* not in great extremity:
16 Therefore doth Job open his mouth in vain; he
multiplieth words without knowledge.

CHAPTER 36

ELIHU also proceeded, and said,
2 Suffer me a little, and I will shew thee that *I*
have yet to speak on God's behalf.
3 I will fetch my knowledge from afar, and will
ascribe righteousness to my Maker.
4 For truly my words *shall* not *be* false: he that is
perfect in knowledge *is* with thee.
5 Behold, God *is* mighty, and despiseth not *any:*
he is mighty in strength *and* wisdom.
6 He preserveth not the life of the wicked: but
giveth right to the poor.
7 He withdraweth not his eyes from the

---

not commit iniquity. God is so pure and unchanging that He cannot even be tempted to sin (James 1:13,17). How might a person be tempted to accuse God of doing wrong? How might you counsel him?

Chapter 35: *Elihu rebukes Job for thinking himself to be righteous and then calls on him to continue to trust God.*

35:2 *My righteousness is more than God's.* An exaggeration and misrepresentation, for though Job often wondered why he was suffering without apparent cause, he never elevated himself above God. Job's dilemma was similar to that of Jeremiah (Jer. 12:1).

35:5–9 God is so far above man that he cannot be benefitted by man's righteousness or harmed by man's sin (22:2–3; 41:11). Indeed, God is absolutely independent of anything outside Himself.

35:10 *who giveth songs in the night.* Communion with God and hope in His salvation lead believers to rejoice and sing His praise (Pss. 42:8; 77:6; 149:5).

35:11 *teacheth us more than the beasts.* The Creator ("maker," v. 10) gave mankind a unique place among all of His creations (Gen. 1:26–31; Ps. 8:4–8).

35:13 *vanity.* Emptiness of speech, that which is uttered without purpose. *regard.* The Hebrew has the idea of looking at something from a bent position. God will not bend or stoop down to listen to meaningless prayers.

35:14 *judgment.* Justice.

35:15 *it is not so.* He accused Job of not trusting. *he hath visited in his anger.* God has paid attention and brought the matter to bear upon Job. *he knoweth it not.* Referring to Job. *extremity.* Arrogance or stupidity. Like those before him, Elihu claimed that Job was suffering because of his sin.

35:16 *Therefore doth Job open his mouth in vain.* Literally, "to no purpose Job moves his mouth with lips." Elihu accused Job of speaking in a way God would not hear (v. 13).

Thoughts for Personal/Family Worship: Chapter 35

The independence of God is an important truth with practical implications. God is not reactionary, constantly plotting His next move on the basis of the creature's actions. The sinful behavior of men does not diminish or detract from His righteousness, nor does the righteous behavior of men add anything to Him (vv. 6–7). On the other hand, God is our strength and song for He has created mankind, exalting us above the animals (vv. 10–11). All men are accountable to God, but God is accountable to no one. God owes no man anything. That He is righteous means that He is always in conformity with who He is. For Job or Jeremiah (Jer. 12), Asaph (Ps. 73), or us to think we deserve better because we seek to serve the Lord betrays an improper motive. We serve Him for who He is. Therefore, Elihu's admonition to trust Him regardless of what we see is good counsel (v. 14). How does a view of God's glory and independence help us to trust Him?

Elihu's Proclamation of God (36:1—37:24)

Chapter 36: *Elihu continues to show that God's ways should not be despised even if they are not understood.*

36:2 *Suffer me a little.* Literally, "be patient with me a short time." *shew thee.* Inform you or make you to know. *have yet to speak on God's behalf.* Literally, there are "still words for or of God."

36:3 *fetch my knowledge from afar.* Literally, "Lift up my knowledge from a great distance," presumably claiming God to be the source.

36:4 *he that is perfect in knowledge is with thee.* Elihu refers to himself and his complete (*perfect*) knowledge that he will reveal to Job. His claims are bold and a bit arrogant.

36:6 *the poor.* Those who are in a needy or desperate

righteous: but with kings *are they* on the throne; yea, he doth establish them for ever, and they are exalted.
8 And if *they be* bound in fetters, *and* be holden in cords of affliction;
9 Then he sheweth them their work, and their transgressions that they have exceeded.
10 He openeth also their ear to discipline, and commandeth that they return from iniquity.
11 If they obey and serve *him*, they shall spend their days in prosperity, and their years in pleasures.
12 But if they obey not, they shall perish by the sword, and they shall die without knowledge.
13 But the hypocrites in heart heap up wrath: they cry not when he bindeth them.
14 They die in youth, and their life *is* among the unclean.
15 He delivereth the poor in his affliction, and openeth their ears in oppression.
16 Even so would he have removed thee out of the strait *into* a broad place, where *there is* no straitness; and that which should be set on thy table *should be* full of fatness.
17 But thou hast fulfilled the judgment of the wicked: judgment and justice take hold *on thee.*
18 Because *there is* wrath, *beware* lest he take thee away with *his* stroke: then a great ransom cannot deliver thee.
19 Will he esteem thy riches? *no*, not gold, nor all the forces of strength.
20 Desire not the night, when people are cut off in their place.
21 Take heed, regard not iniquity: for this hast thou chosen rather than affliction.
22 Behold, God exalteth by his power: who teacheth like him?
23 Who hath enjoined him his way? or who can say, Thou hast wrought iniquity?
24 Remember that thou magnify his work, which men behold.
25 Every man may see it; man may behold *it* afar off.
26 Behold, God *is* great, and we know *him* not, neither can the number of his years be searched out.
27 For he maketh small the drops of water: they pour down rain according to the vapour thereof:
28 Which the clouds do drop *and* distil upon man abundantly.
29 Also can *any* understand the spreadings of the clouds, *or* the noise of his tabernacle?
30 Behold, he spreadeth his light upon it, and covereth the bottom of the sea.
31 For by them judgeth he the people; he giveth meat in abundance.
32 With clouds he covereth the light; and commandeth it *not to shine* by *the cloud* that cometh betwixt.
33 The noise thereof sheweth concerning it, the cattle also concerning the vapour.

CHAPTER 37

AT this also my heart trembleth, and is moved out of his place.

condition, not necessarily referring to those in poverty.
36:8 *fetters.* Bonds or shackles. *holden in cords of affliction.* Captured with ropes of affliction.
36:11–12 *if they obey . . . prosperity . . . if they obey not . . . perish.* Elihu believed the same simplistic, cause-effect prosperity theology as Job's friends.
36:13 *hypocrites.* Godless and profane persons.
36:14 *unclean.* The term elsewhere refers to cultic male prostitutes, homosexual "sodomites" (Deut. 23:17; 1 Kings 14:24; 15:12; 22:46; 2 Kings 23:7).
36:16 *strait.* Narrow place. *straitness.* Place without constraints. *full of fatness.* Refers to luxurious or succulent fare.
36:17 *hast fulfilled the judgment of the wicked.* Literally, "are full of the condemnation of the wicked."
36:18 *Because . . . stroke.* Or "Indeed, lest wrath entice you with mockery."
36:23 *enjoined.* Commissioned or appointed. *hast wrought.* Has done.
36:26 *God is great, and we know him not.* God is incomprehensible, beyond man's limited understanding (11:7–9; 26:14). *his years be searched out.* God is eternal, having no beginning or end (Pss. 90:2; 93:2).
36:27–33 *he maketh small the drops of water . . . commandeth it.* The Lord controls the weather by His ordinary providence (37:1–24; Ps. 147:8,15–18).
36:28 *distil.* To drip or trickle.
36:29 *tabernacle.* Tent or dwelling place.
36:31 *meat.* Any kind of food.
36:33 *the vapour.* Literally, "that which goes up," perhaps referring to the approaching storm (38:1).

Thoughts for Personal/Family Worship: Chapter 36

1. **Verse 26 declares an essential truth about God that magnifies both His infinite being and His amazing grace. God is incomprehensible because He is infinite in all His perfections, whereas we are finite. There is no limit to God's greatness, but there is serious limitation to our ability to understand. Our knowledge of anything can go only so far. Although we can never understand all that is true about God, He has chosen to reveal Himself to us in ways that allow us to understand some things. The very fact that God reveals Himself magnifies His grace. To know God as He has revealed Himself is to fear Him.**
2. **The most significant way in which God has revealed Himself is in the incarnation of the second person of the Trinity (John 1:1,14,18). Jesus Christ is the express image or manifestation of God, and the glory of God is found in the face of Jesus. Hence, Christ says that seeing Him is seeing the Father. Wesley's hymn of the incarnation, "Hark, the Herald Angels Sing," has a line that says it well: "Veiled in flesh the Godhead see—Hail the incarnate Deity." So as we contemplate how infinitely great God is, let us stand in wonder and awe at His marvelous grace by which He makes Himself known to us.**

2 Hear attentively the noise of his voice, and the
sound *that* goeth out of his mouth.
3 He directeth it under the whole heaven, and his
lightning unto the ends of the earth.
4 After it a voice roareth: he thundereth with the
voice of his excellency; and he will not stay them
when his voice is heard.
5 God thundereth marvellously with his
voice; great things doeth he, which we cannot
comprehend.
6 For he saith to the snow, Be thou *on* the earth;
likewise to the small rain, and to the great rain of
his strength.
7 He sealeth up the hand of every man; that all
men may know his work.
8 Then the beasts go into dens, and remain in
their places.
9 Out of the south cometh the whirlwind: and
cold out of the north.
10 By the breath of God frost is given: and the
breadth of the waters is straitened.
11 Also by watering he wearieth the thick cloud:
he scattereth his bright cloud:
12 And it is turned round about by his counsels:
that they may do whatsoever he commandeth
them upon the face of the world in the earth.
13 He causeth it to come, whether for correction,
or for his land, or for mercy.
14 Hearken unto this, O Job: stand still, and
consider the wondrous works of God.
15 Dost thou know when God disposed them,
and caused the light of his cloud to shine?
16 Dost thou know the balancings of the clouds,
the wondrous works of him which is perfect in
knowledge?
17 How thy garments *are* warm, when he qui-
eteth the earth by the south *wind*?
18 Hast thou with him spread out the sky, *which*
is strong, *and* as a molten looking glass?
19 Teach us what we shall say unto him; *for* we
cannot order *our speech* by reason of darkness.
20 Shall it be told him that I speak? if a man
speak, surely he shall be swallowed up.
21 And now *men* see not the bright light which *is*
in the clouds: but the wind passeth, and cleans-
eth them.
22 Fair weather cometh out of the north: with
God *is* terrible majesty.
23 *Touching* the Almighty, we cannot find him
out: *he is* excellent in power, and in judgment, and
in plenty of justice: he will not afflict.
24 Men do therefore fear him: he respecteth not
any *that are* wise of heart.

CHAPTER 38

THEN the LORD answered Job out of the whirl-
wind, and said,
2 Who *is* this that darkeneth counsel by words
without knowledge?
3 Gird up now thy loins like a man; for I will de-
mand of thee, and answer thou me.

Chapter 37: *Elihu focuses on God's control over nature to demonstrate His power and man's weakness.*

37:1 *is moved out of his place.* His heart "leaps from its place."
37:2 *noise of his voice.* Thunder (Ps. 29).
37:4 *excellency.* Majesty. *stay.* Hamper, hinder, or hold back.
37:5 *marvellously.* Wondrously, in extraordinary ways.
37:10 *straitened.* Narrow, restrained. God sets the borders of the seas.
37:11 *by watering he wearieth the thick cloud.* Literally, "with a water supply he loads a cloud."
37:12 *by his counsels . . . do whatsoever he commandeth.* The winds of storms and spinning tornadoes obey the wise decree of God (Pss. 107:25; 148:8; Jonah 1:4; Matt. 8:27).
37:18 *molten looking glass.* A mirror formed out of melted bronze.
37:22 *Fair weather.* Hebrew, "gold," like sunshine on the clouds. *with God is terrible majesty.* God's glory inspires fear and awe (v. 24), as does a great king (Pss. 47:2; 99:1–4).
37:23 *the Almighty.* Hebrew, *Shaddai*, a title of God used thirty-one times in Job out of forty-eight occurrences in the Old Testament. It is associated with God's revelations to the patriarchs (Gen. 17:1 [see note there]; 28:3; 35:11; 43:14; 48:3; 49:25; Ex. 6:3). The word is of uncertain derivation, being interpreted in the Greek Septuagint translation as "all-powerful" and in the Talmud as "sufficient." Here it is linked to God's infinitely great *power* and righteousness. *we cannot find him out.* His greatness is beyond our understanding (36:26). *in judgment, and in plenty of justice: he will not afflict.* Could be translated, "He will not humiliate justice and abundant righteousness"; that is, not compromise them in the least, but exalt them.

Thoughts for Personal/Family Worship: Chapter 37

Elihu's focus on God's sovereignty over the affairs of nature, and especially the weather, links directly to what we should acknowledge regarding His sovereignty over the affairs of our lives. Few things are less predictable than the weather, and certainly nothing is less controllable, even when forecasts prove to be accurate. Nothing can stop the wind from blowing or the rain and snow from falling. But this all happens according to the will of God. We should learn from looking at the weather that God is in control of all His creation, including all of the circumstances of our lives. It should encourage and comfort us to know that God has a purpose for everything (v. 13) and that nothing happens apart from His providence. What can we learn about God by looking at the weather?

The Lord's Interrogation of Job (38:1—41:34)

The Lord's Questions about Creation (38:1—39:30)

Chapter 38: *God draws Job's attention away from himself by pointing to His greatness over the natural world.*

38:1 *out of the whirlwind.* The Lord appeared to Job in the glory of a thunderstorm (ch. 37).
38:3 *Gird up now thy loins.* An idiom meaning "get ready."

4 Where wast thou when I laid the foundations
of the earth? declare, if thou hast understanding.
5 Who hath laid the measures thereof, if thou
knowest? or who hath stretched the line upon it?
6 Whereupon are the foundations thereof fas-
tened? or who laid the corner stone thereof;
7 When the morning stars sang together, and all
the sons of God shouted for joy?
8 Or *who* shut up the sea with doors, when it
brake forth, *as if* it had issued out of the womb?
9 When I made the cloud the garment thereof,
and thick darkness a swaddlingband for it,
10 And brake up for it my decreed *place*, and set
bars and doors,
11 And said, Hitherto shalt thou come, but no
further: and here shall thy proud waves be stayed?
12 Hast thou commanded the morning since thy
days; *and* caused the dayspring to know his place;
13 That it might take hold of the ends of the
earth, that the wicked might be shaken out of it?
14 It is turned as clay *to* the seal; and they stand
as a garment.
15 And from the wicked their light is withholden,
and the high arm shall be broken.
16 Hast thou entered into the springs of the sea?
or hast thou walked in the search of the depth?
17 Have the gates of death been opened unto
thee? or hast thou seen the doors of the shadow
of death?
18 Hast thou perceived the breadth of the earth?
declare if thou knowest it all.
19 Where *is* the way *where* light dwelleth? and *as
for* darkness, where *is* the place thereof,
20 That thou shouldest take it to the bound
thereof, and that thou shouldest know the paths
to the house thereof?
21 Knowest thou *it*, because thou wast then born?
or *because* the number of thy days *is* great?
22 Hast thou entered into the treasures of the
snow? or hast thou seen the treasures of the hail,
23 Which I have reserved against the time of
trouble, against the day of battle and war?
24 By what way is the light parted, *which*
scattereth the east wind upon the earth?
25 Who hath divided a watercourse for the over-
flowing of waters, or a way for the lightning of
thunder;
26 To cause it to rain on the earth, *where* no man
is; on the wilderness, wherein *there is* no man;
27 To satisfy the desolate and waste *ground*; and to
cause the bud of the tender herb to spring forth?
28 Hath the rain a father? or who hath begotten
the drops of dew?
29 Out of whose womb came the ice? and the
hoary frost of heaven, who hath gendered it?
30 The waters are hid as *with* a stone, and the face
of the deep is frozen.
31 Canst thou bind the sweet influences of Pleia-
des, or loose the bands of Orion?
32 Canst thou bring forth Mazzaroth in his sea-
son? or canst thou guide Arcturus with his sons?
33 Knowest thou the ordinances of heaven? canst
thou set the dominion thereof in the earth?
34 Canst thou lift up thy voice to the clouds, that
abundance of waters may cover thee?
35 Canst thou send lightnings, that they may go,
and say unto thee, Here we *are*?
36 Who hath put wisdom in the inward parts? or
who hath given understanding to the heart?
37 Who can number the clouds in wisdom? or
who can stay the bottles of heaven,
38 When the dust groweth into hardness, and the
clods cleave fast together?
39 Wilt thou hunt the prey for the lion? or fill the
appetite of the young lions,
40 When they couch in *their* dens, *and* abide in
the covert to lie in wait?
41 Who provideth for the raven his food? when

38:4 In His first speech God taught Job that He is the Lord over nature: He is the Creator (vv. 4–15); the Ruler over inanimate nature (vv. 16–38); and the Ruler over animate nature (38:39—39:30). God was teaching Job that man is not the center of things and that all creation is for God's enjoyment and glory.
38:7 *morning stars . . . sons of God.* Angels (1:6; 2:1), whom God created to be joyful, worshiping witnesses to the work of creation (Ps. 148:1–6)—and redemption (Ps. 103:20; Luke 2:13; Eph. 3:9–10; 1 Peter 1:12; Rev. 5:11–12).
38:8 *sea . . . when it brake forth.* Either an allusion to the great flood (Gen. 7:11; 8:2) or to boundaries of the seas, as dictated by creation and providence (Gen. 1:9; Jer. 5:22).
38:11 *stayed.* Stopped or held back.
38:12 *dayspring.* Dawn.
38:20 *the bound.* Its borders or boundary.
38:22 *treasures.* Storehouses.
38:24 *By what way is light parted?* How is the light diffused when it displaces the darkness? *which scattereth the east wind.* Who scatters the east wind (the word "which" is not in the Hebrew).
38:31 *sweet influences.* Delicacies, pleasures. The constellation *Pleiades* (9:9) appeared in the springtime, a season of delights, but *Orion* in the winter as a precursor to the storms of that season.
38:32 *Mazzaroth.* The word occurs only here and seems to refer to a constellation of stars.
38:37 *who can stay the bottles of heaven.* Who can tip the jars of heaven, a picturesque way of asking who can make it rain.
38:40 *covert.* Shelter or hiding place, the den.
38:41 *meat.* Food of any kind.

Thoughts for Personal/Family Worship: Chapter 38

1. The fact that the Lord answered Job "out of the whirlwind" (v. 1) indicates that this manifestation of God was a fearful event not altogether different from the Lord's appearance on Mt. Sinai, where there were thunder and lighting, an exceedingly loud trumpet, and a quaking mountain (Ex. 19:16–19). And yet this appearance of God to Job was also a gracious event, as it was when God revealed Himself to Ezekiel, assuring

his young ones cry unto God, they wander for lack of meat.

CHAPTER 39

KNOWEST thou the time when the wild goats of the rock bring forth? *or* canst thou mark when the hinds do calve?
2 Canst thou number the months *that* they fulfil? or knowest thou the time when they bring forth?
3 They bow themselves, they bring forth their young ones, they cast out their sorrows.
4 Their young ones are in good liking, they grow up with corn; they go forth, and return not unto them.
5 Who hath sent out the wild ass free? or who hath loosed the bands of the wild ass?
6 Whose house I have made the wilderness, and the barren land his dwellings.
7 He scorneth the multitude of the city, neither regardeth he the crying of the driver.
8 The range of the mountains *is* his pasture, and he searcheth after every green thing.
9 Will the unicorn be willing to serve thee, or abide by thy crib?
10 Canst thou bind the unicorn with his band in the furrow? or will he harrow the valleys after thee?
11 Wilt thou trust him, because his strength *is* great? or wilt thou leave thy labour to him?
12 Wilt thou believe him, that he will bring home thy seed, and gather *it into* thy barn?
13 *Gavest thou* the goodly wings unto the peacocks? or wings and feathers unto the ostrich?
14 Which leaveth her eggs in the earth, and warmeth them in dust,
15 And forgetteth that the foot may crush them, or that the wild beast may break them.
16 She is hardened against her young ones, as though *they were* not hers: her labour is in vain without fear;
17 Because God hath deprived her of wisdom, neither hath he imparted to her understanding.
18 What time she lifteth up herself on high, she scorneth the horse and his rider.
19 Hast thou given the horse strength? hast thou clothed his neck with thunder?
20 Canst thou make him afraid as a grasshopper? the glory of his nostrils *is* terrible.
21 He paweth in the valley, and rejoiceth in *his* strength: he goeth on to meet the armed men.
22 He mocketh at fear, and is not affrighted; neither turneth he back from the sword.
23 The quiver rattleth against him, the glittering spear and the shield.
24 He swalloweth the ground with fierceness and rage: neither believeth he that *it is* the sound of the trumpet.
25 He saith among the trumpets, Ha, ha; and he smelleth the battle afar off, the thunder of the captains, and the shouting.
26 Doth the hawk fly by thy wisdom, *and* stretch her wings toward the south?
27 Doth the eagle mount up at thy command, and make her nest on high?
28 She dwelleth and abideth on the rock, upon the crag of the rock, and the strong place.
29 From thence she seeketh the prey, *and* her eyes behold afar off.
30 Her young ones also suck up blood: and where the slain *are*, there *is* she.

him of the divine presence (Ezek. 1:4). We should not be surprised that when God visits His people in grace He still inspires fear (Gen. 28:15–17; Luke 5:8). Even in mercy, He remains God.

2. **The Lord "answered" Job (v. 1). In speaking to Job, God never addressed the problem of suffering, though He gave him the answer he needed. Job and the other men had been trying to answer the question *Why*? But this was the wrong question, which accounts for all their wrong answers. The right question was not *Why*? but *Who*? Once Job understood who he was (v. 2; 42:3) and who God is (vv. 5–6; etc.), all was well. The ultimate answer to all our questions about evil and suffering is not information but a person: the Lord Himself. The heart cry of believers is always to see the glory of their God and Savior; one day that cry will be answered forever (John 17:24; Titus 2:13).**

Chapter 39: *God continues to redirect Job from his suffering to the reality of God's control over lesser creatures.*

39:1 *wild goats.* Perhaps the ibex. *the hinds do calve.* The does of a fallow deer give birth.

39:2 *the months that they fulfil.* The gestation period.

39:3 *their sorrows.* The Hebrew refers to the animal fetus.

39:4 *in good liking.* Healthy.

39:9 *unicorn.* Wild ox, not the mythological one-horned horse.

39:10 *harrow.* Plough.

39:11 *trust.* Put confidence in.

39:13 *peacocks.* Most likely the ostrich, per the behavior described in the following verses.

39:17 *God hath deprived her . . . neither hath he imparted.* All strength and skill (*wisdom*), or the lack thereof, in the animal world are determined by God.

39:20 *glory of his nostrils.* Power of his snorting.

39:22 *affrighted.* Frightened.

39:30 *where the slain are, there is she.* Used as a proverb to express something that is just as certain as finding birds of prey near carrion (Matt. 24:28; Luke 17:37).

Thoughts for Personal/Family Worship: Chapter 39

Since ancient times people have studied the animal world and been fascinated by its biology and behaviors. From the wild donkey to the ostrich to the thundering horse to the soaring eagle, the beauty and mystery of these creatures captures man's imagination. By challenging Job with this series of questions, God drove into his mind the recognition that mankind does not fully

CHAPTER 40

MOREOVER the LORD answered Job, and said,
2 Shall he that contendeth with the Almighty
instruct *him*? he that reproveth God, let him
answer it.
3 ¶ Then Job answered the LORD, and said,
4 Behold, I am vile; what shall I answer thee? I
will lay mine hand upon my mouth.
5 Once have I spoken; but I will not answer: yea,
twice; but I will proceed no further.
6 ¶ Then answered the LORD unto Job out of the
whirlwind, and said,
7 Gird up thy loins now like a man: I will demand
of thee, and declare thou unto me.
8 Wilt thou also disannul my judgment? wilt thou
condemn me, that thou mayest be righteous?
9 Hast thou an arm like God? or canst thou
thunder with a voice like him?
10 Deck thyself now *with* majesty and excellency;
and array thyself with glory and beauty.
11 Cast abroad the rage of thy wrath: and behold
every one *that is* proud, and abase him.
12 Look on every one *that is* proud, *and* bring him
low; and tread down the wicked in their place.
13 Hide them in the dust together; *and* bind their
faces in secret.
14 Then will I also confess unto thee that thine
own right hand can save thee.
15 ¶ Behold now behemoth, which I made with
thee; he eateth grass as an ox.
16 Lo now, his strength *is* in his loins, and his
force *is* in the navel of his belly.
17 He moveth his tail like a cedar: the sinews of
his stones are wrapped together.
18 His bones *are as* strong pieces of brass; his
bones *are* like bars of iron.
19 He *is* the chief of the ways of God: he that made
him can make his sword to approach *unto him*.
20 Surely the mountains bring him forth food,
where all the beasts of the field play.
21 He lieth under the shady trees, in the covert of
the reed, and fens.
22 The shady trees cover him *with* their shadow;
the willows of the brook compass him about.
23 Behold, he drinketh up a river, *and* hasteth
not: he trusteth that he can draw up Jordan into
his mouth.
24 He taketh it with his eyes: *his* nose pierceth
through snares.

CHAPTER 41

CANST thou draw out leviathan with an hook? or
his tongue with a cord *which* thou lettest down?

---

understand and cannot completely control the birds and beasts. This remains true even thousands of years after Job. God, however, created them all, and He determines the strengths and weaknesses of each. Our awe and wonder at the natural world should remind us that if we cannot master God's creatures, how much less can we judge God? What are some of your favorite animals? How do they remind you of the glory of God?

The Lord's Challenge regarding the Great Beasts (40:1—41:34)

Chapter 40: *Job becomes silent before God, who directs Job's attention to His control over the moral realm.*

40:1 *Moreover, the LORD answered Job.* In His second speech God, after challenging Job (41:1–7), shows that He is also the Lord over history and the moral order (40:8–14). The Lord illustrates this by referring to behemoth (vv. 15–24) and leviathan (41:1–34), real creatures that symbolically refer to the forces of evil, even Satan himself, that are subject to God. In this way the end of God's discourse echoes the opening narratives, where it is clear that Satan was allowed to do nothing apart from God's control.
40:2 *contendeth with the Almighty.* Takes the all-powerful God to court to dispute with Him. This, the final use of this divine title in Job (see note at 37:23), highlights the utter foolishness of trying to judge Him who has infinite strength and righteousness.
40:4 *vile.* Small and insignificant. *hand upon my mouth.* A gesture expressing humiliation and speechlessness (21:5; 29:9; Judg. 18:19).
40:7 *Gird up thy loins.* See note at 38:3.
40:8 *disannul.* Cast off or make void. Though Job feared the Lord, in his suffering he sinned insofar as he questioned God's righteousness in order to establish his own against his friends' accusations.
40:10 *Deck thyself . . . array thyself.* Put on beautiful clothing, here with the image of a king putting on royal robes. God invited Job to sit in His seat of judgment to deal with the wicked and proud (vv. 11–12).
40:11 *Cast abroad the rage of thy wrath.* Disperse the outbursts of your anger. *abase.* Humiliate or bring low.
40:14 Job did not have the ability to judge the world or even to *save* himself. God is in an entirely different category from man. Therefore, what right did Job have to judge God or question His righteousness?
40:15 *behemoth.* Large beast (12:7; 18:3; 35:11); interpretations include everything from a dinosaur to an elephant to a hippopotamus. *which I made.* Whatever massive animal is in view, the Lord created it and is its master.
40:16 *navel.* Muscles.
40:17 *like a cedar.* The point of similarity may not be its size but its swaying movement. *stones.* Thighs.
40:19 *ways of God.* His works. *he that made him can make his sword to approach.* A challenge to anyone who claims to have made this animal to attack and kill it.
40:21 *covert.* Cover or shelter. *fens.* Swamps or marshes.
40:22 *compass.* Surround.

Thoughts for Personal/Family Worship: Chapter 40

At the conclusion of God's first speech, Job had learned his lesson. Throughout the book Job had desired to be in God's presence to have the opportunity to question Him regarding his troubles. Now that he is in God's presence and given the opportunity to speak, he has nothing to say. Being overwhelmed with the greatness of God has caused him to stop thinking about himself. He has learned that God controls everything in the universe,

2 Canst thou put an hook into his nose? or bore
his jaw through with a thorn?
3 Will he make many supplications unto thee?
will he speak soft *words* unto thee?
4 Will he make a covenant with thee? wilt thou
take him for a servant for ever?
5 Wilt thou play with him as *with* a bird? or wilt
thou bind him for thy maidens?
6 Shall the companions make a banquet of him?
shall they part him among the merchants?
7 Canst thou fill his skin with barbed irons? or his
head with fish spears?
8 Lay thine hand upon him, remember the battle,
do no more.
9 Behold, the hope of him is in vain: shall not *one*
be cast down even at the sight of him?
10 None *is so* fierce that dare stir him up: who
then is able to stand before me?
11 Who hath prevented me, that I should repay
him? whatsoever is under the whole heaven is
mine.
12 I will not conceal his parts, nor his power, nor
his comely proportion.
13 Who can discover the face of his garment? *or*
who can come *to him* with his double bridle?
14 Who can open the doors of his face? his teeth
are terrible round about.
15 *His* scales *are his* pride, shut up together *as
with* a close seal.
16 One is so near to another, that no air can come
between them.
17 They are joined one to another, they stick to-
gether, that they cannot be sundered.
18 By his neesings a light doth shine, and his eyes
are like the eyelids of the morning.
19 Out of his mouth go burning lamps, *and*
sparks of fire leap out.
20 Out of his nostrils goeth smoke, as *out* of a
seething pot or caldron.
21 His breath kindleth coals, and a flame goeth
out of his mouth.
22 In his neck remaineth strength, and sorrow is
turned into joy before him.
23 The flakes of his flesh are joined together: they
are firm in themselves; they cannot be moved.
24 His heart is as firm as a stone; yea, as hard as a
piece of the nether *millstone*.
25 When he raiseth up himself, the mighty are
afraid: by reason of breakings they purify them-
selves.
26 The sword of him that layeth at him cannot
hold: the spear, the dart, nor the habergeon.
27 He esteemeth iron as straw, *and* brass as rotten
wood.
28 The arrow cannot make him flee: slingstones
are turned with him into stubble.
29 Darts are counted as stubble: he laugheth at
the shaking of a spear.
30 Sharp stones *are* under him: he spreadeth
sharp pointed things upon the mire.
31 He maketh the deep to boil like a pot: he
maketh the sea like a pot of ointment.
32 He maketh a path to shine after him; *one*
would think the deep *to be* hoary.
33 Upon earth there is not his like, who is made
without fear.
34 He beholdeth all high *things*: he *is* a king over
all the children of pride.

including himself. That is the key lesson. The more we can be overwhelmed with God, the less we will be consumed with ourselves. Seeing God's greatness fosters faith in Him, regardless of circumstances. When we are tempted to judge God, we should consider how unqualified we are to sit upon His throne and rule the world for Him.

Chapter 41: *God continues to show His control with a description of leviathan.*

41:1 *leviathan*. Large sea creature (Ps. 104:26); interpretations include a whale, some kind of sea monster, a very large crocodile, and a symbol of the power of evil (Isa. 27:1; cf. Ps. 74:13–14; Isa. 51:9–10); that is, the ancient serpent, Satan (1:1—2:13; Gen. 3; Rev. 12:3,9).
41:4–5 This creature cannot be domesticated to serve a purpose for man.
41:6 *Shall the companions make a banquet of him?* Referring to traders making deals or bartering for him. *part*. Divide.
41:10–11 *stand before me*. If leviathan terrifies men, can they expect to conquer the God who created the beast, indeed the Creator of all things *under the whole heaven* (Pss. 24:1; 50:12)? *prevented*. Went before (Pss. 68:25; 89:14). The Hebrew is difficult, but the idea is that no one gives anything to God or puts Him under obligation, for all things are from Him and belong to Him (Rom. 11:35–36).
41:17 *sundered*. Separated.
41:18 *neesings*. Sneezing.
41:19 *burning lamps*. Flames or flashes of light.
41:20 *seething*. Boiling.
41:23 *flakes*. Folds or hanging parts of his flesh.
41:24 *nether*. Lower.
41:25 *purify themselves*. Or withdraw.
41:26 *layeth at*. Reaches at. *habergeon*. Javelin.
41:32 *path*. The creature's wake as it moves through the water. *hoary*. Gray-haired.
41:34 *king*. Supreme among others. *children*. Literally, "sons." The same Hebrew phrase is used of powerful animals earlier in Job (translated "lion's whelps," 28:8). Though using a different word, the concept of pride appears just before the sections on behemoth and leviathan, namely in God's challenge to Job to prove his greatness by subduing the "proud" (40:11–13).

Thoughts for Personal/Family Worship: Chapter 41

1. **After God had taught lessons to Job through various animals (38:1—39:30), He focused on two enormous creatures, behemoth and leviathan (40:1—41:34). These beasts terrify men, but God made them and controls them. In this way they illustrate the point God had made just before speaking of them, namely, that we do not have the right to judge God because man completely lacks the qualifications to rule the universe (40:8–14). If**

CHAPTER 42

THEN Job answered the LORD, and said,
2 I know that thou canst do every *thing*, and *that*
no thought can be withholden from thee.
3 Who *is* he that hideth counsel without knowl-
edge? therefore have I uttered that I understood
not; things too wonderful for me, which I knew not.
4 Hear, I beseech thee, and I will speak: I will
demand of thee, and declare thou unto me.
5 I have heard of thee by the hearing of the ear:
but now mine eye seeth thee.
6 Wherefore I abhor *myself*, and repent in dust
and ashes.
7 ¶ And it was *so*, that after the LORD had spoken
these words unto Job, the LORD said to Eliphaz the
Temanite, My wrath is kindled against thee, and
against thy two friends: for ye have not spoken of
me *the thing that is* right, as my servant Job *hath*.
8 Therefore take unto you now seven bullocks
and seven rams, and go to my servant Job, and
offer up for yourselves a burnt offering; and my
servant Job shall pray for you: for him will I
accept: lest I deal with you *after your* folly, in that
ye have not spoken of me *the thing which is* right,
like my servant Job.
9 So Eliphaz the Temanite and Bildad the Shuhite
and Zophar the Naamathite went, and did ac-
cording as the LORD commanded them: the LORD
also accepted Job.
10 And the LORD turned the captivity of Job,
when he prayed for his friends: also the LORD gave
Job twice as much as he had before.
11 Then came there unto him all his brethren,
and all his sisters, and all they that had been of
his acquaintance before, and did eat bread with
him in his house: and they bemoaned him, and
comforted him over all the evil that the LORD had
brought upon him: every man also gave him a
piece of money, and every one an earring of gold.
12 So the LORD blessed the latter end of Job more
than his beginning: for he had fourteen thousand
sheep, and six thousand camels, and a thousand
yoke of oxen, and a thousand she asses.
13 He had also seven sons and three daughters.

Job could not master the king of the proud beasts (v. 34), how much less could he sit on God's throne to judge proud and wicked men (40:12)? Therefore, what right did he have to judge Him who does sit on that throne?

2. **Through these real (though difficult to identify) creatures, God also illustrated a great spiritual reality. Leviathan is used in Scripture as a symbol of the powers of evil, specifically the Devil. Like leviathan, this monstrous evil spirit terrifies men but is under God's control. This takes us back to the first two chapters of the book, where Satan attacked Job with terrific power but acted only at the sovereign initiative and will of God. Just as Job's inability to master leviathan called him to humbly submit to the Creator, so also Job's inability to master evil and suffering called him to humbly entrust himself to the Lord, who reigns over Satan.**

Chapter 42: *God vindicates Job, rebukes his friends, and restores his fortunes.*

JOB'S CONFESSION (42:1–6)

42:2 *thou canst do every thing*. God is omnipotent, doing all that He wills (Gen. 18:14). *no thought can be withholden from thee*. No purpose or plan is beyond God's reach (Ps. 33:10–11).
42:3 *wonderful*. Difficult or extraordinary; beyond comprehension.
42:4 *demand of thee*. Literally, "ask you."
42:6 *abhor myself, and repent*. When we, by grace, see God by faith, we cannot but know self-abhorrence and repentance experientially.

GOD'S RESTORATION OF JOB (42:7–17)

42:7 *not spoken of me . . . right*. Misapplication of God's Word is as wrong as misinterpretation. The friends' discourses often expressed sound doctrine, but they used it wrongly against Job and thus misrepresented the Lord. *my servant Job*. A title both of submission and of honor, also given to Abraham, Moses, and David (Gen. 26:24; Josh. 1:2; 2 Sam. 7:5). With these words God reaffirmed that Job was a righteous, God-fearing man (1:8; 2:3).
42:8 *folly*. Spiritual stupidity. *burnt offering . . . Job shall pray for you*. Job acted somewhat like a priest for these men, pleading grace from God for them through sacrifice and intercession, as he had done for his family (1:5). Amazingly, Job performed this ministry for the very people who had falsely accused him of sin. In these respects, Job was a type of Christ.
42:10 *turned the captivity*. An idiom meaning to restore fortunes (Ps. 126:1).
42:11 *bemoaned*. Showed sympathy or consoled. *evil*. Trouble or calamity.
42:12–13 The numbers of livestock are double those recorded in ch. 1, but the number of Job's children is the same. From an eternal perspective Job indeed received double the number of children, his previous children having entered eternity.
42:16 *an hundred and forty years*. An age typical of the patriarchal era, the likely historical context for Job's life (Gen. 11:1–32; 25:7,17; 35:28; 47:28; see Introduction: Date).

Thoughts for Personal/Family Worship: Chapter 42

1. **Having heard the Lord, Job had nothing to say except to confess and submit (vv. 1–6). He made this confession while still in the throes of suffering and loss; the Lord had not even hinted that restoration and vindication were coming. What had bothered him for so long was no longer a concern once he saw the Lord. As far as the Bible informs us, Job never learned the reason for his sufferings, and that was fine once he became overwhelmed with God and His greatness. He affirmed God's sovereignty throughout the book, but at the end he gained an experiential knowledge of the glory of God. Like Job, God's people are called to humbly confess God's sovereignty in the midst of the furnace of suffering, while they wait for Christ to appear in glory and restore them to honor and happiness. In light of the book of Job, consider these questions: Do you have a big enough view of God's glory to accept the mystery of suffering without an explanation? Has your knowledge of God entered into the experience of your heart to make you humble and submissive to His ways? What**

14 And he called the name of the first, Jemima;
and the name of the second, Kezia; and the name
of the third, Keren-happuch.
15 And in all the land were no women found *so*
fair as the daughters of Job: and their father gave
them inheritance among their brethren.
16 After this lived Job an hundred and forty years,
and saw his sons, and his sons' sons, *even* four
generations.
17 So Job died, *being* old and full of days.

does the way you presently respond to suffering say about your relationship with God?

2. When God vindicates His people, He often restores to them more than they lost when in the thick of their trials. He does "exceeding abundantly above all that we ask or think" (Eph. 3:20). This will be exponentially true on Judgment Day. Does this thought make you long for Christ's second coming?

THE LORD IS MY *Shepherd*

I SHALL NOT WANT

PSALM 23:1

INTRODUCTION TO THE BOOK OF PSALMS

Authorship: Hebrew sacred song really began with Israel's birth as a nation, and it then continued for more than one thousand years. The earliest recorded composer of psalms was Moses. His first was a solemn choral song, with musical accompaniment, sung after the crossing of the Red Sea (Ex. 15:1,20–21). He followed this up with other songs, most of which were made for particular occasions (Num. 21:17; Deut. 31:22,30; 32; Ps. 90 [see title]). In the time of the Judges, Deborah and Hannah received the prophetic gift for composing such sacred songs (Judg. 5; 1 Sam. 2). Later, it seems, the art of sacred song was cultivated among the sons of the prophets in those prophetic societies apparently founded by Samuel (1 Sam. 10:5). A society was established at Ramah, where David may have received his first impulse to compose psalms (1 Sam. 19:18,20).

David, whom the Spirit of God eminently qualified for the purpose, brought Israel's psalmody to its highest degree of perfection. He was "the sweet psalmist of Israel," who said, "the Spirit of the LORD spake by me, and his word was in my tongue" (2 Sam. 23:1–2). After arranging psalms for bringing up the ark (1 Chron. 15:16), he appointed psalm singing, with its typical musical accompaniment, for solemn worship (1 Chron. 6:31; 16:4–8). This was evidently under divine direction (2 Chron. 29:25).

Altogether seventy-three of the psalms are ascribed to David (Pss. 3–41; 10; 33; 51–65; 68–70; 86; 101; 103; 108–110; 122; 124; 131; 133; 138–145), but it is clear that he was the author of others (e.g., Ps. 2, cf. Acts 4:25; Ps. 95, cf. Heb. 4:7). Moses composed at least one psalm (Ps. 90); Asaph, the director and seer, composed twelve (Pss. 50; 73–83; cf. 1 Chron. 6:39; 2 Chron. 29:30); Heman, one (Ps. 88; cf. 1 Chron. 15:16–17); Ethan, one (Ps. 89; cf. 1 Chron. 15:17); the sons of Korah, ten, perhaps eleven (Pss. 42; [43]; 44–49; 84–85; 87–88[?]; cf. 1 Chron. 9:19); and Solomon, two (Pss. 72; 127; [128]). It is evident that some of the later prophets also composed lyrical pieces (e.g., Isa. 12; Jonah 2; Hab. 3) and some of their productions *may* have been included in the book of Psalms, albeit anonymously.

Date: Since the book contains psalms by a number of inspired authors, a single date cannot be given for the whole collection. In its chronological range, the book commences with the time of Moses, when the children of Israel experienced judicial calamity in the wilderness (Ps. 90; cf. the title with Num. 21:7); and it possibly concludes with the time of Nehemiah, when the outcasts gathered, Jerusalem was rebuilt, and the bars of its gates strengthened (Ps. 147:2,13; cf. Neh. 3:4 where the same word "strengthened" is translated "repaired"). If this is indeed so, the period in which the book of Psalms was written must have been approximately from 1445 BC (the probable date of the exodus) to 444 BC (when the work on Jerusalem's walls was completed), a period of one thousand years.

Theme: The engagement of the whole soul of man in the worship of God.

Purpose: To direct God's people in their praises and prayers to the Lord.

Synopsis: *The Contribution of the Psalms to Redemptive Revelation*

The Scriptures call this book "the book of Psalms" (Luke 20:42; Acts 1:20). Its Hebrew name is both simple and significant: "Praises" (*tehillim*), or more fully, "Book of Praises" (*sepher tehillim*), which expresses its great and leading characteristic—the praising of Jehovah, the one, living, and true God. "Praise" in the Bible relates to the adoring of the divine excellence (Ps. 63:3). Other words generally relate, not to what God is, but to what He does and to what He gives.

There are, in fact, three names for the various praises in this book: first of all, "psalms," a general term for "praise with musical instruments," from the Greek word, "to strike the lyre" (*psallein*); and "hymns," praises devoted to Almighty God (e.g., Pss. 18; 145); and "spiritual songs," inspired poems containing doctrine, history, or prophecy (e.g., Pss. 45; 78; 102; see Eph. 5:19; Col. 3:16).

The Psalms are divinely inspired patterns for both personal and corporate worship. The book of Psalms itself was intended to be Israel's hymnbook, as is clear from its name, "The Book of Praises," the various titles (e.g., "To the Chief Musician" [the Precentor or Master of Song] which occurs fifty-five times), and from various hints within the Psalms themselves (e.g., Ps. 105:2, "Sing unto him, sing psalms unto him"; Ps. 116:19, "In the courts of the LORD's house, in the midst of thee, O Jerusalem. Praise ye the LORD"). There is also historical evidence to show that the Psalms were used for public worship (1 Chron. 16:7; 2 Chron. 29:30; cf. Neh. 12:24).

The Psalms were also intended for teaching. "Maschil" occurs thirteen times and is derived from the verb "to instruct." The title of Ps. 60 reads, "Michtam of David, to teach." By psalms, the divine Word was a means of instructing children (Ps. 78:3–6). They are also a means of meditation: "Higgaion" or "meditation" (Ps. 9:16; cf. 19:14).

The use of the Psalms in worship continued in New Testament times (1 Cor. 14:15,26; Eph. 5:19; Col. 3:16). The "hymn" sung by Christ and His apostles (Matt. 26:30) would have been, as always at the close of the Passover, the second part of the Hallel (Pss. 115–118). The Psalms were sometimes called "hymns" (Matt. 26:30) and sometimes "songs" (titles of Pss. 45–46; 67–68; 75; etc.; James 5:13).

The Psalms are of great value to the church, for they teach:

1. *A sum and summary of the whole Bible.* The book of Psalms is a Bible within a Bible. Athanasius called it an "epitome of the Bible," while Luther called it "a little Bible, wherein everything contained in the entire Bible is beautifully and briefly comprehended and compacted." It holds the middle place of Scripture, as the very heart of God's written revelation.
2. *Praises of divine perfections.* This book unveils God, in all His perfect and most excellent glories, and it provides an inspired response of praise: "The LORD is great and greatly to be praised" (96:4). It shows us God, as only God can reveal Himself, and it teaches us how to fear and adore His glorious Being.
3. *Insights into our human condition.* This book shows us ourselves, as we really are. John Calvin called it "an anatomy of all parts of the soul, for no one will discover in himself a single feeling, whereof the image is not reflected in this mirror." The Psalms express our inmost feelings: loneliness (102:7); oppression (129:1); abandonment (68:5); uncertainty (77:7); and depression (42:5).
4. *An approach to God.* The Psalms teach penitence and prayer. They provide us with a most excellent pattern showing precisely how these things are experienced and expressed; and they inflame our hearts to greater sorrow for sin and desire for God. They sympathize with the souls of believers in all their feelings, agonies and ecstasies. Sometimes prayers pour forth (86:1–6; cf. 119:94) and sometimes praises (Ps. 148). The great value of the book is that it conducts us into the presence of the King and brings us before the throne of His glory (26:6; 43:3–5).
5. *The nature of spiritual communion.* The Psalms describe the almost indescribable experience of communion with God (63:3–4). It has been said: "The Psalter is the music of the soul's friendship with God," but more excellent still, perhaps, is the language of another when he describes the Psalter as "the whole music of the human heart, swept by the hand of its Maker."
6. *A means to stir vital godliness.* The Psalter stirs in believers a strong affection for God's holy law and a profound recognition of its higher and more deeply spiritual requirements (19:7–9; 119). The law is of great use to believers to show us what Christ has done (Gal. 4:4–5), what service and gratitude we owe (2 Cor. 7:1), our many deficiencies (Rom. 7:24), the rule of sanctification (1 Cor. 9:21), and the excellence of what one day we are to enjoy (Rev. 21).
7. *The voice of the universal church.* The Psalms introduce us to the communion of saints. The Jews were able to recite the Psalms in a national way, so that the "I" became the voice of the worshiping community; but even if we do not take that into account, the Psalter is still the book of the church's song (51:18; 79:8; 85:6).
8. *A book of hope, in life and death.* Arising from great stress and sorrow, there are chants of holy expectation: "As for me, I will behold thy face in righteousness: I shall be satisfied, when I awake, with thy likeness" (17:15; cf. 16:9–10; 49:15; 73:24).

9. *A heaven-drawn picture of Christ.* Finally, the book of Psalms brings our Savior into view. Jerome said, "David on the harp and ten-stringed lute, sings throughout of Christ."

Special Problems of Interpretation:

Titles of the Psalms

Dating individual psalms depends partly, but not entirely, on the authority of the prefixed titles. Altogether, there are 116 psalms with titles or inscriptions: the other thirty-four are sometimes called orphan psalms.

Scholars agree that the titles are ancient, existing when the Septuagint (the Greek version of the Hebrew Old Testament) was written, somewhere around 200 BC. Account should also be taken of the following facts: (1) the information in the titles can hardly have been produced by process of deduction; (2) many of the psalms do not have any superscription, and a later scribe, if at work on these, would surely have been tempted to supply the deficiency; and (3) pious Jews, though conscientious readers and students of the written Word, would never have added to what God had written. It is therefore to be believed that these titles are vital parts of God's inspired Word.

The following considerations argue for counting the titles as parts of Holy Scripture. An inscription of some kind would certainly be expected on lyrical compositions, and they can be found in other Scripture passages (Ex. 15:1; Deut. 33:1; 2 Sam. 1:17; Isa. 38:9). A title appears as part of the inspired prophecy of Habakkuk: "To the chief singer, on my stringed instruments" (Hab. 3:19). The title of Ps. 18 is incorporated into the inspired text of the book of Samuel: "David spake unto the LORD the words of this song in the day that the LORD had delivered him out of the hand of all his enemies, and out of the hand of Saul" (2 Sam. 22:1). We also find a title prefixed to words of "the sweet psalmist of Israel" recorded later in Samuel: "Now these be the last words of David" (2 Sam. 23:1).

References in the historical books confirm the details in the titles. First Samuel 21:13 reads, "And he (David) changed his behaviour before them, and feigned himself mad" and the heading of Ps. 34 is as follows: "A Psalm of David, when he changed his behaviour before Abimelech." The information in the titles often corresponds with the contents of the psalms to which they relate. Psalm 90, for example, has for a title, "A Prayer of Moses the man of God," and he is so described in Deut. 33:1. Moreover, in that psalm there are allusions to, if not actual citations of, Moses' words elsewhere—"refuge" (Deut. 33:27), "all generations" (Ps. 90:1), "repent thee" (Ps. 90:13), "thy work" (Ps. 90:16), and "His glory" (Deut. 33:17).

Our Lord and His apostles treated the titles of psalms as Scripture. Our Lord quotes from Psalm 110, entitled "A Psalm of David," and says, "How then doth David in spirit call him Lord, saying, The LORD said unto my Lord, Sit thou on my right hand, till I make thine enemies thy footstool?" (Matt. 22:43–44); and the apostles, when quoting Pss. 16 and 110, also make reference to the name given in those psalm titles (Acts 2:29–36; 13:34–37).

The meaning of these titles deal with various matters:

1. *Authorship:* e.g., "A psalm of David" or "of Asaph." *Nature:* "Maschil"—meaning "teaching," that is, "a teaching psalm" (cf. 32:8)—is a cognate or kindred verb ("to instruct" as in Pss. 32; 78; 142); "Michtam"—possibly from "to cover"—therefore refers to a psalm with a hidden meaning, or a psalm revealing some great mystery (Pss. 16; 56–60).
2. *Setting:* "A Psalm of David, when he fled from Absalom his son" (Ps. 3); "Upon Mahalath," meaning "sickness" or "disease" (Ps. 53; cf. Ex. 15:26), possibly a spiritual condition (Isa. 1:5). Compare "Upon Mahalath Leannoth," meaning "sickness, or disease, in order to humble" (Ps. 88).
3. *Classification:* "A Song of degrees" or "ascents" (Pss. 120–134), probably sung as pilgrims "went up" to Jerusalem at the time of the annual festivals (1 Sam. 1:3; Ps. 122:4).
4. *Music:* "On Neginoth," meaning, "With music of stringed instruments" (Pss. 4; 6; 54; 55; 67; 76); "Upon Neginah," meaning, "With music of a stringed instrument"; and "Upon Nehiloth," meaning, "with music of wind instruments" (Ps. 5). "Upon Gittith," a feminine adjective of the Philistine town "Gath," and so possibly an instrument or tune which came from there (Pss. 8; 81; 84); "Upon Mahalath," perhaps the name of a musical instrument (although some trace it to a word for "sickness" and "disease" [Ex. 15:26], suggesting that it may refer to sin as the universal "illness") (Pss. 53; 88).
5. *Voice:* "Upon Alamoth," literally, "virgins" and therefore "sung by sopranos" (Ps. 46); "upon Sheminith," meaning, "the eighth," perhaps an octave lower—tenor or, more probably, bass (Pss. 6; 12).

6. *Tune:* "Shiggaion," derived from a verb "to wander," possibly a tune with changing rhythm (Ps. 7); "upon Muth-labben," meaning, "the dying of the son," the name of a mournful tune or the opening words of a song associated with a particular tune, although some think it just may refer to its evangelical theme, the death of Christ (Ps. 9).
7. *Subject:* "Upon Jonath-elem-rechokim" could be the name of a tune called "The silent dove afar off" (Ps. 56), or it could describe the contents, the expression of how David felt when in Gath, far from the sanctuary and silent as to public praise. "Upon Aijeleth Shahar" again could be a tune, "The hind of the morning" (Ps. 22), but it could also be (as Martin Luther thought) a reference to Christ, the innocent and lovely hind, who was hunted and driven to the ground, but who, before daybreak, rose up and leapt to the very heights. "Upon Shoshannim" means "the lilies," and since lilies were the emblem of sacred love (Song 2:1–2; cf. 1 Kings 7:19,22,26), this suggests a psalm concerning the excellence of our Lord's person, beauty, and love (Pss. 45; 69). Thus also "Shoshannim-Eduth" means "Lilies, a testimony" (Ps. 80), and "Shushan-eduth" means "Lily of testimony" (Ps. 60).
8. *Purpose:* "To bring to remembrance" (Pss. 38; 70).
9. *Occasion:* "At the dedication of the house of David" (Ps. 30); "For the sabbath day" (Ps. 92). Jewish authorities tell us there was a psalm for each day in the worship of the temple: Psalm 24 for the first day, 48 for the second, 82 for the third, 94 for the fourth, 81 for the fifth, 93 for the sixth, and 92 for the seventh.

Although "Selah" is not in any actual title, it is a word found 71 times in 39 psalms. "Selah" appears to be derived from a root word which means "to elevate" or "to raise," and it may therefore indicate a lifting up of hearts in a silent pause for meditation.

Collection and Arrangement

The number of psalms increased over the years by degrees; and the need for an authorized collection first arose when David, under divine direction, made psalm singing an essential element of public worship (1 Chron. 16:4). There is indeed evidence of some kind of editorial work (Ps. 72:20); and besides David, there may have been other, later editors.

All inspired psalms were not included in the Book of Psalms, but some were placed in other books (e.g., 2 Sam. 1:19–27; 23:1–7). What then were the principles of selection when it came to inclusion in the book of Psalms? *First*, of course, they had to be inspired by the Holy Spirit (2 Sam. 23:2; 1 Chron. 25:5; 2 Chron. 29:30; Matt. 22:43). *Second*, they had to be sacred and charged with spiritual truth; and *third*, they had to be suited to public worship (Isa. 38:20). It is quite true that many of the psalms are written in the first person, but the "I" of the psalmist often represents the typical pious Israelite and even, in process of development, the entire nation of Israel. In any case, these psalms contain material which the nation or church could easily appropriate to its spiritual need.

The Hebrew Psalter is actually one volume in five parts. Its divisions can be easily identified, for each division ends with a doxology which, in the last, is a whole psalm:

1. *Book 1 (Pss. 1–41):* "Blessed be the LORD God of Israel from everlasting, and to everlasting. Amen, and Amen" (41:13). This section is almost completely Davidic; and, in content, it is *doctrinal*, teaching about God, His glorious name and wonderful works, and about man, his sin and salvation.
2. *Book 2 (Pss. 42–72):* "Blessed be the LORD God, the God of Israel, who only doeth wondrous things. And blessed be his glorious name for ever: and let the whole earth be filled with his glory; Amen, and Amen. The prayers of David the son of Jesse are ended" (72:18–20). This one is mainly Davidic, but eight psalms are ascribed to the sons of Korah; and it is *experimental*, twenty-five psalms dealing with failure and sixteen with victory.
3. *Book 3 (Pss. 73–89):* "Blessed be the LORD for evermore. Amen, and Amen" (89:52). This is Asaphic on the whole, opening with eleven "psalms of Asaph," followed by four Korahite psalms; and these are *historical*, with references to dividing the sea (74:13), the way through the sea (77:19), the cleaving of the rock in the wilderness (78:15), the vine taken from Egypt (80:8), the people given up to sin (81:12), the coalition against Israel (83:5), and David's glorious kingdom (Ps. 89).
4. *Book 4 (Pss. 90–106):* "Blessed be the LORD God of Israel from everlasting to everlasting: and let all the people say, Amen. Praise ye the LORD" (106:48). The psalms in this section are chiefly anonymous, with the following exceptions: Psalm 90 is ascribed to Moses, and

Pss. 101 and 103 to David; and the emphasis is *prophetical* concentrating upon the Lord's reign (as in Pss. 96–98).

5. *Book 5 (Pss. 107–150):* The last five are Hallelujah psalms, each beginning with a "Hallelujah," or "Praise ye the Lord." The doxology at the close of this section is "Praise ye the Lord. Praise God in his sanctuary: praise him in the firmament of his power . . . Let every thing that hath breath praise the Lord. Praise ye the Lord" (150:1–6). This section's psalms are generally anonymous, but fifteen are identified as from David; and these psalms being full of praise, they are throughout evidently *jubilant*.

The Jews saw in these five books (or divisions) some likeness to the Pentateuch, with its five books (Genesis to Deuteronomy). The Hebrew Midrash on Psalm 1 says, "Moses gave the five books of the Law to the Israelites and, as a counterpart to them, David gave the psalms consisting of five books."

Classifications of Psalms

It is helpful to identify different kinds of psalms in the Psalter.

1. *Alphabetical Psalms.* There are nine (Pss. 9; 10; 25; 34; 37; 111; 112; 119; 145). The finest example is Ps. 119, formed of twenty-two stanzas, arranged acrostically according to the twenty-two letters of the Hebrew alphabet. These psalms are mainly didactic and were probably composed in this form to aid the memory.
2. *Penitential Psalms.* There are seven (Pss. 6; 32; 38; 51; 102; 130; 143). They have been so called since Origen's time. Each expresses contrition and contains confession of sin. There are others, however, which have something of this character.
3. *Imprecatory Psalms.* There are four (Pss. 7; 35; 69; 109). Other psalms contain imprecations (e.g., Pss. 5:10; 55:9; 83:9–17; 137:8–9), but these are characterized throughout by curses on enemies. They are useful when referring to judgment. Luther tells of a man driven by these denunciations to seek pardon and safety in Christ.
4. *Thanksgiving Psalms.* There are six (Pss. 113–118), known as the Hallel. These were used on festive occasions, especially the Passover when two were sung before partaking of the lamb and four afterward (Matt. 26:30). They describe God's mercy (Ps. 113), a greater redemption (Ps. 114), the necessity of faith (Ps. 115: "Trust thou in the Lord," v. 9), eternal life in possession (Ps. 116), the universality of the gospel call (Ps. 117), and the kingdom of heaven open to all believers (Ps. 118: "Open to me the gates of righteousness," v. 19).
5. *Psalms (or Songs) of Ascent.* There are fifteen (Pss. 120–134). They were probably sung when making pilgrimage ("ascent" or "going up") to Zion (1 Sam. 1:3; Ps. 122:4; Zech. 14:19). They are also sometimes called "Pilgrim Psalms."
6. *Nature Psalms.* There are four (Pss. 19; 29; 104; 147). Psalm 104 is based on the six days' work of creation, beginning with the breaking forth of light on the first day, and concluding with a Sabbath day's meditation on God's works.
7. *Historical Psalms.* There are six (Pss. 68; 78; 105–106; 135–136). They rest on the principle of the unity of the church in all times and the fact that we should identify ourselves with our forefathers. They are also acted "parables," typical representations of spiritual truth (Ps. 78:1–3).
8. *Judgment Psalms.* There are six (Pss. 9–14). These are psalms of judgment, finding consummation in Ps. 15, a vision of the eternal dwelling place of God and His righteous people.
9. *Sovereignty Psalms.* There are three (Pss. 93; 97; 99). They begin with "The Lord reigneth," and they anticipate the day when all shall be placed under His feet (Rev. 11:17; 19:6).
10. *Hallelujah Psalms.* There are ten (Pss. 106; 111–113; 135; 146–150). All commence with "Praise ye the Lord," and they are ideal for teaching on worship. For example, in Ps. 150: "Praise God," or equivalents, occurs twelve times, representing perhaps all God's people (twelve tribes, twelve apostles).

Christ in the Psalms

The Psalms may be studied as a manual for the devotional life and also as prophecies of our Lord Jesus Christ. Many only regard as "messianic" those which are so in the most obvious sense (Pss. 2; 16; 22; 45; 72; 110). It is therefore important to establish some basic principles for a more biblically consistent interpretation, with a view to seeing Christ in all the Psalms.

David was a prophet (Acts 2:29–30) and, as such, the Spirit of Christ was in him, testifying to "the sufferings of Christ, and the glory that should follow" (1 Peter 1:11; cf. Rev. 19:10). The Psalms, with great propriety, are called "the word of Christ" (Col. 3:16). Christ Himself declared that the Psalms applied to Him: "All things must be fulfilled, which were written . . . in the psalms, concerning me" (Luke 24:44); and the apostles assumed that Christ was speaking in them (Acts 2:25,27,31). The entire collection is known as "the psalms of David," and so, according to the principle of typology, the entire collection belongs to Christ because David is His prophetic name (Jer. 30.9; Ezek. 34:23–24; 37:24; Hos. 3:5).

Though the eternal Son of God, Christ also became fully human in body and soul (John 1:14; 19:5; Heb. 2:16). Indeed, He is "the man" par excellence (Ps. 1:1). He was able to sing the Psalms while here upon the earth. A union exists between Christ and His people, and they are so united as to be regarded as one (1 Cor. 12:12; Heb. 2:11). As a result of this union, the Psalms express His thoughts as well as ours.

Our Lord lived in the Psalms and constantly quoted them (Matt. 16:27; 21:16; 25:41; Luke 20:42; John 13:18; 15:25; 17:12). In fact, four out of the seven words from the cross either quote or fulfill verses in the Psalms: "My God . . ." (22:1); "I thirst . . ." (69:21); "It is finished . . ." (22:31); "Into thy hands . . ." (31:5).

Confessions of sin (e.g., 40:12) present difficulties to the messianic interpretation of the Psalms, yet this example of a confession is found in a psalm evidently messianic (40:6–8; Heb. 10:5–7; see also Ps. 69:5,9; John 2:17). With all such confessions, it is important to recall that, although our Lord was not a sinner and was totally without sin in heart and life, yet as our Head and Representative, the sins of His people were imputed or reckoned to Him (Isa. 53:6; 2 Cor. 5:21; 1 Peter 2:24), so that there was a sense in which He felt the burden of them upon His soul (Matt. 26:37; John 1:29) and, of course, He suffered throughout His life and particularly in His death the punishment due to them (Isa. 53:5; 1 Peter 3:18). It is further to be remembered that, as our great High Priest, a vital part of His ministry was to confess His people's sins in order to secure pardon for them (Lev. 16:21; Isa. 53:12).

The messianic view is most helpful in interpreting difficult statements and passages, such as:

1. *Assertions of innocence (Pss. 7:8; 18:20).* While such words can be applied to God's people who have righteousness imputed to them, who are given a new heart and a new spirit, and who genuinely seek to live obedient lives (unlike "the wicked"), they are uniquely true of Christ, the righteous One (Acts 3:14; 1 John 2:1).
2. *Terrible imprecations (Pss. 40:14–15; 69:22–24).* This language is not altogether inappropriate for the believer, since they are really the outpourings of a heart provoked by evil, righteously indignant, and zealous for God and righteousness (Rom. 12:19; Eph. 4:26); but it is entirely appropriate upon the lips of Christ who, as Judge, is able to pronounce doom upon the wicked (Matt. 11:20–24; 23:13–33; Mark 3:5).

Outline:

I. Book 1 (Pss. 1:1—41:13)
II. Book 2 (Pss. 42:1—72:20)
III. Book 3 (Pss. 73:1—89:52)
IV. Book 4 (Pss. 90:1—106:48)
V. Book 5 (Pss. 107:1—150:6)

THE BOOK OF PSALMS

PSALM 1

1 BLESSED *is* the man that walketh not in the
counsel of the ungodly, nor standeth in the way
of sinners, nor sitteth in the seat of the scornful.
2 But his delight *is* in the law of the LORD; and in
his law doth he meditate day and night.
3 And he shall be like a tree planted by the rivers
of water, that bringeth forth his fruit in his season;
his leaf also shall not wither; and whatsoever he
doeth shall prosper.
4 The ungodly *are* not so: but *are* like the chaff
which the wind driveth away.
5 Therefore the ungodly shall not stand in the
judgment, nor sinners in the congregation of the
righteous.
6 For the LORD knoweth the way of the righteous:
but the way of the ungodly shall perish.

PSALM 2

1 WHY do the heathen rage, and the people imag-
ine a vain thing?
2 The kings of the earth set themselves, and the
rulers take counsel together, against the LORD,
and against his anointed, *saying*,
3 Let us break their bands asunder, and cast away
their cords from us.
4 He that sitteth in the heavens shall laugh: the
Lord shall have them in derision.
5 Then shall he speak unto them in his wrath,

BOOK 1 (PSS. 1:1—41:13)

Psalm 1: ***The psalmist contrasts the way of the godly with the way of the ungodly.***

1:1 *Blessed is*. Literally, "O the benefits of," referring to a position to be desired (2:12; 32:1–2; 33:12; 34:8; 40:4; 41:1; 65:4; etc.). *the man*. The Hebrew is definite, singular, and masculine, focusing on one particular man as the ideal and representative of the godly. He is described first negatively in terms of his separation from the mindset and practices of the wicked, represented by the *ungodly* (those who refuse to acknowledge God), *sinners* (such as miss the mark of God's law), and *the scornful* (those who treat God with contempt).

1:2 The blessed man is also described positively. *law*. A general term for God's Word. *meditate day and night*. Concentrate and think consciously about. This was the ideal for the king or leader of the nation (Deut. 17:18–19; Josh. 1:8).

1:3 Here are the benefits. *planted*. Transplanted, taken from one sphere and placed in another. *rivers of water*. Possibly irrigation ditches dug for the transplant. *fruit*. Often a picture of good works (Prov. 11:30; 31:16,31; Isa. 4:2–3; 5:1–7; 27:6; John 15:5; Rom. 6:22). The imagery of trees, flowing water, and fruit may allude to the garden of Eden (Gen. 2:8–10).

1:4 *chaff*. Unstable and worthless, easily blown away.

1:5 *not stand in the judgment*. Will not be vindicated by God, but condemned (Ps. 130:3).

1:6 *knoweth*. In the sense of intimate knowledge and loving care (Gen. 18:19). *the way of the ungodly shall perish*. The way chosen by unbelieving and impenitent men will prove a path to ruin (Matt. 22:13; 25:30).

Thoughts for Personal/Family Worship: Psalm 1

1. **Believers should be the happiest of people, for we know God, His wonderful love, covenant promises, abundant pardon, strong comfort, and abiding presence. We have sorrows, but no reason to be miserable. Although tempted to enjoy the company and pleasures of worldly people, God's grace makes believers different from them and allows us to derive our enjoyment from Scripture and the Holy Spirit, which promote holiness in us. On judgment day we will escape the wrath of God, and discover how He has watched over us in love all our days. How does this encourage you to follow Christ?**
2. **Christ is supremely the man who is blessed (72:17). He is the ideal king who is separated from sinners (v. 1; Heb. 7:26) and engaged to keep God's law (v. 2; 40:7–8). Accordingly, He becomes like a fruitful and flourishing tree, nurtured by the Holy Spirit (Isa. 11:1–2) and full of good works (Isa. 4:2; Acts 10:38). In union with Him by a Spirit-worked faith, we too can become fruitful out of His fullness. What does this teach you about true prosperity?**

Psalm 2: ***The psalmist declares the certainty of Christ's kingdom and links eternal destiny to trusting Him.***

2:1 *rage*. Assemble in restless commotion. *imagine a vain thing*. Conspire or plot emptiness. This opposition found climactic expression in the days of Christ (Acts 4:25–26).

2:2 *set themselves*. Resist, take a stand. *anointed*. Messiah (in Greek, "Christ"), the divinely chosen and empowered king from the line of David (18:50; 20:6; 28:8; 84:9; 89:38,51; 132:10,17; 1 Sam. 16:6,13).

2:3 *break their bands asunder*. Tear their chains into pieces. A rejection of divine control and restraint (Luke 19:14).

2:4 *derision*. Contempt, mockery.

and vex them in his sore displeasure.
6 Yet have I set my king upon my holy hill of Zion.
7 I will declare the decree: the LORD hath said unto
me, Thou *art* my Son; this day have I begotten thee.
8 Ask of me, and I shall give *thee* the heathen *for*
thine inheritance, and the uttermost parts of the earth *for* thy possession.
9 Thou shalt break them with a rod of iron; thou shalt dash them in pieces like a potter's vessel.
10 Be wise now therefore, O ye kings: be instructed, ye judges of the earth.
11 Serve the LORD with fear, and rejoice with trembling.
12 Kiss the Son, lest he be angry, and ye perish *from* the way, when his wrath is kindled but a little. Blessed *are* all they that put their trust in him.

PSALM 3

A Psalm of David, when he fled from Absalom his son.

1 LORD, how are they increased that trouble me!
many *are* they that rise up against me.
2 Many *there be* which say of my soul, *There is* no help for him in God. Selah.
3 But thou, O LORD, *art* a shield for me; my glory, and the lifter up of mine head.
4 I cried unto the LORD with my voice, and he heard me out of his holy hill. Selah.
5 I laid me down and slept; I awaked; for the LORD sustained me.
6 I will not be afraid of ten thousands of people, that have set *themselves* against me round about.
7 Arise, O LORD; save me, O my God: for thou hast smitten all mine enemies *upon* the cheek bone; thou hast broken the teeth of the ungodly.
8 Salvation *belongeth* unto the LORD: thy blessing *is* upon thy people. Selah.

PSALM 4

To the chief Musician on Neginoth, A Psalm of David.

1 HEAR me when I call, O God of my righteousness: thou hast enlarged me *when I was* in distress;
have mercy upon me, and hear my prayer.
2 O ye sons of men, how long *will ye turn* my glory into shame? *how long* will ye love vanity, *and* seek after leasing? Selah.
3 But know that the LORD hath set apart him that

2:5 *vex them in his sore displeasure.* Terrify them with His burning anger.
2:6 *set my king.* Rebellious opposition cannot frustrate God's plan and purpose which He will fulfill through the Son of David. *hill of Zion.* Location of Jerusalem and God's special presence in the temple—a symbol of God's kingdom (48:2; 87:2–3; 99:1–2; Isa. 2:3; Heb. 12:22).
2:7 *this day have I begotten thee.* Christ's eternal glory as God's Son, infinitely above the angels, was publicly declared when God raised Him from the dead and exalted Him as King (Acts 13:32–33; Heb. 1:5–6; cf. Rom. 1:4).
2:8 *Ask of me.* The Father willed that Christ intercede for His redeemed, so that they will become His *inheritance* and *possession. heathen . . . uttermost parts.* Christ will save people from all nations (22:27; 72:8,11; Dan. 7:14).
2:9 *Thou shalt break.* He conquers either by grace or by force (Rev. 19:15). He should deal severely with those who, in unbelief, refuse to submit to Him (Matt. 21:44).
2:10 *Be wise.* Act wisely. *be instructed.* Allow yourself to be taught.
2:12 *Kiss.* An expression of honor and submission (see Gen. 41:40 where the same Hebrew word is translated "ruled"; 1 Sam. 10:1; 1 Kings 19:18; Hos. 13:2). The word *Son* is not the typical Hebrew term (as in v. 7), but Aramaic, the international language of the Ancient Near East, here used in an appeal to all peoples to submit to the Messiah.

Thoughts for Personal/Family Worship: Psalm 2

1. **The world is full of opposition to Christ. Hence there is need for powerful and efficacious grace, to convict, enlighten, and persuade. Churches should therefore concentrate on gospel preaching and prayer for the work of the Holy Spirit. Whatever the opposition, no human power can ever nullify or undo the divine purpose. Are you allowing pessimism to affect you, or are you hanging on to the hope that Christ's kingdom will prevail in every nation?**
2. **God commands all nations to submit to His Son. Let us begin with ourselves. Have we "kissed the Son"? Have we obeyed His command to repent and believe? One day, maybe very soon, Christ will return as Judge. Will He find us still holding out against Him, or will He find us serving Him? Eternal destiny is linked to the Son. How can a person know that the Son has taken him as His inheritance?**

Psalm 3: *David prays for the security of God's protection.*
Title *Absalom.* David's *son* tried to kill him and take the throne (2 Sam. 15).
3:1 *how are they increased.* Antagonism toward God's people is common (Gen. 3:15; Prov. 29:27; John 15:19).
3:2 *my soul.* Me.
3:6 *set themselves against me.* Taken a stand against me.
3:7 *smitten.* Struck.
3:8 *Salvation belongeth unto the LORD.* God is the source of all salvation from evil, whether physical or spiritual (Prov. 21:31; Jonah 2:9)—the only Savior (Isa. 45:21–22).

Thoughts for Personal/Family Worship: Psalm 3

1. **There will be times when troubles come from every side; but God proves to be our shield, very strong, always ready at hand, and surrounding us in His protecting love. We must never sink into despair. Prayer is absolutely vital. In His sovereignty, God is prepared to respond to prayer and work on our behalf. Committing everything into God's hands, we may rest assured that He will grant both help and peace. Remembering former deliverances, we will find courage to face the unknown future. He is the same as ever He was. We go forward, feeling there is much we do not know, but one thing is**

is godly for himself: the LORD will hear when I
call unto him.
4 Stand in awe, and sin not: commune with your
own heart upon your bed, and be still. Selah.
5 Offer the sacrifices of righteousness, and put
your trust in the LORD.
6 *There be* many that say, Who will shew us *any*
good? LORD, lift thou up the light of thy counte-
nance upon us.
7 Thou hast put gladness in my heart, more
than in the time *that* their corn and their wine
increased.
8 I will both lay me down in peace, and sleep: for
thou, LORD, only makest me dwell in safety.

PSALM 5

To the chief Musician upon Nehiloth,
A Psalm of David.

1 GIVE ear to my words, O LORD, consider my
meditation.
2 Hearken unto the voice of my cry, my King, and
my God: for unto thee will I pray.
3 My voice shalt thou hear in the morning, O
LORD; in the morning will I direct *my prayer* unto
thee, and will look up.
4 For thou *art* not a God that hath pleasure in
wickedness: neither shall evil dwell with thee.
5 The foolish shall not stand in thy sight: thou
hatest all workers of iniquity.
6 Thou shalt destroy them that speak leasing: the
LORD will abhor the bloody and deceitful man.
7 But as for me, I will come *into* thy house in
the multitude of thy mercy: *and* in thy fear will I
worship toward thy holy temple.
8 Lead me, O LORD, in thy righteousness because
of mine enemies; make thy way straight before
my face.
9 For *there is* no faithfulness in their mouth; their
inward part *is* very wickedness; their throat *is* an
open sepulchre; they flatter with their tongue.
10 Destroy thou them, O God; let them fall by
their own counsels; cast them out in the multi-
tude of their transgressions; for they have rebelled
against thee.

sure: "Thy blessing is upon thy people" (v. 8) How has God proven to be your help and peace?

2. **David's troubles foreshadowed the sufferings of Christ. Many people turned against Christ and questioned that God was with Him (vv. 1–2; Matt. 27), but He knew that His Father would keep and deliver Him, and therefore He prayed (vv. 3–4; Matt. 26:39). Answering His prayers, God gave Him victory by raising Him from the dead (v. 7; Heb. 5:7; 8:1). Salvation *for Him* and, through Him, *for us* is of the Lord (v. 8). When troubles surround you, how can you rest by faith in Christ who went ahead of you through distress, and how will He help you endure to the end?**

Psalm 4: *David finds peace and joy in knowing the Lord's protection and practice of answering prayer.*

4:1 *thou hast enlarged me . . . in distress.* Literally, "in straights or a narrow place Thou hast created for me a wide space." *have mercy.* Be gracious, show favor (Gen. 32:10; Ps. 119:132; Dan. 9:18).

4:2 *turn my glory into shame.* David's glory was the Lord (3:3), but men mocked his faith. *vanity.* Emptiness, nothing. *leasing.* Falsehoods and lies.

4:3 *set apart.* Hebrew, "Treated excellently or specially." *him that is godly.* One who is the recipient of covenant loyalty and mercy.

4:4 *Stand in awe.* Tremble in strong emotion (Eph. 4:26). *commune with your own heart.* Literally, "say in your heart," here to reflect on the spiritual state of your mind, emotions, and will.

4:6 *the light of thy countenance.* Literally, "the light of Thy face," referring to the experience of the Lord's presence in grace and peace (31:16; 44:3; 67:1; 80:3,7,19; 89:15; 119:135; Num. 6:22–27).

Thoughts for Personal/Family Worship: Psalm 4

1. **In times of difficulty and distress, we should always quickly go to God in prayer. His past deliverances are so many pledges of future deliverances. Since He has proved to be our faithful heavenly Father, let us always hope in God. Remembering the past provides fuel for faith. We must understand that God, in His grace, has made us for Himself. We are meant to be His: bound in covenant to Him, desiring a closer walk with Him, and serving Him in life and death with a single eye to His glory. What comfort will this provide us as we look ahead to our future in heaven with Him?**
2. **This psalm is indirectly messianic, for Christ too experienced profound distress, even unto death, and was set free (Acts 2:24). On earth men denied His glory and falsely accused Him, but He knew God had set Him apart and would hear His prayers. Through the gospel, He calls upon sinners to fear the Lord, quiet their hearts in submission, and trust in the Lord—offering them peace that passes understanding. Have you heard Christ's gospel call? To what degree do you enjoy His peace?**

Psalm 5: *David seeks the Lord for guidance and deliverance from his enemies.*

5:1 *meditation.* Sighing or a faint utterance, expressing deep and intense emotions.

5:2 *my King.* King David acknowledged God as his King (44:4; 47:6; 68:24; 74:12; 84:3).

5:3 *I direct my prayer.* Arrange or set in order my prayer, perhaps comparing it to an offering to God (cf. 141:2).

5:5 *The foolish shall not stand.* The arrogant or boastful will not be able to maintain their position or hold their ground. *thou hatest.* God rejects impenitent sinners.

5:6 *leasing.* A lie or falsehood. *bloody . . . man.* Literally, "a man of bloods," referring to a person guilty of violence.

5:7 *mercy.* Covenant loyalty and love. *temple.* Most likely the heavenly temple (11:4; 18:6,9), though in David's time the site of the tabernacle was called the temple (1 Sam. 1:9; 3:3).

5:8 *in thy righteousness.* Either "according to" or "in" the way of righteousness, referring to the way outlined in God's Word (23:3; Prov. 12:28).

5:9 *open sepulchre.* Grave or tomb with the corpse exposed. The speech of the wicked is full of death and uncleanness—a mark of mankind's enslavement to sin (Rom. 3:13).

11 But let all those that put their trust in thee
rejoice: let them ever shout for joy, because thou
defendest them: let them also that love thy name
be joyful in thee.
12 For thou, LORD, wilt bless the righteous; with
favour wilt thou compass him as *with* a shield.

PSALM 6

To the chief Musician on Neginoth
upon Sheminith, A Psalm of David.

1 O LORD, rebuke me not in thine anger, neither
chasten me in thy hot displeasure.
2 Have mercy upon me, O LORD; for I *am* weak:
O LORD, heal me; for my bones are vexed.
3 My soul is also sore vexed: but thou, O LORD,
how long?
4 Return, O LORD, deliver my soul: oh save me for
thy mercies' sake.
5 For in death *there is* no remembrance of thee:
in the grave who shall give thee thanks?
6 I am weary with my groaning; all the night
make I my bed to swim; I water my couch with
my tears.
7 Mine eye is consumed because of grief; it
waxeth old because of all mine enemies.
8 Depart from me, all ye workers of iniquity; for
the LORD hath heard the voice of my weeping.
9 The LORD hath heard my supplication; the
LORD will receive my prayer.
10 Let all mine enemies be ashamed and sore
vexed: let them return *and* be ashamed suddenly.

PSALM 7

Shiggaion of David, which he sang unto the LORD,
concerning the words of Cush the Benjamite.

1 O LORD my God, in thee do I put my trust: save
me from all them that persecute me, and deliver
me:

5:11 *thy name.* All of God's perfections or attributes that He has revealed to men. To *love* the name is to love God, willfully, intellectually, and emotionally.
5:12 *compass.* Surround. *shield.* A large shield covering the body. God's protection is complete.

Thoughts for Personal/Family Worship: Psalm 5

1. **Never let us be content with saying our prayers. What God requires of us is not formality but personally drawing near to His presence at the throne of grace. True religion is finding, knowing, and enjoying God—do not be satisfied with anything less than this. True believers have much to be joyful about: God is our portion; we are precious in His sight; and our sins are all forgiven. In addition to all this, God sees our tears, hears our sighs, and is able and willing to answer our prayers. How is it then that we are so often cast down? How can loving God's name lead us into more joy?**
2. **Jesus Christ, though God Himself, was also a man and the Mediator for men, and so was much in prayer (Matt. 26:39; Mark 1:35; 6:41,46; Luke 5:16; John 11:41; 17:1). He called God, "my God," as One in covenant with Him (Matt. 27:46; John 20:17). Through prayer, Christ found strength to overcome His wicked enemies despite their lies and violence. How can we, in union with Christ, find the strength we need as well?**

Psalm 6: *David prays for relief with the confidence that God will answer him.*

6:1 *chasten.* Correct by discipline. This is a penitential psalm. David's predicament is due to sin although it is not specifically identified.
6:2 *Have mercy.* Be gracious, show favor which is not deserved. *weak.* He is conscious of his need, which is crucial in prayer. *my bones are vexed.* My mind is disturbed; *bones* can refer to the seat of perception (35:10). Refusing to confess one's sins often leads to mental distress (32:3; 38:3; 51:8).
6:3 *My soul.* In Hebrew, equivalent to the personal pronoun "I." *sore vexed.* Extremely disturbed or dismayed (also v. 10). *O LORD, how long?* He felt that God was not presently answering his prayers, and the delay doubled the hardship (13:1–2; 35:17; 74:10; 79:5; 80:4; 89:46; 90:13; 94:3).
6:4 *Return.* He called God to reverse His direction and draw near to him; he felt abandoned. *my soul.* Me. *for thy mercies' sake.* Because of God's covenant loyalty and love (31:16; 44:26). God's covenant faithfulness assured David of God's answer.
6:5 *in death . . . no remembrance.* The dead cannot publicly glorify God (88:10–12). This is ultimately a plea for resurrection.
6:6 *all the night.* Or every night. *make I my bed to swim.* I flood my bed.
6:7 *consumed.* Become dark or clouded. *waxeth old.* Grow old and weak.

Thoughts for Personal/Family Worship: Psalm 6

1. **God will not allow sin in His children to go unchecked. When troubles come our way, we do well to examine ourselves to find out if God is correcting us for some sin in conduct or heart. Whatever the case, we must take it to God in prayer and not give up. If we are truly His by faith in the covenant, God has graciously bound Himself to hear when we call on Him. Though the trial drags on and you feel exhausted, cling by faith in Jesus Christ to God's faithful love. How can this psalm help depressed Christians?**
2. **Amazingly, the sinless Lord Jesus experienced God's punishment for sin, for the sins of Christ's people were counted toward Him (Isa. 53:4–5; 2 Cor. 5:21; 1 Peter 2:24). Eternity was compressed into time as Christ bore the curse to redeem sinners from everlasting fire. He felt abandoned by His Father's loving presence, and clung to Him as His faithful, covenant God (Matt. 27:46). However, God did not leave Him in the tomb, but raised Him up to the glory of the Father forever. One day, Christ will return to judge all His enemies who have not repented, and they will "be ashamed and sore vexed" just as Christ was "sore vexed" by sinners (vv. 10,3). Will you be counted among Christ's people? Worship Him for the salvation He procured on our behalf.**

Psalm 7: *David prays for justice against his enemies, trusting the Lord for vindication.*

2 Lest he tear my soul like a lion, rending *it* in
pieces, while *there is* none to deliver.
3 O LORD my God, if I have done this; if there be
iniquity in my hands;
4 If I have rewarded evil unto him that was at
peace with me; (yea, I have delivered him that
without cause is mine enemy:)
5 Let the enemy persecute my soul, and take *it*;
yea, let him tread down my life upon the earth,
and lay mine honour in the dust. Selah.
6 Arise, O LORD, in thine anger, lift up thyself because of the rage of mine enemies: and awake for
me *to* the judgment *that* thou hast commanded.
7 So shall the congregation of the people compass
thee about: for their sakes therefore return thou
on high.
8 The LORD shall judge the people: judge me,
O LORD, according to my righteousness, and
according to mine integrity *that is* in me.
9 Oh let the wickedness of the wicked come to an
end; but establish the just: for the righteous God
trieth the hearts and reins.
10 My defence *is* of God, which saveth the upright
in heart.
11 God judgeth the righteous, and God is angry
with the wicked every day.
12 If he turn not, he will whet his sword; he hath
bent his bow, and made it ready.
13 He hath also prepared for him the instruments
of death; he ordaineth his arrows against the
persecutors.
14 Behold, he travaileth with iniquity, and hath
conceived mischief, and brought forth falsehood.
15 He made a pit, and digged it, and is fallen into
the ditch *which* he made.
16 His mischief shall return upon his own head,
and his violent dealing shall come down upon his
own pate.
17 I will praise the LORD according to his righteousness: and will sing praise to the name of the
LORD most high.

PSALM 8

To the chief Musician upon Gittith,
A Psalm of David.

1 O LORD our Lord, how excellent *is* thy name
in all the earth! who hast set thy glory above the
heavens.
2 Out of the mouth of babes and sucklings hast
thou ordained strength because of thine enemies,
that thou mightest still the enemy and the avenger.
3 When I consider thy heavens, the work of thy
fingers, the moon and the stars, which thou hast
ordained;
4 What is man, that thou art mindful of him? and
the son of man, that thou visitest him?

7:1 *I put my trust.* I take refuge, hide myself. *persecute.* Pursue or hunt down (v. 5).
7:2 *my soul.* Me (v. 5).
7:3 *if I have done this.* Falsely accused of sin, David protested his guilt (1 Sam. 24:9–10; 26:18).
7:4 *evil.* Something hurtful.
7:5 *tread down.* Crush to pieces or trample.
7:6 *Arise . . . awake.* He called on God to publicly shame the accusers and to defend the accused (3:7; 9:19; 10:12; 12:5; 17:13; 44:23; 132:8; Isa. 33:10).
7:7 *compass.* Surround.
7:8 *according to my righteousness.* A claim of innocence regarding whatever charges were against him, though not perfect sinlessness (26:1; 35:24).
7:9 *the righteous God trieth the hearts.* God examines the entirety of inner man according to His perfect righteousness. *reins.* Kidneys, representing the secret thoughts and motives.
7:10 *My defence.* Literally, "my shield."
7:11 *God judgeth the righteous.* He saves and vindicates them.
7:12 *whet.* Sharpen.
7:14 *he travaileth with iniquity.* He is pregnant with sin, a metaphor of bringing evil out of his heart (James 1:15). *mischief.* Trouble (v. 16).
7:16 *pate.* Top of the head.

Thoughts for Personal/Family Worship: Psalm 7

1. **Believers can be misrepresented and even slandered in this world. Thankfully, we can always turn to God who knows everything and never did anyone wrong. In times of trouble, our prayers need to be, as here, not formal and heartless, but serious, fervent, and insistent. This should be followed through with persuasive arguments and earnest appeals, as Abraham, Jacob, Moses and others did in former times, striving with God and ultimately prevailing. What relief might we experience as we pour out our hearts to Him, telling Him all that has been said and just how we presently feel?**
2. **The Lord Jesus Christ patiently endured the slander and abuse of the wicked because he "committed himself to him that judgeth righteously" (1 Peter 2:23). He leaned His human soul upon the righteous character of His God and trusted that the Father would make all things right. Through the Spirit, Christ imparts to His suffering people the patient and prayerful character He forged in the fires of persecution. How can we "put on Christ" when we are in the fire or even before it comes?**

Psalm 8: ***Although man is small in comparison to the vastness of creation, God has elevated him to a position of honor and authority.***

8:1 *O LORD our Lord.* Jehovah, our sovereign Master. *excellent.* Mighty or magnificent. *name.* All that God reveals Himself to be. *glory.* Majesty or splendor (v. 9).
8:2 *sucklings.* Nursing children. God uses the weak to defeat the strong (1 Cor. 1:27). Christ applied this statement to children praising Him in Jerusalem when the leaders despised Him (Matt. 21:16). *still.* Stop or destroy.
8:3 *work of thy fingers.* The stars in vast expanse of space are but the intricate detail work of God (Isa. 40:12). Men use their fingers to artistically craft idols for their worship (Isa. 2:8; 17:8), but God uses His to make the galaxies that we might worship Him (Ps. 19:1). *ordained.* Established.
8:4 *man . . . son of man.* Two different Hebrew expressions, but both underscore man's frailty and weakness. *art mindful.*

5 For thou hast made him a little lower than the
angels, and hast crowned him with glory and
honour.
6 Thou madest him to have dominion over the
works of thy hands; thou hast put all *things* un-
der his feet:
7 All sheep and oxen, yea, and the beasts of the
field;
8 The fowl of the air, and the fish of the sea, *and*
whatsoever passeth through the paths of the seas.
9 O LORD our Lord, how excellent *is* thy name in
all the earth!

PSALM 9

To the chief Musician upon
Muth-labben, A Psalm of David.

1 I WILL praise *thee*, O LORD, with my whole
heart; I will shew forth all thy marvellous works.
2 I will be glad and rejoice in thee: I will sing
praise to thy name, O thou most High.
3 When mine enemies are turned back, they shall
fall and perish at thy presence.
4 For thou hast maintained my right and my
cause; thou satest in the throne judging right.
5 Thou hast rebuked the heathen, thou hast
destroyed the wicked, thou hast put out their
name for ever and ever.
6 O thou enemy, destructions are come to a
perpetual end: and thou hast destroyed cities;
their memorial is perished with them.
7 But the LORD shall endure for ever: he hath
prepared his throne for judgment.
8 And he shall judge the world in righteous-
ness, he shall minister judgment to the people in
uprightness.
9 The LORD also will be a refuge for the op-
pressed, a refuge in times of trouble.
10 And they that know thy name will put their
trust in thee: for thou, LORD, hast not forsaken
them that seek thee.
11 Sing praises to the LORD, which dwelleth in
Zion: declare among the people his doings.
12 When he maketh inquisition for blood, he
remembereth them: he forgetteth not the cry of
the humble.
13 Have mercy upon me, O LORD; consider my
trouble *which I suffer* of them that hate me, thou
that liftest me up from the gates of death:
14 That I may shew forth all thy praise in the
gates of the daughter of Zion: I will rejoice in thy
salvation.
15 The heathen are sunk down in the pit *that* they
made: in the net which they hid is their own foot
taken.
16 The LORD is known *by* the judgment *which* he
executeth: the wicked is snared in the work of his
own hands. Higgaion. Selah.
17 The wicked shall be turned into hell, *and* all

Remember, in the sense of consideration and action. *visitest.* Inspects or pays attention to. The question here expresses amazement in God's care for mankind (144:3; Job 7:17). The incarnate Christ is the ideal Son of Man who fulfills God's purposes for humanity both in His humiliation and glory (Heb. 2:6–9).

8:5 *a little.* Either somewhat less in status or for a short time.

8:6 *dominion.* Having created man in God's image, the Lord charged him to rule over the world (Gen. 1:26–28). *put all things under his feet.* Lost in the fall of man, but restored in the exaltation of Christ, the God-man (cited in 1 Cor. 15:27; Eph. 1:22).

8:7–8 The animals (*beasts*), birds (*fowl*), and *fish* represent man's dominion over earth, sky, and sea (Gen. 9:2; cf. 1 Kings 4:33).

8:9 *how excellent.* Repeated from v. 1 to show that man's dominion over creation is for God's glory.

Thoughts for Personal/Family Worship: Psalm 8

1. **Human theories about the origins of world and mankind lead to depravity, degradation, and despair. However, the truth is that God gave man high privileges and dignity in His creation. It glorifies the Lord for man to rule the world. Honoring God does not drag men and women down, except from their self-made thrones of arrogance. Though God's people are weak and lowly like children, they have a nobility about them, for they are children of the King, destined to reign with Him. What is one way that you could be mindful to treat every man, woman, and child as a person of dignity?**
2. **This psalm about man finds its fulfillment in the man Jesus Christ. The New Testament four times applies this psalm to Christ, the last Adam (Matt. 21:15–16; 1 Cor. 15:22–27; Eph. 1:20–22; Heb. 2:6–9). He is the glorious Creator, who with His Father fashioned all the universe (John 1:1–3; Heb. 1:2–3). He has regarded our helpless estate and has taken our nature to Himself, so that through His humiliation and exaltation, the Father would be glorified forever (Phil. 2:6–11). How does seeing Christ in this psalm give us hope that God's noble purpose for man will be completely fulfilled?**

Psalm 9: ***David praises the Lord for judging the wicked and preserving the righteous.***

9:1 *shew forth.* Recount, declare. *marvellous works.* Extraordinary, even miraculous acts (26:7; 96:3; 136:4).

9:3 *turned back.* Made to retreat. *shall fall.* Will stumble or stagger.

9:4 *judging right.* Judging righteously.

9:5 *put out.* Obliterated.

9:6 *memorial.* Memory.

9:10 *know thy name will put their trust in thee.* God's character is so reliable and beautiful that to know Him experientially is to be moved to trust Him and thus to be saved by Him.

9:11 *doings.* Actions or deeds.

9:12 *he maketh inquisition for blood.* Literally, "He who is searching bloods," that is, investigating acts of violence to properly and judicially punish the guilty (Gen. 9:5–6). *the humble.* Those brought low by pain and misery.

9:13 *Have mercy.* Be gracious or show favor to one undeserving. *consider my trouble.* See my misery or affliction. *liftest me up from the gates of death.* Preserves my life from death.

9:16 *Higgaion.* Perhaps meaning meditation or some musical term.

the nations that forget God.
18 For the needy shall not alway be forgotten: the
expectation of the poor shall *not* perish for ever.
19 Arise, O LORD; let not man prevail: let the hea-
then be judged in thy sight.
20 Put them in fear, O LORD: *that* the nations may
know themselves *to be but* men. Selah.

PSALM 10

1 WHY standest thou afar off, O LORD? *why* hidest
thou *thyself* in times of trouble?
2 The wicked in *his* pride doth persecute the
poor: let them be taken in the devices that they
have imagined.
3 For the wicked boasteth of his heart's desire,
and blesseth the covetous, *whom* the LORD
abhorreth.
4 The wicked, through the pride of his counte-
nance, will not seek *after God*: God *is* not in all
his thoughts.
5 His ways are always grievous; thy judgments *are*
far above out of his sight: *as for* all his enemies, he
puffeth at them.
6 He hath said in his heart, I shall not be moved:
for *I shall* never *be* in adversity.
7 His mouth is full of cursing and deceit and
fraud: under his tongue *is* mischief and vanity.
8 He sitteth in the lurking places of the villages:
in the secret places doth he murder the innocent:
his eyes are privily set against the poor.
9 He lieth in wait secretly as a lion in his den: he
lieth in wait to catch the poor: he doth catch the
poor, when he draweth him into his net.
10 He croucheth, *and* humbleth himself, that the
poor may fall by his strong ones.
11 He hath said in his heart, God hath forgotten:
he hideth his face; he will never see *it*.
12 Arise, O LORD; O God, lift up thine hand:
forget not the humble.
13 Wherefore doth the wicked contemn God? he
hath said in his heart, Thou wilt not require *it*.
14 Thou hast seen *it*; for thou beholdest mischief
and spite, to requite *it* with thy hand: the poor
committeth himself unto thee; thou art the helper
of the fatherless.
15 Break thou the arm of the wicked and the evil
man: seek out his wickedness *till* thou find none.
16 The LORD *is* King for ever and ever: the hea-
then are perished out of his land.
17 LORD, thou hast heard the desire of the
humble: thou wilt prepare their heart, thou wilt
cause thine ear to hear:
18 To judge the fatherless and the oppressed, that
the man of the earth may no more oppress.

9:17 *hell*. Hebrew, *sheol*, referring to death, the grave, or the place of the punishment of departed wicked spirits (49:14–15). The final punishment of the wicked is in view here (Deut. 32:22; Job 24:17; Prov. 5:5; 15:24; Isa. 14:9–20). *forget God*. Despise God, turning to pride and idolatry instead of constantly directing one's thoughts and love to God in humility and dependence (Deut. 8:11,19; 32:18; Ps. 44:17–21; 50:22; 106:20–21; Hos. 8:14; 13:6).
9:18 *expectation*. Hope or anticipated outcome.

Thoughts for Personal/Family Worship: Psalm 9

1. **It is important to remember that God holds our eternal destiny in His hands. He will judge all mankind in righteousness. Even before judgment day, death snatches people away from this world. If we know the Lord and seek Him, He will never forsake us. However, if we put God behind our backs and forget Him, then He will cast us into hell. Thomas Manton said, "As they cast God out of their mind and affections, so God will cast them out of his presence." Are you prepared for death? Why or why not?**
2. **Christ echoed the thoughts of this psalm when He said, "And fear not them which kill the body, but are not able to kill the soul: but rather fear him which is able to destroy both soul and body in hell" (Matt. 10:28). The greatest people on earth are but men. Christ's life was an embodiment of this principle, as He faced powerful and violent enemies with boldness and determination borne out of a childlike fear of the Lord. As we wait for Christ to return, how can we follow Him in this path?**

Psalm 10: ***Even though the wicked seem to prosper, David is confident that God's justice will prevail.***

10:1 *Why*. Such forsaking by God is only apparent (31:22; Isa. 50:10), yet it is a bitter thing to experience when God seems to us as a stranger (30:7; Job 23:1–7). *trouble*. The Hebrew literally designates a lack of rain or drought, with the figurative sense of trouble.
10:2 *persecute the poor*. Pursue hotly after the afflicted or weak. *let them be taken in the devices that they have imagined*. Let them be trapped in the wicked plans that they devised.
10:3 *blesseth the covetous, whom the LORD abhorreth*. Or "the greedy getter blesses himself; he spurns the LORD."
10:4 *pride of his countenance*. Literally, "haughtiness of his nose." *God is not in all his thoughts*. Literally, "nonexistence of God is all his schemes" (14:1).
10:5 *puffeth*. Snorts or blows heavily.
10:7 *mouth is full*. Mankind's slavery to sin corrupts all his speech (Rom. 3:14). *deceit and fraud*. Treacherous trickery and violence. *mischief and vanity*. Trouble and disaster.
10:8 *in the lurking places*. In ambush. *his eyes are privily set against the poor*. Literally, "his eyes lie in wait or lurk against the helpless."
10:9 *poor*. Afflicted or weak.
10:10 *humbleth himself*. Cowers or bows down. *the poor*. The helpless.
10:11 *forgotten*. Ignored, refused to think about. The wicked miscalculate who God is and what He is like.
10:12 *forget not the humble*. Do not refuse to think about the afflicted.
10:13 *contemn*. View with contempt or treat disrespectfully.
10:14 *mischief and spite*. Trouble and grief or vexation.
10:17 *the humble*. The weak and afflicted. *prepare*. Establish.
10:18 *may no more oppress*. May not behave like a tyrant again.

PSALM 11

To the chief Musician,
A Psalm of David.

1 IN the LORD put I my trust: how say ye to my
soul, Flee *as* a bird to your mountain?
2 For, lo, the wicked bend *their* bow, they make
ready their arrow upon the string, that they may
privily shoot at the upright in heart.
3 If the foundations be destroyed, what can the
righteous do?
4 The LORD *is* in his holy temple, the LORD's
throne *is* in heaven: his eyes behold, his eyelids
try, the children of men.
5 The LORD trieth the righteous: but the wicked
and him that loveth violence his soul hateth.
6 Upon the wicked he shall rain snares, fire and
brimstone, and an horrible tempest: *this shall be*
the portion of their cup.
7 For the righteous LORD loveth righteousness;
his countenance doth behold the upright.

PSALM 12

To the chief Musician upon Sheminith,
A Psalm of David.

1 HELP, LORD; for the godly man ceaseth; for the
faithful fail from among the children of men.
2 They speak vanity every one with his neigh-
bour: *with* flattering lips *and* with a double heart
do they speak.
3 The LORD shall cut off all flattering lips, *and* the
tongue that speaketh proud things:
4 Who have said, With our tongue will we prevail;
our lips *are* our own: who *is* lord over us?
5 For the oppression of the poor, for the sighing
of the needy, now will I arise, saith the LORD; I

Thoughts for Personal/Family Worship: Psalm 10

If in a time of trouble we sometimes feel God is standing at a distance from us, so that we no longer have the comfortable sense of His presence, we must concentrate on prayer. With a holy boldness, we need to lay hold of Him. Although we should never complain *of* Him, we are permitted to complain *to* Him. One of the chief complaints of the godly is the success of the wicked. Sadly, the world in which we live is one where the fear of God is often conspicuous by its absence. Atheism, humanism, and secularism have usurped the place of true religion, producing bitter fruits in society. The church's prayer and hope is that God will arise on behalf of His people. He will bring His kingdom by His Word and Spirit, by His providence, and ultimately by the second coming of His Son. How does this psalm teach us to pray for persecuted believers as we wait for His coming?

Psalm 11: *David trusts the Lord as the only foundation for life.*

11:1 *put I my trust*. I take or seek refuge. *to my soul*. To me. *Flee as a bird*. Escape for all hope of victory is lost.
11:2 *privily*. Secretly; Hebrew, "in darkness."
11:3 *the foundations be destroyed*. The victory of the wicked seems so complete that the righteous have nothing to build upon, as when basic principles of mercy and justice are rejected by the leaders of society (Ps. 82:2–5).
11:4 *his holy temple*. God's palace in *heaven* (see note at 5:7). *try*. Examine, scrutinize or put to the test (v. 5).
11:5 *his soul hateth*. God, by His very nature, opposes, rejects, and punishes sin.
11:6 *snares*. Nets for trapping; alternative translation, "coals." *brimstone*. Sulfur, perhaps an allusion to the destruction of Sodom (Gen. 19:24; Deut. 29:23). *horrible tempest*. A wind of raging heat.
11:7 *the righteous LORD*. The Lord's righteousness is His unchanging moral character (7:9; Deut. 32:4), such that what He *loveth* and what He hates (v. 5) constantly conforms to His law. *his countenance*. His face, an expression for His grace (see note at 4:6).

Thoughts for Personal/Family Worship: Psalm 11

1. Sometimes the powers of evil seem to have swept the field, and the best the godly can hope for is to hide in desperation. The thought may come to us to desert our post and forsake the work to which God has called us, but this is rarely the right thing to do. We must remember that if we are Christians, our foundation is not set upon anything that man can destroy, but upon God's character and His Word. No matter what happens, God is the righteous Judge and He is on the throne. How can faith in who God is give us courage to stand firm against impossible odds?

2. Christ faced death threats (Luke 13:31) and schemes to murder Him (Luke 22:2), and yet He set His face to do His Father's will. He knew that not one of the arrows of the wicked could kill Him until the Father's appointed time, and then His death would glorify God. He trusted that the righteous Lord would glorify Him, but "fire and brimstone" would fall upon the wicked (Luke 17:29–30). Does your heart ever tell you to fly like a bird to the mountains? Pray to find strength in the Lord Jesus and stand firm when those times come.

Psalm 12: *David finds comfort in the fact that God will judge the wicked and preserve the righteous.*

12:1 *Help, LORD*. Literally, "Save, LORD!" An arrow-like prayer, quickly shot to heaven in moments of felt crisis (1 Chron. 5:20; Neh. 2:4). *the godly*. Those under God's covenant love. *fail*. Disappear.
12:2 *vanity*. Falsehood or empty lies. *flattering lips*. A lip of smoothness (v. 3). *with a double heart*. Literally, "with a heart and a heart," a hypocritical lack of sincerity.
12:3 *proud things*. Literally, "great things."
12:4 *our lips are our own*. Literally, "our lips are with us."
12:5 *poor*. Weak and afflicted. *puffeth*. Snorts or blows heavily.
12:6 *purified seven times*. Refined to perfection, without any mixture of error (18:30; 19:8; 119:140,160,172; 2 Sam. 7:28; Prov. 30:5–6; 2 Cor. 1:18–20).
12:7 *them . . . them*. The people that God assuredly will preserve.
12:8 *walk on every side*. Walk back and forth, without restraint or obstacle.

Thoughts for Personal/Family Worship: Psalm 12

Even in times when the church seems to disappear and

will set *him* in safety *from him that* puffeth at him.
6 The words of the LORD *are* pure words: *as* silver
tried in a furnace of earth, purified seven times.
7 Thou shalt keep them, O LORD, thou shalt
preserve them from this generation for ever.
8 The wicked walk on every side, when the vilest
men are exalted.

PSALM 13

To the chief Musician,
A Psalm of David.

1 HOW long wilt thou forget me, O LORD? for
ever? how long wilt thou hide thy face from me?
2 How long shall I take counsel in my soul,
having sorrow in my heart daily? how long shall
mine enemy be exalted over me?
3 Consider *and* hear me, O LORD my God: lighten
mine eyes, lest I sleep the *sleep of* death;
4 Lest mine enemy say, I have prevailed against
him; *and* those that trouble me rejoice when I am
moved.
5 But I have trusted in thy mercy; my heart shall
rejoice in thy salvation.
6 I will sing unto the LORD, because he hath dealt
bountifully with me.

PSALM 14

To the chief Musician,
A Psalm of David.

1 THE fool hath said in his heart, *There is* no God.
They are corrupt, they have done abominable
works, *there is* none that doeth good.
2 The LORD looked down from heaven upon the
children of men, to see if there were any that did
understand, *and* seek God.
3 They are all gone aside, they are *all* together
become filthy: *there is* none that doeth good, no,
not one.
4 Have all the workers of iniquity no knowledge?
who eat up my people *as* they eat bread, and call
not upon the LORD.
5 There were they in great fear: for God *is* in the
generation of the righteous.
6 Ye have shamed the counsel of the poor, because
the LORD *is* his refuge.
7 Oh that the salvation of Israel *were come* out of

the lies of the wicked threaten to drown us, believers can cling to the perfect trustworthiness of the Bible. God's Word is as precious as pure silver. It contains no error in anything it teaches. If we have a right estimate of its worth, we shall surely treasure it in our hearts, follow its pure precepts, and trust its pure promises. Thank God for His infallible truth, especially in this time of mass falling away and confusion. It is confidence in Holy Scripture that will enable you to pray with hope, "Help, Lord!" How can the trustworthiness of God's Word strengthen you in times of spiritual darkness?

Psalm 13: *David pleads that God would come to his aid without further delay.*

13:1–2 Psalm 13 is often called the *how long* psalm, since the expression occurs four times, suggesting David felt confounded over God's delay in helping him (see note at 6:3). *hide thy face.* A gesture showing displeasure or lack of favor (27:9; 30:7). *take counsel in my soul.* The more he talked to himself, the worse he felt. He was perplexed, dejected, and near despair (77:3–6).

13:3 *Consider.* Look at, show regard to, pay attention to. *hear me.* Hebrew, "answer me." *lighten mine eyes.* Give me insight and understanding (19:8; 119:105; Prov. 6:23) that leads to life and joy (1 Sam. 14:27,29; Ezra 9:8; Prov. 29:13). *lest . . . death.* An expression of desperation unless the Lord would intervene. The perplexing question moved him to supplication.

13:4 *I am moved.* I am made to stagger or overthrown.

13:5–6 The prayer gives way to a song of praise. *mercy.* Covenant loyalty and love. *rejoice.* Shout in exultation. *dealt bountifully.* The Hebrew word elsewhere means "to wean." God had caused him to grow up, to come to a mature faith.

Thoughts for Personal/Family Worship: Psalm 13

1. **The Lord's people sometimes experience spiritual desertion when they feel abandoned in their afflictions without His presence, yet that desertion is never total or final. Jehovah is always there for believers. And so although their troubles may last long, they will not last forever. It is always best to cast our burdens on the Lord rather than mulling them over in our hearts trying to find solutions on our own. God's delays in answering us are not His rejection. When heaven seems silent to our prayers, how can we continue to cling to God's faithful love?**
2. **Christ also cried out, "How long?" as He endured the faithlessness and perversity of the human race in its slavery to the Devil (Matt. 17:17–18). It wearied His human soul to endure the constant presence of evil in our fallen world. Yet Christ did not despair, but persevered in His mission to bring justice to the world (Isa. 42:4). The greater His sorrow, the more He cast Himself upon the Father in prayer. Now, exalted to the right hand of God, He is able to fully sympathize with His weary people and to give them exactly the grace they need to endure (Heb. 2:18; 4:15–16).**

Psalm 14: *David describes man's depravity and corruption and longs for God's salvation.*

14:1–3 This psalm is essentially repeated in Ps. 53, and its first three verses are cited in Rom. 3:10–12.

14:1 *fool.* A person without moral insight or spiritual wisdom, rooted in a practical denial of God (*no God,* 10:4). *heart.* The inner man, including the mind, affections, and will. It is desperately wicked and a liar (Jer. 17:9; Rom. 1:21–31; Eph. 2:1–3).

14:3 *filthy.* Morally corrupt. *none that doeth good.* Mankind is completely under the power of sin (Rom. 3:9–10; cf. Matt. 19:17).

14:6 *poor.* Afflicted or weak.

14:7 *salvation . . . out of Zion.* See Rom. 11:26. *bringeth back the captivity.* Restores the fortunes, released the prisoners. *rejoice.* Shout in exultation.

Zion! when the LORD bringeth back the captivity
of his people, Jacob shall rejoice, *and* Israel shall
be glad.

PSALM 15

A Psalm of David.

1 LORD, who shall abide in thy tabernacle? who
shall dwell in thy holy hill?
2 He that walketh uprightly, and worketh righ-
teousness, and speaketh the truth in his heart.
3 *He that* backbiteth not with his tongue, nor
doeth evil to his neighbour, nor taketh up a
reproach against his neighbour.
4 In whose eyes a vile person is contemned; but
he honoureth them that fear the LORD. *He that*
sweareth to *his own* hurt, and changeth not.
5 *He that* putteth not out his money to usury, nor
taketh reward against the innocent. He that doeth
these *things* shall never be moved.

PSALM 16

Michtam of David.

1 PRESERVE me, O God: for in thee do I put my trust.
2 *O my soul*, thou hast said unto the LORD, Thou
art my Lord: my goodness *extendeth* not to thee;
3 *But* to the saints that *are* in the earth, and *to* the
excellent, in whom *is* all my delight.
4 Their sorrows shall be multiplied *that* hasten *af-
ter* another *god*: their drink offerings of blood will
I not offer, nor take up their names into my lips.

Thoughts for Personal/Family Worship: Psalm 14

1. **Atheism is no mere intellectual problem: it is a manifestation of sin in the naturally deceptive heart. It stands contrary to the light of nature that so evidently reveals the existence and glory of God, not to speak of the clear revelation of God in His Word. In fact the conscious decision to deny God leads invariably to a lifestyle that is corrupt. Sadly there are many who may not profess to be doctrinal atheists but nonetheless live as though God does not exist, a practical atheism. Even some professing Christians approach that kind of atheism. How can we seek to have God in all our thoughts?**
2. **During His ministry, our Lord Jesus spoke of "the fool" who for all practical purposes denied the reality of God (Luke 11:40; 12:20). As the great prophet of the church, Christ revealed not only the goodness of God but also the evils of man, rooted in the corruption of our hearts (Matt. 7:17; 12:33–34; 15:19; 19:17; John 7:7). He taught that men were unable and unwilling to understand and to seek God (Matt. 13:15; John 6:44; 8:43). If we would count ourselves Christians, we must receive Christ's teaching about the corruption of mankind. How should this truth affect us?**

Psalm 15: *David describes the ethical qualifications for dwelling in fellowship with the Lord.*

15:1 *abide*. Dwell as a resident alien. *tabernacle*. Tent. *holy hill*. Mt. Zion, representing God's kingdom and holy presence, ultimately heaven (2:6; 3:4; 24:3; 43:3; 48:1; 99:9). Only those changed by grace will inherit the kingdom of God (1 Cor. 6:9–11).

15:2 *walketh uprightly*. Lives with integrity. *worketh righteousness*. Obeys God's law. *speaketh the truth in his heart*. The evidence of a new or regenerated heart since the natural heart is inherently deceptive (14:1; 36; 58:3).

15:3 *backbiteth*. Slanders. *evil to his neighbour*. Something hurtful to his fellow man. *reproach against his neighbour*. Taunt or reviling against one close to him (a different word than previously).

15:4 *vile*. Contemptible, despised, or despicable, here by contrasting parallelism defined as a person who does not *fear the LORD* (36:1). *contemned*. Despised or rejected. *sweareth . . . changeth not*. He keeps his oath even at risk of personal loss or harm.

15:5 *usury*. Interest on loans, a crime in ancient Israel (Ex. 22:25). *reward*. A bribe. *never be moved*. Will not stagger or be overthrown.

Thoughts for Personal/Family Worship: Psalm 15

1. **While the *ground* of our salvation is the finished work of Jesus Christ, the *evidence* of our faith in Him is a life of godliness and holiness. It is right and good that we subject ourselves to self-examination, so that as we discern marks of grace, we may attain to a good measure of assurance that we will inherit eternal life. Examine your life for these evidences of a true faith: a life of integrity, obedience to God's laws, honesty and sincerity of heart, not seeking to harm others with your words or actions, despising the wicked and honoring those who fear God, and not cheating or exploiting people. What does self-examination reveal about your status in God's kingdom?**
2. **The man described in this psalm is preeminently the Son of God. He lived in pure and sincere righteousness, enduring much slander but always speaking the truth in love (1 Peter 1:19; 2:23). Rather than exploiting others, He became poor in order that they might be made rich forever (2 Cor. 8:9). He reigns in God's heavenly Zion (2:6) as the Father expresses His unending pleasure in His Son's obedient life and death (Phil. 2:8–9). Those who are united with Christ by faith are justified by His righteousness and sanctified by the Spirit to become like Him. How should believers' union with this righteous Lord give them hope that they too will share in His kingdom?**

Psalm 16: *David records by prophecy a prayer of Christ that climaxes in His expressed confidence and assurance of resurrection.*

16:1 This psalm did not find fulfillment in David himself, but was his prophecy of Christ, as the apostles affirmed (see notes at vv. 8–11). *Preserve me*. Watch over Me. *put my trust*. Take or seek refuge. As God's servant, Christ depended upon God's support (Isa. 42:1)

16:2 *Thou art my Lord*. He lived in obedience to God's will (40:6–8). *my goodness extendeth not to thee*. Literally, "my goodness or happiness is not beside you" (*extendeth* is not in the Hebrew). His happiness is in none other than God (v. 11), and He has no good apart from the Lord (73:25).

16:3 His joy in God overflowed into *delight* in His holy people (*saints*).

16:4 *hasten*. Either "rush," or "exchange." He will not join in the

5 The LORD *is* the portion of mine inheritance
and of my cup: thou maintainest my lot.
6 The lines are fallen unto me in pleasant *places*;
yea, I have a goodly heritage.
7 I will bless the LORD, who hath given me coun-
sel: my reins also instruct me in the night seasons.
8 I have set the LORD always before me: because
he is at my right hand, I shall not be moved.
9 Therefore my heart is glad, and my glory rejoic-
eth: my flesh also shall rest in hope.
10 For thou wilt not leave my soul in hell; neither
wilt thou suffer thine Holy One to see corruption.
11 Thou wilt shew me the path of life: in thy
presence *is* fulness of joy; at thy right hand *there*
are pleasures for evermore.

PSALM 17

A Prayer of David.

1 HEAR the right, O LORD, attend unto my cry,
give ear unto my prayer, *that goeth* not out of
feigned lips.
2 Let my sentence come forth from thy presence;
let thine eyes behold the things that are equal.
3 Thou hast proved mine heart; thou hast visited
me in the night; thou hast tried me, *and* shalt find
nothing; I am purposed *that* my mouth shall not
transgress.
4 Concerning the works of men, by the word
of thy lips I have kept *me from* the paths of the
destroyer.
5 Hold up my goings in thy paths, *that* my foot-
steps slip not.
6 I have called upon thee, for thou wilt hear me,
O God: incline thine ear unto me, *and hear* my
speech.
7 Shew thy marvellous lovingkindness, O thou
that savest by thy right hand them which put their
trust *in thee* from those that rise up *against them*.
8 Keep me as the apple of the eye, hide me under
the shadow of thy wings,
9 From the wicked that oppress me, *from* my
deadly enemies, *who* compass me about.
10 They are inclosed in their own fat: with their
mouth they speak proudly.

---

wicked worship of those who seek other gods, for they will suffer great pain (Luke 4:5–8).

16:5 *portion . . . inheritance . . . cup*. He takes no earthly inheritance, but receives and enjoys the Lord as His riches and glory. *maintainest my lot*. Hold my destiny and future prosperity.

16:6 *lines*. Share or portion. *goodly heritage*. Pleasing or beautiful inheritance, namely, the glory of God shared with the people given to Him in the covenant (vv. 2–3).

16:7 *reins*. Kidneys, referring to the mind.

16:8–11 Cited in Acts 2:23–31; 13:35–37 with respect to Christ.

16:8 *shall not be moved*. Will not stagger or be overthrown. The messianic mission cannot fail.

16:9 *rest in hope*. Dwell in security or confidence.

16:10 *thou wilt not leave my soul in hell*. Thou wilt not abandon me to the grave, a reference to resurrection from the dead (Acts 2:31). *my soul*. Me. *hell*. Hebrew, *sheol*, which can refer to death, the grave, or the abode of departed wicked spirits. *suffer . . . to see corruption*. Not allow Him to experience decay.

16:11 *shew me the path of life*. Bring Me out of death, into life *for evermore*. *joy . . . pleasures*. God is the fountain of all good (36:8–9), and He promised to give Christ happiness above all others to share with His people (21:6; 45:7). *at thy right hand*. The place of closeness (v. 8) and honor (110:1; Gen. 48:14).

Thoughts for Personal/Family Worship: Psalm 16

1. **This psalm is directly messianic. David wrote it as a prophet of the Lord, knowing that God would raise Christ from the dead to reign forever in fulfillment of God's covenant with David (1 Chron. 17:11–12; Acts 2:30). It is not about David, who died, was buried, and his body returned to dust (Acts 2:29; 13:36). Thus the Scriptures revealed the resurrection of Christ centuries before He was born. How does this help you to have absolute confidence that the Bible is true, and Jesus is the Christ?**
2. **This psalm sheds light upon the hope that strengthened Christ to endure and "the joy that was set before him" by which He despised the shame of the cross (Heb. 12:2). The incarnate Lord Jesus lived in daily dependence upon God. He believed God's promise to raise Him from the dead and to bring Him and His people into an eternal fullness of life and joy in the manifest glory of God. The Son loves the Father and counts Him to be His eternal portion and delight. How does this encourage your own faith in God?**
3. **The Lord Jesus taught us by His example that in trouble and sorrow we must turn to God and count Him and His people to be all our joy. He is to believers far more than we could ever need, and in His hands is our spiritual and eternal happiness. It is good for Christians to keep in mind what we have in our God, lest we be tempted by the possessions and pleasures of the world. In Him we have a suitable, sufficient, soul-satisfying, secure, and everlasting portion. Compared to Him, the world offers us nothing and cannot harm our true source of happiness. How should that affect the way we view death? How should that affect the way we view this world?**

Psalm 17: *David prays for personal vindication and protection and expresses his confidence in the Lord.*

17:1 *the right*. Righteousness. *attend*. Listen, pay attention. *cry*. Lament or wail. *not out of feigned lips*. Not speaking with deceit or treachery. David prayed for God to act as the Judge, considering his case as an honest man wronged by the wicked.

17:2 *sentence*. Judgment. *behold the things that are equal*. See the straightness or uprightness of my case.

17:3 *proved*. Tested or examined. *visited*. Paid attention to or inspected. *tried*. Refined. Every believer should desire to be examined by God and found innocent (139:23; Job 23:10).

17:4 *destroyer*. Violent one.

17:7 *Shew thy marvellous lovingkindness*. Perform amazing acts of your covenant loyalty.

17:8 *apple of the eye*. Literally, "the pupil of the daughter of the eye," something very delicate and sensitive. *shadow of thy wings*. An image of protection and special provision (36:7; 57:1; 63:7; 91:1,4).

17:9 *compass*. Surround (v. 11).

17:10 *inclosed in their fat*. Wrapped in their fat, a picture of insensitivity (119:70; Isa. 6:10).

11 They have now compassed us in our steps:
they have set their eyes bowing down to the earth;
12 Like as a lion *that* is greedy of his prey, and as it
were a young lion lurking in secret places.
13 Arise, O LORD, disappoint him, cast him
down: deliver my soul from the wicked, *which is*
thy sword:
14 From men *which are* thy hand, O LORD, from
men of the world, *which have* their portion in
this life, and whose belly thou fillest with thy hid
treasure: they are full of children, and leave the
rest of their *substance* to their babes.
15 As for me, I will behold thy face in righteousness: I shall be satisfied, when I awake, with thy likeness.

PSALM 18

To the chief Musician, *A Psalm* of David, the servant of the LORD, who spake unto the LORD the words of this song in the day *that* the LORD delivered him from the hand of all his enemies, and from the hand of Saul: And he said,

1 I WILL love thee, O LORD, my strength.
2 The LORD *is* my rock, and my fortress, and my
deliverer; my God, my strength, in whom I will
trust; my buckler, and the horn of my salvation,
and my high tower.
3 I will call upon the LORD, *who is worthy* to be
praised: so shall I be saved from mine enemies.
4 The sorrows of death compassed me, and the
floods of ungodly men made me afraid.
5 The sorrows of hell compassed me about: the
snares of death prevented me.
6 In my distress I called upon the LORD, and
cried unto my God: he heard my voice out of his
temple, and my cry came before him, *even* into
his ears.
7 Then the earth shook and trembled; the foundations also of the hills moved and were shaken,
because he was wroth.
8 There went up a smoke out of his nostrils,
and fire out of his mouth devoured: coals were
kindled by it.
9 He bowed the heavens also, and came down:
and darkness *was* under his feet.
10 And he rode upon a cherub, and did fly: yea,
he did fly upon the wings of the wind.
11 He made darkness his secret place; his pavilion
round about him *were* dark waters *and* thick
clouds of the skies.
12 At the brightness *that was* before him his thick
clouds passed, hail *stones* and coals of fire.
13 The LORD also thundered in the heavens, and
the Highest gave his voice; hail *stones* and coals
of fire.
14 Yea, he sent out his arrows, and scattered
them; and he shot out lightnings, and discomfited them.
15 Then the channels of waters were seen, and the
foundations of the world were discovered at thy
rebuke, O LORD, at the blast of the breath of thy
nostrils.

17:13 *disappoint*. Confront. *my soul*. Me. *which is thy sword*. By Thy power to judge.
17:14 *From men which are thy hand*. (Save me) from men by Thy power.
17:15 *when I awake*. Either from sleep (4:8; 139:18) or, more likely, death (13:3; Dan. 12:2). In contrast to the wicked who enjoy their rewards in this life (v. 14), David anticipated the reward of seeing God's glory (*likeness*, Num. 12:8) after the resurrection (16:11; Rev. 22:4).

Thoughts for Personal/Family Worship: Psalm 17

1. **While we can never lay claim in this life to sinless perfection, it is greatly to our comfort if before men we have the testimony of a good conscience, especially at times when we are wrongly criticized. We should not be overly troubled by the censures of men. God knows us for what we really are. How can this help us to maintain our constant desire to please Him and wait for His vindication?**
2. **Christ well understands what it was like to be surrounded by wicked men, and to wait quietly upon God's justice as they attacked Him like lions. If ever there was a person with the right to cry out for justice, it was the innocent Son of God. Yet He received insult and injury so very meekly. How does this psalm show us the way to follow in Christ's footsteps?**

Psalm 18: *David expresses his gratitude for God's deliverance in giving victory over his enemies.*

Title *David...who spake unto the LORD*. This psalm is repeated almost exactly in 2 Sam. 22.
18:2 Each title used of God highlights some aspect of His strength as safe refuge for His people. *rock*. The cliff or crag under which one can find shelter. *my strength*. Literally, "my rock," referring to an immovable boulder. *buckler*. Shield. *horn of my salvation*. An image of power to save (Luke 1:69), as a large animal defeats its enemies (92:10).
18:4 *sorrows of death compassed me*. Ropes of death surrounded me (Acts 2:24).
18:5 *sorrows of hell compassed me about*. Ropes of *sheol* (here referring to death) surrounded me. *prevented*. Confronted or met.
18:6 *his temple*. His palace, referring to heaven.
18:7 *the earth shook*. A theophany or appearance of God's glory (114:4–7) as at Mt. Sinai (Ex. 19:16,18) and on the day of the Lord (Isa. 13:13; Hab. 3:6,10; Hag. 2:6). *wroth*. Angry.
18:9 *bowed the heavens*. A Hebrew phrase often used of God as He "stretched out" the skies when He created them (104:2; Isa. 40:22; Jer. 32:17; Zech. 12:1), but here it refers to how He "bent" or disrupted the heavens as He *came down* in glory (144:5; cf. Isa. 64:1; Rev. 6:14). *darkness*. Thick darkness or a cloud.
18:10 *rode upon a cherub...wings of the wind*. The Lord came attended by angelic spirits (68:17; 104:3–4). On cherubim, see note at Ezek. 10:15.
18:11 *pavilion*. Booth or tent.
18:14 *discomfited*. Confused.
18:15 *discovered*. Uncovered, exposed.

16 He sent from above, he took me, he drew me out of many waters.

17 He delivered me from my strong enemy, and from them which hated me: for they were too strong for me.

18 They prevented me in the day of my calamity: but the LORD was my stay.

19 He brought me forth also into a large place; he delivered me, because he delighted in me.

20 The LORD rewarded me according to my righteousness; according to the cleanness of my hands hath he recompensed me.

21 For I have kept the ways of the LORD, and have not wickedly departed from my God.

22 For all his judgments *were* before me, and I did not put away his statutes from me.

23 I was also upright before him, and I kept myself from mine iniquity.

24 Therefore hath the LORD recompensed me according to my righteousness, according to the cleanness of my hands in his eyesight.

25 With the merciful thou wilt shew thyself merciful; with an upright man thou wilt shew thyself upright;

26 With the pure thou wilt shew thyself pure; and with the froward thou wilt shew thyself froward.

27 For thou wilt save the afflicted people; but wilt bring down high looks.

28 For thou wilt light my candle: the LORD my God will enlighten my darkness.

29 For by thee I have run through a troop; and by my God have I leaped over a wall.

30 *As for* God, his way *is* perfect: the word of the LORD is tried: he *is* a buckler to all those that trust in him.

31 For who *is* God save the LORD? or who *is* a rock save our God?

32 *It is* God that girdeth me with strength, and maketh my way perfect.

33 He maketh my feet like hinds' *feet*, and setteth me upon my high places.

34 He teacheth my hands to war, so that a bow of steel is broken by mine arms.

35 Thou hast also given me the shield of thy salvation: and thy right hand hath holden me up, and thy gentleness hath made me great.

36 Thou hast enlarged my steps under me, that my feet did not slip.

37 I have pursued mine enemies, and overtaken them: neither did I turn again till they were consumed.

38 I have wounded them that they were not able to rise: they are fallen under my feet.

39 For thou hast girded me with strength unto the battle: thou hast subdued under me those that rose up against me.

40 Thou hast also given me the necks of mine enemies; that I might destroy them that hate me.

41 They cried, but *there was* none to save *them: even* unto the LORD, but he answered them not.

42 Then did I beat them small as the dust before the wind: I did cast them out as the dirt in the streets.

43 Thou hast delivered me from the strivings of the people; *and* thou hast made me the head of the heathen: a people *whom* I have not known shall serve me.

44 As soon as they hear of me, they shall obey me: the strangers shall submit themselves unto me.

45 The strangers shall fade away, and be afraid out of their close places.

46 The LORD liveth; and blessed *be* my rock; and let the God of my salvation be exalted.

47 *It is* God that avengeth me, and subdueth the people under me.

48 He delivereth me from mine enemies: yea, thou liftest me up above those that rise up against me: thou hast delivered me from the violent man.

49 Therefore will I give thanks unto thee, O LORD, among the heathen, and sing praises unto thy name.

50 Great deliverance giveth he to his king; and sheweth mercy to his anointed, to David, and to his seed for evermore.

18:18 *prevented.* Confronted or met. *stay.* Support or staff.
18:19 *brought . . . into a large place.* Gave freedom, release from pressure and distress.
18:20 *righteousness.* Innocence. *recompensed.* Returned to (v. 24).
18:26 *froward.* Distorted or perverted. *shew thyself froward.* Be tortuous, twisted, winding (two different Hebrew words both translated *froward*).
18:28 *candle.* Lamp.
18:29 *troop.* Either a marauding band or a wall.
18:30 *tried.* Refined, purified. *buckler.* Shield.
18:31 *save.* Except.
18:32 *girdeth.* Secured with a belt, encircled (also v. 39).
18:35 *holden.* Held. *gentleness.* Condescension.
18:43 *a people whom I have not known shall serve me.* God will make the Son of David the ruler (*head*) over distant nations (Isa. 55:3–5).
18:44 *strangers shall submit.* Foreigners will be compelled to give insincere submission.
18:49 *will I give thanks . . . among the heathen.* David, as a type of Christ, calls the nations to worship God for His great salvation (Rom. 15:9).
18:50 *mercy.* Faithful love. *anointed.* Chosen as *king* (see note at 2:2). *to David, and to his seed.* As God promised in His covenant (89:3–4; 132:11; 2 Sam. 7:12–16; 23:5).

Thoughts for Personal/Family Worship: Psalm 18

1. All believers, like David, should confess love for the Lord their God, because they have experienced how He hears and answers their prayers. Our troubles and conflicts become opportunities to experience the many ways the Lord is our strength. When God hears our prayers and rescues us, let us give public testimony for His glory. How has God answered your prayers? How have you glorified Him for it?

PSALM 19

To the chief Musician, A Psalm of David.

1 THE heavens declare the glory of God; and the firmament sheweth his handywork.
2 Day unto day uttereth speech, and night unto night sheweth knowledge.
3 *There is* no speech nor language, *where* their voice is not heard.
4 Their line is gone out through all the earth, and their words to the end of the world. In them hath he set a tabernacle for the sun,
5 Which *is* as a bridegroom coming out of his chamber, *and* rejoiceth as a strong man to run a race.
6 His going forth *is* from the end of the heaven, and his circuit unto the ends of it: and there is nothing hid from the heat thereof.
7 The law of the LORD *is* perfect, converting the soul: the testimony of the LORD *is* sure, making wise the simple.
8 The statutes of the LORD *are* right, rejoicing the heart: the commandment of the LORD *is* pure, enlightening the eyes.
9 The fear of the LORD *is* clean, enduring for ever: the judgments of the LORD *are* true *and* righteous altogether.
10 More to be desired *are they* than gold, yea, than much fine gold: sweeter also than honey and the honeycomb.
11 Moreover by them is thy servant warned: *and* in keeping of them *there is* great reward.
12 Who can understand *his* errors? cleanse thou me from secret *faults*.
13 Keep back thy servant also from presumptuous *sins*; let them not have dominion over me: then shall I be upright, and I shall be innocent from the great transgression.
14 Let the words of my mouth, and the meditation of my heart, be acceptable in thy sight, O LORD, my strength, and my redeemer.

---

2. God's works of salvation center upon the salvation of His anointed king (v. 50). David's song in this way foreshadows Christ's salvation. Though caught in the ropes of death (vv. 4–5; Acts 2:24), the Lord delivered Him because God delights in His righteousness (vv. 19–24). With a great earthquake (v. 7), He was drawn out of the depths of death (v. 16). Therefore, Christ rules over all the nations (vv. 43–44) and is leading them to praise, exalt, and give thanks to the living God (vv. 46,49). How does this psalm help you to see the glory of Christ? How can that move us to love God?

3. David described God's intervention to save him from Saul in terms of an earthquake, fire, cosmic disruption, flying angels, and a violent hailstorm. Such figurative language points forward to the day of the Lord (Ezek. 38:19–23; Matt. 24:27–31). Christ will return as both God and the anointed Son of David to save His people and destroy His enemies. How does God's faithfulness to His covenant in the past assure us of His guarantee to honor it in the future?

Psalm 19: *David describes God's communication through both His creation and His Word and then his communication with God through prayer.*

19:1 *heavens.* Highest part of God's creation, representing all creation. *declare.* Recount. *the glory of God.* God's perfections or attributes (Rom. 1:20). *firmament.* The sky, including the atmosphere and the stars above it (Gen. 1:6–8,14–17,20). *his handywork.* The work of His hands. The universe glorifies God because it reveals its Creator.

19:2 *Day unto day uttereth speech.* Literally, "[One] day bubbles or gushes forth news or information to [the next] day." The communication is ceaseless, going on day and night.

19:3 Creation does not use *speech* or *language* to communicate, but its message is plain to all (Rom. 1:19–20).

19:4–6 *line.* Measuring line or string on an instrument. The communication is universal (Rom. 10:18). *tabernacle.* Dwelling place. The *sun* was worshiped by many people (Deut. 4:19; Job 31:26–28), but it is merely part of God's creation that declares His glory, including His pleasure (*bridegroom . . . rejoiceth,* cf. Acts 14:17), power (*strong man to run,* cf. Rom. 1:20), and presence in all places (*nothing hid,* cf. Acts 17:24).

19:7 *law.* Hebrew, *torah,* not just legislation, but all instruction revealed by God in His Word. *perfect.* Complete. *converting the soul.* Restoring the whole person. *sure.* Trustworthy, faithful, confirmed. *the simple.* A person who is naïve but teachable.

19:8 *heart.* The whole inner man (mind, will, affections). *pure.* Clear. *enlightening the eyes.* Giving understanding.

19:9 *fear.* By a figure of speech (effect for cause), here it is used as a title of special revelation because the Word produces reverence for God.

19:12 *cleanse.* Acquit, set free from guilt and punishment. A prayer for justification.

19:13 *from the great transgression.* From great transgression (no article), thus not referring to a particular sin. A prayer for sanctification.

19:14 A prayer for *acceptable* adoration. *strength.* Rock, the huge immovable boulder. *my redeemer.* The justification, sanctification, and pleasing adoration of a sinner in the sight of the Creator are only possible by God's redeeming grace in Christ (130:7–8).

Thoughts for Personal/Family Worship: Psalm 19

1. God graciously reveals Himself. This is grace to us, for our knowledge of Him is completely dependent on what He chooses to reveal. God constantly reveals to all mankind His being and basic attributes through the natural revelation of what He created. No one has any excuse for not worshiping the Lord. Yet nature conveys no saving message: it justly condemns man for refusing to glorify God but it does not point to the remedy. God's special revelation of His Word is the means of grace that reveals the wonderful remedy to condemnation. The Scripture is more precious than gold and sweeter than honey. Nowhere else do we learn of the Lord as the Redeemer of sinners—God in Christ reconciling the world to Himself (2 Cor. 5:19). Praise God for His creation and the Bible which are both means of revelation. Are you taking time each day to read what God has caused to be written?

2. Significantly, David communes with God in response to God's communication. There is always a link between God's Word and prayer. It is a link that we should use daily. While creation should fill us with awe toward God, only the Bible can teach us how to draw near to God as a

THE MEANS OF GRACE

The apostle Paul declares, "By grace are ye saved through faith, and that not of yourselves: it is the gift of God: not of works, lest any man should boast" (Eph. 2:8–9). Where does this faith come from? How is this gift of God imparted? The answer of historic Christianity is that it comes from God and by the means of grace that Christ has appointed in His church. All the ordinances, or things commanded by Christ (Matt. 28:20), are in view in this answer, but the primary means is the Word of God, the Holy Scriptures, "which are able to make thee wise unto salvation" (2 Tim. 3:15). David extols the saving power of the Word, declaring that "the law of the LORD is perfect, converting the soul" (Ps 19:7).

There is no conflict between faith in the sovereignty of God and use of His appointed means to obtain what He promises to us. As God, the Holy Spirit is free to work when, where, and how He pleases, with or without the use of means. Nevertheless, the means of grace are commended to us by the very fact that the sovereign God commands us to use them.

A distinction must be made between the kindness of God shown to all creatures, by which He showers good gifts upon all mankind, just and unjust alike, and that special or saving grace imparted only to God's elect. The Bible affirms, "The LORD is good to all: and his tender mercies are over all his works" (Ps. 145:9). However, "he sheweth his word unto Jacob, his statutes and his judgments unto Israel. He hath not dealt so with any nation: and as for his judgments, they have not known them" (Ps. 147:19–20).

Scripture's uniqueness as a means of grace lies in its very nature: "The word of God is quick, and powerful, and sharper than any twoedged sword . . . a discerner of the thoughts and intents of the heart" (Heb. 4:12). However, because of the unbelief, ignorance, and darkness of our fallen, corrupted hearts, the Holy Spirit alone makes the reading and preaching of the Word effectual as a means of grace, using the Word to enlighten our darkness, working faith in our hearts, and enabling us to receive Christ as Savior and to serve Him as Lord.

Other means of grace are subordinate to God's Word. Holy baptism and the Lord's Supper are the Word of God made visible to confirm the truth of God's promises to us. Prayer is a means by which those promises are invoked by believers, to "obtain mercy, and find grace to help in time of need" (Heb. 4:16). Praise is a means by which God's grace, the Word of Christ dwelling in our hearts, is poured forth in thanksgiving to God as we sing the "psalms and hymns and spiritual songs" included in the canon of Scripture at the direction of the Holy Spirit (Eph. 5:18–21; Col. 3:16).

We must never attribute efficacy to the means themselves and the bare use of them. The water of baptism cannot wash away sins. The bread and wine of the Lord's Supper are not and cannot become the life-giving flesh and blood of Christ. A man's Christianity is not to be measured by the number of sermons he has heard or prayers he has recited. It is possible to do all the right things without a believing heart: "Whatsoever is not of faith is sin" (Rom. 14:23). Even so, those who believe that God has instituted these means of grace make diligent use of them.

The church must give first place to the sound preaching of the Word. Her members should hear such preaching with faith and submission, desiring to know, believe, and obey the will of God revealed therein. The sacraments should be administered only in conjunction with such preaching, and must be received in faith by all who would profit from them. To pray effectively, our minds must be filled with the truth of God's Word. To praise acceptably, our hearts must be filled with the Word of Christ and with the Holy Spirit.

PSALM 20

To the chief Musician, A Psalm of David.

1 THE LORD hear thee in the day of trouble; the
name of the God of Jacob defend thee;
2 Send thee help from the sanctuary, and
strengthen thee out of Zion;
3 Remember all thy offerings, and accept thy
burnt sacrifice; Selah.
4 Grant thee according to thine own heart, and
fulfil all thy counsel.
5 We will rejoice in thy salvation, and in the name
of our God we will set up *our* banners: the LORD
fulfil all thy petitions.
6 Now know I that the LORD saveth his anointed;
he will hear him from his holy heaven with the
saving strength of his right hand.
7 Some *trust* in chariots, and some in horses: but
we will remember the name of the LORD our God.
8 They are brought down and fallen: but we are
risen, and stand upright.
9 Save, LORD: let the king hear us when we call.

PSALM 21

To the chief Musician, A Psalm of David.

1 THE king shall joy in thy strength, O LORD; and
in thy salvation how greatly shall he rejoice!
2 Thou hast given him his heart's desire, and hast
not withholden the request of his lips. Selah.
3 For thou preventest him with the blessings of
goodness: thou settest a crown of pure gold on
his head.
4 He asked life of thee, *and* thou gavest *it* him,
even length of days for ever and ever.
5 His glory *is* great in thy salvation: honour and
majesty hast thou laid upon him.
6 For thou hast made him most blessed for ever:
thou hast made him exceeding glad with thy
countenance.
7 For the king trusteth in the LORD, and through
the mercy of the most High he shall not be moved.
8 Thine hand shall find out all thine enemies: thy
right hand shall find out those that hate thee.
9 Thou shalt make them as a fiery oven in the
time of thine anger: the LORD shall swallow them
up in his wrath, and the fire shall devour them.
10 Their fruit shalt thou destroy from the earth,
and their seed from among the children of men.
11 For they intended evil against thee: they imag-
ined a mischievous device, *which* they are not able
to perform.
12 Therefore shalt thou make them turn their
back, *when* thou shalt make ready *thine arrows*
upon thy strings against the face of them.
13 Be thou exalted, LORD, in thine own strength:
so will we sing and praise thy power.

---

forgiven and transformed people in acceptable worship. How can we use each benefit of Scripture (vv. 7–11) as a means of guiding our prayers?

Psalm 20: ***David prays for the success of the king in the day of trouble and expresses confidence in the Lord's help.***

20:1 A royal psalm, a prayer concerning the welfare of the king (v. 6), thought to have been one sung when the king went forth to war (v. 7). *name*. All that God reveals Himself to be. *God of Jacob*. The Lord who keeps His covenant with His people. *defend*. Make inaccessible, protect by setting on high.
20:2 *strengthen*. Support or sustain.
20:5 *rejoice*. Exult or give a ringing cry. *set up our banners*. Put up our flag or standard.
20:6 Every king in David's line was *anointed* to royal office ("messiah," see note at 2:2), anticipating and pointing to the coming of the ideal King, Jesus Christ.
20:7 *chariots . . . horses*. Conventional instruments of war. *remember*. Acknowledge and purposefully think about. *name*. See note at v. 1.
20:9 *hear*. Hebrew, "answer." This verse may be understood as, "O LORD, save the king! Answer us when we call." The same Hebrew words—*save*, *king*, and *hear*—appear in v. 6.

Thoughts for Personal/Family Worship: Psalm 20

1. **Warfare is part of the Christian life, and believers are called to fight the battles of the Lord (Eph. 6:10–18). It is important that the weapons of our warfare are not carnal but spiritual (2 Cor. 10:4). We often use human means, but they will do nothing apart from the power of God's Spirit and the victory of Jesus Christ. How can we make better use of the greatest means of victory in our spiritual battles—prayer and faith in God's Word?**
2. **The troubles and victories of Israel's kings foreshadowed the great crisis and victory of Christ. Christ knew His day of trouble, especially toward the end of His life. He prayed to His Father to grant Him strength. He offered His righteous life and sacrificial death to God for sinners—and God fulfilled all of Christ's holy desires. His people rejoice in His victory, for they do not trust in themselves, but in the character of their Lord. How does this psalm help explain what it means for us to pray, "Thy kingdom come"?**

Psalm 21: ***The psalmist gives thanks to the Lord for answering prayer on behalf of the king and for granting victory.***

21:1 *rejoice*. Shout in exultation.
21:2 *hast not withholden*. Have not withheld or refused. The king obtains his *heart's desire* by prayer to God (2:8).
21:3 *thou preventest him*. Thou didst come to meet him.
21:4 *life . . . for ever and ever*. Complete victory over death and enjoyment of eternal life (16:10–11; 61:6).
21:6 *thy countenance*. Thy face or presence.
21:7 *mercy*. Covenant loyalty and love. *moved*. Made to stagger or overthrown.
21:9 *fiery oven . . . wrath*. The king is an instrument of God's anger against the wicked, which burns like a consuming fire (2:12; 11:6; Matt. 13:41–42; 25:31,41; 2 Thess. 1:7–8).
21:11 *evil*. Something hurtful. *imagined a mischievous device*. Devised a wicked plan (2:1–3).

PSALM 22

To the chief Musician upon Aijeleth Shahar, A Psalm of David.

1 MY God, my God, why hast thou forsaken me? *why art thou so* far from helping me, *and from* the words of my roaring?

2 O my God, I cry in the daytime, but thou hearest not; and in the night season, and am not silent.

3 But thou *art* holy, *O thou* that inhabitest the praises of Israel.

4 Our fathers trusted in thee: they trusted, and thou didst deliver them.

5 They cried unto thee, and were delivered: they trusted in thee, and were not confounded.

6 But I *am* a worm, and no man; a reproach of men, and despised of the people.

7 All they that see me laugh me to scorn: they shoot out the lip, they shake the head, *saying,*

8 He trusted on the LORD *that* he would deliver him: let him deliver him, seeing he delighted in him.

9 But thou *art* he that took me out of the womb: thou didst make me hope *when I was* upon my mother's breasts.

10 I was cast upon thee from the womb: thou *art* my God from my mother's belly.

11 Be not far from me; for trouble *is* near; for *there is* none to help.

12 Many bulls have compassed me: strong *bulls* of Bashan have beset me round.

13 They gaped upon me *with* their mouths, *as* a ravening and a roaring lion.

14 I am poured out like water, and all my bones are out of joint: my heart is like wax; it is melted in the midst of my bowels.

15 My strength is dried up like a potsherd; and my tongue cleaveth to my jaws; and thou hast brought me into the dust of death.

16 For dogs have compassed me: the assembly of the wicked have inclosed me: they pierced my hands and my feet.

17 I may tell all my bones: they look *and* stare upon me.

18 They part my garments among them, and cast lots upon my vesture.

19 But be not thou far from me, O LORD: O my strength, haste thee to help me.

20 Deliver my soul from the sword; my darling from the power of the dog.

21 Save me from the lion's mouth: for thou hast heard me from the horns of the unicorns.

22 I will declare thy name unto my brethren: in the midst of the congregation will I praise thee.

23 Ye that fear the LORD, praise him; all ye the seed of Jacob, glorify him; and fear him, all ye the seed of Israel.

24 For he hath not despised nor abhorred the

Thoughts for Personal/Family Worship: Psalm 21

The royal psalms point to Christ, the ideal King. Supported by the strength of God, Christ rejoices in the salvation given to Him and His people from their enemies. He obtains these blessings by prayer and intercession, and now reigns with great honor and joy upon His heavenly throne. One day He will return to judge the wicked with devouring fire so that all their schemes against His kingdom will fail. The ultimate purpose of His reign is the exaltation of the Lord in the praises of His people. Christ's victories are the victories of all who belong to Him by faith. How does this psalm encourage you and give you hope?

Psalm 22: *As a prophet, David describes the suffering of the Messiah and the glory that will follow throughout the earth.*

22:1 *why hast thou forsaken me?* The cry of dereliction from a person trusting in the covenant (*my God*) but experiencing abandonment by God. It has been appropriately labeled the Crucifixion Psalm or the Psalm of the Cross (Matt. 27:46; Mark 15:34). Such a detailed prophecy, written nearly one thousand years before Christ, gives remarkable confirmation of our belief that God inspired the Holy Scriptures. *roaring.* Groaning as in prayer.

22:5 *confounded.* Put to shame (Rom. 5:5).

22:6 *worm.* Grub, maggot, or other insect; an image of lowliness and worthlessness. *reproach . . . despised.* A disgrace, someone treated with contempt (Isa. 53:3; Mark 9:12).

22:7 *shoot out the lip.* They open the mouth widely as a gesture of derision. *shake the head.* A gesture expressing astonishment or mockery (Matt. 27:39; Mark 15:29).

22:8 *trusted.* Literally, "rolled," an expression of total reliance (Matt. 27:43).

22:9–10 The sufferer has been faithful to the Lord, having rested all hope and *cast* all cares (55:22) upon God since the earliest days of childhood.

22:12 *compassed.* Surrounded. *strong bulls of Bashan have beset me round.* Powerful cattle have encircled me. Bashan was proverbial for luxuriant pastures. The comparison of the wicked to animals throughout this psalm depicts their power and savage violence.

22:13 *gaped upon me with their mouths.* Literally, "they opened against me their mouth." *ravening.* Tearing.

22:14 *bowels.* Organs of the body.

22:15 *potsherd.* A piece of broken pottery. *tongue cleaveth.* In terrible thirst (John 19:28).

22:16 *dogs have compassed me.* Wild dogs encircled me. *inclosed.* Surrounded.

22:17 *tell.* Count.

22:18 *cast lots.* A typical means by which soldiers would divide up the spoils of victory (John 19:23–24; cf. Matt. 27:35; Mark 15:24; Luke 23:34). *vesture.* Clothing.

22:20 *my soul.* Me. *my darling.* My only one, referring to His precious life.

22:21 *unicorns.* Wild bulls or oxen. The Hebrew word order marks this verse as the transition from suffering to glory: "Save me from the lion's mouth and from the horns of the wild bulls. Thou hast answered me!"

22:22 *declare thy name unto my brethren.* The psalmist is promising to call others to adore God for His glorious attributes revealed in the work of salvation (Heb. 2:12; cf. 40:9–10).

affliction of the afflicted; neither hath he hid his
face from him; but when he cried unto him, he
heard.
25 My praise *shall be* of thee in the great congre-
gation: I will pay my vows before them that fear
him.
26 The meek shall eat and be satisfied: they shall
praise the LORD that seek him: your heart shall
live for ever.
27 All the ends of the world shall remember and
turn unto the LORD: and all the kindreds of the
nations shall worship before thee.
28 For the kingdom *is* the LORD's: and he *is* the
governor among the nations.
29 All *they that be* fat upon earth shall eat and
worship: all they that go down to the dust shall
bow before him: and none can keep alive his own
soul.
30 A seed shall serve him; it shall be accounted to
the Lord for a generation.
31 They shall come, and shall declare his righ-
teousness unto a people that shall be born, that
he hath done *this*.

PSALM 23

A Psalm of David.

1 THE LORD *is* my shepherd; I shall not want.
2 He maketh me to lie down in green pastures: he
leadeth me beside the still waters.
3 He restoreth my soul: he leadeth me in the
paths of righteousness for his name's sake.
4 Yea, though I walk through the valley of the
shadow of death, I will fear no evil: for thou *art*
with me; thy rod and thy staff they comfort me.
5 Thou preparest a table before me in the pres-
ence of mine enemies: thou anointest my head
with oil; my cup runneth over.
6 Surely goodness and mercy shall follow me all
the days of my life: and I will dwell in the house of
the LORD for ever.

22:25 *pay my vows.* The writer pledges to keep his solemn commitments to the Lord.
22:26 *The meek.* The humble and poor (10:12,17; Matt. 5:3–5).
22:27 *all the kindreds.* God will draw all the peoples of the world into His blessing, as He promised to Abraham and His seed (Gen. 12:3; 28:14).
22:28 *kingdom . . . among the nations.* God's kingdom will spread to all the world (Zech. 14:9; Obad. 21) through the victory He gives to His suffering servant (Isa. 52:13–15).
22:29 Every kind of person will glorify God, from the prosperous (*fat*) to the perishing (*go down to the dust*).
22:30 *seed.* The true covenant people, those who fear the Lord (v. 23; Isa. 53:10).
22:31 *he hath done this.* The good news will be proclaimed to future generations that redemption had been accomplished; it was finished.

Thoughts for Personal/Family Worship: Psalm 22

1. **The first part of this psalm concerns the suffering Savior (vv. 1–21). This is holy ground, allowing us to enter in a small way into the experience of Christ. Here is the man who has faithfully kept covenant with God since His birth (vv. 9–10). And yet He cries out in anguish, "Why hast thou forsaken me?" (v. 1). The answer to this question addresses the very heart of the atonement. God does not forsake the faithful, but the wicked that break His covenant (9:10; 37:28; 94:14; Deut. 31:16–17). Why then did Christ suffer? Christ died for sinners. God withdrew all sense of His gracious presence from His faithful Son and placed upon Him all the guilt and punishment due to the sins of His people (Isa. 53:5–6,8). On this basis, Christ can save sinners from all the penalty of their sins. How does this psalm humble us? How does it call us to place all our trust in Christ?**
2. **The second part of this psalm concerns the successful Savior (vv. 22–31). God answered the prayers of His afflicted Son and delivered Him from evil (v. 24). Therefore, the Son proclaims God's glory to the world and calls people to praise the Lord. The testimony of His salvation will effectively turn people from every nation to repent and seek God in humble faith and worship (vv. 26–27). This worldwide mission will continue for generations (v. 31). How is Christ doing this today?**

Psalm 23: *David expresses confidence in the Lord's providential provision and protection.*

23:1 *my shepherd.* The One who is shepherding me, stressing His constant activity. The title *shepherd* was commonly used for kings (see note at 2 Sam. 5:2). Some of the imagery of the psalm is pastoral, but the focus is on the Lord's gracious sovereignty. *not want.* Lack nothing.
23:2 *green pastures.* Grazing places of grass. *still waters.* Waters of rest or quietness, as an oasis in the wilderness (Rev. 7:17).
23:3 *He restoreth my soul.* Either He causes me to return (as sheep would tend to stray), or He renews me (as with food and drink, v. 2; cf. Lam. 1:11,19). *paths.* Trails clearly marked by the tracks of wagon wheels, a metaphor for a life of obedience to God's Word (*righteousness*). *for his name's sake.* Because of His glory (31:3).
23:4 *shadow of death.* Places of deep darkness, including but not limited to death. *no evil.* No harm. *thou art with me.* Faith in God's presence dispels fears of all potential dangers in the uncertain places of life (Luke 12:32). *rod . . . staff.* A club to powerfully fight off threats (2:9; Isa. 11:4) and a crook to lovingly pull back from danger and keep the sheep nearby.
23:5 *Thou preparest a table.* The image shifts to a gracious host (though the message remains the same as the shepherd), responsible to provide for (*table*) and protect (*mine enemies*) the guests in his house (v. 6). *anointest my head with oil.* Literally, "Thou dost make my head fat with oil," a gesture of sharing prosperity and giving honor (Luke 7:46).
23:6 *mercy.* Covenant loyalty and love. *follow.* Pursue. *dwell in the house of the LORD.* The experience and joy of being in God's presence in fellowship with Him.

Thoughts for Personal/Family Worship: Psalm 23

1. **The title of Shepherd belongs to Christ as the God-man, the Lord, and the Son of David (Isa. 40:11; Ezek. 34:12–16,23,31; Zech. 13:7; John 10:1–16,27–30). He fulfills this role with very special care for His people's souls (Luke 15:3–7; 1 Peter 2:25). It is no small comfort, especially in difficult and sad times, to realize that the Lord**

PSALM 24

A Psalm of David.

1 THE earth *is* the LORD's, and the fulness thereof; the world, and they that dwell therein.
2 For he hath founded it upon the seas, and established it upon the floods.
3 Who shall ascend into the hill of the LORD? or who shall stand in his holy place?
4 He that hath clean hands, and a pure heart; who hath not lifted up his soul unto vanity, nor sworn deceitfully.
5 He shall receive the blessing from the LORD, and righteousness from the God of his salvation.
6 This *is* the generation of them that seek him, that seek thy face, O Jacob. Selah.
7 Lift up your heads, O ye gates; and be ye lift up, ye everlasting doors; and the King of glory shall come in.
8 Who *is* this King of glory? The LORD strong and mighty, the LORD mighty in battle.
9 Lift up your heads, O ye gates; even lift *them* up, ye everlasting doors; and the King of glory shall come in.
10 Who is this King of glory? The LORD of hosts, he *is* the King of glory. Selah.

PSALM 25

A Psalm of David.

1 UNTO thee, O LORD, do I lift up my soul.
2 O my God, I trust in thee: let me not be ashamed, let not mine enemies triumph over me.
3 Yea, let none that wait on thee be ashamed: let them be ashamed which transgress without cause.
4 Shew me thy ways, O LORD; teach me thy paths.
5 Lead me in thy truth, and teach me: for thou *art* the God of my salvation; on thee do I wait all the day.
6 Remember, O LORD, thy tender mercies and thy lovingkindnesses; for they *have been* ever of old.
7 Remember not the sins of my youth, nor my transgressions: according to thy mercy remember

Jesus is looking after us as our wise and gentle leader, provider, and protector. How can the promises of this psalm give comfort and peace to believers in Christ?

2. Without distracting from Christ's loving work as the Shepherd of His people, it is also possible to see Jesus experiencing in His humanity the blessings of knowing God as *His* shepherd. Christ followed the will of God meekly like a lamb, even to the death (Isa. 53:7). He looked to the Father to protect Him and provide for His needs. Even in the presence of enemies, the Father granted Him the satisfaction of doing His will by the anointing of the Spirit. Now the Lord Jesus dwells in His Father's house forever. How would Christ's experience as a sheep help Him to care for us as our Shepherd?

Psalm 24: *God is the glorious king who rules over all and is worthy of worship.*

24:1–2 *The earth is the LORD's.* He owns all things (Deut. 10:14) because He made all things (v. 2; Col. 1:16–17). Therefore, all of creation is good and to be received with thanksgiving (1 Cor. 10:25–26; 1 Tim. 4:4).

24:2 *floods.* Rivers.

24:3 *Who shall.* Who will be able to. *hill . . . holy place.* God's presence with His people, ultimately heaven itself (see notes at 2:6; 15:1).

24:4 *clean hands.* Literally, "innocent of hands," meaning righteous in actions. *lifted up his soul unto vanity.* Set his trust and hope upon something deceitful and worthless (25:1; 86:4; 143:8). *pure heart.* Not sinless perfection, but sincere love springing from faith in the Lord (73:1; Matt. 5:8; Acts 15:9; 1 Tim. 1:15; 2 Tim. 2:22; 1 Peter 1:22).

24:5 *God of his salvation.* God who rescues him.

24:6 *seek him . . . seek thy face.* See note at 105:3–4. *O Jacob.* Some Hebrew manuscripts, with the Greek Septuagint, read "the God of Jacob".

24:7–10 *Lift up . . . gates . . . doors.* Addressed to the Levites who guarded the entrances into the tabernacle or temple (118:19–20; Ex. 40:5,33; 1 Chron. 9:23; 2 Chron. 4:22; 23:19), a type of the angels guarding the gates of heaven (Rev. 21:12). *King of glory.* A title repeated five times here but found nowhere else in Scripture (cf. 29:3; Acts 7:2; 1 Cor. 2:8; James 2:1). He is the Commander (*the LORD of hosts*) of all the forces of creation (vv. 1–2), returning victorious after proving Himself to be a warrior *mighty in battle* (68:1,24–25; Ex. 15:3; Num. 10:35–36; 2 Chron. 6:41). The great blessing of entering God's holy presence (v. 3) is dwelling with the King of glory (John 17:24).

Thoughts for Personal/Family Worship: Psalm 24

1. This psalm found glorious fulfillment in the ascension of Christ to heaven. Truly the Lord Jesus had fought a bitter war against sin at the cost of His own blood. But He proved Himself mighty in battle and went up into heaven as the risen King of glory. What must it have been like for the angels and saints to greet Him on that day? How does it comfort believers on earth to know that the Crucified One is now the Lord of glory?

2. Like Ps. 15, this psalm reminds us that only those purified by grace will enter into God's holy presence. Justification by faith alone gives us our title to heaven, but the sanctification of our lives gives us a fitness to enter and enjoy it, for heaven is a holy place. Those who desire to dwell with the King of glory must begin submitting themselves to His reign even now. How do vv. 3–4 teach us what that means in practical terms?

Psalm 25: *David prays for protection, guidance, and pardon.*

25:1 *lift up my soul.* An expression of total dependence (see note at 24:4).

25:2 *let me not be ashamed.* Includes the idea of not being disappointed (v. 20).

25:3 *wait.* Hope with confident expectation not mere resignation (vv. 5,21).

25:4 *Shew me.* Cause me to know (v. 14).

25:5 *in thy truth.* Or by your truth. God's Word is a means by which He leads His people.

25:6 *Remember.* Give attention and take action (v. 7). *tender mercies . . . lovingkindnesses.* Feelings of tender compassion and demonstrations of covenant loyalty and love.

25:7 *mercy.* Covenant loyalty and love.

thou me for thy goodness' sake, O LORD.
8 Good and upright *is* the LORD: therefore will he
teach sinners in the way.
9 The meek will he guide in judgment: and the
meek will he teach his way.
10 All the paths of the LORD *are* mercy and truth
unto such as keep his covenant and his testimonies.
11 For thy name's sake, O LORD, pardon mine in-
iquity; for it *is* great.
12 What man *is* he that feareth the LORD? him
shall he teach in the way *that* he shall choose.
13 His soul shall dwell at ease; and his seed shall
inherit the earth.
14 The secret of the LORD *is* with them that fear
him; and he will shew them his covenant.
15 Mine eyes *are* ever toward the LORD; for he
shall pluck my feet out of the net.
16 Turn thee unto me, and have mercy upon me;
for I *am* desolate and afflicted.
17 The troubles of my heart are enlarged: *O* bring
thou me out of my distresses.
18 Look upon mine affliction and my pain; and
forgive all my sins.
19 Consider mine enemies; for they are many;
and they hate me with cruel hatred.
20 O keep my soul, and deliver me: let me not be
ashamed; for I put my trust in thee.
21 Let integrity and uprightness preserve me; for
I wait on thee.
22 Redeem Israel, O God, out of all his troubles.

PSALM 26

A Psalm of David.

1 JUDGE me, O LORD; for I have walked in mine
integrity: I have trusted also in the LORD; *therefore*
I shall not slide.
2 Examine me, O LORD, and prove me; try my
reins and my heart.
3 For thy lovingkindness *is* before mine eyes: and
I have walked in thy truth.
4 I have not sat with vain persons, neither will I
go in with dissemblers.
5 I have hated the congregation of evil doers; and
will not sit with the wicked.
6 I will wash mine hands in innocency: so will I
compass thine altar, O LORD:
7 That I may publish with the voice of thanksgiv-
ing, and tell of all thy wondrous works.
8 LORD, I have loved the habitation of thy house,
and the place where thine honour dwelleth.
9 Gather not my soul with sinners, nor my life
with bloody men:
10 In whose hands *is* mischief, and their right
hand is full of bribes.
11 But as for me, I will walk in mine integrity:
redeem me, and be merciful unto me.

25:10 *mercy and truth.* Covenant loyalty and love joined with dependable faithfulness, commonly paired in Scripture as attributes of God and His ways (26:3; 40:10–11; 57:3,10; 61:7; 69:13; 85:10; 86:15; 89:14; 108:4; 115:1; 117:2; 138:2; Gen. 24:27; 32:10; Ex. 34:6; see note at 26:3).
25:11 *For thy name's sake.* God forgives sinners not because of who they are or what they do, but because of who He is (1 John 2:12).
25:12 *him shall he teach.* Fearing God, living in a profound awareness of God's glory, is a prerequisite to learning God's will (111:10).
25:13 *His soul.* "He," a Hebrew expression for the personal pronoun.
25:14 *secret.* Confidential conversation or intimate advice.
25:16 *have mercy.* Be gracious or show undeserved favor.
25:17 *troubles.* Anxiety (v. 22).
25:20 *my soul.* Me. *trust.* Seek refuge or find refuge.

Thoughts for Personal/Family Worship: Psalm 25

This psalm sets a pattern for praying to know God's will. Since He is good, delighting in our well-being, He will give directions if we humbly seek Him with a teachable spirit. A key element in discerning God's will is to submit to it even before we know it (John 7:17). We shall find that He will fulfill His promise according to His rich mercy and unchanging truth. If we fear Him, He will lead us. To fear God is to factor Him into every thought and situation, to live in the reality of God. It is not a terror that keeps us distant from God, but a friendship that brings us under His intimate guidance. God's Son lived in daily dependence and reverence for His Father, seeking to do His will because it was His will (Isa. 50:4–5). If we seek to trust in Christ, His Spirit will enable us to do the same. How does this psalm illuminate what it means to live as God's *child*?

Psalm 26: *David expresses confidence in his integrity before the Lord and prays for divine deliverance.*

26:1 *Judge me.* Misunderstood and slandered by others, David appealed to God, confident that the accusations are without foundation.
26:2 *prove.* Put to the test (139:23–24). *try.* Refine. *reins.* Kidneys, used figuratively of the mind. *my heart.* The whole of inner man (mind, will, affections).
26:3 *lovingkindness.* Covenant loyalty and love (often translated "mercy").
26:4 *vain persons.* Deceptive or worthless people. *dissemblers.* Those who are hidden, most likely hypocrites.
26:5 *sit with the wicked.* Join with them in their sinful thoughts and activities (1:1).
26:6 *wash mine hands.* A figure of speech for cleansing one's actions from sin (Isa. 1:15–16), drawn from the washings of priests (Ex. 30:19–21). *compass.* Go around.
26:7 *publish.* Cause to hear. *tell.* Recount.
26:8 *habitation.* Dwelling place, the temple in Jerusalem as a type of heaven (2 Chron. 30:17; 36:15).
26:9 *my soul.* Me. *bloody men.* Literally, "men of bloods," those guilty of violence or murder.
26:10 *mischief.* Infamy or shameful behavior.
26:11 *be merciful.* Be gracious, show undeserved favor.
26:12 *even place.* Level ground.

Thoughts for Personal/Family Worship: Psalm 26

1. The person who professes to trust in the Lord must live

12 My foot standeth in an even place: in the
congregations will I bless the LORD.

PSALM 27

A Psalm of David.

1 THE LORD *is* my light and my salvation; whom
shall I fear? the LORD *is* the strength of my life; of
whom shall I be afraid?
2 When the wicked, *even* mine enemies and
my foes, came upon me to eat up my flesh, they
stumbled and fell.
3 Though an host should encamp against me,
my heart shall not fear: though war should rise
against me, in this *will I be* confident.
4 One *thing* have I desired of the LORD, that will
I seek after; that I may dwell in the house of the
LORD all the days of my life, to behold the beauty
of the LORD, and to enquire in his temple.
5 For in the time of trouble he shall hide me in
his pavilion: in the secret of his tabernacle shall he
hide me; he shall set me up upon a rock.
6 And now shall mine head be lifted up above
mine enemies round about me: therefore will I
offer in his tabernacle sacrifices of joy; I will sing,
yea, I will sing praises unto the LORD.
7 Hear, O LORD, *when* I cry with my voice: have
mercy also upon me, and answer me.
8 *When thou saidst*, Seek ye my face; my heart
said unto thee, Thy face, LORD, will I seek.
9 Hide not thy face *far* from me; put not thy
servant away in anger: thou hast been my help;
leave me not, neither forsake me, O God of my
salvation.
10 When my father and my mother forsake me,
then the LORD will take me up.
11 Teach me thy way, O LORD, and lead me in a
plain path, because of mine enemies.
12 Deliver me not over unto the will of mine en-
emies: for false witnesses are risen up against me,
and such as breathe out cruelty.
13 *I had fainted*, unless I had believed to see the
goodness of the LORD in the land of the living.
14 Wait on the LORD: be of good courage, and
he shall strengthen thine heart: wait, I say, on the
LORD.

PSALM 28

A Psalm of David.

1 UNTO thee will I cry, O LORD my rock; be not
silent to me: lest, *if* thou be silent to me, I become
like them that go down into the pit.
2 Hear the voice of my supplications, when I cry

---

a consistent godly life. But being aware of the deceitfulness of our hearts even when we have a clear conscience, we should be willing, not only to examine ourselves, but for the great searcher of hearts to examine us. We may pray for God to judge us, not to be condemned, but that we might repent of sins and walk in the good way that pleases God. How often do you pray for God to show you your sins? How often should you?

2. **David's resolve to walk with integrity is a mirror of Christ's absolute determination to avoid all sin (101:2–4; John 8:46; 14:30; 2 Cor. 5:21). Though the Lord Jesus loved sinners, He kept Himself separate and unstained from the world's corruption (Heb. 7:26). This is the basis of our salvation, for believers are in union with Him. How and why do we pursue holiness in our own lives?**

Psalm 27: *David expresses his confidence in the Lord's protection and longing for His presence, and prays for His continuing grace and assistance.*

27:1 *my light*. The source of my wisdom and hope (Mic. 7:8; 2 Sam. 22:29; Isa. 60:19–20).

27:3 *host*. An army camp. *will I be confident*. I will be trusting or feeling secure.

27:4 *desired*. Asked. *dwell in the house of the LORD*. Reside with the Lord, enjoying His presence and protection. As the host, the Lord would be obligated to provide and protect (23:5–6). *behold the beauty of the LORD*. Enjoy His goodness and glory in close fellowship with Him (29:2; 96:6; Isa. 33:17; John 17:24; Rev. 22:4).

27:5 *hide me in his pavilion*. Shelter me in his booth or tent. *in the secret of his tabernacle*. Literally, "in the shelter or protection of his tent." *rock*. A huge immovable boulder.

27:7 *have mercy*. Be gracious or show undeserved favor.

27:9 *Hide not thy face*. This would be a gesture of disfavor.

27:10 *When*. If.

27:11 *plain path*. A level way, without obstacles (26:12).

27:14 *Wait*. Hope with anticipation and expectancy, not resignation (Isa. 25:9; Mic. 7:7; Zeph. 3:8).

Thoughts for Personal/Family Worship: Psalm 27

The Lord is our light in the sense that He reveals to us our sin through the law and our Savior through the gospel. Then in our experience He becomes our salvation. He then proves to be our strength, enabling us to persevere. The Lord Jesus found His own strength in God's presence with Him (Isa. 50:6–9), and His strength becomes ours through the Spirit (Phil. 1:18–19). Christ is thus everything to the believer, and the believer's great desire is to be with Him and see His beauty. He taught us to make Him our "one thing" above all earthly treasures and activities (v. 4; Luke 10:42; 18:22). The apostle Paul likewise made Christ the "one thing" he pursued (Phil. 3:8,13). Let us seek Him in all that we do, and view all His good gifts as valuable only insofar as they help us to glorify and enjoy Him. What practical difference would it make in your life if you began to pursue Christ with this single-minded focus?

Psalm 28: *David prays for God's help in the midst of troubles and thanks the Lord for the help received.*

28:1 *my rock*. A huge, immovable boulder. *be not silent*. Do not be deaf. *if thou be silent*. A different Hebrew word, "to be silent or unresponsive." *pit*. Death or the grave. David knew that if he did not receive grace and strength from God, he had no hope.

unto thee, when I lift up my hands toward thy
holy oracle.
3 Draw me not away with the wicked, and with
the workers of iniquity, which speak peace to their
neighbours, but mischief *is* in their hearts.
4 Give them according to their deeds, and ac-
cording to the wickedness of their endeavours:
give them after the work of their hands; render to
them their desert.
5 Because they regard not the works of the LORD,
nor the operation of his hands, he shall destroy
them, and not build them up.
6 Blessed *be* the LORD, because he hath heard the
voice of my supplications.
7 The LORD *is* my strength and my shield; my
heart trusted in him, and I am helped: therefore
my heart greatly rejoiceth; and with my song will
I praise him.
8 The LORD *is* their strength, and he *is* the saving
strength of his anointed.
9 Save thy people, and bless thine inheritance:
feed them also, and lift them up for ever.

PSALM 29

A Psalm of David.

1 GIVE unto the LORD, O ye mighty, give unto the
LORD glory and strength.
2 Give unto the LORD the glory due unto his
name; worship the LORD in the beauty of holiness.
3 The voice of the LORD *is* upon the waters: the
God of glory thundereth: the LORD *is* upon many
waters.
4 The voice of the LORD *is* powerful; the voice of
the LORD *is* full of majesty.
5 The voice of the LORD breaketh the cedars; yea,
the LORD breaketh the cedars of Lebanon.
6 He maketh them also to skip like a calf; Leba-
non and Sirion like a young unicorn.
7 The voice of the LORD divideth the flames of
fire.
8 The voice of the LORD shaketh the wilderness;
the LORD shaketh the wilderness of Kadesh.
9 The voice of the LORD maketh the hinds to
calve, and discovereth the forests: and in his

28:2 *lift up my hands.* A gesture of calling upon the Lord in dependent prayer (63:4; 134:2; 141:2; Lev. 9:22; Luke 24:50; 1 Tim. 2:8; cf. note at 24:4). *thy holy oracle.* The Holy of Holies or innermost part of the sanctuary, symbolic of the immediate presence of God.
28:3 They are hypocrites, talking as if they desired the well-being (*peace*) of their neighbor, but secretly planning to harm them (*mischief*).
28:4 *according to their deeds.* A fearful prospect to get from God what they deserve (Rom. 2:6–11; Rev. 20:11–15).
28:5 *operation of his hands.* The work of His power.
28:7 *my strength and my shield.* The Lord empowers and defends His people (3:3; 18:2; 33:20; 59:17; 62:7; 144:1–2; Eph. 6:10,16).
28:8 *saving strength.* Literally, "strength of salvations or victories." *his anointed.* God's appointed king, ultimately Christ Himself (20:6).
28:9 *feed.* Shepherd, as a loving king (23:1).

Thoughts for Personal/Family Worship: Psalm 28

1. **In the troubles of this life, men react in different ways, but the godly man will turn to the living and true God who, like a massive rock, is a shelter in the storm and a shade in the heat. This God is everything we need. Yet we must not approach Him as hypocrites, who may say fine prayers to God and nice words to people while their lives cry out for punishment from God's justice. Rather, we must draw near to God as those coming under His shepherding care, submitting to His sovereign authority. Why do we often turn to other sources for the help and strength we need?**
2. **The salvation of God's people is inseparably bound up with God's power with His anointed king (vv. 7–8). God's power for believers is precisely the power by which He raised Christ and exalted Him to the highest place (Eph. 1:19–21). Our strength to fight Satan is to be strong in the Lord Jesus (Eph. 6:10–12). This has two great implications. First, we must have a real union with Christ by faith, or we will never be saved. Second, we must enjoy regular communion with Christ by daily exercising our faith in Him, or our experience of salvation will be crippled. How does David's example (v. 1) teach us to cling to Christ with holy desperation?**

Psalm 29: *David praises the Lord for His power, providence over all creation, and protection of His people.*

29:1 *Give.* In the sense of declaring what belongs to Him (v. 2). *ye mighty.* Literally, "you sons of gods," a reference to supernatural beings, angels (89:6). As created beings, they are obligated to glorify Him.
29:3 *voice of the LORD.* God's power revealed in the thunderstorm (seven times in this psalm).
29:6 *unicorn.* A wild bull or ox.
29:9 *discovereth.* Strips or lays bare.
29:10 *flood.* Word used of the worldwide flood in Noah's day (Gen. 6–9), perhaps here of the ocean. *sitteth King.* He sits enthroned as king. God rules over all things and therefore deserves all praise, worship, and obedience.

Thoughts for Personal/Family Worship: Psalm 29

1. **Nature can be very impressive, but when confronted with its power and might, we should raise our thoughts to the God behind it who is the cause of its great wonders. How great He is! We should bow in fear before Him, ever showing profound reverence. If a mighty thunderstorm raging over the ocean can inspire fear and awe, how much more should the Lord who controls it by His mere word (Matt. 8:26–27). What things in nature produce awe in you? What do they show you about God?**
2. **The voice of natural revelation can produce fear, but true worship only arises among the people who have God's Word (v. 9). The wonders of the natural world need not terrify them, for the God of the storm is also the Lord who speaks peace to His people (v. 11). They view God's power with joyful awe and reverent comfort, for He is their God in Christ. How should faith in Christ affect the way we face the frightening power of storms and other potentially dangerous things?**

temple doth every one speak of *his* glory.
10 The LORD sitteth upon the flood; yea, the LORD
sitteth King for ever.
11 The LORD will give strength unto his people;
the LORD will bless his people with peace.

PSALM 30

A Psalm *and* Song *at* the dedication of the house of David.

1 I WILL extol thee, O LORD; for thou hast lifted me
up, and hast not made my foes to rejoice over me.
2 O LORD my God, I cried unto thee, and thou
hast healed me.
3 O LORD, thou hast brought up my soul from
the grave: thou hast kept me alive, that I should
not go down to the pit.
4 Sing unto the LORD, O ye saints of his, and give
thanks at the remembrance of his holiness.
5 For his anger *endureth but* a moment; in his
favour *is* life: weeping may endure for a night, but
joy *cometh* in the morning.
6 And in my prosperity I said, I shall never be
moved.
7 LORD, by thy favour thou hast made my moun-
tain to stand strong: thou didst hide thy face, *and*
I was troubled.
8 I cried to thee, O LORD; and unto the LORD I
made supplication.
9 What profit *is there* in my blood, when I go
down to the pit? Shall the dust praise thee? shall it
declare thy truth?
10 Hear, O LORD, and have mercy upon me:
LORD, be thou my helper.
11 Thou hast turned for me my mourning into
dancing: thou hast put off my sackcloth, and
girded me with gladness;
12 To the end that *my* glory may sing praise to
thee, and not be silent. O LORD my God, I will give
thanks unto thee for ever.

PSALM 31

To the chief Musician, A Psalm of David.

1 IN thee, O LORD, do I put my trust; let me never
be ashamed: deliver me in thy righteousness.
2 Bow down thine ear to me; deliver me speedily:
be thou my strong rock, for an house of defence
to save me.
3 For thou *art* my rock and my fortress; therefore
for thy name's sake lead me, and guide me.
4 Pull me out of the net that they have laid privily
for me: for thou *art* my strength.
5 Into thine hand I commit my spirit: thou hast

Psalm 30: *God's temporary discipline causes David to praise the Lord for His gracious deliverance.*

Title *Song at the dedication of the house of David.* Perhaps a reference to his royal palace (2 Sam. 5:11; cf. Deut. 20:5). Alternatively, it could be understood, "Song at the dedication of the house; [a psalm] of David," referring to David's purchase of Ornan's threshingfloor as the future site of the house of the Lord (1 Chron. 21:18–22:1; cf. 1 Kings 8:63).
30:1 *extol.* Lift up.
30:2 *cried.* Called for help.
30:3 *my soul.* Me. *grave.* The Hebrew, *sheol*, refers to death, the grave, or abode of departed wicked spirits. Here referring to deliverance from death (*thou hast kept me alive*).
30:4 *remembrance.* Declaring His *holiness* as an act of worship (6:5).
30:5 *his anger . . . life.* Literally, "a short while in His anger; life in His pleasure." Perhaps a reference to the plague God sent on Israel for David's census (2 Sam. 24:1; 1 Chron. 21:14). *endure.* Lodge. *joy.* A cry of jubilation.
30:6 *prosperity.* Quietness or ease. *I shall never be moved.* Self-satisfied pride (10:6), perhaps as he was glorying in his kingdom, led to the numbering of the people (1 Chron. 21:2).
30:7 *thou hast made . . . to stand.* His strength came from God's grace. *mountain.* Kingdom. *hide thy face.* A sign of displeasure. *troubled.* Horrified or out of one's senses.
30:8 *made supplication.* Asked for grace or undeserved favor (another form of the same verb translated "have mercy" (v. 10).
30:10 *have mercy.* Be gracious or show undeserved favor.
30:11 *sackcloth.* Clothing associated with grief or repentance. *girded.* Clothed with a belt, encircled.

Thoughts for Personal/Family Worship: Psalm 30

1. **David had grown self-confident, interpreting all that God had done for him as evidence of invincibility. His power had gone to his head, and he looked to the power of man instead of the Lord. God sent judgment to awaken David to his spiritual senses, bringing him back to reality. David's experience warns us not to rest in the blessings of God rather than in the God who blesses. Take time to express your gratitude to God for His discipline of us, for the dependence it instills in us, and for the humility we gain—our pathway to joy.**
2. **Christ never rested His confidence in His human ability, but constantly looked to God for His present and future success (John 14:10). Yet Christ did experience God's anger as He received the curse for the sins of His people (Gal. 3:13), and then entered into the eternal glory and joy for which He was destined (Matt. 25:21; Luke 24:26; Heb. 12:2). How can Christ's experience of sorrow leading to eternal joy give courage and hope to those who follow Him?**

Psalm 31: *David expresses his confidence in the safety the Lord provides and prays for deliverance from further times of stress.*

31:1–3 These words are substantially repeated in 71:1–3.
31:1 *put my trust.* Seek and find refuge and safety. *never be ashamed.* Not be disappointed, not referring to embarrassment (v. 17).
31:2 *rock.* A huge, immovable boulder.
31:3 *rock.* A cliff or crag under which one can find shelter.
31:4 *laid privily.* Set secretly, concealed.
31:5 *Into thine hand.* An expression of absolute trust in God in the face of death; quoted by Jesus as His final words on the cross (Luke 23:46).

redeemed me, O LORD God of truth.
6 I have hated them that regard lying vanities: but
I trust in the LORD.
7 I will be glad and rejoice in thy mercy: for thou
hast considered my trouble; thou hast known my
soul in adversities;
8 And hast not shut me up into the hand of the
enemy: thou hast set my feet in a large room.
9 Have mercy upon me, O LORD, for I am in
trouble: mine eye is consumed with grief, *yea*, my
soul and my belly.
10 For my life is spent with grief, and my years
with sighing: my strength faileth because of mine
iniquity, and my bones are consumed.
11 I was a reproach among all mine enemies, but
especially among my neighbours, and a fear to
mine acquaintance: they that did see me without
fled from me.
12 I am forgotten as a dead man out of mind: I
am like a broken vessel.
13 For I have heard the slander of many: fear *was*
on every side: while they took counsel together
against me, they devised to take away my life.
14 But I trusted in thee, O LORD: I said, Thou *art*
my God.
15 My times *are* in thy hand: deliver me from
the hand of mine enemies, and from them that
persecute me.
16 Make thy face to shine upon thy servant: save
me for thy mercies' sake.
17 Let me not be ashamed, O LORD; for I have
called upon thee: let the wicked be ashamed, *and*
let them be silent in the grave.
18 Let the lying lips be put to silence; which speak
grievous things proudly and contemptuously
against the righteous.
19 *Oh* how great *is* thy goodness, which thou hast
laid up for them that fear thee; *which* thou hast
wrought for them that trust in thee before the
sons of men!
20 Thou shalt hide them in the secret of thy pres-
ence from the pride of man: thou shalt keep them
secretly in a pavilion from the strife of tongues.
21 Blessed *be* the LORD: for he hath shewed me his
marvellous kindness in a strong city.
22 For I said in my haste, I am cut off from before
thine eyes: nevertheless thou heardest the voice of
my supplications when I cried unto thee.
23 O love the LORD, all ye his saints: *for* the LORD
preserveth the faithful, and plentifully rewardeth
the proud doer.
24 Be of good courage, and he shall strengthen
your heart, all ye that hope in the LORD.

PSALM 32

A Psalm of David, Maschil.

1 BLESSED *is he whose* transgression *is* forgiven,
whose sin *is* covered.
2 Blessed *is* the man unto whom the LORD im-
puteth not iniquity, and in whose spirit *there is*
no guile.
3 When I kept silence, my bones waxed old
through my roaring all the day long.
4 For day and night thy hand was heavy upon

31:6 *hated.* Rejected. *lying vanities.* Literally, "breaths of nothingness," sometimes referring to idols (Jonah 2:8).
31:7 *mercy.* Covenant loyalty and love (v. 16). *trouble.* Misery or situation brought about by oppression. *my soul.* Me.
31:8 *large room.* A spacious place.
31:9 *Have mercy.* Be gracious or show undeserved favor. *my soul and my belly.* The totality of his being.
31:13 *fear was on every side.* See Jer. 20:3,10.
31:15 *My times are in thy hand.* God sovereignly controls all the events of his life (Eccl. 3:1–11).
31:16 *face to shine.* Evidence of favor (see note at 4:6).
31:20 *pavilion.* Booth or tent.
31:21 *kindness.* Covenant loyalty and love, same word as "mercy" (v. 7).
31:23 *plentifully rewardeth the proud doer.* Literally, "he repays abundantly the doer of arrogance."
31:24 *hope.* Wait in eager and confident expectation, an expression of faith.

Thoughts for Personal/Family Worship: Psalm 31

1. **If our trust is in God through Christ, we shall never be disappointed; instead, we may have strong confidence to face whatever is before us. We should not only believe in the sovereignty of God, but also apply it when in any trouble. Our times of sorrow and of joy are all in His hands. Though men may attack us with lies, God will hide us in His presence, and He has prepared rich goodness for our future with Him. How does it help you today to know that the best is yet to come for believers in Christ?**
2. **Even when Christ was broken on the cross and insulted by His enemies, He took up the prayer of this psalm and offered it to His Father, "Into thine hand I commit my spirit" (v. 5; Luke 23:46). His whole life was a model of submission to God's sovereign will (vv. 14–15). How does His example stir us to entrust ourselves to God?**

Psalm 32: *David describes the blessings of sins confessed to God and forgiven by God.*

32:1 This is the second of seven penitential psalms (Pss. 6; 32; 38; 51; 102; 130; 143). *transgression is forgiven . . . sin is covered.* A statement of justification in God's sight apart from the worthiness of one's works (Rom. 4:6–8).
32:2 *Blessed is the man.* Literally, "O the benefits of the man," one that is in a desirable position (1:1). *imputeth not iniquity.* Does not count as guilty of sin (2 Sam. 19:19). *guile.* Deception. Sincere repentance is necessary for forgiveness (v. 5; Luke 24:47; Acts 2:38; 5:31).
32:3–4 *waxed old.* Became brittle, wore out. *roaring.* Groaning. Sin in the life of a believer is a hostile presence producing turmoil and distress. Descriptions of physical problems (*bones*) represent the inner pain of the soul afflicted by an awakened conscience (see note at 51:8).

me: my moisture is turned into the drought of summer. Selah.
5 I acknowledged my sin unto thee, and mine iniquity have I not hid. I said, I will confess my transgressions unto the LORD; and thou forgavest the iniquity of my sin. Selah.
6 For this shall every one that is godly pray unto thee in a time when thou mayest be found: surely in the floods of great waters they shall not come nigh unto him.
7 Thou *art* my hiding place; thou shalt preserve me from trouble; thou shalt compass me about with songs of deliverance. Selah.
8 I will instruct thee and teach thee in the way which thou shalt go: I will guide thee with mine eye.
9 Be ye not as the horse, *or* as the mule, *which* have no understanding: whose mouth must be held in with bit and bridle, lest they come near unto thee.
10 Many sorrows *shall be* to the wicked: but he that trusteth in the LORD, mercy shall compass him about.
11 Be glad in the LORD, and rejoice, ye righteous: and shout for joy, all *ye that are* upright in heart.

PSALM 33

1 REJOICE in the LORD, O ye righteous: *for* praise is comely for the upright.
2 Praise the LORD with harp: sing unto him with the psaltery *and* an instrument of ten strings.
3 Sing unto him a new song; play skilfully with a loud noise.
4 For the word of the LORD *is* right; and all his works *are done* in truth.
5 He loveth righteousness and judgment: the earth is full of the goodness of the LORD.
6 By the word of the LORD were the heavens made; and all the host of them by the breath of his mouth.
7 He gathereth the waters of the sea together as an heap: he layeth up the depth in storehouses.
8 Let all the earth fear the LORD: let all the inhabitants of the world stand in awe of him.
9 For he spake, and it was *done*; he commanded, and it stood fast.
10 The LORD bringeth the counsel of the heathen to nought: he maketh the devices of the people of none effect.
11 The counsel of the LORD standeth for ever, the thoughts of his heart to all generations.

32:5 *acknowledged . . . confess.* Honest admission of one's responsibility for breaking God's law and the wrongness of it (51:3; Prov. 28:13). *forgavest the iniquity.* Took away the guilt (86:5; 1 John 1:9).
32:6 *in a time when thou mayest be found.* There is an urgency in seeking the Lord; delay is dangerous (Isa. 55:6).
32:7 *compass.* Surround (v. 10).
32:8 *I will guide thee with mine eye.* Or "I will advise; my eye is upon you."
32:10 *mercy.* Covenant loyalty and love.

Thoughts for Personal/Family Worship: Psalm 32

1. **The gospel of forgiveness is the basis of the repentant sinner's happiness. It is most wonderful to know that our sin is covered and forgiven. Though sin is offensive to God, He is ready to pardon and faithful to forgive sins as soon as we turn back to Him in honest confession. It is a foolish thing to go without confessing, for delay only causes misery of heart to the true Christian, and endangers the unbeliever with unending sorrows. It is pointless to try ourselves to cover our sins before the all-knowing God. However, when we stop making excuses and openly confess our guilt before God, we discover the blessedness of His forgiveness. Why is it so sweet to a sinner to know that he is completely forgiven by God?**
2. **The forgiveness of sinners is possible because of the death of Christ, represented to Old Testament Israel in promises of a suffering Savior (22:1; Gen. 3:15) and the types of the sacrifices (Lev. 4:20). Sin is not counted to believers because it was imputed to Christ (2 Cor. 5:21). The Lord Jesus bore the guilt of sin so that His people would be released from its consequences and its hold upon their consciences (Isa. 53:5–6; Heb. 9:14). God hears our prayers of confession because of Christ's prayers of intercession. How can you better incorporate prayers of confession into your daily habits?**

Psalm 33: *The psalmist commands praise to God for His works of creation and providence and His special care of His people.*
33:1 *Rejoice.* Exult or give a ringing cry. *comely.* Suitable or proper. Praise includes the acknowledgment of our glorious God, the celebration of His being, nature, and divine perfections.
33:2 *sing.* Play a stringed instrument, such as a *harp* (like a lyre) and *psaltery* (like a lute).
33:3 *Sing.* The basic word for singing; a different word than in v. 2. *play skilfully.* Literally, "make your playing good." *loud noise.* Jubilation or a shout of joy. Rejoicing in God is an important part of worship (100:1–2).
33:5 *goodness.* Covenant loyalty and love.
33:6 *By the word of the LORD.* Through His mere command, an evidence of infinite power and wisdom (Gen. 1:3; Heb. 11:3; 2 Peter 3:5), and an act of the personal Word, God's Son (John 1:1–3; Col. 1:16–17; Heb. 1:2–3). *host.* Army, here most likely the stars and planets (Gen. 2:1; Deut. 4:19). *breath of his mouth.* The divine agency fulfilling the word (Isa. 11:4; 34:16; 59:21), the activity of the Holy Spirit, the divine Agent (Gen. 1:2; cf. John 20:22).
33:7 *gathereth the waters.* God separated the waters to form the dry land (Gen. 1:9; Job 38:8–11). He demonstrated the same power to save Israel when He put the Red Sea and the Jordan River in a *heap* (78:13; Ex. 15:8; Josh. 3:13,16).
33:8–9 God's powerful works call *all* nations to give Him reverent worship and obedience.
33:10 *bringeth the counsel . . . to nought: he maketh the devices . . . of none effect.* God frustrates their intentions and nullifies their plans (Job 5:12–13; Isa. 19:3; 44:24–25).
33:11 *counsel . . . thoughts.* God's plan and His sovereign will are unchanging (*standeth for ever*) for they can never be frustrated by anyone (Dan. 4:35; Eph. 1:11).

12 Blessed *is* the nation whose God *is* the LORD;
and the people *whom* he hath chosen for his own
inheritance.
13 The LORD looketh from heaven; he beholdeth
all the sons of men.
14 From the place of his habitation he looketh
upon all the inhabitants of the earth.
15 He fashioneth their hearts alike; he consid-
ereth all their works.
16 There is no king saved by the multitude of
an host: a mighty man is not delivered by much
strength.
17 An horse *is* a vain thing for safety: neither shall
he deliver *any* by his great strength.
18 Behold, the eye of the LORD *is* upon them that
fear him, upon them that hope in his mercy;
19 To deliver their soul from death, and to keep
them alive in famine.
20 Our soul waiteth for the LORD: he *is* our help
and our shield.
21 For our heart shall rejoice in him, because we
have trusted in his holy name.
22 Let thy mercy, O LORD, be upon us, according
as we hope in thee.

PSALM 34

A Psalm of David, when he changed his behaviour before Abimelech; who drove him away, and he departed.

1 I WILL bless the LORD at all times: his praise
shall continually *be* in my mouth.
2 My soul shall make her boast in the LORD: the
humble shall hear *thereof*, and be glad.
3 O magnify the LORD with me, and let us exalt
his name together.
4 I sought the LORD, and he heard me, and
delivered me from all my fears.
5 They looked unto him, and were lightened: and
their faces were not ashamed.
6 This poor man cried, and the LORD heard *him*,
and saved him out of all his troubles.
7 The angel of the LORD encampeth round about
them that fear him, and delivereth them.
8 O taste and see that the LORD *is* good: blessed *is*
the man *that* trusteth in him.
9 O fear the LORD, ye his saints: for *there is* no
want to them that fear him.
10 The young lions do lack, and suffer hunger:

33:12 *the nation whose God is the LORD*. In the new covenant, this is not the theocratic nation of Israel but the church of Christ among all nations, including Jews and Gentiles (Matt. 21:43; 28:19; 1 Peter 2:9–10).
33:13 *sons of men*. All humanity.
33:15 *alike*. Together.
33:17 *vain thing*. A useless, unsubstantial, or deceptive thing.
33:18 *fear him*. This fear of the Lord is not a terror that drives people away from Him, but a trust that He is all He claims to be, resulting in humble worship (v. 8) and *hope in his mercy*.
33:19 *their soul*. Them.
33:20 *Our soul*. We. *waiteth*. Long for with patient yet eager expectancy and anticipation, an expression of faith.
33:21 *our heart*. Our innermost being (mind, will, and affections).
33:22 *mercy*. Covenant loyalty and love. *hope*. Wait with anticipation.

Thoughts for Personal/Family Worship: Psalm 33

1. **Joyful, reverent, and fervent praise springs from knowing God in His power. The denial of the doctrine of creation directly undermines the worship of God, as does the denial of His sovereign control over all things, including the hearts of men. Our God reigns over the whole world and no one can defeat His will. It is no small comfort to the church that His saving plan shall be fulfilled, no matter what mankind may do to thwart it. Faith in God's sovereignty produces both the fear of the Lord and hope in His faithful love. Why is it crucial for us to worship this aspect of Him?**
2. **Christ rejoiced in the sovereignty of God. He taught the doctrine of creation, arguing on that basis that the Creator has the authority to determine the meaning of marriage (Matt. 19:4–6). He revealed the Father's control over the smallest details of His creation (Matt. 6:26,30; 10:29–30). The Son of God also worshiped His Father for determining whom He would save through the gospel (Matt. 11:25–27). Furthermore, in His divine nature, Christ is the sovereign Creator (Heb. 1:2,10), the Son who with the Father and Spirit made all things and rules them for the salvation of God's elect (John 1:1–3; 17:2). Use this psalm as a song of worship for Christ, in whom we trust.**

Psalm 34: *David praises the Lord for the many benefits and privileges that belong to the righteous.*

Title *changed his behaviour before Abimelech*. David's deliverance from the Philistines to whom he retreated when escaping from Saul (1 Sam. 21:10–15).
34:1–7 Note the five words for praise. *bless*. Speak well of God on account of His benefits (103:1). *praise*. Declare His divine perfections (48:9–10). *boast*. Speak of His worth and value (44:4–8). *magnify*. Celebrate His infinite greatness (Job 36:24–26). *exalt*. Raise Him above and beyond all others in our thoughts and words (Isa. 25:1).
34:2 *humble*. Those who are weak or afflicted.
34:3 *magnify*. Make great (35:26); here, declare His greatness (35:27).
34:4 *heard*. Hebrew, "answered." *my fears*. The objects of dread or horror.
34:5 *were lightened*. Sparkled like a flowing river, a picture of radiant joy.
34:6 *poor man*. One in a needy and wretched condition. *troubles*. Needs, distresses, or anxieties (v. 17).
34:7 *The angel of the LORD*. The heavenly messenger sent by the Lord, who often also is the Lord, the second person of the Trinity (Isa. 63:9). *encampeth round about them*. Literally, "sets up his tent in a circle around them," like a protective army (Num. 1:50; 1 Sam. 26:5).
34:8 *taste and see*. These physical senses express spiritual perception and experience (119:103; 1 Peter 2:3). *blessed*. Possessing the many benefits of seeking and taking refuge (*trusteth*) in the Lord (1:1; 2:12; 32:1–2).
34:12–16 Cited in 1 Peter 3:10–12.

but they that seek the LORD shall not want any
good *thing.*
11 Come, ye children, hearken unto me: I will
teach you the fear of the LORD.
12 What man *is he that* desireth life, *and* loveth
many days, that he may see good?
13 Keep thy tongue from evil, and thy lips from
speaking guile.
14 Depart from evil, and do good; seek peace, and
pursue it.
15 The eyes of the LORD *are* upon the righteous,
and his ears *are open* unto their cry.
16 The face of the LORD *is* against them that do evil,
to cut off the remembrance of them from the earth.
17 *The righteous* cry, and the LORD heareth, and
delivereth them out of all their troubles.
18 The LORD *is* nigh unto them that are of a bro-
ken heart; and saveth such as be of a contrite spirit.
19 Many *are* the afflictions of the righteous: but
the LORD delivereth him out of them all.
20 He keepeth all his bones: not one of them is
broken.
21 Evil shall slay the wicked: and they that hate
the righteous shall be desolate.
22 The LORD redeemeth the soul of his servants:
and none of them that trust in him shall be desolate.

PSALM 35

A Psalm of David.

1 PLEAD *my cause,* O LORD, with them that strive
with me: fight against them that fight against me.
2 Take hold of shield and buckler, and stand up
for mine help.
3 Draw out also the spear, and stop *the way*
against them that persecute me: say unto my soul,
I *am* thy salvation.
4 Let them be confounded and put to shame that
seek after my soul: let them be turned back and
brought to confusion that devise my hurt.
5 Let them be as chaff before the wind: and let the
angel of the LORD chase *them.*
6 Let their way be dark and slippery: and let the
angel of the LORD persecute them.
7 For without cause have they hid for me their
net *in* a pit, *which* without cause they have digged
for my soul.
8 Let destruction come upon him at unawares;
and let his net that he hath hid catch himself: into
that very destruction let him fall.
9 And my soul shall be joyful in the LORD: it shall
rejoice in his salvation.
10 All my bones shall say, LORD, who *is* like unto
thee, which deliverest the poor from him that is
too strong for him, yea, the poor and the needy
from him that spoileth him?
11 False witnesses did rise up; they laid to my
charge *things* that I knew not.
12 They rewarded me evil for good *to* the spoiling
of my soul.
13 But as for me, when they were sick, my cloth-
ing *was* sackcloth: I humbled my soul with fasting;
and my prayer returned into mine own bosom.

34:13 *Keep thy tongue.* Guard your speech. *guile.* Fraud, deceit, or treachery.
34:18 *nigh . . . broken heart.* Near to those who are humbled and crushed (*contrite*) over sin (Isa. 57:15; 66:2).
34:21 *be desolate.* Be condemned as guilty, or suffer punishment (v. 22).

Thoughts for Personal/Family Worship: Psalm 34

1. **The title links this psalm to David's retreat to the Philistines in order to escape from Saul. In trying to flee from one enemy he ran to another, only to learn that salvation comes by fearing and trusting the Lord. Now through inspired song he would teach others to turn from sin and to humbly look to the Lord. The key to safety is repenting of sin and praying to God. In moments of crisis do you immediately seek help from the Lord or do you tend to depend on your own schemes? Why?**
2. **The statement, "Many are the afflictions of the righteous" (v. 19), applies to no one more than Jesus Christ. He experienced horrible pain and cried out to God in agony of soul (Heb. 5:7). Considering His sufferings, one may question this psalm's promises of protection for the faithful. How can they be true of anyone if not of God's Son? However, this psalm finds a surprising fulfillment in the crucified Lord, for even on the cross, not one of His bones was broken (v. 20; John 19:31–36). God was still with Christ, guaranteeing to the smallest detail that His mission as the Lamb of God would take place as promised (Ex. 12:46; Num. 9:12). In the same way, God does not promise to shield His faithful ones from all suffering, but He orders our sufferings so that nothing will defeat His good purposes for our lives (Rom. 8:28,35–39). How does this change the way we view the trials we face?**

Psalm 35: *David appeals to the Lord to defend him against those who attack him without cause.*

35:1 *Plead.* Strive or carry on a lawsuit as his advocate. *them that strive.* His adversaries or legal opponents (same root as *plead*). *fight.* The Lord is the divine warrior (Ex. 14:14,25; 2 Chron. 20:17,29). David desired the Lord to defend him legally and physically.
35:2 *shield and buckler.* A large, full-body shield, and a small, more mobile shield (the Hebrew text has these in the opposite order of the English).
35:3 *my soul.* Me (vv. 4,7).
35:4 *put to shame.* Humiliated.
35:5–6 *angel of the LORD.* See note at 34:7. *dark.* Or confusion.
35:8 *at unawares.* Without his knowledge, that is, by surprise.
35:9 *my soul shall . . . it shall.* A Hebrew idiom for "I will."
35:10 *my bones.* A Hebrew expression for "myself" or my total identity. *poor.* The weak or afflicted. *spoileth.* Robs.
35:11 *False witnesses.* Literally, "witnesses of violence or wrong," describing their character. *laid to my charge.* Literally, "asked me."
35:12 *spoiling of my soul.* My loss.
35:13 *sackcloth.* Garments symbolizing grief or sorrow. *my prayer returned into mine own bosom.* He prayed with his head bowed in sadness. David did not respond in kind to those who

14 I behaved myself as though *he had been* my
friend *or* brother: I bowed down heavily, as one
that mourneth *for his* mother.
15 But in mine adversity they rejoiced, and
gathered themselves together: *yea*, the abjects
gathered themselves together against me, and I
knew *it* not; they did tear *me*, and ceased not:
16 With hypocritical mockers in feasts, they
gnashed upon me with their teeth.
17 Lord, how long wilt thou look on? rescue my
soul from their destructions, my darling from the
lions.
18 I will give thee thanks in the great congregation:
I will praise thee among much people.
19 Let not them that are mine enemies wrong-
fully rejoice over me: *neither* let them wink with
the eye that hate me without a cause.
20 For they speak not peace: but they devise
deceitful matters against *them that are* quiet in
the land.
21 Yea, they opened their mouth wide against me,
and said, Aha, aha, our eye hath seen *it*.
22 *This* thou hast seen, O LORD: keep not silence:
O Lord, be not far from me.
23 Stir up thyself, and awake to my judgment,
even unto my cause, my God and my Lord.
24 Judge me, O LORD my God, according to thy
righteousness; and let them not rejoice over me.
25 Let them not say in their hearts, Ah, so would
we have it: let them not say, We have swallowed
him up.
26 Let them be ashamed and brought to
confusion together that rejoice at mine hurt: let
them be clothed with shame and dishonour that
magnify *themselves* against me.
27 Let them shout for joy, and be glad, that favour
my righteous cause: yea, let them say continually,
Let the LORD be magnified, which hath pleasure
in the prosperity of his servant.
28 And my tongue shall speak of thy righteous-
ness *and* of thy praise all the day long.

PSALM 36

To the chief Musician, *A Psalm* of David the servant of the LORD.

1 THE transgression of the wicked saith within my
heart, *that there is* no fear of God before his eyes.
2 For he flattereth himself in his own eyes, until
his iniquity be found to be hateful.
3 The words of his mouth *are* iniquity and deceit:
he hath left off to be wise, *and* to do good.
4 He deviseth mischief upon his bed; he setteth
himself in a way *that is* not good; he abhorreth
not evil.
5 Thy mercy, O LORD, *is* in the heavens; *and* thy
faithfulness *reacheth* unto the clouds.
6 Thy righteousness *is* like the great mountains;
thy judgments *are* a great deep: O LORD, thou
preservest man and beast.
7 How excellent *is* thy lovingkindness, O God!
therefore the children of men put their trust
under the shadow of thy wings.

---

did him wrong, a mark of spiritual love (Rom. 12:17–21; 1 Cor. 13:4–7).

35:15 *in mine adversity*. When I stumbled. *abjects*. Those crippled or beaten down.

35:16 *hypocritical mockers*. Godless ones of mockery. *gnashed . . . teeth*. A gesture of rage (Acts 7:54).

35:17 *my darling*. My only one, referring to his precious life.

35:19 *them . . . that hate me without a cause*. The unjust who persecute the righteous (69:4), especially true of the sinless Lord Jesus (John 15:25).

35:20 *devise deceitful matters*. To plan words of fraud or treachery. *quiet*. Restful, at peace.

35:21 *Aha, aha*. The actual Hebrew words, an interjection expressing malicious joy.

35:25 *Ah*. Same as "aha" (v. 21).

Thoughts for Personal/Family Worship: Psalm 35

1. **One of the most perplexing experiences of the righteous is facing false accusations from those whom we have loved. Such charges can break our hearts, mar our good reputation, and bring down unjust legal and social consequences. In life's troubles and conflicts, we must always remember that God is ready to stand for our defense. If we belong to Jesus Christ, then He is our Judge and Advocate. A desire for vindication is not necessarily selfish or vengeful, for God is glorified in the good of His servants (v. 27). How then should we pray in such circumstances?**
2. **Christ wept over sinners in His compassion (Luke 19:41), but the wicked hated Him without cause (John 15:25). They accused the Innocent One of blasphemy against God and rebellion against the state, producing many false witnesses in their scrambling attempts to condemn Him to death (Matt. 26:59; Mark 14:57). Though He loved them, He also proclaimed the judgment of God against them for murdering the Son of God (Matt. 21:33–44; Luke 19:27,42–44). God raised Him from the dead and is now greatly glorified in the display of His pleasure in His Son. How can Christ's experiences give us comfort and hope when we suffer unjustly for His sake?**

Psalm 36: *David contrasts the ways of the wicked with the mercy of the Lord.*

36:1 *no fear of God*. Fallen mankind has lost all proper reverence for God's majesty (Rom. 3:18), a failure of man's fundamental duty to God (Eccl. 12:13).

36:3 *be wise*. Act prudently.

36:4 *mischief*. Sin, wickedness, injustice. *he abhorreth not*. He does not reject or refuse.

36:5–6 *mercy*. Covenant loyalty and love. *great mountains*. Literally, "the mountains of God." *judgments*. Acts of justice. The comparisons communicate the awe-inspiring majesty and magnitude of God's moral perfections (57:10; 103:11; Eph. 3:18–19).

36:7 *excellent*. Precious or valuable. *lovingkindness*. Covenant loyalty and love (v. 10), same word as "mercy" (v. 5). *put their*

8 They shall be abundantly satisfied with the
fatness of thy house; and thou shalt make them
drink of the river of thy pleasures.
9 For with thee *is* the fountain of life: in thy light
shall we see light.
10 O continue thy lovingkindness unto them that
know thee; and thy righteousness to the upright
in heart.
11 Let not the foot of pride come against me, and
let not the hand of the wicked remove me.
12 There are the workers of iniquity fallen: they
are cast down, and shall not be able to rise.

PSALM 37

A Psalm of David.

1 FRET not thyself because of evildoers, neither
be thou envious against the workers of iniquity.
2 For they shall soon be cut down like the grass,
and wither as the green herb.
3 Trust in the LORD, and do good; *so* shalt thou
dwell in the land, and verily thou shalt be fed.
4 Delight thyself also in the LORD; and he shall
give thee the desires of thine heart.
5 Commit thy way unto the LORD; trust also in
him; and he shall bring *it* to pass.
6 And he shall bring forth thy righteousness as
the light, and thy judgment as the noonday.
7 Rest in the LORD, and wait patiently for him:
fret not thyself because of him who prospereth in
his way, because of the man who bringeth wicked
devices to pass.
8 Cease from anger, and forsake wrath: fret not
thyself in any wise to do evil.
9 For evildoers shall be cut off: but those that
wait upon the LORD, they shall inherit the earth.
10 For yet a little while, and the wicked *shall* not
be: yea, thou shalt diligently consider his place,
and it *shall* not *be*.
11 But the meek shall inherit the earth; and shall
delight themselves in the abundance of peace.
12 The wicked plotteth against the just, and
gnasheth upon him with his teeth.
13 The Lord shall laugh at him: for he seeth that
his day is coming.
14 The wicked have drawn out the sword, and
have bent their bow, to cast down the poor and
needy, *and* to slay such as be of upright conver-
sation.
15 Their sword shall enter into their own heart,
and their bows shall be broken.
16 A little that a righteous man hath *is* better than
the riches of many wicked.
17 For the arms of the wicked shall be broken:
but the LORD upholdeth the righteous.

---

trust. Seek and find refuge or safety. *shadow of thy wings*. See note at 17:8.

36:8 *fatness*. Prosperity, or the best of something (Gen. 27:28). *thy house*. Truly abundant life is found in God's presence (92:12–13).

36:10 *continue*. Hebrew, "keep stretched out."

Thoughts for Personal/Family Worship: Psalm 36

1. **This psalm reveals the horrible corruption of the human heart. Though created by God and living in His world, man does not honor the Lord with true reverence. Instead of glorifying God, he flatters himself. His heart is a constant fountain of lies and evil. Despite all his pride, his destiny is to be cast down, never to rise again. This diagnosis reveals the desperate need of humanity for Jesus Christ. They need Christ to give them a new heart by His Spirit so that they will repent, and receive forgiveness for their sins so that God will not punish them. See in this psalm a description of yourself as you are by nature. How does it affect you?**
2. **In amazing contrast to the wickedness of man, the perfect character of God shines like a thousand diamonds in this text. God's love, faithfulness, righteousness, and justice tower over mankind like an awesome range of mountains, and elude our full comprehension like the depths of the ocean. Yet God does not stand aloof from fallen man, but He draws sinners to Him through faith in Christ so that His goodness becomes their eternal satisfaction. The gospel call is an invitation to a feast, and Christ is both the host and the food for sinners. Are you hungry? Are you eating?**

Psalm 37: *David exhorts trust in God even in the face of apparent inequities in life, particularly regarding the prosperity of the wicked (cf. Pss. 49; 73).*

37:1 *Fret not*. Do not get hot with anger (vv. 7–8). *workers of iniquity*. People characterized by a lifestyle of disobedience to God, and thus on the path to condemnation from God (Matt. 7:23).

37:3 *Trust . . . do good*. Faith produces good works (Matt. 5:16; James 2:14–17). *verily thou shalt be fed*. Literally, "graze on faithfulness."

37:4 *Delight thyself . . . desires of thine heart*. God is the chief pleasure of man (16:11; 36:8–9) and will not withhold Himself from those who seek Him as their joy and desire (105:3–4; Isa. 55:6; James 4:8), together with all that they need (Matt. 6:33).

37:5 *Commit thy way*. Roll your cares and concerns on the Lord (Matt. 6:8,25; 1 Peter 5:7).

37:7 *Rest in the LORD*. Be silent before the Lord. *wait patiently*. Wait longingly with expectant anticipation, an expression of faith.

37:9 *wait*. Hope, not in resignation but expectancy (v. 34; different word than in v. 7).

37:11 *the meek*. The humble, weak, or afflicted. *inherit the earth*. Receive from God a portion in the land promised in God's covenant (vv. 9,22,29,34; Gen. 15:7; 28:4), a type of God's eternal kingdom (v. 18). Christ based one of His Beatitudes on this text (Matt. 5:5).

37:13 *The Lord shall laugh*. The sovereign Master (Hebrew, *adonay*) will despise the puny and foolish attempts of the wicked to fight against Him (2:4; Prov. 1:26).

37:14 *conversation*. Behavior.

37:16 *better than the riches*. God's economy is different from man's, for happiness is not found in material wealth (Prov. 15:16; 16:8; 1 Tim. 6:6).

18 The LORD knoweth the days of the upright:
and their inheritance shall be for ever.
19 They shall not be ashamed in the evil time:
and in the days of famine they shall be satisfied.
20 But the wicked shall perish, and the enemies
of the LORD *shall be* as the fat of lambs: they shall
consume; into smoke shall they consume away.
21 The wicked borroweth, and payeth not again:
but the righteous sheweth mercy, and giveth.
22 For *such as be* blessed of him shall inherit the
earth; and *they that be* cursed of him shall be cut
off.
23 The steps of a *good* man are ordered by the
LORD: and he delighteth in his way.
24 Though he fall, he shall not be utterly cast
down: for the LORD upholdeth *him with* his hand.
25 I have been young, and *now* am old; yet have
I not seen the righteous forsaken, nor his seed
begging bread.
26 *He is* ever merciful, and lendeth; and his seed
is blessed.
27 Depart from evil, and do good; and dwell for
evermore.
28 For the LORD loveth judgment, and forsaketh
not his saints; they are preserved for ever: but the
seed of the wicked shall be cut off.
29 The righteous shall inherit the land, and dwell
therein for ever.
30 The mouth of the righteous speaketh wisdom,
and his tongue talketh of judgment.
31 The law of his God *is* in his heart; none of his
steps shall slide.
32 The wicked watcheth the righteous, and
seeketh to slay him.
33 The LORD will not leave him in his hand, nor
condemn him when he is judged.
34 Wait on the LORD, and keep his way, and he
shall exalt thee to inherit the land: when the
wicked are cut off, thou shalt see *it*.
35 I have seen the wicked in great power, and
spreading himself like a green bay tree.
36 Yet he passed away, and, lo, he *was* not: yea, I
sought him, but he could not be found.
37 Mark the perfect *man*, and behold the upright:
for the end of *that* man *is* peace.
38 But the transgressors shall be destroyed
together: the end of the wicked shall be cut off.
39 But the salvation of the righteous *is* of the
LORD: *he is* their strength in the time of trouble.
40 And the LORD shall help them, and deliver
them: he shall deliver them from the wicked, and
save them, because they trust in him.

PSALM 38

A Psalm of David, to bring to remembrance.

1 O LORD, rebuke me not in thy wrath: neither
chasten me in thy hot displeasure.
2 For thine arrows stick fast in me, and thy hand
presseth me sore.
3 *There is* no soundness in my flesh because of
thine anger; neither *is there any* rest in my bones
because of my sin.

37:18 *knoweth*. Not just in the sense of awareness, but intentional care (1:6).
37:19 *not be ashamed in the evil time*. Not be disappointed in the hard times.
37:20 *fat of lambs*. Could be translated, "excellence of pastures" (cf. 65:13), the beauty of grass and flowers that quickly wither and die (v. 2; Isa. 40:6–8; Matt. 6:30).
37:21 *sheweth mercy*. Gives grace to the needy though they do not deserve it, a characteristic of *the righteous* (Matt. 5:7).
37:23 *ordered*. Established.
37:24 God will not allow the trials of the righteous to ultimately destroy them (Prov. 24:16; Mic. 7:8).
37:26 *is . . . merciful*. See note at v. 21.
37:28 *judgment*. Justice. *his saints*. The recipients of His covenant loyalty and love. *seed*. Offspring, representing their long-term future.
37:29 *inherit the land*. See note at v. 11.
37:31 *law of his God is in his heart*. God's saving grace regenerates sinners and gives them a new desire to obey by union with Christ in the Holy Spirit (40:8; Jer. 31:33; Ezek. 36:27; Titus 3:3–8).
37:35 *green bay tree*. A tree in its native soil.

Thoughts for Personal/Family Worship: Psalm 37

1. **The success of the wicked tests the faith of the righteous. The apparent contradiction between the promises of prosperity to the godly (1:3) and our experiences in a fallen world can provoke us to confusion, anxiety, and bitterness. This psalm encourages believers to look to the Lord in faith, and look forward to the future with hope. Resting in the Lord and seeking happiness in Him provides contentment regardless of life's circumstances. By faith in God's promises, we see the end of all things and know that the wicked, though prospering in this life, have no future, but the righteous will receive a glorious inheritance. How do you need to put these two principles into practice?**
2. **The Lord Jesus used the wisdom of this psalm in the Sermon on the Mount (Matt. 5:5,7,16; 6:8,25,30,33; 7:23). He also exemplified the life recommended here through His trust in His Father, delight in Him, good works, patient endurance of the wicked, meekness and self-restraint, and hope in a future inheritance. Thus His mouth spoke wisdom because the law of God filled His heart (vv. 30–31). This gives Him all the more moral authority to call us to embrace Ps. 37 as well. How does this show us the importance of having a teacher of God's Word who also lives out God's Word in his own life?**

Psalm 38: ***David confesses his sins, acknowledging the cause of his plight, and pleads with God to help him.***

38:1 *chasten*. Discipline, correct.
38:2 *thine arrows*. The imagery of physical and medical harm, though perhaps reflecting the circumstances of divine discipline, point deeper to painful conviction of sin from God upon the conscience (32:3–4). *stick fast*. Go down into. *presseth me sore*. Comes down upon me. Both are forms of the

4 For mine iniquities are gone over mine head: as
an heavy burden they are too heavy for me.
5 My wounds stink *and* are corrupt because of
my foolishness.
6 I am troubled; I am bowed down greatly; I go
mourning all the day long.
7 For my loins are filled with a loathsome *disease*:
and *there is* no soundness in my flesh.
8 I am feeble and sore broken: I have roared by
reason of the disquietness of my heart.
9 Lord, all my desire *is* before thee; and my
groaning is not hid from thee.
10 My heart panteth, my strength faileth me: as
for the light of mine eyes, it also is gone from me.
11 My lovers and my friends stand aloof from my
sore; and my kinsmen stand afar off.
12 They also that seek after my life lay snares *for*
me: and they that seek my hurt speak mischievous
things, and imagine deceits all the day long.
13 But I, as a deaf *man*, heard not; and *I was* as a
dumb man *that* openeth not his mouth.
14 Thus I was as a man that heareth not, and in
whose mouth *are* no reproofs.
15 For in thee, O LORD, do I hope: thou wilt hear,
O Lord my God.
16 For I said, *Hear me*, lest *otherwise* they should
rejoice over me: when my foot slippeth, they
magnify *themselves* against me.
17 For I *am* ready to halt, and my sorrow *is*
continually before me.
18 For I will declare mine iniquity; I will be sorry
for my sin.
19 But mine enemies *are* lively, *and* they are
strong: and they that hate me wrongfully are
multiplied.
20 They also that render evil for good are mine
adversaries; because I follow *the thing that* good *is*.
21 Forsake me not, O LORD: O my God, be not
far from me.
22 Make haste to help me, O Lord my salvation.

PSALM 39

To the chief Musician, *even* to Jeduthun,
A Psalm of David.

1 I SAID, I will take heed to my ways, that I sin
not with my tongue: I will keep my mouth with a
bridle, while the wicked is before me.
2 I was dumb with silence, I held my peace, *even*
from good; and my sorrow was stirred.
3 My heart was hot within me, while I was mus-
ing the fire burned: *then* spake I with my tongue,
4 LORD, make me to know mine end, and the
measure of my days, what it *is; that* I may know
how frail I *am*.
5 Behold, thou hast made my days *as* an
handbreadth; and mine age *is* as nothing before
thee: verily every man at his best state *is* altogether
vanity. Selah.

---

same Hebrew verb, "go down."

38:3 *soundness*. Healthy part (v. 7). *rest*. Peace or health.

38:5 *My wounds stink and are corrupt*. Infection has aggravated my injury.

38:6 *troubled*. Bent, twisted, with the sense of being irritated.

38:7 *loathsome disease*. Literally, "burning," perhaps fever.

38:8 *feeble*. Faint or powerless. *sore broken*. Completely crushed. *roared*. Groaned loudly. *disquietness*. Growls or groanings.

38:10 *panteth*. Palpitates, throbs violently.

38:11 *lovers*. People who loved him. *sore*. Wound or disease. They are treating him like a leper.

38:12 *mischievous things*. Threats. *deceits*. Fraud or treachery.

38:14 *reproofs*. Retorts or contradictions. He could offer no self-defense.

38:15 *hope*. Wait with expectancy. Salvation from sin comes by faith in the Lord.

38:16 *magnify*. Make great.

38:17 *halt*. Stumble or fall.

38:18 *declare mine iniquity . . . sorry for my sin*. Sorrow over how one's sin dishonors and offends God and confession of one's wrongdoings are essential to repentance and receiving God's forgiveness (32:2,5; 2 Cor. 7:9–11).

38:19–20 *lively*. Active. *hate me wrongfully*. When the godly sin, the wicked seize the opportunity to attack them, not because the wicked hate sin, but because they hate godliness (*because I follow . . . good*).

Thoughts for Personal/Family Worship: Psalm 38

1. Without the realization of our sinfulness, we will not feel any need for the Savior. The Holy Spirit applies the law of God to the conscience to produce a piercing conviction of sin, a sense of God's wrath, and a cry for salvation (John 16:8; Acts 2:37; 16:27,30; Rom. 3:20; 4:15). The mark of a believer is turning back to God with hatred of sin and prayers for mercy. Even if our friends turn away from us in our distress, we can rest assured that the Father of our Lord Jesus Christ is full of mercy to repentant sinners (Luke 15:17–24). Is the Lord convicting you of sin? How are you responding?

2. If conviction of sin horrifies sinners, what must it have been like for Christ to experience the guilt of countless sinners placed upon His sinless person (Isa. 53:6)? This troubled Him deeply (John 12:27). In the garden of Gethsemane, Jesus staggered under a fearful apprehension of divine wrath (Mark 14:33). His situation was aggravated further when He was surrounded by those who hated Him without cause (John 15:25). His best friends abandoned Him (Matt. 26:31). Yet as He agonized on the cross, bearing our sins, He entrusted Himself to God (1 Peter 2:23–24). When we come under conviction of sin, we can find relief by faith in Him because He was crushed for sinners. How should this both humble and release us?

Psalm 39: *David reflects on the brevity of life and expresses his hope in the Lord.*

39:1 *take heed*. Guard.

39:2 *I held my peace*. Literally, "I was quiet."

39:4 *frail*. Transient, fleeting.

39:5 *mine age*. My life-span, the duration of my life. *verily*. Indeed, truly. *every man at his best state*. Every man who stands firm. *vanity*. Literally, "a breath" (Eccl. 1:2), that which is

6 Surely every man walketh in a vain shew: surely
they are disquieted in vain: he heapeth up *riches*,
and knoweth not who shall gather them.
7 And now, Lord, what wait I for? my hope *is* in thee.
8 Deliver me from all my transgressions: make me
not the reproach of the foolish.
9 I was dumb, I opened not my mouth; because
thou didst *it*.
10 Remove thy stroke away from me: I am consumed by the blow of thine hand.
11 When thou with rebukes dost correct man for
iniquity, thou makest his beauty to consume away
like a moth: surely every man *is* vanity. Selah.
12 Hear my prayer, O LORD, and give ear unto
my cry; hold not thy peace at my tears: for I *am*
a stranger with thee, *and* a sojourner, as all my
fathers *were*.
13 O spare me, that I may recover strength, before
I go hence, and be no more.

PSALM 40

To the chief Musician, A Psalm of David.

1 I WAITED patiently for the LORD; and he inclined unto me, and heard my cry.
2 He brought me up also out of an horrible pit,
out of the miry clay, and set my feet upon a rock,
and established my goings.
3 And he hath put a new song in my mouth, *even*
praise unto our God: many shall see *it*, and fear,
and shall trust in the LORD.
4 Blessed *is* that man that maketh the LORD his
trust, and respecteth not the proud, nor such as
turn aside to lies.
5 Many, O LORD my God, *are* thy wonderful
works *which* thou hast done, and thy thoughts
which are to us-ward: they cannot be reckoned up
in order unto thee: *if* I would declare and speak *of*
them, they are more than can be numbered.
6 Sacrifice and offering thou didst not desire;
mine ears hast thou opened: burnt offering and
sin offering hast thou not required.
7 Then said I, Lo, I come: in the volume of the
book *it is* written of me,
8 I delight to do thy will, O my God: yea, thy law
is within my heart.
9 I have preached righteousness in the great
congregation: lo, I have not refrained my lips, O
LORD, thou knowest.
10 I have not hid thy righteousness within my
heart; I have declared thy faithfulness and thy salvation: I have not concealed thy lovingkindness
and thy truth from the great congregation.
11 Withhold not thou thy tender mercies from
me, O LORD: let thy lovingkindness and thy truth
continually preserve me.
12 For innumerable evils have compassed me

---

temporal and unsubstantial (v. 11).

39:6 *vain shew*. A fleeting shadow, an empty image. *they are disquieted in vain*. Literally, "a breath, they bustle about." *heapeth up*. Death makes the pursuit of wealth futile (49:10; Eccl. 2:18–19,26; 5:13–16; Luke 12:16–21).

39:7 *wait*. Look eagerly for. *hope*. Expectation.

39:12 *hold not thy peace*. Do not be deaf or silent. *stranger . . . sojourner*. Resident aliens.

39:13 *recover strength*. Become cheerful.

Thoughts for Personal/Family Worship: Psalm 39

1. **Emotional outbursts do not honor God. The believer needs to keep a careful watch of his tongue, for it can be the instrument of many sins. Particularly when under pressure, we must do everything to ensure that what we say is ordered by grace, pleasing to God, and edifying to others. Controlling our mouths also helps us to engage our minds to think about life's uncertainty, brevity, frailty, vanity, futility, anxiety, and stupidity (if we live for this world). As foreigners in this world, how can we, as Christians, discipline ourselves to fix our hope on God?**
2. **Christ was resolved not to sin, not even in His speech when wicked men taunted Him (1 Peter 2:21–23). This was particularly evident at the end of His life when, arraigned before the Jewish and Gentile rulers of the nation, He maintained a dignified silence (Isa. 53:7; Matt. 26:63; Luke 23:9–10; John 19:8–9). However, Christ was human, and we must not forget the holy power He had to exercise in order to control Himself in this way. That same power comes to believers in Christ through the Holy Spirit. How can we draw from Christ's self-control to grow in holy quietness?**

Psalm 40: *David offers praise for God's deliverance, which finds its ultimate expression in the Messiah.*

40:1 *I waited patiently*. I indeed or certainly waited in eager expectancy.

40:2 *horrible pit*. A pit of noise or roaring, a tumultuous place. *miry clay*. Mire of mud. *rock*. A cliff, representing stability and safety. *goings*. Steps.

40:4 *Blessed*. Having great benefits (1:1; 32:1–2). *respecteth not*. Does not face, in the sense of showing favor to.

40:5 *to us-ward*. Toward us. *they cannot be reckoned up in order unto thee*. There is none to compare to Thee.

40:6 *Sacrifice and offering*. The outward rituals were no substitute for obedience to God from the heart (1 Sam. 15:22; Hos. 6:6; Mic. 6:6–8) and pointed to Christ's obedience unto death (Heb. 10:5–10). *mine ears hast thou opened*. Literally, "two ears Thou hast dug out for me," a figure of speech for submission to God as His servant forever (Ex. 21:6; Isa. 50:5). The part (ear) stands for the whole (giving up the whole body or life to God; cf. Heb. 10:5).

40:7 *volume of the book*. Scroll of the writing. David knew that Scripture would be fulfilled in his greatest descendant (Luke 24:27,44; Acts 2:30).

40:8 *thy law is within my heart*. Not just in knowing the teachings and demands of God's Word, but in deeply desiring to obey it because one loves God and it is God's *will* (37:31; 119:11; Deut. 6:5–6; Job 22:22; Isa. 51:7).

40:9 *refrained*. Restrained.

40:10 *lovingkindness*. Covenant loyalty and love (v. 11).

40:12 *evils*. Dangers. *compassed*. Surrounded. *more than the hairs*. Even a godly man must acknowledge that he is guilty of sins beyond counting. *my heart faileth me*. His courage forsakes him.

about: mine iniquities have taken hold upon me,
so that I am not able to look up; they are more
than the hairs of mine head: therefore my heart
faileth me.
13 Be pleased, O LORD, to deliver me: O LORD,
make haste to help me.
14 Let them be ashamed and confounded
together that seek after my soul to destroy it; let
them be driven backward and put to shame that
wish me evil.
15 Let them be desolate for a reward of their
shame that say unto me, Aha, aha.
16 Let all those that seek thee rejoice and be glad
in thee: let such as love thy salvation say continually, The LORD be magnified.
17 But I *am* poor and needy; *yet* the Lord thinketh upon me: thou *art* my help and my deliverer;
make no tarrying, O my God.

PSALM 41

To the chief Musician, A Psalm of David.

1 BLESSED *is* he that considereth the poor: the
LORD will deliver him in time of trouble.
2 The LORD will preserve him, and keep him
alive; *and* he shall be blessed upon the earth:
and thou wilt not deliver him unto the will of his
enemies.
3 The LORD will strengthen him upon the bed
of languishing: thou wilt make all his bed in his
sickness.
4 I said, LORD, be merciful unto me: heal my soul;
for I have sinned against thee.
5 Mine enemies speak evil of me, When shall he
die, and his name perish?
6 And if he come to see *me*, he speaketh vanity:
his heart gathereth iniquity to itself; *when* he
goeth abroad, he telleth *it*.
7 All that hate me whisper together against me:
against me do they devise my hurt.
8 An evil disease, *say they*, cleaveth fast unto him:
and *now* that he lieth he shall rise up no more.
9 Yea, mine own familiar friend, in whom I
trusted, which did eat of my bread, hath lifted up
his heel against me.
10 But thou, O LORD, be merciful unto me, and
raise me up, that I may requite them.
11 By this I know that thou favourest me, because
mine enemy doth not triumph over me.
12 And as for me, thou upholdest me in mine
integrity, and settest me before thy face for ever.
13 Blessed *be* the LORD God of Israel from everlasting, and to everlasting. Amen, and Amen.

40:13–17 These words are largely repeated in Ps. 70.
40:13 *make haste.* Hurry.
40:14 *confounded.* Disappointed. *evil.* Harm.
40:15 *Let them be desolate for a reward.* Let them shudder in consequence of their shame. *Aha, aha.* The actual Hebrew words, an interjection of malicious joy.
40:16 *magnified.* Made great, in the sense of declaring how great He is.
40:17 *make no tarrying.* Do not delay or hesitate.

Thoughts for Personal/Family Worship: Psalm 40

1. **Even in the Old Testament, the righteous understood that animal sacrifices could not please God, who desires sincere and perfect obedience from people (vv. 6–8). However, God had instituted the sacrifices to give people a picture of atonement by substitution. These two great themes of Scripture come together in Christ's work of complete atonement by perfect obedience (Heb. 10:5–10). Christ took up the words of this psalm when He came to do the will of His Father who sent Him to save the world (John 4:34; 5:30; 6:38–40). God's will required His descent into the horrible pit of death under God's curse for sins more numerable than the hairs of His head (John 10:17–18; Gal. 1:4; 3:10,13). The incarnate God willingly humbled Himself and obeyed all the way to the cross (Phil. 2:6–8). Because of Christ's obedience His Father exalted Him to the highest place (Phil. 2:9–11). Take time to extol Him in worship.**
2. **Perfect delight in obeying God's will characterizes Christ alone among all who have walked upon this earth. Yet He shares His heart of obedience by His Spirit with the people in union with Him (119:32; Deut. 30:6,8; 2 Chron. 30:12; Jer. 31:33; Rom. 7:22; 2 Cor. 3:3; Heb. 8:10; 10:7,16). True believers can never be satisfied with merely going through the motions of outward worship. What is the evidence that by grace a person delights to do God's will and that God's law is within his heart?**

Psalm 41: *David prays for God's mercy as he is being betrayed by those close to him.*

41:1 *Blessed.* Possessing great benefits (1:1). *considereth the poor.* Gives attention and assistance to the helpless or weak (Lev. 25:35; John 13:29; Rom. 12:13; Gal. 2:10), a mark of true salvation (Matt. 25:31–36; 1 John 3:14–19).
41:2 *preserve.* Guard or watch over.
41:3 *strengthen.* Sustain or support. *wilt make.* Will overturn, alter, or transform. Overturning the sick bed refers to healing.
41:4 *be merciful.* Be gracious or show undeserved favor (v. 10). *my soul.* Me.
41:6 *vanity.* Emptiness or falsehood.
41:8 *An evil disease.* Literally, "a thing of Belial," referring to something wicked, base, or useless. *cleaveth fast.* Clings to; Hebrew, "is poured out on."
41:9 *mine own familiar friend.* Literally, "the man of my peace." *lifted up his heel against me.* An image of treachery or craftiness, using the root of Jacob's name (Gen. 25:26; 27:36). Christ quoted this verse with regard to His betrayal by the apostle Judas (John 13:18).
41:10 *requite.* Repay or pay back.
41:11 *favourest.* Take pleasure or delight in.
41:13 *Blessed.* A word of praise, not the same word as v. 1. This doxology concludes the first book of the Psalms (see Introduction: Major Problems of Interpretation; Collection and Arrangement).

Thoughts for Personal/Family Worship: Psalm 41

When misunderstood and misrepresented, we should remember that this has always been the experience

PSALM 42

To the chief Musician, Maschil,
for the sons of Korah.

1 As the hart panteth after the water brooks, so
panteth my soul after thee, O God.
2 My soul thirsteth for God, for the living God:
when shall I come and appear before God?
3 My tears have been my meat day and night, while
they continually say unto me, Where *is* thy God?
4 When I remember these *things*, I pour out my
soul in me: for I had gone with the multitude, I
went with them to the house of God, with the
voice of joy and praise, with a multitude that kept
holyday.
5 Why art thou cast down, O my soul? and *why*
art thou disquieted in me? hope thou in God: for I
shall yet praise him *for* the help of his countenance.
6 O my God, my soul is cast down within me:
therefore will I remember thee from the land of
Jordan, and of the Hermonites, from the hill Mizar.
7 Deep calleth unto deep at the noise of thy
waterspouts: all thy waves and thy billows are
gone over me.
8 *Yet* the LORD will command his lovingkindness
in the daytime, and in the night his song *shall be*
with me, *and* my prayer unto the God of my life.
9 I will say unto God my rock, Why hast thou
forgotten me? why go I mourning because of the
oppression of the enemy?
10 *As* with a sword in my bones, mine enemies
reproach me; while they say daily unto me, Where
is thy God?
11 Why art thou cast down, O my soul? and why
art thou disquieted within me? hope thou in God:
for I shall yet praise him, *who is* the health of my
countenance, and my God.

PSALM 43

1 JUDGE me, O God, and plead my cause against
an ungodly nation: O deliver me from the deceit-
ful and unjust man.

of God's people (and was the experience of the Lord Himself). This happens to believers because they have grace, which is no small comfort. In all life's conflicts, they must look up and realize that God, in love, is looking down. The Lord Jesus fully understands the pain of treachery and betrayal, for He experienced it from one of His own apostles. He looks upon Christians with great sympathy as their hearts are broken through unfaithful friends. Through the love of our God, they shall persevere and endure; and one day, set before His face, they shall know that it has been worth it all to behold Him in His glory. In the meantime, how can giving ourselves to serving people in need, strengthen our assurance in God's faithfulness?

BOOK 2 (PSS. 42:1—72:20)

Psalm 42: *The psalmist expresses his desire for the Lord, whose presence is the only hope for depression.*

Title *sons of Korah*. A reminder of the wonder of grace. Korah was a Levite who, along with others, suffered divine judgment for rebellion (Num. 16). However, not all the sons of Korah shared his doom (Num. 26:9–11). Under King David, his descendants became leaders of psalm singing in the house of God (1 Chron. 6:32–37; 9:19,32–33; titles of Pss. 44–49; 84–85; 87–88). God does not hold the sins of the father against the children.

42:1 *hart*. A fallow deer or stag. *panteth*. Longs for or craves. *water brooks*. The deepest part of a valley flowing with water, a streambed. *my soul*. Equivalent to the pronoun "I" (v. 2). The picture is of pursuit and consequent exhaustion and thirst rather than drought.

42:2 *thirsteth*. Hunger can be endured for a time but severe thirst is intolerable; every effort will be made to quench it (63:1–2).

42:3 *meat*. Bread, food for sustenance.

42:4 *remember*. Think about in a focused manner, a fuel for faith. *kept holyday*. Celebrated a festival.

42:5 *cast down*. Dissolved, here a sense of depression (v. 6). *disquieted*. Restless or turbulent. *hope*. Wait with expectancy, an expression of faith. *help of his countenance*. The salvation of His presence, his only relief (v. 11).

42:7 *deep . . . waves . . . billows*. These images describe his sense of abandonment by the Lord, like a man sinking in the ocean (88:6–7; Jonah 2:3–5).

42:8 *lovingkindness*. Covenant loyalty and love—his hope.

42:9 *rock*. A cliff or crag under which there is safety and protection. *forgotten*. Refuse to give attention and help. His depression clouds his reasoning, resulting in a mixture of confidence in God and doubt, the tension between faith and experience. *mourning*. Literally, "being dark or dirty," as one clothed in garments associated with grief.

42:11 *health of my countenance*. The salvation of my face, that is, the One who saves me.

Thoughts for Personal/Family Worship: Psalm 42

1. **There is a natural thirst common to everyone who seeks good and happiness (4:6), but there is also a spiritual thirst produced within them when by the Holy Spirit they taste God's goodness and desire to be fully satisfied with Him (36:8–9; 1 Peter 2:2–3). True believers can only be satisfied by the presence, grace, and comfort of God. Experiencing God's presence should be like a desperate thirst that must be quenched. If depressed, we need to preach to ourselves, even to argue with ourselves, to hope in the Lord and keep seeking Him. In times of spiritual exhaustion, to what lengths are you willing to go to find your satisfaction in the Lord?**
2. **Christ experienced horrible physical thirst on the cross (John 19:28), but far worse was His thirst for the departed presence of God (Matt. 27:46). He suffered the deprivation of good that is the doom of sinners (Isa. 65:13; Luke 16:24). Taking the curse for us, He won for us the blessing. As a result, Christ can now satisfy the deepest thirsts of mankind through the Holy Spirit (John 4:14; 7:37–39; Rev. 21:6; 22:17). The question is, do you thirst for God? How do you know?**

Psalm 43: *The psalmist relies on God's justice and desires to worship the Lord in the sanctuary.*

43:1 *plead my cause*. Argue in a lawsuit or legal dispute. *de-*

2 For thou *art* the God of my strength: why dost
thou cast me off? why go I mourning because of
the oppression of the enemy?
3 O send out thy light and thy truth: let them lead
me; let them bring me unto thy holy hill, and to
thy tabernacles.
4 Then will I go unto the altar of God, unto God
my exceeding joy: yea, upon the harp will I praise
thee, O God my God.
5 Why art thou cast down, O my soul? and why
art thou disquieted within me? hope in God: for
I shall yet praise him, *who is* the health of my
countenance, and my God.

PSALM 44

To the chief Musician for the sons of Korah, Maschil.

1 WE have heard with our ears, O God, our
fathers have told us, *what* work thou didst in their
days, in the times of old.
2 *How* thou didst drive out the heathen with thy
hand, and plantedst them; *how* thou didst afflict
the people, and cast them out.
3 For they got not the land in possession by their
own sword, neither did their own arm save them:
but thy right hand, and thine arm, and the light
of thy countenance, because thou hadst a favour
unto them.
4 Thou art my King, O God: command deliver-
ances for Jacob.
5 Through thee will we push down our enemies:
through thy name will we tread them under that
rise up against us.
6 For I will not trust in my bow, neither shall my
sword save me.
7 But thou hast saved us from our enemies, and
hast put them to shame that hated us.
8 In God we boast all the day long, and praise thy
name for ever. Selah.
9 But thou hast cast off, and put us to shame; and
goest not forth with our armies.
10 Thou makest us to turn back from the enemy:
and they which hate us spoil for themselves.
11 Thou hast given us like sheep *appointed* for
meat; and hast scattered us among the heathen.
12 Thou sellest thy people for nought, and dost
not increase *thy wealth* by their price.
13 Thou makest us a reproach to our neighbours,
a scorn and a derision to them that are round
about us.
14 Thou makest us a byword among the heathen,
a shaking of the head among the people.
15 My confusion *is* continually before me, and
the shame of my face hath covered me,
16 For the voice of him that reproacheth and
blasphemeth; by reason of the enemy and avenger.
17 All this is come upon us; yet have we not
forgotten thee, neither have we dealt falsely in thy
covenant.
18 Our heart is not turned back, neither have our
steps declined from thy way;
19 Though thou hast sore broken us in the place

ceitful and unjust man. Literally, "a man of treachery and malice."

43:2 *strength.* Mountain stronghold or refuge. *cast me off.* Reject me. *go I mourning.* See note at 42:9.

43:3 *light . . . truth.* Favor (4:6–8) and faithfulness (146:5–6).

43:4 *exceeding joy.* The "gladness of joy," the first term associated with the celebration of a festival or victory party (Judg. 16:23; 1 Sam. 18:6; 1 Kings 1:40). *harp.* A zither or some sort of stringed instrument, often associated with joy and rejoicing (Gen. 31:27; 1 Sam. 16:23).

43:5 See 42:5,11. Because of this refrain and similar language throughout the psalm, some regard this as part of Ps. 42. Some Hebrew manuscripts have linked the two into one.

Thoughts for Personal/Family Worship: Psalm 43

Believers may experience inward anxiety and despondency, but they need not settle into despair. They know that God is their festival of joy. Even if they are not feeling joy now, they should stir themselves to hope in God and persevere in prayer for growth in grace and truth. No one experienced deeper darkness than Christ, and no one has entered into richer joy. The Lord Jesus is able to shepherd His people through their times of sorrow. The key for believers is keeping their focus upon God and giving glory to Him. How does this psalm direct the despondent believer to pray?

Psalm 44: ***Remembering God's past acts causes the psalmist to lament the current situation and to pray for a renewal of God's help.***

44:1 *our fathers have told us.* Learning from history (Pss. 105–107; 1 Cor. 10:6,11) and passing on the testimony of God's work is crucial in training the next generation (78:3–8; Ex. 12:26–27; Deut. 6:7).

44:2 *drive out the heathen.* God expelled the Canaanites from the land for their sins (Deut. 7:1–2; 9:3–6). *plantedst.* Perhaps transplanted, taking from Egypt and the wilderness into the Promised Land.

44:3 *thy right hand . . . light of thy countenance.* God's power and grace.

44:4 *command deliverances.* Decree victories. God has only to speak and blessing comes (Deut. 28:8; Ps. 133:3; Eccl. 8:4).

44:5 *push down.* Thrust at or gore.

44:9 *cast off.* Reject. *put us to shame.* Humiliate. *goest not forth with our armies.* The felt absence of God was cause for lamentation and the petition that follows (Ex. 33:15–16).

44:10 *spoil.* Plunder.

44:11 *for meat.* Destined for slaughter (see note at v. 22).

44:12 *sellest.* Give them away (Deut. 32:30). *for nought.* Without a price or high value, a pittance.

44:14 *byword.* An object of scorn or derision. *shaking of the head.* A gesture expressing shock or mockery.

44:15 *confusion.* Insult, reproach, or disgrace.

44:17 *forgotten.* Intentionally neglected. *dealt falsely.* Broken faith with. Their faithfulness stood in tension with their sense of abandonment by God.

44:18 *declined from.* Turned aside from.

44:19 *hast sore broken.* Crushed in pieces. *dragons.* Jackals. *shadow of death.* Can refer to pitch darkness.

of dragons, and covered us with the shadow of death.
20 If we have forgotten the name of our God, or stretched out our hands to a strange god;
21 Shall not God search this out? for he knoweth the secrets of the heart.
22 Yea, for thy sake are we killed all the day long; we are counted as sheep for the slaughter.
23 Awake, why sleepest thou, O Lord? arise, cast *us* not off for ever.
24 Wherefore hidest thou thy face, *and* forgettest our affliction and our oppression?
25 For our soul is bowed down to the dust: our belly cleaveth unto the earth.
26 Arise for our help, and redeem us for thy mercies' sake.

PSALM 45

To the chief Musician upon Shoshannim, for the sons of Korah, Maschil, A Song of loves.

1 MY heart is inditing a good matter: I speak of the things which I have made touching the king: my tongue *is* the pen of a ready writer.
2 Thou art fairer than the children of men: grace is poured into thy lips: therefore God hath blessed thee for ever.
3 Gird thy sword upon *thy* thigh, O *most* mighty, with thy glory and thy majesty.
4 And in thy majesty ride prosperously because of truth and meekness *and* righteousness; and thy right hand shall teach thee terrible things.
5 Thine arrows *are* sharp in the heart of the king's enemies; *whereby* the people fall under thee.
6 Thy throne, O God, *is* for ever and ever: the sceptre of thy kingdom *is* a right sceptre.
7 Thou lovest righteousness, and hatest wickedness: therefore God, thy God, hath anointed thee with the oil of gladness above thy fellows.
8 All thy garments *smell* of myrrh, and aloes, *and* cassia, out of the ivory palaces, whereby they have made thee glad.
9 Kings' daughters *were* among thy honourable women: upon thy right hand did stand the queen in gold of Ophir.
10 Hearken, O daughter, and consider, and incline thine ear; forget also thine own people, and thy father's house;
11 So shall the king greatly desire thy beauty: for he *is* thy Lord; and worship thou him.
12 And the daughter of Tyre *shall be there* with a gift; *even* the rich among the people shall intreat thy favour.
13 The king's daughter *is* all glorious within: her clothing *is* of wrought gold.

44:20 *strange*. Foreign or illicit.
44:21 *knoweth the secrets of the heart*. See 139:1–4.
44:22 *counted as sheep for the slaughter*. Cited by the apostle Paul (Rom. 8:36).
44:23 *Awake*. Take action.
44:24 *hidest thou thy face*. A sign of displeasure.
44:25 *our soul*. We. *belly*. Whole body.

Thoughts for Personal/Family Worship: Psalm 44

1. **The God of then is the God of now. Reflecting on the great works of God in the past, whether in biblical times or in church history, should increase our desires and prayers for God to do great things in our day. When we recognize that God is not with us as He has been with His servants in some periods of history, we should give ourselves to relentless prayer that God would arise for our help. This is not to demand that the extraordinary be experienced every day, but pray for more grace while you persevere in faithfulness today.**
2. **That we should suffer as a consequence of our sins should not surprise us, but it may perplex us when we glorify God and find ourselves as sheep appointed for the slaughter (vv. 11,22). Yet Paul cited this truth as the common experience of God's children (Rom. 8:36). He did so in the context of explaining the consequences of their union with Christ by the Spirit: God's children suffer with God's Son so that we can be glorified with Him (Rom. 8:17). This same union with Christ, however, guarantees that nothing can separate us from God's love (Rom. 8:37–39). Though God may seem to sleep and neglect His children (v. 23), He remains the King who fights for His people (vv. 4,26), and in Him we are more than conquerors. Why is it so hard to live in the tension of this paradox? How can Christians exercise their faith in such trials?**

Psalm 45: *The psalmist sings a song of love describing the royal wedding.*

45:1 *My heart is inditing*. His innermost being is overflowing. *things which I have made touching the king*. Literally, "my works regarding the king." *pen of a ready writer*. The stylus of an experienced or skillful scribe.
45:3 *Gird thy sword*. Arm yourself by fastening the sword on a belt around the waist.
45:4 *ride prosperously*. Literally, "succeed, ride." *terrible*. Awesome.
45:6 *Thy throne, O God*. One of most explicit statements in the Bible declaring the deity of Christ, the human Son of David and divine Son of God (Heb. 1:8–9). *sceptre*. Symbol of kingly authority. *right sceptre*. Scepter of justice (72:1–4; 2 Sam. 23:3).
45:7 *God, thy God*. The Son is God (v. 6), yet distinct from God the Father, who is the covenant Lord of the Mediator. *anointed*. The verbal form of Messiah or Christ, meaning God gave Him the graces of the Holy Spirit to fulfill His mission (1 Sam. 16:13; Isa. 11:2; 61:1). This is the gospel mystery of the Trinity, one God in three Persons cooperating to save sinners.
45:8 *myrrh . . . aloes . . . cassia*. Expensive fragrances appropriate for a royal wedding.
45:9 *queen*. Scripture speaks of the Lord's people as His bride (Isa. 54:5; 61:10; 62:5; Hos. 2:19–20; Mark 2:19–20). *gold of Ophir*. Well known for quality gold (Job 28:16; 1 Kings 9:28).
45:10 *forget also thine own people*. This principle of marriage (Gen. 2:24) is even more significant in spiritual marriage to Christ (Rom. 7:4), who makes all things new (2 Cor. 5:17).
45:11 *king greatly desire thy beauty*. Christ's redeeming love makes the church lovely in His eyes (Eph. 5:25–27). *worship*

14 She shall be brought unto the king in raiment
of needlework: the virgins her companions that
follow her shall be brought unto thee.
15 With gladness and rejoicing shall they be
brought: they shall enter into the king's palace.
16 Instead of thy fathers shall be thy children,
whom thou mayest make princes in all the earth.
17 I will make thy name to be remembered in all
generations: therefore shall the people praise thee
for ever and ever.

PSALM 46

To the chief Musician for the sons of
Korah, A Song upon Alamoth.

1 GOD *is* our refuge and strength, a very present
help in trouble.
2 Therefore will not we fear, though the earth be
removed, and though the mountains be carried
into the midst of the sea;
3 *Though* the waters thereof roar *and* be troubled,
though the mountains shake with the swelling
thereof. Selah.
4 *There is* a river, the streams whereof shall make
glad the city of God, the holy *place* of the taber-
nacles of the most High.
5 God *is* in the midst of her; she shall not be
moved: God shall help her, *and that* right early.
6 The heathen raged, the kingdoms were moved:
he uttered his voice, the earth melted.
7 The LORD of hosts *is* with us; the God of Jacob
is our refuge. Selah.
8 Come, behold the works of the LORD, what
desolations he hath made in the earth.
9 He maketh wars to cease unto the end of the
earth; he breaketh the bow, and cutteth the spear
in sunder; he burneth the chariot in the fire.
10 Be still, and know that I *am* God: I will be ex-
alted among the heathen, I will be exalted in the
earth.
11 The LORD of hosts *is* with us; the God of Jacob
is our refuge. Selah.

PSALM 47

To the chief Musician, A Psalm
for the sons of Korah.

1 O CLAP your hands, all ye people; shout unto

---

thou him. Another evidence of the deity of this royal Husband (Rev. 19:10).

45:13 *glorious within*. Beautifully dressed in the king's palace (Rev. 19:8). *wrought gold*. Checkered work or brocade of gold.

45:14 *raiment of needlework*. A colorful garment.

45:16–17 *thy . . . thou*. The Hebrew is masculine, addressing the king. His union with the bride will produce a royal people (Isa. 53:11; 54:1–5,11–13), and they will worship Him forever.

Thoughts for Personal/Family Worship: Psalm 45

1. **The expressions of this psalm can hardly refer to anyone else but the incarnate Lord Jesus, both God and the human Son of David, as the New Testament confirms (Heb. 1:8–9). Neither Solomon nor any king in Israel's monarchy could be rightly addressed as "God" without further qualification (v. 6), nor receive the eternal praise of the people (v. 17). Even in the Old Testament, believers looked for a coming king who would be God and man (Isa. 9:6). What light does this psalm shed on your understanding of Christ and the church?**
2. **Meditate on Christ as the king-husband and His church as the queen-bride. The King is beautiful beyond words. With His might He protects and defends His bride. His Father delights in His righteousness and anoints Him to reign with joy by the Holy Spirit. The King shares His royal glory with His bride and delights in her. She submits to Him in total adoration. How do the words of this psalm move you to love the Lord Jesus? How do they call us to treat His church?**

Psalm 46: ***The psalmist expresses his confidence in the Lord's help in times of trouble.***

46:1 *God is our refuge and strength*. Literally, "God is for us, a refuge and protection."

46:2 *will not we fear*. Not to fear is an expression of faith (John 14:1; Phil. 4:5–7). *be carried*. Shake, slip, or fall. The collapse of *mountains* into the *sea* may be figurative for wars and national troubles (v. 9; cf. Isa. 17:12; Jer. 51:25).

46:3 *be troubled*. Foam.

46:4 *river*. Metaphor for God's life-giving presence (1:3; 36:8–9; Isa. 43:19–20; 44:3–5; Ezek. 47:1–12).

46:5 *be moved*. Same Hebrew word as "be carried" (v. 2,6).

46:6 *raged*. Were tumultuous.

46:7 *The LORD of hosts*. "Jehovah of armies," stressing absolute authority as the supreme Commander. *with us*. Present to keep His covenant promises of grace to His people (*God of Jacob*).

46:9 *in sunder*. In pieces.

46:10 *Be still*. Stop. Most likely a call to repent of raging against God and warring against people (vv. 6,9).

Thoughts for Personal/Family Worship: Psalm 46

1. **The great reformer Martin Luther claimed this to be his psalm. It provided the inspiration of his well-known hymn, "A Mighty Fortress Is Our God," often called the battle hymn of the Reformation. It expresses a kind of confident security in the Lord that ought to be the experience of every believer when facing or anticipating the crises of life. God is the comfort and salvation of His people in their troubles, even when disasters shake their world.**
2. **The principle of "Immanuel" (God with us) pervades the Old Testament and reaches its climax in the incarnation. The Son of God became our living tabernacle and sanctuary when He took on human flesh (John 1:14). Though ascended into heaven, His Spirit remains with the church as a constant stream of living water (John 7:37–39). Thus Christ is with us in His authority over all things, even to the end of the age (Matt. 28:18–20). If He is with us, who can be against us (Rom. 8:31)? How does this psalm teach us to handle our fears?**

Psalm 47: ***The psalmist enjoins all nations to acknowledge the Lord's universal Kingship.***

47:1 *clap . . . shout*. Expressions of great joy (98:8; Isa. 44:23).

God with the voice of triumph.
2 For the LORD most high *is* terrible; *he is* a great
King over all the earth.
3 He shall subdue the people under us, and the
nations under our feet.
4 He shall choose our inheritance for us, the
excellency of Jacob whom he loved. Selah.
5 God is gone up with a shout, the LORD with the
sound of a trumpet.
6 Sing praises to God, sing praises: sing praises
unto our King, sing praises.
7 For God *is* the King of all the earth: sing ye
praises with understanding.
8 God reigneth over the heathen: God sitteth
upon the throne of his holiness.
9 The princes of the people are gathered together,
even the people of the God of Abraham: for the
shields of the earth *belong* unto God: he is greatly
exalted.

PSALM 48

A Song *and* Psalm for the sons of Korah.

1 GREAT *is* the LORD, and greatly to be praised in
the city of our God, *in* the mountain of his holiness.
2 Beautiful for situation, the joy of the whole
earth, *is* mount Zion, *on* the sides of the north,
the city of the great King.
3 God is known in her palaces for a refuge.
4 For, lo, the kings were assembled, they passed
by together.
5 They saw *it, and* so they marvelled; they were
troubled, *and* hasted away.
6 Fear took hold upon them there, *and* pain, as of
a woman in travail.
7 Thou breakest the ships of Tarshish with an
east wind.
8 As we have heard, so have we seen in the city of
the LORD of hosts, in the city of our God: God will
establish it for ever. Selah.
9 We have thought of thy lovingkindness, O God,
in the midst of thy temple.
10 According to thy name, O God, so *is* thy praise
unto the ends of the earth: thy right hand is full
of righteousness.
11 Let mount Zion rejoice, let the daughters of
Judah be glad, because of thy judgments.
12 Walk about Zion, and go round about her: tell
the towers thereof.
13 Mark ye well her bulwarks, consider her pal-
aces; that ye may tell *it* to the generation following.
14 For this God *is* our God for ever and ever: he
will be our guide *even* unto death.

---

triumph. Jubilation or rejoicing.
47:2 *terrible*. Inspiring fear and awe.
47:4 *excellency*. Pride or majesty, probably referring to the land (*inheritance*) God gave them. *Jacob whom he loved*. God freely chose to place His special love on undeserving Israel (Mal. 1:2).
47:5 *shout*. Jubilation or shout of joy.
47:8 *God reigneth over the heathen*. God's sovereignty does not depend on the consent of His subjects, but extends over people that reject Him.
47:9 *princes of the people*. Could be translated, "willing ones of peoples," or "noblemen of peoples." *people of the God of Abraham*. The nations will be brought into the blessing promised to Abraham by sharing in his faith (Gen. 12:3; Rom. 4:11–17; Gal. 3:8,29). *shields*. Soldiers and their power to fight.

Thoughts for Personal/Family Worship: Psalm 47

1. **There is hardly a more practical truth for daily living than the absolute sovereignty of God. He is the supreme King over all, and merely human kings are under His dominion. The wicked attempt to escape from His authority but in the end will face it with terror. The godly find in God's sovereignty a joyous cause for praise and confidence. There should be no place for pessimism, only glorious optimism. The kingdoms of this world will become the kingdom of God and Christ. How would you describe biblical optimism? How should it affect believers in their daily lives?**
2. **The gospel of Jesus Christ is the good news of God's kingdom (Isa. 52:7; Mark 1:14–15). Thus the gospel announces that Christ is Lord over all and calls all who hear it to enter by faith into covenant relationship with the God of Abraham. How should an optimistic view of God's kingdom affect how Christians approach missions and evangelism? How can faith that God is King strengthen the church when its efforts to reach the lost are frustrated or provoke persecution?**

Psalm 48: The psalmist praises the Lord for being the defender and guide of His people.

48:1 *city of our God*. Jerusalem, the place that God had chosen for His name to dwell (Deut. 12:5) in the sanctuary (*holiness*) on the hill of Zion (*mountain*, v. 2).
48:2 *Beautiful for situation*. Literally, "beautiful of height or elevation," referring to its honor from God (Isa. 2:2). *sides of the north*. Where the temple stood (Isa. 14:13).
48:5 *marvelled*. Froze with fear, became speechless in the face of terror. *troubled*. Horrified out of one's senses. *hasted away*. Ran away in alarm.
48:6 *travail*. Childbirth.
48:9 *lovingkindness*. Covenant loyalty and love.
48:12 *tell*. Count (v. 13).
48:13 *Mark ye well her bulwarks*. Literally, "set your heart on her outer ramparts."
48:14 *For this God is our God*. The figurative language of examining the defenses of Zion (vv. 12–13) is here explained as meditating on the faithfulness of God, for He is the protection of His people (125:1–2). *be our guide*. Lead or shepherd us (78:52; 80:1).

Thoughts for Personal/Family Worship: Psalm 48

The church has her enemies; she has often suffered oppression and persecution, sometimes with physical violence (as in many nations today), sometimes with insults and verbal attacks (as from false religions and atheism). We may tremble for the church but we should remember that God has decreed her establishment and therefore we should take heart. We should be concerned

PSALM 49

To the chief Musician, A Psalm
for the sons of Korah.

1 HEAR this, all *ye* people; give ear, all *ye* inhabi-
tants of the world:
2 Both low and high, rich and poor, together.
3 My mouth shall speak of wisdom; and the
meditation of my heart *shall be* of understanding.
4 I will incline mine ear to a parable: I will open
my dark saying upon the harp.
5 Wherefore should I fear in the days of evil, *when*
the iniquity of my heels shall compass me about?
6 They that trust in their wealth, and boast
themselves in the multitude of their riches;
7 None *of them* can by any means redeem his
brother, nor give to God a ransom for him:
8 (For the redemption of their soul *is* precious,
and it ceaseth for ever:)
9 That he should still live for ever, *and* not see
corruption.
10 For he seeth *that* wise men die, likewise the
fool and the brutish person perish, and leave their
wealth to others.
11 Their inward thought *is, that* their houses *shall*
continue for ever, *and* their dwelling places to all
generations; they call *their* lands after their own
names.
12 Nevertheless man *being* in honour abideth
not: he is like the beasts *that* perish.
13 This their way *is* their folly: yet their posterity
approve their sayings. Selah.
14 Like sheep they are laid in the grave; death shall
feed on them; and the upright shall have domin-
ion over them in the morning; and their beauty
shall consume in the grave from their dwelling.
15 But God will redeem my soul from the power
of the grave: for he shall receive me. Selah.
16 Be not thou afraid when one is made rich,
when the glory of his house is increased;
17 For when he dieth he shall carry nothing away:
his glory shall not descend after him.
18 Though while he lived he blessed his soul:
and *men* will praise thee, when thou doest well
to thyself.
19 He shall go to the generation of his fathers;
they shall never see light.
20 Man *that is* in honour, and understandeth not,
is like the beasts *that* perish.

to tell the rising generation that God has always been faithful to His people, that their hope may be in Him and their confidence be unshaken. The key to resting in the Lord is thinking deeply about His faithful covenant love (vv. 9,14). How has God proven Himself faithful and loving through Jesus Christ? How can that move us to trust and praise Him when threatened?

Psalm 49: ***The psalmist declares the folly of trusting earthly riches and shows the eternal advantages of trusting the Lord.***

49:1–2 The invitation to *hear this* message is to people everywhere, in every age (the significance of *world*), and of every social strata.
49:3 *wisdom . . . understanding.* In Hebrew the words are plural to indicate keen wisdom and understanding, stressing the vital importance of the message.
49:4 *parable . . . dark saying.* Both words refer to matters of wisdom for life.
49:5 *evil.* Trouble or calamity. *my heels.* A figurative reference to his enemies that pursue him; the root word for the name Jacob (see note at 41:9). *compass.* Surround.
49:6 *trust in.* Put confidence, find security, or seek salvation in. The object of faith determines the value of faith (Jer. 17:5–8).
49:7 *redeem . . . ransom.* Pay a price to release a person from trouble or death (Ex. 21:30), associated with atonement for sin and satisfaction of justice (Ex. 21:30; 30:11–16; Num. 35:31–32; Prov. 6:35).
49:8 *precious.* Costly. *it ceaseth for ever.* The efforts of redemption are always frustrated; they come to an end without achieving their purpose—a parenthetical digression explaining why redeeming himself or another is impossible (v. 7).
49:9 *That.* "In order that," the purpose of paying a ransom (v. 7).
49:10 *brutish.* Senseless. Death is the great equalizer (hence, the universal invitation to pay attention to the message, vv. 1–2).
49:11 *call . . . names.* An expression claiming ownership.
49:12 *abideth not.* Only spends the night, expressing the brevity of life as nothing more than an overnight lodging. *like the beasts.* Like domesticated cattle raised for slaughter. Death is certain for all in Adam (1 Cor. 15:22; Heb. 9:27). This refrain is repeated in v. 20, dividing the psalm into two sections.
49:13 *folly.* Self-confident stupidity. *posterity approve.* Those that follow them agree and perpetuate the false notion.
49:14 *grave.* The Hebrew, *sheol*, can refer to death, the grave, or the abode of departed wicked spirits; grave is appropriate here (v. 15). *death shall feed.* A sinister picture of death as shepherd. *the upright shall have dominion.* The turning of the tables in the next life (*morning*). Status in eternity is infinitely more important than time. *their beauty shall consume in the grave from their dwelling.* The text is difficult; possible meaning: "their form will decay in the grave away from their home."
49:15 *my soul.* Me. The beauty of the gospel is that *God* does for man what man cannot do for himself (vv. 7–9): *redeem* him from death. *receive.* Take, the word used of God taking Enoch and Elijah to eternal life (Gen. 5:24; 2 Kings 2:3,5,9–11), here an anticipation of entering God's glorious presence after death (73:24; cf. 2 Cor. 5:8).
49:16–17 *glory.* Substantial assets.
49:20 The refrain is repeated (v. 12), with a slight alteration (*understandeth* differs from "abideth" by only one letter in Hebrew).

Thoughts for Personal/Family Worship: Psalm 49

1. **There are so many who think that wealth is all-important, but death will test people and their beliefs. Such men will then bitterly regret placing confidence in the things of this world. Only the living and true God can save in that dread hour. Many rich men now suffer in hell for their sins, without a single one of the comforts they enjoyed on earth (Luke 16:19–26). Unlike the**

PSALM 50

A Psalm of Asaph.

1 THE mighty God, *even* the LORD, hath spoken,
and called the earth from the rising of the sun
unto the going down thereof.
2 Out of Zion, the perfection of beauty, God hath
shined.
3 Our God shall come, and shall not keep silence:
a fire shall devour before him, and it shall be very
tempestuous round about him.
4 He shall call to the heavens from above, and to
the earth, that he may judge his people.
5 Gather my saints together unto me; those that
have made a covenant with me by sacrifice.
6 And the heavens shall declare his righteousness:
for God *is* judge himself. Selah.
7 Hear, O my people, and I will speak; O Israel,
and I will testify against thee: I *am* God, *even* thy
God.
8 I will not reprove thee for thy sacrifices or thy
burnt offerings, *to have been* continually before
me.
9 I will take no bullock out of thy house, *nor* he
goats out of thy folds.
10 For every beast of the forest *is* mine, *and* the
cattle upon a thousand hills.
11 I know all the fowls of the mountains: and the
wild beasts of the field *are* mine.
12 If I were hungry, I would not tell thee: for the
world *is* mine, and the fulness thereof.
13 Will I eat the flesh of bulls, or drink the blood
of goats?
14 Offer unto God thanksgiving; and pay thy
vows unto the most High:
15 And call upon me in the day of trouble: I will
deliver thee, and thou shalt glorify me.
16 But unto the wicked God saith, What hast
thou to do to declare my statutes, or *that* thou
shouldest take my covenant in thy mouth?
17 Seeing thou hatest instruction, and castest my
words behind thee.
18 When thou sawest a thief, then thou con-
sentedst with him, and hast been partaker with
adulterers.
19 Thou givest thy mouth to evil, and thy tongue
frameth deceit.
20 Thou sittest *and* speakest against thy brother;
thou slanderest thine own mother's son.
21 These *things* hast thou done, and I kept silence;
thou thoughtest that I was altogether *such an one*
as thyself: *but* I will reprove thee, and set *them* in
order before thine eyes.
22 Now consider this, ye that forget God, lest I
tear *you* in pieces, and *there be* none to deliver.
23 Whoso offereth praise glorifieth me: and to

unbelieving, believers possess the hope and expectation that, when they die, they shall see light—the light of God and the light of all the glories and beauties of the heavenly kingdom. Rest assured that those now in God's everlasting kingdom have no regrets at all over the fact that, through grace, they once came to know God in Christ as their Redeemer and King. How can we strive to keep wealth in its proper perspective?

2. **Christ speaks as the great prophet and the voice of all true prophets, having authority to declare wisdom and truth to all people of this world (vv. 1–3). His teaching alone can enable us to view life and death, riches and poverty, in the right way. Christ said, "What shall it profit a man, if he shall gain the whole world, and lose his own soul?" (Mark 8:36). Are you listening to Christ? One test is whether you view the rich with awe and admiration (vv. 16–17), or set your hope upon the Lord and His redemption (v. 15). You cannot serve both God and money, and you cannot seek both earthly treasure and heavenly treasure (Matt. 6:19–24). What does this test show about your heart?**

Psalm 50: *The psalmist shows that external rituals without sincerity are not acceptable to God.*

50:1 *The mighty God, even the LORD.* Literally, "God, God, Jehovah," designating the transcendent, powerful, and faithful covenant God. *rising . . . going down.* East and west, the whole earth.

50:3 *fire shall devour before him.* God's anger will destroy His enemies (21:9; 97:3).

50:5 *made a covenant with me by sacrifice.* See Ex. 24:3–8; Zech. 9:11; Luke 22:20; Heb. 9:15–20; 13:20.

50:6 *the heavens shall declare his righteousness.* God will publicly display His glory as *judge* to punish His enemies and save His people (97:6).

50:12 *the world is mine.* God owns all things because He created them (24:1–2; 95:4–5).

50:14 *Offer unto God thanksgiving.* Sincere praise from the heart and faithfulness to one's commitments (*pay thy vows*) are more important than external rituals such as animal sacrifices (Hos. 14:2).

50:17 *hatest instruction.* Reject correction, training, or discipline.

50:18 *consentedst with.* Became friends with or favorable toward.

50:19 *frameth.* Harnesses or fits together.

50:21 *thoughtest that I was altogether such an one as thyself.* Thought that I was like you.

50:22 *forget God.* Refuse to acknowledge or think about God. Note that thinking of God in human terms (v. 21) is to intentionally forget who He really is.

50:23 *ordereth his conversation.* Sets or directs his way of life (cf. 119:133).

Thoughts for Personal/Family Worship: Psalm 50

1. **One of our chief faults in life is to think that God is like ourselves (v. 21). People tend to be satisfied with religious rites, so they assume God will be satisfied as well. But ritual by itself, even those rituals commanded by God, mean nothing apart from a genuine heart of praise and obedience. To think of God as He has revealed Himself is to view Him as the God of power, authority, glory, wrath, righteousness, and faithfulness (vv. 1–6). Such thoughts of God will lead us to worship Him in spirit and truth. What habits will encourage this kind of humble attentiveness to His Word and sincere repentance of sin?**

him that ordereth *his* conversation *aright* will I shew the salvation of God.

PSALM 51

To the chief Musician, A Psalm of David, when Nathan the prophet came unto him, after he had gone in to Bath-sheba.

1 HAVE mercy upon me, O God, according to thy
lovingkindness: according unto the multitude of
thy tender mercies blot out my transgressions.
2 Wash me throughly from mine iniquity, and
cleanse me from my sin.
3 For I acknowledge my transgressions: and my
sin *is* ever before me.
4 Against thee, thee only, have I sinned, and done
this evil in thy sight: that thou mightest be justified when thou speakest, *and* be clear when thou
judgest.
5 Behold, I was shapen in iniquity; and in sin did
my mother conceive me.
6 Behold, thou desirest truth in the inward parts:
and in the hidden *part* thou shalt make me to
know wisdom.
7 Purge me with hyssop, and I shall be clean:
wash me, and I shall be whiter than snow.
8 Make me to hear joy and gladness; *that* the
bones *which* thou hast broken may rejoice.
9 Hide thy face from my sins, and blot out all
mine iniquities.
10 Create in me a clean heart, O God; and renew
a right spirit within me.
11 Cast me not away from thy presence; and take
not thy holy spirit from me.
12 Restore unto me the joy of thy salvation; and
uphold me *with thy* free spirit.
13 *Then* will I teach transgressors thy ways; and
sinners shall be converted unto thee.
14 Deliver me from bloodguiltiness, O God, thou
God of my salvation: *and* my tongue shall sing
aloud of thy righteousness.
15 O Lord, open thou my lips; and my mouth
shall shew forth thy praise.
16 For thou desirest not sacrifice; else would I
give *it*: thou delightest not in burnt offering.
17 The sacrifices of God *are* a broken spirit: a
broken and a contrite heart, O God, thou wilt not
despise.
18 Do good in thy good pleasure unto Zion: build
thou the walls of Jerusalem.
19 Then shalt thou be pleased with the sacrifices

---

2. In Christ, God has spoken to men (Heb. 1:2), calling them everywhere to the gospel that is preached in the world. His glory shines in the gospel (2 Cor. 4:3–6). Christ shall one day come again with fire (2 Thess. 1:8). He will gather His saints (Matt. 24:31; 2 Thess. 2:1) and punish the wicked, including religious hypocrites (Matt. 7:21–23). Does this frighten you or comfort you? Why?

Psalm 51: *David confesses his sin, pleading for forgiveness and spiritual renewal, and promising praise.*

Title *gone in to Bath-sheba*. In this penitential psalm, David confessed his sins of adultery and murder (2 Sam. 11).

51:1 *Have mercy*. Be gracious or show undeserved favor. True confession makes no excuses, but immediately appeals to God's goodness. *lovingkindness*. Covenant loyalty and love; a prayer of faith. *multitude of thy tender mercies*. Abundance of Thy compassion to those in trouble. *blot out*. Obliterate, an image of wiping the record clear or acquitting from a crime. *transgressions*. Acts of rebellion against law and authority.

51:2 *Wash*. Scrub out a stain from a garment (v. 7), a picture of forgiving guilt (*iniquity*). *cleanse*. Remove ceremonial uncleanness, a picture of restoring fellowship with God.

51:3 *my sin is ever before me*. The believer's conscience will not give him rest while he continues in unrepentant sin (32:3–4).

51:4 *that thou*. Understand as, "I confess that in order that." An ellipsis (something omitted but to be understood) is common in poetry. *justified*. Confession of our sin requires admitting that God is righteous (Rom. 3:4; cf. Neh. 9:33).

51:5 *shapen in iniquity . . . in sin . . . conceive me*. Not a statement about the actions leading to his mother's pregnancy, but to his spiritual condition in the womb. The fall of man (Gen. 3) has corrupted all people from their youngest days (58:3; Gen. 8:21; Prov. 22:15).

51:6 *inward parts*. Innermost being.

51:7 *Purge me with hyssop*. A ceremony of cleansing, symbolizing restoration of an unclean person to fellowship with the holy God by the application of a blood sacrifice (Lev. 14:6–7,49,52; Num. 19:1–10,18–20; cf. Heb. 9:13–14,19).

51:8 *Make me to hear joy and gladness*. Cause me to hear the word assuring forgiveness, so that I will rejoice. *bones which thou hast broken*. Not physical fractures, but painful conviction of sin and guilt (32:3–4).

51:10 *Create*. The same word used of the original creation (148:5; Gen. 1:1). *right spirit*. A heart that is standing firm and steady, with integrity.

51:11 *thy holy spirit*. Praying for the Spirit's personal presence and preservation, and empowerment for his duties as king (1 Sam. 16:13). He did not want to be set aside from being king as Saul was.

51:12 *free spirit*. God's Spirit, who is very willing to sustain repentant sinners.

51:14 *bloodguiltiness*. Literally, "bloods," the plural Hebrew use refers to the guilt of violence, such as David's murder of Uriah (2 Sam. 11:15).

51:16–17 Sincere heart worship is more important than ritual, especially worship springing from being crushed over one's sins (*contrite*) and offering oneself to God in repentance as a living sacrifice for new obedience (40:6; Isa. 1:11–20; 66:1–3; Hos. 6:6).

Thoughts for Personal/Family Worship: Psalm 51

1. Nathan's word of rebuke brought David to confession, but it was not required to remind David of his sin. A battle was raging inside that no one else could see. David saw his sin as a criminal offense, a ruinous stain, and ceremonial uncleanness. He was guilty, worthless, and unfit for worship. Although others were impacted by his sin, David acknowledged that he had primarily offended

of righteousness, with burnt offering and whole burnt offering: then shall they offer bullocks upon thine altar.

PSALM 52

To the chief Musician, Maschil, *A Psalm* of David, when Doeg the Edomite came and told Saul, and said unto him, David is come to the house of Ahimelech.

1 WHY boastest thou thyself in mischief, O mighty man? the goodness of God *endureth* continually.
2 Thy tongue deviseth mischiefs; like a sharp razor, working deceitfully.
3 Thou lovest evil more than good; *and* lying rather than to speak righteousness. Selah.
4 Thou lovest all devouring words, O *thou* deceitful tongue.
5 God shall likewise destroy thee for ever, he shall take thee away, and pluck thee out of *thy* dwelling place, and root thee out of the land of the living. Selah.
6 The righteous also shall see, and fear, and shall laugh at him:
7 Lo, *this is* the man *that* made not God his strength; but trusted in the abundance of his riches, *and* strengthened himself in his wickedness.
8 But I *am* like a green olive tree in the house of God: I trust in the mercy of God for ever and ever.
9 I will praise thee for ever, because thou hast done *it*: and I will wait on thy name; for *it is* good before thy saints.

PSALM 53

To the chief Musician upon Mahalath, Maschil, *A Psalm* of David.

1 THE fool hath said in his heart, *There is* no God. Corrupt are they, and have done abominable iniquity: *there is* none that doeth good.
2 God looked down from heaven upon the children of men, to see if there were *any* that did understand, that did seek God.
3 Every one of them is gone back: they are altogether become filthy; *there is* none that doeth good, no, not one.
4 Have the workers of iniquity no knowledge? who eat up my people *as* they eat bread: they have not called upon God.
5 There were they in great fear, *where* no fear

God and thus appealed to Him for mercy. His prayer is a model for believers seeking forgiveness and restoration through God's mercy in Christ (1 John 1:5–10). What motivations does this psalm give to Christians to confess their sins? How does it teach us about how to confess our sins? Though it was written by a believer, how might it guide an unbeliever to seek salvation from his sins?

2. **The mention of "hyssop" beautifully connects repentance with faith in the cleansing power of the blood of a sacrifice for sins (v. 7). The stalk of this plant was used to apply the sacrifice directly to the unclean person. Hyssop was also used to put the blood of the Passover lamb upon the doorposts, so that death would not enter the home (Ex. 12:21–22). Faith seeks the particular application of Christ's blood to our sins, so that we may escape God's wrath and draw near to His holy presence to worship Him. Has Christ's blood been applied to your soul?**

Psalm 52: *David praises the Lord and rejoices over the certain destruction of the wicked.*

Title After *David* fled from *Saul* to the priests and then moved on, *Doeg* betrayed the priests to King *Saul* and slaughtered eighty-five of them (1 Sam. 21:1–7; 22:7–23).
52:1 *mischief*. Evil or malicious acts. *goodness*. Covenant loyalty and love (often translated "mercy," v. 8). *endureth continually*. Literally, His love "is all the day."
52:2 *mischiefs*. Threats or engulfing ruin and destruction (different word than in v. 1). *deceitfully*. With trickery or treachery.
52:3 *lovest*. Sinners not only do acts of sin, they love *evil* and *lying* (4:2; Isa. 5:20; Mic. 3:2).
52:5 *destroy*. Pull down. *pluck . . . out*. Tear away.
52:6 *shall see, and fear, and shall laugh*. God's judgments against sinners produce awe and reverence in *the righteous* and reveal how foolish and futile sin is (2:1–4).
52:7 *wickedness*. Either desire or destruction.
52:8–9 *green olive tree*. An image of vibrancy and fruitfulness in God's gracious presence (92:12–13). *mercy*. Covenant loyalty and love. *wait*. Hope or wait with eager expectancy, not in resignation but faith.

Thoughts for Personal/Family Worship: Psalm 52

1. **The perversity of man is astonishing. The wicked do much harm with their lies, sometimes resulting in the death of many righteous people while the wicked grow in their power and wealth. Fallen mankind takes a horrible delight in its sins, actually choosing evil instead of good. The corruption of our race showed itself in the persecutions of David, and even more in the sufferings of Christ. Jesus felt the full force of unjust human hatred, and His cross should humble us with its declaration of how evil mankind has become, that we would do such a thing when God came to us. How can we learn to hate wickedness like God does?**
2. **Though the wicked may seem to succeed and prosper, the Lord will rip them out of His world like noxious weeds. However, the righteous will flourish in the presence of their God. His judgments of the wicked will move the righteous to worship. How does knowing that God will punish the wicked encourage us to trust His goodness now?**

Psalm 53: *David describes man's depravity and corruption and longs for God's salvation.*

53:1–6 See the notes at Ps. 14, which is essentially its duplicate.
53:5 *where no fear was . . . despised them*. This is the principal difference between this psalm and its predecessor (14:5–6).

was: for God hath scattered the bones of him that
encampeth *against* thee: thou hast put *them* to
shame, because God hath despised them.
6 Oh that the salvation of Israel *were come* out
of Zion! When God bringeth back the captivity
of his people, Jacob shall rejoice, *and* Israel shall
be glad.

PSALM 54

To the chief Musician on Neginoth, Maschil, *A Psalm* of David, when the Ziphims came and said to Saul, Doth not David hide himself with us?

1 SAVE me, O God, by thy name, and judge me by
thy strength.
2 Hear my prayer, O God; give ear to the words
of my mouth.
3 For strangers are risen up against me, and op-
pressors seek after my soul: they have not set God
before them. Selah.
4 Behold, God *is* mine helper: the Lord *is* with
them that uphold my soul.
5 He shall reward evil unto mine enemies: cut
them off in thy truth.
6 I will freely sacrifice unto thee: I will praise thy
name, O LORD; for *it is* good.
7 For he hath delivered me out of all trouble: and
mine eye hath seen *his desire* upon mine enemies.

PSALM 55

To the chief Musician on Neginoth, Maschil, *A Psalm* of David.

1 GIVE ear to my prayer, O God; and hide not
thyself from my supplication.
2 Attend unto me, and hear me: I mourn in my
complaint, and make a noise;
3 Because of the voice of the enemy, because
of the oppression of the wicked: for they cast
iniquity upon me, and in wrath they hate me.
4 My heart is sore pained within me: and the
terrors of death are fallen upon me.
5 Fearfulness and trembling are come upon me,
and horror hath overwhelmed me.
6 And I said, Oh that I had wings like a dove! *for*
then would I fly away, and be at rest.
7 Lo, *then* would I wander far off, *and* remain in
the wilderness. Selah.
8 I would hasten my escape from the windy
storm *and* tempest.
9 Destroy, O Lord, *and* divide their tongues: for I
have seen violence and strife in the city.
10 Day and night they go about it upon the walls
thereof: mischief also and sorrow *are* in the midst
of it.
11 Wickedness *is* in the midst thereof: deceit and
guile depart not from her streets.
12 For *it was* not an enemy *that* reproached me;
then I could have borne *it*: neither *was it* he that

God's curse on the wicked puts them in anxiety even when no visible danger threatens (Lev. 26:17,36; Prov. 28:1). *scattered the bones.* He defeated and disgraced them (Jer. 8:1–2).

Thoughts for Personal/Family Worship: Psalm 53

The teaching of Ps. 14 is repeated in Ps. 53, and appears again in Rom. 3:10–12. This implies that we need to pay careful attention to the doctrine of sin. Apart from a piercing sense of our sinfulness, we will not care much about the gospel of Christ. This psalm reveals that by nature fallen human beings are practical atheists. They are corrupt. Though they may do some good in society, not one of them does true spiritual good. They might be religious, but they do not desire God or seek after Him. They do not know Him in their hearts. As a result, they do not really pray to the Lord, and they persecute God's people. Despite all their boasting, they feel guilty and afraid, sometimes for no apparent reason, and God will punish them severely. What does this show you about your need for Jesus Christ? What specifically do you need Him to do for you in order to rescue you from this dreadful condition?

Psalm 54: *David prays for deliverance from his enemies and promises praise, being confident in the Lord's deliverance.*

Title *the Ziphims.* The people of Ziph were part of the tribe of Judah (Josh. 15:20,24), however they betrayed *David* to *Saul*, but he escaped (1 Sam. 23:19–24; cf. 26:1).
54:1 *thy name.* All that God has revealed Himself to be (v. 6). *judge me.* Plead my cause, vindicate.
54:3 *strangers.* Foreigners. *my soul.* Me (v. 4).
54:5 *He shall reward evil.* He will return the calamity.
54:6 *freely sacrifice.* Offer voluntarily without compulsion.

Thoughts for Personal/Family Worship: Psalm 54

David knew what it was to be betrayed by his kinsmen. Trouble is bad enough when it comes from expected sources, but it always feels worse when it comes from those with whom we have some relationship. How painful it must have been for the Lord Jesus for His fellow Israelites to hand Him over to the Gentiles to be crucified! Although we may be hurt or even betrayed by those close to us, there is one who has promised never to forsake us in adversity. We can wholly rely on Him, and He will not fail us. Since we are safe in God's keeping, let us not give way to unrestrained anxiety. Rather, let us praise the Lord that He is with us and that soon we shall be both free and triumphant.

Psalm 55: *David complains about his trouble and comforts himself in God's preservation.*

55:2 *Attend.* Listen attentively. *I mourn in my complaint, and make a noise.* Literally, "I show restlessness in my lament and am in an uproar."
55:3 *oppression.* Pressure. *cast iniquity upon me.* Drop trouble or sorrow on me.
55:4 *is sore pained.* Trembles or writhes. *terrors.* Or dread.
55:9 *Destroy.* Either to swallow up or to confuse.
55:10 *mischief . . . and sorrow.* Looming disaster and trouble.
55:11 *Wickedness.* Destruction or engulfing ruin. *deceit and guile.* Violence and treachery.

hated me *that* did magnify *himself* against me;
then I would have hid myself from him:
13 But *it was* thou, a man mine equal, my guide,
and mine acquaintance.
14 We took sweet counsel together, *and* walked
unto the house of God in company.
15 Let death seize upon them, *and* let them go
down quick into hell: for wickedness *is* in their
dwellings, *and* among them.
16 As for me, I will call upon God; and the LORD
shall save me.
17 Evening, and morning, and at noon, will I
pray, and cry aloud: and he shall hear my voice.
18 He hath delivered my soul in peace from the
battle *that was* against me: for there were many
with me.
19 God shall hear, and afflict them, even he
that abideth of old. Selah. Because they have no
changes, therefore they fear not God.
20 He hath put forth his hands against such as be
at peace with him: he hath broken his covenant.
21 *The words* of his mouth were smoother than
butter, but war *was* in his heart: his words were
softer than oil, yet *were* they drawn swords.
22 Cast thy burden upon the LORD, and he shall
sustain thee: he shall never suffer the righteous to
be moved.
23 But thou, O God, shalt bring them down into
the pit of destruction: bloody and deceitful men
shall not live out half their days; but I will trust
in thee.

PSALM 56

To the chief Musician upon
Jonath-elem-rechokim, Michtam of David,
when the Philistines took him in Gath.

1 BE merciful unto me, O God: for man would
swallow me up; he fighting daily oppresseth me.
2 Mine enemies would daily swallow *me* up: for
they be many that fight against me, O thou most
High.
3 What time I am afraid, I will trust in thee.
4 In God I will praise his word, in God I have put
my trust; I will not fear what flesh can do unto me.
5 Every day they wrest my words: all their
thoughts *are* against me for evil.
6 They gather themselves together, they hide
themselves, they mark my steps, when they wait
for my soul.
7 Shall they escape by iniquity? in *thine* anger cast
down the people, O God.
8 Thou tellest my wanderings: put thou my tears
into thy bottle: *are they* not in thy book?
9 When I cry *unto thee*, then shall mine enemies
turn back: this I know; for God *is* for me.
10 In God will I praise *his* word: in the LORD will
I praise *his* word.
11 In God have I put my trust: I will not be afraid
what man can do unto me.
12 Thy vows *are* upon me, O God: I will render
praises unto thee.
13 For thou hast delivered my soul from death:

55:15 *quick into hell.* Alive into the grave (Hebrew, *sheol*, can refer to death, the grave, or the abode of departed wicked spirits).
55:17 *Evening, and morning, and at noon.* Not three specific times but continually.
55:18 *my soul.* Me.
55:22 *Cast thy burden upon the LORD.* Depend on God to help you with it (v. 23; 22:10; cf. 37:5; 1 Peter 5:7). *suffer . . . to be moved.* Cause to fall.
55:23 *bloody . . . men shall not live out half their days.* Men of violence and murder will die by violence (Matt. 26:52).

Thoughts for Personal/Family Worship: Psalm 55

A believer can experience heart-wrenching trouble that overwhelms him with fear and horror. The Lord Jesus Himself felt this way (John 12:27; Mark 14:33–35). When the believer is in trouble, it is always possible for him to flee to God, in whose presence he will find a place of quiet rest far away from the reach of those who have given him grief. Sometimes in life it is a best friend, even an apparently godly friend, who lets us down badly, causing us a great deal of pain. We do well to rely upon the Lord Jesus, "a friend that sticketh closer than a brother" (Prov. 18:24). In prayer, we should roll the burden of suffering or sorrow upon the Lord, and although He may not remove it altogether, He will uphold us and strengthen us to bear it. As a sympathetic friend and High Priest, He knows exactly how to sustain His servants in their greatest trials.

Psalm 56: ***David expresses his trust in God in the midst of trouble which dispels his fear of man.***

Title *Philistines took him in Gath.* See 1 Sam. 21:10—22:2 for the historical context.
56:1 *Be merciful.* Be gracious or show undeserved favor. *swallow me up.* Trample upon or crush (v. 2). *oppresseth.* Or torments.
56:3 *What time.* When.
56:5 *wrest.* Twist or distort; Hebrew, "find fault with." *evil.* Harm.
56:6 *mark my steps.* Watch my heels or footprints.
56:8 *Thou tellest my wanderings.* Literally, "Thou dost count the changeable circumstances of my life"; the Lord keeps track of everything (Mal. 3:16). *my tears into thy bottle.* God gives compassionate attention to His people's sufferings and will not forget them (Ex. 2:23–24; Judg. 10:16).
56:9 *God is for me.* No one can therefore effectively be against him (Rom. 8:31).
56:12 *Thy vows.* God's covenant promises (2 Sam. 7), which were unconditionally guaranteed since the coming Christ, were the fulfillment. There had to be a David if there was going to be Christ; therefore, David was confident in deliverance.
56:13 *delivered . . . from death.* See 18:16–19. *my soul.* Me.

Thoughts for Personal/Family Worship: Psalm 56

1. **We must understand that this world is no friend to God or the people of God. However the world treats us, the trial will be used for our sanctification if it drives us to the Lord in prayer. In all our troubles, God's Word provides comfort, strength, peace, and hope. Long indeed may be the time of sorrow, but even if we are tempted to think that God is unmindful of our sufferings, the truth is that He knows all about them and is moved with compassion.**

wilt not *thou deliver* my feet from falling, that I may walk before God in the light of the living?

PSALM 57

To the chief Musician,
Al-taschith, Michtam of David, when
he fled from Saul in the cave.

1 BE merciful unto me, O God, be merciful unto me: for my soul trusteth in thee: yea, in the shadow of thy wings will I make my refuge, until *these* calamities be overpast.

2 I will cry unto God most high; unto God that performeth *all things* for me.

3 He shall send from heaven, and save me *from* the reproach of him that would swallow me up. Selah. God shall send forth his mercy and his truth.

4 My soul *is* among lions: *and* I lie *even among* them that are set on fire, *even* the sons of men, whose teeth *are* spears and arrows, and their tongue a sharp sword.

5 Be thou exalted, O God, above the heavens; *let* thy glory *be* above all the earth.

6 They have prepared a net for my steps; my soul is bowed down: they have digged a pit before me, into the midst whereof they are fallen *themselves*. Selah.

7 My heart is fixed, O God, my heart is fixed: I will sing and give praise.

8 Awake up, my glory; awake, psaltery and harp: I *myself* will awake early.

9 I will praise thee, O Lord, among the people: I will sing unto thee among the nations.

10 For thy mercy *is* great unto the heavens, and thy truth unto the clouds.

11 Be thou exalted, O God, above the heavens: *let* thy glory *be* above all the earth.

PSALM 58

To the chief Musician,
Al-taschith, Michtam of David.

1 DO ye indeed speak righteousness, O congregation? do ye judge uprightly, O ye sons of men?

2 Yea, in heart ye work wickedness; ye weigh the violence of your hands in the earth.

3 The wicked are estranged from the womb: they go astray as soon as they be born, speaking lies.

4 Their poison *is* like the poison of a serpent: *they are* like the deaf adder *that* stoppeth her ear;

5 Which will not hearken to the voice of charmers, charming never so wisely.

6 Break their teeth, O God, in their mouth: break out the great teeth of the young lions, O LORD.

Have you witnessed God's provision in your own life or the life of another? How has this impacted you?

2. Since the Lord became incarnate as a real human, the One who has put "my tears into thy bottle" (v. 8) has Himself wept tears (Luke 19:41; John 11:35; Heb. 5:7). Fear, grief, and the opposition of malicious liars were quite familiar to Him. Christ is able to show us sympathy, yet in a way that does not leave us in a self-centered pity party. He will lead us instead in the pathway of this psalm: enduring evil by faith in His Word, resulting in the praise of His glorious grace. Why do we need to know that Jesus Christ can empathize with us?

Psalm 57: *David relies on God's faithfulness and help when threatened by the enemy.*

Title *Al-taschith.* "Destroy not" (Deut. 9:26; Pss. 58–59; 75). *the cave.* Adullam or En-gedi (1 Sam. 22:1; 24:1–3).

57:1 *Be merciful.* Be gracious or show undeserved favor. *my soul trusteth in thee.* I take refuge in Thee. *shadow of thy wings.* An image expressing safety and protection, either by the wings of a parent bird (Deut. 32:10–12) or by the wings of the cherubim overshadowing the mercy seat (Ex. 25:20). *make my refuge.* Same word translated *trusteth.*

57:2 *performeth.* Avenge or accomplish.

57:3 *send forth.* Take action according to these attributes (43:3). *his mercy and his truth.* The words are frequently paired to express the absolute fidelity of God's covenant loyalty and love.

57:4 *My soul is.* I am.

57:7–11 These words are substantially repeated in 108:1–5.

57:7 *My heart is fixed.* My thoughts, desires, and will are firmly focused on the Lord (78:7–8,37; 108:1; 112:7).

57:8 *psaltery and harp.* Stringed instruments often used in praise.

57:10 *mercy.* Covenant loyalty.

57:11 *Be thou exalted . . . above all the earth.* The refrain repeated from v. 5.

Thoughts for Personal/Family Worship: Psalm 57

1. Calamities tend to come and go. David being delivered from one trouble soon finds himself praying his way out of another. In the middle of trouble, it is always best to draw near to God and find that place of quiet rest near to His heart. This requires us to fix our hearts' desires and hopes upon His love and His glory. There we shall find the shelter of divine mercy. Recall a difficult time, when your comfort was found in the assurance of God's love.

2. In all of Christ's troubles, the cry of His heart was, "Be thou exalted, O God" (vv. 5,11; see John 12:27–28). The aim of Christ's humiliation and exaltation was the glory of God the Father (Phil. 2:6–11). Christ taught His disciples to seek the glory of God's holy name first and foremost in their prayers (Matt. 6:9). How can the Lord Jesus enable us to fix our hearts more firmly upon the glory of the Lord?

Psalm 58: *David puts the judgment of the wicked into God's hands.*

58:2 *in heart ye work wickedness.* Our propensity to sin begins in our innermost beliefs, affections, and motives (Gen. 6:5).

58:3 *estranged.* Alienated from God. *from the womb . . . as soon as they be born.* Man is a sinner by nature from conception and a sinner in behavior at the first opportunity to speak.

58:4–5 *deaf adder . . . not hearken.* A poisonous snake, perhaps a cobra, that is not affected by the one seeking to control its behavior. Sinners reject all attempts to turn them back to God until their very nature is changed (Jer. 13:23; Matt. 19:25–26).

58:6 *Break their teeth.* Imprecations, prayers for God's justice

7 Let them melt away as waters *which* run
continually: *when* he bendeth *his bow to shoot* his
arrows, let them be as cut in pieces.
8 As a snail *which* melteth, let *every one of them*
pass away: *like* the untimely birth of a woman,
that they may not see the sun.
9 Before your pots can feel the thorns, he shall
take them away as with a whirlwind, both living,
and in *his* wrath.
10 The righteous shall rejoice when he seeth the
vengeance: he shall wash his feet in the blood of
the wicked.
11 So that a man shall say, Verily *there is* a reward
for the righteous: verily he is a God that judgeth
in the earth.

PSALM 59

To the chief Musician, Al-taschith,
Michtam of David; when Saul sent, and
they watched the house to kill him.

1 DELIVER me from mine enemies, O my God:
defend me from them that rise up against me.
2 Deliver me from the workers of iniquity, and
save me from bloody men.
3 For, lo, they lie in wait for my soul: the mighty
are gathered against me; not *for* my transgression,
nor *for* my sin, O LORD.
4 They run and prepare themselves without *my*
fault: awake to help me, and behold.
5 Thou therefore, O LORD God of hosts, the God
of Israel, awake to visit all the heathen: be not
merciful to any wicked transgressors. Selah.
6 They return at evening: they make a noise like a
dog, and go round about the city.
7 Behold, they belch out with their mouth: swords
are in their lips: for who, *say they*, doth hear?
8 But thou, O LORD, shalt laugh at them; thou
shalt have all the heathen in derision.
9 *Because of* his strength will I wait upon thee: for
God *is* my defence.
10 The God of my mercy shall prevent me: God
shall let me see *my desire* upon mine enemies.
11 Slay them not, lest my people forget: scatter
them by thy power; and bring them down, O Lord
our shield.
12 *For* the sin of their mouth *and* the words of
their lips let them even be taken in their pride:
and for cursing and lying *which* they speak.
13 Consume *them* in wrath, consume *them*, that
they *may* not *be*: and let them know that God
ruleth in Jacob unto the ends of the earth. Selah.
14 And at evening let them return; *and* let them
make a noise like a dog, and go round about the
city.
15 Let them wander up and down for meat, and
grudge if they be not satisfied.
16 But I will sing of thy power; yea, I will sing aloud
of thy mercy in the morning: for thou hast been my

against sinners, often use figurative and hyperbolic language. This is not to be taken literally, but as an appeal to God to disarm them like *lions* without teeth.

58:8 *untimely birth.* A miscarriage.

58:10 *wash . . . in the blood.* Not literally, but figuratively, implying a complete victory over the enemy.

58:11 *Verily.* Indeed, truly.

Thoughts for Personal/Family Worship: Psalm 58

1. **People have become sinful and wretched creatures by the fall in Adam. One of the worst manifestations of this is hatred against truth, so that we are quick to lie. It is tragic when sin reigns in us to the point that we refuse to listen to powerful warnings and sweet arguments. Why do children tell lies? What does this teach us about our fallen human nature?**
2. **Mankind's propensity to sin and lie moves us to resist the gospel of salvation. The Lord Jesus taught that sinners *cannot* listen to His Word because they do not belong to God but to the Devil, and he is the father of lies (John 8:43–47). Though people may hear the Word of God from the mouth of Jesus Christ Himself, they are not willing to come to Christ in faith (John 5:38–40). Only the sheep of the Lord will listen to His voice (John 10:26–27), not because they are inherently better than others, but because God draws them to Christ by the inner teaching of the Holy Spirit (John 6:37,44,63,65). How should these truths affect the way we seek salvation for ourselves? For others?**

Psalm 59: *David petitions the Lord for deliverance from violent men and praises the Lord as his sure defense.*

Title *when Saul sent . . . to kill him.* King Saul, in his jealousy, sent messengers to kill David in his home, but he escaped (1 Sam. 19:11–18).

59:1 *defend . . . from them that rise up.* Literally, "make me high or inaccessible to those who make themselves high against me."

59:2 *bloody men.* Men of bloods; the use of the plural in Hebrew refers to bloodshed or murder.

59:3 *my soul.* Me.

59:5 *God of hosts.* God of armies, designating God as having all authority, the Commander-in-Chief over His creation. *visit.* Pay attention to, with a view to punishing. *be not merciful.* Do not be gracious or show favor.

59:6 *make a noise.* Growl or bark. *dog.* Not a pet, but wild scavengers prowling around (v. 14).

59:7 *belch out with their mouth.* Their words pour out to attack him (*swords*).

59:8 *laugh at them.* An expression of the foolishness of their rebellion (2:4; Prov. 1:26).

59:9 *wait.* Not in resignation, but hopeful expectancy. *defence.* High place or cliff where one may safely hide (from the same Hebrew root as "defend," v. 1).

59:10 *my mercy.* Covenant loyalty and love for me. *prevent.* Come to meet.

59:15 *meat.* Food in general. *grudge.* Literally, "spend the night."

59:16–17 *defence . . . strength . . . mercy.* Terms repeated from vv. 9–10.

Thoughts for Personal/Family Worship: Psalm 59

The world is not neutral to believers but constantly opposes righteousness and sometimes actively conspires to destroy them. Some of the world's most powerful weap-

defence and refuge in the day of my trouble.
17 Unto thee, O my strength, will I sing: for God
is my defence, *and* the God of my mercy.

PSALM 60

To the chief Musician upon Shushan-eduth,
Michtam of David, to teach; when he strove
with Aram-naharaim and with Aram-zobah,
when Joab returned, and smote of Edom
in the valley of salt twelve thousand.

1 O GOD, thou hast cast us off, thou hast scat-
tered us, thou hast been displeased; O turn thyself
to us again.
2 Thou hast made the earth to tremble; thou hast
broken it: heal the breaches thereof; for it shaketh.
3 Thou hast shewed thy people hard things: thou
hast made us to drink the wine of astonishment.
4 Thou hast given a banner to them that fear
thee, that it may be displayed because of the truth.
Selah.
5 That thy beloved may be delivered; save *with*
thy right hand, and hear me.
6 God hath spoken in his holiness; I will rejoice,
I will divide Shechem, and mete out the valley of
Succoth.
7 Gilead *is* mine, and Manasseh *is* mine; Ephraim
also *is* the strength of mine head; Judah *is* my
lawgiver;
8 Moab *is* my washpot; over Edom will I cast out
my shoe: Philistia, triumph thou because of me.
9 Who will bring me *into* the strong city? who
will lead me into Edom?
10 *Wilt* not thou, O God, *which* hadst cast us off?
and *thou*, O God, *which* didst not go out with our
armies?
11 Give us help from trouble: for vain *is* the help
of man.
12 Through God we shall do valiantly: for he *it is*
that shall tread down our enemies.

PSALM 61

To the chief Musician upon Neginah,
A Psalm of David.

1 HEAR my cry, O God; attend unto my prayer.
2 From the end of the earth will I cry unto thee,
when my heart is overwhelmed: lead me to the
rock *that* is higher than I.
3 For thou hast been a shelter for me, *and* a
strong tower from the enemy.
4 I will abide in thy tabernacle for ever: I will

ons are evil words. Christians may find themselves in the frightening position of being under attack by a group of wicked and violent people. In such times, this psalm teaches us to cling to God. He is the "strength" of the believer, giving him power to keep hoping and obeying. He is his "defense," a high cliff where the believer may hide himself and find peace. His "mercy" or faithful love assures the ultimate salvation of His people, and the punishment of their wicked enemies. This confidence gives the people of Jesus Christ the ability to say that even if they are being slaughtered, they are more than overcomers, for nothing can separate them from the love of God in Christ (Rom. 8:31–39). How can we build up our confidence in our God?

Psalm 60: *David acknowledges God's sovereignty over all nations and trusts Him to defeat every enemy.*

Title *smote of Edom in the valley of salt.* David, seeking to establish Israel's supremacy, eventually conquered Edom (2 Sam. 8:13–14; 1 Chron. 18:12).
60:1 *cast us off.* Rejected us. *scattered.* Broke through in judgment. *displeased.* Angry. *turn . . . to us again.* Show us favor.
60:2 *made the earth to tremble.* Figurative for disruptions of ordinary life (18:7).
60:3 *wine of astonishment.* Judgments causing reeling or staggering.
60:5–12 These words are substantially repeated in 108:6–13.
60:6–7 *divide.* Apportion. *mete out.* Measure. All territories of David's kingdom that are subject to God's authority.
60:8 *washpot.* Specifically, a tub for washing feet, an image of humiliation, being reduced to service. *cast out my shoe.* An image of taking possession, claiming ownership. *triumph.* Shout in jubilation (41:11). Each of these nations were traditional enemies of Israel immediately surrounding David's kingdom. They were under God's authority as well.
60:11 *vain.* Worthless.
60:12 *do valiantly.* Perform a mighty work, that is, conquer their *enemies* by the power of the Lord (*through God*).

Thoughts for Personal/Family Worship: Psalm 60

1. **God's people, because of their sins, may incur His fatherly displeasure and be brought to a sad condition. Yet they are never reduced to hopelessness because God is still true to His promise in Christ. However formidable the task and however great the difficulty, we are still by prayer within reach of God. When He hears us, He will confirm and fulfill to us the promises He has made. The Lord is sovereign over all the world, and therefore we may always hope in Him.**
2. **God's promises should particularly give us confidence to make disciples of all nations, for Christ has received authority over heaven and earth and will be with us (Matt. 28:18–20). His gospel is like a banner of His love over us. Although we are to expect God to work for us, we are not to sit down and do nothing. "Through God *we shall do valiantly*" (v. 12). How should we be getting up and getting busy doing His will by His grace?**

Psalm 61: *Feeling isolated and overwhelmed, David prays for God's presence and help.*

61:1 *attend.* Pay attention.
61:2 *From the end of the earth.* David felt remote, far from God's house and people. *my heart is overwhelmed.* His inner being is without strength, feeble, or faint. *rock.* A huge, immovable boulder, a place of stability.
61:4 *thy tabernacle.* God's tent, not the sacred tabernacle into which only priests could enter, but a symbol of dwelling in fellowship with God, claiming Him as his Host to protect and provide for him (23:6). *covert.* Shelter.

trust in the covert of thy wings. Selah.
5 For thou, O God, hast heard my vows: thou
hast given *me* the heritage of those that fear thy
name.
6 Thou wilt prolong the king's life: *and* his years
as many generations.
7 He shall abide before God for ever: O prepare
mercy and truth, *which* may preserve him.
8 So will I sing praise unto thy name for ever, that
I may daily perform my vows.

PSALM 62

To the chief Musician, to Jeduthun,
A Psalm of David.

1 TRULY my soul waiteth upon God: from him
cometh my salvation.
2 He only *is* my rock and my salvation; *he is* my
defence; I shall not be greatly moved.
3 How long will ye imagine mischief against a
man? ye shall be slain all of you: as a bowing wall
shall ye be, and as a tottering fence.
4 They only consult to cast *him* down from his
excellency: they delight in lies: they bless with
their mouth, but they curse inwardly. Selah.
5 My soul, wait thou only upon God; for my
expectation *is* from him.
6 He only *is* my rock and my salvation: *he is* my
defence; I shall not be moved.
7 In God *is* my salvation and my glory: the rock
of my strength, *and* my refuge, *is* in God.
8 Trust in him at all times; ye people, pour out
your heart before him: God *is* a refuge for us.
Selah.
9 Surely men of low degree *are* vanity, *and* men
of high degree *are* a lie: to be laid in the balance,
they *are* altogether *lighter* than vanity.
10 Trust not in oppression, and become not vain
in robbery: if riches increase, set not your heart
upon them.
11 God hath spoken once; twice have I heard this;
that power *belongeth* unto God.
12 Also unto thee, O Lord, *belongeth* mercy: for
thou renderest to every man according to his
work.

61:5 *heritage.* Possession or inheritance. *thy name.* All the Lord has revealed Himself to be.
61:6 *prolong the king's life.* Literally, "add days upon the days of the king." *as many generations.* The ultimate Son of David will possess eternal life (21:4).
61:7 *prepare.* Apportion, appoint, or ordain. *mercy and truth.* These words are often paired to express the fidelity of covenant loyalty and love. *preserve.* Guard from dangers.

Thoughts for Personal/Family Worship: Psalm 61

David's prayer looked ahead to the day when Jesus Christ would rise from the dead to live forever as the king of Israel (v. 6). Christ sought refuge in God during His many trials, and now the risen Christ is the solid rock and strong tower of His people. God's loyal love and faithfulness belong to all who are in union with Christ by a living faith. Believers do well to remember that whatever their outward situation or inward condition, they are always able to turn to God in prayer. Although we may feel totally inadequate, God is stronger than we are, and bigger than any problem we may face. Christ's kingdom cannot fail, and even now His Spirit covers and shelters us with joy and peace. How can knowing that Christ will live forever, and that believers are joined to Him, give comfort and peace to the Christian when he cries out to God in prayer?

Psalm 62: *David testifies of his exclusive trust in God and exhorts others to trust Him as well.*

62:1 *Truly.* The same Hebrew word occurs six times in this psalm, also translated "only" (vv. 2,4–6) and "surely" (v. 9). Hence, it is called the "only" psalm and sets the theme of trusting in the Lord alone. *my soul waiteth.* "I am silent," expressing a quiet and reverent trust in God as the only source of *salvation* (vv. 2,6; Isa. 45:21).
62:2 *rock.* Huge, immovable boulder, a picture of a firm and stable foundation. *defence.* Refuge for safety. *not be greatly moved.* Not made to stagger or be overthrown (vv. 6–7).
62:3 *imagine mischief.* Attack (this Hebrew word occurs only here). *bowing wall . . . tottering fence.* Walls about to collapse; an image of weakness and future failure.
62:4 *consult to cast him down from his excellency.* Literally, "from his elevation or dignity they plan to banish or thrust [him] out."
62:5 *My soul.* He is addressing himself. *wait.* Hebrew, "keep quiet," serenely reliant and quietly expectant upon God. *expectation.* Hope.
62:8 *Trust.* Put confidence in for security (v. 10). *pour out your heart before him.* A picture of fervent prayer (1 Sam. 1:15). His personal experience leads to public exhortation.
62:9 *men of low degree.* Literally, "sons of Adam," underscoring weakness or frailty. *vanity.* Breath, that which is fleeting and unsubstantial. *men of high degree.* Literally, "sons of man," highlighting a man's nobility (49:2).
62:10 *oppression.* Extortion. *become not vain in robbery.* Literally, "do not put empty confidence in loot."
62:11 *once; twice.* Not literally, but using ascending numbers to express the idea of totality or certainty (Amos 1–2; Prov. 6:16).
62:12 *mercy.* Covenant loyalty and love. *thou renderest to every man according to his work.* God's judgment will use men's works to reveal their true character, bringing the rewards of grace to believers but damnation to the wicked (Matt. 12:33–37; 16:27; 25:31–46).

Thoughts for Personal/Family Worship: Psalm 62

1. **The psalm's theme of exclusive trust is vital and far-reaching. The value of faith is determined by its object; and faith is worthless unless it rests upon the Lord alone. Trusting in mankind and human resources is foolish, for the greatest and the least of men are all lighter than a feather in the balances of God. Instead, we must trust in the Lord at all times, building our lives upon His power, reliability, love, and justice. How do we see these divine attributes in Jesus Christ?**
2. **Such faith in the Lord alone will express itself. First, it will move a person to pour out his heart to God in prayer.**

PSALM 63

A Psalm of David, when he was
in the wilderness of Judah.

1 O GOD, thou *art* my God; early will I seek thee:
my soul thirsteth for thee, my flesh longeth for
thee in a dry and thirsty land, where no water is;
2 To see thy power and thy glory, so *as* I have seen
thee in the sanctuary.
3 Because thy lovingkindness *is* better than life,
my lips shall praise thee.
4 Thus will I bless thee while I live: I will lift up
my hands in thy name.
5 My soul shall be satisfied as *with* marrow and
fatness; and my mouth shall praise *thee* with joy-
ful lips:
6 When I remember thee upon my bed, *and*
meditate on thee in the *night* watches.
7 Because thou hast been my help, therefore in
the shadow of thy wings will I rejoice.
8 My soul followeth hard after thee: thy right
hand upholdeth me.
9 But those *that* seek my soul, to destroy *it*, shall
go into the lower parts of the earth.
10 They shall fall by the sword: they shall be a
portion for foxes.
11 But the king shall rejoice in God; every one
that sweareth by him shall glory: but the mouth
of them that speak lies shall be stopped.

PSALM 64

To the chief Musician, A Psalm of David.

1 HEAR my voice, O God, in my prayer: preserve
my life from fear of the enemy.
2 Hide me from the secret counsel of the wicked;
from the insurrection of the workers of iniquity:
3 Who whet their tongue like a sword, *and* bend
their bows to shoot their arrows, *even* bitter words:
4 That they may shoot in secret at the perfect:
suddenly do they shoot at him, and fear not.
5 They encourage themselves *in* an evil matter:
they commune of laying snares privily; they say,
Who shall see them?
6 They search out iniquities; they accomplish a
diligent search: both the inward *thought* of every
one *of them*, and the heart, *is* deep.

Second, it will cause a person to think lightly of men and their wealth. Third, it will create a heart that is open and eager to listen to God's Word. Such a person can truly say that his soul hopes in God alone for salvation. Is this true of you? What evidence is there of it in your life?

Psalm 63: *David expresses his desire for God's presence and protection regardless of location or circumstance of life.*

Title *in the wilderness of Judah*. David often hid in desolate places (1 Sam. 23:14,24; 24:1; 25:1; 26:2–3) when his enemies sought to kill him (v. 9).

63:1 *early will I seek thee*. Not a temporal reference but descriptive of the manner, "to seek with earnest desire or diligence." Seeking the Lord in this way finds Him (2 Chron. 15:15). *my soul thirsteth*. A vivid image to describe desperate desire and relentless pursuit for the Lord's presence (42:1).

63:2 *see thy power*. Being in the wilderness was no hindrance to experiencing God's presence.

63:3 *lovingkindness*. Covenant loyalty and love.

63:4 *lift up my hands*. A gesture expressing dependence, often associated with prayer (see note at 28:2).

63:5 *My soul*. Equates to the personal pronoun, "I." *marrow and fatness*. The best portions, a feast. The dry place became a banquet table when he was conscious of the divine presence. An experiential knowledge of God is a satisfying, exceptional, and never-failing portion (84:11; Jer. 31:14).

63:6 *remember*. Think about intentionally to engage one's heart.

63:7 *shadow of thy wings*. An image of protection and provision.

63:8 *My soul followeth hard after thee*. I cling to Thee.

63:9 *my soul*. Me.

63:10 *foxes*. Jackals. To become the food (*portion*) of scavengers by not receiving a proper burial was to die in shame and disgrace (1 Kings 14:11; 16:4; 21:23–24).

63:11 *the king*. David and his royal sons, ultimately Christ. This implies that David wrote this psalm after his coronation, perhaps when fleeing from Absalom (2 Sam. 15:23; 17:29).

Thoughts for Personal/Family Worship: Psalm 63

1. **David's desire for the presence of God in the wilderness sets a pattern for responding properly to trials and troubles. First, no trial should distract us from contemplating and desiring God's presence (vv. 1–5). God's glory is not limited to any location or circumstance. Second, no trial should keep us from remembering God's faithfulness that we have experienced so many times in the past (vv. 6–8). Third, no trial should cause us to forget God's justice as sooner or later those who would seek our hurt will receive from God what they deserve (vv. 9–11). So if we seek the Lord with all our heart, regardless of where we are or what we are going through, we will find Him. True religion is found where we are satisfied in God and pour forth God's praise. How can a believer cultivate such God-centered joy every day?**
2. **"The king shall rejoice in God" (v. 11). No man or angel has more joy than the Lord Jesus Christ, exalted to God's right hand and given the fullness of the Holy Spirit (16:11; 45:7; 110:1). Amazingly, Christ desires to share His joy with His followers, so that their joy will be full (Matt. 25:21; John 15:11). How can we taste His joy even in this world as we wait for His kingdom to come?**

Psalm 64: *David prays and expresses his confidence that God will fight his enemies for him.*

64:1 *in my prayer*. Specifically, "in my lament or complaint." *preserve*. Keep watch over, guard from dangers. *fear*. Dread or trembling.

64:2 *insurrection*. Unrest or agitation.

64:3 *whet*. Sharpen.

64:4 *in secret*. From a hiding place (11:2). *perfect*. The one with moral integrity.

64:5 *commune of laying snares privily*. Talk about hiding traps.

64:6 *search out iniquities . . . accomplish a diligent search*. Devise malicious plans and complete the plot they devised.

THE SOUL

In the wilderness of Judah David experiences thirst and hunger that go far beyond any physical need for drink and food. His is a thirsting of the soul, a hunger of the body for God, "to see thy power and thy glory, so as I have seen thee in the sanctuary" (Ps. 63:1–2). As a seasoned warrior, David can do without food and drink if need be. Deprived of access to God's house, however, he cries out in his isolation and emptiness.

David uses the terms *soul* and *flesh* to describe his whole being. Paul uses similar terms: "Though our outward man perish, yet the inward man is renewed day by day" (2 Cor. 4:16). In both cases the idea is that the human constitution has two aspects, the visible "outward man" of flesh and blood, and the "inward man" or "soul" or, as Peter says, "the hidden man of the heart" (1 Peter 3:4).

The Hebrew word *nephesh* is used hundreds of times in the Old Testament, where it is most often translated "soul" (428 times). However, depending on context, the translators render it as "life" (119 times), "person" (30 times), "heart" (15 times), and "mind" (15 times). In the New Testament the Greek word *psuche* is translated "soul" (58 times), "life" (40 times), "mind" (3 times), and "heart" (1 time). With such a wide range of meanings, it is unwise to define the word too narrowly or precisely.

Scripture teaches that the human body was a special creation of God, formed from the dust of the earth and brought to life when God breathed "the breath of life" into it: "Man became a living soul" (Gen. 2:7). The human soul is immaterial and immortal, the seat of knowledge and understanding, memory and meditation, conscience and consciousness, will and emotion. It is the unique identity of each person or "self." Each human soul is a gift from the hand of God (Eccl. 12:7).

Interaction between soul and body is so seamless that it is often impossible to distinguish whether a given effect is produced by one or the other. Certainly the soul gives life to the body, and what happens in the soul registers in the body. David records the physical effects of his guilty silence: "My bones waxed old through my roaring all the day long" (Ps. 32:3).

Death is the rending asunder of soul and body. The body succumbs to corruption. The souls of the righteous are made perfect in holiness and received into the highest heavens, to behold the face of God in light and glory, awaiting the resurrection of their bodies. The souls of the wicked are cast into hell, to remain in torments and utter darkness, reserved for judgment at the last day. Scripture does not support such erroneous beliefs as "soul sleep," a second chance to receive Christ and be saved after death, salvation through suffering in purgatory, reincarnation, or annihilation of the souls of the wicked.

Some have proposed a distinction between "soul" and "spirit" based on Paul's prayer in 1 Thessalonians 5:13: "And I pray God your whole spirit and soul and body be preserved blameless." Any distinction between "soul" and "spirit" fails because the words are used interchangeably elsewhere (see Luke 1:46–47), and they denote the same thing, namely, the "inward man." Paul is using a periphrasis or circumlocution to emphasize the totality of preservation he desires for his readers.

Scripture does not denigrate the human body, since it is the creation of God, although its original beauty and perfection have been greatly marred by sin. However, Christ teaches us to put the needs of the soul above the claims of the body: "For what is a man profited, if he shall gain the whole world, and lose his own soul?" (Matt. 16:26). Paul says the same thing, in positive terms: "Bodily exercise profiteth for a little time: but godliness is profitable unto all things, having the promise of the life that now is, and of that which is to come."

7 But God shall shoot at them *with* an arrow;
suddenly shall they be wounded.
8 So they shall make their own tongue to fall
upon themselves: all that see them shall flee away.
9 And all men shall fear, and shall declare the
work of God; for they shall wisely consider of his
doing.
10 The righteous shall be glad in the LORD, and
shall trust in him; and all the upright in heart
shall glory.

PSALM 65

To the chief Musician,
A Psalm *and* Song of David.

1 PRAISE waiteth for thee, O God, in Sion: and
unto thee shall the vow be performed.
2 O thou that hearest prayer, unto thee shall all
flesh come.
3 Iniquities prevail against me: *as for* our trans-
gressions, thou shalt purge them away.
4 Blessed *is the man whom* thou choosest, and
causest to approach *unto thee, that* he may dwell
in thy courts: we shall be satisfied with the good-
ness of thy house, *even* of thy holy temple.
5 *By* terrible things in righteousness wilt thou
answer us, O God of our salvation; *who art* the
confidence of all the ends of the earth, and of
them that are afar off *upon* the sea:
6 Which by his strength setteth fast the moun-
tains; *being* girded with power:
7 Which stilleth the noise of the seas, the noise of
their waves, and the tumult of the people.
8 They also that dwell in the uttermost parts are
afraid at thy tokens: thou makest the outgoings of
the morning and evening to rejoice.
9 Thou visitest the earth, and waterest it: thou
greatly enrichest it with the river of God, *which*
is full of water: thou preparest them corn, when
thou hast so provided for it.
10 Thou waterest the ridges thereof abundantly:
thou settlest the furrows thereof: thou makest
it soft with showers: thou blessest the springing
thereof.
11 Thou crownest the year with thy goodness;
and thy paths drop fatness.
12 They drop *upon* the pastures of the wilderness:
and the little hills rejoice on every side.
13 The pastures are clothed with flocks; the
valleys also are covered over with corn; they shout
for joy, they also sing.

64:7 *shoot . . . with an arrow.* He gives to the wicked what they aim to do to the righteous (vv. 3–4).
64:8 *their own tongue to fall upon themselves.* They will be caught in the trap they set for others by their sinful speech (v. 5).
64:9–10 God's punishment of the wicked produces awe and reverence (*fear*), reflection and wisdom (*wisely consider*), and joy and boasting in God (*be glad . . . glory*).

Thoughts for Personal/Family Worship: Psalm 64

Let us not be naïve; the wicked hate the righteous and implement careful plans to destroy them. On the other hand, let the righteous not live in fear. God is their ally, ready to enter the field for their cause (9:4; 35:23; 140:12). The wicked may aim their bows at people of integrity, but God has a bow too. They have lies, slander, and false accusations, but the godly have a Witness to the truth. In fact, the Lord uses the very schemes of the wicked to destroy them. If you doubt this, consider Satan's attack upon Christ, for through His crucifixion Jesus conquered the Devil (Col. 2:15; Heb. 2:14). Christ's victory belongs to all who believe in Him, and all that sinners say and do against them will ultimately harm only the sinner. How should this change the way we view the hard words and violence that the church must endure from the world?

Psalm 65: *David praises the Lord for His abundant provisions.*
65:1 *Praise waiteth for thee.* Literally, "Praise is silence to Thee," expressing profound reverence (62:1; Eccl. 5:1–3).
65:2 *all flesh.* Mankind.
65:3 *purge them away.* Make atonement for sin.
65:4 *Blessed.* Having great benefits (1:1). *choosest.* God, in His free and sovereign grace, selects whom He will bless (Neh. 9:7). *courts.* Areas outside the holy places where the worshipers would gather (100:4; Ex. 27:9). *temple.* Or palace, representing the presence of God (27:4). The temple was not yet constructed, though this term could be used of the site of the tabernacle (1 Sam. 1:9; 3:3).
65:5 *terrible things.* Awe-inspiring things.
65:6 *setteth fast.* Establishes. *girded.* Clothed as with a belt (93:1).
65:7 *tumult.* Turmoil or roaring.
65:8 *uttermost parts.* Distant places. *tokens.* Signs, often miraculous. *outgoings of the morning and evening.* East and west.
65:9 *visitest.* Pay attention and thus provide what is necessary. *waterest.* Send rain, sometimes a metaphor for the blessing of Christ through the Word and the Spirit (72:6; Deut. 32:2; 2 Sam. 23:4; Isa. 55:10–11; Ezek. 34:26; Hos. 6:3). *corn.* Grain (v. 13).
65:10 *settlest.* Press down or smooth. *springing.* Sprouting or growth.
65:11 *paths.* Trails marked by wheeled wagon traffic (23:3). *drop.* Overflow (v. 12). *fatness.* Abundant provision (36:8; 63:5).

Thoughts for Personal/Family Worship: Psalm 65

The mighty power of the Creator and the goodness of God's providence in watering the earth and producing crops teach us that the best gift of all is closeness to God. The Giver is greater than the gifts. Therefore, the greatest benefits in the universe belong to the person whom God chooses, draws near to Him by the Holy Spirit, forgives of his sins by the blood of Christ, and satisfies with His goodness and holiness. There is nothing sweeter than the sovereign grace of Jesus Christ. Sadly, nothing is more common than for people to enjoy the gifts of creation and providence but have no desire for Christ. In our gratitude, we must look beyond earthly blessings to the deepest blessing, seeking the presence of God

PSALM 66

To the chief Musician, A Song *or* Psalm.

1 MAKE a joyful noise unto God, all ye lands:
2 Sing forth the honour of his name: make his
praise glorious.
3 Say unto God, How terrible *art thou in* thy
works! through the greatness of thy power shall
thine enemies submit themselves unto thee.
4 All the earth shall worship thee, and shall sing
unto thee; they shall sing *to* thy name. Selah.
5 Come and see the works of God: *he is* terrible *in*
his doing toward the children of men.
6 He turned the sea into dry *land*: they went
through the flood on foot: there did we rejoice in
him.
7 He ruleth by his power for ever; his eyes behold
the nations: let not the rebellious exalt them-
selves. Selah.
8 O bless our God, ye people, and make the voice
of his praise to be heard:
9 Which holdeth our soul in life, and suffereth
not our feet to be moved.
10 For thou, O God, hast proved us: thou hast
tried us, as silver is tried.
11 Thou broughtest us into the net; thou laidst
affliction upon our loins.
12 Thou hast caused men to ride over our heads;
we went through fire and through water: but thou
broughtest us out into a wealthy *place*.
13 I will go into thy house with burnt offerings: I
will pay thee my vows,
14 Which my lips have uttered, and my mouth
hath spoken, when I was in trouble.
15 I will offer unto thee burnt sacrifices of
fatlings, with the incense of rams; I will offer
bullocks with goats. Selah.
16 Come *and* hear, all ye that fear God, and I will
declare what he hath done for my soul.
17 I cried unto him with my mouth, and he was
extolled with my tongue.
18 If I regard iniquity in my heart, the Lord will
not hear *me*:
19 *But* verily God hath heard *me*; he hath at-
tended to the voice of my prayer.
20 Blessed *be* God, which hath not turned away
my prayer, nor his mercy from me.

PSALM 67

To the chief Musician on Neginoth,
A Psalm *or* Song.

1 GOD be merciful unto us, and bless us; *and*
cause his face to shine upon us; Selah.
2 That thy way may be known upon earth, thy

through Christ. We must seek Him in quiet reverence and believing prayer. Why is nearness to God the greatest blessing?

Psalm 66: *The wonderful works of God and His gracious benefits are reasons for praise.*

66:3 *terrible.* Inspiring fear and awe (v. 5). *submit themselves.* Come cringing, compelled to an outward show of obedience.
66:4 *worship.* Bow down.
66:6 *the sea into dry land.* Salvation at the Red Sea (Ex. 14). *flood.* Literally, "the river," alluding to the crossing of the Jordan (Josh. 3:14–17).
66:9 *holdeth our soul in life.* The one who puts us in life; He gives and preserves life. *suffereth not.* Does not allow. Hebrew, "He does not appoint our feet to staggering."
66:10 *proved.* Put to the test. *tried.* Refined.
66:11–12 *Thou hast caused . . . thou broughtest.* God's providence brings His people through troubles to a place of superabundance (*wealthy*).
66:13–14 *pay thee my vows.* Solemn commitments to God must be kept, not forgotten after the crisis has passed (Eccl. 5:4–5).
66:15 *fatlings.* Fat sheep.
66:16 *for my soul.* For me.
66:18 *regard.* See, in the sense of enjoying (27:13; 34:8; Gen. 1:31; 3:6; 6:2). Hypocritical prayers while loving sin in the *heart* can expect no answer from God.
66:19 *verily.* Indeed, truly. That God heard means sin was not cherished in the heart.
66:20 *mercy.* Covenant loyalty and love.

Thoughts for Personal/Family Worship: Psalm 66

1. **God's works of power for Israel at the Red Sea and the Jordan River called all nations to praise Him. Even the wicked were compelled to give Him some honor. Much more do God's works of redemption in Jesus Christ call all nations to worship Him. The death of God's Son for sinners declares God's love, wisdom, mercy, justice, and wrath against sin like no other event in history. His resurrection and exaltation to supreme glory reveal God's unspeakable power and faithfulness. Now, through the gospel, Christ calls the world to come and see (John 1:39), for He has made known God's name (John 17:6). When Christ returns, even His enemies will be forced to bow before Him and confess that He is Lord (Phil. 2:10–11). Have you become a true worshiper of God through faith in Christ? If so, how are you working with the church to declare the gospel to everyone on earth?**
2. **God despises hypocrisy. He is very tender and forgiving toward those who fear Him and hope in His love, despite their many faults. However, hypocrites say prayers with their lips while in their hearts they look to sin as their great delight. How can we be careful to pray with our thoughts and desires fixed upon God, acknowledging His faithful love but despising our own sin?**

Psalm 67: *The psalmist prays for the universal extension of God's kingdom.*

67:1 *be merciful . . . bless . . . shine.* This is the language of the blessing by the priests (Num. 6:24–26). Ordinarily invoking "the LORD," here it addresses *God*, the Creator of all things (Gen. 1:1), which fits the psalm's theme of the advance of God's kingdom in all the earth.
67:2 *saving health.* Salvation. *among all nations.* This prayer for missions stands upon God's promise to Abraham to bless all peoples through him and his seed (Gen. 12:3; 22:18).

saving health among all nations.
3 Let the people praise thee, O God; let all the
people praise thee.
4 O let the nations be glad and sing for joy: for
thou shalt judge the people righteously, and
govern the nations upon earth. Selah.
5 Let the people praise thee, O God; let all the
people praise thee.
6 *Then* shall the earth yield her increase; *and*
God, *even* our own God, shall bless us.
7 God shall bless us; and all the ends of the earth
shall fear him.

PSALM 68

To the chief Musician, A Psalm *or* Song of David.

1 LET God arise, let his enemies be scattered: let
them also that hate him flee before him.
2 As smoke is driven away, *so* drive *them* away:
as wax melteth before the fire, *so* let the wicked
perish at the presence of God.
3 But let the righteous be glad; let them rejoice
before God: yea, let them exceedingly rejoice.
4 Sing unto God, sing praises to his name: extol
him that rideth upon the heavens by his name
JAH, and rejoice before him.
5 A father of the fatherless, and a judge of the
widows, *is* God in his holy habitation.
6 God setteth the solitary in families: he bringeth
out those which are bound with chains: but the
rebellious dwell in a dry *land*.
7 O God, when thou wentest forth before thy
people, when thou didst march through the wil-
derness; Selah:
8 The earth shook, the heavens also dropped at
the presence of God: *even* Sinai itself *was moved* at
the presence of God, the God of Israel.
9 Thou, O God, didst send a plentiful rain,
whereby thou didst confirm thine inheritance,
when it was weary.
10 Thy congregation hath dwelt therein: thou, O
God, hast prepared of thy goodness for the poor.
11 The Lord gave the word: great *was* the com-
pany of those that published *it*.
12 Kings of armies did flee apace: and she that
tarried at home divided the spoil.
13 Though ye have lien among the pots, *yet shall*
ye be as the wings of a dove covered with silver,
and her feathers with yellow gold.
14 When the Almighty scattered kings in it, it was
white as snow in Salmon.
15 The hill of God *is as* the hill of Bashan; an high
hill *as* the hill of Bashan.

67:3 *people.* The Hebrew is plural, referring to the Gentiles. The purpose of missions is that all nations would worship the true God.
67:4 *judge.* Rule as a king (1 Sam. 8:5–6,20; 2 Chron. 1:11). *govern.* Lead as a shepherd (23:2), also an image of a king. The reign of God as king is the joy of the nations.
67:5–7 The repeated prayers for all the world to *praise* God (v. 3) and for God to *bless* His people (v. 1) wraps this psalm in patterns of grace-fueled worship centering upon the joyful kingdom of God (v. 4).
67:6 *earth yield her increase.* A sign of divine blessing for keeping the covenant (Lev. 26:3–4). This psalm may have been sung in the celebration of the harvest at the feast of Pentecost (Lev. 23:9–22; Acts 2). Minus the title, the psalm has forty-nine Hebrew words, the number of days of the season leading up to Pentecost (Lev. 23:15).

Thoughts for Personal/Family Worship: Psalm 67

Through this psalm, godly Jews prayed for centuries that God would so bless His covenant people that through them the Gentile nations of the world would come gladly under the Lord's reign and give Him the praise He deserves. It may be that they did so as they celebrated God's provision of another harvest at the Feast of Pentecost. With the coming of the Messiah of Israel, the psalm took on an even richer significance. Jesus the great High Priest now blesses believers, for He has fulfilled the law and brought the covenant blessing by His death on the cross. Christ the risen King rules His people by the Spirit so that they rejoice in obeying Him. At Pentecost He poured out that Spirit, so that a harvest of souls began to be gathered from all nations. The church now prays and labors so that all people will join in the worship of God, as Christ the Prophet preaches God's salvation through the gospel that the church proclaims. Christians must pray toward this today, longing for the full harvest to come in from every nation. As a largely Gentile church, we can rejoice in the blessing promised to Abraham and pray for missions and specifically pray also for the salvation of the Jewish people, through whom this blessing came.

Psalm 68: *David celebrates God's power and providence over the affairs of His people.*

68:1 *Let God arise.* The words of Moses when the ark was taken up, signaling the nation to move (Num. 10:35).
68:4 *JAH.* A shortened form of the divine name Jehovah (as in the last syllable of "hallelujah," praise the LORD).
68:5 *father of the fatherless, and a judge of the widows.* God's compassion and justice are engaged to care for those without the provision and protection of a father or husband (10:14, 17–18; 27:10; Deut. 10:18; 27:19). Israel's slavery in Egypt and sins in the wilderness produced many orphans and widows, but the Lord adopted Israel as His son (Ex. 4:22).
68:6 *solitary.* The lonely (113:9).
68:8 *dropped.* Dripped. The Lord showed His glory on Mt. *Sinai* with an earthquake and thunderstorm (Ex. 19:16,18; Judg. 5:4–5; Isa. 64:3). Nothing remains the same when God appears.
68:11 *great was the company of those that published it.* The ones who heralded the good news were a great army.
68:12 *flee apace.* Literally, "retreated, retreated." Hebrew uses repetition for emphasis: the kings of armies were completely routed and thrown into full retreat.
68:13 *have lien.* Have lain down. *pots.* Either a sheepfold or saddlebags; the Hebrew term is rare. The verse pictures conversion, from filth to beauty (*dove . . . silver . . . gold*).
68:15–16 The *hill* of *Bashan* was the highest in the region but nothing in comparison to the hill where *God* chose to

16 Why leap ye, ye high hills? *this is* the hill *which*
God desireth to dwell in; yea, the LORD will dwell
in it for ever.
17 The chariots of God *are* twenty thousand, *even*
thousands of angels: the Lord *is* among them, *as*
in Sinai, in the holy *place*.
18 Thou hast ascended on high, thou hast led
captivity captive: thou hast received gifts for men;
yea, *for* the rebellious also, that the LORD God
might dwell *among them*.
19 Blessed *be* the Lord, *who* daily loadeth us *with*
benefits, even the God of our salvation. Selah.
20 *He that is* our God *is* the God of salvation; and
unto GOD the Lord *belong* the issues from death.
21 But God shall wound the head of his enemies,
and the hairy scalp of such an one as goeth on still
in his trespasses.
22 The Lord said, I will bring again from Bashan,
I will bring *my people* again from the depths of
the sea:
23 That thy foot may be dipped in the blood of
thine enemies, *and* the tongue of thy dogs in the
same.
24 They have seen thy goings, O God; *even* the
goings of my God, my King, in the sanctuary.
25 The singers went before, the players on in-
struments *followed* after; among *them were* the
damsels playing with timbrels.
26 Bless ye God in the congregations, *even* the
Lord, from the fountain of Israel.
27 There *is* little Benjamin *with* their ruler, the
princes of Judah *and* their council, the princes of
Zebulun, *and* the princes of Naphtali.
28 Thy God hath commanded thy strength:
strengthen, O God, that which thou hast wrought
for us.
29 Because of thy temple at Jerusalem shall kings
bring presents unto thee.
30 Rebuke the company of spearmen, the
multitude of the bulls, with the calves of the
people, *till every one* submit himself with pieces of
silver: scatter thou the people *that* delight in war.
31 Princes shall come out of Egypt; Ethiopia shall
soon stretch out her hands unto God.
32 Sing unto God, ye kingdoms of the earth; O
sing praises unto the Lord; Selah:
33 To him that rideth upon the heavens of
heavens, *which were* of old; lo, he doth send out
his voice, *and that* a mighty voice.
34 Ascribe ye strength unto God: his excellency *is*
over Israel, and his strength *is* in the clouds.
35 O God, *thou art* terrible out of thy holy places:
the God of Israel *is* he that giveth strength and
power unto *his* people. Blessed *be* God.

PSALM 69

To the chief Musician upon Shoshannim,
A Psalm of David.

1 SAVE me, O God; for the waters are come in
unto *my* soul.
2 I sink in deep mire, where *there is* no standing:
I am come into deep waters, where the floods
overflow me.
3 I am weary of my crying: my throat is dried:
mine eyes fail while I wait for my God.
4 They that hate me without a cause are more

dwell, Zion, which is not high in size but significance.

68:18 *ascended on high*. Having come down to save His people, the Lord went up in victory—applied to Christ's ascension into heaven (Eph. 4:8). *received gifts*. The spoils of the Lord's victory, which He shares with His people for their salvation (vv. 19,35). *for men*. Literally, "in the man."

68:20 *issues*. Ways of escape.

68:23 *may be dipped*. Or "may strike, wound."

68:24 *goings*. Procession or progress. *my King, in the sanctuary*. The Lord returns victorious to His house (24:7–10).

68:25 *damsels*. Virgins. *timbrels*. Drums or tambourines.

68:27 *princes*. Leaders, not royal sons.

68:28 *wrought*. Performed or done.

68:29 *temple*. Or palace, the royal residence.

68:30 *company of spearmen*. Or wild animals of the reeds.

68:31 *Princes*. Envoys.

68:35 *terrible*. Inspiring fear and awe.

Thoughts for Personal/Family Worship: Psalm 68

1. This psalm speaks of the victory of Christ. The apostle Paul quoted it with reference to the ascension of Christ to bless His people (v. 18; Eph. 4:8–10). Christ is exalted and, as Captain of the Lord's hosts, He leads His people to victory over all His enemies, which is a cause for great rejoicing in His church (Josh. 5:13–15; Isa. 55:4; Rev. 6:2). Christ has ascended to the heavenly Zion, and He has sent down His many blessings in the Holy Spirit (Acts 2:33; 5:30–32). Give thanks to the Lord for today's daily load of blessings (v. 19)!

2. Our greatest need today is for the Lord, in answer to our prayers, to arise and display His power, reviving His church, promoting His cause, and overcoming His many enemies. Lest we lose heart, we should remember in discouraging days that Christ rules on high over heaven and earth. As the God of salvation, He is able to do wonderful things for His church. There can be no room for pessimism. The victory of the Lord belongs to His people. How can we take hold of the strength that Christ has for us?

Psalm 69: ***In distress, David prays for deliverance and devotes his enemies to destruction in a manner that points to the sorrows of Christ.***

69:1 *waters . . . unto my soul*. Danger threatened to engulf his very life. This psalm is quoted no less than five times in the New Testament with reference to the rejection and sufferings of Jesus Christ (see notes at vv. 4,9,22–23,25), and it foreshadows Christ in many ways. His sorrows would overwhelm Him (Luke 12:50).

69:2 *no standing*. No firm ground or foothold.

69:3 *is dried*. Become hoarse or parched. *wait*. Hope for with expectancy, an expression of faith.

than the hairs of mine head: they that would
destroy me, *being* mine enemies wrongfully, are
mighty: then I restored *that* which I took not
away.
5 O God, thou knowest my foolishness; and my
sins are not hid from thee.
6 Let not them that wait on thee, O Lord GOD of
hosts, be ashamed for my sake: let not those that
seek thee be confounded for my sake, O God of
Israel.
7 Because for thy sake I have borne reproach;
shame hath covered my face.
8 I am become a stranger unto my brethren, and
an alien unto my mother's children.
9 For the zeal of thine house hath eaten me up;
and the reproaches of them that reproached thee
are fallen upon me.
10 When I wept, *and chastened* my soul with
fasting, that was to my reproach.
11 I made sackcloth also my garment; and I
became a proverb to them.
12 They that sit in the gate speak against me; and
I *was* the song of the drunkards.
13 But as for me, my prayer *is* unto thee, O LORD,
in an acceptable time: O God, in the multitude of
thy mercy hear me, in the truth of thy salvation.
14 Deliver me out of the mire, and let me not
sink: let me be delivered from them that hate me,
and out of the deep waters.
15 Let not the waterflood overflow me, neither let
the deep swallow me up, and let not the pit shut
her mouth upon me.
16 Hear me, O LORD; for thy lovingkindness *is*
good: turn unto me according to the multitude of
thy tender mercies.
17 And hide not thy face from thy servant; for I
am in trouble: hear me speedily.
18 Draw nigh unto my soul, *and* redeem it:
deliver me because of mine enemies.
19 Thou hast known my reproach, and my
shame, and my dishonour: mine adversaries *are*
all before thee.
20 Reproach hath broken my heart; and I am full
of heaviness: and I looked *for some* to take pity,
but *there was* none; and for comforters, but I
found none.
21 They gave me also gall for my meat; and in my
thirst they gave me vinegar to drink.
22 Let their table become a snare before them:
and *that which should have been* for *their* welfare,
let it become a trap.
23 Let their eyes be darkened, that they see not;
and make their loins continually to shake.
24 Pour out thine indignation upon them, and let
thy wrathful anger take hold of them.
25 Let their habitation be desolate; *and* let none
dwell in their tents.
26 For they persecute *him* whom thou hast
smitten; and they talk to the grief of those whom
thou hast wounded.
27 Add iniquity unto their iniquity: and let them
not come into thy righteousness.
28 Let them be blotted out of the book of the
living, and not be written with the righteous.
29 But I *am* poor and sorrowful: let thy salvation,
O God, set me up on high.
30 I will praise the name of God with a song, and
will magnify him with thanksgiving.
31 *This* also shall please the LORD better than an
ox *or* bullock that hath horns and hoofs.
32 The humble shall see *this, and* be glad: and
your heart shall live that seek God.

69:4 *hate me without a cause.* Supremely fulfilled in the world's hatred of the sinless Lord Jesus (John 15:25). *restored that which I took not away.* Required to repay what he did not steal.

69:5 *sins.* Guilt, debts, offenses.

69:6 *wait.* A different word (v. 3) but the same idea of hopeful expectancy. *confounded.* Dishonored.

69:8 *stranger.* One estranged. *alien.* One unknown or unfamiliar.

69:9 *zeal of thine house.* Christ showed this zeal by driving merchants from the temple (John 2:17; cf. Matt. 21:12–13). *reproaches.* Christ did not live for His own immediate gratification, but suffered for God's glory (Rom. 15:3).

69:10 *When I wept . . . fasting.* Literally, "I myself wept in the period of fasting." *chastened.* Not in the Hebrew text.

69:11 *sackcloth.* Associated with grief and sorrow.

69:13 *mercy.* Covenant loyalty and love.

69:15 *waterflood.* Torrent or flow. *pit.* Well of underground water.

69:16 *lovingkindness.* Covenant loyalty and love. *tender mercies.* Compassion or pity from the heart that moves to the appropriate action to solve the problem.

69:17 *hide . . . thy face.* A gesture expressing displeasure. *hear me.* Hebrew, "answer me."

69:18 *my soul.* Me. *redeem it.* To act as the near kinsman, doing whatever is necessary to help.

69:20 *full of heaviness.* Sick. *take pity.* Show sympathy.

69:21 *gall for my meat.* Bitterness for my food. Christ was given bitter drink as He died on the cross (Matt. 27:34,48; Mark 15:23,36; Luke 23:36; John 19:28–30).

69:22–23 *table become a snare . . . eyes be darkened.* God's judgment on the wicked begins by trapping them in their own evil desires and giving them over to spiritual blindness so they will not repent and believe, for example as with Israel's rejection of their Messiah (Rom. 11:9–10; cf. Isa. 6:10; John 12:39–40; 2 Cor. 3:14).

69:25 *Let their habitation be desolate.* May their home become empty and ruined. This judgment fell upon Israel for its general failure to receive Christ (Matt. 23:38; Luke 13:35) and especially upon Judas for betraying Christ (Acts 1:20).

69:26 *they persecute him whom thou hast smitten.* God struck the sufferer, but the wicked sinfully took advantage of the opportunity, as happened with Christ (Luke 22:22; Acts 2:23).

69:27 *iniquity unto their iniquity.* Or punishment for their guilt.

69:28 *blotted out.* Sentenced to death (Ex. 32:32).

69:29 *poor and sorrowful.* Afflicted and in pain.

69:32 *humble.* Weak or afflicted.

33 For the LORD heareth the poor, and despiseth
not his prisoners.
34 Let the heaven and earth praise him, the seas,
and every thing that moveth therein.
35 For God will save Zion, and will build the
cities of Judah: that they may dwell there, and
have it in possession.
36 The seed also of his servants shall inherit it:
and they that love his name shall dwell therein.

PSALM 70

To the chief Musician, *A Psalm* of
David, to bring to remembrance.

1 *MAKE haste*, O God, to deliver me; make haste
to help me, O LORD.
2 Let them be ashamed and confounded that
seek after my soul: let them be turned backward,
and put to confusion, that desire my hurt.
3 Let them be turned back for a reward of their
shame that say, Aha, aha.
4 Let all those that seek thee rejoice and be glad
in thee: and let such as love thy salvation say
continually, Let God be magnified.
5 But I *am* poor and needy: make haste unto me,
O God: thou *art* my help and my deliverer; O
LORD, make no tarrying.

PSALM 71

1 IN thee, O LORD, do I put my trust: let me never
be put to confusion.
2 Deliver me in thy righteousness, and cause me
to escape: incline thine ear unto me, and save me.
3 Be thou my strong habitation, whereunto I may
continually resort: thou hast given command-
ment to save me; for thou *art* my rock and my
fortress.
4 Deliver me, O my God, out of the hand of the
wicked, out of the hand of the unrighteous and
cruel man.
5 For thou *art* my hope, O Lord GOD: *thou art* my
trust from my youth.
6 By thee have I been holden up from the womb:
thou art he that took me out of my mother's
bowels: my praise *shall be* continually of thee.
7 I am as a wonder unto many; but thou *art* my
strong refuge.
8 Let my mouth be filled *with* thy praise *and with*
thy honour all the day.
9 Cast me not off in the time of old age; forsake
me not when my strength faileth.
10 For mine enemies speak against me; and they
that lay wait for my soul take counsel together,
11 Saying, God hath forsaken him: persecute and
take him; for *there is* none to deliver *him*.

69:33 *the poor*. Those needing help.

Thoughts for Personal/Family Worship: Psalm 69

1. This is one of the psalms most frequently quoted in the New Testament. Though it resonates in some ways with the experience of believers, it especially embodies Christ's love for the glory of God and His unjust sufferings at the hands of His own countrymen who were hardened in their unbelief. We often suffer as a consequence of our own sins, but Christ suffered because He took the guilt of other people's sins, making payment for a debt He did not personally incur (2 Cor. 5:21; Col. 2:14; 1 Peter 2:24). As a result, the deep waters of divine wrath flooded his life, overwhelming Him (Matt. 26:38; Luke 12:50) until the Lord answered His humble cry (Heb. 5:7). Reading this psalm should profoundly humble believers as they consider what their sin did to the Son of God. How can it also bring deep comfort to those who experience unjust persecution?
2. Unbelievers should see in these words a warning against the incredible evil of sin, that it would move men to do such things to the innocent and loving Lord. They should fear lest they also be hardened in unbelief and quickly run to Christ to save them from the wrath of God. What promises does this psalm give to sinners who seek the Lord?

Psalm 70: *David is in need of urgent care as he prays for God's immediate help.*

70:1–5 This psalm is essentially a repetition of 40:13–17. See the notes there for explanation.

Thoughts for Personal/Family Worship: Psalm 70

David prayed this prayer more than once because his troubles kept returning. In this world, surrounded by dangers, we are totally dependent upon God and we need to constantly turn to Him in prayer. We cannot live safely and happily without prayer. Therefore prayer must not be neglected. Our prayers do not always need to be long; sometimes the most effective prayer is a desperate cry for help. Our God can come to us in any and every time of crisis. God does not tire of hearing our prayers for His help even if we repeat the petitions, just as long as we seek Him sincerely and not out of thoughtless routine. Christ understands what it means to be poor and needy (v. 5), for He embraced poverty that He might make us rich (2 Cor. 8:9). Now, out of His riches, He is glad to bless those who call upon the name of the Lord (Rom. 10:12–13). How does that encourage you to pray more often and with more hope?

Psalm 71: *The psalmist reflects on God's faithfulness in the past and prays for continuing help into his old age.*

71:1 *trust*. Confidence and security (31:1–3).
71:3 *Be thou my strong habitation*. Become for me a rock where I can dwell. The rock is the huge, immovable boulder, an image of stability. *whereunto*. To which. *resort*. Come. *rock*. Cliff or crag, a place to find shelter. *fortress*. Mountain stronghold, a place inaccessible to the enemy.
71:5 *hope*. Ground of expectancy. *trust*. Object of confidence and security.
71:6 *holden up*. Supported. *bowels*. Womb.
71:10 *my soul*. Me (v. 13).
71:12 *make haste for my help*. Hurry to assist me, a frequent

12 O God, be not far from me: O my God, make
haste for my help.
13 Let them be confounded *and* consumed that
are adversaries to my soul; let them be covered
with reproach and dishonour that seek my hurt.
14 But I will hope continually, and will yet praise
thee more and more.
15 My mouth shall shew forth thy righteousness
and thy salvation all the day; for I know not the
numbers *thereof*.
16 I will go in the strength of the Lord GOD: I will
make mention of thy righteousness, *even* of thine
only.
17 O God, thou hast taught me from my youth:
and hitherto have I declared thy wondrous works.
18 Now also when I am old and grayheaded, O
God, forsake me not; until I have shewed thy
strength unto *this* generation, *and* thy power to
every one *that* is to come.
19 Thy righteousness also, O God, *is* very high,
who hast done great things: O God, who *is* like
unto thee!
20 *Thou*, which hast shewed me great and sore
troubles, shalt quicken me again, and shalt bring
me up again from the depths of the earth.
21 Thou shalt increase my greatness, and comfort
me on every side.
22 I will also praise thee with the psaltery, *even*
thy truth, O my God: unto thee will I sing with the
harp, O thou Holy One of Israel.
23 My lips shall greatly rejoice when I sing unto
thee; and my soul, which thou hast redeemed.
24 My tongue also shall talk of thy righteousness
all the day long: for they are confounded, for they
are brought unto shame, that seek my hurt.

PSALM 72

A Psalm for Solomon.

1 GIVE the king thy judgments, O God, and thy
righteousness unto the king's son.
2 He shall judge thy people with righteousness,
and thy poor with judgment.
3 The mountains shall bring peace to the people,
and the little hills, by righteousness.
4 He shall judge the poor of the people, he shall
save the children of the needy, and shall break in
pieces the oppressor.
5 They shall fear thee as long as the sun and
moon endure, throughout all generations.
6 He shall come down like rain upon the mown
grass: as showers *that* water the earth.
7 In his days shall the righteous flourish; and
abundance of peace so long as the moon endureth.
8 He shall have dominion also from sea to sea,
and from the river unto the ends of the earth.
9 They that dwell in the wilderness shall bow
before him; and his enemies shall lick the dust.
10 The kings of Tarshish and of the isles shall
bring presents: the kings of Sheba and Seba shall
offer gifts.
11 Yea, all kings shall fall down before him: all
nations shall serve him.
12 For he shall deliver the needy when he crieth;
the poor also, and *him* that hath no helper.
13 He shall spare the poor and needy, and shall
save the souls of the needy.
14 He shall redeem their soul from deceit and vio-
lence: and precious shall their blood be in his sight.
15 And he shall live, and to him shall be given of
the gold of Sheba: prayer also shall be made for

petition (40:13; 70:1).

71:14 *hope*. Wait with expectancy, an expression of faith.

71:19 *who is like unto thee*. God is incomparably great (Ex. 15:11; Mic. 7:18).

71:20 *sore troubles*. Severe or hurtful anxieties. *quicken*. Make alive, revive, or preserve. *depths of the earth*. A unique expression in the Hebrew Old Testament, probably referring to death or the grave (63:9; Rom. 10:7; Eph. 4:9).

71:22 *psaltery . . . harp*. Stringed instruments.

71:23 *my soul*. Me.

Thoughts for Personal/Family Worship: Psalm 71

When in serious trouble, we feel the need of God as never before, and in such a time, it is no small comfort to realize that He is there for us, ready to hear our prayers. This truth delivers us from reaching the point of desperation and hopelessness. What is most encouraging is the thought of God's continuing and unchanging faithfulness throughout every season of life. It is a fact of life that we transition from youth to old age, but Jesus Christ is the same yesterday, today, and forever (Heb. 13:8). He has been raised from the dead, ever lives to intercede for His people, and is the forerunner who has gone ahead of them into eternal glory (Heb. 6:19–20; 7:25). Spend time praising Him for His presence in your life.

Psalm 72: *David prays for the ideal King and His kingdom.*

Title This psalm was written *for Solomon*, but as a type of Christ, and soon transitions to statements applicable only to Jesus Christ, the One greater than Solomon (Matt. 12:42).

72:2 *judge*. Rule with justice. *thy poor*. Those who look to God in their need.

72:6 *like rain*. His kingdom will bring life, growth, and happiness (2 Sam. 23:4).

72:7–8 *as the moon endureth . . . unto the ends of the earth*. The long duration and universal extent of this *dominion* applies uniquely to Christ's mediatorial kingdom (2:6,8; Isa. 9:6–7; Jer. 31:35–36; 33:20–21; John 17:2; Col. 1:18).

72:9 *lick the dust*. A figure of speech for defeat, humiliation, and subjugation (Gen. 3:14–15).

72:10 *isles*. Distant lands.

72:11 *all kings . . . all nations*. Christ is the King of kings and Lord of lords (Phil. 2:10–11; Rev. 17:14; 19:16).

72:14 *He shall redeem . . . violence*. Like a close relative, the king will set the poor free from injury and wrong. *precious shall their blood be*. He regards their lives as valuable.

72:15 *prayer . . . made for him continually*. God's people should constantly pray for the kingdom of Christ to advance (Matt. 6:10). *praised*. Same verb as "blessed" (vv. 17–19).

him continually; *and* daily shall he be praised.
16 There shall be an handful of corn in the earth
upon the top of the mountains; the fruit thereof
shall shake like Lebanon: and *they* of the city shall
flourish like grass of the earth.
17 His name shall endure for ever: his name shall
be continued as long as the sun: and *men* shall be
blessed in him: all nations shall call him blessed.
18 Blessed *be* the LORD God, the God of Israel,
who only doeth wondrous things.
19 And blessed *be* his glorious name for ever: and
let the whole earth be filled *with* his glory; Amen,
and Amen.
20 The prayers of David the son of Jesse are ended.

PSALM 73

A Psalm of Asaph.

1 TRULY God *is* good to Israel, *even* to such as are
of a clean heart.
2 But as for me, my feet were almost gone; my
steps had well nigh slipped.
3 For I was envious at the foolish, *when* I saw the
prosperity of the wicked.
4 For *there are* no bands in their death: but their
strength *is* firm.
5 They *are* not in trouble *as other* men; neither
are they plagued like *other* men.
6 Therefore pride compasseth them about as a
chain; violence covereth them *as* a garment.
7 Their eyes stand out with fatness: they have
more than heart could wish.
8 They are corrupt, and speak wickedly *concern-
ing* oppression: they speak loftily.
9 They set their mouth against the heavens, and
their tongue walketh through the earth.
10 Therefore his people return hither: and waters
of a full *cup* are wrung out to them.
11 And they say, How doth God know? and is
there knowledge in the most High?
12 Behold, these *are* the ungodly, who prosper in
the world; they increase *in* riches.
13 Verily I have cleansed my heart *in* vain, and
washed my hands in innocency.
14 For all the day long have I been plagued, and
chastened every morning.
15 If I say, I will speak thus; behold, I should
offend *against* the generation of thy children.
16 When I thought to know this, it *was* too pain-
ful for me;
17 Until I went into the sanctuary of God; *then*
understood I their end.
18 Surely thou didst set them in slippery places:

72:16 *handful of corn . . . upon the top of the mountains.* An abundance of grain will grow in the least arable land, a picture of great prosperity. *shake.* Wave like a field of grain in the wind. *they of the city.* The agricultural imagery is applied to the flourishing and fruitfulness of the people in Christ's kingdom (v. 6; Isa. 27:6; Hos. 14:5–8; John 15:1–8).
72:17 *name.* Glory, fame. *as long as the sun . . . all nations.* Uniquely messianic (see note at vv. 7–8). *be blessed in him.* Christ is the fulfillment of God's promise to Abraham to bless all the peoples of the world (Gen. 12:3; 22:18; Gal. 3:8,13–14; Eph. 1:3).
72:18–20 *Blessed be the LORD God . . . Amen.* A doxology concluding the second book of the Psalms. *prayers of David . . . are ended.* Other psalms attributed to David follow, but this ends a major collection of them (see Introduction: Special Problems of Interpretation; Collection and Arrangement).

Thoughts for Personal/Family Worship: Psalm 72

1. **No royal descendant of David, other than the ultimate Son of David, ever ruled over an eternal kingdom without borders with universal subjects. This psalm celebrates the reign of Jesus Christ. We should always remember that Christ is on His throne. Though the church may be attacked or in a state of decline, He is well able to restore it and cause it to thrive and prosper once again. In these sad days, too many think in terms only of survival, whereas they should be thinking of reformation, recovery, and revival. Believers do well to have a vision for the success and advance of Christ's kingdom. The gospel calls for optimism, for it announces, "Jesus reigns!" How does this encourage you as one of God's ambassadors (see 2 Cor. 5:20)?**
2. **Gospel optimism leads to kingdom prayer. This psalm should move us to pray—and to pray with great hope and expectation—that the kingdom of Christ will prevail against the powers of evil and that all His elect will be brought in and made holy. As we are instructed, let's pray for Christ's kingdom to come and for His will to be done (v. 15; Matt. 6:9–13).**

BOOK 3 (PSS. 73:1—89:52)

Psalm 73: ***The psalmist wrestles with the prosperity of the wicked until he understands their ultimate destiny.***

73:1 This is one of a trilogy of psalms (Pss. 37; 49) that address the inequities of life, particularly the prosperity of the wicked. *clean heart.* Pure of heart, not sinless, but sincere in love for God, not just outwardly and ritually clean (24:4; Matt. 5:8; 1 Tim. 1:5; 2 Tim. 2:22; 1 Peter 1:22).
73:2 *well nigh.* Nearly.
73:3 *foolish.* Boastful. *prosperity.* Peace, referring to overall welfare.
73:4 *bands.* Pains or pangs. *their strength is firm.* Literally, "fat is their body or belly," an image of prosperity.
73:6 *pride compasseth them about as a chain.* Literally, "pride adorns their neck as a necklace."
73:7 *Their eyes stand out with fatness.* Their eyes bulge from abundance.
73:10 *hither.* Here, to this place.
73:13 *Verily.* Truly, indeed. *cleansed my heart in vain.* Purified my thoughts, feelings, and choices for no purpose or gain (Mal. 3:14). *washed my hands.* A metaphor for repentance and obedience in his actions (26:6; Isa. 1:15–17).
73:14 *plagued.* Hurt or buffeted. *chastened.* Corrected, disciplined.
73:16 *too painful.* Hard labor or anxious toil.
73:17 *sanctuary.* The holy place, where God dwelt and the priests offered sacrifices to Him (74:7; 96:6; Ex. 25:8).

thou castedst them down into destruction.
19 How are they *brought* into desolation, as in a
moment! they are utterly consumed with terrors.
20 As a dream when *one* awaketh; *so*, O Lord,
when thou awakest, thou shalt despise their image.
21 Thus my heart was grieved, and I was pricked
in my reins.
22 So foolish *was* I, and ignorant: I was *as* a beast
before thee.
23 Nevertheless I *am* continually with thee: thou
hast holden *me* by my right hand.
24 Thou shalt guide me with thy counsel, and
afterward receive me *to* glory.
25 Whom have I in heaven *but thee*? and *there is*
none upon earth *that* I desire beside thee.
26 My flesh and my heart faileth: *but* God *is* the
strength of my heart, and my portion for ever.
27 For, lo, they that are far from thee shall perish:
thou hast destroyed all them that go a whoring
from thee.
28 But *it is* good for me to draw near to God: I
have put my trust in the Lord GOD, that I may
declare all thy works.

PSALM 74

Maschil of Asaph.

1 O GOD, why hast thou cast *us* off for ever? *why*
doth thine anger smoke against the sheep of thy
pasture?
2 Remember thy congregation, *which* thou hast
purchased of old; the rod of thine inheritance,
which thou hast redeemed; this mount Zion,
wherein thou hast dwelt.
3 Lift up thy feet unto the perpetual desolations;
even all *that* the enemy hath done wickedly in the
sanctuary.
4 Thine enemies roar in the midst of thy congre-
gations; they set up their ensigns *for* signs.
5 *A man* was famous according as he had lifted
up axes upon the thick trees.
6 But now they break down the carved work
thereof at once with axes and hammers.
7 They have cast fire into thy sanctuary, they have
defiled *by casting down* the dwelling place of thy
name to the ground.
8 They said in their hearts, Let us destroy them
together: they have burned up all the synagogues
of God in the land.
9 We see not our signs: *there is* no more any
prophet: neither *is there* among us any that
knoweth how long.
10 O God, how long shall the adversary reproach?
shall the enemy blaspheme thy name for ever?
11 Why withdrawest thou thy hand, even thy
right hand? pluck *it* out of thy bosom.
12 For God *is* my King of old, working salvation
in the midst of the earth.
13 Thou didst divide the sea by thy strength: thou
brakest the heads of the dragons in the waters.
14 Thou brakest the heads of leviathan in pieces,
and gavest him *to be* meat to the people inhabit-
ing the wilderness.

73:21 *I was pricked in my reins*. Literally, "I was pierced through my kidneys," referring to his innermost emotional being.
73:23 *holden*. Seized or grasped. *right hand*. Associated with power and favor.
73:24 *afterward receive me to glory*. Take him to God's presence in heaven after death (see note at 49:15).
73:26 *My flesh and my heart*. The totality of his being, outer and inner self, body and soul. *strength*. Literally, "rock," the huge, immovable boulder, an image of stability. *my portion for ever*. His eternal inheritance, life and joy.
73:27 *go a whoring*. Commit fornication, here as spiritual unfaithfulness to the Lord.
73:28 *to draw near to God*. Literally, "the approach of God" (84:1–4; James 4:8). *put my trust*. Sought and found refuge. *declare*. Recount.

Thoughts for Personal/Family Worship: Psalm 73

The tension between faith and experience is common in Christian life. We believe that the faithful man is blessed (1:1–3), but sometimes it appears that the opposite is true. Asaph, like many before and after him, wrestled with the problem and found the answer in the sanctuary. There the priestly work of sacrifice reminded him of the holiness of God, the doom to fall on sinners, and the grace of God to believers. There he was reminded that the life of the wicked will end in grief and their prosperity will vanish like the dream of a waking man. What will follow is divine retribution. God will show them neither love nor pity. It will be so different for believers. They enjoy the life of grace, knowing God's presence, support, and guidance, and one day they will be introduced to the life of glory to enjoy God forever. How can we use an eternal perspective to overcome doubts and questions about the goodness of God?

Psalm 74: ***The psalmist laments the seeming absence of God and longs for new demonstrations of God's power and presence.***

74:1 *sheep of thy pasture*. People to whom God had committed Himself as their benevolent king (23:1; 77:20; 78:52; 79:13; 80:1; 95:7; 100:3).
74:2 *Remember*. Give attention and take action (vv. 18,22). *rod*. Or tribe. *redeemed*. Rescued them from loss, slavery, or death at His own expense because of a close relationship.
74:4 *ensigns*. Banners or standards.
74:5–7 *cast fire into thy sanctuary*. The psalm seems to describe the scene in 587–586 BC, when Nebuchadnezzar burned the temple (2 Kings 25:8–9), decorated with *trees* and *carved work* (1 Kings 6:29,32,35).
74:8 *synagogues*. Meeting places.
74:9 *signs*. Banners or standards.
74:10 *blaspheme*. Treat disrespectfully (v. 18).
74:11 *right hand*. Associated with honor and favor, which now seemed to be gone. *bosom*. Pocket-like folds in a garment.
74:13 *dragons*. Huge sea creatures.
74:14 *brakest*. Crushed in pieces. *leviathan*. A monstrous sea creature, most likely here symbolic of God's defeat of Egypt (Isa. 27:1; 51:9; Ezek. 29:3). *meat*. Food of any kind.

15 Thou didst cleave the fountain and the flood:
thou driedst up mighty rivers.
16 The day *is* thine, the night also *is* thine: thou
hast prepared the light and the sun.
17 Thou hast set all the borders of the earth: thou
hast made summer and winter.
18 Remember this, *that* the enemy hath re-
proached, O LORD, and *that* the foolish people
have blasphemed thy name.
19 O deliver not the soul of thy turtledove
unto the multitude *of the wicked*: forget not the
congregation of thy poor for ever.
20 Have respect unto the covenant: for the dark
places of the earth are full of the habitations of
cruelty.
21 O let not the oppressed return ashamed: let
the poor and needy praise thy name.
22 Arise, O God, plead thine own cause: remem-
ber how the foolish man reproacheth thee daily.
23 Forget not the voice of thine enemies: the
tumult of those that rise up against thee increaseth
continually.

PSALM 75

To the chief Musician, Al-taschith,
A Psalm *or* Song of Asaph.

1 UNTO thee, O God, do we give thanks, *unto*
thee do we give thanks: for *that* thy name is near
thy wondrous works declare.
2 When I shall receive the congregation I will
judge uprightly.
3 The earth and all the inhabitants thereof are
dissolved: I bear up the pillars of it. Selah.
4 I said unto the fools, Deal not foolishly: and to
the wicked, Lift not up the horn:
5 Lift not up your horn on high: speak *not with*
a stiff neck.
6 For promotion *cometh* neither from the east,
nor from the west, nor from the south.
7 But God *is* the judge: he putteth down one, and
setteth up another.
8 For in the hand of the LORD *there is* a cup,
and the wine is red; it is full of mixture; and he
poureth out of the same: but the dregs thereof, all
the wicked of the earth shall wring *them* out, *and*
drink *them*.
9 But I will declare for ever; I will sing praises to
the God of Jacob.
10 All the horns of the wicked also will I cut off;
but the horns of the righteous shall be exalted.

PSALM 76

To the chief Musician on Neginoth,
A Psalm *or* Song of Asaph.

1 IN Judah *is* God known: his name *is* great in
Israel.

74:15 *cleave.* Break open. *fountain.* Headwaters. *flood.* The streambeds that become torrents during the rainy season.
74:19 *soul.* Life. *turtledove.* A symbol for God's beloved people (68:13; Song 2:12,14). *forget.* Ignore, despise (v. 23). *the congregation of thy poor.* Literally, "the life of Thy afflicted ones."
74:20 *dark places.* Hiding places.
74:21 *ashamed.* Humiliated, dishonored, or disappointed. *poor.* Afflicted.
74:23 *tumult.* Noise, roar, or din. *increaseth.* Goes up or ascends.

Thoughts for Personal/Family Worship: Psalm 74

At times God gives His people over to their enemies, and the church is shattered. It seems that God has rejected them. In such times of desolation, we may still cry out to the good shepherd who laid down His life for the sheep (John 10:14–15). We can gather courage and faith by remembering God's past acts of salvation for His people, just as Israel turned back to their salvation from Egypt when Babylon destroyed them (vv. 12–15). The greatest of these acts are the death and resurrection of Christ. We can find refuge in His infinite power as the Creator (vv. 16–17). We can appeal to God's love for His glory (vv. 18,21), His tenderness for His people ("thy turtledove," v. 19), and His commitment to keep His covenant (v. 20). How can leaning on such supports, enable Christians to pray with faith? How can these truths give us the strength to wait with enduring hope for the Lord to intervene on our behalf?

Psalm 75: *The psalmist praises God, looking to that time when God will judge the wicked and vindicate the righteous.*

75:1 *thy name.* All that God has revealed Himself to be in His attributes or perfections. *is near.* A period should go after *near*, marking the end of a sentence. *thy wondrous works declare.* Thy miraculous acts are recounted.
75:2 *receive the congregation.* Take an appointed time (102:13).
75:3 *dissolved.* Swayed back and forth. *bear up.* Keep steady.
75:4–5 *horn.* A symbol of power and strength (v. 10). *stiff neck.* Arrogant attitude.
75:6 *promotion.* Exaltation.
75:8 *cup.* An image of judgment (11:6; Isa. 51:17; Jer. 25:15; Rev. 14:9–10; 16:19). *wine is red . . . full of mixture.* It is a foaming cocktail, an image of full fury. *wring them out.* Slurp or drain dry.

Thoughts for Personal/Family Worship: Psalm 75

1. **This psalm celebrates the hope that at His own appointed time God, who now sustains the earth and all that is in it, will come in all the fury of His righteous wrath to judge the wicked. In that day there will be no escape, and no defense will be possible. Sinners will drink the cup of wrath down to its last drop. The Judge will take away their strength ("horns") so that they can do no more harm, and He will lift up the righteous with power and glory. While this is good news for the godly, it is a dire warning to the wicked. It admonishes them to be arrogant no longer. What will it be like for unrepentant sinners on judgment day?**
2. **One amazing link between this psalm and the New Testament is Christ's prayers in the garden of Gethsemane, "O my Father, if it be possible, let this cup pass from**

2 In Salem also is his tabernacle, and his dwelling
place in Zion.
3 There brake he the arrows of the bow, the
shield, and the sword, and the battle. Selah.
4 Thou *art* more glorious *and* excellent than the
mountains of prey.
5 The stouthearted are spoiled, they have slept
their sleep: and none of the men of might have
found their hands.
6 At thy rebuke, O God of Jacob, both the chariot
and horse are cast into a dead sleep.
7 Thou, *even* thou, *art* to be feared: and who may
stand in thy sight when once thou art angry?
8 Thou didst cause judgment to be heard from
heaven; the earth feared, and was still,
9 When God arose to judgment, to save all the
meek of the earth. Selah.
10 Surely the wrath of man shall praise thee: the
remainder of wrath shalt thou restrain.
11 Vow, and pay unto the LORD your God: let all
that be round about him bring presents unto him
that ought to be feared.
12 He shall cut off the spirit of princes: *he is*
terrible to the kings of the earth.

PSALM 77

To the chief Musician, to Jeduthun,
A Psalm of Asaph.

1 I CRIED unto God with my voice, *even* unto
God with my voice; and he gave ear unto me.
2 In the day of my trouble I sought the Lord: my
sore ran in the night, and ceased not: my soul
refused to be comforted.
3 I remembered God, and was troubled: I com-
plained, and my spirit was overwhelmed. Selah.
4 Thou holdest mine eyes waking: I am so
troubled that I cannot speak.
5 I have considered the days of old, the years of
ancient times.
6 I call to remembrance my song in the night: I
commune with mine own heart: and my spirit
made diligent search.
7 Will the Lord cast off for ever? and will he be
favourable no more?
8 Is his mercy clean gone for ever? doth *his*
promise fail for evermore?
9 Hath God forgotten to be gracious? hath he in
anger shut up his tender mercies? Selah.
10 And I said, This *is* my infirmity: *but I will
remember* the years of the right hand of the most
High.
11 I will remember the works of the LORD: surely
I will remember thy wonders of old.
12 I will meditate also of all thy work, and talk of
thy doings.
13 Thy way, O God, *is* in the sanctuary: who *is so*
great a God as *our* God?
14 Thou *art* the God that doest wonders: thou
hast declared thy strength among the people.
15 Thou hast with *thine* arm redeemed thy

me: nevertheless not as I will, but as thou wilt. . . . O my Father, if this cup may not pass away from me, except I drink it, thy will be done" (Matt. 26:39,42). The Lord Jesus took the cup of God's wrath against sinners and, in submission to His Father's will, drained it dry so that His people would never have to taste it. How does this affect your view of God's love for sinners? How does it affect your view of Christ's cross?

Psalm 76: *The psalmist extols God as the mighty Warrior for His people.*

76:1 *his name is great.* God has revealed that He is glorious in all His perfections.
76:2 *Salem.* Jerusalem. *tabernacle.* Tent or dwelling place.
76:4 *mountains.* Strongholds where supplies of food (*prey*) would be stored.
76:5 *stouthearted.* The valiant of heart, the courageous. *spoiled.* Plundered. *found their hands.* In the sense of being able to function or use their hands.
76:6 *cast into a dead sleep.* Dazed or stunned.
76:9 *meek.* The weak, afflicted, or humble. God's people are often weaker than the wicked, but their humility and meekness mark them as those whom God will save (37:11; Matt. 5:3–5).
76:10 *wrath of man shall praise thee.* Even the sinful rage of the wicked will serve to accomplish God's purposes for His glory (Acts 4:24–28). *restrain.* Gird or bind up.
76:12 *terrible.* Fearsome or awe-inspiring.

Thoughts for Personal/Family Worship: Psalm 76

The church is at times under serious attack, but in vain do Satan and evil men seek her destruction. Greater is He who is in us than he who is in the world. God Himself is her indwelling Sovereign and Protector. In due time, He will take up her cause and arise for her help. Whatever evil may be allowed to overtake the church, it shall all be overruled to God's greater praise, and any further evil will be harnessed and rendered ineffective. Thus, in His keeping, the Lord's people are both safe and well. How does this enable believers to remain humble, quiet, and meek in affliction?

Psalm 77: *The psalmist finds hope for the present by remembering what God has done in the past.*

77:1 *gave ear.* Listened.
77:2 *trouble.* Anxiety or distress. *my sore ran.* Or, my hand was stretched out, as a gesture of dependent prayer (88:9). *my soul.* I.
77:3 *remembered.* Set my mind and affections on (v. 11). *troubled.* Restless. *complained.* Or lamented. *was overwhelmed.* Felt weak or as if it might faint away.
77:4 *Thou holdest mine eyes waking.* Literally, "Thou dost take hold of the eyelids of my eyes." *troubled.* Disturbed, specifically by sleeplessness.
77:6 *commune with mine own heart.* Meditate.
77:8 *mercy.* Covenant loyalty and love. *clean gone.* Ceased or failed.
77:9 *tender mercies.* Compassion and pity that moves to appropriate action to meet the need.
77:10 *right hand.* A position associated with honor and favor.
77:15 *redeemed.* Rescued from trouble at one's own expense because of a close relationship (Ex. 6:5–7).

people, the sons of Jacob and Joseph. Selah.
16 The waters saw thee, O God, the waters saw
thee; they were afraid: the depths also were
troubled.
17 The clouds poured out water: the skies sent
out a sound: thine arrows also went abroad.
18 The voice of thy thunder *was* in the heaven:
the lightnings lightened the world: the earth
trembled and shook.
19 Thy way *is* in the sea, and thy path in the great
waters, and thy footsteps are not known.
20 Thou leddest thy people like a flock by the
hand of Moses and Aaron.

PSALM 78

Maschil of Asaph.

1 GIVE ear, O my people, *to* my law: incline your
ears to the words of my mouth.
2 I will open my mouth in a parable: I will utter
dark sayings of old:
3 Which we have heard and known, and our
fathers have told us.
4 We will not hide *them* from their children,
shewing to the generation to come the praises
of the LORD, and his strength, and his wonderful
works that he hath done.
5 For he established a testimony in Jacob, and
appointed a law in Israel, which he commanded
our fathers, that they should make them known
to their children:
6 That the generation to come might know *them*,
even the children *which* should be born; *who*
should arise and declare *them* to their children:
7 That they might set their hope in God, and
not forget the works of God, but keep his
commandments:
8 And might not be as their fathers, a stubborn
and rebellious generation; a generation *that* set
not their heart aright, and whose spirit was not
stedfast with God.
9 The children of Ephraim, *being* armed, *and*
carrying bows, turned back in the day of battle.
10 They kept not the covenant of God, and re-
fused to walk in his law;
11 And forgat his works, and his wonders that he
had shewed them.
12 Marvellous things did he in the sight of their
fathers, in the land of Egypt, *in* the field of Zoan.
13 He divided the sea, and caused them to pass
through; and he made the waters to stand as an
heap.
14 In the daytime also he led them with a cloud,
and all the night with a light of fire.
15 He clave the rocks in the wilderness, and gave
them drink as *out of* the great depths.
16 He brought streams also out of the rock, and
caused waters to run down like rivers.
17 And they sinned yet more against him by
provoking the most High in the wilderness.
18 And they tempted God in their heart by asking
meat for their lust.
19 Yea, they spake against God; they said, Can
God furnish a table in the wilderness?
20 Behold, he smote the rock, that the waters

77:16–20 The picture is of the Lord coming to the Red Sea in a storm cloud to save Israel by judging Egypt (Ex. 14).
77:17 *went abroad.* Literally, "walked about," meaning that lightning (*thine arrows*) struck in various places.
77:19 *Thy way is in the sea . . . thy footsteps are not known.* Men cannot trace God's paths, for His ways are beyond our limited understanding (Rom. 11:33–34).

Thoughts for Personal/Family Worship: Psalm 77

1. **When stress robs us of sleep, our difficulty is doubled by physical and emotional fatigue. Yet in that situation, we may devote ourselves to prayer and meditation. It is striking that precisely when the disciples were dozing off from grief and exhaustion, Christ was fervently seeking God in prayer though His soul was burdened far worse than theirs (Mark 14:33–40). Let us follow the Master in this too: turn sleepless nights into opportunities for earnest prayer, meditation on Scripture, and intercession. What tends to rob you of sleep? How can you make spiritual use of this opportunity?**
2. **When it seems like God has forgotten us, it is time for us to remember His works. Biblical history is full of marvelous displays of God's power and faithfulness to redeem His people. If you are a believer, your personal history is also a rich resource for meditating on the kindnesses of God's providence and saving grace. How can a Christian make use of these things to find strength and comfort?**

Psalm 78: *The psalmist recounts Israel's history from the Exodus to David's monarchy.*
78:2 *parable . . . dark sayings.* Words of wisdom with deeper meaning beyond the surface (Matt. 13:35 regarding Christ's parables). Since what follows in this psalm is history, we are to learn spiritual lessons from redemptive history (1 Cor. 10:11).
78:5 *law.* More than legislation, it refers to all of God's instruction (v. 10).
78:6 *the generation to come.* Every generation of believers has the responsibility to teach their children the Word of God (Deut. 4:9; 6:6–7; 11:19; Eph. 6:4), lest the next generation not know the Lord or His works and turn to sin and idolatry (Judg. 2:10–12).
78:7 *hope.* Confidence. *forget.* Reject and ignore (v. 11). The aim of teaching the Bible to children is that by God's grace they would trust in the Lord and obey *his commandments.*
78:8 *stedfast with.* Faithful to (v. 37).
78:12 *in the land of Egypt.* God's redemption of Israel from Egypt, the history of which forms the core of this psalm (vv. 12–55), is a prototype for salvation.
78:15 *clave.* Split.
78:16 *rock.* Cliff or crag.
78:18 *tempted.* Put to the test (vv. 41,56). *for their lust.* Literally, "for their soul" or "for themselves."
78:20 *rock.* A huge, immovable boulder (v. 35).
78:21–22 *wroth.* Angry. *believed not . . . trusted not.* Salvation

gushed out, and the streams overflowed; can he give bread also? can he provide flesh for his people?

21 Therefore the LORD heard *this*, and was wroth: so a fire was kindled against Jacob, and anger also came up against Israel;

22 Because they believed not in God, and trusted not in his salvation:

23 Though he had commanded the clouds from above, and opened the doors of heaven,

24 And had rained down manna upon them to eat, and had given them of the corn of heaven.

25 Man did eat angels' food: he sent them meat to the full.

26 He caused an east wind to blow in the heaven: and by his power he brought in the south wind.

27 He rained flesh also upon them as dust, and feathered fowls like as the sand of the sea:

28 And he let *it* fall in the midst of their camp, round about their habitations.

29 So they did eat, and were well filled: for he gave them their own desire;

30 They were not estranged from their lust. But while their meat *was* yet in their mouths,

31 The wrath of God came upon them, and slew the fattest of them, and smote down the chosen *men* of Israel.

32 For all this they sinned still, and believed not for his wondrous works.

33 Therefore their days did he consume in vanity, and their years in trouble.

34 When he slew them, then they sought him: and they returned and enquired early after God.

35 And they remembered that God *was* their rock, and the high God their redeemer.

36 Nevertheless they did flatter him with their mouth, and they lied unto him with their tongues.

37 For their heart was not right with him, neither were they stedfast in his covenant.

38 But he, *being* full of compassion, forgave *their* iniquity, and destroyed *them* not: yea, many a time turned he his anger away, and did not stir up all his wrath.

39 For he remembered that they *were but* flesh; a wind that passeth away, and cometh not again.

40 How oft did they provoke him in the wilderness, *and* grieve him in the desert!

41 Yea, they turned back and tempted God, and limited the Holy One of Israel.

42 They remembered not his hand, *nor* the day when he delivered them from the enemy.

43 How he had wrought his signs in Egypt, and his wonders in the field of Zoan:

44 And had turned their rivers into blood; and their floods, that they could not drink.

45 He sent divers sorts of flies among them, which devoured them; and frogs, which destroyed them.

46 He gave also their increase unto the caterpiller, and their labour unto the locust.

47 He destroyed their vines with hail, and their sycomore trees with frost.

48 He gave up their cattle also to the hail, and their flocks to hot thunderbolts.

49 He cast upon them the fierceness of his anger, wrath, and indignation, and trouble, by sending evil angels *among them*.

50 He made a way to his anger; he spared not their soul from death, but gave their life over to the pestilence;

51 And smote all the firstborn in Egypt; the chief of *their* strength in the tabernacles of Ham:

52 But made his own people to go forth like sheep, and guided them in the wilderness like a flock.

53 And he led them on safely, so that they feared not: but the sea overwhelmed their enemies.

54 And he brought them to the border of his sanctuary, *even to* this mountain, *which* his right hand had purchased.

55 He cast out the heathen also before them, and divided them an inheritance by line, and made the tribes of Israel to dwell in their tents.

56 Yet they tempted and provoked the most high God, and kept not his testimonies:

57 But turned back, and dealt unfaithfully like their fathers: they were turned aside like a deceitful bow.

58 For they provoked him to anger with their high places, and moved him to jealousy with their graven images.

---

from God's wrath and our enemies is by faith; destruction falls on unbelievers (v. 32; Eph. 2:8).

78:24 *corn.* Grain; the "bread of heaven" (105:40; Ex. 16:4; Neh. 9:15), used by Christ as a parable for Himself (John 6:31–33,48–51).

78:25 *meat.* Food of any kind (v. 30).

78:33 *vanity.* Breath, something worthless and unsubstantial.

78:34 *enquired early.* Idiom for sought earnestly.

78:35 *remembered.* Directed their minds toward Him (vv. 39, 42). *redeemer.* Term for a near kinsman who would act to rescue or defend a family member in trouble at his own expense.

78:36–37 *flatter.* Attempt to convince. *heart was not right.* Israel's persistent rebellion and hypocrisy reveals that mankind needs God to change their deepest motives and beliefs, implanting obedience into the very nature of their innermost being (v. 8; 37:31; 86:11; 119:32).

78:41 *limited.* Caused distress or pain.

78:43 *wrought his signs.* Set His miracles.

78:45 *divers.* Various.

78:47 *frost.* Meaning uncertain.

78:49 *evil angels.* Angels of destruction, the agents of the plagues.

78:50 *their soul.* Them. *their life over to the pestilence.* Or their cattle to the plague (Ex. 9:3–6).

78:51 *tabernacles.* Dwelling places (v. 67). *Ham.* Egypt.

78:53 *overwhelmed.* Covered.

78:57 *deceitful bow.* A bow whose string was loose or slack, unusable.

59 When God heard *this*, he was wroth, and
greatly abhorred Israel:
60 So that he forsook the tabernacle of Shiloh, the
tent *which* he placed among men;
61 And delivered his strength into captivity, and
his glory into the enemy's hand.
62 He gave his people over also unto the sword;
and was wroth with his inheritance.
63 The fire consumed their young men; and their
maidens were not given to marriage.
64 Their priests fell by the sword; and their
widows made no lamentation.
65 Then the Lord awaked as one out of sleep,
and like a mighty man that shouteth by reason
of wine.
66 And he smote his enemies in the hinder parts:
he put them to a perpetual reproach.
67 Moreover he refused the tabernacle of Joseph,
and chose not the tribe of Ephraim:
68 But chose the tribe of Judah, the mount Zion
which he loved.
69 And he built his sanctuary like high *palaces*,
like the earth which he hath established for ever.
70 He chose David also his servant, and took him
from the sheepfolds:
71 From following the ewes great with young he
brought him to feed Jacob his people, and Israel
his inheritance.
72 So he fed them according to the integrity of
his heart; and guided them by the skilfulness of
his hands.

PSALM 79

A Psalm of Asaph.

1 O GOD, the heathen are come into thine
inheritance; thy holy temple have they defiled;
they have laid Jerusalem on heaps.
2 The dead bodies of thy servants have they given
to be meat unto the fowls of the heaven, the flesh
of thy saints unto the beasts of the earth.
3 Their blood have they shed like water round
about Jerusalem; and *there was* none to bury *them*.
4 We are become a reproach to our neighbours, a
scorn and derision to them that are round about us.
5 How long, LORD? wilt thou be angry for ever?
shall thy jealousy burn like fire?
6 Pour out thy wrath upon the heathen that have
not known thee, and upon the kingdoms that
have not called upon thy name.
7 For they have devoured Jacob, and laid waste
his dwelling place.
8 O remember not against us former iniquities:
let thy tender mercies speedily prevent us: for we
are brought very low.
9 Help us, O God of our salvation, for the glory
of thy name: and deliver us, and purge away our
sins, for thy name's sake.
10 Wherefore should the heathen say, Where *is*
their God? let him be known among the heathen
in our sight *by* the revenging of the blood of thy
servants *which is* shed.
11 Let the sighing of the prisoner come before

78:59 *wroth*. Angry (v. 62).
78:71–72 *feed . . . fed*. Literally, "shepherd," a pastoral image of ruling them in justice and love as a good king and God's representative (v. 52; Ezek. 34:23–24; 37:24).

Thoughts for Personal/Family Worship: Psalm 78

1. **Biblical history teaches reliable facts about real people and events, and yet its purpose is to communicate spiritual truth and to call for a spiritual response. It is good to teach the Bible's stories to children and adults, but if we do not draw doctrine out of the story and apply it to the heart then we have not been faithful to God. He calls each generation to train future generations to hope in God and obey His commands. What implications does this have for family worship and church classes?**
2. **The history of Israel teaches us that God is faithful to His covenant and works powerfully to save His people. However, humanity is not faithful to God, but rebellious at heart, even when this rebellion is cloaked in the religious flattery of hypocrisy. As a result, God's wrath burns against them. God's loving solution to man's problem centers upon the household of David, giving Israel a king to shepherd them in kindness and righteousness. Yet even David's line failed, resulting in the exile among the Gentiles. This psalm thus implies that Israel's hope lies in a coming Son of David who will keep covenant with the Lord so as to gain His blessing on the people. This King must also have the ability by God's grace to change the hearts of sinners so that they repent of sin and trust in God's promises. The salvation that this King brings will be like Israel's exodus from Egypt, only it must be a spiritual exodus. How are the expectations of this psalm fulfilled in Jesus Christ and His Spirit?**

Psalm 79: *The psalmist laments the desolation of Jerusalem, prays for deliverance, and promises praise.*

79:1 *the heathen*. The Gentile nations (vv. 6,10). *temple . . . defiled . . . laid Jerusalem on heaps*. Perhaps referring to Babylon's destruction of the city (2 Kings 25).
79:2 *meat*. Food of any sort.
79:6 *not known thee . . . not called upon thy name*. Those under God's *wrath* are characterized by a refusal to know God (Rom. 1:18–23,28; Gal. 4:8; 1 Thess. 4:5; 2 Thess. 1:8) and a failure to pray to Him (14:4; Jer. 10:25; Hos. 7:7).
79:8 *remember*. Set one's mind on something and take action; for God to remember sin is to punish the guilty (Jer. 14:10; Hos. 9:9). *tender mercies*. Compassion or pity that motivates one to take the appropriate action to help. *prevent*. Come to meet.
79:9 *purge*. Make atonement for.
79:12 *sevenfold*. An idiom expressing completeness or totality.

Thoughts for Personal/Family Worship: Psalm 79

Great damage, disgrace, and distress can come upon God's church (Rev. 13:15; 17:6). Sometimes God gives the wicked victory over the professing church because of its sins. In such times of disaster, we must give ourselves to prayer for His compassion and forgiveness. Even when the Lord is disciplining His people, we may

thee; according to the greatness of thy power
preserve thou those that are appointed to die;
12 And render unto our neighbours sevenfold
into their bosom their reproach, wherewith they
have reproached thee, O Lord.
13 So we thy people and sheep of thy pasture will
give thee thanks for ever: we will shew forth thy
praise to all generations.

PSALM 80

To the chief Musician upon Shoshannim-Eduth,
A Psalm of Asaph.

1 GIVE ear, O Shepherd of Israel, thou that lead-
est Joseph like a flock; thou that dwellest *between*
the cherubims, shine forth.
2 Before Ephraim and Benjamin and Manasseh
stir up thy strength, and come *and* save us.
3 Turn us again, O God, and cause thy face to
shine; and we shall be saved.
4 O LORD God of hosts, how long wilt thou be
angry against the prayer of thy people?
5 Thou feedest them with the bread of tears; and
givest them tears to drink in great measure.
6 Thou makest us a strife unto our neighbours:
and our enemies laugh among themselves.
7 Turn us again, O God of hosts, and cause thy
face to shine; and we shall be saved.
8 Thou hast brought a vine out of Egypt: thou
hast cast out the heathen, and planted it.
9 Thou preparedst *room* before it, and didst
cause it to take deep root, and it filled the land.
10 The hills were covered with the shadow of it,
and the boughs thereof *were like* the goodly cedars.
11 She sent out her boughs unto the sea, and her
branches unto the river.
12 Why hast thou *then* broken down her hedges,
so that all they which pass by the way do pluck her?
13 The boar out of the wood doth waste it, and
the wild beast of the field doth devour it.
14 Return, we beseech thee, O God of hosts: look
down from heaven, and behold, and visit this vine;
15 And the vineyard which thy right hand hath
planted, and the branch *that* thou madest strong
for thyself.
16 *It is* burned with fire, *it is* cut down: they perish
at the rebuke of thy countenance.
17 Let thy hand be upon the man of thy right
hand, upon the son of man *whom* thou madest
strong for thyself.
18 So will not we go back from thee: quicken us,
and we will call upon thy name.
19 Turn us again, O LORD God of hosts, cause thy
face to shine; and we shall be saved.

PSALM 81

To the chief Musician upon Gittith,
A Psalm of Asaph.

1 SING aloud unto God our strength: make a
joyful noise unto the God of Jacob.
2 Take a psalm, and bring hither the timbrel, the

appeal to His justice to punish the wicked oppressors if they will not repent (Rev. 6:9–11). Christ is ever the shepherd of His sheep (v. 13), and He will never abandon them. When God rescues His church from troubles, or if we do not live in a time of severe persecution, we should give public thanks and praise to the Lord for the peace we enjoy. How do the church's present circumstances call it to prayer and praise?

Psalm 80: *The psalmist prays for revival and restoration after experiencing destruction.*

80:1 *O Shepherd.* Pastoral care of a *flock* was a common image of a good king (23:1; 28:9; 78:71–72). *between the cherubims.* An allusion to the ark of the covenant, a symbol of God's presence with Israel like a king on his throne (99:1; Ex. 25:17–22).
80:3 *Turn.* Reverse, restore, or revive. *cause thy face to shine.* An expression of favor, a recurring refrain, with an expanding title for the Lord: *O God* (here), "O God of hosts" (v. 7), "O LORD God of hosts" (v. 19).
80:6 *strife.* Or object of contention; the surrounding nations fight over them. *laugh.* Mock.
80:8 *vine out of Egypt.* A symbol for Israel (Isa. 5:1–7; 27:3–6; Matt. 21:33–41). *heathen.* Nations.
80:9 *preparedst room.* Cleared ground.
80:10 *goodly cedars.* Cedars of God or mighty cedars.
80:14 *visit.* Pay attention and take the appropriate action.
80:15 *right hand.* An expression of honor and favor (v. 17).
80:16 *countenance.* Face.
80:17 *son of man.* Human being, not yet a messianic term (8:4), though here referring to the royal Son of David.
80:18 *quicken.* Make alive or preserve.

Thoughts for Personal/Family Worship: Psalm 80

When the tears of God's people flow, they can remind themselves that Christ is the divine shepherd of His chosen flock, present with them as an enthroned king by the Holy Spirit. He is the Lord God of hosts, the all-powerful Commander of all creation. His face shines upon believers, indeed shines within their hearts, through the gospel (2 Cor. 4:6). They are God's vineyard, and Christ Himself is the vine whose sap gives life to all branches that abide in Him (John 15:1–8), for He has joined Himself to us by taking our human nature as the Son of Man so that we might be joined to Him by His Spirit. Therefore, when the church suffers defeat, believers should call upon Christ to revive them so that they may bear the fruit God desires. How often are you praying for the revival of Christ's church? How can this psalm help you to pray?

Psalm 81: *The Lord reminds His people of the exodus and all the blessings that could have been theirs had they not rebelled.*

81:1 *God our strength . . . the God of Jacob.* The Lord has both the power and faithful love to save His people.
81:2 *psalm.* A melody or song, not identical to the word for

pleasant harp with the psaltery.
3 Blow up the trumpet in the new moon, in the
time appointed, on our solemn feast day.
4 For this *was* a statute for Israel, *and* a law of the
God of Jacob.
5 This he ordained in Joseph *for* a testimony,
when he went out through the land of Egypt:
where I heard a language *that* I understood not.
6 I removed his shoulder from the burden: his
hands were delivered from the pots.
7 Thou calledst in trouble, and I delivered thee;
I answered thee in the secret place of thunder: I
proved thee at the waters of Meribah. Selah.
8 Hear, O my people, and I will testify unto thee:
O Israel, if thou wilt hearken unto me;
9 There shall no strange god be in thee; neither
shalt thou worship any strange god.
10 I *am* the LORD thy God, which brought thee
out of the land of Egypt: open thy mouth wide,
and I will fill it.
11 But my people would not hearken to my voice;
and Israel would none of me.
12 So I gave them up unto their own hearts' lust:
and they walked in their own counsels.
13 Oh that my people had hearkened unto me,
and Israel had walked in my ways!
14 I should soon have subdued their enemies,
and turned my hand against their adversaries.
15 The haters of the LORD should have submitted
themselves unto him: but their time should have
endured for ever.
16 He should have fed them also with the finest of
the wheat: and with honey out of the rock should
I have satisfied thee.

PSALM 82

A Psalm of Asaph.

1 GOD standeth in the congregation of the
mighty; he judgeth among the gods.
2 How long will ye judge unjustly, and accept the
persons of the wicked? Selah.
3 Defend the poor and fatherless: do justice to
the afflicted and needy.
4 Deliver the poor and needy: rid *them* out of the
hand of the wicked.
5 They know not, neither will they understand;
they walk on in darkness: all the foundations of
the earth are out of course.
6 I have said, Ye *are* gods; and all of you *are*
children of the most High.
7 But ye shall die like men, and fall like one of
the princes.
8 Arise, O God, judge the earth: for thou shalt
inherit all nations.

"Psalm" (as in the title for Ps. 82) though from the same root. *hither*. Here. *timbrel*. A hand drum or tambourine. *pleasant harp with the psaltery*. A sweet-sounding zither and lute, or other stringed instruments. The Levites played musical instruments to accompany and assist worship (1 Chron. 15:16,28).
81:3 *Blow up the trumpet in the new moon*. The priests sounded the call to worship at monthly feasts and other occasions (Num. 10:8,10; 1 Sam. 20:5,24–26).
81:6 *pots*. Baskets. God saved them from the hard labor (*burden*) of slavery.
81:7 *secret place*. Covering or hiding place. *proved*. Examined or put to the test (Ex. 17:2–7; Num. 20:13).
81:9 *strange . . . strange*. Illicit and foreign (two different words in Hebrew).
81:10 *open thy mouth wide*. Come to God trusting in His faithfulness and power as the Savior (*thy God . . . brought thee out*) and desiring Him to satisfy you with His goodness (v. 16; 36:8; 37:3–4; Matt. 7:7–11).
81:11 *Israel would none of me*. Literally, "Israel would not consent or yield to Me."
81:12 *their own hearts' lust*. Literally, "the stubbornness of their heart." *counsels*. Plans.
81:15 *submitted*. Come cringing, been compelled to honor (18:44; 66:3).
81:16 *honey out of the rock*. God's miraculous provision for Israel (Deut. 32:13; cf. Ex. 3:8; 16:31), a type of Christ's spiritual nourishment of His people (1 Cor. 10:4).

Thoughts for Personal/Family Worship: Psalm 81

Through the Psalms the Lord Jesus Christ teaches us to worship God according to His will. God's people must worship Him by singing with energy and joy (v. 1), exercising faith in His power and faithful love (v. 1), offering God psalms with music (vv. 2–3), following the instructions of Scripture (v. 4), remembering God's great works of salvation in Jesus Christ (vv. 5–7), listening to the preaching of the Word (v. 8), renouncing the gods of this world (v. 9), drawing near to God with expectant desire for Him to satisfy us with Christ (vv. 10,16), and repenting of our sins (vv. 11–15). How are you following each of these directions in your public worship? How do you need to change?

Psalm 82: The psalmist laments the failures of human judges and desires God's righteous judgment.

82:1 *mighty*. A term for god (Hebrew, *el*), which here, together with *gods* (Hebrew, *elohim*), refers to human rulers or judges (Ex. 21:6; 22:8–9; 1 Sam. 2:25), for they exercise authority delegated by God (Rom. 13:1; cf. Ex. 7:1–2).
82:2 *accept the persons*. Lift up the faces, an idiom for showing favoritism or partiality.
82:3 *poor*. The helpless or weak (v. 4). God holds those in authority especially responsible for defending the helpless (Deut. 1:16–18; Prov. 31:8–9).
82:5 *are out of course*. Are made to stagger or are shaken. The proper use of authority for justice and mercy is fundamental to the stability of human society (*foundations of the earth*).
82:6 *Ye are gods*. They are powerful rulers representing God and thus accountable to Him to do justice (see note at v. 1). Christ quoted this psalm in His rebuke of the Jews for unjustly condemning Him to death for saying He is the Son of God (John 10:34–36).
82:7 *ye shall die*. The most powerful of men are still mortal (49:12), a reminder of our accountability to God for our sins (90:7–10; Eccl. 12:7; Heb. 9:27). *like men*. Literally, "as Adam"

PSALM 83

A Song *or* Psalm of Asaph.

1 KEEP not thou silence, O God: hold not thy
peace, and be not still, O God.
2 For, lo, thine enemies make a tumult: and they
that hate thee have lifted up the head.
3 They have taken crafty counsel against thy
people, and consulted against thy hidden ones.
4 They have said, Come, and let us cut them off
from *being* a nation; that the name of Israel may
be no more in remembrance.
5 For they have consulted together with one
consent: they are confederate against thee:
6 The tabernacles of Edom, and the Ishmaelites;
of Moab, and the Hagarenes;
7 Gebal, and Ammon, and Amalek; the Philis-
tines with the inhabitants of Tyre;
8 Assur also is joined with them: they have
holpen the children of Lot. Selah.
9 Do unto them as *unto* the Midianites; as *to*
Sisera, as *to* Jabin, at the brook of Kison:
10 *Which* perished at Endor: they became *as*
dung for the earth.
11 Make their nobles like Oreb, and like Zeeb:
yea, all their princes as Zebah, and as Zalmunna:
12 Who said, Let us take to ourselves the houses
of God in possession.
13 O my God, make them like a wheel; as the
stubble before the wind.
14 As the fire burneth a wood, and as the flame
setteth the mountains on fire;
15 So persecute them with thy tempest, and make
them afraid with thy storm.
16 Fill their faces with shame; that they may seek
thy name, O LORD.
17 Let them be confounded and troubled for
ever; yea, let them be put to shame, and perish:
18 That *men* may know that thou, whose name
alone *is* JEHOVAH, *art* the most high over all the
earth.

PSALM 84

To the chief Musician upon Gittith,
A Psalm for the sons of Korah.

1 HOW amiable *are* thy tabernacles, O LORD of
hosts!

(Job 31:33; Hos. 6:7), perhaps an allusion to the fall of the first man, appointed to rule the earth (Gen. 1–3).

82:8 *inherit*. Hold as a possession.

Thoughts for Personal/Family Worship: Psalm 82

God has given men great authority in the world to rule as His representatives (Gen. 1:26–28), but with this authority comes accountability. People, especially people with power, tend to confuse themselves with God. Instead of defending the weak against the wicked, they show favoritism and overthrow the fundamental principles undergirding society. The injustice of human courts reached its pinnacle of perversity when the Jewish council condemned Christ to death, and the Gentile ruler authorized Christ's crucifixion even after finding Him innocent. Nevertheless, when justice miscarries, we may look to the Judge of all the earth to do right. The Lord reminds rulers that they are mere men, fallen and mortal in Adam. If the rulers of this earth do not follow God's principles of justice, then God will judge the judges, for He is the Owner of all nations. How does this psalm teach the officials of civil government to walk in the fear of God?

Psalm 83: *The psalmist prays for God's intervention against a confederacy of enemies.*

83:1 *Keep not thou silence*. Do not rest. *hold not thy peace*. Do not be deaf or silent. *be not still*. Do not be quiet or inactive.

83:2 *tumult*. Noise.

83:3 *consulted against thy hidden ones*. Conspired against the ones God treasured.

83:5 *they are confederate*. Literally, "they cut a covenant," forming an alliance or league against the Lord.

83:6–8 *tabernacles*. Tents or dwelling places. Ten nations (indicating totality) are listed as representative of militant enemies that surround Israel. To the south were *Edom, Ishmaelites*, and *Amalek*; to the east were *Moab, Hagarenes*, and *Ammon*; to the west were *Gebal*, the *Philistines*, and *Tyre*; to the north was *Assur* (Assyria). *holpen the children of Lot*. Literally, they were "an arm to the sons of Lot," helping the Moabites and Ammonites.

83:9 *Midianites*. People against whom Israel warred as early as the days of Moses (Num. 31:1–12). *Sisera*. Canaanite commander defeated by Barak and Deborah (Judg. 4:15–24; 5:19–20).

83:11 *Oreb . . . Zeeb*. Midianite princes defeated by Gideon (Judg. 7:25; 8:1,6,12–21).

83:13 *like a wheel*. Thus to be in a whirl.

83:15 *persecute them with thy tempest*. Pursue them with Thy storm.

83:17 *troubled*. Horrified, terrified out of one's senses.

83:18 *may know that thou . . . art the most high*. God's judgments against the wicked glorify Him as the supreme and sovereign Lord (59:13; 97:1,3,7; Isa. 5:15–16).

Thoughts for Personal/Family Worship: Psalm 83

God's enemies often attack His people, and they should not be surprised if they find themselves surrounded by the wicked seeking their ruin. The comfort of the church is that God will arise to help in answer to prayer. Christians can rest assured of the final victory, because God has shown His power and will to save repeatedly through history. The wicked, however, should fear, because the Lord will fill His enemies with shame and torment them with fire. While God's judgments may seem harsh, in reality they are good and necessary, for they demonstrate to the world that the Lord alone is the sovereign King over all the earth. Judgment serves God's glory. How does this encourage believers to pray for justice? How does it admonish unbelievers to repent?

Psalm 84: *The psalmist expresses his longing to worship the Lord in the temple.*

84:1 *amiable*. Lovely (cf. 27:4). *tabernacles*. Dwelling places. *O LORD of hosts*. Jehovah, who commands all the armies of heaven and earth. This title appears repeatedly in this song of desire and delight (vv. 3,8,12), implying that God's loveliness is

2 My soul longeth, yea, even fainteth for the
courts of the LORD: my heart and my flesh crieth
out for the living God.
3 Yea, the sparrow hath found an house, and the
swallow a nest for herself, where she may lay her
young, *even* thine altars, O LORD of hosts, my
King, and my God.
4 Blessed *are* they that dwell in thy house: they
will be still praising thee. Selah.
5 Blessed *is* the man whose strength *is* in thee; in
whose heart *are* the ways *of them*.
6 *Who* passing through the valley of Baca make it
a well; the rain also filleth the pools.
7 They go from strength to strength, *every one of*
them in Zion appeareth before God.
8 O LORD God of hosts, hear my prayer: give ear,
O God of Jacob. Selah.
9 Behold, O God our shield, and look upon the
face of thine anointed.
10 For a day in thy courts *is* better than a thou-
sand. I had rather be a doorkeeper in the house of
my God, than to dwell in the tents of wickedness.
11 For the LORD God *is* a sun and shield: the
LORD will give grace and glory: no good *thing* will
he withhold from them that walk uprightly.
12 O LORD of hosts, blessed *is* the man that
trusteth in thee.

PSALM 85

To the chief Musician, A Psalm
for the sons of Korah.

1 LORD, thou hast been favourable unto thy land:
thou hast brought back the captivity of Jacob.
2 Thou hast forgiven the iniquity of thy people,
thou hast covered all their sin. Selah.
3 Thou hast taken away all thy wrath: thou hast
turned *thyself* from the fierceness of thine anger.
4 Turn us, O God of our salvation, and cause
thine anger toward us to cease.
5 Wilt thou be angry with us for ever? wilt thou
draw out thine anger to all generations?
6 Wilt thou not revive us again: that thy people
may rejoice in thee?
7 Shew us thy mercy, O LORD, and grant us thy
salvation.
8 I will hear what God the LORD will speak: for he
will speak peace unto his people, and to his saints:
but let them not turn again to folly.
9 Surely his salvation *is* nigh them that fear him;
that glory may dwell in our land.
10 Mercy and truth are met together; righteous-
ness and peace have kissed *each other*.
11 Truth shall spring out of the earth; and
righteousness shall look down from heaven.

inseparable from His sovereignty as King (v. 3; 96:6; Isa. 33:17).

84:2 *My soul*. I. *courts of the LORD*. See note at 65:4. *my heart and my flesh*. His whole person, inside and out.

84:4–5 *Blessed*. Possessing great benefits from God (v. 12; 1:1). *in whose heart are the ways*. Who knows how to draw near to God's presence and desires to do so (122:1).

84:6 *Baca*. Translated, means "lush vegetation." *rain also filleth the pools*. Literally, "rain wraps blessings."

84:9 *thine anointed*. God's appointed king, ultimately Christ (2:6).

84:10 *be a doorkeeper*. Unique Hebrew verb related to "threshold" or "gate," but of uncertain meaning; possibly a Levite guarding the entrances to the temple courts (1 Chron. 9:22), a worshiper seeking to enter (100:4), or a beggar lying at the entrance (Acts 3:2).

84:12 *trusteth*. Place confidence in or to find security in, a principal word for faith in the Old Testament.

Thoughts for Personal/Family Worship: Psalm 84

1. **In the new covenant, the house of God is not a building, but the congregation of people united in Christ by the Holy Spirit (1 Cor. 3:16; Eph. 2:22; 1 Peter 2:5). There is great blessing in going up to worship in the house of God. God's Word calls us to that holy gathering (99:9) and the Holy Spirit draws us (Ezra 1:5). There believers see God's beauty and are satisfied in Him (63:1–2). Love for God's church and its worship of God is a sign of God's saving blessing upon a person. How much do we value the meetings of the church? How frequently do we attend them? What do we seek when we go—God or something from man?**
2. **No one is more zealous for God's house than Jesus Christ (John 2:17). Even as a twelve-year-old child He loved to be there (Luke 2:46–49). As an adult He was often in the temple teaching (Luke 22:53; John 10:23). He especially delights in being with His believing people, who are God's spiritual house. To them He has promised His special presence (Matt. 18:20; 28:20). The risen Lord is our great temple, and He shines like the sun with the beauty of the triune God (John 2:19–22; Rev. 21:22–23). Better is one day with the church in the presence of Christ than a thousand elsewhere. What often hinders our own attitudes from being Christlike in this matter?**

Psalm 85: ***The psalmist acknowledges God's past favors and desires to experience even more.***

85:1 *favourable*. Pleased with, a friend of. *brought back the captivity*. An idiom for reversing fortunes.

85:2–3 *forgiven the iniquity . . . taken away . . . wrath*. God is angry against all sin (Rom. 1:18). His forgiveness comes through the propitiation or appeasement of His anger by the satisfaction of His justice through Christ's sacrifice on the cross (Rom. 3:25).

85:4 *Turn us*. A prayer for reversal and restoration (80:3; Jer. 31:18; Acts 3:19,26).

85:6 *revive us again*. Literally, "return, cause us to live," meaning a renewal of strength and vitality or even resurrection from the dead (71:20; Judg. 15:19; 1 Kings 17:22; Hos. 14:7).

85:7 *mercy*. Covenant loyalty and love.

85:8 *I will hear*. A form of verb expressing resolve or determination, "I am determined to hear." *peace*. Welfare in general, not just cessation of hostility. *folly*. Or stupidity.

85:9 *nigh*. Near to.

85:10 *Mercy and truth*. Two terms frequently linked to refer to the fidelity of covenant love.

Thoughts for Personal/Family Worship: Psalm 85

Thinking about the past ways God has dealt with us is a good way to increase our desire for God to continue to show His grace. As you meditate through this psalm, follow the logic. First, we remember the past, thinking

12 Yea, the LORD shall give *that which is* good; and
our land shall yield her increase.
13 Righteousness shall go before him; and shall
set *us* in the way of his steps.

PSALM 86

A Prayer of David.

1 BOW down thine ear, O LORD, hear me: for I *am*
poor and needy.
2 Preserve my soul; for I *am* holy: O thou my
God, save thy servant that trusteth in thee.
3 Be merciful unto me, O Lord: for I cry unto thee
daily.
4 Rejoice the soul of thy servant: for unto thee, O
Lord, do I lift up my soul.
5 For thou, Lord, *art* good, and ready to forgive;
and plenteous in mercy unto all them that call
upon thee.
6 Give ear, O LORD, unto my prayer; and attend
to the voice of my supplications.
7 In the day of my trouble I will call upon thee:
for thou wilt answer me.
8 Among the gods *there is* none like unto thee,
O Lord; neither *are there any works* like unto thy
works.
9 All nations whom thou hast made shall come
and worship before thee, O Lord; and shall glorify
thy name.
10 For thou *art* great, and doest wondrous things:
thou *art* God alone.
11 Teach me thy way, O LORD; I will walk in thy
truth: unite my heart to fear thy name.
12 I will praise thee, O Lord my God, with all my
heart: and I will glorify thy name for evermore.
13 For great *is* thy mercy toward me: and thou
hast delivered my soul from the lowest hell.
14 O God, the proud are risen against me, and the
assemblies of violent *men* have sought after my
soul; and have not set thee before them.
15 But thou, O Lord, *art* a God full of compas-
sion, and gracious, longsuffering, and plenteous
in mercy and truth.
16 O turn unto me, and have mercy upon me;
give thy strength unto thy servant, and save the
son of thine handmaid.
17 Shew me a token for good; that they which
hate me may see *it*, and be ashamed: because
thou, LORD, hast holpen me, and comforted me.

PSALM 87

A Psalm *or* Song for the sons of Korah.

1 HIS foundation *is* in the holy mountains.

---

about God's mercies, restoration, forgiveness, and peace (vv. 1–3). Then, we pray for the future that God might revive us and show His mercy or covenant loyalty (vv. 4–6). Finally, we express faith for the present by resolving to listen to the Lord's Word, hoping in His salvation and glory, and admonishing ourselves and each other to not return to the old ways of folly but to follow in the way of peace provided (vv. 7–13). How would you apply this pattern specifically to your own situation or that of your church?

Psalm 86: *David prays for God's help in the time of trouble desiring a sign for good.*

86:1 *Bow down thine ear.* A figurative image of God bending down to listen (113:5–6; 2 Kings 19:16). *poor and needy.* Weak or afflicted and needing help, the kind of people God gladly helps (12:5).
86:2 *my soul.* Me (vv. 13–14). *holy.* The recipient of covenant loyalty and love. *my God . . . thy servant.* David was particularly God's servant (vv. 4,16; title of Ps. 36; 78:70; 89:3,20), because the Lord had made a covenant with him (1 Chron. 17:4,7,17–19,23–27). In this he foreshadowed Christ, God's servant par excellence (Isa. 42:1; 49:3–7; 52:13—53:12).
86:3 *Be merciful.* Be gracious or show undeserved favor (v. 16). *daily.* He prayed regularly, not just in moments of crisis.
86:4 *Rejoice the soul.* Make him content. *I lift up my soul.* An idiom expressing dependence (25:1; 143:8).
86:5 *plenteous in mercy.* Great or abundant in covenant loyalty and love (v. 13).
86:6 *attend.* Listen attentively.
86:7–10 *thou art God alone.* There is one God and no other (Deut. 4:35,39; 6:4). The Lord's great *works* show His absolute superiority to all other *gods* that men worship (2 Sam. 7:22–23), therefore His people pray to Him alone for His glory alone among *all nations* (67:2).
86:11 *unite my heart to fear thy name.* Since there is only one God (v. 10), we must pray for God's Spirit to remove all the false gods that divide our loyalty and to focus our mind, affections, and will exclusively on the Lord with holy awe and reverence (Deut. 6:4–5; 30:6).
86:13 *delivered my soul from the lowest hell.* Rescued me from my worst troubles.
86:15 *compassion.* Pity that moves one to help the needy. *gracious.* Giving favor to the undeserving. *longsuffering.* Literally, "long of nostrils," an image of the nose being slow to turn red, expressing patience. *mercy and truth.* The two words are often linked to refer to the fidelity of covenant love. David recited the goodness of the Lord that He revealed to Moses (Ex. 34:6).
86:16 *turn unto me.* Literally, "face me," an expression of favor. *handmaid.* Female servant.
86:17 *token.* Sign. *holpen.* Helped.

Thoughts for Personal/Family Worship: Psalm 86

Biblical prayer is driven by meditation upon God. God's covenant in Christ attracts us to approach Him with humility and trust (vv. 1–2). God's goodness and forgiveness draw us to seek Him in prayer regularly despite our sinfulness (v. 5). God's greatness turns us from all other gods to seek Him alone in our need (vv. 8–10). God's love, compassion, grace, and faithfulness give us hope to call upon Him even when proud sinners work to destroy us (vv. 13–15). God's mercies to us in the past encourage us to boldly ask Him to give us signs of His goodness in the present (v. 17). What concerns do you have to take to the Lord in prayer? Which of God's attributes seen in God's covenant through Christ allow us to pray with confidence?

2 The LORD loveth the gates of Zion more than
all the dwellings of Jacob.
3 Glorious things are spoken of thee, O city of
God. Selah.
4 I will make mention of Rahab and Babylon to
them that know me: behold Philistia, and Tyre,
with Ethiopia; this *man* was born there.
5 And of Zion it shall be said, This and that man
was born in her: and the highest himself shall
establish her.
6 The LORD shall count, when he writeth up the
people, *that* this *man* was born there. Selah.
7 As well the singers as the players on instru-
ments *shall be there*: all my springs *are* in thee.

PSALM 88

A Song *or* Psalm for the sons of Korah,
to the chief Musician upon Mahalath Leannoth,
Maschil of Heman the Ezrahite.

1 O LORD God of my salvation, I have cried day
and night before thee:
2 Let my prayer come before thee: incline thine
ear unto my cry;
3 For my soul is full of troubles: and my life
draweth nigh unto the grave.
4 I am counted with them that go down into the
pit: I am as a man *that hath* no strength:
5 Free among the dead, like the slain that lie in
the grave, whom thou rememberest no more: and
they are cut off from thy hand.
6 Thou hast laid me in the lowest pit, in darkness,
in the deeps.
7 Thy wrath lieth hard upon me, and thou hast
afflicted *me* with all thy waves. Selah.
8 Thou hast put away mine acquaintance far
from me; thou hast made me an abomination
unto them: *I am* shut up, and I cannot come
forth.
9 Mine eye mourneth by reason of affliction:
LORD, I have called daily upon thee, I have
stretched out my hands unto thee.
10 Wilt thou shew wonders to the dead? shall the
dead arise *and* praise thee? Selah.
11 Shall thy lovingkindness be declared in the
grave? *or* thy faithfulness in destruction?
12 Shall thy wonders be known in the dark? and
thy righteousness in the land of forgetfulness?
13 But unto thee have I cried, O LORD; and in the
morning shall my prayer prevent thee.
14 LORD, why castest thou off my soul? *why* hidest
thou thy face from me?
15 *I am* afflicted and ready to die from *my* youth

Psalm 87: *The psalmist describes the blessings of being a citizen of Zion.*

87:1 *His foundation.* The foundation of God's house or *holy* city.
87:2–3 *loveth the gates of Zion.* Though God is in all places and hears prayers spoken in private homes (*dwellings of Jacob*), He chose Jerusalem (*city of God*) as the primary place for His worshipers to encounter His glory (78:68–69; Deut. 12:5; 2 Chron. 5:14—6:6).
87:4–6 *them that know me.* The people of nations like Egypt (*Rahab*, cf. 89:10; Isa. 51:9) generally did not know the Lord (79:6), so this implies conversion from false religion to serve the true God (96:1–5; Isa. 19:18–25; Jer. 31:34). *this man was born there.* Birth represents entrance into citizenship in the holy city (Isa. 54:1–3; 66:8–12; Gal. 4:26–29), and thus being recorded as a member of God's people (*count . . . writeth up the people*; Isa. 4:3; Ezek. 13:9).
87:5 *the highest himself.* The Most High, a title referring to God in His majesty.
87:7 *all my springs are in thee.* Symbolism for God's life-giving presence with His people (36:8; 46:4; John 4:14), which moves them to rejoice and sing His praises (Isa. 12:3; 43:19–21).

Thoughts for Personal/Family Worship: Psalm 87

In the new covenant, the church is God's spiritual Zion, the heavenly Jerusalem, and His living temple among people (Gal. 4:26; Heb. 12:22; 1 Peter 2:5–6; Rev. 3:12; 21:2,10). God's promises to Israel are being fulfilled in the church through faith in His Son, whose person and work is the foundation of God's dwelling with sinners (1 Cor. 3:11; 1 Peter 2:6–7). The church of Jesus Christ is more beautiful, precious, and holy than any other institution on earth (Isa. 60–62). Her citizens are of a heavenly birth by the Holy Spirit (John 3:1–8; Gal. 4:29–31). The Lord knows each of them by name (2 Tim. 2:19). God has promised His special presence to her gatherings in a way that surpasses even private communion with God (Matt. 18:20; 28:20; Eph. 2:18–22). How precious is the meeting of the church! How does this psalm gives us reasons to love the church and her public worship? What changes do you need to make in your attitudes and habits to reflect the importance of the church in God's sight?

Psalm 88: *The psalmist laments his misery with no apparent relief in sight.*

Title *Heman the Ezrahite.* A Levite appointed to oversee part of the temple's instrumental music, a prophet noted for his wisdom (1 Kings 4:31; 1 Chron. 25:1–6).
88:3 *my soul is full of troubles.* I am weary of or I have had enough of calamities. *grave.* The Hebrew, *sheol*, referring to death, the grave, or abode of departed wicked spirits. Here either death or the grave is in view.
88:4 *pit.* Or grave, a different word from *sheol* (v. 6).
88:5 *grave.* Yet another word for grave (v. 11). *rememberest no more.* Rejects.
88:7 *lieth hard upon.* Rests on, puts its weight on. His greatest affliction was not physical, but a sense of God's anger (*wrath*) against sin that lay with crushing weight upon the soul.
88:8 *far from me.* He was isolated (Luke 23:49). *shut up.* Imprisoned.
88:9 *I have stretched out my hands.* A gesture expressing dependence.
88:11 *lovingkindness.* Covenant loyalty and love. *declared in the grave.* The dead cannot publicly glorify God. *destruction.* Hebrew, *abaddon*, the place or power of death.
88:12 *forgetfulness.* Or oblivion.
88:13 *prevent.* Come to meet.
88:14 *my soul.* Me. *hidest thou thy face.* A gesture of displeasure.

up: *while* I suffer thy terrors I am distracted.
16 Thy fierce wrath goeth over me; thy terrors
have cut me off.
17 They came round about me daily like water;
they compassed me about together.
18 Lover and friend hast thou put far from me,
and mine acquaintance into darkness.

PSALM 89

Maschil of Ethan the Ezrahite.

1 I WILL sing of the mercies of the LORD for ever:
with my mouth will I make known thy faithful-
ness to all generations.
2 For I have said, Mercy shall be built up for ever:
thy faithfulness shalt thou establish in the very
heavens.
3 I have made a covenant with my chosen, I have
sworn unto David my servant,
4 Thy seed will I establish for ever, and build up
thy throne to all generations. Selah.
5 And the heavens shall praise thy wonders, O
LORD: thy faithfulness also in the congregation of
the saints.
6 For who in the heaven can be compared unto
the LORD? *who* among the sons of the mighty can
be likened unto the LORD?
7 God is greatly to be feared in the assembly of
the saints, and to be had in reverence of all *them
that are* about him.
8 O LORD God of hosts, who *is* a strong LORD
like unto thee? or to thy faithfulness round about
thee?
9 Thou rulest the raging of the sea: when the
waves thereof arise, thou stillest them.
10 Thou hast broken Rahab in pieces, as one that
is slain; thou hast scattered thine enemies with thy
strong arm.
11 The heavens *are* thine, the earth also *is* thine:
as for the world and the fulness thereof, thou hast
founded them.
12 The north and the south thou hast created
them: Tabor and Hermon shall rejoice in thy name.
13 Thou hast a mighty arm: strong is thy hand,
and high is thy right hand.
14 Justice and judgment *are* the habitation of thy
throne: mercy and truth shall go before thy face.
15 Blessed *is* the people that know the joyful
sound: they shall walk, O LORD, in the light of thy
countenance.
16 In thy name shall they rejoice all the day: and
in thy righteousness shall they be exalted.
17 For thou *art* the glory of their strength: and in
thy favour our horn shall be exalted.
18 For the LORD *is* our defence; and the Holy One
of Israel *is* our king.
19 Then thou spakest in vision to thy holy

88:17 *compassed.* Surrounded.
88:18 *Lover.* Someone who loves him.

Thoughts for Personal/Family Worship: Psalm 88

1. **The Lord may bring a crushing sense of His wrath upon the soul of a sinner, causing the conscience to pierce and the affections to burn with fear. If so, then the right response is to cry out to God for salvation from sin (v. 1; Acts 2:37; 16:29–30). Everyone who calls upon the name of the Lord, trusting in the risen Christ, will be saved (Rom. 10:9–13). Have you ever sensed the wrath of God against your sin? Are you trusting Christ alone to save you?**
2. **God may withdraw a comforting sense of His fatherly love from the believer, and the Christian enters into a time of darkness and horror from the guilt of his sins. Though objectively the believer remains justified in God's sight, subjectively he may lose his sense of assurance and peace of conscience, feeling that God is against him (38:1–8). Such seasons may be compounded by physical illness and isolation from friends. They call the Christian to patient endurance and continual prayer (88:1–2,9,13).**
3. **Though the spiritual desolation of Christians may disturb us, we should be most moved by the sufferings of the sinless Son of God, in whom this psalm is fulfilled. He experienced divine abandonment in the highest degree, though faithful to God from His youngest days (22:1,9–10). He suffered for the sins of others and was crushed for their guilt (Isa. 53:5–6,10). He propitiated God's wrath for sinners by bearing the curse Himself (Rom. 3:25; Gal. 3:13). As a result, though we may feel abandoned by God, the Lord will never truly forsake the believer. How can meditating on Christ's time of horrible darkness help believers to endure times of darkness themselves?**

Psalm 89: *The psalmist praises God for His covenant mercies and faithfulness to David and his kingdom: a commentary on the Davidic covenant.*

89:1–2 *mercies.* The demonstrations and acts of covenant loyalty and love. *faithfulness.* Or trustworthiness (v. 24).
89:3 *covenant with . . . David.* See 2 Sam. 7:8–16.
89:4 *Thy seed will I establish.* The promise to David's offspring was unconditional because it was to be fulfilled in Christ (vv. 29,33,36–37; 2 Sam. 23:5; Isa. 55:3).
89:6 *sons of the mighty.* Sons of gods, referring to angels (see note at 29:1).
89:10 *Rahab.* A symbolic reference to Egypt, the arrogant afflicter.
89:11 God's kingdom must prevail over all because He created all things.
89:12 *north . . . south.* A literary devise that uses extremes to refer to the whole: God made everything. *name.* All that God has revealed Himself to be (vv. 16,24).
89:14 *Justice and judgment.* Righteousness and justice, the basis (*habitation*) of the reign (*throne*) of a good king (72:2). *mercy and truth.* The two terms are often linked to refer to fidelity of covenant loyalty and love.
89:15 *Blessed.* Possessing great benefits from the Lord (1:1). *joyful sound.* Jubilation, sometimes in connection with a theophany or appearance of God's glory. *countenance.* Face, referring to the blessing of God's presence and favor.
89:17 *horn.* A symbol of power (v. 24).
89:18 *defence.* Literally, "shield."
89:19 *vision.* A common means of divine revelation in the Old Testament (Heb. 1:1).

one, and saidst, I have laid help upon *one that*
is mighty; I have exalted *one* chosen out of the
people.
20 I have found David my servant; with my holy
oil have I anointed him:
21 With whom my hand shall be established:
mine arm also shall strengthen him.
22 The enemy shall not exact upon him; nor the
son of wickedness afflict him.
23 And I will beat down his foes before his face,
and plague them that hate him.
24 But my faithfulness and my mercy *shall be*
with him: and in my name shall his horn be
exalted.
25 I will set his hand also in the sea, and his right
hand in the rivers.
26 He shall cry unto me, Thou *art* my father, my
God, and the rock of my salvation.
27 Also I will make him *my* firstborn, higher than
the kings of the earth.
28 My mercy will I keep for him for evermore,
and my covenant shall stand fast with him.
29 His seed also will I make *to endure* for ever,
and his throne as the days of heaven.
30 If his children forsake my law, and walk not in
my judgments;
31 If they break my statutes, and keep not my
commandments;
32 Then will I visit their transgression with the
rod, and their iniquity with stripes.
33 Nevertheless my lovingkindness will I not ut-
terly take from him, nor suffer my faithfulness
to fail.
34 My covenant will I not break, nor alter the
thing that is gone out of my lips.
35 Once have I sworn by my holiness that I will
not lie unto David.
36 His seed shall endure for ever, and his throne
as the sun before me.
37 It shall be established for ever as the moon,
and *as* a faithful witness in heaven. Selah.
38 But thou hast cast off and abhorred, thou hast
been wroth with thine anointed.
39 Thou hast made void the covenant of thy
servant: thou hast profaned his crown *by casting*
it to the ground.
40 Thou hast broken down all his hedges; thou
hast brought his strong holds to ruin.
41 All that pass by the way spoil him: he is a
reproach to his neighbours.
42 Thou hast set up the right hand of his adver-
saries; thou hast made all his enemies to rejoice.
43 Thou hast also turned the edge of his sword,
and hast not made him to stand in the battle.
44 Thou hast made his glory to cease, and cast his
throne down to the ground.
45 The days of his youth hast thou shortened:
thou hast covered him with shame. Selah.
46 How long, LORD? wilt thou hide thyself for
ever? shall thy wrath burn like fire?
47 Remember how short my time is: wherefore
hast thou made all men in vain?
48 What man *is he that* liveth, and shall not see
death? shall he deliver his soul from the hand of
the grave? Selah.
49 Lord, where *are* thy former lovingkindnesses,
which thou swarest unto David in thy truth?
50 Remember, Lord, the reproach of thy servants;
how I do bear in my bosom *the reproach of* all the
mighty people;

89:20 *I have found David my servant.* God chose David's family line to bring forth Christ (Acts 13:22–23). *anointed.* Designated as king by anointing with oil (1 Sam. 16:13); the verb form for Messiah and a type of Christ's anointing with the Spirit (45:6–7; Isa. 61:1).
89:22 *exact.* Treat badly.
89:23 *plague.* Strike or smite.
89:26 *my father.* Just as God adopted Israel as His son (Ex. 4:22), so God adopted the royal line of David (2 Sam. 7:14), making it a type of the eternal Son of God in His resurrected kingship (see note at 2:7). *rock.* The huge, immovable boulder, an image of stability.
89:27 *firstborn.* Not necessarily about birth, but a designation of rank and privilege (*higher than the kings*); ultimately fulfilled in Christ (Rom. 8:29; Col. 1:15,18; Heb. 1:6; Rev. 1:5).
89:28 *mercy.* Covenant loyalty and love.
89:32 *visit.* Give attention and take action, here to discipline (*rod*).
89:33 *lovingkindness.* Covenant loyalty and love (v. 49).
89:35 *have I sworn.* God's commitment to exalt the Son of David forever is sealed with a solemn oath, communicating its unchangeable nature (110:4; Heb. 6:17–18).
89:38–45 *thou hast.* After celebrating God's promises to David's line, the psalm suddenly turns to a series of surprising actions by God to destroy the monarchy. The covenant included the provision for divine discipline for sin (vv. 30–32), but promised unfailing love (vv. 33–34). Though the monarchy was never restored to Israel after the exile, the great Son of David, Jesus Christ, brought the kingdom of God in a more extensive, lasting, and spiritual manner (Isa. 9:6–7; 11:1–5).
89:38 *wroth.* Angry.
89:39 *made void.* Rejected. *profaned.* Broken or defiled the sacred; same Hebrew word as "break" (vv. 31,34). The crown of David would be profaned until Christ takes it and exalts in heaven (110:1; Ezek. 21:25–27).
89:40 *hedges.* Walls, defensive devices.
89:46 *hide thyself.* An expression of displeasure.
89:47 *Remember.* Set one's mind on something and take appropriate action (v. 50). *in vain.* Without use or worth. If God does not keep His promises to the Son of David, the purpose for all mankind will fail.
89:52 *Blessed be . . . Amen.* This doxology concludes the third book of the Psalms (see Introduction: Special Problems of Interpretation; Collection and Arrangement).

Thoughts for Personal/Family Worship: Psalm 89

1. This psalm is a commentary on the Davidic covenant (2 Sam. 7), which marked a significant advance in God's revelation of redemption. The Lord told David that through his royal offspring, God's presence and kingdom

51 Wherewith thine enemies have reproached,
O LORD; wherewith they have reproached the
footsteps of thine anointed.
52 Blessed *be* the LORD for evermore. Amen, and
Amen.

PSALM 90

A Prayer of Moses the man of God.

1 LORD, thou hast been our dwelling place in all
generations.
2 Before the mountains were brought forth, or
ever thou hadst formed the earth and the world,
even from everlasting to everlasting, thou *art* God.
3 Thou turnest man to destruction; and sayest,
Return, ye children of men.
4 For a thousand years in thy sight *are but* as yes-
terday when it is past, and *as* a watch in the night.
5 Thou carriest them away as with a flood; they
are *as* a sleep: in the morning *they are* like grass
which groweth up.
6 In the morning it flourisheth, and groweth up;
in the evening it is cut down, and withereth.
7 For we are consumed by thine anger, and by thy
wrath are we troubled.
8 Thou hast set our iniquities before thee, our
secret *sins* in the light of thy countenance.
9 For all our days are passed away in thy wrath:
we spend our years as a tale *that is told*.
10 The days of our years *are* threescore years and
ten; and if by reason of strength *they be* fourscore
years, yet *is* their strength labour and sorrow; for
it is soon cut off, and we fly away.
11 Who knoweth the power of thine anger? even
according to thy fear, *so is* thy wrath.
12 So teach *us* to number our days, that we may
apply *our* hearts unto wisdom.
13 Return, O LORD, how long? and let it repent
thee concerning thy servants.
14 O satisfy us early with thy mercy; that we may
rejoice and be glad all our days.
15 Make us glad according to the days *wherein*
thou hast afflicted us, *and* the years *wherein* we
have seen evil.
16 Let thy work appear unto thy servants, and thy
glory unto their children.
17 And let the beauty of the LORD our God be
upon us: and establish thou the work of our
hands upon us; yea, the work of our hands estab-
lish thou it.

---

would be established on earth forever. David's sons, beginning with Solomon, in one way or another failed. Their sins seemed to put the promise in jeopardy, bringing down God's judgment and finally destroying the kingdom of Judah. Believers in that time lived in the tension of the promise of a kingdom and the reality of desolation and foreign domination. How does this psalm teach us to pray when life's reality seems to contradict God's promises? How does it encourage both faith and honesty?

2. **Though God had threatened discipline upon the line of David if they broke His law, he also guaranteed that His faithful love and reliable covenant could not be nullified. This called Israel to hope that God would raise up a righteous Son of David whose obedience to God's laws would bring the everlasting kingdom. The failure of Israel's kings reflected the fall of man in the first Adam from his blessed and royal position on earth. Therefore God's promise held out the hope of the last Adam, God's Son. All the hope of believers rests upon Him. Already His kingdom has begun in Christ's coming, death, resurrection, ascension, and pouring out of the Holy Spirit to begin worldwide missions. Yet the church still waits for His coming to reign in glory and lives under the cross of persecution. How can this psalm help us to seek His kingdom in prayer as we live in the "already but not yet"?**

BOOK 4 (PSS. 90:1—106:48)

Psalm 90: ***Moses contrasts God's eternity with man's transience and prays for contentment in light of God's good providence.***

Title *Moses.* This psalm may reflect the experience of God's judgments upon Israel in the wilderness after leaving Mt. Sinai. *man of God.* Prophet.

90:1 *dwelling place.* A place of refuge and safety, also translated "habitation" (71:3; 91:9).

90:2 *earth . . . world.* The planet generally and the continents specifically. *from everlasting to everlasting.* The Lord is eternal, having no beginning or end, and not limited by time in any way (45:6; 93:2; 102:25–27; Gen. 1:1; 21:33; Isa. 40:28).

90:3 *destruction.* Dust, as in death (Gen. 3:19; Eccl. 12:7).

90:4 *thousand years . . . as yesterday.* God's experience of time is not like ours, for He is fully present in all times, being the Lord of time and not subject to it (31:15; 2 Peter 3:8). *watch.* A quarter or third of the *night*, hence three to four hours (Ex. 14:24; Judg. 7:19; Matt. 14:25; Luke 12:38). By this comparison, a man's life would last about twenty minutes or less.

90:5–6 These vivid images describe the irresistibility of death (*flood*) and the brevity of life (a night's *sleep* and *grass*).

90:7–8 Moses saw the wilderness generation forfeit the Promised Land and perish under God's *anger* within a forty-year period because of their unbelief and disobedience (95:7–11; Num. 14:28–35). In the same way, all mankind has lost paradise and fallen under the sentence of death because of Adam's sin in the garden of Eden (Gen. 2:17; 3:19; Rom. 5:12).

90:9 *tale.* Groan or sigh.

90:10 *threescore years and ten.* Seventy. *fourscore.* Eighty.

90:12 *apply our hearts unto wisdom.* Obtain hearts of wisdom.

90:13 *let it repent thee.* Relent, have pity.

90:14 *early.* Literally, "in the morning." *mercy.* Covenant loyalty and love.

90:15 *evil.* Calamity or hard times.

90:17 *beauty.* Kindness.

Thoughts for Personal/Family Worship: Psalm 90

1. **Death is not a natural event to which we should resign ourselves, but a sign of God's anger upon mankind for our sins. Though we would rather not think about it, we gain much wisdom by meditating on the brevity of life, the certainty of death, and the eternity of the God who rules both life and death. The reality of death strips away our pretenses of pride and independence and reminds us of God's absolute power over us and wrath against**

GOD'S ETERNITY

The word *eternity* is easily pronounced but hardly understood. This is due in part to man's frailty of nature, as a creature bound to time. Eternity, being in conflict with time, is an attribute of God that largely exceeds man's mind. Eternity is a perpetual duration, having neither beginning nor end; time has both. Eternity and time differ in much the same way as the sea and rivers: the sea never changes place and is always one water, but the rivers glide along and are swallowed up by the sea. Such is time in relation to eternity.

This difficulty in understanding eternity is increased because the term is used to describe things that are only partially perpetual and not properly eternal. *Eternity* can be used of something having a long duration but possessing an end (Gen. 17:8; Lev. 6:20; Deut. 15:17) or of something having no end though having a beginning—such as angels and souls. Nonetheless, when *eternity* is used of God, it means something further; as the Scriptures attest "even from everlasting to everlasting, thou art God" (Ps. 90:2). Therefore, *eternity* in this sense refers to the duration of God's essence. When God is called *eternal*, all possibility of beginning and ending—any flux and change—is excluded. Consequently, the eternity of God is best understood negatively, as a denial that God has any measure of beginning, end, or succession.

God is *without beginning* as the everlasting God (Gen. 21:33; Rom. 16:26; cf. Gen. 1:1; Dan. 7:9). This is necessary according to God's existence and status as Creator, for, if God does exist, and He has not received His being from another, then He must exist from eternity.

God is *without end*. This aspect refers to *immortality*, which is spoken of in Scripture more frequently than the other aspects of God's eternity. He shall endure forever (Ps. 9:7; James 1:17; Rev. 4:9–10). His years are numberless (Job 36:26–27). This is evident by the name He gives Himself (Ex. 3:14) and the fact that He is life in His own essence (Dan. 6:26; John 5:26; cf. Acts 17:28; 1 Tim. 6:16).

God is *without succession*. He is always the same (Ps. 102:27; Heb. 1:10–12) and has no new progression of quantities or qualities in Himself. Of a creature, it may be said that "he was," "he is," or "he will be," but of God it can only be said that "He is." There is no increase in His knowledge (Acts 15:18) or fluctuation in His decrees (Eph. 1:4). There is no abrogation of any of His attributes. Furthermore, if God were not eternal, all His other attributes would be maimed beyond recognition. God would not be immutable (cf. Job 37:23; Mal. 3:6), infinitely perfect (cf. Job 11:7; Ps. 41:13), omnipotent (cf. Isa. 2:22; Rev. 1:8), or the first cause of all.

The eternity of God holds a word for both the unbeliever and the Christian. For the former, God's eternity is a terror. What a folly and boldness there is in sin, since an eternal God is offended thereby! All sin is aggravated by God's eternity. The blackness of the pagan idolatry was in exchanging the glory of the incorruptible God for things contrary to His immortal nature (Rom. 1:23). It is dreadful to lie under the stroke of this eternal God, who is the "living God, and an everlasting king . . . the nations shall not be able to abide his indignation" (Jer. 10:10). God's eternity makes His punishment more dreadful than His power alone: His power makes it sharp, but His eternity renders it perpetual—ever to endure is the sting at the end of every lash.

But for the Christian the reality that God "remainest forever" (Lam. 5:19–20) is the fountain of comfort. Peace is found in fellowship with the ever merciful, good, wise, and faithful God. His eternity governs His covenant with His people—thereby He swears by Himself (Heb. 6:13,16,17; Rev. 14:6; cf. Rev. 4:3), and so the believer may proclaim, "This God is our God for ever and ever" (Ps. 48:14) and "Thou hast been our dwelling place in all generations" (Ps. 90:1; cf. Gen. 49:26). Moreover, the eternity of God ensures that the enjoyment of God in heaven will be as fresh and glorious after many ages as it was at first.

—adapted from Stephen Charnock, "A Discourse upon the Eternity of God," in *The Existence and Attributes of God*

PSALM 91

1 He that dwelleth in the secret place of the most
High shall abide under the shadow of the Almighty.
2 I will say of the Lord, *He is* my refuge and my
fortress: my God; in him will I trust.
3 Surely he shall deliver thee from the snare of the
fowler, *and* from the noisome pestilence.
4 He shall cover thee with his feathers, and under
his wings shalt thou trust: his truth *shall be thy*
shield and buckler.
5 Thou shalt not be afraid for the terror by night;
nor for the arrow *that* flieth by day;
6 *Nor* for the pestilence *that* walketh in darkness;
nor for the destruction *that* wasteth at noonday.
7 A thousand shall fall at thy side, and ten thousand
at thy right hand; *but* it shall not come nigh thee.
8 Only with thine eyes shalt thou behold and see
the reward of the wicked.
9 Because thou hast made the Lord, *which is* my
refuge, *even* the most High, thy habitation;
10 There shall no evil befall thee, neither shall any
plague come nigh thy dwelling.
11 For he shall give his angels charge over thee, to
keep thee in all thy ways.
12 They shall bear thee up in *their* hands, lest
thou dash thy foot against a stone.
13 Thou shalt tread upon the lion and adder: the
young lion and the dragon shalt thou trample
under feet.
14 Because he hath set his love upon me, therefore
will I deliver him: I will set him on high, because
he hath known my name.
15 He shall call upon me, and I will answer him: I
will be with him in trouble; I will deliver him, and
honour him.
16 With long life will I satisfy him, and shew him
my salvation.

PSALM 92

A Psalm *or* Song for the sabbath day.

1 *It is a* good *thing* to give thanks unto the Lord,
and to sing praises unto thy name, O most High:
2 To shew forth thy lovingkindness in the

---

sin. How should these truths humble us?

2. **The reality of death also moves us to find a dwelling place in God that will outlast this life. This world loses its charm when we see it as a temporary home, but God is eternal. This is the great wisdom given to us by the gospel, to trust in the Lord Jesus Christ for eternal life (2 Tim. 3:15). Pray that God would have mercy upon you for your sins, give you eternal joy and satisfaction in His love, and work in you so that your works will have lasting value.**

Psalm 91: *The psalmist describes the security and protection the Lord provides for His own.*

91:1 Though anonymous, some attribute this psalm to Moses (see the title of Ps. 90). *abide*. Lodge or take up residence. *under the shadow*. A common image for protection (36:7; 57:1; 63:7; 121:5; Gen. 19:8; Judg. 9:15; Song 2:3; Isa. 4:6; 25:4–5; 30:2–3; 32:2; 34:15; 49:2; 51:16; Lam. 4:20; Ezek. 17:23; 31:6; Hos. 14:7).
91:2 *trust*. Place confidence for security, a principal word for faith in the Old Testament.
91:3 *snare of the fowler*. The net or trap of one who catches birds. *noisome pestilence*. Destruction.
91:4 *under his wings*. Literally, "in His pinion He provides cover for you." *trust*. Seek and find refuge. *shield*. A large shield covering the body. *buckler*. Small shield; the Hebrew means simply "defensive protection."
91:6 *wasteth*. Devastates.
91:8 *reward*. Retribution.
91:10 *evil*. Hurtful thing or calamity. *plague*. Affliction or stroke.
91:11–12 The *angels* are God's servants who praise Him and work as the invisible protectors of His people (34:7; 103:20; 104:4; 148:2; 2 Kings 6:16–17; Heb. 1:14). Satan cited this Scripture in his temptation of Christ (Matt. 4:6; Luke 4:10–11).
91:13 *adder*. Venomous serpent. *dragon*. Serpent. The dangerous animals symbolize enemies, especially the great spiritual enemy of mankind (Gen. 3:1; Isa. 27:1; Rev. 12:9).
91:14 *set his love*. Become very attached. *name*. God's glory in all the attributes or perfections He has revealed through His words and works.
91:15 *trouble*. Distress, anxiety, straits.
91:16 *long life*. Length of days.

Thoughts for Personal/Family Worship: Psalm 91

1. **God's people have long cherished this psalm as a promise of God's protective presence. It should not be interpreted to say that no harm can come to believers (v. 10), but rather that God will work all things to the good of those who love Him, making them more than conquerors over Satan and this evil world (Rom. 8:28,37). God's ordinary way is to answer the prayers of Christians by sustaining them in the trouble, then rescuing them from the trouble, and ultimately giving them glory and eternal life (vv. 15–16). What do the images of the first part of the psalm (vv. 1–4) teach us about trusting the Lord?**
2. **Satan abused this Scripture in his temptation of Christ in an attempt to get Jesus to test God in an extraordinary way by leaping from the temple so that angels could carry Him down (vv. 11–12; Luke 4:9–11). The Devil omitted the words, "in all thy ways," perhaps because they imply trusting in God's ordinary providence over all our life, not forcing His hand to some extraordinary show. Christ refused to test the promised angelic protection, and then angels came and cared for the ordinary needs of His weary humanity (Matt. 4:11). What lessons can we learn from Christ about how we should and should not use God's promises of protection?**

Psalm 92: *The psalmist exhorts people to praise the Lord for His greatness and goodness.*

Title *for the sabbath day*. This psalm teaches us how to enjoy the Lord's Day.
92:1 *give thanks*. The general word for praise. *sing praises*. Play an instrument or sing. *name*. All that God has revealed about His glory and perfections.
92:2 *shew forth*. Declare. *lovingkindness*. Covenant loyalty and love. *faithfulness*. Trustworthiness. *morning … night*. A pair of opposites designates totality: all the time, continually (1:2).

morning, and thy faithfulness every night,
3 Upon an instrument of ten strings, and upon
the psaltery; upon the harp with a solemn sound.
4 For thou, LORD, hast made me glad through thy
work: I will triumph in the works of thy hands.
5 O LORD, how great are thy works! *and* thy
thoughts are very deep.
6 A brutish man knoweth not; neither doth a fool
understand this.
7 When the wicked spring as the grass, and when
all the workers of iniquity do flourish; *it is* that
they shall be destroyed for ever:
8 But thou, LORD, *art most* high for evermore.
9 For, lo, thine enemies, O LORD, for, lo, thine
enemies shall perish; all the workers of iniquity
shall be scattered.
10 But my horn shalt thou exalt like *the horn of* an
unicorn: I shall be anointed with fresh oil.
11 Mine eye also shall see *my desire* on mine
enemies, *and* mine ears shall hear *my desire* of the
wicked that rise up against me.
12 The righteous shall flourish like the palm tree:
he shall grow like a cedar in Lebanon.
13 Those that be planted in the house of the LORD
shall flourish in the courts of our God.
14 They shall still bring forth fruit in old age;
they shall be fat and flourishing;
15 To shew that the LORD *is* upright: *he is* my
rock, and *there is* no unrighteousness in him.

PSALM 93

1 THE LORD reigneth, he is clothed with majesty;
the LORD is clothed with strength, *wherewith* he
hath girded himself: the world also is stablished,
that it cannot be moved.
2 Thy throne *is* established of old: thou *art* from
everlasting.
3 The floods have lifted up, O LORD, the floods
have lifted up their voice; the floods lift up their
waves.
4 The LORD on high *is* mightier than the noise of
many waters, *yea, than* the mighty waves of the sea.
5 Thy testimonies are very sure: holiness becom-
eth thine house, O LORD, for ever.

PSALM 94

1 O LORD God, to whom vengeance belongeth; O
God, to whom vengeance belongeth, shew thyself.

92:3 *psaltery . . . harp.* Stringed instruments, perhaps a lute and a zither, used by the Levites in the public worship of the temple (1 Chron. 25:1,6; 2 Chron. 5:12). In the new covenant, Spirit-filled people are the instruments God desires to hear (Eph. 5:19). *solemn sound.* Hebrew, *higgaion*, a musical term (9:16) of uncertain meaning.
92:4 *triumph.* Exult or give a ringing cry.
92:5 *very deep.* Mysterious.
92:6 *brutish.* Stupid, in the sense of spiritual blindness and foolishness (1 Cor. 2:14).
92:10 *horn.* A symbol of power. *unicorn.* Wild bull or ox. *anointed.* Moistened, symbol of refreshment and prosperity.
92:12–13 *palm tree . . . cedar.* Emblems of fruitfulness and long life. *planted.* Transplanted (1:3). The temple was decorated with images of palm trees, perhaps reminiscent of the garden of Eden (1 Kings 6:29,32,35; cf. Gen. 2:8–9). The imagery here is of God's people experiencing life and growth by worshiping in God's holy presence (*house . . . courts*).
92:14 *fat and flourishing.* Idioms of prosperity.
92:15 *rock.* A huge, immovable boulder, an image of stability.

Thoughts for Personal/Family Worship: Psalm 92

As the title of this psalm implies, it teaches us about how to keep the Lord's Day holy. The Sabbath is a day devoted to praising God for who He is and what He has done in the public worship of God's house. We should sing His praise morning and evening—as much as possible. Life can be brutal as we are surrounded by the wicked, but the Lord's Day offers a unique opportunity to renew our perspective by faith in the promises of God's sovereignty, judgment of the wicked, and blessing on believers. Thus the preaching of the Word is central to the day. By worshiping in God's presence, God's people flourish and grow like trees. Even into their old age they are renewed in strength and declare God's righteousness for others to hear. Truly, the Sabbath is a blessed day! How does this psalm call you to change the way you spend your Sabbaths?

Psalm 93: ***The psalmist describes the majesty and power of God's kingdom.***

93:1 *The LORD reigneth.* A declaration of God's unqualified sovereignty as King over His creation (96:10; 97:1; 99:1; 146:10; Ex. 15:18; Isa. 52:7; Rev. 11:15; 19:6). *clothed.* An outward display of His glory. *girded himself.* Encircled himself as with a belt. *world.* Specifically, the continents. *cannot be moved.* Cannot be made to stagger or sway. God's creation has a stability that comes from God's power guaranteeing the fulfillment of His purposes for the blessing of His chosen people (33:10–12).
93:2 *throne.* Symbol of God's kingdom. God and His sovereignty have always been (90:2).
93:3 *floods.* Rivers, symbolizing the political empires built around them such as Egypt (Jer. 46:7–8) and Assyria (Isa. 8:7–8), powers that threaten God's people (124:4–5).
93:5 *very sure.* Firm, reliable, confirmed. *becometh.* Is fitting for.

Thoughts for Personal/Family Worship: Psalm 93

Unwelcome, unexpected, and unexplained things happen in our experience. There is hardly a more comforting truth for God's people than that God is the absolute Sovereign ruling His kingdom unfailingly for purposes of His glory and His people's good. The Lord God only is King, ruling in power, justice, and wisdom over the entire world (Isa. 46:10–11; Eph. 1:11). The triune God reigns through the Mediator, Jesus Christ (2:6; 110:1–2; Matt. 28:18). As absolute monarch, God guides everything by His Son to His predetermined goal (Prov. 16:4; Rom. 11:36; Heb. 1:3). What does this teach us about how to respond to the threats of powerful people

2 Lift up thyself, thou judge of the earth: render a
reward to the proud.
3 LORD, how long shall the wicked, how long
shall the wicked triumph?
4 *How long* shall they utter *and* speak hard things?
and all the workers of iniquity boast themselves?
5 They break in pieces thy people, O LORD, and
afflict thine heritage.
6 They slay the widow and the stranger, and
murder the fatherless.
7 Yet they say, The LORD shall not see, neither
shall the God of Jacob regard *it*.
8 Understand, ye brutish among the people: and
ye fools, when will ye be wise?
9 He that planted the ear, shall he not hear? he
that formed the eye, shall he not see?
10 He that chastiseth the heathen, shall not he
correct? he that teacheth man knowledge, *shall
not he know*?
11 The LORD knoweth the thoughts of man, that
they *are* vanity.
12 Blessed *is* the man whom thou chastenest, O
LORD, and teachest him out of thy law;
13 That thou mayest give him rest from the days
of adversity, until the pit be digged for the wicked.
14 For the LORD will not cast off his people,
neither will he forsake his inheritance.
15 But judgment shall return unto righteousness:
and all the upright in heart shall follow it.
16 Who will rise up for me against the evildoers?
or who will stand up for me against the workers
of iniquity?
17 Unless the LORD *had been* my help, my soul
had almost dwelt in silence.
18 When I said, My foot slippeth; thy mercy, O
LORD, held me up.
19 In the multitude of my thoughts within me
thy comforts delight my soul.
20 Shall the throne of iniquity have fellowship
with thee, which frameth mischief by a law?
21 They gather themselves together against the
soul of the righteous, and condemn the innocent
blood.
22 But the LORD is my defence; and my God *is* the
rock of my refuge.
23 And he shall bring upon them their own iniq-
uity, and shall cut them off in their own wicked-
ness; *yea*, the LORD our God shall cut them off.

PSALM 95

1 O COME, let us sing unto the LORD: let us make
a joyful noise to the rock of our salvation.
2 Let us come before his presence with thanksgiv-
ing, and make a joyful noise unto him with psalms.

(vv. 3–4)? How should this affect the way we approach His Word and worship (v. 5)?

Psalm 94: *The psalmist prays for the execution of divine justice against the wicked, because he knows that God defends His afflicted servants.*

94:1 *O LORD God, to whom vengeance belongeth*. Literally, "A God of retribution is the LORD." *shew thyself*. Shine forth (50:2; 80:1; Deut. 33:2). When Christ returns to pay back the wicked for harming His church, His glory will shine (Matt. 24:27,30; 2 Thess. 1:6–9).
94:2 *reward*. Payback or recompense.
94:4 *utter*. Gush, babble. *hard*. Arrogant. *boast*. Brag.
94:6 *stranger*. A resident alien.
94:7 *The LORD shall not see*. A common misconception of the wicked (10:11,13; Ezek. 8:12; 9:9), but they are sadly mistaken (11:4; 33:13–15; Heb. 4:13).
94:8 *brutish*. Stupid, dull-hearted, unreceptive. *fools*. Insolent dullards.
94:10 *chastiseth*. Disciplines. *correct*. Rebuke for sin.
94:11 *vanity*. A breath, empty and unsubstantial.
94:12 *Blessed*. Having great benefits from the Lord (1:1). *chastenest*. Disciplines. God lovingly trains men through painful discipline to keep His *law* (Job 5:17–18; Prov. 3:11–12; 1 Cor. 11:32; Heb. 12:5–11; Rev. 3:19).
94:13 *rest*. Peace and quiet. *pit*. Trap.
94:14 *cast off*. Forsake, abandon.
94:17 *my soul*. I (v. 19). *dwelt in silence*. Died.
94:18 *mercy*. Covenant loyalty and love.
94:20 *throne of iniquity have fellowship*. Sinful rulers be allies. *frameth mischief*. Devise trouble.
94:21 *soul*. The person.
94:22 *rock*. A huge, immovable boulder, an image of stability.

Thoughts for Personal/Family Worship: Psalm 94

1. **This is a psalm for the persecuted church. Whenever believers suffer unjustly, they can appeal to the God who occupies the seat of supreme power and jurisdiction. He is able to intervene, righting apparent wrongs, and bringing relief to His troubled people. It is solemn to reflect on the truth that God takes account of everything that happens in this world. Even now, all things are clearly seen by the eyes of the Judge before whom all will stand. This gave Christ the strength to patiently endure injustice and malicious persecution, and Christians are called to walk in His footsteps (1 Peter 2:19–23). What injustices trouble you now? How can this truth help you?**
2. **As God's people wait for the Lord to rescue them from their oppressors, they can find comfort in knowing that God has a purpose in this for them. First, He is blessing them through the teaching of His chastening and discipline (v. 12). Even persecutors are God's instruments to make believers holy. Second, He is bringing them into deeper communion with Himself. The sorrows of persecution drive us to drink more deeply of the secret comforts of God's Spirit (vv. 18–19). Do you know the soul-delighting comforts of Christ? If not, why not? If so, how can you grow in them?**

Psalm 95: *The psalmist exhorts people to praise God for His greatness and providence and warns against the sins of Israel's wilderness generation.*

95:1 *let us sing*. Exult or give a ringing cry. *let us make a joyful noise*. Shout (v. 2). *rock*. Huge, immovable boulder, a symbol of stability.
95:2 *thanksgiving*. A song of praise. *psalms*. Songs.

3 For the LORD *is* a great God, and a great King above all gods.
4 In his hand *are* the deep places of the earth: the strength of the hills *is* his also.
5 The sea *is* his, and he made it: and his hands formed the dry *land*.
6 O come, let us worship and bow down: let us kneel before the LORD our maker.
7 For he *is* our God; and we *are* the people of his pasture, and the sheep of his hand. To day if ye will hear his voice,
8 Harden not your heart, as in the provocation, *and* as *in* the day of temptation in the wilderness:
9 When your fathers tempted me, proved me, and saw my work.
10 Forty years long was I grieved with *this* generation, and said, It *is* a people that do err in their heart, and they have not known my ways:
11 Unto whom I sware in my wrath that they should not enter into my rest.

PSALM 96

1 O SING unto the LORD a new song: sing unto the LORD, all the earth.
2 Sing unto the LORD, bless his name; shew forth his salvation from day to day.
3 Declare his glory among the heathen, his wonders among all people.
4 For the LORD *is* great, and greatly to be praised: he *is* to be feared above all gods.
5 For all the gods of the nations *are* idols: but the LORD made the heavens.
6 Honour and majesty *are* before him: strength and beauty *are* in his sanctuary.
7 Give unto the LORD, O ye kindreds of the people, give unto the LORD glory and strength.
8 Give unto the LORD the glory *due unto* his name: bring an offering, and come into his courts.
9 O worship the LORD in the beauty of holiness: fear before him, all the earth.
10 Say among the heathen *that* the LORD reigneth: the world also shall be established that it shall not be moved: he shall judge the people righteously.
11 Let the heavens rejoice, and let the earth be glad; let the sea roar, and the fulness thereof.
12 Let the field be joyful, and all that *is* therein: then shall all the trees of the wood rejoice
13 Before the LORD: for he cometh, for he cometh to judge the earth: he shall judge the world with righteousness, and the people with his truth.

95:4–5 *deep places.* The unexplored depths. *strength.* The heights or peaks. Opposites like depths and heights indicate totality; everything is in His hand, for He created everything.

95:7–11 *pasture . . . sheep.* The picture of a shepherd depicts God as the good king ruling His people (80:1). *To day if ye will hear.* The *voice* of God continues to speak in the church whenever the Bible is read and preached (Eph. 2:17). This text is cited in Heb. 3:7–11 as the Holy Spirit's warning against hardening your heart against God's Word and falling away after making a profession of faith.

95:8 *Harden not.* Do not stiffen or make stubborn. *provocation . . . temptation.* Hebrew, *Meribah* and *Massah*, places where Israel rebelled against the Lord (Ex. 17:7; Num. 27:14).

95:9 *tempted . . . proved.* Tested.

95:10 *grieved.* Felt disgust, loathed. *do err.* Stagger or are confused. *not known.* Did not acknowledge from the heart.

95:11 *enter into my rest.* The people had already entered into the Promised Land (Josh. 23:1), but God's *rest* went beyond that to enjoying lasting peace in God's presence, which was foreshadowed from creation in the Sabbath (Heb. 4:3–11). We see a type of this rest in Solomon's temple and kingdom (132:8,14; Deut. 12:9; 1 Chron. 22:9,18; 23:25; 28:2), but the reality comes through the Prince of Peace and His kingdom of peace (Isa. 9:6–7; 11:10), even heaven itself (Isa. 57:1–2).

Thoughts for Personal/Family Worship: Psalm 95

1. **Worship engages people to sing God's praise as the trustworthy Savior, supreme King, and only Creator of the entire universe. We hear God's voice in the reading and preaching of the Word. What do vv. 1–7 teach us about our response to God's Word in true worship?**
2. **In the worship service, there really are only two options: either we gladly glorify God through Jesus Christ, or we harden our hearts and put Him to the test. If we refuse to believe God's Word, then even seeing miracles would not help us—Israel saw many miracles, but most of the congregation in the wilderness rebelled against God. The tragic reality is that many come to worship services only to fall under God's wrath. The only way to enter the blessing of God's rest is by faith in Christ. Therefore, do not deceive yourself, thinking you can remain neutral. Which of the two options do you find your heart taking? Flee from the wrath of God, place yourself under the care of the Good Shepherd who laid down His life for the sheep, and engage your heart to worship God.**

Psalm 96: ***The psalmist gives reasons and instructions for praising the Lord.***

96:1 *sing.* Recount in song, as an expression of praise and worship.

96:2 *bless his name.* Declare the greatness of God in all the perfections of who He has shown us that He is.

96:3 *Declare his glory.* List and celebrate His great works (v. 5) and beautiful attributes (vv. 6–7) that demonstrate His uniqueness and supremacy (v. 4). *heathen.* The Gentile nations. *wonders.* Miraculous and extraordinary acts. *people.* Hebrew is plural referring to all nations. This is a universal call to praise.

96:5 *idols.* The Hebrew refers to insignificant, mute things. *the LORD made.* Creation testifies to God's unique right to be worshiped.

96:6 *beauty.* Splendor or radiance.

96:7–8 *Give.* Ascribe, declare what belongs to Him.

96:9 *beauty of holiness.* Not the same Hebrew word for "beauty" used in v. 6. This phrase (29:2; 1 Chron. 16:29; 2 Chron. 20:21) may allude to the holy priestly garments (Ex. 28:2,40) as an image of the holy self-dedication by which God's people willingly offer themselves to the Lord (110:3). *fear.* Tremble in recognition of His greatness.

96:10 *the world . . . not be moved.* The stability of the continents that God set in place. *judge . . . righteously.* Not just punish sin, but rule as a righteous king over the world (v. 13).

PSALM 97

1 THE LORD reigneth; let the earth rejoice; let the
multitude of isles be glad *thereof*.
2 Clouds and darkness *are* round about him:
righteousness and judgment *are* the habitation of
his throne.
3 A fire goeth before him, and burneth up his
enemies round about.
4 His lightnings enlightened the world: the earth
saw, and trembled.
5 The hills melted like wax at the presence of the
LORD, at the presence of the Lord of the whole earth.
6 The heavens declare his righteousness, and all
the people see his glory.
7 Confounded be all they that serve graven
images, that boast themselves of idols: worship
him, all *ye* gods.
8 Zion heard, and was glad; and the daughters of
Judah rejoiced because of thy judgments, O LORD.
9 For thou, LORD, *art* high above all the earth:
thou art exalted far above all gods.
10 Ye that love the LORD, hate evil: he preserveth
the souls of his saints; he delivereth them out of
the hand of the wicked.
11 Light is sown for the righteous, and gladness
for the upright in heart.
12 Rejoice in the LORD, ye righteous; and give
thanks at the remembrance of his holiness.

PSALM 98

A Psalm.

1 O SING unto the LORD a new song; for he hath
done marvellous things: his right hand, and his
holy arm, hath gotten him the victory.
2 The LORD hath made known his salvation: his
righteousness hath he openly shewed in the sight
of the heathen.
3 He hath remembered his mercy and his truth
toward the house of Israel: all the ends of the
earth have seen the salvation of our God.
4 Make a joyful noise unto the LORD, all the earth:

96:11–12 All creation joins in praise in testimony to God's glory (19:1–6; 98:7–8).

Thoughts for Personal/Family Worship: Psalm 96

1. **This psalm teaches that praise and worship is God-centered, with every component of praise, whether in song, speech, conduct, or appearance, directed to His glory. Worship responds to His holiness, that is, the radiant majesty, glory, and beauty that display Him as the only true God. Therefore, worship revolves around the preaching of God's glory from the Word. How can we keep our worship centered on God?**
2. **Worship must be missional, that is, calling all people regardless of ethnic or cultural background to join in knowing and adoring this one God. Biblical evangelism is a call to worship God. Authentic worship fuels a longing for all nations to glorify this great God and Savior. How can we reach out to the nations through our worship?**
3. **Worship must be in the beauty of holiness, that is, by people clothed in Christ's perfect obedience and sanctified by the influences of the Holy Spirit to obey God's commands. In our public worship services, our resolve must be to promote His glory and to please Him, not to entertain ourselves and others. Cheapening the holiness of God and His worship does not assist evangelism, but robs it of its core attraction: God Himself. How can we strive toward a worship that is beautiful in holiness?**

Psalm 97: *The Lord's sovereign reign over all creation is reason for praise and uncompromising holiness.*

97:1 *multitude of isles.* The far distant coasts, used to refer to the extremities of the world.
97:2 *Clouds and darkness.* Associated with the majesty and mystery of His presence (2 Sam. 22:12; 1 Kings 8:12; Heb. 12:18). *habitation.* Support, basis.
97:5 *melted like wax.* God's coming in glory disrupts this fallen world (Isa. 64:1–3; Mic. 1:4; Nah. 1:5).
97:6 *people.* The Hebrew is plural, referring to all nations. *his glory.* The weightiness of His assets and accomplishments, displayed in His works (19:1; Rom. 1:18–21).
97:7 *worship him.* Cited in Heb. 1:6 as a call to worship God's Son. *gods.* Supernatural beings, most likely the angels.
97:10 *love . . . hate.* Terms that engage the whole person to choose or reject (Rom. 12:9). Loving God and sin are mutually exclusive (Matt. 6:24).

Thoughts for Personal/Family Worship: Psalm 97

1. **God is enthroned. His people should rejoice, for the world is not governed by random chance or fate. There is Someone in sovereign control; right and righteousness will prevail. Life does have purpose. Wicked men cannot overcome the Lord, evil will be judged at last, and the future lies entirely with God. If you are in the midst of adversities, remember that all things are being directed from on high, by Someone too wise to err and too good to cause needless grief. Pray for others you know who may be facing struggles at this time as well.**
2. **God reigns in His Son, who is the Lord (2:6–8; 110:1–3). This psalm's graphic imagery will ultimately find fulfillment in the return of Jesus Christ in the skies to judge the world, disrupting this creation to bring in a new creation and bringing believers into everlasting joy. How could this psalm motivate Christians to turn from sin with wholehearted hatred and love the Lord with all their hearts? Why should it move unbelievers to turn from their idols to serve the Lord alone?**

Psalm 98: *The psalmist urgently calls all the earth to rejoice because the Lord is coming.*

98:1 *Sing . . . a new song.* See 96:1. *marvellous.* Miraculous, extraordinary. *right hand . . . holy arm.* Symbols of God's grace and power (Ex. 3:20; Isa. 52:10). *gotten him the victory.* Worked salvation (1 Chron. 29:11).
98:2 *openly shewed.* Revealed or uncovered. *heathen.* Nations.
98:3 *remembered.* Considered and taken action. *mercy . . . truth.* Covenant loyalty and love, and trustworthiness and faithfulness (see note at 86:15).
98:4 *Make a joyful noise.* Cheer, shout in triumph (v. 6). *make a loud noise.* Be cheerful, break forth with happiness. *rejoice.*

make a loud noise, and rejoice, and sing praise.
5 Sing unto the LORD with the harp; with the
harp, and the voice of a psalm.
6 With trumpets and sound of cornet make a
joyful noise before the LORD, the King.
7 Let the sea roar, and the fulness thereof; the
world, and they that dwell therein.
8 Let the floods clap *their* hands: let the hills be
joyful together
9 Before the LORD; for he cometh to judge the
earth: with righteousness shall he judge the world,
and the people with equity.

PSALM 99

1 THE LORD reigneth; let the people tremble: he
sitteth *between* the cherubims; let the earth be
moved.
2 The LORD *is* great in Zion; and he *is* high above
all the people.
3 Let them praise thy great and terrible name; *for*
it *is* holy.
4 The king's strength also loveth judgment; thou
dost establish equity, thou executest judgment
and righteousness in Jacob.
5 Exalt ye the LORD our God, and worship at his
footstool; *for* he *is* holy.
6 Moses and Aaron among his priests, and
Samuel among them that call upon his name; they
called upon the LORD, and he answered them.
7 He spake unto them in the cloudy pillar: they
kept his testimonies, and the ordinance *that* he
gave them.
8 Thou answeredst them, O LORD our God: thou
wast a God that forgavest them, though thou
tookest vengeance of their inventions.
9 Exalt the LORD our God, and worship at his
holy hill; for the LORD our God *is* holy.

PSALM 100

A Psalm of praise.

1 MAKE a joyful noise unto the LORD, all ye lands.
2 Serve the LORD with gladness: come before his
presence with singing.
3 Know ye that the LORD he *is* God: *it is* he *that*

Exult, give a ringing cry. *sing praise.* Sing or play an instrument.

98:5 *harp.* Zither or some sort of stringed instrument. *psalm.* Melody or song.

98:6 *cornet.* Some sort of horn.

98:7 *world.* Specifically, the continents (v. 9).

98:8 *floods.* Rivers. *clap their hands.* A figure of speech for the blessing that God's coming brings to creation (96:11–12). Though God's glory disrupts this fallen world (97:5), He also will regenerate it as a new creation (Isa. 65:17–19; 2 Peter 3:12–13).

98:9 *equity.* Straightness.

Thoughts for Personal/Family Worship: Psalm 98

1. **Consider the marvelous things done by God. In creation, He made, by a mere word and out of nothing, the substance of the entire universe (Rom. 4:17; Heb. 11:3). In providence, He preserves, governs, and directs everything according to His will (Neh. 9:6; Isa. 46:10; Eph. 1:11). In redemption, His greatest work, He delivers at great cost to Himself those imprisoned in sin and misery (Ex. 6:6–7; Deut. 7:7–8). How do each of these great works give us reasons to praise the Lord?**
2. **God's great works of salvation are not meant to be celebrated by a few, but to be broadcast among all nations, so that all creation will be filled with His praise. What reasons does this psalm give us for evangelism and missions?**

Psalm 99: *The Lord's reign as the holy King demands our worship.*

99:1 *tremble.* Quake with emotion. *between the cherubims.* The mercy seat over the ark of the covenant symbolizes God's throne, guarded by angelic beings (Ex. 25:22; Ps. 80:1; Ezek. 1; 10:15; cf. Gen. 3:24). *moved.* Made to stagger or sway.

99:2 *people.* Hebrew is plural referring to all nations.

99:3 *terrible name.* All God's attributes or divine qualities that He has revealed in order to inspire awe, reverence, and fear. *holy.* God's unique glory that makes Him completely distinct from anyone and everything else (vv. 5,9).

99:4 *king's strength . . . loveth judgment.* Powerful, divine King delights in justice (11:7).

99:5 *worship at his footstool.* Bow down at the base of His throne, symbolized by the ark (v. 1; 1 Chron. 28:2).

99:6–8 God's infinite holiness is not a barrier to His grace in answering prayer, communicating His will, forgiving sin, and disciplining His people. The examples of God's past dealings with *Moses, Aaron,* and *Samuel* encourage us to worship Him today.

99:7 *cloudy pillar.* A visible sign of God's presence with Israel (78:14; Ex. 13:21).

99:8 *tookest vengeance.* Justly punished sin, but not in the sense of malicious revenge (Deut. 32:4,35). *inventions.* Deeds or acts.

Thoughts for Personal/Family Worship: Psalm 99

1. **When approaching God in worship, men should tremble in awe of His infinite majesty and holiness. There is no place for casual familiarity, much less flippancy, for God is above us in every way. He is God and not mere man. Although He is so infinitely different from the creature, He nonetheless is approachable, to which Moses, Aaron, and Samuel bear witness. So let us rely on His forgiveness and worship with fear and also joy. Why is it no contradiction to worship God with fear and joy?**
2. **God gave people limited access to Him through the pillar of cloud, the priests, and the temple on "his holy hill" in Zion, yet these were but types of how the King would dwell with His people in Jesus Christ. How does God's holiness shine in His Son?**

Psalm 100: *The psalmist issues a call to serve and worship the Lord because He is God and He is good.*

100:1 *Make a joyful noise.* Cheer or shout in triumph. *all ye lands.* The call to worship is international in scope, driving the mission of the church (96:1–5).

100:2 *singing.* Jubilation, public triumph, and rejoicing.

hath made us, and not we ourselves; *we are* his
people, and the sheep of his pasture.
4 Enter into his gates with thanksgiving, *and* into
his courts with praise: be thankful unto him, *and*
bless his name.
5 For the LORD *is* good; his mercy *is* everlasting;
and his truth *endureth* to all generations.

PSALM 101

A Psalm of David.

1 I WILL sing of mercy and judgment: unto thee,
O LORD, will I sing.
2 I will behave myself wisely in a perfect way. O
when wilt thou come unto me? I will walk within
my house with a perfect heart.
3 I will set no wicked thing before mine eyes: I
hate the work of them that turn aside; *it* shall not
cleave to me.
4 A froward heart shall depart from me: I will not
know a wicked *person*.
5 Whoso privily slandereth his neighbour, him
will I cut off: him that hath an high look and a
proud heart will not I suffer.
6 Mine eyes *shall be* upon the faithful of the land,
that they may dwell with me: he that walketh in a
perfect way, he shall serve me.
7 He that worketh deceit shall not dwell within my
house: he that telleth lies shall not tarry in my sight.
8 I will early destroy all the wicked of the land;
that I may cut off all wicked doers from the city
of the LORD.

PSALM 102

A Prayer of the afflicted, when he is overwhelmed, and poureth out his complaint before the LORD.

1 HEAR my prayer, O LORD, and let my cry come
unto thee.
2 Hide not thy face from me in the day *when* I am
in trouble; incline thine ear unto me: in the day
when I call answer me speedily.
3 For my days are consumed like smoke, and my
bones are burned as an hearth.

100:3 *not we ourselves.* Could be read, "we belong to Him." God owns us because He made us. *his people . . . sheep.* An image of God's benevolent kingship over His people (23:1).
100:4 *his gates.* The entrances to the temple area (*courts*); a call to public worship. *bless his name.* Declare the greatness of who He is in all His perfections, an expression of praise.
100:5 *mercy.* Covenant loyalty and love (see Ps. 136).

Thoughts for Personal/Family Worship: Psalm 100

1. **Worship is a duty required of all mankind. God's works of creation all around us summon us to it (Rom. 1:19–21). God's gospel message calls the nations to glorify Him (Rev. 14:6–7). Nor is it enough for people to go through the outward acts of worship, but we must serve Him with joy and energetic praise (vv. 1–2), springing from the knowledge of who He is (v. 3), and expressed in the public gathering of His church (v. 4). Why is joyless worship an insult to God? Why is ignorance a barrier to worship? Why must we worship God in the public assembly of the church instead of merely praising Him at home or on a private walk?**
2. **The worship of God is fueled by the knowledge of Him as the covenant Lord of His people (v. 3), the God who is eternally and faithfully good in His covenant love and loyalty (v. 5). How does the person and work of Jesus Christ reveal these things about God? How does the gospel of Christ fuel the kind of worship this psalm commands?**

Psalm 101: *David determines to behave with integrity before the Lord.*

Title *David* writes here of his resolve to seek righteousness in his private life (vv. 1–4) and to do justice in his public office as king (vv. 5–8).
101:1 *mercy.* Covenant loyalty and love. *judgment.* Justice.
101:2 *I will behave myself wisely in a perfect way.* Literally, "I will closely attend to a way of wholesomeness or innocence" (v. 6). *perfect heart.* Integrity in thoughts and motives.
101:3 *wicked.* Useless, worthless. *I hate the work of them that turn aside.* Literally, "I reject to do deviation or a deed that swerves."
101:4 *froward.* Twisted, false, or perverted. *know a wicked person.* Literally, "know evil" (*person* is not in the Hebrew text), in the sense of loving and engaging in sin (Jer. 4:22).
101:5 *privily.* In secret. *neighbour.* Fellow man. *suffer.* Endure. A ruler has the responsibility to punish (*cut off*) those under his authority who do wrong (Rom. 13:4).
101:7 *tarry.* Be established.
101:8 *early.* Literally, "in the mornings," an expression for earnest or urgent resolve.

Thoughts for Personal/Family Worship: Psalm 101

1. **When we reflect upon God's perfections, we can only be profoundly grateful that He is the God He is, worthy of our sacred songs and worthy of our sanctified lives. To that end it is good for us to have resolution and purpose of heart to behave in a way that is above and beyond reproach, testifying to the power of His grace. How can we live in such a way that we avoid temptations as much as possible, avoid association with those who would lead us astray, and use whatever authority we have to oppose sin?**
2. **This has been called "the householder's psalm" for its resolutions to live with integrity in the home and to exercise authority righteously. As such it has application to every head of household. However, it applies yet more directly to the resolution of the king of Israel to live a righteous life and govern a righteous kingdom. It is fulfilled in the perfect purity of Jesus Christ, His kingdom, and the coming judgment. How can Christ's absolute resolve to be the righteous king of His people give believers hope and comfort? How is it a dire warning to those who continue unrepentant in sin?**

Psalm 102: *The psalmist complains about his afflictions and puts his hope in God's unchanging character.*

102:2 *Hide not thy face.* A gesture expressing displeasure. *trouble.* Distress.
102:3 *hearth.* Or fire.

4 My heart is smitten, and withered like grass; so
that I forget to eat my bread.
5 By reason of the voice of my groaning my bones
cleave to my skin.
6 I am like a pelican of the wilderness: I am like
an owl of the desert.
7 I watch, and am as a sparrow alone upon the
house top.
8 Mine enemies reproach me all the day; *and* they
that are mad against me are sworn against me.
9 For I have eaten ashes like bread, and mingled
my drink with weeping,
10 Because of thine indignation and thy wrath:
for thou hast lifted me up, and cast me down.
11 My days *are* like a shadow that declineth; and I
am withered like grass.
12 But thou, O LORD, shalt endure for ever; and
thy remembrance unto all generations.
13 Thou shalt arise, *and* have mercy upon Zion:
for the time to favour her, yea, the set time, is
come.
14 For thy servants take pleasure in her stones,
and favour the dust thereof.
15 So the heathen shall fear the name of the
LORD, and all the kings of the earth thy glory.
16 When the LORD shall build up Zion, he shall
appear in his glory.
17 He will regard the prayer of the destitute, and
not despise their prayer.
18 This shall be written for the generation to
come: and the people which shall be created shall
praise the LORD.
19 For he hath looked down from the height of
his sanctuary; from heaven did the LORD behold
the earth;
20 To hear the groaning of the prisoner; to loose
those that are appointed to death;
21 To declare the name of the LORD in Zion, and
his praise in Jerusalem;
22 When the people are gathered together, and
the kingdoms, to serve the LORD.
23 He weakened my strength in the way; he
shortened my days.
24 I said, O my God, take me not away in the midst
of my days: thy years *are* throughout all generations.
25 Of old hast thou laid the foundation of the
earth: and the heavens *are* the work of thy hands.
26 They shall perish, but thou shalt endure: yea, all
of them shall wax old like a garment; as a vesture
shalt thou change them, and they shall be changed:
27 But thou *art* the same, and thy years shall have
no end.
28 The children of thy servants shall continue,
and their seed shall be established before thee.

PSALM 103

A Psalm of David.

1 BLESS the LORD, O my soul: and all that is
within me, *bless* his holy name.
2 Bless the LORD, O my soul, and forget not all
his benefits:
3 Who forgiveth all thine iniquities; who healeth
all thy diseases;
4 Who redeemeth thy life from destruction; who
crowneth thee with lovingkindness and tender
mercies;
5 Who satisfieth thy mouth with good *things; so
that* thy youth is renewed like the eagle's.

102:6–7 *pelican*. Some unclean species of bird (Deut. 14:17). Such a bird in the *wilderness*, like an *owl* in the *desert* or *a sparrow alone*, is out of place—just as the psalmist feels.
102:8 *are mad against me*. Make a mockery of me.
102:11 *shadow that declineth*. As in the evening.
102:13 *have mercy*. Have pity or show compassion through appropriate action to give help. *favour*. Be gracious or show undeserved favor toward (v. 14). *set time*. The appointed or determined time.
102:15 *heathen*. The nations. *name*. All of God's attributes or perfections that He has made known.
102:17 *regard*. Face, give attention.
102:22 *people*. The Hebrew is plural, referring to the Gentile nations (v. 15). All peoples will join the true Israel in worshiping the Lord (22:27).
102:25–27 *wax old*. Wear out. *vesture*. Clothing. The Creator is eternal (90:2), already existing in the beginning when He made all things (Gen. 1:1), and continuing forever (v. 12; 92:8) even after this creation is *changed* into a new creation (97:5; 98:8). *thou art the same*. Literally, "Thou art He." The Lord is immutable or unchangeable, always remaining the same in His nature and plans (33:11; Mal. 3:6). These verses are cited in Heb. 1:10–12 and applied to the Son of God, who is the eternal and immutable "I am" (John 8:58), who together with the Father created the universe (John 1:1–3).

Thoughts for Personal/Family Worship: Psalm 102

Trouble drives many onto the rocks of unbelief but it drives true believers into the harbor of God's presence. In the worst of times it is best to draw near to Him in prayer. Whatever happens to us in life, there should be no place for despair. In our hearts there should spring up the grace of hope, which assures us that beyond the gloomy present is a bright and glorious future. God's kingdom will fill the world and all nations will join God's worshipers. How can we know this with certainty? The hope of the Christian rests upon God's unchanging nature. He is always the same God, and therefore we know that He will do what He promised to do in Jesus Christ. Christ is the unchanging Lord, and so believers can know that He will never abandon them (Heb. 13:5,8). How can we find contentment in Christ even as we groan?

Psalm 103: *David praises God for all the benefits of salvation.*

103:1–2 *Bless*. Declare what belongs to Him, an expression of praise. *O my soul*. David exhorted himself (v. 22). *forget not*. Do not refuse to consider.
103:3 *forgiveth*. The verb form suggests that this is God's habitual activity. *iniquities*. Or guilt (v. 10). God alone can

6 The LORD executeth righteousness and judg-
ment for all that are oppressed.
7 He made known his ways unto Moses, his acts
unto the children of Israel.
8 The LORD *is* merciful and gracious, slow to
anger, and plenteous in mercy.
9 He will not always chide: neither will he keep
his anger for ever.
10 He hath not dealt with us after our sins; nor
rewarded us according to our iniquities.
11 For as the heaven is high above the earth, *so*
great is his mercy toward them that fear him.
12 As far as the east is from the west, *so* far hath he
removed our transgressions from us.
13 Like as a father pitieth *his* children, *so* the
LORD pitieth them that fear him.
14 For he knoweth our frame; he remembereth
that we *are* dust.
15 *As for* man, his days *are* as grass: as a flower of
the field, so he flourisheth.
16 For the wind passeth over it, and it is gone; and
the place thereof shall know it no more.
17 But the mercy of the LORD *is* from everlasting
to everlasting upon them that fear him, and his
righteousness unto children's children;
18 To such as keep his covenant, and to those that
remember his commandments to do them.
19 The LORD hath prepared his throne in the
heavens; and his kingdom ruleth over all.
20 Bless the LORD, ye his angels, that excel in
strength, that do his commandments, hearkening
unto the voice of his word.
21 Bless ye the LORD, all *ye* his hosts; *ye* ministers
of his, that do his pleasure.
22 Bless the LORD, all his works in all places of his
dominion: bless the LORD, O my soul.

PSALM 104

1 BLESS the LORD, O my soul. O LORD my God,
thou art very great; thou art clothed with honour
and majesty.
2 Who coverest *thyself* with light as *with* a
garment: who stretchest out the heavens like a
curtain:
3 Who layeth the beams of his chambers in the
waters: who maketh the clouds his chariot: who
walketh upon the wings of the wind:
4 Who maketh his angels spirits; his ministers a
flaming fire:
5 *Who* laid the foundations of the earth, *that* it
should not be removed for ever.
6 Thou coveredst it with the deep as *with* a
garment: the waters stood above the mountains.
7 At thy rebuke they fled; at the voice of thy
thunder they hasted away.
8 They go up by the mountains; they go down
by the valleys unto the place which thou hast
founded for them.
9 Thou hast set a bound that they may not pass
over; that they turn not again to cover the earth.
10 He sendeth the springs into the valleys, *which*
run among the hills.

forgive the guilt of sin (51:1–4; Isa. 43:25; Mark 2:7).

103:4 *redeemeth*. Rescue from trouble at His own expense because of a close relationship. *destruction*. Or the grave. *lovingkindness and tender mercies*. Covenant loyalty and love, and pity or compassion that leads to action to help.

103:8 *merciful*. Compassionate. *mercy*. Covenant loyalty and love (vv. 11,17).

103:9 *chide*. Contest a lawsuit.

103:10 *rewarded*. Recompensed, repaid.

103:11 *as the heaven is high*. God's faithful love (*mercy*) is infinitely great (36:5; 57:10) toward those who worship, trust, and obey Him from a childlike heart (*fear him*; v. 13).

103:12 *as the east is from the west*. God's forgiveness is complete, removing all legal guilt from the sinner (Isa. 38:17; Mic. 7:18–19; Col. 2:13–14; 1 John 1:7,9).

103:13 *pitieth*. Has compassion on those in misery and takes appropriate action.

103:14 *frame*. Form or shape. *remembereth*. Considers and takes to heart (v. 18).

103:17 *unto children's children*. God displays covenant loyalty to the following generations, a key covenant promise (105:8; Deut. 7:9).

103:20 *angels*. Powerful spirits created by God to worship Him in heaven (*Bless the LORD*, cf. 148:1–6) and to obediently execute His plans on earth (*hearkening unto . . . his word*, cf. 68:17; 78:49; 91:11; 104:4).

103:21 *hosts*. Armies. *ministers*. Servants. Both terms most likely refer to the angels (v. 20).

Thoughts for Personal/Family Worship: Psalm 103

1. **How richly and abundantly God has blessed His people. We are prone to forget the good things He has lavished upon us and therefore we need to reflect and recall the wonderful blessings He has given. We need to engage in holy argument with ourselves to stir up our hearts to praise the Lord. What does this psalm teach us about the reasons why we should praise God?**
2. **The wonder and infinite glory of God's love and forgiveness shine brightly in the death of His Son. Nothing could communicate the heights of God's love for sinners more than the words, "For God so love the world, that he gave his only begotten Son" (John 3:16). Nothing could make God's forgiveness more secure or complete than the fact that God placed all the sins of His people upon His Son and punished those sins there (Isa. 53:5–6).**

Psalm 104: *God's power in creation and providence is reason for praise.*

104:1 *Bless*. Declare the good things that are His, an expression of praise. *O my soul*. A reference to himself (v. 35).

104:2–3 *garment . . . curtain . . . chambers . . . chariot*. Metaphors describing the universe as God's house and property.

104:4 The *angels* are God's heavenly servants (*ministers*) to whom He gives power comparable to the wind (*spirits*) and lightning (*fire*). This verse is cited in Heb. 1:7 to show the superiority of Christ, who is God's Son, over the angels.

11 They give drink to every beast of the field: the wild asses quench their thirst.
12 By them shall the fowls of the heaven have their habitation, *which* sing among the branches.
13 He watereth the hills from his chambers: the earth is satisfied with the fruit of thy works.
14 He causeth the grass to grow for the cattle, and herb for the service of man: that he may bring forth food out of the earth;
15 And wine *that* maketh glad the heart of man, *and* oil to make *his* face to shine, and bread *which* strengtheneth man's heart.
16 The trees of the LORD are full *of sap*; the cedars of Lebanon, which he hath planted;
17 Where the birds make their nests: *as for* the stork, the fir trees *are* her house.
18 The high hills *are* a refuge for the wild goats; *and* the rocks for the conies.
19 He appointed the moon for seasons: the sun knoweth his going down.
20 Thou makest darkness, and it is night: wherein all the beasts of the forest do creep *forth*.
21 The young lions roar after their prey, and seek their meat from God.
22 The sun ariseth, they gather themselves together, and lay them down in their dens.
23 Man goeth forth unto his work and to his labour until the evening.
24 O LORD, how manifold are thy works! in wisdom hast thou made them all: the earth is full of thy riches.
25 *So is* this great and wide sea, wherein *are* things creeping innumerable, both small and great beasts.
26 There go the ships: *there is* that leviathan, *whom* thou hast made to play therein.
27 These wait all upon thee; that thou mayest give *them* their meat in due season.
28 *That* thou givest them they gather: thou openest thine hand, they are filled with good.
29 Thou hidest thy face, they are troubled: thou takest away their breath, they die, and return to their dust.
30 Thou sendest forth thy spirit, they are created: and thou renewest the face of the earth.
31 The glory of the LORD shall endure for ever: the LORD shall rejoice in his works.
32 He looketh on the earth, and it trembleth: he toucheth the hills, and they smoke.
33 I will sing unto the LORD as long as I live: I will sing praise to my God while I have my being.
34 My meditation of him shall be sweet: I will be glad in the LORD.
35 Let the sinners be consumed out of the earth, and let the wicked be no more. Bless thou the LORD, O my soul. Praise ye the LORD.

PSALM 105

1 O GIVE thanks unto the LORD; call upon his name: make known his deeds among the people.
2 Sing unto him, sing psalms unto him: talk ye of all his wondrous works.
3 Glory ye in his holy name: let the heart of them rejoice that seek the LORD.
4 Seek the LORD, and his strength: seek his face evermore.

104:13–14 *He watereth . . . He causeth*. All natural processes, including the water cycle and food production, are sustained and directed by God's secret providence (136:25; 147:8; Matt. 6:26,30).

104:15 *maketh glad the heart of man*. All the good things of earth testify to men that there is a good God who loves them despite their sins (Matt. 5:45; Acts 14:17).

104:17 *stork*. Exact identity uncertain, perhaps a heron.

104:18 *conies*. Exact identity uncertain, perhaps a rock badger or hyrax (Prov. 30:26).

104:21 *meat*. Food of any kind (v. 27).

104:24 *manifold*. Many. The wonders of creation, including the vast array of living creatures in sky, sea, and land, demonstrate the infinite *wisdom* of the God who made them (136:5; Prov. 3:19; Jer. 10:12; 51:15).

104:26 *leviathan*. Some sort of large sea creature.

104:29 *hidest thy face*. A sign of displeasure. *troubled*. Horrified, disturbed, or terrified.

104:34 *meditation*. Musing. *sweet*. Pleasing.

104:35 *Praise ye the LORD*. Hebrew, *hallelujah*.

Thoughts for Personal/Family Worship: Psalm 104

This psalm describes the divine works of creation and providence. In fact, it is like a poetic version of Gen. 1. A true, biblical understanding of creation moves us to admire and adore God's attributes of power, wisdom, and love. Failure to maintain the doctrine of creation diminishes God's glory. In our thoughts, we should rise from creation to the Creator and meditate often upon Him. We shall find our meditation to be a sweet antidote to all the trouble and cares of life. We should also rejoice in the daily demonstrations of God's providential care for what He has created. Yet as great as God's creations are, the Lord is far greater. Spend time, even now worshiping the triune God alone, honoring the Father, the Son, and the Holy Spirit far above even the angels.

Psalm 105: *The psalmist reviews the history of God's dealings with the patriarchs and the exodus of Israel as reasons for praise.*

105:1 *his name*. Who God is, as He has revealed Himself in all His perfections (v. 3). *people*. The Hebrew is plural, referring to the nations. There is more to Hebrew history than concerns just Israel.

105:2 *sing psalms*. Play an instrument. *wondrous works*. Miraculous, extraordinary acts (v. 5).

105:3–4 *seek*. The verb form suggests habitual activity. To seek or pursue after God means to draw near to the Lord with faith (9:10), humility (22:26; 69:32–33), repentance over sin (83:16), prayer for salvation from evil and provision of good (34:4,10; 40:16; 77:2), and desire for His lovely presence (27:4). Lost sinners may seek God in an external way but not truly (14:2–3; 78:34–37); the true pursuit of God must come from

5 Remember his marvellous works that he hath
done; his wonders, and the judgments of his mouth;
6 O ye seed of Abraham his servant, ye children
of Jacob his chosen.
7 He *is* the LORD our God: his judgments *are* in
all the earth.
8 He hath remembered his covenant for ever,
the word *which* he commanded to a thousand
generations.
9 Which *covenant* he made with Abraham, and
his oath unto Isaac;
10 And confirmed the same unto Jacob for a law,
and to Israel *for* an everlasting covenant:
11 Saying, Unto thee will I give the land of Canaan, the lot of your inheritance:
12 When they were *but* a few men in number; yea,
very few, and strangers in it.
13 When they went from one nation to another,
from *one* kingdom to another people;
14 He suffered no man to do them wrong: yea, he
reproved kings for their sakes;
15 *Saying*, Touch not mine anointed, and do my
prophets no harm.
16 Moreover he called for a famine upon the
land: he brake the whole staff of bread.
17 He sent a man before them, *even* Joseph, *who*
was sold for a servant:
18 Whose feet they hurt with fetters: he was laid
in iron:
19 Until the time that his word came: the word of
the LORD tried him.
20 The king sent and loosed him; *even* the ruler
of the people, and let him go free.
21 He made him lord of his house, and ruler of
all his substance:
22 To bind his princes at his pleasure; and teach
his senators wisdom.
23 Israel also came into Egypt; and Jacob sojourned in the land of Ham.
24 And he increased his people greatly; and made
them stronger than their enemies.
25 He turned their heart to hate his people, to
deal subtilly with his servants.
26 He sent Moses his servant; *and* Aaron whom
he had chosen.
27 They shewed his signs among them, and
wonders in the land of Ham.
28 He sent darkness, and made it dark; and they
rebelled not against his word.
29 He turned their waters into blood, and slew
their fish.
30 Their land brought forth frogs in abundance,
in the chambers of their kings.
31 He spake, and there came divers sorts of flies,
and lice in all their coasts.
32 He gave them hail for rain, *and* flaming fire in
their land.
33 He smote their vines also and their fig trees;
and brake the trees of their coasts.
34 He spake, and the locusts came, and caterpillers, and that without number,
35 And did eat up all the herbs in their land, and
devoured the fruit of their ground.
36 He smote also all the firstborn in their land,
the chief of all their strength.
37 He brought them forth also with silver and
gold: and *there was* not one feeble *person* among
their tribes.
38 Egypt was glad when they departed: for the
fear of them fell upon them.
39 He spread a cloud for a covering; and fire to
give light in the night.
40 *The people* asked, and he brought quails, and
satisfied them with the bread of heaven.
41 He opened the rock, and the waters gushed
out; they ran in the dry places *like* a river.
42 For he remembered his holy promise, *and*
Abraham his servant.
43 And he brought forth his people with joy, *and*
his chosen with gladness:
44 And gave them the lands of the heathen: and
they inherited the labour of the people;

---

the heart (27:8; 119:2,10). *evermore*. Continually.

105:5 *Remember*. Give thought and take to heart (vv. 8,42). *wonders*. Or signs.

105:8–11 *covenant…with Abraham*. See Gen. 12–22, especially chs. 12; 15; and 17.

105:11 *lot*. A measured portion of a field.

105:12 *strangers*. Those living as dependent aliens.

105:14 *suffered*. Allowed.

105:15 *Touch not*. Do not harm (Gen. 20:3–7). *anointed*. Designated for sacred office by the empowerment of the Spirit, such as receiving and proclaiming God's Word (*prophets*, cf. 1 Kings 19:16).

105:16 *whole staff of bread*. Supply of food.

105:17–23 *Joseph*. See Gen. 37–50.

105:18 *fetters*. Shackles. This is information not supplied in the Genesis narrative.

105:19 *tried*. Refined.

105:21 *substance*. Possessions.

105:22 *senators*. Elders.

105:23 *sojourned*. Lived as a resident alien.

105:25 *turned their heart*. The Lord sovereignly ruled over the beginning of Israel's oppression in Egypt. *subtilly*. Treacherously or cunningly.

105:27–38 *shewed his signs*. Worked miracles by God's power in the ten plagues on Egypt (Ex. 7–12).

105:31 *divers*. Diverse or various. *coasts*. Borders (v. 33).

105:32 *flaming fire*. Lightning.

105:40 *bread of heaven*. The manna supernaturally supplied by God to feed Israel in the wilderness (78:24–25; Ex. 16), a type of Christ in His giving of life to all who receive Him by faith (John 6:31–35).

105:41 *rock*. A huge, immovable boulder. *The waters gushed out* to quench the thirst of Israel in the wilderness (78:15–16; Ex. 17:6), a type of Christ satisfying believers by the Spirit (1 Cor. 10:4; 12:12–13; cf. John 4:14; 7:37–39).

105:44 *heathen*. The Gentile nations.

45 That they might observe his statutes, and keep
his laws. Praise ye the LORD.

PSALM 106

1 PRAISE ye the LORD. O give thanks unto the
LORD; for *he is* good: for his mercy *endureth* for
ever.
2 Who can utter the mighty acts of the LORD?
who can shew forth all his praise?
3 Blessed *are* they that keep judgment, *and* he
that doeth righteousness at all times.
4 Remember me, O LORD, with the favour *that
thou bearest unto* thy people: O visit me with thy
salvation;
5 That I may see the good of thy chosen, that I
may rejoice in the gladness of thy nation, that I
may glory with thine inheritance.
6 We have sinned with our fathers, we have
committed iniquity, we have done wickedly.
7 Our fathers understood not thy wonders in
Egypt; they remembered not the multitude of thy
mercies; but provoked *him* at the sea, *even* at the
Red sea.
8 Nevertheless he saved them for his name's
sake, that he might make his mighty power to be
known.
9 He rebuked the Red sea also, and it was dried
up: so he led them through the depths, as through
the wilderness.
10 And he saved them from the hand of him that
hated *them*, and redeemed them from the hand
of the enemy.
11 And the waters covered their enemies: there
was not one of them left.
12 Then believed they his words; they sang his
praise.
13 They soon forgat his works; they waited not
for his counsel:
14 But lusted exceedingly in the wilderness, and
tempted God in the desert.
15 And he gave them their request; but sent lean-
ness into their soul.
16 They envied Moses also in the camp, *and*
Aaron the saint of the LORD.
17 The earth opened and swallowed up Dathan,
and covered the company of Abiram.
18 And a fire was kindled in their company; the
flame burned up the wicked.
19 They made a calf in Horeb, and worshipped
the molten image.
20 Thus they changed their glory into the simili-
tude of an ox that eateth grass.
21 They forgat God their saviour, which had
done great things in Egypt;
22 Wondrous works in the land of Ham, *and*
terrible things by the Red sea.
23 Therefore he said that he would destroy them,
had not Moses his chosen stood before him in
the breach, to turn away his wrath, lest he should
destroy *them*.

105:45 *Praise ye the LORD*. Hebrew, *hallelujah*.

Thoughts for Personal/Family Worship: Psalm 105

1. **Thinking about God's mighty works in the past is a good way to fuel faith and generate praise. Biblical history is not just a list of facts and dates, but a testimony to God's faithfulness to His covenant and His power to keep His promises. Knowing that His Word cannot fail is a great comfort to believers in life and death and gives them ample reason to praise the Lord. How can the history of God's people encourage us to seek the Lord, His strength, and His presence?**
2. **God still keeps His covenant with Abraham today, for Jesus Christ is the blessed seed of Abraham (Matt. 1:1; Gal. 3:16). Those who are joined to Christ by a living faith are also heirs of the promise, the spiritual offspring of Abraham (Rom. 4:16; Gal. 3:29). The Lord's mighty acts in judging Egypt, bringing out His people, and preserving them in the wilderness prepared the way for Christ's coming in the flesh and foreshadowed the power by which King Jesus saves His people through the gospel and ultimately in His glorious coming. How is Old Testament history a book of comfort for Christians?**

Psalm 106: *The psalmist rehearses the history of God's salvation of Israel at the Red Sea, His faithfulness in the wilderness and conquest, and Israel's sins.*

106:1 *Praise ye the LORD*. Hebrew, *hallelujah* (v. 48). *mercy*. Covenant loyalty and love.

106:3 *Blessed*. Possessing great benefits from God (1:1); not the same term used of the praise of God (v. 48). *judgment*. Justice.

106:4 *Remember*. Set one's mind and heart upon intentionally (vv. 7,45). *favour*. Goodwill or pleasure. *visit*. Give attention to and act accordingly toward, take care of.

106:5 *good*. Prosperity or welfare. *glory*. Boast or praise.

106:7 *wonders*. Miraculous, extraordinary acts. *mercies*. Acts of covenant loyalty and love (v. 45). *provoked*. Behaved rebelliously, disobeyed.

106:8 *for his name's sake*. For the sake of His reputation, according to who He has revealed Himself to be in His perfections.

106:9 *rebuked the Red sea*. See Ex. 14.

106:10 *redeemed*. Rescued them at His expense like a kinsman, faithful to his family.

106:13 *forgat*. Refused to think about, neglected, ignored (v. 21).

106:14 *lusted exceedingly*. Literally, "craved a craving." *tempted*. Put to the test. *sent leanness into their soul*. Sent consumption or wasting to them. See Num. 11:4–6,31–33.

106:16–17 *envied…swallowed up*. See Num. 16:1–3,30–35.

106:18 *was kindled*. Blazed up. See Num. 16:35,46.

106:19 *calf in Horeb*. See Ex. 32.

106:20 *changed*. Exchanged. *their glory*. God (Rom. 1:23). *similitude*. Resemblance.

106:22 *Wondrous works*. Miraculous or extraordinary acts. *terrible*. Fearful or awe-inspiring.

106:23 *breach*. Gap. See Ex. 32:10–32; Deut. 9:19.

24 Yea, they despised the pleasant land, they
believed not his word:
25 But murmured in their tents, *and* hearkened
not unto the voice of the LORD.
26 Therefore he lifted up his hand against them,
to overthrow them in the wilderness:
27 To overthrow their seed also among the
nations, and to scatter them in the lands.
28 They joined themselves also unto Baal-peor,
and ate the sacrifices of the dead.
29 Thus they provoked *him* to anger with their
inventions: and the plague brake in upon them.
30 Then stood up Phinehas, and executed judg-
ment: and *so* the plague was stayed.
31 And that was counted unto him for righteous-
ness unto all generations for evermore.
32 They angered *him* also at the waters of strife,
so that it went ill with Moses for their sakes:
33 Because they provoked his spirit, so that he
spake unadvisedly with his lips.
34 They did not destroy the nations, concerning
whom the LORD commanded them:
35 But were mingled among the heathen, and
learned their works.
36 And they served their idols: which were a snare
unto them.
37 Yea, they sacrificed their sons and their daugh-
ters unto devils,
38 And shed innocent blood, *even* the blood of
their sons and of their daughters, whom they
sacrificed unto the idols of Canaan: and the land
was polluted with blood.
39 Thus were they defiled with their own works,
and went a whoring with their own inventions.
40 Therefore was the wrath of the LORD kindled
against his people, insomuch that he abhorred his
own inheritance.
41 And he gave them into the hand of the hea-
then; and they that hated them ruled over them.
42 Their enemies also oppressed them, and they
were brought into subjection under their hand.
43 Many times did he deliver them; but they
provoked *him* with their counsel, and were
brought low for their iniquity.
44 Nevertheless he regarded their affliction, when
he heard their cry:
45 And he remembered for them his covenant,
and repented according to the multitude of his
mercies.
46 He made them also to be pitied of all those
that carried them captives.
47 Save us, O LORD our God, and gather us from
among the heathen, to give thanks unto thy holy
name, *and* to triumph in thy praise.
48 Blessed *be* the LORD God of Israel from
everlasting to everlasting: and let all the people
say, Amen. Praise ye the LORD.

106:24 *despised.* Refused or rejected. *pleasant land.* "Land of desirable things," a reference to the Promised Land of Canaan. *they believed not.* The root of Israel's rebellion was a refusal to believe God's Word (Heb. 3:9–19; 4:2).
106:25 *murmured.* See Num. 14. *hearkened not.* Did not listen.
106:28 *joined themselves also unto Baal-peor.* See Num. 25:2–5.
106:29 *inventions.* Deeds or practices (v. 39).
106:30 *stayed.* Brought to a halt, restrained.
106:31 *for righteousness.* A righteous act, the right thing to do. Not a reference to justification in God's sight, which is by faith alone (Gen. 15:6; Hab. 2:4).
106:32 *ill.* Badly. See Num. 20:2–13.
106:33 *unadvisedly.* Impetuously, thoughtlessly, rashly. See Num. 20:10. As the prophet of God, he did not represent or speak well of God.
106:34 *not destroy the nations.* See Judg. 1:21—2:3.
106:35 *were mingled.* They mixed themselves up with and had fellowship with. *heathen.* The Gentile nations (vv. 41,47).
106:37 *devils.* Or demons (1 Cor. 10:20).
106:38 *polluted.* Defiled. *blood.* Hebrew is plural, referring to bloodshedding, murders, and consequent guilt.
106:39 *went a whoring.* Engaged in sexual immorality or prostitution, a metaphor for spiritual unfaithfulness to the Lord by worshiping other gods.
106:43–44 *Many times.* See the cycle of sin and deliverance in Judges. *counsel.* Plan. *brought low.* Humiliated.
106:45 *repented.* Relented or was grieved.
106:47 *name.* All that God revealed Himself to be. *triumph.* Boast.
106:48 *Blessed be the LORD God.* Praise Him, declare the blessings that belong to Him.

Thoughts for Personal/Family Worship: Psalm 106

1. **This psalm teaches again how important it is to remember the past as a guide for the present. The history of Israel's sins against the Lord is not an occasion to despise the Jews, but to consider the corruption within us all, to go beyond external religion to real union with Christ, to recognize how easily we can fall, and to flee from lust and idolatry (1 Cor. 10:1–14). Miracles, great acts of salvation from earthly troubles, the presence of godly prophets to declare God's Word, and painful defeats from God's hand of discipline should have turned Israel back to God, but the wickedness of fallen mankind is too deep for external means to root it out. Our only hope for salvation is God's love and faithfulness to His covenant. Seeing our sinfulness reflected in the history of Israel should move us pray, "Save us, O LORD our God" (Ps. 106:47). Then His salvation will move us to praise Him forever for His goodness and mercy. How could you use this psalm to prove that people cannot save themselves?**
2. **What do we need from God to avoid repeating Israel's history in our own lives? God must provide a spiritual salvation beginning with the gift of faith (v. 24), not a superficial belief that passes away (vv. 12–13), but an enduring trust that produces a lifelong practice of justice and righteousness (v. 3). Rather than forgetting God (vv. 13,21), sinners need God to give them an experiential knowledge of Him. Furthermore, to atone for their sins God must provide them with an eternal righteousness through an intercessor greater than Moses (v. 23) or Phineas (vv. 30–31). Jesus Christ turned aside**

PSALM 107

1 O GIVE thanks unto the LORD, for *he is* good:
for his mercy *endureth* for ever.
2 Let the redeemed of the LORD say *so*, whom he
hath redeemed from the hand of the enemy;
3 And gathered them out of the lands, from the
east, and from the west, from the north, and from
the south.
4 They wandered in the wilderness in a solitary
way; they found no city to dwell in.
5 Hungry and thirsty, their soul fainted in them.
6 Then they cried unto the LORD in their trouble,
and he delivered them out of their distresses.
7 And he led them forth by the right way, that
they might go to a city of habitation.
8 Oh that *men* would praise the LORD *for* his
goodness, and *for* his wonderful works to the
children of men!
9 For he satisfieth the longing soul, and filleth the
hungry soul with goodness.
10 Such as sit in darkness and in the shadow of
death, *being* bound in affliction and iron;
11 Because they rebelled against the words of God,
and contemned the counsel of the most High:
12 Therefore he brought down their heart with
labour; they fell down, and *there was* none to help.
13 Then they cried unto the LORD in their trou-
ble, *and* he saved them out of their distresses.
14 He brought them out of darkness and the
shadow of death, and brake their bands in sunder.
15 Oh that *men* would praise the LORD *for* his
goodness, and *for* his wonderful works to the
children of men!
16 For he hath broken the gates of brass, and cut
the bars of iron in sunder.
17 Fools because of their transgression, and
because of their iniquities, are afflicted.
18 Their soul abhorreth all manner of meat; and
they draw near unto the gates of death.
19 Then they cry unto the LORD in their trouble,
and he saveth them out of their distresses.
20 He sent his word, and healed them, and deliv-
ered *them* from their destructions.
21 Oh that *men* would praise the LORD *for* his
goodness, and *for* his wonderful works to the
children of men!
22 And let them sacrifice the sacrifices of thanks-
giving, and declare his works with rejoicing.
23 They that go down to the sea in ships, that do
business in great waters;
24 These see the works of the LORD, and his
wonders in the deep.
25 For he commandeth, and raiseth the stormy
wind, which lifteth up the waves thereof.
26 They mount up to the heaven, they go down
again to the depths: their soul is melted because
of trouble.
27 They reel to and fro, and stagger like a drunken
man, and are at their wits' end.
28 Then they cry unto the LORD in their trouble,
and he bringeth them out of their distresses.
29 He maketh the storm a calm, so that the waves
thereof are still.
30 Then are they glad because they be quiet; so he
bringeth them unto their desired haven.
31 Oh that *men* would praise the LORD *for* his
goodness, and *for* his wonderful works to the
children of men!
32 Let them exalt him also in the congregation of
the people, and praise him in the assembly of the
elders.
33 He turneth rivers into a wilderness, and the
watersprings into dry ground;
34 A fruitful land into barrenness, for the wicked-
ness of them that dwell therein.
35 He turneth the wilderness into a standing
water, and dry ground into watersprings.
36 And there he maketh the hungry to dwell, that
they may prepare a city for habitation;
37 And sow the fields, and plant vineyards, which
may yield fruits of increase.

God's wrath by receiving God's judgment upon Himself (Gal. 3:13). The Spirit of Jesus Christ works faith (1 Cor. 12:3). The only hope of the human race is Christ, the one Mediator of the triune God. Have you known God's gifts of salvation and intercession as your own? If so, you can "come boldly unto the throne of grace" (Heb. 4:16).

BOOK 5 (PSS. 107:1—150:6)

Psalm 107: *The redeemed praise God for His goodness and works.*

107:1 *good.* Doing acts of kindness to others generally. *mercy.* Covenant loyalty and love specifically.
107:2 *redeemed.* Rescued from severe troubles by the intervention of a near kinsman acting at his own expense.
107:4 *solitary way.* A desert waste.
107:7 *right.* Straight.
107:8 *goodness.* Covenant loyalty and love (same word as "mercy" in v. 1). *wonderful.* Extraordinary, often miraculous, beyond human ability. This call to *praise the LORD* is the recurring refrain of the psalm (vv. 15,21,31).
107:9 *goodness.* See note at v. 1 regarding "good."
107:10 *bound in affliction and iron.* Miserable prisoners in chains or confinement (vv. 14,16; 105:18).
107:11 *contemned.* Despised.
107:14 *brake their bands in sunder.* Tore their bonds in pieces.
107:16 *brass.* Bronze. *in sunder.* In pieces.
107:18 *Their soul abhorreth . . . meat.* They had no appetite, regarding all food as disgusting.
107:24 *wonders.* Same word as "wonderful works" (v. 8).
107:26 *their soul is melted.* They begin to move or come apart.
107:27 *are at their wits' end.* Literally, "all their wisdom is swallowed up," meaning they are confused.
107:35 *standing water.* A pool of water.

38 He blesseth them also, so that they are mul-
tiplied greatly; and suffereth not their cattle to
decrease.
39 Again, they are minished and brought low
through oppression, affliction, and sorrow.
40 He poureth contempt upon princes, and caus-
eth them to wander in the wilderness, *where there
is* no way.
41 Yet setteth he the poor on high from affliction,
and maketh *him* families like a flock.
42 The righteous shall see *it*, and rejoice: and all
iniquity shall stop her mouth.
43 Whoso *is* wise, and will observe these *things*,
even they shall understand the lovingkindness of
the LORD.

PSALM 108

A Song *or* Psalm of David.

1 O GOD, my heart is fixed; I will sing and give
praise, even with my glory.
2 Awake, psaltery and harp: I *myself* will awake
early.
3 I will praise thee, O LORD, among the people:
and I will sing praises unto thee among the nations.
4 For thy mercy *is* great above the heavens: and
thy truth *reacheth* unto the clouds.
5 Be thou exalted, O God, above the heavens: and
thy glory above all the earth;
6 That thy beloved may be delivered: save *with*
thy right hand, and answer me.
7 God hath spoken in his holiness; I will rejoice,
I will divide Shechem, and mete out the valley of
Succoth.
8 Gilead *is* mine; Manasseh *is* mine; Ephraim also
is the strength of mine head; Judah *is* my lawgiver;
9 Moab *is* my washpot; over Edom will I cast out
my shoe; over Philistia will I triumph.
10 Who will bring me into the strong city? who
will lead me into Edom?
11 *Wilt* not *thou*, O God, *who* hast cast us off? and
wilt not thou, O God, go forth with our hosts?
12 Give us help from trouble: for vain *is* the help
of man.
13 Through God we shall do valiantly: for he *it is*
that shall tread down our enemies.

PSALM 109

To the chief Musician,
A Psalm of David.

1 HOLD not thy peace, O God of my praise;
2 For the mouth of the wicked and the mouth
of the deceitful are opened against me: they have
spoken against me with a lying tongue.
3 They compassed me about also with words of
hatred; and fought against me without a cause.
4 For my love they are my adversaries: but I *give
myself unto* prayer.
5 And they have rewarded me evil for good, and
hatred for my love.
6 Set thou a wicked man over him: and let Satan
stand at his right hand.

107:38 *suffereth.* Cause or allow.
107:39 *minished.* Made few.
107:43 *lovingkindness.* Covenant loyalty and love, also translated "mercy" (v. 1) and "goodness" (vv. 8,15,21,31).

Thoughts for Personal/Family Worship: Psalm 107

1. If redeemed, we should be willing and eager to say so, telling others about the Savior. Whenever God acts for our deliverance and displays His covenant love, it is that we might praise His name. We must therefore learn never to neglect this, for it is our duty and delight. Whenever God answers our prayers or saves us from the consequences of our sins, let us give Him public thanks for His amazing grace and power. However, it requires wisdom and watchfulness to observe God's goodness at work, or we will take it for granted in our self-righteousness and pass it by without a word. How can we develop an attitude of watchfulness for mercies and a quickness to praise the Lord?
2. Mercy and goodness flows to sinners through Jesus Christ. He is the only Mediator between God and sinners. He is the Redeemer who has delivered men from their fearful bondage to sin and its horrifying consequences in the wrath of God. Therefore, give thanks and praise to God *for* Christ and *through* Christ.

Psalm 108: ***David praises God for His assistance and prays for renewed help.***

108:1–5 The same as 57:7–11; see notes there.
108:6–13 The same as 60:5–12; see notes there.

Thoughts for Personal/Family Worship: Psalm 108

1. Having a heart that is fixed and steadfast is important for "a double minded man is unstable in all his ways" (James 1:8). Having our hearts focused on the Lord and being sensitive to all His faithfulness are the means of having such a fixed mind. Follow David's pattern by being quick to praise God for His goodness and to pray for His renewed help daily. What makes it hard to fix your heart on God? How can you overcome these distractions?
2. The salvation of God's beloved leads to His praises among the nations and the demonstration of His sovereignty over all peoples. This took place supremely when God conquered Satan through the death and resurrection of Jesus Christ, exalted Christ to the highest place, and initiated the mission of evangelizing the world. The success of this mission depends upon the past victory of God's Son, and the present assistance of the Holy Spirit. "Through God we shall do valiantly" (v. 13). How can the Holy Spirit's work in your life lead to God being glorified and praised?

Psalm 109: ***David complains of betrayal and slander and devotes his enemies to destruction.***

109:1 *Hold not thy peace.* Do not be silent.
109:3 *compassed.* Surrounded. *hatred . . . without a cause.* See note at 69:4.
109:4 *For my love.* Instead of my friend.
109:5 *evil.* Hurtful things.
109:6 *Satan.* An accuser, adversary. *at his right hand.* See

7 When he shall be judged, let him be con-
demned: and let his prayer become sin.
8 Let his days be few; *and* let another take his
office.
9 Let his children be fatherless, and his wife a
widow.
10 Let his children be continually vagabonds,
and beg: let them seek *their bread* also out of their
desolate places.
11 Let the extortioner catch all that he hath; and
let the strangers spoil his labour.
12 Let there be none to extend mercy unto him:
neither let there be any to favour his fatherless
children.
13 Let his posterity be cut off; *and* in the genera-
tion following let their name be blotted out.
14 Let the iniquity of his fathers be remembered
with the LORD; and let not the sin of his mother
be blotted out.
15 Let them be before the LORD continually, that
he may cut off the memory of them from the earth.
16 Because that he remembered not to shew
mercy, but persecuted the poor and needy man,
that he might even slay the broken in heart.
17 As he loved cursing, so let it come unto him: as
he delighted not in blessing, so let it be far from
him.
18 As he clothed himself with cursing like as with
his garment, so let it come into his bowels like
water, and like oil into his bones.
19 Let it be unto him as the garment *which*
covereth him, and for a girdle wherewith he is
girded continually.
20 *Let* this *be* the reward of mine adversaries from
the LORD, and of them that speak evil against my
soul.
21 But do thou for me, O GOD the Lord, for thy
name's sake: because thy mercy *is* good, deliver
thou me.
22 For I *am* poor and needy, and my heart is
wounded within me.
23 I am gone like the shadow when it declineth: I
am tossed up and down as the locust.
24 My knees are weak through fasting; and my
flesh faileth of fatness.
25 I became also a reproach unto them: *when*
they looked upon me they shaked their heads.
26 Help me, O LORD my God: O save me accord-
ing to thy mercy:
27 That they may know that this *is* thy hand; *that*
thou, LORD, hast done it.
28 Let them curse, but bless thou: when they arise,
let them be ashamed; but let thy servant rejoice.
29 Let mine adversaries be clothed with shame,
and let them cover themselves with their own
confusion, as with a mantle.
30 I will greatly praise the LORD with my mouth;
yea, I will praise him among the multitude.
31 For he shall stand at the right hand of the poor,
to save *him* from those that condemn his soul.

PSALM 110

A Psalm of David.

1 THE LORD said unto my Lord, Sit thou at
my right hand, until I make thine enemies thy
footstool.

Zech. 3:1; John 13:2,27.

109:7 *let him be condemned.* Literally, "let him go out guilty."

109:8 *office.* Commission or appointment. Cited in Acts 1:20 and applied to and fulfilled by Judas Iscariot, the apostle who betrayed Christ. See Matt. 27:3–5; Acts 1:24–26.

109:11 *extortioner.* The creditor or professional money-lender. *let the strangers spoil his labour.* Literally, "let foreigners plunder his property or product of labor."

109:12 *extend mercy.* One who will prolong or continue covenant loyalty and love.

109:14 *iniquity . . . remembered.* Guilt considered and punished (v. 16).

109:16 *remembered not.* Did not give thought or take to heart. *mercy.* Covenant loyalty and love (vv. 21,26).

109:18 *into his bowels.* Literally, "in his midst" or "inside him."

109:19 *girdle.* Waistband or belt. *girded.* Encircled.

109:23 *like the shadow when it declineth.* Like the evening shadow when it stretches out.

109:24 *faileth.* Grows lean.

109:25 *shaked their heads.* A gesture expressing astonishment or mockery. See Matt. 27:39.

109:29 *confusion.* Shame or disgrace. *mantle.* A coat-like outer garment.

Thoughts for Personal/Family Worship: Psalm 109

1. This is one of the outstanding imprecatory psalms where the psalmist prays for God's direct judgment on the enemy who is hostile to the operations of God's purposes and kingdom. It is not a prayer for personal vengeance but for the advancing of God's cause through His judgment upon those who refuse to repent of sin. Pray for God to turn your enemies from their sins (Matt. 5:44), but then also pray for God to punish those who persecute the church and refuse to repent (Rev. 6:10).

2. The righteousness of this kind of prayer is confirmed by its direct application to Judas who betrayed Christ (Acts 1:20). Christ was surrounded by enemies who hated Him without cause (Matt. 26:60; John 15:18,25). Judas's betrayal of Christ into their hands was decreed by God and foretold in Scripture (John 17:12; cf. 41:9; 55:12–14,21; 69:4), but Christ still held him responsible and pronounced God's "woe" upon him (Matt. 26:24). God inflicted severe punishment on Judas, who died in suicidal despair and utter humiliation (Matt. 27:3–5). It should be a warning to all enemies of God's kingdom and Christ's church that God will hear the cries of His people and will judge their enemies. How can this hope release Christians from taking revenge?

Psalm 110: ***David points to Christ as the ideal King and Priest.***

Title *David.* David's prophecy of Christ is one of the most

2 The LORD shall send the rod of thy strength out
of Zion: rule thou in the midst of thine enemies.
3 Thy people *shall be* willing in the day of thy
power, in the beauties of holiness from the womb
of the morning: thou hast the dew of thy youth.
4 The LORD hath sworn, and will not repent,
Thou *art* a priest for ever after the order of
Melchizedek.
5 The Lord at thy right hand shall strike through
kings in the day of his wrath.
6 He shall judge among the heathen, he shall fill
the places with the dead bodies; he shall wound
the heads over many countries.
7 He shall drink of the brook in the way: there-
fore shall he lift up the head.

PSALM 111

1 PRAISE ye the LORD. I will praise the LORD with
my whole heart, in the assembly of the upright,
and *in* the congregation.
2 The works of the LORD *are* great, sought out of
all them that have pleasure therein.
3 His work *is* honourable and glorious: and his
righteousness endureth for ever.
4 He hath made his wonderful works to be re-
membered: the LORD *is* gracious and full of
compassion.
5 He hath given meat unto them that fear him: he
will ever be mindful of his covenant.
6 He hath shewed his people the power of his
works, that he may give them the heritage of the
heathen.
7 The works of his hands *are* verity and judgment;
all his commandments *are* sure.
8 They stand fast for ever and ever, *and are* done
in truth and uprightness.
9 He sent redemption unto his people: he hath
commanded his covenant for ever: holy and
reverend *is* his name.
10 The fear of the LORD *is* the beginning of

---

quoted and alluded to texts in the New Testament.

110:1 *my Lord.* David's master or king. David, the earthly ruler of God's kingdom, acknowledged that his descendant, Christ, would be sovereign over him (Matt. 22:42–45; Mark 12:35–37; Luke 20:41–44). *my right hand.* The place of supreme honor and authority over all things in heaven and earth (cited in Matt. 26:64; Mark 14:62; 16:19; Luke 22:69; Acts 2:34–35; Rom. 8:34; Eph. 1:20–21; Col. 3:1; Heb. 1:3,13; 8:1; 10:12; 12:2). This implies that the earthly kingdom, centered upon Jerusalem, would be replaced with a universal kingdom, based in heaven itself. *enemies thy footstool.* Complete victory and utter subjection (1 Cor. 15:24–25; Heb. 10:13).

110:2 *rod.* Or scepter. *Zion.* Symbol of God's kingdom and presence (see note at 2:6). *in the midst of thine enemies.* Christ's mediatorial kingdom invades the kingdoms of this world, overcoming them by His Word, Spirit, providence, and return in glory.

110:3 *willing.* A freewill or voluntary offering, indicating the complete self-dedication of His people. *beauties of holiness.* On a similar expression, see note at 96:9.

110:4 *sworn . . . not repent.* An irrevocable decree (Heb. 6:17–18). *priest for ever.* Christ, having risen from the dead, has no successor, but intercedes through the ages for His people (Heb. 7:16–17,24–25). *Melchizedek.* The name means "king of righteousness" (Heb. 7:2). He was king of Salem and a priest of the Most High God before David's kingship and Aaron's priesthood, and thus a type of Christ (Gen. 14:18–20; Heb. 7). Christ unites the offices of *priest* and king in one person (Heb. 5:6,10; 7:17,21; cf. Zech. 6:13), implying that the old covenant and Aaronic priesthood would become obsolete (Heb. 7:11–12).

110:5 *Lord.* A slightly different form of the word used in v. 1. This form is uniquely used of God. *strike through.* Smash or shatter.

110:6 *heathen.* Nations. *wound.* Smash. *heads.* Singular "head," perhaps alluding to the promise of victory over Satan (Gen. 3:15).

110:7 *drink . . . lift up the head.* Christ draws from divine resources for His refreshment, and therefore He will not fail to fully accomplish His royal mission in the world (Isa. 42:1,4).

Thoughts for Personal/Family Worship: Psalm 110

1. Our Savior reigns. Jesus is Lord of all. He wields the scepter of His Word across the world and we are either made His subjects or we remain His enemies. Those who claim to be Christ's should be distinguished by true holiness. The power of Christ's Spirit causes His true people to willingly offer themselves to Him as living sacrifices. Those who persist in rebellion against Him will be smashed when He returns to destroy the kingdom of Satan. Are you in submission to King Jesus? Do you obey Him from the heart?

2. Not only should we yield to Christ's sovereignty, we should submit to His priesthood. We do this by trusting in the sacrifice that He offered and by relying on His intercession that He conducts in His session at God's right hand. We have all sinned against this great King, and therefore need His priestly forgiveness and grace. Are you trusting in Christ alone to save you from the guilt and punishment of your sins against God?

Psalm 111: *The psalmist exhorts people to praise God for His grace and marks the fear of the Lord as the beginning of wisdom.*

111:1 *Praise ye the LORD.* Hebrew, *hallelujah* (112:1; 113:1). *I will praise.* A different word, with the idea of giving thanks. *whole heart.* The totality of the inner man, including the mind, affections, and will.

111:2 *sought out.* Pursued with mind and heart; those who love God delight to study His great works and meditate upon His Word (1:2).

111:4 *wonderful works.* Extraordinary, often miraculous acts beyond human ability. *remembered.* Intentionally thought about so as to stir affection and action.

111:5 *meat.* Food. *be mindful.* Same root and meaning as "remembered" (v. 4).

111:6 *heathen.* Gentile nations.

111:7 *verity and judgment.* Truth and justice. *sure.* Firm, reliable. See 19:7–8; 105:8.

111:8 *stand fast.* Are established.

111:9 *redemption.* Salvation from sin and the miseries it brings (130:7), pictured dramatically in the exodus from Egypt (Deut. 7:8). *his covenant for ever.* Though God made promises to Abraham, Israel, and David at distinct points of history,

wisdom: a good understanding have all they that do *his commandments*: his praise endureth for ever.

PSALM 112

1 PRAISE ye the LORD. Blessed *is* the man *that* feareth the LORD, *that* delighteth greatly in his commandments.
2 His seed shall be mighty upon earth: the generation of the upright shall be blessed.
3 Wealth and riches *shall be* in his house: and his righteousness endureth for ever.
4 Unto the upright there ariseth light in the darkness: *he is* gracious, and full of compassion, and righteous.
5 A good man sheweth favour, and lendeth: he will guide his affairs with discretion.
6 Surely he shall not be moved for ever: the righteous shall be in everlasting remembrance.
7 He shall not be afraid of evil tidings: his heart is fixed, trusting in the LORD.
8 His heart *is* established, he shall not be afraid, until he see *his desire* upon his enemies.
9 He hath dispersed, he hath given to the poor; his righteousness endureth for ever; his horn shall be exalted with honour.
10 The wicked shall see *it*, and be grieved; he shall gnash with his teeth, and melt away: the desire of the wicked shall perish.

PSALM 113

1 PRAISE ye the LORD. Praise, O ye servants of the LORD, praise the name of the LORD.
2 Blessed be the name of the LORD from this time forth and for evermore.
3 From the rising of the sun unto the going down

Scripture indicates the essential unity of God's promises by summing them all up in the enduring, singular *covenant* (v. 5; 105:8). *reverend*. Fearful, awe-inspiring. *his name*. Who God has revealed Himself to be in all His attributes and perfections.
111:10 *fear of the LORD . . . wisdom*. A right perspective to guide one through life begins with seeing all things in light of the holiness of God (Job 28:28; Prov. 1:7; 9:10).

Thoughts for Personal/Family Worship: Psalm 111

1. **In worship, it is of paramount importance that our hearts be engaged, right, and true. It is also most essential that we take our places in congregations of faithful people who embrace sound doctrine. Corporate worship is God's design for His church. The Sabbath is especially well suited for us to meditate on the divine works, both of creation and of redemption. There is so much to discover in them that will fill our souls with wonder and joy. The fear of God is a grace that today is conspicuous by its absence in so much of modern worship. In church, we should not tolerate anything worldly, casual, or flippant. How can we encourage an awe of our God?**
2. **The themes of this psalm point to the Son of God: His glory, righteousness, mighty works, faithfulness to His covenant, and redemption of sinners. God intends for His people to think much about the work of Jesus Christ. Those who love the works of our Lord will delight to meditate on them. Therefore, Christian worship revolves around engaging our thoughts and feelings with the doctrines of the gospel. How are you privately meditating on Christ's work so as to grow in your understanding, faith, love, joy, and peace? How are you doing this in public worship?**

Psalm 112: ***The psalmist describes the advantages of the godly and the demise of the wicked.***

112:1 *Blessed*. Possessing many benefits from God (1:1). *delighteth*. Takes pleasure in.
112:2 *His seed . . . generation*. As part of God's covenant, He promises to do good to the offspring of the godly. *blessed*. Granted favor and good from the Lord; a different Hebrew word than v. 1 (Gen. 1:28; 12:2–3).
112:4 *gracious, and full of compassion*. The same Hebrew words commonly used as attributes of God (86:15; 103:8; 111:4; 145:8; Ex. 34:6). The *righteous* man is a living image of God (Gen. 1:27; Eph. 4:24).
112:5 *sheweth favour*. Gives undeserved grace to the needy. *guide*. Conduct or sustain.
112:6 *moved*. Made to stagger or overthrown.
112:7 *evil tidings*. Bad news. *fixed*. Established or steady. *trusting*. Placing confidence in Him for safety and security.
112:8 *established*. Firm.
112:9 *dispersed*. Distributed freely, lavished (2 Cor. 9:9). *given to the poor*. See 37:21,26; Prov. 14:31. *horn*. Symbol of power.
112:10 *grieved*. Indignant. *melt away*. Become weak.

Thoughts for Personal/Family Worship: Psalm 112

1. **Note the contrast between "feareth the LORD" (v. 1) and "shall not be afraid" (v. 7). Everyone fears something. What we fear is what we are most conscious of and allow to dictate our attitudes and actions—whatever is biggest in our hearts and dominates our lives. The fear of God and the fear of man or things are mutually exclusive. If the consciousness of God is our predominant mindset and we factor Him into all the situations that surround us, we will know blessedness indeed. In essence this is what it is to walk by faith and not sight. How can we learn to live as those convinced that the One we cannot see with the physical eye is more real than what we see around us?**
2. **This psalm gives us a beautiful picture of Jesus Christ. In His human nature, the Son of God fears the Lord (Isa. 11:2; Heb. 5:7) and delights in His commandments (40:8; John 4:34). He is gracious, compassionate, and righteous (Isa. 53:11; Luke 7:13; John 1:14). He is glad to disperse His riches to poor sinners (Rom. 10:12; 2 Cor. 8:9). Therefore, Jesus is the most blessed of men (21:6) and exalted to the right hand of God (110:1). His blessings overflow to His spiritual family (22:30; Isa. 53:10; Gal. 3:29), and though the wicked rage they shall perish under His wrath (2:1,12).**

Psalm 113: ***The psalmist praises the Lord for His mercy to the poor and oppressed.***

113:1 *name*. All of God's perfections and attributes that He has revealed (vv. 2–3).
113:2 *Blessed*. Praised.
113:3 *rising . . . going down*. Morning and evening, or possi-

of the same the LORD's name *is* to be praised.
4 The LORD *is* high above all nations, *and* his glory above the heavens.
5 Who *is* like unto the LORD our God, who dwelleth on high,
6 Who humbleth *himself* to behold *the things that are* in heaven, and in the earth!
7 He raiseth up the poor out of the dust, *and* lifteth the needy out of the dunghill;
8 That he may set *him* with princes, *even* with the princes of his people.
9 He maketh the barren woman to keep house, *and to be* a joyful mother of children. Praise ye the LORD.

PSALM 114

1 WHEN Israel went out of Egypt, the house of Jacob from a people of strange language;
2 Judah was his sanctuary, *and* Israel his dominion.
3 The sea saw *it*, and fled: Jordan was driven back.
4 The mountains skipped like rams, *and* the little hills like lambs.
5 What *ailed* thee, O thou sea, that thou fleddest? thou Jordan, *that* thou wast driven back?
6 Ye mountains, *that* ye skipped like rams; *and* ye little hills, like lambs?
7 Tremble, thou earth, at the presence of the Lord, at the presence of the God of Jacob;
8 Which turned the rock *into* a standing water, the flint into a fountain of waters.

PSALM 115

1 NOT unto us, O LORD, not unto us, but unto thy name give glory, for thy mercy, *and* for thy truth's sake.
2 Wherefore should the heathen say, Where *is* now their God?
3 But our God *is* in the heavens: he hath done whatsoever he hath pleased.

---

bly east and west, referring to every time or every place (50:1; Mal. 1:11).

113:5 *dwelleth on high.* A spatial metaphor for God's holiness by which He is more excellent than everything else in every way (Isa. 6:1; 57:15).

113:6 *humbleth.* Condescends, lowers. God is so great that He must lower Himself to consider the most glorious parts of creation.

113:7–8 *raiseth up the poor . . . set him with princes.* God's very holiness inclines Him to honor and bless the humble who look to Him in faith (1 Sam. 2:1–10; Isa. 66:1–2; Luke 1:46–55).

113:9 *maketh . . . to keep house.* Causes to dwell, in the sense of having a home and family. This is a picture of God's compassion on the solitary (68:6), and perhaps an allusion to His covenant promise to Abraham and Sarah, the *barren woman* who typified God's people (Gen. 17:15–21; Isa. 54).

Thoughts for Personal/Family Worship: Psalm 113

Exalted in majesty, God has to stoop to consider the angels and the sun, moon, and stars, yet He actually reaches down to lowly men and women to deliver them from their fallen state and place them among the princes of His people. The Son of God is infinitely glorious, equal to the Father in His deity, and yet He lowered Himself by taking on a human nature so that He could lift up poor sinners into glory and bring outsiders into the family of God. Now this is grace: love to the loveless, the unlovely, and the unlovable, to give to them inconceivable privilege and dignity. If you have experienced His grace, then you have cause to say "Hallelujah" every day. For what mercies should you bless the Lord today?

Psalm 114: *The psalmist reflects on the mighty acts of God in the exodus event.*

114:1 *When Israel went out of Egypt.* When the Lord saved His people from slavery (Ex. 12–14). *strange language.* Speech that cannot be understood.

114:2 *sanctuary.* Holy place. *dominion.* Realm or kingdom. The Lord saved Israel to make it into a kingdom of priests and a holy nation (Ex. 19:5–6).

114:3–7 Inanimate objects are treated as persons or animals to portray how God's glory shook the earth and drove back the waters (68:16; 74:15; Ex. 14:21; 19:18; Josh. 3:13–16).

114:8 *turned.* Transformed. *standing water.* Pool of water. *flint.* Hard stone. *fountain.* Or source or spring.

Thoughts for Personal/Family Worship: Psalm 114

1. **God has power to turn obstacles into blessings for His people, even in the most unexpected ways. Egypt was the most powerful nation on earth, but it was nothing before God. Man exerts massive efforts to control the least part of the seas, rivers, and mountains, but the Creator so easily manipulates them. Rocks are dry and lifeless but God can transform them into life-giving fountains. God can turn obstacles into stepping-stones. How can this encourage us to rely upon God the next time we find ourselves in a seemingly hopeless situation?**
2. **The redemption of Israel from Egypt was a shadow of Christ's spiritual redemption of His chosen people of all nations from sin, Satan, and hell (Luke 1:68,73–74; 1 Cor. 5:7). The greatest obstacles to our happiness—sin, death, and divine judgment—became the means of our salvation when sinners killed Christ and He died under the curse of God for our sins. What can we learn from this when our own spiritual condition seems hopeless? How have you turned to the Lord in trust? How have you experienced His grace that is greater than any obstacle?**

Psalm 115: *The psalmist magnifies God's greatness in part by showing the worthlessness of idols.*

115:1 *name.* The Lord's perfections that He has revealed to men. *mercy.* Covenant loyalty and love.

115:2 *heathen.* Gentile nations.

115:3 *in the heavens.* Not communicating God's distance from us, but His supremacy (2:4). *whatsoever he hath pleased.* God's will is not hindered in the least bit, for He fully accomplishes all that He has decreed to take place (33:10–11; 135:6; Job 23:13).

4 Their idols *are* silver and gold, the work of
men's hands.
5 They have mouths, but they speak not: eyes
have they, but they see not:
6 They have ears, but they hear not: noses have
they, but they smell not:
7 They have hands, but they handle not: feet
have they, but they walk not: neither speak they
through their throat.
8 They that make them are like unto them; *so is*
every one that trusteth in them.
9 O Israel, trust thou in the LORD: he *is* their help
and their shield.
10 O house of Aaron, trust in the LORD: he *is* their
help and their shield.
11 Ye that fear the LORD, trust in the LORD: he *is*
their help and their shield.
12 The LORD hath been mindful of us: he will
bless *us*; he will bless the house of Israel; he will
bless the house of Aaron.
13 He will bless them that fear the LORD, *both*
small and great.
14 The LORD shall increase you more and more,
you and your children.
15 Ye *are* blessed of the LORD which made heaven
and earth.
16 The heaven, *even* the heavens, *are* the LORD's:
but the earth hath he given to the children of men.
17 The dead praise not the LORD, neither any that
go down into silence.
18 But we will bless the LORD from this time forth
and for evermore. Praise the LORD.

PSALM 116

1 I LOVE the LORD, because he hath heard my
voice *and* my supplications.
2 Because he hath inclined his ear unto me, there-
fore will I call upon *him* as long as I live.
3 The sorrows of death compassed me, and the
pains of hell gat hold upon me: I found trouble
and sorrow.
4 Then called I upon the name of the LORD; O
LORD, I beseech thee, deliver my soul.
5 Gracious *is* the LORD, and righteous; yea, our
God *is* merciful.
6 The LORD preserveth the simple: I was brought
low, and he helped me.
7 Return unto thy rest, O my soul; for the LORD
hath dealt bountifully with thee.
8 For thou hast delivered my soul from death,
mine eyes from tears, *and* my feet from falling.
9 I will walk before the LORD in the land of the
living.
10 I believed, therefore have I spoken: I was
greatly afflicted:
11 I said in my haste, All men *are* liars.
12 What shall I render unto the LORD *for* all his
benefits toward me?

115:4–7 *idols.* Images of divine beings, which unlike the living God are unable to give any wisdom or power to those who worship them.
115:8 *like unto them.* Idolatry makes people as spiritually dead, powerless, and mindless as the things they worship (Isa. 44:9–11,20; Jer. 10:1–16). *trusteth.* Places confidence in them for safety and security (v. 9).
115:9–11 *trust.* Same word as in v. 8, a reminder that salvation is by faith, but the value of faith lies in its object. *shield.* Symbol of protection.
115:12 *hath been mindful of us.* Has remembered or intentionally set His mind and heart upon His people.
115:14 *increase you.* Add to you.
115:16 *children of men.* Literally, "sons of Adam." The Lord displays His glory in the skies and heaven (19:1–3; 103:19), but gave dominion over the earth to mankind when He created them so that they would rule it in His image (Gen. 1:27–28; Ps. 8).

Thoughts for Personal/Family Worship: Psalm 115

1. **Ironically, just as genuine believers are to be conformed to the image of the Lord, the unregenerate resemble the gods of their own making and imagination (v. 8). Sinners may look impressive outwardly (v. 4), but they have no spiritual mouths to cry out for His grace or confess His praises (vv. 5,7), no spiritual senses to experience the beauty of God in Christ (vv. 5–6), no spiritual hands to offer Him worship (v. 7), and no spiritual feet to walk with Him in faith and obedience (v. 7). They are as spiritually dead as the wood or stone they worship (Eph. 2:1), utterly incapable of pleasing God (14:1–3; Rom. 8:6–8; 2 Cor. 4:4). Ultimately God will also remove all their natural abilities as well, leaving them powerless and hollow as vessels for everlasting fire. Therefore flee idolatry, and fervently pray for Christ to save you from its soul-killing influences.**
2. **The hinge upon which true worship turns is faith. Idolaters are like their idols because they trust in them (v. 8). Salvation is by faith in the Lord (vv. 9–11). This also suggests that if we trust in the Lord alone for salvation, we will become like Him (112:4). Why would exercising trust in Christ make you more like God?**

Psalm 116: *The psalmist praises the Lord for deliverance from death.*

116:1 *love the LORD.* Choose to make the Lord central and supreme in all one's thoughts, feelings, and actions because of His unique goodness and greatness (Deut. 6:4–5; 30:19–20).
116:2 *inclined his ear.* Listened attentively (86:1). *therefore will I call.* Answered prayer generates more prayer.
116:3 *sorrows of death compassed me.* Literally, "the cords or snares of death surrounded me." *pains of hell.* The distress of *sheol*, here explained by its parallelism with *death* (in other contexts referring to the grave or the abode of departed wicked spirits). *gat hold upon me.* Literally, "found me."
116:4 *name.* All that God has revealed Himself to be, often summarized in His attributes or perfections. *my soul.* Me, the person himself (v. 8).
116:5 *merciful.* Compassionate.
116:6 *preserveth.* Watches over. *simple.* Naïve, but teachable.
116:10 *I believed, therefore have I spoken.* Faith in the Lord

13 I will take the cup of salvation, and call upon
the name of the LORD.
14 I will pay my vows unto the LORD now in the
presence of all his people.
15 Precious in the sight of the LORD *is* the death
of his saints.
16 O LORD, truly I *am* thy servant; I *am* thy
servant, *and* the son of thine handmaid: thou hast
loosed my bonds.
17 I will offer to thee the sacrifice of thanksgiving,
and will call upon the name of the LORD.
18 I will pay my vows unto the LORD now in the
presence of all his people,
19 In the courts of the LORD's house, in the midst
of thee, O Jerusalem. Praise ye the LORD.

PSALM 117

1 O PRAISE the LORD, all ye nations: praise him,
all ye people.
2 For his merciful kindness is great toward us:
and the truth of the LORD *endureth* for ever. Praise
ye the LORD.

PSALM 118

1 O GIVE thanks unto the LORD; for *he is* good:
because his mercy *endureth* for ever.
2 Let Israel now say, that his mercy *endureth* for
ever.
3 Let the house of Aaron now say, that his mercy
endureth for ever.
4 Let them now that fear the LORD say, that his
mercy *endureth* for ever.
5 I called upon the LORD in distress: the LORD
answered me, *and set me* in a large place.
6 The LORD *is* on my side; I will not fear: what can
man do unto me?
7 The LORD taketh my part with them that help
me: therefore shall I see *my desire* upon them that
hate me.
8 *It is* better to trust in the LORD than to put
confidence in man.
9 *It is* better to trust in the LORD than to put
confidence in princes.
10 All nations compassed me about: but in the
name of the LORD will I destroy them.
11 They compassed me about; yea, they

moves believers to bear witness to others (2 Cor. 4:13).

116:12 *render.* Return.

116:13 *cup of salvation.* A metaphor for the good portion received from the Savior (16:5; 23:5). *call upon the name of the LORD.* Ironically, repaying the Lord (v. 12) consists in receiving more from Him through faith and prayer.

116:14 *pay my vows.* Keep my solemn commitments to the Lord, such as presenting a freewill offering (66:13–15; 116:18; Deut. 23:21–23).

116:15 *Precious.* Highly valued. *saints.* The people of God's faithful love.

116:16 *handmaid.* Female servant. *loosed my bonds.* Set me free.

116:17 *sacrifice of thanksgiving.* An offering of praise (Heb. 13:15).

Thoughts for Personal/Family Worship: Psalm 116

1. **Such is the blessing of salvation, in this life and in the next, that our praises and thanksgivings should never ever cease. True believers feel that it is just impossible to tell the Lord how much they appreciate His loving-kindness and tender mercies. They will need eternity to tell Him what they feel and how much they love Him. However, the greatest way they express their gratitude is by drinking deeply of the joys of His salvation and praying for yet more grace (vv. 12–13). God is glorified not by receiving (as if we could give Him anything) but by giving all (1 Chron. 29:10–16). How does that encourage us to pray great prayers?**
2. **No one loves the Father more than the Son (John 14:31), and no one has had a more earnest and effective prayer life than Christ (John 11:41–42; Heb. 5:7). He entered fully into the sorrows of death, but was raised up and entered His heavenly rest. Today He drinks from the cup of salvation and intercedes for all His redeemed to enter into His glory. He will never fail to keep His commitments to the Father, whose will is for Christ to bring everyone given to Him by the Father to resurrection glory (John 6:37–40). How does this psalm shows us the joys that belong to Jesus Christ?**

Psalm 117: ***The psalmist briefly calls for universal praise for God's faithful love.***

117:1 *nations . . . people.* Gentile nations and tribes of people from everywhere. Paul cited this text to show that Christ came so that the Gentiles would glorify God for His mercy (Rom. 15:11).

117:2 *merciful kindness.* Covenant loyalty and love (often translated "mercy"). *is great.* Prevails, is strong. *truth.* Fidelity, dependability; often paired with covenant loyalty to underscore its certainty and steadfastness (Ex. 34:6).

Thoughts for Personal/Family Worship: Psalm 117

God is not the God of the Jews only but also of the Gentiles. His love extends to the world, His covenant provides for the nations, and His redemption is effective for sinners everywhere. Christ came to draw people of all nations to worship God for His saving grace. The church must therefore be committed to world missions. Our meditations on Christ and praises to the Savior should be mingled with fervent prayers for the success of the gospel in all nations. How are you regularly praying for missions in your private or family devotions? How could you do so more?

Psalm 118: ***The psalmist praises God for the certainty of His unchanging love in the sufferings and exaltation of Christ.***

118:1–4 *good.* Doing acts of kindness generally. *mercy.* Covenant loyalty and love specifically (v. 29).

118:6 *The LORD is on my side.* Literally, "Jehovah is for me," which implies that nothing can effectively do me harm (Rom. 8:31).

118:8 *trust.* Seek and find refuge. *put confidence in.* Trust in for safety and security (usually translated "trust").

118:10 *compassed.* Surrounded (vv. 11–12).

compassed me about: but in the name of the
LORD I will destroy them.
12 They compassed me about like bees; they are
quenched as the fire of thorns: for in the name of
the LORD I will destroy them.
13 Thou hast thrust sore at me that I might fall:
but the LORD helped me.
14 The LORD *is* my strength and song, and is
become my salvation.
15 The voice of rejoicing and salvation *is* in the
tabernacles of the righteous: the right hand of the
LORD doeth valiantly.
16 The right hand of the LORD is exalted: the
right hand of the LORD doeth valiantly.
17 I shall not die, but live, and declare the works
of the LORD.
18 The LORD hath chastened me sore: but he hath
not given me over unto death.
19 Open to me the gates of righteousness: I will
go into them, *and* I will praise the LORD:
20 This gate of the LORD, into which the righ-
teous shall enter.
21 I will praise thee: for thou hast heard me, and
art become my salvation.
22 The stone *which* the builders refused is become
the head *stone* of the corner.
23 This is the LORD's doing; it *is* marvellous in our
eyes.
24 This *is* the day *which* the LORD hath made; we
will rejoice and be glad in it.
25 Save now, I beseech thee, O LORD: O LORD, I
beseech thee, send now prosperity.
26 Blessed *be* he that cometh in the name of the
LORD: we have blessed you out of the house of the
LORD.
27 God *is* the LORD, which hath shewed us light:
bind the sacrifice with cords, *even* unto the horns
of the altar.
28 Thou *art* my God, and I will praise thee: *thou*
art my God, I will exalt thee.
29 O give thanks unto the LORD; for *he is* good:
for his mercy *endureth* for ever.

PSALM 119

ALEPH

1 BLESSED *are* the undefiled in the way, who walk
in the law of the LORD.
2 Blessed *are* they that keep his testimonies, *and*
that seek him with the whole heart.
3 They also do no iniquity: they walk in his ways.
4 Thou hast commanded *us* to keep thy precepts
diligently.
5 O that my ways were directed to keep thy
statutes!
6 Then shall I not be ashamed, when I have
respect unto all thy commandments.
7 I will praise thee with uprightness of heart,
when I shall have learned thy righteous judgments.

118:13 *thrust sore.* Pushed down forcefully.
118:14 *strength and song . . . salvation.* See Ex. 15:2; Isa. 12:2.
118:15 *tabernacles.* Tents or dwelling places.
118:18 *chastened me sore.* Disciplined me severely.
118:19–20 *gates of righteousness . . . gate of the LORD.* Entrances into the temple courts, where worshipers drew near to the Lord.

118:22–23 *stone.* A reference to Christ, rejected by the leaders of Israel (*builders*) but made by God into the cornerstone upon which His people are built (Matt. 21:42; Mark 12:10–11; Luke 20:17; Acts 4:11; 1 Peter 2:7; cf. Eph. 2:20). *This is the LORD's doing.* Literally, "from the LORD is this." *marvellous.* Extraordinary, often miraculous, beyond human ability.
118:24 *This is the day which the LORD hath made.* True of every day, but specifically in view is the time of Christ's coming.
118:25–26 *Save now, I beseech thee.* Hebrew, *hosanna. he that cometh in the name of the LORD.* God's representative, the messianic king. This was the cry of the crowds at Christ's triumphal entry into Jerusalem (Matt. 21:9; Mark 11:9–10; Luke 19:38; John 12:13). Christ also cited it with respect to His second coming (Matt. 23:39).

Thoughts for Personal/Family Worship: Psalm 118

1. **One of our greatest comforts is knowing that the Lord is on our side and taking part with them that help us. There is no reason to fear anyone or anything because, with the Lord at our side, we shall be kept both strong and safe. Paul summed it well: "If God be for us, who can be against us?" (Rom. 8:31). How can a person know that God is on his side? How can that knowledge give him hope and boldness?**
2. **Long before Jesus came to Jerusalem on His last Passover, God had revealed that the Christ would be rejected by the leaders of His people, but would be exalted by God in an amazing way to become the foundation for the church. This calls for two responses. First, we must pray, "Hosanna," not just with our lips like the crowds on Palm Sunday, but with hearts crying out for the Lord to save us from our sins. Second, we must rejoice in Christ's coming to be the sacrifice for sins (v. 27), and His resurrection and ascension to heaven (v. 22). God's faithful love will last forever for those in union with Jesus Christ. How can you incorporate these practices and heart attitudes into your life?**

Psalm 119: ***In the longest psalm and longest chapter in Scripture, the psalmist celebrates the beauties and benefits of the Bible in an acrostic of twenty-two stanzas, where each verse of a given stanza begins with the same letter of the Hebrew alphabet.***

119:1 *Blessed.* Possessing great benefits from God (v. 2). *the undefiled.* Those with integrity. *law.* Not just legislation, but instruction (throughout the psalm). It is the most general word for special revelation from God in the Old Testament.
119:2 *seek him.* See note at 105:3–4. *heart.* Inner man, including the mind, will, and emotions (throughout the psalm). God does not bless hypocrisy or legalism, but the sincere pursuit of Him through a life of faith and obedience to His Word.
119:6 *have respect unto.* Have regard for or pay attention to (v. 15).

8 I will keep thy statutes: O forsake me not utterly.

BETH

9 Wherewithal shall a young man cleanse his
way? by taking heed *thereto* according to thy word.
10 With my whole heart have I sought thee: O let
me not wander from thy commandments.
11 Thy word have I hid in mine heart, that I
might not sin against thee.
12 Blessed *art* thou, O LORD: teach me thy
statutes.
13 With my lips have I declared all the judgments
of thy mouth.
14 I have rejoiced in the way of thy testimonies, as
much as in all riches.
15 I will meditate in thy precepts, and have re-
spect unto thy ways.
16 I will delight myself in thy statutes: I will not
forget thy word.

GIMEL

17 Deal bountifully with thy servant, *that* I may
live, and keep thy word.
18 Open thou mine eyes, that I may behold
wondrous things out of thy law.
19 I *am* a stranger in the earth: hide not thy
commandments from me.
20 My soul breaketh for the longing *that it hath*
unto thy judgments at all times.
21 Thou hast rebuked the proud *that are* cursed,
which do err from thy commandments.
22 Remove from me reproach and contempt; for
I have kept thy testimonies.
23 Princes also did sit *and* speak against me: *but*
thy servant did meditate in thy statutes.
24 Thy testimonies also *are* my delight *and* my
counsellors.

DALETH

25 My soul cleaveth unto the dust: quicken thou
me according to thy word.
26 I have declared my ways, and thou heardest
me: teach me thy statutes.
27 Make me to understand the way of thy
precepts: so shall I talk of thy wondrous works.
28 My soul melteth for heaviness: strengthen
thou me according unto thy word.
29 Remove from me the way of lying: and grant
me thy law graciously.
30 I have chosen the way of truth: thy judgments
have I laid *before me*.
31 I have stuck unto thy testimonies: O LORD, put
me not to shame.
32 I will run the way of thy commandments,
when thou shalt enlarge my heart.

HE

33 Teach me, O LORD, the way of thy statutes; and
I shall keep it *unto* the end.
34 Give me understanding, and I shall keep thy
law; yea, I shall observe it with *my* whole heart.
35 Make me to go in the path of thy command-
ments; for therein do I delight.
36 Incline my heart unto thy testimonies, and not
to covetousness.
37 Turn away mine eyes from beholding vanity;
and quicken thou me in thy way.
38 Stablish thy word unto thy servant, who *is*
devoted to thy fear.
39 Turn away my reproach which I fear: for thy
judgments *are* good.
40 Behold, I have longed after thy precepts:
quicken me in thy righteousness.

VAU

41 Let thy mercies come also unto me, O LORD,
even thy salvation, according to thy word.
42 So shall I have wherewith to answer him that
reproacheth me: for I trust in thy word.
43 And take not the word of truth utterly out of
my mouth; for I have hoped in thy judgments.
44 So shall I keep thy law continually for ever and
ever.
45 And I will walk at liberty: for I seek thy precepts.

119:9 *Wherewithal.* How, by what means. *taking heed thereto.* Guarding it.
119:12 *Blessed.* Praised; a different word than in vv. 1–2.
119:16 *forget.* Refuse to think about, neglect, ignore (throughout the psalm).
119:18 *Open thou mine eyes.* Remove the spiritual blindness that hinders me from seeing God's glory and beauty in the Word (Deut. 29:4; 1 Cor. 2:14; 2 Cor. 3:14–18; 4:4–6). *wondrous things.* Extraordinary, often miraculous things, beyond human ability (v. 27).
119:20 *My soul breaketh.* I am worn down or languish (*soul* refers to the person throughout the psalm).
119:25 *quicken thou me.* Cause me to live (throughout the psalm).
119:28 *melteth.* Weep or shed tears. *heaviness.* Grief.
119:31 *stuck.* Held to.
119:32 *run the way.* Eagerly and energetically pursue a life of obedience to God's *commandments* (40:8). *enlarge my heart.* Give me strong and unhindered desires and delight in doing God's will (cf. Isa. 60:5; Hab. 2:5).
119:33–34 *Teach me, O LORD . . . Give me understanding.* We need God to instruct us by His Word and through the working of the Spirit to illuminate our hearts (v. 18; Isa. 54:13; Jer. 31:33–34; 2 Cor. 3:3). This is the continuing need even of believers (v. 66; Eph. 1:15–19).
119:36–37 *Incline.* Stretch out, thus here draw out and focus the thoughts, affections, and choices (vv. 51,112,157; 141:4). In addition to illumination, we need God's Spirit to give spiritual life (*quicken*; John 6:63) and *turn away* our desires from sin to love His Word (v. 133; Jer. 31:18; Ezek. 36:27). Obedience to God's law is entirely by grace (Phil. 2:12–13).
119:37 *vanity.* Deceit or emptiness.
119:38 *Stablish.* Establish or raise up.
119:41 *mercies.* Covenant loyalty and love (vv. 64,124); also

46 I will speak of thy testimonies also before
kings, and will not be ashamed.
47 And I will delight myself in thy command-
ments, which I have loved.
48 My hands also will I lift up unto thy
commandments, which I have loved; and I will
meditate in thy statutes.

ZAIN

49 Remember the word unto thy servant, upon
which thou hast caused me to hope.
50 This *is* my comfort in my affliction: for thy
word hath quickened me.
51 The proud have had me greatly in derision: *yet*
have I not declined from thy law.
52 I remembered thy judgments of old, O LORD;
and have comforted myself.
53 Horror hath taken hold upon me because of
the wicked that forsake thy law.
54 Thy statutes have been my songs in the house
of my pilgrimage.
55 I have remembered thy name, O LORD, in the
night, and have kept thy law.
56 This I had, because I kept thy precepts.

CHETH

57 *Thou art* my portion, O LORD: I have said that
I would keep thy words.
58 I intreated thy favour with *my* whole heart: be
merciful unto me according to thy word.
59 I thought on my ways, and turned my feet
unto thy testimonies.
60 I made haste, and delayed not to keep thy
commandments.
61 The bands of the wicked have robbed me: *but*
I have not forgotten thy law.
62 At midnight I will rise to give thanks unto thee
because of thy righteous judgments.
63 I *am* a companion of all *them* that fear thee,
and of them that keep thy precepts.
64 The earth, O LORD, is full of thy mercy: teach
me thy statutes.

TETH

65 Thou hast dealt well with thy servant, O LORD,
according unto thy word.
66 Teach me good judgment and knowledge: for
I have believed thy commandments.
67 Before I was afflicted I went astray: but now
have I kept thy word.
68 Thou *art* good, and doest good; teach me thy
statutes.
69 The proud have forged a lie against me: *but* I
will keep thy precepts with *my* whole heart.
70 Their heart is as fat as grease; *but* I delight in
thy law.
71 *It is* good for me that I have been afflicted; that
I might learn thy statutes.
72 The law of thy mouth *is* better unto me than
thousands of gold and silver.

JOD

73 Thy hands have made me and fashioned me:
give me understanding, that I may learn thy
commandments.
74 They that fear thee will be glad when they see
me; because I have hoped in thy word.
75 I know, O LORD, that thy judgments *are* right,
and *that* thou in faithfulness hast afflicted me.
76 Let, I pray thee, thy merciful kindness be for
my comfort, according to thy word unto thy
servant.
77 Let thy tender mercies come unto me, that I
may live: for thy law *is* my delight.
78 Let the proud be ashamed; for they dealt
perversely with me without a cause: *but* I will
meditate in thy precepts.
79 Let those that fear thee turn unto me, and
those that have known thy testimonies.
80 Let my heart be sound in thy statutes; that I be
not ashamed.

CAPH

81 My soul fainteth for thy salvation: *but* I hope
in thy word.
82 Mine eyes fail for thy word, saying, When wilt
thou comfort me?
83 For I am become like a bottle in the smoke; *yet*
do I not forget thy statutes.
84 How many *are* the days of thy servant? when
wilt thou execute judgment on them that perse-
cute me?

---

translated "merciful kindness" (v. 76), and "lovingkindness" (vv. 88,149,159). The plural indicates multiple acts.

119:47–48 *loved.* Chosen with one's whole being (throughout the psalm).

119:49 *Remember.* Think about on purpose and take to heart (vv. 52,55). *hope.* Wait with confident expectation (vv. 74,81).

119:51 *declined.* Turned from, bent away (v. 157).

119:53 *Horror.* Or hot anger. Love for God's law produces profound grief and holy anger over the prevalence of sin in this fallen world (v. 136).

119:55 *thy name.* What the Lord has revealed Himself to be in all His perfections.

119:57 *Thou art my portion.* Delight in God's laws and promises springs from taking God as one's great desire and treasure (16:5; 73:25–26).

119:58 *be merciful.* Be gracious, show undeserved favor.

119:61 *bands.* Snares or cords. *robbed.* Surrounded.

119:70 *fat as grease.* Insensitive.

119:71 *good for me that I have been afflicted.* Suffering is the rod of God's loving discipline to bless His children with growing obedience to His Word (Prov. 3:11–12).

119:77 *tender mercies.* Demonstrations of compassion or pity (v. 156).

119:83 *bottle.* Wineskin.

85 The proud have digged pits for me, which *are*
not after thy law.
86 All thy commandments *are* faithful: they
persecute me wrongfully; help thou me.
87 They had almost consumed me upon earth;
but I forsook not thy precepts.
88 Quicken me after thy lovingkindness; so shall
I keep the testimony of thy mouth.

LAMED

89 For ever, O LORD, thy word is settled in heaven.
90 Thy faithfulness *is* unto all generations: thou
hast established the earth, and it abideth.
91 They continue this day according to thine
ordinances: for all *are* thy servants.
92 Unless thy law *had been* my delights, I should
then have perished in mine affliction.
93 I will never forget thy precepts: for with them
thou hast quickened me.
94 I *am* thine, save me; for I have sought thy
precepts.
95 The wicked have waited for me to destroy me:
but I will consider thy testimonies.
96 I have seen an end of all perfection: *but* thy
commandment *is* exceeding broad.

MEM

97 O how love I thy law! it *is* my meditation all
the day.
98 Thou through thy commandments hast made
me wiser than mine enemies: for they *are* ever
with me.
99 I have more understanding than all my teach-
ers: for thy testimonies *are* my meditation.
100 I understand more than the ancients, because
I keep thy precepts.
101 I have refrained my feet from every evil way,
that I might keep thy word.
102 I have not departed from thy judgments: for
thou hast taught me.
103 How sweet are thy words unto my taste! *yea,*
sweeter than honey to my mouth!
104 Through thy precepts I get understanding:
therefore I hate every false way.

NUN

105 Thy word *is* a lamp unto my feet, and a light
unto my path.
106 I have sworn, and I will perform *it*, that I will
keep thy righteous judgments.
107 I am afflicted very much: quicken me, O LORD,
according unto thy word.
108 Accept, I beseech thee, the freewill offerings of
my mouth, O LORD, and teach me thy judgments.
109 My soul *is* continually in my hand: yet do I not
forget thy law.
110 The wicked have laid a snare for me: yet I
erred not from thy precepts.
111 Thy testimonies have I taken as an heritage for
ever: for they *are* the rejoicing of my heart.
112 I have inclined mine heart to perform thy
statutes alway, *even unto* the end.

SAMECH

113 I hate *vain* thoughts: but thy law do I love.
114 Thou *art* my hiding place and my shield: I
hope in thy word.
115 Depart from me, ye evildoers: for I will keep
the commandments of my God.
116 Uphold me according unto thy word, that I
may live: and let me not be ashamed of my hope.
117 Hold thou me up, and I shall be safe: and I will
have respect unto thy statutes continually.
118 Thou hast trodden down all them that err
from thy statutes: for their deceit *is* falsehood.
119 Thou puttest away all the wicked of the earth
like dross: therefore I love thy testimonies.
120 My flesh trembleth for fear of thee; and I am
afraid of thy judgments.

AIN

121 I have done judgment and justice: leave me
not to mine oppressors.
122 Be surety for thy servant for good: let not the
proud oppress me.
123 Mine eyes fail for thy salvation, and for the
word of thy righteousness.
124 Deal with thy servant according unto thy
mercy, and teach me thy statutes.
125 I *am* thy servant; give me understanding, that
I may know thy testimonies.
126 *It is* time for *thee*, LORD, to work: *for* they have
made void thy law.
127 Therefore I love thy commandments above
gold; yea, above fine gold.
128 Therefore I esteem all *thy* precepts *concerning*
all *things to be* right; *and* I hate every false way.

PE

129 Thy testimonies *are* wonderful: therefore

119:89 *is settled.* Stands firm.
119:90 *abideth.* Stands.
119:95 *waited.* Ambushed.
119:100 *ancients.* Elders.
119:103 *sweet . . . honey.* The Spirit gives to the godly a spiritual sense that enables them to taste God's goodness in the Word, and thus they crave more (v. 131; 19:10; 1 Peter 2:2–3).
119:104 *hate.* Rejected in thought, feeling, and deed (vv. 113, 128,163).
119:113 *vain.* Divided, disunited, futile, or halfhearted.
119:117 *have respect.* Gaze upon or regard.
119:122 *Be surety for.* Take responsibility for, like a man who pledges himself to fulfill the debts or obligations of another (Prov. 6:1; Heb. 7:22).
119:126 *made void.* Suspended or violated.
119:129 *wonderful.* Extraordinary, beyond human ability or

doth my soul keep them.
130 The entrance of thy words giveth light; it
giveth understanding unto the simple.
131 I opened my mouth, and panted: for I longed
for thy commandments.
132 Look thou upon me, and be merciful unto me,
as thou usest to do unto those that love thy name.
133 Order my steps in thy word: and let not any
iniquity have dominion over me.
134 Deliver me from the oppression of man: so
will I keep thy precepts.
135 Make thy face to shine upon thy servant; and
teach me thy statutes.
136 Rivers of waters run down mine eyes, because
they keep not thy law.

TZADDI

137 Righteous *art* thou, O LORD, and upright *are*
thy judgments.
138 Thy testimonies *that* thou hast commanded
are righteous and very faithful.
139 My zeal hath consumed me, because mine
enemies have forgotten thy words.
140 Thy word *is* very pure: therefore thy servant
loveth it.
141 I *am* small and despised: *yet* do not I forget
thy precepts.
142 Thy righteousness *is* an everlasting righteous-
ness, and thy law *is* the truth.
143 Trouble and anguish have taken hold on me:
yet thy commandments *are* my delights.
144 The righteousness of thy testimonies *is* ever-
lasting: give me understanding, and I shall live.

KOPH

145 I cried with *my* whole heart; hear me, O LORD:
I will keep thy statutes.
146 I cried unto thee; save me, and I shall keep thy
testimonies.
147 I prevented the dawning of the morning, and
cried: I hoped in thy word.
148 Mine eyes prevent the *night* watches, that I
might meditate in thy word.
149 Hear my voice according unto thy loving-
kindness: O LORD, quicken me according to thy
judgment.
150 They draw nigh that follow after mischief:
they are far from thy law.
151 Thou *art* near, O LORD; and all thy command-
ments *are* truth.
152 Concerning thy testimonies, I have known of
old that thou hast founded them for ever.

RESH

153 Consider mine affliction, and deliver me: for I
do not forget thy law.
154 Plead my cause, and deliver me: quicken me
according to thy word.
155 Salvation *is* far from the wicked: for they seek
not thy statutes.
156 Great *are* thy tender mercies, O LORD: quicken
me according to thy judgments.
157 Many *are* my persecutors and mine enemies;
yet do I not decline from thy testimonies.
158 I beheld the transgressors, and was grieved;
because they kept not thy word.
159 Consider how I love thy precepts: quicken me,
O LORD, according to thy lovingkindness.
160 Thy word *is* true *from* the beginning: and
every one of thy righteous judgments *endureth*
for ever.

SCHIN

161 Princes have persecuted me without a cause:
but my heart standeth in awe of thy word.
162 I rejoice at thy word, as one that findeth great
spoil.
163 I hate and abhor lying: *but* thy law do I love.
164 Seven times a day do I praise thee because of
thy righteous judgments.
165 Great peace have they which love thy law: and
nothing shall offend them.
166 LORD, I have hoped for thy salvation, and
done thy commandments.
167 My soul hath kept thy testimonies; and I love
them exceedingly.
168 I have kept thy precepts and thy testimonies:
for all my ways *are* before thee.

TAU

169 Let my cry come near before thee, O LORD:
give me understanding according to thy word.

---

comprehension.

119:130 *simple.* Naïve, foolish, but teachable.

119:132 *Look thou upon me.* Face me or turn to me. *be merciful.* Be gracious or show undeserved favor.

119:135 *Make thy face to shine.* A gesture communicating grace and peace (Num. 6:25–26).

119:137–38 *Righteous . . . upright . . . righteous.* God's laws of justice (*judgments*) express His own righteous nature (19:8; Deut. 32:4).

119:140 *very pure.* Refined (12:6; 18:30).

119:147 *prevented.* Went before, anticipated (v. 148).

119:150 *mischief.* Cunning, evil device.

119:161 *persecuted me.* Delight in God's Word leads a person into a lifestyle contrary to the world, provoking its insult and opposition (vv. 22–23,69,78,85; Matt. 5:10–12).

119:162 *spoil.* Plunder or booty.

119:164 *Seven times.* Not literally, but throughout the day.

119:165 *nothing shall offend them.* They will not have a hindrance or stumbling block.

119:166 *hoped.* Waited with expectancy, an expression of faith.

Thoughts for Personal/Family Worship: Psalm 119

1. This psalm, as an Alphabetical Psalm, was evidently meant to be laid up in the memory and heart. God's Word is a great treasure and it is good, not only to meditate

170 Let my supplication come before thee: deliver
me according to thy word.
171 My lips shall utter praise, when thou hast
taught me thy statutes.
172 My tongue shall speak of thy word: for all thy
commandments *are* righteousness.
173 Let thine hand help me; for I have chosen thy
precepts.
174 I have longed for thy salvation, O LORD; and
thy law *is* my delight.
175 Let my soul live, and it shall praise thee; and
let thy judgments help me.
176 I have gone astray like a lost sheep; seek thy
servant; for I do not forget thy commandments.

PSALM 120

A Song of degrees.

1 IN my distress I cried unto the LORD, and he
heard me.
2 Deliver my soul, O LORD, from lying lips, *and*
from a deceitful tongue.
3 What shall be given unto thee? or what shall be
done unto thee, thou false tongue?
4 Sharp arrows of the mighty, with coals of
juniper.
5 Woe is me, that I sojourn in Mesech, *that* I
dwell in the tents of Kedar!
6 My soul hath long dwelt with him that hateth
peace.
7 I *am for* peace: but when I speak, they *are* for
war.

PSALM 121

A Song of degrees.

1 I WILL lift up mine eyes unto the hills, from
whence cometh my help.
2 My help *cometh* from the LORD, which made
heaven and earth.

---

on, but also to commit to memory (v. 11), so that, in a time of need, it can be readily recalled. Since in nearly every verse God is addressed, we are reminded that along with reading the Bible we need to be praying. Our prayer should be that God, by His Holy Spirit, will reveal wonderful things to us, so that we derive from Scripture great and lasting profit. Although believers pass through many changes in this life, it is important to realize that God's written Word is settled and remains forever the same. To our great comfort, it is truth unchanged and unchanging. What is one verse in this psalm that especially comforts or challenges you? How can you make it a prayer?

2. **The psalmist wrote of himself over a dozen times here as "thy servant." The great Servant of the Lord is His Son (Isa. 42:1). The Lord Jesus loved God's Word (40:6–8; Isa. 50:5; Matt. 5:17–18; John 10:35; 17:8,17), for He is God's eternal Word (John 1:1). Just as the fullness of this psalm reflects the fullness and completeness of the Holy Scriptures, so Christ is the fullness of God in bodily form, and in Him we are complete (Col. 2:9–10). Always read the Bible with this desire and prayer: "Father, open my eyes by Thy Spirit that I might see the glories of Thy Son."**
3. **In all but a few of the 176 verses of this psalm, reference is made to words like law, testimonies, ways, precepts, statutes, commandments, judgments, and word. Most of these words refer directly or indirectly to God's law. Why does the psalmist have such deep respect and love for God's law? Should we have that same love for God's law today? Why or why not? How should a Christian use God's law today?**

Psalm 120: *The psalmist prays for deliverance from false accusers.*

Title *Song of degrees*. Or, "song of ascents." The fifteen psalms with this superscription (Pss. 120–134) are called the Pilgrimage Songs and have traditionally been understood to be part of the liturgy associated with pilgrims going up to Jerusalem for the three great feasts of the old covenant religious calendar (Ex. 34:22–23; Deut. 16:16).

120:2 *my soul*. Me, my whole person, not to be confused with one's inner being (v. 6). *lying lips . . . deceitful tongue*. The psalmist was being slandered (52:2–4; 140:1–11).

120:4 *coals of juniper*. Charcoal from burning wood of the broom shrub, an image of God's fiery anger punishing sinners (18:8,12–13; 140:10).

120:5 *Woe*. An interjection expressing anxiety. *sojourn*. Live as a resident alien. *Mesech*. A typically ruthless nation north of Israel (Gen. 10:2, from Japheth). *Kedar*. A typically ruthless nation southeast of Israel (Gen. 25:13, from Ishmael). Both are used figuratively to represent the psalmist's feeling of isolation in a hostile world, even though he resided in Israel.

120:6–7 *peace . . . war*. Godliness leads people to live quiet lives of work and devotion (Rom. 12:18; 1 Thess. 4:11; 1 Tim. 2:2), but Satan provokes sinners to lies and hatred (John 8:44).

Thoughts for Personal/Family Worship: Psalm 120

1. **There is a sense in which all Christians live in Meshech and Kedar as the world is no friend to grace or to God. It is easy to feel out of place in a world where values are the opposite of truth. God, the gift of salvation, the hope of eternal life, and our obedience to God's laws receive mockery. But we should expect this because although we are in the world we are not of it (John 17:14). What example can we follow (vv. 1–2) when we find ourselves opposed?**
2. **Christ came unto His own, but they did not receive Him (John 1:11). Exposed to malice and cruelty, our Lord felt isolated and rejected even among those who should have welcomed Him (Matt. 12:39; Luke 17:25; John 8:23; 15:23–25). He spoke a gospel of peace purchased by His blood (Luke 7:50; 10:5; John 14:27; 20:19–21,26). Nevertheless, His words brought division and conflict with sinners (Matt. 10:34–38). What does this teach us to expect if we follow Him?**

Psalm 121: *The psalmist expresses his confidence in God's protecting providence.*

121:1 *lift up mine eyes*. A gesture of prayerful dependence (25:1; 123:1; 143:8; Lam. 3:41; Mark 7:34; John 11:41; 17:1). *hills*. Or, "mountains," probably a reference to Jerusalem (125:2). *from whence cometh my help*. This is a question, "Where does my help come from?"

121:2 This answers the question of v. 1: my help comes from

3 He will not suffer thy foot to be moved: he that
keepeth thee will not slumber.
4 Behold, he that keepeth Israel shall neither
slumber nor sleep.
5 The LORD *is* thy keeper: the LORD *is* thy shade
upon thy right hand.
6 The sun shall not smite thee by day, nor the
moon by night.
7 The LORD shall preserve thee from all evil: he
shall preserve thy soul.
8 The LORD shall preserve thy going out and
thy coming in from this time forth, and even for
evermore.

PSALM 122

A Song of degrees of David.

1 I WAS glad when they said unto me, Let us go
into the house of the LORD.
2 Our feet shall stand within thy gates, O Jerusalem.
3 Jerusalem is builded as a city that is compact
together:
4 Whither the tribes go up, the tribes of the LORD,
unto the testimony of Israel, to give thanks unto
the name of the LORD.
5 For there are set thrones of judgment, the
thrones of the house of David.
6 Pray for the peace of Jerusalem: they shall
prosper that love thee.
7 Peace be within thy walls, *and* prosperity within
thy palaces.
8 For my brethren and companions' sakes, I will
now say, Peace *be* within thee.
9 Because of the house of the LORD our God I
will seek thy good.

PSALM 123

A Song of degrees.

1 UNTO thee lift I up mine eyes, O thou that
dwellest in the heavens.
2 Behold, as the eyes of servants *look* unto the
hand of their masters, *and* as the eyes of a maiden
unto the hand of her mistress; so our eyes *wait*

---

the almighty Creator (124:8).

121:3 *not suffer thy foot to be moved.* Give you stability.

121:6 *day . . . night.* Opposites designate totality. The Lord's protection is continuous without interruption against all kinds of dangers (91:5–6).

121:7 *preserve.* Watch over or keep (v. 8). *evil.* Harm. *thy soul.* You. The promise of protection against *all evil* (91:10) does not mean that believers will never suffer, but that God's providence will guard them from anything that would truly do them harm, and He will work all things for their good (34:10; 84:11; Rom. 8:28).

121:8 *going out . . . coming in.* Again, opposites designate totality. The Lord's protection covers all activities.

Thoughts for Personal/Family Worship: Psalm 121

One of our greatest comforts is to know that God is always acting as the guardian of believers, so that even in the greatest trouble they have no reason to fear. Faith assures the Christian that all will be well. God is always there for us, never asleep, always vigilant, and without fatigue. He will never fail and therefore we shall never fall. If believers in ancient times could cling to this promise, how much more should we who trust in the incarnate Lord Jesus. If God did not spare His Son, but gave Him up for all His elect, then surely He is totally for them and will work all things to their good and ultimate glory in Christ (Rom. 8:28–32). When do you feel most in need of this assurance? How can you use this psalm to find peace in those times?

Psalm 122: ***The psalmist expresses joy for being in Jerusalem and solicits prayers in its behalf.***

122:1 *house of the LORD.* In David's day the tabernacle, which was replaced by Solomon's temple, God's dwelling place, which foreshadowed His coming in Christ's humanity, dwelling in His people as His living temple, and ultimately His glory filling the new creation (John 2:19–21; 1 Peter 2:5; Rev. 21:1–3,22–23).

122:3 *compact together.* Joined as one, perhaps referring to the unity of the various tribes when they worshiped together in Jerusalem (v. 4; 133). Christ unites the church through His Spirit applying His blood (Eph. 2:14–22; 4:4–6).

122:4 *Whither.* Where, to which place. *testimony.* The ark of the covenant (Ex. 16:34; 26:33–34). *name.* The totality of God's perfections that He has revealed.

122:5 *thrones of judgment.* The authority of the king and his servants to lead the people in justice (2 Chron. 9:8; Prov. 20:8), a type of the kingdom of Christ (Isa. 9:7; 16:5; Rev. 20:4).

122:6 *peace.* Overall well-being (vv. 7–8). *prosper.* Be secure and at ease.

122:7 *prosperity.* Security or quietness.

Thoughts for Personal/Family Worship: Psalm 122

1. **Going to God's house is the occasion for joy. As that was true in the Old Testament economy, so should it be true today. Corporate worship in the visible and local church should be the delight of every Christian. To experience fellowship with those of like precious faith and to join in praise and worship of the Lord should be the highlight of the week as the church gathers on the Lord's Day. Love for the church should also motivate prayer for it (v. 6). Do you prepare for the Lord's Day with prayer, delight, and expectation? How can you make a habit of doing this?**
2. **The joy of public worship revolves around the presence of God. For Israel this was the temple and throne of David and his sons. For Christians, this is the Lord Jesus Christ, reigning through His Word and Spirit. Our joy in worship comes from exercising faith in the gospel of Jesus Christ by the power of the Holy Spirit (Rom. 15:8–13). When you engage in worship with the church, are you drawing near to the Father by faith in Christ in the power of the Spirit? How can you tell?**

Psalm 123: ***The psalmist looks to God's mercy in the trial of mockery.***

123:2 *eyes . . . unto the hand.* The waiting of *servants* for *their masters* to provide their portion (Prov. 31:15) provides an illustration of dependence that is needy, expectantly attentive, and yet submissive (69:14; 119:81–82; 145:15). *have mercy.* Be

upon the LORD our God, until that he have mercy
upon us.
3 Have mercy upon us, O LORD, have mercy upon
us: for we are exceedingly filled with contempt.
4 Our soul is exceedingly filled with the scorning
of those that are at ease, *and* with the contempt
of the proud.

PSALM 124

A Song of degrees of David.

1 IF *it had* not *been* the LORD who was on our
side, now may Israel say;
2 If *it had* not *been* the LORD who was on our
side, when men rose up against us:
3 Then they had swallowed us up quick, when
their wrath was kindled against us:
4 Then the waters had overwhelmed us, the
stream had gone over our soul:
5 Then the proud waters had gone over our soul.
6 Blessed *be* the LORD, who hath not given us *as* a
prey to their teeth.
7 Our soul is escaped as a bird out of the snare of
the fowlers: the snare is broken, and we are escaped.
8 Our help *is* in the name of the LORD, who made
heaven and earth.

PSALM 125

A Song of degrees.

1 THEY that trust in the LORD *shall be* as mount
Zion, *which* cannot be removed, *but* abideth for
ever.
2 *As* the mountains *are* round about Jerusa-
lem, so the LORD *is* round about his people from
henceforth even for ever.
3 For the rod of the wicked shall not rest upon
the lot of the righteous; lest the righteous put
forth their hands unto iniquity.
4 Do good, O LORD, unto *those that be* good, and
to *them that are* upright in their hearts.
5 As for such as turn aside unto their crooked
ways, the LORD shall lead them forth with the
workers of iniquity: *but* peace *shall be* upon Israel.

---

gracious or show undeserved favor (v. 3).

123:3 *exceedingly filled with contempt.* Wearied and overwhelmed (88:3) by the mockery and disrespect of proud and wicked people (v. 4).

123:4 *Our soul is.* We are (soul referring to the persons).

Thoughts for Personal/Family Worship: Psalm 123

One of the most difficult trials in the world is to face disrespect and contempt for following Christ. We inherently sense that doing right should bring honor, yet this corrupt world turns things upside down. The unfairness of it grinds against our consciences, especially when our mockers are at ease in their pride and success. The scorn of the world is one of Satan's great weapons to turn people back from godliness and to weary and embitter the faithful. What are we to do? This psalm teaches us that we must take the posture of servants before our Lord, fixing our eyes upon His sovereign grace, expecting His provision and vindication, and yet submissively waiting on His timing because He is the Master. Christ carried the cross before He entered His glory, and we must follow Him. What practical steps can we take to fix our eyes upon Jesus (Heb. 12:2) when we experience trials?

Psalm 124: *The psalmist reviews God's deliverances from enemies.*

124:1–2 *the LORD who was on our side.* The basis of the believer's confidence (118:6; Rom. 8:31).

124:3 *swallowed us up quick.* Eaten us alive (v. 6).

124:4 *our soul.* Us, soul referring to the person not just the inner being.

124:5 *proud waters.* Raging water, like foaming waves, a picture of the power and violence of the wicked (18:4; 46:3; 93:3–4).

124:6 *Blessed.* Praised.

124:7 *fowlers.* Bird hunters.

124:8 *name.* Who God has revealed Himself to be. *made heaven and earth.* All the power of sinners cannot destroy the church because the infinite strength of the Creator defends them (33:6–12). This verse is used in many Reformed churches to open their worship services.

Thoughts for Personal/Family Worship: Psalm 124

Apart from divine support, the church of Christ would quickly fall before its raging enemies. They would devour believers like ravenous lions, wipe them out like a tsunami wave, and catch them like a professional trapper in the woods. The only reason the people of God continue in this world is the almighty power of their Savior. His strength is more than sufficient. Believers can revel in the promise of Christ, "I will build my church; and the gates of hell shall not prevail against it" (Matt. 16:18), for all authority in heaven and earth belong to Him (Matt. 28:18). How does the world threaten to destroy the church today? How does it comfort you to say, "Our help is in the name of the LORD, who made heaven and earth"?

Psalm 125: *The psalmist describes the safety of those who trust the Lord.*

125:1 *trust.* Put confidence for safety and security, one of the principal words in the Old Testament for faith. *as mount Zion.* Not a very impressive mountain, but the place of God's temple and earthly throne. Thus God's people must abide in Him because they are the kingdom of the Lord. *removed.* Made to totter, stagger, or be overthrown.

125:2 The hilly terrain (*mountains*) in the area of *Jerusalem* provided a natural obstacle to invading armies, and thus it is an image of God's protection, for His righteousness is like great mountains (36:6), and He is the great rocky cliff where believers can hide (31:2–3; 71:3).

125:3 *lot of the righteous.* The portion or inheritance of God's people, which consists of the Lord and His kingdom in the land (16:5; Num. 26:55–56).

125:4 *Do good . . . unto . . . good.* See 34:9–10; 84:11; Rom. 8:28.

Thoughts for Personal/Family Worship: Psalm 125

Whether we need protection against an evil that we

PSALM 126

A Song of degrees.

1 WHEN the LORD turned again the captivity of
Zion, we were like them that dream.
2 Then was our mouth filled with laughter, and
our tongue with singing: then said they among the
heathen, The LORD hath done great things for them.
3 The LORD hath done great things for us; *whereof*
we are glad.
4 Turn again our captivity, O LORD, as the streams
in the south.
5 They that sow in tears shall reap in joy.
6 He that goeth forth and weepeth, bearing
precious seed, shall doubtless come again with
rejoicing, bringing his sheaves *with him.*

PSALM 127

A Song of degrees for Solomon.

1 EXCEPT the LORD build the house, they labour
in vain that build it: except the LORD keep the city,
the watchman waketh *but* in vain.
2 *It is* vain for you to rise up early, to sit up late,
to eat the bread of sorrows: *for* so he giveth his
beloved sleep.
3 Lo, children *are* an heritage of the LORD: *and*
the fruit of the womb *is his* reward.
4 As arrows *are* in the hand of a mighty man; so
are children of the youth.
5 Happy *is* the man that hath his quiver full of
them: they shall not be ashamed, but they shall
speak with the enemies in the gate.

PSALM 128

A Song of degrees.

1 BLESSED *is* every one that feareth the LORD; that
walketh in his ways.
2 For thou shalt eat the labour of thine hands:
happy *shalt* thou *be*, and *it shall be* well with thee.
3 Thy wife *shall be* as a fruitful vine by the sides of

fear, or provision of some good that we desire, the Lord is sufficient for all our needs. His power and righteousness surround His people like impassable mountains. He will give peace to those whose hearts trust in Him and do good. However, those who live in sin will be led away to destruction. How can this psalm help Christians when their lives are shaken by difficulties? How can it help people who are tempted to run to sin or worldly security when trouble threatens?

Psalm 126: *The psalmist reflects on the blessings of God in restoration.*

126:1 *turned again the captivity*. Restored the fortunes (14:7; 53:6; 85:1), not necessarily a reference to a particular captivity or exile (v. 4).

126:2 *heathen*. Gentile nations. *The LORD hath done great things for them*. The Lord has magnified Himself to work for them (v. 3).

126:4 *streams in the south*. Perhaps the wadis of the arid Negev, streambeds that stand dry for long periods until rain fills them, a picture of heavenly renewal.

126:5 *joy*. A cry of jubilation. God will change all the sorrows of His people into gladness (30:5,11).

126:6 *He that goeth forth and weepeth*. Literally, "going he goes and weeping," expressing the idea of continually weeping. *precious seed*. A leather pouch of seed. *sheaves*. Harvested and bundled plants. The imagery suggests that the sorrows of believers are like God's seeds by which He will produce a harvest of happiness for them (Heb. 12:11).

Thoughts for Personal/Family Worship: Psalm 126

Many are the tears of God's children, but God promises them that their mouths will be filled with laughter. This is gospel optimism, for Christ has taken the curse of sin and won the promised blessing (Gal. 3:13–14). Whenever the Lord has done great things for us, we should praise Him for the glory of His grace. One day all our sowing will come back in the harvest, and we will shout for joy. How can we cultivate an optimistic view of life that is based upon God and the gospel?

Psalm 127: *Every facet of life must be founded on God.*

127:1 *vain*. Futility, uselessness (v. 2). God works through means and often blesses human diligence with success, but all created means can accomplish nothing apart from God.

127:2 *to rise up early, to sit up late*. The pair of opposites refers to the whole range of human labor. *bread of sorrows*. Food earned by strenuous work. *giveth . . . sleep*. Trusting in the Lord gives inner peace and rest instead of constant anxiety (3:5; 4:8).

127:3–4 The Bible portrays *children* as a great blessing from God (Gen. 33:5; 48:9), to be sought by married couples, welcomed, and cherished, for they are powerful agents (*arrows*) to fulfill our mandate from the Creator to rule this world in His image (Gen. 1:28; 9:1).

127:5 *Happy*. Having many benefits from God (commonly translated "blessed," 1:1), here the joy of having a large family (*quiver full*). *they shall speak*. Or will drive away. *gate*. Location in the ancient city where business and legal transactions took place.

Thoughts for Personal/Family Worship: Psalm 127

1. **This psalm calls for a balance between hard work and trusting God. Both are essential. Work without trust is self-sufficiency; trust without work is presumption. As Christians, we must recognize that nothing in life can succeed, whether business or family, without the Lord. Trusting God does not make the believer passive or inactive. On the contrary it should make him faithful, diligent, and hopeful in his calling, believing that the will to work, as well as our abilities, opportunities, and successes are gifts of God. In which direction are you tempted to become unbalanced? What can you do to help keep the balance in focus?**
2. **If manual labor and physical procreation cannot succeed without the Lord, how much more do we need His grace to build the living house of the Lord, construct the city of God, and multiply the family of God. Apart from Christ we can do nothing (John 15:5). What reasons can you give why Christian service requires both prayer and work?**

thine house: thy children like olive plants round about thy table.
4 Behold, that thus shall the man be blessed that
feareth the LORD.
5 The LORD shall bless thee out of Zion: and thou
shalt see the good of Jerusalem all the days of thy
life.
6 Yea, thou shalt see thy children's children, *and*
peace upon Israel.

PSALM 129

A Song of degrees.

1 MANY a time have they afflicted me from my
youth, may Israel now say:
2 Many a time have they afflicted me from my
youth: yet they have not prevailed against me.
3 The plowers plowed upon my back: they made
long their furrows.
4 The LORD *is* righteous: he hath cut asunder the
cords of the wicked.
5 Let them all be confounded and turned back
that hate Zion.
6 Let them be as the grass *upon* the housetops,
which withereth afore it groweth up:
7 Wherewith the mower filleth not his hand; nor
he that bindeth sheaves his bosom.
8 Neither do they which go by say, The blessing of
the LORD *be* upon you: we bless you in the name
of the LORD.

PSALM 130

A Song of degrees.

1 OUT of the depths have I cried unto thee, O
LORD.
2 Lord, hear my voice: let thine ears be attentive
to the voice of my supplications.
3 If thou, LORD, shouldest mark iniquities, O
Lord, who shall stand?
4 But *there is* forgiveness with thee, that thou
mayest be feared.

Psalm 128: *The Lord promises to bless the home that fears Him.*

128:1 *Blessed.* Possessing great benefits from the Lord (1:1). *feareth the LORD.* The essence of true religion: knowing God with reverence so that you desire to honor Him and please Him with obedience and dread to offend Him by sin (v. 4; Job 1:1; 28:28; Prov. 2:5; 9:10; Jer. 32:40; 2 Cor. 7:1).
128:2 *happy.* Same word as "blessed" (v. 1).
128:3 *fruitful vine.* An image of beauty, refreshment, delight, and shade. *olive plants.* A picture of preciousness, thriving under gracious influences, and great potential.
128:4 *be blessed.* Receive benefits from the Lord (a different word than v. 1). Better a home with the fear of God and love than one full of wealth and fighting (Prov. 15:16–17).
128:5 *good of Jerusalem.* The psalm's vision of blessing broadens from the household to all of God's people.
128:6 *see thy children's children.* A full and honorable life and rich legacy (Prov. 17:6).

Thoughts for Personal/Family Worship: Psalm 128

Strange as it is to this unbelieving world, those who fear God are the genuinely happy people. This fear of God will lead us in the right and best way, and it will bring upon us the favor and great goodness of God. In many ways, the home is where the sincerity and reality of true religion should be the most evident. In fact, the home becomes an index to how real our fear of the Lord is. Yet this psalm is not limited to domestic families. Christ never married or had physical children, yet He experiences God's blessing in the deepest way. In union with Christ, single people, childless people, and all kinds of people can enjoy deep happiness and fruitfulness in the family of God. Why does the fear of God bring blessing and make us a blessing to others?

Psalm 129: *The psalmist reflects on God's goodness in delivering His people from afflictions.*

129:1 *afflicted.* Treated with hostility, harassed (v. 2).
129:3 *plowers.* A picture of inflicting deep wounds as the ridges of a plowed field.
129:4 *cut asunder.* Chop up or cut in two.
129:6 *grass upon the housetops.* Tufts of grass that spring up on flat mud roofs and quickly come to nothing. *afore.* Before.
129:7 *bosom.* The fold in a garment to hold what has been gathered.
129:8 *The blessing of the LORD be upon you.* A greeting (Ruth 2:4).

Thoughts for Personal/Family Worship: Psalm 129

Suffering is the believer's lot in this world. Sometimes it cuts us deeply. Yet in the most grievous times, know that the Lord is righteous. He will release believers from the power of the wicked and cause sinners to wither and forfeit their blessings. Christ knows this: the Roman soldiers truly plowed His back with horrible wounds (Isa. 50:6; 53:5; Matt. 27:26; John 19:1). Yet in it all, God was righteous, carrying out His plan for the salvation of His church, the exaltation of His Son, and the destruction of His enemies. Therefore we can trust the Lord in many afflictions. What afflictions are you or your loved ones enduring? How can this psalm help?

Psalm 130: *The Lord is merciful and ready to forgive those who confess their sins.*

130:1 *Out of the depths.* A position of helplessness and great need (40:2; 42:7; Jonah 2:2,4). In this context, it refers to guilt, the objective result of sin that brings a person under God's condemnation (Ex. 34:7), and the subjective or experiential sense of His wrath (38:2; Gen. 4:5; 1 John 3:20).
130:2 *supplications.* Pleadings for grace and favor. The guilty must pray for salvation (Joel 2:32; Acts 2:21; 9:11; Rom. 10:13).
130:3 *mark.* Literally, "watch over, keep in custody, or keep a record of." *who shall stand?* Who will be able to defend himself? No sinner can be justified before God by his own efforts (143:2).
130:4 *forgiveness with thee.* God alone can pardon the guilt of sin (Mic. 7:9; Luke 5:21). *that thou mayest be feared.* Childlike reverence and submission to the Lord springs from knowing His grace (Hos. 3:5; Jer. 32:40), for His grace is glorious and

5 I wait for the LORD, my soul doth wait, and in
his word do I hope.
6 My soul *waiteth* for the Lord more than they
that watch for the morning: *I say, more than* they
that watch for the morning.
7 Let Israel hope in the LORD: for with the LORD *there*
is mercy, and with him *is* plenteous redemption.
8 And he shall redeem Israel from all his
iniquities.

PSALM 131

A Song of degrees of David.

1 LORD, my heart is not haughty, nor mine eyes
lofty: neither do I exercise myself in great matters,
or in things too high for me.
2 Surely I have behaved and quieted myself, as a
child that is weaned of his mother: my soul *is* even
as a weaned child.
3 Let Israel hope in the LORD from henceforth
and for ever.

PSALM 132

A Song of degrees.

1 LORD, remember David, *and* all his afflictions:
2 How he sware unto the LORD, *and* vowed unto
the mighty *God* of Jacob;
3 Surely I will not come into the tabernacle of my
house, nor go up into my bed;
4 I will not give sleep to mine eyes, *or* slumber to
mine eyelids,
5 Until I find out a place for the LORD, an habita-
tion for the mighty *God* of Jacob.
6 Lo, we heard of it at Ephratah: we found it in
the fields of the wood.
7 We will go into his tabernacles: we will worship
at his footstool.
8 Arise, O LORD, into thy rest; thou, and the ark
of thy strength.
9 Let thy priests be clothed with righteousness;
and let thy saints shout for joy.
10 For thy servant David's sake turn not away the
face of thine anointed.

---

awe-inspiring (Gen. 28:15–17; Eph. 1:6).

130:5 *wait.* Hope with eager anticipation, an act of faith (27:14; 40:1; Isa. 26:8). *my soul.* Myself (v. 6). *hope.* A different word than *wait*, but the same sense (v. 7).

130:6 *watch for the morning.* Illustrates the expectant anticipation.

130:7 *mercy.* Covenant loyalty and love. God is faithful to forgive repentant sinners who trust in Him (1 John 1:9), and so God is the basis of hope. *plenteous redemption.* Great and abundant salvation from sin and its consequences (see note at 111:9).

130:8 *redeem.* Ransom from the full guilt and punishment of sin (*all his iniquities*) by the payment of a ransom price to satisfy God's justice (Ex. 21:30; Mark 10:45; Rom. 3:24; Eph. 1:7; Titus 2:14; Heb. 9:11–15).

Thoughts for Personal/Family Worship: Psalm 130

1. **Affliction and guilt can bring men very low indeed, but in the worst of depths sinners must not abandon themselves to despair. They should pray with great earnestness to the One who alone can rescue them. They must acknowledge that they cannot stand before God on their own merits. They must look to God as the God who forgives sin through Christ. They must rest their hope entirely in Him. What about you? Do you think you can stand before God on your own? He knows all your sins. Do you fear your sins are too great? God's salvation is abundant. Do you think your sins are too many or you have sinned too long? God will save His people from all their guilt.**
2. **The great means by which God saves the guilty sinner is the redemption in Christ Jesus. Christ paid the ransom to satisfy God's justice. Sinners need not suffer for their sins because Christ suffered and died in the place of sinners (1 Cor. 15:3). Faith focuses its hope and desire upon Jesus Christ. He is the only Mediator between God and men, for He gave Himself as "a ransom for all" (1 Tim. 2:5–6). Are you trusting in Christ alone for salvation from sin? If so, then how has your faith evidenced itself in a childlike fear of the Lord?**

Psalm 131: *David confesses and exhorts us to a childlike faith.*

131:1 *haughty . . . lofty.* Lifted up in pride (101:5; Prov. 16:5,18). *neither do I exercise.* Literally, "I do not walk," referring to the habits and manners of life. *too high.* Wonderful or difficult. His mind is humble, not proud or selfishly ambitious (Jer. 45:5).

131:2 *behaved.* Laid down or composed himself. *quieted.* Became still. *as a weaned child.* Not a child hungrily seeking milk, but one resting contentedly in the embrace of *his mother.* This is a picture of trust, submission, and peaceful rest.

131:3 *hope.* Confidently expect. It is a hope that shall never disappoint. *henceforth.* Now.

Thoughts for Personal/Family Worship: Psalm 131

Pride causes great trouble, but humility brings right thinking, speaking, and living. It is a grace most pleasing to God. True humility expresses itself in confident reliance on the Lord. It releases a person from the strife of arrogance and personal ambition. It quiets the heart with contentment to live near to God. It makes us like Christ, who did not use His equality with the Father for selfish pursuits, but became a humble and crucified servant to obey His Father (Phil. 2:5–8). Yet He counted it His food to do His Father's will (John 4:34), living in joyful hope (Heb. 12:2). Why is humility so essential to peace and hope?

Psalm 132: *David expresses his zeal for the ark of God that it might be in its rightful place.*

132:1 *remember.* Give attention, take to heart in a manner that leads to action (Gen. 8:1).

132:3 *tabernacle.* Tent, not the sacred tabernacle, but a personal home.

132:5 *habitation.* Dwelling place for God (Ex. 25:9; same word as *tabernacles* in v. 7).

132:6 *Ephratah.* The location of Bethlehem (Ruth 4:11; Mic. 5:2). *fields of the wood.* Perhaps Kirjath-jearim ("city of woods"), where the ark temporarily stayed (1 Sam. 7:1–2).

11 The LORD hath sworn *in* truth unto David; he will not turn from it; Of the fruit of thy body will I set upon thy throne.

12 If thy children will keep my covenant and my testimony that I shall teach them, their children shall also sit upon thy throne for evermore.

13 For the LORD hath chosen Zion; he hath desired *it* for his habitation.

14 This *is* my rest for ever: here will I dwell; for I have desired it.

15 I will abundantly bless her provision: I will satisfy her poor with bread.

16 I will also clothe her priests with salvation: and her saints shall shout aloud for joy.

17 There will I make the horn of David to bud: I have ordained a lamp for mine anointed.

18 His enemies will I clothe with shame: but upon himself shall his crown flourish.

PSALM 133

A Song of degrees of David.

1 BEHOLD, how good and how pleasant *it is* for brethren to dwell together in unity!

2 *It is* like the precious ointment upon the head, that ran down upon the beard, *even* Aaron's beard: that went down to the skirts of his garments;

3 As the dew of Hermon, *and as the dew* that descended upon the mountains of Zion: for there the LORD commanded the blessing, *even* life for evermore.

132:7 *footstool.* The ark, like an earthly footrest for the throne of the heavenly king (99:5; 1 Chron. 28:2; cf. Isa. 66:1).

132:8 *Arise, O LORD.* A request for God's presence to dwell in the temple as King (68:1; Num. 10:35–36). *rest.* A word associated with the peace of the kingdom and establishment of God's presence with Israel (v. 14; Deut. 12:9–11; 1 Kings 8:56; 1 Chron. 22:9; 28:2).

132:9 *clothed with righteousness.* Sometimes an expression for putting on godly habits (Job 29:14), but here meaning enjoying the blessings of God's righteous acts of salvation (v. 16; Isa. 61:10). *saints.* Those who are the recipients of covenant love and thus holy (v. 16).

132:10 *anointed.* God's appointed king (literally, "messiah") of the line of David (v. 17; 2:2; 18:50; 20:6; 28:8; 84:9; 89:38,51).

132:11 *sworn . . . unto David.* God made a covenant or solemn promise that David's offspring (*fruit of thy body*) would reign over an eternal kingdom (89:3–4; 2 Sam. 7:12; 1 Kings 8:25; 2 Chron. 6:16), a promise fulfilled in Christ (Acts 2:30; cf. Luke 1:32,69).

132:15 *provision.* Specifically, food supply.

132:17 *horn.* A symbol of strength and power. *bud.* Sprout with life (Jer. 33:15). *lamp for mine anointed.* An image of David's continuing dynasty by God's faithfulness to His covenant (see notes at 2 Sam. 21:17; 1 Kings 11:36).

132:18 *clothe with shame.* In contrast to vv. 9,16.

Thoughts for Personal/Family Worship: Psalm 132

David's resolution to establish a place for God's holy presence (vv. 4–5) reminds us that one great purpose of God's king is to build God's temple. Nothing is more important to the kingdom of God than worshiping the Lord. His presence with His people is their joy and His glory. Jesus Christ is the anointed Son of David and the fulfillment of these promises (Acts 2:29–30). He was born in Bethlehem Ephratah (Mic. 5:2). He declared, "I will build my church" (Matt. 16:18). Christ is Lord of heaven and earth, and in Him the presence of God is coming to all nations (Matt. 28:18–20). God's worshipers no longer gather around a physical location, but worship God through Christ in the Holy Spirit regardless of where they meet for public worship, for they are the temple of the living God (John 4:21–24; Eph. 2:18–22). How does God's covenant with David encourage us to pray, "Thy kingdom come"? How does it help us understand what we are asking for in those words?

Psalm 133: *David describes the beauty of unity among God's people.*

133:1 *Behold.* A word calling for attention. *pleasant.* Lovely, delightful, agreeable, or harmonious. *brethren.* Fellow members of the people of God. *in unity.* Literally, "even together." Such unity and fellowship is authorized by divine command and by approved holy example (Lev. 23:2; Acts 1:4; 2:1–2; 4:31–32; 20:7); and although impossible to nature, divine grace amazingly makes the impossible, possible (2 Chron. 30:12; Jer. 32:39; John 17:23; Eph. 2:11–22).

133:2 *precious ointment . . . Aaron's beard.* The holy anointing oil used to consecrate the priests (Ex. 30:25,30), a symbol of the Holy Spirit empowering people for sacred work (1 Sam. 16:13; Isa. 61:1; Luke 4:18; Acts 10:38). *skirts.* Literally, "mouth" or "edge," referring to the borders of the garment, either the collar area or hem. Thus unity equips God's holy people to serve Him.

133:3 *dew.* A symbol of God's power to give and renew life (110:3; Isa. 26:19; Hos. 14:5). *Zion.* Center of God's kingdom and home to His presence in the temple. The gathering of God's people to worship in spiritual unity is a means of experiencing God's life-giving presence (Eph. 2:18). The images in vv. 2–3 picture that which is excellent descending from top to bottom and affecting everything touched, for spiritual unity in Christ is a gift of the Holy Spirit (Eph. 4:3). *life for evermore.* The Spirit-worked *blessing* God gives to His unified church on earth is just a foretaste of the fullness of blessing they will know in the kingdom (Rom. 8:23; 2 Cor. 1:22).

Thoughts for Personal/Family Worship: Psalm 133

1. **Unity, based on truth, is most desirable. It is to God's glory and His people's good, and therefore we must never do anything to produce discord or division. Since the Holy Spirit is the source of love and peace, we must constantly pray to be filled with the Spirit, and the whole church needs to pray for further outpourings of the Spirit. Is this a petition in your daily prayers? Is it a petition regularly heard in our prayer meetings?**
2. **Just as the unity of Israel was compared to the anointing oil that flowed from Aaron's head down to his garments, so the spiritual unity of the church consists of the Holy Spirit who anointed Christ and now overflows to every member of His body (1 Cor. 12:12–13). Our unity is found not by ignoring doctrine, but in knowing and trusting Jesus Christ (Eph. 4:13). He is our great High Priest, and our worship revolves around drawing near to God through Him and confessing our hope in Him**

PSALM 134

A Song of degrees.

1 BEHOLD, bless ye the LORD, all *ye* servants of the
LORD, which by night stand in the house of the
LORD.
2 Lift up your hands *in* the sanctuary, and bless
the LORD.
3 The LORD that made heaven and earth bless
thee out of Zion.

PSALM 135

1 PRAISE ye the LORD. Praise ye the name of the
LORD; praise *him*, O ye servants of the LORD.
2 Ye that stand in the house of the LORD, in the
courts of the house of our God,
3 Praise the LORD; for the LORD *is* good: sing
praises unto his name; for *it is* pleasant.
4 For the LORD hath chosen Jacob unto himself,
and Israel for his peculiar treasure.
5 For I know that the LORD *is* great, and *that* our
Lord *is* above all gods.
6 Whatsoever the LORD pleased, *that* did he in
heaven, and in earth, in the seas, and all deep places.
7 He causeth the vapours to ascend from the ends
of the earth; he maketh lightnings for the rain;
he bringeth the wind out of his treasuries.
8 Who smote the firstborn of Egypt, both of man
and beast.
9 *Who* sent tokens and wonders into the midst
of thee, O Egypt, upon Pharaoh, and upon all his
servants.
10 Who smote great nations, and slew mighty
kings;
11 Sihon king of the Amorites, and Og king of
Bashan, and all the kingdoms of Canaan:
12 And gave their land *for* an heritage, an heritage
unto Israel his people.
13 Thy name, O LORD, *endureth* for ever; *and* thy
memorial, O LORD, throughout all generations.
14 For the LORD will judge his people, and he will
repent himself concerning his servants.
15 The idols of the heathen *are* silver and gold,
the work of men's hands.
16 They have mouths, but they speak not; eyes
have they, but they see not;
17 They have ears, but they hear not; neither is
there *any* breath in their mouths.
18 They that make them are like unto them: *so is*
every one that trusteth in them.
19 Bless the LORD, O house of Israel: bless the
LORD, O house of Aaron:
20 Bless the LORD, O house of Levi: ye that fear
the LORD, bless the LORD.

(Heb. 10:19–22). How does making Christ the center of our worship promote unity in the church?

Psalm 134: ***The psalmist exhorts God's servants to praise Him.***

134:1 *Behold.* A word calling for attention. *bless.* Declare the praise and honor belonging to Him. When God blesses us, He does well for us; when we bless God, we speak well of Him (vv. 2–3).

134:2 *Lift up your hands.* A gesture of prayer, expressive of reaching up in dependence to God, imploring Him for a gracious response (see notes at 24:4; 28:2).

134:3 *made heaven and earth.* See 115:15; 124:8; 146:5–6. *bless thee out of Zion.* See note at 128:5.

Thoughts for Personal/Family Worship: Psalm 134

1. **Very special attention should be given to public worship since man's chief end is to glorify and enjoy God. Just how much do we love God's house and how devoted are we to Sabbath worship? Tiredness can sometimes hinder us in worship, but it should never be an excuse to leave it off altogether. Godly priests saw it as their duty to worship even at night, and we do well to be as zealous and keen as they were.**
2. **Just as the priests led Israel's praise and declared God's blessing upon the people (Lev. 9:22; Num. 6:22–27), so the Lord Christ, our great High Priest, leads the spiritual Israel to praise God and receive His blessings (Luke 24:50; Rom. 15:8–13; Heb. 2:11–13). As the King reigning in the heavenly Zion, Christ applies God's blessing to His people. In practical terms, how can Christians bless God *through Christ* and receive God's blessing *through Christ* when they meet for worship?**

Psalm 135: ***The psalmist exhorts God's people to praise Him and extols God's unique power in contrast to the worthlessness of idols.***

135:1 *Praise . . . Praise . . . praise.* The repetition calls for superlative praise (vv. 19–20; Isa. 6:3). *Praise ye the LORD.* Hebrew, *hallelujah* (also vv. 3,21). *name.* All of God's perfections that He has revealed (v. 13).

135:3 *pleasant.* See note at 133:1.

135:4 *peculiar treasure.* Personal and valuable property; prized possession (Ex. 19:5; Mal. 3:17). Jacob's being *chosen* underscores God's sovereignty in election since Jacob had no virtue or merit (Mal. 1:2; Rom. 9:10–13).

135:6 *Whatsoever the LORD pleased, that did he.* God fully accomplishes all that He wills, for no one can frustrate His plans (see note at 115:3).

135:7 *causeth the vapours . . . maketh . . . bringeth.* God's providence controls all natural events (see note at 104:13–14). *treasuries.* Storehouses.

135:8 *smote the firstborn.* See Ex. 11–12.

135:9 *tokens.* Signs, often miraculous. *Egypt.* See Ex. 7–11.

135:11 *Sihon . . . Og.* See Num. 21:21–35.

135:14 *judge.* Rule as king with justice and salvation (54:1; 72:2; 96:10). These words are cited in Heb. 10:30. *repent himself.* Have compassion on, relent of punishing. This truth, based upon Deut. 32:36 and cited in Heb. 10:30, comforts the true believer but should terrify the hypocrite and those who fall away from the Lord.

135:15–18 Repeated from 115:4–8 (see notes there).

135:19–20 *Bless the LORD.* Speak well of Him, declare the praises that belong to Him. *fear the LORD.* True biblical religion consists of worshiping the true God with reverence and obeying Him with submission.

21 Blessed be the LORD out of Zion, which
dwelleth at Jerusalem. Praise ye the LORD.

PSALM 136

1 O GIVE thanks unto the LORD; for *he is* good:
for his mercy *endureth* for ever.
2 O give thanks unto the God of gods: for his
mercy *endureth* for ever.
3 O give thanks to the Lord of lords: for his mercy
endureth for ever.
4 To him who alone doeth great wonders: for his
mercy *endureth* for ever.
5 To him that by wisdom made the heavens: for
his mercy *endureth* for ever.
6 To him that stretched out the earth above the
waters: for his mercy *endureth* for ever.
7 To him that made great lights: for his mercy
endureth for ever:
8 The sun to rule by day: for his mercy *endureth*
for ever:
9 The moon and stars to rule by night: for his
mercy *endureth* for ever.
10 To him that smote Egypt in their firstborn: for
his mercy *endureth* for ever:
11 And brought out Israel from among them: for
his mercy *endureth* for ever:
12 With a strong hand, and with a stretched out
arm: for his mercy *endureth* for ever.
13 To him which divided the Red sea into parts:
for his mercy *endureth* for ever:
14 And made Israel to pass through the midst of
it: for his mercy *endureth* for ever:
15 But overthrew Pharaoh and his host in the
Red sea: for his mercy *endureth* for ever.
16 To him which led his people through the
wilderness: for his mercy *endureth* for ever.
17 To him which smote great kings: for his mercy
endureth for ever:
18 And slew famous kings: for his mercy *endureth*
for ever:
19 Sihon king of the Amorites: for his mercy
endureth for ever:
20 And Og the king of Bashan: for his mercy
endureth for ever:
21 And gave their land for an heritage: for his
mercy *endureth* for ever:
22 *Even* an heritage unto Israel his servant: for his
mercy *endureth* for ever.
23 Who remembered us in our low estate: for his
mercy *endureth* for ever:
24 And hath redeemed us from our enemies: for
his mercy *endureth* for ever.
25 Who giveth food to all flesh: for his mercy
endureth for ever.
26 O give thanks unto the God of heaven: for his
mercy *endureth* for ever.

Thoughts for Personal/Family Worship: Psalm 135

1. **God is good and the source of all the good we enjoy. He is also great and able to do anything and everything for His people. Therefore He is most worthy of our praise. The psalmist praises God for His election, redemption, and preservation. Praise must go forth from the church to the world that men might come to know and fear the Lord, turning from their idols to the true God. It is solemn to reflect on the fact that the matter and manner of our praise are means of instructing unbelievers. Does our worship impress men with God's greatness, sovereignty, and holiness, or is it mere entertainment to soothe the worshipers?**
2. **The promise that God will judge His people (v. 14) is a fearful warning to those who profess faith in Jesus Christ but later turn away from Him forever (Heb. 10:29–31). They have known the true God but have chosen worthless idols, provoking God's eternal wrath. What reasons does this psalm give for why it is foolish to reject the Lord?**

Psalm 136: ***The psalmist repeats many of the thoughts of the previous psalm, but with a constant refrain of praise to God for His eternal love.***

136:1 *his mercy endureth for ever.* Literally, "forever is His covenant love and loyalty" (106:1; 107:1; 118:1–4,29). This refrain occurs in every verse. God's faithful love that He demonstrates in goodness, kindness, and mercy is a fountain that never runs dry (103:17; Lam. 3:22–23).
136:2–3 *God of gods . . . Lord of lords.* A Hebrew construction expressing a superlative; He is the absolute, supreme, sovereign, infinite, and unique God and Lord over all.
136:4 *great wonders.* Extraordinary, miraculous acts beyond human ability or comprehension.
136:5 God's infinite *wisdom* is displayed in the creation He made (104:24; 147:4–5; Job 12:13). *made the heavens.* See 33:6; Gen. 1:1.
136:6 *stretched out the earth.* See 24:2; Gen. 1:9–10; Isa. 42:5; 44:24.
136:7–9 *made great lights . . . sun . . . moon.* See Gen. 1:14–19.
136:10–22 *smote . . . overthrew . . . smote . . . slew.* God's acts of *mercy* to Israel included many deadly acts of judgment against their enemies. This shows that God's faithful love, while showering blessings on all creation (v. 25), has a particular focus on His covenant people and is consistent with His wrath against the wicked (Mal. 1:1–5).
136:12 *strong hand . . . stretched out arm.* Metaphors for His active power to save and destroy (Ex. 6:1,6; 7:5; 13:3,9,14,16).
136:15 *host.* Army.
136:22 *Israel his servant.* The covenant relationship places the people under God's faithful lordship (Isa. 41:8).
136:23 *remembered us in our low estate.* Gave intentional attention to His people when they were in a pitiful condition. This is amazing grace, considering God's transcendence, independence, self-sufficiency, infinite greatness, holiness, and justice (8:3–4; Job 7:17).

Thoughts for Personal/Family Worship: Psalm 136

1. **This psalm provides a pattern for praising God's faithful love. It begins by reflecting on who God is both in His goodness and greatness (vv. 1–3). The psalmist enumerates His amazing works (v. 4) of creation (vv. 5–9), redemption (vv. 10–15), and leading His people to their inheritance (vv. 16–22). It concludes by considering the**

PSALM 137

1 By the rivers of Babylon, there we sat down,
yea, we wept, when we remembered Zion.
2 We hanged our harps upon the willows in the
midst thereof.
3 For there they that carried us away captive
required of us a song; and they that wasted us
required of us mirth, *saying*, Sing us *one* of the
songs of Zion.
4 How shall we sing the LORD's song in a strange
land?
5 If I forget thee, O Jerusalem, let my right hand
forget *her cunning*.
6 If I do not remember thee, let my tongue cleave
to the roof of my mouth; if I prefer not Jerusalem
above my chief joy.
7 Remember, O LORD, the children of Edom in
the day of Jerusalem; who said, Rase *it*, rase *it*,
even to the foundation thereof.
8 O daughter of Babylon, who art to be de-
stroyed; happy *shall he be*, that rewardeth thee as
thou hast served us.
9 Happy *shall he be*, that taketh and dasheth thy
little ones against the stones.

PSALM 138

A Psalm of David.

1 I will praise thee with my whole heart: before
the gods will I sing praise unto thee.
2 I will worship toward thy holy temple, and
praise thy name for thy lovingkindness and for
thy truth: for thou hast magnified thy word above
all thy name.
3 In the day when I cried thou answeredst me,
and strengthenedst me *with* strength in my soul.
4 All the kings of the earth shall praise thee, O
LORD, when they hear the words of thy mouth.
5 Yea, they shall sing in the ways of the LORD: for
great *is* the glory of the LORD.

---

gracious and compassionate nature of His love to the lowly, and the breadth of its blessings (vv. 23–25). Why is it good to praise God with songs that recount His great works in history and highlight His attributes?

2. **The refrain repeated in every verse implies that all God does throughout the world is soaked in His faithful love. Yet the focus of the psalm is upon the salvation of Israel, which is a type of salvation through Christ. In Him the love of God comes to its grandest expression and accomplishes its eternal purpose toward His elect people. What reasons from God's work in your own life motivate you to say to God, "Thy mercy endureth forever"?**

Psalm 137: *The psalmist laments the bitterness of being in exile.*

137:1 *remembered.* Chose to consider, took to heart (vv. 6–7). In captivity, they turned their minds back toward home. Babylon was a land of *rivers* (Euphrates, Tigris, Chebar, Ulai; see Jer. 51:13).

137:2 *harps.* Some sort of stringed instruments such as zithers or lyres.

137:3 *required of us a song*. Literally, they "asked us the words of a song." *they that wasted us.* Our mockers or tormenters. *mirth.* Jubilation.

137:4 *strange*. Foreign.

137:5 *forget.* Refuse to think about, primarily a volitional word. *cunning.* Art or skill.

137:7 *children of Edom.* Descendants of Esau of all ages. The Edomites were traditional enemies of Israel and often representative of all those who are hostile to God and His people (see Obadiah). *Rase.* Tear down.

137:8 *happy.* Possessing many benefits from God; often translated "blessed" (v. 9). Cyrus, who led the Medes and Persians to conquer Babylon, was specially helped by God to avenge His people (Isa. 45:1–4). *rewardeth thee as thou hast served us.* Pays you back according to what you did to us (94:23; Jer. 50:15; 51:56).

137:9 *dasheth thy little ones.* The murder of infants was not uncommon when one nation conquered a despised enemy (2 Kings 8:12; Hos. 10:14; 13:16; Nah. 3:10)—the fate of Babylon when the Medes and Persians conquered it (Isa. 13:16). This is a cry for justice against the cruelty of Babylon (2 Kings 25:7; Lam. 5:11–12), an implicit prayer that the wicked should receive what they have done to others (v. 8). Though God has a special kindness for children (Matt. 19:13–15), children are not exempt from the consequences of sin (Ex. 11:5; Matt. 24:19; Luke 23:27–29).

Thoughts for Personal/Family Worship: Psalm 137

1. **Sin brings inevitable consequences. Vengeance is the Lord's. Though the enemies of God's people may mock at their sufferings, one day the Lord will bring back on the wicked what they have done. Even as believers may weep over the persecuted church, they can also rejoice that Christ is coming and will make all things right. How can this hope enable us to wait patiently and not take personal revenge?**
2. **When God finally deals with sinners on judgment day, it will mean far worse than anything written here, for the Lord will banish them from all enjoyment of His goodness into the everlasting fires of hell. The Lord does not take lightly the persecution of His children. If you have harmed or mocked believers in Jesus Christ, repent quickly before it is too late. Pray for others who have fallen into this sin.**

Psalm 138: *David praises God for answered prayer and expresses confidence in the Lord's continuing mercy.*

138:1 *my whole heart.* The entirety of inner man, including the mind, affections, and will. *gods.* The word can refer to a divine being, but also human authorities (see note at 82:1). David resolved to sing God's praises before rulers (119:46).

138:2 *name.* All that God has revealed Himself to be. *lovingkindness.* Covenant love and loyalty. *magnified.* Exalted or made great. *above all thy name.* The Hebrew preposition can mean "according to" or "in addition to." God has honored His Word with His own glory so that people will receive it with absolute trust and humble fear (Isa. 66:1–2).

138:4 *All the kings . . . shall praise thee.* Christ's kingdom will encompass every nation and the greatest of men will honor the Lord (72:11; 102:15; Isa. 52:15; 53:12; Rev. 21:24).

6 Though the LORD *be* high, yet hath he respect
unto the lowly: but the proud he knoweth afar off.
7 Though I walk in the midst of trouble, thou
wilt revive me: thou shalt stretch forth thine hand
against the wrath of mine enemies, and thy right
hand shall save me.
8 The LORD will perfect *that which* concerneth
me: thy mercy, O LORD, *endureth* for ever: forsake
not the works of thine own hands.

PSALM 139

To the chief Musician, A Psalm of David.

1 O LORD, thou hast searched me, and known
me.
2 Thou knowest my downsitting and mine upris-
ing, thou understandest my thought afar off.
3 Thou compassest my path and my lying down,
and art acquainted *with* all my ways.
4 For *there is* not a word in my tongue, *but,* lo, O
LORD, thou knowest it altogether.
5 Thou hast beset me behind and before, and laid
thine hand upon me.
6 *Such* knowledge *is* too wonderful for me; it is
high, I cannot *attain* unto it.
7 Whither shall I go from thy spirit? or whither
shall I flee from thy presence?
8 If I ascend up into heaven, thou *art* there: if I
make my bed in hell, behold, thou *art there.*
9 *If* I take the wings of the morning, *and* dwell in
the uttermost parts of the sea;
10 Even there shall thy hand lead me, and thy
right hand shall hold me.
11 If I say, Surely the darkness shall cover me;
even the night shall be light about me.
12 Yea, the darkness hideth not from thee; but
the night shineth as the day: the darkness and the
light *are* both alike *to thee.*
13 For thou hast possessed my reins: thou hast
covered me in my mother's womb.
14 I will praise thee; for I am fearfully *and*
wonderfully made: marvellous *are* thy works; and
that my soul knoweth right well.
15 My substance was not hid from thee, when I
was made in secret, *and* curiously wrought in the
lowest parts of the earth.
16 Thine eyes did see my substance, yet being
unperfect; and in thy book all *my members* were
written, *which* in continuance were fashioned,
when *as yet there was* none of them.
17 How precious also are thy thoughts unto me,
O God! how great is the sum of them!
18 *If* I should count them, they are more in

138:6 *high . . . lowly.* God's very majesty moves Him to give grace to the humble (Isa. 57:15).
138:7 *revive.* Keep alive.
138:8 *perfect.* Bring to completion His purposes. *mercy.* Same word as "lovingkindness" (v. 2). *works of thine own hands.* God's people are His workmanship (100:3; Eph. 2:10).

Thoughts for Personal/Family Worship: Psalm 138

1. **Christians must not fear to confess Christ before the world, and give praise to God in the presence of great men and women (Matt. 10:18,26,32–33). Though the rich, powerful, and celebrities of the world may be regarded as gods, they will die like all other men (82:6–7). They need to hear of the glories of the only true God, so that they can be saved and give Him the praise that He deserves. Is there anyone around whom you find it very hard to speak to about the Lord? Why is this? How can you overcome that fear?**
2. **God has chosen to invest His glory in His Word, not to make the Bible into God, but so that people will honor the Lord in the way they honor His Word. A mark of true conversion is receiving the Holy Scriptures not as the word of men, but as the powerful and authoritative Word of God (1 Thess. 2:13). How should this affect our attitude when we hear the preaching of God's Word? How should this affect the way that preachers study and proclaim the Word?**

Psalm 139: *David acknowledges God's infinite perfections and expresses his desire for their personal application.*

139:1 *searched.* Examined, studied.
139:2 *downsitting . . . uprising.* A pair of opposites expresses totality: God knows all our activities.
139:3 *compassest.* Surround. Hebrew, "winnow or sift," referring to God's evaluation. *art acquainted with.* Know intimately.
139:5 *beset.* Encircled or enclosed. *hand.* God's power, active in providence to rule all things.
139:6 *too wonderful.* God's *knowledge* is incomprehensible, beyond his ability to understand, because it is infinite (147:5; Job 21:22; Isa. 40:14,28).
139:7 *Whither.* Where, to what place.
139:8 *heaven . . . hell.* The opposite extremes of height and depth express all places; God is omnipresent or present in all places (1 Kings 8:27; Isa. 66:1; Jer. 23:23–24).
139:9 *morning . . . sea.* The east and west, another pair of opposites. *uttermost.* Most distant.
139:13 *possessed my reins.* Formed, created, and owns the kidneys, referring to the innermost being. *covered.* Wove or shaped, referring to God's creation of the embryo in the *womb.*
139:14 *fearfully and wonderfully made: marvellous.* A consideration of artistry and intricate design of each human being should provoke reverence, amazement, and praise to the Creator.
139:15 *My substance.* My bones or frame. *in secret.* In the secret place, referring to the womb. *curiously wrought.* Skillfully formed. *lowest parts of the earth.* Contrasting the lowly place of a woman's womb to the glorious heights of heaven where God dwells.
139:16 *my substance.* A different word than v. 15, here referring to the embryo. *unperfect.* Not yet formed completely. Life begins at conception. *thy book.* An image of God's knowledge and personal attention (56:8; Dan. 7:10; Mal. 3:16). *all my members were written, which in continuance were fashioned.* Literally, "all of them were written, the days formed" (*my members* is not in the Hebrew text). Before he was born, his life was already like a story completely written out by God (Jer. 1:5; Gal. 1:15).

number than the sand: when I awake, I am still with thee.
19 Surely thou wilt slay the wicked, O God: depart from me therefore, ye bloody men.
20 For they speak against thee wickedly, *and* thine enemies take *thy name* in vain.
21 Do not I hate them, O LORD, that hate thee? and am not I grieved with those that rise up against thee?
22 I hate them with perfect hatred: I count them mine enemies.
23 Search me, O God, and know my heart: try me, and know my thoughts:
24 And see if *there be any* wicked way in me, and lead me in the way everlasting.

PSALM 140

To the chief Musician, A Psalm of David.

1 DELIVER me, O LORD, from the evil man: preserve me from the violent man;
2 Which imagine mischiefs in *their* heart; continually are they gathered together *for* war.
3 They have sharpened their tongues like a serpent; adders' poison *is* under their lips. Selah.
4 Keep me, O LORD, from the hands of the wicked; preserve me from the violent man; who have purposed to overthrow my goings.
5 The proud have hid a snare for me, and cords; they have spread a net by the wayside; they have set gins for me. Selah.
6 I said unto the LORD, Thou *art* my God: hear the voice of my supplications, O LORD.
7 O GOD the Lord, the strength of my salvation, thou hast covered my head in the day of battle.
8 Grant not, O LORD, the desires of the wicked: further not his wicked device; *lest* they exalt themselves. Selah.
9 *As for* the head of those that compass me about, let the mischief of their own lips cover them.
10 Let burning coals fall upon them: let them be cast into the fire; into deep pits, that they rise not up again.
11 Let not an evil speaker be established in the earth: evil shall hunt the violent man to overthrow *him*.
12 I know that the LORD will maintain the cause of the afflicted, *and* the right of the poor.
13 Surely the righteous shall give thanks unto thy name: the upright shall dwell in thy presence.

139:19 *bloody men*. Men of bloods, the plural referring to their acts of violence and murder.
139:20 *take . . . in vain*. Treat as worthless or empty.
139:21–22 *hate*. Reject. The psalmist took sides with God against all who rejected Him.
139:23 *Search . . . know*. He prays for God to do what he already acknowledged God does (v. 1). This reflects his willing submission to God's will and his desire for divinely directed self-examination.
139:24 *lead me in the way everlasting*. The proper response to God's infinite knowledge is to pray submissively for God's leading—the inward teaching of the Spirit through the Word unto eternal life (23:3,6; 43:3; 73:24; 119:18).

Thoughts for Personal/Family Worship: Psalm 139

1. **This psalm is a wonderful example of the connection between theology and life. Doctrine should impact our hearts and affect the way that we live. Believing that God sees and knows everything comforts us because He therefore knows our needs and can supply them. However, this same truth challenges us, for nothing escapes His glance, not even our secret sins. Therefore we should be careful, walking in the fear of God. Here is the sum. Since God is omnipresent, He knows me personally. Since God is omnipresent, He is with me constantly. Since God is the Creator, He owns me completely. Since God is righteous, He demands my loyalty. Learn to factor God into all of life. Pick one of God's attributes mentioned in this psalm. What difference should it make in your life today?**
2. **Before Christ left to ascend into heaven, He sent His church to make disciples of all nations, and He promised, "I am with you alway, even unto the end of the world" (Matt. 28:20). Knowing that Christ is with us, indeed that His special presence is promised to every gathering of the true church (Matt. 18:20), is a great comfort as we do His work in the world. How could that encourage people to move to other locations, even to other nations, in order to advance the kingdom of God there?**

Psalm 140: *David prays for protection and expresses his confidence in God's vindication.*

140:2 *Which imagine mischiefs*. Who plan evil things.
140:3 *adders' poison is under their lips*. The corruption of fallen mankind infects human speech with hidden evil such as hatred, deceit, and pride (cited Rom. 3:13; cf. James 3:2–12).
140:5 *gins*. Traps.
140:8 *further not his wicked device*. Literally, "do not allow him to accomplish his plan."
140:9 *compass*. Surround. *mischief*. Trouble or evil.
140:11 *evil speaker*. Hebrew, "a man of tongue."
140:13 *name*. All that God has revealed Himself to be in His perfections.

Thoughts for Personal/Family Worship: Psalm 140

1. **Given that we live in a world where Satan is very active, we should at all times be vigilant. Believers cannot do without God for a single day, for only He can keep us in the evil day when we feel particularly under attack. He alone is a sovereign Protector. It is the greatest of comforts to have God on our side, maintaining our cause. Since He does not change, nor ever will, we have confidence for the future, even for the eternal future. Instead of being cast down, we should be abounding in hope. Spiritual alertness and optimistic hope are key motives to a life of continual prayer. If we rarely pray for God to defend us against evil, what does that say about us?**
2. **The words of fallen man are full of secret poison (v. 3; Rom. 3:13). One of the earliest signs of human depravity is sinful speech (58:3). Though many would deny it, Christ taught that our speech reveals our heart, and God will judge our spiritual condition in part by the patterns**

PSALM 141

A Psalm of David.

1 LORD, I cry unto thee: make haste unto me; give
ear unto my voice, when I cry unto thee.
2 Let my prayer be set forth before thee *as*
incense; *and* the lifting up of my hands *as* the
evening sacrifice.
3 Set a watch, O LORD, before my mouth; keep
the door of my lips.
4 Incline not my heart to *any* evil thing, to prac-
tise wicked works with men that work iniquity:
and let me not eat of their dainties.
5 Let the righteous smite me; *it shall be* a kindness:
and let him reprove me; *it shall be* an excellent oil,
which shall not break my head: for yet my prayer
also *shall be* in their calamities.
6 When their judges are overthrown in stony
places, they shall hear my words; for they are sweet.
7 Our bones are scattered at the grave's mouth,
as when one cutteth and cleaveth *wood* upon the
earth.
8 But mine eyes *are* unto thee, O GOD the Lord:
in thee is my trust; leave not my soul destitute.
9 Keep me from the snares *which* they have laid
for me, and the gins of the workers of iniquity.
10 Let the wicked fall into their own nets, whilst
that I withal escape.

PSALM 142

Maschil of David; A Prayer
when he was in the cave.

1 I CRIED unto the LORD with my voice; with my
voice unto the LORD did I make my supplication.
2 I poured out my complaint before him; I
shewed before him my trouble.
3 When my spirit was overwhelmed within me,
then thou knewest my path. In the way wherein I
walked have they privily laid a snare for me.
4 I looked on *my* right hand, and beheld, but
there was no man that would know me: refuge
failed me; no man cared for my soul.
5 I cried unto thee, O LORD: I said, Thou *art* my
refuge *and* my portion in the land of the living.
6 Attend unto my cry; for I am brought very
low: deliver me from my persecutors; for they are
stronger than I.
7 Bring my soul out of prison, that I may praise
thy name: the righteous shall compass me about;
for thou shalt deal bountifully with me.

of our talk (Matt. 12:34–37). Examine how you talk to people, praying that God will reveal to you any pride, sexual lust, greed, sinful anger, hatred, and lying. How does the way we talk to each other show that we need Jesus Christ to save us from sin?

Psalm 141: *David prays for God to hear his petitions and for protection from the wicked.*

141:1 *make haste.* Hurry. *give ear.* Take notice.
141:2 *as incense.* Sweet-smelling smoke rose from the altar of incense just outside the most holy place, near the ark of the covenant (Ex. 30:1–10). This was symbolic of prayer (Rev. 5:8; 8:3–4). *lifting up of my hands.* A gesture associated with dependent prayer (28:2; Ex. 17:11).
141:4 *Incline not my heart.* Turn my thoughts, desires, and choices away from sin and draw them out toward obedience (119:36). *dainties.* Delicacies. A prayer that he will not be led to temptation (Matt. 6:13).
141:5 David acknowledges the benefits of criticism from the godly (Lev. 19:17; Prov. 27:5–6).
141:8 *my trust.* My place of refuge.
141:9 *gins.* Traps.
141:10 *I withal escape.* I pass by altogether or safely.

Thoughts for Personal/Family Worship: Psalm 141

1. **Prayer is vital and must never be neglected, particularly in difficult times. The storms of life should always drive us into the harbor of God's presence. Notice what David asked God to give him: salvation from sin, accountability from godly friends, rescue from the traps of the world, and judgment upon the wicked. How often do you pray for such things?**
2. **Comparing prayer to incense is most instructive and encouraging. The smoke arising from the altar would waft over the veil entering the inner sanctuary that represented the immediate presence of God. So it is that prayer is the earthly means whereby we may enter into God's presence. Prayer takes us as close to God as we can get this side of the veil, in this life. The comparison of prayer to incense also reminds us that all our prayers depend upon the intercession of the High Priest, Jesus Christ. His intercessions fill the prayers of a believer with a delightful fragrance to God, for Christ obeyed God perfectly and paid for our sins completely. True prayer must always be offered to God by faith in Him. What confidence does it give you to know that Christ is interceding for you (Rom. 8:31–39)?**

Psalm 142: *David acknowledges the Lord's help and prays for renewed deliverance from trouble.*

Title *David . . . in the cave.* Composed either in Adullum or Engedi where David took refuge from Saul (1 Sam. 22:1–2; 24:3)
142:1 *make my supplication.* Plead for favor or grace.
142:2 *complaint.* Or lament.
142:3 *privily laid a snare.* Hid or concealed a trapping net.
142:5 *Thou art my refuge and my portion.* When our friends fail us, the believer may rest in knowing that the Lord is all the protection and provision that he needs (27:10; 73:25–26).
142:7 *out of prison.* Perhaps a reference to the cave, but more likely figuratively of his distressed condition. *compass.* Surround.

Thoughts for Personal/Family Worship: Psalm 142

In the worst of life's troubles, God is only a prayer away from us and if we turn to Him, He will make known to us His power and comfort. Remember, God is a present help in times of trouble. It is a relief to realize that God knows our path and feels concern and sympathy for us in this state. Furthermore, knowing exactly where and how we are, He

PSALM 143

A Psalm of David.

1 HEAR my prayer, O LORD, give ear to my
supplications: in thy faithfulness answer me, *and*
in thy righteousness.
2 And enter not into judgment with thy servant:
for in thy sight shall no man living be justified.
3 For the enemy hath persecuted my soul; he
hath smitten my life down to the ground; he hath
made me to dwell in darkness, as those that have
been long dead.
4 Therefore is my spirit overwhelmed within me;
my heart within me is desolate.
5 I remember the days of old; I meditate on all
thy works; I muse on the work of thy hands.
6 I stretch forth my hands unto thee: my soul
thirsteth after thee, as a thirsty land. Selah.
7 Hear me speedily, O LORD: my spirit faileth:
hide not thy face from me, lest I be like unto them
that go down into the pit.
8 Cause me to hear thy lovingkindness in the
morning; for in thee do I trust: cause me to know
the way wherein I should walk; for I lift up my
soul unto thee.
9 Deliver me, O LORD, from mine enemies: I flee
unto thee to hide me.
10 Teach me to do thy will; for thou *art* my God: thy
spirit *is* good; lead me into the land of uprightness.
11 Quicken me, O LORD, for thy name's sake:
for thy righteousness' sake bring my soul out of
trouble.
12 And of thy mercy cut off mine enemies, and
destroy all them that afflict my soul: for I *am* thy
servant.

PSALM 144

A Psalm of David.

1 BLESSED *be* the LORD my strength, which
teacheth my hands to war, *and* my fingers to fight:
2 My goodness, and my fortress; my high tower,
and my deliverer; my shield, and *he* in whom I
trust; who subdueth my people under me.
3 LORD, what *is* man, that thou takest knowledge
of him! *or* the son of man, that thou makest
account of him!
4 Man is like to vanity: his days *are* as a shadow
that passeth away.
5 Bow thy heavens, O LORD, and come down:
touch the mountains, and they shall smoke.
6 Cast forth lightning, and scatter them: shoot
out thine arrows, and destroy them.
7 Send thine hand from above; rid me, and de-
liver me out of great waters, from the hand of
strange children;

will draw near to help. Friends may let us down; but God will never fail those who trust in Him. Christ understands exactly how it feels to be alone (Matt. 26:31,56), and in His sympathy He helps all who come to God through Him (Heb. 4:15–16). How will hoping in God's faithfulness to His covenant promises affect the attitude of our prayers?

Psalm 143: *In apparent hopelessness, David prays for speedy help and divine guidance.*

143:1 *supplications.* Pleas for grace or favor.

143:2 *shall no man living be justified.* If God judged us by our works or personal worthiness according to the rigor of His law, then He would declare no one righteous (130:3; Rom. 3:20; Gal. 2:16). Justification is by grace alone through faith in Christ alone (Gen. 15:6; Rom. 3:22–26).

143:3 *my soul.* The whole person, "me" (vv. 6,11–12).

143:5 *remember.* Choose to consider and take to heart. *meditate . . . muse on.* Think about, talk to oneself about.

143:6 *stretch forth my hands.* A gesture of prayer (44:20; Ex. 9:29,33; 1 Kings 8:22)

143:7 *hide not thy face.* A gesture expressing displeasure.

143:8 *lovingkindness.* Covenant loyalty and love. *trust.* Place confidence in for safety and security. *I lift up my soul.* An expression of total dependence (25:1).

143:10 *Teach me to do thy will.* Not only are we unable to justify ourselves (v. 2), but we also cannot sanctify ourselves apart from the leading of the Holy Spirit (*thy spirit*) who teaches the inner person to obey (Rom. 8:7–9,12–14; Gal. 5:16–26).

143:11 *Quicken.* Cause to live, or preserve alive.

143:12 *mercy.* Same word as "lovingkindness" in v. 8.

Thoughts for Personal/Family Worship: Psalm 143

We pray with hands stretched out to heaven (v. 6) and souls lifted up to God (v. 8) because we are like beggars seeking everything from Him. As human beings who fell into sin with our first father, Adam, all our prayers are ultimately prayers for Christ, to whom the Father joins sinners when He calls them to faith in Him (1 Cor. 1:23–24,30). We need wisdom from God, and so we must set our minds upon God's Word (v. 5) with prayers for Christ to be our *wisdom*. We need justification in God's sight and cannot obtain a righteous status by our own merit (v. 2), so we must pray for Christ to be our *righteousness*. We need to become obedient to God's will, so we must pray for Christ to be our *sanctification* through the Holy Spirit (v. 10). We pray for deliverance from enemies, persecutors, and death (vv. 3,7,9,12), and Christ is our *redemption*. Of which of these do you most feel in need right now? How can you seek for what you need in Christ?

Psalm 144: *Amazed at God's concern for man, David prays for protection and promises praise.*

144:1 *Blessed.* A declaration of the praises belonging to Him. *teacheth my hands to war.* God is the source of all military power and skill (v. 10; 18:34).

144:2 *goodness.* Covenant loyalty and love, elsewhere translated mercy, kindness, or lovingkindness. *trust.* Seek or take refuge.

144:3 *what is man.* Man's smallness and brevity of life shows the greatness of God's love that He would be concerned about such a creature (8:4; Job 7:17).

144:4 *vanity.* Breath, that which is unsubstantial and temporary (James 4:14).

144:5 *Bow thy heavens.* See note at 18:9. *they shall smoke.* God's holy presence disrupts this fallen and sin-cursed world (97:5; Isa. 64:1–2).

8 Whose mouth speaketh vanity, and their right hand *is* a right hand of falsehood.
9 I will sing a new song unto thee, O God: upon a psaltery *and* an instrument of ten strings will I sing praises unto thee.
10 *It is he* that giveth salvation unto kings: who delivereth David his servant from the hurtful sword.
11 Rid me, and deliver me from the hand of strange children, whose mouth speaketh vanity, and their right hand *is* a right hand of falsehood:
12 That our sons *may be* as plants grown up in their youth; *that* our daughters *may be* as corner stones, polished *after* the similitude of a palace:
13 *That* our garners *may be* full, affording all manner of store: *that* our sheep may bring forth thousands and ten thousands in our streets:
14 *That* our oxen *may be* strong to labour; *that there be* no breaking in, nor going out; that *there be* no complaining in our streets.
15 Happy *is that* people, that is in such a case: *yea,* happy *is that* people, whose God *is* the LORD.

PSALM 145

David's *Psalm* of praise.

1 I WILL extol thee, my God, O king; and I will bless thy name for ever and ever.
2 Every day will I bless thee; and I will praise thy name for ever and ever.
3 Great *is* the LORD, and greatly to be praised; and his greatness *is* unsearchable.
4 One generation shall praise thy works to another, and shall declare thy mighty acts.
5 I will speak of the glorious honour of thy majesty, and of thy wondrous works.
6 And *men* shall speak of the might of thy terrible acts: and I will declare thy greatness.
7 They shall abundantly utter the memory of thy great goodness, and shall sing of thy righteousness.
8 The LORD *is* gracious, and full of compassion; slow to anger, and of great mercy.
9 The LORD *is* good to all: and his tender mercies *are* over all his works.
10 All thy works shall praise thee, O LORD; and thy saints shall bless thee.
11 They shall speak of the glory of thy kingdom, and talk of thy power;
12 To make known to the sons of men his mighty acts, and the glorious majesty of his kingdom.
13 Thy kingdom *is* an everlasting kingdom, and thy dominion *endureth* throughout all generations.
14 The LORD upholdeth all that fall, and raiseth up all *those that be* bowed down.
15 The eyes of all wait upon thee; and thou givest

144:7 *strange children.* Literally, "sons of a foreigner," referring to Gentile unbelievers (v. 11).
144:8 *vanity.* Worthlessness or emptiness of speech (v. 11), a different word than v. 4.
144:9 *psaltery.* Some sort of stringed instrument.
144:10 *salvation.* Or victory. *David his servant.* The language of the covenant relationship between the anointed king and his Lord (1 Chron. 17:4,7,17–19,23–27).
144:12 *sons . . . as plants.* See note at 128:3. *polished after the similitude.* Carved according to the model. The images communicate vitality, strength, and beauty.
144:13 *garners.* Granaries or barns. *affording.* Producing or furnishing. These blessings were promised to Israel if it kept God's covenant (Lev. 26:3–13; Deut. 28:1–14).
144:14 *complaining.* Cries of lamentation.
144:15 *Happy.* Possessing great benefits from God; elsewhere translated "blessed" (1:1; 33:12).

Thoughts for Personal/Family Worship: Psalm 144

1. **Trust in the Lord goes hand in hand with a sense of how small and insignificant we are (vv. 2–4). When our hearts and mouths are full of boasts about ourselves, it is hard to sing God's praises with much interest. However, when we see ourselves as sinners quickly passing from this earth to face judgment, then we will count ourselves blessed only if the Lord is our God and we are in covenant relationship with Him through faith in Jesus Christ. How can meditating on the vanity of man (v. 4) help you to trust in the Lord and give all the glory to Him?**
2. **David, the divinely empowered warrior (v. 1), was a shadow and type of Christ. In an amazing act of condescension, the Son of God became a mortal man (v. 4). He placed Himself in a position of complete dependence upon the Father (v. 2), who amply supplied Him with the Spirit to overcome the Devil. Christ is the Servant of the Lord (v. 10). The Lord Jesus perfectly obeyed the law of God, winning the riches of glory promised to covenant keepers as Israel never could (vv. 12–15). Now His spiritual offspring inherit the blessings He deserves. Christ will tear open the skies and come down with fire and glory to destroy His enemies, save believers from their persecutors, and bring them into His blessing. Can you say with the church of Jesus Christ, "Happy is that people, whose God is the LORD" (v. 15)?**

Psalm 145: *David praises God extolling His manifold perfections.*
145:1 *extol.* Exalt. *bless.* Declare the praises and honors belonging to Him (v. 10). *name.* All that God has revealed Himself to be in the totality of His perfections (also vv. 2,21).
145:3 *unsearchable.* Beyond human comprehension (147:5; Job 36:26).
145:4 *One generation . . . to another.* Believers must teach their children about the Lord (78:1–8), and one way to do this is for children to hear their parents *praise* the Lord.
145:5 *wondrous works.* Extraordinary, miraculous acts.
145:6 *terrible.* Inspiring fear and awe. *declare.* Recount.
145:7 *abundantly utter.* Hebrew, "to gush forth" (45:1).
145:8 *slow to anger.* Hebrew idiom for patience, literally, "long of nostrils," expressing the long time for the nose to turn red in anger. *mercy.* Covenant loyalty and love. The psalmist confesses God's nature as He revealed Himself to Moses (Ex. 34:6).
145:9 *tender mercies.* Expressions of compassion.
145:10 *thy saints.* Those made holy by God's covenant love.
145:15 *wait.* Hope expectantly, not in resignation. *meat.* Food of any kind.

them their meat in due season.
16 Thou openest thine hand, and satisfiest the
desire of every living thing.
17 The LORD *is* righteous in all his ways, and holy
in all his works.
18 The LORD *is* nigh unto all them that call upon
him, to all that call upon him in truth.
19 He will fulfil the desire of them that fear him:
he also will hear their cry, and will save them.
20 The LORD preserveth all them that love him:
but all the wicked will he destroy.
21 My mouth shall speak the praise of the LORD:
and let all flesh bless his holy name for ever and
ever.

PSALM 146

1 PRAISE ye the LORD. Praise the LORD, O my
soul.
2 While I live will I praise the LORD: I will sing
praises unto my God while I have any being.
3 Put not your trust in princes, *nor* in the son of
man, in whom *there is* no help.
4 His breath goeth forth, he returneth to his
earth; in that very day his thoughts perish.
5 Happy *is he* that *hath* the God of Jacob for his
help, whose hope *is* in the LORD his God:
6 Which made heaven, and earth, the sea, and all
that therein *is*: which keepeth truth for ever:
7 Which executeth judgment for the oppressed:
which giveth food to the hungry. The LORD
looseth the prisoners:
8 The LORD openeth *the eyes of* the blind: the
LORD raiseth them that are bowed down: the
LORD loveth the righteous:
9 The LORD preserveth the strangers; he relieveth
the fatherless and widow: but the way of the
wicked he turneth upside down.
10 The LORD shall reign for ever, *even* thy God,
O Zion, unto all generations. Praise ye the LORD.

PSALM 147

1 PRAISE ye the LORD: for *it is* good to sing praises
unto our God; for *it is* pleasant; *and* praise is
comely.
2 The LORD doth build up Jerusalem: he gathereth
together the outcasts of Israel.
3 He healeth the broken in heart, and bindeth up
their wounds.

145:18 *nigh.* Near. God is present with those who seek Him in humble faith in order that He may comfort and rescue them (34:18; James 4:8).
145:20 *love.* Choose to set affections and desires on.
145:21 *all flesh.* All mankind.

146:5 *Happy.* Possessing great benefits from God; elsewhere translated "blessed" (1:1). *hope.* Confident expectation.
146:6 *keepeth truth.* Acts faithfully according to His Word.
146:9 *strangers.* Those living as resident aliens (Deut. 10:18–19).

Thoughts for Personal/Family Worship: Psalm 145

1. **Meditation upon God is vital to spiritual life, for as we comprehend more of God, the knowledge of Him will provide matter for more excellent praise. This psalm offers a lyrical catalog of God's attributes. In what verses do you find reference to the following attributes: greatness, incomprehensibility, power, majesty, fearsomeness, goodness, righteousness, grace, compassion, patience, faithful love, glory, kingdom, eternality, presence, and holiness? Focus on one of these. What does it mean? How has God displayed it through His works in Jesus Christ?**
2. **Singing praise is a means of instruction and edification. It is good for this generation to sing God's praise to the next; and therefore we should encourage little children to be present in the congregation. Let them know how His love for us draws forth our love for Him and how we have learned to look to Him for all our needs. Then shall the prayer of the ages be answered: "Hallowed be thy name." What opportunities do you have to pass on the joy of worship to the next generation?**

Psalm 146: *The psalmist praises God and warns against putting confidence in man.*

146:1 *Praise ye the LORD.* Hebrew, *hallelujah.* Each of the remaining psalms begins and ends with this exhortation. *O my soul.* Refers to the whole person (103:1).
146:3 *trust.* Confidence for security and safety. *princes.* Noblemen, not necessarily royalty.

Thoughts for Personal/Family Worship: Psalm 146

Only believers know true happiness. The world thinks our religion is gloomy and miserable, but they could not be more mistaken. We are the happiest people. God is our God. He is the all-powerful Lord of all His creation. He is faithful to all His promises. He acts with justice and compassion for the oppressed. He loves those who walk in faith and obedience. His kingdom will never end. In every way, the Lord is the hope and joy of believers. For all His qualities belong to them and serve their good if they are joined to Jesus Christ by a living faith. As a result, their happiness is far deeper, more stable, and more satisfying than that of those who trust in man. One of the best ways for believers to enjoy their happiness and demonstrate it to the watching world is by praising the Lord. Do you have a habit of praising God? Why or why not? How can you develop a habit of praising Him as long as you live?

Psalm 147: *The psalmist praises God for the many demonstrations of His goodness and power; this praise delights the Lord.*

147:1 *Praise ye the LORD.* Hebrew, *hallelujah* (v. 20). *pleasant.* Lovely, delightful, agreeable, or harmonious. *comely.* Beautiful.
147:2 *outcasts.* Those who have been scattered or banished.
147:3 *healeth the broken in heart.* The coming of the Lord to heal His people is closely connected to the ministry of Christ (Isa. 35:5–6; 61:1–3; Ezek. 34:16,23–24; Luke 7:19–23).

4 He telleth the number of the stars; he calleth them all by *their* names.
5 Great *is* our Lord, and of great power: his understanding *is* infinite.
6 The LORD lifteth up the meek: he casteth the wicked down to the ground.
7 Sing unto the LORD with thanksgiving; sing praise upon the harp unto our God:
8 Who covereth the heaven with clouds, who prepareth rain for the earth, who maketh grass to grow upon the mountains.
9 He giveth to the beast his food, *and* to the young ravens which cry.
10 He delighteth not in the strength of the horse: he taketh not pleasure in the legs of a man.
11 The LORD taketh pleasure in them that fear him, in those that hope in his mercy.
12 Praise the LORD, O Jerusalem; praise thy God, O Zion.
13 For he hath strengthened the bars of thy gates; he hath blessed thy children within thee.
14 He maketh peace *in* thy borders, *and* filleth thee with the finest of the wheat.
15 He sendeth forth his commandment *upon* earth: his word runneth very swiftly.
16 He giveth snow like wool: he scattereth the hoarfrost like ashes.
17 He casteth forth his ice like morsels: who can stand before his cold?
18 He sendeth out his word, and melteth them: he causeth his wind to blow, *and* the waters flow.
19 He sheweth his word unto Jacob, his statutes and his judgments unto Israel.
20 He hath not dealt so with any nation: and *as for his* judgments, they have not known them. Praise ye the LORD.

PSALM 148

1 PRAISE ye the LORD. Praise ye the LORD from the heavens: praise him in the heights.
2 Praise ye him, all his angels: praise ye him, all his hosts.
3 Praise ye him, sun and moon: praise him, all ye stars of light.
4 Praise him, ye heavens of heavens, and ye waters that *be* above the heavens.
5 Let them praise the name of the LORD: for he commanded, and they were created.

147:4 *telleth.* Recounts.
147:5 *his understanding is infinite.* Literally, "for His intelligence, there is no number." God's knowledge is off the scale, and thus beyond human calculation (Isa. 40:28).
147:6 *lifteth up the meek.* Relieves or restores the humiliated or afflicted.
147:7 *harp.* Some sort of stringed instrument such as a zither.
147:8–9 *rain . . . food.* The Lord governs the course of nature by His providence (104:10–23), and therefore should be praised and thanked for all He gives us (vv. 12–14).
147:10 *horse . . . legs.* Sources of human strength, often relied upon by the self-sufficient; the images may point to the cavalry and infantry of an army.
147:11 *fear him.* Reverence and worship God for who He is and seek to live all of life in a way that pleases Him. *hope in his mercy.* Wait with confident expectation in His covenant love and loyalty; an expression of faith.
147:13 *strengthened the bars of thy gates.* Secured the locking mechanism on the entrance of the city, an image of safety.
147:15 *his commandment . . . his word.* Not the Scriptures, but God's providential will that powerfully controls all things, including the weather (vv. 16–18), just as He made them (148:5).
147:17 *morsels.* Fragments, most likely referring to hailstones.
147:20 *judgments.* Laws of justice. *have not known them.* Though the general revelation of God's creation testifies to all mankind of His greatness and goodness (19:1–6; 104:14–15), the special revelation of His Word was given only to Israel ("Jacob," v. 19), and thus most nations perished in ignorance of God (Rom. 2:12; 10:14). The selectiveness of His revelation highlights the wonder of His grace to His people, for they are no better than others (cf. Deut. 9:4–6; Eph. 2:1–5; Titus 3:3–5).

Thoughts for Personal/Family Worship: Psalm 147

1. **If the Lord has blessed us, praise is the most suitable response; and the more blessed we feel, the more our hearts will well up with gratitude and the more we will want to find vent in greater praise. The Lord is looking after the whole world and since His people are more precious to Him than everything else, we can be assured that He will take special care of us. Since His compassions are new every morning, what do you need to stop worrying about, and for what should you start trusting God?**
2. **The greatest gift from God is His Word. Even today many millions of peoples do not have access to the Scriptures in a language they can understand. Yet how precious is His Word. It is powerful, for it is the Word of Him who rules all things. It is full of wisdom, for it is the Word of Him who is infinite in understanding. It is a message of hope and salvation, for it is the Word of the compassionate and merciful God. If you have a Bible that you can read in your own language, then thank God for it, read it daily, attend the worship service of a church where it is faithfully preached, and pray that God would use you to help others to receive this invaluable gift of God's Word.**

Psalm 148: *The psalmist calls for universal praise to the Lord.*

148:1 *Praise ye the LORD.* Hebrew, *hallelujah* (also v. 14). Scripture recognizes three *heavens* (2 Cor. 12:2): the air with its clouds and birds (78:26; 104:12); the region of sun, moon, and stars in outer space (8:3; 19:1–6); and the place where God dwells in His glory with the angels (2:4; 11:4; 103:19–20; 123:1).
148:2 *hosts.* Armies, either referring to the angels specifically or all creation generally. All serve Him and are under His command.
148:3–4 *Praise ye him, sun and moon.* The psalmist rejoices that even God's nonhuman creation glorifies Him (19:1–6; 98:7–8; 150:6; Rev. 5:13). *waters . . . above the heavens.* Clouds in the sky from which comes rain (Gen. 1:6–8).
148:5 *name.* All that God has revealed Himself to be in the totality of His perfections (v. 13). *he commanded, and they were created.* God made the universe by the mere power of His will (33:6,9; Gen. 1; Heb. 11:3).

6 He hath also stablished them for ever and ever:
he hath made a decree which shall not pass.
7 Praise the LORD from the earth, ye dragons, and
all deeps:
8 Fire, and hail; snow, and vapour; stormy wind
fulfilling his word:
9 Mountains, and all hills; fruitful trees, and all
cedars:
10 Beasts, and all cattle; creeping things, and
flying fowl:
11 Kings of the earth, and all people; princes, and
all judges of the earth:
12 Both young men, and maidens; old men, and
children:
13 Let them praise the name of the LORD: for
his name alone is excellent; his glory *is* above the
earth and heaven.
14 He also exalteth the horn of his people, the
praise of all his saints; *even* of the children of
Israel, a people near unto him. Praise ye the LORD.

PSALM 149

1 PRAISE ye the LORD. Sing unto the LORD a new
song, *and* his praise in the congregation of saints.
2 Let Israel rejoice in him that made him: let the
children of Zion be joyful in their King.
3 Let them praise his name in the dance: let them
sing praises unto him with the timbrel and harp.
4 For the LORD taketh pleasure in his people: he
will beautify the meek with salvation.
5 Let the saints be joyful in glory: let them sing
aloud upon their beds.
6 *Let* the high *praises* of God *be* in their mouth,
and a twoedged sword in their hand;
7 To execute vengeance upon the heathen, *and*
punishments upon the people;
8 To bind their kings with chains, and their
nobles with fetters of iron;
9 To execute upon them the judgment written:
this honour have all his saints. Praise ye the LORD.

148:6 *stablished.* Established. *not pass.* It will not pass away or be altered (89:37; 119:90–91).
148:7 *dragons.* Some sort of large sea creature. *deeps.* The seas.
148:11 *princes.* Those in authority, not sons of royalty.
148:13 *his glory is above the earth and heaven.* Creation testifies that the Creator must be greater than all we see (8:1,9). Since we are part of creation, God is greater than the highest praise we can give Him (Neh. 9:5–6).
148:14 *horn.* A symbol of power, pointing to Christ as a horn of salvation (Luke 1:69). *saints.* Those who are the recipients of covenant love and loyalty and thus holy.

Thoughts for Personal/Family Worship: Psalm 148

1. **All creation praises God and testifies to His glory, from the mightiest angel to the smallest bird. How much more should mankind, the apex of creation, praise Him! Even more so, His redeemed people ought to praise His name. Let us seek to excel in this most excellent work. Praise should be integral to both private and public worship. When in private prayer, begin with praise and not with a list of your needs and requests. In the worship of God's house, make a joyful noise. We should never be at a loss in the praise of His name. Are you eager to praise the Lord?**
2. **A fundamental belief of Christianity is the absolute distinction between the Creator and His creation. There are great differences among what God has created, whether angels, stars, sea monsters, mountains, cattle, kings, or infants. However, they all fall into one category: those which were made by God and therefore should praise Him (v. 5). Worship belongs to God alone, for "his name alone is excellent; his glory is above the earth and heaven" (v. 13). On the one hand, this should impress us with a humbling realization that we exist for His glory. On the other hand, it shows us that Christ our Savior is God, for He is to be worshiped (Heb. 1:6; Rev. 5:8–14). How are we tempted to worship part of God's creation rather than the Creator?**

Psalm 149: *The psalmist exhorts God's people to praise because He saves and protects them.*

149:1 *Praise ye the LORD.* Hebrew, *hallelujah* (v. 9). *new song.* See 33:3; 40:3; 96:1; 98:1; 144:9; 149:1; Isa. 42:10; Rev. 5:9; 14:3. *saints.* Those made holy by God's covenant love and loyalty (vv. 5,9).
149:2 *children of Zion.* Idiomatic expression for the people of God's kingdom.
149:3 *name.* All that God has revealed about Himself, often expressed as His attributes or perfections. *dance.* Not an expression of sensuality, but a feature of Israel's old covenant worship on occasions of great joy (Ex. 15:20–21; 2 Sam. 6:14,16). *timbrel.* Some sort of hand drum or tambourine. *harp.* A zither or some sort of stringed instrument.
149:4 *beautify.* Make lovely or glorious. *meek.* Weak, afflicted, humble. The Lord takes pleasure in taking those with nothing but needs and making them beautiful and honored (Isa. 61:3,10; Eph. 5:25–27).
149:5 *beds.* Can refer to a place of lodging.
149:8 *fetters.* Shackles.

Thoughts for Personal/Family Worship: Psalm 149

1. **We find delight in people who already appear beautiful or honorable. It is a notable mark of God's grace that He delights to take the poor, humiliated, and ugly who trust in Him and make them lovely and glorious (v. 4). He is a King who does not take riches from His people, but joyfully gives to them. How does Christ beautify His people with the graces of justification, sanctification, and glorification? How should this motivate us to praise Him?**
2. **Zeal for God's praise motivates God's people to fight against all powers that oppose His kingdom (vv. 6–9). In the old covenant, this required physical violence to preserve the nation of Israel and bring God's judgments on the wicked (18:34–44; 101:5,8; 144:1). Since Christ abolished Israel's earthly theocracy (Matt. 21:43) and established a heavenly and spiritual kingdom (John 18:36–37), this zeal expresses itself not in physical force but in sacrificial efforts to bring the Word of God to all nations (2 Cor. 10:3–6; Eph. 6:10–18; Heb. 4:12), until Christ returns to destroy His enemies (Rev. 19:15–21). How does your praise of God translate into zealous action to spread His Word throughout the world? If you are not a preacher, how are you using your vocation for His glory and working with the church to fulfill the gospel mission?**

PSALM 150

1 PRAISE ye the LORD. Praise God in his sanctuary:
praise him in the firmament of his power.
2 Praise him for his mighty acts: praise him ac-
cording to his excellent greatness.
3 Praise him with the sound of the trumpet:
praise him with the psaltery and harp.
4 Praise him with the timbrel and dance: praise
him with stringed instruments and organs.
5 Praise him upon the loud cymbals: praise him
upon the high sounding cymbals.
6 Let every thing that hath breath praise the
LORD. Praise ye the LORD.

Psalm 150: ***The psalmist calls for praise with music.***

150:1 *Praise ye the LORD.* Hebrew, *hallelujah* (v. 6). *sanctuary.* The temple, the symbolic dwelling place of God. *firmament.* Expanse, the heavens (19:1; Gen. 1:6–8, 14–17). The earthly temple and heaven are counterparts as centers of God's praise.
150:2 The two great reasons to worship God which form the twin focal points of our praise are God's works (*mighty acts*) and His nature (*excellent greatness*; cf. Ex. 15:10–11).
150:3–5 *sound of the trumpet.* The blast of the horn. *psaltery and harp.* Some sorts of stringed instruments. *timbrel.* Some sort of hand drum or tambourine. *dance.* See note at 149:3. *organs.* A long flute or some sort of wind instrument. *cymbals.* Clanging pans or some sort of percussion instruments.
150:6 *every thing that hath breath.* The call to worship goes out to all mankind, indeed all of God's creation (Ps. 148).

Thoughts for Personal/Family Worship: Psalm 150

1. Song is an integral component of worship and should be offered to God with joy and reverence. The command that God be praised with a orchestra of instruments (vv. 3–5) reflects the old covenant economy of temple worship instituted by David, who appointed the Levites to serve as musicians (1 Chron. 15:16,24). No such requirement is made in the new covenant, where God's sanctuary is not a building where a nation meets, but a people gathered in local congregations (1 Cor. 3:16; Eph. 2:21–22). The New Testament directs its instructions for worship at the hearts and voices of the people as they are moved by God's Spirit (Eph. 5:18–20). Just as the Levites played a variety of instruments in harmony, so God's people are diverse but worship in one Spirit through Christ (Eph. 2:18). How is your church like a spiritual orchestra, with each believer an instrument played by the Holy Spirit to praise the Father through the Son?
2. Our worship of God must revolve around His personal glory and amazing works (v. 2). This should shape the content of our songs, which should primarily focus upon the triune God and not our works or feelings. It should also direct the feeling with which we sing, for the glory of God should impress us with reverent fear and awe even as we rejoice in Him. There is no place for superficial lyrics, mindless repetition, or casual attitudes in the worship of God. Pray for a heart to praise Him and for such a filling of the Holy Spirit that this sacred work will be performed in a way that truly glorifies God.
3. It is fitting that the Psalter ends with a climactic call to praise God (v. 6). The Psalms take us through the full range of human experiences, but they center upon the glory of the Lord. They recount the history of God's people from creation through the second coming of Christ, yet in a way that constantly reminds us that all God does in Christ He does to the praise of His glory (Eph. 1:6,12,14). This is God's ultimate purpose for His creation. Have you embraced God's glory and praise as your ultimate purpose in life? If not, then your first act of worship must be to repent of your self-centeredness and idols, turn back to the living God, and trust in the Lord Jesus Christ to save you from your sins. If by grace God's glory has become your great aim, then devote yourself with all your might to living for His praise.

TRUST
IN
THE LORD
WITH
All Thine
HEART
&
LEAN NOT
UNTO
Thine Own
UNDERSTANDING

PROVERBS 3:5

INTRODUCTION TO THE BOOK OF PROVERBS

Authorship: The principal author of this book is King Solomon, the son of David (1:1; 10:1; 25:1). Solomon spoke no less than 3,000 proverbs (1 Kings 4:32), and this book contains about 800 of the ones which were divinely inspired. The section in chs. 25–29 is a compiled and edited selection of Solomon's proverbs, published over 240 years later by a committee of men appointed by King Hezekiah (Prov. 25:1).

However, Solomon was not the only author of the Proverbs. Internal evidence mentions those who are called collectively, "the wise" (22:17—24:34). Solomon may have collected these sayings from the godly wise men who came before him. Two further contributors are named as Agur the son of Jakeh (ch. 30) and the words of King Lemuel and his mother (ch. 31) though some interpreters identify him as Solomon.

Wisdom literature including proverbs and other genres was produced by various cultures in the Ancient Near East, such as the Egyptian texts *The Instruction of Ptahhotep* and *The Instruction of Amenemope*. However, the book of Proverbs is no mere compilation of sayings from other nations. The Lord gave to King Solomon great wisdom beyond that of any other man of his time (1 Kings 3:5–14; 4:29–34; 5:7,12; 10:1–9,23–24; 11:41). Proverbs consists of divine wisdom revealed by the "mouth" of God (Prov. 2:6). Although Proverbs contains some truths generally recognized by people, it presents these truths in a perspective where the Lord is central and supreme (1:7) and with a perfection of truth guaranteed by God (30:5–6). The New Testament quotes the book of Proverbs as Holy Scripture (compare 3:11–12 with Heb. 12:5–6; Prov. 3:34 with James 4:6 and 1 Peter 5:5; Prov. 11:31 with 1 Peter 4:18; Prov. 25:21–22 with Rom. 12:20; and Prov. 26:11 with 2 Peter 2:22).

Date: Solomon ruled Israel from about 970 to 931 BC, during which he would have spoken his proverbs. The compiled part by the committee of King Hezekiah's men would have been done during his reign, from about 716 to 687 BC.

Theme: The wise life governed by the fear of God and the aim to please Him (1:7; 9:10).

Purpose: To guide God's people in practical religion that applies faith in God's promises and obedience to God's law to every sphere of life.

Synopsis: *The Contribution of Proverbs to Redemptive Revelation*

Proverbs is instruction for the covenant people of God, addressing the individual rather than the nation as a whole. This means the national matters connected to Israel do not often surface. Often framed as a father's instructions to a youthful son, Proverbs greatly assists Christian parents in training their children (Eph. 6:4) and also leaders in training the church as the family of God. It is filled with instructions to preserve God's people individually and their testimony. In many ways, Proverbs is a primer for sanctification, giving directions and illustrations of how to die to sin and live to righteousness. It shows how true religion integrates into our attitudes and actions in a way that touches family, friends, the workplace, etc.

Overriding everything is living in the fear of God, which can be summed up as living in the conscious awareness of God as He has revealed Himself in His holiness, factoring Him into every situation and circumstance of life. To live in the fear of God is to live in the reality of God, which has a profound effect both on worship and ethics. Proverbs is a blueprint for the practice of true religion. Significantly, this is summed up in terms of wisdom. In Hebrew, the word "wisdom" means "skill" or "ability" and has application in various spheres (Ex. 28:3; 31:3–6). In Proverbs, wisdom is the skill or ability to live in a way that pleases God and allows us to enjoy His blessing.

The starting place of this kind of wisdom is Christ (Col. 2:3; 2 Tim. 3:15), and like every book of the Old Testament, Proverbs speaks of Jesus Christ (Luke 24:44). Christ identified Himself as the divine wisdom (Luke 7:34–35; 11:49), the One greater than Solomon (Luke 11:31) who gives wisdom to His people (Luke 21:15). God has united His people to Christ by their effectual calling so that He is their wisdom, particularly in His crucifixion for their sins (1 Cor. 1:23–24,30). God's wisdom in Christ is alien to this world and only received through the Holy Spirit (1 Cor. 2).

Christ's presence in Proverbs is especially evident in its presentation of Wisdom as a living person (chs. 1; 8–9). Wisdom is God, having divine qualities as the source of all human wisdom, power, justice, and glory (8:14–19), and performing divine activities as the Creator (8:27–31). Yet Wisdom is a distinct person in relationship to God (8:22,30), just as John later said that the Word was God and yet was with God (John 1:1). Thus the identity of Wisdom reveals a personal plurality in the one God who created all things and said of man, "Let *us* make man in *our* image" (Gen. 1:26).

That the pronouns used of Wisdom ("she," "her") are feminine in Proverbs has nothing to do with the reality of Christ but is a grammatical issue (the Hebrew word for "wisdom" is feminine). In ch. 9 this is developed into a literary device, presenting the divine Wisdom as a wise and pure woman calling people to herself in contrast to the wicked and immoral woman Folly, just as Christ used the parable of a woman searching for a coin (Luke 15:8–10) to depict His seeking after lost sinners (Luke 15:1–2; 19:10). In fact, it is in His preaching and sending out preachers to call sinners to repent and learn of Him that Christ appears most prominently as Wisdom (Luke 7:29–35; 11:49).

Therefore "Wisdom" is Christ, the Son of God and Mediator of life. Wisdom is eternal, cooperating with God in the creation of the world and mankind (8:22–31; John 1:1–3; Col. 1:16–17; Heb. 1:2). Wisdom preaches the gospel, calling sinners to repent, receive the Spirit of wisdom, learn the ways of wisdom, escape God's judgment, and enjoy His peace (Prov. 1:20–33; Matt. 4:17; Acts 2:38). Proverbs teaches, "He that covereth his sins shall not prosper: but whoso confesseth and forsaketh them shall have mercy" (Prov. 28:13). Whoever finds Wisdom finds life (8:35; 1 John 5:12,20). Wisdom invites people to the banquet of life (Prov. 9:1–6; Matt. 22:1–14; Luke 14:16–24). It is only after life is found in Wisdom that the road of sanctification is mapped out in detail (chs. 10–31). It is only in union with Christ that practical holiness is possible.

Issues of Interpretation: Proverbs is Hebrew poetry and must be interpreted accordingly. The principal feature is the parallelism of thought. Three types of parallel structure are common in Proverbs.

- *Identity Form (Synonymous Parallelism):* the parallel statements say the same thing in different ways by way of repetition, for example, "Then shalt thou understand the fear of the LORD, and find the knowledge of God" (2:5).
- *Contrast Form (Antithetic Parallelism):* the parallel statements say the opposite of each other, contrasting the first clause with an opposite thought in the second, for example, "The fear of the LORD is the beginning of knowledge: but fools despise wisdom and instruction" (1:7).
- *Amplification Form (Synthetic Parallelism):* the parallel statements form one complete thought, with the second clause often expanding or explaining the first, for example, "In the fear of the LORD is strong confidence: and his children shall have a place of refuge" (14:26).

We must remember that Proverbs instructs primarily by stating universal observations. These statements are not always to be taken as specific promises that, following a given procedure, result in a certain outcome. If one takes some statements as definite promises, they might face disappointments in their life. However, exceptions do not disprove the rule, for the proverb remains true. These observations state general principles or patterns to guide one's life.

General Topical Index: As many topics are scattered throughout Proverbs, it is helpful to study the book thematically by collating the topics together. To help get the reader started, a select sample of topics and references are given below.

First, one can see how central the Lord is to a life of wisdom by tracing the following themes:

- *Fear of the Lord:* 1:7,29; 2:5; 3:7; 8:13; 9:10; 10:27; 13:13; 14:2,16,26–27; 15:16,33; 16:6; 19:23; 22:4; 23:17; 24:21; 28:14; 31:30
- *God's attributes/actions:* 2:6–8; 3:3–4; 5:21; 9:10; 14:31; 15:3; 16:1,4,9–10; 17:5; 19:21; 20:24;

21:1–2,30; 22:2,12; 23:10–11; 25:2; 26:10; 30:3,5–6

- *Humility before God:* 3:7; 6:17; 8:13; 11:2; 12:15; 15:12,25,32–33; 16:5,18–19; 18:12; 21:4,24; 22:4; 26:12,16; 27:1; 29:1,23; 30:1–4
- *Love for God's revealed wisdom:* 4:6; 8:17,21,36; 12:1; 22:11; 29:3
- *Prayer/worship toward God:* 3:9; 15:8,29; 17:1; 20:25; 21:3,27; 28:9; 30:7–9
- *Trust and hope in the Lord, not in man:* 3:5,26; 10:28; 14:26,32; 16:3,20; 18:10–11; 20:22; 22:19; 26:12; 28:25–26; 29:25; 30:5

Second, one can find much wisdom about relationships and activities among men, women, and children by exploring the following themes:

- *Adultery/fornication:* 5:1–23; 6:20—7:27; 22:14; 23:26–28; 29:3
- *Alcohol:* 20:1; 21:17; 23:19–21,29–35; 31:4–7
- *Anger/wrath:* 12:16; 14:17,29; 15:1,18; 16:14,32; 19:3,11–12,19; 20:2; 21:14,19; 22:24–25; 25:23; 27:3–4; 29:8,22
- *Contentment:* 13:25; 14:30; 15:15–17; 16:8; 19:23; 23:4–5; 25:16; 30:15–16
- *Corporal discipline:* 3:11–12; 10:13; 13:24; 17:10; 19:18,25; 20:30; 22:15; 23:13–14; 26:3; 29:15,17,19
- *Courage:* 24:10–12; 25:26; 28:1
- *Debt/financial obligation:* 6:1–5; 11:15; 17:18; 20:16; 22:7,26–27; 27:13
- *Emotional distress:*12:25; 13:12; 14:10,13,30; 15:4,13,30; 17:22; 25:20
- *Envy of the wicked:* 3:31–32; 12:12; 23:17–18; 24:1–2,19–20
- *Fools/folly:* 1:32–33; 9:13–18; 11:29; 12:15,23; 13:16; 14:1,7–8,16,18,24,29; 15:2,5,14,21; 17:10,12; 18:2,13; 20:3; 24:8–9; 26:4–5,11; 27:22; 28:26; 29:9,11
- *Friends/neighbors:* 3:27–31; 6:1–5; 11:9,12; 13:20; 14:20–21; 16:28–29; 17:9,17–18; 18:24; 19:4,6–7; 20:6; 22:11,24–25; 23:10–11; 24:28–29; 25:8–10,17–18; 27:6,9–10,14,17; 29:5
- *Gossip:* 10:18; 11:13; 16:28; 18:8; 20:19; 25:8–10,23; 26:20,22; 30:10
- *Haste:* 19:2; 21:5; 28:8,20; 29:20
- *Health/sickness:* 3:7–8; 12:4; 13:12; 14:30; 15:30; 16:24; 17:22; 18:14
- *Kings/authorities:* 8:15–16; 14:28,35; 16:10,12–15; 17:7; 19:12; 20:2,8,26,28; 21:1; 22:11; 23:1–3; 24:21–22; 25:2–7; 27:18; 28:2,12,15–16; 29:2,4,12,14,26; 30:21–23; 31:4–9
- *Listening to advice or correction:* 3:11–12; 9:7–9; 12:1,15; 13:1,10,13–14; 15:5,10,12,31–33; 17:10; 18:2,15; 19:25,27; 21:11; 23:9; 24:5–6; 25:12; 27:5–6,22; 28:23; 29:1,9
- *Love for people/mercy for the poor:* 3:3; 9:8; 10:12; 11:17,24–26; 14:21–22,31; 15:17; 16:6,13; 17:9,17; 19:17,22; 20:6,28; 21:13,21,26; 25:21–22; 27:5–6; 28:27; 29:7; 31:20,26
- *Marriage:* 5:15–19; 15:17; 18:22; 19:13; 21:9,19; 27:15–16; 30:21–23; 31:10–12
- *Meekness/seeking honor from men:* 12:9; 25:6–7,27; 27:1–2,21
- *Money/business practices:* 1:10–19; 3:9–10; 8:18–19; 10:15; 11:1,4,26,28; 12:9; 13:7–8,11, 22–23; 14:31; 15:15–17,27; 16:8,11; 17:1,5; 18:11,23; 19:1,4,22; 20:21; 21:6,17,20; 22:2,4,16, 22–23,28; 23:4–5,10–11,20–21; 24:3–4; 27:13,23–27; 28:3,6,8,11,16,20; 30:7–9 (see Debt/ financial obligation and Work/laziness)
- *Old age:* 16:31; 17:6; 20:29; 22:6; 23:22
- *Parents/children:* 3:11–12; 4:3–4; 10:1; 13:1,24; 14:26; 15:20; 17:6,21,25; 19:13,18,26; 20:7,11,20; 22:6,15; 23:13–14,22–25; 28:7,24; 29:15,17; 30:17
- *Self-control in speech:* 10:14; 11:12–13; 12:18; 13:3,16; 15:1,28; 17:27–28; 26:4–5
- *Strife/conflicts:* 6:19; 10:12; 15:18; 16:28; 17:14,19; 18:6,19; 19:11; 20:3; 22:10; 23:29–30; 26:17, 20–21; 28:25; 29:22
- *Truth/lies:* 6:16–19; 10:18; 11:1; 12:17,19,22; 13:5; 14:5,25; 16:11,13,30; 17:4,7; 18:17; 19:5, 9,22,28; 20:10,14,17,23; 21:6,28; 24:28–29; 25:14,18; 26:18–19,23–28; 28:13
- *Work/laziness:* 6:6–11; 10:4–5,26; 12:11,14,24,27; 13:4; 14:23; 15:19; 16:26; 18:9; 19:15,24; 20:4,13; 21:5,25; 22:13,29; 24:27,30–34; 26:13–16; 27:18,23; 28:19; 31:27

We also encourage the reader to perform keyword searches in Proverbs with Bible software to generate helpful lists of references on themes not listed here.

Outline:

I. Introduction (1:1–7)
   A. Title (1:1)
   B. Purpose of Proverbs (1:2–6)
   C. Theme of Proverbs (1:7)

- II. Invitation to Wisdom (1:8—9:18)
  - A. An Appeal from a Wise Father (1:8–19)
    1. Listen to Your Father and Mother (1:8–9)
    2. Do Not Comply with Violent Sinners (1:10–19)
  - B. Wisdom's Call to Repentance (1:20–33)
  - C. Further Appeals from a Wise Father (2:1—7:27)
    1. Seek Wisdom from God (2:1–9)
    2. Wisdom Will Save You from the Evil Man and Woman (2:10–22)
    3. Trust, Fear, and Honor the Lord (3:1–12)
    4. Wisdom Brings Blessing from the Creator (3:13–35)
    5. Get the Wisdom of Former Generations (4:1–9)
    6. Follow the Way of Wisdom, Not the Way of the Wicked (4:10–19)
    7. Keep Wisdom in Your Heart and Directing All of Your Life (4:20–27)
    8. Avoid the Immoral Woman and Enjoy Your Wife (5:1–23)
    9. Beware of Being a Surety, Sluggard, or Proud Sinner (6:1–19)
    10. Embrace Instruction, Not an Adulterous Woman (6:20–35)
    11. Keep the Commandments and Flee the Adulteress (7:1–27)
  - D. Wisdom's Call to Fear the Creator and Find Life (8:1—9:18)
    1. Wisdom's Public Call to Learn the Fear of the Lord (8:1–21)
    2. Wisdom's Role in God's Creation of the World (8:22–36)
    3. Wisdom's and Folly's Competing Invitations to Dinner (9:1–18)
- III. Collections of Wise Sayings (10:1—31:9)
  - A. Proverbs of Solomon (10:1—22:16)
  - B. Words of the Wise (22:17—24:34)
  - C. Proverbs of Solomon Collected by Hezekiah's Men (25:1—29:27)
  - D. Words of Agur (30:1–33)
  - E. Words of Lemuel from His Mother (31:1–9)
- IV. Conclusion: The Wise and Virtuous Woman (31:10–31)

THE PROVERBS

CHAPTER 1

THE proverbs of Solomon the son of David, king
of Israel;
2 To know wisdom and instruction; to perceive
the words of understanding;
3 To receive the instruction of wisdom, justice,
and judgment, and equity;
4 To give subtilty to the simple, to the young man
knowledge and discretion.
5 A wise *man* will hear, and will increase learning;
and a man of understanding shall attain unto
wise counsels:
6 To understand a proverb, and the interpreta-
tion; the words of the wise, and their dark sayings.
7 ¶ The fear of the LORD *is* the beginning of
knowledge: *but* fools despise wisdom and
instruction.
8 My son, hear the instruction of thy father, and
forsake not the law of thy mother:
9 For they *shall be* an ornament of grace unto thy
head, and chains about thy neck.
10 ¶ My son, if sinners entice thee, consent thou
not.
11 If they say, Come with us, let us lay wait for
blood, let us lurk privily for the innocent with-
out cause:
12 Let us swallow them up alive as the grave; and
whole, as those that go down into the pit:
13 We shall find all precious substance, we shall
fill our houses with spoil:
14 Cast in thy lot among us; let us all have one
purse:
15 My son, walk not thou in the way with them;
refrain thy foot from their path:
16 For their feet run to evil, and make haste to
shed blood.
17 Surely in vain the net is spread in the sight of
any bird.
18 And they lay wait for their *own* blood; they
lurk privily for their *own* lives.
19 So *are* the ways of every one that is greedy of
gain; *which* taketh away the life of the owners
thereof.
20 ¶ Wisdom crieth without; she uttereth her
voice in the streets:
21 She crieth in the chief place of concourse, in

Chapter 1: *True wisdom and knowledge begins with fearing God.*

INTRODUCTION (1:1–7)

Title (1:1)

1:1 *proverbs.* Short and pithy sayings, not promises but true observations about the general principles and patterns of life. *Solomon.* See Introduction: Authorship.

Purpose of Proverbs (1:2–6)

1:2 *wisdom.* Skill or ability, a general word that encompasses *instruction* (training or discipline) and *understanding* (perceptiveness).

1:3 *wisdom.* Insight or comprehension; a different word than in v. 2. *justice.* Righteousness. *judgment.* Justice. *equity.* Integrity, rectitude, uprightness.

1:4 *subtilty.* Cleverness or prudence. *simple.* One who is naïve, but often teachable.

1:6 *interpretation.* A figure of speech or expression alluding to something not openly stated. *dark sayings.* Riddles or allegorical sayings.

Theme of Proverbs (1:7)

1:7 *fear of the LORD.* The heart awareness of the true God that affects attitudes and actions. To fear God is to know Him in His holiness by His Word (2:5; 9:10; 13:13), resulting in humility, a soft and teachable spirit, turning from sin, rejecting the ways of sinners, walking in sincere obedience, and confident hope (3:7; 8:13; 14:2,26; 15:33; 23:17; 28:14). Fearing the Lord in this sense does not harm a person mentally or emotionally, but is a fountain of life and satisfaction (14:27; 19:23). *beginning.* The chief or principal part, the essence (9:10; Job 28:28; Ps. 111:10). *fools.* See note at v. 22.

INVITATION TO WISDOM (1:8—9:18)

An Appeal from a Wise Father (1:8–19)

Listen to Your Father and Mother (1:8–9)

1:8 *law.* Not merely legislation but teaching of all sorts.

1:9 *ornament.* Wreath or garland.

Do Not Comply with Violent Sinners (1:10–19)

1:11 *lay wait for blood.* Ambush to kill. *lurk privily.* Lie hidden (v. 18).

1:13 *precious substance.* Costly property. *spoil.* Booty or plunder.

1:15 *refrain.* Restrain, withhold.

1:17 *in vain.* For nothing or for no purpose.

Wisdom's Call to Repentance (1:20–33)

1:20–21 *Wisdom.* Plural form of the Hebrew term used in

the openings of the gates: in the city she uttereth
her words, *saying*,
22 How long, ye simple ones, will ye love simplic-
ity? and the scorners delight in their scorning, and
fools hate knowledge?
23 Turn you at my reproof: behold, I will pour
out my spirit unto you, I will make known my
words unto you.
24 ¶ Because I have called, and ye refused; I have
stretched out my hand, and no man regarded;
25 But ye have set at nought all my counsel, and
would none of my reproof:
26 I also will laugh at your calamity; I will mock
when your fear cometh;
27 When your fear cometh as desolation, and
your destruction cometh as a whirlwind; when
distress and anguish cometh upon you.
28 Then shall they call upon me, but I will not
answer; they shall seek me early, but they shall not
find me:
29 For that they hated knowledge, and did not
choose the fear of the LORD:
30 They would none of my counsel: they despised
all my reproof.
31 Therefore shall they eat of the fruit of their
own way, and be filled with their own devices.
32 For the turning away of the simple shall slay
them, and the prosperity of fools shall destroy
them.
33 But whoso hearkeneth unto me shall dwell
safely, and shall be quiet from fear of evil.

CHAPTER 2

MY son, if thou wilt receive my words, and hide
my commandments with thee;
2 So that thou incline thine ear unto wisdom,
and apply thine heart to understanding;
3 Yea, if thou criest after knowledge, *and* liftest up
thy voice for understanding;
4 If thou seekest her as silver, and searchest for
her as *for* hid treasures;
5 Then shalt thou understand the fear of the
LORD, and find the knowledge of God.
6 For the LORD giveth wisdom: out of his mouth
cometh knowledge and understanding.
7 He layeth up sound wisdom for the righteous:
he is a buckler to them that walk uprightly.
8 He keepeth the paths of judgment, and preserv-
eth the way of his saints.

v. 2, indicating superlative or excellent skill. The Hebrew word is feminine and thus too the pronouns used (*she, her*). Wisdom represents Christ (1 Cor. 1:24,30; Col. 2:3), and the call of Wisdom is a gospel call (2 Tim. 3:15). For more information on interpreting Wisdom as Christ, see Introduction: Synopsis. *without*. Outside. *streets*. Broad places. *place of concourse*. Noisy places. The call is open and public, where the people are.
1:22 *simple ones*. The naïve, ignorant, thoughtless, careless, negligent, easily-misled people, who still may be teachable (vv. 22,32; 7:7; 8:5; 9:4,13,16; 14:15,18; 19:25; 21:11; 22:3; 27:12). *scorners*. Those who proudly mock at godliness, unwilling to change, who glory in their impiety, infidelity, and blasphemy (3:34; 9:7–8,12; 13:1; 14:6,9; 15:12; 19:25,28–29; 20:1; 21:11,24; 22:10; 24:9). *fools*. Not the same term as in v. 7, but similar in meaning: those who lack wisdom (though perhaps intelligent or educated) yet are insensitive to their need. These three characters appear often in this book, together with a fourth: the "sluggard" or "slothful" (see note at 6:6).
1:23 *Turn*. Repent. *I will pour out my spirit . . . I will make known*. To those who repent and trust in His wisdom, God gives the presence of His Spirit to lead them into deeper spiritual knowledge (John 14:15–17; 16:13–15; Acts 2:38).
1:25 *set at nought*. Neglected or been unconcerned about. *would none*. Would not accept or consent to (v. 30).
1:28 *seek me early*. Not a reference to time but manner, to pursue earnestly or diligently. The gospel call is urgent (Isa. 55:6–7).
1:29 *hated*. Rejected.
1:31 *devices*. Schemes.
1:32 *turning away*. Turning back or falling away in apostasy. *prosperity*. Security or self-confidence.
1:33 *whoso hearkeneth*. Whoever listens. *safely*. Securely. *quiet*. Without anxiety. *evil*. Calamity or destruction. They will be secure from the fate of those who reject Wisdom.

Thoughts for Personal/Family Worship: Chapter 1

1. **God's inspired oracles are designed to give solid and precious instruction about things that relate to time and eternity. Therefore, they are to be studied and carefully observed, by all groups of people, the mature adults, but even more so the youth. In youth, the physical and mental faculties are more quick and retentive, and the direction of one's life is being shaped. Hence, for those who want true wisdom, it is necessary to cultivate deep regard for God and for parental counsels, especially the teaching of godly, Christian parents. Are you seeking the wisdom of more mature believers in your life?**
2. **One's relationship to Christ is a matter of eternal life and death because He is the Wisdom of God. This is a good opportunity to press home the gospel call to repent before it is too late. There is a point when judgment comes and repentance is no longer possible. The gospel call is urgent. If this message is missed, nothing else in Proverbs will matter. Why would it be a tragic mistake to try to live by the Proverbs without first receiving Christ to be your wisdom, righteousness, sanctification, and redemption from God?**

Further Appeals from a Wise Father (2:1—7:27)

Chapter 2: *Wisdom leads to godliness and away from temptation.*

Seek Wisdom from God (2:1–9)

2:1 *hide*. Keep or treasure up.
2:2 *incline thine ear*. Cause yourself to pay attention. *apply thine heart*. Stretch out your inner man, in the sense of directing your mind, emotions, and will toward God's Word.
2:4 *seekest . . . searchest*. Terms expressing constant and diligent effort.
2:7 *sound wisdom*. Literally, "abiding success." *buckler*. Shield for protection.
2:8 *keepeth the paths of judgment*. Protects those living according to His justice (Pss. 1:6; 5:8; 23:3; 25:9). *his saints*. The recipients of His covenant mercy.

9 Then shalt thou understand righteousness, and
judgment, and equity; *yea*, every good path.
10 ¶ When wisdom entereth into thine heart, and
knowledge is pleasant unto thy soul;
11 Discretion shall preserve thee, understanding
shall keep thee:
12 To deliver thee from the way of the evil *man*,
from the man that speaketh froward things;
13 Who leave the paths of uprightness, to walk in
the ways of darkness;
14 Who rejoice to do evil, *and* delight in the
frowardness of the wicked;
15 Whose ways *are* crooked, and *they* froward in
their paths:
16 To deliver thee from the strange woman, *even*
from the stranger *which* flattereth with her words;
17 Which forsaketh the guide of her youth, and
forgetteth the covenant of her God.
18 For her house inclineth unto death, and her
paths unto the dead.
19 None that go unto her return again, neither
take they hold of the paths of life.
20 That thou mayest walk in the way of good
men, and keep the paths of the righteous.
21 For the upright shall dwell in the land, and the
perfect shall remain in it.
22 But the wicked shall be cut off from the earth,
and the transgressors shall be rooted out of it.

CHAPTER 3

MY son, forget not my law; but let thine heart
keep my commandments:
2 For length of days, and long life, and peace,
shall they add to thee.
3 Let not mercy and truth forsake thee: bind
them about thy neck; write them upon the table
of thine heart:
4 So shalt thou find favour and good under-
standing in the sight of God and man.
5 ¶ Trust in the LORD with all thine heart; and
lean not unto thine own understanding.
6 In all thy ways acknowledge him, and he shall
direct thy paths.
7 ¶ Be not wise in thine own eyes: fear the LORD,
and depart from evil.
8 It shall be health to thy navel, and marrow to
thy bones.
9 Honour the LORD with thy substance, and with
the firstfruits of all thine increase:
10 So shall thy barns be filled with plenty, and thy
presses shall burst out with new wine.
11 ¶ My son, despise not the chastening of the
LORD; neither be weary of his correction:
12 For whom the LORD loveth he correcteth; even
as a father the son *in whom* he delighteth.
13 ¶ Happy *is* the man *that* findeth wisdom, and
the man *that* getteth understanding.

Wisdom Will Save You from the Evil Man and Woman (2:10–22)

2:12 *froward.* Perverse, twisted (v. 14).

2:15 *ways are crooked.* Behavior is twisted or perverse. *froward in their paths.* Their regular lifestyle is crooked or devious (a different word than "froward" in v. 12).

2:16 *strange.* Unlawful or forbidden, referring to a prostitute or an adulteress. *flattereth with her words.* Sexual immorality often begins with flattering or sensual words (5:3; 6:24; 7:13–21)

2:17 *guide.* A close or intimate friend, here her husband. *forgetteth.* Refuses to think about or to give serious consideration. *covenant of her God.* The marriage bond, a solemn promise between husband and wife in the presence of God (Mal. 2:14; Matt. 19:5–6).

2:18 *inclineth unto.* Sinks or collapses into.

2:21 *dwell in the land.* Symbolic of peace and protection in God's kingdom (Ps. 37:3,9,18,29). *perfect.* Those with integrity or wholehearted faithfulness to the Lord.

2:22 *cut off.* Destroyed by God's judgment (Ps. 104:35).

Thoughts for Personal/Family Worship: Chapter 2

Our heart is where our treasure is (Matt. 6:21,33). It is natural to expend effort and energy in the pursuit and enjoyment of what we treasure. That is how we ought to estimate the wisdom of fearing and knowing God. It is like digging for hidden treasure. One does not normally just stumble over treasure as he shuffles along. It requires diligent and sometime difficult digging, but finding the treasure is worth it (Job 28:1–11). So our reading and studying in God's Word should not be casual, but serious. The Lord is ready to bless those who sincerely and diligently seek His revealed will with great success, satisfaction, and protection. God's Word must rule our heart as an antidote against the multitude of corrupt principles and lustful temptations. What practical actions will you take to seek God's wisdom like silver?

Chapter 3: ***The wise father gives various practical instructions for walking in wisdom.***

Trust, Fear, and Honor the Lord (3:1–12)

3:1 *My son.* A loving phrase, marking at least six fatherly lessons with encouragements and motivating promises (vv. 1–2,3–4,5–6,7–8,9–10,11–12). *forget not.* Don't refuse to give one's thoughts and affections to. *law.* Teaching or instruction, not just legislation or rules.

3:2 *For length of days.* See Ex. 20:12; Deut. 30:20; Eph. 6:1–3. *peace.* Overall well-being.

3:3 *mercy and truth.* Covenant loyalty and love or fidelity—two words often paired. *table.* Tablet.

3:4 *understanding.* Or success.

3:5 *Trust.* Place confidence for safety and security. *all thine heart.* The totality of your inner person (mind, will, and emotion). *lean not unto.* Do not support yourself with or depend on.

3:7 *fear the LORD . . . depart from evil.* The awareness of God affects moral behavior, putting temptation to sin in proper perspective (Job 1:1).

3:8 *health.* Recovery or healing. *marrow.* Drink or refreshment. *Navel* and *bones* represent the physical body, parts for the whole.

3:10 *presses.* Wine vats. *burst out.* Overflow.

3:11–12 *chastening.* Training or correction. *correction.* Chiding. God disciplines His children for their good out of His great love (cited in Heb. 12:5–11; see 1 Cor. 11:32; Rev. 3:19).

Wisdom Brings Blessing from the Creator (3:13–35)

3:13 *Happy.* Not a subjective feeling, but a state of possessing

14 For the merchandise of it *is* better than the
merchandise of silver, and the gain thereof than
fine gold.
15 She *is* more precious than rubies: and all the
things thou canst desire are not to be compared
unto her.
16 Length of days *is* in her right hand; *and* in her
left hand riches and honour.
17 Her ways *are* ways of pleasantness, and all her
paths *are* peace.
18 She *is* a tree of life to them that lay hold upon
her: and happy *is every one* that retaineth her.
19 The LORD by wisdom hath founded the earth;
by understanding hath he established the heavens.
20 By his knowledge the depths are broken up,
and the clouds drop down the dew.
21 ¶ My son, let not them depart from thine eyes:
keep sound wisdom and discretion:
22 So shall they be life unto thy soul, and grace
to thy neck.
23 Then shalt thou walk in thy way safely, and thy
foot shall not stumble.
24 When thou liest down, thou shalt not be
afraid: yea, thou shalt lie down, and thy sleep shall
be sweet.
25 Be not afraid of sudden fear, neither of the
desolation of the wicked, when it cometh.
26 For the LORD shall be thy confidence, and shall
keep thy foot from being taken.
27 ¶ Withhold not good from them to whom it is
due, when it is in the power of thine hand to do *it*.
28 Say not unto thy neighbour, Go, and come
again, and to morrow I will give; when thou hast
it by thee.
29 Devise not evil against thy neighbour, seeing
he dwelleth securely by thee.
30 ¶ Strive not with a man without cause, if he
have done thee no harm.
31 ¶ Envy thou not the oppressor, and choose
none of his ways.
32 For the froward *is* abomination to the LORD:
but his secret *is* with the righteous.
33 ¶ The curse of the LORD *is* in the house of the
wicked: but he blesseth the habitation of the just.
34 Surely he scorneth the scorners: but he giveth
grace unto the lowly.
35 The wise shall inherit glory: but shame shall be
the promotion of fools.

CHAPTER 4

HEAR, ye children, the instruction of a father, and
attend to know understanding.
2 For I give you good doctrine, forsake ye not my
law.
3 For I was my father's son, tender and only
beloved in the sight of my mother.
4 He taught me also, and said unto me, Let thine
heart retain my words: keep my commandments,
and live.
5 Get wisdom, get understanding: forget *it* not;
neither decline from the words of my mouth.

great benefits from God. *getteth.* Draws out as from a hidden place.

3:14 *merchandise.* Gain or profit from trading.

3:15 *precious.* Valuable.

3:18 *happy.* Different form but same root as v. 13 with the same meaning. *retaineth.* Takes hold of.

3:19 *by wisdom hath founded.* God created the vast and intricate world and all that is in it through His infinite insight and skill (Pss. 104:24; 136:5; Isa. 40:28; Jer. 10:12; 51:15)

3:27–28 Timely payments of obligations (Lev. 19:13; Deut. 24:15; James 2:15–16) and gifts to the needy (Matt. 5:42; Eph. 4:28) are acts of obedience to the second greatest commandment (Lev. 19:18; Matt. 22:37–39).

3:29 *evil.* Anything hurtful. *securely.* Confidently, without care or anxiety. However distant or close one may be to anyone else, treachery and hurt of others is always wrong (Rom. 13:10). Bad examples are found in Haman (Est. 3) and Judas (Matt. 26:14–16).

3:31 *oppressor.* Literally, "man of violence."

3:32 *the froward.* Those who are crooked or devious. *his secret.* Intimacy with Him.

3:34 *scorneth.* Disdains or mocks. *lowly.* Literally, "one who bends himself," referring to the humble (cited in James 4:6; 1 Peter 5:5).

3:35 *shall be the promotion of.* Raises up.

Thoughts for Personal/Family Worship: Chapter 3

1. **How we keep the commandment to love our neighbor is an index to how we keep the greatest commandment to love the Lord. Therefore, we should prayerfully plan how to help those in need. In so doing, we are serving the cause of God. Let us use the finances and gifts that God has given to us for His glory. Be consistent and regular in this service. Trust in God's provision for your life, and give, knowing you can never outgive God. To whom should you be giving assistance now?**
2. **Think about how you should respond to afflictions. Ask: "What can I learn from this chastening of the Lord?" The Hebrew word, "chasten," is also translated "instruction" (8:33), "correction" (22:15), and "rebuke" (Hos. 5:2). Although the experience is not pleasant, it is for good and is evidence of God's love. As God so deals with His children, so should parents, in patiently instructing their children, tenderly reproving them, and at the last resort using the rod of punishment. What can parents learn from God's example of discipline?**

Chapter 4: *Wisdom is the ancient way to life.*

Get the Wisdom of Former Generations (4:1–9)

4:1 *attend.* Listen attentively, pay attention (v. 20).

4:2 *doctrine.* Teaching. *law.* Instruction, not just rules.

4:3–4 *my father's son . . . He taught me.* The good paths are old paths (Jer. 6:16), and though we should reject religious traditions based on merely human teachings (Isa. 29:13; Col. 2:8), there are traditions and a heritage of faithfulness to the Lord that we should take hold of (*retain*) and pass on to others (2 Tim. 1:5,13–14; 2:2; 3:10–11,14–15; Heb. 13:7–8).

4:5 *forget it not.* Don't refuse to think about it or intentionally neglect it. *decline.* Bend away or turn aside.

6 Forsake her not, and she shall preserve thee:
love her, and she shall keep thee.
7 Wisdom *is* the principal thing; *therefore* get wis-
dom: and with all thy getting get understanding.
8 Exalt her, and she shall promote thee: she shall
bring thee to honour, when thou dost embrace her.
9 She shall give to thine head an ornament of
grace: a crown of glory shall she deliver to thee.
10 Hear, O my son, and receive my sayings; and
the years of thy life shall be many.
11 I have taught thee in the way of wisdom; I have
led thee in right paths.
12 When thou goest, thy steps shall not be strait-
ened; and when thou runnest, thou shalt not
stumble.
13 Take fast hold of instruction; let *her* not go:
keep her; for she *is* thy life.
14 ¶ Enter not into the path of the wicked, and go
not in the way of evil *men*.
15 Avoid it, pass not by it, turn from it, and pass
away.
16 For they sleep not, except they have done
mischief; and their sleep is taken away, unless they
cause *some* to fall.
17 For they eat the bread of wickedness, and
drink the wine of violence.
18 But the path of the just *is* as the shining light,
that shineth more and more unto the perfect day.
19 The way of the wicked *is* as darkness: they
know not at what they stumble.
20 ¶ My son, attend to my words; incline thine
ear unto my sayings.
21 Let them not depart from thine eyes; keep
them in the midst of thine heart.
22 For they *are* life unto those that find them, and
health to all their flesh.
23 ¶ Keep thy heart with all diligence; for out of it
are the issues of life.
24 Put away from thee a froward mouth, and
perverse lips put far from thee.
25 Let thine eyes look right on, and let thine
eyelids look straight before thee.
26 Ponder the path of thy feet, and let all thy ways
be established.
27 Turn not to the right hand nor to the left:
remove thy foot from evil.

CHAPTER 5

MY son, attend unto my wisdom, *and* bow thine
ear to my understanding:
2 That thou mayest regard discretion, and *that*
thy lips may keep knowledge.
3 ¶ For the lips of a strange woman drop *as* an
honeycomb, and her mouth *is* smoother than oil:
4 But her end is bitter as wormwood, sharp as a
twoedged sword.
5 Her feet go down to death; her steps take hold
on hell.
6 Lest thou shouldest ponder the path of life,
her ways are moveable, *that* thou canst not know
them.
7 Hear me now therefore, O ye children, and
depart not from the words of my mouth.

4:6 *love*. Choose to set your thoughts and affections upon as your good.
4:7 *principal thing*. Literally, "the beginning," the chief thing.
4:8 *Exalt*. Esteem or prize highly. *promote*. Raise up.
4:9 *ornament*. Garland or wreath (see 3:21–22).

Follow the Way of Wisdom, Not the Way of the Wicked (4:10–19)

4:10 *years of thy life . . . many*. Great in quality as well as long in duration.
4:11 *right paths*. Hebrew, "the steps of righteousness or uprightness."
4:12 *straitened*. Closely restricted or hemmed in.
4:16 *mischief*. Evil, injury, or hurt.
4:18 *perfect day*. Literally, "the standing of the day," referring to the day at its full brightness.

Keep Wisdom in Your Heart and Directing All of Your Life (4:20–27)

4:20 *incline thine ear*. Stretch out your ear, an image of careful listening.
4:23 *Keep thy heart with all diligence*. Literally, "Above all protection guard your heart." *issues of life*. The origin or source of life's activity (Matt. 12:34–35; 15:19).
4:24 *froward mouth*. Perversity or crookedness of speech.
4:25 *look right . . . look straight*. Keep your thoughts and affections focused on God, His wisdom, and His will.

Thoughts for Personal/Family Worship: Chapter 4

This chapter puts much emphasis on the heart, the place of feeling, thinking, and choosing what to do or not to do. We are to guard the heart above all else for it is the index to what we really are and the source of all our attitudes and actions. The best way to keep the heart is by seeking from the Lord Jesus that living water, the sanctifying Spirit, from whom comes everlasting life. It is by His strength and wisdom that we are given help to put away rebellious words and attitudes, to keep our eyes from looking at vanity. In everything always look to the Lord and do not be sidetracked. What steps can you take to get wisdom and guard your heart?

Chapter 5: ***Wisdom warns against the destructive nature of immorality and promotes the satisfying beauty of faithfulness in the marriage union.***

Avoid the Immoral Woman and Enjoy Your Wife (5:1–23)

5:1 *attend unto*. Pay attention to. *bow thine ear*. Cause yourself to listen.
5:3 *strange*. Foreign, here referring to an immoral woman as an outsider or intruder (v. 20).
5:4 *her end*. The short-lived pleasure is followed by long, bitter pain. *wormwood*. A bitter, oil-yielding plant, symbolic of suffering (Deut. 29:18).
5:5 *hell*. Hebrew, *sheol*, referring to *death* (as here), the grave or abode of departed wicked spirits.
5:6 *are moveable*. Roam or are unstable.

8 Remove thy way far from her, and come not
nigh the door of her house:
9 Lest thou give thine honour unto others, and
thy years unto the cruel:
10 Lest strangers be filled with thy wealth; and thy
labours *be* in the house of a stranger;
11 And thou mourn at the last, when thy flesh
and thy body are consumed,
12 And say, How have I hated instruction, and my
heart despised reproof;
13 And have not obeyed the voice of my teachers,
nor inclined mine ear to them that instructed me!
14 I was almost in all evil in the midst of the
congregation and assembly.
15 ¶ Drink waters out of thine own cistern, and
running waters out of thine own well.
16 Let thy fountains be dispersed abroad, *and*
rivers of waters in the streets.
17 Let them be only thine own, and not strang-
ers' with thee.
18 Let thy fountain be blessed: and rejoice with
the wife of thy youth.
19 *Let her be as* the loving hind and pleasant roe;
let her breasts satisfy thee at all times; and be thou
ravished always with her love.
20 And why wilt thou, my son, be ravished with
a strange woman, and embrace the bosom of a
stranger?
21 For the ways of man *are* before the eyes of the
LORD, and he pondereth all his goings.
22 ¶ His own iniquities shall take the wicked
himself, and he shall be holden with the cords of
his sins.
23 He shall die without instruction; and in the
greatness of his folly he shall go astray.

CHAPTER 6

MY son, if thou be surety for thy friend, *if* thou
hast stricken thy hand with a stranger,
2 Thou art snared with the words of thy mouth,
thou art taken with the words of thy mouth.
3 Do this now, my son, and deliver thyself, when
thou art come into the hand of thy friend; go,
humble thyself, and make sure thy friend.
4 Give not sleep to thine eyes, nor slumber to
thine eyelids.
5 Deliver thyself as a roe from the hand *of the
hunter*, and as a bird from the hand of the fowler.
6 ¶ Go to the ant, thou sluggard; consider her
ways, and be wise:
7 Which having no guide, overseer, or ruler,
8 Provideth her meat in the summer, *and*
gathereth her food in the harvest.
9 How long wilt thou sleep, O sluggard? when
wilt thou arise out of thy sleep?

5:10 *strangers.* Foreigners (v. 17). *stranger.* A different Hebrew word, here referring to a prostitute.
5:11 *mourn.* Groan, perhaps as animals in distress. *thy body.* Or physical power.
5:12 *hated . . . despised.* Rejected in one's will, mind, and feelings.
5:13 *inclined mine ear.* Intentionally given attention.
5:15 *Drink waters.* Draw satisfaction and refreshment from your own wife alone.
5:19 *loving hind.* A charming doe of a fallow deer. *pleasant roe.* A graceful or elegant female mountain goat. The point of comparison is not with the wife's appearance so much as the passionate desires displayed by such creatures. *ravished.* Intoxicated as one drunk with love. The sexual pleasure and intimacy shared by a husband and wife were created by God and are blessed by Him as an important dimension of marriage (Gen. 1:26–28; 2:18–25; 1 Cor. 7:1–5; 1 Tim. 4:1–5).
5:21 *pondereth.* Either examines or makes level. *goings.* Literally, "the tracks" or "ruts" left by wheels.
5:22 *holden with the cords of his sins.* Caught in the chains of his sin.

Thoughts for Personal/Family Worship: Chapter 5

1. **The chapter contains warnings about the dangers of temptation. So often when temptation comes there is no time to seek advice, but response must be immediate. It is important to remember what has been taught from God's Word to be able to use it when needed. The eyes and ears must be guarded to not allow lustful and tempting words to enter the mind and to stir the sexual passions for wrong things. Avoid the people and media that use sensual words and sexual provocations. Fill the mind rather with things that are virtuous (Phil. 4:8), and remember the great disgrace and pain that comes with giving yourself away to immorality. What are some lies commonly believed about immorality today? What is God's contrasting truth?**
2. **God's definition and purpose of marriage is radically different from worldly notions and norms. Marriage is the God-ordained means by which one man is to be united to one woman. Marriage is itself a safeguard against sinful vices. Those united together, who honor the Lord and His Word, can truly enjoy one another. Husbands and wives should enjoy a mutual admiration and be intoxicated with each other's love. Do not merely strive against temptation. Labor and pray for your sexual desires to focus entirely on your spouse.**

Chapter 6: *Important warnings and exhortations of practical wisdom are given.*

Beware of Being a Surety, Sluggard, or Proud Sinner (6:1–19)

6:1 *be surety.* Pledge oneself to guarantee a loan for another (see warnings at 11:15; 17:18; 20:16; 22:7; 27:13). *stricken thy hand.* Given a handshake in making a pledge. *stranger.* Foreigner.
6:2 *taken.* Captured.
6:3 *make sure.* Press or urge forcefully. Every effort should be made to reverse the suretyship.
6:5 *roe . . . bird.* The imagery of escaping animals from the hunter illustrates the urgency to escape from the creditor's control. *fowler.* Bird hunter.
6:6 *Go to the ant.* God teaches us lessons through things He created. *sluggard.* Habitually slothful or lazy person (v. 9; 10:26; 13:4; 15:19; 19:24; 20:4; 21:25; 22:13; 24:30; 26:13–16).
6:8 *meat.* Food of any kind.

10 *Yet* a little sleep, a little slumber, a little folding
of the hands to sleep:
11 So shall thy poverty come as one that travel-
leth, and thy want as an armed man.
12 ¶ A naughty person, a wicked man, walketh
with a froward mouth.
13 He winketh with his eyes, he speaketh with his
feet, he teacheth with his fingers;
14 Frowardness *is* in his heart, he deviseth
mischief continually; he soweth discord.
15 Therefore shall his calamity come suddenly;
suddenly shall he be broken without remedy.
16 ¶ These six *things* doth the LORD hate: yea,
seven *are* an abomination unto him:
17 A proud look, a lying tongue, and hands that
shed innocent blood,
18 An heart that deviseth wicked imaginations,
feet that be swift in running to mischief,
19 A false witness *that* speaketh lies, and he that
soweth discord among brethren.
20 ¶ My son, keep thy father's commandment,
and forsake not the law of thy mother:
21 Bind them continually upon thine heart, *and*
tie them about thy neck.
22 When thou goest, it shall lead thee; when
thou sleepest, it shall keep thee; and *when* thou
awakest, it shall talk with thee.
23 For the commandment *is* a lamp; and the law *is*
light; and reproofs of instruction *are* the way of life:
24 To keep thee from the evil woman, from the
flattery of the tongue of a strange woman.
25 Lust not after her beauty in thine heart; neither
let her take thee with her eyelids.
26 For by means of a whorish woman *a man is*
brought to a piece of bread: and the adulteress will
hunt for the precious life.
27 Can a man take fire in his bosom, and his
clothes not be burned?
28 Can one go upon hot coals, and his feet not
be burned?
29 So he that goeth in to his neighbour's wife;
whosoever toucheth her shall not be innocent.
30 *Men* do not despise a thief, if he steal to satisfy
his soul when he is hungry;
31 But *if* he be found, he shall restore sevenfold;
he shall give all the substance of his house.
32 *But* whoso committeth adultery with a woman
lacketh understanding: he *that* doeth it destroyeth
his own soul.
33 A wound and dishonour shall he get; and his
reproach shall not be wiped away.
34 For jealousy *is* the rage of a man: therefore he
will not spare in the day of vengeance.
35 He will not regard any ransom; neither will he
rest content, though thou givest many gifts.

CHAPTER 7

MY son, keep my words, and lay up my com-
mandments with thee.
2 Keep my commandments, and live; and my law
as the apple of thine eye.

6:9 *How long.* Something inappropriate has continued for a while.
6:11 *one that travelleth.* A vagabond or wanderer. *want.* Need, lack, or poverty. *an armed man.* Either "a man of a shield" or perhaps "a shameless man."
6:12 *naughty.* Worthless, good-for-nothing, or wicked. *froward mouth.* Crookedness of speech.
6:13 *winketh.* Instead of using honest and straightforward speech, he communicates sinful intentions through signs and gestures with *his eyes, feet,* and *fingers.*
6:14 *Frowardness.* Perversion or crookedness. *mischief.* Evil or hurtful things (v. 18). *discord.* Controversies, quarrels, contention.
6:15 *without remedy.* Literally, "without healing," no escape from his doom.
6:16 *hate.* Reject. *an abomination.* Disgusting or detestable. *six . . . seven.* Hebrew uses ascending numbers to express completeness (see Amos 1–2).
6:18 *imaginations.* Plans or intentions.

Embrace Instruction, Not an Adulterous Woman (6:20–35)

6:20 *law.* Instruction not just rules (v. 23).
6:23 *lamp . . . light.* God's Word is His means to illuminate a person and guide him with knowledge (Ps. 119:105).
6:24–25 *strange woman.* Here an adulteress. Her two main weapons for conquering and destroying men are words that stroke their egos (*flattery of the tongue*; 2:16) and an appearance that incites his sexual appetite (*her beauty*; 7:10). *lust . . . in thine heart.* Adultery begins in the heart with sinful desire (Matt. 5:28). *take . . . eyelids.* Capture with her flirtatious looks (Isa. 3:16).
6:26 *piece of bread.* All he has left after spending his money on illicit sexual pleasure.
6:32–35 Unlike theft, there is no restitution possible in adultery.

Thoughts for Personal/Family Worship: Chapter 6

1. **The ant is a positive example to follow. Industry, entrepreneurship and hard work are every person's wisdom and duty. As believers we should redeem our time and work effectively, so that we will not be a burden to others and will be able to promote and use our income for the kingdom of God, which will not perish. In what areas of life are you called to diligence?**
2. **Proverbs again warns against sexual sin. The frequent warnings need to be heeded particularly in our day when temptations abound on every hand. Immorality and its many promoters and snares are seen all around us. It is a multimillion dollar industry that grows by enticing men (and sometimes women too). The entertainment industry is the greatest promoters of it in the world. Christians should use great caution as they use the world's media and should beware of relationships with people who flatter and attract them. Which temptations do you most need to guard against?**

Chapter 7: *Further warnings against the beguiling ways of the strange woman are listed.*

Keep the Commandments and Flee the Adulteress (7:1–27)

7:2 *apple of thine eye.* The eye's pupil, a sensitive and precious

3 Bind them upon thy fingers, write them upon the table of thine heart.
4 Say unto wisdom, Thou *art* my sister; and call understanding *thy* kinswoman:
5 That they may keep thee from the strange woman, from the stranger *which* flattereth with her words.
6 ¶ For at the window of my house I looked through my casement,
7 And beheld among the simple ones, I discerned among the youths, a young man void of understanding,
8 Passing through the street near her corner; and he went the way to her house,
9 In the twilight, in the evening, in the black and dark night:
10 And, behold, there met him a woman *with* the attire of an harlot, and subtil of heart.
11 (She *is* loud and stubborn; her feet abide not in her house:
12 Now *is she* without, now in the streets, and lieth in wait at every corner.)
13 So she caught him, and kissed him, *and* with an impudent face said unto him,
14 *I have* peace offerings with me; this day have I payed my vows.
15 Therefore came I forth to meet thee, diligently to seek thy face, and I have found thee.
16 I have decked my bed with coverings of tapestry, with carved *works*, with fine linen of Egypt.
17 I have perfumed my bed with myrrh, aloes, and cinnamon.
18 Come, let us take our fill of love until the morning: let us solace ourselves with loves.
19 For the goodman *is* not at home, he is gone a long journey:
20 He hath taken a bag of money with him, *and* will come home at the day appointed.
21 With her much fair speech she caused him to yield, with the flattering of her lips she forced him.
22 He goeth after her straightway, as an ox goeth to the slaughter, or as a fool to the correction of the stocks;
23 Till a dart strike through his liver; as a bird hasteth to the snare, and knoweth not that it *is* for his life.
24 ¶ Hearken unto me now therefore, O ye children, and attend to the words of my mouth.
25 Let not thine heart decline to her ways, go not astray in her paths.
26 For she hath cast down many wounded: yea, many strong *men* have been slain by her.
27 Her house *is* the way to hell, going down to the chambers of death.

CHAPTER 8

DOTH not wisdom cry? and understanding put forth her voice?

---

part guarded from all harm (Deut. 32:10; Ps. 17:8; Zech. 2:8).

7:3 *table.* Tablet. The moral law (vv. 1–2) of the Ten Commandments which God wrote on tablets of stone (Deut. 4:13; 10:4) must be written upon the *heart*, that is, received with understanding and a desire to do God's will (Ps. 40:8). This is only possible by God's sovereign grace (Jer. 31:33; 2 Cor. 3:3).

7:5 *strange woman.* Foreigner, here referring to the immoral woman.

7:6 *casement.* Window lattice.

7:7 *simple.* See notes at 1:4,22.

7:8 *Passing . . . near her corner.* Contrary to the advice in 4:14–15.

7:9 *In the twilight.* Assuming that darkness hides sin, forgetting God (Ps. 139:11–12).

7:10 *with the attire of an harlot.* Dressed like a prostitute. *subtil of heart.* Cunning, guarded, concealing her true agenda.

7:11 *her feet abide not in her house.* She is not content to devote herself to her husband, children, and household work (31:10–12,27; Titus 2:4–5).

7:12 *without.* Outside her home.

7:14–20 Like the men who enticed a young man to join their violent scheme (1:10–14), the immoral woman promises satisfaction and safety as if she were a trustworthy friend instead of a destroyer.

7:14 She speaks as a spiritual woman, but they are mere words and hypocrisy (2 Tim. 3:5). The leftover meat of the *peace offerings* were to be eaten before the end of day (Lev. 7:11–18).

7:16 *carved works.* Multicolored, embroidered cloth.

7:18 *let us solace ourselves with loves.* Literally, "let us delight ourselves with acts of love."

7:19 *goodman.* Husband.

7:21 *fair speech.* Enticing words. *flattering of her lips.* Smooth speech. *forced.* Seduced.

7:22 *straightway.* Suddenly or surprisingly. *stocks.* Chains locked on the ankles.

7:23 *hasteth.* Rushes. *snare.* Trap.

7:24 *Hearken.* Listen.

7:25 *decline.* Turn aside.

7:26 *many strong men . . . slain.* The immoral woman is like a warrior who defeats and kills an army of powerful soldiers—a warning to beware and fear this danger and not assume you can resist.

7:27 *hell.* Hebrew, *sheol*, referring to death, the grave or abode of departed wicked spirits. Here parallel to the general word *death*.

Thoughts for Personal/Family Worship: Chapter 7

This chapter gives good direction to avoid impurity. Keep the mind pure from any kinds of media that generate fantasies or desires. Stay away from places where temptations are likely. Limit or break off relationships with flattering and enticing people. Avoid flattering and enticing others to win their affection and learn contentment in your calling. Focus on the future rather than on momentary experiences. The daily careful intake of the Word of God, by searching its teachings, will be a key component for resisting temptation. View and discern the world and your life through the spectacle of the Scriptures. Occupy your time with righteous and good things (Phil. 4:8). How can you use this chapter to guide you in your prayers for yourself and others that God would save you from sexual sin?

2 She standeth in the top of high places, by the
way in the places of the paths.
3 She crieth at the gates, at the entry of the city, at
the coming in at the doors.
4 Unto you, O men, I call; and my voice *is* to the
sons of man.
5 O ye simple, understand wisdom: and, ye fools,
be ye of an understanding heart.
6 Hear; for I will speak of excellent things; and
the opening of my lips *shall be* right things.
7 For my mouth shall speak truth; and wicked-
ness *is* an abomination to my lips.
8 All the words of my mouth *are* in righteous-
ness; *there is* nothing froward or perverse in them.
9 They *are* all plain to him that understandeth,
and right to them that find knowledge.
10 Receive my instruction, and not silver; and
knowledge rather than choice gold.
11 For wisdom *is* better than rubies; and all the
things that may be desired are not to be compared
to it.
12 I wisdom dwell with prudence, and find out
knowledge of witty inventions.
13 The fear of the LORD *is* to hate evil: pride,
and arrogancy, and the evil way, and the froward
mouth, do I hate.
14 Counsel *is* mine, and sound wisdom: I *am*
understanding; I have strength.
15 By me kings reign, and princes decree justice.
16 By me princes rule, and nobles, *even* all the
judges of the earth.
17 I love them that love me; and those that seek
me early shall find me.
18 Riches and honour *are* with me; *yea,* durable
riches and righteousness.
19 My fruit *is* better than gold, yea, than fine gold;
and my revenue than choice silver.
20 I lead in the way of righteousness, in the midst
of the paths of judgment:
21 That I may cause those that love me to inherit
substance; and I will fill their treasures.
22 The LORD possessed me in the beginning of
his way, before his works of old.
23 I was set up from everlasting, from the begin-
ning, or ever the earth was.
24 When *there were* no depths, I was brought
forth; when *there were* no fountains abounding
with water.
25 Before the mountains were settled, before the
hills was I brought forth:
26 While as yet he had not made the earth, nor the
fields, nor the highest part of the dust of the world.
27 When he prepared the heavens, I *was* there:
when he set a compass upon the face of the depth:
28 When he established the clouds above: when
he strengthened the fountains of the deep:
29 When he gave to the sea his decree, that the
waters should not pass his commandment: when
he appointed the foundations of the earth:
30 Then I was by him, *as* one brought up *with
him*: and I was daily *his* delight, rejoicing always
before him;

Wisdom's Call to Fear the Creator and Find Life (8:1—9:18)

Chapter 8: *Wisdom appears as a divine person, calling like a wise woman for people to learn the fear of the Lord, and revealing Wisdom's eternality and involvement in creation.*

Wisdom's Public Call to Learn the Fear of the Lord (8:1–21)

8:1 Although some interpreters see *wisdom* here as a mere personification of God's insight and instruction, it is best to see it as a title of Christ, the divine Mediator calling mankind to Himself (1:20; Luke 7:34–35; 11:49; see Introduction: Synopsis).

8:2–3 *high places . . . paths . . . gates . . . doors.* The Lord calls to men publicly, not with a secret knowledge limited to an elite few but in a public proclamation (1:20–21)

8:4 *men . . . sons of man.* The call of wisdom is to all men, from high to low, upon all the paths of life (Ps. 49:1–3), for the good news of God's wisdom must be proclaimed to all people universally (1 Cor. 1:26–27).

8:5 *simple.* See notes at 1:4,22.

8:8 *froward or perverse.* Twisted or false.

8:12 *witty inventions.* Discretion.

8:13 *fear of the LORD is to hate evil.* Living in the heartfelt awareness of God's glory and holiness moves a person to reject everything that rebels or rises against Him. *froward.* Perverse.

8:14–15 *strength . . . reign . . . justice.* This Wisdom is not a bare attribute of the mind or intellect but possesses divine power and righteousness (Isa. 11:2) and is the source of all ability and justice among men.

8:17 *love them that love me.* God's love is always first (1 John 4:10,19), but when His love stirs our love in response, then He delights in our love and draws near to bless us (John 14:21–23). *seek . . . early.* Pursue diligently or earnestly.

8:20 *lead.* Walk, meaning that wisdom consistently does what is right and just (*judgment*).

8:21 *treasures.* Storehouses or storerooms.

Wisdom's Role in God's Creation of the World (8:22–36)

8:22 *possessed.* The verb literally means "got" (4:5); it could be understood as a relationship of belonging (Ruth 4:10; Eccl. 2:7), or begetting a child (Gen. 4:1; cf. Prov. 8:24–25). *in the beginning . . . before his works.* God had an eternal relationship with Wisdom prior to creation (Gen. 1:1). Christ was not created (John 1:1–3; Col. 1:17; 1 John 1:2).

8:23 *set up.* Literally, "poured," used here of the anointing of a person to an office of authority (same word as in Ps. 2:6). *from everlasting.* Without beginning (Pss. 90:2; 93:2; 103:17). The Father gave to His Son the commission to be the Mediator of life before time began (Eph. 1:4; 2 Tim. 1:9; Titus 1:2).

8:24–25 *no depths . . . before the hills.* Before the creation of oceans or the land (Gen. 1:1–2,9). *brought forth.* Born, a metaphor for God's eternal generation of the person of Wisdom, for Christ is God's eternal, begotten Son (30:4; John 1:1,14,18; 3:16,18; 1 John 4:9; cf. Ps. 2:7).

8:27 *I was there.* God by wisdom created all things (Col. 1:15–16). *set a compass.* Like a craftsman, He marked or cut out the circular shape of the earth (Isa. 40:22).

8:30 *I was by him, as one brought up.* Literally, "I was beside Him [as] an architect or master workman." He along with the Father and Spirit was a co-Creator of all things. *daily his delight.*

31 Rejoicing in the habitable part of his earth;
and my delights *were* with the sons of men.
32 Now therefore hearken unto me, O ye children:
for blessed *are they that* keep my ways.
33 Hear instruction, and be wise, and refuse it
not.
34 Blessed *is* the man that heareth me, watching
daily at my gates, waiting at the posts of my doors.
35 For whoso findeth me findeth life, and shall
obtain favour of the LORD.
36 But he that sinneth against me wrongeth his
own soul: all they that hate me love death.

CHAPTER 9

WISDOM hath builded her house, she hath hewn
out her seven pillars:
2 She hath killed her beasts; she hath mingled her
wine; she hath also furnished her table.
3 She hath sent forth her maidens: she crieth
upon the highest places of the city,
4 Whoso *is* simple, let him turn in hither: *as for*
him that wanteth understanding, she saith to him,
5 Come, eat of my bread, and drink of the wine
which I have mingled.
6 Forsake the foolish, and live; and go in the
way of understanding.
7 He that reproveth a scorner getteth to himself
shame: and he that rebuketh a wicked *man getteth*
himself a blot.
8 Reprove not a scorner, lest he hate thee: rebuke
a wise man, and he will love thee.
9 Give *instruction* to a wise *man*, and he will be
yet wiser: teach a just *man*, and he will increase in
learning.
10 The fear of the LORD *is* the beginning of
wisdom: and the knowledge of the holy *is* under-
standing.
11 For by me thy days shall be multiplied, and the
years of thy life shall be increased.
12 If thou be wise, thou shalt be wise for thyself:
but *if* thou scornest, thou alone shalt bear *it*.
13 ¶ A foolish woman *is* clamorous: *she is* simple,
and knoweth nothing.
14 For she sitteth at the door of her house, on a
seat in the high places of the city,
15 To call passengers who go right on their ways:
16 Whoso *is* simple, let him turn in hither: and
as for him that wanteth understanding, she saith
to him,
17 Stolen waters are sweet, and bread *eaten* in
secret is pleasant.

The persons of the triune God work together with joy because of their mutual love (John 5:19–20).

8:31 *my delights were with the sons of men.* Mankind was the object of My special joy. Here we have a clue to the meaning behind God's mysterious, "Let us make man in our image" (Gen. 1:26).

8:32 *blessed.* A descriptive term of the benefits belonging to those in view (v. 34), here those who choose Wisdom.

8:35 *findeth life.* As the Creator of all life, Wisdom is also the Mediator of eternal life (John 1:3–4; 1 John 5:12,20).

8:36 *hate . . . love.* To reject Wisdom is to choose death. One's eternal destiny depends on how one relates to Wisdom (Ps. 2:12).

Thoughts for Personal/Family Worship: Chapter 8

1. **In this chapter we have a remarkable revelation of the Son of God as Wisdom. Wisdom is God's eternal offspring, not just His attribute of wisdom but a divine person who is the living expression of divine wisdom, power, and righteousness. Wisdom exists in a relationship with God of mutual love and joyful cooperation in His greatest works, including the creation of the universe. Wisdom especially delighted in the creation of mankind. How does this beautiful picture we have here of God's only begotten Son help you to know and worship Him?**
2. **Though humanity rebelled against the Lord, this same Wisdom still communicates with fallen man, publicly proclaiming the fear of the Lord and calling people to a treasure more valuable than gold—the gift of life. In Jesus Christ, the person of Wisdom has come to us in the flesh. In order to be saved from eternal death, you must submit to Him and receive Him as the Wisdom of God. How should knowing that Christ is God's living Wisdom affect how we listen to His teachings in the Bible?**

Chapter 9: ***Wisdom invites men to take of her life-giving provisions, while folly invites them to her deadly ways.***

Wisdom's and Folly's Competing Invitations to Dinner (9:1–18)

9:1 *Wisdom.* The Hebrew is plural to intensify the idea. Christ's depiction as Wisdom continues (1:20; 8:1), here developed as a parable of a wise woman (cf. 14:1; 31:26; 2 Sam. 14:2; 20:16) sending out invitations to her feast (Luke 14:15–24). *hewn.* Cut. *seven pillars.* Seven is the number of completion and perfection. The house is fully supported.

9:2 *killed her beasts.* Butchered animals and prepared meat for eating. *mingled.* Mixed (v. 5), diluting the strength of the wine with water and spices for smell and flavor (Song 8:2).

9:4 *simple.* The naïve, but sometimes teachable person (see note at 1:22; also vv. 6,13). *hither.* Here, to this place. *wanteth understanding.* Literally, "lacks heart," spiritually deficient in thoughts, feelings, and choices (v. 16).

9:5 *eat . . . drink.* Metaphors for the gospel call to find satisfaction and life in Christ through repentance and faith (Isa. 55:1–8; John 6:35; 7:37).

9:6 *foolish.* Same root as "simple" (v. 4).

9:7–8 *scorner.* Proud mockers who disdain correction (see note at 1:22).

9:10 *fear of the LORD . . . wisdom.* See note at 1:7. *the holy.* God, the Holy One (30:3; Isa. 1:4; 6:3). The Hebrew is plural, amplifying the idea. The parallelism of the two halves of this verse implies that the fear of the Lord is an experiential knowledge of Him in His supreme holiness.

9:12 *scornest.* Brag or speak boastfully.

9:13 *clamorous.* Noisy or boisterous. Here *simple* refers to spiritual ignorance but not teachableness.

9:15 *passengers.* Those passing by.

9:17 *Stolen waters are sweet.* Figurative language for the pleasures of sin; perhaps alluding to sexual immorality (*waters*; 5:15) and wealth obtained by deceit or oppression (*bread*; 20:17).

18 But he knoweth not that the dead *are* there;
and that her guests *are* in the depths of hell.

CHAPTER 10

THE proverbs of Solomon. A wise son maketh a
glad father: but a foolish son *is* the heaviness of
his mother.
2 Treasures of wickedness profit nothing: but
righteousness delivereth from death.
3 The LORD will not suffer the soul of the righ-
teous to famish: but he casteth away the substance
of the wicked.
4 He becometh poor that dealeth *with* a slack
hand: but the hand of the diligent maketh rich.
5 He that gathereth in summer *is* a wise son: *but*
he that sleepeth in harvest *is* a son that causeth
shame.
6 Blessings *are* upon the head of the just: but
violence covereth the mouth of the wicked.
7 The memory of the just *is* blessed: but the name
of the wicked shall rot.
8 The wise in heart will receive commandments:
but a prating fool shall fall.
9 He that walketh uprightly walketh surely: but
he that perverteth his ways shall be known.
10 He that winketh with the eye causeth sorrow:
but a prating fool shall fall.
11 The mouth of a righteous *man is* a well of life:
but violence covereth the mouth of the wicked.
12 Hatred stirreth up strifes: but love covereth all
sins.
13 In the lips of him that hath understanding
wisdom is found: but a rod *is* for the back of him
that is void of understanding.
14 Wise *men* lay up knowledge: but the mouth of
the foolish *is* near destruction.
15 The rich man's wealth *is* his strong city: the
destruction of the poor *is* their poverty.
16 The labour of the righteous *tendeth* to life: the
fruit of the wicked to sin.
17 He *is in* the way of life that keepeth instruc-
tion: but he that refuseth reproof erreth.
18 He that hideth hatred *with* lying lips, and he
that uttereth a slander, *is* a fool.
19 In the multitude of words there wanteth not
sin: but he that refraineth his lips *is* wise.
20 The tongue of the just *is as* choice silver: the
heart of the wicked *is* little worth.
21 The lips of the righteous feed many: but fools
die for want of wisdom.
22 The blessing of the LORD, it maketh rich, and
he addeth no sorrow with it.
23 *It is* as sport to a fool to do mischief: but a man
of understanding hath wisdom.
24 The fear of the wicked, it shall come upon
him: but the desire of the righteous shall be
granted.
25 As the whirlwind passeth, so *is* the wicked
no *more*: but the righteous *is* an everlasting
foundation.
26 As vinegar to the teeth, and as smoke to the
eyes, so *is* the sluggard to them that send him.
27 The fear of the LORD prolongeth days: but the

9:18 *the dead.* Dead spirits. *hell.* Hebrew, *sheol,* referring to death, the grave, or the abode of departed wicked spirits, here the abode of wicked dead would be in view since it refers to the foolish.

Thoughts for Personal/Family Worship: Chapter 9

1. **Wisdom's call to the banquet parallels Christ's parable in Luke 14:15–24. Many are invited, and many have excuses why they cannot attend. Ultimately, nothing is more important than being part of the feast prepared by Christ, the provision He has made for His people. No excuse is legitimate; and the consequences for refusing to come are eternally severe. Which banquet are you dining at, that of Wisdom or Folly? How do you know?**
2. **No one likes to be corrected or rebuked, but how one responds to legitimate criticism says a lot about your character. The contrasts in vv. 8–9 are instructive. We should be open to criticism, receiving it for our welfare rather than responding in anger or in such a way as to turn the criticism to others. That is the way of wisdom. How do you respond to correction and criticism? How can you learn to respond better?**

COLLECTIONS OF WISE SAYINGS (10:1—31:9)

Proverbs of Solomon (10:1—22:16)

Chapter 10: ***These proverbs are maxims mainly for righteousness, piety, industry, and government of the tongue.***

10:1 *heaviness.* Grief. Much of a parent's earthly sorrow or joy revolves around the moral and spiritual conduct of their children (15:20; 17:21,25; 19:26; 23:15–16; 28:7; 29:3).
10:3 *suffer…to famish.* Allow to hunger. *soul of the righteous.* The righteous person. *casteth away the substance.* Thrusts away the desire.
10:4–5 *slack.* Literally, "deceitful" or "treacherous," referring to one who is sluggish, slow, lazy, inactive. The dangers of laziness and the blessings of being *diligent* are recurring themes (6:6; 13:4; 19:15; 24:30–34; 28:19–20; 30:24–25).
10:8 *prating fool.* Literally, "a fool of lips," one given to chattering or babbling. *fall.* Come to ruin (v. 10).
10:9 *surely.* Securely. *perverteth his ways.* Behaves crookedly.
10:12 *love covereth all sins.* Love moves us to forgive sin and protect the sinner from unnecessary shame (17:9; 1 Peter 4:8).
10:13 *understanding.* Hebrew, "heart." *rod.* Painful discipline is an appropriate corrective to men who reject the teachings of wisdom (19:25,29; 20:30; 26:3; Deut. 25:2–3).
10:14 *lay up knowledge.* There are times when it is wise to be silent and not speak all that one knows (11:12; 26:4–5; Job 38:2; 42:1–6)
10:16 *labour.* Wages. *fruit.* Profit or income.
10:19 *there wanteth not sin.* Sin is not lacking.
10:21 *want of wisdom.* Lack of heart.
10:22 *addeth no sorrow.* Strenuous work cannot add to it.
10:23 *mischief.* Wickedness or shameful behavior.
10:26 *sluggard.* See note at 6:6.
10:27 *fear of the LORD.* See note at 1:7. *years…shortened.* Sin is detrimental to physical and spiritual health.

years of the wicked shall be shortened.
28 The hope of the righteous *shall be* gladness:
but the expectation of the wicked shall perish.
29 The way of the LORD *is* strength to the
upright: but destruction *shall be* to the workers
of iniquity.
30 The righteous shall never be removed: but the
wicked shall not inhabit the earth.
31 The mouth of the just bringeth forth wisdom:
but the froward tongue shall be cut out.
32 The lips of the righteous know what is
acceptable: but the mouth of the wicked *speaketh*
frowardness.

CHAPTER 11

A FALSE balance *is* abomination to the LORD: but
a just weight *is* his delight.
2 *When* pride cometh, then cometh shame: but
with the lowly *is* wisdom.
3 The integrity of the upright shall guide them:
but the perverseness of transgressors shall destroy
them.
4 Riches profit not in the day of wrath: but righ-
teousness delivereth from death.
5 The righteousness of the perfect shall direct
his way: but the wicked shall fall by his own
wickedness.
6 The righteousness of the upright shall deliver
them: but transgressors shall be taken in *their own*
naughtiness.
7 When a wicked man dieth, *his* expectation shall
perish: and the hope of unjust *men* perisheth.
8 The righteous is delivered out of trouble, and
the wicked cometh in his stead.
9 An hypocrite with *his* mouth destroyeth his
neighbour: but through knowledge shall the just
be delivered.
10 When it goeth well with the righteous, the city
rejoiceth: and when the wicked perish, *there is*
shouting.
11 By the blessing of the upright the city is exalted:
but it is overthrown by the mouth of the wicked.
12 He that is void of wisdom despiseth his
neighbour: but a man of understanding holdeth
his peace.
13 A talebearer revealeth secrets: but he that is of
a faithful spirit concealeth the matter.
14 Where no counsel *is*, the people fall: but in the
multitude of counsellors *there is* safety.
15 He that is surety for a stranger shall smart *for*
it: and he that hateth suretiship is sure.
16 A gracious woman retaineth honour: and
strong *men* retain riches.
17 The merciful man doeth good to his own soul:
but *he that is* cruel troubleth his own flesh.
18 The wicked worketh a deceitful work: but
to him that soweth righteousness *shall be* a sure
reward.
19 As righteousness *tendeth* to life: so he that
pursueth evil *pursueth it* to his own death.
20 They that are of a froward heart *are* abomina-

10:30 *removed.* Made to stagger or overthrown.
10:31 *froward.* Perverse or scheming.
10:32 *frowardness.* Perversion.

Thoughts for Personal/Family Worship: Chapter 10

1. **Loving one another is a Christian grace that seeks to promote peace rather than strife (v. 12; 1 Cor. 13:6; 1 Peter 4:8). We must learn to bear with others in patience and seek to stir up love and harmony with those in the family, church, and society. Expressing that love requires control of the tongue. As Christians we should learn to use our speech to promote and foster life and help for others rather than stirring up contention or spreading slander. How do you use your tongue? Does your speech give wisdom? Is it true? Does it do good to men?**
2. **It is part of godly wisdom to redeem the time, to use it appropriately. To slumber during the harvest time is foolish (v. 5). There is only so much time in life to accomplish the tasks that God has given us to do. Let us be productive, taking advantage of every opportunity the Lord has given to us to serve Him. How can you use your time better for the Lord?**

Chapter 11: ***Maxims of wisdom, mainly honesty, humility, faithfulness, and liberality, are contrasted against their contrary vices.***

11:1 *false balance.* Balances of fraud, referring to inaccurately calibrated scales used to cheat in business transactions (16:11; 20:10,23). *abomination.* A disgusting, detestable thing (v. 20). *just weight.* Literally, "a full" or "perfect stone," one that would accurately balance the object being weighed.
11:2 *pride.* An arrogant, presumptuous, and overly confident attitude or behavior. *shame.* Disgrace, dishonor, and reproach (13:18; 16:18). *lowly.* Humble, modest.
11:3 *integrity.* Wholeness, sincerity. *perverseness.* Crookedness, twistedness, subversion (1 Tim. 6:5).
11:5 *righteousness of the perfect.* The right behavior of a man of integrity. *direct.* Make smooth or straight.
11:6 *taken in their own naughtiness.* Those behaving deceitfully will become trapped or captured by their own desires.
11:8 *stead.* place. See an example in Mordecai (Est. 7:9).
11:9 *hypocrite.* A godless, profane person (Job 8:13).
11:12 *void of wisdom.* Hebrew, "destitute of heart." A heartless person shows contempt for others. *holdeth his peace.* He knows when to be silent (10:19; 1 Peter 2:23).
11:13 *talebearer.* A gossip spreads slander with intention of harm (Lev. 19:16).
11:14 *counsel.* Making plans based on wise guidance and direction.
11:15 *is surety.* Gives his pledge to pay someone's obligation. *smart.* Suffer (6:1–2). *hateth.* Rejects.
11:16 *retaineth honour.* Holds on to a good reputation, like *strong men* who will not let their riches be taken (31:28,30).
11:17 *merciful.* Having a character of covenant loyalty and love.
11:18 *work.* Or wages. *sure.* Dependable (Hos. 10:12; Gal. 6:8–9; James 3:18)
11:19 *life.* Not mere existence, but the full quality of life is in view (vv. 5–6; 10:16).

tion to the LORD: but *such as are* upright in *their*
way *are* his delight.
21 *Though* hand *join* in hand, the wicked shall
not be unpunished: but the seed of the righteous
shall be delivered.
22 *As* a jewel of gold in a swine's snout, *so is* a fair
woman which is without discretion.
23 The desire of the righteous *is* only good: *but*
the expectation of the wicked *is* wrath.
24 There is that scattereth, and yet increaseth;
and *there is* that withholdeth more than is meet,
but *it tendeth* to poverty.
25 The liberal soul shall be made fat: and he that
watereth shall be watered also himself.
26 He that withholdeth corn, the people shall
curse him: but blessing *shall be* upon the head of
him that selleth *it*.
27 He that diligently seeketh good procureth
favour: but he that seeketh mischief, it shall come
unto him.
28 He that trusteth in his riches shall fall: but the
righteous shall flourish as a branch.
29 He that troubleth his own house shall inherit
the wind: and the fool *shall be* servant to the wise
of heart.
30 The fruit of the righteous *is* a tree of life; and
he that winneth souls *is* wise.
31 Behold, the righteous shall be recompensed in
the earth: much more the wicked and the sinner.

CHAPTER 12

WHOSO loveth instruction loveth knowledge: but
he that hateth reproof *is* brutish.
2 A good *man* obtaineth favour of the LORD: but
a man of wicked devices will he condemn.
3 A man shall not be established by wickedness:
but the root of the righteous shall not be moved.
4 A virtuous woman *is* a crown to her husband:
but she that maketh ashamed *is* as rottenness in
his bones.
5 The thoughts of the righteous *are* right: *but* the
counsels of the wicked *are* deceit.
6 The words of the wicked *are* to lie in wait for
blood: but the mouth of the upright shall deliver
them.
7 The wicked are overthrown, and *are* not: but
the house of the righteous shall stand.
8 A man shall be commended according to his
wisdom: but he that is of a perverse heart shall
be despised.
9 *He that is* despised, and hath a servant, *is* better
than he that honoureth himself, and lacketh bread.
10 A righteous *man* regardeth the life of his beast:
but the tender mercies of the wicked *are* cruel.
11 He that tilleth his land shall be satisfied with
bread: but he that followeth vain *persons is* void
of understanding.
12 The wicked desireth the net of evil *men*: but
the root of the righteous yieldeth *fruit*.

11:20 *froward.* Crooked or perverse as opposed to the sincerity and purity of the *upright* in their attitudes and behavior. *such as are upright.* People of integrity and sincere truthfulness.
11:21 *hand join in hand.* The fortification of the wicked will not avoid God's punishment (16:5).
11:22 *jewel.* A precious ornament for the body. *fair.* Beautiful and pleasant in appearance. *without discretion.* Lacking sound judgment, reason and guidance.
11:24 *scattereth.* Distributes freely. *meet.* What is due or right.
11:25–26 *liberal soul.* A generous person. *fat.* Prosperous (Ps. 112:9; Eccl. 11:1; John 12:24–25; Acts 20:35; 2 Cor. 9:6–9).
11:27 *favour.* Acceptance, goodwill. *mischief.* Evil or something hurtful (Est. 7:10; Ps. 7:15–16; 57:6).
11:28 *trusteth.* Places confidence in for security or safety (Ps. 49:6). *flourish as a branch.* Sprout or bud like foliage (Ps. 1:3; Jer. 17:8).
11:29 *troubleth.* Disturbs and mismanages. *He . . . shall inherit the wind.* What he gains is of no use or value.
11:30 *winneth souls.* Literally, "takes" or "captures lives," by influencing them in wisdom's ways (Luke 5:10; James 5:20).

Thoughts for Personal/Family Worship: Chapter 11

1. **As God is just and fair in His dealings with us, the life of a true child of God should be marked by honesty, fairness, and faithfulness in business and relationships (v. 1). Be aware of the uncertain riches of this world, and do not be dazzled by their golden baits. In the hour of death, riches will not be the source of our comfort. Make it your daily resolution that by God's grace, you will seek first the kingdom of God and His righteousness! How can keeping your eyes on the Lord protect you against dishonesty and injustice?**
2. **Whatever your status or position, live with integrity before God and man, then you will not be ashamed if your life is laid open before the world. When faced with critical decisions, call upon godly, serious, experienced people to give you counsel and advice (v. 14). Give to those in need and to the Lord's cause cheerfully and generously, as the Lord prospers you (vv. 24–26). Remember how the Father gave His Son, and His Son gave His life, and the Holy Spirit gives of Himself to His people's everlasting happiness, grace, mercy, pardon, and peace. How can you imitate God (Matt. 5:44–48)?**

Chapter 12: *Descriptions of the conduct and the end of the wise and the unwise are contrasted.*
12:1 *hateth reproof.* A large part of man's wisdom is the humility to gladly learn from others (3:11–12; Ps. 141:5; Heb. 12:10–11). *brutish.* Stupid or irrational, beast-like.
12:2 *devices.* Plots or evil practices.
12:3 *root.* Firm and deep grounding in the Lord by faith and love (Isa. 27:6; Jer. 17:8; Eph. 3:17; Col. 2:7).
12:4 *virtuous woman.* Literally, "woman of excellence or strength," here referring to strength of godliness (31:10–31; Ruth 3:11). *crown.* Chief ornament.
12:5–7 Three contrasts are made between the righteous and the wicked: their intentions (v. 5), words (v. 6), and destiny (v. 7). *house . . . shall stand.* An image of blessing and stability (Matt. 7:24–27).
12:9 *despised.* Lightly esteemed, a low social status.
12:10 *regardeth the life of his beast.* Shows mercy even to his animals (Lev. 22:28; Deut. 25:4). *tender mercies . . . cruel.* Sarcasm: even the good things done by the wicked are bad.
12:11 *tilleth.* Cultivates. *vain persons.* Idle or worthless ones.

13 The wicked is snared by the transgression of
his lips: but the just shall come out of trouble.
14 A man shall be satisfied with good by the fruit
of *his* mouth: and the recompence of a man's
hands shall be rendered unto him.
15 The way of a fool *is* right in his own eyes: but
he that hearkeneth unto counsel *is* wise.
16 A fool's wrath is presently known: but a
prudent *man* covereth shame.
17 *He that* speaketh truth sheweth forth righ-
teousness: but a false witness deceit.
18 There is that speaketh like the piercings of a
sword: but the tongue of the wise *is* health.
19 The lip of truth shall be established for ever:
but a lying tongue *is* but for a moment.
20 Deceit *is* in the heart of them that imagine evil:
but to the counsellors of peace *is* joy.
21 There shall no evil happen to the just: but the
wicked shall be filled with mischief.
22 Lying lips *are* abomination to the LORD: but
they that deal truly *are* his delight.
23 A prudent man concealeth knowledge: but the
heart of fools proclaimeth foolishness.
24 The hand of the diligent shall bear rule: but
the slothful shall be under tribute.
25 Heaviness in the heart of man maketh it stoop:
but a good word maketh it glad.
26 The righteous *is* more excellent than his neigh-
bour: but the way of the wicked seduceth them.
27 The slothful *man* roasteth not that which he
took in hunting: but the substance of a diligent
man *is* precious.
28 In the way of righteousness *is* life; and *in* the
pathway *thereof there is* no death.

CHAPTER 13

A WISE son *heareth* his father's instruction: but a
scorner heareth not rebuke.
2 A man shall eat good by the fruit of *his* mouth:
but the soul of the transgressors *shall eat* violence.
3 He that keepeth his mouth keepeth his life:
but he that openeth wide his lips shall have
destruction.
4 The soul of the sluggard desireth, and *hath*
nothing: but the soul of the diligent shall be made
fat.
5 A righteous *man* hateth lying: but a wicked
man is loathsome, and cometh to shame.
6 Righteousness keepeth *him that is* upright in
the way: but wickedness overthroweth the sinner.
7 There is that maketh himself rich, yet *hath*
nothing: *there is* that maketh himself poor, yet
hath great riches.
8 The ransom of a man's life *are* his riches: but
the poor heareth not rebuke.
9 The light of the righteous rejoiceth: but the
lamp of the wicked shall be put out.

---

void of understanding. Literally, "lacking of heart."
12:12 *net*. Or mountain stronghold.
12:16 *presently*. Literally, "in the day," expressing immediacy. *coveteth shame*. Ignores the insults of others (10:12; 17:9).
12:17–19 Three contrasts of the speech of the righteous and the wicked. The words of the righteous are true, healing, helpful, unchanging, and permanent (14:5; Eph. 4:29–30). The words of the wicked are deceitful, hurtful, and transitory (19:9; Pss. 57:4; 106:33).
12:20 *imagine*. Devise or plan.
12:21 *no evil*. No harm. *mischief*. Evil or calamity.
12:22 *abomination*. That which is disgusting and detestable.
12:23 *concealeth*. The wise man has self-control and humility, knowing the appropriate time to speak or to keep silent (26:4–5; Eccl. 3:7; James 3:17–18). *proclaimeth*. The fool has to show off and make all hear his folly.
12:24 *slothful*. Literally, "the deceitful" or "treacherous," referring to one who is lazy (10:4).
12:25 *Heaviness*. Worry, concern, anxiety. *maketh it stoop*. Subdues or depresses (15:13).
12:26 *seduceth*. Leads astray (1 Cor. 15:33).
12:27 *roasteth not*. Opportunities are lost by those who are lazy (v. 11). *substance*. Wealth or property. *precious*. Valuable.
12:28 *life . . . no death*. Since the righteous die physically, the reference must be to spiritual and eternal life.

Thoughts for Personal/Family Worship: Chapter 12

1. **We love what we value; our heart is with our treasure (Matt. 6:21). The person who desires wisdom and abundant life values the Word and ordinances of God; he is thankful for any corrections and is patient and diligent in applying its truths. A wise man loves God's instruction and the knowledge that is gained from it. Knowing God is the most precious treasure we can have. What does the way *you* listen and speak reveal about *your* heart?**
2. **Be aware of self-sufficiency and self-confidence, as they are the attitudes of the foolish. Those who are to make a difference and leave a good inheritance for the future are those who exercise diligence, modesty, prudence, constancy, and integrity, which are fueled by a saving relationship and love for God and His glory. The wise Christian does not make a show of his knowledge. How can your conduct lift up those who are dejected and give hope to those who wait upon the Lord?**

Chapter 13: *Various maxims on life and discipline are given.*

13:2 *transgressors*. Those who act treacherously or deceitfully.
13:3 *keepeth his mouth*. Guards, watches over, and controls his speech. *keepeth his life*. A different word, but the same idea of guarding or keeping watch. *openeth wide his lips*. Speaks much, rashly, boldly, without care of consequences.
13:4 *sluggard*. Lazy and unfaithful person (6:6). *fat*. Blessed, satisfied, prosperous.
13:5 *hateth*. Rejects. *loathsome*. Literally, "odious."
13:6 *keepeth*. Watches over or preserves.
13:8 *ransom*. Riches rescue from some earthly troubles. *poor heareth not rebuke*. This could mean that the poor do not receive the criticism or threats that the rich do or that their poverty comes from proudly refusing to listen to wise counsel (v. 1).
13:9 *light*. Prosperity, happiness, peace, and blessedness

10 Only by pride cometh contention: but with
the well advised *is* wisdom.
11 Wealth *gotten* by vanity shall be diminished:
but he that gathereth by labour shall increase.
12 Hope deferred maketh the heart sick: but
when the desire cometh, *it is* a tree of life.
13 Whoso despiseth the word shall be destroyed:
but he that feareth the commandment shall be
rewarded.
14 The law of the wise *is* a fountain of life, to
depart from the snares of death.
15 Good understanding giveth favour: but the
way of transgressors *is* hard.
16 Every prudent *man* dealeth with knowledge:
but a fool layeth open *his* folly.
17 A wicked messenger falleth into mischief: but
a faithful ambassador *is* health.
18 Poverty and shame *shall be to* him that refuseth
instruction: but he that regardeth reproof shall be
honoured.
19 The desire accomplished is sweet to the soul:
but *it is* abomination to fools to depart from evil.
20 He that walketh with wise *men* shall be wise:
but a companion of fools shall be destroyed.
21 Evil pursueth sinners: but to the righteous
good shall be repayed.
22 A good *man* leaveth an inheritance to his
children's children: and the wealth of the sinner *is*
laid up for the just.
23 Much food *is in* the tillage of the poor: but
there is *that is* destroyed for want of judgment.
24 He that spareth his rod hateth his son: but he
that loveth him chasteneth him betimes.
25 The righteous eateth to the satisfying of his
soul: but the belly of the wicked shall want.

CHAPTER 14

EVERY wise woman buildeth her house: but the
foolish plucketh it down with her hands.
2 He that walketh in his uprightness feareth the
LORD: but *he that is* perverse in his ways despiseth
him.
3 In the mouth of the foolish *is* a rod of pride: but
the lips of the wise shall preserve them.
4 Where no oxen *are*, the crib *is* clean: but much
increase *is* by the strength of the ox.
5 A faithful witness will not lie: but a false witness
will utter lies.
6 A scorner seeketh wisdom, and *findeth*
it not: but knowledge *is* easy unto him that
understandeth.
7 Go from the presence of a foolish man, when
thou perceivest not *in him* the lips of knowledge.
8 The wisdom of the prudent *is* to understand his
way: but the folly of fools *is* deceit.
9 Fools make a mock at sin: but among the
righteous *there is* favour.
10 The heart knoweth his own bitterness; and a
stranger doth not intermeddle with his joy.

(4:18; Pss. 97:11; 112:4). *the lamp.* The little glimmer of prosperity that the wicked possess will soon go out (Job 18:5; 21:17).

13:11 *vanity.* A breath, that which is unsubstantial, perhaps even an idol.

13:12 *Hope.* Expectation. *deferred.* Postponed or delayed.

13:14 *law.* Instruction, not just legislation.

13:17 *wicked.* Disloyal, negligent, and careless. *mischief.* Calamity or trouble.

13:18 *regardeth.* Keeps.

13:20 *walketh ... companion.* Association shapes character, making us like those whose company we keep (1:10; 2:12; 4:14; 5:8; 14:7; 22:24–25; Ps. 1).

13:23 *tillage.* Cultivated ground.

13:24 *spareth.* Hebrew, "withhold what is due." *rod.* Corporal punishment is to be judiciously and lovingly used in the correction and training of children (22:15; 23:13–14; 29:15). *chasteneth him betimes.* Disciplines him early, that is, quickly or promptly.

Thoughts for Personal/Family Worship: Chapter 13

1. **Disciplining children is never pleasant, either for the parent or the child, but it is an important part of raising children in the nurture and admonition of the Lord (Eph. 6:4). It shows the parent's genuine love for the child (Prov. 13:24). It teaches the vital truth that sin has consequences. It is an opportunity to point children to the gospel as the only means of avoiding sin's ultimate punishment. Discipline should not be administered with impatient anger but always lovingly and in self-control with a view to instructing children in behavior that pleases the Lord. Why is it an act of hatred *not* to discipline your children?**
2. **Remember that many contentions among people in families, churches, and nations are the result of pride in one or both of the parties (v. 10). Esteeming others more highly than we esteem ourselves (Phil. 2:3) will prevent a lot of quarreling and will imitate the humble spirit of the Lord Jesus (Phil. 2:5). Are you involved in a conflict? How should you humble yourself and fight against your pride?**

Chapter 14: *The fear of the Lord should govern our daily conduct and relationships.*

14:1 *wise woman.* See 31:10–31. *her house.* Her family and prosperity. *plucketh.* Tears or throws.

14:3 *mouth.* Offense and hurt are caused by the unbridled and arrogant speech of fools (Job 5:21). *rod.* Branch or switch, an instrument of punishment (not the same word as in 13:24).

14:4 *crib is clean.* Feeding trough is empty.

14:7 *Go from.* Keep away from associating with those who do not speak wise and godly things, causing you to be infected by them or seem to approve them.

14:9 *make a mock at.* Treat with contempt (the verbal form of the noun translated "scorner"). *sin.* Guilt or the guilt offering. This could mean either that fools think nothing of sinning or that they despise God's provision of sacrificial atonement and thus forfeit His grace (*favour*).

14:10 *heart knoweth.* The only true and faithful judge of one's joys and sorrows is the person himself (1 Sam. 1:10; 1 Kings 8:38). *stranger.* Simply refers here to another person. *intermeddle.* Either interfere or share.

11 The house of the wicked shall be overthrown: but the tabernacle of the upright shall flourish.
12 There is a way which seemeth right unto a man, but the end thereof *are* the ways of death.
13 Even in laughter the heart is sorrowful; and the end of that mirth *is* heaviness.
14 The backslider in heart shall be filled with his own ways: and a good man *shall be satisfied* from himself.
15 The simple believeth every word: but the prudent *man* looketh well to his going.
16 A wise *man* feareth, and departeth from evil: but the fool rageth, and is confident.
17 *He that is* soon angry dealeth foolishly: and a man of wicked devices is hated.
18 The simple inherit folly: but the prudent are crowned with knowledge.
19 The evil bow before the good; and the wicked at the gates of the righteous.
20 The poor is hated even of his own neighbour: but the rich *hath* many friends.
21 He that despiseth his neighbour sinneth: but he that hath mercy on the poor, happy *is* he.
22 Do they not err that devise evil? but mercy and truth *shall be* to them that devise good.
23 In all labour there is profit: but the talk of the lips *tendeth* only to penury.
24 The crown of the wise *is* their riches: *but* the foolishness of fools *is* folly.
25 A true witness delivereth souls: but a deceitful *witness* speaketh lies.
26 In the fear of the LORD *is* strong confidence: and his children shall have a place of refuge.
27 The fear of the LORD *is* a fountain of life, to depart from the snares of death.
28 In the multitude of people *is* the king's honour: but in the want of people *is* the destruction of the prince.
29 *He that is* slow to wrath *is* of great understanding: but *he that is* hasty of spirit exalteth folly.
30 A sound heart *is* the life of the flesh: but envy the rottenness of the bones.
31 He that oppresseth the poor reproacheth his Maker: but he that honoureth him hath mercy on the poor.
32 The wicked is driven away in his wickedness: but the righteous hath hope in his death.
33 Wisdom resteth in the heart of him that hath understanding: but *that which is* in the midst of fools is made known.
34 Righteousness exalteth a nation: but sin *is* a reproach to any people.
35 The king's favour *is* toward a wise servant: but his wrath is *against* him that causeth shame.

CHAPTER 15

A SOFT answer turneth away wrath: but grievous words stir up anger.
2 The tongue of the wise useth knowledge aright: but the mouth of fools poureth out foolishness.
3 The eyes of the LORD *are* in every place,

14:11 *tabernacle.* Tent or dwelling place.
14:12 *seemeth right.* The undiscerning and rash person is confident in his own perceptions of what is best for him, but he is headed for destruction (2:18,20–22; 3:18; Jer. 21:8; Matt. 7:13–14).
14:13 *mirth is heaviness.* Joy is grief.
14:14 *backslider in heart.* The one who turns back or turns away from the right path in his thoughts, choices, and motivations (Ps. 78:57).
14:15 *simple.* Easily misled, naïve, not skillful in reason (1:4).
14:16 *feareth, and departeth from evil.* The fear of the Lord produces a thoughtful life that carefully avoids sin (Job 1:1). *rageth.* Flares up, shows himself angry. *confident.* Careless or unsuspecting.
14:17 *wicked devices.* Plots.
14:21 *hath mercy.* Graciously shows undeserved favor to those in need (v. 31). *happy.* Possessing great benefits from God; a status, not necessarily a feeling (elsewhere translated "blessed," Ps. 1:1).
14:22 *mercy and truth.* An expression of God's steadfast covenant loyalty and love toward His people (Ps. 86:15).
14:23 *penury.* Extreme poverty; lack of necessities.
14:25 *souls.* Persons.
14:26 *confidence.* Security.
14:29 *hasty of spirit.* Hebrew, "short of spirit." *exalteth.* Hebrew, "lifts up like a banner," to be seen by all (v. 17).
14:31 *reproacheth his Maker.* Shows contempt for God who is the Creator of all human beings in His image, whether rich or *poor*, who therefore should be honored and valued (17:5). This proverb links the two greatest commandments of loving God and loving neighbor.
14:32 *hath hope.* Hebrew, "seeks and finds refuge." Even when dying, the *righteous* have reason to trust God, implying resurrection and eternal life (Job 19:25–26; Ps. 49:15; Dan. 12:1–2).
14:34 *reproach.* Shame.

Thoughts for Personal/Family Worship: Chapter 14

1. **Whatever position you hold in your home (v. 11), seek to build others up in godliness. Do not seek worldly joys, which are neither solid nor lasting, but seek the joys of the Spirit, which are unmixed and everlasting. Backsliding from the Lord begins in the heart (v. 14); therefore, guard your heart. How are your heart attitudes toward the Lord demonstrated? . . . through deep meditation and prayer, as well as sincere obedience?**
2. **Be thankful for godly and righteous laws in your nation and those godly men and women who serve in the public sphere (vv. 34–35). Aim to support and encourage them. In what ways does your society honor justice and godliness, and in what ways do the laws and practices of your people offend God?**

Chapter 15: ***Axioms are given dealing with the use of the tongue, submission, God's providence, and receiving parental instruction.***

15:1 *soft.* Mild, gentle, and soothing. *grievous.* Harsh, severe, and hurtful. Relationships are built or destroyed through words.
15:3 *eyes of the LORD.* God's presence to know and act faithfully (5:21; 22:12; 2 Chron. 16:9; Ps. 34:15). God is omniscient,

beholding the evil and the good.
4 A wholesome tongue *is* a tree of life: but perverseness therein *is* a breach in the spirit.
5 A fool despiseth his father's instruction: but he that regardeth reproof is prudent.
6 In the house of the righteous *is* much treasure: but in the revenues of the wicked is trouble.
7 The lips of the wise disperse knowledge: but the heart of the foolish *doeth* not so.
8 The sacrifice of the wicked *is* an abomination to the LORD: but the prayer of the upright *is* his delight.
9 The way of the wicked *is* an abomination unto the LORD: but he loveth him that followeth after righteousness.
10 Correction *is* grievous unto him that forsaketh the way: *and* he that hateth reproof shall die.
11 Hell and destruction *are* before the LORD: how much more then the hearts of the children of men?
12 A scorner loveth not one that reproveth him: neither will he go unto the wise.
13 A merry heart maketh a cheerful countenance: but by sorrow of the heart the spirit is broken.
14 The heart of him that hath understanding seeketh knowledge: but the mouth of fools feedeth on foolishness.
15 All the days of the afflicted *are* evil: but he that is of a merry heart *hath* a continual feast.
16 Better *is* little with the fear of the LORD than great treasure and trouble therewith.
17 Better *is* a dinner of herbs where love is, than a stalled ox and hatred therewith.
18 A wrathful man stirreth up strife: but *he that is* slow to anger appeaseth strife.
19 The way of the slothful *man is* as an hedge of thorns: but the way of the righteous *is* made plain.
20 A wise son maketh a glad father: but a foolish man despiseth his mother.
21 Folly *is* joy to *him that is* destitute of wisdom: but a man of understanding walketh uprightly.
22 Without counsel purposes are disappointed: but in the multitude of counsellors they are established.
23 A man hath joy by the answer of his mouth: and a word *spoken* in due season, how good *is it!*
24 The way of life *is* above to the wise, that he may depart from hell beneath.
25 The LORD will destroy the house of the proud: but he will establish the border of the widow.
26 The thoughts of the wicked *are* an abomination to the LORD: but *the words* of the pure *are* pleasant words.
27 He that is greedy of gain troubleth his own house; but he that hateth gifts shall live.
28 The heart of the righteous studieth to answer: but the mouth of the wicked poureth out evil things.
29 The LORD *is* far from the wicked: but he heareth the prayer of the righteous.
30 The light of the eyes rejoiceth the heart: *and* a good report maketh the bones fat.
31 The ear that heareth the reproof of life abideth among the wise.
32 He that refuseth instruction despiseth his own soul: but he that heareth reproof getteth understanding.
33 The fear of the LORD *is* the instruction of wisdom; and before honour *is* humility.

knowing all things, including all the actions and words of every person, as well as the intents of the heart (v. 11; Ps. 33:13–14; Jer. 17:10).

15:4 *wholesome tongue*. Gentle and healing speech. *breach*. Collapse.

15:8 *abomination*. That which is disgusting and detestable, often refers to idolatry (vv. 9,26). Hypocritical religion is useless; acts of worship (*sacrifice, prayer*) must be joined with a life of sincere obedience to God's Word (*upright*; Isa. 1:10–20; 29:13).

15:10 *Correction*. Discipline or instruction. *hateth*. Chooses to reject.

15:11 *Hell*. Hebrew, *sheol*, referring to death, the grave, or the abode of departed wicked spirits. *destruction*. Hebrew, *abaddon*, God's judgment on the wicked so that they perish (27:20; Job 26:6; 31:12; cf. Rev. 9:11). The pairing of the two words suggests the place where the spirits of the wicked dead are punished. If God sees into the depths of the invisible spiritual world, then much more does His omniscience penetrate into the secrets of the heart (Ps. 139:8,23–24).

15:13 *merry*. Joyful. *countenance*. Face.

15:16–17 *Better . . . than*. See the same kind of comparison in 12:9; 16:8,19; 17:1; 19:1; 27:5,10; 28:6. *dinner of herbs*. Food of the poor. *stalled*. Fattened, well-fed.

15:18 *appeaseth*. Soothes, pacifies (26:21; 28:25; 29:22).

15:20 *despiseth*. Regards with contempt (see note at 10:1).

15:22 *multitude of counsellors*. Many wise givers of advice (11:14).

15:24 *above*. Going upward, toward heavenly life (Phil. 3:20; Col. 3:1). *hell beneath*. See note at v. 11.

15:25 *establish the border of the widow*. God will defend the rights of the poor and weak to their inheritance.

15:26 *the pure*. Those who are ethically clean.

15:27 *hateth gifts*. Rejects bribes (18:5; 24:23; 29:4; Ex. 23:8; Deut. 16:19; Eccl. 7:7; Isa. 1:23).

15:28 *studieth to answer*. The wise will patiently consider, meditate, and ponder the matter carefully before responding.

15:30 *maketh the bones fat*. Refreshes the inner being.

15:31 *ear that heareth*. The person who allows himself to be admonished by the life-giving Word of God (*reproof of life*) will have a lasting place among the wise.

15:32 *despiseth his own soul*. Refuses sound teaching; is self-destructive.

15:33 *fear of the LORD*. See note at 1:7. *honour is humility*. See James 4:10.

Thoughts for Personal/Family Worship: Chapter 15

1. A sanctified tongue is an important component of Christlikeness—conformity to Christ, the goal of predestination. Our communication can honor God or harm

CHAPTER 16

THE preparations of the heart in man, and the answer of the tongue, *is* from the LORD.
2 All the ways of a man *are* clean in his own eyes; but the LORD weigheth the spirits.
3 Commit thy works unto the LORD, and thy thoughts shall be established.
4 The LORD hath made all *things* for himself: yea, even the wicked for the day of evil.
5 Every one *that is* proud in heart *is* an abomination to the LORD: *though* hand *join* in hand, he shall not be unpunished.
6 By mercy and truth iniquity is purged: and by the fear of the LORD *men* depart from evil.
7 When a man's ways please the LORD, he maketh even his enemies to be at peace with him.
8 Better *is* a little with righteousness than great revenues without right.
9 A man's heart deviseth his way: but the LORD directeth his steps.
10 A divine sentence *is* in the lips of the king: his mouth transgresseth not in judgment.
11 A just weight and balance *are* the LORD's: all the weights of the bag *are* his work.
12 *It is* an abomination to kings to commit wickedness: for the throne is established by righteousness.
13 Righteous lips *are* the delight of kings; and they love him that speaketh right.
14 The wrath of a king *is as* messengers of death: but a wise man will pacify it.
15 In the light of the king's countenance *is* life; and his favour *is* as a cloud of the latter rain.
16 How much better *is it* to get wisdom than gold! and to get understanding rather to be chosen than silver!
17 The highway of the upright *is* to depart from evil: he that keepeth his way preserveth his soul.
18 Pride *goeth* before destruction, and an haughty spirit before a fall.
19 Better *it is to be* of an humble spirit with the lowly, than to divide the spoil with the proud.
20 He that handleth a matter wisely shall find good: and whoso trusteth in the LORD, happy *is* he.

others. Ironically, words communicated in private often have greater power than those in public. Controlling and guarding the tongue and using it well are no small matters in the cultivation of godliness. Weigh all things carefully and from God's viewpoint before you respond. Make sure that your responses are loving, being given gently for the benefit and building up of the hearers. It is a wicked and condemning thing to use our God-given tongues to cause damage or to speak idle words. How can you cultivate a habit of wise and self-controlled speech?

2. God is omniscient (vv. 3,11), knowing everything, and searching all our hearts and seeing all our ways. We should aim to bring Him worship with a heart that is humble and right in His sight. God is also sovereign, in His creating, sustaining, and planning all that goes on in the world. This knowledge should fill our hearts with worship and encourage us, since nothing is overlooked in our lives. To the unconverted, this truth should be humbling and produce dread, as they cannot hide from Him. Has this truth driven you to trust Him with a repentant heart? How can it be a source of encouragement in your daily life?

Chapter 16: *God watches over us and our dealings in human affairs.*

16:1 *preparations.* Arrangements, reflections, or plans. Human effort is always subject to God's sovereign will (vv. 2,9,33; 3:6; 19:21; 20:24; Jer. 10:23; John 11:49–51).
16:2 *weigheth.* Examines. *spirits.* The thoughts and motives (21:2; 1 Sam. 16:7; 1 Cor. 4:4; Heb. 4:12).
16:3 *Commit.* Literally, "to roll upon," referring to the total surrender of our plans and cares to God (Pss. 22:9; 37:5; Matt. 6:26; Luke 12:22; 1 Peter 5:7). *thoughts . . . established.* Plans are best accomplished by making and executing them in submission to the Lord, for He always accomplishes His will (Pss. 90:17; 115:3).
16:4 *made all things for himself.* All of God's creations serve His will and are for His glory (Rom. 11:36; Rev. 4:11). *day of evil.* The day of calamity, referring to judgment day (Job 21:30). God rules even over the wicked, for He will glorify Himself through them in His justice (Rom. 9:17–23).
16:5 *abomination.* That which is disgusting and detestable (v. 12). *though hand join in hand.* Man's unified efforts cannot thwart God's sentence of judgment (11:21).
16:6 *mercy and truth.* Covenant loyalty and love, or fidelity; these words are often paired to stress the reliability of God's faithful love (Ex. 34:6). Here it refers to human faithfulness (3:3), parallel to the *fear* of God. *purged.* The Hebrew term refers to the atoning of sin or appeasement of anger by a gift or sacrifice (v. 14; Gen. 32:20; Lev. 1:4; 4:20). Only those who repent of sin and turn back to God's ways of faithful love are forgiven through Christ's blood (Luke 24:46–47; Acts 2:38; 1 John 1:5–7).
16:7 *even his enemies.* The godly are peacemakers, though they still suffer persecution from the wicked (Matt. 5:9–10; Rom. 12:17–18).
16:9 *deviseth his way.* Man makes plans, but all the means, occasions, conduct, and success depend solely upon God's will and providence.
16:10 *divine sentence.* A decision or verdict; sometimes referring to divination. The *king* is represented in an ideal manner (20:8), as speaking words from God, full of justice.
16:11 *just weight and balance.* Accurate scale, representing fair and honest ethics in business (11:1). *weights.* The stones used in the balance to offset the commodity being weighed. All justice and right dealing among men comes from the Lord (*his work*).
16:15 *light of . . . countenance.* The shining face expresses favor (Ps. 4:6). *latter rain.* The late spring rain before the harvest played a key role in ripening the crop (Deut. 11:14). The favor of the king is a blessing crucial for the well-being of the people (2 Sam 23:3–4; Ps. 72:6).
16:16 *better . . . than gold.* God's wisdom is more precious than any earthly treasure (2:4; 8:10–11,18–19).
16:17 *highway.* Conduct or behavior. *keepeth.* Watches or guards. *preserveth his soul.* Guards himself (a different word than *keepeth*, but with the same sense).
16:18 *destruction.* Collapse. *fall.* Stumbling, calamity. Self-confidence produces carelessness.
16:19 *spoil.* Goods that have been plundered.
16:20 *handleth.* Ponders or gives attention to, considers wisely, mainly by God's Word (13:13). *trusteth.* Places con-

21 The wise in heart shall be called prudent: and
the sweetness of the lips increaseth learning.
22 Understanding *is* a wellspring of life unto him
that hath it: but the instruction of fools *is* folly.
23 The heart of the wise teacheth his mouth, and
addeth learning to his lips.
24 Pleasant words *are as* an honeycomb, sweet to
the soul, and health to the bones.
25 There is a way that seemeth right unto a man,
but the end thereof *are* the ways of death.
26 He that laboureth laboureth for himself; for
his mouth craveth it of him.
27 An ungodly man diggeth up evil: and in his
lips *there is* as a burning fire.
28 A froward man soweth strife: and a whisperer
separateth chief friends.
29 A violent man enticeth his neighbour, and
leadeth him into the way *that is* not good.
30 He shutteth his eyes to devise froward things:
moving his lips he bringeth evil to pass.
31 The hoary head *is* a crown of glory, *if* it be
found in the way of righteousness.
32 *He that is* slow to anger *is* better than the
mighty; and he that ruleth his spirit than he that
taketh a city.
33 The lot is cast into the lap; but the whole
disposing thereof *is* of the LORD.

CHAPTER 17

BETTER *is* a dry morsel, and quietness therewith,
than an house full of sacrifices *with* strife.
2 A wise servant shall have rule over a son
that causeth shame, and shall have part of the
inheritance among the brethren.
3 The fining pot *is* for silver, and the furnace for
gold: but the LORD trieth the hearts.
4 A wicked doer giveth heed to false lips; *and* a
liar giveth ear to a naughty tongue.
5 Whoso mocketh the poor reproacheth his
Maker: *and* he that is glad at calamities shall not
be unpunished.
6 Children's children *are* the crown of old men;
and the glory of children *are* their fathers.
7 Excellent speech becometh not a fool: much
less do lying lips a prince.
8 A gift *is as* a precious stone in the eyes of
him that hath it: whithersoever it turneth, it
prospereth.
9 He that covereth a transgression seeketh love;

fidence for safety and security, a word of faith (Pss. 2:12; 118:8–9). *happy.* Having great benefits from God; elsewhere translated "blessed" (Ps. 1:1).

16:21 *sweetness of the lips.* Eloquent words of the wise that proceed intelligently and discerningly will persuade and instruct others (v. 24).

16:23 The *heart* is the source of wisdom which flows into words (4:21–23).

16:24 *Pleasant words.* Gentle and kind words which sooth the mind, having healing values for relationships and well-being (15:1). *honeycomb.* Honey was the sweetest substance of the ancient world and thus a picture of joy and refreshment (24:13–14; Ps. 19:10).

16:25 See 14:12.

16:26 *his mouth craveth.* His hunger presses him. Self-preservation is a motive for diligent labor (Eccl. 6:7; 2 Thess. 3:10–12).

16:27 *evil.* Trouble or hurt (v. 30). *burning fire.* A picture of the destructive power of vindictive and slanderous words (James 3:6).

16:28 *froward.* Perverse (v. 30; 6:14; 8:8). *whisperer.* A talebearer or gossip (26:20,22).

16:30 *shutteth his eyes.* An image of deep thought. *moving his lips.* Pinching his lips, showing determination and concentration (v. 13).

16:31 *hoary.* Gray or white with age. *crown.* Showing honor and respect for elders (20:29; Lev. 19:32).

16:32 *slow to anger.* See 14:17; James 1:19–20. *taketh a city.* See 25:28; Eccl. 9:17–18.

16:33 *lot.* Casting of lots was an ancient practice of determining God's will in various matters (Josh. 14:1–2; 1 Sam. 14:38–43; Jonah 1:7; Acts 1:26). *whole disposing.* What might seem to be the result of random chance is ordered by the sovereign God.

Thoughts for Personal/Family Worship: Chapter 16

1. **The chapter begins and ends with God's sovereignty (vv. 1,33). He is pleased to order the affairs of men; therefore, we must always live in full trust of His wisdom in ordering our ways and be comforted that even the mundane things of life are ordered by the Lord. Yet, resting in God's sovereignty does not breed passivity. Seek the Lord and labor in all you do with the purpose of glorifying God, who will show you the way forward. Have you committed your plans and actions unto the Lord (v. 3) allowing Him to conform your will to His? There is nothing better or more satisfying than knowing what we want is what God wants for us.**
2. **In contrast to so much of modern thought that glamorizes youth and modern efforts to delay the aging process, the Bible places a premium on the gray head of old age. Reaching old age should be regarded as evidence of God's favor and should be venerated by the young who, if the Lord so grants, will one day be old themselves. Godly, elderly people have much to offer in way of warnings and advice. What ways have you found to honor the elderly and listen to their wisdom?**

Chapter 17: *God's wisdom regarding home, friends, and fools is shared.*

17:1 *dry morsel.* An old piece of bread. *therewith.* With it. *sacrifices with strife.* Feasting on meat from a recent sacrifice to God, while fighting among themselves. A peaceful home is more desirable than a hypocritical, prosperous house (15:17).

17:3 *fining pot.* A crucible for refining metals. *hearts.* Man's innermost being, including his mind, affections, and will.

17:4 *naughty tongue.* Destructive speech.

17:5 *mocketh the poor.* The lowliest of human beings is created by God, and contempt for any man is contempt for God (14:31; James 3:9–10).

17:7 *becometh not.* Is not suitable or appropriate (16:12–13).

17:8 *gift.* A bribe (v. 23; 15:27).

17:9 *covereth . . . repeateth.* Contrast between a peacemaker and a talebearer (10:12; 16:28; 18:8).

but he that repeateth a matter separateth *very*
friends.
10 A reproof entereth more into a wise man than
an hundred stripes into a fool.
11 An evil *man* seeketh only rebellion: therefore a
cruel messenger shall be sent against him.
12 Let a bear robbed of her whelps meet a man,
rather than a fool in his folly.
13 Whoso rewardeth evil for good, evil shall not
depart from his house.
14 The beginning of strife *is as* when one letteth
out water: therefore leave off contention, before it
be meddled with.
15 He that justifieth the wicked, and he that condemneth the just, even they both *are* abomination
to the LORD.
16 Wherefore *is there* a price in the hand of a fool
to get wisdom, seeing *he hath* no heart *to it?*
17 A friend loveth at all times, and a brother is
born for adversity.
18 A man void of understanding striketh hands,
and becometh surety in the presence of his friend.
19 He loveth transgression that loveth strife: *and*
he that exalteth his gate seeketh destruction.
20 He that hath a froward heart findeth no good:
and he that hath a perverse tongue falleth into
mischief.
21 He that begetteth a fool *doeth it* to his sorrow:
and the father of a fool hath no joy.
22 A merry heart doeth good *like* a medicine: but
a broken spirit drieth the bones.
23 A wicked *man* taketh a gift out of the bosom to
pervert the ways of judgment.
24 Wisdom *is* before him that hath understanding;
but the eyes of a fool *are* in the ends of the earth.
25 A foolish son *is* a grief to his father, and
bitterness to her that bare him.
26 Also to punish the just *is* not good, *nor* to
strike princes for equity.
27 He that hath knowledge spareth his words:
and a man of understanding is of an excellent
spirit.
28 Even a fool, when he holdeth his peace, is
counted wise: *and* he that shutteth his lips *is*
esteemed a man of understanding.

CHAPTER 18

THROUGH desire a man, having separated himself,
seeketh *and* intermeddleth with all wisdom.
2 A fool hath no delight in understanding, but
that his heart may discover itself.
3 When the wicked cometh, *then* cometh also
contempt, and with ignominy reproach.
4 The words of a man's mouth *are as* deep waters,
and the wellspring of wisdom *as* a flowing brook.
5 *It is* not good to accept the person of the wicked,
to overthrow the righteous in judgment.
6 A fool's lips enter into contention, and his
mouth calleth for strokes.

17:10 *entereth.* Makes a deep impression (9:7–9).
17:11 *a cruel messenger.* One who is sent to inflict punishment. Those who do wickedly invite just retribution from the authorities (1 Kings 2:25; Rom. 13:1–5).
17:12 *whelps.* Cubs.
17:13 *evil.* Something bad, trouble, or calamity.
17:14 *letteth out water.* Causes an uncontrollable flood by a breach in a dam. *before it be meddled with.* Before it breaks out.
17:15 Miscarriages of justice are disgusting and detestable (an *abomination)* to the Lord (Deut. 25:1).
17:18 *void of understanding.* Lacking heart. *striketh hands.* Confirms an arrangement or deal, here the obligation to pay another's debt (*surety,* see 6:1–5).
17:19 *exalteth his gate.* A picture of the proud person who extravagantly shows off his wealth.
17:20 *froward.* Perverse or crooked. *mischief.* Evil or calamity.
17:21 *begetteth.* Has for a child. *a fool.* A person without wisdom and blind to his need (see note at 1:22). *sorrow . . . joy.* See note at 10:1.
17:22 The state of the mind affects the body in health, power, and motivation (14:30; 15:13,30; 16:14; Job 29:24).
17:23 *gift . . . bosom.* Money or other valuables carried in a fold of the clothing to be used as a bribe to distort (*pervert*) justice (v. 8).
17:24 *eyes . . . in the ends of the earth.* Foolishly daydreaming and fantasizing.
17:25 See note at v. 21.
17:27 *spareth his words.* Uses prudence in controlling his speech. *excellent spirit.* Literally, "cold or cool of spirit," referring to being controlled and calm.
17:28 *holdeth his peace.* Is silent (15:2; Job 13:5; Eccl. 10:3,14).

Thoughts for Personal/Family Worship: Chapter 17

1. **Knowing that God tries or searches our hearts ought to be a powerful motive for right thinking and behaving (v. 3; see Ps. 139). All things are naked and open before His eyes (Heb. 4:12–13), and each of us will give an account before Him. Can you stand before God with the confidence of David when God examines you knowing that you have purposed not to transgress (Ps. 17:3; 2 Cor. 5:21)?**
2. **God's law is a unity, and to refuse to love our neighbor is to reject God (v. 5). An offense against one commandment results in guilt in all (James 2:10). How we treat others is an index to how we really view God. Professing to love Him while at the same time mistreating others is evidence that our love for God is not in keeping with His demand. If we love Him as we ought, we will love and treat others as we should. Consider your relationships with people who are less powerful and prosperous than you are. How does the way you treat them reflect what you think about the Lord?**

Chapter 18: ***The perils and blessings of life are compared.***

18:1 *intermeddleth.* Breaks out against.
18:2 *discover.* Reveal, expose, uncover.
18:3 *with ignominy reproach.* Public shame or disgrace produces hateful expressions in others.
18:5 *accept the person.* Literally, "lift the face," an idiom for showing favoritism (28:21). *righteous.* Those who are innocent in regard to the issue being adjudicated. *judgment.* Justice (17:15,26).
18:6 *strokes.* Blows or beatings (19:29).

7 A fool's mouth *is* his destruction, and his lips
are the snare of his soul.
8 The words of a talebearer *are* as wounds, and
they go down into the innermost parts of the belly.
9 He also that is slothful in his work is brother to
him that is a great waster.
10 The name of the LORD *is* a strong tower: the
righteous runneth into it, and is safe.
11 The rich man's wealth *is* his strong city, and as
an high wall in his own conceit.
12 Before destruction the heart of man is haughty,
and before honour *is* humility.
13 He that answereth a matter before he heareth
it, it *is* folly and shame unto him.
14 The spirit of a man will sustain his infirmity;
but a wounded spirit who can bear?
15 The heart of the prudent getteth knowledge;
and the ear of the wise seeketh knowledge.
16 A man's gift maketh room for him, and
bringeth him before great men.
17 *He that is* first in his own cause *seemeth* just;
but his neighbour cometh and searcheth him.
18 The lot causeth contentions to cease, and
parteth between the mighty.
19 A brother offended *is harder to be won* than a
strong city: and *their* contentions *are* like the bars
of a castle.
20 A man's belly shall be satisfied with the fruit of
his mouth; *and* with the increase of his lips shall
he be filled.
21 Death and life *are* in the power of the tongue:
and they that love it shall eat the fruit thereof.
22 *Whoso* findeth a wife findeth a good *thing*, and
obtaineth favour of the LORD.
23 The poor useth intreaties; but the rich an-
swereth roughly.
24 A man *that hath* friends must shew himself
friendly: and there is a friend *that* sticketh closer
than a brother.

CHAPTER 19

BETTER *is* the poor that walketh in his integrity,
than *he that is* perverse in his lips, and is a fool.
2 Also, *that* the soul *be* without knowledge, *it is*
not good; and he that hasteth with *his* feet sinneth.
3 The foolishness of man perverteth his way: and
his heart fretteth against the LORD.
4 Wealth maketh many friends; but the poor is
separated from his neighbour.

18:7 People who are quarrelsome bring trouble upon themselves; their rash language ensnares them (12:13; 17:14,19,28; 20:3).

18:8 *talebearer.* The one who slanders or backbites. *wounds.* Words have the power to deeply hurt.

18:9 *slothful.* Lazy (6:9–11). *great waster.* Literally, "master of destruction."

18:10 *name of the LORD.* The only place this phrase occurs in Proverbs, referring to all that God reveals Himself to be in His person and perfections (Ex. 3:13–15; 15:3; 34:5–7). *strong tower.* Safety and salvation (Ps. 18:2).

18:11 The *rich* often trust in *wealth* for security (10:15; Ps. 49:6; Luke 12:13–21) instead of in the Lord (v. 10; 1 Tim. 6:17). *conceit.* Delusion or imagination.

18:12 *haughty.* Lifted up in pride (15:33; 16:18).

18:16 *gift.* Not a bribe to pervert justice, but a gift to win favor.

18:17 *searcheth.* Questions, cross-examines, or examines thoroughly. Avoid making judgments before all the evidence is heard (v. 13; 29:20).

18:18 *lot.* See note at 16:33. A decision without bias should satisfy the parties.

18:19 *bars of a castle.* The mechanisms used to secure the gate.

18:20 *fruit of his mouth . . . increase of his lips.* It is satisfying and fulfilling to see constructive and fruitful results of one's speech.

18:21 *Death and life.* One can do the greatest harm or greatest good by what he says (James 1:19; 3:6–10).

18:23 *intreaties.* Pleadings and supplications. *roughly.* Rudely or fiercely.

18:24 *must shew himself friendly.* The Hebrew could be translated "comes to ruin." The idea is either that to have friends one must make friends, or that having multiple friends, without a close one, will result in disappointments. *sticketh closer than a brother.* Clings more tenaciously than a family member and does not abandon you. One faithful friend is more advantageous than many surface, fair-weather friendships. The best friend is the Lord (Isa. 41:8–9; Matt. 11:19; Luke 7:34; John 15:13–15).

Thoughts for Personal/Family Worship: Chapter 18

1. **There is a striking contrast between trusting in the Lord and trusting in wealth (vv. 10–11). Where one finds security and safety spiritually has eternal consequences. To trust the Lord is a certain and inviolable place of safety forever; to trust one's own resources is nothing more than a delusion (Ps. 49; Matt. 6:19–24). The object of faith always determines the value of faith, and the only infinitely valuable object is the Lord. What does it mean to run to the Lord as your strong tower, instead of seeking security in wealth?**
2. **The advice given in vv. 13,15,17 is crucial and should be followed in all matters of dispute and controversy. It is common sense, but far too often ignored. Do not make any judgments until all the facts are known; factor in both sides of the story before taking sides. Jumping to conclusions is not only unwise, but it has the potential of doing great harm. Ask many questions before giving any answers. How are these manifestations of humility?**

Chapter 19: *Foolish and wise behavior are contrasted.*

19:1 *Better is the poor.* See 15:16–17; 16:8.

19:2 *soul . . . without knowledge . . . hasteth with his feet.* One who rushes on without any mature and proper planning brings trouble (21:5; 28:8,20; 29:20; Rom. 10:2). *sinneth.* Misses the mark or standard of God.

19:3 *perverteth his way.* Distorts and ruins his life (13:6) *fretteth.* Rages. He blames God for his own failures and misfortunes (Gen. 4:5; Isa. 8:21; Lam. 3:39–41; James 1:13).

19:4 *separated from his neighbour.* Poverty isolates people as their friends abandon them (14:20). This implicitly warns against showing partiality to the rich (James 2:1–4).

5 A false witness shall not be unpunished, and *he that* speaketh lies shall not escape.
6 Many will intreat the favour of the prince: and every man *is* a friend to him that giveth gifts.
7 All the brethren of the poor do hate him: how much more do his friends go far from him? he pursueth *them with* words, *yet* they *are* wanting *to him*.
8 He that getteth wisdom loveth his own soul: he that keepeth understanding shall find good.
9 A false witness shall not be unpunished, and *he that* speaketh lies shall perish.
10 Delight is not seemly for a fool; much less for a servant to have rule over princes.
11 The discretion of a man deferreth his anger; and *it is* his glory to pass over a transgression.
12 The king's wrath *is* as the roaring of a lion; but his favour *is* as dew upon the grass.
13 A foolish son *is* the calamity of his father: and the contentions of a wife *are* a continual dropping.
14 House and riches *are* the inheritance of fathers: and a prudent wife *is* from the LORD.
15 Slothfulness casteth into a deep sleep; and an idle soul shall suffer hunger.
16 He that keepeth the commandment keepeth his own soul; *but* he that despiseth his ways shall die.
17 He that hath pity upon the poor lendeth unto the LORD; and that which he hath given will he pay him again.
18 Chasten thy son while there is hope, and let not thy soul spare for his crying.
19 A man of great wrath shall suffer punishment: for if thou deliver *him*, yet thou must do it again.
20 Hear counsel, and receive instruction, that thou mayest be wise in thy latter end.
21 *There are* many devices in a man's heart; nevertheless the counsel of the LORD, that shall stand.
22 The desire of a man *is* his kindness: and a poor man *is* better than a liar.
23 The fear of the LORD *tendeth* to life: and *he that hath it* shall abide satisfied; he shall not be visited with evil.
24 A slothful *man* hideth his hand in *his* bosom, and will not so much as bring it to his mouth again.
25 Smite a scorner, and the simple will beware: and reprove one that hath understanding, *and* he will understand knowledge.
26 He that wasteth *his* father, *and* chaseth away *his* mother, *is* a son that causeth shame, and bringeth reproach.
27 Cease, my son, to hear the instruction *that causeth* to err from the words of knowledge.
28 An ungodly witness scorneth judgment: and the mouth of the wicked devoureth iniquity.

19:5 *false witness.* See v. 9; 6:19; 12:17; 14:5,25; ; Ex. 20:16; Deut. 19:18–21.
19:6 *intreat.* Entreat, beg, beseech, implore. *friend.* See v. 4.
19:7 *pursueth them with words.* Constantly and persistently asks for help. *wanting to him.* Literally, "not for him."
19:8 *He that getteth wisdom.* Literally, "he who acquires a heart," referring to godly understanding and desires. The pursuit of wisdom is a holy seeking of our own good (*loveth his own soul*).
19:10 *Delight.* Specifically, a life of luxury. *seemly.* Fitting, pleasing, or appropriate.
19:11 *deferreth his anger.* Makes him slow to act in anger (14:17,29; 16:32). A forgiving spirit shows that true religion exists (Matt. 5:22).
19:12 *roaring of a lion . . . dew upon the grass.* Death and life: good reasons to submit to lawful authorities (16:14–15; 20:2; Rom 13:1–4; 1 Peter 2:13–17).
19:13 *contentions of a wife.* Her quarrels and strife (21:9,19; 25:24). *continual dropping.* The constant annoyance of a leaking roof can ruin the house (27:15; Job 14:19; Eccl. 10:18).
19:15 *Slothfulness.* Laziness (6:6–11; 10:4; 12:24). *deep sleep.* A state of utter indifference.
19:16 *despiseth his ways.* Regards God's laws with contempt (10:17; 13:13; 16:17).
19:17 *hath pity.* Shows undeserved grace to those in need. *lendeth unto the LORD.* He need not look to man to repay him, for God will reward him for loving the poor (14:21,31; Matt. 10:42; 25:40; Luke 14:12–14; 2 Cor. 9:6–7).
19:18 *Chasten.* Discipline (3:11–12; 13:24; 22:6; 23:13).
19:19 *suffer.* Experience. *must do it again.* Repeated efforts of kindness are lost on ill-natured persons.
19:21 *devices.* Thoughts or plans. *counsel of the LORD . . . shall stand.* God's plans cannot fail or be frustrated by human beings (16:1,9; Job 23:13; Ps. 33:10–11; Isa. 46:10).
19:23 *evil.* Calamity or ruin, here as the consequence of judgment (Ps. 89:32; Jer. 6:15).
19:24 *bosom.* A wide food dish in which the hand was plunged in eating (26:15; Matt. 26:23). The image describes a necessary task begun but not finished.
19:26 *wasteth.* Assaults or mistreats. *chaseth away.* Injures. Those who abuse their parents bring great *shame* on themselves (20:20; Deut. 21:18–21) and their family (see note at 10:1).
19:29 *stripes.* Lashes of a whip or long welts (see note at 10:13).

Thoughts for Personal/Family Worship: Chapter 19

1. **We are to be tenderhearted and fair toward those who do not have the privileges and blessings that we enjoy (v. 17). Too often treatment of others is motivated by selfish concerns of what might be received in return. That kind of partiality does not reflect the kind of gospel love that God requires of His people (1 John 3:16–18). Our love for others should mirror our love for God and how God loves us. He treats us graciously in spite of our unworthiness. God is not a respecter of persons and neither should we be. Whom do you know in financial difficulty? How can you show them love and respect?**
2. **There must be respect for all earthly authorities, as they are ordained of God and can do us much harm or good (v. 12; Rom. 13:1–5). However, we should not forget that ultimately Jesus Christ is the King of kings. We are to have the greatest respect, faith, and love for Him, and remember that the One who is called love is also the Judge of all the earth. He displays His wrath upon all His enemies like a roaring lion (Ps. 2:12; Amos 1:2; Rev. 5:5; 10:3). If we were to fear and honor Christ, knowing that we are**

29 Judgments are prepared for scorners, and
stripes for the back of fools.

CHAPTER 20

WINE *is* a mocker, strong drink *is* raging: and
whosoever is deceived thereby is not wise.
2 The fear of a king *is* as the roaring of a lion:
whoso provoketh him to anger sinneth *against* his
own soul.
3 *It is* an honour for a man to cease from strife:
but every fool will be meddling.
4 The sluggard will not plow by reason of the cold;
therefore shall he beg in harvest, and *have* nothing.
5 Counsel in the heart of man *is like* deep water;
but a man of understanding will draw it out.
6 Most men will proclaim every one his own
goodness: but a faithful man who can find?
7 The just *man* walketh in his integrity: his
children *are* blessed after him.
8 A king that sitteth in the throne of judgment
scattereth away all evil with his eyes.
9 Who can say, I have made my heart clean, I am
pure from my sin?
10 Divers weights, *and* divers measures, both of
them *are* alike abomination to the LORD.
11 Even a child is known by his doings, whether
his work *be* pure, and whether *it be* right.
12 The hearing ear, and the seeing eye, the LORD
hath made even both of them.
13 Love not sleep, lest thou come to poverty;
open thine eyes, *and* thou shalt be satisfied with
bread.
14 *It is* naught, *it is* naught, saith the buyer: but
when he is gone his way, then he boasteth.
15 There is gold, and a multitude of rubies: but
the lips of knowledge *are* a precious jewel.
16 Take his garment that is surety *for* a stranger:
and take a pledge of him for a strange woman.
17 Bread of deceit *is* sweet to a man; but
afterwards his mouth shall be filled with gravel.
18 *Every* purpose is established by counsel: and
with good advice make war.
19 He that goeth about *as* a talebearer revealeth
secrets: therefore meddle not with him that flat-
tereth with his lips.
20 Whoso curseth his father or his mother, his
lamp shall be put out in obscure darkness.
21 An inheritance *may be* gotten hastily at the be-
ginning; but the end thereof shall not be blessed.
22 Say not thou, I will recompense evil; *but* wait
on the LORD, and he shall save thee.
23 Divers weights *are* an abomination unto the
LORD; and a false balance *is* not good.
24 Man's goings *are* of the LORD; how can a man
then understand his own way?
25 *It is* a snare to the man *who* devoureth *that
which is* holy, and after vows to make enquiry.
26 A wise king scattereth the wicked, and bringeth
the wheel over them.
27 The spirit of man *is* the candle of the LORD,
searching all the inward parts of the belly.
28 Mercy and truth preserve the king: and his
throne is upholden by mercy.
29 The glory of young men *is* their strength: and
the beauty of old men *is* the gray head.
30 The blueness of a wound cleanseth away evil:
so *do* stripes the inward parts of the belly.

accountable to Him, then we and the society around us would live more soberly and godly under God's blessing.

Chapter 20: *Self-control, honesty, and trust in God are enjoined.*

20:1 *mocker.* Same word as scorner or scoffer (19:25,29). *strong drink.* Alcoholic drink produced from grain whereas *wine* is the product of the vine. Being intoxicated or under the control of any intoxicating drink is forbidden (Isa. 28:7; Eph. 5:18).
20:3 *be meddling.* Break out in quarreling.
20:4 *sluggard.* Lazy person (6:6–11).
20:8 *scattereth away.* Sifts or winnows, as in separating grain from chaff. A wise king can discriminate between right and wrong, good and evil (14:35; 16:10).
20:9 *Who can say.* No one is entirely *clean* in motives or pure of *sin* (1 Kings 8:46; 1 John 1:8,10).
20:10 *Divers.* Various. *abomination.* That which is disgusting and detestable. The differing weights refers to dishonest, unethical business practices in general (v. 23; 11:1; 16:11).
20:13 *Love not sleep.* Sleep is a blessing, but the work of one's vocation demands getting up to labor through the day (6:9–10; 10:5; 19:14; 24:33–34).
20:14 *naught.* Worthless, useless.
20:15 *lips of knowledge.* Wise speech. *precious jewel.* See 3:14–16; 8:10–11,18–21; 16:16; Matt. 13:45–46.
20:16 *surety.* See note at 6:1. *stranger . . . strange.* Different words that both refer typically to foreigners, but here most likely just to another person.
20:17 *Bread of deceit.* Wealth gained dishonestly.
20:18 *purpose is established by counsel.* For plans to be realistic and likely to succeed, they must be based on careful research, wise *advice,* and counting the cost (15:22; Luke 14:28–32).
20:19 *talebearer.* A slanderer or gossip. *meddle not.* Don't get involved with or have fellowship with.
20:20 *lamp . . . put out.* Happiness and life taken away in disgrace (Job 18:5–6,18; Matt. 22:13; 25:30; Jude 13).
20:22 *I will recompense.* One is not to take the law into one's own hand to avenge evil, but leave the matter to God, who will finally deliver (Deut. 32:35; Rom. 12:17,19; Heb. 10:30).
20:23 *Divers weights . . . false balance.* See v. 10; 11:1.
20:25 *snare.* Noose-like trap. *after vows to make enquiry.* Then to reflect or consider whether the vow is viable. Rash vows which cannot be fulfilled are worse than no vows (Eccl. 5:1–7).
20:26 *scattereth.* See v. 8. *wheel.* Implement for threshing grain, symbolic of severe punishment (Amos 1:3).
20:27 *spirit . . . candle.* The mind or conscience, sometimes called the light of nature, by which God calls to account our secret and inmost thoughts (16:2; 21:2; 24:12; Rom. 2:14–16; 1 Cor. 2:11).
20:28 *Mercy and truth.* Faithful loyalty and love, especially to a covenant (3:3; 16:6,12). *upholden.* Supported, sustained (16:12).
20:30 *blueness.* Bruise. *cleanseth . . . stripes the inward parts.* Corporal punishment must be executed wisely to train in

CHAPTER 21

THE king's heart *is* in the hand of the LORD, *as*
the rivers of water: he turneth it whithersoever he
will.
2 Every way of a man *is* right in his own eyes: but
the LORD pondereth the hearts.
3 To do justice and judgment *is* more acceptable
to the LORD than sacrifice.
4 An high look, and a proud heart, *and* the
plowing of the wicked, *is* sin.
5 The thoughts of the diligent *tend* only to
plenteousness; but of every one *that is* hasty only
to want.
6 The getting of treasures by a lying tongue *is* a
vanity tossed to and fro of them that seek death.
7 The robbery of the wicked shall destroy them;
because they refuse to do judgment.
8 The way of man *is* froward and strange: but *as*
for the pure, his work *is* right.
9 *It is* better to dwell in a corner of the housetop,
than with a brawling woman in a wide house.
10 The soul of the wicked desireth evil: his
neighbour findeth no favour in his eyes.
11 When the scorner is punished, the simple is
made wise: and when the wise is instructed, he
receiveth knowledge.
12 The righteous *man* wisely considereth the
house of the wicked: *but God* overthroweth the
wicked for *their* wickedness.
13 Whoso stoppeth his ears at the cry of the poor,
he also shall cry himself, but shall not be heard.
14 A gift in secret pacifieth anger: and a reward in
the bosom strong wrath.
15 *It is* joy to the just to do judgment: but
destruction *shall be* to the workers of iniquity.
16 The man that wandereth out of the way of
understanding shall remain in the congregation
of the dead.
17 He that loveth pleasure *shall be* a poor man: he
that loveth wine and oil shall not be rich.
18 The wicked *shall be* a ransom for the righteous,
and the transgressor for the upright.
19 *It is* better to dwell in the wilderness, than with
a contentious and an angry woman.
20 *There is* treasure to be desired and oil in the
dwelling of the wise; but a foolish man spendeth
it up.
21 He that followeth after righteousness and
mercy findeth life, righteousness, and honour.
22 A wise *man* scaleth the city of the mighty,
and casteth down the strength of the confidence
thereof.
23 Whoso keepeth his mouth and his tongue
keepeth his soul from troubles.

---

godly behavior and deter from evil courses (19:25; 22:15; Heb. 12:10).

Thoughts for Personal/Family Worship: Chapter 20

1. **Our society is increasingly poisoning itself by excess, and one of the destructive and enticing excesses is the abuse of alcoholic beverages and other mind-altering drugs. We must take to heart the many warnings associated with wine and alcoholic drink, which can affect the emotions and can control our judgment in ways that lead to sin. Be aware of the entanglements of addiction that come with such intoxicating drinks. How might you be tempted to sin with regard to alcohol or drugs? How can you resist?**
2. **To know that our daily experiences are of the Lord must encourage our continual trust of Him and submission to His mysterious ways (v. 24). He will provide for all His people who follow Him. Think of your past and how you have been guided and carried through to this point in your life. Praise the One who has richly sustained you. Look to the future glory that will follow those who have trusted and continue to live "looking unto Jesus the author and finisher of our faith" (Heb. 12:2). Walking by faith rather than by sight is the theme of much of Scripture and Christian experience. Though we may not fully understand the meaning of our lives, how can we build up our faith and trust in the God who rules over us?**

Chapter 21: ***God is sovereign, but man is helpless, needy, and wicked at heart.***

21:1 *rivers.* Irrigation channels (Ps. 1:3), whose course was easily turned. *he turneth it.* Showing God's absolute sovereignty over the most powerful men in the world (16:9; Ps. 33:15). *whithersoever.* Wherever.

21:2 *pondereth.* Examines (16:2). Repetition of such maxims emphasizes their importance.

21:3 External rituals without the spiritual reality in heart and practice is worthless (15:8; 1 Sam. 15:22; Isa. 1:11,17; Hos. 6:6; Mic. 6:6–8).

21:4 *high look.* Hebrew, "haughtiness of eyes," a gesture or sign of pride (6:17). *proud heart.* Or, "heart of breadth," one that is swollen with pride (Ps. 101:5). *plowing.* The Hebrew word can refer to either plowing or a lamp, which would designate prosperity or joy. Even the indifferent or benign actions or states of the wicked are sin before God (Gen. 6:5).

21:5 *plenteousness.* Profit or advantage. *hasty . . . to want.* Rushing to action without wise thought leads to poverty (19:2; 28:20).

21:6 *vanity.* A breath, referring to what is unsubstantial and temporal (13:11).

21:7 *robbery.* All sorts of violent actions (1:18–19; 12:6; Jer. 7:9–11,15). *judgment.* Justice.

21:8 *froward and strange.* Crooked and dishonest.

21:9 *brawling woman.* Woman of contention or strife, one given to arguing and fighting (v. 19; 19:13; 25:24; 27:15–16).

21:12 *wisely considereth.* Regards or gives attention to (Pss. 37:35–38; 73:17,20).

21:14 *A gift in secret.* A bribe. *pacifieth.* Subdues or soothes. *reward.* Another word for a bribe (17:8,23; 18:16; 19:6).

21:17 *loveth wine and oil.* Such things are good gifts of God for our enjoyment (Deut. 14:26; Neh. 8:12; Ps. 104:15), but not to be loved and pursued in extravagant luxury (Amos 6:6).

21:19 *contentious . . . woman.* See note at v. 9.

21:20 The wise, by diligence and care, store and increase in wealth; fools unwisely *spendeth it*, literally, "swallow it up."

21:22 *scaleth.* Goes up, like a soldier who climbs the wall and penetrates the fortress. Wisdom is more effective than force or strength (Eccl. 7:19; 9:15–16; 10:10).

21:23 *keepeth his mouth.* Watches what he says (12:13; 13:2–3; James 1:26).

24 Proud *and* haughty scorner *is* his name, who dealeth in proud wrath.
25 The desire of the slothful killeth him; for his hands refuse to labour.
26 He coveteth greedily all the day long: but the righteous giveth and spareth not.
27 The sacrifice of the wicked *is* abomination: how much more, *when* he bringeth it with a wicked mind?
28 A false witness shall perish: but the man that heareth speaketh constantly.
29 A wicked man hardeneth his face: but *as for* the upright, he directeth his way.
30 *There is* no wisdom nor understanding nor counsel against the LORD.
31 The horse *is* prepared against the day of battle: but safety *is* of the LORD.

CHAPTER 22

A GOOD name *is* rather to be chosen than great riches, *and* loving favour rather than silver and gold.
2 The rich and poor meet together: the LORD *is* the maker of them all.
3 A prudent *man* foreseeth the evil, and hideth himself: but the simple pass on, and are punished.
4 By humility *and* the fear of the LORD *are* riches, and honour, and life.
5 Thorns *and* snares *are* in the way of the froward: he that doth keep his soul shall be far from them.
6 Train up a child in the way he should go: and when he is old, he will not depart from it.
7 The rich ruleth over the poor, and the borrower *is* servant to the lender.
8 He that soweth iniquity shall reap vanity: and the rod of his anger shall fail.
9 He that hath a bountiful eye shall be blessed; for he giveth of his bread to the poor.
10 Cast out the scorner, and contention shall go out; yea, strife and reproach shall cease.
11 He that loveth pureness of heart, *for* the grace of his lips the king *shall be* his friend.
12 The eyes of the LORD preserve knowledge, and he overthroweth the words of the transgressor.
13 The slothful *man* saith, *There is* a lion without, I shall be slain in the streets.
14 The mouth of strange women *is* a deep pit: he that is abhorred of the LORD shall fall therein.
15 Foolishness *is* bound in the heart of a child; *but* the rod of correction shall drive it far from him.
16 He that oppresseth the poor to increase his

21:26 *coveteth greedily.* Hebrew, "craves for a craving or lusts after a lust." *spareth not.* Does not withhold or keep back for self.

21:27 *abomination.* That which is disgusting and detestable. See v. 3.

21:28 *heareth.* Listens to instruction. *speaketh constantly.* He and his witness will endure (12:19; 19:5).

21:29 *hardeneth his face.* Becomes obstinate and impertinent. *directeth . . . way.* Considers and acts advisedly.

21:30–31 Men's best plans can neither defeat God's will (*against the LORD*) nor win the victory (*safety* or literally, "salvation") without His aid (19:21; Pss. 20:7; 33:17; Jer. 9:23).

Thoughts for Personal/Family Worship: Chapter 21

It is a source of great comfort to know that all the governments of earth are subject to God, who rules and manipulates them according to His purpose and pleasure (v. 1). Reasoning from the greater to lesser leads to the conclusion that the Lord governs everything else as well. Nothing can stand against His will (v. 30). Take comfort from the truth that all hearts and all the ways of men flow according to divine direction. This drives us to ask for greater and childlike faith in His dealings with us and that we may not sin against Him, by hardening ourselves against His providences. Trusting the Lord is always the wise thing to do. How can you grow in humility and fear before this sovereign Lord?

Chapter 22: *The function of instruction and training is presented.*

22:1 *good name.* Reputation (Eccl. 7:1).

22:2 *rich and poor.* Referring to opposites is a means of expressing totality. Every class of humanity is on the same level before God; He is no respecter of persons (14:31; 17:5).

22:3 *evil.* Danger or calamity. *hideth.* Seeks protection in God, his strong tower (18:10; cf. 14:16; 27:12). *are punished.* Come to grief.

22:5 *Thorns and snares.* Symbolic of the dangers and misfortunes that come upon the wicked. *the froward.* Those who are twisted or perverted (3:32; 6:12).

22:6 *Train up.* Dedicate (Deut. 20:5; cf. Neh. 12:27), a Hebrew root used for dedicating the temple or its altar for sacred use (Num. 7:10–11,84,88; 1 Kings 8:63; 2 Chron. 7:5,9; Ezra 6:16–17). Parents must train their children to serve the Lord in holiness (Deut. 4:9; 6:6–8; 11:18–21; Josh. 24:15; Eph. 6:4). *in the way he should go.* According to his way; training and education should fit the child's needs, interests, and abilities.

22:8 *soweth . . . reap.* The principle of the harvest (Job 4:8; Hos. 10:12; 2 Cor. 9:6; Gal. 6:7–8) illustrates that God will give to each man according to his works (Ps. 109:16–20). *vanity.* Trouble.

22:9 *bountiful eye.* Hebrew, "a good eye," an idiom for mercy and generosity to the needy.

22:10 *scorner.* The proud mocker (1:22; 9:7). *contention.* Strife, conflict (6:14; 15:18; 16:28).

22:11 The wise character is attractive and wins the respect of all, even the most powerful and influential people (Eccl. 10:12).

22:12 *eyes of the LORD.* God's presence to know all things and act accordingly. *preserve.* Protect or guard.

22:13 *without.* Outside. Frivolous excuses and irrational fears satisfy the lazy man's conscience (26:13).

22:14 *mouth of strange women.* The flattering and seductive speech of immoral women (see note at 2:16).

22:15 *bound.* Firmly fixed or settled, as being born and rooted in the deepest motives and beliefs (*heart*) of a child's nature. *rod of correction.* Judicious, controlled, and loving physical discipline deters from sin and makes one watchful against it (13:24).

22:16 *oppresseth.* Wrongs by fraud or force (14:31). *giveth to*

riches, and he that giveth to the rich, *shall* surely
come to want.
17 Bow down thine ear, and hear the words of the
wise, and apply thine heart unto my knowledge.
18 For *it is* a pleasant thing if thou keep them
within thee; they shall withal be fitted in thy lips.
19 That thy trust may be in the LORD, I have made
known to thee this day, even to thee.
20 Have not I written to thee excellent things in
counsels and knowledge,
21 That I might make thee know the certainty of
the words of truth; that thou mightest answer the
words of truth to them that send unto thee?
22 Rob not the poor, because he *is* poor: neither
oppress the afflicted in the gate:
23 For the LORD will plead their cause, and spoil
the soul of those that spoiled them.
24 Make no friendship with an angry man; and
with a furious man thou shalt not go:
25 Lest thou learn his ways, and get a snare to thy
soul.
26 Be not thou *one* of them that strike hands, *or*
of them that are sureties for debts.
27 If thou hast nothing to pay, why should he take
away thy bed from under thee?
28 Remove not the ancient landmark, which thy
fathers have set.
29 Seest thou a man diligent in his business? he
shall stand before kings; he shall not stand before
mean *men*.

CHAPTER 23

WHEN thou sittest to eat with a ruler, consider
diligently what *is* before thee:
2 And put a knife to thy throat, if thou *be* a man
given to appetite.
3 Be not desirous of his dainties: for they *are*
deceitful meat.
4 Labour not to be rich: cease from thine own
wisdom.
5 Wilt thou set thine eyes upon that which is not?
for *riches* certainly make themselves wings; they
fly away as an eagle toward heaven.
6 Eat thou not the bread of *him that hath* an evil
eye, neither desire thou his dainty meats:
7 For as he thinketh in his heart, so *is* he: Eat and
drink, saith he to thee; but his heart *is* not with
thee.
8 The morsel *which* thou hast eaten shalt thou
vomit up, and lose thy sweet words.
9 Speak not in the ears of a fool: for he will
despise the wisdom of thy words.
10 Remove not the old landmark; and enter not

---

the rich. Bribes the rich. These two vices show selfishness and incur God's displeasure and punishment. *want.* Lack, poverty.

Words of the Wise (22:17—24:34)

22:17 *Bow down thine ear.* Intentionally listen (5:1). *words of the wise.* See Introduction: Authorship. *apply thine heart.* Think carefully, give diligent study (23:12; Ps. 90:12; Eccl. 7:25; 8:9,16).

22:18 *withal be fitted.* Be established together, referring to the readiness to respond with wise speech (*lips*; 8:6; 10:13; Ps. 119:13,171; Mal. 2:7; Heb. 13:15).

22:19 *trust.* Confidence for security and safety.

22:20 *excellent things.* The principal and great things of God's law (8:6; Hos. 8:12). *counsels and knowledge.* Advice and instruction (Ps. 12:6; 2 Tim. 3:15–17; 2 Peter 1:19–21).

22:22–23 *Rob not the poor . . . the LORD will plead.* Though men fail to defend the poor, God will do so (17:5; Ps. 12:5). *gate.* Place of public gathering for matters of law and justice, but also the place where beggars would sit (Job 5:4; Ps. 69:12).

22:24–25 *no friendship . . . learn his ways.* The company we keep shapes our lives (see note at 13:20).

22:26–27 *strike hands.* Give a handshake to confirm a transaction. *sureties for debts.* A person pledged to guarantee a contractual loan (6:1–5; 17:18). *take away thy bed.* The creditor will not spare your most precious possessions to recoup his losses for an unpaid loan.

22:28 *landmark.* The boundary mark for the land. One is not to get gain by injury to others and invading their rights (23:10; Lev. 25:23; Deut. 19:14; 27:17).

22:29 *mean.* Common, obscure, insignificant, or low in position and influence. Success rewards diligence (10:4; 21:5).

Thoughts for Personal/Family Worship: Chapter 22

1. **Guard your character and name by a godly life (v. 1). Christians must be concerned for their reputations because their lives should mirror that of Christ. We should live in such a way that no reproach is brought to the name of Christ because of our sinful behavior. Just a little folly has the power to destroy a whole life of good (Eccl. 10:1). How does a person develop and protect a good reputation?**
2. **When rearing children in the nurture and admonition of the Lord, parents must be sensitive to a child's God-given traits and abilities (v. 6). They should dedicate their children to the kind of training that will do them good for life. At the core of all training must be the religious and spiritual education that will teach children the gospel and way of life that is pleasing to the Lord (1:7–9). It is that kind of life that will do them good both for this life and the life to come. Why is it important to craft child training to the individual and yet to teach all our children the common calling of fearing the Lord?**

Chapter 23: *Warnings are given against being controlled by things or people; and godliness is encouraged.*

23:1–3 This is a warning against deception and an exhortation for self-control and discernment before people of high position. These are the representative sins of man's fallen nature: the lust of the flesh (*man given to appetite*) and the pride of life (*sittest . . . with a ruler*).

23:2 *put a knife.* Forcefully restrain your desires (Matt. 18:8–9; 1 Cor. 9:27; Phil. 3:19).

23:3 *dainties.* Choice food, delicacies. *deceitful.* The offer of a feast appears generous, but is driven by a secret agenda (v. 7). *meat.* Food of any sort.

23:4–5 Do not weary yourself by aiming to simply accumulate wealth which is as temporary as a bird that flies away

into the fields of the fatherless:
11 For their redeemer *is* mighty; he shall plead
their cause with thee.
12 Apply thine heart unto instruction, and thine
ears to the words of knowledge.
13 Withhold not correction from the child: for *if*
thou beatest him with the rod, he shall not die.
14 Thou shalt beat him with the rod, and shalt
deliver his soul from hell.
15 My son, if thine heart be wise, my heart shall
rejoice, even mine.
16 Yea, my reins shall rejoice, when thy lips speak
right things.
17 Let not thine heart envy sinners: but *be thou* in
the fear of the LORD all the day long.
18 For surely there is an end; and thine expecta-
tion shall not be cut off.
19 Hear thou, my son, and be wise, and guide
thine heart in the way.
20 Be not among winebibbers; among riotous
eaters of flesh:
21 For the drunkard and the glutton shall come
to poverty: and drowsiness shall clothe *a man*
with rags.
22 Hearken unto thy father that begat thee, and
despise not thy mother when she is old.
23 Buy the truth, and sell *it* not; *also* wisdom, and
instruction, and understanding.
24 The father of the righteous shall greatly
rejoice: and he that begetteth a wise *child* shall
have joy of him.
25 Thy father and thy mother shall be glad, and
she that bare thee shall rejoice.
26 My son, give me thine heart, and let thine eyes
observe my ways.
27 For a whore *is* a deep ditch; and a strange
woman *is* a narrow pit.
28 She also lieth in wait as *for* a prey, and increas-
eth the transgressors among men.
29 Who hath woe? who hath sorrow? who hath
contentions? who hath babbling? who hath
wounds without cause? who hath redness of eyes?
30 They that tarry long at the wine; they that go
to seek mixed wine.
31 Look not thou upon the wine when it is red,
when it giveth his colour in the cup, *when* it
moveth itself aright.
32 At the last it biteth like a serpent, and stingeth
like an adder.
33 Thine eyes shall behold strange women, and
thine heart shall utter perverse things.
34 Yea, thou shalt be as he that lieth down in the
midst of the sea, or as he that lieth upon the top
of a mast.

(11:28; 28:20; John 6:27; 1 Tim. 6:8–10).

23:6 *evil eye.* A hurtful purpose, particularly a heart of greed and stinginess (22:9; 28:22; Deut. 15:9; Matt. 6:23; 20:15). *dainty meats.* Tasty or savory food.

23:9 *fool . . . will despise the wisdom.* See 9:8; Matt. 7:6.

23:10–11 See notes at 15:25; 22:22–23,28. *redeemer.* The near kinsman who acts to rescue and defend family members in need at his own expense (Lev. 25:25–26; Num. 35:12; Job 19:25).

23:13–14 *rod . . . deliver his soul from hell.* If done judiciously and out of love, corporal discipline will achieve spiritual good, turning the child from sin and death (13:24; 19:18; 29:15,17). *hell.* The Hebrew word, *sheol*, refers to death, the grave, or the abode of departed wicked spirits.

23:15–16 The wise conduct of the well-trained child (vv. 13–14) brings joy to the parents (vv. 24–25; see note at 10:1).

23:16 *reins.* Hebrew, "kidneys," figuratively referring to the spirit as the seat of thoughts and feelings.

23:17–18 *not . . . envy sinners.* The lifestyle of wickedness may seem appealing until seen in the light of God's majesty and the future (24:19–20; Pss. 37; 49; 73).

23:20 *winebibbers.* Drunkards (vv. 29–35; Rom. 13:13; Eph. 5:18; 1 Peter 4:3–4). *riotous eaters.* Gluttons (v. 21; 28:7). *flesh.* Meat. Drunkenness and gluttony are linked together in Scripture as a summary of a life of rebellion against authority and wild pursuit of luxury and pleasure instead of wisdom, hard work, and service to others (Deut. 21:18–21; Luke 7:34; 16:19–20; 21:34).

23:21 *drowsiness.* The dreamy sleep of the lazy (6:9–11; 19:15; 24:30–34).

23:23 *Buy.* Literally, "get." Spare no pains nor cost to get *the truth* (4:5–7; Matt. 13:44–46). *sell it not.* Do not forget or forsake it for any worldly advantages or any price (Dan. 1:8; Matt. 16:26; Acts 20:23; Heb. 11:26; Rev. 12:11).

23:24–25 See note at vv. 15–16.

23:27–28 *whore.* Prostitute. *strange woman.* An adulterous or immoral woman, as an intruder into one's marriage (2:16; 5:3–5; 7:6–27; 9:13–18; 22:14).

23:29–35 A convincing and emphatic warning against drunkenness and coming under the control of intoxicating drink.

23:29 *babbling.* Much unwise talking, loud noise, or clamor (20:1).

23:30 *tarry long.* Stay, loiter, implying drinking over a period of time resulting in drunkenness (1 Tim. 3:3; Titus 1:7). *mixed wine.* See note at 9:2.

23:31 *Look not.* In the sense of not experiencing it. *when . . . red.* The color denotes undiluted wine with greater strength to intoxicate.

23:33 The moral effects and experiences of intoxication include: uncontrolled passions which leave the heart open to sin, confused thinking, and a warped vision and perception of reality (Gen. 19:35; 1 Cor. 6:12).

23:34 Sea metaphors are used to describe the dizziness, sickness, and confusion of the drunkard. *top of a mast.* The most unstable and dangerous part of the ship, especially to one asleep.

23:35 *felt it not.* The drunkard lacks sense. *awake.* Get up after being drunk (Gen. 9:24). *I will seek it yet again.* Even though he is in pain and is suffering, yet he convinces himself to return to more drinking—evidence of the addictive power of substance abuse.

Thoughts for Personal/Family Worship: Chapter 23

1. In a society that increases in wealth and luxury, it is essential to cultivate godly contentment, to be thankful and satisfied with all that God has provided, and not to be lured by anyone or anything that seems to offer

35 They have stricken me, *shalt thou say, and* I
was not sick; they have beaten me, *and* I felt *it* not:
when shall I awake? I will seek it yet again.

CHAPTER 24

BE not thou envious against evil men, neither
desire to be with them.
2 For their heart studieth destruction, and their
lips talk of mischief.
3 Through wisdom is an house builded; and by
understanding it is established:
4 And by knowledge shall the chambers be filled
with all precious and pleasant riches.
5 A wise man *is* strong; yea, a man of knowledge
increaseth strength.
6 For by wise counsel thou shalt make thy war:
and in multitude of counsellors *there is* safety.
7 Wisdom *is* too high for a fool: he openeth not
his mouth in the gate.
8 He that deviseth to do evil shall be called a
mischievous person.
9 The thought of foolishness *is* sin: and the
scorner *is* an abomination to men.
10 *If* thou faint in the day of adversity, thy
strength *is* small.
11 If thou forbear to deliver *them that are* drawn
unto death, and *those that are* ready to be slain;
12 If thou sayest, Behold, we knew it not; doth
not he that pondereth the heart consider *it*? and
he that keepeth thy soul, doth *not* he know *it*? and
shall *not* he render to *every* man according to his
works?
13 My son, eat thou honey, because *it is* good; and
the honeycomb, *which is* sweet to thy taste:
14 So *shall* the knowledge of wisdom *be* unto thy
soul: when thou hast found *it*, then there shall be
a reward, and thy expectation shall not be cut off.
15 Lay not wait, O wicked *man*, against the dwell-
ing of the righteous; spoil not his resting place:
16 For a just *man* falleth seven times, and riseth
up again: but the wicked shall fall into mischief.
17 Rejoice not when thine enemy falleth, and let
not thine heart be glad when he stumbleth:
18 Lest the LORD see *it*, and it displease him, and
he turn away his wrath from him.
19 Fret not thyself because of evil *men*, neither be
thou envious at the wicked;
20 For there shall be no reward to the evil *man*;
the candle of the wicked shall be put out.
21 My son, fear thou the LORD and the king: *and*
meddle not with them that are given to change:
22 For their calamity shall rise suddenly; and who
knoweth the ruin of them both?
23 These *things* also *belong* to the wise. *It is* not
good to have respect of persons in judgment.
24 He that saith unto the wicked, Thou *art*
righteous; him shall the people curse, nations
shall abhor him:
25 But to them that rebuke *him* shall be delight,

us greater advantages. Let us not "envy sinners" (v. 17), but live conscientiously in the fear of God all the day long, and wait "for the mercy of our Lord Jesus Christ unto eternal life" (Jude 21). Remember that when the end of your life comes, your expectation in God will fully be answered, you will find that true "godliness with contentment is great gain" (1 Tim. 6:6). How can we develop more self-control and contentment regarding our physical desires and possessions?

2. Listen to the warnings of Scripture against drunkenness and addiction, which destroy the body, harden the heart to spiritual things, and bring condemnation upon the soul. Instead of being filled with things that will take control of your life and lead to sin, fill your life with God's Word and Spirit, so that you may joyfully give yourself to praise, thanksgiving, submission to authority, and wise living (Eph. 5:15–21). How does your society attempt to make drunkenness or drug abuse acceptable and desirable? How does this chapter help us to see the truth?

Chapter 24: *God sees the personal emotions and motives of both the wise and the unwise.*

24:1–2 *envious against evil men.* See v. 19; 3:31–32; 23:17–18; Ps. 37.

24:2 *studieth destruction.* Plotted violence or havoc. *mischief.* Harm or trouble.

24:4 *chambers.* Storerooms.

24:5–6 See 11:14; 21:22; Eccl. 9:16,18.

24:7 *gate.* Place of public justice and business transaction (22:22).

24:8 *deviseth to do evil.* Plans sin or harm (vv. 2,9; 6:14,18; 14:22; Ps. 21:11; Nah. 1:11; Rom. 1:30). *mischievous person.* Hebrew, "a master of wickedness or wicked schemes."

24:9 *thought.* Plan. *abomination.* That which is disgusting and detestable.

24:10 *faint.* Become discouraged and give up. The character of a person is shown during trials (Job 4:5; Isa. 40:28–31; 2 Cor. 4:1; Eph. 3:13; Heb. 12:3–5; Rev. 2:3,13).

24:11–12 *forbear to deliver.* Refuse to rescue. Neglect of known duty is sin (James 4:17). *pondereth the heart.* God sees our motives (5:21; 21:2; 1 Sam. 16:7). *according to his works.* By His divine justice (Job 34:11; Jer. 25:14; 50:29; Matt. 16:27; Rom. 2:6; 2 Cor. 5:10).

24:13–14 As *sweet* and delicious food is nourishing and pleasant, so should a man seek wisdom (16:24; Pss. 19:10–11; 119:103, 111; Jer. 15:16). *expectation.* Outcome or thing hoped for.

24:15–16 *Lay not wait.* Do not ambush. *spoil.* Rob, plunder, ravage. The plots of the wicked against the righteous may cause them many troubles (*falleth seven times*), but the righteous will ultimately prosper (Ps. 37:24). The wicked, however, will finally fall into suffering (*mischief*).

24:17–18 *Rejoice not when thine enemy falleth.* God requires us to love our enemies and not rejoice in anyone's calamity (17:5; 25:21–22; Ex. 23:4–5; Job 31:29; Matt. 5:44).

24:19–20 *Fret not.* Don't become hot, agitated, and vexed (see note at vv. 1–2). *candle.* Life and prosperity (13:9; 20:20).

24:21–22 *fear thou the LORD and the king.* The fear of the Lord (1:7) leads us to respect proper human authority (Rom. 13:1–7; 1 Peter 2:17). *meddle not with them that . . . change.* Avoid the company of restless and unstable people.

24:23–25 *have respect.* Literally, "discern faces," meaning,

and a good blessing shall come upon them.
26 *Every man* shall kiss *his* lips that giveth a right
answer.
27 Prepare thy work without, and make it fit for
thyself in the field; and afterwards build thine
house.
28 Be not a witness against thy neighbour without
cause; and deceive *not* with thy lips.
29 Say not, I will do so to him as he hath done to
me: I will render to the man according to his work.
30 I went by the field of the slothful, and by the
vineyard of the man void of understanding;
31 And, lo, it was all grown over with thorns, *and*
nettles had covered the face thereof, and the stone
wall thereof was broken down.
32 Then I saw, *and* considered *it* well: I looked
upon *it, and* received instruction.
33 *Yet* a little sleep, a little slumber, a little folding
of the hands to sleep:
34 So shall thy poverty come *as* one that travel-
leth; and thy want as an armed man.

CHAPTER 25

THESE *are* also proverbs of Solomon, which the
men of Hezekiah king of Judah copied out.
2 *It is* the glory of God to conceal a thing: but the
honour of kings *is* to search out a matter.
3 The heaven for height, and the earth for depth,
and the heart of kings *is* unsearchable.
4 Take away the dross from the silver, and there
shall come forth a vessel for the finer.
5 Take away the wicked *from* before the king, and
his throne shall be established in righteousness.
6 Put not forth thyself in the presence of the king,
and stand not in the place of great *men*:
7 For better *it is* that it be said unto thee, Come
up hither; than that thou shouldest be put lower
in the presence of the prince whom thine eyes
have seen.
8 Go not forth hastily to strive, lest *thou know not*
what to do in the end thereof, when thy neigh-
bour hath put thee to shame.
9 Debate thy cause with thy neighbour *himself*;
and discover not a secret to another:
10 Lest he that heareth *it* put thee to shame, and
thine infamy turn not away.
11 A word fitly spoken *is like* apples of gold in
pictures of silver.
12 *As* an earring of gold, and an ornament of fine
gold, *so is* a wise reprover upon an obedient ear.
13 As the cold of snow in the time of harvest, *so is*
a faithful messenger to them that send him: for he
refresheth the soul of his masters.
14 Whoso boasteth himself of a false gift *is like*
clouds and wind without rain.
15 By long forbearing is a prince persuaded, and
a soft tongue breaketh the bone.

---

to show partiality (18:5; 28:21; Lev. 19:15; John 7:24; 1 Tim. 5:20–21; James 2:4–6).

24:26 *kiss his lips.* An expression of love (Song 8:1) or submission (Ps. 2:12). *right answer.* Literally, "plain words" or "right words" (8:9; 27:6), as opposed to being deceptive or obscure.

24:27 *without.* Outside, out-of-doors. Give first priority to securing what is necessary to support your life (*field*) before seeking what is for your comfort and pleasure (*house*).

24:28–29 *without cause.* Or falsely. Do not speak lies against any (14:5; 19:5) and especially avoid retaliation (6:16–19; 20:22; Rom. 12:17).

24:30–34 *slothful.* The lazy man (6:6–11; 15:19).

Thoughts for Personal/Family Worship: Chapter 24

1. **We should not desire the destruction of people, neither should we rejoice when our enemy falls (v. 17). Regardless of how we might have been treated by someone, we must not allow any emotion of revenge to rise and embitter us, for our Lord will see it and will be displeased by it. He is not pleased when His people have a malignant spirit. Christian love never rejoices at another's sin or calamity, but delights in mercy. What is the difference between desiring personal vengeance and desiring divine justice?**
2. **The overgrown and ruined state of the field of the slothful is a testimony to the foolishness of laziness (vv. 30–34). What is true in the physical realm applies as well to the spiritual. Far too often people neglect the care and cultivation of their hearts and spiritual life. For many, all their faculties are thrown open to the delusions of the world and suggestions of the Devil, and they are slothful about their sinful soul. How can you be more diligent to watch and pray, and daily trust in Christ and His finished work on our behalf?**

Proverbs of Solomon Collected by Hezekiah's Men (25:1—29:27)

Chapter 25: *The ways of humility and kindness are extolled.*

25:1 *proverbs of Solomon . . . men of Hezekiah.* See Introduction: Authorship; Date.

25:2 God shows His *glory* by only revealing some truths to men's limited minds (Deut. 29:29), but men get glory (*honour* is the same Hebrew word as *glory*) by seeking God's wisdom (3:16,35; 8:15,18; 2 Chron. 1:11–12).

25:4–5 Separating impurities (*dross*) from ore as by a refiner (*finer*) leaves pure silver; so removing *wicked* counselors establishes a nation (14:34; 16:12; Est. 7:10; 8:11–17).

25:6–7 *Put not forth thyself.* Do not magnify or glorify yourself. Self-elevation is most unwise (Luke 14:8–10; James 4:7–10). *hither.* Here, to this place.

25:8–10 *strive . . . Debate.* Contest a lawsuit or conduct a legal case (3:30). *neighbour.* Another person, not necessarily the resident next door. *discover.* Reveal or expose. *infamy.* Shame, disgrace, bad reputation. Instead of rushing to legal action, work to resolve a dispute privately first (Matt. 5:25–26; 18:15).

25:11 *fitly.* At the proper time and right circumstance. *pictures.* Beautiful engraving and artistic work in *silver*.

25:13 *messenger.* An important means of long-distance communication in the ancient world (v. 25; 13:17; 26:6).

25:14 *false gift.* Most likely, a gift promised, but not given. *clouds.* Literally, "vapors" or "rising mist" (Jude 12).

25:15 *long forbearing.* Self-restraint, patience, slowness to

16 Hast thou found honey? eat so much as is
sufficient for thee, lest thou be filled therewith,
and vomit it.
17 Withdraw thy foot from thy neighbour's
house; lest he be weary of thee, and *so* hate thee.
18 A man that beareth false witness against his
neighbour *is* a maul, and a sword, and a sharp
arrow.
19 Confidence in an unfaithful man in time of
trouble *is like* a broken tooth, and a foot out of
joint.
20 *As* he that taketh away a garment in cold
weather, *and as* vinegar upon nitre, so *is* he that
singeth songs to an heavy heart.
21 If thine enemy be hungry, give him bread to
eat; and if he be thirsty, give him water to drink:
22 For thou shalt heap coals of fire upon his head,
and the LORD shall reward thee.
23 The north wind driveth away rain: so *doth* an
angry countenance a backbiting tongue.
24 *It is* better to dwell in the corner of the house-
top, than with a brawling woman and in a wide
house.
25 *As* cold waters to a thirsty soul, so *is* good news
from a far country.
26 A righteous man falling down before the wick-
ed *is as* a troubled fountain, and a corrupt spring.
27 *It is* not good to eat much honey: so *for men* to
search their own glory *is not* glory.
28 He that *hath* no rule over his own spirit *is like* a
city *that is* broken down, *and* without walls.

CHAPTER 26

As snow in summer, and as rain in harvest, so
honour is not seemly for a fool.
2 As the bird by wandering, as the swallow by
flying, so the curse causeless shall not come.
3 A whip for the horse, a bridle for the ass, and a
rod for the fool's back.
4 Answer not a fool according to his folly, lest
thou also be like unto him.
5 Answer a fool according to his folly, lest he be
wise in his own conceit.
6 He that sendeth a message by the hand of a fool
cutteth off the feet, *and* drinketh damage.
7 The legs of the lame are not equal: so *is* a
parable in the mouth of fools.
8 As he that bindeth a stone in a sling, so *is* he that
giveth honour to a fool.
9 *As* a thorn goeth up into the hand of a drunkard,
so *is* a parable in the mouth of fools.
10 The great *God* that formed all *things* both
rewardeth the fool, and rewardeth transgressors.

anger. *soft tongue*. Patient and kind speech which has the power of a great weapon (14:29; 15:1,18; 16:32).

25:17 *Withdraw thy foot from*. Do not always be at.

25:18 *maul*. Very heavy hammer, club, or mallet used in combat (24:28).

25:20 *nitre*. Sodium nitrate, baking soda. Vinegar reacts with baking soda producing bubbling and boiling, rendering it useless. So is a song without sympathy to the sorrowful (Ps. 137:3–4).

25:21–22 *coals of fire*. Hot coals were heaped upon metals to cause melting. Through such kindness and love the hard hearts of enemies may soften (cited in Rom. 12:20).

25:23 *driveth away*. Or brings forth, describing cause and effect. A slandering tongue produces anger (26:20; Pss. 15:3; 101:5).

25:24 *brawling woman*. See note at 21:9.

25:25 *good news from a far country*. Such as news about a business success (31:14) or military victory.

25:26 *falling down*. Slipping or tottering morally or ethically, not physically. *troubled fountain*. Headwaters which are muddied or polluted.

25:27 See vv. 6–7; 27:2.

25:28 *broken down*. Exposed and vulnerable to the enemy. So one who does not have self-control is open to many dangers (16:32).

Thoughts for Personal/Family Worship: Chapter 25

1. **To call attention to self and to seek attention from others is foolish (v. 27) and potentially embarrassing (vv. 6–7). Humility is a godly virtue, and true honor comes to those who wait on the Lord. It is better to assume the lowly place without expecting or desiring the praise of man. Wait on the Lord to honor you as He sees fit. How can you make your life the pursuit of His glory and not of your own glory?**
2. **Fighting fire with fire or answering in kind is not the best way to treat those who mistreat us. Soft words and gestures of kindness are more effective than force (vv. 21–22). When we see our enemy in need or in trouble, we should be proactive in showing kindness to him by doing what we can to help and relieve him. This may melt him to be kind in the future or even to turn to the Lord for forgiveness and salvation. How have the loving responses of other people helped you to turn from sin and anger?**

Chapter 26: *Advice is given for the conduct of the wise toward fools.*

26:1 *seemly*. Suitable or proper. The comparison illustrates that some things are mutually exclusive.

26:2 *curse causeless*. An undeserved curse. The birds that fly are harmless in their flight, so are unmerited anathemas over the innocent.

26:4–5 *Answer not . . . Answer*. These two seemingly contradictory proverbs highlight the great discernment needed to speak with a *fool* (see note at 1:22). Do not allow a fool to drag you into a useless argument (29:9) or provoke you to sin (22:24–25). There are times when it is best to walk away (14:7). Yet it is also good to expose his foolishness so that he will not continue to be confident that he is wise. *in his own conceit*. Literally, "in his eyes," his opinion of himself.

26:6 *damage*. Violence. Harm comes to those who depend on fools (10:26; 25:13).

26:7 *are not equal*. Hang limp or dangle. A wise saying (*parable*) can be repeated by fools, but they lack the wisdom to apply it for the benefit of others, and so it is useless and harmful (v. 9).

26:8 *sling*. Weapon for throwing stones. Tying up a stone in the sling renders it useless.

26:10 *rewardeth*. Pays the wages of or hires.

11 As a dog returneth to his vomit, *so* a fool
returneth to his folly.
12 Seest thou a man wise in his own conceit?
there is more hope of a fool than of him.
13 The slothful *man* saith, *There is* a lion in the
way; a lion *is* in the streets.
14 *As* the door turneth upon his hinges, so *doth*
the slothful upon his bed.
15 The slothful hideth his hand in *his* bosom; it
grieveth him to bring it again to his mouth.
16 The sluggard *is* wiser in his own conceit than
seven men that can render a reason.
17 He that passeth by, *and* meddleth with strife
belonging not to him, *is like* one that taketh a dog
by the ears.
18 As a mad *man* who casteth firebrands, arrows,
and death,
19 So *is* the man *that* deceiveth his neighbour,
and saith, Am not I in sport?
20 Where no wood is, *there* the fire goeth out: so
where *there is* no talebearer, the strife ceaseth.
21 *As* coals *are* to burning coals, and wood to fire;
so *is* a contentious man to kindle strife.
22 The words of a talebearer *are* as wounds, and
they go down into the innermost parts of the
belly.
23 Burning lips and a wicked heart *are like* a
potsherd covered with silver dross.
24 He that hateth dissembleth with his lips, and
layeth up deceit within him;
25 When he speaketh fair, believe him not: for
there are seven abominations in his heart.
26 *Whose* hatred is covered by deceit, his
wickedness shall be shewed before the *whole*
congregation.
27 Whoso diggeth a pit shall fall therein: and he
that rolleth a stone, it will return upon him.
28 A lying tongue hateth *those that are* afflicted by
it; and a flattering mouth worketh ruin.

CHAPTER 27

Boast not thyself of to morrow; for thou knowest
not what a day may bring forth.
2 Let another man praise thee, and not thine own
mouth; a stranger, and not thine own lips.
3 A stone *is* heavy, and the sand weighty; but a
fool's wrath *is* heavier than them both.
4 Wrath *is* cruel, and anger *is* outrageous; but
who *is* able to stand before envy?
5 Open rebuke *is* better than secret love.
6 Faithful *are* the wounds of a friend; but the
kisses of an enemy *are* deceitful.
7 The full soul loatheth an honeycomb; but to the
hungry soul every bitter thing is sweet.
8 As a bird that wandereth from her nest, so *is* a
man that wandereth from his place.
9 Ointment and perfume rejoice the heart: so
doth the sweetness of a man's friend by hearty
counsel.

26:11 *dog returneth to his vomit.* Disgusting image of failing to learn one's lesson (cited in 2 Peter 2:22). Dogs in the Ancient Near East were often despised as useless and unclean scavengers (v. 17; Ex. 22:31; 1 Sam. 17:43; 1 Kings 14:11).
26:12 *in his own conceit.* Literally, "in his eyes," referring to his opinion (v. 16; 3:7; 12:15; 28:11; Isa. 5:21).
26:13–16 *slothful . . . sluggard.* Lazy person (see note at 6:6).
26:15 *his bosom.* A dish or bowl. *grieveth.* He is too weary.
26:17 *taketh a dog by the ears.* Most likely referring to a wild dog.
26:18–19 *firebrands.* Pieces of burning wood. *neighbour.* Another person, not necessarily next door resident. *sport.* Joke or jest. To deceive someone and dismiss it, by making light of it, causes serious harm.
26:20 *talebearer.* Slanderer or gossip (16:28; 18:8).
26:23 *Burning lips.* A fake show of warmth and affection, when the motives are evil (*wicked heart*), is as worthless and deceptive as a shiny coating on a vessel of common clay (*potsherd*).
26:24 *dissembleth.* Disguises oneself, acts hypocritically.
26:25 *seven abominations.* Many disgusting, hateful, detestable, and loathsome things.
26:26–27 Deceit will at last be exposed, and the wicked by their own actions often bring retribution upon themselves (12:13; Ps. 7:16).
26:28 Lies are acts of hatred.

Thoughts for Personal/Family Worship: Chapter 26

1. **The old saying that "sticks and stones may break my bones but words will never hurt me" is far from being true. At least bone-breaking sticks and stones are direct; so often hurtful words are behind the back and capable of hurting deeply (v. 22). Gossipers delight in spreading their "news" to as many as will listen; they are like a wildfire. The best way to stop a fire is to remove the fuel (v. 21); the best way to silence the backbiter is not to listen. When are you tempted to gossip? How can you keep yourself silent in those times?**
2. **Minding one's own business is wise. To interfere in the disputes of others without knowing all the facts or taking sides is asking for trouble, like yanking on a dog's ears (v. 17). It is best to wait for the parties to request input or arbitration before barging in. This is common sense, but also divinely revealed wisdom. When you are tempted to interfere, what could you do to pursue wisdom?**

Chapter 27: *Lessons are presented about friends and friendship.*

27:1 *Boast not.* You are not in control of your future (16:9; 19:21; Luke 12:19–20; James 4:13–16).
27:2 *stranger.* Someone unknown or unfamiliar. Self-praise is empty (25:27; 1 Cor. 13:4–5).
27:5–6 *secret love.* A friend who remains silent when a rebuke is in order. *Faithful . . . wounds.* Correction is painful to receive but does much good and is a mark of true love (9:8; 28:23; Lev. 19:17; Ps. 141:5; Matt. 18:15; Rev. 3:19).
27:7 *full soul.* A satisfied person. *loatheth.* Rejects. The luxury of wealth gives less happiness than the healthy appetite of a hard-working person (Eccl. 5:12). The proverb has implications beyond food.
27:9 *hearty counsel.* Earnest advice.

10 Thine own friend, and thy father's friend, forsake not; neither go into thy brother's house in the day of thy calamity: *for* better *is* a neighbour *that is* near than a brother far off.

11 My son, be wise, and make my heart glad, that I may answer him that reproacheth me.

12 A prudent *man* foreseeth the evil, *and* hideth himself; *but* the simple pass on, *and* are punished.

13 Take his garment that is surety for a stranger, and take a pledge of him for a strange woman.

14 He that blesseth his friend with a loud voice, rising early in the morning, it shall be counted a curse to him.

15 A continual dropping in a very rainy day and a contentious woman are alike.

16 Whosoever hideth her hideth the wind, and the ointment of his right hand, *which* bewrayeth *itself.*

17 Iron sharpeneth iron; so a man sharpeneth the countenance of his friend.

18 Whoso keepeth the fig tree shall eat the fruit thereof: so he that waiteth on his master shall be honoured.

19 As in water face *answereth* to face, so the heart of man to man.

20 Hell and destruction are never full; so the eyes of man are never satisfied.

21 *As* the fining pot for silver, and the furnace for gold; so *is* a man to his praise.

22 Though thou shouldest bray a fool in a mortar among wheat with a pestle, *yet* will not his foolishness depart from him.

23 Be thou diligent to know the state of thy flocks, *and* look well to thy herds.

24 For riches *are* not for ever: and doth the crown *endure* to every generation?

25 The hay appeareth, and the tender grass sheweth itself, and herbs of the mountains are gathered.

26 The lambs *are* for thy clothing, and the goats *are* the price of the field.

27 And *thou shalt have* goats' milk enough for thy food, for the food of thy household, and *for* the maintenance for thy maidens.

CHAPTER 28

THE wicked flee when no man pursueth: but the righteous are bold as a lion.

2 For the transgression of a land many *are* the princes thereof: but by a man of understanding *and* knowledge the state *thereof* shall be prolonged.

3 A poor man that oppresseth the poor *is like* a

27:10 Rely upon friends who have been true and tried over a long time. Family ties may be less reliable than those of genuine friendship (17:17; 18:24).

27:12 *evil.* Calamity or trouble. *pass on.* Keep going without precaution. *are punished.* Come to grief, referring to the consequences of his carelessness.

27:13 *is surety for.* Taken as a guarantee against a debt. *strange.* Foreign. See 20:16. Caution is necessary in money matters concerning high risk individuals.

27:14 Timing is important (25:20).

27:15–16 *bewrayeth.* Hebrew, "meets or encounters," referring to grasping the oil with the hand. Holding back the wind or grasping oil are futile efforts, as is restraining an argumentative woman.

27:17 *sharpeneth iron.* Perhaps an image of increasing skill and wisdom by mutual conversation (v. 9), resulting in more success (Eccl. 10:10).

27:18 *waiteth on.* Keeps, guards, attends to. This verse contrasts the consequence of work with the folly of laziness (26:13–16).

27:19 You are able to see a reflection of your *face* in a pool of *water*, and by considering the thoughts, feelings, and motives of your *heart* you can see who you truly are. However, it is not easy to see deeply into the heart (20:5; Jer. 17:9).

27:20 *Hell and destruction.* See note at 15:11. *eyes of man.* His desires. The parallel suggests that man's insatiable lusts are destructive, even demonic.

27:21 *fining pot.* The crucible or smelting pot (17:3; Job 28:1). How one responds to *praise* is a test of character.

27:22. *pestle.* Instrument used to crush or grind (*bray*) hard materials in a vessel or bowl (*mortar*). *wheat.* A general term for grain. Foolishness is so deeply embedded in a fool that the most severe experiences are insufficient to remove it (Jer. 13:23; 17:1).

27:23 *look well.* Hebrew, "set your heart," referring to caring for or giving attention to. The *flocks* were the main element of wealth and security in work and life. It is only by care and diligence that the most solid possessions can be preserved, for they tend to fly away (23:5).

Thoughts for Personal/Family Worship: Chapter 27

1. **Good friends can sometimes be closer than family. A good friend will tell you the truth even when it hurts (v. 6) and will be a means of a making you a better person (v. 17). It is important, therefore, to cultivate friendships that will be mutually beneficial and edifying. Rather than waiting for someone to be a good friend to you, make an effort to be a good friend to those whom God has put in your life who are open to His wisdom. How can you sharpen one another?**
2. **Foolishness is so stubbornly rooted in fallen human nature that the worst suffering cannot break it loose from us (v. 22). This implies that when such external means such as parental correction (22:15) or a friend's rebuke (v. 5) prove effective, it is only because of the powerful grace of God acting through them as divine discipline (3:11–12). Some people go through great sorrows but only come out more bitter, proud, and evil. Therefore, pray for yourself or people you know who are going through trials, that God's grace would soften the heart and that foolishness would be rejected and Christ's wisdom would be embraced.**

Chapter 28: *Keeping the law and fearing the Lord put life in perspective.*

28:1 *flee when no man pursueth.* A fearful conscience is a consequence of God's curse on lawbreakers (Lev. 26:17,36; Deut. 28:7,25; Ps. 53:5). *bold as a lion.* A good conscience gives courage, for one knows that the Lord is with him (14:26; Ps. 27:1; Acts 23:1; 24:16).

28:2 *many are the princes.* Sin brings fragmentation and instability to a nation, but wisdom brings order, unity, and

sweeping rain which leaveth no food.
4 They that forsake the law praise the wicked: but
such as keep the law contend with them.
5 Evil men understand not judgment: but they
that seek the LORD understand all *things*.
6 Better *is* the poor that walketh in his upright-
ness, than *he that is* perverse *in his* ways, though
he *be* rich.
7 Whoso keepeth the law *is* a wise son: but he
that is a companion of riotous *men* shameth his
father.
8 He that by usury and unjust gain increaseth his
substance, he shall gather it for him that will pity
the poor.
9 He that turneth away his ear from hearing the
law, even his prayer *shall be* abomination.
10 Whoso causeth the righteous to go astray in an
evil way, he shall fall himself into his own pit: but
the upright shall have good *things* in possession.
11 The rich man *is* wise in his own conceit; but
the poor that hath understanding searcheth him
out.
12 When righteous *men* do rejoice, *there is* great
glory: but when the wicked rise, a man is hidden.
13 He that covereth his sins shall not prosper: but
whoso confesseth and forsaketh *them* shall have
mercy.
14 Happy *is* the man that feareth alway: but he
that hardeneth his heart shall fall into mischief.
15 *As* a roaring lion, and a ranging bear; *so is* a
wicked ruler over the poor people.
16 The prince that wanteth understanding *is* also
a great oppressor: *but* he that hateth covetousness
shall prolong *his* days.
17 A man that doeth violence to the blood of *any*
person shall flee to the pit; let no man stay him.
18 Whoso walketh uprightly shall be saved: but
he that is perverse *in his* ways shall fall at once.
19 He that tilleth his land shall have plenty of
bread: but he that followeth after vain *persons*
shall have poverty enough.
20 A faithful man shall abound with blessings:
but he that maketh haste to be rich shall not be
innocent.
21 To have respect of persons *is* not good: for for
a piece of bread *that* man will transgress.
22 He that hasteth to be rich *hath* an evil eye, and
considereth not that poverty shall come upon
him.
23 He that rebuketh a man afterwards shall find
more favour than he that flattereth with the
tongue.
24 Whoso robbeth his father or his mother,
and saith, *It is* no transgression; the same *is* the
companion of a destroyer.
25 He that is of a proud heart stirreth up strife:
but he that putteth his trust in the LORD shall be
made fat.
26 He that trusteth in his own heart is a fool: but
whoso walketh wisely, he shall be delivered.
27 He that giveth unto the poor shall not lack: but
he that hideth his eyes shall have many a curse.

---

enduring peace to a society.

28:3 *sweeping rain which leaveth no food.* Just as one would expect rain to nourish crops and would be greatly disappointed when a storm destroys them, so one expects a *poor man* to show compassion and justice to the poor (Matt. 18:28–30).

28:4 *law.* The most general word referring to special revelation; not just commandments but the whole body of divine instruction (v. 7).

28:5 *judgment.* Justice.

28:7 *companion of riotous men.* One who associates with those who are thoughtless, rash, or lavish (also translated "gluttons," 23:20–21). *shameth his father.* See note at 10:1.

28:8 *usury.* Interest charged on loans. God instructed His people to use their income from usury to help the poor around them (Ex. 22:25).

28:9 *abomination.* That which is disgusting or detestable. God rejects religious activity done without a heart for Him (15:8; Pss. 66:18; 109:7).

28:10 *fall . . . into his own pit.* God will bring the sins back on the sinner (26:27; Eccl. 10:8).

28:11 *in his own conceit.* Literally, "in his own eyes," referring to his opinion.

28:13 *have mercy.* Receive compassion.

28:14 *Happy.* Blessed, possessing many benefits from God. *feareth.* Fears the Lord with a soft and responsive heart (see note at 1:7; Pss. 112:1; 128:1). *mischief.* Evil or calamity.

28:15 *ranging bear.* A charging or attacking bear.

28:16 *wanteth.* Lacks.

28:17 *flee to the pit.* He will be a fugitive unto death. *stay him.* Give help or support to him.

28:19 *tilleth.* Cultivates, Hebrew, "work or serve." *vain.* Empty or unprofitable.

28:20 *innocent.* Blameless or exempt from punishment.

28:21 *respect of persons.* Favoritism. *a piece of bread.* The least of bribes.

28:22 *evil eye.* Greed or stinginess, a perspective corrupted by the love of money (23:6).

28:23 *afterwards.* That is, after the rebuke.

28:24 *robbeth.* Plunder.

28:25 *proud heart.* Literally, "large soul," referring to greedy desires. *trust.* Confidence for security and safety (v. 26). *fat.* An image of prosperity.

28:26 *his own heart.* To trust in one's own wisdom or feelings is to trust in a liar (3:5; Jer. 9:23; 17:9).

28:27 *hideth his eyes.* Shuts his eyes, refuses to consider the needs of *the poor*.

Thoughts for Personal/Family Worship: Chapter 28

1. **God is never satisfied with external religion that is not the expression of a true heart of faith and devotion (v. 9). Even praying, a most spiritual endeavor, can be idolatrous (the word for abomination commonly applies to idolatry and false worship). Turning from God's law or instruction reveals the true condition of the heart and renders prayer as something detestable before God. How we view God's Word is an index to how we view the Lord Himself. Give genuine attention and obedience to His Word so that He will hear your prayers. Spend time confessing your sins to God, knowing that He shows compassion and forgiveness to those who confess and**

28 When the wicked rise, men hide themselves: but when they perish, the righteous increase.

CHAPTER 29

HE, that being often reproved hardeneth *his* neck, shall suddenly be destroyed, and that without remedy.
2 When the righteous are in authority, the people rejoice: but when the wicked beareth rule, the people mourn.
3 Whoso loveth wisdom rejoiceth his father: but he that keepeth company with harlots spendeth *his* substance.
4 The king by judgment establisheth the land: but he that receiveth gifts overthroweth it.
5 A man that flattereth his neighbour spreadeth a net for his feet.
6 In the transgression of an evil man *there is* a snare: but the righteous doth sing and rejoice.
7 The righteous considereth the cause of the poor: *but* the wicked regardeth not to know *it*.
8 Scornful men bring a city into a snare: but wise *men* turn away wrath.
9 *If* a wise man contendeth with a foolish man, whether he rage or laugh, *there is* no rest.
10 The bloodthirsty hate the upright: but the just seek his soul.
11 A fool uttereth all his mind: but a wise *man* keepeth it in till afterwards.
12 If a ruler hearken to lies, all his servants *are* wicked.
13 The poor and the deceitful man meet together: the LORD lighteneth both their eyes.
14 The king that faithfully judgeth the poor, his throne shall be established for ever.
15 The rod and reproof give wisdom: but a child left *to himself* bringeth his mother to shame.
16 When the wicked are multiplied, transgression increaseth: but the righteous shall see their fall.
17 Correct thy son, and he shall give thee rest; yea, he shall give delight unto thy soul.
18 Where *there is* no vision, the people perish: but he that keepeth the law, happy *is* he.
19 A servant will not be corrected by words: for though he understand he will not answer.
20 Seest thou a man *that is* hasty in his words? *there is* more hope of a fool than of him.
21 He that delicately bringeth up his servant from a child shall have him become *his* son at the length.
22 An angry man stirreth up strife, and a furious man aboundeth in transgression.
23 A man's pride shall bring him low: but honour shall uphold the humble in spirit.
24 Whoso is partner with a thief hateth his own soul: he heareth cursing, and bewrayeth *it* not.
25 The fear of man bringeth a snare: but whoso putteth his trust in the LORD shall be safe.
26 Many seek the ruler's favour; but *every* man's

forsake sin (v. 13; 1 John 1:9).

2. How we treat those less fortunate than ourselves is the essence of pure, undefiled religion and the fulfillment of the royal law (vv. 21,27). James was echoing Proverbs when he taught us not to show favoritism to people and that helping others is a source of blessing (James 1:27; 2:8). On the other hand, being stingy and greedy is selfishness and ultimately self-defeating (vv. 8,20,22). How we love others says much about how we love God since the two great commandments of loving God totally and loving one's neighbor as one's self are inseparably linked. Whom do you know in need? How should you be compassionately and wisely involved to help?

Chapter 29: *The effects of the conduct of the righteous and the wicked on those around them are compared.*

29:1 *reproved.* Verbally corrected or rebuked (1:30; 5:12; 9:7–8; 10:17; 12:1). *hardeneth his neck.* As oxen that will not be turned by their master. *suddenly be destroyed . . . without remedy.* Broken forever, wounded without cure, receiving the eternal judgment of God (Matt. 25:46).

29:3 *rejoiceth his father.* See note at 10:1. *spendeth his substance.* See Luke 15:13,30.

29:4 *judgment.* Justice. *gifts.* Bribes (15:27; 28:21).

29:5 *flattereth.* Deals smoothly. *spreadeth a net.* His flattering words are a trap (26:28; 28:23).

29:7 *considereth.* Knows, observes, acquaints himself with, gives due attention (v. 14; Job 29:16).

29:8 *Scornful men.* Those who proudly disregard and mock God's Word (see note at 1:22). *bring . . . into a snare.* Or set on fire. They fan the flame of strife but the wise bring peace (26:21).

29:10 *bloodthirsty.* Literally, "men of bloods," referring to murderers (Pss. 5:6; 26:9) *seek his soul.* Preserve the life of the godly person.

29:13 *deceitful man.* Or creditor, a man of violence. *lighteneth both their eyes.* Despite their differences, God has given life to both and both are accountable to Him (22:2; Ps. 145:9; Matt. 5:45).

29:15 *rod.* An instrument of corporal discipline, which when used with loving words of correction (*reproof*) is often effective in training *a child* in *wisdom* (13:24; 22:6,15; 23:13–14). *left to himself.* Not restrained.

29:16 The success of the wicked increases public sin (vv. 2, 12), but the righteous will triumph in the end (Pss. 12:1–8; 37:34–38; 58:10–11).

29:18 *vision.* God's truth revealed through the prophets (1 Sam. 3:1), paralleled with God's *law* or spiritual and moral instruction. The lack of knowledge of God's Word is a great curse (Amos 8:11–12). *perish.* They are let loose without restraint. *happy.* Possessing many blessings from God, here the result of keeping God's law (14:11,34; 28:14; Ps. 19:11).

29:20 *hasty in his words.* Wisdom, humility, and self-control lead us to listen and think before we form opinions and speak (10:19; 18:13,17; James 1:19). *more hope of a fool.* These words link this saying to the warning against considering yourself wise (26:12).

29:21 *delicately bringeth up.* Pampers or over indulges. *shall have him become his son at the length.* Literally, "[in] the final end, he will be thankless or insolent."

29:22 *stirreth up strife.* See 15:18.

29:24 *cursing.* The doom publicly declared on those who refuse to disclose information about a crime (Lev. 5:1).

judgment *cometh* from the LORD.
27 An unjust man *is* an abomination to the just:
and *he that is* upright in the way *is* abomination
to the wicked.

CHAPTER 30

THE words of Agur the son of Jakeh, *even* the
prophecy: the man spake unto Ithiel, even unto
Ithiel and Ucal,
2 Surely I *am* more brutish than *any* man, and
have not the understanding of a man.
3 I neither learned wisdom, nor have the knowl-
edge of the holy.
4 Who hath ascended up into heaven, or
descended? who hath gathered the wind in his
fists? who hath bound the waters in a garment?
who hath established all the ends of the earth?
what *is* his name, and what *is* his son's name, if
thou canst tell?
5 Every word of God *is* pure: he *is* a shield unto
them that put their trust in him.
6 Add thou not unto his words, lest he reprove
thee, and thou be found a liar.
7 Two *things* have I required of thee; deny me
them not before I die:
8 Remove far from me vanity and lies: give me
neither poverty nor riches; feed me with food
convenient for me:
9 Lest I be full, and deny *thee*, and say, Who *is*
the LORD? or lest I be poor, and steal, and take the
name of my God *in vain*.
10 Accuse not a servant unto his master, lest he
curse thee, and thou be found guilty.
11 *There is* a generation *that* curseth their father,
and doth not bless their mother.
12 *There is* a generation *that are* pure in their own
eyes, and *yet* is not washed from their filthiness.
13 *There is* a generation, O how lofty are their
eyes! and their eyelids are lifted up.
14 *There is* a generation, whose teeth *are as*
swords, and their jaw teeth *as* knives, to devour
the poor from off the earth, and the needy from
among men.
15 The horseleach hath two daughters, *crying*,
Give, give. There are three *things that* are never
satisfied, *yea*, four *things* say not, *It is* enough:
16 The grave; and the barren womb; the earth
that is not filled with water; and the fire *that* saith
not, *It is* enough.
17 The eye *that* mocketh at *his* father, and despis-
eth to obey *his* mother, the ravens of the valley
shall pick it out, and the young eagles shall eat it.
18 There be three *things which* are too wonderful

---

bewrayeth. Divulges, reveals, betrays.
29:25 *snare*. Trap. Fearing man and fearing God are mutually exclusive.
29:27 *abomination*. That which is disgusting and detestable.

Thoughts for Personal/Family Worship: Chapter 29

1. **One of the severest judgments of God upon a rebellious and hardened nation is to give them unjust rulers who will do injustice in order to retain power or increase in it (vv. 2,4). This should cause the child of God to cling to and follow the King of Zion, the Lord Jesus Christ, whose throne is established forever in righteousness (Ps. 45:6; Heb. 1:8). How can the believer's hope in Christ give him comfort and strength to do right in a corrupt society?**
2. **Without divine revelation, man has no hope (v. 18). Faith comes by hearing and hearing by the Word of God. It is God's grace that He has revealed truth to us. It should be our desire to be under the faithful preaching of God's Word that exalts Christ in all things. We should receive it in meekness and faith. Pray as well that the Lord of the harvest would send forth faithful ministers and Christian workers throughout the world, because without the Word of God, men will perish. How are you assisting in this great work?**

Chapter 30: *Agur prophesies about the humble and wise. Words of Agur (30:1–33)*

30:1 *Agur*. Meaning "collector." Could refer to his name or his character, that is, a gatherer of wise sayings. Apart from this reference, all the names here are otherwise unknown in Scripture except for *Ithiel* (Neh. 11:7). *prophecy*. Literally, "burden," often used of the oracle or word of a prophet (31:1; Hab. 1:1).
30:2 *brutish*. Stupid.
30:3 This may confirm Agur as collector of wise sayings, rather than composer of such.
30:4 *Who hath ascended . . . descended*. Man cannot grasp hold of divine wisdom unless God comes down to reveal His Word (Deut. 30:12–13; Job 28:12–14), an anticipation of Christ's coming (John 3:13; Rom. 10:6–7; Eph. 4:8–10). *who hath gathered the wind . . . bound . . . established*. The Creator is infinitely greater than us (Job 38:1–11; Isa. 40:12–14). *what is his name*. God partially reveals His glorious perfections in Scripture but ultimately they are beyond our limited minds (Ps. 145:3). *his son's name*. God reveals His wisdom through His Son (John 1:18), who also is incomprehensible in His glory (*if thou canst tell*), just as the person of Wisdom earlier was said to be eternally begotten by God and co-Creator with Him (see notes at 8:22–36).
30:5 *pure*. Refined and thus free from all falsehood and error. *shield*. A protector (2 Sam. 22:3; Pss. 28:7; 115:9). *put their trust*. Seek and find their refuge, a word of faith.
30:6 *Add thou not*. God's Word is sufficient for the faith, obedience, and worship of His people (Deut. 4:2; 12:32; 2 Tim. 3:16–17; Rev. 22:18).
30:7 *required*. Asked or requested.
30:8 *vanity*. Deceitfulness or emptiness of speech. *convenient*. Suitable, from a Hebrew word meaning, "that which is appointed," that is, according to God's will (Eccl. 3:1–13).
30:12 *pure in their own eyes*. Self-righteousness is a hypocritical cloak for sin (14:12; 21:2; Jer. 2:22–23; Matt. 23:26–28).
30:13 *lofty*. High, in the sense of being haughty.
30:15 *horseleach*. A blood-sucking worm. *three . . . four*. Hebrew uses ascending numbers to represent an indefinite number or representative list, indicating it is not a complete list (vv. 18,21,29; Amos 1–2).
30:16 *grave*. Hebrew, *sheol*, here referring to death which comes to all men without exception (27:20) until it is finally destroyed (1 Cor. 15:26). *barren womb*. A woman who desires children may be impatient until the Lord grants them (Gen. 30:1). *earth*. Parched soil will soak in all the water available.

THE AUTHORITY AND INERRANCY OF SCRIPTURE

The authority and inerrancy of Holy Scripture are the bedrock upon which true Christianity stands. We depend upon Scripture's witness for all that we hold true concerning God, man, and the way of salvation in Christ. The great events of redemptive history, such as the incarnation of the Son of God in the person of Jesus Christ, His atoning death, His glorious resurrection, and His ascension into heaven, are recorded only in Scripture. If the witness of Scripture is not reliable and compelling, then we have no basis for our faith and nothing to command our obedience.

Scripture has authority because it is the Word of God. God is first revealed as the Creator who speaks with compelling authority to call creation into being out of nothing (Gen. 1). That creative word was executed by the Holy Spirit, who secured the result intended by the words that were spoken. From that time until Christ came, God continued to speak through His servants, the prophets. In the person of His Son, God has spoken His final word, offering grace, forgiveness, and eternal life to all who believe in Christ (Heb. 1:1–3).

Moved by the testimony of the Holy Spirit, Christians confess that God's Word is true and trustworthy in all that it affirms. If the basic tenets of our faith are challenged by anyone, our reply must be, "Thus saith the LORD." This is equally so whether it concerns what man is to believe concerning God or what duty God requires of man. As a rule or authority for faith and life, Scripture has no equal or rival, but stands alone and supreme.

This authority extends equally to all sixty-six books of Scripture. Though revealed "at sundry times and in diverse manners" (Heb. 1:1) and mediated through an astonishing array of human writers, "all Scripture is given by inspiration of God" (2 Tim. 3:16). It comes forth from God as breath proceeds from the body. Scripture is the product of one divine mind and speaks with one divine voice: "Prophecy of old came not by the will of man: but holy men of God spake as they were moved by the Holy Ghost" (2 Peter 1:21).

The authority of Scripture implies its inerrancy. As the Word of "God that cannot lie" (Titus 1:2), it cannot err or stray from the path of truth: "Thy word is true from the beginning" (Ps. 119:160). Such was the faith of the church of the Old Testament, and zealous care was taken by her scribes to preserve every word and letter of the text of Scripture. Christ Himself confessed, "Thy word is truth" (John 17:17).

A vain attempt has been made to distinguish inerrancy from infallibility by those who wish to maintain the authority of Scripture while granting the claim of unbelieving scholars that Scripture contains many errors by the writers of the books and those who transmitted the text. This attempt fails because the two words are synonymous, and because if the Bible errs at any point, it may err at every point and cannot be trusted.

While affirming the infallibility and inerrancy of the Holy Scriptures, we do not attribute either quality to mere human beings whose task it is to read, translate, or expound them. There is no office in the church high enough to confer infallibility on the man who holds it. There is no degree of learning in the languages of Scripture and the history of their interpretation sufficient to ensure inerrancy on the part of the church's Bible scholars and teachers, much less their secular counterparts. No translation of the Hebrew and Greek Scriptures is absolutely perfect as a representation of the inspired Word of God; none is so good that it cannot be improved. Because our understanding is limited in so many ways, reading and interpreting the Bible must be an enterprise of faith. We must trust in Christ as our Chief Prophet to open our eyes to the wondrous things taught in Scripture and to lead us to a right understanding and faithful application of them.

for me, yea, four which I know not:
19 The way of an eagle in the air; the way of a
serpent upon a rock; the way of a ship in the midst
of the sea; and the way of a man with a maid.
20 Such *is* the way of an adulterous woman; she
eateth, and wipeth her mouth, and saith, I have
done no wickedness.
21 For three *things* the earth is disquieted, and for
four *which* it cannot bear:
22 For a servant when he reigneth; and a fool
when he is filled with meat;
23 For an odious *woman* when she is married;
and an handmaid that is heir to her mistress.
24 There be four *things which are* little upon the
earth, but they *are* exceeding wise:
25 The ants *are* a people not strong, yet they
prepare their meat in the summer;
26 The conies *are but* a feeble folk, yet make they
their houses in the rocks;
27 The locusts have no king, yet go they forth all
of them by bands;
28 The spider taketh hold with her hands, and is
in kings' palaces.
29 There be three *things* which go well, yea, four
are comely in going:
30 A lion *which is* strongest among beasts, and
turneth not away for any;
31 A greyhound; an he goat also; and a king,
against whom *there is* no rising up.
32 If thou hast done foolishly in lifting up thyself,
or if thou hast thought evil, *lay* thine hand upon
thy mouth.
33 Surely the churning of milk bringeth forth
butter, and the wringing of the nose bringeth
forth blood: so the forcing of wrath bringeth
forth strife.

CHAPTER 31

THE words of king Lemuel, the prophecy that his
mother taught him.
2 What, my son? and what, the son of my womb?
and what, the son of my vows?
3 Give not thy strength unto women, nor thy
ways to that which destroyeth kings.
4 *It is* not for kings, O Lemuel, *it is* not for kings
to drink wine; nor for princes strong drink:
5 Lest they drink, and forget the law, and pervert
the judgment of any of the afflicted.
6 Give strong drink unto him that is ready to per-
ish, and wine unto those that be of heavy hearts.
7 Let him drink, and forget his poverty, and
remember his misery no more.
8 Open thy mouth for the dumb in the cause of
all such as are appointed to destruction.
9 Open thy mouth, judge righteously, and plead
the cause of the poor and needy.
10 ¶ Who can find a virtuous woman? for her
price *is* far above rubies.
11 The heart of her husband doth safely trust in

fire. Flames will continue as long as there is fuel.

30:18 *too wonderful.* Things beyond comprehension, too difficult to grasp.

30:19 *maid.* A virgin, the only word in the Old Testament that refers to virgin without further qualification or definition (Isa. 7:14).

30:20 *she eateth, and wipeth her mouth.* An image depicting skill in hiding the evidences of her adultery.

30:21 *disquieted.* Quivered or quaked in restless motion.

30:22 *meat.* Food of any kind (v. 25).

30:23 *odious.* Hated or unloved.

30:24–28 *four things which are little.* They are models for those who desire to live godly: *ants* for their labor and preparation (6:6–8), *conies* or hyraxes for their diligence in seeking safety, *locusts* for their order and working together in harmonious ranks (*by bands*), and the *spider* (Hebrew uncertain), perhaps for its skillful and constant work (*kings' palaces*; cf. 22:29).

30:29 *comely in going.* Walking in a stately manner.

30:31 *greyhound.* Hebrew is uncertain, referring to something that struts such as a war-horse or rooster.

30:33 *churning . . . wringing . . . forcing.* In Hebrew, the same word for each, with the general meaning "pressing." Each statement reasons from cause to effect.

Thoughts for Personal/Family Worship: Chapter 30

Agur was a wise man, who did not think too highly of himself or his wisdom. His wisdom lay in the fact that he placed all his trust in God and His revealed wisdom, rather than in his own learning. He sought to lift the reader's thoughts heavenward to the infinite glory of God and His Son, the Creator of the vast universe. He gives great credence to the Bible being the inspired, pure Word of God, always and in all places the most relevant truth. In this he is a model for us of humility before God, complete dependence upon God's Son and His Word for true wisdom, and absolute confidence in the Scriptures as the infallible truth of God. Why does humility before God lead to dependence on the Bible? Why does pride entangle people in foolish speculations and in adding human ideas to Scripture?

Chapter 31: ***A mother counsels her son, the king, and a virtuous woman, who is a paragon of wise living, is celebrated through poetry.***

Words of Lemuel from His Mother (31:1–9)

31:1 *king Lemuel.* Some interpret this to refer to King Solomon, possibly the name his mother used for him, meaning "one who is devoted to God." *prophecy.* See note at 30:1.

31:4–6 *wine . . . strong drink.* The alcoholic product of the vine and of grain (20:1). *princes.* Rulers or kings. The ruler must avoid anything that would impair judgment.

31:7 *drink, and forget.* This could refer to the medicinal value of alcohol for those in great physical pain or the terminally ill ("ready to perish," v. 6), or it could refer to cheering the hearts of the poor with a feast granted of sincere generosity (9:2,5; Eccl. 9:7–8; 10:19; contrast Prov. 23:6–7).

31:8 *dumb.* Those unable to speak.

CONCLUSION: THE WISE AND VIRTUOUS WOMAN (31:10–31)

31:10 *virtuous woman.* Literally, "a woman of excellence or strength," here referring to strength of godliness (12:4; Ruth 3:11). *above rubies.* An allusion to the precious value of

her, so that he shall have no need of spoil.
12 She will do him good and not evil all the days of her life.
13 She seeketh wool, and flax, and worketh willingly with her hands.
14 She is like the merchants' ships; she bringeth her food from afar.
15 She riseth also while it is yet night, and giveth meat to her household, and a portion to her maidens.
16 She considereth a field, and buyeth it: with the fruit of her hands she planteth a vineyard.
17 She girdeth her loins with strength, and strengtheneth her arms.
18 She perceiveth that her merchandise *is* good: her candle goeth not out by night.
19 She layeth her hands to the spindle, and her hands hold the distaff.
20 She stretcheth out her hand to the poor; yea, she reacheth forth her hands to the needy.
21 She is not afraid of the snow for her household: for all her household *are* clothed with scarlet.
22 She maketh herself coverings of tapestry; her clothing *is* silk and purple.
23 Her husband is known in the gates, when he sitteth among the elders of the land.
24 She maketh fine linen, and selleth *it*; and delivereth girdles unto the merchant.
25 Strength and honour *are* her clothing; and she shall rejoice in time to come.
26 She openeth her mouth with wisdom; and in her tongue *is* the law of kindness.
27 She looketh well to the ways of her household, and eateth not the bread of idleness.
28 Her children arise up, and call her blessed; her husband *also*, and he praiseth her.
29 Many daughters have done virtuously, but thou excellest them all.
30 Favour *is* deceitful, and beauty *is* vain: *but* a woman *that* feareth the LORD, she shall be praised.
31 Give her of the fruit of her hands; and let her own works praise her in the gates.

---

wisdom (3:15; 8:11; 20:15), of which this woman is the living embodiment. The 22 verses of this poem are an acrostic, with each successive verse beginning with the next letter of the Hebrew alphabet.

31:11–12 *trust.* Place confidence for security or safety. *have no need of spoil.* Not lack gain. *evil.* Harm. The virtuous wife loves her husband in many practical ways, truly a helper suitable for him (Gen. 2:18–23; Titus 2:4).

31:13–15 *worketh willingly . . . riseth also while it is yet night.* She cheerfully and sacrificially works in the home (Titus 2:5), managing the resources of the *household* so that every member receives what is needed (v. 27).

31:15 *meat.* Food of any kind.

31:16 *considereth a field, and buyeth it.* Her submission to her husband's authority does not hinder her from exercising her own authority to engage in business for the sake of the household.

31:17 *girdeth her loins.* To put on or clothe with a belt around the waist, symbolizing preparation for action or work. She is not a weak woman, but a competent and strong person (v. 25).

31:18 *merchandise.* Or profit from trading.

31:19 *distaff.* The spindle whorl, a rod to hold the wool for spinning.

31:20 *stretcheth out her hand to the poor.* She not only cares for her family, but reaches out in practical acts of compassion to the *needy* (14:21,31).

31:21 *scarlet.* Or perhaps, double garments.

31:23 *known in the gates.* Publicly honored because of his wife's wisdom and work.

31:24 *girdles.* Sashes.

31:25 *honour.* Splendor or beauty. *rejoice in time to come.* Literally, "she laughs at the latter day," an expression of her confident hope in the future (3:21–26; 10:28; 14:26).

31:26 *law.* Teaching. Her words instruct others in the qualities that her life exemplifies: *wisdom* and faithful love (*kindness*; 3:3).

31:28 *call her blessed.* Everyone has the duty of honoring one's mother, but this obligation is magnified all the more when one's mother is faithful and godly. *he praiseth her.* Husbands should publicly honor their wives for their character and work (v. 31).

31:30 *Favour.* Charm or elegance. *beauty is vain.* Physical attractiveness is a breath, unsubstantial and temporary (11:22; James 4:14). *feareth the LORD.* Just as Proverbs opened with the theme that wisdom consists of the fear of God (see note at 1:7), so it closes by revealing that this is the key ingredient in a virtuous woman's character.

31:31 *praise her in the gates.* Society should not despise the labor of God-fearing wives and mothers, but publicly honor them for their service and its good results (*fruit of her hands*).

Thoughts for Personal/Family Worship: Chapter 31

1. Lemuel's mother is a model for parenting. The concern and wisdom of a godly mother causes her to admonish and give wise counsel to her son concerning the temptations and responsibilities of his calling in life. The love that parents have toward God and toward their children encourages them to do likewise. It is the responsibility of parents to judge their children rightly and not to turn a blind eye to their sin. Parents should, with loving admonition, help the child understand the law of God and give due warnings to practical and spiritual dangers. To be warned of the dangers is to be prepared, and a wise man will hear wise counsels. What wisdom that you received from your parents do you especially treasure? What wisdom does each of your children need?

2. Proverbs says much about the kind of women to avoid, so it is significant that it ends with a most noble example. The description of the virtuous woman is a paradigm for every Christian woman. Her virtue is evident both in character and action. What is striking is the selflessness of this wife and mother. Everything she does, whether in the home or out of the home, is for the good of her family. And even more striking is the spiritual motive behind all she does. She fears the Lord, living in awareness of Him and serving Him in what may otherwise seem to be just mundane affairs. For the Christian everything in life must be directed by this great aim: to please the God who has saved us. Whether you are a man or woman, adult or child, married or single, what are some specific qualities about the virtuous woman portrayed here that you should imitate? How does her example teach you what it means to fear the Lord?

INTRODUCTION TO THE BOOK OF

ECCLESIASTES

Authorship: Ecclesiastes 1:1 identifies the author as "the Preacher, the son of David, king in Jerusalem." Although opinions differ even among conservatives, this most likely refers to Solomon. The word "Preacher" in Hebrew is *Qoheleth*, a title designating one who either summons or addresses an assembly. The verb form occurs in 1 Kings 8:1 where Solomon assembled the people for the dedication of the temple. Comparing Ecclesiastes with Solomon's biography in 1 Kings identifies significant parallels between the Preacher and Solomon: unique wisdom, unsurpassed riches, many servants, extensive building projects, writing of proverbs, etc. If not written by Solomon, the book was certainly written in the spirit of Solomon. Significantly, regardless of the identity of the human author, Ecclesiastes claims that the words written were "upright" and "true" and "given from one shepherd" (12:10–11). That one shepherd is God Himself. Although every biblical book is inspired, Ecclesiastes is one of the few that directly states the truth.

Date: 970–930 BC. These are the dates of Solomon's reign, sometime during which he wrote the book, most likely toward the end of his career.

Theme: Living in the light of and with a view to eternity. Ecclesiastes 3:11–14 and 12:13–14 sum up the message.

Purpose: To provide believers with a biblical worldview or theology of life, marked by fearing and obeying God and designed to give contentment during life and certain hope for after life.

Synopsis: *The Contribution of Ecclesiastes to Redemptive Revelation*

Although Ecclesiastes is often described as being pessimistic, fatalistic, or cynical, it is, rather, a book that realistically examines the issues and questions of life with the intent of directing all to God. To that end, the book is evangelistic, bringing man to total dependence on God, who is the powerful creator, sovereign ruler, infallible judge, and supreme reality. A proper understanding of God makes possible a proper use of life. While the Preacher directs both saints and sinners to the Lord, Ecclesiastes is primarily a divinely inspired and revealed philosophy of life for believers.

A biblical, Christian worldview requires recognizing and submitting to who the Lord is. How we view God will determine our view of life, and how we view life mirrors how we view the Lord. The unmistakable premise of the book is the brevity of life. Since life is like a breath ("vanity"), the things of this temporary, earthly life ("under the sun") can never bring ultimate satisfaction. Trying to find contentment in whatever is temporary is like chasing after the wind ("vexation of spirit"). So we are to take full advantage of what life entails, recognizing that our lot in life is God's gift for our good. But we must never view the gift apart from the Giver.

Understanding the message depends on defining key expressions. "Vanity of vanities" is literally, "breath of breaths," which is a figure of speech primarily designating transience, something that is only momentary. It does not suggest the idea of uselessness. The Hebrew construction expresses a superlative idea and effectively conveys the message of the brevity of life. "Under the sun" identifies the sphere of physical life (where we live and experience life)—the only place we can employ our senses. "Vexation of spirit" is literally, "a striving for or chasing after wind;" the phrase refers to the futility of an action not the depression of one's soul. "Eat . . . drink . . . enjoy" does not advise hedonism, but rather contentment and full use of what God has given to sustain life. See the notes for the full significance of these repeated expressions.

Outline:

I. The Investigation of Life (1:1—6:12)
   A. A Poem on Life's Cycles (1:1–11)
   B. Vanity of Striving after Knowledge (1:12–18)
   C. Vanity of Striving after Pleasure (2:1–11)
   D. Vanity of Striving after Wisdom (2:12–17)
   E. Vanity of Striving after the Results of Labor (2:18—6:12)
      1. Everything Is Temporary (2:18–26)
      2. Everything Is Predetermined (3:1–15)
      3. Everything Is Liable to Injustice (3:16–22)
      4. Everything Is Subject to Oppression and Envy (4:1–6)
      5. Everything Is Prone to Loss (4:7–16)
      6. Everything Is Subservient to the Fear of God (5:1–7)
      7. Everything Is a Potential Frustration (5:8—6:12)

II. The Evaluation of Life (7:1—12:7)
   A. The Inability to Know What to Do (7:1—8:17)
      1. Because the Better Things Are Contrary to Expectation (7:1–14)
      2. Because Life Is Unpredictable (7:15–24)
      3. Because Foolishness Abounds (7:25–29)
      4. Because Life Is Full of Incongruities (8:1–17)
   B. The Inability to Know the Future (9:1—11:6)
      1. Because Life Is Uncertain and Brief (9:1–10)
      2. Because Wisdom Does Not Guarantee Success (9:11—10:15)
      3. Because Evil Happens (10:16—11:6)
   C. A Poem on Youth (11:7–10)
   D. An Allegory on Old Age (12:1–7)

III. The Counsel for Life (12:8–14)

THE BOOK OF ECCLESIASTES

CHAPTER 1

THE words of the Preacher, the son of David, king
in Jerusalem.
2 Vanity of vanities, saith the Preacher, vanity of
vanities; all *is* vanity.
3 What profit hath a man of all his labour which
he taketh under the sun?
4 *One* generation passeth away, and *another*
generation cometh: but the earth abideth for ever.
5 The sun also ariseth, and the sun goeth down,
and hasteth to his place where he arose.
6 The wind goeth toward the south, and
turneth about unto the north; it whirleth about
continually, and the wind returneth again
according to his circuits.
7 All the rivers run into the sea; yet the sea *is* not
full; unto the place from whence the rivers come,
thither they return again.
8 All things *are* full of labour; man cannot utter
it: the eye is not satisfied with seeing, nor the ear
filled with hearing.
9 The thing that hath been, it *is that* which shall
be; and that which is done *is* that which shall be
done: and *there is* no new *thing* under the sun.
10 Is there *any* thing whereof it may be said, See,
this *is* new? it hath been already of old time, which
was before us.
11 *There is* no remembrance of former *things*;
neither shall there be *any* remembrance of *things*
that are to come with *those* that shall come after.
12 ¶ I the Preacher was king over Israel in
Jerusalem.
13 And I gave my heart to seek and search out by
wisdom concerning all *things* that are done un-
der heaven: this sore travail hath God given to the
sons of man to be exercised therewith.
14 I have seen all the works that are done under the
sun; and, behold, all *is* vanity and vexation of spirit.
15 *That which is* crooked cannot be made straight:
and that which is wanting cannot be numbered.
16 I communed with mine own heart, saying, Lo,
I am come to great estate, and have gotten more
wisdom than all *they* that have been before me in
Jerusalem: yea, my heart had great experience of
wisdom and knowledge.
17 And I gave my heart to know wisdom, and to
know madness and folly: I perceived that this also
is vexation of spirit.

THE INVESTIGATION OF LIFE (1:1—6:12)

Chapter 1: *After describing the seeming monotony of life, the Preacher sums up his investigation of the issues of life, concluding that all is vanity.*

A Poem on Life's Cycles (1:1–11)

1:1 *the Preacher.* The Hebrew term is an official title of one who summons or addresses an assembly, not a gospel minister. See Introduction: Authorship.

1:2 *Vanity of vanities.* "Breath of breaths"—see Introduction: Synopsis. The opening poem sets the tone of monotony, restlessness, and ultimate inability to understand the world.

1:3 *What profit.* What advantage does a man have or what is the result of man's labor. *under the sun.* Where life occurs. See Introduction: Synopsis.

1:4 The cycles of life continue regardless of who populates the earth.

1:5 *hasteth to his place.* Literally, the sun "presses on" or "pants." The imagery pictures the relentlessness with which even inanimate creation does its divinely assigned task.

1:6 *according to his circuits.* The wind blows back and forth according to its patterns around the world.

1:8 *All things are full of labour.* Literally, "all things are striving or weariness."

1:9–11 The poem's conclusion points to the timeless and universal relevance of the message. Generations pass away, but the circumstances, problems, and issues of life remain the same. The characters change but the plot is the same.

Vanity of Striving after Knowledge (1:12–18)

1:12 *was king.* Some have interpreted this to mean that the Preacher was no longer king. The Hebrew can be translated, "I have been king," which would designate the current status.

1:13 *I gave my heart.* An idiom expressing determination. *by wisdom.* Wisdom involves the idea of skill or ability. The Preacher was well qualified for the proposed task. *this sore travail.* The hard task or business. *to be exercised.* To be occupied with. The hardness of labor, but not labor itself, was the consequence of the fall.

1:14 The initial conclusion was that the activities of life are temporary (*vanity*) and futile in and of themselves (*vexation of spirit*; see Introduction: Synopsis).

1:15 *that which is wanting.* A deficit or what is lacking. The Preacher admits man's inability to change whatever is.

1:17 *to know wisdom, and to know madness and folly.* An

18 For in much wisdom *is* much grief: and he that
increaseth knowledge increaseth sorrow.

CHAPTER 2

I SAID in mine heart, Go to now, I will prove thee
with mirth, therefore enjoy pleasure: and, behold,
this also *is* vanity.
2 I said of laughter, *It is* mad: and of mirth, What
doeth it?
3 I sought in mine heart to give myself unto wine,
yet acquainting mine heart with wisdom; and to
lay hold on folly, till I might see what *was* that
good for the sons of men, which they should do
under the heaven all the days of their life.
4 I made me great works; I builded me houses; I
planted me vineyards:
5 I made me gardens and orchards, and I planted
trees in them of all *kind of* fruits:
6 I made me pools of water, to water therewith
the wood that bringeth forth trees:
7 I got *me* servants and maidens, and had servants
born in my house; also I had great possessions
of great and small cattle above all that were in
Jerusalem before me:
8 I gathered me also silver and gold, and the
peculiar treasure of kings and of the provinces:
I gat me men singers and women singers, and
the delights of the sons of men, *as* musical
instruments, and that of all sorts.
9 So I was great, and increased more than all that
were before me in Jerusalem: also my wisdom
remained with me.
10 And whatsoever mine eyes desired I kept not
from them, I withheld not my heart from any joy;
for my heart rejoiced in all my labour: and this
was my portion of all my labour.
11 Then I looked on all the works that my hands
had wrought, and on the labour that I had laboured
to do: and, behold, all *was* vanity and vexation of
spirit, and *there was* no profit under the sun.
12 ¶ And I turned myself to behold wisdom, and
madness, and folly: for what *can* the man *do* that
cometh after the king? *even* that which hath been
already done.
13 Then I saw that wisdom excelleth folly, as far
as light excelleth darkness.
14 The wise man's eyes *are* in his head; but the
fool walketh in darkness: and I myself perceived
also that one event happeneth to them all.
15 Then said I in my heart, As it happeneth to the
fool, so it happeneth even to me; and why was I
then more wise? Then I said in my heart, that this
also *is* vanity.
16 For *there is* no remembrance of the wise more
than of the fool for ever; seeing that which now
is in the days to come shall all be forgotten. And
how dieth the wise *man*? as the fool.

---

alternate translation: "to know wisdom and knowledge, madness and folly." This puts in pairs two sets of synonyms which stand as opposites of each other. Linking opposites is a literary devise to express totality. Simply, the Preacher is saying that he looked at everything; no stone was left unturned.

1:18 *grief.* Vexation or frustration. *sorrow.* Pain. A well-known adage says that "ignorance is bliss." The Preacher is saying the same: learning removes the ignorance and its accompanying bliss.

Thoughts for Personal/Family Worship: Chapter 1

1. **The opening poem about the endless and monotonous cycles of life and nature reminds us of our insignificance in the whole scheme of creation. That generations come and go without remembrance by the next is a sober reminder that life will go on without us and that none of us is the center of the universe. Yet notwithstanding our insignificance in comparison to all creation, God has given us His special attention and cares for us graciously (Ps. 8). Our contentment in this life will never come from the things in this world but only from the Lord Himself.**
2. **No one in his day had more God-given wisdom and more material resources than Solomon, and yet he was not able to find the answer to all the questions of life no matter how diligently he sought for those answers. That there are things about life that we will never understand is a fact of life. The inability to understand everything about the present is reason for us to find the ultimate reason for everything in God who knows the why of everything because He has ordained all things.**

Chapter 2: ***Solomon concludes that amusements and accomplishments are only temporary and that the best course of action is to use and enjoy what God has given with contentment.***

Vanity of Striving after Pleasure (2:1–11)

2:1 *I will prove thee with mirth.* I will conduct a test regarding joy or pleasure. *enjoy pleasure.* Literally, "see" or "look on good." Seeing has the idea of experiencing.

2:2 *mad.* Foolish or senseless.

2:3 *to give myself unto wine.* Literally, "to cheer with wine my flesh." *yet acquainting mine heart with wisdom.* My heart was behaving wisely. He did not give himself to drunkenness. *folly.* Here, it most likely refers to some sort of revelry.

2:6 *the wood that bringeth forth trees.* The forest that sprouts trees.

2:8 *peculiar treasure.* Prized or personal treasure. *I gat me.* I acquired for myself. *delights.* Luxurious things.

2:10 *my portion.* My profit or reward. The ability to enjoy labor is greater reward than amassing possessions from it.

2:11 *no profit under the sun.* Nothing remains of what labor accomplishes, so enjoy labor for its own sake.

Vanity of Striving after Wisdom (2:12–17)

2:12 *to behold wisdom, and madness, and folly.* The idea is that he observed wisdom to be the same as both madness and folly in regard to providing ultimate answers. *what can the man do.* The Preacher, *the king*, claims that his investigation was so thorough and done with such expertise that duplicating his efforts would be of no avail.

2:13–16 Wisdom has advantages over foolishness, but it is not the key to life's meaning and purpose. It certainly does not remove the brevity of life, for the wise and foolish both die. Life is temporary for both.

17 Therefore I hated life; because the work that is
wrought under the sun *is* grievous unto me: for
all *is* vanity and vexation of spirit.
18 ¶ Yea, I hated all my labour which I had taken
under the sun: because I should leave it unto the
man that shall be after me.
19 And who knoweth whether he shall be a wise
man or a fool? yet shall he have rule over all my
labour wherein I have laboured, and wherein I have
shewed myself wise under the sun. This *is* also vanity.
20 Therefore I went about to cause my heart to despair of all the labour which I took under the sun.
21 For there is a man whose labour *is* in wisdom,
and in knowledge, and in equity; yet to a man that
hath not laboured therein shall he leave it *for* his
portion. This also *is* vanity and a great evil.
22 For what hath man of all his labour, and of the
vexation of his heart, wherein he hath laboured
under the sun?
23 For all his days *are* sorrows, and his travail
grief; yea, his heart taketh not rest in the night.
This is also vanity.
24 ¶ *There is* nothing better for a man, *than* that
he should eat and drink, and *that* he should make
his soul enjoy good in his labour. This also I saw,
that it *was* from the hand of God.
25 For who can eat, or who else can hasten
hereunto, more than I?
26 For *God* giveth to a man that *is* good in his
sight wisdom, and knowledge, and joy: but to the
sinner he giveth travail, to gather and to heap up,
that he may give to *him that is* good before God.
This also *is* vanity and vexation of spirit.

CHAPTER 3

TO every *thing there is* a season, and a time to
every purpose under the heaven:
2 A time to be born, and a time to die; a time to
plant, and a time to pluck up *that which is* planted;
3 A time to kill, and a time to heal; a time to break
down, and a time to build up;
4 A time to weep, and a time to laugh; a time to
mourn, and a time to dance;
5 A time to cast away stones, and a time to gather
stones together; a time to embrace, and a time to
refrain from embracing;
6 A time to get, and a time to lose; a time to keep,
and a time to cast away;
7 A time to rend, and a time to sew; a time to keep
silence, and a time to speak;
8 A time to love, and a time to hate; a time of war,
and a time of peace.
9 What profit hath he that worketh in that
wherein he laboureth?
10 I have seen the travail, which God hath given

2:17 *I hated life.* He rejected life as being an end in itself. Rather than a statement of pessimism, it is the sound conclusion that something is more important than mere physical existence.

Vanity of Striving after the Results of Labor (2:18—6:12)

Everything Is Temporary (2:18–26)

2:18 *I hated all my labour.* He rejected it as the ultimate answer. That labor's profit goes to the next generation is one of its limitations. It is a reminder not to be obsessed with things that we cannot take with us after life.

2:19–21 Part of the frustration is that what he gained through wisdom may be squandered by the carelessness of those who did not labor for it.

2:22–23 The attention is on the curse associated with labor, not the labor itself. It is sin that caused all the adverse circumstances of labor (Gen. 3:17–19).

2:24 Man should recognize that the provisions for life (*eat . . . drink*) are from the hand of God. The *eat, drink, enjoy* refrain refers to being content with whatever is one's lot in life, realizing that it is God's gift and therefore good.

2:25 *who else can hasten.* Literally, "Who can be delighted with?"

2:26 All that God gives is ultimately for good. Those who know God have been given the ability to enjoy life; but sinners have been given the task (*travail*) without the ability to enjoy it. That inability should drive sinners to God.

Thoughts for Personal/Family Worship: Chapter 2

1. **The Preacher's counsel against the folly of seeking pleasure and possessions is most relevant for this day that is so consumed with momentary experiences and materialism. So many today pursue happiness by living for the moment and by trying to get as many things as possible. Such is an imaginary happiness that really does not exist. Pleasure and things can never ultimately satisfy because they are unsubstantial and temporary. It is an endless cycle that only breeds frustration and disappointment.**
2. **The refrain in 2:24 occurs again in 3:12–13; 3:22; 5:18–19; 8:15; and 9:7–9. In each instance, the sense is the same. It is the Preacher's way of instructing us to recognize that the provisions we have for life are God's gift that He has intended for our enjoyment. That enjoyment entails being content and satisfied with what God has given and to use gifts to their fullest potentials. In many ways, this refrain parallels Paul's testimony that he was content in whatever state God put him (Phil. 4:11).**

Chapter 3: ***God determines the times and circumstances of life as well as the time for a future judgment so that men might fear Him.***

Everything Is Predetermined (3:1–15)

3:1 *a season.* An appointed time. *purpose.* Matter or affair. *under the heaven.* Equivalent to the more frequent expression, "under the sun."

3:2–8 By listing 28 specific times that occur in 14 pairs of opposite circumstances, the Preacher employs literary devices designed to express totality. Both numbers are multiples of seven, which are frequently used to represent completeness. The 28 times is an example of brachylogy, the use of a partial list to designate totality. The 14 pairs of opposites is an example of merismus, the use of polar terms to designate entirety. The point is clear even without considering the individual statements: There is a determined time for everything. Life unfolds according to divine providence (everything from birth to death).

3:9 *What profit.* What is the result of all the labor?

3:10 *travail.* Business, task, or occupation.

to the sons of men to be exercised in it.
11 He hath made every *thing* beautiful in his time:
also he hath set the world in their heart, so that no
man can find out the work that God maketh from
the beginning to the end.
12 I know that *there is* no good in them, but for *a*
man to rejoice, and to do good in his life.
13 And also that every man should eat and drink,
and enjoy the good of all his labour, it *is* the gift
of God.
14 I know that, whatsoever God doeth, it shall be
for ever: nothing can be put to it, nor any thing
taken from it: and God doeth *it*, that *men* should
fear before him.
15 That which hath been is now; and that which
is to be hath already been; and God requireth that
which is past.
16 ¶ And moreover I saw under the sun the place
of judgment, *that* wickedness *was* there; and the
place of righteousness, *that* iniquity *was* there.
17 I said in mine heart, God shall judge the righ-
teous and the wicked: for *there is* a time there for
every purpose and for every work.
18 I said in mine heart concerning the estate of
the sons of men, that God might manifest them,
and that they might see that they themselves are
beasts.
19 For that which befalleth the sons of men
befalleth beasts; even one thing befalleth them: as
the one dieth, so dieth the other; yea, they have all
one breath; so that a man hath no preeminence
above a beast: for all *is* vanity.
20 All go unto one place; all are of the dust, and
all turn to dust again.
21 Who knoweth the spirit of man that goeth
upward, and the spirit of the beast that goeth
downward to the earth?
22 Wherefore I perceive that *there is* nothing
better, than that a man should rejoice in his own
works; for that *is* his portion: for who shall bring
him to see what shall be after him?

CHAPTER 4

SO I returned, and considered all the oppressions
that are done under the sun: and behold the
tears of *such as were* oppressed, and they had no
comforter; and on the side of their oppressors
there was power; but they had no comforter.
2 Wherefore I praised the dead which are already

3:11 *He hath made every thing beautiful.* He has made everything right or appropriate in its time. This equates to Rom. 8:28 which declares that God is working everything to good. Life does not happen haphazardly by blind fate but according to God's all-wise plan. *the world in their heart.* Almost everywhere else, the Hebrew term translated "world" refers to eternity. This is a key to understanding why the temporal things of life under the sun cannot ultimately satisfy. Although every man is mortal under the sun, he will live someplace forever. The only source of satisfaction for the eternity within us is the eternal God. *no man can find out.* God's plan is beautiful but its scope is incomprehensible to us.

3:12–14 Here is the sum of responding properly to God's unfrustratable plan: do not deny it nor rebel against it, but rather fear God and enjoy life with full contentment in the will of God.

3:15 The future is as certain as the past. *God requireth.* Literally, "God seeks what has been sought." It declares God's consistency and immutability: His standards never change.

Everything Is Liable to Injustice (3:16–22)

3:16–17 The injustices in life can create a tension between faith and experience, causing doubts as to how inequities can be if God has a beautiful plan for everything. Faith triumphs knowing that God is the infallible judge and that there is a set time for judgment. Therefore, we are not to judge before the time.

3:18 *the estate of the sons of men.* The affairs of mankind. *God might manifest them . . . beasts.* God might test or prove to men that they are like the beasts. The point of similarity will be explained in terms of the certainty of death. The word *beasts* usually refers to large domesticated cattle whose existence is for the purpose of eventual slaughter. This reminder of the brevity of life is a means of removing the tension regarding life's inequities.

3:19 *befalleth.* This means such is the condition of all; what happens to one happens to all. Death, the terrible consequence of man's sin, was the curse for every living thing. Humankind and animal kind all die. *no preeminence.* No advantage. Death is the great equalizer of all life.

3:20 The *one place* refers to the dust to which all flesh returns. It refers to the body and not the spirit.

3:21 *Who knoweth.* Not an expression of doubt but of experience. What happens to the body is visible; what happens to the spirit, while real, is unseen to the physical eye.

3:22 True contentment and joy in life is possible only by living in the light of eternity.

Thoughts for Personal/Family Worship: Chapter 3

1. **Recognizing that all the times and circumstances of life are ordained by a good, wise, and sovereign God should encourage us to use correctly the times that God has purposed. For instance, God brings times of both weeping and laughing into life. He expects us, therefore, to weep in weeping times. As believers, we do not sorrow like the world which has no hope, but we do sorrow in times of grief. It is not distrust but rather a contented belief in God's sovereignty that allows us to experience all His appropriate times for our ultimate good.**
2. **Verse 11 is the key verse that explains why all the temporary things of life under the sun cannot bring ultimate satisfaction. Since God has put eternity in our hearts, only the eternal God can satisfy. Living now with a view to eternity is the essence of a Christian worldview. The Preacher's references to death are not intended to be pessimistic but realistic. Certain death makes life temporary. We are not to be morbid, but we are to live under the sun with a view of life "beyond the sun."**

Chapter 4: ***The Preacher identifies problems that seem incongruous to providence and offers practical advice.***

dead more than the living which are yet alive.
3 Yea, better *is he* than both they, which hath not
yet been, who hath not seen the evil work that is
done under the sun.
4 ¶ Again, I considered all travail, and every right
work, that for this a man is envied of his neigh-
bour. This *is* also vanity and vexation of spirit.
5 The fool foldeth his hands together, and eateth
his own flesh.
6 Better *is* an handful *with* quietness, than both
the hands full *with* travail and vexation of spirit.
7 ¶ Then I returned, and I saw vanity under the sun.
8 There is one *alone*, and *there is* not a second;
yea, he hath neither child nor brother: yet *is there*
no end of all his labour; neither is his eye satisfied
with riches; neither *saith he*, For whom do I
labour, and bereave my soul of good? This *is* also
vanity, yea, it *is* a sore travail.
9 ¶ Two *are* better than one; because they have a
good reward for their labour.
10 For if they fall, the one will lift up his fellow:
but woe to him *that is* alone when he falleth; for
he hath not another to help him up.
11 Again, if two lie together, then they have heat:
but how can one be warm *alone*?
12 And if one prevail against him, two shall with-
stand him; and a threefold cord is not quickly
broken.
13 ¶ Better *is* a poor and a wise child than an old
and foolish king, who will no more be admonished.
14 For out of prison he cometh to reign; whereas
also *he that is* born in his kingdom becometh poor.
15 I considered all the living which walk under
the sun, with the second child that shall stand up
in his stead.
16 *There is* no end of all the people, *even* of all
that have been before them: they also that come
after shall not rejoice in him. Surely this also *is*
vanity and vexation of spirit.

CHAPTER 5

KEEP thy foot when thou goest to the house of
God, and be more ready to hear, than to give the
sacrifice of fools: for they consider not that they
do evil.
2 Be not rash with thy mouth, and let not thine
heart be hasty to utter *any* thing before God: for
God *is* in heaven, and thou upon earth: therefore
let thy words be few.
3 For a dream cometh through the multitude of
business; and a fool's voice *is known* by multitude
of words.
4 When thou vowest a vow unto God, defer not
to pay it; for *he hath* no pleasure in fools: pay that
which thou hast vowed.

Everything Is Subject to Oppression and Envy (4:1–6)

4:1–3 Oppression, exploitation, or injustices are facts of life. Death or nonexistence is the only way to escape. Sometimes suffering can be so intense that life is no longer attractive (Job 3:3–10). *the evil work.* That which is harmful or hurtful.

4:4 *travail.* Business, task, or occupation. *every right work.* Every successful work. *a man is envied of his neighbour.* Literally, "the rivalry or competitive spirit of a man with his fellow." Competition, the desire to get ahead at the expense of another, is an all too common motivator.

4:5 *eateth his own flesh.* Not literally, but an image of self-destruction. The answer to competition is not laziness.

4:6 *quietness.* A calm and patient attitude. Moderation and contentment is the answer to envy.

Everything Is Prone to Loss (4:7–16)

4:8 *bereave my soul of good.* Deprive self of good. The Preacher describes a recluse who exerts all his energy on self without a thought beyond himself. Such isolation is not the answer to life's vanity. His wealth is prone to loss in spite of his oblivion.

4:9–12 Companionship has advantages: assistance (v. 10), comfort (v. 11), and defense (v. 12).

4:13–16 Most likely an illustration about the transitory nature of fame rather than a specific historical situation. Fame is prone to loss—first regarding the foolish king (v. 14) and then regarding the wise child himself (v. 16).

4:15 *with the second child.* Only two characters are in view in vv. 13–15. This should be rendered "the child, the second one"—the wise child that replaced the foolish king.

Thoughts for Personal/Family Worship: Chapter 4

1. **Diligence in labor is a virtue; laziness is self-destructive (4:5). God has given us the ability to labor both for its inherent enjoyment and for its provisions for life. However, laboring just to get ahead of someone else (v. 4), or laboring in order to hoard what is earned (v. 8), is an abuse of what God has given for good. Although work is good, to be motivated to work out of envy or greed violates God's law (the tenth commandment). Christians should work hard but not with the tension and pressure of trying to keep up with someone else. Moderation and contentment with what one has is attainable, but always striving for more is chasing after the wind.**
2. **God has made us to be social creatures (vv. 9–12), and there is blessing and advantage attached with companionship, including marriage, family, and friends. We should be thankful for those God has brought into our lives and let family and friends know of our gratitude. Thinking of family and friends should also direct our hearts to Christ who is our husband, our elder brother, and friend that sticks closer than any brother could.**

Chapter 5: *Recognizing the sovereignty of God influences practices of worship and perceptions of problems in life.*

Everything Is Subservient to the Fear of God (5:1–7)

5:1 *Keep thy foot.* An idiom for guarding steps or being careful. Careless worship must be avoided. Imperatives for worship include self-restraint, submission, and sincerity.

5:2 Entering God's presence in prayer is a privilege not to be abused with thoughtless and rambling words.

5:3 Although dreams were often a means of divine revelation, they could also be the consequence of restlessness. The much speaking of the fool confirms the latter.

5:4 *defer not to pay it.* Do not delay to fulfill it.

5 Better *is it* that thou shouldest not vow, than
that thou shouldest vow and not pay.
6 Suffer not thy mouth to cause thy flesh to sin;
neither say thou before the angel, that it *was* an
error: wherefore should God be angry at thy
voice, and destroy the work of thine hands?
7 For in the multitude of dreams and many
words *there are* also *divers* vanities: but fear thou
God.
8 ¶ If thou seest the oppression of the poor, and
violent perverting of judgment and justice in a
province, marvel not at the matter: for *he that is*
higher than the highest regardeth; and *there be*
higher than they.
9 ¶ Moreover the profit of the earth is for all: the
king *himself* is served by the field.
10 He that loveth silver shall not be satisfied with
silver; nor he that loveth abundance with increase:
this *is* also vanity.
11 When goods increase, they are increased that
eat them: and what good *is there* to the owners
thereof, saving the beholding *of them* with their
eyes?
12 The sleep of a labouring man *is* sweet, whether
he eat little or much: but the abundance of the
rich will not suffer him to sleep.
13 There is a sore evil *which* I have seen under the
sun, *namely*, riches kept for the owners thereof to
their hurt.
14 But those riches perish by evil travail: and he
begetteth a son, and *there is* nothing in his hand.
15 As he came forth of his mother's womb, naked
shall he return to go as he came, and shall take
nothing of his labour, which he may carry away
in his hand.
16 And this also *is* a sore evil, *that* in all points as
he came, so shall he go: and what profit hath he
that hath laboured for the wind?
17 All his days also he eateth in darkness, and *he
hath* much sorrow and wrath with his sickness.
18 ¶ Behold *that* which I have seen: *it is* good and
comely *for one* to eat and to drink, and to enjoy
the good of all his labour that he taketh under the
sun all the days of his life, which God giveth him:
for it *is* his portion.
19 Every man also to whom God hath given
riches and wealth, and hath given him power to
eat thereof, and to take his portion, and to rejoice
in his labour; this *is* the gift of God.
20 For he shall not much remember the days of
his life; because God answereth *him* in the joy of
his heart.

CHAPTER 6

THERE is an evil which I have seen under the sun,
and it *is* common among men:
2 A man to whom God hath given riches, wealth,
and honour, so that he wanteth nothing for his
soul of all that he desireth, yet God giveth him not
power to eat thereof, but a stranger eateth it: this
is vanity, and it *is* an evil disease.

5:5 Do not trifle with God. Avoid making hasty bargains with God. A vow is a solemn promise and should never be thoughtless or impetuous.
5:6 *Suffer not.* Do not allow.
5:7 *fear thou God.* Being consciously and actively aware of God is a remedy for sin.

Everything Is a Potential Frustration (5:8—6:12)

5:8 Do not think that injustice will prevail. The highest judge of all is watching (*regardeth*), and He will bring all to account in highest court.
5:10 *he that loveth abundance with increase.* The one who loves wealth will never be satisfied with his income. The desire for things is never satisfied because things cannot satisfy.
5:12 *not suffer.* Not allow.
5:13 *a sore evil.* A severe problem.
5:14 Riches can be lost by bad business, leaving no inheritance for the heir. Wealth is always uncertain.
5:17 *in darkness.* In distress.
5:18 *comely.* Beautiful. In spite of all the potential frustrations, God has given man the ability to use and enjoy the things of life.
5:19 *hath given him power.* Has given him the opportunity.
5:20 *remember.* To consciously and willfully to think about something. *God answereth.* God corresponds to the joy. Simply, God Himself is the joy of the heart. It is only as we regard God as the ultimate joy or satisfaction that everything else in life falls in place. We will not be thinking about the days of life when God is preeminent in our thoughts.

Thoughts for Personal/Family Worship: Chapter 5

1. **A proper view of God's greatness will govern how we approach Him in worship. That He is in heaven and that we are on earth means that we should be cautious and reverent as we enter into His holy presence. That we can approach Him is itself a wonderful privilege that must not be abused with triteness or triviality. Self-restraint, submission, sincerity, and spiritual sacrifice (heart-generated praise) should characterize the place and practice of worship.**
2. **The instructions regarding vows are important reminders of how seriously God regards the promises we make. Some carelessly try to make bargains with God, promising to do something for Him if He does the special something they desire from Him. Then they forget all about it. In every situation, but most certainly before God, our yeas should be yeas and our nays nays. This is not a prohibition of vows, for there are legitimate vows, such as swearing truth before tribunals or pledging faithfulness to marriage bonds. It is a solemn reminder that God does and therefore we ought to take vows seriously and to make them thoughtfully.**

Chapter 6: ***The Preacher shows that prosperity is not always good, warning that things are not always as they appear.***

6:1 *evil.* Not sin, but misery or trouble. *common.* Abundantly plentiful.
6:2 *wealth,* which appears to be a good thing, without the

3 ¶ If a man beget an hundred *children*, and live
many years, so that the days of his years be many,
and his soul be not filled with good, and also *that*
he have no burial; I say, *that* an untimely birth *is*
better than he.
4 For he cometh in with vanity, and departeth
in darkness, and his name shall be covered with
darkness.
5 Moreover he hath not seen the sun, nor known
any thing: this hath more rest than the other.
6 ¶ Yea, though he live a thousand years twice *told*,
yet hath he seen no good: do not all go to one place?
7 All the labour of man *is* for his mouth, and yet
the appetite is not filled.
8 For what hath the wise more than the fool?
what hath the poor, that knoweth to walk before
the living?
9 ¶ Better *is* the sight of the eyes than the
wandering of the desire: this *is* also vanity and
vexation of spirit.
10 That which hath been is named already, and it
is known that it *is* man: neither may he contend
with him that is mightier than he.
11 ¶ Seeing there be many things that increase
vanity, what *is* man the better?
12 For who knoweth what *is* good for man in *this*
life, all the days of his vain life which he spendeth
as a shadow? for who can tell a man what shall be
after him under the sun?

CHAPTER 7

A GOOD name *is* better than precious ointment;
and the day of death than the day of one's birth.
2 ¶ *It is* better to go to the house of mourning,
than to go to the house of feasting: for that *is* the
end of all men; and the living will lay *it* to his heart.
3 Sorrow *is* better than laughter: for by the sad-
ness of the countenance the heart is made better.
4 The heart of the wise *is* in the house of mourn-
ing; but the heart of fools *is* in the house of mirth.
5 *It is* better to hear the rebuke of the wise, than
for a man to hear the song of fools.
6 For as the crackling of thorns under a pot, so *is*
the laughter of the fool: this also *is* vanity.
7 ¶ Surely oppression maketh a wise man mad;
and a gift destroyeth the heart.
8 Better *is* the end of a thing than the beginning
thereof: *and* the patient in spirit *is* better than the
proud in spirit.

---

ability to enjoy it, is in reality a cause of suffering (*evil disease*).

6:3 *untimely birth*. A miscarriage. Long life and many children would appear to be good, but death at birth would be preferable to a life without satisfaction or children who did not care for end of life issues.

6:4–5 Although the stillborn does not experience the activities of life, he experiences a calmness (*rest*) exceeding those who do. His missing life under the sun does not exclude his life "beyond the sun." This is a clear statement of the personhood of the fetus.

6:6 Long life by itself cannot satisfy, and eventually the longest of lives end and all go to the grave (the *one place*).

6:7 *appetite*. The word is most often translated "soul" and designates the whole person.

6:8 *that knoweth to walk*. Even though the poor person may know how best to behave (*walk*), his poverty leaves him no advantage and robs him of influence.

6:9 *the sight of the eyes*. Refers to the actual experiences of life. *the wandering of the desire*. Literally, "the walking of the person." It is better to enjoy the life that you have than to daydream about another. Again, the Preacher advises contentment in whatever our state.

6:10 God has determined all that exists. For man to dispute with God about it is useless (Rom. 9:20).

6:12 The inability to know the future is one of life's limitations designed to lead to the fear and trust of God who not only knows but has also determined all of time.

Thoughts for Personal/Family Worship: Chapter 6

1. **Too often it is easy to look at someone who seems to have everything and to become envious. Even apart from such envy being a transgression of the tenth commandment, the Preacher shows the folly by highlighting the difference between appearance and reality. Although a lot of money, a big family, and a long life may appear to be ideal, the reality is that having those things is no guarantee that all is well. In fact many who appear to have it all are in reality most miserable. It is best to trust the wisdom of God who has determined our times and circumstances and learn to be content.**
2. **The Preacher's reminder that life is but a shadow reinforces the frequent and important theme of life's brevity. A shadow is unsubstantial and fleeting. It is particularly vivid given the hypothetical example of one who may live for two thousand years (6:6). Even for him, life comes to an end and most likely before he expected. In the light of eternity, the longest of lives is just a passing moment. The vital issue in this life, therefore, is to be ready for eternity. Being ready for eternity requires looking to God and the provision for eternal life He has given in His Son.**

THE EVALUATION OF LIFE (7:1—12:7)

The Inability to Know What to Do (7:1—8:17)

Chapter 7: *The Preacher shows that adversity is not always bad, warning that things are not always as they appear.*

Because the Better Things Are Contrary to Expectation (7:1–14)

7:1 *A good name*. A good reputation. *day of death . . . birth*. The apparently pessimistic statement must be understood in the context of one's reputation. Since a reputation is earned and subject to change throughout life, only death secures it by removing any further possibility of tarnishing it (v. 8).

7:2 Compare the words of Christ in the Sermon on the Mount (Matt. 5:4). The sight of death is sobering and brings to focus the real issues of life (Heb. 9:27).

7:3–6 Although not as pleasant, times of sorrow are of greater profit than shallow happiness.

7:7 *maketh a wise man mad*. Makes a wise man look foolish. *a gift*. A bribe.

9 Be not hasty in thy spirit to be angry: for anger
resteth in the bosom of fools.
10 Say not thou, What is *the cause* that the former
days were better than these? for thou dost not
enquire wisely concerning this.
11 ¶ Wisdom *is* good with an inheritance: and *by
it there is* profit to them that see the sun.
12 For wisdom *is* a defence, *and* money *is* a
defence: but the excellency of knowledge *is, that*
wisdom giveth life to them that have it.
13 Consider the work of God: for who can make
that straight, which he hath made crooked?
14 In the day of prosperity be joyful, but in the
day of adversity consider: God also hath set the
one over against the other, to the end that man
should find nothing after him.
15 All *things* have I seen in the days of my vanity:
there is a just *man* that perisheth in his righteous-
ness, and there is a wicked *man* that prolongeth
his life in his wickedness.
16 Be not righteous over much; neither make
thyself over wise: why shouldest thou destroy
thyself?
17 Be not over much wicked, neither be thou
foolish: why shouldest thou die before thy time?
18 *It is* good that thou shouldest take hold of this;
yea, also from this withdraw not thine hand: for
he that feareth God shall come forth of them all.
19 Wisdom strengtheneth the wise more than ten
mighty *men* which are in the city.
20 For *there is* not a just man upon earth, that
doeth good, and sinneth not.
21 Also take no heed unto all words that are
spoken; lest thou hear thy servant curse thee:
22 For oftentimes also thine own heart knoweth
that thou thyself likewise hast cursed others.
23 ¶ All this have I proved by wisdom: I said, I
will be wise; but it *was* far from me.
24 That which is far off, and exceeding deep, who
can find it out?
25 I applied mine heart to know, and to search,
and to seek out wisdom, and the reason *of things*,
and to know the wickedness of folly, even of
foolishness *and* madness:
26 And I find more bitter than death the woman,
whose heart *is* snares and nets, *and* her hands *as*
bands: whoso pleaseth God shall escape from her;
but the sinner shall be taken by her.
27 Behold, this have I found, saith the preacher,
counting one by one, to find out the account:
28 Which yet my soul seeketh, but I find not:
one man among a thousand have I found; but a

7:10 Nothing new under the sun (1:9) means that the *former days* were no better than the present.

7:11–12 Wisdom has its limitations but also its potentials. *defence.* Literally, "a shadow," which is a common image for protection.

7:13 What God has done is unalterable.

7:14 God puts good days (*prosperity*) and bad days (*adversity*) together in order to teach man to depend on Him completely always. *after him.* Him, referring to God. It sometimes takes adversity to remind us of our dependence on God.

Because Life Is Unpredictable (7:15–24)

7:15 *just . . . righteousness.* Though these words meaning "straight" and "straightness" often have moral and theological significance, here they refer to one who lives by a rigid set of self-imposed standards. *wicked . . . wickedness.* Though usually designating moral sin, here it is simply the opposite of righteous. The man who lives according to strict rules and habits dies in spite of his plans, and the one who lives capriciously prolongs his life in spite of his carelessness. Life is unpredictable and contrary to expectation.

7:16–17 *Be not righteous over much.* Do not be overly rigid. *Be not over much wicked.* Do not be overly impulsive or careless. The Preacher is not saying to sin in moderation. The Bible never contradicts itself. Morally, we are to live as righteously as possible and to avoid sinning in every instance. But practically, we are to be flexible because we do not know what will happen next.

7:18 *come forth of them all.* Fearing God will avoid both extremes and evidence moderation and flexibility.

7:20 Sin is the universal failure of man in every sphere of life.

Because Foolishness Abounds (7:25–29)

7:26 The Hebrew often personifies abstract ideas in the feminine gender. Here folly is personified as a woman. Compare Prov. 1 and 8 where wisdom is feminine.

7:27 *account.* The conclusion of the matter.

7:28 *one man among a thousand . . . a woman . . . not found.* A pointed statement of the universal presence of folly in all humanity. The "one man" exception points to the coming of the only perfect man, Christ Himself.

7:29 *inventions.* Plans or schemes, referring to man's fall into sin after God's creating him *upright*.

Thoughts for Personal/Family Worship: Chapter 7

1. **Coffins are powerful sermons (7:2). Mourning the loss of life is one of the times God has ordained (3:4), but through and beyond the tears are important life lessons. As we experience life under the sun, death is always something that happens to someone else. But the Preacher reminds us of the sobering reality that sooner or later we will be the "someone else" that will be preaching the message of the brevity of life to others by our own death. The place of mourning, therefore, ought to be an occasion to face reality and to be sure that we are ready for eternity. The only way to be ready is Christ.**
2. **It is not a hard thing to be joyful in the day of prosperity (7:14). But all too often there is a tendency to forget God when everything is going well. Moses warned Israel about the potential of forgetting God when they entered the Promised Land and would enjoy all the bounty (Deut. 8). It was going to be so different from the wilderness wanderings when they were forced to depend on God for daily bread (the manna). Although the days of adversity are not as enjoyable, they serve to teach a vital spiritual lesson. It often takes the trials and troubles of life to remind us of how much we need the Lord. Trouble does not mean that God no longer cares about us; on the contrary, it shows His concern for us by bringing us again to the realization of how much we depend on Him for everything.**

woman among all those have I not found.
29 Lo, this only have I found, that God hath made
man upright; but they have sought out many
inventions.

CHAPTER 8

WHO *is* as the wise *man*? and who knoweth the
interpretation of a thing? a man's wisdom maketh
his face to shine, and the boldness of his face shall
be changed.
2 I *counsel thee* to keep the king's commandment,
and *that* in regard of the oath of God.
3 Be not hasty to go out of his sight: stand not
in an evil thing; for he doeth whatsoever pleaseth
him.
4 Where the word of a king *is, there is* power: and
who may say unto him, What doest thou?
5 Whoso keepeth the commandment shall feel
no evil thing: and a wise man's heart discerneth
both time and judgment.
6 ¶ Because to every purpose there is time and
judgment, therefore the misery of man *is* great
upon him.
7 For he knoweth not that which shall be: for
who can tell him when it shall be?
8 *There is* no man that hath power over the spirit
to retain the spirit; neither *hath he* power in the
day of death: and *there is* no discharge in *that* war;
neither shall wickedness deliver those that are
given to it.
9 All this have I seen, and applied my heart unto
every work that is done under the sun: *there is* a
time wherein one man ruleth over another to his
own hurt.
10 And so I saw the wicked buried, who had come
and gone from the place of the holy, and they
were forgotten in the city where they had so done:
this *is* also vanity.
11 Because sentence against an evil work is not
executed speedily, therefore the heart of the sons
of men is fully set in them to do evil.
12 ¶ Though a sinner do evil an hundred times,
and his *days* be prolonged, yet surely I know that
it shall be well with them that fear God, which
fear before him:
13 But it shall not be well with the wicked, neither
shall he prolong *his* days, *which are* as a shadow;
because he feareth not before God.
14 There is a vanity which is done upon the earth;
that there be just *men*, unto whom it happeneth
according to the work of the wicked; again, there
be wicked *men*, to whom it happeneth according
to the work of the righteous: I said that this also
is vanity.
15 Then I commended mirth, because a man
hath no better thing under the sun, than to eat,
and to drink, and to be merry: for that shall abide
with him of his labour the days of his life, which
God giveth him under the sun.
16 ¶ When I applied mine heart to know wisdom,
and to see the business that is done upon the
earth: (for also *there is that* neither day nor night
seeth sleep with his eyes:)
17 Then I beheld all the work of God, that a man
cannot find out the work that is done under the
sun: because though a man labour to seek *it* out,
yet he shall not find *it*; yea further; though a wise
man think to know *it*, yet shall he not be able to
find *it*.

Chapter 8: ***The Preacher recommends obeying the king and fearing God in spite of all of life's incongruities.***

Because Life Is Full of Incongruities (8:1–17)

8:1 *interpretation.* Explanation. *maketh his face to shine.* An idiom for being gracious toward another. See the explicit link to grace with reference to God in the Aaronic blessing (Num. 6:25). *the boldness of his face . . . changed.* Being gracious will make beautiful what may be otherwise a harsh appearance.
8:2 Obedience to the civil authority is evidence of allegiance to God. This connection is established in the fifth commandment.
8:3 *Be not hasty to go out of his sight.* Most likely, an idiom for not rebelling against the king. *stand not in an evil thing.* Do not persist in that wrong behavior.
8:5 *feel.* Literally, "know."
8:6 *to every purpose there is time and judgment.* The idea is that every purpose has its appropriate time.
8:11–13 Delay in justice convinces some that they can sin with impunity. But the fact is that regardless of how many sins are committed and how long justice is delayed, there is a day of reckoning that is certain. Fearing God in life is the only protection in that day.
8:15 *I commended mirth.* Literally, "I sang the praises of joy or contentment." *to be merry.* To rejoice or be content.
8:16–17 God's ways are incomprehensible.

Thoughts for Personal/Family Worship: Chapter 8

1. **The Preacher's counsel to obey the king parallels the New Testament's teaching regarding the Christian's submission to civil authority (Rom. 13:1–7; 1 Peter 2:13–17). This is a component of the fifth commandment, which defines the duties and responsibilities between inferiors and superiors. How much we agree with the state is not an issue. Unless the state legislates contrary to the law and government of God, good citizenship is the Christian's duty (Acts 4:19).**
2. **Fearing God defines the essence of Christian living, encompassing both our attitude of reverence toward God and our behavior before God. Verses 12 and 13 make it clear that fearing or not fearing God will be a crucial factor in the day of judgment. The true fear of God is the essence of true religion and includes, therefore, saving faith in Christ.**

The Inability to Know the Future (9:1—11:6)

Chapter 9: ***In spite of the frustrations and mysteries of life, life should be lived to its fullest by taking***

CHAPTER 9

FOR all this I considered in my heart even to declare
all this, that the righteous, and the wise, and their
works, *are* in the hand of God: no man knoweth
either love or hatred *by* all *that is* before them.
2 All *things come* alike to all: *there is* one event
to the righteous, and to the wicked; to the good
and to the clean, and to the unclean; to him that
sacrificeth, and to him that sacrificeth not: as *is*
the good, so *is* the sinner; *and* he that sweareth, as
he that feareth an oath.
3 This *is* an evil among all *things* that are done
under the sun, that *there is* one event unto all: yea,
also the heart of the sons of men is full of evil, and
madness *is* in their heart while they live, and after
that *they go* to the dead.
4 ¶ For to him that is joined to all the living there
is hope: for a living dog is better than a dead lion.
5 For the living know that they shall die: but
the dead know not any thing, neither have they
any more a reward; for the memory of them is
forgotten.
6 Also their love, and their hatred, and their envy,
is now perished; neither have they any more a portion
for ever in any *thing* that is done under the sun.
7 ¶ Go thy way, eat thy bread with joy, and
drink thy wine with a merry heart; for God now
accepteth thy works.
8 Let thy garments be always white; and let thy
head lack no ointment.
9 Live joyfully with the wife whom thou lovest
all the days of the life of thy vanity, which he
hath given thee under the sun, all the days of thy
vanity: for that *is* thy portion in *this* life, and in
thy labour which thou takest under the sun.
10 Whatsoever thy hand findeth to do, do *it* with
thy might; for *there is* no work, nor device, nor
knowledge, nor wisdom, in the grave, whither
thou goest.
11 ¶ I returned, and saw under the sun, that the
race *is* not to the swift, nor the battle to the strong,
neither yet bread to the wise, nor yet riches to
men of understanding, nor yet favour to men of
skill; but time and chance happeneth to them all.
12 For man also knoweth not his time: as the
fishes that are taken in an evil net, and as the birds
that are caught in the snare; so *are* the sons of men
snared in an evil time, when it falleth suddenly
upon them.
13 ¶ This wisdom have I seen also under the sun,
and it *seemed* great unto me:
14 *There was* a little city, and few men within
it; and there came a great king against it, and
besieged it, and built great bulwarks against it:
15 Now there was found in it a poor wise man,
and he by his wisdom delivered the city; yet no
man remembered that same poor man.
16 Then said I, Wisdom *is* better than strength:
nevertheless the poor man's wisdom *is* despised,
and his words are not heard.
17 The words of wise *men are* heard in quiet
more than the cry of him that ruleth among fools.
18 Wisdom *is* better than weapons of war: but
one sinner destroyeth much good.

advantage of all God's gifts and realizing that life's end is certain.

Because Life Is Uncertain and Brief (9:1–10)

9:1 *either love or hatred.* Using opposite terms is a literary device to express totality. The idea simply is that man does not know the whole scope of circumstances that will come into life, whether good or bad. Therefore, it is assuring to know that all is in the hand of God.
9:2–3 The *evil* (trouble) that happens to all regardless of who they are or what they are like is death.
9:4–6 This is no denial of life after death; just the observation that death is the end of life as we know it. Only the living can experience the things of life; hence, the *living dog* versus *dead lion* comparison.
9:7 God has commanded us to enjoy what He has given for life, and He is pleased (*accepteth*) with that obedience.
9:8 Images of joy.
9:9 *Live joyfully.* Literally, "see or experience life." One's spouse is a gift from God to be enjoyed throughout life.
9:10 This is no denial of life after death; just the observation that death is the end of life as we know it. The Preacher parallels Paul in 1 Cor. 10:31 and Col. 3:23.

Because Wisdom Does Not Guarantee Success (9:11—10:15)

9:11 *chance.* An event or circumstance. Some things happen contrary to expectation. Even the best planning, preparation, or skill cannot guarantee success.
9:12 *his time.* Specifically, the time of his death. *evil.* Harmful or dangerous. In spite of natural instincts to avoid danger, animals often fall prey to the hunter. So man falls prey to death; it is so often unexpected but unavoidable.
9:14–16 *great bulwarks.* Siege works, a ramp to enter the city. The parable illustrates both wisdom's potential and its limitations.

Thoughts for Personal/Family Worship: Chapter 9

1. **That God holds the lives of His people in His hand (9:1) is a most comforting truth given all the events and circumstances of life that appear to be so random and contrary to expectation. Without this assurance we would be subject to frustrations and disappointments when the unexpected happens (like the events described in vv. 11–12). Not knowing the future is not a problem when we know the One who holds the future in His hand. We must trust Him that in His infinite wisdom all things happen according to His plan for His glory and our good.**
2. **That a living dog is better than a dead lion (v. 4) is a vivid way of saying there is hope so long as there is life. This truth has evangelistic application regarding the urgency of the gospel call. If conversion occurs, it must occur during life for there are no chances after death. Today is the day of salvation.**

Chapter 10: *Wisdom has advantages over foolishness but is still not a guarantee of success.*

10:1 *Dead flies.* Literally, "flies of death," which some interpret

CHAPTER 10

DEAD flies cause the ointment of the apothecary
to send forth a stinking savour: *so doth* a little folly
him that is in reputation for wisdom *and* honour.
2 A wise man's heart *is* at his right hand; but a
fool's heart at his left.
3 Yea also, when he that is a fool walketh by the
way, his wisdom faileth *him*, and he saith to every
one *that* he *is* a fool.
4 If the spirit of the ruler rise up against thee,
leave not thy place; for yielding pacifieth great
offences.
5 There is an evil *which* I have seen under the sun,
as an error *which* proceedeth from the ruler:
6 Folly is set in great dignity, and the rich sit in
low place.
7 I have seen servants upon horses, and princes
walking as servants upon the earth.
8 He that diggeth a pit shall fall into it; and whoso
breaketh an hedge, a serpent shall bite him.
9 Whoso removeth stones shall be hurt therewith;
and he that cleaveth wood shall be endangered
thereby.
10 If the iron be blunt, and he do not whet the
edge, then must he put to more strength: but
wisdom *is* profitable to direct.
11 Surely the serpent will bite without enchant-
ment; and a babbler is no better.
12 The words of a wise man's mouth *are* gracious;
but the lips of a fool will swallow up himself.
13 The beginning of the words of his mouth *is*
foolishness: and the end of his talk *is* mischievous
madness.
14 A fool also is full of words: a man cannot tell
what shall be; and what shall be after him, who
can tell him?
15 The labour of the foolish wearieth every one
of them, because he knoweth not how to go to
the city.
16 ¶ Woe to thee, O land, when thy king *is* a child,
and thy princes eat in the morning!
17 Blessed *art* thou, O land, when thy king *is* the
son of nobles, and thy princes eat in due season,
for strength, and not for drunkenness!
18 ¶ By much slothfulness the building decayeth;
and through idleness of the hands the house
droppeth through.
19 ¶ A feast is made for laughter, and wine
maketh merry: but money answereth all *things*.
20 ¶ Curse not the king, no not in thy thought;
and curse not the rich in thy bedchamber: for a
bird of the air shall carry the voice, and that which
hath wings shall tell the matter.

CHAPTER 11

CAST thy bread upon the waters: for thou shalt
find it after many days.
2 Give a portion to seven, and also to eight; for
thou knowest not what evil shall be upon the earth.

---

to be poisonous flies causing death; they are more likely flies which are about to die or are already dead. *cause the ointment of the apothecary . . . savour*. Literally, the dead flies "turn rancid; they cause to bubble or ferment the oil of the perfumer." Flies are small but they ruin the whole batch; in such a way a little folly can ruin a whole life's testimony.

10:2 *at his right hand . . . at his left*. An idiom expressing advantage and disadvantage.

10:3 *his wisdom faileth*. Literally, "his heart is lacking." Even an activity as innocuous as walking is an opportunity for a fool to show his foolishness.

10:4 *yielding pacifieth*. Calmness puts to rest or assuages.

10:5–7 More of life's incongruities.

10:8–9 Every activity involves risks but that should not preclude the activity. *breaketh an hedge*. Breaks down a hedge.

10:10 *wisdom is profitable to direct*. Using skill in any job factors into being successful, and being prepared is a component in that skill.

10:11 *a babbler is no better*. There is no advantage in the "master of the tongue" once the snake has bitten. This is another illustration of the importance of being prepared.

10:15 *he knoweth not how to go to the city*. The precise imagery is not clear but most likely refers to extreme stupidity.

Because Evil Happens (10:16—11:6)

10:16–17 *child*. Though age may be in view, the primary idea is inexperience. *princes eat in the morning*. Refers to revelry, not breakfast, as is clear from contrast in the next verse. But the fact is that sometimes rulers selfishly abuse their powers.

10:18 *the house droppeth through*. The roof leaks.

10:19 *money answereth*. Money is able to provide for things.

10:20 Instruction to keep the fifth and tenth commandments. Even secret transgressions will be known, certainly by God.

Thoughts for Personal/Family Worship: Chapter 10

1. **The opening verse is a powerful reminder of how careful we must be to guard and preserve our reputations and testimonies. Regardless of the fact that most of the vat was filled with the pleasant perfume, those floating dead flies ruined the whole batch. So a reputation that has been earned through a lifetime can be easily destroyed by a single sin. We should, therefore, be diligent to walk circumspectly, relying on the Holy Spirit to guide us through the Word of God to a life of consistent holiness. A good testimony is something that takes time to earn but can be so easily lost in a moment.**
2. **The closing verse illustrates the spiritual and internal aspect of God's moral law. Obedience is more than external behavior. The proper relationship and attitude regarding civil authorities is a component of the fifth commandment that deals with relationships between superiors and inferiors. It may be possible to pledge allegiance and to perform all the duties the state requires while at the same time disrespecting and dishonoring the authorities in our hearts. This too is a violation of God's holy law, and He knows it even if no one else does.**

Chapter 11: *The Preacher offers practical advice on getting the most out of life while keeping eternity in view.*

11:1–2 Although the principle has application in various

3 If the clouds be full of rain, they empty
themselves upon the earth: and if the tree fall
toward the south, or toward the north, in the
place where the tree falleth, there it shall be.
4 He that observeth the wind shall not sow; and
he that regardeth the clouds shall not reap.
5 As thou knowest not what *is* the way of the
spirit, *nor* how the bones *do grow* in the womb of
her that is with child: even so thou knowest not
the works of God who maketh all.
6 In the morning sow thy seed, and in the evening
withhold not thine hand: for thou knowest not
whether shall prosper, either this or that, or
whether they both *shall be* alike good.
7 ¶ Truly the light *is* sweet, and a pleasant *thing it*
is for the eyes to behold the sun:
8 But if a man live many years, *and* rejoice in them
all; yet let him remember the days of darkness; for
they shall be many. All that cometh *is* vanity.
9 ¶ Rejoice, O young man, in thy youth; and let
thy heart cheer thee in the days of thy youth, and
walk in the ways of thine heart, and in the sight of
thine eyes: but know thou, that for all these *things*
God will bring thee into judgment.
10 Therefore remove sorrow from thy heart, and
put away evil from thy flesh: for childhood and
youth *are* vanity.

CHAPTER 12

REMEMBER now thy Creator in the days of thy
youth, while the evil days come not, nor the years
draw nigh, when thou shalt say, I have no pleasure
in them;
2 While the sun, or the light, or the moon, or the
stars, be not darkened, nor the clouds return after
the rain:
3 In the day when the keepers of the house shall
tremble, and the strong men shall bow them-
selves, and the grinders cease because they are
few, and those that look out of the windows be
darkened,
4 And the doors shall be shut in the streets, when
the sound of the grinding is low, and he shall rise
up at the voice of the bird, and all the daughters
of musick shall be brought low;
5 Also *when* they shall be afraid of *that which is*
high, and fears *shall be* in the way, and the almond
tree shall flourish, and the grasshopper shall be a
burden, and desire shall fail: because man goeth
to his long home, and the mourners go about the
streets:
6 Or ever the silver cord be loosed, or the golden
bowl be broken, or the pitcher be broken at the
fountain, or the wheel broken at the cistern.
7 Then shall the dust return to the earth as it was:

spheres, the most likely reference is to investments. *knowest not*. Because of life's uncertainties, diversifying is the best strategy.

11:3–4 What happens happens, and if one waits around speculating on what may happen nothing is accomplished.

11:5–6 Admitting the mysteries of life and of divine providence should generate diligent activity resting in the assurance that the success or failure of a venture is in God's hand. Demanding certainty prevents any activity.

A Poem on Youth (11:7–10)

11:8 *yet let him*. He should. Interpreters differ as to whether *darkness* refers to times of adversity or to the days of youth. In the latter case, the darkness refers to the color of the hair in contrast to the gray hair that often designates age. *All . . . vanity*. Youth and old age both are fleeting.

11:9–10 Sums up the book's message: live now with a view to eternity.

Thoughts for Personal/Family Worship: Chapter 11

1. **That the opening verses address very mundane issues of how to handle money and go about daily tasks illustrates the inclusiveness of God's Word that speaks to every area of life. Psalm 19:7 says the law is complete having an effect on every part of man's being. If God regards the unplowed fields of the wicked to be sin (Prov. 21:4), it would seem to follow that He will be pleased with the mundane activities of His people. As Christians, we should realize that there is no part of our lives exempt from God's grace and concern for us. We should live wisely in every sphere of life being conscious that all our times and circumstances are in His hands.**
2. **The closing verses provide pointed application to youth. Godly living is not something that can be put off until old age. Youth is gone before we know it, and the time of youth should not be wasted with carelessness and godlessness. There are experiences that only youth can fully enjoy, and they should be experienced with contentment to their fullest, but always with God and eternity in view. The best way to enjoy youth is to live consciously before the Lord.**

Chapter 12: ***Various images describe the aging process that leads ultimately to death and to the final advice to fear and obey God with a view to eternity.***

An Allegory on Old Age (12:1–7)

12:1 *Remember*. To remember is a conscious willful determination to think about something. This must become the habit of life during youth because old age has the potential of obscuring thought.

12:2–7 Although some of the specific images are obscure, the overall meaning is clear. The aging process involves a deterioration of bodily functions and strength. The notes will highlight some of the images that are more obvious.

12:3 *keepers . . . strong men*. Probably a reference to the arms and legs that weaken. *grinders cease*. The teeth decay. *those that look out*. The eyesight fails.

12:4 Situations that suggest the failing of hearing.

12:5 The weakness of legs and loss of stamina cause fear of activity. *the almond tree*. The white blossoms picture the graying of the hair. *grasshoppers*. Things associated with spring and rejuvenation lose attractiveness. *mourners go about*. Life seems to be filled more with sadness than happiness, a tendency to depression.

12:6–7 Death comes at the end of the deteriorating process. *Dust return to the earth*. The allusion to Gen. 2:7 and 3:19 is significant. The allegory illustrates a thematic inclusio (beginning and ending the same). The spirit's returning to God after death parallels remembering the Creator during life.

and the spirit shall return unto God who gave it.
8 ¶ Vanity of vanities, saith the preacher; all *is*
vanity.
9 And moreover, because the preacher was wise,
he still taught the people knowledge; yea, he gave
good heed, and sought out, *and* set in order many
proverbs.
10 The preacher sought to find out acceptable
words: and *that which was* written *was* upright,
even words of truth.
11 The words of the wise *are* as goads, and as nails
fastened *by* the masters of assemblies, *which* are
given from one shepherd.
12 And further, by these, my son, be admonished:
of making many books *there is* no end; and much
study *is* a weariness of the flesh.
13 ¶ Let us hear the conclusion of the whole
matter: Fear God, and keep his commandments:
for this *is* the whole *duty* of man.
14 For God shall bring every work into judgment,
with every secret thing, whether *it be* good, or
whether *it be* evil.

THE COUNSEL FOR LIFE (12:8–14)

12:8 *Vanity of vanities.* The conclusion is the same as the introduction (1:2). The thoroughness of the Preacher's investigation did not alter the verdict that life is as brief as a breath.
12:9 *he gave good heed.* He proved.
12:10 *acceptable words.* Words of joy or delight.
12:11 *goads.* These are pointed wooden sticks used to drive cattle. *masters of assemblies.* Most likely referring to the experts of the words of truth, which had been assembled into a collection. *given from one shepherd.* A reference to God, who revealed the words of truth to the Preacher.
12:13–14 Sums up the whole message of the book. We are to live now with eternity always in view.

Thoughts for Personal/Family Worship: Chapter 12

1. The imagery of the words of the wise being as goads and fastened nails describe important functions of Scripture. God's Word is often like a goad to prod us and to direct us to the proper course of behavior. It sometimes hurts the flesh but it is always designed to adjust our actions in such a way to cause us to follow the paths of righteousness. The Word is also like a nail that is fixed in a sure and solid place upon which we can hang our hope. It is for us to walk according to all of God's commandments and to rest confidently in His certain promises.
2. Fearing God involves both an attitude of awe that generates worship and actions that reflect the kind of behavior pleasing to God. For instance, Job feared God and turned away from evil (Job 1:1); that is always the pattern. Fearing the Lord is the consequence of knowing Him as He reveals Himself in His Word where He prescribes the kind of life that is pleasing to Him. To fear God is to factor Him into every situation and circumstance of life. To live in that awareness of God is a powerful motivator to proper living. According to Jesus, loving God is the same motivation to obedience as fearing Him (John 14:15). In many ways, fearing God and loving Him are exactly the same. This is the kind of life that God demands of us, and if, by God's grace, we can fulfill this duty on earth we will be fit for the judgment then. Only in and through the Lord Jesus is such a life possible.

MY BELOVED IS *Mine* & I AM HIS HE FEEDETH AMONG *the Lilies*

SONG OF SOLOMON 2:16

INTRODUCTION TO THE BOOK OF THE SONG OF SOLOMON

Authorship: The opening words of the book ascribe it to King Solomon, the son of David (1:1). It often makes reference to Solomon (1:5; 3:7,9,11; 8:11–12) and the "king" (1:4,12; 3:9,11; 7:5). Several considerations confirm the identification of Solomon as the author. The frequent addresses to the daughters of Jerusalem (1:5; 2:7; 3:5,10; 5:8,16; 8:4) or Zion (3:11), together with positive references to locations in the north, such as Carmel (7:5), Sharon (2:1), and Hermon (4:8), suggest that it was written in the period of the unified kingdom before the northern tribes departed from the son of David. The bride is compared in a single breath to both Jerusalem and Tirzah (6:4), which is not likely to have happened after the division of the kingdom when the two cities were capitals of rival nations (1 Kings 14:17; 15:21,33). Solomon's kingdom was known for the abundance of spices available in Israel (1 Kings 10:2,10,25), and a variety of spices are prominent in the love songs of this book. This was also a time of the flourishing of wisdom and wise sayings (1 Kings 4:29–34). Solomon is most famous for his proverbs but also composed many songs (1 Kings 4:32).

Date: Solomon reigned from 970 to 931 BC.

Theme: The union and communion of love between Jesus Christ and His church.

Purpose: To stir up the affections of believers to seek experiential fellowship with their King.

Synopsis: *The Contribution of the Song of Solomon to Redemptive Revelation*

The Song of Solomon is given by the Spirit of God to stir up the affections of believers, whether of the Old Testament or of the New, to seek to cultivate secret communion with Christ in prayer and in all the other means of grace. Such spiritual delight was enjoyed by such Old Testament saints as Abraham, Moses, David, and the prophets. This book uses the language of love to draw Christians to yearn for experiences in our heart of assurance, joy, and rapture of soul as we taste something of Christ's love for us, even here in this world.

Although believers, symbolized by the fair young woman (1:8), have weaknesses and sins (5:2–3), they genuinely love Jesus as Lord and Savior and yearn for a taste of His love as something "better than wine" (1:2). This book uses the language of physical beauty to express the mutual delight that Christ and the believer have one in the other. This delight will be consummated one day in heaven, when Christ will at long last present His church to Himself as "a glorious church, not having spot, or wrinkle, or any such thing" (Eph. 5:27). So this lovely book aims to stir up Christians to seek communion now with Christ and to yearn for His second coming in glory.

The inward delights that a true believer may at times enjoy exceed the pleasures that worldly men find in such material things as "wine" (1:2). The pleasures of believers are not sensual but spiritual, and they are poured into their hearts by Christ, whom they love.

Christ's presence is not felt by the believer at all times in the same measure of intensity. At times the believer senses that Jesus has "withdrawn himself" (5:6). At such times he or she earnestly seeks once again for the felt presence of Christ. When Jesus again draws near, the believer's soul is like "the chariots of Ammi-nadib" (6:12)—alive with excitement and energy to live and fight for our blessed Lord.

The best experiences of Christ's love in this world are all too short. The souls of the saints yearn for the day when their Lord will come at last in all His glory to lift them from the grave and bestow endless divine affection upon them. The Song ends fitly with the anguished cry, "Make haste, my beloved, and be thou like to a roe or to a young hart upon the mountains of spices" (8:14). The Bible voices this same yearning cry as it closes: "Even so, come, Lord Jesus" (Rev. 22:20).

Special Problems of Interpretation: For centuries the dominant view of this book took it as a poetic representation of the spiritual relationship between the Lord and His people. This view appears in the ancient Jewish traditions and also in the Christian writings spanning the early church, the medieval church, the Reformation, and the Puritan and modern eras.

However, since the nineteenth century the *romantic* reading has gained popularity, taking the Song as a collection of entirely human love poetry. At times this is a reaction against the fanciful allegorizing by some traditional interpreters who did not root their interpretation in the text and context. There are still considerable variations among interpreters of this school as to who the characters are, whether Solomon and an unnamed bride, an unnamed shepherd and shepherdess, or a more complex cast of characters. There is also a lot of debate as to what the interactions of the characters signify. Some interpreters in this school see the Song merely as a collection of poems that do not present any coherent storyline. The romantic reading in its various forms sees the Song as divine wisdom for human romantic relationships, marriage, and sexuality.

Several arguments may be advanced against the romantic reading in favor of the traditional, Christ-centered interpretation of the Song. *First*, the Lord Jesus taught His disciples to read all of the Old Testament as a revelation of Christ (Luke 24:27,44–47). To say that an entire book of the Old Testament says nothing of Christ conflicts with the apostolic approach to Scripture. *Second*, the Song presents itself as "the song of songs" (Song 1:1), a Hebrew idiom meaning the supreme or greatest song. While the Bible has a high view of marriage and the sexual love between a husband and wife (Gen. 2:18–25; Prov. 5:15–23), it is difficult to understand how a song on romance would rank above the songs of God's glory and love. *Third*, the Song identifies itself as "Solomon's" (Song 1:1). Christ spoke of Solomon as a type of Himself, for Jesus is the great Son of David (Matt. 1:1; 12:42). The name "Solomon" means "peace" (see notes at 1 Chron. 22:8 and 9), and thus he represents the Prince of peace (Isa. 9:6). The term "Shulamite" (Song 6:13) is the feminine form of Solomon, representing his counterpart in peace.

As a *fourth* argument we may consider that Scripture often uses marriage as a metaphor for the Lord's union with His beloved people (Isa. 54; 61:10; 62:5; Ezek. 16:1–63; Hos. 2:1–23; Matt. 22:1–2; 2 Cor. 11:1–4; Eph. 5:22–33; Rev. 19:7–8; 21:9). Christ referred to Himself simply as "the bridegroom" (Matt. 9:15; cf. Matt. 25:1–10; John 3:29). *Fifth*, it may well be that Christ alluded to the Song when He said to a church, "Behold, I stand at the door, and knock: if any man hear my voice, and open the door, I will come in to him, and will sup with him, and he with me" (Rev. 3:20; cf. Song 5:1–2). *Sixth*, Psalm 45 provides a significant parallel to the Song in the way it points to Christ, as the New Testament teaches (Heb. 1:8–9). The psalm is titled "A Song of loves"; depicts the King who is both God and in covenant with God; speaks, as does the Song, of oil, spices, ivory, and gold; and exhorts His bride to give herself entirely to Him. *Seventh*, a Christ-centered reading of the Song need not indulge in wild, highly imaginative interpretations that may rightly offend thoughtful readers. The Song is poetry, and its figures of speech and doctrines are to be understood in the context of Scripture as a whole.

There are two basic approaches to the Song that take it as a revelation of Christ: the typological and the allegorical.

The *typological* reading begins with the recognition that a significant person in the Bible may be by divine design a "figure [or type] of him that was to come" (Rom. 5:14). Typology begins with a real, historical person, event, or institution and recognizes the shadow of Christ in him or it (Col. 2:16–17; Heb. 7:1–17; 10:1). The typical view is based on a proper, literal interpretation because all true types are based in history. While recognizing that the Song is rooted in the historical figure of Solomon and presents the beauty and sanctity of human marriage, we understand that it looks ahead to the One greater than Solomon. Just as Paul took Adam's paradigmatic marriage with Eve as a foreshadowing of Christ's union with the church (Gen. 2:24; Eph. 5:31), so we should read the Song of Solomon as the Song of Christ. As we think of the most precious love relationships, we must think also of that love that supersedes all human love. An alternative typological reading held by Martin Luther sees the Song as a poem celebrating the love between Solomon and the people of his kingdom, foreshadowing the love between Christ and the people of His kingdom. In either case, the typological reading starts with Solomon and ends with Christ.

The *allegorical* reading is the traditional reading, which has dominated among both the Jewish and Christian interpreters throughout the centuries. It holds much in common with the typological approach but believes that the Song refers directly to the Lord, not to Solomon. The language of love is entirely symbolic, as it is in the story of the Lord and His bride in Ezek. 16. There is a difference between interpreting an allegory and allegorizing a text. An allegory is a form of writing in which the author intended to write an extended comparison, such as Christ's parable of the soils (Mark 4:1–20). John Bunyan's *Pilgrim's Progress* is a well-known example of an allegory. Allegorizing, in contrast, means reading all sorts of hidden meanings into what was never meant to be an allegory.

Both the typological and the allegorical interpretations end in the love that exists between the Lord Jesus Christ and His precious, blood-bought people who, in this life and the next, are in union and communion with Him as their beloved Savior and Lord. This deeply spiritual and beautiful book uses the language of marital affection and delight to express the love that our Savior has for all true believers and that they, notwithstanding their many sins and failings, have for Christ in this life. The book looks wistfully to the future day when our Lord will return in all His glory to marry His beloved church and take her home to everlasting glory. Such is the meaning of the sigh, "Until the day break, and the shadows flee away" (Song 2:17).

These study notes approach the Song according to the allegorical reading, where the bridegroom is understood as Christ and the bride as His church. The "virgins" (1:3), also called "daughters of Zion" (3:11) and "daughters of Jerusalem" (1:5), are godly, converted people who love Christ (2 Cor. 11:2; Rev. 14:1–4). The "watchmen" (Song 3:3; 5:7) represent ministers and pastors of the church (Ezek. 3:16–21; Heb. 13:17). The "mother's" (Song 1:6; 3:4,11; 6:9; 8:1–2,5) is the universal church of Christ in which are to be found the means of grace and of salvation (Isa. 54:1–3,13; Gal. 4:26; Rev. 12:1–6,13–17).

Outline: The recurring themes and expressions of the poetry make it difficult to structure the Song of Solomon. However, the refrain charging the daughters of Jerusalem seems to mark the conclusions of sections (2:7; 3:5; 8:4). Also 5:2 and 6:11 seem to start new units of personal reflection set off from the preceding. This yields the following:

I. Heading (1:1)
II. The Longing Bride and Her Bridegroom (1:2—2:7)
   A. The Church Longs for Christ Her Lord (1:2–4)
   B. The Church Laments Her Present State and Past and Desires Christ (1:5–7)
   C. Christ Declares His Love for His Church, Her Beauty, and His Promises (1:8–11)
   D. The Church Praises Christ and His House (1:12–17)
   E. Christ and His Church Delight in Each Other (2:1–7)
III. The Seeking Bride and Her Bridegroom (2:8—3:5)
   A. The Church Compares Christ's Coming to Springtime (2:8–13)
   B. Christ Expresses His Care for His Church (2:14–15)
   C. The Church Longs for His Second Coming (2:16–17)
   D. The Church Seeks Christ, Finds Him, and Is Fearful of Offending Him (3:1–5)
IV. A Communing Bride and Her Bridegroom (3:6—5:1)
   A. We See Christ Coming Up Out of the World to Be Married (3:6–11)
   B. Christ Speaks of the Beauty He Sees in His Church (4:1–7)
   C. He Invites Her to Come with Him (4:8)
   D. Christ Loves His Church (4:9–15)
   E. The Church Prays for the Holy Spirit to Enhance Her Graces (4:16)
   F. Christ Delights in His Church (5:1)
V. The Negligent Bride and Her Bridegroom (5:2—6:10)
   A. The Church's Failure to Welcome Christ and Her Distress (5:2–6)
   B. The Church Suffers a Painful Rebuke and Desires Christ (5:7–8)
   C. The Church Loves and Esteems Christ (5:9–16)
   D. Her Love for Christ Stirs Others to Seek Him with Her (6:1–3)
   E. Christ Expresses His Love for His Church in Exquisite Language (6:4–10)
VI. A Communing Bride and Bridegroom (6:11—8:4)
   A. Christ Reviews the Church's Graces and Is Stirred with Love and Longing (6:11–13)
   B. Christ Further Describes the Beauty of His Church (7:1–9)
   C. The Church Redoubles Her Zeal to Seek Christ after Her Earlier Laziness (7:10–13)
   D. The Church Expresses Her Love for Christ's Fellowship (8:1–4)
VII. Conclusion (8:5–14)

THE SONG OF SOLOMON

CHAPTER 1

THE song of songs, which *is* Solomon's.
2 Let him kiss me with the kisses of his mouth:
for thy love *is* better than wine.
3 Because of the savour of thy good ointments
thy name *is as* ointment poured forth, therefore
do the virgins love thee.
4 Draw me, we will run after thee: the king hath
brought me into his chambers: we will be glad
and rejoice in thee, we will remember thy love
more than wine: the upright love thee.
5 I *am* black, but comely, O ye daughters of
Jerusalem, as the tents of Kedar, as the curtains
of Solomon.
6 Look not upon me, because I *am* black, because
the sun hath looked upon me: my mother's
children were angry with me; they made me the
keeper of the vineyards; *but* mine own vineyard
have I not kept.
7 Tell me, O thou whom my soul loveth, where
thou feedest, where thou makest *thy flock* to rest
at noon: for why should I be as one that turneth
aside by the flocks of thy companions?
8 ¶ If thou know not, O thou fairest among
women, go thy way forth by the footsteps of the
flock, and feed thy kids beside the shepherds' tents.
9 I have compared thee, O my love, to a company
of horses in Pharaoh's chariots.
10 Thy cheeks are comely with rows *of jewels*, thy
neck with chains *of gold*.
11 We will make thee borders of gold with studs
of silver.

Chapter 1: *The bride longs for Christ, who encourages her and confirms His love for her.*

HEADING (1:1)

1:1 *song of songs*. A Hebrew idiom for the best and highest of songs (cf. Ps. 136:2–3). This song is superlatively good because its subject is the communion between Christ and His church. The author is King *Solomon* (1 Kings 4:32), son of David, who writes of Christ (cf. Ps. 45).

THE LONGING BRIDE AND HER BRIDEGROOM (1:2—2:7)

The Church Longs for Christ Her Lord (1:2–4)

1:2 *Let him kiss me*. A common expression of affection (8:1; Gen. 29:11,13). *kisses*. The plural implies a display of great affection. The church speaks here of her longing for experiences of Christ's *love* in the soul (Rom. 5:5; 15:13). *better than wine*. Christ's love satisfies more than the sweetest earthly pleasure (v. 4; Ps. 4:6–7; Eph. 3:19; 5:18–19).

1:3 *savour*. Fragrant smell. *ointments*. Oil, as for anointing (4:10; Ps. 45:7–8), symbolizing the gracious influences of the Holy Spirit (1 Sam. 16:13; Isa. 61:1–3). *thy name*. Who He is in His perfections, which satisfies as no earthly experience can. *virgins*. Believers in their spiritual purity and devotion to Christ (2 Cor. 11:2; Rev. 14:4); not a rebuke of marriage (Heb. 13:4).

1:4 *Draw me . . . run*. All our devotions need God to stir them up into life (Ps. 119:32; John 6:44). *chambers*. Inner rooms, a picture of joyful intimacy with *the king*.

The Church Laments Her Present State and Past and Desires Christ (1:5–7)

1:5–6 *black*. Either a picture of inherent sin (Jer. 13:23) or not a picture of natural skin color but of suffering persecution, as one forced to work long under the hot *sun*; compared to the dwellings of nomadic Arabians in the desert (*tents of Kedar*; Ps. 120:5). *comely*. Beautiful (v. 10; 2:14; 4:3; 6:4), compared to the decorations of the royal palace (*curtains of Solomon*). *my mother*['s]. The universal church, portrayed like Sarah as the mother of all God's people (Isa. 54:1–3,13; Gal. 4:26; Rev. 12:1–6,13–17). *children were angry*. Persecution from within the professing church (Ps. 69:7–8). *vineyard*. A metaphor for God's people (v. 14; 2:15; 7:12; 8:11–12; Isa. 5:1–7; 27:2–6; Matt. 21:33–46; John 15:1–8). Outwardly, the true church is not glorious but suffers in this world, especially from hypocrites, yet it has true, inward beauty.

1:7 *feedest*. Literally, "shepherd" (v. 8; 2:16; 4:5; 6:2–3), a figure of speech often used of a king (see note at 2 Sam. 5:2). *makest thy flock to rest*. See Ps. 23:1–2. Believers seek Christ *where* He tends His sheep with the Word and the Spirit (Matt. 18:20; 28:18–20).

Christ Declares His Love for His Church, Her Beauty, and His Promises (1:8–11)

1:8 *fairest*. Most lovely. Here is Christ's answer to the church's query in the previous verse. *footsteps of the flock*. Answering the question of v. 7, Christ directs the church to seek Him by following the old paths of faithful believers of the past (1 Cor. 11:1). *feed thy kids*. Shepherd your young female goats, an image of feeding the rising generation with truth and righteousness.

1:9 *compared thee*. The point of comparisons in the Song is not physical appearance but qualities or attributes. *horses of Solomon in Pharaoh's chariots*. The best steeds on earth (2 Chron. 1:16–17; Isa. 31:1). So God's saints are the excellent ones of the earth (Ps. 16:3).

1:10–11 *rows . . . borders*. Same Hebrew word, referring to jewelry of precious metals. *We will make thee*. The beauty of God's people is not from themselves but from God (Ps. 149:4;

12 ¶ While the king *sitteth* at his table, my spikenard sendeth forth the smell thereof.
13 A bundle of myrrh *is* my wellbeloved unto me; he shall lie all night betwixt my breasts.
14 My beloved *is* unto me *as* a cluster of camphire in the vineyards of En-gedi.
15 Behold, thou *art* fair, my love; behold, thou *art* fair; thou *hast* doves' eyes.
16 Behold, thou *art* fair, my beloved, yea, pleasant: also our bed *is* green.
17 The beams of our house *are* cedar, *and* our rafters of fir.

CHAPTER 2

I *AM* the rose of Sharon, *and* the lily of the valleys.
2 As the lily among thorns, so *is* my love among the daughters.
3 As the apple tree among the trees of the wood,
so *is* my beloved among the sons. I sat down under his shadow with great delight, and his fruit *was* sweet to my taste.
4 He brought me to the banqueting house, and his banner over me *was* love.
5 Stay me with flagons, comfort me with apples: for I *am* sick of love.
6 His left hand *is* under my head, and his right hand doth embrace me.
7 I charge you, O ye daughters of Jerusalem, by the roes, and by the hinds of the field, that ye stir not up, nor awake *my* love, till he please.
8 ¶ The voice of my beloved! behold, he cometh leaping upon the mountains, skipping upon the hills.
9 My beloved is like a roe or a young hart: behold, he standeth behind our wall, he looketh forth at the windows, shewing himself through the lattice.
10 My beloved spake, and said unto me, Rise up,

Isa. 61:10; Eph. 5:27), who speaks in the plural as the Trinity (Gen. 1:26; Isa. 6:8).

The Church Praises Christ and His House (1:12–17)

1:12 *king . . . at his table.* Here the church speaks, confessing that she enjoys fellowship with Christ in the means of grace. *spikenard.* Fragrant perfume (4:13–14) representing the bride's delightful graces of devotion and love to Him (Ps. 141:2; John 12:3; Eph. 5:2).

1:13 *myrrh.* A spice used in fragrant oils (3:6; 4:6,14; 5:1,5,13; Ex. 30:23; Est. 2:12; Ps. 45:8; Prov. 7:17). *all night.* Continual companionship. *breasts.* See 4:5; 7:3,7–8; 8:1,8,10.

1:14 *camphire.* Henna, a flowering plant (4:13). *En-gedi.* Oasis in the wilderness (1 Sam. 23:29; 24:1).

1:15 Christ now speaks, commending His church for her spiritual beauty (*fair*). *doves.* Birds associated with purity, meekness, and mourning (2:14; 4:1; 5:2,12; 6:9; cf. 2:12; Lev. 1:14; 5:7,11; Ps. 74:19; Isa. 38:14; 59:11; Nah. 2:7; Matt. 3:16; 10:16).

1:16 The church now speaks again here. *our bed is green.* A symbol of their fruitful union (Hos. 14:8; Rom. 7:4).

1:17 *our house.* Believers love God's dwelling with them (Ps. 84:1–12). *cedar.* Fragrant wood, used in constructing the temple (1 Kings 6) and abundant in Solomon's kingdom (1 Kings 10:27).

Thoughts for Personal/Family Worship: Chapter 1

1. **The relationship between Christ and His people is not merely one of faith or service, important as these aspects are. Believers are loved by Christ, and they in turn love their Lord. The gospel reveals God's love, and the greatest commandment is to love the Lord. Why is it important to make divine love the center of our religion?**
2. **The expressions used in this wonderful book of the Bible speak of physical love and describe gestures and attitudes that are familiar to us in our human understanding of marital love. God has seen fit to represent His love for His people in the institution of Christian marriage (Eph. 5:22–33). Yet the love of God in Christ transcends all earthly relationships, for His love is infinite, eternal, and unchangeable in His being, wisdom, power, holiness, justice, goodness, and truth. Why does that make this the Song of all songs?**

Chapter 2: ***The bride and Christ delight in each other, Christ calling His bride away to Himself.***

Christ and His Church Delight in Each Other (2:1–7)

2:1 *rose of Sharon.* Flower from a fertile plain in northern Israel, an emblem of glory, beauty, and life likely referring to Christ (Isa. 35:1–2). *lily.* See vv. 2,16; 4:5; 5:13; 6:2–3; 7:2. An image of flourishing life (Hos. 14:5) used in art of the temple (1 Kings 7:19,22,26).

2:2 *lily among thorns.* Christ here commends His church above all other peoples or institutions. *daughters.* A symbol of peoples or nations (Pss. 45:12; 48:11; 137:8).

2:3 *apple tree.* An image of protection (*shadow*) and nourishment and refreshment (*his fruit was sweet*) found in the *beloved* Lord (v. 5; 7:8; 8:5). Trees could represent kingdoms (Ezek. 31:3–6; Dan. 4:10–12; Matt. 13:32). *among the trees . . . among the sons.* Christ is unique in the spiritual safety and life He provides (John 14:6; Rev. 7:14–17).

2:4 *banqueting house.* Literally, "house of wine," a place of feasting (8:2; Est. 5:6; 7:7–8; Job 1:13,18) where believers feast upon the *love* of Christ (1:2). *banner.* Flag, rallying point for an army (6:4,10); here, hope in the gospel of Christ's love (Ps. 20:5; Isa. 11:10; Rom. 15:12).

2:5 *Stay.* Sustain. *flagons.* Some kind of nourishment. *apples.* See v. 3. *sick.* Either weak from missing the Lord's presence (5:8; Pss. 42:1–2; 63:1; 84:1–2) or overwhelmed with His love.

2:6 *under my head.* When we cry to Christ He comes to support us (Deut. 33:27). Hebrew uses pairs of opposites (here *left* and *right*) to communicate totality (2 Kings 11:11; Job 23:9); Christ gives the church His full support in all her trials.

2:7 *I charge you.* An exhortation repeated as a refrain (3:5; 8:4; cf. 5:8). *stir not up, nor awake my love.* Do not disturb the One I love. Church members (*daughters of Jerusalem*) are urged never to offend the Lord (Eph. 4:30). *roes . . . hinds.* Deer, animals of strength and beauty (vv. 9,17; 8:14), are still easily chased away. Communion with Christ should be carefully guarded.

THE SEEKING BRIDE AND HER BRIDEGROOM (2:8—3:5)

The Church Compares Christ's Coming to Springtime (2:8–13)

2:8–9 *voice of my beloved . . . he cometh.* The church always rejoices at the prospect of Christ's coming, whether at His incarnation, in the Spirit, or in His future glory. *leaping . . . skipping . . . like a roe or a young hart.* The Lord's coming like a young deer: quick, energetic, graceful, and sudden (v. 17). *Windows . . . lattice.* Like a young man calling upon a young lady.

2:10 *Rise up, my love.* Christ coaxes His dear people to awaken,

my love, my fair one, and come away.
11 For, lo, the winter is past, the rain is over *and*
gone;
12 The flowers appear on the earth; the time of
the singing *of birds* is come, and the voice of the
turtle is heard in our land;
13 The fig tree putteth forth her green figs, and
the vines *with* the tender grape give a *good* smell.
Arise, my love, my fair one, and come away.
14 ¶ O my dove, *that art* in the clefts of the rock,
in the secret *places* of the stairs, let me see thy
countenance, let me hear thy voice; for sweet *is*
thy voice, and thy countenance *is* comely.
15 Take us the foxes, the little foxes, that spoil the
vines: for our vines *have* tender grapes.
16 ¶ My beloved *is* mine, and I *am* his: he feedeth
among the lilies.
17 Until the day break, and the shadows flee
away, turn, my beloved, and be thou like a roe or a
young hart upon the mountains of Bether.

CHAPTER 3

BY night on my bed I sought him whom my soul
loveth: I sought him, but I found him not.
2 I will rise now, and go about the city in the
streets, and in the broad ways I will seek him
whom my soul loveth: I sought him, but I found
him not.
3 The watchmen that go about the city found
me: *to whom I said*, Saw ye him whom my soul
loveth?
4 *It was* but a little that I passed from them, but
I found him whom my soul loveth: I held him,
and would not let him go, until I had brought him
into my mother's house, and into the chamber of
her that conceived me.
5 I charge you, O ye daughters of Jerusalem, by
the roes, and by the hinds of the field, that ye stir
not up, nor awake *my* love, till he please.
6 ¶ Who *is* this that cometh out of the wilderness
like pillars of smoke, perfumed with myrrh and

---

shake off their laziness, and walk with Him (Rom. 13:11; Eph. 5:14; repeated in v. 13).

2:11–13 The images of springtime invite the church to leave behind the times of darkness and death and walk with the Lord in flourishing life and joy because the times of darkness and death are past. *fig tree . . . vines*. Images of prosperity in the kingdom of the Son of David (1 Kings 4:25; Mic. 4:4; Zech. 3:8–10), ultimately fulfilled in His second coming (Matt. 24:32–33).

Christ Expresses His Care for His Church (2:14–15)

2:14 *dove*. See note at 1:15. *clefts of the rock . . . secret places of the stairs*. Places where birds hide from danger (Jer. 48:28). Again, the church is identified by the paradoxical marks of suffering and beauty (1:5–6). *let me hear thy voice*. Christ calls them to speak both to Him and of Him (8:13).

2:15 *foxes*. Wild scavengers that destroy crops before harvest, an image of false teachers who undermine the fruitfulness of the church (Ezek. 13:4).

The Church Longs for His Second Coming (2:16–17)

2:16 *My beloved is mine, and I am his*. The essence of assurance, the foundation of spiritual comfort, is knowing one's union with the Lord (6:3; 7:10). *feedeth*. Or shepherds (1:7). *lilies*. Emblem of the spiritual beauties of His dear believing people (v. 2).

2:17 The church longs for her Lord to return, for His coming is like the dawn of the day after a long night (Mal. 4:2; Rom. 13:12). *Bether*. Division, picturing Christ leaping like a deer (*hart*) across impassable mountains so that nothing separates Him from His dear people any longer (1 Thess. 4:17–18).

Thoughts for Personal/Family Worship: Chapter 2

1. **None but a true Christian knows the inward experiences of delight that may be enjoyed in fellowship with the blessed Jesus (vv. 4–6). These are elsewhere in Scripture called "the love of Christ; which passeth knowledge" (Eph. 3:19); "the peace of God; which passeth all understanding" (Phil. 4:7); "joy unspeakable and full of glory" (1 Peter 1:8); and similar expressions. Have you tasted the supernatural happiness in Christ? Has it awakened you to long for more?**
2. **The believer needs to be careful not to do anything that might offend or grieve his Lord (v. 7). This means that we need to attend to our lives so as to do nothing that might disturb or displease Him. To displease Jesus might mean to lose some of His sweet presence and blessing. We must therefore keep watch against sin, resist temptation, and quickly confess and repent of sin, seeking renewal of fellowship with Christ.**
3. **The believer's comfort in this sad world is that one day he or she will be beyond all sorrow and all care. Hence Christians, while in this life, look forward to the happy day when they will be with Christ in glory. This is expressed beautifully here: "Until the day break; and the shadows flee away" (v. 17).**

Chapter 3: *The bride seeks Christ and finds Him, and expresses His glory.*

The Church Seeks Christ, Finds Him, and Is Fearful of Offending Him (3:1–5)

3:1–2 *on my bed I sought him*. God's people pray without ceasing, both by day and by night (Pss. 42:8; 63:6). *found him not*. At times believers do not have a felt sense of His presence.

3:3 *watchmen*. Ministers and office bearers of the church (Ezek. 3:16–21; Heb. 13:17).

3:4 *would not let him go*. See Gen. 32:26. *my mother's house*. The gathering of the church (see note at 1:5–6). Private experiences of Christ fuel the desire to glorify Him in public worship.

3:5 *stir not up*. When we have rediscovered Christ's presence we are above all to be concerned that nothing be done to offend Him (see note at 2:7).

A COMMUNING BRIDE AND HER BRIDEGROOM (3:6—5:1)

We See Christ Coming Up Out of the World to Be Married (3:6–11)

3:6 *Who is this that cometh out of the wilderness*. The language alludes to God's leading of Israel to the Promised Land (Ex. 13:18; Jer. 2:6; Amos 2:10). The King is bringing His bride, the church, out of this fallen and sad world to spend eternity with her Lord and Savior (8:5). *pillars of smoke*. The dust raised by the King and his attendants (3:7–10) is used as an image of God's presence coming in glory (Ex. 13:21; 19:18; Joel 2:30–32). *myrrh*. See note at 1:13. *frankincense*. Fragrant spice used by priests in burning incense and grain offerings (4:6,14; Ex. 30:34; Lev. 2:1–2). *powders*. Spices.

frankincense, with all powders of the merchant?
7 Behold his bed, which *is* Solomon's; threescore
valiant men *are* about it, of the valiant of Israel.
8 They all hold swords, *being* expert in war: every
man *hath* his sword upon his thigh because of
fear in the night.
9 King Solomon made himself a chariot of the
wood of Lebanon.
10 He made the pillars thereof *of* silver, the
bottom thereof *of* gold, the covering of it *of*
purple, the midst thereof being paved *with* love,
for the daughters of Jerusalem.
11 Go forth, O ye daughters of Zion, and behold
king Solomon with the crown wherewith his
mother crowned him in the day of his espousals,
and in the day of the gladness of his heart.

CHAPTER 4

BEHOLD, thou *art* fair, my love; behold, thou *art*
fair; thou *hast* doves' eyes within thy locks: thy
hair *is* as a flock of goats, that appear from mount
Gilead.
2 Thy teeth *are* like a flock *of sheep that are even*
shorn, which came up from the washing; whereof
every one bear twins, and none *is* barren among
them.
3 Thy lips *are* like a thread of scarlet, and thy
speech *is* comely: thy temples *are* like a piece of a
pomegranate within thy locks.
4 Thy neck *is* like the tower of David builded
for an armoury, whereon there hang a thousand
bucklers, all shields of mighty men.
5 Thy two breasts *are* like two young roes that are
twins, which feed among the lilies.
6 Until the day break, and the shadows flee away,
I will get me to the mountain of myrrh, and to the
hill of frankincense.
7 Thou *art* all fair, my love; *there is* no spot in
thee.
8 ¶ Come with me from Lebanon, *my* spouse,
with me from Lebanon: look from the top of

3:7 *bed.* A palanquin or portable couch/throne carried by servants (v. 9). *Solomon*['s]. His name means "peace" (see note at 1 Chron. 22:8–9), pointing to the Prince of peace (Isa. 9:6; cf. Mic. 5:5; Eph. 2:14). *threescore valiant men.* Sixty soldiers. The ark of the covenant, carried by priests and portraying angelic figures (Ex. 25:10–22), was a symbol of the King attended by heavenly and earthly servants (Heb. 1:6,14). The Lord comes for His wedding (v. 11).
3:8 *all hold swords.* The angels are God's heavenly army (2 Kings 2:11; 6:17; Matt. 26:53).
3:9–10 *chariot.* Or royal palanquin (v. 7). *wood of Lebanon.* Material used to build the temple and Solomon's palace (2 Chron. 2). *pillars.* Holding up its canopy. *midst thereof being paved.* Its middle or interior is decorated with *love. for.* Because of. Christ rides forth presently in the gospel message and will ride forth in glory when He returns (Ps. 45:3–5; Rev. 6:2; 19:11).
3:11 *Go forth.* If we wish to see Christ and His glory we must separate ourselves from the world and its mindset and practices (Isa. 52:11; 2 Cor. 6:14—7:1). *espousals.* The wedding as the *day* of the culmination of the betrothal (Isa. 62:5; Rev. 19:7).

Thoughts for Personal/Family Worship: Chapter 3

1. **Those who have the grace of God in their heart value communion with Christ above all earthly experiences. They are ready to do all in their power to enjoy again their fellowship Christ when they lose a sense of it (vv. 1–5). Believers should organize their time and their life so as to seek after the felt enjoyment of Christ's love. What does it mean to seek Him, and when finding Him not to let Him go?**
2. **Christ is most glorious and powerful. A sight of Him will change you. The unbelievers in Jerusalem wondered at the changed lives of the apostles: "They took knowledge of them; that they had been with Jesus" (Acts 4:13). This alteration will be perfect at last in glory, when believers will "shine forth as the sun in the kingdom of their Father" (Matt. 13:43). The happiness of heaven will very much consist of gazing upon Christ and appreciating His love and His divine beauty. The Day is coming when all His people, being spiritually espoused to Him, will rejoice with joy unspeakable at the sight of His glorious majesty as He comes upon the clouds to marry His church to Himself forever. How can this give hope?**

Chapter 4: *Christ expresses the beauty of the bride.*

Christ Speaks of the Beauty He Sees in His Church (4:1–7)

4:1 *fair.* Beautiful. In vv. 1–5 the Lord describes several features of the inward loveliness of His bride, using physical metaphors. *doves' eyes.* Purity, meekness, and mourning (see note at 1:15). *hair . . . flock of goats.* A woman's hair is her special beauty (Isa. 3:24; 1 Cor. 11:15; 1 Tim. 2:9; 1 Peter 3:3). The pastures of *Gilead* were rich for grazing (Mic. 7:14), implying a full and healthy inner beauty (1 Peter 3:3–4).
4:2 *teeth . . . flock.* White teeth with none missing (6:6) are an image of health and prosperity (Gen. 49:12). Teeth can represent speech (Ps. 57:4; Prov. 30:14; Lam. 2:16); her talk is sound and wholesome in its truth (Prov. 31:26; Eph. 4:29; Titus 1:9,13; 2:1–2,8).
4:3 *lips . . . speech.* Her talk is also attractive and beautiful (*comely*). The *thread of scarlet* may allude to the sign by which Rahab's family was saved from Jericho (Josh. 2:18), indicating speech salted with God's grace for sinners (Col. 4:6). *temples . . . pomegranate.* Her face reflects a heart rejoicing in the Lord (Ps. 34:5,8). The fruit's sweet red seeds were among the prized products of the Promised Land (Num. 13:23) and symbols of God's life-giving presence in the tabernacle/temple (Ex. 28:33–34; 1 Kings 7:18,20). Yet she is meek and modest (covered with *locks* or a veil; Gen. 24:65) and humble (Isa. 57:15).
4:4 *neck . . . tower of David.* The posture of the neck communicates one's attitude (Ex. 32:9; Ps. 75:5; Prov. 29:1); comparing it to a tower (7:4) with *shields* implying a militant mindset ready to fight against evil (Eph. 6:10,16).
4:5 *breasts.* As with the teeth, there is a sense of beauty (*roes,* deer or gazelle, 7:3) and completeness (*twins*) in this picture. A woman's breasts are the means of motherly nourishment and consolation of her children (8:1; Isa. 66:10–13). The church's spiritual beauty enables her to *feed* believers for comfort and growth into maturity (1 Cor. 3:2; 1 Peter 2:2).
4:6 *Until the day break.* Christ will dwell with His bride until He comes in glory (see note at 2:17). *mountain of myrrh . . . hill of frankincense.* See note at 8:14.
4:7 *all fair . . . no spot.* He counts her as perfect in beauty and

Amana, from the top of Shenir and Hermon, from the lions' dens, from the mountains of the leopards.
9 Thou hast ravished my heart, my sister, *my* spouse; thou hast ravished my heart with one of thine eyes, with one chain of thy neck.
10 How fair is thy love, my sister, *my* spouse! how much better is thy love than wine! and the smell of thine ointments than all spices!
11 Thy lips, O *my* spouse, drop *as* the honeycomb: honey and milk *are* under thy tongue; and the smell of thy garments *is* like the smell of Lebanon.
12 A garden inclosed *is* my sister, *my* spouse; a spring shut up, a fountain sealed.
13 Thy plants *are* an orchard of pomegranates, with pleasant fruits; camphire, with spikenard,
14 Spikenard and saffron; calamus and cinnamon, with all trees of frankincense; myrrh and aloes, with all the chief spices:
15 A fountain of gardens, a well of living waters, and streams from Lebanon.
16 ¶ Awake, O north wind; and come, thou south; blow upon my garden, *that* the spices thereof may flow out. Let my beloved come into his garden, and eat his pleasant fruits.

CHAPTER 5

I AM come into my garden, my sister, *my* spouse: I have gathered my myrrh with my spice; I have eaten my honeycomb with my honey; I have drunk my wine with my milk: eat, O friends; drink, yea, drink abundantly, O beloved.
2 ¶ I sleep, but my heart waketh: *it is* the voice of my beloved that knocketh, *saying*, Open to me, my sister, my love, my dove, my undefiled: for my head is filled with dew, *and* my locks with the drops of the night.
3 I have put off my coat; how shall I put it on? I have washed my feet; how shall I defile them?
4 My beloved put in his hand by the hole *of the door*, and my bowels were moved for him.

---

overlooks all her flaws. The church now is perfectly justified by Christ's obedience and death and will at last be also perfectly sanctified (Ps. 130:4,8; Rom. 4:5; 8:29; Eph. 1:4; 5:27).

He Invites Her to Come with Him (4:8)

4:8 *Come with me.* Christ calls His *spouse* to follow Him so that He may take her out of the land of danger, savage persecution, and death (*lions* and *leopards*). *look.* As Moses viewed the Promised Land from the top of Mt. Nebo (Deut. 34:1–5), so the church is invited to view by faith its future inheritance with Christ (Rev. 21:2). *Amana . . . Shenir . . . Hermon.* Mountains.

Christ Loves His Church (4:9–15)

4:9 *ravished my heart.* His love for her is greater than words can express.
4:10 *my sister.* The church is "sister" to Christ, who shares our human nature, being bone of our bone and flesh of our flesh (Matt. 12:50; Rom. 8:29).
4:11 *Thy lips.* The teaching that Christ's church gives is sweeter than *honey* to a spiritual man (Ps. 19:10). *smell of Lebanon.* Symbol of life, beauty, and growth (Hos. 14:6).
4:12 *garden.* A place of beauty, delight, and food (vv. 15–16; 5:1; 6:2; 8:13), perhaps alluding to God's presence with man in the Paradise of Eden (Gen. 2; Isa. 51:3) *inclosed.* Enclosed, locked. The church excludes false teachers and others who would disrupt its fruitfulness to the Lord.
4:13–14 *plants.* Or branches; believers within Christ's church (Ps. 128:3; Isa. 5:1; 27:2–6; John 15:5), compared to an *orchard* of diverse yet fruitful and fragrant flora. *pomegranates . . . camphire . . . spikenard . . . frankincense; myrrh.* See notes at v. 3; 1:14; 1:12; 3:6; 1:13, respectively. *saffron.* Crocus flower used for spice. *calamus and cinnamon.* Spices used in perfume and holy anointing oil (Ex. 30:23). *aloes.* Spice (Ps. 45:8).
4:15 *fountain . . . well . . . streams.* Living waters are a sign of God's life-giving presence within the church (Ps. 46:4; Isa. 44:1–4; John 4:14; 7:37–39).

The Church Prays for the Holy Spirit to Enhance Her Graces (4:16)

4:16 *Awake.* Here the church speaks in the light of what Christ has said. *wind.* She wishes for the Holy Spirit (*blow*, Ezek. 37:9,14) to sanctify her so that she may be pleasing to her Lord.

Thoughts for Personal/Family Worship: Chapter 4

1. **It is a very great strength to the Christian to know how greatly Christ loves him. The Devil would have believers despair at the thought of our sinfulness and failure in so many ways. But Christ, though so well aware of believers' failings, does not hesitate to tell them plainly that He has this immense love for all who believe in Him. He tells His church "Thou hast ravished my heart" (v. 9). How can believers use this text to defend themselves when Satan comes to accuse them?**
2. **The church prays for the wind to blow. This is a reference to the Holy Spirit. God's people need the Holy Spirit to blow on them. He blows like the chilling north wind so as to convict us in our carelessness (John 16:8). He touches our hearts as a warm south wind to cause our lives to bring forth the fruits of the Spirit (Gal. 5:22–24). All the graces of the Christian are the gift of Christ by His Spirit. Are you part of the garden of God? How often are you praying for the Spirit to cause you to grow for Christ's pleasure?**

Chapter 5: ***The bride fails to respond to Christ's knocks but subsequently affirms her love for Him by expressing His exquisite beauty.***

Christ Delights in His Church (5:1)

5:1 *I am come.* Christ responds to the church's welcome (4:16). *gathered . . . eaten . . . drunk.* Christ enjoys spiritual communion with His dear people (Zeph. 3:17; John 14:21,23; Rev. 3:20).

THE NEGLIGENT BRIDE AND HER BRIDEGROOM (5:2—6:10)

The Church's Failure to Welcome Christ and Her Distress (5:2–6)

5:2 *sleep.* A picture of a lack of spiritual alertness (Matt. 25:5; 26:38–41; 1 Thess. 5:6). *knocketh.* Christ calls the church to repentance (Rev. 3:19–20). *Open to me.* Welcome His companionship and love.
5:3 *put off my coat.* The church, being in a lazy state of mind, makes excuses for not rushing to open the door to admit Him (cf. Luke 11:7)—a picture of spiritual laziness.
5:4 *bowels.* Affections. The church now at last feels her need for her Lord.

5 I rose up to open to my beloved; and my hands
dropped *with* myrrh, and my fingers *with* sweet
smelling myrrh, upon the handles of the lock.
6 I opened to my beloved; but my beloved had
withdrawn himself, *and* was gone: my soul failed
when he spake: I sought him, but I could not find
him; I called him, but he gave me no answer.
7 The watchmen that went about the city found
me, they smote me, they wounded me; the keepers
of the walls took away my veil from me.
8 I charge you, O daughters of Jerusalem, if ye find
my beloved, that ye tell him, that I *am* sick of love.
9 ¶ What *is* thy beloved more than *another*
beloved, O thou fairest among women? what *is*
thy beloved more than *another* beloved, that thou
dost so charge us?
10 My beloved *is* white and ruddy, the chiefest
among ten thousand.
11 His head *is as* the most fine gold, his locks *are*
bushy, *and* black as a raven.
12 His eyes *are* as *the eyes* of doves by the rivers of
waters, washed with milk, *and* fitly set.
13 His cheeks *are* as a bed of spices, *as* sweet
flowers: his lips *like* lilies, dropping sweet smelling
myrrh.
14 His hands *are as* gold rings set with the beryl:
his belly *is as* bright ivory overlaid *with* sapphires.
15 His legs *are as* pillars of marble, set upon
sockets of fine gold: his countenance *is* as
Lebanon, excellent as the cedars.
16 His mouth *is* most sweet: yea, he *is* altogether
lovely. This *is* my beloved, and this *is* my friend, O
daughters of Jerusalem.

CHAPTER 6

WHITHER is thy beloved gone, O thou fairest
among women? whither is thy beloved turned
aside? that we may seek him with thee.
2 My beloved is gone down into his garden, to the
beds of spices, to feed in the gardens, and to gather
lilies.
3 I *am* my beloved's, and my beloved *is* mine: he
feedeth among the lilies.
4 ¶ Thou *art* beautiful, O my love, as Tirzah, come-
ly as Jerusalem, terrible as *an army* with banners.

5:5–6 The bride rises up *to open*, but Christ has *withdrawn* Himself and is *gone*. Laziness on the believer's part has resulted in spiritual loss. *dropped . . . sweet smelling myrrh.* Dripped with liquid myrrh; the Lord's knocking left the church with a sense of the goodness of His presence.

The Church Suffers a Painful Rebuke and Desires Christ (5:7–8)

5:7 *watchmen.* The bride seeks help from ministers of the church (see note at 3:3), but they treat her harshly instead of sympathetically leading her back to her Beloved.

5:8 *daughters of Jerusalem.* The bride next goes to seek help for her wounded soul from private Christians. She experiences deep yearning after Christ (*sick of love*; 2:5).

The Church Loves and Esteems Christ (5:9–16)

5:9 *What is thy beloved more.* These Christians now draw out the bride by asking her to speak about her beloved Savior. Meditation on Christ's excellence and praise of His attributes are great means of recovering His felt presence (Ps. 22:3; Col. 3:1–3).

5:10 *white and ruddy.* Radiant and red, colors of youthful health symbolizing personal excellence (1 Sam. 16:12; 17:42; Lam. 4:7). *chiefest among ten thousand.* Like one who raises a banner for an army (same root as "banners" in 6:4,10): their leader and focus of their attention.

5:11–16 As throughout the Song of Solomon, the comparisons are not according to physical appearance so much as in the qualities suggested by the images. The materials described here communicate joy, riches, and glory in every facet of His person, work, and words—the infinite glory of Christ, who is *altogether lovely* (Pss. 27:4; 45:2; Isa. 33:17). *my beloved . . . my friend.* This glory of Christ is not considered abstractly but as the personal possession of believers for their happiness.

Thoughts for Personal/Family Worship: Chapter 5

1. **Christians have experiences from which they may benefit all their lives. Here the church recounts an experience she has of failing her Lord (vv. 1–4). We must expect to pay a price when we are too slow to rise to meet Christ when He calls. The bride longs for the felt presence of Christ but fails for a time to experience it. Her laziness has taught her an important lesson. Christ never forsakes His people completely in this life (Matt. 28:20; Heb. 13:5, 8). However, Christ may teach us a needed lesson if we do not seek Him as we should. He may hide His face from us for a time. Let us never rest in such a condition but earnestly seek Him through the public means of grace, the help of godly friends, and especially meditation and praise regarding His beauties. How are you seeking Christ's presence in your regular habits?**
2. **God frequently brings good out of our evil. This is no reason for us to do what is foolish. But it comforts us when we make mistakes and go astray, as we too often do. So here, the bride's failure to open to her Beloved is a means whereby she is roused to confess her heartfelt love for her Lord: "Yea, he is altogether lovely" (v. 16). Believers, we must never despair. No matter how wrongly we may have behaved, we must not give up hope of finding again the love of Christ. Even when we fall badly we are to return to Christ with tears of repentance and expect to find Him ready to bless us still.**

Chapter 6: *The bride expresses her love for Christ, while He in turn praises her beauty.*

Her Love for Christ Stirs Others to Seek Him with Her (6:1–3)

6:1 *Whither is thy beloved gone?* The church's praise of her Lord rouses others to *seek him with* her (Pss. 96:1–9; 105:1–4).

6:2–3 *into his garden.* Among His people (4:12—5:1). *feed.* Shepherd (1:7). *gather.* Often "glean," as in picking up things scattered. *my beloved's . . . mine.* The assurance of union with Him (2:16). Christ calls His elect to Himself out of the world, knows each personally, cares for them as the good shepherd, and leads them to glory (John 10:4,14–16,27–29).

Christ Expresses His Love for His Church in Exquisite Language (6:4–10)

6:4–9 Christ again manifests Himself to His beloved bride, expressing His love for her.

5 Turn away thine eyes from me, for they have
overcome me: thy hair *is* as a flock of goats that
appear from Gilead.
6 Thy teeth *are* as a flock of sheep which go up
from the washing, whereof every one beareth
twins, and *there is* not one barren among them.
7 As a piece of a pomegranate *are* thy temples
within thy locks.
8 There are threescore queens, and fourscore
concubines, and virgins without number.
9 My dove, my undefiled is *but* one; she *is* the *only*
one of her mother, she *is* the choice *one* of her
that bare her. The daughters saw her, and blessed
her; *yea*, the queens and the concubines, and they
praised her.
10 ¶ Who *is* she *that* looketh forth as the morning,
fair as the moon, clear as the sun, *and* terrible as
an army with banners?
11 I went down into the garden of nuts to see the
fruits of the valley, *and* to see whether the vine
flourished, *and* the pomegranates budded.
12 Or ever I was aware, my soul made me *like* the
chariots of Ammi-nadib.
13 Return, return, O Shulamite; return, return,
that we may look upon thee. What will ye see in the
Shulamite? As it were the company of two armies.

CHAPTER 7

How beautiful are thy feet with shoes, O prince's
daughter! the joints of thy thighs *are* like jewels,
the work of the hands of a cunning workman.
2 Thy navel *is like* a round goblet, *which* wanteth
not liquor: thy belly *is like* an heap of wheat set
about with lilies.
3 Thy two breasts *are* like two young roes *that are*
twins.
4 Thy neck *is* as a tower of ivory; thine eyes *like* the
fishpools in Heshbon, by the gate of Bath-rabbim:
thy nose *is* as the tower of Lebanon which looketh
toward Damascus.
5 Thine head upon thee *is* like Carmel, and the

6:4 *Tirzah.* Means "delightful"; a lovely (*comely*) city later chosen by the kings of the northern kingdom as the capital (1 Kings 14:17; 15:21,33; 16:6,8–9,15,23). *terrible.* Inspiring fear for her militant resolve to fight for good and truth against evil and lies (v. 10; 4:4).
6:5 *eyes . . . overcome me.* Her beauty and love fill His heart with desire to bless her (4:9).
6:6–7 Our Lord repeats the language of love that He had earlier used (4:2–3).
6:8–9 *threescore . . . fourscore.* Sixty and eighty. Hebrew uses ascending numbers for a representative but incomplete list (Prov. 30:15). Even if surrounded by an infinite number of competitors (symbolized by a king's harem, 1 Kings 11:3), the church appears unique (*one*) to Christ because of His love (Deut. 7:6–8; Eph. 5:25).
6:10 *Who is she.* These words of admiration express again the excellence of Christ's church. *fair as the moon, clear as the sun.* God's people are beautiful and glorious (Gen. 37:9; Rev. 12:1), shining now with spiritual graces on earth and one day radiant with open glory (Isa. 60:1–3,19–20; Rev. 21:1–2,11,23). *terrible . . . banners.* See note at v. 4.

A COMMUNING BRIDE AND BRIDEGROOM (6:11—8:4)
Christ Reviews the Church's Graces and Is Stirred with Love and Longing (6:11–13)

6:11 *went down . . . to see.* Christ examines the spiritual state of His people to see if they are bringing forth the *fruits* of holiness (Rev. 2:1—3:22)
6:12 *ever I was aware, my soul.* Literally, "before I knew it, my desire," an expression of how quickly Christ desires His people when He sees their sincere holiness. *chariots of Ammi-nadib.* Probably a metaphor for great speed.
6:13 *Return, return.* Here Christ calls to His bride to come to Him after his absence. *Shulamite.* Perhaps the feminine counterpart to "Solomon" (Hebrew, *shelōmō*), meaning peaceful. *company.* Or dance. *two armies.* Hebrew, *Mahanaim*, either another military metaphor (vv. 4,10) or a location associated with Jacob, Ish-bosheth, and David (Gen. 32:2; 2 Sam. 2:8; 19:32).

Thoughts for Personal/Family Worship: Chapter 6

1. Christ greatly values the devotion of His people to Him (v. 5). Some believers suffer the contempt of men for His sake, some financial loss, and some martyrdom. Our Lord well knows the motive of love in the hearts of His own dear people. No sacrifice that we can make could ever be too great for Him who died for us. Christ is looking for fruit (v. 11). He will reward every faithful act of His people in the Great Day. What comfort it will then be to hear Him say, "Well done, then good and faithful servant" (Matt. 25:21)!

2. Christ describes His church in words that indicate her excellence in His eyes: "Fair as the moon, clear as the sun, and terrible as an army with banners" (v. 10). There are excellencies in Christ's church that are not to be found elsewhere in this world. She shines as a light in the darkness of this world's sin and superstition. She is ever rising higher in the sky as God's providence unfolds, just as the sun soars higher and higher till it reaches its zenith. She is a powerful force for good, ever conquering in the name of Christ till at last all nations shall be blessed in her and call her blessed. How can this encourage believers to serve God zealously even in sorrow?

Chapter 7: *Christ further describes the bride's beauty while she seeks communion with Him.*
Christ Further Describes the Beauty of His Church (7:1–9)

7:1–3 *How beautiful.* Christ's love for the church is unchanging. As elsewhere, these comparisons pertain especially to spiritual qualities suggested by the imagery. *feet with shoes.* Literally, "footsteps in sandals," an image of walking in a lifestyle of obedience (Pss. 17:5; 119:133; Col. 1:10; 1 Thess. 2:12). *navel . . . belly . . . breasts.* Most likely references to the bride's ability to bear and nourish children by union with her Lord (see notes at 4:5; Isa. 54:1,5; Rom. 7:4).
7:4 *neck . . . tower.* Beauty and wealth (*ivory*; 5:14; Ps. 45:8) combined with strength and determination (see note at 4:4). *fishpools.* Reservoirs of water, symbolic of life. *Heshbon.* City about fifteen miles east of the Jordan River. *Damascus.* Capital city of Syria, a beautiful area well supplied by rivers (2 Kings 5:12).
7:5 *Carmel.* A lovely hill, well known for its fertility (Isa. 35:2; Jer. 50:19). *purple.* The color of wealth and royalty (3:10; Judg.

hair of thine head like purple; the king *is* held in
the galleries.
6 How fair and how pleasant art thou, O love, for
delights!
7 This thy stature is like to a palm tree, and thy
breasts to clusters *of grapes*.
8 I said, I will go up to the palm tree, I will take
hold of the boughs thereof: now also thy breasts
shall be as clusters of the vine, and the smell of thy
nose like apples;
9 And the roof of thy mouth like the best wine for
my beloved, that goeth *down* sweetly, causing the
lips of those that are asleep to speak.
10 ¶ I *am* my beloved's, and his desire *is* toward
me.
11 Come, my beloved, let us go forth into the
field; let us lodge in the villages.
12 Let us get up early to the vineyards; let us see if
the vine flourish, *whether* the tender grape appear,
and the pomegranates bud forth: there will I give
thee my loves.
13 The mandrakes give a smell, and at our gates
are all manner of pleasant *fruits*, new and old,
which I have laid up for thee, O my beloved.

CHAPTER 8

O THAT thou *wert* as my brother, that sucked the
breasts of my mother! *when* I should find thee
without, I would kiss thee; yea, I should not be
despised.
2 I would lead thee, *and* bring thee into my
mother's house, *who* would instruct me: I would
cause thee to drink of spiced wine of the juice of
my pomegranate.
3 His left hand *should be* under my head, and his
right hand should embrace me.
4 I charge you, O daughters of Jerusalem, that ye
stir not up, nor awake *my* love, until he please.
5 Who *is* this that cometh up from the wilder-
ness, leaning upon her beloved? I raised thee up
under the apple tree: there thy mother brought
thee forth: there she brought thee forth *that* bare
thee.

8:26; Prov. 31:22). *held in the galleries.* Captivated by the beauty of her *hair* (4:1; 6:5).

7:7 *palm tree.* A picture of uprightness and flourishing growth (Ps. 92:12–14). *breasts.* An image of feminine love and motherhood (see v. 3; 1:13; 4:5; 8:1).

7:8 *take hold of the boughs.* Either to harvest its fruit or to prune the tree for more fruitfulness (John 15:2). *clusters of the vine.* An emblem of fruitfulness (Num. 13:23–24). *smell of thy nose.* Fragrance of your breath, an indicator of health, specifically health by feasting on Christ's love (*apples*; 2:3–4).

7:9 *roof of thy mouth.* Palate. *causing the lips of those that are asleep to speak.* Or gliding smoothly over the lips of sleepers.

The Church Redoubles Her Zeal to Seek Christ after Her Earlier Laziness (7:10–13)

7:10 *I am my beloved's.* The believer knows what no one else knows, the love that passes knowledge (2:16; Eph. 3:19). *his desire is toward me.* Having chosen her for His bride, the King longs for perfect communion with the church (Ps. 45:11).

7:11–12 *Come, my beloved.* Through prayer believers invite the Lord to draw near so that Christ and His people enjoy communion by exercises of the fruit of the Spirit (*grape . . . pomegranates*). *get up early.* An expression of eagerness. *loves.* Plural to communicate acts or intensity of love.

7:13 *mandrakes.* Plants associated with conceiving children (Gen. 30:14–17). The images of fertility and motherhood throughout this chapter remind us that the church's desire to please Christ leads it to work toward conversions and growth in holiness, both by His grace (Gal. 4:19,23,26–29; 5:22–24).

Thoughts for Personal/Family Worship: Chapter 7

1. **Christ takes note of the way in which believers walk. "How beautiful are thy feet with shoes, O prince's daughter" (v. 1). This is a lesson to us of great practical importance. We are called upon to walk in the light of God's Word, the Holy Scriptures. This includes walking by faith in the gospel and in obedience to the Ten Commandments. The believer should take every care to walk in the light of God's Word and to honor Him in thought, word, and deed.**
2. **The word "come" is often on the lips of Christ and of His church (e.g., v. 11). The gospel invites sinners often with this word (e.g., Matt. 11:28). Christ welcomes all sinners who hear His gospel to come to Him and be saved. Those who have already walked with Christ for a long time are still invited with that same call. Has this word become necessary, suitable, and precious to you?**

Chapter 8: *The bride expresses her love to Christ and looks toward the future.*

The Church Expresses Her Love for Christ's Fellowship (8:1–4)

8:1–2 *O that thou wert as my brother.* Literally, "I wish you were like my brother," to allow for greater freedom for open displays of affection that were permitted for members of the same family (*kiss thee*; Gen. 27:26; 29:11,13; 33:4; 45:15). This longing for family-like closeness was fulfilled in Christ's incarnation, in which the eternal Son of God became the brother of His people so that He might save them (Heb. 2:11–18; cf. John 20:17; Rom. 8:29). *my mother's house.* Believers desire to carry their communion with Christ into the public worship of God's church (3:4), pictured as a spiritual mother (see note at 1:6), particularly in responding to the preaching of God's Word (*instruct me*).

8:3 *left hand . . . right hand.* Christ is nearer to His dear, believing people than we usually suppose. He is ready to support and help us in all our trials (see note at 2:6).

8:4 *stir not . . . my love.* The church's main concern ought always to be, as here, never to offend or displease her beloved Lord (see note at 2:7).

CONCLUSION (8:5–14)

8:5–14 The conclusion of the Song of Solomon includes parting words from the bride and Bridegroom. They concern the depth of love, conquering death (vv. 6–7); the breadth of love, extending to the Gentiles, (vv. 8–12); and the future of their love (vv. 13–14).

8:5 *Who is this that cometh up from the wilderness.* Just as earlier the King had appeared with His royal attendants for His wedding day, so now the bride appears with Him like Israel being led to the Promised Land (see note at 3:6). *leaning.* A posture of affection, closeness, and dependence. *apple tree.*

6 ¶ Set me as a seal upon thine heart, as a seal
upon thine arm: for love *is* strong as death; jeal-
ousy *is* cruel as the grave: the coals thereof *are*
coals of fire, *which hath* a most vehement flame.
7 Many waters cannot quench love, neither can
the floods drown it: if a man would give all the
substance of his house for love, it would utterly
be contemned.
8 ¶ We have a little sister, and she hath no breasts:
what shall we do for our sister in the day when she
shall be spoken for?
9 If she *be* a wall, we will build upon her a palace
of silver: and if she *be* a door, we will inclose her
with boards of cedar.
10 I *am* a wall, and my breasts like towers: then
was I in his eyes as one that found favour.
11 Solomon had a vineyard at Baal-hamon; he
let out the vineyard unto keepers; every one for
the fruit thereof was to bring a thousand *pieces*
of silver.
12 My vineyard, which *is* mine, *is* before me: thou,
O Solomon, *must have* a thousand, and those that
keep the fruit thereof two hundred.
13 Thou that dwellest in the gardens, the com-
panions hearken to thy voice: cause me to hear *it*.
14 ¶ Make haste, my beloved, and be thou like to
a roe or to a young hart upon the mountains of
spices.

Christ speaks, reminding the church that it was His life-giving influence (2:3) that awakened them to sense their spiritual need (*raised thee up*; 5:2) and brought them to the new birth (*brought thee forth . . . bare thee*; Ps. 87:6; John 3:1–8).

8:6–7 *Set me as a seal.* An image of security (4:12); a seal marks something as authentically belonging to an important person (1 Kings 21:8; Est. 8:8). The people of God, since they profoundly value Christ, desire to know that His love (*heart*) and power (*arm*) are permanently committed to their good (Isa. 54:5–10; Jer. 32:40–41; 2 Cor. 1:22; Eph. 1:13–14; 4:30). *jealousy.* The burning zeal shared by God and His people that He alone be glorified among them (Ex. 20:5; 34:14; Deut. 4:24). *cruel.* Fierce, severe. *vehement flame.* Literally, "flame of Jehovah," the only explicit naming of God in the book. Divine love is stronger than death, hotter than fire, unquenchable, and more valuable than any earthly treasures (Pss. 36:5; 103:17; Rom. 5:8; 8:31,35,39).

8:8 *little sister . . . no breasts.* Sexual immaturity represents people not ready for spiritual fruitfulness. It may refer to the Gentile nations (cf. Ezek. 16:46) who for the most part had not yet been brought into the church before Christ's ascension (Hos. 2:1,23; Rom. 9:25–26). The church seeking Christ's love leads it to pray for others to be brought into union with Him.

8:9 Christ answers the church's prayer (v. 8), promising that if recent converts are well established in the faith (*wall*) He will give them glory (*silver*; 1:11), but that if they remain open to His teaching and vulnerable to sin and error (*door*) He will protect them (*inclose her with boards*; 4:12).

8:10 *wall . . . towers.* Again, the comparison refers not to physical similarity but to qualities implied by the images. The true church must always remain in a state of wartime readiness, strong in the Lord to resist the powers of evil (4:4; 7:4; Ps. 48:12–14).

8:11–12 *Solomon.* The King of peace (see note at 3:7). *vineyard.* An image for the church (see note at 1:6). *keepers.* Leaders, especially teachers, appointed to care for the people (Matt. 21:33,45). *thousand pieces of silver.* Cost of the rent for a very productive vineyard (Isa. 7:23). *keep the fruit.* Christ's ministers will receive their reward (1 Cor. 3:5–8).

8:13 *dwellest in the gardens.* Here Christ speaks to His church, giving to His people this last command. *thy voice.* He commands the church to speak (2:14) to Him in prayer (*cause me to hear it*) and of Him in proclamation to men (*the companions hearken*). Christ's last commission before ascending into heaven spurred the church to devote itself to prayer for the Spirit and the preaching of the Word (Acts 1:4,8,14; 2:42; 3:1,12; 4:31; 6:4; 12:5,12,24; 13:1–3).

8:14 *Make haste.* Run. Like the last book of the Bible, Song of Solomon ends with a prayer for Christ to come quickly (Rev. 22:20). *hart . . . mountains of spices.* The images of Christ leaping across the mountains like a deer (2:8–9) and delighting in the spiritual fragrance of His bride (1:12) merge into a single invitation for Christ to come to her with eager desire (4:6).

Thoughts for Personal/Family Worship: Chapter 8

1. **We know that Christ's love for His bride went so deep that He was willing to go to death and the grave for her (v. 6). There is no doubt but that Christ has His church on His heart and has her engraved on the palms of His hands (Isa. 49:16). He cannot leave her or abandon her. Therefore, the greatest source of peace and joy a person can have is to know that he is sealed by the Spirit and belongs to Christ's eternal love. If you have that assurance, cherish it and pursue a deeper communion with Christ. If you do not have it, seek it through faith in the gospel, prayer, and the use of the means of grace.**
2. **The church prays for elect persons who have not yet been called to salvation but who will be called in the course of God's providence (v. 8). Believers should always have a deep desire to be of help to those who are not yet saved. The Lord commands the church to be diligent in prayer and in witness (v. 13). We should particularly long for the salvation of the Jews, just as believing Jews longed for Christ to save the Gentiles (Luke 2:25–32). We should long for God to transform ethnic Israel into spiritual Israel again (Rom. 11:23). How are you praying for the salvation of unconverted people, both Jews and Gentiles?**
3. **"Make haste, my beloved" (v.14). With these words of hope and expectation the Lord's people look forward to the coming of their blessed Savior. The practical import of these words is that we should seek to be a people given to watching and praying. We do not know the hour when our Lord will return. As our Savior Himself tells us, "Behold, I come quickly; and my reward is with me, to give every man according as his work shall be" (Rev. 22:12). How should this give believers an incentive to serve Christ faithfully?**

INTRODUCTION TO

THE PROPHETS

Prophets were one of the three "messianic" or anointed offices or occupations in the Old Testament, along with priests and kings. By simple definition, the prophet was God's representative to the people whereas the priest served as man's representative before God. Whereas legitimate priests were limited to the tribe of Levi and the family of Aaron and Judah's kings were to be from David's line, prophets could be from any tribe and occupation. But they served by direct call and commission from the Lord; the service was not a voluntary ministry.

As God's representative, the prophet functioned as God's mouthpiece and had authority as he spoke only what God had revealed to him. This is highlighted by the principal titles used to refer to the office. Common in the time of Samuel and David, though not limited to this period, was the title "Seer." The KJV translates two different Hebrew words as "Seer," but both express the thought of receiving a vision from the Lord that was then passed on to the people. The title "man of God" occurs throughout the Old Testament to underscore the fact that these were men who knew the Lord and were sent on special missions by God. By far the most common term is translated "prophet." Opinions differ regarding the basic meaning, but most likely the verb form means simply "to speak." Although the prophet was certainly one who spoke God's word, the noun form in Hebrew is actually passive. The prophet, then, is first one who has been spoken to and then in turn speaks the message to others. The prophet's only authority was as he proclaimed "thus saith the Lord" (Ezek. 2:4). All of the principal terms highlight the revelational reception of the message. It was God's word, not human opinion, that had authority.

The prophets employed various methods of delivering God's message. Obeying God's instruction, they often performed symbolic acts to illustrate or reinforce truth. For instance, Hosea's family life pictured God's unfailing love in spite of the people's unfaithfulness. Jeremiah's wearing a yoke to symbolize captivity (Jer. 28) and Ezekiel's constructing a model city (Ezek. 4) to picture the siege are examples of the specific enactments commanded by God. Many of the prophets did similar and sometimes strange things, but always as instructed by God. Because the symbols were commanded by God, they were authoritative.

But the prophets were primarily preachers who directed God's word to the entire man including the mind, emotions, and will. They preached to the heart, not just the head. They did not simply impart information but sought to stir emotions and illicit responses. To that end, the prophets were essentially reformers who preached against specific sins (Mic. 3:8), both religious and social transgressions of God's moral law. In addition to exposing and condemning sin, they issued calls to repentance and pleas for conformity to God's covenant demands (Jer. 6:16). The theology of Moses, particularly in the book of Deuteronomy, was the biblical foundation of virtually every prophetic sermon. There is little hope of understanding the prophets apart from Deuteronomy, the prophet's creed. In addition to being reformers, the prophets were also intercessors for the people (Amos 7:2) and watchmen who warned of judgment unless there was repentance (Ezek. 3; 33).

An essential part of their reformed and experiential preaching was the preaching of the gospel, the preaching of Christ. Christ confirmed that He was the topic of prophetic preaching (Luke 24:27) as did Peter when he wrote, "Searching what, or what manner of time the Spirit of Christ which was in them did signify, when it testified beforehand the sufferings of Christ, and the glory that should follow" (1 Peter 1:11). Part of that preaching about Christ involved predictions of both Christ's first and second advents.

In considering the prophetic predictions, there are some key things to keep in mind about predictive prophecy, a significant yet comparatively small component of the prophet's preaching. Even the predictions were ultimately directed to the heart and not just the head. God revealed the future to affect the present; a proper use of predictive prophecy always brings the future to bear on the present. As you read the prophets and encounter their predictions, keep in mind these principles of prophetic purpose.

1. *To glorify God.*
   Prophecy indicates that God is in control. God's absolute control over time and circumstance evidences His complete sovereignty over all. Predictive prophecy is a dramatic way of displaying that control and of bringing glory to God. He knows the end from the beginning because He has decreed it; and thus, it is guaranteed. Nothing can frustrate or alter what He has determined. This is a vital component of the gospel ever since God promised Christ in the Garden of Eden (Gen. 3:15) and governed all the moments from Eden to Bethlehem. Christ came in the fullness of time as predicted. And so Christ continues to govern until all moments disappear into eternity when He will come again.

2. *To encourage believers.*
   Prophecy inspires confidence. This confidence is the inevitable corollary to the assurance that God controls time and that, therefore, regardless of appearances, the present is part of the execution of God's program. Looking in faith to God's revealed future should inspire confidence for present service and duty by assuring that the present fits precisely on the way to the future. A proper application of prophecy produces an active, bold, fervent, and confident performance of duty until God fulfills the promise.

3. *To intensify desire for God's will.*
   Prophecy increases expectant hope. Knowing what God has promised intensifies the desire to experience and possess the promise. The more we contemplate the promise, the more we want the promise to materialize. Predictive prophecy is a means whereby God keeps hope alive and increases trust and dependence on Him. Simeon and Anna certainly had that anticipation regarding the predictions about Christ's coming (Luke 2:25–26,38).

4. *To motivate sinners to repentance and saints to purity.*
   Prophecy encourages holiness. The coming of Christ is not without consequence; it behooves us to be ready for His appearing. If the Old Testament prophets teach anything about the use of prophecy, it is that prophecy is a motive to repentance and purity. Joel, for instance, after describing the great and terrible day of the Lord issued a classic call to repentance (Joel 2:11–13). The Scripture is clear that any use of prophecy which does not influence the present is inappropriate. The Old Testament prophets always applied the future; it was simply part of their preaching.

Finally, as you read the prophets be aware of their special genre and style. *First*, prophecy tends to use *symbolic language* that needs to be interpreted figuratively. Interpreting symbolism requires that you determine the point of relevance between the symbol and the actual referent without attempting to find a tit-for-tat parallel. The meaning of symbolism is not on the surface; discerning the meaning requires careful thought. There is a degree of subjectivism, so exercise caution about going too far. *Second*, prophecy tends to use the *language of imminency.* This means that regardless of how distant the actual prophecy is from its fulfillment, the prediction is made as though the fulfillment is about to occur. This intentional temporal ambiguity is one of the most significant features of prophetic language. Since the time of fulfillment is not specified, the application is not limited. *Third*, prophecy tends to link distinct epoch events into *single predictive contexts*, giving the appearance of a single event. This is called progressive prediction or prophetic telescoping by which the prophet juxtaposes events without any indication of time intervals between them. The focus is on the certain fact of the epochs, not the timing of them. In this way the prophets often linked what we now know to be the two advents of Christ (for example, compare Isa. 61:2 with Luke 4:17–21, noting particularly where Christ ends His reading before proclaiming the fulfillment).

INTRODUCTION TO THE BOOK OF THE PROPHET ISAIAH

Authorship: Isaiah, whose name means "Jehovah is salvation," is the sole author of the prophecy that bears his name (1:1). He is identified as the son of Amoz and ministered as a prophet in the southern kingdom, although the scope of his prophecy extended beyond Judah's borders (including Syria, Moab, Egypt, Tyre, Assyria, and Babylonia). The grandeur of his writing style and the access he had to the kings of Judah imply that he was well-educated and a member of an influential family in the nation. Jewish tradition suggests that his father, Amoz, was the brother of King Amaziah. If this is true, it would make Isaiah a young cousin of King Uzziah. The prophet's writings reveal a man of great learning and intellect, as well as a man of real courage. Legend has it that Isaiah was martyred during the early part of Manasseh's reign, but the Scriptures are silent on the matter.

With the rise of rationalism and biblical skepticism in the eighteenth century, some scholars have questioned the unity of the prophecy and generated theories of multiple authorship, some arguing for two authors (Deutero-Isaiah, ch. 40 onward) and some for three (Trito-Isaiah, ch. 56 onward) based on alleged differences in language and style, theological ideas, and subject matter. At the core of these theories is the denial of supernatural prophecy of future events, leading to the assumption that the later chapters must have been written by someone long after Isaiah. Particularly problematic for the skeptic are the references to Cyrus (44:28; 45:1), who dates almost two hundred years after the events of the first part of the book. Those who believe in divine inspiration have no problem with predictive prophecy, for God, the ultimate Author, knows the end from the beginning (46:10). The Lord Jesus confirmed that the prophet who wrote the first part of the book also wrote the latter, attributing the words from ch. 6 and ch. 53 to a single author, the prophet Isaiah (John 12:37–41).

Date: Isaiah 1:1 dates Isaiah's ministry during the administrations of Uzziah, Jotham, Ahaz, and Hezekiah. At the latest, Isaiah began his ministry in 740 BC, the year that King Uzziah died (6:1), but he may have started preaching toward the end of Uzziah's reign. The last historical reference records the death of Sennacherib (37:38), which occurred in 680 BC. Thus 740 to 680 BC marks the general period of Isaiah's ministry and composition, although it may extend beyond those dates. This makes him contemporary with Micah (a fellow southern prophet), Hosea, Amos, and perhaps even Jonah from the north.

The period in which Isaiah wrote was one of great change. Under Uzziah and Jotham, Judah expanded its borders and engaged in significant building projects. That prosperity had the effect of making the people less dependent upon the Lord, and they began to descend into great sinfulness by turning away from God, who had so richly blessed them. That spiritual decline reached its climax during the reign of Ahaz, who acted foolishly, both religiously and politically. Religiously, he failed to follow God and introduced abominable pagan practices, desecrating even the temple. Politically, his conflicts with Israel and Syria led him to appeal to Assyria for help. The godly king Hezekiah sought to turn things around, but the root of apostasy had taken hold, and there would be no preventing the inevitable judgment that was to come. That coming judgment was a constant theme in Isaiah's preaching.

The world scene was changing as well, as the Assyrians were expanding their borders by ruthless military means in the creation of an empire. The Assyrians were the agents used by God to punish Israel, and they were a threat to Judah as well. In the mercy and providence of God Judah was spared exile at this time, but Babylonia was coming.

Theme: Judgment for sin and salvation by grace in the coming Messiah for the glory of God.

Purpose: To warn of impending judgment against those who persisted in sin in Judah, and to comfort those who sought the Lord, for God had not repudiated His covenant.

Synopsis: *The Contribution of Isaiah to Redemptive Revelation*

The genius of Isaiah is without parallel. From any perspective this book is a literary masterpiece; the language is rich and the imagery beautiful. But beyond the majesty of the style is the majesty of the message of the everlasting gospel. With theological precision equal to that of the apostle Paul, this evangelical prophet proclaims a message of free and sovereign grace. As a gospel preacher, Isaiah puts man's need of a savior squarely before him. Without the knowledge of sin there is no sense of need. But man's sins have separated him from God (59:2), and he is without hope unless God intervenes.

The horror of man's condition becomes apparent in light of Isaiah's revelation that we have despised the Holy One (1:4), the King of infinite majesty and glory (6:1–5). When the day of the Lord comes, God will flatten every attempt by man to glorify himself instead of God, for the Lord alone will be exalted on that day (2:10–22). Notwithstanding man's rebellion and corruption in the face of the Holy One, God offers a gospel and commands repentance. It is a gospel founded in the Messiah, God's elect Servant, the only Mediator between God and men. Isaiah defines the gospel in terms of Christ's substitutionary death and victorious resurrection. The narratives of the four Gospels are no more vivid in detailing the history of Christ's death and resurrection than Isaiah's prediction (53:1–12), and Christ's gracious invitation, "Come unto me" (Matt. 11:28), finds its counterpart in the call of Isaiah's message (Isa. 55:1–13).

Isaiah makes clear both who the Messiah will be and what He will do in order to accomplish redemption. In what is sometimes called Isaiah's Immanuel trilogy, he disclosed that the Savior would be the virgin-born God-with-us, the Son born to rule, and the Spirit-empowered King who would administer perfect justice (7:14; 9:6–7; 11:1–5). He would also be the Spirit-anointed preacher of good news (61:1–3). He would be God's ideal and elect Servant who would fulfill every function of the Mediator (42:1–7; 49:1–12; 50:4–10; 52:13—53:12). Isaiah expounds details of what we now know to be the first and second advents of Christ. To say the least, Isaiah's contribution to the message of redemption is profound. If Isaiah were the only revelation of God's gracious gospel of Christ, we would have all the gospel we needed.

Isaiah's vision of the coming of Christ revolves around the kingdom of God, symbolized by Zion, the holy mountain of the Lord, yet including all things in the grand hope of a new heaven and a new earth (65:17–18; 66:22). This kingdom comes in God's righteousness and salvation, and yet also with judgment and destruction. In fact, Isaiah teaches us that we cannot separate the three realities of salvation, judgment, and the glory of God. Even the Servant Himself must fall under divine judgment if He will save His people from their sins (53:4–6).

The intertwining of judgment, salvation, and divine glory had immediate relevance for Isaiah's first audience. Judah would not be exempt from the kind of judgment that Israel experienced. The themes of judgment and salvation are woven together in such a way as to show that the two were not mutually exclusive. Rather, God used judgment as a means to purify and to bring forth a remnant who would exemplify God's covenant purpose. They are given a wonderful hope that would come through the Messiah. However, there are clear warnings to those who reject the ways of the Lord, warnings culminating in some of the most sobering images of hell contained in the Bible (34:10; 66:24).

Outline:

I. Introduction (1:1)

II. Judgment and Salvation for Zion (1:2—12:6)

- A. Children or Rebels? Zion or Sodom? (1:2–31)
- B. The Lord Alone Exalted (2:1–22)
- C. God against Great Men and Rich Women (3:1—4:1)
- D. Fruitful Branch, Worthless Vineyard (4:2—5:7)
- E. Six Woes on the Worldly Hedonists (5:8–30)
- F. Isaiah's Vision of the Holy King (6:1–13)
- G. Ahaz and the Promise of Immanuel (7:1–25)
- H. Assyria's Flood and the Land of Immanuel (8:1–22)
- I. The Reign of the Messiah (9:1–7)
- J. His Hand Is Stretched Out Still (9:8—10:4)
- K. God's Use and Judgment of Assyria (10:5–34)

- L. The Spirit-Filled King and the Joy of Israel (11:1—12:6)
- III. Oracles against the Nations (13:1—23:18)
  - A. The Day of the Lord against Babylon (13:1—14:23)
  - B. Oracles on Assyria and Philistia (14:24–32)
  - C. Oracle on Moab (15:1—16:14)
  - D. Oracles on Syria, Jacob, and Ethiopia (17:1—18:7)
  - E. Oracle on Egypt (19:1–25)
  - F. Isaiah's Sign against Egypt and Ethiopia (20:1–6)
  - G. Oracles on Babylon, Edom, and Arabia (21:1–17)
  - H. The Valley of Vision for Judah (22:1–25)
  - I. Oracle on Tyre (23:1–18)
- IV. The Little Apocalypse (24:1—27:13)
  - A. The Ruin of the Heavens and Earth and the Coming of God's Kingdom (24:1–23)
  - B. Songs of Resurrection and Feasting on Eternal Life (25:1—26:19)
  - C. The Day of Judgment and Fruitfulness (26:20—27:13)
- V. Woes and Hope for Israel, Judah, and Edom (28:1—35:10)
  - A. Woes and Promises for Ephraim and Jerusalem (28:1—29:24)
  - B. The Call to Trust in the Lord, Not in Egypt (30:1—31:9)
  - C. The King and the Spirit (32:1–20)
  - D. The King and Everlasting Fire (33:1–24)
  - E. The Sword of the Lord against All Nations, Especially Edom (34:1–17)
  - F. The Coming of God's Glory to Heal the Redeemed (35:1–10)
- VI. Salvation for Judah and Judgment on Assyria (36:1—39:8)
  - A. Thus Saith the King of Assyria against the Lord (36:1–22)
  - B. Thus Saith the Lord against the King of Assyria (37:1–38)
  - C. Hezekiah's Prayer and Healing (38:1–22)
  - D. Hezekiah's Boasting to Babylon (39:1–8)
- VII. Restoration through the Servant of the Lord (40:1—55:13)
  - A. God's Comfort and Greatness for Israel (40:1—41:29)
  - B. The Lord's Servant and Jacob's Blindness (42:1–25)
  - C. The Redeemer of Israel and His Witnesses (43:1—44:28)
  - D. The Calling of Cyrus and the Destruction of Babylon (45:1—47:15)
  - E. The Lord's Appeal to Israel (48:1–22)
  - F. The Lord's Servant and the Salvation of Israel and the Gentiles (49:1–26)
  - G. The Submissive Servant and the Unbelievers (50:1–11)
  - H. The Good News of Salvation (51:1—52:12)
  - I. The Suffering Servant and the Substitute for Sinners (52:13—53:12)
  - J. The Reconciled Wife and Her Children (54:1–17)
  - K. The Call of the Gospel (55:1–13)
- VIII. Preparation for Salvation and Righteousness (56:1—66:24)
  - A. Promises to Faithful Outsiders and Rebukes to Blind Leaders (56:1–12)
  - B. Exhortations to Sinners in Jacob (57:1—59:21)
  - C. The Coming of the Lord to Zion with Glory (60:1—62:12)
  - D. The Coming of the Heavenly Warrior (63:1—64:12)
  - E. Judgment and the New Creation (65:1—66:24)

THE BOOK OF THE PROPHET

ISAIAH

CHAPTER 1

THE vision of Isaiah the son of Amoz, which he
saw concerning Judah and Jerusalem in the days
of Uzziah, Jotham, Ahaz, *and* Hezekiah, kings of
Judah.
2 Hear, O heavens, and give ear, O earth: for the
LORD hath spoken, I have nourished and brought
up children, and they have rebelled against me.
3 The ox knoweth his owner, and the ass his
master's crib: *but* Israel doth not know, my people
doth not consider.
4 Ah sinful nation, a people laden with iniquity,
a seed of evildoers, children that are corrupters:
they have forsaken the LORD, they have provoked
the Holy One of Israel unto anger, they are gone
away backward.
5 ¶ Why should ye be stricken any more? ye will
revolt more and more: the whole head is sick, and
the whole heart faint.
6 From the sole of the foot even unto the head *there*
is no soundness in it; *but* wounds, and bruises, and
putrifying sores: they have not been closed, neither
bound up, neither mollified with ointment.
7 Your country *is* desolate, your cities *are* burned
with fire: your land, strangers devour it in your
presence, and *it is* desolate, as overthrown by
strangers.
8 And the daughter of Zion is left as a cottage in
a vineyard, as a lodge in a garden of cucumbers,
as a besieged city.
9 Except the LORD of hosts had left unto us a very
small remnant, we should have been as Sodom,
and we should have been like unto Gomorrah.
10 ¶ Hear the word of the LORD, ye rulers of
Sodom; give ear unto the law of our God, ye
people of Gomorrah.
11 To what purpose *is* the multitude of your
sacrifices unto me? saith the LORD: I am full of the
burnt offerings of rams, and the fat of fed beasts;
and I delight not in the blood of bullocks, or of
lambs, or of he goats.
12 When ye come to appear before me, who hath
required this at your hand, to tread my courts?
13 Bring no more vain oblations; incense is an

Chapter 1: *God is dismayed at the sinful state of Judah, yet in mercy He pleads with them to be willing and obedient.*

INTRODUCTION (1:1)

1:1 *vision.* The whole book is a revelation of truth by God (1 Sam. 3:1; 1 Chron. 17:15; 2 Chron. 32:32). *Uzziah.* One of the most accomplished of Judah's kings (2 Chron. 26:3–15). *Hezekiah.* One of the most godly kings (2 Chron. 29–32).

JUDGMENT AND SALVATION FOR ZION (1:2—12:6)

Children or Rebels? Zion or Sodom? (1:2–31)

1:2 *Hear.* A call to be attentive. *heavens . . . earth.* Witnesses to God's covenant (Deut. 4:26; 31:28; 30:19; 32:1). *brought up children . . . rebelled against me.* The Lord had given tender, fatherly care to the people (Ex. 4:22; Deut. 14:1), but they responded to material prosperity with self-sufficiency and a willful forgetfulness of God (Deut. 8:10–20).

1:3 *crib.* A manger or stall providing food, rest, and safety for animals. Judah displayed an ignorance not shared even by dumb animals.

1:4 *Ah.* Also translated "woe" or "alas," a common prophetic interjection expressing lamentation and warning of doom (v. 24; 5:8,11,18,20–22; 10:1,5; 17:12; 18:1; 28:1; 29:1,14; 30:1; 31:1; 33:1; 45:9–10; 55:1). *laden with iniquity.* Heavy with guilt. *provoked.* Treated disrespectfully, discarded, or rejected. *Holy One of Israel.* A divine title expressing both God's transcendence and His gracious immanence with His people (twenty-five times in Isaiah; only five times in the rest of the Old Testament). *gone away.* Estranged.

1:5 *Why.* Or where; literally, "upon what." They had been beaten so many times that there was no place left to strike them. *stricken.* Beaten; painful discipline had no effect in bringing them to repentance. *ye will revolt more and more.* Yet you will add obstinacy.

1:6 *wounds . . . sores.* Injuries inflicted by slashes or blows. *ointment.* Oil. The focus is not on total depravity (Gen. 6:5) but on the greatness of their suffering and yet their continuing insensitivity and refusal to repent (Amos 4:6–11).

1:7 *strangers.* Foreigners.

1:8 *cottage.* A hut or booth for shelter. *lodge.* Specifically, an overnight hut.

1:9 *remnant.* The Old Testament designation for true believers. *Sodom . . . Gomorrah.* It was only the Lord's mercy that prevented their utter destruction (Gen. 19; cited in Rom. 9:29).

1:11–15 External religion without sincerity of heart before God is an abomination. When the heart is not right, sacrifice serves no purpose (Ps. 51:16).

1:12 *required.* Sought.

1:13 *oblations.* Gifts or sacrifices. *abomination.* A detestable,

abomination unto me; the new moons and sab-
baths, the calling of assemblies, I cannot away
with; *it is* iniquity, even the solemn meeting.
14 Your new moons and your appointed feasts
my soul hateth: they are a trouble unto me; I am
weary to bear *them*.
15 And when ye spread forth your hands, I will
hide mine eyes from you: yea, when ye make
many prayers, I will not hear: your hands are full
of blood.
16 ¶ Wash you, make you clean; put away the evil
of your doings from before mine eyes; cease to do
evil;
17 Learn to do well; seek judgment, relieve the
oppressed, judge the fatherless, plead for the
widow.
18 Come now, and let us reason together, saith
the LORD: though your sins be as scarlet, they
shall be as white as snow; though they be red like
crimson, they shall be as wool.
19 If ye be willing and obedient, ye shall eat the
good of the land:
20 But if ye refuse and rebel, ye shall be devoured
with the sword: for the mouth of the LORD hath
spoken *it*.
21 ¶ How is the faithful city become an harlot! it
was full of judgment; righteousness lodged in it;
but now murderers.
22 Thy silver is become dross, thy wine mixed
with water:
23 Thy princes *are* rebellious, and companions of
thieves: every one loveth gifts, and followeth after
rewards: they judge not the fatherless, neither
doth the cause of the widow come unto them.
24 Therefore saith the Lord, the LORD of hosts, the
mighty One of Israel, Ah, I will ease me of mine
adversaries, and avenge me of mine enemies:
25 ¶ And I will turn my hand upon thee, and
purely purge away thy dross, and take away all thy
tin:
26 And I will restore thy judges as at the first, and
thy counsellors as at the beginning: afterward
thou shalt be called, The city of righteousness, the
faithful city.
27 Zion shall be redeemed with judgment, and
her converts with righteousness.
28 ¶ And the destruction of the transgressors
and of the sinners *shall be* together, and they that
forsake the LORD shall be consumed.
29 For they shall be ashamed of the oaks which ye
have desired, and ye shall be confounded for the
gardens that ye have chosen.
30 For ye shall be as an oak whose leaf fadeth, and
as a garden that hath no water.
31 And the strong shall be as tow, and the maker
of it as a spark, and they shall both burn together,
and none shall quench *them*.

CHAPTER 2

THE word that Isaiah the son of Amoz saw
concerning Judah and Jerusalem.

disgusting thing; God here views their temple worship as though it were idolatry. *I cannot away with*. Literally, "I am not able." God finds their sinful worship intolerable.

1:14 *my soul*. Used for the personal pronoun "I." *hateth*. Reject. *trouble*. A burden. *weary to bear*. Bold imagery to describe divine omnipotence as being tired; this is a means of underscoring the degree to which God detests heartless religion.

1:15 *spread forth your hands*. The outward gesture of prayer. True sacrifice is accompanied by a broken and contrite heart (Ps. 51:17) without which God will not hear prayer (Ps. 66:18; John 9:31). *blood*. The Hebrew is plural, referring to acts of violence and bloodshed.

1:16–17 *Wash you*. Repentance for sin in heart and action is necessary to draw near to God (Ps. 24:3–4; James 4:8). *cease to do evil . . . Learn to do well*. Repentance involves both a stopping of bad things and a doing of good things (Eph. 4:22–24). *judgment*. Justice in all relationships, what God desires from man and produces in His kingdom (v. 21; 4:4; 5:7; 9:7; 16:6; 28:6; 32:1,16; 33:5; 42:1,3–4; 56:1; 61:8).

1:18 *reason together*. Repentance begins by learning a new way of thinking from God. *Scarlet* and *crimson* represent sin as being of the deepest dye, the stain of which cannot be removed except by the grace of God. He offered cleansing from all their sins (1 John 1:7,9).

1:22 *silver . . . dross*. Their former purity had become worthless. *wine . . . water*. Their former joy in the Lord had become diluted and tasteless.

1:23 *princes*. Leaders. They were self-seeking and covetous, accepting bribes (*gifts*) rather than upholding justice for the weak and vulnerable (contrast with v. 17).

1:24 *ease me of*. Obtain satisfaction from.

1:29 *oaks . . . gardens*. Places associated with pagan rites.

1:31 *tow*. Flax fibers used for tinder.

Thoughts for Personal/Family Worship: Chapter 1

1. **In our folly we often view sin lightly, but God hates it. We need to impress this thought upon our own hearts and confess with David, "My wounds stink and are corrupt because of my foolishness" (Ps. 38:5). How foolish we can be in failing to consider the effect sin has upon us! We can so easily be influenced by worldly opinion that we forget that God is dishonored when our outward profession is not matched with heartfelt love for His Word and His ways. What do vv. 2–4 teach us about how God views sin?**
2. **The wickedness of Israel was so great that they deserved to be punished as Sodom and Gomorrah had been. Yet in spite of their heinous sins, they were going to the temple and offering all the appropriate sacrifices as though all were well between them and God. They had a form of religion but knew nothing of its power or reality. They were satisfied with themselves, but God regarded their religion as idolatry. It is tragically possible to be frequent in church and to go through all the motions of worship without sincerity and truth. What does this teach us about worship that pleases God?**

Chapter 2: ***God reveals what Jerusalem ought to be and then exposes them for what they had in reality become.***

The Lord Alone Exalted (2:1–22)

2 And it shall come to pass in the last days,
that the mountain of the LORD's house shall be
established in the top of the mountains, and shall
be exalted above the hills; and all nations shall
flow unto it.
3 And many people shall go and say, Come ye,
and let us go up to the mountain of the LORD, to
the house of the God of Jacob; and he will teach
us of his ways, and we will walk in his paths: for
out of Zion shall go forth the law, and the word of
the LORD from Jerusalem.
4 And he shall judge among the nations, and
shall rebuke many people: and they shall beat
their swords into plowshares, and their spears
into pruninghooks: nation shall not lift up sword
against nation, neither shall they learn war any
more.
5 O house of Jacob, come ye, and let us walk in
the light of the LORD.
6 ¶ Therefore thou hast forsaken thy people the
house of Jacob, because they be replenished from
the east, and *are* soothsayers like the Philistines,
and they please themselves in the children of
strangers.
7 Their land also is full of silver and gold, neither
is there any end of their treasures; their land is
also full of horses, neither *is there any* end of their
chariots:
8 Their land also is full of idols; they worship the
work of their own hands, that which their own
fingers have made:
9 And the mean man boweth down, and the great
man humbleth himself: therefore forgive them
not.
10 ¶ Enter into the rock, and hide thee in the
dust, for fear of the LORD, and for the glory of his
majesty.
11 The lofty looks of man shall be humbled, and
the haughtiness of men shall be bowed down, and
the LORD alone shall be exalted in that day.
12 For the day of the LORD of hosts *shall be* upon
every *one that is* proud and lofty, and upon every
one that is lifted up; and he shall be brought low:
13 And upon all the cedars of Lebanon, *that*
are high and lifted up, and upon all the oaks of
Bashan,
14 And upon all the high mountains, and upon
all the hills *that are* lifted up,
15 And upon every high tower, and upon every
fenced wall,
16 And upon all the ships of Tarshish, and upon
all pleasant pictures.
17 And the loftiness of man shall be bowed down,
and the haughtiness of men shall be made low:
and the LORD alone shall be exalted in that day.
18 And the idols he shall utterly abolish.
19 And they shall go into the holes of the rocks,
and into the caves of the earth, for fear of the
LORD, and for the glory of his majesty, when he
ariseth to shake terribly the earth.
20 In that day a man shall cast his idols of silver,
and his idols of gold, which they made *each one* for
himself to worship, to the moles and to the bats;
21 To go into the clefts of the rocks, and into the
tops of the ragged rocks, for fear of the LORD, and
for the glory of his majesty, when he ariseth to
shake terribly the earth.
22 Cease ye from man, whose breath *is* in his
nostrils: for wherein is he to be accounted of?

2:2–4 God's purpose for *all nations* is to gather them into His kingdom (*mountain*) in order to worship Him (11:9–12; 18:7; 19:18–25; 25:6–7; 42:1,6; 49:6; 56:6–7; 60:3; 66:18). The same text appears in Mic. 4:1–3.

2:2 *last days*. The time of Christ's exaltation, beginning in the New Testament era (Acts 2:17; Heb. 1:2). *exalted above the hills*. Not speaking literally of topographical alterations but figuratively of status and honor. *all nations*. God purposes to save Gentiles as well as Israel.

2:4 A picture of peace (9:7; 11:6–9): *swords* and *spears* (weapons of war) will be turned into *plowshares* and *pruninghooks* (tools for cultivation).

2:5 *walk in the light of the LORD*. Live in submission to the truth and righteousness of His Word (5:20; 8:20; 9:2; 42:6; 49:6; 60:1–3; Eph. 5:8–9; 1 John 1:7)

2:6 *replenished from the east*. Filled with influences from eastern nations. *soothsayers*. Those who practice divination. *please themselves in the children of strangers*. Make agreements with foreigners.

2:9 *mean man . . . great man*. Two different words for man in the Hebrew; the first can refer to man as frail, the second as noble.

2:10 *for fear . . . glory of his majesty*. God will reveal His glory in a way that destroys His enemies (vv. 19,21). The Septuagint's Greek rendering appears almost exactly in Paul's description of Christ's return (2 Thess. 1:9).

2:11 *the LORD alone shall be exalted*. God's acts of judgment are to the glory of God alone (v. 17; 5:15–16; Ps. 83:17–18).

2:12 *day of the LORD*. A technical term referring to the direct and manifest interventions of God into the affairs of time for the purposes of judgment and salvation (13:6,9; 34:8; Joel 2:31), culminating in the great day at the end of the age (1 Thess. 5:2; 2 Peter 3:10).

2:13–15 *cedars . . . mountains . . . every high tower*. Symbols of every way in which man lifts himself up in pride and self-reliance instead of honoring the Lord (2 Cor. 10:4).

2:16 *pleasant pictures*. Most likely "the ships of precious things," referring to their cargo.

2:20 When God's judgment begins, men's *idols* are useless despite all the precious resources (*silver* and *gold*) that they have invested in them. *moles . . . bats*. Creatures living in the dark that cannot see, suggesting the blindness of idolaters (44:18).

2:22 *Cease ye from man*. Stop depending on mortal men (Ps. 146:3; Jer. 17:5–6); salvation is found only in the Lord.

Thoughts for Personal/Family Worship: Chapter 2

1. Judah had become extremely prosperous during the reign of Uzziah, and this turned their hearts away from God. We too live in a very materialistic society, where

CHAPTER 3

For, behold, the Lord, the LORD of hosts, doth
take away from Jerusalem and from Judah the
stay and the staff, the whole stay of bread, and the
whole stay of water,
2 The mighty man, and the man of war, the
judge, and the prophet, and the prudent, and the
ancient,
3 The captain of fifty, and the honourable man,
and the counsellor, and the cunning artificer, and
the eloquent orator.
4 And I will give children *to be* their princes, and
babes shall rule over them.
5 And the people shall be oppressed, every one
by another, and every one by his neighbour: the
child shall behave himself proudly against the
ancient, and the base against the honourable.
6 When a man shall take hold of his brother of
the house of his father, *saying*, Thou hast clothing,
be thou our ruler, and *let* this ruin *be* under thy
hand:
7 In that day shall he swear, saying, I will not be
an healer; for in my house *is* neither bread nor
clothing: make me not a ruler of the people.
8 For Jerusalem is ruined, and Judah is fallen:
because their tongue and their doings *are* against
the LORD, to provoke the eyes of his glory.
9 ¶ The shew of their countenance doth witness
against them; and they declare their sin as Sodom,
they hide *it* not. Woe unto their soul! for they have
rewarded evil unto themselves.
10 Say ye to the righteous, that *it shall be* well *with*
him: for they shall eat the fruit of their doings.
11 Woe unto the wicked! *it shall be* ill *with him*:
for the reward of his hands shall be given him.
12 ¶ *As for* my people, children *are* their
oppressors, and women rule over them. O my
people, they which lead thee cause *thee* to err, and
destroy the way of thy paths.
13 The LORD standeth up to plead, and standeth
to judge the people.
14 The LORD will enter into judgment with the
ancients of his people, and the princes thereof:
for ye have eaten up the vineyard; the spoil of the
poor *is* in your houses.
15 What mean ye *that* ye beat my people to
pieces, and grind the faces of the poor? saith the
Lord GOD of hosts.
16 ¶ Moreover the LORD saith, Because the
daughters of Zion are haughty, and walk with
stretched forth necks and wanton eyes, walking
and mincing *as* they go, and making a tinkling
with their feet:
17 Therefore the Lord will smite with a scab the
crown of the head of the daughters of Zion, and
the LORD will discover their secret parts.
18 In that day the Lord will take away the bravery
of *their* tinkling ornaments *about their feet*, and
their cauls, and *their* round tires like the moon,
19 The chains, and the bracelets, and the mufflers,

wealth and riches have become the idols of many. By God's grace we need to guard ourselves against the love of riches. The antidote to such excesses is surely found in v. 5: "Come ye, and let us walk in the light of the LORD." The apostle John reminds us, "If we walk in the light, as he is in the light, we have fellowship one with another, and the blood of Jesus Christ his Son cleanseth us from all sin" (1 John 1:7).

2. **An important exhortation is given in v. 22, "Cease ye from man." In other words, do not put your trust in man, not even the greatest of men, for man is an unreliable and often false guide. Those who would rather trust in man show contempt toward God; therefore the believer is warned against such folly, which in the end leads only to great disappointment, sorrow, and shame. How does believing in the coming day of the Lord (vv. 10–21) help us to stop relying on mere men?**

God against Great Men and Rich Women (3:1—4:1)

Chapter 3: *The effects of corrupt religion manifested in society make the whole nation corrupt and ripe for judgment.*

3:1 *stay . . . staff*. Supplies and support. The Lord would take away everything Judah was relying upon, even the essentials for survival.

3:2 *prudent*. One who predicts by enchantment. *ancient*. The elder.

3:3 *cunning artificer*. Skilled craftsman, referring to a skilled magician or sorcerer. *eloquent orator*. A skilled enchanter or snake charmer.

3:4 *princes*. Rulers in general, not necessarily children of royalty. *children . . . babes*. See Eccl. 10:16, a woeful situation.

3:5 *ancient*. Elderly. *base*. Worthless.

3:6–8 The collapse would be so great that none would want to assume the responsibility of leadership. *healer*. One who would bind up or govern. *tongue*. Words, what they say.

3:9 *shew of their countenance*. The look on their faces; they were unashamed of their sin, flaunting it publicly. *rewarded evil*. They dealt out or brought calamity upon themselves.

3:11 *reward of his hands*. Literally, "what was dealt out [by] his hands will be done to him." The principle of *lex talionis* (law of retaliation; eye-for-eye justice).

3:13 *plead*. Contest a lawsuit or enter a legal controversy.

3:14 *ancients*. The elders, referring to those in authority. *princes*. Rulers. *eaten up*. Or set on fire. *spoil of the poor*. The loot or what was seized from the weak.

3:16 *haughty*. Lifted up in pride. *stretched forth necks*. Holding heads up high. *wanton eyes*. Eyes that wink with seductive glances. *mincing*. Skipping along. *tinkling with their feet*. Walking with jingling anklets.

3:17 *smite with a scab*. Lay bare the scalp or cause a scab on the head, an embarrassing disgrace. *discover*. Expose.

3:18–23 God's judgment on the fine clothes and jewelry of wealthy women in Jerusalem reflects His will that women should pursue inner beauty, not outward glory (Prov. 31:30; 1 Tim. 2:9–10; 1 Peter 3:2–3).

3:18 *that day*. A shortened expression for the day of the Lord (see note at 2:12). *tinkling ornaments*. Anklets or bangles. *cauls*. Hairnets or headbands. *round tires like the moon*. Crescent shaped adornments.

3:19 *chains*. Ear pendants. *mufflers*. Veils or scarves.

20 The bonnets, and the ornaments of the legs, and
the headbands, and the tablets, and the earrings,
21 The rings, and nose jewels,
22 The changeable suits of apparel, and the
mantles, and the wimples, and the crisping pins,
23 The glasses, and the fine linen, and the hoods,
and the vails.
24 And it shall come to pass, *that* instead of sweet
smell there shall be stink; and instead of a girdle
a rent; and instead of well set hair baldness; and
instead of a stomacher a girding of sackcloth; *and*
burning instead of beauty.
25 Thy men shall fall by the sword, and thy
mighty in the war.
26 And her gates shall lament and mourn; and
she *being* desolate shall sit upon the ground.

CHAPTER 4

AND in that day seven women shall take hold of one man, saying, We will eat our own bread, and wear our own apparel: only let us be called by thy name, to take away our reproach.
2 In that day shall the branch of the LORD be
beautiful and glorious, and the fruit of the earth
shall be excellent and comely for them that are
escaped of Israel.
3 And it shall come to pass, *that he that is* left in
Zion, and *he that* remaineth in Jerusalem, shall be
called holy, *even* every one that is written among
the living in Jerusalem:
4 When the Lord shall have washed away the filth
of the daughters of Zion, and shall have purged the
blood of Jerusalem from the midst thereof by the
spirit of judgment, and by the spirit of burning.
5 And the LORD will create upon every dwelling
place of mount Zion, and upon her assemblies,
a cloud and smoke by day, and the shining of a
flaming fire by night: for upon all the glory *shall
be* a defence.
6 And there shall be a tabernacle for a shadow
in the daytime from the heat, and for a place of
refuge, and for a covert from storm and from rain.

CHAPTER 5

NOW will I sing to my wellbeloved a song of my beloved touching his vineyard. My wellbeloved

3:20 *bonnets*. Turban-like headdresses. *headbands*. Sashes for the upper body. *tablets*. Literally, "house of the person," referring most likely to a perfume box. *earrings*. Or amulets or charms.
3:22 *changeable suits of apparel*. Fine white garments, festive dress. *mantles*. Tunics or outer garments. *wimples*. Shawls or cloaks. *crisping pins*. Bags or purses.
3:23 *glasses*. Mirrors.
3:24 *girdle . . . rent*. Instead of a loin-covering, just a cord or encircling rope. *stomacher*. A magnificent garment. *girding*. A robe.
3:26 *desolate*. Emptied or cleaned out.

Thoughts for Personal/Family Worship: Chapter 3

The materialism with its outward display that characterized Isaiah's day is the trademark of much of society today. Part of God's judgment on that pretentious people was His removal of all their trinkets and His sentencing them to a government of weak and ineffective leadership. If society today is guilty of the same sins, it is liable to the same punishments. In many ways reading this chapter is like reading the newspaper and then looking in the mirror. In government, there is a display of foolish and irresponsible action in the overturning of God's laws and their replacement with the whims of godless and immature politicians whose unholy statutes can only drag our societies down further into sin and poverty. How can this chapter guide Christians in their prayers for their nation?

Chapter 4: *The Branch is revealed as the Redeemer of His people.*

4:1 *seven women . . . one man*. Concluding the judgment against the arrogant women of Jerusalem (3:16–26), the Lord will give women over to such desperation that they will allow men to use them while the men abdicate their responsibility to provide.

Fruitful Branch, Worthless Vineyard (4:2—5:7)

4:2 *branch of the LORD*. The sprout who is the Lord, a key title for the divine Messiah (see notes at Jer. 23:5; 33:15; Zech. 3:8; 6:12), depicting him as a new shoot of life that will sprout up out of the apparently dead stump of the Davidic line (6:13; 11:1; 53:1–2; Ps. 132:17). *fruit*. Righteousness for God's pleasure and man's peace (Isa. 5:1–7; 27:2–6; John 15:1–8). *comely*. Beautiful. *them that are escaped*. Those saved, the remnant.
4:3 *he that is left*. The remnant, the spiritual seed. *written among the living*. Those whose names are in God's decree of election (Dan. 12:1) will be made *holy* by grace (Eph. 1:4).
4:4 *purged*. Cleansed. *blood*. The Hebrew is plural, referring to the guilt of bloodshed. *spirit of judgment*. The power of the Holy Spirit to do justice (28:6; cf. 11:2,4; 42:1; Ezek. 36:27; Mic. 3:8). *spirit of burning*. The Spirit of Christ purifies like a refining fire (cf. 6:6; Mal. 3:2–4; Matt. 3:11).
4:5 *cloud . . . fire*. Visible manifestations of God's presence (Ex. 13:21). *defence*. A canopy or covering, used elsewhere of the intimacy of a bridal chamber (Ps. 19:5; Joel 2:16).
4:6 *tabernacle for a shadow*. A hut or booth for protection. *covert*. A shelter. The Lord's presence protects His people (Ps. 91:1–2; Rev. 7:15–17).

Thoughts for Personal/Family Worship: Chapter 4

This short chapter, though beginning with judgment, quickly moves to the wondrous subject of salvation. It speaks of Christ and of the great comfort that stems from Him. He is the Branch who is at once the Son of God and the Son of David. He is the One in whom all our hopes lie. It is a great blessing to know that one's name is written in the Book of Life, to be cleansed and purified from the filth of sin, and to bear luscious fruit by union with Jesus Christ. Believers in Christ can know the God of all comfort in times of trial and adversity, for He is our refuge from the heat and the storm.

Chapter 5: *Judah is described as an unfruitful vineyard, ripe for destruction.*

hath a vineyard in a very fruitful hill:

2 And he fenced it, and gathered out the stones thereof, and planted it with the choicest vine, and built a tower in the midst of it, and also made a winepress therein: and he looked that it should bring forth grapes, and it brought forth wild grapes.

3 And now, O inhabitants of Jerusalem, and men of Judah, judge, I pray you, betwixt me and my vineyard.

4 What could have been done more to my vineyard, that I have not done in it? wherefore, when I looked that it should bring forth grapes, brought it forth wild grapes?

5 And now go to; I will tell you what I will do to my vineyard: I will take away the hedge thereof, and it shall be eaten up; *and* break down the wall thereof, and it shall be trodden down:

6 And I will lay it waste: it shall not be pruned, nor digged; but there shall come up briers and thorns: I will also command the clouds that they rain no rain upon it.

7 For the vineyard of the LORD of hosts *is* the house of Israel, and the men of Judah his pleasant plant: and he looked for judgment, but behold oppression; for righteousness, but behold a cry.

8 ¶ Woe unto them that join house to house, *that* lay field to field, till *there be* no place, that they may be placed alone in the midst of the earth!

9 In mine ears *said* the LORD of hosts, Of a truth many houses shall be desolate, *even* great and fair, without inhabitant.

10 Yea, ten acres of vineyard shall yield one bath, and the seed of an homer shall yield an ephah.

11 ¶ Woe unto them that rise up early in the morning, *that* they may follow strong drink; that continue until night, *till* wine inflame them!

12 And the harp, and the viol, the tabret, and pipe, and wine, are in their feasts: but they regard not the work of the LORD, neither consider the operation of his hands.

13 ¶ Therefore my people are gone into captivity, because *they have* no knowledge: and their honourable men *are* famished, and their multitude dried up with thirst.

14 Therefore hell hath enlarged herself, and opened her mouth without measure: and their glory, and their multitude, and their pomp, and he that rejoiceth, shall descend into it.

15 And the mean man shall be brought down, and the mighty man shall be humbled, and the eyes of the lofty shall be humbled:

16 But the LORD of hosts shall be exalted in judgment, and God that is holy shall be sanctified in righteousness.

17 Then shall the lambs feed after their manner, and the waste places of the fat ones shall strangers eat.

18 Woe unto them that draw iniquity with cords of vanity, and sin as it were with a cart rope:

19 That say, Let him make speed, *and* hasten his work, that we may see *it*: and let the counsel of the Holy One of Israel draw nigh and come, that we may know *it*!

20 ¶ Woe unto them that call evil good, and good evil; that put darkness for light, and light for darkness; that put bitter for sweet, and sweet for bitter!

21 Woe unto *them that are* wise in their own eyes, and prudent in their own sight!

22 Woe unto *them that are* mighty to drink wine, and men of strength to mingle strong drink:

23 Which justify the wicked for reward, and take away the righteousness of the righteous from him!

24 Therefore as the fire devoureth the stubble, and the flame consumeth the chaff, *so* their root

---

5:1 *My wellbeloved.* Speaks of the intimate relationship between husband and wife (Song 1:14; 2:8–10,16; 5:4–6). *very fruitful hill.* Literally, "a horn, a son of oil," referring to a hillside or mountain spur that was located to provide the best exposure to the sun and the elements.

5:2 *fenced.* Or dug over by hoeing and weeding. Special effort was given to assure productivity. *tower.* To watch for intruders. *winepress.* Or vat, in anticipation of the fruit. *wild grapes.* Sour, worthless fruit of wild growth; contrary to expectation.

5:3 *betwixt.* Between.

5:5–6 *take away the hedge . . . wall.* The withdrawal of special care and protection. *briers and thorns.* An allusion to the fall of man into sin and death (Gen. 3:18).

5:7 *looked.* Waited in eager anticipation and expectancy. *judgment.* Justice. *oppression.* Breach of law.

Six Woes on the Worldly Hedonists (5:8–30)

5:8 *Woe.* Alas; see note at 1:4 (throughout the chapter). *join house to house.* The greedy taking of land (Mic. 2:2) that left many without their ancient inheritance (Num. 33:54) and thus exploited them.

5:9–10 Increasing holdings proved futile as God took away their profit. *bath.* About nine gallons. *homer.* Almost ten bushels. *ephah.* Almost one bushel.

5:11 *strong drink . . . wine.* Beverage produced from grain and the vine, respectively (v. 22).

5:12 *harp . . . viol.* Some sorts of stringed instruments. *tabret.* A hand-drum or tambourine. *pipe.* Or flute, a wind instrument. These people were self-indulgent pleasure seekers, having no thought for God and no concern for others.

5:14 *hell.* Hebrew, *sheol,* referring to death, the grave, or the abode of departed wicked spirits. The imagery here likely alludes to the episode of Korah (Num. 16:31–33). *enlarged.* Opened wide. *he that rejoiceth.* Exultant one. Ironically, those who loved to feast insatiably would find themselves metaphorically swallowed up by a ravenous earth.

5:15–16 *mean man . . . mighty man.* See note at 2:9. *the LORD of hosts . . . exalted.* God displays His absolute supremacy (*holy . . . sanctified;* 6:1–4), justice (*judgment*), and *righteousness* by humbling rebellious sinners.

5:17 *manner.* Pasture. *strangers.* Resident aliens.

5:18 *vanity.* Worthlessness.

5:23 *justify the wicked for reward.* Declare the guilty innocent for a bribe (Prov. 17:15; 24:24).

shall be as rottenness, and their blossom shall go
up as dust: because they have cast away the law of
the LORD of hosts, and despised the word of the
Holy One of Israel.
25 Therefore is the anger of the LORD kindled
against his people, and he hath stretched forth his
hand against them, and hath smitten them: and
the hills did tremble, and their carcases *were* torn
in the midst of the streets. For all this his anger is
not turned away, but his hand *is* stretched out still.
26 ¶ And he will lift up an ensign to the nations
from far, and will hiss unto them from the end of
the earth: and, behold, they shall come with speed
swiftly:
27 None shall be weary nor stumble among
them; none shall slumber nor sleep; neither shall
the girdle of their loins be loosed, nor the latchet
of their shoes be broken:
28 Whose arrows *are* sharp, and all their bows
bent, their horses' hoofs shall be counted like flint,
and their wheels like a whirlwind:
29 Their roaring *shall be* like a lion, they shall roar
like young lions: yea, they shall roar, and lay hold
of the prey, and shall carry *it* away safe, and none
shall deliver *it.*
30 And in that day they shall roar against them
like the roaring of the sea: and if *one* look unto the
land, behold darkness *and* sorrow, and the light is
darkened in the heavens thereof.

CHAPTER 6

IN the year that king Uzziah died I saw also the
Lord sitting upon a throne, high and lifted up,
and his train filled the temple.
2 Above it stood the seraphims: each one had six
wings; with twain he covered his face, and with
twain he covered his feet, and with twain he did fly.
3 And one cried unto another, and said, Holy,
holy, holy, *is* the LORD of hosts: the whole earth *is*
full of his glory.
4 And the posts of the door moved at the voice
of him that cried, and the house was filled with
smoke.
5 ¶ Then said I, Woe *is* me! for I am undone;
because I *am* a man of unclean lips, and I dwell
in the midst of a people of unclean lips: for mine
eyes have seen the King, the LORD of hosts.
6 Then flew one of the seraphims unto me,
having a live coal in his hand, *which* he had taken
with the tongs from off the altar:
7 And he laid *it* upon my mouth, and said, Lo,

5:24 *despised the word of the Holy One of Israel.* The root of their many sins was a rejection of the Lord and contempt for His Word (1:4); the beginning of repentance is trembling at the Word (66:2).
5:25 *hills did tremble.* Possibly an earthquake in the days of Uzziah (Amos 1:1; Zech. 14:5). *their carcases were torn.* Their corpses were as rubbish or dung.
5:26 *ensign.* A flag or standard. *hiss.* Summon by whistling.
5:27 *neither . . . girdle . . . be loosed.* The waistcloth will not be loosened. *latchet of their shoes.* The straps of their sandals. The agents of God's judgment will be tireless and prepared.
5:30 *in that day.* See 2:12; 3:18; 4:1–2.

Thoughts for Personal/Family Worship: Chapter 5

1. **The song of the vineyard illustrates Christ's teaching that "unto whomsoever much is given, of him shall be much required" (Luke 12:42). The song describes the great privileges of care, attention, and cultivation that the Lord provided. But notwithstanding the fact that every advantage was supplied, the vine produced wild and sour grapes. As a consequence the Lord left them vulnerable. In particular, this is a warning to all who grow up in a Christian environment to take advantage of the spiritual benefits. What kind of fruit are you producing: justice and righteousness or sin and oppression?**
2. **It would be profitable and sobering to compare the six woes in this chapter to the situation that exists in society today. Selfishness, hedonism, self-sufficiency, perverted thinking, arrogance, and a perverted legal system are as prevalent now as then. It is the sad fact that nearly all sense of right and wrong has been turned upside down as man has rejected God's law and authority (vv. 20,24). Yet the believer must never be discouraged. Our God reigns, and He will glorify His holiness and justice by humbling proud sinners. Though many admire proud rebels against God, this chapter teaches us to pity them and pray for their conversion.**

Chapter 6: *Isaiah sees the Lord and is informed that his message will go unheeded by the people.*

Isaiah's Vision of the Holy King (6:1–13)

6:1 *In the year that king Uzziah died.* Perhaps not the time of Isaiah's prophetic calling (1:1) but a special time of crisis. *Lord.* Not the divine name Jehovah but a title of sovereignty. *sitting upon a throne.* The earthly king was dead, but the heavenly King ruled. *high and lifted up.* A sign of absolute supremacy and superiority. *train.* The long, flowing robe symbolizing His presence. *temple.* The word also means "palace," which is more fitting for this scene.
6:2 *seraphims.* The "burning ones," the angelic attendants of the throne. *twain.* Two. They covered the *face* as a sign of reverence, the *feet* as a sign of humility, and *did fly* as sign of willing service.
6:3 *Holy, holy, holy.* The Hebrew uses repetition to express superlatives: infinite holiness is attributed to Him. God's holiness is not just His moral purity but His limitless superiority over all things in every way (40:25; Ex. 15:11), pictured in His being "high and lifted up" (v. 1; 57:15; Ps. 99:1–3). *full of his glory.* God's infinite majesty is fully present in every place, pictured in His royal "train" filling the temple (66:1).
6:4 *house was filled with smoke.* Another sign of God's glorious presence (Ex. 19:18).
6:5 *undone.* Either "silenced" or "ruined." *unclean lips.* The sin of the prophet and His people made them unfit to worship in God's presence, for holiness is utterly incompatible with uncleanness (Lev. 15:31; 16:16). *mine eyes have seen the King.* The New Testament indicates that He saw Christ (John 12:38–41).
6:6 *live coal . . . from off the altar.* The bronze altar of burnt offerings was the place where the priests killed sacrifices and burnt them before the Lord to make atonement for sin (Lev. 1).

this hath touched thy lips; and thine iniquity is
taken away, and thy sin purged.
8 Also I heard the voice of the Lord, saying,
Whom shall I send, and who will go for us? Then
said I, Here *am* I; send me.
9 ¶ And he said, Go, and tell this people, Hear ye
indeed, but understand not; and see ye indeed,
but perceive not.
10 Make the heart of this people fat, and make their
ears heavy, and shut their eyes; lest they see with
their eyes, and hear with their ears, and understand
with their heart, and convert, and be healed.
11 Then said I, Lord, how long? And he answered,
Until the cities be wasted without inhabitant, and
the houses without man, and the land be utterly
desolate,
12 And the LORD have removed men far away,
and *there be* a great forsaking in the midst of the
land.
13 ¶ But yet in it *shall be* a tenth, and *it* shall
return, and shall be eaten: as a teil tree, and as an
oak, whose substance *is* in them, when they cast
their leaves: so the holy seed *shall be* the substance
thereof.

CHAPTER 7

AND it came to pass in the days of Ahaz the son
of Jotham, the son of Uzziah, king of Judah, *that*
Rezin the king of Syria, and Pekah the son of Rem-
aliah, king of Israel, went up toward Jerusalem to
war against it, but could not prevail against it.
2 And it was told the house of David, saying,
Syria is confederate with Ephraim. And his heart
was moved, and the heart of his people, as the
trees of the wood are moved with the wind.
3 Then said the LORD unto Isaiah, Go forth now
to meet Ahaz, thou, and Shear-jashub thy son, at
the end of the conduit of the upper pool in the
highway of the fuller's field;
4 And say unto him, Take heed, and be quiet; fear
not, neither be fainthearted for the two tails of
these smoking firebrands, for the fierce anger of
Rezin with Syria, and of the son of Remaliah.
5 Because Syria, Ephraim, and the son of Rema-
liah, have taken evil counsel against thee, saying,
6 Let us go up against Judah, and vex it, and let us
make a breach therein for us, and set a king in the
midst of it, *even* the son of Tabeal:
7 Thus saith the Lord GOD, It shall not stand,
neither shall it come to pass.
8 For the head of Syria *is* Damascus, and the head
of Damascus *is* Rezin; and within threescore and
five years shall Ephraim be broken, that it be not
a people.
9 And the head of Ephraim *is* Samaria, and the
head of Samaria *is* Remaliah's son. If ye will not
believe, surely ye shall not be established.
10 ¶ Moreover the LORD spake again unto Ahaz,
saying,
11 Ask thee a sign of the LORD thy God; ask it
either in the depth, or in the height above.

6:7 *iniquity*. Guilt. *purged*. Atoned for.
6:8 *Whom shall I send . . . go for us*. This is the voice of the Lord; the use of the singular (*I*) and plural (*us*) implies that there is more than one person in the one God (Gen. 1:26).
6:10 *heart . . . fat*. Unresponsive to God and His Word. *ears heavy*. Dull of hearing. *shut their eyes*. Blind to spiritual truths (42:19–20). All these are the operations of God's judicial abandonment of the sinner to his own ways (Mark 4:12; John 12:39–40; Acts 28:25–27; cf. 29:10; Rom. 9:17–18; 11:7–10).
6:13 *teil*. A massive tree of some sort. *holy seed*. A remnant of the offspring of Abraham (Gen. 17:7; Ezra 9:2), chosen by God's grace (Rom. 11:5). *substance*. Stock or trunk of the tree, implying new growth (11:1). There is hope in the midst of gloom.

Thoughts for Personal/Family Worship: Chapter 6

Nothing is more necessary in times of crisis than a fresh experience of the Lord. Uzziah had ruled for more than fifty years, and now he was dead. The future was uncertain, and God had a special word for Isaiah that directed his ministry from that day forward. What God showed Isaiah is good for us to see as well. As you meditate through his vision, note the directions Isaiah received and the lessons he learned. First, he looked up to see that God is absolutely holy, sovereignly ruling from His glorious throne. Worshiping and serving Him are essential, as exemplified by the seraphim. Second, he looked inside himself to see his own uncleanness and unworthiness. Third, he looked to God's altar to see the greatness of God's grace that provided the cleansing and atonement for his sin. Finally, he looked outside to the world into which the Lord had sent him to preach. Though most people would reject Him, this too was God's will, but some would be saved as God's holy seed. How does each aspect of this vision apply to the church of Christ today?

Chapter 7: *Isaiah warns Ahaz against an ungodly alliance and encourages him with a sign to trust the Lord.*

Ahaz and the Promise of Immanuel (7:1–25)

7:2 *is confederate*. Has an alliance with; Hebrew, "rest or encamp with." *was moved*. Trembled.
7:3 *Shear-jashub*. Translated, "a remnant will return." *conduit*. A man-made aqueduct or channel. *highway*. A track or public road. *fuller's field*. The field of the one who washes clothes by beating or treading them.
7:4 *be quiet*. Be still and do not fret. *two tails of these smoking firebrands*. Two stumps or ends of the burning logs.
7:5 *taken evil counsel*. Planned to do you harm.
7:6 *vex*. Frighten, horrify, or cause a sickening dread. *make a breach*. Take by assault.
7:8 *threescore and five*. Sixty-five.
7:9 *not believe . . . not be established*. This has been called the prophet's thesis: the necessity of faith. In Hebrew, *believe* and *be established* are different forms of the same word: "if you do not trust the Lord's Word as being firmly established, indeed you will not be established."
7:11 *thee*. Singular, addressing Ahaz individually. *sign*. Or

12 But Ahaz said, I will not ask, neither will I
tempt the LORD.
13 And he said, Hear ye now, O house of David; *Is*
it a small thing for you to weary men, but will ye
weary my God also?
14 Therefore the Lord himself shall give you a
sign; Behold, a virgin shall conceive, and bear a
son, and shall call his name Immanuel.
15 Butter and honey shall he eat, that he may
know to refuse the evil, and choose the good.
16 For before the child shall know to refuse the
evil, and choose the good, the land that thou
abhorrest shall be forsaken of both her kings.
17 ¶ The LORD shall bring upon thee, and upon
thy people, and upon thy father's house, days
that have not come, from the day that Ephraim
departed from Judah; *even* the king of Assyria.
18 And it shall come to pass in that day, *that* the
LORD shall hiss for the fly that *is* in the uttermost
part of the rivers of Egypt, and for the bee that *is*
in the land of Assyria.
19 And they shall come, and shall rest all of them
in the desolate valleys, and in the holes of the
rocks, and upon all thorns, and upon all bushes.
20 In the same day shall the Lord shave with a
razor that is hired, *namely*, by them beyond the
river, by the king of Assyria, the head, and the hair
of the feet: and it shall also consume the beard.
21 And it shall come to pass in that day, *that* a
man shall nourish a young cow, and two sheep;
22 And it shall come to pass, for the abundance
of milk *that* they shall give he shall eat butter: for
butter and honey shall every one eat that is left in
the land.
23 And it shall come to pass in that day, *that* every
place shall be, where there were a thousand vines
at a thousand silverlings, it shall *even* be for briers
and thorns.
24 With arrows and with bows shall *men* come
thither; because all the land shall become briers
and thorns.
25 And *on* all hills that shall be digged with the
mattock, there shall not come thither the fear of
briers and thorns: but it shall be for the sending
forth of oxen, and for the treading of lesser cattle.

CHAPTER 8

MOREOVER the LORD said unto me, Take thee
a great roll, and write in it with a man's pen
concerning Maher-shalal-hash-baz.
2 And I took unto me faithful witnesses to
record, Uriah the priest, and Zechariah the son of
Jeberechiah.
3 And I went unto the prophetess; and she
conceived, and bare a son. Then said the LORD to
me, Call his name Maher-shalal-hash-baz.
4 For before the child shall have knowledge
to cry, My father, and my mother, the riches of
Damascus and the spoil of Samaria shall be taken
away before the king of Assyria.
5 ¶ The LORD spake also unto me again, saying,

---

omen, often supernatural. A sign functions either as a present persuader (Ex. 4:6–9) or as a confirmation after the fact (Ex. 3:12).

7:12 *tempt.* Put to the test.

7:13 *weary.* Exhaust the patience of. *my God.* Instead of "our God," implying that though Ahaz was a son of *David* his refusal to believe excluded him from the covenant of the Lord.

7:14 *you.* Plural (contrast v. 11). Since Ahaz rejected the sign God offered him individually for the present, God would *give* a sign to a far greater audience to confirm the truth of all that He has said. *virgin.* The only word used in the Old Testament to refer to a virgin in the strictest sense without any other qualification (Gen. 24:43); another word translated "virgin" requires the qualifying statement that the woman had not known a man (Gen. 24:16). That the word means "virgin" is confirmed by its translation by the Greek Septuagint. *Immanuel.* Translated, "God with us" (8:8,10; 41:10; 43:5). Like the miraculous birth of Isaac, to whom God said, "I am with thee" (Gen. 26:24), the birth of this child to a virgin would be a *sign* of God's grace and faithfulness to His people. This prophecy was fulfilled when God the Son became a man, Jesus, the son of Mary (9:6; Matt. 1:18–23; cf. Luke 1:31–35).

7:15 *Butter and honey.* Sometimes viewed as a diet of captivity, since these require no cultivation (vv. 21–22).

7:16 *child.* Perhaps one of Isaiah's children (v. 3; 8:3–4). By the time this boy reached the age of discernment the kings Ahaz feared would be gone.

7:18 *hiss.* Summon by whistling.

7:20 *shave.* Gesture of humiliation and embarrassment.

7:21–22 *abundance of milk.* An indication not of blessing but of the sparseness of inhabitants (the majority having been killed or taken into captivity); therefore, those few *left* have plenty.

7:23 *silverlings.* Silver coins, probably shekels.

7:25 *mattock.* A plow or hoe. *lesser cattle.* Small livestock like sheep or goats.

Thoughts for Personal/Family Worship: Chapter 7

What a blessed promise is conveyed in v. 14, and it is all the more wonderful to us, who view it from the perspective of the New Testament. The promise has been gloriously fulfilled: Immanuel, "God with us," has come, and we who are the recipients of His grace have the joy of Christ within us. What confidence this ought to bring to our souls; what consolation during times of troubles and trials! Our God is with us every step of the way and will lead us safely to our eternal rest. Let us therefore adore Him and praise Him. How can knowing that God's Son took our own flesh and blood assure believers that He will never leave nor forsake them?

Chapter 8: *Isaiah predicts the coming Assyrian invasion of Syria and Israel.*

Assyria's Flood and the Land of Immanuel (8:1–22)

8:1 *great roll.* A tablet, perhaps of metal, wood, leather, or papyrus. *pen.* Stylus for writing. *Maher-shalal-hash-baz.* Translated, "hasten [to the] spoil, swift [to the] prey" (v. 3).

8:4 *before the child shall have.* The time principle of 7:16.

8:6 *Forasmuch.* Because. *Shiloah.* A pool into which water

6 Forasmuch as this people refuseth the waters
of Shiloah that go softly, and rejoice in Rezin and
Remaliah's son;
7 Now therefore, behold, the Lord bringeth up
upon them the waters of the river, strong and
many, *even* the king of Assyria, and all his glory:
and he shall come up over all his channels, and go
over all his banks:
8 And he shall pass through Judah; he shall over-
flow and go over, he shall reach *even* to the neck;
and the stretching out of his wings shall fill the
breadth of thy land, O Immanuel.
9 ¶ Associate yourselves, O ye people, and ye
shall be broken in pieces; and give ear, all ye of far
countries: gird yourselves, and ye shall be broken
in pieces; gird yourselves, and ye shall be broken
in pieces.
10 Take counsel together, and it shall come to
nought; speak the word, and it shall not stand: for
God *is* with us.
11 ¶ For the LORD spake thus to me with a strong
hand, and instructed me that I should not walk in
the way of this people, saying,
12 Say ye not, A confederacy, to all *them to* whom
this people shall say, A confederacy; neither fear
ye their fear, nor be afraid.
13 Sanctify the LORD of hosts himself; and *let* him
be your fear, and *let* him *be* your dread.
14 And he shall be for a sanctuary; but for a stone
of stumbling and for a rock of offence to both the
houses of Israel, for a gin and for a snare to the
inhabitants of Jerusalem.
15 And many among them shall stumble, and fall,
and be broken, and be snared, and be taken.
16 Bind up the testimony, seal the law among my
disciples.
17 And I will wait upon the LORD, that hideth his
face from the house of Jacob, and I will look for
him.
18 Behold, I and the children whom the LORD
hath given me *are* for signs and for wonders in
Israel from the LORD of hosts, which dwelleth in
mount Zion.
19 ¶ And when they shall say unto you, Seek unto
them that have familiar spirits, and unto wizards
that peep, and that mutter: should not a people
seek unto their God? for the living to the dead?
20 To the law and to the testimony: if they speak
not according to this word, *it is* because *there is* no
light in them.
21 And they shall pass through it, hardly bestead
and hungry: and it shall come to pass, that when
they shall be hungry, they shall fret themselves,
and curse their king and their God, and look
upward.
22 And they shall look unto the earth; and behold
trouble and darkness, dimness of anguish; and
they shall be driven to darkness.

---

from the spring of Gihon flows. *go softly*. Flow gently.

8:7 *waters of the river*. Assyria was based around the Euphrates River, and thus this is an image of its king's *glory*.

8:8 *overflow*. The Lord brought Assyria to invade Judah, as a flooding river bursting its banks. *stretching out of his wings*. Like a bird of prey (Job 39:26); Judah would be a prey to the Assyrians. *Immanuel*. The virgin-born Lord (7:14) would come to a nation broken and impoverished by conquest, inheriting the suffering of His sinful people.

8:9 *Associate yourselves*. Close ranks, unite, or perhaps raise a war cry. *gird yourselves*. To secure oneself with a belt, an image for preparing for action.

8:10 *God is with us*. Hebrew, *immanuel* (v. 8; 7:14). God's presence remains their hope.

8:12–13 *confederacy*. Conspiracy. *Sanctify*. Treat Him as holy (6:1–4) by fearing Him with one's whole heart. Believers should not allow the fear of man to toss them about but should be steady in hope because they fear the Lord (1 Peter 3:14–15).

8:14 *sanctuary*. The holy place of God's presence in the temple. For the Lord to become the sanctuary implies that He will be with His people in a new and greater way (7:14; John 1:14; 2:19–21). *stone of stumbling*. An obstacle that makes people fall. *gin*. A trapping net for birds. *snare*. A concealed trap. The same Lord who is the confidence of believers is the obstacle that destroys unbelievers (Rom. 9:33; 1 Peter 2:8; cf. Luke 2:34)

8:15 *snared*. Caught by bait.

8:16 *my disciples*. My pupils or those who are taught by Me.

8:17 *wait*. Long for. *hideth his face*. A gesture expressing displeasure. *look*. Wait or hope with eager expectation.

8:18 *children whom the LORD hath given me*. Most likely the disciples (v. 16) whom God drew to the prophet to listen to and follow him (59:21; 2 Kings 2:12; 1 Tim. 1:2; 3 John 4). Christ, who spoke through the prophets (1 Peter 2:11), received His disciples as His spiritual family (Heb. 2:13). *signs and for wonders*. Or symbols and tokens (20:3). Their faithfulness to God's Word was a visible demonstration of the truth of His coming judgment and salvation (Phil. 1:27–28; 2 Thess. 1:4–5), like the plagues of Egypt (Ex. 7:3).

8:19 *familiar spirits*. Demons supposedly under the influence of man. *wizards*. Soothsayers or those who had a spirit of divination. *peep*. Chirp or whisper.

8:20 *law . . . testimony*. The Holy Scriptures are the only source of spiritual *light* (2:5; Ps. 119:105). Therefore we should not listen to messages purportedly from spirits (v. 19).

8:21–22 *hardly bestead*. Hard pressed or greatly distressed. *fret themselves*. To put themselves in a rage. *trouble*. Distress or anxiety. *dimness of anguish*. Gloom of distress or pressure. *driven to darkness*. Thrust into calamity. Even as God casts the wicked into the darkness of His wrath, they continue to curse Him (Rev. 16:10–11).

Thoughts for Personal/Family Worship: Chapter 8

1. **As believers, when the Lord appears to hide His face from us in difficult times, we must say with Isaiah, "I will wait upon the LORD" (v. 17). Let us remember that He is with us. This is not resignation to whatever will be but a vibrant and expectant faith. Rather than fear what the plans and conspiracies of men may do, let us fear the Lord alone. Let us call upon Him in prayer and plead with Him, for if we wait with patience He will surely come to us and guide us every step of the way.**
2. **"To the law and to the testimony" should be our regular**

CHAPTER 9

NEVERTHELESS the dimness *shall* not *be* such as
was in her vexation, when at the first he lightly
afflicted the land of Zebulun and the land of
Naphtali, and afterward did more grievously
afflict *her by* the way of the sea, beyond Jordan, in
Galilee of the nations.
2 The people that walked in darkness have seen
a great light: they that dwell in the land of the
shadow of death, upon them hath the light shined.
3 Thou hast multiplied the nation, *and* not
increased the joy: they joy before thee according
to the joy in harvest, *and* as *men* rejoice when they
divide the spoil.
4 For thou hast broken the yoke of his burden,
and the staff of his shoulder, the rod of his
oppressor, as in the day of Midian.
5 For every battle of the warrior *is* with confused
noise, and garments rolled in blood; but *this* shall
be with burning *and* fuel of fire.
6 For unto us a child is born, unto us a son is
given: and the government shall be upon his
shoulder: and his name shall be called Wonderful,
Counsellor, The mighty God, The everlasting
Father, The Prince of Peace.
7 Of the increase of *his* government and peace
there shall be no end, upon the throne of David,
and upon his kingdom, to order it, and to
establish it with judgment and with justice from
henceforth even for ever. The zeal of the LORD of
hosts will perform this.
8 ¶ The Lord sent a word into Jacob, and it hath
lighted upon Israel.
9 And all the people shall know, *even* Ephraim
and the inhabitant of Samaria, that say in the
pride and stoutness of heart,
10 The bricks are fallen down, but we will build
with hewn stones: the sycomores are cut down,
but we will change *them into* cedars.
11 Therefore the LORD shall set up the adversar-
ies of Rezin against him, and join his enemies
together;
12 The Syrians before, and the Philistines behind;
and they shall devour Israel with open mouth.
For all this his anger is not turned away, but his
hand *is* stretched out still.
13 ¶ For the people turneth not unto him that
smiteth them, neither do they seek the LORD of
hosts.
14 Therefore the LORD will cut off from Israel
head and tail, branch and rush, in one day.
15 The ancient and honourable, he *is* the head;
and the prophet that teacheth lies, he *is* the tail.
16 For the leaders of this people cause *them* to
err; and *they that are* led of them *are* destroyed.
17 Therefore the Lord shall have no joy in
their young men, neither shall have mercy on
their fatherless and widows: for every one *is* an
hypocrite and an evildoer, and every mouth
speaketh folly. For all this his anger is not turned
away, but his hand *is* stretched out still.
18 ¶ For wickedness burneth as the fire: it shall

---

practice (v. 20). Christians believe that the Bible is our only divine rule for what we are to believe and do. The Bible must be the touchstone for everything. It is our lamp enabling us to see and our guide to follow. God's Word will teach us how to discern; its counsel may go contrary to popular opinions and practices, but it is the absolute truth. In a world caught up in all kinds of false spirituality, how can we walk in the light of the Bible every day?

Chapter 9: *The child to be born shines light into the darkness.*

The Reign of the Messiah (9:1–7)

9:1–2 *Nevertheless the dimness . . . vexation.* Literally, "But no gloom to the one who had distress." *lightly afflicted.* Belittled or treated with contempt. *more grievously afflict.* Or honor. *Galilee.* A region in northern Israel, its name meaning "district," often influenced or ruled by Gentiles (*nations*; 1 Kings 9:11; 2 Kings 15:29; 17:6). *shadow of death.* Total, extreme darkness. Christ fulfilled this prophecy (Matt. 4:12–16).

9:3 *not increased the joy.* Or "increased joy to it," referring to the nation.

9:4 *day of Midian.* See Judg. 7–8.

9:5 *every battle . . . confused noise.* Literally, "every boot of the one marching in roar or din." *rolled.* Stained.

9:6 *unto us.* For our benefit. *a child is born.* The virgin-born Immanuel (7:14). *a son is given.* God appointed and sent His Son to be the promised Son of David (v. 7; 2 Sam. 7:12–15; Ps. 2:7; John 3:16; Gal. 4:4). Four titles reflect His deity and gracious work as Mediator. *Wonderful, Counsellor.* Extraordinary revealer of divine wisdom (25:1; 28:29), of whom Solomon was a shadow (1 Kings 10:23–24). *The mighty God.* God, the powerful defender (42:13); a phrase used only of the Lord God (10:20–21; Deut. 10:17; Neh. 9:32; Jer. 32:18; Zeph. 3:17). *everlasting Father.* "The Father of eternity," not referring to the Son's relationship to the Father in the Trinity but to the Son's benevolent authority and eternal care of His people (22:21; 63:16). *The Prince of Peace.* Not a king-in-waiting but the chief ruler and administrator of peace; His work of reconciling sinners into harmony with God and each other (48:22; 53:5; 59:7–8).

9:7 *judgment . . . justice.* Justice and righteousness, key qualities of the reign of the Son of *David* (2 Sam. 8:15; 1 Kings 10:9; Jer. 23:5; see note at Isa. 1:16–17). *no end.* In contrast to the quickly passing reigns of earthly kings (1:1; 6:1), this King will reign forever (Luke 1:32–33). *zeal of the LORD.* God's burning love for His own glory (42:8; 48:11).

His Hand Is Stretched Out Still (9:8—10:4)

9:8 *lighted.* Fell.

9:9 *stoutness.* Arrogance or insolence.

9:10 *hewn.* Cut.

9:12 *his anger is not turned away, but his hand is stretched out still.* This repeated refrain indicates that despite all God's discipline the people remained unrepentant and under His wrath (vv. 12,17,21; 10:4; cf. 5:25).

9:13 *turneth not.* See note at 1:6.

9:15 *ancient.* The elder, as a representative leader.

9:17 *neither shall have mercy.* Will not pity or show compassion. *hypocrite.* A godless or profane person. *folly.* Willful sin or sacrilege.

CHRIST'S KINGDOM

The kingdom of God is His rule and reign over all things; it arises from His nature as King (Ps. 99:1–5; 1 Tim. 1:17). God is staggeringly majestic (Isa. 6:1–7). He is the incomparable King of glory, all-sufficient, controlling life and death, infinitely holy, a boundless ocean of love (2 Sam. 2:2–10; Ps. 136:1–3). God created the world in order to make a kingdom for His Son (Heb. 1:2). Since Christ is the heir of the world, His kingdom will gather all nations together through the gospel (Matt. 24:14).

Christ brings His kingdom step by step in history. God's promise of the universal extension of Christ's kingdom (Dan. 7:13–14) is realized through progressive fulfillment every time Christ acts in the world for salvation and judgment. The kingdom of Christ opposes and overcomes the kingdom of Satan (Luke 11:18–22). Satan attempted to set up a rival kingdom, usurping the Creator's dominion on earth (Gen. 3:1–6; Job 1:7; cf. Isa. 14:12–14). Christ took up His office immediately upon the fall of man (Gen. 3:15), and whenever God appeared to men it was the Son who came (John 1:18). David was the greatest personal type of Christ (Ezek. 34:24), and the establishment of the kingdom of David and his sons was God's planting of the root from which the messianic Branch would come (2 Sam. 7:12–14; Isa. 11:1; Jer. 23:5). The Old Testament as a whole was preparation for the arrival of the kingdom when the great King and Savior came in the flesh (Isa. 9:6–7).

The kingdom springs from Christ's work in dying and rising again. By His death on the cross Christ conquered the powers of evil, slaying the spiritual Goliath with his own sword (John 12:31; 16:11; Col. 2:15; Heb. 2:14). Yet Christ's redemption is not first and foremost a victory over Satan but a purchase (Mark 10:45); His humiliation was the price necessary to satisfy God's law (Gal. 3:10,13; 4:4–5). The kingdom officially began after Christ's resurrection, when He ascended into heaven, sat down at God's right hand, and poured out the Spirit to empower His church to take the gospel to all nations (Acts 1:6–9; 2:23–36).

The essence of Christ's redemptive kingdom is the Spirit (Isa. 11:1–2). The Father gave the Redeemer, the Son purchased redemption, and the Spirit is the blessing purchased (Gal. 3:13–14; 4:4–6)—Trinitarian redemption. In His Spirit the exalted King is conquering the Devil on earth, especially in converting and sanctifying the elect (Rom. 5:17,21; 14:17; Rev. 17:14). Conversion delivers a sinner out of the kingdom of the Devil and sin and translates him into the kingdom of Christ (Rom. 6:14,17; Col. 1:13).

The context of the kingdom is the church, where Christ's royal power operates (Matt. 16:16–19; 18:20; 1 Cor. 4:19–21; 5:3–5; 2 Cor. 13:1–4). Christ rules His people externally through His Word and officers (John 18:36–37; Eph. 4:10–11) and internally by the influences of His grace, which make His people willing to obey by His power (Ps. 110:3). When Christ revives His church, believers rejoice to see the goings of their God and King in His sanctuary (Ps. 68:24). However, not all in the visible kingdom of Christ, the church, belong there; some are like bad fish caught in the net, which will be thrown away in the final judgment (Matt. 13:47–50).

God promised to extend Christ's kingdom over every nation (Ps. 72:8–11). The satanic kingdoms of this world and its false religions will all ultimately fail (Dan. 2:44; 7:9–14), and Christ will reign as "King of kings and Lord of lords" (Rev. 19:16). The kingdom will reach its ultimate realization in the happiness and holiness of eternal life when Christ returns in glory (Matt. 13:43). In one sense Christ's mediatorial work will be done and He will hand over the kingdom to His Father (1 Cor. 15:28). However, in another sense He will reign as never before in the hearts of His people, who will be with Him to behold the King in His glory to their eternal delight (Isa. 33:17; John 17:24; Titus 2:13).

—adapted from Jonathan Edwards, *A History of the Work of Redemption*

devour the briers and thorns, and shall kindle in
the thickets of the forest, and they shall mount up
like the lifting up of smoke.
19 Through the wrath of the LORD of hosts is the
land darkened, and the people shall be as the fuel
of the fire: no man shall spare his brother.
20 And he shall snatch on the right hand, and be
hungry; and he shall eat on the left hand, and they
shall not be satisfied: they shall eat every man the
flesh of his own arm:
21 Manasseh, Ephraim; and Ephraim, Manasseh:
and they together *shall be* against Judah. For all
this his anger is not turned away, but his hand *is*
stretched out still.

CHAPTER 10

WOE unto them that decree unrighteous decrees,
and that write grievousness *which* they have
prescribed;
2 To turn aside the needy from judgment, and to
take away the right from the poor of my people,
that widows may be their prey, and *that* they may
rob the fatherless!
3 And what will ye do in the day of visitation, and
in the desolation *which* shall come from far? to
whom will ye flee for help? and where will ye leave
your glory?
4 Without me they shall bow down under the
prisoners, and they shall fall under the slain. For
all this his anger is not turned away, but his hand
is stretched out still.
5 ¶ O Assyrian, the rod of mine anger, and the
staff in their hand is mine indignation.
6 I will send him against an hypocritical nation,
and against the people of my wrath will I give him
a charge, to take the spoil, and to take the prey, and
to tread them down like the mire of the streets.
7 Howbeit he meaneth not so, neither doth his
heart think so; but *it is* in his heart to destroy and
cut off nations not a few.
8 For he saith, *Are* not my princes altogether
kings?
9 *Is* not Calno as Carchemish? *is* not Hamath as
Arpad? *is* not Samaria as Damascus?
10 As my hand hath found the kingdoms of the
idols, and whose graven images did excel them of
Jerusalem and of Samaria;
11 Shall I not, as I have done unto Samaria and
her idols, so do to Jerusalem and her idols?
12 Wherefore it shall come to pass, *that* when
the Lord hath performed his whole work upon
mount Zion and on Jerusalem, I will punish the
fruit of the stout heart of the king of Assyria, and
the glory of his high looks.
13 For he saith, By the strength of my hand I have
done *it*, and by my wisdom; for I am prudent: and
I have removed the bounds of the people, and
have robbed their treasures, and I have put down
the inhabitants like a valiant *man*:
14 And my hand hath found as a nest the riches
of the people: and as one gathereth eggs *that are*
left, have I gathered all the earth; and there was
none that moved the wing, or opened the mouth,
or peeped.
15 Shall the axe boast itself against him that
heweth therewith? *or* shall the saw magnify itself
against him that shaketh it? as if the rod should
shake *itself* against them that lift it up, *or* as if the
staff should lift up *itself*, *as if it were* no wood.

9:19 *the LORD of hosts.* God as the Commander of all things in heaven and earth, especially of His armies of angels and believers.

Thoughts for Personal/Family Worship: Chapter 9

1. **The heart of Isaiah's Immanuel trilogy (v. 6) details the amazing difference Christ's presence makes in the world. When Isaiah issued this prophecy, the nation was in the darkness of Assyrian domination and oppression. With prophetic insight he saw a time when those in darkness would see a great light. The presence of Christ changes everything; He always shines light into darkness. What was true for Galilee during Christ's earthly ministry is true in every individual to whom the light of the glorious gospel shines. Christ makes a difference. Is He shining in your heart?**
2. **Jesus is the wise counselor to the foolish and ignorant, bringing them the very wisdom of God. He is the powerful defender of the weak and oppressed, rescuing them from their enemies. He is the loving father of the orphans and isolated, caring for them forever. He is the peaceful ruler over those who have known only conflict with God, others, and themselves. Which of the four titles for Christ (v. 6) is most helpful to you now? How can you take hold of it and use it to walk by faith in Him?**

Chapter 10: *The Lord humbles Assyria after they fulfilled His purpose of chastising Israel.*

10:3 *day of visitation.* Day of vengeance or punishment.
10:4 *his hand is stretched out still.* See note at 9:12.

God's Use and Judgment of Assyria (10:5–34)

10:5 *rod of mine anger.* Assyria was an instrument of justice and discipline in the Lord's hands (2 Sam. 7:14).
10:6 *hypocritical.* Godless or profane. *give him a charge.* Command him. God did not communicate this command through His prophets to the Assyrians but decreed it in His eternal will (Lam. 3:37–38). *prey.* Plunder or booty.
10:7 *meaneth not.* Does not intend. Though he was an instrument of God's providence, he acted not out of obedience to God but out of his own sinful ambitions (Gen. 50:20).
10:9 *Calno . . . Damascus.* Already conquered cities; now boasting that others are sure to fall.
10:12 *stout.* Arrogant or insolent. The Lord's use of Assyria for His holy purposes does not excuse their sins (Rom. 9:19); they will suffer His just punishment (Luke 22:22).
10:13 *bounds.* Borders.
10:14 *peeped.* Twittered or chirped.
10:15 *Shall the axe boast.* The greatest men on earth are just tools in the Lord's hands and have no power in themselves (Dan. 2:20–21). Therefore the glory for all ability and success

16 Therefore shall the Lord, the Lord of hosts,
send among his fat ones leanness; and under his
glory he shall kindle a burning like the burning
of a fire.
17 And the light of Israel shall be for a fire, and
his Holy One for a flame: and it shall burn and
devour his thorns and his briers in one day;
18 And shall consume the glory of his forest, and
of his fruitful field, both soul and body: and they
shall be as when a standardbearer fainteth.
19 And the rest of the trees of his forest shall be
few, that a child may write them.
20 ¶ And it shall come to pass in that day, *that*
the remnant of Israel, and such as are escaped
of the house of Jacob, shall no more again stay
upon him that smote them; but shall stay upon
the LORD, the Holy One of Israel, in truth.
21 The remnant shall return, *even* the remnant of
Jacob, unto the mighty God.
22 For though thy people Israel be as the sand
of the sea, *yet* a remnant of them shall return:
the consumption decreed shall overflow with
righteousness.
23 For the Lord GOD of hosts shall make a con-
sumption, even determined, in the midst of all
the land.
24 ¶ Therefore thus saith the Lord GOD of hosts,
O my people that dwellest in Zion, be not afraid
of the Assyrian: he shall smite thee with a rod, and
shall lift up his staff against thee, after the manner
of Egypt.
25 For yet a very little while, and the indignation
shall cease, and mine anger in their destruction.
26 And the LORD of hosts shall stir up a scourge
for him according to the slaughter of Midian at
the rock of Oreb: and *as* his rod *was* upon the sea,
so shall he lift it up after the manner of Egypt.
27 And it shall come to pass in that day, *that* his
burden shall be taken away from off thy shoulder,
and his yoke from off thy neck, and the yoke shall
be destroyed because of the anointing.
28 He is come to Aiath, he is passed to Migron; at
Michmash he hath laid up his carriages:
29 They are gone over the passage: they have
taken up their lodging at Geba; Ramah is afraid;
Gibeah of Saul is fled.
30 Lift up thy voice, O daughter of Gallim: cause
it to be heard unto Laish, O poor Anathoth.
31 Madmenah is removed; the inhabitants of
Gebim gather themselves to flee.
32 As yet shall he remain at Nob that day: he shall
shake his hand *against* the mount of the daughter
of Zion, the hill of Jerusalem.
33 Behold, the Lord, the LORD of hosts, shall
lop the bough with terror: and the high ones of
stature *shall be* hewn down, and the haughty shall
be humbled.
34 And he shall cut down the thickets of the forest
with iron, and Lebanon shall fall by a mighty
one.

CHAPTER 11

AND there shall come forth a rod out of the stem
of Jesse, and a Branch shall grow out of his roots:
2 And the spirit of the LORD shall rest upon him,

must go to God. *heweth*. Cuts down. *shaketh*. Moves back and forth.

10:18 *standardbearer fainteth*. Hebrew, "one who is sick wastes away."

10:20 *stay*. Lean or depend.

10:21 *remnant*. A designation for true believers. *mighty God*. The context makes it clear that this refers to the Lord, Jehovah (v. 20).

10:22–23 *sand of the sea*. An allusion to God's promise to Abraham that He would greatly multiply His offspring (Gen. 22:17; 32:12), physically fulfilled in the early monarchy (1 Kings 4:20). *consumption*. Destruction. God seemingly reverses His promise here, as He judges most of the physical offspring of Abraham for their sins while saving a godly *remnant* (Rom. 9:27–28; cf. 48:19–20; Hos. 1:10).

10:26 *stir up a scourge*. Set a whip in motion. *Midian*. See Judg. 7:25; 9:4.

10:27 *anointing*. The face of fat, picturing the fattened neck of the ox that breaks off the yoke.

10:28 *carriages*. Vessels, burdens, or baggage.

10:29 *passage*. Gorge or mountain pass.

10:34 *iron*. Axe.

Thoughts for Personal/Family Worship: Chapter 10

There are many things happening in the world that are a great discouragement to the Lord's people, and these things become all the more difficult when they affect us personally. It is at such times that we must remember that our lives are in God's hands and that "all things work together for good to them that love God" (Rom. 8:28). The Lord reigns over the most wicked of men. They can only do His will, though they do not intend it, and in the end He will punish them for their sins. Let us take great comfort in this when trials and tribulations come upon us. The Lord chastens us only for our good. We may face the rod, which may be in the form of an enemy, just as Israel faced the Assyrian army, but let us remember that the rod is in the Lord's hand. He is ultimately in control. The heaviness of our trials is but for "a season" (1 Peter 1:6).

The Spirit-Filled King and the Joy of Israel (11:1—12:6)

Chapter 11: *The coming of the Messiah, Israel's true King, will bring peace and prosperity to His people.*

11:1 *rod*. Twig or shoot. *stem of Jesse*. Bypassing the connection to royal David and linking Him to pre-royal Jesse intensifies the lowly life and humble origin of the Messiah. *Branch*. A different word from the one in 4:2 (see note there) but much the same idea, referring to the offshoot or suckling that is usually discarded. The Hebrew spelling of this word (*nêtzer*) may be the basis for Matthew's reference to Christ as a Nazarene (Matt. 2:23). Each term speaks to the humanity and humiliation of the Messiah.

11:2 *spirit of the LORD*. Evidence of messianic anointing (61:1; Matt. 3:16; John 1:32–33; 3:34; Acts 10:38).

the spirit of wisdom and understanding, the spirit
of counsel and might, the spirit of knowledge and
of the fear of the LORD;
3 And shall make him of quick understanding
in the fear of the LORD: and he shall not judge
after the sight of his eyes, neither reprove after the
hearing of his ears:
4 But with righteousness shall he judge the poor,
and reprove with equity for the meek of the earth:
and he shall smite the earth with the rod of his
mouth, and with the breath of his lips shall he slay
the wicked.
5 And righteousness shall be the girdle of his
loins, and faithfulness the girdle of his reins.
6 The wolf also shall dwell with the lamb, and the
leopard shall lie down with the kid; and the calf
and the young lion and the fatling together; and a
little child shall lead them.
7 And the cow and the bear shall feed; their
young ones shall lie down together: and the lion
shall eat straw like the ox.
8 And the sucking child shall play on the hole of
the asp, and the weaned child shall put his hand
on the cockatrice' den.
9 They shall not hurt nor destroy in all my holy
mountain: for the earth shall be full of the knowl-
edge of the LORD, as the waters cover the sea.
10 ¶ And in that day there shall be a root of Jesse,
which shall stand for an ensign of the people;
to it shall the Gentiles seek: and his rest shall be
glorious.
11 And it shall come to pass in that day, *that* the
Lord shall set his hand again the second time to
recover the remnant of his people, which shall
be left, from Assyria, and from Egypt, and from
Pathros, and from Cush, and from Elam, and
from Shinar, and from Hamath, and from the
islands of the sea.
12 And he shall set up an ensign for the nations,
and shall assemble the outcasts of Israel, and
gather together the dispersed of Judah from the
four corners of the earth.
13 The envy also of Ephraim shall depart, and
the adversaries of Judah shall be cut off: Ephraim
shall not envy Judah, and Judah shall not vex
Ephraim.
14 But they shall fly upon the shoulders of the
Philistines toward the west; they shall spoil them
of the east together: they shall lay their hand upon
Edom and Moab; and the children of Ammon
shall obey them.
15 And the LORD shall utterly destroy the tongue
of the Egyptian sea; and with his mighty wind
shall he shake his hand over the river, and shall
smite it in the seven streams, and make *men* go
over dryshod.
16 And there shall be an highway for the remnant
of his people, which shall be left, from Assyria;
like as it was to Israel in the day that he came up
out of the land of Egypt.

CHAPTER 12

AND in that day thou shalt say, O LORD, I will
praise thee: though thou wast angry with me,
thine anger is turned away, and thou comfortedst
me.
2 Behold, God *is* my salvation; I will trust, and not
be afraid: for the LORD JEHOVAH *is* my strength
and *my* song; he also is become my salvation.

11:3 *make him of quick understanding.* Literally, "his smelling is in/by the fear of the Lord," referring either to His discernment or His delight. Not judging by sight (*eyes*) or sound (*ears*) suggests discernment.
11:4 *breath.* The Hebrew word also means "spirit"; the Holy Spirit is the divine agent of both salvation and judgment through the words (*mouth* and *lips*) of the Messiah (34:16; 59:21).
11:5 *girdle.* A waistcloth around the hips secured with a belt, a symbol of being prepared. The Messiah is ready for any adversary. *reins.* Loins or waist.
11:6–9 *wolf . . . lamb.* A symbolic and idyllic scene of peace and tranquility, paradise restored, and the curse removed.
11:8 *cockatrice.* Viper or adder.
11:10 *ensign.* A banner to rally the nations together around Him (v. 12).
11:11 *second time.* A new or second exodus. Note the imagery that follows (v. 15).
11:13 *vex.* Cause hostility.
11:15 *tongue.* A gulf or bay. *dryshod.* In sandals, meaning with dry feet.

Thoughts for Personal/Family Worship: Chapter 11
This is the third part of Isaiah's Immanuel trilogy and provides another opportunity to worship Christ for His person and work. Think of Christ along these lines. First, consider the mystery of the God-man. The focus is principally on the humiliation of the incarnation. For God to be with us (Immanuel) meant that God in the Person of the Son condescended very low (v. 1). What a mystery in His mercy! Second, consider the power of the God-man. The Father has fully equipped Him for all His mediatorial duties by the Holy Spirit (v. 2). Third, consider the work of the God-man. He saves His people, destroys sinners, and judges infallibly (vv. 3–5). Our destiny is directly linked to our response to Him. Surely we can trust this Savior completely. What reasons does this chapter give us to trust the Lord Jesus with all our hearts?

Chapter 12: *Experiencing God's salvation is reason to praise Him.*

12:1 *in that day.* The day of deliverance. *thine anger is turned away.* See 54:9–10.
12:2 *trust.* Place confidence in, find security. *the LORD JEHOVAH.* The Hebrew is *Yah Jehovah*, where the first word is an abbreviation for the same divine name (26:4), as in the end of *Hallelujah*, or "Praise ye the *LORD*" (Ps. 104:35). *my strength . . . song . . . salvation.* The praise of Moses after God saved Israel at the Red Sea (Ex. 15:2). Isaiah proclaims a second exodus that is just as much cause for praise as the first (11:11,15).

3 Therefore with joy shall ye draw water out of
the wells of salvation.
4 And in that day shall ye say, Praise the LORD,
call upon his name, declare his doings among the
people, make mention that his name is exalted.
5 Sing unto the LORD; for he hath done excellent
things: this *is* known in all the earth.
6 Cry out and shout, thou inhabitant of Zion: for
great *is* the Holy One of Israel in the midst of thee.

CHAPTER 13

THE burden of Babylon, which Isaiah the son of
Amoz did see.
2 Lift ye up a banner upon the high mountain,
exalt the voice unto them, shake the hand, that
they may go into the gates of the nobles.
3 I have commanded my sanctified ones, I have
also called my mighty ones for mine anger, *even*
them that rejoice in my highness.
4 The noise of a multitude in the mountains, like
as of a great people; a tumultuous noise of the
kingdoms of nations gathered together: the LORD
of hosts mustereth the host of the battle.
5 They come from a far country, from the end
of heaven, *even* the LORD, and the weapons of his
indignation, to destroy the whole land.
6 ¶ Howl ye; for the day of the LORD *is* at hand;
it shall come as a destruction from the Almighty.
7 Therefore shall all hands be faint, and every
man's heart shall melt:
8 And they shall be afraid: pangs and sorrows
shall take hold of them; they shall be in pain as a
woman that travaileth: they shall be amazed one
at another; their faces *shall be as* flames.
9 Behold, the day of the LORD cometh, cruel
both with wrath and fierce anger, to lay the land
desolate: and he shall destroy the sinners thereof
out of it.
10 For the stars of heaven and the constellations
thereof shall not give their light: the sun shall be
darkened in his going forth, and the moon shall
not cause her light to shine.
11 And I will punish the world for *their* evil, and
the wicked for their iniquity; and I will cause the
arrogancy of the proud to cease, and will lay low
the haughtiness of the terrible.
12 I will make a man more precious than fine
gold; even a man than the golden wedge of Ophir.
13 Therefore I will shake the heavens, and the
earth shall remove out of her place, in the wrath
of the LORD of hosts, and in the day of his fierce
anger.
14 And it shall be as the chased roe, and as a sheep
that no man taketh up: they shall every man turn
to his own people, and flee every one into his own
land.
15 Every one that is found shall be thrust through;
and every one that is joined *unto them* shall fall by
the sword.
16 Their children also shall be dashed to pieces
before their eyes; their houses shall be spoiled,
and their wives ravished.
17 Behold, I will stir up the Medes against them,
which shall not regard silver; and *as for* gold, they
shall not delight in it.
18 *Their* bows also shall dash the young men to
pieces; and they shall have no pity on the fruit of

12:3 *wells.* Headwaters or spring.
12:4 *name.* Who God has revealed Himself to be in all His perfections. *doings.* Acts or deeds.

Thoughts for Personal/Family Worship: Chapter 12

How wonderful it is for the believer to know that God's anger is turned away because Christ has stood in the sinner's place! He has done for us what we could never have done for ourselves. He has delivered and "hath triumphed gloriously" (Ex. 15:1). What a comfort it ought to be to our souls that we can declare with Isaiah, "Behold, God is my salvation; I will trust, and not be afraid" (v. 2) When the Word of God speaks to our hearts it should thrill us. We ought to be like those two disciples on the road to Emmaus who declared, "Did not our heart burn within us, while he [Jesus] talked with us by the way, and while he opened to us the scriptures?" (Luke 24:32). Do you have a desire to praise God and declare His great works to others? Why or why not? What motives does this chapter give believers to stir such a desire?

ORACLES AGAINST THE NATIONS (13:1—23:18)

The Day of the Lord against Babylon (13:1—14:23)

Chapter 13: ***Isaiah's prophecies concerning the fall of Babylon by the Medes.***

13:1 *burden.* Oracle or utterance.
13:2 *shake.* Wave, so as to attract attention.
13:3 *sanctified ones.* Those set apart by God for a particular task.
13:4 *mustereth the host.* Assembles the troops or army for battle.
13:6 *Howl.* Or lament. *day of the LORD.* The time of divine intervention (v. 9; see note at 2:12). Isaiah particularly focuses here on God's judgment on Babylon (v. 19) for the salvation of Israel (14:1), which was a type of the final "day" at the end of the age.
13:8 *travaileth.* Is in labor. *be amazed.* Stare at each other in astonishment.
13:10 *stars . . . sun shall be darkened.* Cosmic disruptions ultimately fulfilled at Christ's second coming (Matt. 24:29; Rev. 6:12–13).
13:11 *terrible.* The ruthless tyrant.
13:12 *precious.* Rare or scarce. *Ophir.* A region thought to be in what is now Saudi Arabia that was famous for the quality of its gold (1 Kings 9:28; 10:11; 22:48).
13:14 *chased roe.* A gazelle being hunted. *sheep that no man taketh up.* Like sheep without a shepherd (1 Kings 22:17).
13:15 *every one that is joined.* Those who were carried away or captured.
13:17 *Medes.* Babylonia fell to the Medo-Persian forces in 539 BC (21:2; Jer. 51:11,28). Isaiah had predicted this almost

the womb; their eye shall not spare children.
19 ¶ And Babylon, the glory of kingdoms, the
beauty of the Chaldees' excellency, shall be as
when God overthrew Sodom and Gomorrah.
20 It shall never be inhabited, neither shall it be
dwelt in from generation to generation: neither
shall the Arabian pitch tent there; neither shall the
shepherds make their fold there.
21 But wild beasts of the desert shall lie there;
and their houses shall be full of doleful creatures;
and owls shall dwell there, and satyrs shall dance
there.
22 And the wild beasts of the islands shall cry
in their desolate houses, and dragons in *their*
pleasant palaces: and her time *is* near to come,
and her days shall not be prolonged.

CHAPTER 14

FOR the LORD will have mercy on Jacob, and will
yet choose Israel, and set them in their own land:
and the strangers shall be joined with them, and
they shall cleave to the house of Jacob.
2 And the people shall take them, and bring them
to their place: and the house of Israel shall possess
them in the land of the LORD for servants and
handmaids: and they shall take them captives,
whose captives they were; and they shall rule over
their oppressors.
3 And it shall come to pass in the day that the
LORD shall give thee rest from thy sorrow, and
from thy fear, and from the hard bondage wherein
thou wast made to serve,
4 ¶ That thou shalt take up this proverb against
the king of Babylon, and say, How hath the
oppressor ceased! the golden city ceased!
5 The LORD hath broken the staff of the wicked,
and the sceptre of the rulers.
6 He who smote the people in wrath with a
continual stroke, he that ruled the nations in
anger, is persecuted, *and* none hindereth.
7 The whole earth is at rest, *and* is quiet: they
break forth into singing.
8 Yea, the fir trees rejoice at thee, *and* the cedars
of Lebanon, *saying*, Since thou art laid down, no
feller is come up against us.
9 Hell from beneath is moved for thee to meet
thee at thy coming: it stirreth up the dead for thee,
even all the chief ones of the earth; it hath raised
up from their thrones all the kings of the nations.
10 All they shall speak and say unto thee, Art
thou also become weak as we? art thou become
like unto us?
11 Thy pomp is brought down to the grave, *and*
the noise of thy viols: the worm is spread under
thee, and the worms cover thee.
12 How art thou fallen from heaven, O Lucifer,
son of the morning! *how* art thou cut down to the
ground, which didst weaken the nations!
13 For thou hast said in thine heart, I will ascend
into heaven, I will exalt my throne above the stars
of God: I will sit also upon the mount of the
congregation, in the sides of the north:
14 I will ascend above the heights of the clouds; I
will be like the most High.
15 Yet thou shalt be brought down to hell, to the
sides of the pit.
16 They that see thee shall narrowly look upon

two hundred years before the event.
13:19–21 The fall of *Babylon* foreshadows God's judgment upon the world (Rev. 18:2).
13:21 *doleful creatures*. Howling desert animals, perhaps jackals. *owls*. Or ostriches. *satyrs shall dance*. Wild goats shall play or leap.
13:22 *desolate houses*. Or fortified towers. *dragons*. Jackals. *be prolonged*. Hesitate.

Thoughts for Personal/Family Worship: Chapter 13

Here is a warning against the arrogance and pride of those who seek to ignore God and challenge His rule. Babylon represents the height of worldly hostility toward the Lord. Yet we see how easily such a haughty spirit is crushed by the might of the Lord. None can stand against Him. The enemies of the gospel may be powerful and threatening, but Christians need not fear. We have One who is mightier. The wicked have but an allotted time, and when it is over they are taken from the scene of this life. As the psalmist reminds us, "Surely thou didst set them in slippery places: thou castedst them down into destruction. How are they brought into desolation, as in a moment! They are utterly consumed with terrors" (Ps. 73:18–19). How should unbelievers respond to the news of the coming day of the Lord? How should believers respond?

Chapter 14: *The Lord promises mercy to Israel and assures them that they will triumph over both Babylonia and Assyria.*

14:1 *have mercy*. Show compassion or pity. *strangers*. Resident aliens. *cleave*. Cling to or hold firmly.
14:4 *proverb*. A prophetic, figurative discourse. *king of Babylon*. Not specific to one king, but representing those powers hostile to the Lord and His people.
14:5 *the staff . . . sceptre*. Symbols of power and rule.
14:6 *continual stroke*. Unceasing blows.
14:7 *at rest . . . quiet*. At peace.
14:8 *feller*. A lumberjack, one who cuts down trees.
14:9 *Hell*. Hebrew, *sheol*, referring to death, the grave, or the realm of departed wicked spirits. *is moved*. Is perturbed, in restless motion. The activity indicates that the place of punishment for the wicked spirits is in view. *stirreth up the dead*. Agitates the dead spirits. *chief ones*. Former tyrants and kings.
14:11 *grave*. Hebrew, *sheol* (see v. 9). *viols*. Some sort of stringed instruments.
14:12–14 *Lucifer*. Literally, "morning-star, son of dawn." The Babylonian king in all his arrogance is in view. It was common for ancient kings to be regarded as divine and to claim divinity for themselves (Acts 12:22). Some suggest that this king is typical of or analogous to Satan; others suggest that Satan is uniquely in view (Ezek. 28:11–19; Luke 10:18; Rev. 12:9).
14:15 *hell*. See note at v. 9. *sides of the pit*. The recesses of the

thee, *and* consider thee, *saying, Is* this the man
that made the earth to tremble, that did shake
kingdoms;
17 *That* made the world as a wilderness, and
destroyed the cities thereof; *that* opened not the
house of his prisoners?
18 All the kings of the nations, *even* all of them,
lie in glory, every one in his own house.
19 But thou art cast out of thy grave like an
abominable branch, *and as* the raiment of those
that are slain, thrust through with a sword, that go
down to the stones of the pit; as a carcase trodden
under feet.
20 Thou shalt not be joined with them in burial,
because thou hast destroyed thy land, *and* slain
thy people: the seed of evildoers shall never be
renowned.
21 Prepare slaughter for his children for the iniqui-
ty of their fathers; that they do not rise, nor possess
the land, nor fill the face of the world with cities.
22 For I will rise up against them, saith the LORD
of hosts, and cut off from Babylon the name, and
remnant, and son, and nephew, saith the LORD.
23 I will also make it a possession for the bittern,
and pools of water: and I will sweep it with the
besom of destruction, saith the LORD of hosts.
24 ¶ The LORD of hosts hath sworn, saying, Surely
as I have thought, so shall it come to pass; and as I
have purposed, *so* shall it stand:
25 That I will break the Assyrian in my land,
and upon my mountains tread him under foot:
then shall his yoke depart from off them, and his
burden depart from off their shoulders.
26 This *is* the purpose that is purposed upon the
whole earth: and this *is* the hand that is stretched
out upon all the nations.
27 For the LORD of hosts hath purposed, and who
shall disannul *it*? and his hand *is* stretched out,
and who shall turn it back?
28 In the year that king Ahaz died was this burden.
29 ¶ Rejoice not thou, whole Palestina, because
the rod of him that smote thee is broken: for out
of the serpent's root shall come forth a cockatrice,
and his fruit *shall be* a fiery flying serpent.
30 And the firstborn of the poor shall feed, and
the needy shall lie down in safety: and I will kill thy
root with famine, and he shall slay thy remnant.
31 Howl, O gate; cry, O city; thou, whole Pales-
tina, *art* dissolved: for there shall come from the
north a smoke, and none *shall be* alone in his
appointed times.
32 What shall *one* then answer the messengers of
the nation? That the LORD hath founded Zion,
and the poor of his people shall trust in it.

CHAPTER 15

THE burden of Moab. Because in the night Ar
of Moab is laid waste, *and* brought to silence;
because in the night Kir of Moab is laid waste, *and*
brought to silence;
2 He is gone up to Bajith, and to Dibon, the high
places, to weep: Moab shall howl over Nebo, and
over Medeba: on all their heads *shall be* baldness,
and every beard cut off.
3 In their streets they shall gird themselves with
sackcloth: on the tops of their houses, and in their
streets, every one shall howl, weeping abundantly.
4 And Heshbon shall cry, and Elealeh: their voice
shall be heard *even* unto Jahaz: therefore the
armed soldiers of Moab shall cry out; his life shall
be grievous unto him.

---

pit, perhaps a reference to the world of the departed wicked spirits, like *sheol*.

14:16 *narrowly look upon*. Gaze upon or stare at.

14:19 *branch*. A sprout or offshoot to be discarded; the same word that describes the Messiah's humiliation (11:1). *raiment*. Clothing. *trodden*. Trampled.

14:20 *never be renowned*. Not be mentioned again.

14:22 *nephew*. Grandson or offspring in general.

14:23 *bittern*. Either a type of owl or a porcupine. *pools of water*. Swamps or marshes. *besom*. A broom.

Oracles on Assyria and Philistia (14:24–32)

14:24 *thought . . . come to pass . . . purposed . . . stand*. God's plans cannot fail, and mankind cannot frustrate His decree (46:10–11; Ps. 33:10–11).

14:27 *who shall turn it back*. No one can stop God's decree from being fulfilled, for He is the Commander of all creation (*the LORD of hosts*) with infinite power (*hand*; 43:13; Dan. 4:35).

14:29 *Palestina*. The Philistines. *cockatrice*. Viper. *fruit*. Offspring. *fiery flying serpent*. Poisonous serpents crawling around.

Thoughts for Personal/Family Worship: Chapter 14

It is a tragic thought that multitudes of religious men and women now reside in the terrible place of torment because they never leaned wholly upon Christ. Oh, how this question from the place of torment ought to stir us up to truly examine ourselves: "Art thou become like unto us?" (v. 10)? If we would avoid hearing these words from the pit, we must ask ourselves questions now: Are we in Christ? Is our house built upon the solid rock that is the Lord Jesus, or have we built our religion upon the shifting sands of pride and foolishness? Let us pray with the psalmist, "Search me, O God, and know my heart: try me, and know my thoughts: and see if there be any wicked way in me, and lead me in the way everlasting" (Ps. 139:23–24).

Oracle on Moab (15:1—16:14)

Chapter 15: *Moab is threatened with certain destruction because of its selfishness and pride.*

15:1 *burden*. Oracle or utterance. *Moab*. A nation descended, like Ammon, from Lot's incest (Gen. 19:30–38). *laid waste*. Devastated. *brought to silence*. Cut off or ruined.

15:2 *Bajith*. Translated "house." *baldness . . . beard cut off*. Symbols of grief or shame.

15:3 *gird themselves with sackcloth*. Dress in special clothing as a further sign of mourning.

15:4 *be grievous*. Quiver or be apprehensive.

5 My heart shall cry out for Moab; his fugitives
shall flee unto Zoar, an heifer of three years old:
for by the mounting up of Luhith with weeping
shall they go it up; for in the way of Horonaim
they shall raise up a cry of destruction.
6 For the waters of Nimrim shall be desolate: for
the hay is withered away, the grass faileth, there is
no green thing.
7 Therefore the abundance they have gotten, and
that which they have laid up, shall they carry away
to the brook of the willows.
8 For the cry is gone round about the borders of
Moab; the howling thereof unto Eglaim, and the
howling thereof unto Beer-elim.
9 For the waters of Dimon shall be full of
blood: for I will bring more upon Dimon, lions
upon him that escapeth of Moab, and upon the
remnant of the land.

CHAPTER 16

SEND ye the lamb to the ruler of the land from
Sela to the wilderness, unto the mount of the
daughter of Zion.
2 For it shall be, *that*, as a wandering bird cast out
of the nest, *so* the daughters of Moab shall be at
the fords of Arnon.
3 Take counsel, execute judgment; make thy
shadow as the night in the midst of the noonday;
hide the outcasts; bewray not him that wandereth.
4 Let mine outcasts dwell with thee, Moab; be
thou a covert to them from the face of the spoiler:
for the extortioner is at an end, the spoiler ceas-
eth, the oppressors are consumed out of the land.
5 And in mercy shall the throne be established:
and he shall sit upon it in truth in the tabernacle
of David, judging, and seeking judgment, and
hasting righteousness.
6 ¶ We have heard of the pride of Moab; *he is* very
proud: *even* of his haughtiness, and his pride, and
his wrath: *but* his lies *shall* not *be* so.
7 Therefore shall Moab howl for Moab, every one
shall howl: for the foundations of Kir-hareseth
shall ye mourn; surely *they are* stricken.
8 For the fields of Heshbon languish, *and* the
vine of Sibmah: the lords of the heathen have
broken down the principal plants thereof, they
are come *even* unto Jazer, they wandered *through*
the wilderness: her branches are stretched out,
they are gone over the sea.
9 ¶ Therefore I will bewail with the weeping of
Jazer the vine of Sibmah: I will water thee with my
tears, O Heshbon, and Elealeh: for the shouting
for thy summer fruits and for thy harvest is fallen.
10 And gladness is taken away, and joy out of the
plentiful field; and in the vineyards there shall be
no singing, neither shall there be shouting: the
treaders shall tread out no wine in *their* presses; I
have made *their vintage* shouting to cease.
11 Wherefore my bowels shall sound like an harp
for Moab, and mine inward parts for Kir-haresh.
12 ¶ And it shall come to pass, when it is seen
that Moab is weary on the high place, that he shall
come to his sanctuary to pray; but he shall not
prevail.
13 This *is* the word that the LORD hath spoken
concerning Moab since that time.
14 But now the LORD hath spoken, saying, Within
three years, as the years of an hireling, and the
glory of Moab shall be contemned, with all that

15:5 *Zoar.* Ironically, the place where Lot and his daughters sought refuge (Gen.19:23–24). *heifer of three years old.* An image referring to Moab, perhaps also to an animal not used to the yoke.

Thoughts for Personal/Family Worship: Chapter 15

Moab was a nation that overindulged itself. The Moabites had lived in peace and prosperity for many years and were overconfident that things would continue to go well for them. They were blinded by the foolish philosophy that says there will be no judgment to come. They carried on in their own selfish lifestyles, till all of a sudden they were caught unawares. Let us never envy those who prosper in this world through ungodly ways, for their end is destruction. Rather, let Christians thank God that He has worked a miracle of grace within their hearts so that they are born again (1 Peter 1:3–4). Let us also pray for God to awaken sinners to their need before destruction comes.

Chapter 16: Moab is exhorted to submit to David's throne or face impending doom.

16:2 *wandering bird.* A bird that flees or escapes.
16:3 *bewray.* Betray; literally, "do not uncover or expose the one who is escaping."
16:4 *outcasts.* Those banished or thrust out. *covert.* A hidden place of safety. *spoiler.* The destroyer. *extortioner.* Oppressor; literally, "one who squeezes or presses."
16:5 *throne . . . David.* A promise ultimately fulfilled in the kingdom of Christ (9:6–7). David had family connections with the Moabites (Ruth 4:13–22; 1 Sam. 22:3–4). *mercy . . . truth.* Covenant loyalty, love, and faithfulness, reflecting the character of God (Ex. 34:6). *tabernacle.* Tent or dwelling place, representing the family line and kingdom (Amos 9:11). *hasting righteousness.* Is quick to do right (11:1–5).
16:9 *shouting.* The war cry.
16:10 *vintage.* The time of grape gathering.
16:11 *bowels.* Inner feelings of compassion (Jer. 48:36).
16:14 *contemned.* Degraded, despised, or lightly esteemed.

Thoughts for Personal/Family Worship: Chapter 16

Pride is such a destructive sin because it fails to listen to sound advice. The proud think they have all the answers. They will not be told by others. Hence, we read in Prov. 16:18, "Pride goeth before destruction, and an haughty spirit before a fall." What a blessing it is to have a teachable spirit, especially concerning the things of God! Moab was offered refuge, but their pride would not allow them to accept the gracious offer from the Lord of submission to a good and righteous King. There are

great multitude; and the remnant *shall be* very
small *and* feeble.

CHAPTER 17

THE burden of Damascus. Behold, Damascus
is taken away from *being* a city, and it shall be a
ruinous heap.
2 The cities of Aroer *are* forsaken: they shall be
for flocks, which shall lie down, and none shall
make *them* afraid.
3 The fortress also shall cease from Ephraim, and
the kingdom from Damascus, and the remnant of
Syria: they shall be as the glory of the children of
Israel, saith the LORD of hosts.
4 And in that day it shall come to pass, *that* the
glory of Jacob shall be made thin, and the fatness
of his flesh shall wax lean.
5 And it shall be as when the harvestman
gathereth the corn, and reapeth the ears with his
arm; and it shall be as he that gathereth ears in the
valley of Rephaim.
6 ¶ Yet gleaning grapes shall be left in it, as the
shaking of an olive tree, two *or* three berries in the
top of the uppermost bough, four *or* five in the
outmost fruitful branches thereof, saith the LORD
God of Israel.
7 At that day shall a man look to his Maker, and his
eyes shall have respect to the Holy One of Israel.
8 And he shall not look to the altars, the work of
his hands, neither shall respect *that* which his fin-
gers have made, either the groves, or the images.
9 ¶ In that day shall his strong cities be as a
forsaken bough, and an uppermost branch,
which they left because of the children of Israel:
and there shall be desolation.
10 Because thou hast forgotten the God of thy
salvation, and hast not been mindful of the rock
of thy strength, therefore shalt thou plant pleasant
plants, and shalt set it with strange slips:
11 In the day shalt thou make thy plant to grow,
and in the morning shalt thou make thy seed to
flourish: *but* the harvest *shall be* a heap in the day
of grief and of desperate sorrow.
12 ¶ Woe to the multitude of many people, *which*
make a noise like the noise of the seas; and to the
rushing of nations, *that* make a rushing like the
rushing of mighty waters!
13 The nations shall rush like the rushing of
many waters: but *God* shall rebuke them, and they
shall flee far off, and shall be chased as the chaff of
the mountains before the wind, and like a rolling
thing before the whirlwind.
14 And behold at eveningtide trouble; *and* before
the morning he *is* not. This *is* the portion of them
that spoil us, and the lot of them that rob us.

CHAPTER 18

WOE to the land shadowing with wings, which *is*
beyond the rivers of Ethiopia:
2 That sendeth ambassadors by the sea, even in
vessels of bulrushes upon the waters, *saying*, Go,
ye swift messengers, to a nation scattered and

---

many like Moab today, whose pride ruins them because they refuse to submit to the Son of David, King Jesus. Why is our pride such a bitter enemy of the kingdom of Christ?

Oracles on Syria, Jacob, and Ethiopia (chs. 17:1—18:7)

Chapter 17: *Isaiah pronounces judgment on Damascus.*

17:1 *burden.* Oracle or utterance. *Damascus.* The capital of Syria (7:8,16; 8:4; 2 Kings 16:1–9).
17:3 *Ephraim.* The northern kingdom that had allied with Syria (7:1–2).
17:4 *made thin.* Faded or became tiny. *wax lean.* Become lean or dwindle. Prosperity becomes poverty.
17:5–6 *gleaning.* The little remaining after harvesters have gone through the field. The wealth and power of both these nations would be stripped bare, just as the wheat is cut down and the ears of corn are stripped during the harvest. Yet there would be a remnant.
17:7 *have respect.* Look, an expression of dependence.
17:8 *groves.* The Asherah, cultic wooden poles erected near altars, common in Canaanite rituals. *images.* Specifically, sun-pillars.
17:9 *strong.* Fortified, walled. *forsaken bough.* A solitary branch left when rest of the tree is stripped—a picture of the remnant.
17:10 *forgotten.* Intentionally refused to think about. They rejected the Lord as their hope for *salvation. rock.* A huge, immovable boulder, an image of stability and a common designation for the Lord (26:4; Deut. 32:4,18). *strange slips.* Illicit shoots used for planting.
17:13 *rolling thing.* Wheel-shaped thistle.
17:14 *rob.* Plunder.

Thoughts for Personal/Family Worship: Chapter 17

The enemy of our souls is always subtle in his approaches, seeking to convince men and women that the Lord's demands are unjust. Ephraim listened to such a lie and turned their backs upon their covenant God, associating themselves with a pagan people. The Lord caused them to prosper, but in their prosperity they listened to the voice of evil. Imagining they would do much better without God, they turned away from Him. Do we not see the same foolishness in society today? Lust for self-interest has brought misery and heartache to countless multitudes who have been stripped of all that is good and left vulnerable—all because they have forgotten the Lord. Blessed are they who set their minds on Him as their true rock and salvation. How can we develop an attitude of always remembering God as our only hope?

Chapter 18: *Isaiah pronounces judgment on Ethiopia.*

18:1 *Woe.* See note at 1:4. *shadowing with wings.* Perhaps referring to winged crickets, symbolic of Ethiopia's armies.
18:2 *ambassadors.* Envoys. *vessels of bulrushes.* Boats or ships made from papyrus, more suited to inland waterways than to

peeled, to a people terrible from their beginning
hitherto; a nation meted out and trodden down,
whose land the rivers have spoiled!
3 All ye inhabitants of the world, and dwellers on
the earth, see ye, when he lifteth up an ensign on
the mountains; and when he bloweth a trumpet,
hear ye.
4 For so the LORD said unto me, I will take my
rest, and I will consider in my dwelling place like
a clear heat upon herbs, *and* like a cloud of dew in
the heat of harvest.
5 For afore the harvest, when the bud is perfect,
and the sour grape is ripening in the flower, he
shall both cut off the sprigs with pruning hooks,
and take away *and* cut down the branches.
6 They shall be left together unto the fowls of the
mountains, and to the beasts of the earth: and the
fowls shall summer upon them, and all the beasts
of the earth shall winter upon them.
7 ¶ In that time shall the present be brought unto
the LORD of hosts of a people scattered and peeled,
and from a people terrible from their beginning
hitherto; a nation meted out and trodden under
foot, whose land the rivers have spoiled, to the
place of the name of the LORD of hosts, the mount
Zion.

CHAPTER 19

THE burden of Egypt. Behold, the LORD rideth
upon a swift cloud, and shall come into Egypt:
and the idols of Egypt shall be moved at his
presence, and the heart of Egypt shall melt in the
midst of it.
2 And I will set the Egyptians against the
Egyptians: and they shall fight every one against
his brother, and every one against his neighbour;
city against city, *and* kingdom against kingdom.
3 And the spirit of Egypt shall fail in the midst
thereof; and I will destroy the counsel thereof: and
they shall seek to the idols, and to the charmers,
and to them that have familiar spirits, and to the
wizards.
4 And the Egyptians will I give over into the hand
of a cruel lord; and a fierce king shall rule over
them, saith the Lord, the LORD of hosts.
5 And the waters shall fail from the sea, and the
river shall be wasted and dried up.
6 And they shall turn the rivers far away; *and* the
brooks of defence shall be emptied and dried up:
the reeds and flags shall wither.
7 The paper reeds by the brooks, by the mouth of
the brooks, and every thing sown by the brooks,
shall wither, be driven away, and be no *more*.
8 The fishers also shall mourn, and all they that
cast angle into the brooks shall lament, and they
that spread nets upon the waters shall languish.
9 Moreover they that work in fine flax, and they
that weave networks, shall be confounded.
10 And they shall be broken in the purposes
thereof, all that make sluices *and* ponds for fish.
11 ¶ Surely the princes of Zoan *are* fools, the
counsel of the wise counsellors of Pharaoh is
become brutish: how say ye unto Pharaoh, I *am*
the son of the wise, the son of ancient kings?
12 Where *are* they? where *are* thy wise *men*? and
let them tell thee now, and let them know what
the LORD of hosts hath purposed upon Egypt.
13 The princes of Zoan are become fools, the
princes of Noph are deceived; they have also

---

sea travel. *nation scattered . . . spoiled.* Could be translated "a nation tall and smooth, a fearsome people from their beginning to this day, a strong and dominating nation whose land is divided by the rivers."

18:3 *ensign.* Banner.

18:4 *take my rest.* Maintain a quiet attitude. *clear heat upon herbs.* Or a dazzling heat in the light.

18:5 *afore.* Before.

18:6 *fowls.* Specifically, birds of prey. *summer . . . winter.* Spend the summer and winter.

18:7 *present.* A gift offered as homage. *hitherto.* To this day. *place of the name.* The temple, implying that they would become worshipers of the true God (Jer. 38:7–13; 39:15–18; Acts 8:26–39), His purpose for all nations (see note at 2:2–4).

Thoughts for Personal/Family Worship: Chapter 18

God's purposes for the Ethiopian people were judgment and salvation. Isaiah's prophecy intertwines these two in all of God's dealings. On the one hand we must fear the Lord because of the woes He sends upon the wicked nations. On the other hand, we must hope in the Lord because He is gathering worshipers to Himself from all nations. Judgment and salvation will come upon all the world for the glory of God. This is the driving motive for missions and evangelism. Whenever you hear of the nations in the news, or meet people from other countries, view them through the twin lenses of judgment and salvation. How should this change the way you live?

Chapter 19: *Egypt is put to confusion and turns to the Lord.*

Oracle on Egypt (19:1–25)

19:1 *burden.* Oracle or utterance.

19:2 *set.* Provoke, prick, or spur.

19:3 *fail.* Be disturbed. *destroy.* Swallow up or confuse. *charmers.* Those using incantations. *them that have familiar spirits.* Mediums of supernatural powers. *wizards.* Sorcerers or magicians.

19:5 *wasted.* Drained or dried up.

19:6 *turn the rivers far way.* Make the rivers stink, become foul-smelling. *defence.* Or Egypt. *flags.* Rushes, some sort of water-plant.

19:7 *paper reeds.* Papyrus or a bare place.

19:8 *fishers.* Fishermen. *cast angle.* Fish with a hook and line.

19:9 *networks.* Fine, white cloth.

19:10 *purposes.* Foundations. *sluices.* Water channels controlled by gates. The hired workers in these trades would be grieved.

19:11 *brutish.* Stupid.

19:13 *Noph.* Otherwise known as Memphis, an ancient city in Egypt. *the stay.* The cornerstone.

seduced Egypt, *even they that are* the stay of the
tribes thereof.
14 The LORD hath mingled a perverse spirit in
the midst thereof: and they have caused Egypt to
err in every work thereof, as a drunken *man* stag-
gereth in his vomit.
15 Neither shall there be *any* work for Egypt,
which the head or tail, branch or rush, may do.
16 In that day shall Egypt be like unto women:
and it shall be afraid and fear because of the
shaking of the hand of the LORD of hosts, which
he shaketh over it.
17 And the land of Judah shall be a terror unto
Egypt, every one that maketh mention thereof
shall be afraid in himself, because of the counsel
of the LORD of hosts, which he hath determined
against it.
18 ¶ In that day shall five cities in the land of
Egypt speak the language of Canaan, and swear
to the LORD of hosts; one shall be called, The city
of destruction.
19 In that day shall there be an altar to the LORD
in the midst of the land of Egypt, and a pillar at
the border thereof to the LORD.
20 And it shall be for a sign and for a witness unto
the LORD of hosts in the land of Egypt: for they
shall cry unto the LORD because of the oppressors,
and he shall send them a saviour, and a great one,
and he shall deliver them.
21 And the LORD shall be known to Egypt, and
the Egyptians shall know the LORD in that day,
and shall do sacrifice and oblation; yea, they shall
vow a vow unto the LORD, and perform *it*.
22 And the LORD shall smite Egypt: he shall smite
and heal *it*: and they shall return *even* to the LORD,
and he shall be intreated of them, and shall heal
them.
23 ¶ In that day shall there be a highway out of
Egypt to Assyria, and the Assyrian shall come
into Egypt, and the Egyptian into Assyria, and the
Egyptians shall serve with the Assyrians.
24 In that day shall Israel be the third with Egypt
and with Assyria, *even* a blessing in the midst of
the land:
25 Whom the LORD of hosts shall bless, saying,
Blessed *be* Egypt my people, and Assyria the work
of my hands, and Israel mine inheritance.

CHAPTER 20

IN the year that Tartan came unto Ashdod, (when
Sargon the king of Assyria sent him,) and fought
against Ashdod, and took it;
2 At the same time spake the LORD by Isaiah the
son of Amoz, saying, Go and loose the sackcloth
from off thy loins, and put off thy shoe from thy
foot. And he did so, walking naked and barefoot.
3 And the LORD said, Like as my servant Isaiah
hath walked naked and barefoot three years *for* a
sign and wonder upon Egypt and upon Ethiopia;
4 So shall the king of Assyria lead away the
Egyptians prisoners, and the Ethiopians captives,
young and old, naked and barefoot, even with
their buttocks uncovered, to the shame of Egypt.
5 And they shall be afraid and ashamed of Ethiopia
their expectation, and of Egypt their glory.
6 And the inhabitant of this isle shall say in that
day, Behold, such *is* our expectation, whither

19:14 *perverse spirit.* Spirit of confusion.
19:18–22 This section moves from warnings of judgment to promises of restoration.
19:18 *language of Canaan.* Perhaps the Hebrew language, or a figure of speech for pure and holy speech glorifying the Lord (Zeph. 3:9).
19:19 *altar to the LORD.* There would be true worship of God in Egypt. *pillar.* A memorial stone.
19:21 *oblation.* Offering.
19:23–25 *Israel . . . Egypt . . . Assyria.* Here is something marvelous: a demonstration of the power of grace to unite former enemies in the worship of the true God (Eph. 2:11–22).

Thoughts for Personal/Family Worship: Chapter 19

This chapter reveals the wonderful grace of God toward the Gentiles. In Christ, we who were once strangers and foreigners and at enmity with Him are brought into sweet communion. In Him we speak the holy language of Scripture; for the new heart within us, given by our gracious God, has changed our speech. We no longer ought to have interest in the worldly and the vile, for our thoughts are now toward the Lord who has redeemed us and healed us of our iniquities. What a privilege to be blessed by God, to be the work of His hands, and to have our inheritance in Him. How amazing is the grace of the gospel that transforms former enemies into a fellowship of saints! How have you experienced the way God unites very different people through a shared love and worship for Him?

Chapter 20: *Isaiah prophesies the defeat of Egypt and Ethiopia at the hands of the Assyrians.*

Isaiah's Sign against Egypt and Ethiopia (20:1–6)

20:1 *Tartan.* A title rather than a name of a person; most likely the military commander appointed by the Assyrian king (2 Kings 18:17).
20:2–3 *naked.* The Hebrew term can refer to being lightly dressed, probably in undergarments. This was an embarrassing object lesson of the humiliating defeat coming for Egypt and Ethiopia, though it falls short of total nakedness.
20:5 *their expectation . . . glory.* They had made these nations their hope and boasting, and therefore the Lord would disappoint them.
20:6 *isle.* Coast or border. *whither.* Where, to which place.

Thoughts for Personal/Family Worship: Chapter 20

We learn from this short chapter the folly of trusting in human resources and power. Such things will always let us down and cause us to be ashamed. You have a responsibility to "trust in the LORD with all thine heart" (Prov. 3:5). If you lean on your own understanding, you will not succeed. Resting your hope in man will lead to

we flee for help to be delivered from the king of
Assyria: and how shall we escape?

CHAPTER 21

THE burden of the desert of the sea. As whirlwinds
in the south pass through; *so* it cometh from the
desert, from a terrible land.
2 A grievous vision is declared unto me; the
treacherous dealer dealeth treacherously, and the
spoiler spoileth. Go up, O Elam: besiege, O Media;
all the sighing thereof have I made to cease.
3 Therefore are my loins filled with pain: pangs
have taken hold upon me, as the pangs of a
woman that travaileth: I was bowed down at the
hearing *of it*; I was dismayed at the seeing *of it*.
4 My heart panted, fearfulness affrighted me:
the night of my pleasure hath he turned into fear
unto me.
5 Prepare the table, watch in the watchtower, eat,
drink: arise, ye princes, *and* anoint the shield.
6 For thus hath the Lord said unto me, Go, set a
watchman, let him declare what he seeth.
7 And he saw a chariot *with* a couple of horsemen,
a chariot of asses, *and* a chariot of camels; and he
hearkened diligently with much heed:
8 And he cried, A lion: My lord, I stand
continually upon the watchtower in the daytime,
and I am set in my ward whole nights:
9 And, behold, here cometh a chariot of men, *with*
a couple of horsemen. And he answered and said,
Babylon is fallen, is fallen; and all the graven im-
ages of her gods he hath broken unto the ground.
10 O my threshing, and the corn of my floor: that
which I have heard of the LORD of hosts, the God
of Israel, have I declared unto you.
11 ¶ The burden of Dumah. He calleth to me out
of Seir, Watchman, what of the night? Watchman,
what of the night?
12 The watchman said, The morning cometh,
and also the night: if ye will enquire, enquire ye:
return, come.
13 ¶ The burden upon Arabia. In the forest in
Arabia shall ye lodge, O ye travelling companies
of Dedanim.
14 The inhabitants of the land of Tema brought
water to him that was thirsty, they prevented with
their bread him that fled.
15 For they fled from the swords, from the drawn
sword, and from the bent bow, and from the
grievousness of war.
16 For thus hath the Lord said unto me, Within a
year, according to the years of an hireling, and all
the glory of Kedar shall fail:
17 And the residue of the number of archers,
the mighty men of the children of Kedar, shall
be diminished: for the LORD God of Israel hath
spoken *it*.

CHAPTER 22

THE burden of the valley of vision. What aileth
thee now, that thou art wholly gone up to the
housetops?

---

disappointment and ultimately to a divine curse (Jer. 17:5–6). Trust the Savior, Jesus Christ; lean on Him with all your weight. "For the scripture saith, Whosoever believeth in him shall not be ashamed" (Rom. 10:11). The Egypts of this world will always fail, but the Lord cannot fail. What are some ways in which you are tempted to trust in man's help? How can you place your confidence fully in the Lord?

Chapter 21: *Isaiah predicts the fall of Babylon and warns both Edom and Arabia.*
Oracles on Babylon, Edom, and Arabia (21:1–17)

21:1 *burden.* Oracle or utterance. *desert of the sea.* A symbolic reference to Babylon, situated in the region near the Persian Gulf. *terrible.* Fearsome.
21:2 *grievous.* Harsh or severe. *Elam . . . Media.* See note at 13:17.
21:3 *travaileth.* Is in labor.
21:4 *panted.* Staggered. *fearfulness affrighted.* Horror terrified or overwhelmed.
21:5 *Prepare the table.* Babylon was conquered while she was feasting (Dan. 5; cf. Jer. 51:39). *anoint the shield.* Oil the shield to make it ready for use.
21:7 *hearkened diligently with much heed.* Listened carefully with attention.
21:8 *am set in my ward.* Standing firmly on guard.
21:9 *Babylon is fallen.* A cry of victory over the enemy of the Lord and His people (Jer. 51:8; Rev. 14:8; 18:1–2).
21:10 *threshing.* A figure of speech for downtrodden people (Amos 1:3). *corn of my floor.* Literally, "the son of my threshing floor," a Hebraic idiom for someone threshed and winnowed; that is, someone severely oppressed.
21:11 *Dumah . . . Seir.* Edom.
21:13 *forest.* Thicket. *travelling companies.* Caravans.
21:14 *prevented.* Went to meet.
21:16 *hireling.* Either a day-laborer or a mercenary.
21:17 *for the LORD . . . hath spoken it.* Their destruction is certain because God has decreed it. This assures His people that His covenant with them cannot fail ("God of Israel"; v. 10).

Thoughts for Personal/Family Worship: Chapter 21

Although God's people sometimes suffer severe persecution, even akin to being threshed and winnowed, they may still wait with confident hope in the God of Israel. The sovereign Lord will overthrow the empires of this world, and one day His people will cry "Babylon is fallen!" while Christ's glory fills the skies. God has decreed it, and therefore it will certainly come to be. Christians, therefore, may suffer with expectation that God's justice will prevail. How can this hope protect us from being attracted to this world's ways and intimidated by its threats?

Chapter 22: *Isaiah laments over Judah and pronounces Shebna's downfall.*
The Valley of Vision for Judah (2:1–252)

22:1 *burden.* Oracle or utterance. *valley of vision.* Most likely

2 Thou that art full of stirs, a tumultuous city, a
joyous city: thy slain *men are* not slain with the
sword, nor dead in battle.
3 All thy rulers are fled together, they are bound
by the archers: all that are found in thee are bound
together, *which* have fled from far.
4 Therefore said I, Look away from me; I will
weep bitterly, labour not to comfort me, because
of the spoiling of the daughter of my people.
5 For *it is* a day of trouble, and of treading down,
and of perplexity by the Lord GOD of hosts in the
valley of vision, breaking down the walls, and of
crying to the mountains.
6 And Elam bare the quiver with chariots of men
and horsemen, and Kir uncovered the shield.
7 And it shall come to pass, *that* thy choicest
valleys shall be full of chariots, and the horsemen
shall set themselves in array at the gate.
8 ¶ And he discovered the covering of Judah, and
thou didst look in that day to the armour of the
house of the forest.
9 Ye have seen also the breaches of the city of
David, that they are many: and ye gathered
together the waters of the lower pool.
10 And ye have numbered the houses of
Jerusalem, and the houses have ye broken down
to fortify the wall.
11 Ye made also a ditch between the two walls for
the water of the old pool: but ye have not looked
unto the maker thereof, neither had respect unto
him that fashioned it long ago.
12 And in that day did the Lord GOD of hosts call
to weeping, and to mourning, and to baldness,
and to girding with sackcloth:
13 And behold joy and gladness, slaying oxen,
and killing sheep, eating flesh, and drinking wine:
let us eat and drink; for to morrow we shall die.
14 And it was revealed in mine ears by the LORD
of hosts, Surely this iniquity shall not be purged
from you till ye die, saith the Lord GOD of hosts.
15 ¶ Thus saith the Lord GOD of hosts, Go, get
thee unto this treasurer, *even* unto Shebna, which
is over the house, *and say*,
16 What hast thou here? and whom hast thou here,
that thou hast hewed thee out a sepulchre here, *as*
he that heweth him out a sepulchre on high, *and*
that graveth an habitation for himself in a rock?
17 Behold, the LORD will carry thee away with a
mighty captivity, and will surely cover thee.
18 He will surely violently turn and toss thee *like*
a ball into a large country: there shalt thou die,
and there the chariots of thy glory *shall be* the
shame of thy lord's house.
19 And I will drive thee from thy station, and
from thy state shall he pull thee down.
20 ¶ And it shall come to pass in that day, that I
will call my servant Eliakim the son of Hilkiah:
21 And I will clothe him with thy robe, and
strengthen him with thy girdle, and I will commit
thy government into his hand: and he shall be a
father to the inhabitants of Jerusalem, and to the
house of Judah.
22 And the key of the house of David will I lay
upon his shoulder; so he shall open, and none
shall shut; and he shall shut, and none shall open.
23 And I will fasten him *as* a nail in a sure place;
and he shall be for a glorious throne to his father's
house.
24 And they shall hang upon him all the glory of
his father's house, the offspring and the issue, all
vessels of small quantity, from the vessels of cups,
even to all the vessels of flagons.
25 In that day, saith the LORD of hosts, shall the
nail that is fastened in the sure place be removed,
and be cut down, and fall; and the burden that *was*
upon it shall be cut off: for the LORD hath spoken *it*.

referring to Jerusalem (v. 5).

22:2 *stirs.* Noise. *tumultuous city.* City of commotion. *slain.* Or pierced.

22:3 *bound.* Captured.

22:4 *spoiling.* Destruction.

22:5 *trouble.* Dismay, consternation, or panic. *perplexity.* Confusion.

22:7 *set themselves in array.* Took up their position to fight.

22:8 *discovered the covering.* Removed the protection.

22:12 *baldness . . . girding with sackcloth.* Expressions of mourning.

22:13 *eat and drink . . . die.* The philosophy of hedonistic despair (1 Cor. 15:32).

22:15 *treasurer.* Administrator, a high-ranking official. *Shebna.* On this man and Eliakim (v. 20), see 36:3–4,11,22; 37:2. *over the house.* A position second to that of the king.

22:16 *hewed.* Cut. *sepulchre.* Tomb. His preparation for a lavish burial and prominent grave site was a manifestation of pride and worldliness (*here . . . here . . . here*).

22:17 *the LORD will carry . . . captivity.* Literally, "The Lord will hurl you away with a mighty and violent hurling."

22:18 *He will surely . . . ball.* Literally, "He will certainly whirl you about and throw you like a ball."

22:19 *drive thee from thy station.* Remove him forcibly from office.

22:21 *girdle.* Sash. *father.* A leader who does good, a loving authority.

22:22 *key . . . open . . . shut.* A symbol of authority in the kingdom of the son of *David*, pointing ultimately to Christ's supreme authority (Rev. 1:18; 3:7–8)

22:24 *flagons.* Jars or pitchers.

22:25 *removed.* Even faithful Eliakim could not save the kingdom from falling.

Thoughts for Personal/Family Worship: Chapter 22

Shebna is an illustration of foolish pride. He enjoyed a position of honor, and it went to his head. He lost his vision of mission to the king and desired his own legacy. His concern was how he could be remembered in this world (v. 16), and so he devoted his efforts toward creating a memorial for himself. But God had different plans and showed how dispensable Shebna was by replacing him with Eliakim. God's work is more important than any one man, and it will go on. Let us

CHAPTER 23

THE burden of Tyre. Howl, ye ships of Tarshish;
for it is laid waste, so that there is no house, no
entering in: from the land of Chittim it is revealed
to them.
2 Be still, ye inhabitants of the isle; thou whom
the merchants of Zidon, that pass over the sea,
have replenished.
3 And by great waters the seed of Sihor, the har-
vest of the river, *is* her revenue; and she is a mart
of nations.
4 Be thou ashamed, O Zidon: for the sea hath
spoken, *even* the strength of the sea, saying, I
travail not, nor bring forth children, neither do I
nourish up young men, *nor* bring up virgins.
5 As at the report concerning Egypt, *so* shall they
be sorely pained at the report of Tyre.
6 Pass ye over to Tarshish; howl, ye inhabitants
of the isle.
7 *Is* this your joyous *city*, whose antiquity *is* of
ancient days? her own feet shall carry her afar off
to sojourn.
8 Who hath taken this counsel against Tyre, the
crowning *city*, whose merchants *are* princes,
whose traffickers *are* the honourable of the earth?
9 The LORD of hosts hath purposed it, to stain the
pride of all glory, *and* to bring into contempt all
the honourable of the earth.
10 Pass through thy land as a river, O daughter of
Tarshish: *there is* no more strength.
11 He stretched out his hand over the sea, he
shook the kingdoms: the LORD hath given a
commandment against the merchant *city*, to
destroy the strong holds thereof.
12 And he said, Thou shalt no more rejoice, O
thou oppressed virgin, daughter of Zidon: arise,
pass over to Chittim; there also shalt thou have
no rest.
13 Behold the land of the Chaldeans; this people
was not, *till* the Assyrian founded it for them that
dwell in the wilderness: they set up the towers
thereof, they raised up the palaces thereof; *and* he
brought it to ruin.
14 Howl, ye ships of Tarshish: for your strength
is laid waste.
15 And it shall come to pass in that day, that Tyre
shall be forgotten seventy years, according to the
days of one king: after the end of seventy years
shall Tyre sing as an harlot.
16 Take an harp, go about the city, thou harlot
that hast been forgotten; make sweet melody, sing
many songs, that thou mayest be remembered.
17 ¶ And it shall come to pass after the end of
seventy years, that the LORD will visit Tyre, and
she shall turn to her hire, and shall commit
fornication with all the kingdoms of the world
upon the face of the earth.
18 And her merchandise and her hire shall be
holiness to the LORD: it shall not be treasured nor
laid up; for her merchandise shall be for them that
dwell before the LORD, to eat sufficiently, and for
durable clothing.

CHAPTER 24

BEHOLD, the LORD maketh the earth empty, and
maketh it waste, and turneth it upside down, and
scattereth abroad the inhabitants thereof.

---

learn from Shebna that God looks to him who is contrite in spirit (66:2), and He knows the proud only afar off (Ps. 138:6). How might you be tempted to be like Shebna? How can you live entirely for the kingdom of Christ?

Chapter 23: *Tyre is overthrown.*

Oracle on Tyre (23:1–18)

23:1 *burden.* Oracle or utterance. *Tyre.* A principal coastal city of Phoenicia (Ezek. 26–28). *Howl.* Lament. *Chittim.* Cyprus (v. 12).

23:2 *Be still.* Either be struck dumb or wail. *isle.* Coast (v. 6). *Zidon.* Or Sidon, representing the whole of Phoenicia rather than simply the city.

23:3 *Sihor.* Another name for the Nile. The grain of Egypt was shipped throughout the Mediterranean by the Phoenician fleet, thus providing wealth for both Egypt and Tyre. *mart.* Marketplace or profit.

23:4 *travail.* Labor in childbirth.

23:5 *sorely pained.* Writhed.

23:7 *sojourn.* Live as a resident alien.

23:15–16 *seventy years.* See Jer. 25:9-22; 27:3–7; 29:10. *sing as an harlot.* A means of attracting her clients and building up her trade.

23:17 *visit.* Give attention with appropriate action; here to punish. *commit fornication with all the kingdoms.* Seduce many nations to live for worldly prestige, possessions, and pleasures; a form of idolatry (Rev. 17:2; 18:3,9). *turn to her hire.* Return to her pay.

23:18 *holiness to the LORD.* Possibly a prophecy of the conversion of the Phoenicians to worship the true God (Acts 11:19; 15:3).

Thoughts for Personal/Family Worship: Chapter 23

This chapter brings a severe warning to all who would make money and possessions their main goal in life. Such things are easily taken away by the Lord, and they must be ultimately given up and left behind when death comes. The Savior declares, "For what shall it profit a man, if he shall gain the whole world, and lose his own soul?" (Mark 8:36). Let us, therefore, get our priorities in order. Rather than setting our hearts on material possessions, we must seek God's kingdom first by obeying His will and trust that He will care for our needs (Matt. 6:31–33). How can we avoid being seduced by the allure of money and what it can buy?

THE LITTLE APOCALYPSE (24:1—27:13)

Chapter 24: *The Lord declares judgment upon the world.*

The Ruin of the Heavens and Earth and the Coming of God's Kingdom (24:1–23)

2 And it shall be, as with the people, so with the
priest; as with the servant, so with his master; as
with the maid, so with her mistress; as with the
buyer, so with the seller; as with the lender, so
with the borrower; as with the taker of usury, so
with the giver of usury to him.
3 The land shall be utterly emptied, and utterly
spoiled: for the LORD hath spoken this word.
4 The earth mourneth *and* fadeth away, the world
languisheth *and* fadeth away, the haughty people
of the earth do languish.
5 The earth also is defiled under the inhabitants
thereof; because they have transgressed the laws,
changed the ordinance, broken the everlasting
covenant.
6 Therefore hath the curse devoured the earth,
and they that dwell therein are desolate: therefore
the inhabitants of the earth are burned, and few
men left.
7 The new wine mourneth, the vine languisheth,
all the merryhearted do sigh.
8 The mirth of tabrets ceaseth, the noise of them
that rejoice endeth, the joy of the harp ceaseth.
9 They shall not drink wine with a song; strong
drink shall be bitter to them that drink it.
10 The city of confusion is broken down: every
house is shut up, that no man may come in.
11 *There is* a crying for wine in the streets; all joy
is darkened, the mirth of the land is gone.
12 In the city is left desolation, and the gate is
smitten with destruction.
13 ¶ When thus it shall be in the midst of the land
among the people, *there shall be* as the shaking of
an olive tree, *and* as the gleaning grapes when the
vintage is done.
14 They shall lift up their voice, they shall sing for
the majesty of the LORD, they shall cry aloud from
the sea.
15 Wherefore glorify ye the LORD in the fires, *even*
the name of the LORD God of Israel in the isles of
the sea.
16 ¶ From the uttermost part of the earth have we
heard songs, *even* glory to the righteous. But I said,
My leanness, my leanness, woe unto me! the treach-
erous dealers have dealt treacherously; yea, the
treacherous dealers have dealt very treacherously.
17 Fear, and the pit, and the snare, *are* upon thee,
O inhabitant of the earth.
18 And it shall come to pass, *that* he who fleeth
from the noise of the fear shall fall into the pit;
and he that cometh up out of the midst of the
pit shall be taken in the snare: for the windows
from on high are open, and the foundations of
the earth do shake.
19 The earth is utterly broken down, the earth is
clean dissolved, the earth is moved exceedingly.
20 The earth shall reel to and fro like a drunkard,
and shall be removed like a cottage; and the
transgression thereof shall be heavy upon it; and
it shall fall, and not rise again.
21 And it shall come to pass in that day, *that* the
LORD shall punish the host of the high ones *that*
are on high, and the kings of the earth upon the
earth.
22 And they shall be gathered together, *as*
prisoners are gathered in the pit, and shall be shut
up in the prison, and after many days shall they
be visited.
23 Then the moon shall be confounded, and the
sun ashamed, when the LORD of hosts shall reign

24:1 *turneth it upside down.* Twists or distorts its face (2 Peter 3:10).
24:2 *servant . . . master.* No class of people will be spared this judgment. *taker of usury.* The creditor who charges interest on loans. *giver of usury.* The debtor.
24:3 *utterly spoiled.* Thoroughly plundered.
24:5–6 *earth also is defiled.* Man's sin brought God's *curse* upon all earthly creation (Gen. 3:17–18; Rom. 8:19–22). *broken the everlasting covenant.* Violated God's unchanging laws (33:8; Lev. 26:15; Jer. 31:32), implying that God made a covenant with all mankind which man has broken (Gen. 2:15–17; Hos. 6:7; Rom. 5:12–15).
24:7 *new wine mourneth.* The vines fail because of the curse, and there is no drinking or making merry.
24:8 *tabrets.* Hand-drums or tambourines. God's judgment will remove all delights (*mirth*) from sinners (Rev. 18:22).
24:9 *wine . . . strong drink.* The alcoholic products of the vine and grain, respectively.
24:10 *confusion.* Chaos or formlessness.
24:11 *joy is darkened.* Happiness turns to gloom.
24:13 *shaking of.* What has fallen or been knocked off. *vintage.* The time of grape gathering. The number of people left is so small that they are likened to plants after the harvest, where only a few fruits remain on the branches.
24:14 *sing for the majesty of the LORD.* Although the destruction of the world will end the joy of the wicked, the righteous will greet Him with praise and adoration (2 Thess. 1:10; Rev. 19:1–5).
24:15 *fires.* Literally, "lights," most likely the east, where the light rises. *sea.* The west, where the sun sets. The worshipers will come from all places and nations.
24:17 *snare.* Trapping net (Luke 21:35).
24:18 *fleeth . . . shall fall.* Judgment is inescapable (Amos 5:19).
24:19 *clean dissolved.* Split or cracked through. *moved exceedingly.* Thoroughly shaken.
24:20 *reel to and fro.* Tremble. *be removed like a cottage.* Totter like a hut.
24:21 *host of the high ones.* Literally, "the army of the height in the height," referring to the spiritual wickedness in high places, the wicked angels (Eph. 6:12; Jude 6).
24:22 *visited.* Given attention to with the appropriate action, here punishment.
24:23 *moon . . . sun ashamed.* Cosmic disruption of the universe, a sign of the day of the Lord (13:10). *ancients.* Elders.

Thoughts for Personal/Family Worship: Chapter 24

There is a day coming when the Lord will bring this present world to an end. The Christian should always be ready for this by watching and waiting in prayer. We

in mount Zion, and in Jerusalem, and before his
ancients gloriously.

CHAPTER 25

O LORD, thou *art* my God; I will exalt thee, I will
praise thy name; for thou hast done wonderful
things; thy counsels of old *are* faithfulness *and*
truth.
2 For thou hast made of a city an heap; *of* a
defenced city a ruin: a palace of strangers to be no
city; it shall never be built.
3 Therefore shall the strong people glorify thee,
the city of the terrible nations shall fear thee.
4 For thou hast been a strength to the poor, a
strength to the needy in his distress, a refuge from
the storm, a shadow from the heat, when the blast
of the terrible ones *is* as a storm *against* the wall.
5 Thou shalt bring down the noise of strangers,
as the heat in a dry place; *even* the heat with the
shadow of a cloud: the branch of the terrible ones
shall be brought low.
6 ¶ And in this mountain shall the LORD of hosts
make unto all people a feast of fat things, a feast
of wines on the lees, of fat things full of marrow,
of wines on the lees well refined.
7 And he will destroy in this mountain the face of
the covering cast over all people, and the vail that
is spread over all nations.
8 He will swallow up death in victory; and the
Lord GOD will wipe away tears from off all faces;
and the rebuke of his people shall he take away
from off all the earth: for the LORD hath spoken *it*.
9 ¶ And it shall be said in that day, Lo, this *is* our
God; we have waited for him, and he will save us:
this *is* the LORD; we have waited for him, we will
be glad and rejoice in his salvation.
10 For in this mountain shall the hand of the LORD
rest, and Moab shall be trodden down under him,
even as straw is trodden down for the dunghill.
11 And he shall spread forth his hands in the
midst of them, as he that swimmeth spreadeth
forth *his hands* to swim: and he shall bring down
their pride together with the spoils of their hands.
12 And the fortress of the high fort of thy walls
shall he bring down, lay low, *and* bring to the
ground, *even* to the dust.

CHAPTER 26

IN that day shall this song be sung in the land of
Judah; We have a strong city; salvation will *God*
appoint *for* walls and bulwarks.
2 Open ye the gates, that the righteous nation

need to diligently observe the days we are living in. The wickedness upon the earth is becoming ripe for harvest. All too suddenly the Lord will send His angels as reapers into the world, and none shall escape who live unrepentant lives. Let us ensure that we are walking in the ways of the Lord and that we are bearing fruit that is pleasing in His sight. For then that day will be filled with joy, and we shall join the heavenly host in praising our blessed Redeemer who loved us and washed us from our sins with His blood (Rev. 1:5). However, if we are not saved by Christ's blood, His coming will cause us to wail in terror (Rev. 1:7). If Christ were to come today, how would you greet Him, with praise or in horror?

Songs of Resurrection and Feasting on Eternal Life (25:1—26:19)

Chapter 25: *The people rejoice in God's glorious salvation and give thanks for His mercy.*

25:1 *thy name.* Who God is in the totality of the perfections that He has revealed. *wonderful things.* Supernatural and extraordinary acts.
25:2 *defenced.* Inaccessible, unassailable. *palace of strangers.* A citadel of foreigners.
25:3 *terrible.* Violently acting or awe-inspiring (v. 4).
25:4 *poor.* Helpless.
25:5 *strangers.* Foreigners.
25:6 *this mountain.* Zion, a symbol of God's kingdom (11:9; 24:23). *wines on the lees.* Refined, mature wine. The whole fare pictures a luxuriant feast, the best (*fat*) of everything.
25:7 *destroy.* Swallow up (same Hebrew word as in v. 8). *vail.* The woven hanging or covering.
25:8 *swallow up death in victory.* God will raise His people from the dead, never again to suffer death (26:19; Hos. 13:14; 1 Cor. 15:54). *wipe away tears.* He will remove sadness and provide perfect comfort for all previous hurts (Rev. 7:17; 21:4). *rebuke of his people.* Their disgrace and shame (Isa. 54:4).
25:9 *waited.* Hoped with confident expectation.
25:10 *Moab.* As representative of all those hostile to God and His people.
25:11 *together with the spoils of their hands.* "In spite of the skillful movements of his hands," picturing the tragi-comical scene of their swimming, to no avail, through dung to escape.

Thoughts for Personal/Family Worship: Chapter 25

1. **There is much in this chapter to encourage the believer. When the enemies of the gospel seem to have the upper hand, we must look with expectancy beyond the present to that glorious and certain event when the Lord will be seen to reign in Zion. On that great day we shall surely declare with Isaiah, "O LORD, thou art my God; I will exalt thee, I will praise thy name; for thou hast done wonderful things; thy counsels of old are faithfulness and truth" (v. 1).**
2. **In this tragic and sinful world, death and weeping are the inevitable consequences of the fall. Yet how blessed will that day be when death is swallowed up in victory, God will wipe away all tears, and believers will feast with Christ (vv. 6–8)! The thought of this should spur us on to live for Christ now with steady perseverance in good works (1 Cor. 15:58). If the anticipation of the destruction of this world can help us to reject worldly lusts and fears (ch. 24), how can the hope of the resurrection help us to set our affections on Christ and His kingdom?**

Chapter 26: *Isaiah incites us to confidence in the Lord for all of His righteous works.*

26:1 *that day.* The Day of the Lord (see note at 13:6). *bulwarks.* Ramparts or defensive walls. The Lord's salvation

which keepeth the truth may enter in.
3 Thou wilt keep *him* in perfect peace, *whose*
mind *is* stayed *on thee*: because he trusteth in thee.
4 Trust ye in the LORD for ever: for in the LORD
JEHOVAH *is* everlasting strength:
5 ¶ For he bringeth down them that dwell on
high; the lofty city, he layeth it low; he layeth it low,
even to the ground; he bringeth it *even* to the dust.
6 The foot shall tread it down, *even* the feet of the
poor, *and* the steps of the needy.
7 The way of the just *is* uprightness: thou, most
upright, dost weigh the path of the just.
8 Yea, in the way of thy judgments, O LORD, have
we waited for thee; the desire of *our* soul *is* to thy
name, and to the remembrance of thee.
9 With my soul have I desired thee in the night;
yea, with my spirit within me will I seek thee
early: for when thy judgments *are* in the earth, the
inhabitants of the world will learn righteousness.
10 Let favour be shewed to the wicked, *yet*
will he not learn righteousness: in the land of
uprightness will he deal unjustly, and will not
behold the majesty of the LORD.
11 LORD, *when* thy hand is lifted up, they will not
see: *but* they shall see, and be ashamed for *their*
envy at the people; yea, the fire of thine enemies
shall devour them.
12 ¶ LORD, thou wilt ordain peace for us: for thou
also hast wrought all our works in us.
13 O LORD our God, *other* lords beside thee have
had dominion over us: *but* by thee only will we
make mention of thy name.
14 *They are* dead, they shall not live; *they are*
deceased, they shall not rise: therefore hast thou
visited and destroyed them, and made all their
memory to perish.
15 Thou hast increased the nation, O LORD, thou
hast increased the nation: thou art glorified: thou
hadst removed *it* far *unto* all the ends of the earth.
16 LORD, in trouble have they visited thee, they
poured out a prayer *when* thy chastening *was*
upon them.
17 Like as a woman with child, *that* draweth near
the time of her delivery, is in pain, *and* crieth out
in her pangs; so have we been in thy sight, O LORD.
18 We have been with child, we have been in pain,
we have as it were brought forth wind; we have
not wrought any deliverance in the earth; neither
have the inhabitants of the world fallen.
19 Thy dead *men* shall live, *together with* my dead
body shall they arise. Awake and sing, ye that
dwell in dust: for thy dew *is as* the dew of herbs,
and the earth shall cast out the dead.
20 ¶ Come, my people, enter thou into thy
chambers, and shut thy doors about thee: hide
thyself as it were for a little moment, until the
indignation be overpast.
21 For, behold, the LORD cometh out of his place
to punish the inhabitants of the earth for their
iniquity: the earth also shall disclose her blood,
and shall no more cover her slain.

CHAPTER 27

IN that day the LORD with his sore and great and
strong sword shall punish leviathan the piercing

---

is the protection of His people.

26:3 *perfect peace.* Literally, "peace, peace," using repetition the convey the superlative. God can give supernatural peace to those who trust Him (Phil. 4:6–7). *stayed.* Propped up, leaned upon (36:6; 48:2).

26:4 *Trust.* Place confidence in for security; one of the principal words for faith in the Old Testament. *the LORD JEHOVAH.* See note at 12:2. *everlasting strength.* Literally, "the rock of ages or eternity," picturing God as a huge, immovable boulder that never changes (17:10).

26:6 *poor.* The afflicted.

26:7 *weigh the path.* Make the path level.

26:8 *waited.* Hoped with confident expectation. *name.* Who God is in all His revealed perfections (v. 13).

26:9 *soul.* Whole person. *seek thee early.* Pursue God earnestly and eagerly, a reference to manner, not time.

26:11 *thy hand is lifted up.* The Lord exercises great power. *fire of thine enemies shall devour them.* God's anger against His adversaries is like a devouring fire (Heb. 10:27).

26:12 *ordain.* Accomplish or establish. *wrought.* Performed or done.

26:16 *visited.* Gave attention to.

26:18 *in pain.* As a woman about to give birth, yet with no show but *wind*, a picture of disappointment.

26:19 *dead men shall live.* An explicit declaration of the resurrection of the body (Job 19:25–27; Dan. 12:2; John 5:28–29; 1 Cor. 15). *Awake and sing.* The future resurrection calls for a present spiritual resurrection into a life of worship (Eph. 5:14,19). *dew.* An image of renewed life (Deut. 32:2; Ps. 110:3; Prov. 19:12; Hos. 14:5).

The Day of Judgment and Fruitfulness (26:20—27:13)

26:20 *hide . . . until the indignation be overpast.* As in the first Passover (Ex. 12:22–23).

26:21 *disclose her blood.* Reveal the acts of violence and murder committed on it: judgment day.

Thoughts for Personal/Family Worship: Chapter 26

1. **The Lord Jehovah is the Rock of ages (v. 4). In Him we need not fear. In Him is all our hope. Therefore, we must trust Him in every situation. The trials of life often bring doubts to our minds, but these we must cast off. It is only when our mind and thoughts are propped up upon the Lord, thinking of Him, that we will experience peace regardless of circumstances. What anxieties trouble you? How can you lean upon the Lord?**
2. **The resurrection of the dead is a strange doctrine to this world, but it is the center of the Christian hope. Christ's resurrection raises His elect spiritually to a living hope and will raise them one day to physical glory and immortality. What practical difference should the doctrine of the resurrection make in our lives?**

Chapter 27: *The world and its wickedness are defeated, and the Lord's people are gathered in.*

27:1 *that day.* The day of the Lord (see note at 13:6; also

serpent, even leviathan that crooked serpent; and
he shall slay the dragon that *is* in the sea.
2 In that day sing ye unto her, A vineyard of red
wine.
3 I the LORD do keep it; I will water it every moment: lest *any* hurt it, I will keep it night and day.
4 Fury *is* not in me: who would set the briers *and*
thorns against me in battle? I would go through
them, I would burn them together.
5 Or let him take hold of my strength, *that* he
may make peace with me; *and* he shall make
peace with me.
6 He shall cause them that come of Jacob to take
root: Israel shall blossom and bud, and fill the face
of the world with fruit.
7 ¶ Hath he smitten him, as he smote those
that smote him? *or* is he slain according to the
slaughter of them that are slain by him?
8 In measure, when it shooteth forth, thou wilt
debate with it: he stayeth his rough wind in the
day of the east wind.
9 By this therefore shall the iniquity of Jacob be
purged; and this *is* all the fruit to take away his
sin; when he maketh all the stones of the altar as
chalkstones that are beaten in sunder, the groves
and images shall not stand up.
10 Yet the defenced city *shall be* desolate, *and* the
habitation forsaken, and left like a wilderness:
there shall the calf feed, and there shall he lie
down, and consume the branches thereof.
11 When the boughs thereof are withered, they shall
be broken off: the women come, *and* set them on
fire: for it *is* a people of no understanding: therefore
he that made them will not have mercy on them,
and he that formed them will shew them no favour.
12 ¶ And it shall come to pass in that day, *that* the
LORD shall beat off from the channel of the river
unto the stream of Egypt, and ye shall be gathered
one by one, O ye children of Israel.
13 And it shall come to pass in that day, *that* the
great trumpet shall be blown, and they shall come
which were ready to perish in the land of Assyria,
and the outcasts in the land of Egypt, and shall
worship the LORD in the holy mount at Jerusalem.

CHAPTER 28

WOE to the crown of pride, to the drunkards
of Ephraim, whose glorious beauty *is* a fading
flower, which *are* on the head of the fat valleys of
them that are overcome with wine!
2 Behold, the Lord hath a mighty and strong one,
which as a tempest of hail *and* a destroying storm,
as a flood of mighty waters overflowing, shall cast
down to the earth with the hand.
3 The crown of pride, the drunkards of Ephraim,
shall be trodden under feet:
4 And the glorious beauty, which *is* on the head
of the fat valley, shall be a fading flower, *and* as
the hasty fruit before the summer; which *when* he
that looketh upon it seeth, while it is yet in his
hand he eateth it up.

27:12–13). *sore.* Relentless or fierce. *leviathan . . . piercing serpent . . . crooked serpent . . . dragon.* All descriptions of the same entity as a huge, twisting sea serpent, most likely referring to Satan (Gen. 3:1; Rev. 12:3,9).

27:2 *vineyard of red wine.* A vineyard that produced the desired fruit (v. 6; 4:2; 37:31; John 15:1–7), a symbol of God's people doing good works, in contrast to Israel's failure to respond with righteousness to God's covenant and provisions (5:1–7).

27:4–5 *Fury is not in me.* God's anger against the sins of His people has been propitiated (12:1; 54:8–9; Hos. 14:4), and He is at *peace* with all who will grasp His gospel by faith (*take hold of my strength*; 53:5).

27:8 *debate.* Contend. *stayeth.* Drives away or removes. *rough.* Fierce.

27:9 *purged.* Atoned for. *take away his sin.* See Rom. 11:27. *chalkstones . . . beaten in sunder.* Stones easily broken into powder or pulverized. *groves.* The wooden poles erected near altars, common in pagan rituals.

27:10 *defenced.* Fortified.

27:11 *have mercy.* Show compassion or pity. *shew them no favour.* Not be gracious.

27:12 *beat off from the channel.* Or possibly thresh out the ears of corn.

27:13 *great trumpet shall be blown.* To signal the return of the exiles (Num. 10:1–10; Matt. 24:31; 1 Cor. 15:52; 1 Thess. 4:16; Rev. 8:2), perhaps an allusion to the Jubilee (Lev. 25:9).

Thoughts for Personal/Family Worship: Chapter 27

The Lord gives His people a double grace in Christ. First He pacifies His righteous anger against their sins and establishes a relationship of peace with them (vv. 4–5). Second, He purifies their souls of sin and idolatry so that they bear the fruit of good works for His pleasure and the good of the world (vv. 2,6). Justification and sanctification are distinct but inseparable, and we need both to be saved. Through both of these graces the Lord gives His people victory over their ancient enemy, Satan, their tempter and accuser (v. 1). One day grace will become glory when the trumpet calls Christians to the side of their King (v. 13). However, these great blessings belong only to those who receive God's offer of peace by taking hold of Christ (v. 5). Faith is the hand that receives Him. Are you trusting in Christ alone for these blessings?

WOES AND HOPE FOR ISRAEL, JUDAH, AND EDOM (2:1—35:10)

Woes and Promises for Ephraim and Jerusalem (28:1—29:24)

Chapter 28: *Isaiah pronounces judgment on Ephraim.*

28:1 *Woe.* See note at 1:4. *crown of pride.* Samaria (Hos. 5:5). *Ephraim.* The northern kingdom of Israel (Isa. 1:3). *fat.* Fruitful or fertile (v. 4).

28:4 *hasty fruit.* The early or first-ripe fig. *yet in his hand.* Picturing the eagerness and swiftness with which it will be devoured.

28:5 *that day.* See 27:1. *diadem.* Or wreath, as a head-dress. The Lord will honor and glorify His beloved people with His glory (61:10; 62:3), for they are united to Him. *residue.* The

5 ¶ In that day shall the LORD of hosts be for a
crown of glory, and for a diadem of beauty, unto
the residue of his people,
6 And for a spirit of judgment to him that sitteth
in judgment, and for strength to them that turn
the battle to the gate.
7 ¶ But they also have erred through wine, and
through strong drink are out of the way; the priest
and the prophet have erred through strong drink,
they are swallowed up of wine, they are out of the
way through strong drink; they err in vision, they
stumble *in* judgment.
8 For all tables are full of vomit *and* filthiness, *so*
that there is no place *clean*.
9 ¶ Whom shall he teach knowledge? and whom
shall he make to understand doctrine? *them that*
are weaned from the milk, *and* drawn from the
breasts.
10 For precept *must be* upon precept, precept
upon precept; line upon line, line upon line; here
a little, *and* there a little:
11 For with stammering lips and another tongue
will he speak to this people.
12 To whom he said, This *is* the rest *wherewith*
ye may cause the weary to rest; and this *is* the
refreshing: yet they would not hear.
13 But the word of the LORD was unto them
precept upon precept, precept upon precept; line
upon line, line upon line; here a little, *and* there a
little; that they might go, and fall backward, and
be broken, and snared, and taken.
14 ¶ Wherefore hear the word of the LORD, ye
scornful men, that rule this people which *is* in
Jerusalem.
15 Because ye have said, We have made a covenant
with death, and with hell are we at agreement;
when the overflowing scourge shall pass through,
it shall not come unto us: for we have made lies
our refuge, and under falsehood have we hid
ourselves:
16 ¶ Therefore thus saith the Lord GOD, Behold, I
lay in Zion for a foundation a stone, a tried stone,
a precious corner *stone*, a sure foundation: he that
believeth shall not make haste.
17 Judgment also will I lay to the line, and righ-
teousness to the plummet: and the hail shall
sweep away the refuge of lies, and the waters shall
overflow the hiding place.
18 ¶ And your covenant with death shall be
disannulled, and your agreement with hell shall
not stand; when the overflowing scourge shall
pass through, then ye shall be trodden down by it.
19 From the time that it goeth forth it shall take
you: for morning by morning shall it pass over, by
day and by night: and it shall be a vexation only *to*
understand the report.
20 For the bed is shorter than that *a man* can
stretch himself *on it*: and the covering narrower
than that he can wrap himself *in it*.
21 For the LORD shall rise up as *in* mount Perazim,
he shall be wroth as *in* the valley of Gibeon, that
he may do his work, his strange work; and bring
to pass his act, his strange act.
22 Now therefore be ye not mockers, lest your
bands be made strong: for I have heard from the
Lord GOD of hosts a consumption, even deter-
mined upon the whole earth.
23 ¶ Give ye ear, and hear my voice; hearken, and
hear my speech.
24 Doth the plowman plow all day to sow? doth
he open and break the clods of his ground?
25 When he hath made plain the face thereof,

---

remnant; evidence of hope that the judgment will not be total in its destruction.

28:6 *spirit of judgment*. The enabling power of the Holy Spirit to exercise authority with justice (4:4; 42:1).

28:7 *wine . . . strong drink*. Alcoholic products of the vine and grain, respectively. It is particularly grievous for leaders to allow intoxication to cloud their judgment (56:10–12; Lev. 10:9; Prov. 31:4–5).

28:9–12 This section appears to be a jeering, scornful response against the faithful ministry of Isaiah.

28:10 *precept . . . line*. The Hebrew terms are simple, one-syllable words that mockingly describe Isaiah's preaching—similar to the English expression "blah, blah, blah."

28:11 *stammering lips*. Mocking or derisive speech. *another tongue*. A foreign language, a sign of God's judgment on sinners (Deut. 28:47–50; 1 Cor. 14:21–22).

28:13 Isaiah turns their mockery into condemnation for their inexcusable rejection of such a simple message. *fall backward*. Totter or stumble backward. *broken*. Crushed or smashed. *snared*. Caught by bait. *taken*. Captured.

28:15 *covenant*. Probably their trust in Egypt to save them from Assyria (30:1–7; 31:1–3; 36:6,9). *death . . . lies*. Ironic statements of how worthless their hope is. *hell*. Hebrew, *sheol*, meaning the grave; the abode of departed, wicked spirits; or, as the parallelism shows it to mean here, *death*. *overflowing scourge*. An invading army, most likely the Assyrians (8:7–8).

28:16 In remarkable contrast to their worthless covenant and trust in mere man, the Lord declares that Christ, pictured as a *stone* (8:14; Ps. 118:22; Rom. 9:33; 10:11; 1 Peter 2:3–8; cf. 1 Cor. 3:11; Eph. 2:20), is the only One worthy of their faith. *I lay . . . for a foundation*. The Hebrew implies a past action; the Lord has already established Christ as the basis of the covenant of grace (2 Tim. 1:9). Christ is proven and reliable (*tried*), extremely valuable (*precious*), fundamental and necessary (*corner stone*), and solid and stable (*sure foundation*). *he that believeth*. The verbal form indicates constant, habitual believing. *not make haste*. Not yield or hurry away. True faith perseveres.

28:17 *line*. A cord used for measuring. *plummet*. A weight attached to a cord, used to ensure that a wall is built straight and upright. *hail . . . waters shall overflow*. See Matt. 7:24–27.

28:19 *vexation*. Trembling or terror.

28:21 *wroth*. Angry. *mount Perazim*. The location of a great victory for David (2 Sam. 5:20). *Strange . . . strange*. Two different words meaning peculiar and disturbing, respectively.

28:22 *bands*. Fetters or bonds. *consumption*. Complete destruction, annihilation.

28:24 *break the clods*. Harrow the ground.

doth he not cast abroad the fitches, and scatter the
cummin, and cast in the principal wheat and the
appointed barley and the rie in their place?
26 For his God doth instruct him to discretion,
and doth teach him.
27 For the fitches are not threshed with a threshing
instrument, neither is a cart wheel turned about
upon the cummin; but the fitches are beaten out
with a staff, and the cummin with a rod.
28 Bread *corn* is bruised; because he will not ever
be threshing it, nor break *it with* the wheel of his
cart, nor bruise it *with* his horsemen.
29 This also cometh forth from the LORD of hosts,
which is wonderful in counsel, *and* excellent in
working.

CHAPTER 29

WOE to Ariel, to Ariel, the city *where* David dwelt!
add ye year to year; let them kill sacrifices.
2 Yet I will distress Ariel, and there shall be heavi-
ness and sorrow: and it shall be unto me as Ariel.
3 And I will camp against thee round about, and
will lay siege against thee with a mount, and I will
raise forts against thee.
4 And thou shalt be brought down, *and* shalt
speak out of the ground, and thy speech shall be
low out of the dust, and thy voice shall be, as of
one that hath a familiar spirit, out of the ground,
and thy speech shall whisper out of the dust.
5 Moreover the multitude of thy strangers shall
be like small dust, and the multitude of the
terrible ones *shall be* as chaff that passeth away:
yea, it shall be at an instant suddenly.
6 Thou shalt be visited of the LORD of hosts
with thunder, and with earthquake, and great
noise, with storm and tempest, and the flame of
devouring fire.
7 ¶ And the multitude of all the nations that fight
against Ariel, even all that fight against her and
her munition, and that distress her, shall be as a
dream of a night vision.
8 It shall even be as when an hungry *man*
dreameth, and, behold, he eateth; but he awaketh,
and his soul is empty: or as when a thirsty man
dreameth, and, behold, he drinketh; but he
awaketh, and, behold, *he is* faint, and his soul hath
appetite: so shall the multitude of all the nations
be, that fight against mount Zion.
9 ¶ Stay yourselves, and wonder; cry ye out, and
cry: they are drunken, but not with wine; they
stagger, but not with strong drink.
10 For the LORD hath poured out upon you the
spirit of deep sleep, and hath closed your eyes: the
prophets and your rulers, the seers hath he covered.
11 And the vision of all is become unto you as the
words of a book that is sealed, which *men* deliver
to one that is learned, saying, Read this, I pray
thee: and he saith, I cannot; for it *is* sealed:
12 And the book is delivered to him that is not
learned, saying, Read this, I pray thee: and he
saith, I am not learned.
13 ¶ Wherefore the Lord said, Forasmuch as this
people draw near *me* with their mouth, and with

28:25 *fitches.* Fennel flowers or dill. *cummin.* An herb, the seeds of which are used as seasoning (v. 27). *principal.* Set in place or in rows. *appointed.* In its own plot. *rie in their place.* Rye in its boundary.

28:26 *his God doth instruct . . . teach him.* If all workers in agriculture receive their skill from God, then surely we can trust Him to know how to use severe methods to cultivate His people.

28:29 *wonderful in counsel, and excellent in working.* God is supernatural and amazing in His wisdom and understanding when He makes His plans (9:6; 40:13–14; Rom. 11:33–34).

Thoughts for Personal/Family Worship: Chapter 28

1. **It is important to have a teachable spirit and to willingly be taught from the Word of God. We should never think so highly of ourselves as to regard the instruction of God as childish and beneath us. In reality, we are far beneath Him, for God's wisdom is infinitely beyond our understanding (v. 29). Therefore, we should gladly submit to being taught like children. There is great benefit in the sincere milk of the Word (1 Peter 2:2), and our faith is built up "precept upon precept; line upon line" (vv. 10,13). How can we approach the Word with true humility and openness?**
2. **The believer has a "sure foundation" in Jesus Christ (v. 16). He alone is our hope and stay. If we build on anything else, our structure will fall. Meditate upon each aspect of the description of Christ as the stone upon which our faith must stand. How is Christ proven and reliable? Extremely valuable? Fundamental and necessary? Solid and stable? How does seeing these qualities in Christ draw out your faith in Him? How does it fan into flame your love for Him?**

Chapter 29: *The Lord inflicts punishment upon Jerusalem.*

29:1 *Woe.* See note at 1:4 (v. 15). *Ariel.* A special name for Jerusalem, perhaps meaning "lion of God" or "hearth of God," where sacrifices were offered. *let them kill sacrifices.* Or let the feasts recur.

29:3 *mount.* A siege wall or entrenchment. *forts.* Siege works.

29:4 *one that hath a familiar spirit.* One communicating with a spirit of the dead. *whisper.* Peep or chirp.

29:5 *strangers.* Foreigners. *terrible ones.* Formidable adversaries, ruthless tyrants. *suddenly.* Perhaps referring to Sennacherib's defeat (37:33–37).

29:6 *visited.* Called to account.

29:7 *munition.* Fortress or stronghold.

29:9 *Stay yourselves.* Tarry or linger. *wonder.* Be horrified or paralyzed with fear. *cry ye out, and cry.* Literally, "blind yourselves and be blind" (v. 10).

29:10 *seers.* Prophets.

29:11 *vision.* The revelation from God. *sealed.* Fastened or closed up.

29:12 *not learned.* Does not know how to read.

29:13 *Forasmuch.* Because. *with their lips.* Outward forms of worship mean nothing to the Lord when the *heart* is not engaged (Matt. 5:8; 23:25–28). *their fear toward me . . . the precept of men.* Their worship and obedience are based on human teachings, not on God's Word (Matt. 15:7–9;

their lips do honour me, but have removed their
heart far from me, and their fear toward me is
taught by the precept of men:
14 Therefore, behold, I will proceed to do a
marvellous work among this people, *even* a
marvellous work and a wonder: for the wisdom of
their wise *men* shall perish, and the understanding
of their prudent *men* shall be hid.
15 Woe unto them that seek deep to hide their
counsel from the LORD, and their works are in
the dark, and they say, Who seeth us? and who
knoweth us?
16 Surely your turning of things upside down
shall be esteemed as the potter's clay: for shall the
work say of him that made it, He made me not?
or shall the thing framed say of him that framed
it, He had no understanding?
17 *Is* it not yet a very little while, and Lebanon
shall be turned into a fruitful field, and the fruit-
ful field shall be esteemed as a forest?
18 ¶ And in that day shall the deaf hear the words
of the book, and the eyes of the blind shall see out
of obscurity, and out of darkness.
19 The meek also shall increase *their* joy in the
LORD, and the poor among men shall rejoice in
the Holy One of Israel.
20 For the terrible one is brought to nought, and
the scorner is consumed, and all that watch for
iniquity are cut off:
21 That make a man an offender for a word, and
lay a snare for him that reproveth in the gate, and
turn aside the just for a thing of nought.
22 Therefore thus saith the LORD, who redeemed
Abraham, concerning the house of Jacob, Jacob
shall not now be ashamed, neither shall his face
now wax pale.
23 But when he seeth his children, the work
of mine hands, in the midst of him, they shall
sanctify my name, and sanctify the Holy One of
Jacob, and shall fear the God of Israel.
24 They also that erred in spirit shall come to
understanding, and they that murmured shall
learn doctrine.

CHAPTER 30

WOE to the rebellious children, saith the LORD,
that take counsel, but not of me; and that cover
with a covering, but not of my spirit, that they
may add sin to sin:
2 That walk to go down into Egypt, and have
not asked at my mouth; to strengthen themselves
in the strength of Pharaoh, and to trust in the
shadow of Egypt!
3 Therefore shall the strength of Pharaoh be your
shame, and the trust in the shadow of Egypt *your*
confusion.
4 For his princes were at Zoan, and his ambassa-
dors came to Hanes.
5 They were all ashamed of a people *that* could
not profit them, nor be an help nor profit, but a
shame, and also a reproach.
6 The burden of the beasts of the south: into
the land of trouble and anguish, from whence
come the young and old lion, the viper and fiery
flying serpent, they will carry their riches upon
the shoulders of young asses, and their treasures
upon the bunches of camels, to a people *that* shall
not profit *them*.
7 For the Egyptians shall help in vain, and to no
purpose: therefore have I cried concerning this,
Their strength *is* to sit still.

Mark 7:6–7). Worship that pleases God is always a response of faith and obedience to God's Word and not invented by men (Ex. 25:9, 40; Lev. 10:1–3; Col. 2:23).

29:14 *marvellous work and a wonder*. The same Hebrew root word is used for both, referring to that which is supernatural or extraordinary. *for the wisdom . . . shall perish*. When men rely on their wisdom for their religion, God makes them into fools (1 Cor. 1:19; cf. Matt. 11:25; Rom. 1:21–22).

29:16 *framed*. Formed.

29:18 *obscurity*. Gloom.

29:19 *meek*. Afflicted and humbled. *poor*. Helpless and dependent.

29:20 *terrible one*. Ruthless tyrant. *brought to nought*. Be no more.

29:21 *for a thing of nought*. For emptiness.

29:22 *wax*. Become or grow.

29:23 *sanctify*. Set apart or honored as holy. *name*. Who God has revealed Himself to be in all His perfections.

29:24 *erred*. Staggered, wavered. *doctrine*. Instruction.

Thoughts for Personal/Family Worship: Chapter 29

The Lord's indictment against hypocritical and man-made worship (v. 13) is a sobering reminder of the importance of worshiping the Lord in spirit and in truth (John 4:24). It is all too possible to be in a religious environment and to go through all the routines of worship and yet have a heart that is far from God and a form of worship never commanded by God. God rejects both heartless worship and humanly invented worship, for true worshipers worship God as the Holy Spirit engages their hearts with the truth of His Word. Those raised in the church must ask themselves two questions. First, am I giving God mere lip-service or worshiping Him with love and fear in my heart? Second, are the forms of worship we use in our service commanded by God's Word or based merely in human ideas?

The Call to Trust in the Lord, Not in Egypt (30:1—31:9)

Chapter 30: *The Lord denounces those who seek help from Egypt rather than seeking Him.*

30:1 *Woe*. See note at 1:4.

30:2 *trust*. Seek and find refuge. *shadow*. An image for protection or safety (v. 3).

30:4 *princes*. Rulers. *ambassadors*. Messengers.

30:6 *burden*. The oracle or prophetic pronouncement. *south*. The Negev, a desert region. *fiery flying serpent*. Some sort of swift venomous snake. *bunches*. Humps.

8 ¶ Now go, write it before them in a table, and
note it in a book, that it may be for the time to
come for ever and ever:
9 That this *is* a rebellious people, lying children,
children *that* will not hear the law of the LORD:
10 Which say to the seers, See not; and to the
prophets, Prophesy not unto us right things,
speak unto us smooth things, prophesy deceits:
11 Get you out of the way, turn aside out of the
path, cause the Holy One of Israel to cease from
before us.
12 Wherefore thus saith the Holy One of Israel,
Because ye despise this word, and trust in
oppression and perverseness, and stay thereon:
13 Therefore this iniquity shall be to you as a
breach ready to fall, swelling out in a high wall,
whose breaking cometh suddenly at an instant.
14 And he shall break it as the breaking of the
potters' vessel that is broken in pieces; he shall
not spare: so that there shall not be found in the
bursting of it a sherd to take fire from the hearth,
or to take water *withal* out of the pit.
15 For thus saith the Lord GOD, the Holy One
of Israel; In returning and rest shall ye be saved;
in quietness and in confidence shall be your
strength: and ye would not.
16 But ye said, No; for we will flee upon horses;
therefore shall ye flee: and, We will ride upon the
swift; therefore shall they that pursue you be swift.
17 One thousand *shall flee* at the rebuke of one;
at the rebuke of five shall ye flee: till ye be left as
a beacon upon the top of a mountain, and as an
ensign on an hill.
18 ¶ And therefore will the LORD wait, that he
may be gracious unto you, and therefore will he
be exalted, that he may have mercy upon you: for
the LORD *is* a God of judgment: blessed *are* all
they that wait for him.
19 For the people shall dwell in Zion at Jerusalem:
thou shalt weep no more: he will be very gracious
unto thee at the voice of thy cry; when he shall
hear it, he will answer thee.
20 And *though* the Lord give you the bread of
adversity, and the water of affliction, yet shall not
thy teachers be removed into a corner any more,
but thine eyes shall see thy teachers:
21 And thine ears shall hear a word behind thee,
saying, This *is* the way, walk ye in it, when ye turn
to the right hand, and when ye turn to the left.
22 Ye shall defile also the covering of thy graven
images of silver, and the ornament of thy molten
images of gold: thou shalt cast them away as a
menstruous cloth; thou shalt say unto it, Get thee
hence.
23 Then shall he give the rain of thy seed, that thou
shalt sow the ground withal; and bread of the in-
crease of the earth, and it shall be fat and plenteous:
in that day shall thy cattle feed in large pastures.
24 The oxen likewise and the young asses that ear
the ground shall eat clean provender, which hath
been winnowed with the shovel and with the fan.
25 And there shall be upon every high mountain,
and upon every high hill, rivers *and* streams of
waters in the day of the great slaughter, when the
towers fall.
26 Moreover the light of the moon shall be as the
light of the sun, and the light of the sun shall be
sevenfold, as the light of seven days, in the day
that the LORD bindeth up the breach of his people,
and healeth the stroke of their wound.
27 ¶ Behold, the name of the LORD cometh from
far, burning *with* his anger, and the burden *thereof*
is heavy: his lips are full of indignation, and his
tongue as a devouring fire:
28 And his breath, as an overflowing stream, shall
reach to the midst of the neck, to sift the nations
with the sieve of vanity: and *there shall be* a bridle
in the jaws of the people, causing *them* to err.
29 Ye shall have a song, as in the night *when* a holy
solemnity is kept; and gladness of heart, as when
one goeth with a pipe to come into the mountain
of the LORD, to the mighty One of Israel.
30 And the LORD shall cause his glorious voice to
be heard, and shall shew the lighting down of his
arm, with the indignation of *his* anger, and *with*
the flame of a devouring fire, *with* scattering, and
tempest, and hailstones.
31 For through the voice of the LORD shall the

30:8 *table.* Tablet.
30:10 *seers . . . prophets.* The same class of people. *smooth things.* Falsehood or flattery.
30:12 *trust in oppression and perverseness.* Put confidence in that which is gained by extortion and craftiness. *stay.* Depend on.
30:13 *breach.* Gap or crack (v. 26).
30:14 *sherd.* Fragment of pottery. *the pit.* The cistern.
30:15 *returning.* Repentance. Turning from sin back to the Lord and trusting in Him is the only way to salvation (Mark 1:15; Acts 20:21; Heb. 6:1). *and ye would not.* But you were not willing (John 5:40).
30:17 *beacon.* Signal post or flagstaff. *ensign.* Banner or flag.
30:18 *will the LORD wait.* God patiently and yet eagerly intends to give grace at the right time. *be exalted, that he may have mercy.* He glorifies Himself by showing compassion (48:9). *God of judgment.* The God who does justice, which includes keeping His promises to give grace to the humble who hope (*wait*) in Him (1 John 1:9).
30:20 *removed into a corner.* Hidden.
30:22 *covering.* The metal plating decorating the *images.*
30:23 *withal.* With it. *be fat.* A sign of prosperity.
30:24 *ear the ground.* Work the ground. *clean provender.* Seasoned fodder. *fan.* A fork-like tool for winnowing the harvest to separate the grain from the chaff.
30:26 *sevenfold.* A figure of speech for intensity or completeness. The sunlight will be overwhelmingly bright.
30:29 *holy solemnity.* A sacred festival. *pipe.* Some sort of wind instrument. *the mighty One.* The Rock, a huge, immovable boulder as an image of stability.

Assyrian be beaten down, *which* smote with a rod.
32 And *in* every place where the grounded staff
shall pass, which the LORD shall lay upon him, *it*
shall be with tabrets and harps: and in battles of
shaking will he fight with it.
33 For Tophet *is* ordained of old; yea, for the king
it is prepared; he hath made *it* deep *and* large: the
pile thereof *is* fire and much wood; the breath of
the LORD, like a stream of brimstone, doth kindle it.

CHAPTER 31

WOE to them that go down to Egypt for help; and
stay on horses, and trust in chariots, because *they*
are many; and in horsemen, because they are very
strong; but they look not unto the Holy One of
Israel, neither seek the LORD!
2 Yet he also *is* wise, and will bring evil, and will
not call back his words: but will arise against the
house of the evildoers, and against the help of
them that work iniquity.
3 Now the Egyptians *are* men, and not God; and
their horses flesh, and not spirit. When the LORD
shall stretch out his hand, both he that helpeth
shall fall, and he that is holpen shall fall down, and
they all shall fail together.
4 For thus hath the LORD spoken unto me, Like
as the lion and the young lion roaring on his prey,
when a multitude of shepherds is called forth
against him, *he* will not be afraid of their voice,
nor abase himself for the noise of them: so shall
the LORD of hosts come down to fight for mount
Zion, and for the hill thereof.
5 As birds flying, so will the LORD of hosts defend
Jerusalem; defending also he will deliver *it; and*
passing over he will preserve *it*.
6 ¶ Turn ye unto *him from* whom the children of
Israel have deeply revolted.
7 For in that day every man shall cast away his
idols of silver, and his idols of gold, which your
own hands have made unto you *for* a sin.
8 ¶ Then shall the Assyrian fall with the sword,
not of a mighty man; and the sword, not of a mean
man, shall devour him: but he shall flee from the
sword, and his young men shall be discomfited.
9 And he shall pass over to his strong hold for
fear, and his princes shall be afraid of the ensign,
saith the LORD, whose fire *is* in Zion, and his fur-
nace in Jerusalem.

CHAPTER 32

BEHOLD, a king shall reign in righteousness, and
princes shall rule in judgment.

30:32 *grounded staff.* Literally, "decreed rod," the punishment God appointed. *tabrets.* Hand-drums or tambourines. *harps.* Some sort of stringed instrument. *battles of shaking.* The brandishing of weapons in battle.

30:33 *Tophet.* The valley of Hinnom, where children were offered in the flames to idols. It became a symbol of severe judgment and punishment. *brimstone.* Sulfur, alluding to God's destruction of Sodom (34:9; Gen. 19:24; Deut. 29:23).

Thoughts for Personal/Family Worship: Chapter 30

1. **There is "a time to keep silence" (Eccl. 3:7). Great comfort is found in the words "In quietness and in confidence shall be your strength" (v. 15). When we are in quiet trust before the Lord, we are better placed to hear Him speaking through His Word and to submit to His will for us. We receive confidence through the promises of God. They strengthen us in times of trial. Faith is always the best way, but too often the Lord must say "yet ye would not" (v. 15).**
2. **We are often impatient and find waiting hard. Why do our prayers seem to go unanswered for so long? Verse 18 gives us some of the answer: we are waiting because God Himself is waiting for the right time to give us the blessing He desires for us. We must trust that He is faithful and just to bless those who humbly hope in Him. We must also learn to desire that He will be glorified in the way He shows us mercy more than we desire to have the mercy exactly when and how we want it. How does this help you understand what it means to find strength in quietness and confidence (v. 15)?**

Chapter 31: ***Isaiah warns of the folly of trusting in Egypt and predicts the fall of Assyria.***

31:1 *Woe.* See note at 1:4. *stay.* Depend. *trust.* Place confidence in for safety.

31:2 *he also is wise.* A reference to God. *evil.* Calamity, referring to judgment. *evildoers.* Those who behave ruinously.

31:3 *men, and not God.* The Lord is in a different category from mankind and is the only proper object of our supreme love and trust (40:17,25; Pss. 118:6–9; 146:3–6). *flesh . . . spirit.* Contrasting the weakness, mortality, and transience of all creatures in this fallen world with God's powerful, eternal, and boundless life (40:6–8,28–31; Ps. 78:39; Jer. 17:5–6). *holpen.* Helped.

31:4 *abase himself.* Be disturbed or cringe. *noise.* Multitude.

31:5 *flying.* Hovering in order to protect.

31:6 *Turn.* Reverse direction; the principal word in the Old Testament for repentance.

31:8 *mighty man . . . mean man.* Two different words translated elsewhere as "man," the first being man in strength and the second common man in his frailty. *be discomfited.* Become forced labor.

31:9 *ensign.* Banner.

Thoughts for Personal/Family Worship: Chapter 31

The destructive nature of sin is such that it drives men and women to foolish would-be remedies. Judah's sin kept them away from the only One who could help. They preferred to seek help from the nation that had once enslaved them and vainly opted for the support of Egypt's horses and chariots rather than submitting to the will of the Lord and trusting in Him. Oh, that God would save us from such foolishness and hardness of heart! He alone can deliver us. Let us therefore always be looking unto Him. Why is it foolish to trust in men and their resources instead of in God?

Chapter 32: ***Isaiah prophesies about the coming King and the blessing of His kingdom.***

The King and the Spirit (32:1–20)

32:1 *a king shall reign in righteousness.* A promise of Christ

2 And a man shall be as an hiding place from the
wind, and a covert from the tempest; as rivers of
water in a dry place, as the shadow of a great rock
in a weary land.
3 And the eyes of them that see shall not be dim,
and the ears of them that hear shall hearken.
4 The heart also of the rash shall understand
knowledge, and the tongue of the stammerers
shall be ready to speak plainly.
5 The vile person shall be no more called liberal,
nor the churl said *to be* bountiful.
6 For the vile person will speak villany, and his
heart will work iniquity, to practise hypocrisy,
and to utter error against the LORD, to make
empty the soul of the hungry, and he will cause
the drink of the thirsty to fail.
7 The instruments also of the churl *are* evil: he
deviseth wicked devices to destroy the poor with
lying words, even when the needy speaketh right.
8 But the liberal deviseth liberal things; and by
liberal things shall he stand.
9 ¶ Rise up, ye women that are at ease; hear my
voice, ye careless daughters; give ear unto my speech.
10 Many days and years shall ye be troubled,
ye careless women: for the vintage shall fail, the
gathering shall not come.
11 Tremble, ye women that are at ease; be
troubled, ye careless ones: strip you, and make
you bare, and gird *sackcloth* upon *your* loins.
12 They shall lament for the teats, for the pleasant
fields, for the fruitful vine.
13 Upon the land of my people shall come up
thorns *and* briers; yea, upon all the houses of joy
in the joyous city:
14 Because the palaces shall be forsaken; the
multitude of the city shall be left; the forts and
towers shall be for dens for ever, a joy of wild
asses, a pasture of flocks;
15 Until the spirit be poured upon us from on
high, and the wilderness be a fruitful field, and
the fruitful field be counted for a forest.
16 Then judgment shall dwell in the wilderness,
and righteousness remain in the fruitful field.
17 And the work of righteousness shall be peace;
and the effect of righteousness quietness and
assurance for ever.
18 And my people shall dwell in a peaceable
habitation, and in sure dwellings, and in quiet
resting places;
19 When it shall hail, coming down on the forest;
and the city shall be low in a low place.
20 Blessed *are* ye that sow beside all waters, that
send forth *thither* the feet of the ox and the ass.

CHAPTER 33

WOE to thee that spoilest, and thou *wast* not
spoiled; and dealest treacherously, and they dealt

(9:6–7; 11:1–5; Pss. 2:6; 45:1–7; 72:1–4; Dan. 7:13–14; Jer. 23:5–6; Ezek. 34:23–24; Zech. 9:9). *princes.* The servants of Christ will share His royal and righteous character. *judgment.* Justice.

32:2 *covert.* A shelter for protection. *rivers of water.* Sources of life, an image of the Holy Spirit (v. 15; 44:3). *shadow.* An image of protection and provision. *great rock.* A large crag or cliff.

32:3 *be dim.* Look away. *hearken.* Be fully alert.

32:4 *rash.* Impetuous. *stammerers.* Those unable to speak well.

32:5 *vile person.* A fool (v. 6). *liberal.* Noble (v. 8). *churl.* A knave or miserly person (v. 7). *bountiful.* Honorable.

32:6 *villany.* Disgraceful folly or sacrilege. *hypocrisy.* Ungodliness.

32:9 *at ease.* Carefree, careless, or arrogant. *careless.* Those feeling secure and confident (vv. 10–11).

32:10 *vintage.* The grape harvest.

32:11 *gird sackcloth upon your loins.* Put on uncomfortable clothing as a sign of mourning.

32:12 *lament for the teats.* Beat the breasts, an expression of grief.

32:13 *thorns and briers.* Emblems of the curse (Gen. 3:18; Heb. 6:8).

32:14 *forts.* Fortified hills within cities. *dens.* Or clear fields, empty spaces.

32:15 *spirit be poured . . . fruitful field.* The Holy Spirit comes with transforming, life-giving power through the promised King and His servants (vv. 1–2; John 7:37–39) in a renewal of God's creation (51:3; 65:17–18).

32:16–17 The images of agricultural prosperity (v. 15) are applied to spiritual and moral changes in God's people, who by the Holy Spirit become fruitful in justice (*judgment*; 4:4; 28:6), *righteousness*, and *peace* (5:7; 27:2,6; Rom. 14:17; Gal. 5:22–24).

32:18 *sure dwellings.* Dwellings of security. *quiet resting places.* Places that are undisturbed.

32:19 *hail.* Image of judgment on the wicked (28:2,17; 30:30), as upon Egypt (Ex. 9:18–35).

32:20 *Blessed.* Possessing great benefits from the Lord (Pss. 1:1; 32:1–2). *ye that sow beside all waters.* Those seeking to produce and spread the fruit of the Spirit (Gal. 6:7–8; James 3:18).

Thoughts for Personal/Family Worship: Chapter 32

1. **Christ's reign in the world is wonderful, and believers ought to rejoice that Christ reigns in their hearts by the Holy Spirit. Child of God, there was once a time when you could not see spiritual things, but now your eyes are opened to see the truth. Your ears were once deaf to the gospel, but now they hear. Your heart was once rash and foolish, but now the Lord has given knowledge so that you can speak plainly of what God has done through Christ. Take time now to praise and thank Him for His grace!**
2. **Peace is illusive to the world. It is impossible to find true peace from this passing world because sin ruins any possibility of doing so. Yet how blessed is the Christian, for the promise of God is, "My people shall dwell in . . . quiet resting places" (32:18). The child of God rests in the peace the Savior brings to the soul. He says, "Peace I leave with you, my peace I give unto you: not as the world giveth, give I unto you. Let not your heart be troubled, neither let it be afraid" (John 14:27). In what ways do you need peace today? How can you seek it from God through Christ?**

Chapter 33: ***The Lord judges the enemies of Zion.***

not treacherously with thee! when thou shalt
cease to spoil, thou shalt be spoiled; *and* when
thou shalt make an end to deal treacherously, they
shall deal treacherously with thee.
2 O LORD, be gracious unto us; we have waited
for thee: be thou their arm every morning, our
salvation also in the time of trouble.
3 At the noise of the tumult the people fled; at
the lifting up of thyself the nations were scattered.
4 And your spoil shall be gathered *like* the
gathering of the caterpiller: as the running to and
fro of locusts shall he run upon them.
5 The LORD is exalted; for he dwelleth on high: he
hath filled Zion with judgment and righteousness.
6 And wisdom and knowledge shall be the
stability of thy times, *and* strength of salvation:
the fear of the LORD *is* his treasure.
7 Behold, their valiant ones shall cry without: the
ambassadors of peace shall weep bitterly.
8 The highways lie waste, the wayfaring man
ceaseth: he hath broken the covenant, he hath
despised the cities, he regardeth no man.
9 The earth mourneth *and* languisheth: Lebanon
is ashamed *and* hewn down: Sharon is like a
wilderness; and Bashan and Carmel shake off
their fruits.
10 Now will I rise, saith the LORD; now will I be
exalted; now will I lift up myself.
11 Ye shall conceive chaff, ye shall bring forth
stubble: your breath, *as* fire, shall devour you.
12 And the people shall be *as* the burnings of
lime: *as* thorns cut up shall they be burned in the
fire.
13 ¶ Hear, ye *that are* far off, what I have done;
and, ye *that are* near, acknowledge my might.
14 The sinners in Zion are afraid; fearfulness
hath surprised the hypocrites. Who among us
shall dwell with the devouring fire? who among
us shall dwell with everlasting burnings?
15 He that walketh righteously, and speaketh
uprightly; he that despiseth the gain of
oppressions, that shaketh his hands from holding
of bribes, that stoppeth his ears from hearing of
blood, and shutteth his eyes from seeing evil;
16 He shall dwell on high: his place of defence
shall be the munitions of rocks: bread shall be
given him; his waters *shall be* sure.
17 Thine eyes shall see the king in his beauty: they
shall behold the land that is very far off.
18 Thine heart shall meditate terror. Where *is*
the scribe? where *is* the receiver? where *is* he that
counted the towers?
19 Thou shalt not see a fierce people, a people of a
deeper speech than thou canst perceive; of a stam-
mering tongue, *that thou canst* not understand.
20 Look upon Zion, the city of our solemnities:
thine eyes shall see Jerusalem a quiet habitation,
a tabernacle *that* shall not be taken down; not
one of the stakes thereof shall ever be removed,
neither shall any of the cords thereof be broken.
21 But there the glorious LORD *will be* unto us a
place of broad rivers *and* streams; wherein shall
go no galley with oars, neither shall gallant ship
pass thereby.
22 For the LORD *is* our judge, the LORD *is* our
lawgiver, the LORD *is* our king; he will save us.
23 Thy tacklings are loosed; they could not well
strengthen their mast, they could not spread the
sail: then is the prey of a great spoil divided; the
lame take the prey.

The King and Everlasting Fire (33:1–24)

33:1 *Woe.* See note at 1:4. *spoilest.* Destroys or deals violently.
33:2 *waited.* Hoped with confident expectation. *arm.* Symbolic of power for protection.
33:3 *tumult.* Noise, din, or roar.
33:4 *spoil.* Plunder or booty. *running to and fro of locusts.* An infestation of insects that devour everything, another plague on Egypt (32:19; Ps 78:46; cf. Joel 2:3–10).
33:7 *valiant ones.* The inhabitants of Jerusalem. *ambassadors.* Messengers.
33:8 *wayfaring man.* Traveler.
33:9 *languisheth.* Is sick or weak. *Lebanon . . . Sharon . . . Bashan . . . Carmel.* Each location represented productivity, whether in terms of cedars, agricultural, or cattle. *hewn.* Cut.
33:12 *burnings of lime.* Calcium oxide, a white powder that burns.
33:14 *hypocrites.* Godless, profane people. *devouring fire.* God's holiness expressed in His destructive anger against sinners (vv. 11–12; 30:27,30,33; Ex. 24:17; Lev. 10:2; Num. 11:1; 16:35; Deut. 32:22; Heb. 12:29). *everlasting burnings.* God's wrath will punish the wicked forever (34:10; Matt. 25:41,46).
33:15 *oppressions.* Extortions. *blood.* The Hebrew is plural, referring to blood-shedding.
33:16 *munitions of rocks.* Inaccessible heights.
33:17 *king in his beauty.* The Messiah (32:1; Ps. 45:2). The great hope of God's people is to see the glory and splendor of their Lord (35:2; John 17:24; Titus 2:13; 1 John 3:2).
33:18 *meditate terror.* Consider the things that formerly terrified God's people but now are gone (*where is he*). *receiver.* One who calculates the weight of something, such as tax or tribute.
33:19 *fierce.* Barbarous. *deeper.* Incomprehensible or unintelligible.
33:20 *solemnities.* Solemn feasts. *tabernacle.* Tent or dwelling place.
33:21 God will dwell with His people in His majesty (*glorious*, 40:5), and in His presence will be found abundant life in the Spirit (*rivers and streams*; 32:2,15) and safety from all enemies, symbolized by warships (*galley . . . gallant ship*).
33:22 *judge . . . lawgiver . . . king.* The divine ruler in his functions of exercising justice, making laws, and defending His kingdom (*save us*). The Messiah (v. 17) is here identified as Jehovah God (*the LORD*).
33:23 *tacklings.* Ropes or cords, referring to the ship's riggings. *prey.* Spoil, plunder.

Thoughts for Personal/Family Worship: Chapter 33

1. Let us never doubt the Lord's ability to provide for our needs. He promises to be our hiding place and to provide all we need (v. 16). If God cares for the sparrow that falls to the ground, will He not also care for His

24 And the inhabitant shall not say, I am sick: the
people that dwell therein *shall be* forgiven *their*
iniquity.

CHAPTER 34

COME near, ye nations, to hear; and hearken, ye
people: let the earth hear, and all that is therein;
the world, and all things that come forth of it.
2 For the indignation of the LORD *is* upon all
nations, and *his* fury upon all their armies: he
hath utterly destroyed them, he hath delivered
them to the slaughter.
3 Their slain also shall be cast out, and their
stink shall come up out of their carcases, and the
mountains shall be melted with their blood.
4 And all the host of heaven shall be dissolved,
and the heavens shall be rolled together as a scroll:
and all their host shall fall down, as the leaf falleth
off from the vine, and as a falling *fig* from the fig
tree.
5 For my sword shall be bathed in heaven: behold,
it shall come down upon Idumea, and upon the
people of my curse, to judgment.
6 The sword of the LORD is filled with blood, it
is made fat with fatness, *and* with the blood of
lambs and goats, with the fat of the kidneys of
rams: for the LORD hath a sacrifice in Bozrah, and
a great slaughter in the land of Idumea.
7 And the unicorns shall come down with them,
and the bullocks with the bulls; and their land
shall be soaked with blood, and their dust made
fat with fatness.
8 For *it is* the day of the LORD's vengeance, *and*
the year of recompences for the controversy of
Zion.
9 And the streams thereof shall be turned into
pitch, and the dust thereof into brimstone, and
the land thereof shall become burning pitch.
10 It shall not be quenched night nor day;
the smoke thereof shall go up for ever: from
generation to generation it shall lie waste; none
shall pass through it for ever and ever.
11 ¶ But the cormorant and the bittern shall
possess it; the owl also and the raven shall dwell
in it: and he shall stretch out upon it the line of
confusion, and the stones of emptiness.
12 They shall call the nobles thereof to the king-
dom, but none *shall be* there, and all her princes
shall be nothing.
13 And thorns shall come up in her palaces,
nettles and brambles in the fortresses thereof: and
it shall be an habitation of dragons, *and* a court
for owls.
14 The wild beasts of the desert shall also meet
with the wild beasts of the island, and the satyr
shall cry to his fellow; the screech owl also shall
rest there, and find for herself a place of rest.
15 There shall the great owl make her nest, and
lay, and hatch, and gather under her shadow:
there shall the vultures also be gathered, every one
with her mate.
16 ¶ Seek ye out of the book of the LORD, and
read: no one of these shall fail, none shall want
her mate: for my mouth it hath commanded, and
his spirit it hath gathered them.
17 And he hath cast the lot for them, and his
hand hath divided it unto them by line: they shall

---

children? Sometimes trials are brought upon us to shake us from our complacency in order that we might flee to the Lord, depend solely on Him, and renew our commitment to fear Him (v. 6) and obey His laws as the highest priority of our lives (v. 15). Rather than fretting over earthly concerns, let us seek above all to escape the fires of hell (v. 14) and praise the Savior.

2. **We easily fix our eyes upon this passing world. We need to remind ourselves of this promise: "Thine eyes shall see the king in his beauty" (v. 17). This is the blessed hope of every Christian. Surely Christ should be the center of our thoughts. The most joyful heart is the one that delights to meditate upon the Savior, and the more we meditate on Him the more of His beauty we shall see. How can you work to set your mind upon things above, where Christ is seated?**

The Sword of the Lord against All Nations, Especially Edom (34:1–17)

Chapter 34: *The Lord announces judgment upon the world, singling out Edom because of their enmity against His people.*

34:4 *host of heaven.* The armies of heaven, here referring to the heavenly bodies. *rolled together as a scroll.* The disruption of the heavens (13:10; 24:23; Matt. 24:29; 2 Peter 3:10,12), an image suggesting the closing of the "book" of this age (Rev. 6:13–14).

34:5 *Idumea.* Edom, the nation descended from Esau and consistently hostile to Israel, often representative of all enemies of God's people (See Obadiah.).

34:7 *unicorns.* Wild oxen.

34:8 *day of the LORD's vengeance.* See note at 13:6. *recompenses.* Retaliation. *controversy.* A legal contest, cause, quarrel, or struggle.

34:9 *brimstone.* See note at 30:33. The burning land is a direct contrast to the inheritance of those whose king is the Lord, which is like a land full of rivers and streams (33:21–22).

34:10 *not be quenched night nor day . . . smoke . . . go up for ever.* God's anger will burn without end against the wicked (Rev. 14:10–11; 19:3; see note at Isa. 33:14).

34:11 *cormorant.* Some sort of owl or pelican. *bittern.* Either a hedgehog, porcupine, or short-eared owl. *confusion . . . emptiness.* Without form and void, referring to an uninhabited desolation and suggesting a reversal of God's blessing on creation (Gen. 1:2).

34:13 *dragons.* Jackals. *owls.* Or ostriches.

34:14 *wild beasts of the island.* Perhaps hyenas. *satyr.* A wild goat. *screech owl.* A night creature.

34:16 *no one . . . fail.* Scripture will prove true in every detail (Matt. 5:18), for the Holy Spirit (*his spirit*) will bring to pass all that God has spoken. The Spirit is the agent of the Word.

possess it for ever, from generation to generation
shall they dwell therein.

CHAPTER 35

THE wilderness and the solitary place shall be
glad for them; and the desert shall rejoice, and
blossom as the rose.
2 It shall blossom abundantly, and rejoice even
with joy and singing: the glory of Lebanon shall
be given unto it, the excellency of Carmel and
Sharon, they shall see the glory of the LORD, *and*
the excellency of our God.
3 ¶ Strengthen ye the weak hands, and confirm
the feeble knees.
4 Say to them *that are* of a fearful heart, Be
strong, fear not: behold, your God will come *with*
vengeance, *even* God *with* a recompence; he will
come and save you.
5 Then the eyes of the blind shall be opened, and
the ears of the deaf shall be unstopped.
6 Then shall the lame *man* leap as an hart, and
the tongue of the dumb sing: for in the wilderness
shall waters break out, and streams in the desert.
7 And the parched ground shall become a pool,
and the thirsty land springs of water: in the
habitation of dragons, where each lay, *shall be*
grass with reeds and rushes.
8 And an highway shall be there, and a way, and
it shall be called The way of holiness; the unclean
shall not pass over it; but it *shall be* for those: the
wayfaring men, though fools, shall not err *therein*.
9 No lion shall be there, nor *any* ravenous beast
shall go up thereon, it shall not be found there;
but the redeemed shall walk *there*:
10 And the ransomed of the LORD shall return,
and come to Zion with songs and everlasting
joy upon their heads: they shall obtain joy and
gladness, and sorrow and sighing shall flee away.

CHAPTER 36

NOW it came to pass in the fourteenth year of king
Hezekiah, *that* Sennacherib king of Assyria came
up against all the defenced cities of Judah, and
took them.

Thoughts for Personal/Family Worship: Chapter 34

1. **God is remarkably patient, having waited thousands of years already to gather in His elect. However, the day of the Lord will come and completely destroy the heavens and the earth. All that worldly men have labored to accumulate and build as their treasures will be gone. The masses of wicked people that fill the earth will be exterminated. God will summon all mankind before His judgment throne and cast the wicked into the fire of His wrath, where they will suffer burning pain forever and ever. Therefore, do not presume upon God's kindness. Repent of your sins now, and live for the kingdom of Christ that will endure forever. Receive Christ as your King and look to Him for the forgiveness of your sins.**
2. **The Lord's judgment will come true, both in time and in eternity, exactly as He has promised in the Bible (v. 17). God's almighty Spirit will see to it that this happens. So devote yourself to reading the Bible, studying it, and seeking the Lord in it.**

Chapter 35: *The Lord declares the way of holiness.*

The Coming of God's Glory to Heal the Redeemed (35:1–10)

35:1 *solitary place*. A dry region.
35:2 *excellency*. Majesty.
35:3 *weak*. Slack or feeble. *feeble*. Staggering or tottering. *confirm*. Strengthen or make firm. The imagery here is of finding courage, strength, and hope (Heb. 12:12).
35:4 *fearful*. Hurried, unsettled.
35:5–6 *blind . . . deaf . . . lame . . . dumb*. This was the significance of Christ's miracles: God has come to heal all the consequences of the fall of man (Luke 7:22). The greatest healing is the giving of spiritual sense and ability to a sinner's heart (6:10; 42:17–20; 44:17–18; Acts 26:18).
35:6 *hart*. Deer.
35:7 *dragons*. Jackals.
35:8 *way of holiness*. The lifestyle of one separating himself from sin and dedicating himself to the Lord, pictured as the road home from exile (v. 10; 19:23; cf. Prov. 4:11; Matt. 7:13–14). *wayfaring men*. Literally, "He who walks a path," referring to travelers. *shall not err*. Will not wander off or go astray because the way is so clearly marked.
35:9 *redeemed*. The word generally refers to rescuing or defending a person or property at one's own expense based on an existing family relationship (Lev. 25:24–26, 47–49; Ruth 4:1–8). The prototypical redemption was God's salvation of Israel from slavery in Egypt (Ex. 6:6; 15:13; Pss. 77:15; 78:35). Isaiah uses the term often (41:14; 43:1,14; 44:6,22–24; 47:4; 48:17,20; 49:7,26; 51:10; 52:3,9; 54:5,8; 59:20; 60:16; 62:12; 63:4,9,16).
35:10 *ransomed*. Another term for redeemed (1:27; 29:22; 51:11; Deut. 7:8; Ps. 78:42; cf. v. 9).

Thoughts for Personal/Family Worship: Chapter 35

This chapter paints a wonderful picture of what it is to be redeemed. Our sin and separation from the Lord caused us to become dry and parched like a barren desert, but the grace of God has been poured into His people. His Spirit satiates the soul, causing the good seed that He has planted to spring up and blossom. What a transformation God brings to the hearts of His people, yet He does much more: He prepares a highway of holiness to walk on, where His people are kept safe. When we stay on that highway, no harm can come to us. The path is so clearly marked that it is impossible to go astray except by deliberate detour. Let us be careful to follow the path with joy for what God has done for us. What in this chapter is most attractive or delightful to you? How does it encourage you to a life of hope and holiness?

SALVATION FOR JUDAH AND JUDGMENT ON ASSYRIA (36:1—39:8)

(Note: The material in chs. 36–39 also appears in 2 Kings 18:13—20:21.)

Chapter 36: *Assyria invades Judah and Sennacherib makes threats to Hezekiah.*

Thus Saith the King of Assyria against the Lord (36:1–22)

36:1 *defenced*. Fortified. *took*. Layed hold of, seized possession.

2 And the king of Assyria sent Rab-shakeh from
Lachish to Jerusalem unto king Hezekiah with a
great army. And he stood by the conduit of the
upper pool in the highway of the fuller's field.
3 Then came forth unto him Eliakim, Hilkiah's
son, which was over the house, and Shebna the
scribe, and Joah, Asaph's son, the recorder.
4 ¶ And Rab-shakeh said unto them, Say ye now
to Hezekiah, Thus saith the great king, the king
of Assyria, What confidence *is* this wherein thou
trustest?
5 I say, *sayest thou*, (but *they are but* vain words) *I
have* counsel and strength for war: now on whom
dost thou trust, that thou rebellest against me?
6 Lo, thou trustest in the staff of this broken reed,
on Egypt; whereon if a man lean, it will go into his
hand, and pierce it: so *is* Pharaoh king of Egypt to
all that trust in him.
7 But if thou say to me, We trust in the LORD our
God: *is it* not he, whose high places and whose
altars Hezekiah hath taken away, and said to
Judah and to Jerusalem, Ye shall worship before
this altar?
8 Now therefore give pledges, I pray thee, to my
master the king of Assyria, and I will give thee two
thousand horses, if thou be able on thy part to set
riders upon them.
9 How then wilt thou turn away the face of
one captain of the least of my master's servants,
and put thy trust on Egypt for chariots and for
horsemen?
10 And am I now come up without the LORD
against this land to destroy it? the LORD said unto
me, Go up against this land, and destroy it.
11 ¶ Then said Eliakim and Shebna and Joah unto
Rab-shakeh, Speak, I pray thee, unto thy servants
in the Syrian language; for we understand *it*: and
speak not to us in the Jews' language, in the ears of
the people that *are* on the wall.
12 ¶ But Rab-shakeh said, Hath my master sent
me to thy master and to thee to speak these words?
hath he not *sent me* to the men that sit upon the
wall, that they may eat their own dung, and drink
their own piss with you?
13 Then Rab-shakeh stood, and cried with a loud
voice in the Jews' language, and said, Hear ye the
words of the great king, the king of Assyria.
14 Thus saith the king, Let not Hezekiah deceive
you: for he shall not be able to deliver you.
15 Neither let Hezekiah make you trust in the
LORD, saying, The LORD will surely deliver us: this
city shall not be delivered into the hand of the
king of Assyria.
16 Hearken not to Hezekiah: for thus saith the
king of Assyria, Make *an agreement* with me *by* a
present, and come out to me: and eat ye every one
of his vine, and every one of his fig tree, and drink
ye every one the waters of his own cistern;
17 Until I come and take you away to a land like
your own land, a land of corn and wine, a land of
bread and vineyards.
18 *Beware* lest Hezekiah persuade you, saying,
The LORD will deliver us. Hath any of the gods of
the nations delivered his land out of the hand of
the king of Assyria?
19 Where *are* the gods of Hamath and Arphad?
where *are* the gods of Sepharvaim? and have they
delivered Samaria out of my hand?
20 Who *are they* among all the gods of these
lands, that have delivered their land out of my
hand, that the LORD should deliver Jerusalem out
of my hand?
21 But they held their peace, and answered him
not a word: for the king's commandment was,
saying, Answer him not.
22 ¶ Then came Eliakim, the son of Hilkiah, that
was over the household, and Shebna the scribe,
and Joah, the son of Asaph, the recorder, to
Hezekiah with *their* clothes rent, and told him the
words of Rab-shakeh.

36:2 *Rab-shakeh.* Not a name but a title of a government official, the chief spokesman. *conduit.* A raised water channel or aqueduct (7:3). *fuller's field.* The field of the one washing clothes by kneading and beating.

36:3 *Eliakim . . . over the house.* See 22:20–24. *Shebna.* Most likely the same as in ch. 22, now demoted. *scribe.* The state secretary.

36:4 *Thus saith the great king.* This royal formula of speech (37:3; Ex. 5:10; Num. 22:16) is repeated here (vv. 14,16) as *the king of Assyria* asserts his supremacy and mocks the Lord (vv. 15,18–20), who often uses the same formula ("Thus saith the LORD") in His royal declarations (44:6). In this way the conflict is set up as a contest between two kings, one human and the other divine (Ex. 5:2).

36:5 *vain words.* Literally, "words of two lips," referring to empty talk.

36:8 *give pledges.* Make a wager. *I will give . . . if thou be able.* The details of the wager, intended as boasting and mockery.

36:10 *the LORD said unto me.* A common tactic of ancient warfare was to claim that the people's own deity had sanctioned the invasion.

36:11 *Syrian language.* Aramaic, which was becoming the language of international communication. The intent was to keep the general population from hearing the intimidating words.

36:12 *eat . . . drink.* Revolting language used to indicate terrible hunger and thirst while under siege.

36:16 *Hearken not.* Do not listen. *Make an agreement with me by a present.* Give a goodwill gesture or make peace with me.

36:20 *all the gods . . . the LORD.* The Assyrians insulted God as having no more power to save than the idols of the nations, challenging the biblical view of His sovereignty (Ps. 96:4–5).

36:22 *clothes rent.* A gesture of grief and sorrow.

Thoughts for Personal/Family Worship: Chapter 36

The proud and overconfident Rab-shakeh instructed the men on Jerusalem's walls to ask Hezekiah in whom he trusted (v. 5). This is a question to which each of us needs to give a clear and unequivocal answer, and this

CHAPTER 37

AND it came to pass, when king Hezekiah heard *it*,
that he rent his clothes, and covered himself with
sackcloth, and went into the house of the LORD.
2 And he sent Eliakim, who *was* over the house-
hold, and Shebna the scribe, and the elders of the
priests covered with sackcloth, unto Isaiah the
prophet the son of Amoz.
3 And they said unto him, Thus saith Hezekiah,
This day *is* a day of trouble, and of rebuke, and of
blasphemy: for the children are come to the birth,
and *there is* not strength to bring forth.
4 It may be the LORD thy God will hear the words
of Rab-shakeh, whom the king of Assyria his
master hath sent to reproach the living God, and
will reprove the words which the LORD thy God
hath heard: wherefore lift up *thy* prayer for the
remnant that is left.
5 So the servants of king Hezekiah came to Isaiah.
6 ¶ And Isaiah said unto them, Thus shall ye
say unto your master, Thus saith the LORD, Be
not afraid of the words that thou hast heard,
wherewith the servants of the king of Assyria have
blasphemed me.
7 Behold, I will send a blast upon him, and he
shall hear a rumour, and return to his own land;
and I will cause him to fall by the sword in his
own land.
8 ¶ So Rab-shakeh returned, and found the king
of Assyria warring against Libnah: for he had
heard that he was departed from Lachish.
9 And he heard say concerning Tirhakah king
of Ethiopia, He is come forth to make war with
thee. And when he heard *it*, he sent messengers to
Hezekiah, saying,
10 Thus shall ye speak to Hezekiah king of Judah,
saying, Let not thy God, in whom thou trustest,
deceive thee, saying, Jerusalem shall not be given
into the hand of the king of Assyria.
11 Behold, thou hast heard what the kings of
Assyria have done to all lands by destroying them
utterly; and shalt thou be delivered?
12 Have the gods of the nations delivered them
which my fathers have destroyed, *as* Gozan, and
Haran, and Rezeph, and the children of Eden
which *were* in Telassar?
13 Where *is* the king of Hamath, and the king of
Arphad, and the king of the city of Sepharvaim,
Hena, and Ivah?
14 ¶ And Hezekiah received the letter from the
hand of the messengers, and read it: and Hezekiah
went up unto the house of the LORD, and spread
it before the LORD.
15 And Hezekiah prayed unto the LORD, saying,
16 O LORD of hosts, God of Israel, that dwellest
between the cherubims, thou *art* the God, *even*
thou alone, of all the kingdoms of the earth: thou
hast made heaven and earth.
17 Incline thine ear, O LORD, and hear; open thine
eyes, O LORD, and see: and hear all the words of
Sennacherib, which hath sent to reproach the
living God.
18 Of a truth, LORD, the kings of Assyria have laid
waste all the nations, and their countries,
19 And have cast their gods into the fire: for they
were no gods, but the work of men's hands, wood
and stone: therefore they have destroyed them.
20 Now therefore, O LORD our God, save us from
his hand, that all the kingdoms of the earth may
know that thou *art* the LORD, *even* thou only.
21 ¶ Then Isaiah the son of Amoz sent unto
Hezekiah, saying, Thus saith the LORD God of
Israel, Whereas thou hast prayed to me against
Sennacherib king of Assyria:
22 This *is* the word which the LORD hath spoken
concerning him; The virgin, the daughter of Zion,
hath despised thee, *and* laughed thee to scorn; the
daughter of Jerusalem hath shaken her head at thee.

---

is especially so when we are in the midst of severe trials. The world may challenge our faith in the Lord and mock Him as weak and worthless (v. 20). Or it may claim that He is against us, an evil and fickle God (v. 10). The mockery of the wicked is all the harder to bear when they are more powerful or successful than we are. Our King teaches us to bear it quietly and patiently, as He did when He went to the cross for our sins (v. 21; 1 Peter 2:19–25). Let us trust in the Lord, persevere in doing good, turn away from anger, and wait for Him (Ps. 37:1–11). The Lord will save us and glorify His holy name. Whom do you hear mocking the Lord and His people? How do you need to respond?

Chapter 37: ***Isaiah assures Hezekiah of divine intervention against the Assyrian threat.***

Thus Saith the Lord against the King of Assyria (37:1–38)

37:1 *rent his clothes . . . covered himself with sackcloth.* Gestures of humiliation and penitence.

37:2 *sent . . . unto Isaiah the prophet.* Hezekiah desired a word from God in addition to prayer support.

37:3 *rebuke.* Or correction, punishment. *blasphemy.* Humiliation or contempt.

37:4 *reproach.* Taunt (vv. 17,24).

37:6 *Thus saith the LORD.* Just as the Rab-shekah issued three royal declarations of the king of Assyria in this form (36:4, 14,16), so the Lord responds with three declarations from the King of kings (vv. 21,33).

37:7 *send a blast.* Literally, "give in him a spirit." *rumour.* A report or news.

37:16 *dwellest between the cherubims.* Alludes to the ark of the covenant, the symbol of God's presence (Pss. 80:1; 99:1).

37:19 *they were no gods.* The reason the gods of the nations could not save their peoples from Assyria (36:18) was that they were worthless idols, but the Lord is not so (Ps. 115:1–11).

37:20 *know that thou art the LORD.* His motive and argument in prayer were God's glory and honor as the only true God (42:8).

37:22 *despised.* Showed contempt. *laughed thee to scorn.* Mocked. *shaken her head.* A gesture of ridicule.

23 Whom hast thou reproached and blasphemed?
and against whom hast thou exalted *thy* voice,
and lifted up thine eyes on high? *even* against the
Holy One of Israel.
24 By thy servants hast thou reproached the Lord,
and hast said, By the multitude of my chariots
am I come up to the height of the mountains, to
the sides of Lebanon; and I will cut down the tall
cedars thereof, *and* the choice fir trees thereof:
and I will enter into the height of his border, *and*
the forest of his Carmel.
25 I have digged, and drunk water; and with the
sole of my feet have I dried up all the rivers of the
besieged places.
26 Hast thou not heard long ago, *how* I have done
it; *and* of ancient times, that I have formed it? now
have I brought it to pass, that thou shouldest be to
lay waste defenced cities *into* ruinous heaps.
27 Therefore their inhabitants *were* of small
power, they were dismayed and confounded: they
were *as* the grass of the field, and *as* the green
herb, *as* the grass on the housetops, and *as corn*
blasted before it be grown up.
28 But I know thy abode, and thy going out, and
thy coming in, and thy rage against me.
29 Because thy rage against me, and thy tumult,
is come up into mine ears, therefore will I put my
hook in thy nose, and my bridle in thy lips, and
I will turn thee back by the way by which thou
camest.
30 And this *shall be* a sign unto thee, Ye shall eat
this year such as groweth of itself; and the second
year that which springeth of the same: and in the
third year sow ye, and reap, and plant vineyards,
and eat the fruit thereof.
31 And the remnant that is escaped of the house
of Judah shall again take root downward, and
bear fruit upward:
32 For out of Jerusalem shall go forth a remnant,
and they that escape out of mount Zion: the zeal
of the LORD of hosts shall do this.
33 Therefore thus saith the LORD concerning the
king of Assyria, He shall not come into this city,
nor shoot an arrow there, nor come before it with
shields, nor cast a bank against it.
34 By the way that he came, by the same shall he
return, and shall not come into this city, saith the
LORD.
35 For I will defend this city to save it for mine
own sake, and for my servant David's sake.
36 Then the angel of the LORD went forth, and
smote in the camp of the Assyrians a hundred
and fourscore and five thousand: and when they
arose early in the morning, behold, they *were* all
dead corpses.
37 ¶ So Sennacherib king of Assyria departed,
and went and returned, and dwelt at Nineveh.
38 And it came to pass, as he was worshipping in
the house of Nisroch his god, that Adrammelech
and Sharezer his sons smote him with the sword;
and they escaped into the land of Armenia: and
Esarhaddon his son reigned in his stead.

CHAPTER 38

IN those days was Hezekiah sick unto death. And
Isaiah the prophet the son of Amoz came unto him,
and said unto him, Thus saith the LORD, Set thine
house in order: for thou shalt die, and not live.
2 Then Hezekiah turned his face toward the wall,
and prayed unto the LORD,
3 And said, Remember now, O LORD, I beseech

37:25 *besieged places.* Fortifications in general, or Egypt specifically.
37:26 *defenced.* Fortified.
37:29 *tumult.* Self-confident arrogance. *hook in thy nose.* A technique commonly used by the Assyrians to parade their captives.
37:33 *bank.* Mound or assault ramp.
37:36 *angel of the LORD.* Often this phrase refers to the messenger who is the Lord and yet is sent by the Lord, a preincarnate appearance of Christ (Gen. 16:7–14; 22:11–18). *a hundred and fourscore and five thousand.* 185,000.
37:38 *in the house of . . . his god.* Hezekiah went to the house of the Lord and found salvation (v. 1), but Sennacherib went to his temple and found death, showing again that the Lord is sovereign but that the gods of this world cannot save. *his sons smote him.* Secular history records Sennacherib's campaigns against Judah (ca. 700 BC) and his death (ca. 680 BC). Twenty years passed after Isaiah's prophecy, but it was fulfilled precisely. *stead.* Place.

Thoughts for Personal/Family Worship: Chapter 37

1. **Hezekiah provides a pattern to follow in dealing with our problems. First, he recognized the seriousness of his need (vv. 1,3). Second, he sought a word from the Lord (v. 2). He had Isaiah; we have the complete Bible. Third, he spread the matter before the Lord in prayer (v. 14). Note that his prayer begins with worship (v. 16), proceeds to petition (v. 17), and argues for God's glory (v. 20). Fourth, he receives the answer (v. 21), assuring him of deliverance even though he would have to wait twenty years for the full outworking. How can you follow this pattern in dealing with your problems?**
2. **Though the great men and women of the earth mock at the Lord, the Lord will have the last laugh. He is the supreme King and the only God. Other gods are worthless and cannot save, but the Lord both saves and destroys. Therefore our greatest ambition should be that "all the kingdoms of the earth may know that thou art the LORD, even thou only" (v. 20). Make this your guiding principle and constant prayer.**

Chapter 38: ***On his deathbed Hezekiah prays for healing and is restored to health and life.***

Hezekiah's Prayer and Healing (38:1–22)

38:1 *In those days.* The events of chs. 38–39 most likely do not follow those of chs. 36–37 in chronological order.
38:3 *Remember.* Intentionally give thought and take to heart.

thee, how I have walked before thee in truth and
with a perfect heart, and have done *that which is*
good in thy sight. And Hezekiah wept sore.
4 ¶ Then came the word of the LORD to Isaiah,
saying,
5 Go, and say to Hezekiah, Thus saith the LORD,
the God of David thy father, I have heard thy
prayer, I have seen thy tears: behold, I will add
unto thy days fifteen years.
6 And I will deliver thee and this city out of the
hand of the king of Assyria: and I will defend this
city.
7 And this *shall be* a sign unto thee from the
LORD, that the LORD will do this thing that he
hath spoken;
8 Behold, I will bring again the shadow of the
degrees, which is gone down in the sun dial of
Ahaz, ten degrees backward. So the sun returned
ten degrees, by which degrees it was gone down.
9 ¶ The writing of Hezekiah king of Judah, when
he had been sick, and was recovered of his sickness:
10 I said in the cutting off of my days, I shall go to
the gates of the grave: I am deprived of the residue
of my years.
11 I said, I shall not see the LORD, *even* the LORD,
in the land of the living: I shall behold man no
more with the inhabitants of the world.
12 Mine age is departed, and is removed from me
as a shepherd's tent: I have cut off like a weaver my
life: he will cut me off with pining sickness: from
day *even* to night wilt thou make an end of me.
13 I reckoned till morning, *that*, as a lion, so will
he break all my bones: from day *even* to night wilt
thou make an end of me.
14 Like a crane *or* a swallow, so did I chatter: I did
mourn as a dove: mine eyes fail *with looking* up-
ward: O LORD, I am oppressed; undertake for me.
15 What shall I say? he hath both spoken unto
me, and himself hath done *it*: I shall go softly all
my years in the bitterness of my soul.
16 O Lord, by these *things men* live, and in all
these *things is* the life of my spirit: so wilt thou
recover me, and make me to live.
17 Behold, for peace I had great bitterness: but
thou hast in love to my soul *delivered it* from the
pit of corruption: for thou hast cast all my sins
behind thy back.
18 For the grave cannot praise thee, death can
not celebrate thee: they that go down into the pit
cannot hope for thy truth.
19 The living, the living, he shall praise thee, as I
do this day: the father to the children shall make
known thy truth.
20 The LORD *was ready* to save me: therefore we
will sing my songs to the stringed instruments all
the days of our life in the house of the LORD.
21 For Isaiah had said, Let them take a lump of
figs, and lay *it* for a plaister upon the boil, and he
shall recover.
22 Hezekiah also had said, What *is* the sign that I
shall go up to the house of the LORD?

CHAPTER 39

AT that time Merodach-baladan, the son of
Baladan, king of Babylon, sent letters and a
present to Hezekiah: for he had heard that he had
been sick, and was recovered.
2 And Hezekiah was glad of them, and shewed
them the house of his precious things, the silver,

perfect heart. Not sinlessness but whole-hearted dedication. *wept sore.* Literally, "wept a great weeping."

38:7 *sign.* Something miraculous as a present persuader or convincer.

38:10 *grave.* Hebrew, *sheol*, here death or the grave (v. 18). *the residue.* The rest.

38:12 *with pining sickness.* Literally, "from the loom or warp," continuing the image of the *weaver*.

38:14 *mourn.* Groan or moan. *undertake.* Accept responsibility for someone else, often translated "be surety" (Ps. 119:122); take on the accountability to fulfill another's obligations (Gen. 43:9; 44:32; Prov. 6:1).

38:15 *go softly.* Walk deliberately, perhaps in the sense of humbly. *bitterness of my soul.* Not anger but suffering (1 Sam. 1:10; Job 3:20).

38:17 *thou has cast all my sins behind thy back.* A marvelous picture of the complete forgiveness God gives believers (Pss. 32:1–2; 103:12; Mic. 7:19) based on Christ's work as our surety (v. 14; Heb. 7:22–27).

38:21 *Isaiah had said.* Chronologically this took place earlier, about the time of vv. 4–8. *plaister upon the boil.* Ointment on the inflamed area.

Thoughts for Personal/Family Worship: Chapter 38

Hezekiah was going to die, and he was told to set his house in order. This was fearful news to him, and he pleaded with the Lord that it would not be so. God heard his cry and granted him another fifteen years. Hezekiah therefore voiced this testimony: "The LORD was ready to save me" (v. 20). Surely this is the testimony of every true child of God. The Lord has saved His people, and He will continue to keep us unto the end, saving us from all that would destroy us. Are there not many times that we can look back to in our lives when He saved us from harm and delivered us from all our fears? Cannot we be sure that He will save us to the end since He has already cast all our sins behind His back? Therefore, like Hezekiah we should give the Lord praise and thanksgiving, even in writing if we have the skill. Believer, how are you glorifying God for answering your prayers, especially your prayers for salvation?

Chapter 39: *Hezekiah foolishly shows all of his wealth to the emissaries from Babylon.*

Hezekiah's Boasting to Babylon (39:1–8)

39:1 *Babylon.* Presently revolting against Assyrian King Sennacherib and thus sympathetic to Hezekiah.

39:2 *precious things.* Treasures. *armour.* Vessels or instruments, perhaps referring to jewelry. *there was nothing . . . that*

and the gold, and the spices, and the precious
ointment, and all the house of his armour, and
all that was found in his treasures: there was
nothing in his house, nor in all his dominion, that
Hezekiah shewed them not.
3 ¶ Then came Isaiah the prophet unto king
Hezekiah, and said unto him, What said these
men? and from whence came they unto thee? And
Hezekiah said, They are come from a far country
unto me, *even* from Babylon.
4 Then said he, What have they seen in thine
house? And Hezekiah answered, All that *is* in mine
house have they seen: there is nothing among my
treasures that I have not shewed them.
5 Then said Isaiah to Hezekiah, Hear the word of
the LORD of hosts:
6 Behold, the days come, that all that *is* in thine
house, and *that* which thy fathers have laid up in
store until this day, shall be carried to Babylon:
nothing shall be left, saith the LORD.
7 And of thy sons that shall issue from thee, which
thou shalt beget, shall they take away; and they shall
be eunuchs in the palace of the king of Babylon.
8 Then said Hezekiah to Isaiah, Good *is* the word
of the LORD which thou hast spoken. He said more-
over, For there shall be peace and truth in my days.

CHAPTER 40

COMFORT ye, comfort ye my people, saith your
God.
2 Speak ye comfortably to Jerusalem, and cry
unto her, that her warfare is accomplished, that
her iniquity is pardoned: for she hath received of
the LORD's hand double for all her sins.
3 ¶ The voice of him that crieth in the wilderness,
Prepare ye the way of the LORD, make straight in
the desert a highway for our God.
4 Every valley shall be exalted, and every moun-
tain and hill shall be made low: and the crooked
shall be made straight, and the rough places plain:
5 And the glory of the LORD shall be revealed,
and all flesh shall see *it* together: for the mouth of
the LORD hath spoken *it*.
6 The voice said, Cry. And he said, What shall
I cry? All flesh *is* grass, and all the goodliness
thereof *is* as the flower of the field:
7 The grass withereth, the flower fadeth: because
the spirit of the LORD bloweth upon it: surely the
people *is* grass.
8 The grass withereth, the flower fadeth: but the
word of our God shall stand for ever.
9 ¶ O Zion, that bringest good tidings, get thee
up into the high mountain; O Jerusalem, that
bringest good tidings, lift up thy voice with
strength; lift *it* up, be not afraid; say unto the cities
of Judah, Behold your God!
10 Behold, the Lord GOD will come with strong
hand, and his arm shall rule for him: behold, his
reward *is* with him, and his work before him.
11 He shall feed his flock like a shepherd: he shall
gather the lambs with his arm, and carry *them*
in his bosom, *and* shall gently lead those that are
with young.

Hezekiah shewed them not. He became proud and boastful (2 Chron. 32:25), forgetting that all He had was of the Lord's grace (note the repetition of "his" here and "my" and "mine" in v. 4).
39:6 *laid up in store.* The stored treasures.
39:7 *issue from.* To come from or descend from. *eunuchs.* Most likely referring to high level officers serving in the royal court.

Thoughts for Personal/Family Worship: Chapter 39

This chapter provides a somber lesson to us all. Hezekiah, one of the most godly kings to ever sit on the throne in Jerusalem, in a moment of weakness became puffed up in his pride, revealing to the Babylonians all of his treasures. How easily the human heart behaves unwisely! No wonder the exhortation comes, "Wherefore let him that thinketh he standeth take heed lest he fall" (1 Cor. 10:12). We need to be on our guard, watching and praying vigilantly against pride, especially after experiencing great success. How can we recognize the first motions of pride in our hearts? How can we put them to death by the blood and Spirit of Christ?

RESTORATION THROUGH THE SERVANT OF THE LORD (40:1—55:13)

God's Comfort and Greatness for Israel (40:1—41:29)

Chapter 40: *The Lord comforts His people by revealing His purpose of grace and His incomparable glory.*

40:1 *Comfort ye.* God will console His people with His compassion and salvation (v. 1; 12:1; 49:13; 51:3,12,19; 52:9; 54:11; 61:2; 66:13). The comfort of Israel is Christ (Luke 2:25–26).
40:2 *Speak ye comfortably.* Literally, "Speak to the heart." *double.* Not literally, but in the sense of an equivalent, that which is enough for her discipline.
40:3 *voice of him that crieth.* Fulfilled in John the Baptist, who came before the revealing of the divine Messiah (Matt. 3:4; Mark 1:3; Luke 3:4–6; John 1:23; cf. Mal. 3:1; Luke 1:76). *Prepare ye the way.* The picture is of clearing obstacles for a road (Isa. 40:4; 57:14; 62:10), symbolizing the repentance of the people so that they are ready to welcome their Lord (Matt. 3:1–3).
40:4 *exalted.* Lifted up. *crooked . . . straight.* Uneven, bumpy terrain becomes level country. *rough places . . . plain.* Rocky mountain chains become a level plain. Each change pictures a removing of obstacles.
40:5 *all flesh.* The Gentiles will also see God's *glory* when He comes in Christ (42:6; 60:3).
40:6–8 *goodliness.* Covenant loyalty and love; man has no enduring faithfulness in his own fallen nature. *grass.* A picture of transience; man's life is quickly and easily ended (Pss. 37:2; 90:5; 103:15–16; 129:6; James 1:11). *spirit of the LORD.* The image here is of a withering wind, but the phrase points to the Holy Spirit (v. 13; 11:2), who is the divine agent of judgment (11:4; 34:16). *word of our God shall stand for ever.* The gospel is eternal truth, and it is God's means for giving eternal life to sinful and mortal men (1 Peter 1:23–25).
40:10 *his reward is with him.* The Lord will come to judge men by their works and repay each accordingly (Rev. 22:12).
40:11 *feed his flock like a shepherd.* The King will come

12 ¶ Who hath measured the waters in the hol-
low of his hand, and meted out heaven with the
span, and comprehended the dust of the earth in
a measure, and weighed the mountains in scales,
and the hills in a balance?
13 Who hath directed the Spirit of the LORD, or
being his counsellor hath taught him?
14 With whom took he counsel, and *who* in-
structed him, and taught him in the path of judg-
ment, and taught him knowledge, and shewed to
him the way of understanding?
15 Behold, the nations *are* as a drop of a bucket,
and are counted as the small dust of the balance:
behold, he taketh up the isles as a very little thing.
16 And Lebanon *is* not sufficient to burn, nor the
beasts thereof sufficient for a burnt offering.
17 All nations before him *are* as nothing; and they
are counted to him less than nothing, and vanity.
18 ¶ To whom then will ye liken God? or what
likeness will ye compare unto him?
19 The workman melteth a graven image, and the
goldsmith spreadeth it over with gold, and casteth
silver chains.
20 He that *is* so impoverished that he hath no ob-
lation chooseth a tree *that* will not rot; he seeketh
unto him a cunning workman to prepare a graven
image, *that* shall not be moved.
21 Have ye not known? have ye not heard? hath
it not been told you from the beginning? have
ye not understood from the foundations of the
earth?
22 *It is* he that sitteth upon the circle of the earth,
and the inhabitants thereof *are* as grasshoppers;
that stretcheth out the heavens as a curtain, and
spreadeth them out as a tent to dwell in:
23 That bringeth the princes to nothing; he mak-
eth the judges of the earth as vanity.
24 Yea, they shall not be planted; yea, they shall
not be sown: yea, their stock shall not take root in
the earth: and he shall also blow upon them, and
they shall wither, and the whirlwind shall take
them away as stubble.
25 To whom then will ye liken me, or shall I be
equal? saith the Holy One.
26 Lift up your eyes on high, and behold who
hath created these *things*, that bringeth out their
host by number: he calleth them all by names by
the greatness of his might, for that *he is* strong in
power; not one faileth.
27 Why sayest thou, O Jacob, and speakest, O
Israel, My way is hid from the LORD, and my
judgment is passed over from my God?
28 ¶ Hast thou not known? hast thou not heard,
that the everlasting God, the LORD, the Creator
of the ends of the earth, fainteth not, neither is
weary? *there is* no searching of his understanding.
29 He giveth power to the faint; and to *them that*
have no might he increaseth strength.
30 Even the youths shall faint and be weary, and
the young men shall utterly fall:
31 But they that wait upon the LORD shall renew
their strength; they shall mount up with wings as
eagles; they shall run, and not be weary; *and* they
shall walk, and not faint.

with tender love for His people (Ezek. 34:11–16,23–24; John 10:1–16).

40:12 *meted out heaven with the span.* Measured the size of the heavens with a hand. *comprehended.* Contained or calculated. Each statement highlights the immensity of God, to whom the universe is a small thing.

40:13–14 *directed.* Measured (same Hebrew word translated "meted," v. 12). God is infinite and far beyond man's comprehension (v. 28). Therefore, man is always in the position of a learner and never a teacher with respect to God (Rom. 11:34; 1 Cor. 2:16).

40:15 *isles.* The distant shores, the extremities of the world.

40:17 *vanity.* Emptiness, nothingness (v. 23).

40:18–19 *liken God . . . image.* It is impossible to represent God in a physical image crafted by artists because His nature is infinitely more glorious than creation (Acts 17:29).

40:20 *oblation.* Offering. *cunning.* Skillful.

40:22 *sitteth upon the circle of the earth.* Figurative language describing God's exalted position as He controls and upholds His creation.

40:24 *stock.* Stem or trunk.

40:26 *on high . . . their host.* The stars and planets created and sustained in their motions by Him (Ps. 147:4). *not one faileth.* Not one is missing by His providence.

40:28 God is infinite with regard to time (*everlasting*; Ps. 90:2), power (*Creator . . . fainteth not*; Jer. 32:17), and knowledge and wisdom (*understanding*; Ps. 147:5); therefore He is incomprehensible or far beyond our understanding (*no searching*, Ps. 145:3).

40:31 *wait.* Hope with confident expectation. *renew.* Change or receive anew. *eagles.* Or griffin-vultures. The point of the image is the ability to soar high.

Thoughts for Personal/Family Worship: Chapter 40

1. **In this ever-changing world it is good to know that "The word of our God shall stand for ever" (v. 8). That Word is reliable in every circumstance of life. When we are facing trials and affliction, it is good for us to rest upon the certain promises of God. When we fall into sin, what a comfort it is to know the way to confession and forgiveness. The immutable Word of God stands firm for every situation. The Lord will never change His mind or go back on a promise. How is that a solid ground for comfort?**
2. **It is good to reflect on the absolute greatness of God, who is infinite in all His perfections and beyond our highest thoughts of Him. In an uncertain world we have confidence in the God who made the world and all that is in it and governs even the things that may cause us to fear His own glory. This infinite Lord has come to us in human flesh in the person of Jesus Christ. Though no man-made image suffices to honor Him, the fullness of His deity now dwells in a man who is His living image. Thus we have a divine and sympathetic Shepherd. If Christ is all this to us, it makes sense to wait on the Lord with the full anticipation and confident expectation that He will supply our needs, enabling us to soar as the eagle. What does it mean, practically, to wait upon the Lord by faith in Christ?**

CHAPTER 41

KEEP silence before me, O islands; and let the
people renew *their* strength: let them come near;
then let them speak: let us come near together to
judgment.
2 Who raised up the righteous *man* from the east,
called him to his foot, gave the nations before him,
and made *him* rule over kings? he gave *them* as the
dust to his sword, *and* as driven stubble to his bow.
3 He pursued them, *and* passed safely; *even* by
the way *that* he had not gone with his feet.
4 Who hath wrought and done *it*, calling the
generations from the beginning? I the LORD, the
first, and with the last; I *am* he.
5 The isles saw *it*, and feared; the ends of the
earth were afraid, drew near, and came.
6 They helped every one his neighbour; and *every
one* said to his brother, Be of good courage.
7 So the carpenter encouraged the goldsmith,
and he that smootheth *with* the hammer him
that smote the anvil, saying, It *is* ready for the
sodering: and he fastened it with nails, *that* it
should not be moved.
8 But thou, Israel, *art* my servant, Jacob whom I
have chosen, the seed of Abraham my friend.
9 *Thou* whom I have taken from the ends of the
earth, and called thee from the chief men thereof,
and said unto thee, Thou *art* my servant; I have
chosen thee, and not cast thee away.
10 ¶ Fear thou not; for I *am* with thee: be not
dismayed; for I *am* thy God: I will strengthen
thee; yea, I will help thee; yea, I will uphold thee
with the right hand of my righteousness.
11 Behold, all they that were incensed against
thee shall be ashamed and confounded: they shall
be as nothing; and they that strive with thee shall
perish.
12 Thou shalt seek them, and shalt not find them,
even them that contended with thee: they that war
against thee shall be as nothing, and as a thing of
nought.
13 For I the LORD thy God will hold thy right
hand, saying unto thee, Fear not; I will help thee.
14 Fear not, thou worm Jacob, *and* ye men of
Israel; I will help thee, saith the LORD, and thy
redeemer, the Holy One of Israel.
15 Behold, I will make thee a new sharp threshing
instrument having teeth: thou shalt thresh the
mountains, and beat *them* small, and shalt make
the hills as chaff.
16 Thou shalt fan them, and the wind shall carry
them away, and the whirlwind shall scatter them:
and thou shalt rejoice in the LORD, *and* shalt glory
in the Holy One of Israel.
17 *When* the poor and needy seek water, and
there is none, *and* their tongue faileth for thirst, I
the LORD will hear them, *I* the God of Israel will
not forsake them.
18 I will open rivers in high places, and fountains in
the midst of the valleys: I will make the wilderness
a pool of water, and the dry land springs of water.
19 I will plant in the wilderness the cedar, the
shittah tree, and the myrtle, and the oil tree; I will
set in the desert the fir tree, *and* the pine, and the
box tree together:
20 That they may see, and know, and consider,
and understand together, that the hand of the
LORD hath done this, and the Holy One of Israel
hath created it.
21 Produce your cause, saith the LORD; bring
forth your strong *reasons*, saith the King of Jacob.
22 Let them bring *them* forth, and shew us what
shall happen: let them shew the former things,
what they *be*, that we may consider them, and
know the latter end of them; or declare us things
for to come.

Chapter 41: *The great power of the Lord is contrasted with the utter weakness of man-made gods.*

41:1 *islands.* Distant shores, the extremities of the world ("isles"; v. 5).

41:2 *raised up the righteous man from the east.* Literally, "awakened righteousness from the east," where "righteousness" refers to God's righteous work of salvation (45:8; 51:5) and "from the east" refers to Cyrus, the man God used to punish Babylon and save Israel (44:28; 45:1; 46:11).

41:4 *wrought.* Accomplished or done. *first . . . last.* A pair of opposites is an idiom for totality: God is Lord of everything throughout history (44:6–7; 48:12; Rev. 1:11,17; 2:8; 22:13).

41:7 *carpenter.* Craftsman. *sodering.* Soldering.

41:8–9 *my servant.* An honorific title given to God's appointed leaders, like prophets and kings (20:3; 22:10; 37:35; 44:26), here applied to Israel as God's *chosen* people in a relationship of privilege with the Lord and responsibility to represent Him (43:10; 44:1–2; 45:4; 48:20; 54:17; 56:6; 63:17; 65:8–9,13–15; 66:14; Luke 1:54). Israel's failure as the servant of the Lord (42:19) leads to Isaiah's revelation of the ideal Servant (v. 1). *seed of Abraham my friend.* A reminder of God's covenant of love (2 Chron. 20:7; James 2:23; cf. Gen. 26:24).

41:10 *Fear thou not.* The gospel calls men from fear to faith (vv. 13–14; 7:4; 35:4; 43:1,5; 44:2,8; 54:4; Jer. 30:10; 46:27–28). *I am with thee.* God is present with believers through Christ (7:14) to enable them to keep His covenant (*thy God*); this includes His promise to *strengthen* and *help* them in their troubles (Ps. 91:15).

41:11 *incensed against.* Angry with. *confounded.* Humiliated or dishonored. *they that strive.* Men of contention, who enter into controversy.

41:14 *redeemer.* See note at 35:9.

41:17 *poor and needy.* The weak and helpless.

41:21 *Produce your cause.* Come to court to present evidence in a legal controversy. This is sometimes referred to as a trial speech where God summons the idols to court to prove they really exist as divine beings.

41:22–23 *shew us what shall happen . . . the former things.* Declaring the future and the past are evidence of deity. *do evil.* Cause some calamity.

41:24 The inability to speak or to act proved the verdict that idols were nothing (v. 29). *abomination.* That which is disgusting and detestable, often associated with idolatry.

23 Shew the things that are to come hereafter,
that we may know that ye *are* gods: yea, do good,
or do evil, that we may be dismayed, and behold
it together.
24 Behold, ye *are* of nothing, and your work of
nought: an abomination *is he that* chooseth you.
25 I have raised up *one* from the north, and he
shall come: from the rising of the sun shall he call
upon my name: and he shall come upon princes
as *upon* morter, and as the potter treadeth clay.
26 Who hath declared from the beginning, that
we may know? and beforetime, that we may say,
He is righteous? yea, *there is* none that sheweth,
yea, *there is* none that declareth, yea, *there is* none
that heareth your words.
27 The first *shall say* to Zion, Behold, behold
them: and I will give to Jerusalem one that bring-
eth good tidings.
28 For I beheld, and *there was* no man; even
among them, and *there was* no counsellor, that,
when I asked of them, could answer a word.
29 Behold, they *are* all vanity; their works *are* noth-
ing: their molten images *are* wind and confusion.

CHAPTER 42

BEHOLD my servant, whom I uphold; mine elect,
in whom my soul delighteth; I have put my spirit
upon him: he shall bring forth judgment to the
Gentiles.
2 He shall not cry, nor lift up, nor cause his voice
to be heard in the street.
3 A bruised reed shall he not break, and the
smoking flax shall he not quench: he shall bring
forth judgment unto truth.
4 He shall not fail nor be discouraged, till he have
set judgment in the earth: and the isles shall wait
for his law.
5 ¶ Thus saith God the LORD, he that created the
heavens, and stretched them out; he that spread
forth the earth, and that which cometh out of it;
he that giveth breath unto the people upon it, and
spirit to them that walk therein:
6 I the LORD have called thee in righteousness,
and will hold thine hand, and will keep thee, and
give thee for a covenant of the people, for a light
of the Gentiles;
7 To open the blind eyes, to bring out the
prisoners from the prison, *and* them that sit in
darkness out of the prison house.
8 I *am* the LORD: that *is* my name: and my glory
will I not give to another, neither my praise to
graven images.
9 Behold, the former things are come to pass, and
new things do I declare: before they spring forth I
tell you of them.

41:25–27 The Lord now gives the irrefutable evidence that He is God by declaring the future and bringing it into reality (46:8–11).

41:29 *vanity.* Deception or nothingness. *confusion.* Emptiness, what is unreal.

Thoughts for Personal/Family Worship: Chapter 41

Christians may fear when they fail to appreciate the wonderful relationship they have with the Lord. Child of God, there are many precious promises in the Word that we need to appropriate to ourselves; how wonderful is the promise that the One who is incomparably great is always with His people (v. 10). The nations of this world are "as a drop of a bucket" (40:15), so what have we to fear when the Lord says "I will uphold thee" (v. 10)? Not only is the Lord's presence with His people, but so is His strength. He says, "I will strengthen thee" (v. 10.) Fearlessness is appropriated by faith in the promises. If you are a believer, how do you need to apply these promises today? How does this show to unbelievers how good it is to be a Christian?

Chapter 42: *The Lord's Servant is the remedy to the plight of Israel and the nations.*

The Lord's Servant and Jacob's Blindness (42:1–25)

42:1–4 This text, cited in Matt. 12:17–21, introduces Christ as the ideal *servant* of the Lord (49:1–12; 50:4–11; 52:13—53:12; cf. 61:1–3) who fulfills God's every expectation and demand for Israel (see note at 41:8–9).

42:1 *my servant.* This title of honor and commission for special service is used of God's prophets (20:3; 44:26; Num. 12:7–8), but especially of the Davidic king in covenant with the Lord (37:35; 2 Sam. 3:18; 7:5,8; Zech. 3:8). It highlights the work of Christ as obedience to the Father's will (Ps. 40:6–8; Mark 14:36; John 4:34; 6:38; Phil. 2:8). *my soul.* Referring to God's person; hence, "I delight" (Matt. 3:17; Luke 9:35). *put my spirit upon him.* The divine anointing to empower Christ in His human nature for service (11:2; 61:1; Ps. 45:7), fulfilled at His baptism (Matt. 3:16) and again at His ascension, to overflow to His people (32:2,15; John 1:33; Acts 2:32–33). *judgment.* Justice, the goal of His work (vv. 3–4; see note at 1:16–17). *Gentiles.* The nations; the Messiah comes not only for the Jews but for all peoples (vv. 4,6).

42:2 *not cry.* He will act in a humble and unassuming manner.

42:3 *smoking flax . . . . not quench.* He will not extinguish the dimly glowing wick. He is compassionate and gracious, knowing the frailty and weakness of men (Heb. 4:15–16).

42:4 *not fail.* Literally, "not grow dim." *discouraged.* Crushed. Note the parallelism to His not crushing the reed or putting out the dim flame (v. 3). *isles.* The distant shores, the extremities of the world (vv. 10,12). The Messiah's mission is universal. *wait for his law.* Hope in His teaching or instruction.

42:6 *hold thine hand.* God supported Christ's humanity with all the power of the Creator (v. 5) and faithfulness of the covenant Lord (41:13). *given thee for a covenant of the people.* In Christ God confirmed His faithfulness to all His promises to Israel (Rom. 15:8; 2 Cor. 1:20), and Christ Himself is the essence of what God gives sinners in the covenant of grace. *light of the Gentiles.* God's truth and salvation in Christ will reach all nations (49:6; Luke 2:32; Acts 26:23; see note at 2:2–4).

42:7 *open the blind eyes.* See note at 35:5–6. *darkness . . . prison house.* The greatest freedom comes when Christ releases a sinner from spiritual blindness (Acts 26:18; 2 Cor. 4:4–6) and leads him home to glory (v. 16).

42:8 *my glory . . . my praise.* Christ's mission ultimately aims at the glory of God, and Him alone (44:23; 48:9–11; John 17:4; Eph. 1:6,12,14; Phil. 2:11).

10 Sing unto the LORD a new song, *and* his praise
from the end of the earth, ye that go down to
the sea, and all that is therein; the isles, and the
inhabitants thereof.
11 Let the wilderness and the cities thereof lift up
their voice, the villages *that* Kedar doth inhabit: let
the inhabitants of the rock sing, let them shout
from the top of the mountains.
12 Let them give glory unto the LORD, and declare
his praise in the islands.
13 The LORD shall go forth as a mighty man, he
shall stir up jealousy like a man of war: he shall
cry, yea, roar; he shall prevail against his enemies.
14 I have long time holden my peace; I have been
still, *and* refrained myself: *now* will I cry like a tra-
vailing woman; I will destroy and devour at once.
15 I will make waste mountains and hills, and
dry up all their herbs; and I will make the rivers
islands, and I will dry up the pools.
16 And I will bring the blind by a way *that* they
knew not; I will lead them in paths *that* they have
not known: I will make darkness light before
them, and crooked things straight. These things
will I do unto them, and not forsake them.
17 ¶ They shall be turned back, they shall be
greatly ashamed, that trust in graven images, that
say to the molten images, Ye *are* our gods.
18 Hear, ye deaf; and look, ye blind, that ye may see.
19 Who *is* blind, but my servant? or deaf, as my
messenger *that* I sent? who *is* blind as *he that is*
perfect, and blind as the LORD's servant?
20 Seeing many things, but thou observest not;
opening the ears, but he heareth not.
21 The LORD is well pleased for his righteous-
ness' sake; he will magnify the law, and make *it*
honourable.
22 But this *is* a people robbed and spoiled; *they*
are all of them snared in holes, and they are hid
in prison houses: they are for a prey, and none
delivereth; for a spoil, and none saith, Restore.
23 Who among you will give ear to this? *who* will
hearken and hear for the time to come?
24 Who gave Jacob for a spoil, and Israel to the
robbers? did not the LORD, he against whom we
have sinned? for they would not walk in his ways,
neither were they obedient unto his law.
25 Therefore he hath poured upon him the fury
of his anger, and the strength of battle: and it hath
set him on fire round about, yet he knew not; and
it burned him, yet he laid *it* not to heart.

CHAPTER 43

BUT now thus saith the LORD that created thee, O
Jacob, and he that formed thee, O Israel, Fear not:
for I have redeemed thee, I have called *thee* by thy
name; thou *art* mine.
2 When thou passest through the waters, I *will be*
with thee; and through the rivers, they shall not
overflow thee: when thou walkest through the
fire, thou shalt not be burned; neither shall the
flame kindle upon thee.
3 For I *am* the LORD thy God, the Holy One of
Israel, thy Saviour: I gave Egypt *for* thy ransom,
Ethiopia and Seba for thee.
4 Since thou wast precious in my sight, thou hast
been honourable, and I have loved thee: therefore
will I give men for thee, and people for thy life.
5 Fear not: for I *am* with thee: I will bring thy
seed from the east, and gather thee from the west;
6 I will say to the north, Give up; and to the
south, Keep not back: bring my sons from far, and

42:13 *jealousy.* Zeal.
42:14 *holden my peace.* Keep quiet. *travailing.* In labor pains.
42:19 *blind . . . my servant.* Israel failed to keep their covenantal responsibilities because of spiritual blindness (v. 7). *perfect.* Complete or whole, referring to the totality of covenant blessings given to them.
42:21 *law.* All His revelation, not just the commandments.
42:22 *robbed and spoiled.* Both words have the idea of being plundered (v. 24). *prey.* Plunder. *spoil.* Sack of booty.

Thoughts for Personal/Family Worship: Chapter 42

1. **Here we have a rich mine full of the sparkling gems of Christ's glory. Let us meditate on just two precious truths. First, God sent Christ to produce justice ("judgment") in the world (vv. 1,3,4). This means that He came to change the way we relate to each other, so that our relationships conform to His laws (Ex. 21:1; Lev. 19:37). If we would claim Christ as our King and His Spirit as our life, we must demonstrate the reality of Christ's saving work in our lives by walking in obedience to His commands. Christians bear the mark of the Servant of the Lord. What evidence do you see in your life of being a servant of God like Christ?**
2. **Second, Christ will not break the bruised reed or quench the smoking wick (v. 3). He is tender and compassionate with those broken by suffering, especially those contrite under sorrows over their sins (57:15; 66:2). He will not snuff out the faith of weak Christians but will work in them that their faith and love may burn brightly. How can this promise encourage believers going through times of spiritual darkness?**

The Redeemer of Israel and His Witnesses (43:1—44:28)

Chapter 43: ***The Lord exhorts His people to be witnesses of His uniqueness.***

43:1 *Fear not.* See note at 41:10. *redeemed.* Term used of a kinsman who rescues or defends the family at his own expense (see note at 35:9). Israel belongs to God by virtue both of creation and His covenant.
43:2 *waters . . . fire.* Symbols of afflictions and tribulations.
43:3 *gave Egypt . . . for thee.* Alluding to the final plague, when God took the lives of the firstborn (Ex. 12). *ransom.* A price to redeem one's life (Job 33:24; Ps. 49:7), often implying the satisfaction of justice (Ex. 21:30; Num. 35:31–32).
43:4 *precious.* Highly valued or esteemed. *loved.* God chose freely to set His love upon them (Deut. 7:6–8).
43:5–6 *Fear not: for I am with thee.* God's presence with His

my daughters from the ends of the earth;
7 *Even* every one that is called by my name: for I
have created him for my glory, I have formed him;
yea, I have made him.
8 ¶ Bring forth the blind people that have eyes,
and the deaf that have ears.
9 Let all the nations be gathered together, and
let the people be assembled: who among them
can declare this, and shew us former things? let
them bring forth their witnesses, that they may
be justified: or let them hear, and say, *It is* truth.
10 Ye *are* my witnesses, saith the LORD, and my
servant whom I have chosen: that ye may know
and believe me, and understand that I *am* he:
before me there was no God formed, neither shall
there be after me.
11 I, *even* I, *am* the LORD; and beside me *there is*
no saviour.
12 I have declared, and have saved, and I have
shewed, when *there was* no strange *god* among
you: therefore ye *are* my witnesses, saith the LORD,
that I *am* God.
13 Yea, before the day *was* I *am* he; and *there is*
none that can deliver out of my hand: I will work,
and who shall let it?
14 ¶ Thus saith the LORD, your redeemer, the
Holy One of Israel; For your sake I have sent to
Babylon, and have brought down all their nobles,
and the Chaldeans, whose cry *is* in the ships.
15 I *am* the LORD, your Holy One, the creator of
Israel, your King.
16 Thus saith the LORD, which maketh a way in
the sea, and a path in the mighty waters;
17 Which bringeth forth the chariot and horse,
the army and the power; they shall lie down
together, they shall not rise: they are extinct, they
are quenched as tow.
18 ¶ Remember ye not the former things, neither
consider the things of old.
19 Behold, I will do a new thing; now it shall
spring forth; shall ye not know it? I will even make
a way in the wilderness, *and* rivers in the desert.
20 The beast of the field shall honour me, the
dragons and the owls: because I give waters in the
wilderness, *and* rivers in the desert, to give drink
to my people, my chosen.
21 This people have I formed for myself; they
shall shew forth my praise.
22 ¶ But thou hast not called upon me, O Jacob;
but thou hast been weary of me, O Israel.
23 Thou hast not brought me the small cattle of
thy burnt offerings; neither hast thou honoured
me with thy sacrifices. I have not caused thee to
serve with an offering, nor wearied thee with
incense.
24 Thou hast bought me no sweet cane with
money, neither hast thou filled me with the fat
of thy sacrifices: but thou hast made me to serve
with thy sins, thou hast wearied me with thine
iniquities.
25 I, *even* I, *am* he that blotteth out thy transgres-
sions for mine own sake, and will not remember
thy sins.
26 Put me in remembrance: let us plead together:
declare thou, that thou mayest be justified.
27 Thy first father hath sinned, and thy teachers
have transgressed against me.
28 Therefore I have profaned the princes of the
sanctuary, and have given Jacob to the curse, and
Israel to reproaches.

---

people should make them confident that He will gather His elect (*bring thy seed*) to Himself (Acts 18:9–10). *east . . . west . . . north . . . south.* Everywhere. *my sons . . . my daughters.* The spiritual offspring of Jacob are the adopted children of God (2 Cor. 6:18; Gal. 3:26,29).

43:8–13 Another trial speech to identify the one true God (see note at 41:21).

43:9 *justified.* Vindicated.

43:10–11 *my witnesses.* God calls His people to publicly stand for the truth that He is the only God and Savior, like those who testify in a courtroom (44:8; Acts 1:8). Their witness is linked to their public praise of the Lord (v. 21).

43:12 *strange.* Foreign.

43:13 *who shall let it.* "Who shall hinder or reverse it?"

43:14 *redeemer.* See note at v. 1.

43:16 *maketh a way in the sea.* An allusion to the exodus deliverance (Ex. 14).

43:17 *quenched as tow.* Put out or extinguished like a wick (contrast 42:3).

43:18 *Remember ye not the former things.* Though they are not to forget the warnings and examples of the past (v. 16), they must not dwell on the past but look ahead to the fulfillment of God's promises.

43:19 *I will do a new thing.* A new exodus (v. 16; 11:11; 12:2), which is a new creation (45:8; 48:6–7; 57:19; 65:17–18; 2 Cor. 5:17; Eph. 2:10).

43:20 *dragons.* Jackals. *owls.* Or ostriches.

43:21 *shew forth my praise.* God created His people to glorify Himself (1 Peter 2:9).

43:23 *small cattle.* Sheep.

43:24 *made me to serve with thy sins.* Burdened me with your sins.

43:25 *I, even I, am he.* The Lord alone has the authority to forgive (*blotteth out*) the guilt of sin (Mark 2:7), and He does so for His glory (*for mine own sake*; 1 John 2:12). *remember.* Think about on purpose, take to heart and take action (Jer. 17:10). After the Lord has forgiven sins, His attitude and treatment of the person is no longer colored by his guiltiness and worthiness of punishment (Jer. 31:34).

43:26 *Put me in remembrance.* Summon me to court. *justified.* Vindicated.

43:27 *Thy first father hath sinned.* Either a reference to Adam or to Jacob. *teachers.* Interpreters.

43:28 *profaned.* Polluted, treated the holy as common.

Thoughts for Personal/Family Worship: Chapter 43

1. It is both a blessing and a challenge that God says to His people, "Ye are my witnesses" (v. 12). It is a blessing that the Lord's people have tasted of His goodness and have experienced His saving power. It is a blessing to speak

CHAPTER 44

YET now hear, O Jacob my servant; and Israel,
whom I have chosen:
2 Thus saith the LORD that made thee, and
formed thee from the womb, *which* will help thee;
Fear not, O Jacob, my servant; and thou, Jesurun,
whom I have chosen.
3 For I will pour water upon him that is thirsty,
and floods upon the dry ground: I will pour my
spirit upon thy seed, and my blessing upon thine
offspring:
4 And they shall spring up *as* among the grass, as
willows by the water courses.
5 One shall say, I *am* the LORD's; and another shall
call *himself* by the name of Jacob; and another
shall subscribe *with* his hand unto the LORD, and
surname *himself* by the name of Israel.
6 Thus saith the LORD the King of Israel, and his
redeemer the LORD of hosts; I *am* the first, and I
am the last; and beside me *there is* no God.
7 And who, as I, shall call, and shall declare it,
and set it in order for me, since I appointed the
ancient people? and the things that are coming,
and shall come, let them shew unto them.
8 Fear ye not, neither be afraid: have not I told
thee from that time, and have declared *it*? ye *are*
even my witnesses. Is there a God beside me? yea,
there is no God; I know not *any*.
9 ¶ They that make a graven image *are* all of them
vanity; and their delectable things shall not profit;
and they *are* their own witnesses; they see not, nor
know; that they may be ashamed.
10 Who hath formed a god, or molten a graven
image *that* is profitable for nothing?
11 Behold, all his fellows shall be ashamed: and
the workmen, they *are* of men: let them all be
gathered together, let them stand up; *yet* they shall
fear, *and* they shall be ashamed together.
12 The smith with the tongs both worketh in
the coals, and fashioneth it with hammers, and
worketh it with the strength of his arms: yea, he
is hungry, and his strength faileth: he drinketh no
water, and is faint.
13 The carpenter stretcheth out *his* rule; he mark-
eth it out with a line; he fitteth it with planes, and
he marketh it out with the compass, and mak-
eth it after the figure of a man, according to the
beauty of a man; that it may remain in the house.
14 He heweth him down cedars, and taketh the
cypress and the oak, which he strengtheneth for
himself among the trees of the forest: he planteth
an ash, and the rain doth nourish *it*.
15 Then shall it be for a man to burn: for he will
take thereof, and warm himself; yea, he kindleth
it, and baketh bread; yea, he maketh a god, and
worshippeth *it*; he maketh it a graven image, and
falleth down thereto.
16 He burneth part thereof in the fire; with part
thereof he eateth flesh; he roasteth roast, and is
satisfied: yea, he warmeth *himself*, and saith, Aha,
I am warm, I have seen the fire:
17 And the residue thereof he maketh a god, *even*
his graven image: he falleth down unto it, and
worshippeth *it*, and prayeth unto it, and saith,
Deliver me; for thou *art* my god.
18 They have not known nor understood: for
he hath shut their eyes, that they cannot see; *and*
their hearts, that they cannot understand.
19 And none considereth in his heart, neither *is*
there knowledge nor understanding to say, I have
burned part of it in the fire; yea, also I have baked
bread upon the coals thereof; I have roasted flesh,
and eaten *it*: and shall I make the residue thereof
an abomination? shall I fall down to the stock of
a tree?
20 He feedeth on ashes: a deceived heart hath
turned him aside, that he cannot deliver his soul,
nor say, *Is there* not a lie in my right hand?

of His goodness and faithfulness. However, it is also a great challenge, for we have a responsibility to tell the lost and perishing that there is hope in Christ. How do we measure up to this challenge? How can this chapter help us to be His witnesses?

2. **God says to His people, "I . . . will not remember thy sins" (v. 25). We may look back on our own lives with shame that we could ever have done the wicked things we did. We may find it difficult to get such shameful thoughts out of our minds and find ourselves confessing the same sins over and over again. Our heart may condemn us, but God is greater than our heart. How can believers rest their consciences in the truth that their forgiveness is complete?**

Chapter 44: *The Lord shows the folly of idolatry and exhorts His people to trust Him.*

44:2 *Jesurun*. A term of endearment for Israel, perhaps meaning "upright one" (Deut. 32:15; 33:5,26).
44:3 *I will pour water . . . my spirit*. God will give new life to His people (*seed*) by an abundant work of the Holy Spirit (32:15; 43:19–21; 45:8; Prov. 1:23; Ezek. 39:29; Joel 2:28; Zech. 12:10).
44:5 *subscribe*. Write. *surname*. Use a title. The work of God's Spirit (v. 4) will cause people to willingly and publically belong to the Lord and His covenant people.
44:6 *redeemer*. See note at 35:9. *first . . . last*. See note at 41:4.
44:8 *no God*. Literally, "no rock"; a huge, immovable boulder as an image of stability (Deut. 32:4).
44:9–20 The Lord shows how ridiculous it is to worship idols and look to them for salvation (37:19; 40:18–20; 46:5–7).
44:9 *vanity*. Emptiness, nothingness. *delectable*. Desirable, here referring to the idols.
44:13 *carpenter*. Craftsman. *fitteth it with planes*. Forms with chisels.
44:14 *heweth*. Cuts.
44:15 *kindleth*. Makes a fire.
44:17 *residue*. Remainder (v. 19).
44:18 *shut*. Smear.
44:19 *abomination*. A detestable or disgusting thing, used here to refer to the idol. *stock of a tree*. A block of wood.
44:20 *his soul*. Himself.
44:21 *Remember*. Think about on purpose, bring to mind.

21 ¶ Remember these, O Jacob and Israel; for
thou *art* my servant: I have formed thee; thou *art*
my servant: O Israel, thou shalt not be forgotten
of me.
22 I have blotted out, as a thick cloud, thy trans-
gressions, and, as a cloud, thy sins: return unto
me; for I have redeemed thee.
23 Sing, O ye heavens; for the LORD hath done *it*:
shout, ye lower parts of the earth: break forth into
singing, ye mountains, O forest, and every tree
therein: for the LORD hath redeemed Jacob, and
glorified himself in Israel.
24 Thus saith the LORD, thy redeemer, and he
that formed thee from the womb, I *am* the LORD
that maketh all *things*; that stretcheth forth the
heavens alone; that spreadeth abroad the earth by
myself;
25 That frustrateth the tokens of the liars, and
maketh diviners mad; that turneth wise *men*
backward, and maketh their knowledge foolish;
26 That confirmeth the word of his servant, and
performeth the counsel of his messengers; that
saith to Jerusalem, Thou shalt be inhabited; and
to the cities of Judah, Ye shall be built, and I will
raise up the decayed places thereof:
27 That saith to the deep, Be dry, and I will dry
up thy rivers:
28 That saith of Cyrus, *He is* my shepherd, and
shall perform all my pleasure: even saying to
Jerusalem, Thou shalt be built; and to the temple,
Thy foundation shall be laid.

CHAPTER 45

THUS saith the LORD to his anointed, to Cyrus,
whose right hand I have holden, to subdue
nations before him; and I will loose the loins of
kings, to open before him the two leaved gates;
and the gates shall not be shut;
2 I will go before thee, and make the crooked
places straight: I will break in pieces the gates of
brass, and cut in sunder the bars of iron:
3 And I will give thee the treasures of darkness,
and hidden riches of secret places, that thou
mayest know that I, the LORD, which call *thee* by
thy name, *am* the God of Israel.
4 For Jacob my servant's sake, and Israel mine
elect, I have even called thee by thy name: I have
surnamed thee, though thou hast not known me.
5 ¶ I *am* the LORD, and *there is* none else, *there*
is no God beside me: I girded thee, though thou
hast not known me:
6 That they may know from the rising of the sun,
and from the west, that *there is* none beside me. I
am the LORD, and *there is* none else.
7 I form the light, and create darkness: I make
peace, and create evil: I the LORD do all these
things.

forgotten. Neglected, intentionally ignored.

44:22 *return*. Repent. *for I have redeemed thee*. Redemption brings repentance and forgiveness of sins (Ps. 130:4,7–8; Luke 24:46–47; Acts 5:30–31).

44:23 *lower parts of the earth*. The earth itself, in contrast to the *heavens*.

44:24 *maketh all things . . . by myself*. There is only one God and Creator; no other being assisted Him in making the universe. Thus, when Scripture attributes the work of creation to God's Son (John 1:3; Col. 1:16; Heb. 1:2) and God's Spirit (Gen. 1:2; Job 33:4), it is not describing three gods but one God in three persons. *spreadeth abroad*. Spreads out.

44:25 *tokens of the liars*. Signs or omens of those who predict by magic (*diviners*).

44:28 *Cyrus*. The Medo-Persian king who conquered Babylon in 539 BC, about two centuries after Isaiah began to prophesy (45:1; Ezra 1:1–11). *my shepherd*. The ordained or selected ruler. God is the Lord of history: past, present, and future. He knows the name of each person and has planned what he will do centuries before he is born (1 Kings 13:2).

Thoughts for Personal/Family Worship: Chapter 44

1. **God's Spirit is poured down from heaven through the ascended Mediator, Jesus Christ. He comes like a heavenly river to give life to dead souls. He satisfies all the thirsts of God's elect and causes them to prosper in the inner man, and one day in visible glory. There is nothing more important than having the Spirit of God dwell in you, for if anyone does not have the Spirit of Christ, he does not belong to Him (Rom. 8:9). A defining mark of the people renewed by the Spirit is their public and personal confession, "I am the Lord's." They belong to the Lord and identify with His church. What practical effects does this produce in your life?**
2. **Isaiah's diatribe against idolatry (vv. 9–20) shows the incredible stupidity and blindness of giving our adoration to objects (v. 18). This applies not just to images and statues of divine beings but also to sinful lusts after riches and pleasures. Why is it foolish and degrading to give your heart to any mere object instead of to God?**

The Calling of Cyrus and the Destruction of Babylon (45:1—47:15)

Chapter 45: *Cyrus is addressed by the Lord and given his commission.*

45:1 *anointed*. Hebrew, *messiah* (2 Sam. 23:1; Ps. 2:2); placing oil on the head was a sign of appointing to an office such as king (1 Sam. 10:1; 16:13). God's selecting of this pagan king (*Cyrus*; see note at 44:28) to save Israel from its Babylonian exile is a type of Christ, the true Savior. *holden*. Strengthened. *loose the loins of kings*. Disarm opposing kings. *leaved gates*. Double doors.

45:2 *make the crooked places straight*. Make an easy path for him. *sunder*. In pieces. *bars*. The mechanism for barring the gates.

45:4 *surnamed thee*. Gave a title of honor. *not known me*. Evidence of God's absolute sovereignty even over pagans (Prov. 21:1).

45:5 *girded*. Dressed for action, an image of being equipped and ready.

45:6 *rising of the sun . . . west*. Pairs of opposites designate totality: all places (Mal. 1:11).

45:7 *peace . . . evil*. The first refers to well-being and harmony, the second to disaster or harm.

8 Drop down, ye heavens, from above, and let the
skies pour down righteousness: let the earth open,
and let them bring forth salvation, and let righteous-
ness spring up together; I the LORD have created it.
9 Woe unto him that striveth with his Maker! *Let*
the potsherd *strive* with the potsherds of the earth.
Shall the clay say to him that fashioneth it, What
makest thou? or thy work, He hath no hands?
10 Woe unto him that saith unto *his* father, What
begettest thou? or to the woman, What hast thou
brought forth?
11 Thus saith the LORD, the Holy One of Israel,
and his Maker, Ask me of things to come con-
cerning my sons, and concerning the work of my
hands command ye me.
12 I have made the earth, and created man
upon it: I, *even* my hands, have stretched out the
heavens, and all their host have I commanded.
13 I have raised him up in righteousness, and
I will direct all his ways: he shall build my city,
and he shall let go my captives, not for price nor
reward, saith the LORD of hosts.
14 Thus saith the LORD, The labour of Egypt, and
merchandise of Ethiopia and of the Sabeans, men of
stature, shall come over unto thee, and they shall be
thine: they shall come after thee; in chains they shall
come over, and they shall fall down unto thee, they
shall make supplication unto thee, *saying*, Surely
God *is* in thee; and *there is* none else, *there is* no God.
15 Verily thou *art* a God that hidest thyself, O
God of Israel, the Saviour.
16 They shall be ashamed, and also confounded,
all of them: they shall go to confusion together
that are makers of idols.
17 *But* Israel shall be saved in the LORD with an
everlasting salvation: ye shall not be ashamed nor
confounded world without end.
18 For thus saith the LORD that created the
heavens; God himself that formed the earth and
made it; he hath established it, he created it not in
vain, he formed it to be inhabited: I *am* the LORD;
and *there is* none else.
19 I have not spoken in secret, in a dark place of
the earth: I said not unto the seed of Jacob, Seek
ye me in vain: I the LORD speak righteousness, I
declare things that are right.
20 ¶ Assemble yourselves and come; draw near
together, ye *that are* escaped of the nations: they
have no knowledge that set up the wood of their
graven image, and pray unto a god *that* cannot save.
21 Tell ye, and bring *them* near; yea, let them take
counsel together: who hath declared this from
ancient time? *who* hath told it from that time? *have*
not I the LORD? and *there is* no God else beside me;
a just God and a Saviour; *there is* none beside me.
22 Look unto me, and be ye saved, all the ends
of the earth: for I *am* God, and *there is* none else.
23 I have sworn by myself, the word is gone out of
my mouth *in* righteousness, and shall not return,
That unto me every knee shall bow, every tongue
shall swear.
24 Surely, shall *one* say, in the LORD have I righ-
teousness and strength: *even* to him shall *men*
come; and all that are incensed against him shall
be ashamed.
25 In the LORD shall all the seed of Israel be
justified, and shall glory.

CHAPTER 46

BEL boweth down, Nebo stoopeth, their idols
were upon the beasts, and upon the cattle: your

45:8 *Drop down, ye heavens.* The pouring out of the Holy Spirit through Christ will bring *righteousness* and *salvation* to earth (32:15–18). The two terms are often paralleled in this prophecy (46:12–13; 51:5–6,8; 56:1; 59:16–17; 61:10; 62:1) because God's works of saving His people display His faithfulness to glorify Himself according to His law and promises (vv. 23–25; 5:16; 33:5; 63:1).

45:9 *potsherds.* Clay pots or fragments. *What makest thou?* The Creator has the right to do as He sees fit with His creations (Rom. 9:20–22).

45:14 *Surely God is in thee.* God's presence to bless His people will bring honor to both Himself and them (Zech. 8:23; 1 Cor. 14:25; Rev. 3:9).

45:15 *Verily.* Surely or truly. *God that hidest thyself.* God's ways are incomprehensible, and some things He intentionally does not reveal to men (Deut. 29:29).

45:16 *go to confusion.* Face humiliation.

45:17 *world without end.* To eternity, literally, "unto ages of ever."

45:18 *in vain.* Empty.

45:19 *in vain.* In futility.

45:23 *sworn by myself.* God cannot swear by any greater or offer any higher confirmation (Gen. 22:16; Jer. 22:5; Heb. 6:13–20). *unto me every knee shall bow, every tongue shall swear.* God will be glorified in all the world. In a remarkable demonstration of Christ's deity and worthiness of worship, Paul applies this statement to Christ (Rom. 14:10–11; Phil. 2:10–11).

45:24 *incensed.* Angry.

45:25 *seed.* Spiritual Israel, all those redeemed through the work of the Messiah (Rom. 4:13–16; 9:6; Gal. 3:29; 6:16). They seek their righteousness and place their boasting in the Lord alone (1 Cor. 1:30–31; Phil. 3:3).

Thoughts for Personal/Family Worship: Chapter 45

A wonderful promise is found in v. 22: "Look unto me, and be ye saved, all the ends of the earth: for I am God, and there is none else." Faith is a look of utter dependence and need, and this is the only way to be healed of our sins and their just punishment (Num. 21:8; John 3:14–15). God's gospel call goes out to all nations, for there is no other name under heaven by which we must be saved besides that of Jesus Christ (Acts 4:12). God will be glorified. We may either turn to Him now and be saved or His glory will compel us to honor Him even when He punishes us for our sins. How should this motivate us to repent and believe now? How should it motivate us to work together to bring the gospel to all nations?

carriages *were* heavy loaden; *they are* a burden to
the weary *beast*.
2 They stoop, they bow down together; they
could not deliver the burden, but themselves are
gone into captivity.
3 ¶ Hearken unto me, O house of Jacob, and all
the remnant of the house of Israel, which are
borne *by me* from the belly, which are carried
from the womb:
4 And *even* to *your* old age I *am* he; and *even* to
hoar hairs will I carry *you*: I have made, and I will
bear; even I will carry, and will deliver *you*.
5 ¶ To whom will ye liken me, and make *me*
equal, and compare me, that we may be like?
6 They lavish gold out of the bag, and weigh
silver in the balance, *and* hire a goldsmith; and he
maketh it a god: they fall down, yea, they worship.
7 They bear him upon the shoulder, they carry
him, and set him in his place, and he standeth;
from his place shall he not remove: yea, *one* shall
cry unto him, yet can he not answer, nor save him
out of his trouble.
8 Remember this, and shew yourselves men:
bring *it* again to mind, O ye transgressors.
9 Remember the former things of old: for I *am*
God, and *there is* none else; *I am* God, and *there*
is none like me,
10 Declaring the end from the beginning, and
from ancient times *the things* that are not *yet*
done, saying, My counsel shall stand, and I will do
all my pleasure:
11 Calling a ravenous bird from the east, the man
that executeth my counsel from a far country: yea,
I have spoken *it*, I will also bring it to pass; I have
purposed *it*, I will also do it.
12 ¶ Hearken unto me, ye stouthearted, that *are*
far from righteousness:
13 I bring near my righteousness; it shall not be
far off, and my salvation shall not tarry: and I will
place salvation in Zion for Israel my glory.

CHAPTER 47

COME down, and sit in the dust, O virgin daughter
of Babylon, sit on the ground: *there is* no throne,
O daughter of the Chaldeans: for thou shalt no
more be called tender and delicate.
2 Take the millstones, and grind meal: uncover
thy locks, make bare the leg, uncover the thigh,
pass over the rivers.
3 Thy nakedness shall be uncovered, yea, thy
shame shall be seen: I will take vengeance, and I
will not meet *thee as* a man.
4 *As for* our redeemer, the LORD of hosts *is* his
name, the Holy One of Israel.
5 Sit thou silent, and get thee into darkness,
O daughter of the Chaldeans: for thou shalt no
more be called, The lady of kingdoms.
6 ¶ I was wroth with my people, I have polluted
mine inheritance, and given them into thine
hand: thou didst shew them no mercy; upon the
ancient hast thou very heavily laid thy yoke.
7 ¶ And thou saidst, I shall be a lady for ever: *so*
that thou didst not lay these *things* to thy heart,

Chapter 46: *The Lord's might is contrasted with the weakness and inability of Babylon's idols.*

46:1–2 *Bel.* The god Marduk, chief of the Babylonian pantheon. *Nebo.* A son of Marduk. *carriages.* Things that were lifted up, referring to baggage. The idols were powerless to help and would be part of the load or booty carried captive.
46:3 *Hearken.* Listen. *borne . . . from the belly.* Carried from birth. Note the contrast: idols had to be carried, but God carries along His people.
46:4 *hoar.* Gray.
46:5–7 God is unique and incomprehensible, whereas idols are the designs of man's imagination and the work of man's hands, lifeless and powerless (44:9–20). *not remove.* Cannot leave wherever it is placed.
46:8 *Remember.* Intentionally consider (v. 9). *shew yourselves men.* Be brave.
46:10 *Declaring the end from the beginning.* God knew all the future at the first moment of creation because He had decreed it (*my counsel*) from eternity (44:28). *my pleasure.* My will.
46:11 *ravenous bird.* A bird of prey, referring to Cyrus, who would hunt Babylon down swiftly (45:1). *I have spoken . . . I will . . . I have purposed . . . I will.* God is the One who decrees His plan and makes it happen (14:24; Eph. 1:4,11). Cyrus was simply God's instrument.
46:12 *stouthearted.* Stubborn in heart.

Thoughts for Personal/Family Worship: Chapter 46

1. **God will glorify Himself against all the idols of man. The things the nations worship are burdens for them to carry, but God is not so. He is the Lord of all events, carrying out His eternal plans without fail. Even pagan kings serve Him without realizing it. Certainly then we can be confident that He will bring complete salvation and glory to His people. Why do people tend to trust in idols? Why should they trust in the Lord?**
2. **There are many times when discouragement springs from our many failings and weaknesses and the difficulty of our way. The Lord promises His people, "And even to your old age I am he; and even to hoar hairs will I carry you: I have made, and I will bear; even I will carry, and will deliver you" (v. 4). Believers can persevere because the Lord will persevere with them.**

Chapter 47: *The Lord punishes Babylon for its arrogance.*

47:1 *tender and delicate.* Coddled and pampered.
47:2–3 *meal.* Flour. *locks.* Veil. *make bare the leg.* Strip off the flowing skirt. All these are gestures of humiliation. *I will not meet thee as a man.* I will not spare a man.
47:4 *redeemer.* See note at 35:9.
47:6 *wroth.* Angry. *polluted.* Treated as ordinary or common. *mercy.* Compassion or pity. *ancient.* Aged.
47:7–9 The arrogance and self-sufficiency pictured here is not unique to Babylon but characterizes the wicked and provokes God's judgment on the world (Rev. 18:7–8).
47:7 *lady.* A queen or queen-mother. *remember.* Choose to give thought to.

neither didst remember the latter end of it.
8 Therefore hear now this, *thou that art* given to
pleasures, that dwellest carelessly, that sayest in thine
heart, I *am*, and none else beside me; I shall not sit
as a widow, neither shall I know the loss of children:
9 But these two *things* shall come to thee in a
moment in one day, the loss of children, and
widowhood: they shall come upon thee in their
perfection for the multitude of thy sorceries, *and*
for the great abundance of thine enchantments.
10 ¶ For thou hast trusted in thy wickedness: thou
hast said, None seeth me. Thy wisdom and thy
knowledge, it hath perverted thee; and thou hast
said in thine heart, I *am*, and none else beside me.
11 ¶ Therefore shall evil come upon thee; thou
shalt not know from whence it riseth: and
mischief shall fall upon thee; thou shalt not be
able to put it off: and desolation shall come upon
thee suddenly, *which* thou shalt not know.
12 Stand now with thine enchantments, and with
the multitude of thy sorceries, wherein thou hast
laboured from thy youth; if so be thou shalt be
able to profit, if so be thou mayest prevail.
13 Thou art wearied in the multitude of thy
counsels. Let now the astrologers, the stargazers,
the monthly prognosticators, stand up, and save
thee from *these things* that shall come upon thee.
14 Behold, they shall be as stubble; the fire shall
burn them; they shall not deliver themselves from
the power of the flame: *there shall* not *be* a coal to
warm at, *nor* fire to sit before it.
15 Thus shall they be unto thee with whom thou
hast laboured, *even* thy merchants, from thy
youth: they shall wander every one to his quarter;
none shall save thee.

CHAPTER 48

HEAR ye this, O house of Jacob, which are called
by the name of Israel, and are come forth out of
the waters of Judah, which swear by the name of
the LORD, and make mention of the God of Israel,
but not in truth, nor in righteousness.
2 For they call themselves of the holy city, and
stay themselves upon the God of Israel; The LORD
of hosts *is* his name.
3 I have declared the former things from the
beginning; and they went forth out of my mouth,
and I shewed them; I did *them* suddenly, and they
came to pass.
4 Because I knew that thou *art* obstinate, and thy
neck *is* an iron sinew, and thy brow brass;
5 I have even from the beginning declared *it* to
thee; before it came to pass I shewed *it* thee: lest
thou shouldest say, Mine idol hath done them,
and my graven image, and my molten image, hath
commanded them.
6 Thou hast heard, see all this; and will not ye
declare *it*? I have shewed thee new things from
this time, even hidden things, and thou didst not
know them.
7 They are created now, and not from the begin-
ning; even before the day when thou heardest
them not; lest thou shouldest say, Behold, I knew
them.
8 Yea, thou heardest not; yea, thou knewest
not; yea, from that time *that* thine ear was not
opened: for I knew that thou wouldest deal very
treacherously, and wast called a transgressor from
the womb.
9 ¶ For my name's sake will I defer mine anger,
and for my praise will I refrain for thee, that I cut
thee not off.
10 Behold, I have refined thee, but not with silver;
I have chosen thee in the furnace of affliction.
11 For mine own sake, *even* for mine own sake,
will I do *it*: for how should *my name* be polluted?
and I will not give my glory unto another.
12 ¶ Hearken unto me, O Jacob and Israel, my
called; I *am* he; I *am* the first, I also *am* the last.

47:8 *given to pleasures.* Used to the good life. *carelessly.* With a sense of safety or security.
47:9 *perfection.* Fullness. *enchantments.* Charms or spells (v. 12).
47:11 *evil.* Calamity or disaster. *mischief.* Disaster or ruin. *put it off.* Make atonement.
47:13 *monthly prognosticators.* Those who make predictions by the moon.

Thoughts for Personal/Family Worship: Chapter 47

Babylon had become used to the good life (v. 8) and lived as though it would last forever, feeling safe and secure. Nebuchadnezzar expressed such pride before God humbled him (Dan. 4), and Belshazzar hosted a party on the very night of destruction (Dan. 5). It is easy to grow comfortable with the things of life and assume that nothing will ever interrupt the flow of pleasure and contentment. Such is the presumption of horrendous pride. Babylon did not bring to heart or mind the latter end (v. 7)—and suffered extreme consequences. Let us all be warned that security is not in the things of this life but only in God. Thinking about our latter end should lead us to trust the Lord, for the things of this world will surely pass away.

Chapter 48: *The Lord rebukes Israel because of their refusal to trust Him, yet in mercy He assures them that He will deliver them.*

The Lord's Appeal to Israel (48:1–22)

48:2 *stay.* Support or brace.
48:3 *I have declared . . . I did them.* See notes at 46:10–11.
48:4 *neck . . . iron . . . brow* and *brass.* Symbols of being stubborn (*obstinate*).
48:6 *hidden things.* Things kept secret.
48:9–11 God's grace for Israel was not brought about by anything in them but only by His love for His own *glory* and His will to make Himself known (*name*) and adored (*praise*; 2:11,17; 5:16; 30:18; 33:10; 44:23; 49:3; 60:21; 61:3; Pss. 25:11; 31:1; Ezek. 20:9,14,22,44; 36:21–24; Dan. 9:19).
48:9 *refrain.* Restrain oneself.

13 Mine hand also hath laid the foundation of
the earth, and my right hand hath spanned the
heavens: *when* I call unto them, they stand up
together.
14 All ye, assemble yourselves, and hear; which
among them hath declared these *things*? The
LORD hath loved him: he will do his pleasure on
Babylon, and his arm *shall be on* the Chaldeans.
15 I, *even* I, have spoken; yea, I have called him:
I have brought him, and he shall make his way
prosperous.
16 ¶ Come ye near unto me, hear ye this; I have
not spoken in secret from the beginning; from
the time that it was, there *am* I: and now the Lord
GOD, and his Spirit, hath sent me.
17 Thus saith the LORD, thy Redeemer, the Holy
One of Israel; I *am* the LORD thy God which
teacheth thee to profit, which leadeth thee by the
way *that* thou shouldest go.
18 O that thou hadst hearkened to my command-
ments! then had thy peace been as a river, and thy
righteousness as the waves of the sea:
19 Thy seed also had been as the sand, and the
offspring of thy bowels like the gravel thereof; his
name should not have been cut off nor destroyed
from before me.
20 ¶ Go ye forth of Babylon, flee ye from the
Chaldeans, with a voice of singing declare ye, tell
this, utter it *even* to the end of the earth; say ye,
The LORD hath redeemed his servant Jacob.
21 And they thirsted not *when* he led them
through the deserts: he caused the waters to flow
out of the rock for them: he clave the rock also,
and the waters gushed out.
22 *There is* no peace, saith the LORD, unto the
wicked.

CHAPTER 49

LISTEN, O isles, unto me; and hearken, ye people,
from far; The LORD hath called me from the
womb; from the bowels of my mother hath he
made mention of my name.
2 And he hath made my mouth like a sharp
sword; in the shadow of his hand hath he hid me,
and made me a polished shaft; in his quiver hath
he hid me;
3 And said unto me, Thou *art* my servant, O
Israel, in whom I will be glorified.
4 Then I said, I have laboured in vain, I have
spent my strength for nought, and in vain: *yet*
surely my judgment *is* with the LORD, and my
work with my God.
5 ¶ And now, saith the LORD that formed me
from the womb *to be* his servant, to bring Jacob
again to him, Though Israel be not gathered, yet
shall I be glorious in the eyes of the LORD, and my
God shall be my strength.

48:10 *refined*. Smelted or tested (1 Peter 1:7).
48:11 *polluted*. Treated or regarded as common or ordinary; the opposite of being set apart as holy.
48:12 *first . . . last*. See note at 41:4.
48:13 *spanned*. Spread out.
48:14 *The LORD hath loved him*. God sovereignly chose Cyrus; not an expression of affection.
48:15 *prosperous*. Successful.
48:16 *not spoken in secret from the beginning*. The words of the Lord (vv. 15,17; 40:21; 45:19). *there am I: and now the Lord GOD, and his Spirit, hath sent me*. Mysteriously, the Lord was sent by the Lord and His Spirit: a reference to Christ and the Trinity (42:1).
48:17 *Redeemer*. See note at 35:9 (v. 20).
48:19 *the offspring of thy bowels*. Descendants of the womb.
48:20 *Go ye forth of Babylon*. See note at 52:11.
48:21 *clave*. Split. See Ex. 17:6.
48:22 *no peace . . . unto the wicked*. Though sinners may feel safe and content at times, they are out of harmony with God and His world, and their sin constantly disrupts their lives (57:21).

Thoughts for Personal/Family Worship: Chapter 48

1. **The great motive and highest aim of all God's actions is to make people know and praise His glory (vv. 9–11). He does not seek this out of any need, for He is all-sufficient in Himself. However, it is right for Him to glorify Himself, it is His delight, and it is the most loving gift He can give to His people.**
2. **Afflictions should bring us nearer to the Lord, for they are His furnace to refine believers like precious metal (v. 10). We should not fear the fire, for He will be with us (43:2). His purpose is to make us pure and holy, so that our peace may be like a river and God's children may multiply and fill the earth (vv. 18–19). When we face the furnace of affliction we do not walk alone, any more than Daniel's three friends were alone in the fire (Dan. 3:1–30). How can viewing suffering as refining help believers to endure it?**

Chapter 49: *The Lord's Servant will be a light and comfort to the people.*

The Lord's Servant and the Salvation of Israel and the Gentiles (49:1–26)

49:1 *isles*. The distant shores, the extremities of the world. The promise of the Servant of the Lord concerns the whole world, not just Israel (v. 6). *hearken*. Listen. *womb . . . bowels*. Different words but both referring to the womb. God had predestined Him to this purpose before He was born (Ps. 22:9–10; Jer. 1:5; Gal. 1:15; 1 Peter 1:19).
49:2 *mouth like a sharp sword*. His words are powerful to judge sin (Eph. 6:17; Heb. 4:12; Rev. 1:16; 2:12,16; 19:15). *polished shaft*. A sharpened arrow (Ps. 45:5; Rev. 6:2).
49:3 *my servant, O Israel*. Christ is the ideal and fulfillment of all God desires in His covenant people for His glory. The Servant here cannot be the people themselves because He restores the people (v. 6).
49:4 *laboured in vain*. Toiled in futility. *nought*. Nothing. *in vain*. A breath, referring to that which is without substance. The Servant expresses the apparent frustration and futility of His mission (53:1–3; John 1:11). *my judgment is with the LORD*. He entrusted Himself to God's justice to make all things right (1 Peter 2:23). *work*. Reward.
49:5 *Though Israel be not gathered, yet shall I be glorious.*

6 And he said, It is a light thing that thou should-
est be my servant to raise up the tribes of Jacob,
and to restore the preserved of Israel: I will also
give thee for a light to the Gentiles, that thou
mayest be my salvation unto the end of the earth.
7 Thus saith the LORD, the Redeemer of Israel,
and his Holy One, to him whom man despiseth,
to him whom the nation abhorreth, to a servant of
rulers, Kings shall see and arise, princes also shall
worship, because of the LORD that is faithful, *and*
the Holy One of Israel, and he shall choose thee.
8 Thus saith the LORD, In an acceptable time
have I heard thee, and in a day of salvation have
I helped thee: and I will preserve thee, and give
thee for a covenant of the people, to establish the
earth, to cause to inherit the desolate heritages;
9 That thou mayest say to the prisoners, Go forth;
to them that *are* in darkness, Shew yourselves.
They shall feed in the ways, and their pastures
shall be in all high places.
10 They shall not hunger nor thirst; neither
shall the heat nor sun smite them: for he that
hath mercy on them shall lead them, even by the
springs of water shall he guide them.
11 And I will make all my mountains a way, and
my highways shall be exalted.
12 Behold, these shall come from far: and, lo,
these from the north and from the west; and these
from the land of Sinim.
13 ¶ Sing, O heavens; and be joyful, O earth; and
break forth into singing, O mountains: for the
LORD hath comforted his people, and will have
mercy upon his afflicted.
14 But Zion said, The LORD hath forsaken me,
and my Lord hath forgotten me.
15 Can a woman forget her sucking child, that
she should not have compassion on the son of her
womb? yea, they may forget, yet will I not forget
thee.
16 Behold, I have graven thee upon the palms of
my hands; thy walls *are* continually before me.
17 Thy children shall make haste; thy destroyers
and they that made thee waste shall go forth of thee.
18 ¶ Lift up thine eyes round about, and behold:
all these gather themselves together, *and* come to
thee. *As* I live, saith the LORD, thou shalt surely
clothe thee with them all, as with an ornament,
and bind them *on thee*, as a bride *doeth*.
19 For thy waste and thy desolate places, and the
land of thy destruction, shall even now be too
narrow by reason of the inhabitants, and they that
swallowed thee up shall be far away.
20 The children which thou shalt have, after thou
hast lost the other, shall say again in thine ears,
The place *is* too strait for me: give place to me that
I may dwell.
21 Then shalt thou say in thine heart, Who hath
begotten me these, seeing I have lost my children,
and am desolate, a captive, and removing to and
fro? and who hath brought up these? Behold, I
was left alone; these, where *had* they *been*?
22 Thus saith the Lord GOD, Behold, I will lift
up mine hand to the Gentiles, and set up my
standard to the people: and they shall bring thy
sons in *their* arms, and thy daughters shall be
carried upon *their* shoulders.
23 And kings shall be thy nursing fathers, and
their queens thy nursing mothers: they shall bow
down to thee with *their* face toward the earth, and
lick up the dust of thy feet; and thou shalt know
that I *am* the LORD: for they shall not be ashamed
that wait for me.
24 ¶ Shall the prey be taken from the mighty, or
the lawful captive delivered?
25 But thus saith the LORD, Even the captives of
the mighty shall be taken away, and the prey of
the terrible shall be delivered: for I will contend
with him that contendeth with thee, and I will
save thy children.
26 And I will feed them that oppress thee with

Alternative translation, "and that Israel may be gathered to Him, and I may be glorious."

49:6 *light*. Trivial or trifling. *preserved of Israel*. Those being protected or watched over, referring to the remnant. *light to the Gentiles*. The Lord had far greater plans for Christ than the saving of one nation, for He aimed to save all the nations (see note at 42:6; Acts 13:47).

49:7 *Redeemer*. See note at 35:9 (v. 26).

49:8 *acceptable time*. A time of delight or favor. *day of salvation*. The coming of Christ has made this the time of gospel opportunity (2 Cor. 5:20—6:2).

49:9–10 *prisoners, Go forth*. Christ came to set men free (61:1; John 8:31–36). *feed . . . lead*. Christ will care for them like a shepherd (40:11; Ps. 23; Rev. 7:16–17). *mercy*. Compassion or pity.

49:12 *from far*. From all parts of the world. *Sinim*. Unknown location. The gospel has universal success in gathering Christ's sheep to Himself.

49:13 *have mercy*. Show compassion or pity.

49:14 *hath forgotten*. Refuses to think about, intentionally ignores (v. 15).

49:15 *forget her sucking child*. The Lord's love for His people surpasses the closest and most tender of human bonds.

49:16 *graven*. Inscribed or carved. God's people are permanently held in the power and knowledge of His love, like a precious signet ring on the hand (cf. Song 8:6). This text is sometimes taken to refer to the wounds of Christ (Ps. 22:16; John 20:25,27).

49:19–20 *strait*. Constricted. *give place*. Make room for. She has so many children that they need more space (54:1–3).

49:22 *standard*. Banner or ensign.

49:23 *nursing fathers*. Nourishing fathers; those acting as foster-fathers, using a different word for *nursing* than that used of *mothers* (v. 7; 60:16; 1 Tim. 2:1–2).

49:24 *prey*. Plunder or spoil of war (v. 25). *taken from the mighty*. Christ has conquered the strong man and is plundering his house (Matt. 12:29).

49:26 *feed them . . . with their own flesh*. Perhaps an image of

their own flesh; and they shall be drunken with
their own blood, as with sweet wine: and all flesh
shall know that I the LORD *am* thy Saviour and thy
Redeemer, the mighty One of Jacob.

CHAPTER 50

THUS saith the LORD, Where *is* the bill of your
mother's divorcement, whom I have put away?
or which of my creditors *is it* to whom I have
sold you? Behold, for your iniquities have ye sold
yourselves, and for your transgressions is your
mother put away.
2 Wherefore, when I came, *was there* no man?
when I called, *was there* none to answer? Is my
hand shortened at all, that it cannot redeem? or
have I no power to deliver? behold, at my rebuke
I dry up the sea, I make the rivers a wilderness:
their fish stinketh, because *there is* no water, and
dieth for thirst.
3 I clothe the heavens with blackness, and I make
sackcloth their covering.
4 The Lord GOD hath given me the tongue of
the learned, that I should know how to speak a
word in season to *him that is* weary: he wakeneth
morning by morning, he wakeneth mine ear to
hear as the learned.
5 ¶ The Lord GOD hath opened mine ear, and I
was not rebellious, neither turned away back.
6 I gave my back to the smiters, and my cheeks to
them that plucked off the hair: I hid not my face
from shame and spitting.
7 ¶ For the Lord GOD will help me; therefore
shall I not be confounded: therefore have I set
my face like a flint, and I know that I shall not be
ashamed.
8 *He is* near that justifieth me; who will contend
with me? let us stand together: who *is* mine
adversary? let him come near to me.
9 Behold, the Lord GOD will help me; who *is* he
that shall condemn me? lo, they all shall wax old
as a garment; the moth shall eat them up.
10 ¶ Who *is* among you that feareth the LORD,
that obeyeth the voice of his servant, that walketh
in darkness, and hath no light? let him trust in the
name of the LORD, and stay upon his God.
11 Behold, all ye that kindle a fire, that compass
yourselves about with sparks: walk in the light of

---

desperate hunger (9:20; 65:13), or repaying them according to their killing of others (Rev. 16:6).

Thoughts for Personal/Family Worship: Chapter 49

Christ was fully qualified and powerfully gifted to do His Father's will, but His glory was hidden and His ministry strangely wrapped in weakness, frustration, and rejection. Nevertheless, God not only saved His elect among the Jewish nation through Him but also redeemed people from all over the world. Under Christ as their shepherd, the international church experiences deliverance from its former imprisonment and is beginning to enjoy the satisfaction of His kingdom. If believers ever question Christ's love for them, they should remember that He is more closely united to them than a mother is to her nursing child. Just as surely as His wounds pierced His hands for their sins, so they themselves are engraved upon His loving heart forever. Therefore, let us never despair, even if our lives are strangely wrapped in suffering and rejection. Let each Christian learn to say, "Christ loved me and died for me, and nothing can separate me from His love" (cf. Rom. 8:35,39; Gal. 2:20).

Chapter 50: *Israel's sins are in stark contrast to the obedience of the Servant.*

The Submissive Servant and the Unbelievers (50:1–11)

50:1 *Where is the bill of . . . divorcement?* The covenant relationship between the Lord and Judah was as a marriage, but the nation deserved to be cut off for its sins. *creditors . . . to whom I have sold you.* Under the law, if a man was in debt and had no means to pay, he could sell his children into indentured service (Ex. 21:7). However, the Lord is no man's debtor; He did not sell His people to Babylon based on any need but because of their sins.

50:2 *Is my hand shortened . . . cannot redeem?* Is my power unable to reach out to provide a ransom? *dry up the sea.* God's salvation is a second exodus (Ex. 14).

50:3 *blackness . . . sackcloth.* Signs of mourning.

50:4–9 The Servant of the Lord speaks (see note at 42:1–4).

50:4 *tongue of the learned.* The ability to speak as one taught by God. The Servant is the ideal Prophet, the Mediator of God's truth (Deut. 18:18; Acts 3:22–23). *word . . . weary.* The words of Christ are the means by which God strengthens those who wait on Him (40:29). *wakeneth morning by morning.* The Spirit constantly instructs Christ's human mind in wisdom (11:2).

50:5 *opened mine ear.* A figure of speech for the humble and loving submission of the divine Servant to His divine Master (Ex. 21:5–6; Ps. 40:6–8; see note at 42:1). *not rebellious.* Completely obedient to the One who sent Him, in contrast to Israel (63:10; cf. 1:2,23; 30:1,9).

50:6 *I gave my back . . . my cheeks . . . hid not my face.* The Servant willingly offered Himself to receive suffering without resistance (53:7; Matt. 26:67; 27:26,30; John 18:22).

50:7 *set my face like a flint.* An image expressing adamant resolve to fulfill His mission to speak the Word and to suffer (Ezek. 3:8–9; Luke 9:51).

50:8 *justifieth me.* Vindicates me as righteous. What applies to the Messiah also applies to His people in union with Him (54:17; Rom. 8:31–34).

50:9 *the Lord GOD will help me.* See note at 42:6. *wax old.* Wear out.

50:10 *feareth the LORD . . . obeyeth the voice of his servant.* True piety requires submission to the words of Christ. *walketh in darkness.* Believers will experience suffering, frustration, and tests of faith as God's judgments come upon the world (v. 3), like the Servant whom they follow (v. 6; 49:4). *trust in the name.* Place confidence in who God has revealed Himself to be as one's hope and security. *stay upon his God.* Lean on the promises of the covenant for support.

50:11 *all ye that kindle a fire.* Everyone who follows the *light* of human wisdom instead of the Word of God. *compass.* Surround.

Thoughts for Personal/Family Worship: Chapter 50

1. Christ is the Mediator of God's truth and a model of

your fire, and in the sparks *that* ye have kindled.
This shall ye have of mine hand; ye shall lie down
in sorrow.

CHAPTER 51

HEARKEN to me, ye that follow after righteous-
ness, ye that seek the LORD: look unto the rock
whence ye are hewn, and to the hole of the pit
whence ye are digged.
2 Look unto Abraham your father, and unto
Sarah *that* bare you: for I called him alone, and
blessed him, and increased him.
3 For the LORD shall comfort Zion: he will
comfort all her waste places; and he will make her
wilderness like Eden, and her desert like the gar-
den of the LORD; joy and gladness shall be found
therein, thanksgiving, and the voice of melody.
4 ¶ Hearken unto me, my people; and give ear
unto me, O my nation: for a law shall proceed
from me, and I will make my judgment to rest for
a light of the people.
5 My righteousness *is* near; my salvation is gone
forth, and mine arms shall judge the people; the
isles shall wait upon me, and on mine arm shall
they trust.
6 Lift up your eyes to the heavens, and look upon
the earth beneath: for the heavens shall vanish
away like smoke, and the earth shall wax old like
a garment, and they that dwell therein shall die
in like manner: but my salvation shall be for ever,
and my righteousness shall not be abolished.
7 ¶ Hearken unto me, ye that know righteous-
ness, the people in whose heart *is* my law; fear ye
not the reproach of men, neither be ye afraid of
their revilings.
8 For the moth shall eat them up like a garment,
and the worm shall eat them like wool: but my
righteousness shall be for ever, and my salvation
from generation to generation.
9 ¶ Awake, awake, put on strength, O arm of the
LORD; awake, as in the ancient days, in the genera-
tions of old. *Art* thou not it that hath cut Rahab,
and wounded the dragon?
10 *Art* thou not it which hath dried the sea, the
waters of the great deep; that hath made the
depths of the sea a way for the ransomed to pass
over?
11 Therefore the redeemed of the LORD shall
return, and come with singing unto Zion; and
everlasting joy *shall be* upon their head: they
shall obtain gladness and joy; *and* sorrow and
mourning shall flee away.
12 I, *even* I, *am* he that comforteth you: who *art*
thou, that thou shouldest be afraid of a man *that*
shall die, and of the son of man *which* shall be
made *as* grass;
13 And forgettest the LORD thy maker, that
hath stretched forth the heavens, and laid
the foundations of the earth; and hast feared
continually every day because of the fury of the
oppressor, as if he were ready to destroy? and
where *is* the fury of the oppressor?
14 The captive exile hasteneth that he may be

---

patient suffering and persistent witness. He willingly gave His human body to the torments of His enemies, and yet did so with an unflinching determination to declare the Word of God and an unwavering hope that His Father would vindicate Him in the end. How does Christ's suffering assure us that His message is true? How does He set an example for believers?

2. **The closing verses teach important lessons about faith. The object of faith determines its value. Saving faith puts all its trust (confidence) in Christ, leaning on Him for support and safety. Trusting in Christ never fails. So many spend their efforts trying to kindle their own light that would give the appearance of safety and calm. But all those who trust their own efforts are doomed, regardless of the sincerity or fervency with which they have worked up their own religion. Make sure that you are trusting the only sure Savior. To walk in the true light is salvation and fellowship with God. To walk in one's own light leads to eternal darkness.**

The Good News of Salvation (51:1—52:12)

Chapter 51: *The Lord comforts and helps those who are faithful in seeking Him and following after righteousness.*

51:1 *Hearken*. Listen. *look*. Consider or look with confidence (, v. 2). *rock*. A huge, immovable boulder. *whence ye are hewn*. From which you are cut.

51:2 *Look unto Abraham*. Remember the covenant, at the heart of which was the gospel of the promised seed, the Christ (Gen. 15; cf. Gen. 3:15).

51:3 *comfort Zion*. See note at 40:1 (vv. 12,19). *like Eden . . . garden of the LORD*. The Lord will reverse the curse from the fall of man and restore His people to paradise (Gen. 2; Rev. 22:1–5).

51:4 *law*. The general word for special revelation; instruction, not just legislation (v. 7).

51:5 *righteousness . . . salvation*. See note at 45:8 (v. 6). *isles*. Distant shores, the extremities of the earth. God's redemptive purpose is worldwide, not just for the nation of Israel. *wait*. Hope with confident expectation. *on mine arm*. In My saving power (v. 9; 33:2; 40:10–11; 52:10; 53:1; 59:16; 62:8; 63:5,12).

51:6 *vanish*. Be dissipated (2 Peter 3:7,10–12). *wax old like a garment*. Wear out like clothing (Ps. 102:25–27).

51:7 *revilings*. Insults.

51:8 *worm*. The Hebrew word occurs only here. The meaning is uncertain but may refer to a grub.

51:9 *Rahab*. Some sort of sea creature meaning "surger" or "storm" that symbolizes Egypt in her pride (Pss. 87:4; 89:10). *dragon*. Serpent or sea creature.

51:10 *dried the sea*. An allusion to the exodus (43:16; 50:2; Ex. 14:1–31). God's deliverance from the future enemy is often described in terms of a second or new exodus (v. 15).

51:11 Repeated from 35:10.

51:13 *forgettest*. Intentionally refuses to think about, ignores.

51:14 *pit*. Prison or dungeon.

51:16 *shadow of mine hand*. God's powerful protection.

loosed, and that he should not die in the pit, nor
that his bread should fail.
15 But I *am* the LORD thy God, that divided the
sea, whose waves roared: The LORD of hosts *is* his
name.
16 And I have put my words in thy mouth, and
I have covered thee in the shadow of mine hand,
that I may plant the heavens, and lay the founda-
tions of the earth, and say unto Zion, Thou *art*
my people.
17 ¶ Awake, awake, stand up, O Jerusalem, which
hast drunk at the hand of the LORD the cup of his
fury; thou hast drunken the dregs of the cup of
trembling, *and* wrung *them* out.
18 *There is* none to guide her among all the sons
whom she hath brought forth; neither *is there any*
that taketh her by the hand of all the sons *that* she
hath brought up.
19 These two *things* are come unto thee; who shall
be sorry for thee? desolation, and destruction,
and the famine, and the sword: by whom shall I
comfort thee?
20 Thy sons have fainted, they lie at the head of all
the streets, as a wild bull in a net: they are full of
the fury of the LORD, the rebuke of thy God.
21 ¶ Therefore hear now this, thou afflicted, and
drunken, but not with wine:
22 Thus saith thy Lord the LORD, and thy God
that pleadeth the cause of his people, Behold, I
have taken out of thine hand the cup of trembling,
even the dregs of the cup of my fury; thou shalt no
more drink it again:
23 But I will put it into the hand of them that
afflict thee; which have said to thy soul, Bow
down, that we may go over: and thou hast laid thy
body as the ground, and as the street, to them that
went over.

CHAPTER 52

AWAKE, awake; put on thy strength, O Zion; put
on thy beautiful garments, O Jerusalem, the holy
city: for henceforth there shall no more come into
thee the uncircumcised and the unclean.
2 Shake thyself from the dust; arise, *and* sit down,
O Jerusalem: loose thyself from the bands of thy
neck, O captive daughter of Zion.
3 For thus saith the LORD, Ye have sold yourselves
for nought; and ye shall be redeemed without
money.
4 For thus saith the Lord GOD, My people went
down aforetime into Egypt to sojourn there; and
the Assyrian oppressed them without cause.
5 Now therefore, what have I here, saith the
LORD, that my people is taken away for nought?
they that rule over them make them to howl, saith
the LORD; and my name continually every day *is*
blasphemed.
6 Therefore my people shall know my name:
therefore *they shall know* in that day that I *am* he
that doth speak: behold, *it is* I.
7 ¶ How beautiful upon the mountains are
the feet of him that bringeth good tidings, that
publisheth peace; that bringeth good tidings of
good, that publisheth salvation; that saith unto
Zion, Thy God reigneth!
8 Thy watchmen shall lift up the voice; with the
voice together shall they sing: for they shall see eye
to eye, when the LORD shall bring again Zion.
9 ¶ Break forth into joy, sing together, ye waste
places of Jerusalem: for the LORD hath comforted
his people, he hath redeemed Jerusalem.
10 The LORD hath made bare his holy arm in
the eyes of all the nations; and all the ends of the
earth shall see the salvation of our God.
11 ¶ Depart ye, depart ye, go ye out from thence,

51:17 *cup.* An image of punishment or judgment (Ps. 75:8; Mark 14:36; Rev. 14:10; 16:19). *wrung them out.* Slurp or drain out (Ps. 73:10).
51:20 *wild bull.* Or some sort of antelope.

Thoughts for Personal/Family Worship: Chapter 51

1. **It ought to be a great source of encouragement to every believer that the Lord says, "On mine arm shall they trust" (v. 5). There is no mightier arm than the Lord's. His strength can never fail or diminish. When we lean upon Him we shall never fall; hence Jude writes, "Now unto him that is able to keep you from falling" (Jude 24). What a folly it is, then, when we seek to walk in our own strength or depend upon those in the world rather than leaning wholly upon the Lord. Remember that He commands us to depend and lean upon Him.**
2. **It is surely a sad affair when Christians suffer and yet fail to go to the One who has said, "I am he that comforteth you" (v. 12). Why suffer and mourn alone? Why seek the help of those who cannot alleviate your sorrows, when there is One who bids you come and be comforted? Remember this: "He that spared not his own Son, but delivered him up for us all, how shall he not with him also freely give us all things?" (Rom. 8:32). Does this not bring comfort to your soul?**

Chapter 52: *The Lord exhorts Zion that they might be encouraged.*
52:2 *bands.* Chains.
52:3 *for nought.* Without compensation (v. 5).
52:4 *aforetime.* At the first or before. *sojourn.* Live as a resident alien.
53:5 *howl.* Or lament. *my name . . . is blasphemed.* The sins and sufferings of Israel dishonored their covenant God in the eyes of the nations (Rom. 2:24; cf. 2 Peter 2:2).
52:7 *How beautiful . . . the feet.* An expression of delight in the messengers who bring good news (*tidings*; Nah. 1:15), ultimately referring to gospel preachers (Rom. 10:15). *publisheth peace.* Proclaims reconciliation and harmony with God and His people (Acts 10:36; Eph. 2:17). *Thy God reigneth.* The gospel announces the coming of God's kingdom in the person of the King (9:6–7; Matt. 4:24; 9:35; 24:14).
52:9 *redeemed.* See note at 35:9.
52:10 *made bare his holy arm.* Revealed His power to glorify Himself by saving sinners (53:1; Ps. 98:1–2).
52:11 *Depart ye . . . be ye clean.* The hope of God's coming

touch no unclean *thing*; go ye out of the midst of
her; be ye clean, that bear the vessels of the LORD.
12 For ye shall not go out with haste, nor go by
flight: for the LORD will go before you; and the
God of Israel *will be* your rereward.
13 ¶ Behold, my servant shall deal prudently, he
shall be exalted and extolled, and be very high.
14 As many were astonied at thee; his visage was
so marred more than any man, and his form
more than the sons of men:
15 So shall he sprinkle many nations; the kings
shall shut their mouths at him: for *that* which had
not been told them shall they see; and *that* which
they had not heard shall they consider.

CHAPTER 53

WHO hath believed our report? and to whom is
the arm of the LORD revealed?
2 For he shall grow up before him as a tender
plant, and as a root out of a dry ground: he hath
no form nor comeliness; and when we shall see
him, *there is* no beauty that we should desire him.
3 He is despised and rejected of men; a man of
sorrows, and acquainted with grief: and we hid as
it were *our* faces from him; he was despised, and
we esteemed him not.
4 ¶ Surely he hath borne our griefs, and carried
our sorrows: yet we did esteem him stricken,
smitten of God, and afflicted.
5 But he *was* wounded for our transgressions, *he*
was bruised for our iniquities: the chastisement
of our peace *was* upon him; and with his stripes
we are healed.
6 All we like sheep have gone astray; we have
turned every one to his own way; and the LORD
hath laid on him the iniquity of us all.
7 He was oppressed, and he was afflicted, yet he

---

kingdom of holiness (v. 1) motivates believers to purify themselves and separate from the sins of the world that God will destroy (2 Cor. 6:17; cf. 2 Peter 3:11–13; 1 John 3:2–3; Rev. 18:4).

52:12 *haste.* Tepidation. *rereward.* Rear guard. Literally, "the One gathering you," referring to the stragglers.

The Suffering Servant and the Substitute for Sinners (52:13—53:12)

52:13–15 The end of this chapter introduces Isaiah's great exposition of the humiliation and exaltation of the Suffering Servant (53:1–12). It consists of five units of three verses each.

52:13 *my servant.* See note at 42:1. *prudently.* Wisely or successfully. *exalted and extolled.* High and lifted up, the same words used of the holy Lord (6:1; 57:15). *very high.* The threefold expression of exaltation implies supremacy over all (Ps. 110:1; Phil. 2:9–11).

52:14 *astonied.* Astonished, being either appalled or startled. *visage.* Appearance. *marred.* Disfigured. The Servant's exaltation was preceded by deep humiliation and horrible suffering.

52:15 *So . . . many.* Parallel to "As many" (v. 14): the Servant will minister to many *nations* on the basis of His suffering. *sprinkle.* Cleanse the unclean as a priest applying the death of a sacrifice (53:10–12; Lev. 4:6; 14:7; 16:14–15,30; Num. 19:4, 18–21; 1 Peter 1:2). *shut their mouths.* In awe and perhaps defeat (Ps. 107:42). *not been told them . . . had not heard.* The good news of Christ's work must be preached to all the world (Rom. 15:20–21). The preaching of the gospel is the means by which Christ saves sinners (v. 7; Rom. 10:13–15).

Thoughts for Personal/Family Worship: Chapter 52

1. **The gospel announces that God rescues sinners from the slavery and oppression into which the guilt of their sins has plunged them and brings them into peace with Himself. Just as the Lord promised to save Israel from its exile in Babylon, so He promises today to save believers in Christ out of this present wicked world. The preachers of this gospel are precious gifts from God. How are you supporting and encouraging them in their labors?**
2. **Though Christ humbled Himself as God's servant, His very sufferings won Him the ability to cleanse unclean sinners from every nation. God the Father has exalted Him to the highest place, declaring that Jesus is our Lord and God. The kingdom of God is invading this dark world with the good news that our God reigns! Has Christ washed you with His blood? Are you trusting in Him and confessing Him as Lord?**

Chapter 53: *The Suffering Servant was despised and rejected by the people but owned and loved by God for offering Himself as a sacrifice for sinners.*

53:1–3 The Servant came in a hidden way, not recognized or respected by most people.

53:1 *Who hath believed our report?* Few respond to the gospel with faith (John 12:38; Rom. 10:16). *arm of the LORD.* God's saving power that came in Christ (see note at Isa. 51:5). *revealed.* Sinners are blind to God's salvation in Christ unless the Spirit reveals it to them (see notes at 35:5–6; 42:7; cf. 1 Cor. 1:18—2:16).

53:2 *tender plant.* A suckling, a worthless twig. *form nor comeliness.* Visible royalty or majesty. Christ looked like an ordinary, common man. *beauty.* Appearance, translated "visage" (52:14). His sufferings made him unattractive.

53:3 *despised.* Regarded as having no value, irrelevant, unworthy of attention. *acquainted with grief.* Experienced physical troubles such as weakness, fatigue, or wounds (v. 4). *hid . . . faces.* A gesture of displeasure or disgust.

53:4–6 The Servant suffered as the substitute for sinners to bring them peace.

53:4 *borne . . . carried.* The many sorrows of the Servant actually belonged to His people, but He took them as His burden (Matt. 8:16–17). *esteem him . . . smitten of God.* People assumed that His sufferings were God's punishment for His sins.

53:5 *wounded . . . bruised.* Pierced and crushed, a violent death. *for our transgressions . . . for our iniquities.* God punished Him for the guilt of His people (vv. 6,8). *chastisement of our peace.* His suffering reconciled God's enemies to God, replacing God's anger with a relationship of harmony (12:1; 54:9–10; 57:17–19; Rom. 5:1,10). *with his stripes we are healed.* His wounds heal the miseries brought about by man's fall, beginning by healing the inner corruption of sin (1 Peter 2:24).

53:6 *All we like sheep have gone astray.* We all rebel against the Lord, our Shepherd-King (40:11; 49:9–10; 1 Peter 2:25). *iniquity.* Or guilt. God counted against or imputed to His Servant the guilt of sinners and laid the punishment for their sins upon Him (Gal. 3:10,13). *us all.* The "we" in this context consists of sinners (*all we*) who once thought little of the

opened not his mouth: he is brought as a lamb to
the slaughter, and as a sheep before her shearers is
dumb, so he openeth not his mouth.
8 He was taken from prison and from judgment:
and who shall declare his generation? for he
was cut off out of the land of the living: for the
transgression of my people was he stricken.
9 And he made his grave with the wicked, and
with the rich in his death; because he had done
no violence, neither *was any* deceit in his mouth.
10 ¶ Yet it pleased the LORD to bruise him; he
hath put *him* to grief: when thou shalt make his
soul an offering for sin, he shall see *his* seed, he
shall prolong *his* days, and the pleasure of the
LORD shall prosper in his hand.
11 He shall see of the travail of his soul, *and* shall
be satisfied: by his knowledge shall my righteous
servant justify many; for he shall bear their
iniquities.
12 Therefore will I divide him *a portion* with the
great, and he shall divide the spoil with the strong;
because he hath poured out his soul unto death:
and he was numbered with the transgressors; and
he bare the sin of many, and made intercession for
the transgressors.

CHAPTER 54

SING, O barren, thou *that* didst not bear; break
forth into singing, and cry aloud, thou *that* didst
not travail with child: for more *are* the children of
the desolate than the children of the married wife,
saith the LORD.
2 Enlarge the place of thy tent, and let them

Servant (vv. 2–3) but were redeemed and healed by His death (vv. 4–6) and now confess the gospel to others (v. 1). Christ suffered "for the transgression of my people" (v. 8), the spiritual Israel (vv. 10–11).

53:7–9 The Servant suffered meekly under unjust oppression (vv. 7–8, Acts 8:32–35).

53:7 *afflicted.* He allowed himself to be humbled; the verb form may indicate His voluntary submission. *opened not his mouth.* Quietly and meekly accepted His death (42:2; 50:6). *brought as a lamb.* The verb can be used of bringing an offering to God (Ps. 76:11; Zeph. 3:10). Christ is the Lamb of God, offered to God to atone for sin (John 1:29; Rev. 5:6–10).

53:8 *from prison and from judgment.* By force and judicial action. *who shall declare.* None concerned themselves; nobody cared. *his generation . . . he was cut off.* He died without children, sometimes a sign of God's curse on sinners (Ps. 37:22,28).

53:9 *grave with the wicked . . . the rich.* A remarkably precise prophecy of His burial; literally, "his grave was assigned to be with wicked people but [he was] with a rich man in his death" (cf. Matt. 27:57–60). *because.* Or although. *no violence . . . deceit.* Though killed like a law-breaker, Christ was innocent of all sin and falsehood (v. 1; 1 Peter 2:22).

53:10–12 The Servant fulfilled God's plan and received God's blessing for His people.

53:10 *pleased the LORD . . . pleasure of the LORD.* Surprisingly, the unjust murder of the Servant fulfilled God's sovereign plan to His delight (Luke 22:22; Acts 2:23; 4:28). *bruise.* Crush (v. 5). *when thou shalt make.* Or, "if He makes." *offering for sin.* A "trespass offering" or sacrifice to God to compensate for dishonoring His holiness (Lev. 5:1–19). *see his seed.* Though dying without physical offspring (v. 8), He would have the joy of spiritual offspring, a family born of His sufferings, fulfilling the ancient covenant with Abraham and his seed (41:8; 45:25; 54:1–5). *prolong his days.* This is God's blessing on the one who keeps His law (Deut. 4:40; 5:16; 17:20). Long life after his death and burial (vv. 8–9) implies His resurrection (Rev. 1:17–18). Before Christ came, the Father promised to raise Him from the dead and give Him a spiritual family, if He would die for them (2 Tim. 1:9; Titus 1:2).

53:11 *of the travail of his soul.* Because of His suffering. *by his knowledge.* By knowing Him (through faith), or by His knowledge of God (righteous relationship). *righteous . . . justify.* The same Hebrew root, implying that His obedience (*servant*), which makes Him right with God, is counted to *many* sinners so that they too are right with God (Rom. 5:19), just as their guilt (*iniquities*) was counted or imputed to Him (vv. 5–6; 2 Cor. 5:21). The glory God will receive from this blessing of justification on the spiritual Israel (45:24–25) will make the Servant completely *satisfied* that His sufferings were worthwhile (Heb. 12:2).

53:12 *divide him a portion . . . the spoil.* Like a conquering warrior returning with the plunder of victory, the Servant will share the riches of His glory with many people (v. 11). *because . . . death.* All the blessings of the Messiah depend upon His voluntary death for sinners. *numbered with the transgressors.* Counted as a criminal (Luke 22:37). *bare the sin . . . made intercession.* Carried the guilt and prays for God's blessing on sinners. The verb forms imply that His atoning death is past but that His intercession continues (Heb. 7:25). Like His offering of Himself as a lamb for sins, His intercession implies His office as priest.

Thoughts for Personal/Family Worship: Chapter 53

This chapter presents one of the most wonderful declarations of the gospel in all the Bible. It should affect us deeply and eternally. We should be amazed that the holy, pure, and loving Lord was despised and rejected by men. How blind we are to the things that really matter! We should tremble that the horrors of Christ's cross reflect God's hatred of our sins, and that Christ willingly carried them at His Father's command. Truly this is a love beyond all human comprehension. We should rejoice that Christ's perfect obedience is counted to believers as their righteousness before God and that they are welcomed into His spiritual family to enjoy the riches of His glory forever. Most importantly, we should trust in Christ alone to save us from our sins and misery. If He has done all this in order to save sinners, will we dare to ignore Him? Far be it from us to insult Him in such a way. Let us instead rest our entire hope and confidence in Christ, the righteous Servant of the Lord. How does this chapter help you to trust Him more now than ever before?

Chapter 54: ***The Lord comforts Zion with promises of expansion, deliverance, and preservation.***

The Reconciled Wife and Her Children (54:1–17)

54:1 *barren.* Israel is pictured as being like Sarah, an allusion to the covenant with Abraham (Gen. 11:30; 15:5; 22:17–18). *travail.* Labor in childbirth. The universal church is like a mother to God's children, and God promised that despite her sins she would have many offspring by supernatural grace (49:18–21; Gal. 4:26–29).

54:2 *Enlarge . . . thy tent.* An image of needing a bigger home

stretch forth the curtains of thine habitations: spare not, lengthen thy cords, and strengthen thy stakes;
3 For thou shalt break forth on the right hand and on the left; and thy seed shall inherit the Gentiles, and make the desolate cities to be inhabited.
4 Fear not; for thou shalt not be ashamed: neither be thou confounded; for thou shalt not be put to shame: for thou shalt forget the shame of thy youth, and shalt not remember the reproach of thy widowhood any more.
5 For thy Maker *is* thine husband; the LORD of hosts *is* his name; and thy Redeemer the Holy One of Israel; The God of the whole earth shall he be called.
6 For the LORD hath called thee as a woman forsaken and grieved in spirit, and a wife of youth, when thou wast refused, saith thy God.
7 For a small moment have I forsaken thee; but with great mercies will I gather thee.
8 In a little wrath I hid my face from thee for a moment; but with everlasting kindness will I have mercy on thee, saith the LORD thy Redeemer.
9 For this *is as* the waters of Noah unto me: for *as* I have sworn that the waters of Noah should no more go over the earth; so have I sworn that I would not be wroth with thee, nor rebuke thee.
10 For the mountains shall depart, and the hills be removed; but my kindness shall not depart from thee, neither shall the covenant of my peace be removed, saith the LORD that hath mercy on thee.
11 ¶ O thou afflicted, tossed with tempest, *and* not comforted, behold, I will lay thy stones with fair colours, and lay thy foundations with sapphires.
12 And I will make thy windows of agates, and thy gates of carbuncles, and all thy borders of pleasant stones.
13 And all thy children *shall be* taught of the LORD; and great *shall be* the peace of thy children.
14 In righteousness shalt thou be established: thou shalt be far from oppression; for thou shalt not fear: and from terror; for it shall not come near thee.
15 Behold, they shall surely gather together, *but* not by me: whosoever shall gather together against thee shall fall for thy sake.
16 Behold, I have created the smith that bloweth the coals in the fire, and that bringeth forth an instrument for his work; and I have created the waster to destroy.
17 ¶ No weapon that is formed against thee shall prosper; and every tongue *that* shall rise against thee in judgment thou shalt condemn. This *is* the heritage of the servants of the LORD, and their righteousness *is* of me, saith the LORD.

CHAPTER 55

HO, every one that thirsteth, come ye to the waters, and he that hath no money; come ye, buy, and eat; yea, come, buy wine and milk without money and without price.

because of multiplied children.
54:3 *thy seed.* Your offspring.
54:4 *forget.* Refuse to think about. *remember.* Intentionally set one's mind and heart upon.
54:5 *For . . . thine husband.* The reason they will be fruitful and multiply is their spiritual union with the Lord (see note at 62:4–5). *Redeemer.* See note at 35:9 (v. 8).
54:6 *wast refused.* Were rejected.
54:7 *small moment.* A brief period. *mercies.* Demonstrations of compassion and pity (vv. 8,10).
54:8 *hid my face.* A gesture expressing displeasure. *kindness.* Covenant loyalty and love.
54:9 *sworn . . . Noah.* God made an unconditional promise in His covenant with Noah to never again flood the whole earth for man's sins (Gen. 9:8–11). *wroth.* Angry.
54:10 *kindness.* Covenant loyalty and love. *covenant of my peace.* Also called the "everlasting covenant" (55:3; 61:8) made in Christ (42:6; 49:8) through the reconciliation of His death (*peace*, 53:5).
54:11–12 *I will lay thy stones with fair colours.* Literally, "I am setting precious stones with hard mortar." *agates.* Crystals. *carbuncles.* Some sort of sparkling jewels. *pleasant.* Precious. The Lord promises to make His people glorious and invincible (Rev. 21:19).
54:13 *all thy children.* All the elect in the true church (8:18; 43:5–6; 59:21). *taught of the LORD.* Inwardly drawn to trust in Christ and transformed to obey God's Word (Jer. 31:34; John 6:44–45).
54:17 *No weapon . . . every tongue.* All things work together for the good of God's elect, and there is no condemnation for those in Christ Jesus (Rom. 8:1,28,34). *their righteousness is of me.* They are justified and vindicated by the grace of Christ (53:11).

Thoughts for Personal/Family Worship: Chapter 54

1. **Israel's sins and covenant-breaking could not stop the purpose of God's covenant love to multiply a people for Himself. He would fill the world with the children born of His spiritual union with the church, and they would inherit righteousness and glory. How does this chapter look back to the finished work of Christ described in chapter 53? How does it look forward to a glorious hope?**
2. **Believers are in a blessed state, for they are the bride of Christ (v. 5) and the heirs of beauty and riches (vv. 11–12). Their future is secure beyond the reach of any enemy or accuser (v. 17) because God's covenant of grace is unconditional and everlasting (vv. 9–10). God Himself will teach the hearts of His elect to believe and obey (v. 13). How should these promises motivate the church to sing (v. 1)?**

Chapter 55: ***The Lord bids all who are thirsty to come to Him for salvation, which He offers freely.***
The Call of the Gospel (55:1–13)
55:1 *every one that thirsteth.* The command to come is as universal as human need (Matt. 11:28; Rev. 21:6; 22:17). *no*

2 Wherefore do ye spend money for *that which*
is not bread? and your labour for *that which*
satisfieth not? hearken diligently unto me, and eat
ye *that which is* good, and let your soul delight
itself in fatness.
3 Incline your ear, and come unto me: hear, and
your soul shall live; and I will make an everlasting
covenant with you, *even* the sure mercies of David.
4 Behold, I have given him *for* a witness to the
people, a leader and commander to the people.
5 Behold, thou shalt call a nation *that* thou know-
est not, and nations *that* knew not thee shall run
unto thee because of the LORD thy God, and for
the Holy One of Israel; for he hath glorified thee.
6 ¶ Seek ye the LORD while he may be found, call
ye upon him while he is near:
7 Let the wicked forsake his way, and the unrigh-
teous man his thoughts: and let him return unto
the LORD, and he will have mercy upon him; and
to our God, for he will abundantly pardon.
8 ¶ For my thoughts *are* not your thoughts,
neither *are* your ways my ways, saith the LORD.
9 For *as* the heavens are higher than the earth,
so are my ways higher than your ways, and my
thoughts than your thoughts.
10 For as the rain cometh down, and the snow
from heaven, and returneth not thither, but
watereth the earth, and maketh it bring forth and
bud, that it may give seed to the sower, and bread
to the eater:
11 So shall my word be that goeth forth out of
my mouth: it shall not return unto me void, but it
shall accomplish that which I please, and it shall
prosper *in the thing* whereto I sent it.
12 For ye shall go out with joy, and be led forth
with peace: the mountains and the hills shall
break forth before you into singing, and all the
trees of the field shall clap *their* hands.
13 Instead of the thorn shall come up the fir tree,
and instead of the brier shall come up the myrtle
tree: and it shall be to the LORD for a name, for an
everlasting sign *that* shall not be cut off.

CHAPTER 56

THUS saith the LORD, Keep ye judgment, and do
justice: for my salvation *is* near to come, and my
righteousness to be revealed.
2 Blessed *is* the man *that* doeth this, and the son
of man *that* layeth hold on it; that keepeth the
sabbath from polluting it, and keepeth his hand
from doing any evil.
3 ¶ Neither let the son of the stranger, that hath
joined himself to the LORD, speak, saying, The

---

money . . . without price. Salvation is free for sinners, obtained without worthiness or merit because Christ has already paid the price (53:1–12).

55:2 *hearken diligently.* Listen intently with faith, the means of eating this spiritual feast (John 6:35). *fatness.* Abundance.

55:3 *your soul.* You, *soul* referring to the person. *sure mercies of David.* The enduring or firm covenant loyalties and love given to David and his offspring (2 Sam. 7:12–16) and fulfilled in Christ (Acts 13:34). *everlasting covenant.* The eternal promises made to Abraham (Ps. 105:8–10) and David (2 Sam. 23:5) come to fruition in Christ (42:6; 49:8; 54:10); all believers are included in the new covenant (Jer. 32:40; Ezek. 16:60; 37:26; Heb. 13:20).

55:4 *I have given him.* God sent Christ (v. 3) for His people (9:6) to fulfill the offices of a prophet, in order to reveal God's unique glory (*witness*; 43:10–12), and as a king, to bring God's kingdom (*leader and commander*). *people . . . people.* Both are plural in the Hebrew: Christ came for the nations (42:6).

55:5 *call a nation that thou knowest not.* Having received universal authority, Christ calls not just Israel but also foreign nations to serve Him (Ps. 18:43; Matt. 28:18–19).

55:6 *while he may be found.* Hebrew, "when He permits Himself to be found," implying that He will not always allow Himself to be found. Hence there is urgency in the call (Prov. 1:24–28).

55:7 *have mercy.* Show compassion or pity through appropriate action to alleviate the problem. Here the appropriate action is the abundant *pardon.*

55:8–9 *my thoughts are not your thoughts.* The point is not that God is beyond comprehension (40:13–14,28) but that sinners must turn from their sinful *thoughts* and *ways* to God's holy *thoughts* and *ways* in order to be saved.

55:10–11 *void.* Without success. Just as the rains and snows accomplish their purpose, so will God's Word succeed in accomplishing its purpose by the Spirit's power (34:16).

55:13 *tree . . . tree.* God will restore man to the Paradise of the garden of Eden (51:3), reversing the curse (*thorn . . . brier*; Gen. 3:17–18) for His *everlasting* glory (*name*).

Thoughts for Personal/Family Worship: Chapter 55

This whole chapter is full of encouragement to come to the Lord. Man cannot earn God's grace but must turn back to the Lord in humble faith and repentance in order to receive life and forgiveness without cost. At the heart of the gospel is the Son of David, who has paid the price for salvation and now serves as the great Prophet and King, calling the nations to Himself. He promises nothing less to believers than a return to paradise. His very words are powerful to give life, though we are barren and fruitless. Why not come to Him now? If you are not yet a Christian, what holds you back? How does this chapter answer that with its call?

PREPARATION FOR SALVATION AND RIGHTEOUSNESS (56:1—66:24)

Chapter 56: ***The Lord promises blessing for the holy and exposes the greed of the watchmen.***

Promises to Faithful Outsiders and Rebukes to Blind Leaders (56:1–12)

56:1 *judgment . . . justice.* Justice and righteousness, key elements of Christ's kingdom (9:7). *salvation . . . righteousness.* God's intervention into the fallen world to rescue His people for His glory, ultimately looking to Christ's second coming (see note at 45:8).

56:2 *Blessed.* Possessing great benefits from God. *keepeth the sabbath from polluting it.* Treats the Sabbath as a holy day of rest and worship, not an ordinary day (Ex. 20:8–11; v. 6).

56:3 *stranger.* Foreigner. *joined himself to the LORD.* A proselyte, one converted to true religion (v. 6). *eunuch.* A government

LORD hath utterly separated me from his people:
neither let the eunuch say, Behold, I *am* a dry tree.
4 For thus saith the LORD unto the eunuchs that
keep my sabbaths, and choose *the things* that
please me, and take hold of my covenant;
5 Even unto them will I give in mine house and
within my walls a place and a name better than
of sons and of daughters: I will give them an
everlasting name, that shall not be cut off.
6 Also the sons of the stranger, that join themselves
to the LORD, to serve him, and to love the name of
the LORD, to be his servants, every one that keepeth
the sabbath from polluting it, and taketh hold of
my covenant;
7 Even them will I bring to my holy mountain,
and make them joyful in my house of prayer:
their burnt offerings and their sacrifices *shall be*
accepted upon mine altar; for mine house shall be
called an house of prayer for all people.
8 The Lord GOD which gathereth the outcasts of
Israel saith, Yet will I gather *others* to him, beside
those that are gathered unto him.
9 ¶ All ye beasts of the field, come to devour, *yea*,
all ye beasts in the forest.
10 His watchmen *are* blind: they are all ignorant,
they *are* all dumb dogs, they cannot bark; sleeping,
lying down, loving to slumber.
11 Yea, *they are* greedy dogs *which* can never
have enough, and they *are* shepherds *that* cannot
understand: they all look to their own way, every
one for his gain, from his quarter.
12 Come ye, *say they*, I will fetch wine, and we will
fill ourselves with strong drink; and to morrow
shall be as this day, *and* much more abundant.

CHAPTER 57

THE righteous perisheth, and no man layeth *it*
to heart: and merciful men *are* taken away, none
considering that the righteous is taken away from
the evil *to come*.
2 He shall enter into peace: they shall rest in their
beds, *each one* walking *in* his uprightness.
3 ¶ But draw near hither, ye sons of the sorceress,
the seed of the adulterer and the whore.
4 Against whom do ye sport yourselves? against
whom make ye a wide mouth, *and* draw out the
tongue? *are* ye not children of transgression, a
seed of falsehood,
5 Enflaming yourselves with idols under every
green tree, slaying the children in the valleys
under the clifts of the rocks?
6 Among the smooth *stones* of the stream *is* thy
portion; they, they *are* thy lot: even to them hast
thou poured a drink offering, thou hast offered a
meat offering. Should I receive comfort in these?
7 Upon a lofty and high mountain hast thou set
thy bed: even thither wentest thou up to offer
sacrifice.
8 Behind the doors also and the posts hast thou
set up thy remembrance: for thou hast discovered
thyself to another than me, and art gone up; thou
hast enlarged thy bed, and made thee *a covenant*
with them; thou lovedst their bed where thou
sawest *it*.
9 And thou wentest to the king with ointment,
and didst increase thy perfumes, and didst send
thy messengers far off, and didst debase *thyself*
even unto hell.
10 Thou art wearied in the greatness of thy way;

official, sometimes but not always a castrated male who cannot have offspring (*dry tree*).
56:6 *name of the LORD.* Who God has revealed Himself to be in the totality of His perfections.
56:7 *holy mountain.* Zion, a symbol of God's kingdom (11:9; 25:6–8). *house of prayer for all people.* God's temple is a place for repentant sinners to find God's grace by prayer (1 Kings 8:27–53; this includes people of all nations (Isa. 2:1–3; Matt. 21:13; Mark 11:17; Luke 19:46).
56:8 *gather others.* See Hos. 2:23; John 10:16; Rom. 9:24–25; Eph. 2:11–13.
56:10 *watchmen.* Religious leaders and prophets.
56:11 *greedy dogs.* Fierce of soul or appetite. *shepherds.* Rulers, usually civil authorities. *quarter.* Territory or border.

Thoughts for Personal/Family Worship: Chapter 56

Leaders, both religious and civil, have significant responsibility and are liable for their failures. Isaiah indicts those who are blind, dumb, and sleeping. They are not watching for signs of danger. Sadly, there are many in the ministry today who are like this, and they must bear a large measure of responsibility for the weakness and ineffectiveness of much of the professing church today. We need to pray that the Lord would deal with those in leadership, that either He would awaken them and give them a holy zeal for the gospel or remove them from office. If the Lord has blessed you with a faithful pastor, pray for him continually.

Exhortations to Sinners in Jacob (57:1—59:21)

Chapter 57: ***The Lord issues a strong rebuke to Judah because of their continuing idolatry.***

57:1 *no man layeth it to heart.* No one cares or takes it to heart. *merciful men.* Men of covenant loyalty and love. *evil.* Calamity.
57:2 Death (v. 1) brings the godly into *peace*, releasing their spirits from this evil world as their bodies wait for the resurrection (*rest in their beds*; 26:19).
57:3 *draw near hither.* Come close to this place.
57:4 *sport yourselves.* Amuse yourselves or make fun at another's expense. *draw out the tongue.* A gesture of derision (Pss. 22:7; 35:21; Lam. 2:16).
57:5 *Enflaming.* Burning with lust. *under every green tree.* Public places associated with pagan rituals, including fornication. *slaying the children.* Sacrificing their offspring to idols (Jer. 32:35; Ezek. 20:26–31).
57:6 *meat offering.* Grain offering.
57:8 *remembrance.* Pagan symbols. *discovered.* Uncovered or exposed. *where thou sawest it.* Literally, "a hand you saw," a euphemism for the male organ. Descriptions of the depth of their depravity, in imitation of the pagans.
57:9 *debase . . . hell.* Hebrew, *sheol*, here used figuratively to

yet saidst thou not, There is no hope: thou hast
found the life of thine hand; therefore thou wast
not grieved.
11 And of whom hast thou been afraid or feared,
that thou hast lied, and hast not remembered me,
nor laid *it* to thy heart? have not I held my peace
even of old, and thou fearest me not?
12 I will declare thy righteousness, and thy works;
for they shall not profit thee.
13 ¶ When thou criest, let thy companies deliver
thee; but the wind shall carry them all away;
vanity shall take *them*: but he that putteth his
trust in me shall possess the land, and shall inherit
my holy mountain;
14 And shall say, Cast ye up, cast ye up, prepare
the way, take up the stumblingblock out of the
way of my people.
15 For thus saith the high and lofty One that
inhabiteth eternity, whose name *is* Holy; I dwell
in the high and holy *place*, with him also *that is* of
a contrite and humble spirit, to revive the spirit of
the humble, and to revive the heart of the contrite
ones.
16 For I will not contend for ever, neither will I be
always wroth: for the spirit should fail before me,
and the souls *which* I have made.
17 For the iniquity of his covetousness was I
wroth, and smote him: I hid me, and was wroth,
and he went on frowardly in the way of his heart.
18 I have seen his ways, and will heal him: I will
lead him also, and restore comforts unto him and
to his mourners.
19 I create the fruit of the lips; Peace, peace to *him*
that is far off, and to *him that is* near, saith the
LORD; and I will heal him.
20 But the wicked *are* like the troubled sea, when
it cannot rest, whose waters cast up mire and dirt.
21 *There is* no peace, saith my God, to the wicked.

CHAPTER 58

CRY aloud, spare not, lift up thy voice like a
trumpet, and shew my people their transgression,
and the house of Jacob their sins.
2 Yet they seek me daily, and delight to know
my ways, as a nation that did righteousness, and
forsook not the ordinance of their God: they ask
of me the ordinances of justice; they take delight
in approaching to God.
3 ¶ Wherefore have we fasted, *say they*, and thou
seest not? *wherefore* have we afflicted our soul,
and thou takest no knowledge? Behold, in the day
of your fast ye find pleasure, and exact all your
labours.
4 Behold, ye fast for strife and debate, and to smite
with the fist of wickedness: ye shall not fast as *ye do*
this day, to make your voice to be heard on high.
5 Is it such a fast that I have chosen? a day for
a man to afflict his soul? *is it* to bow down his
head as a bulrush, and to spread sackcloth and
ashes *under him*? wilt thou call this a fast, and an
acceptable day to the LORD?
6 *Is* not this the fast that I have chosen? to loose
the bands of wickedness, to undo the heavy

underscore the depths to which they have sunk in their sinful ways.

57:11 *not remembered.* Refused to think about the Lord. *held my peace.* Have been silent.

57:13 *companies.* Idols. *vanity.* A breath, that which is unsubstantial.

57:15 *high and lofty . . . Holy.* The supreme King (6:1). *inhabiteth eternity.* Though God is fully present in every moment of time, His infinite being transcends time and cannot be limited by it (Ps. 90:1–4). *contrite.* Crushed over a sense of their sins (Isa. 66:2). *revive.* Cause to live.

57:16 *contend.* Enter into legal proceedings. *wroth.* Angry (v. 17).

57:17 *I hid.* A gesture of displeasure. *frowardly.* Turning back, backsliding.

57:19 *I create.* The worship of the redeemed is the result of God's sovereign grace producing a new creation (43:7; 45:8; 65:17–18). *fruit of the lips.* Praise (Hos. 14:2; Heb. 13:15). *Peace, peace.* Total or completed peace; Hebrew uses repetition to express superlatives. *far . . . near.* The message of reconciliation with God goes to every nation on earth (Eph. 2:17).

57:20 *troubled.* Churning or tossed. *mire and dirt.* Grime and muck.

57:21 *no peace . . . to the wicked.* See 48:22.

Thoughts for Personal/Family Worship: Chapter 57

This is a chapter of great contrast between the depths of man's sin and the greatness of God's grace. Were it not for God's grace, sinners would have no hope. The statement in v. 18 highlights the wonder of grace as God says, "I have seen his ways, and will heal him." What God sees is sin and depravity, nothing worthy of His love and goodness. But in spite of what He sees, He is willing to save and make peace. That is what makes grace what it is: God's favor that He gives to those who are so undeserving of it. It is not by works of righteousness that any are saved but only because of His grace. How does God's grace motivate believers to praise Him?

Chapter 58: ***The prophet contrasts true and false fasting and directs to the proper keeping of the sabbath.***

58:1 *Cry aloud.* Literally, "call with the throat," meaning to shout at the top of one's voice.

58:2 *they seek me.* They had a formal outward religion that they zealously practiced.

58:3 *Wherefore.* Why. This exposes their mercantile motive; when they *fasted*, they sought to manipulate God to their advantage (Luke 18:11–12). *afflicted our soul.* An expression for a fast, as in the Day of Atonement, the only divinely ordered fast (Lev. 16:29). *exact all your labours.* Oppress your workers.

58:4 *strife and debate, and to smite.* Their religion was marred by pride and fighting.

58:5 *bulrush.* Reed; even plants can bow down, so outward acts of worship are insufficient.

58:6–7 *bands.* Chains. True fasting, and true religion in general, must move people to treat others with justice and compassion; this applies particularly to the vulnerable in

burdens, and to let the oppressed go free, and that
ye break every yoke?
7 *Is it* not to deal thy bread to the hungry, and
that thou bring the poor that are cast out to thy
house? when thou seest the naked, that thou cover
him; and that thou hide not thyself from thine
own flesh?
8 ¶ Then shall thy light break forth as the
morning, and thine health shall spring forth
speedily: and thy righteousness shall go before
thee; the glory of the LORD shall be thy rereward.
9 Then shalt thou call, and the LORD shall
answer; thou shalt cry, and he shall say, Here I *am*.
If thou take away from the midst of thee the yoke,
the putting forth of the finger, and speaking
vanity;
10 And *if* thou draw out thy soul to the hungry,
and satisfy the afflicted soul; then shall thy light
rise in obscurity, and thy darkness *be* as the
noonday:
11 And the LORD shall guide thee continually,
and satisfy thy soul in drought, and make fat thy
bones: and thou shalt be like a watered garden,
and like a spring of water, whose waters fail not.
12 And *they that shall be* of thee shall build the old
waste places: thou shalt raise up the foundations
of many generations; and thou shalt be called,
The repairer of the breach, The restorer of paths
to dwell in.
13 ¶ If thou turn away thy foot from the sabbath,
from doing thy pleasure on my holy day; and
call the sabbath a delight, the holy of the LORD,
honourable; and shalt honour him, not doing
thine own ways, nor finding thine own pleasure,
nor speaking *thine own* words:
14 Then shalt thou delight thyself in the LORD;
and I will cause thee to ride upon the high places
of the earth, and feed thee with the heritage of
Jacob thy father: for the mouth of the LORD hath
spoken *it*.

CHAPTER 59

BEHOLD, the LORD's hand is not shortened, that it
cannot save; neither his ear heavy, that it cannot
hear:
2 But your iniquities have separated between you
and your God, and your sins have hid *his* face
from you, that he will not hear.
3 For your hands are defiled with blood, and your
fingers with iniquity; your lips have spoken lies,
your tongue hath muttered perverseness.
4 None calleth for justice, nor *any* pleadeth for
truth: they trust in vanity, and speak lies; they
conceive mischief, and bring forth iniquity.
5 They hatch cockatrice' eggs, and weave the
spider's web: he that eateth of their eggs dieth, and
that which is crushed breaketh out into a viper.
6 Their webs shall not become garments, neither
shall they cover themselves with their works:
their works *are* works of iniquity, and the act of
violence *is* in their hands.
7 Their feet run to evil, and they make haste to
shed innocent blood: their thoughts *are* thoughts

---

society (1:11–17,23; 10:2; Matt. 5:7; 25:34–40; James 1:27). Love for one's neighbor is an index of one's love for God.

58:8 *light break forth . . . glory of the LORD*. They will experience the kingdom of Christ if they seek first His *righteousness* (9:2; 60:1–3). *rereward.* Rear guard to protect them.

58:9 *yoke*. Of oppression. *putting forth of the finger*. Pointing the finger in an act of contempt. *vanity*. Wickedness.

58:10 *obscurity*. Darkness.

58:11 *make fat thy bones*. Give prosperity and health.

58:13–14 The proper keeping of the Sabbath is a safeguard to true worship.

58:13 *turn away thy foot*. An idiom for guarding and controlling oneself because of (*from*) the special day (Ps. 119:59,101; Eccl. 5:1). *sabbath*. A day of rest from ordinary work in order to devote oneself to holy things (Gen. 2:1–3; Ex. 20:8–11; Lev. 23:3). *my holy day*. The sabbath is the Lord's day (Rev. 1:10), a time when He especially calls us to *honour him* in public and private worship. *call the sabbath a delight*. Keep or observe it out of love for the Lord.

58:14 Keeping the Sabbath is not a legalistic observance of rules but a means of grace for the enjoyment of God's presence (*delight thyself in the LORD*), His loving care and provision (*ride upon the high places of the earth*; Deut. 32:12–13), and our inheritance promised in the covenant (*feed thee with the heritage of Jacob*).

Thoughts for Personal/Family Worship: Chapter 58

It may seem strange that the Lord should rebuke His people for seeking daily to know His ways and delight in Him (v. 2). However, this seeking was not being done from right motives but in proud hypocrisy. They were not taking care of the poor, who lacked food and clothing. They were oppressing those in servitude (Ex. 21:2; Deut. 15:12). We learn here that outward devotion without a true change of heart is worthless in the sight of the Lord. Let us ensure that our worship is real and born out of a heart of gratitude to God for His grace and mercy to us. To that end, learn how keeping the Sabbath is a safeguard to spiritual worship. If we observe the Sabbath as the day of rest and spiritual delight that God has designed for our good, our worship will be spiritual and not perfunctory show. What does it mean to call the Sabbath a delight?

Chapter 59: ***The prophet describes the heinous nature of sin and points to the only Savior of sinners.***

59:1 *shortened*. Diminished in power. *ear heavy*. Dull of hearing.

59:2 *your iniquities have separated . . . your God*. The guilt of sin breaks the bond of God's friendship with men, stirs His anger, and makes their prayers futile (*he will not hear*).

59:4 *trust in vanity*. Put confidence for safety in that which is unreal or nothing. *mischief*. Trouble.

59:5–6 *cockatrice*. Viper or adder. *weave the spider's web . . . garments*. Vivid images to describe the futility of their works.

59:7–8 *feet run to evil*. They are eager to sin and do harm. *wasting*. Violence or destruction. *way of peace*. Lifestyle of harmony with others. *no judgment in their goings*. No justice

of iniquity; wasting and destruction *are* in their
paths.
8 The way of peace they know not; and *there is* no
judgment in their goings: they have made them
crooked paths: whosoever goeth therein shall not
know peace.
9 ¶ Therefore is judgment far from us, neither doth
justice overtake us: we wait for light, but behold
obscurity; for brightness, *but* we walk in darkness.
10 We grope for the wall like the blind, and we
grope as if *we had* no eyes: we stumble at noon-
day as in the night; *we are* in desolate places as
dead *men*.
11 We roar all like bears, and mourn sore like
doves: we look for judgment, but *there is* none;
for salvation, *but* it is far off from us.
12 For our transgressions are multiplied before
thee, and our sins testify against us: for our trans-
gressions *are* with us; and *as for* our iniquities, we
know them;
13 In transgressing and lying against the LORD,
and departing away from our God, speaking
oppression and revolt, conceiving and uttering
from the heart words of falsehood.
14 And judgment is turned away backward, and
justice standeth afar off: for truth is fallen in the
street, and equity cannot enter.
15 Yea, truth faileth; and he *that* departeth from
evil maketh himself a prey: and the LORD saw *it*,
and it displeased him that *there was* no judgment.
16 ¶ And he saw that *there was* no man, and
wondered that *there was* no intercessor: therefore
his arm brought salvation unto him; and his
righteousness, it sustained him.
17 For he put on righteousness as a breastplate,
and an helmet of salvation upon his head; and he
put on the garments of vengeance *for* clothing,
and was clad with zeal as a cloke.
18 According to *their* deeds, accordingly he will
repay, fury to his adversaries, recompence to his
enemies; to the islands he will repay recompence.
19 So shall they fear the name of the LORD from the
west, and his glory from the rising of the sun. When
the enemy shall come in like a flood, the Spirit of
the LORD shall lift up a standard against him.
20 ¶ And the Redeemer shall come to Zion, and
unto them that turn from transgression in Jacob,
saith the LORD.
21 As for me, this *is* my covenant with them, saith
the LORD; My spirit that *is* upon thee, and my
words which I have put in thy mouth, shall not
depart out of thy mouth, nor out of the mouth of
thy seed, nor out of the mouth of thy seed's seed,
saith the LORD, from henceforth and for ever.

CHAPTER 60

ARISE, shine; for thy light is come, and the glory
of the LORD is risen upon thee.
2 For, behold, the darkness shall cover the earth,
and gross darkness the people: but the LORD shall
arise upon thee, and his glory shall be seen upon
thee.
3 And the Gentiles shall come to thy light, and

---

or treating others rightly in their conduct. Sin has poisoned every aspect of fallen mankind's existence (Rom. 3:15–17).

59:9–15 *us . . . we.* The prophet identifies himself with the people, acknowledging their spiritual blindness and deadness.

59:9 *judgment . . . justice.* Justice and righteousness (v. 14). *obscurity.* Darkness.

59:11 *mourn sore.* Coo or moan greatly. *judgment.* Justice (also v. 15).

59:15 *prey.* Spoil or plunder.

59:16 *no man . . . no intercessor.* Only the Lord can save, for no other being in all creation is sufficient for the task (43:11; 45:21–22; Rev. 5:1–5). *wondered.* Was appalled.

59:17 *breastplate . . . helmet.* God comes clothed in armor as a warrior, but His armor consists of His own glory in action (*righteousness . . . salvation . . . vengeance . . . zeal*), and He comes in the person of Christ (v. 20; 11:4–5). Believers also can conquer in God's armor because of their union with Christ (61:10; Rom. 13:12–14; Eph. 6:11,14–17; 1 Thess. 5:8).

59:18 *According to their deeds.* God's justice repays people according to what they have done, a terrifying prospect of *fury* for sinners. *islands.* The distant shores, the ends of the world.

59:19 *name.* God's *glory*, who He reveals Himself to be in all His attributes. *west . . . rising of the sun* [east]. Pairs of opposites designate totality: all the world. *lift up a standard.* Literally, the Spirit of the Lord "will drive him onward or away."

59:20 *Redeemer.* See note at 35:9. Here specifically Christ (Rom. 11:26–27).

59:21 In God's everlasting *covenant* in Christ (42:6; 49:8; 54:10; 55:3), God promises that the Holy Spirit (*My spirit*) will perpetually preserve a remnant, spiritual Israel (*thy seed*; Jer. 31:31–34; 32:40), that holds to the gospel of Christ (*my words . . . in thy mouth*; 50:4; 51:16).

Thoughts for Personal/Family Worship: Chapter 59

Sin separates us from God because He can have nothing to do with iniquity. Do not think that God will bless you if you continue unrepentant in sin. Sadly, mankind is conquered by sin. No one seeks justice and truth, but the entire race is quick to sin, meditating on iniquity, and in constant strife with God and each other. No one in the entire human race is qualified to save himself or another person from sin. The Lord saw this, and He took on the full responsibility to come and work salvation and judgment as the divine warrior. Christ, the Son of God, is the only Redeemer of God's elect. If you are trusting in yourself or in another person to save you from evil and bring you happiness, you are like one leaning on a spider's web to keep you out of hell. How does this chapter call us to trust in Christ alone for salvation?

The Coming of the Lord to Zion with Glory (60:1—62:12)

Chapter 60: *The Lord promises great blessings and glory for His people.*

60:1 *shine.* Become light or be enlightened. God's *glory* comes shining in Christ to save and transform His people (9:2; 35:2; 40:5; 42:6–7; Mal. 4:2; Luke 1:78–79; John 8:12; 12:36; 2 Cor. 4:6; Eph. 5:8; Rev. 21:11).

kings to the brightness of thy rising.
4 Lift up thine eyes round about, and see: all they
gather themselves together, they come to thee: thy
sons shall come from far, and thy daughters shall
be nursed at *thy* side.
5 Then thou shalt see, and flow together, and
thine heart shall fear, and be enlarged; because
the abundance of the sea shall be converted unto
thee, the forces of the Gentiles shall come unto
thee.
6 The multitude of camels shall cover thee,
the dromedaries of Midian and Ephah; all they
from Sheba shall come: they shall bring gold and
incense; and they shall shew forth the praises of
the LORD.
7 All the flocks of Kedar shall be gathered together
unto thee, the rams of Nebaioth shall minister
unto thee: they shall come up with acceptance on
mine altar, and I will glorify the house of my glory.
8 Who *are* these *that* fly as a cloud, and as the
doves to their windows?
9 Surely the isles shall wait for me, and the ships
of Tarshish first, to bring thy sons from far, their
silver and their gold with them, unto the name of
the LORD thy God, and to the Holy One of Israel,
because he hath glorified thee.
10 And the sons of strangers shall build up thy
walls, and their kings shall minister unto thee: for
in my wrath I smote thee, but in my favour have I
had mercy on thee.
11 Therefore thy gates shall be open continually;
they shall not be shut day nor night; that *men* may
bring unto thee the forces of the Gentiles, and
that their kings *may be* brought.
12 For the nation and kingdom that will not serve
thee shall perish; yea, *those* nations shall be utterly
wasted.
13 The glory of Lebanon shall come unto thee,
the fir tree, the pine tree, and the box together,
to beautify the place of my sanctuary; and I will
make the place of my feet glorious.
14 The sons also of them that afflicted thee
shall come bending unto thee; and all they that
despised thee shall bow themselves down at the
soles of thy feet; and they shall call thee, The city
of the LORD, The Zion of the Holy One of Israel.
15 Whereas thou hast been forsaken and hated, so
that no man went through *thee*, I will make thee
an eternal excellency, a joy of many generations.
16 Thou shalt also suck the milk of the Gentiles,
and shalt suck the breast of kings: and thou shalt
know that I the LORD *am* thy Saviour and thy
Redeemer, the mighty One of Jacob.
17 For brass I will bring gold, and for iron I will
bring silver, and for wood brass, and for stones
iron: I will also make thy officers peace, and thine
exactors righteousness.
18 Violence shall no more be heard in thy land,
wasting nor destruction within thy borders; but
thou shalt call thy walls Salvation, and thy gates
Praise.
19 The sun shall be no more thy light by day;
neither for brightness shall the moon give light
unto thee: but the LORD shall be unto thee an
everlasting light, and thy God thy glory.
20 Thy sun shall no more go down; neither shall
thy moon withdraw itself: for the LORD shall
be thine everlasting light, and the days of thy
mourning shall be ended.
21 Thy people also *shall be* all righteous: they
shall inherit the land for ever, the branch of my
planting, the work of my hands, that I may be
glorified.
22 A little one shall become a thousand, and a

60:3 *Gentiles shall come.* God's redemptive purpose for the world (see note at 49:6).
60:5 *flow together.* Or shine or be radiant. *fear.* Be filled with awe and excitement. *abundance of the sea.* The noise or wealth of the sea, referring to the nations. *converted.* Turned over to. *forces of the Gentiles.* The wealth or riches of the nations (v. 11; Rev. 21:24,26).
60:6 *gold and incense.* See Matt. 2:11.
60:7 *minister.* Serve (v. 10).
60:9 *the isles shall wait.* The ends of the earth will hope with confident expectancy. *name.* The Lord Himself in all His perfections.
60:10 *strangers.* Foreigners. *had mercy.* Showed compassion or pity.
60:11 *gates . . . open continually.* An image of complete safety because all danger is gone (Rev. 21:25).
60:13 *box.* Type of tree.
60:15 *excellency.* Pride or loftiness.
60:16 *suck the milk . . . breast of kings.* The nations will give their wealth (Deut. 33:19) and loving care to God's people (49:23). *Redeemer.* See note at 35:9.
60:17 *brass.* Bronze. *officers.* Overseers. *exactors.* Rulers or taskmasters.
60:19 *sun shall be no more thy light.* So great is the brilliance of the Lord in the midst of His people (v. 1) that there is no need for the light of the sun in the heavenly Jerusalem (Rev. 21:23; 22:5).
60:20 *days of thy mourning shall be ended.* There will be no more sadness, death, or pain (Rev. 21:4).
60:21 *branch.* Shoot or sprig. *my planting.* Created by God's grace (Matt. 15:13).

Thoughts for Personal/Family Worship: Chapter 60

What glorious prospects there are for every child of God! How wonderful that day will be when we truly walk in the full Light of the Lord, where no shadow of sin can fall upon us and where no darkness of any kind can hinder us. On that great day all sorrowing and mourning shall cease. How this thought ought to lift us up out of any present sorrows and fill us with the hope of that which is to come. Such thoughts of future bliss should therefore encourage us now to be faithful to the Lord and not hiding the light He has given us under a bushel (Matt. 5:15). Whatever light we have let us by God's grace display for all to see. How has the light of God's glory already come to the church? How does it draw the nations to the Lord?

small one a strong nation: I the LORD will hasten
it in his time.

CHAPTER 61

THE Spirit of the Lord GOD *is* upon me; because
the LORD hath anointed me to preach good tidings
unto the meek; he hath sent me to bind up the bro-
kenhearted, to proclaim liberty to the captives, and
the opening of the prison to *them that are* bound;
2 To proclaim the acceptable year of the LORD,
and the day of vengeance of our God; to comfort
all that mourn;
3 To appoint unto them that mourn in Zion, to
give unto them beauty for ashes, the oil of joy for
mourning, the garment of praise for the spirit
of heaviness; that they might be called trees of
righteousness, the planting of the LORD, that he
might be glorified.
4 ¶ And they shall build the old wastes, they shall
raise up the former desolations, and they shall
repair the waste cities, the desolations of many
generations.
5 And strangers shall stand and feed your flocks,
and the sons of the alien *shall be* your plowmen
and your vinedressers.
6 But ye shall be named the Priests of the LORD:
men shall call you the Ministers of our God: ye
shall eat the riches of the Gentiles, and in their
glory shall ye boast yourselves.
7 ¶ For your shame *ye shall have* double; and
for confusion they shall rejoice in their portion:
therefore in their land they shall possess the
double: everlasting joy shall be unto them.
8 For I the LORD love judgment, I hate robbery for
burnt offering; and I will direct their work in truth,
and I will make an everlasting covenant with them.
9 And their seed shall be known among the
Gentiles, and their offspring among the people:
all that see them shall acknowledge them, that
they *are* the seed *which* the LORD hath blessed.
10 I will greatly rejoice in the LORD, my soul shall
be joyful in my God; for he hath clothed me with
the garments of salvation, he hath covered me
with the robe of righteousness, as a bridegroom
decketh *himself* with ornaments, and as a bride
adorneth *herself* with her jewels.
11 For as the earth bringeth forth her bud, and
as the garden causeth the things that are sown
in it to spring forth; so the Lord GOD will cause
righteousness and praise to spring forth before all
the nations.

CHAPTER 62

FOR Zion's sake will I not hold my peace, and
for Jerusalem's sake I will not rest, until the
righteousness thereof go forth as brightness, and
the salvation thereof as a lamp *that* burneth.
2 And the Gentiles shall see thy righteousness,

Chapter 61: *The prophet details the work of the Messiah and the blessedness of His kingdom.*

61:1–3 Although not a servant song, this text clearly presents the Messiah, as Christ affirmed (Luke 4:18–19; 7:22). It highlights His office as the prophet of salvation and judgment (*preach . . . proclaim*). Its language is reflected in the Beatitudes (Matt. 5:3–5).

61:1 *Spirit . . . is upon me.* God anointed (the verbal form of the word "messiah") Him in that He empowered Him for the special work that God *sent* Him to do (48:16; 1 Sam. 16:13; John 3:34; Acts 4:27; 10:38). *meek.* The afflicted. *liberty . . . opening of the prison.* The messianic freedom from sin and its misery (42:7; 49:9).

61:2 *acceptable year . . . day of vengeance.* The time of grace and of judgment (63:4). When Christ said that this prophecy was fulfilled, He stopped at the *acceptable year* (Luke 4:19–21) because while Isaiah's prophecy links the two advents of Christ, now is still the time of grace when sinners can be saved (see note at 49:8).

61:3 *ashes.* Sign of grief (58:5). Note the reversals accomplished by the gospel. *trees of righteousness, the planting of the LORD.* God's new creation of people who are strong, stable, and fruitful in doing what is right (v. 11; 60:21).

61:4 *old wastes.* Ruins. *desolations.* Uninhabited, deserted places. *waste cities.* Cities of devastation.

61:5 *strangers . . . alien.* Two Hebrew words, both referring to foreigners.

61:6 *Priests of the LORD.* There would no longer be a priestly class in the line of Aaron, but all of the Lord's people would be priests (1 Peter 2:5,9; Rev. 1:6; 5:9–10). *Ministers of our God.* Those who serve the Lord.

61:7 *For your shame . . . double.* Instead of disgrace, a double blessing or portion.

61:8 *judgment.* Justice. *everlasting covenant.* See note at 55:3.

61:9 *seed.* Descendants.

61:10 *my soul.* I; *soul* refers to the person or self. *clothed me with . . . salvation . . . covered me with . . . righteousness.* Whereas earlier the Lord had clothed Himself in these qualities in order to work salvation by Himself (59:16–17), now He clothes His people with His own glory so that they may enjoy His salvation—a picture of union with Christ and justification by imputed righteousness (53:11). *decketh himself with ornaments.* Dresses to serve as a priest.

Thoughts for Personal/Family Worship: Chapter 61

In considering the wonder of salvation, Isaiah breaks forth with rejoicing (v. 10), and we should as well. Christ's blood has cleansed us and clothed us in the garments of salvation. We have been covered with the robe of righteousness, which is Christ Himself. So when God the Father looks upon us, wretched, unworthy sinners as we are, He remembers our sins no more and instead sees the absolute perfection of Christ covering us. Beloved in Christ, how blessed we are! Believers ought to praise God with joyful adoration. We should draw near to the Lord with boldness, for Christians are priests in Christ. How can you use this chapter as fuel for heartfelt praise?

Chapter 62: *The Lord declares to His people that their salvation is drawing near.*

62:1 *hold my peace.* Be silent. *not rest.* Not be inactive. *lamp*

and all kings thy glory: and thou shalt be called by
a new name, which the mouth of the LORD shall
name.
3 Thou shalt also be a crown of glory in the hand
of the LORD, and a royal diadem in the hand of
thy God.
4 Thou shalt no more be termed Forsaken;
neither shall thy land any more be termed
Desolate: but thou shalt be called Hephzi-bah,
and thy land Beulah: for the LORD delighteth in
thee, and thy land shall be married.
5 ¶ For *as* a young man marrieth a virgin, *so*
shall thy sons marry thee: and *as* the bridegroom
rejoiceth over the bride, *so* shall thy God rejoice
over thee.
6 I have set watchmen upon thy walls, O
Jerusalem, *which* shall never hold their peace day
nor night: ye that make mention of the LORD,
keep not silence,
7 And give him no rest, till he establish, and till he
make Jerusalem a praise in the earth.
8 The LORD hath sworn by his right hand, and
by the arm of his strength, Surely I will no more
give thy corn *to be* meat for thine enemies; and the
sons of the stranger shall not drink thy wine, for
the which thou hast laboured:
9 But they that have gathered it shall eat it, and
praise the LORD; and they that have brought it to-
gether shall drink it in the courts of my holiness.
10 ¶ Go through, go through the gates; prepare
ye the way of the people; cast up, cast up the
highway; gather out the stones; lift up a standard
for the people.
11 Behold, the LORD hath proclaimed unto the
end of the world, Say ye to the daughter of Zion,
Behold, thy salvation cometh; behold, his reward
is with him, and his work before him.
12 And they shall call them, The holy people, The
redeemed of the LORD: and thou shalt be called,
Sought out, A city not forsaken.

CHAPTER 63

WHO *is* this that cometh from Edom, with dyed
garments from Bozrah? this *that is* glorious in his
apparel, travelling in the greatness of his strength?
I that speak in righteousness, mighty to save.
2 Wherefore *art thou* red in thine apparel, and thy
garments like him that treadeth in the winefat?
3 I have trodden the winepress alone; and of the
people *there was* none with me: for I will tread
them in mine anger, and trample them in my
fury; and their blood shall be sprinkled upon my
garments, and I will stain all my raiment.
4 For the day of vengeance *is* in mine heart, and
the year of my redeemed is come.
5 And I looked, and *there was* none to help;
and I wondered that *there was* none to uphold:

that burneth. Flaming torch (60:1–3).

62:3 *crown of glory.* A garland of beauty. *royal diadem.* A turban of royalty.

62:4–5 *Hephzi-bah.* Translated, "my delight is in her." *Beulah.* Translated, "married." *as the bridegroom rejoiceth . . . so shall thy God.* The Lord's everlasting covenant with Israel guarantees that she will never again be *forsaken* for her sins but is now bound to Christ in spiritual marriage forever for their mutual delight (54:4–10; Ps. 45:11; Song 7:10; Hos. 2:19–23; Matt. 9:15; 25:1; John 3:29; Rom. 7:4; 2 Cor. 11:2; Eph. 5:22–33; Rev. 19:7–8; 21:2,9; 22:17).

62:6 *watchmen.* Those given oversight of the church (56:10; Ezek. 3:17; Heb. 13:17). *never hold their peace.* Never be silent. *keep not silence.* Do not be quiet, a different Hebrew word.

62:7 *give him no rest.* Pressing urgency in prayer (Luke 11:8–9; 1 Thess. 5:17).

62:8 *The LORD hath sworn.* Though God cannot lie, for the sake of confirming the faith of His people He sometimes seals His words with an oath (Heb. 6:16–18). *meat.* Food of any kind. *stranger.* Foreigner.

62:10 *standard.* Flag or banner.

62:11 *end of the world.* The extremity of the earth, showing the universal intent of the gospel message. *Say ye to the daughter of Zion.* Proclaim the gospel of Christ's coming to judge and to save (cited together with Zech. 9:9 in Matt. 21:5).

62:12 *Sought out.* See Zech. 8:22–23.

Thoughts for Personal/Family Worship: Chapter 62

1. One of the most beautiful pictures given to us of Christ's relationship with His people is that of a marriage of mutual love and delight (vv. 4–5). Salvation is not just a matter of legal verdicts and rescue from danger but of bringing people to the Lord so that He may love them forever. One of the fruits of the Spirit is joy in the Lord. How should the Christian life reflect this spiritual marriage?

2. In their prayers to God Christians should "give him no rest" until He builds up His kingdom and church throughout the earth (v. 7). Before we even ask for our daily needs, we should pray "Thy kingdom come" (Luke 11:2). God welcomes such bold prayers for revival and missions; indeed, He commands them. Why is this the duty of every believer? Why is it especially the duty of those whom He calls to be the "watchmen" of His people (v. 6), their office-bearers?

The Coming of the Heavenly Warrior (63:1—64:12)

Chapter 63: *The prophet declares the Lord's vengeance on the enemy and then prays for fresh displays of God's faithfulness for His people.*

63:1 *Who is this.* The answer is Christ the Lord (Rev. 19:13). *Edom . . . Bozrah.* The nation descended from Esau, frequently representative of all peoples hostile to God and His people (34:6). *dyed garments.* Garments red with the blood of His enemies (63:3). *glorious in his apparel.* Clothed majestically.

63:2–3 *winefat.* Winepress, an image of crushing the wicked in His wrath (Joel 3:13; Rev. 14:19–20; 19:15). *winepress.* Tub or trough. *raiment.* Clothing.

63:4 *day of vengeance.* The day of the Lord (34:8; 61:2), when He brings justice against His enemies (see note at 2:12). *year of my redeemed.* The time when God brings full salvation to His people (see note at 35:9). God's judgment upon the wicked coincides with His salvation for the righteous.

63:5 *wondered . . . mine own arm brought salvation.* This

therefore mine own arm brought salvation unto
me; and my fury, it upheld me.
6 And I will tread down the people in mine anger,
and make them drunk in my fury, and I will bring
down their strength to the earth.
7 ¶ I will mention the lovingkindnesses of the
LORD, *and* the praises of the LORD, according to
all that the LORD hath bestowed on us, and the
great goodness toward the house of Israel, which
he hath bestowed on them according to his
mercies, and according to the multitude of his
lovingkindnesses.
8 For he said, Surely they *are* my people, children
that will not lie: so he was their Saviour.
9 In all their affliction he was afflicted, and the
angel of his presence saved them: in his love and
in his pity he redeemed them; and he bare them,
and carried them all the days of old.
10 ¶ But they rebelled, and vexed his holy Spirit:
therefore he was turned to be their enemy, *and* he
fought against them.
11 Then he remembered the days of old, Moses,
and his people, *saying*, Where *is* he that brought
them up out of the sea with the shepherd of his
flock? where *is* he that put his holy Spirit within
him?
12 That led *them* by the right hand of Moses with
his glorious arm, dividing the water before them,
to make himself an everlasting name?
13 That led them through the deep, as an horse
in the wilderness, *that* they should not stumble?
14 As a beast goeth down into the valley, the
Spirit of the LORD caused him to rest: so didst
thou lead thy people, to make thyself a glorious
name.
15 ¶ Look down from heaven, and behold from
the habitation of thy holiness and of thy glory:
where *is* thy zeal and thy strength, the sounding of
thy bowels and of thy mercies toward me? are they
restrained?
16 Doubtless thou *art* our father, though Abraham
be ignorant of us, and Israel acknowledge us not:
thou, O LORD, *art* our father, our redeemer; thy
name *is* from everlasting.
17 ¶ O LORD, why hast thou made us to err from
thy ways, *and* hardened our heart from thy fear?
Return for thy servants' sake, the tribes of thine
inheritance.
18 The people of thy holiness have possessed *it*
but a little while: our adversaries have trodden
down thy sanctuary.
19 We are *thine*: thou never barest rule over them;
they were not called by thy name.

CHAPTER 64

OH that thou wouldest rend the heavens, that
thou wouldest come down, that the mountains

language, repeated from 59:16, identifies this bloodstained figure as the divine warrior, the only Savior.

63:6 *tread down.* Trample upon.

63:7 *lovingkindnesses.* Multiple demonstrations of covenant loyalty and love. *mercies.* Multiple acts of compassion or pity.

63:8 *lie.* Break faith or deal falsely.

63:9 *he was afflicted.* Literally, "in all their distress, he had distress." This points to the sympathy of Christ (Heb. 4:15). *angel of his presence.* Most likely the angel of the Lord, the Messenger who is the Lord, the pre-incarnate Christ.

63:10–11 *holy Spirit.* The main title of the third person of the Trinity in the New Testament, but a title rarely used of "the Spirit of the LORD" (v. 14) in the Old Testament (Ps. 51:11). Just as the Spirit dwells in each believer in Christ, leading the sons of God in holiness (Rom. 8:9,14), so the Spirit was God's guiding presence with Israel as a nation from the exodus onward (Hag. 2:4–5). *vexed.* Grieved or hurt the feelings. The Holy Spirit is a person whose company must be cultivated with a desire not to offend Him by resisting the preaching of His Word (Acts 7:51) or harming His church with sin and division (Eph. 4:29–32).

63:12–13 *dividing the water . . . through the deep.* See Ex. 14.

63:14 *beast.* Livestock. *lead thy people.* The Spirit of the Lord is the Shepherd of Israel, who brings His sheep to *rest* (49:10; Pss. 78:52; 80:1).

63:15 *sounding of thy bowels.* Stirrings of tenderness, an expression of deep love and sympathy. *mercies.* Demonstrations of compassion or pity. *are they restrained.* Isaiah desired to experience in his time what previous generations had experienced from the Lord.

63:16 *our father.* God adopted Israel as His firstborn son (Ex. 4:22; Deut. 14:1; Hos. 1:10; 11:1). *our redeemer; thy name is from everlasting.* Or "our redeemer is your name from everlasting." The Lord is ever the kinsman-defender of His people (see note at 35:9).

63:17 *why hast thou made us to err . . . hardened our heart.* Though man is responsible for his sins, the Lord is sovereign and may withhold transforming grace, giving sinners over to sin's power instead of turning them back (6:10). Therefore, Isaiah prayed for grace to intervene.

63:19 *thou never barest rule over them.* Not a denial of God's absolute sovereignty over all but a recognition that no other nation enjoyed the privilege of being His chosen kingdom and people, His special possession (Ex. 19:5–6; Deut. 4:20; 1 Kings 8:51; Ps. 147:19–20).

Thoughts for Personal/Family Worship: Chapter 63

Verse 9 makes this marvelous statement: "In all their affliction he was afflicted." How tender is the union between Christ and His church! When the Lord's people suffer, His compassion is deeply stirred too, "For we have not an high priest which cannot be touched with the feeling of our infirmities; but was in all points tempted like as we are, yet without sin" (Heb. 4:15). Not only is the Lord able to sympathize, but He is able to help us in the time of anxiety and needs. We can cast our care upon Him because He cares. We never suffer alone, for the Lord is always with us in our afflictions. How can we find comfort and strength in this truth when we are suffering?

Chapter 64: ***Isaiah prays for a manifestation of God's presence and power.***

64:1–3 The image is similar to God's coming in glory upon Sinai (Ex. 19:18–20; Deut. 5:25–27). This prayer is answered

might flow down at thy presence,
2 As *when* the melting fire burneth, the fire
causeth the waters to boil, to make thy name
known to thine adversaries, *that* the nations may
tremble at thy presence!
3 When thou didst terrible things *which* we
looked not for, thou camest down, the mountains
flowed down at thy presence.
4 For since the beginning of the world *men* have
not heard, nor perceived by the ear, neither hath
the eye seen, O God, beside thee, *what* he hath
prepared for him that waiteth for him.
5 Thou meetest him that rejoiceth and worketh
righteousness, *those that* remember thee in thy
ways: behold, thou art wroth; for we have sinned:
in those is continuance, and we shall be saved.
6 But we are all as an unclean *thing*, and all our
righteousnesses *are* as filthy rags; and we all do
fade as a leaf; and our iniquities, like the wind,
have taken us away.
7 And *there is* none that calleth upon thy name,
that stirreth up himself to take hold of thee: for
thou hast hid thy face from us, and hast consumed
us, because of our iniquities.
8 But now, O LORD, thou *art* our father; we *are*
the clay, and thou our potter; and we all *are* the
work of thy hand.
9 ¶ Be not wroth very sore, O LORD, neither
remember iniquity for ever: behold, see, we
beseech thee, we *are* all thy people.
10 Thy holy cities are a wilderness, Zion is a
wilderness, Jerusalem a desolation.
11 Our holy and our beautiful house, where our
fathers praised thee, is burned up with fire: and all
our pleasant things are laid waste.
12 Wilt thou refrain thyself for these *things*, O
LORD? wilt thou hold thy peace, and afflict us very
sore?

CHAPTER 65

I AM sought of *them that* asked not *for me*; I am
found of *them that* sought me not: I said, Behold
me, behold me, unto a nation *that* was not called
by my name.
2 I have spread out my hands all the day unto a
rebellious people, which walketh in a way *that was*
not good, after their own thoughts;
3 A people that provoketh me to anger contin-
ually to my face; that sacrificeth in gardens, and
burneth incense upon altars of brick;
4 Which remain among the graves, and lodge
in the monuments, which eat swine's flesh, and
broth of abominable *things is in* their vessels;

in Christ's resurrection with an earthquake (Matt. 28:2), the Spirit's coming with fire and an earthquake to fill and revive the church (Acts 2:3; 4:31), and ultimately Christ's second coming with fire to shake all things (Heb. 12:26–29).

64:1 *rend.* Tear open. *flow down.* Quake or shake, the dramatic consequence of God's presence (v. 3). Things are different when God makes Himself known.

64:2 *melting fire.* Fire kindling brushwood, hence crackling fire. *thy name.* Who God has revealed Himself to be in all the divine perfections (v. 7).

64:3 *terrible things.* Fearful or awesome things.

64:4 *not heard, nor perceived . . . what he hath prepared.* The gospel hope is known only by divine revelation (1 Cor. 2:9). *waiteth.* Longs for with expectation.

64:5 *remember.* Think about on purpose (v. 9). *wroth.* Angry. *in those is continuance.* Literally, "in them a long time," signifying that they had sinned for a long time.

64:6 *unclean thing.* Ceremonial impurity (Lev. 5:2; 7:19; 11:31, etc.) symbolizes the manner in which sin breaks fellowship with God (59:2; Lev. 15:31). *filthy rags.* Garments of menstruation.

64:7 *hid thy face.* A gesture expressing displeasure. *consumed us, because of our iniquities.* Literally, "you caused us to melt by the hand of our iniquities."

64:8 *our father.* An image of compassion and authority (63:16). *clay . . . potter.* Images of sovereignty (Jer. 18:6; Rom. 9:20–23).

64:9 *wroth very sore.* Extremely angry.

64:10 *Thy holy cities.* All the cities of the Promised Land, but particularly *Jerusalem*, which would be desolate and laid waste because of their sins.

64:11 *Our holy and our beautiful house.* The temple.

64:12 *refrain.* Restrain oneself. *hold thy peace.* Be silent. *sore.* Exceedingly.

Thoughts for Personal/Family Worship: Chapter 64

The Lord's presence and power ought to be the desire of every believer. There are times when the Lord seems to have hidden His face from us, and that ought to drive us to prayer, as it did Isaiah. In the previous chapter the prophet prayed for God to look down from heaven (63:15). Now he prays for God to tear the heavens apart and come down. We should plead with God to remove every impediment to knowing the fullness of His presence. Things will be remarkably different when God appears in His glory and power. Let us wait upon the Lord, earnestly expecting Him to bless His people, that by faith in the gospel we may see what God "hath prepared for him that waiteth for him" (v. 4). How does this kind of prayer seek awakening and revival by the Holy Spirit? How does it ultimately seek nothing less than the return of Christ?

Judgment and the New Creation (65:1—66:24)

Chapter 65: ***The prophet declares the salvation of the Gentiles and a remnant of Israel and then predicts the new Jerusalem.***

65:1 *sought . . . asked not . . . found . . . sought me not.* The nations had no desire for the Lord, but the Lord of His own sovereign initiative gathered the Gentiles into the church by the grace of Christ (Rom. 10:20).

65:2 *spread out my hands.* A gesture of welcome. The Lord continually appealed to Israel through the prophets (2 Kings 17:13–14; Ezek. 33:11) but was rejected by most of the people (Rom. 10:21).

65:4 *lodge in the monuments.* Spend the night in secret places. *swine's flesh.* Forbidden as unclean for eating under the ceremonial law (Lev. 11:7–8). *abominable things.* Sacrificial

5 Which say, Stand by thyself, come not near to
me; for I am holier than thou. These *are* a smoke
in my nose, a fire that burneth all the day.
6 Behold, *it is* written before me: I will not keep
silence, but will recompense, even recompense
into their bosom,
7 Your iniquities, and the iniquities of your
fathers together, saith the LORD, which have
burned incense upon the mountains, and
blasphemed me upon the hills: therefore will I
measure their former work into their bosom.
8 ¶ Thus saith the LORD, As the new wine is found
in the cluster, and *one* saith, Destroy it not; for a
blessing *is* in it: so will I do for my servants' sakes,
that I may not destroy them all.
9 And I will bring forth a seed out of Jacob, and
out of Judah an inheritor of my mountains: and
mine elect shall inherit it, and my servants shall
dwell there.
10 And Sharon shall be a fold of flocks, and the
valley of Achor a place for the herds to lie down
in, for my people that have sought me.
11 ¶ But ye *are* they that forsake the LORD, that
forget my holy mountain, that prepare a table for
that troop, and that furnish the drink offering
unto that number.
12 Therefore will I number you to the sword, and
ye shall all bow down to the slaughter: because
when I called, ye did not answer; when I spake, ye
did not hear; but did evil before mine eyes, and
did choose *that* wherein I delighted not.
13 Therefore thus saith the Lord GOD, Behold,
my servants shall eat, but ye shall be hungry:
behold, my servants shall drink, but ye shall be
thirsty: behold, my servants shall rejoice, but ye
shall be ashamed:
14 Behold, my servants shall sing for joy of heart,
but ye shall cry for sorrow of heart, and shall howl
for vexation of spirit.
15 And ye shall leave your name for a curse unto
my chosen: for the Lord GOD shall slay thee, and
call his servants by another name:
16 That he who blesseth himself in the earth shall
bless himself in the God of truth; and he that
sweareth in the earth shall swear by the God of
truth; because the former troubles are forgotten,
and because they are hid from mine eyes.
17 ¶ For, behold, I create new heavens and a new
earth: and the former shall not be remembered,
nor come into mind.
18 But be ye glad and rejoice for ever *in that*
which I create: for, behold, I create Jerusalem a
rejoicing, and her people a joy.
19 And I will rejoice in Jerusalem, and joy in my
people: and the voice of weeping shall be no more
heard in her, nor the voice of crying.
20 There shall be no more thence an infant of days,
nor an old man that hath not filled his days: for the
child shall die an hundred years old; but the sinner
being an hundred years old shall be accursed.
21 And they shall build houses, and inhabit *them*;
and they shall plant vineyards, and eat the fruit
of them.
22 They shall not build, and another inhabit; they
shall not plant, and another eat: for as the days of
a tree *are* the days of my people, and mine elect
shall long enjoy the work of their hands.
23 They shall not labour in vain, nor bring forth
for trouble; for they *are* the seed of the blessed of
the LORD, and their offspring with them.
24 And it shall come to pass, that before they call,
I will answer; and while they are yet speaking, I
will hear.
25 The wolf and the lamb shall feed together, and

meat that has become unclean; something foul, refuse.
65:5 *nose.* Or anger.
65:7 *measure.* Deal out.
65:8 *cluster.* The image pictures God's saving a remnant.
65:10 *Achor.* Where Achan was stoned (Josh. 7:26). The place of trouble becomes a place of hope (Hos. 2:15).
65:11 *forget.* Refuse to think about, choose to ignore (v. 16). *my holy mountain.* Zion, symbolic of God's holy presence and kingdom. *troop.* Gad, the god of fortune or luck. *number.* Meni, the god of fate.
65:13–14 *my servants.* The godly (56:6), the spiritual Israel (vv. 9,23) redeemed by the Servant (54:17). *eat . . . drink . . . rejoice . . . sing.* Those faithful to the Lord will experience the satisfaction of all desire (Luke 6:20–23). *hungry . . . thirsty . . . ashamed . . . cry.* Those unfaithful to the Lord will experience the suffering of desires never met and great disgrace and sadness (Luke 6:24–26; 16:24). *vexation of spirit.* The breaking of the heart by despair (Prov. 13:12).
65:16 *God of truth.* Literally, "the God of Amen," the faithful Lord.
65:17–18 *create new heavens and a new earth.* The finished work of the Messiah results in a new creation as the old creation, cursed by sin, is replaced by a new, Eden-like order of righteousness and salvation (4:5–6; 45:8; 51:3,6; Rom. 8:19–22; 2 Peter 3:13; Rev. 21:1). *not be remembered.* The sins and miseries of the past will no longer dominate one's experience, but the hearts of believers will be full of hope and joy. *weeping shall be no more.* See 25:8; 60:20. *I create Jerusalem . . . her people.* The new creation begins not with outward and universal glory but with the transformation of sinners with a new, inward peace and *joy* in the Lord (57:19; 2 Cor. 5:17; Gal. 6:15; Eph. 2:10,15; 4:24).
65:20–23 Various scenarios describing the reversing of the curse upon law-breakers threatened against Israel in the old covenant (Deut. 28:15,30–33). *blessed of the LORD.* The spiritual offspring of Abraham, believers in Christ (Gen. 12:1–3; Gal. 3:8,14,29).
65:24 *before they call . . . while they are yet speaking.* God's people will no longer have to wait for God to answer their prayers but will experience the immediate satisfaction of every desire.
65:25 *meat.* Food of any kind. This verse repeats the idyllic view of the peaceful kingdom of Christ given in 11:6–9.

Thoughts for Personal/Family Worship: Chapter 65

God's redemption of sinners will ultimately result in the transformation of the universe into a new creation

the lion shall eat straw like the bullock: and dust
shall be the serpent's meat. They shall not hurt nor
destroy in all my holy mountain, saith the LORD.

CHAPTER 66

THUS saith the LORD, The heaven *is* my throne,
and the earth *is* my footstool: where *is* the house
that ye build unto me? and where *is* the place of
my rest?
2 For all those *things* hath mine hand made, and
all those *things* have been, saith the LORD: but to
this *man* will I look, *even* to *him that is* poor and
of a contrite spirit, and trembleth at my word.
3 He that killeth an ox *is as if* he slew a man; he
that sacrificeth a lamb, *as if* he cut off a dog's neck;
he that offereth an oblation, *as if he offered* swine's
blood; he that burneth incense, *as if* he blessed an
idol. Yea, they have chosen their own ways, and
their soul delighteth in their abominations.
4 I also will choose their delusions, and will bring
their fears upon them; because when I called,
none did answer; when I spake, they did not hear:
but they did evil before mine eyes, and chose *that*
in which I delighted not.
5 ¶ Hear the word of the LORD, ye that tremble at
his word; Your brethren that hated you, that cast
you out for my name's sake, said, Let the LORD be
glorified: but he shall appear to your joy, and they
shall be ashamed.
6 A voice of noise from the city, a voice from
the temple, a voice of the LORD that rendereth
recompence to his enemies.
7 Before she travailed, she brought forth; before
her pain came, she was delivered of a man child.
8 Who hath heard such a thing? who hath seen
such things? Shall the earth be made to bring
forth in one day? *or* shall a nation be born at
once? for as soon as Zion travailed, she brought
forth her children.
9 Shall I bring to the birth, and not cause to bring
forth? saith the LORD: shall I cause to bring forth,
and shut *the womb*? saith thy God.
10 Rejoice ye with Jerusalem, and be glad with
her, all ye that love her: rejoice for joy with her, all
ye that mourn for her:
11 That ye may suck, and be satisfied with the
breasts of her consolations; that ye may milk out,
and be delighted with the abundance of her glory.
12 For thus saith the LORD, Behold, I will extend
peace to her like a river, and the glory of the
Gentiles like a flowing stream: then shall ye suck,
ye shall be borne upon *her* sides, and be dandled
upon *her* knees.
13 As one whom his mother comforteth, so
will I comfort you; and ye shall be comforted in
Jerusalem.
14 And when ye see *this*, your heart shall rejoice,
and your bones shall flourish like an herb: and
the hand of the LORD shall be known toward his
servants, and *his* indignation toward his enemies.
15 For, behold, the LORD will come with fire, and
with his chariots like a whirlwind, to render his
anger with fury, and his rebuke with flames of fire.
16 For by fire and by his sword will the LORD
plead with all flesh: and the slain of the LORD shall
be many.
17 They that sanctify themselves, and purify
themselves in the gardens behind one *tree* in the
midst, eating swine's flesh, and the abomination,

---

unharmed by the curse against man's sin. If this fallen world retains much beauty and pleasure, to a much greater degree will the new heavens and the new earth be a paradise of happiness for the church. All our desires will be satisfied by the God who made us. However, before we can enter into the new creation, the new creation must enter into us. We must be created anew in Christ by the work of the Holy Spirit. One fruit of this new creation is a new joy in the Lord Jesus, a spiritual delight in the loveliness of Christ. Another fruit is that we truly become one of the servants of the Lord, doing His will. Are you part of God's new creation? How do you know?

Chapter 66: ***The Lord declares judgment upon all who are unrepentant of their sins, but He promises great blessings upon Zion.***

66:1 *heaven is my throne.* God displays His glory and majesty supremely in heaven (6:1; Pss. 11:4; 103:19; Matt. 5:34–35; Rev. 4). *earth is my footstool.* The Lord reigns over the world. *where is the house.* We must never identify God's holy presence with a building (1 Kings 8:27), lest our religion degenerate into mere externals (Acts 7:48–50).

66:2 *but to this man will I look.* True worship does not require a special building but a heart that is humble (*poor*), wounded over sin (*contrite spirit*), and fearful and reverent toward the Word of the Lord (*trembleth at my word*; v. 5; 57:15; Pss. 34:18; 51:17).

66:3 *killeth an ox . . . slew a man.* God gave man the right to kill animals for food (Gen. 9:3); this refers to God's hatred of their hypocritical offerings (*oblation*; 1:11–17).

66:4 *delusions.* Ill treatment, punishments.

66:7–10 *travailed.* Had labor pains (v. 8). The Lord will supernaturally produce spiritual children for the *joy* of the true church (42:19–21; 54:1–2).

66:11 *ye may suck, and be satisfied.* As the infant finds comfort at his mother's breasts, so likewise shall the saints be comforted in the *glory* of the church. *milk out.* Slurp or drain out.

66:12 *peace . . . like a river.* By Christ's righteousness and death (53:5,11) they will enjoy the blessings that belong to those who keep God's commandments (48:18). *borne upon her sides.* Carried. *dandled.* Fondled.

66:14 *your bones shall flourish.* You will be strengthened.

66:15 *come with fire . . . chariots . . . whirlwind.* The Lord will come with His heavenly armies of angels to destroy the wicked (2 Kings 2:11; 6:17).

66:16 *plead with.* Judge.

66:17 *abomination.* A disgusting or detestable thing, often referring to idolatry.

and the mouse, shall be consumed together, saith
the LORD.
18 For I *know* their works and their thoughts:
it shall come, that I will gather all nations and
tongues; and they shall come, and see my glory.
19 And I will set a sign among them, and I will
send those that escape of them unto the nations,
to Tarshish, Pul, and Lud, that draw the bow, *to*
Tubal, and Javan, *to* the isles afar off, that have not
heard my fame, neither have seen my glory; and
they shall declare my glory among the Gentiles.
20 And they shall bring all your brethren *for*
an offering unto the LORD out of all nations
upon horses, and in chariots, and in litters, and
upon mules, and upon swift beasts, to my holy
mountain Jerusalem, saith the LORD, as the
children of Israel bring an offering in a clean
vessel into the house of the LORD.
21 And I will also take of them for priests *and* for
Levites, saith the LORD.
22 For as the new heavens and the new earth,
which I will make, shall remain before me, saith the
LORD, so shall your seed and your name remain.
23 And it shall come to pass, *that* from one
new moon to another, and from one sabbath to
another, shall all flesh come to worship before me,
saith the LORD.
24 And they shall go forth, and look upon the
carcases of the men that have transgressed
against me: for their worm shall not die, neither
shall their fire be quenched; and they shall be an
abhorring unto all flesh.

66:18 *thoughts.* Intentions. *tongues.* Languages.
66:19 *sign.* Perhaps a reference to Christ (7:14). *send those that escape . . . declare my glory among the Gentiles.* Out of the godly remnant of Israel the Lord will raise up preachers to take the gospel to the most distant parts of the earth (*isles;* Ps. 96:3; Luke 24:45–47).
66:20–21 *litters.* Covered wagons. The imagery here communicates that large numbers of people will join Israel in worshiping the Lord and be included in the spiritual priesthood (61:6,10).
66:22 *new heavens and the new earth.* God will transform all things (see note at 65:17–18), and His blessings upon His people will *remain* forever (1 Peter 1:4).
66:23–24 *new moon.* Worship is expressed in terms of the old covenant. *all flesh.* All mankind, that is, some from every nation and language (v. 18). *look . . . abhorring unto all flesh.* The punishment of the wicked will be an eternal witness to all the redeemed of the horrible evil of sinning against God. *their worm shall not die . . . fire be quenched.* An image picturing everlasting torment in a constant state of decay and pain (33:14; 34:10; Mark 9:43–48). This is the twofold destiny of mankind, either to join in the worship of the only God or to experience eternal death (Rev. 21:7–8).

Thoughts for Personal/Family Worship: Chapter 66

Isaiah concludes his prophecy with an awe-inspiring vision of the eternal state of all mankind (vv. 22–24). Every human being will either end up worshiping the Lord in the new creation forever or suffering horribly in hell without intermission or end. There is no third option. This reality presses upon us two other great truths of this chapter.

1. **First, it calls us to consider whether we are saved by grace. Salvation is not about external things like being in a church building or bringing an offering. It is a matter of a heart humbled by God's majesty, broken under the weight of one's sins, and submissive to God's Word (vv. 1–2). Is this a description of you? Are you headed for eternal worship and joy or for eternal damnation?**
2. **Second, it calls us to consider the great mission of the church to all nations (vv. 18–21). It began with faithful Jews, the apostles, and other disciples of Jesus Christ, who gave themselves to bring the gospel to the Gentiles. Yet the mission continues for the church today. The only way for sinners to escape hell and gain heaven is by the gospel of Christ. How are you using your abilities and resources to send the gospel to all nations?**

Behold
THOU HAST MADE
THE
HEAVEN
AND
The Earth
BY THY
GREAT
POWER
AND
Stretched
OUT ARM
AND THERE IS
Nothing
TOO HARD
FOR THEE

JEREMIAH 32:17

INTRODUCTION TO THE BOOK OF THE PROPHET

JEREMIAH

Authorship: The author of the book is Jeremiah (whose name means "Jehovah appoints or establishes"), a prophet of the living God who came from a priestly family (1:1–2; 2 Chron. 35:25; 36:12,21–22).

Date: Jeremiah's ministry began in the thirteenth year of the reign of Josiah, king of Judah (1:2), which most accept as being 627 BC, and it lasted for about forty-seven years, covering the reigns of several kings and the first part of the captivity (chs. 40–44). Jeremiah's writings are not in chronological order, so the reader may find it helpful to bear in mind a general outline of the history of the time as he finds references to various kings in this book.

1. *Josiah*, a godly king, brought spiritual reformation to Judah. However, those who reigned after him returned to the sins of their forefathers. During his reign Babylon rose in power, conquering Nineveh, the capital of Assyria, in 612 BC. Josiah died in battle against Egypt in 609 BC (2 Kings 22:1—23:29).
2. *Jehoahaz*, son of Josiah, reigned only three months before being deposed by the Egyptian pharaoh, who replaced him with his brother (23:30–34).
3. *Jehoiakim*, another son of Josiah, reigned next for eleven years (609–598 BC). Nebuchadnezzar of Babylon came south in 605 BC, defeating Assyria and Egypt at the battle of Carchemish, subjugating Judah, and taking away the first group of exiles, including Daniel. Jehoiakim later rebelled against Babylon and died under God's curse (Jer. 36:29–31; 2 Kings 23:34—24:7).
4. *Jehoiachin*, also known as *Jeconiah* and *Coniah*, son of Jehoiakim, reigned three months before Nebuchadnezzar took him into exile in 597 BC, carrying away the treasures of the temple and many captives, including Ezekiel (24:8–16). Thirty-seven years later Jehoiachin was given liberty and honor by a new king of Babylon (25:27–30).
5. *Zedekiah*, an uncle of Jehoiachin, was installed as king by the Babylonians. He reigned for eleven years (597–586 BC) until Nebuchadnezzar destroyed Jerusalem for its continued rebellion, killed Zedekiah's sons, put out his eyes, and took him and others as prisoners to Babylon (24:17—25:21).
6. *Gedaliah*, whose godly father Ahikam (26:24) and grandfather Shaphan had served in the administration of Josiah (22:1–20), was appointed governor of Judah by the Babylonians (Jer. 40:5; 2 Kings 25:22–24). Some wicked Judeans murdered him (v. 25), and the people, fearing retaliation from Babylon, forced Jeremiah to flee with them to Egypt (Jer. 43:5–7; 2 Kings 25:26), where the prophet appears to have died.

Theme: Judgment for breaking the covenant and restoration by God's faithfulness (Jer. 1:10).

Purpose: To encourage repentance from sin because of impending judgment and trust in the Lord as the only hope for salvation.

Synopsis: *The Contribution of Jeremiah to Redemptive Revelation*
Although the writings of Jeremiah are perhaps not as eloquent as the writings of Isaiah, they are splendid in their zeal and in presenting a unified message. Jeremiah is the longest of the prophetic books, and is written in both poetry and prose. The book contains various literary types, including sermons and visions. A large portion is autobiographical, describing various incidents in Jeremiah's life. We are, therefore, given a great deal of insight into his character,

enabling us to identify much more readily with him as a man. Like Moses, he made excuses and was reluctant to accept the call and commission of God (Jer. 1:6; cf. Ex. 4:10). Whereas Moses ministered before the nation entered the Promised Land, Jeremiah was a teacher of the people before they were removed from that land into exile.

There are also parallels between Jeremiah and the apostle Paul (Jer. 1:5; cf. Gal. 1:15–16). Both had a love for the lost and desired the salvation of their nation but were rejected by their own people. Both felt an agony of soul as they contemplated the fact that those who rejected them and their message also rejected Almighty God, who had called them and sent them to preach. However, unlike Paul, Jeremiah had no faithful friends who eagerly supported his work. He did not have the encouragement of seeing growing and flourishing churches, as Paul did. His solitude and lack of apparent success explain why he is often referred to as "the weeping prophet."

Although much of Jeremiah's preaching was negative, he was by no means a pessimist, though he *was* a realist. He lived in an age when the Jewish nation had departed from the Lord, and they thought nothing of the consequences. Punishment was soon to come upon them because of their sin, and Jeremiah was called of God to warn them. The false prophets spoke of peace when there was no peace (Jer. 6:14; 8:11) but Jeremiah spoke honestly. When he spoke in strong terms, it was out of love and concern for the souls he addressed. He sought to stir them out of their spiritual apathy and to awaken their consciences that they might see the gravity of their sins. He preached such things in the hope that the people might turn away from wickedness. In stark contrast to the disobedience of the children of Israel, Jeremiah presented the faithfulness of God.

Jeremiah was committed to the work of the Lord. The message given to him by God was not an easy one to deliver. Human nature wants to be liked, but Jeremiah thought only of his duty toward God. He preached an unpopular message and was prepared to suffer the consequences of being faithful to the Lord. Oh for men like him today! His spirituality is evidenced throughout the long ministry that the Lord gave to him.

Jeremiah's twofold message of judgment and restoration is rich in gospel significance. His declaration to the unrepentant people of Judah is a graphic illustration of the consequences of sin in the exile and fall of Jerusalem. His frequent appeals for conversion show that the terms for receiving salvation have always been the same. His pointing to the coming Messiah as "the Lord Our Righteousness" (23:6; 33:16) and to the new covenant (31:1–40) show that the only basis and hope of salvation have always been through God's grace in His Christ. This surely ought to bring joy to the heart of every true Christian! In addition to his message, Jeremiah himself, as a type or picture-prophecy, points to the Lord Jesus in that he, like the Savior, was a suffering servant. No one except the Lord Jesus was ever treated with more contempt by Israel.

Outline: I. Introduction (1:1–19)

- A. Setting the Scene (1:1–3)
- B. The Call of Jeremiah: The Span and Purpose of His Ministry (1:4–10)
- C. The Two Visions (1:11–16)
- D. The Sovereign Charge and Promise (1:17–19)

II. God's Judgment upon Judah and Jerusalem (2:1—25:38)

- A. The Backslidden Nature of the Nation (2:1–37)
- B. A Call to Repentance (3:1—4:4)
- C. Judgment Is Coming (4:5—6:30)
- D. The Futility of Believing False Promises and Rejecting Truth (7:1—8:17)
- E. Jeremiah's Mourning over the Nation's Sins (8:18—9:26)
- F. A Further Appeal to Return to the Lord (10:1–25)
- G. A Proclamation of God's Covenant and the Penalties for Disobedience (11:1—12:17)
- H. The Lesson of the Linen Girdle (13:1–27)
- I. A Terrible Drought (14:1–22)
- J. God's Rejection of Judah Contrasted with His Promise to Jeremiah (15:1–21)
- K. Judah's Utter Ruin Declared (16:1–21)
- L. The Sin of Judah Written with a Pen of Iron (17:1–27)
- M. Lessons Drawn from the Potter (18:1—20:18)
- N. Rulers and False Prophets Denounced (21:1—23:40)
- O. Two Further Visions (24:1—25:38)

III. Jeremiah and the False Prophets (26:1—29:32)
   A. Diminish Not a Word (26:1–24)
   B. Surrender to the Yoke or Perish by the Sword (27:1–22)
   C. The False Prophet Hananiah (28:1–17)
   D. Jeremiah's Letter to the Captives in Babylon (29:1–32)

IV. The Book of Consolation (30:1—33:26)
   A. Be Not Dismayed (30:1–24)
   B. Loved with an Everlasting Love (31:1–26)
   C. Behold, the Days Come (31:27–40)
   D. A Test of Faith (32:1–44)
   E. Call unto Me (33:1–8)
   F. The Lord is Good (33:9–14)
   G. The Branch of Righteousness (33:15–18)
   H. The Strength of the Covenant (33:19–26)

V. Invaders at the City Gates (34:1—38:28)
   A. A Message for Zedekiah (34:1–7)
   B. A Wicked Act against Servants (34:8–22)
   C. The Rechabites Blessed for their Obedience (35:1–19)
   D. Jeremiah's Writings Brought before the King (36:1–32)
   E. Zedekiah Seeks Jeremiah (37:1–10)
   F. Jeremiah Thrown into Prison (37:11–21)
   G. Sunk in the Mire (38:1–6)
   H. The Prophet Released (38:7–13)
   I. Zedekiah's Last Talk with Jeremiah (38:14–28)

VI. The Fall of Jerusalem (39:1–18)
   A. Zedekiah Captured (39:1–7)
   B. Jeremiah Shown Favor (39:8–14)
   C. Ebed-melech Delivered (39:15–18)

VII. Events after Jerusalem's Fall (40:1—43:7)
   A. Gedaliah's Period as Governor (40:1—41:18)
   B. A Foolish Flight to Egypt (42:1—43:7)

VIII. Events in Egypt (43:8—45:5)
   A. Jeremiah Prophesies Babylon's Invasion of Egypt (43:8–13)
   B. The Punishment of the Jews in Egypt (44:1–30)
   C. The Despairing Baruch Is Comforted (45:1–5)

IX. Warnings to the Nations (46:1—51:64)
   A. The Defeat of Egypt (46:1–28)
   B. The Destruction of the Philistines (47:1–7)
   C. The Horn of Moab Cut Off (48:1–47)
   D. The Captivity of Ammon (49:1–6)
   E. The Desolation of Edom (49:7–22)
   F. The Confounding of Damascus (49:23–27)
   G. The Smiting of Kedar and Hazor (49:28–33)
   H. The Elamites Made Outcasts (49:34–39)
   I. The Judgment and Fall of Babylon (50:1—51:64)

X. Final Thoughts in Conclusion (52:1–34)
   A. Jerusalem Laid Waste and Zedekiah Imprisoned in Babylon (52:1–11)
   B. The Temple Sacked and Burned (52:12–23)
   C. Captives Deported to Babylon (52:24–30)
   D. Jehoiachin Released from Prison and Honored (52:31–34)

THE BOOK OF THE PROPHET JEREMIAH

CHAPTER 1

THE words of Jeremiah the son of Hilkiah, of
the priests that *were* in Anathoth in the land of
Benjamin:
2 To whom the word of the LORD came in the
days of Josiah the son of Amon king of Judah, in
the thirteenth year of his reign.
3 It came also in the days of Jehoiakim the son of
Josiah king of Judah, unto the end of the eleventh
year of Zedekiah the son of Josiah king of Judah,
unto the carrying away of Jerusalem captive in the
fifth month.
4 Then the word of the LORD came unto me,
saying,
5 Before I formed thee in the belly I knew thee;
and before thou camest forth out of the womb
I sanctified thee, *and* I ordained thee a prophet
unto the nations.
6 Then said I, Ah, Lord GOD! behold, I cannot
speak: for I *am* a child.
7 ¶ But the LORD said unto me, Say not, I *am* a
child: for thou shalt go to all that I shall send thee,
and whatsoever I command thee thou shalt speak.
8 Be not afraid of their faces: for I *am* with thee to
deliver thee, saith the LORD.
9 Then the LORD put forth his hand, and touched
my mouth. And the LORD said unto me, Behold, I
have put my words in thy mouth.
10 See, I have this day set thee over the nations
and over the kingdoms, to root out, and to pull
down, and to destroy, and to throw down, to
build, and to plant.
11 ¶ Moreover the word of the LORD came unto
me, saying, Jeremiah, what seest thou? And I said,
I see a rod of an almond tree.
12 Then said the LORD unto me, Thou hast well
seen: for I will hasten my word to perform it.
13 And the word of the LORD came unto me the
second time, saying, What seest thou? And I said,
I see a seething pot; and the face thereof *is* toward
the north.
14 Then the LORD said unto me, Out of the north
an evil shall break forth upon all the inhabitants
of the land.
15 For, lo, I will call all the families of the king-
doms of the north, saith the LORD; and they shall

Chapter 1: *God calls Jeremiah to the prophetic office, giving him both instructions and promises for his ministry.*

INTRODUCTION (1:1–19)

Setting the Scene (1:1–3)

1:1–3 *the son of Hilkiah the priests.* Jeremiah may have been too young (v. 6) to exercise the priestly office at the time of his calling. *Anathoth.* A small town about three miles northeast of Jerusalem, given to the priests (Josh. 21:18). *Josiah.* One of the godliest of all Judah's kings (2 Kings 23:25)—yet how sad was the spiritual decline of Judah after Josiah's death.

The Call of Jeremiah: The Span and Purpose of His Ministry (1:4–10)

1:4 *the word of the LORD came unto me.* God speaks personally to His servant.

1:5 *Before I formed thee . . . I knew thee.* To know involves the idea of selection as well as comprehension—chosen before the foundation of the world (Gal. 1:15; Eph. 1:4). *sanctified.* Consecrated or dedicated. *ordained.* Appointed. *the nations.* Gentile nations as well as Judah.

1:6 *A child* refers to his inexperience rather than to his age.

1:7–8 *Say not, I am a child.* The Lord reveals His sovereignty. Though difficult and fearful situations lay ahead, God's servant need not worry (Acts 18:10; 26:17). The Lord possesses infinite power and wisdom. He is on the throne (Isa. 40:22–23; Rom. 8:31).

1:9 *put my words in thy mouth.* The words of the prophet are the words of God.

1:10 *See, I have . . . set thee.* The Lord uses agricultural and architectural terminology to outline the objectives of Jeremiah's message, both destructive and constructive.

The Two Visions (1:11–16)

1:11–12 *I see a rod of an almond tree.* The word *almond* literally means "awake." The almond blossoms as early as January, being the first tree to awaken from winter, the harbinger of the certain spring. The symbol aptly describes the Word of God and the certainty of its fulfillment. Jeremiah sees the Word of God as not only awake but active, fulfilling the Lord's purposes. The word *hasten* has the same root as *almond.* God is watchful over His Word to fulfill it.

1:13–15 Judah's sin had become an abomination unto the Lord. *seething.* Literally, "blown upon." A pot is boiling outside on a fire; the wind suddenly blows upon it so that it is tilted to one side and pours out. *north.* Babylon would use the traditional invasion route, avoiding the hostile desert terrain. *set . . . his throne.* Subjection by conquerors.

come, and they shall set every one his throne at
the entering of the gates of Jerusalem, and against
all the walls thereof round about, and against all
the cities of Judah.
16 And I will utter my judgments against them
touching all their wickedness, who have forsaken
me, and have burned incense unto other gods,
and worshipped the works of their own hands.
17 ¶ Thou therefore gird up thy loins, and arise,
and speak unto them all that I command thee: be
not dismayed at their faces, lest I confound thee
before them.
18 For, behold, I have made thee this day a
defenced city, and an iron pillar, and brasen walls
against the whole land, against the kings of Judah,
against the princes thereof, against the priests
thereof, and against the people of the land.
19 And they shall fight against thee; but they shall
not prevail against thee; for I *am* with thee, saith
the LORD, to deliver thee.

CHAPTER 2

MOREOVER the word of the LORD came to me,
saying,
2 Go and cry in the ears of Jerusalem, saying,
Thus saith the LORD; I remember thee, the
kindness of thy youth, the love of thine espousals,
when thou wentest after me in the wilderness, in
a land *that was* not sown.
3 Israel *was* holiness unto the LORD, *and* the first-
fruits of his increase: all that devour him shall of-
fend; evil shall come upon them, saith the LORD.
4 Hear ye the word of the LORD, O house of Jacob,
and all the families of the house of Israel:
5 ¶ Thus saith the LORD, What iniquity have your
fathers found in me, that they are gone far from
me, and have walked after vanity, and are become
vain?
6 Neither said they, Where *is* the LORD that
brought us up out of the land of Egypt, that led us
through the wilderness, through a land of deserts
and of pits, through a land of drought, and of
the shadow of death, through a land that no man
passed through, and where no man dwelt?
7 And I brought you into a plentiful country, to
eat the fruit thereof and the goodness thereof; but
when ye entered, ye defiled my land, and made
mine heritage an abomination.
8 The priests said not, Where *is* the LORD? and
they that handle the law knew me not: the pastors
also transgressed against me, and the prophets
prophesied by Baal, and walked after *things that*
do not profit.
9 ¶ Wherefore I will yet plead with you, saith
the LORD, and with your children's children will
I plead.
10 For pass over the isles of Chittim, and see; and
send unto Kedar, and consider diligently, and see
if there be such a thing.
11 Hath a nation changed *their* gods, which *are*
yet no gods? but my people have changed their
glory for *that which* doth not profit.
12 Be astonished, O ye heavens, at this, and be
horribly afraid, be ye very desolate, saith the
LORD.
13 For my people have committed two evils; they
have forsaken me the fountain of living waters,

The Sovereign Charge and Promise (1:17–19)

1:17–19 Hard times were ahead, but Jeremiah must get on with the task. *gird up thy loins.* To secure with a belt the long flowing clothes that would hinder freedom of movement over rough terrain, a metaphor for spiritual preparation (Luke 12:35; 1 Peter 1:13). Like an impregnable *city*, Jeremiah would withstand every assault against him because the Lord was with Him.

Thoughts for Personal/Family Worship: Chapter 1

1. **Though we may not be prophets, our call is personal and effectual (Rom. 8:29–30). Every Christian has been consecrated by divine grace to be in the service of the Lord, and as such every believer is the object of His love. Whatever service we are given, it is a calling. Perhaps if we had a better grasp of this, we would not be so despondent in times of difficulty and hardship. Let us therefore serve the Lord with gladness.**
2. **The children of God are engaged in spiritual warfare; the battle is raging. Let us "fight a good fight" (2 Tim. 4:7), not as defeated Christians but as "more than conquerors through him that loved us" (Rom. 8:37). Upholding the Word of God will never make us popular. We will be hated by many, yet one person with God is a majority! How does this chapter encourage you to stand up for the Lord?**

GOD'S JUDGMENT UPON JUDAH AND JERUSALEM (2:1—25:28)

Chapter 2: ***Judah's sins are set out in the form of an indictment that would be brought before a court of law.***

The Backslidden Nature of the Nation (2:1–37)

2:1–7 This chapter resembles a legal document, based on the covenant between God and His people. *espousals.* Their betrothal when love was freshly new. *plentiful country.* Literally, "land of Carmel," indicating fruitfulness and luxurious growth.

2:8 Note the four groups identified. *priests.* They whose duty was service to the Lord (Deut. 33:10) had become a disgrace, mingling pagan idolatry with the worship of God. *they that handle the law.* The scribes, who had responsibility for interpreting the law, are admonished for their lack of knowledge concerning God's law. *pastors.* Shepherds, here the rulers who defied the Lord. *prophets.* False prophets with no true calling from God.

2:9 *plead.* Strive or contend, as in a legal sense of bringing an indictment.

2:11 Judah's crime had no parallel in any of the heathen nations surrounding her.

2:13 God is the *fountain* of life springing from the unfathomable depths of His being (Ps. 36:8–9; John 4:10,14; 7:37–39; Rev. 7:17; 21:6; 22:1). The people rejected that which was free, pure, refreshing, and abundant. Instead, they labored and

and hewed them out cisterns, broken cisterns,
that can hold no water.
14 ¶ *Is* Israel a servant? *is* he a homeborn *slave*?
why is he spoiled?
15 The young lions roared upon him, *and* yelled,
and they made his land waste: his cities are burned
without inhabitant.
16 Also the children of Noph and Tahapanes have
broken the crown of thy head.
17 Hast thou not procured this unto thyself, in
that thou hast forsaken the LORD thy God, when
he led thee by the way?
18 And now what hast thou to do in the way of
Egypt, to drink the waters of Sihor? or what hast
thou to do in the way of Assyria, to drink the
waters of the river?
19 Thine own wickedness shall correct thee, and
thy backslidings shall reprove thee: know there-
fore and see that *it is* an evil *thing* and bitter, that
thou hast forsaken the LORD thy God, and that my
fear *is* not in thee, saith the Lord GOD of hosts.
20 ¶ For of old time I have broken thy yoke, *and*
burst thy bands; and thou saidst, I will not trans-
gress; when upon every high hill and under every
green tree thou wanderest, playing the harlot.
21 Yet I had planted thee a noble vine, wholly
a right seed: how then art thou turned into the
degenerate plant of a strange vine unto me?
22 For though thou wash thee with nitre, and
take thee much soap, *yet* thine iniquity is marked
before me, saith the Lord GOD.
23 How canst thou say, I am not polluted, I have
not gone after Baalim? see thy way in the valley,
know what thou hast done: *thou art* a swift
dromedary traversing her ways;
24 A wild ass used to the wilderness, *that* snuffeth
up the wind at her pleasure; in her occasion who
can turn her away? all they that seek her will not
weary themselves; in her month they shall find her.
25 Withhold thy foot from being unshod, and
thy throat from thirst: but thou saidst, There is
no hope: no; for I have loved strangers, and after
them will I go.
26 As the thief is ashamed when he is found, so
is the house of Israel ashamed; they, their kings,
their princes, and their priests, and their prophets,
27 Saying to a stock, Thou *art* my father; and to a
stone, Thou hast brought me forth: for they have
turned *their* back unto me, and not *their* face: but
in the time of their trouble they will say, Arise,
and save us.
28 But where *are* thy gods that thou hast made
thee? let them arise, if they can save thee in the
time of thy trouble: for *according to* the number
of thy cities are thy gods, O Judah.
29 Wherefore will ye plead with me? ye all have
transgressed against me, saith the LORD.
30 In vain have I smitten your children; they
received no correction: your own sword hath
devoured your prophets, like a destroying lion.
31 ¶ O generation, see ye the word of the LORD.
Have I been a wilderness unto Israel? a land of
darkness? wherefore say my people, We are lords;
we will come no more unto thee?
32 Can a maid forget her ornaments, *or* a bride
her attire? yet my people have forgotten me days
without number.
33 Why trimmest thou thy way to seek love?

---

toiled to cut (*hew*) cisterns that could not retain even stale water. Such is the futility of idolatry (Jer. 17:11–13).

2:14 *spoiled.* Plundered.

2:15–18 *young lions.* Picture of the fierce strength of Judah's enemies. *Noph.* Memphis, an ancient Egyptian capital. *Broken.* Literally, "graze upon," a reference to shaving the head, a gesture of shame and disgrace.

2:17–18 *procured this unto thyself.* Judah was responsible for everything that had come upon her. *Sihor.* Perhaps a canal, but most likely the Nile. Judah had sought not only after Egypt but after Assyria as well (the Euphrates *river*).

2:19 *Thine own wickedness shall correct* (chastise) *thee.* Chastisement comes solely as a result of their wickedness (Isa. 59:12). *my fear is not in thee.* They were destitute of any sense of true worship and faith, and therefore would receive no pardon.

2:20 *I have broken.* The Greek Septuagint reads the verb as second person: "*thou* hast broken"—the nation's rebellion. Retaining the first person refers to the Lord's liberating them from bondage in Egypt, in response to which Israel promised they would not *transgress* against His law by *playing the harlot*. Tragically, they broke the promise.

2:21 Israel had been planted as *a noble vine*. The Lord made every provision for His people to be spiritually fruitful (Isa. 5:1–4), but they became a *strange vine* (wild or foreign).

2:22 *nitre.* Alkaline mineral such as saltpeter or carbonate of soda. Their attempts at self-cleansing would avail them nothing (4:14; Mal. 3:2).

2:23–24 Two animals picture Judah's treachery and idolatry: the *dromedary*, a young female camel, running here and there in a fickle manner (*traversing her ways*), and the female *wild ass* in heat (*in her month*) aggressively pursuing every male she smells (*snuffeth*).

2:25 Judah had deserted the Lord, so when trouble came they looked to foreign powers (*strangers*) for help; they would eventually go barefoot (*unshod*) and thirsty into the captivity.

2:26 Judah is depicted as a publically disgraced *thief*. Yet the sense of the word "ashamed" indicates that they were not truly repentant.

2:27–28 *stock.* Wooden block made into an idol. How foolish to imagine that a piece of wood or stone, fashioned by men, could possibly hear and answer prayers (Ps. 115:4–8).

2:29 Having rejected God in times of peace, they now seek Him when in trouble, hoping He will forget their sins and help them. The unrepentant pray in vain (Ps. 66:18; Prov. 15:8).

2:31 The *wilderness* (v. 6) is an uncomfortable place, lacking in water and devoid of edible vegetation, a place where it is easy to lose one's way, a place of danger.

2:32 A young woman on her wedding day would not forget her bridal *attire*, yet Judah had forgotten the Lord, while clinging to outward religion (Pss. 78:10–11; 106:13).

2:33 *Why trimmest thou thy way.* Literally, "How do you make

therefore hast thou also taught the wicked ones
thy ways.
34 Also in thy skirts is found the blood of the
souls of the poor innocents: I have not found it by
secret search, but upon all these.
35 Yet thou sayest, Because I am innocent, surely
his anger shall turn from me. Behold, I will plead
with thee, because thou sayest, I have not sinned.
36 Why gaddest thou about so much to change
thy way? thou also shalt be ashamed of Egypt, as
thou wast ashamed of Assyria.
37 Yea, thou shalt go forth from him, and thine
hands upon thine head: for the LORD hath rejected
thy confidences, and thou shalt not prosper in
them.

CHAPTER 3

THEY say, If a man put away his wife, and she go
from him, and become another man's, shall he re-
turn unto her again? shall not that land be greatly
polluted? but thou hast played the harlot with
many lovers; yet return again to me, saith the LORD.
2 Lift up thine eyes unto the high places, and see
where thou hast not been lien with. In the ways
hast thou sat for them, as the Arabian in the
wilderness; and thou hast polluted the land with
thy whoredoms and with thy wickedness.
3 Therefore the showers have been withholden,
and there hath been no latter rain; and thou hadst
a whore's forehead, thou refusedst to be ashamed.
4 Wilt thou not from this time cry unto me, My
father, thou *art* the guide of my youth?
5 Will he reserve *his anger* for ever? will he keep
it to the end? Behold, thou hast spoken and done
evil things as thou couldest.
6 ¶ The LORD said also unto me in the days
of Josiah the king, Hast thou seen *that* which
backsliding Israel hath done? she is gone up upon
every high mountain and under every green tree,
and there hath played the harlot.
7 And I said after she had done all these *things*,
Turn thou unto me. But she returned not. And
her treacherous sister Judah saw *it*.
8 And I saw, when for all the causes whereby
backsliding Israel committed adultery I had put
her away, and given her a bill of divorce; yet her
treacherous sister Judah feared not, but went and
played the harlot also.
9 And it came to pass through the lightness of
her whoredom, that she defiled the land, and
committed adultery with stones and with stocks.
10 And yet for all this her treacherous sister Judah
hath not turned unto me with her whole heart,
but feignedly, saith the LORD.
11 And the LORD said unto me, The backsliding
Israel hath justified herself more than treacher-
ous Judah.

---

good (or adorn) your way?" an allusion to women who seek to make themselves attractive to other men besides their husbands. Israel's spiritual adultery even went beyond the sins of adulterous women (*taught the wicked ones*).

2:34 This may refer to Manasseh's crimes (2 Kings 21:16) or, more likely, to the shed blood of the prophets (v. 30). *by secret search.* Literally, "by breaking in." The guilt was obvious.

2:35 Judah was guilty of rejecting God's covenant and of hostility toward His prophets; yet they declared they had not sinned, thus revealing that the truth was not in them (1 John 1:8). *Behold, I will plead with thee.* The Hebrew means "to judge in order to bring justice"; to condemn or contend with the notion of punishing.

2:36 *gaddest . . . about.* Go about. Turning away from the Lord only ends in disaster. *Assyria* and *Egypt* were fickle, unreliable as allies, acting only in self-interest.

2:37 *hands upon thine head.* As mourners or prisoners. *confidences.* Those on whom they relied.

Thoughts for Personal/Family Worship: Chapter 2

1. **When we backslide from the Lord, He brings to remembrance the love that we had at first (vv. 2–3; Rev. 2:4). If we feel our love for the Lord and His people cooling, let us remember former days when it burned hot and bright. What zeal we once had and what gratitude for His forgiveness and love! Such remembering can stir the backslidden heart to desire repentance, that it may taste again of God's living waters.**
2. **How foolish it is to reject the Lord. If we have the fountain, we need nothing more. Blessing and salvation are freely available to those who would come (Rev. 22:17). Come to the Lord Jesus, for He says, "Whosoever drinketh of the water that I shall give him shall never thirst; but the water that I shall give him shall be in him a well of water springing up into everlasting life" (John 4:14). In what ways do you need Him today?**

A Call to Repentance (3:1—4:4)

Chapter 3: ***After a description of the nation's sin, the Lord commands repentance and gives promises to the penitent.***

3:1 Judah's breaking of the covenant is depicted in terms of a wife who has been unfaithful to her husband (Hos. 1–3). *but thou hast played the harlot.* God had set them apart to be His own, and yet they are defiled and polluted by their spiritual adultery. *Yet return again to me.* In mercy, patience, and love the Lord invites them to return (Isa. 1:18–19).

3:2 *where thou has not been lien with.* Literally, "where you have not been ravished." When the human heart becomes promiscuous and wanton, it becomes oblivious to any wrongdoing.

3:3 Sin causes the *showers* of God's blessing to dry up (1 Kings 17:1). The *latter rain* fell in March and April and was vital for a fruitful crop. Ironically, Judah turned to Baal in the hope of plentiful rain, but by withholding the rain the Lord revealed that false religion was a delusion. *whore's forehead.* Blatant sin rendered the conscience insensitive (6:15).

3:4 When the nation was young they looked to God as their *guide*, literally, "friend."

3:6 *backsliding.* Falling away or apostasy. *high mountain . . . green tree.* Places associated with pagan and sensual worship.

3:9 *lightness.* Frivolity or thoughtlessness. *stones . . . stocks.* Idols made from stone and wood.

3:10 *feignedly.* With falsehood.

12 ¶ Go and proclaim these words toward the
north, and say, Return, thou backsliding Israel,
saith the LORD; *and* I will not cause mine anger to
fall upon you: for I *am* merciful, saith the LORD,
and I will not keep *anger* for ever.
13 Only acknowledge thine iniquity, that thou
hast transgressed against the LORD thy God, and
hast scattered thy ways to the strangers under
every green tree, and ye have not obeyed my voice,
saith the LORD.
14 Turn, O backsliding children, saith the LORD;
for I am married unto you: and I will take you
one of a city, and two of a family, and I will bring
you to Zion:
15 And I will give you pastors according to mine
heart, which shall feed you with knowledge and
understanding.
16 And it shall come to pass, when ye be multi-
plied and increased in the land, in those days,
saith the LORD, they shall say no more, The ark of
the covenant of the LORD: neither shall it come to
mind: neither shall they remember it; neither shall
they visit *it*; neither shall *that* be done any more.
17 At that time they shall call Jerusalem the
throne of the LORD; and all the nations shall be
gathered unto it, to the name of the LORD, to
Jerusalem: neither shall they walk any more after
the imagination of their evil heart.
18 In those days the house of Judah shall walk
with the house of Israel, and they shall come to-
gether out of the land of the north to the land that
I have given for an inheritance unto your fathers.
19 But I said, How shall I put thee among the
children, and give thee a pleasant land, a goodly
heritage of the hosts of nations? and I said, Thou
shalt call me, My father; and shalt not turn away
from me.
20 ¶ Surely *as* a wife treacherously departeth
from her husband, so have ye dealt treacherously
with me, O house of Israel, saith the LORD.
21 A voice was heard upon the high places,
weeping *and* supplications of the children of
Israel: for they have perverted their way, *and* they
have forgotten the LORD their God.
22 Return, ye backsliding children, *and* I will heal
your backslidings. Behold, we come unto thee; for
thou *art* the LORD our God.
23 Truly in vain *is salvation hoped for* from the
hills, *and from* the multitude of mountains: truly
in the LORD our God *is* the salvation of Israel.
24 For shame hath devoured the labour of our
fathers from our youth; their flocks and their
herds, their sons and their daughters.
25 We lie down in our shame, and our confusion
covereth us: for we have sinned against the LORD
our God, we and our fathers, from our youth even
unto this day, and have not obeyed the voice of
the LORD our God.

CHAPTER 4

IF thou wilt return, O Israel, saith the LORD,
return unto me: and if thou wilt put away thine
abominations out of my sight, then shalt thou not
remove.
2 And thou shalt swear, The LORD liveth, in
truth, in judgment, and in righteousness; and the
nations shall bless themselves in him, and in him
shall they glory.
3 ¶ For thus saith the LORD to the men of Judah
and Jerusalem, Break up your fallow ground, and
sow not among thorns.
4 Circumcise yourselves to the LORD, and take
away the foreskins of your heart, ye men of Judah

3:12–14 The words *return* and *turn* are the same in Hebrew; this Hebrew word is the principal word for "repentance." The Lord tenderly calls sinners to repent and promises to receive all who do.
3:16 See Ezek. 36:11; Hos. 1:10. The *ark* was the only furniture in the Holy of Holies. However, the type and shadow were to give way to the glorious reality of Christ Himself, who is the true tabernacle (John 1:14) and mercy seat (Rom. 3:25).
3:17–18 *imagination.* Stubbornness. *land of the north.* Babylon, the place of exile. This prophecy seems to point to the spiritual, heavenly *Jerusalem* rather than to a physical place (John 4:21–24; Gal. 4:26; Rev. 21:2–3) where nothing that corrupts is permitted to enter (1 Peter 1:3–4).
3:23 *from the hills . . . mountains.* The supposed places of residence for the pagan gods.
3:25 *confusion.* Shame or disgrace. Recognizing that Jehovah is the only source of salvation (v. 23) involves confession of sin.

Thoughts for Personal/Family Worship: Chapter 3

1. **Many professing Christians behave as Judah did. They assume that as long as they pay lip service to God, they can live as they please and all will still be well. But becoming a true child of God results in a true change (Ezek. 36:25–27). Those united to Christ cannot live in sin any longer (Rom. 6:1–4).**
2. **Idolatry, greed, selfishness, and immorality are all fruits that find their root in the hardness and sinfulness of an unregenerate heart. Godly reformation, the kind that Josiah enforced, may strip away evil fruits, but it cannot reach the root or source of the problem, which is the hardened heart of unbelief. We learn from Judah's treachery the depravity of the human heart. The Lord Jesus says in Matt. 15:19, "For out of the heart proceed evil thoughts, murders, adulteries, fornications, thefts, false witness, blasphemies." How then can people ever change?**

Chapter 4: ***A graphic account of the inevitable consequences of sin follows a further plea to return to the Lord.***

4:1 *abominations.* Detestable, hateful things, here idols. *not remove.* Not be homeless or wander aimlessly.
4:2 *The nations shall bless themselves.* As promised to Abraham (Gen. 12:3).
4:3 *Break up your fallow ground.* Plough that ground that has never been tilled.

and inhabitants of Jerusalem: lest my fury come
forth like fire, and burn that none can quench *it*,
because of the evil of your doings.
5 Declare ye in Judah, and publish in Jerusalem;
and say, Blow ye the trumpet in the land: cry,
gather together, and say, Assemble yourselves, and
let us go into the defenced cities.
6 Set up the standard toward Zion: retire, stay
not: for I will bring evil from the north, and a
great destruction.
7 The lion is come up from his thicket, and the
destroyer of the Gentiles is on his way; he is gone
forth from his place to make thy land desolate;
and thy cities shall be laid waste, without an
inhabitant.
8 For this gird you with sackcloth, lament and
howl: for the fierce anger of the LORD is not
turned back from us.
9 And it shall come to pass at that day, saith the
LORD, *that* the heart of the king shall perish, and
the heart of the princes; and the priests shall be
astonished, and the prophets shall wonder.
10 Then said I, Ah, Lord GOD! surely thou hast
greatly deceived this people and Jerusalem,
saying, Ye shall have peace; whereas the sword
reacheth unto the soul.
11 At that time shall it be said to this people and
to Jerusalem, A dry wind of the high places in the
wilderness toward the daughter of my people, not
to fan, nor to cleanse,
12 *Even* a full wind from those *places* shall come
unto me: now also will I give sentence against
them.
13 Behold, he shall come up as clouds, and
his chariots *shall be* as a whirlwind: his horses
are swifter than eagles. Woe unto us! for we are
spoiled.
14 O Jerusalem, wash thine heart from wicked-
ness, that thou mayest be saved. How long shall
thy vain thoughts lodge within thee?
15 For a voice declareth from Dan, and publisheth
affliction from mount Ephraim.
16 Make ye mention to the nations; behold,
publish against Jerusalem, *that* watchers come
from a far country, and give out their voice against
the cities of Judah.
17 As keepers of a field, are they against her round
about; because she hath been rebellious against
me, saith the LORD.
18 Thy way and thy doings have procured these
things unto thee; this *is* thy wickedness, because
it is bitter, because it reacheth unto thine heart.
19 ¶ My bowels, my bowels! I am pained at my
very heart; my heart maketh a noise in me; I
cannot hold my peace, because thou hast heard,
O my soul, the sound of the trumpet, the alarm
of war.
20 Destruction upon destruction is cried; for
the whole land is spoiled: suddenly are my tents
spoiled, *and* my curtains in a moment.
21 How long shall I see the standard, *and* hear the
sound of the trumpet?
22 For my people *is* foolish, they have not known
me; they *are* sottish children, and they have none
understanding: they *are* wise to do evil, but to do
good they have no knowledge.
23 I beheld the earth, and, lo, *it was* without
form, and void; and the heavens, and they *had*
no light.
24 I beheld the mountains, and, lo, they trembled,
and all the hills moved lightly.
25 I beheld, and, lo, *there was* no man, and all the
birds of the heavens were fled.
26 I beheld, and, lo, the fruitful place *was* a
wilderness, and all the cities thereof were broken
down at the presence of the LORD, *and* by his
fierce anger.
27 For thus hath the LORD said, The whole land
shall be desolate; yet will I not make a full end.
28 For this shall the earth mourn, and the heavens

4:4 The outward sign of circumcision reveals the need for an inward work of grace (9:26; Lev. 26:41; Deut. 10:16; 30:6; Acts 7:51; Rom. 2:28–29; Phil. 3:3; Col. 2:11–13).

Judgment Is Coming (4:5—6:30)

4:5–6 *trumpet.* An alarm (Ezek. 33:4), warning of emergency and causing fear of impending doom. *set up the standard.* Raise the flag. *evil from the north.* Calamity from Babylon.

4:7 *lion.* Fierce invader. *destroyer of the Gentiles.* One who ruins nations.

4:8 *gird.* Secure with a belt. *sackcloth.* Uncomfortable clothing worn in mourning. The people would not weep over their sins and repent, therefore they would cry bitterly over their destruction (Lam. 1:2). *fierce.* Literally, "fierce heat"; describes God's anger (Heb. 12:29).

4:10 *deceived this people.* A hard statement to interpret. Most likely it reflects the delusion of false prophets and those who followed them (6:14; 8:11; Ezek. 14:9–10; 2 Thess. 2:10–12).

4:11–13 The invading Chaldeans are portrayed as a hot, destructive *wind*, and as fierce storm *clouds* that cause great suffering (Isa. 5:28; 66:15; Ezek. 38:16).

4:14 *heart.* The inner being, including the mind, affections, and will, must be cleansed (Acts 15:9).

4:16 *watchers.* The Babylonians who would lay siege to the city.

4:19 *bowels.* Internal organs, representing deep emotions, here extreme pain.

4:20 Their feeble dwellings (*tents*) would be violently blown away.

4:22 *sottish.* Stupid. Ignorance of God and lack of moral discernment are the height of folly.

4:23 *without form and void . . . no light.* Judgment is a reversal of creation (Gen. 1:2–3), especially the final judgment (Rev. 6:12,14; 20:11).

4:27 *not make a full end.* The Lord will always have a remnant (Isa. 1:9). This should comfort believers.

4:28 *will not repent.* Will not relent. God's purpose stands firm.

above be black: because I have spoken *it*, I have
purposed *it*, and will not repent, neither will I
turn back from it.
29 The whole city shall flee for the noise of
the horsemen and bowmen; they shall go into
thickets, and climb up upon the rocks: every city
shall be forsaken, and not a man dwell therein.
30 And *when* thou *art* spoiled, what wilt thou
do? Though thou clothest thyself with crimson,
though thou deckest thee with ornaments of
gold, though thou rentest thy face with painting,
in vain shalt thou make thyself fair; *thy* lovers will
despise thee, they will seek thy life.
31 For I have heard a voice as of a woman in
travail, *and* the anguish as of her that bringeth
forth her first child, the voice of the daughter
of Zion, *that* bewaileth herself, *that* spreadeth
her hands, *saying*, Woe *is* me now! for my soul is
wearied because of murderers.

CHAPTER 5

Run ye to and fro through the streets of Jerusalem,
and see now, and know, and seek in the broad
places thereof, if ye can find a man, if there be *any*
that executeth judgment, that seeketh the truth;
and I will pardon it.
2 And though they say, The LORD liveth; surely
they swear falsely.
3 O LORD, *are* not thine eyes upon the truth? thou
hast stricken them, but they have not grieved;
thou hast consumed them, *but* they have refused
to receive correction: they have made their faces
harder than a rock; they have refused to return.
4 Therefore I said, Surely these *are* poor; they are
foolish: for they know not the way of the LORD,
nor the judgment of their God.
5 I will get me unto the great men, and will speak
unto them; for they have known the way of the
LORD, *and* the judgment of their God: but these
have altogether broken the yoke, *and* burst the
bonds.
6 Wherefore a lion out of the forest shall slay
them, *and* a wolf of the evenings shall spoil them,
a leopard shall watch over their cities: every one
that goeth out thence shall be torn in pieces:
because their transgressions are many, *and* their
backslidings are increased.
7 ¶ How shall I pardon thee for this? thy children
have forsaken me, and sworn by *them that are* no
gods: when I had fed them to the full, they then
committed adultery, and assembled themselves
by troops in the harlots' houses.
8 They were *as* fed horses in the morning: every
one neighed after his neighbour's wife.
9 Shall I not visit for these *things?* saith the LORD:
and shall not my soul be avenged on such a nation
as this?
10 ¶ Go ye up upon her walls, and destroy; but
make not a full end: take away her battlements;
for they *are* not the LORD's.
11 For the house of Israel and the house of Judah
have dealt very treacherously against me, saith the
LORD.

4:30 *thou rentest thy face with painting.* Literally, "you enlarged your eyes with eye make-up." The picture is of Judah acting as a prostitute, seeking to entice favor in the hope of avoiding calamity, only to be despised and rejected.

Thoughts for Personal/Family Worship: Chapter 4

1. **The warnings of judgment given to Judah look forward to that great and terrible day of the Lord when Christ returns in glory. It is a great blessing when God gives us such warnings and makes us willing to listen to them. There is no greater comfort in the day of wrath than to know that we are in Christ Jesus (Rom. 8:1; 1 Thess. 1:10; 5:9). What reasons does this chapter give us to flee to Christ and cling to Him by faith?**
2. **God's judgment of reversing creation begins in the spiritual disorder of those who claim to be His people. This judgment can be seen in churches today that once had order in worship and the light of the gospel but have descended into disorder and darkness. Let us be careful to cling to God's Word by faith and obedience, and then we can take great comfort that the Lord will not make "a full end" of His church.**

Chapter 5: ***The Lord announces His judgment against Judah for their atrocious sins.***

5:1 *broad places.* Public meeting places, such as markets and streets. *executeth judgment.* Does what is just. Very few were willing to publicly stand for righteousness and truth.

5:2 *The LORD liveth.* Common oath formula. *swear falsely.* Lie under oath.

5:3 *refused to return.* In spite of the Lord's chastening, they refused to repent (Amos 4:6–11).

5:4 *poor.* The Hebrew can mean "small" or "insignificant." *foolish.* Specifically wicked folly.

5:5–6 *great men.* Leaders who, although knowing the way of the Lord, in utter defiance and rebellion have chosen to ignore God's decrees. *broken the yoke.* Set aside the Lord's restraints (Ps. 2:1–3), like rebellious livestock. *wolf of the evenings.* Literally, "a wolf of the deserts," where they roam. *watch.* Lurk or lie in wait. Their escape from the Lord's yoke forgoes the protection of the stall, and they become the prey of wicked men.

5:7 *assembled themselves by troops.* The Hebrew means "they gash themselves," a common ritual in Baal worship (1 Kings 18:28). *harlots' houses.* Most likely places of cultic prostitution. Their rejection of the Lord and desiring of false gods resulted in unbridled lust.

5:8 *fed horses.* The Hebrew word occurs only here and mostly likely refers to horses roaming around in the time of rut (*the morning*)—a graphic image of lustful promiscuity.

5:9 *visit.* Inspect or examine, frequently used of God's knowledge and judgment.

5:10 *destroy.* Devastate by pulling down. *battlements.* The Hebrew word means "tendril" or "offshoot"; here it most likely refers to the offshoot of a wall.

5:11 *dealt very treacherously.* The verb designates unfaithful

12 They have belied the LORD, and said, *It is* not
he; neither shall evil come upon us; neither shall
we see sword nor famine:
13 And the prophets shall become wind, and the
word *is* not in them: thus shall it be done unto them.
14 Wherefore thus saith the LORD God of hosts,
Because ye speak this word, behold, I will make
my words in thy mouth fire, and this people
wood, and it shall devour them.
15 Lo, I will bring a nation upon you from far,
O house of Israel, saith the LORD: it *is* a mighty
nation, it *is* an ancient nation, a nation whose
language thou knowest not, neither understandest
what they say.
16 Their quiver *is* as an open sepulchre, they *are*
all mighty men.
17 And they shall eat up thine harvest, and thy
bread, *which* thy sons and thy daughters should
eat: they shall eat up thy flocks and thine herds:
they shall eat up thy vines and thy fig trees: they
shall impoverish thy fenced cities, wherein thou
trustedst, with the sword.
18 Nevertheless in those days, saith the LORD, I
will not make a full end with you.
19 ¶ And it shall come to pass, when ye shall say,
Wherefore doeth the LORD our God all these
things unto us? then shalt thou answer them, Like
as ye have forsaken me, and served strange gods
in your land, so shall ye serve strangers in a land
that is not yours.
20 Declare this in the house of Jacob, and publish
it in Judah, saying,
21 Hear now this, O foolish people, and without
understanding; which have eyes, and see not;
which have ears, and hear not:
22 Fear ye not me? saith the LORD: will ye not
tremble at my presence, which have placed the
sand *for* the bound of the sea by a perpetual decree,
that it cannot pass it: and though the waves thereof
toss themselves, yet can they not prevail; though
they roar, yet can they not pass over it?
23 But this people hath a revolting and a
rebellious heart; they are revolted and gone.
24 Neither say they in their heart, Let us now
fear the LORD our God, that giveth rain, both the
former and the latter, in his season: he reserveth
unto us the appointed weeks of the harvest.
25 ¶ Your iniquities have turned away these
things, and your sins have withholden good *things*
from you.
26 For among my people are found wicked *men*:
they lay wait, as he that setteth snares; they set a
trap, they catch men.
27 As a cage is full of birds, so *are* their houses
full of deceit: therefore they are become great, and
waxen rich.
28 They are waxen fat, they shine: yea, they over-
pass the deeds of the wicked: they judge not the
cause, the cause of the fatherless, yet they prosper;
and the right of the needy do they not judge.
29 Shall I not visit for these *things?* saith the LORD:
shall not my soul be avenged on such a nation as
this?
30 ¶ A wonderful and horrible thing is commit-
ted in the land;
31 The prophets prophesy falsely, and the priests
bear rule by their means; and my people love *to
have it* so: and what will ye do in the end thereof?

acts (spiritual adultery), and the grammar removes all doubt about the certainty of the accusation.

5:12 *belied.* Denied. *Evil.* Disaster or danger, not sin.

5:13 Denying the Lord included denying the prophetic word.

5:14 *make my words in thy mouth fire.* An image of the power of God's Word to condemn those who reject it (Rev. 11:5).

5:15 *I will bring.* The Babylonians were the instruments of the Lord's judgment.

5:17 *wherein thou trustedst.* Jeremiah repeatedly highlights the object of a people's trust as the decisive factor in their salvation or destruction (7:4,8,14; 9:4; 12:5; 13:25; 17:5,7; 28:15; 29:31; 39:18; 46:25; 48:7; 49:4,11).

5:18 Some regard these words as a token of mercy (4:27; 5:10). Others, including John Calvin, interpret them as meaning the calamities will have no end.

5:19 *strange.* Foreign. *strangers.* Foreign people. *Like as . . . so.* Their punishment corresponded to their sin—poetic justice.

5:21 *eyes, and see not.* Spiritual blindness (Deut. 29:4; Isa. 6:10; Mark 8:18).

5:22 There is nothing more foolish than a failure to *fear* the Almighty. As the powerful *sea* cannot alter God's established borders for it, so sinners cannot escape His judgment.

5:23–25 *revolting . . . rebellious.* The heart is stubborn and recalcitrant. In their rebellion they fail to acknowledge God's provision (Acts 14:17; Rom. 2:4), so they will not experience His kindness.

5:26–28 As the fowler uses *snares* and a *trap* to catch *birds*, so the wicked use similar methods to catch unsuspecting men and women (Prov. 7:21–23).

5:29 *visit.* See note at v. 9.

5:30 *wonderful.* Horrific or atrocious.

5:31 A terrible indictment (2 Peter 2:1–2) and an urgent question.

Thoughts for Personal/Family Worship: Chapter 5

1. **In a time of great spiritual decline, the Lord challenged Jeremiah to find just one man who publicly stood for truth and righteousness so that the Lord would pardon the city. We see the mercy of God wonderfully revealed here. He would have spared Sodom if *ten* righteous men could have been found there (Gen. 18:23–32); yet though Jerusalem's sins exceed those of Sodom (Ezek. 16:48) the Lord asks for just *one* man. How are you standing in the gap (22:30) by advocating for and doing justice in society?**
2. **The nation of Judah behaved despicably toward the Lord, yet they still thought highly of themselves. We see the same thing today. The judgment of God is coming, and it will be a terrifying thing (Rev. 20:11–15). Sadly, many will not believe this until it comes upon them. Repent of every sin now, before it is too late.**

CHAPTER 6

O YE children of Benjamin, gather yourselves to
flee out of the midst of Jerusalem, and blow the
trumpet in Tekoa, and set up a sign of fire in Beth-
haccerem: for evil appeareth out of the north, and
great destruction.
2 I have likened the daughter of Zion to a comely
and delicate *woman*.
3 The shepherds with their flocks shall come unto
her; they shall pitch *their* tents against her round
about; they shall feed every one in his place.
4 Prepare ye war against her; arise, and let us go
up at noon. Woe unto us! for the day goeth away,
for the shadows of the evening are stretched out.
5 Arise, and let us go by night, and let us destroy
her palaces.
6 ¶ For thus hath the LORD of hosts said, Hew ye
down trees, and cast a mount against Jerusalem:
this *is* the city to be visited; she *is* wholly oppres-
sion in the midst of her.
7 As a fountain casteth out her waters, so she
casteth out her wickedness: violence and spoil is
heard in her; before me continually *is* grief and
wounds.
8 Be thou instructed, O Jerusalem, lest my soul
depart from thee; lest I make thee desolate, a land
not inhabited.
9 ¶ Thus saith the LORD of hosts, They shall
throughly glean the remnant of Israel as a vine:
turn back thine hand as a grapegatherer into the
baskets.
10 To whom shall I speak, and give warning, that
they may hear? behold, their ear *is* uncircumcised,
and they cannot hearken: behold, the word of
the LORD is unto them a reproach; they have no
delight in it.
11 Therefore I am full of the fury of the LORD; I am
weary with holding in: I will pour it out upon the
children abroad, and upon the assembly of young
men together: for even the husband with the wife
shall be taken, the aged with *him that is* full of days.
12 And their houses shall be turned unto others,
with their fields and wives together: for I will
stretch out my hand upon the inhabitants of the
land, saith the LORD.
13 For from the least of them even unto the great-
est of them every one *is* given to covetousness;
and from the prophet even unto the priest every
one dealeth falsely.
14 They have healed also the hurt *of the daughter*
of my people slightly, saying, Peace, peace; when
there is no peace.
15 Were they ashamed when they had committed
abomination? nay, they were not at all ashamed,
neither could they blush: therefore they shall fall
among them that fall: at the time *that* I visit them
they shall be cast down, saith the LORD.
16 Thus saith the LORD, Stand ye in the ways, and
see, and ask for the old paths, where *is* the good
way, and walk therein, and ye shall find rest for
your souls. But they said, We will not walk *therein*.
17 Also I set watchmen over you, *saying*, Hearken
to the sound of the trumpet. But they said, We
will not hearken.
18 ¶ Therefore hear, ye nations, and know, O
congregation, what *is* among them.
19 Hear, O earth: behold, I will bring evil upon
this people, *even* the fruit of their thoughts,
because they have not hearkened unto my words,
nor to my law, but rejected it.
20 To what purpose cometh there to me incense
from Sheba, and the sweet cane from a far
country? your burnt offerings *are* not acceptable,
nor your sacrifices sweet unto me.
21 Therefore thus saith the LORD, Behold, I will
lay stumblingblocks before this people, and the
fathers and the sons together shall fall upon them;
the neighbour and his friend shall perish.
22 Thus saith the LORD, Behold, a people cometh
from the north country, and a great nation shall
be raised from the sides of the earth.
23 They shall lay hold on bow and spear; they *are*

Chapter 6: *The Lord continues to warn the sinful and rebellious people that judgment is surely coming.*

6:1 *trumpet.* Ram's horn used to sound alarms. *sign of fire.* An ancient means of long-distance communication. *evil.* Disaster. *of the north.* From Babylon.

6:2–3 Note that *woman* is in italics, signifying that it is not in the original Hebrew text. The reference may not be to *a comely and delicate woman* but to "a tenderly cared-for meadow (or pasture)" to which the *shepherds* (the enemies) will come and feed.

6:4–6 The enemy is eager to destroy. *cast a mount.* Construct an assault ramp.

6:7 A picture of a corrupt heart, from which all iniquities and evils flow unchecked by conscience (Prov. 4:23; Matt. 15:19–20).

6:10 *uncircumcised.* Incapable of hearing God (Acts 7:51).

6:11 *full of the fury of the LORD.* God's Spirit fills His servants with His holy zeal to preach against sin (20:9; Ps. 39:3; Mic. 3:8).

6:13 *the prophet . . . the priest . . . dealeth falsely.* It is a crime of the worst kind when men entrusted with the leadership of God's people seek to turn them away from the truth.

6:14 See notes at 4:10; 8:11.

6:16 *old paths.* The fundamental principles of true religion revealed in Scripture. Jeremiah, like every true prophet since Moses, was a reformer, not an innovator. *rest for your souls.* See Matt. 11:28–29.

6:19 *evil.* Disastrous punishment. *fruit of their thoughts.* Punishment is the natural product of what they have devised. They get what they deserve—always a fearful prospect.

6:20 *Sheba*, in southwest Arabia, was a center for expensive spices, precious stones, and gold (Ezek. 27:22). *far country.* Most likely India. Worship can be expensive but worthless (Ps. 51:16–17).

6:22 *from the north.* Babylon. *from the sides of the earth.* From the remote parts of the earth.

cruel, and have no mercy; their voice roareth like
the sea; and they ride upon horses, set in array
as men for war against thee, O daughter of Zion.
24 We have heard the fame thereof: our hands
wax feeble: anguish hath taken hold of us, *and*
pain, as of a woman in travail.
25 Go not forth into the field, nor walk by the
way; for the sword of the enemy *and* fear *is* on
every side.
26 ¶ O daughter of my people, gird *thee* with
sackcloth, and wallow thyself in ashes: make
thee mourning, *as for* an only son, most bitter
lamentation: for the spoiler shall suddenly come
upon us.
27 I have set thee *for* a tower *and* a fortress among
my people, that thou mayest know and try their
way.
28 They *are* all grievous revolters, walking with
slanders: *they are* brass and iron; they *are* all
corrupters.
29 The bellows are burned, the lead is consumed
of the fire; the founder melteth in vain: for the
wicked are not plucked away.
30 Reprobate silver shall *men* call them, because
the LORD hath rejected them.

CHAPTER 7

THE word that came to Jeremiah from the LORD,
saying,
2 Stand in the gate of the LORD's house, and
proclaim there this word, and say, Hear the word
of the LORD, all *ye of* Judah, that enter in at these
gates to worship the LORD.
3 Thus saith the LORD of hosts, the God of Israel,
Amend your ways and your doings, and I will
cause you to dwell in this place.
4 Trust ye not in lying words, saying, The temple
of the LORD, The temple of the LORD, The temple
of the LORD, *are* these.
5 For if ye throughly amend your ways and your
doings; if ye throughly execute judgment between
a man and his neighbour;
6 *If* ye oppress not the stranger, the fatherless,
and the widow, and shed not innocent blood in
this place, neither walk after other gods to your
hurt:
7 Then will I cause you to dwell in this place, in
the land that I gave to your fathers, for ever and
ever.
8 ¶ Behold, ye trust in lying words, that cannot
profit.
9 Will ye steal, murder, and commit adultery, and
swear falsely, and burn incense unto Baal, and
walk after other gods whom ye know not;
10 And come and stand before me in this house,
which is called by my name, and say, We are
delivered to do all these abominations?
11 Is this house, which is called by my name,
become a den of robbers in your eyes? Behold,
even I have seen *it*, saith the LORD.
12 But go ye now unto my place which *was* in

6:24 *the fame thereof.* The news or report about Babylon.
6:25 *fear is on every side.* The taunting name Jeremiah gave to Pashur (20:1–3).
6:26 *gird.* Secure with a belt.
6:27 The Lord reminds Jeremiah of His initial promise and commission (1:18).
6:29–30 *founder.* Person who casts metal in a mold. *are not plucked away.* Dross that is not separated from the pure metal, so that the whole is rejected (*reprobate*).

Thoughts for Personal/Family Worship: Chapter 6

1. It was a terrible ordeal for the Jews to fall into the hands of Nebuchadnezzar, but "it is a fearful thing to fall into the hands of the living God" (Heb. 10:31). Like an erupting volcano, the wrath of God will be poured out upon the impenitent. What a comfort it is, then, to be able to say with the apostle Paul, "I know whom I have believed, and am persuaded that he is able to keep that which I have committed unto him against that day" (2 Tim. 1:12). Do you know this comfort? Why or why not?
2. The "old paths" are not the way of mere tradition but the fundamental truths of revealed religion (Col. 2:6–8). Jeremiah is not bidding us to live in the past, for we are to live in the present where God has placed us (Eccl. 7:10). To be in the "old paths" is to be in Christ and to abide in His Word; it is to walk after the Savior in holiness, meekness, obedience, and self-denial. Such is the way of peace and happiness.

The Futility of Believing False Promises and Rejecting Truth (7:1—8:17)

Chapter 7: *At the temple, the prophet warns against hypocritical religion, exposes sin, and warns of certain judgment.*

7:2 *Stand in the gate.* This is known as the Temple Sermon.
7:3 *Amend your ways and your doings.* Make good your habits of life and specific acts. Their sinful ways made their worship a sham.
7:4 *Trust.* Be confident or find security in: a principal word for faith in the Old Testament. Lies are worthless; therefore trusting them is foolish. *The temple of the LORD.* Its threefold repetition intensifies their feeling of confidence in an external place with its external rituals.
7:5–6 The two greatest commandments are addressed in reverse order: loving one's neighbor and loving God.
7:7 See Deut. 4:40.
7:8 *ye trust in lying words.* Literally, "you are trusting constantly for yourselves upon words of deception." The very thing Jeremiah commanded them not to do (v. 4) became their habitual practice.
7:9 The list of sins touches both parts of the moral law, as revealed in the Ten Commandments: first the sins against man and then those against God.
7:10–11 Although guilty of sin, they came to the Lord's house as if all was well. *den of robbers.* Cave or hideout where criminals felt safe—a picture of hypocrisy cloaked in outward piety (Mark 11:17). *I have seen.* The temple would be no hiding place for those who despised the Lord's covenant.

Shiloh, where I set my name at the first, and see
what I did to it for the wickedness of my people
Israel.
13 And now, because ye have done all these works,
saith the LORD, and I spake unto you, rising up
early and speaking, but ye heard not; and I called
you, but ye answered not;
14 Therefore will I do unto *this* house, which is
called by my name, wherein ye trust, and unto the
place which I gave to you and to your fathers, as I
have done to Shiloh.
15 And I will cast you out of my sight, as I have
cast out all your brethren, *even* the whole seed of
Ephraim.
16 Therefore pray not thou for this people,
neither lift up cry nor prayer for them, neither
make intercession to me: for I will not hear thee.
17 ¶ Seest thou not what they do in the cities of
Judah and in the streets of Jerusalem?
18 The children gather wood, and the fathers
kindle the fire, and the women knead *their* dough,
to make cakes to the queen of heaven, and to pour
out drink offerings unto other gods, that they
may provoke me to anger.
19 Do they provoke me to anger? saith the LORD:
do they not *provoke* themselves to the confusion
of their own faces?
20 Therefore thus saith the Lord GOD; Behold,
mine anger and my fury shall be poured out
upon this place, upon man, and upon beast, and
upon the trees of the field, and upon the fruit of
the ground; and it shall burn, and shall not be
quenched.
21 ¶ Thus saith the LORD of hosts, the God
of Israel; Put your burnt offerings unto your
sacrifices, and eat flesh.
22 For I spake not unto your fathers, nor
commanded them in the day that I brought
them out of the land of Egypt, concerning burnt
offerings or sacrifices:
23 But this thing commanded I them, saying,
Obey my voice, and I will be your God, and ye
shall be my people: and walk ye in all the ways
that I have commanded you, that it may be well
unto you.
24 But they hearkened not, nor inclined their ear,
but walked in the counsels *and* in the imagination
of their evil heart, and went backward, and not
forward.
25 Since the day that your fathers came forth out
of the land of Egypt unto this day I have even sent
unto you all my servants the prophets, daily rising
up early and sending *them*:
26 Yet they hearkened not unto me, nor inclined
their ear, but hardened their neck: they did worse
than their fathers.
27 Therefore thou shalt speak all these words
unto them; but they will not hearken to thee: thou
shalt also call unto them; but they will not answer
thee.
28 But thou shalt say unto them, This *is* a nation
that obeyeth not the voice of the LORD their God,
nor receiveth correction: truth is perished, and is
cut off from their mouth.
29 ¶ Cut off thine hair, *O Jerusalem*, and cast *it*
away, and take up a lamentation on high places;
for the LORD hath rejected and forsaken the
generation of his wrath.
30 For the children of Judah have done evil
in my sight, saith the LORD: they have set their
abominations in the house which is called by my
name, to pollute it.
31 And they have built the high places of Tophet,
which *is* in the valley of the son of Hinnom, to
burn their sons and their daughters in the fire;
which I commanded *them* not, neither came it
into my heart.
32 ¶ Therefore, behold, the days come, saith the
LORD, that it shall no more be called Tophet, nor
the valley of the son of Hinnom, but the valley of
slaughter: for they shall bury in Tophet, till there
be no place.
33 And the carcases of this people shall be meat
for the fowls of the heaven, and for the beasts of

7:12–15 *Shiloh.* Home of the tabernacle (Josh. 18:1) and the ark of the covenant. When the people regarded it almost as a lucky charm, the Lord delivered them into the hands of the Philistines (1 Sam. 4:3–11; Ps. 78:56–61). In Jeremiah's day, Shiloh was nothing but a pile of rubble. If the people did not repent, the Lord would destroy the temple, just as He had destroyed Shiloh. *rising up early and speaking.* Idiom for speaking earnestly.

7:16 When Israel rebelled in the wilderness, the Lord's wrath was kindled, but Moses interceded for them (Ex. 32:9–13). Yet the Lord forbade Jeremiah to pray for the people.

7:18 Idolatry had so infected the nation that it had become part of family life. *queen of heaven.* The Canaanite goddess Ashteroth, or Asherah (Persian Ishtar), which represents the whole of pagan worship so often connected to astrology (8:2).

7:22 *I spake not.* Though God commanded sacrifices, external religion without a genuine heart of faith, repentance, and obedience was never sufficient (Ps. 51:17; Hos. 6:6).

7:24 *imagination.* Hard-heartedness or stubbornness.

7:25 *daily rising up early and sending.* Idiom expressing earnestness and persistence. The Lord sent prophets over and again; the people had no excuse.

7:29 *thine hair.* Literally, "consecration or dedication," referring to the Nazirite vow not to cut their hair (Num. 6:5; Judg. 16:17). Jerusalem was no longer consecrated to the Lord.

7:30 *abominations.* Images of Baal and Ashteroth in the temple. The Jews purported to serve the Lord, but they thought the worshiping of other gods would also benefit them.

7:31 *high places.* Shrines and altars of sacrifice on elevated platforms of stones. *Tophet.* Perhaps a fireplace. The pagan practice of sacrificing children in the fire was directly forbidden under the law (Lev. 18:21; 20:2–5) but practiced by Manasseh (2 Kings 23:10).

7:33 *fray.* Frighten.

the earth; and none shall fray *them* away.
34 Then will I cause to cease from the cities of Ju-
dah, and from the streets of Jerusalem, the voice
of mirth, and the voice of gladness, the voice of
the bridegroom, and the voice of the bride: for the
land shall be desolate.

CHAPTER 8

AT that time, saith the LORD, they shall bring out
the bones of the kings of Judah, and the bones
of his princes, and the bones of the priests, and
the bones of the prophets, and the bones of the
inhabitants of Jerusalem, out of their graves:
2 And they shall spread them before the sun, and
the moon, and all the host of heaven, whom they
have loved, and whom they have served, and after
whom they have walked, and whom they have
sought, and whom they have worshipped: they
shall not be gathered, nor be buried; they shall be
for dung upon the face of the earth.
3 And death shall be chosen rather than life by
all the residue of them that remain of this evil
family, which remain in all the places whither I
have driven them, saith the LORD of hosts.
4 ¶ Moreover thou shalt say unto them, Thus
saith the LORD; Shall they fall, and not arise? shall
he turn away, and not return?
5 Why *then* is this people of Jerusalem slidden
back by a perpetual backsliding? they hold fast
deceit, they refuse to return.
6 I hearkened and heard, *but* they spake not
aright: no man repented him of his wickedness,
saying, What have I done? every one turned to his
course, as the horse rusheth into the battle.
7 Yea, the stork in the heaven knoweth her
appointed times; and the turtle and the crane and
the swallow observe the time of their coming; but
my people know not the judgment of the LORD.
8 How do ye say, We *are* wise, and the law of the
LORD *is* with us? Lo, certainly in vain made he *it*;
the pen of the scribes *is* in vain.
9 The wise *men* are ashamed, they are dismayed
and taken: lo, they have rejected the word of the
LORD; and what wisdom *is* in them?
10 Therefore will I give their wives unto others,
and their fields to them that shall inherit *them*:
for every one from the least even unto the greatest
is given to covetousness, from the prophet even
unto the priest every one dealeth falsely.
11 For they have healed the hurt of the daughter
of my people slightly, saying, Peace, peace; when
there is no peace.
12 Were they ashamed when they had committed
abomination? nay, they were not at all ashamed,
neither could they blush: therefore shall they
fall among them that fall: in the time of their
visitation they shall be cast down, saith the LORD.
13 ¶ I will surely consume them, saith the LORD:
there shall be no grapes on the vine, nor figs on
the fig tree, and the leaf shall fade; and *the things*
that I have given them shall pass away from them.
14 Why do we sit still? assemble yourselves, and
let us enter into the defenced cities, and let us
be silent there: for the LORD our God hath put
us to silence, and given us water of gall to drink,
because we have sinned against the LORD.
15 We looked for peace, but no good *came; and*
for a time of health, and behold trouble!
16 The snorting of his horses was heard from
Dan: the whole land trembled at the sound of the

7:34 *voice of mirth . . . voice of the bride*. God will remove all joy (Rev. 18:23).

Thoughts for Personal/Family Worship: Chapter 7

1. **The Temple Sermon is a warning against the danger of external religion without a sincere heart for the Lord. Judah thought that attending the temple and going through all the prescribed rituals would satisfy God. They were like so many today who think that simply going to church is enough. The Lord does not ask for a mere form of godliness. He requires true adoration from a contrite heart and a reverent, humble spirit. When sincerity is absent from the heart, then all religion and worship are a lie.**
2. **It was a terrible tragedy that Judah's sin had become so ingrained and widespread that the day of grace was over for them, so that further intercession on their behalf was pointless. God had been patient and longsuffering, but they would not hear His voice and must therefore face His judgment. Oh that the Lord would have mercy on our own generation, for if things continue as they are the day of grace may soon be over!**

Chapter 8: ***The prophet describes the horrors of judgment to come because of the perpetual sins of the nation.***

8:1–3 *They shall bring*. The Babylonians would break open the sepulchers of Judah's former rulers and spread the bones before the astral deities that Judah had chosen to worship (Acts 7:42)—evidence that their so-called gods had no interest in or ability to aid their worshipers, even when they would rather die than live (Rev. 9:6).
8:5 *perpetual backsliding*. Ongoing apostasy. *return*. The principal Hebrew word for "repent." Refusal to repent marks the apostate.
8:7 *turtle*. Turtle-dove. Birds by instinct know their appointed seasons, but Judah lacked any sensitivity to God's law.
8:11 *They have healed the hurt . . . slightly*. Literally, "they have treated the fracture . . . superficially." A false assurance of *peace* only brings sorrow in the end (1 Thess. 5:3). Sin has terrible consequences, and to say otherwise is a blatant lie. Only true repentance and the humble acceptance of God's gracious remedy can bring true peace.
8:12 *the time of their visitation*. When they are examined and judged accordingly.
8:14 *silent*. Destroyed. *hath put us to silence*. Has caused us to perish. *gall*. Bitter and poisonous herb.

neighing of his strong ones; for they are come,
and have devoured the land, and all that is in it;
the city, and those that dwell therein.
17 For, behold, I will send serpents, cockatrices,
among you, which *will* not *be* charmed, and they
shall bite you, saith the LORD.
18 ¶ *When* I would comfort myself against
sorrow, my heart *is* faint in me.
19 Behold the voice of the cry of the daughter
of my people because of them that dwell in a far
country: *Is* not the LORD in Zion? *is* not her king
in her? Why have they provoked me to anger with
their graven images, *and* with strange vanities?
20 The harvest is past, the summer is ended, and
we are not saved.
21 For the hurt of the daughter of my people am
I hurt; I am black; astonishment hath taken hold
on me.
22 *Is there* no balm in Gilead; *is there* no physician
there? why then is not the health of the daughter
of my people recovered?

CHAPTER 9

OH that my head were waters, and mine eyes a
fountain of tears, that I might weep day and night
for the slain of the daughter of my people!
2 Oh that I had in the wilderness a lodging place
of wayfaring men; that I might leave my people,
and go from them! for they *be* all adulterers, an
assembly of treacherous men.
3 And they bend their tongues *like* their bow *for*
lies: but they are not valiant for the truth upon the
earth; for they proceed from evil to evil, and they
know not me, saith the LORD.
4 Take ye heed every one of his neighbour, and
trust ye not in any brother: for every brother will
utterly supplant, and every neighbour will walk
with slanders.
5 And they will deceive every one his neighbour,
and will not speak the truth: they have taught
their tongue to speak lies, *and* weary themselves
to commit iniquity.
6 Thine habitation *is* in the midst of deceit;
through deceit they refuse to know me, saith the
LORD.
7 Therefore thus saith the LORD of hosts, Behold,
I will melt them, and try them; for how shall I do
for the daughter of my people?
8 Their tongue *is as* an arrow shot out; it speaketh
deceit: *one* speaketh peaceably to his neighbour
with his mouth, but in heart he layeth his wait.
9 ¶ Shall I not visit them for these *things*? saith
the LORD: shall not my soul be avenged on such
a nation as this?
10 For the mountains will I take up a weeping and
wailing, and for the habitations of the wilderness
a lamentation, because they are burned up, so
that none can pass through *them*; neither can *men*
hear the voice of the cattle; both the fowl of the
heavens and the beast are fled; they are gone.
11 And I will make Jerusalem heaps, *and* a den
of dragons; and I will make the cities of Judah
desolate, without an inhabitant.
12 ¶ Who *is* the wise man, that may understand
this? and *who is he* to whom the mouth of the
LORD hath spoken, that he may declare it, for
what the land perisheth *and* is burned up like a

8:15 *We looked.* Literally, "we hoped or looked eagerly for."
8:17 *serpents.* Compare the "fiery serpents" in the wilderness (Num. 21:6). *cockatrices.* Adders or vipers.

Jeremiah's Mourning over the Nation's Sins (8:18—9:26)

8:18–22 Jeremiah agonizes over this fearful message of judgment he must now deliver to the people.
8:19 *strange vanities.* Literally, "breaths or vapors of a foreign land," a fitting designation for pagan idols that have no substance.
8:21 *am black.* Dressed for mourning.
8:22 *why then is not.* The question assumes that a *balm* (medicinal ointment) is indeed in *Gilead* (46:11; Gen. 37:25), but the sinful wounds of the nation were beyond cure.

Thoughts for Personal/Family Worship: Chapter 8

1. **It is sad that scribes should be rebuked for falsehood and misinterpretation of the law. Those who ought to have rightly instructed the people had failed to do so. They valued their own wisdom too highly. There is an important lesson here for us as Christians. While scholarship can be of great value when it comes from believing hearts that seek to reverence the Lord, it can also become a snare and a danger when scholarship is seen as the supreme authority. How can we give scholarship its rightful place without making an idol of it?**
2. **It is the greatest of tragedies that the vast majority of people have rejected Christ, the Physician of souls. Yet He alone can heal people from their sins. Let us, therefore, who know the Lord, seek to proclaim the good news of Jesus Christ to those who are lost and perishing. There is indeed a balm in Gilead to heal the sin-sick soul.**

Chapter 9: *Jeremiah laments over a people who would not repent and who failed to see the catastrophic end that awaited them.*

9:1 Jeremiah can only weep at the tragedy of his people's sin and misery; hence his reputation as the "weeping prophet."
9:2 *go from them.* His compassion did not alleviate the weariness caused by their sin and unbelief. It is often a natural thing to desire escape from our calling when we are facing opposition. Yet Christians must endure hardship as good soldiers of Jesus Christ (2 Tim. 2:3).
9:3 As a bow is drawn to shoot arrows, so their tongue is drawn to shoot lies. Their bent to lies reflects the fact that they *know not* the righteous and true God (vv. 6,24).
9:4 *supplant.* Seize by the heel, or betray; the root word for "Jacob."
9:9 *such a nation.* Rejecting spiritual privileges from God is a dreadful crime by any nation, not just Judah (5:9,29).
9:11 *dragons.* Jackals or wolves, predators in deserted ruins.
9:12–16 The events in the book of Jeremiah are not in chronological order. These words were either uttered prophetically

wilderness, that none passeth through?
13 And the LORD saith, Because they have
forsaken my law which I set before them, and
have not obeyed my voice, neither walked therein;
14 But have walked after the imagination of their
own heart, and after Baalim, which their fathers
taught them:
15 Therefore thus saith the LORD of hosts, the
God of Israel; Behold, I will feed them, *even* this
people, with wormwood, and give them water of
gall to drink.
16 I will scatter them also among the heathen,
whom neither they nor their fathers have known:
and I will send a sword after them, till I have
consumed them.
17 ¶ Thus saith the LORD of hosts, Consider ye,
and call for the mourning women, that they may
come; and send for cunning *women*, that they
may come:
18 And let them make haste, and take up a wailing
for us, that our eyes may run down with tears, and
our eyelids gush out with waters.
19 For a voice of wailing is heard out of Zion,
How are we spoiled! we are greatly confounded,
because we have forsaken the land, because our
dwellings have cast *us* out.
20 Yet hear the word of the LORD, O ye women,
and let your ear receive the word of his mouth,
and teach your daughters wailing, and every one
her neighbour lamentation.
21 For death is come up into our windows, *and*
is entered into our palaces, to cut off the children
from without, *and* the young men from the
streets.
22 Speak, Thus saith the LORD, Even the carcases
of men shall fall as dung upon the open field, and
as the handful after the harvestman, and none
shall gather *them*.
23 ¶ Thus saith the LORD, Let not the wise *man*
glory in his wisdom, neither let the mighty *man*
glory in his might, let not the rich *man* glory in
his riches:
24 But let him that glorieth glory in this, that he
understandeth and knoweth me, that I *am* the
LORD which exercise lovingkindness, judgment,
and righteousness, in the earth: for in these *things*
I delight, saith the LORD.
25 ¶ Behold, the days come, saith the LORD, that
I will punish all *them which are* circumcised with
the uncircumcised;
26 Egypt, and Judah, and Edom, and the children
of Ammon, and Moab, and all *that are* in the
utmost corners, that dwell in the wilderness: for
all *these* nations *are* uncircumcised, and all the
house of Israel *are* uncircumcised in the heart.

CHAPTER 10

HEAR ye the word which the LORD speaketh unto
you, O house of Israel:
2 Thus saith the LORD, Learn not the way of the
heathen, and be not dismayed at the signs of
heaven; for the heathen are dismayed at them.
3 For the customs of the people *are* vain: for *one*
cutteth a tree out of the forest, the work of the
hands of the workman, with the axe.
4 They deck it with silver and with gold; they
fasten it with nails and with hammers, that it
move not.
5 They *are* upright as the palm tree, but speak

or perhaps after the exile has already happened.

9:14 *imagination.* Stubbornness.

9:15 *wormwood.* From the root "to curse," here relating to a poisonous drink. *gall.* Poisonous plant made into a drink, a figure of speech for the bitter consequences of sin (Lam. 3:15,19; Rev. 8:11).

9:17 An appeal is made to professional women mourners because the calamity will be great. *cunning women.* Those who are skillful at mourning.

9:21 *death is come up into our windows.* A sinister description of death's irresistible and inescapable power; even the *children* and vigorous *young men* are susceptible.

9:23–24 *glory.* The recurring verb means "to boast." Knowing God in Christ is the only legitimate reason for boasting (1 Cor. 1:19–31). The heart knowledge of God in His sovereignty and love is the only true wisdom, power, and wealth (Hos. 2:20; 4:1; 6:6).

9:25–26 It is useless to plead a covenant relationship with God by external rituals like circumcision when the heart is far from Him (Acts 7:51; Rom. 2:25–29).

Thoughts for Personal/Family Worship: Chapter 9

1. Jeremiah is moved to tears over the persistent sin and unbelief of his people. God had reasoned and pleaded with the people through His prophets to turn unto Him, but they would not. As we look around us today, we see the terrible effects of sin and the misery it has caused. However, the greatest tragedy is that the gospel is rejected. Every provision for cleansing and healing is provided in and through Christ, yet the great majority choose to reject and despise the Savior. How do sin and unbelief in your neighbors affect you? Do they move you to great sorrow? Why or why not?

2. Great mischief and trouble come from unbridled tongues (v. 8; James 3:3–12). If a work of grace has taken place in our hearts, then surely we will say with the psalmist, "Set a watch, O LORD, before my mouth; keep the door of my lips" (Ps. 141:3).

Chapter 10: ***The contrast between lifeless idols and the one true and living God leads to the prophet's lament over the nation's sin and impending judgment.***

A Further Appeal to Return to the Lord (10:1–25)

10:1–9 Here is an almost comical description of the worthlessness of idols: they must be constructed and cared for by those who worship them.

10:3 *customs.* Statutes or ordinances. *vain.* Worthless or unsubstantial.

10:4 *deck.* Decorate or beautify.

not: they must needs be borne, because they
cannot go. Be not afraid of them; for they cannot
do evil, neither also *is it* in them to do good.
6 Forasmuch as *there is* none like unto thee, O
LORD; thou *art* great, and thy name *is* great in
might.
7 Who would not fear thee, O King of nations?
for to thee doth it appertain: forasmuch as among
all the wise *men* of the nations, and in all their
kingdoms, *there is* none like unto thee.
8 But they are altogether brutish and foolish: the
stock *is* a doctrine of vanities.
9 Silver spread into plates is brought from
Tarshish, and gold from Uphaz, the work of the
workman, and of the hands of the founder: blue
and purple *is* their clothing: they *are* all the work
of cunning *men*.
10 But the LORD *is* the true God, he *is* the living
God, and an everlasting king: at his wrath the
earth shall tremble, and the nations shall not be
able to abide his indignation.
11 Thus shall ye say unto them, The gods that
have not made the heavens and the earth, *even*
they shall perish from the earth, and from under
these heavens.
12 He hath made the earth by his power, he hath
established the world by his wisdom, and hath
stretched out the heavens by his discretion.
13 When he uttereth his voice, *there is* a multitude
of waters in the heavens, and he causeth the
vapours to ascend from the ends of the earth; he
maketh lightnings with rain, and bringeth forth
the wind out of his treasures.
14 Every man is brutish in *his* knowledge: every
founder is confounded by the graven image: for
his molten image *is* falsehood, and *there is* no
breath in them.
15 They *are* vanity, *and* the work of errors: in the
time of their visitation they shall perish.
16 The portion of Jacob *is* not like them: for he *is*
the former of all *things*; and Israel *is* the rod of his
inheritance: The LORD of hosts *is* his name.
17 ¶ Gather up thy wares out of the land, O
inhabitant of the fortress.
18 For thus saith the LORD, Behold, I will sling out
the inhabitants of the land at this once, and will
distress them, that they may find *it so*.
19 ¶ Woe is me for my hurt! my wound is grievous:
but I said, Truly this *is* a grief, and I must bear it.
20 My tabernacle is spoiled, and all my cords are
broken: my children are gone forth of me, and
they *are* not: *there is* none to stretch forth my tent
any more, and to set up my curtains.
21 For the pastors are become brutish, and have
not sought the LORD: therefore they shall not
prosper, and all their flocks shall be scattered.
22 Behold, the noise of the bruit is come, and a
great commotion out of the north country, to
make the cities of Judah desolate, *and* a den of
dragons.
23 ¶ O LORD, I know that the way of man *is* not
in himself: *it is* not in man that walketh to direct
his steps.
24 O LORD, correct me, but with judgment; not in
thine anger, lest thou bring me to nothing.
25 Pour out thy fury upon the heathen that
know thee not, and upon the families that call
not on thy name: for they have eaten up Jacob,
and devoured him, and consumed him, and have
made his habitation desolate.

10:5 *palm tree.* Perhaps an actual tree, but more likely a palm-shaped pillar. *needs be borne.* Must be lifted up; without life. *Be not afraid of them.* An inanimate object cannot do anything, either good or evil.

10:6 Contrast lifeless idols and the Lord. *thy name.* God's person and perfections, including His power (*might*).

10:7 *to thee doth it appertain.* It is fitting for the Lord to be feared and worshiped by all *nations* (Rev. 15:4).

10:8 *brutish.* Stupid or dull-hearted. Idolatry is not rational. *the stock is a doctrine of vanities.* Literally, "instruction of worthlessness (or an idol) is the tree."

10:9 *founder.* Person who casts metal in a mold. *cunning.* Skillful.

10:11 This verse is in Aramaic (the international language at the time) rather than Hebrew, probably so that the exiles could confess their faith to the Babylonians when confronted with pagan gods.

10:12 Creation is uniquely the work of the true God, testifying to His *power*, *wisdom*, ownership, and sovereignty (27:5–6; 32:17; 33:2; 51:15–16; Gen. 1:1; Job 9:8; Ps. 33:6–9; 95:5; Isa. 40:28; 42:5; 45:18).

10:14 *brutish.* Ignorant. *founder.* See note at v. 9. *confounded.* Ashamed. *graven.* Carved from wood or chiseled from stone. *molten.* Cast in metal.

10:15 *their visitation.* In the day when they are examined, they will come to nothing.

10:16 *the portion of Jacob.* God, in contrast to the lifeless and worthless idols. *the former.* The Creator.

10:17–18 Jeremiah returns to the coming invasion. Jerusalem is depicted here as under siege. The people are to pack up their belongings (*wares*). There is little time to prepare for exile. *sling.* Weapon designed to hurl stones. The Lord is going to throw out the inhabitants of Jerusalem with great force and speed.

10:20 *tabernacle.* Tent, a temporary dwelling place. *my cords are broken.* The tent ropes have snapped. The absence of children to help pitch the tent again emphasizes the extent of the exile.

10:21 *pastors.* Shepherds, here the leaders of Judah who had deliberately rejected the ways of the Lord. *brutish.* Ignorant, without sense or reason.

10:22 *bruit.* Something heard, an announcement, report, or news. *dragons.* Jackals or wolves (9:11).

10:24 *judgment.* Justice. God's justice includes His mercy to those who hope in him (Isa. 30:18). The *but* is restrictive; there would be no hope of survival if God acted in *anger*.

10:25 Jeremiah implores the Lord to pour out His wrath upon the pagans who do not *know* God (Ps. 79:6–7; 1 Thess. 4:5; 2 Thess. 1:8). God's chastisement of His people differs from His *fury* against the wicked (Jer. 30:11; 46:28).

CHAPTER 11

THE word that came to Jeremiah from the LORD,
saying,
2 Hear ye the words of this covenant, and speak
unto the men of Judah, and to the inhabitants of
Jerusalem;
3 And say thou unto them, Thus saith the LORD
God of Israel; Cursed *be* the man that obeyeth not
the words of this covenant,
4 Which I commanded your fathers in the day
that I brought them forth out of the land of Egypt,
from the iron furnace, saying, Obey my voice, and
do them, according to all which I command you:
so shall ye be my people, and I will be your God:
5 That I may perform the oath which I have
sworn unto your fathers, to give them a land
flowing with milk and honey, as *it is* this day.
Then answered I, and said, So be it, O LORD.
6 Then the LORD said unto me, Proclaim all these
words in the cities of Judah, and in the streets
of Jerusalem, saying, Hear ye the words of this
covenant, and do them.
7 For I earnestly protested unto your fathers in
the day *that* I brought them up out of the land
of Egypt, *even* unto this day, rising early and
protesting, saying, Obey my voice.
8 Yet they obeyed not, nor inclined their ear, but
walked every one in the imagination of their evil
heart: therefore I will bring upon them all the
words of this covenant, which I commanded *them*
to do; but they did *them* not.
9 And the LORD said unto me, A conspiracy is
found among the men of Judah, and among the
inhabitants of Jerusalem.
10 They are turned back to the iniquities of their
forefathers, which refused to hear my words; and
they went after other gods to serve them: the
house of Israel and the house of Judah have bro-
ken my covenant which I made with their fathers.
11 ¶ Therefore thus saith the LORD, Behold, I will
bring evil upon them, which they shall not be able
to escape; and though they shall cry unto me, I
will not hearken unto them.
12 Then shall the cities of Judah and inhabi-
tants of Jerusalem go, and cry unto the gods unto
whom they offer incense: but they shall not save
them at all in the time of their trouble.
13 For *according to* the number of thy cities were
thy gods, O Judah; and *according to* the number
of the streets of Jerusalem have ye set up altars to
that shameful thing, *even* altars to burn incense
unto Baal.
14 Therefore pray not thou for this people,
neither lift up a cry or prayer for them: for I will
not hear *them* in the time that they cry unto me
for their trouble.
15 What hath my beloved to do in mine house,
seeing she hath wrought lewdness with many, and
the holy flesh is passed from thee? when thou
doest evil, then thou rejoicest.
16 The LORD called thy name, A green olive tree,
fair, *and* of goodly fruit: with the noise of a great

Thoughts for Personal/Family Worship: Chapter 10

1. **The religion of Judah was molded by worldly thought practices. The human race was created to worship God. When He is not worshiped there is a void quickly filled by idols, but idols cannot think, see, hear, speak, or take action. Modern idols, such as celebrities or wealth, are equally helpless. The true follower of Jesus Christ is to reject all idols (1 John 5:21). If we are to escape the vanities of this world we must know God (9:24), which will give us great energy to serve Him (Dan. 11:32).**
2. **Jeremiah was a man prepared for his trials, yet when the shadow of darkness fell on his life he said, "Woe is me for my hurt! My wound is grievous" (v. 19). He felt the intense agony of it. However, he was nonetheless able to say, "Truly this is a grief, and I must bear it." Jeremiah was able to quickly compose himself and put aside his personal fear by bowing to the sovereign will of God. How can a Christian prepare himself so that when troubles come he can cast his cares on the Lord (1 Peter 5:7)?**

A Proclamation of God's Covenant and the Penalties for Disobedience (chs. 11–12)

Chapter 11: ***Jeremiah links God's judgment on Judah to their breaking the covenant and then prays for specific judgment on those who have conspired against him.***

11:2 *this covenant.* Most likely the covenant God had made with Israel at Sinai (Ex. 19), including the ceremonies that prefigured the work of the coming Messiah and so declared the gospel.

11:3 *Cursed.* Paid back for disobedience with great calamity (Deut. 27:26; Gal. 3:10). *obeyeth not.* Disobeying this covenant equates to disbelieving the gospel, since that message was at the heart of the covenant revelation (2 Thess. 1:8).

11:5 *so be it.* Hebrew, "*amen*," meaning "surely" or "truly."

11:7 *earnestly protested.* Certainly admonished, or exhorted. *rising early.* Expression of urgency.

11:8 *the imagination.* the stubbornness. *I will bring . . . this covenant.* God's curse was the consequence for breaking the covenant (Lev. 26:14–39; Deut. 28:15–68; 29:18–28; 32:15–27).

11:11 *evil.* Disaster. God warns against the foolish dismissal of His decrees. *not be able to escape.* Even though they may *cry* unto the Lord with many tears, the day of opportunity is gone (Prov. 1:24–31).

11:13 *the number of thy cities . . . thy gods.* Following pagan custom, each city had its own patron deity. *Baal.* Title meaning "lord" or "master," applied to whatever god they designated supreme.

11:14 See note at 7:16.

11:15 The Hebrew is difficult, but the meaning clearly expresses the incompatibility between Judah's sinful behavior and their hypocritical rituals in the temple. *holy flesh.* Sacrifices that could neither cover their sins nor avert the calamities that awaited them.

11:16 *green olive tree.* The flourishing olive tree is a picture of what Israel ought to have been (Ps. 52:8; Hos. 14:6; Matt. 3:10). *great tumult.* A storm in which lightning would strike the tree and set fire to it—a picture of judgment.

tumult he hath kindled fire upon it, and the
branches of it are broken.
17 For the LORD of hosts, that planted thee, hath
pronounced evil against thee, for the evil of the
house of Israel and of the house of Judah, which
they have done against themselves to provoke me
to anger in offering incense unto Baal.
18 ¶ And the LORD hath given me knowledge *of it*,
and I know *it*: then thou shewedst me their doings.
19 But I *was* like a lamb *or* an ox *that* is brought
to the slaughter; and I knew not that they had
devised devices against me, *saying*, Let us destroy
the tree with the fruit thereof, and let us cut him
off from the land of the living, that his name may
be no more remembered.
20 But, O LORD of hosts, that judgest righteously,
that triest the reins and the heart, let me see thy
vengeance on them: for unto thee have I revealed
my cause.
21 Therefore thus saith the LORD of the men of
Anathoth, that seek thy life, saying, Prophesy not
in the name of the LORD, that thou die not by our
hand:
22 Therefore thus saith the LORD of hosts, Behold,
I will punish them: the young men shall die by the
sword; their sons and their daughters shall die by
famine:
23 And there shall be no remnant of them: for I
will bring evil upon the men of Anathoth, *even*
the year of their visitation.

CHAPTER 12

RIGHTEOUS *art* thou, O LORD, when I plead with
thee: yet let me talk with thee of *thy* judgments:
Wherefore doth the way of the wicked prosper?
wherefore are all they happy that deal very
treacherously?
2 Thou hast planted them, yea, they have taken
root: they grow, yea, they bring forth fruit: thou
art near in their mouth, and far from their reins.
3 But thou, O LORD, knowest me: thou hast seen
me, and tried mine heart toward thee: pull them
out like sheep for the slaughter, and prepare them
for the day of slaughter.
4 How long shall the land mourn, and the herbs
of every field wither, for the wickedness of them
that dwell therein? the beasts are consumed, and
the birds; because they said, He shall not see our
last end.
5 ¶ If thou hast run with the footmen, and they
have wearied thee, then how canst thou contend
with horses? and *if* in the land of peace, *wherein*
thou trustedst, *they wearied thee*, then how wilt
thou do in the swelling of Jordan?
6 For even thy brethren, and the house of thy fa-

11:17 *evil . . . evil.* the first occurrence refers to a divine sentence of judgment, a disastrous event; the second refers to Israel's sin, disastrous behavior.

11:18–23 The context abruptly shifts to Jeremiah's imprecatory prayer against those who have rejected his message and conspired against his life. However, these people were not his personal enemies but the Lord's. His prayer for divine judgment against them illustrates Ps. 139:21–22.

11:19 *a lamb or an ox.* This could be rendered "a tame or docile lamb," indicating Jeremiah's innocence. *devised devices.* Schemed.

11:20 Instead of fleeing, Jeremiah prayed and committed the matter to the Lord, trusting in His promises (1:18–19). *triest.* Examines or puts to the test. *reins and the heart.* Literally, "the kidneys and the heart," a reference to man's innermost being, including motives (17:10; Rev. 2:23). Jeremiah was confident of God's infallible knowledge of both himself and the conspirators. *my cause.* Legal dispute.

11:21–23 The Lord answers Jeremiah's prayer with the assurance that He will punish them and preserve him to continue proclaiming God's Word.

Thoughts for Personal/Family Worship: Chapter 11

1. **The curse of the law is the fearful destiny of all who disobey God's covenant (Gal. 3:10). But blessed are all who trust in God's Son (Ps. 2:12), for Christ redeemed sinners from the law by receiving its curse upon the cross (Gal. 3:13). He paid the penalty to satisfy God's justice in the shedding of His own precious blood. Therefore there is no condemnation for those in Christ Jesus (Rom. 8:1).**
2. **How patient is the love of God! Though the Jews despised His ways, He still calls them "beloved" (v. 15; Rom. 11:28). If this is the case, how patient is He with Jews and Gentiles who belong to Christ, despite their remaining sins and stumbling?**
3. **Taking a stand for truth can result in hostility. At such times we must trust in the promises of God, as Jeremiah did. Many stumble, because they are fearful of the possible consequences of taking such a stand. Do you have faith that God will keep His promises, or do you grow weak at the thought of opposition?**

Chapter 12: ***Jeremiah complains about the prosperity of the wicked and learns that it is only apparent because they are under the sentence of judgment unless they repent.***

12:1–4 Jeremiah addresses the common tension between creed and experience, specifically the prosperity of the wicked in contrast to the condition of the righteous (Pss. 37; 49; 73).

12:1 *plead.* Present a legal complaint. *happy.* At rest or at ease. He acknowledges that God does all things right (his creed) but complains that the prospering of the wicked seems contradictory (his experience).

12:2 What should be the marks of the blessed man seem instead to characterize the wicked (Ps. 1:1–3). *reins.* Kidneys, representing desire and longing.

12:3 *day of slaughter.* Just as an animal may be fattened only for butchering, so the wicked are blessed by God only for judgment if they do not repent (James 5:5).

12:5–6 The Lord's answer is not expected; if Jeremiah thinks the situation is tough now, it is going to get much harder. He is portrayed as a foot soldier fighting against other infantrymen, but he will soon have to fight against cavalry. *swelling of Jordan.* Most likely the thickets on the banks of the Jordan.

12:7 The wicked appeared to prosper but in reality were under the sentence of divine wrath, abandoned by God (Matt.

ther, even they have dealt treacherously with thee; yea, they have called a multitude after thee: believe them not, though they speak fair words unto thee.
7 ¶ I have forsaken mine house, I have left mine heritage; I have given the dearly beloved of my soul into the hand of her enemies.
8 Mine heritage is unto me as a lion in the forest; it crieth out against me: therefore have I hated it.
9 Mine heritage *is* unto me *as* a speckled bird, the birds round about *are* against her; come ye, assemble all the beasts of the field, come to devour.
10 Many pastors have destroyed my vineyard, they have trodden my portion under foot, they have made my pleasant portion a desolate wilderness.
11 They have made it desolate, *and being* desolate it mourneth unto me; the whole land is made desolate, because no man layeth *it* to heart.
12 The spoilers are come upon all high places through the wilderness: for the sword of the LORD shall devour from the *one* end of the land even to the *other* end of the land: no flesh shall have peace.
13 They have sown wheat, but shall reap thorns: they have put themselves to pain, *but* shall not profit: and they shall be ashamed of your revenues because of the fierce anger of the LORD.
14 ¶ Thus saith the LORD against all mine evil neighbours, that touch the inheritance which I have caused my people Israel to inherit; Behold, I will pluck them out of their land, and pluck out the house of Judah from among them.
15 And it shall come to pass, after that I have plucked them out I will return, and have compassion on them, and will bring them again, every man to his heritage, and every man to his land.
16 And it shall come to pass, if they will diligently learn the ways of my people, to swear by my name, The LORD liveth; as they taught my people to swear by Baal; then shall they be built in the midst of my people.
17 But if they will not obey, I will utterly pluck up and destroy that nation, saith the LORD.

CHAPTER 13

THUS saith the LORD unto me, Go and get thee a linen girdle, and put it upon thy loins, and put it not in water.
2 So I got a girdle according to the word of the LORD, and put *it* on my loins.
3 And the word of the LORD came unto me the second time, saying,
4 Take the girdle that thou hast got, which *is* upon thy loins, and arise, go to Euphrates, and hide it there in a hole of the rock.
5 So I went, and hid it by Euphrates, as the LORD commanded me.
6 And it came to pass after many days, that the LORD said unto me, Arise, go to Euphrates, and take the girdle from thence, which I commanded thee to hide there.
7 Then I went to Euphrates, and digged, and took the girdle from the place where I had hid it: and, behold, the girdle was marred, it was profitable for nothing.
8 Then the word of the LORD came unto me, saying,
9 Thus saith the LORD, After this manner will I mar the pride of Judah, and the great pride of Jerusalem.

23:38). *forsaken . . . left . . . given.* Past tense of events yet to take place, but so certain that they are to be viewed as having already occurred.

12:8 *hated.* Rejected—volitional, not emotional.

12:9 The Lord's people had become a *speckled bird* (or bird of prey), but the speckled appearance marked Judah as being different from the other birds (nations) that would therefore gather around and peck her into submission.

12:10 *pastors.* Literally, "shepherds," the kings and leaders of the nations. *my vineyard.* See Isa. 5:1–7.

12:13 *put themselves to pain.* Exhausted themselves, but got nothing in return (*profit*). *revenues.* Products.

12:14 *touch.* Harm. *Pluck . . . pluck.* The evil neighbors of Judah would be plucked out of their lands, but Judah would be plucked from exile.

12:15–17 In His wrath He remembers mercy (Isa. 54:8; Hab. 3:2).

Thoughts for Personal/Family Worship: Chapter 12

1. **Jeremiah saw the corrupt worship of God seemingly prospering, while the true faith was making no apparent headway at all. We look at many churches that have corrupted their worship with worldly practices and have watered down the gospel, yet they seem to be growing. We sometimes, like Jeremiah, have difficulty reconciling God's promises with our own experiences. However, we need to understand that God sees the whole picture, and we do not. The Christian life involves taking up our cross (Matt.10:38; Acts 14:22) and waiting on the Lord (Ps. 37:7).**
2. **The grace of God is held out to people of every nation through the gospel, but it also gives a final warning (vv. 16–17). The Lord sets before people life and death. How foolish it is to reject such great salvation, but how blessed we are who trust in Jesus Christ!**

Chapter 13: *The linen girdle and wine bottles picture the sin of the nation and its consequent punishment.*

The Lesson of the Linen Girdle (13:1–27)

13:1–2 *linen girdle.* Either a short, thigh-length skirt wrapped around the waist or a simple wrapping around the waist. It is part of the priestly attire (Lev. 16:4) and a fitting symbol for God's special people, a priestly nation bound close to the Lord, reminding the people of their initial pure and untarnished relationship with the Lord.

13:3–5 God commands Jeremiah to go to the Euphrates, a round-trip journey of about 700 miles, and hide the girdle in a crack in a cliff (*hole of the rock*).

13:7 *marred.* Ruined.

13:8–10 The divine interpretation of the symbol is that the

10 This evil people, which refuse to hear my
words, which walk in the imagination of their
heart, and walk after other gods, to serve them,
and to worship them, shall even be as this girdle,
which is good for nothing.
11 For as the girdle cleaveth to the loins of a man,
so have I caused to cleave unto me the whole
house of Israel and the whole house of Judah,
saith the LORD; that they might be unto me for a
people, and for a name, and for a praise, and for a
glory: but they would not hear.
12 ¶ Therefore thou shalt speak unto them this
word; Thus saith the LORD God of Israel, Every
bottle shall be filled with wine: and they shall say
unto thee, Do we not certainly know that every
bottle shall be filled with wine?
13 Then shalt thou say unto them, Thus saith the
LORD, Behold, I will fill all the inhabitants of this
land, even the kings that sit upon David's throne,
and the priests, and the prophets, and all the
inhabitants of Jerusalem, with drunkenness.
14 And I will dash them one against another,
even the fathers and the sons together, saith the
LORD: I will not pity, nor spare, nor have mercy,
but destroy them.
15 ¶ Hear ye, and give ear; be not proud: for the
LORD hath spoken.
16 Give glory to the LORD your God, before he
cause darkness, and before your feet stumble
upon the dark mountains, and, while ye look for
light, he turn it into the shadow of death, *and*
make *it* gross darkness.
17 But if ye will not hear it, my soul shall weep
in secret places for *your* pride; and mine eye shall
weep sore, and run down with tears, because the
LORD's flock is carried away captive.
18 Say unto the king and to the queen, Humble
yourselves, sit down: for your principalities shall
come down, *even* the crown of your glory.
19 The cities of the south shall be shut up, and
none shall open *them*: Judah shall be carried away
captive all of it, it shall be wholly carried away
captive.
20 Lift up your eyes, and behold them that come
from the north: where *is* the flock *that* was given
thee, thy beautiful flock?
21 What wilt thou say when he shall punish thee?
for thou hast taught them *to be* captains, *and* as
chief over thee: shall not sorrows take thee, as a
woman in travail?
22 ¶ And if thou say in thine heart, Wherefore
come these things upon me? For the greatness of
thine iniquity are thy skirts discovered, *and* thy
heels made bare.
23 Can the Ethiopian change his skin, or the
leopard his spots? *then* may ye also do good, that
are accustomed to do evil.
24 Therefore will I scatter them as the stubble
that passeth away by the wind of the wilderness.
25 This *is* thy lot, the portion of thy measures
from me, saith the LORD; because thou hast
forgotten me, and trusted in falsehood.
26 Therefore will I discover thy skirts upon thy
face, that thy shame may appear.
27 I have seen thine adulteries, and thy neighings,
the lewdness of thy whoredom, *and* thine

Lord would mar the pride of Judah, bringing them into exile because of their sins. *imagination*. Stubbornness. Judah's corruption was contrary to expectation and privilege.

13:11 *cleave*. Cling. God intended His relationship with His people to be as intimate as that between husband and wife (Gen. 2:24), but they would cling to Him in faith (*hear*).

13:12–14 The impending judgment of Judah is likened to wine *bottles* (storage jars) that will be shattered. *drunkenness*. Picture of judgment as a loss of wisdom and control.

13:16 Judgment is pictured as the terrors of darkness coming upon the people. *shadow of death*. The Hebrew can refer to pitch darkness. *gross darkness*. Thick darkness, or heavy cloud.

13:17 *sore*. Exceedingly. The weeping prophet reveals his pastor's heart in not wanting to see his people perish.

13:18 *queen*. Possibly "lady" or, more likely, the queen mother, Nehushta, the mother of Jehoiachin (2 Kings 24:8). *your principalities*. Literally, "what is at your head," here specified as *the crown of your glory*, meaning the loss of all regal authority and status.

13:19–20 *cities of the south . . . from the north*. While coming from the north, the Babylonians would first take the land to the south of Jerusalem, so as to cut off all means of escape.

13:21 *travail*. Labor pains.

13:22 *discovered*. Uncovered. Judah would be treated like disgraced prostitutes, who had their *skirts* torn from their legs and their bare *heels* beaten with rods or sticks. This may also have reference to the shame of being stripped and taken barefoot into captivity (Isa. 20:4).

13:23 Just as it is impossible for a person to change his natural skin color, so it is impossible for a sinner to repent and do good (Rom. 3:12; 8:7–8). Nature determines behavior (Matt. 12:33–34). Man cannot save himself from the sin he inherited from Adam; only God can save sinners (19:26).

13:25 *lot*. The retribution the Lord allotted to them because of their sin.

13:26 *I discover thy skirts*. See note at v. 22.

13:27 *wilt thou not . . . once be?* An alternate translation is, "How long will you yet be unclean?"

Thoughts for Personal/Family Worship: Chapter 13

1. **The symbolism of the linen girdle provides a tragic picture of the effects of sin. Israel was God's special people, who enjoyed a unique relationship with Him. Yet against all privilege they transgressed the covenant and defiled themselves, becoming useless to God and deprived of His presence. Jeremiah's prophecy warns all in the church: those who outwardly enjoy great spiritual privileges must guard against the corruption of the world, lest they become so marred that privilege is replaced with judgment.**
2. **Sin is as deeply engrained in mankind as the genetics of our skin color. However, whereas God delights in various colors of skin, His wrath is provoked by our sin. How then can anyone be saved from sin and wrath? Reflect upon Titus 3:3–7.**

abominations on the hills in the fields. Woe unto
thee, O Jerusalem! wilt thou not be made clean?
when *shall it* once *be?*

CHAPTER 14

THE word of the LORD that came to Jeremiah
concerning the dearth.
2 Judah mourneth, and the gates thereof
languish; they are black unto the ground; and the
cry of Jerusalem is gone up.
3 And their nobles have sent their little ones to
the waters: they came to the pits, *and* found no
water; they returned with their vessels empty;
they were ashamed and confounded, and covered
their heads.
4 Because the ground is chapt, for there was no
rain in the earth, the plowmen were ashamed,
they covered their heads.
5 Yea, the hind also calved in the field, and
forsook *it*, because there was no grass.
6 And the wild asses did stand in the high places,
they snuffed up the wind like dragons; their eyes
did fail, because *there was* no grass.
7 ¶ O LORD, though our iniquities testify against
us, do thou *it* for thy name's sake: for our back-
slidings are many; we have sinned against thee.
8 O the hope of Israel, the saviour thereof in time
of trouble, why shouldest thou be as a stranger
in the land, and as a wayfaring man *that* turneth
aside to tarry for a night?
9 Why shouldest thou be as a man astonied, as a
mighty man *that* cannot save? yet thou, O LORD,
art in the midst of us, and we are called by thy
name; leave us not.
10 ¶ Thus saith the LORD unto this people, Thus
have they loved to wander, they have not refrained
their feet, therefore the LORD doth not accept
them; he will now remember their iniquity, and
visit their sins.
11 Then said the LORD unto me, Pray not for this
people for *their* good.
12 When they fast, I will not hear their cry; and
when they offer burnt offering and an oblation, I
will not accept them: but I will consume them by
the sword, and by the famine, and by the pestilence.
13 ¶ Then said I, Ah, Lord GOD! behold, the
prophets say unto them, Ye shall not see the
sword, neither shall ye have famine; but I will give
you assured peace in this place.
14 Then the LORD said unto me, The prophets
prophesy lies in my name: I sent them not, neither
have I commanded them, neither spake unto
them: they prophesy unto you a false vision and
divination, and a thing of nought, and the deceit
of their heart.
15 Therefore thus saith the LORD concerning the
prophets that prophesy in my name, and I sent
them not, yet they say, Sword and famine shall not
be in this land; By sword and famine shall those
prophets be consumed.
16 And the people to whom they prophesy shall
be cast out in the streets of Jerusalem because of
the famine and the sword; and they shall have
none to bury them, them, their wives, nor their
sons, nor their daughters: for I will pour their
wickedness upon them.
17 ¶ Therefore thou shalt say this word unto
them; Let mine eyes run down with tears night
and day, and let them not cease: for the virgin
daughter of my people is broken with a great
breach, with a very grievous blow.
18 If I go forth into the field, then behold the
slain with the sword! and if I enter into the city,
then behold them that are sick with famine! yea,
both the prophet and the priest go about into a
land that they know not.
19 Hast thou utterly rejected Judah? hath thy soul
lothed Zion? why hast thou smitten us, and *there*
is no healing for us? we looked for peace, and

Chapter 14: ***Jeremiah, after lamenting the drought in the land and pronouncing judgment on the false prophets, confesses the sin of the nation to the Lord.***

A Terrible Drought (14:1–22)

14:1 *dearth.* Drought.

14:2 *gates.* Places of commerce, where people tended to gather. *they are black unto the ground.* The people were dirty, or in black mourning garments.

14:3 *pits.* Cisterns or ditches, normally holding water, are empty. *covered their heads.* Expression of grief or embarrassment (2 Sam. 15:30).

14:4 *chapt.* Cracked or shattered.

14:5 *hind.* Female deer, usually most tender toward their young; yet in this case they forsook them, indicating how desperate the drought was.

14:6 *the high places.* Most likely a barren plain. *snuffed up the wind like dragons.* Gasped or panted like jackals.

14:7–9 Jeremiah identifies with his people, reverently arguing their cause with God. He acknowledges sin as the cause, and the Lord as the only hope.

14:10–12 God's reply offers no hope, and for the third time Jeremiah is told not to pray for the people (7:16; 11:14). Judah's religious efforts were without heart repentance and therefore worthless (Prov. 1:24–28). God is never satisfied with purely external religion.

14:13–16 Conformity to God's revealed Word was a test to determine true or false prophets (Deut. 13:1–5). Consequently, both the false prophets and the people who believed them were culpable.

14:17 *broken with a great breach, with a very grievous blow.* Shattered with a great shattering or collapse, having an incurable wound.

14:18 *go about into a land that they know not.* Wander around not knowing where they are.

14:19 *thy soul.* Expression equivalent to the personal pronoun "you." God does not have a soul as in human terms. *lothed.* Detested. The questions express the prophet's hope

there is no good; and for the time of healing, and
behold trouble!
20 We acknowledge, O LORD, our wickedness,
and the iniquity of our fathers: for we have sinned
against thee.
21 Do not abhor *us*, for thy name's sake, do not
disgrace the throne of thy glory: remember, break
not thy covenant with us.
22 Are there *any* among the vanities of the
Gentiles that can cause rain? or can the heavens
give showers? *art* not thou he, O LORD our God?
therefore we will wait upon thee: for thou hast
made all these *things*.

CHAPTER 15

THEN said the LORD unto me, Though Moses and
Samuel stood before me, *yet* my mind *could* not
be toward this people: cast *them* out of my sight,
and let them go forth.
2 And it shall come to pass, if they say unto
thee, Whither shall we go forth? then thou shalt
tell them, Thus saith the LORD; Such as *are* for
death, to death; and such as *are* for the sword, to
the sword; and such as *are* for the famine, to the
famine; and such as *are* for the captivity, to the
captivity.
3 And I will appoint over them four kinds, saith
the LORD: the sword to slay, and the dogs to tear,
and the fowls of the heaven, and the beasts of the
earth, to devour and destroy.
4 And I will cause them to be removed into all
kingdoms of the earth, because of Manasseh the
son of Hezekiah king of Judah, for *that* which he
did in Jerusalem.
5 For who shall have pity upon thee, O Jerusalem?
or who shall bemoan thee? or who shall go aside
to ask how thou doest?
6 Thou hast forsaken me, saith the LORD, thou
art gone backward: therefore will I stretch out my
hand against thee, and destroy thee; I am weary
with repenting.
7 And I will fan them with a fan in the gates of
the land; I will bereave *them* of children, I will
destroy my people, *since* they return not from
their ways.
8 Their widows are increased to me above the
sand of the seas: I have brought upon them
against the mother of the young men a spoiler
at noonday: I have caused *him* to fall upon it
suddenly, and terrors upon the city.
9 She that hath borne seven languisheth: she
hath given up the ghost; her sun is gone down
while *it was* yet day: she hath been ashamed and
confounded: and the residue of them will I deliver
to the sword before their enemies, saith the LORD.
10 ¶ Woe is me, my mother, that thou hast borne
me a man of strife and a man of contention to

---

that, even in wrath, God will remember mercy (Hab. 3:2).

14:20–22 A well-reasoned prayer: confession and petition motivated by dependence on God's promises and desire for God's glory. *vanities of the Gentiles.* Idols or false gods that cannot do anything. Believers wait upon Him who alone can give what we need.

Thoughts for Personal/Family Worship: Chapter 14

1. **The physical famine Judah faced was but a reflection of the spiritual famine within. Their hearts were hard, dry, and resistant to both plow and seed. So too, when God's children foolishly harden their hearts, there comes a period of loving chastening that will end only when there is heartfelt repentance (Heb. 12:6; Rev. 3:19). Has God disciplined you? How have you responded?**
2. **Jeremiah saw the tragedy of all that had happened to his people, and he wanted God to act. Do we ever come to the Lord with such passion? The prophet wept when he saw the state of the people. It grieved him to see them brought so low. Do we have the same concern for people today? Are we moved to tears that many who profess Christ as Lord have become so worldly and have moved so far from their moorings?**

Chapter 15: *After describing Judah's judgment, Jeremiah complains about the problems he has endured, and God responds by reminding him of His promises.*

God's Rejection of Judah Contrasted with His Promise to Jeremiah (15:1–21)

15:1 *Moses and Samuel* proved powerful intercessors in their generations (Ex. 32:11–14; 1 Sam. 12:23; Ps. 99:6), yet such was the sin of Judah that even these great prophets would not be heard now. The time for intercession was over; the moment of judgment had arrived.

15:2 *for the captivity, to the captivity.* God sovereignly determined the specific sorrow to fall on each person (Rev. 13:10).

15:4 *because of Manasseh.* Manasseh's sin led the nation into great depravity and atrocities, but his repentance did not lead them out (2 Kings 21; 2 Chron. 33). This testifies to the terrible power of sin's influence and consequences. However, this statement in no way excuses the people in Jeremiah's day. They were fully responsible for their sins.

15:6 *weary with repenting.* Literally, "Tired of relenting." God's ungrateful and undeserving people had abused His mercy and would now feel the terror of His wrath.

15:7 *fan them with a fan.* Winnow them with a pitchfork, a method of separating grain from chaff; here an image of judgment (51:2; Matt. 3:12). *gates.* Places where people congregated. *return not.* Do not repent.

15:8 Judah was so weak and vulnerable that the destroyer (*spoiler*) attacked at midday rather than waiting for night.

15:9 *She that hath borne seven* usually signified a wonderful blessing (Ruth 4:15), but here the blessing is turned to heartfelt sorrow as the offspring are taken away. *given up the ghost.* Literally, "soul gasped or expired."

15:10–21 Jeremiah complains twice about the problems he faces because of his ministry, each complaint followed by God's answer.

15:10 *usury.* Interest. Jeremiah's first lament is that the world is against him through no fault of his own. Lamenting the day of his birth (20:14; Job 3:3) was tantamount to his lamenting his ministry, since he had been set apart from conception (1:5).

the whole earth! I have neither lent on usury, nor
men have lent to me on usury; *yet* every one of
them doth curse me.
11 The LORD said, Verily it shall be well with thy
remnant; verily I will cause the enemy to entreat
thee *well* in the time of evil and in the time of
affliction.
12 Shall iron break the northern iron and the
steel?
13 Thy substance and thy treasures will I give to
the spoil without price, and *that* for all thy sins,
even in all thy borders.
14 And I will make *thee* to pass with thine
enemies into a land *which* thou knowest not: for
a fire is kindled in mine anger, *which* shall burn
upon you.
15 ¶ O LORD, thou knowest: remember me, and
visit me, and revenge me of my persecutors; take
me not away in thy longsuffering: know that for
thy sake I have suffered rebuke.
16 Thy words were found, and I did eat them; and
thy word was unto me the joy and rejoicing of
mine heart: for I am called by thy name, O LORD
God of hosts.
17 I sat not in the assembly of the mockers, nor
rejoiced; I sat alone because of thy hand: for thou
hast filled me with indignation.
18 Why is my pain perpetual, and my wound
incurable, *which* refuseth to be healed? wilt thou
be altogether unto me as a liar, *and as* waters *that*
fail?
19 ¶ Therefore thus saith the LORD, If thou
return, then will I bring thee again, *and* thou
shalt stand before me: and if thou take forth
the precious from the vile, thou shalt be as my
mouth: let them return unto thee; but return not
thou unto them.
20 And I will make thee unto this people a fenced
brasen wall: and they shall fight against thee, but
they shall not prevail against thee: for I *am* with
thee to save thee and to deliver thee, saith the
LORD.
21 And I will deliver thee out of the hand of the
wicked, and I will redeem thee out of the hand of
the terrible.

CHAPTER 16

THE word of the LORD came also unto me, saying,
2 Thou shalt not take thee a wife, neither shalt
thou have sons or daughters in this place.
3 For thus saith the LORD concerning the sons
and concerning the daughters that are born in
this place, and concerning their mothers that bare
them, and concerning their fathers that begat
them in this land;
4 They shall die of grievous deaths; they shall
not be lamented; neither shall they be buried; *but*
they shall be as dung upon the face of the earth:
and they shall be consumed by the sword, and by
famine; and their carcases shall be meat for the
fowls of heaven, and for the beasts of the earth.
5 For thus saith the LORD, Enter not into the house
of mourning, neither go to lament nor bemoan

15:11–14 Jeremiah's lament is answered by God's rebuke and promise of personal protection. The text is difficult, but the sense is clear. Jeremiah is to look away from his own perceived problems and focus on the foe coming against Judah. This is not a time for self-pity. When disaster (*evil*) comes upon the nation, God will ensure Jeremiah's personal safety. *steel*. Literally, "bronze."

15:15–21 The second complaint is bold, detailing the inner struggles of the prophet and expressing his desire for vengeance and his feeling of betrayal.

15:15 *take me not away*. Jeremiah saw God's patience with the wicked as a threat to his well-being.

15:16–18 The main complaint was that in spite of his faithfulness he experienced nothing but rejection and failure. He was a willing, joyful servant (v. 16) who followed the pattern of the blessed man of Ps. 1 (v. 17) yet knew nothing but trouble (v. 18). In his despair He accused God of deception. Distressing experiences and discontentment can distort our views of God.

15:19–21 God's answer is a call to repentance and a repetition of an old promise.

15:19 *return*. Repent. *bring thee again*. Restore, same Hebrew word as *return*. *vile*. Worthless, a reference to his complaining utterances. *my mouth*. God's prophet, a role dependent on his repentance.

15:20–21 *brasen wall*. God repeats His promise (1:18–19), giving Jeremiah renewed perspective. The Lord had not forsaken him, and therefore his enemies cannot prevail against him. It is a blessed thing to rest upon the promises of God.

Thoughts for Personal/Family Worship: Chapter 15

1. **There are occasions when even the fervent prayers of a righteous man are not enough (v. 1). God will answer the prayer for blessing upon the church only after there has been true reformation. Before we pray for the church's prosperity, let us pray for its repentance. And let us repent ourselves before praying for others.**
2. **The ways of the Lord are hard for us to understand when we have immersed ourselves in the Lord's work and sought to be faithful, yet all of our labors appear to have achieved nothing except to provoke hostility. We might be tempted to say to ourselves, "Why did I ever bother? Life would have been so much easier if I had done nothing." How would you counsel a Christian experiencing a situation like that of Jeremiah?**

Chapter 16: *Restrictions on Jeremiah's personal life represent the extent of the ruin coming on Judah, yet the Lord points to a future restoration.*

Judah's Utter Ruin Declared (16:1–21)

16:1–4 God prohibits Jeremiah from marrying in order to spare his prospective wife the terrible circumstances of the coming judgment (cf. 1 Cor. 7:26), as well as to publically foreshadow the doom ahead.

16:5–7 *house of mourning*. Most likely a funeral feast involving pagan cultic practices, which many in Judah adopted. Instead of turning to the Lord, they *cut themselves*

them: for I have taken away my peace from this people, saith the LORD, *even* lovingkindness and mercies.

6 Both the great and the small shall die in this land: they shall not be buried, neither shall *men* lament for them, nor cut themselves, nor make themselves bald for them:

7 Neither shall *men* tear *themselves* for them in mourning, to comfort them for the dead; neither shall *men* give them the cup of consolation to drink for their father or for their mother.

8 Thou shalt not also go into the house of feasting, to sit with them to eat and to drink.

9 For thus saith the LORD of hosts, the God of Israel; Behold, I will cause to cease out of this place in your eyes, and in your days, the voice of mirth, and the voice of gladness, the voice of the bridegroom, and the voice of the bride.

10 ¶ And it shall come to pass, when thou shalt shew this people all these words, and they shall say unto thee, Wherefore hath the LORD pronounced all this great evil against us? or what *is* our iniquity? or what *is* our sin that we have committed against the LORD our God?

11 Then shalt thou say unto them, Because your fathers have forsaken me, saith the LORD, and have walked after other gods, and have served them, and have worshipped them, and have forsaken me, and have not kept my law;

12 And ye have done worse than your fathers; for, behold, ye walk every one after the imagination of his evil heart, that they may not hearken unto me:

13 Therefore will I cast you out of this land into a land that ye know not, *neither* ye nor your fathers; and there shall ye serve other gods day and night; where I will not shew you favour.

14 ¶ Therefore, behold, the days come, saith the LORD, that it shall no more be said, The LORD liveth, that brought up the children of Israel out of the land of Egypt;

15 But, The LORD liveth, that brought up the children of Israel from the land of the north, and from all the lands whither he had driven them: and I will bring them again into their land that I gave unto their fathers.

16 ¶ Behold, I will send for many fishers, saith the LORD, and they shall fish them; and after will I send for many hunters, and they shall hunt them from every mountain, and from every hill, and out of the holes of the rocks.

17 For mine eyes *are* upon all their ways: they are not hid from my face, neither is their iniquity hid from mine eyes.

18 And first I will recompense their iniquity and their sin double; because they have defiled my land, they have filled mine inheritance with the carcases of their detestable and abominable things.

19 O LORD, my strength, and my fortress, and my refuge in the day of affliction, the Gentiles shall come unto thee from the ends of the earth, and shall say, Surely our fathers have inherited lies, vanity, and *things* wherein *there is* no profit.

20 Shall a man make gods unto himself, and they *are* no gods?

21 Therefore, behold, I will this once cause them to know, I will cause them to know mine hand and my might; and they shall know that my name *is* The LORD.

---

and shaved their heads, as was the practice of Baal worshipers.

16:9 *voice of mirth.* See note at 7:34.

16:10 *evil.* Disaster. *what is our iniquity?* Their sin had so engulfed them that they had become oblivious to guilt (5:19; Mal. 3:8–9).

16:12 *imagination.* Stubbornness. To follow one's heart is to reject God (17:1).

16:13 Exile was the consequence of breaking the covenant (by serving pagan gods; see Deut. 4:25–28). *I will not shew you favour.* Literally, "I will not give to you grace or pity."

16:14–15 *The LORD liveth.* Literally, "the life of the Lord," used as an oath. *the land of the north.* Babylon. *I will bring them again.* The reversal of exile in terms of a second exodus greater than the first exodus *out of the land of Egypt* (Isa. 43:16–21; 48:20–21).

16:18 *I will recompense.* The Lord will repay them the equivalent (*double*) of what they deserve—always a fearful thought.

16:19–21 This second exodus will include Gentiles (4:2; 12:16) who turn from their empty idols to the Lord, a promise fulfilled in the gathering of God's elect from all nations through the saving work of Jesus Christ (Rev. 5:9–10).

Thoughts for Personal/Family Worship: Chapter 16

1. God's knows every sin committed against Him, and in due season He will use whatever means He chooses to search out sinners and gather them for judgment (vv. 16–18). Have you sought the Lord in repentance? You hide from Him in vain, for even your secret sins are in His plain view (Ps. 90:8; Heb. 4:13). Only the blood of Christ can remove sin from God's sight. Are you trusting in that blood?

2. The nations will come to the Lord from the ends of the earth (v. 19; Ps. 22:27). The gospel will experience worldwide success. It is a great mercy to us if God has brought home the gospel to our hearts so that we turn from idols to serve the living God (1 Thess. 1:3–10). However, if we have been saved by the gospel we must also join with the church in its mission: "Go ye into all the world and preach the gospel to every creature" (Mark 16:15). What are you doing to help reach the world for Christ?

Chapter 17: ***The prophet contrasts false and true faith and explains that the proper observance of the Sabbath will bring blessing.***

The Sin of Judah Written with a Pen of Iron (17:1–27)

17:1 *pen of iron.* An iron stylus used for engraving or chiseling. *heart.* Man's inner being, including the mind, emotions, and will. Sin is permanently and deeply written upon the soul of man, contrary to the holy law God gave to Israel on tablets (*table*) of stone (Ex. 24:12; 34:28). *horns of your altars.* Place for binding the sacrifice and putting the blood from the sin

CHAPTER 17

THE sin of Judah *is* written with a pen of iron, *and*
with the point of a diamond: *it is* graven upon the
table of their heart, and upon the horns of your
altars;
2 Whilst their children remember their altars and
their groves by the green trees upon the high hills.
3 O my mountain in the field, I will give thy
substance *and* all thy treasures to the spoil, *and*
thy high places for sin, throughout all thy borders.
4 And thou, even thyself, shalt discontinue from
thine heritage that I gave thee; and I will cause
thee to serve thine enemies in the land which
thou knowest not: for ye have kindled a fire in
mine anger, *which* shall burn for ever.
5 ¶ Thus saith the LORD; Cursed *be* the man that
trusteth in man, and maketh flesh his arm, and
whose heart departeth from the LORD.
6 For he shall be like the heath in the desert, and
shall not see when good cometh; but shall inhabit
the parched places in the wilderness, *in* a salt land
and not inhabited.
7 Blessed *is* the man that trusteth in the LORD,
and whose hope the LORD is.
8 For he shall be as a tree planted by the waters,
and *that* spreadeth out her roots by the river, and
shall not see when heat cometh, but her leaf shall
be green; and shall not be careful in the year of
drought, neither shall cease from yielding fruit.
9 ¶ The heart *is* deceitful above all *things*, and
desperately wicked: who can know it?
10 I the LORD search the heart, *I* try the reins,
even to give every man according to his ways, *and*
according to the fruit of his doings.
11 *As* the partridge sitteth *on eggs*, and hatcheth
them not; *so* he that getteth riches, and not by
right, shall leave them in the midst of his days,
and at his end shall be a fool.
12 ¶ A glorious high throne from the beginning *is*
the place of our sanctuary.
13 O LORD, the hope of Israel, all that forsake thee
shall be ashamed, *and* they that depart from me
shall be written in the earth, because they have
forsaken the LORD, the fountain of living waters.
14 Heal me, O LORD, and I shall be healed; save
me, and I shall be saved: for thou *art* my praise.
15 ¶ Behold, they say unto me, Where *is* the word
of the LORD? let it come now.
16 As for me, I have not hastened from *being* a
pastor to follow thee: neither have I desired the
woeful day; thou knowest: that which came out
of my lips was *right* before thee.
17 Be not a terror unto me: thou *art* my hope in
the day of evil.
18 Let them be confounded that persecute
me, but let not me be confounded: let them be
dismayed, but let not me be dismayed: bring
upon them the day of evil, and destroy them with
double destruction.
19 ¶ Thus said the LORD unto me; Go and stand
in the gate of the children of the people, whereby
the kings of Judah come in, and by the which they
go out, and in all the gates of Jerusalem;
20 And say unto them, Hear ye the word of the
LORD, ye kings of Judah, and all Judah, and all the
inhabitants of Jerusalem, that enter in by these
gates:
21 Thus saith the LORD; Take heed to yourselves,
and bear no burden on the sabbath day, nor bring
it in by the gates of Jerusalem;
22 Neither carry forth a burden out of your
houses on the sabbath day, neither do ye any work,
but hallow ye the sabbath day, as I commanded
your fathers.

---

offering. Even Judah's worship and means of atonement were corrupted by sin.

17:2 *groves.* Wooden poles erected for pagan rituals; evidence of combining the worship of Jehovah with that of Baal.

17:4 *discontinue from thine heritage.* Drop or lose their inheritance in the land as a consequence of sin (Deut. 4:25–28).

17:5–8 The theme and imagery are similar to those of Ps. 1. The essential difference between the cursed man and the blessed man is their object of trust. Trusting in man brings sorrow and death, but trusting God brings life.

17:5 *trusteth.* Key Old Testament word for faith, with the idea of finding security, safety, or confidence (see note at 5:17). *his arm.* His strength. *whose heart departeth from the LORD.* Trust in man and trust in God are mutually exclusive.

17:6 *heath.* Perhaps a juniper or some sort of shrub.

17:7 The verb *trusteth* and the noun *hope* come from the same Hebrew root. The blessed man rests in *the LORD* alone for security and safety. God saves by grace through faith (Eph. 2:8).

17:8 See Ps. 1:3. *not see when the heat cometh.* Not experience the destructive power of the heat; alternative reading, "not fear." *careful.* Anxious.

17:9 *deceitful.* Sly, insidious, crooked; root for the name Jacob. *desperately wicked.* Incurable (15:18). Not only is man's soul corrupted by sin, but it is wrapped in layers of lies and beyond earthly help.

17:10 *search the heart.* The Lord can see what man cannot discern. *reins.* Literally, "kidneys," referring to the emotions (11:20; 12:2). God knows all about us (Pss. 44:21; 94:11; 139:1–4) and will judge each person accordingly (Rev. 2:23; 22:12).

17:11 As the partridge purportedly hatches eggs it did not lay, only to lose its efforts, so the ungodly get rich from wealth they did not earn, only to forfeit it under divine judgment.

17:13 *written in the earth.* The names of the wicked will be brought low to the ground in humiliation. *fountain of living waters.* See note at 2:13.

17:15–18 is another of Jeremiah's complaints. He prays for deliverance from his adversaries who mocked him because his message was not yet fulfilled. He prays for the judgment (*day of evil*) to come speedily for his vindication.

17:19–27 Blessing or curse was conditioned upon the keeping of the *sabbath day.*

17:19 *gate.* Place of commerce and public gathering.

17:22 *hallow ye the sabbath day.* Make it holy, or distinctly separate from all the other days as a time to rest from ordinary labor, so that people may give themselves to worship (Ex. 20:8–11; Isa. 58:13–14).

TOTAL DEPRAVITY

When Adam and Eve sinned, they fell from their state of original righteousness into a state of spiritual, moral, emotional, and physical corruption. Our first parents "became dead in sin, and wholly defiled in all the parts and faculties of soul and body" (Westminster Confession of Faith, 6.2). The guilt of this "original sin" was imputed, and the resulting corruption of soul and body was transmitted, to all their natural descendants.

This inherited corruption is described as "total depravity," from the Latin word *depravatio*, meaning the wickedness (*pravitas*) that is rooted in our hearts and reaches to every aspect of our persons and lives. We bring forth the fruits of this depravity in our lives every day: "Sin issues forth from this woeful source, as water from a fountain" (Belgic Confession, Art. 15).

God's Word to Jeremiah identifies this "woeful source" as the heart of man, meaning the seat of our intellect, will, and emotions, that is, all that makes us distinctly human, forms our personalities, and determines our outward conduct (Jer. 17:1,9). Sin cannot be blamed on environment, upbringing, education, or bad examples set for us by others. We are sinners at heart.

That is not to say that human beings are as wicked as they could possibly be. In the kindness of God, "there remain . . . in man since the fall, glimmerings of natural light, whereby he retains some knowledge of God, of natural things, and of the differences between good and evil, and discovers some regard for virtue, good order in society, and for maintaining an orderly external deportment." This natural light is limited, however, and only explains why men are not more wicked than they are at present, since fallen man "is incapable of using it aright even in things natural and civil" (Canons of Dort, III–IV, Art. 4).

Without the restraint of "natural light," the human race would soon have destroyed itself. We are prone by nature to hate God and our neighbor (Heidelberg Catechism, Q. 6). We defy the living God, go our own way in life, and make war on one another. So "natural darkness" coexists in us alongside "natural light."

Profound in depth, human depravity is comprehensive in its reach and effects. No part of our being, no time in our earthly pilgrimage, no facet of life and work in the world, no relationship with God or man, and nothing we think, feel, say, or do is left uncorrupted or unimpaired by our depravity.

New Christians soon discover that depravity, as "the law of sin" in their members, still wars against the "law" of their minds, that is, the things they consciously believe and know to be God's will for their lives (Rom. 7:23). They say with Paul, "I find then a law, that, when I would do good, evil is present with me" (Rom. 7:21).

God's remedy for the total depravity of His people is a threefold salvation in Christ. *First*, in regeneration, new life is implanted in the believer. *Second*, by the process of sanctification, this new life is nourished, increased, and made fruitful. *Third*, it is brought to final perfection or glorification at death, when the believer's soul is made perfect, and at the last day, when his resurrected body is changed and made like the glorious body of the risen Christ.

Our comfort meanwhile is that our sins are forgiven for the sake of Christ and our remaining infirmities are covered by His passion and death. These infirmities include weakness of understanding with regard to knowledge of the truth; weakness of faith in the face of doubts and difficulties; and weakness of will with regard to obeying God's commandments and resisting temptations to sin. All such infirmities are covered by the grant and imputation of Christ's righteousness to the believer, "as if I never had had, nor committed any sin; yea, as if I had fully accomplished all that obedience which Christ has accomplished for me" (Heidelberg Catechism, Q. 60).

23 But they obeyed not, neither inclined their
ear, but made their neck stiff, that they might not
hear, nor receive instruction.
24 And it shall come to pass, if ye diligently
hearken unto me, saith the LORD, to bring in
no burden through the gates of this city on the
sabbath day, but hallow the sabbath day, to do no
work therein;
25 Then shall there enter into the gates of this
city kings and princes sitting upon the throne
of David, riding in chariots and on horses, they,
and their princes, the men of Judah, and the
inhabitants of Jerusalem: and this city shall
remain for ever.
26 And they shall come from the cities of Judah,
and from the places about Jerusalem, and from
the land of Benjamin, and from the plain,
and from the mountains, and from the south,
bringing burnt offerings, and sacrifices, and meat
offerings, and incense, and bringing sacrifices of
praise, unto the house of the LORD.
27 But if ye will not hearken unto me to hallow
the sabbath day, and not to bear a burden, even
entering in at the gates of Jerusalem on the sabbath
day; then will I kindle a fire in the gates thereof,
and it shall devour the palaces of Jerusalem, and it
shall not be quenched.

CHAPTER 18

THE word which came to Jeremiah from the
LORD, saying,
2 Arise, and go down to the potter's house, and
there I will cause thee to hear my words.
3 Then I went down to the potter's house, and,
behold, he wrought a work on the wheels.
4 And the vessel that he made of clay was marred
in the hand of the potter: so he made it again
another vessel, as seemed good to the potter to
make *it*.
5 Then the word of the LORD came to me, saying,
6 O house of Israel, cannot I do with you as this
potter? saith the LORD. Behold, as the clay *is* in the
potter's hand, so *are* ye in mine hand, O house of
Israel.
7 *At what* instant I shall speak concerning a
nation, and concerning a kingdom, to pluck up,
and to pull down, and to destroy *it*;
8 If that nation, against whom I have pronounced,
turn from their evil, I will repent of the evil that I
thought to do unto them.
9 And *at what* instant I shall speak concerning a
nation, and concerning a kingdom, to build and
to plant *it*;
10 If it do evil in my sight, that it obey not my
voice, then I will repent of the good, wherewith I
said I would benefit them.
11 ¶ Now therefore go to, speak to the men of
Judah, and to the inhabitants of Jerusalem, saying,
Thus saith the LORD; Behold, I frame evil against
you, and devise a device against you: return ye
now every one from his evil way, and make your
ways and your doings good.
12 And they said, There is no hope: but we will
walk after our own devices, and we will every one
do the imagination of his evil heart.
13 Therefore thus saith the LORD; Ask ye now
among the heathen, who hath heard such things:
the virgin of Israel hath done a very horrible
thing.
14 Will *a man* leave the snow of Lebanon *which*
cometh from the rock of the field? *or* shall the cold

17:27 Their failure to honor the Lord's Day resulted in the wrath of God coming upon them like a *fire* that *shall not be quenched* (4:4; 7:20; 21:12; Matt. 3:12; Mark 9:43–48).

Thoughts for Personal/Family Worship: Chapter 17

1. **The human heart is hard like stone and engraved with rebellion against God (v.1). It is hostile to God, leading man to depart from the Lord (v. 5). It is utterly deceitful and wholly untrustworthy; the effects of sin make it incurably malignant, and it is unfathomable (v. 9). Man has no hope of curing his own sin. How then can we have hope (24:7; 31:33)?**
2. **The contrast between the cursed man and the blessed man (vv. 5–8) emphasizes an essential element about the nature of true faith. While both the cursed man and the blessed man may express the same degree of trust, the vital difference between them is in the object of their faith. The only faith that saves is faith in Christ.**
3. **One of the first signs of apostasy is the abandonment of the Lord's Day. We need to come aside from the world and worship the Lord. Keeping the Lord's Day reveals a longing for Christ to return and affords us a foretaste of heaven, our eternal rest. In the meantime, let us by God's grace seek to hallow this blessed one day in seven. God promises blessing for those who delight in His day (Isa. 58:13–14).**

Lessons Drawn from the Potter (18:1—20:18)

Chapter 18: ***The work of the potter illustrates God's sovereign right and power to judge Judah for their sins, and Jeremiah again prays for deliverance from conspirators.***

18:1–10 As the divine Potter, God has the prerogative to do as He pleases with His own creation (Isa. 29:16; 64:8; Rom. 9:20–23).

18:8 *turn from their evil, I will repent of the evil.* If they repent of their sin, I will relent of disaster. God in His sovereignty has determined not to punish anyone who truly repents.

18:10 *repent.* Relent. God's blessing is reserved for the obedient.

18:11 *frame evil.* Create disaster. The Hebrew word for *frame* is the same as the word for "potter." *devise a device.* Make or plan a plan.

18:12 *devices.* Plans. *Imagination.* Stubbornness.

18:13–14 Whereas the elements of nature act according to

flowing waters that come from another place be
forsaken?
15 Because my people hath forgotten me, they
have burned incense to vanity, and they have
caused them to stumble in their ways *from* the an-
cient paths, to walk in paths, *in* a way not cast up;
16 To make their land desolate, *and* a perpetual
hissing; every one that passeth thereby shall be
astonished, and wag his head.
17 I will scatter them as with an east wind before
the enemy; I will shew them the back, and not the
face, in the day of their calamity.
18 ¶ Then said they, Come, and let us devise
devices against Jeremiah; for the law shall not
perish from the priest, nor counsel from the wise,
nor the word from the prophet. Come, and let
us smite him with the tongue, and let us not give
heed to any of his words.
19 Give heed to me, O LORD, and hearken to the
voice of them that contend with me.
20 Shall evil be recompensed for good? for they
have digged a pit for my soul. Remember that I
stood before thee to speak good for them, *and* to
turn away thy wrath from them.
21 Therefore deliver up their children to the
famine, and pour out their *blood* by the force of
the sword; and let their wives be bereaved of their
children, and *be* widows; and let their men be put
to death; *let* their young men *be* slain by the sword
in battle.
22 Let a cry be heard from their houses, when
thou shalt bring a troop suddenly upon them: for
they have digged a pit to take me, and hid snares
for my feet.
23 Yet, LORD, thou knowest all their counsel
against me to slay *me*: forgive not their iniquity,
neither blot out their sin from thy sight, but let
them be overthrown before thee; deal *thus* with
them in the time of thine anger.

CHAPTER 19

THUS saith the LORD, Go and get a potter's earthen
bottle, and *take* of the ancients of the people, and
of the ancients of the priests;
2 And go forth unto the valley of the son of
Hinnom, which *is* by the entry of the east gate,
and proclaim there the words that I shall tell thee,
3 And say, Hear ye the word of the LORD, O kings
of Judah, and inhabitants of Jerusalem; Thus saith
the LORD of hosts, the God of Israel; Behold, I will
bring evil upon this place, the which whosoever
heareth, his ears shall tingle.
4 Because they have forsaken me, and have es-
tranged this place, and have burned incense in
it unto other gods, whom neither they nor their
fathers have known, nor the kings of Judah, and
have filled this place with the blood of innocents;
5 They have built also the high places of Baal,
to burn their sons with fire *for* burnt offerings
unto Baal, which I commanded not, nor spake *it*,
neither came *it* into my mind:
6 Therefore, behold, the days come, saith the
LORD, that this place shall no more be called

---

expectation, Judah's behavior is contrary to expectation, given its privileges.

18:15 *vanity*. A worthless idol. *not cast up*. Not prepared for travel.

18:16 *hissing*. Whistling in scorn or derision at the foolishness of Judah in forsaking their God.

18:17 *shew them the back*. Gesture of rejection.

18:19–23 Jeremiah learns of a plot against him and prays for deliverance and vengeance. He had so identified himself with the Lord that he saw attacks against him as ultimately against God.

18:18 *devise devices*. Scheme plans. *smite him with the tongue*. Bring accusations against him.

18:20 *my soul*. Literally, "me," referring to his person, not his immaterial being.

18:21 The calamities parallel the covenant curses (Lev. 26; Deut. 28), thus implying not personal vindictiveness but the punishment of those who had rejected God (Ps. 139:21–22).

18:23 *thou knowest*. This speaks of a special relationship that would have brought comfort to the prophet at this difficult time.

Thoughts for Personal/Family Worship: Chapter 18

1. Every one of us is as clay in the hands of God. God "formed" the body of Adam out of the ground (Gen. 2:7), the same word used by Jeremiah for "potter." He formed us, and therefore He owns us and has the right to do with us as He wills. It should be our prayer that He will mold us more and more into the image of His Son.

2. Just as Judah dismissed God's Word as irrelevant, so people today do the same, saying, "We will walk after our own devices" (v. 12). They are so engrossed in themselves that they have no time for God or for His messengers. Even within the professing church there are many who ignore the Word of God on vital issues, preferring the stubbornness of their own hearts. What is the opposite of stubbornly walking in our own plans and desires? How can you cultivate that in your life?

Chapter 19: *The breaking of the clay pot provides a grim picture of the desolation that would come upon Judah.*

19:1 *earthen bottle*. Clay vessel fired in a kiln; it cannot be remolded. *ancients*. Elders, the leaders of the people.

19:2 *east gate*. Also called the "potsherd gate," for broken pottery was carried through it to be discarded.

19:3 *evil*. Calamity or disaster.

19:4 *estranged*. Defaced or profaned, made it into an alien place. *blood of innocents*. Pagan rites were practiced there, such as burning child sacrifices (2 Chron. 28:3; 33:6).

19:6 Changing the name of *Tophet, the valley of the son of Hinnom,* to *the valley of slaughter* signifies that the place of pagan ritual would become a place of divine judgment. King Josiah defiled it as an unclean place, and Isaiah used it as an image of God's wrath (2 Kings 23:10; Isa. 30:33). The "valley of Hinnom" (Hebrew *gey-hinnom*) is the basis for the New Testament term for "hell" (Greek, *gehenna*), eternity's fiery

Tophet, nor The valley of the son of Hinnom, but
The valley of slaughter.
7 And I will make void the counsel of Judah and
Jerusalem in this place; and I will cause them to
fall by the sword before their enemies, and by
the hands of them that seek their lives: and their
carcases will I give to be meat for the fowls of the
heaven, and for the beasts of the earth.
8 And I will make this city desolate, and an hiss-
ing; every one that passeth thereby shall be aston-
ished and hiss because of all the plagues thereof.
9 And I will cause them to eat the flesh of their
sons and the flesh of their daughters, and they
shall eat every one the flesh of his friend in the
siege and straitness, wherewith their enemies, and
they that seek their lives, shall straiten them.
10 Then shalt thou break the bottle in the sight of
the men that go with thee,
11 And shalt say unto them, Thus saith the LORD
of hosts; Even so will I break this people and this
city, as *one* breaketh a potter's vessel, that cannot
be made whole again: and they shall bury *them* in
Tophet, till *there be* no place to bury.
12 Thus will I do unto this place, saith the LORD,
and to the inhabitants thereof, and *even* make this
city as Tophet:
13 And the houses of Jerusalem, and the houses
of the kings of Judah, shall be defiled as the place
of Tophet, because of all the houses upon whose
roofs they have burned incense unto all the host
of heaven, and have poured out drink offerings
unto other gods.
14 Then came Jeremiah from Tophet, whither the
LORD had sent him to prophesy; and he stood in
the court of the LORD's house; and said to all the
people,
15 Thus saith the LORD of hosts, the God of Israel;
Behold, I will bring upon this city and upon all
her towns all the evil that I have pronounced
against it, because they have hardened their necks,
that they might not hear my words.

CHAPTER 20

NOW Pashur the son of Immer the priest, who
was also chief governor in the house of the LORD,
heard that Jeremiah prophesied these things.
2 Then Pashur smote Jeremiah the prophet, and
put him in the stocks that *were* in the high gate of
Benjamin, which *was* by the house of the LORD.
3 And it came to pass on the morrow, that Pashur
brought forth Jeremiah out of the stocks. Then
said Jeremiah unto him, The LORD hath not called
thy name Pashur, but Magor-missabib.
4 For thus saith the LORD, Behold, I will make
thee a terror to thyself, and to all thy friends: and
they shall fall by the sword of their enemies, and
thine eyes shall behold *it*: and I will give all Judah
into the hand of the king of Babylon, and he shall
carry them captive into Babylon, and shall slay
them with the sword.
5 Moreover I will deliver all the strength of
this city, and all the labours thereof, and all the
precious things thereof, and all the treasures of
the kings of Judah will I give into the hand of their
enemies, which shall spoil them, and take them,
and carry them to Babylon.
6 And thou, Pashur, and all that dwell in thine
house shall go into captivity: and thou shalt come
to Babylon, and there thou shalt die, and shalt be
buried there, thou, and all thy friends, to whom
thou hast prophesied lies.
7 ¶ O LORD, thou hast deceived me, and I was
deceived: thou art stronger than I, and hast

---

garbage dump (Matt. 5:22; Mark 9:47–48).

19:8 *hissing.* Whistling at the sight of something astonishing (1 Kings 9:8; Lam. 2:15,16; Ezek. 27:36; Zeph. 2:15). *plagues.* Wounds.

19:9 *straitness.* Distress or hardship. *straiten.* Harass.

19:10–15 The breaking of the jar was an object lesson of the judgment to come. The nation was to be smashed and discarded.

19:13 *all the host of heaven.* Astral deities of Mesopotamia and Canaan that were commonly worshiped from housetops (Zeph. 1:5).

Thoughts for Personal/Family Worship: Chapter 19

1. **The shedding of the blood of the innocents brought the condemnation of God upon Judah. Sadly, the same atrocity is prevalent today when people sacrifice unborn children on the altar of self. There is very little difference between our day and Jeremiah's, which teaches a grim lesson to us about the judgment to come.**
2. **The fierce anger of the Lord, revealed against Judah, will inevitably fall upon all who harden their hearts and refuse to listen to the Word of the Lord. Therefore, it is a great comfort to know that God has provided a way of escape by giving His only begotten Son (John 3:16). The Lord Jesus has stood in the sinner's place (1 Cor. 15:3), enduring the wrath of God on Calvary's cross for all His blood-bought people. Do not neglect so great a salvation (Heb. 2:3). Repent and believe.**

Chapter 20: *Pashur's opposition to Jeremiah leads to his own doom and to Jeremiah's struggle about his calling.*

20:1–2 *chief governor.* Literally, "an overseer, a high official." *stocks.* Restraints to confine a prisoner in a stooped position.

20:3 The Lord changes his name to *Magor-missabib*, meaning "terror on every side," personalizing the word of judgment against the wicked (Prov. 28:1).

20:5 *strength.* Wealth. *labours.* Products of labor.

20:7–18 Jeremiah confesses his inner struggles and feelings of despair over his persecution.

20:7 *deceived.* Persuaded or seduced. *I was deceived.* Literally, "let myself be taken for a fool." God most certainly did not deceive, but in his frustration over his circumstances Jeremiah speaks rashly. *thou art stronger than I.* Literally, "you overpowered me," meaning that God forced him.

prevailed: I am in derision daily, every one
mocketh me.
8 For since I spake, I cried out, I cried violence
and spoil; because the word of the LORD was
made a reproach unto me, and a derision, daily.
9 Then I said, I will not make mention of him,
nor speak any more in his name. But *his word*
was in mine heart as a burning fire shut up in
my bones, and I was weary with forbearing, and
I could not *stay*.
10 ¶ For I heard the defaming of many, fear on ev-
ery side. Report, *say they*, and we will report it. All
my familiars watched for my halting, *saying*, Per-
adventure he will be enticed, and we shall prevail
against him, and we shall take our revenge on him.
11 But the LORD *is* with me as a mighty terrible
one: therefore my persecutors shall stumble,
and they shall not prevail: they shall be greatly
ashamed; for they shall not prosper: *their*
everlasting confusion shall never be forgotten.
12 But, O LORD of hosts, that triest the righteous,
and seest the reins and the heart, let me see thy
vengeance on them: for unto thee have I opened
my cause.
13 Sing unto the LORD, praise ye the LORD: for he
hath delivered the soul of the poor from the hand
of evildoers.
14 ¶ Cursed *be* the day wherein I was born: let not
the day wherein my mother bare me be blessed.
15 Cursed *be* the man who brought tidings to
my father, saying, A man child is born unto thee;
making him very glad.
16 And let that man be as the cities which the
LORD overthrew, and repented not: and let him
hear the cry in the morning, and the shouting at
noontide;
17 Because he slew me not from the womb; or
that my mother might have been my grave, and
her womb *to be* always great *with me*.
18 Wherefore came I forth out of the womb to
see labour and sorrow, that my days should be
consumed with shame?

CHAPTER 21

THE word which came unto Jeremiah from the
LORD, when king Zedekiah sent unto him Pashur
the son of Melchiah, and Zephaniah the son of
Maaseiah the priest, saying,
2 Enquire, I pray thee, of the LORD for us; for
Nebuchadrezzar king of Babylon maketh war
against us; if so be that the LORD will deal with us
according to all his wondrous works, that he may
go up from us.
3 ¶ Then said Jeremiah unto them, Thus shall ye
say to Zedekiah:
4 Thus saith the LORD God of Israel; Behold,
I will turn back the weapons of war that *are* in
your hands, wherewith ye fight against the king
of Babylon, and *against* the Chaldeans, which

20:8 The word was God's, but Jeremiah suffered the consequence of the people's rejection.
20:9 *I was weary . . . stay.* Literally, "I struggled to contain it but I was not able." God gave him an inner compulsion to speak what he could not deny (Rom. 1:14; 1 Cor. 9:16).
20:10 *defaming.* Rumor, or whispering. *fear on every side.* Hebrew, *magor-missabib* (v. 3). They turned his own message into a taunt against him. *Report.* Most likely, "denounce." *All my familiars.* Literally, "every man of my peace," all his friends. *halting.* Stumbling. *Peradventure.* Perhaps. *enticed.* Same word as "deceived" in v. 7.
20:11–12 In his complaint, Jeremiah acknowledges God as his only hope. *terrible.* Awe-inspiring. *confusion.* Reproach or shame. *Reins.* Literally, "kidneys," referring to the seat of emotions, which with *heart* portrays the entire inner man. *cause.* Legal case or suit.
20:13 *poor.* Those who are defenseless.
20:14–18 Expressions of deep despair. To curse the day he was born was to despise his calling by God.
20:16 *cities.* Sodom and Gomorrah (Gen. 19:24–28), which the Lord overthrew without relenting (*repented not*). God gave him no answer, but the initial promises stood firm.

Thoughts for Personal/Family Worship: Chapter 20

1. **We would expect Jeremiah to praise God for delivering him from Pashur, but he does not. Instead he starts to imagine the terrible things that could have happened to him. We learn here how subtle is the enemy of our souls. At the very time that Jeremiah should have been depending upon God, he gives in to the weakness of the flesh (1 Kings 19:2–4). Let us learn that at such times of trial we need to trust in the Lord rather than leaning on our own understanding of the situation (Prov. 3:5–6).**
2. **The chapter ends with Jeremiah full of self-pity. Sadly, this is a common experience for Christians when we take our eyes off the Lord and focus on our troubles (Job 3:1–13). On the one hand, let us remember that such times of darkness do not disqualify a person from salvation. On the other hand, let us stir ourselves up to take hold of God and cling to His promises when we are in the darkness. Christ was truly forsaken by God in the darkness, bearing the sins of all His elect (Ps. 22:1; Matt. 27:45–46). If we are in Christ, God will never, ever forsake us, even in our darkest times (Heb. 13:5).**

Rulers and False Prophets Denounced (21:1—23:40)

Chapter 21: *Jeremiah is commanded to tell Zedekiah that he must either surrender to Babylon or perish.*

21:1–2 *Zedekiah.* Judah's last king, whose name ironically means "The Lord is my righteousness." *Nebuchadrezzar.* Alternate spelling of Nebuchadnezzar. *maketh war.* Although Zedekiah was set up as a puppet king, his rebellion brought Nebuchadnezzar to Jerusalem to besiege the city. *wondrous works.* Past extraordinary divine interventions that rescued the city from destruction (2 Kings 19:35–36).
21:4 *I will turn back.* The Lord would render ineffective any resistance against the Babylonians. Judah's defeat was divinely determined and certain.
21:5–6 Judah's sins made the Lord Himself their enemy (Lam. 2:5). Babylon was simply the weapon in His hand (cf. Isa. 10:5).

besiege you without the walls, and I will assemble
them into the midst of this city.
5 And I myself will fight against you with an
outstretched hand and with a strong arm, even in
anger, and in fury, and in great wrath.
6 And I will smite the inhabitants of this city, both
man and beast: they shall die of a great pestilence.
7 And afterward, saith the LORD, I will deliver
Zedekiah king of Judah, and his servants, and the
people, and such as are left in this city from the
pestilence, from the sword, and from the famine,
into the hand of Nebuchadrezzar king of Babylon,
and into the hand of their enemies, and into
the hand of those that seek their life: and he shall
smite them with the edge of the sword; he shall
not spare them, neither have pity, nor have mercy.
8 ¶ And unto this people thou shalt say, Thus
saith the LORD; Behold, I set before you the way
of life, and the way of death.
9 He that abideth in this city shall die by the
sword, and by the famine, and by the pestilence:
but he that goeth out, and falleth to the Chaldeans
that besiege you, he shall live, and his life shall be
unto him for a prey.
10 For I have set my face against this city for evil,
and not for good, saith the LORD: it shall be given
into the hand of the king of Babylon, and he shall
burn it with fire.
11 ¶ And touching the house of the king of Judah,
say, Hear ye the word of the LORD;
12 O house of David, thus saith the LORD; Execute
judgment in the morning, and deliver *him that
is* spoiled out of the hand of the oppressor, lest
my fury go out like fire, and burn that none can
quench *it*, because of the evil of your doings.
13 Behold, I *am* against thee, O inhabitant of
the valley, *and* rock of the plain, saith the LORD;
which say, Who shall come down against us? or
who shall enter into our habitations?
14 But I will punish you according to the fruit of
your doings, saith the LORD: and I will kindle a
fire in the forest thereof, and it shall devour all
things round about it.

CHAPTER 22

THUS saith the LORD; Go down to the house of
the king of Judah, and speak there this word,
2 And say, Hear the word of the LORD, O king of
Judah, that sittest upon the throne of David, thou,
and thy servants, and thy people that enter in by
these gates:
3 Thus saith the LORD; Execute ye judgment and
righteousness, and deliver the spoiled out of the
hand of the oppressor: and do no wrong, do no
violence to the stranger, the fatherless, nor the
widow, neither shed innocent blood in this place.
4 For if ye do this thing indeed, then shall there
enter in by the gates of this house kings sitting
upon the throne of David, riding in chariots and
on horses, he, and his servants, and his people.
5 But if ye will not hear these words, I swear
by myself, saith the LORD, that this house shall
become a desolation.
6 For thus saith the LORD unto the king's house of
Judah; Thou *art* Gilead unto me, *and* the head of
Lebanon: *yet* surely I will make thee a wilderness,
and cities *which* are not inhabited.
7 And I will prepare destroyers against thee, every
one with his weapons: and they shall cut down
thy choice cedars, and cast *them* into the fire.
8 And many nations shall pass by this city, and
they shall say every man to his neighbour, Wherefore
hath the LORD done thus unto this great city?
9 Then they shall answer, Because they have
forsaken the covenant of the LORD their God, and
worshipped other gods, and served them.
10 ¶ Weep ye not for the dead, neither bemoan

21:9 *falleth*. Surrenders. *prey*. Possession. Surrendering is the only way to escape death.

21:10 *evil*. Disaster or calamity. This is a startling contrast to 29:11.

21:12 *none can quench*. See note at 17:27.

21:14 *according to the fruit of your doings*. Judgment is by works (Rom. 2:6); the punishment will fit Judah's crime.

Thoughts for Personal/Family Worship: Chapter 21

1. **There are many like Zedekiah today who refuse to be in subjection to the Lord. Yet when their rebellion brings calamity upon them, they hope that God will get them out of the mess *they* have created. They do not come in contrition and sorrow for their sins; they merely want to escape the consequences of their sins. Such insincerity only heightens the anger of the Lord against the violators of His law.**
2. **The Lord said, "I will punish you according to the fruit of your doings" (v. 14). These are fearful and sobering words. To rebel against God and reject His message leaves one alone on the day of judgment. God's justice will be satisfied, and those who refuse to repent are storing up wrath for themselves that will be unleashed on the day of God's wrath and righteous judgment (Rom. 2:5). Do not fool yourself if you continue unrepentant in your sins; God will not be mocked (Gal. 6:7).**

Chapter 22: *The royal house is exhorted to do their duty or face the consequences.*

22:1–2 These verses give no indication as to which of the last four kings of Judah is being addressed. However, in one sense they apply to all who sat on David's throne.

22:3 *judgment*. Justice. *spoiled*. One who has been plundered.

22:5 *I swear by myself*. The divine oath intensifies the certainty of the coming judgment (Heb. 6:13).

22:6–7 *Gilead . . . the head of Lebanon*. God likens Judah to a verdant forest that would be cut down in judgment and laid waste. The invaders are described as woodcutters.

22:10–12 *weep ye not for the dead*. Josiah, who died at the Battle of Megiddo (2 Kings 23:29–30). *sore*. Exceedingly. *him that goeth away*. Josiah's son, *Shallum* (Jehoahaz), removed

him: *but* weep sore for him that goeth away: for he
shall return no more, nor see his native country.
11 For thus saith the LORD touching Shallum the
son of Josiah king of Judah, which reigned instead
of Josiah his father, which went forth out of this
place; He shall not return thither any more:
12 But he shall die in the place whither they have
led him captive, and shall see this land no more.
13 ¶ Woe unto him that buildeth his house by
unrighteousness, and his chambers by wrong;
that useth his neighbour's service without wages,
and giveth him not for his work;
14 That saith, I will build me a wide house and
large chambers, and cutteth him out windows;
and *it is* cieled with cedar, and painted with
vermilion.
15 Shalt thou reign, because thou closest *thyself*
in cedar? did not thy father eat and drink, and do
judgment and justice, *and* then *it was* well with
him?
16 He judged the cause of the poor and needy;
then *it was* well *with him: was* not this to know
me? saith the LORD.
17 But thine eyes and thine heart *are* not but for
thy covetousness, and for to shed innocent blood,
and for oppression, and for violence, to do *it*.
18 Therefore thus saith the LORD concerning
Jehoiakim the son of Josiah king of Judah; They
shall not lament for him, *saying*, Ah my brother!
or, Ah sister! they shall not lament for him, *saying*,
Ah lord! or, Ah his glory!
19 He shall be buried with the burial of an
ass, drawn and cast forth beyond the gates of
Jerusalem.
20 ¶ Go up to Lebanon, and cry; and lift up thy
voice in Bashan, and cry from the passages: for all
thy lovers are destroyed.
21 I spake unto thee in thy prosperity; *but* thou
saidst, I will not hear. This *hath been* thy manner
from thy youth, that thou obeyedst not my voice.
22 The wind shall eat up all thy pastors, and thy
lovers shall go into captivity: surely then shalt
thou be ashamed and confounded for all thy
wickedness.
23 O inhabitant of Lebanon, that makest thy nest
in the cedars, how gracious shalt thou be when
pangs come upon thee, the pain as of a woman
in travail!
24 *As* I live, saith the LORD, though Coniah the
son of Jehoiakim king of Judah were the signet
upon my right hand, yet would I pluck thee
thence;
25 And I will give thee into the hand of them that
seek thy life, and into the hand *of them* whose face
thou fearest, even into the hand of Nebuchadrez-
zar king of Babylon, and into the hand of the
Chaldeans.
26 And I will cast thee out, and thy mother that
bare thee, into another country, where ye were
not born; and there shall ye die.
27 But to the land whereunto they desire to
return, thither shall they not return.
28 *Is* this man Coniah a despised broken idol? *is*
he a vessel wherein *is* no pleasure? wherefore are
they cast out, he and his seed, and are cast into a
land which they know not?
29 O earth, earth, earth, hear the word of the
LORD.
30 Thus saith the LORD, Write ye this man child-
less, a man *that* shall not prosper in his days: for

from the throne by Pharaoh Necho and taken into captivity in Egypt.

22:13 *Woe unto him* refers to Jehoiakim, Josiah's other son who became king after Shallum's exile. *by wrong*. Unjustly.

22:14 *cieled*. Paneled or overlaid. *vermilion*. Bright red pigment.

22:16 *To know* God is more than head knowledge; it is heart knowledge leading to acts of justice and compassion, and that is what delights God (9:24).

22:19 *drawn*. Dragged away. Jehoiakim was extravagantly selfish in life and most disgraced in death (36:30).

22:20 *the passages*. More likely "Abarim," a mountain range in Moab, Mount Nebo being the main peak, where Moses died (Num. 27:12; 33:47,48; Deut. 32:49). *thy lovers*. Their allies (v. 22).

22:21 *prosperity*. Security. *manner*. Habit or custom.

22:22 *pastors*. Shepherds, indicating the pastoral care kings should provide for their people.

22:23 *gracious*. The Hebrew can mean "groaning" or "being pitied."

22:24 *Coniah*. Jeconiah or Jehoiachin, whose wicked reign lasted only three months. *signet*. Ring representing the king's ownership and authority. God rejected Coniah as His representative but later revealed His acceptance of Zerubbabel, Coniah's grandson (Hag. 2:23).

22:25 Coniah was part of the second stage of Babylonian exile (about 597 BC; see 2 Kings 24:10–16; Ezek. 1:2).

22:28 *idol*. More likely a broken pottery vessel that is worthless.

22:30 *childless*. Not without children, but without offspring on the throne (1 Chron. 3:17).

Thoughts for Personal/Family Worship: Chapter 22

1. **The sins and failures of Judah's kings are in stark contrast to David's divinely inspired mandate: that rulers must be just, ruling in the fear of God (2 Sam. 23:2–3). However, even the failure of David's offspring points to God's everlasting covenant anticipating David's greater Son, who would fulfill every qualification (v. 5). Do not hope in human leadership but in Christ, the King of kings.**
2. **Like father like son is not always true. Josiah set a fine example for Jehoiakim, but Jehoiakim despised his godly home and wise father, foolishly loving outward grandeur rather than inner holiness. As he saw his new palace being built, he no doubt thought to himself how much better his life was than his father's. The Savior says, "For what is a man profited, if he shall gain the whole world, and lose his own soul? or what shall a man give in exchange for his soul?" (Matt. 16:26).**

no man of his seed shall prosper, sitting upon the
throne of David, and ruling any more in Judah.

CHAPTER 23

WOE be unto the pastors that destroy and scatter
the sheep of my pasture! saith the LORD.
2 Therefore thus saith the LORD God of Israel
against the pastors that feed my people; Ye have
scattered my flock, and driven them away, and
have not visited them: behold, I will visit upon
you the evil of your doings, saith the LORD.
3 And I will gather the remnant of my flock out
of all countries whither I have driven them, and
will bring them again to their folds; and they shall
be fruitful and increase.
4 And I will set up shepherds over them which
shall feed them: and they shall fear no more, nor
be dismayed, neither shall they be lacking, saith
the LORD.
5 ¶ Behold, the days come, saith the LORD, that
I will raise unto David a righteous Branch, and
a King shall reign and prosper, and shall execute
judgment and justice in the earth.
6 In his days Judah shall be saved, and Israel shall
dwell safely: and this *is* his name whereby he shall
be called, THE LORD OUR RIGHTEOUSNESS.
7 Therefore, behold, the days come, saith the
LORD, that they shall no more say, The LORD
liveth, which brought up the children of Israel out
of the land of Egypt;
8 But, The LORD liveth, which brought up and
which led the seed of the house of Israel out of
the north country, and from all countries whither
I had driven them; and they shall dwell in their
own land.
9 ¶ Mine heart within me is broken because
of the prophets; all my bones shake; I am like a
drunken man, and like a man whom wine hath
overcome, because of the LORD, and because of
the words of his holiness.
10 For the land is full of adulterers; for because of
swearing the land mourneth; the pleasant places
of the wilderness are dried up, and their course is
evil, and their force *is* not right.
11 For both prophet and priest are profane; yea,
in my house have I found their wickedness, saith
the LORD.
12 Wherefore their way shall be unto them as
slippery *ways* in the darkness: they shall be driven
on, and fall therein: for I will bring evil upon them,
even the year of their visitation, saith the LORD.
13 And I have seen folly in the prophets of
Samaria; they prophesied in Baal, and caused my
people Israel to err.
14 I have seen also in the prophets of Jerusalem
an horrible thing: they commit adultery, and walk
in lies: they strengthen also the hands of evildoers,
that none doth return from his wickedness:
they are all of them unto me as Sodom, and the
inhabitants thereof as Gomorrah.
15 Therefore thus saith the LORD of hosts
concerning the prophets; Behold, I will feed them
with wormwood, and make them drink the water
of gall: for from the prophets of Jerusalem is
profaneness gone forth into all the land.
16 Thus saith the LORD of hosts, Hearken not unto
the words of the prophets that prophesy unto you:
they make you vain: they speak a vision of their
own heart, *and* not out of the mouth of the LORD.
17 They say still unto them that despise me, The
LORD hath said, Ye shall have peace; and they say

Chapter 23: *The Lord pronounces His verdict on the failing shepherds and prophets and promises deliverance through His faithful King.*

23:1 *pastors.* See note at 22:22; most likely a reference to Judah's last four kings.
23:2 *visit.* Inspect or examine closely. The leaders did not pay attention to the flock; therefore God would pay attention to them by calling them to account for their sins.
23:3 *remnant.* Regardless of its size, the Old Testament term denoting God's spiritual people. He always has His "remnant according to the election of grace" (Rom. 11:5).
23:4 *shepherds.* Same word as pastors (v. 1). With the passing of Judah's earthly kings, God would raise up sufficient leaders to care for His people. The ultimate fulfillment is seen in the coming of Christ as the Good Shepherd (John 10:1–18).
23:5 The covenant promise to *David* remained (2 Sam. 7:12–16). Though his house fell to Babylon, God would raise up a new *King* as a living *Branch* out of what appeared to be a dead stump (33:15–16; Isa. 4:2; 11:1 [different word, but same sense]; Zech. 3:8; 6:12; cf. Job 14:7–9). *execute judgment and justice.* The divine ideal for a king (22:3,15; 2 Sam. 8:15; 23:3–4; 1 Kings 10:9; Ps. 72:1).
23:6 *THE LORD OUR RIGHTEOUSNESS.* Though a human descendant of David (v. 5), this King would also be the *LORD* God, the incarnate *Jehovah* (Isa. 9:6). *Righteousness* in this context first refers to God's judgment on Babylon and salvation of Judah from exile (51:9–11) but ultimately points to Christ as *our righteousness* in the presence of God (1 Cor. 1:30). Just as the sincere obedience of David brought God's blessing on him and the people (22:2–4,15–16), so the perfect obedience of Christ, even unto death on the cross, brings God's acceptance and blessing on all in Christ (Rom. 5:18–19; 2 Cor. 5:21).
23:7–8 The Messianic deliverance is seen as a second and far greater exodus (16:14–15). *north country.* Babylon, representing all the enemies of God's people.
23:10 *swearing.* A curse. *pleasant places.* Pastures or meadows. *their course.* Literally, "the place of running," the paths they follow. *their force is not right.* Their strength is not legitimate.
23:11 *profane.* Ungodly or defiled.
23:12 *evil.* Disaster. *visitation.* Punishment.
23:13 *folly.* The Hebrew refers to offensiveness. *err.* Go astray, morally and spiritually.
23:15 *wormwood.* Bitter, oil-yielding plant (9:15). *Gall.* Bitter and poisonous herb. *profaneness.* Ungodliness.
23:16 *make you vain.* Literally, "delude you."
23:17 *imagination.* Stubbornness.

unto every one that walketh after the imagination
of his own heart, No evil shall come upon you.
18 For who hath stood in the counsel of the LORD,
and hath perceived and heard his word? who hath
marked his word, and heard *it*?
19 Behold, a whirlwind of the LORD is gone forth
in fury, even a grievous whirlwind: it shall fall
grievously upon the head of the wicked.
20 The anger of the LORD shall not return, until
he have executed, and till he have performed the
thoughts of his heart: in the latter days ye shall
consider it perfectly.
21 I have not sent these prophets, yet they ran: I
have not spoken to them, yet they prophesied.
22 But if they had stood in my counsel, and had
caused my people to hear my words, then they
should have turned them from their evil way, and
from the evil of their doings.
23 *Am* I a God at hand, saith the LORD, and not a
God afar off?
24 Can any hide himself in secret places that I
shall not see him? saith the LORD. Do not I fill
heaven and earth? saith the LORD.
25 I have heard what the prophets said, that
prophesy lies in my name, saying, I have dreamed,
I have dreamed.
26 How long shall *this* be in the heart of the
prophets that prophesy lies? yea, *they are* proph-
ets of the deceit of their own heart;
27 Which think to cause my people to forget my
name by their dreams which they tell every man
to his neighbour, as their fathers have forgotten
my name for Baal.
28 The prophet that hath a dream, let him tell a
dream; and he that hath my word, let him speak
my word faithfully. What *is* the chaff to the wheat?
saith the LORD.
29 *Is* not my word like as a fire? saith the LORD;
and like a hammer *that* breaketh the rock in
pieces?
30 Therefore, behold, I *am* against the prophets,
saith the LORD, that steal my words every one
from his neighbour.
31 Behold, I *am* against the prophets, saith the
LORD, that use their tongues, and say, He saith.
32 Behold, I *am* against them that prophesy false
dreams, saith the LORD, and do tell them, and
cause my people to err by their lies, and by their
lightness; yet I sent them not, nor commanded
them: therefore they shall not profit this people at
all, saith the LORD.
33 ¶ And when this people, or the prophet, or a
priest, shall ask thee, saying, What *is* the burden
of the LORD? thou shalt then say unto them, What
burden? I will even forsake you, saith the LORD.
34 And *as for* the prophet, and the priest, and the
people, that shall say, The burden of the LORD, I
will even punish that man and his house.
35 Thus shall ye say every one to his neighbour,
and every one to his brother, What hath the LORD
answered? and, What hath the LORD spoken?
36 And the burden of the LORD shall ye mention
no more: for every man's word shall be his burden;
for ye have perverted the words of the living God,
of the LORD of hosts our God.
37 Thus shalt thou say to the prophet, What hath
the LORD answered thee? and, What hath the
LORD spoken?
38 But since ye say, The burden of the LORD;
therefore thus saith the LORD; Because ye say this
word, The burden of the LORD, and I have sent
unto you, saying, Ye shall not say, The burden of
the LORD;
39 Therefore, behold, I, even I, will utterly forget
you, and I will forsake you, and the city that I
gave you and your fathers, *and cast you* out of my
presence:
40 And I will bring an everlasting reproach upon
you, and a perpetual shame, which shall not be
forgotten.

CHAPTER 24

THE LORD shewed me, and, behold, two baskets of
figs *were* set before the temple of the LORD, after
that Nebuchadrezzar king of Babylon had carried

23:18 *counsel*. Secret or intimate circle. *marked*. Listened attentively. True prophecy comes by direct revelation from God. **23:19** *grievous whirlwind*. Whirling tempest. *fall grievously*. Whirl on the head. **23:20** *return*. Turn back. *consider*. Understand. **23:23–24** God is present everywhere (omnipresent) and knows everything (omniscient). This is a comfort to the godly (12:3; 15:15; Ps. 139:1–12) but a terror to those seeking to escape accountability for their sins (Jer. 16:17; 32:19; Ps. 94:7–11). **23:32** *lightness*. Boasting. **23:33–40** *burden*. An utterance or oracle, something taken up. The burden of the Lord seems to be this sinful people, who would be laid aside and forsaken (v. 33). This burden was to be of no more concern to Jeremiah (v. 36). The Lord would cast aside these ungrateful people, and they would bear the reproach (vv. 39–40).

Thoughts for Personal/Family Worship: Chapter 23

1. **God's omnipresence and omniscience (vv. 23–34) should bring a perspective of sober clarity to all our lives. All our thoughts and actions are open to the God with whom we have to do (Heb. 4:13). All our troubles and trials are noticed by Him. Do these two attributes of God frighten you? Do they comfort you? Why?**
2. **To enjoy God's salvation, we must have Christ as both our King and our righteousness (vv. 5–6). He came to rule as God in justice. To participate in His kingdom you must bow to His divine authority and obey His holy will (Matt. 7:21–23). Yet He also came to give a sinful, guilty people righteousness to stand before God. Your obedience will never be sufficient to atone for your sins or achieve for you acceptance in God's sight. You must**

away captive Jeconiah the son of Jehoiakim king
of Judah, and the princes of Judah, with the
carpenters and smiths, from Jerusalem, and had
brought them to Babylon.
2 One basket *had* very good figs, *even* like the figs
that are first ripe: and the other basket *had* very
naughty figs, which could not be eaten, they were
so bad.
3 Then said the LORD unto me, What seest thou,
Jeremiah? And I said, Figs; the good figs, very
good; and the evil, very evil, that cannot be eaten,
they are so evil.
4 ¶ Again the word of the LORD came unto me,
saying,
5 Thus saith the LORD, the God of Israel; Like
these good figs, so will I acknowledge them
that are carried away captive of Judah, whom
I have sent out of this place into the land of the
Chaldeans for *their* good.
6 For I will set mine eyes upon them for good,
and I will bring them again to this land: and I will
build them, and not pull *them* down; and I will
plant them, and not pluck *them* up.
7 And I will give them an heart to know me, that
I *am* the LORD: and they shall be my people, and
I will be their God: for they shall return unto me
with their whole heart.
8 ¶ And as the evil figs, which cannot be eaten,
they are so evil; surely thus saith the LORD, So will
I give Zedekiah the king of Judah, and his princes,
and the residue of Jerusalem, that remain in this
land, and them that dwell in the land of Egypt:
9 And I will deliver them to be removed into all
the kingdoms of the earth for *their* hurt, *to be* a
reproach and a proverb, a taunt and a curse, in all
places whither I shall drive them.
10 And I will send the sword, the famine, and the
pestilence, among them, till they be consumed
from off the land that I gave unto them and to
their fathers.

CHAPTER 25

THE word that came to Jeremiah concerning all the
people of Judah in the fourth year of Jehoiakim
the son of Josiah king of Judah, that *was* the first
year of Nebuchadrezzar king of Babylon;
2 The which Jeremiah the prophet spake unto all
the people of Judah, and to all the inhabitants of
Jerusalem, saying,
3 From the thirteenth year of Josiah the son of
Amon king of Judah, even unto this day, that
is the three and twentieth year, the word of the
LORD hath come unto me, and I have spoken
unto you, rising early and speaking; but ye have
not hearkened.
4 And the LORD hath sent unto you all his
servants the prophets, rising early and sending

trust entirely in Christ's work, not your own, and then God will count you as righteous in His sight (Phil. 3:8–9).

Two Further Visions (24:1—25:38)

Chapter 24: *Baskets of good and bad figs symbolize restoration for some and desolation for others.*

24:1 *The LORD shewed me.* The vision became an object lesson. *Nebuchadrezzar.* Alternate spelling of Nebuchadnezzar. *carpenters and smiths.* Craftsmen and metalworkers.

24:2 *naughty.* Of bad quality; word typically translated "evil" (23:3).

24:5 *good figs.* Captives who had surrendered to Babylon per Jeremiah's instructions.

24:6 See 1:10 for the same imagery.

24:7 *I will give them an heart . . . they shall return unto me.* Regeneration and the consequent experience of conversion, exercised in faith and repentance (31:33; Deut. 30:6; Ezek. 36:26; John 3:3). *to know me.* The essence of true godliness (9:24; 22:16; 31:34; John 17:3). *their whole heart.* Conversion involves the whole inner person: the emotions are affected, the mind earnestly turns to thoughts of God, and the will is conformed to His Word.

24:8 *evil figs.* Those who resisted or tried to escape Babylon in disobedience to Jeremiah.

24:9 *to be removed.* More literally, "to become an object of terror" to all the kingdoms.

24:10 *pestilence.* Plague. The consequences for disobedience are severe.

Thoughts for Personal/Family Worship: Chapter 24

1. **Many good people suffer terrible adversity, but God has a purpose that will ultimately work for their good (Rom. 8:28). Indeed, the Lord said of the captives, "I have sent [them] out of this place into the land of the Chaldeans *for their good*" (v. 5, emphasis added). What may have appeared to be a catastrophe would ultimately be seen as a blessing. We should not, therefore, be overwhelmed when apparent calamity overtakes us. Rather, we should remember captives like Daniel and Ezekiel who served God through it all.**
2. **Appearances often belie the facts. As the captives were carried away in chains, no doubt many who were left felt a sense of pride and self-esteem over God having chosen them to remain in the Promised Land. Instead of seeing this as a warning to turn away from their wicked practices, they imagined that all was fine with them. They would soon discover that they were under the wrath of God and marked for severe judgment. When we see the wicked prospering, let us not despair (Ps. 73).**

Chapter 25: *Jeremiah announces the seventy-year captivity and then the pouring out of the cup of divine wrath against all nations.*

25:1 *fourth year of Jehoiakim.* Jeremiah's prophecy is not in chronological order. The events of ch. 24 occurred in 597 BC, whereas ch. 25 dates to 605–604 BC.

25:3 *rising early and speaking.* Jeremiah had been prophesying with fervency for twenty-three years. *not hearkened.* Disobeyed, stubbornly resisted the truth.

25:4 *rising early and sending.* See note at v. 3. Here it speaks of the Lord's fervency in sending prophets and emphasizes how patiently He had dealt with Judah.

them; but ye have not hearkened, nor inclined
your ear to hear.
5 They said, Turn ye again now every one from
his evil way, and from the evil of your doings, and
dwell in the land that the LORD hath given unto
you and to your fathers for ever and ever:
6 And go not after other gods to serve them, and
to worship them, and provoke me not to anger
with the works of your hands; and I will do you
no hurt.
7 Yet ye have not hearkened unto me, saith the
LORD; that ye might provoke me to anger with the
works of your hands to your own hurt.
8 ¶ Therefore thus saith the LORD of hosts;
Because ye have not heard my words,
9 Behold, I will send and take all the families of
the north, saith the LORD, and Nebuchadrezzar
the king of Babylon, my servant, and will bring
them against this land, and against the inhabi-
tants thereof, and against all these nations round
about, and will utterly destroy them, and make
them an astonishment, and an hissing, and
perpetual desolations.
10 Moreover I will take from them the voice of
mirth, and the voice of gladness, the voice of the
bridegroom, and the voice of the bride, the sound
of the millstones, and the light of the candle.
11 And this whole land shall be a desolation, *and*
an astonishment; and these nations shall serve the
king of Babylon seventy years.
12 ¶ And it shall come to pass, when seventy years
are accomplished, *that* I will punish the king of
Babylon, and that nation, saith the LORD, for their
iniquity, and the land of the Chaldeans, and will
make it perpetual desolations.
13 And I will bring upon that land all my words
which I have pronounced against it, *even* all that
is written in this book, which Jeremiah hath
prophesied against all the nations.
14 For many nations and great kings shall serve
themselves of them also: and I will recompense
them according to their deeds, and according to
the works of their own hands.
15 ¶ For thus saith the LORD God of Israel unto
me; Take the wine cup of this fury at my hand,
and cause all the nations, to whom I send thee,
to drink it.
16 And they shall drink, and be moved, and be
mad, because of the sword that I will send among
them.
17 Then took I the cup at the LORD's hand, and
made all the nations to drink, unto whom the
LORD had sent me:
18 *To wit*, Jerusalem, and the cities of Judah, and
the kings thereof, and the princes thereof, to make
them a desolation, an astonishment, an hissing,
and a curse; as *it is* this day;
19 Pharaoh king of Egypt, and his servants, and
his princes, and all his people;
20 And all the mingled people, and all the kings
of the land of Uz, and all the kings of the land
of the Philistines, and Ashkelon, and Azzah, and
Ekron, and the remnant of Ashdod,
21 Edom, and Moab, and the children of Ammon,
22 And all the kings of Tyrus, and all the kings of
Zidon, and the kings of the isles which *are* beyond
the sea,
23 Dedan, and Tema, and Buz, and all *that are* in
the utmost corners,
24 And all the kings of Arabia, and all the kings of
the mingled people that dwell in the desert,
25 And all the kings of Zimri, and all the kings of
Elam, and all the kings of the Medes,
26 And all the kings of the north, far and near,
one with another, and all the kingdoms of the
world, which *are* upon the face of the earth: and
the king of Sheshach shall drink after them.
27 Therefore thou shalt say unto them, Thus saith
the LORD of hosts, the God of Israel; Drink ye, and
be drunken, and spue, and fall, and rise no more,
because of the sword which I will send among
you.
28 And it shall be, if they refuse to take the cup
at thine hand to drink, then shalt thou say unto
them, Thus saith the LORD of hosts; Ye shall
certainly drink.

25:6–7 *works of your hands*. Man-made idols. *Yet ye have not hearkened*. One can be exposed to the Word of God regularly, without effect.

25:9 *the north*. Babylon. *my servant*. Although Nebuchadnezzar had no knowledge of God, he was God's instrument to carry out His will. The Lord is absolutely sovereign and rules over *all* without exception (Isa. 10:5–7; Dan. 2:21; 4:34–35). *hissing*. Whistling as a gesture of contempt or astonishment.

25:11 *seventy years*. This is the average span of human life (Ps. 90:10). Thus, most of those going into captivity would not return. The seventy years symbolized the land's keeping the sabbath (2 Chron. 36:21). The span is most likely an approximation, since the captivity began at three different points (605, 597, and 586 BC).

25:12 God's using Babylon as His instrument of judgment did not exempt them from responsibility for their own sinful atrocities (Zech. 1:15, "they help forward the affliction").

25:14 *recompense*. Repay. Nothing is more fearful than receiving from God what is deserved (Rom. 2:6–11; 6:23).

25:15 *cup of . . . fury*. Image of being forced to receive and experience God's wrath (Ps. 75:8; Isa. 51:17,22; Rev. 14:10–11).

25:16 *moved*. Shaken violently, reel to and fro, or vomit loudly—a picture of a staggering drunk.

25:18 Of all the nations, Judah would be the first to face divine judgment. Those given the greatest privileges have the greatest responsibility. *hissing*. See note at v. 9.

25:19–26 Nations that did not know the true God were nonetheless accountable to His sovereign will.

25:22 *isles*. Coastlands or regions.

25:26 *Sheshach*. A cryptic reference to Babylon.

25:27 *spue*. Be sick or vomit.

25:28 The judgment is irresistible.

29 For, lo, I begin to bring evil on the city which
is called by my name, and should ye be utterly
unpunished? Ye shall not be unpunished: for I
will call for a sword upon all the inhabitants of
the earth, saith the LORD of hosts.
30 Therefore prophesy thou against them all
these words, and say unto them, The LORD shall
roar from on high, and utter his voice from his
holy habitation; he shall mightily roar upon his
habitation; he shall give a shout, as they that tread
the grapes, against all the inhabitants of the earth.
31 A noise shall come *even* to the ends of the
earth; for the LORD hath a controversy with the
nations, he will plead with all flesh; he will give
them *that are* wicked to the sword, saith the LORD.
32 Thus saith the LORD of hosts, Behold, evil
shall go forth from nation to nation, and a great
whirlwind shall be raised up from the coasts of
the earth.
33 And the slain of the LORD shall be at that day
from *one* end of the earth even unto the *other* end
of the earth: they shall not be lamented, neither
gathered, nor buried; they shall be dung upon the
ground.
34 ¶ Howl, ye shepherds, and cry; and wallow
yourselves *in the ashes*, ye principal of the flock:
for the days of your slaughter and of your
dispersions are accomplished; and ye shall fall like
a pleasant vessel.
35 And the shepherds shall have no way to flee,
nor the principal of the flock to escape.
36 A voice of the cry of the shepherds, and an
howling of the principal of the flock, *shall be
heard*: for the LORD hath spoiled their pasture.
37 And the peaceable habitations are cut down
because of the fierce anger of the LORD.
38 He hath forsaken his covert, as the lion: for
their land is desolate because of the fierceness of
the oppressor, and because of his fierce anger.

CHAPTER 26

IN the beginning of the reign of Jehoiakim the son
of Josiah king of Judah came this word from the
LORD, saying,
2 Thus saith the LORD; Stand in the court of
the LORD's house, and speak unto all the cities
of Judah, which come to worship in the LORD's
house, all the words that I command thee to speak
unto them; diminish not a word:
3 If so be they will hearken, and turn every man
from his evil way, that I may repent me of the evil,
which I purpose to do unto them because of the
evil of their doings.
4 And thou shalt say unto them, Thus saith the
LORD; If ye will not hearken to me, to walk in my
law, which I have set before you,
5 To hearken to the words of my servants the
prophets, whom I sent unto you, both ris-
ing up early, and sending *them*, but ye have not
hearkened;
6 Then will I make this house like Shiloh, and
will make this city a curse to all the nations of the
earth.
7 So the priests and the prophets and all the
people heard Jeremiah speaking these words in
the house of the LORD.
8 ¶ Now it came to pass, when Jeremiah had

25:29 *bring evil.* To inflict injury. Judgment begins in the household of God (1 Peter 4:17).
25:31 *controversy.* Legal dispute.
25:32 *evil.* Disaster, the effects of the judgment.
25:33 *slain of.* Killed by.
25:34 *shepherds.* Rulers of the nations who had been forced to drink the bitter cup. *ye principal.* You mighty ones. *the days. . . are accomplished.* The time has come. *pleasant.* Choice or precious.
25:38 *covert.* Lair.

Thoughts for Personal/Family Worship: Chapter 25

1. **The godly king Josiah did all he could to drive idolatry out of Judah. Yet how different was his son, Jehoiakim. Grace is not inherited. The Lord Jesus declares, "Ye must be born again" (John 3:7). This applies just as much to the children of believing parents as it does to any other person. New birth is "not of blood, nor of the will of the flesh, nor of the will of man, but of God" (John 1:13).**
2. **Scripture compares God's judgment to a cup of wrath and fury that is to be given to sinners (v. 15). Just as believers will drink forever from the fountain of living waters (2:13), delighting in God's limitless love, so also the wicked and unbelieving will choke forever on the molten fire of God's righteous anger. This should fill us with wonder at what Christ did to save sinners, when He drank the bitter cup of wrath to the very last drop (Luke 22:42–44). Who can say what it cost Him?**

JEREMIAH AND THE FALSE PROPHETS (26:1—29:32)

Chapter 26: *Jeremiah's second Temple Sermon leads to his arrest and subsequent acquittal.*

Diminish Not a Word (26:1–24)

26:1–6 This is the prophet's second Temple Sermon exposing the hypocrisy of those who claimed to worship the Lord (ch. 7). Hypocrisy can exist in the best of environments. External religion without a sincere heart before God is never acceptable to Him.
26:2 *diminish not.* Do not omit. He was to preach the whole counsel of God; the preacher has no authority to edit God's Word (Acts 20:20,27; 2 Tim. 4:1–5).
26:3 *the evil.* The disastrous nature of Judah's sin. In reference to God, it designates the disastrous consequences of His judgment. If they would repent (*turn*), He would relent (*repent*) and not bring the judgment.
26:5 *rising up early and sending.* The Lord warned Judah with consistency and earnestness through His prophets.
26:6 *like Shiloh.* The mere presence of the tabernacle did not preserve Shiloh, and neither could the mere presence of the temple preserve Jerusalem. What takes place in the heart of worshipers is more important than any building (Isa. 29:13).

made an end of speaking all that the LORD had
commanded *him* to speak unto all the people,
that the priests and the prophets and all the
people took him, saying, Thou shalt surely die.
9 Why hast thou prophesied in the name of the
LORD, saying, This house shall be like Shiloh, and
this city shall be desolate without an inhabitant?
And all the people were gathered against Jeremiah
in the house of the LORD.
10 ¶ When the princes of Judah heard these
things, then they came up from the king's house
unto the house of the LORD, and sat down in the
entry of the new gate of the LORD's *house*.
11 Then spake the priests and the prophets unto
the princes and to all the people, saying, This man
is worthy to die; for he hath prophesied against
this city, as ye have heard with your ears.
12 ¶ Then spake Jeremiah unto all the princes
and to all the people, saying, The LORD sent me to
prophesy against this house and against this city
all the words that ye have heard.
13 Therefore now amend your ways and your
doings, and obey the voice of the LORD your God;
and the LORD will repent him of the evil that he
hath pronounced against you.
14 As for me, behold, I *am* in your hand: do with
me as seemeth good and meet unto you.
15 But know ye for certain, that if ye put me to
death, ye shall surely bring innocent blood upon
yourselves, and upon this city, and upon the
inhabitants thereof: for of a truth the LORD hath
sent me unto you to speak all these words in your
ears.
16 ¶ Then said the princes and all the people
unto the priests and to the prophets; This man *is*
not worthy to die: for he hath spoken to us in the
name of the LORD our God.
17 Then rose up certain of the elders of the land,
and spake to all the assembly of the people, saying,
18 Micah the Morasthite prophesied in the days
of Hezekiah king of Judah, and spake to all the
people of Judah, saying, Thus saith the LORD
of hosts; Zion shall be plowed *like* a field, and
Jerusalem shall become heaps, and the mountain
of the house as the high places of a forest.
19 Did Hezekiah king of Judah and all Judah
put him at all to death? did he not fear the LORD,
and besought the LORD, and the LORD repented
him of the evil which he had pronounced against
them? Thus might we procure great evil against
our souls.
20 And there was also a man that prophesied in
the name of the LORD, Urijah the son of Shema-
iah of Kirjath-jearim, who prophesied against
this city and against this land according to all the
words of Jeremiah:
21 And when Jehoiakim the king, with all his
mighty men, and all the princes, heard his words,
the king sought to put him to death: but when
Urijah heard it, he was afraid, and fled, and went
into Egypt;
22 And Jehoiakim the king sent men into Egypt,
namely, Elnathan the son of Achbor, and *certain*
men with him into Egypt.
23 And they fetched forth Urijah out of Egypt,
and brought him unto Jehoiakim the king; who
slew him with the sword, and cast his dead body
into the graves of the common people.
24 Nevertheless the hand of Ahikam the son of
Shaphan was with Jeremiah, that they should not
give him into the hand of the people to put him
to death.

CHAPTER 27

IN the beginning of the reign of Jehoiakim the
son of Josiah king of Judah came this word unto
Jeremiah from the LORD, saying,

26:10 *princes.* Persons of rank and authority over others, not the king's sons (vv. 11,16).
26:11 Confronting false confidence in holy places and rituals may provoke murderous anger from those who hope in them (Acts 6:13; 7:54–58).
26:13 *amend.* Literally, "make good." Nothing less than genuine sorrow for sin and true repentance could save them. *The LORD will repent.* Relent; see note at v. 3.
26:14 *meet unto you.* Suitable or fit, literally, "the right thing in your eyes."
26:18 See Mic. 3:12.
26:19 *besought.* Prayed to. *repented.* relented. *evil.* Disaster.

Thoughts for Personal/Family Worship: Chapter 26

1. **Jeremiah's exhortation to repent, delivered to the temple worshipers, is a vivid reminder that just going to church has no merit before God. It is possible to be in the most holy of environments, and to go through all the motions of worship, without a sincere heart before God. Many today hear the gospel and profess it to be the Word of God, yet go no further. What are the distinctive marks of truly believing the Word?**
2. **Jeremiah and Urijah faithfully preached the same message (v. 20), and both of their lives were threatened because of what they preached. In the providence of God Jeremiah was delivered, but Urijah was not. Some who live by faith are delivered from their enemies, and some are killed (Acts 12:1–11; Heb. 11:33–37). We are to be faithful to God and His Word, regardless of the consequences.**
3. **The rejection of the prophet points to the ultimate rejection of the ideal Prophet, Jesus Christ. How was Jeremiah an imperfect but true picture of Christ? How are the two different?**

Chapter 27: ***Using the object lesson of a yoke, Jeremiah warns that surrendering to Babylon is the only hope for survival.***

Surrender to the Yoke or Perish by the Sword (27:1–22)

27:1–3 God's word through Jeremiah was consistent. He

2 Thus saith the LORD to me; Make thee bonds
and yokes, and put them upon thy neck,
3 And send them to the king of Edom, and to the
king of Moab, and to the king of the Ammonites,
and to the king of Tyrus, and to the king of Zidon,
by the hand of the messengers which come to
Jerusalem unto Zedekiah king of Judah;
4 And command them to say unto their masters,
Thus saith the LORD of hosts, the God of Israel;
Thus shall ye say unto your masters;
5 I have made the earth, the man and the beast
that *are* upon the ground, by my great power and
by my outstretched arm, and have given it unto
whom it seemed meet unto me.
6 And now have I given all these lands into the
hand of Nebuchadnezzar the king of Babylon, my
servant; and the beasts of the field have I given
him also to serve him.
7 And all nations shall serve him, and his son, and
his son's son, until the very time of his land come:
and then many nations and great kings shall serve
themselves of him.
8 And it shall come to pass, *that* the nation
and kingdom which will not serve the same
Nebuchadnezzar the king of Babylon, and that
will not put their neck under the yoke of the king
of Babylon, that nation will I punish, saith the
LORD, with the sword, and with the famine, and
with the pestilence, until I have consumed them
by his hand.
9 Therefore hearken not ye to your prophets,
nor to your diviners, nor to your dreamers, nor
to your enchanters, nor to your sorcerers, which
speak unto you, saying, Ye shall not serve the king
of Babylon:
10 For they prophesy a lie unto you, to remove
you far from your land; and that I should drive
you out, and ye should perish.
11 But the nations that bring their neck under the
yoke of the king of Babylon, and serve him, those
will I let remain still in their own land, saith the
LORD; and they shall till it, and dwell therein.
12 ¶ I spake also to Zedekiah king of Judah
according to all these words, saying, Bring your
necks under the yoke of the king of Babylon, and
serve him and his people, and live.
13 Why will ye die, thou and thy people, by the
sword, by the famine, and by the pestilence, as the
LORD hath spoken against the nation that will not
serve the king of Babylon?
14 Therefore hearken not unto the words of the
prophets that speak unto you, saying, Ye shall not
serve the king of Babylon: for they prophesy a lie
unto you.
15 For I have not sent them, saith the LORD, yet
they prophesy a lie in my name; that I might drive
you out, and that ye might perish, ye, and the
prophets that prophesy unto you.
16 Also I spake to the priests and to all this people,
saying, Thus saith the LORD; Hearken not to the
words of your prophets that prophesy unto you,
saying, Behold, the vessels of the LORD's house
shall now shortly be brought again from Babylon:
for they prophesy a lie unto you.
17 Hearken not unto them; serve the king of
Babylon, and live: wherefore should this city be
laid waste?
18 But if they *be* prophets, and if the word of the
LORD be with them, let them now make interces-
sion to the LORD of hosts, that the vessels which
are left in the house of the LORD, and *in* the house
of the king of Judah, and at Jerusalem, go not to
Babylon.
19 ¶ For thus saith the LORD of hosts concerning
the pillars, and concerning the sea, and concern-
ing the bases, and concerning the residue of the
vessels that remain in this city,
20 Which Nebuchadnezzar king of Babylon took
not, when he carried away captive Jeconiah the
son of Jehoiakim king of Judah from Jerusalem
to Babylon, and all the nobles of Judah and
Jerusalem;

---

gave a commandment at the beginning of Jehoiakim's reign, and it remained relevant to the reign of Zedekiah.

27:3 *Edom . . . Zidon*. Jeremiah's message to foreign nations was part of his commission (1:10).

27:5 *meet unto me*. Literally, "that which is right or pleasing in my eyes." Being the Creator (see note at 10:12), God determines all national borders (Acts 17:24–26).

27:6 *my servant*. See note at 25:9. Nebuchadnezzar was the most powerful king on earth, yet he was nothing more than an agent of divine providence.

27:9 *diviners*. Those who use magic to make predictions.

27:11 *till*. Cultivate.

27:19 *pillars . . . sea . . . bases*. Components of the temple (1 Kings 7:15–37). *the residue*. The rest. For the fulfillment of this prophecy, see 52:17.

Thoughts for Personal/Family Worship: Chapter 27

1. Zedekiah's foolish refusal of the Lord's easy yoke of obedience resulted in divine justice coming heavily upon him. Zedekiah refused to see the truth, and his eyes were put out, and he was shackled in irons, never to be released (39:7; 2 Kings 25:7). Here is a picture of what happens when God gives a person over to a reprobate mind. The Lord Jesus lovingly calls the slaves of Satan to come unto Him and take His easy yoke upon them (Matt. 11:28–30). The reprobate, however, refuse the message of grace and despise God's salvation. Eventually, all light is taken from them and they perish. Do not resist the light you have been given, or you may end up in total darkness.

2. The contrast between the words of the true and the false prophets was a matter of life and death. False prophecy naturally appeals to us. "There is a way that seemeth right unto a man, but the end thereof are the ways of death" (Prov. 14:12). The true Word calls us to humbly surrender to Christ, God's great Prophet and Servant. Listen to Him!

21 Yea, thus saith the LORD of hosts, the God of
Israel, concerning the vessels that remain *in* the
house of the LORD, and *in* the house of the king of
Judah and of Jerusalem;
22 They shall be carried to Babylon, and there
shall they be until the day that I visit them, saith
the LORD; then will I bring them up, and restore
them to this place.

CHAPTER 28

AND it came to pass the same year, in the
beginning of the reign of Zedekiah king of Judah,
in the fourth year, *and* in the fifth month, *that*
Hananiah the son of Azur the prophet, which
was of Gibeon, spake unto me in the house of the
LORD, in the presence of the priests and of all the
people, saying,
2 Thus speaketh the LORD of hosts, the God of
Israel, saying, I have broken the yoke of the king
of Babylon.
3 Within two full years will I bring again into
this place all the vessels of the LORD's house, that
Nebuchadnezzar king of Babylon took away from
this place, and carried them to Babylon:
4 And I will bring again to this place Jeconiah
the son of Jehoiakim king of Judah, with all the
captives of Judah, that went into Babylon, saith
the LORD: for I will break the yoke of the king of
Babylon.
5 ¶ Then the prophet Jeremiah said unto the
prophet Hananiah in the presence of the priests,
and in the presence of all the people that stood in
the house of the LORD,
6 Even the prophet Jeremiah said, Amen: the
LORD do so: the LORD perform thy words which
thou hast prophesied, to bring again the vessels
of the LORD's house, and all that is carried away
captive, from Babylon into this place.
7 Nevertheless hear thou now this word that
I speak in thine ears, and in the ears of all the
people;
8 The prophets that have been before me and
before thee of old prophesied both against many
countries, and against great kingdoms, of war,
and of evil, and of pestilence.
9 The prophet which prophesieth of peace, when
the word of the prophet shall come to pass, *then*
shall the prophet be known, that the LORD hath
truly sent him.
10 ¶ Then Hananiah the prophet took the yoke
from off the prophet Jeremiah's neck, and brake
it.
11 And Hananiah spake in the presence of all
the people, saying, Thus saith the LORD; Even so
will I break the yoke of Nebuchadnezzar king of
Babylon from the neck of all nations within the
space of two full years. And the prophet Jeremiah
went his way.
12 ¶ Then the word of the LORD came unto
Jeremiah *the prophet*, after that Hananiah the
prophet had broken the yoke from off the neck of
the prophet Jeremiah, saying,
13 Go and tell Hananiah, saying, Thus saith the
LORD; Thou hast broken the yokes of wood; but
thou shalt make for them yokes of iron.
14 For thus saith the LORD of hosts, the God of
Israel; I have put a yoke of iron upon the neck of
all these nations, that they may serve Nebuchad-
nezzar king of Babylon; and they shall serve him:
and I have given him the beasts of the field also.
15 ¶ Then said the prophet Jeremiah unto Hana-
niah the prophet, Hear now, Hananiah; The LORD
hath not sent thee; but thou makest this people to
trust in a lie.
16 Therefore thus saith the LORD; Behold, I will

Chapter 28: *Hananiah contradicts Jeremiah, who in turn identifies him as a false prophet and predicts his imminent death.*

The False Prophet Hananiah (28:1–17)

28:1 *Hananiah . . . of Gibeon.* Ironically, his name means "the Lord is gracious," yet he comes from Gibeon, a territory of Benjamin historically associated with deception (Josh. 9).
28:3–4 Claiming divine authority, Hananiah's prediction contradicts Jeremiah's of seventy years of captivity (22:26–27; 25:1). Both could not be right.
28:6 *Amen.* Surely or truly. Some interpreters suggest that this was spoken with sarcasm, others in sincerity. Hananiah's was the more pleasant prophecy, but Jeremiah knew it was false.
28:9 One test of a true prophet is whether his message comes to pass (Deut. 18:22). Another test is whether the word confirms or contradicts what God has already said (Deut. 13:1–3). Hananiah, in contradicting Jeremiah, was already marked as a false prophet, which the non-fulfillment of his prediction would confirm.
28:10 Hananiah reinforces his message by symbolically breaking Jeremiah's yoke, the symbol of his message.
28:16 After confirming Jeremiah's word (26:12–14), the Lord gives him a short-term prophecy to validate his ministry: the imminent death of Hananiah.
28:17 Hananiah's death confirmed Jeremiah as a true prophet (see note at v. 9).

Thoughts for Personal/Family Worship: Chapter 28

1. **Jeremiah's message was one of gloom and hardship. Hananiah's was upbeat and positive. There can be little doubt which was the more popular. We must not, therefore, be surprised when false religion is more popular than the truth. Liberalism falsely declares what people want to hear: that God is love and that everyone will enjoy heaven. Such lies cause people to live without any regard for their sins, or for the holiness and justice of God. Why should we be so foolish as to ignore God's Word? "It is a fearful thing to fall into the hands of the living God" (Heb. 10:31).**
2. **That both the false prophet and the true prophet claimed to have a word from the Lord reminds us of how important it is to "try the spirits whether they are of**

cast thee from off the face of the earth: this year
thou shalt die, because thou hast taught rebellion
against the LORD.
17 So Hananiah the prophet died the same year
in the seventh month.

CHAPTER 29

NOW these *are* the words of the letter that
Jeremiah the prophet sent from Jerusalem unto
the residue of the elders which were carried away
captives, and to the priests, and to the prophets,
and to all the people whom Nebuchadnezzar had
carried away captive from Jerusalem to Babylon;
2 (After that Jeconiah the king, and the queen,
and the eunuchs, the princes of Judah and
Jerusalem, and the carpenters, and the smiths,
were departed from Jerusalem;)
3 By the hand of Elasah the son of Shaphan, and
Gemariah the son of Hilkiah, (whom Zedekiah
king of Judah sent unto Babylon to Nebuchadnez-
zar king of Babylon) saying,
4 Thus saith the LORD of hosts, the God of Israel,
unto all that are carried away captives, whom I
have caused to be carried away from Jerusalem
unto Babylon;
5 Build ye houses, and dwell *in them*; and plant
gardens, and eat the fruit of them;
6 Take ye wives, and beget sons and daughters;
and take wives for your sons, and give your
daughters to husbands, that they may bear sons
and daughters; that ye may be increased there,
and not diminished.
7 And seek the peace of the city whither I have
caused you to be carried away captives, and pray
unto the LORD for it: for in the peace thereof shall
ye have peace.
8 ¶ For thus saith the LORD of hosts, the God of
Israel; Let not your prophets and your diviners,
that *be* in the midst of you, deceive you, neither
hearken to your dreams which ye cause to be
dreamed.
9 For they prophesy falsely unto you in my name:
I have not sent them, saith the LORD.
10 ¶ For thus saith the LORD, That after seventy
years be accomplished at Babylon I will visit
you, and perform my good word toward you, in
causing you to return to this place.
11 For I know the thoughts that I think toward
you, saith the LORD, thoughts of peace, and not of
evil, to give you an expected end.
12 Then shall ye call upon me, and ye shall go and
pray unto me, and I will hearken unto you.
13 And ye shall seek me, and find *me*, when ye
shall search for me with all your heart.
14 And I will be found of you, saith the LORD:
and I will turn away your captivity, and I will
gather you from all the nations, and from all the
places whither I have driven you, saith the LORD;
and I will bring you again into the place whence I
caused you to be carried away captive.
15 ¶ Because ye have said, The LORD hath raised
us up prophets in Babylon;
16 *Know* that thus saith the LORD of the king
that sitteth upon the throne of David, and of all
the people that dwelleth in this city, *and* of your
brethren that are not gone forth with you into
captivity;
17 Thus saith the LORD of hosts; Behold, I will
send upon them the sword, the famine, and the
pestilence, and will make them like vile figs, that
cannot be eaten, they are so evil.
18 And I will persecute them with the sword,
with the famine, and with the pestilence, and will
deliver them to be removed to all the kingdoms of
the earth, to be a curse, and an astonishment, and

God, because many false prophets are gone out into the world" (1 John 4:1; cf. 2 Peter 2:1–3). In our day, the key test is conformity to what God has already revealed. We know that God's Word will never be self-contradictory. We must be like the Bereans, who "searched the scriptures daily, whether those things were so" (Acts 17:11).

Chapter 29: ***Jeremiah writes to the captives in Babylon, instructing them to live normally, with a view to future deliverance, and declares the destruction coming on Jerusalem and the false prophets.***

Jeremiah's Letter to the Captives in Babylon (29:1–32)

29:1–2 This letter dates sometime between the second wave of the Babylonian captivity (597 BC; see 2 Kings 24:12–16) and the final destruction of the city (586 BC). The first wave was 605 BC when Daniel was exiled. *Eunuchs . . . princes.* High officials; the two words refer to just one group of leaders. *smiths.* Metalworkers.

29:4 *I have caused.* It was the Lord, not Nebuchadnezzar, who ordained Judah's captivity. Babylon was merely the tool God used to accomplish His purpose.

29:5–6 The captives must settle down and live normal lives while in Babylon.

29:7 They are instructed to seek *peace* in Babylon and pray for that peace to remain.

29:8 *diviners.* Those who made predictions using magic. *your dreams.* Dreams were a means of divine revelation, but these were self-generated by false prophets and not from God.

29:11 A remarkably beautiful statement of grace. *the thoughts . . . I think.* The plans I plan. *peace.* Overall well-being. *evil.* Harm or hurt. *to give you an expected end.* Literally, "to give to you a future and hope." Though the Lord was punishing Judah, their chastisement was for their good.

29:13 *with all your heart.* Not sinless perfection but wholehearted sincerity engaging the mind, affections, and will. The Lord assures genuine seekers that they will find Him (2 Chron. 15:2). This new disposition of the heart is the gift of God (Deut. 30:6).

29:14 *I will be found.* The Hebrew has the idea of God's allowing Himself to be found (Isa. 55:6).

29:17–18 points to the final siege against Jerusalem in 586 BC. *pestilence.* Plague. *vile.* Horrid or offensive. *evil.* Of bad quality. *hissing.* Whistling as a gesture of scorn or ridicule.

an hissing, and a reproach, among all the nations
whither I have driven them:
19 Because they have not hearkened to my words,
saith the LORD, which I sent unto them by my
servants the prophets, rising up early and sending
them; but ye would not hear, saith the LORD.
20 ¶ Hear ye therefore the word of the LORD, all ye
of the captivity, whom I have sent from Jerusalem
to Babylon:
21 Thus saith the LORD of hosts, the God of Israel,
of Ahab the son of Kolaiah, and of Zedekiah the
son of Maaseiah, which prophesy a lie unto you
in my name; Behold, I will deliver them into the
hand of Nebuchadrezzar king of Babylon; and he
shall slay them before your eyes;
22 And of them shall be taken up a curse by
all the captivity of Judah which *are* in Babylon,
saying, The LORD make thee like Zedekiah and
like Ahab, whom the king of Babylon roasted in
the fire;
23 Because they have committed villany in
Israel, and have committed adultery with their
neighbours' wives, and have spoken lying words
in my name, which I have not commanded them;
even I know, and *am* a witness, saith the LORD.
24 ¶ *Thus* shalt thou also speak to Shemaiah the
Nehelamite, saying,
25 Thus speaketh the LORD of hosts, the God of
Israel, saying, Because thou hast sent letters in thy
name unto all the people that *are* at Jerusalem,
and to Zephaniah the son of Maaseiah the priest,
and to all the priests, saying,
26 The LORD hath made thee priest in the stead
of Jehoiada the priest, that ye should be officers
in the house of the LORD, for every man *that is*
mad, and maketh himself a prophet, that thou
shouldest put him in prison, and in the stocks.
27 Now therefore why hast thou not reproved
Jeremiah of Anathoth, which maketh himself a
prophet to you?
28 For therefore he sent unto us *in* Babylon,
saying, This *captivity is* long: build ye houses, and
dwell *in them*; and plant gardens, and eat the fruit
of them.
29 And Zephaniah the priest read this letter in the
ears of Jeremiah the prophet.
30 ¶ Then came the word of the LORD unto
Jeremiah, saying,
31 Send to all them of the captivity, saying, Thus
saith the LORD concerning Shemaiah the Ne-
helamite; Because that Shemaiah hath prophesied
unto you, and I sent him not, and he caused you
to trust in a lie:
32 Therefore thus saith the LORD; Behold, I will
punish Shemaiah the Nehelamite, and his seed: he
shall not have a man to dwell among this people;
neither shall he behold the good that I will do for
my people, saith the LORD; because he hath taught
rebellion against the LORD.

CHAPTER 30

THE word that came to Jeremiah from the LORD,
saying,
2 Thus speaketh the LORD God of Israel, saying,
Write thee all the words that I have spoken unto
thee in a book.
3 For, lo, the days come, saith the LORD, that I will
bring again the captivity of my people Israel and
Judah, saith the LORD: and I will cause them to
return to the land that I gave to their fathers, and
they shall possess it.
4 ¶ And these *are* the words that the LORD spake
concerning Israel and concerning Judah.
5 For thus saith the LORD; We have heard a voice
of trembling, of fear, and not of peace.
6 Ask ye now, and see whether a man doth travail
with child? wherefore do I see every man with his
hands on his loins, as a woman in travail, and all
faces are turned into paleness?

29:19 *rising up early and sending.* Expression of fervency or earnestness.
29:23 *villany.* Willful, sacrilegious sin or disgraceful folly.
29:26 *mad.* Crazy or behaving like a madman. Here is Shemaiah's contemptuous description of prophetic behavior, particularly Jeremiah's.

Thoughts for Personal/Family Worship: Chapter 29

1. **Like the exiles of Judah in Babylon, so Christians are exiles in this world (Heb. 11:13; 1 Peter 1:1; 2:11). Our citizenship is in heaven, not here (Phil. 3:20). However, Christians are not to be detached from society but should live in the world in such a way as to set forth the beauty of Christ. We too must seek the peace of our community (v. 7), letting our good works shine before men (Matt. 5:16). How can you do that?**
2. **As God had plans of peace for the people of Judah in their captivity, so He has plans of peace toward all His people in Christ, though they are still exiles in this world.**

God is not playing hide and seek with His people. He will not forsake any who genuinely and wholeheartedly seek Him. Christians, therefore, should be people of great optimism, enduring their trials with confident hope.

THE BOOK OF CONSOLATION (30:1—33:26)

Chapter 30: *Jeremiah predicts the end of the captivity, giving assurance of God's presence, the punishment of the enemy, and the renewal of covenant blessings.*

Be Not Dismayed (30:1–24)

30:2 *Write.* A vivid example of God inspiring the Scriptures (2 Peter 1:20–21).
30:3 Significantly, the promise was not only to Judah but also to *Israel*. The northern kingdom had been displaced a hundred years earlier.
30:5 *fear.* Specifically, "trembling" or "dread."
30:6 *a man doth travail with child.* Literally, "a male is giving birth." *every man with his hands.* Literally, "every strong man." *travail.* Giving birth, a graphic image of intense pain.

7 Alas! for that day *is* great, so that none *is* like it:
it *is* even the time of Jacob's trouble; but he shall
be saved out of it.
8 For it shall come to pass in that day, saith the
LORD of hosts, *that* I will break his yoke from off
thy neck, and will burst thy bonds, and strangers
shall no more serve themselves of him:
9 But they shall serve the LORD their God, and
David their king, whom I will raise up unto them.
10 ¶ Therefore fear thou not, O my servant Jacob,
saith the LORD; neither be dismayed, O Israel: for,
lo, I will save thee from afar, and thy seed from the
land of their captivity; and Jacob shall return, and
shall be in rest, and be quiet, and none shall make
him afraid.
11 For I *am* with thee, saith the LORD, to save thee:
though I make a full end of all nations whither I
have scattered thee, yet will I not make a full end
of thee: but I will correct thee in measure, and will
not leave thee altogether unpunished.
12 For thus saith the LORD, Thy bruise *is* incur-
able, *and* thy wound *is* grievous.
13 *There is* none to plead thy cause, that thou
mayest be bound up: thou hast no healing
medicines.
14 All thy lovers have forgotten thee; they seek
thee not; for I have wounded thee with the wound
of an enemy, with the chastisement of a cruel one,
for the multitude of thine iniquity; *because* thy
sins were increased.
15 Why criest thou for thine affliction? thy sorrow
is incurable for the multitude of thine iniquity:
because thy sins were increased, I have done these
things unto thee.
16 Therefore all they that devour thee shall be
devoured; and all thine adversaries, every one of
them, shall go into captivity; and they that spoil
thee shall be a spoil, and all that prey upon thee
will I give for a prey.
17 For I will restore health unto thee, and I will
heal thee of thy wounds, saith the LORD; because
they called thee an Outcast, *saying*, This *is* Zion,
whom no man seeketh after.
18 ¶ Thus saith the LORD; Behold, I will bring
again the captivity of Jacob's tents, and have
mercy on his dwellingplaces; and the city shall be
builded upon her own heap, and the palace shall
remain after the manner thereof.
19 And out of them shall proceed thanksgiving
and the voice of them that make merry: and I will
multiply them, and they shall not be few; I will
also glorify them, and they shall not be small.
20 Their children also shall be as aforetime, and
their congregation shall be established before me,
and I will punish all that oppress them.
21 And their nobles shall be of themselves, and
their governor shall proceed from the midst of
them; and I will cause him to draw near, and
he shall approach unto me: for who *is* this that
engaged his heart to approach unto me? saith the
LORD.
22 And ye shall be my people, and I will be your
God.
23 Behold, the whirlwind of the LORD goeth forth

30:7 *that day*. The day of the Lord, whenever God comes in salvation and judgment, especially at the end of the age. *time of Jacob's trouble*. What our Lord Jesus speaks of in Matt. 24:21–22. Although this time will be fearful, the Lord will save His people *out of it*.
30:8 *strangers shall no more serve themselves of him*. Foreigners will no longer keep them in slavery.
30:9 *the LORD their God, and David their king*. Or "the Lord their God, even David their King," a direct reference to Christ, God incarnate (23:5; 33:15). Christ is both the heir of David's kingdom (Isa. 9:7) and the ideal *David* who would come (Ezek. 34:23–24; 37:24–25; Hos. 3:5).
30:11 *I am with thee*. He is Immanuel (God with us). *a full end*. Complete destruction. *correct thee in measure*. Literally, "chasten you according to justice, or according to what is due."
30:12–17 Their sin and misery were so severe as to be humanly *incurable*, but the Lord says, *I will heal thee of thy wounds*. He is the great Physician for sinners (3:22; 17:14; 33:6; Hos. 14:4; Luke 5:30–32). What is impossible for man is possible with God (Mark 10:27).
30:16 *all that prey upon thee will I give for a prey*. All that plunder you I will make plunder or booty. What the enemy has done will, in turn, be done to them in retaliation.
30:18 *heap*. Mound of rubble. Cities would typically build on the ruins of previous settlements. *manner*. Custom. The fortified *palace* would be restored to its usual function.
30:19 *small*. Lowly or insignificant.
30:20 *aforetime*. Previously.
30:21 *nobles*. The Hebrew is singular ("noble"), referring to a mighty or majestic one. *governor*. One who rules or reigns. *approach unto me*. As a priest (Num. 3:10; 16:5,10). The linking of kingly and priestly functions in one person implies that this is Christ, the priest-king (Ps. 110:1,4; Heb. 7:1). In Him believers are also kings and priests (Rev. 1:6; 5:10).
30:22 *my people . . . your God*. The consequence of the coming of Christ is the fulfillment of God's covenant promise of union and communion between Him and His people (24:7; 31:1,33; 32:28; Gen. 17:7; Ex. 6:7).

Thoughts for Personal/Family Worship: Chapter 30

1. **It is surely the greatest comfort to have a real assurance that the Lord is with us (v. 9). This assuring promise runs throughout Scripture, particularly in times of crisis, or special work in advancing the kingdom: to Jacob (Gen. 28:15), Moses (Ex. 3:12), Joshua (Josh. 1:9), Gideon (Judg. 6:12), and believers today (Matt. 28:20). How blessed we are if our trust is in the Lord! Let this thought be to your continual comfort, for God is the great healer.**
2. **Judah suffered greatly because they would not obey the Word of the Lord; but God used their suffering to chastise them, with a view of bringing them back to Himself. It is a wonderful assurance to know that though there are times when the Lord chastises His people, it is nonetheless always for our good (Rom. 8:28). How much better it would be to hear God's Word and avoid His chastisement altogether. May the Lord grant us teachable spirits and the humility to walk in obedience before Him.**

with fury, a continuing whirlwind: it shall fall
with pain upon the head of the wicked.
24 The fierce anger of the LORD shall not return,
until he have done *it*, and until he have performed
the intents of his heart: in the latter days ye shall
consider it.

CHAPTER 31

AT the same time, saith the LORD, will I be the
God of all the families of Israel, and they shall be
my people.
2 Thus saith the LORD, The people *which were* left
of the sword found grace in the wilderness; *even*
Israel, when I went to cause him to rest.
3 The LORD hath appeared of old unto me, *say-*
ing, Yea, I have loved thee with an everlasting love:
therefore with lovingkindness have I drawn thee.
4 Again I will build thee, and thou shalt be built,
O virgin of Israel: thou shalt again be adorned
with thy tabrets, and shalt go forth in the dances
of them that make merry.
5 Thou shalt yet plant vines upon the mountains
of Samaria: the planters shall plant, and shall eat
them as common things.
6 For there shall be a day, *that* the watchmen
upon the mount Ephraim shall cry, Arise ye, and
let us go up to Zion unto the LORD our God.
7 For thus saith the LORD; Sing with gladness for
Jacob, and shout among the chief of the nations:
publish ye, praise ye, and say, O LORD, save thy
people, the remnant of Israel.
8 Behold, I will bring them from the north coun-
try, and gather them from the coasts of the earth,
and with them the blind and the lame, the woman
with child and her that travaileth with child
together: a great company shall return thither.
9 They shall come with weeping, and with
supplications will I lead them: I will cause them
to walk by the rivers of waters in a straight way,
wherein they shall not stumble: for I am a father
to Israel, and Ephraim *is* my firstborn.
10 ¶ Hear the word of the LORD, O ye nations,
and declare *it* in the isles afar off, and say, He that
scattered Israel will gather him, and keep him, as
a shepherd *doth* his flock.
11 For the LORD hath redeemed Jacob, and
ransomed him from the hand of *him that was*
stronger than he.
12 Therefore they shall come and sing in the
height of Zion, and shall flow together to the
goodness of the LORD, for wheat, and for wine,
and for oil, and for the young of the flock and
of the herd: and their soul shall be as a watered
garden; and they shall not sorrow any more at all.
13 Then shall the virgin rejoice in the dance, both
young men and old together: for I will turn their
mourning into joy, and will comfort them, and
make them rejoice from their sorrow.
14 And I will satiate the soul of the priests with
fatness, and my people shall be satisfied with my
goodness, saith the LORD.
15 ¶ Thus saith the LORD; A voice was heard in
Ramah, lamentation, *and* bitter weeping; Rahel
weeping for her children refused to be comforted
for her children, because they *were* not.
16 Thus saith the LORD; Refrain thy voice from
weeping, and thine eyes from tears: for thy work
shall be rewarded, saith the LORD; and they shall
come again from the land of the enemy.
17 And there is hope in thine end, saith the LORD,
that thy children shall come again to their own
border.
18 ¶ I have surely heard Ephraim bemoaning
himself *thus*; Thou hast chastised me, and I was
chastised, as a bullock unaccustomed *to the yoke*:
turn thou me, and I shall be turned; for thou *art*
the LORD my God.
19 Surely after that I was turned, I repented; and
after that I was instructed, I smote upon *my* thigh:

Chapter 31: *Israel's restoration is explained in terms of God's everlasting love and covenant renewal.*

Loved with an Everlasting Love (31:1–26)

31:1 The renewing of the covenant between *God* and His *people* (see note at 30:22) also heals the rift between the northern and southern kingdoms (*all the families of Israel*).

31:2 *left of the sword*. Those who survived the sword. *grace in the wilderness*. God's deliverance of the people at the exodus, and particularly from defeat at the Red Sea.

31:3 *with lovingkindness have I drawn thee*. The idea is that God in His sovereignty has extended, or stretched out, His covenant loyalty to those He has eternally loved.

31:4 *virgin of Israel*. The people pictured as a young woman (18:13; Isa. 47:1). *tabrets*. Hand-drums or tambourines.

31:5 *the planters . . . shall eat as common things*. Literally, "the planters planted and will profane or treat as common" most likely refers to the normal expectation of eating what was planted; hence the KJV translation. Some take this to mean that the vineyard would be defiled.

31:7 *remnant*. See note at 23:3.

31:8 *north country*. Perhaps Assyria and Babylon; general designation of hostile nations. *coasts*. Literally, "remote parts." The Lord will bring His people from distant lands in the second exodus.

31:11 *redeemed*. Set free by payment. *ransomed*. Restored by a kinsman-redeemer who does whatever is necessary for the one with whom he has a relationship (Mark 10:45; Gal. 3:13).

31:14 *I will satiate . . . with fatness*. Symbolic of prosperity.

31:15 *Ramah*. Place of Benjamin's birth and, ironically, the staging place where the Babylonians brought their Jewish captives to prepare them for the long march to Babylon (40:1). *Rahel*. Rachel, an ancestor to those in both the northern and southern kingdoms, representing the whole of Israel lamenting the sorrow of oppression by foreign powers, even to the days of Christ (Matt. 2:18).

31:16–17 This sorrow would end with the return from exile.

31:18–21 *bullock*. Calf. God's purpose in chastening Israel is

I was ashamed, yea, even confounded, because I
did bear the reproach of my youth.
20 *Is* Ephraim my dear son? *is he* a pleasant
child? for since I spake against him, I do earnestly
remember him still: therefore my bowels are
troubled for him; I will surely have mercy upon
him, saith the LORD.
21 Set thee up waymarks, make thee high heaps:
set thine heart toward the highway, *even* the way
which thou wentest: turn again, O virgin of Israel,
turn again to these thy cities.
22 ¶ How long wilt thou go about, O thou back-
sliding daughter? for the LORD hath created a new
thing in the earth, A woman shall compass a man.
23 Thus saith the LORD of hosts, the God of
Israel; As yet they shall use this speech in the land
of Judah and in the cities thereof, when I shall
bring again their captivity; The LORD bless thee,
O habitation of justice, *and* mountain of holiness.
24 And there shall dwell in Judah itself, and in all
the cities thereof together, husbandmen, and they
that go forth with flocks.
25 For I have satiated the weary soul, and I have
replenished every sorrowful soul.
26 Upon this I awaked, and beheld; and my sleep
was sweet unto me.
27 ¶ Behold, the days come, saith the LORD, that
I will sow the house of Israel and the house of
Judah with the seed of man, and with the seed of
beast.
28 And it shall come to pass, *that* like as I have
watched over them, to pluck up, and to break
down, and to throw down, and to destroy, and to
afflict; so will I watch over them, to build, and to
plant, saith the LORD.
29 In those days they shall say no more, The
fathers have eaten a sour grape, and the children's
teeth are set on edge.
30 But every one shall die for his own iniquity:
every man that eateth the sour grape, his teeth
shall be set on edge.
31 ¶ Behold, the days come, saith the LORD, that I
will make a new covenant with the house of Israel,
and with the house of Judah:
32 Not according to the covenant that I made
with their fathers in the day *that* I took them by
the hand to bring them out of the land of Egypt;
which my covenant they brake, although I was an
husband unto them, saith the LORD:
33 But this *shall be* the covenant that I will make
with the house of Israel; After those days, saith the
LORD, I will put my law in their inward parts, and
write it in their hearts; and will be their God, and
they shall be my people.
34 And they shall teach no more every man his
neighbour, and every man his brother, saying,
Know the LORD: for they shall all know me, from
the least of them unto the greatest of them, saith
the LORD: for I will forgive their iniquity, and I
will remember their sin no more.
35 ¶ Thus saith the LORD, which giveth the sun
for a light by day, *and* the ordinances of the moon
and of the stars for a light by night, which divideth
the sea when the waves thereof roar; The LORD of
hosts *is* his name:
36 If those ordinances depart from before me,

---

fulfilled in their contrition and seeking His grace (Hos. 5:15).

31:20 *my bowels are troubled.* My inner being is churning. Vivid human emotion is used to express the Lord's yearning for Ephraim.

31:21 *Waymarks* and *high heaps* are synonyms referring to road signs or guideposts.

31:22 *go about.* Literally, "turn here and there or waver." *compass a man.* Encircle a man or mighty one, a sign interpreted to be either of the virgin birth of Christ or of Israel (pictured as a woman) clinging to the Lord in repentance.

31:24 *husbandmen.* Farmers.

31:25 *satiated.* Satisfied, quenched the thirst.

Behold, the Days Come (31:27–40)

31:28 God accomplishes His purposes and fulfills His promises (1:10,12).

31:29–30 *sour grape.* Common proverb (Ezek. 18:1–4). In this day of repentance, all accept their own guilt; there is no casting blame.

31:31–34 Salvation always requires initiation by God (*I will make*). The *new covenant* is the heart of Jeremiah's Book of Consolation (chs. 30–33). The phrase is unique among the Hebrew prophets to Jeremiah, but the concept is not (Isa. 42:6; 49:8; 54:10; 55:3; 61:8; Ezek. 34:25; 37:26). This is the largest Old Testament text quoted in its entirety in the New Testament (Heb. 8:8–12; 10:16–17). Since much of the covenant is a repetition of earlier promises, it is best to understand this as a renewed covenant rather than as brand new. Whereas the old covenant had a shadowy character, with types and ceremonies, the new covenant brings a greater clarity, a more abundant measure of the Spirit, and freedom from ceremonies and the rigor of the law. Each promise is a precious declaration of sovereign grace. God will *write* the law *in their hearts*, which is to shatter the hardened mindset of sin (17:1) and create a new desire to do God's will by the Spirit (Ps. 40:8; 2 Cor. 3:3,6). God promises to take them as *my people* and be *their God*, which is to establish a lasting union and loving fellowship between the Lord and redeemed sinners (vv. 1–3; Ex. 6:6–7; 29:45–56; Ezek. 37:27). In this spiritual communion, even *the least* of the new covenant people *know the LORD* with a heart knowledge that enriches the soul and transforms the life (9:24; 22:16; 24:7). These promises are grounded upon God's foundational work (*for I will*) of atoning for the guilt of their sins (Isa. 53) so that He will *remember their sin no more*; i.e., He will never approach them in wrath or punish them again (14:10; Isa. 54:9–10). Though Jeremiah looked forward to a future restoration, the essence of the grace promised in the new covenant operates every time an individual, whether Jew or Gentile, in the old or new dispensation, is regenerated. The new covenant rests upon Christ's finished work of redemption by His death (Luke 22:20; 1 Cor. 11:25; Heb. 9:15–16).

31:35–37 *ordinances.* Statutes or inviolable principles. The consistency and predictability of nature illustrate God's

saith the LORD, *then* the seed of Israel also shall
cease from being a nation before me for ever.
37 Thus saith the LORD; If heaven above can
be measured, and the foundations of the earth
searched out beneath, I will also cast off all the
seed of Israel for all that they have done, saith the
LORD.
38 ¶ Behold, the days come, saith the LORD, that
the city shall be built to the LORD from the tower
of Hananeel unto the gate of the corner.
39 And the measuring line shall yet go forth over
against it upon the hill Gareb, and shall compass
about to Goath.
40 And the whole valley of the dead bodies, and
of the ashes, and all the fields unto the brook of
Kidron, unto the corner of the horse gate toward
the east, *shall be* holy unto the LORD; it shall not be
plucked up, nor thrown down any more for ever.

CHAPTER 32

THE word that came to Jeremiah from the LORD
in the tenth year of Zedekiah king of Judah, which
was the eighteenth year of Nebuchadrezzar.
2 For then the king of Babylon's army besieged
Jerusalem: and Jeremiah the prophet was shut up
in the court of the prison, which *was* in the king
of Judah's house.
3 For Zedekiah king of Judah had shut him up,
saying, Wherefore dost thou prophesy, and say,
Thus saith the LORD, Behold, I will give this city
into the hand of the king of Babylon, and he shall
take it;
4 And Zedekiah king of Judah shall not escape
out of the hand of the Chaldeans, but shall surely
be delivered into the hand of the king of Babylon,
and shall speak with him mouth to mouth, and
his eyes shall behold his eyes;
5 And he shall lead Zedekiah to Babylon, and
there shall he be until I visit him, saith the LORD:
though ye fight with the Chaldeans, ye shall not
prosper.
6 ¶ And Jeremiah said, The word of the LORD
came unto me, saying,
7 Behold, Hanameel the son of Shallum thine
uncle shall come unto thee, saying, Buy thee
my field that *is* in Anathoth: for the right of
redemption *is* thine to buy *it*.
8 So Hanameel mine uncle's son came to me in
the court of the prison according to the word of
the LORD, and said unto me, Buy my field, I pray
thee, that *is* in Anathoth, which *is* in the country
of Benjamin: for the right of inheritance *is* thine,
and the redemption *is* thine; buy *it* for thyself.
Then I knew that this *was* the word of the LORD.
9 And I bought the field of Hanameel my uncle's
son, that *was* in Anathoth, and weighed him the
money, *even* seventeen shekels of silver.
10 And I subscribed the evidence, and sealed *it*,
and took witnesses, and weighed *him* the money
in the balances.
11 So I took the evidence of the purchase, *both*
that which was sealed *according* to the law and
custom, and that which was open:
12 And I gave the evidence of the purchase unto
Baruch the son of Neriah, the son of Maaseiah,
in the sight of Hanameel mine uncle's *son*, and in
the presence of the witnesses that subscribed the
book of the purchase, before all the Jews that sat
in the court of the prison.
13 ¶ And I charged Baruch before them, saying,
14 Thus saith the LORD of hosts, the God of
Israel; Take these evidences, this evidence of the
purchase, both which is sealed, and this evidence
which is open; and put them in an earthen vessel,
that they may continue many days.

irreversible purpose for His people.

31:38–40 Not all of the exact locations mentioned are known, but together they represent the totality of the city that would be rebuilt on the ruins.

Thoughts for Personal/Family Worship: Chapter 31

1. **The word "love" is often used too casually. "In love" is the common term for those who are attracted to each other. However, when the Lord of glory says, "I have loved thee" to fallen men and women, it is amazing. We tend to love what we consider to be lovable, but God loved His people while they were still sinners, with nothing attractive about them. It is even more amazing that God bound Himself in a covenant commitment to sinners and promised not just to love them but also to win their love for Himself. Take time now and through the day to praise God for His amazing, sovereign grace.**
2. **Another wonderful statement appears at the end of v. 9: "I am a father to Israel and Ephraim is my firstborn." Israel had squandered their blessings and gone astray, yet the Lord chastised them to bring them back to Himself. Every child of God is like the prodigal who journeyed far from his father. We lived for ourselves and had no thought of God. Yet the Lord brings sinners back. Does your heart echo the words of repentance (vv. 18–19)? If so, then God rejoices over you as his dear son or daughter (v. 20).**

Chapter 32: *The Lord instructs Jeremiah while he is in prison to purchase property, as a symbolic guarantee that the captivity will end.*

A Test of Faith (32:1–44)

32:1–2 *the tenth year . . . besieged.* The beginning of Jerusalem's end. The city fell to the Babylonians in Zedekiah's eleventh year (39:2; 52:5). *Nebuchadrezzar.* Alternate spelling of Nebuchadnezzar.

32:7 *right of redemption.* Obligation of redemption. Jeremiah was to fulfill the role of kinsman-redeemer (Lev. 25:24–32; Ruth 4:4).

32:9 *seventeen shekels.* About seven ounces of silver.

32:10 *subscribed the evidence.* Literally, "wrote in the book."

32:14 *earthen vessel.* Clay pot.

15 For thus saith the LORD of hosts, the God of
Israel; Houses and fields and vineyards shall be
possessed again in this land.
16 ¶ Now when I had delivered the evidence of
the purchase unto Baruch the son of Neriah, I
prayed unto the LORD, saying,
17 Ah Lord GOD! behold, thou hast made the
heaven and the earth by thy great power and
stretched out arm, *and* there is nothing too hard
for thee:
18 Thou shewest lovingkindness unto thousands,
and recompensest the iniquity of the fathers
into the bosom of their children after them: the
Great, the Mighty God, the LORD of hosts, *is* his
name,
19 Great in counsel, and mighty in work: for
thine eyes *are* open upon all the ways of the sons
of men: to give every one according to his ways,
and according to the fruit of his doings:
20 Which hast set signs and wonders in the land
of Egypt, *even* unto this day, and in Israel, and
among *other* men; and hast made thee a name,
as at this day;
21 And hast brought forth thy people Israel out
of the land of Egypt with signs, and with wonders,
and with a strong hand, and with a stretched out
arm, and with great terror;
22 And hast given them this land, which thou
didst swear to their fathers to give them, a land
flowing with milk and honey;
23 And they came in, and possessed it; but they
obeyed not thy voice, neither walked in thy law;
they have done nothing of all that thou commandedst them to do: therefore thou hast caused
all this evil to come upon them:
24 Behold the mounts, they are come unto the
city to take it; and the city is given into the hand of
the Chaldeans, that fight against it, because of the
sword, and of the famine, and of the pestilence:
and what thou hast spoken is come to pass; and,
behold, thou seest *it*.
25 And thou hast said unto me, O Lord GOD, Buy
thee the field for money, and take witnesses; for
the city is given into the hand of the Chaldeans.
26 ¶ Then came the word of the LORD unto
Jeremiah, saying,
27 Behold, I *am* the LORD, the God of all flesh: is
there any thing too hard for me?
28 Therefore thus saith the LORD; Behold, I will
give this city into the hand of the Chaldeans, and
into the hand of Nebuchadrezzar king of Babylon,
and he shall take it:
29 And the Chaldeans, that fight against this city,
shall come and set fire on this city, and burn it
with the houses, upon whose roofs they have
offered incense unto Baal, and poured out drink
offerings unto other gods, to provoke me to anger.
30 For the children of Israel and the children
of Judah have only done evil before me from
their youth: for the children of Israel have only
provoked me to anger with the work of their
hands, saith the LORD.
31 For this city hath been to me *as* a provocation
of mine anger and of my fury from the day that
they built it even unto this day; that I should
remove it from before my face,
32 Because of all the evil of the children of Israel
and of the children of Judah, which they have
done to provoke me to anger, they, their kings,
their princes, their priests, and their prophets,
and the men of Judah, and the inhabitants of
Jerusalem.
33 And they have turned unto me the back, and
not the face: though I taught them, rising up early
and teaching *them*, yet they have not hearkened to
receive instruction.
34 But they set their abominations in the house,
which is called by my name, to defile it.
35 And they built the high places of Baal, which
are in the valley of the son of Hinnom, to cause
their sons and their daughters to pass through *the*
fire unto Molech; which I commanded them not,
neither came it into my mind, that they should do
this abomination, to cause Judah to sin.
36 ¶ And now therefore thus saith the LORD, the
God of Israel, concerning this city, whereof ye say,
It shall be delivered into the hand of the king of
Babylon by the sword, and by the famine, and by
the pestilence;
37 Behold, I will gather them out of all countries,
whither I have driven them in mine anger, and
in my fury, and in great wrath; and I will bring
them again unto this place, and I will cause them
to dwell safely:
38 And they shall be my people, and I will be their
God:
39 And I will give them one heart, and one way,
that they may fear me for ever, for the good of

32:15 Though, humanly speaking, buying a field in a land about to be conquered was foolish, God used this as a sign of restoration by His amazing grace.
32:17 *nothing too hard*. God, being omnipotent, can do anything He wills (v. 27; Gen. 18:14; Job 42:1; Luke 1:37), and He accomplishes all that He wills (Pss. 115:3; 135:6). Creation is evidence of God's unlimited power (Job 9:4–10; Ps. 33:6–8; Amos 4:13; 5:8; see note at 10:12).
32:18 *recompensest*. Repays.
32:20 *name*. Reputation.
32:23 *evil*. Disaster.
32:24 *mounts*. Assault ramps or mounds.
32:27 See note at v. 17.
32:33 *back*. Neck, picturing the turning of the face away from the Lord. *rising up early and teaching*. The Lord teaches with zeal. There was no excuse for not hearing or obeying.
32:34 *abominations*. Things detestable or monstrous, here idols.

them, and of their children after them:
40 And I will make an everlasting covenant with
them, that I will not turn away from them, to do
them good; but I will put my fear in their hearts,
that they shall not depart from me.
41 Yea, I will rejoice over them to do them good,
and I will plant them in this land assuredly with
my whole heart and with my whole soul.
42 For thus saith the LORD; Like as I have brought
all this great evil upon this people, so will I bring
upon them all the good that I have promised
them.
43 And fields shall be bought in this land, whereof
ye say, *It is* desolate without man or beast; it is
given into the hand of the Chaldeans.
44 Men shall buy fields for money, and subscribe
evidences, and seal *them*, and take witnesses in
the land of Benjamin, and in the places about
Jerusalem, and in the cities of Judah, and in the
cities of the mountains, and in the cities of the
valley, and in the cities of the south: for I will
cause their captivity to return, saith the LORD.

CHAPTER 33

MOREOVER the word of the LORD came unto
Jeremiah the second time, while he was yet shut
up in the court of the prison, saying,
2 Thus saith the LORD the maker thereof, the
LORD that formed it, to establish it; the LORD *is*
his name;
3 Call unto me, and I will answer thee, and shew
thee great and mighty things, which thou knowest
not.
4 For thus saith the LORD, the God of Israel,
concerning the houses of this city, and concerning
the houses of the kings of Judah, which are
thrown down by the mounts, and by the sword;
5 They come to fight with the Chaldeans, but *it is*
to fill them with the dead bodies of men, whom
I have slain in mine anger and in my fury, and
for all whose wickedness I have hid my face from
this city.
6 Behold, I will bring it health and cure, and
I will cure them, and will reveal unto them the
abundance of peace and truth.
7 And I will cause the captivity of Judah and the
captivity of Israel to return, and will build them,
as at the first.
8 And I will cleanse them from all their iniquity,
whereby they have sinned against me; and I will
pardon all their iniquities, whereby they have
sinned, and whereby they have transgressed
against me.
9 ¶ And it shall be to me a name of joy, a praise
and an honour before all the nations of the earth,
which shall hear all the good that I do unto them:
and they shall fear and tremble for all the goodness
and for all the prosperity that I procure unto it.
10 Thus saith the LORD; Again there shall be
heard in this place, which ye say *shall be* desolate
without man and without beast, *even* in the cities
of Judah, and in the streets of Jerusalem, that are
desolate, without man, and without inhabitant,
and without beast,
11 The voice of joy, and the voice of gladness,
the voice of the bridegroom, and the voice of the
bride, the voice of them that shall say, Praise the
LORD of hosts: for the LORD *is* good; for his mercy
endureth for ever: *and* of them that shall bring the

32:39–40 *I will give them one heart.* Regeneration (24:7), promised in the new and *everlasting covenant* (31:33). *my fear.* Reverence for and submission to the Lord. *they shall not depart from me.* God's grace guarantees that the saints will persevere to the end.
32:41 *assuredly.* Literally, "in truth." *with my whole heart . . . soul.* Since God is a Spirit without body parts (John 4:24), this statement refers to His entire being.
32:42 *great evil.* The devastating disaster of the judgment.

Thoughts for Personal/Family Worship: Chapter 32

1. **Tests of faith often come in the midst of trials. Jeremiah was shut up in prison when, just as Jerusalem was about to fall, God told him to purchase a field. Yet this command points to God's promise: that Judah's captivity would end and that they would return. Jeremiah's only hope was in God's Word, but that was enough for him, so he bought the land. Faith often appears beyond reason, but it is never unreasonable. Let us walk by faith in God's sure Word, even when circumstances seem to be contrary.**
2. **Jeremiah's praying after purchasing the property (vv. 16–25) illustrates that prayer arises from and is fueled by faith in the Word. We know and believe that God's will shall be done, so we pray as Christ taught us, "Thy will be done" (Matt. 6:10). Jeremiah's prayer focused on God's perfections (32:17–19) and past acts (vv. 20–23). Why does meditating on God and His works give us power to pray in faith?**

Chapter 33: ***The Lord renews His promise of restoration and gives assurance regarding the certainty of His covenant.***

Call unto Me (33:1–8)

33:1 *the second time.* See 32:1–2 for the first time.
33:2 References to God's creating activities emphasize His absolute power (32:17).
33:3 *mighty things.* Things beyond natural human understanding (Rom. 11:33–34; 1 Cor. 2:9–10). It is in God's grace and mercy that He reveals to us His salvation.
33:4 *mounts.* Siege ramps erected by the enemy to enter the city.
33:5 *hid my face.* Gesture expressing displeasure.
33:8 *iniquity . . . iniquities.* Perhaps referring to both original sin (inward corruption) and actual sins.

The Lord Is Good (33:9–14)

33:9 *fear and tremble.* To shake or shiver with emotion.
33:10–11 The reversal of divine judgment (7:34; 16:9; 25:10) results in genuine biblical worship (1 Chron. 16:34,41; Ps. 136).

THE PERSEVERANCE OF THE SAINTS

In the context of the Old Testament, no promise of God is more astonishing than the one recorded in Jeremiah 32:40: "I will not turn away from them, to do them good . . . they shall not depart from me." As summarized in Psalms 78 and 106, Israel's history reveals that they often departed from the living God, turning aside to idols and falling into grievous sin, so He turned away from them in His wrath until they repented and cried out to Him in their misery.

Jeremiah must have rejoiced to hear of a day when this endless cycle of human unfaithfulness and divine chastisement would give way to a very different relationship between God and His people in the form of a new and everlasting covenant. The law graven on tablets of stone would be written on the very hearts of the people, and all would know the Lord and be forgiven, restored, and renewed by His grace. God would then continue to persevere with His people, and His people with Him.

This promise embodies the doctrine of the perseverance of the saints. But who are these saints? Why do they continue or persevere as saints? In what things do they persevere?

Much depends on what is meant by "saints." In the pre-Reformation church (and in the Roman Catholic Church today), a saint was defined as "one whose holiness of life and heroic virtue have been confirmed and recognized by the church's official process of beatification and canonization" (*Catholic Dictionary*, 469). Though deceased, they are remembered, venerated, and invoked in public worship and private devotion as though they could hear and answer prayers.

In this view, saints were exceptional in the membership of the church. They were better than they had to be and did more than duty required, so they acquired a store of merit to bring to the aid of less holy or less virtuous Christians (the false concept of supererogation). Therefore, they are accorded feast days and shrines and fill a substantial place in the devotion of those who invoke them.

Nothing could be more contrary to the biblical idea of sainthood. Simply put, all Christians are saints. They have been sanctified or set apart by God as His people. Biblical sainthood depends not on what we do but on what God does in us by His Word and Holy Spirit.

God the Father has made an everlasting covenant of grace with us and has adopted us as His children and heirs. God the Son has washed us in His blood from all our sins and has incorporated us into the fellowship of His death and resurrection. God the Holy Spirit dwells in us, sanctifies us to be members of Christ, and applies to us that which we have in Christ, namely, the washing away of our sins and the daily renewing of our lives. Such is the portion of all who belong to Christ and are joined to Him by a true faith.

As such, all believers are "kept by the power of God unto salvation" (1 Peter 1:5). God perseveres with us, and so we persevere with Him. God's sovereignty means that what God does stays done. We are safe in His hands, under His protection, calling on His name and resting in His love.

In what do we persevere? We persevere in faith, believing in God, trusting in His Word, and hoping in His promises; in repenting from sin; in denying ourselves and following Christ, striving for holiness of life; and in seeking to know God's will and to do those things that please Him. Such are the fruits that accompany justifying faith. It is a disturbing sign when such fruits are lacking in a professing Christian. Christ warns of temporary faith (Matt. 13:18–22); Paul denounces those "having a form of godliness, but denying the power thereof" (2 Tim. 3:5); and James declares that "faith, if it hath not works, is dead, being alone" (James 2:17). So Paul exhort us, "Examine yourselves, whether ye be in the faith; prove your own selves" (2 Cor. 13:5).

sacrifice of praise into the house of the LORD. For
I will cause to return the captivity of the land, as
at the first, saith the LORD.
12 Thus saith the LORD of hosts; Again in this
place, which is desolate without man and without
beast, and in all the cities thereof, shall be an
habitation of shepherds causing *their* flocks to lie
down.
13 In the cities of the mountains, in the cities
of the vale, and in the cities of the south, and in
the land of Benjamin, and in the places about
Jerusalem, and in the cities of Judah, shall the
flocks pass again under the hands of him that
telleth *them*, saith the LORD.
14 Behold, the days come, saith the LORD, that
I will perform that good thing which I have
promised unto the house of Israel and to the
house of Judah.
15 ¶ In those days, and at that time, will I cause
the Branch of righteousness to grow up unto
David; and he shall execute judgment and
righteousness in the land.
16 In those days shall Judah be saved, and
Jerusalem shall dwell safely: and this *is the name*
wherewith she shall be called, The LORD our
righteousness.
17 ¶ For thus saith the LORD; David shall never
want a man to sit upon the throne of the house
of Israel;
18 Neither shall the priests the Levites want a
man before me to offer burnt offerings, and
to kindle meat offerings, and to do sacrifice
continually.
19 ¶ And the word of the LORD came unto
Jeremiah, saying,
20 Thus saith the LORD; If ye can break my
covenant of the day, and my covenant of the
night, and that there should not be day and night
in their season;
21 *Then* may also my covenant be broken with
David my servant, that he should not have a son
to reign upon his throne; and with the Levites the
priests, my ministers.
22 As the host of heaven cannot be numbered,
neither the sand of the sea measured: so will I
multiply the seed of David my servant, and the
Levites that minister unto me.
23 Moreover the word of the LORD came to
Jeremiah, saying,
24 Considerest thou not what this people have
spoken, saying, The two families which the LORD
hath chosen, he hath even cast them off? thus they
have despised my people, that they should be no
more a nation before them.
25 Thus saith the LORD; If my covenant *be* not
with day and night, *and if* I have not appointed
the ordinances of heaven and earth;
26 Then will I cast away the seed of Jacob, and
David my servant, *so* that I will not take *any* of his
seed *to be* rulers over the seed of Abraham, Isaac,
and Jacob: for I will cause their captivity to return,
and have mercy on them.

CHAPTER 34

THE word which came unto Jeremiah from the
LORD, when Nebuchadnezzar king of Babylon,
and all his army, and all the kingdoms of the
earth of his dominion, and all the people, fought
against Jerusalem, and against all the cities
thereof, saying,
2 Thus saith the LORD, the God of Israel; Go and
speak to Zedekiah king of Judah, and tell him,
Thus saith the LORD; Behold, I will give this city
into the hand of the king of Babylon, and he shall
burn it with fire:
3 And thou shalt not escape out of his hand, but
shalt surely be taken, and delivered into his hand;
and thine eyes shall behold the eyes of the king of
Babylon, and he shall speak with thee mouth to
mouth, and thou shalt go to Babylon.
4 Yet hear the word of the LORD, O Zedekiah king

33:13 *telleth.* Counts.

The Branch of Righteousness (33:15–18)

33:15–16 *Branch.* See note at 23:5 and 6. *the name wherewith she shall be called.* Literally, "this is that which will be called, with respect to her." The *righteousness* of Christ is imputed to and declared over His people.

33:17–18 Even though David's throne would be empty, and there would be no temple during the exile, God ensures the continuation of a legitimate kingship and priesthood, joined together in Christ. The shadows of the Levitical priesthood are now fulfilled in Christ and His people (Heb. 7:11–17; see note at Jer. 30:21).

The Strength of the Covenant (33:19–26)

33:19–26 The laws of the universe, established by God, are so constant that we have no reason to doubt their certainty. So likewise the believer should never doubt the promises of God.

33:24–26 *the two families.* The northern and southern kingdoms (Israel and Judah). God would bring them from *their captivity to return* to the land as a united people.

Thoughts for Personal/Family Worship: Chapter 33

1. **Verse 3 is surely one of the great prayer promises in the Bible. The Lord invites—indeed, commands—us to call unto Him, with the assurance that He will answer in ways that exceed our expectations (Eph. 3:20). He is a God who loves to hear and answer prayer. This is a great incentive for us to love Him and call upon Him habitually (Ps. 116:1–2). He does not say "I might" but "I will answer thee." He will not refuse when we ask aright (Luke 11:9–10).**
2. **The promises of the Branch (vv. 15–16; 23:5–6) sum up the great gospel truth of justification by the righteousness of Christ alone. He satisfied every demand of the law for us and paid the penalty for our transgression.**

of Judah; Thus saith the LORD of thee, Thou shalt
not die by the sword:
5 *But* thou shalt die in peace: and with the
burnings of thy fathers, the former kings which
were before thee, so shall they burn *odours* for
thee; and they will lament thee, *saying*, Ah lord!
for I have pronounced the word, saith the LORD.
6 Then Jeremiah the prophet spake all these
words unto Zedekiah king of Judah in Jerusalem,
7 When the king of Babylon's army fought
against Jerusalem, and against all the cities of
Judah that were left, against Lachish, and against
Azekah: for these defenced cities remained of the
cities of Judah.
8 ¶ *This is* the word that came unto Jeremiah
from the LORD, after that the king Zedekiah had
made a covenant with all the people which *were* at
Jerusalem, to proclaim liberty unto them;
9 That every man should let his manservant, and
every man his maidservant, *being* an Hebrew or
an Hebrewess, go free; that none should serve
himself of them, *to wit*, of a Jew his brother.
10 Now when all the princes, and all the people,
which had entered into the covenant, heard that
every one should let his manservant, and every
one his maidservant, go free, that none should
serve themselves of them any more, then they
obeyed, and let *them* go.
11 But afterward they turned, and caused the
servants and the handmaids, whom they had
let go free, to return, and brought them into
subjection for servants and for handmaids.
12 ¶ Therefore the word of the LORD came to
Jeremiah from the LORD, saying,
13 Thus saith the LORD, the God of Israel; I made
a covenant with your fathers in the day that I
brought them forth out of the land of Egypt, out
of the house of bondmen, saying,
14 At the end of seven years let ye go every man
his brother an Hebrew, which hath been sold unto
thee; and when he hath served thee six years, thou
shalt let him go free from thee: but your fathers
hearkened not unto me, neither inclined their ear.
15 And ye were now turned, and had done right
in my sight, in proclaiming liberty every man to
his neighbour; and ye had made a covenant be-
fore me in the house which is called by my name:
16 But ye turned and polluted my name, and
caused every man his servant, and every man his
handmaid, whom ye had set at liberty at their plea-
sure, to return, and brought them into subjection,
to be unto you for servants and for handmaids.
17 Therefore thus saith the LORD; Ye have not
hearkened unto me, in proclaiming liberty,
every one to his brother, and every man to his
neighbour: behold, I proclaim a liberty for you,
saith the LORD, to the sword, to the pestilence, and
to the famine; and I will make you to be removed
into all the kingdoms of the earth.
18 And I will give the men that have transgressed
my covenant, which have not performed the
words of the covenant which they had made
before me, when they cut the calf in twain, and
passed between the parts thereof,
19 The princes of Judah, and the princes of
Jerusalem, the eunuchs, and the priests, and all
the people of the land, which passed between the
parts of the calf;
20 I will even give them into the hand of their
enemies, and into the hand of them that seek
their life: and their dead bodies shall be for meat
unto the fowls of the heaven, and to the beasts of
the earth.
21 And Zedekiah king of Judah and his princes
will I give into the hand of their enemies, and into
the hand of them that seek their life, and into the
hand of the king of Babylon's army, which are
gone up from you.

His name is our only hope of salvation, for His righteousness covers believers with His beauty in God's sight (Isa. 61:10). We are accepted in the Beloved (Eph. 1:6)! How can that give you joy?

INVADERS AT THE CITY GATES (34:1—38:28)

Chapter 34: ***Jeremiah declares Zedekiah's personal fate in the coming captivity and denounces the people for breaking the covenant to release their servants.***

A Message for Zedekiah (34:1–7)

34:5 *burnings*. Most likely the burning of spices in the burial ceremony of kings. Contrary to expectation, given the dire circumstances, Zedekiah would be honored with a king's burial.

A Wicked Act against Servants (34:8–22)

34:8 *liberty*. Release or emancipation. That such a proclamation was necessary indicates a failure to follow the law, which provided for the regular release of slaves every seven years (v. 14; Ex. 21:2–4; Lev. 25:10; Deut. 15:12).

34:9 *manservant*. Male slave. *maidservant*. Female slave.

34:16 *polluted my name*. Treated His holiness as common or ordinary.

34:17 *I proclaim a liberty for you*. With biting irony, the Lord describes their punishment in terms of emancipation.

34:18–19 *cut the calf in twain*. Cut it in two, a symbol of the punishment for covenant breakers. *passed between the parts*. Symbol of the oath taken by the covenant parties (Gen. 15:9–10). Those who violate a covenant with the Lord shall not go unpunished.

Thoughts for Personal/Family Worship: Chapter 34

1. **What an insult to Almighty God that these slave owners, having released their slaves with an oath to the Lord, should quickly change their minds when the thought of danger appears to have passed. Sadly, it is often the case that men and women make promises to God when their troubles confront them, yet as soon as there is a respite go back to their sinful lifestyles. There was no true repentance in their lives. Let us be very careful to keep any promise that we make to the Lord.**

22 Behold, I will command, saith the LORD, and
cause them to return to this city; and they shall
fight against it, and take it, and burn it with fire:
and I will make the cities of Judah a desolation
without an inhabitant.

CHAPTER 35

THE word which came unto Jeremiah from the
LORD in the days of Jehoiakim the son of Josiah
king of Judah, saying,
2 Go unto the house of the Rechabites, and speak
unto them, and bring them into the house of the
LORD, into one of the chambers, and give them
wine to drink.
3 Then I took Jaazaniah the son of Jeremiah, the
son of Habaziniah, and his brethren, and all his
sons, and the whole house of the Rechabites;
4 And I brought them into the house of the
LORD, into the chamber of the sons of Hanan,
the son of Igdaliah, a man of God, which *was*
by the chamber of the princes, which *was* above
the chamber of Maaseiah the son of Shallum, the
keeper of the door:
5 And I set before the sons of the house of the
Rechabites pots full of wine, and cups, and I said
unto them, Drink ye wine.
6 But they said, We will drink no wine: for
Jonadab the son of Rechab our father commanded
us, saying, Ye shall drink no wine, *neither* ye, nor
your sons for ever:
7 Neither shall ye build house, nor sow seed, nor
plant vineyard, nor have *any*: but all your days ye
shall dwell in tents; that ye may live many days in
the land where ye *be* strangers.
8 Thus have we obeyed the voice of Jonadab
the son of Rechab our father in all that he hath
charged us, to drink no wine all our days, we, our
wives, our sons, nor our daughters;
9 Nor to build houses for us to dwell in: neither
have we vineyard, nor field, nor seed:
10 But we have dwelt in tents, and have obeyed,
and done according to all that Jonadab our father
commanded us.
11 But it came to pass, when Nebuchadrezzar
king of Babylon came up into the land, that we
said, Come, and let us go to Jerusalem for fear
of the army of the Chaldeans, and for fear of the
army of the Syrians: so we dwell at Jerusalem.
12 ¶ Then came the word of the LORD unto
Jeremiah, saying,
13 Thus saith the LORD of hosts, the God of Israel;
Go and tell the men of Judah and the inhabitants
of Jerusalem, Will ye not receive instruction to
hearken to my words? saith the LORD.
14 The words of Jonadab the son of Rechab, that
he commanded his sons not to drink wine, are
performed; for unto this day they drink none,
but obey their father's commandment: notwith-
standing I have spoken unto you, rising early and
speaking; but ye hearkened not unto me.
15 I have sent also unto you all my servants the
prophets, rising up early and sending *them*, saying,
Return ye now every man from his evil way, and
amend your doings, and go not after other gods to
serve them, and ye shall dwell in the land which I
have given to you and to your fathers: but ye have
not inclined your ear, nor hearkened unto me.
16 Because the sons of Jonadab the son of
Rechab have performed the commandment of
their father, which he commanded them; but this
people hath not hearkened unto me:
17 Therefore thus saith the LORD God of hosts,
the God of Israel; Behold, I will bring upon Judah
and upon all the inhabitants of Jerusalem all the
evil that I have pronounced against them: because
I have spoken unto them, but they have not heard;
and I have called unto them, but they have not
answered.
18 ¶ And Jeremiah said unto the house of
the Rechabites, Thus saith the LORD of hosts,
the God of Israel; Because ye have obeyed the
commandment of Jonadab your father, and kept
all his precepts, and done according unto all that
he hath commanded you:
19 Therefore thus saith the LORD of hosts, the
God of Israel; Jonadab the son of Rechab shall not
want a man to stand before me for ever.

2. What a contrast there is between these wicked men, who went back on their promise, and the Lord Jesus, who kept His covenant promise even to a bloody death. He came to set free those who were held fast by the chains of sin (Luke 4:16–21). He says of Himself, "If the Son therefore shall make you free, ye shall be free indeed" (John 8:36). If God did not spare His own Son, how much more can we trust Him to keep His promises?

Chapter 35: *The obedient faithfulness of the Rechabites contrasts with the disobedient unfaithfulness of Judah.*

The Rechabites Blessed for their Obedience (35:1–19)

35:2–10 *Rechabites.* Kenites, the people of Moses' father-in-law, Jethro, a priest of Midian. They became allies of Israel and embraced the ways of the Lord (Judg. 1:16; 1 Chron. 2:55). *Jonadab.* See 2 Kings 10:15,23. Their refusal to drink wine proved their integrity. The Lord used them as an object lesson in loyalty and fidelity for the people of Jerusalem.

35:14–15 *rising early.* Expresses the consistency, fervency, and zeal with which God had commanded Israel through the succession of prophets.

35:17 *evil.* Disastrous judgment.

35:19 *for ever.* Literally, "all the days," perhaps referring to the days of the captivity. There is evidence of a Rechabite presence after the exile (Neh. 3:14).

Thoughts for Personal/Family Worship: Chapter 35

There are practical lessons for Christians from the

CHAPTER 36

AND it came to pass in the fourth year of Jehoia-
kim the son of Josiah king of Judah, *that* this word
came unto Jeremiah from the LORD, saying,
2 Take thee a roll of a book, and write therein all
the words that I have spoken unto thee against
Israel, and against Judah, and against all the
nations, from the day I spake unto thee, from the
days of Josiah, even unto this day.
3 It may be that the house of Judah will hear all
the evil which I purpose to do unto them; that
they may return every man from his evil way; that
I may forgive their iniquity and their sin.
4 Then Jeremiah called Baruch the son of Neriah:
and Baruch wrote from the mouth of Jeremiah all
the words of the LORD, which he had spoken unto
him, upon a roll of a book.
5 And Jeremiah commanded Baruch, saying,
I *am* shut up; I cannot go into the house of the
LORD:
6 Therefore go thou, and read in the roll, which
thou hast written from my mouth, the words of
the LORD in the ears of the people in the LORD's
house upon the fasting day: and also thou shalt
read them in the ears of all Judah that come out
of their cities.
7 It may be they will present their supplication
before the LORD, and will return every one from
his evil way: for great *is* the anger and the fury that
the LORD hath pronounced against this people.
8 And Baruch the son of Neriah did according to
all that Jeremiah the prophet commanded him,
reading in the book the words of the LORD in the
LORD's house.
9 And it came to pass in the fifth year of
Jehoiakim the son of Josiah king of Judah, in the
ninth month, *that* they proclaimed a fast before
the LORD to all the people in Jerusalem, and to
all the people that came from the cities of Judah
unto Jerusalem.
10 Then read Baruch in the book the words of
Jeremiah in the house of the LORD, in the cham-
ber of Gemariah the son of Shaphan the scribe,
in the higher court, at the entry of the new gate
of the LORD's house, in the ears of all the people.
11 ¶ When Michaiah the son of Gemariah, the
son of Shaphan, had heard out of the book all the
words of the LORD,
12 Then he went down into the king's house, into
the scribe's chamber: and, lo, all the princes sat
there, *even* Elishama the scribe, and Delaiah the
son of Shemaiah, and Elnathan the son of Achbor,
and Gemariah the son of Shaphan, and Zedekiah
the son of Hananiah, and all the princes.
13 Then Michaiah declared unto them all the
words that he had heard, when Baruch read the
book in the ears of the people.
14 Therefore all the princes sent Jehudi the son
of Nethaniah, the son of Shelemiah, the son of
Cushi, unto Baruch, saying, Take in thine hand
the roll wherein thou hast read in the ears of the
people, and come. So Baruch the son of Neriah
took the roll in his hand, and came unto them.
15 And they said unto him, Sit down now, and
read it in our ears. So Baruch read *it* in their ears.
16 Now it came to pass, when they had heard all
the words, they were afraid both one and other,
and said unto Baruch, We will surely tell the king
of all these words.
17 And they asked Baruch, saying, Tell us now,
How didst thou write all these words at his
mouth?
18 Then Baruch answered them, He pronounced
all these words unto me with his mouth, and I
wrote *them* with ink in the book.
19 Then said the princes unto Baruch, Go, hide

example of the Rechabites. If they kept the command of their father for generations, how much more should we live in sober faithfulness to the commands of God through His prophets and apostles? The Rechabites may have seemed like a poor people to others, living as they did in tents and abstaining from the pleasure of wine, but God blessed them for their faithfulness in an inconsistent and unfaithful generation (34:10–11). May we also be people whose yes means yes, and no means no, a people who cling to the faithfulness of God whose promises are all yes in Jesus Christ—even if it makes us seem poor and deprived to the world. What is one point at which it is hard for you to be faithful and consistent? How can the faithfulness of the Rechabites and the Lord encourage you?

Chapter 36: *Jeremiah's prophecy is recorded, destroyed, and restored.*

Jeremiah's Writings Brought before the King (36:1–32)

36:2 *roll.* scroll. *all the words.* Recurring theme (vv. 4,11,13, 16–18,24,28,32).

36:3 *evil.* God's disastrous judgment (v. 31) or man's disastrous sin. *that I may forgive.* The purpose of the divinely given Word was to lead Judah to repentance and pardon.

36:4 *Baruch wrote.* Compare Paul's use of Tertius (Rom. 16:22).

36:5 *shut up.* Can mean to restrain or hinder. Since Jeremiah later went into hiding (v. 19), this seems not to refer to imprisonment but to his being barred from public ministry.

36:6 *from my mouth, the words of the LORD.* The words written were not originated by Jeremiah but by the Lord (1:9; 2 Peter 1:20–21). The *fasting day* was not a day designated by God but practiced in times of emergency, often used as a ploy for divine aid (Isa. 58:3–5).

36:9 This *fast before the LORD* took place in December 604 BC, shortly after the first wave of captivity in 605 BC—a time of emergency. However, God is not manipulated by rituals.

36:10–11 The written *words of Jeremiah* are the *words of the LORD,* human language of which every word came from God with divine authority, accuracy, and trustworthiness (Ps. 12:6; Prov. 30:5–6; 1 Thess. 2:13).

36:16 *were afraid.* Trembled in terror, a proper response to God's word of judgment.

thee, thou and Jeremiah; and let no man know where ye be.

20 ¶ And they went in to the king into the court, but they laid up the roll in the chamber of Elishama the scribe, and told all the words in the ears of the king.

21 So the king sent Jehudi to fetch the roll: and he took it out of Elishama the scribe's chamber. And Jehudi read it in the ears of the king, and in the ears of all the princes which stood beside the king.

22 Now the king sat in the winterhouse in the ninth month: and *there was a fire* on the hearth burning before him.

23 And it came to pass, *that* when Jehudi had read three or four leaves, he cut it with the penknife, and cast *it* into the fire that *was* on the hearth, until all the roll was consumed in the fire that *was* on the hearth.

24 Yet they were not afraid, nor rent their garments, *neither* the king, nor any of his servants that heard all these words.

25 Nevertheless Elnathan and Delaiah and Gemariah had made intercession to the king that he would not burn the roll: but he would not hear them.

26 But the king commanded Jerahmeel the son of Hammelech, and Seraiah the son of Azriel, and Shelemiah the son of Abdeel, to take Baruch the scribe and Jeremiah the prophet: but the LORD hid them.

27 ¶ Then the word of the LORD came to Jeremiah, after that the king had burned the roll, and the words which Baruch wrote at the mouth of Jeremiah, saying,

28 Take thee again another roll, and write in it all the former words that were in the first roll, which Jehoiakim the king of Judah hath burned.

29 And thou shalt say to Jehoiakim king of Judah, Thus saith the LORD; Thou hast burned this roll, saying, Why hast thou written therein, saying, The king of Babylon shall certainly come and destroy this land, and shall cause to cease from thence man and beast?

30 Therefore thus saith the LORD of Jehoiakim king of Judah; He shall have none to sit upon the throne of David: and his dead body shall be cast out in the day to the heat, and in the night to the frost.

31 And I will punish him and his seed and his servants for their iniquity; and I will bring upon them, and upon the inhabitants of Jerusalem, and upon the men of Judah, all the evil that I have pronounced against them; but they hearkened not.

32 ¶ Then took Jeremiah another roll, and gave it to Baruch the scribe, the son of Neriah; who wrote therein from the mouth of Jeremiah all the words of the book which Jehoiakim king of Judah had burned in the fire: and there were added besides unto them many like words.

CHAPTER 37

AND king Zedekiah the son of Josiah reigned instead of Coniah the son of Jehoiakim, whom Nebuchadrezzar king of Babylon made king in the land of Judah.

2 But neither he, nor his servants, nor the people of the land, did hearken unto the words of the LORD, which he spake by the prophet Jeremiah.

3 And Zedekiah the king sent Jehucal the son of Shelemiah and Zephaniah the son of Maaseiah the priest to the prophet Jeremiah, saying, Pray now unto the LORD our God for us.

4 Now Jeremiah came in and went out among the people: for they had not put him into prison.

5 Then Pharaoh's army was come forth out of

36:20–23 The same Word that is a savor of life unto life for some is a savor of death unto death for others, worthy only to be destroyed.

36:24 *not afraid.* Sinners can be remarkably callous to God's Word.

36:27–32 Jehoiakim's cutting up and burning the Word of God was futile. God's Word is indestructible (Ps. 119:89), but those who oppose it will be destroyed.

Thoughts for Personal/Family Worship: Chapter 36

1. **Baruch's writing of Jeremiah's prophetic words illustrates the creation of the Bible. The Lord gave the words to Jeremiah (1:5), who faithfully spoke them. Baruch faithfully recorded them in writing. Each step of this process was governed by the Spirit of God so that the product, the Scriptures, is the inspired Word of God (2 Tim. 3:16). When we read the words of the prophets and apostles, we may rest assured that these are the very words of the Lord (vv. 4,6,8,11,27).**
2. **There are many like Jehoiakim who are determined to destroy God's Word. Tragically, even those who make an outward profession of belief in Christ often make the greatest efforts to blot out parts of Scripture, whether miracles or moral laws or some teaching they deem to be offensive. Yet such efforts by these enemies of God are ultimately all in vain. God's Word will triumph. It cannot be destroyed. Let us therefore open our hearts to receive His Word that it may be our constant companion through life.**

Chapter 37: *Egypt diverts Babylon from Jerusalem's siege, but Jeremiah warns that the respite will be short-lived because the city will certainly fall to Babylon.*

Zedekiah Seeks Jeremiah (37:1–10)

37:1 *Zedekiah* was Judah's last king, and a puppet of Babylon. He came to the throne after the removal of *Coniah, the son of Jehoiakim*, after just three months, in fulfillment of Jeremiah's prophecy (22:24–26; 2 Kings 24:8–18).

37:5 At this time Egypt (seeking to regain power) posed a threat to Babylon and forced Nebuchadnezzar to divert his attention away from Jerusalem. However, God's purpose to use Babylon as His servant could not be frustrated. Egypt

Egypt: and when the Chaldeans that besieged
Jerusalem heard tidings of them, they departed
from Jerusalem.
6 ¶ Then came the word of the LORD unto the
prophet Jeremiah, saying,
7 Thus saith the LORD, the God of Israel; Thus
shall ye say to the king of Judah, that sent you
unto me to enquire of me; Behold, Pharaoh's
army, which is come forth to help you, shall
return to Egypt into their own land.
8 And the Chaldeans shall come again, and fight
against this city, and take it, and burn it with fire.
9 Thus saith the LORD; Deceive not yourselves,
saying, The Chaldeans shall surely depart from
us: for they shall not depart.
10 For though ye had smitten the whole army of
the Chaldeans that fight against you, and there
remained *but* wounded men among them, *yet*
should they rise up every man in his tent, and
burn this city with fire.
11 ¶ And it came to pass, that when the army of
the Chaldeans was broken up from Jerusalem for
fear of Pharaoh's army,
12 Then Jeremiah went forth out of Jerusalem to
go into the land of Benjamin, to separate himself
thence in the midst of the people.
13 And when he was in the gate of Benjamin, a
captain of the ward *was* there, whose name *was*
Irijah, the son of Shelemiah, the son of Hananiah;
and he took Jeremiah the prophet, saying, Thou
fallest away to the Chaldeans.
14 Then said Jeremiah, *It is* false; I fall not away
to the Chaldeans. But he hearkened not to him:
so Irijah took Jeremiah, and brought him to the
princes.
15 Wherefore the princes were wroth with
Jeremiah, and smote him, and put him in prison
in the house of Jonathan the scribe: for they had
made that the prison.
16 ¶ When Jeremiah was entered into the
dungeon, and into the cabins, and Jeremiah had
remained there many days;
17 Then Zedekiah the king sent, and took him
out: and the king asked him secretly in his house,
and said, Is there *any* word from the LORD? And
Jeremiah said, There is: for, said he, thou shalt be
delivered into the hand of the king of Babylon.
18 Moreover Jeremiah said unto king Zedekiah,
What have I offended against thee, or against thy
servants, or against this people, that ye have put
me in prison?
19 Where *are* now your prophets which proph-
esied unto you, saying, The king of Babylon shall
not come against you, nor against this land?
20 Therefore hear now, I pray thee, O my lord the
king: let my supplication, I pray thee, be accepted
before thee; that thou cause me not to return to
the house of Jonathan the scribe, lest I die there.
21 Then Zedekiah the king commanded that
they should commit Jeremiah into the court of
the prison, and that they should give him daily
a piece of bread out of the bakers' street, until all
the bread in the city were spent. Thus Jeremiah
remained in the court of the prison.

CHAPTER 38

THEN Shephatiah the son of Mattan, and Gedaliah
the son of Pashur, and Jucal the son of Shelemiah,
and Pashur the son of Malchiah, heard the words
that Jeremiah had spoken unto all the people,
saying,
2 Thus saith the LORD, He that remaineth in this
city shall die by the sword, by the famine, and
by the pestilence: but he that goeth forth to the
Chaldeans shall live; for he shall have his life for a
prey, and shall live.
3 Thus saith the LORD, This city shall surely be
given into the hand of the king of Babylon's army,
which shall take it.

was ultimately of no help to Judah, being destined also to fall (46:1–28).

Jeremiah Thrown into Prison (37:11–21)

37:13 *ward.* Guard. *fallest away to the Chaldeans.* Surrenders or deserts to the Babylonians.
37:15 *the princes were wroth.* The officials were angry. *smote.* Struck. Jeremiah, like other prophets, endured this persecution by faith in the Lord (Heb. 11:32–33,36).
37:16 *cabins.* Vaults or cells.
37:20 *supplication.* Humble request.

Thoughts for Personal/Family Worship: Chapter 37

1. **Zedekiah's request for prayer reveals a peculiar irony among many who will not listen to God's Word and pray, yet they will ask true believers to intercede for them during difficult times. Of course, if such people ask us to pray for them we should, because in the providence of God this may lead to their salvation. However, such requests from unbelievers are usually a last resort, highlighting their own spiritual deadness. Sadly, when such prayers are answered these people usually return to their former rejection of God. Let us therefore pray for the circumstances and their souls.**
2. **Jeremiah was hated because he told the truth. Let us also remember that the gospel will always cause offense to the unbeliever. People do not want to hear that they are sinners (John 3:19–20; 15:18,22). Yet unless they hear what their true state is before God, they will never desire the remedy for their sins. Let us therefore seek to be courageous for the truth and pray that the Lord will bless our labors in the gospel.**

Chapter 38: ***Ebed-melech rescues Jeremiah from a miry dungeon, and Jeremiah gives private counsel to the king.***
Sunk in the Mire (38:1–6)

38:2 *prey.* Possession. Surrendering was the only way to keep one's life.

4 Therefore the princes said unto the king, We be-
seech thee, let this man be put to death: for thus
he weakeneth the hands of the men of war that
remain in this city, and the hands of all the people,
in speaking such words unto them: for this man
seeketh not the welfare of this people, but the hurt.
5 Then Zedekiah the king said, Behold, he *is* in
your hand: for the king *is* not *he that* can do *any*
thing against you.
6 Then took they Jeremiah, and cast him into the
dungeon of Malchiah the son of Hammelech, that
was in the court of the prison: and they let down
Jeremiah with cords. And in the dungeon *there was*
no water, but mire: so Jeremiah sunk in the mire.
7 ¶ Now when Ebed-melech the Ethiopian, one
of the eunuchs which was in the king's house,
heard that they had put Jeremiah in the dungeon;
the king then sitting in the gate of Benjamin;
8 Ebed-melech went forth out of the king's
house, and spake to the king, saying,
9 My lord the king, these men have done evil in
all that they have done to Jeremiah the prophet,
whom they have cast into the dungeon; and he is
like to die for hunger in the place where he is: for
there is no more bread in the city.
10 Then the king commanded Ebed-melech the
Ethiopian, saying, Take from hence thirty men
with thee, and take up Jeremiah the prophet out
of the dungeon, before he die.
11 So Ebed-melech took the men with him,
and went into the house of the king under the
treasury, and took thence old cast clouts and old
rotten rags, and let them down by cords into the
dungeon to Jeremiah.
12 And Ebed-melech the Ethiopian said unto
Jeremiah, Put now *these* old cast clouts and rotten
rags under thine armholes under the cords. And
Jeremiah did so.
13 So they drew up Jeremiah with cords, and
took him up out of the dungeon: and Jeremiah
remained in the court of the prison.
14 ¶ Then Zedekiah the king sent, and took
Jeremiah the prophet unto him into the third
entry that *is* in the house of the LORD: and the
king said unto Jeremiah, I will ask thee a thing;
hide nothing from me.
15 Then Jeremiah said unto Zedekiah, If I declare
it unto thee, wilt thou not surely put me to death?
and if I give thee counsel, wilt thou not hearken
unto me?
16 So Zedekiah the king sware secretly unto Jere-
miah, saying, *As* the LORD liveth, that made us this
soul, I will not put thee to death, neither will I give
thee into the hand of these men that seek thy life.
17 Then said Jeremiah unto Zedekiah, Thus saith
the LORD, the God of hosts, the God of Israel;
If thou wilt assuredly go forth unto the king of
Babylon's princes, then thy soul shall live, and this
city shall not be burned with fire; and thou shalt
live, and thine house:
18 But if thou wilt not go forth to the king of
Babylon's princes, then shall this city be given into
the hand of the Chaldeans, and they shall burn it
with fire, and thou shalt not escape out of their
hand.
19 And Zedekiah the king said unto Jeremiah,
I am afraid of the Jews that are fallen to the
Chaldeans, lest they deliver me into their hand,
and they mock me.
20 But Jeremiah said, They shall not deliver *thee*.
Obey, I beseech thee, the voice of the LORD, which
I speak unto thee: so it shall be well unto thee, and
thy soul shall live.
21 But if thou refuse to go forth, this *is* the word
that the LORD hath shewed me:
22 And, behold, all the women that are left in the
king of Judah's house *shall be* brought forth to
the king of Babylon's princes, and those *women*
shall say, Thy friends have set thee on, and have
prevailed against thee: thy feet are sunk in the
mire, *and* they are turned away back.
23 So they shall bring out all thy wives and thy

38:4 *princes*. Not royal sons but government officials (v. 25).
38:6 *dungeon*. Pit or cistern. *Hammelech*. Translated, means "the king."

The Prophet Released (38:7–13)

38:7 *eunuchs*. High court officials.
38:11 *treasury*. Storehouse for supplies, not just treasures. Here they found some worn-out clothes (*cast clouts*) and *rags*.
38:13 *court of the prison*. The court of the guard.

Zedekiah's Last Talk with Jeremiah (38:14–28)

38:14 *third entry*. Mentioned only here, perhaps a private or secret entryway.
38:19–23 It should have been obvious that God was with Nebuchadnezzar, yet Zedekiah was too embarrassed to face up to what he regarded as humiliation. All he had to do was trust the Word of the Lord, but he was too ashamed and afraid to trust God. Those whom Zedekiah regarded as friends were certainly not. His only true friend was Jeremiah, for he alone was concerned for the king's well-being and for his soul.
38:22 *Thy friends have set thee on*. Literally, "the men of your peace have misled you."

Thoughts for Personal/Family Worship: Chapter 38

1. **Jeremiah, a man of sorrows, typifies the Lord Jesus (Isa. 53:3). It can be said of both that "He came unto his own, and his own received him not" (John 1:11). The princes or court officials called for Jeremiah to be put to death. Likewise, they said of the Lord Jesus, "He is guilty of death" (Matt. 26:66). Zedekiah's words are reminiscent of what Pilate would later say when prevailed upon to put Jesus to death: "I am innocent of the blood of this just person: see ye to it" (Matt. 27:24). Jeremiah's sinking into the mire is reminiscent of that messianic psalm of David: "I sink in the deep mire, where there is no standing" (Ps. 69:2; cf. vv.15,20; 40:1–2).**
2. **There are many like Zedekiah who are too proud to repent and to trust in the Lord, even though they see**

children to the Chaldeans: and thou shalt not
escape out of their hand, but shalt be taken by the
hand of the king of Babylon: and thou shalt cause
this city to be burned with fire.
24 ¶ Then said Zedekiah unto Jeremiah, Let no
man know of these words, and thou shalt not die.
25 But if the princes hear that I have talked with
thee, and they come unto thee, and say unto thee,
Declare unto us now what thou hast said unto the
king, hide it not from us, and we will not put thee
to death; also what the king said unto thee:
26 Then thou shalt say unto them, I presented my
supplication before the king, that he would not
cause me to return to Jonathan's house, to die there.
27 Then came all the princes unto Jeremiah, and
asked him: and he told them according to all these
words that the king had commanded. So they left
off speaking with him; for the matter was not
perceived.
28 So Jeremiah abode in the court of the prison
until the day that Jerusalem was taken: and he was
there when Jerusalem was taken.

CHAPTER 39

IN the ninth year of Zedekiah king of Judah, in
the tenth month, came Nebuchadrezzar king of
Babylon and all his army against Jerusalem, and
they besieged it.
2 *And* in the eleventh year of Zedekiah, in the
fourth month, the ninth *day* of the month, the
city was broken up.
3 And all the princes of the king of Babylon
came in, and sat in the middle gate, *even* Nergal-
sharezer, Samgar-nebo, Sarsechim, Rab-saris,
Nergal-sharezer, Rab-mag, with all the residue of
the princes of the king of Babylon.
4 ¶ And it came to pass, *that* when Zedekiah the
king of Judah saw them, and all the men of war,
then they fled, and went forth out of the city by
night, by the way of the king's garden, by the gate
betwixt the two walls: and he went out the way of
the plain.
5 But the Chaldeans' army pursued after them,
and overtook Zedekiah in the plains of Jericho:
and when they had taken him, they brought him
up to Nebuchadnezzar king of Babylon to Riblah
in the land of Hamath, where he gave judgment
upon him.
6 Then the king of Babylon slew the sons of
Zedekiah in Riblah before his eyes: also the king
of Babylon slew all the nobles of Judah.
7 Moreover he put out Zedekiah's eyes, and
bound him with chains, to carry him to Babylon.
8 ¶ And the Chaldeans burned the king's house,
and the houses of the people, with fire, and brake
down the walls of Jerusalem.
9 Then Nebuzar-adan the captain of the guard
carried away captive into Babylon the remnant
of the people that remained in the city, and those
that fell away, that fell to him, with the rest of the
people that remained.
10 But Nebuzar-adan the captain of the guard left
of the poor of the people, which had nothing, in
the land of Judah, and gave them vineyards and
fields at the same time.
11 ¶ Now Nebuchadrezzar king of Babylon gave
charge concerning Jeremiah to Nebuzar-adan the
captain of the guard, saying,
12 Take him, and look well to him, and do him
no harm; but do unto him even as he shall say
unto thee.
13 So Nebuzar-adan the captain of the guard
sent, and Nebushasban, Rab-saris, and Nergal-
sharezer, Rab-mag, and all the king of Babylon's
princes;
14 Even they sent, and took Jeremiah out of the
court of the prison, and committed him unto
Gedaliah the son of Ahikam the son of Shaphan,
that he should carry him home: so he dwelt
among the people.
15 ¶ Now the word of the LORD came unto
Jeremiah, while he was shut up in the court of the
prison, saying,
16 Go and speak to Ebed-melech the Ethiopian,
saying, Thus saith the LORD of hosts, the God of

---

everything collapsing around them. They see the truth of God's Word coming to pass and they fear for the future, yet they cannot humble themselves before the Lord. The Scripture says, "Seek ye the LORD while he may be found, call ye upon him while he is near" (Isa. 55:6). That day of opportunity will come to an end, as it did for Zedekiah, and then all hope is lost. How are you seeking God now?

Chapter 39: *Jerusalem falls to the Babylonians, who treat Zedekiah harshly but show favor to Jeremiah.*

THE FALL OF JERUSALEM (39:1–18)

Zedekiah Captured (39:1–7)

39:1–2 *Nebuchadrezzar.* Alternate spelling of Nebuchadnezzar. The year-long siege ends with the city's destruction in 587/586 BC.

39:3 *princes.* Government or military officials.

39:4–7 Zedekiah sought to flee for his life, but there was no hiding place for him. He was forced to watch his sons being killed, after which his eyes were put out and he was led away into captivity. His tragic end is a vivid picture of the horror, darkness, bondage, and despair that fall upon the damned.

Jeremiah Shown Favor (39:8–14)

39:10 Only the poor are left behind. Some kindness is shown to them: Nebuzar-adan gives them vineyards and fields that they might survive (Zeph. 3:12).

39:11–14 Jeremiah is released from prison and put in the care of the godly family of *Shaphan.*

Ebed-melech Delivered (39:15–18)

39:16 *Ebed-melech.* A protector of Jeremiah (38:7–13). His name means "servant of the king." *evil.* Harm.

Israel; Behold, I will bring my words upon this
city for evil, and not for good; and they shall be
accomplished in that day before thee.
17 But I will deliver thee in that day, saith the
LORD: and thou shalt not be given into the hand
of the men of whom thou *art* afraid.
18 For I will surely deliver thee, and thou shalt
not fall by the sword, but thy life shall be for a prey
unto thee: because thou hast put thy trust in me,
saith the LORD.

CHAPTER 40

THE word that came to Jeremiah from the LORD,
after that Nebuzar-adan the captain of the guard
had let him go from Ramah, when he had taken
him being bound in chains among all that were
carried away captive of Jerusalem and Judah,
which were carried away captive unto Babylon.
2 And the captain of the guard took Jeremiah,
and said unto him, The LORD thy God hath
pronounced this evil upon this place.
3 Now the LORD hath brought *it*, and done
according as he hath said: because ye have sinned
against the LORD, and have not obeyed his voice,
therefore this thing is come upon you.
4 And now, behold, I loose thee this day from the
chains which *were* upon thine hand. If it seem
good unto thee to come with me into Babylon,
come; and I will look well unto thee: but if it
seem ill unto thee to come with me into Babylon,
forbear: behold, all the land *is* before thee:
whither it seemeth good and convenient for thee
to go, thither go.
5 Now while he was not yet gone back, *he said*,
Go back also to Gedaliah the son of Ahikam the
son of Shaphan, whom the king of Babylon hath
made governor over the cities of Judah, and dwell
with him among the people: or go wheresoever
it seemeth convenient unto thee to go. So the
captain of the guard gave him victuals and a
reward, and let him go.
6 Then went Jeremiah unto Gedaliah the son of
Ahikam to Mizpah; and dwelt with him among
the people that were left in the land.
7 ¶ Now when all the captains of the forces which
were in the fields, *even* they and their men, heard
that the king of Babylon had made Gedaliah the
son of Ahikam governor in the land, and had
committed unto him men, and women, and
children, and of the poor of the land, of them that
were not carried away captive to Babylon;
8 Then they came to Gedaliah to Mizpah, even
Ishmael the son of Nethaniah, and Johanan and
Jonathan the sons of Kareah, and Seraiah the
son of Tanhumeth, and the sons of Ephai the
Netophathite, and Jezaniah the son of a Maacha-
thite, they and their men.
9 And Gedaliah the son of Ahikam the son of
Shaphan sware unto them and to their men,
saying, Fear not to serve the Chaldeans: dwell in
the land, and serve the king of Babylon, and it
shall be well with you.
10 As for me, behold, I will dwell at Mizpah to
serve the Chaldeans, which will come unto us:
but ye, gather ye wine, and summer fruits, and oil,
and put *them* in your vessels, and dwell in your
cities that ye have taken.
11 Likewise when all the Jews that *were* in Moab,
and among the Ammonites, and in Edom, and
that *were* in all the countries, heard that the king
of Babylon had left a remnant of Judah, and that
he had set over them Gedaliah the son of Ahikam
the son of Shaphan;
12 Even all the Jews returned out of all places
whither they were driven, and came to the land

39:18 *prey.* Possession. Ebed-melech is assured that no harm shall come to him because he has put his *trust* in the Lord. Salvation is by faith in the Lord (17:7), even for Gentiles like this godly Ethiopian. Ironically, the king of Israel falls, but his Gentile servant stands by faith.

Thoughts for Personal/Family Worship: Chapter 39

1. **The people of Judah did not believe that the wrath of God would come upon them, even when the warning signs were there. There are many people today like this who scoff at Christ's return to judge the world in holy wrath. Yet we should not be surprised at His coming (see 2 Peter 3:1–4). Let us believe and humble ourselves before the Lord. Let us be watching and waiting in prayer, for the day of wrath will come.**
2. **There is a great contrast between Zedekiah and Ebed-melech. They heard the same word, but with vastly different responses. Ebed-melech trusted God's Word and cared for God's prophet. He did what was right in the eyes of the Lord; therefore, God delivered him. By God's grace, this is what will happen to every believer on the day of judgment. Which would you rather be, a rich king who does not trust the Lord or a servant who places his faith in Him? Why?**

EVENTS AFTER JERUSALEM'S FALL (40:1—43:7)

Gedaliah's Period as Governor (40:1—41:18)

Chapter 40: *Jeremiah is set free, and Gedaliah becomes governor over Judah.*

40:2 *evil.* Disaster or calamity.

40:3 *done according as he hath said.* Even the Babylonian commander acknowledged the truth of God's Word against Judah. God is glorified through His judgments, for they display the truth of His Word.

40:4 *convenient.* Literally, "the right thing in your eyes," preferable or suitable to him.

40:5 *Gedaliah* had a good heritage. His father, *Ahikam*, intervened to protect Jeremiah in one of the plots against him (26:24). His grandfather, *Shaphan*, an official under Josiah, brought the scroll to the king that led to his reforms (2 Kings 22:3–13). *victuals.* Food. *reward.* Gift.

40:9–10 *serve the Chaldeans.* As the Lord had commanded

of Judah, to Gedaliah, unto Mizpah, and gathered
wine and summer fruits very much.
13 ¶ Moreover Johanan the son of Kareah, and all
the captains of the forces that *were* in the fields,
came to Gedaliah to Mizpah,
14 And said unto him, Dost thou certainly know
that Baalis the king of the Ammonites hath sent
Ishmael the son of Nethaniah to slay thee? But
Gedaliah the son of Ahikam believed them not.
15 Then Johanan the son of Kareah spake to
Gedaliah in Mizpah secretly, saying, Let me go,
I pray thee, and I will slay Ishmael the son of
Nethaniah, and no man shall know *it:* wherefore
should he slay thee, that all the Jews which are
gathered unto thee should be scattered, and the
remnant in Judah perish?
16 But Gedaliah the son of Ahikam said unto
Johanan the son of Kareah, Thou shalt not do this
thing: for thou speakest falsely of Ishmael.

CHAPTER 41

NOW it came to pass in the seventh month, *that*
Ishmael the son of Nethaniah the son of Elish-
ama, of the seed royal, and the princes of the king,
even ten men with him, came unto Gedaliah the
son of Ahikam to Mizpah; and there they did eat
bread together in Mizpah.
2 Then arose Ishmael the son of Nethaniah,
and the ten men that were with him, and smote
Gedaliah the son of Ahikam the son of Shaphan
with the sword, and slew him, whom the king of
Babylon had made governor over the land.
3 Ishmael also slew all the Jews that were with
him, *even* with Gedaliah, at Mizpah, and the Chal-
deans that were found there, *and* the men of war.
4 And it came to pass the second day after he had
slain Gedaliah, and no man knew *it,*
5 That there came certain from Shechem, from
Shiloh, and from Samaria, *even* fourscore men,
having their beards shaven, and their clothes rent,
and having cut themselves, with offerings and
incense in their hand, to bring *them* to the house
of the LORD.
6 And Ishmael the son of Nethaniah went forth
from Mizpah to meet them, weeping all along as he
went: and it came to pass, as he met them, he said
unto them, Come to Gedaliah the son of Ahikam.
7 And it was *so,* when they came into the midst
of the city, that Ishmael the son of Nethaniah slew
them, *and cast them* into the midst of the pit, he,
and the men that *were* with him.
8 But ten men were found among them that said
unto Ishmael, Slay us not: for we have treasures in
the field, of wheat, and of barley, and of oil, and of
honey. So he forbare, and slew them not among
their brethren.
9 Now the pit wherein Ishmael had cast all the
dead bodies of the men, whom he had slain
because of Gedaliah, *was* it which Asa the king
had made for fear of Baasha king of Israel: *and*
Ishmael the son of Nethaniah filled it with *them*
that were slain.
10 Then Ishmael carried away captive all the
residue of the people that *were* in Mizpah, *even* the
king's daughters, and all the people that remained
in Mizpah, whom Nebuzar-adan the captain of
the guard had committed to Gedaliah the son
of Ahikam: and Ishmael the son of Nethaniah
carried them away captive, and departed to go
over to the Ammonites.
11 ¶ But when Johanan the son of Kareah,
and all the captains of the forces that *were* with
him, heard of all the evil that Ishmael the son of
Nethaniah had done,
12 Then they took all the men, and went to fight
with Ishmael the son of Nethaniah, and found
him by the great waters that *are* in Gibeon.
13 Now it came to pass, *that* when all the people
which *were* with Ishmael saw Johanan the son of
Kareah, and all the captains of the forces that *were*
with him, then they were glad.

---

through Jeremiah (21:9).

40:12 *gathered wine . . . very much.* Tokens of blessing and prosperity. Grace is greater than sin.

40:13–14 *Johanan.* Unknown other than that he was a military commander who supported Gedaliah. *Ishmael.* Unknown other than that he was of the royal family (41:1), that he was allied with the Ammonites, and that he was sent to assassinate Gedaliah.

Thoughts for Personal/Family Worship: Chapter 40

The blessing of much fruit in the midst of destruction reveals the grace of God, a sign that He offered blessings to His people if they would submit to the Babylonians as He had commanded (vv. 9–10,12). As long as we live, God's judgments are mingled with mercy, calling sinners to submit to His discipline and instruction. Even in the midst of pronouncing judgment after man's fall, God announced the grace of Christ (Gen. 3:15). Yet His call is hard, just as hard as it was for the Jews to serve the Babylonians. Christ calls us to take our crosses, deny ourselves, and follow Him (Matt. 16:24).

Chapter 41: ***Ishmael slays Gedaliah and many others and then retreats to the Ammonites, taking captives with him, who are then rescued by Johanan.***

41:1–2 Although he was in alliance with Ammon, Ishmael's treachery may have been motivated by his aspiration to govern, since he was of the king's family (*seed royal*).

41:5 *beards shaven, and their clothes rent.* Typical gestures of grief. *having cut themselves.* Practiced by pagans like Baal worshipers (47:5; 48:37; 1 Kings 18:28) but forbidden by God (Deut. 14:1). Though judgment had fallen upon them, some still foolishly mixed religions.

41:9 *which Asa the king had made.* See 1 Kings 15:22; 2 Chron. 16:6.

41:12 *great waters . . . in Gibeon.* Scene of confrontation

14 So all the people that Ishmael had carried away
captive from Mizpah cast about and returned,
and went unto Johanan the son of Kareah.
15 But Ishmael the son of Nethaniah escaped
from Johanan with eight men, and went to the
Ammonites.
16 Then took Johanan the son of Kareah, and
all the captains of the forces that *were* with him,
all the remnant of the people whom he had
recovered from Ishmael the son of Nethaniah,
from Mizpah, after *that* he had slain Gedaliah
the son of Ahikam, *even* mighty men of war, and
the women, and the children, and the eunuchs,
whom he had brought again from Gibeon:
17 And they departed, and dwelt in the habitation
of Chimham, which is by Beth-lehem, to go to
enter into Egypt,
18 Because of the Chaldeans: for they were afraid
of them, because Ishmael the son of Nethaniah
had slain Gedaliah the son of Ahikam, whom the
king of Babylon made governor in the land.

CHAPTER 42

THEN all the captains of the forces, and Johanan
the son of Kareah, and Jezaniah the son of Hosh-
aiah, and all the people from the least even unto
the greatest, came near,
2 And said unto Jeremiah the prophet, Let, we
beseech thee, our supplication be accepted before
thee, and pray for us unto the LORD thy God, *even*
for all this remnant; (for we are left *but* a few of
many, as thine eyes do behold us:)
3 That the LORD thy God may shew us the way
wherein we may walk, and the thing that we
may do.
4 Then Jeremiah the prophet said unto them, I
have heard *you*; behold, I will pray unto the LORD
your God according to your words; and it shall
come to pass, *that* whatsoever thing the LORD
shall answer you, I will declare *it* unto you; I will
keep nothing back from you.
5 Then they said to Jeremiah, The LORD be a true
and faithful witness between us, if we do not even
according to all things for the which the LORD thy
God shall send thee to us.
6 Whether *it be* good, or whether *it be* evil, we will
obey the voice of the LORD our God, to whom we
send thee; that it may be well with us, when we
obey the voice of the LORD our God.
7 ¶ And it came to pass after ten days, that the
word of the LORD came unto Jeremiah.
8 Then called he Johanan the son of Kareah, and
all the captains of the forces which *were* with
him, and all the people from the least even to the
greatest,
9 And said unto them, Thus saith the LORD, the
God of Israel, unto whom ye sent me to present
your supplication before him;
10 If ye will still abide in this land, then will I
build you, and not pull *you* down, and I will plant
you, and not pluck *you* up: for I repent me of the
evil that I have done unto you.
11 Be not afraid of the king of Babylon, of whom
ye are afraid; be not afraid of him, saith the LORD:
for I *am* with you to save you, and to deliver you
from his hand.
12 And I will shew mercies unto you, that he may
have mercy upon you, and cause you to return to
your own land.
13 ¶ But if ye say, We will not dwell in this land,
neither obey the voice of the LORD your God,
14 Saying, No; but we will go into the land of
Egypt, where we shall see no war, nor hear the
sound of the trumpet, nor have hunger of bread;
and there will we dwell:
15 And now therefore hear the word of the LORD,
ye remnant of Judah; Thus saith the LORD of
hosts, the God of Israel; If ye wholly set your faces
to enter into Egypt, and go to sojourn there;
16 Then it shall come to pass, *that* the sword,
which ye feared, shall overtake you there in the

---

between the men of Saul and those of David (2 Sam. 2:12–16).
41:14 *cast about*. Turned around.
41:16 *eunuchs*. High-ranking court officials.

Thoughts for Personal/Family Worship: Chapter 41

1. **While believers must seek to be as "harmless as doves," they are also exhorted to be as "wise as serpents" (Matt. 10:16). Gedaliah made a huge error of judgment in his trust of Ishmael. How important it is to have discernment in our dealings with others, especially with those in the world. To trust human nature is to give way to folly. We must always be on our guard against the subtle actions of those who despise the Lord's ways. What are areas in which you need discernment now? How can you seek it?**
2. **Ishmael's eating of bread with Gedaliah under the guise of friendship is suggestive of Judas Iscariot's betrayal of the Lord Jesus at the Last Supper. However, whereas Gedaliah was ignorant of Ishmael's intentions, the Lord Jesus was fully aware of Judas's plot (John 13:21,25–26). Gedaliah's naive trust allowed the betrayal to succeed and resulted not only in his own death but also in the deaths of many others. However, Christ willingly allowed His betrayal to take place, for His death gives life to all who will trust in Him.**

A Foolish Flight to Egypt (42:1—43:7)

Chapter 42: ***Jeremiah warns against fleeing to Egypt and assures safety for those who remain in Judea.***

42:6 *evil*. Not in the sense of sinful but of harmful or unpleasant.
42:10 *build . . . not pluck*. Words reminiscent of the call of Jeremiah (1:10). *I repent me of the evil*. The Lord relented regarding the calamity He had brought in judgment.
42:15 *sojourn*. Take up residence as a foreigner (vv. 17,22).

land of Egypt, and the famine, whereof ye were
afraid, shall follow close after you there in Egypt;
and there ye shall die.
17 So shall it be with all the men that set their
faces to go into Egypt to sojourn there; they
shall die by the sword, by the famine, and by the
pestilence: and none of them shall remain or
escape from the evil that I will bring upon them.
18 For thus saith the LORD of hosts, the God
of Israel; As mine anger and my fury hath been
poured forth upon the inhabitants of Jerusalem;
so shall my fury be poured forth upon you,
when ye shall enter into Egypt: and ye shall be an
execration, and an astonishment, and a curse, and
a reproach; and ye shall see this place no more.
19 ¶ The LORD hath said concerning you, O ye
remnant of Judah; Go ye not into Egypt: know
certainly that I have admonished you this day.
20 For ye dissembled in your hearts, when ye sent
me unto the LORD your God, saying, Pray for us
unto the LORD our God; and according unto all
that the LORD our God shall say, so declare unto
us, and we will do *it*.
21 And *now* I have this day declared *it* to you; but
ye have not obeyed the voice of the LORD your
God, nor any *thing* for the which he hath sent me
unto you.
22 Now therefore know certainly that ye shall
die by the sword, by the famine, and by the
pestilence, in the place whither ye desire to go
and to sojourn.

CHAPTER 43

AND it came to pass, *that* when Jeremiah had
made an end of speaking unto all the people all
the words of the LORD their God, for which the
LORD their God had sent him to them, *even* all
these words,
2 Then spake Azariah the son of Hoshaiah, and
Johanan the son of Kareah, and all the proud
men, saying unto Jeremiah, Thou speakest falsely:
the LORD our God hath not sent thee to say, Go
not into Egypt to sojourn there:
3 But Baruch the son of Neriah setteth thee on
against us, for to deliver us into the hand of the
Chaldeans, that they might put us to death, and
carry us away captives into Babylon.
4 So Johanan the son of Kareah, and all the
captains of the forces, and all the people, obeyed
not the voice of the LORD, to dwell in the land of
Judah.
5 But Johanan the son of Kareah, and all the cap-
tains of the forces, took all the remnant of Judah,
that were returned from all nations, whither they
had been driven, to dwell in the land of Judah;
6 *Even* men, and women, and children, and the
king's daughters, and every person that Nebuzar-
adan the captain of the guard had left with
Gedaliah the son of Ahikam the son of Shaphan,
and Jeremiah the prophet, and Baruch the son of
Neriah.
7 So they came into the land of Egypt: for they
obeyed not the voice of the LORD: thus came they
even to Tahpanhes.
8 ¶ Then came the word of the LORD unto
Jeremiah in Tahpanhes, saying,
9 Take great stones in thine hand, and hide them
in the clay in the brickkiln, which *is* at the entry of
Pharaoh's house in Tahpanhes, in the sight of the
men of Judah;
10 And say unto them, Thus saith the LORD of

42:17 *evil.* Calamity.
42:18 *execration.* Curse. *astonishment.* An horrific, atrocious event. *curse.* A curse formula. *reproach.* Disgrace.
42:20 *ye dissembled in your hearts.* Literally, "you misled in your souls" (in yourselves).

Thoughts for Personal/Family Worship: Chapter 42

1. **God always requires obedience to His will. The people were right to go to Jeremiah in order to discover God's will, for he was the prophet from whom the Word of the Lord would be revealed. Their professed commitment to do His will seemed commendable (v. 6) but ultimately proved hypocritical, for when His will was declared they did not want to hear, because it was contrary to their own plans. Too often, even professing Christians tend to be selective in their obedience, thus revealing that they sometimes prefer their own desires to God's will. We must believe that the Lord's way is always best, even when it seems to go against what we may perceive to be better (Prov. 3:5).**
2. **The Jews' desire to return to Egypt is equivalent to Christians wanting to go back into the world; it is to forget the powerful blood of Christ and that the believer is separated from this vain and passing world. Let us never lose sight of the blessedness we have in Christ; neither should we ever doubt that God always knows what is best for us. May we therefore always seek to be obedient to His Word.**

Chapter 43: ***In defiance of Jeremiah's word, the people go to Egypt and take Jeremiah with them, where he symbolically declares the destruction of Egypt.***

43:2 *proud.* Presumptuous and insolent. *sojourn.* Take up residence as a foreigner.
43:3 *Baruch . . . setteth thee on against us.* Literally, "Baruch . . . incites you against us."
43:7 *Tahpanhes.* Most likely in the eastern part of the Nile delta, on the border of Goshen. Ironically, they thought their safety would be in the place of their historic bondage.

EVENTS IN EGYPT (43:8—45:5)

Jeremiah Prophesies Babylon's Invasion of Egypt (43:8–13)

43:9–10 *in the clay in the brickkiln.* The Hebrew is uncertain but seems to refer to the clay floor of a brick terrace. This represents the pedestal on which Nebuchadnezzar would erect his throne. *pavilion.* Also uncertain; some suggest "carpet of the throne" and others a "state tent." Either way, the symbol is one of royal power. *my servant.* See note at 25:9.

hosts, the God of Israel; Behold, I will send and
take Nebuchadrezzar the king of Babylon, my
servant, and will set his throne upon these stones
that I have hid; and he shall spread his royal
pavilion over them.
11 And when he cometh, he shall smite the land
of Egypt, *and deliver* such *as are* for death to
death; and such *as are* for captivity to captivity;
and such *as are* for the sword to the sword.
12 And I will kindle a fire in the houses of the
gods of Egypt; and he shall burn them, and carry
them away captives: and he shall array himself
with the land of Egypt, as a shepherd putteth on
his garment; and he shall go forth from thence in
peace.
13 He shall break also the images of Beth-she-
mesh, that *is* in the land of Egypt; and the houses
of the gods of the Egyptians shall he burn with fire.

CHAPTER 44

THE word that came to Jeremiah concerning all
the Jews which dwell in the land of Egypt, which
dwell at Migdol, and at Tahpanhes, and at Noph,
and in the country of Pathros, saying,
2 Thus saith the LORD of hosts, the God of Israel;
Ye have seen all the evil that I have brought upon
Jerusalem, and upon all the cities of Judah; and,
behold, this day they *are* a desolation, and no man
dwelleth therein,
3 Because of their wickedness which they have
committed to provoke me to anger, in that they
went to burn incense, *and* to serve other gods,
whom they knew not, *neither* they, ye, nor your
fathers.
4 Howbeit I sent unto you all my servants the
prophets, rising early and sending *them*, saying,
Oh, do not this abominable thing that I hate.
5 But they hearkened not, nor inclined their ear
to turn from their wickedness, to burn no incense
unto other gods.
6 Wherefore my fury and mine anger was poured
forth, and was kindled in the cities of Judah and
in the streets of Jerusalem; and they are wasted
and desolate, as at this day.
7 Therefore now thus saith the LORD, the God
of hosts, the God of Israel; Wherefore commit ye
this great evil against your souls, to cut off from
you man and woman, child and suckling, out of
Judah, to leave you none to remain;
8 In that ye provoke me unto wrath with the
works of your hands, burning incense unto other
gods in the land of Egypt, whither ye be gone to
dwell, that ye might cut yourselves off, and that
ye might be a curse and a reproach among all the
nations of the earth?
9 Have ye forgotten the wickedness of your
fathers, and the wickedness of the kings of Judah,
and the wickedness of their wives, and your own
wickedness, and the wickedness of your wives,
which they have committed in the land of Judah,
and in the streets of Jerusalem?
10 They are not humbled *even* unto this day,
neither have they feared, nor walked in my law,
nor in my statutes, that I set before you and before
your fathers.
11 ¶ Therefore thus saith the LORD of hosts, the
God of Israel; Behold, I will set my face against
you for evil, and to cut off all Judah.
12 And I will take the remnant of Judah, that

43:11 *for captivity to captivity*. See note at 15:2.
43:12 *array . . . putteth on*. Literally, "to delouse." Just as a shepherd would pick lice from off his clothing, so would Babylon pick Egypt clean of its wealth.
43:13 *Beth-shemesh*. The house of the sun, better known as Heliopolis (sun-city). Ra, the sun god, was a principal deity in Egypt.

Thoughts for Personal/Family Worship: Chapter 43

1. **Hebrews 1:1 mentions various ways in which God communicated through His prophets. This chapter reveals two of them: first, through the prophet's preaching, and second, through his symbolic actions, such as burying the stones. This portrayed the message in a way that should have been easy for all to understand. It was gracious of God to reinforce His Word in this way, but it also left them without excuse. The Bible presents Christ to us in many ways in order to make Him clear; we have no excuse for not trusting and following Him.**
2. **The safe haven Israel hoped to find proved anything but secure, and their folly provides us with a cautionary tale. It is utter foolishness to go against the revealed will of God. This Jewish remnant knew what He required of them. Yet they proved to be more fearful of man than of God; hence, they made a fateful mistake (Prov. 14:12). The safest place on earth is the place of obedience to God's will (Ps. 37:3–6).**

Chapter 44: ***Jeremiah threatens severe judgment on those who have fled to Egypt for their persistent idolatry and declares the fall of Egypt to Babylon.***

The Punishment of the Jews in Egypt (44:1–30)

44:1 *The word that came*. Most likely the last public message of Jeremiah. The remaining chapters fall chronologically earlier in his ministry.
44:2–5 *Ye have seen all the evil . . . hearkened not*. They saw the calamity caused by sin, but it did not deter them from the same sins.
44:4 *rising early*. Expression of the fervency and priority the Lord showed in giving prophetic warnings.
44:7 *your souls*. Hebrew expression meaning "yourselves."
44:9 *the wickedness*. The Hebrew is plural for intensification, "the extreme wickedness."
44:10 *They are not humbled*. Literally, "they have not been crushed," in the sense of being contrite and broken over sin (Isa. 57:15).
44:11 *I will set my face against you for evil*. The Lord resolved to bring calamitous judgment.
44:12 *sojourn*. Take up permanent residence as a foreigner

have set their faces to go into the land of Egypt
to sojourn there, and they shall all be consumed,
and fall in the land of Egypt; they shall *even* be
consumed by the sword *and* by the famine: they
shall die, from the least even unto the greatest, by
the sword and by the famine: and they shall be
an execration, *and* an astonishment, and a curse,
and a reproach.
13 For I will punish them that dwell in the land
of Egypt, as I have punished Jerusalem, by the
sword, by the famine, and by the pestilence:
14 So that none of the remnant of Judah, which
are gone into the land of Egypt to sojourn there,
shall escape or remain, that they should return
into the land of Judah, to the which they have
a desire to return to dwell there: for none shall
return but such as shall escape.
15 ¶ Then all the men which knew that their
wives had burned incense unto other gods, and
all the women that stood by, a great multitude,
even all the people that dwelt in the land of Egypt,
in Pathros, answered Jeremiah, saying,
16 *As for* the word that thou hast spoken unto
us in the name of the LORD, we will not hearken
unto thee.
17 But we will certainly do whatsoever thing
goeth forth out of our own mouth, to burn in-
cense unto the queen of heaven, and to pour out
drink offerings unto her, as we have done, we, and
our fathers, our kings, and our princes, in the cit-
ies of Judah, and in the streets of Jerusalem: for
then had we plenty of victuals, and were well, and
saw no evil.
18 But since we left off to burn incense to the
queen of heaven, and to pour out drink offerings
unto her, we have wanted all *things*, and have been
consumed by the sword and by the famine.
19 And when we burned incense to the queen of
heaven, and poured out drink offerings unto her,
did we make her cakes to worship her, and pour
out drink offerings unto her, without our men?
20 ¶ Then Jeremiah said unto all the people, to
the men, and to the women, and to all the people
which had given him *that* answer, saying,
21 The incense that ye burned in the cities of
Judah, and in the streets of Jerusalem, ye, and
your fathers, your kings, and your princes, and the
people of the land, did not the LORD remember
them, and came it *not* into his mind?
22 So that the LORD could no longer bear,
because of the evil of your doings, *and* because
of the abominations which ye have committed;
therefore is your land a desolation, and an
astonishment, and a curse, without an inhabitant,
as at this day.
23 Because ye have burned incense, and because
ye have sinned against the LORD, and have not
obeyed the voice of the LORD, nor walked in his
law, nor in his statutes, nor in his testimonies;
therefore this evil is happened unto you, as at this
day.
24 Moreover Jeremiah said unto all the people,
and to all the women, Hear the word of the LORD,
all Judah that *are* in the land of Egypt:
25 Thus saith the LORD of hosts, the God of
Israel, saying; Ye and your wives have both spoken
with your mouths, and fulfilled with your hand,
saying, We will surely perform our vows that
we have vowed, to burn incense to the queen of
heaven, and to pour out drink offerings unto her:
ye will surely accomplish your vows, and surely
perform your vows.
26 Therefore hear ye the word of the LORD, all
Judah that dwell in the land of Egypt; Behold, I
have sworn by my great name, saith the LORD,
that my name shall no more be named in the
mouth of any man of Judah in all the land of
Egypt, saying, The Lord GOD liveth.
27 Behold, I will watch over them for evil, and
not for good: and all the men of Judah that *are* in
the land of Egypt shall be consumed by the sword
and by the famine, until there be an end of them.
28 Yet a small number that escape the sword shall
return out of the land of Egypt into the land of
Judah, and all the remnant of Judah, that are
gone into the land of Egypt to sojourn there, shall
know whose words shall stand, mine, or theirs.
29 ¶ And this *shall be* a sign unto you, saith the

(vv. 14,28). They made Egypt their home. *execration.* Curse.

44:17–18 *queen of heaven.* See note at 7:18. *plenty of victuals.* Literally, "we ate our fill." They falsely claimed that their previous worship of a pagan god had brought prosperity and that the present calamity resulted from their failure to worship her. Pagan worship involves a mercenary attitude of giving the gods what they want so the worshipers can get what they desire.

44:21 *remember.* Consider and punish their sin (14:10).

44:22 *the LORD could no longer bear.* God's patience does not delay His judgment forever—a warning to unrepentant sinners (Gen. 6:3; Prov. 1:24–33).

44:27 *watch.* Literally, "be awake and vigilant." The Lord will be vigilant in fulfilling His word of judgment (*evil*). The Lord's declaration at the end of Jeremiah's ministry was the same as at the beginning (1:12), for His Word and purpose never change.

44:29–30 *sign.* Confirmation or affirmation. The fall of Pharaoh would confirm all that God had said.

Thoughts for Personal/Family Worship: Chapter 44

1. **The Jewish exiles in Egypt failed to have teachable spirits. They had witnessed the calamity God had inflicted upon Jerusalem because of their idolatry. Their previous worship of the queen of heaven had caused God to make their land "a desolation" (v. 22). However, their hearts were so hardened they would not learn the lesson. Their repeated refusal to repent led into spiritual stupidity and dullness. The vast majority of those who fled to Egypt would never return. They would be "consumed**

LORD, that I will punish you in this place, that
ye may know that my words shall surely stand
against you for evil:
30 Thus saith the LORD; Behold, I will give
Pharaoh-hophra king of Egypt into the hand of
his enemies, and into the hand of them that seek
his life; as I gave Zedekiah king of Judah into the
hand of Nebuchadrezzar king of Babylon, his
enemy, and that sought his life.

CHAPTER 45

THE word that Jeremiah the prophet spake unto
Baruch the son of Neriah, when he had written
these words in a book at the mouth of Jeremiah,
in the fourth year of Jehoiakim the son of Josiah
king of Judah, saying,
2 Thus saith the LORD, the God of Israel, unto
thee, O Baruch;
3 Thou didst say, Woe is me now! for the LORD
hath added grief to my sorrow; I fainted in my
sighing, and I find no rest.
4 ¶ Thus shalt thou say unto him, The LORD saith
thus; Behold, *that* which I have built will I break
down, and that which I have planted I will pluck
up, even this whole land.
5 And seekest thou great things for thyself? seek
them not: for, behold, I will bring evil upon all
flesh, saith the LORD: but thy life will I give unto
thee for a prey in all places whither thou goest.

CHAPTER 46

THE word of the LORD which came to Jeremiah
the prophet against the Gentiles;
2 Against Egypt, against the army of Pharaoh-
necho king of Egypt, which was by the river
Euphrates in Carchemish, which Nebuchadrezzar
king of Babylon smote in the fourth year of
Jehoiakim the son of Josiah king of Judah.
3 Order ye the buckler and shield, and draw near
to battle.
4 Harness the horses; and get up, ye horsemen,
and stand forth with *your* helmets; furbish the
spears, *and* put on the brigandines.
5 Wherefore have I seen them dismayed *and*
turned away back? and their mighty ones are
beaten down, and are fled apace, and look not
back: *for* fear *was* round about, saith the LORD.
6 Let not the swift flee away, nor the mighty man
escape; they shall stumble, and fall toward the
north by the river Euphrates.
7 Who *is* this *that* cometh up as a flood, whose
waters are moved as the rivers?
8 Egypt riseth up like a flood, and *his* waters are
moved like the rivers; and he saith, I will go up,
and will cover the earth; I will destroy the city and
the inhabitants thereof.
9 Come up, ye horses; and rage, ye chariots; and
let the mighty men come forth; the Ethiopians
and the Libyans, that handle the shield; and the
Lydians, that handle *and* bend the bow.

---

by the sword and by the famine" (v. 27). Therefore, let us be quick to repent as soon as God's Word reveals our sin, lest we too fall into hardness and then destruction.

2. Even in judgment, God spared some in mercy. He says, "Yet a small number that escape the sword shall return out of the land of Egypt into the land of Judah" (v. 28). This blessed thought should never cause us to be presumptuous; rather, it should spur us on to desire a life of righteousness and obedience unto Him.

Chapter 45: *Baruch receives a personal word from the Lord for his instruction and comfort.*

The Despairing Baruch Is Comforted (45:1–5)

45:1 Chronologically, these events follow chapter 36, where Jeremiah dictated all his prophecies to *Baruch*. That this whole chapter is addressed to a single person reveals that Scripture speaks to individual needs and concerns and that the Lord cares for each individual who belongs to Him (Ps. 1:6).
45:3 *Woe is me.* Although the message he wrote down concerned the nation as a whole, Baruch focused only on the personal implications.
45:5 *evil.* Calamitous judgment. *prey.* Plunder. Calamity (*evil*) will come, but his life will be his possession (*prey*); he will be spared.

Thoughts for Personal/Family Worship: Chapter 45

Baruch faithfully recorded Jeremiah's message of doom and destruction; nevertheless, his response was inappropriate. While not disagreeing with the prophecy, he seems to have grieved that the judgment of the nation would take away the great things he sought for himself. Self-seeking and self-pity only bring distress. Christians sometimes hope that God will hold back His judgment of the world until all their earthly goals have been achieved. This special word to Baruch teaches us that if believers would know real peace they must submit unreservedly to the will of God and rejoice to know that their own persons will be saved from the wrath of God.

WARNINGS TO THE NATIONS (46:1—51:64)

Chapter 46: *Egypt's days are numbered; the defeat of Pharaoh's army is foretold.*

The Defeat of Egypt (46:1–28)

46:1 *against the Gentiles.* Chapters 46–51, "The Warnings to the Nations," fulfill part of Jeremiah's commission as "a prophet unto the nations" (1:5). The warnings testify to God's sovereignty over the nations and their accountability to Him.
46:2 The battle of *Carchemish* in 605 BC marked the beginning of the Babylonian Empire and the demise of Egypt and Assyria. *Nebuchadrezzar.* Alternate spelling of Nebuchadnezzar.
46:3 *buckler.* Small shield. *shield.* Large shield covering the whole body.
46:4 *furbish.* Polish or sharpen. *brigandines.* Coats of mail or armor.
46:8 *I will go up . . . I will destroy.* Pharaoh's boasting reveals his sinful self-confidence; pride goes before a fall (Prov. 11:2; 16:18).
46:10 *the day of the Lord God.* The time of direct divine intervention in human affairs to save and judge. Although the events at Carchemish had political and military explanations,

10 For this *is* the day of the Lord GOD of hosts,
a day of vengeance, that he may avenge him of
his adversaries: and the sword shall devour, and it
shall be satiate and made drunk with their blood:
for the Lord GOD of hosts hath a sacrifice in the
north country by the river Euphrates.
11 Go up into Gilead, and take balm, O virgin,
the daughter of Egypt: in vain shalt thou use
many medicines; *for* thou shalt not be cured.
12 The nations have heard of thy shame, and thy
cry hath filled the land: for the mighty man hath
stumbled against the mighty, *and* they are fallen
both together.
13 ¶ The word that the LORD spake to Jeremiah
the prophet, how Nebuchadrezzar king of
Babylon should come *and* smite the land of Egypt.
14 Declare ye in Egypt, and publish in Migdol,
and publish in Noph and in Tahpanhes: say ye,
Stand fast, and prepare thee; for the sword shall
devour round about thee.
15 Why are thy valiant *men* swept away? they
stood not, because the LORD did drive them.
16 He made many to fall, yea, one fell upon
another: and they said, Arise, and let us go again
to our own people, and to the land of our nativity,
from the oppressing sword.
17 They did cry there, Pharaoh king of Egypt *is*
but a noise; he hath passed the time appointed.
18 *As* I live, saith the King, whose name *is* the LORD
of hosts, Surely as Tabor *is* among the mountains,
and as Carmel by the sea, *so* shall he come.
19 O thou daughter dwelling in Egypt, furnish
thyself to go into captivity: for Noph shall be
waste and desolate without an inhabitant.
20 Egypt *is like* a very fair heifer, *but* destruction
cometh; it cometh out of the north.
21 Also her hired men *are* in the midst of her like
fatted bullocks; for they also are turned back, *and*
are fled away together: they did not stand, because
the day of their calamity was come upon them,
and the time of their visitation.
22 The voice thereof shall go like a serpent; for
they shall march with an army, and come against
her with axes, as hewers of wood.
23 They shall cut down her forest, saith the LORD,
though it cannot be searched; because they are
more than the grasshoppers, and *are* innumerable.
24 The daughter of Egypt shall be confounded;
she shall be delivered into the hand of the people
of the north.
25 The LORD of hosts, the God of Israel, saith; Be-
hold, I will punish the multitude of No, and Pha-
raoh, and Egypt, with their gods, and their kings;
even Pharaoh, and *all* them that trust in him:
26 And I will deliver them into the hand of
those that seek their lives, and into the hand of
Nebuchadrezzar king of Babylon, and into the
hand of his servants: and afterward it shall be
inhabited, as in the days of old, saith the LORD.
27 ¶ But fear not thou, O my servant Jacob, and
be not dismayed, O Israel: for, behold, I will save
thee from afar off, and thy seed from the land of
their captivity; and Jacob shall return, and be in
rest and at ease, and none shall make *him* afraid.
28 Fear thou not, O Jacob my servant, saith the
LORD: for I *am* with thee; for I will make a full
end of all the nations whither I have driven thee:
but I will not make a full end of thee, but correct
thee in measure; yet will I not leave thee wholly
unpunished.

CHAPTER 47

THE word of the LORD that came to Jeremiah
the prophet against the Philistines, before that
Pharaoh smote Gaza.

God orchestrated them all to accomplish His purpose for history. Egypt and Babylon were merely pawns in God's hand. *hosts*. Army; God is the Commander-in-Chief.

46:13 Egypt's defeat here would be followed by Babylon's invasion of Egypt itself.

46:20 *fair heifer*. Perhaps an allusion to the bull god worshiped by the Egyptians, who would be powerless to help.

46:22 *like a serpent*. The imagery is of a snake that can do nothing but hiss when moved from its covering by the wood cutters (*hewers of wood*). Since serpents were common in Egyptian art, this graphically portrays Egypt's helplessness before her enemy.

46:24 *people of the north*. Babylon, whose invasion came from the north.

46:25 *multitude*. Literally, "Amun," one of the chief Egyptian deities. *No*. Thebes, the capital of Upper Egypt (the south). *them that trust in him*. A warning to Judah not to hope in men.

46:26 *afterward it shall be inhabited*. Hints of a future restoration for Egypt.

46:27–28 *Fear thou not, O Jacob my servant . . . for I am with thee*. God speaks an amazing word of grace to His backslidden people, again calling them to trust His covenant mercies and to experience His salvation (30:10–11; 42:11; Gen. 26:24; Deut. 31:6,8; Isa. 41:10; 43:5).

Thoughts for Personal/Family Worship: Chapter 46

1. **God used Babylon as an instrument to accomplish His will (v. 26). Let us remember that the events of our era are also still under His control. If we hear of wars, nations rising against nations, and other disasters, we must not view them merely as the results of human factors. The Lord reigns, and His people can rejoice that all things serve for His glory and their good.**
2. **The principal application Jeremiah draws from the coming judgment on Egypt is directed toward Judah (vv. 27–28). They had foolishly trusted in Egypt (v. 25), but the Lord of glory called them to trust in Him alone (Isa. 30:1–3; 31:1–5). How might you be tempted to trust in yourself or other people? How can you make the Lord alone your hope in all things?**

Chapter 47: *God declares judgment on the Philistines.*

The Destruction of the Philistines (47:1–7)

2 Thus saith the LORD; Behold, waters rise up out
of the north, and shall be an overflowing flood,
and shall overflow the land, and all that is therein;
the city, and them that dwell therein: then the
men shall cry, and all the inhabitants of the land
shall howl.
3 At the noise of the stamping of the hoofs of his
strong *horses*, at the rushing of his chariots, *and at*
the rumbling of his wheels, the fathers shall not
look back to *their* children for feebleness of hands;
4 Because of the day that cometh to spoil all the
Philistines, *and* to cut off from Tyrus and Zidon
every helper that remaineth: for the LORD will
spoil the Philistines, the remnant of the country
of Caphtor.
5 Baldness is come upon Gaza; Ashkelon is cut
off *with* the remnant of their valley: how long wilt
thou cut thyself?
6 O thou sword of the LORD, how long *will it be*
ere thou be quiet? put up thyself into thy scabbard,
rest, and be still.
7 How can it be quiet, seeing the LORD hath given
it a charge against Ashkelon, and against the sea
shore? there hath he appointed it.

CHAPTER 48

AGAINST Moab thus saith the LORD of hosts, the
God of Israel; Woe unto Nebo! for it is spoiled:
Kiriathaim is confounded *and* taken: Misgab is
confounded and dismayed.
2 *There shall be* no more praise of Moab: in Hesh-
bon they have devised evil against it; come, and let
us cut it off from *being* a nation. Also thou shalt be
cut down, O Madmen; the sword shall pursue thee.
3 A voice of crying *shall be* from Horonaim,
spoiling and great destruction.
4 Moab is destroyed; her little ones have caused
a cry to be heard.
5 For in the going up of Luhith continual weep-
ing shall go up; for in the going down of Horo-
naim the enemies have heard a cry of destruction.
6 Flee, save your lives, and be like the heath in the
wilderness.
7 ¶ For because thou hast trusted in thy works
and in thy treasures, thou shalt also be taken: and
Chemosh shall go forth into captivity *with* his
priests and his princes together.
8 And the spoiler shall come upon every city, and
no city shall escape: the valley also shall perish,
and the plain shall be destroyed, as the LORD hath
spoken.
9 Give wings unto Moab, that it may flee and
get away: for the cities thereof shall be desolate,
without any to dwell therein.
10 Cursed *be* he that doeth the work of the LORD
deceitfully, and cursed *be* he that keepeth back his
sword from blood.
11 ¶ Moab hath been at ease from his youth, and
he hath settled on his lees, and hath not been
emptied from vessel to vessel, neither hath he
gone into captivity: therefore his taste remained
in him, and his scent is not changed.
12 Therefore, behold, the days come, saith the
LORD, that I will send unto him wanderers, that
shall cause him to wander, and shall empty his
vessels, and break their bottles.
13 And Moab shall be ashamed of Chemosh, as
the house of Israel was ashamed of Beth-el their
confidence.
14 ¶ How say ye, We *are* mighty and strong men
for the war?
15 Moab is spoiled, and gone up *out of* her cities,
and his chosen young men are gone down to the
slaughter, saith the King, whose name *is* the LORD
of hosts.

47:1 *before that Pharoah smote Gaza.* The date is uncertain, but most likely associated with Necho's northern campaigns, leading to his confrontation with Babylon.
47:2 *waters . . . out of the north.* The Babylonians, whose invasion route was from the north. Their power is compared to an overwhelming *flood* (46:7–8; Isa. 8:7–8; 17:12).
47:4 *Tyrus and Zidon.* Phoenician cities that could provide no aid to Philistia. *Caphtor.* Possibly Crete, the original home of the Philistines (Amos 9:7).
47:5 *Baldness.* From shaving heads during times of mourning. *cut thyself.* See note at 41:5.
47:6 *sword of the LORD.* Human armies were just a tool in God's hand to punish the wicked in Philistia (Isa. 10:5,15).

Thoughts for Personal/Family Worship: Chapter 47

The Philistines had been a thorn in Israel's side since the times of the judges. On occasions Israel was able to subdue them (e.g., Samson and David), yet they persisted as enemies of God's people. The Lord's judgment may sometimes be slow in coming, but it will come. It is a most wonderful attribute of God that He is slow to anger. In mercy He grants time for repentance (Rom. 2:4), but when that repentance does not come His patience gives way to judgment. That time had now come for Philistia. If you do not know the Lord, then seek Him while He may be found.

Chapter 48: *The Lord announces judgment on Moab because of their sins, yet offers a word of hope.*

The Horn of Moab Cut Off (48:1–47)

48:1 *Moab.* The nation born out of the incestuous relationship between Lot and his eldest daughter (Gen. 19:37). From the time of the exodus Moab was hostile toward Israel (Num. 22:4–7; 25:1; Deut. 23:3–4). *Misgab.* No known city; better translated as "high place" or "fortress."
48:6 *heath.* Juniper tree, a plant of stark appearance.
48:7 *trusted in thy works and in thy treasures.* See notes at 5:17; 17:5–8. *Chemosh.* Moab's national deity.
48:10 *deceitfully.* Here "negligently" or "with laxness." God commanded Moab's destroyer to perform his task with diligence as an agent of the Lord.
48:11 *settled on his lees.* When the sediment at the bottom

16 The calamity of Moab *is* near to come, and his
affliction hasteth fast.
17 All ye that are about him, bemoan him; and all
ye that know his name, say, How is the strong staff
broken, *and* the beautiful rod!
18 Thou daughter that dost inhabit Dibon, come
down from *thy* glory, and sit in thirst; for the
spoiler of Moab shall come upon thee, *and* he
shall destroy thy strong holds.
19 O inhabitant of Aroer, stand by the way, and
espy; ask him that fleeth, and her that escapeth,
and say, What is done?
20 Moab is confounded; for it is broken down:
howl and cry; tell ye it in Arnon, that Moab is
spoiled,
21 And judgment is come upon the plain coun-
try; upon Holon, and upon Jahazah, and upon
Mephaath,
22 And upon Dibon, and upon Nebo, and upon
Beth-diblathaim,
23 And upon Kiriathaim, and upon Beth-gamul,
and upon Beth-meon,
24 And upon Kerioth, and upon Bozrah, and
upon all the cities of the land of Moab, far or near.
25 The horn of Moab is cut off, and his arm is
broken, saith the LORD.
26 ¶ Make ye him drunken: for he magnified
himself against the LORD: Moab also shall wallow
in his vomit, and he also shall be in derision.
27 For was not Israel a derision unto thee? was he
found among thieves? for since thou spakest of
him, thou skippedst for joy.
28 O ye that dwell in Moab, leave the cities, and
dwell in the rock, and be like the dove *that* maketh
her nest in the sides of the hole's mouth.
29 We have heard the pride of Moab, (he is
exceeding proud) his loftiness, and his arrogancy,
and his pride, and the haughtiness of his heart.
30 I know his wrath, saith the LORD; but *it shall*
not *be* so; his lies shall not so effect *it*.
31 Therefore will I howl for Moab, and I will cry
out for all Moab; *mine heart* shall mourn for the
men of Kir-heres.
32 O vine of Sibmah, I will weep for thee with
the weeping of Jazer: thy plants are gone over the
sea, they reach *even* to the sea of Jazer: the spoiler
is fallen upon thy summer fruits and upon thy
vintage.
33 And joy and gladness is taken from the
plentiful field, and from the land of Moab; and
I have caused wine to fail from the winepresses:
none shall tread with shouting; *their* shouting
shall be no shouting.
34 From the cry of Heshbon *even* unto Elealeh,
and even unto Jahaz, have they uttered their voice,
from Zoar *even* unto Horonaim, *as* an heifer of
three years old: for the waters also of Nimrim
shall be desolate.
35 Moreover I will cause to cease in Moab, saith
the LORD, him that offereth in the high places,
and him that burneth incense to his gods.
36 Therefore mine heart shall sound for Moab
like pipes, and mine heart shall sound like pipes
for the men of Kir-heres: because the riches *that*
he hath gotten are perished.
37 For every head *shall be* bald, and every beard
clipped: upon all the hands *shall be* cuttings, and
upon the loins sackcloth.
38 *There shall be* lamentation generally upon all
the housetops of Moab, and in the streets thereof:
for I have broken Moab like a vessel wherein *is* no
pleasure, saith the LORD.
39 They shall howl, *saying*, How is it broken down!
how hath Moab turned the back with shame! so
shall Moab be a derision and a dismaying to all
them about him.
40 For thus saith the LORD; Behold, he shall fly as
an eagle, and shall spread his wings over Moab.
41 Kerioth is taken, and the strong holds are
surprised, and the mighty men's hearts in Moab
at that day shall be as the heart of a woman in her
pangs.
42 And Moab shall be destroyed from *being* a
people, because he hath magnified *himself* against
the LORD.
43 Fear, and the pit, and the snare, *shall be* upon
thee, O inhabitant of Moab, saith the LORD.
44 He that fleeth from the fear shall fall into the pit;
and he that getteth up out of the pit shall be taken
in the snare: for I will bring upon it, *even* upon

---

of wine bottles was left undisturbed the wine became bitter; hence, the wine was usually decanted from bottle to bottle. Like undisturbed wine, Moab was left undisturbed for its wickedness to mature.

48:13 *Beth-el*. Allusion to the apostate religion of the northern kingdom, initiated by Jeroboam (1 Kings 12:28–33). As Beth-el did not secure Israel from the Assyrians, Chemosh will not deliver Moab from Babylon.

48:17 *staff . . . rod*. Symbols of authority and influence.

48:19 *espy*. To be on the lookout for, or to watch closely.

48:25 *horn*. Symbol of strength. As the removal of an animal's horn leaves it weakened, so will Moab be left weak and unable to prevent its own destruction.

48:32 *plants*. Tendrils or shoots of a vine. *vintage*. The time of grape gathering.

48:34 *heifer of three years old*. Possibly a location (see Isa. 15:4–6).

48:36 *pipes*. Reed instruments used for both festive and mourning occasions. Since the Lord does not take pleasure in the death of the wicked (Ezek. 33:11), it refers to lamentations (Isa. 16:11).

48:37 Relates common gestures for mourners.

48:40 *eagle*. From the root meaning "to lacerate," pictures a large bird of prey getting ready to swoop down on Moab.

48:44–45 The imagery reveals that there is no escape from God's wrath (Amos 9:1–4).

Moab, the year of their visitation, saith the LORD.
45 They that fled stood under the shadow of Hes-
hbon because of the force: but a fire shall come
forth out of Heshbon, and a flame from the midst
of Sihon, and shall devour the corner of Moab,
and the crown of the head of the tumultuous ones.
46 Woe be unto thee, O Moab! the people of
Chemosh perisheth: for thy sons are taken
captives, and thy daughters captives.
47 ¶ Yet will I bring again the captivity of Moab
in the latter days, saith the LORD. Thus far *is* the
judgment of Moab.

CHAPTER 49

CONCERNING the Ammonites, thus saith the
LORD; Hath Israel no sons? hath he no heir? why
then doth their king inherit Gad, and his people
dwell in his cities?
2 Therefore, behold, the days come, saith the
LORD, that I will cause an alarm of war to be heard
in Rabbah of the Ammonites; and it shall be a
desolate heap, and her daughters shall be burned
with fire: then shall Israel be heir unto them that
were his heirs, saith the LORD.
3 Howl, O Heshbon, for Ai is spoiled: cry, ye
daughters of Rabbah, gird you with sackcloth;
lament, and run to and fro by the hedges; for their
king shall go into captivity, *and* his priests and his
princes together.
4 Wherefore gloriest thou in the valleys, thy flow-
ing valley, O backsliding daughter? that trusted in
her treasures, *saying*, Who shall come unto me?
5 Behold, I will bring a fear upon thee, saith
the Lord GOD of hosts, from all those that be
about thee; and ye shall be driven out every man
right forth; and none shall gather up him that
wandereth.
6 And afterward I will bring again the captivity of
the children of Ammon, saith the LORD.
7 ¶ Concerning Edom, thus saith the LORD of
hosts; *Is* wisdom no more in Teman? is counsel per-
ished from the prudent? is their wisdom vanished?
8 Flee ye, turn back, dwell deep, O inhabitants of
Dedan; for I will bring the calamity of Esau upon
him, the time *that* I will visit him.
9 If grapegatherers come to thee, would they not
leave *some* gleaning grapes? if thieves by night,
they will destroy till they have enough.
10 But I have made Esau bare, I have uncovered
his secret places, and he shall not be able to hide
himself: his seed is spoiled, and his brethren, and
his neighbours, and he *is* not.
11 Leave thy fatherless children, I will preserve
them alive; and let thy widows trust in me.
12 For thus saith the LORD; Behold, they whose
judgment *was* not to drink of the cup have
assuredly drunken; and *art* thou he *that* shall
altogether go unpunished? thou shalt not go
unpunished, but thou shalt surely drink *of it*.
13 For I have sworn by myself, saith the LORD,
that Bozrah shall become a desolation, a reproach,
a waste, and a curse; and all the cities thereof shall
be perpetual wastes.
14 I have heard a rumour from the LORD, and
an ambassador is sent unto the heathen, *saying*,
Gather ye together, and come against her, and rise
up to the battle.
15 For, lo, I will make thee small among the
heathen, *and* despised among men.
16 Thy terribleness hath deceived thee, *and* the
pride of thine heart, O thou that dwellest in the

48:47 In wrath, God remembers mercy (Hab. 3:2).

Thoughts for Personal/Family Worship: Chapter 48

1. **The Lord judges the nations for their sins. God named three reasons why He destroyed Moab. First, they trusted in their strength, riches, and false gods instead of trusting in Him (vv. 7,13). Second, they were proud and arrogant instead of humble before Him (vv. 26,29). Third, they mocked at Israel instead of having compassion for the people of the Lord (v. 27). How are these sins evident in your own nation? What does this text say to your people today?**
2. **The Lord shows wonderful mercy to undeserving sinners! Even the remnant of Moab shall return (v. 47). God humbled those who had puffed themselves up in arrogance against Him, but then He set them free. Though the Lord is a God of wrath, still He delights in mercy. If God has humbled you for your sins, be encouraged to return to Him through Jesus Christ. He is a gracious God, quick to bless all who repent.**

Chapter 49: *The Lord announces the judgment of more Gentile nations.*

The Captivity of Ammon (49:1–6)

49:1 *Ammonites*. The nation born out of the incestuous relationship between Lot and his youngest daughter (Gen. 19:38). Like Moab, Ammon was an enemy of Israel. *their king*. Hebrew, *malcom*; perhaps Ammon's national deity, "Milcom" (1 Kings 11:5, 33; 2 Kings 23:13), one of the vilest pagan deities in the Middle East. Some of the ancestral lands of Ammon had become the possession of Reuben and *Gad*, and now they attempted to reclaim them.

49:3 *gird*. Encircle, or secure with a belt.

49:6 There is a future hope for Ammon.

The Desolation of Edom (49:7–22)

49:7 *Edom*. The nation descended from Esau; enemies of Israel, representing all nations hostile to God's people. Jeremiah seems to rely directly on his predecessor, Obadiah (compare vv. 9,14–16 with Obad. 1–5).

49:9–10 *gleaning grapes*. Those missed by the reapers. God's judgment would miss nothing, and Edom would be stripped *bare*.

49:11 *let thy widows trust in me*. God is the defender of widows and orphans (Pss. 10:14; 68:5; Hos. 14:3). Again, Jeremiah emphasizes the centrality of faith in godliness (see note at 5:17).

clefts of the rock, that holdest the height of the hill: though thou shouldest make thy nest as high as the eagle, I will bring thee down from thence, saith the LORD.

17 Also Edom shall be a desolation: every one that goeth by it shall be astonished, and shall hiss at all the plagues thereof.

18 As in the overthrow of Sodom and Gomorrah and the neighbour *cities* thereof, saith the LORD, no man shall abide there, neither shall a son of man dwell in it.

19 Behold, he shall come up like a lion from the swelling of Jordan against the habitation of the strong: but I will suddenly make him run away from her: and who *is* a chosen *man, that* I may appoint over her? for who *is* like me? and who will appoint me the time? and who *is* that shepherd that will stand before me?

20 Therefore hear the counsel of the LORD, that he hath taken against Edom; and his purposes, that he hath purposed against the inhabitants of Teman: Surely the least of the flock shall draw them out: surely he shall make their habitations desolate with them.

21 The earth is moved at the noise of their fall, at the cry the noise thereof was heard in the Red sea.

22 Behold, he shall come up and fly as the eagle, and spread his wings over Bozrah: and at that day shall the heart of the mighty men of Edom be as the heart of a woman in her pangs.

23 ¶ Concerning Damascus. Hamath is confounded, and Arpad: for they have heard evil tidings: they are fainthearted; *there is* sorrow on the sea; it cannot be quiet.

24 Damascus is waxed feeble, *and* turneth herself to flee, and fear hath seized on *her*: anguish and sorrows have taken her, as a woman in travail.

25 How is the city of praise not left, the city of my joy!

26 Therefore her young men shall fall in her streets, and all the men of war shall be cut off in that day, saith the LORD of hosts.

27 And I will kindle a fire in the wall of Damascus, and it shall consume the palaces of Benhadad.

28 ¶ Concerning Kedar, and concerning the kingdoms of Hazor, which Nebuchadrezzar king of Babylon shall smite, thus saith the LORD; Arise ye, go up to Kedar, and spoil the men of the east.

29 Their tents and their flocks shall they take away: they shall take to themselves their curtains, and all their vessels, and their camels; and they shall cry unto them, Fear *is* on every side.

30 ¶ Flee, get you far off, dwell deep, O ye inhabitants of Hazor, saith the LORD; for Nebuchadrezzar king of Babylon hath taken counsel against you, and hath conceived a purpose against you.

31 Arise, get you up unto the wealthy nation, that dwelleth without care, saith the LORD, which have neither gates nor bars, *which* dwell alone.

32 And their camels shall be a booty, and the multitude of their cattle a spoil: and I will scatter into all winds them *that are* in the utmost corners; and I will bring their calamity from all sides thereof, saith the LORD.

33 And Hazor shall be a dwelling for dragons, *and* a desolation for ever: there shall no man abide there, nor *any* son of man dwell in it.

34 ¶ The word of the LORD that came to Jeremiah the prophet against Elam in the beginning of the reign of Zedekiah king of Judah, saying,

35 Thus saith the LORD of hosts; Behold, I will break the bow of Elam, the chief of their might.

36 And upon Elam will I bring the four winds from the four quarters of heaven, and will scatter them toward all those winds; and there shall be no nation whither the outcasts of Elam shall not come.

37 For I will cause Elam to be dismayed before their enemies, and before them that seek their life: and I will bring evil upon them, *even* my fierce anger, saith the LORD; and I will send the sword after them, till I have consumed them:

38 And I will set my throne in Elam, and will destroy from thence the king and the princes, saith the LORD.

39 ¶ But it shall come to pass in the latter days,

49:13 *Bozrah.* Capital of Edom.
49:14 *rumour.* Report, or news.
49:17 *hiss.* Whistle in astonishment and mockery.
49:19 *swelling of Jordan.* Height or flooding of the river.
49:22 *eagle.* See note at 48:40.

The Confounding of Damascus (49:23–27)

49:23 *Damascus.* Capital of Syria, another enemy of Israel. *sorrow on the sea.* Agitation or anxiety, like that caused by boisterous waves that churn the sea.

The Smiting of Kedar and Hazor (49:28–33)

49:28 *Kedar . . . Hazor.* Arab tribes (bedouin nomads) who often attacked people and then escaped into the desert to avoid detection. They would not escape the judgment of God coming through Nebuchadnezzar, His instrument.
49:29 *curtains.* Tent curtains.
49:33 *dragons.* Jackals, creatures of the wilderness.

The Elamites Made Outcasts (49:34–39)

49:34 *Elam.* Associated with the Medo-Persian Empire that conquered Babylon.
49:36 *four winds.* Similar to the language of Dan. 7:2 that sums up the rise and fall of kingdoms from Babylon to Rome, including that of the Medes and Persians.
49:39 God gives hope for Elam. Interestingly, Elamites were among those who heard the gospel on the day of Pentecost (Acts 2:9,11).

Thoughts for Personal/Family Worship: Chapter 49

When God judges the nations, He announces hope for some, but not for all. Why does the Lord show mercy to Egypt (46:26), Moab (48:47), Ammon (49:6), and Elam

that I will bring again the captivity of Elam, saith
the LORD.

CHAPTER 50

THE word that the LORD spake against Babylon
and against the land of the Chaldeans by Jeremiah
the prophet.
2 Declare ye among the nations, and publish, and
set up a standard; publish, *and* conceal not: say,
Babylon is taken, Bel is confounded, Merodach is
broken in pieces; her idols are confounded, her
images are broken in pieces.
3 For out of the north there cometh up a nation
against her, which shall make her land desolate,
and none shall dwell therein: they shall remove,
they shall depart, both man and beast.
4 ¶ In those days, and in that time, saith the
LORD, the children of Israel shall come, they and
the children of Judah together, going and weep-
ing: they shall go, and seek the LORD their God.
5 They shall ask the way to Zion with their
faces thitherward, *saying*, Come, and let us join
ourselves to the LORD in a perpetual covenant *that*
shall not be forgotten.
6 My people hath been lost sheep: their shepherds
have caused them to go astray, they have turned
them away *on* the mountains: they have gone
from mountain to hill, they have forgotten their
restingplace.
7 All that found them have devoured them: and
their adversaries said, We offend not, because they
have sinned against the LORD, the habitation of
justice, even the LORD, the hope of their fathers.
8 Remove out of the midst of Babylon, and go
forth out of the land of the Chaldeans, and be as
the he goats before the flocks.
9 ¶ For, lo, I will raise and cause to come up
against Babylon an assembly of great nations
from the north country: and they shall set
themselves in array against her; from thence she
shall be taken: their arrows *shall be* as of a mighty
expert man; none shall return in vain.
10 And Chaldea shall be a spoil: all that spoil her
shall be satisfied, saith the LORD.
11 Because ye were glad, because ye rejoiced, O ye
destroyers of mine heritage, because ye are grown
fat as the heifer at grass, and bellow as bulls;
12 Your mother shall be sore confounded; she
that bare you shall be ashamed: behold, the
hindermost of the nations *shall be* a wilderness, a
dry land, and a desert.
13 Because of the wrath of the LORD it shall not
be inhabited, but it shall be wholly desolate: every
one that goeth by Babylon shall be astonished,
and hiss at all her plagues.
14 Put yourselves in array against Babylon round
about: all ye that bend the bow, shoot at her, spare
no arrows: for she hath sinned against the LORD.
15 Shout against her round about: she hath given
her hand: her foundations are fallen, her walls are
thrown down: for it *is* the vengeance of the LORD:
take vengeance upon her; as she hath done, do
unto her.
16 Cut off the sower from Babylon, and him that
handleth the sickle in the time of harvest: for fear
of the oppressing sword they shall turn every one
to his people, and they shall flee every one to his
own land.
17 ¶ Israel *is* a scattered sheep; the lions have

(v. 39) but not to Philistia, Edom, Damascus, Kedar, and Hazor? Here we come to the mystery of God's grace. God chose Jacob for mercy, but not Esau (Rom. 9:10–16). There were two thieves crucified with Christ at Calvary, but only one was convicted of his sins and turned to Christ in humility and hope (Luke 23:39–43). On the one hand, this teaches us not to despair, for God has grace for His enemies. On the other hand, it warns us not to presume upon His grace, for the Lord saves only some. Let us humbly and earnestly seek God's grace, trusting in His promise to save all who come to Him.

The Judgment and Fall of Babylon (50:1—51:64)

Chapter 50: *Babylon, the Lord's instrument of justice against Judah, is now judged for her own crimes.*

50:1 *against Babylon*. The language of this chapter and the next is taken up again by John in the visions of Revelation to pronounce God's doom on the world and to call believers to flee worldliness (see notes at Rev. 17:1–6; 18:4–8 and 21–24).

50:2 *set up a standard*. Lift up a flag or banner. *Bel* and *Merodach* were principal deities of Babylon (51:44). *confounded*. The Hebrew can mean "to be shattered," more appropriately with reference to idols.

50:3 *out of the north*. The Medes and Persians (vv. 9,41). Ironically Babylon, the "north country" as the instrument of judgment against Judah, was now subject to another "north country" as the instrument for its judgment.

50:4 *Israel . . . Judah*. Babylon's destruction leads to a restoration of the previously divided kingdom. Judgment of the enemy equates to blessing for God's people. *going and weeping*. They wept constantly as they went.

50:6 *lost sheep*. See Matt. 9:36; 10:6.

50:7 The enemies used Israel's sins to justify their own atrocious behavior.

50:8 *Remove*. Literally, "become homeless." Babylon would be their residence for seventy years, but the time would come to leave that temporary home and return to Zion (51:6,9,45). The call to depart from Babylon is a call to flee all worldliness (Rev. 18:4).

50:9 *a mighty expert man*. Literally, "a mighty man who makes childless," a vivid description of the ruthlessness and thoroughness of the military action. *none shall return in vain*. The army will have complete success.

50:11–12 Though Babylon was the Lord's instrument of justice, it was culpable for its crimes against Judah. *sore*. Exceedingly. *hindermost*. Least important.

50:13 *hiss*. Whistle or hiss as a gesture of astonishment or mockery.

50:14 *Put yourselves in array*. Line up to enter into battle (v. 42).

driven *him* away: first the king of Assyria hath
devoured him; and last this Nebuchadrezzar king
of Babylon hath broken his bones.
18 Therefore thus saith the LORD of hosts, the God
of Israel; Behold, I will punish the king of Babylon
and his land, as I have punished the king of Assyria.
19 And I will bring Israel again to his habitation,
and he shall feed on Carmel and Bashan, and his
soul shall be satisfied upon mount Ephraim and
Gilead.
20 In those days, and in that time, saith the LORD,
the iniquity of Israel shall be sought for, and *there*
shall be none; and the sins of Judah, and they shall
not be found: for I will pardon them whom I
reserve.
21 ¶ Go up against the land of Merathaim, *even*
against it, and against the inhabitants of Pekod:
waste and utterly destroy after them, saith the
LORD, and do according to all that I have com-
manded thee.
22 A sound of battle *is* in the land, and of great
destruction.
23 How is the hammer of the whole earth cut
asunder and broken! how is Babylon become a
desolation among the nations!
24 I have laid a snare for thee, and thou art also
taken, O Babylon, and thou wast not aware: thou
art found, and also caught, because thou hast
striven against the LORD.
25 The LORD hath opened his armoury, and hath
brought forth the weapons of his indignation: for
this *is* the work of the Lord GOD of hosts in the
land of the Chaldeans.
26 Come against her from the utmost border,
open her storehouses: cast her up as heaps, and
destroy her utterly: let nothing of her be left.
27 Slay all her bullocks; let them go down to the
slaughter: woe unto them! for their day is come,
the time of their visitation.
28 The voice of them that flee and escape out
of the land of Babylon, to declare in Zion the
vengeance of the LORD our God, the vengeance
of his temple.
29 Call together the archers against Babylon:
all ye that bend the bow, camp against it round
about; let none thereof escape: recompense her
according to her work; according to all that she
hath done, do unto her: for she hath been proud
against the LORD, against the Holy One of Israel.
30 Therefore shall her young men fall in the
streets, and all her men of war shall be cut off in
that day, saith the LORD.
31 Behold, I *am* against thee, *O thou* most proud,
saith the Lord GOD of hosts: for thy day is come,
the time *that* I will visit thee.
32 And the most proud shall stumble and fall, and
none shall raise him up: and I will kindle a fire in
his cities, and it shall devour all round about him.
33 ¶ Thus saith the LORD of hosts; The children
of Israel and the children of Judah *were* oppressed
together: and all that took them captives held
them fast; they refused to let them go.
34 Their Redeemer *is* strong; the LORD of hosts
is his name: he shall throughly plead their cause,
that he may give rest to the land, and disquiet the
inhabitants of Babylon.
35 ¶ A sword *is* upon the Chaldeans, saith the
LORD, and upon the inhabitants of Babylon, and
upon her princes, and upon her wise *men*.
36 A sword *is* upon the liars; and they shall dote:
a sword *is* upon her mighty men; and they shall
be dismayed.
37 A sword *is* upon their horses, and upon their
chariots, and upon all the mingled people that
are in the midst of her; and they shall become as
women: a sword *is* upon her treasures; and they
shall be robbed.
38 A drought *is* upon her waters; and they shall
be dried up: for it *is* the land of graven images,
and they are mad upon *their* idols.
39 Therefore the wild beasts of the desert with
the wild beasts of the islands shall dwell *there*,
and the owls shall dwell therein: and it shall be no
more inhabited for ever; neither shall it be dwelt
in from generation to generation.
40 As God overthrew Sodom and Gomorrah and
the neighbour *cities* thereof, saith the LORD; *so*
shall no man abide there, neither shall any son of
man dwell therein.
41 Behold, a people shall come from the north,

50:15 *given her hand*. Gesture indicating surrender. *as she hath done, do*. Poetic justice or retribution (v. 29).
50:18 See Isa. 10:5–19.
50:20 Compare Balaam's assessment (Num. 23:21). *I reserve*. The verb form of the root typically translated "remnant," thus indicating true believers.
50:21 *Merathaim*. Literally, "double bitterness" or "double rebellion," the land surrounding the point where the rivers Tigris and Euphrates meet. *Pekod*. Literally, "land under punishment" or "land of doom," situated in the eastern part of Babylonia.
50:26 *cast her up*. Pile her up.
50:27 *their visitation*. Judgment (v. 31).
50:29 *hath been proud*. Has acted insolently or presumptuously against God.
50:31 *most proud*. Most presumptuous, or overly confident (v. 32).
50:34 *Redeemer*. Specifically the kinsman-redeemer, who is obligated to act on behalf of those with whom there is a relationship. *plead their cause*. Legal language: the Lord will defend them, arguing their case as their Advocate.
50:36 *dote*. Become a fool or act foolishly.
50:37 *mingled people*. Mixed company, or mixture of races. Such a population would be expected, given Babylon's policy to deport the peoples they conquered and to bring them captive to Babylon.
50:38 *they are mad upon their idols*. Literally, "in their dread(ful idols) they act like madmen."
50:41 *the coasts*. The remotest parts.

and a great nation, and many kings shall be raised
up from the coasts of the earth.
42 They shall hold the bow and the lance: they *are*
cruel, and will not shew mercy: their voice shall
roar like the sea, and they shall ride upon horses,
every one put in array, like a man to the battle,
against thee, O daughter of Babylon.
43 The king of Babylon hath heard the report of
them, and his hands waxed feeble: anguish took
hold of him, *and* pangs as of a woman in travail.
44 Behold, he shall come up like a lion from the
swelling of Jordan unto the habitation of the
strong: but I will make them suddenly run away
from her: and who *is* a chosen *man, that* I may
appoint over her? for who *is* like me? and who will
appoint me the time? and who *is* that shepherd
that will stand before me?
45 Therefore hear ye the counsel of the LORD, that
he hath taken against Babylon; and his purposes,
that he hath purposed against the land of the
Chaldeans: Surely the least of the flock shall draw
them out: surely he shall make *their* habitation
desolate with them.
46 At the noise of the taking of Babylon the earth
is moved, and the cry is heard among the nations.

CHAPTER 51

THUS saith the LORD; Behold, I will raise up
against Babylon, and against them that dwell
in the midst of them that rise up against me, a
destroying wind;
2 And will send unto Babylon fanners, that shall
fan her, and shall empty her land: for in the day
of trouble they shall be against her round about.
3 Against *him that* bendeth let the archer bend
his bow, and against *him that* lifteth himself up in
his brigandine: and spare ye not her young men;
destroy ye utterly all her host.
4 Thus the slain shall fall in the land of the
Chaldeans, and *they that are* thrust through in
her streets.
5 For Israel *hath* not *been* forsaken, nor Judah of
his God, of the LORD of hosts; though their land
was filled with sin against the Holy One of Israel.
6 Flee out of the midst of Babylon, and deliver
every man his soul: be not cut off in her iniquity;
for this *is* the time of the LORD's vengeance; he
will render unto her a recompence.
7 Babylon *hath been* a golden cup in the LORD's
hand, that made all the earth drunken: the
nations have drunken of her wine; therefore the
nations are mad.
8 Babylon is suddenly fallen and destroyed: howl
for her; take balm for her pain, if so be she may
be healed.
9 We would have healed Babylon, but she is not
healed: forsake her, and let us go every one into
his own country: for her judgment reacheth unto
heaven, and is lifted up *even* to the skies.
10 The LORD hath brought forth our righteous-
ness: come, and let us declare in Zion the work of
the LORD our God.
11 Make bright the arrows; gather the shields:
the LORD hath raised up the spirit of the kings of
the Medes: for his device *is* against Babylon, to
destroy it; because it *is* the vengeance of the LORD,
the vengeance of his temple.
12 Set up the standard upon the walls of Babylon,
make the watch strong, set up the watchmen,
prepare the ambushes: for the LORD hath both
devised and done that which he spake against the
inhabitants of Babylon.
13 O thou that dwellest upon many waters,
abundant in treasures, thine end is come, *and* the
measure of thy covetousness.
14 The LORD of hosts hath sworn by himself, *say-
ing*, Surely I will fill thee with men, as with cater-

50:42 *lance*. Spear or javelin.
50:44 *swelling of Jordan*. Height or flooding of the Jordan. *appoint me the time*. Or summon me.
50:46 The fall of a future Babylon generates a similar response (Rev. 18:9,15,19).

Thoughts for Personal/Family Worship: Chapter 50

1. **Jeremiah gives us a wonderful picture of conversion (v. 4). In the mercy and providence of Almighty God, He brings about true contrition in the hearts of His people. They weep over their sins and return not simply to their land but to their God. Conversion is not a movement of the body but a motion of the heart, turning away from sin in humility, brokenness, and grief and turning to the Lord in desire and hope (Matt. 5:3–6; James 4:8–10).**
2. **God's judgment of Babylon gives occasion to reflect upon the mysterious relationship between divine sovereignty and human responsibility. Although men often tend to deny one to support the other, Scripture always unites them. God used Babylon to inflict judgment upon His people, and then He judged Babylon for their sins in doing so. Babylon, while being God's instrument, acted without reference to Him, transgressing His laws in the process. What lessons do these twin truths teach us?**

Chapter 51: ***Jeremiah describes more of Babylon's judgment and ends with an object lesson picturing the irreversibility of Babylon's destruction.***

51:1 *destroying wind*. Enemies will tear through the nation, blowing it away like chaff.
51:2 *fanners; that shall fan her*. Winnowers who scatter the chaff.
51:3 *brigandine*. Coat of chainmail or armor. *host*. Army.
51:6 *his soul*. Hebrew expression meaning "himself."
51:7 On the *cup*. See 25:15–16; Rev. 14:8; 17:2,6; 18:3.
51:11 *Make bright*. Polish or sharpen.
51:12 *standard*. Flag or banner. *the ambushes*. Those who will lie in wait to ambush.
51:14 *hath sworn*. The Lord's swearing by Himself is an emphatic confirmation of the word (Heb. 6:13).
51:15–19 This section repeats 10:12–16 (see notes at 10:12;

pillers; and they shall lift up a shout against thee.
15 He hath made the earth by his power, he hath
established the world by his wisdom, and hath
stretched out the heaven by his understanding.
16 When he uttereth *his* voice, *there is* a multi-
tude of waters in the heavens; and he causeth the
vapours to ascend from the ends of the earth: he
maketh lightnings with rain, and bringeth forth
the wind out of his treasures.
17 Every man is brutish by *his* knowledge; every
founder is confounded by the graven image: for
his molten image *is* falsehood, and *there is* no
breath in them.
18 They *are* vanity, the work of errors: in the time
of their visitation they shall perish.
19 The portion of Jacob *is* not like them; for he *is*
the former of all things: and *Israel is* the rod of his
inheritance: the LORD of hosts *is* his name.
20 Thou *art* my battle axe *and* weapons of war:
for with thee will I break in pieces the nations,
and with thee will I destroy kingdoms;
21 And with thee will I break in pieces the horse
and his rider; and with thee will I break in pieces
the chariot and his rider;
22 With thee also will I break in pieces man and
woman; and with thee will I break in pieces old
and young; and with thee will I break in pieces the
young man and the maid;
23 I will also break in pieces with thee the shep-
herd and his flock; and with thee will I break in
pieces the husbandman and his yoke of oxen; and
with thee will I break in pieces captains and rulers.
24 And I will render unto Babylon and to all the
inhabitants of Chaldea all their evil that they have
done in Zion in your sight, saith the LORD.
25 Behold, I *am* against thee, O destroying
mountain, saith the LORD, which destroyest all
the earth: and I will stretch out mine hand upon
thee, and roll thee down from the rocks, and will
make thee a burnt mountain.
26 And they shall not take of thee a stone for a
corner, nor a stone for foundations; but thou
shalt be desolate for ever, saith the LORD.
27 Set ye up a standard in the land, blow the
trumpet among the nations, prepare the nations
against her, call together against her the kingdoms
of Ararat, Minni, and Ashchenaz; appoint a
captain against her; cause the horses to come up
as the rough caterpillers.
28 Prepare against her the nations with the kings
of the Medes, the captains thereof, and all the
rulers thereof, and all the land of his dominion.
29 And the land shall tremble and sorrow: for
every purpose of the LORD shall be performed
against Babylon, to make the land of Babylon a
desolation without an inhabitant.
30 The mighty men of Babylon have forborn
to fight, they have remained in *their* holds: their
might hath failed; they became as women: they
have burned her dwellingplaces; her bars are
broken.
31 One post shall run to meet another, and one
messenger to meet another, to shew the king of
Babylon that his city is taken at *one* end,
32 And that the passages are stopped, and the
reeds they have burned with fire, and the men of
war are affrighted.
33 For thus saith the LORD of hosts, the God
of Israel; The daughter of Babylon *is* like a
threshingfloor, *it is* time to thresh her: yet a little
while, and the time of her harvest shall come.
34 Nebuchadrezzar the king of Babylon hath
devoured me, he hath crushed me, he hath made
me an empty vessel, he hath swallowed me up like
a dragon, he hath filled his belly with my delicates,
he hath cast me out.
35 The violence done to me and to my flesh *be*
upon Babylon, shall the inhabitant of Zion say;
and my blood upon the inhabitants of Chaldea,
shall Jerusalem say.
36 Therefore thus saith the LORD; Behold, I will
plead thy cause, and take vengeance for thee; and
I will dry up her sea, and make her springs dry.
37 And Babylon shall become heaps, a dwell-
ingplace for dragons, an astonishment, and an
hissing, without an inhabitant.
38 They shall roar together like lions: they shall
yell as lions' whelps.
39 In their heat I will make their feasts, and I will
make them drunken, that they may rejoice, and

14; and 16), for God's glory is demonstrated in the destruction of the idol-worshiping world powers like Babylon.

51:20–23 *with thee.* By means of you. God could do His work immediately Himself but often chooses to use secondary means. Just as He used Babylon as His weapon, so He will use the Medes and Persians against Babylon. *husbandman.* Farmer.

51:27 *standard.* Flag or banner. Raising the flag and blowing the trumpets was a call to arms. *rough caterpillers.* Some kind of locust, indicating a devouring army.

51:30 *forborn to fight.* Refrained from fighting. *holds.* Military strongholds, virtually inaccessible to an enemy. *bars.* Crossbeams used to secure gates.

51:31 *One post shall run to meet another.* Literally, "a runner to meet a runner will run."

51:32 *affrighted.* Horrified.

51:34 Judah, identified by the first person pronouns, makes complaint against *Nebuchadrezzar. dragon.* The identity of the creature is uncertain, but this is often used as an image to express power. *delicates.* Dainties or delicacies. *cast me out.* The Hebrew is uncertain, meaning either "to expel," in the sense of vomiting, or "to rinse," in the sense of cleaning the plate; either fits the imagery of the gluttony described.

51:37 *dragons.* Jackals (different word from that used in v. 34).

51:39 *In their heat.* Their being provoked, agitated or excited. *I will make them drunken.* A common imagery describing the stupefying effects of God's judgment (25:15–18).

sleep a perpetual sleep, and not wake, saith the
LORD.
40 I will bring them down like lambs to the
slaughter, like rams with he goats.
41 How is Sheshach taken! and how is the praise
of the whole earth surprised! how is Babylon
become an astonishment among the nations!
42 The sea is come up upon Babylon: she is
covered with the multitude of the waves thereof.
43 Her cities are a desolation, a dry land, and a
wilderness, a land wherein no man dwelleth,
neither doth *any* son of man pass thereby.
44 And I will punish Bel in Babylon, and I will
bring forth out of his mouth that which he hath
swallowed up: and the nations shall not flow
together any more unto him: yea, the wall of
Babylon shall fall.
45 My people, go ye out of the midst of her, and
deliver ye every man his soul from the fierce anger
of the LORD.
46 And lest your heart faint, and ye fear for the
rumour that shall be heard in the land; a rumour
shall both come *one* year, and after that in *another*
year *shall come* a rumour, and violence in the
land, ruler against ruler.
47 Therefore, behold, the days come, that I will
do judgment upon the graven images of Babylon:
and her whole land shall be confounded, and all
her slain shall fall in the midst of her.
48 Then the heaven and the earth, and all that
is therein, shall sing for Babylon: for the spoilers
shall come unto her from the north, saith the
LORD.
49 As Babylon *hath caused* the slain of Israel to
fall, so at Babylon shall fall the slain of all the
earth.
50 Ye that have escaped the sword, go away, stand
not still: remember the LORD afar off, and let
Jerusalem come into your mind.
51 We are confounded, because we have heard
reproach: shame hath covered our faces: for
strangers are come into the sanctuaries of the
LORD's house.
52 Wherefore, behold, the days come, saith the
LORD, that I will do judgment upon her graven
images: and through all her land the wounded
shall groan.
53 Though Babylon should mount up to heaven,
and though she should fortify the height of her
strength, *yet* from me shall spoilers come unto
her, saith the LORD.
54 A sound of a cry *cometh* from Babylon, and
great destruction from the land of the Chaldeans:
55 Because the LORD hath spoiled Babylon, and
destroyed out of her the great voice; when her
waves do roar like great waters, a noise of their
voice is uttered:
56 Because the spoiler is come upon her, *even*
upon Babylon, and her mighty men are taken,
every one of their bows is broken: for the LORD
God of recompences shall surely requite.
57 And I will make drunk her princes, and her
wise *men*, her captains, and her rulers, and her
mighty men: and they shall sleep a perpetual
sleep, and not wake, saith the King, whose name
is the LORD of hosts.
58 Thus saith the LORD of hosts; The broad walls
of Babylon shall be utterly broken, and her high
gates shall be burned with fire; and the people
shall labour in vain, and the folk in the fire, and
they shall be weary.
59 ¶ The word which Jeremiah the prophet
commanded Seraiah the son of Neriah, the son of
Maaseiah, when he went with Zedekiah the king
of Judah into Babylon in the fourth year of his
reign. And *this* Seraiah *was* a quiet prince.
60 So Jeremiah wrote in a book all the evil that
should come upon Babylon, *even* all these words
that are written against Babylon.
61 And Jeremiah said to Seraiah, When thou
comest to Babylon, and shalt see, and shalt read
all these words;
62 Then shalt thou say, O LORD, thou hast spoken
against this place, to cut it off, that none shall
remain in it, neither man nor beast, but that it
shall be desolate for ever.
63 And it shall be, when thou hast made an end of
reading this book, *that* thou shalt bind a stone to

51:43 *son of man.* Hebrew term referring to a human being.
51:44 *Bel.* See note at 50:2.
51:45 *go ye out of the midst of her.* See Zech. 2:6–7 for a similar appeal. *his soul.* A Hebrew expression meaning "himself."
51:46 *rumour.* news or report.
51:48 *sing for Babylon.* See Rev. 18:20; 19:1–7.
51:49 *caused the slain . . . to fall . . . shall fall.* The principle of retaliation: the punishment fits the crime.
51:51 *strangers.* Foreigners.
51:55 *spoiled.* Devastated or dealt violently with.
51:59 *quiet prince.* Literally, "the officer of a resting place." Not a reference to his personality but rather to his job as a quartermaster.
51:60 *evil.* Calamity.
51:63–64 Throwing the stone-weighted scroll into the Euphrates was a vivid symbol of the message declaring Babylon's irreversible destruction (Rev. 18:21). Historic Babylon, which fell to the Medes and Persians, is representative of that quintessential enemy of God, who faces the Lord's inescapable and unquenchable wrath (Rev. 17–18).

Thoughts for Personal/Family Worship: Chapter 51

1. **Poetic justice characterized Babylon's judgment (v. 49). Just as they had done to others, so it would be done to them. The prospect of receiving from God what we justly deserve is a terrifying thought. Outside of Christ it is the certain consequence of sin (Gal. 6:7–8). The beauty of the gospel is that Christ took what we deserve (our condemnation) so that we might receive what He deserves (His righteousness, 2 Cor. 5:21). This should be a**

it, and cast it into the midst of Euphrates:

64 And thou shalt say, Thus shall Babylon sink, and shall not rise from the evil that I will bring upon her: and they shall be weary. Thus far *are* the words of Jeremiah.

CHAPTER 52

ZEDEKIAH *was* one and twenty years old when he began to reign, and he reigned eleven years in Jerusalem. And his mother's name *was* Hamutal the daughter of Jeremiah of Libnah.

2 And he did *that which was* evil in the eyes of the LORD, according to all that Jehoiakim had done.

3 For through the anger of the LORD it came to pass in Jerusalem and Judah, till he had cast them out from his presence, that Zedekiah rebelled against the king of Babylon.

4 ¶ And it came to pass in the ninth year of his reign, in the tenth month, in the tenth *day* of the month, *that* Nebuchadrezzar king of Babylon came, he and all his army, against Jerusalem, and pitched against it, and built forts against it round about.

5 So the city was besieged unto the eleventh year of king Zedekiah.

6 And in the fourth month, in the ninth *day* of the month, the famine was sore in the city, so that there was no bread for the people of the land.

7 Then the city was broken up, and all the men of war fled, and went forth out of the city by night by the way of the gate between the two walls, which *was* by the king's garden; (now the Chaldeans *were* by the city round about:) and they went by the way of the plain.

8 ¶ But the army of the Chaldeans pursued after the king, and overtook Zedekiah in the plains of Jericho; and all his army was scattered from him.

9 Then they took the king, and carried him up unto the king of Babylon to Riblah in the land of Hamath; where he gave judgment upon him.

10 And the king of Babylon slew the sons of Zedekiah before his eyes: he slew also all the princes of Judah in Riblah.

11 Then he put out the eyes of Zedekiah; and the king of Babylon bound him in chains, and carried him to Babylon, and put him in prison till the day of his death.

12 ¶ Now in the fifth month, in the tenth *day* of the month, which *was* the nineteenth year of Nebuchadrezzar king of Babylon, came Nebuzar-adan, captain of the guard, *which* served the king of Babylon, into Jerusalem,

13 And burned the house of the LORD, and the king's house; and all the houses of Jerusalem, and all the houses of the great *men*, burned he with fire:

14 And all the army of the Chaldeans, that *were* with the captain of the guard, brake down all the walls of Jerusalem round about.

15 Then Nebuzar-adan the captain of the guard carried away captive *certain* of the poor of the people, and the residue of the people that remained in the city, and those that fell away, that fell to the king of Babylon, and the rest of the multitude.

16 But Nebuzar-adan the captain of the guard left *certain* of the poor of the land for vinedressers and for husbandmen.

17 Also the pillars of brass that *were* in the house of the LORD, and the bases, and the brasen sea that *was* in the house of the LORD, the Chaldeans brake, and carried all the brass of them to Babylon.

18 The caldrons also, and the shovels, and the snuffers, and the bowls, and the spoons, and all the vessels of brass wherewith they ministered, took they away.

19 And the basons, and the firepans, and the bowls, and the caldrons, and the candlesticks, and the spoons, and the cups; *that* which *was* of gold *in* gold, and *that* which *was* of silver *in* silver, took the captain of the guard away.

20 The two pillars, one sea, and twelve brasen bulls that *were* under the bases, which king Solomon had made in the house of the LORD: the brass of all these vessels was without weight.

21 And *concerning* the pillars, the height of one pillar *was* eighteen cubits; and a fillet of twelve

pressing motive to flee to Christ as the only hope for life.

2. Living with sin all around us can affect our spiritual vitality. It was not easy to remember Jerusalem when the Jews saw the splendor of Babylon. It is easy today for Christians to be enticed by earthly ambition and pleasure. We are not to love the things of this world, because they are destined to pass away just like Babylon (1 John 2:15–17). It is much better to set our affections on things above (Col. 3:1–2).

Chapter 52: ***Jeremiah's overview of the events surrounding the final destruction of Jerusalem by the Babylonians.***

FINAL THOUGHTS IN CONCLUSION (52:1–34)

52:1–34 See the parallel passage in 2 Kings 24:18—25:30.

Jerusalem Laid Waste and Zedekiah Imprisoned in Babylon (52:1–11)

52:3 *through the anger of the LORD*. The events in Jerusalem happened not because Babylon was a mighty force but rather as a judgment from God.

52:4 *Nebuchadrezzar*. Alternate spelling of Nebuchadnezzar.

52:6 *sore*. Extreme or severe.

The Temple Sacked and Burned (52:12–23)

52:16 *husbandmen*. Farmers.

52:17 *brass*. Bronze (vv. 18,20,22). The carrying away of the bronze from the temple took place in fulfillment of the word of the Lord (27:19–22).

52:21 *cubits*. Each approximately 18 inches in length. *fillet*. Thread. *compass*. Surround. *fingers*. Each a quarter of the

cubits did compass it; and the thickness thereof
was four fingers: *it was* hollow.
22 And a chapiter of brass *was* upon it; and
the height of one chapiter *was* five cubits, with
network and pomegranates upon the chapiters
round about, all *of* brass. The second pillar also
and the pomegranates *were* like unto these.
23 And there were ninety and six pomegranates
on a side; *and* all the pomegranates upon the
network *were* an hundred round about.
24 ¶ And the captain of the guard took Seraiah
the chief priest, and Zephaniah the second priest,
and the three keepers of the door:
25 He took also out of the city an eunuch, which
had the charge of the men of war; and seven men
of them that were near the king's person, which
were found in the city; and the principal scribe
of the host, who mustered the people of the land;
and threescore men of the people of the land, that
were found in the midst of the city.
26 So Nebuzar-adan the captain of the guard
took them, and brought them to the king of
Babylon to Riblah.
27 And the king of Babylon smote them, and put
them to death in Riblah in the land of Hamath.
Thus Judah was carried away captive out of his
own land.
28 This *is* the people whom Nebuchadrezzar
carried away captive: in the seventh year three
thousand Jews and three and twenty:
29 In the eighteenth year of Nebuchadrezzar
he carried away captive from Jerusalem eight
hundred thirty and two persons:
30 In the three and twentieth year of Nebu-
chadrezzar Nebuzar-adan the captain of the
guard carried away captive of the Jews seven
hundred forty and five persons: all the persons
were four thousand and six hundred.
31 ¶ And it came to pass in the seven and thirtieth
year of the captivity of Jehoiachin king of Judah,
in the twelfth month, in the five and twentieth
day of the month, *that* Evil-merodach king of
Babylon in the *first* year of his reign lifted up the
head of Jehoiachin king of Judah, and brought
him forth out of prison,
32 And spake kindly unto him, and set his throne
above the throne of the kings that *were* with him
in Babylon,
33 And changed his prison garments: and he did
continually eat bread before him all the days of
his life.
34 And *for* his diet, there was a continual diet giv-
en him of the king of Babylon, every day a portion
until the day of his death, all the days of his life.

breadth of a hand, or less than an inch.

52:22 *chapiter.* Capital of the pillar, the ornamentation at the top. *network.* Latticework (v. 23).

Captives Deported to Babylon (52:24–30)

52:25 *eunuch.* High ranking official. *threescore.* Sixty.
52:27 *smote.* Struck.

Jehoiachin Released from Prison and Honored (52:31–34)

52:31 *Jehoiachin.* Also called Jeconiah or Coniah, the king carried earlier into exile by Nebuchadnezzar (22:24–26; 29:2; 37:1; 2 Kings 24:8–18). *Evil-merodach.* Son and heir of Nebuchadnezzar. His name here seems to be a corrupted transliteration of the Babylonian Amel-marduk, meaning "man of Marduk." *Evil* in this name would mean "stupid" or "foolish."

52:32–33 The surprising exaltation of Jehoiachin implies that God remained faithful to the covenant with David even after the end of the monarchy for its sins (2 Sam. 7:12–14). Jehoiachin's son was Shealtiel or Salathiel (1 Chron. 3:17). Jehoiachin's grandson, Zerubbabel or Zorobabel, became the governor of Judah when the exiles returned under the Medo-Persian Empire (Ezra 2:2; 3:2; Hag. 1:1). He was a godly man, empowered by the Spirit and accepted by God (vv. 12–14; 2:4,23; Zech. 4:6–10). The preservation of the line of David paved the way for the coming of Christ (Matt. 1:1,12).

52:34 *diet.* His daily allowance or provisions.

Thoughts for Personal/Family Worship: Chapter 52

1. **The events of Jerusalem's destruction confirm what God assured Jeremiah at the start of His ministry: "I will hasten my word to perform it" (1:12). Every part of Jeremiah's hard prophecy of judgment was fulfilled in his day, giving confidence that the glorious and hopeful elements would also be fulfilled, as they were in the coming of Christ, the righteous Branch (23:5–6; 33:15–16). Seeing prophecy fulfilled is wonderfully encouraging, and it energizes our faith. All of God's promises will just as certainly come to pass: "Even so, come, Lord Jesus" (Rev. 22:20).**
2. **Jehoiachin's preservation served God's redemptive purpose for when Christ would come. There needed to be a royal line of the seed of David in order for Christ to be his greater son and thereby display all the fullness of God's grace. When everything seemed hopeless, the Lord did not forget His promises, all of which are yea (yes) and amen in Christ (2 Cor. 1:20). Hoping in God's providences and promises means hoping in Jesus Christ, for they all revolve around Him. How has reading Jeremiah encouraged you to hope in Jesus Christ, and Him alone?**

INTRODUCTION TO THE BOOK OF LAMENTATIONS

Authorship: The book gives no hint as to the author; neither do any of the later books of the Old or New Testaments. However, the writer was obviously an eyewitness to the fall of Jerusalem and to the captivity of Judah. The events recorded in the book are written in vivid language indicating firsthand experience. Jewish tradition points to the prophet Jeremiah as being the man most likely to have written it. Some suggest the book was originally part of the book of Jeremiah, but was separated from that book and included in the Megilloth to be read at one of the Jewish feasts. (The *Megilloth*, or five scrolls, were read in the following order: the Song of Solomon on the eighth day of the Feast of Passover; Ruth on the second day of the Feast of Pentecost; Lamentations at *Tisha B'av*, a fast commemorating the destruction of the temple; Ecclesiastes on the third day of the Feast of Tabernacles; and Esther at the Feast of Purim.) The earliest external witness to Jeremiah's authorship comes from the Septuagint which has the following preface: "And it came to pass, after Israel was led into captivity and Jerusalem laid waste, that Jeremiah sat weeping and lamented over Jerusalem and said . . . ." The Vulgate concurs. This tradition has been endorsed and maintained by the majority of commentators down through the ages. Jeremiah 9:1 anticipates that the prophet would write a tearful lament after Jerusalem's fall: "Oh that my head were waters, and mine eyes a fountain of tears, that I might weep day and night for the slain of the daughter of my people!" Compare this with Lam. 1:16; 3:48–49. Hence the title in the King James Version reads, "The Lamentations of Jeremiah."

Date: The fall of Jerusalem took place in the summer of 586 BC, when the Babylonian army finally broke through the city walls after a long siege. Lamentations must have been written very soon after.

Theme: The terrible effects of a nation's rejection of God and the inevitable sorrow that comes as a result.

Purpose: To vindicate God's justice and righteous indignation in bringing judgment on Judah because of sin, thereby teaching God's people to avoid the sins and judgment of Judah by looking to the Lord as the only hope.

Synopsis: *The Contribution of Lamentations to Redemptive Revelation*

While Lamentations is not primarily intended to be messianic, there are nonetheless certain aspects of it that may legitimately be applied to the ministry of the Lord Jesus Christ. Indeed a number of references to the Lord (*Jehovah*) can equally be seen as referring to Christ as the second person of the Godhead. The circumstances also point to the second destruction of Jerusalem in AD 70, after the Jews' tragic rejection of Christ. Lamentations depicts the effects that the first devastation of Jerusalem had upon the Jewish nation, and it reveals the tragic consequences of sin. The focus on sin and its consequences contributes to Scripture's redemptive message by underscoring the need for the gospel and the Redeemer. The book, therefore, anticipates Christ as the only hope. The gospel means little to those unaware of their need for it. Jeremiah is a compassionate pastor, identifying with his people, and seeking to encourage them to confess their sins. He points them to the God of mercy and exhorts them to put all their hope and trust in the Lord. It has been aptly stated that in Lamentations, Jeremiah turns from "warning to mourning." The Lord's design in chastisement is to remove the dross and to refine His church.

Outline: The first four chapters are tragic poems or sad songs, written to express heartfelt sorrow and grief. They are written in the style of an alphabetic acrostic: each has twenty-two sections beginning with a consecutive letter of the Hebrew alphabet. Chapter 3 is the most complex consisting of sixty-six verses divided into twenty-two sections of three lines with each line beginning with the same consecutive letter of the alphabet. The fifth chapter is a prayer, which although not an acrostic has twenty-two sections. The outline of the book may be viewed in the following manner:

- I. Four Laments (1:1—4:22)
  - A. The Loneliness of the Sinner when Abandoned by God (1:1–22)
    1. The Widow's Constant Weeping over Her Loss (1:1–11)
    2. Her Appeal to the Reader (1:12–17)
    3. An Acknowledgment of God's Righteousness and Her Grief (1:18–22)
  - B. The Lord's Punishment (2:1–22)
    1. God's Righteous Anger Revealed (2:1–9)
    2. The Need for Spiritual Healing Develops a Prayerful Heart (2:10–19)
    3. A Crisis of Faith (2:20–22)
  - C. The Finite Nature of Man and the Greatness of God (3:1–66)
    1. Suffering under the Rod of God (3:1–21)
    2. The Great Faithfulness of God (3:22–25)
    3. Resignation to God's Will (3:26–66)
  - D. The Sadness of Faded Glory (4:1–22)
    1. How Gold Has Lost Its Luster (4:1–2)
    2. Only Faithful Ministry Satisfies Spiritual Need (4:3–5)
    3. The Terrible Cost of Following Arrogant Leadership (4:6–20)
    4. God's Judgment upon His Enemies (4:21–22)
- II. Plea for the Lord to Remember (5:1–22)
  - A. A Prayer Begun (5:1)
  - B. The Inheritance Is Lost (5:2–3)
  - C. The Emptiness of Life without God (5:4–22)

THE LAMENTATIONS OF JEREMIAH

CHAPTER 1

HOW doth the city sit solitary, *that was* full of
people! *how* is she become as a widow! she *that*
was great among the nations, *and* princess among
the provinces, *how* is she become tributary!
2 She weepeth sore in the night, and her tears *are*
on her cheeks: among all her lovers she hath none
to comfort *her*: all her friends have dealt treacher-
ously with her, they are become her enemies.
3 Judah is gone into captivity because of afflic-
tion, and because of great servitude: she dwelleth
among the heathen, she findeth no rest: all her
persecutors overtook her between the straits.
4 The ways of Zion do mourn, because none
come to the solemn feasts: all her gates are
desolate: her priests sigh, her virgins are afflicted,
and she *is* in bitterness.
5 Her adversaries are the chief, her enemies
prosper; for the LORD hath afflicted her for the
multitude of her transgressions: her children are
gone into captivity before the enemy.
6 And from the daughter of Zion all her beauty
is departed: her princes are become like harts
that find no pasture, and they are gone without
strength before the pursuer.
7 Jerusalem remembered in the days of her
affliction and of her miseries all her pleasant
things that she had in the days of old, when her
people fell into the hand of the enemy, and none
did help her: the adversaries saw her, *and* did
mock at her sabbaths.
8 Jerusalem hath grievously sinned; therefore
she is removed: all that honoured her despise her,
because they have seen her nakedness: yea, she
sigheth, and turneth backward.
9 Her filthiness *is* in her skirts; she remembereth
not her last end; therefore she came down wonder-
fully: she had no comforter. O LORD, behold my
affliction: for the enemy hath magnified *himself*.
10 The adversary hath spread out his hand upon
all her pleasant things: for she hath seen *that* the
heathen entered into her sanctuary, whom thou
didst command *that* they should not enter into
thy congregation.
11 All her people sigh, they seek bread; they have
given their pleasant things for meat to relieve the
soul: see, O LORD, and consider; for I am become
vile.
12 ¶ *Is it* nothing to you, all ye that pass by? behold,
and see if there be any sorrow like unto my sorrow,

FOUR LAMENTS (1:1—4:22)

Chapter 1: *Jerusalem is seen as a widow in great distress, desiring all who pass by to behold the extent of her sorrow.*

The Loneliness of the Sinner when Abandoned by God (1:1–22)

The Widow's Constant Weeping over Her Loss (1:1–11)

1:1 *How.* Not a question, but an exclamation of bewilderment (Jer. 8:8; 48:17). The nation had turned from God, refusing to heed His warnings, thus provoking Him to anger. As the Lord allowed the ark to fall into the hands of the Philistines because of Israel's sins (1 Sam. 4), so here He allows Jerusalem to fall into the hands of the Babylonians. "Ichabod" (the glory is departed) is written over the city. *become as a widow.* She no longer has communion with the Lord, her Husband. *tributary.* Forced to pay tribute service.

1:2 *She weepeth sore.* Literally, "weeping she weeps," an idiom for intense weeping. Weeping in the *night*, normally the time of sleep, indicates the overwhelming nature of her sorrow.

1:3 *Judah is gone into captivity . . . no rest.* The Promised Land was the place of rest, which in the Old Testament was symbolic of enjoying God's presence and conditioned by obedience. Now continued sin deprives them of rest, returning them to captivity under a foreign power. Sin is the hardest of taskmasters. Its yoke is exceedingly heavy and its affliction is great. *heathen.* Literally, "nations," referring specifically to Gentile nations. *straits.* Narrow place from where escape is impossible.

1:4 *desolate.* Indicating destruction.

1:5 Although the Babylonians were the means of judgment, God was the primary agent and sin was the primary cause.

1:6 *her beauty is departed.* When the glory is departed nothing of spiritual beauty is beheld (Isa. 1:5–6). She who should have been "all glorious within: her clothing of wrought gold" (Ps. 45:13) is now marred by sin and stripped of her apparel (v. 8). She is without food becoming like *harts that find no pasture*—hungry stags or male deer.

1:7 *pleasant things.* Desirable things (vv. 10–11).

1:8 *turneth backward.* Hiding because of shame.

1:9 *wonderfully.* Here relates to astonishment.

1:11 *meat.* Food of any kind. *vile.* Worthless.

Her Appeal to the Reader (1:12–17)

1:12 *Is it nothing to you, all ye that pass by?* This verse, while

which is done unto me, wherewith the LORD hath
afflicted *me* in the day of his fierce anger.
13 From above hath he sent fire into my bones,
and it prevaileth against them: he hath spread a
net for my feet, he hath turned me back: he hath
made me desolate *and* faint all the day.
14 The yoke of my transgressions is bound by his
hand: they are wreathed, *and* come up upon my
neck: he hath made my strength to fall, the Lord
hath delivered me into *their* hands, *from whom* I
am not able to rise up.
15 The Lord hath trodden under foot all my
mighty *men* in the midst of me: he hath called
an assembly against me to crush my young men:
the Lord hath trodden the virgin, the daughter of
Judah, *as* in a winepress.
16 For these *things* I weep; mine eye, mine eye
runneth down with water, because the comforter
that should relieve my soul is far from me:
my children are desolate, because the enemy
prevailed.
17 Zion spreadeth forth her hands, *and there is*
none to comfort her: the LORD hath commanded
concerning Jacob, *that* his adversaries *should be*
round about him: Jerusalem is as a menstruous
woman among them.
18 ¶ The LORD is righteous; for I have rebelled
against his commandment: hear, I pray you, all
people, and behold my sorrow: my virgins and
my young men are gone into captivity.
19 I called for my lovers, *but* they deceived me:
my priests and mine elders gave up the ghost in
the city, while they sought their meat to relieve
their souls.
20 Behold, O LORD; for I *am* in distress: my
bowels are troubled; mine heart is turned within
me; for I have grievously rebelled: abroad the
sword bereaveth, at home *there is* as death.
21 They have heard that I sigh: *there is* none to
comfort me: all mine enemies have heard of my
trouble; they are glad that thou hast done *it*: thou
wilt bring the day *that* thou hast called, and they
shall be like unto me.
22 Let all their wickedness come before thee; and
do unto them, as thou hast done unto me for all
my transgressions: for my sighs *are* many, and my
heart *is* faint.

CHAPTER 2

HOW hath the Lord covered the daughter of Zion
with a cloud in his anger, *and* cast down from

not primarily referring to Christ, nonetheless presents aspects of His life and work. Many have put these words into the mouth of Christ while on the cross. No one ever suffered as He did. On Calvary, He endured the wrath of the Father, and few understood that Jesus was dying to redeem His people from their sins. Although the question suggests a line to Christ, the context does not refer to Him and there are significant differences. On the Cross He did not draw attention to His suffering (Luke 23:27–28). The tone in Lamentations is very different: it is a call for sympathy, pointing to self-pity.

1:13 *he sent fire into my bones.* Pain in the innermost parts (Ps. 6:2). Sin incurs the fiery displeasure of the Lord. Judah felt the burning anger of the Lord kindled against them. Attempts to free themselves were of no avail. Sins not repented of became a heavy yoke which could not be thrown off.

1:14 *wreathed.* Wrapped or entwined together as foliage.

1:15–17 *The Lord hath trodden under foot.* The first step to spiritual healing comes from a recognition that suffering is not without design. God has a purpose to every sorrow (Heb. 12:5). However, thus far the weeping is not sorrow for sin, but at the lack of spiritual comfort. Without God's presence there is an aching void that can never be filled. Yet the comfort of God cannot come while the people remain in their sins.

An Acknowledgment of God's Righteousness and Her Grief (1:18–22)

1:18–22 *The LORD is righteous; for I have rebelled.* A contrite heart is pleasing to the Lord. Acknowledgment of the Lord's perfect righteousness is an admission that God can do no wrong. He is absolutely just and fair in all His dealings. It is sin that brings suffering and distress. The people were now ready to admit this (v. 20; see Ps. 32:4–5).

1:19 *gave up the ghost.* The Hebrew word means "to perish" or expire. *meat.* Food of any kind.

1:20 *bowels.* Literally, "intestines"; here refers to the seat of the emotions. *bereaveth.* Literally, "to miscarry" or "lose children." Here in relation to the *sword*, it seems to refer to killing children by the sword.

Thoughts for Personal/Family Worship: Chapter 1

1. **In the midst of national suffering, Jeremiah reveals a true pastor's heart. He does not turn from the people, but rather, he identifies with them in their sorrow. His tears mingle with theirs. How can you identify, grieve with, and support someone you know who is suffering?**
2. **What sorrow sin brings in its wake! Let us, therefore, heed the Word of God and seek to follow God's ways rather than our own desires. Remember, our sufficiency is in Christ alone!**
3. **Sadly, the world often takes great delight in the sufferings of the Lord's people, and here, in Lamentations, we have such a case before us in v. 21. What should be our response, when such taunting is directed at us in our sorrows? First, we are to remember that a day of judgment is coming. Secondly, we should remember that though the enemies of God may take much delight in the present sufferings of His people, they are completely ignorant of the fact that He chastens us "for our profit" (Heb. 12:10) in order that we might escape what will be their tragic end.**

Chapter 2: *The Lord's devastating punishment is seen, displaying the terrifying consequences of sin.*

The Lord's Punishment (2:1–22)

God's Righteous Anger Revealed (2:1–9)

2:1–9 Note the repetitive statement that God Himself is the agent of judgment, reaching a climax with the declaration that *the Lord was an enemy* (v. 5).

2:1 *How hath the Lord.* This second lament begins with the same word as the first and repeats many of the same calamities. *covered.* To make dark, cover with a cloud, or to

heaven unto the earth the beauty of Israel, and remembered not his footstool in the day of his anger!
2 The Lord hath swallowed up all the habitations of Jacob, and hath not pitied: he hath thrown down in his wrath the strong holds of the daughter of Judah; he hath brought *them* down to the ground: he hath polluted the kingdom and the princes thereof.
3 He hath cut off in *his* fierce anger all the horn of Israel: he hath drawn back his right hand from before the enemy, and he burned against Jacob like a flaming fire, *which* devoureth round about.
4 He hath bent his bow like an enemy: he stood with his right hand as an adversary, and slew all *that were* pleasant to the eye in the tabernacle of the daughter of Zion: he poured out his fury like fire.
5 The Lord was as an enemy: he hath swallowed up Israel, he hath swallowed up all her palaces: he hath destroyed his strong holds, and hath increased in the daughter of Judah mourning and lamentation.
6 And he hath violently taken away his tabernacle, as *if it were of* a garden: he hath destroyed his places of the assembly: the LORD hath caused the solemn feasts and sabbaths to be forgotten in Zion, and hath despised in the indignation of his anger the king and the priest.
7 The Lord hath cast off his altar, he hath abhorred his sanctuary, he hath given up into the hand of the enemy the walls of her palaces; they have made a noise in the house of the LORD, as in the day of a solemn feast.
8 The LORD hath purposed to destroy the wall of the daughter of Zion: he hath stretched out a line, he hath not withdrawn his hand from destroying: therefore he made the rampart and the wall to lament; they languished together.
9 Her gates are sunk into the ground; he hath destroyed and broken her bars: her king and her princes *are* among the Gentiles: the law *is* no *more*; her prophets also find no vision from the LORD.
10 The elders of the daughter of Zion sit upon the ground, *and* keep silence: they have cast up dust upon their heads; they have girded themselves with sackcloth: the virgins of Jerusalem hang down their heads to the ground.
11 Mine eyes do fail with tears, my bowels are troubled, my liver is poured upon the earth, for the destruction of the daughter of my people; because the children and the sucklings swoon in the streets of the city.
12 They say to their mothers, Where *is* corn and wine? when they swooned as the wounded in the streets of the city, when their soul was poured out into their mothers' bosom.
13 What thing shall I take to witness for thee? what thing shall I liken to thee, O daughter of Jerusalem? what shall I equal to thee, that I may comfort thee, O virgin daughter of Zion? for thy breach *is* great like the sea: who can heal thee?
14 Thy prophets have seen vain and foolish things for thee: and they have not discovered thine iniquity, to turn away thy captivity; but have seen for thee false burdens and causes of banishment.
15 All that pass by clap *their* hands at thee; they hiss and wag their head at the daughter of Jerusalem, *saying, Is* this the city that *men* call The perfection of beauty, The joy of the whole earth?
16 All thine enemies have opened their mouth against thee: they hiss and gnash the teeth: they say, We have swallowed *her* up: certainly this *is* the day that we looked for; we have found, we have seen *it*.
17 The LORD hath done *that* which he had

scorn. *daughter of Zion* and *beauty of Israel* speak of privilege but such privilege brings responsibilities (Amos 3:2). Judah despised their unique relationship with God. *footstool.* Ark of the covenant (1 Chron. 28:2; Pss. 99:5; 132:7; Isa. 60:13).

2:2 *polluted.* The Hebrew means "to make common or ordinary." Because of Judah's covenant violations, God treated them as an ordinary nation. They forfeited their privilege.

2:3 *horn.* Symbol of strength. The Lord renders them powerless and helpless.

2:4 *all that were pleasant to the eye.* What was desirable or pleasing to the eye. *tabernacle.* Tent, referring to their dwelling places.

2:6 *tabernacle.* An enclosure, hut, or pavilion. Such structures were common in agricultural fields.

2:7 See Jeremiah's temple sermon (Jer. 7) where he makes it clear that the presence of the sanctuary was not a safeguard against God's judgment.

2:8 *rampart.* Raised bank of dirt for defense.

2:9 *bars.* The mechanism used to keep gates closed and secure. The Lord removed every means of defense. *no vision.* God no longer revealed Himself.

The Need for Spiritual Healing Develops a Prayerful Heart (2:10–19)

2:10 *elders.* Ruling body of men who sat in the city gate to pass judgment. They are now humiliated and humbled. *dust upon their heads . . . sackcloth.* Outward signs of mourning.

2:11 *bowels.* Emotion of anguish (1:20). *swoon.* To faint or be overwhelmed.

2:13 *breach.* A hurt or wound. *who can heal thee?* This poignant question parallels what Jeremiah asked before: "Is there no balm in Gilead?" (Jer. 8:22). Only One can heal, and that is the Lord Himself (Song 1:3; Mal. 4:2).

2:14 *Thy prophets.* False prophets, who stood against Jeremiah. *discovered.* Revealed or disclosed. *false burdens.* Literally, "oracles or utterances of deceit." *causes of banishment.* Literally, "things to draw aside" or "enticements."

2:15 *they hiss and wag their head.* Gestures expressing astonishment. Similar gestures were directed to Christ (Ps. 22:6–8; Isa. 53:3; Matt. 27:39; Luke 23:35–36).

2:16 *hiss and gnash the teeth.* Gestures expressing astonishment as well as rage.

2:17 *The Lord hath done that which he had devised.* There was

devised; he hath fulfilled his word that he had
commanded in the days of old: he hath thrown
down, and hath not pitied: and he hath caused
thine enemy to rejoice over thee, he hath set up
the horn of thine adversaries.
18 Their heart cried unto the Lord, O wall of the
daughter of Zion, let tears run down like a river
day and night: give thyself no rest; let not the
apple of thine eye cease.
19 Arise, cry out in the night: in the beginning of
the watches pour out thine heart like water before
the face of the Lord: lift up thy hands toward him
for the life of thy young children, that faint for
hunger in the top of every street.
20 ¶ Behold, O LORD, and consider to whom thou
hast done this. Shall the women eat their fruit, *and*
children of a span long? shall the priest and the
prophet be slain in the sanctuary of the Lord?
21 The young and the old lie on the ground in the
streets: my virgins and my young men are fallen
by the sword; thou hast slain *them* in the day of
thine anger; thou hast killed, *and* not pitied.
22 Thou hast called as in a solemn day my terrors
round about, so that in the day of the LORD's
anger none escaped nor remained: those that I
have swaddled and brought up hath mine enemy
consumed.

CHAPTER 3

I *AM* the man *that* hath seen affliction by the rod
of his wrath.
2 He hath led me, and brought *me into* darkness,
but not *into* light.
3 Surely against me is he turned; he turneth his
hand *against me* all the day.
4 My flesh and my skin hath he made old; he hath
broken my bones.
5 He hath builded against me, and compassed *me*
with gall and travail.
6 He hath set me in dark places, as *they that be*
dead of old.
7 He hath hedged me about, that I cannot get
out: he hath made my chain heavy.
8 Also when I cry and shout, he shutteth out my
prayer.
9 He hath inclosed my ways with hewn stone, he
hath made my paths crooked.
10 He *was* unto me *as* a bear lying in wait, *and as*
a lion in secret places.
11 He hath turned aside my ways, and pulled me
in pieces: he hath made me desolate.
12 He hath bent his bow, and set me as a mark
for the arrow.
13 He hath caused the arrows of his quiver to
enter into my reins.

---

recognition that this was the Lord's doing. *horn.* An image of power and strength.

2:18 *O wall.* A figurative reference to the Lord as the defense of His people. *apple of thine eye.* The pupil of the eye, that part which is most sensitive and thus protected.

2:19 *beginning of the watches.* The Jews divided the night into three watches, the first beginning at sunset; the second from about ten o'clock; the third from about two o'clock until sunrise. The expression may refer to sunset, but most probably to the beginning of each watch (Pss. 63:6; 119:148). *top of every street.* Literally, "the head of every street."

A Crisis of Faith (2:20–22)

2:20–22 This last section of the second lament is more of a complaint than a prayer, perhaps reflecting the feelings of the people in their suffering.

2:20 *Shall the women eat their fruit . . . ?* The prophet is not asking whether such a thing is inevitable but is asserting it was not right that women should eat their offspring. *children of a span long.* Referring to the size of the child—just a handbreadth—or to the loveliness of a newborn.

2:22 *swaddled.* Carried or nursed.

Thoughts for Personal/Family Worship: Chapter 2

1. **Lamentations reveals how the Lord deals with His unrepentant people, "How hath the Lord covered the daughter of Zion with a cloud in his anger" (v. 1). When the Egyptians pursued after Israel at the Red Sea, the fiery, cloudy pillar came between Israel and the Egyptians (Ex. 14:19–20), yet now the cloud of God's anger confronts Judah. Let us therefore endeavor, by God's grace, to stay close to the Savior, for He says, "I am the light of the world: he that followeth me shall not walk in darkness, but shall have the light of life" (John 8:12).**
2. **Judah was suffering the consequence of their sin. Yet sometimes calamities come into life for no apparent reason. Our faith can at times be tested severely. We may find these trials hard to square with the love of a heavenly Father. We may ask, concerning our circumstances, "Why is this thing happening? Why am I suffering so much? What good can come from this? Has God deserted me?" At times like this, we have plenty of questions, but few or no answers. Yet often we can do nothing in our grief, other than ask God these questions even as we bow under His sovereign will. Such was the situation concerning Judah after the fall of Jerusalem. However, "Shall not the Judge of all the earth do right?" (Gen. 18:25).**

Chapter 3: ***The illuminating greatness and mercy of God is wonderfully contrasted against the bitter darkness of sin and its consequences.***

The Finite Nature of Man and the Greatness of God (3:1–66)

Suffering under the Rod of God (3:1–21)

3:1–21 This section shows Jeremiah as the suffering servant, a type of the Lord Jesus. No one, except the Savior, was ever treated with more contempt by Israel. Jeremiah feels God has afflicted him and allowed his ministry to fail.

3:5 *compassed.* Surrounded. *gall.* A bitter and poisonous herb (v. 19). *travail.* Hardship, weariness, or distress.

3:9 *inclosed.* The Hebrew means "to block a road."

3:13 *reins.* Specifically, the kidneys, but generally designating the vital organs.

3:15 *wormwood.* A bitter oil-yielding plant (v. 19).

3:16 *covered me with ashes.* The Hebrew has the idea of making someone cower in the dust.

3:21 *therefore have I hope.* The beginning of a glorious turning point, which leads to the high point of Lamentations.

14 I was a derision to all my people; *and* their
song all the day.
15 He hath filled me with bitterness, he hath
made me drunken with wormwood.
16 He hath also broken my teeth with gravel
stones, he hath covered me with ashes.
17 And thou hast removed my soul far off from
peace: I forgat prosperity.
18 And I said, My strength and my hope is
perished from the LORD:
19 Remembering mine affliction and my misery,
the wormwood and the gall.
20 My soul hath *them* still in remembrance, and
is humbled in me.
21 This I recall to my mind, therefore have I hope.
22 ¶ *It is of* the LORD's mercies that we are not
consumed, because his compassions fail not.
23 *They are* new every morning: great *is* thy
faithfulness.
24 The LORD *is* my portion, saith my soul; there-
fore will I hope in him.
25 The LORD *is* good unto them that wait for him,
to the soul *that* seeketh him.
26 *It is* good that *a man* should both hope and
quietly wait for the salvation of the LORD.
27 *It is* good for a man that he bear the yoke in
his youth.
28 He sitteth alone and keepeth silence, because
he hath borne *it* upon him.
29 He putteth his mouth in the dust; if so be there
may be hope.
30 He giveth *his* cheek to him that smiteth him:
he is filled full with reproach.
31 For the Lord will not cast off for ever:
32 But though he cause grief, yet will he have com-
passion according to the multitude of his mercies.
33 For he doth not afflict willingly nor grieve the
children of men.
34 To crush under his feet all the prisoners of the
earth,
35 To turn aside the right of a man before the face
of the most High,
36 To subvert a man in his cause, the Lord
approveth not.
37 ¶ Who *is* he *that* saith, and it cometh to pass,
when the Lord commandeth *it* not?
38 Out of the mouth of the most High pro-
ceedeth not evil and good?
39 Wherefore doth a living man complain, a man
for the punishment of his sins?
40 Let us search and try our ways, and turn again
to the LORD.
41 Let us lift up our heart with *our* hands unto
God in the heavens.
42 We have transgressed and have rebelled: thou
hast not pardoned.
43 Thou hast covered with anger, and persecuted
us: thou hast slain, thou hast not pitied.
44 Thou hast covered thyself with a cloud, that
our prayer should not pass through.
45 Thou hast made us *as* the offscouring and
refuse in the midst of the people.
46 All our enemies have opened their mouths
against us.
47 Fear and a snare is come upon us, desolation
and destruction.

It is good to turn away thoughts from afflictions and to focus upon the Lord.

The Great Faithfulness of God (3:22–25)

3:22 *It is of the LORD'S mercies.* See Ps. 103:9–10; Jude 21. Whereas *mercies* underscore God's covenant obligations, *compassions* highlight His feelings of love and pity for those in need.

3:23 *new every morning.* God's mercies never fail; they are continuous and ever fresh. *faithfulness.* The Hebrew refers to trustworthiness, steadfastness, reliability, and fidelity. Regardless of circumstances, God proves Himself to be worthy of trust.

3:24 *my portion.* The Hebrew refers to the share that has been allotted; often used figuratively of the relationship between God and His people. That He allots Himself to His people is incomprehensible and should be ground for contentment and as well as expectant *hope*.

Resignation to God's Will (3:26–66)

3:26 Afflictions are designed to drive us to the throne of grace. *hope and quietly wait.* Not in fatalistic resignation, but in confident, eager anticipation. There is great spiritual benefit when we wait upon the Lord (1 Peter 1:7,9). *salvation.* The Lord's deliverance.

3:27 *bear the yoke in his youth.* Bearing affliction is best learned early, for it better equips us for later trials; such trials strengthen our faith to depend upon God for the future.

3:29 *He putteth his mouth in the dust.* The reference seems to be to the ancient practice of falling down in prostration before rulers, so as to lie with one's face to the ground. Such should be our spiritual posture before the Lord, submitting ourselves to the trials He has decreed. Yet this submission is founded on *hope* in the Lord, the manifestation of faith toward the future.

3:30 *giveth his cheek to him that smiteth him.* See Matt. 5:39. We may also see something of the Savior's suffering (Matt. 26:67; 27:30).

3:32 *according to the multitude of his mercies.* God's discipline is tempered and controlled by His covenant love and self-imposed obligations to His people.

3:33 *willingly.* Literally, "from His heart." God does not delight in disciplining.

3:37–54 The focus is on God's sovereign right in executing judgment. It is self-defeating to murmur against that which God has ordained in providence. When suffering is deserved, it is confession rather than complaint that the Lord desires to hear.

3:38 *evil.* Calamity or disaster.

3:40–41 *Let us search and try our ways.* To test and examine thoroughly. Self-examination must never end with self, which can lead to despair, but should be a motivation to look away from self to the Lord (*turn again . . . lift up our heart*).

3:42 *thou hast not pardoned.* The Hebrew can have the idea of being indulgent toward. God is ready to forgive, but He is not capriciously lenient regarding sin.

3:46 *opened their mouths.* A gesture of astonishment and mockery.

GOD'S FAITHFULNESS

Surveying the ruins of Jerusalem, Jeremiah is overwhelmed with grief. Nonetheless, he sees evidence that God keeps truth and covenant forever and will in no wise forsake the works of His hands. A remnant has been spared. The prophet sees that God has not cast off His people nor forgotten to be gracious (cf. Ps. 77:5–9). A new day has dawned, and with it new mercies for those who hope in the Lord.

God's faithfulness is the outworking of His infinite, eternal, and unchangeable being, wisdom, power, holiness, justice, goodness, and truth. What He says can be trusted. What He promises can be sought after and obtained. All His works are done in wisdom and in love. So David exhorts us to "trust in him at all times; ye people, pour out your heart before him: God is a refuge for us" (Ps. 62:8).

Truth stands at the heart of the biblical idea of faithfulness. The Westminster Divines root the authority of Scripture in "God, who is truth itself" (Westminster Confession of Faith, 1.4). Much of the Bible is history that shows that God keeps His Word, blessing where He promises to bless, punishing where He threatens to punish, sending judgment on wicked people who do not repent, and saving those who cry out to Him for salvation and life. Central to this history of divine faithfulness is the promise of a Savior (Gen. 3:15), which was confirmed by the prophets and fulfilled in the coming of Christ the Lord (Luke 1:54–55,68–75).

In ancient times the gods of the pagans were seen as capricious and self-serving. Their favor, such as it was, had to be courted with vows and sacrifices of all kinds, and they were not reliable, since their own conduct was described as amoral, if not immoral. They followed the lusts of their own hearts; committed atrocious crimes of murder, adultery, and rape; played favorites among the children of men; and broke out in blind rage if their desires were thwarted. They were greatly to be feared but could not be loved or trusted.

Moses proclaims a radically different view of God, recording God's faithful dealings with Abraham and his seed as He keeps covenant through many generations. Invoking the same record of divine faithfulness, Malachi proclaims these words of God: "I am the LORD, I change not; therefore ye sons of Jacob are not consumed" (Mal. 3:6). The epistle to the Hebrews likewise exalts "Jesus Christ the same yesterday, and to day, and for ever" (13:8).

Christians err concerning God's faithfulness in at least two ways. One is taking God's promises for granted, as though nothing were required of us in God's covenant. But in all covenants there are two parts: covenant promises and covenant obligations. All the promises of God are made to "faith which worketh by love" (Gal. 5:6). So David declares that "the mercy of the LORD is from everlasting to everlasting upon them that fear him, and his righteousness to children's children; to such as keep his covenant, and to those who remember his commandments to do them" (Ps. 103:17–18). We must cleave to this God and trust in Him with heart, soul, mind, and strength, forsaking the world, crucifying the old nature, and walking in a new and godly life (cf. Dutch Reformed Form for the Administration of Baptism).

The other error is limiting God's faithfulness only to things we view as positive and beneficial. This is to "despise the chastening of the Lord" (Heb. 12:5–6). The crosses we bear in this life come not by chance, but by God's fatherly hand (vv. 7–13). "Many are the afflictions of the righteous: but the LORD delivereth him out of them all" (Ps. 34:19). Bad things happen to good people as part of the will of God for those who love Him and are the called according to His purpose in Christ, and nothing can separate them from His love (Rom. 8:28–29,38–39).

48 Mine eye runneth down with rivers of water
for the destruction of the daughter of my people.
49 Mine eye trickleth down, and ceaseth not,
without any intermission,
50 Till the LORD look down, and behold from
heaven.
51 Mine eye affecteth mine heart because of all
the daughters of my city.
52 Mine enemies chased me sore, like a bird,
without cause.
53 They have cut off my life in the dungeon, and
cast a stone upon me.
54 Waters flowed over mine head; *then* I said, I
am cut off.
55 ¶ I called upon thy name, O LORD, out of the
low dungeon.
56 Thou hast heard my voice: hide not thine ear
at my breathing, at my cry.
57 Thou drewest near in the day *that* I called
upon thee: thou saidst, Fear not.
58 O Lord, thou hast pleaded the causes of my
soul; thou hast redeemed my life.
59 O LORD, thou hast seen my wrong: judge thou
my cause.
60 Thou hast seen all their vengeance *and* all their
imaginations against me.
61 Thou hast heard their reproach, O LORD, *and*
all their imaginations against me;
62 The lips of those that rose up against me, and
their device against me all the day.
63 Behold their sitting down, and their rising up;
I *am* their musick.
64 ¶ Render unto them a recompence, O LORD,
according to the work of their hands.
65 Give them sorrow of heart, thy curse unto
them.
66 Persecute and destroy them in anger from
under the heavens of the LORD.

CHAPTER 4

HOW is the gold become dim! *how* is the most
fine gold changed! the stones of the sanctuary are
poured out in the top of every street.
2 The precious sons of Zion, comparable to fine
gold, how are they esteemed as earthen pitchers,
the work of the hands of the potter!
3 Even the sea monsters draw out the breast, they
give suck to their young ones: the daughter of my
people *is become* cruel, like the ostriches in the
wilderness.
4 The tongue of the sucking child cleaveth to the
roof of his mouth for thirst: the young children
ask bread, *and* no man breaketh *it* unto them.
5 They that did feed delicately are desolate in
the streets: they that were brought up in scarlet
embrace dunghills.
6 For the punishment of the iniquity of the
daughter of my people is greater than the punish-
ment of the sin of Sodom, that was overthrown as

3:48 *Mine eye runneth down*. Jeremiah's weeping prefigures Christ's weeping over Jerusalem (Matt. 23:37–38; Luke 19:41–42).
3:52 *chased me sore*. Literally, "dealt with me severely."
3:55–66 *I called upon thy name*. In v. 44 there seemed no answer to the petition, yet the true petitioner is not put off by apparent rebuff (Luke 18:6–8).
3:60 *imaginations*. Schemes or plans.
3:63 *musick*. Specifically, a mocking song.
3:64 *recompence*. The Hebrew refers to an equivalent dealing. It is a fearful thing to get from God what is deserved.
3:65 *sorrow*. Literally, "a plague" or "torment."

Thoughts for Personal/Family Worship: Chapter 3

1. **Jeremiah's counsel is appropriate for every circumstance of life yet particularly in times of trouble: "The LORD is good unto them that wait for him, to the soul that seeketh him" (v. 25). When the apostle Paul was severely troubled by his "thorn in the flesh," he writes: "For this thing I besought the Lord thrice, that it might depart from me. And he said unto me, My grace is sufficient for thee: for my strength is made perfect in weakness" (2 Cor. 12:7–9). What a blessing, in times of trial, to be able to say, "Most gladly therefore will I glory in my infirmities, that the power of Christ may rest upon me" (2 Cor. 12:9)!**
2. **Although there are times when prayer seems to be powerless and empty (v. 44), the reality is that God draws near when His people call (v. 57). Prayer is often not easy. Sometimes we must wrestle as Jacob did, but what an incentive to keep on praying—God hears us and will answer! Take comfort in this: our God says, "Fear not" (v. 57). Remember what Christ has done for believers! The closing verses of this third lament reveal God as the Vindicator of His people. Jeremiah knows that the Lord sees and hears all that the enemies of God's people have done to them, and he cries to the One who "though he bear long with them . . . will avenge them speedily" (Luke 18:7–8).**

Chapter 4: ***The effects of unfaithful ministry are here revealed in horrific detail.***

The Sadness of Faded Glory (4:1–22)

How Gold Has Lost Its Luster (4:1–2)

4:1 *How*. An exclamation of bewilderment. The days of former glory have departed. *poured out*. The stones are lying in piles. In its construction, each stone of the temple was carefully cut to size, but now the once beautiful stones and golden interior are blackened through fire and cast into the streets as worthless rubble.
4:2 Similarly, the glory has departed from the priesthood—now regarded (*esteemed*) as a clay pot rather than a highly valued golden vessel.

Only Faithful Ministry Satisfies Spiritual Need (4:3–5)

4:3 *the sea monsters*. The Hebrew term refers to jackals. The religious leaders should have fed the people with God's Word, but they had *become cruel, like the ostriches*. See Job 39:14–17 for an illustration of the cruelness.
4:5 *delicately*. Delicacies.

The Terrible Cost of Following Arrogant Leadership (4:6–20)

4:6 *greater than the punishment of the sin of Sodom*. The

in a moment, and no hands stayed on her.
7 Her Nazarites were purer than snow, they were
whiter than milk, they were more ruddy in body
than rubies, their polishing *was* of sapphire:
8 Their visage is blacker than a coal; they are not
known in the streets: their skin cleaveth to their
bones; it is withered, it is become like a stick.
9 *They that be* slain with the sword are better
than *they that be* slain with hunger: for these pine
away, stricken through for *want of* the fruits of
the field.
10 The hands of the pitiful women have sodden
their own children: they were their meat in the
destruction of the daughter of my people.
11 The LORD hath accomplished his fury; he hath
poured out his fierce anger, and hath kindled a
fire in Zion, and it hath devoured the foundations
thereof.
12 The kings of the earth, and all the inhabitants
of the world, would not have believed that the
adversary and the enemy should have entered
into the gates of Jerusalem.
13 ¶ For the sins of her prophets, *and* the iniqui-
ties of her priests, that have shed the blood of the
just in the midst of her,
14 They have wandered *as* blind *men* in the
streets, they have polluted themselves with blood,
so that men could not touch their garments.
15 They cried unto them, Depart ye; *it is* unclean;
depart, depart, touch not: when they fled away
and wandered, they said among the heathen,
They shall no more sojourn *there*.
16 The anger of the LORD hath divided them;
he will no more regard them: they respected not
the persons of the priests, they favoured not the
elders.
17 As for us, our eyes as yet failed for our vain
help: in our watching we have watched for a
nation *that* could not save *us*.
18 They hunt our steps, that we cannot go in our
streets: our end is near, our days are fulfilled; for
our end is come.
19 Our persecutors are swifter than the eagles of
the heaven: they pursued us upon the mountains,
they laid wait for us in the wilderness.
20 The breath of our nostrils, the anointed of
the LORD, was taken in their pits, of whom we
said, Under his shadow we shall live among the
heathen.
21 ¶ Rejoice and be glad, O daughter of Edom,
that dwellest in the land of Uz; the cup also shall
pass through unto thee: thou shalt be drunken,
and shalt make thyself naked.
22 ¶ The punishment of thine iniquity is accom-
plished, O daughter of Zion; he will no more carry
thee away into captivity: he will visit thine iniquity,
O daughter of Edom; he will discover thy sins.

CHAPTER 5

REMEMBER, O LORD, what is come upon us:
consider, and behold our reproach.
2 Our inheritance is turned to strangers, our
houses to aliens.

---

cities of the plain were destroyed in an instant with fire and brimstone (Gen. 19:24). *no hands stayed on her*. Literally, "no hands whirled around on her." In contrast, Judah's suffering was slow and lingering at the hands of a cruel enemy.

4:7 *Nazarites*. Those "separated or dedicated."

4:8 *visage*. Appearance.

4:10 *pitiful*. Compassionate and sensitive. *sodden*. Boiled. *meat*. Food of any kind.

4:13 *For the sins of her prophets*. The terrible affliction was as a direct result of a corrupt religious establishment (Isa. 9:16; Ezek. 22:26,28; Zeph. 3:3–4).

4:15 *sojourn*. To dwell as an alien and dependent.

4:19 *eagles*. Most likely the griffin vulture, giving a grim picture of buzzards circling the doomed.

God's Judgment upon His Enemies (4:21–22)

4:21–22 Edom historically was hostile to Israel. Though actually insignificant, Edom represents all those hostile to God and His people. They rejoiced at Judah's downfall but themselves were under sentence of judgment (see Obadiah). *he will discover thy sins*. Literally, "He will exile because of your sins."

Thoughts for Personal/Family Worship: Chapter 4

1. **What a tragedy when the Lord's people lose their usefulness in His service. Just as the temple was constructed of fine stones perfectly fitted together to the glory of God, so believers as "lively [or living] stones, are built up a spiritual house, an holy priesthood, to offer up spiritual sacrifices, acceptable to God by Jesus Christ" (1 Peter 2:5). Remember, Christian, you are chosen to "shew forth the praises of him who hath called you out of darkness into his marvellous light" (1 Pet. 2:9).**
2. **The failures of the religious leaders had terrible consequences for the entire nation. The connection between the pulpit and the welfare of people remains strong. In a real sense, "how goes the pulpit, so goes the nation." Let us, therefore, understand the vital importance of sitting under faithful ministry where our spiritual needs are satisfied in Christ alone. May we earnestly seek after faithful ministry that preaches Christ in all His beauty and declares His wonderful merits. May we delight in the gospel and shun that which is harmful to our souls. O that we might be delivered from sinful religious leadership in our day!**

Chapter 5: ***A prayer for renewal longs for mercy to replace chastisement, yet it is uncertain as to how God will respond.***

PLEA FOR THE LORD TO REMEMBER (5:1–22)

A Prayer Begun (5:1)

5:1 The prayer is an honest acknowledgment of reproach and disgrace, the necessary approach to trouble (James 5:13). *Remember*. An appeal for God to purposefully set His mind to think about. *consider, and behold*. Literally, "look and see."

The Inheritance Is Lost (5:2–3)

5:2 *Our inheritance is turned to strangers*. Possessing the

3 We are orphans and fatherless, our mothers *are*
as widows.
4 We have drunken our water for money; our
wood is sold unto us.
5 Our necks *are* under persecution: we labour,
and have no rest.
6 We have given the hand *to* the Egyptians, *and to*
the Assyrians, to be satisfied with bread.
7 Our fathers have sinned, *and are* not; and we
have borne their iniquities.
8 Servants have ruled over us: *there is* none that
doth deliver *us* out of their hand.
9 We gat our bread with *the peril of* our lives
because of the sword of the wilderness.
10 Our skin was black like an oven because of the
terrible famine.
11 They ravished the women in Zion, *and* the
maids in the cities of Judah.
12 Princes are hanged up by their hand: the faces
of elders were not honoured.
13 They took the young men to grind, and the
children fell under the wood.
14 The elders have ceased from the gate, the
young men from their musick.
15 The joy of our heart is ceased; our dance is
turned into mourning.
16 The crown is fallen *from* our head: woe unto
us, that we have sinned!
17 For this our heart is faint; for these *things* our
eyes are dim.
18 Because of the mountain of Zion, which is
desolate, the foxes walk upon it.
19 Thou, O LORD, remainest for ever; thy throne
from generation to generation.
20 Wherefore dost thou forget us for ever, *and*
forsake us so long time?
21 Turn thou us unto thee, O LORD, and we shall
be turned; renew our days as of old.
22 But thou hast utterly rejected us; thou art very
wroth against us.

Promised Land was conditioned by faith and obedience (Lev. 26; Deut. 27–28). Judah broke that condition in a dreadful manner, and the people are therefore cast out of the land. Sin brings terrible consequences. *strangers* refers to foreigners.

5:3 *We are orphans and fatherless*. Literally, "we are fatherless and there is no father." Those who once proudly considered themselves sons and daughters of Jerusalem are now in great distress.

The Emptiness of Life without God (5:4–22)

5:6 *Egyptians . . . Assyrians*. Historic enemies of Israel. Here used figuratively to represent Babylon, the actual enemy in this context.

5:7 *borne their iniquities*. The Hebrew term also designates punishment. The sins of preceding generations affected the subsequent generations. Sin always has far-reaching effects either by example or consequence.

5:9 *gat*. Got.

5:13 *to grind*. To work at the grinding mill. *fell under the wood*. To stumble or stagger under the weight of wood. The young were forced to hard labor.

5:14 *ceased from the gate*. The city gate was the place of commerce and judgments. The elders were removed from any official duties. *musick*. Specifically, music played on stringed instruments.

5:18 *foxes*. Either foxes or jackals, both wild creatures. The city had become like a wilderness.

5:21 See Ps. 80:3,7,19; Jer. 31:18.

5:22 *But thou hast utterly rejected us*. The final words underscore the severity of the reality of the current state of God's judgment and highlights the magnitude of mercy desired for God's gracious restoration. *wroth*. Angry.

Thoughts for Personal/Family Worship: Chapter 5

1. **It is a difficult thing for God's people to bear reproach because it poorly reflects upon the honor of the Lord Himself. Therefore, when we feel such reproach, we must come with all haste to the throne of grace and find our refuge in Christ. Judah's inheritance was lost through sin, and while it is the Christian's privilege to have an inheritance that cannot be lost (1 Peter 1:4), nonetheless, our being the Lord's is revealed by obedience to Him (1 Peter 1:14–15). Let us therefore greatly value our inheritance won at such tremendous cost through the supreme sacrifice of our Savior, Jesus Christ.**
2. **Judah's sin took them to the depths, and it was not until they realized that depth that they came to their senses and sought the Lord. When we stubbornly go our own way, God allows us to come to an end of ourselves; only then shall we realize our foolishness (Luke 15:17–19). What a blessing that God has a design for our suffering—it brings us to the place of prayer! Let us learn this lesson well: there is no true joy when living distant from the Lord.**

I WILL TAKE THE
Stony
HEART
OUT OF
THEIR FLESH
&
WILL GIVE THEM
AN
Heart
OF
FLESH

EZEKIEL 11:19

INTRODUCTION TO THE BOOK OF EZEKIEL

Authorship: Ezekiel is the author of this prophecy. He is identified by name on two separate occasions (1:3; 24:24), and throughout the prophecy the first person singular ("I") is used. The prophecy is stamped with clear unity, which supports the assertion that Ezekiel is the human penman. Ezekiel's name means "God strengthens," and he served God as both an ordained priest (1:3) and a prophet (2:5).

Date: The prophecy came in the "thirtieth year," which was also "the fifth year of king Jehoiachin's captivity" (1:1–2; see 2 Kings 24:12–16). This marked the second stage of the Babylonian captivity (which began in 597 BC). The thirtieth year most probably refers to Ezekiel's age, the age when Levites commenced their service for God (Num. 4:35). Ezekiel had come of age and, although not at Jerusalem, had a special work to do. He commenced his prophetic work at this time. The fact that this coincided with the fifth year of the captivity reveals that Ezekiel was twenty-five years old when he was taken captive and brought to Babylon. His ministry continued until the twenty-seventh year of the captivity (Ezek. 29:17). This gives the prophet a twenty-two year ministry, extending from 592 to 570 BC. His wife died on the first day of the siege of Jerusalem (24:1,15–18), which ultimately fell in 587 BC. He was contemporary with Daniel (14:14,20; 28:3), who was exiled at the first stage of captivity in 605 BC.

Ezekiel introduces each of the literary units or specific prophetic utterances with chronological statements (1:1; 8:1; 20:1; 24:1; 26:1; 29:1,17; 30:20; 31:1; 32:1,17; 33:21; 40:1).

Theme: Destruction and restoration for the sake of God's holiness and glory.

Purpose: To call Israel to grief and shame over its horrible crimes, and to hope and wonder over God's saving grace by placing its history in the light of God's supreme holiness.

Synopsis: *The Contribution of Ezekiel to Redemptive Revelation*

Ezekiel's ministry was not an easy one; he lived in dark days with seemingly no hope for a better future, although many of his contemporaries in exile failed to comprehend the gravity of the situation. They believed that the captivity would be short-lived and that God would never permit Jerusalem to be completely destroyed.

The people failed to see how holy God was and how heinous their sins were. Ezekiel addressed both of those issues and in so doing underscored essential gospel truths. He did so by developing and intermingling five principal themes: (1) the holiness and glory of God, (2) the sinfulness of the nation, (3) the necessity of judgment, (4) individual responsibility, and (5) restoration made possible by the Messiah.

Ezekiel made it clear that God's holiness and glory are the chief motives for both divine judgment and salvation. Israel's sin had profaned God's holy name, which required judgment. Ezekiel is a master of analogy in describing sin, and thus the necessity of the gospel. The people are described as a rebellious house (2:5–8, etc.), a worthless vine (15:1–8), an orphan turned adulterous (16:1–63), two sister harlots (23:1–49), those with stony hearts (11:9), etc. Perhaps one of the most significant points he makes regarding sin is individual responsibility and accountability: "all souls are mine . . . the soul that sinneth, it shall die" (18:4). Personalizing sin personalizes repentance as well; salvation is ultimately an individual matter.

Although much of Ezekiel's preaching focused on the reasons for judgment, he pointed to a great hope as well. He described a restoration in terms of a new exodus, a spiritual renewal

(37:1–28) that would be accomplished by the Good Shepherd, a new David who would rule justly and rescue His lost people (34:1–31)—a message precisely paralleled by Christ's teaching (John 10). Similarly, Ezekiel's exposition of regeneration (Ezek. 36:22–27) explains Christ's amazement that Nicodemus did not seem to know about the necessity of the new birth (John 3:3–8). Notwithstanding some of the complex visions and the sometimes strange object lessons Ezekiel used to illustrate the message, his prophecy is clear, with both gospel warnings and hope.

In both judgment and grace, God reveals through Ezekiel that He does all things for His glory. Over sixty times in this book the Lord declares that He acts so that people will "know that I am the LORD," picking up one of the great themes of Exodus (Ex. 6:7; 7:5, etc.). The Lord does His mighty works of salvation and judgment for the sake of His great and holy name (Ezek. 20:9,14,39,44; 36:20–23; 39:7,25; 43:7–8). He is "the Lord GOD," a combined title appearing 210 times in Ezekiel (over seventy percent of all its occurrences in the Old Testament). The first word (*Adonai*) of the title means "Lord" or "Master," and the second (*Yahweh* or *Jehovah*) is God's name, the great "I AM" (Ex. 3:14–15).

These elements come together in God's declaration of why He will save Israel: "Therefore say unto the house of Israel, Thus saith *the Lord GOD*; I do not this for your sakes, O house of Israel, but *for mine holy name's sake*, which ye have profaned among the heathen, whither ye went. And I will *sanctify my great name*, which was profaned among the heathen, which ye have profaned in the midst of them; and the heathen *shall know that I am the LORD*, saith *the Lord GOD*, when *I shall be sanctified in you before their eyes*" (36:22–23, emphasis added). Thus the plotline of the book revolves around the glory of the sovereign God, opening with a vision of His majesty (1:1–28), describing the departure of His glory from His temple (8:1—11:25), and promising the return of His glory to a new temple (43:1–5; 44:4). The ultimate hope of Israel is for God's glory to dwell with them through His work of sovereign grace.

Major Problems of Interpretation:

Ezekiel's Symbolic Actions

In addition to using parables and common sayings to drive home his message, the prophet was also directed by God to engage in many symbolic actions, visible words, or enacted parables. Below are listed ten and their significance.

1. Making a model of Jerusalem (4:1–3): the siege of Jerusalem.
2. Lying on the ground (4:4–8): the time and discomforts of captivity for the northern and southern kingdoms.
3. Eating a strange diet (4:9–17): the scarcity of food during the siege of Jerusalem, and contamination of the nation during exile.
4. Shaving and disposing of his hair (5:1–4): dishonor coming to the nation and the manner in which people would be destroyed (plague, battle, and exile).
5. Packing and leaving home (12:3–7): the attempted escape and exile of Zedekiah (2 Kings 25:4–5).
6. Eating rations with anxiety (12:17–20): the horror of conquest and exile.
7. Crying and striking his thighs (21:11–12): alarm and grief because of judgment.
8. Making a model of a road (21:19–21): the approach of Nebuchadnezzar and his assault on Jerusalem.
9. Not openly mourning his wife's death (24:15–24): grief coming on Judah so deeply that external mourning would be impossible and inadequate.
10. Writing on two sticks (37:15–17): God gathering Israel and Judah together again.

Ezekiel's Vision of a New Temple and Land

Chapters 40–48 are considered to be among the most difficult chapters to interpret in Ezekiel's prophecy, indeed in the whole Bible. Various interpretations have been offered of this final vision, and the details have engendered debate among Bible scholars. There are generally four views held concerning this vision:

1. The historical-literal view: the vision relates to the times immediately prior to the captivity and focuses on Solomon's temple.
2. The ideal or conditional view: the vision outlines what should have been after the return from captivity, but because of the disobedience of the people it was never realized.

3. The Jewish view: the description given in this vision was followed by the returning captives as far as circumstances allowed them, and Herod copied the same pattern when he renovated and enlarged the temple.
4. The spiritual view: the vision symbolically represents God's good plan for His people, especially after Christ's incarnation, when His glory shall dwell within His people as His living temple by the life-giving work of the Holy Spirit (37:14,27–28; Eph. 2:18–22).

The spiritual view has been the most common in church history and was reflected in the interpretations of the Reformers. Several considerations from the text favor this interpretation. *First*, chs. 40–48 are a vision (40:2), and this form of revelation commonly uses symbolism (such as the visions of Zechariah and Daniel). *Second*, elements of the vision clearly run contrary to normal experience, such as the river that comes out of the temple and grows deeper as it flows, changing quickly from a trickle to an impassable flood several feet deep over the course of less than a mile and a half. *Third*, the idea of this river appears again in the apostle John's vision of the New Jerusalem in Revelation, which is also a book full of symbolism (Rev. 22:1–2).

Fourth, the physical dimensions of the temple and division of the land in this vision were never fulfilled in Israel's history, nor did the Lord ever rebuke His people after the exile for failing to implement them. *Fifth*, if the instructions of this vision pertain to some future temple, then this mandates animal sacrifices for the sins of the people (Ezek. 40:38–39, etc.). However, Christ has offered Himself once for all as the sufficient sacrifice for sinners, and all other sacrifices for sin have ceased (Heb. 10:10–18). The reply that the sacrifices in Ezekiel's vision will function as mere remembrances of Christ's work fails to take the text literally, for it says that these sacrifices will "make reconciliation" or atonement for them (Ezek. 45:15,17). Therefore, it is best to understand the vision of chs. 40–48 as a symbolic representation of Israel's hope.

However, the symbolism in the closing vision of the temple and land does not encourage the reader to engage in wild allegory, assigning a spiritual meaning to every dimension of the architecture. Just like the opening vision of God's glory riding the chariot of the cherubim (1:1–28), the message is not in every detail but in the overall impressions the vision makes.

Ezekiel's prophecy closes with a vision of overwhelming hope, that though the descendants of Abraham forfeited God's presence, the means of atoning for sin, and their inheritance by their idolatry, God would certainly restore all of these to believers for the sake of His holy name. Christians can rejoice that this restoration is found in Jesus Christ, for by His Spirit God's presence is with His people forever. Christ our Priest has offered the perfect sacrifice for their sins, and they will enjoy a glorious inheritance with Christ the King in a new world without end.

Outline:

I. The Vision of Glory and the Call to Prophesy (1:1—3:27)
II. Messages of Judgment against Jerusalem (4:1—7:27)
  A. Signs of Jerusalem's Siege and Doom (4:1—5:17)
  B. Oracles against the Mountains and Land (6:1—7:27)
III. The Vision of Glory Departing from the Temple (8:1—11:25)
IV. Parables and Teachings against Jerusalem (12:1—24:27)
  A. Signs and Warnings of the Coming Exile (12:1–28)
  B. False Prophets (13:1–23)
  C. People of Idolatry beyond Intercession (14:1–23)
  D. Parables of the Vine, the Wife, and the Eagles (15:1—17:24)
  E. Principle of Responsibility (18:1–32)
  F. Parables of the Lioness and the Vine (19:1–14)
  G. Israel's History and God's Name (20:1–44)
  H. Fire and Sword (20:45—21:32)
  I. The Defiled City (22:1–31)
  J. Parable of the Immoral Sisters (23:1–49)
  K. Signs of the Cauldron and the Death of Ezekiel's Wife (24:1–27)
V. Messages of Judgment against Gentile Nations (25:1—32:32)
  A. Judgment against Ammon, Moab, Edom, and Philistia (25:1–17)
  B. Judgment against Tyre and Sidon (26:1—28:26)
  C. Judgment against Egypt (29:1—32:32)
VI. The Fall and Restoration of Jerusalem (33:1—37:28)
  A. The Fall and Exile of Jerusalem (33:1–33)

B. Parable of the Shepherds and the Sheep (34:1–31)
C. Judgment against Edom (35:1–15)
D. Restoration of Land and People for God's Holy Name (36:1–38)
E. The Vision of Resurrection and the Sign of Reunification (37:1–28)

VII. The Great Conflict with Gog (38:1—39:29)

VIII. The Vision of Glory Returning to the Land (40:1—48:35)
A. The Temple and the Ceremonies of Worship (40:1—46:24)
B. The River and the Land (47:1—48:35)

THE BOOK OF THE PROPHET

EZEKIEL

CHAPTER 1

NOW it came to pass in the thirtieth year, in the fourth *month*, in the fifth *day* of the month, as I *was* among the captives by the river of Chebar, *that* the heavens were opened, and I saw visions of God.

2 In the fifth *day* of the month, which *was* the fifth year of king Jehoiachin's captivity,

3 The word of the LORD came expressly unto Ezekiel the priest, the son of Buzi, in the land of the Chaldeans by the river Chebar; and the hand of the LORD was there upon him.

4 ¶ And I looked, and, behold, a whirlwind came out of the north, a great cloud, and a fire infolding itself, and a brightness *was* about it, and out of the midst thereof as the colour of amber, out of the midst of the fire.

5 Also out of the midst thereof *came* the likeness of four living creatures. And this *was* their appearance; they had the likeness of a man.

6 And every one had four faces, and every one had four wings.

7 And their feet *were* straight feet; and the sole of their feet *was* like the sole of a calf's foot: and they sparkled like the colour of burnished brass.

8 And *they had* the hands of a man under their wings on their four sides; and they four had their faces and their wings.

9 Their wings *were* joined one to another; they turned not when they went; they went every one straight forward.

10 As for the likeness of their faces, they four had the face of a man, and the face of a lion, on the right side: and they four had the face of an ox on the left side; they four also had the face of an eagle.

11 Thus *were* their faces: and their wings *were* stretched upward; two *wings* of every one *were* joined one to another, and two covered their bodies.

12 And they went every one straight forward: whither the spirit was to go, they went; *and* they turned not when they went.

13 As for the likeness of the living creatures, their appearance *was* like burning coals of fire, *and* like the appearance of lamps: it went up and down among the living creatures; and the fire was bright, and out of the fire went forth lightning.

14 And the living creatures ran and returned as the appearance of a flash of lightning.

THE VISION OF GLORY AND THE CALL TO PROPHESY (1:1—3:27)

Chapter 1: *Ezekiel is a captive in Babylon when God reveals Himself to him by the river Chebar.*

1:1 *thirtieth year.* Most likely Ezekiel's age, and the time when he should have commenced his priestly work. However, he was in exile away from the temple, and so without a ministry (see Introduction: Date). *the heavens were opened . . . visions of God.* Ezekiel's exile did not hinder God from drawing near to reveal Himself; God is not limited to any one location.

1:3 *The word of the LORD.* The vision equates to the divinely given word. *the hand of the LORD.* An anthropomorphism (speaking of God as though He were a man) signifying the Lord's setting Ezekiel apart for his prophetic ministry.

1:4 The beginning of the vision that unfolds in four stages: the cloud, the four living creatures, the chariot throne, and the Lord on the throne. *whirlwind.* Communicating a sense of urgency, expectancy, and awe. *north.* Frequently not so much about geography but used as a reference to an enemy (Zech. 2:6), as here to Babylon. *great cloud.* A symbol of divine presence. *fire infolding itself.* Literally, "fire taking itself," meaning that the fire was flashing here and there.

1:5 *four living creatures.* Angelic beings, later identified as cherubim (see note at 10:15). All angels are servants of divine providence (Heb. 1:14).

1:6–11 The description of the living creatures is strange and complex, being a set of symbols about the function and power of angels, heavenly spirits that have no bodies.

1:7 *Straight feet . . . calf's foot.* Images of faithfulness, surefootedness, or stability. *they sparkled like the colour of burnished brass.* Literally, "they sparkled like an eye of shining bronze."

1:8 *hands . . . under their wings.* Denotes activity and work to promote God's glory.

1:10 *man.* Symbolic of intelligence. *lion.* Symbolic of strength and majesty. *ox.* Symbolic of service and loyalty. *eagle.* Symbolic of swiftness to do God's will.

1:11 *two wings . . . joined.* Symbolic of their unity and harmony of service. *two covered their bodies.* Symbolic of humility (Isa. 6:2–3).

1:12 *straight forward.* The living creatures were submissive to God, willingly and immediately carrying out His will. *whither.* Wherever. *they turned not.* With four faces, they went in every direction. God's providence is universal.

1:14 *ran and returned as . . . of a flash of lightning.* They acted with swiftness; promptly and precisely serving the Lord.

15 ¶ Now as I beheld the living creatures, behold
one wheel upon the earth by the living creatures,
with his four faces.
16 The appearance of the wheels and their work
was like unto the colour of a beryl: and they four
had one likeness: and their appearance and their
work *was* as it were a wheel in the middle of a wheel.
17 When they went, they went upon their four
sides: *and* they turned not when they went.
18 As for their rings, they were so high that they
were dreadful; and their rings *were* full of eyes
round about them four.
19 And when the living creatures went, the wheels
went by them: and when the living creatures were
lifted up from the earth, the wheels were lifted up.
20 Whithersoever the spirit was to go, they went,
thither *was their* spirit to go; and the wheels were
lifted up over against them: for the spirit of the
living creature *was* in the wheels.
21 When those went, *these* went; and when those
stood, *these* stood; and when those were lifted
up from the earth, the wheels were lifted up over
against them: for the spirit of the living creature
was in the wheels.
22 And the likeness of the firmament upon the
heads of the living creature *was* as the colour
of the terrible crystal, stretched forth over their
heads above.
23 And under the firmament *were* their wings
straight, the one toward the other: every one had
two, which covered on this side, and every one
had two, which covered on that side, their bodies.
24 And when they went, I heard the noise of their
wings, like the noise of great waters, as the voice
of the Almighty, the voice of speech, as the noise
of an host: when they stood, they let down their
wings.
25 And there was a voice from the firmament that
was over their heads, when they stood, *and* had let
down their wings.
26 ¶ And above the firmament that *was* over
their heads *was* the likeness of a throne, as the
appearance of a sapphire stone: and upon the
likeness of the throne *was* the likeness as the
appearance of a man above upon it.
27 And I saw as the colour of amber, as the
appearance of fire round about within it, from
the appearance of his loins even upward, and
from the appearance of his loins even downward,
I saw as it were the appearance of fire, and it had
brightness round about.
28 As the appearance of the bow that is in the
cloud in the day of rain, so *was* the appearance
of the brightness round about. This *was* the
appearance of the likeness of the glory of the
LORD. And when I saw *it*, I fell upon my face, and
I heard a voice of one that spake.

1:15 Just as the angels are the agents of providence, so the chariot represents the works of providence. *one wheel upon the earth.* God's sovereign will is accomplished not just in heaven but also on earth (Ps. 135:6).

1:16–17 *a wheel in the middle of a wheel.* Perhaps a wheel at right angles within a wheel. *turned not when they went.* Not the wheels' rotation but to their direction. At right angles, the wheels pointed in every direction (north, south, east, and west). So it is with God's providence; it operates everywhere (Ps. 139:9–10).

1:18 *rings.* The circumference, the curves or rims of the wheels. *dreadful.* Awe-inspiring, inducing fear. *full of eyes.* The eyes were around the entire circumference, symbolizing that God's works of providence are not the accidents of blind fate but rather the workings of an all-wise and all-knowing God, accomplishing the best possible ends by the best possible means.

1:19–21 *The Spirit of the living creature was in the wheels.* The unity of the Spirit, the living creatures, and the wheels confirms the perfect harmony of the purposes of God (Rom. 8:28).

1:22–23 *firmament.* Sky. *terrible crystal.* Exceedingly clear and bright crystal. All things are transparent to God, so nothing hinders His providence (Pss. 33:13–15; 139:11–12; Heb. 4:13).

1:24–25 *as the voice of the Almighty.* The works of providence reveal God, as do His words.

1:26 *above the firmament . . . upon the likeness of the throne.* The focus moves step-by-step upward to One who is high and lifted up in sovereignty and glory (Isa. 6:1). *a man above upon it.* A Christophany, a preincarnate revelation of the Christ. Even in the Old Testament the only way to see God was to see Him in the Son (John 1:18; 12:41).

1:28 *bow.* Rainbow, a sign of the covenant promises of God testifying to the mercy, faithfulness, and grace of God in the midst of a world cursed by sin (Gen. 9:12–17). *brightness.* The covenant promises had lost none of their significance or power since they were first given. *fell upon my face.* The sight of the God of *glory* humbled and overwhelmed Ezekiel. Falling on his face in submission and worship was the appropriate response (Rev. 1:17). This vision of glory reappears later (3:23; 8:1—11:25; 43:1–5; 44:4).

Thoughts for Personal/Family Worship: Chapter 1

1. **God brings His people into difficult circumstances, but He is with them. Ezekiel was a priest, ready and of age to enter upon the Lord's work, but God had ordered the situation so that he had been taken as a captive into Babylon (vv. 1–3). How distressing it must have been for Ezekiel to lose his opportunity to serve in the temple! Yet God had a plan for Ezekiel even greater than he had anticipated. Although Ezekiel was far from Jerusalem, God was not far from His servant. Christians must remember that great trials and pagan neighbors or coworkers cannot separate us from our God or frustrate His purposes for us. He will not waste our lives but will be with us and use us for His glory if we follow Him.**
2. **Though Ezekiel's vision is dazzling and some of its details are hard to interpret, the big picture it presents reveals truths about God that are most encouraging. Behind the visible world of politics, wars, and personal tragedies there sits One upon a throne of glory (vv. 26–28), ruling the world by His power and His servants, the spirits of heaven. Christians must live with their eyes open to the unseen world (2 Kings 6:15–17; Eph. 6:12).**

CHAPTER 2

AND he said unto me, Son of man, stand upon thy
feet, and I will speak unto thee.
2 And the spirit entered into me when he spake
unto me, and set me upon my feet, that I heard
him that spake unto me.
3 And he said unto me, Son of man, I send thee
to the children of Israel, to a rebellious nation that
hath rebelled against me: they and their fathers
have transgressed against me, *even* unto this very
day.
4 For *they are* impudent children and stiff-
hearted. I do send thee unto them; and thou shalt
say unto them, Thus saith the Lord GOD.
5 And they, whether they will hear, or whether
they will forbear, (for they *are* a rebellious house,)
yet shall know that there hath been a prophet
among them.
6 ¶ And thou, son of man, be not afraid of them,
neither be afraid of their words, though briers
and thorns *be* with thee, and thou dost dwell
among scorpions: be not afraid of their words,
nor be dismayed at their looks, though they *be* a
rebellious house.
7 And thou shalt speak my words unto them,
whether they will hear, or whether they will for-
bear: for they *are* most rebellious.
8 But thou, son of man, hear what I say unto thee;
Be not thou rebellious like that rebellious house:
open thy mouth, and eat that I give thee.
9 ¶ And when I looked, behold, an hand *was* sent
unto me; and, lo, a roll of a book *was* therein;
10 And he spread it before me; and it *was* written
within and without: and *there was* written therein
lamentations, and mourning, and woe.

CHAPTER 3

MOREOVER he said unto me, Son of man, eat that
thou findest; eat this roll, and go speak unto the
house of Israel.
2 So I opened my mouth, and he caused me to
eat that roll.
3 And he said unto me, Son of man, cause thy
belly to eat, and fill thy bowels with this roll that
I give thee. Then did I eat *it*; and it was in my
mouth as honey for sweetness.
4 ¶ And he said unto me, Son of man, go, get thee

Be assured that God's rule is universal (vv. 15–25). The chariot throne with its complexity and harmony teaches that God's providence, though hidden in mystery, rules all things through an amazingly wise design (Eph. 1:11). We should learn to look beyond circumstances to the One on the throne. How can you seek a spiritual awareness of the glory of Christ that gives you courage and hope?

Chapter 2: *God calls Ezekiel to a prophetic ministry.*

2:1 *Son of man.* "Son of Adam, or mankind." The expression occurs over ninety times in the prophecy, either as God's designation of the prophet or the prophet's designation of himself. It expresses weakness, inability, and insufficiency—a good way for every Christian to see himself. *stand upon thy feet.* He did right to fall down in worship, but worship does not breed passivity. Following the service of worship is the service of activity for the kingdom.

2:2 *spirit entered into me.* In the sense of empowering for service, the aspect of the Holy Spirit's ministry most commonly revealed in the Old Testament (see note at 1 Sam. 10:6). *set me upon my feet.* Literally, "stood me up," as one ready to serve (same verb as in 1:1). What God commands He enables, so the "Son of Man" is sufficient for his task.

2:3 *send.* A term expressing the divine commission. *rebellious nation.* Though Jews by birth, they had behaved as Gentiles in their rebellion against God, turning their backs on Him.

2:4 *impudent.* Literally, "hard of face," stubborn, obstinate, and cruel. *stiffhearted.* Literally, "hard ones of heart," refusing to submit and inflexible like a stone. *the Lord GOD.* Hebrew, *Adonai Yahweh*, or Master *Jehovah*, the divine title that pervades this book (210 times) with a sense of God's glorious sovereignty (see Introduction: Synopsis).

2:5 *forbear.* Stop listening. The way in which people would respond to the message was not the prophet's responsibility.

2:6–7 The Lord informed Ezekiel up front that his ministry would be met with opposition. He was to counter the opposition with the faithful proclamation of God's Word. Ultimately, the opposition was against God, not the prophet.

2:8 *open thy mouth, and eat.* Receive the message into your soul. He could preach to others only what he had first received and digested for himself. That remains true for preachers today.

2:9 *roll of a book.* Scroll of writing.

2:10 *spread.* Stretched out so as to reveal its contents. *within and without.* On both sides. Normally writing was only on one side of a scroll, but this scroll contains a full message from God, with no room left for human addition. *lamentations . . . woe.* The message was not a happy one, but it was from start to finish God's Word.

Thoughts for Personal/Family Worship: Chapter 2

1. **Ezekiel had no supernatural qualities of his own. He was a man, a son of Adam, with all the frailties and fears common to fallen men. However, God called him, filled him with the Spirit, and commissioned him to a great work. His power to preach came from God. God still chooses weak human instruments to serve Him (2 Cor. 4:7). Every servant of the Lord must rely on the Spirit's empowering to fulfill his task. How often do you pray for your pastor that God's Spirit would enable him to speak God's Word boldly?**
2. **God's Word is a hard message, for it is a message to sinners. People have rebelled against God, turned their backs on God, hardened their faces, and become stony-hearted toward Him. God is rightly offended at their rebellion, but in His mercy He calls sinners to repentance through the preaching of the Word. When you hear a hard message against sin from a preacher, do not despise him for his faithfulness. Welcome it and repent.**

Chapter 3: *Ezekiel is called and equipped for ministry.*

3:1 *eat this roll.* Receive the truths of this scroll into your heart (v. 10; see note at 2:8).

3:3 *honey for sweetness.* Although the words were full of lamentations and warnings against sinners (2:9), they were

unto the house of Israel, and speak with my words
unto them.
5 For thou *art* not sent to a people of a strange
speech and of an hard language, *but* to the house
of Israel;
6 Not to many people of a strange speech and of
an hard language, whose words thou canst not
understand. Surely, had I sent thee to them, they
would have hearkened unto thee.
7 But the house of Israel will not hearken unto
thee; for they will not hearken unto me: for all the
house of Israel *are* impudent and hardhearted.
8 Behold, I have made thy face strong against
their faces, and thy forehead strong against their
foreheads.
9 As an adamant harder than flint have I made
thy forehead: fear them not, neither be dismayed
at their looks, though they *be* a rebellious house.
10 Moreover he said unto me, Son of man, all my
words that I shall speak unto thee receive in thine
heart, and hear with thine ears.
11 And go, get thee to them of the captivity, unto
the children of thy people, and speak unto them,
and tell them, Thus saith the Lord GOD; whether
they will hear, or whether they will forbear.
12 Then the spirit took me up, and I heard behind
me a voice of a great rushing, *saying*, Blessed *be*
the glory of the LORD from his place.
13 *I heard* also the noise of the wings of the living
creatures that touched one another, and the noise
of the wheels over against them, and a noise of a
great rushing.
14 So the spirit lifted me up, and took me away,
and I went in bitterness, in the heat of my spirit;
but the hand of the LORD was strong upon me.
15 ¶ Then I came to them of the captivity at Tel-
abib, that dwelt by the river of Chebar, and I sat
where they sat, and remained there astonished
among them seven days.
16 And it came to pass at the end of seven days,
that the word of the LORD came unto me, saying,
17 Son of man, I have made thee a watchman
unto the house of Israel: therefore hear the word
at my mouth, and give them warning from me.
18 When I say unto the wicked, Thou shalt surely
die; and thou givest him not warning, nor speak-
est to warn the wicked from his wicked way, to
save his life; the same wicked *man* shall die in his
iniquity; but his blood will I require at thine hand.
19 Yet if thou warn the wicked, and he turn not
from his wickedness, nor from his wicked way, he
shall die in his iniquity; but thou hast delivered
thy soul.
20 Again, When a righteous *man* doth turn from
his righteousness, and commit iniquity, and I
lay a stumblingblock before him, he shall die:
because thou hast not given him warning, he shall
die in his sin, and his righteousness which he hath
done shall not be remembered; but his blood will
I require at thine hand.
21 Nevertheless if thou warn the righteous *man*,
that the righteous sin not, and he doth not sin, he
shall surely live, because he is warned; also thou
hast delivered thy soul.
22 ¶ And the hand of the LORD was there upon
me; and he said unto me, Arise, go forth into the
plain, and I will there talk with thee.
23 Then I arose, and went forth into the plain:
and, behold, the glory of the LORD stood there, as
the glory which I saw by the river of Chebar: and
I fell on my face.
24 Then the spirit entered into me, and set me
upon my feet, and spake with me, and said unto
me, Go, shut thyself within thine house.
25 But thou, O son of man, behold, they shall put
bands upon thee, and shall bind thee with them,

nutritious and delightful to the prophet's soul. Those with a heart for God's Word are satisfied with the Word, regardless of the message (Pss. 19:10; 119:103).

3:5 *of a strange speech and . . . hard language.* Literally, "deep or unfathomable of lip" and "heavy or thick of tongue" (v. 6). The prophet was not sent to those who had an unknown language, whose words would be difficult to understand.

3:6 *they would have hearkened.* They were not as hardhearted but would have listened (Matt. 11:21–23).

3:7 *impudent.* Literally, "hard of forehead." *hardhearted.* Literally, "stiff or stubborn of heart."

3:8 The Lord had equipped him with the necessary defenses to withstand their attacks and rebellion.

3:9 *adamant.* The hardest stone or diamond, signifying resolve and strength to minister to an obstinate and rebellious people.

3:11 *whether they will hear, or . . . forbear.* See 2:4–5.

3:12 *the spirit took me up.* Like Philip the evangelist (Acts 8:39).

3:14 *bitterness.* Great heaviness, sadness, and sorrow. *heat of my spirit.* Hot displeasure and anger (not in the sense of anger toward God but conscious of the difficulties that awaited him).

3:15 *Tel-abib.* A city in Babylon, near the river Chebar. *sat where they sat.* With other captives, a gesture to identify and sympathize with them, perhaps to win a hearing from them. *seven days.* A week of silence (Job 2:13).

3:17 *watchman.* One who keeps guard or watches attentively for news or danger (2 Kings 9:17). The term is used metaphorically for leaders and prophets (Isa. 56:10–11; Jer. 6:17; Hos. 9:8).

3:18 *die in his iniquity.* Each person is responsible for his own sins (18:4). *his blood will I require at thine hand.* You are accountable for his death (Acts 20:26). The prophet-watchman will bear responsibility, not for the sins of others but for his own failure to *warn* the ungodly of the coming judgment (33:1–9).

3:20 *righteous man.* A person who so far had conducted himself in integrity, straightness, and uprightness. *turn . . . and commit iniquity.* Reject the path of obedience and pursue a lifestyle of sin. *stumblingblock.* Obstacle, cause of ruin (Lev. 19:14; Jer. 6:21; see note at 7:19).

3:23 *the glory of the LORD . . . which I saw.* See ch. 1.

3:24 *the spirit entered.* The Holy Spirit gave fresh strength to serve (2:2).

3:25 *bands.* Cords or ropes.

and thou shalt not go out among them:
26 And I will make thy tongue cleave to the roof
of thy mouth, that thou shalt be dumb, and shalt
not be to them a reprover: for they *are* a rebellious
house.
27 But when I speak with thee, I will open thy
mouth, and thou shalt say unto them, Thus saith
the Lord GOD; He that heareth, let him hear; and
he that forbeareth, let him forbear: for they *are* a
rebellious house.

CHAPTER 4

THOU also, son of man, take thee a tile, and lay it
before thee, and pourtray upon it the city, *even*
Jerusalem:
2 And lay siege against it, and build a fort against
it, and cast a mount against it; set the camp also
against it, and set *battering* rams against it round
about.
3 Moreover take thou unto thee an iron pan, and
set it *for* a wall of iron between thee and the city:
and set thy face against it, and it shall be besieged,
and thou shalt lay siege against it. This *shall be* a
sign to the house of Israel.
4 Lie thou also upon thy left side, and lay the
iniquity of the house of Israel upon it: *according*
to the number of the days that thou shalt lie upon
it thou shalt bear their iniquity.
5 For I have laid upon thee the years of their
iniquity, according to the number of the days,
three hundred and ninety days: so shalt thou bear
the iniquity of the house of Israel.
6 And when thou hast accomplished them, lie
again on thy right side, and thou shalt bear the
iniquity of the house of Judah forty days: I have
appointed thee each day for a year.
7 Therefore thou shalt set thy face toward
the siege of Jerusalem, and thine arm *shall be*
uncovered, and thou shalt prophesy against it.
8 And, behold, I will lay bands upon thee, and
thou shalt not turn thee from one side to another,
till thou hast ended the days of thy siege.
9 ¶ Take thou also unto thee wheat, and barley,
and beans, and lentiles, and millet, and fitches,
and put them in one vessel, and make thee bread
thereof, *according* to the number of the days that
thou shalt lie upon thy side, three hundred and
ninety days shalt thou eat thereof.
10 And thy meat which thou shalt eat *shall be* by
weight, twenty shekels a day: from time to time
shalt thou eat it.
11 Thou shalt drink also water by measure, the
sixth part of an hin: from time to time shalt thou
drink.
12 And thou shalt eat it *as* barley cakes, and thou
shalt bake it with dung that cometh out of man,
in their sight.

3:26 *I will make thy tongue cleave to the roof of thy mouth.* He would be silent (*dumb*), a sign of judgment from the Lord. *reprover.* One who speaks a reprimand or chides.

Thoughts for Personal/Family Worship: Chapter 3

1. **The Lord's instruction to Ezekiel to eat the words He gave him (v. 3) and to receive them in his heart (v. 10) has pointed application for preachers and also for all Christians. To eat something is to receive its nutrients so that it becomes part of the body and fuels its activity. Unless ministers who preach the Word first feed their own souls, they are simply spouting theory. They must preach God's truth from their hearts. Every Christian should receive the Word of God the same way, whether as they hear it in a sermon or read it in the Scripture. Take time to "chew" on the Word, to prayerfully meditate so that its truths will become a part of your mind and heart and give the necessary strength for spiritual activity. When do you regularly meditate on the Word?**
2. **Whenever God gives authority to one person over others, He also holds that leader accountable as a "watchman" over them. This person has a responsibility to promote good, speak against evil, and warn of sin's consequences. This is especially true of the elders of the church, who "watch for your souls, as they that must give account" (Heb. 13:17). God does not hold His watchmen accountable for how people respond to the truth, but He does require watchmen to faithfully speak the truth to those under their charge. How can we encourage God's watchmen to serve well in their callings? What would motivate someone to be a good watchman, even when this task is far from popular?**

MESSAGES OF JUDGMENT AGAINST JERUSALEM (4:1—7:27)

Signs of Jerusalem's Siege and Doom (4:1—5:17)

Chapter 4: ***The Lord instructs Ezekiel to enact four signs picturing Jerusalem's sin and judgment.***

4:1–3 It was not uncommon for prophets to use object lessons to illustrate the message. These symbolic acts were commanded by God and were a component of the prophet's proclaiming the Word of the Lord. *tile.* A sunbaked brick. *Pourtray.* To inscribe. *fort.* A bulwark or siege wall. *cast a mount.* Raise up or build an assault ramp. *iron pan.* An iron cooking pan or plate used to represent a wall. The model of the city pictured the impending siege against Jerusalem.

4:4–6 Lying on the ground was an object lesson of the time and discomforts of the captivity: 390 days on the left side represented the northern kingdom's captivity; 40 days on the right side that of the southern kingdom, which would not last as long. The total of 430 days may be an allusion to the 430 years of Israel's sojourn in Egypt before the exodus (Ex. 12:40).

4:7 *arm . . . uncovered.* Symbolizing the might that would be arrayed against Jerusalem.

4:8 *bands upon thee.* Ropes or cords, suggesting that the siege of Jerusalem would be firm and immovable. *Not turn thee from one side to another.* Most likely Ezekiel did not lie down continuously, but for some period of time every day during those 430 consecutive days he lay down in the presence of the people without turning.

4:9–11 *fitches.* Spelt, like a cereal. *meat.* Food of any kind. *twenty shekels a day.* Approximately nine ounces, a small portion of food common during a famine. *by measure, the sixth part of an hin.* Approximately one-half pint.

4:12 *barley cakes.* Lower quality bread. *bake it with dung*

13 And the LORD said, Even thus shall the
children of Israel eat their defiled bread among
the Gentiles, whither I will drive them.
14 Then said I, Ah Lord GOD! behold, my soul
hath not been polluted: for from my youth up
even till now have I not eaten of that which dieth
of itself, or is torn in pieces; neither came there
abominable flesh into my mouth.
15 Then he said unto me, Lo, I have given thee
cow's dung for man's dung, and thou shalt
prepare thy bread therewith.
16 Moreover he said unto me, Son of man,
behold, I will break the staff of bread in Jerusalem:
and they shall eat bread by weight, and with care;
and they shall drink water by measure, and with
astonishment:
17 That they may want bread and water, and be
astonied one with another, and consume away for
their iniquity.

CHAPTER 5

AND thou, son of man, take thee a sharp knife,
take thee a barber's razor, and cause *it* to pass
upon thine head and upon thy beard: then take
thee balances to weigh, and divide the *hair*.
2 Thou shalt burn with fire a third part in the
midst of the city, when the days of the siege are
fulfilled: and thou shalt take a third part, *and*
smite about it with a knife: and a third part thou
shalt scatter in the wind; and I will draw out a
sword after them.
3 Thou shalt also take thereof a few in number,
and bind them in thy skirts.
4 Then take of them again, and cast them into the
midst of the fire, and burn them in the fire; *for*
thereof shall a fire come forth into all the house
of Israel.
5 ¶ Thus saith the Lord GOD; This *is* Jerusalem:
I have set it in the midst of the nations and
countries *that are* round about her.
6 And she hath changed my judgments into
wickedness more than the nations, and my
statutes more than the countries that *are* round
about her: for they have refused my judgments
and my statutes, they have not walked in them.
7 Therefore thus saith the Lord GOD; Because ye
multiplied more than the nations that *are* round
about you, *and* have not walked in my statutes,
neither have kept my judgments, neither have
done according to the judgments of the nations
that *are* round about you;
8 Therefore thus saith the Lord GOD; Behold, I,
even I, *am* against thee, and will execute judgments
in the midst of thee in the sight of the nations.
9 And I will do in thee that which I have not done,
and whereunto I will not do any more the like,
because of all thine abominations.
10 Therefore the fathers shall eat the sons in the
midst of thee, and the sons shall eat their fathers;
and I will execute judgments in thee, and the whole
remnant of thee will I scatter into all the winds.
11 Wherefore, *as* I live, saith the Lord GOD; Surely,
because thou hast defiled my sanctuary with all

---

that cometh out of man. The oven was to be fueled by human excrement, a graphic picture of desperate times.

4:13 *defiled.* Unclean according to the ceremonial law.

4:14 *my soul hath not been polluted.* I have not caused myself to be ceremonially unclean. This would have been particularly horrible to one of the priestly line, as Ezekiel was.

4:16 *staff of bread.* A bread pole to stack bread and keep it away from mice. Breaking it signifies famine (Ps. 105:16), a curse of breaking God's covenant (Lev. 26:26). *eat bread by weight.* By careful measure, rationing in order to prolong its availability. *care.* Worry or anxiety. *astonishment.* Horror or shuddering.

4:17 *be astonied one with another.* To be appalled or made to tremble with each other. *consume away.* Pine away.

Thoughts for Personal/Family Worship: Chapter 4

1. **Why did God send a series of strange signs to the captives? It was to teach by repetition. God was instructing them line by line. He was emphasizing His will, patiently showing them the consequences of sin. God is patient with sinners. How good God is! This gives us all the more reason to listen humbly to His Word.**
2. **Although there were many signs, the message they conveyed was the same: Israel's sin was going to be followed by judgment. When God speaks, we should take note. He has a message for us that is worthy of our attention and reception. He does not change. His warning to Judah of siege and famine was the same warning He had given over 800 years earlier through Moses. Let no one deceive you with empty words. The wrath of God is coming on sinners who do not repent.**

Chapter 5: *God instructs Ezekiel to cut his hair to point to the different ways that God will judge.*

5:1 *sharp knife . . . barber's razor.* Cutting of hair was associated with catastrophe (Deut. 21:12; Job 1:20; Isa. 7:20). *balances.* Scales.

5:2 *burn . . . smite . . . scatter.* To symbolize the threefold fate of the inhabitants of Jerusalem (v. 12).

5:3 *take thereof a few in number.* That is, a few hairs. *skirts.* The hem or edge of a garment, perhaps to symbolize temporary safety and preservation.

5:4 *take of them again.* There would be no escaping after all; the judgment would affect the entire nation.

5:5 *Jerusalem.* The capital city, standing for the entire nation.

5:6 *changed.* Rebelled against. *judgments.* Ordinances and laws. *refused.* Despised or hated. *not walked in.* Not followed with ongoing obedience.

5:7 *ye multiplied more than the nations.* Literally, "your turmoil [is] more than the nations," referring to their tumultuous rage against God.

5:8 *Behold.* An interjection meaning to take note or pay attention. *I, even I, am against thee.* If God is against us, who can be for us? The wrath of God is the worst of dooms.

5:9 *abominations.* Things that are offensive and disgusting before the Lord (v. 11).

5:10 *fathers shall eat the sons . . . and the sons shall eat their*

thy detestable things, and with all thine abomina-
tions, therefore will I also diminish *thee*; neither
shall mine eye spare, neither will I have any pity.
12 ¶ A third part of thee shall die with the pes-
tilence, and with famine shall they be consumed
in the midst of thee: and a third part shall fall by
the sword round about thee; and I will scatter a
third part into all the winds, and I will draw out a
sword after them.
13 Thus shall mine anger be accomplished,
and I will cause my fury to rest upon them, and
I will be comforted: and they shall know that I
the LORD have spoken *it* in my zeal, when I have
accomplished my fury in them.
14 Moreover I will make thee waste, and a
reproach among the nations that *are* round about
thee, in the sight of all that pass by.
15 So it shall be a reproach and a taunt, an
instruction and an astonishment unto the nations
that *are* round about thee, when I shall execute
judgments in thee in anger and in fury and in
furious rebukes. I the LORD have spoken *it*.
16 When I shall send upon them the evil arrows
of famine, which shall be for *their* destruction,
and which I will send to destroy you: and I will
increase the famine upon you, and will break your
staff of bread:
17 So will I send upon you famine and evil beasts,
and they shall bereave thee; and pestilence and
blood shall pass through thee; and I will bring the
sword upon thee. I the LORD have spoken *it*.

CHAPTER 6

AND the word of the LORD came unto me, saying,
2 Son of man, set thy face toward the mountains
of Israel, and prophesy against them,
3 And say, Ye mountains of Israel, hear the word
of the Lord GOD; Thus saith the Lord GOD to the
mountains, and to the hills, to the rivers, and to
the valleys; Behold, I, *even* I, will bring a sword
upon you, and I will destroy your high places.
4 And your altars shall be desolate, and your
images shall be broken: and I will cast down your
slain *men* before your idols.
5 And I will lay the dead carcases of the children
of Israel before their idols; and I will scatter your
bones round about your altars.
6 In all your dwellingplaces the cities shall be laid
waste, and the high places shall be desolate; that
your altars may be laid waste and made desolate,
and your idols may be broken and cease, and your
images may be cut down, and your works may be
abolished.
7 And the slain shall fall in the midst of you, and
ye shall know that I *am* the LORD.
8 ¶ Yet will I leave a remnant, that ye may have *some*
that shall escape the sword among the nations,
when ye shall be scattered through the countries.
9 And they that escape of you shall remember me
among the nations whither they shall be carried
captives, because I am broken with their whor-
ish heart, which hath departed from me, and with
their eyes, which go a whoring after their idols:
and they shall lothe themselves for the evils which

---

fathers. The horrific results of famine (Lev. 26:29; Deut. 28:53–57; 2 Kings 6:29). *the whole remnant.* Whatever is left.

5:11 *defiled my sanctuary.* Intentionally and intensively profaned or made unclean God holy temple. *detestable.* Idols as impure. *diminish.* Shaved, an allusion to Ezekiel's object lesson (v. 1). *neither shall mine eye spare.* Ironically, God's eye often refers to His mercy (20:17; 2 Chron. 16:9; Pss. 33:18–19; 34:15) but here expresses judgment without mercy (7:4,9; 8:18; 9:5,10; cf. Deut. 7:16).

5:12 The threefold fate of Jerusalem symbolized by the hair is here explained (v. 2).

5:14 *waste.* A desolation or a dry place. *reproach.* Scorn or contempt (v. 15).

5:15 *taunt.* Reviling. *instruction.* An example of correction. *astonishment.* Amazement that leads to silence or dumbness. *furious rebukes.* Punishments or reproofs.

5:16 *evil.* Hurtful. *staff of bread.* See note at 4:16.

5:17 *evil beasts.* Those that do harm.

Thoughts for Personal/Family Worship: Chapter 5

One of the most striking truths to emerge from Ezekiel is the severity of the judgment upon the people for their sin. The cutting and division of Ezekiel's hair portray intense judgment. With emphatic tone God stated, "Behold, I, even I, am against thee, and will execute judgments in the midst of thee" (v. 8). This declaration is supported by the repeated phrase "I the LORD have spoken it" (vv. 13,15,17). In a world that makes light of God's wrath upon sin, we must remember that by nature we are all sinners under the fury and condemnation of God. His wrath abides upon unbelievers. Only Christ can save from the judgment of God. How does this truth make Christ precious to your soul?

Oracles against the Mountains and Land (6:1—7:27)

Chapter 6: *Ezekiel warns of judgment and gives the promise of a remnant.*

6:3 *the mountains . . . hills . . . rivers . . . valleys.* These four geographical features represent the topography of the whole land. Addressing these inanimate objects constitutes a figure of speech referring to all the inhabitants of the land. *high places.* Places of idolatry and illegitimate worship.

6:7 *ye shall know that I am the LORD.* God's judgments against sinners display His glory—a key theme of Ezekiel (see Introduction: Synopsis).

6:8 *leave a remnant.* Save or preserve a portion.

6:9 *remember me.* Think about who God is, what He has done for His people, and how we have sinned against Him, so that fear and love affect the heart and obedience directs the behavior (16:22,43,61,63; 20:43; 36:31; cf. 22:12; Deut. 5:15; 7:18; 8:2,18; 9:7; 15:5; 16:3,12; 24:9,18,22; 32:7). *I am broken.* A graphic description of God's grief over their sin, comparing Him to a man whose wife repeatedly commits adultery (16:1–63). *their whorish heart.* Their heart, which acts as a harlot, an ugly image of loving *their idols* instead of loving their covenant God (14:3–5; 20:16; Jer. 17:1–2). *lothe themselves.* Detest themselves.

they have committed in all their abominations.
10 And they shall know that I *am* the LORD, *and*
that I have not said in vain that I would do this
evil unto them.
11 ¶ Thus saith the Lord GOD; Smite with thine
hand, and stamp with thy foot, and say, Alas for
all the evil abominations of the house of Israel!
for they shall fall by the sword, by the famine, and
by the pestilence.
12 He that is far off shall die of the pestilence; and
he that is near shall fall by the sword; and he that
remaineth and is besieged shall die by the famine:
thus will I accomplish my fury upon them.
13 Then shall ye know that I *am* the LORD, when
their slain *men* shall be among their idols round
about their altars, upon every high hill, in all the
tops of the mountains, and under every green
tree, and under every thick oak, the place where
they did offer sweet savour to all their idols.
14 So will I stretch out my hand upon them, and
make the land desolate, yea, more desolate than
the wilderness toward Diblath, in all their habi-
tations: and they shall know that I *am* the LORD.

CHAPTER 7

MOREOVER the word of the LORD came unto me,
saying,
2 Also, thou son of man, thus saith the Lord GOD
unto the land of Israel; An end, the end is come
upon the four corners of the land.
3 Now *is* the end *come* upon thee, and I will
send mine anger upon thee, and will judge thee
according to thy ways, and will recompense upon
thee all thine abominations.
4 And mine eye shall not spare thee, neither will
I have pity: but I will recompense thy ways upon
thee, and thine abominations shall be in the midst
of thee: and ye shall know that I *am* the LORD.
5 Thus saith the Lord GOD; An evil, an only evil,
behold, is come.
6 An end is come, the end is come: it watcheth for
thee; behold, it is come.
7 The morning is come unto thee, O thou that
dwellest in the land: the time is come, the day of
trouble *is* near, and not the sounding again of the
mountains.
8 Now will I shortly pour out my fury upon
thee, and accomplish mine anger upon thee: and
I will judge thee according to thy ways, and will
recompense thee for all thine abominations.
9 And mine eye shall not spare, neither will I have
pity: I will recompense thee according to thy ways
and thine abominations *that* are in the midst of
thee; and ye shall know that I *am* the LORD that
smiteth.
10 Behold the day, behold, it is come: the morning
is gone forth; the rod hath blossomed, pride hath
budded.
11 Violence is risen up into a rod of wickedness:
none of them *shall remain*, nor of their multitude,
nor of any of theirs: neither *shall there be* wailing
for them.
12 The time is come, the day draweth near: let not
the buyer rejoice, nor the seller mourn: for wrath
is upon all the multitude thereof.
13 For the seller shall not return to that which is
sold, although they were yet alive: for the vision
is touching the whole multitude thereof, *which*
shall not return; neither shall any strengthen

6:10 *not . . . in vain.* Not without purpose or cause. *evil.* The calamity of judgment.
6:11 *Smite with thine hand, and stamp with thy foot.* Gestures indicating earnestness and authority.
6:12 *He that is far off . . . he that is near . . . and he that remaineth and is besieged.* Three classes of people: those who try to escape by fleeing, those who try to escape by hiding, and those who remain.

Thoughts for Personal/Family Worship: Chapter 6

Idolatry is a common sin. However, idolatry is not confined to worshiping before a statue or picture; it is a disposition of the soul that turns away from God to replace Him with created things, what Ezekiel called a "whorish heart." By nature the human heart is idolatrous (Rom. 1:21–23). It loves itself and this world instead of God and His will (1 John 2:15–17). Idolatry can take many forms and is often a secret sin. God is against all idolatry, for He deserves and demands our worship. He is jealous over our wholehearted love. We are to have no other gods before him, not even the god of self. To what forms of idolatry are you most attracted? How do you need to repent of idolatry?

Chapter 7: ***Ezekiel multiplies warnings of certain judgments as the end is foretold.***

7:2 *four corners of the land.* The entire land.
7:3 *according to thy ways.* On account of the manner or course of life. *recompense.* Hebrew, "give" (v. 8).
7:4 *mine eye shall not spare thee.* See note at 5:11 (also v. 9).
7:5 *An evil, an only evil.* One calamity shall come upon another.
7:6 *watcheth.* is awakened or aroused.
7:7 *morning.* Literally, "a circle or circuit," as in the coming of an event and referring to the day of trouble (v. 10). *not the sounding again.* The Hebrew is uncertain, having the idea either of a thunderclap or of a joyous sound.
7:10 *rod hath blossomed, pride hath budded.* Perhaps Nebuchadnezzar, a proud king whom God used as a rod to punish Israel (cf. Isa. 10:5), or the pride and sin of Israel (v. 11). The blossoming and budding signify that the time has come, that judgment is impending. Aaron's rod budded and blossomed as a sign of God's choice of His family for the priesthood (Num. 17), but now, with tragic irony, the same image declares God's destruction of Jerusalem and its temple.
7:11 *Violence is risen up into a rod of wickedness.* Either a violent man (Nebuchadnezzar) had risen to punish Israel's wickedness, or Israel's own violence was the cause of their punishment from God.
7:12 *let not the buyer rejoice, nor the seller mourn.* A figure of speech using opposites to designate all classes of people. Normal social life and commerce would cease.

himself in the iniquity of his life.
14 They have blown the trumpet, even to make
all ready; but none goeth to the battle: for my
wrath *is* upon all the multitude thereof.
15 The sword *is* without, and the pestilence and
the famine within: he that *is* in the field shall die
with the sword; and he that *is* in the city, famine
and pestilence shall devour him.
16 ¶ But they that escape of them shall escape,
and shall be on the mountains like doves of the
valleys, all of them mourning, every one for his
iniquity.
17 All hands shall be feeble, and all knees shall be
weak *as* water.
18 They shall also gird *themselves* with sackcloth,
and horror shall cover them; and shame *shall be*
upon all faces, and baldness upon all their heads.
19 They shall cast their silver in the streets, and
their gold shall be removed: their silver and their
gold shall not be able to deliver them in the day
of the wrath of the LORD: they shall not satisfy
their souls, neither fill their bowels: because it is
the stumblingblock of their iniquity.
20 ¶ As for the beauty of his ornament, he set
it in majesty: but they made the images of their
abominations *and* of their detestable things
therein: therefore have I set it far from them.
21 And I will give it into the hands of the strangers
for a prey, and to the wicked of the earth for a
spoil; and they shall pollute it.
22 My face will I turn also from them, and they
shall pollute my secret *place*: for the robbers shall
enter into it, and defile it.
23 ¶ Make a chain: for the land is full of bloody
crimes, and the city is full of violence.
24 Wherefore I will bring the worst of the
heathen, and they shall possess their houses: I will
also make the pomp of the strong to cease; and
their holy places shall be defiled.
25 Destruction cometh; and they shall seek peace,
and *there shall be* none.
26 Mischief shall come upon mischief, and ru-
mour shall be upon rumour; then shall they seek
a vision of the prophet; but the law shall perish
from the priest, and counsel from the ancients.
27 The king shall mourn, and the prince shall
be clothed with desolation, and the hands of the
people of the land shall be troubled: I will do
unto them after their way, and according to their
deserts will I judge them; and they shall know that
I *am* the LORD.

CHAPTER 8

AND it came to pass in the sixth year, in the sixth
month, in the fifth *day* of the month, *as* I sat in
mine house, and the elders of Judah sat before me,
that the hand of the Lord GOD fell there upon me.
2 Then I beheld, and lo a likeness as the appearance
of fire: from the appearance of his loins even down-
ward, fire; and from his loins even upward, as the
appearance of brightness, as the colour of amber.

7:15 *The sword is without, and the pestilence and the famine within.* The threefold judgment foretold (5:2,12).
7:16 They might escape one form of punishment only to suffer another that would be worse. Valley *doves* could not survive in the mountains.
7:18 *gird . . . with sackcloth.* A gesture symbolizing mourning and distress. *baldness.* Associated with mourning.
7:19 *silver . . . gold.* Specifically, their idols were made of these metals (v. 20; 16:17). *not be able to deliver them.* See Zeph. 1:18. *stumblingblock of their iniquity.* The idols by which Judah fell into sin and destruction (14:3–4,7; 18:30; 21:15; 44:12; cf. note at 3:20).
7:20 *beauty of his ornament.* The silver and gold that God gave them for His glory. *images.* They misused the gifts of God for idolatrous purposes that He hates (*abominations*). *set it far from.* Literally, "have given it to them for garbage."
7:21 *strangers.* Foreigners, specifically the Babylonians. *for a prey.* As spoil. *pollute.* Desecrate or defile something holy by treating it as common or ordinary (vv. 22,24).
7:22 *secret place.* Hidden place, a reference to the Holy of Holies. *robbers.* Violent oppressors. *defile.* Same word as *pollute* (see note at v. 21).
7:23 *Make a chain.* So as to bind those who are guilty of crimes.
7:24 *the worst of the heathen.* The Babylonians (Hab. 1:6–11). *pomp.* Pride.
7:26 *Mischief shall come upon mischief.* Disaster shall follow disaster. *rumour . . . upon rumour.* Report will follow report. *vision.* A revelation from God. *ancients.* Elders.
7:27 *their deserts.* What they deserved from God—a fearful prospect that should point us to Christ, who took what sinners deserved so that they might receive what He deserved (2 Cor. 5:21).

Thoughts for Personal/Family Worship: Chapter 7

1. **The intensity of the language in this chapter and the repetition of the words "the time is come" (vv. 7,12) emphasize the certainty of God's judgment upon sin. His time for judgment upon all sin will come at His appointed hour (Eccl. 8:11–13). It is imperative to be ready to meet the Lord. Have you turned from sin to the Savior? If not, why not? The time of judgment is coming.**
2. **No man will be able to deliver himself from the judgment of God. No amount of gold or human effort will provide safety from the wrath of God (v. 19). If souls do not escape to Christ and find deliverance in Him, they will not be delivered. There is no salvation through riches or "being religious" but only through the Lord Jesus Christ, the only Redeemer of God's elect. Cast away your idols now, for they cannot save you, and flee to the Lord.**

THE VISION OF GLORY DEPARTING FROM THE TEMPLE (8:1—11:25)

Chapter 8: ***In a vision Ezekiel tours the temple and sees the secret idolatry and abomination as God sees it.***

8:1 *sixth year.* The date is the year of Jehoiachin's captivity.
8:2 *likeness as the appearance of fire.* The dazzling figure was either an angelic messenger or, more likely, another manifestation of God's glory (1:4,27).

3 And he put forth the form of an hand, and took
me by a lock of mine head; and the spirit lifted
me up between the earth and the heaven, and
brought me in the visions of God to Jerusalem, to
the door of the inner gate that looketh toward the
north; where *was* the seat of the image of jealousy,
which provoketh to jealousy.
4 And, behold, the glory of the God of Israel *was*
there, according to the vision that I saw in the
plain.
5 ¶ Then said he unto me, Son of man, lift up
thine eyes now the way toward the north. So
I lifted up mine eyes the way toward the north,
and behold northward at the gate of the altar this
image of jealousy in the entry.
6 He said furthermore unto me, Son of man, seest
thou what they do? *even* the great abominations
that the house of Israel committeth here, that
I should go far off from my sanctuary? but
turn thee yet again, *and* thou shalt see greater
abominations.
7 ¶ And he brought me to the door of the court;
and when I looked, behold a hole in the wall.
8 Then said he unto me, Son of man, dig now
in the wall: and when I had digged in the wall,
behold a door.
9 And he said unto me, Go in, and behold the
wicked abominations that they do here.
10 So I went in and saw; and behold every form
of creeping things, and abominable beasts, and all
the idols of the house of Israel, pourtrayed upon
the wall round about.
11 And there stood before them seventy men
of the ancients of the house of Israel, and in
the midst of them stood Jaazaniah the son of
Shaphan, with every man his censer in his hand;
and a thick cloud of incense went up.
12 Then said he unto me, Son of man, hast thou
seen what the ancients of the house of Israel do
in the dark, every man in the chambers of his
imagery? for they say, The LORD seeth us not; the
LORD hath forsaken the earth.
13 ¶ He said also unto me, Turn thee yet again,
and thou shalt see greater abominations that they
do.
14 Then he brought me to the door of the
gate of the LORD's house which *was* toward the
north; and, behold, there sat women weeping for
Tammuz.
15 ¶ Then said he unto me, Hast thou seen *this*,
O son of man? turn thee yet again, *and* thou shalt
see greater abominations than these.
16 And he brought me into the inner court of
the LORD's house, and, behold, at the door of the
temple of the LORD, between the porch and the
altar, *were* about five and twenty men, with their
backs toward the temple of the LORD, and their
faces toward the east; and they worshipped the
sun toward the east.
17 ¶ Then he said unto me, Hast thou seen *this*,
O son of man? Is it a light thing to the house of
Judah that they commit the abominations which
they commit here? for they have filled the land
with violence, and have returned to provoke me

8:3 *brought me in the visions.* A vision was a vehicle of divine revelation, the prophet often being in a trancelike state. Ezekiel was not physically transported, but this describes what he saw within himself as God communicated to him. *image of jealousy, which provoketh to jealousy.* Idol provoking God's anger, perhaps an image of Asherah erected by Manasseh (2 Kings 21:7). It was physically removed by Josiah, but its offense remained before God (2 Kings 23:6,26–27; 24:3), and Jehoiakim returned to his forefathers' evil ways (2 Kings 23:32,37; 24:9).

8:5 The *altar* was located at the northern gate, where the sacrifices were offered (Lev. 1:11). They substituted an idol for a type of Christ's atoning blood.

8:6 *great abominations.* Things disgusting and detestable before God, a common designation for idols. *go far off from my sanctuary.* Withdraw from the sacred place. *thou shalt see greater abominations.* The further into the temple he would go, the worse things would become (vv. 13,15).

8:10 *every form of creeping things.* Images of various venomous and poisonous creatures that were worshiped by the heathen; creeping, cultic abominations. *pourtrayed.* Carved all over the room. Animal worship represents the degradation of the unregenerate heart (Rom. 1:23).

8:11 *seventy men of the ancients.* Prominent elders or leaders, as representatives of the people (v. 12). *Jaazaniah.* His father, *Shaphan*, played a leading role in Josiah's reforms (2 Kings 22:3–20). Having godly parents is no assurance that all will be well. *censer.* For burning incense, indicating that the elders were actively engaged in idolatry.

8:12 *in the dark.* In secret (John 3:19). *chambers of his imagery.* The dark room of his idols. *The LORD seeth us not.* The practical atheism of sinners (Ps. 94:7)—but God sees (see note at 1:22–23).

8:14 *weeping.* Strong weeping, wailing, or lamenting. *Tammuz.* A fertility god. The notion was that in time of drought and famine he was held in the underworld; his coming back to the realm of the living resulted in prosperity. This was nature worship for profit.

8:16 *inner court of the LORD's house.* The interior before the Holy of Holies. *between the porch and the altar.* The porch that led to the brazen altar, a sacred place. *backs toward the temple of the LORD.* A graphic demonstration that true worship and false worship are mutually exclusive.

8:17 *light thing.* Something to treat with contempt. *branch to their nose.* Most likely the pagan rite of putting a laurel, olive, or vine branch to their nose in honor of the idol they worshiped.

Thoughts for Personal/Family Worship: Chapter 8

Even today many people represent divine beings with visible objects, or direct their worship to or through images. Millions still engage in gross idolatry. However, people in secularized nations may have difficulty identifying idol worship in their culture. In such societies, idols may take other forms, such as pornography, captivation by video entertainment, or the love of money, but secular idols no less rule the souls of those who adore them. God sees all idolatry, and He views it with disgust. It is particularly offensive to Him when

to anger: and, lo, they put the branch to their nose.
18 Therefore will I also deal in fury: mine eye
shall not spare, neither will I have pity: and
though they cry in mine ears with a loud voice,
yet will I not hear them.

CHAPTER 9

HE cried also in mine ears with a loud voice,
saying, Cause them that have charge over the city
to draw near, even every man *with* his destroying
weapon in his hand.
2 And, behold, six men came from the way of the
higher gate, which lieth toward the north, and
every man a slaughter weapon in his hand; and
one man among them *was* clothed with linen,
with a writer's inkhorn by his side: and they went
in, and stood beside the brasen altar.
3 And the glory of the God of Israel was gone
up from the cherub, whereupon he was, to the
threshold of the house. And he called to the
man clothed with linen, which *had* the writer's
inkhorn by his side;
4 And the LORD said unto him, Go through the
midst of the city, through the midst of Jerusalem,
and set a mark upon the foreheads of the men
that sigh and that cry for all the abominations
that be done in the midst thereof.
5 ¶ And to the others he said in mine hearing, Go
ye after him through the city, and smite: let not
your eye spare, neither have ye pity:
6 Slay utterly old *and* young, both maids, and
little children, and women: but come not near any
man upon whom *is* the mark; and begin at my
sanctuary. Then they began at the ancient men
which *were* before the house.
7 And he said unto them, Defile the house, and
fill the courts with the slain: go ye forth. And they
went forth, and slew in the city.
8 ¶ And it came to pass, while they were slaying
them, and I was left, that I fell upon my face, and
cried, and said, Ah Lord GOD! wilt thou destroy
all the residue of Israel in thy pouring out of thy
fury upon Jerusalem?
9 Then said he unto me, The iniquity of the house
of Israel and Judah *is* exceeding great, and the land
is full of blood, and the city full of perverseness:
for they say, The LORD hath forsaken the earth,
and the LORD seeth not.
10 And as for me also, mine eye shall not spare,
neither will I have pity, *but* I will recompense their
way upon their head.

those who participate in public worship with His people profane His holy presence with their wicked idols. What are the most common idols worshiped by people around you? How does God view these idols? How are you fleeing this idolatry?

Chapter 9: *Ezekiel sees the man with a writer's inkhorn and witnesses God's discriminating judgment.*

9:1 *destroying weapon in his hand.* A sword or something similar, drawn and ready for use.

9:2 *six men.* Most likely angelic executioners. *the way of the higher gate, which lieth toward the north.* Where idolatrous practices were committed (8:14). *slaughter weapon.* A weapon of his shattering, to be used for destruction. *one man among them.* Most likely, in addition to the six. *linen.* Priestly attire (Lev. 16:4); it was the priest's work to distinguish the clean from the unclean (Lev. 10:10; 14:7). *writer's inkhorn.* Scribal equipment, a vessel used to hold ink (v. 3). This seventh figure is central to the vision and most likely a representation of Christ. *brazen altar.* The place of sacrifice, where sin was atoned for by the blood of a substitute (Lev. 1:4–5).

9:3 *gone up from the cherub.* God removed His *glory* from over the mercy seat, where He dwelt between the cherubim, and began to depart from the temple. On cherubim, see note at 10:15.

9:4 *set a mark.* "Mark a mark." In Hebrew, to put the letter *tau*, which at that time looked like an "x," on the foreheads. This symbolizes the Lord's perfect knowledge of those who belong to Him (Nah. 1:7). The mark identified those who mourned and grieved over the sin of the nation as evidence of their love for the Lord (Matt. 5:4) and protected them from the slaughter (v. 6). The implication is that the wicked do not have godly sorrow over sin (2 Cor. 7:10).

9:5 *the others.* The six men with the weapons.

9:6 Regardless of age or gender, all were under the sentence of death except those with the *mark* on their forehead, those sealed by God as His (Rev. 7:3; 14:1). *begin at my sanctuary.* Where the abominations were most offensive to God's holiness (Amos 3:2; 1 Peter 4:17–18).

9:8 *fell upon my face.* A posture of humility and brokenness. *all the residue.* Those who were left. The prophet interceded in Abraham-like fashion (Gen. 18:23–33).

9:9 *iniquity.* Refers principally to guilt. *full of blood.* In Hebrew blood is plural, designating the guilt of violence. *perverseness.* Describes sin as behavior that is twisted or warped.

9:10 *I will recompense their way upon their head.* Literally, "their way or manner of life on their head I have given." They have received from the Lord what they deserve—always a terrifying prospect.

Thoughts for Personal/Family Worship: Chapter 9

1. **This vision suggests four important truths to consider about God's judgment. (1) Divine judgment is justified. The text shows that sinners are completely defiled and deluded, being complacent in sin. (2) Divine judgment is comprehensive. None were to be spared, regardless of age or gender, because all have sinned. (3) Divine judgment is infallible. That it began at the sanctuary shows that the religious hypocrites are known by God, who looks through religion to the heart. (4) Divine judgment is escapable. God has marked those who belong to Him, redeeming them through Christ's blood, sealing them with the Holy Spirit, and enabling them to evidence their salvation in holy grief and repentance for sin.**
2. **Christ the Priest is the Mediator charged by God to distinguish between those who will fall under divine judgment and those who will be saved. The central figure described in this vision is the one clothed in linen like a priest, standing beside the altar of burnt offerings in the temple. Christ is the High Priest of His people (Heb. 8:1). He has offered Himself once for all their sins (Heb. 10:12). He alone has the authority to mark people**

11 And, behold, the man clothed with linen,
which *had* the inkhorn by his side, reported
the matter, saying, I have done as thou hast
commanded me.

CHAPTER 10

THEN I looked, and, behold, in the firmament
that was above the head of the cherubims there
appeared over them as it were a sapphire stone, as
the appearance of the likeness of a throne.
2 And he spake unto the man clothed with linen,
and said, Go in between the wheels, *even* under
the cherub, and fill thine hand with coals of fire
from between the cherubims, and scatter *them*
over the city. And he went in in my sight.
3 Now the cherubims stood on the right side of
the house, when the man went in; and the cloud
filled the inner court.
4 Then the glory of the LORD went up from the
cherub, *and stood* over the threshold of the house;
and the house was filled with the cloud, and the
court was full of the brightness of the LORD's
glory.
5 And the sound of the cherubims' wings was
heard *even* to the outer court, as the voice of the
Almighty God when he speaketh.
6 And it came to pass, *that* when he had
commanded the man clothed with linen, saying,
Take fire from between the wheels, from between
the cherubims; then he went in, and stood beside
the wheels.
7 And *one* cherub stretched forth his hand from
between the cherubims unto the fire that *was*
between the cherubims, and took *thereof*, and
put *it* into the hands of *him that was* clothed with
linen: who took *it*, and went out.
8 ¶ And there appeared in the cherubims the
form of a man's hand under their wings.
9 And when I looked, behold the four wheels
by the cherubims, one wheel by one cherub,
and another wheel by another cherub: and the
appearance of the wheels *was* as the colour of a
beryl stone.
10 And *as for* their appearances, they four had
one likeness, as if a wheel had been in the midst
of a wheel.
11 When they went, they went upon their four
sides; they turned not as they went, but to the
place whither the head looked they followed it;
they turned not as they went.
12 And their whole body, and their backs, and
their hands, and their wings, and the wheels, *were*
full of eyes round about, *even* the wheels that they
four had.
13 As for the wheels, it was cried unto them in my
hearing, O wheel.
14 And every one had four faces: the first face *was*
the face of a cherub, and the second face *was* the
face of a man, and the third the face of a lion, and
the fourth the face of an eagle.
15 And the cherubims were lifted up. This *is* the
living creature that I saw by the river of Chebar.
16 And when the cherubims went, the wheels
went by them: and when the cherubims lifted up
their wings to mount up from the earth, the same
wheels also turned not from beside them.
17 When they stood, *these* stood; and when they
were lifted up, *these* lifted up themselves *also*: for
the spirit of the living creature *was* in them.
18 Then the glory of the LORD departed from off
the threshold of the house, and stood over the
cherubims.
19 And the cherubims lifted up their wings, and

---

as saved. Whom does He mark? He marks only those who sorrow over sin and cry out to God. Is Christ your priest? Are you looking to Him by faith in His saving death and resurrection? Is your heart broken and contrite over sin, crying out to God for mercy?

Chapter 10: *Ezekiel sees in a vision the cherubim and God's glory moving away from the temple.*

10:1 Many of the elements of this vision are the same as his in the first vision at the river Chebar (see notes at ch. 1). *firmament.* Sky.

10:2 *the man clothed with linen.* The same figure as in ch. 9, Christ, who again is assigned a work of judgment. *scatter them over the city.* To symbolize judgment and the purging necessary because of sin.

10:3 *the cloud.* A symbol of the Lord's presence.

10:4 *the glory of the LORD.* The dwelling glory, the glorious presence of the Lord, left the inner sanctuary and moved to the threshold. The Lord's departure was Israel's greatest loss, for His presence with His people was the purpose of redemption (Ex. 29:45–46; 33:15–16).

10:11 *they turned not as they went.* As with the wheels in ch. 1, this refers not to rotation but to direction; they moved in every direction simultaneously.

10:12 *full of eyes.* The divine wisdom by which they operated.

10:15 *This is the living creature . . . Chebar.* The angelic beings seen carrying God's chariot in ch. 1 are now identified as *cherubims* (the KJV plural of "cherub"). The cherubim are closely associated with the majesty and glory of God and are the guardians of His holiness in the garden of Eden and the tabernacle/temple of Israel (28:13–14; 41:18,20,25; Gen. 3:24; Ex. 25:18–20; 26:1; 2 Sam. 6:2; 1 Kings 6:23–35; Pss. 18:10; 80:1; 99:1; Heb. 9:5).

10:18 *departed.* Part of judgment is the Lord's withdrawal of His presence.

Thoughts for Personal/Family Worship: Chapter 10

This vision could well have the title "Ichabod," which means either "there is no glory" or "where is the glory?" (1 Sam. 4:21). The glory of God had descended on the temple at its dedication, overwhelming all those who were there (1 Kings 8:10–11). But now the glory of God departed, and soon the temple would be destroyed. However, God's purpose of grace cannot be frustrated. The temple would be rebuilt, and that second temple

mounted up from the earth in my sight: when
they went out, the wheels also *were* beside them,
and *every one* stood at the door of the east gate
of the LORD's house; and the glory of the God of
Israel *was* over them above.
20 This *is* the living creature that I saw under the
God of Israel by the river of Chebar; and I knew
that they *were* the cherubims.
21 Every one had four faces apiece, and every one
four wings; and the likeness of the hands of a man
was under their wings.
22 And the likeness of their faces *was* the same
faces which I saw by the river of Chebar, their
appearances and themselves: they went every one
straight forward.

CHAPTER 11

MOREOVER the spirit lifted me up, and brought
me unto the east gate of the LORD's house, which
looketh eastward: and behold at the door of the
gate five and twenty men; among whom I saw
Jaazaniah the son of Azur, and Pelatiah the son of
Benaiah, princes of the people.
2 Then said he unto me, Son of man, these *are*
the men that devise mischief, and give wicked
counsel in this city:
3 Which say, *It is* not near; let us build houses:
this *city is* the caldron, and we *be* the flesh.
4 ¶ Therefore prophesy against them, prophesy,
O son of man.
5 And the Spirit of the LORD fell upon me, and said
unto me, Speak; Thus saith the LORD; Thus have ye
said, O house of Israel: for I know the things that
come into your mind, *every one of* them.
6 Ye have multiplied your slain in this city, and ye
have filled the streets thereof with the slain.
7 Therefore thus saith the Lord GOD; Your slain
whom ye have laid in the midst of it, they *are* the
flesh, and this *city is* the caldron: but I will bring
you forth out of the midst of it.
8 Ye have feared the sword; and I will bring a
sword upon you, saith the Lord GOD.
9 And I will bring you out of the midst thereof,
and deliver you into the hands of strangers, and
will execute judgments among you.
10 Ye shall fall by the sword; I will judge you in
the border of Israel; and ye shall know that I *am*
the LORD.
11 This *city* shall not be your caldron, neither
shall ye be the flesh in the midst thereof; *but* I will
judge you in the border of Israel:
12 And ye shall know that I *am* the LORD: for ye
have not walked in my statutes, neither executed
my judgments, but have done after the manners
of the heathen that *are* round about you.
13 ¶ And it came to pass, when I prophesied, that
Pelatiah the son of Benaiah died. Then fell I down
upon my face, and cried with a loud voice, and
said, Ah Lord GOD! wilt thou make a full end of
the remnant of Israel?
14 Again the word of the LORD came unto me,
saying,
15 Son of man, thy brethren, *even* thy brethren,
the men of thy kindred, and all the house of Israel
wholly, *are* they unto whom the inhabitants of
Jerusalem have said, Get you far from the LORD:
unto us is this land given in possession.
16 Therefore say, Thus saith the Lord GOD;
Although I have cast them far off among the hea-
then, and although I have scattered them among
the countries, yet will I be to them as a little sanc-
tuary in the countries where they shall come.
17 Therefore say, Thus saith the Lord GOD; I will
even gather you from the people, and assemble
you out of the countries where ye have been
scattered, and I will give you the land of Israel.
18 And they shall come thither, and they shall

would know a greater glory than the first. God would come to it, not in a mysterious cloud but in the person of the Son (Mal. 3:1). In union with Christ, the church is now the temple of the living God (1 Cor. 3:16–17). How tragic it is for a church today to have "Ichabod" written over it! Nothing is worse than to be a church without His presence, thinking of itself as rich and wise even while Christ is outside knocking to enter and calling it to repent (Rev. 3:17–20). How can a church avoid this tragedy?

Chapter 11: ***Ezekiel assures that judgment is coming in spite of some denials and looks to a time when God will restore from captivity.***

11:2 *devise.* Design, think, or contrive with studied thinking. *mischief.* Wickedness or evil.

11:3 *It.* The judgment of God. *this city is the caldron, and we be the flesh.* An image suggesting that the city was a sure defense: as flesh or meat remains in the pot, so the inhabitants believed they would remain unharmed in the city.

11:5 *fell upon.* empowered and enabled (2:2).

11:7 *flesh . . . cauldron.* The Lord turns their analogy against them. The only meat in the pot consisted of those already slain. The dead would remain, but the living were subject to exile.

11:9 *strangers.* Foreigners, referring specifically to the Babylonians.

11:11 *This city shall not be your caldron.* You will not be safe in the city.

11:13 *Pelatiah.* One of the leaders who denied the coming judgment (vv. 1–2).

11:15–16 The inhabitants of Jerusalem assessed the situation differently from the prophet. They thought they were the faithful to whom the land belonged. God claimed the opposite, as His presence was with those who had been scattered. *little sanctuary.* Or "sanctuary for a little while." The *sanctuary* or holy place ordinarily referred to the temple (5:11), but surprisingly God Himself promised to be the sanctuary of those exiled far from the sacred building until they returned. The essence of the sanctuary was not a building but God's

take away all the detestable things thereof and all
the abominations thereof from thence.
19 And I will give them one heart, and I will put
a new spirit within you; and I will take the stony
heart out of their flesh, and will give them an
heart of flesh:
20 That they may walk in my statutes, and keep
mine ordinances, and do them: and they shall be
my people, and I will be their God.
21 But *as for them* whose heart walketh after
the heart of their detestable things and their
abominations, I will recompense their way upon
their own heads, saith the Lord GOD.
22 ¶ Then did the cherubims lift up their wings,
and the wheels beside them; and the glory of the
God of Israel *was* over them above.
23 And the glory of the LORD went up from the
midst of the city, and stood upon the mountain
which *is* on the east side of the city.
24 ¶ Afterwards the spirit took me up, and
brought me in a vision by the Spirit of God into
Chaldea, to them of the captivity. So the vision
that I had seen went up from me.
25 Then I spake unto them of the captivity all the
things that the LORD had shewed me.

CHAPTER 12

THE word of the LORD also came unto me, saying,
2 Son of man, thou dwellest in the midst of a
rebellious house, which have eyes to see, and see
not; they have ears to hear, and hear not: for they
are a rebellious house.
3 Therefore, thou son of man, prepare thee stuff
for removing, and remove by day in their sight;
and thou shalt remove from thy place to another
place in their sight: it may be they will consider,
though they *be* a rebellious house.
4 Then shalt thou bring forth thy stuff by day in
their sight, as stuff for removing: and thou shalt
go forth at even in their sight, as they that go forth
into captivity.
5 Dig thou through the wall in their sight, and
carry out thereby.
6 In their sight shalt thou bear *it* upon *thy* shoul-
ders, *and* carry *it* forth in the twilight: thou shalt
cover thy face, that thou see not the ground: for
I have set thee *for* a sign unto the house of Israel.
7 And I did so as I was commanded: I brought
forth my stuff by day, as stuff for captivity, and
in the even I digged through the wall with mine
hand; I brought *it* forth in the twilight, *and* I bare
it upon *my* shoulder in their sight.

---

presence with His people by His Spirit (36:27; 37:14,26–28; Isa. 8:14; Hag. 2:4–5,9; Rev. 21:22).

11:18 Those who returned to the land after captivity would rid the land of idolatry.

11:19–20 The *heart* in Scripture is the center of the person's thoughts, motives, and identity and the source of his actions. God promised a work of sovereign grace (*I will give*) to radically transform people from the inside out unto true repentance (*new spirit*; 18:30–32). He would rescue them from spiritual death and take away their stubborn enslavement to idolatry (*stony heart*; cf. v. 21; 6:9; 14:3). He would give them spiritual life (*heart of flesh*) that would unify the people of God (*one heart*; Jer. 32:38–40) around a desire to obey the law of God (*walk in my statutes*; Deut. 30:6–8). This work of renewal fulfills the purpose of the covenant by bringing people into right relationship with God (*my people . . . their God*; see note at 36:28). The promise is later repeated (11:25–27) and vividly illustrated (37:1–28).

11:21 See note at 9:10.

11:22–23 *The glory of the LORD* departed from the threshold of the inner sanctuary (9:3) and went completely outside the city, abandoning Jerusalem and its temple. Yet He remained *the God of Israel* and would keep His covenant promises through the spiritual renewal of the people.

11:24 *into Chaldea*. To the captives in Babylon. *vision . . .went up from me*. The end of the vision.

11:25 *I spake all . . . the things that the LORD had shewed me*. The function of the prophet was to declare to others what God had revealed to him.

Thoughts for Personal/Family Worship: Chapter 11

1. **That God promised to be a "sanctuary" for His scattered people is precious and encouraging. God is full of mercy, and that mercy is often seen in the darkest and deepest trials. Fellowshipping with God does not depend on any location or special building. David desired to see the Lord's power and glory in the dry and thirsty land, just as he had seen it in the sanctuary (Ps. 63:1–2). In Christ, God's glory is no longer located at a particular building, but with all who worship Him in spirit and truth (John 4:21–24). Providence often takes the church to hard places, but God does not abandon her. No matter where you may be, draw near to God through Christ in unity with His people, and through His Spirit the Lord will be your sanctuary (Eph. 2:18).**
2. **Regeneration is a work that we need but only God can do (vv. 19–20). The old heart is stone cold, lifeless, insensitive, incapable of doing anything in the direction of God. God transforms the dead heart into a heart of flesh with vitality and spiritual impulses. This is the new birth (John 3:3–8; Titus 3:3–8) that produces obedience to God's Word (1 John 2:29; 3:9). Without this new heart man is doomed (v. 21). You must be born again. Are you? If so, rejoice in God's amazing grace. If not, then feel the danger of your impending damnation and cry out to Jesus Christ to save you from your sins.**

PARABLES AND TEACHINGS AGAINST JERUSALEM (12:1—24:27)

Chapter 12: *The Lord instructs Ezekiel to enact aspects of the coming captivity to refute those who denied the Word.*

Signs and Warnings of the Coming Exile (12:1–28)

12:2 This blindness and deafness were in themselves components of divine judgment (Isa. 6:9–10).

12:3 *stuff*. Vessels or instruments (vv. 4,7). *remove*. Move, as though going into exile.

12:4 *by day . . . go forth at even*. Suggesting a day-long process finishing at twilight.

12:6 *sign*. The prophet's actions were to be a visible object lesson to confirm the spoken word.

8 ¶ And in the morning came the word of the
LORD unto me, saying,
9 Son of man, hath not the house of Israel, the re-
bellious house, said unto thee, What doest thou?
10 Say thou unto them, Thus saith the Lord GOD;
This burden *concerneth* the prince in Jerusalem,
and all the house of Israel that *are* among them.
11 Say, I *am* your sign: like as I have done, so shall
it be done unto them: they shall remove *and* go
into captivity.
12 And the prince that *is* among them shall bear
upon *his* shoulder in the twilight, and shall go
forth: they shall dig through the wall to carry out
thereby: he shall cover his face, that he see not the
ground with *his* eyes.
13 My net also will I spread upon him, and he
shall be taken in my snare: and I will bring him to
Babylon *to* the land of the Chaldeans; yet shall he
not see it, though he shall die there.
14 And I will scatter toward every wind all that
are about him to help him, and all his bands; and
I will draw out the sword after them.
15 And they shall know that I *am* the LORD,
when I shall scatter them among the nations, and
disperse them in the countries.
16 But I will leave a few men of them from the
sword, from the famine, and from the pestilence;
that they may declare all their abominations
among the heathen whither they come; and they
shall know that I *am* the LORD.
17 ¶ Moreover the word of the LORD came to me,
saying,
18 Son of man, eat thy bread with quaking,
and drink thy water with trembling and with
carefulness;
19 And say unto the people of the land, Thus
saith the Lord GOD of the inhabitants of Jerusa-
lem, *and* of the land of Israel; They shall eat their
bread with carefulness, and drink their water with
astonishment, that her land may be desolate from
all that is therein, because of the violence of all
them that dwell therein.
20 And the cities that are inhabited shall be laid
waste, and the land shall be desolate; and ye shall
know that I *am* the LORD.
21 ¶ And the word of the LORD came unto me,
saying,
22 Son of man, what *is* that proverb *that* ye
have in the land of Israel, saying, The days are
prolonged, and every vision faileth?
23 Tell them therefore, Thus saith the Lord GOD;
I will make this proverb to cease, and they shall
no more use it as a proverb in Israel; but say unto
them, The days are at hand, and the effect of every
vision.
24 For there shall be no more any vain vision nor
flattering divination within the house of Israel.
25 For I *am* the LORD: I will speak, and the word
that I shall speak shall come to pass; it shall be
no more prolonged: for in your days, O rebellious
house, will I say the word, and will perform it,
saith the Lord GOD.
26 ¶ Again the word of the LORD came to me,
saying,
27 Son of man, behold, *they of* the house of Israel
say, The vision that he seeth *is* for many days *to
come*, and he prophesieth of the times *that are* far
off.
28 Therefore say unto them, Thus saith the Lord
GOD; There shall none of my words be prolonged
any more, but the word which I have spoken shall
be done, saith the Lord GOD.

CHAPTER 13

AND the word of the LORD came unto me, saying,
2 Son of man, prophesy against the prophets of
Israel that prophesy, and say thou unto them that

12:10 *prince.* A general title used of kings and leaders, not necessarily of the son of royalty (v. 12).
12:13 *yet shall he not see it, though he shall die there.* Zedekiah was blinded after witnessing the death of his sons (2 Kings 25:7; Jer. 32:5; 34:3–4; 52:10–11).
12:14 *bands.* Forces or army, a word found only in this prophecy.
12:15 *scatter.* Disperse violently.
12:18 *quaking.* Trembling. *trembling.* Fear and anxiety. *Carefulness.* Fear, dread, and anxious care (v. 19).
12:20 *laid waste.* Desolate.
12:22 *proverb.* Saying. *every vision faileth.* God's revelation or prophecy is not happening.
12:23 *effect of every vision.* The word of every prophecy, which will certainly and soon be fulfilled. God will not let His words fail (1 Kings 8:56; Matt. 5:18).
12:24 *vain.* Empty. *flattering divination.* Slippery or deceitful oracle, often connected with magic.
12:27 *far off.* They mocked at the prophecies (2 Peter 3:4).
12:28 *none . . . prolonged.* No more delay; fulfillment is impending.

Thoughts for Personal/Family Worship: Chapter 12

From the beginning of the nation's existence God had raised up prophets to warn the people of certain judgment if they broke the covenant and did not repent. For hundreds of years prophets were preaching the same message. Those who needed to repent rejected prophet after prophet and denied the threatened judgment because it had not yet happened. That is the same attitude expressed by the generation that would perish in the flood, and it will also be expressed by deniers of the second coming (2 Peter 3:4). Though God's judgments appear to move slowly, they move certainly. Justice delayed is not justice denied. The judgments of God should cause fear and trembling in the hearts of men. Sinners should take advantage of God's patience, which is designed to lead to repentance (Rom. 2:4), and flee the wrath to come. If judgment came today, would you be ready? Why or why not?

Chapter 13: *Ezekiel reproves the false prophets.*
False Prophets (13:1–23)

prophesy out of their own hearts, Hear ye the
word of the LORD;
3 Thus saith the Lord GOD; Woe unto the foolish
prophets, that follow their own spirit, and have
seen nothing!
4 O Israel, thy prophets are like the foxes in the
deserts.
5 Ye have not gone up into the gaps, neither made
up the hedge for the house of Israel to stand in the
battle in the day of the LORD.
6 They have seen vanity and lying divination,
saying, The LORD saith: and the LORD hath not
sent them: and they have made *others* to hope that
they would confirm the word.
7 Have ye not seen a vain vision, and have ye not
spoken a lying divination, whereas ye say, The
LORD saith *it*; albeit I have not spoken?
8 Therefore thus saith the Lord GOD; Because
ye have spoken vanity, and seen lies, therefore,
behold, I *am* against you, saith the Lord GOD.
9 And mine hand shall be upon the prophets that
see vanity, and that divine lies: they shall not be
in the assembly of my people, neither shall they
be written in the writing of the house of Israel,
neither shall they enter into the land of Israel; and
ye shall know that I *am* the Lord GOD.
10 ¶ Because, even because they have seduced my
people, saying, Peace; and *there was* no peace; and
one built up a wall, and, lo, others daubed it with
untempered *morter*:
11 Say unto them which daub *it* with untempered
morter, that it shall fall: there shall be an overflow-
ing shower; and ye, O great hailstones, shall fall;
and a stormy wind shall rend *it*.
12 Lo, when the wall is fallen, shall it not be said
unto you, Where *is* the daubing wherewith ye
have daubed *it*?
13 Therefore thus saith the Lord GOD; I will even
rend *it* with a stormy wind in my fury; and there
shall be an overflowing shower in mine anger, and
great hailstones in *my* fury to consume *it*.
14 So will I break down the wall that ye have
daubed with untempered *morter*, and bring
it down to the ground, so that the foundation
thereof shall be discovered, and it shall fall, and
ye shall be consumed in the midst thereof: and ye
shall know that I *am* the LORD.
15 Thus will I accomplish my wrath upon the
wall, and upon them that have daubed it with
untempered *morter*, and will say unto you, The
wall *is* no *more*, neither they that daubed it;
16 *To wit*, the prophets of Israel which prophesy
concerning Jerusalem, and which see visions of
peace for her, and *there is* no peace, saith the Lord
GOD.
17 ¶ Likewise, thou son of man, set thy face
against the daughters of thy people, which
prophesy out of their own heart; and prophesy
thou against them,
18 And say, Thus saith the Lord GOD; Woe to the
women that sew pillows to all armholes, and make
kerchiefs upon the head of every stature to hunt
souls! Will ye hunt the souls of my people, and
will ye save the souls alive *that come* unto you?
19 And will ye pollute me among my people for
handfuls of barley and for pieces of bread, to slay
the souls that should not die, and to save the souls
alive that should not live, by your lying to my
people that hear *your* lies?
20 Wherefore thus saith the Lord GOD; Behold, I
am against your pillows, wherewith ye there hunt
the souls to make *them* fly, and I will tear them
from your arms, and will let the souls go, *even* the
souls that ye hunt to make *them* fly.
21 Your kerchiefs also will I tear, and deliver my
people out of your hand, and they shall be no
more in your hand to be hunted; and ye shall
know that I *am* the LORD.

13:2–3 *out of their own hearts.* Prophets had authority to speak only what God had put into their mouths to speak (2:4–5; Ex. 4:14–15; 7:1–2). Speaking from their own imagination marked them as senseless (*foolish*) prophets.
13:4 *like the foxes in the deserts.* Most likely referring to jackals, scavengers. The simile stresses the selfish, greedy, and callous nature of the false prophets.
13:5 *gaps.* Breaches in the wall. *hedge.* Stone wall or fence that they left in disrepair. The prophets provided no defense for the people for the day of judgment.
13:6 *vanity.* Nothingness or emptiness. *lying divination.* Literally, "prediction of falsehood," a false forecast of the future (vv. 7,23).
13:8 *I am against you.* The sovereign Lord opposed the false prophets and their ministry (5:8).
13:9 *mine hand shall be upon the prophets.* In the sense of judgment and retribution. *divine.* Use omens or magic to seek hidden wisdom.
13:10–11 *seduced.* Led astray. *daubed it with untempered morter.* Plastered it with whitewash, expressing something that is attractive on the outside but lacking the strength to withstand the elements that will buffet it. *overflowing shower.* Torrential, gushing rain. *rend.* Tear apart.
13:14 *discovered.* Uncovered or revealed.
13:16 *To wit.* That is.
13:17 *daughters . . . which prophesy out of their own heart.* False prophetesses.
13:18 *pillows.* Bands for magic. *armholes.* Joints, perhaps of the wrist or elbow. These most likely refer to bracelets as a magic charm. *kerchiefs upon the head of every stature.* Scarfs or long veils covering the whole body that would fit any size (vv. 20,21). *hunt souls.* Capture people. The false prophetesses made these items to captivate the people.
13:19 *pollute.* Dishonor or profane the holy by bringing it down to the level of the ordinary. *handfuls of barley.* Perhaps meager wages.
13:20 *make them fly.* The Hebrew is uncertain; perhaps capture them like birds.
13:22 *sad.* Fearful or faint-hearted.

Thoughts for Personal/Family Worship: Chapter 13

It is part of a faithful ministry to expose error (Titus 1:9).

22 Because with lies ye have made the heart of
the righteous sad, whom I have not made sad;
and strengthened the hands of the wicked, that
he should not return from his wicked way, by
promising him life:
23 Therefore ye shall see no more vanity, nor
divine divinations: for I will deliver my people
out of your hand: and ye shall know that I *am* the
LORD.

CHAPTER 14

THEN came certain of the elders of Israel unto me,
and sat before me.
2 And the word of the LORD came unto me,
saying,
3 Son of man, these men have set up their idols
in their heart, and put the stumblingblock of their
iniquity before their face: should I be enquired of
at all by them?
4 Therefore speak unto them, and say unto them,
Thus saith the Lord GOD; Every man of the house
of Israel that setteth up his idols in his heart, and
putteth the stumblingblock of his iniquity before
his face, and cometh to the prophet; I the LORD
will answer him that cometh according to the
multitude of his idols;
5 That I may take the house of Israel in their own
heart, because they are all estranged from me
through their idols.
6 ¶ Therefore say unto the house of Israel, Thus
saith the Lord GOD; Repent, and turn *yourselves*
from your idols; and turn away your faces from
all your abominations.
7 For every one of the house of Israel, or of
the stranger that sojourneth in Israel, which
separateth himself from me, and setteth up his
idols in his heart, and putteth the stumblingblock
of his iniquity before his face, and cometh to a
prophet to enquire of him concerning me; I the
LORD will answer him by myself:
8 And I will set my face against that man, and
will make him a sign and a proverb, and I will cut
him off from the midst of my people; and ye shall
know that I *am* the LORD.
9 And if the prophet be deceived when he hath
spoken a thing, I the LORD have deceived that
prophet, and I will stretch out my hand upon
him, and will destroy him from the midst of my
people Israel.
10 And they shall bear the punishment of their
iniquity: the punishment of the prophet shall be
even as the punishment of him that seeketh *unto*
him;
11 That the house of Israel may go no more astray
from me, neither be polluted any more with all
their transgressions; but that they may be my peo-
ple, and I may be their God, saith the Lord GOD.
12 ¶ The word of the LORD came again to me,
saying,
13 Son of man, when the land sinneth against me
by trespassing grievously, then will I stretch out
mine hand upon it, and will break the staff of the
bread thereof, and will send famine upon it, and
will cut off man and beast from it:
14 Though these three men, Noah, Daniel, and
Job, were in it, they should deliver *but* their own
souls by their righteousness, saith the Lord GOD.
15 ¶ If I cause noisome beasts to pass through the
land, and they spoil it, so that it be desolate, that

Ezekiel's preaching stood in sharp contrast to the words of many of his fellow ministers in Babylon. Their lying words and empty visions lulled the people into a false sense of security. People naturally seek to hide from truths that expose sin and warn of judgment. But Ezekiel preached in such a way as to expose the false prophets for what they were, regardless of the consequences to his own popularity. False prophets appear in every age, and God is always against them. We must be careful to test what they say and not listen to those who do not speak according to God's Word. What false prophets does the church need to beware of in our day?

Chapter 14: *God exposes heart idolatry and promises a remnant.*

People of Idolatry beyond Intercession (14:1–23)

14:3 *idols in their heart.* The heart refers to the inner man, including the mind, will, and affections. An idol in the heart was no less serious than one set up in the temple (see note at 6:9). *the stumblingblock of their iniquity.* See note at 7:19 (vv. 4,7). *should I be enquired of at all by them.* Literally, "Should I indeed allow myself to be sought by them?" The Lord welcomes people to seek Him, but seeking God is a farce if it is done without repentance (Isa. 55:6–7).

14:5 *estranged.* Turned aside or gone away.
14:6 *Repent.* Turn or reverse "direction," the principal Old Testament word for repentance. *turn.* Withdraw from. *abominations.* Disgusting and detestable things, a frequent designation for idols.
14:7 *stranger.* Foreigner or alien. *sojourneth.* To dwell as a resident alien. *separateth.* To turn aside.
14:9 *I . . . have deceived that prophet.* The Lord gave the false prophet over to delusion as the first step toward destroying him (1 Kings 22:19–22; Jer. 4:10). God cannot lie (Num. 23:19).
14:10 *bear.* Carry, take, or endure.
14:11 *go . . . astray.* Wander sinfully. *polluted.* Defiled. *transgressions.* Sins and iniquities.
14:13–19 *famine . . . sword . . . pestilence.* The threefold judgment already pronounced by Ezekiel (5:1–17).
14:13 *staff of the bread.* A pole for stacking bread.
14:14 *Noah, Daniel, and Job.* Evidence that these men, known for their righteousness, were real, historical persons. Daniel was contemporary with Ezekiel but nonetheless had already earned an impeccable reputation for his testimony. *deliver . . . their own souls by their righteousness.* Each individual is accountable before God, but only Christ can save others by His own righteousness (vv. 16,20; Isa. 53:11; 2 Cor. 5:21).
14:15 *noisome.* Hurtful or deadly (v. 21). *spoil.* Depopulate or bereave.

no man may pass through because of the beasts:
16 *Though* these three men *were* in it, *as* I live,
saith the Lord GOD, they shall deliver neither sons
nor daughters; they only shall be delivered, but
the land shall be desolate.
17 ¶ Or *if* I bring a sword upon that land, and say,
Sword, go through the land; so that I cut off man
and beast from it:
18 Though these three men *were* in it, *as* I live,
saith the Lord GOD, they shall deliver neither sons
nor daughters, but they only shall be delivered
themselves.
19 ¶ Or *if* I send a pestilence into that land, and
pour out my fury upon it in blood, to cut off from
it man and beast:
20 Though Noah, Daniel, and Job, *were* in it, *as* I
live, saith the Lord GOD, they shall deliver neither
son nor daughter; they shall *but* deliver their own
souls by their righteousness.
21 For thus saith the Lord GOD; How much
more when I send my four sore judgments upon
Jerusalem, the sword, and the famine, and the
noisome beast, and the pestilence, to cut off from
it man and beast?
22 ¶ Yet, behold, therein shall be left a remnant
that shall be brought forth, *both* sons and
daughters: behold, they shall come forth unto
you, and ye shall see their way and their doings:
and ye shall be comforted concerning the evil that
I have brought upon Jerusalem, *even* concerning
all that I have brought upon it.
23 And they shall comfort you, when ye see their
ways and their doings: and ye shall know that I
have not done without cause all that I have done
in it, saith the Lord GOD.

CHAPTER 15

AND the word of the LORD came unto me, saying,
2 Son of man, What is the vine tree more than
any tree, *or than* a branch which is among the
trees of the forest?
3 Shall wood be taken thereof to do any work?
or will *men* take a pin of it to hang any vessel
thereon?
4 Behold, it is cast into the fire for fuel; the fire
devoureth both the ends of it, and the midst of it
is burned. Is it meet for *any* work?
5 Behold, when it was whole, it was meet for no
work: how much less shall it be meet yet for *any*
work, when the fire hath devoured it, and it is
burned?
6 ¶ Therefore thus saith the Lord GOD; As the
vine tree among the trees of the forest, which I
have given to the fire for fuel, so will I give the
inhabitants of Jerusalem.
7 And I will set my face against them; they shall
go out from *one* fire, and *another* fire shall devour
them; and ye shall know that I *am* the LORD, when
I set my face against them.
8 And I will make the land desolate, because they
have committed a trespass, saith the Lord GOD.

14:21 *sore.* Severe.
14:22 *remnant.* A small group of faithful people. *evil.* Calamity.

Thoughts for Personal/Family Worship: Chapter 14

We must flee from idolatry (1 Cor. 10:14; 1 John 5:21). Yet this is more subtle than we may realize. Although idolatry revolves around objects and images, it is rooted in the human heart (vv. 3–4,7). Therefore it is not enough to get rid of the physical thing we have made into an idol, although this must often be done (Matt. 5:28–29). As John Calvin said, the human heart is an idol factory. To put idolatry to death, we must deal with fears and desires that have grown far larger than any created thing deserves (Col. 3:5). Whenever we love something or someone in a way that is not dominated by love for God, that love has degenerated into a proud and idolatrous lust (1 John 2:15–16). At the heart of the gospel is the call to turn away from all such idols and to give our obedience and hope to the living God (1 Thess. 1:9–10). That is the only way to escape God's wrath. Trusting in Christ requires us to turn from our deepest idolatry: the false god of our self-righteousness. Why is this so hard? Why is it so good?

Parables of the Vine, the Wife, and the Eagles (15:1—17:24)
Chapter 15: *The Lord compares the nation to a worthless vine.*
15:2 *vine tree.* A creeping or climbing plant, often a wild growth but sometimes a grapevine.
15:3 *pin.* A peg for hanging something.
15:4 *meet.* Suitable or useful (v. 5). The wood of a vine is useless for construction work. If the vine produces no good fruit, the wood serves only as kindling (John 15:6; Heb. 6:7–8).
15:6 *so will I give the inhabitants of Jerusalem.* The Lord explained the analogy: Jerusalem, as the vine, was good for nothing but the fire of judgment.
15:7 *go out from one fire, and another fire . . . devour them.* Escape would be impossible; they would be like dry kindling to feed the flame.
15:8 *committed a trespass.* Literally, "treacherously performed a treacherous act." This describes sin—disloyalty and infidelity—as a violation of legal and covenant obligations, a fitting description of the nation's idolatry and forsaking the Lord (16:1–63).

Thoughts for Personal/Family Worship: Chapter 15

The nation's description as a wild and useless growth explains why judgment was necessary: sin had left the people spiritually fruitless and consequently suitable only as fuel for the fire. To see the full tragedy, compare this with Isaiah's song of the vineyard (Isa. 5:1–7). The Lord had planted His people as a noble vine and made every provision for them to produce the fruit of righteousness and justice. However, in spite of all the privileges given and much patience, they produced only the bad fruit of sin. They had spurned their privileges and had become good for nothing but kindling. This sounds a sober warning to all whom God has placed in a

CHAPTER 16

AGAIN the word of the LORD came unto me,
saying,
2 Son of man, cause Jerusalem to know her
abominations,
3 And say, Thus saith the Lord GOD unto Jeru-
salem; Thy birth and thy nativity *is* of the land
of Canaan; thy father *was* an Amorite, and thy
mother an Hittite.
4 And *as for* thy nativity, in the day thou wast
born thy navel was not cut, neither wast thou
washed in water to supple *thee*; thou wast not
salted at all, nor swaddled at all.
5 None eye pitied thee, to do any of these unto
thee, to have compassion upon thee; but thou
wast cast out in the open field, to the lothing of
thy person, in the day that thou wast born.
6 ¶ And when I passed by thee, and saw thee
polluted in thine own blood, I said unto thee
when thou wast in thy blood, Live; yea, I said unto
thee *when thou wast* in thy blood, Live.
7 I have caused thee to multiply as the bud of the
field, and thou hast increased and waxen great,
and thou art come to excellent ornaments: *thy*
breasts are fashioned, and thine hair is grown,
whereas thou *wast* naked and bare.
8 Now when I passed by thee, and looked upon
thee, behold, thy time *was* the time of love; and
I spread my skirt over thee, and covered thy
nakedness: yea, I sware unto thee, and entered
into a covenant with thee, saith the Lord GOD,
and thou becamest mine.
9 Then washed I thee with water; yea, I throughly
washed away thy blood from thee, and I anointed
thee with oil.
10 I clothed thee also with broidered work, and
shod thee with badgers' skin, and I girded thee
about with fine linen, and I covered thee with silk.
11 I decked thee also with ornaments, and I put
bracelets upon thy hands, and a chain on thy neck.
12 And I put a jewel on thy forehead, and earrings
in thine ears, and a beautiful crown upon thine
head.
13 Thus wast thou decked with gold and silver;
and thy raiment *was of* fine linen, and silk, and
broidered work; thou didst eat fine flour, and
honey, and oil: and thou wast exceeding beautiful,
and thou didst prosper into a kingdom.
14 And thy renown went forth among the
heathen for thy beauty: for it *was* perfect through
my comeliness, which I had put upon thee, saith
the Lord GOD.
15 ¶ But thou didst trust in thine own beauty,
and playedst the harlot because of thy renown,
and pouredst out thy fornications on every one
that passed by; his it was.
16 And of thy garments thou didst take, and
deckedst thy high places with divers colours, and
playedst the harlot thereupon: *the like things* shall
not come, neither shall it be *so*.
17 Thou hast also taken thy fair jewels of my
gold and of my silver, which I had given thee,
and madest to thyself images of men, and didst
commit whoredom with them,

position of spiritual privileges, such as a godly home or a gospel-preaching church. Do not despise what God has given you, or your judgment will be all the worse. How can those with such privileges use them well?

Chapter 16: ***The Lord uses an allegory to trace the nation's history, highlighting their heinous sins against the backdrop of God's grace.***

16:2 *abominations.* Disgusting and detestable things; a fitting designation for idolatry, which is so offensive to the Lord (vv. 22,36). What follows is allegory, an extended analogy to teach literal truths. The details are symbolic, not literal, though they convey actual facts.

16:3 *Thy birth and thy nativity.* The origin and circumstances of birth. *Canaan . . . Amorite . . . Hittite.* They were born foreigners to grace, morally depraved, and enemies of God. Everyone is born a spiritual heathen, even if a physical descendant of Abraham (Acts 7:51; Rom. 2:29).

16:4–5 *navel.* Umbilical cord. *neither wast thou washed in water to supple.* Literally, "you were not washed for purification." *salted.* Done for antiseptic protection of a newborn. *swaddled.* Wrapped. *lothing.* Disgust or disdain. The pitiful picture of a child exposed to die shows the helpless state of fallen man in his sin and misery.

16:6 *polluted in thine own blood.* Literally, "kicking about or wallowing in your blood," struggling in the fluids from the birth. *Live.* A command of divine and irresistible power that gives the life that it commands (37:5,9–10; John 5:25–26; 11:43–44).

16:7 *waxen great.* Grew great and important. The Lord's gracious intervention not only spared the infant's life but provided for growth and maturity.

16:8 *spread my skirt.* A sign of covenant love, as in betrothal and marriage (Ruth 3:9). The allegory has shifted its imagery to depict a grown woman. The point is not chronology but spiritual reality: the Lord graciously changed her relationship from a Canaanite to His bride.

16:9 *washed I thee . . . anointed thee with oil.* Made you attractive (Ruth 3:3), symbolic of God's graces in forgiving sins, cleansing guilt, and bestowing righteousness and honor.

16:10 *broidered work.* Something that is colorfully woven (vv. 13,18). *shod thee with badgers' skin.* Provided you with leather sandals. The animal from which the leather is made is uncertain. *girded . . . fine linen.* Wrapped you in linen. *silk.* Some sort of fine and costly material used for garments.

16:11 *decked.* Adorned (vv. 13,16).

16:12 *jewel on thy forehead.* Most likely a ring for the nose (Isa. 3:21). *beautiful crown.* Literally, "a garland of beauty."

16:14 *renown.* Reputation, fame, or glory. *through my comeliness.* On account of my majesty.

16:15 *trust.* Feel secure or confident. *playedst the harlot.* Participated in sinful sexual activity. *pouredst out.* Exercised no restraint in obscene behavior.

16:16 *high places.* The places of idolatry. *divers.* Diverse or various.

16:17 *my gold . . . my silver . . . madest to thyself images of men.* The horrible irony of idolatry is that people take God's creations, which He gives them for their thankful enjoyment

18 And tookest thy broidered garments, and
coveredst them: and thou hast set mine oil and
mine incense before them.
19 My meat also which I gave thee, fine flour, and
oil, and honey, *wherewith* I fed thee, thou hast
even set it before them for a sweet savour: and
thus it was, saith the Lord GOD.
20 Moreover thou hast taken thy sons and thy
daughters, whom thou hast borne unto me,
and these hast thou sacrificed unto them to be
devoured. *Is this* of thy whoredoms a small matter,
21 That thou hast slain my children, and delivered
them to cause them to pass through *the fire* for
them?
22 And in all thine abominations and thy
whoredoms thou hast not remembered the days
of thy youth, when thou wast naked and bare, *and*
wast polluted in thy blood.
23 And it came to pass after all thy wickedness,
(woe, woe unto thee! saith the Lord GOD;)
24 *That* thou hast also built unto thee an eminent
place, and hast made thee an high place in every
street.
25 Thou hast built thy high place at every head of
the way, and hast made thy beauty to be abhorred,
and hast opened thy feet to every one that passed
by, and multiplied thy whoredoms.
26 Thou hast also committed fornication with
the Egyptians thy neighbours, great of flesh; and
hast increased thy whoredoms, to provoke me to
anger.
27 Behold, therefore I have stretched out my hand
over thee, and have diminished thine ordinary
food, and delivered thee unto the will of them that
hate thee, the daughters of the Philistines, which
are ashamed of thy lewd way.
28 Thou hast played the whore also with the
Assyrians, because thou wast unsatiable; yea, thou
hast played the harlot with them, and yet couldest
not be satisfied.
29 Thou hast moreover multiplied thy fornica-
tion in the land of Canaan unto Chaldea; and yet
thou wast not satisfied herewith.
30 How weak is thine heart, saith the Lord GOD,
seeing thou doest all these *things*, the work of an
imperious whorish woman;
31 In that thou buildest thine eminent place in
the head of every way, and makest thine high
place in every street; and hast not been as an
harlot, in that thou scornest hire;
32 *But as* a wife that committeth adultery, *which*
taketh strangers instead of her husband!
33 They give gifts to all whores: but thou givest
thy gifts to all thy lovers, and hirest them, that
they may come unto thee on every side for thy
whoredom.
34 And the contrary is in thee from *other* women
in thy whoredoms, whereas none followeth thee
to commit whoredoms: and in that thou givest
a reward, and no reward is given unto thee,
therefore thou art contrary.
35 ¶ Wherefore, O harlot, hear the word of the
LORD:
36 Thus saith the Lord GOD; Because thy filthiness
was poured out, and thy nakedness discovered
through thy whoredoms with thy lovers, and with
all the idols of thy abominations, and by the blood
of thy children, which thou didst give unto them;
37 Behold, therefore I will gather all thy lovers,
with whom thou hast taken pleasure, and all
them that thou hast loved, with all *them* that thou
hast hated; I will even gather them round about
against thee, and will discover thy nakedness unto
them, that they may see all thy nakedness.
38 And I will judge thee, as women that break
wedlock and shed blood are judged; and I will

(1 Tim. 4:4; 6:17), and pervert them into replacements for God (Rom. 1:23). *whoredom.* Sinful sexual activity.

16:18 *set mine oil and mine incense before them.* What was intended for holy purposes was set on the idolatrous altars.

16:19 *meat.* Food of any kind.

16:20 *unto them.* To the images of false gods, to which they sacrificed their children.

16:21 *slain.* Killed as in sacrifice. *delivered.* Given. *cause them to pass through the fire for them.* The pagan custom of placing children in the arms of images for burning as child sacrifices.

16:22 *not remembered.* They refused to think about and take to heart God's works of salvation in their history as a nation (see note at 6:9). Thinking guides behavior. Thinking rightly about God leads to proper living; thinking wrongly or not thinking at all leads to sin.

16:24 *eminent place.* A mound or rounded molding on an altar. *high place in every street.* A pagan shrine in the broad or open places, indicating the public nature of the idolatry (vv. 31,39).

16:25 *opened thy feet.* A euphemism for promiscuity and eagerness to engage in spiritual adultery.

16:27 *diminished thine ordinary food.* Literally, "cut down your boundaries." Shameful behavior. So horrific was their behavior that even pagans were embarrassed by them.

16:29 *Canaan unto Chaldea.* Their idolatry extended from the land of Canaan to Babylonia.

16:30 *How weak is thine heart.* The heart was hot with fever. *imperious whorish.* Domineering and adulterous.

16:31–34 Their harlotry was not for payment but out of unabashed and insatiable lust. So perverse were their desires that although they played the harlot, they paid for services rather than receiving payment, behavior that was out of the ordinary. Israel pursued false gods and idols at their own expense, even when they received no perceived benefit. Such is the slavery of idolatry.

16:32 *instead of her husband.* Israel's idolatry was more aggravated because they were in covenant with God.

16:36 *filthiness was poured out.* They abandoned feminine modesty in their lust. *discovered.* Uncovered by obscene practice.

16:37 *discover thy nakedness.* God would give them over to the shame of their sins.

16:38 *break wedlock.* Commit adultery (Lev. 20:10; Deut. 22:22). *shed blood.* Commit murder (Gen. 9:6; Ex. 21:12).

give thee blood in fury and jealousy.
39 And I will also give thee into their hand, and
they shall throw down thine eminent place, and
shall break down thy high places: they shall strip
thee also of thy clothes, and shall take thy fair
jewels, and leave thee naked and bare.
40 They shall also bring up a company against
thee, and they shall stone thee with stones, and
thrust thee through with their swords.
41 And they shall burn thine houses with fire,
and execute judgments upon thee in the sight of
many women: and I will cause thee to cease from
playing the harlot, and thou also shalt give no hire
any more.
42 So will I make my fury toward thee to rest, and
my jealousy shall depart from thee, and I will be
quiet, and will be no more angry.
43 Because thou hast not remembered the days of
thy youth, but hast fretted me in all these *things*;
behold, therefore I also will recompense thy way
upon *thine* head, saith the Lord GOD: and thou
shalt not commit this lewdness above all thine
abominations.
44 ¶ Behold, every one that useth proverbs shall
use *this* proverb against thee, saying, As *is* the
mother, *so is* her daughter.
45 Thou *art* thy mother's daughter, that lotheth
her husband and her children; and thou *art* the
sister of thy sisters, which lothed their husbands
and their children: your mother *was* an Hittite,
and your father an Amorite.
46 And thine elder sister *is* Samaria, she and her
daughters that dwell at thy left hand: and thy
younger sister, that dwelleth at thy right hand, *is*
Sodom and her daughters.
47 Yet hast thou not walked after their ways, nor
done after their abominations: but, as *if that were*
a very little *thing*, thou wast corrupted more than
they in all thy ways.
48 *As* I live, saith the Lord GOD, Sodom thy sister
hath not done, she nor her daughters, as thou hast
done, thou and thy daughters.
49 Behold, this was the iniquity of thy sister
Sodom, pride, fulness of bread, and abundance of
idleness was in her and in her daughters, neither
did she strengthen the hand of the poor and needy.
50 And they were haughty, and committed
abomination before me: therefore I took them
away as I saw *good*.
51 Neither hath Samaria committed half of thy
sins; but thou hast multiplied thine abominations
more than they, and hast justified thy sisters in all
thine abominations which thou hast done.
52 Thou also, which hast judged thy sisters,
bear thine own shame for thy sins that thou
hast committed more abominable than they:
they are more righteous than thou: yea, be thou
confounded also, and bear thy shame, in that
thou hast justified thy sisters.
53 When I shall bring again their captivity, the
captivity of Sodom and her daughters, and the
captivity of Samaria and her daughters, then *will
I bring again* the captivity of thy captives in the
midst of them:
54 That thou mayest bear thine own shame, and
mayest be confounded in all that thou hast done,
in that thou art a comfort unto them.
55 When thy sisters, Sodom and her daughters,
shall return to their former estate, and Samaria
and her daughters shall return to their former
estate, then thou and thy daughters shall return
to your former estate.
56 For thy sister Sodom was not mentioned by
thy mouth in the day of thy pride,
57 Before thy wickedness was discovered, as at
the time of *thy* reproach of the daughters of Syria,
and all *that are* round about her, the daughters of
the Philistines, which despise thee round about.
58 Thou hast borne thy lewdness and thine
abominations, saith the LORD.
59 For thus saith the Lord GOD; I will even deal
with thee as thou hast done, which hast despised
the oath in breaking the covenant.
60 ¶ Nevertheless I will remember my covenant
with thee in the days of thy youth, and I will
establish unto thee an everlasting covenant.
61 Then thou shalt remember thy ways, and be
ashamed, when thou shalt receive thy sisters,
thine elder and thy younger: and I will give them
unto thee for daughters, but not by thy covenant.

16:40 *company.* A group assembled for war or invasion.
16:41 *I will cause thee to cease from playing the harlot.* Judgment would bring Israel's open idolatry to an end.
16:43 *not remembered.* See note at v. 22. *fretted.* Disturbed or made to tremble.
16:44–49 The Israelites were worse than the Canaanites and more corrupt than even *Samaria* and *Sodom*. Israel's sin was more aggravated and abominable because of God's covenant with them.
16:44 *every one that useth proverbs shall use this proverb.* They would become infamous for their sins.
16:45 *thy mother's daughter.* See note at v. 3. *lotheth.* Detests, rejects.
16:46 *Samaria.* The northern kingdom, already judged for its sins. *Sodom.* The ancient wicked city judged for its gross immorality (Gen. 19).
16:51–52 *justified thy sisters.* Their sins made Samaria appear innocent by comparison.
16:54 *confounded.* Humiliated or ashamed.
16:59 *despised the oath in breaking the covenant.* Israel had held God's Word in contempt and violated His covenant with them.
16:60 *remember my covenant.* God's remembering means that He will faithfully keep His promises (Gen. 9:15–16; Ex. 2:24; 6:5; Lev. 26:42,45; Pss. 105:8; 106:45; Jer. 14:21; Luke 1:72). *everlasting covenant.* See 37:26; Jer. 32:40.
16:61 *not by thy covenant.* Not by any covenant the Jews would impose but by God's own covenant.

62 And I will establish my covenant with thee;
and thou shalt know that I *am* the LORD:
63 That thou mayest remember, and be con-
founded, and never open thy mouth any more
because of thy shame, when I am pacified toward
thee for all that thou hast done, saith the Lord GOD.

CHAPTER 17

AND the word of the LORD came unto me, saying,
2 Son of man, put forth a riddle, and speak a
parable unto the house of Israel;
3 And say, Thus saith the Lord GOD; A great eagle
with great wings, longwinged, full of feathers,
which had divers colours, came unto Lebanon,
and took the highest branch of the cedar:
4 He cropped off the top of his young twigs, and
carried it into a land of traffick; he set it in a city
of merchants.
5 He took also of the seed of the land, and planted
it in a fruitful field; he placed *it* by great waters,
and set it *as* a willow tree.
6 And it grew, and became a spreading vine
of low stature, whose branches turned toward
him, and the roots thereof were under him: so it
became a vine, and brought forth branches, and
shot forth sprigs.
7 There was also another great eagle with great
wings and many feathers: and, behold, this vine
did bend her roots toward him, and shot forth her
branches toward him, that he might water it by
the furrows of her plantation.
8 It was planted in a good soil by great waters,
that it might bring forth branches, and that it
might bear fruit, that it might be a goodly vine.
9 Say thou, Thus saith the Lord GOD; Shall it pros-
per? shall he not pull up the roots thereof, and cut
off the fruit thereof, that it wither? it shall wither in
all the leaves of her spring, even without great power
or many people to pluck it up by the roots thereof.
10 Yea, behold, *being* planted, shall it prosper? shall
it not utterly wither, when the east wind toucheth
it? it shall wither in the furrows where it grew.
11 ¶ Moreover the word of the LORD came unto
me, saying,
12 Say now to the rebellious house, Know ye not
what these *things mean*? tell *them*, Behold, the
king of Babylon is come to Jerusalem, and hath
taken the king thereof, and the princes thereof,
and led them with him to Babylon;
13 And hath taken of the king's seed, and made
a covenant with him, and hath taken an oath of
him: he hath also taken the mighty of the land:
14 That the kingdom might be base, that it
might not lift itself up, *but* that by keeping of his
covenant it might stand.
15 But he rebelled against him in sending his
ambassadors into Egypt, that they might give him
horses and much people. Shall he prosper? shall
he escape that doeth such *things*? or shall he break
the covenant, and be delivered?
16 *As* I live, saith the Lord GOD, surely in the

16:63 *pacified toward thee.* Reconciled and at peace.

Thoughts for Personal/Family Worship: Chapter 16

1. **Idolatry is a personal attack upon the honor of God, just as adultery is a personal attack upon the honor of one's spouse, for in both cases one despises the person to whom one owes great love and wastes that love on one to whom it does not belong. The horrors of "whoredom," with its disgraceful behavior and betrayal of one's closest companion, should move us to grieve over our sins against God. Beneath the conflicts and lusts of men is a corrupt heart that should provoke us all to cry out, "We have been spiritual adulterers!" Therefore let us humble ourselves, as James exhorts us, and submit to God with mourning over our unfaithfulness to Him who has loved us most (James 4:1–10).**
2. **The solution to spiritual adultery is summed up in the word "remember" (vv. 22,43,61,63). We must remember God's past acts of love in creating us, sustaining us, and performing great deeds of mercy, supremely the death of His Son, and we must respond to His love with amazed and grateful love. We must remember our horrible sins against God, and we must respond with grief and hatred for sin, along with a sincere desire for new obedience. If we remember these things with faith, love, and repentance, we will discover that God also will "remember" His covenant promises and establish an everlasting relationship with us so that we may truly know Him. Indeed, our gratitude and love will overflow as we realize that our remembering Him was caused by His first remembering us (vv. 60–63).**

Chapter 17: *Using a parable of two eagles, Ezekiel addresses Zedekiah's rebellion and the promise of a glorious kingdom.*

17:2 *riddle.* A puzzle or hard question. *Parable.* A proverb often involving comparisons.
17:3 *divers.* Diverse or varied. *Lebanon.* The land north of Israel, noted for its magnificent *cedar* trees.
17:4 *cropped.* Plucked or cut off. *land of traffick.* Literally, "the land of Canaan," which can refer to a place of commerce. *city of merchants.* A place of trade.
17:6 *spreading vine of low stature.* The transplant grew profusely but without height.
17:7 *water it by the furrows of her plantation.* Irrigate the garden where it was planted.
17:8 *planted.* Specifically, transplanted (v. 10).
17:10 *east wind.* Usually hot and destructive (Jonah 4:8).
17:12 *Know ye not what these things mean?* A rhetorical question designed to introduce the explanation of the parable. *king of Babylon.* Nebuchadnezzar, depicted by the first great eagle (2 Kings 24:11–16). *the king thereof.* Jeconiah, the king of Jerusalem. *princes.* Nobles or leaders, not sons of royalty. The king and nobles correspond to the transplanted branch.
17:13 *made a covenant with him.* Nebuchadnezzar set up Zedekiah as a puppet king (2 Kings 24:17–20).
17:14 *base.* Kept in a low or dependent state (this is the significance of the low vine). *by keeping of his covenant it might stand.* By keeping the covenant or agreement, it would continue a kingdom.
17:15 *rebelled.* See 2 Kings 24:20. This relates to the branches

place *where* the king *dwelleth* that made him king,
whose oath he despised, and whose covenant he
brake, *even* with him in the midst of Babylon he
shall die.
17 Neither shall Pharaoh with *his* mighty army
and great company make for him in the war, by
casting up mounts, and building forts, to cut off
many persons:
18 Seeing he despised the oath by breaking the
covenant, when, lo, he had given his hand, and
hath done all these *things*, he shall not escape.
19 Therefore thus saith the Lord GOD; *As* I live,
surely mine oath that he hath despised, and
my covenant that he hath broken, even it will I
recompense upon his own head.
20 And I will spread my net upon him, and he
shall be taken in my snare, and I will bring him
to Babylon, and will plead with him there for his
trespass that he hath trespassed against me.
21 And all his fugitives with all his bands shall
fall by the sword, and they that remain shall be
scattered toward all winds: and ye shall know that
I the LORD have spoken *it*.
22 ¶ Thus saith the Lord GOD; I will also take
of the highest branch of the high cedar, and will
set *it*; I will crop off from the top of his young
twigs a tender one, and will plant *it* upon an high
mountain and eminent:
23 In the mountain of the height of Israel will I
plant it: and it shall bring forth boughs, and bear
fruit, and be a goodly cedar: and under it shall
dwell all fowl of every wing; in the shadow of the
branches thereof shall they dwell.
24 And all the trees of the field shall know that I
the LORD have brought down the high tree, have
exalted the low tree, have dried up the green tree,
and have made the dry tree to flourish: I the LORD
have spoken and have done *it*.

CHAPTER 18

THE word of the LORD came unto me again,
saying,
2 What mean ye, that ye use this proverb
concerning the land of Israel, saying, The fathers
have eaten sour grapes, and the children's teeth
are set on edge?
3 *As* I live, saith the Lord GOD, ye shall not have
occasion any more to use this proverb in Israel.
4 Behold, all souls are mine; as the soul of the
father, so also the soul of the son is mine: the soul
that sinneth, it shall die.
5 ¶ But if a man be just, and do that which is
lawful and right,
6 *And* hath not eaten upon the mountains,
neither hath lifted up his eyes to the idols of

---

of the vine turning toward the second eagle and seeking assistance.

17:17 *casting up mounts, and building forts.* Building ramparts and fortifications in order to resist the Babylonians and their siege of Jerusalem.

17:18 *given his hand.* Confirmed the promise, which he later broke.

17:19 The Lord calls it His *oath* and *covenant* because it was established before Him and sworn in His name (2 Chron. 36:13). *recompense.* Repay or requite.

17:20 *I will spread my net upon him.* God sovereignly gave Zedekiah to the Babylonians (cf. Dan. 1:2). *plead with him.* Enter into controversy, a legal expression.

17:21 *fugitives.* Refugees. *bands.* Troops or soldiers.

17:22 *I will also take of the highest branch . . . and will set it.* As Nebuchadnezzar had taken people from Judah and planted them in Babylon (vv. 3–4,12), so the Lord promised that He would sovereignly make a planting of His own. *high mountain.* An image of God's kingdom (20:40; 28:14; 40:2; Isa. 2:2–3; 11:9; Dan. 2:34–35,44; Rev. 21:10). *eminent.* High, exalted.

17:23 *goodly.* Large or excellent. *under it . . . in the shadow of the branches.* A picture of safety and protection.

17:24 *dried up the green . . . made the dry tree to flourish.* It seemed with the Babylonian exile that the kingdom of David had dried up and become defunct, but God had promised to David unconditionally that a king would be forever on the throne (2 Sam. 7:12–15). With the coming of Jesus, the dried-up tree of David's dynasty flourished (Isa. 11:1). *I the LORD have spoken and have done it.* God performs His decree so that His Word will prove true.

Thoughts for Personal/Family Worship: Chapter 17

1. God expects people to keep their word and fulfill their promises, even promises made with unbelievers and pagans (vv. 16–19). While no promise or oath can bind us to commit sin, we must never violate our commitments just because a better opportunity comes alone (vv. 7,17).

2. "I the LORD have spoken and have done it" (v. 24). God controls all events for His own glory. Nebuchadnezzar was a great eagle from every human perspective; his kingdom was majestic and his power unmatched. Yet he was nothing apart from God. Babylon was the means God used to inflict His purposed judgment on Judah. The God who ordered all the events in the sixth century BC still sits on the same throne governing the affairs of states throughout the world. In His own sovereign way God advances the kingdom of Christ. How does that encourage you today?

Chapter 18: *Ezekiel underscores personal responsibility and shows that God's justice is always equitable.*

Principle of Responsibility (18:1–32)

18:2 *The fathers have eaten sour grapes, and the children's teeth are set on edge.* A proverb indicating that one person or one generation suffers from the sins of those of an earlier generation. Ezekiel's contemporaries blamed preceding generations for the calamity they were experiencing. Verses 5–18 illustrate the error of their thinking.

18:4 *all souls are mine.* Every person belongs to God and is personally accountable to Him (Rom. 14:12). *the soul that sinneth, it shall die.* The person who sins earns death (Rom. 6:23).

18:6 *eaten upon the mountains.* Where temples and altars were raised to false gods. *defiled.* Made unclean or impure with adultery of fornication. *menstruous woman.* A woman ceremonially unclean in her monthly cycle (Lev. 15:19).

the house of Israel, neither hath defiled his
neighbour's wife, neither hath come near to a
menstruous woman,
7 And hath not oppressed any, *but* hath restored
to the debtor his pledge, hath spoiled none by
violence, hath given his bread to the hungry, and
hath covered the naked with a garment;
8 He *that* hath not given forth upon usury, neither
hath taken any increase, *that* hath withdrawn his
hand from iniquity, hath executed true judgment
between man and man,
9 Hath walked in my statutes, and hath kept my
judgments, to deal truly; he *is* just, he shall surely
live, saith the Lord GOD.
10 ¶ If he beget a son *that is* a robber, a shedder
of blood, and *that* doeth the like to *any* one of
these *things*,
11 And that doeth not any of those *duties*, but
even hath eaten upon the mountains, and defiled
his neighbour's wife,
12 Hath oppressed the poor and needy, hath
spoiled by violence, hath not restored the pledge,
and hath lifted up his eyes to the idols, hath
committed abomination,
13 Hath given forth upon usury, and hath taken
increase: shall he then live? he shall not live: he
hath done all these abominations; he shall surely
die; his blood shall be upon him.
14 ¶ Now, lo, *if* he beget a son, that seeth all his
father's sins which he hath done, and considereth,
and doeth not such like,
15 *That* hath not eaten upon the mountains,
neither hath lifted up his eyes to the idols of the
house of Israel, hath not defiled his neighbour's
wife,
16 Neither hath oppressed any, hath not
withholden the pledge, neither hath spoiled by
violence, *but* hath given his bread to the hungry,
and hath covered the naked with a garment,
17 *That* hath taken off his hand from the poor,
that hath not received usury nor increase, hath
executed my judgments, hath walked in my
statutes; he shall not die for the iniquity of his
father, he shall surely live.
18 *As for* his father, because he cruelly oppressed,
spoiled his brother by violence, and did *that*
which *is* not good among his people, lo, even he
shall die in his iniquity.
19 ¶ Yet say ye, Why? doth not the son bear the
iniquity of the father? When the son hath done
that which is lawful and right, *and* hath kept all
my statutes, and hath done them, he shall surely
live.
20 The soul that sinneth, it shall die. The son shall
not bear the iniquity of the father, neither shall the
father bear the iniquity of the son: the righteous-
ness of the righteous shall be upon him, and the
wickedness of the wicked shall be upon him.
21 But if the wicked will turn from all his sins that
he hath committed, and keep all my statutes, and
do that which is lawful and right, he shall surely
live, he shall not die.
22 All his transgressions that he hath committed,
they shall not be mentioned unto him: in his
righteousness that he hath done he shall live.
23 Have I any pleasure at all that the wicked
should die? saith the Lord GOD: *and* not that he
should return from his ways, and live?
24 ¶ But when the righteous turneth away from
his righteousness, and committeth iniquity, *and*
doeth according to all the abominations that the
wicked *man* doeth, shall he live? All his righteous-
ness that he hath done shall not be mentioned: in
his trespass that he hath trespassed, and in his sin
that he hath sinned, in them shall he die.
25 ¶ Yet ye say, The way of the Lord is not equal.
Hear now, O house of Israel; Is not my way equal?
are not your ways unequal?
26 When a righteous *man* turneth away from
his righteousness, and committeth iniquity, and
dieth in them; for his iniquity that he hath done
shall he die.
27 Again, when the wicked *man* turneth away
from his wickedness that he hath committed, and

18:7 *not oppressed.* Not treated violently or maltreated by fraud. *restored to the debtor his pledge.* Returned what was pawned. *spoiled none by violence.* Did not commit robbery.
18:8 *usury . . . increase.* Lending with interest. In an ancient agricultural society, loans were generally a form of charity to the very poor, and interest was oppressive (Ex. 22:25).
18:10 *robber.* A violent or rapacious one. *shedder of blood.* Murderer.
18:11 *any of those.* Those acts of righteousness mentioned, which his father did.
18:12 *abomination.* That which is disgusting and detestable before God, usually idolatry.
18:13 *his blood.* The Hebrew is plural, referring to the guilt of violence and bloodshed.
18:19 *iniquity.* The guilt of sin (v. 20).
18:21–22 *turn.* The principal Old Testament word for repentance, picturing a reversal of direction. *mentioned.* Remembered. For God to remember sin is for Him to punish it, and not remembering sin is forgiving it (Jer. 14:10; 31:34). *in his righteousness.* Not justification by his works, but in the pathway of repentance and new obedience. This text teaches that God is not demanding perfect obedience to the law but promising forgiveness to those who repent, even after many years of sinning (*all his sins*).
18:23 *pleasure.* Delight. God is not cruel and bloodthirsty to rejoice in the destruction of the people He created in His image (v. 32; 33:11; Lam. 3:33). However, God does delight in justice (Jer. 9:24), hates sin (Ps. 5:4–6), and is pleased to punish sinners for their crimes (Deut. 28:63). Therefore God is utterly sincere, both in His calls to repentance and His warnings of judgment.
18:24 *righteous.* Not in the sense of justification, but outwardly doing what appear to be good things.
18:25 *is not equal.* Does not measure up or is incorrect.

doeth that which is lawful and right, he shall save
his soul alive.
28 Because he considereth, and turneth away
from all his transgressions that he hath commit-
ted, he shall surely live, he shall not die.
29 Yet saith the house of Israel, The way of the
Lord is not equal. O house of Israel, are not my
ways equal? are not your ways unequal?
30 Therefore I will judge you, O house of Israel,
every one according to his ways, saith the Lord
GOD. Repent, and turn *yourselves* from all your
transgressions; so iniquity shall not be your ruin.
31 ¶ Cast away from you all your transgressions,
whereby ye have transgressed; and make you a
new heart and a new spirit: for why will ye die, O
house of Israel?
32 For I have no pleasure in the death of him
that dieth, saith the Lord GOD: wherefore turn
yourselves, and live ye.

CHAPTER 19

MOREOVER take thou up a lamentation for the
princes of Israel,
2 And say, What *is* thy mother? A lioness: she lay
down among lions, she nourished her whelps
among young lions.
3 And she brought up one of her whelps: it
became a young lion, and it learned to catch the
prey; it devoured men.
4 The nations also heard of him; he was taken in
their pit, and they brought him with chains unto
the land of Egypt.
5 Now when she saw that she had waited, *and*
her hope was lost, then she took another of her
whelps, *and* made him a young lion.
6 And he went up and down among the lions,
he became a young lion, and learned to catch the
prey, *and* devoured men.
7 And he knew their desolate palaces, and he laid
waste their cities; and the land was desolate, and
the fulness thereof, by the noise of his roaring.
8 Then the nations set against him on every side
from the provinces, and spread their net over
him: he was taken in their pit.
9 And they put him in ward in chains, and
brought him to the king of Babylon: they brought
him into holds, that his voice should no more be
heard upon the mountains of Israel.
10 ¶ Thy mother *is* like a vine in thy blood,
planted by the waters: she was fruitful and full of
branches by reason of many waters.
11 And she had strong rods for the sceptres of
them that bare rule, and her stature was exalted
among the thick branches, and she appeared in
her height with the multitude of her branches.

18:30 *Repent . . . turn.* The same Hebrew word (v. 21). *iniquity shall not be your ruin.* Literally, "it will not be for you a stumbling block of iniquity" (cf. 7:19).
18:31 *Cast away . . . why will ye die.* Texts like these authorize preachers to command all men to turn from sin to God and to make urgent appeals to them based on eternal consequences. *make you a new heart and a new spirit.* Repentance (vv. 30,32) requires every sinner to change not merely his behavior but also his deepest beliefs and motives. This is the duty of everyone (Acts 17:30), but it is possible only by the regenerating grace of God (11:19–20; 36:25–27).
18:32 *I have no pleasure in the death of him that dieth.* See note at v. 23.

Thoughts for Personal/Family Worship: Chapter 18

1. **God is the Owner of all men: "all souls are mine" (v. 4). Since God created us, we are accountable to Him. Each individual is responsible before God for his own sin. To ignore personal responsibility to God is to dishonor God and degrade men to the level of beasts. We must not attempt to blame others for our wrongdoings, even if they tempted us (Gen. 3:12) or set an evil example for us, such as the case with wicked parents. Christ will not accept such excuses when He summons each person before Him on the judgment day (2 Cor. 5:10).**
2. **This chapter answers three key questions about repentance: (1) *Why should sinners repent?* They must repent because God owns every person, knows the true condition of every person, and inflicts death on every sinner. (2) *How must sinners repent?* They must repent by turning from all their sins back to God with their hearts and behavior. (3) *What do repentant sinners receive?* They receive the forgiveness of sin and life. So the urgent question goes to every unrepentant sinner, "Why will you die?" What reasons and motives hold back sinners from repenting? How would you answer them?**

Chapter 19: *Using the imagery of lions and a vine, Ezekiel laments the leaders and the nation.*
Parables of the Lioness and the Vine (19:1–14)

19:1 *lamentation.* A dirge or funeral song. *princes of Israel.* The civil leaders, not necessarily the sons of royalty.
19:2 In the parable the *lioness* refers to the nation of Judah and the *whelps* (cubs) to two of the kings, probably Jehoahaz (taken captive to Egypt, 2 Kings 23:31–33) and either Jehoiachin (who was already captive in Babylon, along with Ezekiel; 1:2) or Zedekiah (the puppet king who soon would be deposed, 2 Kings 25:7). The kings could not prevent the captivity.
19:4 *nations.* Gentile nations. *he was taken in their pit.* Alluding to hunting or capturing prey. *brought him with chains unto the land of Egypt.* A reference to Jehoahaz's capture by Pharaoh-nechoh (2 Kings 23:31–33).
19:8 *Then the nations set against him on every side from the provinces . . . spread their net over him.* See 2 Kings 24:1,2.
19:9 *ward.* Cage. *chains.* A collar with hooks. *brought him to the king of Babylon.* Carried him to Nebuchadnezzar. Although Jehoiakim followed Jehoahaz, this seems to be more in keeping with the fate of Jehoiachin.
19:10 *in thy blood.* Perhaps used figuratively for the vineyard, the point of similarity being the color of the grapes. *planted by the waters.* Transplanted beside the waters to ensure the necessary moisture.
19:11 *strong rods for the sceptres of them that bare rule.* Some of Judah's strong and able rulers. *her stature was exalted.* There were times when Judah was a prominent nation.

HUMAN RESPONSIBILITY

Since the gospel was first preached in the world, men have objected that God is unjust to require in His law what they cannot perform, because, as sinners, they are wholly incapable of doing any good and are inclined to all wickedness. In a similar vein, men have argued that if God is sovereign in salvation, they cannot be blamed for their lack of faith or grace: "Why doth he yet find fault? For who hath resisted his will?" (Rom. 9:19). In other words, lack of ability is held to imply lack of responsibility.

Both lines of argument are exposed as false when man's present fallen state is contrasted with his original state of knowledge, holiness, freedom, and communion with God as his Creator. As a creature made in God's image, Adam knew and loved God and had the power, will, and freedom to do God's will.

Adam threw away these gifts when he yielded to lies and fell into sin. His knowledge of the truth was suppressed in unrighteousness; his fallen heart was turned away from God; the purposes and desires of his heart became only evil continually; and his will was enslaved to sin (Gen. 6:5).

Adam inflicted these terrible losses on himself and his offspring. However, such losses could not free him from the terms of the covenant of works, by which he was bound to obey the law of God written in his heart: "This do, and thou shalt live" (Luke 10:28). Though blurred and defaced by sin, that law is still written in the human heart today, and all men are bound to obey it, whether they will or not, whether they can or not. Theologians sometimes speak of conscience, or "the light of nature," when referring to this law written in the heart (Rom. 2:13–15).

God called Cain to account for his sin in murdering his brother, Abel (Gen. 4:9–12). According to His severe judgment, God punished the unbelieving and unrepentant world with the flood, while in His great mercy He saved and protected believing Noah and his family (Gen. 7). Later, because the cry of Sodom and Gomorrah was great and their sin very grievous, God destroyed these prosperous and proud cities, raining brimstone and fire from heaven upon them (Gen. 18:20; 19:24–25).

All of these punishments were inflicted by God upon human beings long before the giving of the law to Israel at Sinai. But, as Paul observes, "Where no law is, there is no transgression" (Rom. 4:15). The very fact that God punished human transgression before Sinai, even from the dawn of human history, implies that there always has been a divine law known to mankind; therefore, all men are bound to obey it or face the consequences if they do not.

The gospel itself, as preached by Christ, comes to us as a command: "The time is fulfilled, and the kingdom of God is at hand: repent ye, and believe the gospel" (Mark 1:15; cf. Acts 17:30). This gospel imperative is rooted in the fact that the gospel is indeed good news that men ought to believe. If the minds of men were not darkened, their desires not corrupted, and their wills not enslaved, they would believe it. The fault is not with Christ or with His gospel but with men who love darkness and will not come to the light (John 3:19).

Moreover, Christ has not left anyone who hears the gospel without access to the means of grace. The gospel must be preached to all nations, and therefore no one can say that this good news is not addressed to him: "Whosoever shall call upon the name of the Lord shall be saved" (Rom. 10:13). Those who truly know their need of grace will seek it from God, who alone can bestow it, by using the means He has appointed to obtain it: "He that cometh to God must believe that he is, and that he is a rewarder of them that diligently seek him" (Heb. 11:7). The way to Christ and salvation is open to all (John 6:37).

12 But she was plucked up in fury, she was cast
down to the ground, and the east wind dried
up her fruit: her strong rods were broken and
withered; the fire consumed them.
13 And now she *is* planted in the wilderness, in a
dry and thirsty ground.
14 And fire is gone out of a rod of her branches,
which hath devoured her fruit, so that she hath
no strong rod *to be* a sceptre to rule. This *is* a
lamentation, and shall be for a lamentation.

CHAPTER 20

AND it came to pass in the seventh year, in the fifth
month, the tenth *day* of the month, *that* certain of
the elders of Israel came to enquire of the LORD,
and sat before me.
2 Then came the word of the LORD unto me,
saying,
3 Son of man, speak unto the elders of Israel, and
say unto them, Thus saith the Lord GOD; Are ye
come to enquire of me? *As* I live, saith the Lord
GOD, I will not be enquired of by you.
4 Wilt thou judge them, son of man, wilt thou
judge *them*? cause them to know the abominations
of their fathers:
5 ¶ And say unto them, Thus saith the Lord
GOD; In the day when I chose Israel, and lifted up
mine hand unto the seed of the house of Jacob,
and made myself known unto them in the land
of Egypt, when I lifted up mine hand unto them,
saying, I *am* the LORD your God;
6 In the day *that* I lifted up mine hand unto them,
to bring them forth of the land of Egypt into a
land that I had espied for them, flowing with milk
and honey, which *is* the glory of all lands:
7 Then said I unto them, Cast ye away every
man the abominations of his eyes, and defile not
yourselves with the idols of Egypt: I *am* the LORD
your God.
8 But they rebelled against me, and would not
hearken unto me: they did not every man cast away
the abominations of their eyes, neither did they
forsake the idols of Egypt: then I said, I will pour
out my fury upon them, to accomplish my anger
against them in the midst of the land of Egypt.
9 But I wrought for my name's sake, that it should
not be polluted before the heathen, among whom
they *were*, in whose sight I made myself known
unto them, in bringing them forth out of the land
of Egypt.
10 ¶ Wherefore I caused them to go forth out
of the land of Egypt, and brought them into the
wilderness.
11 And I gave them my statutes, and shewed
them my judgments, which *if* a man do, he shall
even live in them.
12 Moreover also I gave them my sabbaths, to
be a sign between me and them, that they might
know that I *am* the LORD that sanctify them.
13 But the house of Israel rebelled against me in
the wilderness: they walked not in my statutes,
and they despised my judgments, which *if* a man
do, he shall even live in them; and my sabbaths

19:12 *cast down to the ground.* Thrown down, a phrase expressing the overthrow of the nation. *east wind.* Fierce and destructive forces.
19:13 *planted in the wilderness.* Transplanted in Babylon. *in a dry and thirsty ground.* Suggesting barrenness and emptiness.

Thoughts for Personal/Family Worship: Chapter 19

Pride comes before a fall. The young lions, representing the kings of Israel, felt invincible but were eventually taken in the snare. Their disregard for God paved the way for their downfall. In the parable, the second young lion behaved exactly as the first one and was taken in the pit exactly as the first one had been. Insensitivity to the results of sin betrays a hard and callous heart. Sin has terrible consequences for both individuals and nations. Like Ezekiel, Christians have good cause to take up a lamentation against the sins that plague their nation and pray that God will be favorable and raise up righteous rulers before it becomes too late, as it did for Judah. How are you praying for your nation?

Chapter 20: *Ezekiel reviews Israel's history, noting the nation's rebellion and God's patience.*

Israel's History and God's Name (20:1–44)

20:3 *enquire.* Seek. *I will not be enquired of by you.* I will not permit Myself to be sought (v. 31). The Lord saw through their hypocrisy into the idolatry of their hearts (14:3).
20:4 *abomination of their fathers.* The idolatry and wickedness their fathers had committed, which the Lord regarded as disgusting and detestable.
20:5 *lifted up mine hand.* A gesture signifying a covenant or commitment, swearing an oath (Gen. 14:22; Dan. 12:7). *I am the LORD your God.* Expressive of the covenant relationship (Ex. 6:7).
20:6 *espied.* Searched out. *the glory of all lands.* A land that surpasses all others, the most glorious (v. 15).
20:7 *abominations of his eyes.* The images he looked on; the Hebrew refers to an object of hatred and disgust. God viewed the idols far differently from those who worshiped them.
20:8 *would not hearken.* Literally, "were not willing to hear."
20:9 *wrought for my name's sake.* Worked so that people would see My glory. This statement occurs throughout the chapter (vv. 14,22,44). *polluted.* Treated as common or ordinary, the opposite of "holy" (vv. 13–14,16,21–22,24,39). To treat the holy God as ordinary is the ultimate profanity.
20:11 *statutes . . . which if a man do, he shall even live.* See Lev. 18:5; Deut. 4:1; Neh. 9:29 (vv. 13,21). *judgments.* God's just laws (vv. 13,16,18–19,21,24–25)
20:12 *my sabbaths.* Days set apart for holy rest, including both the weekly Sabbath, as part of the unchangeable moral law (Gen. 2:1–3; Ex. 20:8–11), and the ritual Sabbaths of the ceremonial law (like the day of Passover). *sign between me and them.* A token of their relationship. *that they might know that I am the LORD.* To know His sovereign glory in an experiential way (repeated frequently; vv. 20,26,38,42,44).
20:13 *despised.* Profaned or refused. Jeremiah also links breaking the Sabbath to judgment and keeping the Sabbath as a safeguard (Jer. 17:19–27).

they greatly polluted: then I said, I would pour
out my fury upon them in the wilderness, to
consume them.
14 But I wrought for my name's sake, that it
should not be polluted before the heathen, in
whose sight I brought them out.
15 Yet also I lifted up my hand unto them in the
wilderness, that I would not bring them into the
land which I had given *them*, flowing with milk
and honey, which *is* the glory of all lands;
16 Because they despised my judgments, and
walked not in my statutes, but polluted my
sabbaths: for their heart went after their idols.
17 Nevertheless mine eye spared them from
destroying them, neither did I make an end of
them in the wilderness.
18 But I said unto their children in the wilderness,
Walk ye not in the statutes of your fathers, neither
observe their judgments, nor defile yourselves
with their idols:
19 I *am* the LORD your God; walk in my statutes,
and keep my judgments, and do them;
20 And hallow my sabbaths; and they shall be a
sign between me and you, that ye may know that
I *am* the LORD your God.
21 Notwithstanding the children rebelled against
me: they walked not in my statutes, neither kept
my judgments to do them, which *if* a man do, he
shall even live in them; they polluted my sabbaths:
then I said, I would pour out my fury upon them,
to accomplish my anger against them in the
wilderness.
22 Nevertheless I withdrew mine hand, and
wrought for my name's sake, that it should not
be polluted in the sight of the heathen, in whose
sight I brought them forth.
23 I lifted up mine hand unto them also in the
wilderness, that I would scatter them among
the heathen, and disperse them through the
countries;
24 Because they had not executed my judgments,
but had despised my statutes, and had polluted
my sabbaths, and their eyes were after their
fathers' idols.
25 Wherefore I gave them also statutes *that were*
not good, and judgments whereby they should
not live;
26 And I polluted them in their own gifts, in
that they caused to pass through *the fire* all that
openeth the womb, that I might make them
desolate, to the end that they might know that I
am the LORD.
27 ¶ Therefore, son of man, speak unto the house
of Israel, and say unto them, Thus saith the Lord
GOD; Yet in this your fathers have blasphemed me,
in that they have committed a trespass against me.
28 *For* when I had brought them into the land,
for the which I lifted up mine hand to give it to
them, then they saw every high hill, and all the
thick trees, and they offered there their sacrifices,
and there they presented the provocation of their
offering: there also they made their sweet savour,
and poured out there their drink offerings.
29 Then I said unto them, What *is* the high place
whereunto ye go? And the name thereof is called
Bamah unto this day.
30 Wherefore say unto the house of Israel,
Thus saith the Lord GOD; Are ye polluted after
the manner of your fathers? and commit ye
whoredom after their abominations?
31 For when ye offer your gifts, when ye make
your sons to pass through the fire, ye pollute
yourselves with all your idols, even unto this day:
and shall I be enquired of by you, O house of
Israel? *As* I live, saith the Lord GOD, I will not be
enquired of by you.
32 And that which cometh into your mind shall
not be at all, that ye say, We will be as the heathen,
as the families of the countries, to serve wood and
stone.
33 ¶ *As* I live, saith the Lord GOD, surely with a
mighty hand, and with a stretched out arm, and
with fury poured out, will I rule over you:
34 And I will bring you out from the people, and
will gather you out of the countries wherein ye
are scattered, with a mighty hand, and with a
stretched out arm, and with fury poured out.
35 And I will bring you into the wilderness of

20:17 *mine eye spared them.* The Lord had compassion and restrained judgment.
20:20 *hallow.* Set apart as holy and sacred.
20:22 *I withdrew mine hand.* Symbolizing the withdrawing of His favor, mercy, and help.
20:23 *scatter.* Literally, "to break in pieces and then scatter." *disperse . . . through the countries.* Cast away as in the winnowing process.
20:24 *executed my judgments.* Done or obeyed God's laws.
20:25 *I gave them also statutes that were not good.* The consequences were not good to those who disobeyed them.
20:26 *polluted them.* Pronounced them unclean or defiled in their offerings. *to pass through . . . all that openeth the womb.* The sacrificing of their firstborn children to idols.
20:28 *every high hill.* Places of pagan worship. *thick trees.* Trees with thick, intertwining branches and heavy foliage. Most likely places of false worship. *provocation of their offering.* Offering that provoked the Lord. *sweet savour.* Fragrances offered with a view to appeasement (also v. 41, where used of legitimate offerings).
20:29 *Bamah.* The Hebrew word for "high place."
20:30 *whoredom.* Sinful sexual activity. *abominations.* Horrific or monstrous things.
20:32 *wood and stone.* The material from which idols are made; here referring to the idols themselves.
20:33 *mighty hand . . . stretched out arm.* Indicating invincible strength.
20:34 *bring you out.* Out of those places and from among those people to whom you had looked for safety.
20:35 *plead with you face to face.* Judge you directly, as

the people, and there will I plead with you face
to face.
36 Like as I pleaded with your fathers in the
wilderness of the land of Egypt, so will I plead
with you, saith the Lord GOD.
37 And I will cause you to pass under the rod, and
I will bring you into the bond of the covenant:
38 And I will purge out from among you the
rebels, and them that transgress against me: I will
bring them forth out of the country where they
sojourn, and they shall not enter into the land of
Israel: and ye shall know that I *am* the LORD.
39 As for you, O house of Israel, thus saith the
Lord GOD; Go ye, serve ye every one his idols, and
hereafter *also*, if ye will not hearken unto me: but
pollute ye my holy name no more with your gifts,
and with your idols.
40 For in mine holy mountain, in the mountain
of the height of Israel, saith the Lord GOD, there
shall all the house of Israel, all of them in the land,
serve me: there will I accept them, and there will I
require your offerings, and the firstfruits of your
oblations, with all your holy things.
41 I will accept you with your sweet savour, when
I bring you out from the people, and gather
you out of the countries wherein ye have been
scattered; and I will be sanctified in you before
the heathen.
42 And ye shall know that I *am* the LORD, when
I shall bring you into the land of Israel, into the
country *for* the which I lifted up mine hand to
give it to your fathers.
43 And there shall ye remember your ways, and
all your doings, wherein ye have been defiled; and
ye shall lothe yourselves in your own sight for all
your evils that ye have committed.
44 And ye shall know that I *am* the LORD, when
I have wrought with you for my name's sake, not
according to your wicked ways, nor according to
your corrupt doings, O ye house of Israel, saith
the Lord GOD.
45 ¶ Moreover the word of the LORD came unto
me, saying,
46 Son of man, set thy face toward the south, and
drop *thy word* toward the south, and prophesy
against the forest of the south field;
47 And say to the forest of the south, Hear the
word of the LORD; Thus saith the Lord GOD; Be-
hold, I will kindle a fire in thee, and it shall devour
every green tree in thee, and every dry tree: the
flaming flame shall not be quenched, and all faces
from the south to the north shall be burned therein.
48 And all flesh shall see that I the LORD have
kindled it: it shall not be quenched.
49 Then said I, Ah Lord GOD! they say of me,
Doth he not speak parables?

CHAPTER 21

AND the word of the LORD came unto me, saying,
2 Son of man, set thy face toward Jerusalem,
and drop *thy word* toward the holy places, and
prophesy against the land of Israel,
3 And say to the land of Israel, Thus saith the
LORD; Behold, I *am* against thee, and will draw
forth my sword out of his sheath, and will cut off
from thee the righteous and the wicked.
4 Seeing then that I will cut off from thee the
righteous and the wicked, therefore shall my
sword go forth out of his sheath against all flesh
from the south to the north:
5 That all flesh may know that I the LORD have

in court (v. 36).

20:37 *pass under the rod.* An image of sheep under the care of a shepherd (Lev. 27:32). *into the bond.* Under the terms or obligation.

20:38 *sojourn.* To live temporarily or as a resident alien.

20:39 *Go ye, serve ye every one his idols.* The Lord is abandoning them to their sin (Amos 4:4–5). Sin is often punished with further sin.

20:41 *I will be sanctified in you before the heathen.* God will show Himself to be holy so that the Gentiles will know that He is the Lord.

Fire and Sword (20:45—21:32)

20:46 *the south.* Most likely Jerusalem, compared to a *forest* in the *field* because of its many people.

20:47 Joining pairs of opposites (*green tree* and *dry tree, south* and *north*) expresses totality. Judgment will come on everyone throughout the land.

20:49 *parables.* Riddles or proverbs (Ps. 78:2).

Thoughts for Personal/Family Worship: Chapter 20

1. **Do not play games with God. He has no interest in the prayers of those who cling to idols in their hearts (vv. 3,31). He is not impressed with worship on Sunday without faithfulness on Monday through Saturday. He despises the study of the Bible without obedience to the Bible. He welcomes sinners, but only sinners repenting of sin, for He will not save sinners in a way that profanes His holy name (v. 39).**
2. **The hinge upon which salvation turns is the glory of God's name. When Israel's sins provoked the Lord to anger, He saved them for the sake of His name (vv. 9, 14,22,44). His works all aim at the goal that the world may know He is the Lord (vv. 5,9,12,20,26,38,42,44). God does not save believers for anything in them but simply for the praise of His glory (Eph. 1:6,12,14). Why is this a great source of consolation and peace to those broken over their sins? How then should Christians respond to their salvation?**

Chapter 21: ***Ezekiel shows God's sovereignty in directing the Babylonians against Judah and Ammon.***

21:2 *drop.* Literally, "drip," a word referring to prophetic preaching (20:46; Amos 7:16).

21:3–4 Joining pairs of opposites (*righteous* and *wicked, south* and *north*) expresses totality of the extent of judgment (20:47).

drawn forth my sword out of his sheath: it shall
not return any more.
6 Sigh therefore, thou son of man, with the break-
ing of *thy* loins; and with bitterness sigh before
their eyes.
7 And it shall be, when they say unto thee,
Wherefore sighest thou? that thou shalt answer,
For the tidings; because it cometh: and every
heart shall melt, and all hands shall be feeble, and
every spirit shall faint, and all knees shall be weak
as water: behold, it cometh, and shall be brought
to pass, saith the Lord GOD.
8 ¶ Again the word of the LORD came unto me,
saying,
9 Son of man, prophesy, and say, Thus saith the
LORD; Say, A sword, a sword is sharpened, and
also furbished:
10 It is sharpened to make a sore slaughter; it is
furbished that it may glitter: should we then make
mirth? it contemneth the rod of my son, *as* every
tree.
11 And he hath given it to be furbished, that it
may be handled: this sword is sharpened, and it
is furbished, to give it into the hand of the slayer.
12 Cry and howl, son of man: for it shall be upon
my people, it *shall be* upon all the princes of Israel:
terrors by reason of the sword shall be upon my
people: smite therefore upon *thy* thigh.
13 Because *it is* a trial, and what if *the sword*
contemn even the rod? it shall be no *more*, saith
the Lord GOD.
14 Thou therefore, son of man, prophesy, and
smite *thine* hands together, and let the sword be
doubled the third time, the sword of the slain: it
is the sword of the great *men that are* slain, which
entereth into their privy chambers.
15 I have set the point of the sword against all
their gates, that *their* heart may faint, and *their*
ruins be multiplied: ah! *it is* made bright, *it is*
wrapped up for the slaughter.
16 Go thee one way or other, *either* on the right
hand, *or* on the left, whithersoever thy face *is* set.
17 I will also smite mine hands together, and I
will cause my fury to rest: I the LORD have said *it*.
18 ¶ The word of the LORD came unto me again,
saying,
19 Also, thou son of man, appoint thee two ways,
that the sword of the king of Babylon may come:
both twain shall come forth out of one land: and
choose thou a place, choose *it* at the head of the
way to the city.
20 Appoint a way, that the sword may come
to Rabbath of the Ammonites, and to Judah in
Jerusalem the defenced.
21 For the king of Babylon stood at the parting
of the way, at the head of the two ways, to
use divination: he made *his* arrows bright, he
consulted with images, he looked in the liver.
22 At his right hand was the divination for
Jerusalem, to appoint captains, to open the mouth
in the slaughter, to lift up the voice with shouting,
to appoint *battering* rams against the gates, to cast
a mount, *and* to build a fort.
23 And it shall be unto them as a false divination
in their sight, to them that have sworn oaths: but
he will call to remembrance the iniquity, that they
may be taken.
24 Therefore thus saith the Lord GOD; Because
ye have made your iniquity to be remembered,
in that your transgressions are discovered, so that
in all your doings your sins do appear; because, *I
say*, that ye are come to remembrance, ye shall be
taken with the hand.
25 ¶ And thou, profane wicked prince of Israel,
whose day is come, when iniquity *shall have* an end,
26 Thus saith the Lord GOD; Remove the diadem,

21:5 *it shall not return any more.* Until its work of judgment has been completed.
21:6 *Sigh.* Groan as in mourning. *breaking of thy loins.* Deep and intense sighs, as though in great pain.
21:7 *tidings.* Report. *every heart shall melt.* As melting wax, expressing fear.
21:9 *A sword, a sword.* Repeated to signify the certainly of the impending judgment. *furbished.* Polished (vv. 10–11,28).
21:10 *sore.* Very great or severe. *should we then make mirth? it contemneth the rod of my son, as every tree.* The Hebrew is difficult, possibly with the meaning "Should we rejoice in the scepter of my son? The sword has no respect for a scepter."
21:12 *princes.* Leaders in general, not sons of royalty. *smite therefore upon thy thigh.* A gesture indicating deep grief and sorrow of heart.
21:13 *contemn even the rod.* Despise the scepter.
21:14 *smite thine hands together.* Strike hand to hand, an action suggesting great agony. *doubled.* Repeated. *the third time.* Either the threefold decree of judgment (5:2,12) or Nebuchadnezzar taking the king, the city, and also the people. *privy chambers.* Private or secure rooms.
21:15 *made bright.* Polished and sharpened. *wrapped up.* Thinned or sharpened in preparation for the slaughter.
21:17 *I will cause my fury to rest.* When the judgment is finished and justice is satisfied, God will cause His anger to cease.
21:19–20 The prophet was to mark two (*twain*) ways for the king of Babylon to take, one to the *Ammonites* and the other *to Judah*.
21:21 *the parting of the way.* Literally, "the mother of the way," the crossroads or the fork in the road. *use divination.* Seek secret knowledge by omens or magic, such as by examining the *liver* of an animal. *made his arrows bright.* Perhaps firing arrows inscribed with the names of the cities into the sky and determining which to attack depending on how the arrows fell.
21:22 *cast a mount.* Build an assault ramp. *fort.* A bulwark or siege wall.
21:23 *a false divination in their sight.* The Jews would dismiss the decision, trusting in what they regarded as promises made to them.
21:24 *discovered.* Revealed or uncovered. *taken with the hand.* Snared or taken captive.
21:25 *profane wicked prince.* Literally, "dishonored, wicked, exalted one," referring to Zedekiah.
21:26 *Remove the diadem.* Take off the official, turban-like

and take off the crown: this *shall* not *be* the same:
exalt *him that is* low, and abase *him that is* high.
27 I will overturn, overturn, overturn, it: and it
shall be no *more*, until he come whose right it is;
and I will give it *him*.
28 ¶ And thou, son of man, prophesy and say,
Thus saith the Lord GOD concerning the Ammon-
ites, and concerning their reproach; even say thou,
The sword, the sword *is* drawn: for the slaughter *it*
is furbished, to consume because of the glittering:
29 Whiles they see vanity unto thee, whiles they
divine a lie unto thee, to bring thee upon the
necks of *them that are* slain, of the wicked, whose
day is come, when their iniquity *shall have* an end.
30 Shall I cause *it* to return into his sheath? I will
judge thee in the place where thou wast created,
in the land of thy nativity.
31 And I will pour out mine indignation upon
thee, I will blow against thee in the fire of my
wrath, and deliver thee into the hand of brutish
men, *and* skilful to destroy.
32 Thou shalt be for fuel to the fire; thy blood
shall be in the midst of the land; thou shalt be no
more remembered: for I the LORD have spoken *it*.

CHAPTER 22

MOREOVER the word of the LORD came unto me,
saying,
2 Now, thou son of man, wilt thou judge, wilt
thou judge the bloody city? yea, thou shalt shew
her all her abominations.
3 Then say thou, Thus saith the Lord GOD, The
city sheddeth blood in the midst of it, that her
time may come, and maketh idols against herself
to defile herself.
4 Thou art become guilty in thy blood that thou
hast shed; and hast defiled thyself in thine idols
which thou hast made; and thou hast caused thy
days to draw near, and art come *even* unto thy
years: therefore have I made thee a reproach unto
the heathen, and a mocking to all countries.
5 *Those that be* near, and *those that be* far from
thee, shall mock thee, *which art* infamous *and*
much vexed.
6 Behold, the princes of Israel, every one were in
thee to their power to shed blood.
7 In thee have they set light by father and mother:
in the midst of thee have they dealt by oppression
with the stranger: in thee have they vexed the
fatherless and the widow.
8 Thou hast despised mine holy things, and hast
profaned my sabbaths.
9 In thee are men that carry tales to shed blood:
and in thee they eat upon the mountains: in the
midst of thee they commit lewdness.
10 In thee have they discovered their fathers'
nakedness: in thee have they humbled her that
was set apart for pollution.
11 And one hath committed abomination with

headband. *take off the crown.* Thus deposing him from the royal throne. *abase.* Humiliate.
21:27 *I will overturn, overturn, overturn it.* The triple reference indicates certainty and completeness. *it shall be no more, until he come whose right it is; and I will give it him.* Refers to Christ, whose right to reign is established. There would be no Davidic king until Christ appeared, and the kingdom belongs to Him (Luke 1:33).
21:28 *The sword, the sword is drawn.* Repetition indicates the certainty of judgment.
21:29 *Whiles they see vanity.* The deceptive visions of false prophets.
21:30 *cause it to return into his sheath.* Put away the sword.
21:31 *brutish.* Cruel or barbaric. *skilful to destroy.* Literally, "craftsmen of destruction."

Thoughts for Personal/Family Worship: Chapter 21

1. **God sovereignly used the Babylonians to accomplish His purpose of judgment against both Judah and Ammon. The pagan king made the decision by various means of divination. But just as the Lord superintends the disposing of lots (Prov. 16:33), so He does even the pagan's looking into a liver. There is no such thing as fate or chance. All things operate according to God's will.**
2. **God's message of judgment contains a word of hope centered on Christ (v. 27). God promised through Jacob that kingship would not depart from Judah until the rightful King would come (Gen. 49:10). For years there was never a scepter belonging to Judah, and then there was David. Then, again, because of the sins of David's sons there was no king for centuries. But in the fullness of time Jesus, David's ideal son, appeared and forever reigns. No matter how dark things become for you or for your nation, hope in Christ, for His kingdom will never fail.**

Chapter 22: *The prophet delineates Judah's sins that deserve judgment.*

The Defiled City (22:1–31)

22:2 *the bloody city.* Literally, "the city of bloods." Hebrew uses the plural for the violence of bloodshed. *shew her.* Cause her to know. *abominations.* Disgusting or detestable things, often idolatry.
22:3 *her time.* The judgment that her sin brings (v. 4).
22:4–5 *reproach.* An object of scorn or taunt. *infamous.* Literally, "unclean of name," a shameful reputation. *much vexed.* "Great of consternation or panic." It is not uncommon for the ungodly to mock those who have fallen away after professing to follow the Lord.
22:6 *princes.* Leaders in general, not necessarily royalty. *were in thee to their power.* Literally, "to their necks they were in you"—up to their necks in the crimes.
22:7 *set light.* Treat with contempt. *dealt by oppression with the stranger.* Treated foreigners with brutality and extortion. *vexed.* Oppressed or mistreated.
22:8 *despised.* Regarded with contempt. *profaned my sabbaths.* Treated the Sabbaths, days that were to be set apart for holy rest, as ordinary or regular days.
22:9 *men that carry tales.* Men of slander. *upon the mountains.* At mountain shrines. *lewdness.* All sorts of shameful behavior.
22:10 *discovered.* Uncovered or revealed. *humbled her that was set apart for pollution.* Abused her during the time of uncleanness (Lev. 18:19).

his neighbour's wife; and another hath lewdly
defiled his daughter in law; and another in thee
hath humbled his sister, his father's daughter.
12 In thee have they taken gifts to shed blood;
thou hast taken usury and increase, and thou hast
greedily gained of thy neighbours by extortion,
and hast forgotten me, saith the Lord GOD.
13 ¶ Behold, therefore I have smitten mine hand
at thy dishonest gain which thou hast made, and
at thy blood which hath been in the midst of thee.
14 Can thine heart endure, or can thine hands be
strong, in the days that I shall deal with thee? I the
LORD have spoken *it*, and will do *it*.
15 And I will scatter thee among the heathen, and
disperse thee in the countries, and will consume
thy filthiness out of thee.
16 And thou shalt take thine inheritance in
thyself in the sight of the heathen, and thou shalt
know that I *am* the LORD.
17 And the word of the LORD came unto me,
saying,
18 Son of man, the house of Israel is to me
become dross: all they *are* brass, and tin, and iron,
and lead, in the midst of the furnace; they are *even*
the dross of silver.
19 Therefore thus saith the Lord GOD; Because
ye are all become dross, behold, therefore I will
gather you into the midst of Jerusalem.
20 *As* they gather silver, and brass, and iron, and
lead, and tin, into the midst of the furnace, to
blow the fire upon it, to melt *it*; so will I gather
you in mine anger and in my fury, and I will leave
you there, and melt you.
21 Yea, I will gather you, and blow upon you in
the fire of my wrath, and ye shall be melted in the
midst thereof.
22 As silver is melted in the midst of the furnace,
so shall ye be melted in the midst thereof; and ye
shall know that I the LORD have poured out my
fury upon you.
23 ¶ And the word of the LORD came unto me,
saying,
24 Son of man, say unto her, Thou *art* the land
that is not cleansed, nor rained upon in the day
of indignation.
25 *There is* a conspiracy of her prophets in the
midst thereof, like a roaring lion ravening the
prey; they have devoured souls; they have taken
the treasure and precious things; they have made
her many widows in the midst thereof.
26 Her priests have violated my law, and have
profaned mine holy things: they have put no
difference between the holy and profane, neither
have they shewed *difference* between the unclean
and the clean, and have hid their eyes from my
sabbaths, and I am profaned among them.
27 Her princes in the midst thereof *are* like wolves
ravening the prey, to shed blood, *and* to destroy
souls, to get dishonest gain.
28 And her prophets have daubed them with
untempered *morter*, seeing vanity, and divining
lies unto them, saying, Thus saith the Lord GOD,
when the LORD hath not spoken.
29 The people of the land have used oppression,
and exercised robbery, and have vexed the poor
and needy: yea, they have oppressed the stranger
wrongfully.
30 And I sought for a man among them, that
should make up the hedge, and stand in the gap
before me for the land, that I should not destroy
it: but I found none.
31 Therefore have I poured out mine indignation

22:11 *abomination with his neighbour's wife.* Adultery. *lewdly defiled.* Made unclean by sexual sin. *humbled.* Sexually abused.
22:12 *taken gifts.* Accepted bribes. *usury and increase.* See note at 18:8. *forgotten me.* Failed to meditate on God's Word and ways, resulting in a lack of the fear of the Lord, and thus also in pride, sin, and idolatry (23:35; Deut. 4:9,23,31; 6:12; 8:11,14,19; 32:18); this is the opposite of remembering the Lord (see note at 6:9).
22:13 *I have smitten mine hand.* Either in the sense of indignation or in preparation to smite with the hand.
22:14 *Can thine heart endure.* No man has the strength to endure God's judgment (Isa. 33:14).
22:16 *thou shalt take thine inheritance in thyself.* Irony, meaning they will forfeit their inheritance; or may be translated "thou shalt be profaned by thy own doing."
22:18 *dross.* The useless and unprofitable residue after refining.
22:24 *cleansed.* Purged or cleared. *nor rained upon.* A curse for breaking God's covenant (Lev. 26:18–20) and provoking His anger (*indignation*). Contrast 34:26; Ps. 68:9.
22:25 *ravening.* Tearing in pieces (v. 27). *devoured souls.* Consumed lives.
22:26 *profaned.* Treated as common or ordinary. God commissioned the priests to distinguish between *the holy and profane* (ordinary) and *the unclean and the clean* (Lev. 10:10).
22:27 *princes.* Leaders.
22:28 *daubed them with untempered morter.* Whitewashed their sins in the sense of covering them up (Matt. 23:27). *seeing vanity, and divining lies.* A double reference to dishonesty.
22:29 *oppression . . . robbery.* Extortion and plundering. *vexed.* Oppressed or mistreated.
22:30 *make up the hedge.* Build up a wall or fence. *stand in the gap.* To block the entrance through the breach. There were none righteous to spare the city from judgment (Gen. 18:23–32).
22:31 *I recompensed.* The Lord gave them what they deserved, a fearful prospect.

Thoughts for Personal/Family Worship: Chapter 22

1. **The catalog of corruptions in this chapter teaches that man's depravity is such that there is no sin he is incapable of committing. Both private sins and public sins flow from wicked hearts. We must not imagine that we are any different. God knows the depth of corruption that belongs to each one of us. God would have us know our sin and therefore the Holy Spirit convinces and convicts. Sin is exposed in order that we might repent of it and that God's justice would be clearly observed.**

upon them; I have consumed them with the fire
of my wrath: their own way have I recompensed
upon their heads, saith the Lord GOD.

CHAPTER 23

THE word of the LORD came again unto me,
saying,
2 Son of man, there were two women, the daugh-
ters of one mother:
3 And they committed whoredoms in Egypt;
they committed whoredoms in their youth: there
were their breasts pressed, and there they bruised
the teats of their virginity.
4 And the names of them *were* Aholah the elder,
and Aholibah her sister: and they were mine,
and they bare sons and daughters. Thus *were*
their names; Samaria *is* Aholah, and Jerusalem
Aholibah.
5 And Aholah played the harlot when she was
mine; and she doted on her lovers, on the Assyr-
ians *her* neighbours,
6 *Which were* clothed with blue, captains and
rulers, all of them desirable young men, horsemen
riding upon horses.
7 Thus she committed her whoredoms with
them, with all them *that were* the chosen men of
Assyria, and with all on whom she doted: with all
their idols she defiled herself.
8 Neither left she her whoredoms *brought* from
Egypt: for in her youth they lay with her, and they
bruised the breasts of her virginity, and poured
their whoredom upon her.
9 Wherefore I have delivered her into the hand of
her lovers, into the hand of the Assyrians, upon
whom she doted.
10 These discovered her nakedness: they took
her sons and her daughters, and slew her with the
sword: and she became famous among women;
for they had executed judgment upon her.
11 And when her sister Aholibah saw *this*, she
was more corrupt in her inordinate love than she,
and in her whoredoms more than her sister in *her*
whoredoms.
12 She doted upon the Assyrians *her* neighbours,
captains and rulers clothed most gorgeously,
horsemen riding upon horses, all of them
desirable young men.
13 Then I saw that she was defiled, *that* they *took*
both one way,
14 And *that* she increased her whoredoms: for
when she saw men pourtrayed upon the wall,
the images of the Chaldeans pourtrayed with
vermilion,
15 Girded with girdles upon their loins, exceeding
in dyed attire upon their heads, all of them princes
to look to, after the manner of the Babylonians of
Chaldea, the land of their nativity:
16 And as soon as she saw them with her eyes,
she doted upon them, and sent messengers unto
them into Chaldea.
17 And the Babylonians came to her into the bed
of love, and they defiled her with their whoredom,
and she was polluted with them, and her mind
was alienated from them.
18 So she discovered her whoredoms, and
discovered her nakedness: then my mind was
alienated from her, like as my mind was alienated
from her sister.
19 Yet she multiplied her whoredoms, in calling
to remembrance the days of her youth, wherein
she had played the harlot in the land of Egypt.
20 For she doted upon their paramours, whose
flesh *is as* the flesh of asses, and whose issue *is like*
the issue of horses.
21 Thus thou calledst to remembrance the

---

2. The parts played by both the civil and religious leaders in contributing to Judah's litany of sins remind us of the importance of having godly men in authority, both in the state and in the church. Wickedness at the top drips to the bottom. Christians are often quick to complain about leaders, but how often do they pray for them? How could you cultivate a habit of regularly praying for the leaders of your church and civil government?

Chapter 23: *The sins of Judah and Israel are described in the allegory of two sisters, Aholah and Aholibah.*

Parable of the Immoral Sisters (23:1–49)

23:2 *two women.* Symbols of the northern and southern kingdoms, Israel and Judah. What follows is an allegory, a story with a moral lesson in symbolic language. The language is graphic and shocking to underscore the hateful and horrible nature of their sins.

23:3 *whoredoms.* Sinful sexual activity (throughout the chapter). *pressed.* Touched or squeezed. *bruised the teats of their virginity.* Fondled their virgin breasts (vv. 8,21).

23:4 *Aholah.* Translated, "his tent," representing Samaria, capital city of Israel. *Aholibah.* Translated, "my tent in her," representing Jerusalem, the capital of Judah.

23:5 *doted.* Desired sensuously or with extreme affection (throughout the chapter).

23:8 *poured.* Gushed, signifying excessiveness.

23:10 *discovered.* Uncovered (vv. 18,29).

23:11 *inordinate love.* Lustfulness.

23:13 *they took both one way.* The two nations went the same path into idolatry and sin.

23:14 *men pourtrayed upon the wall.* Images of men carved upon the wall. *vermilion.* Red.

23:15 *Girded with girdles.* Covered with undergarments. *exceeding in dyed attire.* The men had turbans of various colors, in imitation of the Babylonians.

23:17 *her mind was alienated.* She turned away from them in disgust (vv. 18,22,28).

23:19 *multiplied.* Increased. *calling to remembrance the days of her youth.* Remembering and repeating the sins of the Israelites in *Egypt*.

23:20 *paramours.* Lovers. *asses . . . horses.* Symbolic depictions of Israel's and Judah's insatiable desire for idolatry.

lewdness of thy youth, in bruising thy teats by the
Egyptians for the paps of thy youth.
22 ¶ Therefore, O Aholibah, thus saith the Lord
GOD; Behold, I will raise up thy lovers against
thee, from whom thy mind is alienated, and I will
bring them against thee on every side;
23 The Babylonians, and all the Chaldeans,
Pekod, and Shoa, and Koa, *and* all the Assyrians
with them: all of them desirable young men,
captains and rulers, great lords and renowned, all
of them riding upon horses.
24 And they shall come against thee with chariots,
wagons, and wheels, and with an assembly of
people, *which* shall set against thee buckler and
shield and helmet round about: and I will set
judgment before them, and they shall judge thee
according to their judgments.
25 And I will set my jealousy against thee, and
they shall deal furiously with thee: they shall take
away thy nose and thine ears; and thy remnant
shall fall by the sword: they shall take thy sons and
thy daughters; and thy residue shall be devoured
by the fire.
26 They shall also strip thee out of thy clothes,
and take away thy fair jewels.
27 Thus will I make thy lewdness to cease from
thee, and thy whoredom *brought* from the land
of Egypt: so that thou shalt not lift up thine eyes
unto them, nor remember Egypt any more.
28 For thus saith the Lord GOD; Behold, I will
deliver thee into the hand *of them* whom thou
hatest, into the hand *of them* from whom thy
mind is alienated:
29 And they shall deal with thee hatefully, and
shall take away all thy labour, and shall leave
thee naked and bare: and the nakedness of thy
whoredoms shall be discovered, both thy lewdness
and thy whoredoms.
30 I will do these *things* unto thee, because
thou hast gone a whoring after the heathen, *and*
because thou art polluted with their idols.
31 Thou hast walked in the way of thy sister;
therefore will I give her cup into thine hand.
32 Thus saith the Lord GOD; Thou shalt drink
of thy sister's cup deep and large: thou shalt
be laughed to scorn and had in derision; it
containeth much.
33 Thou shalt be filled with drunkenness and
sorrow, with the cup of astonishment and
desolation, with the cup of thy sister Samaria.
34 Thou shalt even drink it and suck *it* out, and
thou shalt break the sherds thereof, and pluck off
thine own breasts: for I have spoken *it*, saith the
Lord GOD.
35 Therefore thus saith the Lord GOD; Because
thou hast forgotten me, and cast me behind thy
back, therefore bear thou also thy lewdness and
thy whoredoms.
36 ¶ The LORD said moreover unto me; Son of
man, wilt thou judge Aholah and Aholibah? yea,
declare unto them their abominations;
37 That they have committed adultery, and blood
is in their hands, and with their idols have they
committed adultery, and have also caused their
sons, whom they bare unto me, to pass for them
through *the fire*, to devour *them*.
38 Moreover this they have done unto me: they
have defiled my sanctuary in the same day, and
have profaned my sabbaths.
39 For when they had slain their children to
their idols, then they came the same day into my
sanctuary to profane it; and, lo, thus have they
done in the midst of mine house.
40 And furthermore, that ye have sent for men to
come from far, unto whom a messenger *was* sent;
and, lo, they came: for whom thou didst wash
thyself, paintedst thy eyes, and deckedst thyself
with ornaments,
41 And satest upon a stately bed, and a table
prepared before it, whereupon thou hast set mine
incense and mine oil.
42 And a voice of a multitude being at ease *was*
with her: and with the men of the common sort
were brought Sabeans from the wilderness, which

23:21 *paps.* Breasts.
23:23 *Pekod.* A tribe southeast of Babylon. *Shoa.* Nomads from Mesopotamia. *Koa.* People from a region in Mesopotamia.
23:24 *buckler.* The Hebrew refers to a large shield covering the body.
23:25 *jealousy.* Anger or wrath. *take away thy nose and thine ears.* Signifying ruin or disfigurement, a typical Babylonian practice; cruel punishment.
23:27 *lewdness.* Adultery and immorality.
23:29 *take away all thy labour.* Seize all the results of your work.
23:31 *cup.* Often symbolic of judgment (vv. 32–33; Ps. 11:6; Jer. 25:15–18).
23:32 *it containeth much.* The cup was full.
23:33 *filled with drunkenness and sorrow.* The fullness of sin and the sadness that accompanies it. *cup.* God's judgment against them, which could bring *astonishment and desolation*, for God would judge Judah in a similar way as He did *Samaria*.
23:34 *suck it out.* Slurp or drain it dry. *sherds.* Shards or broken pieces of the cup, signifying the intensity of the judgment. *pluck off thine own breasts.* Tear at oneself in despair or anguish.
23:35 *forgotten me.* See note at 22:12.
23:38 *defiled.* Made unclean. *profaned.* Treated the holy as common.
23:39 They mixed pagan practices with their hypocritical worship in the temple (*mine house*). Thus they *profan*(ed) or brought the Lord down to the level of the pagan gods.
23:40 *thou didst wash thyself.* Meticulous preparation and readiness to engage in idolatry.
23:41 *stately bed.* A magnificent or glorious bed.
23:42 *of the common sort.* Literally, "from a multitude of men," referring to all sorts of people. *Sabeans.* Not an ethnic

put bracelets upon their hands, and beautiful
crowns upon their heads.
43 Then said I unto *her that was* old in adulteries,
Will they now commit whoredoms with her, and
she *with them*?
44 Yet they went in unto her, as they go in unto
a woman that playeth the harlot: so went they in
unto Aholah and unto Aholibah, the lewd women.
45 ¶ And the righteous men, they shall judge
them after the manner of adulteresses, and after
the manner of women that shed blood; because
they *are* adulteresses, and blood *is* in their hands.
46 For thus saith the Lord GOD; I will bring up
a company upon them, and will give them to be
removed and spoiled.
47 And the company shall stone them with
stones, and dispatch them with their swords; they
shall slay their sons and their daughters, and burn
up their houses with fire.
48 Thus will I cause lewdness to cease out of the
land, that all women may be taught not to do after
your lewdness.
49 And they shall recompense your lewdness
upon you, and ye shall bear the sins of your idols:
and ye shall know that I *am* the Lord GOD.

CHAPTER 24

AGAIN in the ninth year, in the tenth month, in
the tenth *day* of the month, the word of the LORD
came unto me, saying,
2 Son of man, write thee the name of the day,
even of this same day: the king of Babylon set
himself against Jerusalem this same day.
3 And utter a parable unto the rebellious house,
and say unto them, Thus saith the Lord GOD; Set
on a pot, set *it* on, and also pour water into it:
4 Gather the pieces thereof into it, *even* every
good piece, the thigh, and the shoulder; fill *it* with
the choice bones.
5 Take the choice of the flock, and burn also the
bones under it, *and* make it boil well, and let them
seethe the bones of it therein.
6 ¶ Wherefore thus saith the Lord GOD; Woe to
the bloody city, to the pot whose scum *is* therein,
and whose scum is not gone out of it! bring it out
piece by piece; let no lot fall upon it.
7 For her blood is in the midst of her; she set it
upon the top of a rock; she poured it not upon the
ground, to cover it with dust;
8 That it might cause fury to come up to take
vengeance; I have set her blood upon the top of a
rock, that it should not be covered.
9 Therefore thus saith the Lord GOD; Woe to the
bloody city! I will even make the pile for fire great.
10 Heap on wood, kindle the fire, consume the
flesh, and spice it well, and let the bones be burned.
11 Then set it empty upon the coals thereof, that
the brass of it may be hot, and may burn, and *that*
the filthiness of it may be molten in it, *that* the
scum of it may be consumed.
12 She hath wearied *herself* with lies, and her
great scum went not forth out of her: her scum
shall be in the fire.
13 In thy filthiness *is* lewdness: because I have
purged thee, and thou wast not purged, thou shalt
not be purged from thy filthiness any more, till I
have caused my fury to rest upon thee.
14 I the LORD have spoken *it*: it shall come to pass,
and I will do *it*; I will not go back, neither will I

term here but refers specifically to drunkards.

23:43 *old in adulteries.* Involved in adultery and idolatry over a long period.

23:45 *righteous men.* Not in the sense that they were godly but that they acted rightly or correctly in judging.

23:46 *to be removed and spoiled.* Literally, "[to be] a terror and plunder."

23:47 *dispatch.* Cut down.

23:49 *recompense.* Repaid. *bear the sins of your idols.* Suffer the consequences of your idolatry.

Thoughts for Personal/Family Worship: Chapter 23

The degrading and defiling nature of sin is vividly portrayed here. The details and language are shocking because sin against God is shocking. One sin leads to another, and wicked habits are formed, thus resulting in a desensitized mind and a readiness to entertain wicked thoughts and engage in wicked actions. That these explicit details are recorded is not without significance. God speaks so as to convince sinners of the dreadfulness of their sin and their misery and the danger on account of that sin. If we find this chapter offensive, how much more offensive does God find our sin! How should this vivid portrayal of idolatry move us to grieve and repent of our own idols?

Chapter 24: *Ezekiel compares Jerusalem to a boiling pot, and he is forbidden to mourn the death of his wife.*

Signs of the Cauldron and the Death of Ezekiel's Wife (24:1–27)

24:4 *pieces.* Of flesh or meat. *choice bones.* The best bones with marrow.

24:5 *burn also the bones under it.* Heap up a pile of bones under the pot. *seethe.* Boil or cook.

24:6 *bloody city.* City of bloods, the plural designating the guilt of violent bloodshed. *scum.* Rust (vv. 11–12). *no lot fall upon it.* In order to spare some.

24:7 *her blood.* The innocent blood shed in the city. *upon the top of a rock.* The blood was shed in an open place, with no attempt to hide the evidence.

24:8 *I have set her blood.* The Lord avenges the shedding of blood according to the principle of *lex talionis* (the law of retaliation, eye-for-eye), where the penalty corresponds to the crime.

24:9 *pile for fire.* The pile of wood for kindling and fuel.

24:10 *spice.* Mix.

24:11 *brass.* Bronze. *molten.* Brought to the melting point or poured out.

24:13 *filthiness.* Uncleanness. *lewdness.* Immorality and idolatry. *I have purged thee.* God often used means designed to bring them to repentance, which they ignored, confirming

spare, neither will I repent; according to thy ways,
and according to thy doings, shall they judge thee,
saith the Lord GOD.
15 ¶ Also the word of the LORD came unto me,
saying,
16 Son of man, behold, I take away from thee the
desire of thine eyes with a stroke: yet neither shalt
thou mourn nor weep, neither shall thy tears run
down.
17 Forbear to cry, make no mourning for the
dead, bind the tire of thine head upon thee, and
put on thy shoes upon thy feet, and cover not *thy*
lips, and eat not the bread of men.
18 So I spake unto the people in the morning: and
at even my wife died; and I did in the morning as I
was commanded.
19 ¶ And the people said unto me, Wilt thou not
tell us what these *things are* to us, that thou doest
so?
20 Then I answered them, The word of the LORD
came unto me, saying,
21 Speak unto the house of Israel, Thus saith the
Lord GOD; Behold, I will profane my sanctuary,
the excellency of your strength, the desire of your
eyes, and that which your soul pitieth; and your
sons and your daughters whom ye have left shall
fall by the sword.
22 And ye shall do as I have done: ye shall not
cover *your* lips, nor eat the bread of men.
23 And your tires *shall be* upon your heads, and
your shoes upon your feet: ye shall not mourn nor
weep; but ye shall pine away for your iniquities,
and mourn one toward another.
24 Thus Ezekiel is unto you a sign: according to
all that he hath done shall ye do: and when this
cometh, ye shall know that I *am* the Lord GOD.
25 Also, thou son of man, *shall it* not *be* in the
day when I take from them their strength, the joy
of their glory, the desire of their eyes, and that
whereupon they set their minds, their sons and
their daughters,
26 *That* he that escapeth in that day shall come
unto thee, to cause *thee* to hear *it* with *thine* ears?
27 In that day shall thy mouth be opened to him
which is escaped, and thou shalt speak, and be no
more dumb: and thou shalt be a sign unto them;
and they shall know that I *am* the LORD.

CHAPTER 25

THE word of the LORD came again unto me, saying,
2 Son of man, set thy face against the Ammon-
ites, and prophesy against them;
3 And say unto the Ammonites, Hear the word of
the Lord GOD; Thus saith the Lord GOD; Because
thou saidst, Aha, against my sanctuary, when it
was profaned; and against the land of Israel, when
it was desolate; and against the house of Judah,
when they went into captivity;
4 Behold, therefore I will deliver thee to the men
of the east for a possession, and they shall set their
palaces in thee, and make their dwellings in thee:

---

their uncleanness and sealing their judgment (Amos 4:6–12).

24:14 *neither will I repent.* Will not relent from judgment. *thy doings.* What you deserve.

24:16 *the desire of thine eyes.* Your beloved wife. *stroke.* A plague or some sort of sickness. The Lord directly controls (*I take away*) the life and death of each person (Deut. 32:39; Job 1:21).

24:17 *Forbear to cry.* Sigh silently. *bind the tire of thine head.* Keep on the head-dress or turban. *cover not thy lips.* Not cover the face with a veil. *eat not the bread of men.* Not consume customary food. God prohibited Ezekiel from the normal cultural expressions of grief, such as wailing, putting on special clothing, and eating special foods (vv. 22–23).

24:19–23 *tell us what these things are to us.* The answer is that so many people will die when the judgment comes that ordinary mourning rites will not be possible.

24:23 *pine away.* Rot or dissolve (4:17; 33:10; Ps. 38:5; Isa. 34:4; Zech. 14:12), a term used in the covenant curses upon Israel if the nation breaks God's law and suffers exile (Lev. 26:39).

24:24 *unto you a sign.* Ezekiel's behavior at the loss of his wife was an object lesson.

24:27 *dumb.* Mute.

Thoughts for Personal/Family Worship: Chapter 24

1. **Jerusalem's description as a rusty pot beyond salvage is a tragic picture and a fearful warning. Throughout her history God had given multiple opportunities for the pot to be cleansed, but the people had refused to receive the divine scouring and scrubbing. The time had come to meet the Lord in judgment. This is a warning, particularly to people who hear God's Word over and over again without responding with genuine faith and repentance. The heart is becoming hard with unrepentant hearing. What are the signs that a person is hardening under the gospel instead of responding rightly?**
2. **God is our Maker, and He has the right to take our lives when He sees fit, and even to regulate how we grieve for His glory (Lev. 10:1–3). Ordinarily God permits His people to express their grief in appropriate ways (Gen. 50:10; 2 Sam. 1:17; Acts 8:2), though not as those without hope (1 Thess. 4:13). However, Ezekiel was a sign from God that His wrath would bring bereavement beyond grieving, desolation so absolute that even the healing process of mourning would be denied the people. This sign points to hell itself, where the wicked will never find peace but will weep and gnash their teeth forever (Matt. 8:12; 22:13; 24:51; 25:30), which is their eternal punishment (Matt. 25:46).**

MESSAGES OF JUDGMENT AGAINST GENTILE NATIONS (25:1—32:32)

Chapter 25: *God's judgment extends to heathen nations.*

Judgment against Ammon, Moab, Edom, and Philistia (25:1–17)

25:2 *Ammonites.* The descendants of Lot through incest (Gen. 19:30–38).

25:3 *Aha.* This is the Hebrew word; it is an interjection of malicious joy.

25:4 *men of the east.* The Babylonians (v. 10). *palaces.*

they shall eat thy fruit, and they shall drink thy
milk.
5 And I will make Rabbah a stable for camels, and
the Ammonites a couchingplace for flocks: and ye
shall know that I *am* the LORD.
6 For thus saith the Lord GOD; Because thou hast
clapped *thine* hands, and stamped with the feet,
and rejoiced in heart with all thy despite against
the land of Israel;
7 Behold, therefore I will stretch out mine hand
upon thee, and will deliver thee for a spoil to the
heathen; and I will cut thee off from the people,
and I will cause thee to perish out of the countries:
I will destroy thee; and thou shalt know that I *am*
the LORD.
8 ¶ Thus saith the Lord GOD; Because that Moab
and Seir do say, Behold, the house of Judah *is* like
unto all the heathen;
9 Therefore, behold, I will open the side of Moab
from the cities, from his cities *which are* on his
frontiers, the glory of the country, Beth-jeshi-
moth, Baal-meon, and Kiriathaim,
10 Unto the men of the east with the Ammonites,
and will give them in possession, that the Ammon-
ites may not be remembered among the nations.
11 And I will execute judgments upon Moab; and
they shall know that I *am* the LORD.
12 ¶ Thus saith the Lord GOD; Because that
Edom hath dealt against the house of Judah by
taking vengeance, and hath greatly offended, and
revenged himself upon them;
13 Therefore thus saith the Lord GOD; I will also
stretch out mine hand upon Edom, and will cut
off man and beast from it; and I will make it
desolate from Teman; and they of Dedan shall fall
by the sword.
14 And I will lay my vengeance upon Edom by
the hand of my people Israel: and they shall do in
Edom according to mine anger and according to
my fury; and they shall know my vengeance, saith
the Lord GOD.
15 ¶ Thus saith the Lord GOD; Because the
Philistines have dealt by revenge, and have taken
vengeance with a despiteful heart, to destroy *it* for
the old hatred;
16 Therefore thus saith the Lord GOD; Behold, I
will stretch out mine hand upon the Philistines,
and I will cut off the Cherethims, and destroy the
remnant of the sea coast.
17 And I will execute great vengeance upon them
with furious rebukes; and they shall know that I
am the LORD, when I shall lay my vengeance upon
them.

CHAPTER 26

AND it came to pass in the eleventh year, in the
first *day* of the month, *that* the word of the LORD
came unto me, saying,
2 Son of man, because that Tyrus hath said
against Jerusalem, Aha, she is broken *that was* the
gates of the people: she is turned unto me: I shall
be replenished, *now* she is laid waste:
3 Therefore thus saith the Lord GOD; Behold, I
am against thee, O Tyrus, and will cause many
nations to come up against thee, as the sea causeth
his waves to come up.
4 And they shall destroy the walls of Tyrus, and
break down her towers: I will also scrape her dust
from her, and make her like the top of a rock.
5 It shall be *a place for* the spreading of nets in the
midst of the sea: for I have spoken *it*, saith the Lord

Encampments or battlements. Ironically, Ammon fell to the same people who brought them joy when Judah fell.

25:5 *Rabbah.* The capital city. *couchingplace for flocks.* A place to lie down, a resting place.

25:6 *clapped thine hands.* Gestures of expressing glee. *despite.* Spite or contempt.

25:8 *Moab.* Also descendants of Lot through incest (v. 2). *Seir.* A mountain of Idumea.

25:9 *the side of Moab.* Its shoulder, signifying the strongest cities. *frontiers.* The borders of the land.

25:12 *Edom.* The descendants of Esau. Edom was often treated as typical or representative of all the nations hostile to Israel. See Obadiah.

25:13 *Teman . . . Dedan.* The northernmost and southernmost cities, referring to the entirety of the land.

25:15 *Philistines.* Ancient enemies of Israel. *despiteful heart.* A heart full of spite and contempt. *old hatred.* Ancient conflict climaxing in the days of the judges and early monarchy.

25:17 *furious rebukes.* Raging punishments.

Thoughts for Personal/Family Worship: Chapter 25

God has a great jealousy for His own glory and worship. He knows when He is mocked and His holiness is profaned. He does not ignore sin, wherever it appears or whoever is guilty. God will cause all men to know that He is the Lord (vv. 5,7,11,17). There is no other God beside Him. He will judge all nations, whether or not they have acknowledged Him as God. He will call every person to account for his sins against His moral law. On judgment day every knee will bow and every tongue will confess that Jesus is Lord, to the glory of the Father (Isa. 45:22–23; Phil. 2:9–11). How should this truth shape our lives? How should it motivate us to support missions?

Judgment against Tyre and Sidon (26:1—28:26)

Chapter 26: *God threatens Tyre with judgment.*

26:1 *the eleventh year.* This marked the year of Jerusalem's fall.

26:2 *Tyrus.* Tyre, a Phoenician city on the Mediterranean coast. *Aha.* See note at 25:3. Tyre interpreted Jerusalem's fall to be an open door to self-enrichment.

26:3 *Therefore.* God will punish those who rejoice over the disaster of others (Prov. 17:5).

26:4 *scrape her dust from her; and make her like the top of a rock.* Complete destruction so that nothing remains, like a polished rock.

26:5 *the spreading of nets in the midst of the sea.* A desolate place used only by fishermen to dry their nets (v. 14).

GOD: and it shall become a spoil to the nations.
6 And her daughters which *are* in the field shall
be slain by the sword; and they shall know that I
am the LORD.
7 ¶ For thus saith the Lord GOD; Behold, I will
bring upon Tyrus Nebuchadrezzar king of
Babylon, a king of kings, from the north, with
horses, and with chariots, and with horsemen,
and companies, and much people.
8 He shall slay with the sword thy daughters in
the field: and he shall make a fort against thee,
and cast a mount against thee, and lift up the
buckler against thee.
9 And he shall set engines of war against thy walls,
and with his axes he shall break down thy towers.
10 By reason of the abundance of his horses their
dust shall cover thee: thy walls shall shake at the
noise of the horsemen, and of the wheels, and of
the chariots, when he shall enter into thy gates, as
men enter into a city wherein is made a breach.
11 With the hoofs of his horses shall he tread
down all thy streets: he shall slay thy people by the
sword, and thy strong garrisons shall go down to
the ground.
12 And they shall make a spoil of thy riches, and
make a prey of thy merchandise: and they shall
break down thy walls, and destroy thy pleasant
houses: and they shall lay thy stones and thy
timber and thy dust in the midst of the water.
13 And I will cause the noise of thy songs to cease;
and the sound of thy harps shall be no more heard.
14 And I will make thee like the top of a rock:
thou shalt be *a place* to spread nets upon; thou
shalt be built no more: for I the LORD have spoken
it, saith the Lord GOD.
15 ¶ Thus saith the Lord GOD to Tyrus; Shall not
the isles shake at the sound of thy fall, when the
wounded cry, when the slaughter is made in the
midst of thee?
16 Then all the princes of the sea shall come down
from their thrones, and lay away their robes, and
put off their broidered garments: they shall clothe
themselves with trembling; they shall sit upon the
ground, and shall tremble at *every* moment, and
be astonished at thee.
17 And they shall take up a lamentation for thee,
and say to thee, How art thou destroyed, *that*
wast inhabited of seafaring men, the renowned
city, which wast strong in the sea, she and her
inhabitants, which cause their terror *to be* on all
that haunt it!
18 Now shall the isles tremble in the day of thy
fall; yea, the isles that *are* in the sea shall be trou-
bled at thy departure.
19 For thus saith the Lord GOD; When I shall
make thee a desolate city, like the cities that are
not inhabited; when I shall bring up the deep
upon thee, and great waters shall cover thee;
20 When I shall bring thee down with them that
descend into the pit, with the people of old time,
and shall set thee in the low parts of the earth, in
places desolate of old, with them that go down to
the pit, that thou be not inhabited; and I shall set
glory in the land of the living;
21 I will make thee a terror, and thou *shalt be* no
more: though thou be sought for, yet shalt thou
never be found again, saith the Lord GOD.

CHAPTER 27

THE word of the LORD came again unto me,
saying,

26:6 *daughters which are in the field.* A general reference to the inhabitants (v. 8).
26:7 *king of kings.* A Hebrew way of expressing a superlative; a supreme king or emperor (Ezra 7:12; Dan. 2:37). A title of God only when coupled with "Lord of lords" (1 Tim. 6:15; Rev. 17:14; 19:16; cf. Deut. 10:17; Ps. 136:2–3). *horses . . . chariots . . . horsemen . . . companies . . . much people.* The vast numbers, power, and intensity of the armies of *Nebuchadrezzar*.
26:8 *fort.* A bulwark or siege wall. *cast a mount.* Construct an assault ramp. *buckler.* The Hebrew refers to a large, full-body shield.
26:9 *engines of war.* Something like battering rams.
26:12 *make a prey.* Plunder.
26:15 *the isles.* Or coastlands (v. 18).
26:16 *princes of the sea.* The kings of other coastline nations. *broidered garments.* The colorfully woven robes of rulers or rich men.
26:17 *lamentation.* Dirge or funeral song. *strong in the sea.* Wealthy by virtue of trade and safe with the sea itself as a defense. *all that haunt it.* All the ones inhabiting it. The grief of men over the fall of this wealthy city foreshadows the grief of all the world when God's judgment falls upon it, impoverishing all sinners by taking away the objects of their lusts (Rev. 18:9–19).
26:20 *pit.* The grave. *I shall set glory in the land of the living.* The Hebrew is difficult, perhaps referring to loss of place in the land of the living.
26:21 *never be found again.* Tyre would disappear—not its physical location (Mark 3:8) but its wicked people (Ps. 37:10,36), who would descend into death (v. 20).

Thoughts for Personal/Family Worship: Chapter 26

Riches offer no security in the day of God's judgment. Tyre was a wealthy place, full of merchandise and commerce, but none of that was able to deliver it in the days of God's wrath. Once it rejoiced over Jerusalem's fall as an opportunity for profit, but its joy turned to horror and destruction. Rich people may look down on the suffering and exploit the weak, but their days are numbered. Their wealth cannot save them (Ps. 49:6–7). We cannot be redeemed with silver and gold but only by the precious blood of Christ (1 Peter 1:18–19). Consider Christ's searching question of "What shall it profit a man, if he shall gain the whole world, and lose his own soul?" (Mark 8:36). Losing our wealth and fame is nothing in comparison to losing our soul and facing the wrath of God.

Chapter 27: ***Ezekiel sings a funeral song for Tyre.***

2 Now, thou son of man, take up a lamentation for Tyrus;
3 And say unto Tyrus, O thou that art situate at the entry of the sea, *which art* a merchant of the people for many isles, Thus saith the Lord GOD; O Tyrus, thou hast said, I *am* of perfect beauty.
4 Thy borders *are* in the midst of the seas, thy builders have perfected thy beauty.
5 They have made all thy *ship* boards of fir trees of Senir: they have taken cedars from Lebanon to make masts for thee.
6 *Of* the oaks of Bashan have they made thine oars; the company of the Ashurites have made thy benches *of* ivory, *brought* out of the isles of Chittim.
7 Fine linen with broidered work from Egypt was that which thou spreadest forth to be thy sail; blue and purple from the isles of Elishah was that which covered thee.
8 The inhabitants of Zidon and Arvad were thy mariners: thy wise *men*, O Tyrus, *that* were in thee, were thy pilots.
9 The ancients of Gebal and the wise *men* thereof were in thee thy calkers: all the ships of the sea with their mariners were in thee to occupy thy merchandise.
10 They of Persia and of Lud and of Phut were in thine army, thy men of war: they hanged the shield and helmet in thee; they set forth thy comeliness.
11 The men of Arvad with thine army *were* upon thy walls round about, and the Gammadims were in thy towers: they hanged their shields upon thy walls round about; they have made thy beauty perfect.
12 Tarshish *was* thy merchant by reason of the multitude of all *kind of* riches; with silver, iron, tin, and lead, they traded in thy fairs.
13 Javan, Tubal, and Meshech, they *were* thy merchants: they traded the persons of men and vessels of brass in thy market.
14 They of the house of Togarmah traded in thy fairs with horses and horsemen and mules.
15 The men of Dedan *were* thy merchants; many isles *were* the merchandise of thine hand: they brought thee *for* a present horns of ivory and ebony.
16 Syria *was* thy merchant by reason of the multitude of the wares of thy making: they occupied in thy fairs with emeralds, purple, and broidered work, and fine linen, and coral, and agate.
17 Judah, and the land of Israel, they *were* thy merchants: they traded in thy market wheat of Minnith, and Pannag, and honey, and oil, and balm.
18 Damascus *was* thy merchant in the multitude of the wares of thy making, for the multitude of all riches; in the wine of Helbon, and white wool.
19 Dan also and Javan going to and fro occupied in thy fairs: bright iron, cassia, and calamus, were in thy market.
20 Dedan *was* thy merchant in precious clothes for chariots.
21 Arabia, and all the princes of Kedar, they occupied with thee in lambs, and rams, and goats: in these *were they* thy merchants.
22 The merchants of Sheba and Raamah, they *were* thy merchants: they occupied in thy fairs with chief of all spices, and with all precious stones, and gold.
23 Haran, and Canneh, and Eden, the merchants of Sheba, Asshur, *and* Chilmad, *were* thy merchants.
24 These *were* thy merchants in all sorts *of things*, in blue clothes, and broidered work, and in chests of rich apparel, bound with cords, and made of cedar, among thy merchandise.
25 The ships of Tarshish did sing of thee in thy market: and thou wast replenished, and made very glorious in the midst of the seas.
26 ¶ Thy rowers have brought thee into great waters: the east wind hath broken thee in the midst of the seas.
27 Thy riches, and thy fairs, thy merchandise, thy mariners, and thy pilots, thy calkers, and the occupiers of thy merchandise, and all thy men of war, that *are* in thee, and in all thy company which *is* in the midst of thee, shall fall into the midst of the seas in the day of thy ruin.
28 The suburbs shall shake at the sound of the cry of thy pilots.
29 And all that handle the oar, the mariners, *and* all the pilots of the sea, shall come down from

27:2 *lamentation.* A dirge or funeral song (v. 32).
27:3 *art situate.* Is located. *at the entry of the sea.* A port city. *many isles.* Large coasts. *of perfect beauty.* Entirely beautiful.
27:4 *borders are in the midst of the seas.* The sea was within its domain and under its control.
27:6 *benches.* The Hebrew is uncertain; either the deck of a ship, a cabin wall, or a ship's pole.
27:8 *pilots.* Sailors (vv. 27–29).
27:9 *calkers.* Repairmen who fixed the leaks. *occupy thy merchandise.* Barter or trade your goods (v. 27).
27:10 *Lud . . . Phut.* Most likely locations in North Africa. *hanged the shield and helmet in thee.* Used as a military base. *set forth thy comeliness.* Literally, "gave your splendor" (v. 11).
27:12–24 The extensive details signify the richness of the trade and the variety of items involved, thus indicating how important a place Tyre was in ancient times. Its influence and commercial activities stretched across the Mediterranean.
27:12 *fairs.* Merchandise or wares (vv. 14,16,19,22,27).
27:25 *glorious.* Exceedingly honorable.
27:26 *east wind.* A fearful wind for sailors, full of peril and danger.
27:28 *suburbs.* The outlying districts under the jurisdiction of the city.

their ships, they shall stand upon the land;
30 And shall cause their voice to be heard against
thee, and shall cry bitterly, and shall cast up dust
upon their heads, they shall wallow themselves in
the ashes:
31 And they shall make themselves utterly bald
for thee, and gird them with sackcloth, and they
shall weep for thee with bitterness of heart *and*
bitter wailing.
32 And in their wailing they shall take up a
lamentation for thee, and lament over thee,
saying, What *city is* like Tyrus, like the destroyed
in the midst of the sea?
33 When thy wares went forth out of the seas,
thou filledst many people; thou didst enrich the
kings of the earth with the multitude of thy riches
and of thy merchandise.
34 In the time *when* thou shalt be broken by the
seas in the depths of the waters thy merchandise
and all thy company in the midst of thee shall fall.
35 All the inhabitants of the isles shall be
astonished at thee, and their kings shall be sore
afraid, they shall be troubled in *their* countenance.
36 The merchants among the people shall hiss at
thee; thou shalt be a terror, and never *shalt be* any
more.

CHAPTER 28

THE word of the LORD came again unto me,
saying,
2 Son of man, say unto the prince of Tyrus, Thus
saith the Lord GOD; Because thine heart *is* lifted
up, and thou hast said, I *am* a God, I sit *in* the
seat of God, in the midst of the seas; yet thou *art*
a man, and not God, though thou set thine heart
as the heart of God:
3 Behold, thou *art* wiser than Daniel; there is no
secret that they can hide from thee:
4 With thy wisdom and with thine understand-
ing thou hast gotten thee riches, and hast gotten
gold and silver into thy treasures:
5 By thy great wisdom *and* by thy traffick hast
thou increased thy riches, and thine heart is lifted
up because of thy riches:
6 Therefore thus saith the Lord GOD; Because
thou hast set thine heart as the heart of God;
7 Behold, therefore I will bring strangers upon
thee, the terrible of the nations: and they shall
draw their swords against the beauty of thy
wisdom, and they shall defile thy brightness.
8 They shall bring thee down to the pit, and thou
shalt die the deaths of *them that are* slain in the
midst of the seas.
9 Wilt thou yet say before him that slayeth thee, I
am God? but thou *shalt be* a man, and no God, in
the hand of him that slayeth thee.
10 Thou shalt die the deaths of the uncircum-
cised by the hand of strangers: for I have spoken
it, saith the Lord GOD.
11 ¶ Moreover the word of the LORD came unto
me, saying,
12 Son of man, take up a lamentation upon
the king of Tyrus, and say unto him, Thus saith
the Lord GOD; Thou sealest up the sum, full of
wisdom, and perfect in beauty.
13 Thou hast been in Eden the garden of God;
every precious stone *was* thy covering, the sardius,

27:30 *cast up dust upon.* Gestures indicating deep mourning or sorrow.
27:31 *utterly bald.* Either by shaving or tearing out their hair in despair. *gird . . . sackcloth.* A sign of great grief.
27:35 *isles.* Coastlands. *sore afraid.* Very terrified.
27:36 *hiss.* Express shock or mockery.

Thoughts for Personal/Family Worship: Chapter 27

Tyre was the epitome of pride and stands as a warning to all against the dangers of this sin. The city of Tyre boasted of its own beauty and was convinced of its superiority. Pride is the forerunner of judgment and trouble. God brought the proud city low. "Every one that is proud in heart is an abomination to the LORD: though hand join in hand, he shall not be unpunished" (Prov. 16:5). The cause of pride is irrelevant; God hates it. We must remember that all we are and have we owe to God. He distributes gifts, talents, and abilities according to His sovereign good pleasure. There is absolutely no legitimate cause for boasting, but only for thanksgiving. How can we beware of pride and kill it?

Chapter 28: *Ezekiel pronounces judgment on the king of Tyre because of the king's pride.*

28:2 *prince.* The king or ruler, not a prince waiting for a throne. *lifted up.* Proud (v. 17). *I am a God.* A most ungodly and arrogant claim.
28:3 *wiser than Daniel.* Daniel was contemporary with Ezekiel and a fellow captive in Babylon (14:14,20). Daniel, because of his God-given wisdom, had become a part of the Babylonian bureaucracy (Dan. 1:17; 2:23,48).
28:4 *wisdom.* Shrewdness or skill. *gotten.* Obtained. *treasures.* Storehouses.
28:5 *traffick.* Trade (v. 18).
28:7 *strangers.* Foreigners (v. 10). *terrible.* Powerful or tyrannical.
28:8 *pit.* Destruction or grave. *die the deaths of them that are slain in the midst of the seas.* Die as those thrown overboard to drown in the ocean.
28:11–19 Ezekiel spoke of the king of Tyre as the pinnacle of glory who had fallen into the depths of disgrace and destruction for his pride. Some interpret this text as a highly symbolic description of the king's earthly majesty. Others read it as going beyond any earthly king to describe the fall of the angel who is now the Devil or Satan (cf. Isa. 14:12–14).
28:12 *lamentation.* Dirge or funeral song. *sealest up the sum.* Sealed up the model of perfection.
28:13 *Eden the garden of God.* Man's original dwelling place, a paradise of beauty and pleasure (31:9,16,18; 36:35; Gen. 2:1–25). *every precious stone.* Immense wealth and loveliness. All nine gemstones listed here also appeared among the

topaz, and the diamond, the beryl, the onyx, and
the jasper, the sapphire, the emerald, and the
carbuncle, and gold: the workmanship of thy
tabrets and of thy pipes was prepared in thee in
the day that thou wast created.
14 Thou *art* the anointed cherub that covereth;
and I have set thee *so*: thou wast upon the holy
mountain of God; thou hast walked up and down
in the midst of the stones of fire.
15 Thou *wast* perfect in thy ways from the day
that thou wast created, till iniquity was found in
thee.
16 By the multitude of thy merchandise they have
filled the midst of thee with violence, and thou
hast sinned: therefore I will cast thee as profane
out of the mountain of God: and I will destroy
thee, O covering cherub, from the midst of the
stones of fire.
17 Thine heart was lifted up because of thy
beauty, thou hast corrupted thy wisdom by
reason of thy brightness: I will cast thee to the
ground, I will lay thee before kings, that they may
behold thee.
18 Thou hast defiled thy sanctuaries by the
multitude of thine iniquities, by the iniquity of
thy traffick; therefore will I bring forth a fire from
the midst of thee, it shall devour thee, and I will
bring thee to ashes upon the earth in the sight of
all them that behold thee.
19 All they that know thee among the people
shall be astonished at thee: thou shalt be a terror,
and never *shalt* thou *be* any more.
20 ¶ Again the word of the LORD came unto me,
saying,
21 Son of man, set thy face against Zidon, and
prophesy against it,
22 And say, Thus saith the Lord GOD; Behold, I
am against thee, O Zidon; and I will be glorified
in the midst of thee: and they shall know that I *am*
the LORD, when I shall have executed judgments
in her, and shall be sanctified in her.
23 For I will send into her pestilence, and blood
into her streets; and the wounded shall be judged
in the midst of her by the sword upon her on every
side; and they shall know that I *am* the LORD.
24 ¶ And there shall be no more a pricking brier
unto the house of Israel, nor *any* grieving thorn of
all *that are* round about them, that despised them;
and they shall know that I *am* the Lord GOD.
25 Thus saith the Lord GOD; When I shall have
gathered the house of Israel from the people
among whom they are scattered, and shall be
sanctified in them in the sight of the heathen,
then shall they dwell in their land that I have given
to my servant Jacob.
26 And they shall dwell safely therein, and shall
build houses, and plant vineyards; yea, they shall
dwell with confidence, when I have executed
judgments upon all those that despise them
round about them; and they shall know that I *am*
the LORD their God.

CHAPTER 29

IN the tenth year, in the tenth *month*, in the
twelfth *day* of the month, the word of the LORD
came unto me, saying,
2 Son of man, set thy face against Pharaoh king

---

twelve stones set in *gold* upon the breastplate worn by the high priest of Israel (Ex. 28:17–20). Both *gold* and *onyx* were associated with the garden of Eden as well (Gen. 2:12). *tabrets.* Tambourines or some sort of hand drums, a sign of joy (Gen. 31:27; Ex. 15:20; Jer. 31:4). *pipes.* Hebrew uncertain, something with holes. *created.* Same word used in Gen. 1:1.

28:14 *anointed.* Hebrew term used only here, possibly related to "anoint" for special office or service like a priest or a king. *cherub.* An angelic being, a heavenly servant of God (see note at 10:15) and guardian of the garden of Eden (Gen. 3:24). *that covereth.* Same Hebrew term used of the cherubim covering the ark of the covenant with their wings as guardians of God's holiness (Ex. 25:20; 37:9; 1 Kings 8:7; 1 Chron. 28:18). *holy mountain of God.* Symbol for God's kingdom (see note at 17:22). *stones of fire.* Most likely decorative stones with a dazzling appearance as of fire (v. 16).

28:15 *perfect in thy ways.* Blameless in moral conduct (Ps. 101:2,6).

28:16 *multitude.* Abundance. *merchandise.* Trade (26:12; same word as "traffick," vv. 5,18; from same root as "merchants" throughout ch. 27). *profane.* Common or ordinary, opposite of holy and set apart.

28:17 *lifted up.* Proud. *cast.* Throw down. *lay.* Set or place.

28:18 *defiled.* Profaned, treated the holy as common. *traffick.* Trade.

28:21 *Zidon.* Sidon, an ancient Phoenician city north of Tyre and often associated with it.

28:23 *pestilence.* Plagues or epidemics.

28:24 *pricking brier.* An irritation or pain. *grieving thorn.* That which causes hurt or pain.

28:26 *safely.* Confidently.

Thoughts for Personal/Family Worship: Chapter 28

When God gives honor, ability, or beauty to one of His creations, too often that creature becomes puffed up with wicked and foolish pride instead of lowering himself in grateful worship to God. So it was with Satan, with Adam in the garden, and with many kings and other people since then. We must all be careful because pride is an insidious sin that dwells in the hearts of all men. Natural man seeks to take the place of God. Let us be quick to acknowledge that God sovereignly distributes gifts and abilities according to His will, and that we have nothing apart from what God has given. Whenever we find ourselves in a position of prosperity or prestige, let us resolve to humbly serve God by His grace in Christ for His glory alone.

Judgment against Egypt (29:1—32:32)

Chapter 29: ***Ezekiel pronounces God's judgment on Egypt.***

of Egypt, and prophesy against him, and against
all Egypt:
3 Speak, and say, Thus saith the Lord GOD;
Behold, I *am* against thee, Pharaoh king of Egypt,
the great dragon that lieth in the midst of his
rivers, which hath said, My river *is* mine own, and
I have made *it* for myself.
4 But I will put hooks in thy jaws, and I will cause
the fish of thy rivers to stick unto thy scales, and
I will bring thee up out of the midst of thy rivers,
and all the fish of thy rivers shall stick unto thy
scales.
5 And I will leave thee *thrown* into the wilderness,
thee and all the fish of thy rivers: thou shalt fall
upon the open fields; thou shalt not be brought
together, nor gathered: I have given thee for meat
to the beasts of the field and to the fowls of the
heaven.
6 And all the inhabitants of Egypt shall know that
I *am* the LORD, because they have been a staff of
reed to the house of Israel.
7 When they took hold of thee by thy hand, thou
didst break, and rend all their shoulder: and when
they leaned upon thee, thou brakest, and madest
all their loins to be at a stand.
8 ¶ Therefore thus saith the Lord GOD; Behold, I
will bring a sword upon thee, and cut off man and
beast out of thee.
9 And the land of Egypt shall be desolate and
waste; and they shall know that I *am* the LORD:
because he hath said, The river *is* mine, and I have
made *it*.
10 Behold, therefore I *am* against thee, and
against thy rivers, and I will make the land of
Egypt utterly waste *and* desolate, from the tower
of Syene even unto the border of Ethiopia.
11 No foot of man shall pass through it, nor foot
of beast shall pass through it, neither shall it be
inhabited forty years.
12 And I will make the land of Egypt desolate in
the midst of the countries *that are* desolate, and
her cities among the cities *that are* laid waste
shall be desolate forty years: and I will scatter the
Egyptians among the nations, and will disperse
them through the countries.
13 ¶ Yet thus saith the Lord GOD; At the end of
forty years will I gather the Egyptians from the
people whither they were scattered:
14 And I will bring again the captivity of Egypt,
and will cause them to return *into* the land of
Pathros, into the land of their habitation; and
they shall be there a base kingdom.
15 It shall be the basest of the kingdoms; neither
shall it exalt itself any more above the nations: for
I will diminish them, that they shall no more rule
over the nations.
16 And it shall be no more the confidence of the
house of Israel, which bringeth *their* iniquity to
remembrance, when they shall look after them:
but they shall know that I *am* the Lord GOD.
17 ¶ And it came to pass in the seven and
twentieth year, in the first *month*, in the first *day*
of the month, the word of the LORD came unto
me, saying,
18 Son of man, Nebuchadrezzar king of Babylon
caused his army to serve a great service against
Tyrus: every head *was* made bald, and every
shoulder *was* peeled: yet had he no wages, nor his
army, for Tyrus, for the service that he had served
against it:
19 Therefore thus saith the Lord GOD; Behold, I
will give the land of Egypt unto Nebuchadrezzar
king of Babylon; and he shall take her multitude,
and take her spoil, and take her prey; and it shall
be the wages for his army.
20 I have given him the land of Egypt *for* his
labour wherewith he served against it, because
they wrought for me, saith the Lord GOD.
21 ¶ In that day will I cause the horn of the house
of Israel to bud forth, and I will give thee the
opening of the mouth in the midst of them; and
they shall know that I *am* the LORD.

29:3 *great dragon.* Huge sea creature of some sort; sometimes also translated "serpent" or "whale" (32:2; Gen. 1:21; Job 7:12; Ps. 148:7; Isa. 27:1). The Lord's victory over Egypt was pictured as the killing of such a sea serpent (Pss. 74:12–15; 89:9–10; Isa. 51:9–10). *My river is mine own . . . made it for myself.* A boastful claim over the Nile, similar to boasts of the king of Tyre and later those of Nebuchadnezzar (Dan. 4:30). This was for his punishment (v. 9)

29:5 *meat.* Food.

29:6–7 *a staff of reed . . . didst break.* Egypt's lack of effective support for Israel, despite her faith in Pharaoh (Isa. 36:6; cf. Isa. 30:3; 31:1,3). *madest all their loins to be at a stand.* The significance is unclear; perhaps they shook because of a lack of support.

29:10 *Syene . . . Ethiopia.* The western and eastern borders, and thus the entire country.

29:13 Unlike the irreversible destruction of Tyre (27:36), Egypt would be restored.

29:14 *bring again the captivity.* Restore the fortunes. *habitation.* Birth or origin. *base kingdom.* A humbled or low kingdom, but a kingdom nonetheless (v. 15).

29:16 *no more the confidence.* Israel would no longer look to them for help.

29:17 *seven and twentieth year.* The latest dated prophecy of Ezekiel, most likely dated from his captivity; therefore 571/570 BC.

29:18 *Nebuchadrezzar.* Nebuchadnezzar. *bald . . . peeled.* Rubbed raw, the cost upon his soldiers of prosecuting the long siege. *no wages, nor his army.* Indicating no spoil for his efforts or the vast expense involved in the war.

29:19–20 The Lord would give Egypt to Babylon in compensation for the long siege against Tyre. *they wrought for me.* Babylon was God's weapon against Tyre, just as against Egypt.

29:21 *horn.* A symbol of power or strength. *bud forth.* Increase or flourish. *the opening of the mouth.* An occasion for speaking.

CHAPTER 30

THE word of the LORD came again unto me,
saying,
2 Son of man, prophesy and say, Thus saith the
Lord GOD; Howl ye, Woe worth the day!
3 For the day *is* near, even the day of the LORD
is near, a cloudy day; it shall be the time of the
heathen.
4 And the sword shall come upon Egypt, and
great pain shall be in Ethiopia, when the slain shall
fall in Egypt, and they shall take away her multi-
tude, and her foundations shall be broken down.
5 Ethiopia, and Libya, and Lydia, and all the min-
gled people, and Chub, and the men of the land
that is in league, shall fall with them by the sword.
6 Thus saith the LORD; They also that uphold
Egypt shall fall; and the pride of her power shall
come down: from the tower of Syene shall they
fall in it by the sword, saith the Lord GOD.
7 And they shall be desolate in the midst of the
countries *that are* desolate, and her cities shall be
in the midst of the cities *that are* wasted.
8 And they shall know that I *am* the LORD, when
I have set a fire in Egypt, and *when* all her helpers
shall be destroyed.
9 In that day shall messengers go forth from me
in ships to make the careless Ethiopians afraid,
and great pain shall come upon them, as in the
day of Egypt: for, lo, it cometh.
10 Thus saith the Lord GOD; I will also make
the multitude of Egypt to cease by the hand of
Nebuchadrezzar king of Babylon.
11 He and his people with him, the terrible of the
nations, shall be brought to destroy the land: and
they shall draw their swords against Egypt, and fill
the land with the slain.
12 And I will make the rivers dry, and sell the land
into the hand of the wicked: and I will make the
land waste, and all that is therein, by the hand of
strangers: I the LORD have spoken *it*.
13 Thus saith the Lord GOD; I will also destroy
the idols, and I will cause *their* images to cease out
of Noph; and there shall be no more a prince of
the land of Egypt: and I will put a fear in the land
of Egypt.
14 And I will make Pathros desolate, and will set
fire in Zoan, and will execute judgments in No.
15 And I will pour my fury upon Sin, the strength
of Egypt; and I will cut off the multitude of No.
16 And I will set fire in Egypt: Sin shall have great
pain, and No shall be rent asunder, and Noph
shall have distresses daily.
17 The young men of Aven and of Pi-beseth shall
fall by the sword: and these *cities* shall go into
captivity.
18 At Tehaphnehes also the day shall be darkened,
when I shall break there the yokes of Egypt: and
the pomp of her strength shall cease in her: as for
her, a cloud shall cover her, and her daughters
shall go into captivity.
19 Thus will I execute judgments in Egypt: and
they shall know that I *am* the LORD.
20 ¶ And it came to pass in the eleventh year, in
the first *month*, in the seventh *day* of the month,
that the word of the LORD came unto me, saying,
21 Son of man, I have broken the arm of Pharaoh
king of Egypt; and, lo, it shall not be bound up
to be healed, to put a roller to bind it, to make it
strong to hold the sword.
22 Therefore thus saith the Lord GOD; Behold, I
am against Pharaoh king of Egypt, and will break
his arms, the strong, and that which was broken;

Thoughts for Personal/Family Worship: Chapter 29

We are reminded by this passage not to trust in princes or in human power but in God. Egypt was a mighty nation, and some in Israel had put their confidence in her. But this creature confidence was misplaced. Egypt could no more save Israel than save herself. The people of Egypt gloried in their power and in their self-made prosperity, but their boasting was in vain. All that they had was due to God's common grace, yet they failed to acknowledge Him. In His time they were shown to be powerless and poor. God raises up nations and brings down nations according to His will. In what powers of man do people commonly trust today? How can you trust in God alone for those concerns?

Chapter 30: *Ezekiel identifies the judgment of Egypt as a day of the Lord.*

30:2 *Howl.* Lament. *Woe worth the day!* "O unhappy day!"
30:3 *near.* Impending. *the day of the LORD.* The time of God's direct and extraordinary intervention in human affairs, either for judgment or blessing, here judgment. *cloudy day.* A day of darkness (Joel 2:1–2; Zeph. 1:15).
30:4 *pain.* Trembling or anguish (v. 9).
30:5 *mingled people.* Foreign mercenaries, a mixed company. *league.* Covenant or alliance.
30:6 *Syene.* See 29:10.
30:9 *to make the careless Ethiopians afraid.* To startle the Ethiopians, who were carefree and living in security.
30:10 *make . . . to cease.* Put an end to (v. 13).
30:11 *terrible of the nations.* Violent nations.
30:12 *strangers.* Foreigners.
30:13 *Noph.* Memphis, a capital city in Egypt (v. 16). *prince.* A leader or ruler.
30:14 *Pathros.* A part of Egypt. *Zoan.* Tanis, a city in lower (northern) Egypt. *No.* Thebes, an ancient capital city (vv. 15–16).
30:15 *Sin.* A town in eastern Egypt rather than the tract of wilderness between Sinai and Elim.
30:16 *rent asunder.* Torn apart.
30:17 *Aven.* Meaning vanity, the name of various places connected with idolatry. *Pi-beseth.* A town in lower (northern) Egypt.
30:18 *Tehaphnehes.* A city in Egypt. *darkened.* Restrained.
30:20 *in the eleventh year.* Of Zedekiah's reign and Jehoiachin's captivity (31:1).
30:21 *arm.* Power or strength (vv. 22,24–25). *roller.* A bandage or splint.

and I will cause the sword to fall out of his hand.
23 And I will scatter the Egyptians among the na-
tions, and will disperse them through the countries.
24 And I will strengthen the arms of the king of
Babylon, and put my sword in his hand: but I will
break Pharaoh's arms, and he shall groan before
him with the groanings of a deadly wounded *man*.
25 But I will strengthen the arms of the king of
Babylon, and the arms of Pharaoh shall fall down;
and they shall know that I *am* the LORD, when I
shall put my sword into the hand of the king of
Babylon, and he shall stretch it out upon the land
of Egypt.
26 And I will scatter the Egyptians among the
nations, and disperse them among the countries;
and they shall know that I *am* the LORD.

CHAPTER 31

AND it came to pass in the eleventh year, in the
third *month*, in the first *day* of the month, *that* the
word of the LORD came unto me, saying,
2 Son of man, speak unto Pharaoh king of Egypt,
and to his multitude; Whom art thou like in thy
greatness?
3 ¶ Behold, the Assyrian *was* a cedar in Lebanon
with fair branches, and with a shadowing shroud,
and of an high stature; and his top was among the
thick boughs.
4 The waters made him great, the deep set him
up on high with her rivers running round about
his plants, and sent out her little rivers unto all the
trees of the field.
5 Therefore his height was exalted above all the
trees of the field, and his boughs were multiplied,
and his branches became long because of the
multitude of waters, when he shot forth.
6 All the fowls of heaven made their nests in his
boughs, and under his branches did all the beasts
of the field bring forth their young, and under his
shadow dwelt all great nations.
7 Thus was he fair in his greatness, in the length
of his branches: for his root was by great waters.
8 The cedars in the garden of God could not hide
him: the fir trees were not like his boughs, and
the chesnut trees were not like his branches; nor
any tree in the garden of God was like unto him
in his beauty.
9 I have made him fair by the multitude of his
branches: so that all the trees of Eden, that *were* in
the garden of God, envied him.
10 ¶ Therefore thus saith the Lord GOD; Because
thou hast lifted up thyself in height, and he hath
shot up his top among the thick boughs, and his
heart is lifted up in his height;
11 I have therefore delivered him into the hand of
the mighty one of the heathen; he shall surely deal
with him: I have driven him out for his wickedness.
12 And strangers, the terrible of the nations,
have cut him off, and have left him: upon the
mountains and in all the valleys his branches are
fallen, and his boughs are broken by all the rivers
of the land; and all the people of the earth are
gone down from his shadow, and have left him.
13 Upon his ruin shall all the fowls of the heaven
remain, and all the beasts of the field shall be
upon his branches:
14 To the end that none of all the trees by the waters
exalt themselves for their height, neither shoot up
their top among the thick boughs, neither their
trees stand up in their height, all that drink water:
for they are all delivered unto death, to the nether
parts of the earth, in the midst of the children of
men, with them that go down to the pit.
15 Thus saith the Lord GOD; In the day when he
went down to the grave I caused a mourning: I

30:24 *I will strengthen the arms of the king . . . but I will break Pharaoh's arms.* The weakness or strength of each man comes directly from God, and therefore He determines every victory or defeat (1 Chron. 29:12; Ps. 33:16–19).

Thoughts for Personal/Family Worship: Chapter 30

1. **That Egypt's judgment is called the day of the Lord (v. 3) is a reminder of God's control of all the affairs of time. From the perspective of history, Babylon's invasion and subjection of Egypt in the sixth century BC could be explained by political and military causes. However, there is more to history than meets the eye. God's providence rules and orchestrates all things to achieve His glory through judgment and salvation.**
2. **The day of the Lord against Egypt and every other declaration of it in the Old Testament points to that final day when Christ will come and bring ultimate judgment and salvation. That time is set, and it will display perfect justice. All who have trusted in idols or mere men will be put to shame. All unforgiven sin and unrepentant sinners will be punished. How can we prepare for the day of the Lord so that we can greet it with joy?**

Chapter 31: *Ezekiel reviews Assyria's greatness and fall to confirm the same destruction on Egypt.*

31:3 *a cedar in Lebanon.* An image of Assyria as stately and powerful. *fair.* Beautiful. *shadowing shroud.* Literally, "a forest that gives shade."

31:5 *shot forth.* Spread out branches.

31:6 *in his boughs . . . under his branches . . . under his shadow.* The kingdom was able to rule, protect, and provide for many (17:23; Dan. 4:12,21–22; Mark 4:30–32).

31:7 *fair.* Bright, beautiful, or splendid.

31:8 *not like.* Assyria was unique among the nations.

31:10 *lifted up thyself.* Became haughty or arrogant. *shot up his top.* Literally, "gave his top," indicating that this tree was taller than any other.

31:11 *the mighty one of the heathen.* Literally, "the ram of nations," symbolic of power.

31:12 *strangers.* Foreigners. *the terrible of the nations.* The violent among the nations. *cut him off.* Literally, "cut him down." *shadow.* Protection (v. 17).

31:14 *nether.* Lower. *pit.* The grave (vv. 16–18).

31:15 *grave.* Hebrew, *sheol* (vv. 16–17; 32:21,27), sometimes

covered the deep for him, and I restrained the floods thereof, and the great waters were stayed: and I caused Lebanon to mourn for him, and all the trees of the field fainted for him.

16 I made the nations to shake at the sound of his fall, when I cast him down to hell with them that descend into the pit: and all the trees of Eden, the choice and best of Lebanon, all that drink water, shall be comforted in the nether parts of the earth.

17 They also went down into hell with him unto *them that be* slain with the sword; and *they that were* his arm, *that* dwelt under his shadow in the midst of the heathen.

18 ¶ To whom art thou thus like in glory and in greatness among the trees of Eden? yet shalt thou be brought down with the trees of Eden unto the nether parts of the earth: thou shalt lie in the midst of the uncircumcised with *them that be* slain by the sword. This *is* Pharaoh and all his multitude, saith the Lord GOD.

CHAPTER 32

AND it came to pass in the twelfth year, in the twelfth month, in the first *day* of the month, *that* the word of the LORD came unto me, saying,

2 Son of man, take up a lamentation for Pharaoh king of Egypt, and say unto him, Thou art like a young lion of the nations, and thou *art* as a whale in the seas: and thou camest forth with thy rivers, and troubledst the waters with thy feet, and fouledst their rivers.

3 Thus saith the Lord GOD; I will therefore spread out my net over thee with a company of many people; and they shall bring thee up in my net.

4 Then will I leave thee upon the land, I will cast thee forth upon the open field, and will cause all the fowls of the heaven to remain upon thee, and I will fill the beasts of the whole earth with thee.

5 And I will lay thy flesh upon the mountains, and fill the valleys with thy height.

6 I will also water with thy blood the land wherein thou swimmest, *even* to the mountains; and the rivers shall be full of thee.

7 And when I shall put thee out, I will cover the heaven, and make the stars thereof dark; I will cover the sun with a cloud, and the moon shall not give her light.

8 All the bright lights of heaven will I make dark over thee, and set darkness upon thy land, saith the Lord GOD.

9 I will also vex the hearts of many people, when I shall bring thy destruction among the nations, into the countries which thou hast not known.

10 Yea, I will make many people amazed at thee, and their kings shall be horribly afraid for thee, when I shall brandish my sword before them; and they shall tremble at *every* moment, every man for his own life, in the day of thy fall.

11 ¶ For thus saith the Lord GOD; The sword of the king of Babylon shall come upon thee.

12 By the swords of the mighty will I cause thy multitude to fall, the terrible of the nations, all of them: and they shall spoil the pomp of Egypt, and all the multitude thereof shall be destroyed.

13 I will destroy also all the beasts thereof from beside the great waters; neither shall the foot of man trouble them any more, nor the hoofs of beasts trouble them.

14 Then will I make their waters deep, and cause their rivers to run like oil, saith the Lord GOD.

15 When I shall make the land of Egypt desolate, and the country shall be destitute of that whereof it was full, when I shall smite all them that dwell therein, then shall they know that I *am* the LORD.

---

translated "hell." The term can refer to death, the grave, or the place of departed wicked spirits. *fainted.* Languished.

31:17 *his arm.* A symbol of strength. *dwelt.* Remained or abided. *shadow.* Rule and dominion.

31:18 *uncircumcised.* The wicked who are not in covenant with God.

Thoughts for Personal/Family Worship: Chapter 31

The sight of a great tree being cut down reminds us of how the high and lofty can quickly become firewood. Great men are nothing without God. The king of Assyria was noted for his stature and splendor. His kingdom was vast, and he was filled with pride, but God humbled him and judged him according to his wickedness. In the time of judgment his greatness counted for nothing. No man, however great, can stand against the power and wrath of God. The proud sinner will be brought to shame and ruin, but God gives grace to the humble. What men and women are commonly viewed as great ones or celebrities? How will it go for them on judgment day if they do not follow Christ?

Chapter 32: *Ezekiel laments the fall of Pharaoh and Egypt.*

32:2 *lamentation.* Dirge or funeral song (v. 16). *whale.* The picture in this text is the catching and killing of a great sea monster (see note at 29:3). *troubledst.* Disturbs or stirs up. *fouledst.* Makes muddy by stamping.

32:4 *fill the beasts of the whole earth with thee.* The monster's flesh would feed many scavengers, and perhaps be filled with the flesh of the dead men from Egypt's army.

32:6 *I will . . . water . . . swimmest.* The land would be irrigated by the monster's *blood*, and the *rivers* would be full of blood—an allusion to the first plague on Egypt through Moses (Ex. 7:14–25).

32:7 *put thee out.* Quench or extinguish you.

32:8 *darkness upon thy land.* An allusion to the ninth plague on Egypt (Ex. 10:21–23).

32:9 *vex.* Trouble or provoke.

32:10 *amazed.* Appalled. *brandish.* To whirl about.

32:12 *the terrible.* The violent ones. *the pomp of Egypt.* That which Egypt is proud of.

32:13 *neither shall the foot of man trouble them.* Egypt would become depopulated (29:11).

16 This *is* the lamentation wherewith they shall
lament her: the daughters of the nations shall
lament her: they shall lament for her, *even* for
Egypt, and for all her multitude, saith the Lord
GOD.
17 ¶ It came to pass also in the twelfth year, in the
fifteenth *day* of the month, *that* the word of the
LORD came unto me, saying,
18 Son of man, wail for the multitude of Egypt,
and cast them down, *even* her, and the daughters
of the famous nations, unto the nether parts of
the earth, with them that go down into the pit.
19 Whom dost thou pass in beauty? go down, and
be thou laid with the uncircumcised.
20 They shall fall in the midst of *them that are*
slain by the sword: she is delivered to the sword:
draw her and all her multitudes.
21 The strong among the mighty shall speak to
him out of the midst of hell with them that help
him: they are gone down, they lie uncircumcised,
slain by the sword.
22 Asshur *is* there and all her company: his graves
are about him: all of them slain, fallen by the
sword:
23 Whose graves are set in the sides of the pit, and
her company is round about her grave: all of them
slain, fallen by the sword, which caused terror in
the land of the living.
24 There *is* Elam and all her multitude round
about her grave, all of them slain, fallen by the
sword, which are gone down uncircumcised into
the nether parts of the earth, which caused their
terror in the land of the living; yet have they borne
their shame with them that go down to the pit.
25 They have set her a bed in the midst of the
slain with all her multitude: her graves *are* round
about him: all of them uncircumcised, slain by
the sword: though their terror was caused in the
land of the living, yet have they borne their shame
with them that go down to the pit: he is put in the
midst of *them that be* slain.
26 There *is* Meshech, Tubal, and all her multi-
tude: her graves *are* round about him: all of them
uncircumcised, slain by the sword, though they
caused their terror in the land of the living.
27 And they shall not lie with the mighty *that are*
fallen of the uncircumcised, which are gone down
to hell with their weapons of war: and they have
laid their swords under their heads, but their iniq-
uities shall be upon their bones, though *they were*
the terror of the mighty in the land of the living.
28 Yea, thou shalt be broken in the midst of the
uncircumcised, and shalt lie with *them that are*
slain with the sword.
29 There *is* Edom, her kings, and all her princes,
which with their might are laid by *them that were*
slain by the sword: they shall lie with the uncir-
cumcised, and with them that go down to the pit.
30 There *be* the princes of the north, all of them,
and all the Zidonians, which are gone down with
the slain; with their terror they are ashamed of
their might; and they lie uncircumcised with
them that be slain by the sword, and bear their
shame with them that go down to the pit.
31 Pharaoh shall see them, and shall be comforted
over all his multitude, *even* Pharaoh and all his
army slain by the sword, saith the Lord GOD.
32 For I have caused my terror in the land of the
living: and he shall be laid in the midst of the
uncircumcised with *them that are* slain with the
sword, *even* Pharaoh and all his multitude, saith
the Lord GOD.

CHAPTER 33

AGAIN the word of the LORD came unto me,
saying,
2 Son of man, speak to the children of thy people,

32:18 *wail.* Lament or mourn. *famous nations.* Mighty or magnificent nations. *nether parts.* Lower parts. *pit.* The grave (vv. 24–25).
32:19 *uncircumcised.* The ungodly or wicked; here those in the realm of the dead.
32:20 *draw.* Seize and drag.
32:21 *hell.* See note at 31:15.
32:22 *company.* Congregation or assembly (v. 3).
32:24 *Elam.* The king of Elam and his armies. *borne their shame.* Endured their disgrace and reproach.
32:25 *They have set her a bed.* This is where she rests and remains.
32:26 *Meshech.* The descendants of the son of Japheth, a people to the north of Israel. *Tubal.* A people descended from Tubal, from east Asia Minor.
32:27 *hell.* See note at 31:15. They were buried with their weapons of war, a typical custom.

Thoughts for Personal/Family Worship: Chapter 32

The powers of this world can seem like massive dragons and beasts that can never be overcome (Rev. 13). However, the Lord will slaughter them when He pleases, just as He broke Egypt at the Red Sea and again by the Babylonians. Many mighty empires have had their day in history, but when God had fulfilled His purposes for them they fell. With their fall, great leaders have joined the vast crowd of spirits of the damned in hell, powerless to do anything on earth and consigned to wait until the judgment day. How very different is the path of the righteous! Death brings them to peace (Isa. 57:1–2), and the judgment day will bring them to unspeakable honor and joy (Dan. 12:3). Which path are you walking, the path of worldly glory and hell or the path of Christ and heaven?

THE FALL AND RESTORATION OF JERUSALEM (33:1—37:28)

Chapter 33: ***Ezekiel is admonished about being a watchman, and God explains His dealings with the righteous and sinners.***

The Fall and Exile of Jerusalem (33:1–33)

and say unto them, When I bring the sword upon
a land, if the people of the land take a man of their
coasts, and set him for their watchman:
3 If when he seeth the sword come upon the land,
he blow the trumpet, and warn the people;
4 Then whosoever heareth the sound of the
trumpet, and taketh not warning; if the sword
come, and take him away, his blood shall be upon
his own head.
5 He heard the sound of the trumpet, and took
not warning; his blood shall be upon him. But he
that taketh warning shall deliver his soul.
6 But if the watchman see the sword come,
and blow not the trumpet, and the people be
not warned; if the sword come, and take *any*
person from among them, he is taken away in
his iniquity; but his blood will I require at the
watchman's hand.
7 ¶ So thou, O son of man, I have set thee a
watchman unto the house of Israel; therefore
thou shalt hear the word at my mouth, and warn
them from me.
8 When I say unto the wicked, O wicked *man*,
thou shalt surely die; if thou dost not speak to
warn the wicked from his way, that wicked *man*
shall die in his iniquity; but his blood will I
require at thine hand.
9 Nevertheless, if thou warn the wicked of his
way to turn from it; if he do not turn from his
way, he shall die in his iniquity; but thou hast de-
livered thy soul.
10 Therefore, O thou son of man, speak unto
the house of Israel; Thus ye speak, saying, If our
transgressions and our sins *be* upon us, and we
pine away in them, how should we then live?
11 Say unto them, *As* I live, saith the Lord GOD, I
have no pleasure in the death of the wicked; but
that the wicked turn from his way and live: turn
ye, turn ye from your evil ways; for why will ye
die, O house of Israel?
12 Therefore, thou son of man, say unto the
children of thy people, The righteousness of the
righteous shall not deliver him in the day of his
transgression: as for the wickedness of the wicked,
he shall not fall thereby in the day that he turneth
from his wickedness; neither shall the righteous
be able to live for his *righteousness* in the day that
he sinneth.
13 When I shall say to the righteous, *that* he shall
surely live; if he trust to his own righteousness,
and commit iniquity, all his righteousnesses shall
not be remembered; but for his iniquity that he
hath committed, he shall die for it.
14 Again, when I say unto the wicked, Thou shalt
surely die; if he turn from his sin, and do that
which is lawful and right;
15 *If* the wicked restore the pledge, give again that
he had robbed, walk in the statutes of life, without
committing iniquity; he shall surely live, he shall
not die.
16 None of his sins that he hath committed shall
be mentioned unto him: he hath done that which
is lawful and right; he shall surely live.
17 ¶ Yet the children of thy people say, The way of
the Lord is not equal: but as for them, their way
is not equal.
18 When the righteous turneth from his righ-
teousness, and committeth iniquity, he shall even
die thereby.
19 But if the wicked turn from his wickedness,
and do that which is lawful and right, he shall live
thereby.
20 ¶ Yet ye say, The way of the Lord is not equal.
O ye house of Israel, I will judge you every one
after his ways.
21 ¶ And it came to pass in the twelfth year of our
captivity, in the tenth *month*, in the fifth *day* of the
month, *that* one that had escaped out of Jerusalem
came unto me, saying, The city is smitten.
22 Now the hand of the LORD was upon me in
the evening, afore he that was escaped came; and
had opened my mouth, until he came to me in the
morning; and my mouth was opened, and I was
no more dumb.

33:2 *children of thy people.* Fellow countrymen. *coasts.* Borders or regions. *watchman.* One who keeps guard or watches attentively for news or danger. This chapter returns to the themes of the responsibilities of prophets and people before God (3:1–27; 18:1–32).
33:4 *his blood shall be upon his own head.* He shall be responsible.
33:5 *his soul.* The Hebrew means "himself."
33:6 *in his iniquity.* In his guilt or punishment; he bears his own guilt. *his blood will I require at the watchman's hand.* The watchman will be responsible for his own failure to warn the sinner, though he is not responsible for another's sin.
33:7 *I have set thee a watchman.* The prophet's ministry is patterned after the work of a watchman (see notes at 3:17–18).
33:10 *pine away.* Rot (see note at 24:23).
33:11 *I have no pleasure.* God does not delight in the destruction of His creations (see note at 18:23). *turn.* To reverse direction, the principal Old Testament word for repentance (v. 12).
33:12 *The righteousness of the righteous.* His former good conduct.
33:13 *trust to his own righteousness.* Self-righteousness can lead to moral carelessness and to falling away. *shall not be remembered.* Perseverance in faith and sincere (though imperfect) obedience are necessary for ultimate salvation (Matt. 10:22; 24:13; Col. 1:23; Heb. 3:14).
33:15 *pledge.* What had been pawned as a security for a debt.
33:16 *shall be mentioned.* Will be acknowledged or brought to mind.
33:17 *equal.* Fair or just.
33:21 *escaped.* A refugee from Jerusalem informed those already in captivity of Jerusalem's destruction (*smitten*).
33:22 *afore.* Before. *opened my mouth.* Given me a message (24:25–27).

23 Then the word of the LORD came unto me,
saying,
24 Son of man, they that inhabit those wastes of
the land of Israel speak, saying, Abraham was one,
and he inherited the land: but we *are* many; the
land is given us for inheritance.
25 Wherefore say unto them, Thus saith the Lord
GOD; Ye eat with the blood, and lift up your eyes
toward your idols, and shed blood: and shall ye
possess the land?
26 Ye stand upon your sword, ye work abomina-
tion, and ye defile every one his neighbour's wife:
and shall ye possess the land?
27 Say thou thus unto them, Thus saith the Lord
GOD; *As* I live, surely they that *are* in the wastes
shall fall by the sword, and him that *is* in the open
field will I give to the beasts to be devoured, and
they that *be* in the forts and in the caves shall die
of the pestilence.
28 For I will lay the land most desolate, and
the pomp of her strength shall cease; and the
mountains of Israel shall be desolate, that none
shall pass through.
29 Then shall they know that I *am* the LORD,
when I have laid the land most desolate because
of all their abominations which they have
committed.
30 ¶ Also, thou son of man, the children of thy
people still are talking against thee by the walls
and in the doors of the houses, and speak one to
another, every one to his brother, saying, Come, I
pray you, and hear what is the word that cometh
forth from the LORD.
31 And they come unto thee as the people
cometh, and they sit before thee *as* my people,
and they hear thy words, but they will not do
them: for with their mouth they shew much love,
but their heart goeth after their covetousness.
32 And, lo, thou *art* unto them as a very lovely
song of one that hath a pleasant voice, and can
play well on an instrument: for they hear thy
words, but they do them not.
33 And when this cometh to pass, (lo, it will
come,) then shall they know that a prophet hath
been among them.

CHAPTER 34

AND the word of the LORD came unto me, saying,
2 Son of man, prophesy against the shepherds of
Israel, prophesy, and say unto them, Thus saith
the Lord GOD unto the shepherds; Woe *be* to
the shepherds of Israel that do feed themselves!
should not the shepherds feed the flocks?
3 Ye eat the fat, and ye clothe you with the wool,
ye kill them that are fed: *but* ye feed not the flock.
4 The diseased have ye not strengthened, neither
have ye healed that which was sick, neither have
ye bound up *that which was* broken, neither have
ye brought again that which was driven away,

33:24 *wastes of the land.* The site of ruins (v. 27).
33:25 *eat with the blood.* In opposition to the law of God (Lev. 17:10).
33:26 *stand upon your sword.* They trusted in their military strength. *abomination.* Disgusting things connected with idolatry (v. 29). *defile every one his neighbour's wife.* Adultery.
33:27 *forts.* An almost inaccessible place used by soldiers. *pestilence.* Plague or epidemic.
33:28 *pomp of her strength.* The riches, majesty, and power in which they took pride.
33:30 *against thee.* Or about you. *Come . . . and hear.* They were curious what the prophet might reveal concerning the state of affairs back in Jerusalem.
33:31 *they hear thy words, but they will not do them.* Hearing God's Word without faith and obedience is worthless (Matt. 7:24–27; Luke 6:46; Heb. 4:2; James 1:21–25). *with their mouth they shew much love.* They pretend to be passionate about the Word. *covetousness.* Unlawful gain made by violence.
33:32 *a very lovely song.* A song of beautiful love. Unbelievers were able to take even the strong words of the prophet and twist them into a kind of pleasant entertainment.
33:33 *when this cometh to pass.* The mark of a true prophet is that his words are not just interesting or pleasant sayings but divine revelation of what must certainly come to pass (Deut. 18:21–22). Even though Israel did not believe Ezekiel's words, they will *know that a prophet hath been among them* (2:5) when God's judgments fall.

Thoughts for Personal/Family Worship: Chapter 33

1. **The Lord sincerely calls sinners to repent and come back to Him (v. 11). God is good and kind, even to those who hate Him. Through His preachers He urges and even pleads with His enemies so that they might escape His righteous judgment (2 Cor. 5:20). What amazing grace and mercy to wicked sinners! We should marvel at His gospel, run into His open arms, and seek to be His voice by spreading the gospel to whomever we can. How does the gospel call reveal the loving heart of Christ?**
2. **Sinners hear God's Word but respond out of their hatred for God. In some cases, instead of repenting of their sins they accuse God of sin (v. 17). People are sometimes offended when God welcomes sinners who turn back to His ways and when He judges seemingly good people who commit sin and refuse to repent. In other cases, people rejoice in the Word but only because they find it interesting or entertaining. They give it no more credence or obedience than a beautiful love song (vv. 30–33). We must repent of our sin and our self-righteousness and believe God's Word with total submission.**

Chapter 34: ***The Lord rebukes the shepherds of Israel and promises to set up the ideal shepherd.***

Parable of the Shepherds and the Sheep (34:1–31)

34:2 *shepherds.* A common designation in the Bible and in other ancient Near Eastern literature for rulers and kings (37:24; Num. 27:17). *feed themselves.* They rule the subjects of their kingdom (*flocks*) only for their own profit.
34:3 *the fat.* The best portions, sometimes referring to milk.
34:4 They neglected every duty of a shepherd. *force and . . . cruelty.* Violence and harshness. *ruled.* Dominated or subjugated.

neither have ye sought that which was lost; but
with force and with cruelty have ye ruled them.
5 And they were scattered, because *there is* no
shepherd: and they became meat to all the beasts
of the field, when they were scattered.
6 My sheep wandered through all the mountains,
and upon every high hill: yea, my flock was
scattered upon all the face of the earth, and none
did search or seek *after them.*
7 ¶ Therefore, ye shepherds, hear the word of the
LORD;
8 *As* I live, saith the Lord GOD, surely because my
flock became a prey, and my flock became meat
to every beast of the field, because *there was* no
shepherd, neither did my shepherds search for my
flock, but the shepherds fed themselves, and fed
not my flock;
9 Therefore, O ye shepherds, hear the word of the
LORD;
10 Thus saith the Lord GOD; Behold, I *am* against
the shepherds; and I will require my flock at their
hand, and cause them to cease from feeding the
flock; neither shall the shepherds feed themselves
any more; for I will deliver my flock from their
mouth, that they may not be meat for them.
11 ¶ For thus saith the Lord GOD; Behold, I, *even*
I, will both search my sheep, and seek them out.
12 As a shepherd seeketh out his flock in the day
that he is among his sheep *that are* scattered; so
will I seek out my sheep, and will deliver them out
of all places where they have been scattered in the
cloudy and dark day.
13 And I will bring them out from the people,
and gather them from the countries, and will
bring them to their own land, and feed them
upon the mountains of Israel by the rivers, and in
all the inhabited places of the country.
14 I will feed them in a good pasture, and upon
the high mountains of Israel shall their fold be:
there shall they lie in a good fold, and *in* a fat pas-
ture shall they feed upon the mountains of Israel.
15 I will feed my flock, and I will cause them to lie
down, saith the Lord GOD.
16 I will seek that which was lost, and bring again
that which was driven away, and will bind up *that
which was* broken, and will strengthen that which
was sick: but I will destroy the fat and the strong;
I will feed them with judgment.
17 And *as for* you, O my flock, thus saith the Lord
GOD; Behold, I judge between cattle and cattle,
between the rams and the he goats.
18 *Seemeth it* a small thing unto you to have eaten
up the good pasture, but ye must tread down with
your feet the residue of your pastures? and to have
drunk of the deep waters, but ye must foul the
residue with your feet?
19 And *as for* my flock, they eat that which ye
have trodden with your feet; and they drink that
which ye have fouled with your feet.
20 ¶ Therefore thus saith the Lord GOD unto
them; Behold, I, *even* I, will judge between the fat
cattle and between the lean cattle.
21 Because ye have thrust with side and with
shoulder, and pushed all the diseased with your
horns, till ye have scattered them abroad;
22 Therefore will I save my flock, and they shall
no more be a prey; and I will judge between cattle
and cattle.
23 And I will set up one shepherd over them, and
he shall feed them, *even* my servant David; he
shall feed them, and he shall be their shepherd.
24 And I the LORD will be their God, and my
servant David a prince among them; I the LORD
have spoken *it.*
25 And I will make with them a covenant of
peace, and will cause the evil beasts to cease out
of the land: and they shall dwell safely in the
wilderness, and sleep in the woods.
26 And I will make them and the places round
about my hill a blessing; and I will cause the
shower to come down in his season; there shall be
showers of blessing.

34:5 *meat.* Food (vv. 8,10).
34:8 *prey.* Spoil or booty.
34:10 *require.* Seek or demand. *cause them to cease from feeding the flock.* Remove the kingship from Jerusalem.
34:11 *search.* Pursue. *seek.* Search.
34:14 *fat pasture.* Rich or plenteous place with abundant provision.
34:15 *lie down.* Recline in rest (Ps. 23:2).
34:16 *destroy the fat and the strong.* Punish the prosperous and the mighty. *feed them with judgment.* Shepherd them with justice; they will receive what they deserve.
34:17 *I judge.* The Lord discriminates between true Israelites and the wicked by their works (vv. 20,22), exercising infallible discernment (Nah. 1:7; Matt. 25:31–46; John 10:14; 2 Tim. 2:19). *cattle.* The Hebrew word refers to sheep or goats.
34:18 *small.* Light or insignificant. *tread down . . . the residue of your pastures.* Trample or crush the remainder of your pastures. *deep.* Or clear. *foul.* Make muddy by trampling (v. 19). The wicked in Israel are like Pharaoh (32:2).
34:21 *thrust with side and with shoulder.* As livestock push and jostle other livestock.
34:22 *save.* Rescue. *a prey.* A spoil to their enemies (v. 28).
34:23 *David.* The ideal David, a reference to the Messiah (37:24–25; Jer. 30:9; Hos. 3:5). God will fulfill His covenant with David through his offspring (2 Sam. 7; Jer. 33:15–26). David was a *shepherd* both literally, as a young man (1 Sam. 16:11), and figuratively, as the king of Israel ("feed" in 2 Sam. 5:2; 7:7; Ps. 78:70–72).
34:24 *my servant David.* The language of the covenant (2 Sam. 7:5,8; 1 Kings 11:32). *prince.* An exalted one or king.
34:25 *evil.* Dangerous, able to cause hurt.
34:26 *showers of blessing.* In the metaphor of the shepherd and sheep, rain is crucial to provide good pasture for the flocks. The old covenant promised abundant rains for obedience to the law (Lev. 26:3–4; Jer. 5:24; Hos. 6:3), but Israel utterly failed to keep covenant with God and received

27 And the tree of the field shall yield her fruit,
and the earth shall yield her increase, and they
shall be safe in their land, and shall know that I
am the LORD, when I have broken the bands of
their yoke, and delivered them out of the hand of
those that served themselves of them.
28 And they shall no more be a prey to the
heathen, neither shall the beast of the land devour
them; but they shall dwell safely, and none shall
make *them* afraid.
29 And I will raise up for them a plant of renown,
and they shall be no more consumed with hunger
in the land, neither bear the shame of the heathen
any more.
30 Thus shall they know that I the LORD their
God *am* with them, and *that* they, *even* the house
of Israel, *are* my people, saith the Lord GOD.
31 And ye my flock, the flock of my pasture, *are*
men, *and* I *am* your God, saith the Lord GOD.

CHAPTER 35

MOREOVER the word of the LORD came unto me,
saying,
2 Son of man, set thy face against mount Seir, and
prophesy against it,
3 And say unto it, Thus saith the Lord GOD;
Behold, O mount Seir, I *am* against thee, and I
will stretch out mine hand against thee, and I will
make thee most desolate.
4 I will lay thy cities waste, and thou shalt be
desolate, and thou shalt know that I *am* the LORD.
5 Because thou hast had a perpetual hatred, and
hast shed *the blood of* the children of Israel by the
force of the sword in the time of their calamity, in
the time *that their* iniquity *had* an end:
6 Therefore, *as* I live, saith the Lord GOD, I will
prepare thee unto blood, and blood shall pursue
thee: sith thou hast not hated blood, even blood
shall pursue thee.
7 Thus will I make mount Seir most desolate, and
cut off from it him that passeth out and him that
returneth.
8 And I will fill his mountains with his slain *men*:
in thy hills, and in thy valleys, and in all thy rivers,
shall they fall that are slain with the sword.
9 I will make thee perpetual desolations, and thy
cities shall not return: and ye shall know that I *am*
the LORD.
10 Because thou hast said, These two nations and
these two countries shall be mine, and we will
possess it; whereas the LORD was there:
11 Therefore, *as* I live, saith the Lord GOD, I will
even do according to thine anger, and according
to thine envy which thou hast used out of thy
hatred against them; and I will make myself
known among them, when I have judged thee.
12 And thou shalt know that I *am* the LORD,
and that I have heard all thy blasphemies which
thou hast spoken against the mountains of Israel,
saying, They are laid desolate, they are given us to
consume.
13 Thus with your mouth ye have boasted against
me, and have multiplied your words against me: I
have heard *them*.
14 Thus saith the Lord GOD; When the whole

---

the curse. With the coming of Christ (vv. 23–24), God's law was fulfilled, and Christ's kingdom brings gospel blessings like abundant rain (2 Sam. 23:4; Ps. 72:6–7; Isa. 55:3,10–11).

34:29 *plant of renown.* Literally, "planting for a name" referring to something famous.

Thoughts for Personal/Family Worship: Chapter 34

1. **Of all the analogies to describe God's saving work, the shepherd image is one of the most precious. Christ alluded to this chapter in His teaching on the good shepherd (John 10). As the good shepherd He loves, cares for, guides, guards, and feeds His sheep. He willingly laid down His life to save His sheep. Consider the good shepherd as He revealed Himself in this chapter of Ezekiel. The Lord God is the shepherd (v. 11). And yet the Son of David is the one and only shepherd (v. 23). Thus the good shepherd is the incarnate Lord, the God-man, the Son who is one with His Father (John 10:30).**
2. **Consider too the condition of His sheep. They are scattered (v. 12), lost, and sick (v. 16). They have suffered much from the wicked (v. 21). They cannot save themselves but depend entirely upon their shepherd to rescue, provide for, and protect them.**
3. **Consider finally the work of the shepherd. He seeks and saves the lost (v. 12). He heals them and feeds them (vv. 14,16). He also judges them (vv. 17,20), so that they will be rescued from the wicked hidden among them. How do these truths show us the beauty of Jesus Christ? How do they attract people to desire to be a sheep of this shepherd?**

Chapter 35: *The prophet pronounces judgment against Edom for their hatred of Israel.*

Judgment against Edom (35:1–15)

35:2 *mount Seir.* The country of Edom, the descendants of Esau. What began as a struggle in the womb between Esau and Jacob (Gen. 25:19–26) escalated throughout the history of the two nations.

35:4 *lay.* Set or make. *waste.* Desolate.

35:5 *perpetual hatred.* Long-lasting hostility.

35:6 *sith.* Since. Their judgments fit their sin; blood for blood. This is poetic justice or *lex talionis* (law of retaliation). Obadiah develops the same principle of judgment for Edom.

35:7 *him that passeth out and him that returneth.* Those who travel to and from the city.

35:9 *perpetual.* Long-lasting.

35:10 *These two nations and these two countries.* Either Israel and Edom or Judah and Israel.

35:11 *I will do . . . according to thine anger, and according to thine envy.* As Edom had dealt with Israel, so God would deal with them, another statement of poetic justice.

35:13 *with your mouth ye have boasted.* Literally, "you made great against me with your lip."

earth rejoiceth, I will make thee desolate.
15 As thou didst rejoice at the inheritance of the
house of Israel, because it was desolate, so will I
do unto thee: thou shalt be desolate, O mount
Seir, and all Idumea, *even* all of it: and they shall
know that I *am* the LORD.

CHAPTER 36

ALSO, thou son of man, prophesy unto the
mountains of Israel, and say, Ye mountains of
Israel, hear the word of the LORD:
2 Thus saith the Lord GOD; Because the enemy
hath said against you, Aha, even the ancient high
places are ours in possession:
3 Therefore prophesy and say, Thus saith the
Lord GOD; Because they have made *you* desolate,
and swallowed you up on every side, that ye might
be a possession unto the residue of the heathen,
and ye are taken up in the lips of talkers, and *are*
an infamy of the people:
4 Therefore, ye mountains of Israel, hear the word
of the Lord GOD; Thus saith the Lord GOD to the
mountains, and to the hills, to the rivers, and to the
valleys, to the desolate wastes, and to the cities that
are forsaken, which became a prey and derision to
the residue of the heathen that *are* round about;
5 Therefore thus saith the Lord GOD; Surely in
the fire of my jealousy have I spoken against the
residue of the heathen, and against all Idumea,
which have appointed my land into their posses-
sion with the joy of all *their* heart, with despiteful
minds, to cast it out for a prey.
6 Prophesy therefore concerning the land of
Israel, and say unto the mountains, and to the
hills, to the rivers, and to the valleys, Thus saith
the Lord GOD; Behold, I have spoken in my
jealousy and in my fury, because ye have borne
the shame of the heathen:
7 Therefore thus saith the Lord GOD; I have lifted
up mine hand, Surely the heathen that *are* about
you, they shall bear their shame.
8 ¶ But ye, O mountains of Israel, ye shall shoot
forth your branches, and yield your fruit to my
people of Israel; for they are at hand to come.
9 For, behold, I *am* for you, and I will turn unto
you, and ye shall be tilled and sown:
10 And I will multiply men upon you, all the
house of Israel, *even* all of it: and the cities shall be
inhabited, and the wastes shall be builded:
11 And I will multiply upon you man and beast;
and they shall increase and bring fruit: and I will
settle you after your old estates, and will do better
unto you than at your beginnings: and ye shall
know that I *am* the LORD.
12 Yea, I will cause men to walk upon you, *even*
my people Israel; and they shall possess thee, and
thou shalt be their inheritance, and thou shalt no
more henceforth bereave them *of men*.
13 Thus saith the Lord GOD; Because they say
unto you, Thou *land* devourest up men, and hast
bereaved thy nations;
14 Therefore thou shalt devour men no more,
neither bereave thy nations any more, saith the
Lord GOD.
15 Neither will I cause *men* to hear in thee the
shame of the heathen any more, neither shalt
thou bear the reproach of the people any more,
neither shalt thou cause thy nations to fall any
more, saith the Lord GOD.
16 ¶ Moreover the word of the LORD came unto
me, saying,
17 Son of man, when the house of Israel dwelt in
their own land, they defiled it by their own way

35:15 *As . . . so.* Another example of poetic justice. *Idumea.* Edom.

Thoughts for Personal/Family Worship: Chapter 35

The law of the harvest is an inviolable law. We reap what we sow (Gal. 6:7–9). The people of mount Seir had lived by the sword and were going to die by the sword. They had scorned Israel for her desolation, but they also would be brought to desolation. God's justice always gives what is deserved. This is why the gospel is such good news, for Christ took the full guilt and penalty of the sins of His people. He took what His people deserved, and His people receive what He deserves. Justice is served, and His people are saved. Be warned not to be like Edom, who stood before God on its own.

Chapter 36: *Ezekiel extends hope that the nation will be restored to blessing for the sake of God's name.*

Restoration of Land and People for God's Holy Name (36:1–38)

36:1 *mountains of Israel.* Addressing the mountains (35:2) as a person is a figure of speech referring to the nation (vv. 4,6).

36:2 *the Lord GOD.* This phrase "Lord Jehovah" is Ezekiel's favorite title for God (see Introduction: Synopsis). It appears no fewer than fifteen times in this chapter, more than in any other in the book, emphasizing the sovereignty and glory of His grace. *Aha.* This is the Hebrew word, an interjection expressing malicious joy. *high places.* Places associated with idolatrous shrines.

36:3 *swallowed you up on every side.* Crushed you completely or totally. *in the lips of talkers.* In the speech of the talkers, signifying the subject of conversation. *infamy.* The subject of a bad report.

36:5 *fire of my jealousy.* The anger of God's zeal. *Idumea.* Edom, often referring to the totality of those hostile to God's people. *despiteful.* Contemptuous or malicious. *prey.* Spoil.

36:6 *borne the shame of the heathen.* Carried the reproach of the heathen.

36:7 *lifted up mine hand.* Sworn an oath or made a solemn promise.

36:9 *tilled and sown.* Cultivated and planted.

36:10 *multiply men.* Increase the population.

36:11 *after your old estates.* According to your former state.

36:12–14 *bereave.* Make childless.

36:17 *defiled.* Made unclean. *a removed woman.* A woman in her menstrual impurity.

and by their doings: their way was before me as
the uncleanness of a removed woman.
18 Wherefore I poured my fury upon them for
the blood that they had shed upon the land, and
for their idols *wherewith* they had polluted it:
19 And I scattered them among the heathen,
and they were dispersed through the countries:
according to their way and according to their
doings I judged them.
20 And when they entered unto the heathen,
whither they went, they profaned my holy name,
when they said to them, These *are* the people of
the LORD, and are gone forth out of his land.
21 ¶ But I had pity for mine holy name, which the
house of Israel had profaned among the heathen,
whither they went.
22 Therefore say unto the house of Israel, Thus
saith the Lord GOD; I do not *this* for your sakes,
O house of Israel, but for mine holy name's sake,
which ye have profaned among the heathen,
whither ye went.
23 And I will sanctify my great name, which was
profaned among the heathen, which ye have pro-
faned in the midst of them; and the heathen shall
know that I *am* the LORD, saith the Lord GOD,
when I shall be sanctified in you before their eyes.
24 For I will take you from among the heathen,
and gather you out of all countries, and will bring
you into your own land.
25 ¶ Then will I sprinkle clean water upon you,
and ye shall be clean: from all your filthiness, and
from all your idols, will I cleanse you.
26 A new heart also will I give you, and a new
spirit will I put within you: and I will take away
the stony heart out of your flesh, and I will give
you an heart of flesh.
27 And I will put my spirit within you, and cause
you to walk in my statutes, and ye shall keep my
judgments, and do *them*.
28 And ye shall dwell in the land that I gave to
your fathers; and ye shall be my people, and I will
be your God.
29 I will also save you from all your uncleannesses:
and I will call for the corn, and will increase it, and
lay no famine upon you.
30 And I will multiply the fruit of the tree, and
the increase of the field, that ye shall receive no
more reproach of famine among the heathen.
31 Then shall ye remember your own evil ways,
and your doings that *were* not good, and shall
lothe yourselves in your own sight for your
iniquities and for your abominations.
32 Not for your sakes do I *this*, saith the Lord
GOD, be it known unto you: be ashamed and
confounded for your own ways, O house of Israel.
33 Thus saith the Lord GOD; In the day that I shall
have cleansed you from all your iniquities I will
also cause *you* to dwell in the cities, and the wastes
shall be builded.
34 And the desolate land shall be tilled, whereas it
lay desolate in the sight of all that passed by.
35 And they shall say, This land that was desolate
is become like the garden of Eden; and the waste
and desolate and ruined cities *are become* fenced,
and are inhabited.
36 Then the heathen that are left round about

36:20 *profaned.* Treated the *holy* as common or ordinary, the opposite of setting apart or sanctifying (vv. 21–23).
36:23 *sanctify.* Set apart or honor as a sacred thing. *my great name.* God's name is His glory (Pss. 72:19; 102:15; Isa. 42:8; 48:9,11; 59:19), which He causes people to *know* (20:9,44).
36:24 *take.* Get or fetch. *gather.* Bring together as in an assembly. *bring.* Lead in or carry in.
36:25 Ceremonial uncleanness (*filthiness*) was symbolic of being incapable of fellowship with God. Ceremonial cleanness (*clean*) allowed fellowship and participation in worship. God had provided a ceremony of sprinkling with *water* mixed with the ashes of a sacrifice for ritual cleansing from external uncleanness (Num. 19). Jerusalem's love for *idols* was its real, spiritual uncleanness. God Himself would spiritually *sprinkle* His people to cleanse them from their idolatry so that they would draw near to Him in worship with clear consciences (Heb. 9:13–14).
36:26 *A new heart will I give you, and new spirit.* God regenerates sinners by the Holy Spirit (John 3:3–8; Titus 3:3–8; 1 Peter 1:3, 23), resulting in a new creation in Christ (2 Cor. 5:17; Eph. 2:10). The *new heart* is the transformation of the whole inner man (mind, emotions, and will). The *new spirit* is the implantation of a new principle of life to animate one's personality and conduct. God takes a *heart* that was lifeless, hard, and obstinate against Him (*stony*) and makes it alive, soft, and responsive to Him (*flesh*). See note at 11:19–20.
36:27 *my spirit.* The Holy Spirit, who dwells in the regenerated heart (John 14:16–17; Rom. 8:9; 1 Cor. 6:19). *cause you to walk in my statutes . . . keep my judgments.* Spiritual life produces spiritual living, that is, obedience to God's just and righteous laws (1 John 5:1–5).
36:28 *my people . . . your God.* God and people bound together in covenant love, the great covenant promise that runs through all the covenants and unifies the Bible (11:20; 14:11; 34:30; 37:23,27; Gen. 17:7–8; Ex. 6:7; 29:45; Lev. 26:12; Ruth 1:16; 2 Sam. 7:24; Isa. 40:1; Jer. 24:7; 30:22; 31:1,33; 32:38; Joel 2:27; Zech. 8:8; 2 Cor. 6:16; Heb. 8:10; Rev. 21:3).
36:29–30 *increase . . . multiply.* The covenant blessings promised to Israel if they kept God's law (Lev. 26:3–13; Deut. 28:1–14), implying that the Lord would not only forgive their sins but also satisfy the demands of His law. This He did through the obedience of Christ (Rom. 5:19), and these blessings find their ultimate fulfillment in His glorious kingdom (37:24–28).
36:31 *remember.* Consider in a way that moves the heart and changes the behavior. *lothe.* Detest or despise. *abominations.* Disgusting and detestable things, usually idols. God's gracious gifts of justification and sanctification do not cause His people to take sin lightly but to grieve over it and hate it all the more (16:60–63).
36:32 *confounded.* Humiliated.
36:33 *wastes.* Ruined places. *builded.* Rebuilt or reestablished.
36:34 *tilled.* Cultivated, worked to make fruitful.
36:35 *like the garden of Eden.* The Lord will restore His people to the beauties and pleasures of Paradise for which mankind

you shall know that I the LORD build the ruined
places, and plant that that was desolate: I the LORD
have spoken *it*, and I will do *it*.
37 Thus saith the Lord GOD; I will yet *for* this be
enquired of by the house of Israel, to do *it* for
them; I will increase them with men like a flock.
38 As the holy flock, as the flock of Jerusalem in
her solemn feasts; so shall the waste cities be filled
with flocks of men: and they shall know that I *am*
the LORD.

CHAPTER 37

THE hand of the LORD was upon me, and carried
me out in the spirit of the LORD, and set me down
in the midst of the valley which *was* full of bones,
2 And caused me to pass by them round about:
and, behold, *there were* very many in the open
valley; and, lo, *they were* very dry.
3 And he said unto me, Son of man, can these
bones live? And I answered, O Lord GOD, thou
knowest.
4 Again he said unto me, Prophesy upon these
bones, and say unto them, O ye dry bones, hear
the word of the LORD.
5 Thus saith the Lord GOD unto these bones;
Behold, I will cause breath to enter into you, and
ye shall live:
6 And I will lay sinews upon you, and will bring
up flesh upon you, and cover you with skin, and
put breath in you, and ye shall live; and ye shall
know that I *am* the LORD.
7 So I prophesied as I was commanded: and as
I prophesied, there was a noise, and behold a
shaking, and the bones came together, bone to his
bone.
8 And when I beheld, lo, the sinews and the flesh
came up upon them, and the skin covered them
above: but *there was* no breath in them.
9 Then said he unto me, Prophesy unto the wind,
prophesy, son of man, and say to the wind, Thus
saith the Lord GOD; Come from the four winds,
O breath, and breathe upon these slain, that they
may live.
10 So I prophesied as he commanded me, and the
breath came into them, and they lived, and stood
up upon their feet, an exceeding great army.
11 ¶ Then he said unto me, Son of man, these
bones are the whole house of Israel: behold, they
say, Our bones are dried, and our hope is lost: we
are cut off for our parts.
12 Therefore prophesy and say unto them, Thus
saith the Lord GOD; Behold, O my people, I will
open your graves, and cause you to come up out
of your graves, and bring you into the land of
Israel.
13 And ye shall know that I *am* the LORD, when
I have opened your graves, O my people, and
brought you up out of your graves,
14 And shall put my spirit in you, and ye shall
live, and I shall place you in your own land: then
shall ye know that I the LORD have spoken *it*, and
performed *it*, saith the LORD.
15 ¶ The word of the LORD came again unto me,
saying,
16 Moreover, thou son of man, take thee one

was originally created (Gen. 2:8–14; Isa. 51:3; Rev. 22:1–3). *fenced.* Fortified.
36:37 *be enquired of.* Sought as in prayer.
36:38 *holy flock.* A flock of holy things. *solemn.* Appointed.

Thoughts for Personal/Family Worship: Chapter 36

1. **Sinners cannot save themselves. Salvation is all of God's grace and for His glory (Eph. 1:3–14). Repeatedly God said "I will" in this chapter. The Lord changes filthy idolaters into cleansed worshipers. He makes stubborn enemies into submissive servants and takes estranged outsiders and draws them into covenant friendship. Salvation is begun by God's initiative, is effective by His power, and is completed by His determination. What is impossible with man is possible with God. While we should despair of saving ourselves, we should hope confidently in the Lord's salvation.**
2. **Real salvation cannot be separated from practical holiness of life. Grace does not enable hypocrisy. If God saved a person but did not make that person holy, then salvation would not glorify God but would pollute His holy name. Real, saving grace produces a new heart and a new spirit. Obstinate clinging to idols gives way to brokenhearted repentance over sin. Everyone in whom the Spirit dwells will show it by a life of obedience to God's moral law. This is the great test of whether a person is born again. No emotional experience or rational belief can take the place of a new heart that produces new obedience. What is the evidence that God gave you a new heart toward Him?**

Chapter 37: ***Ezekiel sees a valley of dry bones that come to life and two sticks that unite.***

The Vision of Resurrection and the Sign of Reunification (37:1–28)

37:1 *in the spirit.* This was a prophetic vision.
37:2 *open valley.* On the face of the valley, on the surface, unburied. *very dry.* Dried and bleached from exposure to the sun. The image is of the remains of a massacre many years earlier, such that God's people were long dead (Rom. 5:12; 8:6; Eph. 2:1–3).
37:3 *can these bones live?* An amazing question that only God can answer (*thou knowest*).
37:4 *Prophesy.* Preach or proclaim. On the surface, this appeared to be futile.
37:7 *shaking.* A rustling, a commotion; sometimes refers to an earthquake.
37:9 *wind.* Spirit. *from the four winds.* Signifying the four corners of the earth.
37:10 *breath.* The Spirit.
37:11 *the whole house of Israel.* The entire nation, including both the northern and southern kingdoms. *hope.* Expectation.
37:14 *put my spirit in you, and ye shall live.* The gift of the Holy Spirit (36:27; 39:29) is depicted as a resurrection of God's people from the dead (Eph. 2:4–7). *place you in your own land.*

stick, and write upon it, For Judah, and for the
children of Israel his companions: then take
another stick, and write upon it, For Joseph, the
stick of Ephraim, and *for* all the house of Israel
his companions:
17 And join them one to another into one stick;
and they shall become one in thine hand.
18 ¶ And when the children of thy people shall
speak unto thee, saying, Wilt thou not shew us
what thou *meanest* by these?
19 Say unto them, Thus saith the Lord GOD;
Behold, I will take the stick of Joseph, which *is* in
the hand of Ephraim, and the tribes of Israel his
fellows, and will put them with him, *even* with the
stick of Judah, and make them one stick, and they
shall be one in mine hand.
20 ¶ And the sticks whereon thou writest shall be
in thine hand before their eyes.
21 And say unto them, Thus saith the Lord GOD;
Behold, I will take the children of Israel from
among the heathen, whither they be gone, and
will gather them on every side, and bring them
into their own land:
22 And I will make them one nation in the land
upon the mountains of Israel; and one king shall
be king to them all: and they shall be no more two
nations, neither shall they be divided into two
kingdoms any more at all:
23 Neither shall they defile themselves any more
with their idols, nor with their detestable things,
nor with any of their transgressions: but I will
save them out of all their dwellingplaces, wherein
they have sinned, and will cleanse them: so shall
they be my people, and I will be their God.
24 And David my servant *shall be* king over
them; and they all shall have one shepherd: they
shall also walk in my judgments, and observe my
statutes, and do them.
25 And they shall dwell in the land that I have
given unto Jacob my servant, wherein your
fathers have dwelt; and they shall dwell therein,
even they, and their children, and their children's
children for ever: and my servant David *shall be*
their prince for ever.
26 Moreover I will make a covenant of peace with
them; it shall be an everlasting covenant with
them: and I will place them, and multiply them,
and will set my sanctuary in the midst of them
for evermore.
27 My tabernacle also shall be with them: yea, I
will be their God, and they shall be my people.
28 And the heathen shall know that I the LORD do
sanctify Israel, when my sanctuary shall be in the
midst of them for evermore.

CHAPTER 38

AND the word of the LORD came unto me, saying,
2 Son of man, set thy face against Gog, the land
of Magog, the chief prince of Meshech and Tubal,
and prophesy against him,
3 And say, Thus saith the Lord GOD; Behold, I *am*
against thee, O Gog, the chief prince of Meshech
and Tubal:

Restore you from exile to prepare the way for Christ (v. 24) and ultimately bring those renewed by the Spirit to the kingdom of which the land was a type (John 3:3; Heb. 11:13–16; 1 Peter 1:3–4).

37:16 *stick.* Tree or wood. *companions.* Fellows or associates.

37:17 *join.* Bring together.

37:19 *one stick.* A picture of the reunification of the nation (v. 22) for the first time after its division in the days of Rehoboam (1 Kings 12).

37:22 *one king shall be king to them all.* Just as their worship will not be divided between God and idols, so their allegiance will not be divided between the thrones of the northern and southern kingdoms.

37:23 *my people . . . their God.* See note at 36:28.

37:24 *David my servant . . . one shepherd.* The ideal David, God's covenant servant (see notes at 34:23–24) Jesus Christ (John 10:14). Submission to Christ is the unity of His people (11:19; Eph. 4:5,13). His kingdom or reign over them by the Holy Spirit produces their obedience to God's laws (*judgments . . . statutes*; 36:27).

37:25 *prince.* Exalted ruler or king.

37:26–27 *I will make a covenant of peace . . . everlasting covenant.* What Jeremiah designates the "new covenant" (Jer. 31:31–34). *my sanctuary . . . My tabernacle.* God's holy dwelling place with His people. The dwelling of God's Spirit in them (v. 14; 36:27) suggests that the sanctuary will be the people, not a physical building. The fact that it will remain forever and never depart again (8:1—11:25) implies that God's wrath is propitiated and His people's sins are forgiven.

Thoughts for Personal/Family Worship: Chapter 37

1. **Man's hopeless state without God is clearly portrayed in this passage. The picture of death and desolation highlights the devastating results of man's fall into sin. Satan has slaughtered the human race, and all mankind is dead in sin, utterly without spiritual life. Preachers can preach with all their heart, and we can move bones around, but until the Spirit of the Lord comes there will be no life. How should this move us to pray for the lost? How should it move us to praise God for our salvation?**
2. **Christ's kingdom will flourish despite every apparent obstacle. He is the servant-king (v. 24) who perfectly does His Father's will and rules with omnipotent power in heaven and on earth. His church shall be built and His people shall all be eternally saved. This truth should fill even the most troubled believer with hope and confidence. The church should never have a defeatist mindset. Christ reigns and will reign forever and forever!**

THE GREAT CONFLICT WITH GOG (38:1—39:29)

Chapter 38: *Ezekiel pronounces judgment against Gog for their planned invasion of Israel.*

38:2 *Gog.* Outside of chs. 38–39, named only once elsewhere in Scripture (Rev. 20:8). *chief prince.* The ruler or, literally, "the exalted head" of an unidentified northern nation. *Magog . . . Meshech . . . Tubal.* All descendants of Japheth (Gen. 10:2), as well as Gomer (v. 6). Most likely referring to territories in

4 And I will turn thee back, and put hooks into
thy jaws, and I will bring thee forth, and all thine
army, horses and horsemen, all of them clothed
with all sorts *of armour, even* a great company
with bucklers and shields, all of them handling
swords:
5 Persia, Ethiopia, and Libya with them; all of
them with shield and helmet:
6 Gomer, and all his bands; the house of Togar-
mah of the north quarters, and all his bands: *and*
many people with thee.
7 Be thou prepared, and prepare for thyself, thou,
and all thy company that are assembled unto thee,
and be thou a guard unto them.
8 ¶ After many days thou shalt be visited: in the
latter years thou shalt come into the land *that is*
brought back from the sword, *and is* gathered out
of many people, against the mountains of Israel,
which have been always waste: but it is brought
forth out of the nations, and they shall dwell
safely all of them.
9 Thou shalt ascend and come like a storm, thou
shalt be like a cloud to cover the land, thou, and
all thy bands, and many people with thee.
10 Thus saith the Lord GOD; It shall also come to
pass, *that* at the same time shall things come into
thy mind, and thou shalt think an evil thought:
11 And thou shalt say, I will go up to the land of
unwalled villages; I will go to them that are at rest,
that dwell safely, all of them dwelling without
walls, and having neither bars nor gates,
12 To take a spoil, and to take a prey; to turn
thine hand upon the desolate places *that are now*
inhabited, and upon the people *that are* gathered
out of the nations, which have gotten cattle and
goods, that dwell in the midst of the land.
13 Sheba, and Dedan, and the merchants of
Tarshish, with all the young lions thereof, shall
say unto thee, Art thou come to take a spoil? hast
thou gathered thy company to take a prey? to
carry away silver and gold, to take away cattle and
goods, to take a great spoil?
14 ¶ Therefore, son of man, prophesy and say
unto Gog, Thus saith the Lord GOD; In that day
when my people of Israel dwelleth safely, shalt
thou not know *it*?
15 And thou shalt come from thy place out of the
north parts, thou, and many people with thee, all
of them riding upon horses, a great company, and
a mighty army:
16 And thou shalt come up against my people of
Israel, as a cloud to cover the land; it shall be in
the latter days, and I will bring thee against my
land, that the heathen may know me, when I shall
be sanctified in thee, O Gog, before their eyes.
17 Thus saith the Lord GOD; *Art* thou he of
whom I have spoken in old time by my servants
the prophets of Israel, which prophesied in those
days *many* years that I would bring thee against
them?
18 And it shall come to pass at the same time
when Gog shall come against the land of Israel,
saith the Lord GOD, *that* my fury shall come up
in my face.
19 For in my jealousy *and* in the fire of my wrath
have I spoken, Surely in that day there shall be a
great shaking in the land of Israel;
20 So that the fishes of the sea, and the fowls of
the heaven, and the beasts of the field, and all
creeping things that creep upon the earth, and all
the men that *are* upon the face of the earth, shall
shake at my presence, and the mountains shall be
thrown down, and the steep places shall fall, and
every wall shall fall to the ground.
21 And I will call for a sword against him
throughout all my mountains, saith the Lord GOD:

Asia Minor, north of Israel.
38:4 *put hooks into thy jaws.* A humiliating means of bringing into subjection. *bucklers.* The Hebrew refers to large, body-covering shields.
38:5–6 *Persia, Ethiopia . . . Libya . . . Gomer.* Locations surrounding Israel to the east, south, west, and north. These together represent the "four corners of the earth," or all the nations gathered for war against the Lord and His people (Rev. 16:14; 19:19; 20:8).
38:7 *guard.* Or a lookout.
38:8 *visited.* Punished. *latter years.* In due course, "finally" or "at the end" (v. 16).
38:9 *like a storm.* Suddenly and with devastating effect.
38:10 *things come into thy mind.* Words or ideas shall enter into your thoughts. *think an evil thought.* Devise a plan to bring calamity.
38:11 *unwalled.* Defenseless. *rest.* Peace and quiet. *neither bars nor gates.* Without fortification.
38:12 *take a spoil.* Seize goods that have been plundered. *take a prey.* Plunder booty (same terms in v. 13). *gotten.* Obtained.
38:13 *Sheba, and Dedan.* Important trading centers in Arabia. *Tarshish.* An important trading center in the west, identified by some as Spain.
38:15 *out of the north parts.* Although it seems as though Gog's kingdom was actually north of Israel, it should be noted that virtually every invasion of Israel came from the north; hence the enemy was typically viewed as coming from that direction regardless of geographical location. For instance, Babylon was known as the land of the north, even though it was actually east of Israel (Zech. 2:6–7).
38:16 *sanctified.* Set apart or acknowledged as holy.
38:17 The Lord had predicted Gog's attack against His people through His *prophets* long before Ezekiel (*in old time*). The person or power named Gog does not appear in any previous prophecy, but since the fall God had predicted conflict between the seed of the godly and the seed of Satan (Gen. 3:15), and Gog's invasion and defeat may represent that conflict, particularly in its final manifestation (Rev. 20:7–10).
38:18 *my fury shall come up in my face.* My indignation or wrath will rise in my nose, picturing the heat and redness of anger.
38:19 *great shaking.* An earthquake.
38:20 *shake.* Tremble like an earthquake. *steep places.* Cliffs or mountain passes.

every man's sword shall be against his brother.
22 And I will plead against him with pestilence
and with blood; and I will rain upon him, and
upon his bands, and upon the many people that
are with him, an overflowing rain, and great
hailstones, fire, and brimstone.
23 Thus will I magnify myself, and sanctify
myself; and I will be known in the eyes of many
nations, and they shall know that I *am* the LORD.

CHAPTER 39

THEREFORE, thou son of man, prophesy against
Gog, and say, Thus saith the Lord GOD; Behold,
I *am* against thee, O Gog, the chief prince of
Meshech and Tubal:
2 And I will turn thee back, and leave but the
sixth part of thee, and will cause thee to come up
from the north parts, and will bring thee upon the
mountains of Israel:
3 And I will smite thy bow out of thy left hand,
and will cause thine arrows to fall out of thy right
hand.
4 Thou shalt fall upon the mountains of Israel,
thou, and all thy bands, and the people that *is*
with thee: I will give thee unto the ravenous birds
of every sort, and *to* the beasts of the field to be
devoured.
5 Thou shalt fall upon the open field: for I have
spoken *it*, saith the Lord GOD.
6 And I will send a fire on Magog, and among
them that dwell carelessly in the isles: and they
shall know that I *am* the LORD.
7 So will I make my holy name known in the
midst of my people Israel; and I will not *let them*
pollute my holy name any more: and the heathen
shall know that I *am* the LORD, the Holy One in
Israel.
8 ¶ Behold, it is come, and it is done, saith the
Lord GOD; this *is* the day whereof I have spoken.
9 And they that dwell in the cities of Israel shall go
forth, and shall set on fire and burn the weapons,
both the shields and the bucklers, the bows and
the arrows, and the handstaves, and the spears,
and they shall burn them with fire seven years:
10 So that they shall take no wood out of the field,
neither cut down *any* out of the forests; for they
shall burn the weapons with fire: and they shall
spoil those that spoiled them, and rob those that
robbed them, saith the Lord GOD.
11 ¶ And it shall come to pass in that day, *that* I
will give unto Gog a place there of graves in Israel,
the valley of the passengers on the east of the sea:
and it shall stop the *noses* of the passengers: and
there shall they bury Gog and all his multitude:
and they shall call *it* The valley of Hamon-gog.
12 And seven months shall the house of Israel be
burying of them, that they may cleanse the land.
13 Yea, all the people of the land shall bury *them*;
and it shall be to them a renown the day that I
shall be glorified, saith the Lord GOD.
14 And they shall sever out men of continual

38:22 *plead against.* Judge. *pestilence.* Plague. *blood.* Signifying violent death. *bands.* Troops or armies. *hailstones.* See Josh. 10:10–11. *brimstone.* Sulfur. Blood, pestilence, and hail all featured in God's plagues upon Egypt (Ex. 7:14–25; 9:1–7,18–35). This imagery also appears in the book of Revelation (Rev. 8:7–8; 16:3–4), particularly in climactic visions of a devastating earthquake and hailstorm (Rev. 11:19; 16:17–21).
38:23 *magnify myself.* Show my greatness. *sanctify myself.* Set myself apart as holy.

Thoughts for Personal/Family Worship: Chapter 38

After revelations of resurrection from spiritual death to serve the Christ (36:1—37:28), Ezekiel prophesied of the worldwide opposition that would come against the peaceful kingdom of the Messiah, and its ultimate victory by supernatural, divine intervention. This vision finds partial fulfillment whenever the wicked attack the church of Christ and the gospel triumphs. Its ultimate fulfillment will arrive when Christ returns. Christians should not be surprised when the world declares war on them; this is an ancient battle. However, Christians should also be optimistic: all the world will know that our God is the Lord!

Chapter 39: *Ezekiel gives details of God's destruction of Gog.*

39:1 *chief prince . . . Tubal.* See note at 38:2.
39:2–3 *leave but the sixth part of thee.* Literally, "lead you along with a rope," perhaps with the hook with six teeth (38:4). *north parts.* The far northern border, the typical direction from which invasions to Israel came. *I will.* God is sovereign in the whole event, drawing out His enemies to the place where He will defeat them (Ex. 14:4,17).
39:4 *bands.* Troops or armies. *birds . . . to be devoured.* Like Egypt (29:5; 31:4).
39:6 *carelessly.* Without care in assumed safety. *in the isles.* On the borders.
39:7 *pollute.* Profane by treating the holy as common or ordinary.
39:8 *the day.* The appointed time, most likely the day of the Lord that marks His special intervention for judgment and salvation (cf. "that day," v. 11).
39:9 *bucklers.* Large shields covering the body. *handstaves.* Sticks, possibly javelins. *burn them with fire seven years.* Perhaps figurative to represent the complete destruction of a very large group.
39:10 *no wood.* So many weapons to burn that further kindling would be unnecessary. *rob . . . robbed.* Plunder those who had plundered them (Ex. 3:22).
39:11 *passengers on the east of the sea.* The travelers on the east coast of the Mediterranean. *stop the noses of the passengers.* Literally, "block the way of the travelers" (*noses* is in italic in the KJV text, and thus not in the original Hebrew). *Hamon-gog.* Translated, "the multitude of Gog" (v. 15).
39:12 *cleanse.* Purify.
39:13 *renown.* Literally, "for a name," for fame or honor. The Lord God will *be glorified* through the defeat of the enemies of His people.
39:14 *sever out.* Separate or choose. *of continual employment.* With the standing responsibility.

employment, passing through the land to bury
with the passengers those that remain upon the
face of the earth, to cleanse it: after the end of
seven months shall they search.
15 And the passengers *that* pass through the land,
when *any* seeth a man's bone, then shall he set up
a sign by it, till the buriers have buried it in the
valley of Hamon-gog.
16 And also the name of the city *shall be*
Hamonah. Thus shall they cleanse the land.
17 ¶ And, thou son of man, thus saith the Lord
GOD; Speak unto every feathered fowl, and to
every beast of the field, Assemble yourselves,
and come; gather yourselves on every side to my
sacrifice that I do sacrifice for you, *even* a great
sacrifice upon the mountains of Israel, that ye
may eat flesh, and drink blood.
18 Ye shall eat the flesh of the mighty, and drink
the blood of the princes of the earth, of rams,
of lambs, and of goats, of bullocks, all of them
fatlings of Bashan.
19 And ye shall eat fat till ye be full, and drink
blood till ye be drunken, of my sacrifice which I
have sacrificed for you.
20 Thus ye shall be filled at my table with horses
and chariots, with mighty men, and with all men
of war, saith the Lord GOD.
21 And I will set my glory among the heathen,
and all the heathen shall see my judgment that I
have executed, and my hand that I have laid upon
them.
22 So the house of Israel shall know that I *am* the
LORD their God from that day and forward.
23 ¶ And the heathen shall know that the house
of Israel went into captivity for their iniquity:
because they trespassed against me, therefore hid
I my face from them, and gave them into the hand
of their enemies: so fell they all by the sword.
24 According to their uncleanness and according
to their transgressions have I done unto them,
and hid my face from them.
25 Therefore thus saith the Lord GOD; Now will
I bring again the captivity of Jacob, and have
mercy upon the whole house of Israel, and will be
jealous for my holy name;
26 After that they have borne their shame, and
all their trespasses whereby they have trespassed
against me, when they dwelt safely in their land,
and none made *them* afraid.
27 When I have brought them again from the
people, and gathered them out of their enemies'
lands, and am sanctified in them in the sight of
many nations;
28 Then shall they know that I *am* the LORD their
God, which caused them to be led into captivity
among the heathen: but I have gathered them
unto their own land, and have left none of them
any more there.
29 Neither will I hide my face any more from
them: for I have poured out my spirit upon the
house of Israel, saith the Lord GOD.

CHAPTER 40

IN the five and twentieth year of our captivity, in
the beginning of the year, in the tenth *day* of the
month, in the fourteenth year after that the city
was smitten, in the selfsame day the hand of the
LORD was upon me, and brought me thither.
2 In the visions of God brought he me into the

39:15 *passengers.* Travelers. *set up a sign.* Place a marker.
39:16 *Hamonah.* Translated, "the multitude."
39:17 *feathered fowl.* Bird. *sacrifice.* Referring to the slaughter. *that ye may eat flesh.* This image of a gruesome dinner for scavengers is taken up in John's vision of Christ coming like a warrior on a white horse (Rev. 19:17–21).
39:18 *the princes.* The exalted ones or rulers. *them fatlings of Bashan.* The well-fed from the region east of Jordan, known for luxuriant pastures.
39:21–22 *the heathen shall see . . . house of Israel shall know.* God will glorify Himself among the nations and Israel, the Gentiles and the Jews.
39:24 *hid my face.* Concealed or withdrew my presence (Hos. 5:15).
39:25 *bring again.* Turn again or restore. *jealous.* Zealous. God is zealous or has a strong and energetic love for His name, His law, and His people.
39:26 *borne their shame.* Carried or endured disgrace, reproach, and dishonor.
39:27 *sanctified in them.* Set apart or honored as holy.
39:29 *poured out my spirit.* The abundant gift of the Holy Spirit (36:27; 37:14; Isa. 44:3; Joel 2:28).

Thoughts for Personal/Family Worship: Chapter 39

The Lord God's victory over the enemies of His people will be total. The wicked will be judged in overwhelming numbers, as is clear from the graphic references to their slaughter and the disposal of their bodies and equipment. All nations will know that King Jesus is Lord (vv. 13,21; Phil. 2:10). Even now God has poured out the Spirit of Christ upon His people (v. 29). Therefore, the great question is where you will stand on that great day. Will you be among His enemies or His people? The answer to that question about the future resolves into a question about the present. Do you have His Spirit working faith and obedience in you today?

THE VISION OF GLORY RETURNING TO THE LAND (40:1—48:35)

The Temple and the Ceremonies of Worship (40:1—46:24)

Chapter 40: ***Ezekiel receives a vision of a model temple, beginning with its outer courtyard and gates.***

40:1 *five and twentieth year of our captivity.* Twenty years after Ezekiel's ministry began (1:1–2), approximately 572 BC. *the city.* Jerusalem, which had lain in ruins, with its temple destroyed, for fourteen years.
40:2 *visions of God.* The mode of this revelation from God, often involving symbolic images. On various approaches to chs. 40–48, see Introduction: Major Problems of Interpretation; Ezekiel's Vision of a New Temple and Land. *into the land of*

land of Israel, and set me upon a very high moun-
tain, by which *was* as the frame of a city on the
south.
3 And he brought me thither, and, behold, *there*
was a man, whose appearance *was* like the ap-
pearance of brass, with a line of flax in his hand,
and a measuring reed; and he stood in the gate.
4 And the man said unto me, Son of man, behold
with thine eyes, and hear with thine ears, and set
thine heart upon all that I shall shew thee; for to
the intent that I might shew *them* unto thee *art*
thou brought hither: declare all that thou seest to
the house of Israel.
5 And behold a wall on the outside of the house
round about, and in the man's hand a measuring
reed of six cubits *long* by the cubit and an hand
breadth: so he measured the breadth of the
building, one reed; and the height, one reed.
6 ¶ Then came he unto the gate which looketh
toward the east, and went up the stairs thereof,
and measured the threshold of the gate, *which*
was one reed broad; and the other threshold *of*
the gate, which was one reed broad.
7 And *every* little chamber *was* one reed long, and
one reed broad; and between the little chambers
were five cubits; and the threshold of the gate by
the porch of the gate within *was* one reed.
8 He measured also the porch of the gate within,
one reed.
9 Then measured he the porch of the gate, eight
cubits; and the posts thereof, two cubits; and the
porch of the gate *was* inward.
10 And the little chambers of the gate eastward
were three on this side, and three on that side;
they three *were* of one measure: and the posts had
one measure on this side and on that side.
11 And he measured the breadth of the entry of
the gate, ten cubits; *and* the length of the gate,
thirteen cubits.
12 The space also before the little chambers *was*
one cubit *on this side*, and the space *was* one cubit
on that side: and the little chambers *were* six
cubits on this side, and six cubits on that side.
13 He measured then the gate from the roof of *one*
little chamber to the roof of another: the breadth
was five and twenty cubits, door against door.
14 He made also posts of threescore cubits, even
unto the post of the court round about the gate.
15 And from the face of the gate of the entrance
unto the face of the porch of the inner gate *were*
fifty cubits.
16 And *there were* narrow windows to the little
chambers, and to their posts within the gate
round about, and likewise to the arches: and
windows *were* round about inward: and upon
each post *were* palm trees.
17 Then brought he me into the outward court,
and, lo, *there were* chambers, and a pavement
made for the court round about: thirty chambers
were upon the pavement.
18 And the pavement by the side of the gates
over against the length of the gates *was* the lower
pavement.
19 Then he measured the breadth from the
forefront of the lower gate unto the forefront
of the inner court without, an hundred cubits
eastward and northward.
20 ¶ And the gate of the outward court that
looked toward the north, he measured the length
thereof, and the breadth thereof.
21 And the little chambers thereof *were* three
on this side and three on that side; and the posts
thereof and the arches thereof were after the mea-
sure of the first gate: the length thereof *was* fifty
cubits, and the breadth five and twenty cubits.
22 And their windows, and their arches, and their
palm trees, *were* after the measure of the gate that
looketh toward the east; and they went up unto it
by seven steps; and the arches thereof *were* before
them.
23 And the gate of the inner court *was* over
against the gate toward the north, and toward
the east; and he measured from gate to gate an
hundred cubits.
24 ¶ After that he brought me toward the south,
and behold a gate toward the south: and he
measured the posts thereof and the arches thereof
according to these measures.
25 And *there were* windows in it and in the arches
thereof round about, like those windows: the
length *was* fifty cubits, and the breadth five and
twenty cubits.

Israel. Not physically, but as a part of the vision. *very high mountain.* A symbol of God's kingdom (see note at 17:22). John used similar language of his vision of the New Jerusalem (Rev. 21:10). *frame.* Structure.

40:3 *brass.* Bronze. *line of flax.* A cord or thread twine. *measuring reed.* A rod for measuring.

40:5 *cubits.* A cubit measured approximately eighteen inches, but these cubits were extended by a *hand breadth* or three inches (43:13), so *one reed* or six of such cubits was about ten-and-a-half feet (throughout the whole section). *measured.* Measuring the dimensions of this visionary temple communicates God's careful attention to His people to guarantee their hope and holiness (Zech. 2:1–5; Rev. 11:1–2; 21:15).

40:7 *little chamber.* Apartment or guardroom. *porch.* Vestibule.

40:9 *posts.* Door posts or pillars.

40:10 *one measure.* All the same length.

40:11 *entry.* Opening or entrance.

40:12 *space.* Boundary, territory, or space.

40:14 *posts.* Pillars or door posts. *court.* Enclosure.

40:15 *face.* The front of.

40:16 *narrow.* Literally, "closed," signifying small. *arches.* Porches, vestibules, or galleries (throughout the whole section).

40:17 *chambers.* Rooms.

40:18 *over against.* Alongside of or parallel to.

26 And *there were* seven steps to go up to it, and
the arches thereof *were* before them: and it had
palm trees, one on this side, and another on that
side, upon the posts thereof.
27 And *there was* a gate in the inner court toward
the south: and he measured from gate to gate
toward the south an hundred cubits.
28 And he brought me to the inner court by
the south gate: and he measured the south gate
according to these measures;
29 And the little chambers thereof, and the posts
thereof, and the arches thereof, according to these
measures: and *there were* windows in it and in
the arches thereof round about: *it was* fifty cubits
long, and five and twenty cubits broad.
30 And the arches round about *were* five and
twenty cubits long, and five cubits broad.
31 And the arches thereof *were* toward the utter
court; and palm trees *were* upon the posts thereof:
and the going up to it *had* eight steps.
32 ¶ And he brought me into the inner court
toward the east: and he measured the gate
according to these measures.
33 And the little chambers thereof, and the posts
thereof, and the arches thereof, *were* according to
these measures: and *there were* windows therein
and in the arches thereof round about: *it was* fifty
cubits long, and five and twenty cubits broad.
34 And the arches thereof *were* toward the
outward court; and palm trees *were* upon the
posts thereof, on this side, and on that side: and
the going up to it *had* eight steps.
35 ¶ And he brought me to the north gate, and
measured *it* according to these measures;
36 The little chambers thereof, the posts thereof,
and the arches thereof, and the windows to it
round about: the length *was* fifty cubits, and the
breadth five and twenty cubits.
37 And the posts thereof *were* toward the utter
court; and palm trees *were* upon the posts thereof,
on this side, and on that side: and the going up to
it *had* eight steps.
38 And the chambers and the entries thereof *were*
by the posts of the gates, where they washed the
burnt offering.
39 ¶ And in the porch of the gate *were* two tables
on this side, and two tables on that side, to slay
thereon the burnt offering and the sin offering
and the trespass offering.
40 And at the side without, as one goeth up to the
entry of the north gate, *were* two tables; and on
the other side, which *was* at the porch of the gate,
were two tables.
41 Four tables *were* on this side, and four tables
on that side, by the side of the gate; eight tables,
whereupon they slew *their sacrifices*.
42 And the four tables *were* of hewn stone for the
burnt offering, of a cubit and an half long, and
a cubit and an half broad, and one cubit high:
whereupon also they laid the instruments where-
with they slew the burnt offering and the sacrifice.
43 And within *were* hooks, an hand broad,
fastened round about: and upon the tables *was*
the flesh of the offering.
44 ¶ And without the inner gate *were* the cham-
bers of the singers in the inner court, which *was* at
the side of the north gate; and their prospect *was*
toward the south: one at the side of the east gate
having the prospect toward the north.
45 And he said unto me, This chamber, whose
prospect *is* toward the south, *is* for the priests, the
keepers of the charge of the house.
46 And the chamber whose prospect *is* toward the
north *is* for the priests, the keepers of the charge
of the altar: these *are* the sons of Zadok among
the sons of Levi, which come near to the LORD to
minister unto him.
47 So he measured the court, an hundred cubits
long, and an hundred cubits broad, foursquare;
and the altar *that was* before the house.
48 ¶ And he brought me to the porch of the
house, and measured *each* post of the porch, five
cubits on this side, and five cubits on that side:
and the breadth of the gate *was* three cubits on
this side, and three cubits on that side.
49 The length of the porch *was* twenty cubits, and
the breadth eleven cubits; and *he brought me* by
the steps whereby they went up to it: and *there
were* pillars by the posts, one on this side, and
another on that side.

40:37 *utter.* Outer.
40:38 *entries.* Openings or doorways. *burnt offering.* The animal for the burnt offering.
40:42 *hewn.* Cut. *instruments.* Implements or utensils.
40:43 *hooks.* Lips or hook-shaped pegs.
40:44 *prospect.* Face, the direction they faced (vv. 45–46).
40:45 *the keepers of the charge of the house.* Those with responsibility to keep the temple.
40:46 *the keepers of the charge of the altar.* Those with responsibility to keep and tend to the altar. *sons of Zadok.* The priestly family.

Thoughts for Personal/Family Worship: Chapter 40

As a godly man of the priestly line, Ezekiel must have been deeply distressed at his vision of the departure of God's glory from the temple (8:1—11:25) and the news that the holy city had been destroyed (33:21). God's special presence with Israel distinguished them from all other nations (Ex. 33:15–16) and was the life and joy of the godly (Pss. 46; 84). This vision of measuring out a new temple would have filled him with hope, for it was a pledge that God would see to everything necessary so that His presence would remain forever with His people (37:26–27). However, God was not concerned about buildings, for He had revealed that His presence would dwell by the Spirit in a transformed heart (11:16,19–20; 36:26–27; 37:14; 39:29). The meaning of the vision lies in its symbolism of God's restored presence with His

CHAPTER 41

AFTERWARD he brought me to the temple, and
measured the posts, six cubits broad on the one
side, and six cubits broad on the other side, *which*
was the breadth of the tabernacle.
2 And the breadth of the door *was* ten cubits;
and the sides of the door *were* five cubits on the
one side, and five cubits on the other side: and he
measured the length thereof, forty cubits: and the
breadth, twenty cubits.
3 Then went he inward, and measured the post of
the door, two cubits; and the door, six cubits; and
the breadth of the door, seven cubits.
4 So he measured the length thereof, twenty
cubits; and the breadth, twenty cubits, before the
temple: and he said unto me, This *is* the most holy
place.
5 After he measured the wall of the house, six
cubits; and the breadth of *every* side chamber,
four cubits, round about the house on every side.
6 And the side chambers *were* three, one over
another, and thirty in order; and they entered
into the wall which *was* of the house for the side
chambers round about, that they might have hold,
but they had not hold in the wall of the house.
7 And *there was* an enlarging, and a winding
about still upward to the side chambers: for the
winding about of the house went still upward
round about the house: therefore the breadth of
the house *was still* upward, and so increased *from*
the lowest *chamber* to the highest by the midst.
8 I saw also the height of the house round about:
the foundations of the side chambers *were* a full
reed of six great cubits.
9 The thickness of the wall, which *was* for the side
chamber without, *was* five cubits: and *that* which
was left *was* the place of the side chambers that
were within.
10 And between the chambers *was* the wideness
of twenty cubits round about the house on every
side.
11 And the doors of the side chambers *were*
toward *the place that was* left, one door toward
the north, and another door toward the south:
and the breadth of the place that was left *was* five
cubits round about.
12 Now the building that *was* before the separate
place at the end toward the west *was* seventy
cubits broad; and the wall of the building *was* five
cubits thick round about, and the length thereof
ninety cubits.
13 So he measured the house, an hundred cubits
long; and the separate place, and the building,
with the walls thereof, an hundred cubits long;
14 Also the breadth of the face of the house, and
of the separate place toward the east, an hundred
cubits.
15 And he measured the length of the building
over against the separate place which *was* behind
it, and the galleries thereof on the one side and on
the other side, an hundred cubits, with the inner
temple, and the porches of the court;
16 The door posts, and the narrow windows, and
the galleries round about on their three stories,
over against the door, cieled with wood round
about, and from the ground up to the windows,
and the windows *were* covered;
17 To that above the door, even unto the inner
house, and without, and by all the wall round
about within and without, by measure.
18 And *it was* made with cherubims and palm
trees, so that a palm tree *was* between a cherub
and a cherub; and *every* cherub had two faces;
19 So that the face of a man *was* toward the palm
tree on the one side, and the face of a young lion
toward the palm tree on the other side: *it was*
made through all the house round about.
20 From the ground unto above the door *were*
cherubims and palm trees made, and *on* the wall
of the temple.
21 The posts of the temple *were* squared, *and* the
face of the sanctuary; the appearance *of the one* as
the appearance *of the other*.
22 The altar of wood *was* three cubits high, and
the length thereof two cubits; and the corners
thereof, and the length thereof, and the walls
thereof, *were* of wood: and he said unto me, This
is the table that *is* before the LORD.

worshipers. What does it mean to hope in and seek after God's spiritual presence?

Chapter 41: ***Ezekiel's vision of a new temple continues as he stands in the inner court and hears the measuring of the holy places.***

41:1 *temple.* Can designate the main room, as well as the whole temple. *tabernacle.* Dwelling place.

41:2 *door.* The opening or entrance (throughout the chapter).

41:3 *inward.* Inside.

41:4 *most holy place.* The center point of God's holy presence, built as a perfect thirty-foot cube (Ex. 26:33–34; 1 Kings 6:16,20; 8:6; Rev. 21:16).

41:5 *chamber.* Room (throughout the chapter).

41:6 *have hold.* Be made secure or fastened.

41:7 *enlarging.* Widening on the way up. *winding.* Most likely a winding staircase.

41:12 *separate place.* A cut-out place, signifying the holiest place (also vv. 14–15).

41:14 *face of.* The front of.

41:15 *galleries.* Walkways with pillars.

41:16 *cieled.* Covered or overlaid.

41:18–20 *cherubims.* Angelic beings (see note at 10:15). *palm trees.* Symbols of flourishing life in God's presence (1 Kings 6:29; Ps. 92:12–13), perhaps alluding to the garden of Eden (Gen. 2:8–9). These trees appear thirteen times in 40:1—41:26.

41:21 *squared.* Made square.

41:22 *walls.* The sides of the altar.

23 And the temple and the sanctuary had two
doors.
24 And the doors had two leaves *apiece,* two
turning leaves; two *leaves* for the one door, and
two leaves for the other *door.*
25 And *there were* made on them, on the doors of
the temple, cherubims and palm trees, like as *were*
made upon the walls; and *there were* thick planks
upon the face of the porch without.
26 And *there were* narrow windows and palm
trees on the one side and on the other side, on the
sides of the porch, and *upon* the side chambers of
the house, and thick planks.

CHAPTER 42

THEN he brought me forth into the utter court,
the way toward the north: and he brought me into
the chamber that *was* over against the separate
place, and which *was* before the building toward
the north.
2 Before the length of an hundred cubits *was* the
north door, and the breadth *was* fifty cubits.
3 Over against the twenty *cubits* which *were* for
the inner court, and over against the pavement
which *was* for the utter court, *was* gallery against
gallery in three *stories.*
4 And before the chambers *was* a walk of ten
cubits breadth inward, a way of one cubit; and
their doors toward the north.
5 Now the upper chambers *were* shorter: for the
galleries were higher than these, than the lower,
and than the middlemost of the building.
6 For they *were* in three *stories,* but had not pillars
as the pillars of the courts: therefore *the building*
was straitened more than the lowest and the
middlemost from the ground.
7 And the wall that *was* without over against the
chambers, toward the utter court on the forepart
of the chambers, the length thereof *was* fifty
cubits.
8 For the length of the chambers that *were* in the
utter court *was* fifty cubits: and, lo, before the
temple *were* an hundred cubits.
9 And from under these chambers *was* the entry
on the east side, as one goeth into them from the
utter court.
10 The chambers *were* in the thickness of the
wall of the court toward the east, over against the
separate place, and over against the building.
11 And the way before them *was* like the
appearance of the chambers which *were* toward
the north, as long as they, *and* as broad as they:
and all their goings out *were* both according to
their fashions, and according to their doors.
12 And according to the doors of the chambers
that *were* toward the south *was* a door in the head
of the way, *even* the way directly before the wall
toward the east, as one entereth into them.
13 ¶ Then said he unto me, The north chambers
and the south chambers, which *are* before the
separate place, they *be* holy chambers, where the
priests that approach unto the LORD shall eat the
most holy things: there shall they lay the most
holy things, and the meat offering, and the sin
offering, and the trespass offering; for the place *is*
holy.
14 When the priests enter therein, then shall they
not go out of the holy *place* into the utter court,
but there they shall lay their garments wherein
they minister; for they *are* holy; and shall put on
other garments, and shall approach to *those things*
which *are* for the people.
15 Now when he had made an end of measuring
the inner house, he brought me forth toward
the gate whose prospect *is* toward the east, and
measured it round about.
16 He measured the east side with the measuring
reed, five hundred reeds, with the measuring reed
round about.
17 He measured the north side, five hundred
reeds, with the measuring reed round about.

41:24 *two leaves.* Two doors to each door opening.

Thoughts for Personal/Family Worship: Chapter 41

The symbolism of the holy places in the new temple would have reminded Ezekiel that the God who dwells with His people is the holy King (v. 4), whose servants are mighty spirits (vv. 18,20). His presence inspires fear and awe and commands reverence. Yet the images of palm trees frequently appearing in this vision (v. 18) imply that His holiness does not bring death to His people but abundant life. This is the hope of believers: that the Lord God will so dwell among them by the Spirit that they will rejoice with trembling. How will this hope be gloriously fulfilled when Christ returns?

Chapter 42: *Ezekiel hears of chambers in the outer court of the temple and observes the measuring of the whole temple complex.*

42:1 *utter.* Outer (throughout the section). *chamber.* Room used in the work of the priests and Levites (40:38,44–46; 1 Chron. 9:26,33). *separate place.* Either a space in the courtyard or the most holy place (vv. 10,13).

42:3 *gallery against gallery in three stories.* Porches in all three levels.

42:4 *a walk.* A place to walk.

42:6 *straitened.* Recessed or narrowed.

42:7 *on the forepart.* In front of.

42:10 *in the thickness of the wall.* In the expanse or breadth of the wall.

42:11 *fashions.* Its plans.

42:13 *eat the most holy things.* The priests were permitted to eat portions of the offerings brought to God for their own sustenance (Lev. 2:3,10; 6:16,26; 10:14; 24:9).

42:15 *prospect is toward the east.* Facing east.

18 He measured the south side, five hundred
reeds, with the measuring reed.
19 ¶ He turned about to the west side, *and* mea-
sured five hundred reeds with the measuring reed.
20 He measured it by the four sides: it had a wall
round about, five hundred *reeds* long, and five
hundred broad, to make a separation between the
sanctuary and the profane place.

CHAPTER 43

AFTERWARD he brought me to the gate, *even* the
gate that looketh toward the east:
2 And, behold, the glory of the God of Israel
came from the way of the east: and his voice *was*
like a noise of many waters: and the earth shined
with his glory.
3 And *it was* according to the appearance of the
vision which I saw, *even* according to the vision
that I saw when I came to destroy the city: and the
visions *were* like the vision that I saw by the river
Chebar; and I fell upon my face.
4 And the glory of the LORD came into the house
by the way of the gate whose prospect *is* toward
the east.
5 So the spirit took me up, and brought me into
the inner court; and, behold, the glory of the
LORD filled the house.
6 And I heard *him* speaking unto me out of the
house; and the man stood by me.
7 ¶ And he said unto me, Son of man, the place
of my throne, and the place of the soles of my feet,
where I will dwell in the midst of the children of
Israel for ever, and my holy name, shall the house
of Israel no more defile, *neither* they, nor their
kings, by their whoredom, nor by the carcases of
their kings in their high places.
8 In their setting of their threshold by my
thresholds, and their post by my posts, and the
wall between me and them, they have even defiled
my holy name by their abominations that they
have committed: wherefore I have consumed
them in mine anger.
9 Now let them put away their whoredom, and
the carcases of their kings, far from me, and I will
dwell in the midst of them for ever.
10 ¶ Thou son of man, shew the house to the
house of Israel, that they may be ashamed of their
iniquities: and let them measure the pattern.
11 And if they be ashamed of all that they have
done, shew them the form of the house, and the
fashion thereof, and the goings out thereof, and
the comings in thereof, and all the forms thereof,
and all the ordinances thereof, and all the forms
thereof, and all the laws thereof: and write *it* in
their sight, that they may keep the whole form
thereof, and all the ordinances thereof, and do
them.
12 This *is* the law of the house; Upon the top
of the mountain the whole limit thereof round
about *shall be* most holy. Behold, this *is* the law
of the house.
13 ¶ And these *are* the measures of the altar
after the cubits: The cubit *is* a cubit and an hand
breadth; even the bottom *shall be* a cubit, and the
breadth a cubit, and the border thereof by the
edge thereof round about *shall be* a span: and this
shall be the higher place of the altar.
14 And from the bottom *upon* the ground *even*
to the lower settle *shall be* two cubits, and the

42:20 *profane place.* A common area, not set apart as holy.

Thoughts for Personal/Family Worship: Chapter 42

The temple, including its courts, was a holy space that was separated from the common (vv. 14,20). Yet this was a place of human activity, requiring "chambers" for God's servants to work and to eat the holy food of their portion of the offerings (v. 13). These aspects of Ezekiel's vision would have assured him that God would not only give His presence but would also provide for the needs of the ministers who would serve Him there. This reminds us that the church must provide for the physical needs of its pastors (1 Cor. 9:13–14). It also reminds us that God provides for His priesthood. The priests of Aaron's line had largely failed to honor the Lord (7:26; 22:26), but in Christ God's people have all become priests who eat from the benefits of Christ's sacrifice (Isa. 61:6; Heb. 13:8–9). How does God feed His people with His holy things as they worship Him today?

Chapter 43: ***The glory of God returns to His people, and Ezekiel hears a call to repentance and instructions for consecrating the altar.***

43:2 *the glory of the God of Israel.* Having departed from the temple in Jerusalem (9:3; 10:19; 11:22–23), the manifest presence of God returns to this new temple.

43:3 *the vision which I saw.* See chs. 1; 10. *fell upon my face.* In fear and worship.

43:4 *prospect.* The direction it faces.

43:5 *the spirit took me up.* As part of the vision, not physically. *the glory of the LORD filled the house.* As it did when Solomon first dedicated the temple (1 Kings 8:10–11).

43:6 *the man.* Most likely the same man as in 40:3.

43:7 *place of the soles of my feet.* The ark of the covenant was like the footstool of God's throne (1 Chron. 28:2; Ps. 99:1,5; Isa. 60:13). *whoredom . . . carcases of their kings in their high places.* Spiritually unfaithful conduct and dead idolatrous images in places of idolatry and pagan ritual (v. 9).

43:8 *their post by my posts.* They had incorporated the pagan gods and rituals with worship in the temple (ch. 8), earning God's judgment.

43:9 *put away their whoredom . . . I will dwell.* Repenting from the idolatry would result in God's gracious presence.

43:10 *ashamed.* Humiliated.

43:11–12 *if they be ashamed.* The promise implied by the temple vision belonged only to those who would repent of idolatry. *the law of the house.* Revelation or instruction about the temple.

43:13 *altar.* The altar of burnt offering in the outer court.

breadth one cubit; and from the lesser settle *even*
to the greater settle *shall be* four cubits, and the
breadth *one* cubit.
15 So the altar *shall be* four cubits; and from the
altar and upward *shall be* four horns.
16 And the altar *shall be* twelve *cubits* long, twelve
broad, square in the four squares thereof.
17 And the settle *shall be* fourteen *cubits* long
and fourteen broad in the four squares thereof;
and the border about it *shall be* half a cubit; and
the bottom thereof *shall be* a cubit about; and his
stairs shall look toward the east.
18 ¶ And he said unto me, Son of man, thus saith
the Lord GOD; These *are* the ordinances of the altar
in the day when they shall make it, to offer burnt
offerings thereon, and to sprinkle blood thereon.
19 And thou shalt give to the priests the Levites
that be of the seed of Zadok, which approach
unto me, to minister unto me, saith the Lord
GOD, a young bullock for a sin offering.
20 And thou shalt take of the blood thereof, and
put *it* on the four horns of it, and on the four
corners of the settle, and upon the border round
about: thus shalt thou cleanse and purge it.
21 Thou shalt take the bullock also of the sin
offering, and he shall burn it in the appointed
place of the house, without the sanctuary.
22 And on the second day thou shalt offer a kid of
the goats without blemish for a sin offering; and
they shall cleanse the altar, as they did cleanse *it*
with the bullock.
23 When thou hast made an end of cleansing *it*,
thou shalt offer a young bullock without blemish,
and a ram out of the flock without blemish.
24 And thou shalt offer them before the LORD,
and the priests shall cast salt upon them, and they
shall offer them up *for* a burnt offering unto the
LORD.
25 Seven days shalt thou prepare every day a goat
for a sin offering: they shall also prepare a young
bullock, and a ram out of the flock, without
blemish.
26 Seven days shall they purge the altar and purify
it; and they shall consecrate themselves.
27 And when these days are expired, it shall be,
that upon the eighth day, and *so* forward, the
priests shall make your burnt offerings upon the
altar, and your peace offerings; and I will accept
you, saith the Lord GOD.

CHAPTER 44

THEN he brought me back the way of the gate of
the outward sanctuary which looketh toward the
east; and it *was* shut.
2 Then said the LORD unto me; This gate shall
be shut, it shall not be opened, and no man shall
enter in by it; because the LORD, the God of Israel,
hath entered in by it, therefore it shall be shut.
3 *It is* for the prince; the prince, he shall sit in it
to eat bread before the LORD; he shall enter by the
way of the porch of *that* gate, and shall go out by
the way of the same.
4 ¶ Then brought he me the way of the north gate
before the house: and I looked, and, behold, the
glory of the LORD filled the house of the LORD:
and I fell upon my face.
5 And the LORD said unto me, Son of man, mark
well, and behold with thine eyes, and hear with
thine ears all that I say unto thee concerning all
the ordinances of the house of the LORD, and
all the laws thereof; and mark well the entering
in of the house, with every going forth of the
sanctuary.
6 And thou shalt say to the rebellious, *even* to
the house of Israel, Thus saith the Lord GOD; O
ye house of Israel, let it suffice you of all your
abominations,

span. About nine inches.
43:14 *settle.* Ledge or pedestal (vv. 17,20).
43:18 *ordinances of.* Statutes or rules concerning.
43:19 *seed of Zadok.* The priestly family (1 Chron. 6:49–53).
43:20 *cleanse.* Purify. *purge.* Cover.
43:21 *without.* Outside.
43:24 *cast.* Throw or pour.
43:26 *consecrate.* Literally, "to fill his hands," an idiom expressing ordination to priestly office (Ex. 28:41; Lev. 8:33).
43:27 *expired.* Accomplished or ended. *I will accept you.* I will be pleased and accept you favorably.

Thoughts for Personal/Family Worship: Chapter 43

God's grace does not diminish His holiness. Ezekiel's vision depicts God's presence returning to His people, a work of amazing grace to those guilty of idolatry and other horrible sins. Yet His presence did not return in a soft or mild way but as "glory" that cast the prophet upon his face (vv. 2–3). The most glorious and holy place on earth was still a mere footstool for the feet of the heavenly King (v. 7). The gospel still shines with glory, the glory of grace (2 Cor. 4:6; Eph. 1:6). The Lord's presence will always require us to humble ourselves and repent of our sins with appropriate shame (vv. 7–11). Why do people resist this and prefer another approach to worship, whether it be casual or formal? How can we cultivate a deeper sense of God's glory in our worship?

Chapter 44: ***The return of God's glory introduces the presence of the king in the temple and prompts renewed instructions for an obedient priesthood.***

44:2 *shut . . . because the LORD . . . hath entered in by it.* The coming of God's glory to Israel would be a once-for-all event.
44:3 *prince.* The king, earlier identified as the ideal David, the Messiah (34:23–24; 37:24–25). His sitting and eating bread at the closed gate symbolize unique access to and fellowship with God (Matt. 11:27; John 1:1,18).
44:4 *glory . . . filled . . . fell upon my face.* See notes at 43:2,3,5.
44:5 *mark well.* Take careful note. *ordinances.* Manners or customs.
44:6 *let it suffice you of all your abominations.* Literally,

7 In that ye have brought *into my sanctuary*
strangers, uncircumcised in heart, and uncircum-
cised in flesh, to be in my sanctuary, to pollute it,
even my house, when ye offer my bread, the fat
and the blood, and they have broken my covenant
because of all your abominations.
8 And ye have not kept the charge of mine holy
things: but ye have set keepers of my charge in my
sanctuary for yourselves.
9 ¶ Thus saith the Lord GOD; No stranger, un-
circumcised in heart, nor uncircumcised in flesh,
shall enter into my sanctuary, of any stranger that
is among the children of Israel.
10 And the Levites that are gone away far from me,
when Israel went astray, which went astray away
from me after their idols; they shall even bear their
iniquity.
11 Yet they shall be ministers in my sanctuary,
having charge at the gates of the house, and
ministering to the house: they shall slay the burnt
offering and the sacrifice for the people, and they
shall stand before them to minister unto them.
12 Because they ministered unto them before
their idols, and caused the house of Israel to fall
into iniquity; therefore have I lifted up mine hand
against them, saith the Lord GOD, and they shall
bear their iniquity.
13 And they shall not come near unto me, to do
the office of a priest unto me, nor to come near to
any of my holy things, in the most holy *place*: but
they shall bear their shame, and their abomina-
tions which they have committed.
14 But I will make them keepers of the charge of
the house, for all the service thereof, and for all
that shall be done therein.
15 ¶ But the priests the Levites, the sons of Zadok,
that kept the charge of my sanctuary when the
children of Israel went astray from me, they shall
come near to me to minister unto me, and they
shall stand before me to offer unto me the fat and
the blood, saith the Lord GOD:
16 They shall enter into my sanctuary, and they
shall come near to my table, to minister unto me,
and they shall keep my charge.
17 ¶ And it shall come to pass, *that* when they
enter in at the gates of the inner court, they shall
be clothed with linen garments; and no wool shall
come upon them, whiles they minister in the
gates of the inner court, and within.
18 They shall have linen bonnets upon their
heads, and shall have linen breeches upon their
loins; they shall not gird *themselves* with any thing
that causeth sweat.
19 And when they go forth into the utter court,
even into the utter court to the people, they shall
put off their garments wherein they ministered,
and lay them in the holy chambers, and they shall
put on other garments; and they shall not sanctify
the people with their garments.
20 Neither shall they shave their heads, nor suffer
their locks to grow long; they shall only poll their
heads.
21 Neither shall any priest drink wine, when they
enter into the inner court.
22 Neither shall they take for their wives a widow,
nor her that is put away: but they shall take
maidens of the seed of the house of Israel, or a
widow that had a priest before.
23 And they shall teach my people *the difference*
between the holy and profane, and cause them to
discern between the unclean and the clean.
24 And in controversy they shall stand in
judgment; *and* they shall judge it according to
my judgments: and they shall keep my laws and
my statutes in all mine assemblies; and they shall
hallow my sabbaths.
25 And they shall come at no dead person to de-
file themselves: but for father, or for mother, or for
son, or for daughter, for brother, or for sister that
hath had no husband, they may defile themselves.
26 And after he is cleansed, they shall reckon unto
him seven days.
27 And in the day that he goeth into the sanctuary,
unto the inner court, to minister in the sanctuary,
he shall offer his sin offering, saith the Lord GOD.
28 And it shall be unto them for an inheritance:

"enough to you from all your detestable things."
44:7 *strangers.* Foreigners. *uncircumcised in heart.* Unclean and unchanged in heart, and thus spiritually outside the covenant (6:9). *uncircumcised in flesh.* Physically outside the covenant. *pollute.* To treat as ordinary and common.
44:8 *charge.* Custody or service (v. 11).
44:11 *ministers.* Attendants or worshipers.
44:12 *to fall into iniquity.* Literally, "stumbling block of iniquity," the same Hebrew phrase used earlier (7:19).
44:15 *sons of Zadok.* The priestly family.
44:17 *linen garments.* Holy clothing for priestly work (Ex. 28:39–43; 39:27–29; Lev. 16:4).
44:18 *bonnets.* Turban-like head coverings. *breeches.* Priestly undergarments. *gird.* Wrap themselves as with a belt.
44:20 *suffer.* Permit or allow. *locks.* Hair. *poll their heads.* Trim their hair.
44:22 *put away.* Divorced. *maidens.* Virgins. *seed.* The families of Israel.
44:23 *holy and profane . . . unclean and the clean.* Two pairs of opposites the priests must teach Israel to distinguish (22:26; Lev. 10:10–11). The first distinction is between the sacred and the ordinary, and the second pertains to contamination by contact with corruption or death. *discern.* Know.
44:24 *controversy.* A legal contest. *stand in judgment.* Rise as a prosecutor or defender. *judge.* Pronounce sentence. *hallow.* To reverence or set apart as holy.
44:25 *defile.* Make ceremonially unclean—forbidden to priests because of their participation in the holy (Lev. 19:28; 21:1–3,11; 22:3).
44:26 *reckon unto him seven days.* The waiting period before approaching the holy (Num. 6:10; 19:11,12).
44:28 *I am their inheritance.* The priests enjoyed communion

I *am* their inheritance: and ye shall give them no
possession in Israel: I *am* their possession.
29 They shall eat the meat offering, and the sin
offering, and the trespass offering; and every
dedicated thing in Israel shall be theirs.
30 And the first of all the firstfruits of all *things*,
and every oblation of all, of every *sort* of your
oblations, shall be the priest's: ye shall also give
unto the priest the first of your dough, that he
may cause the blessing to rest in thine house.
31 The priests shall not eat of any thing that is
dead of itself, or torn, whether it be fowl or beast.

CHAPTER 45

MOREOVER, when ye shall divide by lot the land
for inheritance, ye shall offer an oblation unto the
LORD, an holy portion of the land: the length *shall*
be the length of five and twenty thousand *reeds*,
and the breadth *shall be* ten thousand. This *shall*
be holy in all the borders thereof round about.
2 Of this there shall be for the sanctuary five
hundred *in length*, with five hundred *in breadth*,
square round about; and fifty cubits round about
for the suburbs thereof.
3 And of this measure shalt thou measure the
length of five and twenty thousand, and the breadth
of ten thousand: and in it shall be the sanctuary *and*
the most holy *place*.
4 The holy *portion* of the land shall be for the
priests the ministers of the sanctuary, which shall
come near to minister unto the LORD: and it shall
be a place for their houses, and an holy place for
the sanctuary.
5 And the five and twenty thousand of length,
and the ten thousand of breadth, shall also the
Levites, the ministers of the house, have for
themselves, for a possession for twenty chambers.
6 ¶ And ye shall appoint the possession of the city
five thousand broad, and five and twenty thou-
sand long, over against the oblation of the holy
portion: it shall be for the whole house of Israel.
7 ¶ And *a portion shall be* for the prince on the
one side and on the other side of the oblation of
the holy *portion*, and of the possession of the city,
before the oblation of the holy *portion*, and before
the possession of the city, from the west side west-
ward, and from the east side eastward: and the
length *shall be* over against one of the portions,
from the west border unto the east border.
8 In the land shall be his possession in Israel: and
my princes shall no more oppress my people; and
the rest of the land shall they give to the house of
Israel according to their tribes.
9 ¶ Thus saith the Lord GOD; Let it suffice you,
O princes of Israel: remove violence and spoil,
and execute judgment and justice, take away your
exactions from my people, saith the Lord GOD.
10 Ye shall have just balances, and a just ephah,
and a just bath.
11 The ephah and the bath shall be of one
measure, that the bath may contain the tenth
part of an homer, and the ephah the tenth part
of an homer: the measure thereof shall be after
the homer.
12 And the shekel *shall be* twenty gerahs: twenty
shekels, five and twenty shekels, fifteen shekels,
shall be your maneh.
13 This *is* the oblation that ye shall offer; the sixth
part of an ephah of an homer of wheat, and ye
shall give the sixth part of an ephah of an homer
of barley:
14 Concerning the ordinance of oil, the bath of
oil, *ye shall offer* the tenth part of a bath out of the

---

with God and sustenance from the offerings in place of a portion of the land (Num. 18:20–21; Deut. 10:9; Josh. 13:14,33).
44:29 *dedicated.* Devoted to the Lord.
44:30 *oblations.* Offerings or sacrifices. *dough.* Whole-grain flour.

Thoughts for Personal/Family Worship: Chapter 44

1. **The presence of the king ("prince") in the temple was another symbol of great hope for Israel (v. 3). The Lord had shattered the monarchy of David's line because it had been corrupted through idolatry. However, the Lord promised through this vision that not only would He give Israel a king again but that this king would be a true worshiper with special intimacy with God. Jesus Christ in His mediatorial office is both the supreme worshiper and the great worship leader of the church (Ps. 22:22–27; Matt. 11:25; Heb. 2:12). How does He lead His people in worship as their king?**
2. **The Lord reasserted the necessity that His priests serve in purity and obedience to His Word, excluding the unfit from the privileges of His worship. Though the ceremonies of the old covenant have ceased, the Lord remains zealous for His worship. How must the church, especially its elders, guard the purity of God's worship?**

Chapter 45: *Laws concerning land and offerings*
45:1 *oblation.* A contribution or offering (throughout the section), here a portion of the land.
45:2 *suburbs.* Land outside the walls of a city or structure but under its jurisdiction.
45:7 *prince.* The king (throughout the section).
45:8 *oppress.* Mistreat.
45:9 *Let it suffice you.* Literally, "enough to you." *judgment and justice.* Key terms describing the reign of a righteous king (2 Sam. 8:15; 1 Kings 10:9; Ps. 72:1; Isa. 9:7; Jer. 22:2–3,15; 23:5; 33:15). *exactions.* Extortions and oppressive demands.
45:10 *just balances . . . ephah . . . bath.* Scales for weight and dry and liquid measures were to be accurate for righteous commerce. The leaders must repent of dishonest gain (22:27).
45:11 *homer.* A unit of dry measure, approximately 9.5 bushels or 340 liters.
45:12 *shekel.* A chief unit of weight or measure. *gerahs.* A small weight, the twentieth part of a shekel. *maneh.* Sixty shekels.
45:13 *ephah.* Almost a bushel.
45:14 *bath.* A liquid measure of about nine gallons. *cor.* A dry or liquid measure equal to ten ephahs or baths.

cor, *which is* an homer of ten baths; for ten baths
are an homer:
15 And one lamb out of the flock, out of two
hundred, out of the fat pastures of Israel; for a
meat offering, and for a burnt offering, and for
peace offerings, to make reconciliation for them,
saith the Lord GOD.
16 All the people of the land shall give this
oblation for the prince in Israel.
17 And it shall be the prince's part *to give* burnt
offerings, and meat offerings, and drink offerings,
in the feasts, and in the new moons, and in the
sabbaths, in all solemnities of the house of Israel:
he shall prepare the sin offering, and the meat
offering, and the burnt offering, and the peace
offerings, to make reconciliation for the house of
Israel.
18 Thus saith the Lord GOD; In the first *month*,
in the first *day* of the month, thou shalt take a
young bullock without blemish, and cleanse the
sanctuary:
19 And the priest shall take of the blood of the sin
offering, and put *it* upon the posts of the house,
and upon the four corners of the settle of the
altar, and upon the posts of the gate of the inner
court.
20 And so thou shalt do the seventh *day* of the
month for every one that erreth, and for *him that
is* simple: so shall ye reconcile the house.
21 In the first *month*, in the fourteenth day of the
month, ye shall have the passover, a feast of seven
days; unleavened bread shall be eaten.
22 And upon that day shall the prince prepare
for himself and for all the people of the land a
bullock *for* a sin offering.
23 And seven days of the feast he shall prepare a
burnt offering to the LORD, seven bullocks and
seven rams without blemish daily the seven days;
and a kid of the goats daily *for* a sin offering.
24 And he shall prepare a meat offering of an
ephah for a bullock, and an ephah for a ram, and
an hin of oil for an ephah.
25 In the seventh *month*, in the fifteenth day
of the month, shall he do the like in the feast
of the seven days, according to the sin offering,
according to the burnt offering, and according to
the meat offering, and according to the oil.

CHAPTER 46

THUS saith the Lord GOD; The gate of the inner
court that looketh toward the east shall be shut
the six working days; but on the sabbath it shall be
opened, and in the day of the new moon it shall
be opened.
2 And the prince shall enter by the way of the
porch of *that* gate without, and shall stand by
the post of the gate, and the priests shall prepare
his burnt offering and his peace offerings, and he
shall worship at the threshold of the gate: then he
shall go forth; but the gate shall not be shut until
the evening.
3 Likewise the people of the land shall worship
at the door of this gate before the LORD in the
sabbaths and in the new moons.
4 And the burnt offering that the prince shall
offer unto the LORD in the sabbath day *shall be*
six lambs without blemish, and a ram without
blemish.
5 And the meat offering *shall be* an ephah for a
ram, and the meat offering for the lambs as he
shall be able to give, and an hin of oil to an ephah.
6 And in the day of the new moon *it shall be* a
young bullock without blemish, and six lambs,
and a ram: they shall be without blemish.
7 And he shall prepare a meat offering, an ephah

45:15 *fat.* The best pasture. *reconciliation.* Propitiation of God's wrath for forgiveness of sins (v. 17).
45:17 *the prince's part.* It was not unusual for godly kings to supply animals for the priests to sacrifice (2 Chron. 30:24; 35:7). *new moons.* The beginning of the month was a special day of priestly activity (Num. 10:10; 28:11). *solemnities.* Appointed seasons.
45:18 *first month . . . first day.* This statute does not match the ceremonial law of Moses, which commanded that the priests ritually cleanse "purify" the holy places on the Day of Atonement in the seventh month (Lev. 16:16,30). Instead, it closely links cleansing to Passover (v. 21).
45:19 *settle.* Ledge.
45:20 *erreth.* Goes astray or sins. *simple.* Foolish or ignorant.
45:24 *hin.* A unit of about five quarts or six liters.

Thoughts for Personal/Family Worship: Chapter 45

1. **The symbolism of the division of the land (vv. 1–7) reinforces again the promise that God's holy dwelling place would be with His people and would be closely connected to the king ("prince"). The future king would not be a greedy and unjust oppressor but a ruler of impeccable righteousness and truth (vv. 8–10). Jesus Christ is the King of His people, God's incarnate presence with them, and He leads them in justice and holiness.**
2. **Ezekiel's vision of the temple portrayed the offering of sacrifices for sin in order to accomplish "reconciliation" between God and His sinful worshipers (vv. 15,17). Christ offered Himself as the sacrifice for sin once and for all, abolishing all other sacrifices for sin (Heb. 10:10, 12,14,18). Therefore, this vision cannot depict a literal future sacrifice. The Lord was symbolically promising Ezekiel that, though God destroyed the temple, He would still provide for the necessary sacrifice for sins through His king (v. 17). If the Jews in exile could hope in God's promise of atonement, how much more can Jews and Gentiles today trust in Christ's finished work upon the cross?**

Chapter 46: *Further ordinances and laws*

46:1 *new moon.* See note at 45:17.
46:5 *as he shall be able to give.* Literally, "the gift of his hand," where "hand" represents power.

for a bullock, and an ephah for a ram, and for the
lambs according as his hand shall attain unto, and
an hin of oil to an ephah.
8 And when the prince shall enter, he shall go in
by the way of the porch of *that* gate, and he shall
go forth by the way thereof.
9 ¶ But when the people of the land shall come
before the LORD in the solemn feasts, he that
entereth in by the way of the north gate to worship
shall go out by the way of the south gate; and he
that entereth by the way of the south gate shall go
forth by the way of the north gate: he shall not
return by the way of the gate whereby he came in,
but shall go forth over against it.
10 And the prince in the midst of them, when
they go in, shall go in; and when they go forth,
shall go forth.
11 And in the feasts and in the solemnities the
meat offering shall be an ephah to a bullock, and
an ephah to a ram, and to the lambs as he is able
to give, and an hin of oil to an ephah.
12 Now when the prince shall prepare a voluntary
burnt offering or peace offerings voluntarily unto
the LORD, *one* shall then open him the gate that
looketh toward the east, and he shall prepare his
burnt offering and his peace offerings, as he did
on the sabbath day: then he shall go forth; and
after his going forth *one* shall shut the gate.
13 Thou shalt daily prepare a burnt offering
unto the LORD *of* a lamb of the first year without
blemish: thou shalt prepare it every morning.
14 And thou shalt prepare a meat offering for it
every morning, the sixth part of an ephah, and the
third part of an hin of oil, to temper with the fine
flour; a meat offering continually by a perpetual
ordinance unto the LORD.
15 Thus shall they prepare the lamb, and the
meat offering, and the oil, every morning *for* a
continual burnt offering.
16 ¶ Thus saith the Lord GOD; If the prince give a
gift unto any of his sons, the inheritance thereof
shall be his sons'; it *shall be* their possession by
inheritance.
17 But if he give a gift of his inheritance to one
of his servants, then it shall be his to the year of
liberty; after it shall return to the prince: but his
inheritance shall be his sons' for them.
18 Moreover the prince shall not take of the
people's inheritance by oppression, to thrust
them out of their possession; *but* he shall give his
sons inheritance out of his own possession: that
my people be not scattered every man from his
possession.
19 ¶ After he brought me through the entry,
which *was* at the side of the gate, into the holy
chambers of the priests, which looked toward the
north: and, behold, there *was* a place on the two
sides westward.
20 Then said he unto me, This *is* the place where
the priests shall boil the trespass offering and
the sin offering, where they shall bake the meat
offering; that they bear *them* not out into the utter
court, to sanctify the people.
21 Then he brought me forth into the utter court,
and caused me to pass by the four corners of the
court; and, behold, in every corner of the court
there was a court.
22 In the four corners of the court *there were*
courts joined of forty *cubits* long and thirty broad:
these four corners *were* of one measure.
23 And *there was* a row *of building* round about
in them, round about them four, and *it was* made
with boiling places under the rows round about.
24 Then said he unto me, These *are* the places of
them that boil, where the ministers of the house
shall boil the sacrifice of the people.

CHAPTER 47

AFTERWARD he brought me again unto the door
of the house; and, behold, waters issued out from
under the threshold of the house eastward: for the

46:9 *solemn feasts.* Appointed times (v. 11).
46:10 The king (*prince*) will accompany the people in all their processions to worship God.
46:12 *voluntary burnt offering.* A freewill offering.
46:14 *temper.* Mix.
46:16 *possession by inheritance.* Possession that cannot be taken away.
46:18 *oppression.* Violence or mistreatment. The point of vv. 16–18 reiterates the idea that the king will not harm the people by injustice but will be completely content with his portion in the inheritance (45:7–9).
46:23 *boiling places under the rows round about.* Places to boil the sacrifices, located under rows of stones.

Thoughts for Personal/Family Worship: Chapter 46

The King worships God (v. 2), walking with His people in all their feasts of worship (vv. 9–10) and leading them in offering voluntary sacrifices of praise to God (v. 12). Christ is the Mediator of the church's worship. Whenever even the smallest congregation gathers in His name, He is there with them (Matt. 18:20). Through Him believers offer to God sacrifices of praise, thanksgiving, and financial gifts (Heb. 13:15–16). In response to His great sacrifice, Christians offer themselves as living sacrifices to God (Rom. 12:1). How can knowing that Jesus Christ is directly involved in your church's worship change the way you participate in the service?

The River and the Land (47:1—48:35)

Chapter 47: ***Ezekiel's vision reveals a river of healing flowing from the temple and the promise of a restoration of Israel's inheritance in the land.***

47:1 *issued.* Came out or flowed. *forefront.* Front. The image of waters flowing from the temple symbolizes life coming from God's presence to bless His people (Joel 3:18; Zech. 14:8;

forefront of the house *stood toward* the east, and
the waters came down from under from the right
side of the house, at the south *side* of the altar.
2 Then brought he me out of the way of the gate
northward, and led me about the way without
unto the utter gate by the way that looketh
eastward; and, behold, there ran out waters on
the right side.
3 And when the man that had the line in his hand
went forth eastward, he measured a thousand
cubits, and he brought me through the waters;
the waters *were* to the ankles.
4 Again he measured a thousand, and brought me
through the waters; the waters *were* to the knees.
Again he measured a thousand, and brought me
through; the waters *were* to the loins.
5 Afterward he measured a thousand; *and it was*
a river that I could not pass over: for the waters
were risen, waters to swim in, a river that could
not be passed over.
6 ¶ And he said unto me, Son of man, hast thou
seen *this*? Then he brought me, and caused me to
return to the brink of the river.
7 Now when I had returned, behold, at the bank
of the river *were* very many trees on the one side
and on the other.
8 Then said he unto me, These waters issue out
toward the east country, and go down into the
desert, and go into the sea: *which being* brought
forth into the sea, the waters shall be healed.
9 And it shall come to pass, *that* every thing that
liveth, which moveth, whithersoever the rivers
shall come, shall live: and there shall be a very
great multitude of fish, because these waters shall
come thither: for they shall be healed; and every
thing shall live whither the river cometh.
10 And it shall come to pass, *that* the fishers shall
stand upon it from En-gedi even unto En-eglaim;
they shall be a *place* to spread forth nets; their fish
shall be according to their kinds, as the fish of the
great sea, exceeding many.
11 But the miry places thereof and the marishes
thereof shall not be healed; they shall be given to salt.
12 And by the river upon the bank thereof, on
this side and on that side, shall grow all trees for
meat, whose leaf shall not fade, neither shall the
fruit thereof be consumed: it shall bring forth
new fruit according to his months, because their
waters they issued out of the sanctuary: and the
fruit thereof shall be for meat, and the leaf thereof
for medicine.
13 ¶ Thus saith the Lord GOD; This *shall be* the
border, whereby ye shall inherit the land accord-
ing to the twelve tribes of Israel: Joseph *shall have*
two portions.
14 And ye shall inherit it, one as well as another:
concerning the which I lifted up mine hand to give
it unto your fathers: and this land shall fall unto
you for inheritance.
15 And this *shall be* the border of the land toward
the north side, from the great sea, the way of
Hethlon, as men go to Zedad;
16 Hamath, Berothah, Sibraim, which *is* between
the border of Damascus and the border of Hamath;
Hazar-hatticon, which *is* by the coast of Hauran.
17 And the border from the sea shall be Hazar-
enan, the border of Damascus, and the north
northward, and the border of Hamath. And *this*
is the north side.
18 And the east side ye shall measure from
Hauran, and from Damascus, and from Gilead,
and from the land of Israel *by* Jordan, from the
border unto the east sea. And *this is* the east side.
19 And the south side southward, from Tamar
even to the waters of strife *in* Kadesh, the river to
the great sea. And *this is* the south side southward.
20 The west side also *shall be* the great sea from
the border, till a man come over against Hamath.
This *is* the west side.
21 So shall ye divide this land unto you according
to the tribes of Israel.
22 ¶ And it shall come to pass, *that* ye shall divide
it by lot for an inheritance unto you, and to the
strangers that sojourn among you, which shall

Rev. 22:1) and may allude to the river of the garden of Eden (Gen. 2:10).
47:3 *line.* Measuring line.
47:4 *loins.* The waist area.
47:5 *could not be passed over.* The image of a river that deepens from a trickle to a depth that cannot be crossed in fewer than 1.5 miles, like that of a rock growing into a mountain that fills the world (Dan. 2:35), indicates that it has a supernatural source.
47:6 *brink.* The edge or bank.
47:7 *very many trees.* An allusion to the garden of Eden (v. 12; see notes at 36:35; 41:18–20).
47:8 *the waters shall be healed.* The Dead Sea will be made wholesome and full of life. This was the location of Sodom and Gomorrah and so represents the healing of a world cursed for sin.
47:9 *shall live.* Earlier, the gift of life to the dead was attributed to the Spirit (37:14; cf. Isa. 44:3).
47:10 *from En-gedi . . . unto En-eglaim.* Places on either side of the Dead Sea. *the great sea.* The Mediterranean Sea (vv. 19–20).
47:11 *miry.* Swampy. *marishes.* Marshland. *given to salt.* An image of falling under God's anger (Gen. 19:26; Deut. 29:23; Jer. 17:5–6; Zeph. 2:9). Not all will enjoy the blessings of grace.
47:12 *be consumed.* Come to an end; it will constantly bear. *meat.* Food, here specifically fruit. *medicine.* For healing. The image of the fruitful trees symbolizes the restoration of mankind to paradise and the removal of the curse for sin (Rev. 22:2–3).
47:14 *one as well as another.* Each one shall inherit. *I lifted up mine hand.* As a sign of the covenant promise.
47:15 *this shall be the border.* The territory generally followed the boundaries described in Num. 34:1–12.
47:19 *waters of strife.* So called because of the strife of Israel (Num. 20:1–13).

beget children among you: and they shall be unto
you as born in the country among the children
of Israel; they shall have inheritance with you
among the tribes of Israel.
23 And it shall come to pass, *that* in what tribe
the stranger sojourneth, there shall ye give *him* his
inheritance, saith the Lord GOD.

CHAPTER 48

NOW these *are* the names of the tribes. From the
north end to the coast of the way of Hethlon, as
one goeth to Hamath, Hazar-enan, the border of
Damascus northward, to the coast of Hamath; for
these are his sides east *and* west; a *portion for* Dan.
2 And by the border of Dan, from the east side
unto the west side, a *portion for* Asher.
3 And by the border of Asher, from the east side
even unto the west side, a *portion for* Naphtali.
4 And by the border of Naphtali, from the east
side unto the west side, a *portion for* Manasseh.
5 And by the border of Manasseh, from the east
side unto the west side, a *portion for* Ephraim.
6 And by the border of Ephraim, from the east
side even unto the west side, a *portion for* Reuben.
7 And by the border of Reuben, from the east side
unto the west side, a *portion for* Judah.
8 ¶ And by the border of Judah, from the east side
unto the west side, shall be the offering which ye
shall offer of five and twenty thousand *reeds in*
breadth, and *in* length as one of the *other* parts,
from the east side unto the west side: and the
sanctuary shall be in the midst of it.
9 The oblation that ye shall offer unto the LORD
shall be of five and twenty thousand in length, and
of ten thousand in breadth.
10 And for them, *even* for the priests, shall be
this holy oblation; toward the north five and
twenty thousand *in length*, and toward the west
ten thousand in breadth, and toward the east ten
thousand in breadth, and toward the south five
and twenty thousand in length: and the sanctuary
of the LORD shall be in the midst thereof.
11 *It shall be* for the priests that are sanctified of
the sons of Zadok; which have kept my charge,
which went not astray when the children of Israel
went astray, as the Levites went astray.
12 And *this* oblation of the land that is offered
shall be unto them a thing most holy by the
border of the Levites.
13 And over against the border of the priests the
Levites *shall have* five and twenty thousand in
length, and ten thousand in breadth: all the length
shall be five and twenty thousand, and the breadth
ten thousand.
14 And they shall not sell of it, neither exchange,
nor alienate the firstfruits of the land: for *it is* holy
unto the LORD.
15 ¶ And the five thousand, that are left in
the breadth over against the five and twenty
thousand, shall be a profane *place* for the city, for
dwelling, and for suburbs: and the city shall be in
the midst thereof.
16 And these *shall be* the measures thereof; the
north side four thousand and five hundred, and
the south side four thousand and five hundred,
and on the east side four thousand and five
hundred, and the west side four thousand and
five hundred.
17 And the suburbs of the city shall be toward
the north two hundred and fifty, and toward the
south two hundred and fifty, and toward the east
two hundred and fifty, and toward the west two
hundred and fifty.
18 And the residue in length over against the
oblation of the holy *portion shall be* ten thousand
eastward, and ten thousand westward: and it shall
be over against the oblation of the holy *portion*;

47:22–23 *strangers.* Foreigners. *sojourn.* To live as resident aliens.

Thoughts for Personal/Family Worship: Chapter 47

The vision of the river flowing from the temple promises that the Lord's holy presence will come to His people as a supernatural source of life. He will bring them healing and transform them from a salty wasteland to a people of flourishing life. The images of this chapter take us back to the garden of Eden. That this vision leads into a description of the boundaries of Israel's inheritance implies that God's people will inherit nothing less than paradise. How beautiful is this picture! Yet the giving of the marshes "to salt" reminds us that not all people will enjoy its fulfillment. Jesus said that we must come to Him with spiritual thirst and ask for the living water (John 4:14; 7:37–39). Why must we have the Spirit of Christ in this life if we would enjoy the river of His delights forever?

Chapter 48: ***Ezekiel's vision concludes with a new division of the land and a promise of God's presence.***

48:1–7 The land was divided into inheritances for seven of the twelve tribes (on the others, see vv. 23–29). This vision pictures the inheritance of Israel as including all the tribes but in a new arrangement, not according to the portions of land that they received from the Lord through Moses and Joshua (Josh. 13:1—19:51). This implies both a fulfillment of the ancient promises to Abraham and a change compared to the old covenant inheritance.

48:8 *offering.* A portion of territory offered to the Lord (45:1–6).

48:9 *oblation.* Same word as offering (v. 8; so throughout the chapter.)

48:11 *sanctified.* Set apart or consecrated as holy.

48:12 *a thing most holy.* That which has been set apart.

48:13 The Levites would be located next to the priests.

48:14 *alienate.* Take away.

48:15 *profane place.* An area not set apart as holy. *suburbs.* Land outside the walls but under the jurisdiction of the city (v. 17).

48:18 *residue.* Remainder. *over against.* Close by or side by side with.

and the increase thereof shall be for food unto
them that serve the city.
19 And they that serve the city shall serve it out of
all the tribes of Israel.
20 All the oblation *shall be* five and twenty
thousand by five and twenty thousand: ye shall
offer the holy oblation foursquare, with the
possession of the city.
21 ¶ And the residue *shall be* for the prince, on
the one side and on the other of the holy oblation,
and of the possession of the city, over against the
five and twenty thousand of the oblation toward
the east border, and westward over against the
five and twenty thousand toward the west border,
over against the portions for the prince: and it
shall be the holy oblation; and the sanctuary of
the house *shall be* in the midst thereof.
22 Moreover from the possession of the Levites,
and from the possession of the city, *being* in the
midst *of that* which is the prince's, between the
border of Judah and the border of Benjamin, shall
be for the prince.
23 As for the rest of the tribes, from the east side
unto the west side, Benjamin *shall have* a *portion.*
24 And by the border of Benjamin, from the east
side unto the west side, Simeon *shall have* a *portion.*
25 And by the border of Simeon, from the east
side unto the west side, Issachar a *portion.*
26 And by the border of Issachar, from the east
side unto the west side, Zebulun a *portion.*
27 And by the border of Zebulun, from the east
side unto the west side, Gad a *portion.*
28 And by the border of Gad, at the south side
southward, the border shall be even from Tamar
unto the waters of strife *in* Kadesh, *and* to the
river toward the great sea.
29 This *is* the land which ye shall divide by lot
unto the tribes of Israel for inheritance, and these
are their portions, saith the Lord GOD.
30 ¶ And these *are* the goings out of the city on
the north side, four thousand and five hundred
measures.
31 And the gates of the city *shall be* after the names
of the tribes of Israel: three gates northward; one
gate of Reuben, one gate of Judah, one gate of
Levi.
32 And at the east side four thousand and five
hundred: and three gates; and one gate of Joseph,
one gate of Benjamin, one gate of Dan.
33 And at the south side four thousand and five
hundred measures: and three gates; one gate of
Simeon, one gate of Issachar, one gate of Zebulun.
34 At the west side four thousand and five
hundred, *with* their three gates; one gate of Gad,
one gate of Asher, one gate of Naphtali.
35 *It was* round about eighteen thousand
measures: and the name of the city from *that* day
shall be, The LORD *is* there.

48:23–29 Details specifying the territories of the five remaining tribes.
48:30 *goings out.* Borders or extremities.
48:31–34 *gates of the city.* Entrances for each of the twelve tribes (Rev. 21:12–13), indicating that all of God's chosen people will enter into it.
48:35 *The LORD is there.* Hebrew, *Jehovah-Shammah.* The book, which revolves around the presence of God's glory with His people, concludes with the promise that God will be with His people (35:10; Rev. 21:3). Their very identity (*name*) will be bound up with His presence.

Thoughts for Personal/Family Worship: Chapter 48

The inheritance of God's people centers around being with God. Already Christians have a foretaste of God's presence in the Spirit of God. Still, the best is yet to come. Too often we think of heaven in terms of the absence of pain, but the essence of heaven is the presence of Christ. When God fulfills all His covenant promises, the true children of Abraham will dwell with Him and see His glory. Even if someone could come back from heaven to earth, the best he could do to describe its wonders would boil down to the statement "The Lord is there." This is what gave the apostle Paul the courage to face death, indeed the joy to call it gain (2 Cor. 5:8; Phil. 1:21–23). This is what makes the second coming of Christ the great hope of believers, because then they will be with the Lord (1 Thess. 4:17). How does your hope of being with Christ compare with your desires for the things and relationships of this world? This is the test of your heart.

INTRODUCTION TO THE BOOK OF DANIEL

Authorship: Daniel, whose name means "God is Judge," is the sole author of the book. A youth at the beginning of the book and an old man at the end, Daniel's life spans the entire period from the preexilic to the postexilic eras of Judah's history. No doubt because of the book's many predictions, the English Bible locates Daniel as the fourth of the Major Prophets. The Hebrew Bible, which is divided in three principal sections (the Law, the Prophets, and the Writings), however, places the book in the Writings section because the criterion for inclusion in the second section was occupation in the prophetic office. Prophets were more than "tellers of the future"; they were principally preachers of God's Word. Although inspired by the Holy Spirit to record a divine message that included revelations of the future, Daniel was not a prophet by profession. Rather, he was a bureaucrat, who, in the providence of God, was so entrenched in the government system that he kept his job throughout the entire Babylonian Empire and even into the Persian regime. Unlike modern caricatures of bureaucrats, Daniel served his Lord with integrity and virtue as he served the state. Ezekiel, for a while his contemporary in Babylon, linked Daniel with Noah and Job and identified him as a model of righteousness (Ezek. 14:14,20). This should be an encouragement to laymen, as well as ministers, to live godly lives in whatever occupation God has placed them. One does not have to be an ordained minister to be used by God.

Date: Conservatives date Daniel to the sixth century BC, most likely about 530 BC, toward the end of Daniel's career and life. Most liberal scholars date the book to the second century BC, usually 168 BC, in the Maccabean period of Jewish history. This late date would obviously preclude the historic Daniel from being the author. The significant discrepancy reflects a fundamental difference in presuppositions regarding the nature of supernatural inspiration and prophecy. Particularly troubling for those who deny inspiration is Dan. 11, that so minutely predicts events involving the Seleucid and Ptolemaic dynasties of the divided Greek Empire that occurred in the third to second centuries BC. The liberal critics refer to this as *vaticinium post eventum* (prophecy after the event), claiming that whoever wrote it deceptively portrayed it as prediction. Those who believe in supernatural inspiration and revelation have no difficulty accepting Daniel's predictions and are not surprised at the accuracy of fulfillment.

Theme: God's sovereignty over time, circumstances, nations, and individuals. Daniel 4:34–35, Nebuchadnezzar's confession, is a key text summing up the theme.

Purpose: To inspire God's people during difficult or uncertain times, whether nationally and individually, to have confidence in God's unfailing purpose to govern the world to the end of His glory and their good.

Synopsis: *The Contribution of Daniel to Redemptive Revelation*

Daniel is a theology of time. Since all history (the progression of time) is redemptive in its purpose, Daniel's message contributes significantly to God's revelation of His redemptive plan, His unfailing purpose. A theology of time centers on the divine work of providence, the temporal operation of the eternal God whereby He preserves and governs His creation to the designed end of His glory and the good of His people. The inviolable truth is that God is the sovereign King whose kingdom is universal, subsuming every earthly kingdom regardless of how powerful and hostile it is. Daniel's tracing the kingdoms of the world from Babylon to Persia to Greece to Rome was designed to show that God's kingdom is coming and His will is being done in earth just as in heaven. From every human perspective, it appeared that the pagan powers of the world would triumph over righteousness and redemption. In reality, God was manipulating them and using them to set all in place for the fullness of time when He would send His Son into the world. So the affairs of the world do not happen by blind chance; they happen as the all-wise God, who knows and determines the end from the beginning, orchestrates them in perfect harmony. Not only was that a reassuring message to Daniel's contemporaries that all was on track for the coming of Christ, it should be a reassuring message that even today in spite of appearances to the contrary all is divinely under control and on course to the second fullness of time when Christ will come again.

In addition to Daniel's overarching contribution to the redemptive message, the book has significant specific texts with Christological focus. Christ is the stone cut without hands that smashes the kingdoms of the world (2:34); He is the Son of Man who receives the everlasting kingdom from the Ancient of days (7:13–14); He is the Messiah that would be cut off but not for Himself (9:26), a reference to His atoning death. The preincarnate Christ appeared with the three Hebrews in the fiery furnace (3:25). The closing chapter's revelation of the certain resurrection of both the just and unjust underscores Daniel's evangelistic focus as well.

Outline: Note: Beginning in 2:4 and continuing through 7:28, Daniel writes in Aramaic. Aramaic was the international language at this time and was the appropriate vehicle for communicating the message with worldwide significance. Note also the concentric symmetry: chs. 2 and 7 concern the world; chs. 3 and 6 concern righteous individuals; chs. 4 and 5 concern pagan kings. The message converges on the pagan kings who represented what appeared to be the greatest threat to God's purpose but were in reality subject to God's sovereign rule.

I. Introduction to Daniel (1:1–21)
  A. Daniel's Predicament (1:1–7)
  B. Daniel's Purity (1:8–16)
  C. Daniel's Wisdom (1:17–21)
II. The Message for the World (2:1—7:28)
  A. The King's Dream about the World (2:1–49)
    1. The Dilemma of the Magicians (2:1–11)
    2. The Decree of the King (2:12–18)
    3. The Deliverance through Prayer (2:19–30)
    4. The Description of the Dream (2:31–35)
    5. The Details of the Interpretation (2:36–45)
    6. The Declaration of the King (2:46–49)
  B. Deliverance from the Fiery Furnace (3:1–30)
    1. The Pressure of Compromise (3:1–7)
    2. The Courage of Convictions (3:8–18)
    3. The Experience of Vindication (3:19–30)
  C. The King's Dream about Himself (4:1–37)
    1. The King's Reflections (4:1–9)
    2. The King's Dream (4:10–18)
    3. Daniel's Interpretation (4:19–27)
    4. The King's Humiliation (4:28–33)
    5. The King's Confession (4:34–37)
  D. The Handwriting on the Wall (5:1–31)
    1. The King's Feast (5:1–4)
    2. The Lord's Message (5:5–9)
    3. Daniel's Interpretation (5:10–28)
    4. The Message Fulfilled (5:29–31)
  E. Deliverance from the Den of Lions (6:1–28)
    1. The Preeminence of Daniel (6:1–3)
    2. The Plot against Daniel (6:4–9)
    3. The Prayer of Daniel (6:10–11)
    4. The Punishment of Daniel (6:12–17)
    5. The Vindication of Daniel (6:18–28)
  F. Daniel's Vision about the World (7:1–28)
    1. The Four Great Beasts (7:1–8)

2. The Ancient of Days and Son of Man (7:9–14)
3. The Interpretation of the Vision (7:15–28)

III. The Implications of the Message for God's People (8:1—12:13)
   A. The Vision of Persia and Greece (8:1–27)
      1. The Ram and Goat (8:1–7)
      2. The Little Horn (8:8–14)
      3. The Angelic Interpretation (8:15–27)
   B. Daniel's Prayer and God's Answer (9:1–27)
      1. The Prayer (9:1–19)
      2. The Answer (9:20–27)
   C. A Personal Revelation to Daniel (10:1–21)
      1. The Circumstances of the Revelation (10:1–4)
      2. The Revelation (10:5–9)
      3. The Encouraging Explanation (10:10–21)
   D. History to the Fullness of Time and Beyond (11:1–45)
   E. Final Prophecies and Instructions (12:1–13)

THE BOOK OF

DANIEL

CHAPTER 1

In the third year of the reign of Jehoiakim king
of Judah came Nebuchadnezzar king of Babylon
unto Jerusalem, and besieged it.
2 And the Lord gave Jehoiakim king of Judah into
his hand, with part of the vessels of the house of
God: which he carried into the land of Shinar to
the house of his god; and he brought the vessels
into the treasure house of his god.
3 ¶ And the king spake unto Ashpenaz the master
of his eunuchs, that he should bring *certain* of the
children of Israel, and of the king's seed, and of
the princes;
4 Children in whom *was* no blemish, but well
favoured, and skilful in all wisdom, and cunning
in knowledge, and understanding science, and
such as *had* ability in them to stand in the king's
palace, and whom they might teach the learning
and the tongue of the Chaldeans.
5 And the king appointed them a daily provision
of the king's meat, and of the wine which he
drank: so nourishing them three years, that at the
end thereof they might stand before the king.
6 Now among these were of the children of
Judah, Daniel, Hananiah, Mishael, and Azariah:
7 Unto whom the prince of the eunuchs gave
names: for he gave unto Daniel *the name* of
Belteshazzar; and to Hananiah, of Shadrach;
and to Mishael, of Meshach; and to Azariah, of
Abed-nego.
8 ¶ But Daniel purposed in his heart that he
would not defile himself with the portion of the
king's meat, nor with the wine which he drank:
therefore he requested of the prince of the
eunuchs that he might not defile himself.
9 Now God had brought Daniel into favour and
tender love with the prince of the eunuchs.
10 And the prince of the eunuchs said unto
Daniel, I fear my lord the king, who hath ap-
pointed your meat and your drink: for why
should he see your faces worse liking than the
children which *are* of your sort? then shall ye
make *me* endanger my head to the king.
11 Then said Daniel to Melzar, whom the prince

Chapter 1: ***Although captives in Babylon are under great pressure to conform to pagan practices, Daniel and his companions maintain their purity before God, who rewards their faithfulness by causing them to prosper and by granting them skills that set them apart from all others in the kingdom.***

INTRODUCTION TO DANIEL (1:1–21)

Daniel's Predicament (1:1–7)

1:1 *the third year.* Jeremiah 25:1 records the same event as the fourth year, but there is no contradiction, just different ways of reckoning reigns. The accession year method, used in Babylon by Daniel, does not calculate the king's reign until his first full year after his coronation. The nonaccession year method, used in Palestine by Jeremiah, includes the year of coronation in the calculation. The year is 605 BC when Nebuchadnezzar, in celebration after his victory over the Egyptians at Carchemish, initiates the first wave of Judah's exile. This was followed in 597 BC with his exiling 10,000 more including Ezekiel and then in 586 BC with the destruction of Jerusalem and the temple.

1:2 *the Lord gave. Lord* (Adonai) is a divine title declaring God's kingly authority and power. In spite of Nebuchadnezzar's superior military power, it was not his might but the Lord who gave Jerusalem into his hands. Nebuchadnezzar was simply God's instrument to inflict His chastisement on Judah. *Shinar.* An old name for Babylon.

1:3 *eunuchs.* A term designating court officials, not necessarily emasculated men.

1:4 *Chaldeans.* Here referring to the inhabitants of Babylon as a whole, whose native language would have been Akkadian. Elsewhere in the book, the term refers specifically to the professional class of the magicians and astrologers who served as advisors to the king (2:4–5).

1:7 *prince.* The leader or head.

Daniel's Purity (1:8–16)

1:8 *Daniel purposed in his heart.* Literally, "Daniel set upon his heart," an idiom meaning to determine or take heed. *defile himself.* The word has religious implications. Daniel recognized something about the provisions that countered his system of belief and practice. Whether the food and drink had been part of pagan rituals or whether it violated the Levitical dietary laws is a matter of speculation, but Daniel regarded it as against his religious convictions.

1:9 *God had brought.* Directed by God's sovereign control, the head eunuch took special interest in Daniel showing him *favour* (loyalty based on a relationship) and *tender love* (expressions of compassion).

1:11 *Melzar.* Not a proper name, but a word meaning overseer or guardian.

of the eunuchs had set over Daniel, Hananiah, Mishael, and Azariah,
12 Prove thy servants, I beseech thee, ten days; and let them give us pulse to eat, and water to drink.
13 Then let our countenances be looked upon before thee, and the countenance of the children that eat of the portion of the king's meat: and as thou seest, deal with thy servants.
14 So he consented to them in this matter, and proved them ten days.
15 And at the end of ten days their countenances appeared fairer and fatter in flesh than all the children which did eat the portion of the king's meat.
16 Thus Melzar took away the portion of their meat, and the wine that they should drink; and gave them pulse.
17 ¶ As for these four children, God gave them knowledge and skill in all learning and wisdom: and Daniel had understanding in all visions and dreams.
18 Now at the end of the days that the king had said he should bring them in, then the prince of the eunuchs brought them in before Nebuchadnezzar.
19 And the king communed with them; and among them all was found none like Daniel, Hananiah, Mishael, and Azariah: therefore stood they before the king.
20 And in all matters of wisdom *and* understanding, that the king enquired of them, he found them ten times better than all the magicians *and* astrologers that *were* in all his realm.
21 And Daniel continued *even* unto the first year of king Cyrus.

CHAPTER 2

AND in the second year of the reign of Nebuchadnezzar Nebuchadnezzar dreamed dreams, wherewith his spirit was troubled, and his sleep brake from him.
2 Then the king commanded to call the magicians, and the astrologers, and the sorcerers, and the Chaldeans, for to shew the king his dreams. So they came and stood before the king.
3 And the king said unto them, I have dreamed a dream, and my spirit was troubled to know the dream.
4 Then spake the Chaldeans to the king in

1:12 *Prove.* To try or put to the test. *pulse.* Vegetables.
1:13 *countenances.* Literally, "faces," but refers to overall appearance. Daniel claims that after the test, he and his companions will appear healthier than the others who ate the royal diet.
1:15 *fatter in flesh.* The expression refers to a healthy appearance not necessarily weight gain.

Daniel's Wisdom (1:17–21)

1:17 The God-given *knowledge* included both *skill in all learning* (understanding of literature) and *wisdom* (the skill and ability to apply knowledge properly). *visions and dreams.* Both were means of divine revelation, and both were internal. Visions were limited to those with spiritual maturity, and the recipients were often engaged in the process (like Daniel in ch. 8). Dreams were usually for those who were either spiritually immature or without spiritual sensitivity or life at all and were always completely passive (like Nebuchadnezzar in ch. 2).
1:20 *ten times better.* Literally, "ten hands over," not an actual measurement but an idiom expressing superiority.

Thoughts for Personal/Family Worship: Chapter 1

1. **Daniel's being taken captive to Babylon illustrates the mystery and divine wisdom of providence. The captivity was the consequence of and chastisement for the nation's sin. It is clear from Daniel's character that he was not guilty of the sins that precipitated the judgment, but he was nonetheless affected by it. God made the event that was judgment for the nation to be a means of testing, purifying, and using Daniel for His glory. What Daniel did in service to the Lord could not have been done if he had remained back in Judah. It had to have been a traumatic experience for the young teen to be snatched from home and taken to a strange and foreign land, but God used the trauma for ultimate good. This should be a lesson in trusting the providence of God that sometimes leads to difficult and uncertain situations. But, His way and purpose is always best. It often takes the hard providences to bring us to the place of our best opportunities to be used by God for His glory and our good.**
2. **The stand taken by Daniel and his companions regarding their diet is a powerful example to young people. They were teenagers in a strange place. For teenage boys to refuse a hearty meal for a plate of vegetables was most remarkable. No one there would have suspected that their eating the king's provision would have been a compromise of their convictions. They were in a place far from home where it would have been easy just to do what everybody else was doing. But God's law was written on their hearts, and they obeyed the Lord in the face of the pressure to conform. They were firm in their convictions but not obnoxious in their stand. First Timothy 4:12 sums up Daniel's life as it should every Christian young person.**

THE MESSAGE FOR THE WORLD (2:1—7:28)

Chapter 2: *Nebuchadnezzar's dream of a colossal statue is interpreted by Daniel to represent the kingdoms of the world that will be destroyed by God's indestructible kingdom.*

The King's Dream about the World (2:1–49)

The Dilemma of the Magicians (2:1–11)

2:1 *his sleep brake from him.* So real and troubling were the God-directed dreams that his sleep went away; he awoke startled.
2:2 *magicians . . . Chaldeans.* The king's advisors or wise men that included soothsayers, sorcerers, astrologers, and necromancers. The term "Chaldean" often designates the whole group. *to shew.* To tell or to report.
2:3 *to know the dream.* To understand the dream. For the advisors to give understanding of the dream without knowing the dream would assure the king of their accurate interpretation.
2:4 *in Syriak.* The Aramaic language, which had become the

Syriack, O king, live for ever: tell thy servants the
dream, and we will shew the interpretation.
5 The king answered and said to the Chaldeans,
The thing is gone from me: if ye will not make
known unto me the dream, with the interpretation
thereof, ye shall be cut in pieces, and your houses
shall be made a dunghill.
6 But if ye shew the dream, and the interpretation
thereof, ye shall receive of me gifts and rewards
and great honour: therefore shew me the dream,
and the interpretation thereof.
7 They answered again and said, Let the king
tell his servants the dream, and we will shew the
interpretation of it.
8 The king answered and said, I know of certainty
that ye would gain the time, because ye see the
thing is gone from me.
9 But if ye will not make known unto me the
dream, *there is but* one decree for you: for ye have
prepared lying and corrupt words to speak before
me, till the time be changed: therefore tell me the
dream, and I shall know that ye can shew me the
interpretation thereof.
10 ¶ The Chaldeans answered before the king,
and said, There is not a man upon the earth that
can shew the king's matter: therefore *there is* no
king, lord, nor ruler, *that* asked such things at any
magician, or astrologer, or Chaldean.
11 And *it is* a rare thing that the king requireth,
and there is none other that can shew it before
the king, except the gods, whose dwelling is not
with flesh.
12 For this cause the king was angry and very
furious, and commanded to destroy all the wise
men of Babylon.
13 And the decree went forth that the wise *men*
should be slain; and they sought Daniel and his
fellows to be slain.
14 ¶ Then Daniel answered with counsel and
wisdom to Arioch the captain of the king's guard,
which was gone forth to slay the wise *men* of
Babylon:
15 He answered and said to Arioch the king's
captain, Why *is* the decree *so* hasty from the king?
Then Arioch made the thing known to Daniel.
16 Then Daniel went in, and desired of the king
that he would give him time, and that he would
shew the king the interpretation.
17 Then Daniel went to his house, and made the
thing known to Hananiah, Mishael, and Azariah,
his companions:
18 That they would desire mercies of the God of
heaven concerning this secret; that Daniel and his
fellows should not perish with the rest of the wise
men of Babylon.
19 ¶ Then was the secret revealed unto Daniel in
a night vision. Then Daniel blessed the God of
heaven.
20 Daniel answered and said, Blessed be the name
of God for ever and ever: for wisdom and might
are his:
21 And he changeth the times and the seasons: he
removeth kings, and setteth up kings: he giveth
wisdom unto the wise, and knowledge to them
that know understanding:
22 He revealeth the deep and secret things: he
knoweth what *is* in the darkness, and the light
dwelleth with him.
23 I thank thee, and praise thee, O thou God
of my fathers, who hast given me wisdom and

---

official language for international communication. This begins the Aramaic section of the book that continues through ch. 7. *tell thy servants the dream, and we will shew the interpretation.* The wise men requested the facts of the dream as prerequisite to their interpretation.

2:5 *The thing is gone from me.* The king is not saying that he had forgotten the dream, but literally, "the command is irrevocable." He would not alter the decree demanding their recounting the dream along with its interpretation. *cut in pieces . . . dunghill.* The penalty was severe but in keeping with the kinds of punishment literally and actually inflicted in that society.

2:8–9 Nebuchadnezzar accuses them of stalling (*gain the time*) and expresses his suspicion that they might make up an interpretation just to save themselves. If they could tell the dream, he would trust their interpretation.

2:10–11 The Chaldeans charge the king with making an unreasonable request and protest that no mere human could meet his demands.

The Decree of the King (2:12–18)

2:13 Although Daniel and his companions were not privy to the king's demands, by their association with the Chaldeans they were under the same sentence of death. The providence of God that brought them into favor with this elite group (1:19) now seemed to turn against them. But in reality, providence was once again putting Daniel in a position to use him for God's glory—a reminder not to make hasty judgments about the course of God's government.

2:15 *Why . . . so hasty.* "Why so harsh?"

2:16–18 *desired . . . time.* Literally, he "requested" time, not as a stalling technique but for an opportunity to pray. The king's demand was humanly impossible, but Daniel knew the God of the impossible.

The Deliverance through Prayer (2:19–30)

2:19 The king's dream (divine revelation to one spiritually insensitive) is revealed to Daniel in a vision (divine revelation to one spiritually mature). Since time was of the essence, God answered the prayer immediately.

2:20–23 Daniel thanks God for answering prayer and hints at the dream's message of God's sovereignty over time and seasons as well as over the rise and fall of kings. The whole course of history leading to the fullness of time when Christ would come is in God's hands; this is the key redemptive message of Daniel.

2:24–30 Before revealing the dream and its interpretation to the king, Daniel testifies that all the credit belongs to God, who gave the dream about *the latter days* to Nebuchadnezzar and who gave to Daniel the knowledge of the dream and its meaning. The failure of the wise men's divination to

might, and hast made known unto me now
what we desired of thee: for thou hast *now* made
known unto us the king's matter.
24 ¶ Therefore Daniel went in unto Arioch,
whom the king had ordained to destroy the wise
men of Babylon: he went and said thus unto him;
Destroy not the wise *men* of Babylon: bring me in
before the king, and I will shew unto the king the
interpretation.
25 Then Arioch brought in Daniel before the
king in haste, and said thus unto him, I have
found a man of the captives of Judah, that will
make known unto the king the interpretation.
26 The king answered and said to Daniel, whose
name *was* Belteshazzar, Art thou able to make
known unto me the dream which I have seen, and
the interpretation thereof?
27 Daniel answered in the presence of the king,
and said, The secret which the king hath demanded
cannot the wise *men*, the astrologers, the
magicians, the soothsayers, shew unto the king;
28 But there is a God in heaven that revealeth
secrets, and maketh known to the king Nebuchadnezzar
what shall be in the latter days. Thy
dream, and the visions of thy head upon thy bed,
are these;
29 As for thee, O king, thy thoughts came *into
thy mind* upon thy bed, what should come to pass
hereafter: and he that revealeth secrets maketh
known to thee what shall come to pass.
30 But as for me, this secret is not revealed to me
for *any* wisdom that I have more than any living,
but for *their* sakes that shall make known the
interpretation to the king, and that thou mightest
know the thoughts of thy heart.
31 ¶ Thou, O king, sawest, and behold a great
image. This great image, whose brightness *was*
excellent, stood before thee; and the form thereof
was terrible.
32 This image's head *was* of fine gold, his breast
and his arms of silver, his belly and his thighs of
brass,
33 His legs of iron, his feet part of iron and part
of clay.
34 Thou sawest till that a stone was cut out
without hands, which smote the image upon his
feet *that were* of iron and clay, and brake them to
pieces.
35 Then was the iron, the clay, the brass, the
silver, and the gold, broken to pieces together,
and became like the chaff of the summer
threshingfloors; and the wind carried them away,
that no place was found for them: and the stone
that smote the image became a great mountain,
and filled the whole earth.
36 ¶ This *is* the dream; and we will tell the
interpretation thereof before the king.
37 Thou, O king, *art* a king of kings: for the God
of heaven hath given thee a kingdom, power, and
strength, and glory.
38 And wheresoever the children of men dwell,
the beasts of the field and the fowls of the heaven
hath he given into thine hand, and hath made
thee ruler over them all. Thou *art* this head of
gold.
39 And after thee shall arise another kingdom
inferior to thee, and another third kingdom of
brass, which shall bear rule over all the earth.
40 And the fourth kingdom shall be strong as
iron: forasmuch as iron breaketh in pieces and
subdueth all *things*: and as iron that breaketh all
these, shall it break in pieces and bruise.
41 And whereas thou sawest the feet and toes,
part of potters' clay, and part of iron, the kingdom
shall be divided; but there shall be in it of the
strength of the iron, forasmuch as thou sawest the
iron mixed with miry clay.
42 And *as* the toes of the feet *were* part of iron,
and part of clay, *so* the kingdom shall be partly
strong, and partly broken.
43 And whereas thou sawest iron mixed with
miry clay, they shall mingle themselves with the
seed of men: but they shall not cleave one to
another, even as iron is not mixed with clay.

---

discern the futuristic dream is evidence of God's uniqueness in contrast to the man-made gods of Babylon. The inability to declare the future reveals the nothingness of false gods in contrast to the one true and living God, who knows the end from the beginning (Isa. 41:21–29; 46:9–11).

The Description of the Dream (2:31–35)

2:31 *a great image.* Not an idol, but a colossal statue. *whose brightness was excellent.* Literally, "whose splendor was extraordinary." *the form thereof was terrible.* Literally, "its appearance was causing fear."

2:32–33 From the head to the legs, the giant structure decreases in value but increases in strength (gold to iron). The feet, however, with their mixture of the iron and clay would render it weak as well as worthless.

2:34–35 The magnitude of the colossus pales in comparison to the uncarved stone that smashes and replaces it.

The Details of the Interpretation (2:36–45)

2:37–38 *a king of kings.* An idiom expressing a superlative idea, the greatest king. *the God of heaven hath given . . . hath made thee ruler.* Even though Nebuchadnezzar was the greatest of all earthly kings, he was subservient to God and ruled only because God had ordained him to rule. All earthly authorities, even the pagan ones, are subject to God and rule only by His sovereign decree.

2:38–43 Daniel identifies the components of the statue to be Babylon and successive kingdoms, with the primary focus being on the fourth. Most agree that the head represents Babylon, the chest and arms Persia, the belly and thighs Greece, and the legs Rome. The form of government represented by these successive empires from total dictatorship to republic to democracy (*mingle themselves with the seed of men*) relates to the decreasing value and increasing strength of the statue.

44 And in the days of these kings shall the God of
heaven set up a kingdom, which shall never be de-
stroyed: and the kingdom shall not be left to other
people, *but* it shall break in pieces and consume
all these kingdoms, and it shall stand for ever.
45 Forasmuch as thou sawest that the stone was
cut out of the mountain without hands, and
that it brake in pieces the iron, the brass, the
clay, the silver, and the gold; the great God hath
made known to the king what shall come to
pass hereafter: and the dream *is* certain, and the
interpretation thereof sure.
46 ¶ Then the king Nebuchadnezzar fell upon his
face, and worshipped Daniel, and commanded
that they should offer an oblation and sweet
odours unto him.
47 The king answered unto Daniel, and said, Of
a truth *it is*, that your God *is* a God of gods, and
a Lord of kings, and a revealer of secrets, seeing
thou couldest reveal this secret.
48 Then the king made Daniel a great man, and
gave him many great gifts, and made him ruler
over the whole province of Babylon, and chief of
the governors over all the wise *men* of Babylon.
49 Then Daniel requested of the king, and he
set Shadrach, Meshach, and Abed-nego, over the
affairs of the province of Babylon: but Daniel *sat*
in the gate of the king.

CHAPTER 3

NEBUCHADNEZZAR the king made an image of
gold, whose height *was* threescore cubits, *and* the
breadth thereof six cubits: he set it up in the plain
of Dura, in the province of Babylon.
2 Then Nebuchadnezzar the king sent to
gather together the princes, the governors,
and the captains, the judges, the treasurers, the
counsellors, the sheriffs, and all the rulers of the
provinces, to come to the dedication of the image
which Nebuchadnezzar the king had set up.
3 Then the princes, the governors, and captains,
the judges, the treasurers, the counsellors, the
sheriffs, and all the rulers of the provinces,

That they *bear rule over all the earth* is hyperbole, referring specifically to the regions associated with biblical history.

2:44 The indestructible and everlasting kingdom designates the rule of God Himself and particularly the mediatorial rule of Christ, the stone cut without hands.

2:45 Daniel tells Nebuchadnezzar that God has revealed to him the summation of history from his time until the end. *the interpretation thereof sure.* It is trustworthy; the word "amen" is from the word for "sure."

The Declaration of the King (2:46–49)

2:46 *worshipped Daniel.* Paid homage to him. *oblation and sweet odours.* An offering and incense.

2:47 *God of gods.* An idiom expressing a superlative, the supreme God. *a Lord of kings.* In Babylonian "theology," a designation and attribute of deity. It was customary in that polytheistic culture to acknowledge any god that they assumed proved to be powerful in a particular situation. This was not Nebuchadnezzar's conversion to true monotheism, but just his recognizing that Daniel's God was able to do something that the others could not.

2:49 *the affairs.* The administration. *the gate of the king.* The court of the king, where the affairs of state took place. In the providence of God, Daniel became an embedded bureaucrat, whose tenure extended throughout the duration of the Babylonian Empire into the early years of the Persian.

Thoughts for Personal/Family Worship: Chapter 2

1. **The response of Daniel and his friends to the king's threat provides a lesson in the importance and power of prayer. Seemingly without panic or a second thought, they immediately took the matter to the Lord casting their cares and concerns upon Him. It was a crisis prayer, and God answered them according to their need. Upon receiving the answer, Daniel was careful before doing anything else to return in prayer expressing his praise, thanksgiving, and worship to God who so graciously answered their specific request. This episode should remind us that prayer is never to be a last resort when all else fails but should be the first impulse when faced with any crisis. It also exemplifies the importance of thanksgiving for answered prayer.**
2. **Daniel's initial conversation with the king is a great example of godly humility. He could have immediately interpreted the dream to Nebuchadnezzar and taken all the credit for himself, posturing for some reward or recognition by the king. But rather, even though the king was pressing for the interpretation and much more delay would put all the wise men in jeopardy, Daniel took the time to give all the credit to God. We should always be more interested in God's glory than we are in our own.**
3. **It may be profitable to compare Nebuchadnezzar's dream with Daniel's vision in ch. 7. They are two revelations with a single message. Chapter 2 is a view of human power from man's perspective. The four metals suggest value and strength, and an inanimate stone destroyed the statue for no apparent reason. Chapter 7 views the same from God's perspective. The beasts have no moral conscience and are destroyed for their terrible acts by the Son of man. Together they demonstrate God's absolute control in the rise and fall of kings. Governments are in His hands, and that is just as true today as it was in Daniel's day. No matter how uncertain things seem, they are certain in God's unfailing purpose.**

Chapter 3: *Defying the king's command to worship the golden image, Daniel's companions are thrown into a fiery furnace but escape death by divine intervention.*

Deliverance from the Fiery Furnace (3:1–30)

The Pressure of Compromise (3:1–7)

3:1 *an image of gold.* A statue most likely inspired by and erected immediately following the dream in which Nebuchadnezzar learned he was the head of gold. *threescore cubits . . . six cubits.* Ninety feet high by nine feet wide, perhaps including the pedestal. It would have been an imposing sight towering over everything in the otherwise flat *plain of Dura*.

3:2 The exact duty of each is not clear, but all the officials of state were summoned to celebrate the dedication of the

were gathered together unto the dedication of
the image that Nebuchadnezzar the king had
set up; and they stood before the image that
Nebuchadnezzar had set up.
4 Then an herald cried aloud, To you it is com-
manded, O people, nations, and languages,
5 *That* at what time ye hear the sound of the
cornet, flute, harp, sackbut, psaltery, dulcimer,
and all kinds of musick, ye fall down and worship
the golden image that Nebuchadnezzar the king
hath set up:
6 And whoso falleth not down and worshippeth
shall the same hour be cast into the midst of a
burning fiery furnace.
7 Therefore at that time, when all the people
heard the sound of the cornet, flute, harp,
sackbut, psaltery, and all kinds of musick, all
the people, the nations, and the languages, fell
down *and* worshipped the golden image that
Nebuchadnezzar the king had set up.
8 ¶ Wherefore at that time certain Chaldeans
came near, and accused the Jews.
9 They spake and said to the king Nebuchadnez-
zar, O king, live for ever.
10 Thou, O king, hast made a decree, that every
man that shall hear the sound of the cornet, flute,
harp, sackbut, psaltery, and dulcimer, and all
kinds of musick, shall fall down and worship the
golden image:
11 And whoso falleth not down and worshippeth,
that he should be cast into the midst of a burning
fiery furnace.
12 There are certain Jews whom thou hast set
over the affairs of the province of Babylon,
Shadrach, Meshach, and Abed-nego; these men,
O king, have not regarded thee: they serve not thy
gods, nor worship the golden image which thou
hast set up.
13 ¶ Then Nebuchadnezzar in *his* rage and fury
commanded to bring Shadrach, Meshach, and
Abed-nego. Then they brought these men before
the king.
14 Nebuchadnezzar spake and said unto them,
Is it true, O Shadrach, Meshach, and Abed-nego,
do not ye serve my gods, nor worship the golden
image which I have set up?
15 Now if ye be ready that at what time ye hear the
sound of the cornet, flute, harp, sackbut, psaltery,
and dulcimer, and all kinds of musick, ye fall down
and worship the image which I have made; *well:*
but if ye worship not, ye shall be cast the same hour
into the midst of a burning fiery furnace; and who
is that God that shall deliver you out of my hands?
16 Shadrach, Meshach, and Abed-nego, answered
and said to the king, O Nebuchadnezzar, we *are*
not careful to answer thee in this matter.
17 If it be *so*, our God whom we serve is able to
deliver us from the burning fiery furnace, and he
will deliver *us* out of thine hand, O king.
18 But if not, be it known unto thee, O king, that
we will not serve thy gods, nor worship the golden
image which thou hast set up.
19 ¶ Then was Nebuchadnezzar full of fury,
and the form of his visage was changed against
Shadrach, Meshach, and Abed-nego: *therefore* he
spake, and commanded that they should heat the
furnace one seven times more than it was wont
to be heated.
20 And he commanded the most mighty men
that *were* in his army to bind Shadrach, Meshach,
and Abed-nego, *and* to cast *them* into the burning
fiery furnace.

---

statue. Shadrach, Meshach, and Abed-nego were among the invited dignitaries (2:49).

3:5 *fall down and worship*. The sound of the music was the call to unified worship. To bow and pay homage to the statue was more than an expression of allegiance to the king; it had religious implications. For Shadrach, Meshach, and Abed-nego this would have been a perversion, compromise, and concealment of their faith.

3:6–7 The pressure to comply and conform was great. There was the threat of death (*fiery furnace*) and the fear of being different (*all the people*). At the sound of the music, all bowed—or almost all.

The Courage of Convictions (3:8–18)

3:8 *accused the Jews*. Literally, "they ate their pieces, the Jews"—a graphic description of vitriol. The pagan reaction is the first indication that the three Jews did not bow. The ungodly hate what they cannot understand about spiritual matters.

3:9–12 The Chaldeans remind the king of his clear command and then level their charges against the three Jews. The accusation removes any doubt that bowing to the statue was not our equivalent of saluting the flag but indeed was regarded as religious worship.

3:13–15 Nebuchadnezzar was furious, but he offered the three a second chance to conform just in case they misunderstood the instructions and to reevaluate whether it was worth it to take their stand, given the negative responses. The king repeated and intensified the threat of fiery execution by claiming that no God—not even theirs—could rescue them from his power.

3:16 *we are not careful to answer*. Literally, "we do not need to answer you concerning this thing." In other words, their minds were made up; the issue was settled. God's Word was so clear in prohibiting the worshiping of other gods that they did not need to think twice about it.

3:17–18 They had no doubt about God's ability to deliver them, but they did not know His will to deliver. Their personal welfare was not the criterion for their obedience; they were not serving God in order to get something in return. This kind of courage is not natural; it is faith and resolution to do what is right regardless of personal consequence.

The Experience of Vindication (3:19–30)

3:19 *the form of his visage was changed*. The appearance of his face changed, showing his anger against the three who defied his command and refused his offer to recant. *one seven times more than . . . wont to be heated.* Using an idiom

21 Then these men were bound in their coats,
their hosen, and their hats, and their *other*
garments, and were cast into the midst of the
burning fiery furnace.
22 Therefore because the king's commandment
was urgent, and the furnace exceeding hot, the
flame of the fire slew those men that took up
Shadrach, Meshach, and Abed-nego.
23 And these three men, Shadrach, Meshach, and
Abed-nego, fell down bound into the midst of the
burning fiery furnace.
24 Then Nebuchadnezzar the king was astonied,
and rose up in haste, *and* spake, and said unto his
counsellors, Did not we cast three men bound
into the midst of the fire? They answered and said
unto the king, True, O king.
25 He answered and said, Lo, I see four men
loose, walking in the midst of the fire, and they
have no hurt; and the form of the fourth is like
the Son of God.
26 ¶ Then Nebuchadnezzar came near to the
mouth of the burning fiery furnace, *and* spake,
and said, Shadrach, Meshach, and Abed-nego, ye
servants of the most high God, come forth, and
come *hither*. Then Shadrach, Meshach, and Abed-
nego, came forth of the midst of the fire.
27 And the princes, governors, and captains, and
the king's counsellors, being gathered together,
saw these men, upon whose bodies the fire had
no power, nor was an hair of their head singed,
neither were their coats changed, nor the smell of
fire had passed on them.
28 *Then* Nebuchadnezzar spake, and said, Blessed
be the God of Shadrach, Meshach, and Abed-
nego, who hath sent his angel, and delivered his
servants that trusted in him, and have changed
the king's word, and yielded their bodies, that
they might not serve nor worship any god, except
their own God.
29 Therefore I make a decree, That every people,
nation, and language, which speak any thing
amiss against the God of Shadrach, Meshach,
and Abed-nego, shall be cut in pieces, and their
houses shall be made a dunghill: because there is

expressing intensity, the king commanded to stoke up the furnace making it hotter than customary (*wont*), to make it as hot as they could.

3:21 Their being thrown in the furnace fully clothed suggests the immediacy of their execution and the provision of more fuel for the fire.

3:22 *the king's commandment was urgent.* It was harsh and overbearing, cruel even by Babylonian standards. The death of the executioners from the extreme heat emanating from the furnace only affirms how much more intense was the heat in the furnace itself.

3:23 After this verse, the Septuagint (the ancient Greek translation of the Old Testament) inserts "The Prayer of Azariah and the Song of the Three Youths," in praise of God's righteousness while they were in the flames.

3:24 *the king was astonied.* The verb includes the idea not only of astonishment, but of horror and startling alarm. The Septuagint adds the thought that he heard them singing.

3:25 The alarm is caused by his sight of four men walking around in the flames without any sign of injury. *the form of the fourth is like the Son of God.* Literally, "the appearance of the fourth resembles a son of gods." The statement begs two questions: Who was the fourth and whom did Nebuchadnezzar think was the fourth? Nebuchadnezzar, as a pagan, would not have known the true God and certainly nothing of the Trinity. His statement merely indicates that the fourth appeared to be a supernatural being, one that was in the class of (significance of *son*) of supernatural beings (note he calls the fourth God's "angel" or messenger in v. 28). That was enough to horrify him. But in reality, the fourth was a Christophany, a preincarnate appearance of the Son of God, hence the use of the capital letters in the KJV. That was more than enough to protect the three, who in a most literal way experienced Isa. 43:2.

3:26–27 The three came out of the fire completely unharmed and unaffected by the flames, a miraculous demonstration of God's care and deliverance. Though they did not know it on the way into the furnace, it was indeed God's will to bring them out. They knew He could.

3:28–29 Nebuchadnezzar was forced to acknowledge the one true God. What started as a solitary witness by three seemingly insignificant young men spread by the decree of a pagan king to the whole realm. This is an example of God's using the wrath of man to get praise for Himself (Ps. 76:10).

Thoughts for Personal/Family Worship: Chapter 3

1. **This familiar story of the fiery furnace, set in a world system that was both ignorant of and hostile to truth, teaches us that we must stand firm and faithful regardless of pressures to compromise. Shadrach, Meshach, and Abed-nego illustrate a kind of courage and resolve to stand firm that comes from faith in God and His Word. Knowing that whatever happened in time was God's will enabled them to face their situation with confidence, resisting the world's pressure and resting on the Lord. It is that kind of total dependence on God that empowers believers to stand on the promises. Courage alone is not a uniquely spiritual virtue, but when that courage flows from an unwavering conviction of the unchangeable truth of God's Word and from the personal resolve to take God at His Word, it is the spiritual virtue of walking by faith.**
2. **One way or another, God achieves His glory and His people's good, but He doesn't always do it the way we might expect. For Shadrach, Meshach, and Abed-nego that purpose did not mean preventing adversity: they were thrown into the fire. Although it was God's will to place His servants in the furnace, it was not His will to leave them alone. Their Savior was present with them. Regardless of how horrific the circumstances, God has promised to be the constant company of His people. Whereas the Lord's presence with His people is a guaranteed promise, physical deliverance from danger is not (Heb. 11:36–38). The Lord's presence may not be visible as in the case of the three youths, but it is always the reality of faith.**

Chapter 4: *Nebuchadnezzar dreams of a huge tree that is cut down which Daniel interprets as*

no other God that can deliver after this sort.
30 Then the king promoted Shadrach, Meshach,
and Abed-nego, in the province of Babylon.

CHAPTER 4

NEBUCHADNEZZAR the king, unto all people,
nations, and languages, that dwell in all the earth;
Peace be multiplied unto you.
2 I thought it good to shew the signs and won-
ders that the high God hath wrought toward me.
3 How great *are* his signs! and how mighty *are*
his wonders! his kingdom *is* an everlasting king-
dom, and his dominion *is* from generation to
generation.
4 ¶ I Nebuchadnezzar was at rest in mine house,
and flourishing in my palace:
5 I saw a dream which made me afraid, and the
thoughts upon my bed and the visions of my
head troubled me.
6 Therefore made I a decree to bring in all the
wise *men* of Babylon before me, that they might
make known unto me the interpretation of the
dream.
7 Then came in the magicians, the astrologers,
the Chaldeans, and the soothsayers: and I told the
dream before them; but they did not make known
unto me the interpretation thereof.
8 ¶ But at the last Daniel came in before me,
whose name *was* Belteshazzar, according to the
name of my god, and in whom *is* the spirit of
the holy gods: and before him I told the dream,
saying,
9 O Belteshazzar, master of the magicians,
because I know that the spirit of the holy gods
is in thee, and no secret troubleth thee, tell me
the visions of my dream that I have seen, and the
interpretation thereof.
10 Thus *were* the visions of mine head in my bed;
I saw, and behold a tree in the midst of the earth,
and the height thereof *was* great.
11 The tree grew, and was strong, and the height
thereof reached unto heaven, and the sight
thereof to the end of all the earth:
12 The leaves thereof *were* fair, and the fruit
thereof much, and in it *was* meat for all: the beasts
of the field had shadow under it, and the fowls of
the heaven dwelt in the boughs thereof, and all
flesh was fed of it.
13 I saw in the visions of my head upon my bed,
and, behold, a watcher and an holy one came
down from heaven;
14 He cried aloud, and said thus, Hew down the
tree, and cut off his branches, shake off his leaves,
and scatter his fruit: let the beasts get away from
under it, and the fowls from his branches:
15 Nevertheless leave the stump of his roots in the
earth, even with a band of iron and brass, in the
tender grass of the field; and let it be wet with the
dew of heaven, and *let* his portion *be* with the beasts
in the grass of the earth:
16 Let his heart be changed from man's, and let
a beast's heart be given unto him; and let seven
times pass over him.
17 This matter *is* by the decree of the watchers,
and the demand by the word of the holy ones: to
the intent that the living may know that the most
High ruleth in the kingdom of men, and giveth it
to whomsoever he will, and setteth up over it the
basest of men.
18 This dream I king Nebuchadnezzar have
seen. Now thou, O Belteshazzar, declare the

referring to the king's humiliation, after which the king acknowledges the absolute supremacy and sovereignty of the true God.

The King's Dream about Himself (4:1–37)

The King's Reflections (4:1–9)

4:1–3 The order of events in the chapter is potentially confusing. The whole chapter is Nebuchadnezzar's own testimony after the events have taken place. The chapter begins with a doxology in retrospect of what God has done to him (4:1–3, which is 3:31–33 in the Hebrew Bible). This is followed by a detailed account of the dream and Daniel's interpretation and warning (4:4–27). Verses 28–33 record the actualization of the dream, and the chapter ends with the king's first-person profession of faith in 4:34–37.

4:4 *at rest.* At ease. *flourishing.* Happy and prosperous. Most likely, this was toward the end of his reign after he had finished his extensive building projects, ranging from the restored palace, the famous hanging gardens, and multiple temples dedicated to Marduk.

4:5 *a dream . . . made me afraid . . . troubled me.* The dream both startled and terrified him.

4:6–7 Notwithstanding their previous inability, the king summons the same group of advisors to interpret it. But again, they are unable even though this time he tells them the dream. Since the dream was divine revelation, it is not surprising that pagans could not understand it. The natural man can never understand things of the Spirit (1 Cor. 2:14).

4:8 *at the last Daniel.* Daniel was the last resort, perhaps because the king suspected he would not like the interpretation. *in whom is the spirit of the holy gods.* The king simply acknowledges that Daniel possessed some supernatural aid to interpret dreams, not that he was indwelt by the Holy Spirit.

The King's Dream (4:10–18)

4:10–12 The first part of the dream is of a huge and flourishing tree. It filled the earth, its foliage was beautiful, its branches provided shade for animals and lodging for birds, and its fruit was sufficient to provide nourishment (*meat*) for all.

4:13–18 The dream becomes ominous with the appearance and announcement of the *watcher and an holy one.* The expression designates a single entity ("a watcher even a holy one") and refers to an angel or supernatural being, who hints at the interpretation and reveals the purpose of the dream. The magnificent tree is reduced to a stump unable to support all its dependents. The angel hints that the stump represents one who through extreme humiliation is forced to admit the absolute supremacy of God.

interpretation thereof, forasmuch as all the wise
men of my kingdom are not able to make known
unto me the interpretation: but thou *art* able; for
the spirit of the holy gods *is* in thee.
19 ¶ Then Daniel, whose name *was* Belteshazzar,
was astonied for one hour, and his thoughts trou-
bled him. The king spake, and said, Belteshazzar,
let not the dream, or the interpretation thereof,
trouble thee. Belteshazzar answered and said, My
lord, the dream *be* to them that hate thee, and the
interpretation thereof to thine enemies.
20 The tree that thou sawest, which grew, and was
strong, whose height reached unto the heaven,
and the sight thereof to all the earth;
21 Whose leaves *were* fair, and the fruit thereof
much, and in it *was* meat for all; under which the
beasts of the field dwelt, and upon whose branches
the fowls of the heaven had their habitation:
22 It *is* thou, O king, that art grown and become
strong: for thy greatness is grown, and reacheth
unto heaven, and thy dominion to the end of the
earth.
23 And whereas the king saw a watcher and an
holy one coming down from heaven, and saying,
Hew the tree down, and destroy it; yet leave the
stump of the roots thereof in the earth, even with
a band of iron and brass, in the tender grass of the
field; and let it be wet with the dew of heaven, and
let his portion *be* with the beasts of the field, till
seven times pass over him;
24 This *is* the interpretation, O king, and this *is*
the decree of the most High, which is come upon
my lord the king:
25 That they shall drive thee from men, and thy
dwelling shall be with the beasts of the field, and
they shall make thee to eat grass as oxen, and they
shall wet thee with the dew of heaven, and seven
times shall pass over thee, till thou know that the
most High ruleth in the kingdom of men, and
giveth it to whomsoever he will.
26 And whereas they commanded to leave the
stump of the tree roots; thy kingdom shall be sure
unto thee, after that thou shalt have known that
the heavens do rule.
27 Wherefore, O king, let my counsel be
acceptable unto thee, and break off thy sins by
righteousness, and thine iniquities by shewing
mercy to the poor; if it may be a lengthening of
thy tranquillity.
28 ¶ All this came upon the king Nebuchadnezzar.
29 At the end of twelve months he walked in the
palace of the kingdom of Babylon.
30 The king spake, and said, Is not this great
Babylon, that I have built for the house of the
kingdom by the might of my power, and for the
honour of my majesty?
31 While the word *was* in the king's mouth,
there fell a voice from heaven, *saying*, O king
Nebuchadnezzar, to thee it is spoken; The
kingdom is departed from thee.
32 And they shall drive thee from men, and thy
dwelling *shall be* with the beasts of the field: they
shall make thee to eat grass as oxen, and seven
times shall pass over thee, until thou know that
the most High ruleth in the kingdom of men, and
giveth it to whomsoever he will.
33 The same hour was the thing fulfilled upon
Nebuchadnezzar: and he was driven from men,
and did eat grass as oxen, and his body was wet
with the dew of heaven, till his hairs were grown
like eagles' *feathers*, and his nails like birds' *claws*.
34 And at the end of the days I Nebuchadnezzar
lifted up mine eyes unto heaven, and mine
understanding returned unto me, and I blessed
the most High, and I praised and honoured
him that liveth for ever, whose dominion *is* an
everlasting dominion, and his kingdom *is* from
generation to generation:

Daniel's Interpretation (4:19–27)

4:19 *was astonied.* Was appalled.

4:22 Daniel identifies the king as the great tree and uses hyperbolic language to describe the greatness of his majesty and kingdom. Although Daniel says his dominion was to the end of the earth, in reality Babylon was geographically the smallest of the kingdoms that followed it (ch. 2).

4:23–26 The chopping down of the tree and the remaining stump represented God's intent to remove sovereignty from Nebuchadnezzar personally, forcing him to live like an ox for a period of *seven times*, most likely seven years. Nebuchadnezzar was going to lose his mind; God would sovereignly drive him crazy that he might ultimately come to his senses. His condition is sometimes termed "boanthropy," a condition in which a man lives like a cow.

4:27 Having given the interpretation providing the information requested of the king, Daniel presses Nebuchadnezzar to repent before it is too late. God's Word always demands a heart response.

The King's Humiliation (4:28–33)

4:28–29 *All this came . . . at the end of twelve months.* God delayed the actualization of the dream to give the king sufficient time to repent, but His longsuffering, which should have led to repentance (Rom. 2:4), ended.

4:30–33 At the very moment the king was bragging about his accomplishments, God removed the kingdom from him. Every detail of the symbolic dream became reality in the insanity of the king. For seven years, he was confined to his personal pasture, eating grass, exposed to the elements, and ungroomed so that his hair was matted and his nails grotesquely long. God brought down the mighty.

The King's Confession (4:34–37)

4:34 *at the end of the days.* The end of the humiliation was just as certain as its beginning. *eyes unto heaven . . . understanding returned.* In his irrational condition, the king realized what he never had before in his rational state: God rules. The only feasible explanation for this transition from irrationality to spiritually rational understanding is the gracious intervention of God. Without such divine intervention, every sinner is doomed; with it sinners are wondrously converted.

35 And all the inhabitants of the earth *are*
reputed as nothing: and he doeth according to
his will in the army of heaven, and *among* the
inhabitants of the earth: and none can stay his
hand, or say unto him, What doest thou?
36 At the same time my reason returned unto
me; and for the glory of my kingdom, mine
honour and brightness returned unto me; and my
counsellors and my lords sought unto me; and I
was established in my kingdom, and excellent
majesty was added unto me.
37 Now I Nebuchadnezzar praise and extol and
honour the King of heaven, all whose works *are*
truth, and his ways judgment: and those that walk
in pride he is able to abase.

CHAPTER 5

BELSHAZZAR the king made a great feast to a
thousand of his lords, and drank wine before the
thousand.
2 Belshazzar, whiles he tasted the wine,
commanded to bring the golden and silver
vessels which his father Nebuchadnezzar had
taken out of the temple which *was* in Jerusalem;
that the king, and his princes, his wives, and his
concubines, might drink therein.
3 Then they brought the golden vessels that were
taken out of the temple of the house of God which
was at Jerusalem; and the king, and his princes,
his wives, and his concubines, drank in them.
4 They drank wine, and praised the gods of gold,
and of silver, of brass, of iron, of wood, and of
stone.
5 ¶ In the same hour came forth fingers of a
man's hand, and wrote over against the candle-
stick upon the plaister of the wall of the king's
palace: and the king saw the part of the hand that
wrote.
6 Then the king's countenance was changed, and
his thoughts troubled him, so that the joints of
his loins were loosed, and his knees smote one
against another.
7 The king cried aloud to bring in the astrologers,
the Chaldeans, and the soothsayers. *And* the king
spake, and said to the wise *men* of Babylon,

4:35 *reputed as nothing.* All men, regardless of how powerful, are considered to be of no account; they neither can nor do threaten the accomplishing of God's will. *none can stay his hand.* God's hand represents His activity. None can hinder Him from doing what He wants to do.
4:36 His humiliation led to spiritual understanding and ultimately back to the throne of his kingdom. This is a vivid illustration of 1 Sam. 2:7, God "bringeth low, and lifteth up."
4:37 Not all interpreters agree, and ultimately only God knows, but Nebuchadnezzar's profession seems to indicate a genuine spiritual conversion. One of the evidences of saving grace is the ability to comprehend spiritual truth (1 Cor. 2:10–14). After his humiliation, the king uttered a confession of unquestionable orthodoxy. He acknowledged the Most High God as the one true and living God whose sovereign authority both in heaven and earth was eternal, incontestable, and irresistible and whose works were always right and just. That is quite a creed.

Thoughts for Personal/Family Worship: Chapter 4

1. **Although Nebuchadnezzar's manifestation of pride was unique, his self-absorbed pride is the common malady of all sinners. The unchanging spiritual law is that God "resisteth the proud, and giveth grace to the humble" (1 Peter 5:5). Nebuchadnezzar stood in need of grace. Without divine intervention to change his heart, the king's prosperous time would surely lead to a tragic eternity. So it is for every sinner: divine intervention is necessary to change his destiny.**
2. **Conversion is marked by faith toward God and repentance from sin. It is the first conscious response to the grace of God that irresistibly invades the heart, implanting spiritual life and enabling spiritual perception. The story of Nebuchadnezzar's conversion illustrates Paul's theological proposition that "faith cometh by hearing, and hearing by the word of God" (Rom. 10:17) and that "there is no difference between the Jew and the Greek: for the same Lord over all is rich unto all that call upon him" (Rom. 10:12). The Lord graciously gave the Word and governed all the circumstances that led the pagan king to salvation.**

Chapter 5: *God interrupts Belshazzar's irreverent celebration with a mysterious message written on the wall, which only Daniel can interpret, announcing the imminent end of the Babylonian kingdom.*

The Handwriting on the Wall (5:1–31)

The King's Feast (5:1–4)

5:1 *Belshazzar the king.* Not a significant figure from either secular or sacred accounts. Archaeological records explain his coregency with his father, Nabonidus, Babylon's last head of state. Belshazzar had only minor political status as a secondary official who administered the affairs of the city during frequent absences of his father. He had position but little power, living in luxury with more time on his hands than he knew what to do with. God's message was going to make it clear he did not have the time he thought. Indeed, no one does.
5:2–4 The presence of wives and concubines indicates that this was not an official state affair but a party that soon degenerated into drunken debauchery and sacrilege against God. Sins of the flesh far too often express themselves in irreverence. Profaning the temple artifacts that had been consecrated to God was blasphemous.

The Lord's Message (5:5–9)

5:5 Out of nowhere, fingers appeared writing a cryptic message on the wall. In ancient palaces, walls were often decorated with reliefs depicting the exploits and conquests of the regime. Ironically, the Lord wrote the message of doom over the record of triumph; the temporal achievements were nothing in comparison to the greater issues of eternity.
5:6 *countenance was changed.* The brightness or radiance of his appearance changed. He sobered up quickly. *his thoughts troubled him.* They terrified him. *the joints of his loins were loosed.* The joints of his hips shook.
5:7 The king summoned the same incompetent group of advisors who had failed the previous interpretation

Whosoever shall read this writing, and shew me
the interpretation thereof, shall be clothed with
scarlet, and *have* a chain of gold about his neck,
and shall be the third ruler in the kingdom.
8 Then came in all the king's wise *men*: but they
could not read the writing, nor make known to
the king the interpretation thereof.
9 Then was king Belshazzar greatly troubled, and
his countenance was changed in him, and his
lords were astonied.
10 ¶ *Now* the queen, by reason of the words of the
king and his lords, came into the banquet house:
and the queen spake and said, O king, live for
ever: let not thy thoughts trouble thee, nor let thy
countenance be changed:
11 There is a man in thy kingdom, in whom *is*
the spirit of the holy gods; and in the days of thy
father light and understanding and wisdom, like
the wisdom of the gods, was found in him; whom
the king Nebuchadnezzar thy father, the king,
I say, thy father, made master of the magicians,
astrologers, Chaldeans, *and* soothsayers;
12 Forasmuch as an excellent spirit, and knowl-
edge, and understanding, interpreting of dreams,
and shewing of hard sentences, and dissolving of
doubts, were found in the same Daniel, whom
the king named Belteshazzar: now let Daniel be
called, and he will shew the interpretation.
13 Then was Daniel brought in before the king.
And the king spake and said unto Daniel, *Art*
thou that Daniel, which *art* of the children of
the captivity of Judah, whom the king my father
brought out of Jewry?
14 I have even heard of thee, that the spirit of the
gods *is* in thee, and *that* light and understanding
and excellent wisdom is found in thee.
15 And now the wise *men*, the astrologers, have
been brought in before me, that they should
read this writing, and make known unto me the
interpretation thereof: but they could not shew
the interpretation of the thing:
16 And I have heard of thee, that thou canst make
interpretations, and dissolve doubts: now if thou
canst read the writing, and make known to me
the interpretation thereof, thou shalt be clothed
with scarlet, and *have* a chain of gold about thy
neck, and shalt be the third ruler in the kingdom.
17 ¶ Then Daniel answered and said before
the king, Let thy gifts be to thyself, and give thy
rewards to another; yet I will read the writing
unto the king, and make known to him the
interpretation.
18 O thou king, the most high God gave
Nebuchadnezzar thy father a kingdom, and
majesty, and glory, and honour:
19 And for the majesty that he gave him, all people,
nations, and languages, trembled and feared
before him: whom he would he slew; and whom
he would he kept alive; and whom he would he set
up; and whom he would he put down.
20 But when his heart was lifted up, and his
mind hardened in pride, he was deposed from his
kingly throne, and they took his glory from him:
21 And he was driven from the sons of men; and
his heart was made like the beasts, and his dwelling
was with the wild asses: they fed him with grass
like oxen, and his body was wet with the dew of
heaven; till he knew that the most high God ruled
in the kingdom of men, and *that* he appointeth
over it whomsoever he will.
22 And thou his son, O Belshazzar, hast not
humbled thine heart, though thou knewest all this;
23 But hast lifted up thyself against the Lord of
heaven; and they have brought the vessels of his
house before thee, and thou, and thy lords, thy
wives, and thy concubines, have drunk wine in
them; and thou hast praised the gods of silver, and
gold, of brass, iron, wood, and stone, which see
not, nor hear, nor know: and the God in whose
hand thy breath *is*, and whose *are* all thy ways,
hast thou not glorified:
24 Then was the part of the hand sent from him;
and this writing was written.
25 ¶ And this *is* the writing that was written,

---

challenges (chs. 2, 4) and promised to promote the interpreter to administrative status. *scarlet*. Purple or reddish purple, a color associated with royalty. *third ruler*. Evidence of his own position as second in command.

5:8–9 The wise men were unable to read the message, let alone tell what it meant. That only intensified the king's fright and perplexed (*astonied*) the nobles who witnessed the events along with the king.

Daniel's Interpretation (5:10–28)

5:10 *the queen*. Most likely, the queen-mother, either the wife of Nabonidus or perhaps even of Nebuchadnezzar, who certainly would have known of Daniel.

5:11 *Nebuchadnezzar thy father*. The Hebrew uses the word "father" to refer to an ancestor or predecessor, not just the biological parent.

5:12 *excellent spirit*. A reference to extraordinary insight. *shewing of hard sentences*. The interpretation of riddles. *dissolving of doubts*. Solving a knotty problem, or difficult task.

5:14–16 Belshazzar lists Daniel's reputed credentials as including supernatural influence (*spirit of the gods*), illumination (*light*), insight (*understanding*), and extraordinary skill (*excellent wisdom*). He then makes Daniel the same offer as he did to the wise men, who were incapable of deciphering the message.

5:17 Daniel agrees to read and interpret the writing but rejects the king's offer. Most likely, he had already read what was on the wall and knew that being third in line in the kingdom was not an attractive position.

5:18–23 Before reading the text, Daniel rebukes the king for his pride, his blasphemy against the Lord, and his willful refusal to learn the lesson that God taught Nebuchadnezzar (ch. 4). Throughout his ministry, Daniel always linked experiential application to the Word that God revealed, and there was no doubt the handwriting on the wall was God's Word.

MENE, MENE, TEKEL, UPHARSIN.
26 This *is* the interpretation of the thing: MENE;
God hath numbered thy kingdom, and finished it.
27 TEKEL; Thou art weighed in the balances, and
art found wanting.
28 PERES; Thy kingdom is divided, and given to
the Medes and Persians.
29 Then commanded Belshazzar, and they
clothed Daniel with scarlet, and *put* a chain of
gold about his neck, and made a proclamation
concerning him, that he should be the third ruler
in the kingdom.
30 ¶ In that night was Belshazzar the king of the
Chaldeans slain.
31 And Darius the Median took the kingdom,
being about threescore and two years old.

CHAPTER 6

It pleased Darius to set over the kingdom an
hundred and twenty princes, which should be
over the whole kingdom;
2 And over these three presidents; of whom Daniel
was first: that the princes might give accounts
unto them, and the king should have no damage.
3 Then this Daniel was preferred above the
presidents and princes, because an excellent spirit
was in him; and the king thought to set him over
the whole realm.
4 ¶ Then the presidents and princes sought to
find occasion against Daniel concerning the
kingdom; but they could find none occasion nor
fault; forasmuch as he *was* faithful, neither was
there any error or fault found in him.
5 Then said these men, We shall not find any
occasion against this Daniel, except we find *it*
against him concerning the law of his God.
6 Then these presidents and princes assembled
together to the king, and said thus unto him, King
Darius, live for ever.
7 All the presidents of the kingdom, the
governors, and the princes, the counsellors, and
the captains, have consulted together to establish
a royal statute, and to make a firm decree, that
whosoever shall ask a petition of any God or man
for thirty days, save of thee, O king, he shall be
cast into the den of lions.
8 Now, O king, establish the decree, and sign the

5:25 *MENE . . . UPHARSIN*. The word of condemnation was brief but powerful, a terse and simple Aramaic statement literally translated: "Having been counted, having been counted, having been weighed, and having been divided." Why the wise men could not read it remains a mystery. Perhaps it was written in an archaic script or vertically rather than horizontally, or perhaps God confused their minds.
5:26–28 Daniel skips the translation and immediately gives the grim interpretation. Time was up for Belshazzar personally (*MENE* and *TEKEL* are singular referring directly to him) and the kingdom corporately (*UPHARSIN* is plural referring to the empire).

The Message Fulfilled (5:29–31)

5:29–30 The king kept his word regarding Daniel, and God kept His Word regarding the king.
5:31 The identity of *Darius* the Mede is disputed. It most likely refers to Gubaru, who was appointed governor of Babylon by Cyrus. According to the Nabonidus Chronicle, he played a significant role in Babylon's fall. The term "Darius" can be used as a title as well as being a proper name.

Thoughts for Personal/Family Worship: Chapter 5

1. **The opening scene stands as a warning against the dangers of drunkenness. The more the wine flowed, the more they abandoned themselves to sensual and irreverent debauchery. All sin is ultimately a direct affront against God.**
2. **The immediacy of Belshazzar's punishment is a most sobering lesson. A night that started with a party ended in death. When that night began, it is most certain that he had no idea it would be his last. It is a common human thought, even of believers, that death is way in the future, for now something that happens only to others. The Bible is explicit that death comes to all (Heb. 9:27). Only God knows the date, time, and place of that appointment, but notwithstanding our ignorance of those details, it will be an appointment that we will not miss. It is imperative, therefore, to take advantage of the time God has given us and to make sure that we are right with Him through Jesus Christ.**

Chapter 6: ***The target of a conspiracy, Daniel is thrown into a den of lions for his faithfulness to God, who vindicates him by a miraculous preservation from the lions and a sovereign execution of justice against the conspirators.***

Deliverance from the Den of Lions (6:1–28)

The Preeminence of Daniel (6:1–3)

6:1 *over the kingdom*. Just the district of Babylon, now only a part of the newly formed Medo-Persian Empire. *an hundred and twenty princes*. Satraps or administrative assistants within the province.
6:2 *presidents*. Overseers or high-ranking officials. *the king should have no damage*. They protected the king from suffering injury or coming to grief. In Aramaic, the term "king" can designate the highest official in a particular location and not necessarily the supreme and sovereign head of state. In English, "governor" might be more appropriate for Darius.
6:3 *Daniel was preferred*. Literally, he "distinguished himself." *the king thought*. He planned or intended. So distinguished was Daniel that even though he was entrenched in the Babylonian regime he rose to preeminence in the Persian. God took him to Babylon on purpose as a young man, and God still had purpose for him in his elderly years.

The Plot against Daniel (6:4–9)

6:4 *occasion*. A cause or reason for making a complaint.
6:5 Daniel's publicly consistent and predictable devotion to God is an example for every believer to live according to biblical principles regardless of consequence.
6:7 The trap against Daniel was set under the pretext of flattering the king.
6:8 *which altereth not*. The law could not be annulled or revoked.

writing, that it be not changed, according to the
law of the Medes and Persians, which altereth not.
9 Wherefore king Darius signed the writing and
the decree.
10 ¶ Now when Daniel knew that the writing was
signed, he went into his house; and his windows
being open in his chamber toward Jerusalem, he
kneeled upon his knees three times a day, and
prayed, and gave thanks before his God, as he did
aforetime.
11 Then these men assembled, and found Daniel
praying and making supplication before his God.
12 Then they came near, and spake before the
king concerning the king's decree; Hast thou not
signed a decree, that every man that shall ask *a
petition* of any God or man within thirty days,
save of thee, O king, shall be cast into the den
of lions? The king answered and said, The thing
is true, according to the law of the Medes and
Persians, which altereth not.
13 Then answered they and said before the
king, That Daniel, which *is* of the children of the
captivity of Judah, regardeth not thee, O king, nor
the decree that thou hast signed, but maketh his
petition three times a day.
14 Then the king, when he heard *these* words,
was sore displeased with himself, and set *his* heart
on Daniel to deliver him: and he laboured till the
going down of the sun to deliver him.
15 Then these men assembled unto the king,
and said unto the king, Know, O king, that the
law of the Medes and Persians *is*, That no decree
nor statute which the king establisheth may be
changed.
16 Then the king commanded, and they brought
Daniel, and cast *him* into the den of lions. *Now* the
king spake and said unto Daniel, Thy God whom
thou servest continually, he will deliver thee.
17 And a stone was brought, and laid upon the
mouth of the den; and the king sealed it with his
own signet, and with the signet of his lords; that
the purpose might not be changed concerning
Daniel.
18 ¶ Then the king went to his palace, and passed
the night fasting: neither were instruments of
musick brought before him: and his sleep went
from him.
19 Then the king arose very early in the morning,
and went in haste unto the den of lions.
20 And when he came to the den, he cried with a
lamentable voice unto Daniel: *and* the king spake
and said to Daniel, O Daniel, servant of the living
God, is thy God, whom thou servest continually,
able to deliver thee from the lions?
21 Then said Daniel unto the king, O king, live
for ever.
22 My God hath sent his angel, and hath shut the
lions' mouths, that they have not hurt me: foras-
much as before him innocency was found in me;
and also before thee, O king, have I done no hurt.
23 Then was the king exceeding glad for him,
and commanded that they should take Daniel up
out of the den. So Daniel was taken up out of the
den, and no manner of hurt was found upon him,
because he believed in his God.
24 ¶ And the king commanded, and they brought
those men which had accused Daniel, and they
cast *them* into the den of lions, them, their
children, and their wives; and the lions had the
mastery of them, and brake all their bones in
pieces or ever they came at the bottom of the den.
25 ¶ Then king Darius wrote unto all people,

The Prayer of Daniel (6:10–11)

6:10 *toward Jerusalem.* A symbolic gesture reflecting obedience to God's instruction for those in captivity (2 Chron. 6:36–39). Daniel's prayer was courageous, pious, scriptural, and habitual.

6:11 *these men assembled.* Waiting for the appropriate moment, the men barged in as a crowd to catch Daniel in his prayers.

The Punishment of Daniel (6:12–17)

6:14 When the king learned the intent of the law and its consequence for Daniel, he determined (*set his heart*) to find some way to deliver him. But Darius was unwillingly subject to his own law, perhaps evidence of his own subordinate position in the kingdom (see note at 5:31).

6:16 *den of lions.* A pit. *Thy God . . . will deliver.* Daniel's testimony was such that even the pagan king acknowledged God's ability to rescue Daniel from the punishment that he himself was forced to administer.

6:17 *mouth of the den.* The entrance or opening of the pit.

The Vindication of Daniel (6:18–28)

6:18–20 After a long and restless night, the king hurried to the pit and shrieked to Daniel with a sad or troubled voice (*he cried with a lamentable voice*).

6:21 *O king, live for ever.* A typical greeting, expressing desire for the king's well-being.

6:24 *which had accused Daniel.* Literally, "who had eaten his pieces"—a graphic picture of bitter hatred. *the lions had the mastery of them.* I.e., overpowered them. The fate of the conspirators illustrates *lex talionis*, the law of retaliation (eye-for-eye principle). *or ever.* Before.

6:25 *that dwell in all the earth.* Not a reference to the planet but to the land, specifically the province of Babylon over which Darius governed. Once again, a pagan authority is forced to acknowledge the absolute authority of the true God.

Thoughts for Personal/Family Worship: Chapter 6

1. In his old age as in his youth, Daniel is a model for living a consistently godly life in a hostile world. The temptation to conform to what everyone is doing is as much a temptation for the old as the young. Even at the risk of death, Daniel had the conviction that it was better to obey God rather than men (Acts 5:29). It is not surprising that Ezekiel, for a while Daniel's contemporary, pointed to Daniel as a model of righteous living (Ezek. 14:14,20). The world today is no less hostile to grace and God as

nations, and languages, that dwell in all the earth;
Peace be multiplied unto you.
26 I make a decree, That in every dominion of my
kingdom men tremble and fear before the God
of Daniel: for he *is* the living God, and stedfast
for ever, and his kingdom *that* which shall not be
destroyed, and his dominion *shall be even* unto
the end.
27 He delivereth and rescueth, and he worketh
signs and wonders in heaven and in earth, who
hath delivered Daniel from the power of the lions.
28 So this Daniel prospered in the reign of Darius,
and in the reign of Cyrus the Persian.

CHAPTER 7

IN the first year of Belshazzar king of Babylon
Daniel had a dream and visions of his head upon
his bed: then he wrote the dream, *and* told the
sum of the matters.
2 Daniel spake and said, I saw in my vision by
night, and, behold, the four winds of the heaven
strove upon the great sea.
3 And four great beasts came up from the sea,
diverse one from another.
4 The first *was* like a lion, and had eagle's wings:
I beheld till the wings thereof were plucked, and
it was lifted up from the earth, and made stand
upon the feet as a man, and a man's heart was
given to it.
5 And behold another beast, a second, like to a
bear, and it raised up itself on one side, and *it had*
three ribs in the mouth of it between the teeth of
it: and they said thus unto it, Arise, devour much
flesh.
6 After this I beheld, and lo another, like a
leopard, which had upon the back of it four
wings of a fowl; the beast had also four heads; and
dominion was given to it.
7 After this I saw in the night visions, and behold
a fourth beast, dreadful and terrible, and strong
exceedingly; and it had great iron teeth: it devoured and brake in pieces, and stamped the residue with the feet of it: and it *was* diverse from all
the beasts that *were* before it; and it had ten horns.
8 I considered the horns, and, behold, there came
up among them another little horn, before whom
there were three of the first horns plucked up
by the roots: and, behold, in this horn *were* eyes
like the eyes of man, and a mouth speaking great
things.
9 ¶ I beheld till the thrones were cast down, and
the Ancient of days did sit, whose garment *was*
white as snow, and the hair of his head like the

Daniel's world. Regardless of consequences, we should learn from Daniel to maintain a consistent and God-honoring testimony. Every believer should dare to stand like Daniel.

2. **Daniel's response after learning about the prayer injunction provides important lessons about prayer (6:10). Even though the temple in Jerusalem was no longer standing, his praying in that direction symbolically expressed his attitude of worship. His kneeling posture pictured the necessary humility before God. His doing it three times a day as he did aforetime shows that prayer should be a regular habit and not just the last resort in crisis. His praying and giving thanks indicates that prayer involves both petition and praise.**

Chapter 7: ***Daniel's vision of four great beasts represents the kingdoms of the world that will be destroyed by the indestructible kingdom of the Son of man.***

Daniel's Vision about the World (7:1–28)

The Four Great Beasts (7:1–8)

7:1 *In the first year of Belshazzar.* Daniel's vision occurs approximately fifty years after Nebuchadnezzar's dream of the statue. These are two separate revelations but one essential message. God's Word does not change with the passing of time.

7:2 *four winds . . . strove upon the sea.* Winds from every direction churned up the sea.

7:3 *four great beasts . . . from the sea.* The sea represents the nations of the world out of which four different kingdoms are going to come, the same four kingdoms as represented in Nebuchadnezzar's dream (ch. 2): Babylon, Persia, Greece, and Rome.

7:4 Both the lion and eagle were symbols of regal power and glory, corresponding to the head of gold (ch. 2). The wings being torn off suggests humiliation, and the beast's receiving the heart of a man suggests transformation. This parallels Nebuchadnezzar's career from glory to humiliation to conversion (ch. 4).

7:5 The lopsided bear represents the Medo-Persians, with Persia's preeminence over Media. Although less majestic than the lion, the bear is larger and stronger, and the three ribs symbolize the insatiable appetite driving the kingdom to conquest.

7:6 The four-winged and four-headed leopard represents Greece. The speed of the leopard points to the swiftness of Alexander's conquests, and the four wings and heads represent the division of the kingdom after his death among his four principal generals: Lysimachus (Thrace and Bithynia); Antipater or Cassander (Macedonia and Greece); Seleucus (Syria and east to India); Ptolemy (Palestine and Egypt).

7:7 The fourth beast represents Rome and was so grotesque that it was without comparison in the real animal world. Its teeth and ten horns (symbolic of superlative power) represent the violence that marked Rome's quest for territory.

7:8 Eventually, a portion (*three of the first horns*) of Rome's total power was dominated and replaced by another power (*little horn*) with special intelligence and eloquence (*eyes* and *mouth*).

The Ancient of Days and Son of Man (7:9–14)

7:9 *thrones were cast down.* Literally, "thrones were set." In Aramaic, the word for *thrones* is most likely an intensive plural referring to the one exquisitely grand and glorious throne upon which *the Ancient of days* sat. This is a divine title, referring to God's dignity and eternity. Earthly kingdoms come and go, but God is eternally on His throne. *garment . . . as snow.* Symbol of purity. *hair . . . like . . . wool.* Symbol of majesty. *fiery*

pure wool: his throne *was like* the fiery flame, *and*
his wheels *as* burning fire.
10 A fiery stream issued and came forth from
before him: thousand thousands ministered unto
him, and ten thousand times ten thousand stood
before him: the judgment was set, and the books
were opened.
11 I beheld then because of the voice of the great
words which the horn spake: I beheld *even* till the
beast was slain, and his body destroyed, and given
to the burning flame.
12 As concerning the rest of the beasts, they had
their dominion taken away: yet their lives were
prolonged for a season and time.
13 I saw in the night visions, and, behold, *one* like
the Son of man came with the clouds of heaven,
and came to the Ancient of days, and they brought
him near before him.
14 And there was given him dominion, and
glory, and a kingdom, that all people, nations,
and languages, should serve him: his dominion
is an everlasting dominion, which shall not pass
away, and his kingdom *that* which shall not be
destroyed.
15 ¶ I Daniel was grieved in my spirit in the midst
of *my* body, and the visions of my head troubled
me.
16 I came near unto one of them that stood by,
and asked him the truth of all this. So he told
me, and made me know the interpretation of the
things.
17 These great beasts, which are four, *are* four
kings, *which* shall arise out of the earth.
18 But the saints of the most High shall take the
kingdom, and possess the kingdom for ever, even
for ever and ever.
19 Then I would know the truth of the fourth
beast, which was diverse from all the others,
exceeding dreadful, whose teeth *were of* iron, and
his nails *of* brass; *which* devoured, brake in pieces,
and stamped the residue with his feet;
20 And of the ten horns that *were* in his head, and
of the other which came up, and before whom
three fell; even *of* that horn that had eyes, and a
mouth that spake very great things, whose look
was more stout than his fellows.
21 I beheld, and the same horn made war with
the saints, and prevailed against them;
22 Until the Ancient of days came, and judgment
was given to the saints of the most High; and the
time came that the saints possessed the kingdom.
23 Thus he said, The fourth beast shall be the
fourth kingdom upon earth, which shall be
diverse from all kingdoms, and shall devour the
whole earth, and shall tread it down, and break
it in pieces.
24 And the ten horns out of this kingdom *are* ten
kings *that* shall arise: and another shall rise after
them; and he shall be diverse from the first, and
he shall subdue three kings.
25 And he shall speak *great* words against the
most High, and shall wear out the saints of the
most High, and think to change times and laws:
and they shall be given into his hand until a time
and times and the dividing of time.
26 But the judgment shall sit, and they shall take
away his dominion, to consume and to destroy *it*
unto the end.

---

flame . . . burning fire. Fire often accompanies God's presence symbolizing both His majesty and power to consume. The *wheels* represent the moving of His providence.

7:10 *thousand thousands . . . ten thousand times ten thousand*. Not intended to be literally calculated but to highlight the incalculable number of His servants ready to do His bidding. *the judgment was set*. The judicial assembly was seated. The heavenly court over which the absolutely sovereign God presided was in session, and the divine sentence against the earthly kingdoms was about to be announced (*the books were opened*).

7:11–12 The little horn received the death sentence from the heavenly throne whereas the remaining beasts only lost their kingdoms.

7:13–14 Ironically, the Ancient of days takes the kingdoms (sovereignty) away from beasts and gives them to the Son of man. This is the only time the Old Testament uses this designation for Messiah, but it is the basis of the common New Testament use of the title for Christ. Whereas the kingdoms of the beasts were localized and temporary, Christ's rule is *universal, everlasting*, and *indestructible*. The Roman Empire started something that only Christ can finish.

The Interpretation of the Vision (7:15–28)

7:15–16 *grieved*. Distressed. *troubled*. Frightened or terrified. The vision staggered Daniel. He needed help understanding, and an angelic interpreter explained the vision to him.

7:17–18 The short answer to Daniel's question was that kingdoms of man will fail, and the kingdom of God will prevail.

7:19–20 Daniel's principal questions concerned the fourth beast. *whose look was more stout*. Whose appearance was greater.

7:21–25 The angelic explanation gives some new details about the little horn: he wages war against saints; he blasphemes God; he attempts to alter *times and laws* (most likely, a reference to religious traditions and holy days), he persecutes the saints for *a time and times and the dividing of time*. This is most likely a three and a half year period (42 months) paralleling the same time period associated with the beast of Revelation (11:2—13:5, particularly 12:6,14).

7:26 *the judgment shall sit*. The judicial assembly will sit, a reference to the heavenly court over which God presides.

7:28 *my cogitations*. My thoughts. *my countenance*. My appearance.

Thoughts for Personal/Family Worship: Chapter 7

1. **Daniel's preview of world history testifies to God's absolute sovereignty. Kingdoms rise and fall according to His will, and each one accomplishes His purpose. Knowing that God is in control ought to produce comfort, hope, and purity in God's people, even when it appears that powers hostile to God and His people seem**

27 And the kingdom and dominion, and the
greatness of the kingdom under the whole heaven,
shall be given to the people of the saints of the
most High, whose kingdom *is* an everlasting king-
dom, and all dominions shall serve and obey him.
28 Hitherto *is* the end of the matter. As for me
Daniel, my cogitations much troubled me, and
my countenance changed in me: but I kept the
matter in my heart.

CHAPTER 8

IN the third year of the reign of king Belshazzar
a vision appeared unto me, *even unto* me Daniel,
after that which appeared unto me at the first.
2 And I saw in a vision; and it came to pass, when
I saw, that I *was* at Shushan *in* the palace, which *is*
in the province of Elam; and I saw in a vision, and
I was by the river of Ulai.
3 Then I lifted up mine eyes, and saw, and, behold,
there stood before the river a ram which had *two*
horns: and the *two* horns *were* high; but one *was*
higher than the other, and the higher came up last.
4 I saw the ram pushing westward, and
northward, and southward; so that no beasts
might stand before him, neither *was there any*
that could deliver out of his hand; but he did
according to his will, and became great.
5 And as I was considering, behold, an he goat
came from the west on the face of the whole earth,
and touched not the ground: and the goat *had* a
notable horn between his eyes.
6 And he came to the ram that had *two* horns,
which I had seen standing before the river, and
ran unto him in the fury of his power.
7 And I saw him come close unto the ram, and
he was moved with choler against him, and smote
the ram, and brake his two horns: and there was
no power in the ram to stand before him, but he
cast him down to the ground, and stamped upon
him: and there was none that could deliver the
ram out of his hand.
8 Therefore the he goat waxed very great: and
when he was strong, the great horn was broken;
and for it came up four notable ones toward the
four winds of heaven.
9 And out of one of them came forth a little horn,
which waxed exceeding great, toward the south,
and toward the east, and toward the pleasant *land*.
10 And it waxed great, *even* to the host of heaven;
and it cast down *some* of the host and of the stars
to the ground, and stamped upon them.
11 Yea, he magnified *himself* even to the prince of
the host, and by him the daily *sacrifice* was taken
away, and the place of his sanctuary was cast
down.
12 And an host was given *him* against the daily
sacrifice by reason of transgression, and it cast

---

to have the upper hand. God uses the wrath of man to get praise, and all is working without frustration to the ultimate manifestation of His glory and kingdom.

2. **The link between the little horn's blaspheming God and his persecution of the saints is not surprising. Remember Christ said that the world would hate us because it hates Him (John 15:18) and that we would have tribulation in this world (John 16:33). The enemy cannot get to the Head so it attacks the body. But Christ has overcome the world (John 16:33). It is far better to share in the ultimate triumph of Christ than to be on the side of the world. Daniel's vision assures us that saints will reign with Christ (Dan. 7:18).**

THE IMPLICATIONS OF THE MESSAGE FOR GOD'S PEOPLE (8:1—12:13)

Chapter 8: *Daniel's vision of the ram and goat symbolizes the fall of Persia to Greece and Greece's domination over the land of Israel.*

The Vision of Persia and Greece (8:1–27)

The Ram and Goat (8:1–7)

8:1 Daniel switches back to writing in Hebrew at this point, suggesting the particular relevance of the message for Israel. *In the third year.* Two years after the vision of ch. 7, about twelve years before the fall of Babylon to the Medes and Persians.

8:2 *Shushan.* Daniel's being in this principal Persian city was part of the vision. Physically, he was still in Babylon.

8:3 See v. 20 for the interpretation. Horns typically represent strength or power. The two horns represent the powers of Media and Persia. One horn's being higher symbolizes the ultimate supremacy of Persia due to the rise of Cyrus.

8:4 The ram's charging in three directions corresponds to the three ribs in the bear's mouth (7:5), both of which picture unrelenting conquests.

8:5 *he goat.* Literally, the buck of the goats. *touched not the ground.* Pictures the speed of movement. Verse 21 interprets this as referring to Greece and its first king, who would be Alexander the Great. He conquered in less than four years what took Persia twenty-five years.

8:7 *moved with choler against him.* Became enraged against him.

The Little Horn (8:8–14)

8:8 See 8:22 for the interpretation and note at 7:6 for the specific identifications.

8:9 The focus is on an individual coming from one of the four horns or powers, most likely from the Seleucid line. *south . . . east . . . pleasant land.* The Seleucids originally governed the territory of Syria, but this king will expand his rule not only eastward toward India, but south toward Egypt and the *pleasant land,* a reference to Palestine (Jer. 3:19), both of which were under the Ptolemies. This would put Israel directly in the middle. The little horn is to be identified with Antiochus IV Epiphanes, the Seleucid ruler from 175 to 164 BC who caused such turmoil in Israel during the Maccabean era.

8:10 God gave Daniel a preview of what the little horn would do against Israel. *host.* Army. *stars.* A symbolic reference to God's people (Gen. 15:5; Dan. 12:3).

8:11 *magnified . . . the prince of the host.* He considered himself to be equal with God, hence his nickname, Epiphanes, "God manifest."

down the truth to the ground; and it practised,
and prospered.
13 ¶ Then I heard one saint speaking, and
another saint said unto that certain *saint* which
spake, How long *shall be* the vision *concerning* the
daily *sacrifice*, and the transgression of desolation,
to give both the sanctuary and the host to be
trodden under foot?
14 And he said unto me, Unto two thousand and
three hundred days; then shall the sanctuary be
cleansed.
15 ¶ And it came to pass, when I, *even* I Daniel,
had seen the vision, and sought for the meaning,
then, behold, there stood before me as the
appearance of a man.
16 And I heard a man's voice between *the banks*
of Ulai, which called, and said, Gabriel, make this
man to understand the vision.
17 So he came near where I stood: and when he
came, I was afraid, and fell upon my face: but he
said unto me, Understand, O son of man: for at
the time of the end *shall be* the vision.
18 Now as he was speaking with me, I was in a
deep sleep on my face toward the ground: but he
touched me, and set me upright.
19 And he said, Behold, I will make thee know
what shall be in the last end of the indignation:
for at the time appointed the end *shall be*.
20 The ram which thou sawest having *two* horns
are the kings of Media and Persia.
21 And the rough goat *is* the king of Grecia: and
the great horn that *is* between his eyes *is* the first
king.
22 Now that being broken, whereas four stood
up for it, four kingdoms shall stand up out of the
nation, but not in his power.
23 And in the latter time of their kingdom, when
the transgressors are come to the full, a king of
fierce countenance, and understanding dark
sentences, shall stand up.
24 And his power shall be mighty, but not by his
own power: and he shall destroy wonderfully, and
shall prosper, and practise, and shall destroy the
mighty and the holy people.
25 And through his policy also he shall cause
craft to prosper in his hand; and he shall magnify
himself in his heart, and by peace shall destroy
many: he shall also stand up against the Prince
of princes; but he shall be broken without hand.
26 And the vision of the evening and the morning
which was told *is* true: wherefore shut thou up the
vision; for it *shall be* for many days.
27 And I Daniel fainted, and was sick *certain* days;
afterward I rose up, and did the king's business;
and I was astonished at the vision, but none
understood *it*.

CHAPTER 9

In the first year of Darius the son of Ahasuerus, of
the seed of the Medes, which was made king over
the realm of the Chaldeans;

8:12 *him.* Not in the Hebrew. It's better to read the first clause as: "An army was set against the daily sacrifice." *it practised.* The idea is that it, the little horn, did whatever it wanted to do.
8:13 *saint.* A "holy one," most likely an angel. *the transgression of desolation.* The devastating cultic violation.
8:14 *Unto two thousand and three hundred days.* The exact significance of the number is uncertain, but it does indicate an end to the desolation. No matter how long or severe the opposition, God's glory and His people will be vindicated.

The Angelic Interpretation (8:15–27)

8:15–16 *the appearance of a man . . . Gabriel.* The interpreting angel is Gabriel, one of the few named angels in Scripture. The word for "man" is part of his name, which means "the strong man of God."
8:19 *in the last end of the indignation.* Although the details of the vision describe events of the Persian and Greek periods of history, Gabriel points the significance to the end times. As the sovereign controller of time, God uses the events of history to prefigure as picture prophecies things yet to come.
8:22 *not in his power.* None of the leaders of the divided Greek Empire will equal the dominance of Alexander.
8:23 *fierce countenance.* Literally, "strong of face." *understanding dark sentences.* Refers to one of high intelligence either with the ability to interpret riddles or as a master of intrigue or double-dealer. This refers to Antiochus IV.
8:24 *destroy wonderfully.* Destroy in extraordinary ways.
8:25 *through his policy.* Through his cunning. *cause craft to prosper.* He will cause treachery or fraud to flourish. *by peace shall destroy.* Rather, by guile he shall destroy. *broken without hand.* A shameful end. History records Antiochus became irrational and died insane.
8:26 *shut thou up the vision.* An idiom meaning to safeguard it or keep it secure.

Thoughts for Personal/Family Worship: Chapter 8

The precision with which Daniel's vision predicts events hundreds of years in the future testifies to the uniqueness of the one true and living God who knows the end from the beginning. Isaiah records God's challenge to the dead idols to prove they are gods by telling the future (Isa. 40:21–24). They, of course, are silent but the Lord repeatedly gives ample proof of His deity. Seeing how precisely His predictions have been fulfilled should increase our confidence that those prophecies yet to be fulfilled have the same certainty. Without fail, God will fulfill His Word. As Christ said, "Heaven and earth shall pass away, but my words shall not pass away" (Matt. 24:35). It is imperative, therefore, to heed His warnings and be prepared for the judgment ahead.

Chapter 9: ***Daniel's prayer for God to fulfill His Word regarding the end of the captivity is answered with a more glorious Word regarding the coming of Christ.***

Daniel's Prayer and God's Answer (9:1–27)

The Prayer (9:1–19)

9:2 Jeremiah's prediction about the duration of captivity was

2 In the first year of his reign I Daniel understood
by books the number of the years, whereof the
word of the LORD came to Jeremiah the prophet,
that he would accomplish seventy years in the
desolations of Jerusalem.
3 ¶ And I set my face unto the Lord God, to seek
by prayer and supplications, with fasting, and
sackcloth, and ashes:
4 And I prayed unto the LORD my God, and made
my confession, and said, O Lord, the great and
dreadful God, keeping the covenant and mercy
to them that love him, and to them that keep his
commandments;
5 We have sinned, and have committed iniquity,
and have done wickedly, and have rebelled, even
by departing from thy precepts and from thy
judgments:
6 Neither have we hearkened unto thy servants
the prophets, which spake in thy name to our
kings, our princes, and our fathers, and to all the
people of the land.
7 O Lord, righteousness *belongeth* unto thee,
but unto us confusion of faces, as at this day;
to the men of Judah, and to the inhabitants of
Jerusalem, and unto all Israel, *that are* near, and
that are far off, through all the countries whither
thou hast driven them, because of their trespass
that they have trespassed against thee.
8 O Lord, to us *belongeth* confusion of face, to our
kings, to our princes, and to our fathers, because
we have sinned against thee.
9 To the Lord our God *belong* mercies and for-
givenesses, though we have rebelled against him;
10 Neither have we obeyed the voice of the LORD
our God, to walk in his laws, which he set before
us by his servants the prophets.
11 Yea, all Israel have transgressed thy law, even
by departing, that they might not obey thy voice;
therefore the curse is poured upon us, and the
oath that *is* written in the law of Moses the ser-
vant of God, because we have sinned against him.
12 And he hath confirmed his words, which he
spake against us, and against our judges that
judged us, by bringing upon us a great evil: for
under the whole heaven hath not been done as
hath been done upon Jerusalem.
13 As *it is* written in the law of Moses, all this
evil is come upon us: yet made we not our prayer
before the LORD our God, that we might turn
from our iniquities, and understand thy truth.
14 Therefore hath the LORD watched upon the
evil, and brought it upon us: for the LORD our
God *is* righteous in all his works which he doeth:
for we obeyed not his voice.
15 And now, O Lord our God, that hast brought
thy people forth out of the land of Egypt with a
mighty hand, and hast gotten thee renown, as at
this day; we have sinned, we have done wickedly.
16 ¶ O Lord, according to all thy righteousness,
I beseech thee, let thine anger and thy fury be
turned away from thy city Jerusalem, thy holy
mountain: because for our sins, and for the
iniquities of our fathers, Jerusalem and thy people
are become a reproach to all *that are* about us.
17 Now therefore, O our God, hear the prayer of
thy servant, and his supplications, and cause thy
face to shine upon thy sanctuary that is desolate,
for the Lord's sake.
18 O my God, incline thine ear, and hear; open
thine eyes, and behold our desolations, and the
city which is called by thy name: for we do not
present our supplications before thee for our
righteousnesses, but for thy great mercies.
19 O Lord, hear; O Lord, forgive; O Lord, heark-
en and do; defer not, for thine own sake, O my
God: for thy city and thy people are called by thy
name.
20 ¶ And whiles I *was* speaking, and praying, and
confessing my sin and the sin of my people Israel,
and presenting my supplication before the LORD
my God for the holy mountain of my God;
21 Yea, whiles I *was* speaking in prayer, even the
man Gabriel, whom I had seen in the vision at the
beginning, being caused to fly swiftly, touched me
about the time of the evening oblation.
22 And he informed *me*, and talked with me, and

definite, but it is uncertain when to begin the counting: 605 BC (the initial stage when Daniel was exiled); 597 BC (the second stage when Ezekiel and 10,000 of the upper society were exiled); or 586 BC (the final stage when Jerusalem fell and the temple was destroyed). Daniel, taken captive at the beginning of the exile and now an old man, was able to calculate from his age that Jeremiah's prophecy was about to be fulfilled, and so he prays. Significantly, Jeremiah's prophecy, written in Judah, had made its way to Babylon and was regarded as the Word of God. There should always be a link between God's Word and prayer, both of which are means of grace.

9:3 *fasting . . . ashes*. External displays of inward contrition.

9:4 *dreadful*. Fearful. *mercy*. Covenant love, loyalty, and faithfulness. Daniel begins his prayer with worship, focusing on God's person—a good pattern to follow.

9:7–8 *confusion*. Shame.

9:9 *mercies*. Feelings of compassion.

9:12 *confirmed*. Literally, "made to stand." *a great evil*. A great calamity.

9:14 *watched upon the evil*. The Lord was vigilant regarding the calamity, the judgment He brought. It was not capricious but divinely calculated to accomplish its purpose.

9:15 *hast gotten thee renown*. Literally, "Thou hast made a name for Thyself."

9:18 *great mercies*. See note at 9:9.

9:19 *defer not*. Do not delay.

The Answer (9:20–27)

9:20–23 *Gabriel*, Daniel's interpreting angel, appears to announce an answer far greater than the petition and gives Daniel the *skill* (insight) to understand.

said, O Daniel, I am now come forth to give thee
skill and understanding.
23 At the beginning of thy supplications the
commandment came forth, and I am come to
shew *thee*; for thou *art* greatly beloved: therefore
understand the matter, and consider the vision.
24 Seventy weeks are determined upon thy
people and upon thy holy city, to finish the
transgression, and to make an end of sins, and
to make reconciliation for iniquity, and to bring
in everlasting righteousness, and to seal up the
vision and prophecy, and to anoint the most Holy.
25 Know therefore and understand, *that* from the
going forth of the commandment to restore and
to build Jerusalem unto the Messiah the Prince
shall be seven weeks, and threescore and two
weeks: the street shall be built again, and the wall,
even in troublous times.
26 And after threescore and two weeks shall
Messiah be cut off, but not for himself: and the
people of the prince that shall come shall destroy
the city and the sanctuary; and the end thereof
shall be with a flood, and unto the end of the war
desolations are determined.
27 And he shall confirm the covenant with many
for one week: and in the midst of the week he
shall cause the sacrifice and the oblation to cease,
and for the overspreading of abominations he
shall make *it* desolate, even until the consumma-
tion, and that determined shall be poured upon
the desolate.

CHAPTER 10

In the third year of Cyrus king of Persia a thing
was revealed unto Daniel, whose name was called
Belteshazzar; and the thing *was* true, but the time
appointed *was* long: and he understood the thing,
and had understanding of the vision.
2 In those days I Daniel was mourning three full
weeks.
3 I ate no pleasant bread, neither came flesh nor

9:24 *Seventy weeks.* Literally, "seventy sevens." The "sevens" most likely refer to periods of seven years; therefore, seventy periods of seven years each (490 years). Interpretations vary as to how literal or how symbolic is the time, but without question the weeks provide a preview of God's plan for His people, summed up in the sixfold purpose. The symbolic interpretation sees this as playing on the covenant language that multiplies the curse by seven times (see Lev. 26:18,21,24,28). There the seventy-year exile would be multiplied by seven, designating the severity of the seventy-year captivity. The literal view interprets this as referring to an actual duration of time culminating with the coming of Christ (*to anoint the most Holy*).
9:25 *from the going forth.* The command to rebuild Jerusalem marks the beginning of the seventy weeks. Opinions differ as to when that command was issued: Cyrus's decree to rebuild the temple (538 BC); Darius's decree confirming Cyrus's (520 BC); Artaxerxes's decree granting provisions for Ezra's return (458 BC); or Artaxerxes's decree giving Nehemiah authority to rebuild Jerusalem (445 BC). *the street . . . the wall.* This would seem to reference Nehemiah's work. Note that the first 69 weeks are divided into *seven weeks* (49 years) and *threescore and two* (62) *weeks* (434 years). Most likely the division suggests the relatively short time before the city's restoration in comparison to the waiting time for *Messiah the Prince*. Taking into consideration a prophetic year of 360 days and the various differences between Jewish and Roman dating, the 69 weeks would end somewhere between AD 26 and 33. The prophecy concerns the end of Christ's ministry.
9:26 Two major events follow the 69 weeks: *Messiah* will *be cut off* (a reference to His death) and the destruction of Jerusalem (opinions differ as to whether it refers to Jerusalem's destruction by Titus in AD 70 or to a yet future destruction). *not for himself.* Most likely referring to the substitutionary death of Messiah.
9:27 Adherents of the literal view differ as to whether the last week is continuous with the first 69, referring to events associated with Christ's first advent or after some interval, associated with the activity of a future Antichrist. The symbolic view typically sees the first 49 years to represent the postexilic period, the next 62 to represent the current church, and the final 7 to refer to the end times.

Thoughts for Personal/Family Worship: Chapter 9

1. **Throughout His Word, God commands us to pray, invites us to pray, and shows us how to pray. Daniel's prayer provides a pattern to follow. As you read through the prayer, note the following: (1) prayer is based on God's Word; (2) it focuses on God's person and character; (3) it involves the confession of sin; (4) it makes great supplications; and (5) it makes God's glory the supreme motive.**
2. **Praying God's Word is a sure way to pray for God's will to be done. Jeremiah prophesied that the captivity would last for seventy years, and it would have lasted for seventy years whether Daniel prayed or not. But Daniel's praying that promise was an expression of his faith in God's unfailing Word and his appropriation of the promise knowing that the time was at hand. His praying for the Word to be fulfilled corresponds to Christ's model prayer, "Thy will be done (Matt. 6)."**
3. **Notwithstanding the interpretational difficulties and disagreements regarding the seventy weeks, this prophecy, which was God's answer to Daniel's prayer, illustrates a wonderful truth: God is "able to do exceeding abundantly above all that we ask or think" (Eph. 3:20). Daniel prayed that God might end the captivity; God answered by pointing him to Christ, who would accomplish far greater things than ending an exile. It is a wonderful thought that God's purpose for His people is always greater than their expectations.**

Chapter 10: ***Daniel's vision of the preincarnate Christ and the reality of spiritual warfare encourages him in a time of personal distress.***

A Personal Revelation to Daniel (10:1–21)

The Circumstances of the Revelation (10:1–4)

10:1–2 *In the third year . . . was mourning.* At the beginning of Cyrus's reign, he issued a decree allowing Jews to return to Palestine and rebuild the temple. By this time, they began to encounter the opposition that led to the cessation of work, which most likely was the reason for Daniel's grief.
10:3 *pleasant bread.* Literally, "bread (food) of desirable

wine in my mouth, neither did I anoint myself at
all, till three whole weeks were fulfilled.
4 And in the four and twentieth day of the first
month, as I was by the side of the great river,
which *is* Hiddekel;
5 Then I lifted up mine eyes, and looked, and
behold a certain man clothed in linen, whose
loins *were* girded with fine gold of Uphaz:
6 His body also *was* like the beryl, and his face as
the appearance of lightning, and his eyes as lamps
of fire, and his arms and his feet like in colour to
polished brass, and the voice of his words like the
voice of a multitude.
7 And I Daniel alone saw the vision: for the men
that were with me saw not the vision; but a great
quaking fell upon them, so that they fled to hide
themselves.
8 Therefore I was left alone, and saw this great
vision, and there remained no strength in me: for
my comeliness was turned in me into corruption,
and I retained no strength.
9 Yet heard I the voice of his words: and when I
heard the voice of his words, then was I in a deep
sleep on my face, and my face toward the ground.
10 ¶ And, behold, an hand touched me, which
set me upon my knees and *upon* the palms of my
hands.
11 And he said unto me, O Daniel, a man greatly
beloved, understand the words that I speak unto
thee, and stand upright: for unto thee am I now
sent. And when he had spoken this word unto me,
I stood trembling.
12 Then said he unto me, Fear not, Daniel: for
from the first day that thou didst set thine heart
to understand, and to chasten thyself before thy
God, thy words were heard, and I am come for
thy words.
13 But the prince of the kingdom of Persia
withstood me one and twenty days: but, lo,
Michael, one of the chief princes, came to help
me; and I remained there with the kings of Persia.
14 Now I am come to make thee understand what
shall befall thy people in the latter days: for yet the
vision *is* for *many* days.
15 And when he had spoken such words unto me,
I set my face toward the ground, and I became
dumb.
16 And, behold, *one* like the similitude of the sons
of men touched my lips: then I opened my mouth,
and spake, and said unto him that stood before
me, O my lord, by the vision my sorrows are
turned upon me, and I have retained no strength.
17 For how can the servant of this my lord talk
with this my lord? for as for me, straightway there
remained no strength in me, neither is there
breath left in me.
18 Then there came again and touched me *one* like
the appearance of a man, and he strengthened me,
19 And said, O man greatly beloved, fear not:
peace *be* unto thee, be strong, yea, be strong. And
when he had spoken unto me, I was strength-
ened, and said, Let my lord speak; for thou hast
strengthened me.
20 Then said he, Knowest thou wherefore I come

---

things," a reference to delicacies. *neither did I anoint myself.* Literally, it refers to smearing grease, a reference to some grooming practice not a religious anointing. Daniel was so overwhelmed with grief that he set aside the normal routines of life to devote himself to prayer.

The Revelation (10:5–9)

10:5–6 *a certain man.* Very likely, a vision of the preincarnate Christ. The description parallels Ezekiel's vision in Ezek. 1:26 and 9:2 as well as John's vision of the exalted incarnate Christ in Rev. 1:12–20. Whether one is an Old Testament or New Testament saint, seeing Christ is always the best solution to discouragement.

10:8 *my comeliness . . . into corruption.* His vigor turned to nothing. He lost all strength. He was brought to an end of himself when he saw the Lord, the common and expected response (Isa. 6; Ezek. 1; Rev. 1).

The Encouraging Explanation (10:10–21)

10:11 *greatly beloved.* The same word as "pleasant" in v. 3. Daniel was regarded as a most special person.

10:12 *chasten thyself.* To bow humbly or humble oneself.

10:13 *the prince of the kingdom of Persia.* The supernatural demonic power behind the pagan gods (1 Cor. 10:20). A mysterious scene of spiritual battle in the spiritual realm (Eph. 6:11–12), in which Christ Himself makes war on behalf of His people against the hostile spirits. He is the mediatorial King who conquers all of His and our enemies. As the Lord of hosts or armies, He commands the angelic host. Here *Michael,* one of the named angels, is present as having particular interest in Israel (10:21).

10:14 *what shall befall.* What will happen in the end identifies the scope of the prophecy.

10:15 *I became dumb.* I was made to be silent.

10:16 *my sorrows.* Pangs or spasms, referring more to the physical effects of the vision than the emotional.

10:20 *the prince of Grecia shall come.* The supernatural demonic power associated with the next pagan nation. Satanic opposition to Christ will continue until once and for all the Lord makes all Christ's enemies to be His footstool (Ps. 110:1).

10:21 *scripture of truth.* Not the Bible per se, but the book of truth, what God has revealed to Daniel about His decreed will for the future. *none that holdeth with me.* No one is showing himself strong or being courageous with me, except Michael (see note at 10:13).

Thoughts for Personal/Family Worship: Chapter 10

1. **The warfare in the spiritual realm is real even though it occurs beyond our natural sight. Although beyond our sight, believers are often in the field of battle. What Job experienced, for instance, was the consequence of the challenge between God and Satan. It is imperative, therefore, that we arm ourselves with the armor and weaponry that God has given to us because we do fight against unworldly foes (Eph. 6:10–18). But victory is assured because the battle is the Lord's.**

unto thee? and now will I return to fight with the
prince of Persia: and when I am gone forth, lo, the
prince of Grecia shall come.
21 But I will shew thee that which is noted in the
scripture of truth: and *there is* none that holdeth
with me in these things, but Michael your prince.

CHAPTER 11

ALSO I in the first year of Darius the Mede, *even* I,
stood to confirm and to strengthen him.
2 And now will I shew thee the truth. Behold,
there shall stand up yet three kings in Persia; and
the fourth shall be far richer than *they* all: and by
his strength through his riches he shall stir up all
against the realm of Grecia.
3 And a mighty king shall stand up, that shall rule
with great dominion, and do according to his will.
4 And when he shall stand up, his kingdom shall
be broken, and shall be divided toward the four
winds of heaven; and not to his posterity, nor
according to his dominion which he ruled: for
his kingdom shall be plucked up, even for others
beside those.
5 ¶ And the king of the south shall be strong, and
one of his princes; and he shall be strong above
him, and have dominion; his dominion *shall be* a
great dominion.
6 And in the end of years they shall join
themselves together; for the king's daughter of the
south shall come to the king of the north to make
an agreement: but she shall not retain the power
of the arm; neither shall he stand, nor his arm: but
she shall be given up, and they that brought her,
and he that begat her, and he that strengthened
her in *these* times.
7 But out of a branch of her roots shall *one* stand
up in his estate, which shall come with an army, and
shall enter into the fortress of the king of the north,
and shall deal against them, and shall prevail:
8 And shall also carry captives into Egypt their
gods, with their princes, *and* with their precious
vessels of silver and of gold; and he shall continue
more years than the king of the north.
9 So the king of the south shall come into *his*
kingdom, and shall return into his own land.
10 But his sons shall be stirred up, and shall
assemble a multitude of great forces: and *one* shall
certainly come, and overflow, and pass through:
then shall he return, and be stirred up, *even* to his
fortress.
11 And the king of the south shall be moved with
choler, and shall come forth and fight with him,
even with the king of the north: and he shall set
forth a great multitude; but the multitude shall be
given into his hand.
12 *And* when he hath taken away the multitude,
his heart shall be lifted up; and he shall cast
down *many* ten thousands: but he shall not be
strengthened *by it.*
13 For the king of the north shall return, and
shall set forth a multitude greater than the former,
and shall certainly come after certain years with a
great army and with much riches.
14 And in those times there shall many stand up
against the king of the south: also the robbers of
thy people shall exalt themselves to establish the
vision; but they shall fall.
15 So the king of the north shall come, and cast
up a mount, and take the most fenced cities: and
the arms of the south shall not withstand, neither
his chosen people, neither *shall there be any*
strength to withstand.
16 But he that cometh against him shall do
according to his own will, and none shall stand
before him: and he shall stand in the glorious
land, which by his hand shall be consumed.
17 He shall also set his face to enter with the
strength of his whole kingdom, and upright ones
with him; thus shall he do: and he shall give him
the daughter of women, corrupting her: but she
shall not stand *on his side*, neither be for him.

---

2. That the prince of Greece followed the prince of Persia (10:20) is a reminder that we can never let down our guard in the spiritual war. Victory in one battle does not cause the next enemy to surrender. Sin does not have dominion over us, but we must resist every temptation that comes our way every time it comes.

Chapter 11: *Daniel prophetically and precisely details the history of the Near East from his day to the intertestamental period to the end times.*

History to the Fullness of Time and Beyond (11:1–45)

11:2 *the truth.* The truth Daniel explains falls into three parts: Persia and Greece, particularly the Ptolemaic and Seleucid dynasties (vv. 2–20); the Seleucid Antiochus IV (vv. 21–35); the future Antichrist (vv. 36–45). The detailed precision with which Daniel previews this history has caused critics to deny his authorship, claiming it was written after the fact. Secular histories, such as the apocryphal books of 1 and 2 Maccabees and Book 12 of *The Antiquities of the Jews* by Josephus add to Daniel's preview by supplying the actual names of the characters involved.

11:3–4 Alexander and the subsequent division of his kingdom (see note at 7:6).

11:5–6 *south.* Egypt, the principal part of the Ptolemaic kingdom. *north.* Syria, the principal part of the Seleucid kingdom.

11:7 *branch of her roots.* An idiom designating kinship, most likely a sibling.

11:10 *overflow.* Cascade like a flood, a picture of force and fury.

11:11 *moved with choler.* Enraged or furious.

11:14 *the robbers.* The violent ones.

11:15 *cast up a mount.* Erect an assault ramp.

11:16 *the glorious land.* The land of beauty, a reference to land of Palestine.

18 After this shall he turn his face unto the isles,
and shall take many: but a prince for his own
behalf shall cause the reproach offered by him to
cease; without his own reproach he shall cause *it*
to turn upon him.
19 Then he shall turn his face toward the fort of
his own land: but he shall stumble and fall, and
not be found.
20 Then shall stand up in his estate a raiser of
taxes *in* the glory of the kingdom: but within few
days he shall be destroyed, neither in anger, nor
in battle.
21 And in his estate shall stand up a vile person,
to whom they shall not give the honour of the
kingdom: but he shall come in peaceably, and
obtain the kingdom by flatteries.
22 And with the arms of a flood shall they be
overflown from before him, and shall be broken;
yea, also the prince of the covenant.
23 And after the league *made* with him he shall
work deceitfully: for he shall come up, and shall
become strong with a small people.
24 He shall enter peaceably even upon the fattest
places of the province; and he shall do *that* which
his fathers have not done, nor his fathers' fathers;
he shall scatter among them the prey, and spoil,
and riches: *yea*, and he shall forecast his devices
against the strong holds, even for a time.
25 And he shall stir up his power and his courage
against the king of the south with a great army;
and the king of the south shall be stirred up to
battle with a very great and mighty army; but
he shall not stand: for they shall forecast devices
against him.
26 Yea, they that feed of the portion of his meat
shall destroy him, and his army shall overflow:
and many shall fall down slain.
27 And both these kings' hearts *shall be* to do
mischief, and they shall speak lies at one table; but
it shall not prosper: for yet the end *shall be* at the
time appointed.
28 Then shall he return into his land with great
riches; and his heart *shall be* against the holy
covenant; and he shall do *exploits*, and return to
his own land.
29 At the time appointed he shall return, and
come toward the south; but it shall not be as the
former, or as the latter.
30 ¶ For the ships of Chittim shall come against
him: therefore he shall be grieved, and return,
and have indignation against the holy covenant:
so shall he do; he shall even return, and have intel-
ligence with them that forsake the holy covenant.
31 And arms shall stand on his part, and they
shall pollute the sanctuary of strength, and shall
take away the daily *sacrifice*, and they shall place
the abomination that maketh desolate.
32 And such as do wickedly against the cov-
enant shall he corrupt by flatteries: but the people
that do know their God shall be strong, and do
exploits.
33 And they that understand among the people
shall instruct many: yet they shall fall by the
sword, and by flame, by captivity, and by spoil,
many days.
34 Now when they shall fall, they shall be holpen
with a little help: but many shall cleave to them
with flatteries.
35 And *some* of them of understanding shall
fall, to try them, and to purge, and to make *them*
white, *even* to the time of the end: because *it is* yet
for a time appointed.
36 And the king shall do according to his will;
and he shall exalt himself, and magnify himself
above every god, and shall speak marvellous
things against the God of gods, and shall prosper
till the indignation be accomplished: for that that
is determined shall be done.
37 Neither shall he regard the God of his fathers,
nor the desire of women, nor regard any god: for
he shall magnify himself above all.
38 But in his estate shall he honour the God of

11:21 *vile person.* A despicable, despised, and contemptible person, here referring to Antiochus IV, the little horn of 8:8–14 (see notes). *by flatteries.* Intrigue. Antiochus was not the legitimate heir, but through shrewd politicking he gained the throne.
11:22 *And with the arms of a flood shall they be overthrown.* The armies will be overwhelmingly swept away.
11:23 *a small people.* A few people.
11:24–25 *the fattest places of the province.* The most fertile or most prosperous places in the district. *he shall forecast his devices.* He will calculate his plans (v. 25 also).
11:25 *forecast devices.* See 11:24.
11:26 *they that feed . . . shall destroy him.* An image of betrayal. *his army shall overflow.* Be swept away.
11:27 *mischief.* Wickedness.
11:30 *Chittim.* A reference to Rome. *and have intelligence with.* He will give heed to the covenant breakers.
11:31 *And arms shall stand on his part.* And a military force will rise from him. *the sanctuary of strength.* The sanctuary, which is the temple or fortress. *the abomination that maketh desolate.* The detested thing that appalls.
11:32 *flatteries.* Falsehood.
11:34 *holpen.* Helped. *Many shall cleave to them with flatteries.* Many will join themselves to them in hypocrisy.
11:35 *to try.* To refine. *to purge.* To sift or sort out.
11:36 *marvellous things.* Amazingly dreadful things. *God of gods.* A superlative expression designating the absolutely supreme God. Many see Daniel transitioning to a yet-to-come Antichrist at this point.
11:37 *God of his fathers.* Probably better "god," referring to an ancestral deity rather than the one true God. *the desire of women.* Very likely referring to the coming Christ, who according to prophecy would be virgin-born, the seed of the woman. *nor regard any god.* This one will be completely atheistic.
11:38 *the God of forces.* Likely referring to his considering his military forces to be his god, what he trusted.

forces: and a god whom his fathers knew not
shall he honour with gold, and silver, and with
precious stones, and pleasant things.
39 Thus shall he do in the most strong holds with
a strange god, whom he shall acknowledge *and*
increase with glory: and he shall cause them to
rule over many, and shall divide the land for gain.
40 And at the time of the end shall the king of the
south push at him: and the king of the north shall
come against him like a whirlwind, with chariots,
and with horsemen, and with many ships; and he
shall enter into the countries, and shall overflow
and pass over.
41 He shall enter also into the glorious land, and
many *countries* shall be overthrown: but these
shall escape out of his hand, *even* Edom, and
Moab, and the chief of the children of Ammon.
42 He shall stretch forth his hand also upon the
countries: and the land of Egypt shall not escape.
43 But he shall have power over the treasures of
gold and of silver, and over all the precious things
of Egypt: and the Libyans and the Ethiopians *shall
be* at his steps.
44 But tidings out of the east and out of the north
shall trouble him: therefore he shall go forth
with great fury to destroy, and utterly to make
away many.
45 And he shall plant the tabernacles of his palace
between the seas in the glorious holy mountain;
yet he shall come to his end, and none shall help
him.

CHAPTER 12

AND at that time shall Michael stand up, the great
prince which standeth for the children of thy
people: and there shall be a time of trouble, such
as never was since there was a nation *even* to that
same time: and at that time thy people shall be
delivered, every one that shall be found written
in the book.
2 And many of them that sleep in the dust of the
earth shall awake, some to everlasting life, and
some to shame *and* everlasting contempt.
3 And they that be wise shall shine as the bright-
ness of the firmament; and they that turn many to
righteousness as the stars for ever and ever.
4 But thou, O Daniel, shut up the words, and seal
the book, *even* to the time of the end: many shall
run to and fro, and knowledge shall be increased.
5 ¶ Then I Daniel looked, and, behold, there
stood other two, the one on this side of the bank
of the river, and the other on that side of the bank
of the river.
6 And *one* said to the man clothed in linen, which
was upon the waters of the river, How long *shall it
be to* the end of these wonders?
7 And I heard the man clothed in linen, which

11:39 *strange god.* God of a foreign land. Although atheistic, he will use religion to his advantage to advance his cause.
11:40 *shall overflow and pass over.* He will go through countries like a cascade of water, destroying whatever is in the path.
11:41 *glorious land.* A reference to Palestine.
11:43 *his steps.* Perhaps meaning they will follow in his steps.
11:44 *tidings out of the east.* Evidence that his power is not universal. He has enemies that God will use to bring his defeat.
11:45 *plant the tabernacles of his palace.* He will pitch his royal tents or pavilions somewhere in Palestine, perhaps in Zion itself (*the glorious holy mountain*). Notwithstanding his power, he is destroyed. None can frustrate God's purpose.

Thoughts for Personal/Family Worship: Chapter 11

On the surface, it may appear that this prewritten history has little practical or devotional application. Yet, the fact that Daniel writes with such precision about things that would happen hundreds of years after him suggests two important thoughts that should be encouraging to believers. First, it teaches us that God is not just a distant observer or someone reacting to what happens on earth; rather, He is the orchestrator of all. Since He knows the end from the beginning, it is no difficulty for Him to reveal things prior to their occurrence. His will guarantees the fulfillment of His Word. Second, the precision with which some of the prophecies were fulfilled gives confidence that God's will for what is still to come is just as certain. So even though the world at times would appear to be out of control, all is moving steadily to that time when the great enemy of God and His people will come to his end.

Chapter 12: *Daniel receives a final vision detailing great trouble but ultimate triumph for God's people and a final assurance that all will be fulfilled.*

Final Prophecies and Instructions (12:1–13)

12:1 *a time of trouble.* Mostly likely, this is the time Christ referred to as a "great tribulation" (Matt. 24:21). *in the book.* Most likely, an allusion to the book of life (Rev. 13:8; 20:12).
12:2 Along with Job 19:25 and Isa. 26:19, this is a key Old Testament text for the resurrection. *many of them.* This does not imply that some are excluded; it is a way of expressing the incalculable number. This is the resurrection of both the just and unjust (Matt. 25:46; John 5:28–29).
12:3 *firmament.* The expanse of the sky.
12:4 *shut . . . and seal.* Safeguard the message. It will endure until its certain fulfillment.
12:6 *man clothed in linen.* Very likely, a preincarnate view of Christ.
12:7 *time, times, and an half.* See note at 7:21–25. *when he shall have accomplished to scatter.* Literally, "when smashing the power of the holy people is finished."
12:11–12 *the abomination that maketh desolate.* Parallels 9:27 and seems to be what Christ refers to in Matt. 24:15. *a thousand two hundred and ninety days . . . thousand three hundred and five and thirty days.* The significance of the numbers is obscure.
12:13 *shalt rest . . . and stand in thy lot.* Daniel will die before the events are fulfilled, but he will be part of that future resurrection and receive his lot or inheritance.

Thoughts for Personal/Family Worship: Chapter 12

1. The classic text on the resurrection (12:2) is occasion

was upon the waters of the river, when he held up
his right hand and his left hand unto heaven, and
sware by him that liveth for ever that *it shall be* for
a time, times, and an half; and when he shall have
accomplished to scatter the power of the holy
people, all these *things* shall be finished.
8 And I heard, but I understood not: then said I,
O my Lord, what *shall be* the end of these *things*?
9 And he said, Go thy way, Daniel: for the words
are closed up and sealed till the time of the end.
10 Many shall be purified, and made white, and
tried; but the wicked shall do wickedly: and none
of the wicked shall understand; but the wise shall
understand.
11 And from the time *that* the daily *sacrifice* shall
be taken away, and the abomination that maketh
desolate set up, *there shall be* a thousand two hun-
dred and ninety days.
12 Blessed *is* he that waiteth, and cometh to the
thousand three hundred and five and thirty days.
13 But go thou thy way till the end *be*: for thou
shalt rest, and stand in thy lot at the end of the days.

to reflect on this vital doctrine. For the believer, the resurrection is a glorious hope that the body will be delivered from sin as well as the soul, and that forever we will enjoy the completeness of our redemption in a body like Christ's. For the unbeliever, the bodily resurrection is a terrible thought—to be in a body capable of being tormented forever. It is incentive to repent in order to be among the wise that will shine like stars in that day.

2. **Verse 12 sums up how the Christian is to live in the light of God's certain revelation. After Daniel sealed up the book, life would go on as normal with people going about and knowledge advancing (v. 4). The passing of time, however, should not dull the spiritual senses. God promises blessing to those who wait and patiently endure the troubles of life in eager anticipation of God's purpose. In spite of the uncertain meaning of the 1290 days versus the 1,335 days (vv. 11–12), the point, in part, is that sometimes the waiting may be longer than expected. But God is never late in His timing, and the end will come as He has purposed. Christians should always live with a view to the certain future.**

Thou Art
MY PEOPLE
&
THEY SHALL SAY
THOU ART
My God

HOSEA 2:23

INTRODUCTION TO THE BOOK OF HOSEA

Authorship: Hosea 1:1 identifies the author as "Hosea, the son of Beeri." Apart from his father's identification, nothing else is known about Hosea's lineage, unless Beeri is to be identified with the Beerah of 1 Chron. 5:6. If these are the same, Hosea would be of the tribe of Reuben. Although speculative, this would confirm his northern roots. Hosea's uniqueness is that he was a prophet from the north ministering to the north. Hosea's name means "salvation."

Date: The list of kings in Hos. 1:1 spans just over a century—a period of time obviously longer than Hosea's ministry. The internal evidence suggests that Hosea's ministry began prior to Jeroboam II's death in 753 BC and ended around 725 BC, after Hezekiah's ascension but before Samaria's fall. Hosea's ministry was in part contemporary with Isaiah and Micah, both of whom ministered to the southern kingdom, and Amos, who although from the south preached principally to the northern kingdom.

Although Hosea's ministry commenced during a time of prosperity during the administration of Jeroboam II, that prosperity soon gave way to decline. The history of Hosea's world delineates the fulfillment of his prophecy that the Lord would bring first the demise of Jehu's dynasty and then the end of the whole kingdom of Israel (1:4), and that He would do so at the hand of the Assyrians (11:5). Hosea lived and ministered during most of that history and, therefore, preached to a people on the brink of national disaster. There was a sense of urgency to his message, but the nation was oblivious. What the nation experienced in the swirling demise of their national sovereignty and standard of living consistently affirmed the veracity and authority of Hosea's message.

Ironically, the tragic consequences of Israel's rejection of Hosea's message anticipated the grace of the gospel. The territory of Israel that first experienced God's judgment (all the land of Naphtali, 2 Kings 15:29) was by God's grace the first region of Israel to witness the ministry of Christ (Matt. 4:12–16). The darkness of Hosea's day would give way to the light of Christ. The time of darkness was a providentially ordered step toward the fullness of time in which the Light would shine.

Theme: God's love, spurned but constant.

Purpose: To highlight God's unfailing love that guarantees His covenant faithfulness both in terms of judgment and mercy.

Synopsis: *The Contribution of Hosea to Redemptive Revelation*

The message of marriage is an integral part of the prophecy of Hosea. God intended Hosea's family life to be a symbol, a visible picture or object lesson, of the message he was to preach to Israel. Hosea 3:1 is the key verse of the book and explicitly links Hosea's marriage to Gomer with God's marriage to Israel. Hosea's relationship with Gomer and God's relationship with Israel were initiated by love, spurned by sin, and maintained by loyalty. Hosea's constant love and loyalty to Gomer was a beautiful picture of the Lord's unfailing love and loyalty to Israel. Gomer's unfaithfulness to Hosea was a tragically clear picture of Israel's treacherous unfaithfulness to the Lord. On several levels, Hosea's experience parallels God's relationship with Israel, which in turn is paradigmatic of God's salvific acts for the church.

Major Problem of Interpretation: Hosea's marriage to Gomer, crucial to the message of the book, constitutes a major problem for interpreters. The crux of the problem concerns the initial command of God to marry a wife of whoredoms (1:2). On the surface this creates a moral and ethical dilemma because it seems to counter the clear instructions and restrictions for marriage that God gave to priests prohibiting them from marrying harlots (Lev. 21:7,13). If it would be a disgrace for a priest to marry a harlot, it would seem to follow that it would be a disgrace for a prophet as well. In addition, Deut. 22:13,20–21 sentences to death any woman proven to be unchaste at the time of marriage. The dilemma, therefore, is twofold: Would the Lord lower the standards for a prophet, and would He overlook the impurity of the wife of whoredoms?

The solutions to the problem fall into two major categories: those that regard the marriage as hypothetical and those that regard the marriage as literal.

Hypothetical Marriage

The hypothetical view denies a real historical marriage between Hosea and Gomer and interprets Hosea's use of the marriage imagery as simply a means of figuratively communicating God's relationship to Israel and Israel's spiritual unfaithfulness to God. According to this view, the best way to resolve the moral and theological tension is to disallow the fact but not the significance of the marriage. The marriage conveyed a message even if there were no actual nuptials. It is as though Hosea introduced his ministry with a "what if."

Literal Marriage

There are several versions of the literal marriage interpretation, all agreeing that a real marriage took place but disagreeing on the nature or timing of the harlotry ascribed to Gomer.

First, the harlot view maintains that Gomer was in fact impure, perhaps a temple prostitute, when Hosea married her. This view recognizes the moral difficulty but suggests that for the sake of the message, God overruled His previously stated standards. Hosea's marriage to the harlot would emphasize God's gracious love for an undeserving people. Gomer's continuing adultery was an affront to Hosea's kindness as Israel's was to God's.

Second, the idolatress view claims that Gomer was an idol worshiper when she married Hosea. The word "whoredom" would then refer to spiritual rather than sexual fornication.

Third, the proleptic view claims that Gomer was sexually pure at the beginning of the marriage but soon became unfaithful. Prolepsis is the use of a descriptive word in anticipation of a later occurrence that will make the term appropriate. Accordingly, though pure at marriage, Gomer was identified as a "wife of whoredoms" in anticipation of what she would become. God, who knows the end from the beginning, could certainly reveal to Hosea what his bride would do before she actually committed acts of fornication.

Fourth, the hybrid view, which is followed in these notes, is a cross between the harlot view that takes the initial command at face value and the proleptic view that postpones Gomer's infidelity. The word "whoredoms" is an abstract plural that would more likely describe an inner characteristic than an outward behavior. It most likely refers to Gomer's latent bent toward immorality that surfaced not long after the marriage. God revealed to Hosea up front something about Gomer's inner self that would potentially jeopardize the sanctity of the marriage. At the beginning of the marriage she was innocent of any physical fornication, but Hosea knew both what she was capable of doing and most likely would do. It was just a matter of time before propensity became practice. This is a key link to the spiritual parallel for believers: God loves us in spite of what He knows about us.

Outline:

I. Introduction (1:1)

II. Hosea's Personal Life: His Symbolic Message (1:2—3:5)
  - A. The Marriage and Children (1:2—2:1)
    1. Marriage to Gomer as a Symbol of the Nation's Sin (1:2)
    2. Birth and Names of Children as Symbols of Judgment (1:3–9)
    3. Renaming of the Children as a Symbol of Hope (1:10—2:1)
  - B. Application of Hosea's Family Life to Israel (2:2–23)
    1. Sin and Punishment (2:2–13)
    2. Restoration (2:14–23)
  - C. Hosea's Reunion with Gomer and Application to Israel (3:1–5)
    1. The Terms for Reunion (3:1–3)

        2. The Application to the Nation (3:4–5)
- III. Hosea's Prophetic Discourses: His Direct Message (4:1—14:9)
    - A. Synopsis of the Charges against the Nation (4:1–5)
    - B. Sin of Ignorance and Statement of Hope (4:6—6:3)
        1. Deserved Destruction of the Nation (4:6–19)
        2. Guilt of the Nation Follows the Guilt of Its Leaders (5:1–7)
        3. Doom of the Nation (5:8–15)
        4. Statement of Hope and Invitation to Repent (6:1–3)
    - C. Sin of Unfaithfulness and Statement of Hope (6:4—11:11)
        1. Refusal to Repent of Manifold Sins (6:4—8:14)
            - a) Transgression of the Covenant (6:4–11)
            - b) Obstinacy (7:1–16)
            - c) Idolatry (8:1–14)
        2. Deserved Judgment (9:1—10:15)
            - a) Dispersion (9:1–5)
            - b) Barrenness (9:6–17)
            - c) Destruction (10:1–15)
        3. Statement of Hope Springing from God's Love (11:1–11)
    - D. Sin of Faithlessness and Statement of Hope (11:12—14:9)
        1. Sin Described (11:12—13:16)
        2. Repentance and Hope (14:1–9)

THE BOOK OF HOSEA

CHAPTER 1

THE word of the LORD that came unto Hosea, the
son of Beeri, in the days of Uzziah, Jotham, Ahaz,
and Hezekiah, kings of Judah, and in the days of
Jeroboam the son of Joash, king of Israel.
2 The beginning of the word of the LORD by
Hosea. And the LORD said to Hosea, Go, take
unto thee a wife of whoredoms and children of
whoredoms: for the land hath committed great
whoredom, *departing* from the LORD.
3 So he went and took Gomer the daughter of
Diblaim; which conceived, and bare him a son.
4 And the LORD said unto him, Call his name
Jezreel; for yet a little *while*, and I will avenge the
blood of Jezreel upon the house of Jehu, and will
cause to cease the kingdom of the house of Israel.
5 And it shall come to pass at that day, that I will
break the bow of Israel in the valley of Jezreel.
6 ¶ And she conceived again, and bare a daughter.
And *God* said unto him, Call her name Lo-
ruhamah: for I will no more have mercy upon the
house of Israel; but I will utterly take them away.

Chapter 1: *Hosea's family life is used as a portrait of God's relationship with Israel.*

INTRODUCTION (1:1)

1:1 *The word of the LORD that came.* Hosea's timeline sets his ministry in a context of religious pluralism. His parish was ecumenical in the worst way: the state religion inaugurated by Jeroboam I was entrenched and Baal worship lingered. That God raised up Hosea to minister in such a day should give hope to Christians who live in a world that is at odds with the exclusive claims of Christianity. It should be our prayer that God would raise up ministers today with prophetic boldness to declare His Word. In His grace, God has given His Word as the answer to any crisis. The authority and relevance of God's Word is not restricted by either time or borders.

HOSEA'S PERSONAL LIFE: HIS SYMBOLIC MESSAGE (1:2—3:5)

The Marriage and Children (1:2—2:1)

Marriage to Gomer as a Symbol of the Nation's Sin (1:2)

1:2 *wife of whoredoms.* Whoredoms most likely refer to the inward propensity and bent to fornication rather than the actual transgression (see Introduction: Major Problem of Interpretation). Hosea's bride, therefore, was physically pure at the time of the marriage, but the issues of her heart would soon surface. God revealed to Hosea the nature of Gomer's heart, something that otherwise only God would have known. That Hosea married Gomer in spite of what he knew about her parallels God's grace in loving His people in spite of their sins. *children of whoredoms.* Hosea uses a figure of speech involving ellipsis (zeugma) that requires supplying a verb like "beget" before children, which would place the birth of the children after the marriage. The children born subsequently to the marriage shared their mother's wicked heart, which only added to Hosea's grief. The three children symbolize aspects of God's judgment upon the nation (see explanations below). *for the land hath committed . . . LORD.* The Hebrew says, "because the land is certainly committing fornication from after the Lord." Hosea's generation had forsaken the Lord and owned no claim to God's promise. Consequently, judgment was inevitable.

Birth and Names of Children as Symbols of Judgment (1:3–9)

1:3 *bare him a son.* The Hebrew says literally, "bare a son to him," indicating that Hosea was the father of the first child.

1:4 *Jezreel* means "God scatters." The focus here is not on the meaning of the name but on the historical significance of the location, a place frequently associated with murders (1 Kings 21:8–14), assassinations (2 Kings 9:24), and even massacres (2 Kings 10:11). Jezreel pictures the irony of judgment, particularly upon the dynasty of Jehu. Jehu's dynasty commenced with his execution of Ahab's house in Jezreel. According to 2 Kings 10:30, God commended him for his actions. So although Hos. 1:4 places no blame on Jehu, it does preview the bloodshed that would end Jehu's dynasty. Ironically, what was an act of obedience that initiated his house will become an act of punishment because of sins as heinous as those associated with Ahab. *avenge the blood.* The word *avenge* means to inspect or give attention. In Hebrew, *blood* is plural, which always refers to bloodshed and often bloodguilt. God will see the guilt of bloodshed that took place at Jezreel to be upon Jehu's house. Jehu's dynasty will end with the same kind of violence as Ahab's. The Jezreel symbolism juxtaposes two aspects of the coming judgment in one predictive context. First, the Lord announces the end of Jehu's dynasty, which from its inception was limited to four generations (2 Kings 10:30). That prophecy was fulfilled when Shallum assassinated Zechariah (2 Kings 15:8–10). Second, God announces the fall of the whole northern kingdom (2 Kings 17:6,23). Forty-two years separated the two components of the prophecy.

1:5 *break the bow . . . in the valley of Jezreel.* By metonymy, *bow* represents the totality of Israel's military arsenal and strength. Both historically and prophetically, the valley of Jezreel has strategic importance militarily. Megiddo is a key site commanding the valley, which accounts for its identification as the valley of Armageddon.

1:6 *Lo-ruhamah* means "no mercy." The absence of any reference to Hosea may indicate this child was born through

7 But I will have mercy upon the house of Judah,
and will save them by the LORD their God, and
will not save them by bow, nor by sword, nor by
battle, by horses, nor by horsemen.
8 ¶ Now when she had weaned Lo-ruhamah, she
conceived, and bare a son.
9 Then said *God*, Call his name Lo-ammi: for ye
are not my people, and I will not be your *God*.
10 ¶ Yet the number of the children of Israel
shall be as the sand of the sea, which cannot be
measured nor numbered; and it shall come to
pass, *that* in the place where it was said unto
them, Ye *are* not my people, *there* it shall be said
unto them, *Ye are* the sons of the living God.
11 Then shall the children of Judah and the chil-
dren of Israel be gathered together, and appoint
themselves one head, and they shall come up out
of the land: for great *shall be* the day of Jezreel.

CHAPTER 2

SAY ye unto your brethren, Ammi; and to your
sisters, Ru-hamah.
2 Plead with your mother, plead: for she *is* not my
wife, neither *am* I her husband: let her therefore
put away her whoredoms out of her sight, and her
adulteries from between her breasts;
3 Lest I strip her naked, and set her as in the day
that she was born, and make her as a wilderness,
and set her like a dry land, and slay her with thirst.

---

fornication. The symbolism regarding judgment is transparent; it marks the forfeiture of God's compassionate pity.

1:9 *Lo-ammi* means "not my people." The absence of any reference to Hosea may indicate this child also was born through fornication. The symbolism regarding judgment is transparent; the Lord will deal with them as though they were heathens. Lo-ruhamah and Lo-ammi together symbolize the tragedy of the judgment. The Lord would show no mercy in the national disaster and would seemingly set aside the covenant, as they would no longer be His people. Although the covenant is ultimately unconditional because of Christ, individual participation was always conditioned on or, perhaps better, evidenced by faith in the promise. *your God.* The word *God* is not in the Hebrew, but was added by the translators. The addition of *God* in the statement *I will not be your God* logically and contextually corresponds to "not my people" as the opposite of the normal "your God . . . my people" covenant formula. However, the Hebrew text could be rendered either, "and I myself will not be for you" or "even I, I will not be yours." God's not being for them would make them susceptible to any and all opposition. Judgment was inevitable. All of this is in keeping with the covenant curses and blessings of Deut. 27–28.

Renaming of the Children as a Symbol of Hope (1:10—2:1)

1:10 *Yet the number.* Judgment was coming, but restoration was to follow. Peter recognized the full gospel implication of this curse reversal when he applied the promise to believers of the New Testament dispensation (1 Peter 2:9–10).

1:11 *one head.* This looks to a time when the divided kingdom again becomes a united monarchy under the leadership of one head. That one head must be the Messiah-King.

Thoughts for Personal/Family Worship: Chapter 1

1. **The whole message of Hosea ought to generate thoughts of the wonder of God's gracious love for His people. The apostle John declared that "God is love" (1 John 4:16). There is more talk and less understanding about God's love than almost any other divine attribute. Most people define God's love based on their own experience of love as an emotional attachment to something attractive. Even the Christian's love for God is generated by attraction to Him. John says that "we love him, because he first loved us" (1 John 4:19). On this reasoning, people feel that God will love them because they are attractive to God. God, however, does not love because something in the object is worthy or attractive. God loves because He is love. His love springs from His character rather than the character of those He loves. He loves us not because we are what we are, but in spite of what we are. Every Christian must realize that he does not deserve God's favor. It is only possible because God in love sent His Son, the only One worthy of the Father's love, to be the Redeemer of an unlovely people. This realization should arouse humility and gratitude in all who have experienced God's free love revealed and given in Jesus Christ. The prophecy of Hosea is a vivid illustration of the nature of God's free love to an undeserving people.**
2. **Throughout Scripture, God uses marriage as a choice symbol of His relationship with the church, the bride of Christ. This is why every Christian marriage ought to be a living gospel sermon. The marriage analogy puts Israel's apostasy in perspective. The marriage bond assumes, indeed demands, that there be an exclusive union between husband and wife. That must be maintained and guarded. Adultery violates that bond and is a most serious offense against both the spouse and against God (Ex. 20:14). Faithfulness and mutual loyalty between husband and wife are basic to marriage. Unfaithfulness and disloyalty threaten and jeopardize the union. Not surprisingly, then, Scripture often describes Israel's unfaithfulness to the Lord in terms of harlotry or spiritual adultery—a tragically vivid picture of apostasy.**

Chapter 2: ***God outlines His plan to restore His wayward people by isolating them, bringing them to poverty, and alluring them with the prospect of renewed covenant mercy.***

2:1 *Ammi . . . Ru-hamah.* God's withdrawal of His mercy (the significance of Lo-ruhamah) was with a view to the declaration of His mercy again. Though God disowned His people (the significance of Lo-ammi), He reversed this by His announcement that once again He would own them (my people). Again see the covenant theology of Deut. 27–28.

Application of Hosea's Family Life to Israel (2:2–23)

Sin and Punishment (2:2–13)

2:2 Hosea boldly draws the connection between Gomer's adultery and Israel's. *Plead* is usually a legal term designating an accusation or grievance, but here it includes the exhortation to reverse the cause of the grievance, the spiritual adultery. The mother/wife represents Israel whose transgression severed the relationship with the Lord. But He sought to restore it.

2:3 *Lest I strip . . . and slay her with thirst.* Both the imagery of nakedness and barrenness/thirst picture the deprivation from the necessities of life.

4 And I will not have mercy upon her children;
for they *be* the children of whoredoms.
5 For their mother hath played the harlot: she
that conceived them hath done shamefully: for
she said, I will go after my lovers, that give *me* my
bread and my water, my wool and my flax, mine
oil and my drink.
6 ¶ Therefore, behold, I will hedge up thy way
with thorns, and make a wall, that she shall not
find her paths.
7 And she shall follow after her lovers, but she
shall not overtake them; and she shall seek them,
but shall not find *them*: then shall she say, I will
go and return to my first husband; for then *was it*
better with me than now.
8 For she did not know that I gave her corn, and
wine, and oil, and multiplied her silver and gold,
which they prepared for Baal.
9 Therefore will I return, and take away my corn
in the time thereof, and my wine in the season
thereof, and will recover my wool and my flax
given to cover her nakedness.
10 And now will I discover her lewdness in the
sight of her lovers, and none shall deliver her out
of mine hand.
11 I will also cause all her mirth to cease, her feast
days, her new moons, and her sabbaths, and all
her solemn feasts.
12 And I will destroy her vines and her fig trees,
whereof she hath said, These *are* my rewards that
my lovers have given me: and I will make them a
forest, and the beasts of the field shall eat them.
13 And I will visit upon her the days of Baalim,
wherein she burned incense to them, and she
decked herself with her earrings and her jewels,
and she went after her lovers, and forgat me, saith
the LORD.
14 ¶ Therefore, behold, I will allure her, and bring
her into the wilderness, and speak comfortably
unto her.
15 And I will give her her vineyards from thence,
and the valley of Achor for a door of hope: and
she shall sing there, as in the days of her youth,
and as in the day when she came up out of the
land of Egypt.
16 And it shall be at that day, saith the LORD, *that*
thou shalt call me Ishi; and shalt call me no more
Baali.
17 For I will take away the names of Baalim
out of her mouth, and they shall no more be
remembered by their name.
18 And in that day will I make a covenant for
them with the beasts of the field, and with the
fowls of heaven, and *with* the creeping things
of the ground: and I will break the bow and the
sword and the battle out of the earth, and will
make them to lie down safely.
19 And I will betroth thee unto me for ever; yea, I
will betroth thee unto me in righteousness, and in
judgment, and in lovingkindness, and in mercies.
20 I will even betroth thee unto me in faithful-
ness: and thou shalt know the LORD.

2:6–8 *I will hedge up.* God would isolate the nation so that they would recognize His superiority and return to Him.
2:8 *Baal.* Israel committed spiritual whoredoms by switching their devotion from the Lord to Baal. Baal is not so much a proper name of a god as it is a descriptive title, meaning "master," which designated an imagined god to be the head over other imagined gods. There was a commonality in Baal mythology, although the specific identity of the designated Baal would differ from place to place: Hadad, Dagon, Chemosh, etc. Baal worship was essentially a fertility cult involving various rigmaroles of rituals—often lewd ones—to ensure the productivity of the land in each agricultural cycle. It was a religion for profit, worshiping in order to procure things for living. The god whom Israel regarded as their Baal is not specified; neither is it relevant. What is significant is that under the influence of their pagan neighbors and out of selfish motives, they worshiped a god of their own conception.
2:9–13 *take away my corn.* God would impoverish them in order to jog their memory of Him and teach them to depend utterly on Him.

Restoration (2:14–23)

2:14–23 Having gotten their attention through isolation and impoverishment, God would irresistibly entice them to a renewed relationship so that they would really know Him. It appeared that Israel had gone so far away from God that restoration was impossible. But grace is greater than sin and reaches as far as God's intent to maintain His covenant. What Hosea describes corresponds to Jeremiah's new covenant (Jer. 31:31–34). The focus is on a spiritual, unbreakable covenant. Unlike the covenant at Sinai that marked the birth of the nation, the new covenant is individual, internal, irresistible, and irreversible.
2:15 *I will give her her vineyards.* This refers to restoration in the land of promise. The land was God's gift, and enjoying the gift was contingent upon faith and obedience. It also draws a line directly to Christ since dwelling in the land was the experience of rest—a physical rest that was symbolic of the greater spiritual rest that is found solely in Jesus Christ. *The valley of Achor* was a symbol of judgment since the day of Achan's execution after his sin at Jericho (Josh. 7:26). *door of hope.* Judgment would give way to restoration. *she shall sing.* The Hebrew root translated *sing* could also be rendered "answer" or "respond." Either rendering suggests the kind of joy that accompanies the first experiences of grace.
2:16 *Ishi* means "my husband" whereas *Baali* means "my master." The change of names reflects a change of attitude toward the Lord.
2:17 *Baalim* is the plural of Baal.
2:19–20 The Lord's announcement of the renewed marriage reveals that God's love is not impetuous but is based in God's eternal purpose according to His perfect *righteousness*. It is God's covenant loyalty or *lovingkindness* that resolves the apparent tension between divine righteousness and justice with their demands of perfection and God's compassion and faithfulness displayed to those incapable of meeting the demands. There is hope for those prone to wander because the lovingkindness of God endures forever (Ps. 136).

21 And it shall come to pass in that day, I will
hear, saith the LORD, I will hear the heavens, and
they shall hear the earth;
22 And the earth shall hear the corn, and the
wine, and the oil; and they shall hear Jezreel.
23 And I will sow her unto me in the earth; and I
will have mercy upon her that had not obtained
mercy; and I will say to *them which were* not my
people, Thou *art* my people; and they shall say,
Thou art my God.

CHAPTER 3

THEN said the LORD unto me, Go yet, love a
woman beloved of *her* friend, yet an adulteress,
according to the love of the LORD toward the
children of Israel, who look to other gods, and
love flagons of wine.
2 So I bought her to me for fifteen *pieces* of silver,
and *for* an homer of barley, and an half homer of
barley:
3 And I said unto her, Thou shalt abide for me
many days; thou shalt not play the harlot, and
thou shalt not be for *another* man: so *will* I also
be for thee.
4 For the children of Israel shall abide many days
without a king, and without a prince, and without
a sacrifice, and without an image, and without an
ephod, and *without* teraphim:
5 Afterward shall the children of Israel return, and
seek the LORD their God, and David their king;
and shall fear the LORD and his goodness in the
latter days.

CHAPTER 4

HEAR the word of the LORD, ye children of
Israel: for the LORD hath a controversy with the

2:21 *Hear* is literally "answer" and has the idea of responding to something.

2:22–23 The prophet describes the blessing in terms of the children's names. Playing on the name *Jezreel* ("God scatters"), the Lord says that He will *sow . . . in the earth*. This is not a scattering in judgment but an expansion in blessing, an advancing of the kingdom. Similarly, playing on Lo-ruhamah and Lo-ammi, "no mercy" receives *mercy* and "not my people" becomes *my people*. Again see the curse reversal as part of the covenant theology of Deut. 27–28 as well as Peter's application to all believers (1 Peter 2:9–10).

Thoughts for Personal/Family Worship: Chapter 2

1. **God's plan for restoring His sinning people entailed discipline. Love sometimes requires what is not pleasant for the welfare of those loved. According to Scripture, this discipline, although unpleasant, is evidence of love. See Prov. 13:24. We usually call this tough love, but it is love nonetheless. Parents can use this as an opportunity to instruct their children.**
2. **The change of the children's names illustrating Hosea's judgment/hope cycle exemplifies one of the great "buts" of God's grace, paralleling Paul's great "but God" of Eph. 2:4–5. Were it not for these "buts" of grace, there would be no hope of salvation for any. This provides opportunity for reflection and thanksgiving for the personal evidences of God's grace. Asking the question "Where would I be, apart from God's grace?" would be a good way to begin the meditation.**

Chapter 3: *Hosea's reunion with Gomer points to God's restoration of Israel.*

Hosea's Reunion with Gomer and Application to Israel (3:1–5)

The Terms for Reunion (3:1–3)

3:1 *beloved of her friend.* The identity of the friend may refer to one of Gomer's paramours but more likely to Hosea himself. If Hosea, it would underscore his constant love for her in spite of her unfaithfulness. That parallels the gospel truth of God's constant love for His people in spite of their failures. *Adulteress* is actually a verbal form indicating that she had become completely enslaved to this licentious behavior.

3:2–3 *I bought her . . . Thou shalt abide.* Who received the payment and the amount are incidental. The point is that Hosea did what was necessary to restore Gomer and to impose on her restrictions designed to maintain her purity from that point on.

The Application to the Nation (3:4–5)

3:5 The referent of *the LORD their God, and David their king* is the ideal David, David's greater Son, the Messiah. The *and* is explicative and the phrase could be translated "the Lord their God, even David their king." This not only identifies Christ as the object of seeking faith but also links His deity and humanity. The Messiah is the God-Man.

Thoughts for Personal/Family Worship: Chapter 3

Hosea's reunion with Gomer provides another reminder of the wonder of God's gracious love. Gomer gives hope to every sinner. It is not surprising that a book about marriage and family should refer so often to love. The root word for love occurs almost twenty times in Hosea. What is surprising is that the majority of occurrences refer to Israel's illicit love associated with their spiritual adultery and pagan worship. This only highlights the wonder of God's love for them (3:1; 11:1,4; 14:4) and points to the real issue of love. The marriage/family motif certainly speaks of the natural affection that ought to be the experience of every family. Yet the word for love goes far beyond expressions of affection. This love is moved by the will. It designates a compelling inclination of the heart to a chosen object. From the outset, God's love has been a matter of choice; He decides to love His people, and the reason for that loving choice is not in their attractiveness or worthiness. God's love is totally of grace. The motive of God's gracious, electing love is within Himself, not in the objects of His choice. This is what makes grace so amazing.

HOSEA'S PROPHETIC DISCOURSES: HIS DIRECT MESSAGE (4:1—14:9)

Chapter 4: *The Lord indicts Israel and begins to list the charges against them in terms of covenant violations and ignorance of God.*

Synopsis of the Charges against the Nation (4:1–5)

4:1 *the LORD hath a controversy.* Using the imagery of the court,

inhabitants of the land, because *there is* no truth,
nor mercy, nor knowledge of God in the land.
2 By swearing, and lying, and killing, and stealing,
and committing adultery, they break out, and
blood toucheth blood.
3 Therefore shall the land mourn, and every
one that dwelleth therein shall languish, with the
beasts of the field, and with the fowls of heaven;
yea, the fishes of the sea also shall be taken away.
4 Yet let no man strive, nor reprove another: for
thy people *are* as they that strive with the priest.
5 Therefore shalt thou fall in the day, and the
prophet also shall fall with thee in the night, and I
will destroy thy mother.
6 ¶ My people are destroyed for lack of
knowledge: because thou hast rejected knowledge,
I will also reject thee, that thou shalt be no priest
to me: seeing thou hast forgotten the law of thy
God, I will also forget thy children.
7 As they were increased, so they sinned against
me: *therefore* will I change their glory into shame.
8 They eat up the sin of my people, and they set
their heart on their iniquity.
9 And there shall be, like people, like priest: and I
will punish them for their ways, and reward them
their doings.
10 For they shall eat, and not have enough: they
shall commit whoredom, and shall not increase:
because they have left off to take heed to the LORD.
11 Whoredom and wine and new wine take away
the heart.
12 ¶ My people ask counsel at their stocks, and
their staff declareth unto them: for the spirit of
whoredoms hath caused *them* to err, and they
have gone a whoring from under their God.
13 They sacrifice upon the tops of the mountains,
and burn incense upon the hills, under oaks and
poplars and elms, because the shadow thereof
is good: therefore your daughters shall commit
whoredom, and your spouses shall commit
adultery.
14 I will not punish your daughters when they
commit whoredom, nor your spouses when they
commit adultery: for themselves are separated
with whores, and they sacrifice with harlots: there-
fore the people *that* doth not understand shall fall.
15 ¶ Though thou, Israel, play the harlot, *yet* let
not Judah offend; and come not ye unto Gilgal,
neither go ye up to Beth-aven, nor swear, The
LORD liveth.
16 For Israel slideth back as a backsliding heifer:
now the LORD will feed them as a lamb in a large
place.
17 Ephraim *is* joined to idols: let him alone.

---

the Lord summons Israel and brings charges against them. In the following chapters, the Lord irrefutably proves their guilt, justly pronounces sentence against them, and graciously offers restoration. *no truth, nor mercy, nor knowledge.* The threefold charge is summed up by the absence of covenant fidelity in word and deed, of covenant loyalty, and of covenant experience.

4:2 *By swearing.* The general accusations of no truth, mercy, or knowledge are specified in terms of violating the moral law summed up in the Decalogue. By the literary device brachylogy (a partial list to designate totality), the five designated violations of law include the transgression of the whole law. This parallels James's statement in James 2:10–11.

Sin of Ignorance and Statement of Hope (4:6—6:3)

Deserved Destruction of the Nation (4:6–19)

4:6 *lack of knowledge.* The implication is that had they known God, Israel would have avoided the sins and consequent judgment. There is something about knowing God experientially that produces behavior that is pleasing to Him. To know God is to fear God. To fear God is to love God. To love God is to keep His commandments. *forgotten the law ... I will also forget.* Forgetting involves a conscious and willful decision to refuse to acknowledge or think about something. It equates with rejection.

4:8 *They eat up the sin.* Eating sin could refer to consuming the sin offering, but the parallelism to setting their heart on iniquity suggests that sin was the object of their diet, what they thrived on. *they set their heart.* Setting the heart is literally lifting up the soul (or entire being), an idiom expressing dependence. Sin and iniquity were their sustenance.

4:12 *ask counsel at their stocks.* Rather than relying on the Lord and His prophets for revelation, the nation turns to its wooden idols.

4:13 *tops of the mountains.* A reference to the high places associated with pagan shrines.

4:14 *I will not punish.* The withholding of punishment from the daughters and spouses does not imply divine indifference to sin but rather underscores the principal blame for the transgression to be on the males. This is suggested from the causal clause, *for themselves* (masculine gender) *are separated with whores.*

4:15 *Gilgal* and *Beth-aven* were sites associated with Israel's idolatrous worship. Ironically, Beth-aven, meaning "house of idolatry" is the same place as Beth-el, meaning "house of God."

4:16 *Israel slideth back.* To slide back or backslide literally is to be stubborn or rebellious.

4:18 *Their drink is sour.* The word *sour* literally is "turn aside." It could refer either to the drink turning aside in the sense of being depleted (gone) or turning bad (sour). The drink was part of the idolatrous worship and by synecdoche (part for the whole) designates the totality of the ritualistic debauchery. *her rulers with shame do love, Give ye.* The Hebrew is difficult. The idea is that Israel's rulers, literally referred to as shields, were given over to loving shame.

Thoughts for Personal/Family Worship: Chapter 4

1. **As a gospel preacher, Hosea spoke to sin head on. Preaching the gospel always entails preaching against sin, warning of sin's consequences, and announcing sin's remedy. In order to highlight the heinous nature and seriousness of sin, surveying Hosea's terms for sin would be in order. Use this synopsis to guide your meditation. Hosea's sermon provides a casebook of sin. Most of the standard Old Testament words for sin are scattered throughout the prophecy in addition to others that are specifically suited to Hosea's focus on the breach of covenant.**

18 Their drink is sour: they have committed
whoredom continually: her rulers *with* shame do
love, Give ye.
19 The wind hath bound her up in her wings, and
they shall be ashamed because of their sacrifices.

CHAPTER 5

HEAR ye this, O priests; and hearken, ye house of
Israel; and give ye ear, O house of the king; for
judgment *is* toward you, because ye have been a
snare on Mizpah, and a net spread upon Tabor.
2 And the revolters are profound to make slaugh-
ter, though I *have been* a rebuker of them all.
3 I know Ephraim, and Israel is not hid from me:
for now, O Ephraim, thou committest whoredom,
and Israel is defiled.
4 They will not frame their doings to turn unto
their God: for the spirit of whoredoms *is* in the
midst of them, and they have not known the LORD.
5 And the pride of Israel doth testify to his face:
therefore shall Israel and Ephraim fall in their
iniquity; Judah also shall fall with them.
6 They shall go with their flocks and with their
herds to seek the LORD; but they shall not find
him; he hath withdrawn himself from them.
7 They have dealt treacherously against the LORD:
for they have begotten strange children: now shall
a month devour them with their portions.
8 Blow ye the cornet in Gibeah, *and* the trumpet
in Ramah: cry aloud *at* Beth-aven, after thee, O
Benjamin.
9 Ephraim shall be desolate in the day of rebuke:
among the tribes of Israel have I made known
that which shall surely be.
10 The princes of Judah were like them that
remove the bound: *therefore* I will pour out my
wrath upon them like water.
11 Ephraim *is* oppressed *and* broken in judg-
ment, because he willingly walked after the
commandment.
12 Therefore *will* I *be* unto Ephraim as a moth,

Sin: **The word most often translated as "sin" occurs in either verb or noun form at least eleven times (4:7,8; 8:11 [twice],13; 9:9; 10:8,9; 12:8; 13:2,12). This is the word that provides the image of missing a target. It vividly pictures sin as the failure to conform to the standard of God's righteous and inflexible law.**

Iniquity: **The noun usually translated "iniquity" occurs at least as frequently (4:8; 5:5; 7:1; 8:13; 9:7,9; 10:13; 12:8; 13:12; 14:1,2). This word pictures sin as twisted, perverted, or deviant behavior. Significantly, this is the principal word that the Old Testament uses to designate the guilt of sin, and sometimes—although rarely—even the punishment of sin. Thus, when this word occurs, the interpreter must determine whether the text is referring to the actual sin or the guilt that results from the sin.**

Evil: **Another commonly used word for sin usually translated as "evil" or "wickedness" occurs eight times (7:1,2,3,15; 9:15 [twice]; 10:15 [twice]). This word pictures sin as disastrous or calamitous behavior: sin is destructive.**

Rebellion, Harlotry, Etc.: **Other key words, such as "to rebel," occur less frequently (7:13; 8:1; 14:9); some contextually specific words, such as "to play the harlot" and "to commit adultery" occur more frequently (1:2 [twice]; 2:2,4,5; 4:12 [twice]; 5:3,4; 6:10; 9:1 and 2:2; 3:1; 4:2,13,14; 7:4 respectively). But all are instructive, whether picturing sin as corruption (9:9); reproach (12:14); shameful behavior (Hos. 2:5); lewdness (2:10); deceit (6:8; 10:8; 12:12); or stubbornness (9:15).**

2. That Israel was punished in part for a lack of knowledge of God is a sober reminder regarding the importance of knowing God as directive for behavior that is pleasing to Him. Has knowing God changed your life?

Chapter 5: *Israel's sin includes both the religious and civil authorities and extends to the entire congregation.*

Guilt of the Nation Follows the Guilt of Its Leaders (5:1–7)

5:1 *O priests . . . O house of the king.* Both the religious and civil leaders are indicted for their entrapment (*snare*) of the people, compared to bird traps set on high spots. *Mizpah* is a mountain located near Gilead in the Transjordan and *Tabor* the conspicuous hill in the valley of Jezreel.

5:3 *Ephraim* equals Israel. Ephraim, the most notable of the northern tribes, stands for the whole nation.

5:4 *they have not known the LORD.* Knowing God involves both intellectual and experiential aspects. Ignorance of God includes both the lack of apprehension of the truth about God and the nonexistence of any personal relationship with Him. Spiritual ignorance of God and His law is never an excuse; it is, rather, reason for condemnation. So if not knowing God is the problem, knowing Him is the solution. And there is no true knowledge of God apart from Christ.

5:6 *they shall not find.* A solemn reminder of the urgency of seeking the Lord when He allows Himself to be found (Isa. 55:6). Tragically, a time comes when He does not allow Himself to be found (Prov. 1:28); consequentially, there is always an urgency attending invitations to repent.

5:7 *They have dealt treacherously.* Israel's sin is described in terms of marriage violation. Dealing treacherously refers to marital unfaithfulness; *strange children* refer to those born illegitimately. *Month* is literally new moon and refers to the holy day in which special sacrifices were to be offered (Num. 28:11–15). To say it would *devour them* is a vivid way of highlighting the danger of heartless, external rituals (see Hos. 6:6).

Doom of the Nation (5:8–15)

5:8 *Blow ye the cornet.* Blowing the horns and crying aloud were alarm warnings. Sounding the alarm in these cities near Israel's southern border with Benjamin and Judah indicates the extent of the judgment throughout the whole of the northern kingdom.

5:10 *remove the bound.* Removing the boundary lines was one of the covenant violations (Deut. 19:14; 27:17). Such practice was indicative of a pervasive spirit of deceit and selfishness. *I will pour out my wrath.* The image pictures God's overflowing rage.

5:11 *Commandment* is a rare term referring either to vulgar human commands or nonsense statements in mockery of prophetic revelation as in Isa. 28:10,13.

5:12 The *moth* is a symbol of destruction.

and to the house of Judah as rottenness.
13 When Ephraim saw his sickness, and Judah
saw his wound, then went Ephraim to the
Assyrian, and sent to king Jareb: yet could he not
heal you, nor cure you of your wound.
14 For I *will be* unto Ephraim as a lion, and as a
young lion to the house of Judah: I, *even* I, will
tear and go away; I will take away, and none shall
rescue *him*.
15 ¶ I will go *and* return to my place, till they
acknowledge their offence, and seek my face: in
their affliction they will seek me early.

CHAPTER 6

COME, and let us return unto the LORD: for he
hath torn, and he will heal us; he hath smitten,
and he will bind us up.
2 After two days will he revive us: in the third day
he will raise us up, and we shall live in his sight.
3 Then shall we know, *if* we follow on to know the
LORD: his going forth is prepared as the morning;
and he shall come unto us as the rain, as the latter
and former rain unto the earth.
4 ¶ O Ephraim, what shall I do unto thee?
O Judah, what shall I do unto thee? for your
goodness *is* as a morning cloud, and as the early
dew it goeth away.
5 Therefore have I hewed *them* by the prophets;
I have slain them by the words of my mouth: and
thy judgments *are as* the light *that* goeth forth.
6 For I desired mercy, and not sacrifice; and the
knowledge of God more than burnt offerings.
7 But they like men have transgressed the
covenant: there have they dealt treacherously
against me.
8 Gilead *is* a city of them that work iniquity, *and*
is polluted with blood.

5:13 *king Jareb.* The text is literally, "the king of Jareb." Such a place or name is uncertain and most likely is used symbolically with vivid irony. It is related to a verb meaning "to contend." The irony is that the nation sought relief from Assyria, the very place that would soon contend with them to their demise. The nation was guilty of ungodly and unlawful alliances, which reflected their ignorance of God's law and their distrust of Him.
5:15 *I will go and return to my place.* The Lord declared that He would do the hard thing of withdrawing Himself from His people to awaken their senses to their spiritual need of Him. The threat of divine judgment was to be a motive to obedience and repentance. The potential of losing the experience of God's presence should remain an incentive to maintaining personal holiness. *they will seek me early.* Seeking the Lord early refers to the diligence and earnestness of seeking, not the time of seeking.

Thoughts for Personal/Family Worship: Chapter 5

1. **Verse 3 provides an opportunity to underscore the personal application of God's knowledge. Israel's sin was known to God and so is ours. It is impossible to escape His knowledge, and there is a sense in which every sin committed is in His presence. Psalm 139:7 and Heb. 4:13 reinforce this truth.**
2. **Comparing v. 6 with v. 15 provides an opportunity to discuss what it means to seek the Lord with a genuine heart of belief. Not all seeking is successful, yet God promises that those who seek Him with all their heart will find Him. The purpose of the divine discipline was to create that kind of heart.**

Chapter 6: ***After inviting the nation to repent, the Lord contrasts His covenant expectations with their covenant treachery.***

Statement of Hope and Invitation to Repent (6:1–3)

6:1 *let us return.* Return is the principal Old Testament word for repentance and means to turn by reversing directions, by doing an about-face. Repentance requires turning away from sin and turning to the Lord. It involves a change of life. *he will heal.* The invitation to repent rests on the confidence that the Lord's chastening was remedial, designed to motivate repentance (5:15), and that He will graciously restore His people when they genuinely repent. First John 1:9 states that every child of God has this same guarantee.
6:2 *After two days.* The time frame is not to be taken literally but rather idiomatically referring to a brief period. There will be no delay in enjoying the consequences of repentance.
6:3 *Then shall we know.* The Hebrew says literally, "Let us know; let us pursue to know the Lord." It parallels the opening invitation in v. 1 and identifies another principal component of repentance, the knowledge of God, including the certainty of His mercy and grace to the penitent. Since ignorance of God was one of the nation's chief sins (5:4), it follows that pursuing the knowledge of God would be essential to genuine repentance.

Sin of Unfaithfulness and Statement of Hope (6:4—11:11)

Refusal to Repent of Manifold Sins (6:4—8:14)

Transgression of the Covenant (6:4–11)

6:4 *your goodness.* Often translated as mercy or lovingkindness in the KJV, the Hebrew word translated here as *goodness* is a covenant term designating the loyalty of attitude and behavior required from and rightfully expected by the parties in a covenant with one another. It is a covenant obligation. Whereas God's "loyalty" is consistent and everlasting (Ps. 136), Israel's was inconsistent and fleeting. Ultimately, the believer's loyalty to God is exercised in terms of trust and obedience.
6:6 The word *mercy* is the same as "goodness" in v. 4. *the knowledge of God more than burnt offerings.* When religion takes shape without the knowledge of God, it will inevitably and invariably miss the mark of what is acceptable to God and profitable to the soul. Since God is never satisfied with purely external religion, it is imperative for Christians to cultivate and maintain genuine heart devotion before the Lord.
6:7 In Hebrew the word *men* is singular and could refer specifically to Adam and the first transgression of the covenant of works that condemned the whole race of humanity and set the pattern of all other transgressions. Humanity sinned in Adam and like Adam by overstepping or passing over the borders set by the covenant.
6:8 *Gilead* specifically refers to the Transjordan region of Israel but here most likely by synecdoche (part for the whole) designates the entirety of the nation. The word *polluted* comes from a root meaning "heel." The imagery pictures foot tracks of blood.
6:9 *by consent.* Literally, "to Shechem." Some interpreters

9 And as troops of robbers wait for a man, *so* the
company of priests murder in the way by consent:
for they commit lewdness.
10 I have seen an horrible thing in the house of
Israel: there *is* the whoredom of Ephraim, Israel
is defiled.
11 Also, O Judah, he hath set an harvest for thee,
when I returned the captivity of my people.

CHAPTER 7

WHEN I would have healed Israel, then the iniquity
of Ephraim was discovered, and the wickedness
of Samaria: for they commit falsehood; and the
thief cometh in, *and* the troop of robbers spoileth
without.
2 And they consider not in their hearts *that* I
remember all their wickedness: now their own
doings have beset them about; they are before my
face.
3 They make the king glad with their wickedness,
and the princes with their lies.
4 They *are* all adulterers, as an oven heated by
the baker, *who* ceaseth from raising after he hath
kneaded the dough, until it be leavened.
5 In the day of our king the princes have made
him sick with bottles of wine; he stretched out his
hand with scorners.
6 For they have made ready their heart like an
oven, whiles they lie in wait: their baker sleepeth
all the night; in the morning it burneth as a
flaming fire.
7 They are all hot as an oven, and have devoured
their judges; all their kings are fallen: *there is* none
among them that calleth unto me.
8 Ephraim, he hath mixed himself among the
people; Ephraim is a cake not turned.
9 Strangers have devoured his strength, and he
knoweth *it* not: yea, gray hairs are here and there
upon him, yet he knoweth not.
10 And the pride of Israel testifieth to his face:
and they do not return to the LORD their God, nor
seek him for all this.
11 ¶ Ephraim also is like a silly dove without
heart: they call to Egypt, they go to Assyria.
12 When they shall go, I will spread my net upon
them; I will bring them down as the fowls of the
heaven; I will chastise them, as their congregation
hath heard.
13 Woe unto them! for they have fled from me:

---

identify Shechem as the place located between Samaria (the political city) and Beth-el (the principal religious city). The reference would be to the priests' ambushing pilgrims on their way to worship. The translators of the KJV linked the word to the root for "shoulder," suggesting that the priests committed their crimes "shoulder to shoulder" or by consent.

6:11 *he hath set an harvest.* Harvest is a common image of judgment.

Thoughts for Personal/Family Worship: Chapter 6

1. **The opening invitation to repent and the assurance that God will accept genuine repentance give hope and encouragement to every Christian who thinks that he has lost out with God because of his sin. God's grace is greater than sin, and His mercy is infinite.**
2. **God's stated preference for mercy and knowledge of Himself over sacrifice and burnt offerings provides occasion to emphasize the importance of worshiping in spirit and in truth. We have a natural propensity to walk by sight and not by faith. It is possible to go through all the motions of worship without pleasing the Lord or without benefiting the soul. In this sense, think about the dangers of going to church. Remember that while the actions of worship are important, God is always looking at the heart. Today, many without Christ assume that going to church or keeping the Golden Rule will somehow accrue to their favor before God. Even believers sometimes allow their religious routines to substitute for private devotion and a sincere heart. Human reasoning contrasts with the divine preference for heart obedience over manual religion.**

Chapter 7: ***By using various images, the Lord describes Israel's perverse impiety and spiritual insensitivity.***

Obstinacy (7:1–16)

7:1 *Ephraim,* the principal tribe, and *Samaria,* the capital city, stand for the whole nation.

7:2 *they consider not in their hearts.* The Hebrew says literally, "They do not say to their heart." In Hebrew "heart" includes the entirety of inner man—the mind, emotions, and will. Here the focus would be on mental activity; the idea is that they were not giving any thought to the fact that God remembers. In Hebrew, "to remember" is consciously and willfully to think about something. The contrast is stark. They refused to think about what God purposefully and intentionally thought about. The consequences were severe.

7:4 *an oven heated by the baker.* A hot, flaming oven that is not employed for its intended purpose describes the people's misdirected and perverted passions. The following verses play on this imagery of a fire out of control.

7:5 *Scorners* are those who obstinately and contemptuously disdain correction or rebuke. The godly are to disassociate from their attitudes and behavior (Ps. 1:1) rather than joining with them or acting like them.

7:7 *there is none . . . that calleth.* Notwithstanding the evidences of trouble, their failure to call to the Lord in prayer betrayed a spirit of self-reliance. Prayer is always an index of the level of dependence upon the Lord.

7:8 *a cake not turned.* Scorched on one side, raw on the other, the cake would be uneatable. The image describes the failure of the nation to fulfill its purpose. The nation, instituted to be holy (Ex. 19:6), had so allied themselves with the heathen as to be unholy.

7:9 *he knoweth it not.* A reminder that the effects of sin may be gradually imperceptible but ultimately obvious.

7:10 *the pride of Israel.* Ironically, all that the nation presumed to elevate and rely upon (their pride), being without foundation, witnessed against them. Notwithstanding the failure of their self-reliance, they refused to rely on the Lord.

7:11–12 *like a silly dove.* The nation's behavior is compared to the flight patterns of doves in the open sky, movement that appears to be unpredictable, lacking clear direction. But

destruction unto them! because they have trans-
gressed against me: though I have redeemed
them, yet they have spoken lies against me.
14 And they have not cried unto me with their
heart, when they howled upon their beds: they
assemble themselves for corn and wine, *and* they
rebel against me.
15 Though I have bound *and* strengthened their
arms, yet do they imagine mischief against me.
16 They return, *but* not to the most High: they
are like a deceitful bow: their princes shall fall by
the sword for the rage of their tongue: this *shall be*
their derision in the land of Egypt.

CHAPTER 8

SET the trumpet to thy mouth. *He shall come* as an
eagle against the house of the LORD, because they
have transgressed my covenant, and trespassed
against my law.
2 Israel shall cry unto me, My God, we know thee.
3 Israel hath cast off *the thing that is* good: the
enemy shall pursue him.
4 They have set up kings, but not by me: they
have made princes, and I knew *it* not: of their
silver and their gold have they made them idols,
that they may be cut off.
5 ¶ Thy calf, O Samaria, hath cast *thee* off; mine
anger is kindled against them: how long *will it be*
ere they attain to innocency?
6 For from Israel *was* it also: the workman made
it; therefore it *is* not God: but the calf of Samaria
shall be broken in pieces.
7 For they have sown the wind, and they shall
reap the whirlwind: it hath no stalk: the bud shall
yield no meal: if so be it yield, the strangers shall
swallow it up.
8 Israel is swallowed up: now shall they be among
the Gentiles as a vessel wherein *is* no pleasure.
9 For they are gone up to Assyria, a wild ass alone
by himself: Ephraim hath hired lovers.
10 Yea, though they have hired among the nations,
now will I gather them, and they shall sorrow a
little for the burden of the king of princes.
11 Because Ephraim hath made many altars to
sin, altars shall be unto him to sin.
12 I have written to him the great things of my
law, *but* they were counted as a strange thing.

---

notwithstanding their erratic maneuvering that led them to find refuge in Egypt and Assyria, they could not escape the Lord. It is a sober reminder that all our actions and thoughts are open and thoroughly known to God and should therefore motivate holy behavior.

7:14 *they howled upon their beds.* The reference is most likely to the sensuous rituals of Baal worship designed to ensure the harvest.

7:15 To *imagine mischief* is literally to plan or devise evil.

7:16 *A deceitful bow* is one whose string is slack and therefore one whose operation is defective.

Thoughts for Personal/Family Worship: Chapter 7

The principal theme running through the entire chapter concerns the spiritual insensitivity and callousness resulting from sin. The message offers an opportunity to reflect on how deceiving sin can be. The sinning nation was oblivious to God's presence (v. 2), His offers of mercy to them (v. 1), and His past goodness (v. 15). In their self-trust, they never thought to call upon the Lord (v. 7). Failure to pray is always a sign of self-dependence. You can see this whole chapter as an illustration of Jer. 17:5–6 that describes the cursed man in terms of self-trust and spiritual oblivion (the inability to see when the good comes, Jer. 17:6). It demonstrates the danger of following the deceitful and desperately wicked heart (Jer. 17:9).

Chapter 8: *Israel's impending judgment is deserved because of their rebellion against God evident in their idolatry.*

Idolatry (8:1–14)

8:1 *Set the trumpet to thy mouth.* The Hebrew says literally, "to your mouth a horn." The sounding of the horn was to signal an alarm. The absence of the verb tersely underscores the sense of urgency. The word translated *eagle* designates a large bird of prey and can refer to either a carrion vulture or an eagle. If a vulture is in view, the image is that of the Lord's hovering over the temple as though it were a scene of death. If an eagle is in view, the image is of the Lord's swift and swooping attack against the temple because of sin. The KJV, probably because of the opening reference to sounding an alarm, translates it as eagle and sees a reference to impending judgment.

8:2 *Israel shall cry unto me.* A cry of protest and astonishment. Notwithstanding their covenant violations, they assumed that God would not so judge them since they included Him as part of their syncretistic worship. They were satisfied with their external rites; they supposed the Lord would be too.

8:4 *I knew it not.* Since God is omniscient, His not knowing something would be impossible. The Hebrew verb "to know" also has the sense of choosing or selecting. The statements regarding the kings and princes are parallel: just as the kings were not set up according to God's appointment, so the princes were set up without God's approval.

8:5 *Thy calf.* By metonymy, the calf represents the entire system of cultic rituals.

8:6 *but the calf . . . shall be broken in pieces.* The breaking of the calf is evidence of the idol's powerlessness, proof against any claim of deity and confirmation that the whole religious system which the calf symbolized was worthless. Compare the breaking of Dagon before the ark of the covenant in 1 Sam. 5.

8:8 *now shall they be among the Gentiles.* At the beginning of Israel's national existence the Lord declared them to be unique among the nations as His special treasure (Ex. 19:5), but now their sin has obliterated that distinction among the nations. God no longer takes pleasure in them.

8:9 *a wild ass alone.* An image of senseless stupidity.

8:10 The word *a little* is temporal, having the idea of a little while or soon. The gathering for judgment was imminent. *For the burden* is causal. Soon they would sorrow because of the heavy load imposed on them by the foreign king—a reference to the Assyrian captivity.

8:12 The word *law* is the most general word for special revelation, encompassing all of God's Word, not just legislation

13 They sacrifice flesh *for* the sacrifices of mine
offerings, and eat *it; but* the LORD accepteth them
not; now will he remember their iniquity, and
visit their sins: they shall return to Egypt.
14 For Israel hath forgotten his Maker, and
buildeth temples; and Judah hath multiplied
fenced cities: but I will send a fire upon his cities,
and it shall devour the palaces thereof.

CHAPTER 9

REJOICE not, O Israel, for joy, as *other* people: for
thou hast gone a whoring from thy God, thou
hast loved a reward upon every cornfloor.
2 The floor and the winepress shall not feed
them, and the new wine shall fail in her.
3 They shall not dwell in the LORD's land; but
Ephraim shall return to Egypt, and they shall eat
unclean *things* in Assyria.
4 They shall not offer wine *offerings* to the LORD,
neither shall they be pleasing unto him: their
sacrifices *shall be* unto them as the bread of
mourners; all that eat thereof shall be polluted:
for their bread for their soul shall not come into
the house of the LORD.
5 What will ye do in the solemn day, and in the
day of the feast of the LORD?
6 For, lo, they are gone because of destruction:
Egypt shall gather them up, Memphis shall
bury them: the pleasant *places* for their silver,
nettles shall possess them: thorns *shall be* in their
tabernacles.
7 The days of visitation are come, the days of
recompence are come; Israel shall know *it*: the
prophet *is* a fool, the spiritual man *is* mad, for the
multitude of thine iniquity, and the great hatred.
8 The watchman of Ephraim *was* with my God:
but the prophet *is* a snare of a fowler in all his
ways, *and* hatred in the house of his God.
9 They have deeply corrupted *themselves*, as in
the days of Gibeah: *therefore* he will remember
their iniquity, he will visit their sins.
10 I found Israel like grapes in the wilderness;
I saw your fathers as the firstripe in the fig tree

---

or commandments. When God gave His law, it was a means of aiding His people to love Him; it was a gracious thing for Him to do. How one responds to God's Word is an index to one's response to grace.

8:13 *now will he remember.* The Lord had not forgotten their sins but the time had come when He would purposefully think about their iniquity and act accordingly. To *visit* literally has the idea of inspecting or investigating and appropriately parallels to *remember*. God's examination exposes their sins and results in punishment. Together the verbs underscore the priority that God was giving to the matter. *Egypt* should be taken figuratively to refer to the place of bondage regardless of location. For this generation of Israel, Assyria would be that place.

8:14 *Israel hath forgotten.* To forget is a conscious and willful decision to refuse to think about. The Hebrew word translated *temples* can also designate palaces. Since reference is made to Judah's palaces (different word) at the end of the verse, Israel's palaces may be in view here. The *fenced cities* were designed for defense but were ineffective against the Lord's commissioned destruction.

Thoughts for Personal/Family Worship: Chapter 8

1. **Verse 7 speaks of the sowing-reaping principle commonly used in Scripture (Hos. 10:12; Gal. 6:7–8). The law of the harvest rules. Sinful behavior has consequences to avoid, and righteous behavior has consequences to desire. We should strive, therefore, to do those things pleasing to the Lord, for He is the rewarder of those who seek Him (Heb. 11:6).**
2. **Verse 12 reminds us of the wonderful gift of God's Word and how important it is that we properly respond to it. The great things of God's law define how God's children are supposed to live. The law and every other word that God has given are expressions of His love. Israel's disobedience to God's law was a rejection, therefore, of His love. We should be careful to receive God's Word as a gracious gift and respond to it in obedience as evidence of our love to Him.**

Deserved Judgment (9:1—10:15)

Chapter 9: *Israel's judgment will include exile and decrease in population.*

Dispersion (9:1–5)

9:1 *Rejoice not.* The circumstance of the prohibited rejoicing most likely is the harvest, which the heathen and Israel mistakenly attributed to Baal. *thou hast gone a whoring.* Their spiritual adultery that separated them from God is described in the sensuous terms of the fertility rituals of the Baal cult. The word *reward* refers specifically to the wages paid to a harlot and points to the cult prostitution occurring at the threshingfloors of grain as part of the pagan rites.

9:3 *They shall not dwell in the LORD's land.* The land was the Lord's, not Baal's, and exile from the land was the long-warned penalty for violating the covenant (Deut. 28:63). The reference to *Egypt* is metonymical, referring to a place of bondage regardless of location. In this context, the place of bondage was *Assyria*.

9:5 The exile will preclude them from worshiping the Lord according to the prescribed manner. The *solemn day* and the *day of the feast* are the same (literally, "in the day of the appointment, even in the day of the feast") and refer to the special occasions that the Lord set to celebrate various aspects of His goodness and provision (Lev. 23). The question is rhetorical, implying that there is nothing they can do.

Barrenness (9:6–17)

9:6 *Memphis* was one of the cities of Egypt frequently serving as the capital. Again the focus here is not on location but function. Assyria now was the oppressor of Israel—their Egypt.

9:7 The Hebrew word translated *visitation* basically means examination or inspection. Depending on what is observed in the examination, it can refer to either punishment or blessing. Here it refers to the time of punishment as defined in the following reference to the days of recompense or retribution. It was payback time for their transgressions.

9:9 The depth of depravity is compared to the atrocities committed in *Gibeah* by the Benjamites during the days of the judges involving the abuse, death, and subsequent

at her first time: *but* they went to Baal-peor, and
separated themselves unto *that* shame; and *their*
abominations were according as they loved.
11 *As for* Ephraim, their glory shall fly away like
a bird, from the birth, and from the womb, and
from the conception.
12 Though they bring up their children, yet will
I bereave them, *that there shall* not *be* a man *left*:
yea, woe also to them when I depart from them!
13 Ephraim, as I saw Tyrus, *is* planted in a
pleasant place: but Ephraim shall bring forth his
children to the murderer.
14 Give them, O LORD: what wilt thou give? give
them a miscarrying womb and dry breasts.
15 All their wickedness *is* in Gilgal: for there I
hated them: for the wickedness of their doings
I will drive them out of mine house, I will love
them no more: all their princes *are* revolters.
16 Ephraim is smitten, their root is dried up, they
shall bear no fruit: yea, though they bring forth,
yet will I slay *even* the beloved *fruit* of their womb.
17 My God will cast them away, because they
did not hearken unto him: and they shall be
wanderers among the nations.

CHAPTER 10

ISRAEL *is* an empty vine, he bringeth forth fruit
unto himself: according to the multitude of his fruit
he hath increased the altars; according to the good-
ness of his land they have made goodly images.
2 Their heart is divided; now shall they be found
faulty: he shall break down their altars, he shall
spoil their images.
3 For now they shall say, We have no king,
because we feared not the LORD; what then should
a king do to us?
4 They have spoken words, swearing falsely in
making a covenant: thus judgment springeth up
as hemlock in the furrows of the field.
5 The inhabitants of Samaria shall fear because
of the calves of Beth-aven: for the people thereof
shall mourn over it, and the priests thereof *that*
rejoiced on it, for the glory thereof, because it is
departed from it.
6 It shall be also carried unto Assyria *for* a present
to king Jareb: Ephraim shall receive shame, and
Israel shall be ashamed of his own counsel.
7 *As for* Samaria, her king is cut off as the foam
upon the water.

---

dismemberment of the Levite's concubine (Judg. 19).

9:10 *but they went to Baal-peor.* The imagery alludes to Israel's early history when, since God was blessing them, Balaam could not curse them, but they were soon seduced to shameful behavior at Peor (Num. 25:1–18). In their sin of choosing Baal, they became just as detestable as the god they chose to love.

9:11 By metonymy, *their glory* refers to the population of the nation that will be dispersed in judgment and decline in the future generations.

9:12 *there shall not be a man left.* Hyperbole, an intentional exaggeration, to underscore the severity of the Lord's chastisement.

9:13 *Ephraim, as I saw Tyrus.* Both Israel and Tyre were objects of Assyrian aggression. The reference to Tyrus, a pagan Phoenician city and a target of God's judgment (Isa. 23:8–18; Amos 1:9–10), suggests that Israel, by their sin, forfeited their privileges as the covenant nation and had become like any other nation. See a similar thought in Amos 9:7.

9:15 *Gilgal* was one of the cultic centers and refers not so much to the specific location but to all the religious perversions that occurred there and throughout the land. *I hated them . . . I will love them no more.* Hating and loving no more are parallel thoughts. Both hate and love are principally volitional terms referring to matters of choice. The statements here refer to God's rejection of the nation.

9:17 *My God will cast them away.* See Deut. 28:64. Hosea constantly employs covenant imagery in announcing the judgment. What Moses warned, Hosea applies.

Thoughts for Personal/Family Worship: Chapter 9

The description of the judgment in this chapter is summed up in v. 7 as "the days of visitation:" Israel was getting what they deserved. Nothing is more fearful than to get what we deserve from God. The word for visitation, having the basic idea of inspection or examination, often points to God's dealing with people in consequence or in accordance to what He sees about them. That man is so small and God is so infinitely great makes His visitation with man an amazing reality (Ps. 8:3–4). Yet, it is also an awful reality and should therefore be a motive to purity knowing that God will punish iniquity (see Amos 3:2 where the word "punish" is the same Hebrew word as "visit"). Ps. 17:3 expresses the proper response to the fact that God examines all of life: "I am purposed that my mouth shall not transgress." God's involvement in the affairs of man is never neutral.

Chapter 10: *Israel's sin leads to total destruction.*

Destruction (10:1–15)

10:1 *Israel is an empty vine.* That the empty vine brought forth a multitude of fruit means that it was not barren. The image is of a vine overflowing with fruit to be harvested. The tragedy is that Israel employed the fruit for selfish purposes and attributed the affluence to Baal, hence the multiplication of altars and manufacture of images.

10:2 *Their heart is divided.* The Hebrew root could also be translated as "slippery." Whether divided or smooth, it is a heart that is deceptively unstable and desperately wicked (Jer. 17:9; James 1:8). *he shall break down their altars.* Literally, "he shall break the neck of their altars," a vivid picture of the decisive finality of the destruction.

10:4 *Judgment* does not refer to an act of punishment but rather to the exercise of justice. The evidence of their deceit was that justice was like a weed growing where good grain was expected. There was no justice at all.

10:5 *Beth-aven* ("the house of idolatry") was Hosea's sarcastic designation of Beth-el ("house of God"), one of Israel's cultic centers. His reference to *the calves* may be another prophetic sarcasm. There was most likely only a single calf at Beth-el, but the Hebrew often uses the plural to magnify an object, called the plural of excellence or majesty. So, ironically, what they regarded as their supreme object of worship had no power to protect itself from being part of Assyria's spoil (10:6).

10:6 *king Jareb.* See note at 5:13 for an explanation of *Jareb*.

8 The high places also of Aven, the sin of Israel,
shall be destroyed: the thorn and the thistle shall
come up on their altars; and they shall say to the
mountains, Cover us; and to the hills, Fall on us.
9 O Israel, thou hast sinned from the days of
Gibeah: there they stood: the battle in Gibeah
against the children of iniquity did not overtake
them.
10 *It is* in my desire that I should chastise them;
and the people shall be gathered against them,
when they shall bind themselves in their two
furrows.
11 And Ephraim *is as* an heifer *that is* taught,
and loveth to tread out *the corn*; but I passed over
upon her fair neck: I will make Ephraim to ride;
Judah shall plow, *and* Jacob shall break his clods.
12 Sow to yourselves in righteousness, reap
in mercy; break up your fallow ground: for *it
is* time to seek the LORD, till he come and rain
righteousness upon you.
13 Ye have plowed wickedness, ye have reaped
iniquity; ye have eaten the fruit of lies: because
thou didst trust in thy way, in the multitude of
thy mighty men.
14 Therefore shall a tumult arise among thy
people, and all thy fortresses shall be spoiled, as
Shalman spoiled Beth-arbel in the day of battle:
the mother was dashed in pieces upon *her* children.
15 So shall Beth-el do unto you because of your
great wickedness: in a morning shall the king of
Israel utterly be cut off.

CHAPTER 11

WHEN Israel *was* a child, then I loved him, and
called my son out of Egypt.
2 *As* they called them, so they went from them:
they sacrificed unto Baalim, and burned incense
to graven images.
3 I taught Ephraim also to go, taking them by
their arms; but they knew not that I healed them.
4 I drew them with cords of a man, with bands
of love: and I was to them as they that take off
the yoke on their jaws, and I laid meat unto them.
5 ¶ He shall not return into the land of Egypt,
but the Assyrian shall be his king, because they
refused to return.
6 And the sword shall abide on his cities, and

10:8 *The high places also of Aven.* Literally, the high places of idolatry—a reference to the whole of Israel's cultic rituals.
10:9 *Gibeah* was proverbial for moral depravity. See note at 9:9 for the historical context.
10:10 *in their two furrows.* Literally, "to two of their eyes." The idea is that the atrocities of the judgment would be in plain view.
10:11 *Ephraim is as an heifer.* The contrast is between the unbridled and yoked beast. By analogy, the freedom of the nation was going to transition to the yoke and burden of foreign bondage.
10:12 *it is time to seek the LORD.* Notwithstanding the certain judgment, Hosea admonishes the nation to fulfill their covenant demands in order to experience covenant benefits.
10:13 The sowing-reaping imagery is clear (Gal. 6:7). It is always tragic when God gives what is deserved.
10:14 *Shalman.* Perhaps a reference to the Assyrian king Shalmeneser, infamous for his battle atrocities.
10:15 *Beth-el,* representing the cause of judgment (the religious syncretism), is viewed as the agent of judgment. *In a morning* refers not so much to the time of day but to the sudden swiftness in which the kingdom will fall.

Thoughts for Personal/Family Worship: Chapter 10

1. **The invitation to repent and seek the Lord (v. 12) stands in stark contrast to what appears to be a helpless and hopeless situation of sin and punishment. The invitation itself testifies to God's grace being greater than man's sin. Yet it is a sober reminder that men must come to God on His terms and at His time. It was time to seek the Lord, but Isaiah indicates that the seeking must occur "while he may be found" (Isa. 55:6). The force of that verb is "while He permits Himself to be found." The implication is that He is not always findable (Prov. 1:28). There is always urgency in heeding the Word of God.**
2. **The contrast between vv. 12 and 13 illustrates the sowing-reaping principle both positively and negatively. Righteousness reaps mercy, but wickedness reaps iniquity (a word that can refer to punishment as well as sin). This law of the harvest ought to be one of the motives for us to live in purity and holiness.**

Chapter 11: *In spite of God's tender love and compassion for Israel, they continue to spurn Him.*

Statement of Hope Springing from God's Love (11:1–11)

11:1 *out of Egypt.* The exodus marked the beginning of Israel's national identity and throughout the Old Testament was evidence of God's covenant and electing love. The exodus was a paradigm of God's gracious salvation. Matthew 2:15 forthrightly declares the Christological import of Hosea's statement by applying Israel's exodus to Jesus' deliverance from Herod's plot. By analogy, just as God delivered Israel from bondage to ensure the progression of redemptive history leading to Christ, so God delivered Christ from Herod, thus preserving His Son to accomplish His redemptive purpose.
11:2 *As they called them, so they went from them.* Israel's response to God's call was contrary to expectation. Rather than heeding the call, they went into idolatry. The plural subject of the calling most likely refers to the frequent call of the prophets, sent by God to reiterate the Exodus message. That prophetic witness was repeatedly rejected (Jer. 7:25–26).
11:3 *I taught Ephraim also to go.* In Hebrew, the root for the verb "to teach to go" means "feet" and thus refers specifically to teaching to walk. It is a tender image of a parent holding up the arms of a toddler, supporting his first steps.
11:4 *I laid meat unto them.* Literally, "I bent down to him, I fed"—another image of a parent's tender care of spoon-feeding the child.
11:5 The link between *Egypt* and *Assyria* is now explicit. What Egypt had been, Assyria was about to become—the place of bondage.
11:6 *Branches* translates a word that refers to something extending, such as a limb. Here it most likely refers to that which extends from a gate to keep it locked, its bar or bolt. The point is that the city under attack cannot be secured.

shall consume his branches, and devour *them*,
because of their own counsels.
7 And my people are bent to backsliding from
me: though they called them to the most High,
none at all would exalt *him*.
8 How shall I give thee up, Ephraim? *how* shall
I deliver thee, Israel? how shall I make thee as
Admah? *how* shall I set thee as Zeboim? mine
heart is turned within me, my repentings are
kindled together.
9 I will not execute the fierceness of mine anger, I
will not return to destroy Ephraim: for I *am* God,
and not man; the Holy One in the midst of thee:
and I will not enter into the city.
10 They shall walk after the LORD: he shall roar
like a lion: when he shall roar, then the children
shall tremble from the west.
11 They shall tremble as a bird out of Egypt, and
as a dove out of the land of Assyria: and I will
place them in their houses, saith the LORD.
12 Ephraim compasseth me about with lies, and
the house of Israel with deceit: but Judah yet
ruleth with God, and is faithful with the saints.

CHAPTER 12

EPHRAIM feedeth on wind, and followeth after the
east wind: he daily increaseth lies and desolation;
and they do make a covenant with the Assyrians,
and oil is carried into Egypt.
2 The LORD hath also a controversy with Judah,
and will punish Jacob according to his ways;
according to his doings will he recompense him.
3 ¶ He took his brother by the heel in the womb,
and by his strength he had power with God:
4 Yea, he had power over the angel, and prevailed:
he wept, and made supplication unto him: he
found him *in* Beth-el, and there he spake with us;

11:7 The word translated *backsliding* is a principal word for apostasy. *though they called.* The plural subject of "call" again refers to the ministry of the prophets whose message was spurned.
11:8 *Admah* and *Zeboim* were allies of Sodom and Gomorrah (Gen. 14:8) who suffered the same annihilation (Deut. 29:23). The destruction of these cities was proverbial of total and irreversible destruction. Although judgment was coming to Israel, it would not match the annihilation of these ancient cities. *mine heart . . . my repentings.* These are bold anthropopathisms, human emotions attributed to God to emphasize the intensity of His compassion.
11:9 *I will not return to destroy.* This is an idiom meaning that God will not destroy again. His chastisement of the nation is reasoned and controlled—not a temper out of control like what is common among men. *I will not enter into the city.* Entering the city has military connotations. The Lord's refusal to enter is another evidence of His restraint in judgment.
11:10–11 Together these verses depict the time of restoration when the Lord irresistibly reassembles the dispersed in their own land. This is the prospect of hope.

Sin of Faithlessness and Statement of Hope (11:12—14:9)
Sin Described (11:12—13:16)

11:12 The contrast between Israel and Judah is pronounced. Judah had not yet degenerated to the depth and blatancy of Israel's sin. *compasseth me about.* The deceit and treachery that surrounded the Lord graphically describes the extent of the sin; it was everywhere. *Judah yet ruleth with God.* In contrast, Judah's ruling with God has the idea of fellowship, a walking with the Lord. The word translated *saints* literally is "holy ones." It could well refer to God's people, but it may be a plural of majesty referring to God Himself. This would parallel the specific reference to God. See Prov. 9:10, for instance, for an example of this sense for "holy ones" (or "the holy").

Thoughts for Personal/Family Worship: Chapter 11

Remembering our redemption is a good motive for proper living. The opening reference to the exodus is a reminder of God's grace, power, and provision of effective atonement in saving His people. The more we reflect on God's grace in saving us through faith in Christ's finished and effective atoning work, the more we should be moved to live in gratitude the new life we have in Christ. When Israel spurned God's love, it was contrary to what would be expected in view of what He had done for them.

Chapter 12: *Notwithstanding the Lord's consistent prophetic witness to the nation, they are oblivious to His Word and persist in their sins.*

12:1 *Ephraim feedeth on wind.* Feeding or grazing on the wind and pursuing the *east wind* are vivid images of futility used to describe the foolish foreign alliances Israel assumed would be to their advantage. *they do make a covenant with the Assyrians.* Second Kings 17:1–6 may record the actual historical event to which Hosea refers.
12:2 *Controversy* is a legal term. The Lord is bringing an indictment against Judah. Although the southern kingdom had not yet matched Israel's sin, they were not exempt from divine justice. God would deal justly with Jacob *according to his ways* (his overall character and way of life) and *his doings* (his specific acts of behavior). The prospect of getting what we deserve from God is fearful.
12:3 *He took his brother by the heel.* Israel's character and behavior are traced to their covenant ancestor and events of his birth and life (Gen. 25–35). In fact, Jacob's name is derived from the word "heel," a key factor in the birth narrative. It has the idea of supplanting or overtaking and suggests Jacob's propensity to control and manipulate his own circumstances. In the life of the patriarch, his bent to control and dominate led to both bad and beneficial consequences. It is most likely this domineering character trait that is the point of similarity between the patriarch and the nation.
12:4 *power over the angel.* The angel with whom Jacob wrestled was the angel of the Lord, a Christophany or preincarnate appearance of Christ. Hosea's reference to Jacob's weeping is not found in the Genesis account (Gen. 32:24–28) but adds significant insight into the means by which Jacob *prevailed.* His prevailing with God involved his humble submission to Him. The reference to Jacob's finding the Lord in *Beth-el* ("house of God") is a pointed irony in view of Hosea's frequent reference to Beth-el's becoming Beth-aven ("house of idolatry"). National Jacob lost out with God in the very place the patriarch Jacob had found Him.

5 Even the LORD God of hosts; the LORD *is* his
memorial.
6 Therefore turn thou to thy God: keep mercy
and judgment, and wait on thy God continually.
7 ¶ *He is* a merchant, the balances of deceit *are*
in his hand: he loveth to oppress.
8 And Ephraim said, Yet I am become rich, I have
found me out substance: *in* all my labours they
shall find none iniquity in me that *were* sin.
9 And I *that am* the LORD thy God from the land
of Egypt will yet make thee to dwell in tabernacles,
as in the days of the solemn feast.
10 I have also spoken by the prophets, and I have
multiplied visions, and used similitudes, by the
ministry of the prophets.
11 *Is there* iniquity *in* Gilead? surely they are
vanity: they sacrifice bullocks in Gilgal; yea, their
altars *are* as heaps in the furrows of the fields.
12 And Jacob fled into the country of Syria, and
Israel served for a wife, and for a wife he kept
sheep.
13 And by a prophet the LORD brought Israel out
of Egypt, and by a prophet was he preserved.
14 Ephraim provoked *him* to anger most bitterly:
therefore shall he leave his blood upon him, and
his reproach shall his Lord return unto him.

CHAPTER 13

WHEN Ephraim spake trembling, he exalted him-
self in Israel; but when he offended in Baal, he died.
2 And now they sin more and more, and have
made them molten images of their silver, *and*
idols according to their own understanding, all of
it the work of the craftsmen: they say of them, Let
the men that sacrifice kiss the calves.
3 Therefore they shall be as the morning cloud,
and as the early dew that passeth away, as the chaff
that is driven with the whirlwind out of the floor,
and as the smoke out of the chimney.
4 Yet I *am* the LORD thy God from the land of
Egypt, and thou shalt know no god but me: for
there is no saviour beside me.
5 ¶ I did know thee in the wilderness, in the land
of great drought.
6 According to their pasture, so were they filled;
they were filled, and their heart was exalted;
therefore have they forgotten me.
7 Therefore I will be unto them as a lion: as a
leopard by the way will I observe *them*:
8 I will meet them as a bear *that is* bereaved *of her*
whelps, and will rend the caul of their heart, and
there will I devour them like a lion: the wild beast
shall tear them.

12:5 The title *God of hosts* has a military connotation. The Lord is the God of armies, the Commander-in-Chief. Jacob, the controller, learned that Jehovah was the ultimate controller and commander of all.

12:6 *turn . . . keep mercy . . . wait.* The prophet implores the nation to learn what their ancestor learned and pursue God's favor by repenting, maintaining covenant obligations, and persistently looking to Him in faith.

12:7 That the word translated *merchant* is the pejorative word "Canaan" in the Hebrew adds to the opprobrium of the indictment.

12:8 *they shall find none iniquity in me.* Notwithstanding all the evidence of the nation's transgression, they regarded themselves as innocent. It is a spiritual law that the further a person is from God the less sensitive to sin he will be. The converse is true as well: the closer to God a person is, the more sensitive to sin he will be.

12:9 *I . . . am the LORD thy God from the land of Egypt.* A reminder that God has remained consistently the same from the beginning of His relationship with the nation when He delivered them from Egypt and provided for them in their wilderness wanderings.

12:10 *spoken by the prophets.* See Jer. 7:23–26. As God consistently speaks, He testifies to His grace and to the nation's hardness.

12:11 In 6:8, the prophet singled out *Gilead* as a place associated with violent social crimes, and here it is clear that *Gilgal* was a religious site. Together the cities represent the entire nation, guilty of both social and religious sins. The two spheres of sin connect the two divisions of the law of God, evincing the inviolable principle that transgression against true worship always couples with transgressions against society.

12:12 *Jacob fled.* Hosea abruptly alludes to the patriarchal narrative of Jacob's escape from Esau and his service to Laban (Gen. 29). His exile to Syria was the consequence of his deceitful actions. In Laban, he found his manipulative match. Hosea's point is that just as Jacob's sin caused these circumstances, so the nation's sin caused the reproach the Lord would bring upon them (12:14).

12:13 *by a prophet.* A reference to Moses, the most significant of the Old Testament prophets foreshadowing the coming of the Messiah, the ideal Prophet (Deut. 18:15,18).

12:14 In Hebrew *blood* is plural, a figure used to designate guilt.

Thoughts for Personal/Family Worship: Chapter 12

Just as Paul directs attention to Old Testament history to teach spiritual lessons, so does Hosea in speaking to his generation about the history of the patriarch Jacob. Central to the lesson is Jacob's wrestling with the angel, which is a vivid illustration of earnest and prevailing prayer. Too often our prayers are casual and unthinking. This reminds us of the energy and diligence that ought to mark our praying. Notwithstanding the struggle and how injurious it was to his flesh, Jacob would not let go until he received the blessing (Gen. 32:24–28). So we must keep on asking until we receive the answer. This is a reminder that prayer is an arduous exercise of faith.

Chapter 13: *Israel's persistent sin in spite of God's past redemption from Egypt and His promised redemption from death results in devastating judgment.*

13:1 Hosea contrasts Ephraim's rise to prominence among the tribes of Israel with their demise because of their guilt in worshiping Baal.

13:2 *kiss the calves.* The imagery of kissing the calves suggests submission and homage. The gesture required to be directed to the messianic Son to escape His anger (Ps. 2:12), they offered to idols.

13:8 The Hebrew word translated *caul* literally means "enclosure" and refers to the chest cavity.

9 ¶ O Israel, thou hast destroyed thyself; but in
me *is* thine help.
10 I will be thy king: where *is any other* that may
save thee in all thy cities? and thy judges of whom
thou saidst, Give me a king and princes?
11 I gave thee a king in mine anger, and took *him*
away in my wrath.
12 The iniquity of Ephraim *is* bound up; his sin
is hid.
13 The sorrows of a travailing woman shall come
upon him: he *is* an unwise son; for he should
not stay long in *the place of* the breaking forth of
children.
14 I will ransom them from the power of the
grave; I will redeem them from death: O death, I
will be thy plagues; O grave, I will be thy destruc-
tion: repentance shall be hid from mine eyes.
15 ¶ Though he be fruitful among *his* brethren,
an east wind shall come, the wind of the LORD
shall come up from the wilderness, and his spring
shall become dry, and his fountain shall be dried
up: he shall spoil the treasure of all pleasant
vessels.
16 Samaria shall become desolate; for she hath
rebelled against her God: they shall fall by the
sword: their infants shall be dashed in pieces, and
their women with child shall be ripped up.

CHAPTER 14

O ISRAEL, return unto the LORD thy God; for thou
hast fallen by thine iniquity.
2 Take with you words, and turn to the LORD: say
unto him, Take away all iniquity, and receive *us*
graciously: so will we render the calves of our lips.
3 Asshur shall not save us; we will not ride upon
horses: neither will we say any more to the work
of our hands, *Ye are* our gods: for in thee the
fatherless findeth mercy.
4 ¶ I will heal their backsliding, I will love them

13:11 *I gave thee a king.* Given the historical situation, the singular *king* most likely is a collective noun, referring not to a specific king but to a whole series of kings. During the closing years of Israel's kingdom, there was great political instability evidenced by the rise and fall of several kings. This absence of good and stable leadership was itself indication of God's displeasure.
13:12 *bound up . . . hid.* The image is of Ephraim's sin being packaged and stored, implying that it was being held in reserve for its time of reckoning.
13:13 The image suggests that when the time for birth arrives, the *unwise son* does not come to the mouth of the womb, to the birth canal. He refuses to be born, to come to the new beginning.
13:14 *I will ransom them from the power of the grave.* In stark contrast to man's refusal and inability to be born, God declares His purpose to deliver from death, both spiritual and physical. Hope for life resides in God alone. The New Testament quotes this text in regard to the resurrection of the body (1 Cor. 15:55), applying it directly to God's purpose and power to deliver from physical death. *repentance shall be hid from mine eyes.* The idea is that God will not relent or change His mind regarding the promised redemption from and destruction of death. The promise of the gospel is sure and cannot be frustrated.
13:15–16 These verses abruptly shift from the declaration of hope in v. 14 to the pronouncement of horrific judgment on the nation. God's ultimate purpose in delivering His people is certain, but that unchanging purpose does not excuse or exempt the current generation of Israel from the consequences of rebellion against the Lord.

Thoughts for Personal/Family Worship: Chapter 13

1. **The chapter begins with a warning of the dangers of idolatry. Israel exchanged true spiritual worship for sight worship. That God regards idolatry of any sort as an abomination and a personal insult is obvious from the most cursory reading of the Bible (Rom.1:18,23,25). Idolatry facilitates worship since it is always easier to operate by sight instead of faith, but it is a dark and serious sin. Idolatry goes beyond just images, statues, or paintings. Since the heart, as Calvin said, "is a perpetual factory of idols," it is easy to turn legitimate practices of worship into perversions. We must be careful to worship in spirit and in truth.**
2. **Verse 14 underscores the absolute certainty of the gospel. The promised resurrection, the necessary consequence of Christ's resurrection (1 Cor. 15:12–22), is based on the immutability of God. Changing His mind regarding His redemptive purpose for His people is impossible. This parallels Malachi's statement linking God's unchangeableness to Jacob's not being consumed (Mal. 3:6). This should generate praise and thanksgiving for our salvation, knowing that even though we may be unfaithful, He never is. He always keeps His word.**

Chapter 14: *The call to repent includes instructions for repentance and a description of the blessings and benefits of restored relationship with the Lord.*

Repentance and Hope (14:1–9)

14:2 *Take with you words.* "Taking words" refers to the prayer of confession that should accompanying true repentance. See David's prayer of confession in Ps. 51 for an example. The word translated *iniquity* has three senses in the Old Testament: the actual sin, consequent guilt, and punishment for sin. In this context, it designates guilt. *receive us graciously.* Literally, "accept [the] good." The petition involves offering to God what He requires with the expectancy that He will receive what is offered. A commitment of self in obedience is the essence of what God demands (Mic. 6:8). *so will we render the calves of our lips.* Literally, "we resolve to repay young bulls, our lips." The imagery points to the votive or peace offerings, which were offered to the Lord in payment of a vow or in thanksgiving for grace and salvation (Ps. 116:16–18; Heb. 13:15). A believer at peace with God will be full of praise, thanksgiving, and gratitude for grace.
14:3 This verse expresses the forsaking of every empty hope in exchange for dependence upon the Lord. The orphan is a vivid example of one who is destitute and incapable of self-preservation, one who is completely dependent on another. Thus, repentance involves abandonment to the mercies of God.
14:4 *I will heal . . . I will love them freely.* Accompanying the invitation to repent is the assurance that God will forgive

freely: for mine anger is turned away from him.
5 I will be as the dew unto Israel: he shall grow as
the lily, and cast forth his roots as Lebanon.
6 His branches shall spread, and his beauty shall
be as the olive tree, and his smell as Lebanon.
7 They that dwell under his shadow shall return;
they shall revive *as* the corn, and grow as the vine:
the scent thereof *shall be* as the wine of Lebanon.
8 Ephraim *shall say*, What have I to do any more
with idols? I have heard *him*, and observed him:
I *am* like a green fir tree. From me is thy fruit
found.
9 Who *is* wise, and he shall understand these
things? prudent, and he shall know them? for the
ways of the LORD *are* right, and the just shall walk
in them: but the transgressors shall fall therein.

those who genuinely confess their sins. Hosea's assurance parallels John's guarantee in 1 John 1:9. When God loves freely, it means that He loves on His own accord. Had God not loved Israel of His own accord, He would never have had reason to love them. As amazing as His love was to Israel, it was not unique, for His love for us is graciously free as well.

14:5–8 In a series of similes (comparisons), these verses detail the benefits resulting from God's dew-like provision, which is evidence of His favor (Prov. 19:12): growth like a lily, stability like a deep-rooted cedar, attractiveness in appearance and aroma like the cedar and olive trees, and fruitfulness. To put all this in New Testament terms, God gives His people richly all things to enjoy (1 Tim. 6:17) as He lavishes on them all the riches of His grace found and enjoyed in Christ (Eph. 1:3–14).

14:9 *The just shall walk . . . transgressors shall fall.* The book concludes according to the covenant pattern of two opposing options typically found in Deuteronomy. The walking of the just and the staggering of the transgressor parallels the choice between life and death, blessing and cursing (Deut. 30:15,19).

Thoughts for Personal/Family Worship: Chapter 14

1. **The opening verses are most instructive in charting the marks of genuine repentance. There must be confession of sin, commitment to God, praise for grace, forsaking of everything else in exclusive dependence on God. The Lord's invitation to repent is not ineffective, for God seeks the sinner with grace before the sinner seeks Him. Therefore, with the invitation comes the assurance of God's free love. There is something wonderfully consistent about God's promise to forgive those who genuinely confess their sins.**
2. **For any Christian troubled and disappointed with the level of his spiritual experience and enjoyment, the closing words of Hosea are encouraging and instructive. There is a remedy to spiritual dryness, a way to reverse a path littered with disobedience and sin. For those far from God, there is a way back to Him; for those near God, there is a way to be nearer still.**

I WILL

Pour Out

MY SPIRIT

UPON ALL FLESH

&

YOUR SONS

AND

Your Daughters

SHALL

PROPHESY

YOUR OLD MEN

Shall Dream

DREAMS

YOUR YOUNG MEN

Shall See

VISIONS

JOEL 2:28

INTRODUCTION TO THE BOOK OF JOEL

Authorship: Joel means "Jehovah is God." Although the Scripture does not mention his ministry elsewhere, it appears from references to Judah (3:1,6) and Jerusalem (2:1,15) that he prophesied in the southern kingdom.

Date: Although Joel did not directly date his prophecy like other prophets by listing the kings during whose reigns he ministered, the circumstantial evidence points to the ninth century BC—either during the illegal renegade rule of Queen Athaliah or the early days of the boy king Joash, who had providentially escaped Athaliah's deadly plot against the royal seed (2 Kings 11–12). Dating Joel's prophecy to about 830 BC would mark him along with Obadiah among the first of the writing prophets. Notwithstanding the circumstantial evidence, even some conservatives would date Joel to the postexilic period.

Theme: The day of the Lord: judgment and restoration.

Purpose: To call the nation to repentance in order to escape judgment and to experience God's gracious revival.

Synopsis: *The Contribution of Joel to Redemptive Revelation*

The days were dark, both politically and spiritually. With the slaying of the royal seed, it appeared that God's redemptive purpose in Christ was in jeopardy. There seemed to be little prospect for hope, but not even wicked Athaliah could frustrate God's purpose and plan. The Lord raised up the prophet Joel to provide the theological interpretation of all the tragic events of the day and to announce details of God's fixed plans for the future. Joel made it clear that what to sight seemed to be a natural disaster—the locust plague—was in reality a manifestation of the day of the Lord. God had directly, supernaturally, and unmistakably intervened into human affairs to accomplish His purpose of judgment against the nation's sin. The locusts were dedicated and obedient soldiers under the command of the Lord Himself.

Joel declared not only that God had punished, but that He would punish again with even greater severity and devastation unless the people repented. Using both the past and future day of the Lord as the incentive, the prophet issued two great calls for repentance (1:13–14; 2:12–17). Turning to the Lord was the only hope. But it was a real hope because God does not turn away those who turn to Him. Not only was there going to be an Israel preserved for the messianic fullness of time, there was going to be a magnificent outpouring of the Holy Spirit to advance God's kingdom to the ends of the earth.

Outline:

- I. Introduction (1:1)
- II. Invasion of Locusts: Disaster Explained (1:2–20)
  - A. Extent and Effects of the Invasion (1:2–12)
  - B. Call to Repentance in Light of the Disaster (1:13–14)
  - C. Recognition of Divine Agency in the Disaster (1:15–20)
- III. Day of the Lord: Destruction Threatened (2:1–17)
  - A. The Destruction as Imminent and Irresistible (2:1–11)
  - B. The Call to Repentance in Light of Impending Destruction (2:12–17)
- IV. Restoration: Conditions Reversed (2:18–32)
  - A. Physical Restoration of the Land (2:18–27)
  - B. Spiritual Revival of the People (2:28–32)
- V. Judgment of God: Justice Executed (3:1–21)
  - A. Judgment against the Nations (3:1–15)
  - B. Judgment in Behalf of Israel (3:16–21)

THE BOOK OF JOEL

CHAPTER 1

THE word of the LORD that came to Joel the son
of Pethuel.
2 Hear this, ye old men, and give ear, all ye
inhabitants of the land. Hath this been in your
days, or even in the days of your fathers?
3 Tell ye your children of it, and *let* your children
tell their children, and their children another
generation.
4 That which the palmerworm hath left hath the
locust eaten; and that which the locust hath left
hath the cankerworm eaten; and that which the
cankerworm hath left hath the caterpiller eaten.
5 Awake, ye drunkards, and weep; and howl, all
ye drinkers of wine, because of the new wine; for
it is cut off from your mouth.
6 For a nation is come up upon my land, strong,
and without number, whose teeth *are* the teeth of
a lion, and he hath the cheek teeth of a great lion.
7 He hath laid my vine waste, and barked my fig
tree: he hath made it clean bare, and cast *it* away;
the branches thereof are made white.
8 ¶ Lament like a virgin girded with sackcloth for
the husband of her youth.
9 The meat offering and the drink offering is cut
off from the house of the LORD; the priests, the
LORD's ministers, mourn.
10 The field is wasted, the land mourneth; for the
corn is wasted: the new wine is dried up, the oil
languisheth.
11 Be ye ashamed, O ye husbandmen; howl, O
ye vinedressers, for the wheat and for the barley;
because the harvest of the field is perished.
12 The vine is dried up, and the fig tree
languisheth; the pomegranate tree, the palm tree
also, and the apple tree, *even* all the trees of the
field, are withered: because joy is withered away
from the sons of men.
13 Gird yourselves, and lament, ye priests: howl,
ye ministers of the altar: come, lie all night in
sackcloth, ye ministers of my God: for the meat
offering and the drink offering is withholden
from the house of your God.
14 ¶ Sanctify ye a fast, call a solemn assembly,

Chapter 1: *Joel interprets the devastating locust invasion as direct evidence of God's judgment and issues the invitation to repent.*

INTRODUCTION (1:1)

1:1 *The word of the LORD that came.* If Joel is to be dated to the reign of the wicked queen Athaliah, this is a reminder that in times of crisis God always has a word for His people. That principle still operates and should encourage believers to find help, direction, and comfort in the Scripture in times of need.

INVASION OF LOCUSTS: DISASTER EXPLAINED (1:2–20)

Extent and Effects of the Invasion (1:2–12)

1:2 *ye old men.* This most likely refers to the representatives of the people rather than a specific age group. The parallel reference to *all ye inhabitants* would suggest this. *Hath this been.* The rhetorical question would highlight the uniqueness of the situation.

1:4 *palmerworm . . . locust . . . cankerworm . . . caterpiller.* Most interpreters agree that these terms designate different stages in the life cycle of the insect from larvae to maturity. Each stage had its own appetite that combined to devastate the entire land. Deuteronomy 28:38 identifies this same locust as an instrument of divine judgment for covenant unfaithfulness. All of nature is at God's disposal to accomplish His will.

1:5 Commanding the *drunkards* to *awake* or sober up underscores the extent of the devastation. Even those whose stupor would render them oblivious to reality could not miss the extent of the disaster, particularly when their supply of wine dwindled away due to the loss of grapes.

1:7 *vine . . . fig tree.* These were common images of prosperity, so their destruction would represent the economic consequences of the locust invasion.

1:8 *Lament like a virgin girded with sackcloth.* The death of the husband before the marriage consummation turned the time of celebration to an occasion for mourning, symbolized by the sackcloth.

1:9–12 The complete loss of harvest was cause for sorrow. All of society, both sacred and secular, felt the consequences of the disaster. *Joy is withered* is an example of metonymy. The word designating the effect (joy) is used for the cause (the harvest). The consequences of sin are always severe. The temporal effects should awaken us to the more serious eternal consequences.

Call to Repentance in Light of the Disaster (1:13–14)

1:13 *Gird yourselves.* Putting on sackcloth was an outward gesture of inward repentance. That the imperative is directed to the *priests*, the *ministers of the altar*, is a solemn reminder of the responsibility of spiritual leaders not only to sorrow over

gather the elders *and* all the inhabitants of the
land *into* the house of the LORD your God, and
cry unto the LORD,
15 Alas for the day! for the day of the LORD *is* at
hand, and as a destruction from the Almighty
shall it come.
16 Is not the meat cut off before our eyes, *yea*, joy
and gladness from the house of our God?
17 The seed is rotten under their clods, the
garners are laid desolate, the barns are broken
down; for the corn is withered.
18 How do the beasts groan! the herds of cattle
are perplexed, because they have no pasture; yea,
the flocks of sheep are made desolate.
19 O LORD, to thee will I cry: for the fire hath
devoured the pastures of the wilderness, and the
flame hath burned all the trees of the field.
20 The beasts of the field cry also unto thee: for
the rivers of waters are dried up, and the fire hath
devoured the pastures of the wilderness.

CHAPTER 2

BLOW ye the trumpet in Zion, and sound an alarm
in my holy mountain: let all the inhabitants of the
land tremble: for the day of the LORD cometh, for
it is nigh at hand;
2 A day of darkness and of gloominess, a day of
clouds and of thick darkness, as the morning spread
upon the mountains: a great people and a strong;
there hath not been ever the like, neither shall be any
more after it, *even* to the years of many generations.
3 A fire devoureth before them; and behind
them a flame burneth: the land *is* as the garden
of Eden before them, and behind them a desolate
wilderness; yea, and nothing shall escape them.
4 The appearance of them *is* as the appearance of
horses; and as horsemen, so shall they run.
5 Like the noise of chariots on the tops of moun-
tains shall they leap, like the noise of a flame of
fire that devoureth the stubble, as a strong people
set in battle array.

---

the consequent conditions of sin but to lead the people to repentance. If the clergy is oblivious and insensitive to sin, so will be the laity.

1:14 *Sanctify ye a fast.* Literally, "make holy a fast." The idea is to set aside time from fleshly concerns and pursuits so that attention can be devoted to spiritual matters. *solemn assembly.* A sacred day, the special time set apart for the fast. Setting time aside from all the normal concerns of life to deal with spiritual issues is important. *cry unto the LORD.* Literally, to "cry out to Him for help." It expresses the sense of absolute dependence on God. If He does not help, there is no help possible. This attitude is essential for true repentance and, in fact, ought to be the constant mindset of believers.

Recognition of Divine Agency in the Disaster (1:15–20)

1:15 *the day of the LORD.* A technical expression designating God's direct intervention into the affairs of time either for judgment or for blessing. God controls all of time and circumstance, but the day of the Lord refers to special and unusual manifestations of God's works. Providence is His ordinary work; the various days of the Lord are extraordinary works. *at hand.* This expression can refer to either temporal or spatial nearness. Here it is most likely spatial, identifying the locust plague as a direct divine intervention rather than just the normal cycle of nature. What was being witnessed throughout the land was the unmistakable judgment of God.

1:16 *meat.* An archaic use of the term referring to food in general. There was widespread famine. *joy and gladness.* Synonyms that combine to intensify the sense of jubilation that would expectedly accompany the offering of sacrifices to the Lord. So extensive was the devastation that there was nothing that could be offered as sacrifice.

1:17 *corn.* A general word referring to grain.

1:18 *groan . . . perplexed.* A figure of speech in which animals are engaged in actions usually associated with people (see also v. 20 where "the beasts of the field cry").

Thoughts for Personal/Family Worship: Chapter 1

1. **Disasters happen by divine appointment. Throughout the world there are earthquakes, floods, and storms of every sort that destroy property and claim lives. Rather than these being random occurrences with purely natural explanations, they are the workings of divine providence, all of which declares the glory of God. It is a source of comfort to Christians to know that regardless of how terrible circumstances may be, there is a good and all-wise God who is working His purpose.**
2. **The knowledge that disasters happen by divine appointment ought to generate a conscious awareness or fear of God and motivate repentance and dependence on the Lord. Natural disasters are a means that God uses to knock out every prop of self-reliance.**

Chapter 2: ***Joel predicts a more severe judgment, issues an invitation to repent, and then describes the prospect of great blessing including both physical restoration and spiritual revival.***

DAY OF THE LORD: DESTRUCTION THREATENED (2:1–17)

The Destruction as Imminent and Irresistible (2:1–11)

2:1–11 Note the references to the *day of the LORD* in vv. 1 and 11. This forms an inclusio, or verbal parenthesis, that marks the theme of the intervening verses. The day of the Lord, one of those times when God directly intervenes into the affairs of time, is a powerful incentive to repentance. Joel describes the day as impending, terrible, and irresistible. Interpreters differ as to whether the invading army under God's direct command refers literally to another wave of locusts more destructive than the first, or figuratively either to a coming invasion by a foreign enemy, or by the Lord's heavenly army that will bring the final judgment. Regardless of the specific identity of the army, the invasion is unstoppable, the consequences severe and the call to repent urgent.

2:1 *Blow ye the trumpet . . . sound an alarm.* Military terms to warn of impending attack and to signal for war. Zion and my holy mountain refer specifically to Jerusalem.

2:2 Zephaniah 1:15 describes the darkness of the day of the Lord with the same expressions. Ironically, the same manifestations of God's judgment against Egypt in delivering Israel (Ex. 10:14–15,21–23) are now directed against Israel. It reveals that God is no respecter of persons as He metes out justice righteously.

2:3 *Eden.* The allusion to paradise lost is vivid imagery of total devastation.

2:4 *Horsemen* is parallel to *horses* in the first part of the verse.

6 Before their face the people shall be much
pained: all faces shall gather blackness.
7 They shall run like mighty men; they shall
climb the wall like men of war; and they shall
march every one on his ways, and they shall not
break their ranks:
8 Neither shall one thrust another; they shall
walk every one in his path: and *when* they fall
upon the sword, they shall not be wounded.
9 They shall run to and fro in the city; they shall
run upon the wall, they shall climb up upon the
houses; they shall enter in at the windows like a
thief.
10 The earth shall quake before them; the heavens
shall tremble: the sun and the moon shall be dark,
and the stars shall withdraw their shining:
11 And the LORD shall utter his voice before his
army: for his camp *is* very great: for *he is* strong
that executeth his word: for the day of the LORD
is great and very terrible; and who can abide it?
12 ¶ Therefore also now, saith the LORD, turn ye
even to me with all your heart, and with fasting,
and with weeping, and with mourning:
13 And rend your heart, and not your garments,
and turn unto the LORD your God: for he *is*
gracious and merciful, slow to anger, and of great
kindness, and repenteth him of the evil.
14 Who knoweth *if* he will return and repent, and
leave a blessing behind him; *even* a meat offering
and a drink offering unto the LORD your God?
15 ¶ Blow the trumpet in Zion, sanctify a fast, call
a solemn assembly:
16 Gather the people, sanctify the congregation,
assemble the elders, gather the children, and those
that suck the breasts: let the bridegroom go forth
of his chamber, and the bride out of her closet.
17 Let the priests, the ministers of the LORD, weep
between the porch and the altar, and let them say,
Spare thy people, O LORD, and give not thine
heritage to reproach, that the heathen should rule
over them: wherefore should they say among the
people, Where *is* their God?
18 ¶ Then will the LORD be jealous for his land,
and pity his people.

The term refers specifically to male horses or steeds and so emphasizes the endurance and strength with which the invading army advances.

2:6 A description of the fear and panic caused by the invading army. *blackness*. Literally, heat or glowing redness. A reference either to the scorching caused by heat, hence the black appearance, or to a flushed complexion expressing fear. The panic shows on their faces.

2:7–9 Descriptions of the discipline, invincibility, and destructiveness of the army.

2:10 So devastating is the judgment that it reverses the order of creation. At creation light dispelled darkness; here the darkness shadows the light.

2:11 *who can abide it?* A rhetorical question with an obvious answer: none can endure or escape God's judgment. The question continues to serve as a solemn warning.

The Call to Repentance in Light of Impending Destruction (2:12–17)

2:12 *turn*. Reverse direction. This is the principal word in the Old Testament for evangelical repentance. It vividly expresses the transformation of life that marks true repentance. Before repentance, God was behind and sin was in front. Repentance involves a following after God and forsaking of sin. *Heart* in the Old Testament designates the entirety of inner man: the mind, emotion, and will. True repentance requires the apprehension of the grievous nature of sin, contrition over it, and the resolute turning from it to God for mercy. *Fasting . . . mourning*. External evidences of inward repentance.

2:13 *rend your heart, and not your garments*. Given a natural tendency to externalize rather than internalize, the prophet warns not to confuse or substitute outward displays for inward reality. *for he is gracious*. God's character is encouragement to repent. *repenteth him of the evil*. An anthropopathism (a human emotion applied to God) to express the assurance that God will relent by withdrawing His calamitous judgment (*the evil*) from those who turn to Him. The Hebrew word for *evil* often refers to harm or disaster without any moral connotation of wickedness.

2:14 *Who knoweth if*. Although the character of God encourages repentance, there can be no presumption by man that his actions obligate God: God remains sovereign. *meat offering and a drink offering*. The prospect of the food and drink offerings is evidence of God's blessing of restoration since the locust invasion had made these impossible (1:9).

2:15–16 None were exempt from the call to repent. Everyone from the old to the young was expected to participate in the religious services associated with the national repentance.

2:16 *Closet* designates the bride's nuptial chamber.

2:17 *between the porch and the altar*. The porch was directly adjacent to the holy place, and the altar was at the front of the inner court. This refers to that part of the inner court of the temple where the priests congregated to conduct their intercessory ministry, most likely "the court of the priests" (2 Chron. 4:9). Significantly, Joel records the intercession offered from this designated place of prayer. *Where is their God?* The chief argument in prayer was the glory of God: the heathen would have occasion to mock if God did not spare His people.

RESTORATION: CONDITIONS REVERSED (2:18–32)

2:18–32 The blessing would involve both a restoration of the land and a revival of the people. Joel details the restoration in two distinct stages. The "at the first" blessing would involve the physical (v. 23) and the "afterward" blessing (v. 28) would focus on the spiritual. Note that in v. 23 the word *month* is italicized, indicating its absence from the Hebrew text. Rather than referring to the month in which the rain comes, it would be better to see it as a temporal indication of the immediate blessing after which will come the spiritual blessing.

Physical Restoration of the Land (2:18–27)

2:18–19 These verses mark a key transition in Joel's argument. In Hebrew the verbs *be jealous*, *pity*, *answer*, and *say* are in the past tense, suggesting that there has been some positive response to the two calls to repent (1:13 and 2:12–13) to which the Lord has answered with the two declarations of promise (2:21–27 and 2:28–32).

2:18 *jealous for his land*. God's jealousy refers to His fervent zeal that acts appropriately to ensure the honor of His own name or reputation, His word, and His people. *His land* refers to Israel, the land of *his people*, who are the special object of His jealousy.

19 Yea, the LORD will answer and say unto his
people, Behold, I will send you corn, and wine,
and oil, and ye shall be satisfied therewith: and
I will no more make you a reproach among the
heathen:
20 But I will remove far off from you the northern
army, and will drive him into a land barren and
desolate, with his face toward the east sea, and his
hinder part toward the utmost sea, and his stink
shall come up, and his ill savour shall come up,
because he hath done great things.
21 ¶ Fear not, O land; be glad and rejoice: for the
LORD will do great things.
22 Be not afraid, ye beasts of the field: for the
pastures of the wilderness do spring, for the tree
beareth her fruit, the fig tree and the vine do yield
their strength.
23 Be glad then, ye children of Zion, and rejoice
in the LORD your God: for he hath given you
the former rain moderately, and he will cause to
come down for you the rain, the former rain, and
the latter rain in the first *month*.
24 And the floors shall be full of wheat, and the
fats shall overflow with wine and oil.
25 And I will restore to you the years that the
locust hath eaten, the cankerworm, and the
caterpiller, and the palmerworm, my great army
which I sent among you.
26 And ye shall eat in plenty, and be satisfied, and
praise the name of the LORD your God, that hath
dealt wondrously with you: and my people shall
never be ashamed.
27 And ye shall know that I *am* in the midst of
Israel, and *that* I *am* the LORD your God, and
none else: and my people shall never be ashamed.
28 ¶ And it shall come to pass afterward, *that* I
will pour out my spirit upon all flesh; and your
sons and your daughters shall prophesy, your old
men shall dream dreams, your young men shall
see visions:
29 And also upon the servants and upon the
handmaids in those days will I pour out my spirit.
30 And I will shew wonders in the heavens and
in the earth, blood, and fire, and pillars of smoke.
31 The sun shall be turned into darkness, and the
moon into blood, before the great and the terrible
day of the LORD come.
32 And it shall come to pass, *that* whosoever shall

2:19 *I will send.* The Hebrew uses a special construction for the future tense that underscores both the certainty and the imminence of the event: I am about to send.

2:20 *northern army.* Since the majority of Israel's enemies attacked from the north, this reference does not aid in identifying the invading army. Regardless of the identity, the army is divinely forced to retreat. *utmost sea.* Literally, "western sea." *done great things.* Referring to the quantity not the quality of what was done.

2:21–23 The locust devastation affected the land, animals, and men (1:16–20). The restoration would be just as inclusive. *O land . . . beasts.* To highlight the extent of the physical restoration, Joel uses apostrophe, a type of personification in which nonpersons are addressed as persons or engaged in personal activity.

2:21 *the LORD will do great things.* Contrast with the army doing great things (v. 20). Whereas the activity of the army was great in terms of quantity, the Lord's activity would be as wonderful as it was extensive. The locust devastation had removed the cause of joy (1:16), but the Lord's reversal of the devastation would restore joy.

2:23 *the former rain.* Literally, "the rain of righteousness." The Lord would give the necessary rain in the right amount at the right time. In Hebrew the word *rain* is a homonym meaning "teacher." Some interpreters identify the "teacher of righteousness" as a messianic reference. Notwithstanding the attractiveness of a messianic prophecy, the idea of appropriate rainfall fits the context of physical restoration better.

2:24 *floors . . . fats.* The threshingfloors and the wine vats.

2:25 *And I will restore to you the years that the locust hath eaten.* A beautiful synopsis of God's promise to reverse the devastating waste. Its application extends to those burdened by a wasted life—if they repent God has a way of making up the losses.

2:26–27 These verses highlight the healing results of divine discipline: contentment, praise, and consciousness of God's uniqueness and presence. The causes of reproach and shame would be removed.

Spiritual Revival of the People (2:28–32)

2:28–32 This section is ch. 3 in the Hebrew Bible. Although it is a single predictive unit, it contains three distinct prophecies. Verses 28, 30, and 32 each begin with the future tense, suggesting the beginning of a new paragraph. The units beginning with vv. 28 and 32 each contain an inclusio, a verbal parenthesis that sets off discourse units. The first unit begins and ends with *I will pour out my spirit*; the last unit begins and ends with the word *call*. The middle section (vv. 30–31) does not use the device, but it follows that if the first and last units are set apart, what is in between must itself be a separate unit. These are separate prophecies that would be fulfilled sometime after the restoration of the locust plague, but not necessarily at the same time. From the perspective of the New Testament, it is clear that aspects of this prophecy were fulfilled on the day of Pentecost and others wait to be fulfilled when the Lord returns at the end of the age. Without specifying time intervals, Joel prophesies concerning spiritual power, supernatural signs, and salvation guarantees.

2:28–29 *I will pour out my spirit.* This refers to the outpouring of the Spirit resulting in spiritual power and enabling for service. *All flesh* refers to all classes of people, including both Jews and Gentiles. *Your sons, your daughters, your old men, your young men, the servants,* and *the handmaids* illustrate the inclusiveness of the recipients of this spiritual power. Peter recognized the events of Pentecost to be what Joel predicted when all those in the upper room (not just the apostles) received power from the Holy Spirit to minister (Acts 2:4,16). What happened at Pentecost marked an important transition regarding the work of the Holy Spirit. In the Old Testament era, the Spirit's empowering for service was limited almost exclusively to religious and civil leaders. After Pentecost, the outpouring of the Spirit became available to every believer.

2:30–31 *And I will shew wonders.* The celestial and terrestrial signs associated with the final manifestation of the day of the Lord will be supernatural. It is vain to speculate concerning the essence or mechanics of such signs but their function as

call on the name of the LORD shall be delivered:
for in mount Zion and in Jerusalem shall be
deliverance, as the LORD hath said, and in the
remnant whom the LORD shall call.

CHAPTER 3

FOR, behold, in those days, and in that time, when
I shall bring again the captivity of Judah and
Jerusalem,
2 I will also gather all nations, and will bring
them down into the valley of Jehoshaphat, and
will plead with them there for my people and
for my heritage Israel, whom they have scattered
among the nations, and parted my land.
3 And they have cast lots for my people; and have
given a boy for an harlot, and sold a girl for wine,
that they might drink.
4 Yea, and what have ye to do with me, O Tyre,
and Zidon, and all the coasts of Palestine? will ye
render me a recompence? and if ye recompense
me, swiftly *and* speedily will I return your
recompence upon your own head;
5 Because ye have taken my silver and my gold,
and have carried into your temples my goodly
pleasant things:
6 The children also of Judah and the children of
Jerusalem have ye sold unto the Grecians, that ye
might remove them far from their border.
7 Behold, I will raise them out of the place
whither ye have sold them, and will return your
recompence upon your own head:

---

ominous warnings of judgment is clear. To miss the blessing of the outpouring of the Spirit is to experience the curse of judgment.

2:32 *whosoever shall call . . . shall be delivered.* This third unit is a timeless declaration of salvation. Calling on the Lord equates to approaching Him in saving faith (Rom. 10:9–13). Being delivered has both physical and spiritual significance and refers to the rescue from God's wrath and condemnation. *the remnant* (literally, "survivors") *whom the LORD shall call.* Significantly, those who call on the Lord are identified as those the Lord calls. Those whom God sovereignly calls respond by calling on Him for salvation.

Thoughts for Personal/Family Worship: Chapter 2

1. **Joel 2:12–13 provides occasion to reflect on the nature of evangelical repentance. As the Hebrew word "turn" implies, repentance involves a reversal of direction, demanding a new way of thinking and living. The Westminster Shorter Catechism's definition would be a good place to start: "Repentance unto life is a saving grace whereby a sinner, out of a true sense of his sin, and apprehension of the mercy of God in Christ, doth, with grief and hatred of his sin, turn from it unto God, with full purpose of, and endeavor after, new obedience" (Q. 87). Joel's invitation encompasses most of these elements. It stresses particularly the inward focus. Sometimes people doubt the reality of their own repentance on the basis of outward manifestations of contrition (weeping and mourning). There must be the contrition over sin, but how that contrition is shown often depends on personality. This is why Joel stresses the rending of the heart rather than the outward shows of rending garments. What God sees is more important than what man sees.**
2. **God's promise to restore what the locusts had eaten (2:25) is an encouragement. The consequences of sin are a tragic reality, but where sin abounds grace superabounds (Rom. 5:20). Sometimes people convince themselves that their sin has been so great or so much of life has been wasted that God would never save them or ever use them. The locusts had so consumed the land that nothing was left, but God said He would restore it all. So God's power and grace is sufficient to restore His people to usefulness.**
3. **On the day of Pentecost, the Holy Spirit came upon every believer, who then in the power of the Spirit evangelized Jerusalem (Acts 2:4). Peter explained the wonders of Pentecost by saying "this is that" which Joel prophesied concerning, the outpouring of the Holy Spirit (Acts 2:16). What Pentecost started continues, and every Christian has the power of the Spirit available to serve Christ and His church.**

Chapter 3: *Joel predicts the judgment that God will bring on the whole world, punishing every enemy and showing special favor to His people.*

JUDGMENT OF GOD: JUSTICE EXECUTED (3:1–21)
(ch. 4 in the Hebrew Bible)

Judgment against the Nations (3:1–15)

3:1 *in those days, and in that time.* Designations of the day of the Lord, most likely here referring to the final eschatological day. *I shall bring again the captivity.* Literally, "I will turn around (or reverse) the captivity." The Lord would restore Judah and Jerusalem.

3:2 *the valley of Jehoshaphat.* Opinions differ regarding the exact location. The significance is in the meaning of Jehoshaphat ("Jehovah judges") rather than the precise location. God summons the nations to the place of judgment. *Plead* is the same root as occurs in the second part of Jeho-*shaphat*; the Lord will judge the nations for their acts against His people. *parted my land.* Their apportioning the land among themselves.

3:3 *they have cast lots.* A common practice of victors for dividing the spoils of their conquests. *a boy for an harlot . . . a girl for wine.* Such was the cruelty and low regard of human life; boys and girls became currency. They were given in exchange for a prostitute and for wine.

3:4 *Tyre . . . Zidon . . . all the coasts of Palestine.* Historic enemies of God's people; most likely representative of Gentile enemies collectively. *Recompense.* An act of repaying or getting even. What they attempted against God, God would rapidly execute against them. This illustrates lex talionis (the law of retaliation; eye for eye, tooth for tooth concept), a common principle of divine judgment.

3:5 *temples.* The Hebrew word also refers to palaces, the more likely reference. *pleasant things.* Precious or desirable objects.

3:6 *Grecians.* Some see this as evidence of a postexilic date for Joel. However, since there is evidence of contact and commerce between Greece and Mesopotamia as early as the second millennium BC, this gives no indication regarding the date of Joel.

3:7–8 Another vivid illustration of the judgment principle of lex talionis. Not only will God rescue the sons and daughters of His people, He will "get even" (*recompence upon your own head*) by selling the children of the enemy to Judah, who

8 And I will sell your sons and your daughters
into the hand of the children of Judah, and they
shall sell them to the Sabeans, to a people far off:
for the LORD hath spoken *it*.
9 ¶ Proclaim ye this among the Gentiles; Prepare
war, wake up the mighty men, let all the men of
war draw near; let them come up:
10 Beat your plowshares into swords, and your
pruninghooks into spears: let the weak say, I *am*
strong.
11 Assemble yourselves, and come, all ye heathen,
and gather yourselves together round about: thither
cause thy mighty ones to come down, O LORD.
12 Let the heathen be wakened, and come up to
the valley of Jehoshaphat: for there will I sit to
judge all the heathen round about.
13 Put ye in the sickle, for the harvest is ripe:
come, get you down; for the press is full, the fats
overflow; for their wickedness *is* great.
14 Multitudes, multitudes in the valley of
decision: for the day of the LORD *is* near in the
valley of decision.
15 The sun and the moon shall be darkened, and
the stars shall withdraw their shining.
16 The LORD also shall roar out of Zion, and utter
his voice from Jerusalem; and the heavens and the
earth shall shake: but the LORD *will be* the hope of
his people, and the strength of the children of Israel.
17 So shall ye know that I *am* the LORD your God
dwelling in Zion, my holy mountain: then shall
Jerusalem be holy, and there shall no strangers
pass through her any more.
18 ¶ And it shall come to pass in that day, *that*
the mountains shall drop down new wine, and
the hills shall flow with milk, and all the rivers of
Judah shall flow with waters, and a fountain shall
come forth of the house of the LORD, and shall
water the valley of Shittim.
19 Egypt shall be a desolation, and Edom shall
be a desolate wilderness, for the violence *against*
the children of Judah, because they have shed
innocent blood in their land.
20 But Judah shall dwell for ever, and Jerusalem
from generation to generation.
21 For I will cleanse their blood *that* I have not
cleansed: for the LORD dwelleth in Zion.

---

in turn will sell them to the *Sabeans* (an Arabian merchant people). To get from God what is deserved is a fearful thought.

3:9–10 *Beat your plowshares.* The Lord summons to battle and such would be the magnitude of the conflict that farming implements would have to be transformed to weapons. Note that the opposite transition would mark the time of universal peace (Isa. 2:4; Mic. 4:3).

3:13 *harvest is ripe.* A frequent image describing judgment (Rev. 14:14–20). *Press . . . fats.* The wine press and wine vat.

3:14 *valley of decision.* Literally, "valley of what has been decided." It is not the place for the gathered multitudes to decide but to learn the verdict of God's decree.

3:15 See note at 2:10.

Judgment in Behalf of Israel (3:16–21)

3:16 See Nah. 1:2–7 for the same contrast. While the Lord takes vengeance on the wicked, He is a refuge for His people. *hope . . . strength.* God's presence makes Zion an inviolable sanctuary.

3:17 *Strangers* refers to foreigners, who will no longer trespass against Zion's borders.

3:18 *in that day.* The day of the Lord, here most likely referring to the final eschatological judgment. What is disaster for the wicked is blessing for God's people. Agricultural productivity is a common biblical image for divine blessing. Significantly, whereas Joel began with a description of agricultural failure, he ends with a description of bounty. *valley of Shittim.* Most likely not the name of a particular valley but refers to a place where acacia trees grow. What is normally arid territory will have an abundance of water in this time of blessing.

3:19 *Egypt . . . Edom.* Representative of all the enemies of God and His people who are justly punished and no longer a threat.

3:20–21 Although opinions differ regarding the eschatological (end-time) implications and details of the whole section, it is indisputably clear that God's presence with His people guarantees their perpetual existence. This truth applies to the present as well as future experience of the church. *I will cleanse their blood.* See Ps. 9:11–12 for the connection between God's presence and His role as the avenger of blood.

Thoughts for Personal/Family Worship: Chapter 3

1. **Use 3:14 as a solemn reminder of the importance of conversion before it is too late. A day of judgment is coming when God will declare His guilty verdict and pronounce His sentence upon the wicked, who will have no recourse or way to escape.**
2. **Reflect on vv. 16–21 regarding the safety and security that God's presence offers believers regardless of external circumstances. Notwithstanding the eschatological (end-time) implications of these verses, they sum up a timeless and universal truth. Psalm 91 would be a good parallel passage: the Lord is our security; He provides our safety; and He promises our salvation.**

INTRODUCTION TO THE BOOK OF AMOS

Authorship: Amos means "burden" or "burden bearer." Although a herdsman from Tekoa just south of Bethlehem in the southern kingdom, Amos was commissioned by the Lord to preach to the northern tribes.

Date: Amos dates his prophecy in 1:1 as during the reigns of Uzziah and Jeroboam II, specifically two years before the earthquake. That Zech. 14:5 also mentions this earthquake indicates that it was a significant event. Archaeological data from sites such as Hazor give evidence of an earthquake in the mid-eighth century BC, within the general time frame allowed by the two kings mentioned. Given that the reigns of Uzziah and Jeroboam II overlapped approximately from 767 to 753 BC, Amos most likely prophesied between 760 and 755 BC.

Theme: Judgment for social and religious sins.

Purpose: To warn the nation of impending divine judgment because of the abuse and neglect of covenant privileges (Amos 3:2).

Synopsis: *The Contribution of Amos to Redemptive Revelation*

Peace and prosperity marked the first half of the eighth century BC. However, there was as much corruption as wealth. Moral, social, and religious decay were eating away at the nation and would eventually destroy it. Profiteering, injustice, and immorality were the rule of the day. Money was more influential than truth. The selfish passion to preserve or increase the standard of living defined a code of ethics used to justify any means to the desired end. In spite of vast spiritual problems, the people interpreted their prosperity as evidence of God's blessing and assumed that they were immune from divine displeasure. In reality they were far from God, and God was anything but pleased. Amos was called and burdened by God to make the nation face reality. He exposed the social and religious sins and warned of impending judgment if there was no genuine repentance. His message underscores the heinous nature of sin and spiritual deadness that can only be remedied by heeding God's gracious invitation to seek Him in order to live (5:4,6). Within forty years of Amos's preaching, the nation, refusing to repent, fell under God's judgment. Nonetheless, God's redemptive plan was on course to certain fulfillment as Amos pointed to a time when Gentiles as well as Jews would enjoy the blessings of Christ's kingdom (9:11–15). Significantly, James appealed to Amos to justify the inclusion of Gentiles in the first-century church (Acts 15:16–17).

Outline:

I. Introduction (1:1–2)

II. Oracles of Judgment (1:3—2:16)

- A. Judgments against Heathen Nations and Judah (1:3—2:5)
- B. Judgments against Israel (2:6–16)

III. Warnings of Judgment (3:1—6:14)

- A. Judgment Is Impending (3:1–15)
  1. Origin of the Judgment (3:1–8)
  2. Causes of the Judgment (3:9–10)
  3. Extent of the Judgment (3:11–15)
- B. Judgment Is Inevitable (4:1–13)
  1. Social and Religious Causes of Judgment (4:1–5)
  2. Spiritual Callousness to Past Judgments (4:6–11)
  3. Ominous Threat of Final Judgment (4:12–13)
- C. Judgment Is Escapable (5:1–15)
  1. Lamentation for Fallen State (5:1–3)
  2. Invitations to Repent (5:4–15)
- D. Judgment Is Certain (5:16—6:14)
  1. Woe against Carnal Confidence (5:16–27)
  2. Woe against Religious Complacency (6:1–6)
  3. Divine Determination in Judgment (6:7–14)

IV. Visions of Judgment (7:1—9:10)

- A. Locusts and Fire Picture Prevented Judgment (7:1–6)
- B. A Plumbline Pictures Inevitable Judgment (7:7–9)
- C. Parenthesis: Confrontation with a False Priest (7:10–17)
- D. A Basket of Summer Fruit Pictures the Imminence of Judgment (8:1–14)
- E. The Lord at the Altar Pictures the Inescapability and Discrimination of Judgment (9:1–10)

V. Restoration after Judgment (9:11–15)

- A. Restoration of the Kingdom (9:11–12)
- B. Universal Prosperity (9:13–15)

THE BOOK OF AMOS

CHAPTER 1

THE words of Amos, who was among the herdmen
of Tekoa, which he saw concerning Israel in the
days of Uzziah king of Judah, and in the days
of Jeroboam the son of Joash king of Israel, two
years before the earthquake.
2 And he said, The LORD will roar from Zion,
and utter his voice from Jerusalem; and the
habitations of the shepherds shall mourn, and the
top of Carmel shall wither.
3 Thus saith the LORD; For three transgressions
of Damascus, and for four, I will not turn away *the
punishment* thereof; because they have threshed
Gilead with threshing instruments of iron:
4 But I will send a fire into the house of Hazael,
which shall devour the palaces of Ben-hadad.
5 I will break also the bar of Damascus, and cut
off the inhabitant from the plain of Aven, and him
that holdeth the sceptre from the house of Eden:
and the people of Syria shall go into captivity
unto Kir, saith the LORD.
6 ¶ Thus saith the LORD; For three transgressions
of Gaza, and for four, I will not turn away *the
punishment* thereof; because they carried away
captive the whole captivity, to deliver *them* up to
Edom:

Chapter 1: *Amos announces God's judgment of heathen nations, who although ignorant of God and His law were nonetheless accountable to Him and subject to His rule and discipline.*

INTRODUCTION (1:1–2)

1:1 Although not the usual word for shepherd, *herdmen* identifies Amos as either a shepherd or sheep dealer/breeder. His authority did not derive from his credentials of birthright or background but in the call of God. Since *Tekoa* was known for its rich pastureland, Amos, most likely, left a lucrative business to obey God's call. *he saw.* A technical word referring to the reception of the prophetic message. Therefore *the words of Amos* were in reality the very words of God.

1:2 The lion's *roar,* a sound of imminent danger. Ironically, the shepherd Amos would have responded to the lion's roar with special vigilance for the welfare of his flock; so the prophet Amos warns his audience of the impending danger of judgment from the Lord. As it was his duty as a shepherd, so was it as a prophet. *from Zion . . . from Jerusalem.* Where God had especially caused His name to dwell, the symbolic place of His presence among His covenant people. Although the northern kingdom had become a separate political entity, it was still part of the covenant nation and still subject to covenant stipulations. This truth is crucial to Amos's right to preach in the northern kingdom even though he was a citizen of the southern kingdom. *mourn . . . wither.* Expressions often associated with drought and famine which were evidences of covenant judgments (Deut. 28:22–24; Jer. 12:4; 23:10).

ORACLES OF JUDGMENT (1:3—2:16)

Judgments against Heathen Nations and Judah (1:3—2:5)

1:3—2:3 The prophet's declaration of these judgments not only revealed God's sovereign right over all nations, but also gave Amos a platform for his ultimate message against Israel. A southern prophet would not have a receptive audience immediately, but he gained a favorable hearing by preaching a message with which they agreed before directing the word against them directly.

1:3,6,9,11,13; 2:1,4,6 *For three transgressions . . . and for four* introduces each of the judgments and is an idiom expressing an indefinite number. Persistent and habitual sin deserves and earns judgment. It highlights both the long-suffering of God that withholds immediate judgment and the justice of God that ensures certain judgment. *I will not turn away the punishment.* Literally, "I will not return it," meaning that the Lord will not reverse the punishment. Judgment was divinely determined, inevitable, and irreversible.

1:3 *Damascus.* Capital of Syria, the nation just north of Israel. *threshed Gilead.* A graphic image of cruelty against this Israelite city on the border with Syria. Second Kings 13:7 uses the same imagery to describe Syria's destruction of Israel during the days of Jehoahaz.

1:4 *I will send a fire* (also 1:7,10,12,14 "kindle;" 2:2,5). The summary statement of divine judgment.

1:5 *bar of Damascus.* A reference to the large bars used to secure the city gates. Breaking the bar would "unlock" the door to the city, compromise its security, and expose it to invasion. The punishment would be extensive; not only would the capital city fall but the entire territory would experience upheaval. *him that holdeth the sceptre.* A reference to the king. *Eden* does not refer to the garden of paradise, but to a city a couple hundred miles northeast of Damascus. *Kir.* Amos 9:7 identifies this as the original home of the Syrians. Their return there would mark their loss of territory and independence.

1:6 *Gaza.* One of the principal cities of Philistia; the following references to Ashdod, Ashkelon, and Ekron (1:8) indicate that the judgment is against the entire nation of Philistia, Israel's historic enemy located on the Mediterranean coast. *They carried away captive the whole captivity* identifies their principal

7 But I will send a fire on the wall of Gaza, which
shall devour the palaces thereof:
8 And I will cut off the inhabitant from Ashdod,
and him that holdeth the sceptre from Ashkelon,
and I will turn mine hand against Ekron: and the
remnant of the Philistines shall perish, saith the
Lord GOD.
9 ¶ Thus saith the LORD; For three transgressions
of Tyrus, and for four, I will not turn away *the
punishment* thereof; because they delivered up
the whole captivity to Edom, and remembered
not the brotherly covenant:
10 But I will send a fire on the wall of Tyrus,
which shall devour the palaces thereof.
11 ¶ Thus saith the LORD; For three transgres-
sions of Edom, and for four, I will not turn away
the punishment thereof; because he did pursue his
brother with the sword, and did cast off all pity,
and his anger did tear perpetually, and he kept his
wrath for ever:
12 But I will send a fire upon Teman, which shall
devour the palaces of Bozrah.
13 ¶ Thus saith the LORD; For three transgressions
of the children of Ammon, and for four, I will not
turn away *the punishment* thereof; because they
have ripped up the women with child of Gilead,
that they might enlarge their border:
14 But I will kindle a fire in the wall of Rabbah,
and it shall devour the palaces thereof, with
shouting in the day of battle, with a tempest in
the day of the whirlwind:
15 And their king shall go into captivity, he and
his princes together, saith the LORD.

CHAPTER 2

THUS saith the LORD; For three transgressions
of Moab, and for four, I will not turn away *the
punishment* thereof; because he burned the bones
of the king of Edom into lime:
2 But I will send a fire upon Moab, and it shall
devour the palaces of Kerioth: and Moab shall die
with tumult, with shouting, *and* with the sound
of the trumpet:
3 And I will cut off the judge from the midst
thereof, and will slay all the princes thereof with
him, saith the LORD.
4 ¶ Thus saith the LORD; For three transgressions

---

transgression as slave trading with Edom, most likely referring to those of Israel that they had taken as prisoners of war. One occasion of this crime is given in 2 Chron. 2:16–17.

1:8 *the remnant of the Philistines.* The specific judgments against the principal Philistine cities climax in the perishing of whatever else remains. Philistia was going to lose not only its independence but its very identity as a nation.

1:9 *Tyrus.* Along with Sidon one of the chief cities of Phoenicia and here represents the entire nation. *they delivered up the whole captivity.* Another reference to slave trading (Ezek. 27:13; Joel 3:6). Ironically, when Tyre fell to the Greeks in the fourth century BC, many of its inhabitants became slaves.

1:11 *Edom.* The nation descending from Esau, Jacob's brother. The tension and conflict between the two brothers marked the entire history of the two nations, so much so that Edom became representative of all the nations hostile to Israel. Significantly, they were complicit in the transgressions of Philistia and Phoenicia. *his anger did tear.* Imagery of savagery, just like a lion tearing apart its prey (Ps. 7:2).

1:12 *Teman* in the north and *Bozrah* in the south show the extensiveness of the judgment that will cover the whole country.

1:13 *Ammon.* The nation descending from Lot's incestuous relationship with his younger daughter (Gen. 19:30–38). *ripped up the women with child.* Although this was barbaric and heinous, it was not an uncommon tactic in war (2 Kings 8:12, by Syria; Hos. 13:16, by Assyria; 2 Kings 15:16, by Israel itself).

1:14 *Rabbah.* The capital of Ammon, modern day Amman in Jordan.

Thoughts for Personal/Family Worship: Chapter 1

1. **Amos's call to be a prophet should encourage all believers that God can use them in His service regardless of their status, vocation, or background. Amos was a layman with no heritage in Christian service (7:14). But when God called him, He equipped him for a special ministry. So every Christian should be willing to submit to God's call to service even if that sphere of service counters what had been planned for life. Nothing is more important than doing God's will.**
2. **The series of judgments pronounced against the various heathen nations testifies to God's absolute sovereignty over all; He is the King of kings, and His law rules supreme. The ignorance of heathens concerning God, His law, and His gospel does not exempt them from being accountable to God. His judgments are just and always according to righteousness. What was true in Amos's day remains true today. It seems as though the wickedness of nations reigns unchecked, but God who rules over all holds them accountable for their transgressions. The day will come when "for three transgressions and for four," He will no longer withhold His judgment.**

Chapter 2: ***After finishing his pronouncements against neighboring nations, including Judah, Amos directs his message to Israel, exposing their sins and announcing God's intended judgment against them.***

2:1 *Moab.* The nation descending from Lot's incestuous relationship with his older daughter (Gen. 19:30–38). *burned the bones… into lime.* An act demonstrating extreme contempt and hatred. Josiah burned the bones of idolaters in demonstration of righteous anger (2 Kings 23:16), but Moab's so treating the bones of the king of Edom was a desecration worthy of divine retribution. Each of the preceding nations was judged for particular crimes against Israel, but Moab was to be punished for crimes against *Edom.* God's demand for justice is not limited to behavior toward His people, but extends to all humanity. In regard to His righteous demands, God is no respecter of persons.

2:2 *Kerioth.* A principal city of Moab, here standing for the nation as a whole. The following words indicate Moab's defeat in battle: *tumult,* the noise of panic; *shouting,* a war cry or alarm; *trumpet,* the horn used in battle, most likely a ram's horn.

2:3 *judge . . . princes.* Terms referring generally to ruling officials, not just to adjudicators or royal heirs.

2:4–5 *Judah.* The divine judgment of the southern kingdom

of Judah, and for four, I will not turn away *the*
punishment thereof; because they have despised
the law of the LORD, and have not kept his
commandments, and their lies caused them to
err, after the which their fathers have walked:
5 But I will send a fire upon Judah, and it shall
devour the palaces of Jerusalem.
6 ¶ Thus saith the LORD; For three transgressions
of Israel, and for four, I will not turn away *the*
punishment thereof; because they sold the righ-
teous for silver, and the poor for a pair of shoes;
7 That pant after the dust of the earth on the head
of the poor, and turn aside the way of the meek:
and a man and his father will go in unto the *same*
maid, to profane my holy name:
8 And they lay *themselves* down upon clothes laid
to pledge by every altar, and they drink the wine
of the condemned *in* the house of their god.
9 ¶ Yet destroyed I the Amorite before them,
whose height *was* like the height of the cedars,
and he *was* strong as the oaks; yet I destroyed his
fruit from above, and his roots from beneath.
10 Also I brought you up from the land of Egypt,
and led you forty years through the wilderness, to
possess the land of the Amorite.
11 And I raised up of your sons for prophets, and
of your young men for Nazarites. *Is it* not even
thus, O ye children of Israel? saith the LORD.
12 But ye gave the Nazarites wine to drink; and
commanded the prophets, saying, Prophesy not.
13 Behold, I am pressed under you, as a cart is
pressed *that is* full of sheaves.
14 Therefore the flight shall perish from the swift,
and the strong shall not strengthen his force,
neither shall the mighty deliver himself:
15 Neither shall he stand that handleth the
bow; and *he that is* swift of foot shall not deliver
himself: neither shall he that rideth the horse
deliver himself.
16 And *he that is* courageous among the mighty
shall flee away naked in that day, saith the LORD.

CHAPTER 3

HEAR this word that the LORD hath spoken
against you, O children of Israel, against the

would come years after that of the north, but it would certainly come because of their covenant violations. *despised the law . . . not kept his commandments.* They rejected the whole of divine revelation and disobeyed God's statutes, the prescriptions for living. By metonymy, *their lies* (falsehoods) refer not to acts or words of deception but to their idols, their false gods, which caused them to err. Rejecting God's law and following after false gods are covenant violations subject to divine curse (Deut. 28:14–15). In addressing the sin of Judah, Amos focused on the breaking of the first great commandment of loving God totally.

Judgments against Israel (2:6–16)

2:6 *Israel.* The northern kingdom and principal target of Amos's preaching. In addressing the sin of Israel, Amos first focused on the breaking of the second great commandment, "love thy neighbour as thyself." The social sins were symptoms of deep-rooted sins against God. *sold the righteous for silver, and the poor for a pair of shoes.* A reference to selling innocent victims, the poor or needy ones, into slavery in exchange for money because of a debt as minimal as the cost of shoes.

2:7 *pant . . . head.* A reference to crushing the head of the poor into the dust, similar to our idiom of taking advantage of someone by walking all over them. *turn aside the way of the meek.* Preventing the poor and meek from attaining justice. *to profane my holy name.* The word *profane* (common) is the antonym to *holy* (separate/distinct). The consequence of the social injustice and sexual sin described was to cause the Lord's unique name/person to be regarded as common or ordinary.

2:8 *they lay . . . upon clothes laid to pledge.* A violation of Ex. 22:25–26 and Deut. 24:12–13 and evidence of their selfishness and lack of humanitarian concern, a failure to love their neighbor as themselves. *condemned.* Those required to pay a fine which was used to purchase wine for a sacrilegious ordeal.

2:9–10 *Amorite.* The people who lived on Jordan's west bank, but generally a designation of all the inhabitants of Canaan, whom God expelled from the land when their iniquity had become full and whose territory God gave to Israel in keeping His covenant promise (Gen. 15:16).

2:11 *And I raised up.* The prophets, as representatives of God to the people and declarers of His will, and the Nazarites, as illustrative of those whose lives were consecrated to God's service, were evidences of the Lord's gracious dealings with the nation.

2:12 *But.* Contrary to expectation, Israel mocked God's grace by causing the Nazarites to violate their vows and by prohibiting the prophets from declaring God's word.

2:13 *Behold, I am pressed under you.* An announcement of judgment, the grammar suggesting imminent action. Literally, "I am about to make a furrow under you." The image is that of pressing down with such weight to render movement difficult or impossible like an overloaded cart.

2:14–16 These verses illustrate the inescapability and irresistibility of the judgment. Advantages that normally provide some defense in warfare are ineffective against *that day*, an expression designating the day of the Lord, a time of the special divine intervention.

Thoughts for Personal/Family Worship: Chapter 2

1. **Amos exposes the social sins of the nation before addressing its religious sins against God. Since the people were not right with their fellow man, there could be no claim of being right with God. There is an inseparable link between the two greatest commandments to love God totally and to love one's neighbor as one's self, which summarize the two main divisions of the Decalogue. To break one commandment is to be guilty of breaking them all. This provides good opportunity for reflection: how we treat others is an index to our relationship with God.**
2. **Despising grace deserves divine judgment. Although Israel had many spiritual advantages (vv. 10–11), they rejected the means of grace (v. 12) and earned divine judgment (vv. 13–16). This is a solemn reminder that with privilege comes responsibility (Luke 12:48).**

WARNINGS OF JUDGMENT (3:1—6:14)

Chapter 3: *Amos authoritatively declares the divine*

whole family which I brought up from the land
of Egypt, saying,
2 You only have I known of all the families of
the earth: therefore I will punish you for all your
iniquities.
3 Can two walk together, except they be agreed?
4 Will a lion roar in the forest, when he hath no
prey? will a young lion cry out of his den, if he
have taken nothing?
5 Can a bird fall in a snare upon the earth, where
no gin *is* for him? shall *one* take up a snare from
the earth, and have taken nothing at all?
6 Shall a trumpet be blown in the city, and the
people not be afraid? shall there be evil in a city,
and the LORD hath not done *it*?
7 Surely the Lord GOD will do nothing, but he re-
vealeth his secret unto his servants the prophets.
8 The lion hath roared, who will not fear? the
Lord GOD hath spoken, who can but prophesy?
9 ¶ Publish in the palaces at Ashdod, and in the
palaces in the land of Egypt, and say, Assemble
yourselves upon the mountains of Samaria, and
behold the great tumults in the midst thereof, and
the oppressed in the midst thereof.
10 For they know not to do right, saith the LORD,
who store up violence and robbery in their palaces.
11 Therefore thus saith the Lord GOD; An
adversary *there shall be* even round about the
land; and he shall bring down thy strength from
thee, and thy palaces shall be spoiled.
12 Thus saith the LORD; As the shepherd taketh
out of the mouth of the lion two legs, or a piece of
an ear; so shall the children of Israel be taken out
that dwell in Samaria in the corner of a bed, and
in Damascus *in* a couch.
13 Hear ye, and testify in the house of Jacob, saith
the Lord GOD, the God of hosts,
14 That in the day that I shall visit the transgres-
sions of Israel upon him I will also visit the altars
of Beth-el: and the horns of the altar shall be cut
off, and fall to the ground.
15 And I will smite the winter house with the
summer house; and the houses of ivory shall
perish, and the great houses shall have an end,
saith the LORD.

---

judgment deserved because of sin and devastating in its extent and effects.

Judgment Is Impending (3:1–15)

Origin of the Judgment (3:1–8)

3:2 *You only have I known.* Since God is omniscient, He knows all there is to know about every nation. This knowledge refers to His special, selective, caring knowledge. It is a word of election. *therefore.* The consequence of election is increased responsibility and accountability before God. That God had chosen them did not exempt them from discipline.

3:3–6 Each question anticipates a negative answer. The series of questions is a rhetorical device establishing a cause-effect relationship and leading to the principal question underscoring the divine origin of judgment: the judgment will not come unless the Lord brings it.

3:3 *Agreed* does not refer to philosophical or theological agreement but literally, to making an appointment. Going someplace with someone is not a haphazard occurrence. Arrangements are made, agreeing on a time and place to meet.

3:5 *gin.* A baited trap to lure the bird; continues the cause-effect logic and suggests the similar cause-effect between the allurements of sin and falling into the actual sin. It is a warning against the seductive nature of temptation.

3:6 *trumpet.* Refers to the warning sound of impending invasion certain to generate fear. *Evil* does not refer to sin but danger or disaster.

3:7–8 These verses mark the conclusion intended by the preceding questions. The Lord is the agent of judgment and has graciously revealed His *secret* (His plan or purposed scheme) to the prophet who is under compulsion to declare God's Word. The fact that God issues the warning of judgment through His servant is itself a token of His grace designed to lead to repentance (Rom. 2:4).

Causes of the Judgment (3:9–10)

3:9 Israel's sin and judgment will be on public display even for the pagans (represented by *Ashdod* and *Egypt*). *Tumults* refer to the panic and disorder in the land.

3:10 This verse sums up the nation's sin as not knowing *to do right*, a reference to their covenant violations, evident in *violence* (crimes against men) and *robbery* (crimes against property).

Extent of the Judgment (3:11–15)

3:12 *As the shepherd . . . an ear.* An analogy to illustrate the extent of judgment. That only two legs and a piece of an ear are rescued from the lion pictures total destruction, yet the prospect of a remnant. So Israel's destruction will be extensive with just a remnant being preserved (what could fit on *the corner of a bed* or *couch*).

3:14 *visit.* The word means to inspect or examine and often has the idea of punishment. As the Lord sees the sins of Israel, He will punish them accordingly. The *horns of the altar*, often a last resort for those trying to escape execution (1 Kings 1:50), would be removed, indicating a judgment so extensive that escape would be impossible.

3:15 The multiple houses, evidence of the affluence of the nation, will be totally devastated in the judgment.

Thoughts for Personal/Family Worship: Chapter 3

1. **Israel's national election (3:2) teaches significant truths about God's gracious election of individuals to salvation. It is an amazing display of God's grace to those undeserving of the least of any divine favor. The elect enjoy a position of unique privilege. Reflecting on the many benefits and blessings of salvation is always an appropriate theme in worship. Yet, with the privilege comes increased responsibility, "For unto whomsoever much is given, of him shall be much required" (Luke 12:48). Rather than creating pride and carelessness, election should produce a sense of humility and increased incentive to live holy and blameless lives before God and men.**
2. **Amos 3:12 suggests that God's judgment of sinners is also a means of revealing the righteous remnant. The remaining legs and part of an ear were not much, but it was something. Often God's people go through the same trouble as others, but for them it is a purifying and strengthening process rather than chastening. Daniel**

CHAPTER 4

HEAR this word, ye kine of Bashan, that *are* in the
mountain of Samaria, which oppress the poor,
which crush the needy, which say to their masters,
Bring, and let us drink.
2 The Lord GOD hath sworn by his holiness, that,
lo, the days shall come upon you, that he will take
you away with hooks, and your posterity with
fishhooks.
3 And ye shall go out at the breaches, every *cow*
at that which is before her; and ye shall cast *them*
into the palace, saith the LORD.
4 ¶ Come to Beth-el, and transgress; at Gilgal
multiply transgression; and bring your sacrifices
every morning, *and* your tithes after three years:
5 And offer a sacrifice of thanksgiving with leaven,
and proclaim *and* publish the free offerings: for
this liketh you, O ye children of Israel, saith the
Lord GOD.
6 ¶ And I also have given you cleanness of teeth
in all your cities, and want of bread in all your
places: yet have ye not returned unto me, saith the
LORD.
7 And also I have withholden the rain from you,
when *there were* yet three months to the harvest:
and I caused it to rain upon one city, and caused
it not to rain upon another city: one piece was
rained upon, and the piece whereupon it rained
not withered.
8 So two *or* three cities wandered unto one city, to
drink water; but they were not satisfied: yet have
ye not returned unto me, saith the LORD.
9 I have smitten you with blasting and mildew:
when your gardens and your vineyards and
your fig trees and your olive trees increased, the
palmerworm devoured *them*: yet have ye not
returned unto me, saith the LORD.
10 I have sent among you the pestilence after the
manner of Egypt: your young men have I slain
with the sword, and have taken away your horses;
and I have made the stink of your camps to come
up unto your nostrils: yet have ye not returned
unto me, saith the LORD.
11 I have overthrown *some* of you, as God
overthrew Sodom and Gomorrah, and ye were as
a firebrand plucked out of the burning: yet have
ye not returned unto me, saith the LORD.
12 Therefore thus will I do unto thee, O Israel:
and because I will do this unto thee, prepare to
meet thy God, O Israel.
13 For, lo, he that formeth the mountains, and
createth the wind, and declareth unto man what

---

was righteous but he was taken captive. What was judgment for his nation was means of his spiritual growth and usefulness. We should let every circumstance, even chastening, foster our sanctification.

Chapter 4: *Israel's sins and spiritual insensitivity lead to certain judgment.*

Judgment Is Inevitable (4:1–13)

Social and Religious Causes of Judgment (4:1–5)

4:1 *Kine* (cows) *of Bashan* is an unflattering image designating the women or wives of Samaria. Bashan, located east of the Jordan, was proverbial for its verdant pastures. As the cows of Bashan fed on the best of grasses, so the wives of Samaria were accustomed to a luxuriant lifestyle and selfishly pressured their *masters* (husbands) to maintain that lifestyle even at the expense of the *poor* and *needy*. Selfishness violates the second greatest commandment to love our neighbors as we love ourselves.

4:2 *hath sworn by his holiness.* Every word of God is sure but His swearing underscores the absolute certainty of what He says. *lo, the days shall come.* The Hebrew indicates that these days are impending; they are about to come. *hooks . . . fishhooks.* Symbols of the instruments of judgment. It was a common Assyrian practice to lead captives with a rope secured to a ring that had pierced the nose or lip. This physical judgment was severe but only a harbinger of the more serious and eternal judgment awaiting the unrepentant (Matt. 10:28).

4:3 The text refers to the breaching of the city and the leading to captivity of the inhabitants. The word *palace* occurs only here and could refer either to a place to which the captives will be cast or to the idea of dominion, which the captives will cast away or forfeit. Their wealth acquired through their injustice to others was no defense against the certain judgment.

4:4–5 God's command to transgress at Beth-el and Gilgal and to offer the various sacrifices in manners contrary to Mosaic prescription is sarcastically ironic to highlight the folly and unacceptability of their religious practices. The political division between the northern and southern kingdoms did not abrogate the law of the central sanctuary that limited the rituals of sacrifice to the place of God's choosing, then the temple in Jerusalem (Deut. 12:1–8). Seeing they had erected altars in the wrong places, they might as well add violation to violation. None of it was acceptable to the Lord anyway.

Spiritual Callousness to Past Judgments (4:6–11)

4:6–11 Note the refrain *yet have ye not returned unto me, saith the LORD* (4:6,8,9,10,11). Regardless of the numerous divine disciplines, they refused to repent. This section illustrates Paul's argument in Rom. 2:4–6.

4:6 *cleanness of teeth.* A graphic picture of famine; lack of food to chew kept the teeth clean.

4:9 *blasting and mildew.* The blight and disease upon the fruit-bearing trees preventing the production of fruit. Significantly, this marks a component of the covenant curses (Deut. 28:22).

4:10 *the stink of your camps.* The stench of death from the decaying bodies of the unburied slain (Isa. 34:3).

4:11 This verse reveals something of God's mercy in judgment. Although some judgment was as devastating as that let loose on Sodom and Gomorrah, there was nonetheless a remnant preserved (*firebrand*, that is a stick, *plucked out of the burning*).

Ominous Threat of Final Judgment (4:12–13)

4:12 *thus will I do.* Not just a *will* of future time but of personal resolve and determination: I am resolved to do. What the Lord resolves to do is not specified, which only intensifies the dread. The word *meet* is often used in contexts of war in which opposing armies face off against each other. Such a hostile meeting with the Lord is a fearful thing.

4:13 This description of God's creative power and sovereign authority heightens the dread of facing Him in the day of judgment.

is his thought, that maketh the morning darkness,
and treadeth upon the high places of the earth,
The LORD, The God of hosts, *is* his name.

CHAPTER 5

HEAR ye this word which I take up against you,
even a lamentation, O house of Israel.
2 The virgin of Israel is fallen; she shall no more
rise: she is forsaken upon her land; *there is* none
to raise her up.
3 For thus saith the Lord GOD; The city that went
out *by* a thousand shall leave an hundred, and
that which went forth *by* an hundred shall leave
ten, to the house of Israel.
4 ¶ For thus saith the LORD unto the house of
Israel, Seek ye me, and ye shall live:
5 But seek not Beth-el, nor enter into Gilgal, and
pass not to Beer-sheba: for Gilgal shall surely go
into captivity, and Beth-el shall come to nought.
6 Seek the LORD, and ye shall live; lest he break
out like fire in the house of Joseph, and devour *it*,
and *there be* none to quench *it* in Beth-el.
7 Ye who turn judgment to wormwood, and leave
off righteousness in the earth,
8 *Seek him* that maketh the seven stars and
Orion, and turneth the shadow of death into the
morning, and maketh the day dark with night:
that calleth for the waters of the sea, and poureth
them out upon the face of the earth: The LORD *is*
his name:
9 That strengtheneth the spoiled against the strong,
so that the spoiled shall come against the fortress.
10 They hate him that rebuketh in the gate, and
they abhor him that speaketh uprightly.
11 Forasmuch therefore as your treading *is* upon
the poor, and ye take from him burdens of wheat:
ye have built houses of hewn stone, but ye shall
not dwell in them; ye have planted pleasant
vineyards, but ye shall not drink wine of them.
12 For I know your manifold transgressions and
your mighty sins: they afflict the just, they take
a bribe, and they turn aside the poor in the gate
from their right.
13 Therefore the prudent shall keep silence in
that time; for it *is* an evil time.

Thoughts for Personal/Family Worship: Chapter 4

1. **The negative example of the selfishness and self-indulgence of the women of Samaria provides the opportunity to reflect on what Christ identifies as the second great commandment: to love one's neighbor as one's self. You could contrast the women of Samaria, who were willing to harm others in order to help themselves, with the Good Samaritan, who was willing to sacrifice his own possessions to help another (Luke 10:30–36).**
2. **The Lord's ironic command to transgress at Beth-el (4:4–5) teaches some important lessons about worship. First, it is important to worship the Lord in the way that He has prescribed (the regulative principle). We are not left to our own imagination or devices to worship Him. Second, it is important to worship the Lord with a genuine heart of faith, in spirit and in truth. The multiplication of all the rituals without a heart for God meant nothing. God is never satisfied with a purely external religion without faith.**
3. **Amos 4:6–11 warns of the danger of not responding to God's gracious dealings. In spite of all of the gracious warnings the Lord had given, the people persisted in their sin and became more and more calloused to spiritual things. There are great advantages to being in a Christian home where the evidences of God's grace abound. But we must be careful not to become oblivious and insensitive to His goodness and longsuffering. We must warn our children not to take their spiritual privileges for granted and not to turn from His dealings in their lives.**

Chapter 5: ***Genuine repentance was Israel's only hope to avert the divine judgment warranted by their social and religious sins.***

Judgment Is Escapable (5:1–15)

Lamentation for Fallen State (5:1–3)

5:1 *lamentation.* Literally, a funeral song or dirge. Ironically, Amos offers the lament in anticipation of Israel's tragic end.

5:2 *The virgin of Israel* is an appositional statement identifying Israel as the virgin, a term reflecting the nation's special covenant standing with the Lord that they had violated. Israel's fall and abandonment earned by their covenant disobedience was sadly contrary to expectation.

5:3 This verse describes a thorough decimation of the population but yet holds hope of a remnant.

Invitations to Repent (5:4–15)

5:4–6 *Seek . . . live.* Genuinely seeking the Lord involves turning to Him in faith and repentance. The consequence of so seeking Him is finding Him (Deut. 4:29) and receiving the benefits of His grace for He is "a rewarder of them that diligently seek him" (Heb. 11:6).

5:5 *Beth-el . . . Gilgal . . . Beer-sheba.* Places with significant religious tradition, but tradition or ritual could not substitute for a genuine and spiritual experience with the Lord Himself. Hope is in the Lord, not external religion.

5:6 *lest.* The consequences of not seeking the Lord were certain, severe, and irreversible.

5:7 *judgment.* The ethical display of justice that they distorted into poisonous acts against others (*wormwood*, a bitter plant). *leave off righteousness in the earth.* They abandoned proper and acceptable behavior as though they left it in the dirt.

5:8–9 Attention to God's creative and providential activity over the natural sphere (v. 8) and human affairs (v. 9) shows the sensibility of seeking Him. A more literal reading of v. 9 shows the folly of thinking God's judgment is resistible: "He causes destruction to flash against the strong, and destruction comes against a stronghold."

5:10 *They hate . . . they abhor.* Impersonal subjects, a way of expressing a passive idea: "the one rebuking is hated; the one speaking is abhorred." *rebuketh in the gate.* Arbitrates in the place where court was held.

5:11 This verse expresses the irony of judgment. They would not benefit from their ill-gotten gain.

5:12 *gate.* See note at 5:10.

14 Seek good, and not evil, that ye may live: and
so the LORD, the God of hosts, shall be with you,
as ye have spoken.
15 Hate the evil, and love the good, and establish
judgment in the gate: it may be that the LORD
God of hosts will be gracious unto the remnant
of Joseph.
16 Therefore the LORD, the God of hosts, the
Lord, saith thus; Wailing *shall be* in all streets; and
they shall say in all the highways, Alas! alas! and
they shall call the husbandman to mourning, and
such as are skilful of lamentation to wailing.
17 And in all vineyards *shall be* wailing: for I will
pass through thee, saith the LORD.
18 Woe unto you that desire the day of the LORD!
to what end *is* it for you? the day of the LORD *is*
darkness, and not light.
19 As if a man did flee from a lion, and a bear met
him; or went into the house, and leaned his hand
on the wall, and a serpent bit him.
20 *Shall* not the day of the LORD *be* darkness,
and not light? even very dark, and no brightness
in it?
21 ¶ I hate, I despise your feast days, and I will not
smell in your solemn assemblies.
22 Though ye offer me burnt offerings and your
meat offerings, I will not accept *them*: neither will
I regard the peace offerings of your fat beasts.
23 Take thou away from me the noise of thy
songs; for I will not hear the melody of thy viols.
24 But let judgment run down as waters, and
righteousness as a mighty stream.
25 Have ye offered unto me sacrifices and offerings
in the wilderness forty years, O house of
Israel?
26 But ye have borne the tabernacle of your
Moloch and Chiun your images, the star of your
god, which ye made to yourselves.
27 Therefore will I cause you to go into captivity
beyond Damascus, saith the LORD, whose name *is*
The God of hosts.

CHAPTER 6

WOE to them *that are* at ease in Zion, and trust
in the mountain of Samaria, *which are* named

5:15 *Hate . . . love.* Primarily volitional terms; hence, reject evil and choose good. *it may be.* The Hebrew expresses hope, not doubt. Repentance is the only hope that sinners will experience God's grace in escaping judgment.

Judgment Is Certain (5:16—6:14)

Woe against Carnal Confidence (5:16–27)

5:16–17 So devastating will be the judgment that those in the city (*streets . . . highways*) and those in the country (*husbandman*, i.e., farmer) will be joined by professional mourners (*skilful of lamentation*) in lamenting the effects. *I will pass through thee.* As the Lord passed through to strike the Egyptians on the night of Passover (Ex. 12:23) so will He pass through Israel.

5:18–20 *the day of the LORD.* God's direct intervention into human affairs either to bless His people or judge the wicked. Amos contradicts Israel's false sense of security that the day would be blessing for them. Not only was it going to be fearful darkness (vv. 18,20) but also inescapable (v. 19).

5:21–26 These verses detail Israel's religious practices, which were the grounds for their false security but rejected by God.

5:21 *I hate, I despise.* The Hebrew construction emphasizes the utter rejection of the *feast days*, also designated as the *solemn assemblies* (referring specifically to the pilgrimage feasts of Unleavened Bread, Weeks, and Booths or Tabernacles). *I will not smell* has the idea of delighting in and refers to God's refusal to accept or be pleased with the sweet savor offerings.

5:23 *noise.* As the din or racket of rushing waters or chariots. *viols.* A type of stringed instrument such as harp.

5:24 *judgment.* Justice. In contrast to heartless rituals, God desires spiritual worship that will reveal its genuineness in ethical behavior. A right relationship with God is requisite to right relationships with others.

5:25 *Have ye offered* (rather, did you offer). A rhetorical question expecting a negative answer. The point concerns not the fact of the sacrifices but the spirit with which the sacrifices were offered. Ritual without heart had been a habitual problem in Israel's history, and characterizes much of modern worship as well.

5:26 Heartless worship evolved to idolatry. The word *tabernacle* is perhaps a proper name, Sikkuth, an Assyrian god whom they regarded as their king (*Moloch*); *Chiun* is perhaps a reference to Saturn. Regardless of the identity of the idols, the people worshiped and carried around the products of their imaginations and their hands.

Thoughts for Personal/Family Worship: Chapter 5

1. **The invitations to repent are reminders of the hope extended to the greatest of sinners. God's goodness, forbearance, and longsuffering delayed the earned judgment providing the opportunity to repent (Rom. 2:4). The invitations also testify to God's inflexibility since true repentance is the only way to escape the judgment. Sinners can come to God only on His terms.**
2. **Amos 5:12 ("I know your manifold transgressions") is occasion to reflect on God's infallible knowledge: "All things are naked and opened unto the eyes of him with whom we have to do" (Heb. 4:13). It is a fearful thing and should be a motive to purity to know that God knows all we are and all we do.**
3. **God's rejection of Israel's rituals is a solemn warning about the danger of purely external religion. Because of their worship practices, Israel assumed they were right with God and God was satisfied with them. External religion tends to breed a false confidence and security. The form of external worship is different today, but the attitude persists. Many believe that all is well spiritually simply because they attend church and do "Christian" things. God's view of religion without heart does not change. Those that worship Him must do so in spirit and in truth (John 4:24).**

Chapter 6: *Amos addresses the complacency of the nation and declares the certainty and the extent of coming judgment.*

Woe against Religious Complacency (6:1–6)

6:1 *at ease.* Arrogantly carefree and careless (see 6:4). *Zion.*

chief of the nations, to whom the house of Israel
came!
2 Pass ye unto Calneh, and see; and from thence
go ye to Hamath the great: then go down to Gath
of the Philistines: *be they* better than these king-
doms? or their border greater than your border?
3 Ye that put far away the evil day, and cause the
seat of violence to come near;
4 That lie upon beds of ivory, and stretch
themselves upon their couches, and eat the lambs
out of the flock, and the calves out of the midst
of the stall;
5 That chant to the sound of the viol, *and* invent
to themselves instruments of musick, like David;
6 That drink wine in bowls, and anoint
themselves with the chief ointments: but they are
not grieved for the affliction of Joseph.
7 ¶ Therefore now shall they go captive with the
first that go captive, and the banquet of them that
stretched themselves shall be removed.
8 The Lord GOD hath sworn by himself, saith the
LORD the God of hosts, I abhor the excellency of
Jacob, and hate his palaces: therefore will I deliver
up the city with all that is therein.
9 And it shall come to pass, if there remain ten
men in one house, that they shall die.
10 And a man's uncle shall take him up, and he
that burneth him, to bring out the bones out of
the house, and shall say unto him that *is* by the
sides of the house, *Is there* yet *any* with thee?
and he shall say, No. Then shall he say, Hold thy
tongue: for we may not make mention of the
name of the LORD.
11 For, behold, the LORD commandeth, and he
will smite the great house with breaches, and the
little house with clefts.
12 ¶ Shall horses run upon the rock? will *one*
plow *there* with oxen? for ye have turned judg-
ment into gall, and the fruit of righteousness into
hemlock:
13 Ye which rejoice in a thing of nought, which
say, Have we not taken to us horns by our own
strength?
14 But, behold, I will raise up against you a nation,

The southern kingdom, though not the principal target of the prophet's message, shared the northern kingdom's (*the mountain of Samaria*) false confidence and sense of security (*trust*). *named chief of the nations, to whom . . . came.* Identifies the object of their confidence as the notable or famous men (*named*) in their nation, which they reckoned to be preeminent among the nations.

6:2 *Calneh, Hamath, Gath.* Though the precise locations are disputed, the places designate regions east, north, and west of Israel. *be they.* The KJV adds these words referring to Zion and Samaria. The answer to the rhetorical questions should have been yes given their privileged heritage from the Lord, but ironically, the answer was no.

6:3 They ignored the prophet by thrusting out (*put far away*) any thought of disastrous judgment (*evil day*) and persisted in their sins by allowing violence to reign.

6:5 *chant.* To improvise carelessly, resulting in frivolous songs. *viol.* A stringed instrument, perhaps a harp. *invent to themselves.* Literally, "think to themselves." This refers not to inventing instruments, but to making up songs with instruments.

6:6 Luxurious living (indulging self) is contrasted with insensitivity (not being *grieved* or sickened) to the collapse (*affliction*) of the nation.

Divine Determination in Judgment (6:7–14)

6:7 *Therefore* links the judgment to the sins of complacency. Ironically, those who regarded themselves the first of nations (v. 1) are destined to be the first of the exiles. *the banquet . . . removed.* The cessation of the cry of revelry from those reclining on the couches of ease.

6:8 *GOD hath sworn.* See note at 4:2. *excellency of Jacob.* His pride. *palaces.* Fortified strongholds.

6:10 *uncle.* A kinsman of some relation or even a close friend who extracts the dead found in the house. *burneth.* Either an honorific part of the funeral ceremony or the actual cremation of the body, which though not the normal practice in Israel may have been necessitated by the massive number of corpses. *not make mention.* A recognition of the futility of invoking the Lord since He is the cause of the calamity being experienced.

6:11 *great house . . . little house.* A literary device called merismus that uses polar ideas (*great* and *little*) to represent totality: the calamity will hit all houses. *with breaches . . . with clefts.* The judgment will reduce the houses to ruin and rubbish.

6:12 *the rock.* A craggy cliff. As this would be an unsafe, unlikely, and foolish place for horses to run or oxen to plow, so was Israel's changing justice and righteousness to poison was foolish.

6:13 *thing of nought . . . horns.* Some interpret these as names of locations: Lo-debar (2 Sam. 9:4) and Karnaim (Gen. 14:5). The KJV translates the words and reflects a fitting sense in context. They rejoiced in nothing, perhaps a reference to idols; they claimed by their own strength to increase strength (*horns* are a common symbol of power).

6:14 *entering in of Hemath . . . the river of the wilderness.* The northern and southern borders and thus identifying the total extent of the judgment: no part of the land would be exempt.

Thoughts for Personal/Family Worship: Chapter 6

1. **Material prosperity can distort reality and cause insensitivity to spiritual issues. Israel was accustomed to a lifestyle of luxury and refused to think about the consequences of their self-indulgence. The experience of the moment blinded them to the certain coming of judgment (6:3). Second Peter 3:3–10 similarly speaks of those who deny the coming judgment just because it has not yet come. We should be warned from the fact that judgment did come to Israel. Spiritual insensitivity and obliviousness are dangerous.**
2. **Christ's illustration of the rich man and Lazarus (Luke 16:19–26) parallels the situation described in Amos 6:6 of those engaged in self-indulgence at the neglect of the afflicted. In both contexts, the consequences are severe.**
3. **That God commands the judgment (6:11) is occasion to reflect on His inflexible righteousness that ought to generate the fear of the Lord. For it is, indeed, a fearful thing to fall into the hands of the living God (Heb. 10:31). That God raises up a nation (Assyria) as the agent of judgment (6:14) demonstrates His sovereignty and**

O house of Israel, saith the LORD the God of hosts;
and they shall afflict you from the entering in of
Hemath unto the river of the wilderness.

CHAPTER 7

THUS hath the Lord GOD shewed unto me; and,
behold, he formed grasshoppers in the beginning
of the shooting up of the latter growth; and, lo,
it was the latter growth after the king's mowings.
2 And it came to pass, *that* when they had made
an end of eating the grass of the land, then I said,
O Lord GOD, forgive, I beseech thee: by whom
shall Jacob arise? for he *is* small.
3 The LORD repented for this: It shall not be, saith
the LORD.
4 ¶ Thus hath the Lord GOD shewed unto me:
and, behold, the Lord GOD called to contend by
fire, and it devoured the great deep, and did eat
up a part.
5 Then said I, O Lord GOD, cease, I beseech thee:
by whom shall Jacob arise? for he *is* small.
6 The LORD repented for this: This also shall not
be, saith the Lord GOD.
7 ¶ Thus he shewed me: and, behold, the Lord
stood upon a wall *made* by a plumbline, with a
plumbline in his hand.
8 And the LORD said unto me, Amos, what seest
thou? And I said, A plumbline. Then said the
Lord, Behold, I will set a plumbline in the midst
of my people Israel: I will not again pass by them
any more:
9 And the high places of Isaac shall be desolate,
and the sanctuaries of Israel shall be laid waste;
and I will rise against the house of Jeroboam with
the sword.
10 ¶ Then Amaziah the priest of Beth-el sent
to Jeroboam king of Israel, saying, Amos hath
conspired against thee in the midst of the house
of Israel: the land is not able to bear all his words.
11 For thus Amos saith, Jeroboam shall die by the
sword, and Israel shall surely be led away captive
out of their own land.
12 Also Amaziah said unto Amos, O thou seer, go,
flee thee away into the land of Judah, and there eat
bread, and prophesy there:
13 But prophesy not again any more at Beth-el:
for it *is* the king's chapel, and it *is* the king's court.
14 ¶ Then answered Amos, and said to Amaziah,
I *was* no prophet, neither *was* I a prophet's son;
but I *was* an herdman, and a gatherer of sycomore
fruit:
15 And the LORD took me as I followed the flock,
and the LORD said unto me, Go, prophesy unto
my people Israel.
16 ¶ Now therefore hear thou the word of the

His authority to use secondary causes to accomplish His will. God judged, but the Assyrians were the rod of His anger (Isa. 10:5).

VISIONS OF JUDGMENT (7:1—9:10)

Chapter 7: *In a series of visions, the Lord reveals His longsuffering that ultimately gives way to judgment, and Amos confronts a false priest who opposes his preaching.*

Locusts and Fire Picture Prevented Judgment (7:1–6)

7:1 *the Lord GOD shewed.* A vision was one of the diverse ways God communicated to the prophets (Heb. 1:1). Rich in symbolism, visions were internal to the prophet, who often participated in the revelation. The prophet most likely appeared to be in some ecstatic state during the revelation experience. God revealed visions to those spiritually mature whereas He revealed things in dreams to those spiritually immature or even spiritually dead (Pharaoh, for instance) and who were always passive during the experience. *he formed grasshoppers . . . after the king's mowings.* The first vision is that of the locust invasion, often associated with God's chastening for covenant violations (Deut. 28:42; Joel 1). Its coming after the king had taken his share of the harvest (a form of taxation) would result in a complete and devastating loss.

7:2 Like Moses (e.g., Deut. 9:25–29), Amos interceded asking God to *forgive. by whom shall Jacob arise?* How can Jacob be able to endure? The prophet's argument in prayer was for the nation's weakness and insignificance.

7:3 *The LORD repented.* God answered the prayer by relenting from the judgment, an evidence of His longsuffering. "Repent" means to sorrow and is a bold anthropopathism (human emotion applied to God) to aid our understanding of God's actions.

7:4 *to contend.* A legal term designating a lawsuit. *by fire.* The means of executing the guilty sentence. *devoured the great deep.* The fire's consuming the ocean is hyperbole to emphasize intensity of the flame. *did eat up a part.* Literally, "and it will devour the share," referring specifically to Israel's portion or inheritance.

7:5–6 See notes at vv. 2 and 3.

A Plumbline Pictures Inevitable Judgment (7:7–9)

7:7–8 *plumbline.* Although some interpret this word (rare in Hebrew) to mean tin, symbolizing military strength that will ultimately subdue Israel, more traditionally, as reflected by the KJV, it refers to a lead weight on the end of a line to measure straightness. It would symbolize the perfect standard by which Israel would be evaluated and consequently judged because of their "crookedness." *I will not again pass by.* God's longsuffering would end, resulting in inevitable judgment (Gen. 6:3).

7:9 *high places.* Sites where illegitimate rituals occurred.

Parenthesis: Confrontation with a False Priest (7:10–17)

7:10 *priest of Beth-el.* A renegade priest at one of Israel's chief centers of worship. *conspired.* Amaziah accused Amos of treason.

7:12 *seer.* One of the Old Testament designations of a prophet, appropriate here since Amos was recording the visions he saw from the Lord. Amaziah commands Amos to return home to the south and take his message with him.

7:13 *chapel.* Elsewhere translated "sanctuary" or "holy place." *king's court.* Literally, "house of a kingdom," referring to the royal temple.

7:14 *a prophet's son.* Literally, "a son of a prophet," an idiom referring to one belonging to the class of prophets.

7:16 *drop.* To drool or foam at the mouth. Amaziah's derogatory description of Amos's preaching.

LORD: Thou sayest, Prophesy not against Israel,
and drop not *thy word* against the house of Isaac.
17 Therefore thus saith the LORD; Thy wife shall
be an harlot in the city, and thy sons and thy
daughters shall fall by the sword, and thy land
shall be divided by line; and thou shalt die in a
polluted land: and Israel shall surely go into
captivity forth of his land.

CHAPTER 8

THUS hath the Lord GOD shewed unto me: and
behold a basket of summer fruit.
2 And he said, Amos, what seest thou? And I said,
A basket of summer fruit. Then said the LORD
unto me, The end is come upon my people of
Israel; I will not again pass by them any more.
3 And the songs of the temple shall be howlings
in that day, saith the Lord GOD: *there shall be*
many dead bodies in every place; they shall cast
them forth with silence.
4 ¶ Hear this, O ye that swallow up the needy,
even to make the poor of the land to fail,
5 Saying, When will the new moon be gone, that
we may sell corn? and the sabbath, that we may
set forth wheat, making the ephah small, and the
shekel great, and falsifying the balances by deceit?
6 That we may buy the poor for silver, and the
needy for a pair of shoes; *yea*, and sell the refuse
of the wheat?
7 The LORD hath sworn by the excellency of
Jacob, Surely I will never forget any of their works.
8 Shall not the land tremble for this, and every
one mourn that dwelleth therein? and it shall rise
up wholly as a flood; and it shall be cast out and
drowned, as *by* the flood of Egypt.
9 And it shall come to pass in that day, saith the
Lord GOD, that I will cause the sun to go down at
noon, and I will darken the earth in the clear day:
10 And I will turn your feasts into mourning, and
all your songs into lamentation; and I will bring
up sackcloth upon all loins, and baldness upon
every head; and I will make it as the mourning of
an only *son*, and the end thereof as a bitter day.
11 ¶ Behold, the days come, saith the Lord GOD,
that I will send a famine in the land, not a famine
of bread, nor a thirst for water, but of hearing the
words of the LORD:
12 And they shall wander from sea to sea, and
from the north even to the east, they shall run to
and fro to seek the word of the LORD, and shall
not find *it*.
13 In that day shall the fair virgins and young
men faint for thirst.

7:17 *divided by line.* Part of the judgment of Amaziah would be the parceling out of measured portions of his personal property.

Thoughts for Personal/Family Worship: Chapter 7

1. **The Lord's relenting of the judgment in answer to the prophet's prayer (7:2–3; 5–6) is a lesson in the power of intercessory prayer. Believing that God has decreed the end requires also believing that God has decreed the means to accomplishing His purpose. Prayer is a means whereby God works His will. As effective as Amos's prayer was before God, it pales before the intercessions of the greater prophet, the Lord Jesus Christ. He ever lives to make intercession for us as our Advocate with the Father (Heb. 7:25; 1 John 2:1). Whereas Amos appealed to God from Israel's weakness and insignificance (7:2,5), Christ pleads the merits of His sacrifice. Charles Wesley's hymn sums up nicely the effectiveness of Christ's intercession: "Five bleeding wounds He bears, received on Calvary, they pour effectual prayers, they strongly plead for me: Forgive him, O forgive they cry . . . nor let that ransomed sinner die." And then the wonderful assurance: "The Father hears Him pray, His dear anointed One; He cannot turn away the presence of His Son."**
2. **Amos's preaching in spite of the "official" injunction against him parallels the persistent preaching of the apostles when they too were ordered to stop by the established religious authorities (Acts 4:18–20). Obeying God is always more important than obeying man.**

Chapter 8: *The Lord reveals a vision of impending judgment and then gives details of the judgment that He will impose because of the nation's sins.*

A Basket of Summer Fruit Pictures the Imminence of Judgment (8:1–14)

8:1–2 *summer fruit . . . end.* A pun in Hebrew, the two words sounding similar. As summer fruit is ripe marking the time of harvest, so the nation was ripe for judgment. *I will not again pass by.* See notes at 7:7–8.

8:3 *songs of the temple shall be howlings.* Literally, "songs of the temple will lament." *cast them forth with silence.* The vast number of corpses will preclude normal mourning rites, hence a command for silence.

8:5 This details the greed and dishonest business practices, including disdain for the Sabbath, exorbitant prices for a small amount of goods, and misrepresentation.

8:6 See note at 2:6.

8:7 *The LORD hath sworn.* See note at 4:2. *excellency of Jacob.* His pride, most likely referring to the land, which the nation inherited as part of the covenant promise. Now it had become ironically a component of the divine oath to remove the people from the land because of their unforgettable transgressions.

8:8 *flood.* The Nile, the river of Egypt. Judgment is compared to the devastation caused by the ebb and flow of the flooding river.

8:9 This verse uses the imagery of an eclipse to describe the darkness so often associated with judgment, particularly in consequence of covenant violations (e.g., Deut. 28:29; Joel 2:10,31).

8:10 *baldness.* The result of shaving the head as a gesture of mourning.

8:11 *famine . . . of hearing the words.* God's removing His word marked the climax of judgment and removal of hope, since faith comes by hearing and hearing by the word of God. Without a vision (the prophetic word) the people perish (Prov. 29:18).

8:13 Singling out the effects of judgment on the young and strong underscores how devastating it would be on the rest of the population.

14 They that swear by the sin of Samaria, and say,
Thy god, O Dan, liveth; and, The manner of Beer-
sheba liveth; even they shall fall, and never rise up
again.

CHAPTER 9

I SAW the Lord standing upon the altar: and he
said, Smite the lintel of the door, that the posts
may shake: and cut them in the head, all of them;
and I will slay the last of them with the sword: he
that fleeth of them shall not flee away, and he that
escapeth of them shall not be delivered.
2 Though they dig into hell, thence shall mine
hand take them; though they climb up to heaven,
thence will I bring them down:
3 And though they hide themselves in the top of
Carmel, I will search and take them out thence;
and though they be hid from my sight in the
bottom of the sea, thence will I command the
serpent, and he shall bite them:
4 And though they go into captivity before their
enemies, thence will I command the sword, and
it shall slay them: and I will set mine eyes upon
them for evil, and not for good.
5 And the Lord GOD of hosts *is* he that toucheth
the land, and it shall melt, and all that dwell
therein shall mourn: and it shall rise up wholly
like a flood; and shall be drowned, as *by* the flood
of Egypt.
6 *It is* he that buildeth his stories in the heaven,
and hath founded his troop in the earth; he that
calleth for the waters of the sea, and poureth them
out upon the face of the earth: The LORD *is* his
name.
7 *Are* ye not as children of the Ethiopians unto
me, O children of Israel? saith the LORD. Have
not I brought up Israel out of the land of Egypt?
and the Philistines from Caphtor, and the Syrians
from Kir?
8 Behold, the eyes of the Lord GOD *are* upon the
sinful kingdom, and I will destroy it from off the
face of the earth; saving that I will not utterly
destroy the house of Jacob, saith the LORD.
9 For, lo, I will command, and I will sift the house
of Israel among all nations, like as *corn* is sifted
in a sieve, yet shall not the least grain fall upon
the earth.
10 All the sinners of my people shall die by the
sword, which say, The evil shall not overtake nor
prevent us.
11 ¶ In that day will I raise up the tabernacle of

8:14 *sin of Samaria.* Metonymy for the god of Samaria, the worship of which was sinful shame, a specific reference to the golden calf erected by Jeroboam. *The manner of Beer-sheba.* The way of Beer-sheba, another reference to the practice of pagan idolatry destined to doom.

Thoughts for Personal/Family Worship: Chapter 8

1. **The vision of the basket of summer fruit warns the sinner that the time comes when God's longsuffering, designed to lead to repentance (Rom. 2:4), ends and judgment is inevitable. There is a point of no return, a complete loss of hope. This truth can be illustrated from the flood narrative (Gen. 6:3) and the Lord's dealing with those who refused Wisdom's invitation to life (Prov. 1:24–32). In addition, the physical judgment inflicted on Israel points to the far greater eternal judgment awaiting Christ-rejecters (Matt. 8:12).**
2. **That a famine of hearing the words of the Lord (8:11) is a sign of God's disfavor should generate praise and thanksgiving for His favor in giving and preserving His Word for us in the Bible. Not only should be we be thankful for it, we should feast on it regularly that we might benefit from its bounty for our spiritual welfare.**

Chapter 9: ***After a final vision of divine judgment to come, the Lord gives a wonderful message of hope and blessing based on His covenant promise to David.***

The Lord at the Altar Pictures the Inescapability and Discrimination of Judgment (9:1–10)

9:1 *altar.* One of the altars associated with Israel's idolatry, perhaps at Beth-el but representative of the whole religious system under the sentence of judgment. *lintel.* The top of the column post. *posts.* The threshold base of the door with holes for the column posts. *cut them in the head.* Either cutting off the tops of the doors causing a collapse of the temple structure or heads of people gathered at the temple that will be crushed with the collapse. The rest of the verse detailing the impossibility of escaping the judgment suggests the reference may be to the people.

9:2–3 *hell . . . heaven.* Not referring here to either the abode of the wicked or of God, they are polar expressions to designate totality of space. There is no place too low or too high to escape God's judgment. The *top of Carmel* contrasted with *the bottom of the sea* expresses the same idea.

9:4 *evil.* Harmful or destructive. *good.* Prosperity or well-being.

9:5 *rise up wholly like a flood.* A reference to the flooding of the Nile. *shall be drowned.* Literally, "shall sink or subside"; probably a reference to the receding of the Nile after its rising, exposing the flood damage.

9:6 Referring to God's creative work reinforces the threat of judgment by highlighting His unique power. *stories.* Literally, "stairs" or "ascents": perhaps a figure of speech (part for the whole) referring to His heavenly temple or palace. *founded his troop in the earth.* Literally, "established His vault or storehouse above the earth," perhaps a reference to the firmament or expanse of the heaven which declares His glory (Ps. 19:1).

9:7 Israel was unique not because God allotted them territory since He assigned borders to other nations in His sovereignty as well. The other nations, however, did not possess their lands as part of a covenant. Ironically, because Israel had broken that covenant, they forfeited all distinction from the pagan nations.

9:8–9 *I will not utterly destroy.* Along with the threat of certain and total destruction is the promise of hope in the preservation of a remnant. Genesis 3:15 sets a pattern evident throughout Scripture: included in the statement of the curse is a message of hope and blessing. The imagery of sifting (v. 9) illustrates how the act of judgment identifies the remnant: a separation of the good from the bad.

9:10 *All the sinners* identifies the part *of my people* that

David that is fallen, and close up the breaches
thereof; and I will raise up his ruins, and I will
build it as in the days of old:
12 That they may possess the remnant of Edom,
and of all the heathen, which are called by my
name, saith the LORD that doeth this.
13 Behold, the days come, saith the LORD, that the
plowman shall overtake the reaper, and the treader
of grapes him that soweth seed; and the mountains
shall drop sweet wine, and all the hills shall melt.
14 And I will bring again the captivity of my
people of Israel, and they shall build the waste
cities, and inhabit *them*; and they shall plant
vineyards, and drink the wine thereof; they shall
also make gardens, and eat the fruit of them.
15 And I will plant them upon their land, and
they shall no more be pulled up out of their land
which I have given them, saith the LORD thy God.

will be judged, suggesting that some are not among the condemned sinners. *The evil.* The destruction. *prevent.* Meet or confront. Like so many under the sentence of divine wrath, they ignored the warnings and were oblivious to the impending doom.

RESTORATION AFTER JUDGMENT (9:11–15)

Restoration of the Kingdom (9:11–12)

9:11 *In that day.* A reference to the day of the Lord, a designation of those special times of unmistakable divine intervention into time either for judgment or blessing. *tabernacle of David.* The hut or booth of David, not referring to the place of worship but to David's kingdom or dynasty that had been divided. God declares that He will reunite the kingdom in faithfulness to the covenant with David (2 Sam. 7:4–17), a promise guaranteed by the coming of David's greater Son, the Christ.

9:12 *the remnant of Edom.* God's people possessing Edom was associated with messianic blessing as far back as Balaam's prophecy (Num. 24:17–19). *and of all the heathen.* "Even" all the heathen, an explicative statement defining the significance of Edom as being representative of all the Gentiles. Significantly, James appeals to this prophecy to justify the inclusion of Gentiles in Christ's kingdom (Acts 15:13–17).

Universal Prosperity (9:13–15)

9:13 This verse describes a time of unceasing harvest and productivity. *all the hills shall melt.* The hills will flow with the abundance of the vintage.

9:14–15 These verses describe the complete reversal of the covenant judgments. Interpretations differ regarding the time and mechanics of the prophecy's fulfillment, but the message of hope and blessing is clear. One way or another it points to the enjoyment of the messianic feast (Isa. 25:6–9; Matt. 8:11) that ultimately is beyond comprehension (1 Cor. 2:9).

Thoughts for Personal/Family Worship: Chapter 9

1. **The similarity of Amos 9:2–3 to Psalm 139:7–9 is remarkable. Both texts address God's omnipresence and omniscience. What is a dread to sinners who can never hide from or escape God's hand of judgment is a comfort to saints who can never be out of God's sight and care. It is indeed a thought that is too wonderful (Ps. 139:6). We should, therefore, live in that constant awareness of God and consistently factor Him into all the circumstances of life.**
2. **Amos 9:8–10 teaches that one of the purposes of judgment is to identify the remnant, those who belong to the Lord. God is able to use a single occurrence for multiple purposes. A disaster that may be judgment on sinners can also be a trial to test and strengthen saints. Daniel, for instance, was taken to Babylon as part of Judah's captivity because of sin. But that national chastisement was a means of maturing Daniel to great usefulness in God's kingdom.**
3. **That Christ's kingdom takes possession of Edom, even all the nations, or as James interprets it "the residue of men" declares the absolute success of the gospel (Acts 15:17). It parallels the dramatic heavenly scene in Rev. 7 that describes the redeemed as being comprised of every nation, people, and tongue. It ought to be reason for our praise and thanksgiving that we are included in that great number.**

INTRODUCTION TO THE BOOK OF OBADIAH

Authorship: Obadiah, "the servant of the Lord," is a common name in the Old Testament. Although the exact identity of the prophet is hard to determine, there are indications he ministered in Judah, the southern kingdom (vv. 12,17).

Date: Obadiah preached during a time of national disaster (v. 11). Conservatives disagree as to whether Obadiah is the earliest of the Minor Prophets, ministering during the reign of Jehoram (848–841 BC) or later after Judah's fall to Babylon (586 BC). Babylon's invasion easily explains the extent of the devastation to Judah, but a battle in which Edom may have participated referred to in 2 Chron. 21:16–17 is more likely the historical context. Statements indicating that the northern kingdom had not yet fallen (v. 19) and Jer. 49:9–10,14–16,22 apparently quoting Obad. 1–6,9 would also suggest Obadiah's early date. Dating Obadiah to about 848 BC would make him the first of all the writing prophets.

Theme: The day of the Lord as poetic justice: "as thou hast done, it shall be done unto thee" (v. 15).

Examples of the poetic justice theme

Sin	Punishment
Treachery against Judah (vv. 11–12)	Treachery of its confederates (v. 7)
Robbed Judah (v. 13)	They will be robbed (vv. 5–6)
Violence against Judah (v. 11)	They will perish by sword (v. 9)
Sought Judah's destruction (vv. 12–14)	They will be utterly destroyed (vv. 10,18)
Sought to dispossess Judah (v. 14)	They will be possessed (v. 19)

Purpose: To encourage God's people that no opposition can frustrate the advancing of God's kingdom (v. 21).

Synopsis: *The Contribution of Obadiah to Redemptive Revelation*

The Edomites were the descendants of Esau and historic enemies of Israel. The hatred went back to the conflict between Esau and Jacob and was first evident nationally when Edom refused Israel passage after the exodus. Although Edom was never a serious military threat, they always sided with Israel's enemies. Consequently, they became a fitting representative of all powers that are hostile to God, His people, and His kingdom. The day of the Lord against Edom was fulfilled against Edom, but is also typical of the day against every evil force. The question was whether Edom and other enemies would get away with their behavior to God's people. The book stresses the divine punishment that must come to Edom for its pride and violence against Judah. Obadiah stresses God's sovereignty in such a way as to make it clear that even though the enemy seemed to prosper, it was only temporary. The Lord is a God of moral justice who will right all the wrongs of the world in His time. God is in control, and behind the scenes He works His plan and His people will triumph. Redemptive history cannot be frustrated.

Outline:
I. The Destruction of Edom (vv. 1–9)
II. The Sin of Edom (vv. 10–14)
III. The Punishment of Edom (vv. 15–21)

THE BOOK OF

OBADIAH

THE vision of Obadiah. Thus saith the Lord GOD concerning Edom; We have heard a rumour from the LORD, and an ambassador is sent among the heathen, Arise ye, and let us rise up against her in battle.
2 Behold, I have made thee small among the heathen: thou art greatly despised.
3 ¶ The pride of thine heart hath deceived thee, thou that dwellest in the clefts of the rock, whose habitation *is* high; that saith in his heart, Who shall bring me down to the ground?
4 Though thou exalt *thyself* as the eagle, and though thou set thy nest among the stars, thence will I bring thee down, saith the LORD.
5 If thieves came to thee, if robbers by night, (how art thou cut off!) would they not have stolen till they had enough? if the grapegatherers came to thee, would they not leave *some* grapes?
6 How are *the things* of Esau searched out! *how* are his hidden things sought up!
7 All the men of thy confederacy have brought thee *even* to the border: the men that were at peace with thee have deceived thee, *and* prevailed against thee; *they that eat* thy bread have laid a wound under thee: *there is* none understanding in him.
8 Shall I not in that day, saith the LORD, even destroy the wise *men* out of Edom, and understanding out of the mount of Esau?
9 And thy mighty *men*, O Teman, shall be dismayed, to the end that every one of the mount of Esau may be cut off by slaughter.
10 ¶ For *thy* violence against thy brother Jacob shame shall cover thee, and thou shalt be cut off for ever.
11 In the day that thou stoodest on the other side, in the day that the strangers carried away captive his forces, and foreigners entered into his gates, and cast lots upon Jerusalem, even thou *wast* as one of them.
12 But thou shouldest not have looked on the day of thy brother in the day that he became a stranger; neither shouldest thou have rejoiced over the children of Judah in the day of their destruction; neither shouldest thou have spoken proudly in the day of distress.
13 Thou shouldest not have entered into the gate of my people in the day of their calamity; yea, thou shouldest not have looked on their affliction in the day of their calamity, nor have laid *hands* on their substance in the day of their calamity;

Obadiah: *The prophet describes the day of the Lord that will come against Edom because of its sin against Judah and Judah's triumph over all its enemies.*

THE DESTRUCTION OF EDOM (vv. 1–9)

1 *vision*. Divine revelation. *rumour*. A report or news. *ambassador*. A messenger or envoy. *heathen*. Nations. The Lord establishes His sovereignty over the Gentile nations that would not acknowledge His kingship. God's rule is absolute and does not depend on the consent of the governed.
2 *small*. Lowly and insignificant.
3 *pride*. Presumption, insolence, or overconfidence. Edom's territory was in the mountains of Seir, a rugged region between the Gulf of Aqaba and the Dead Sea. Presuming that their habitation was impenetrable, they were deceived by a false sense of security.
4 This divine threat to Edom's lofty position corresponds to Christ's threat to Capernaum (Matt. 11:23) and illustrates the inviolable spiritual law that God will humble those who exalt themselves (Matt. 23:12).
5–6 The rhetorical questions underscore the totality of Edom's destruction. Whereas thieves take only what they can carry and some grapes remain after the harvest, those that plunder Edom will leave nothing behind. Even the most hidden treasures are sought and found.
7 *have brought thee even to the border*. Sent back home without the solicited aid. *laid a wound under thee*. Literally, "set a trap under you." The whole verse describes the betrayal of Edom by those they trusted.
9 *Teman*. Named after one of Esau's descendants (Gen. 36:15), it was one of Edom's principal cities along with Sela and Bozrah.

THE SIN OF EDOM (vv. 10–14)

10–14 Edom's treatment of Israel is a profound violation of the second great commandment, to love one's neighbor. Contrast their behavior with 1 Cor. 13:4–7 that describes what love is like.
11 *on the other side*. A reference to Edom's hostility against Israel. Even though Edom may not have been the actual aggressor against Israel, they sided with the enemy, "rooting for them."
12 *not have looked on*. Looking on with hostility, perhaps in the sense of gloating. *in the day that he became a stranger*. Literally, "in the day of his calamity (or misfortune)."

14 Neither shouldest thou have stood in the
crossway, to cut off those of his that did escape;
neither shouldest thou have delivered up those of
his that did remain in the day of distress.
15 For the day of the LORD *is* near upon all the
heathen: as thou hast done, it shall be done unto
thee: thy reward shall return upon thine own
head.
16 For as ye have drunk upon my holy mountain,
so shall all the heathen drink continually, yea, they
shall drink, and they shall swallow down, and they
shall be as though they had not been.
17 ¶ But upon mount Zion shall be deliverance,
and there shall be holiness; and the house of Jacob
shall possess their possessions.
18 And the house of Jacob shall be a fire, and the
house of Joseph a flame, and the house of Esau for
stubble, and they shall kindle in them, and devour
them; and there shall not be *any* remaining of the
house of Esau; for the LORD hath spoken *it*.
19 And *they of* the south shall possess the mount
of Esau; and *they of* the plain the Philistines: and
they shall possess the fields of Ephraim, and the
fields of Samaria: and Benjamin *shall possess*
Gilead.
20 And the captivity of this host of the children of
Israel *shall possess* that of the Canaanites, *even* unto
Zarephath; and the captivity of Jerusalem, which *is*
in Sepharad, shall possess the cities of the south.
21 And saviours shall come up on mount Zion to
judge the mount of Esau; and the kingdom shall
be the LORD's.

---

14 *crossway*. A fork in the road or crossroads. Not only did they rejoice in what the enemy did to Israel, they actively participated by blocking any escape routes.

THE PUNISHMENT OF EDOM (vv. 15–21)

15–16 These verses sum up Edom's punishment in terms of lex talionis (the law of retaliation—an eye for an eye). This is poetic justice. It is a fearful thing to receive from God what is deserved (Matt. 7:1–2; Rom. 2:5–6).
15 *Day of the LORD* designates the Lord's direct intervention into the affairs of time. This day of the Lord would be judgment on Edom specifically (and representatively of all God's enemies) and deliverance for God's people (vv. 17–21).
16 Their drinking in celebration would be turned into drinking the cup of judgment (Lam. 4:21).
17 *possess their possessions*. More significant than Israel's possessing what they had lost is the Christian's possessing all that Christ has restored. Possessing and enjoying our inheritance in Christ ought to be the experience of every Christian.
18 *Fire* is a common image of divine judgment. God uses Israel as the agent of judgment against Edom.
19–20 The geographical extent of the nation's possession. It pictures the unification of the nation and its incursion into enemy territory. *The south* refers to the Negev, the southernmost section of Judah west of Edom. *The plain* refers to the Shephelah region east of Philistia. *Ephraim . . . Samaria* designate the regions of the northern kingdom. *Gilead* represents the Transjordan region. *captivity*. The exiles. *Zarephath*. A Phoenician city. *Sepharad*. The exact location is unknown.
21 *saviours shall come up . . . to judge*. This is reminiscent of the time of the judges when God raised up Spirit-empowered persons to deliver the people from oppression. All of the lesser saviors point to the ideal Savior who accomplishes the ultimate deliverance for His people.

Thoughts for Personal/Family Worship

1. **Obadiah's message of doom for Edom has significant relevance for God's people in every age. Some of the details have been historically fulfilled in the distant past, and others await eschatological climax. Yet there is a message that cannot be limited just to the past or the future. Although it may appear at times that evil triumphs, this book makes it clear that God is in control and He will right every wrong. Two central truths are clear: (1) the kingdom of this world will fail; (2) the kingdom of our God will prevail.**
2. **Obadiah's prophecy of the day of the Lord underscores the certainty of divine justice. The most outstanding focus is that judgment is deserved and therefore, fair. It highlights the contrast with God's gracious salvation. In damnation, the sinner receives what he deserves; in salvation, the saved sinner receives what he does not deserve. Judgment is all of merit; salvation is all of grace.**

I CRIED
BY REASON OF MINE
Affliction
UNTO
THE LORD
&
HE HEARD
Me

JONAH 2:2

INTRODUCTION TO THE BOOK OF JONAH

Authorship: Jonah, meaning "dove," was a prophet from Israel, the northern kingdom, but his written prophecy is biographical and concerns his ministry to Nineveh, the capital of Assyria.

Date: Unlike most other prophets, Jonah does not specify the kings during whose reigns he ministered. However, according to 2 Kings 14:23–29, he prophesied during the reign of Jeroboam II, one of Israel's most powerful and prosperous kings—therefore around 760 BC. The duration of his ministry is not known. To some extent he was a contemporary of Hosea and Amos.

Theme: God's absolute sovereignty in both natural and spiritual realms. "Salvation is of the LORD" (2:9) sums up the message evident in both Jonah's undeserved deliverance from death and Nineveh's undeserved deliverance from judgment.

Purpose: To teach God's people their responsibility to deliver the message of salvation to all and to prefigure Christ's death and resurrection in Jonah's experience.

Synopsis: *The Contribution of Jonah to Redemptive Revelation*

Whereas the other Minor Prophets are primarily collections of prophetic oracles, Jonah records only one sermon consisting of five words in Hebrew: "Yet forty days, and Nineveh shall be overthrown" (3:4). The book is more a prophetic narrative comparable to the stories of Elijah and Elisha, although Jonah is certainly no spiritual hero whose ministry is to be emulated. The book narrates his extraordinary call to preach directly to a heathen people and his equally extraordinary refusal to obey the divine command. Notwithstanding the sometimes surprising plot of the narrative that can hold the attention of the youngest child, the book develops significant theological truths. God's deliverance of Nineveh from the announced judgment illustrates God's sovereign grace to the undeserving as well as His acceptance of genuine repentance in response to that grace. The salvation of a city with more than 120,000 citizens was a foreshadowing of God's purpose to include Gentiles in the kingdom; elsewhere in the Old Testament converts had to come under all of Israel's covenant obligations. Jonah was a foretaste of both the great number of conversions on the New Testament day of Pentecost and the synod decision in Acts 15 declaring Gentiles to be part of the church without first converting to "Judaism."

Most significantly, Jonah's experience in the belly of the fish prefigured Christ's death and resurrection. Christ was infinitely greater than Jonah, but both were signs to their respective generations of messengers divinely authorized by deliverance from death (Matt. 12:39–40; 16:4; Luke 11:29). This is one reason to defend the historicity of Jonah against those who say the story of Jonah is allegorical or at best a legend to combat Jewish nationalism by showing the all-inclusive nature of divine love. Since the resurrection of Christ was historically real, so was the experience of Jonah. To regard Jonah as legendary jeopardizes the gospel itself.

Outline: The outline reflects the symmetry and balance of the four episodes in the book's plot. Note in chs. 1 and 3 Jonah is in a public setting in which pagans appeal to God. In chs. 2 and 4 Jonah is in solitude as he prays.

I. God Calls Jonah to Nineveh (1:1–17)
  A. His Call (1:1–2)
  B. His Disobedience (1:3)
  C. The Consequences (1:4–16)
  D. God's Grace (1:17)
II. Jonah Prays and God Answers (2:1–10)
III. God Recalls Jonah to Nineveh (3:1–10)
  A. His Recall (3:1–2)
  B. His Obedience (3:3–4)
  C. The Consequences (3:5–9)
  D. God's Grace (3:10)
IV. Jonah Prays and God Answers (4:1–11)

THE BOOK OF JONAH

CHAPTER 1

NOW the word of the LORD came unto Jonah the
son of Amittai, saying,
2 Arise, go to Nineveh, that great city, and cry
against it; for their wickedness is come up before me.
3 But Jonah rose up to flee unto Tarshish from the
presence of the LORD, and went down to Joppa;
and he found a ship going to Tarshish: so he paid
the fare thereof, and went down into it, to go with
them unto Tarshish from the presence of the LORD.
4 ¶ But the LORD sent out a great wind into the
sea, and there was a mighty tempest in the sea, so
that the ship was like to be broken.
5 Then the mariners were afraid, and cried every
man unto his god, and cast forth the wares that
were in the ship into the sea, to lighten *it* of them.
But Jonah was gone down into the sides of the
ship; and he lay, and was fast asleep.
6 So the shipmaster came to him, and said unto
him, What meanest thou, O sleeper? arise, call
upon thy God, if so be that God will think upon
us, that we perish not.
7 And they said every one to his fellow, Come,
and let us cast lots, that we may know for whose
cause this evil *is* upon us. So they cast lots, and the
lot fell upon Jonah.
8 Then said they unto him, Tell us, we pray thee,
for whose cause this evil *is* upon us; What *is* thine
occupation? and whence comest thou? what *is* thy
country? and of what people *art* thou?
9 And he said unto them, I *am* an Hebrew; and
I fear the LORD, the God of heaven, which hath
made the sea and the dry *land*.
10 Then were the men exceedingly afraid, and
said unto him, Why hast thou done this? For the
men knew that he fled from the presence of the
LORD, because he had told them.
11 ¶ Then said they unto him, What shall we do

Chapter 1: *Jonah disobeys God's call to Nineveh resulting in a catastrophic storm and an unexpected rescue by the great fish.*

GOD CALLS JONAH TO NINEVEH (1:1–17)

His Call (1:1–2)

1:2 *Arise, go.* The two commands without a conjunction express urgency. Although prophets often pronounced judgments against foreign lands, it was normally just for Israel's consolation. It was uncommon for God to send the prophet to the heathen so that they could actually hear the message. This is an evidence of His gracious mercy. *Nineveh.* The capital city of Assyria, great both in size and influence. Ironically, within forty years it would be God's instrument of judgment against Israel. *wickedness.* A word meaning calamity that can refer either to moral behavior or disasters of any kind. *before me.* Even though Nineveh was a pagan city without any knowledge of the true God, their sin was before God and they were accountable to Him.

His Disobedience (1:3)

1:3 *But Jonah.* The prophet's response was unusual and unexpected; other prophets were sometimes reluctant or fearful but not defiant. *Tarshish.* Located in the western Mediterranean, perhaps as far west as Spain; it was in the opposite direction from Nineveh. *From the presence of the LORD* expressed Jonah's unattainable intent in fleeing.

The Consequences (1:4–16)

1:4 *sent.* Literally, "hurled," emphasizing the violent force of the wind. *The ship was like to be broken.* Literally, "the ship thought to be broken," an idiom meaning the ship was about to be smashed.

1:5 *cast forth.* Literally, "hurled." They hurled the cargo overboard with the same fervent force that God used to hurl the wind. Although some interpret this as a pagan attempt to pacify the sea or storm god, it was more likely a desperate attempt to make the ship more manageable, to prevent it from being smashed. *Jonah . . . was fast asleep.* Although the storm was Jonah's fault, sent to get his attention, he was oblivious. His physical sleep was symbolic of his spiritual stupor and insensitivity.

1:6 The captain, along with all the pagan sailors, had a better grasp of divine activity than Jonah. Ironically and no doubt startling to Jonah, the captain's alarm call to *arise* echoed the initial word from the Lord. Tragically, it took the imploring of a heathen to get the prophet to pray.

1:7 Casting *lots* was a common practice in ancient times for making decisions. Although seemingly a matter of random chance, even pagans believed the outcome was controlled by supernatural intervention. The purpose was to discover who was to blame for the *evil*, i.e., the dangerous storm (also v. 8). The lot's identification of Jonah as the culprit confirmed God's superintendence (see Prov. 16:33).

1:9 Jonah's confession of faith is betrayed by his actions. How one behaves often speaks more clearly than what one says.

1:11 *for the sea wrought, and was tempestuous.* Literally, "the

unto thee, that the sea may be calm unto us? for
the sea wrought, and was tempestuous.
12 And he said unto them, Take me up, and cast
me forth into the sea; so shall the sea be calm unto
you: for I know that for my sake this great tempest
is upon you.
13 Nevertheless the men rowed hard to bring *it* to
the land; but they could not: for the sea wrought,
and was tempestuous against them.
14 Wherefore they cried unto the LORD, and said,
We beseech thee, O LORD, we beseech thee, let us
not perish for this man's life, and lay not upon us
innocent blood: for thou, O LORD, hast done as it
pleased thee.
15 So they took up Jonah, and cast him forth into
the sea: and the sea ceased from her raging.
16 Then the men feared the LORD exceedingly, and
offered a sacrifice unto the LORD, and made vows.
17 ¶ Now the LORD had prepared a great fish to
swallow up Jonah. And Jonah was in the belly of
the fish three days and three nights.

CHAPTER 2

THEN Jonah prayed unto the LORD his God out of
the fish's belly,
2 And said, I cried by reason of mine affliction
unto the LORD, and he heard me; out of the belly
of hell cried I, *and* thou heardest my voice.
3 For thou hadst cast me into the deep, in the
midst of the seas; and the floods compassed me
about: all thy billows and thy waves passed over me.
4 Then I said, I am cast out of thy sight; yet I will
look again toward thy holy temple.
5 The waters compassed me about, *even* to the
soul: the depth closed me round about, the weeds
were wrapped about my head.
6 I went down to the bottoms of the mountains;
the earth with her bars *was* about me for ever: yet
hast thou brought up my life from corruption, O
LORD my God.
7 When my soul fainted within me I remembered
the LORD: and my prayer came in unto thee, into
thine holy temple.

---

sea was walking and raging," an idiom meaning the storm was growing worse (also v. 13).

1:12 Although Jonah acknowledged his blame in causing the storm, he expressed no repentance but claimed that to *cast* him overboard would be the only "cargo" sacrifice to save the ship (same word as "hurl" in vv. 4–5).

1:13–14 Yet again, the pagan sailors evidence more humane sensitivity and spiritual concern than the prophet. Their natural reluctance led to their prayer for physical deliverance and absolution from guilt in executing the death sentence. Significantly, perhaps influenced by Jonah's confession of faith, they appeal to God, using His covenant name and confessing His absolute sovereignty.

1:16 The sailors give evidence of genuine faith. God sovereignly used Jonah's disobedience as the occasion for introducing these pagans to the one true and living God. "Salvation is of the LORD" is a principal theme throughout the book.

God's Grace (1:17)

1:17 *prepared.* The great fish that swallowed Jonah was not uniquely created but rather appointed for this particular task. When God ordered this fish's unusual meal, it was another evidence of His overall sovereignty. The fish was a token of God's grace and mercy. Contrary to expectation, Jonah was not swallowed by the waves to a watery death but was spared at the last moment when there appeared to be no hope.

Thoughts for Personal/Family Worship: Chapter 1

1. **We can only speculate as to why Jonah chose to disobey God—perhaps from fear of Nineveh's size or wickedness, or patriotism, knowing the role that Assyria would have as Israel's conqueror. That no reason is given for Jonah's disobedience suggests that there is never a good reason or legitimate excuse for disobeying God.**
2. **Jonah warns against the far-reaching consequences of sin. It brings chastisement to the sinner: the storm was Jonah's fault and designed to deal with his disobedience. But sin's consequences jeopardize others who are not directly responsible. In one way or another sin always affects others: there is no such thing as a private sin. The storm threatened the sailors as well as Jonah. The sailors learned why the storm occurred, but there had to be multiple other ships on the Mediterranean going through the same storm without any knowledge of the fact that their lives were in jeopardy because of Jonah's sin. It is part of Satan's deceit that says sin is without corporate consequence.**
3. **The first chapter says much about God's absolute sovereignty. He controls the weather, the waves, and the fish to achieve His purpose. His sovereignty in the natural sphere is indicative of His sovereignty in the spiritual sphere as well. That becomes clear in the salvation of Nineveh.**
4. **The appointed fish that swallowed Jonah illustrates the wonder of grace. Jonah deserved to die, but God let him live. So it is that we deserve death, but God's amazing grace has saved us and given life. Grace is getting what we do not deserve.**

Chapter 2: *Jonah prays from the belly of the fish, and God delivers him safely to shore.*

JONAH PRAYS AND GOD ANSWERS (2:1–10)

2:1 *Jonah prayed . . . out of the fish's belly.* Notwithstanding the prophet's disobedience, his prayer gives evidence of an otherwise spiritual man. Virtually every line of the prayer is either a quotation or allusion to some line in the Psalms. Even in the solitude, darkness, discomfort, and slime of the fish's belly, he was able to draw from his knowledge of Scripture to frame his petitions. Compare: v. 2 with Pss. 31:22; 120:1; v. 3 with Pss. 42:7; 69:2,15; v. 4 with Pss. 5:7; 31:22; v. 5 with Ps. 69:2; v. 6 with Ps. 30:3; v. 7 with Pss. 88:2; 142:3; v. 8 with Ps. 31:6; v. 9 with Pss. 3:8; 42:5; 50:14.

2:2 *the belly of hell.* The Hebrew word can refer to death, the grave, or the abode of departed wicked spirits. Here, Jonah perceived that the fish's belly was his soon-to-be grave, where his body would decay. At this point, he felt as though he were buried alive.

2:3 *the floods.* The word for river, here referring to the sea currents that surrounded him.

2:5 *to the soul.* To the very extremity of life. Jonah thought that his end had come.

2:6 *Her bars* refers to the bolts of a gate or door. Jonah thought the door of life had been shut forever behind him. *yet*

8 They that observe lying vanities forsake their
own mercy.
9 But I will sacrifice unto thee with the voice of
thanksgiving; I will pay *that* that I have vowed.
Salvation *is* of the LORD.
10 ¶ And the LORD spake unto the fish, and it
vomited out Jonah upon the dry *land*.

CHAPTER 3

AND the word of the LORD came unto Jonah the
second time, saying,
2 Arise, go unto Nineveh, that great city, and
preach unto it the preaching that I bid thee.
3 So Jonah arose, and went unto Nineveh,
according to the word of the LORD. Now Nineveh
was an exceeding great city of three days' journey.
4 And Jonah began to enter into the city a day's
journey, and he cried, and said, Yet forty days, and
Nineveh shall be overthrown.
5 ¶ So the people of Nineveh believed God, and
proclaimed a fast, and put on sackcloth, from the
greatest of them even to the least of them.
6 For word came unto the king of Nineveh, and
he arose from his throne, and he laid his robe
from him, and covered *him* with sackcloth, and
sat in ashes.
7 And he caused *it* to be proclaimed and
published through Nineveh by the decree of the
king and his nobles, saying, Let neither man nor
beast, herd nor flock, taste any thing: let them not
feed, nor drink water:
8 But let man and beast be covered with
sackcloth, and cry mightily unto God: yea, let
them turn every one from his evil way, and from
the violence that *is* in their hands.

---

hast thou brought up my life. Contrary to all expectation, his life was spared. It is almost as though it dawned on Jonah in his thought-to-be grave that he was still alive.

2:8 *lying vanities*. Literally, "breaths of emptiness," a reference to idols. Idolaters forsake God's covenant loyalty (*their own mercy*). Worshiping God and worshiping idols are mutually exclusive.

2:9 *Salvation is of the LORD*. The Lord is the author as well as the agent of salvation, whether physical or spiritual. This statement sums up the whole message of the prophecy.

2:10 As Jonah prayed, the commissioned fish was transporting him back to shore. He arrived safely but not without the sickly smells and slime of where his disobedience had taken him.

Thoughts for Personal/Family Worship: Chapter 2

1. **Prayer is an important means of grace that God has ordained for His people. The Bible commands prayer, invites prayer, and instructs about prayer. Jonah's prayer is a good example of how to pray, as his prayer is comprised of so much from the Psalms. The link between God's Word and prayer is a key component. We are to pray God's Word back to Him in faith that He will perform it in His faithfulness. The Psalms especially provide patterns that we are to follow in prayer. The Psalms are divinely inspired and show the way God wants His people to pray. It is a good practice regularly to pray through the Psalms, applying the petitions to our own needs just as Jonah did to his.**
2. **Jonah's prayer also reminds us how important it is to hide God's Word in our hearts so that we can use it and rely on it even when we don't have a Bible at hand. All that Jonah prayed in the darkness and disgust of the fish's belly came from what he had committed to his memory. Becoming saturated with the Word in times of Bible study and devotion enables us to use and rely upon it in times of crisis.**

Chapter 3: ***Jonah's preaching in Nineveh moves the people to faith and repentance, thus averting God's impending judgment.***

GOD RECALLS JONAH TO NINEVEH (3:1–10)

His Recall (3:1–2)

3:1 *the second time*. Although undeserving, Jonah received another chance to obey the Lord's command.

3:2 *Preach . . . the preaching* refers not to preaching a sermon but proclaiming a proclamation. *that I bid thee*. Literally, "that I am speaking to you." As a prophet, Jonah had authority to speak only what God commanded him to speak.

His Obedience (3:3–4)

3:3 Jonah obeys and goes to Nineveh; later verses reveal his persisting reluctance, but he had learned his lesson that the consequences of disobedience were too severe to experience again. *Three days' journey* is most likely a reference to the time frame of Jonah's short-term mission rather than the size of the city.

3:4 *a day's journey*. Jonah begins his proclamation on the first day of his projected stay in Nineveh. *Yet forty days . . . overthrown*. In Hebrew the proclamation consists of five words, terse and to the point. The form of the verb *overthrown* suggests impending action. The verb, meaning "to turn upside down," most frequently refers to the catastrophic judgment of Sodom and Gomorrah and thus forebodes a terrible end for Nineveh. Unquestionably, the warning of doom was the surface and intended point of the declaration, but ironically the word can be used positively with the sense of reformation or transformation. Nineveh escaped being turned upside down in judgment by being turned upside down in spiritual reformation.

The Consequences (3:5–9)

3:5 This verse is a clear example of Rom. 10:17—faith comes by hearing the Word of God. Many of the Ninevites evidenced true conversion: They *believed God* (faith); *they proclaimed a fast, and put on sackcloth* (gestures of repentance). *From the greatest . . . to the least*. A literary device (merismus) that uses extremes to designate entirety. The conversions in Nineveh were widespread, touching every segment of the population.

3:6 *sackcloth . . . ashes*. Outward actions symbolizing the internal realities of sorrow, grief, and repentance.

3:7–8 The inclusion of the domesticated livestock in the external signs although seemingly odd was not uncommon in that culture. The inclusion of the animals does suggest that the wave of repentance extended beyond the city limits. *Let them turn*. This is the principal Old Testament word for saving repentance; it pictures a complete reversal of direction, an "about face" from both their *evil way* (the whole manner of life characterized by sin) and *violence* (specific acts of sin). True repentance always involves a reversal of direction that moves toward God and away from sin.

9 Who can tell *if* God will turn and repent, and
turn away from his fierce anger, that we perish
not?
10 ¶ And God saw their works, that they turned
from their evil way; and God repented of the evil,
that he had said that he would do unto them; and
he did *it* not.

CHAPTER 4

BUT it displeased Jonah exceedingly, and he was
very angry.
2 And he prayed unto the LORD, and said, I pray
thee, O LORD, *was* not this my saying, when I was
yet in my country? Therefore I fled before unto
Tarshish: for I knew that thou *art* a gracious God,
and merciful, slow to anger, and of great kindness,
and repentest thee of the evil.
3 Therefore now, O LORD, take, I beseech thee,
my life from me; for *it is* better for me to die than
to live.
4 ¶ Then said the LORD, Doest thou well to be
angry?
5 So Jonah went out of the city, and sat on the
east side of the city, and there made him a booth,
and sat under it in the shadow, till he might see
what would become of the city.
6 And the LORD God prepared a gourd, and
made *it* to come up over Jonah, that it might be
a shadow over his head, to deliver him from his
grief. So Jonah was exceeding glad of the gourd.
7 But God prepared a worm when the morning
rose the next day, and it smote the gourd that it
withered.
8 And it came to pass, when the sun did arise,
that God prepared a vehement east wind; and
the sun beat upon the head of Jonah, that he
fainted, and wished in himself to die, and said, *It*

3:9 *Who can tell if God will turn* (reverse the threat of judgment) *and repent* (be moved to pity). The question acknowledges God's sovereignty that He is not obligated to accept their repentance while expressing hope that He will.

God's Grace (3:10)

3:10 God had pity (*repented*) and accepted their repentance from *their evil way*, thus canceling the calamitous judgment (*the evil*) that He had threatened. God's dealings with men are always without partiality. God saves those who are truly repentant.

Thoughts for Personal/Family Worship: Chapter 3

1. **Jonah's second call to Nineveh is instructive. First, it shows God's sovereignty in being merciful to whom He will be merciful. Compare Jonah with the unnamed prophet in 1 Kings 13. God called him to a dangerous mission before Jeroboam I, instructing him to return home immediately after delivering the message. Without reluctance or hesitation, he obeyed God. However, he was seduced by the old prophet to tarry contrary to God's instruction. Because of his disobedience, lions killed him on his way home. In contrast, Jonah was blatantly and willfully disobedient, yet God spared him and gave him the second opportunity to obey. From a human perspective, the bold yet naïve unnamed prophet seemed worthy of a second chance whereas Jonah more reasonably deserved death. But God acted justly regarding the unnamed prophet, but chose to be gracious to Jonah. It should be occasion for thought. How many times have we disobeyed, deserving punishment, yet how many "chances" has God given us to obey?**
2. **Jonah's second call is also a lesson in the invincible power of God's plan and purpose. God had a purpose regarding Jonah and Nineveh that Jonah's disobedience could not frustrate. According to God's plan, Jonah was the chosen messenger to these wicked people. We believe both that God has sovereignly decreed the end of things and that He has decreed the means to accomplish the purposed ends. This has a sobering application to evangelism. God may sovereignly place on a given individual the dreadful responsibility of being the only one who can reach some people. We all are accountable to God and should not rebel against His purpose. God will unfailingly save whom He will but faith comes by hearing and hearing by the Word of God and how will they hear without a preacher (see the ordained logic of evangelism in Rom. 10:13–17)?**
3. **Where sin abounds, grace superabounds (Rom. 5:20). God's mercy toward wicked Nineveh testifies to the amazing power of grace to save sinners and assures that none are too wicked to receive God's salvation. They were objects of divine wrath under the sentence of death, but they were moved by the Word to repent, and God graciously received them. The words of Christ sum up the truth: "Him that cometh to me I will in no wise cast out" (John 6:37).**

Chapter 4: *Jonah complains about God's mercy to Nineveh, and God explains His grace by exposing Jonah's selfishness.*

JONAH PRAYS AND GOD ANSWERS (4:1–11)

4:1 Most prophets would have rejoiced at such a positive response to their preaching, but Jonah was *displeased* (literally, "it was an evil or disastrous thing to him") and *very angry* (literally, "it was hot for him") over Nineveh's repentance.

4:2 Tragically, Jonah appeals to orthodox truths to excuse his disobedience. He refused to go to Nineveh because he knew the real possibility of God's forgiveness toward them and His pity (*repentest*) on them so as to withhold His judgment (*evil*). Whatever Jonah's motive, he desired Nineveh's destruction.

4:3 *I beseech thee.* I.e., please.

4:4 *Doest thou well to be angry*? Literally, "is it well hot for you," i.e., "are you really angry?"

4:5 *booth.* A temporary shelter most likely of interwoven branches. The same word designates the Feast of Tabernacles (booths) that commemorated the wilderness wanderings. Jonah tried to get comfortable in hopeful anticipation of the city's destruction.

4:6 *God prepared.* To appoint or ordain. The same word is used for the fish in 1:17 and the worm in 4:7. *gourd.* Generally assumed to be a castor-oil tree whose broad leaves would provide added shade and relief against the heat of the sun, alleviating some of his *grief* (literally, "evil"). The enjoyment of this physical blessing from the Lord made him *exceeding glad* (literally, "he rejoiced a rejoicing").

4:9 God asks Jonah if he is good and angry, and Jonah

is better for me to die than to live.
9 And God said to Jonah, Doest thou well to be
angry for the gourd? And he said, I do well to
be angry, *even* unto death.
10 Then said the LORD, Thou hast had pity on
the gourd, for the which thou hast not laboured,
neither madest it grow; which came up in a night,
and perished in a night:
11 And should not I spare Nineveh, that great
city, wherein are more than sixscore thousand
persons that cannot discern between their right
hand and their left hand; and *also* much cattle?

---

responds that he is good and angry—so angry that he could die.

4:10 *pity*. To be troubled about or to look with compassion.

4:11 *spare*. The same word as "pity" in v. 10. *Sixscore thousand.* 120,000. *cannot discern*. Either a reference to the children, which would imply an even greater total population, or a reference to the inhabitants as a whole who were incapable of spiritual discernment. By either calculation, the city, filled with living people, was more deserving of compassion than the temporary plant that so concerned Jonah.

Thoughts for Personal/Family Worship: Chapter 4

1. **Jonah's anger over Nineveh's repentance and deliverance illustrates the principal lesson of the book that "salvation is of the LORD." Had Nineveh's salvation depended on Jonah, it would have perished for sure. What a contrast Jonah is to Jeremiah, who loved his people and prayed for their conversion, but saw little positive response. Ironically, a very short sermon by a prophet who hated the people to whom he preached was used by God to save more people on a single occasion than perhaps at any other time in history. The power is in the Word of God. God can use even unclean vessels to accomplish His will.**
2. **Jonah's appeal to God's perfections as the excuse for his disobedience betrays an inappropriate use of truth and theology. Every point of his stated creed about God was right, but his use of truth was terribly wrong. Any understanding or application of theology that breeds coldness or selfishness or any other unspiritual reaction is wrong, but the fault may not be with the theology.**
3. **Jonah's response to the gourd's growth and its subsequent withering exposes his spiritual selfishness. He received God's favor to him with joy and became angry when the favor was withdrawn. It was all about how things affected him. But the thought of God being merciful to Nineveh was contrary to his desire for its destruction. His attitude is similar to the man Christ describes, who was happy when he was forgiven a large debt, but was without sympathy to one who owed him just a small amount (Matt. 18:23–35). We should rejoice in God's blessings to others as much as we do in our own.**
4. **The book ends with an unanswered question: Should not God pity even those who might be enemies? We don't know how Jonah would have answered the question, so the "little Jonah" that resides within us must answer. The question is rhetorical, but the answer is obvious. Do our lives reflect it?**

GOD'S MERCY

The Lord is merciful (Jonah 4:2). God's mercy is His kindness to a person in misery (Matt. 9:27). The apostle Paul wrote, "Blessed be God, even the Father of our Lord Jesus Christ, the Father of mercies, and the God of all comfort" (2 Cor. 1:3). Notice the order. God is first the Father of Jesus Christ, and then our Father if we are in Christ. Christ has everything *first*, and we receive all from Him. He is the first Son, and we are sons. He is the first beloved of God, and we are beloved in Him. He is filled first with all grace, and we are filled from Him (John 1:16).

God must first be the Father of Christ, and then our Father through faith in Christ, so that He may be "the Father of mercies" to us. God's mercy must see God's justice satisfied. One attribute must not devour another in God (Ps. 85:10). God cannot wrong His own justice, but it must be satisfied by Christ (Rom. 3:26). Christ took our nature to die for us (Heb. 2:14,17), so that God could be our Father despite our sins, for He has punished our sins in Christ, our surety (Heb. 7:22). Thus God, out of His heart of mercy, found a way that He might do good to us and bring together His mercy and justice. God is holiness; we are a mass of sin and corruption. But Christ died for us, and God is the Father of mercies to all who are in Christ. Since God's justice has been satisfied for sin, the obstacle is removed and the stream of God's mercy runs freely.

God is merciful by nature. The sea is not more naturally wet, the sun does not more naturally shine, fire does not more naturally burn, and gravity does not more naturally pull weights down, than God naturally shows mercy when His justice is satisfied. God's attributes, such as His wisdom and power, would terrify us apart from His mercy. But if we know Him as the Father of mercies, then all His attributes becomes sweet to us. His wisdom will plan good things for us. His power will free us from our enemies. His justice will vindicate us against those who wrong us.

God glorifies Himself in showing mercy. God is merciful before we are converted. He delays His wrath and does not punish the sinner immediately. God is merciful in forgiving all sin, punishment, and guilt when we trust in Christ. God is merciful in correcting some of the sins of His children (Heb. 12:6), while passing over many sins, and moderating His correction with gentleness and perfect timing. He is merciful in continuing our daily blessings. If we have comfort, it is mercy. If we have strength, it is mercy. His mercies do not fail but are new every morning (Lam. 3:22–23). Everything that comes from God to His children is dipped in mercy.

When God is severe with sinners in His justice, it is their fault. His heart is merciful (Lam. 3:33). He is good in Himself. We provoke Him to be severe in justice. But in His own nature, "he delighteth in mercy" (Mic. 7:18). Therefore He will be merciful to all who repent of their sins and take hold of Christ by a true faith. This is the name by which God wants to be known, "merciful and gracious" (Ex. 34:6). The Psalms tells us the same thing, again and again (Ps. 86:15; 103:8, 13; 111:4; 116:5; 145:8–9).

God's promises are promises of mercy. Whenever a sinner repents, regardless of how many or how bad his sins may be, God will forgive them all (1 John 1:7). The Bible says to the guilty soul, "Let the wicked forsake his way, and the unrighteous man his thoughts: and let him return unto the LORD, and he will have mercy upon him; and to our God, for he will abundantly pardon" (Isa. 55:7). We are vindictive, quick to be offended and seek revenge. Our thoughts of mercy are poor and narrow because we are so unmerciful. But God's thoughts are above our thoughts, and His ways above our ways (Isa. 55:7–8). God's mercy is infinite!

—adapted from Richard Sibbes, *Exposition of 2 Corinthians 1*

INTRODUCTION TO THE BOOK OF MICAH

Authorship: Micah's name means, "Who is like Jehovah?" Coming from the fertile lowlands of Judah, Micah had a strong sense of ethical purity and justice that cried against the social abuses of the elite establishment who set aside God's standards in favor of self-interest. Conservatives have maintained the unity of the book, identifying Micah, a contemporary of Isaiah, as the sole author. Although part of his message concerned the northern kingdom of Israel whose capital was Samaria, his principal preaching was directed to Jerusalem and the whole southern kingdom.

Date: Micah dates his prophecy in 1:1 as during the reigns of Jotham, Ahaz, and Hezekiah. Given that Jotham's reign began in 750 BC and Micah's preaching had some influence on Hezekiah's reforms (Jer. 26:18–19), Micah most likely prophesied between 750 and 700 BC.

Theme: Penalty of judgment and promise of restoration.

Purpose: To expose the sin of the nation, warn of impending judgment, and encourage repentance in light of God's redemptive purpose in the coming Messiah.

Synopsis: *The Contribution of Micah to Redemptive Revelation*

What Amos was to the northern kingdom, Micah was to the southern. The themes and focuses of these two prophets were remarkably similar because the sins of the two nations were remarkably the same. Profiteering, injustice, and immorality ruled the day. Money was more influential than truth. The selfish passion to preserve or increase the style of life defined a code of ethics that justified any means to the desired end. Moral, social, and religious decay were eating away at the nation and would eventually destroy it.

Micah was a prophet called and burdened by God to make the people face the reality of their sins and God's dissatisfaction with them. He exposed social and religious sins and warned of impending judgment unless there was genuine repentance. Whereas in the providence of God, Amos saw little visible success and his predicted judgment came within the next generation, Micah in the same providence saw some fruit (Jer. 26:18–19) and his predicted judgment was delayed. The message of the gospel is always a savor of death to some and of life to others. Ultimately the judgment came as the nation persisted in sin and seemed to jeopardize the promise of restoration. But God's ultimate redemptive purpose in the Messiah could not be frustrated. Micah predicts the birthplace of the coming Redeemer (5:2) and describes the remarkable change He will bring to the world (4:1–5). Salvation is possible because God is a God who pardons sins, casting them away to the depths of the sea (7:18–19).

Outline: Note: The imperative "hear" in 1:2; 3:1; and 6:1 divides the book into three principal sections, each developing the dual theme of penalty and promise.

I. Penalty and Promise (1:1—2:13)
   A. Imminent Judgment on Samaria and Judah (1:1–16)
   B. Indictments Justifying Judgment (2:1–11)
   C. Promise of Restoration (2:12–13)
II. Penalty and Promise (3:1—5:15)
   A. Indictment on Leaders and Imminent Judgment (3:1–12)
   B. Promise of a Glorious Kingdom (4:1–13)
   C. Promise of the Messiah (5:1–15)
III. Penalty and Promise (6:1—7:20)
   A. Indictments against the People (6:1–16)
   B. Promise of Ultimate Victory and Salvation (7:1–20)

THE BOOK OF
MICAH

CHAPTER 1

THE word of the LORD that came to Micah
the Morasthite in the days of Jotham, Ahaz,
and Hezekiah, kings of Judah, which he saw
concerning Samaria and Jerusalem.
2 Hear, all ye people; hearken, O earth, and all
that therein is: and let the Lord GOD be witness
against you, the Lord from his holy temple.
3 For, behold, the LORD cometh forth out of his
place, and will come down, and tread upon the
high places of the earth.
4 And the mountains shall be molten under him,
and the valleys shall be cleft, as wax before the fire,
and as the waters *that are* poured down a steep
place.
5 For the transgression of Jacob *is* all this, and for
the sins of the house of Israel. What *is* the trans-
gression of Jacob? *is it* not Samaria? and what *are*
the high places of Judah? *are they* not Jerusalem?
6 Therefore I will make Samaria as an heap of
the field, *and* as plantings of a vineyard: and I will
pour down the stones thereof into the valley, and
I will discover the foundations thereof.
7 And all the graven images thereof shall be
beaten to pieces, and all the hires thereof shall
be burned with the fire, and all the idols thereof
will I lay desolate: for she gathered *it* of the hire
of an harlot, and they shall return to the hire of
an harlot.
8 Therefore I will wail and howl, I will go stripped
and naked: I will make a wailing like the dragons,
and mourning as the owls.
9 For her wound *is* incurable; for it is come unto
Judah; he is come unto the gate of my people,
even to Jerusalem.
10 ¶ Declare ye *it* not at Gath, weep ye not at all:
in the house of Aphrah roll thyself in the dust.
11 Pass ye away, thou inhabitant of Saphir, having

PENALTY AND PROMISE (1:1—2:13)

Chapter 1: *Micah identifies the Lord as the judge who indicts Israel and Judah of their transgressions and pronounces the sentence of judgment upon them.*

Imminent Judgment on Samaria and Judah (1:1–16)

1:1 *The word . . . which he saw.* A technical expression referring to the revelation received by Micah in prophetic vision. *Samaria and Jerusalem.* By synecdoche (part for whole), the capital cities designate the northern and southern kingdoms. Micah's message is primarily to the south, but references to the northern kingdom's sin and consequent judgment serve to reinforce and illustrate the sobriety of the word to Judah.

1:2 *Hear . . . hearken.* These imperatives introduce the forensic imagery. All are summoned before the bar of divine justice.

1:3 *behold.* An interjection demanding attention to the terror of the Lord's coming to judge.

1:4 Micah uses vivid images to describe the irresistible and inescapable effects of the Lord's judging presence. The extreme topographies, mountains melting (*be molten*) and valleys being split apart (*be cleft*), indicate that no place is exempt. *steep place.* A deep mountain gorge.

1:5 Although *the house of Israel* often designates the northern kingdom, the parallelism in the verse suggests it refers here to Judah. *Jacob* (the northern kingdom) and its transgression are linked to the capital city *Samaria*, and *the house of Israel* or *Judah* is linked to its capital city *Jerusalem*. The *high places* refer to sites of pagan worship. Ironically, the place of the temple where true worship was to be conducted had become a place of perverted idolatry.

1:6 *an heap of the field, and . . . plantings of a vineyard.* The Lord would turn walled cities into rubble so that they became a place to plant vineyards; simply, He would flatten them by hurling down (*pour down*) the stones of the walls exposing the foundations. The walled cities, representing their self-defense, could not stand against the Lord's judgment. This becomes a paradigm of divine judgment: no man can ever defend himself before the bar of divine justice.

1:7 *the hires.* Literally, "gift" or "reward," referring typically to the wages of a prostitute. Its association with the idols suggests the reference to be to the cultic prostitution that had become part of Israel's religion.

1:8 *I will wail.* Micah is the subject of these verbs that describe customary acts of lamentation. *Stripped* likely refers to being barefoot, and *naked* may refer to being lightly dressed in undergarments. *dragons.* Jackals. *owls.* Perhaps, ostriches.

1:9 Micah explains the reason for his lamentation to be the spread of Samaria's calamity to Jerusalem. This is a reminder of the terrible influence of sin and its consequences on others.

1:10–16 Micah concisely describes the doom coming to various small and insignificant cities throughout Judah. If these cities do not escape the coming judgment, it is certain that the larger cities will not either. The judgment will be extensive. Micah exhibits a mastery of language using alliteration, historical allusions, and pun-like statements that cannot be duplicated in translation as he plays on the name of the city and its particular doom.

thy shame naked: the inhabitant of Zaanan came
not forth in the mourning of Beth-ezel; he shall
receive of you his standing.
12 For the inhabitant of Maroth waited carefully
for good: but evil came down from the LORD unto
the gate of Jerusalem.
13 O thou inhabitant of Lachish, bind the chariot
to the swift beast: she *is* the beginning of the sin
to the daughter of Zion: for the transgressions of
Israel were found in thee.
14 Therefore shalt thou give presents to
Moresheth-gath: the houses of Achzib *shall be* a
lie to the kings of Israel.
15 Yet will I bring an heir unto thee, O inhabitant
of Mareshah: he shall come unto Adullam the
glory of Israel.
16 Make thee bald, and poll thee for thy delicate
children; enlarge thy baldness as the eagle; for
they are gone into captivity from thee.

CHAPTER 2

WOE to them that devise iniquity, and work evil
upon their beds! when the morning is light, they
practise it, because it is in the power of their hand.
2 And they covet fields, and take *them* by violence; and houses, and take *them* away: so they
oppress a man and his house, even a man and his
heritage.
3 Therefore thus saith the LORD; Behold, against
this family do I devise an evil, from which ye
shall not remove your necks; neither shall ye go
haughtily: for this time *is* evil.
4 ¶ In that day shall *one* take up a parable against
you, and lament with a doleful lamentation, *and*
say, We be utterly spoiled: he hath changed the
portion of my people: how hath he removed *it*
from me! turning away he hath divided our fields.
5 Therefore thou shalt have none that shall cast a
cord by lot in the congregation of the LORD.
6 Prophesy ye not, *say they to them that* prophesy:
they shall not prophesy to them, *that* they shall
not take shame.
7 ¶ O *thou that art* named the house of Jacob,
is the spirit of the LORD straitened? *are* these his
doings? do not my words do good to him that
walketh uprightly?
8 Even of late my people is risen up as an enemy:

1:11 *having thy shame naked.* Literally, "the nakedness of shame," or "shameful nakedness." *Standing* refers to the place to take a stand; the defensive position will be taken away.
1:12 *evil.* Disaster.
1:16 *poll.* Shave or shear the head. *delicate children.* Literally, "sons of delight," designating children in whom you delight.

Thoughts for Personal/Family Worship: Chapter 1

1. **In 1:2 the Lord is identified as the witness against those He judges. He is the witness who testifies, verifying every accusation against the guilty, and the judge with the authority to execute the deserved penalty. This is an opportunity to reflect on the fearful reality of having to stand before the judge of all the earth with the awareness that "all things are naked and opened unto the eyes of him with whom we have to do" (Heb. 4:13). His judgments, therefore, are always righteous and infallibly just. There are no excuses or self-defenses that can stand before Him. This points directly to the beauty of the gospel of Christ and justifying grace that gives the guilty sinner a perfect standing before God because there can be no condemnation to those who are in Christ Jesus (Rom. 8:1).**
2. **Verse 9 is a reminder of the devastating power of sin to affect others. Although Judah was responsible and accountable before God for its own sin, there is a link between what was happening in the north and what was happening in the south. Jacob's transgression was first, and Judah followed and in some ways became worse (see the allegory of the two sisters in Ezek. 23). It is part of sin's deception that it is a private matter. But in reality there is nothing that can be just a private sin. Either by example or consequence, sin is an infection that spreads.**

Chapter 2: ***Micah pronounces woe on Judah identifying the sins that made judgment necessary, particularly heartless oppression and resistance to God's Word.***

Indictments Justifying Judgment (2:1–11)
2:1 *Woe.* A prophetic expression of threat against those who scheme evil in their nighttime thoughts and execute their plans when the daytime comes.
2:2 *oppress a man and his house . . . his heritage.* A literary device requiring a verb to be supplied to govern the second object: oppress a man and "take" his house, which is identified as his inheritance. The transgression reveals a materialistic selfishness that disregarded the rights of others.
2:3 *family.* Clan, a reference to the entire nation. This would suggest that the materialism and selfish behavior permeated the entire society and was not just a class struggle between the rich and poor. The oppression was widespread and so would be the judgment. *evil.* Disaster, a reference to God's punishment. *not remove your necks.* The imagery of yoking an animal describes the control by foreign domination that would break the pride of the nation. First, Assyria and then Babylon would subdue the nation, but they are not mentioned because the ultimate agent is God.
2:4 *parable.* A proverb or prophetic figurative discourse, here a mocking taunt by outsiders. *he hath changed . . . he removed . . . he hath divided.* Impersonal subjects expressing a passive idea (have been changed, removed, and divided).
2:5 *a cord.* A measuring line. The loss of land appears to be permanent; there will be none to redistribute possessions, an allusion to the original distribution of the land by the priests who cast lots (Num. 26:52–56).
2:6–11 Micah identifies false prophets who attempt to silence true prophets, refusing to preach the truth; he describes the consequences of the false preaching.
2:7 *straitened.* To become short, a reference to becoming impatient. This sums up part of the preaching of the false prophets who had a distorted view of God that contributed to the sins of the people. *do not my words.* The Lord answers the false prophets by declaring that His words prosper the upright.
2:8–9 A description of the social injustices in terms of a hostile army taking the spoils of conquest.

ye pull off the robe with the garment from them
that pass by securely as men averse from war.
9 The women of my people have ye cast out from
their pleasant houses; from their children have ye
taken away my glory for ever.
10 Arise ye, and depart; for this *is* not *your* rest:
because it is polluted, it shall destroy *you*, even
with a sore destruction.
11 If a man walking in the spirit and falsehood
do lie, *saying*, I will prophesy unto thee of wine
and of strong drink; he shall even be the prophet
of this people.
12 ¶ I will surely assemble, O Jacob, all of thee; I
will surely gather the remnant of Israel; I will put
them together as the sheep of Bozrah, as the flock
in the midst of their fold: they shall make great
noise by reason of *the multitude of* men.
13 The breaker is come up before them: they have
broken up, and have passed through the gate, and
are gone out by it: and their king shall pass before
them, and the LORD on the head of them.

CHAPTER 3

AND I said, Hear, I pray you, O heads of Jacob, and
ye princes of the house of Israel; *Is it* not for you
to know judgment?
2 Who hate the good, and love the evil; who
pluck off their skin from off them, and their flesh
from off their bones;
3 Who also eat the flesh of my people, and flay
their skin from off them; and they break their
bones, and chop them in pieces, as for the pot,
and as flesh within the caldron.
4 Then shall they cry unto the LORD, but he
will not hear them: he will even hide his face
from them at that time, as they have behaved
themselves ill in their doings.
5 ¶ Thus saith the LORD concerning the prophets
that make my people err, that bite with their teeth,
and cry, Peace; and he that putteth not into their
mouths, they even prepare war against him.
6 Therefore night *shall be* unto you, that ye shall
not have a vision; and it shall be dark unto you,

2:8 *averse from war.* Returning from war; refers to those who felt secure having returned safely from battle only to be stripped and humiliated by materialistic oppressors at home.
2:9 The oppressors with selfish callousness did not exempt women and children from their schemes. *My glory* refers figuratively to the splendid inheritance and provisions God had given.
2:10 The Lord pronounces His sentence against the offenders. *rest.* Quiet place of peace. Conditioned on the nation's covenant obedience, the land was to be God's gift, a place of rest where there would be a cessation of warfare and enjoyment of God's presence. But since they did not meet the condition, removal from the land was necessary (Lev. 26).
2:11 The sinful people desire the message of false prophets. *Spirit* can mean wind or breath. Here it describes the false prophet who is marked by windy, baseless lies. It is not a reference to the Holy Spirit who inspires true prophets (3:8). *I will prophesy.* Literally, "I will drivel." It was an attractive, pleasant message, but only drivel and foaming at the mouth.

Promise of Restoration (2:12–13)

2:12–13 The first hint of hope after the long exposition of sin and penalty. The Lord gathers the *remnant* (the spiritual ones) of His people like a flock into a fold to protect them. Then as the shepherd-king He breaks through enemy defenses to deliver and lead His people in victory. *The breaker, their king,* and *the LORD* are all one and ultimately refer to the Lord Jesus Christ, the only mediatorial king and savior of His people. Regardless of how great the sin and its penalty, there is hope in Christ.

Thoughts for Personal/Family Worship: Chapter 2

1. **God's condemnation of the nation's social sins highlights the authority and unity of God's law. At the very least the nation was guilty of transgressing the eighth and tenth commandments, prohibiting stealing and coveting of what belongs to others (Ex. 20:15,17). In due course the prophet would expose their religious sins as well. But the prophet's logic is clear. Wronging your neighbor precludes being right with God regardless of religious practice or profession. How will a right relationship with God manifest itself in right relationships with others?**
2. **Preaching the whole counsel of God requires denouncing sin and warning of judgment as well as the message of grace and the gospel. Too often people reject the hard message, wanting only to hear that everything is going to be good—just like Israel (2:11). But the wonder of the gospel of grace in Christ can only be understood in the light of the terror and danger without it. Micah provides a good example exposing and condemning sin on his way to the glorious message of peace and salvation that can be found only in Christ (2:12–13).**

PENALTY AND PROMISE (3:1—5:15)

Chapter 3: ***Micah, being full of the Spirit's power, exposes the sinful abuses of both the civil and religious authorities and blames them for the devastation that will come upon the nation.***

Indictment on Leaders and Imminent Judgment (3:1–12)

3:1 *heads . . . princes . . . is it not for you to know judgment?* Practicing judgment or justice was to be a mark of godly rulers. The ruler over men must be just, fearing God (2 Sam. 23:3). Similarly, Jeremiah links a ruler's just actions with knowing the Lord (Jer. 22:15–16). Micah's question implies the lack of justice and consequently the lack of knowledge of God in the leaders he addresses.
3:2–3 *hate . . . love.* These are primarily volitional words; a rejection of what is good and a choice of what is bad. *who pluck off their skin.* A hyperbolic description of the abuses of the civil leaders in graphic images of cannibalistic behavior.
3:4 Illustrates the principle of lex talionis (the law of retaliation) or poetic justice. The leaders will get from God what they deserve. They ignored the cries of the people they abused, and God will ignore their cries accordingly. Getting from God what is deserved is a fearful thought that should motivate repentance.
3:5 True prophets were to speak only what God instructed them. These false prophets did not have a word from the Lord; rather their pleasant message of peace was against the Lord, misleading the people (*make my people err*). *Bite with their teeth* refers to the biting of a serpent. It is a vivid image describing the venomous message of the false prophets.
3:6–7 The false prophets do not have any revelation from the

that ye shall not divine; and the sun shall go
down over the prophets, and the day shall be dark
over them.
7 Then shall the seers be ashamed, and the
diviners confounded: yea, they shall all cover their
lips; for *there is* no answer of God.
8 ¶ But truly I am full of power by the spirit of
the LORD, and of judgment, and of might, to
declare unto Jacob his transgression, and to Israel
his sin.
9 Hear this, I pray you, ye heads of the house
of Jacob, and princes of the house of Israel, that
abhor judgment, and pervert all equity.
10 They build up Zion with blood, and Jerusalem
with iniquity.
11 The heads thereof judge for reward, and the
priests thereof teach for hire, and the prophets
thereof divine for money: yet will they lean upon
the LORD, and say, *Is* not the LORD among us?
none evil can come upon us.
12 Therefore shall Zion for your sake be plowed
as a field, and Jerusalem shall become heaps, and
the mountain of the house as the high places of
the forest.

CHAPTER 4

BUT in the last days it shall come to pass, *that*
the mountain of the house of the LORD shall be
established in the top of the mountains, and it
shall be exalted above the hills; and people shall
flow unto it.
2 And many nations shall come, and say, Come,
and let us go up to the mountain of the LORD, and
to the house of the God of Jacob; and he will teach
us of his ways, and we will walk in his paths: for
the law shall go forth of Zion, and the word of the
LORD from Jerusalem.
3 ¶ And he shall judge among many people, and
rebuke strong nations afar off; and they shall beat
their swords into plowshares, and their spears
into pruninghooks: nation shall not lift up a
sword against nation, neither shall they learn war
any more.
4 But they shall sit every man under his vine and
under his fig tree; and none shall make *them* afraid:
for the mouth of the LORD of hosts hath spoken *it*.
5 For all people will walk every one in the name
of his god, and we will walk in the name of the
LORD our God for ever and ever.

Lord, even though they are identified as *seers* and *diviners*, designations highlighting a prophet's reception of a divine word. When the Lord does not answer them, they will be proved false.

3:8 As Micah is empowered by the Spirit, he is enabled to boldly expose sin, setting him apart from the false prophets, who without a word from God, preached peace when there was no peace.

3:10 *blood*. The Hebrew word is plural, which always refers to bloodshed or blood guiltiness. Here it would designate the violent disregard of the leaders for life.

3:11 The civil and religious leaders were mercenaries, who used their offices for selfish gain. Yet ironically, they professed to depend on God whose assumed presence would protect them from harm or disaster (*evil*). Such a profession was evidence of their spiritual ignorance.

3:12 *Therefore* links the coming threefold disaster (*field, heaps, forest*) directly to the failures of three kinds of leaders (civil heads, prophets, priests). The holy city would become desolate and abandoned to be inhabited by wild animals of the forest as though it were a pagan city (cf. Isa. 13:21–22; Zeph. 2:13–15).

Thoughts for Personal/Family Worship: Chapter 3

1. **The sins and failures of civil and religious leaders were not unique to Micah's day. Every generation and geographical location has been subject to those who fall short of God's requirement for those who rule over men to be just and to rule in the fear of God (2 Sam. 23:3). On the one hand, it is a grievous matter. Yet, on the other hand, it should be a means of increasing desire for the ideal prophet, priest, and king, the Lord Jesus Christ. His rule is always just and His dominion is universal (Ps. 72). It is a reminder that our hope should never be in men or political or religious systems but only in the Lord. We should be confident as well that even though injustices now exist, God will right all wrongs (Eccl. 3:16–17).**
2. **The principle of judgment illustrated in 3:4 is a terrible warning of the danger of receiving from God according to our own works. Getting from God what is deserved is always awful, since the wages of sin is death (Rom. 6:23). The beauty of the gospel is that we do not get what we deserve but what Christ deserves. On the cross He bore our sins and guilt receiving what we deserved. In our justification, we receive the life and righteousness that He deserved by His perfect obedience to all of God's demands (2 Cor. 5:21).**

Chapter 4: *Micah describes the glories and greatness of God's kingdom marked by true worship, peace, prosperity, vindication, and victory for His people.*

Promise of a Glorious Kingdom (4:1–13)

4:1 *in the last days*. The expression points to the future when the present situation and circumstance will be reversed. It encompasses the progression of God's redemptive plan from the end of the Babylonian exile to Christ's incarnation and the Spirit's Pentecostal fullness to the final consummation of the age at Christ's second coming. *the mountain*. A reference to the place of true worship. This does not involve a literal topographical change but figuratively describes the triumph of the gospel and the centrality of true worship.

4:2 *many nations*. These nations participating in the worship of the one true and living God corresponds to Paul's description of the middle wall of partition between Jew and Gentile being removed by the gospel (Eph. 2:14–18) and the Gentiles being engrafted into the one olive tree (Rom. 11:11–25). From the first revelation of the gospel (Gen. 3:15) God's redemptive purpose has been worldwide in its scope; all the world would be blessed by the promised Messiah (Gen. 12:3).

4:3 *swords . . . pruninghooks*. Images of disarmament and universal peace.

4:4 *every man under his vine and under his fig tree*. An image of individual prosperity and peace. Ultimately and spiritually, it points to that enjoyment of peace in Christ that passes understanding (Phil. 4:7).

4:5 *his god . . . our God*. The two lines of the verse are parallel

6 In that day, saith the LORD, will I assemble her
that halteth, and I will gather her that is driven
out, and her that I have afflicted;
7 And I will make her that halted a remnant, and
her that was cast far off a strong nation: and the
LORD shall reign over them in mount Zion from
henceforth, even for ever.
8 ¶ And thou, O tower of the flock, the strong
hold of the daughter of Zion, unto thee shall it
come, even the first dominion; the kingdom shall
come to the daughter of Jerusalem.
9 Now why dost thou cry out aloud? *is there* no
king in thee? is thy counsellor perished? for pangs
have taken thee as a woman in travail.
10 Be in pain, and labour to bring forth, O
daughter of Zion, like a woman in travail: for
now shalt thou go forth out of the city, and thou
shalt dwell in the field, and thou shalt go *even* to
Babylon; there shalt thou be delivered; there the
LORD shall redeem thee from the hand of thine
enemies.
11 ¶ Now also many nations are gathered against
thee, that say, Let her be defiled, and let our eye
look upon Zion.
12 But they know not the thoughts of the LORD,
neither understand they his counsel: for he shall
gather them as the sheaves into the floor.
13 Arise and thresh, O daughter of Zion: for I will
make thine horn iron, and I will make thy hoofs
brass: and thou shalt beat in pieces many people:
and I will consecrate their gain unto the LORD,
and their substance unto the Lord of the whole
earth.

CHAPTER 5

NOW gather thyself in troops, O daughter of
troops: he hath laid siege against us: they shall
smite the judge of Israel with a rod upon the
cheek.
2 But thou, Beth-lehem Ephratah, *though* thou
be little among the thousands of Judah, *yet* out
of thee shall he come forth unto me *that is* to be
ruler in Israel; whose goings forth *have been* from
of old, from everlasting.
3 Therefore will he give them up, until the time
that she which travaileth hath brought forth: then
the remnant of his brethren shall return unto the
children of Israel.
4 ¶ And he shall stand and feed in the strength of

---

in thought. The context describing the triumph of true religion requires that both refer to the one true and living God: his God is our God. Walking in the name of God refers to maintaining a way of life in keeping with the character of God.

4:6–7 *assemble her that halteth*. Gather the lame. The Lord restores blessing to His people, transforming the lame, scattered, and afflicted into a spiritual body (*remnant*) that prospers under His reign.

4:8 The restoration is described in terms of a revival of Davidic splendor.

4:9–10 The imagery of birth *pangs* describes the distress of the impending Babylonian captivity, and the joy of giving birth describes the subsequent deliverance. Out of judgment comes blessing.

4:11–13 Apparent defeat is turned into ultimate victory in keeping with God's unchanging redemptive purpose (*the thoughts of the LORD*). The covenant nation, so long the object of mockery, would become an agent of judgment against the enemy.

4:13 *horn*. Image of power and strength.

Thoughts for Personal/Family Worship: Chapter 4

1. **The whole chapter is an occasion for reflecting on God's unchanging and unfailing purpose in the covenant of grace. Although at points in history it has appeared evil would triumph, it is certain that the upright will have dominion (Ps. 49:14). It is certain that the church of Christ will advance triumphantly against the very gates of hell (Matt. 16:18).**
2. **That the Gentile nations come to acknowledge and worship the true God is another evidence of God's unfailing redemptive purpose that was never intended to be limited to national Israel. The promised Messiah was from the beginning to be the source of blessing and salvation for the world. The description in Rev. 7:9 of the heavenly throng from every nation and tongue on earth confirms that Christ is the Savior of sinners from every race. Knowing that Christ has a people from all over the world should give confidence in every missionary and evangelistic venture.**

Chapter 5: *Micah predicts the birthplace and victorious rule of the Messiah, who achieves both political peace and religious purity.*

Promise of the Messiah (5:1–15)

5:1 Verse 1 is 4:14 in the Hebrew. Whereas 4:13 describes the victorious offense of a divinely empowered army, this describes the present reality of a meager troop in defensive posture against a superior army, most likely the Assyrian siege by Sennacherib. The reality of the present threat is a fitting transition from the future hope of victory to the identity of the Messiah who is our basis of all hope.

5:2 *Beth-lehem*. The only prophecy of Messiah's birthplace. Being born in Beth-lehem uniquely linked the Messiah directly to David. Of all the kings of the Davidic dynasty, only David, the first, and Jesus, the last, were born in this humble village. His coming forth from Beth-lehem declares the Messiah's humanity; *whose goings forth have been . . . from everlasting* requires His deity. The Messiah is the God-man. His coming forth from Beth-lehem was not the beginning of His existence; there were multiple goings forth from eternity, most likely a reference to the numerous appearances of Christ before His incarnation. His eternal existence and His earthly existence are in view. Only God is eternal.

5:3 *give them up, until*. Expresses the thought of Ezek. 21:26–27 that God would remove kingship from the nation until the coming of the Messiah, the ideal and rightful king from whom redemption would come. *she which travaileth*. A reference to Messiah's birth by a woman, indicating His real humanity and His being the fulfillment of Gen. 3:15, the seed of the woman who would reverse the curse. Because Micah is a contemporary of Isaiah, this links with his prophecy of the virgin birth (Isa. 7:14).

5:4 Pictures Messiah's activity as a shepherd who takes His

the LORD, in the majesty of the name of the LORD
his God; and they shall abide: for now shall he be
great unto the ends of the earth.
5 And this *man* shall be the peace, when the As-
syrian shall come into our land: and when he shall
tread in our palaces, then shall we raise against
him seven shepherds, and eight principal men.
6 And they shall waste the land of Assyria
with the sword, and the land of Nimrod in the
entrances thereof: thus shall he deliver *us* from
the Assyrian, when he cometh into our land, and
when he treadeth within our borders.
7 And the remnant of Jacob shall be in the midst
of many people as a dew from the LORD, as the
showers upon the grass, that tarrieth not for man,
nor waiteth for the sons of men.
8 ¶ And the remnant of Jacob shall be among the
Gentiles in the midst of many people as a lion
among the beasts of the forest, as a young lion
among the flocks of sheep: who, if he go through,
both treadeth down, and teareth in pieces, and
none can deliver.
9 Thine hand shall be lifted up upon thine
adversaries, and all thine enemies shall be cut off.
10 And it shall come to pass in that day, saith
the LORD, that I will cut off thy horses out of the
midst of thee, and I will destroy thy chariots:
11 And I will cut off the cities of thy land, and
throw down all thy strong holds:
12 And I will cut off witchcrafts out of thine
hand; and thou shalt have no *more* soothsayers:
13 Thy graven images also will I cut off, and thy
standing images out of the midst of thee; and
thou shalt no more worship the work of thine
hands.
14 And I will pluck up thy groves out of the midst
of thee: so will I destroy thy cities.
15 And I will execute vengeance in anger and fury
upon the heathen, such as they have not heard.

CHAPTER 6

HEAR ye now what the LORD saith; Arise, contend
thou before the mountains, and let the hills hear
thy voice.
2 Hear ye, O mountains, the LORD's controversy,

stand as guard, protector, and provider of His people. His faithful and kind rule extends to the ends of the earth.

5:5 *peace.* Messiah is the fulfillment of welfare and prosperity for His people. *seven shepherds, and eight principal men* (i.e., princes or leaders). Prior to Messiah's coming, there will be ample leadership to counter the attack of the enemy (*the Assyrian*). Seven and eight does not refer to actual numbers, but is an idiom of expressing completeness.

5:6 They (the undershepherds) will defeat Assyria, but *thus shall he* (the Messiah) *deliver.* Messiah's kingship is both mediate (through His representatives) and immediate (direct). *Assyria* was the specific threat in Micah's day; *Nimrod* (Babylon) was the future threat. They represent all who are hostile to God and His people regardless of specific identification.

5:7 *tarrieth not . . . nor waiteth.* These are words expressing hope and dependence, expressions of faith when God is the object. The *remnant* (the spiritual people) enjoys refreshing supplies (*dew . . . showers*) from the Lord without depending on the help of man.

5:8–9 Just as sheep are defenseless against an unrelenting lion, so the nation's enemies would be defenseless against them.

5:10–14 The Lord will remove everything upon which they might rely (both militarily and religiously) in order that they may trust and depend on Him exclusively. *Horses . . . chariots.* Offensive weapons. *cities . . . strong holds.* Defensive systems. Verses 12–14 refer to the removal of various religious perversions associated with idolatry. *groves.* Literally, cultic poles erected near an altar, associated with Baal worship.

5:15 Having removed every prop of false hope and confidence, the Lord intervenes in direct and unique judgment (*such as they have not heard*) on the enemies. Vengeance belongs to the Lord (Heb. 10:30–31).

Thoughts for Personal/Family Worship: Chapter 5

1. **The birth of Jesus in a barn in Beth-lehem underscores the depth of the humiliation of the incarnation of the Son of God. The eternal Son who in the heavenly glory was surrounded by a chorus of praising angels condescended to enter the virgin's womb to be born in a stall surrounded by brute beasts. From the ivory palaces (Ps. 45:8) He entered the world He created in poverty. Although Beth-lehem was the place of David's birth, it was not the royal city where presumably all the other kings of Judah were born with royal pageantry. His humble birth was followed by a life of humble obedience and humiliation leading to death on the cross. Christ was born that He might accomplish His unique mission of being the only redeemer of God's elect.**
2. **Micah's prophecy of the Messiah's birthplace includes vital truths about the person of Christ that constitute reasons for worship and praise. Both the deity and humanity of Christ are in view; He is the God-man with two distinct natures in one person. His goings forth before His birth indicate the existence of His person prior to the incarnation and thus His deity. His birth indicates that His humanity is real. As the God-man He is the only mediator between God and men. The whole work of redemption depends on this unique person. Christ is mankind's only hope. It is significant that this is a truth revealed in the Old Testament as well as the New.**

PENALTY AND PROMISE (6:1—7:20)

Chapter 6: ***Micah summons the people to court and proves with irrefutable evidence that their religion did not satisfy God's spiritual demands and that rather than appeasing God with their rituals, they merited His just punishment.***

Indictments against the People (6:1–16)

6:1–3 The first two verses constitute the subpoena that identifies the parties of the lawsuit and summons the witnesses. This is a case of the Lord versus Israel. Verse 3 discloses the indictment: Israel had become impatient with God and had stopped performing their covenant duties. The Lord is prosecutor, plaintiff, and judge, and Judah is the accused.

6:1 *contend.* A legal term meaning to argue a case.

6:2 *controversy.* The noun form of the verb "contend," a legal term referring to the lawsuit or complaint. *plead.* Also a legal

and ye strong foundations of the earth: for the
LORD hath a controversy with his people, and he
will plead with Israel.
3 O my people, what have I done unto thee? and
wherein have I wearied thee? testify against me.
4 For I brought thee up out of the land of Egypt,
and redeemed thee out of the house of servants;
and I sent before thee Moses, Aaron, and Miriam.
5 O my people, remember now what Balak king
of Moab consulted, and what Balaam the son of
Beor answered him from Shittim unto Gilgal; that
ye may know the righteousness of the LORD.
6 ¶ Wherewith shall I come before the LORD, *and*
bow myself before the high God? shall I come
before him with burnt offerings, with calves of a
year old?
7 Will the LORD be pleased with thousands of
rams, *or* with ten thousands of rivers of oil? shall
I give my firstborn *for* my transgression, the fruit
of my body *for* the sin of my soul?
8 He hath shewed thee, O man, what *is* good;
and what doth the LORD require of thee, but to
do justly, and to love mercy, and to walk humbly
with thy God?
9 The LORD's voice crieth unto the city, and *the*
man of wisdom shall see thy name: hear ye the
rod, and who hath appointed it.
10 ¶ Are there yet the treasures of wickedness in
the house of the wicked, and the scant measure
that is abominable?
11 Shall I count *them* pure with the wicked
balances, and with the bag of deceitful weights?
12 For the rich men thereof are full of violence,
and the inhabitants thereof have spoken lies, and
their tongue *is* deceitful in their mouth.
13 Therefore also will I make *thee* sick in smiting
thee, in making *thee* desolate because of thy sins.
14 Thou shalt eat, but not be satisfied; and thy
casting down *shall be* in the midst of thee; and
thou shalt take hold, but shalt not deliver; and *that*
which thou deliverest will I give up to the sword.
15 Thou shalt sow, but thou shalt not reap; thou
shalt tread the olives, but thou shalt not anoint
thee with oil; and sweet wine, but shalt not drink
wine.
16 ¶ For the statutes of Omri are kept, and all the
works of the house of Ahab, and ye walk in their
counsels; that I should make thee a desolation,

---

term meaning to answer or testify for or against someone.

6:3 The question becomes the accusation: they had grown tired of the Lord, and He wanted to know why. The question asserts that Israel's attitude was contrary to expectation, for God had given them every reason to obey Him. Israel had no answer or defense, and the trial evidence would make that clear.

6:4–8 The trial begins and includes irrefutable evidence and devastating rebuttal that the nation is guilty.

6:4–5 The Lord presents evidence of His past deliverance (the exodus), His care (the provision of leaders), and His protection (*Balak* and *Balaam*). *from Shittim* (the last place of encampment in the wilderness) *unto Gilgal* (the first place of encampment in the Promised Land). Together they represent the entire wilderness experience and conquest which gave evidence of God's unceasing providential care.

6:6–7 This sums up the nation's self-defense. They assert that they are willing to do whatever God wants; all He has to do is ask. Their defense is that God is to blame for not making His expectations clear. Their quandary is evident in the intensification of their offers ranging from the best of the animals (*calves of a year old*) to the exaggerated quantities of sacrifices (*thousands . . . ten thousands*) to the desperate abomination of child sacrifice (*firstborn . . . fruit of my body*). Ironically, rather than defending themselves, they further incriminated themselves by assuming God wanted things rather than hearts.

6:8 The Lord refutes the nation's argument with a simple yet profound statement defining spiritual life and worship, true ethical religion. Outward behavior is an index to the heart. Three summary statements show that piety encompasses all of life. *To do justly* involves social and ethical behavior in conformity to God's legal requirements. *To love mercy* involves the inclination of the will to the practice of covenant loyalty and affection toward God and men. *To walk humbly* involves a lowly and careful manner of life conscious of God. True religion consists of a whole life lived in awareness of God.

6:9–16 These verses record the decision and enumerate specific counts for which the people were judged guilty and were to hear the punishment sentenced (*rod*). Whereas God demanded justice, the people were guilty of fraud (vv. 10–11). Whereas God demanded covenant loyalty and mercy, they were guilty of violence and falsehood for personal gain (v. 12). Verse 16 sums it up: rather than obeying God, they followed the ways of *Omri* and *Ahab*, each the epitome of wickedness. The sentence of punishment (the *rod* of v. 9) involved several phases: disease and desolation (v. 13), dissatisfaction (eating without satisfying hunger, v. 14), defenselessness and defeat (inability to escape the sword, v. 14), disappointments and frustrations (inability to benefit from the harvest, v. 15), destruction and derision (*hissing*, a mocking whistle, v. 16).

Thoughts for Personal/Family Worship: Chapter 6

1. **Although the court session Micah records concerned ancient Israel, the trial issues are universal and timeless. Religion in one form or another dominated life and in many ways blinded the people to the problem of sin. Religious people are often the hardest to convict of sin because they assume that they are doing what God wants. Many today without Christ assume that going to church and keeping the Golden Rule will somehow balance to their favor in the end. Even many who profess Christ allow their pious routines to substitute for private devotion and a sincere heart. The Scripture is explicitly clear that God has never been nor will ever be satisfied with external religion or empty profession without a true heart of faith on the inside that authenticates itself by true holiness on the outside. The link between behavior and belief is the essence of true religion (James 1:27).**
2. **Unquestionably Christ referred to Mic. 6:8 when He exposed the hypocrisy of the Pharisees by accusing them of omitting the most important matters of the law: judgment, mercy, and faith (Matt. 23:23). What condemned the Jews of Micah's day condemned the Pharisees of Christ's day. Indeed, the requirements of true religion never change, and God's requirement of what is good remains the standard for today. That Micah uses a court scene to make his point reminds us**

and the inhabitants thereof an hissing: therefore
ye shall bear the reproach of my people.

CHAPTER 7

WOE is me! for I am as when they have gathered
the summer fruits, as the grapegleanings of the
vintage: *there is* no cluster to eat: my soul desired
the firstripe fruit.
2 The good *man* is perished out of the earth: and
there is none upright among men: they all lie in
wait for blood; they hunt every man his brother
with a net.
3 ¶ That they may do evil with both hands
earnestly, the prince asketh, and the judge *asketh*
for a reward; and the great *man*, he uttereth his
mischievous desire: so they wrap it up.
4 The best of them *is* as a brier: the most upright
is sharper than a thorn hedge: the day of thy
watchmen *and* thy visitation cometh; now shall
be their perplexity.
5 ¶ Trust ye not in a friend, put ye not confidence
in a guide: keep the doors of thy mouth from her
that lieth in thy bosom.
6 For the son dishonoureth the father, the
daughter riseth up against her mother, the
daughter in law against her mother in law; a
man's enemies *are* the men of his own house.
7 Therefore I will look unto the LORD; I will wait
for the God of my salvation: my God will hear me.
8 ¶ Rejoice not against me, O mine enemy: when
I fall, I shall arise; when I sit in darkness, the LORD
shall be a light unto me.
9 I will bear the indignation of the LORD, because
I have sinned against him, until he plead my
cause, and execute judgment for me: he will
bring me forth to the light, *and* I shall behold his
righteousness.
10 Then *she that is* mine enemy shall see *it*, and
shame shall cover her which said unto me, Where
is the LORD thy God? mine eyes shall behold her:
now shall she be trodden down as the mire of the
streets.
11 *In* the day that thy walls are to be built, *in* that
day shall the decree be far removed.
12 *In* that day *also* he shall come even to thee
from Assyria, and *from* the fortified cities, and
from the fortress even to the river, and from sea to
sea, and *from* mountain to mountain.
13 Notwithstanding the land shall be desolate
because of them that dwell therein, for the fruit
of their doings.
14 ¶ Feed thy people with thy rod, the flock of
thine heritage, which dwell solitarily *in* the wood,
in the midst of Carmel: let them feed *in* Bashan
and Gilead, as in the days of old.
15 According to the days of thy coming out of the
land of Egypt will I shew unto him marvellous
things.
16 ¶ The nations shall see and be confounded at
all their might: they shall lay *their* hand upon *their*
mouth, their ears shall be deaf.

---

of a coming day of judgment when all hearts will be open and naked before the eyes of Him to whom we will answer. The verdicts rendered on that day are eternal, so it behooves us all "to do justly, to love mercy, and to walk humbly with [our] God."

Chapter 7: *Micah bemoans the appalling state of the nation, affirms his personal faith, appeals to the prayer-answering God, and ascribes praise to God's amazing grace.*

Promise of Ultimate Victory and Salvation (7:1–20)

7:1 Micah expresses his disappointment regarding the spiritual condition of the nation using the imagery of a vineyard that has been repeatedly picked so that nothing is left. Compare the parable of the vineyard in Isa. 5 where the Lord found wild grapes instead of good; here Micah finds nothing.

7:2–4 The point of the illustration; there were no good men in the land.

7:2 *good.* The adjective form of the word "mercy" in 6:8. None met the standards of God's requirement. *they all lie in wait . . . with a net.* Images of trickery, treachery, and violence.

7:3 *do evil with both hands earnestly.* Literally, "concerning evil both hands to do well." They were zealous and good at doing bad. *the prince asketh.* Anarchy reigned as there was a conspiracy between the rulers and courts for personal gain. *wrap it up.* Literally, "twist or plot together." It sums up the conspiracy.

7:4 Micah interrupts his description of society's sins by announcing certain judgment on the wicked. *thy watchmen.* Most likely the prophets sent to warn. *and thy visitation.* The retribution that will come.

7:5–6 A description of the complete breakdown of society extending to the family. *guide.* Literally, "closest and most intimate friend"; refers to one's spouse.

7:7–10 Micah turns his attention away from the disappointments of society and expresses his confidence. The ground of his confidence is the Lord; the expression of his confidence is faith; the validity of his confidence is the Lord's hearing; the hope of his confidence is vindication.

7:7 *I will look.* To watch closely or be on the lookout for. *I will wait.* Not in passive resignation but in heart-throbbing expectancy.

7:11 *the decree be far removed.* The word *decree* can refer to a boundary, and the words *far removed* can mean to extend or be distant. The idea would be that the borders of the nation would be enlarged, paralleling the blessing of the walls being rebuilt. The personal vindication described in vv. 8–10 will one day include the entire nation.

7:13 The future vindication follows judgment: Israel cannot escape the consequences of sin.

7:14 Prayer is the evidence of confidence in the Lord. He prays that God would be the good shepherd of His people. *Bashan and Gilead.* Proverbial for the rich pasturelands. Feeding here represents the fullness of blessing.

7:15 The Lord answers the prayer, promising exodus-like wonders. *marvellous.* A word designating extraordinary and even miraculous acts.

7:16–17 These verses detail the confusion of the enemies

17 They shall lick the dust like a serpent, they
shall move out of their holes like worms of the
earth: they shall be afraid of the LORD our God,
and shall fear because of thee.
18 Who *is* a God like unto thee, that pardoneth
iniquity, and passeth by the transgression of the
remnant of his heritage? he retaineth not his
anger for ever, because he delighteth *in* mercy.
19 He will turn again, he will have compassion
upon us; he will subdue our iniquities; and thou
wilt cast all their sins into the depths of the sea.
20 Thou wilt perform the truth to Jacob, *and* the
mercy to Abraham, which thou hast sworn unto
our fathers from the days of old.

when God intervenes in answer to prayer. *hand upon their mouth.* A gesture of humiliation and silence.

7:18–20 Micah ends with a doxology. He draws attention to God's matchless character. The question *Who is a God like unto thee?* plays on Micah's name ("who is like Jehovah?"); it expects no answer, just reflection. He mentions God's matchless acts of pardon, compassion, and covenant loyalty.

Thoughts for Personal/Family Worship: Chapter 7

1. Micah, writing thousands of years ago, describes scenes that could have come from today's news. The presence of good and upright men was rare. Micah longed for the fruit of righteousness but instead found a land filled with crooked leaders, ruthless neighbors, and troubled homes (7:1–6). We, too, live in a day when the unrighteous constitute the immoral majority; they mock God's people and are increasingly willing to vent their full hatred against the Christ of God. Although his days were dark, the prophet did not despair, and he has written for us an inspired pattern for living in an evil day. Micah puts it all in perspective, showing us how to feel, what to pray, and why to rejoice in an evil day. We should feel confident before God because of who He is (v. 7) and before the wicked because God will vindicate us (vv. 8–10). We should pray that God would shepherd His flock in faith that He would do the extraordinary and confound the wicked (vv. 14–17). We should praise Him because there is none like Him who can do what He can do (vv. 18–20).
2. The Old Testament uses various words in the vocabulary for faith. The ideas of looking expectantly and waiting for the Lord are important concepts (7:7). Every word for faith in some way describes confidence in the object of faith. Waiting on the Lord is an expression of hope and confidence. It is not just a passive notion that resigns to whatever happens. It involves an active, vigilant expectancy that what God has promised will come at any moment. It is like sitting on the edge of your seat in eager anticipation. And the wonderful thing is that those who wait on the Lord will never be disappointed.

THE LORD

is Good

A

STRONG

Hold

IN

THE DAY

of Trouble

AND

He

KNOWETH

Them

THAT

TRUST

in Him

NAHUM 1:7

INTRODUCTION TO THE BOOK OF NAHUM

Authorship: Nahum's name means "comfort" or "consolation," a shortened form of Nehemiah, which means "the comfort (or consolation) of Jehovah." Little is known about Nahum apart from his powerful prophecy and his identification as "the Elkoshite." There are three basic theories regarding the location of Elkosh: (1) an Assyrian city "al-Kush" on the Tigris River not far from Nineveh; (2) Capernaum, the well-known city in the northern kingdom, whose name was changed in honor of Nahum; (3) a city of uncertain location in the southern kingdom. If the reference is to a city in Assyria, it would indicate Nahum's family had been part of the Assyrian deportation at the fall of Samaria (722 BC), thus giving him northern roots. Identifying the significance of "the Elkoshite" conclusively is not crucial to the interpretation of the message.

Date: A historic event and a future event mark the time frame for Nahum's prophecy. Nahum 3:8 mentions the fall of No, a chief Egyptian city also known as No-Amon or Thebes. Thebes fell to the Assyrian forces under the leadership of Assurbanipal around 664/663 BC. Nahum's prophecy began after that event but before the fall of Nineveh which was the theme of his message. Nineveh fell to a Medo-Babylonian coalition in 612 BC. The Babylonian Chronicle, a concise record of Nabopolassar's campaigns (616–609 BC) describes a two-month siege against Nineveh that was ultimately aided by the flooding of the Tigris, which enabled the Babylonian forces to breach Nineveh's seemingly impregnable defensive walls. Significantly, Nahum links Nineveh's fall to a flood (1:8; 2:6). In the light of the historic and future event, Nahum's prophecy dates between 663 and 612 BC.

Theme: The doom and destruction of Nineveh.

Purpose: To warn sinners of God's exacting justice and to encourage God's people with His power to save, also to vouchsafe His redemptive purpose by showing that no opposition can frustrate the advancement of God's kingdom. Nahum 1:7–8 sums up the dual purpose.

Synopsis: *The Contribution of Nahum to Redemptive Revelation*

Although there are no explicit references to Christ in Nahum, the prophecy points to Christ and makes a vital contribution to the progression of redemptive history. Nahum reveals God in terms of justice, power, and goodness and artfully intertwines the message of judgment and grace. His message of consolation to Israel was that God would judge Nineveh, a great and bloody city whose savagery was proverbial both in Scripture and its own records. Ironically, this message of certain destruction of Nineveh comes a hundred years after Jonah's message to Nineveh that led to the amazing display of God's grace in sparing the city in the light of its widespread repentance. That repentance under Jonah was short-lived and soon forgotten, and now Nahum pronounces doom on this new generation whose gross iniquities and opposition to God would find no pardon. Great and unrepentant sins bring certain ruin. Significantly, whereas Jonah preached his message of threatened judgment directly to Nineveh, leading to their experience of grace, there is no indication that Nineveh ever heard Nahum's declaration of a certain and irreversible sentence of doom. God is gracious to whom He is gracious, but He withholds His mercy from whom He wills (Rom. 9:14–18). He is sovereign in both grace and judgment. Nahum's oracle contributes to the redemptive message by highlighting the sinner's desperate condition and warning sinners of every age not to trifle with God. His message is indeed a comfort to saints of the certainty of God's unfailing plan and purpose of redemption. Had Assyria successfully persisted in their cruelty and opposition to Israel, the coming of Messiah would have been jeopardized. There had to be an Israel if there was going to be Christ, and God ensured that the Christ was coming. Assyria was just one more member of the serpent's seed that would be defeated in its hostility to the promised Seed of the woman (Gen. 3:15). Nahum assures us that the whole program of redemption is on course. That God defeats this fierce enemy of grace points directly to the mediatorial kingship of Christ that assures the defeat of all of His and our enemies: a victory won on the cross that continues in the church and will be consummated at the end of time.

Outline:

I. Superscription (1:1)

II. The Announcement of Nineveh's Doom (1:2–15)
- A. The Identity of the Judge: The Song of God's Majesty (1:2–8)
- B. The Purpose of the Judgment (1:9–15)
  1. Destruction to Nineveh (1:9–11)
  2. Deliverance for Judah (1:12–15)

III. The Description of Nineveh's Destruction (2:1–13)
- A. Warfare (2:1–6)
- B. Defeat and Plunder (2:7–13)

IV. The Reasons for Nineveh's Destruction (3:1–19)
- A. Great Sins (3:1–10)
- B. Great Weakness (3:11–19)

THE BOOK OF

NAHUM

CHAPTER 1

THE burden of Nineveh. The book of the vision of
Nahum the Elkoshite.
2 God *is* jealous, and the LORD revengeth; the
LORD revengeth, and *is* furious; the LORD will take
vengeance on his adversaries, and he reserveth
wrath for his enemies.
3 The LORD *is* slow to anger, and great in power,
and will not at all acquit *the wicked*: the LORD *hath*
his way in the whirlwind and in the storm, and
the clouds *are* the dust of his feet.
4 He rebuketh the sea, and maketh it dry, and
drieth up all the rivers: Bashan languisheth, and
Carmel, and the flower of Lebanon languisheth.
5 The mountains quake at him, and the hills
melt, and the earth is burned at his presence, yea,
the world, and all that dwell therein.
6 Who can stand before his indignation? and who
can abide in the fierceness of his anger? his fury
is poured out like fire, and the rocks are thrown
down by him.
7 The LORD *is* good, a strong hold in the day of
trouble; and he knoweth them that trust in him.
8 But with an overrunning flood he will make an
utter end of the place thereof, and darkness shall
pursue his enemies.
9 What do ye imagine against the LORD? he will
make an utter end: affliction shall not rise up the
second time.
10 For while *they be* folden together *as* thorns,
and while they are drunken *as* drunkards, they
shall be devoured as stubble fully dry.

Chapter 1: ***After offering a magnificent song of God's majesty, Nahum announces God's irresistible judgment on Nineveh with its corollary consequence of consolation for Judah.***

SUPERSCRIPTION (1:1)

1:1 *burden*. Literally, "pronouncement" or "oracle," a common designation of the prophetic word. *vision*. The prophetic revelation, focusing on the divine message received by the prophet more than the manner of reception. This was the inspired Word from the Lord.

THE ANNOUNCEMENT OF NINEVEH'S DOOM (1:2–15)

The Identity of the Judge: The Song of God's Majesty (1:2–8)

1:2–8 The song is one of grandest descriptions of God in all Scripture, highlighting His inflexible justice (v. 2), His irresistible power (vv. 3–6), and His immeasurable goodness (v. 7).

1:2 That *God is jealous* refers to His zeal for truth, His glory, and His people. His zealous fervency demands exclusive worship and allegiance; He is intolerant of any other allegiance (Ex. 34:14; Deut. 4:24). *revengeth*. The word occurs three times in the verse (*take vengeance* is the same word). In Hebrew, the root word differs from the word for "Nahum" by a single letter, resulting in an interesting verbal play as "consolation" gives way to condemnation. This wrathful action flows from His jealousy. It is not from temper, vindictiveness, or malice, but rather from His just and righteous nature. *furious*. Literally, "a master of wrath." God is proficient in executing wrath; therefore, sinners should be warned not to trifle with Him. *he reserveth… enemies*. Literally, "He is one keeping watch of His enemies." He observes and therefore His judgments are infallible and inescapable because all things are open and naked before Him.

1:3–5 God's power over natural creation illustrates and proves His power over spiritual matters as well. He controls the heavens (v. 3), the seas and rivers, setting their shores (v. 4), and the earth (places noted for fertility are subject to God, v. 4; places noted for stability are nothing before God, v. 5).

1:3 *slow to anger*. Literally, "long of nostrils," an idiom for patience. It takes time for the nose to redden, a symbol of anger. The Lord's just wrath does not flare up uncontrollably or unreasonably. This longsuffering is designed to bring men to repentance (Rom. 2:4). *great in power*. The delays of vengeance are not from weakness but strength: God can be as longsuffering as He is because He is as powerful as He is. The enemy can never gain an advantage.

1:6 If majestic mountains melt before God, puny man certainly cannot stand before Him. Sinners will have no defense, no excuse, and no ground on which to stand at the judgment.

1:7 The Lord Himself is the only defense in the day of judgment for those that *trust* in Him, that seek refuge and find security in a place of safety. *he knoweth*. God's judgments are infallible. See 2 Tim. 2:19: "The Lord knoweth them that are his."

1:8 A tragic contrast to the stability of faith. Sinners, and specifically here the Assyrians, will be completely swept away into darkness, most likely an image of death.

The Purpose of the Judgment (1:9–15)

Destruction to Nineveh (1:9–11)

1:9 The prophet now addresses Assyria directly. The Lord will frustrate all their schemes (Ps. 2:1). The distress (*affliction*) will not need to come a *second time* because it accomplishes its purpose the first time.

1:10 *Thorns* tangled together and *drunkards* picture helplessness and powerlessness; they are as certain for destruction

11 There is *one* come out of thee, that imagineth
evil against the LORD, a wicked counsellor.
12 Thus saith the LORD; Though *they be* quiet,
and likewise many, yet thus shall they be cut
down, when he shall pass through. Though I have
afflicted thee, I will afflict thee no more.
13 For now will I break his yoke from off thee,
and will burst thy bonds in sunder.
14 And the LORD hath given a commandment
concerning thee, *that* no more of thy name be
sown: out of the house of thy gods will I cut off
the graven image and the molten image: I will
make thy grave; for thou art vile.
15 Behold upon the mountains the feet of him
that bringeth good tidings, that publisheth peace!
O Judah, keep thy solemn feasts, perform thy
vows: for the wicked shall no more pass through
thee; he is utterly cut off.

CHAPTER 2

HE that dasheth in pieces is come up before thy
face: keep the munition, watch the way, make *thy*
loins strong, fortify *thy* power mightily.
2 For the LORD hath turned away the excellency of
Jacob, as the excellency of Israel: for the emptiers
have emptied them out, and marred their vine
branches.
3 The shield of his mighty men is made red, the
valiant men *are* in scarlet: the chariots *shall be*
with flaming torches in the day of his preparation,
and the fir trees shall be terribly shaken.

---

as dry straw is in contact with fire.

1:11 Many identify the *wicked counsellor* to be Sennacherib, the Assyrian king during the administration of Hezekiah who schemed to conquer Judah but was thwarted by divine, supernatural intervention.

Deliverance for Judah (1:12–15)

1:12 The prophet abruptly transitions from addressing Assyria to Judah. The doom decreed on Assyria is good news for Judah; it means the end of Assyrian threat. *quiet*. From the root often translated as "peace," the word has the idea of being complete or healthy, referring to general welfare. The following words, *likewise many*, suggest the idea of completeness. Although the Assyrians were a huge and formidable foe and it appeared they were invincible, they are no match against God's wrath; they will perish and pass away (*pass through*). *Though I have afflicted . . . no more.* God had sovereignly used the Assyrians as an instrument of chastisement against His people, but now He would judge the Assyrians for their abuses (Isa. 10:5–19).

1:13 *yoke*. A symbol of manipulating control, slavery, and bondage.

1:14 The message of hopeful deliverance to Judah takes the form of a direct word to the Assyrian king. The Lord pronounces a threefold sentence on the king: (1) He will have no descendants to follow him to the throne (*no more of thy name be sown*); (2) God would remove the idols from the pagan temples (a common gesture marking the defeat showing that the images had no power); (3) He will die (*make thy grave*). *for thou art vile.* Sums up the reason for the severe sentence with a touch of irony. In Hebrew the word for *vile* has the idea of being small or insignificant. Though the king appeared to be mighty, he was nothing before God.

1:15 The image suggests the scene of those waiting to hear the outcome of a battle and then rejoicing in the good news of victory (see 2 Sam. 18:18–27). The consequence of the good news of Assyria's defeat was the peace and the freedom to perform religious duties without threat of interruption. Assyria would never again be a threat (*he is utterly cut off*). Isaiah 52:7 makes a similar declaration regarding God's salvation, and in Rom. 10:15 Paul gives the ultimate application in terms of those who preach the gospel.

Thoughts for Personal/Family Worship: Chapter 1

1. **Nahum's song of God's majesty highlights both the justice and goodness of God, making it clear that these divine perfections are not contradictory but essential in God's nature. It is a foolish, sentimental, and unbiblical notion of God that concludes that His love or goodness requires Him to be gracious to all indiscriminately. In fact, it is the love of God that renders the punishment of sinners just because the supreme object of His love is His Son. To know and experience God's love is to do so in Christ; out of Christ there is nothing but wrath and condemnation. It would be a betrayal of His love to His Son to allow sinners to escape justice. This is why sinners must flee to Christ as the only refuge or stronghold of safety against the day of judgment. No man can stand before God on his own merit, but in Christ there is total acceptance.**
2. **Verse 12 is a reminder that appearance and reality are not the same and that we should, therefore, walk by faith and not sight. It appeared that the enemy remained strong and numerous, but the reality was that God had irreversibly sentenced them to destruction and they were doomed (v. 15). At any given moment it appears that Satan is a roaring lion seeking whom he can devour but the reality is that he was defeated on Calvary, is being defeated with every advance of the church, and will be ultimately defeated at the consummation of the age. Faith must live in the light of the certain reality; faith overcomes sight.**

Chapter 2: *Nahum describes the siege, ransacking, and total destruction of Nineveh.*

THE DESCRIPTION OF NINEVEH'S DESTRUCTION (2:1–13)

Warfare (2:1–6)

2:1 The Lord addresses Nineveh, instructing them to prepare for battle. The instruction is satirical given the decreed and certain outcome. Preparations for this battle would be futile. *He that dasheth in pieces*. Literally, "he that scatters." Historically, a reference to the Medes and Babylonians, but spiritually and really, a reference to God Himself as the principal foe against Nineveh. The Medes and Babylonians were the weapons He used. *keep the munition*. Guard the fortress.

2:2 *hath turned away the excellency of Jacob*. A positive statement meaning that the Lord has restored the eminence or majesty of Israel. This is a positive consequence of Assyria's destruction. *for the emptiers have emptied them*. Because the ravagers ravaged them.

2:3 Most likely describes the appearance of the warriors and weapons, which were intended to intimidate and frighten. The red shields and uniforms along with the flashing glares from the metallic parts of the chariots would be an awesome

4 The chariots shall rage in the streets, they shall
justle one against another in the broad ways: they
shall seem like torches, they shall run like the
lightnings.
5 He shall recount his worthies: they shall
stumble in their walk; they shall make haste to the
wall thereof, and the defence shall be prepared.
6 The gates of the rivers shall be opened, and the
palace shall be dissolved.
7 And Huzzab shall be led away captive, she
shall be brought up, and her maids shall lead *her*
as with the voice of doves, tabering upon their
breasts.
8 But Nineveh *is* of old like a pool of water: yet
they shall flee away. Stand, stand, *shall they cry*;
but none shall look back.
9 Take ye the spoil of silver, take the spoil of gold:
for *there is* none end of the store *and* glory out of
all the pleasant furniture.
10 She is empty, and void, and waste: and the
heart melteth, and the knees smite together, and
much pain *is* in all loins, and the faces of them all
gather blackness.
11 Where *is* the dwelling of the lions, and the
feedingplace of the young lions, where the lion,
even the old lion, walked, *and* the lion's whelp,
and none made *them* afraid?
12 The lion did tear in pieces enough for his
whelps, and strangled for his lionesses, and filled
his holes with prey, and his dens with ravin.
13 Behold, I *am* against thee, saith the LORD of
hosts, and I will burn her chariots in the smoke,

psychological tactic of the invading army. *the day of his preparation*. When he arrays for battle. *fir trees shall be terribly shaken*. Refers to brandishing of the spear shafts, which would have been constructed from fir or cypress.

2:4 Describes the confusion and panic of the chariot cavalry inside the city at the approach of the seemingly blood-drenched army.

2:5 The infantry is in a panic as well. *He shall recount his worthies*. The king will summon his mighty ones or officers, but they will stagger as they try to advance (*in their walk*). *they shall make haste to the wall*. A reference to the advance of the invading army as they prepare to breach the wall. This was a major obstacle. Nineveh's walls were reportedly 100-feet high, wide enough for three chariots, with towers extending 100 feet around the wall itself and surrounded by a moat 150 feet wide and 60 feet deep. Were it not for the Lord's intervention, Nineveh would be impregnable. *the defence shall be prepared*. A reference to a movable shelter called a "mantelet" used to shield those who were building the siege works.

2:6 The flooding of the city aided in the defeat of the city.

Defeat and Plunder (2:7–13)

2:7 *Huzzab*. A difficult and disputed word. The text of the KJV has simply transliterated the word, implying it is a proper name referring either to the actual queen of Nineveh or to the goddess queen commonly known as Ishtar. The removal of either would be a sign of shameful defeat. Some translate the word "that which was established." The idea would be that the defeat of Nineveh has been decreed. Either way, the lamentation was intense. *her maids shall lead her as with the voice of doves*. Her maidservants will moan like the sound of a dove. *tabering upon their breasts*. Repeatedly striking upon their heart.

2:8 Nineveh is compared to a standing pool of water whose dike has given way resulting in a flood of confusion and panic. Instructions to remain calm are ignored as the people try to escape.

2:9 Nineveh's inexhaustible supply of wealth was now booty for the soldiers who now became plunderers. *none end of the store*. No end to the resources of gold and silver. *glory out of all the pleasant furniture*. The assets from all the desirable or precious objects.

2:10 The devastation is total and the reactions express shock and fear. *the faces of them all gather blackness*. The exact significance is unclear but clearly it describes the facial expression when one hears of bad or frightening news.

2:11–12 Nineveh is compared to a lair where the lioness and whelps wait restlessly for the return of the lion with the prey and *ravin* (torn flesh). The rhetorical question implies that the lair is abandoned and the lion does not return. It pictures a complete reversal of Isaiah's description of Assyria as a lion who is unstoppable in its quest (Isa. 5:29). Assyria that once sustained itself by conquest is itself now the object of conquest.

2:13 The description of destruction ends with a judgment oracle explicitly identifying the Lord as being against them and the direct agent of their devastating defeat. The silencing of the messengers means that the once fierce nation will no longer be a threat (for instance, like the threats of the Rabshakeh against Hezekiah, 2 Kings 18).

Thoughts for Personal/Family Worship: Chapter 2

1. **The defeat and destruction of Nineveh provide a good example of the sovereignty of God whereby the Lord accomplishes His purpose either directly or indirectly through secondary agents. From a human perspective the fall of Nineveh at the hands of the Medes and Babylonians had natural, political, and military explanations. It could well have been the topic of the daily news with commentary and analysis. Yet the Medes and Babylonians in reality were merely the instruments or tools God used to achieve His purpose. Consequently, the spiritual explanation for Nineveh's fall is far more significant than the political and military explanations. The secondary agents do not in any way diminish the ultimate agency of God Himself. That these nations were themselves ignorant that they were doing God's will was irrelevant. Their purpose was mercenary; God's purpose was to keep on track His redemptive plan.**
2. **Assyria had amassed extreme wealth, but all their assets could not deliver them. In many ways, the history of Assyria parallels the parable of Christ recorded in Luke 12:16–21 of the man who lived to be rich only to die in spiritual poverty leaving all his assets to another. It is far more important to be rich toward God than to amass possessions that are only temporary. Peter reminds us that we cannot be redeemed with silver or gold but only with the precious blood of Christ (1 Peter 1:18–19).**
3. **The opening statement of Nah. 2:13 is fearful: "I am against thee, saith the LORD." For God to be the enemy spells doom and damnation. But this is the state of every individual outside of Christ. To be outside of Christ is to be under condemnation and subject to God's severe wrath. To be in Christ changes everything. The believer is united to Christ and enjoys security and peace. The**

and the sword shall devour thy young lions: and I
will cut off thy prey from the earth, and the voice
of thy messengers shall no more be heard.

CHAPTER 3

WOE to the bloody city! it *is* all full of lies *and*
robbery; the prey departeth not;
2 The noise of a whip, and the noise of the
rattling of the wheels, and of the pransing horses,
and of the jumping chariots.
3 The horseman lifteth up both the bright sword
and the glittering spear: and *there is* a multitude
of slain, and a great number of carcases; and *there*
is none end of *their* corpses; they stumble upon
their corpses:
4 Because of the multitude of the whoredoms
of the wellfavoured harlot, the mistress of
witchcrafts, that selleth nations through her
whoredoms, and families through her witchcrafts.
5 Behold, I *am* against thee, saith the LORD of
hosts; and I will discover thy skirts upon thy face,
and I will shew the nations thy nakedness, and the
kingdoms thy shame.
6 And I will cast abominable filth upon thee, and
make thee vile, and will set thee as a gazingstock.
7 And it shall come to pass, *that* all they that look
upon thee shall flee from thee, and say, Nineveh
is laid waste: who will bemoan her? whence shall
I seek comforters for thee?
8 Art thou better than populous No, that was
situate among the rivers, *that had* the waters
round about it, whose rampart *was* the sea, *and*
her wall *was* from the sea?
9 Ethiopia and Egypt *were* her strength, and *it*
was infinite; Put and Lubim were thy helpers.
10 Yet *was* she carried away, she went into
captivity: her young children also were dashed in
pieces at the top of all the streets: and they cast
lots for her honourable men, and all her great
men were bound in chains.
11 Thou also shalt be drunken: thou shalt be hid,
thou also shalt seek strength because of the enemy.
12 All thy strong holds *shall be like* fig trees with
the firstripe figs: if they be shaken, they shall even
fall into the mouth of the eater.
13 Behold, thy people in the midst of thee *are*
women: the gates of thy land shall be set wide open
unto thine enemies: the fire shall devour thy bars.
14 Draw thee waters for the siege, fortify thy
strong holds: go into clay, and tread the morter,
make strong the brickkiln.
15 There shall the fire devour thee; the sword
shall cut thee off, it shall eat thee up like the can-
kerworm: make thyself many as the cankerworm,
make thyself many as the locusts.

---

consequence is that God is now for us instead of against us. And the consequence of that is, "If God be for us, who can be against us?" (Rom. 8:31).

Chapter 3: ***The destruction of Nineveh is extensive and embarrassing in the light of its previous strength but thoroughly deserved because of its heinous sins and crimes.***

THE REASONS FOR NINEVEH'S DESTRUCTION (3:1–19)

Great Sins (3:1–10)

3:1 *the bloody city.* Literally, "the city of bloods." The plural of blood always refers to bloodshedding or blood guiltiness. It designates all murderous atrocities committed. *robbery.* Refers to their plundering. *the prey departeth not.* There were always some people they could pursue.

3:2–3 Nahum abruptly moves from Nineveh's crimes to a description of the battle scene of Nineveh's defeat that results in so many deaths that the corpses are piled up without burial.

3:4 Nineveh's sins deserving judgment are described in terms of *whoredoms* and *witchcrafts.* Harlotry and sorcery are common biblical images to epitomize wickedness (Ezek. 16,23; Rev. 17). In their wickedness they bartered in human life (*nations* and *families*) for their own gain.

3:5–7 The prophet describes punishment that was fitting to the sin. *I will discover thy skirts upon thy face.* A euphemistic idiom referring to the exposure of the private parts, a gesture of terrible shame that will be made public. The glory that once belonged to Assyria would change to mockery and scorn. The nation is pelted with disgusting garbage, becomes a spectacle of shame, forsaken without sympathy.

3:8–10 Ironically, *No* or Thebes, a city that seemed to be invincible, was destroyed by the Assyrians and becomes a warning to Nineveh that it, too, is vulnerable. Thebes was *situate among the rivers*, i.e., located on the Nile. The waters of the Nile formed a natural barrier of defense (*rampart* and *wall*). Though just a river, so important and vast was the Nile that native bedouin call it a sea, even to this day. Notwithstanding the boundless strength of Egypt and its allies, Thebes fell and was taken captive, its people becoming the objects of Assyrian cruelties. The question, *Art thou better*, demands a negative response; thus, Assyria will receive just as they gave (eye-for-eye judgment).

Great Weakness (3:11–19)

3:11–19 The prophet issues a series of insults that heighten the scorn as well as the weakness that precludes any defense against coming judgment

3:11 *thou shalt be hid.* The Hebrew word can mean "to become unconscious or deranged"; this meaning would better follow the idea of drunkenness. *seek strength because of the enemy.* Seek a place of safety from the enemy.

3:12 The image is of *figs* easily harvested. The fortified cities, rather than providing security, were "easy picking" for the enemy.

3:13 The ranks of the once invincible army are now filled with women, weak and inexperienced with warfare. *devour thy bars.* The fire will consume the bars that secure the gates, allowing them to open wide to the enemy.

3:14 With obvious sarcasm, the prophet instructs the inhabitants of the doomed city to make preparations for the battle they are destined to lose. *go into clay.* Part of the process of making the clay or mud bricks to be used for bolstering weak places in the wall.

3:15–17 The prophet, again with sarcasm, uses the reference to the cankerworm/locust to ridicule the weakness of

16 Thou hast multiplied thy merchants above the
stars of heaven: the cankerworm spoileth, and
flieth away.
17 Thy crowned *are* as the locusts, and thy
captains as the great grasshoppers, which camp
in the hedges in the cold day, *but* when the sun
ariseth they flee away, and their place is not
known where they *are*.
18 Thy shepherds slumber, O king of Assyria:
thy nobles shall dwell *in the dust*: thy people
is scattered upon the mountains, and no man
gathereth *them*.
19 *There is* no healing of thy bruise; thy wound is
grievous: all that hear the bruit of thee shall clap
the hands over thee: for upon whom hath not thy
wickedness passed continually?

the people. Even if they were to multiply like a swarm of locusts, they would still be brought to nothing. *Thy crowned*. The princes. The point is that all the officials and leaders seem to disappear when the trouble comes: the nation is without leaders.

3:15 The announcement of defeat underscores the sarcasm of v. 14. Their destruction will be as devastating as a locust invasion.

3:18 *Thy shepherds*. Leaders who should be vigilant in oversight. That the people are scattered with no man to assemble them is the consequence of sleeping shepherds.

3:19 *no healing of thy bruise*. No alleviation of the collapse; the destruction was irreversible. *bruit*. Report or news. *for upon whom hath not thy wickedness passed continually?* Who has not been aware of the wickedness of Assyria? The implication is that all who heard the report of Nineveh's fall would rejoice (*clap the hands*) because Assyria's wickedness extended to all nations. Nineveh got what it deserved.

Thoughts for Personal/Family Worship: Chapter 3

1. **The nation of Assyria was destroyed because of its cruel atrocities against other nations. The Assyrians had little regard for human dignity or in their selfish pursuits. The tables were turned and their total destruction was justly proportioned to what they deserved. Although Nineveh suffered defeat at the hands of another nation, its judgment was ultimately decreed and orchestrated by God. But even so, it was the putting down of a kingdom. The principles of this national judgment, however, point to the even more grave judgment of individuals which affects not just the body, but the soul. Christ said to "fear him which is able to destroy both soul and body in hell" (Matt. 10:28). There is nothing more fearful in divine judgment than receiving the sentence from God that is deserved. The terrors of that judgment should be an incentive to flee in faith and repentance to the God of mercy.**
2. **The sleeping shepherds of Nah. 3:18 remind us that we have a good shepherd who never slumbers nor sleeps and who with constant vigilance and care provides for us and protects us from all harm.**
3. **Interestingly, Nahum, whose message concerns Nineveh, ends with a question just like Jonah, whose message also concerned Nineveh. Jonah ended by God asking how can He not spare repentant Nineveh? Nahum's question is essentially how can God not judge wicked Nineveh? God in His mercy receives those who come to Him in faith and repentance. God in His justice must judge the unrepentant. It is eternally better to experience God's grace and mercy than to be sentenced according to His justice.**

I WILL

Rejoice

IN

THE LORD

I WILL JOY IN

THE GOD

OF

My

SALVATION

HABAKKUK 3:18

INTRODUCTION TO THE BOOK OF HABAKKUK

Authorship: Habakkuk's name means "ardent embrace." Although his name does not define his message, in his closing statement he lives up to his name when he confesses his unconditional faith in the Lord, totally embracing God and His Word (3:16–17). Virtually nothing is known about the prophet although the postscript "To the chief singer on my stringed instruments" (3:19) may connect him to the rituals of the temple and therefore to the priestly office. Although an obscure character, few prophets lay bare their personal struggles as clearly as Habakkuk. So notwithstanding the lack of information about him, we know his heart pretty well. The apocryphal *Bel and the Dragon* refers to a Habakkuk of the tribe of Levi who was carried by an angel from Judea to Babylon to minister to Daniel in the lions' den. As interesting as this may be, it is merely fiction with no credibility.

Date: The absence of any explicit data requires dating the book by implicit evidence, the most significant being the imminence of the Babylonian invasion (1:6). Although some of the sins of Judah mentioned in Habakkuk point to the reign of Manasseh (686–640 BC), who bore great responsibility for Judah's guilt, Babylon was not at that time a world power. More likely, Habakkuk preached during the reign of Jehoiakim (609–597 BC), whose wickedness and foolishness led Judah to destruction (2 Kings 23:34; Jer. 22:17). This corresponds to Babylon's rise to world power under the leadership of Nabopolassar (626–605 BC) and his part in overthrowing Nineveh (612 BC). After victory at the battle of Carchemish (605 BC), Nebuchadnezzar became the emperor of the neo-Babylonian Empire and initiated the first stage of Judah's exile. Since Habakkuk is predicting the Babylonian exile, his message would have to be before 605 BC. Conservatives, therefore, tend to date Habakkuk to the eve of the first Babylonian invasion, 607/606 BC.

Theme: Living by faith (2:4 is the key verse that declares the theme: "the just shall live by his faith").

Purpose: To prove the sensibility of trusting God unconditionally. Habakkuk could well be designated a theodicy, a defense of divine justice. Habakkuk questioned God's justice, and God revealed that He would bring justice. Faith accepts what it cannot affirm by mere facts of observation.

Synopsis: *The Contribution of Habakkuk to Redemptive Revelation*

Whereas other prophets record their inspired sermons, Habakkuk records dialogues between himself and God (prayers and answers) and then his song of praise and thanksgiving for what God had taught him about faith. Habakkuk, with bold honesty, admits his personal struggles over the conflict and incongruity between what he believed and what he saw. Things were happening in the nation that to him made no sense, given what he believed about God. Judah was guilty of terrible sin seemingly without consequence; it appeared that the law was powerless and wickedness was unchecked (1:4).

When God assured him that justice was coming and that He was going to use the Babylonians to chastise Judah, Habakkuk's soul struggle intensified. He offered no defense for Judah but could not understand how or why God who was so pure and holy could or would use a nation whose wickedness and idolatry exceeded even sinful Judah's. God was doing something Habakkuk neither understood nor liked; it created a tension between creed and experience, between faith and sight. God graciously dealt with Habakkuk, declaring in a remarkably far-reaching statement, "the just shall live by his faith" (2:4). That declaration not only solved Habakkuk's problem, it became a proposition intimately associated with the explanation and advance of redemption as revealed in the gospel. Paul's use of this text in Rom. 1:17 and Gal. 3:11

is a crucial component in his exposition of saving and justifying grace in Jesus Christ. Similarly, Heb. 10:37–38 links the verse to persevering faith in Jesus Christ. Significantly, the verse was the battle cry of the Reformation. If 2:4 were the only sentence in Habakkuk, the contribution to redemptive revelation and history would be outstanding. But it's not the only contribution.

Although disputed, Hab. 3:13 most likely refers directly to Christ—the word translated "anointed" is Messiah. The context is a synopsis of redemptive history illustrating God's defeat of those hostile to His purpose of saving His people. Significantly, the salvation of His people is linked to the salvation or deliverance of His Messiah and the wounding of "the head out of the house of the wicked." The image is reminiscent of Gen. 3:15 that encapsulates the whole course of redemption's plan consummating in the fatal blow to the head of the serpent. Throughout history, the seed of the serpent attempted to thwart the coming of Christ, but over and again God preserved both the line leading to Christ and Christ Himself. Although the way God counters the hostility is sometimes beyond our understanding, Habakkuk teaches us to walk by faith and not by sight.

Outline: I. The Problems for Faith (1:1—2:20)

- A. The Problem regarding Sin (1:1–11)
  1. The Prophet's Prayer (1:2–4)
  2. The Lord's Answer (1:5–11)
- B. The Problem regarding God's Nature (1:12—2:20)
  1. The Prophet's Prayer (1:12–17)
  2. The Lord's Answer (2:1–4)
  3. The Lord's Gracious Digression (2:5–20)

II. The Praise of Faith (3:1–19)

- A. The Petition of Praise (3:1–2)
- B. The Components of Praise (3:3–15)
  1. God's Glory (3:3–4)
  2. God's Power (3:5–15)
- C. The Peace in Praise (3:16–19)

THE BOOK OF
HABAKKUK

CHAPTER 1

THE burden which Habakkuk the prophet did see.
2 O LORD, how long shall I cry, and thou wilt not
hear! *even* cry out unto thee *of* violence, and thou
wilt not save!
3 Why dost thou shew me iniquity, and cause *me*
to behold grievance? for spoiling and violence *are*
before me: and there are *that* raise up strife and
contention.
4 Therefore the law is slacked, and judgment
doth never go forth: for the wicked doth compass
about the righteous; therefore wrong judgment
proceedeth.
5 ¶ Behold ye among the heathen, and regard,
and wonder marvellously: for *I* will work a work
in your days, *which* ye will not believe, though it
be told *you*.
6 For, lo, I raise up the Chaldeans, *that* bitter
and hasty nation, which shall march through the
breadth of the land, to possess the dwellingplaces
that are not theirs.
7 They *are* terrible and dreadful: their judgment
and their dignity shall proceed of themselves.
8 Their horses also are swifter than the leopards,
and are more fierce than the evening wolves: and
their horsemen shall spread themselves, and their
horsemen shall come from far; they shall fly as the
eagle *that* hasteth to eat.
9 They shall come all for violence: their faces shall
sup up *as* the east wind, and they shall gather the
captivity as the sand.
10 And they shall scoff at the kings, and the princes
shall be a scorn unto them: they shall deride every
strong hold; for they shall heap dust, and take it.
11 Then shall *his* mind change, and he shall pass
over, and offend, *imputing* this his power unto his
god.
12 ¶ *Art* thou not from everlasting, O LORD my
God, mine Holy One? we shall not die. O LORD,
thou hast ordained them for judgment; and,
O mighty God, thou hast established them for
correction.

THE PROBLEMS FOR FAITH (1:1—2:20)

Chapter 1: *Habakkuk expresses his concern over Judah's sinning with impunity and then questions God's justice in using the Babylonians to chastise Judah.*

The Problem regarding Sin (1:1–11)

The Prophet's Prayer (1:2–4)

1:1 *The burden.* The prophetic oracle or pronouncement. The term designates the revelatory nature of prophetic vision. What follows is inspired even though it expresses the prophet's individual concerns.

1:2 *how long.* A question of bewilderment as to the Lord's silence and seeming inactivity. Though not justified, it is a common sentiment (Ps. 13). Verses 3–4 describe the deplorable state of the nation that generated the prophet's question.

1:3 *shew me.* Allow me to see. *iniquity.* Disastrous trouble. *grievance.* Mischief. *spoiling.* Murderous acts. *strife.* Legal disputes. *contention.* Quarreling. The list of sins parallels those Jeremiah associates with Jehoiakim (Jer. 22:17).

1:4 *the law is slacked.* The law has grown numb or cold and therefore inoperative. *judgment.* Justice. *compass.* Surround. *wrong.* Literally, "confused, crooked, or crazy."

The Lord's Answer (1:5–11)

1:5 *wonder marvellously.* An idiomatic translation of "be horrified, freeze with fear." The Hebrew juxtaposes two different forms of the same word. In answer to the prophet's assumption of divine inactivity, the Lord announces that He is about to do something incredible. Interestingly, Paul connects this with the gospel of Christ (Acts 13:41).

1:6 *lo, I raise up.* An idiom of impending action—"I am about to raise up." *bitter and hasty.* Fierce and impetuous. Raising up the Chaldeans or Babylonians was the incredible thing God was going to do to answer Habakkuk's concern.

1:7 *dignity.* Sovereignty or majesty. The verse describes the arrogant self-sufficiency of the Babylonians.

1:8 *their horsemen shall spread themselves.* They will charge along.

1:9 *their faces shall sup up as the east wind.* The Hebrew is difficult and could be translated "all their faces are forward," describing the relenting advance of the army. *the captivity as the sand.* They will take captives as numerous as the sand.

1:10 *they shall deride.* Literally, "they will laugh," referring to their mocking disdain for the strongholds designed to hold them at bay. *they shall heap dust.* Their piling up dirt for siege ramps to capture the strongholds.

1:11 *Then shall his mind change.* Literally, "then he will move like the wind." *he shall pass over.* The changing of direction from one conquest to the next. The Babylonians, ignorant that the true God purposed their conquests, would give credit to the only gods they knew, most especially Marduk.

The Problem regarding God's Nature (1:12—2:20)

The Prophet's Prayer (1:12–17)

13 *Thou art* of purer eyes than to behold evil,
and canst not look on iniquity: wherefore lookest
thou upon them that deal treacherously, *and*
holdest thy tongue when the wicked devoureth
the man that is more righteous than he?
14 And makest men as the fishes of the sea, as the
creeping things, *that have* no ruler over them?
15 They take up all of them with the angle, they
catch them in their net, and gather them in their
drag: therefore they rejoice and are glad.
16 Therefore they sacrifice unto their net, and
burn incense unto their drag; because by them
their portion *is* fat, and their meat plenteous.
17 Shall they therefore empty their net, and not
spare continually to slay the nations?

CHAPTER 2

I WILL stand upon my watch, and set me upon the
tower, and will watch to see what he will say unto
me, and what I shall answer when I am reproved.
2 And the LORD answered me, and said, Write the
vision, and make *it* plain upon tables, that he may
run that readeth it.
3 For the vision *is* yet for an appointed time, but
at the end it shall speak, and not lie: though it
tarry, wait for it; because it will surely come, it will
not tarry.
4 Behold, his soul *which* is lifted up is not upright
in him: but the just shall live by his faith.
5 ¶ Yea also, because he transgresseth by wine,
he is a proud man, neither keepeth at home, who

1:12–17 Habakkuk's second prayer exposes an even deeper tension in his soul: God's use of the wicked Babylonians conflicted with his creed about God. The prayer reveals his orthodoxy and his honesty before the Lord. As such, it stands as an inspired pattern of prayer worthy of imitation.
1:12 He addresses God in terms of His divine eternity, His being the covenant Savior (*LORD*—Jehovah), His holiness, and His stability (*mighty God*—literally, Rock, an immovable boulder). He notes God's actions that reveal His sovereignty (*ordained . . . established*, i.e., destined). He asserts the consequence of these truths: *we shall not die*. This does not refer to personal immortality but to the preservation of the covenant nation, which was essential to the fullness of time in which Christ would come.
1:13 *holdest thy tongue.* The Hebrew verb is simply "to keep silence." To Habakkuk, it seemed that God was letting them get away with sin.
1:14–17 Habakkuk uses the imagery of fishermen who skillfully employ various tactics to gather as many fish as possible. To them he compares the Babylonians who skillfully and ruthlessly capture people. The prophet attributes the whole scenario to God since He is responsible for making *men as the fishes of the sea*.
1:14 *no ruler over them.* Consequently, defenseless.
1:15 *angle.* Hook.
1:16 The fishermen give credit for their catch to their own devices. Just as foolishly the Babylonians take the credit for their conquests, at best acknowledging the god of their own making (1:11).
1:17 Habakkuk asks simply how long this is going to go on. *not spare.* Not have pity to stop the killing.

Thoughts for Personal/Family Worship: Chapter 1

1. **The question "why?" is most perplexing. Parents ask their children this question typically receiving the response "I don't know." When children ask their parents "why," the typical response is "because I said so." Neither of those answers is satisfying. There is seldom a good and satisfying answer to that question. Yet, Christians often ask God "why" when things happen that they don't understand or like. The Bible gives many examples: Job, Jeremiah, various psalmists (e.g., Pss. 37; 49; 73, etc.). Seldom does God answer the question. Over and again, God turns the attention away from the circumstance that generated the question to Himself, who is the ultimate satisfying answer. The tension between what we know about God (our creed) and what we are seeing that bothers us (our experience) can be real, but the resolution is always to look away from the circumstance to the Lord. Faith links our creed and our experience.**
2. **Habakkuk's prayers, though generated by his misunderstanding of and confusion about what God was doing, are most instructive. The Bible records inspired prayers as patterns for us to follow. If anything is on the surface in Habakkuk's praying, it is his honesty and transparency before God. He boldly bares his heart, expressing his bewilderment concerning God's justice. He prays what he thinks. Too often our prayers become routine and rigid with standard platitudes as we try to mask before God our true feelings. Similarly, Jeremiah was so transparent in his praying that he accused God of deception (Jer. 20:7). We would never be so bold to mouth those words. But how often have we had these same feelings when things were not as we thought they should be. We must be reverent, but God knows our hearts and thoughts. Let us learn in our praying to appeal to Him reverently, yet with boldness, knowing that He is a God who loves to hear our prayers.**

Chapter 2: ***God wonderfully answers the waiting prophet by declaring the importance of trusting the certainty of His Word and then assures Habakkuk that His justice will be meted to the Babylonians for their sins.***

The Lord's Answer (2:1–4)

2:1 Habakkuk uses the imagery of a sentinel on duty to watch for a messenger to describe his waiting for the message of God. *when I am reproved.* Literally, "concerning my argument."
2:2 *Write the vision.* Record the word of revelation. *tables.* Tablets. *that he may run that readeth it.* Most likely referring to the legibility of what is written; so clear and large that it can be read at a glance while on the move as though it were on a billboard.
2:3 *it shall speak, and not lie.* The decreed (*for an appointed time*) word of revelation will bear witness and not fail or disappoint. *though it tarry . . . it will not tarry.* The Hebrew uses two different words for "tarry" but they are synonyms. The statement addresses the tension between divine and human "time." What God decrees will happen precisely when He has decreed, even though it seems to delay from man's perspective. Hebrews 10:37 applies the statement to the coming of Christ.
2:4 The stark contrast of the two lines illustrates the difference between leaning on one's own understanding and trusting the Lord with all the heart (Prov. 3:5). *Behold, his soul.* Literally,

enlargeth his desire as hell, and *is* as death, and
cannot be satisfied, but gathereth unto him all
nations, and heapeth unto him all people:
6 Shall not all these take up a parable against him,
and a taunting proverb against him, and say, Woe
to him that increaseth *that which is* not his! how
long? and to him that ladeth himself with thick
clay!
7 Shall they not rise up suddenly that shall bite
thee, and awake that shall vex thee, and thou shalt
be for booties unto them?
8 Because thou hast spoiled many nations, all the
remnant of the people shall spoil thee; because of
men's blood, and *for* the violence of the land, of
the city, and of all that dwell therein.
9 ¶ Woe to him that coveteth an evil covetousness
to his house, that he may set his nest on high, that
he may be delivered from the power of evil!
10 Thou hast consulted shame to thy house by
cutting off many people, and hast sinned *against*
thy soul.
11 For the stone shall cry out of the wall, and the
beam out of the timber shall answer it.
12 ¶ Woe to him that buildeth a town with blood,
and stablisheth a city by iniquity!
13 Behold, *is it* not of the LORD of hosts that the
people shall labour in the very fire, and the people
shall weary themselves for very vanity?
14 For the earth shall be filled with the knowledge
of the glory of the LORD, as the waters cover the sea.
15 ¶ Woe unto him that giveth his neighbour
drink, that puttest thy bottle to *him*, and makest
him drunken also, that thou mayest look on their
nakedness!
16 Thou art filled with shame for glory: drink
thou also, and let thy foreskin be uncovered: the
cup of the LORD's right hand shall be turned unto
thee, and shameful spewing *shall be* on thy glory.
17 For the violence of Lebanon shall cover thee,
and the spoil of beasts, *which* made them afraid,
because of men's blood, and for the violence of
the land, of the city, and of all that dwell therein.
18 ¶ What profiteth the graven image that the
maker thereof hath graven it; the molten image,
and a teacher of lies, that the maker of his work
trusteth therein, to make dumb idols?
19 Woe unto him that saith to the wood, Awake;
to the dumb stone, Arise, it shall teach! Behold,
it *is* laid over with gold and silver, and *there is* no
breath at all in the midst of it.
20 But the LORD *is* in his holy temple: let all the
earth keep silence before him.

"Behold the one who is swollen (i.e., the proud)! His soul is not right in him." On the other hand, the *just* (the righteous one) will live by *faith* (trust that shapes the whole life). The statement broadly includes both the inception of justifying faith and the perseverance of faith. The New Testament uses the statement for both (see Introduction: Synopsis). Walking by faith was the answer Habakkuk needed.

The Lord's Gracious Digression (2:5–20)

2:5–20 Although God did not owe Habakkuk an explanation, He graciously assures the prophet that He holds the Babylonians accountable for their sins and that He will judge them accordingly.

2:5 This verse is a prelude to a series of five woes pronounced against Babylon. Babylon is like a drunkard never satisfied, whose desire for expansion is as greedy as death. In contrast to the faithful man who lives (v. 4), Babylon is as the proud man that will not have a dwelling in which to abide (*keepeth at home*).

2:6–8 The first woe is against Babylon's exploitation of other nations for personal gain. *ladeth himself with thick clay.* Literally, "makes himself heavy with pledges," meaning they assume heavy debts that eventually will come due. *that shall bite thee.* Refers to creditors. The day of payback comes, and Babylon, which had plundered so many others, now becomes booty for them. *because of men's blood.* In Hebrew, *blood* is plural, referring to bloodshed.

2:9–11 The second woe addresses Babylon's abuse of others to achieve personal security. *coveteth an evil covetousness.* Literally "to gain an unjust gain." Making the nest high is an image for security (protection from the *power of evil*, i.e., any danger). It is a fitting imagery since Babylon is elsewhere compared to the eagle (Dan. 7). *Thou hast consulted shame.* You have planned or devised shame. Their actions would have the opposite consequence of their intent: shame instead of security. The constructions they trusted for security would strain with structural tension, suggesting impending collapse (v. 11).

2:12–14 The third woe is against the cruelty and violence by which Babylon built its empire. A kingdom built in this fashion will not last; it is like feeding a flame and working for nothing (*vanity*). Babylon's kingdom will fail, as will every other kingdom of man, but God's kingdom is universal and eternal.

2:15–17 The fourth woe is against Babylon's immorality. Inducing intoxication was a tactic to corrupt morals and to lead to all sorts of debauchery. Drunkenness and debauchery go together. Babylon's conquests are often described with this imagery (Jer. 51:7; Rev. 17:4). In poetic justice, the *cup* leading to shame and death with which they seduced others will be returned to them (Jer. 25:17–29).

2:18–20 The fifth woe addresses Babylon's idolatry. The foolishness of making and worshiping lifeless idols is put in bold by the declaration of the Lord's glory. The call to *silence* before His majesty is paralleled in Isa. 41:1 and Zech. 2:13.

Thoughts for Personal/Family Worship: Chapter 2

1. **God's answer to Habakkuk is instructive (vv. 1–4). Not only does the answer reveal God's pleasure with Habakkuk's prayer, notwithstanding his confessions expressing his confusion about God's actions (no rebuke to the prophet), it reveals the way believers are to live through the times of confusion. That the just are to live by faith encompasses all of life and every experience of life. We are to walk by faith and not by sight. Faith gives the assurance that God is in heaven (v. 20), His glory is in the earth (v. 14), and therefore, all is well regardless of what we see or sense. We may not always understand the reason, but we should live in the confidence that God is sovereignly accomplishing His purpose in all things.**
2. **Babylon was not exempt from accountability before God because she was God's servant to accomplish His work of chastisement on Judah. God was sovereign in**

CHAPTER 3

A PRAYER of Habakkuk the prophet upon
Shigionoth.
2 O LORD, I have heard thy speech, *and* was
afraid: O LORD, revive thy work in the midst of
the years, in the midst of the years make known;
in wrath remember mercy.
3 God came from Teman, and the Holy One
from mount Paran. Selah. His glory covered the
heavens, and the earth was full of his praise.
4 And *his* brightness was as the light; he had
horns *coming* out of his hand: and there *was* the
hiding of his power.
5 Before him went the pestilence, and burning
coals went forth at his feet.
6 He stood, and measured the earth: he beheld,
and drove asunder the nations; and the everlasting
mountains were scattered, the perpetual hills did
bow: his ways *are* everlasting.
7 I saw the tents of Cushan in affliction: *and* the
curtains of the land of Midian did tremble.
8 Was the LORD displeased against the rivers?
was thine anger against the rivers? *was* thy wrath
against the sea, that thou didst ride upon thine
horses *and* thy chariots of salvation?
9 Thy bow was made quite naked, *according* to
the oaths of the tribes, *even thy* word. Selah. Thou
didst cleave the earth with rivers.
10 The mountains saw thee, *and* they trembled:
the overflowing of the water passed by: the deep
uttered his voice, *and* lifted up his hands on high.
11 The sun *and* moon stood still in their
habitation: at the light of thine arrows they went,
and at the shining of thy glittering spear.
12 Thou didst march through the land in indig-
nation, thou didst thresh the heathen in anger.
13 Thou wentest forth for the salvation of thy peo-
ple, *even* for salvation with thine anointed; thou
woundedst the head out of the house of the wicked,
by discovering the foundation unto the neck. Selah.
14 Thou didst strike through with his staves the
head of his villages: they came out as a whirlwind
to scatter me: their rejoicing *was* as to devour the
poor secretly.
15 Thou didst walk through the sea with thine
horses, *through* the heap of great waters.
16 When I heard, my belly trembled; my lips
quivered at the voice: rottenness entered into my
bones, and I trembled in myself, that I might rest
in the day of trouble: when he cometh up unto

---

how He used the pagan nation, and the pagan nation was responsible for their own behavior and liable to just punishment. The only conflict between God's sovereignty and human responsibility is in the mind of man. God is just in all His ways, and it is best that all the earth be in silent subjection before Him (2:20).

Chapter 3: ***Habakkuk prays in faith desiring God's will, praising God's perfections and works, and expressing his satisfaction with God regardless of the circumstances of life.***

THE PRAISE OF FAITH (3:1–19)

The Petition of Praise (3:1–2)

3:1 *Shigionoth.* A musical notation of uncertain meaning.

3:2 *speech.* Report or news, referring to the revelatory visions of the previous chapters. *revive thy work in the midst of the years.* Cause to live or revitalize. The *work* refers to the work of purifying judgment on Judah, even if through the unclean hands of the Babylonians. The prophet who had questioned God's will now desires it. *in wrath remember mercy.* He prays that God would exercise His discipline with a mindset of compassion and pity. He desires that this purifying work be done without delay.

The Components of Praise (3:3–15)

God's Glory (3:3–4)

3:3 The praise consists of reflecting on God's past acts. Habakkuk recalls locations associated with God's glorious presence with His people after the exodus. *Teman* (within the borders of Edom) and *Paran* (between Edom and Sinai) were unlikely places to see God's glory, but they were part of the world *full of his praise.* They represent the whole period of wilderness wanderings with so many displays of God's glory.

3:4 *horns coming out of his hand.* Horns are a symbol designating strength or power. The hand represents activity. This is an anthropomorphism expressing God's mighty acts.

God's Power (3:5–15)

3:5 *burning coals.* The Hebrew words designate a blaze and can refer to a burning disease or plague, which is more likely, given the parallelism with *pestilence.* Perhaps it alludes to the exodus events that revealed God's power.

3:6 God's control over the natural world ensures His control over all.

3:7 *Cushan* and *Midian* were in the Transjordan region.

3:8 An allusion to the crossing of the Red Sea and Jordan, both of which were evidences of God's redemptive power. God's riding *horses* and *chariots* figuratively represent Him as the warrior for His people. See a similar description in Ps. 68:17.

3:9 *Thy bow was made quite naked.* It was made ready for use.

3:10 The description is similar to Deborah's praise in response to God's deliverance from Sisera (Judg. 5:4–5).

3:11 An allusion to Joshua's battle involving the sun and moon (Josh. 10:12–14).

3:12 *the land.* Earth.

3:13 See the Introduction: Synopsis for the messianic significance. *By discovering the foundation unto the neck.* The image is uncertain, but it is clear that it represents total destruction.

3:14 *strike through with his staves the head of his villages.* Rare and uncertain, perhaps, a reference to warriors. The Lord turns the weapons of the enemy against themselves. *their* [the warriors'] *rejoicing was as to devour the poor secretly.* They arrogantly attempted to destroy the weak in their hiding place.

The Peace in Praise (3:16–19)

3:16 *When I heard.* Habakkuk describes the effects he felt upon hearing the word that made him afraid (3:2). *my belly.* A reference to internal organs. *when he cometh up unto the people.* The Hebrew syntax is terse and could be translated, "to come up against the people who will attack us." So Habakkuk will wait and rest in the day of trouble knowing that God will ultimately intervene for His people against the Babylonian invaders. That is the knowledge that gives him peace in the meantime.

the people, he will invade them with his troops.
17 ¶ Although the fig tree shall not blossom,
neither *shall* fruit *be* in the vines; the labour of the
olive shall fail, and the fields shall yield no meat;
the flock shall be cut off from the fold, and *there
shall be* no herd in the stalls:
18 Yet I will rejoice in the LORD, I will joy in the
God of my salvation.
19 The LORD God *is* my strength, and he will
make my feet like hinds' *feet*, and he will make me
to walk upon mine high places. To the chief singer
on my stringed instruments.

3:17 This is a bleak picture of apparent failure on every hand.
3:18 *I will rejoice . . . I will joy*. The words do not describe an emotion of happiness based on present prosperity but rather a contentment and satisfaction that is independent of external circumstances (Phil. 4:11).
3:19 *hinds' feet*. A type of deer noted for surefootedness. So he is well equipped for the *high places* the Lord has for him to walk.

Thoughts for Personal/Family Worship: Chapter 3

1. Habakkuk's prayer provides another important pattern with key lessons. On the surface is the link between prayer and God's Word. Both are means of grace and work together. It is the Word that fuels the praying. Once Habakkuk learned God's will, he prayed for that will to be done. Nothing was more crucial than the will of God even though it would involve painful discipline. But if the hard things were a means for the manifestation of God's glory, then that would be for the best. It is noteworthy as well that the majority of the prayer is praise not petition. Praising God for who He is and what He has done fuels the faith to ask God for great things.
2. Reading the praise section of Habakkuk's prayer illustrates the importance of knowing redemptive history. Many of the statements make no sense apart from what God has preserved in the historical records in Scripture. This ought to be an incentive to know our Bibles so when one part of Scripture alludes to another part we can understand the message. This section also illustrates that what Paul said concerning Israel's history being an example and admonition for us (1 Cor. 10:11) applies to those living in the New Testament times as well. Can you think of more reasons why there is more to biblical history than just names, dates, and events?
3. The closing verses (3:17–19) teach that real contentment is found only in the Lord. This is another facet of living by faith. Too often, we allow circumstances to control our emotions and dictate our feelings. Circumstances change. It is fine to be happy or sad as circumstances dictate (Eccl. 3). But if we find our ultimate contentment and satisfaction in the eternal God who never changes, external stimuli are not the controlling factor. Habakkuk describes a situation in which nothing was good but he was rejoicing because his joy was in the Lord. Do you recall times in your life when you were content in the Lord, by faith, despite being in difficult circumstances?

HE WILL

REJOICE

OVER THEE

With Joy

HE WILL

REST

IN

His Love

HE WILL

JOY

OVER THEE WITH

Singing

ZEPHANIAH 3:17

INTRODUCTION TO THE BOOK OF

ZEPHANIAH

Authorship: Zephaniah's name means "The Lord has hidden." He traces his lineage to four generations, the most extensive genealogy among the prophets but most likely to establish his royal pedigree. Most identify "Hizkiah" (1:1) as Hezekiah, the good king of Judah, whose piety shone brightly between the sins of his father (Ahaz) and the sins of his son (Manasseh). His identification with Hezekiah, whose religious reforms had such a positive impact on Judah, is a subtle link to Josiah, during whose reign he ministered and who like Hezekiah enforced a revival of true religion in the land.

Date: Zephaniah 1:1 dates Zephaniah's ministry "in the days of Josiah . . . king of Judah." Josiah had a lengthy reign from 640 to 609 BC, but the prophet's ministry did not cover that full period. Zephaniah 2:13, for instance, indicates that Nineveh had not yet fallen (612 BC). Many of the sins cited (e.g., 1:3–13) were common before but not after Josiah's reforms. Second Chronicles 34:3—35:19 suggests that there were two stages to Josiah's reforms: in his twelfth and eighteenth years (628 BC and 622/621 BC). Zephaniah's preaching in all likelihood contributed to the revival. This would date his ministry to the first part of Josiah's reign: 640–621 BC. This was a period of political, social, and spiritual corruption that brought the depraved and perverted nation to the brink of disaster. He would have been contemporary with the early days of Jeremiah.

Theme: The day of the Lord: judgment and salvation.

Purpose: To warn sinners of impending, inescapable, and catastrophic judgment, and to encourage sinners to repent as the only possible hope for salvation.

Synopsis: *The Contribution of Zephaniah to Redemptive Revelation*

Zephaniah skillfully employs the theology of the day of the Lord in his preaching of the gospel. The day of the Lord designates those epochal interventions of God into time to accomplish His purpose of judgment against sinners or of blessing for His people. The Old Testament shows that there were multiple days of the Lord, all of which pointed to and were typical (picture prophecies) of the final day that marks the consummation of time, the final judgment of sinners, and the complete salvation of saints at the second coming of the Lord Jesus. To this end, Zephaniah's message finds ultimate reference to Christ.

His dual focus of judgment and salvation also illustrates what it is to preach the whole counsel of God. The good news of salvation is attractive because of the bad news of judgment. Zephaniah's message of the terror of the Lord opened the way for a call to repentance and for the unfolding of the mercy of God. His message also anticipates truths that are more fully developed and realized in the New Testament. His preaching of judgment foreshadows the preaching of Christ, the ideal prophet (Matt. 24). Zephaniah 2:11 looks to a time when Gentiles worship the true God, a time made possible by Christ (Eph. 2:14–22) and commenced in the New Testament church (Gal. 3:26–29). Zephaniah's message of judgment and grace assures that God is in control of time and will vindicate His name in the final victory over sin and ultimate salvation for His people (3:19–20).

Outline

I. The Day of the Lord: Universal Judgment (1:1—3:8)
  A. Judgment of the World (1:2–3)
  B. Judgment of Judah (1:4—2:3)
    1. Because of Sin (1:4–13)
    2. A Day of the Lord (1:14–18)
    3. Invitation to Repent (2:1–3)
  C. Judgment of Gentiles (2:4–15)
    1. Philistia (2:4–7)
    1. Moab and Ammon (2:8–11)
    2. Ethiopia (2:12)
    3. Assyria (2:13–15)
  D. Judgment of Jerusalem (3:1–7)
  E. Judgment of the World (3:8)
II. The Day of the Lord: Gracious Salvation (3:9–20)
  A. Complete Transformation (3:9–13)
  B. Glorious Restoration (3:14–20)

THE BOOK OF ZEPHANIAH

CHAPTER 1

THE word of the LORD which came unto
Zephaniah the son of Cushi, the son of Gedaliah,
the son of Amariah, the son of Hizkiah, in the
days of Josiah the son of Amon, king of Judah.
2 I will utterly consume all *things* from off the
land, saith the LORD.
3 I will consume man and beast; I will consume
the fowls of the heaven, and the fishes of the sea,
and the stumblingblocks with the wicked; and I
will cut off man from off the land, saith the LORD.
4 I will also stretch out mine hand upon Judah,
and upon all the inhabitants of Jerusalem; and I
will cut off the remnant of Baal from this place,
and the name of the Chemarims with the priests;
5 And them that worship the host of heaven upon
the housetops; and them that worship *and* that
swear by the LORD, and that swear by Malcham;
6 And them that are turned back from the LORD;
and *those* that have not sought the LORD, nor
enquired for him.
7 Hold thy peace at the presence of the Lord GOD:
for the day of the LORD *is* at hand: for the LORD
hath prepared a sacrifice, he hath bid his guests.
8 And it shall come to pass in the day of the
LORD's sacrifice, that I will punish the princes,
and the king's children, and all such as are clothed
with strange apparel.
9 In the same day also will I punish all those that
leap on the threshold, which fill their masters'
houses with violence and deceit.
10 And it shall come to pass in that day, saith the
LORD, *that there shall be* the noise of a cry from
the fish gate, and an howling from the second,
and a great crashing from the hills.
11 Howl, ye inhabitants of Maktesh, for all the
merchant people are cut down; all they that bear
silver are cut off.

THE DAY OF THE LORD: UNIVERSAL JUDGMENT (1:1—3:8)

Chapter 1: *Zephaniah announces God's judgment on the world with particular focus on Judah, identifying the sins justifying the judgment and describing its horrors in terms of the day of the Lord.*

Judgment of the World (1:2–3)

1:2 *saith the LORD.* Literally, "the utterance of the Lord," an authoritative declaration.

1:3 The effects of judgment are universal, more devastating than the worldwide destruction of the flood (even the fish are destroyed); it is a reversing of creation (days five and six specifically). *the stumblingblocks with the wicked.* Most likely a reference to idols. Note the anticipation of Christ's description of the final judgment when all offending things will be removed (Matt. 13:41).

Judgment of Judah (1:4—2:3)

Because of Sin (1:4–13)

1:4 The transition to judgment on Judah illustrates Amos 3:2 and Luke 12:48 (privilege increases responsibility and accountability) and 1 Peter 4:17 (judgment begins at God's house). *the remnant of Baal.* Every vestige of Baal worship. *Chemarims.* Black-robed renegade priests, a class of priests associated with frenzied worship, part of the Baal priesthood.

1:5 *the host of heaven upon the housetops.* The astral bodies (sun, moon, stars) that were worshiped openly; a pagan cult common in the Ancient Near East. *swear by the LORD.* Evidence of syncretism, pagan worship but still appealing to Jehovah. *Malcham.* Literally, "their king," either referring to their pagan notion of Jehovah or Baal. Verses 4–5 detail the breaking of the first and greatest commandment: not loving the Lord and replacing Him with gods of the imagination.

1:6 *turned back.* Literally, "have become disloyal" or "turned away from". Not seeking the Lord is typical of sinners, who are alienated from God and find no attraction in spiritual things.

1:7 *Hold thy peace.* Literally, "hush" or "be silent." *the day of the LORD is at hand.* The time of special divine intervention is close. *prepared a sacrifice.* The language of satisfaction; justice will be exacted. *he hath bid his guests.* Literally, "he has consecrated the ones who have been called." These are those who have been consecrated as the victims of the Lord's sacrifice.

1:8 His own royal pedigree may account for his singling out the royal family for judgment. The implication is that any judgment of the royal family will extend to the entire population. *strange apparel.* Foreign attire, evidence of their association with the world.

1:9 *leap on the threshold.* Uncertain, but perhaps refers to the frivolous activity of priests who bring *violence and deceit* (trickery) into *their masters' houses* ("the house of their Lord").

1:10 *that day.* The day of the Lord. *the fish gate.* The main gate on the north of the city. *the second.* Another gate north of the temple opening to the main part of the city. *the hills.* A district within the city. Invasions were typically from the north, so this pictures the breach of the city and its total collapse.

1:11 *Maktesh.* Literally translated, "a shallow hollow." Contrasted with the "hills" (1:10), it suggests the totality of the destruction (high and low).

12 And it shall come to pass at that time, *that* I
will search Jerusalem with candles, and punish
the men that are settled on their lees: that say in
their heart, The LORD will not do good, neither
will he do evil.
13 Therefore their goods shall become a booty,
and their houses a desolation: they shall also build
houses, but not inhabit *them*; and they shall plant
vineyards, but not drink the wine thereof.
14 The great day of the LORD *is* near, *it is* near,
and hasteth greatly, *even* the voice of the day of
the LORD: the mighty man shall cry there bitterly.
15 That day *is* a day of wrath, a day of trouble and
distress, a day of wasteness and desolation, a day
of darkness and gloominess, a day of clouds and
thick darkness,
16 A day of the trumpet and alarm against the
fenced cities, and against the high towers.
17 And I will bring distress upon men, that they
shall walk like blind men, because they have
sinned against the LORD: and their blood shall be
poured out as dust, and their flesh as the dung.
18 Neither their silver nor their gold shall be able
to deliver them in the day of the LORD's wrath; but
the whole land shall be devoured by the fire of his
jealousy: for he shall make even a speedy riddance
of all them that dwell in the land.

CHAPTER 2

GATHER yourselves together, yea, gather together,
O nation not desired;
2 Before the decree bring forth, *before* the day
pass as the chaff, before the fierce anger of the
LORD come upon you, before the day of the LORD's
anger come upon you.
3 Seek ye the LORD, all ye meek of the earth, which
have wrought his judgment; seek righteousness,

1:12 *with candles.* Lights or lamps. *settled on their lees.* Congealed on the dregs. The image is of wine at the bottom of the vat that has thickened with the impurities making it sour and undrinkable. It pictures a people who have sunk down in sinful complacency, accusing God of inactivity.

1:13 The judgment is described in covenant terms (Deut. 28:30). Identifying the sins as covenant violations heightens their seriousness.

A Day of the Lord (1:14–18)

1:14 *near.* No idle threat; it is about to happen. The horrors of the day will cause the mightiest of men to scream shrilly (*cry there bitterly*) in panic and fear.

1:15–16 The prophet crowds into these two verses seemingly all possible words to describe the terror of the day. *A day of* is repeated six times, perhaps an eerie parallel to the days of creation in which God made all good. These six days make all bad.

1:17 *blood . . . as dust.* The point of comparison concerns quality not quantity. Blood (human life) will be as worthless as dust under feet. Ironically, man, formed from dust to become the apex of creation, being corrupted by sin, becomes something without value.

1:18 Human resources avail nothing to avert the judgment. Man cannot redeem himself or another with money (Ps. 49:7–8; 1 Peter 1:18). *fire of his jealousy.* Zeal for His holy name and word that demands the fiery judgment. Peter's description of the day of the Lord's consuming the elements with fervent heat (2 Peter 3:10) links directly to Zephaniah. *for he shall make even a speedy riddance.* Literally, "because a complete destruction—indeed, that which is dreadful—he will make."

Thoughts for Personal/Family Worship: Chapter 1

1. **The great gospel themes of salvation are always attractive, but there is another side of the gospel that is hard. But the hard message of just judgment against sin and sinners highlights and intensifies the beauty of saving grace. God's sovereign love for sinners is understood to be all the more gracious in the light of His just wrath and condemnation of sinners. Zephaniah begins his preaching with the hard message and provides some key points of meditation. (1) Judgment is just because of the heinous nature of sin (1:4–13). (2) Judgment is terrible because of its divine source (day of the Lord) and its fearful features and consequences (vv. 15–17). (3) Judgment is inevitable (v. 18). It is the hard and certain message of God's wrath that transitions so wonderfully to the message of salvation in Christ. It points to the cross where Christ took the full blow of God's justice and wrath in the place of His people. His people can escape judgment, not with silver or gold, but by the precious blood of Christ.**
2. **Zephaniah's judgment on Judah specifically is a sobering warning to those who have an association with and show of religion without the reality of religion. Judah, as the covenant nation, had many spiritual advantages yet they mixed what they knew about the truth with the paganism of the world and thus were far from God. There is a danger that those who have been long in the church can be in heart insensitive to the reality of God and truth. The high level of spiritual advantage increases the responsibility, and it is impossible to fool God who knows infallibly the heart of everyone. Remind the children of the importance of personal faith and repentance and not just association with the church. Judgment begins at the house of God.**

Chapter 2: *Zephaniah extends a gracious offer to repent as the only hope for escaping judgment and then details God's judgment of select Gentile nations.*

Invitation to Repent (2:1–3)

2:1–3 The prophet is still addressing Judah and gives the first glimmer of hope. Escaping judgment is possible.

2:1 *Gather yourselves together.* Image of stooping down to pick up sticks, a picture of humiliation. *O nation not desired.* The Hebrew is uncertain, perhaps "to turn pale"; an image of being "shameless" or "insensitive."

2:2 *Before the decree bring forth.* Literally, "before the bringing forth of the decree," i.e., before the decree of judgment happens. *the day pass as the chaff.* A reference to the suddenness with which the day comes and goes. Like chaff in the wind, the day rushes on. The repetition of *before* suggests the urgency connected to the invitation.

2:3 The three statements of urgency are balanced with three invitations to *seek. all ye meek.* The lowly and humble; the character of those with whom God will dwell (Isa. 57:15). *which have wrought his judgment.* Which have carried out his

seek meekness: it may be ye shall be hid in the day
of the LORD's anger.
4 ¶ For Gaza shall be forsaken, and Ashkelon
a desolation: they shall drive out Ashdod at the
noon day, and Ekron shall be rooted up.
5 Woe unto the inhabitants of the sea coast, the
nation of the Cherethites! the word of the LORD *is*
against you; O Canaan, the land of the Philistines,
I will even destroy thee, that there shall be no
inhabitant.
6 And the sea coast shall be dwellings *and* cottages
for shepherds, and folds for flocks.
7 And the coast shall be for the remnant of the
house of Judah; they shall feed thereupon: in the
houses of Ashkelon shall they lie down in the
evening: for the LORD their God shall visit them,
and turn away their captivity.
8 ¶ I have heard the reproach of Moab, and the
revilings of the children of Ammon, whereby
they have reproached my people, and magnified
themselves against their border.
9 Therefore *as* I live, saith the LORD of hosts, the
God of Israel, Surely Moab shall be as Sodom, and
the children of Ammon as Gomorrah, *even* the
breeding of nettles, and saltpits, and a perpetual
desolation: the residue of my people shall spoil
them, and the remnant of my people shall possess
them.
10 This shall they have for their pride, because
they have reproached and magnified *themselves*
against the people of the LORD of hosts.
11 The LORD *will be* terrible unto them: for he
will famish all the gods of the earth; and *men* shall
worship him, every one from his place, *even* all
the isles of the heathen.
12 ¶ Ye Ethiopians also, ye *shall be* slain by my
sword.
13 And he will stretch out his hand against
the north, and destroy Assyria; and will make
Nineveh a desolation, *and* dry like a wilderness.
14 And flocks shall lie down in the midst of her,
all the beasts of the nations: both the cormorant
and the bittern shall lodge in the upper lintels of
it; *their* voice shall sing in the windows; desolation
shall be in the thresholds: for he shall uncover the
cedar work.
15 This *is* the rejoicing city that dwelt carelessly,
that said in her heart, I *am*, and *there is* none

---

decisions. *meekness.* Humility. *it may be ye shall be hid.* This expresses the only possible hope; it does not presume on the Lord's grace but neither does it doubt.

Judgment of Gentiles (2:4–15)

2:4–15 The prophet announces God's judgment on nations surrounding Judah, all of which at one time or another were enemies of Israel.

Philistia (2:4–7)

2:4 The judgment of the principal cities of Philistia implies the judgment of the whole nation. From the days of the judges to the early years of the monarchy, Philistia and Israel were hostile and active enemies. *they shall drive out.* The subject is impersonal, equal to a passive idea: "Ashdod will be driven out." The Lord is the agent of judgment.

2:5 *Cherethites.* So-called because of Philistia's connection to Crete; they are often referred to as the sea-people.

2:6 Pictures the transformation from a warlike setting to a pastoral and idyllic setting.

2:7 When God judges Philistia, He gives their land as a possession to Judah.

Moab and Ammon (2:8–11)

2:8 Moab and Ammon, the nations descending from Lot's incest. *reproach.* Taunts; highlights the fact that these were never formidable foes but ones that would side with Israel's enemies and rejoice in their troubles.

2:9 *as I live, saith the LORD of hosts.* The language of oath and authoritative utterance from the Lord of armies; the Lord is the Commander-in-Chief with all the resources and authority to accomplish His purpose. *the breeding of nettles.* The Sodom and Gomorrah–like destruction turn them into a bed of weeds, a place abandoned to wild growth. *spoil . . . possess.* God's people will plunder and possess the territories of the enemies.

2:10 Further identifies their judgment-worthy sin as presumptive pride and arrogant taunting against God's people.

2:11 *The LORD will be terrible.* Awesome and worthy to be feared. *he will famish.* He will dominate, rule, or cause to vanish. The remarkable consequence of divine judgment is universal worship of the one true and living God.

Ethiopia (2:12)

2:12 *Ethiopians.* A reference to Cush, a southern part of Egypt, is used to designate Israel's southern enemies who will not escape judgment.

Assyria (2:13–15)

2:13 At the time of Zephaniah, *Assyria* was the most serious and formidable enemy of Judah, but not even *Nineveh* with all of its might, wealth, and splendor would survive God's stretched-out hand of judgment.

2:14 Nineveh being inhabited by flocks and wildlife means that its human population has been removed. *cormorant and the bittern . . . in the upper lintels . . . their voice shall sing in the windows.* Most likely referring to different kinds of owls that nest in the upper parts of the pillars and squawk from holes in the walls. Since these are normally birds of the forest not the city, it pictures the desolation of Nineveh. *he shall uncover the cedar work.* The destruction of the outer walls expose the interior cedar panels.

2:15 *the rejoicing city that dwelt carelessly.* The exultant or arrogant city that lived in security—or so they thought (*that said in her heart*). *hiss . . . wag.* Gestures of derision.

Thoughts for Personal/Family Worship: Chapter 2

1. Verses 1–3 reveal how to escape the inescapable. The call to repentance underscores the irony of hope in contrast to natural reasoning. Common sense would say that the way to escape danger is by fleeing from it (an impossibility, 1:18); the message of the gospel is that the way to escape the danger of certain judgment is to flee to its source to find mercy, to seek the Lord. The Lord is gracious and merciful and has promised to be found of those who seek Him sincerely; those who seek find, and those that come will not be cast out (John 6:37). It

beside me: how is she become a desolation, a place
for beasts to lie down in! every one that passeth by
her shall hiss, *and* wag his hand.

CHAPTER 3

WOE to her that is filthy and polluted, to the
oppressing city!
2 She obeyed not the voice; she received not
correction; she trusted not in the LORD; she drew
not near to her God.
3 Her princes within her *are* roaring lions; her
judges *are* evening wolves; they gnaw not the
bones till the morrow.
4 Her prophets *are* light *and* treacherous persons:
her priests have polluted the sanctuary, they have
done violence to the law.
5 The just LORD *is* in the midst thereof; he will
not do iniquity: every morning doth he bring his
judgment to light, he faileth not; but the unjust
knoweth no shame.
6 I have cut off the nations: their towers are
desolate; I made their streets waste, that none
passeth by: their cities are destroyed, so that there
is no man, that there is none inhabitant.
7 I said, Surely thou wilt fear me, thou wilt
receive instruction; so their dwelling should not
be cut off, howsoever I punished them: but they
rose early, *and* corrupted all their doings.
8 ¶ Therefore wait ye upon me, saith the LORD,
until the day that I rise up to the prey: for my
determination *is* to gather the nations, that I
may assemble the kingdoms, to pour upon them
mine indignation, *even* all my fierce anger: for all
the earth shall be devoured with the fire of my
jealousy.
9 For then will I turn to the people a pure
language, that they may all call upon the name of
the LORD, to serve him with one consent.
10 From beyond the rivers of Ethiopia my
suppliants, *even* the daughter of my dispersed,
shall bring mine offering.
11 In that day shalt thou not be ashamed for
all thy doings, wherein thou hast transgressed
against me: for then I will take away out of the
midst of thee them that rejoice in thy pride, and
thou shalt no more be haughty because of my
holy mountain.
12 I will also leave in the midst of thee an afflicted
and poor people, and they shall trust in the name
of the LORD.
13 The remnant of Israel shall not do iniquity,

is important as well to stress the urgency of the invitation to seek the Lord. Today is the day of salvation, but tomorrow is the day of judgment.

2. **The judgment of the Gentile nations is an opportunity to reflect on God's absolute sovereignty. None of the nations identified worshiped the true God or knew the truth from His special and gracious revelation. Nevertheless, He owned them and held them accountable for their sins, and particularly their sins against His people, which identified them as belonging to the serpent's seed bent on opposing God's redemptive plan. God had the authority and power to judge them; their ignorance of Him provided no excuse. It is significant as well to reflect on how God's judgment on the enemy results in blessing for His people. Divine judgment of the serpent's seed is an essential component in the advancement of God's kingdom.**

Chapter 3: *Zephaniah again denounces Judah and declares God's worldwide judgment, but then describes the wondrous blessings consequent upon His gracious and special presence.*

Judgment of Jerusalem (3:1–7)

3:1 *filthy . . . polluted . . . oppressing.* Rebellious, defiled, and violent.

3:2 Judah sinned by not responding properly to all their spiritual advantages. Unlike the Gentiles, they had God's Word but disobeyed, and it did not profit them because they did not mix it with faith (Heb. 4:2).

3:3–4 The prophet notes the sinful failures of the leadership, both civil and religious. The civil leaders appear bestial: fierce as lions and cruel as wolves of the night that devour their prey before morning arrives. The *prophets are light* (insolent) and the *priests have polluted the sanctuary* (treated the holy place as common or ordinary, thus profaning it).

3:5 The people's sin stands in stark contrast to God's perfect consistency and the privilege of His presence among them.

3:6–7 The Lord reviews all that He has done on behalf of His people to bring them to *fear* Him (the expression of true religion). *but they rose early and corrupted all their doings.* An idiom meaning that they corrupted their deeds again and again.

Judgment of the World (3:8)

3:8 God's judgment on the world would have positive effects for His people, but because of their sin, the universal judgment—although still certain—would be delayed. *with the fire of my jealousy.* See note at 1:18.

THE DAY OF THE LORD: GRACIOUS SALVATION (3:9–20)

Complete Transformation (3:9–13)

3:9 *will I turn to the people a pure language.* Literally, "I will restore . . . a plain lip," or language, perhaps alluding to a reversal of the curse of Babel. This reversal results in universal worship and service to God. *with one consent.* Literally, "one shoulder," an idiom for unified action.

3:10 *from beyond the rivers of Ethiopia.* The rivers of Cush represent far distant places. *my suppliants.* My worshipers, who had been scattered all over (*the daughter of my dispersed*).

3:11 Not only will the day of gracious salvation affect the Gentiles, it will have a positive effect on Judah as well, particularly effecting a removal of religious pride.

3:12 *afflicted and poor.* Humble and dependent.

3:13 *the remnant of Israel.* A reference to spiritual Israel; it is a qualitative rather than quantitative expression. The gracious transformation involves the eradication of sin and enjoyment of idyllic peace.

Glorious Restoration (3:14–20)

3:15 *taken away thy judgments.* Removed all accusations against them. *he hath cast out thine enemy.* Literally, "He has caused the enemy to about face or retreat." The Lord's presence removes all danger (*not see evil any more*). The Lord

nor speak lies; neither shall a deceitful tongue be
found in their mouth: for they shall feed and lie
down, and none shall make *them* afraid.
14 ¶ Sing, O daughter of Zion; shout, O Israel; be
glad and rejoice with all the heart, O daughter of
Jerusalem.
15 The LORD hath taken away thy judgments, he
hath cast out thine enemy: the king of Israel, *even*
the LORD, *is* in the midst of thee: thou shalt not
see evil any more.
16 In that day it shall be said to Jerusalem, Fear
thou not: *and to* Zion, Let not thine hands be
slack.
17 The LORD thy God in the midst of thee *is*
mighty; he will save, he will rejoice over thee with
joy; he will rest in his love, he will joy over thee
with singing.
18 I will gather *them that are* sorrowful for the
solemn assembly, *who* are of thee, *to whom* the
reproach of it *was* a burden.
19 Behold, at that time I will undo all that afflict
thee: and I will save her that halteth, and gather
her that was driven out; and I will get them praise
and fame in every land where they have been put
to shame.
20 At that time will I bring you *again*, even in the
time that I gather you: for I will make you a name
and a praise among all people of the earth, when
I turn back your captivity before your eyes, saith
the LORD.

---

as *the king of Israel* most likely refers specifically to Messiah, the mediatorial king.

3:16 *Let not thine hands be slack.* Don't let the hands hang down, i.e., don't be idle. The occupation of this restored and fearless people will be the service of worship.

3:17 The Lord's rejoicing over His people, resting in His love for them, and singing joyfully over them are incomprehensible but precious truths, illustrated by the response of the father at the return of his prodigal son (Luke 15:32).

3:18 The Hebrew is terse, but the idea is that in that day of pure worship, He will have removed those who had no true heart for Him and spiritual worship: those who grieved (*sorrowful*) and those who regarded it to be a burden.

3:19 *undo all that afflict thee.* The Lord will deal with those who oppressed them. *I will save her that halteth.* The Lord will rescue the lame, who cannot defend themselves.

Thoughts for Personal/Family Worship: Chapter 3

1. **Verse 8 is an opportunity to reflect on God's longsuffering that is designed to bring men to repentance and God's sovereignty that uses even man's sin to accomplish His ultimate redemptive purpose (Rom. 2:4; 9:22–24). The verse is clear that judgment is certain, but it is being delayed because of Israel's sin. Paul's exposition of this truth in Rom. 9 is remarkable. Israel's sin and all of its devastating consequences, rather than annulling God's promise, became a means of bringing in the Gentiles. But all unbelievers must beware; judgment is still coming in all the fury of God's wrath upon those who reject the gospel. Hebrews 12:25,29 puts it in perspective: "See that ye refuse not him that speaketh . . . our God is a consuming fire."**
2. **The final section of Zephaniah reminds us that there is a positive and glorious aspect of the day of the Lord. The day, which executes justice against sinners, also ushers in the time of restoration and full salvation blessing, where every vestige of sin and the curse are gone. The King will come, and He will gather His people to enjoy eternal bliss and peace in His presence (Rev. 19). It is imperative that we seek Him now to escape the wrath to come and to enjoy both the present life in Christ, who took God's wrath for His people, and the prospect of eternal hope. To this end the day of the Lord is a purifying and comforting truth for God's people.**

THE DAY OF THE LORD

The expression "the Day of the Lord" occurs about twenty times in the Old Testament. Related expressions, such as "that day" or "the day of the LORD of hosts," occur about fifty times and refer to the same phenomenon. It is a common prophetic theme. In these expressions the word *day* does not refer to a literal twenty-four hour period; rather, it designates a time when the Lord intervenes directly in human history, the sphere of time, either for judgment or for blessing. By His providence God controls and governs the affairs of history at all times, but the Day of the Lord marks His special, epochal manifestation into time. It is God's intervention in time in spectacular fashion to bring retribution against the wicked and deliverance for the righteous. Eternity breaks into time.

In the Old Testament this day has both historical and a future reference. Many Days of the Lord have already occurred. For instance, Zephaniah 1:7 refers to the destruction of Jerusalem (586 BC) as a Day of the Lord. Isaiah 13:7–13 refers to the capture of Babylon by the Medes and Persians (539 BC); it was future from Isaiah's perspective, but it is past from ours. Joel interprets a devastating locust invasion as a Day of the Lord, not just a natural phenomenon (Joel 1:1—2:17; ninth century BC). Each of these historical days foreshadowed the unparalleled Day of the Lord yet to come, when God will interrupt time for the last time.

Because the Day of the Lord is such a prominent prophetic theme with such far-reaching implications, it deserves attention. Use this outline to direct your study, consulting the relevant study notes for each of the texts below.

I. Key Passages
   A. Major Texts
      1. Isaiah 13; 34–35
      2. Jeremiah 46
      3. Ezekiel 30
      4. Joel
      5. Obadiah
      6. Zephaniah
      7. Zechariah 14
   B. Minor Texts
      1. Isaiah 2:9–22
      2. Lamentations 2:22
      3. Ezekiel 13:5
      4. Amos 5:18–20
      5. Malachi 4:5–6

II. Key Past Days (each is typical, a picture prophecy of the final future day)
   A. Isaiah 13—Babylon
   B. Jeremiah 46 and Ezekiel 30—Egypt
   C. Joel—Locust Invasion
   D. Obadiah and Isaiah 34—Edom
   E. Zephaniah—Judah

III. Key Themes That Mark the Day of the Lord
   A. Judgment
   B. Restoration or Blessing
   C. Messiah

IV. Key Applications of the Day of the Lord
   A. Since the prophets refer to the day as impending, this should be a motivation to us to be ready. There is always an urgency in the gospel message.
   B. The sins that precipitated the historic manifestations of the day parallel the kinds of sins that mark our day and society. God's justice and immutability mean that He will judge all the guilty.
   C. The Day of the Lord was and remains an incentive to repentance. Escaping God's wrath by self-effort is impossible. The only way to escape divine wrath is by fleeing to the source of that wrath and finding security in Christ.
   D. The blessing components of the Day of the Lord, particularly as they find expression in the Messiah, should be hopeful encouragements to every Christian. For believers, the final consummation should not be a day of dread but one of confident expectation. A perfect day is ahead.

INTRODUCTION TO THE BOOK OF HAGGAI

Authorship: Haggai's name means "festal one." Although little is known about the prophet, his authorship of this prophecy is not a matter of dispute. Ezra records the beginning of his ministry to Judah and Jerusalem (Ezra 5:1), and the success of his preaching (Ezra 6:14). Very likely, Haggai was among those who could remember something of the glory of the former temple (Hag. 2:3); thus, he would have been at least in his midseventies when God commissioned him for this particular ministry.

Date: Haggai, a contemporary of Zechariah, is the first in our canonical order of the postexilic prophets, and he explicitly dates his prophecy to the second year of Darius. In fact, his written prophecy is the collection of four messages that he dated by the day, month, and year (1:1; 2:1,10,20). Although his ministry and influence in Jerusalem may have been longer, his entire written prophecy spanned a four-month period from our September to December, 520 BC.

Theme: Rebuilding the temple—putting God first.

Purpose: To inspire the people to renewed dedication and determination for the work of the kingdom; to convince them that nothing is more important than kingdom work.

Synopsis: *The Contribution of Haggai to Redemptive Revelation*

In 537 BC Zerubbabel—a descendant of David and an ancestor of Jesus—led the first wave of exiles back to Israel after the Babylonian captivity in response to the decree of Cyrus (2 Chron. 36:22–23; Ezra 1:1–4). The captivity, the lowest point in Israel's checkered history, was over. Seventy years of retribution and purification had been accomplished, and a new day was dawning. The people returned in faith and in hope that God would keep His promise of restoration and blessing. This was a generation that lived in a crucial moment in the progression of God's unfailing purpose of redemption. So many things had to be in place for the approaching of the incarnation, the climax of redemptive history in the fullness of time. According to prophecy (Hag. 2:9), there had to be a Jerusalem and a temple in place when Messiah came. It was the first and principal order of business for Zerubbabel and the remnant to rebuild the fallen temple.

At first there was good progress; there was the confident expectation that God's promises were certain. But soon there was opposition, beginning with misunderstandings and escalating to rumors, accusations, and threats. The opposition became so intense that the work ceased, and then apathy and carelessness about the kingdom work set in. Loss of hope and the delay of blessing stagnated the work. Then in 520 BC God raised up Haggai and Zechariah to exhort the nation to reevaluate their priorities and to finish the temple; that was a vital contribution Haggai made to redemptive revelation. That the divine name Jehovah, which reveals God as the covenant Savior, occurs in thirty-four of the thirty-eight verses indicates that the theme of salvation is predominant.

In addition, Haggai pointed to the coming Messiah, both directly and indirectly through typology (picture prophecies). Although a disputed interpretation, Haggai's prophecy of the coming of the "desire of all nations" likely refers to the Messiah, whose physical presence in the rebuilt temple would fill it with a glory exceeding that of Solomon's temple (2:7,9) and is preceded by a divine shaking up of things (2:6). Significantly, Heb. 12:26 quotes Haggai 2:6 in a context about rejecting God's Word about Jesus, the Mediator of the new covenant (Heb. 12:24). Typically, the temple, as the symbol of God's dwelling with His people, points to the climax of that dwelling in the incarnation of the Son. Also typically, Zerubbabel prefigures Christ. Hag. 2:23 says that he is a signet ring, that which is used as a seal to ensure or authenticate. Although not officially a king, he was of the royal family and anticipated the certain coming of David's greater Son, the rightful heir to the throne (Ezek. 21:27). Zerubbabel was the ancestor of Jesus that linked Him to David whether through the line of Joseph via Solomon (Matt. 1:12) or of Mary via Nathan (Luke 3:27). Haggai assures his readers that the Christ that must come will come.

Outline: The outline is based on the four dated messages (1:1; 2:1,10,20).

I. Rebuke and Response regarding the Temple Work (1:1–15)
  A. Rebuke for Their Priorities (1:1–11)
  B. Response of Obedience (1:12–15)
II. Reassurances regarding the Temple (2:1–9)
  A. Against Discouragement (2:1–3)
  B. In Anticipation of Greater Glory (2:4–9)
III. Incentives for Obedience (2:10–19)
  A. Consequences of Disobedience (2:10–17)
  B. Consequences of Obedience (2:18–19)
IV. Assurances regarding a Certain Future (2:20–23)
  A. The Overthrow of the World's Kingdoms (2:20–22)
  B. The Establishment of Messiah's Kingdom (2:23)

THE BOOK OF HAGGAI

CHAPTER 1

IN the second year of Darius the king, in the sixth
month, in the first day of the month, came the
word of the LORD by Haggai the prophet unto
Zerubbabel the son of Shealtiel, governor of
Judah, and to Joshua the son of Josedech, the high
priest, saying,
2 Thus speaketh the LORD of hosts, saying, This
people say, The time is not come, the time that the
LORD's house should be built.
3 Then came the word of the LORD by Haggai the
prophet, saying,
4 *Is it* time for you, O ye, to dwell in your cieled
houses, and this house *lie* waste?
5 Now therefore thus saith the LORD of hosts;
Consider your ways.
6 Ye have sown much, and bring in little; ye eat,
but ye have not enough; ye drink, but ye are not
filled with drink; ye clothe you, but there is none
warm; and he that earneth wages earneth wages *to*
put it into a bag with holes.
7 ¶ Thus saith the LORD of hosts; Consider your
ways.
8 Go up to the mountain, and bring wood, and
build the house; and I will take pleasure in it, and
I will be glorified, saith the LORD.
9 Ye looked for much, and, lo, *it came* to little;
and when ye brought *it* home, I did blow upon
it. Why? saith the LORD of hosts. Because of mine
house that *is* waste, and ye run every man unto
his own house.
10 Therefore the heaven over you is stayed from
dew, and the earth is stayed *from* her fruit.
11 And I called for a drought upon the land, and
upon the mountains, and upon the corn, and
upon the new wine, and upon the oil, and upon
that which the ground bringeth forth, and upon
men, and upon cattle, and upon all the labour of
the hands.
12 ¶ Then Zerubbabel the son of Shealtiel, and
Joshua the son of Josedech, the high priest, with
all the remnant of the people, obeyed the voice of
the LORD their God, and the words of Haggai the
prophet, as the LORD their God had sent him, and
the people did fear before the LORD.
13 Then spake Haggai the LORD's messenger in

Chapter 1: ***Haggai rebukes the people for neglecting the work on the temple, attributing their frustrations and failures to their skewed priorities of putting their own concerns above the Lord's, and the people respond in obedience, returning to the work.***

REBUKE AND RESPONSE REGARDING THE TEMPLE WORK (1:1–15)

Rebuke for Their Priorities (1:1–11)

1:2 Claiming that it was not time to rebuild the temple indicates awareness of God's command to rebuild. The opposition (Ezra 4) caused them to reinterpret God's will rather than obeying by faith. Sight prevailed over faith.

1:4 The question addresses the principal issue: personal comfort took precedence over the Lord. *cieled houses*. Paneled, most likely with cedar planks. *waste*. Desolate ruin.

1:5,7 *Consider your ways*. Literally, "set your heart upon your ways," that is, take to heart, in the sense of thinking seriously about what they were doing.

1:6 This verse highlights the futility and frustrations of much work without the desired ends. Although they were back in the land of promise and potential blessing, their disobedience placed them under circumstances associated with the curse (Deut. 28:38–40).

1:8 God is pleased with and will be glorified by the obedience of His people.

1:9–11 Haggai specifically links the lack of blessing and experience of curse (1:6) to the desolate condition of the temple, which persisted while they exerted their energy on self-interests. The seriousness is compounded in the light of the temple's gospel significance, foreshadowing the incarnation. The issue points to Paul's assertion that self-interests must give way in light of what Christ has done (2 Cor. 5:14–15). To put it simply, the people of Haggai's "congregation" were not thinking gospel thoughts.

Response of Obedience (1:12–15)

1:12 In response to Haggai's stern rebuke, the people obeyed, acknowledging the divine authority of his message, just as the Thessalonians responded to Paul's preaching hundred of years later (1 Thess. 2:13). They also feared the Lord. The *fear* of the Lord is that childlike awe and love toward God's majesty which moves us to worship and obey Him as His Word commands (Prov. 9:10; 2 Cor. 6:16–7:1; 1 Pet. 1:13–17).

1:13 *the LORD's messenger in the LORD's message*. A classic statement of prophetic authority. The prophet could speak only what God revealed and commissioned him to speak. God both revealed and inspired.

the LORD's message unto the people, saying, I *am* with you, saith the LORD.
14 And the LORD stirred up the spirit of Zerubbabel the son of Shealtiel, governor of Judah, and the spirit of Joshua the son of Josedech, the high priest, and the spirit of all the remnant of the people; and they came and did work in the house of the LORD of hosts, their God,
15 In the four and twentieth day of the sixth month, in the second year of Darius the king.

CHAPTER 2

IN the seventh *month*, in the one and twentieth *day* of the month, came the word of the LORD by the prophet Haggai, saying,
2 Speak now to Zerubbabel the son of Shealtiel, governor of Judah, and to Joshua the son of Josedech, the high priest, and to the residue of the people, saying,
3 Who *is* left among you that saw this house in her first glory? and how do ye see it now? *is it* not in your eyes in comparison of it as nothing?
4 Yet now be strong, O Zerubbabel, saith the LORD; and be strong, O Joshua, son of Josedech, the high priest; and be strong, all ye people of the land, saith the LORD, and work: for I *am* with you, saith the LORD of hosts:
5 *According to* the word that I covenanted with you when ye came out of Egypt, so my spirit remaineth among you: fear ye not.
6 For thus saith the LORD of hosts; Yet once, it *is*

1:14 *stirred up.* Put into motion, roused. *the spirit of.* Man's spirit refers to his mind or disposition. The Lord Himself moves it, making His people willing to obey. This is an example of Phil. 2:13, "For it is God which worketh in you both to will and to do of his good pleasure."
1:15 Twenty-three days after the sermon, most likely referring to the time required to organize and restart the temple project.

Thoughts for Personal/Family Worship: Chapter 1

1. **In the classic allegory *The Pilgrim's Progress*, John Bunyan illustrates the notions of many who have mistaken views of God and His Word. Early on his journey, Christian encountered two of his neighbors, Obstinate and Pliable. Though both were curious about Christian's journey, Obstinate determined from the beginning not to go and tried to convince Pliable not to go either. But Pliable, interested in the blessings and benefits Christian described, set out on the journey. Along the way, he kept asking Christian about the blessings ahead. All went well until they entered the Slough of Despond. Pliable forgot about all the benefits and returned home as quickly as he could. Unless the way was easy and the blessings clearly in view, he wanted nothing to do with Christian and this journey to the distant city. He would follow God only for what he thought he would get out of it. Bunyan's self-consumed Pliable bears uncanny resemblance to those in the days of Haggai, who allowed the opposition to distract them from what God had commanded. It was easier to redirect their efforts to self-interests, but losing the vision of God's purpose turned life itself into futility—nothing brought fulfillment. Haggai made it clear that self-serving is always self-defeating. This is a poignant message to so many Christians today whose priorities are skewed toward the stuff of temporal life rather than spiritual life.**
2. **How the people responded to Haggai's preaching is a model example. They listened, they acknowledged it as God's Word, and they obeyed. By their returning to the work, they became doers of the Word and not just hearers (James 1:22). That their response was the consequence of the Lord's arousing them is a reminder of how vital it is for the Spirit to be in attendance with the preaching of the Word and to apply that work to the heart. Preachers are able to convince people to do or not to do, but only the Spirit can apply the Word in a living way (see the illustration in Ezek. 37 of the prophet's preaching to the dry bones). Preaching is the method God has ordained for evangelism and edification. Not only are ministers responsible to preach well, the congregation is responsible to listen well.**
3. **Haggai's "congregation" also provides a lesson in fearing the Lord. The fear of God is an expression of faith, which is more aware of the unseen than the seen. The people lost their vision and energy for the work of kingdom when they saw and experienced the hostility. But when they became conscious of God's presence (Hag. 1:13) and feared Him (v. 12), they determined to obey. What we fear always determines behavior. To fear the Lord is to be consciously aware of Him and to consciously factor Him into every part of life.**

Chapter 2: ***In three dated messages, Haggai encourages the people with the prospect of an unprecedented, glorious temple, incites them to continued obedience with the prospect of present blessing, and assures them of the certainty of God's kingdom.***

REASSURANCES REGARDING THE TEMPLE (2:1–9)

Against Discouragement (2:1–3)

2:1 *In the seventh month.* This would be a word in season. This message occurred at the end of Feast of Tabernacles (Lev. 23:34–36), which commemorated God's faithfulness during the wilderness wanderings. Perhaps even more relevant is that Solomon dedicated the first temple in the seventh month (1 Kings 8:2). That anniversary may have precipitated the comparison between the current project and Solomon's temple, which at this point appeared to be so much better.
2:3 Solomon's temple was destroyed in 586 BC, 66 years earlier. Undoubtedly, some, now in their seventies and older, would have vivid memories of the grandeur of that temple.

In Anticipation of Greater Glory (2:4–9)

2:4–5 The assurance of the Lord's presence (*I am with you . . . my spirit remaineth among you*, literally, "is standing in your midst") is reason for confidence (*be strong*), action (*work*), and faith (*fear ye not*). *I covenanted with you.* Literally, "I cut with you." Cutting a covenant was the standard idiom for initiating a covenant; perhaps an allusion to the cutting of a sacrificial animal in a covenant ceremony (Jer. 34:18).
2:6–9 *Yet once, it is a little while.* The temporal expression is to be understood from the perspective of God's eternal plan and timetable and not from human perspective. What seems to man to be delay is always on schedule to God. *I will shake.* An action associated with theophany (an appearance by God), whether past or future. The point is, nothing is

a little while, and I will shake the heavens, and the
earth, and the sea, and the dry *land*;
7 And I will shake all nations, and the desire of all
nations shall come: and I will fill this house with
glory, saith the LORD of hosts.
8 The silver *is* mine, and the gold *is* mine, saith
the LORD of hosts.
9 The glory of this latter house shall be greater
than of the former, saith the LORD of hosts: and
in this place will I give peace, saith the LORD of
hosts.
10 ¶ In the four and twentieth *day* of the ninth
month, in the second year of Darius, came the
word of the LORD by Haggai the prophet, saying,
11 Thus saith the LORD of hosts; Ask now the
priests *concerning* the law, saying,
12 If one bear holy flesh in the skirt of his
garment, and with his skirt do touch bread, or
pottage, or wine, or oil, or any meat, shall it be
holy? And the priests answered and said, No.
13 Then said Haggai, If *one that is* unclean by a
dead body touch any of these, shall it be unclean?
And the priests answered and said, It shall be
unclean.
14 Then answered Haggai, and said, So *is* this
people, and so *is* this nation before me, saith the
LORD; and so *is* every work of their hands; and
that which they offer there *is* unclean.
15 And now, I pray you, consider from this day
and upward, from before a stone was laid upon a
stone in the temple of the LORD:
16 Since those *days* were, when *one* came to an
heap of twenty *measures*, there were *but* ten: when
one came to the pressfat for to draw out fifty
vessels out of the press, there were *but* twenty.
17 I smote you with blasting and with mildew
and with hail in all the labours of your hands; yet
ye *turned* not to me, saith the LORD.
18 Consider now from this day and upward, from
the four and twentieth day of the ninth *month*,
even from the day that the foundation of the
LORD's temple was laid, consider *it*.
19 Is the seed yet in the barn? yea, as yet the vine,
and the fig tree, and the pomegranate, and the
olive tree, hath not brought forth: from this day
will I bless *you*.
20 ¶ And again the word of the LORD came unto
Haggai in the four and twentieth *day* of the
month, saying,
21 Speak to Zerubbabel, governor of Judah,
saying, I will shake the heavens and the earth;
22 And I will overthrow the throne of kingdoms,

---

unaffected when God comes down. This coming refers to the incarnation, when God became manifest in the flesh. *the desire of all nations*. Some interpret "desire" to refer to the wealth of Gentiles that will be brought into the temple. It is best to see this as referring to Christ, the infinitely valuable treasure, who is the object of longing and desire (the One whom all nations desire). It is the coming of Christ into this second temple, then under construction, that would fill it with unsurpassed glory, a glory far superior to adornments of silver or gold, which belonged to the Lord anyway.

INCENTIVES FOR OBEDIENCE (2:10–19)

Consequences of Disobedience (2:10–17)

2:10–14 Haggai returns to his opening message directed to the disobedient. In ch. 1, he addressed misplaced priorities; here, he describes disobedience as violations of ceremonial laws of cleanness and uncleanness.
2:11 *Ask now the priests*. The priests were the teachers, interpreters, and enforcers of the law.
2:12 *holy flesh*. That which was consecrated for offering. *skirt of his garment*. Literally, "the wing of his garment," referring to the hem or the bottom part that would be gathered to act as a sack. *pottage*. Cooked food. The point is that holiness is not transferable; touching something clean to something unclean does not alter the state of the unclean.
2:13 *dead body*. Contact with a dead body constituted ceremonial uncleanness (Num. 19:11,22). The point is that unholiness is transferable; touching something unclean to something clean does alter the state of the clean.
2:14 Haggai applies the illustration from Levitical law to the state of the nation; everything they do will be defiled unless they give themselves in dedication to the Lord for His work.
2:15 This verse describes the consequences of their disobedience of failing to build the temple (*before a stone was laid upon a stone*).
2:16 They did not have the resources to accomplish anything (see imagery of 1:6). *pressfat*. Wine vat.
2:17 Divine activity associated with the curse of covenant violations (Deut. 28:22). *yet ye turned not to me*. Literally, "nonexistence of you to me." They were spiritually insensitive and would have nothing to do with the Lord (Amos 4).

Consequences of Obedience (2:18–19)

2:18–19 They were to take to heart (*consider*) that returning to the work of the temple would reverse the curse—*from this day will I bless you*. Even though the harvest was not yet apparent, the Lord's pledge guaranteed it.

ASSURANCES REGARDING A CERTAIN FUTURE (2:20–23)

The Overthrow of the World's Kingdoms (2:20–22)

2:21 *I will shake*. Again the language of theophany and the unmistakable consequences of divine intervention (Heb. 12:25–29).
2:22 Up to this point, Haggai's message has concerned issues related to Christ's first coming. But God's redemptive purpose in Christ is one unfailing plan, which involves the removal of every obstacle and hindrance to God's kingdom. The final consummation occurs at Christ's second coming. All the kingdoms of this world will fail; Christ's kingdom will prevail. Prophets often link aspects of what we now know are the two advents.

The Establishment of Messiah's Kingdom (2:23)

2:23 God designates Zerubbabel, the civil leader in David's line, as a type of coming Messiah (a real historical person, event, or thing used as a picture prophecy). *signet*. A symbol conveying the authority and privilege of office, here guaranteeing the unconditional certainty of God's covenant with David concerning his "greater Son." When God removed the signet from Jehoiachin (Jer. 22:24), it appeared the promise was in jeopardy. But the Lord transfers it to another of David's sons granting the promise to be realized in Jesus. See Introduction: Synopsis for further comments on Zerubbabel.

and I will destroy the strength of the kingdoms of the heathen; and I will overthrow the chariots, and those that ride in them; and the horses and their riders shall come down, every one by the sword of his brother.

23 In that day, saith the LORD of hosts, will I take thee, O Zerubbabel, my servant, the son of Shealtiel, saith the LORD, and will make thee as a signet: for I have chosen thee, saith the LORD of hosts.

Thoughts for Personal/Family Worship: Chapter 2

1. **If 1:6,8–11 taught that putting yourself in first place is self-defeating, 2:3 teaches that putting yourself down is service defeating. Comparing the first temple with the plans of the second temple led to discouragement and inactivity. The people allowed appearance to influence their thinking and concluded that they were making no real contribution to the work of the Lord. They looked backward instead of forward to what was going to be greater than their expectations. It is always dangerous and defeating to evaluate the value of our service by comparing it with what others are doing or have done. The value of service is always to be measured by conformity to God's will and purpose. Too many Christians tend to compare themselves and their spiritual gifts with others and convince themselves there is nothing they can contribute to the service of the Lord. Consequently, they become idle. There is no better service that we can render to the Lord than being faithful to what He has called us and enabled us to do by the help of His Spirit. All service that is rendered in faithful obedience is pleasing to Him.**
2. **Christ's designation as the "desire of all nations" (v. 7) directs us to Him as the object of our worship. The word "desire" includes the sense of treasure or wealth. This means that Christ with all of His infinite and intrinsic worth ought to be our prized possession. To have Christ is to have everything. If He is our treasure our heart will be with Him (Matt. 6:19–21; Col. 3:1–2). Paul understood this when he testified that he counted everything else to be nothing but rubbish in contrast to knowing Christ (Phil. 3:7–8). That is the example to follow.**
3. **Verses 10–14 are a reminder of how important it is for believers to walk cautiously in this world. There are so many things in the world that rob us of our fellowship with God and our ability to serve Him. This is one reason why we are not to love the things of this world (1 John 2:15–17). Here is an illustration: rubbing a clean shirt on a grease rag will not clean the grease from the rag, but it will stain the shirt. So Christians must be cautious to avoid contact with sinful things and practices.**

INTRODUCTION TO THE BOOK OF ZECHARIAH

Authorship: Zechariah was a common name in the Old Testament, meaning "Jehovah remembers." The prophet was the son of Berechiah, the son of Iddo, and according to the genealogy recorded in Nehemiah 12, was born into the priestly line. That Ezra 5:1 and Neh. 12:16 identify Zechariah as the son of Iddo is no contradiction, just a Hebrew way of saying he was a descendant of Iddo, who was more prominent as one of the priests who returned to Jerusalem with Zerubbabel. Zechariah would have been a young man when he began his prophetic ministry in contrast to Haggai, his much older prophetic colleague. Although his death is not recorded in the Old Testament, Jesus said that he was martyred at the temple (Matt. 23:35), under much the same circumstances as the martyrdom of an earlier Zechariah (2 Chron. 24:20–21).

Date: Zechariah, like Haggai, dates his prophecy in reference to the reign of Darius, although his tenure extended beyond that of his colleague. According to 1:1, his first message (chs. 1–6) dates to the second year of Darius (520 BC) and according to 7:1 his second message (chs. 7–8) dates to Darius's fourth year (518 BC). The message of chs. 9–14, however, is undated, and its references to Greece would indicate a later date. Most conservatives date this section 480–470 BC. All together, Zechariah's ministry spanned about fifty years (520–470 BC).

Theme: Hope in God's unfailing purpose.

Purpose: To encourage God's people to live in victory and serve with diligence in view of the certain blessing God has purposed and promised.

Synopsis: *The Contribution of Zechariah to Redemptive Revelation*

The years of Babylonian bondage were over, but the end of the seventy-year captivity did not initiate the prosperity and blessing anticipated. Those who returned to Israel faced opposition from the Samaritans, desolation of the land, hard work, and hardships. Though they returned with eager hope, the circumstances soon overwhelmed them, the hope faded and progress toward restoration ceased. But the temple had to be in place for the coming of Messiah, so God raised up Haggai and Zechariah to encourage the people to work. Their combined ministries worked, for the second temple was completed in 516/515 BC. Whereas Haggai addressed the problem head on, Zechariah sought to incite the people to rebuild the temple in view of God's overarching redemptive plan. He accomplished this by directing faith to God's covenant promises that He had to fulfill, both concerning the physical needs of the day and the spiritual promises centered in the Messiah. Significantly, the title "the Lord of hosts" occurs approximately fifty times in the prophecy. This title is appropriate for it designates God as the "Commander-in-Chief" who has all authority and power over all His creation to accomplish His will. Consequently, every grand promise He makes is absolutely certain. A confident hope in the guaranteed blessings of the future was effective motivation to encourage present service.

The focus of Zechariah's message of hope was the Messiah. His specific and explicit predictions of the Messiah rank his prophecy as one of the most messianic in the Old Testament. The prophecies detail aspects of each of the Messiah's mediatorial functions as prophet, priest, and king. His prophetic office as the representative of God is evident in 13:7 where the Lord of hosts refers to Messiah as "my shepherd," "my fellow" (the one who is equal), whom He Himself strikes. Matthew 26:31 links this directly to Christ and the cross. It also parallels Christ's exposition of the good shepherd where He declares that He lays down His life for the sheep and that He and

His Father are one (John 10:30). The priestly ministry is most explicit in the significant messianic title, "The BRANCH" that occurs in 3:8 and 6:12 in analogy with Joshua the high priest. Christ's kingship is seen in 9:9, the prophecy so specifically fulfilled on Palm Sunday. Aspects of kingship associated with Christ's second coming are also part of the hope (ch. 14). Other specific messianic texts will be identified in the notes, but it is clear that Zechariah must be read with an eye open for Christ.

Outline:

- I. The Call to Repent (1:1–6)
- II. The Visions to Encourage (1:7—6:15)
  - A. Introduction to Encouraging Visions (1:7)
  - B. Horses and the Myrtle Tree (1:8–17)
  - C. Four Horns (1:18–21)
  - D. Man with the Measuring Line (2:1–13)
  - E. Joshua and the Branch (3:1–10)
  - F. The Candlestick and Olive Trees (4:1–14)
  - G. The Flying Scroll (5:1–4)
  - H. The Woman in the Ephah (5:5–11)
  - I. The Four Chariots (6:1–8)
  - J. The Symbolic Crowning of Joshua (6:9–15)
- III. Questions to Answer (7:1—8:23)
  - A. One Question about Fasting (7:1–3)
  - B. Four Answers (7:4—8:23; marked by "the word of the LORD came")
    - 1. Hypocritical Fasting (7:4–7)
    - 2. Obedience Better (7:8–14)
    - 3. Restoration in the Place of Devastation (8:1–17)
    - 4. Joy in the Place of Mourning (8:18–23)
- IV. Prophetic Oracles to Bless (9:1—14:21)
  - A. The First Oracle (9:1—11:17; marked by "The burden of the word of the LORD")
    - 1. Judgment of Enemies (9:1–8)
    - 2. The Coming King (9:9—10:12)
    - 3. The Rejected Shepherd (11:1–17)
  - B. The Second Oracle (12:1—14:21; marked by "The burden of the word of the LORD")
    - 1. National Deliverance (12:1–9)
    - 2. Spiritual Deliverance (12:10—13:9)
    - 3. The Coming of Messiah (14:1–21)

THE BOOK OF

ZECHARIAH

CHAPTER 1

In the eighth month, in the second year of Darius, came the word of the LORD unto Zechariah, the son of Berechiah, the son of Iddo the prophet, saying,
2 The LORD hath been sore displeased with your fathers.
3 Therefore say thou unto them, Thus saith the LORD of hosts; Turn ye unto me, saith the LORD of hosts, and I will turn unto you, saith the LORD of hosts.
4 Be ye not as your fathers, unto whom the former prophets have cried, saying, Thus saith the LORD of hosts; Turn ye now from your evil ways, and *from* your evil doings: but they did not hear, nor hearken unto me, saith the LORD.
5 Your fathers, where *are* they? and the prophets, do they live for ever?
6 But my words and my statutes, which I commanded my servants the prophets, did they not take hold of your fathers? and they returned and said, Like as the LORD of hosts thought to do unto us, according to our ways, and according to our doings, so hath he dealt with us.
7 ¶ Upon the four and twentieth day of the eleventh month, which *is* the month Sebat, in the second year of Darius, came the word of the LORD unto Zechariah, the son of Berechiah, the son of Iddo the prophet, saying,
8 I saw by night, and behold a man riding upon a red horse, and he stood among the myrtle trees that *were* in the bottom; and behind him *were there* red horses, speckled, and white.
9 Then said I, O my lord, what *are* these? And the angel that talked with me said unto me, I will shew thee what these *be*.

Chapter 1: ***Zechariah begins with a call to repentance issuing a warning not to ignore the prophetic word like former generations and then commences his series of night visions with the man on a red horse among the myrtle trees followed by the four horns and four craftsmen.***

THE CALL TO REPENT (1:1–6)

1:2 *hath been sore displeased with your fathers.* Literally, "has been angry against your fathers with anger," an idiom expressing intense fury or wrath.

1:3 *Turn ye.* The principal word in the Old Testament for repentance; it pictures a reversal of direction. *I will turn.* God does not change directions, but repentant sinners will experience His mercy rather than wrath. God graciously receives those who repent (John 6:37).

1:4 *Former prophets* refers to all the preexilic prophets. *Evil ways... evil doings* refers respectively to the inclinations of life and individual acts. *unto me.* The prophets spoke, but it was the Lord that the former generations ignored and disobeyed. The words of the prophets were the words of the Lord Himself.

1:6 *did they not take hold.* Did they not overtake; a reference to the fulfillment of all the warnings and prophecies. *they returned and said.* Those to whom Zechariah is preaching repented, acknowledging that all the prophetic warnings had been fulfilled and admitting that God had dealt justly.

THE VISIONS TO ENCOURAGE (1:7—6:15)

Introduction to Encouraging Visions (1:7)

1:7 Introduces a series of visions Zechariah received in a single night, giving an overview of God's redemptive plan from the immediate context to the distant future. Both dreams and visions were means of divine revelation. God spoke through dreams to those who were either spiritually dead (e.g., Pharaoh) or spiritually immature (e.g., the young Joseph), and the recipients were passive. Visions were given to the spiritually mature, who were active participants (e.g., Zechariah's communicating with the angel), although the whole revelatory experience was internal. Both dreams and visions were highly symbolic, using images to convey truth. *came the word of the LORD.* That the vision is designated as the *word* underscores its revelatory authority.

Horses and the Myrtle Tree (1:8–17)

1:8–17 The essential point is that God will keep His word in bringing a full end to the seventy-year captivity by restoring Jerusalem and by punishing the nations responsible for the captivity. The salient points of the vision: *A man riding upon a red horse*—the angel of the Lord, a reference to the preincarnate Christ; *the myrtle trees*—Israel; *the horses*—the angels as the agents of divine providence; *the angel that talked with me*—an angel that interpreted the vision for Zechariah.

1:8 *riding... stood.* He was mounted on the horse and had stopped among the myrtles. *in the bottom.* A basin or valley, perhaps a picture of the low estate of the nation represented by the myrtle trees. *red horses.* Reddish brown, perhaps a symbol of judgment. *speckled.* A mixed color like a sorrel or bay, perhaps a symbol of the dual mission of judgment and mercy. *white.* Perhaps, a symbol of victory.

1:9 Zechariah appeals to the interpreting angel who gives him clues as to the meaning of what he sees.

10 And the man that stood among the myrtle
trees answered and said, These *are they* whom
the LORD hath sent to walk to and fro through the
earth.
11 And they answered the angel of the LORD that
stood among the myrtle trees, and said, We have
walked to and fro through the earth, and, behold,
all the earth sitteth still, and is at rest.
12 ¶ Then the angel of the LORD answered and
said, O LORD of hosts, how long wilt thou not
have mercy on Jerusalem and on the cities of Ju-
dah, against which thou hast had indignation
these threescore and ten years?
13 And the LORD answered the angel that talked
with me *with* good words *and* comfortable words.
14 So the angel that communed with me said
unto me, Cry thou, saying, Thus saith the LORD
of hosts; I am jealous for Jerusalem and for Zion
with a great jealousy.
15 And I am very sore displeased with the heathen
that are at ease: for I was but a little displeased,
and they helped forward the affliction.
16 Therefore thus saith the LORD; I am returned
to Jerusalem with mercies: my house shall be built
in it, saith the LORD of hosts, and a line shall be
stretched forth upon Jerusalem.
17 Cry yet, saying, Thus saith the LORD of hosts;
My cities through prosperity shall yet be spread
abroad; and the LORD shall yet comfort Zion, and
shall yet choose Jerusalem.
18 ¶ Then lifted I up mine eyes, and saw, and
behold four horns.
19 And I said unto the angel that talked with me,
What *be* these? And he answered me, These *are*
the horns which have scattered Judah, Israel, and
Jerusalem.
20 And the LORD shewed me four carpenters.
21 Then said I, What come these to do? And he
spake, saying, These *are* the horns which have
scattered Judah, so that no man did lift up his
head: but these are come to fray them, to cast out
the horns of the Gentiles, which lifted up *their*
horn over the land of Judah to scatter it.

CHAPTER 2

I LIFTED up mine eyes again, and looked, and
behold a man with a measuring line in his hand.

1:10 *to walk to and fro through the earth.* To walk around the earth; describes the divine commission to the horses (symbolic of the angelic agents of providence) to discover the affairs of earth. God obviously does not need to discover facts; He knows all things immediately. Symbols are not reality.

1:11 *the angel of the LORD.* The angel or messenger who is the Lord, an Old Testament title for a Christophany, a preincarnate appearance of Christ. *sitteth still . . . at rest.* An idiom meaning "to dwell peacefully or undisturbed."

1:12 The peace and security in the world's kingdom moved the angel of the Lord to pray that God would show pity or compassion (*have mercy*) on Judah against whom He had been indignant for seventy years (*threescore and ten*).

1:13 *comfortable.* From the same root as "have mercy" (v. 12), suggesting a most specific and definite answer to the intercession.

1:14 *I am jealous . . . with a great jealously.* Idiom expressing intensification, "I am really jealous," referring to God's fervent zeal.

1:15 *I am very sore displeased.* Literally, "with great anger I am being angry." *the heathen that are at ease.* The nations that are carefree. *they helped forward the affliction.* Literally, "they themselves helped the disaster." Although God used these nations as His instruments of judgment, they were accountable for their terrible cruelty against Judah (Isa. 47:5–7).

1:16 *with mercies.* The Hebrew often uses the plural for intensification, "great mercy." As a result, the temple will be rebuilt and Jerusalem will be measured (*a line shall be stretched*), evidence of its restoration.

1:17 *my cities . . . shall yet be spread abroad.* They will overflow due to increased population. *comfort . . . choose.* The Lord confirms His covenant promise and purpose that not even Judah's captivity-earning sins could frustrate.

Four Horns (1:18–21)

1:18–21 The essential point is that God has adequate resources to curb and conquer all the powerful enemies of His people. The salient points of the vision: *four horns*—the hostile nations; *four carpenters*—agents of God's providence and judgment. Just as the horns, though powerful, cannot resist the even more powerful smiths, so God's enemies cannot resist or prevail against His superior power.

1:18–19 *four horns.* The horns of bulls are a common image for power. Some interpret *four* to refer to Assyria, Egypt, Babylon, and Medo-Persia, all of which were powerful and hostile enemies. More likely, four represents the "four-quarters" of the earth and thus would include potential enemies worldwide. That the horns were guilty of scattering the covenant nation supports the indefinite identification of the horns. Scattering most likely sums up any sort of hostile treatment rather than just deportations (only Assyria and Babylon employed that tactic).

1:20 *four carpenters.* Craftsmen. There were four to counter each of the four horns.

1:21 *no man did lift up his head.* A gesture of humiliation. *to fray.* To rout in terror.

Thoughts for Personal/Family Worship: Chapter 1

1. **Verse 14 sums up the message of the entire prophecy and suggests key thoughts for meditation. God's jealousy or zeal is His ardent and active love for His name, His glory, His law, and His people. It is His zealous disposition that demonstrates the appropriate action. When offended, it shows itself in just retribution. When stirred by grace, it reveals eternal love. Whereas jealousy and zeal in man can be easily perverted in moments of passion, that is never true of God. Behind His fervent zeal and hot jealousy are His eternal purpose, immutability, omnipotence, and authority. Significantly, this declared jealousy for His people is from the Lord of hosts, a title that highlights His power and authority. As you read through Zechariah, pay attention to this title that occurs over fifty times. Many of the promises are beyond human comprehension, but behind every promise is the God who controls and commands all of creation; that is solid reason for hope. Nothing can hinder or frustrate God's burning zeal.**

2 Then said I, Whither goest thou? And he said
unto me, To measure Jerusalem, to see what *is* the
breadth thereof, and what *is* the length thereof.
3 And, behold, the angel that talked with me
went forth, and another angel went out to meet
him,
4 And said unto him, Run, speak to this young
man, saying, Jerusalem shall be inhabited *as*
towns without walls for the multitude of men and
cattle therein:
5 For I, saith the LORD, will be unto her a wall
of fire round about, and will be the glory in the
midst of her.
6 ¶ Ho, ho, *come forth*, and flee from the land of
the north, saith the LORD: for I have spread you
abroad as the four winds of the heaven, saith the
LORD.
7 Deliver thyself, O Zion, that dwellest *with* the
daughter of Babylon.
8 For thus saith the LORD of hosts; After the glory
hath he sent me unto the nations which spoiled
you: for he that toucheth you toucheth the apple
of his eye.
9 For, behold, I will shake mine hand upon them,
and they shall be a spoil to their servants: and ye
shall know that the LORD of hosts hath sent me.
10 ¶ Sing and rejoice, O daughter of Zion: for, lo,
I come, and I will dwell in the midst of thee, saith
the LORD.
11 And many nations shall be joined to the LORD
in that day, and shall be my people: and I will
dwell in the midst of thee, and thou shalt know
that the LORD of hosts hath sent me unto thee.
12 And the LORD shall inherit Judah his portion
in the holy land, and shall choose Jerusalem again.
13 Be silent, O all flesh, before the LORD: for he is
raised up out of his holy habitation.

CHAPTER 3

AND he shewed me Joshua the high priest
standing before the angel of the LORD, and Satan

---

2. In the opening vision, the man on the red horse represents Christ. Indeed, the vision identifies Him as the angel of the Lord, one of the frequent designations of Christ in His preincarnate appearances in the Old Testament. His activity in the vision is instructive. The fact that He is present with His people in their low estate (among the myrtles in the valley) is evidence of Immanuel theology (God with us). It is always a comfort to know that regardless of our circumstance, as believers we can be assured that our Savior is with us and that He will not leave us alone. His intercession for Israel in their lowly condition is a wonderful reminder of Christ's constant intercessory ministry for us. He saw their need and prayed for resolution. As our faithful high priest, He ever lives to intercede and He does so from the reality of knowing by experience all our infirmities.

Chapter 2: *Zechariah's vision of a man with a measuring line forbidden to measure Jerusalem is the basis of his appeal to the exiles remaining in Babylon to return to Jerusalem because of the great expansion God has purposed for His people.*

Man with the Measuring Line (2:1–13)

2:1–5 The essential point of the third vision is that God's purpose for His people is greater than their expectations. Since the city was still in ruins, measuring Jerusalem was an act of faith in God's promise to restore Jerusalem after the captivity. But measuring a city implies borders, city limits. However, this Jerusalem would be without borders because of a huge population and without defensive walls because God's presence would be its security.

2:6–13 Zechariah exhorts those remaining in Babylon to return to Judah to experience the blessing of growth and security symbolized in the vision.

2:6 *the land of the north.* The typical direction from which hostile armies invaded the land; here a reference to Babylon. *I have spread.* Like the spreading out of a garment; a reference to the worldwide expansion of God's people. *as the four winds.* In every direction.

2:8 *After the glory hath he sent me . . . spoiled you.* Most likely a reference to Christ and His mission to vindicate His people against those who had plundered them and thus display God's glory. *apple of his eye.* The pupil of the eye, which would be so sensitive to touch and therefore protected.

2:9 *I will shake mine hand.* A gesture of hostility, like shaking a fist.

2:11 The inclusion of Gentiles into the covenant community (*my people*) points to the expansion of the church (Eph. 2:14–22).

Thoughts for Personal/Family Worship: Chapter 2

1. **The surface lesson of the third vision is that God's purpose for His people is greater than expectation. This is a vivid illustration of the promise of Eph. 3:20—God is "able to do exceeding abundantly above all that we ask or think." It would have been a wonderful fulfillment of promise had God merely restored Jerusalem to its previous glory. But He had a purpose to dwell with His people and to increase them beyond comprehension. This should encourage us to be bold in our praying. Too often we fear to ask too much lest we become disappointed if He does not answer according to our expectations. Our notions of what is best or how God should answer are always limited by lack of knowledge or of faith. Let us trust Him for the best and know that He will supply our needs according to His riches in Christ Jesus. We should not limit God to our notions of what He should or can do.**
2. **That God regards His people as the pupil of His eye is a precious thought. As the eye is sensitive to touch, so God is sensitive to what may threaten us. To touch a child of God in hostility is tantamount to poking God in the eye. He will protect us with all His resources. It is an amazing truth that we are precious to Him and that He will take care of us.**
3. **This third vision encourages us to think on God's unfailing purpose for the church, His protection, and His gracious presence. It reveals the triumph of grace and assures us that whatever we see in this world (1) God will get the glory, (2) every enemy will be conquered, and (3) every believer will share in covenant promises and blessing. These are good reasons to worship: to hush and to be quiet and reverently calm (v. 13).**

standing at his right hand to resist him.
2 And the LORD said unto Satan, The LORD
rebuke thee, O Satan; even the LORD that hath
chosen Jerusalem rebuke thee: *is* not this a brand
plucked out of the fire?
3 Now Joshua was clothed with filthy garments,
and stood before the angel.
4 And he answered and spake unto those that
stood before him, saying, Take away the filthy
garments from him. And unto him he said,
Behold, I have caused thine iniquity to pass from
thee, and I will clothe thee with change of raiment.
5 And I said, Let them set a fair mitre upon his
head. So they set a fair mitre upon his head, and
clothed him with garments. And the angel of the
LORD stood by.
6 And the angel of the LORD protested unto
Joshua, saying,
7 Thus saith the LORD of hosts; If thou wilt walk
in my ways, and if thou wilt keep my charge, then
thou shalt also judge my house, and shalt also
keep my courts, and I will give thee places to walk
among these that stand by.
8 Hear now, O Joshua the high priest, thou, and
thy fellows that sit before thee: for they *are* men
wondered at: for, behold, I will bring forth my
servant the BRANCH.
9 For behold the stone that I have laid before
Joshua; upon one stone *shall be* seven eyes:
behold, I will engrave the graving thereof, saith
the LORD of hosts, and I will remove the iniquity
of that land in one day.
10 In that day, saith the LORD of hosts, shall ye
call every man his neighbour under the vine and
under the fig tree.

CHAPTER 4

AND the angel that talked with me came again,
and waked me, as a man that is wakened out of
his sleep,
2 And said unto me, What seest thou? And I

Chapter 3: *Zechariah sees Joshua the high priest dressed in filthy garments being accused by Satan but acquitted by God and then the Branch whose coming removes iniquity in a single day.*

Joshua and the Branch (3:1–10)

3:1–10 The essential point concerns the personal issue of salvation from sin and moral defilement. Joshua, the high priest, is in view both in his person and in his office as the representative of men before God. He stands before God filthy and defenseless, but God graciously removes the filthy garments replacing them with splendid ones. This pictures the forgiveness of sins. The salient points of the vision picture in explicit detail the elements of justification: the need (guilt); the act (pardon, provision of righteousness); the ground (the coming and work of the Branch); and the demand (godliness).

3:1 *Satan . . . to resist.* The same root; "the accuser to accuse" or "Satan to be Satan."

3:2 *a brand plucked out of the fire.* A log salvaged from the fire.

3:3 *filthy.* Detestable and disgusting foulness of excrement or vomit; vivid picture of sin (Isa. 64:6).

3:4 Removing the dirty garments pictures pardon. *iniquity.* In the Old Testament, this is the principal word for guilt as the consequence of sin, both the objective fact (the significance here) and subjective feeling. *change of raiment.* Costly, white, and festive garments; pictures the imputation of righteousness.

3:5 *fair mitre.* A ceremonially clean turban or headband, part of the holy and high priestly wardrobe.

3:6 *protested.* Admonished or exhorted.

3:7 *charge.* Obligation or service, referring to obedience to God's requirements. *places to walk.* Free access. *among these that stand by.* Those in v. 4 who did God's bidding, most likely His heavenly attendants.

3:8 *men wondered at.* Literally, "men of a sign." Joshua and his fellow priests were symbolic of *my servant the BRANCH*, a messianic title meaning "shoot" or "sprout." In addition to servant, see the Branch as king (Jer. 23:5–6; 33:15–16); as God (Isa. 4:2; the Branch who is Jehovah); as the man (Zech. 6:12). Note how the Branch relates to how the Gospels portray Christ (Matthew—as king; Mark—as servant; Luke—as man; John—as God).

3:9 *the stone . . . seven eyes.* Either symbolic of Christ and His omniscience or, preferably, of God's kingdom upon which He directs His omniscience and care. *remove the iniquity in one day.* A reference to the sacrifice of Christ, the only means of dealing with guilt.

3:10 *under the vine and . . . fig tree.* Symbolic of the peace and prosperity resulting from the work of the Branch.

Thoughts for Personal/Family Worship: Chapter 3

1. **Justification is one of the great components of our complete salvation in Christ as believers. In a gracious act, God pardons our sin and accepts us as righteous by imputing Christ's righteousness to us, which we receive by faith alone. By reflecting on the picture of Joshua, even little children can understand something of this remarkable truth. The filthy garments picture the terrible stain of guilt we have before God. The removal of the garments pictures God's gracious forgiveness, and receiving the new garments points to the imputation of Christ's righteousness that gives us acceptance with God. This shows that we need more than forgiveness for what we have done in offending God; we need the garment of salvation, the robe of righteousness that Christ provides.**
2. **It is impossible to think about justification without thinking about what Christ has done. The prophecy of the Branch, God's servant, points to Christ in His humanity and life of humble obedience whereby He earned merit before God, weaving for us that robe of righteousness. He was made of woman under the law. His removal of iniquity in a single day points to His cross on which He shed His blood in atonement for our sins. Because of what Christ did in His life and in His death, we can be justified before the Holy God.**
3. **Since priests were man's representatives before God, what was said about Joshua and his colleagues is applicable to all true believers. Their being "men of a sign" (see note at 3:8) is instructive. They were symbolic of something greater than themselves. They were to attract attention to the Branch, to Christ. That sums up what should be true for every believer—to be like Christ, to be conformed to His image.**

said, I have looked, and behold a candlestick all
of gold, with a bowl upon the top of it, and his
seven lamps thereon, and seven pipes to the seven
lamps, which *are* upon the top thereof:
3 And two olive trees by it, one upon the right
side of the bowl, and the other upon the left *side*
thereof.
4 So I answered and spake to the angel that talked
with me, saying, What *are* these, my lord?
5 Then the angel that talked with me answered
and said unto me, Knowest thou not what these
be? And I said, No, my lord.
6 Then he answered and spake unto me, saying,
This *is* the word of the LORD unto Zerubbabel,
saying, Not by might, nor by power, but by my
spirit, saith the LORD of hosts.
7 Who *art* thou, O great mountain? before
Zerubbabel *thou shalt become* a plain: and he shall
bring forth the headstone *thereof with* shoutings,
crying, Grace, grace unto it.
8 Moreover the word of the LORD came unto me,
saying,
9 The hands of Zerubbabel have laid the
foundation of this house; his hands shall also
finish it; and thou shalt know that the LORD of
hosts hath sent me unto you.
10 For who hath despised the day of small things?
for they shall rejoice, and shall see the plummet
in the hand of Zerubbabel *with* those seven; they
are the eyes of the LORD, which run to and fro
through the whole earth.
11 ¶ Then answered I, and said unto him, What
are these two olive trees upon the right *side* of the
candlestick and upon the left *side* thereof?
12 And I answered again, and said unto him,
What *be these* two olive branches which through
the two golden pipes empty the golden *oil* out of
themselves?
13 And he answered me and said, Knowest thou
not what these *be*? And I said, No, my lord.
14 Then said he, These *are* the two anointed ones,
that stand by the Lord of the whole earth.

CHAPTER 5

THEN I turned, and lifted up mine eyes, and
looked, and behold a flying roll.
2 And he said unto me, What seest thou? And I

Chapter 4: *Zechariah sees a candlestick between two olive trees with pipes pouring oil directly from a bowl to picture the Spirit's empowerment of Zerubbabel to finish the temple.*

The Candlestick and Olive Trees (4:1–14)

4:1–14 The essential point is that God will supply Zerubbabel with the power of His Spirit to ensure the completion of the temple regardless of the opposition and discouragements that threaten the work. The salient points of the vision: *the candlestick*—the church and its ministry to bear witness; *two olive trees*—the Messiah from whom the Spirit proceeds; *seven pipes to the seven lamps*—the inexhaustible supply of oil for fueling the lamps, symbolic of the supply of the Holy Spirit. Verse 6 is the key to the interpretation.
4:2 *candlestick.* Lampstand, fueled with oil. *seven pipes to the seven lamps.* The lampstand had seven branches, each of which have a lamp. Each lamp was supplied with oil directly through pipes connected to the bowl on top of the lampstand.
4:6 The interpreting angel interrupts the vision with the interpretation. This word is directly to Zerubbabel, the civil leader, whose principal duty was to supervise the completion of the temple. *Not by might.* A reference to corporate power. *nor by power.* A reference to individual ability. The key principle: the Holy Spirit accomplishes success in God's work, not man.
4:7 *O great mountain . . . a plain.* Figurative for the obstacles that will be removed. *headstone.* The stone which marks the completion of a structure. The temple will be completed with joy (*shoutings*) and prayer for God's favor to rest upon it (*grace*).
4:10 *small things.* Alluding to the size of this temple compared to Solomon's (Hag. 2:3). *for they shall rejoice . . . earth.* Alternate translation: "Those seven, the eyes of the Lord which are roaming about the whole earth, will rejoice and see the plummet in the hand of Zerubbabel." Regardless of how insignificant our kingdom work appears, the omniscient God sees and rejoices in it.
4:14 *the two anointed ones.* Literally, "the two sons of oil." Typically, pointing to the true son of oil or anointed Messiah who unites in one Person each of the mediatorial offices, two of which are in view in Zerubbabel and Joshua, the central figures in visions 4 and 5.

Thoughts for Personal/Family Worship: Chapter 4

1. **The lampstand is a wonderful picture of the Christian's ministry to bear witness to Christ while in union with Him. The lampstand was all of one piece, and the lights from the six branches (symbolic of the church) shone toward the center shaft (symbolic of Christ). Christ is the light of the world, and believers are lights. The ministry of John the Baptist illustrates this (John 1:6–9). These lamps burned with oil, which represents the Holy Spirit. Meditate on this: the Holy Spirit enables believers to glorify Christ in their service. The remarkable point of Zechariah's vision is the pipes that run directly from the olive trees to the lamps, picturing the inexhaustible supply of Holy Spirit power. There is sufficient power for every Christian to fulfill his duty of bearing witness to Christ.**
2. **Verse 6, the key verse, is a humbling reminder that the church can fulfill its mission only in the power of the Spirit. The lamps could not burn without oil; the church cannot function without the Holy Spirit. Too often, the modern church substitutes administrative skills or seminars for success in the effort to advance the kingdom.**
3. **God rejoices when He sees the plummet in the hand of Zerubbabel (v. 10). This should encourage every believer to serve the Lord regardless of how big or small his ministry may appear. Holding a plumbline did not require any skill, but it was an essential task. Every Christian should be confident that however he or others estimate the value of his service, it pleases the Lord when done for Him.**

Chapter 5: *Zechariah sees a scroll flying over the earth on a mission to discover and deal with sinners followed by a woman, a personification of wickedness, who is transported in a basket to a house built for her in Shinar.*

answered, I see a flying roll; the length thereof *is*
twenty cubits, and the breadth thereof ten cubits.
3 Then said he unto me, This *is* the curse that
goeth forth over the face of the whole earth: for
every one that stealeth shall be cut off *as* on this
side according to it; and every one that sweareth
shall be cut off *as* on that side according to it.
4 I will bring it forth, saith the LORD of hosts,
and it shall enter into the house of the thief,
and into the house of him that sweareth falsely
by my name: and it shall remain in the midst of
his house, and shall consume it with the timber
thereof and the stones thereof.
5 ¶ Then the angel that talked with me went
forth, and said unto me, Lift up now thine eyes,
and see what *is* this that goeth forth.
6 And I said, What *is* it? And he said, This *is* an
ephah that goeth forth. He said moreover, This *is*
their resemblance through all the earth.
7 And, behold, there was lifted up a talent of lead:
and this *is* a woman that sitteth in the midst of
the ephah.
8 And he said, This *is* wickedness. And he cast
it into the midst of the ephah; and he cast the
weight of lead upon the mouth thereof.
9 Then lifted I up mine eyes, and looked, and,
behold, there came out two women, and the
wind *was* in their wings; for they had wings like
the wings of a stork: and they lifted up the ephah
between the earth and the heaven.
10 Then said I to the angel that talked with me,
Whither do these bear the ephah?
11 And he said unto me, To build it an house in
the land of Shinar: and it shall be established, and
set there upon her own base.

CHAPTER 6

AND I turned, and lifted up mine eyes, and
looked, and, behold, there came four chariots out
from between two mountains; and the moun-
tains *were* mountains of brass.
2 In the first chariot *were* red horses; and in the
second chariot black horses;
3 And in the third chariot white horses; and in
the fourth chariot grisled and bay horses.

The Flying Scroll (5:1–4)

5:1–4 The essential point is that God will justly and certainly deal with every sinner who has transgressed His law.

5:1 *a flying roll.* A scroll, representing the law of God as the standard of judgment. The fact that it is flying suggests the threat of judgment is in progress.

5:2 *twenty cubits . . . ten cubits.* Approximately 30 feet by 15 feet, corresponding to the dimensions of the holy place in the temple and tabernacle. Judgment will be according to the standard of the sanctuary, God's sacred law.

5:3 The curse on thieves and perjurers does not exclude or exempt other sinners but rather illustrates how specifically the law identifies sinners. *be cut off.* To be cleansed by purging. *This side . . . that side.* Both sides of the scroll, hence the totality of the law.

5:4 *I will bring it . . . it shall enter . . . it shall remain.* Refers to the curse of the broken law. *consume.* Literally, to "finish" or "bring to an end"; the work of judgment will be thorough and irreversible.

The Woman in the Ephah (5:5–11)

5:5–11 The essential point is God's ultimate triumph over evil that not only judges individual sinners (the flying scroll) but removes the every vestige of sin. The salient points of the vision: *the woman* in the *ephah*—the containment of wickedness; *two women* with *wings like . . . a stork*—agents of God's providence to carry out His judgments; *Shinar*—an old name for Babylon, symbolic of wickedness. God contains and confines wickedness to its own special place and thus eradicates its corrupting influence.

5:6 *ephah.* A large dry measure, roughly equivalent to a bushel basket. *their resemblance.* Literally, "their eye"; referring to their worldwide appearance.

5:7 *talent.* A circular disk, here the lead lid for the basket, which when lifted exposes a woman.

5:8 *wickedness.* The identity of the woman, a crucial interpretation of the vision. The Hebrew often uses the feminine gender to personify abstract ideas, whether vice or virtue. *upon the mouth.* The lid covered the opening (mouth) of the basket, securely trapping its content. Wickedness could not escape.

5:9 No specific identification of the two women is necessary; they simply represent the means used to transport the basket. *wings of a stork.* Symbolic of strength required for long-distance flight. Wickedness was going to be taken far away.

5:11 *Shinar.* Symbolic of earthly kingdoms hostile to God, a fitting place to store wickedness permanently (*house* implies fixed and permanent residence). *upon her own base.* In her own place.

Thoughts for Personal/Family Worship: Chapter 5

1. **The flying scroll, representing God's inflexible and unchanging laws, is like a military drone, an eye in the sky, on a mission to discover the enemy's presence and to detect his movements and behavior. So all the world is accountable to God, liable to the just penalty of the broken law, and incapable of escaping the just consequences. It is good to remember that God is no respecter of persons and that none will be exempt from His righteous judgment. To be outside of Christ is to be left with no defense against the curse.**
2. **The vision of the woman in the ephah provides occasion to express praise for the absolute triumph of the gospel. The day will come when every vestige of sin will be gone; there will be a complete reversal of the curse. The new heavens and new earth will be a perfect environment for God's people. Wickedness will be put in its place never again to tempt or to trouble. All of this is possible because Christ crushed the serpent's head.**

Chapter 6: ***Zechariah sees four chariots transporting multicolored horses that give assurance of victory and then uses the crowning of Joshua as an object lesson of the Messiah.***

The Four Chariots (6:1–8)

6:1–8 The essential point concerns the final defeat of Judah's enemies. This last vision parallels the first with similar imagery and an ironic conclusion in that it is the answer to the prayer of 1:12. In the first, horses reported that the nations who

4 Then I answered and said unto the angel that
talked with me, What *are* these, my lord?
5 And the angel answered and said unto me, These
are the four spirits of the heavens, which go forth
from standing before the Lord of all the earth.
6 The black horses which *are* therein go forth
into the north country; and the white go forth
after them; and the grisled go forth toward the
south country.
7 And the bay went forth, and sought to go that
they might walk to and fro through the earth: and
he said, Get you hence, walk to and fro through
the earth. So they walked to and fro through the
earth.
8 Then cried he upon me, and spake unto me,
saying, Behold, these that go toward the north
country have quieted my spirit in the north
country.
9 ¶ And the word of the LORD came unto me,
saying,
10 Take of *them of* the captivity, *even* of Heldai,
of Tobijah, and of Jedaiah, which are come from
Babylon, and come thou the same day, and go
into the house of Josiah the son of Zephaniah;
11 Then take silver and gold, and make crowns,
and set *them* upon the head of Joshua the son of
Josedech, the high priest;
12 And speak unto him, saying, Thus speaketh
the LORD of hosts, saying, Behold the man whose
name *is* The BRANCH; and he shall grow up out
of his place, and he shall build the temple of the
LORD:
13 Even he shall build the temple of the LORD;
and he shall bear the glory, and shall sit and rule
upon his throne; and he shall be a priest upon his
throne: and the counsel of peace shall be between
them both.
14 And the crowns shall be to Helem, and to To-
bijah, and to Jedaiah, and to Hen the son of Zeph-
aniah, for a memorial in the temple of the LORD.
15 And they *that are* far off shall come and build
in the temple of the LORD, and ye shall know that
the LORD of hosts hath sent me unto you. And *this*
shall come to pass, if ye will diligently obey the
voice of the LORD your God.

CHAPTER 7

AND it came to pass in the fourth year of king
Darius, *that* the word of the LORD came unto

---

had spoiled Judah were at rest; in the last horses bring a report that appeases the Lord implying that vengeance had been served. The salient points of the vision: *four chariots*—symbolic of God's might, the absence of drivers suggest God's control; *horses*—agents of divine providence; see notes at vv. 6–7 for significance of colors, but the overlapping of activity suggests that the colors may not be germane to the message.

6:1 *four chariots*. War wagons used for transport rather than battle; they moved mysteriously under divine direction without drivers to guide or beasts to pull. *mountains of brass*. Bronze; perhaps symbolic of judgment.

6:2 *In the first chariot*. The horses were in the cargo wagons.

6:3 *grisled*. Spotted or dappled. *bay*. Literally, "strong"; a reference to their strength and stamina not color.

6:5 *four spirits of the heavens*. Referring to angels (Ps. 104:4). *Spirits* also means "winds," which would suggest their swiftness to conduct their worldwide mission (the significance of *four*). *standing before the Lord*. Ready to serve.

6:6 *north*. A reference to Babylon. Black and white horses there may suggest severe calamity followed by victory. *south*. A reference to Egypt. The spotted horses there may suggest the changing fortunes associated with Egypt (Isa. 19:18–19).

6:7 The *bay* or strong horse went everywhere. Note the red were not commissioned, perhaps illustrating God's unlimited resources.

6:8 *quieted my spirit in the north country*. God's anger has ceased; His displeasure (1:15) has been appeased.

The Symbolic Crowning of Joshua (6:9–15)

6:9–15 The coronation ceremony was an actual enactment to be a picture prophecy of the priestly and kingly offices of the coming Messiah, the only One in whom these offices could unite. After the object lesson, Joshua had to vacate the throne.

6:11 *crowns*. A magnificently splendid crown. The Hebrew uses the plural to intensify.

6:12 *BRANCH*. A messianic title; see note at 3:8. *he shall grow up*. Literally, "he will sprout," the same root as *BRANCH*.

6:13 *rule . . . be a priest*. Uniquely fulfilled in Jesus Christ. *between them both*. Refers to the two offices of priest and king.

6:14 *crowns*. See 6:11. After the symbolic coronation, the crown was taken away from Joshua and kept in the temple as a reminder of the promised Royal Priest.

6:15 *know that . . . sent me*. Zechariah's conclusion to his first message. Widespread work on and completion of the temple would confirm his prophetic authority.

Thoughts for Personal/Family Worship: Chapter 6

1. **The final vision reminds us of the effectual power of the intercessory ministry of Christ. The sight of the hostile nations enjoying peace and security led to His prayer for God to show mercy to His people by executing vengeance on the enemy (1:12–15). The final vision details the answer to the prayer. Christ's prayers are always heard and answered; God will not turn away His Son. So as He sits exalted at God's right hand, He is interceding for believers who should rejoice, and boldly utilize Him as their Advocate.**
2. **The war wagons and angelic forces at God's command in Zechariah's day are still operative as God's providence rules and subdues all forces hostile to the advance of His kingdom. The God of then is the God of now. The fact that we cannot see what is happening in the spiritual realm does not mean that nothing is happening. Beyond our sight God is controlling everything to the certain accomplishment of His redemptive plan. Things had to be done in Zechariah's day for the preparation of the incarnation; things are being done in our day leading to the second coming. We may not understand what is happening at any given time, but faith rests in God's promise.**

QUESTIONS TO ANSWER (7:1—8:23)

Chapter 7: ***Zechariah entertains a question regarding a seventy-year fast and answers by exposing improper***

Zechariah in the fourth *day* of the ninth month,
even in Chisleu;
2 When they had sent unto the house of God
Sherezer and Regem-melech, and their men, to
pray before the LORD,
3 *And* to speak unto the priests which *were* in the
house of the LORD of hosts, and to the prophets,
saying, Should I weep in the fifth month, separat-
ing myself, as I have done these so many years?
4 ¶ Then came the word of the LORD of hosts
unto me, saying,
5 Speak unto all the people of the land, and to
the priests, saying, When ye fasted and mourned
in the fifth and seventh *month*, even those seventy
years, did ye at all fast unto me, *even* to me?
6 And when ye did eat, and when ye did drink,
did not ye eat *for yourselves*, and drink *for your-
selves*?
7 *Should ye* not *hear* the words which the
LORD hath cried by the former prophets, when
Jerusalem was inhabited and in prosperity, and
the cities thereof round about her, when *men*
inhabited the south and the plain?
8 ¶ And the word of the LORD came unto
Zechariah, saying,
9 Thus speaketh the LORD of hosts, saying,
Execute true judgment, and shew mercy and
compassions every man to his brother:
10 And oppress not the widow, nor the fatherless,
the stranger, nor the poor; and let none of you
imagine evil against his brother in your heart.
11 But they refused to hearken, and pulled away
the shoulder, and stopped their ears, that they
should not hear.
12 Yea, they made their hearts *as* an adamant
stone, lest they should hear the law, and the words
which the LORD of hosts hath sent in his spirit by
the former prophets: therefore came a great wrath
from the LORD of hosts.
13 Therefore it is come to pass, *that* as he cried,
and they would not hear; so they cried, and I
would not hear, saith the LORD of hosts:
14 But I scattered them with a whirlwind among
all the nations whom they knew not. Thus the
land was desolate after them, that no man passed
through nor returned: for they laid the pleasant
land desolate.

CHAPTER 8

AGAIN the word of the LORD of hosts came *to me*,
saying,

motives and by explaining God's preference for obedience that would have precluded the occasion for the fast.

One Question about Fasting (7:1–3)

7:3 *weep in the fifth month.* Commemorating the destruction of the temple that occurred in this month (2 Kings 25:8–9). *separating myself.* From food; hence, "to fast." Since the temple was soon to be completed, they questioned whether they should continue to fast in memory of its destruction.

Four Answers (7:4—8:23; marked by "the word of the LORD came")

Hypocritical Fasting (7:4–7)

7:5–6 The captivity generated several fasts, none of which were commanded by God. Whether fasting or eating, they did not factor God into their thinking.

7:7 Had they heeded the preaching of the preexilic prophets, the captivity could have been averted. *the south and the plain.* The geographical districts of the Negev and Shephelah or lowland.

Obedience Better (7:8–14)

7:8–14 The second answer expands on 7:7 by reviewing some of God's righteous demands that were ignored thus justifying the captivity. Obedience to God's demands is better than observing heartless rituals that God did not command.

7:9 *Execute true judgment.* Practice justice consistently. *mercy.* Covenant loyalty shown in acts of kindness. *compassions.* Acts of mercy or pity.

7:10 *imagine evil . . . in your heart.* To scheme or plot harm in your mind.

7:11 *to hearken.* To listen attentively. *pulled away the shoulder.* Literally, "to give a stubborn shoulder"; idiom for unwillingness to submit to authority. *stopped their ears.* "Made their ears heavy" to be unresponsive.

7:12 *their hearts as an adamant stone.* Their inner self (mind, will, and emotions) became as hard as a diamond. *in his spirit.* By His Spirit, the agent of revelation.

7:14 *I scattered them with a whirlwind.* One word in Hebrew, "I blew them away in a storm." *the land was desolate.* Uninhabited.

Thoughts for Personal/Family Worship: Chapter 7

1. God's answer to the question of fasting illustrates the frequent biblical warning that performing perfunctory religious rituals without a genuine heart for the Lord never pleases Him. God is never satisfied with religion without devotion. These fasts commemorating the captivity were of their own devising and were conducted without any thought toward God. Whatever their motive, it was not a service being rendered to God. It is all too easy to be taken up with the liturgical calendar or even routine services and assume that the mere exercise or observance pleases the Lord. Those that worship God must do so with genuine hearts (in spirit and truth), and God looks through the rituals right to the heart.

2. To obey is better than sacrifice (1 Sam. 15:22). Rather than the multiplication of offerings, God has revealed what is good (Mic. 6:6–8). God's explanation that captivity could have been averted if the people had obeyed the prophets and behaved righteously teaches the same truth. It is obedience to God that truly affirms love for Him (1 John 5:3). Once we find acceptance with God in Christ, we please Him when we trust and obey Him.

Chapter 8: ***Zechariah describes a scene of peace, security, and prosperity so marvelous that all the fasts of mourning will be replaced with feasts of celebration.***

Restoration in the Place of Devastation (8:1–17)

8:1–17 Zechariah's message of hope reaches a climax. Note the frequency of *the LORD of hosts*, the divine title expressing

2 Thus saith the LORD of hosts; I was jealous for
Zion with great jealousy, and I was jealous for her
with great fury.
3 Thus saith the LORD; I am returned unto Zion,
and will dwell in the midst of Jerusalem: and
Jerusalem shall be called a city of truth; and the
mountain of the LORD of hosts the holy mountain.
4 Thus saith the LORD of hosts; There shall yet
old men and old women dwell in the streets of
Jerusalem, and every man with his staff in his
hand for very age.
5 And the streets of the city shall be full of boys
and girls playing in the streets thereof.
6 Thus saith the LORD of hosts; If it be marvellous
in the eyes of the remnant of this people in these
days, should it also be marvellous in mine eyes?
saith the LORD of hosts.
7 Thus saith the LORD of hosts; Behold, I will save
my people from the east country, and from the
west country;
8 And I will bring them, and they shall dwell
in the midst of Jerusalem: and they shall be my
people, and I will be their God, in truth and in
righteousness.
9 ¶ Thus saith the LORD of hosts; Let your hands
be strong, ye that hear in these days these words
by the mouth of the prophets, which *were* in the
day *that* the foundation of the house of the LORD
of hosts was laid, that the temple might be built.
10 For before these days there was no hire for
man, nor any hire for beast; neither *was there any*
peace to him that went out or came in because of
the affliction: for I set all men every one against
his neighbour.
11 But now I *will* not *be* unto the residue of this
people as in the former days, saith the LORD of
hosts.
12 For the seed *shall be* prosperous; the vine
shall give her fruit, and the ground shall give her
increase, and the heavens shall give their dew; and
I will cause the remnant of this people to possess
all these *things*.
13 And it shall come to pass, *that* as ye were a
curse among the heathen, O house of Judah, and
house of Israel; so will I save you, and ye shall be
a blessing: fear not, *but* let your hands be strong.
14 For thus saith the LORD of hosts; As I thought
to punish you, when your fathers provoked me to
wrath, saith the LORD of hosts, and I repented not:
15 So again have I thought in these days to do
well unto Jerusalem and to the house of Judah:
fear ye not.
16 ¶ These *are* the things that ye shall do; Speak
ye every man the truth to his neighbour; execute
the judgment of truth and peace in your gates:
17 And let none of you imagine evil in your hearts
against his neighbour; and love no false oath: for
all these *are things* that I hate, saith the LORD.
18 ¶ And the word of the LORD of hosts came
unto me, saying,
19 Thus saith the LORD of hosts; The fast of the
fourth *month*, and the fast of the fifth, and the fast
of the seventh, and the fast of the tenth, shall be to
the house of Judah joy and gladness, and cheerful
feasts; therefore love the truth and peace.
20 Thus saith the LORD of hosts; *It shall* yet *come*
to pass, that there shall come people, and the
inhabitants of many cities:
21 And the inhabitants of one *city* shall go to an-
other, saying, Let us go speedily to pray before the
LORD, and to seek the LORD of hosts: I will go also.
22 Yea, many people and strong nations shall
come to seek the LORD of hosts in Jerusalem, and
to pray before the LORD.
23 Thus saith the LORD of hosts; In those days *it*
shall come to pass, that ten men shall take hold out

Jehovah's covenant faithfulness coupled with power and authority. The promises that seemed to be too fantastic to be possible were certain because of who made the promises.

8:2 *I was jealous . . . with great fury.* Intensive expressions describing God's fervent passion and zeal for His people.

8:3–5 The Lord's presence is protection (see ch. 2). In times of war, streets were dangerous places, but with the Lord present they were places where the most defenseless in wartime (the old and young) would be safe.

8:6 *marvellous.* Difficult, beyond one's power; a word often referring to God's extraordinary miraculous acts. What was incomprehensible to those receiving the promise was not beyond God's ability to do.

8:7 *east . . . west.* Polar expressions used to designate totality; God will retrieve His people from wherever they are.

8:9 In view of the glorious future, those who were still living in the ruins were exhorted to work diligently in rebuilding the temple. Prophecy is an effective motivator to service.

8:10–12 The Lord's presence brings prosperity. The presence of the enemy (*affliction*) made conducting business impossible (*no hire*), but the day was coming when there would be no obstacles to productivity.

8:13 *curse.* Regarded as light, despised. *blessing.* A fulfillment of God's covenant purpose for the nation (Gen. 12:2–3) centered in Messiah. The messianic hope was incentive to the temple work so essential to the fullness of time (*let your hands be strong*).

8:14 *I thought.* Literally, "I planned or purposed" (v. 15). *I repented not.* I did not relent or take pity.

8:16–17 The Lord's presence demands piety. *execute the judgment of truth and peace.* Judge truly, even judgment resulting in peace. *let none . . . imagine evil.* Do not think or devise harm.

Joy in the Place of Mourning (8:18–23)

8:18–23 A worldwide revival of true religion removes every reason for fasting.

8:21 *Let us go speedily to pray.* Let us go earnestly to entreat favor. *I will also go.* I myself also determine to go; an expression of personal resolve and self-interest.

8:22 *strong nations.* Mighty Gentile nations. *to pray.* Specifically, to entreat favor.

8:23 *ten men shall take hold out of all languages.* Ten men from every language group will grasp or hang on. Ten Gentiles to every Jew pictures an indefinitely huge number that will

of all languages of the nations, even shall take hold
of the skirt of him that is a Jew, saying, We will go
with you: for we have heard *that* God *is* with you.

CHAPTER 9

THE burden of the word of the LORD in the land of
Hadrach, and Damascus *shall be* the rest thereof:
when the eyes of man, as of all the tribes of Israel,
shall be toward the LORD.
2 And Hamath also shall border thereby; Tyrus,
and Zidon, though it be very wise.
3 And Tyrus did build herself a strong hold, and
heaped up silver as the dust, and fine gold as the
mire of the streets.
4 Behold, the Lord will cast her out, and he
will smite her power in the sea; and she shall be
devoured with fire.
5 Ashkelon shall see *it*, and fear; Gaza also *shall
see it*, and be very sorrowful, and Ekron; for her
expectation shall be ashamed; and the king shall
perish from Gaza, and Ashkelon shall not be
inhabited.
6 And a bastard shall dwell in Ashdod, and I will
cut off the pride of the Philistines.
7 And I will take away his blood out of his mouth,
and his abominations from between his teeth: but
he that remaineth, even he, *shall be* for our God,
and he shall be as a governor in Judah, and Ekron
as a Jebusite.
8 And I will encamp about mine house because
of the army, because of him that passeth by, and
because of him that returneth: and no oppressor
shall pass through them any more: for now have I
seen with mine eyes.
9 ¶ Rejoice greatly, O daughter of Zion; shout, O
daughter of Jerusalem: behold, thy King cometh
unto thee: he *is* just, and having salvation; lowly,
and riding upon an ass, and upon a colt the foal
of an ass.
10 And I will cut off the chariot from Ephraim,
and the horse from Jerusalem, and the battle bow
shall be cut off: and he shall speak peace unto the
heathen: and his dominion *shall be* from sea *even*
to sea, and from the river *even* to the ends of the
earth.
11 As for thee also, by the blood of thy covenant
I have sent forth thy prisoners out of the pit
wherein *is* no water.
12 ¶ Turn you to the strong hold, ye prisoners of

---

worship the true God—a prophecy of Gentile inclusion in the church and universal expansion of God's kingdom.

Thoughts for Personal/Family Worship: Chapter 8

1. **Zechariah's application of the grand prophecies illustrates a key function of biblical prophecy that is as relevant for us as those to whom Zechariah preached. What God reveals about the future is to affect life in the present. Although those who heard Zechariah's message never personally witnessed the fulfillment of all the details, they were to be encouraged and to engage fervently in serving the Lord—rebuilding the temple. So must we, in view of all the future things associated with Christ's second coming, be diligent and faithful in our service. Christ has told us "to occupy" or to stay busy with God-honoring tasks until He comes (Luke 19:13).**
2. **The prophecy regarding Gentile inclusion in God's kingdom is reason for all Gentile believers in the church to rejoice because in part they represent the fulfillment. Although God had a special purpose for Israel as the human ancestry for Christ, it was His grand design in the gospel that all of the world would be blessed. Let us thank the Lord that Christ tore down the wall of partition giving both Jew and Gentile equal access to the Father through His blood (Eph. 2:14–18).**

PROPHETIC ORACLES TO BLESS (9:1—14:21)

The First Oracle (9:1—11:17; marked by "The burden of the word of the LORD")

Chapter 9: *Zechariah declares God's judgment on nations surrounding Israel, announces the coming messianic king, and assures of God's defense of His people.*

Judgment of Enemies (9:1–8)

9:1 *The burden.* The prophetic oracle or pronouncement. *Hadrach . . . Damascus.* Principal cities in Syria, north of Israel. *shall be the rest.* These cities will be the resting place of the oracle; i.e., the subject of the divine oracle. *when the eyes of man . . . the LORD.* The Hebrew is difficult and could be translated, "The Lord's eye is on mankind and all the tribes of Israel," referring to God's universal knowledge.

9:2 *And Hamath also shall border thereby.* Another Syrian city, whose district borders the others, will be subject to the same message. *Tyrus . . . Zidon.* Phoenician cities whose skills cannot exempt them from the word (*though it be very wise*).

9:5 *Ashkelon . . . Gaza . . . Ekron.* Philistine cities. *her expectation shall be ashamed.* Her hope will dry up.

9:6 *bastard.* Half-breed or child of incest. *the pride.* Majesty or excellence.

9:7 *his blood.* The Hebrew is plural, referring to bloodshed. Its parallelism to *abominations* (something abhorred, associated with idolatry) suggests the blood shed in sacrifices that were part of a pagan sacred meal (hence, *mouth . . . teeth*).

9:8 *I will encamp . . . because of the army.* Rather, "I will encamp as a guard." *passeth by . . . returneth.* Idiom for going back and forth. The Lord is with His people as a guard against all invaders.

The Coming King (9:9—10:12)

9:9 Fulfilled specifically at Christ's triumphal entry to Jerusalem at the beginning of His passion (Matt. 21:4–5). As king, Christ is promised (*cometh*); righteous (*just*, animated with righteousness); victorious (*having salvation*, literally, "being delivered," see Ps. 18:50); humble (*lowly*, afflicted from outside agents). *an ass, and upon a colt.* "And" is explicative; hence "even upon a colt." He rode only one animal.

9:10 Israel will be disarmed because the king will be their defense. *his dominion.* The borderless kingdom is uniquely messianic (Ps. 72:8).

9:11 *by the blood of thy covenant.* Because of it. God's covenant with them guaranteed their preservation (symbolized by rescue from the pit) with a view to the coming king. There had to be an Israel if there was going to be the Christ.

hope: even to day do I declare *that* I will render
double unto thee;
13 When I have bent Judah for me, filled the bow
with Ephraim, and raised up thy sons, O Zion,
against thy sons, O Greece, and made thee as the
sword of a mighty man.
14 And the LORD shall be seen over them, and his
arrow shall go forth as the lightning: and the Lord
GOD shall blow the trumpet, and shall go with
whirlwinds of the south.
15 The LORD of hosts shall defend them; and
they shall devour, and subdue with sling stones;
and they shall drink, *and* make a noise as through
wine; and they shall be filled like bowls, *and* as the
corners of the altar.
16 And the LORD their God shall save them in
that day as the flock of his people: for *they shall
be as* the stones of a crown, lifted up as an ensign
upon his land.
17 For how great *is* his goodness, and how great
is his beauty! corn shall make the young men
cheerful, and new wine the maids.

CHAPTER 10

ASK ye of the LORD rain in the time of the latter
rain; *so* the LORD shall make bright clouds, and
give them showers of rain, to every one grass in
the field.
2 For the idols have spoken vanity, and the
diviners have seen a lie, and have told false
dreams; they comfort in vain: therefore they went
their way as a flock, they were troubled, because
there was no shepherd.
3 Mine anger was kindled against the shepherds,
and I punished the goats: for the LORD of hosts
hath visited his flock the house of Judah, and hath
made them as his goodly horse in the battle.
4 Out of him came forth the corner, out of him
the nail, out of him the battle bow, out of him
every oppressor together.
5 ¶ And they shall be as mighty *men*, which tread
down *their enemies* in the mire of the streets in
the battle: and they shall fight, because the LORD
is with them, and the riders on horses shall be
confounded.
6 And I will strengthen the house of Judah, and
I will save the house of Joseph, and I will bring
them again to place them; for I have mercy upon
them: and they shall be as though I had not cast
them off: for I *am* the LORD their God, and will
hear them.
7 And *they of* Ephraim shall be like a mighty *man*,
and their heart shall rejoice as through wine: yea,
their children shall see *it*, and be glad; their heart
shall rejoice in the LORD.
8 I will hiss for them, and gather them; for I have
redeemed them: and they shall increase as they
have increased.
9 And I will sow them among the people: and

9:12 *prisoners of hope.* Prisoners who have hope (v. 11). *render double.* Restore a double portion; they will gain more than they lost.
9:13 As the Lord used Assyria and Babylon as His instruments of chastisement against Israel, He will use Israel as His chosen weapon against the enemy represented by Greece.
9:14 *whirlwinds of the south.* The roaring southern winds picture the Lord's destruction of the enemy.
9:15 *subdue with sling stones.* Literally, "subdue the stones of sling," suggesting the ease of defense in light of the enemy's meager weaponry. *they shall be filled like bowls . . . altar.* Imagery of the collecting and overflowing of blood from the temple sacrifices; in their victory they would be covered with the blood of their enemies.

Thoughts for Personal/Family Worship: Chapter 9

1. **As Israel was to shout and rejoice over the certain prospect of the coming King, so we should rejoice over the King who has come and is coming again. As that coming King was the message of hope to both Jews and Gentiles (9:10) in Zechariah's day, He remains the only hope for man today.**
2. **That Christ's kingdom is without borders (v. 10) is a source of great confidence. A king's authority is always limited by the borders of His kingdom, so a borderless kingdom speaks of unlimited authority. Kingdoms come and go because kings cannot hold on to what little they govern, but Christ's kingdom is without threat for every human government exists within the borders of His. He rules all for His own glory and the good of His people. To be a citizen of His kingdom is reason for joy (v. 17).**

Chapter 10: *God punishes the useless shepherds and blesses His people with the coming Messiah, strength for battle, and a total restoration described as a new exodus.*
10:1–2 A reminder that blessing comes from the Lord not idols and a warning not to revert to the preexilic sins of idolatry. *the idols have spoken vanity.* "The *teraphim* (a common idol) speak wickedness or iniquitous trouble." *comfort in vain.* To no purpose. Those who listened to them wandered around (*went*) and were afflicted (*troubled*).
10:3 *Shepherds* and *goats* (i.e., he goats) refer to leaders. *punished . . . visited.* Same Hebrew word meaning to inspect or examine. What is discovered in the inspection is cause for punishment or blessing. *his goodly horse.* A horse of majesty or power; God will empower Judah as a war machine.
10:4 The Messiah, sent from God (*out of him*) to be the agent of punishment and blessing, is described with four names. *corner.* The sure and stable foundation. *nail.* The ability to bear the load of support. *battle bow.* The active champion and warrior. *oppressor.* The absolute ruler. The Hebrew is difficult, but the word designates a ruler whether good or bad. Here a designation of Messiah as the ruler whose authority is not oppressive but for sure absolute.
10:6 *Judah . . . Joseph.* God's blessing extends to the whole nation—no more division between northern and southern kingdoms.
10:7 *Ephraim.* Common designation for the northern kingdom that now shares in the blessing of restoration.
10:8 *hiss.* To summon by whistling.
10:9 *sow.* To spread, referring to the expansion of the

they shall remember me in far countries; and they
shall live with their children, and turn again.
10 I will bring them again also out of the land of
Egypt, and gather them out of Assyria; and I will
bring them into the land of Gilead and Lebanon;
and *place* shall not be found for them.
11 And he shall pass through the sea with affliction, and shall smite the waves in the sea, and all
the deeps of the river shall dry up: and the pride
of Assyria shall be brought down, and the sceptre
of Egypt shall depart away.
12 And I will strengthen them in the LORD; and
they shall walk up and down in his name, saith
the LORD.

CHAPTER 11

OPEN thy doors, O Lebanon, that the fire may
devour thy cedars.
2 Howl, fir tree; for the cedar is fallen; because the
mighty are spoiled: howl, O ye oaks of Bashan; for
the forest of the vintage is come down.
3 ¶ *There is* a voice of the howling of the shepherds;
for their glory is spoiled: a voice of the roaring of
young lions; for the pride of Jordan is spoiled.
4 Thus saith the LORD my God; Feed the flock of
the slaughter;
5 Whose possessors slay them, and hold
themselves not guilty: and they that sell them say,
Blessed *be* the LORD; for I am rich: and their own
shepherds pity them not.
6 For I will no more pity the inhabitants of the
land, saith the LORD: but, lo, I will deliver the men
every one into his neighbour's hand, and into the
hand of his king: and they shall smite the land,
and out of their hand I will not deliver *them*.
7 And I will feed the flock of slaughter, *even* you,
O poor of the flock. And I took unto me two
staves; the one I called Beauty, and the other I
called Bands; and I fed the flock.
8 Three shepherds also I cut off in one month;
and my soul lothed them, and their soul also
abhorred me.
9 Then said I, I will not feed you: that that dieth,
let it die; and that that is to be cut off, let it be
cut off; and let the rest eat every one the flesh of
another.
10 ¶ And I took my staff, *even* Beauty, and cut it
asunder, that I might break my covenant which I
had made with all the people.
11 And it was broken in that day: and so the poor
of the flock that waited upon me knew that it *was*
the word of the LORD.
12 And I said unto them, If ye think good, give *me*
my price; and if not, forbear. So they weighed for
my price thirty *pieces* of silver.

---

kingdom. *remember.* To acknowledge, make mention of.

10:10 *out of the land of Egypt.* The imagery of a new exodus. *land of Gilead and Lebanon.* Places proverbial for their fertility; the Lord brings His people to prosperity. *and place shall not be found for them.* Hyperbolic language to express the huge population.

10:11 Allusions to exodus and conquest events portray the total defeat of Assyria and Egypt, representatives of all hostility to God and His people.

Thoughts for Personal/Family Worship: Chapter 10

1. **The word translated "punished" and "visited" in 10:3 means to inspect or examine and is a sobering reminder that God is more than a casual observer of the affairs of man. He is the divine, all-thorough inspector who investigates and examines every man and deals with men according to what He knows. He punishes those not right with Him and blesses those who seek to live without offense to Him. None can escape the all-seeing eye of God and that should encourage piety. We should all strive for the testimony of David in Ps. 17:3.**
2. **Reflecting on the titles of Christ in Zech. 10:4 should generate worship and thanksgiving. As the corner, the sure foundation, He is the only trustworthy object of faith—the only hope for sinners. As the nail, He holds up under any weight and load. He bore the load of our guilt and sin and is able to hold our troubles and cares. We can hang it all on Him. As the battle bow, He subdues all of His and our enemies; He is the able and unfailing defender of His people. As the absolute ruler, He rules either by grace or with iron. It is critical to be a citizen rather than enemy of His kingdom.**

Chapter 11: *Zechariah describes the consequences of rejecting the good shepherd and pronounces judgment on the wicked shepherds who lead the people astray.*

The Rejected Shepherd (11:1–17)

11:1–2 Addressing the trees and forests of their impending destruction sets a foreboding scene of catastrophe. *the forest of the vintage.* The forest of the inaccessible, referring to a dense forest. Most likely, the new wave of oppression refers to the period of Greek and Roman domination.

11:3 *shepherds . . . young lions.* Images referring to the leaders of the people. *pride of Jordan.* Refers to fertility surrounding the river. The *howling* expresses their sense of doom.

11:4 *Feed the flock.* God uses the prophet as an object lesson of shepherds (11:15).

11:5 Describes the haggling between merchants (*possessors* or buyers) and shepherds in the sheep market, each seeking a profit at the expense of the doomed sheep.

11:7 The prophet begins his symbolic ministry by inscribing two sticks, one called *Beauty* (i.e., favor) and the other *Bands* (i.e., that which binds).

11:8–9 Three unidentified leaders, with whom the prophet shared mutual animosity, were expelled from office, but apparently the level of hostility against the prophet caused him to abandon them to the slaughter.

11:10 The breaking of the *staff* symbolized God's giving them over to judgment.

11:11 That the breaking was recognized as the *word of the LORD* demonstrates the divine authority of symbolic acts.

11:12 In keeping with his role of shepherd, the prophet asks for his wages (*price*) for services rendered. *thirty pieces of silver.* That this was the amount of compensation for a slain slave (Ex. 21:32) seems coincidental.

13 And the LORD said unto me, Cast it unto the
potter: a goodly price that I was prised at of them.
And I took the thirty *pieces* of silver, and cast them
to the potter in the house of the LORD.
14 Then I cut asunder mine other staff, *even*
Bands, that I might break the brotherhood
between Judah and Israel.
15 ¶ And the LORD said unto me, Take unto thee
yet the instruments of a foolish shepherd.
16 For, lo, I will raise up a shepherd in the land,
which shall not visit those that be cut off, neither
shall seek the young one, nor heal that that is bro-
ken, nor feed that that standeth still: but he shall
eat the flesh of the fat, and tear their claws in pieces.
17 Woe to the idol shepherd that leaveth the
flock! the sword *shall be* upon his arm, and upon
his right eye: his arm shall be clean dried up, and
his right eye shall be utterly darkened.

CHAPTER 12

THE burden of the word of the LORD for Israel,
saith the LORD, which stretcheth forth the
heavens, and layeth the foundation of the earth,
and formeth the spirit of man within him.
2 Behold, I will make Jerusalem a cup of
trembling unto all the people round about, when
they shall be in the siege both against Judah *and*
against Jerusalem.
3 ¶ And in that day will I make Jerusalem a
burdensome stone for all people: all that burden
themselves with it shall be cut in pieces, though
all the people of the earth be gathered together
against it.
4 In that day, saith the LORD, I will smite every
horse with astonishment, and his rider with
madness: and I will open mine eyes upon the
house of Judah, and will smite every horse of the
people with blindness.
5 And the governors of Judah shall say in their
heart, The inhabitants of Jerusalem *shall be* my
strength in the LORD of hosts their God.
6 ¶ In that day will I make the governors of Judah
like an hearth of fire among the wood, and like a
torch of fire in a sheaf; and they shall devour all
the people round about, on the right hand and on
the left: and Jerusalem shall be inhabited again in
her own place, *even* in Jerusalem.
7 The LORD also shall save the tents of Judah first,
that the glory of the house of David and the glory
of the inhabitants of Jerusalem do not magnify
themselves against Judah.
8 In that day shall the LORD defend the inhabitants
of Jerusalem; and he that is feeble among them at
that day shall be as David; and the house of David
shall be as God, as the angel of the LORD before
them.
9 ¶ And it shall come to pass in that day, *that* I

11:13 *Cast it unto the potter.* A gesture of disgust over the inadequacy of the wage. *a goodly price that I was prised at of them.* "A magnificent sum which I was valued or appraised by them," a sarcastic remark to highlight further the meagerness of the wage. The prophet's being paid off for thirty pieces of silver points to Christ who was betrayed for that price (Matt. 26:15; 27:3,9). The point of similarity is the rejection of both shepherds.
11:14 The nation would not only experience devastation (v. 10) but also disunity.
11:15–16 The prophet becomes an object lesson of the foolish shepherd. *instruments.* Implements. God's raising up abusive and self-serving leaders is one way He punishes.
11:17 God raises up the foolish shepherd as an agent of judgment, and sovereignly holds the shepherd accountable for his behavior.

Thoughts for Personal/Family Worship: Chapter 11

1. **God's judgment on the foolish shepherd's arm and eye is significant because these two body parts are instrumental to a shepherd's work, to attend to and to watch over the flock. The failure of the foolish shepherd puts in bold the wonderful faithfulness of our good shepherd, who loves, guides, guards, feeds, seeks, and cares for His flock. He gathers His lambs in His arms (Isa. 40:11), and with His all-seeing eye He seeks for His sheep (Ezek. 34:11).**
2. **As unfair as it was for the prophet's labors to be valued at such a meager sum, how much more does Christ's betrayal for that same paltry sum add to the shame that He suffered for us. We should be ever amazed at the wonder of His grace that brought Him down from His ivory palace (Ps. 45:8) to be so rejected and scorned by sinners. Let us never get over the extent of His humiliation endured for our sakes.**

The Second Oracle (12:1—14:21; marked by "The burden of the word of the LORD")

Chapter 12: *Zechariah announces God's intent to deliver the nation from every enemy and to bring them to a spiritual awakening and contrition over their rejection of Him.*

National Deliverance (12:1–9)

12:1 Referring to God's creative work emphasizes the unique power and authority underlying His word.
12:2 *a cup of trembling.* Those who attempt a siege against Judah and Jerusalem will stagger and reel like drunkards.
12:3 *in that day.* A technical expression for a day of the Lord, an occasion of direct divine intervention. *a burdensome stone.* A weighty or heavy stone. *all that burden themselves . . . pieces.* Literally, "all who lever it up (in an effort to carry it) will certainly make gashes in themselves." *though all.* Even if the world gathered against them, the result would be the same.
12:4 A picture of mass confusion as the horses are blinded and in panic (*astonishment*).
12:6 *hearth of fire.* A movable stove or pot containing flame. The imagery suggests the ease with which the leaders of the city, being enabled by God, dispose of the enemies.
12:7 The order of deliverance suggests the equality among God's people.
12:8 *the house of David shall be as God.* Significantly, the next king from David's house would be Messiah Himself. *as the angel of the LORD.* The messenger who is the Lord, a designation of the preincarnate Christ.

will seek to destroy all the nations that come
against Jerusalem.
10 And I will pour upon the house of David, and
upon the inhabitants of Jerusalem, the spirit of
grace and of supplications: and they shall look
upon me whom they have pierced, and they shall
mourn for him, as one mourneth for *his* only *son*,
and shall be in bitterness for him, as one that is in
bitterness for *his* firstborn.
11 In that day shall there be a great mourning in
Jerusalem, as the mourning of Hadadrimmon in
the valley of Megiddon.
12 And the land shall mourn, every family apart;
the family of the house of David apart, and their
wives apart; the family of the house of Nathan
apart, and their wives apart;
13 The family of the house of Levi apart, and
their wives apart; the family of Shimei apart, and
their wives apart;
14 All the families that remain, every family apart,
and their wives apart.

CHAPTER 13

IN that day there shall be a fountain opened to
the house of David and to the inhabitants of
Jerusalem for sin and for uncleanness.
2 ¶ And it shall come to pass in that day, saith the
LORD of hosts, *that* I will cut off the names of the
idols out of the land, and they shall no more be
remembered: and also I will cause the prophets
and the unclean spirit to pass out of the land.
3 And it shall come to pass, *that* when any shall
yet prophesy, then his father and his mother that
begat him shall say unto him, Thou shalt not live;
for thou speakest lies in the name of the LORD:
and his father and his mother that begat him shall
thrust him through when he prophesieth.
4 And it shall come to pass in that day, *that* the
prophets shall be ashamed every one of his vision,
when he hath prophesied; neither shall they wear
a rough garment to deceive:
5 But he shall say, I *am* no prophet, I *am* an
husbandman; for man taught me to keep cattle
from my youth.
6 And *one* shall say unto him, What *are* these
wounds in thine hands? Then he shall answer,
Those with which I was wounded *in* the house of
my friends.
7 ¶ Awake, O sword, against my shepherd, and
against the man *that is* my fellow, saith the LORD
of hosts: smite the shepherd, and the sheep shall
be scattered: and I will turn mine hand upon the
little ones.

Spiritual Deliverance (12:10—13:9)

12:10 *I will pour . . . the spirit of grace and of supplications.* Most likely, the Holy Spirit that dispenses grace and generates prayer; a spiritual awakening. *look upon me whom they have pierced . . . mourn for him.* The New Testament confirms the reference to Christ (John 19:37; Rev. 1:7). Note the trinitarian framework: *me* and *him* points to John 10:30, "I and my Father are one." The mourning is evidence of repentance.

12:11–14 The contrition extends to every segment of the nation, perhaps pointing to that universal conversion mentioned by Paul in Rom. 11:26. *as the mourning of Hadadrimmon.* The exact location is uncertain. But being in the valley of Megiddo, the place of so many battles, it would suggest that mourning was common there. *apart.* Alone, indicating that while conversion may be widespread, it is always individual.

Thoughts for Personal/Family Worship: Chapter 12

1. **When God makes Judah and Jerusalem unassailable by any and all invaders, He illustrates the wonderful truth of Rom. 8:31, "If God be for us, who can be against us?" The sight of infantry and cavalry charging would be demoralizing and terrifying, but the sight of God's frustration of every advance would bring confidence, encouragement, and peace. So it should be for every believer to realize that in the face of all that may come our way, "in all these things we are more than conquerors through him that loved us" (Rom. 8:37).**
2. **When God pours out His Spirit, dispensing grace and generating prayer, He shows the power and consequence of regeneration. The Spirit awakens the sinner to look with understanding on Christ (the one who was pierced) and then to seek favor from God. Pleading in prayer is evidence of spiritual life. Remember when Ananias was reticent about ministering to the newly converted Saul, God assured him that the conversion was genuine by informing Ananias that Saul was praying (Acts 9:11). It is a basic truth that Christians pray.**

Chapter 13: ***Zechariah describes a spiritual cleansing that purges the land from all pagan worship and then declares the Lord's gathering of His remnant after the smiting of the shepherd.***

13:1 *In that day.* A time of special divine intervention, here for blessing and salvation. This purging from sin is contextually linked to the one who was pierced (12:10), theologically pointing to the expiatory aspect of the atonement.

13:2 *no more be remembered.* Such will be the cleansing from sin that there will be no mention or acknowledgment of idols: a conscious and willful refusal to think about them.

13:3 Loyalty and devotion to God are greater than family connections.

13:4–5 Knowing their lives are in jeopardy, the false prophets take every precaution to be undetected. *Neither . . . wear a rough garment.* They cease wearing "the garment of hair" that before they wore pretentiously (perhaps to be like Elijah, 2 Kings 2:8).

13:6 Though the false prophet attempted to disguise his occupation, there were some telltale signs that gave him away. *wounds in thine hands.* Between your hands, referring to scars on the chest or back, self-inflicted during pagan rituals (1 Kings 18:28). Nonetheless, he attempts to remove suspicion by claiming they happened among friends.

13:7 The New Testament confirms this as a reference to the cross (Matt. 26:31). *my fellow.* My associate or equal, a profound statement made by the Lord Himself—the shepherd being smitten is Himself God. See comments in the Worship Section below. *I will turn my hand upon the little ones.* The Lord will turn graciously to those who are lowly and insignificant, referring

8 And it shall come to pass, *that* in all the land,
saith the LORD, two parts therein shall be cut off
and die; but the third shall be left therein.
9 And I will bring the third part through the fire,
and will refine them as silver is refined, and will
try them as gold is tried: they shall call on my
name, and I will hear them: I will say, It *is* my
people: and they shall say, The LORD *is* my God.

CHAPTER 14

BEHOLD, the day of the LORD cometh, and thy
spoil shall be divided in the midst of thee.
2 For I will gather all nations against Jerusalem to
battle; and the city shall be taken, and the houses
rifled, and the women ravished; and half of the
city shall go forth into captivity, and the residue
of the people shall not be cut off from the city.
3 Then shall the LORD go forth, and fight against
those nations, as when he fought in the day of
battle.
4 ¶ And his feet shall stand in that day upon the
mount of Olives, which *is* before Jerusalem on
the east, and the mount of Olives shall cleave in
the midst thereof toward the east and toward the
west, *and there shall be* a very great valley; and half
of the mountain shall remove toward the north,
and half of it toward the south.
5 And ye shall flee *to* the valley of the mountains;
for the valley of the mountains shall reach unto
Azal: yea, ye shall flee, like as ye fled from before
the earthquake in the days of Uzziah king of
Judah: and the LORD my God shall come, *and* all
the saints with thee.
6 And it shall come to pass in that day, *that* the
light shall not be clear, *nor* dark:
7 But it shall be one day which shall be known to
the LORD, not day, nor night: but it shall come to
pass, *that* at evening time it shall be light.
8 And it shall be in that day, *that* living waters
shall go out from Jerusalem; half of them toward
the former sea, and half of them toward the
hinder sea: in summer and in winter shall it be.
9 And the LORD shall be king over all the earth:
in that day shall there be one LORD, and his name
one.
10 All the land shall be turned as a plain from
Geba to Rimmon south of Jerusalem: and it

to His purpose to refine and gather His remnant.

13:8–9 The purging is severe, but it reveals a purified remnant. *my people . . . my God.* Covenant language expressing a reconciled relationship.

Thoughts for Personal/Family Worship: Chapter 13

1. **Reflect in worship on what 13:7 says about the atonement. Two thoughts are particularly overwhelming: the identity and the sacrifice of the shepherd. The Lord speaks and designates Christ as "my shepherd," referring to His divine appointment to be the mediator, and "my fellow," speaking of His essential equality with the Lord. Both terms point to His deity, but Christ is also man, thus enabling Him to die. That the Lord Himself commands the sword to smite Christ testifies to the seriousness of sin; God's justice demanded the death of His "fellow," His coequal Son. While the cross is evidence of divine love, it is foremost evidence to divine justice. Ought not the wonder of it all—that Christ died for sinners—bring us to praise?**
2. **Similarly, the reference to the cleansing fountain comes between a reference to Christ being pierced by men (12:10) and being executed by God's sword. That reminds us that the cleansing fountain of Christ's blood is the only means whereby sins can be forgiven. Comparing 12:10 with 13:7 also points to Acts 2:23 that links God's eternal purpose regarding the cross to the sinner's guilt in nailing Him to the tree. The cross was central to God's plan, and it should be in the lives of all who have been redeemed by it.**

Chapter 14: ***Zechariah announces the final day of the Lord when Christ returns in glory to defeat every enemy and to establish the triumph of true religion.***

The Coming of Messiah (14:1–21)

14:1 *the day of the LORD.* The final eschatological moment when God interrupts time to accomplish His purpose, which all the previous "days" anticipated. It introduces the climax of the prophet's message of hope: the absolute triumph of Christ and His kingdom. *thy spoil shall be divided.* The enemy divides what they have plundered. This day of the Lord is about to turn defeat into triumph.

14:2 *I will gather.* The Lord Himself instigates the crisis by sovereignly bringing the hostile nations together. *half of the city . . . the residue of the people.* Half will be exiled, and half will remain.

14:3 When all seems hopeless, the Lord enters the conflict. *as when he fought in the day of battle.* The Hebrew is indefinite and does not refer to some past battle, but rather that God will fight as a warrior in battle.

14:4 The geographical cataclysms associated with the manifestations of God's presence symbolize His awesome power. Nothing remains the same when God appears (Isa. 64:1–3; Mic. 1:2–3). The significance of His coming to the mount of Olives is its location just outside Jerusalem; He comes right where He is needed.

14:5 The details are uncertain, but the message is clear that God has a way of escape and refuge for His people.

14:6 *the light shall not be clear, nor dark.* The Hebrew is difficult; translate rather, "and there will not be light; the precious things (referring to the heavenly bodies) will be reduced." Such cosmic changes are often associated with divine judgment (Joel 2:1–2; Amos 5:20).

14:8 *living waters.* Running water like a river or stream, symbolic of that which sustains life. *former sea.* Eastern, referring to the Dead Sea. *hinder sea.* Western, referring to the Mediterranean Sea. *in summer and in winter.* The benefits of the life-sustaining waters are continuous.

14:9 *one LORD . . . his name one.* According to Deut. 6:4, this is the sum of orthodoxy and points to the universal acknowledgment of the only true God.

14:10–11 The exact locations are uncertain, but seem to designate both the surrounding environs of Jerusalem and the entire circumference of the city that will be secured for habitation.

shall be lifted up, and inhabited in her place,
from Benjamin's gate unto the place of the first
gate, unto the corner gate, and *from* the tower of
Hananeel unto the king's winepresses.
11 And *men* shall dwell in it, and there shall be
no more utter destruction; but Jerusalem shall be
safely inhabited.
12 ¶ And this shall be the plague wherewith the
LORD will smite all the people that have fought
against Jerusalem; Their flesh shall consume
away while they stand upon their feet, and their
eyes shall consume away in their holes, and their
tongue shall consume away in their mouth.
13 And it shall come to pass in that day, *that* a
great tumult from the LORD shall be among them;
and they shall lay hold every one on the hand of
his neighbour, and his hand shall rise up against
the hand of his neighbour.
14 And Judah also shall fight at Jerusalem; and
the wealth of all the heathen round about shall be
gathered together, gold, and silver, and apparel, in
great abundance.
15 And so shall be the plague of the horse, of the
mule, of the camel, and of the ass, and of all the
beasts that shall be in these tents, as this plague.
16 ¶ And it shall come to pass, *that* every one
that is left of all the nations which came against
Jerusalem shall even go up from year to year to
worship the King, the LORD of hosts, and to keep
the feast of tabernacles.
17 And it shall be, *that* whoso will not come up
of *all* the families of the earth unto Jerusalem to
worship the King, the LORD of hosts, even upon
them shall be no rain.
18 And if the family of Egypt go not up, and come
not, that *have* no *rain*; there shall be the plague,
wherewith the LORD will smite the heathen that
come not up to keep the feast of tabernacles.
19 This shall be the punishment of Egypt, and
the punishment of all nations that come not up
to keep the feast of tabernacles.
20 ¶ In that day shall there be upon the bells of
the horses, HOLINESS UNTO THE LORD; and
the pots in the LORD's house shall be like the
bowls before the altar.
21 Yea, every pot in Jerusalem and in Judah shall be
holiness unto the LORD of hosts: and all they that
sacrifice shall come and take of them, and seethe
therein: and in that day there shall be no more the
Canaanite in the house of the LORD of hosts.

14:12 *their holes.* Their eye sockets.
14:13 *neighbour.* Comrade. There is so much confusion in the battle that they begin fighting against themselves.
14:14 *the wealth of all the heathen.* Compared with v. 1, this marks a reversal of fortune: Jerusalem was being plundered; now they are plundering.
14:15 *in these tents.* The encampments of the enemy. Even the livestock that would have been part of the enemy's arsenal will be destroyed.
14:16 *the feast of tabernacles.* The feast commemorating God's presence and providential protection and preservation of His people. Here it represents the whole of divinely prescribed and acceptable worship by both Jew and Gentile (*every one that is left of all the nations*).
14:17 *no rain.* One of the consequences of breaking the covenant (Deut. 28:24).
14:18–19 *if the family of Egypt.* Egypt is representative of all hostile nations. It appears that the conditional statement is hypothetical since God's victory over the heathen has been total. But if it were true, there is no escaping the consequences.
14:20–21 The distinction between the secular and sacred disappears. That every thing is holy points to the complete reversal of the curse. *seethe therein.* To cook in them. *no more Canaanite.* Canaanite is either a vocational term referring to merchants (Hos. 12:7) or an ethnic designation referring to the inhabitants of Palestine, who were both threats and temptations to Israel. Either way, their exclusion speaks to the absence of any corrupting influence.

Thoughts for Personal/Family Worship: Chapter 14

1. **When God gathered the nations to fight against Jerusalem, only to fight against them Himself, we are reminded of the many examples of the mysterious ways of God's sovereign providence. Events and circumstances that we easily interpret as being threatening and fearful prove to be occasions for God to display His mighty power. Remember when the five Amorite kings came together to fight against Joshua. That had to be a fearful sight since up to that point Israel had faced one enemy at a time. But what appeared to be a disaster turned out to be an amazing victory thanks to the divine intervention causing the sun and moon to stand still (Josh. 10). It was God's way of accomplishing multiple victories in a single battle. We should not judge or question God's ways. Rather we should trust Him that He uses even those things that appear to be against us to accomplish our good.**
2. **Although the scene described in this chapter is subject to various views of the end times, it does generate the happy hope for all believers that God, Christ, and truth will triumph. A new heaven and new earth are coming that will be free from every vestige of sin and will manifest the power of the gospel in reversing the curse. The desire of every believer should be "Even so, come, Lord Jesus" (Rev. 22:20). The way Zechariah closes his prophecy justifies his reputation as the prophet of hope.**

INTRODUCTION TO THE BOOK OF MALACHI

Authorship: Malachi's name means "my messenger." Although some think "my messenger" simply designates an anonymous prophet, most conservatives regard Malachi as the personal name of the sole author of the prophecy. Some critics link the prophecy to a series of three anonymous collections introduced with the expression "the burden of the word of the Lord." They claim that two of these were erroneously appended to Zechariah (chs. 9–11 as Deutero-Zechariah and chs. 12–14 as Trito-Zechariah) and that this one called Malachi was erroneously allowed to stand independently.

Date: Though not dated as precisely as Haggai and Zechariah, the other postexilic prophets, there is credible evidence that Malachi prophesied c. 435 BC, sometime during the reign of Artaxerxes between the two administrations of Nehemiah in Palestine. His mention of temple abuses demands a date after 516 BC, the year the temple was restored. Similar themes between Malachi and Nehemiah suggest that they were contemporaries: marriage to heathen wives (2:11–15; Neh. 13:23–27); neglect of tithes (3:8–10; Neh. 13:10–14); disregard for Sabbath (2:8–9; Neh. 13:15–22); and corruption of the priesthood (1:6—2:9; Neh. 13:7–9). Although not the last book composed during the Old Testament era (1 and 2 Chronicles were, c. 424 BC), Malachi's message, inciting the fear of judgment and instilling hope for healing, marks an appropriate end to the Old Testament prophetic order and anticipates the next prophetic word to come from John the Baptist and Christ Himself.

Theme: Exposing and rebuking insincere religion.

Purpose: To awaken a people whose religious cynicism and skepticism of God's promises led to careless and dead worship and to renew hope and revive true religion in view of the certainty of God's purpose.

Synopsis: *The Contribution of Malachi to Redemptive Revelation*

In 520 BC Haggai and Zechariah motivated a discouraged people to be diligent in serving the Lord. Their proclamation of a glorious messianic age inspired the returnees from Babylon to rebuild the temple. But now almost a hundred years had passed, and the nation was still subject to the same foreign power with no prospect of a king on David's throne. The people were not experiencing the blessings they assumed God had promised and that they thought they most certainly deserved. They were growing more and more impatient with God. Because God was not acting according to their agenda or schedule, they began to doubt His Word and His ability to keep His promise. They developed serious misconceptions of God and the nature of true worship: God was someone who owed them things, and religion was a means of manipulating God for a better life. In an artful, unrelenting, irrefutable dialectic, Malachi exposed the worthless religion and arrogance of these people. His logic and precision are impeccable. He made it clear that the blame for any lack of blessing was due to their spiritual deadness and not God's unfaithfulness or injustice. It is as though Malachi as a theological pathologist examined and identified the causes and signs of dead religion and spiritual decay. In so doing, he exposes the human condition that so desperately needs the gospel.

Although written thousands of years ago, Malachi's message is tragically relevant. Though the mechanics of worship are different, the same mercantile, self-focused religion lives on. A perfunctory, dead, formalistic religion cannot satisfy God. Malachi's autopsy of dead religion is a casebook for modern day messengers who must expose the same kind of spiritual death, proclaim the same warning, and prescribe the same remedy.

Malachi preached the gospel in its fullness: condemnation of sinners and salvation for believers. The coming day of Lord would turn the wicked to stubble (4:1). Sinners would not be able to stand on their own in that day (3:2), but the destiny of the righteous would be different as they would experience life through the Sun of righteousness (4:2). Malachi pointed to God's unfailing purpose of redemption in the election of God's people (1:2–3)—a display of His grace that was vouchsafed in His immutability (3:6). Most significantly, he pointed to the messenger of the covenant, the Messiah, who would be the purifier of His people (3:1–3) and who would be preceded by His forerunner (3:1), the second Elijah (4:5). When we turn the page to the New Testament, we see John the Baptist and Jesus just as Malachi predicted. God is faithful to His promise.

Outline: Malachi outlines his message with a series of six cutting propositions followed by a predictable denial and then irrefutable evidence proving the proposition. He employs a dialectical style (a question-answer format reflecting a tension of ideas and coming to the resolution of truth).

I. Introduction (1:1)
II. Insensitivity to Grace (1:2–5)
III. Insincere Worship (1:6—2:9)
IV. Instability in Families (2:10–16)
V. Inaccurate Views of God (2:17—3:7)
VI. Insufficient Giving (3:7–12)
VII. Improper Motives for Service (3:13—4:3)
VIII. Conclusion (4:4–6)

THE BOOK OF

MALACHI

CHAPTER 1

THE burden of the word of the LORD to Israel by
Malachi.
2 I have loved you, saith the LORD. Yet ye say,
Wherein hast thou loved us? *Was* not Esau Jacob's
brother? saith the LORD: yet I loved Jacob,
3 And I hated Esau, and laid his mountains
and his heritage waste for the dragons of the
wilderness.
4 Whereas Edom saith, We are impoverished, but
we will return and build the desolate places; thus
saith the LORD of hosts, They shall build, but I will
throw down; and they shall call them, The border
of wickedness, and, The people against whom the
LORD hath indignation for ever.
5 And your eyes shall see, and ye shall say, The
LORD will be magnified from the border of Israel.
6 ¶ A son honoureth *his* father, and a servant his
master: if then I *be* a father, where *is* mine hon-
our? and if I *be* a master, where *is* my fear? saith
the LORD of hosts unto you, O priests, that despise
my name. And ye say, Wherein have we despised
thy name?
7 Ye offer polluted bread upon mine altar; and ye
say, Wherein have we polluted thee? In that ye say,
The table of the LORD *is* contemptible.
8 And if ye offer the blind for sacrifice, *is it* not
evil? and if ye offer the lame and sick, *is it* not evil?
offer it now unto thy governor; will he be pleased
with thee, or accept thy person? saith the LORD
of hosts.
9 And now, I pray you, beseech God that he
will be gracious unto us: this hath been by your
means: will he regard your persons? saith the
LORD of hosts.
10 Who *is there* even among you that would shut
the doors *for nought*? neither do ye kindle *fire* on
mine altar for nought. I have no pleasure in you,
saith the LORD of hosts, neither will I accept an
offering at your hand.

Chapter 1: *Malachi declares and proves God's love for His people and then rebukes them for their careless and heartless worship.*

INTRODUCTION (1:1)

1:1 *burden.* The prophetic utterance or oracle. *to Israel.* In the postexilic era, refers to the entire nation, not just the northern tribes of the divided kingdom.

INSENSITIVITY TO GRACE (1:2–5)

1:2 *I have loved you.* A declaration of election. Love is an expression of the will and thus a decision to choose. *saith the LORD. Yet ye say.* They deny what God has declared, revealing their insensitivity.

1:3 *I hated Esau.* Hate is an expression of the will and thus a decision to reject. God proves His electing love by contrasting Jacob and Esau, a paradigm of electing grace repeated by Paul in Rom. 9:11–13. *laid . . . waste.* God's turning Esau's inheritance into a deserted wasteland is evidence of His rejection. *dragons.* Jackals.

1:4 *Edom.* The nation descended from Esau. *they shall call them.* The Hebrew uses an impersonal subject to express a passive voice—"they shall be called." *the LORD hath indignation for ever.* The Lord has cursed for ever. Regardless of Edom's efforts for self-improvement, they remain under God's curse and are doomed to failure.

1:5 *from the border.* From beyond the border. In God's sovereign decision to judge Edom, Israel should see evidence of His sovereign election and preservation of Israel.

INSINCERE WORSHIP (1:6—2:9)

1:6—2:9 Failure by the priesthood contributes to irreverence toward God and careless worship by the people.

1:6 *despise my name.* To regard the person and perfections of God with contempt instead of with the honor and respect He deserves.

1:7 *polluted bread.* Desecrated or defiled. *mine altar . . . thee.* Defiling the altar is tantamount to defiling the Lord Himself. Carelessness in worship is irreverence toward God. *contemptible.* Despised, regarded as without value.

1:8 *offer the blind . . . lame and sick.* Not only would such offerings be rejected and offensive to human authorities (*governor*), they betrayed the gospel truths the sacrifices were intended to convey. As the sacrifices point to Messiah's atoning work, the required perfection of the animal victims symbolize Christ's righteousness that rendered Him the only acceptable sacrifice for sin. God will not accept for atonement anything with defect (Lev. 22:20; 1 Peter 1:19).

1:9 *And now, I pray you, beseech God.* Literally, "now flatter God." Malachi uses a bit of sarcasm to highlight the absurdity of their attempting to appease God in light of the sacrifices they have offered. *this hath been by your means.* This has been from your hand. *will he regard your persons?* Literally, "will He lift from faces," an idiom for accepting someone.

1:10 *Who is there . . . nought?* A Hebrew idiom expressing desire, therefore, "O that someone among you would shut the doors (of the temple) so that you do not light my altar in vain."

11 For from the rising of the sun even unto the
going down of the same my name *shall be* great
among the Gentiles; and in every place incense
shall be offered unto my name, and a pure
offering: for my name *shall be* great among the
heathen, saith the LORD of hosts.
12 ¶ But ye have profaned it, in that ye say, The
table of the LORD *is* polluted; and the fruit thereof,
even his meat, *is* contemptible.
13 Ye said also, Behold, what a weariness *is it*! and
ye have snuffed at it, saith the LORD of hosts; and
ye brought *that which was* torn, and the lame, and
the sick; thus ye brought an offering: should I
accept this of your hand? saith the LORD.
14 But cursed *be* the deceiver, which hath in his
flock a male, and voweth, and sacrificeth unto
the Lord a corrupt thing: for I *am* a great King,
saith the LORD of hosts, and my name *is* dreadful
among the heathen.

CHAPTER 2

AND now, O ye priests, this commandment *is* for
you.
2 If ye will not hear, and if ye will not lay *it* to
heart, to give glory unto my name, saith the LORD
of hosts, I will even send a curse upon you, and I
will curse your blessings: yea, I have cursed them
already, because ye do not lay *it* to heart.
3 Behold, I will corrupt your seed, and spread
dung upon your faces, *even* the dung of your
solemn feasts; and *one* shall take you away with it.
4 And ye shall know that I have sent this com-
mandment unto you, that my covenant might be
with Levi, saith the LORD of hosts.
5 My covenant was with him of life and peace;
and I gave them to him *for* the fear wherewith he
feared me, and was afraid before my name.
6 The law of truth was in his mouth, and iniquity
was not found in his lips: he walked with me in
peace and equity, and did turn many away from
iniquity.
7 For the priest's lips should keep knowledge, and
they should seek the law at his mouth: for he *is* the
messenger of the LORD of hosts.
8 But ye are departed out of the way; ye have caused
many to stumble at the law; ye have corrupted the
covenant of Levi, saith the LORD of hosts.
9 Therefore have I also made you contemptible
and base before all the people, according as ye

1:11 The prophet looks to a time when the worship of God will be pure and universal in contrast to the wrong of Israel's worship.
1:12 *But ye have profaned it.* They brought worship down to the common or ordinary, there was nothing special about it. *polluted.* Defiled or desecrated. *contemptible.* Despised, without value.
1:13 *what a weariness.* A hardship or nuisance. *snuffed at it.* To sniff at as an expression of revulsion, to undervalue.
1:14 *the deceiver.* One who acts slickly or deceptively. Although he could offer an appropriate sacrifice, he brings a defective (*corrupt*) one instead evidencing his disrespect for God. *dreadful.* Fearful.

Thoughts for Personal/Family Worship: Chapter 1

1. **If we are believers, the folly of Israel's insensitivity to grace should cause us to be thankfully sensitive to the grace we have received. Nothing will keep religion alive more than being conscious of grace. Sensitivity to grace is always grateful and realizes that God's love is not measured by things but by the reality of a personal, intimate relationship with the Lord Himself. God's love is amazing; it is a truth we could not dare to know apart from His revelation that He loves us. God's love is unmerited, finding its cause in God the Lover and not in us the loved. He loved Jacob, the deceiver who was without virtue or merit to be a candidate for grace. God's love is unfailing and preserving. This sovereign, unchanging love is the banner over all His people.**
2. **Genuine worship flows from the reverential knowledge of who God is. The titles of God in vv. 6 and 14 particularly focus on His authority, honor, and power. A light regard for God is never conducive to worship. Until we see ourselves as little and God as infinitely big we will not worship as we ought or as He deserves. Fearing God, being in awe of Him, is an essential component of worship.**
3. **Israel's casual and careless worship is a vivid reminder of how easy it can be for religion to become routine and empty. It is so easy just to go through the motions of familiar rituals or liturgies thinking that God will be pleased with the trinkets we throw Him. Too often, churches are filled with those who regard worship as a necessary nuisance (v. 13). Christ's words to the woman at the well ring most appropriate: "They that worship him must worship him in spirit and in truth" (John 4:24). God demands a genuine, sincere heart to worship Him and will be pleased with no less.**

Chapter 2: ***Malachi lays the blame for careless worship directly on the failures of the priesthood and then links unfaithfulness in worship to the instability and unfaithfulness in families.***

2:2 *hear.* To listen carefully or to heed. *lay it to heart to give glory.* Idiom for determining or resolving to give glory. Giving glory means to regard as weighty and worthy in contrast to the light regard toward God that was so prevalent.
2:3 *corrupt.* To rebuke. *spread dung . . . of your solemn feasts. Dung* refers to the disgusting contents of the intestines that would have been exposed in the slaying of the sacrificial victims. Spreading it on their faces was symbolic of God's disgust with and rejection of the divinely offensive and insulting sacrifices. *take you away with it.* The humiliated priests will be taken to the disposal site where the refuse from sacrifices were discarded, a place of uncleanness. The priesthood would be out of service.
2:4–7 Alludes to the covenant with the house of Levi that determined the priestly line through Eleazar because of the faithful act of Phinehas (Num. 25:12–13).
2:8 *ye are departed.* The priests of Malachi's day had violated their covenant mandate and heritage. Rather than turning many from sin (v. 6), they contributed to the sin of many (*caused many to stumble*).

have not kept my ways, but have been partial in
the law.
10 Have we not all one father? hath not one God
created us? why do we deal treacherously every
man against his brother, by profaning the cov-
enant of our fathers?
11 ¶ Judah hath dealt treacherously, and an
abomination is committed in Israel and in
Jerusalem; for Judah hath profaned the holiness
of the LORD which he loved, and hath married the
daughter of a strange god.
12 The LORD will cut off the man that doeth this,
the master and the scholar, out of the tabernacles
of Jacob, and him that offereth an offering unto
the LORD of hosts.
13 And this have ye done again, covering the altar
of the LORD with tears, with weeping, and with
crying out, insomuch that he regardeth not the
offering any more, or receiveth *it* with good will
at your hand.
14 ¶ Yet ye say, Wherefore? Because the LORD
hath been witness between thee and the wife
of thy youth, against whom thou hast dealt
treacherously: yet *is* she thy companion, and the
wife of thy covenant.
15 And did not he make one? Yet had he the
residue of the spirit. And wherefore one? That
he might seek a godly seed. Therefore take heed
to your spirit, and let none deal treacherously
against the wife of his youth.
16 For the LORD, the God of Israel, saith that he
hateth putting away: for *one* covereth violence
with his garment, saith the LORD of hosts:
therefore take heed to your spirit, that ye deal not
treacherously.
17 ¶ Ye have wearied the LORD with your words.
Yet ye say, Wherein have we wearied *him*? When
ye say, Every one that doeth evil *is* good in the
sight of the LORD, and he delighteth in them; or,
Where *is* the God of judgment?

CHAPTER 3

BEHOLD, I will send my messenger, and he shall
prepare the way before me: and the Lord, whom
ye seek, shall suddenly come to his temple, even

2:9 *Therefore.* A foreboding thought in view of their failures. *contemptible.* Despised or despicable. *base.* Humiliated, of little value. *partial in the law.* Literally, "to lift up faces in the law," an idiom for showing favoritism. Contrasted with the former priests who walked with fairness ("equity" in v. 6), these priests were unfair in the way they ministered the law.

INSTABILITY IN FAMILIES (2:10–16)

2:10 *one father . . . one God.* God's fatherhood demanding honor and obedience (1:6) and God's creatorship declaring His exclusive ownership and rights underscore the incongruity of Israel's behavior. *treacherously.* Deal faithlessly, by breaking covenant terms, especially the marriage covenant. Family life is in view. *profaning the covenant.* By making it invalid or to treating it as unholy. Most likely the *covenant* refers to the Mosaic covenant that included strict requirements regarding marriage and family.

2:11 Judah's unfaithfulness (*dealt treacherously*) is called *an abomination*, a term often used to refer to pagan idolatry, which was so detestable to God. *profaned the holiness.* Regarded God's holiness as common or ordinary. *strange god.* A foreign god. The first charge was that they engaged in "interfaith" marriages, a religiously dangerous union strictly forbidden (Deut. 7:3–4). Moses and Paul agree that marriage for God's people must be only in the Lord (1 Cor. 7:39).

2:12 *the master and the scholar.* Literally, "the one who awakes and the one who answers." The Hebrew is uncertain but seems to be an idiom expressing inclusiveness: everyone guilty of this transgression will face the consequences.

2:13 The exaggerated outward displays were pagan patterns that they employed under the pretense of worshiping the Lord. God will neither accept (*regardeth not*) nor be pleased (*receiveth it with good will*) with such pretentious shows.

2:14 This is a key text declaring marriage to be a covenant bond. To break the covenant (deal *treacherously*) is to violate a *companion* (from a root meaning "to join or ally together").

2:15 *And did not he make one . . . the spirit.* The Hebrew is ambiguous. Possibly, "Did He not make them to be one" (see Moses' exposition of marriage, Gen. 2:24). Also, "and no one will do this who has the residue (or portion) of the Spirit," that is, no one with the Spirit would violate the covenant with his wife (2:16). This seems to be the point of the application of taking *heed to your spirit* and not dealing *treacherously*.

2:16 *putting away.* Refers to divorce. *covereth violence with his garment.* Rather, "covers his garment (with) violence." The image does not picture an effort to conceal violence, but that the violence is exposed as a stain on a garment.

INACCURATE VIEWS OF GOD (2:17—3:7)

2:17 *wearied the LORD.* A vivid image to describe how they had made the Lord "sick and tired" with their charges of divine injustice and unfairness (*Where is the God of judgment?*). They defined God's justice in terms of personal benefit.

Thoughts for Personal/Family Worship: Chapter 2

1. **Malachi's charge against the priests for their unfaithfulness and bad influence is a sobering reminder of how vital good and faithful ministers are to the welfare of the church. Ministers are God's gift to the church for its edification (Eph. 4:11–12). Certainly ministers must heed the warning and be sure that their preaching and testimony make them good examples. Likewise, the church should pray diligently and faithfully for their ministers that God will preserve them and empower them for the ministry.**
2. **Malachi's exposure of the instability in families and his explanation that God is seeking a godly seed (2:15) through the marriage covenant shows how important the family structure is in God's purpose for His people. God has ordained the family to be an experience of heaven on earth (Deut. 11:21), but too often homes have become battlegrounds. The fact of the matter is that religion is no more real than it is in the home. Christian parents should make it a priority to keep the Lord constantly in the forefront of all the activities of the home (Deut. 6:4–9). Godly homes make for godly churches.**

Chapter 3: ***Malachi announces the coming of Messiah and His forerunner, charges the nation with various***

the messenger of the covenant, whom ye delight
in: behold, he shall come, saith the LORD of
hosts.
2 But who may abide the day of his coming? and
who shall stand when he appeareth? for he *is* like
a refiner's fire, and like fullers' soap:
3 And he shall sit *as* a refiner and purifier of
silver: and he shall purify the sons of Levi, and
purge them as gold and silver, that they may offer
unto the LORD an offering in righteousness.
4 Then shall the offering of Judah and Jerusalem
be pleasant unto the LORD, as in the days of old,
and as in former years.
5 And I will come near to you to judgment; and
I will be a swift witness against the sorcerers, and
against the adulterers, and against false swearers,
and against those that oppress the hireling in *his*
wages, the widow, and the fatherless, and that
turn aside the stranger *from his right*, and fear not
me, saith the LORD of hosts.
6 For I *am* the LORD, I change not; therefore ye
sons of Jacob are not consumed.
7 ¶ Even from the days of your fathers ye are gone
away from mine ordinances, and have not kept
them. Return unto me, and I will return unto you,
saith the LORD of hosts. But ye said, Wherein shall
we return?
8 ¶ Will a man rob God? Yet ye have robbed me.
But ye say, Wherein have we robbed thee? In tithes
and offerings.
9 Ye *are* cursed with a curse: for ye have robbed
me, *even* this whole nation.
10 Bring ye all the tithes into the storehouse, that
there may be meat in mine house, and prove me
now herewith, saith the LORD of hosts, if I will not
open you the windows of heaven, and pour you
out a blessing, that *there shall* not *be room* enough
to receive it.
11 And I will rebuke the devourer for your sakes,
and he shall not destroy the fruits of your ground;
neither shall your vine cast her fruit before the
time in the field, saith the LORD of hosts.
12 And all nations shall call you blessed: for ye shall
be a delightsome land, saith the LORD of hosts.
13 ¶ Your words have been stout against me, saith
the LORD. Yet ye say, What have we spoken *so
much* against thee?
14 Ye have said, It *is* vain to serve God: and what
profit *is it* that we have kept his ordinance, and
that we have walked mournfully before the LORD
of hosts?
15 And now we call the proud happy; yea, they
that work wickedness are set up; yea, *they that*
tempt God are even delivered.
16 ¶ Then they that feared the LORD spake often
one to another: and the LORD hearkened, and
heard *it*, and a book of remembrance was written
before him for them that feared the LORD, and
that thought upon his name.
17 And they shall be mine, saith the LORD of

---

offenses against God, and describes the blessings for those who fear the Lord.

3:1 Verse 1 begins the answer to the question of 2:17. Christ is the evidence of God's unchangeable justice. *Behold, I will send my messenger . . . prepare the way.* The Hebrew asserts both certainty and imminence: "I am about to send." This was fulfilled in John the Baptist. Much is revealed concerning Christ: He is (1) the God of justice (demanded by logic of text—the Lord speaks in answer to 2:17, *before me . . . he shall come*—the One coming is the Lord of hosts), (2) *the LORD*—always deity with the article, refers to His sovereignty, (3) *the messenger of the covenant*—used only here for the mediator of the covenant of grace.

3:2 *who may abide . . . who shall stand.* See Ps. 1:5 for the answer; see the similar question in Nah. 1:6. *refiner's fire . . . fullers'* (i.e., launderers') *soap*. As fire separates slag from metal and soap dirt from clothes, so Christ will do a purifying and cleansing work.

3:3–4 The purifying work of Christ renders the offerings and service of those He has cleansed pleasing and acceptable before God. It is only because of Christ's work that any of our service can please the Lord.

3:5 Another answer to the question of 2:17. Those not cleansed by Christ get the justice they deserve for their sins.

3:6–7 *I change not . . . gone away.* A remarkable declaration of God's immutability and its gracious implications. In spite of the nation's failures that deserved God's finishing them off (*consumed*), God's immutability guaranteed the covenant. His redemptive purpose focused in Christ, and there had to be an Israel if there was to be a Christ (Rom. 9:4–5).

INSUFFICIENT GIVING (3:7–12)

3:10 *storehouse.* The house of the treasure, one of the chambers in the temple. *meat.* Food. *prove me.* To examine or put to the test, God's gracious challenge to their faith to claim the blessings and to experience His abundant provision.

3:11 God will protect them from enemy raids against their crops and ensure a timely harvest.

3:12 *blessed.* A descriptive term designating a fortunate condition that can be observed by others. The nations will see how prosperous Israel is as a result of God's blessing them.

IMPROPER MOTIVES FOR SERVICE (3:13—4:3)

3:13 *Your words have been stout against me.* Literally, "You have strengthened against me your words," meaning they spoke harshly.

3:14 *vain.* Purposeless. *we have walked mournfully.* Dressed in drab mourning attire, professing the soberness of their behavior. But they complained that they got nothing in return (no *profit*, no cut). They were serving God from a mercantile spirit to get something from Him.

3:15 They walked humbly, but the *proud* (the insolent) were *happy* (in that enviable state, same word as "blessed" in v. 12) and the wicked were *set up* (built up or prospered).

3:16–18 Here is reality in contrast to the faulty perceptions of vv. 13–15. Appearance and reality are seldom the same.

3:16 *they that feared the LORD.* "The fearers of the Lord," those who lived in the conscious awareness of God's reality. *the LORD hearkened.* Paid close attention. *that thought upon his name.* Those who took inventory of all His perfections.

3:17 *when I make up my jewels.* When I claim my special

hosts, in that day when I make up my jewels; and I will spare them, as a man spareth his own son that serveth him.
18 Then shall ye return, and discern between the righteous and the wicked, between him that serveth God and him that serveth him not.

CHAPTER 4

FOR, behold, the day cometh, that shall burn as an
oven; and all the proud, yea, and all that do wick-
edly, shall be stubble: and the day that cometh
shall burn them up, saith the LORD of hosts, that
it shall leave them neither root nor branch.
2 ¶ But unto you that fear my name shall the Sun
of righteousness arise with healing in his wings;
and ye shall go forth, and grow up as calves of the
stall.
3 And ye shall tread down the wicked; for they
shall be ashes under the soles of your feet in the
day that I shall do *this*, saith the LORD of hosts.
4 ¶ Remember ye the law of Moses my servant,
which I commanded unto him in Horeb for all
Israel, *with* the statutes and judgments.
5 ¶ Behold, I will send you Elijah the prophet
before the coming of the great and dreadful day
of the LORD:
6 And he shall turn the heart of the fathers to the
children, and the heart of the children to their fa-
thers, lest I come and smite the earth with a curse.

---

property or prized treasure (*jewels* elsewhere is translated "peculiar people").
3:18 *discern*. Literally, "see," an idiom for seeing again.

Thoughts for Personal/Family Worship: Chapter 3

1. **Verse 6 is a key verse for Malachi's argument and for theology as a whole. God's immutability, an objective aspect of God's essence, is a most encouraging and comforting truth. Significantly, Malachi places this proposition in the context of God's certain promise of the coming of Christ. The unchangeable God is the guarantee that every covenant promise will be fulfilled (Ps. 89:28–29,34). Paul sums it up well: "For all the promises of God in him [Jesus Christ] are yea, and in him Amen, unto the glory of God by us" (2 Cor. 1:20).**
2. **Verses 7–12 reminds us of how important it is to return to God a portion of what He has given to us. We are to offer our tithes and offerings in gratitude and in recognition of our dependence on Him. The more we find our satisfaction in God, the more freely we will give what we have to Him. God has promised to bless those who give, but we should never give as a bargaining device or as an investment strategy to get something in return. It is an expression of our enjoyment of the Lord. It is a fact that heartless religion hoards selfishly, and living religion selflessly gives.**
3. **Wrong motives kill good religion. Some of Malachi's congregation did the right things (v. 14) for the wrong reasons. They offered their service to God with the intent of getting something in return and got upset when they did not get it. Our service to God must always be to His glory and never for personal gain or recognition. We cannot live according to self-interests in light of what Christ has done for us (2 Cor. 5:15). Our motive should be like that of John who desired to decrease that Christ might increase (John 3:30).**

Chapter 4 (3:19–24 in Hebrew): *Malachi contrasts the fate of the wicked and the righteous and admonishes obedience to the law with a view to the coming day of the Lord.*

4:1 Although the wicked may enjoy some prosperity in time, their end is tragic, certain, and total (*neither root nor branch*). The fire is destructive and unrelenting.
4:2 *Sun of righteousness*. Though disputed, most likely a messianic reference, since Christ is what makes the difference in the judgment. The fearers of God do not merely escape fiery damnation and destruction, they will thrive with lively energy (*go forth*, i.e., frisk or spring about) like young strong bulls (*calves*).
4:3 Compare Ps. 49:14.

CONCLUSION (4:4–6)

4:4 *Remember*. An act of the will, "consciously to think about." This is a fitting conclusion: adherence to Moses will be a safeguard against the dead religion Malachi has exposed.
4:5 *Elijah*. Fulfilled in the ministry of John the Baptist (Matt. 11:14; 17:12; Mark 9:11–13; Luke 1:17). *before . . . the great and dreadful* [awe-inspiring] *day of the LORD*. A specific reference to the incarnation, the most spectacular entrance of God into the affairs of time. The incarnation was a day of the Lord.
4:6 The hearts of fathers and children will be in the same place in response to "Elijah's" preaching. While it includes the notion of family reconciliation, it points to a bigger picture of widespread conversion through the gospel. *lest . . . a curse*. A final warning to the unconverted. A curse refers to the ban, something devoted to destruction.

Thoughts for Personal/Family Worship: Chapter 4

1. **Verses 1–3 remind us that things are not to be judged before the time. So often we can fall into the same trap as those in Malachi's day thinking that the wicked prosper and are getting away with their wickedness. But the day is coming when the upright will have dominion, and the wicked will perish. This world is the best thing the wicked will ever know; this world is the worst thing the righteous will ever know. Eternity sets everything right, and it is better to be prepared for eternity than to be prosperous in time.**
2. **Significantly, the last Old Testament prophet ends with a message that heightens anticipation for the New Testament. Over four hundred years of prophetic silence were about to begin. But the years of divine silence were not years of divine inactivity. Events would progress on schedule according to God's purpose until that fullness of time when the messenger of the covenant appeared suddenly and not long after His ordained forerunner. The last prophet predicted that Messiah would come, and John, the next prophet, announced His presence. Both preached the fear of judgment for the wicked and hope of healing and salvation for the righteous. Whether in the Old Testament era or the New, Christ is the difference between life and death.**

Behold
I WILL SEND YOU
ELIJAH THE PROPHET
BEFORE THE
COMING
OF
The Great
AND
DREADFUL DAY
OF
The Lord
AND HE SHALL TURN
THE HEART
OF
The Fathers
TO
THE CHILDREN
AND THE HEART
OF
The Children
TO THEIR
FATHERS

MALACHI 4:5-6

WHAT HAPPENED
BETWEEN THE TESTAMENTS?

When we turn the page from Malachi to Matthew, it is helpful to remember that roughly 450 years have taken place. These were centuries in which the Lord made Israel and the nations wait and prepare for the coming of the promised Messiah. There were no new Scriptures during these years. The Old Testament, however, spoke to these waiting generations. It called Israel and the nations to repentance and to wait for the fulfillment of the prophecies. The Scriptures were copied and translated, and the godly attended to their truths. Scribes and doctors of the law studied the deposit of God's Word and in synagogues throughout the Mediterranean world, God's Word was read and taught.

Let's look first at the major changes on the world stage:

1. Politically, Rome succeeded the empires that had ruled the Mediterranean world before it. There had been the Persian Empire (539–332 BC), which had conquered and expanded the Babylonian Empire (620–539 BC). In turn, Alexander the Great conquered it, and after his death the empire fell to various generals and kings. From about 63 BC Rome solidified its power over the whole Mediterranean region.
2. Economically, Rome brought openness and stability to the whole Mediterranean region. Rome ruled with remarkable efficiency, stationing military colonies throughout its empire. It imposed heavy tributes on its provinces, but also used its power to construct many roads and aqueducts (structures conveying water from water sources to areas where there was no water), all of which fostered communication and commerce. Areas given to political unrest, like Judaea, were put under military prefects or procurators, like Pilate. All of these actions gave relative openness and stability, called the Pax Romana, or the Roman Peace. This would eventually under God's direction serve to help spread the Christian faith, or the Christian gospel of peace.
3. Linguistically, the common language was Greek. It helped commerce, education, and ultimately the spread of Christianity. By the mid–second century BC, the Old Testament was translated into Greek, and called the Septuagint. It spread the Word of God throughout the many nations, who would not easily have learned Hebrew.
4. Religiously, paganism prevailed throughout the Roman world. Magic and astrology were popular. Mystery cults attracted many followers during Roman times. In previous centuries, philosophy had enjoyed prominence among intellectuals; however, during the time of the New Testament, it had a therapeutic function for many. Many saw it as a way to advance themselves or find refuge from evil powers.

Next, let's consider the changes for the Jewish people:

1. Politically, Rome ruled the Jews, though various political groups also interfaced with the Romans and exercised some control, especially on religious fronts. In order to understand how this came to be, we need to know about the Maccabean revolt of 167–160 BC. Prior to this, Antiochus IV (Epiphanes), the king who reigned over the Jewish region at this time, defiled the temple by dedicating it to Jupiter. He also forbade the observance of certain laws of Moses, which prompted a revolt spearheaded by Mattathias and his sons, who would come to be referred to as the Maccabees and Hasmoneans. Remarkably, they managed to free Jerusalem and the temple from the grip of their enemies and eventually achieved the independence of the whole country. The apocryphal books of 1 and 2 Maccabees, tell this history, as does the Jewish historian Josephus. Over time the Hasmoneans themselves compromised and embraced many practices that the faithful found repugnant. When the rule of the country fell to Herod, an Idumean, or Edomite in 37 BC, he tried to absorb the Hasmonean claims by marrying a Hasmonean, Mariamne I, and descendants such as Agrippa I (Acts 12) and Agrippa II (Acts 26) could claim descent from the Hasmoneans.

2. In terms of infrastructure, few in the Holy Land were as ambitious a builder as Herod. He built strategic hilltop fortresses, including Masada, Herodium, and Alexandrium. Herod expanded the temple considerably in order to gain the favor of the Jews. The Temple buildings themselves were increased to twice the height of those of Solomon and Zerubbabel. The courtyard was extended southward to include the site of the old palace buildings and was surrounded by massive, pillared porches. The courtyards were paved with marble and parts of the building were overlaid with gold. There was a Court of the Gentiles, a Men's Court, a Court of the Women, a Court for the Priests. The main platform of the Temple was bounded by walls that provided the rear walls for the four porches. The eastern porch, or colonnade, was known as Solomon's Porch (John 10:23; Acts 3:11; 5:12).
3. Besides the temple, the synagogue was now an important institution. As places dedicated to the instruction of the law, synagogues were scattered all over the country, most larger towns having one or more (e.g., Nazareth, Matt. 13:54; Capernaum, Matt. 12:9). In Jerusalem, in spite of the fact that the Temple was there, there were many synagogues, and all parts of the Diaspora were represented by particular synagogues (Acts 6:9). Even in large cities outside of the Holy Land, Jews had their own synagogue: e.g., Damascus (Acts 9:2), Salamis (Acts 13:5), Antioch of Pisidia (Acts 13:14), etc.
4. Though rarely free from violence, Jerusalem continued as a great city till it was destroyed by the Romans in AD 70. Under the leadership of General Vespasian, the Roman armies advanced with considerable power and first conquered Galilee (AD 67). Titus, the son of Vespasian, took the chief command after Vespasian became emperor. Under him, Jerusalem fell to the Romans and was destroyed, temple and all. A few fortified places yet maintained themselves after the fall of Jerusalem, e.g., Masada, a stronghold of the Zealots. The destruction of Jerusalem and the temple had been prophesied by Christ (e.g., Luke 19:41–44).
5. The events between the Testaments produced religious parties and sects, which the New Testament frequently names: e.g., the Pharisees, Sadducees, and Zealots. The Pharisees (literally, "separate ones") had committed themselves to the faithful observance of the Law from the tradition of their fathers. They mostly controlled the synagogue life, though later they even occupied seats on the Sanhedrin (see Acts 5:34). The Sadducees were a party of wealthier, aristocratic, and politically involved members. They had considerable power in the temple and the Sanhedrin. They rejected all tradition other than the Mosaic Pentateuch, and quite readily compromised with the Romans. The Zealots professed great zeal for the law and were dedicated to overthrowing the Romans, and readily turned to military means to do so. In addition to these groups mentioned in the Bible, we have learned quite a bit about another group, namely, the Essenes. The archaeology of Qumran and the Dead Sea Scrolls has done a lot to shed light on these people, who withdrew from society to prepare for the coming of the Lord. They appear to have formed communities, looking for a prince from Aaron's line, who would defeat the forces of darkness. They were deeply concerned about outward purity, as can be seen from their many ritual baths and lavers.
6. Though not a party, the New Testament refers frequently to the Samaritans, whose identity also was shaped by the time between the testaments. Descendants of intermarriages between remnants of ancient Israel and people from other nations who were brought in, the New Testament shows a lot of bias and prejudice between Jews and Samaritans (e.g., John 4:9; Luke 9:51–55). The Samaritans differed with the Jews notably on the place of worship (see John 4:20), which the Samaritans considered Mt. Gerizim.

The NEW TESTAMENT SCRIPTURES

The Time
IS
FULFILLED
&
THE
Kingdom
OF GOD
IS AT HAND
Repent Ye
AND
BELIEVE
The Gospel

MARK 1:15

INTRODUCTION TO THE GOSPELS AND ACTS

The New Testament opens with the four Gospels and Acts. Together these books trace the history of the ministry of Christ from His birth till after His ascension into heaven, from where He governs His church and the world.

The first four books are called the Gospels. The term "gospel" (Mark 1:1,14; see Rom. 1:16) translates a Hebrew word found in Isaiah 40:9 and 52:7, which literally means "glad tidings" or "good news." The four Gospels certainly give us the good news of Christ's life, teaching, death, and resurrection. We might define a gospel as we have come to use the term as an orderly account of Christ's life, death, and resurrection. The four Gospels we have are, in addition, Spirit inspired, historically true accounts, written or verified by eyewitnesses (see 1 John 1:1–4). In addition to our four canonical Gospels, you sometimes hear about the *Gospel of Thomas*, an apocryphal and pseudepigraphal work, not accepted as reliable in the church of Christ.

Various theories have been constructed to account for some of the similarities and differences among the Gospels. Scholars have especially noted the similarities between Matthew, Mark, and Luke, such that they have been called synoptic Gospels (*sun-opsis*: literally, "seeing together"). Scholars have constructed complex theories of interdependence. Much ink has been spilled adjusting the theories to accommodate the evidence. At some level the apostles and other early ministers of the Word no doubt conferred with each other (see Luke 1:2). However, the similarities between the Gospels are owing to the fact that they were eyewitness accounts or based on eyewitness testimony, and that the Spirit inspired the authors to write as they did. The differences of wording or order between the Gospels have to do with the fact that the authors were led to handle the material differently according to their aims and how the eyewitness testimony reached them. In everything, however, the reliability of the Gospels need not be doubted. None of the supposed differences need be contradictions. Good harmonizing has been proposed for every seeming difficulty.

In fact, the veracity of the Scriptures is clearer because there are four written witnesses to the life, teaching, death, and resurrection of Christ. Far from detracting from the reliability of the accounts, the manifold witnesses to the truth of Christ has had a positive effect the world over. We have not just one witness, but more than three. If the truth of something must be tested by two or three witnesses (Deut. 17:6; 19:15), let people examine the claims of these four witnesses. Only those who are bent on caviling will find a problem where believers will find proof.

Matthew appropriately heads up the four Gospels with many references to and connections with the Old Testament Scriptures. Even the way the Gospel begins with a genealogy (Matt. 1:1–18) connects the coming of Christ with the Old Testament history and promises. The Gospel highlights Christ's saving ministry as Teacher and Savior in fulfillment of the Old Testament prophets. After calling His disciples, instructing them, and dying and rising for His church, Christ gave His people the charge to make disciples of all nations (Matt. 28:18–20) to fulfill the covenant with Abraham (Gen. 12:1–3). He promised to be with them to the end of the world (Matt. 28:20).

Mark's Gospel highlights the glory of Christ as the King of the kingdom. His glory is such that devils tremble, adversaries plot and scheme, and yet Christ's disciples are often slow to understand His identity and purpose. Gradually, through Christ's instruction and miracles, the disciples confess Christ as the Son of God. His mission as the Servant of the Lord takes Him to the death on the cross as a ransom for sin (Mark 10:45), and the head of the corner of God's building (Mark 12:10). Gloriously, He rises the third day and ascends to the place of majesty at God's right hand (Mark 16:19).

John's Gospel begins in eternity and focuses on the sublime character of Christ as the Word incarnate, dwelling among a sinful humanity, many of which reject Him as the way, truth, and life, but some of whom receive Him, thereby showing that they were born from above (John 1:12–13). Christ's glory is seen in the seven miracles or signs John selects, as well as the heavenly discourses John records. His death on the cross is to please His Father and to draw many to Himself (John 12:23–34). John's stated purpose is that "ye might believe that Jesus is the Christ, the Son of God, and that believing ye might have life through his name" (John 20:31).

In terms of the historical fabric of the New Testament, Luke and Acts are an important two-volume collection. Essentially, this two-volume work gives to the New Testament its basic historical backbone. Under the inspiration of the Holy Spirit, Luke has organized the history of Christ's life and work into two main phases: one leading up to and culminating with the ascension of Christ (Luke); the other tracing all the events that occur subsequent to and flowing from the ascension of Christ (Acts). In his Gospel, Luke the physician portrays the saving capacity within which Christ lives, ministers, and dies, accomplishing redemption (Luke 1:68–75). In Acts, he shows how Christ applies His accomplished redemption so as to save many from Israel and the nations, gathering a church to Himself, appointed unto everlasting life (Acts 2:47).

The events recorded in Luke through Acts cover almost seventy years. As best as we can surmise, Christ was born between 6 and 4 BC, before the death of Herod I in 4 BC. Acts ends while Paul is still in prison, likely in the early AD 60s. We know quite a bit about the history of Judaea at this time, largely from Josephus, the Jewish historian. Like most eras of political history, it was a time of intrigue, power struggles, murder, plots, and ambition that came up short.

The rise of Herod and his family was a remarkable backdrop for the coming of Christ. Herod was an Idumean, or Edomite, a descendant of Esau. The prominence that Rome saw fit to give him represented all that the world offers. After his death in 4 BC, the Herodian family continued their hold on the Jewish provinces. Three of Herod's sons governed the territories under Rome. Archaelaus was over Judaea (Matt. 2:22); Herod Antipas over Galilee and Perea, and Philip governed the regions across the Jordan (Luke 3:1). Other Herods occur in the book of Acts, including Herod Agrippa I (Acts 12) and Herod Agrippa II (Acts 26). The names seemed to change, but the struggles didn't. Christ summed it up like this: "Ye know that they which are accounted to rule over the Gentiles exercise lordship over them; and their great ones exercise authority upon them" (Mark 10:42).

How different it is in Christ's kingdom! From the loins of Jacob, not Esau, Christ came as God in the flesh. He did not seek His own will, but that of His Father. His kingdom was a glorious kingdom though with humble beginnings. He was meek and gave rest to many (Matt. 11:28–30). His work led to a final triumph, not over political foes and natural forces, but supernatural forces and demonic foes. But the way to this triumph is through death, the dying of the God-appointed Mediator, Christ Jesus the Lord. The Gospels are truly history; however, they are more than history. Thanks be to God, they give us God's transaction of redemption through Jesus Christ. That is truly good news.

INTRODUCTION TO THE BOOK OF SAINT MATTHEW

Authorship: The Gospel According to Matthew does not explicitly credit the apostle Matthew with authorship. Some have questioned the long-standing tradition that Matthew is the author of this gospel bearing his name. Many contemporary scholars believe that this gospel is of a late composition and relies heavily on other sources. There is no good reason, however, to believe that this traditional accreditation of Matthew as the author is not accurate. Internal evidence also alludes to Matthew's authorship, such as his use of the "tribute money" (see note at 22:19) and the story of Jesus and Peter paying the imperial tax (17:24–27)—things well known to a tax collector.

Matthew is mentioned five times throughout the New Testament (9:9; 10:3; Mark 3:18; Luke 6:15; Acts 1:13). He is also known as Levi and was a tax collector before Jesus called him to be a disciple. In Matt. 9:9–13, Jesus called Matthew as he was "sitting at the receipt of custom," and it is believed that Jesus gave Levi the name Matthew, meaning "gift of the Lord." As a tax collector he had good training in the scribal techniques needed to write good literature.

Date: Matthew's gospel was quoted in the late first or early second century in the writings of Ignatius, the *Didache*, Polycarp, the *Epistle of Pseudo-Barnabas*, and the testimony of Papias as cited in Eusebius's writings. In some of these references, Matthew is quoted with as much authority as the Old Testament.

Given the prophetic content of chs. 24 and 25, we are certain that Matthew was not written after AD 70 when Jerusalem was destroyed. Likewise, Matthew references the Sadducees, a political faction that disappeared shortly after AD 70. The early church father Irenaeus dates Matthew to the time when both Peter and Paul were in Rome, thus in the early 60s.

Theme: Jesus is both Christ and Emmanuel, fulfilling the ancient promises and bringing God's reign to earth through His life, death, and resurrection.

Purpose: To show how Jesus is the Messiah promised in the Old Testament, who in His death and resurrection saves His people from their sins.

Synopsis: *The Contribution of Matthew to Redemptive Revelation*
Matthew is centered on Christology, as is seen in the following considerations. *First*, Matthew shows how Jesus is the anticipated Messiah of God's people. The chronology of ch. 1 shows that Jesus belonged to the royal line of "David the king" (v. 6). Jesus' birth disturbs "Herod the king" (2:1) as the scribes speak of a time when a "Governor . . . shall rule my people Israel" (2:6). In His baptism, temptation, teachings, and miracles, Christ announces and brings into view the kingdom of heaven. Over Jesus' head, on the cross, hangs the epithet announcing his kingship (27:37). Jesus' final commission of His disciples, in the Great Commission, rests on Jesus having "All power . . . in heaven and in earth" (28:18). He is the King, the Messiah of God who has come into the world to save His people from their sins.

Second, as the Lord's anointed, Jesus is also Emmanuel, that is, "God with us" (1:23) and "the son of David" (1:1). At His baptism, the heavens are rent open and God proclaims, "This is my beloved Son, in whom I am well pleased" (3:17). Throughout His earthly ministry, Christ shows that the temple will no longer be the place of God meeting with His people, but that God now communes with His people in the person of Christ. Matthew highlights how the veil of the temple was rent in two at the death of Christ (27:51). Jesus is God dwelling in the midst of His people.

Third, Jesus is "the son of Abraham" (1:1). Christ is the culmination of God's promise to

Abraham that all the nations would be blessed through him. John the Baptist exhorts the Pharisees not to depend on their relation with Abraham, but to seek God through repentance (3:8–9). Likewise, Jesus opens the door for salvation to the Gentiles (8:10–12; 15:27–28).

Fourth, Jesus is the new Moses. The many discourses, especially the Sermon on the Mount (chs. 5–7) picture Christ as the Prophet sent by God. He has not come to abolish the law but to fulfill it (5:17). The new covenant is not an abrogation of the Mosaic law. Rather, Jesus' teaching gives the correct interpretation of the Mosaic law, showing the seriousness of the curses and the blessings. At the Mount of Transfiguration, the Father speaks the words: "hear ye him" (17:5), which recalls Moses' words concerning the great Prophet like himself, whom God would "raise up" (Deut. 18:15).

Outline:

- I. The Person of Jesus the Messiah (1:1—4:11)
  - A. Chronology of Jesus, the Son of David and Abraham (1:1–17)
  - B. The Birth of Jesus (1:18—2:23)
  - C. Preparation in the Wilderness (3:1—4:11)
    1. John the Baptist's Preaching (3:1–12)
    2. Christ's Baptism (3:13–17)
    3. Christ's Temptation (4:1–11)
- II. The Proclamation of Jesus the Messiah (4:12—16:28)
  - A. Jesus Begins to Preach (4:12—7:29)
    1. Jesus' First Disciples and First Miracles (4:12–25)
    2. The Sermon on the Mount (5:1—7:29)
  - B. Jesus' Ministry in Galilee: Teachings and Miracles (8:1—11:1)
    1. Miracles Performed in Galilee (8:1—9:38)
    2. Teaching on the Nature of Discipleship (10:1—11:1)
  - C. Jesus' Work as the Messiah (11:2–30)
  - D. The Authority of Jesus Challenged (12:1–50)
  - E. The Parables of the Kingdom of Heaven (13:1–58)
    1. Parable of the Sower (13:1–9)
    2. Purpose of Parables (13:10–17)
    3. Parable of the Sower Explained (13:18–23)
    4. Parable of the Tares (13:24–30)
    5. Parable of the Mustard Seed (13:31–33)
    6. Purpose of Parables (13:34–35)
    7. Parable of the Tares Explained (13:36–43)
    8. Parables of the Treasure and the Pearl (13:44–46)
    9. Parable of the Net (13:47–50)
    10. Jesus the Rejected Prophet (13:51–58)
  - F. John the Baptist's Death Reported to Jesus (14:1–13)
  - G. Several Miracles Performed (14:14–36)
  - H. Further Teaching on Discipleship (15:1–20)
  - I. Several Miracles Performed (15:21–39)
  - J. Jesus' Message Rejected and Accepted (16:1–28)
    1. Pharisees' and Sadducees' Rejection of Jesus (16:1–12)
    2. Peter's Confession of Christ (16:13–20)
    3. Jesus' Foretelling of His Death (16:21–28)
- III. The Passion, Death, and Resurrection of Jesus the Messiah (17:1—28:20)
  - A. Jesus' Transfiguration (17:1–13)
  - B. Jesus' Continued Ministry (17:14–27)
  - C. The Nature and Authority of the Church (18:1–35)
  - D. Jesus' Ministry in Judaea: Teachings and Miracles (19:1—25:46)
    1. Jesus' Teachings Concerning Divorce (19:1–12)
    2. Children in the Kingdom (19:13–15)
    3. Discipleship and Service (19:16—20:28)
    4. Jesus' Healing of Two Blind Men (20:29–34)
    5. Jesus in Jerusalem (21:1—23:39)
    6. The Olivet Discourse (24:1—25:46)
  - E. Jesus' Death and Resurrection (26:1—28:20)

1. Jesus' Feet Anointed (26:1–13)
2. Judas's Betrayal of Jesus (26:14–16)
3. The Last Supper (26:17–29)
4. Jesus' Arrest (26:30–56)
5. Jesus' Trial and Sentence (26:57—27:31)
6. Jesus' Death and Burial (27:32–66)
7. Jesus' Resurrection and the Great Commission (28:1–20)

THE GOSPEL ACCORDING TO SAINT

MATTHEW

CHAPTER 1

THE book of the generation of Jesus Christ, the
son of David, the son of Abraham.
2 Abraham begat Isaac; and Isaac begat Jacob;
and Jacob begat Judas and his brethren;
3 And Judas begat Phares and Zara of Thamar;
and Phares begat Esrom; and Esrom begat Aram;
4 And Aram begat Aminadab; and Aminadab
begat Naasson; and Naasson begat Salmon;
5 And Salmon begat Booz of Rachab; and Booz
begat Obed of Ruth; and Obed begat Jesse;
6 And Jesse begat David the king; and David the
king begat Solomon of her *that had been the wife*
of Urias;
7 And Solomon begat Roboam; and Roboam
begat Abia; and Abia begat Asa;
8 And Asa begat Josaphat; and Josaphat begat
Joram; and Joram begat Ozias;
9 And Ozias begat Joatham; and Joatham begat
Achaz; and Achaz begat Ezekias;
10 And Ezekias begat Manasses; and Manasses
begat Amon; and Amon begat Josias;
11 And Josias begat Jechonias and his brethren,
about the time they were carried away to Babylon:
12 And after they were brought to Babylon,
Jechonias begat Salathiel; and Salathiel begat
Zorobabel;
13 And Zorobabel begat Abiud; and Abiud begat
Eliakim; and Eliakim begat Azor;
14 And Azor begat Sadoc; and Sadoc begat Achim;
and Achim begat Eliud;
15 And Eliud begat Eleazar; and Eleazar begat
Matthan; and Matthan begat Jacob;
16 And Jacob begat Joseph the husband of Mary,
of whom was born Jesus, who is called Christ.
17 So all the generations from Abraham to David
are fourteen generations; and from David until
the carrying away into Babylon *are* fourteen
generations; and from the carrying away into
Babylon unto Christ *are* fourteen generations.
18 ¶ Now the birth of Jesus Christ was on this
wise: When as his mother Mary was espoused to
Joseph, before they came together, she was found
with child of the Holy Ghost.
19 Then Joseph her husband, being a just *man*,
and not willing to make her a publick example,

THE PERSON OF JESUS THE MESSIAH (1:1—4:11)

Chapter 1: *Jesus' genealogy is recorded, showing that He is the fulfillment of Abraham's promised seed. Matthew records His miraculous birth.*

Chronology of Jesus, the Son of David and Abraham (1:1–17)

1:1 *book of the generation.* Similar to Gen. 2:4. *son of David.* A common messianic title (vv. 17,20; 9:27; 12:23; 1 Chron. 17:11–12). *son of Abraham.* Heir of the covenant promises and Mediator of blessing to the nations (Gen. 12:1–3; 22:17–18). These historical roots place Him as fulfilling God's purposes throughout history. Jesus' life resembles the historical account of Israel's history.

1:2 *Abraham begat Isaac.* Matthew traces Jesus' genealogy from a pre-Davidic era to show Jesus' continuity with the promised seed of Abraham. *Judas.* Judah (Gen. 49:10).

1:3 *Thamar.* Tamar (Gen. 38).

1:5 *Rachab.* Rahab. She and her family alone were saved when Jericho fell (Josh. 2; 6:25).

1:16 *of whom.* That is Mary. Joseph is not said to be the father of Jesus, because he was not the biological father, even though he was the legal father. There is no scriptural warrant to think that Mary was without sin when she conceived Jesus. Given the extraordinary genealogy in the first 15 verses, we see that God used sinners, even the worst of sinners, to magnify His grace and power in redemption.

1:17 *fourteen generations . . . fourteen generations . . . fourteen generations.* The literary symmetry that Matthew uses here shows that the history of the Israelites was evidence of God's providential care over His people. Fourteen is the numerical value for David's name in Hebrew, showing the significance of the Son of David throughout the whole genealogy.

The Birth of Jesus (1:18—2:23)

1:18 While Mary and Joseph were *espoused* (or engaged), they were not yet married. For Mary to be with child would have been shocking. But the child was not the result of union with Joseph because it was *before they came together* (Luke 1:35). *with child of the Holy Ghost.* Given conception by the Holy Spirit—the fulfillment of prophecy (vv. 22–23) and the beginning of the new creation (Gen. 1:2).

1:19 *put her away privily.* Divorce her secretly, out of the public eye. On the basis of the Mosaic law, Joseph and Mary were legally bound to one another. Joseph intended to divorce Mary as the law allowed for in the case of infidelity. Thus, given Joseph's assumption that Mary had been unfaithful, he was *just* in what he purposed to do, though he was also compassionate, intending to divorce her privately.

1:20 *son of David.* The angel reminded Joseph that he

was minded to put her away privily.
20 But while he thought on these things, behold,
the angel of the Lord appeared unto him in a
dream, saying, Joseph, thou son of David, fear not
to take unto thee Mary thy wife: for that which is
conceived in her is of the Holy Ghost.
21 And she shall bring forth a son, and thou shalt
call his name JESUS: for he shall save his people
from their sins.
22 Now all this was done, that it might be fulfilled
which was spoken of the Lord by the prophet,
saying,
23 Behold, a virgin shall be with child, and shall
bring forth a son, and they shall call his name Em-
manuel, which being interpreted is, God with us.
24 Then Joseph being raised from sleep did as the
angel of the Lord had bidden him, and took unto
him his wife:
25 And knew her not till she had brought forth
her firstborn son: and he called his name JESUS.

CHAPTER 2

NOW when Jesus was born in Bethlehem of Judaea
in the days of Herod the king, behold, there came
wise men from the east to Jerusalem,
2 Saying, Where is he that is born King of the
Jews? for we have seen his star in the east, and are
come to worship him.
3 When Herod the king had heard *these things*, he
was troubled, and all Jerusalem with him.
4 And when he had gathered all the chief priests
and scribes of the people together, he demanded
of them where Christ should be born.
5 And they said unto him, In Bethlehem of
Judaea: for thus it is written by the prophet,
6 And thou Bethlehem, *in* the land of Juda, art
not the least among the princes of Juda: for out
of thee shall come a Governor, that shall rule my
people Israel.
7 Then Herod, when he had privily called the
wise men, enquired of them diligently what time
the star appeared.
8 And he sent them to Bethlehem, and said, Go
and search diligently for the young child; and
when ye have found *him*, bring me word again,
that I may come and worship him also.
9 When they had heard the king, they departed;
and, lo, the star, which they saw in the east, went
before them, till it came and stood over where the
young child was.
10 When they saw the star, they rejoiced with
exceeding great joy.
11 ¶ And when they were come into the house,

belonged to the house of David, and thus, God's purposes for the line of David were coming to fruition.

1:21 *JESUS.* The Greek equivalent of the Hebrew name Joshua, meaning "the LORD is salvation." *save his people from their sins.* Jesus did not come to overthrow political powers or correct social injustices, but rather to save His people from their moral guilt and spiritual ruin (18:11; 19:25–26; Luke 1:77; John 3:16–17; Acts 4:12).

1:22 *that it might be fulfilled.* Jesus is the fulfillment of the promised son of Isa. 7:14, a sign of both judgment and salvation. This verse is the first of many subsequent "fulfillments" of Scripture that Matthew will highlight in connection with Jesus (2:15,17,23; 4:14; 8:17; 12:17; 13:35; 21:4; 26:54,56; 27:9,35; cf. 3:15; 5:17).

1:23 *virgin.* Christianity maintains the virgin birth as a pillar of faith (Luke 1:34–35). *Emmanuel.* Hebrew, *God with us.* Jesus is God incarnate (Isa. 9:6). What is true of God in His attributes is also true of the person of Jesus.

Thoughts for Personal/Family Worship: Chapter 1

1. **Often it is tempting to skim over the long chronologies in the Bible. However, it helps us to see that the coming of Christ was already foreseen in the Old Testament (Luke 24:44–46). When we read of Abraham, Boaz, David, Solomon, and others we are to see that their greater Son is now coming into the world. Now the time of shadows is over. The Son Himself has now come. How does this fulfilled prophecy strengthen your faith?**
2. **Jesus' saving work is at the forefront of the Gospels. Matthew records the angel's words, "And she shall bring forth a son, and thou shalt call his name JESUS: for he shall save his people from their sins" (v. 21). Sinners of all stripes and dyes can find in this God-man a qualified and able Savior. His spotless life of obedience and His payment of the price for sin resulted in a complete and effective salvation. Are you trusting in Christ to save you from sin?**
3. **Though His personal name is Jesus, Christ's royal title is Emmanuel, "God with us." In the person and work of Jesus, God was coming to dwell or tabernacle among His people. He did this visibly during His life on earth, but He also promises to be with His people forever (28:20). How does Christ continue to be "God with us" even now while He is in heaven?**

Chapter 2: ***The wise men visit Jesus, the newborn king. Jesus' early years are recorded as His parents flee to Egypt and eventually settle in Nazareth.***

2:1 *Now when Jesus was born.* Likely a year or two after Jesus' birth. *Bethlehem of Judaea.* The city of David; Jesus is the true Son of David (1:1). *Herod.* A cruel tyrannical king, murdering several of his sons. *wise men.* These men came from the east around the territory of Babylon. The coming of the wise men fulfilled prophecy, including that the Gentiles would come to be blessed by Abraham's promised Seed (Gen. 22:18; Isa. 60:3; Zech. 8:23).

2:2 *star.* See Num. 24:17; Isa. 60:1–2. It may also have been something like God's glory cloud, which led Israel through the wilderness to the Promised Land.

2:6 *least among the princes.* The Lord's king will arise out of an insignificant city, Bethlehem (Mic. 5:2; cf. 1 Sam. 17:12).

2:7 *privily.* Secretly.

2:8 *that I may come and worship him also.* Herod spoke deceptively, as appeared later in the slaughtering of the children of Israel.

2:10 *exceeding great joy.* Herod and all Jerusalem were troubled at the news of the Davidic king, but the wise men rejoiced. The gospel of Christ is a savor of death unto death, as well as a savor of life unto life (2 Cor. 2:14–17).

they saw the young child with Mary his mother, and fell down, and worshipped him: and when they had opened their treasures, they presented unto him gifts; gold, and frankincense, and myrrh.

12 And being warned of God in a dream that they should not return to Herod, they departed into their own country another way.

13 And when they were departed, behold, the angel of the Lord appeareth to Joseph in a dream, saying, Arise, and take the young child and his mother, and flee into Egypt, and be thou there until I bring thee word: for Herod will seek the young child to destroy him.

14 When he arose, he took the young child and his mother by night, and departed into Egypt:

15 And was there until the death of Herod: that it might be fulfilled which was spoken of the Lord by the prophet, saying, Out of Egypt have I called my son.

16 ¶ Then Herod, when he saw that he was mocked of the wise men, was exceeding wroth, and sent forth, and slew all the children that were in Bethlehem, and in all the coasts thereof, from two years old and under, according to the time which he had diligently enquired of the wise men.

17 Then was fulfilled that which was spoken by Jeremy the prophet, saying,

18 In Rama was there a voice heard, lamentation, and weeping, and great mourning, Rachel weeping *for* her children, and would not be comforted, because they are not.

19 ¶ But when Herod was dead, behold, an angel of the Lord appeareth in a dream to Joseph in Egypt,

20 Saying, Arise, and take the young child and his mother, and go into the land of Israel: for they are dead which sought the young child's life.

21 And he arose, and took the young child and his mother, and came into the land of Israel.

22 But when he heard that Archelaus did reign in Judaea in the room of his father Herod, he was afraid to go thither: notwithstanding, being warned of God in a dream, he turned aside into the parts of Galilee:

23 And he came and dwelt in a city called Nazareth: that it might be fulfilled which was spoken by the prophets, He shall be called a Nazarene.

CHAPTER 3

In those days came John the Baptist, preaching in the wilderness of Judaea,

2 And saying, Repent ye: for the kingdom of heaven is at hand.

2:11 *worshipped him.* An indication of Jesus' deity (14:33). *treasures.* Gifts for royalty, acknowledging the kingship of Christ, and thus fulfilling prophecy (Pss. 45; 72:10–12; 110:3; Isa. 60:1–6).

2:13 Herod's destruction of the Jewish males is strikingly similar to Pharaoh's destruction of the Hebrew males (Ex. 1:22).

2:15 *Out of Egypt have I called my son.* Citing Hos. 11:1, which speaks of Israel being called out of Egypt in the exodus. Jesus is true Israel. This gospel often asserts that Christ is the divine Son of the Father (3:17; 4:3,6; 7:21; 8:29; 10:32–33; 11:25–27; 12:50; 14:33; 16:16–17; 17:5; 18:10–19; 20:23; 21:37–38; 22:2,42; 24:36; 25:34; 26:29,39,42,53,63–64; 27:40,43,54; 28:19).

2:16 *exceeding wroth.* Extremely angry. *coasts thereof.* Region around it. Herod's response to the birth of Jesus is in line with what was prophesied (Ps. 2:1–2).

2:17 *Jeremy the prophet.* Jeremiah.

2:18 Citing Jer. 31:15, a prophecy in connection with the Babylonian exile of Judah. The exile will not be permanent as God will set captives free through God's appointed Redeemer, Christ. While the young males are being killed, God is protecting Christ so that in His death and resurrection He would save His people from their sins.

2:22 *Archelaus.* A tyrant. Joseph was right to fear him. *room.* Place.

2:23 The word *Nazareth* suggests the Hebrew word for branch (*netzer;* Isa. 11:1; cf. Rev. 22:16). Nazareth was likely the place where David's descendants settled during the last two centuries BC, though it was also a city that was regarded as unimportant (John 1:46).

Thoughts for Personal/Family Worship: Chapter 2

1. **Jerusalem's response to the announcement of Christ's birth shows us the reality of our sinful hearts. The good news does not appear to be good until the Holy Ghost opens our ears and hearts to receive it as good news. Our hostility against God by nature runs deep. Like Herod, we would rage against Christ lest He would reveal our sin. Yet in spite of man's exceedingly wicked thoughts, God will fulfill all His counsel (Isa. 46:10). How does man's opposition to Christ appear today?**
2. **Matthew notes several dreams from God given to Joseph (v. 19; 1:20) and the wise men (v. 12). In today's world there are many people who claim to receive dreams from the Lord that reveal His personal will to them. However, now that redemption has been accomplished and God has finally spoken in His Son (Heb. 1:1–4), Scripture is God's means of revealing His gracious plan of redemption as well as His will for our lives.**
3. **Note Joseph's unwavering obedience to God, in both chs. 1 and 2. A sinner himself, Joseph showed this obedience as a fruit of God's work through Christ, his adopted Son. We too need to be ready and willing to obey the commands of God regardless of the personal conflicts this may cause (Heb. 11:26). How might it have been hard for Joseph to obey? How is it hard for you?**

Preparation in the Wilderness (3:1—4:11)

Chapter 3: ***John the Baptist prepares the way for Christ's public ministry by his preaching and by baptizing Jesus.***

John the Baptist's Preaching (3:1–12)

3:1 *In those days.* Nearly three decades have passed since the events of the previous chapter (Luke 3:23). *John the Baptist.* A Nazarite like Samuel and Samson, set apart for special service to God (Num. 6:1–21; Luke 1:15).

3:2 *Repent.* Turn from sin with hatred for it, and turn toward God with trust in His mercy and enduring resolve to new obedience to His will (Acts 26:18–20). *kingdom of heaven.* A

3 For this is he that was spoken of by the prophet Esaias, saying, The voice of one crying in the wilderness, Prepare ye the way of the Lord, make his paths straight.

4 And the same John had his raiment of camel's hair, and a leathern girdle about his loins; and his meat was locusts and wild honey.

5 Then went out to him Jerusalem, and all Judaea, and all the region round about Jordan,

6 And were baptized of him in Jordan, confessing their sins.

7 ¶ But when he saw many of the Pharisees and Sadducees come to his baptism, he said unto them, O generation of vipers, who hath warned you to flee from the wrath to come?

8 Bring forth therefore fruits meet for repentance:

9 And think not to say within yourselves, We have Abraham to *our* father: for I say unto you, that God is able of these stones to raise up children unto Abraham.

10 And now also the axe is laid unto the root of the trees: therefore every tree which bringeth not forth good fruit is hewn down, and cast into the fire.

11 I indeed baptize you with water unto repentance: but he that cometh after me is mightier than I, whose shoes I am not worthy to bear: he shall baptize you with the Holy Ghost, and *with* fire:

12 Whose fan *is* in his hand, and he will throughly purge his floor, and gather his wheat into the garner; but he will burn up the chaff with unquenchable fire.

13 ¶ Then cometh Jesus from Galilee to Jordan unto John, to be baptized of him.

14 But John forbad him, saying, I have need to be baptized of thee, and comest thou to me?

15 And Jesus answering said unto him, Suffer *it to be so* now: for thus it becometh us to fulfil all righteousness. Then he suffered him.

16 And Jesus, when he was baptized, went up straightway out of the water: and, lo, the heavens were opened unto him, and he saw the Spirit of God descending like a dove, and lighting upon him:

17 And lo a voice from heaven, saying, This is my beloved Son, in whom I am well pleased.

---

synonym for the kingdom of God (19:23–24), referring to His reign among men, beginning with God's grace in the hearts of sinners and ending in God's glory. The coming of the kingdom is both the opportunity and necessity of repentance.

3:3 *Esaias.* Isaiah (Isa. 40:3). *Prepare.* John's ministry was preparatory for the coming of Christ, here identified as *the Lord* (*Jehovah* God in Isa. 40). Repentance does not prepare sinners in the sense of making them worthy of God, but is the work of His grace in their souls (Jer. 32:40).

3:4 *raiment.* Clothing. John's appearance was similar to Elijah (2 Kings 1:8), identifying him as the forerunner of the Lord (Mal. 4:5).

3:6 *baptized . . . confessing their sins.* John's baptism was a sign of repentance, implying that the true plight of Israel was not the Roman occupation, but their separation from God because of their sins.

3:7 The populace congregated to receive John's baptism, while the religious leaders disdained John. This foreshadowed and prepared the people for their response to Jesus (Luke 7:29–30). *O generation of vipers.* John exposed the hypocrisy of the Pharisees and Sadducees who were not truly repentant.

3:8 *fruits meet for repentance.* Works fitting for one who has turned from sin to God (7:16). John's baptism was not a guarantee of personal salvation but a call to a new life.

3:9 *Abraham to our father.* Genealogical descent from Abraham, or any godly father or mother, is not sufficient to save anyone (Rom. 9:4–8); true repentance is needed. *God is able of these stones to raise up children unto Abraham.* As hard as it is to imagine stones becoming sons, nevertheless, God's work of grace is such that hearts of stone are changed into hearts of flesh (Ezek. 36:25–26).

3:10 *hewn.* Cut. God's coming kingdom brings with it imminent judgment (Ps. 96:13; Zeph. 2:1–2; Mal. 3:2). *fire.* An image of hell (v. 12; 5:22; 13:40,42,50; 18:8–9; 25:41), the judgment of God's wrath coming on those whose lives do not show evidence of repentance (*fruit*; v. 8; 7:19).

3:11 *baptize you with the Holy Ghost, and with fire.* Christ poured out the Spirit in great abundance upon His people (Acts 1:5; 2:38; 11:16; 1 Cor. 12:13). Baptism is both a proclamation of the gospel as well as a proclamation of judgment to all those who are not united to Christ (Rom. 6:3–6; 1 Cor. 10:2).

3:12 *fan.* Threshing fork used to separate grain from useless parts of the plant. *garner.* Barn used for grain storage. *unquenchable fire.* The wicked will suffer forever (18:8; 25:41,46). The coming of the Messiah will bring salvation and judgment, though what John the Baptist saw as one event is in fact two events (11:2–3). Though Christ's first coming divided people (10:34–35), it did not bring the final judgment (13:41–42) but instead accomplished salvation (John 3:16–21).

Christ's Baptism (3:13–17)

3:15 *Suffer.* Permit. *fulfil all righteousness.* Christ came not to destroy the law, but to fulfill it for His people (5:17), and to satisfy its demand for payment of sin by His death (20:28). This work began by His obedient submission to His Father's mission when He identified with His sinful people (1:21) by entering the waters of confession and repentance (vv. 2,6), though He was without sin (v. 17).

3:16 *Spirit of God descending.* God was anointing Christ with the Holy Spirit to empower Him for His work (Isa. 11:2; 61:1). The coming of the Spirit in the form of *a dove* suggests that Christ's work involved gentleness (10:16), sorrow (Isa. 38:14; 59:11), and new creation (Gen. 1:2; 8:10).

3:17 The Father, Son, and Holy Spirit all manifest themselves here as distinct persons in the Trinity (28:19). *beloved Son . . . well pleased.* God fully approved of the obedience of His Son (see note at 2:15), something which He could never have said in the same way of Israel or David's offspring, whose sonship foreshadowed the coming of the perfect Son (Ex. 4:22; Ps. 89:26–27). The language here alludes to Christ's calling to serve on God's throne as king and servant (Ps. 2:7; Isa. 42:1).

Thoughts for Personal/Family Worship: Chapter 3

1. **Repentance is not merely feeling bad about things we do or say. Nor is it simply forsaking certain bad habits. True repentance stems from the grace of God in the heart of a sinner, which makes him or her mourn over sin, hate it, and turn from it toward God and His ways.**

THE TRINITY

Part of the great inheritance that the church has received from Israel is the conviction that there is one—and only one—God. In numerous places and in various ways, the writers of the New Testament books reaffirm this bedrock confession of the old covenant people, "The LORD our God is one LORD" (Deut. 6:4). To this great confession of monotheism, the New Testament adds two vital affirmations. *First*, the God-breathed New Testament maintains unequivocally that Jesus is the one and only true way to knowing God. *Second*, there is the deep conviction that to know the one true God is also to know him as three Persons. It is none other than Jesus who leads His people along this pathway when He commands His disciples—and, through them, the church—to baptize believers into the one divine "name of the Father, and of the Son, and of the Holy Ghost" (Matt. 28:19). Here we find the names of Father, Son, and Holy Spirit coordinated in such a way as to imply their equality and their distinctness as Persons, but mention is made only of the singular *name* of the three, a distinct indication of their unity.

Then there are numerous passages in the letters of the apostle Paul where these three Persons of the Godhead are linked together as co-sources of the blessings that belong to believers in Christ. For instance, there is the benediction in 2 Cor. 13:14, and there is the way in which Paul, in 1 Cor. 12:4–6, traces the various manifestations of God's grace in the church—first to the Spirit, then to the Lord Jesus, and finally to God the Father.

In other parts of the New Testament the same phenomenon is to be observed. In the letters outside the Pauline corpus, as the Presbyterian theologian B. B. Warfield stressed, it is everywhere assumed that the redemptive activities of God rest on a threefold source in the Persons of the Trinity. Peter can speak of God's saints in various regions of Asia Minor as being "elect according to the foreknowledge of God the Father, through sanctification of the Spirit, unto obedience and sprinkling of the blood of Jesus Christ" (1 Peter 1:2). Jude writes his brief letter to encourage his readers to stand against apostasy by praying in the Holy Spirit, keeping themselves in the love of God, and waiting for the mercy of the Lord Jesus Christ (Jude 20–21). The author of Revelation pronounces upon the seven churches to which he writes "grace . . . and peace, from him which is, and which was, and which is to come; and from the seven Spirits which are before his throne; and from Jesus Christ" (Rev. 1:4–5).

Particularly rich in Trinitarian language is the Gospel of John. Early on in this Gospel we are told that God has given the Spirit in unlimited measure to Jesus, for "the Father loveth the Son, and hath given all things into his hands" (John 3:34–35). In the farewell discourse of John 14–16 Jesus tells his disciples, "the Holy Ghost, whom the Father will send in my name, he shall teach you all things, and bring all things to your remembrance, whatsoever I have said unto you" (John 14:26). Other verses in this section of John's Gospel, however, assert that Jesus is the One who will send the Spirit (John 15:26; 16:7). The Spirit is being sent in the place of Jesus as "*another* Comforter" (John 14:16, emphasis added), but it is only through the Spirit's presence in the disciples' lives that Jesus, and the Father, are also present (John 14:23). Like the other New Testament authors, John does not use the word *Trinity*, but the elements of Trinitarian faith are clearly here.

Thus, over the centuries the church has rightly taught that God is three fully divine, co-equal Persons who share one being. Careful consideration of the Scriptures reveals that this doctrine of the Trinity underlies, shapes, and informs all that the Bible teaches us about God.

CHAPTER 4

THEN was Jesus led up of the Spirit into the wilderness to be tempted of the devil.

2 And when he had fasted forty days and forty nights, he was afterward an hungred.

3 And when the tempter came to him, he said, If thou be the Son of God, command that these stones be made bread.

4 But he answered and said, It is written, Man shall not live by bread alone, but by every word that proceedeth out of the mouth of God.

5 Then the devil taketh him up into the holy city, and setteth him on a pinnacle of the temple,

6 And saith unto him, If thou be the Son of God, cast thyself down: for it is written, He shall give his angels charge concerning thee: and in *their* hands they shall bear thee up, lest at any time thou dash thy foot against a stone.

7 Jesus said unto him, It is written again, Thou shalt not tempt the Lord thy God.

8 Again, the devil taketh him up into an exceeding high mountain, and sheweth him all the kingdoms of the world, and the glory of them;

9 And saith unto him, All these things will I give thee, if thou wilt fall down and worship me.

10 Then saith Jesus unto him, Get thee hence, Satan: for it is written, Thou shalt worship the Lord thy God, and him only shalt thou serve.

11 Then the devil leaveth him, and, behold, angels came and ministered unto him.

12 ¶ Now when Jesus had heard that John was cast into prison, he departed into Galilee;

13 And leaving Nazareth, he came and dwelt in Capernaum, which is upon the sea coast, in the borders of Zabulon and Nephthalim:

14 That it might be fulfilled which was spoken by Esaias the prophet, saying,

15 The land of Zabulon, and the land of Nephthalim, *by* the way of the sea, beyond Jordan, Galilee of the Gentiles;

16 The people which sat in darkness saw great light; and to them which sat in the region and shadow of death light is sprung up.

17 ¶ From that time Jesus began to preach, and to say, Repent: for the kingdom of heaven is at hand.

Like the Pharisees in this chapter, many seem to want to repent or appear to repent, but there is no real fruit, because there is no true root. What fruit of repentance is there in your life?

2. **Christ came to John to be baptized not because He had a need for John's baptism of repentance, but because He would be like His brethren in all things (Heb. 2:17). He became like sinners so that He might make sinners more like Himself. Better yet: He was made sin, that sinners might be made the righteousness of God through Him (2 Cor. 5:21).**

Chapter 4: *Jesus is tempted by Satan in the wilderness. His public ministry commences with His preaching of repentance and the calling of His first disciples.*

Christ's Temptation (4:1–11)

4:1 *led up of the Spirit.* As the Spirit led Israel in the *wilderness* (Isa. 63:10–14; cf. Ex. 13:20–21; 16–17). God does not tempt people to sin (James 1:13), but does test them (Gen. 22:1) by putting them in situations of temptation (6:13). *tempted of the devil.* Jesus is a real human being, and His temptation should be taken as real temptation (Heb. 4:15).

4:2 *forty days and forty nights.* Like Moses on Mt. Sinai (Ex. 24:18; 34:28) and Israel's spies in the Promised Land (Num. 13:25), and Israel's years in the wilderness (Num. 14:33–34; 32:13). *an hungred.* Hungry.

4:3–10 The Devil's tempting of Jesus attacked His messianic mission, questioning whether He was the *Son of God* as the Father had just declared (3:17), and offering Him shortcuts instead of the path of humiliation and suffering. Satan tempted the first Adam in the garden to disbelieve God's Word (Gen. 3:1–6), and here he tempted the second Adam, who resists the tempter with the Word of God.

4:3 *command that these stones be made bread.* Jesus had the ability to miraculously turn the stones into bread. When Israel lacked food in the wilderness, they murmured against God (Ex. 16:2–3).

4:4 *It is written.* Jesus responded to temptations by quoting Scripture, validating the Old Testament as God's profitable Word (5:17–19; 2 Tim. 3:16), and showing that meditation on the Bible is our weapon in the spiritual fight (Isa. 49:2; Eph. 6:17). *not live by bread alone.* The experience of Israel in the wilderness teaches us to look beyond the physical to God's powerful will (Deut. 8:3).

4:6 *it is written.* The Devil twisted the Scripture itself into a means of temptation (Ps. 91:11–12). The Devil tempted Jesus to put God to the test, a sin that Israel had committed in the wilderness (Ex. 17:7).

4:7 Jesus again responded by quoting Scripture (Deut. 6:16). Jesus did not question His Father's ability to protect Him, but submitted to God's will to provide in His time.

4:9 *All . . . will I give thee.* The Devil is the ruler of this world (John 12:31), and seeks its worship (2 Cor. 4:4; Rev. 13), though he is subject to God's sovereignty (Job 1:9–12,21; 2:4–6,10; Ps. 103:19).

4:10 *Get thee hence.* Jesus banished the Devil, exercising His Lordship. *it is written.* Jesus responded with unswerving allegiance to the worship of God alone (Deut. 6:13), showing Himself faithful to keep the first commandment that Israel so often broken. Jesus is the true Israel, the true Son of God.

4:11 *angels . . . ministered unto him.* Ironically, after Jesus refuses to force the angels to act (vv. 6–7), the Father sends them to care for His weary Son, as they do for all His children (Heb. 1:14).

THE PROCLAMATION OF JESUS THE MESSIAH (4:12—16:28)

Jesus Begins to Preach (4:12—7:29)

Jesus' First Disciples and First Miracles (4:12–25)

4:12–16 *Zabulon and Nephthalim.* Zebulun and Naphtali, two of the most northern tribes of Israel, coinciding with Galilee, an area viewed by strict rabbis as of mixed blood. Christ began His ministry in what was perceived as the spiritually darkest region of Israel, as Isaiah had prophesied (Isa. 9:1–2). His preaching of repentance was like rays of *light*, marking the dawning of a new day.

4:17 *Repent: for the kingdom of heaven is at hand.* The same message that John the Baptist preached (see note at 3:2), and

18 ¶ And Jesus, walking by the sea of Galilee, saw
two brethren, Simon called Peter, and Andrew his
brother, casting a net into the sea: for they were
fishers.
19 And he saith unto them, Follow me, and I will
make you fishers of men.
20 And they straightway left *their* nets, and
followed him.
21 And going on from thence, he saw other two
brethren, James *the son* of Zebedee, and John
his brother, in a ship with Zebedee their father,
mending their nets; and he called them.
22 And they immediately left the ship and their
father, and followed him.
23 ¶ And Jesus went about all Galilee, teaching in
their synagogues, and preaching the gospel of the
kingdom, and healing all manner of sickness and
all manner of disease among the people.
24 And his fame went throughout all Syria: and
they brought unto him all sick people that were
taken with divers diseases and torments, and
those which were possessed with devils, and those
which were lunatick, and those that had the palsy;
and he healed them.
25 And there followed him great multitudes
of people from Galilee, and *from* Decapolis,
and *from* Jerusalem, and *from* Judaea, and *from*
beyond Jordan.

CHAPTER 5

AND seeing the multitudes, he went up into a
mountain: and when he was set, his disciples
came unto him:
2 And he opened his mouth, and taught them,
saying,
3 Blessed *are* the poor in spirit: for theirs is the
kingdom of heaven.
4 Blessed *are* they that mourn: for they shall be
comforted.
5 Blessed *are* the meek: for they shall inherit the
earth.
6 Blessed *are* they which do hunger and thirst
after righteousness: for they shall be filled.

---

the same urgent call that the gospel makes to us today (Acts 17:30–31).

4:18–22 *Simon . . . Andrew . . . James . . . John.* Future apostles (10:2), whom Jesus would train to evangelize the world (*make you fishers of men*; 10:7; 28:19).

4:19 *Follow me.* Jesus did not simply invite these men but commanded them to be His disciples. For us as well, this command cannot be negotiated but requires our utmost allegiance (10:24–42; 16:24–26).

4:23 *went about all Galilee.* This is the beginning of Jesus' Galilean ministry.

4:24–25 *divers.* Various. *possessed with devils.* Literally, "demonized," severely afflicted by evil spirits (8:16,28,33; 9:32; 12:22; 15:22; cf. 10:1,8; 12:43). *lunatick.* Suffering from seizures. *palsy.* Paralysis. Jesus' fame spread all around the surrounding region and His followers grew to include many from these different regions, representing both Jews and Gentiles (*Decapolis*). Jesus' messianic authority knows no limits as He healed many afflicted with a variety of ailments.

Thoughts for Personal/Family Worship: Chapter 4

1. **Christ's temptation gives us both the pattern and power for overcoming the Devil. The pattern: recognizing how Satan tempts us to doubt God's Word and goodness and resisting the Devil by exercising faith in specific truths of Scripture. The power: although our first Adam fell under temptation, casting all mankind under the Devil's power, Christ stood firm and therefore can effectively lead us to conquer sin (Heb. 2:18; 4:15; 1 John 3:8). How do we find victory over temptation in Him?**
2. **Though these men would be specially trained by Christ for apostleship (ch. 10), Christ's call is essentially the same in every age: "Follow me." Discipleship involves submission to Christ's teaching, fellowship with His person, imitation of His ways, and setting aside everything that hinders our allegiance to Him (vv. 18–22). He has a right to each of our lives. He alone deserves to be followed. The life of faith is one of following the Lamb wherever He leads (Rev. 14:4). What does this mean in your life right now?**

The Sermon on the Mount (5:1—7:29)

Chapter 5: ***Jesus pronounces His humble disciples to be the blessed heirs of the kingdom of heaven, and teaches the relationship between the moral law and God's kingdom.***

5:1 This is the first of the five great discourses of Christ recorded in this gospel (chs. 5–7; 10; 13; 18; 24–25). *went up into a mountain.* As Moses did when God revealed the law (Ex. 19:3,20; 24:12). Christ is the new and greater Moses, the supreme Prophet (17:3–5; Deut. 18:15). Jesus' message holds together in Himself as King of the kingdom (13:41; 16:28; 21:5; 25:34; 27:37). His kingdom or reign has already begun in His people (vv. 3,10), transforming their lives by changing their nature (7:17; 12:33; 15:13). Christ's standards of obedience are impossible apart from His grace, and His laws constantly press His people to seek more grace from God (6:9–13).

5:3–10 The Beatitudes of Christ are a pithy exposition of repentance in light of the kingdom (4:17). *Blessed.* Rich in the benefits of God's grace, regardless of their present, outward condition (Pss. 1:1; 2:12; 112:1). *theirs is the kingdom of heaven.* The present tense (vv. 3,10) implies that these people already partake of God's reign in this present life by the Spirit (12:28), though the full experience of God's glory is yet to be experienced in the future (*they shall*; cf. 13:43).

5:3 *poor in spirit.* Recognizing their complete spiritual bankruptcy (Isa. 57:15; 66:2; Luke 18:9–14; Rev. 3:17).

5:4 *mourn.* Not the sorrow of the world, but sorrow over sin against God, producing repentance and zeal for the Lord (2 Cor. 7:10–11). *comforted.* Christ's Spirit-anointed preaching announces that God will heal the brokenhearted sinner and replace sorrow with joy (Isa. 61:1–3; cf. Ps. 30:5).

5:5 *meek.* Not weakness or passivity, but humility, gentleness, and patience in doing good as they wait on the Lord for vindication and blessing (Ps. 37:11). *inherit the earth.* Receive the promised covenant inheritance (Rom. 4:13) in the new creation (Isa. 65:17–18; 2 Peter 3:13; Rev. 21:1).

5:6 *hunger and thirst.* Strongly desire to live in a manner pleasing to the Father (*righteousness*; vv. 10,20; Luke 1:75). *be filled.* They will be satisfied with the holiness God gives them (1 John 3:2).

7 Blessed *are* the merciful: for they shall obtain
mercy.
8 Blessed *are* the pure in heart: for they shall see
God.
9 Blessed *are* the peacemakers: for they shall be
called the children of God.
10 Blessed *are* they which are persecuted for
righteousness' sake: for theirs is the kingdom of
heaven.
11 Blessed are ye, when *men* shall revile you, and
persecute *you*, and shall say all manner of evil
against you falsely, for my sake.
12 Rejoice, and be exceeding glad: for great *is*
your reward in heaven: for so persecuted they the
prophets which were before you.
13 ¶ Ye are the salt of the earth: but if the salt have
lost his savour, wherewith shall it be salted? it is
thenceforth good for nothing, but to be cast out,
and to be trodden under foot of men.
14 Ye are the light of the world. A city that is set
on an hill cannot be hid.
15 Neither do men light a candle, and put it
under a bushel, but on a candlestick; and it giveth
light unto all that are in the house.
16 Let your light so shine before men, that they
may see your good works, and glorify your Father
which is in heaven.
17 ¶ Think not that I am come to destroy the law,
or the prophets: I am not come to destroy, but to
fulfil.
18 For verily I say unto you, Till heaven and earth
pass, one jot or one tittle shall in no wise pass
from the law, till all be fulfilled.
19 Whosoever therefore shall break one of these
least commandments, and shall teach men so, he
shall be called the least in the kingdom of heaven:
but whosoever shall do and teach *them*, the same
shall be called great in the kingdom of heaven.
20 For I say unto you, That except your righ-
teousness shall exceed *the righteousness* of the
scribes and Pharisees, ye shall in no case enter
into the kingdom of heaven.
21 ¶ Ye have heard that it was said by them of old
time, Thou shalt not kill; and whosoever shall kill
shall be in danger of the judgment:
22 But I say unto you, That whosoever is angry
with his brother without a cause shall be in
danger of the judgment: and whosoever shall

5:7 *merciful.* Those who respond to human need with compassion and grace (9:27; 15:22) out of a sense of their own need for mercy (18:33). *obtain mercy.* Those who show compassion to others will receive compassion from God on judgment day (Matt. 25:31–40; James 2:12–13).

5:8 *pure in heart.* Not external purity or ceremonial cleanness (15:1–20), but inward sincerity (though not perfection) in faith and love (Pss. 24:4; 73:1; Acts 15:9; 1 Tim. 1:5; 2 Tim. 2:22; 1 Peter 1:22). *see God.* Enjoy close fellowship with God in His glory through Jesus Christ (John 17:24; Rev. 22:3–4).

5:9 *peacemakers.* Not smoothing over disobedience to God's Word, but seeking to restore people to harmony with God and each other (Rom. 12:18–21; 14:19), as Christ did on the cross (Eph. 2:14–17). *children of God.* Literally, "sons of God." God will vindicate and glorify His adopted children for the ways they have shown that they bear His image by grace (v. 45).

5:10 *persecuted.* Jesus makes clear that the lives of His disciples will inevitably invite insult and mistreatment because of the distinctive qualities highlighted in previous verses (*for righteousness' sake*).

5:11–12 *revile.* Insult or mock, which together with making false accusations is the first step of persecution. *reward in heaven.* Joy is possible in the pain of persecution by trusting that all earthly loss will be more than repaid with eternal blessings. *so persecuted they the prophets.* The persecuted church stands in the noble line of Old Testament saints who suffered for the Lord (23:34–35; Heb. 11).

5:13 *salt.* Even in small quantities, it is pleasing in its distinctive flavor (Job 6:6) and powerfully effective as a preservative (Lev. 2:13; Num. 18:19) and antiseptic (Ezek. 16:4). The godliness of Christ's true disciples, though they are few, makes them a potent force to preserve good and restrain evil in the world. *lost his savour.* If the professing people of God lose their distinctive qualities described in the Beatitudes, they become worthless and ineffective.

5:14–26 *light of the world.* The people of God are transformed by knowing God's glory in Christ so that their *good works* attract people to become worshipers of God (Isa. 60:1–3; John 8:12; 12:35–36; 2 Cor. 4:6; Eph. 5:7–14). *city . . . on an hill.* Christ's church is the new Jerusalem (John 4:21–24; Gal. 4:26; Heb. 12:22; Rev. 21:9–10).

5:17 *not . . . to destroy, but to fulfil.* Christ had a high regard for the Old Testament, citing it as the authoritative Word of God (John 10:35). Christ obeyed the law of Moses fully and revealed the true meaning and spirit of its precepts.

5:18 *jot . . . tittle.* The smallest pen strokes in Hebrew script. Divine inspiration extends to the smallest parts of the prophetic writings, and therefore God will bring to completion all He has said in His Word without fail (24:35).

5:19 *these least commandments.* The context shows that Christ was not speaking of the ceremonial law, but the moral teachings of the Old Testament summed up in the Ten Commandments (vv. 21,27,31,33,38,43). Not only does Jesus fulfill the Scriptures, but His people are to follow His example and teach others to do likewise (28:20) so that their reward may be great in the kingdom (v. 12).

5:20 *exceed the righteousness of the scribes and Pharisees.* Much of the remainder of this sermon is showing practically what Jesus meant. The scribes and Pharisees kept the law only in an outward manner distorted by human tradition (15:3–9; 23:26–27). Saving repentance that brings a person to the kingdom engages Christ's disciples in sincere, hearty obedience to the Bible (7:21; 12:50).

5:21–48 Jesus speaks six times concerning what the people have heard and contrasts it with His authoritative explanation of the commandments.

5:21 *Thou shalt not kill . . . danger of the judgment.* Jesus cited the sixth commandment and referred to one of its applications (Ex. 20:13; 21:12–14).

5:22 *Raca.* A transliteration of an Aramaic term that is almost synonymous with the Greek word for *fool*. Jesus traced the beginning of murder to the intention of the heart and said that this alone brought guilt worthy of God's damnation (1 John 3:15). *hell.* Greek, *gehenna*, originally from the Hebrew phrase "valley of Hinnom" (see note at Jer. 19:6), used by Christ for the final and never-ending punishment of the wicked in

say to his brother, Raca, shall be in danger of the
council: but whosoever shall say, Thou fool, shall
be in danger of hell fire.
23 Therefore if thou bring thy gift to the altar,
and there rememberest that thy brother hath
ought against thee;
24 Leave there thy gift before the altar, and go thy
way; first be reconciled to thy brother, and then
come and offer thy gift.
25 Agree with thine adversary quickly, whiles
thou art in the way with him; lest at any time the
adversary deliver thee to the judge, and the judge
deliver thee to the officer, and thou be cast into
prison.
26 Verily I say unto thee, Thou shalt by no means
come out thence, till thou hast paid the uttermost
farthing.
27 ¶ Ye have heard that it was said by them of old
time, Thou shalt not commit adultery:
28 But I say unto you, That whosoever looketh
on a woman to lust after her hath committed
adultery with her already in his heart.
29 And if thy right eye offend thee, pluck it out,
and cast *it* from thee: for it is profitable for thee
that one of thy members should perish, and not
that thy whole body should be cast into hell.
30 And if thy right hand offend thee, cut it off,
and cast *it* from thee: for it is profitable for thee
that one of thy members should perish, and not
that thy whole body should be cast into hell.
31 It hath been said, Whosoever shall put away
his wife, let him give her a writing of divorcement:
32 But I say unto you, That whosoever shall put
away his wife, saving for the cause of fornication,
causeth her to commit adultery: and whosoever
shall marry her that is divorced committeth
adultery.
33 ¶ Again, ye have heard that it hath been said by
them of old time, Thou shalt not forswear thyself,
but shalt perform unto the Lord thine oaths:
34 But I say unto you, Swear not at all; neither by
heaven; for it is God's throne:
35 Nor by the earth; for it is his footstool: neither
by Jerusalem; for it is the city of the great King.
36 Neither shalt thou swear by thy head, because
thou canst not make one hair white or black.
37 But let your communication be, Yea, yea; Nay,
nay: for whatsoever is more than these cometh
of evil.
38 ¶ Ye have heard that it hath been said, An eye
for an eye, and a tooth for a tooth:
39 But I say unto you, That ye resist not evil: but
whosoever shall smite thee on thy right cheek,
turn to him the other also.
40 And if any man will sue thee at the law, and
take away thy coat, let him have *thy* cloke also.
41 And whosoever shall compel thee to go a mile,
go with him twain.
42 Give to him that asketh thee, and from him
that would borrow of thee turn not thou away.
43 ¶ Ye have heard that it hath been said, Thou
shalt love thy neighbour, and hate thine enemy.
44 But I say unto you, Love your enemies, bless
them that curse you, do good to them that hate
you, and pray for them which despitefully use
you, and persecute you;
45 That ye may be the children of your Father
which is in heaven: for he maketh his sun to rise

---

fire (vv. 29–30; 10:28; 18:9; 23:15,33; cf. 3:10,12).

5:23 *bring thy gift to the altar.* The old covenant offering of sacrifices illustrates the act of worship. One cannot serve God while remaining in an unreconciled state with his or her brother (Prov. 15:8). *ought against thee.* Any legitimate offense according to Scripture.

5:25 *Agree . . . quickly.* Jesus stressed the urgency of seeking reconciliation in terms of earthly legal judgments, but with implications for heavenly and eternal judgment. *adversary.* Opponent.

5:27 *Thou shalt not commit adultery.* Jesus next cited the seventh commandment (Ex. 20:14), but He also refers to the tenth commandment against coveting another's wife (Ex. 20:17).

5:28 *lust.* Like hatred, sexual sin begins with evil desires in the *heart* (15:19).

5:29–30 *pluck it out . . . cut it off.* Not a call to self-mutilation, which cannot overcome sin in the heart, but a figure of speech for taking serious and costly action to kill sin (18:7–9; Col. 3:5). *cast into hell.* Sexual lust will condemn a man to eternal damnation, unless truly repented of.

5:31–32 Christ cited Deut. 24:1–4, which did not command divorce, but regulated it as a tragic reality among sinful people (19:7–9). *fornication.* A general term for sexual sin (1 Cor. 5:1; 6:13,18; 7:2), which is such a violation of the bond of "one flesh" that it permits divorce (19:3–9).

5:34–37 Christ referred to the old covenant commands to keep one's oaths (Lev. 19:12; Num. 30:2; Deut. 23:21–23). He condemned the practice of swearing oaths lightly by avoiding direct reference to God (23:16–22) and commended directness, honesty, and integrity in all speech (*Yea, yea; Nay, nay*; James 5:12). The Lord did not forbid all vows, but modeled reverent and truthful speech under oath (26:63–64; cf. Gen. 14:22; 21:24; Josh. 2:12; 2 Cor. 1:23; Heb. 6:16).

5:38 *eye for an eye . . . tooth for a tooth.* Jesus cited the law of retaliation (*lex talionis*), which did not justify personal revenge (Prov. 20:22) but limited judicial punishments (Ex. 21:24–25; Lev. 24:20; Deut. 19:21).

5:39–42 *smite thee . . . cheek.* A humiliating insult (26:67; 2 Cor. 11:20). The disciple of Jesus must be willing to suffer insult and injustice without retaliating in revenge. *coat . . . cloke.* Losing the tunic and cloak would leave a man wearing only a loincloth—Christ spoke in hyperbole (vv. 29–30). Civil authorities have the responsibility to punish the evildoer (Rom. 13:1–7), but individuals should not seek revenge but overcome evil by doing good (Rom. 12:19–21).

5:43 *love thy neighbour.* Christ cited Lev. 19:18. *hate thine enemy.* Not an Old Testament command.

5:44 *Love your enemies.* This principle is also taught in the Old Testament (Ex. 23:4–5; Prov. 25:21–22). *despitefully use.* Insult or slander.

5:45 *children of your Father.* Children reflect the image of their fathers (v. 48). *maketh his sun to rise . . . sendeth rain.*

on the evil and on the good, and sendeth rain on
the just and on the unjust.
46 For if ye love them which love you, what re-
ward have ye? do not even the publicans the same?
47 And if ye salute your brethren only, what do ye
more *than others*? do not even the publicans so?
48 Be ye therefore perfect, even as your Father
which is in heaven is perfect.

CHAPTER 6

TAKE heed that ye do not your alms before men,
to be seen of them: otherwise ye have no reward
of your Father which is in heaven.
2 Therefore when thou doest *thine* alms, do not
sound a trumpet before thee, as the hypocrites do
in the synagogues and in the streets, that they may
have glory of men. Verily I say unto you, They
have their reward.
3 But when thou doest alms, let not thy left hand
know what thy right hand doeth:
4 That thine alms may be in secret: and thy
Father which seeth in secret himself shall reward
thee openly.
5 ¶ And when thou prayest, thou shalt not be as
the hypocrites *are*: for they love to pray standing
in the synagogues and in the corners of the streets,
that they may be seen of men. Verily I say unto
you, They have their reward.
6 But thou, when thou prayest, enter into thy
closet, and when thou hast shut thy door, pray to
thy Father which is in secret; and thy Father which
seeth in secret shall reward thee openly.
7 But when ye pray, use not vain repetitions, as
the heathen *do*: for they think that they shall be
heard for their much speaking.
8 Be not ye therefore like unto them: for your
Father knoweth what things ye have need of,
before ye ask him.
9 After this manner therefore pray ye: Our Father
which art in heaven, Hallowed be thy name.
10 Thy kingdom come. Thy will be done in earth,
as *it is* in heaven.
11 Give us this day our daily bread.

God's providence reveals His goodness in the ordinary events of nature (Acts 14:17). *evil . . . good . . . just . . . unjust.* Though God will sharply distinguish between the righteous and the wicked on judgment day (7:21,23), He presently shows much kindness to His enemies (Rom. 2:4–5).

5:46 *publicans.* Tax collectors, regarded as outsiders to the covenant people (18:17). Even the wicked often love those who treat them well or are part of their group.

5:47 *salute.* Greet.

Thoughts for Personal/Family Worship: Chapter 5

1. **When Christ spoke the Beatitudes, He was not promoting some kind of perfectionism or offering a higher level of spirituality to those already saved, but giving a concise description of the character of those blessed by God. How would you summarize the kind of person Jesus says is a member of His kingdom? How can these traits help believers recognize the work of the Spirit in their hearts and confirm their assurance of salvation?**
2. **There are many people who believe that being a Christian frees one from all moral imperatives or obligations to obey God's laws. This is antinomianism. Some people believe Christians should be directed mostly by spiritual experiences and feelings instead of careful attention to the Bible. This is unbiblical mysticism. Yet others build their lives upon the pride and self-righteousness of keeping a list of rules for behavior that were largely invented by man. This is legalism. Jesus rejects all these errors and teaches us that the core of true godliness is a heart set free by the power of His kingdom in order to seek after obedience to God's laws with humility and love. This is the piety promised and practiced in the Old Testament (Pss. 40:8; 119:16), revealed with even more clarity and power by the ultimate Prophet of the church. How can you seek to resist distortions of God's truth even as you pursue true piety?**
3. **If your heart delights in Christ's teachings even as they humble you over your sins, then it is a sign that you are a Christian. The believer delights in the law of God in the inner man even as he grieves over the rebellion against that law he finds in himself. If this is true of you, what is one way Christ's words challenge you to grow in repentance? If you find Christ's words offensive, foolish, or legalistic, then what does that reveal about your relationship with Him?**

Chapter 6: ***Jesus continues teaching on the kingdom of heaven, especially the inward character of it.***

6:1 *alms.* Acts of charity. *reward.* Faith seeks God's blessing (Heb. 11:6). *Father which is in heaven.* This title for God, used many times throughout chs. 6–7, reminds us both of God's compassionate love and His sovereign majesty (v. 9).

6:2 *when thou doest.* Jesus assumed that His disciples would give alms, pray, and fast (vv. 5,16) and instructs them how to do so correctly. *hypocrites.* A pretender, likely referring to the Pharisees (ch. 23), but hypocrisy can be present in anyone who puts on a religious facade.

6:3–4 *let not thy left hand know what thy right hand doeth.* Rather than giving to impress people, Christ's disciples should give in *secret*, not even thinking much of it themselves, but concerned only to please the *Father*.

6:5 *love to pray standing in the synagogues.* God does not condemn public prayer (2 Chron. 6:13–42; Neh. 9; Acts 4:24–31), but He does condemn a spirit of self-display and self-righteousness (Luke 18:9).

6:7 Prayers are heard not because of their length but when they are offered in faith. There are many examples of short, effective prayers (Ex. 32:31–32; 1 Kings 3:6–9; 1 Chron. 4:10; Luke 23:42; Acts 7:60).

6:9 *After this manner.* Jesus gives a model prayer to His disciples. *Our Father which art in heaven.* Prayer begins by addressing God as He has revealed Himself in the gospel of Christ (see note at v. 1). *Hallowed be thy name.* A request that God would cause people to honor Him as holy.

6:10 *Thy kingdom come.* A request for the Lord to reign as King in grace and glory (see note at 3:2). *Thy will be done.* A petition for people to obey God's will as expressed in His commandments (5:19).

6:11 *daily bread.* Basic needs for each day. This petition underscores man's complete dependence on God's providence

12 And forgive us our debts, as we forgive our
debtors.
13 And lead us not into temptation, but deliver
us from evil: For thine is the kingdom, and the
power, and the glory, for ever. Amen.
14 For if ye forgive men their trespasses, your
heavenly Father will also forgive you:
15 But if ye forgive not men their trespasses,
neither will your Father forgive your trespasses.
16 ¶ Moreover when ye fast, be not, as the hyp-
ocrites, of a sad countenance: for they disfigure
their faces, that they may appear unto men to fast.
Verily I say unto you, They have their reward.
17 But thou, when thou fastest, anoint thine
head, and wash thy face;
18 That thou appear not unto men to fast, but
unto thy Father which is in secret: and thy Father,
which seeth in secret, shall reward thee openly.
19 ¶ Lay not up for yourselves treasures upon
earth, where moth and rust doth corrupt, and
where thieves break through and steal:
20 But lay up for yourselves treasures in heaven,
where neither moth nor rust doth corrupt, and
where thieves do not break through nor steal:
21 For where your treasure is, there will your
heart be also.
22 The light of the body is the eye: if therefore
thine eye be single, thy whole body shall be full
of light.
23 But if thine eye be evil, thy whole body shall
be full of darkness. If therefore the light that is in
thee be darkness, how great *is* that darkness!
24 ¶ No man can serve two masters: for either
he will hate the one, and love the other; or else
he will hold to the one, and despise the other. Ye
cannot serve God and mammon.
25 Therefore I say unto you, Take no thought
for your life, what ye shall eat, or what ye shall
drink; nor yet for your body, what ye shall put on.
Is not the life more than meat, and the body than
raiment?
26 Behold the fowls of the air: for they sow not,
neither do they reap, nor gather into barns; yet
your heavenly Father feedeth them. Are ye not
much better than they?
27 Which of you by taking thought can add one
cubit unto his stature?
28 And why take ye thought for raiment?
Consider the lilies of the field, how they grow;
they toil not, neither do they spin:
29 And yet I say unto you, That even Solomon
in all his glory was not arrayed like one of these.
30 Wherefore, if God so clothe the grass of the
field, which to day is, and to morrow is cast into
the oven, *shall he* not much more *clothe* you, O ye
of little faith?
31 Therefore take no thought, saying, What shall
we eat? or, What shall we drink? or, Wherewithal
shall we be clothed?
32 (For after all these things do the Gentiles seek:)
for your heavenly Father knoweth that ye have
need of all these things.
33 But seek ye first the kingdom of God, and his
righteousness; and all these things shall be added
unto you.
34 Take therefore no thought for the morrow: for

in all areas of life (vv. 25–26; 5:45).

6:12 *forgive us.* Disciples are marked by continual confession of sins to God and dependence on Christ's grace for forgiveness (1 John 1:7,9). *our debts.* Sin is a failure to fulfill our obligation to God, resulting in enormous debts to divine justice (18:24). *as we forgive our debtors.* Our mercy to others does not effect or secure God's forgiveness to us, but it does express a heart truly humbled by one's own sins and grateful for God's grace—marks of a person saved and forgiven by God.

6:13 *lead us not into temptation, but deliver us from evil.* Requests for protection from situations exposing our spiritual weakness (26:41) and for our rescue from the power of sin and Satan (Ps. 19:13; 1 Cor. 10:13).

6:16–18 *when ye fast.* Fasting is a discipline of denying the body its nourishment for a time in order to devote oneself to seeking God (4:2; 9:14–15; 17:21; Neh. 9:1; Dan. 9:3; Joel 2:12; Luke 18:12; Acts 13:2–3; 14:23). Again the emphasis is on doing the spiritual discipline in private so as to be rewarded by *thy Father, which seeth in secret.*

6:19–20 *Heaven* and *earth* are contrasted here as two spheres of existence. Heaven is eternal and incorruptible (1 Peter 1:4), while earth is transitory and corruptible (Heb. 1:11).

6:20 *lay up for yourselves treasures in heaven.* Live for the eternal kingdom (v. 33) by obeying Christ's commands and by having faith in God's promise of reward (Heb. 11:6).

6:22 *eye be single.* A figure of speech for being focused on one thing, namely the King of the kingdom.

6:23 *eye be evil.* A figure of speech for a perspective clouded by greed (see note at Prov. 23:6).

6:24 *two masters.* Just as the eye cannot be divided, neither can the heart be divided. Jesus is calling His disciples to singular trust and obedience (James 4:8). *mammon.* Money, wealth.

6:25–32 The command not to worry (*take no thought*) rests on the fact that God who created life and sustains all things is able and willing to provide for His children's material needs of food (*meat*) and clothing (*raiment*). Confidence arises from a practical application of the doctrine of God's providential care (5:45). This is not teaching us to neglect our work (Eph. 4:28; 2 Thess. 3:12), but to labor faithfully in our callings, with our hearts set not on earthly things but on God's kingdom (v. 33).

6:30 *ye of little faith.* Anxiety about earthly goods is the opposite of trust in the Word of God (13:22).

6:32–33 *the Gentiles seek . . . seek ye first.* Those who do not know God are characterized by their pursuit of earthly needs and pleasures, whether out of fear or greed, but Christ's disciples must give their highest priority and greatest efforts to their pursuit of God's glorious reign (*kingdom*) and obedience to His will (*righteousness;* v. 10), trusting God to provide for their needs.

6:34 *the morrow.* Tomorrow. *Sufficient . . . evil thereof.* Each day has enough trouble for itself.

Thoughts for Personal/Family Worship: Chapter 6

1. Our private prayers, tithing, and fasting should be marked by a veil of privacy or secrecy. This curtails the sinful ambition to be praised by man. God rewards those

the morrow shall take thought for the things of itself. Sufficient unto the day *is* the evil thereof.

CHAPTER 7

JUDGE not, that ye be not judged.
2 For with what judgment ye judge, ye shall be
judged: and with what measure ye mete, it shall
be measured to you again.
3 And why beholdest thou the mote that is in thy
brother's eye, but considerest not the beam that is
in thine own eye?
4 Or how wilt thou say to thy brother, Let me
pull out the mote out of thine eye; and, behold, a
beam *is* in thine own eye?
5 Thou hypocrite, first cast out the beam out of
thine own eye; and then shalt thou see clearly to
cast out the mote out of thy brother's eye.
6 ¶ Give not that which is holy unto the dogs,
neither cast ye your pearls before swine, lest they
trample them under their feet, and turn again and
rend you.
7 ¶ Ask, and it shall be given you; seek, and ye
shall find; knock, and it shall be opened unto you:
8 For every one that asketh receiveth; and he that
seeketh findeth; and to him that knocketh it shall
be opened.
9 Or what man is there of you, whom if his son
ask bread, will he give him a stone?
10 Or if he ask a fish, will he give him a serpent?
11 If ye then, being evil, know how to give good
gifts unto your children, how much more shall
your Father which is in heaven give good things
to them that ask him?
12 Therefore all things whatsoever ye would that
men should do to you, do ye even so to them: for
this is the law and the prophets.
13 ¶ Enter ye in at the strait gate: for wide *is* the
gate, and broad *is* the way, that leadeth to destruc-
tion, and many there be which go in thereat:
14 Because strait *is* the gate, and narrow *is* the
way, which leadeth unto life, and few there be that
find it.
15 ¶ Beware of false prophets, which come to you
in sheep's clothing, but inwardly they are ravening
wolves.
16 Ye shall know them by their fruits. Do men
gather grapes of thorns, or figs of thistles?
17 Even so every good tree bringeth forth good
fruit; but a corrupt tree bringeth forth evil fruit.
18 A good tree cannot bring forth evil fruit,
neither *can* a corrupt tree bring forth good fruit.
19 Every tree that bringeth not forth good fruit is
hewn down, and cast into the fire.

who seek Him in faith by the effectual working of the Holy Spirit. Is it a comforting thought to know that what the Christian does for the glory of Christ is not neglected or forgotten? How will this motivate you in your private worship?

2. **Note the practical implications of faith in this chapter. Jesus warns His disciples that they should not give in to sinful anxiety (vv. 25–32). He states in v. 30 that having such sinful anxiety is the result of having little faith in God's providential care over life. How can you exercise faith in Christ's promises so that you can overcome fear and worry?**
3. **Jesus taught His disciples to call God "our Father." Christ's work results in God's adoption of sinners who place their trust in Him, so that they are part of God's family. How could viewing God as your "Father" change the way you view money, possessions, and your needs?**

Chapter 7: ***Jesus finishes preaching on the law and the kingdom of heaven. Afterward, the crowds marvel at His authority and teaching.***

7:2 *mete.* Measure. Just as God condemns unjust weights in economic transactions (Prov. 11:1), so judging others unfairly will bring sad results in the day of judgment.

7:3–5 *mote.* Speck of dust. Jesus was not condemning all discernment or judgments (v. 6), but rather judgments that elevate oneself and demean another—hypocritical judgment.

7:6 *Give not that which is holy unto the dogs.* While Jesus condemned a spirit of hypocritical judgment, He also warned against having a naïve mindset and a lack of discernment.

7:7 *Ask . . . seek . . . knock.* Synonyms for prayer, each more intensive than the last. Jesus commanded His disciples to pray perseveringly, confident in the promises that the Father would give them His best.

7:8 *asketh . . . seeketh . . . knocketh.* The original Greek here indicates a continual action.

7:9–11 *what man.* Comparatively speaking, an earthly father's love for his children is far less than the love that God has for His children, for the best of fathers is corrupted by sin (*evil*), but God is perfect. *your Father . . . give good things.* God is generous to His children. This, too, underscores the Father's ability to provide for His people and their freedom from the need to worry (6:25–34).

7:12 *Therefore.* Jesus was encouraging His disciples to pray for others. *for this is the law and the prophets.* The "Golden Rule" of loving one's neighbor fulfills the law. This is reminiscent of Jesus' initial statement that He has not come to abolish the law (5:17).

7:13–27 Jesus gave warnings concerning true and false religion—different responses to the kingdom message in images of opposites (narrow and broad gates, good and bad trees, solid and unstable houses, etc.). Christ called for discriminating self-examination. Much that claims to be real is not. Genuine disciples will be diligent to make their calling and election sure (2 Peter 1:10).

7:13–14 *strait.* Narrow. Discipleship to Christ is more difficult and less popular than the alternative, but it is the only way to eternal *life* (5:20).

7:15 *Beware.* A call to watchfulness, because *false prophets* creep into the church disguised as true disciples (*sheep*) but in reality are as dangerous as wolves that come seizing (*ravening*) and killing (Acts 20:29).

7:16–20 Jesus compared all people to one of two trees that produce *fruits* according to their natures (12:33). The wicked (*corrupt tree*) cannot bring forth good works (*good fruit*) and will be cut off (*hewn*) and condemned to hell (*fire*; 3:10). Christ's words imply that sinners cannot save themselves, but God's grace must change their natures so that they produce a new kind of life (John 3:1–8).

20 Wherefore by their fruits ye shall know them.
21 ¶ Not every one that saith unto me, Lord,
Lord, shall enter into the kingdom of heaven; but
he that doeth the will of my Father which is in
heaven.
22 Many will say to me in that day, Lord, Lord,
have we not prophesied in thy name? and in thy
name have cast out devils? and in thy name done
many wonderful works?
23 And then will I profess unto them, I never
knew you: depart from me, ye that work iniquity.
24 ¶ Therefore whosoever heareth these sayings
of mine, and doeth them, I will liken him unto a
wise man, which built his house upon a rock:
25 And the rain descended, and the floods came,
and the winds blew, and beat upon that house;
and it fell not: for it was founded upon a rock.
26 And every one that heareth these sayings of
mine, and doeth them not, shall be likened unto a
foolish man, which built his house upon the sand:
27 And the rain descended, and the floods came,
and the winds blew, and beat upon that house;
and it fell: and great was the fall of it.
28 And it came to pass, when Jesus had ended
these sayings, the people were astonished at his
doctrine:
29 For he taught them as *one* having authority,
and not as the scribes.

CHAPTER 8

WHEN he was come down from the mountain,
great multitudes followed him.
2 And, behold, there came a leper and worshipped
him, saying, Lord, if thou wilt, thou canst make
me clean.
3 And Jesus put forth *his* hand, and touched him,
saying, I will; be thou clean. And immediately his
leprosy was cleansed.
4 And Jesus saith unto him, See thou tell no man;
but go thy way, shew thyself to the priest, and offer
the gift that Moses commanded, for a testimony
unto them.
5 ¶ And when Jesus was entered into Capernaum,
there came unto him a centurion, beseeching
him,
6 And saying, Lord, my servant lieth at home sick
of the palsy, grievously tormented.
7 And Jesus saith unto him, I will come and heal
him.
8 The centurion answered and said, Lord, I am
not worthy that thou shouldest come under my
roof: but speak the word only, and my servant
shall be healed.
9 For I am a man under authority, having soldiers
under me: and I say to this *man*, Go, and he goeth;
and to another, Come, and he cometh; and to my
servant, Do this, and he doeth *it*.

7:21–23 *Lord, Lord.* A basic confession of the Christian faith (Rom. 10:9). *prophesied.* Spoke new revelation from God by the influence of the Holy Spirit (1 Cor. 14:29–30). *wonderful works.* Powerful miracles. Neither a profession of faith, nor ministry, nor supernatural gifts proves one has a place in Christ's kingdom, but only repentance of sin (*iniquity*) and obedience to God's commands (*doeth the will of my Father*) based on a relationship of grace with Christ (*I . . . knew you*). *depart from me.* Christ will reject unrepentant sinners, sending them to eternal punishment (25:41).
7:24–27 Both men *heareth these sayings* but only the wise man *doeth them* (James 1:21–25).
7:28–29 *ended these sayings.* This completes the first discourse and brings us back into the narrative. *astonished at his doctrine . . . one having authority.* Christ's teaching amazed people (13:54; 19:25; 22:22,33), as would His miracles (8:27; 9:8,33; 15:31; 21:20), for He came not only as a messenger of the kingdom, but as its sovereign King (8:8–9; 9:6).

Thoughts for Personal/Family Worship: Chapter 7

1. **A judgmental spirit, that is, judging people hypocritically without having judged our own hearts, is evidence that we have not come off the throne of our lives. The kingdom of grace is a place where God's Spirit uses the Word to help us see the judgment we are under and to encourage us to seek mercy by Christ's death and to show mercy to one another. How are you tempted to judge others? How should you instead judge yourself first?**
2. **While we are not to judge hypocritically, Jesus taught us to recognize that there are two kinds of people, and only one will enjoy eternal life. Christ divided mankind between travelers on the broad and narrow ways, bad trees and good trees, wise and foolish builders. His words press us to not assume all is well. Are you on the narrow way? Are you a good tree by God's grace?**
3. **Christ did not teach the people the way that the Pharisees did—by endless recitation of other men's opinions. Rather, He taught with authority. When we read God's Word, we cannot simply sit back to have our ears tickled. It should expose our sin, show us God in Christ, and drive us outside of ourselves to seek mercy with this King. How have you been convicted to be a "doer" and not a "hearer" only (James 1:21–25).**

Jesus' Ministry in Galilee: Teachings and Miracles (8:1—11:1)

Miracles Performed in Galilee (8:1—9:38)

Chapter 8: *Jesus performs several miracles in His early ministry in Galilee and gives several prominent lessons.*

8:2 *leper.* Leprosy is a term used for a variety of skin diseases and ceremonial uncleanness (Lev. 13:1–46). *if thou wilt, thou canst.* If you will, you are able. God is able to do all He wills (Pss. 115:3; 135:6). The leper in faith exalts Christ's ability, making a bold request of Him.
8:4 *tell no man.* Jesus probably did not want to stir up the crowds to seek for miracles only. Moreover, the leper had to present himself to the priest to keep the ceremonial law (Lev. 14).
8:5 *Capernaum.* Jesus' base for ministry at this time (4:13). *centurion.* A Roman military officer. *came . . . beseeching.* He communicated with Jesus through representatives (Luke 7:1–10).
8:6 *palsy.* Paralysis.

10 When Jesus heard *it*, he marvelled, and said to
them that followed, Verily I say unto you, I have
not found so great faith, no, not in Israel.
11 And I say unto you, That many shall come
from the east and west, and shall sit down with
Abraham, and Isaac, and Jacob, in the kingdom
of heaven.
12 But the children of the kingdom shall be cast
out into outer darkness: there shall be weeping
and gnashing of teeth.
13 And Jesus said unto the centurion, Go thy
way; and as thou hast believed, *so* be it done unto
thee. And his servant was healed in the selfsame
hour.
14 ¶ And when Jesus was come into Peter's house,
he saw his wife's mother laid, and sick of a fever.
15 And he touched her hand, and the fever left
her: and she arose, and ministered unto them.
16 ¶ When the even was come, they brought unto
him many that were possessed with devils: and he
cast out the spirits with *his* word, and healed all
that were sick:
17 That it might be fulfilled which was spoken
by Esaias the prophet, saying, Himself took our
infirmities, and bare *our* sicknesses.
18 ¶ Now when Jesus saw great multitudes about
him, he gave commandment to depart unto the
other side.
19 And a certain scribe came, and said unto him,
Master, I will follow thee whithersoever thou
goest.
20 And Jesus saith unto him, The foxes have
holes, and the birds of the air *have* nests; but the
Son of man hath not where to lay *his* head.
21 And another of his disciples said unto him,
Lord, suffer me first to go and bury my father.
22 But Jesus said unto him, Follow me; and let the
dead bury their dead.
23 ¶ And when he was entered into a ship, his
disciples followed him.
24 And, behold, there arose a great tempest in the
sea, insomuch that the ship was covered with the
waves: but he was asleep.
25 And his disciples came to *him*, and awoke him,
saying, Lord, save us: we perish.
26 And he saith unto them, Why are ye fearful, O
ye of little faith? Then he arose, and rebuked the
winds and the sea; and there was a great calm.
27 But the men marvelled, saying, What manner
of man is this, that even the winds and the sea
obey him!
28 ¶ And when he was come to the other side into
the country of the Gergesenes, there met him two
possessed with devils, coming out of the tombs,
exceeding fierce, so that no man might pass by
that way.
29 And, behold, they cried out, saying, What have
we to do with thee, Jesus, thou Son of God? art
thou come hither to torment us before the time?
30 And there was a good way off from them an
herd of many swine feeding.
31 So the devils besought him, saying, If thou cast

8:10 *Verily.* Truly.

8:11 *sit down with Abraham.* This centurion felt he was unworthy to have Christ under his roof (v. 8); however, Christ gives him a place at His table in the kingdom, an example of the Beatitudes (5:3).

8:12 *children.* Literally, "sons," an idiom here referring to Israel, the people one would expect to inherit God's *kingdom* (21:43). *cast out.* Physical descent from godly parents cannot bring a person into the *kingdom* (3:9); salvation is by faith in Christ alone (v. 10). *outer darkness.* An image of the isolation and deprivation of everything good that will be experienced by the damned (22:13; 25:30). *weeping and gnashing of teeth.* Christ's standard expression for the suffering and frustrated rage of sinners in hell (13:42,50; 22:13; 24:51; 25:30; Luke 13:28; cf. Pss. 35:16; 37:12; 112:10).

8:13 *in the selfsame hour.* At that same time. Jesus healed the centurion's servant from a distance, without even touching him, showing that Christ's word is powerful to save (vv. 26–27).

8:14 *his wife's mother.* The ministers of the Word may be married (1 Cor. 9:5; 1 Tim. 3:2).

8:15 Jesus initiated this healing, unlike the previous two healings where he was first approached. *she arose, and ministered unto them.* This woman's healing was complete, and her response was grateful service. When Christ heals you spiritually, you will serve Him.

8:17 *fulfilled.* See note at 1:22. *Esaias.* Isaiah (Isa. 53:4). *took our infirmities.* Christ's miracles of healing were signs that He would save people from misery by suffering in their place. His atonement does not guarantee present health to Christians (Phil. 2:26–27; 1 Tim. 5:23; 2 Tim. 4:20), but present spiritual restoration (1 Peter 2:24–25) and future healing from all sickness, death, or pain (Rev. 21:4).

8:20 *Son of man.* An idiom for a human being (Num. 23:19; Ps. 8:4) and specifically the title of the ruler of God's universal kingdom (26:64; Dan. 7:13–14). The Son of God took a human nature to Himself to be the Messiah. Christ often used this title of Himself (thirty-two times in Matt.; cf. Acts 7:56; Rev. 1:13; 14:14). *hath not where to lay his head.* Has no permanent home in this world, implying that His followers will also be strangers and exiles on earth (Heb. 11:13). Christ did not hide the cost of discipleship as many have done since then.

8:21 *suffer.* Permit. *first to go and bury my father.* The man's father had probably not yet died, and so the man was asking for a long delay before following Christ (contrast 4:21–22).

8:22 *let the dead bury their dead.* The spiritually dead are preoccupied with the concerns of this life (23:27; John 5:24–25), but the spiritually alive seek first the kingdom (6:33; Col. 3:1).

8:24 *tempest.* Storm.

8:26 *little faith.* Trials uncover the weakness of a believer's faith, but are occasions for growth. *rebuked . . . great calm.* Jesus' miraculous power over creation shows He is Lord (Ps. 107:28–29).

8:27 *What manner of man is this.* The answer is given by the disciples in another miraculous scene on the sea (14:33).

8:29 *they cried out.* Even the demons called Jesus the *Son of God* and believed in the final judgment. *art thou come hither.* Have you come here.

8:31 *besought.* Implored, asked urgently. *swine.* Livestock considered unclean by Jews (Lev. 11:7).

us out, suffer us to go away into the herd of swine.
32 And he said unto them, Go. And when they
were come out, they went into the herd of swine:
and, behold, the whole herd of swine ran violently
down a steep place into the sea, and perished in
the waters.
33 And they that kept them fled, and went their
ways into the city, and told every thing, and what
was befallen to the possessed of the devils.
34 And, behold, the whole city came out to meet
Jesus: and when they saw him, they besought *him*
that he would depart out of their coasts.

CHAPTER 9

AND he entered into a ship, and passed over, and
came into his own city.
2 And, behold, they brought to him a man sick
of the palsy, lying on a bed: and Jesus seeing their
faith said unto the sick of the palsy; Son, be of
good cheer; thy sins be forgiven thee.
3 And, behold, certain of the scribes said within
themselves, This *man* blasphemeth.
4 And Jesus knowing their thoughts said,
Wherefore think ye evil in your hearts?
5 For whether is easier, to say, *Thy* sins be forgiven
thee; or to say, Arise, and walk?
6 But that ye may know that the Son of man hath
power on earth to forgive sins, (then saith he to
the sick of the palsy,) Arise, take up thy bed, and
go unto thine house.
7 And he arose, and departed to his house.
8 But when the multitudes saw *it*, they marvelled,
and glorified God, which had given such power
unto men.
9 ¶ And as Jesus passed forth from thence, he saw
a man, named Matthew, sitting at the receipt of
custom: and he saith unto him, Follow me. And
he arose, and followed him.
10 ¶ And it came to pass, as Jesus sat at meat in
the house, behold, many publicans and sinners
came and sat down with him and his disciples.
11 And when the Pharisees saw *it*, they said
unto his disciples, Why eateth your Master with
publicans and sinners?
12 But when Jesus heard *that*, he said unto them,
They that be whole need not a physician, but they
that are sick.
13 But go ye and learn what *that* meaneth, I will
have mercy, and not sacrifice: for I am not come
to call the righteous, but sinners to repentance.
14 ¶ Then came to him the disciples of John,
saying, Why do we and the Pharisees fast oft, but
thy disciples fast not?

8:32 *Go.* Jesus uttered one word and the demons obeyed (4:10–11). His authority extends over the spiritual forces of darkness (Col. 2:14–15). *whole herd . . . perished.* Jesus counts one human being worth more than hundreds of animals (10:31; 12:12), especially when it comes to saving him from Satan.

8:34 *besought him that he would depart.* The same verb used of the demons begging Christ (v. 31). Sadly, most people have more in common with demons than believers (v. 5). *coasts.* Region.

Thoughts for Personal/Family Worship: Chapter 8

1. **Christ is the exalted King who teaches with authority and confirms His message with miracles. However, Christ is also the lowly servant, who bears His people's sin as a substitute (v. 17) and has nowhere to lay His head (v. 20). He is glorious as a King yet approachable as a servant. How necessary and suitable a Savior Christ is! How does this encourage you to trust in Him?**
2. **Christ can drive away diseases, disasters, and demons with a mere word. His presence and power amaze people. His disciples exclaim, "What manner of man is this, that even the winds and the sea obey him!" (v. 27).The answer is that Christ is God, the glorious Creator. However, recognizing His glory is not the same as trusting in Him. The demons believed and trembled, begging to be sent away. The Gentiles begged Him to go away. Do you know Christ's majesty? How does it affect you, with love and a desire to be with Him, or with a desire to get away?**

Chapter 9: ***Jesus again performs several miracles and teaches His disciples the nature of His mission.***

9:1 *his own city.* Capernaum (4:13; 8:5).

9:2 *palsy.* Paralysis (v. 6). *good cheer.* Courage. *thy sins be forgiven thee.* This is the first time Jesus spoke of the forgiveness of sins in this gospel (see Mark 2:1–12 and Luke 5:17–26 for parallels).

9:3 *blasphemeth.* Only God could forgive sins (Ps. 103:12; Isa. 43:25). Christ would thus prove Himself divine.

9:5–6 *whether.* Which. *power.* Authority. Jesus showed that He has the authority to forgive sins by showing the people He has authority over diseases. *palsy.* Paralysis.

9:8 *marvelled, and glorified God.* See note at 7:28–29.

9:9 *Matthew.* Also known as Levi (Mark 2:14; Luke 5:27). *receipt of custom.* Place where the Jewish tax collectors did business on behalf of the Roman Empire, to the contempt and hatred of many of the Jews (18:17). *Follow me . . . followed him.* Christ's Word is powerful to save, effective by the Spirit to change sinners into disciples despite their former evil desires and habits.

9:10 *sat at meat.* Dined on food of any kind, a meal hosted by Matthew (Luke 5:29). *publicans.* Tax collectors, counted by many Jews as wicked people outside of God's covenant (*sinners*; 18:17). Conquered by divine love, Matthew introduced his friends to his new Master.

9:11 *eateth your Master with . . . sinners.* Sharing fellowship at a table was a sign of friendship (11:19).

9:12 *physician.* Jesus does not approve of the actions of sinners, but as a spiritual doctor, He moves among sick sinners, calling them to repentance (v. 13; 4:17).

9:13 *go ye and learn.* The Pharisees should have comprehended such a foundational biblical truth (Hos. 6:6). *mercy, and not sacrifice.* God's great desire is not outward acts of worship so much as faithful love (12:7). *not come to call the righteous.* The gospel call (4:21; 22:1–14) has nothing for people who do not see and feel their sins.

9:14 *fast oft.* Often deny their bodies food (6:16–18). The only fast commanded in the law was the Day of Atonement (Lev. 23:27), but there were other voluntary fasts (Neh. 1:4; 9:1; Est. 4:16).

15 And Jesus said unto them, Can the children of
the bridechamber mourn, as long as the bride-
groom is with them? but the days will come, when
the bridegroom shall be taken from them, and
then shall they fast.
16 No man putteth a piece of new cloth unto an
old garment, for that which is put in to fill it up ta-
keth from the garment, and the rent is made worse.
17 Neither do men put new wine into old bottles:
else the bottles break, and the wine runneth out,
and the bottles perish: but they put new wine into
new bottles, and both are preserved.
18 ¶ While he spake these things unto them,
behold, there came a certain ruler, and worshipped
him, saying, My daughter is even now dead: but
come and lay thy hand upon her, and she shall live.
19 And Jesus arose, and followed him, and *so did*
his disciples.
20 ¶ And, behold, a woman, which was diseased
with an issue of blood twelve years, came behind
him, and touched the hem of his garment:
21 For she said within herself, If I may but touch
his garment, I shall be whole.
22 But Jesus turned him about, and when he saw
her, he said, Daughter, be of good comfort; thy
faith hath made thee whole. And the woman was
made whole from that hour.
23 And when Jesus came into the ruler's house,
and saw the minstrels and the people making a
noise,
24 He said unto them, Give place: for the maid is
not dead, but sleepeth. And they laughed him to
scorn.
25 But when the people were put forth, he went
in, and took her by the hand, and the maid arose.
26 And the fame hereof went abroad into all that
land.
27 ¶ And when Jesus departed thence, two blind
men followed him, crying, and saying, *Thou* Son
of David, have mercy on us.
28 And when he was come into the house, the
blind men came to him: and Jesus saith unto
them, Believe ye that I am able to do this? They
said unto him, Yea, Lord.
29 Then touched he their eyes, saying, According
to your faith be it unto you.
30 And their eyes were opened; and Jesus straitly
charged them, saying, See *that* no man know *it*.
31 But they, when they were departed, spread
abroad his fame in all that country.
32 ¶ As they went out, behold, they brought to
him a dumb man possessed with a devil.
33 And when the devil was cast out, the dumb
spake: and the multitudes marvelled, saying, It
was never so seen in Israel.
34 But the Pharisees said, He casteth out devils
through the prince of the devils.
35 And Jesus went about all the cities and villages,
teaching in their synagogues, and preaching the
gospel of the kingdom, and healing every sickness
and every disease among the people.
36 ¶ But when he saw the multitudes, he was
moved with compassion on them, because they
fainted, and were scattered abroad, as sheep
having no shepherd.
37 Then saith he unto his disciples, The harvest

9:15 *children of the bridechamber.* Idiom for wedding guests. *bridegroom.* The Lord is the spiritual husband of Israel (25:1; Song 1–8; Isa. 54:5; 62:5; Hos. 2:19–20; John 3:29; Rev. 19:7; 21:2,9; 22:17). Christ's presence with His people was the occasion for rejoicing, not fasting. However, fasting is appropriate while His church waits for Him to return.

9:16–17 Christ did not come simply to patch man-made religion together, but to make things new. *new . . . old.* Christ was not contrasting the Old and New Testaments (5:17), but the legalism of the Pharisees with true biblical piety (5:20). The two are incompatible, just as *new cloth* patched onto *old* clothing will shrink and tear, and *new wine* is still fermenting and would burst *old* wineskins (*bottles*).

9:18–26 Christ performed a double miracle, healing disease and conquering death (see Mark 5:22–43 and Luke 8:41–56 for a fuller account).

9:18 *worshipped him.* Much like the leper (8:2). The ruler believed that Jesus could raise his deceased daughter from the *dead*, a remarkable miracle (2 Kings 4:32–37).

9:20 *diseased . . . issue of blood twelve years.* Her illness was humanly incurable (Luke 8:43), and it made her continually unclean (Lev. 15:25,33). *hem of his garment.* Perhaps the tassel that all Jews were commanded to wear on the corners of their garments to remind them of the law (Num. 15:38–39).

9:21–22 *be whole . . . made whole.* Literally, "saved," the word used for rescue from physical (8:25) or spiritual misery (1:21). *thy faith.* Salvation comes not by physical objects associated with Jesus, but trusting in Him.

9:23 Matthew returns to the narrative of the ruler's daughter. *minstrels.* Flute players. It was Jewish custom to hire professional mourners to lament a death. Many would have gathered for the death of a child of a prominent person.

9:24 *Give place.* Depart, go out. *maid.* Girl. *sleepeth.* Jesus did not doubt the girl's death, but knew He was about to raise her from the dead. *laughed him to scorn.* They incessantly mocked Him.

9:27 *Son of David.* Ironically, the first people in this gospel to call Jesus by this messianic title (1:1,20) are *blind men*; His frequent healing of the blind was a key sign that He is the Christ (11:5; 12:22; 15:30–31; 20:30–34; 21:14).

9:28 *Believe ye that I am able.* See note at 8:2. Their response, *Yea, Lord,* shows they had faith that Jesus had the power to heal them.

9:30–31 *straitly charged.* Told them with stern emotion. It is likely that Jesus did not want to stir up a riotous mob with an insatiable appetite for the miraculous.

9:32 *dumb.* Unable to speak. *possessed.* See note at 4:24–25.

9:33 *never so seen in Israel.* The immediate context of this is the casting out of the demon that caused muteness, but in the larger context this is a response to many miracles by Jesus.

9:34 *prince of the devils.* First or ruler of the demons. The Pharisees accuse Jesus of using the powers of Satan to drive out demons as if He were a sorcerer (12:22–30).

9:35 This is another summary statement of Jesus' ministry (4:23) before this gospel's second major discourse (ch. 10).

9:36 *sheep having no shepherd.* Old Testament imagery for a

truly *is* plenteous, but the labourers *are* few;
38 Pray ye therefore the Lord of the harvest, that
he will send forth labourers into his harvest.

CHAPTER 10

AND when he had called unto *him* his twelve
disciples, he gave them power *against* unclean
spirits, to cast them out, and to heal all manner of
sickness and all manner of disease.
2 Now the names of the twelve apostles are these;
The first, Simon, who is called Peter, and Andrew
his brother; James *the son* of Zebedee, and John
his brother;
3 Philip, and Bartholomew; Thomas, and
Matthew the publican; James *the son* of Alphaeus,
and Lebbaeus, whose surname was Thaddaeus;
4 Simon the Canaanite, and Judas Iscariot, who
also betrayed him.
5 These twelve Jesus sent forth, and commanded
them, saying, Go not into the way of the Gentiles,
and into *any* city of the Samaritans enter ye not:
6 But go rather to the lost sheep of the house of
Israel.
7 And as ye go, preach, saying, The kingdom of
heaven is at hand.
8 Heal the sick, cleanse the lepers, raise the dead,
cast out devils: freely ye have received, freely give.
9 Provide neither gold, nor silver, nor brass in
your purses,
10 Nor scrip for *your* journey, neither two coats,
neither shoes, nor yet staves: for the workman is
worthy of his meat.
11 And into whatsoever city or town ye shall
enter, enquire who in it is worthy; and there abide
till ye go thence.
12 And when ye come into an house, salute it.
13 And if the house be worthy, let your peace
come upon it: but if it be not worthy, let your peace
return to you.
14 And whosoever shall not receive you, nor hear
your words, when ye depart out of that house or
city, shake off the dust of your feet.
15 Verily I say unto you, It shall be more tolerable
for the land of Sodom and Gomorrha in the day
of judgment, than for that city.
16 ¶ Behold, I send you forth as sheep in the
midst of wolves: be ye therefore wise as serpents,
and harmless as doves.
17 But beware of men: for they will deliver you
up to the councils, and they will scourge you in
their synagogues;

---

lack of a good king to lead and protect them (1 Kings 22:17; Ezek. 34:5; Zech. 10:2). As the Good Shepherd, Jesus saves and gathers His sheep (John 10:1–16,26–29).

Thoughts for Personal/Family Worship: Chapter 9

Christ has authority on earth to forgive sins (v. 6). People today speak of forgiving themselves, but they fail to see that they are not the Judge. Christ alone possesses the authority to condemn or to forgive. In this chapter we see Him granting forgiveness to weak and worthless sinners like the paralytic and great sinners like Matthew the tax collector. Obviously His forgiveness is not bought with money or earned with good works. Rather it is received by faith, just as healing was received by faith when Jesus worked miracles (vv. 2,22,28–29). Do you believe that Christ is able to forgive your sins? Are you trusting Him to actually forgive you? Remember, Christ did not come to save the righteous, but as a spiritual doctor for sinners.

Teaching on the Nature of Discipleship (10:1—11:1)

Chapter 10: *Jesus sends out the twelve apostles to preach the kingdom. In addition He teaches the people concerning various issues.*

10:1–4 *twelve apostles.* The men sent by Christ with His delegated authority to carry the message and miracles of the kingdom (Mark 3:13–19; Luke 6:12–16; Acts 1:13) to Israel (v. 6; 15:24), and later throughout the world (28:18–20). Their number suggests a reconstitution of the twelve tribes of Israel centered on the person of Jesus Christ (19:28).

10:7 *kingdom . . . is at hand.* The apostolic message stands in continuity with the message of both John the Baptist and Jesus. It is also the message that the church proclaims to the whole world (24:14).

10:8 *freely ye have received, freely give.* The blessing of the kingdom comes by God's grace alone. The disciples were not to sell it for a profit, though teachers may depend upon the church for their financial support (v. 10; 1 Cor. 9:14; 1 Tim. 5:17).

10:9–10 *neither gold, nor silver.* The apostles were not to accumulate wealth for themselves (Acts 3:6; 20:33). *scrip.* Bag or sack for provisions. *staves.* Staffs. *meat.* Food of any kind. Jesus commanded simplicity and dependence on God.

10:11–13 *worthy.* Those who received the preaching of the apostles. *go thence.* Leave. *salute.* Greet. *your peace.* Their declaration of God's blessing on those who believe the gospel (Acts 10:36). The apostles traveled from house to house with the message of the kingdom and from town to town depending on the hospitality of believers. Those who rejected their message were to be left alone.

10:14–15 *shake off the dust of your feet.* A Jewish custom when reentering the Holy Land from a foreign country, symbolizing separation from those who were unclean and outsiders. *more tolerable.* Though God will punish *Sodom* and Gomorrah (*Gomorrha*) on the day of judgment, those who heard but rejected the gospel of the kingdom will face an even more severe punishment (11:20–24; Luke 12:47–48).

10:16 *I send you.* The verbal form of the word "apostle" (v. 2); their mission comes directly from Christ Himself. *sheep in the midst of wolves.* The kingdom has not yet come in its glorious peace (Isa. 11:6), and therefore God's servants must suffer (Rom. 8:36). *wise as serpents.* A surprising use of an image commonly used for evil (3:7; 12:34; 23:33), perhaps implying exercising watchfulness against the Devil's violent schemes (vv. 17,23; Gen. 3:1; Eph. 6:11). *harmless as doves.* Disciples should not retaliate with force against those who would persecute them (5:44; Rom. 12:17–18).

10:17–18 *beware of men.* Disciples are to be prudent and winsome in their dealings with men so as not to suffer needlessly or fall into sin under persecution. Persecution will arise from both Jews and *Gentiles.*

10:19–20 Jesus did not send them alone but gave the Spirit

18 And ye shall be brought before governors and
kings for my sake, for a testimony against them
and the Gentiles.
19 But when they deliver you up, take no thought
how or what ye shall speak: for it shall be given
you in that same hour what ye shall speak.
20 For it is not ye that speak, but the Spirit of
your Father which speaketh in you.
21 And the brother shall deliver up the brother to
death, and the father the child: and the children
shall rise up against *their* parents, and cause them
to be put to death.
22 And ye shall be hated of all *men* for my name's
sake: but he that endureth to the end shall be saved.
23 But when they persecute you in this city, flee
ye into another: for verily I say unto you, Ye shall
not have gone over the cities of Israel, till the Son
of man be come.
24 The disciple is not above *his* master, nor the
servant above his lord.
25 It is enough for the disciple that he be as his
master, and the servant as his lord. If they have
called the master of the house Beelzebub, how
much more *shall they call* them of his household?
26 Fear them not therefore: for there is nothing
covered, that shall not be revealed; and hid, that
shall not be known.
27 What I tell you in darkness, *that* speak ye in
light: and what ye hear in the ear, *that* preach ye
upon the housetops.
28 And fear not them which kill the body, but are
not able to kill the soul: but rather fear him which
is able to destroy both soul and body in hell.
29 Are not two sparrows sold for a farthing? and
one of them shall not fall on the ground without
your Father.
30 But the very hairs of your head are all numbered.
31 Fear ye not therefore, ye are of more value
than many sparrows.
32 Whosoever therefore shall confess me before
men, him will I confess also before my Father
which is in heaven.
33 But whosoever shall deny me before men,
him will I also deny before my Father which is in
heaven.
34 Think not that I am come to send peace on
earth: I came not to send peace, but a sword.
35 For I am come to set a man at variance against
his father, and the daughter against her mother,
and the daughter in law against her mother in law.
36 And a man's foes *shall be* they of his own
household.
37 He that loveth father or mother more than
me is not worthy of me: and he that loveth son
or daughter more than me is not worthy of me.
38 And he that taketh not his cross, and followeth
after me, is not worthy of me.
39 He that findeth his life shall lose it: and he that
loseth his life for my sake shall find it.
40 ¶ He that receiveth you receiveth me, and he
that receiveth me receiveth him that sent me.
41 He that receiveth a prophet in the name of a
prophet shall receive a prophet's reward; and he that
receiveth a righteous man in the name of a righteous man shall receive a righteous man's reward.

---

to speak God's Word through them, a reminder of the apostles' prophetic office (v. 41; Eph. 3:5). *Spirit of your Father.* A unique title of the Holy Spirit, perhaps to assure His suffering believers that they are God's children (Rom. 8:15–17).

10:21 *brother shall deliver up the brother.* Jesus' kingdom message divides even the closest of all earthly relationships.

10:22 *hated of all men for my name's sake.* This is still a present reality for the disciples of Jesus (5:10–12; 1 John 3:13). *endureth . . . saved.* The true disciple of Christ will persevere to the end and receive eternal glory (19:29; John 10:28).

10:23 *flee.* Disciples need not be passive martyrs (Acts 9:23–25; 17:10). *verily.* Truly. *till the Son of man be come.* Perhaps the coming of Christ's kingdom, with His resurrection and the pouring out of his Spirit (16:28), or the destruction of the temple in Jerusalem.

10:24–25 *disciple . . . master.* Learner and teacher, where the learner not only receives the doctrine of his teacher but also imitates his life, which implies that Christ's disciples will suffer too (16:21,24; 2 Tim. 3:10–14). Jesus does not lead His disciples down a path that He was unwilling to go Himself. *Beelzebub.* A name for Satan (12:24), derived from the pagan god, "Baal-zebub" (2 Kings 1:1–6,16).

10:26 *nothing covered . . . not be revealed.* Jesus' command not to *fear* rests on the final judgment when God will openly judge all men, vindicating the faithful and condemning the wicked (1 Cor. 4:5).

10:28 *fear not . . . fear him.* Freedom from the fear of man comes from fearing the Lord and Judge of all people. Though temporal persecution is difficult, it is little compared to the fires of *hell* (see note at 5:22). *destroy.* The Greek word does not indicate annihilation, but ruin and loss (used of a burst skin in 9:17).

10:29–30 *farthing.* A very small bronze or copper coin. *without your Father.* God's providence rules over the condition of the smallest creatures (*sparrows*), or parts of our bodies (*hairs*), and therefore His children can trust Him.

10:32 *confess . . . before my Father.* On judgment day, when Christ shall give the verdict over each person while surrounded by the glory of God and His angels (16:27; Luke 12:8; Rev. 3:5). Again, Jesus calls us to weigh the present fears induced by men against the fear of the Lord and Judge (v. 28).

10:34–36 *not . . . peace, but a sword.* Jesus' message is not one of false comfort, but of judgment against sin and sinners. *set . . . at variance.* Separate, alienate. *foes.* Enemies. The gospel divides families according to how individuals respond (v. 21), as it divided Israel (Luke 2:34–35).

10:37 Considering the division that the message of the kingdom causes, no one should presume to lean on their family relations. A disciple must love Christ supremely, above all others (Phil. 3:7–9).

10:38 *taketh not his cross.* A sign of rejection, hatred, and death (16:24–25). Jesus' disciples must willingly embrace and endure the cost of following Christ and becoming like Him.

10:39–42 Receiving Christ's apostles, indeed the least of His disciples (*little ones*), is equivalent to receiving Jesus because it is in His authority and commission that they go.

42 And whosoever shall give to drink unto one
of these little ones a cup of cold *water* only in the
name of a disciple, verily I say unto you, he shall
in no wise lose his reward.

CHAPTER 11

AND it came to pass, when Jesus had made an end
of commanding his twelve disciples, he departed
thence to teach and to preach in their cities.
2 Now when John had heard in the prison the
works of Christ, he sent two of his disciples,
3 And said unto him, Art thou he that should
come, or do we look for another?
4 Jesus answered and said unto them, Go and
shew John again those things which ye do hear
and see:
5 The blind receive their sight, and the lame walk,
the lepers are cleansed, and the deaf hear, the
dead are raised up, and the poor have the gospel
preached to them.
6 And blessed is *he*, whosoever shall not be of-
fended in me.
7 ¶ And as they departed, Jesus began to say unto
the multitudes concerning John, What went ye
out into the wilderness to see? A reed shaken with
the wind?
8 But what went ye out for to see? A man clothed
in soft raiment? behold, they that wear soft
clothing are in kings' houses.
9 But what went ye out for to see? A prophet? yea,
I say unto you, and more than a prophet.
10 For this is *he*, of whom it is written, Behold, I
send my messenger before thy face, which shall
prepare thy way before thee.
11 Verily I say unto you, Among them that are
born of women there hath not risen a greater than
John the Baptist: notwithstanding he that is least
in the kingdom of heaven is greater than he.
12 And from the days of John the Baptist until
now the kingdom of heaven suffereth violence,
and the violent take it by force.
13 For all the prophets and the law prophesied
until John.
14 And if ye will receive *it*, this is Elias, which was
for to come.
15 He that hath ears to hear, let him hear.
16 ¶ But whereunto shall I liken this generation?
It is like unto children sitting in the markets, and
calling unto their fellows,
17 And saying, We have piped unto you, and ye
have not danced; we have mourned unto you, and
ye have not lamented.
18 For John came neither eating nor drinking,
and they say, He hath a devil.
19 The Son of man came eating and drinking,
and they say, Behold a man gluttonous, and a
winebibber, a friend of publicans and sinners. But

Thoughts for Personal/Family Worship: Chapter 10

1. **Were it not for Christ and the mission He gave to the apostles, we would all be completely in the darkness of paganism. On the apostles the foundation of the church was built (Eph. 2:20). After Christ's ascension, the church was spread abroad by the apostles as an enlargement of God's nation, Israel, among all peoples. This is what God had promised to Abraham, that in him all the nations would be blessed (Gen. 12:3; see Gal. 3:8). What does this chapter teach us about missions? How are you and your church implementing these principles?**
2. **In these days when people generally want their lives to run smoothly, let us remember that Christ did not hide from His disciples the reality of the suffering they will experience (vv. 24,38). So rooted in pride and rebellion is the human race, that they killed Jesus Christ who went about healing, preaching, and saving lost sinners. So too, the Christian message and the Christian life is likely to arouse persecution and suffering today. In what way will you need to take up the cross if you will follow Jesus? What teachings of Christ in this chapter can give you the courage to follow through?**

Chapter 11: ***The ministries of John the Baptist and Jesus are compared. Christ curses the unrepentant cities and invites the weary sinners to come to Him for rest.***

11:1 *And it came to pass, when Jesus had made an end.* A marker of the completion of a section of Jesus' teaching in this gospel (13:53; 19:1; 26:1). *commanding his twelve disciples.* The instructions to the apostles in ch. 10. *teach . . . preach.* A major component of Christ's ministry (4:17,23; 5:2; 7:29; 9:35; 13:54; 21:23; 26:55), a model for His ministers (10:7; 28:20).

Jesus' Work as the Messiah (11:2–30)

11:3 *Art thou he that should come . . . ?* In prison, John struggled with how Christ's ministry of grace fit with the judgment and coming wrath (3:12). His disappointment tested his hope (Rom. 8:24–25), yet he looked to Christ for help.
11:5 *blind receive their sight.* Jesus pointed to the messianic actions prophesied in the Old Testament (Isa. 29:18; 35:5; 61:1). Jesus was performing these deeds as John's disciples asked Jesus their question (Luke 7:21).
11:6 *blessed is he . . . not be offended.* Ultimate blessing (5:3–9) rests on those who submit to Christ even when they do not understand His ways in their life.
11:7–8 *raiment.* Clothing. Despite John's doubts, Jesus praised him as a solid, resolved, and urgent preacher of the gospel message.
11:9 *more than a prophet.* John's ministry was unique as the bridge from the Old to the New Testament.
11:11 *Verily.* Truly.
11:12 *kingdom . . . suffereth violence.* Many people were striving to enter into the kingdom through repentance and faith (Luke 13:24).
11:13 *all . . . prophesied until John.* All of the Scriptures serve a prophetic role.
11:14 *Elias.* Elijah. *which was for to come.* See Mal. 3:1; 4:5. John the Baptist came in the spirit of Elijah (17:11–12; Luke 1:17).
11:16–19 *whereunto shall I liken.* To what shall I compare. *gluttonous . . . winebibber.* A worthless, rebellious person who seeks pleasure in food and drink but deserves death (Deut.

wisdom is justified of her children.
20 ¶ Then began he to upbraid the cities wherein
most of his mighty works were done, because
they repented not:
21 Woe unto thee, Chorazin! woe unto thee, Beth-
saida! for if the mighty works, which were done in
you, had been done in Tyre and Sidon, they would
have repented long ago in sackcloth and ashes.
22 But I say unto you, It shall be more tolerable
for Tyre and Sidon at the day of judgment, than
for you.
23 And thou, Capernaum, which art exalted unto
heaven, shalt be brought down to hell: for if the
mighty works, which have been done in thee, had
been done in Sodom, it would have remained
until this day.
24 But I say unto you, That it shall be more
tolerable for the land of Sodom in the day of
judgment, than for thee.
25 ¶ At that time Jesus answered and said, I thank
thee, O Father, Lord of heaven and earth, because
thou hast hid these things from the wise and
prudent, and hast revealed them unto babes.
26 Even so, Father: for so it seemed good in thy
sight.
27 All things are delivered unto me of my Father:
and no man knoweth the Son, but the Father; nei-
ther knoweth any man the Father, save the Son,
and *he* to whomsoever the Son will reveal *him*.
28 ¶ Come unto me, all *ye* that labour and are
heavy laden, and I will give you rest.
29 Take my yoke upon you, and learn of me; for I
am meek and lowly in heart: and ye shall find rest
unto your souls.
30 For my yoke *is* easy, and my burden is light.

CHAPTER 12

AT that time Jesus went on the sabbath day through
the corn; and his disciples were an hungred, and

21:20; Prov. 23:21). *publicans*. Tax collectors. Like petulant *children* who find fault with whatever they are offered, people imagined John too remote and Jesus too common. They were not satisfied with either ministry, but Christ spoke of Himself as the divine *wisdom* calling the foolish to Himself (v. 28; 12:42; Prov. 8–9; Luke 11:49). *children*. Christ's works, which publicly vindicated Him as righteous (*justified*).

11:20 *upbraid*. Charge with wrongdoing, reproach.

11:21 *Woe*. The prophetic equivalent of a curse. *Tyre and Sidon*. Two pagan cities, enemies of Israel (Ezek. 26–28). *sackcloth and ashes*. Outward signs of grief (Est. 4:1; Dan. 9:3; Jonah 3:6).

11:22–24 *more tolerable*. With greater revelation comes greater accountability and greater condemnation for unbelief. *Capernaum*. Jesus' hometown. *exalted unto heaven . . . brought down to hell*. Christ's fellow Jews who refused to believe in Him had become like the king of Babylon (Isa. 14:12–15). The Greek term for *hell* (*hades*, also 16:18, but not the same as in 5:22) can refer to death (Acts 2:27,31), the grave (1 Cor. 15:55), or the punishment of the wicked after this life (Luke 16:23). *Sodom*. A model of corruption, yet not as guilty as those who rejected Christ's gospel (10:14–15).

11:25 *At that time*. Likely after the seventy returned from this mission (Luke 10:17–21). *I thank thee*. The Father is worthy of praise for His absolute sovereignty over condemnation and salvation (Eph. 1:3–6). *wise and prudent . . . babes*. God glorifies Himself by reversing human expectations, rejecting the arrogant (v. 23), and blessing the humble (18:3).

11:27 *the Son*. Jesus defined the unique relationship (*knoweth*) that He has with God as *my Father* which distinguishes Him from all men and exalts Him above the angels (3:17; 14:33; John 1:18; 20:17; Heb. 1:4–5; see note at 2:15). On the basis of Christ's divine identity, the Father appointed Him as the only Mediator, so that He alone rules over *all things* with God's authority (28:18; John 17:2), and He alone reveals God to sinners in a saving way (John 14:6–9). *save*. Except. *he to whomsoever the Son will reveal him*. Literally, "the one to whom the Son wills to reveal." Like the Father (v. 25), Christ is free and sovereign to reveal God or not reveal Him to each individual as the Lord chooses.

11:28–30 *Come unto me*. God's sovereignty in saving sinners (vv. 25,27) does not hinder the call of the gospel to all men (Isa. 55:3), the invitation of Wisdom (Prov. 9:5; cf. Matt. 22:4). *laden*. Loaded, burdened with the guilt of sin and fear of judgment (vv. 22,24), only made worse by the legalistic teachings of the Pharisees (23:4). *give you rest*. Christ relieves the burden by saving from sin and guilt (1:21; 9:2–6). *Take my yoke . . . learn of me*. Salvation requires submission to Christ as one's Lord, Master, and Teacher (Jer. 27:8,11–12; 1 Tim. 6:1). *my yoke is easy*. Following Christ is the best life that could ever be lived, for He is a gentle and humble King who serves His people (*meek and lowly*; 20:28; 21:5; contrast 1 Kings 12:4–16). Though hard on our sins, Christ's commandments lead in paths of pleasantness (Prov. 3:17).

Thoughts for Personal/Family Worship: Chapter 11

1. **John, though mighty in the Lord, was weak in himself. Even the best of men are men at best. But Christ is much better than any man. He directed John's fainting heart to Himself. John had to learn that patience works experience; "and experience, hope: and hope maketh not ashamed" (Rom. 5:4–5). Do not be surprised when great servants of Christ fall into seasons of weakness. Instead, pray for them and point them to Christ, who is the answer to all our doubts and fears.**
2. **The gospel brings great accountability to its hearers. Capernaum was privileged above most places in Israel at this time in the sense that Christ spent more time there teaching and performing miracles than anywhere else. Through Christ's ministry it was as if they were "exalted unto heaven"; however, they would be cast down to hell because of their unbelief. We could say that the "hottest" places in hell are reserved for people who have lived the closest to gospel privileges and yet have continued in sin. What implications does this have for those of us in Bible-preaching churches?**
3. **Many find it difficult to hold together God's sovereignty and man's responsibility. Verses 25–30 show God's glorious sovereignty in salvation and also the gentle call of the gospel to all who hear. Rather than arrogantly arguing about sovereignty and responsibility, we need to humble ourselves as spiritual "babes," to believe all that Christ teaches and to see the beauty of God's sovereignty and our responsibility.**

Chapter 12: *Jesus teaches concerning the Sabbath, warns against blasphemy and unbelief, and encourages faith and perseverance among His disciples.*

The Authority of Jesus Challenged (12:1–50)

began to pluck the ears of corn, and to eat.
2 But when the Pharisees saw *it*, they said unto
him, Behold, thy disciples do that which is not
lawful to do upon the sabbath day.
3 But he said unto them, Have ye not read what
David did, when he was an hungred, and they that
were with him;
4 How he entered into the house of God, and did
eat the shewbread, which was not lawful for him
to eat, neither for them which were with him, but
only for the priests?
5 Or have ye not read in the law, how that on the
sabbath days the priests in the temple profane the
sabbath, and are blameless?
6 But I say unto you, That in this place is *one*
greater than the temple.
7 But if ye had known what *this* meaneth, I will
have mercy, and not sacrifice, ye would not have
condemned the guiltless.
8 For the Son of man is Lord even of the sabbath
day.
9 And when he was departed thence, he went into
their synagogue:
10 ¶ And, behold, there was a man which had
his hand withered. And they asked him, saying,
Is it lawful to heal on the sabbath days? that they
might accuse him.
11 And he said unto them, What man shall there
be among you, that shall have one sheep, and if it
fall into a pit on the sabbath day, will he not lay
hold on it, and lift *it* out?
12 How much then is a man better than a sheep?
Wherefore it is lawful to do well on the sabbath
days.
13 Then saith he to the man, Stretch forth
thine hand. And he stretched *it* forth; and it was
restored whole, like as the other.
14 ¶ Then the Pharisees went out, and held a
council against him, how they might destroy him.
15 But when Jesus knew *it*, he withdrew himself
from thence: and great multitudes followed him,
and he healed them all;
16 And charged them that they should not make
him known:
17 That it might be fulfilled which was spoken by
Esaias the prophet, saying,
18 Behold my servant, whom I have chosen;
my beloved, in whom my soul is well pleased: I
will put my spirit upon him, and he shall shew
judgment to the Gentiles.
19 He shall not strive, nor cry; neither shall any
man hear his voice in the streets.
20 A bruised reed shall he not break, and
smoking flax shall he not quench, till he send
forth judgment unto victory.
21 And in his name shall the Gentiles trust.
22 ¶ Then was brought unto him one possessed
with a devil, blind, and dumb: and he healed him,
insomuch that the blind and dumb both spake
and saw.
23 And all the people were amazed, and said, Is
not this the son of David?
24 But when the Pharisees heard *it*, they said,
This *fellow* doth not cast out devils, but by Beelze-
bub the prince of the devils.
25 And Jesus knew their thoughts, and said unto
them, Every kingdom divided against itself is
brought to desolation; and every city or house

12:1 *corn.* A general term for grain, such as barley or wheat. *an hungred.* Hungry.

12:2 *not lawful.* Contrary to the Pharisaic traditions. The disciples were not stealing, for God's law permitted handpicking food from a neighbor's field but not harvesting with a sickle or container (Deut. 23:24–25).

12:3–4 *David . . . did eat the shewbread.* He violated the ceremonial law of the tabernacle (Lev. 24:9) when he was in need of food (1 Sam. 21:1–6), because the sixth commandment transcends ceremonies. Implicitly, Jesus declared Himself to be the greater Son of David. *an hungred.* Hungry.

12:5 *priests . . . profane the sabbath.* They worked on the day of rest in such divinely appointed duties as offering the sacrifices.

12:6 *one greater than the temple.* Christ's body is the true temple (John 2:21).

12:7 *mercy, and not sacrifice.* Faithful love outweighs ceremonial worship (9:13; Hos. 6:6).

12:8 *Lord even of the sabbath day.* David, the Sabbath, and the temple all find their fulfillment in Jesus. God called the Sabbath "my holy day . . . the holy of the LORD" (Isa. 58:13); Christ's claim to be Lord of the Sabbath implies His deity. Jesus did not abolish the day of holy rest, but took it as His own (Rev. 1:10) and fulfilled it by teaching its true meaning and spirit (5:17). Works of necessity, like eating, and works of mercy, like helping those in great need, are permissible on the Sabbath.

12:10 *lawful.* The Pharisees believed it was a sin to heal on the Sabbath, though the Law never condemns such an action.

12:11–12 Jesus argued from a lesser to a greater: if an act of mercy to an animal on the Sabbath is not sin, how much more healing people on the Sabbath is not sin.

12:14 *how they might destroy him.* The ironic tension between Jesus and the unbelieving community continued to grow. Jesus showed how to uphold the sixth commandment on the Sabbath by preserving life, but the Pharisees broke the sixth commandment by conspiring to murder Jesus.

12:16–21 *Behold my servant . . . the Gentiles trust.* Citing Isa. 42:1–4 (Greek Septuagint). Christ's humility, as prophesied by Isaiah (*Esaias*), and the fact that His hour of intense suffering and death had not yet come are a couple of reasons Jesus *charged* the people to not broadcast news of His miracles (8:4; 9:30).

12:18 *shew judgment.* The Servant of the Lord will reveal God's justice in law and the gospel.

12:19–20 *not strive, nor cry.* The Servant of the Lord will not be loud and arrogant in promoting Himself (20:25–28), but will compassionately serve those broken over sin (*bruised reed*) and weak in faith (*smoking flax* or dimly burning wick).

12:22 *dumb.* Mute, unable to speak.

12:23 *amazed.* The Greek indicates that they were out of their mind in amazement. *Is not this the son of David?* The Greek indicates that they expected a negative answer, not

divided against itself shall not stand:
26 And if Satan cast out Satan, he is divided
against himself; how shall then his kingdom stand?
27 And if I by Beelzebub cast out devils, by whom
do your children cast *them* out? therefore they
shall be your judges.
28 But if I cast out devils by the Spirit of God,
then the kingdom of God is come unto you.
29 Or else how can one enter into a strong man's
house, and spoil his goods, except he first bind the
strong man? and then he will spoil his house.
30 He that is not with me is against me; and he
that gathereth not with me scattereth abroad.
31 ¶ Wherefore I say unto you, All manner of sin
and blasphemy shall be forgiven unto men: but
the blasphemy *against* the *Holy* Ghost shall not be
forgiven unto men.
32 And whosoever speaketh a word against
the Son of man, it shall be forgiven him: but
whosoever speaketh against the Holy Ghost, it
shall not be forgiven him, neither in this world,
neither in the *world* to come.
33 Either make the tree good, and his fruit
good; or else make the tree corrupt, and his fruit
corrupt: for the tree is known by *his* fruit.
34 O generation of vipers, how can ye, being evil,
speak good things? for out of the abundance of
the heart the mouth speaketh.
35 A good man out of the good treasure of the
heart bringeth forth good things: and an evil man
out of the evil treasure bringeth forth evil things.
36 But I say unto you, That every idle word that
men shall speak, they shall give account thereof in
the day of judgment.
37 For by thy words thou shalt be justified, and by
thy words thou shalt be condemned.
38 ¶ Then certain of the scribes and of the
Pharisees answered, saying, Master, we would see
a sign from thee.
39 But he answered and said unto them, An evil
and adulterous generation seeketh after a sign;
and there shall no sign be given to it, but the sign
of the prophet Jonas:
40 For as Jonas was three days and three nights in
the whale's belly; so shall the Son of man be three
days and three nights in the heart of the earth.
41 The men of Nineveh shall rise in judgment
with this generation, and shall condemn it:
because they repented at the preaching of Jonas;
and, behold, a greater than Jonas *is* here.
42 The queen of the south shall rise up in
the judgment with this generation, and shall
condemn it: for she came from the uttermost
parts of the earth to hear the wisdom of Solomon;
and, behold, a greater than Solomon *is* here.
43 When the unclean spirit is gone out of a man,
he walketh through dry places, seeking rest, and
findeth none.
44 Then he saith, I will return into my house
from whence I came out; and when he is come, he
findeth *it* empty, swept, and garnished.
45 Then goeth he, and taketh with himself seven
other spirits more wicked than himself, and they
enter in and dwell there: and the last *state* of that
man is worse than the first. Even so shall it be also
unto this wicked generation.
46 ¶ While he yet talked to the people, behold, *his*
mother and his brethren stood without, desiring
to speak with him.
47 Then one said unto him, Behold, thy mother

believing in Him (1:1; 9:27).

12:24 *Beelzebub.* Satan (see note at 10:24–25).

12:28 *by the Spirit of God . . . kingdom of God is come.* Jesus defeats Satan and brings the reign of the Lord into people's lives through the Holy Spirit with whom God anointed Him (v. 18; Isa. 11:1–2; 32:1–2,15; John 3:5; Rom. 14:17).

12:29 *spoil his goods.* Plunder his possessions. The kingdom of God was making a profound impact against the kingdom of darkness, showing that Christ decisively defeated the Devil in His first coming (*bind the strong man*; Rev. 20:1–3; cf. Luke 10:18; John 12:31; 16:11), though Satan is still active in the world (Rev. 12:9).

12:30 *not with me is against me.* There is no neutrality in one's position toward Jesus.

12:31–32 *blasphemy.* Speaking evil, especially about God, His attributes, or His ordinances. *speaketh against the Holy Ghost . . . not be forgiven.* Blasphemy against the Holy Spirit is persistently ascribing to Satan the work of Christ by the Holy Spirit, an act of a profoundly hardened heart like that of Pharaoh. Those who fear the Lord and confess their sins are not guilty of this unforgivable sin (1 John 1:9).

12:33–35 *the tree is known by his fruit.* A person's words and works reveal his nature (7:16–20). *how can ye, being evil, speak good.* It is impossible for sinners to make themselves good (Jer. 13:23; 17:1). Only God's all-powerful grace can convert men to faith and repentance (19:25–26).

12:36 *every idle word.* All useless speech. While a broad application of this would be that we should all watch our words; a more narrow application of this would be that the Pharisees' idle words concerning Jesus will be condemned.

12:37 *by thy words . . . justified.* Though believers are justified by faith alone in terms of God's relationship to them (Luke 18:9–14; Rom. 3:21—4:6), God will publicly vindicate them and declare them righteous on the judgment day according to how their speech and actions show their faith in Christ to be genuine (25:31–46; cf. James 2:14,18).

12:38–40 The Pharisees asked for a *sign* despite the fact that Jesus had already given them many signs and yet they persisted in their unbelief. *adulterous.* Sinners give their supreme love to this world and thus are treacherous to God (Jer. 3:8; Mark 8:36–38; James 4:4). *Jonas.* Jonah. *whale.* Large fish. *three days and three nights.* An idiom for a time period touching three distinct days, even if only a portion of any one of them (thus Friday night, Saturday, and Sunday morning, cf. 16:21; 17:23; 20:19; 27:64).

12:41–42 *Nineveh . . . queen of the south.* These Gentiles believed the words of Jonah and *Solomon* (Jonah 3:5; 1 Kings 10:1–13), but the Pharisees did not believe though One *greater than* both Jonah and *Solomon* was in their midst.

12:46 *his brethren.* Even those of Jesus' own family did not

and thy brethren stand without, desiring to speak
with thee.
48 But he answered and said unto him that told
him, Who is my mother? and who are my brethren?
49 And he stretched forth his hand toward his
disciples, and said, Behold my mother and my
brethren!
50 For whosoever shall do the will of my Father
which is in heaven, the same is my brother, and
sister, and mother.

CHAPTER 13

THE same day went Jesus out of the house, and sat
by the sea side.
2 And great multitudes were gathered together
unto him, so that he went into a ship, and sat; and
the whole multitude stood on the shore.
3 And he spake many things unto them in par-
ables, saying, Behold, a sower went forth to sow;
4 And when he sowed, some *seeds* fell by the way
side, and the fowls came and devoured them up:
5 Some fell upon stony places, where they had
not much earth: and forthwith they sprung up,
because they had no deepness of earth:
6 And when the sun was up, they were scorched;
and because they had no root, they withered away.
7 And some fell among thorns; and the thorns
sprung up, and choked them:
8 But other fell into good ground, and brought
forth fruit, some an hundredfold, some sixtyfold,
some thirtyfold.
9 Who hath ears to hear, let him hear.
10 And the disciples came, and said unto him,
Why speakest thou unto them in parables?
11 He answered and said unto them, Because it
is given unto you to know the mysteries of the
kingdom of heaven, but to them it is not given.
12 For whosoever hath, to him shall be given, and
he shall have more abundance: but whosoever
hath not, from him shall be taken away even that
he hath.
13 Therefore speak I to them in parables: because
they seeing see not; and hearing they hear not,
neither do they understand.
14 And in them is fulfilled the prophecy of Esaias,
which saith, By hearing ye shall hear, and shall not
understand; and seeing ye shall see, and shall not
perceive:
15 For this people's heart is waxed gross, and
their ears are dull of hearing, and their eyes they
have closed; lest at any time they should see with
their eyes, and hear with *their* ears, and should
understand with *their* heart, and should be

believe His messianic claims (Mark 3:21; John 7:1–5). *without.* Outside.

12:49–50 *Behold my mother and my brethren!* Though the gospel divides families (10:35–37), it creates a new spiritual family consisting of those given a new nature to obey God's Word (v. 33).

Thoughts for Personal/Family Worship: Chapter 12

1. **Christ did not declare the Sabbath to be like any other day, but declared Himself to be the Lord of the Sabbath and taught His disciples how to observe it rightly. Legalists ruin the day by their burdensome traditions, but Christ loved the Sabbath and reserved a few of His greatest miracles for the Sabbath day. Christians also should love the Sabbath and keep the Lord's Day. What does Christ's example and teaching show us about how to truly keep the Sabbath?**
2. **Christ will not break the bruised reed or quench the smoking flax (v. 20). God's true people often go through life bruised and assailed. It may seem like everything and everyone is against them, especially their sins. Christ is a tender Savior. He can nurse and nurture the flame of faith in the heart. His work on the cross ensures a full victory for even the weakest believer. How can His gentle spirit encourage you in your own struggle against sin?**
3. **Christ pointed to His true family: "For whosoever shall do the will of my Father which is in heaven, the same is my brother, and sister, and mother" (v. 50). This was a holy rebuke to His brothers, who were later converted. It is not fleshly connections that ultimately matter. However, let those who obey Christ's Word take comfort that Jesus Christ embraces them as the family of God. Why is this a great comfort to believers?**

Chapter 13: *Jesus teaches about the kingdom of heaven by using parables that both conceal and reveal the glory of Jesus.*

The Parables of the Kingdom of Heaven (13:1–58)

Parable of the Sower (13:1–9)

13:1 *same day.* Connected in time with ch. 12.

13:3–9 Though commonly known as the parable of the sower, Jesus focused on the various kinds of soil, all of which received seed, but only one produced a harvest (see vv. 18–23 for the interpretation).

13:4 *way side.* Roadside; untillable, useless ground. *fowls.* Birds.

13:5 *stony places.* Shallow soil with a solid bedrock where the roots could not go deep.

13:8 *good ground.* Fertile ground. *hundredfold . . . sixtyfold . . . thirtyfold.* Even in good soil, the seeds did not all produce the same, but varying amounts of fruit.

Purpose of Parables (13:10–17)

13:10 *them.* The crowds gathered on the shore to hear Jesus' teaching (v. 2). There was a decisive change in Jesus' public ministry at this point as He went from speaking plainly to speaking in parables.

13:11 *given unto you to know.* The knowledge of the kingdom is a gift of God's grace (11:25,27). *mysteries.* Things hidden that are now being revealed.

13:12 *whosoever hath . . . hath not.* Those in whom God is savingly at work will produce fruit. Those who do not, even their privileges such as hearing Christ's Word will be taken away from them.

13:13–15 *Esaias.* Isaiah (Isa. 6:9–10). The parables reveal the truths of the kingdom to the children of the kingdom but conceal these same truths from others as divine judgment

converted, and I should heal them.
16 But blessed *are* your eyes, for they see: and
your ears, for they hear.
17 For verily I say unto you, That many prophets
and righteous *men* have desired to see *those things*
which ye see, and have not seen *them*; and to hear
those things which ye hear, and have not heard
them.
18 ¶ Hear ye therefore the parable of the sower.
19 When any one heareth the word of the kingdom, and understandeth *it* not, then cometh the
wicked *one*, and catcheth away that which was
sown in his heart. This is he which received seed
by the way side.
20 But he that received the seed into stony places,
the same is he that heareth the word, and anon
with joy receiveth it;
21 Yet hath he not root in himself, but dureth for
a while: for when tribulation or persecution ariseth because of the word, by and by he is offended.
22 He also that received seed among the thorns
is he that heareth the word; and the care of this
world, and the deceitfulness of riches, choke the
word, and he becometh unfruitful.
23 But he that received seed into the good ground
is he that heareth the word, and understandeth *it*;
which also beareth fruit, and bringeth forth, some
an hundredfold, some sixty, some thirty.
24 ¶ Another parable put he forth unto them,
saying, The kingdom of heaven is likened unto a
man which sowed good seed in his field:
25 But while men slept, his enemy came and
sowed tares among the wheat, and went his way.
26 But when the blade was sprung up, and
brought forth fruit, then appeared the tares also.
27 So the servants of the householder came and
said unto him, Sir, didst not thou sow good seed
in thy field? from whence then hath it tares?
28 He said unto them, An enemy hath done this.
The servants said unto him, Wilt thou then that we
go and gather them up?
29 But he said, Nay; lest while ye gather up the
tares, ye root up also the wheat with them.
30 Let both grow together until the harvest: and in
the time of harvest I will say to the reapers, Gather
ye together first the tares, and bind them in bundles
to burn them: but gather the wheat into my barn.
31 ¶ Another parable put he forth unto them,
saying, The kingdom of heaven is like to a grain
of mustard seed, which a man took, and sowed
in his field:
32 Which indeed is the least of all seeds: but when
it is grown, it is the greatest among herbs, and
becometh a tree, so that the birds of the air come
and lodge in the branches thereof.
33 ¶ Another parable spake he unto them; The
kingdom of heaven is like unto leaven, which a
woman took, and hid in three measures of meal,
till the whole was leavened.
34 All these things spake Jesus unto the multitude
in parables; and without a parable spake he not
unto them:

---

upon them. This underscores God's sovereign initiative in saving sinners (Mark 4:11).

13:17 *verily.* Truly. Under the *prophets* the mysteries of the kingdom were only partially revealed, but Christ's teaching is their full manifestation (Rom. 16:25–26; Heb. 1:1–4; 1 Peter 1:10–12).

Parable of the Sower Explained (13:18–23)

13:18–23 God had compared Israel to His agriculture, where He sought a harvest of righteousness and justice (Isa. 5:1–7; 27:2–6). Christ here indicated that His Word would produce the desired fruit, but only some of His hearers in Israel would prove themselves to be the spiritual Israel.

13:19 Though the Word was *sown in his heart* it did not reside deeply in his mind with an experiential knowledge of God (*understandeth it not*; vv. 13–15), and so Satan (*the wicked one*; vv. 38–39) takes away its influence by his lies (2 Cor. 4:4; Rev. 12:9) as easily as birds eating seed laying on the surface of the ground (v. 4).

13:20–21 *anon.* Immediately. *dureth.* Endures. *tribulation.* Difficulties and trials. His initial *joy* in the Word does not last and he falls away (*is offended*), because the secret hardness of his yet unconverted heart (*stony places*; Ezek. 36:26) stops the Word from changing His deepest motives (*not root*).

13:22 *care of this world.* Anxiety and fear about earthly things (6:25–34). *deceitfulness of riches.* Desire for earthly things based on false beliefs that they can give and preserve happiness (Eph. 4:22). Attempts to receive God's Word without repenting of worldliness are not profitable.

13:23 The defining characteristic of *good ground* is that it produces *fruit*: the Word changes the heart with experiential knowledge (*understandeth*; contrast v. 19) so that Satan, trials, and worldliness cannot stop it from producing a new life (John 15:5–6; Gal. 5:22–24), though in varying degrees.

Parable of the Tares (13:24–30)

13:24–30 For the interpretation of this parable, see vv. 36–43.

13:25 *tares.* Weeds, probably darnel, which closely resembles *wheat* until grain is produced. Whereas the *enemy* in the earlier parable snatched up the seed, here he sows weeds. The messages of the parable are distinct and not to be confused.

13:27 *householder.* Master or head of the household. *from whence.* By what cause, how.

13:28 *Wilt thou.* Do you will or desire.

13:29 *Nay.* No.

Parable of the Mustard Seed (13:31–33)

13:31–32 *mustard seed.* The smallest seed commonly planted in Palestine. Though the kingdom of God has small beginnings, it will grow into the *greatest* of kingdoms. *tree . . . birds.* An image of safety and prosperity under a king's reign (Ezek. 17:23; 31:6; Dan. 4:11–12,20–22).

13:33 *leaven.* Dough with yeast, a small quantity of which, worked through the *whole* lump of dough, affects every part. The kingdom may seem insignificant, but it will change everything.

Purpose of Parables (13:34–35)

13:34 *unto the multitude.* Christ's teaching to the crowds was cloaked in parables, and He reserved the explanations for those who sincerely sought Him (v. 36).

35 That it might be fulfilled which was spoken
by the prophet, saying, I will open my mouth in
parables; I will utter things which have been kept
secret from the foundation of the world.
36 Then Jesus sent the multitude away, and went
into the house: and his disciples came unto him,
saying, Declare unto us the parable of the tares of
the field.
37 He answered and said unto them, He that
soweth the good seed is the Son of man;
38 The field is the world; the good seed are the
children of the kingdom; but the tares are the
children of the wicked *one*;
39 The enemy that sowed them is the devil; the
harvest is the end of the world; and the reapers
are the angels.
40 As therefore the tares are gathered and burned
in the fire; so shall it be in the end of this world.
41 The Son of man shall send forth his angels,
and they shall gather out of his kingdom all things
that offend, and them which do iniquity;
42 And shall cast them into a furnace of fire: there
shall be wailing and gnashing of teeth.
43 Then shall the righteous shine forth as the sun
in the kingdom of their Father. Who hath ears to
hear, let him hear.
44 ¶ Again, the kingdom of heaven is like unto
treasure hid in a field; the which when a man hath
found, he hideth, and for joy thereof goeth and
selleth all that he hath, and buyeth that field.
45 ¶ Again, the kingdom of heaven is like unto a
merchant man, seeking goodly pearls:
46 Who, when he had found one pearl of great
price, went and sold all that he had, and bought it.
47 ¶ Again, the kingdom of heaven is like unto
a net, that was cast into the sea, and gathered of
every kind:
48 Which, when it was full, they drew to shore,
and sat down, and gathered the good into vessels,
but cast the bad away.
49 So shall it be at the end of the world: the angels
shall come forth, and sever the wicked from among
the just,
50 And shall cast them into the furnace of fire:
there shall be wailing and gnashing of teeth.
51 Jesus saith unto them, Have ye understood all
these things? They say unto him, Yea, Lord.
52 Then said he unto them, Therefore every scribe
which is instructed unto the kingdom of heaven is
like unto a man *that is* an householder, which bring-
eth forth out of his treasure *things* new and old.
53 ¶ And it came to pass, *that* when Jesus had
finished these parables, he departed thence.
54 And when he was come into his own country,
he taught them in their synagogue, insomuch that
they were astonished, and said, Whence hath this
man this wisdom, and *these* mighty works?
55 Is not this the carpenter's son? is not his
mother called Mary? and his brethren, James, and
Joses, and Simon, and Judas?
56 And his sisters, are they not all with us?
Whence then hath this *man* all these things?
57 And they were offended in him. But Jesus said
unto them, A prophet is not without honour, save

13:35 *spoken by the prophet.* Citing Ps. 78:2.

Parable of the Tares Explained (13:36–43)

13:36 *Declare.* Explain.

13:37–39 Christ explained how each element of this parable symbolized something about His kingdom. *Son of man.* Jesus is both the Savior who creates believers by His sovereign grace (*soweth the good seed*) and the Judge of all men (v. 41). *field . . . world.* Interpreted as a picture either of the godly mixed among the wicked in the world or of the righteous and the wicked mingled in the visible church. *children.* Literally, "sons," an idiom for those belonging to God's *kingdom* or those belonging to the *devil*. *end of the world.* Literally, "the completion of the age," the day of judgment and arrival of the new age of righteousness and glory (vv. 40,49; 24:3; 28:20).

13:41 *his angels . . . his kingdom.* Christ is the sovereign Lord of the angels, Judge of all men, and King of the kingdom of God, the divine *Son of man* (Dan. 7:13–14; see note at 8:20). *offend.* Cause others to stumble and fall (16:23; 18:6–9).

13:42 *wailing and gnashing of teeth.* The sufferings of hell (v. 50; see note at 8:12).

Parables of the Treasure and the Pearl (13:44–46)

13:44–46 *treasure hid in a field . . . pearl of great price.* These two brief parables are very similar, illustrating the immense value of the *kingdom*, the *joy* it gives to those who find it by grace, and their willingness to forsake *all* to gain it. They differ slightly in that the first highlights that the value of the *kingdom* is hidden from most people and sometimes discovered as if by accident, and the second portrays a person who is intentionally *seeking* it. God leads people into His *kingdom* along different ways.

Parable of the Net (13:47–50)

13:47–50 This *net* was large, with weights tied to the bottom, to catch many fish. This parable speaks of two separations: first, the net separating the fish from *the sea*, and second, the fishermen separating *the good* fish from *the bad*. The gospel call brings some people out of the world into the church, and the judgment day will distinguish (*sever*) between the converted and the hypocrites in the church.

Jesus the Rejected Prophet (13:51–58)

13:52 *bringeth forth out of his treasure things new and old.* This statement refers to the disciples' task to bring forth new truths out of the truths contained in the treasure house of the Word of God.

13:54–56 *his own country . . . in their synagogue.* Christ taught in Nazareth on the Sabbath (Mark 6:2; Luke 4:16). *Whence.* From what cause, how. The people of His hometown recognized His prophetic *wisdom* and kingly *mighty works*, but still did not believe that the Christ could come from such ordinary beginnings (*carpenter's son*; Isa. 53:1–3).

13:57 *prophet.* Jesus took the title of this office upon Himself, a fulfillment of Moses' prophecy (Deut. 18:15). As the fulfillment of the Old Testament Scriptures, Jesus held the threefold office of Prophet, Priest, and King. *save.* Except.

13:58 *because of their unbelief.* See Mark 6:5–6. Though God

in his own country, and in his own house.
58 And he did not many mighty works there
because of their unbelief.

CHAPTER 14

AT that time Herod the tetrarch heard of the fame
of Jesus,
2 And said unto his servants, This is John the
Baptist; he is risen from the dead; and therefore
mighty works do shew forth themselves in him.
3 ¶ For Herod had laid hold on John, and bound
him, and put *him* in prison for Herodias' sake, his
brother Philip's wife.
4 For John said unto him, It is not lawful for thee
to have her.
5 And when he would have put him to death, he
feared the multitude, because they counted him
as a prophet.
6 But when Herod's birthday was kept, the
daughter of Herodias danced before them, and
pleased Herod.
7 Whereupon he promised with an oath to give
her whatsoever she would ask.
8 And she, being before instructed of her mother,
said, Give me here John Baptist's head in a charger.
9 And the king was sorry: nevertheless for the
oath's sake, and them which sat with him at meat,
he commanded *it* to be given *her*.
10 And he sent, and beheaded John in the prison.
11 And his head was brought in a charger, and
given to the damsel: and she brought *it* to her
mother.
12 And his disciples came, and took up the body,
and buried it, and went and told Jesus.
13 ¶ When Jesus heard *of it*, he departed thence
by ship into a desert place apart: and when the
people had heard *thereof*, they followed him on
foot out of the cities.
14 And Jesus went forth, and saw a great multi-
tude, and was moved with compassion toward
them, and he healed their sick.
15 ¶ And when it was evening, his disciples came
to him, saying, This is a desert place, and the
time is now past; send the multitude away, that
they may go into the villages, and buy themselves
victuals.
16 But Jesus said unto them, They need not
depart; give ye them to eat.
17 And they say unto him, We have here but five
loaves, and two fishes.
18 He said, Bring them hither to me.
19 And he commanded the multitude to sit down
on the grass, and took the five loaves, and the two
fishes, and looking up to heaven, he blessed, and
brake, and gave the loaves to *his* disciples, and the
disciples to the multitude.
20 And they did all eat, and were filled: and they
took up of the fragments that remained twelve
baskets full.
21 And they that had eaten were about five
thousand men, beside women and children.

---

can do as He pleases regardless of man's faithlessness, Jesus' power as Mediator was controlled and limited by His Father's will (20:23), and God would not cast the pearls of His miracles before spiritual swine who refused to believe (7:6).

Thoughts for Personal/Family Worship: Chapter 13

1. **Christ searches our hearts, and His parables call us to search ourselves. Which soil are you? In reality, all the negative influences of Satan, sin, and the world remain in the hearts of believers. But God's grace prevails and they bear a harvest of good works. We must not rest in hearing and reading the Word. Others have enjoyed the same privilege and yet in the end proved to be fruitless. Nor may we rest in it having some influence upon us. Many fish caught in the net were later thrown away. The only sure sign that God's Word has saved a sinner is a changed life. It changes the inner life, for the converted count Christ as their greatest joy and treasure. It changes the outer life, for the converted bear fruit. How has the gospel changed you? How is it changing you now?**
2. **The kingdom of heaven may appear as insignificant as a tiny seed or a little piece of leaven, but at the completion of this age it will tower over all other kingdoms. Nothing else will matter compared to the great question of whether one goes to the fires of hell, where the wicked weep and gnash their teeth, or to the glories of heaven, where the righteous shine like the sun. How should this truth change the way we think about ourselves, other people, and our lives?**

Chapter 14: *John the Baptist dies. Jesus performs several miracles confirming His teachings and declarations as the Son of God.*

John the Baptist's Death Reported to Jesus (14:1–13)

14:1 *Herod.* Herod Antipas, who ruled over Galilee and Perea (4 BC–AD 39). *tetrarch.* Ruler over one-fourth of the kingdom. *fame of Jesus.* Despite Jesus' warning that people not spread the message of His miraculous work, it is clear that word about Him spread quickly.
14:2 *John the Baptist . . . risen.* Apparently a common belief (16:14).
14:3–5 *Herodias.* Herod Antipas had divorced his first wife to marry her, which was forbidden by Old Testament law because she was *his brother Philip's wife* (Lev. 18:16; 20:21).
14:8 *charger.* A platter.
14:10 *beheaded.* A form of death reserved for terrible wrongdoers. John the Baptist died as an accused criminal, much as Jesus would.
14:11 *damsel.* Young woman, girl.

Several Miracles Performed (14:14–36)

14:14–15 Jesus' *compassion* is contrasted with the disciples' wish to *send the multitude away. victuals.* Food.
14:16 *give ye them to eat.* You give them something to eat. Jesus tested His disciples' faith in His sufficiency, but even after His many miracles they still were weak in faith.
14:18 *hither.* Here.
14:20 *twelve baskets.* Likely symbolic that Jesus has come to give a *full* blessing upon Israel.
14:21 *five thousand men.* Feeding such a crowd with such

22 ¶ And straightway Jesus constrained his disci-
ples to get into a ship, and to go before him unto
the other side, while he sent the multitudes away.
23 And when he had sent the multitudes away, he
went up into a mountain apart to pray: and when
the evening was come, he was there alone.
24 But the ship was now in the midst of the sea,
tossed with waves: for the wind was contrary.
25 And in the fourth watch of the night Jesus
went unto them, walking on the sea.
26 And when the disciples saw him walking on
the sea, they were troubled, saying, It is a spirit;
and they cried out for fear.
27 But straightway Jesus spake unto them, saying,
Be of good cheer; it is I; be not afraid.
28 And Peter answered him and said, Lord, if it be
thou, bid me come unto thee on the water.
29 And he said, Come. And when Peter was come
down out of the ship, he walked on the water, to
go to Jesus.
30 But when he saw the wind boisterous, he was
afraid; and beginning to sink, he cried, saying,
Lord, save me.
31 And immediately Jesus stretched forth *his*
hand, and caught him, and said unto him, O thou
of little faith, wherefore didst thou doubt?
32 And when they were come into the ship, the
wind ceased.
33 Then they that were in the ship came and
worshipped him, saying, Of a truth thou art the
Son of God.
34 ¶ And when they were gone over, they came
into the land of Gennesaret.
35 And when the men of that place had knowl-
edge of him, they sent out into all that country
round about, and brought unto him all that were
diseased;
36 And besought him that they might only touch
the hem of his garment: and as many as touched
were made perfectly whole.

CHAPTER 15

THEN came to Jesus scribes and Pharisees, which
were of Jerusalem, saying,
2 Why do thy disciples transgress the tradition
of the elders? for they wash not their hands when
they eat bread.
3 But he answered and said unto them, Why do
ye also transgress the commandment of God by
your tradition?
4 For God commanded, saying, Honour thy
father and mother: and, He that curseth father or
mother, let him die the death.
5 But ye say, Whosoever shall say to *his* father
or *his* mother, *It is* a gift, by whatsoever thou
mightest be profited by me;
6 And honour not his father or his mother, *he*

a small amount was a miracle of the highest order, like the works of the Lord in the days of Moses (Ex. 16) and of Elisha (2 Kings 4:42–44).

14:25 *fourth watch.* Probably between 3:00 and 6:00 a.m. *walking on the sea.* Jesus is greater than Moses, who led Israel through the sea. This story recalls the Old Testament passages where God is said to rule over the seas (Job 9:8; Ps. 77:19; Isa. 43:16).

14:26 *spirit.* The Greek term can refer to the *spirit* of a dead person, an angel, or a demon.

14:27 *Be of good cheer.* Have courage. *it is I.* Literally, "I am," perhaps an allusion to the name of the Lord *Jehovah* (Ex. 3:14; John 8:58).

14:28 *bid.* Command, order. Peter's request to Jesus showed Peter's faith in Christ.

14:30 *boisterous.* Strong, forceful.

14:31 *little faith.* A startling statement considering Peter's willingness to go out to Jesus on the water, but part of the strength of faith consists in its perseverance under trial. *wherefore.* Why, for what reason.

14:32 *wind ceased.* As it had when Christ rebuked the storm (8:26). Jesus' calming of the sea shows His power over the chaotic powers of nature.

14:33 *worshipped him.* A sign that Christ is to be honored as God (4:9–10; Rev. 19:10). *Son of God.* The Christ (26:63; Ps. 2:7), the promised Son of David (2 Sam. 7:16), yet plainly here greater than any mere man but possessing the power of the Creator over His creation.

Thoughts for Personal/Family Worship: Chapter 14

1. **John the Baptist died because of faithfulness to his Lord. He would not hide the truth, and he didn't cease to warn transgressors. His death was not a tragedy. He was immediately translated from the dungeon of Herod to the throne room of God, to the festival of the spirits of righteous men made perfect in the presence of their Lord. How can his example help you to not fear to suffer or die for the Lord?**
2. **Jesus is Lord and God. Though a prophet, like Moses who saw the Lord divide the sea and provide manna to Israel, Jesus is far greater than Moses, for Christ walked upon the sea and enabled Peter to do the same. Therefore, it is right that we worship Him in our prayers and praises. Do you delight to worship Christ with holy fear? If so, then remember that your greatest act of worship is to trust Him. What can we learn from Peter about honoring Christ by faith?**

Chapter 15: ***Jesus teaches about true defilement and the nature of genuine faith, again performing several miracles.***

Further Teaching on Discipleship (15:1–20)

15:2 *tradition of the elders.* Not Old Testament law, but human customs that the disciples were not following.

15:4 Christ cited Ex. 20:12; 21:17.

15:5 *It is a gift.* Consecrated to the service of God (Hebrew, *qorban*; cf. Mark 7:11), yet often kept for one's own use—a hypocritical method of avoiding one's moral obligation to support one's parents.

15:6 *the commandment of God of none effect.* Adding human tradition as an authority alongside God's Word does not complement Scripture but contradicts it.

15:7–9 *Esaias.* Isaiah (Isa. 29:13). *nigh.* Near. God's law

shall be free. Thus have ye made the command-
ment of God of none effect by your tradition.
7 *Ye* hypocrites, well did Esaias prophesy of you,
saying,
8 This people draweth nigh unto me with their
mouth, and honoureth me with *their* lips; but
their heart is far from me.
9 But in vain they do worship me, teaching *for*
doctrines the commandments of men.
10 ¶ And he called the multitude, and said unto
them, Hear, and understand:
11 Not that which goeth into the mouth defileth
a man; but that which cometh out of the mouth,
this defileth a man.
12 Then came his disciples, and said unto him,
Knowest thou that the Pharisees were offended,
after they heard this saying?
13 But he answered and said, Every plant, which
my heavenly Father hath not planted, shall be
rooted up.
14 Let them alone: they be blind leaders of the
blind. And if the blind lead the blind, both shall
fall into the ditch.
15 Then answered Peter and said unto him,
Declare unto us this parable.
16 And Jesus said, Are ye also yet without under-
standing?
17 Do not ye yet understand, that whatsoever
entereth in at the mouth goeth into the belly, and
is cast out into the draught?
18 But those things which proceed out of the
mouth come forth from the heart; and they defile
the man.
19 For out of the heart proceed evil thoughts,
murders, adulteries, fornications, thefts, false
witness, blasphemies:
20 These are *the things* which defile a man: but to
eat with unwashen hands defileth not a man.
21 ¶ Then Jesus went thence, and departed into
the coasts of Tyre and Sidon.
22 And, behold, a woman of Canaan came out
of the same coasts, and cried unto him, saying,
Have mercy on me, O Lord, *thou* Son of David;
my daughter is grievously vexed with a devil.
23 But he answered her not a word. And his
disciples came and besought him, saying, Send
her away; for she crieth after us.
24 But he answered and said, I am not sent but
unto the lost sheep of the house of Israel.
25 Then came she and worshipped him, saying,
Lord, help me.
26 But he answered and said, It is not meet to take
the children's bread, and to cast *it* to dogs.
27 And she said, Truth, Lord: yet the dogs eat of
the crumbs which fall from their masters' table.
28 Then Jesus answered and said unto her, O
woman, great *is* thy faith: be it unto thee even
as thou wilt. And her daughter was made whole
from that very hour.
29 And Jesus departed from thence, and came
nigh unto the sea of Galilee; and went up into a
mountain, and sat down there.
30 And great multitudes came unto him, having
with them *those that were* lame, blind, dumb,
maimed, and many others, and cast them down
at Jesus' feet; and he healed them:

---

requires both inward and outward holiness. Whereas the Pharisees blamed the disciples for being outwardly unholy, Jesus accused the Pharisees of being inwardly unholy (23:25–27). *teaching for doctrines the commandments of men.* Christ affirmed the biblical principle that *worship* only pleases God if done as He commands and not according to human ideas and inventions (Ex. 25:40; 39:43; Lev. 10:1–3; Col. 2:23)

15:13–14 *which my heavenly Father hath not planted.* The only religion acceptable to God is that which He creates by His sovereign grace in Christ (13:37). *rooted up. Let.* The same Greek verbs used in the parable of the tares (13:29–30). For the present time, the righteous must tolerate the presence of wicked hypocrites, but in the final judgment God will separate them to their proper destinies. *blind.* Christ's many miracles of healing the blind (see note at 9:27) were a sign that sinners need Him to heal their spiritual blindness so that they may trust and obey God's Word (6:22–23; 7:3; 13:15; 23:16–17, 19,24,26; Isa. 42:6–7; Acts 26:18).

15:15 *Declare.* Explain (13:36).

15:17 *draught.* Sewer, drain.

15:20 *unwashen hands defileth not a man.* Outward rituals do not directly affect spiritual realities, a suggestion that Christ was about to abolish the ceremonial laws (Mark 7:19; Luke 11:41; John 4:21–24), particularly in His death on the cross (27:51).

Several Miracles Performed (15:21–39)

15:21 *thence.* From there. This is the fifth time that Jesus *departed* from people (2:12–14,22 ["turned aside"]; 4:12; 12:15; 14:13). *coasts.* Region. *Tyre and Sidon.* Gentile cities.

15:22 *Lord . . . Son of David.* These titles illustrate that this Canaanite woman had faith in Christ as the Messiah. *grievously vexed with a devil.* Literally, "badly demonized" (see note at 4:24–25).

15:23 *he answered her not a word.* Jesus ignored her first petition. Unlike the disciples, however, Christ was testing the woman's faith.

15:24 *lost sheep of the house of Israel.* In submission to God's redemptive plan, Christ focused His ministry upon the spiritual needs of the physical offspring of Abraham in the land (9:36; 10:6) before sending the gospel to the Gentiles as well (28:19).

15:26 *dogs.* Unclean scavengers (Ex. 22:31), insulting language for people such as the wicked or Gentiles (7:6; Ps. 22:16; Luke 16:21; Phil. 3:2; Rev. 22:15).

15:27 In humility the woman took hold of Christ's words, not denying her unworthy position (*dogs*), but relying on the graciousness of God to give her grace (*crumbs*).

15:28 *great is thy faith.* As with the centurion (8:10), Jesus highly commended the humble and persistent reliance of this Gentile woman, implying that His people will be gathered from all nations (12:21).

15:30 *great multitudes.* It is uncertain whether this great multitude was comprised of Jews, Gentiles, or both. *dumb.* Mute, unable to speak.

31 Insomuch that the multitude wondered, when
they saw the dumb to speak, the maimed to be
whole, the lame to walk, and the blind to see: and
they glorified the God of Israel.
32 ¶ Then Jesus called his disciples *unto him*, and
said, I have compassion on the multitude, because
they continue with me now three days, and have
nothing to eat: and I will not send them away
fasting, lest they faint in the way.
33 And his disciples say unto him, Whence
should we have so much bread in the wilderness,
as to fill so great a multitude?
34 And Jesus saith unto them, How many loaves
have ye? And they said, Seven, and a few little fishes.
35 And he commanded the multitude to sit down
on the ground.
36 And he took the seven loaves and the fishes,
and gave thanks, and brake *them*, and gave to his
disciples, and the disciples to the multitude.
37 And they did all eat, and were filled: and they
took up of the broken *meat* that was left seven
baskets full.
38 And they that did eat were four thousand men,
beside women and children.
39 And he sent away the multitude, and took
ship, and came into the coasts of Magdala.

CHAPTER 16

THE Pharisees also with the Sadducees came, and
tempting desired him that he would shew them a
sign from heaven.
2 He answered and said unto them, When it is
evening, ye say, *It will be* fair weather: for the sky
is red.
3 And in the morning, *It will be* foul weather
to day: for the sky is red and lowring. O *ye*
hypocrites, ye can discern the face of the sky; but
can ye not *discern* the signs of the times?
4 A wicked and adulterous generation seeketh
after a sign; and there shall no sign be given unto
it, but the sign of the prophet Jonas. And he left
them, and departed.
5 And when his disciples were come to the other
side, they had forgotten to take bread.
6 ¶ Then Jesus said unto them, Take heed and
beware of the leaven of the Pharisees and of the
Sadducees.
7 And they reasoned among themselves, saying,
It is because we have taken no bread.
8 *Which* when Jesus perceived, he said unto them,
O ye of little faith, why reason ye among your-
selves, because ye have brought no bread?
9 Do ye not yet understand, neither remember
the five loaves of the five thousand, and how
many baskets ye took up?
10 Neither the seven loaves of the four thousand,
and how many baskets ye took up?
11 How is it that ye do not understand that I
spake *it* not to you concerning bread, that ye
should beware of the leaven of the Pharisees and
of the Sadducees?
12 Then understood they how that he bade *them*
not beware of the leaven of bread, but of the

15:31 *glorified the God of Israel.* While this could refer to Gentiles, this title of God is often used to designate Israel's praise of the Lord (Ex. 5:1).
15:32–38 This miracle of feeding *four thousand men* plus *women and children* is very similar to the previous feeding of five thousand (14:13–21). However, this one comes after the Canaanite woman asked for a crumb, suggesting that the Lord has a large table filled with bounty for all sorts of people.
15:37 *meat.* Food of any kind.

Thoughts for Personal/Family Worship: Chapter 15

1. **The heart of sin is the sin of the heart. The scribes and the Pharisees focused on external sins, especially the rituals they dictated, but the Lord Jesus said that all the moral evils of mankind proceed out of the heart (v. 19). When God works in our heart, He gives us the ability to see how deeply rooted sin is and how corrupt and deceitful our hearts are. Our salvation cannot simply be dressing up or cleaning up the outside of our lives. Christ must heal our blindness. We need the new birth. God must plant new life within us. How does this humble you? How does it glorify the Savior?**
2. **Christ's dealings with the woman of Canaan appear harsh. However, His silence and apparent objections provoked her faith to shine brightly against the backdrop of this glorious Son of David. William Cowper said it well: "Behind a frowning providence / He hides a smiling face." Let us imitate the persistence and humility of the Canaanite woman's faith. When the Lord is not answering your prayers, acknowledge your unworthiness but cling to Christ all the more.**

Chapter 16: ***Jesus is rejected by the Pharisees and Sadducees and warns His disciples against them. Peter makes the grand confession of faith in Christ, who announces His passion, death, and resurrection.***

Jesus' Message Rejected and Accepted (16:1–28)

Pharisees' and Sadducees' Rejection of Jesus (16:1–12)

16:1 *Pharisees . . . Sadducees.* Typically at odds with each other (Acts 23:6–8), but here united against Jesus Christ. The Sadducees did not believe in the resurrection (22:23) and were associated with the priests (Acts 4:1; 5:17). *tempting.* Testing. *shew them a sign.* Though Christ had already done many signs, unbelief is never satisfied.
16:3 *lowring.* Gloomy. *discern the signs of the times.* His works testified that He is the Christ.
16:4 *there shall no sign be given . . . but the sign of the prophet Jonas.* See note at 12:38–40. Jesus' resurrection should be sufficient for people to believe in Him.
16:6–7 *leaven.* Yeast, fermented dough. Jesus uses the occasion of the disciples' failure to bring bread to warn them about the deceitfulness of the Pharisees and the Sadducees. This again underscores Jesus' wisdom, using everyday things to communicate great and divine realities.
16:9 *Do ye not yet understand . . . ?* The disciples had said they understood His parables (13:51), but continue to show a lack of spiritual insight.

doctrine of the Pharisees and of the Sadducees.
13 ¶ When Jesus came into the coasts of Caesarea
Philippi, he asked his disciples, saying, Whom do
men say that I the Son of man am?
14 And they said, Some *say that thou art* John the
Baptist: some, Elias; and others, Jeremias, or one
of the prophets.
15 He saith unto them, But whom say ye that
I am?
16 And Simon Peter answered and said, Thou art
the Christ, the Son of the living God.
17 And Jesus answered and said unto him,
Blessed art thou, Simon Bar-jona: for flesh and
blood hath not revealed *it* unto thee, but my
Father which is in heaven.
18 And I say also unto thee, That thou art Peter,
and upon this rock I will build my church; and
the gates of hell shall not prevail against it.
19 And I will give unto thee the keys of the king-
dom of heaven: and whatsoever thou shalt bind
on earth shall be bound in heaven: and whatso-
ever thou shalt loose on earth shall be loosed in
heaven.
20 Then charged he his disciples that they should
tell no man that he was Jesus the Christ.
21 ¶ From that time forth began Jesus to shew
unto his disciples, how that he must go unto
Jerusalem, and suffer many things of the elders
and chief priests and scribes, and be killed, and be
raised again the third day.
22 Then Peter took him, and began to rebuke
him, saying, Be it far from thee, Lord: this shall
not be unto thee.
23 But he turned, and said unto Peter, Get thee
behind me, Satan: thou art an offence unto me:
for thou savourest not the things that be of God,
but those that be of men.
24 ¶ Then said Jesus unto his disciples, If any *man*
will come after me, let him deny himself, and take
up his cross, and follow me.
25 For whosoever will save his life shall lose it:
and whosoever will lose his life for my sake shall
find it.
26 For what is a man profited, if he shall gain the
whole world, and lose his own soul? or what shall
a man give in exchange for his soul?

16:11–12 *bade*. Told. *doctrine*. Teaching.

Peter's Confession of Christ (16:13–20)

16:13 *coasts*. Region. *Caesarea Philippi*. A Gentile city located near the beginning of the Jordan River, about twenty-five miles north of the Sea of Galilee.

16:14 *John the Baptist . . . one of the prophets*. The popular messianic claims of the day associated Jesus with different prominent figures throughout Israel's history (14:2).

16:15 *whom say ye that I am?* Regardless of what others say, every individual has to answer who Jesus is for himself or herself. This is a question to which there is no neutral answer.

16:16 *Christ*. Peter is the first person in this gospel to confess this title of Jesus (1:1,16–18; 2:4; 11:2); it means "anointed" and refers to a man whom God has chosen and empowered by His Spirit to serve Him in sacred office such as a prophet (1 Kings 19:16), a priest (Ex. 28:41), and especially a king (1 Sam. 10:1; 16:13–14; 2 Sam. 22:51; 23:1). All three offices are united in Jesus Christ (Ps. 110:1,4; Heb. 1:1–9). *Son of the living God*. Peter's answer unites Jesus' messianic title with His Sonship (John 6:69), a title that in this Gospel indicates Jesus is the ideal Israel (2:15), the King and Servant completely pleasing to God (3:16–17), the One in unique relationship to the Father and thus serving as the unique Mediator of God's power and truth (11:27), the Lord who controls creation and is worthy of worship (14:33), and the person distinct from the Father and Spirit yet sharing one name and nature with them (28:19). This is a great confession of faith regarding the person and work of Jesus, though Peter was just beginning to understand it.

16:17 *Bar-jona*. Son of Jonah. *flesh and blood hath not revealed it . . . but my Father*. The saving knowledge of Christ is a gift of God's grace (11:25,27).

16:18 *Peter* means "a stone"; *rock* is a different word referring to bedrock (7:24–25). Christ, reflecting on Peter's name, affirmed that the confession of Him by Peter and the other apostles is the bedrock on which He builds His church (Eph. 2:20; Rev. 21:14). Nothing here implies that Peter is the first in any apostolic or papal succession. True apostolic succession lies in the confession of the gospel through the ages. *gates of hell shall not prevail*. Jesus' person and work was the decisive blow against Satan and his powers of death (see note on *hell* at 11:22–24), and the church participates in Christ's victory (12:29; Luke 10:17–20; Rom. 16:20; Eph. 6:10–13; Col. 2:15).

16:19 *keys of the kingdom of heaven*. Likely a reference to the church's authority as the agent of God's kingdom (Isa. 22:22; Luke 11:52; Rev. 1:18; 3:7), exercised not through human traditions or arbitrary authority but through the preaching of Christ's Word and exercise of church order and discipline commanded by His Word (Acts 2:38–39; 3:16–20; 4:12; 10:34–43).

16:20 Again Jesus exhorted His disciples not to make His messianic claims known (8:4; 9:30; 12:16; 17:9).

Jesus' Foretelling of His Death (16:21–28)

16:21 *he must*. The verb implies necessity; this is God's plan and there is no other way (26:54). *suffer many things*. The true nature of messianic mission was not to usurp Roman authority, but to suffer and die as one condemned by the law, and then to rise on *the third day* (12:40; 17:23; 20:19).

16:22 *Peter . . . began to rebuke him*. After Peter's climactic confession of Christ (v. 16), Peter fell very low by presuming to rebuke Jesus as if he had greater authority and wisdom than Christ.

16:23 *savourest*. Thinks, grasps. Peter failed to grasp the implications of what he had so admirably confessed several verses before, being to some degree still influenced by the mindset of fallen *men* instead of the truth *of God*, and therefore still influenced by *Satan*.

16:24 *take up his cross, and follow me*. Just as Jesus must be rejected, suffer, and die to fulfill His messianic mission (v. 21), so Christ's disciples must also embrace self-denial, rejection, and suffering in order to follow Him to glory (10:24–25,38–39).

16:25 *save . . . lose*. This is the paradox of the Christian's participation in Christ's death and resurrection: dying to our pride, our sin, and this world is the only way to rise to real life (Phil. 3:8–10).

16:26 *what is a man profited . . . what shall a man give*. These rhetorical questions are meant to be answered negatively. No material wealth can compare to one's salvation, or secure one's position before God.

27 For the Son of man shall come in the glory
of his Father with his angels; and then he shall
reward every man according to his works.
28 Verily I say unto you, There be some standing
here, which shall not taste of death, till they see
the Son of man coming in his kingdom.

CHAPTER 17

AND after six days Jesus taketh Peter, James, and
John his brother, and bringeth them up into an
high mountain apart,
2 And was transfigured before them: and his face
did shine as the sun, and his raiment was white
as the light.
3 And, behold, there appeared unto them Moses
and Elias talking with him.
4 Then answered Peter, and said unto Jesus, Lord,
it is good for us to be here: if thou wilt, let us make
here three tabernacles; one for thee, and one for
Moses, and one for Elias.
5 While he yet spake, behold, a bright cloud
overshadowed them: and behold a voice out of
the cloud, which said, This is my beloved Son, in
whom I am well pleased; hear ye him.
6 And when the disciples heard *it*, they fell on
their face, and were sore afraid.
7 And Jesus came and touched them, and said,
Arise, and be not afraid.
8 And when they had lifted up their eyes, they
saw no man, save Jesus only.
9 And as they came down from the mountain,
Jesus charged them, saying, Tell the vision to no
man, until the Son of man be risen again from
the dead.
10 And his disciples asked him, saying, Why then
say the scribes that Elias must first come?
11 And Jesus answered and said unto them, Elias
truly shall first come, and restore all things.
12 But I say unto you, That Elias is come already,
and they knew him not, but have done unto him
whatsoever they listed. Likewise shall also the Son
of man suffer of them.
13 Then the disciples understood that he spake
unto them of John the Baptist.
14 ¶ And when they were come to the multitude,
there came to him a *certain* man, kneeling down
to him, and saying,

16:27 *Son of man . . . glory . . . with his angels.* Jesus identified Himself as the glorious King who will judge all mankind (13:41; 25:41; Dan. 7:9–14), implying that His sufferings will lead Him to glory (v. 21). *reward . . . according to his works.* Salvation is by grace alone through faith alone, never based on the works or merits of men (Eph. 2:8–9), but God in His grace will recognize and reward His own work of grace in believers (15:13) as evidenced in the works it produces (Eph. 2:10).
16:28 *Verily.* Truly. *not taste of death, till they see.* Christ's *kingdom* was manifested during the lifetime of some of these men in His transfiguration (17:1–8), death (27:35,50–54), resurrection (28:18), and later events including the destruction of Jerusalem in AD 70 (21:40–44).

Thoughts for Personal/Family Worship: Chapter 16

1. **Christ had to unseat the false religion of the Pharisees in the hearts of His disciples (v. 12). Like leaven, false teaching can easily enter and influence all our lives. The church and its ministers must contend for the faith that was once for all delivered to the saints and expose false teachers (Jude 3–4). Why is this an important part of our faithfulness to God?**
2. **The great question of all time is, "But whom say ye that I am?" (v. 15). The world has its opinion of Christ. Religion has its opinion. And our lives are issuing a constant verdict of who Christ is. Perhaps your actions say that Christ is a person you run to in need, but for the rest He has to fit in with your program and life. Perhaps you have an orthodox opinion about Christ but you do not listen to His demands. What does your life declare about who Jesus is?**
3. **Though Peter confessed Jesus as Christ, the Son of the living God, he still foolishly and vainly attempted to thwart Christ's sacrificial suffering and death. The gospel of the cross is foolish and offensive to men. The call of discipleship is a call to die. Do you understand your need for Christ to die an accursed death in your place? Are you taking up your own cross and following Him?**

THE PASSION, DEATH, AND RESURRECTION OF JESUS THE MESSIAH (17:1—28:20)

Chapter 17: ***Jesus is transfigured before His disciples in preparation for His death and subsequent glory. He performs several miracles and teaches about faith in Himself as the Son of God.***

Jesus' Transfiguration (17:1–13)

17:1 *after six days.* This links what follows to Christ's prophecy of His future glory (16:28).
17:2 *transfigured.* Transformed, an unveiling of His divine majesty. *his face did shine as the sun.* As the face of Moses did in God's presence (Ex. 34:29–35), but with far greater glory (Rev. 1:16). *raiment.* Clothing.
17:3 *Moses and Elias.* Likely representing the law (Moses) and the prophets (Elijah), which Christ fulfilled (5:17). Their appearance and conversation with Jesus implies that the deceased Old Testament saints enjoy eternal life in God's glory (22:31–32; Luke 16:19–31), and their hope was and is in Christ (John 8:56).
17:4 *three tabernacles.* Peter may have been thinking this was some new Mt. Sinai experience, which might warrant the Feast of Tabernacles, celebrated in the Old Testament (Lev. 23:42–43).
17:5 *bright cloud.* A sign of God's presence among His people as in the tabernacle and temple (Ex. 40:34; 2 Chron. 5:14). *This is my beloved Son.* The Father reaffirmed Jesus' unique identity and relationship to Him (3:17), confirming the disciples in their confession of faith (16:16). *hear ye him.* Christ is the great Prophet foretold by Moses (Deut. 18:15–19), and the only way to salvation and glory is by submitting to Christ's Word in faith (Acts 3:19–23).
17:6 *sore.* Very, greatly.
17:8 *they saw no man, save Jesus only.* This implies the absolute supremacy of Jesus over Moses and Elijah, and His uniqueness as the only Savior.
17:9 *risen again from the dead.* The resurrection would be the occasion on which the historical event of the transfigura-

15 Lord, have mercy on my son: for he is lunatick,
and sore vexed: for ofttimes he falleth into the fire,
and oft into the water.
16 And I brought him to thy disciples, and they
could not cure him.
17 Then Jesus answered and said, O faithless and
perverse generation, how long shall I be with
you? how long shall I suffer you? bring him hither
to me.
18 And Jesus rebuked the devil; and he departed
out of him: and the child was cured from that
very hour.
19 Then came the disciples to Jesus apart, and
said, Why could not we cast him out?
20 And Jesus said unto them, Because of your
unbelief: for verily I say unto you, If ye have faith as a
grain of mustard seed, ye shall say unto this moun-
tain, Remove hence to yonder place; and it shall
remove; and nothing shall be impossible unto you.
21 Howbeit this kind goeth not out but by prayer
and fasting.
22 ¶ And while they abode in Galilee, Jesus said
unto them, The Son of man shall be betrayed into
the hands of men:
23 And they shall kill him, and the third day he
shall be raised again. And they were exceeding
sorry.
24 ¶ And when they were come to Capernaum,
they that received tribute *money* came to Peter,
and said, Doth not your master pay tribute?
25 He saith, Yes. And when he was come into the
house, Jesus prevented him, saying, What thinkest
thou, Simon? of whom do the kings of the earth
take custom or tribute? of their own children, or
of strangers?
26 Peter saith unto him, Of strangers. Jesus saith
unto him, Then are the children free.
27 Notwithstanding, lest we should offend them,
go thou to the sea, and cast an hook, and take
up the fish that first cometh up; and when thou
hast opened his mouth, thou shalt find a piece of
money: that take, and give unto them for me and
thee.

CHAPTER 18

AT the same time came the disciples unto Jesus,
saying, Who is the greatest in the kingdom of
heaven?
2 And Jesus called a little child unto him, and set
him in the midst of them,
3 And said, Verily I say unto you, Except ye be
converted, and become as little children, ye shall
not enter into the kingdom of heaven.

---

tion might and should have been proclaimed to the world, for Christ then entered His glory.

17:10–13 *Elias must first come.* See notes at 3:4; 11:14.

Jesus' Continued Ministry (17:14–27)

17:14–23 See Mark 9:14–28 for a parallel account.

17:15 *lunatick.* Suffering from seizures. *sore.* Very, greatly.

17:17 *faithless and perverse generation.* Though the denouncement appears to be leveled at the man, it is likely that Jesus is referring to the scribes and Pharisees, and to an extent, His own disciples because of remaining unbelief despite their faith (v. 20). Even in true believers there is still much cause to count them faithless. *hither.* Here.

17:19 *Why could not we.* The disciples did not understand their inability to cast out the demon because Jesus had given them the authority over evil spirits (10:8).

17:20 *Because of your unbelief.* The disciples' problem was that they failed to trust Jesus. *verily.* Truly. *mustard seed.* Jesus indicates that it is not the quantity of faith but the quality of faith that essentially matters. *say unto this mountain, Remove hence.* Symbolic language for overcoming powers that rise up against the Lord and His people (Isa. 40:4; Jer. 51:25; Zech. 4:7; cf. Ps. 46:2).

17:22–23 *betrayed . . . kill him . . . raised again.* See 16:21. *exceeding sorry.* They did not yet understand the full meaning of Jesus' death and subsequent resurrection.

17:24 *tribute money.* Literally, "two drachmas," roughly two days' wages, the taxes or offerings for the temple.

17:25 *prevented.* Spoke first. *custom or tribute.* Tax. *children.* Sons. Jesus is the Son of God and therefore exempt from the temple tax.

17:27 *Notwithstanding, lest we should offend.* Jesus did not demand His rights when it would cause unnecessary offense to the gospel (1 Cor. 9:12). *cast an hook . . . the fish that first cometh up.* Christ displayed His omniscience (knowing all) and omnipotence (controlling all), again showing that as the Son of God (v. 5), He is God, having the same deity as the Father (14:33).

Thoughts for Personal/Family Worship: Chapter 17

1. **Christ's divine glory and majesty shine wonderfully through His humanity, confirming the focus of many Old Testament promises. Yet He came to earth veiled, with His glory largely hidden. Christ's transfiguration took place between announcements of His suffering and death (vv. 22–23; 16:21). If we seek glory with God apart from the humiliation and death of Christ, then we still imagine ourselves to be saved by man's works, wisdom, and glory. Christ did not take the crown apart from the cross, and neither can we. We must listen to Christ's words about the cross and follow in His crucified footsteps. How does this help you understand what it means for a Christian to pursue glory?**
2. **When Christ descended from the mountain of glory, He entered, as it were, the workshop of the Devil. This demon had stymied all the efforts of the child's father and Christ's disciples, but it was no match for the power of Christ (vv. 14–21). Christians need not fear the Devil, so long as they cling to Christ by faith, for greater is He that is in us than he that is in the world. How can this comfort us?**

Chapter 18: ***Jesus gives a teaching concerning the nature of the church and dealing with sinful brothers and sisters.***

The Nature and Authority of the Church (18:1–35)

18:1 *greatest in the kingdom.* Christ's disciples all had selfish ambitions for personal glory (20:20–28).

18:3–4 *Verily.* Truly. *converted.* Turned around, a radical change of orientation and direction. *become as little children.*

4 Whosoever therefore shall humble himself as
this little child, the same is greatest in the king-
dom of heaven.
5 And whoso shall receive one such little child in
my name receiveth me.
6 But whoso shall offend one of these little ones
which believe in me, it were better for him that a
millstone were hanged about his neck, and *that* he
were drowned in the depth of the sea.
7 ¶ Woe unto the world because of offences! for it
must needs be that offences come; but woe to that
man by whom the offence cometh!
8 Wherefore if thy hand or thy foot offend thee,
cut them off, and cast *them* from thee: it is better
for thee to enter into life halt or maimed, rather
than having two hands or two feet to be cast into
everlasting fire.
9 And if thine eye offend thee, pluck it out, and
cast *it* from thee: it is better for thee to enter into
life with one eye, rather than having two eyes to
be cast into hell fire.
10 Take heed that ye despise not one of these
little ones; for I say unto you, That in heaven their
angels do always behold the face of my Father
which is in heaven.
11 For the Son of man is come to save that which
was lost.
12 How think ye? if a man have an hundred
sheep, and one of them be gone astray, doth he
not leave the ninety and nine, and goeth into the
mountains, and seeketh that which is gone astray?
13 And if so be that he find it, verily I say unto
you, he rejoiceth more of that *sheep*, than of the
ninety and nine which went not astray.
14 Even so it is not the will of your Father which
is in heaven, that one of these little ones should
perish.
15 ¶ Moreover if thy brother shall trespass against
thee, go and tell him his fault between thee and
him alone: if he shall hear thee, thou hast gained
thy brother.
16 But if he will not hear *thee, then* take with
thee one or two more, that in the mouth of two
or three witnesses every word may be established.
17 And if he shall neglect to hear them, tell *it* unto
the church: but if he neglect to hear the church,
let him be unto thee as an heathen man and a
publican.
18 Verily I say unto you, Whatsoever ye shall bind
on earth shall be bound in heaven: and whatsoev-
er ye shall loose on earth shall be loosed in heaven.
19 Again I say unto you, That if two of you shall
agree on earth as touching any thing that they
shall ask, it shall be done for them of my Father
which is in heaven.
20 For where two or three are gathered together
in my name, there am I in the midst of them.
21 ¶ Then came Peter to him, and said, Lord, how
oft shall my brother sin against me, and I forgive
him? till seven times?

Jesus was not saying that all children are saved, but He is using a child to depict a person who is *humble*, an essential quality of a member of His *kingdom* (5:3). *greatest*. There are different degrees of glory in Christ's kingdom, but surprisingly, the highest positions will go to those who are lowest in their self-assessment in the presence of God.

18:5–6 *little child . . . little ones.* Christ's humble disciples of any age (v. 3). Jesus stressed the need to welcome (*receive*) the humble into the community of His disciples, and not cause them to stumble (*offend*). How one relates to the humble disciples of Christ reveals his relationship to Christ Himself (*receiveth me*). *millstone.* A very heavy stone used to crush and grind grain. Causing spiritual harm to Christ's disciples instead of loving them results in a fate worse than a horrible death.

18:7 *Woe . . . woe.* The double pronouncement of doom stresses the importance of putting sin to death.

18:8–9 *cut them off . . . pluck it out.* Not a call for literal mutilation, but a vivid way of demanding forceful efforts to avoid temptation and put sin to death (5:29–30). *halt.* Lame. *everlasting fire . . . hell fire.* Eternal suffering under the righteous anger of God (see notes at 3:10,12; 5:22).

18:10 *their angels.* Angels serve the heirs of salvation (Heb. 1:14).

18:11 *save that which was lost.* Christ's mission was one of compassion to sinners, to rescue them from their sins and the miseries caused by sin (1:21; Luke 19:10).

18:12–14 The parable here is applied not to sinners in general (as in Luke 15:1–7) but to Christ's humble disciples (*little ones*; vv. 3–6) when they stray from the obedience of the church, showing the *will* of the *Father* to preserve them in salvation (John 10:27–29), and the necessity of faithful disciples to pursue them and bring them back (Ezek. 34:1–6). Jesus explained the method next (vv. 15–17).

18:13 *verily.* Truly.

18:15–17 *trespass against thee.* Even when a *brother* sins against you personally, you are not to despise him, but seek to win him back to love and obedience. *alone.* The first step is to seek reconciliation and repentance in private, for love desires to cover sin (Prov. 10:12; 17:9). *two or three witnesses.* The next step is to bring more disciples to confront the sinner, enough to testify publicly of what happened if necessary (Deut. 17:6; 19:15). *tell it unto the church.* Refusal to repent after repeated private confrontation results in public censure so that the whole church may exhort the sinner (2 Thess. 3:14–15). *let him be unto thee as an heathen.* The final step is excommunication, putting the sinner outside the church and treating him as such until he repents. *publican.* Tax collector.

18:18 *bind on earth . . . bound in heaven.* Church discipline derives its authority from God when administered with faithful preaching and obedience to God's Word. Through faithful preaching and administration of church discipline, the kingdom of heaven is opened to believers and shut to unbelievers (16:19).

18:19–20 *two of you shall agree . . . ask.* Christ's church should be a house of prayer (21:13), and united prayer especially receives God's blessing (Acts 12:5,12). *gathered together . . . there am I.* Jesus promised His special presence to the church when it meets in humility and love to use the means of grace by faith in His Lordship (v. 5; 28:18–20). *two or three.* Perhaps alluding to church discipline (v. 16), promising Christ's presence in the most difficult duties of the church. This ought to encourage and admonish church officers not to exert authority on the basis of their own strength.

22 Jesus saith unto him, I say not unto thee, Until
seven times: but, Until seventy times seven.
23 ¶ Therefore is the kingdom of heaven likened
unto a certain king, which would take account of
his servants.
24 And when he had begun to reckon, one was
brought unto him, which owed him ten thousand
talents.
25 But forasmuch as he had not to pay, his lord
commanded him to be sold, and his wife, and chil-
dren, and all that he had, and payment to be made.
26 The servant therefore fell down, and
worshipped him, saying, Lord, have patience with
me, and I will pay thee all.
27 Then the lord of that servant was moved with
compassion, and loosed him, and forgave him the
debt.
28 But the same servant went out, and found one
of his fellowservants, which owed him an hun-
dred pence: and he laid hands on him, and took
him by the throat, saying, Pay me that thou owest.
29 And his fellowservant fell down at his feet, and
besought him, saying, Have patience with me,
and I will pay thee all.
30 And he would not: but went and cast him into
prison, till he should pay the debt.
31 So when his fellowservants saw what was
done, they were very sorry, and came and told
unto their lord all that was done.
32 Then his lord, after that he had called him,
said unto him, O thou wicked servant, I forgave
thee all that debt, because thou desiredst me:
33 Shouldest not thou also have had compassion
on thy fellowservant, even as I had pity on thee?
34 And his lord was wroth, and delivered him to
the tormentors, till he should pay all that was due
unto him.
35 So likewise shall my heavenly Father do also
unto you, if ye from your hearts forgive not every
one his brother their trespasses.

CHAPTER 19

AND it came to pass, *that* when Jesus had finished
these sayings, he departed from Galilee, and came
into the coasts of Judaea beyond Jordan;
2 And great multitudes followed him; and he
healed them there.
3 ¶ The Pharisees also came unto him, tempting
him, and saying unto him, Is it lawful for a man to
put away his wife for every cause?
4 And he answered and said unto them, Have ye

18:22 *seventy times seven.* An expression for perfect and unlimited forgiveness.
18:24 *ten thousand talents.* An astronomical sum of money, unable to be repaid in many lifetimes (1 Chron. 29:7; Est. 3:9). One talent equaled 6,000 denarii (v. 28; 25:15). Our sin against God puts us in debt to His justice that we would spend eternity paying, unless it is forgiven.
18:25 *forasmuch.* Since.
18:26 *I will pay thee all.* The man knew his need but had not faced his inability to save himself from his predicament and thus retained his pride.
18:28 *hundred pence.* A hundred denarii, about four months wages, a significant amount but a tiny fraction of what the first man owed.
18:32 *thou wicked servant.* The same words later used in a parable describing judgment day (25:26).
18:33 *compassion . . . pity.* The same Greek word, literally, "show mercy" (5:7). His heart remained proud, ungrateful, and unloving despite the mercy of his king (Luke 15:25–32).
18:34 *wroth.* Angry.
18:35 *likewise shall my heavenly Father do.* God does not annul His forgiveness toward a repentant believer, but He will judge those who show their faith to be hypocritical by failing to show grace and forgiveness to others (James 2:13). *from your hearts.* Just as evil thoughts begin in the heart (15:19), so too forgiveness begins with a heart of kindness and compassion (Eph. 4:32). However, complete forgiveness involving restoration of relationship depends on the sinner's repentance (Luke 17:3).

Thoughts for Personal/Family Worship: Chapter 18

1. **Conversion is absolutely necessary if we are to be saved. This applies to us, our children, our parents, our friends and neighbors, those who have grown up in the church, and those who have not. Christ described conversion here in terms of turning around and childlike humility (vv. 3–4). Every true disciple of Christ has a root of repentance and humility planted in his heart by grace. But as believers we must continually work to put our pride to death. How are you working at this in your own life?**
2. **Much of our humility comes from realizing that the guilt of our sins is like a debt of billions of dollars that we owe to God's justice (v. 24). A true sense of our sin shows us both that we deserve horrible punishment from God and, unlike the servant in the parable, that we cannot possibly save ourselves from it no matter how long and hard we work. This puts us in the position of a beggar before God (5:3), whose only hope is free and lavish grace. How bad do you really believe your sins are against God? How much do you value the grace of Christ?**
3. **The practical effect of true Christian humility is hatred of sin (vv. 7–9) and love for other Christians (v. 5) that especially shows itself in seeking to make peace with those who wrong us (v. 15), working to preserve the purity of the body of Christ (vv. 16–20), and forgiving others for their sins against us (vv. 21–35). How is the Holy Spirit convicting you regarding these heart issues?**

Jesus' Ministry in Judaea: Teachings and Miracles (19:1—25:46)

Chapter 19: ***Jesus teaches on various practical and eternal matters.***

Jesus' Teachings Concerning Divorce (19:1–12)

19:1 *And it came to pass, that when Jesus had finished.* Matthew concludes another section of his book (see note at 11:1)—the *sayings* of Jesus (ch. 18)—and returns to the narrative. *coasts.* Region.
19:2 *great multitudes.* Crowds often followed Jesus seeking to be healed.
19:3 *The Pharisees* sought to put Christ to the test (*tempting*) by attempting to show that He was opposed to the law of Moses (*Is it lawful*; 12:10; 22:17).

not read, that he which made *them* at the begin-
ning made them male and female,
5 And said, For this cause shall a man leave father
and mother, and shall cleave to his wife: and they
twain shall be one flesh?
6 Wherefore they are no more twain, but one
flesh. What therefore God hath joined together,
let not man put asunder.
7 They say unto him, Why did Moses then
command to give a writing of divorcement, and
to put her away?
8 He saith unto them, Moses because of the
hardness of your hearts suffered you to put away
your wives: but from the beginning it was not so.
9 And I say unto you, Whosoever shall put away
his wife, except *it be* for fornication, and shall
marry another, committeth adultery: and whoso
marrieth her which is put away doth commit
adultery.
10 ¶ His disciples say unto him, If the case of the
man be so with *his* wife, it is not good to marry.
11 But he said unto them, All *men* cannot receive
this saying, save *they* to whom it is given.
12 For there are some eunuchs, which were so
born from *their* mother's womb: and there are
some eunuchs, which were made eunuchs of
men: and there be eunuchs, which have made
themselves eunuchs for the kingdom of heaven's
sake. He that is able to receive *it*, let him receive *it*.
13 ¶ Then were there brought unto him little
children, that he should put *his* hands on them,
and pray: and the disciples rebuked them.
14 But Jesus said, Suffer little children, and forbid
them not, to come unto me: for of such is the
kingdom of heaven.
15 And he laid *his* hands on them, and departed
thence.
16 ¶ And, behold, one came and said unto him,
Good Master, what good thing shall I do, that I
may have eternal life?
17 And he said unto him, Why callest thou me
good? *there is* none good but one, *that is*, God: but
if thou wilt enter into life, keep the command-
ments.
18 He saith unto him, Which? Jesus said, Thou
shalt do no murder, Thou shalt not commit adul-
tery, Thou shalt not steal, Thou shalt not bear
false witness,
19 Honour thy father and *thy* mother: and, Thou
shalt love thy neighbour as thyself.
20 The young man saith unto him, All these
things have I kept from my youth up: what lack
I yet?
21 Jesus said unto him, If thou wilt be perfect, go
and sell that thou hast, and give to the poor, and
thou shalt have treasure in heaven: and come *and*
follow me.
22 But when the young man heard that saying, he

19:4–6 *made them.* Christ affirmed a literal understanding of Gen. 1–2, teaching that God created man, and did so *at the beginning* of creation (Mark 10:6). *male and female.* Citing Gen. 1:27. *For this cause . . . one flesh.* Citing Gen. 2:24. *twain.* Two. *put asunder.* Separate. The law of marriage between one man and one woman until death separates them is embedded in creation itself. Jesus' citation from the creation narrative of the Torah should have resonated with the Pharisees.
19:7–9 Though Moses allowed (*suffered*) for a certificate of divorce (Deut. 24:1), divorce was never commanded in the Old Testament, and Christ only sanctioned it in cases of sexual immorality (*fornication*; 5:31–32).
19:11 *save.* Except.
19:12 *eunuchs.* Sexually inactive men, whether by birth defect (*so born*), surgical procedure (*made . . . of men*), or their choice to fully consecrate themselves to serving God's *kingdom* (1 Cor. 7:7–9). *He that is able . . . let him receive it.* The life of celibacy should not be imposed on a Christian minister or anyone else (1 Cor. 7:2), unless he willingly takes it up by the enabling gift of God's grace (v. 11).

Children in the Kingdom (19:13–15)

19:13–15 Though singleness can be useful for the kingdom (vv. 10–12), marriage is still a divine institution, and children are a great blessing from the Lord.
19:14 *Suffer.* Permit. *for of such is the kingdom.* Jesus was not teaching that *the kingdom of heaven* belongs to all *children*, but that childlikeness is essential to participating in it (18:3–4), and therefore God gives *children* an important place in His church and *kingdom* (Acts 2:39; Eph. 6:1–3).
19:15 *laid his hands on them.* Jesus was blessing these children (Gen. 48:14–15).

Discipleship and Service (19:16—20:28)

19:16 *Master.* Literally, "teacher," quite a meager title for Jesus in Matthew (8:19; 12:38), implying the man's inadequate view of the Son of God. *Good . . . good thing shall I do.* The man believed that mere men could be righteous by their works and failed to understand that salvation was a gift of grace.
19:17 *Why callest thou me good . . . none good.* Though Jesus is perfectly righteous (3:17; Heb. 4:15), He challenged the man's assumptions about human goodness. God's people have a new nature such that they can be called "good" in a qualified sense (5:45; 7:17–18; 12:35; 25:21,23; Luke 8:15), but in a strict sense all men are evil and God alone is good (7:11; Rom. 3:10–12). *if thou wilt.* If you desire or choose to. *keep the commandments.* Perfect obedience to the law of God would grant life (Rom. 10:5). Christ had not come to abolish the law (5:17), and here He used it to search the man's conscience to reveal sin and the inability of sinners to merit eternal life (Rom. 3:19–20).
19:18–19 Christ cited the fifth through ninth commandments (Ex. 20:12–16) and the second greatest love commandment (22:39; Lev. 19:18), highlighting the Ten Commandments and love as a summary of the moral law. If this man could not keep the law's second table, how could he keep the law's first table?
19:20 *All these . . . have I kept from my youth.* Tragic spiritual blindness to the law's demands upon the heart and his own condition (5:21–22,27–28).
19:21 *perfect.* The law demands perfect conformity to the will of God (5:48). *sell . . . give . . . come.* Not Christ's ordinary demand for discipleship, but His way to uncover the man's idolatrous attachment to his possessions (6:24) and violation of the greatest and tenth commandments (22:37–38; Ex. 20:17).

went away sorrowful: for he had great possessions.
23 ¶ Then said Jesus unto his disciples, Verily I say
unto you, That a rich man shall hardly enter into
the kingdom of heaven.
24 And again I say unto you, It is easier for a
camel to go through the eye of a needle, than for a
rich man to enter into the kingdom of God.
25 When his disciples heard *it*, they were exceed-
ingly amazed, saying, Who then can be saved?
26 But Jesus beheld *them*, and said unto them,
With men this is impossible; but with God all
things are possible.
27 ¶ Then answered Peter and said unto him,
Behold, we have forsaken all, and followed thee;
what shall we have therefore?
28 And Jesus said unto them, Verily I say unto
you, That ye which have followed me, in the
regeneration when the Son of man shall sit in the
throne of his glory, ye also shall sit upon twelve
thrones, judging the twelve tribes of Israel.
29 And every one that hath forsaken houses,
or brethren, or sisters, or father, or mother, or
wife, or children, or lands, for my name's sake,
shall receive an hundredfold, and shall inherit
everlasting life.
30 But many *that are* first shall be last; and the last
shall be first.

CHAPTER 20

FOR the kingdom of heaven is like unto a man
that is an householder, which went out early in
the morning to hire labourers into his vineyard.
2 And when he had agreed with the labourers for
a penny a day, he sent them into his vineyard.
3 And he went out about the third hour, and saw
others standing idle in the marketplace,
4 And said unto them; Go ye also into the
vineyard, and whatsoever is right I will give you.
And they went their way.
5 Again he went out about the sixth and ninth
hour, and did likewise.
6 And about the eleventh hour he went out, and
found others standing idle, and saith unto them,
Why stand ye here all the day idle?
7 They say unto him, Because no man hath hired

19:22 *went away sorrowful.* He represents the opposite of the man in the parable of the hidden treasure (13:44), implying that the infinite value of Christ and His kingdom were hidden to him.

19:23–24 *hardly.* With difficulty. *kingdom of heaven . . . kingdom of God.* The parallel implies that the two phrases refer to the same reality. *camel . . . through the eye of a needle.* A ridiculous impossibility (v. 26). Money is not inherently sinful or damning, but sinners generally respond to possessing riches with self-sufficiency and self-righteousness (Prov. 18:10–11,23; 28:11).

19:25–26 *Who then can be saved?* The disciples were probably accustomed to hearing riches connected with God's favor and so wondered with surprise how anyone will enter the kingdom. *With men this is impossible.* Neither the rich nor the poor can save themselves. Conversion to faith and repentance is beyond the ability of fallen mankind (John 6:44). *with God all things are possible.* God's infinite power (Jer. 32:17; Luke 1:37) can save anyone, but He does not give this grace to everyone, as the rich young man illustrates.

19:27 *what shall we have.* What reward will the apostles receive in the kingdom for their self-denying service of Christ—a question that anticipates the parable (20:1–16).

19:28 *regeneration.* The new creation, Christ's kingdom at His second coming (*throne of his glory*; 25:31). Alternatively, the whole phrase may be rendered without a comma as "followed me in the regeneration," and the *thrones* taken symbolically of Christ's kingdom after His ascension, when the apostles led the church in Christ's spiritual victory and power (cf. Ps. 122:5).

19:30 *first shall be last; and the last shall be first.* God's ways of grace often reverse human expectations, and so we should not presume (20:16).

Thoughts for Personal/Family Worship: Chapter 19

1. **Marriage is not a contract that we may define as we please, but a sovereign act of the Creator, defined by His will. Despite attempts to make it normal to have sexual relations outside of marriage, engage in homosexuality, and divorce at will, God's standards for marriage remain unchanged. If we desire His blessing, we must repent of our failures and live in the joy of sexual faithfulness. How can you honor this sacred relationship, whether you are single or married?**
2. **Children have an important place in the church of God. God's promises belong to Abraham's seed, that is, to the children of believing parents (Acts 2:39). This does not remove their need to be born again. Jesus' words to His disciples—"Suffer little children, and forbid them not" (v. 14)—encourage believers to bring children to the Lord through prayer and teaching and to watch that we do not hinder their coming to Christ. How can you bring children to Jesus?**
3. **The rich young man's response to Christ reveals a deadly spiritual illness that infects many people. Though they may have respect for Jesus and a desire for eternal life, they see mankind as essentially good, themselves as obedient to God's laws, and Christ as a mere teacher to show them what to do to gain heaven for themselves. They operate as if still under the covenant of works in Paradise before Adam's fall (Gen. 2). However, the last Adam is able to expose our sin with His Word and Spirit. If the rich man took Christ's words to heart and returned to Him, how might he approach Christ differently? What might he say?**

Chapter 20: *Jesus again predicts His death and prepares Himself and His disciples for His upcoming death and resurrection.*

20:1 *householder.* Master or head of the household. *went out early in the morning.* It was common for employers to seek daily employees to help in their vineyards, depending on the amount of work needed that day.

20:2–7 The master offers a *penny* (denarius, a coin worth one day's wage for a laborer) for the workers he finds at the start of the day, and then *whatsoever is right* each time he goes out and hires more laborers throughout the day.

us. He saith unto them, Go ye also into the vine-
yard; and whatsoever is right, *that* shall ye receive.
8 So when even was come, the lord of the vineyard
saith unto his steward, Call the labourers, and give
them *their* hire, beginning from the last unto the
first.
9 And when they came that *were hired* about the
eleventh hour, they received every man a penny.
10 But when the first came, they supposed that
they should have received more; and they likewise
received every man a penny.
11 And when they had received *it*, they mur-
mured against the goodman of the house,
12 Saying, These last have wrought *but* one hour,
and thou hast made them equal unto us, which
have borne the burden and heat of the day.
13 But he answered one of them, and said, Friend,
I do thee no wrong: didst not thou agree with me
for a penny?
14 Take *that* thine *is*, and go thy way: I will give
unto this last, even as unto thee.
15 Is it not lawful for me to do what I will with
mine own? Is thine eye evil, because I am good?
16 So the last shall be first, and the first last: for
many be called, but few chosen.
17 ¶ And Jesus going up to Jerusalem took the
twelve disciples apart in the way, and said unto
them,
18 Behold, we go up to Jerusalem; and the Son of
man shall be betrayed unto the chief priests and
unto the scribes, and they shall condemn him to
death,
19 And shall deliver him to the Gentiles to mock,
and to scourge, and to crucify *him*: and the third
day he shall rise again.
20 ¶ Then came to him the mother of Zebedee's
children with her sons, worshipping *him*, and de-
siring a certain thing of him.
21 And he said unto her, What wilt thou? She
saith unto him, Grant that these my two sons may
sit, the one on thy right hand, and the other on
the left, in thy kingdom.
22 But Jesus answered and said, Ye know not what
ye ask. Are ye able to drink of the cup that I shall
drink of, and to be baptized with the baptism that I
am baptized with? They say unto him, We are able.
23 And he saith unto them, Ye shall drink indeed
of my cup, and be baptized with the baptism that I
am baptized with: but to sit on my right hand, and
on my left, is not mine to give, but *it shall be given
to them* for whom it is prepared of my Father.
24 And when the ten heard *it*, they were moved
with indignation against the two brethren.
25 But Jesus called them *unto him*, and said, Ye
know that the princes of the Gentiles exercise
dominion over them, and they that are great
exercise authority upon them.
26 But it shall not be so among you: but who-
soever will be great among you, let him be your
minister;
27 And whosoever will be chief among you, let
him be your servant:
28 Even as the Son of man came not to be min-
istered unto, but to minister, and to give his life a
ransom for many.
29 And as they departed from Jericho, a great
multitude followed him.
30 ¶ And, behold, two blind men sitting by the
way side, when they heard that Jesus passed by,
cried out, saying, Have mercy on us, O Lord, *thou*
Son of David.
31 And the multitude rebuked them, because

20:11 *goodman.* Master.

20:12 *wrought.* Worked.

20:13 *Friend, I do thee no wrong.* Not only had the master and laborers agreed on the payment beforehand, but it was also His undeserved kindness to have called them in the first place. Even when we know that salvation is by grace alone, we still often think we deserve more than others.

20:15 *eye evil.* An idiom for greed (6:23; see note at Prov. 23:6). The selfish and self-righteous take offense at God's grace to the undeserving (*I am good*). This may allude to the rich man and to some degree even the disciples (19:20,27).

20:16 *last shall be first, and the first last.* In God's kingdom of grace, we must not presume that we are superior to others (19:30).

20:17 *going up to Jerusalem.* This was Jesus' final trip to Jerusalem. He was preparing to go and be killed.

20:18–19 *Gentiles.* Not mentioned in Christ's earlier predictions of His passion (16:21; 17:22–23). Christ was rejected and killed not just by the Jews but by the nations as well. *scourge.* Flog, whip.

20:20 *Zebedee's children.* James and John.

20:21 *right hand . . . left.* Positions of honor near a king.

20:22 *drink of the cup.* Share in Jesus' suffering. *baptized with the baptism.* A figure of speech for being plunged into an overwhelming experience (Luke 12:50; cf. Ps. 69:1–2).

20:23 *not mine to give.* The position of each person in the kingdom was *prepared* by God the *Father* before the foundation of the world (25:34), a statement of God's predestination of individuals (v. 16; 22:14). Though the King, Christ is also the submissive Servant to His Father's will.

20:26–27 *minister.* Servant. The path to greatness in the kingdom is downward into humility and service (18:4). God reverses human expectations (v. 16; 19:30).

20:28 *Son of man.* A title associated with sovereignty (Dan. 7:13–14), but here with humble service (*minister*) and self-sacrifice. *give his life a ransom for many.* Christ died in the place of His people (1:21), His death being the price for their redemption from the vast debt of their guilt toward God (18:24; 26:28; cf. Ex. 21:30; Ps. 130:3–4,7–8). This verse clearly teaches Jesus' substitutionary atonement (Isa. 53:4–6; Rom. 3:24–25; Gal. 3:13).

Jesus' Healing of Two Blind Men (20:29–34)

20:29 *they departed from Jericho.* The city had been rebuilt about a mile from its original site. The journey from Jericho to Jerusalem is about fifteen miles, and the terrain descends some 3,500 feet in elevation. Luke's Gospel indicates that Christ healed a blind man when approaching Jericho (Luke

they should hold their peace: but they cried the
more, saying, Have mercy on us, O Lord, *thou* Son
of David.
32 And Jesus stood still, and called them, and
said, What will ye that I shall do unto you?
33 They say unto him, Lord, that our eyes may
be opened.
34 So Jesus had compassion *on them*, and touched
their eyes: and immediately their eyes received
sight, and they followed him.

CHAPTER 21

AND when they drew nigh unto Jerusalem, and
were come to Bethphage, unto the mount of
Olives, then sent Jesus two disciples,
2 Saying unto them, Go into the village over
against you, and straightway ye shall find an ass
tied, and a colt with her: loose *them*, and bring
them unto me.
3 And if any *man* say ought unto you, ye shall say,
The Lord hath need of them; and straightway he
will send them.
4 All this was done, that it might be fulfilled
which was spoken by the prophet, saying,
5 Tell ye the daughter of Sion, Behold, thy King
cometh unto thee, meek, and sitting upon an
ass, and a colt the foal of an ass.
6 And the disciples went, and did as Jesus commanded them,
7 And brought the ass, and the colt, and put on
them their clothes, and they set *him* thereon.
8 And a very great multitude spread their
garments in the way; others cut down branches
from the trees, and strawed *them* in the way.
9 And the multitudes that went before, and that
followed, cried, saying, Hosanna to the Son of
David: Blessed *is* he that cometh in the name of
the Lord; Hosanna in the highest.
10 And when he was come into Jerusalem, all the
city was moved, saying, Who is this?
11 And the multitude said, This is Jesus the
prophet of Nazareth of Galilee.
12 ¶ And Jesus went into the temple of God,
and cast out all them that sold and bought in the
temple, and overthrew the tables of the moneychangers, and the seats of them that sold doves,
13 And said unto them, It is written, My house
shall be called the house of prayer; but ye have
made it a den of thieves.
14 And the blind and the lame came to him in the
temple; and he healed them.
15 And when the chief priests and scribes saw the
wonderful things that he did, and the children

18:35–43; cf. Mark 10:46–52). One proposed solution is that Christ healed one blind man when entering the city, and two more men when departing; a second is that the healings took place between the old city and the new; and a third solution is that the blind men began crying to Christ as He approached the city, and He healed them when He departed.

20:30–31 *Have mercy . . . Son of David*. A common cry to Christ for help (9:27; 15:22; cf. 21:9). *multitude rebuked them . . . they cried the more*. Faith persists in seeking grace (15:22–28).

20:32 *What will ye that I shall do unto you?* The blind men had already made their request known clearly enough, but Jesus questioned them to draw out their faith.

Thoughts for Personal/Family Worship: Chapter 20

1. **Christ announces the basic kingdom pattern as one of servanthood. Christ is the great Servant, who gives His life as a ransom (v. 28). His disciples must also pursue greatness by humbling themselves to serve others. We must renounce our tendency to envy others and criticize God's ways, and instead receive whatever He gives us with gratitude. Are you able to have joy and contentment in serving God however and wherever God determines to use you?**
2. **Christ asked the same question of the mother of James and John, and the blind men: what do you want? (vv. 21,32). Their answers are a study in contrasts, for one sought personal glory out of pride and ambition, and the others sought mercy and sight. Ironically, it was the disciples who were blind to what really mattered. What are you seeking from God in your prayers? What does that reveal about your soul?**

Jesus in Jerusalem (21:1—23:39)

Chapter 21: ***Jesus enters into Jerusalem and cleanses the temple. He answers a challenge to His authority. The crowds receive Him as a prophet.***

21:1 *drew nigh*. Came near. *unto Jerusalem*. Thus begins the fulfillment of Christ's predictions of His sufferings (16:21; 17:22–23). *mount of Olives*. A north-south ridge that extends for about two and one-half miles on the east side of Jerusalem.

21:5 *Tell ye the daughter of Sion*. A citation of Isa. 62:11, using a common biblical expression for Jerusalem (Zion) and her inhabitants (2 Kings 19:21; Ps. 9:14; Isa. 1:8; etc.). *thy King cometh . . . upon an ass*. A citation of Zech. 9:9. Christ intentionally approached the city in a manner that publicly announced the coming of salvation to God's people in the promised King as foretold by the prophets.

21:8 *very great multitude*. Crowds of pilgrims came to celebrate the Passover. *spread their garments in the way*. Laying their cloaks on the road was a form of public recognition of Jesus' kingship (2 Kings 9:13) *strawed*. Scattered.

21:9 *Hosanna . . . Blessed is he*. A citation of Ps. 118:25–26 (cf. v. 15), literally praying, "Please save," and applied to the promised king (*Son of David*). What the people may have interpreted as a deliverance from Rome, we need to see as salvation from sin (1:21).

21:12 *cast out all them that sold*. Jesus was angered by how temple worship had been corrupted into a money-making business, from which the true service was all but entirely gone.

21:13 *house of prayer*. The temple was to be a center for seeking God's grace in repentance (Isa. 56:7). *den of thieves*. They used outward worship to cloak their unrepentant sins and injustice with religious hypocrisy (Jer. 7:11).

21:14 *the blind and the lame came to him*. The last healing miracles of Jesus performed in this gospel, again highlighting that the true worship of God (*in the temple*) involves mercy to the needy (12:7,12).

crying in the temple, and saying, Hosanna to the
Son of David; they were sore displeased,
16 And said unto him, Hearest thou what these
say? And Jesus saith unto them, Yea; have ye never
read, Out of the mouth of babes and sucklings
thou hast perfected praise?
17 ¶ And he left them, and went out of the city
into Bethany; and he lodged there.
18 Now in the morning as he returned into the
city, he hungered.
19 And when he saw a fig tree in the way, he
came to it, and found nothing thereon, but leaves
only, and said unto it, Let no fruit grow on thee
henceforward for ever. And presently the fig tree
withered away.
20 And when the disciples saw *it*, they marvelled,
saying, How soon is the fig tree withered away!
21 Jesus answered and said unto them, Verily I say
unto you, If ye have faith, and doubt not, ye shall
not only do this *which is done* to the fig tree, but
also if ye shall say unto this mountain, Be thou
removed, and be thou cast into the sea; it shall be
done.
22 And all things, whatsoever ye shall ask in
prayer, believing, ye shall receive.
23 ¶ And when he was come into the temple, the
chief priests and the elders of the people came unto
him as he was teaching, and said, By what authority
doest thou these things? and who gave thee this
authority?
24 And Jesus answered and said unto them, I also
will ask you one thing, which if ye tell me, I in
like wise will tell you by what authority I do these
things.
25 The baptism of John, whence was it? from
heaven, or of men? And they reasoned with them-
selves, saying, If we shall say, From heaven; he will
say unto us, Why did ye not then believe him?
26 But if we shall say, Of men; we fear the people;
for all hold John as a prophet.
27 And they answered Jesus, and said, We cannot
tell. And he said unto them, Neither tell I you by
what authority I do these things.
28 ¶ But what think ye? A *certain* man had two
sons; and he came to the first, and said, Son, go
work to day in my vineyard.
29 He answered and said, I will not: but afterward
he repented, and went.
30 And he came to the second, and said likewise.
And he answered and said, I *go*, sir: and went not.
31 Whether of them twain did the will of *his* fa-
ther? They say unto him, The first. Jesus saith unto
them, Verily I say unto you, That the publicans and
the harlots go into the kingdom of God before you.
32 For John came unto you in the way of
righteousness, and ye believed him not: but the
publicans and the harlots believed him: and ye,
when ye had seen *it*, repented not afterward, that
ye might believe him.
33 ¶ Hear another parable: There was a certain
householder, which planted a vineyard, and
hedged it round about, and digged a winepress in
it, and built a tower, and let it out to husbandmen,
and went into a far country:
34 And when the time of the fruit drew near, he
sent his servants to the husbandmen, that they
might receive the fruits of it.
35 And the husbandmen took his servants, and
beat one, and killed another, and stoned another.
36 Again, he sent other servants more than the
first: and they did unto them likewise.
37 But last of all he sent unto them his son,
saying, They will reverence my son.
38 But when the husbandmen saw the son, they

21:15 *Hosanna.* See note at v. 9. *sore displeased.* Indignant, very upset.

21:16 *Out of the mouth of babes.* God uses little children to glorify Him and to defeat His enemies (Ps. 8:2). Jesus' use of the psalm implies that He believes He is worthy of the *praise* that was credited to the Lord alone in the Old Testament (Ps. 8:1).

21:17 *Bethany.* Jesus likely retired to the house of Lazarus where His feet were anointed (John 12:1–12).

21:19 *fig tree.* Often an emblem of Israel in its prosperity (24:32; Deut. 8:8; 1 Kings 4:25; Jer. 8:13; Zech. 3:10). *found nothing . . . but leaves only.* This was the season for small figs (large figs would develop later, Mark 11:13). Just as Christ inspected the temple and found it full of corruption instead of devotion to God, so He inspected Israel for fruit and pronounced divine judgment on it (3:10). *Let no fruit grow.* Christ's prophetic curse symbolized the withering of Israel for its formal, hypocritical religion. *presently.* Immediately.

21:20 *when the disciples saw it.* Matthew telescoped into one account what took place over two days (Mark 11:11–14,19–21). *they marvelled.* Though they may not have understood its prophetic meaning, the disciples were amazed at the supernatural power of Christ's word (8:27).

21:21 *Verily.* Truly. *say unto this mountain . . . into the sea.* Figurative speech (see note at 17:20), probably referring to speaking prophetically of the coming destruction of the physical city of God (an ironic adaptation of Ps. 46:2–4).

21:23 *By what authority.* Jesus already had demonstrated His surpassing authority in many ways (7:29; 8:8–9; 9:6–8; 10:1).

21:25–27 Jesus' question exposed their lack of concern for the truth and their actual motives of pleasing people (*we fear the people*; 6:1). *Neither tell I you.* Christ will not waste His teaching on those who will only play games with the truth (7:6).

21:31 *Whether of them twain.* Which of the two of them. The parable shows that the repentant sinner is more obedient to the *will* of God than the hypocrite. *publicans.* Tax collectors. *harlots.* Prostitutes.

21:33 *householder.* Master, head of the household. *planted a vineyard.* A prophetic parable of God's care for Israel so that they should produce righteousness and justice, but they refused (Isa. 5:1–7). *let it out to husbandmen.* Leased it to tenant farmers.

21:34–36 *servants.* The prophets of the Old Testament who suffered persecution (5:12; 23:29–32).

21:37–39 *his son.* Jesus placed Himself in a different category than the prophets, not a mere servant but the Son

said among themselves, This is the heir; come, let
us kill him, and let us seize on his inheritance.
39 And they caught him, and cast *him* out of the
vineyard, and slew *him.*
40 When the lord therefore of the vineyard com-
eth, what will he do unto those husbandmen?
41 They say unto him, He will miserably destroy
those wicked men, and will let out *his* vineyard
unto other husbandmen, which shall render him
the fruits in their seasons.
42 Jesus saith unto them, Did ye never read in the
scriptures, The stone which the builders rejected,
the same is become the head of the corner: this is
the Lord's doing, and it is marvellous in our eyes?
43 Therefore say I unto you, The kingdom of God
shall be taken from you, and given to a nation
bringing forth the fruits thereof.
44 And whosoever shall fall on this stone shall
be broken: but on whomsoever it shall fall, it will
grind him to powder.
45 And when the chief priests and Pharisees had
heard his parables, they perceived that he spake
of them.
46 But when they sought to lay hands on him,
they feared the multitude, because they took him
for a prophet.

CHAPTER 22

AND Jesus answered and spake unto them again
by parables, and said,
2 The kingdom of heaven is like unto a certain
king, which made a marriage for his son,
3 And sent forth his servants to call them that
were bidden to the wedding: and they would not
come.
4 Again, he sent forth other servants, saying, Tell
them which are bidden, Behold, I have prepared
my dinner: my oxen and *my* fatlings *are* killed,
and all things *are* ready: come unto the marriage.
5 But they made light of *it*, and went their ways,
one to his farm, another to his merchandise:
6 And the remnant took his servants, and
entreated *them* spitefully, and slew *them.*
7 But when the king heard *thereof*, he was wroth:
and he sent forth his armies, and destroyed those
murderers, and burned up their city.
8 Then saith he to his servants, The wedding
is ready, but they which were bidden were not
worthy.
9 Go ye therefore into the highways, and as many
as ye shall find, bid to the marriage.
10 So those servants went out into the highways,
and gathered together all as many as they found,

---

of God and *heir* of God's kingdom. *cast him out . . . and slew him.* An implicit prophecy concerning His rejection and death at the hands of the religious leaders.

21:41 *destroy those wicked men.* The people unwittingly foretold the doom of Jerusalem (22:7).

21:42 *the scriptures.* Literally, "the writings," a technical term for the Bible as the written Word of God (22:29; 26:54,56; 2 Tim. 3:16; 2 Peter 1:20–21). *stone which the builders rejected.* The Old Testament prophesied Christ's rejection by the leaders of Israel and His exaltation by God to the honor of being the cornerstone of the new people of God (Ps. 118:22–23; see v. 9).

21:43 *kingdom . . . taken from you.* Agreeing with the people's response to His parable (v. 41), Christ declared God's judgment on national Israel, the end of its theocracy and temple (24:1–2; 27:51), and the formation of a new people of God defined by repentance and obedience to the divine King (*nation bringing forth the fruits*).

21:44 *fall on this stone . . . powder.* Jesus drew upon other "stone" prophecies (Isa. 8:14–15; Dan. 2:34–35,44–45; see Rom. 9:33; 1 Cor. 1:23; 1 Peter 2:8) to indicate that He and His kingdom will shatter those who stumble over Him in unbelief (Ps. 2:9).

Thoughts for Personal/Family Worship: Chapter 21

1. **Christ came riding into Jerusalem as a glorious, yet meek and lowly King, as prophesied by Zechariah. Sinners need such a Savior! Just as He came to Jerusalem, so He comes in the preaching of the gospel. Do we come to hear the Word, praying, "Hosanna," that is, "Lord, please save us"?**
2. **The fig tree with beautiful leaves, but no fruit, represents hypocritical religion among any professing people of God. The hypocrite loves to make himself or herself look nice to the outside world. However, when God comes to pluck the fruits of true repentance, there are none. For all the hypocrite's fine words to the Lord, he remains disobedient. Far better to confess our sinfulness to the Lord with honesty, and then repent and turn to obedience with sincerity. What can we learn from the publicans and harlots, of whom Christ said, they "go into the kingdom of God" before many other religious people (v. 31)?**

Chapter 22: ***Jesus again teaches with parables. He is challenged by the religious elite. Finally, He presents a challenge concerning His person, which they are unable to answer.***

22:2 *marriage for his son.* Christ is the Son of God (see notes at 2:15; 16:16) and the bridegroom of the church (9:15; 25:1–13).

22:3 *servants.* The prophets, apostles, and other ministers of the Word. *bidden.* Called (vv. 4,8–9; the noun appears in v. 14). Through the gospel preaching of His ambassadors, God is calling a lost world to Himself (2 Cor. 5:18–21).

22:4 *dinner.* The kingdom is like a banquet or feast (8:11; Isa. 25:6; 55:1–3; Luke 14:15–24). The imagery here resonates with that used of divine Wisdom (Prov. 9:1–6; cf. Matt. 11:19,28). *fatlings.* Grain-fed livestock, raised for delicious meat.

22:5–6 *made light of it.* Had no interest and paid no attention. *merchandise.* Trade, commerce. *entreated . . . spitefully.* Abused, attacked. Some people passively neglected the invitation, and others aggressively attacked the messengers, but neither response was acceptable (v. 8).

22:7 *wroth.* Angry. *destroyed . . . burned up their city.* Another warning of the destruction of Jerusalem, fulfilled in AD 70 (21:41; ch. 24), and perhaps ultimately fulfilled in all the world at Christ's second coming (Rev. 18:18).

22:8 *not worthy.* Though the call is all of grace, deserved by none, some prove themselves unfit to receive its blessing by their refusal to come (Acts 13:46).

22:9–10 *as many as ye shall find . . . both bad and good.* Preachers of the gospel must call all people who hear their

both bad and good: and the wedding was
furnished with guests.
11 ¶ And when the king came in to see the guests,
he saw there a man which had not on a wedding
garment:
12 And he saith unto him, Friend, how camest
thou in hither not having a wedding garment?
And he was speechless.
13 Then said the king to the servants, Bind him
hand and foot, and take him away, and cast *him*
into outer darkness; there shall be weeping and
gnashing of teeth.
14 For many are called, but few *are* chosen.
15 ¶ Then went the Pharisees, and took counsel
how they might entangle him in *his* talk.
16 And they sent out unto him their disciples
with the Herodians, saying, Master, we know
that thou art true, and teachest the way of God in
truth, neither carest thou for any *man*: for thou
regardest not the person of men.
17 Tell us therefore, What thinkest thou? Is it
lawful to give tribute unto Caesar, or not?
18 But Jesus perceived their wickedness, and said,
Why tempt ye me, *ye* hypocrites?
19 Shew me the tribute money. And they brought
unto him a penny.
20 And he saith unto them, Whose *is* this image
and superscription?
21 They say unto him, Caesar's. Then saith he
unto them, Render therefore unto Caesar the
things which are Caesar's; and unto God the
things that are God's.
22 When they had heard *these words*, they
marvelled, and left him, and went their way.
23 ¶ The same day came to him the Sadducees,
which say that there is no resurrection, and asked
him,
24 Saying, Master, Moses said, If a man die,
having no children, his brother shall marry his
wife, and raise up seed unto his brother.
25 Now there were with us seven brethren: and
the first, when he had married a wife, deceased,
and, having no issue, left his wife unto his brother:
26 Likewise the second also, and the third, unto
the seventh.
27 And last of all the woman died also.
28 Therefore in the resurrection whose wife shall
she be of the seven? for they all had her.
29 Jesus answered and said unto them, Ye do err,
not knowing the scriptures, nor the power of God.
30 For in the resurrection they neither marry, nor
are given in marriage, but are as the angels of God
in heaven.
31 But as touching the resurrection of the dead,
have ye not read that which was spoken unto you
by God, saying,
32 I am the God of Abraham, and the God of
Isaac, and the God of Jacob? God is not the God
of the dead, but of the living.
33 And when the multitude heard *this*, they were
astonished at his doctrine.
34 ¶ But when the Pharisees had heard that
he had put the Sadducees to silence, they were
gathered together.

---

message to repent and believe in Christ, regardless of their morals. *furnished.* Filled.

22:11 *wedding garment.* The salvation and righteousness given by God to believers (Isa. 61:10; Zech. 3:4). Since guests of all kinds were brought in from the highways without time to prepare, the parable assumes that the king would have provided wedding garments, but this man evidently thought himself able to attend the wedding on his own terms and not those of the king.

22:12 *in hither.* In here, into this place.

22:13 *outer darkness . . . weeping and gnashing of teeth.* The suffering of hell (see note at 8:12).

22:14 *many are called, but few are chosen.* The gospel calls all who hear it to life (vv. 3,9–10), but God has elected only certain individuals to salvation, and they alone will respond rightly to the gospel and come to Christ (11:25,27–28; John 6:37,44,65; 17:2,6). Christ saves many in number (20:28), but few relative to all mankind (7:13–14).

22:16 *thou art true.* They attempted to flatter Jesus with their words. *Herodians.* The servants and supporters of Herod Antipas (14:1,3; Mark 3:6). They were pro-Roman.

22:17 The *tribute* given to Caesar was different than mandatory tax to support the temple (17:24–27).

22:18 *tempt.* Test.

22:19 *tribute money.* The particular Greek phrase used here, unique in the Gospels to Matthew, refers to the Roman coin currently used for taxes, which Matthew as a former tax collector would well know. *penny.* Denarius, one day's wage for a laborer.

22:20–21 *superscription.* The words written or engraved on the coin. *Caesar's.* The emperor's *image* was on the coin and it likely referred to Tiberius as divine and a high priest—blasphemy to the Jews. *Render.* Give or pay back. *unto Caesar . . . Caesar's . . . unto God . . . God's.* Christ neither rejected civil government and its taxes (Rom. 13:1–7) nor did He encourage absolute submission to civil government and its idolatries (Dan. 3:18). While we must pay taxes to rulers, even pagan rulers, we must offer all things to God in worship and obedience, especially offering ourselves as human beings created in His *image* (Gen. 1:26).

22:23 *Sadducees.* A party of the Jews (see note at 16:1).

22:24 *raise up seed.* Produce offspring to continue the family line. The hypothetical situation builds upon the practice of levirate marriage (Deut. 25:5) in an attempt to trap Jesus in His words.

22:28 *in the resurrection whose wife shall she be.* The Sadducees attempted to show that the resurrection is inconsistent with the law of God and results in absurd situations.

22:30 *neither marry, nor are given in marriage.* Marriage is a blessing for creation but will be obsolete in the glories of the age to come, when the resurrected saints possess glorious and heavenly bodies (*as the angels*) of a different order than our present existence (13:43; Dan. 12:3; 1 Cor. 15:35–50).

22:32 *I am the God of Abraham.* Jesus argued by inference from Scripture (Ex. 3:6), that if God still had a covenant relationship with the patriarchs when He spoke to Moses, they must still be alive with Him, waiting to enjoy the fulfillment of God's promises when He raises them from the dead.

35 Then one of them, *which was* a lawyer, asked
him a question, tempting him, and saying,
36 Master, which *is* the great commandment in
the law?
37 Jesus said unto him, Thou shalt love the Lord
thy God with all thy heart, and with all thy soul,
and with all thy mind.
38 This is the first and great commandment.
39 And the second *is* like unto it, Thou shalt love
thy neighbour as thyself.
40 On these two commandments hang all the law
and the prophets.
41 ¶ While the Pharisees were gathered together,
Jesus asked them,
42 Saying, What think ye of Christ? whose son is
he? They say unto him, *The Son* of David.
43 He saith unto them, How then doth David in
spirit call him Lord, saying,
44 The LORD said unto my Lord, Sit thou on my
right hand, till I make thine enemies thy footstool?
45 If David then call him Lord, how is he his son?
46 And no man was able to answer him a word,
neither durst any *man* from that day forth ask
him any more *questions*.

CHAPTER 23

THEN spake Jesus to the multitude, and to his
disciples,
2 Saying, The scribes and the Pharisees sit in
Moses' seat:
3 All therefore whatsoever they bid you observe,
that observe and do; but do not ye after their
works: for they say, and do not.
4 For they bind heavy burdens and grievous to
be borne, and lay *them* on men's shoulders; but
they *themselves* will not move them with one of
their fingers.
5 But all their works they do for to be seen of
men: they make broad their phylacteries, and
enlarge the borders of their garments,
6 And love the uppermost rooms at feasts, and
the chief seats in the synagogues,
7 And greetings in the markets, and to be called
of men, Rabbi, Rabbi.
8 But be not ye called Rabbi: for one is your
Master, *even* Christ; and all ye are brethren.
9 And call no *man* your father upon the earth: for
one is your Father, which is in heaven.
10 Neither be ye called masters: for one is your
Master, *even* Christ.
11 But he that is greatest among you shall be your
servant.
12 And whosoever shall exalt himself shall be
abased; and he that shall humble himself shall be
exalted.
13 ¶ But woe unto you, scribes and Pharisees,
hypocrites! for ye shut up the kingdom of heaven

22:35 *tempting.* Testing.
22:37–40 *love the Lord . . . love thy neighbour.* Jesus quotes Deut. 6:5 and Lev. 19:18 to sum up the entire moral teaching of the Old Testament (*all the law and the prophets*) in the principle of love (Rom. 13:9; Gal. 5:6,14; James 2:8). Love for God is first and supreme and must engage all the powers and activities of our being. Love for other people is second and must be an extension of our love for God.
22:42 *Christ.* God's anointed (see note at 16:16). *whose son is he?* The Pharisees answered rightly that He is the promised King of David's offspring (2 Sam. 7:12). The question was simple and easily answered, but it set up the Pharisees for what He would say next.
22:43 *David in spirit call.* The prophets wrote the Scriptures by the Holy Spirit so that the words of the Bible are the words of the Spirit (Heb. 3:7; 9:8; 10:15; see note at 21:42).
22:44–45 *the LORD said unto my Lord.* Both times (*LORD*) is translated from the same Greek word, but in the Hebrew text of Ps. 110:1, which Jesus quoted, the first is God's name, *Jehovah*, and the second is a title meaning, "my Master." David, anointed by God as king of Israel, addressed the Messiah as his king, exalted to share in the very glory of God at the *right hand* of *Jehovah*. Therefore, "the Son of David" (v. 42), though human, must be far more than a man. The question, "Whose son is he?" requires the answer, "The Son of God." Jesus was proving from the Scriptures His unique status as the God-man, the same claim for which they would condemn Him to death (26:63–66).
22:46 *durst.* Dared.

Thoughts for Personal/Family Worship: Chapter 22

1. **God's call to the marriage supper of His Son is remarkably open and indiscriminate. However, all who inherit salvation have come through the narrow gate, namely, through Jesus (John 14:6). Those who do not come by way of repentance and faith in Jesus Christ are not found dressed in His righteousness alone. At the last, they will be cast out as those who would not submit to the righteousness of God. How do you know if you are clothed with wedding garment?**
2. **Many people use religion as a cloak to keep away from Christ. They love arguments. They love to identify with this party or that sect. In the end their basic attitude is "tempting" Christ (v. 35). It is one thing to know Scripture or even debate aspects of Scripture. It is another thing to listen to Scripture and submit to the Son (Ps. 2:12). How can you tell which you are doing?**

Chapter 23: *Jesus denounces the scribes and Pharisees with eight woes of judgment proving Himself to be the Lord and Judge.*

23:2 *Moses' seat.* The office with the authority to interpret the law. Jesus does not mean that the Pharisees were just like Moses.
23:3 *observe and do.* Some take this to be sarcastic; others as simply stating a fact. In either case, Jesus is pointing out the severe hypocrisy of the Pharisees (*they say, and do not*).
23:5 *phylacteries.* Small leather boxes that contained portions of the law in them. Jews would wear them from their garments indicating their love of the law in a literal fulfillment of Ex. 13:9,16.
23:7 *Rabbi.* In Jesus' day this term meant something akin to "master" or "teacher" (John 1:38).

against men: for ye neither go in *yourselves*,
neither suffer ye them that are entering to go in.
14 Woe unto you, scribes and Pharisees,
hypocrites! for ye devour widows' houses, and for
a pretence make long prayer: therefore ye shall
receive the greater damnation.
15 Woe unto you, scribes and Pharisees, hypo-
crites! for ye compass sea and land to make one
proselyte, and when he is made, ye make him
twofold more the child of hell than yourselves.
16 Woe unto you, *ye* blind guides, which say,
Whosoever shall swear by the temple, it is
nothing; but whosoever shall swear by the gold of
the temple, he is a debtor!
17 *Ye* fools and blind: for whether is greater, the
gold, or the temple that sanctifieth the gold?
18 And, Whosoever shall swear by the altar, it is
nothing; but whosoever sweareth by the gift that
is upon it, he is guilty.
19 *Ye* fools and blind: for whether *is* greater, the
gift, or the altar that sanctifieth the gift?
20 Whoso therefore shall swear by the altar,
sweareth by it, and by all things thereon.
21 And whoso shall swear by the temple, sweareth
by it, and by him that dwelleth therein.
22 And he that shall swear by heaven, sweareth by
the throne of God, and by him that sitteth thereon.
23 Woe unto you, scribes and Pharisees,
hypocrites! for ye pay tithe of mint and anise and
cummin, and have omitted the weightier *matters*
of the law, judgment, mercy, and faith: these
ought ye to have done, and not to leave the other
undone.
24 *Ye* blind guides, which strain at a gnat, and
swallow a camel.
25 Woe unto you, scribes and Pharisees,
hypocrites! for ye make clean the outside of the
cup and of the platter, but within they are full of
extortion and excess.
26 *Thou* blind Pharisee, cleanse first that *which*
is within the cup and platter, that the outside of
them may be clean also.
27 Woe unto you, scribes and Pharisees, hypo-
crites! for ye are like unto whited sepulchres, which
indeed appear beautiful outward, but are within
full of dead *men's* bones, and of all uncleanness.
28 Even so ye also outwardly appear righteous
unto men, but within ye are full of hypocrisy and
iniquity.
29 Woe unto you, scribes and Pharisees, hypo-
crites! because ye build the tombs of the proph-
ets, and garnish the sepulchres of the righteous,
30 And say, If we had been in the days of our
fathers, we would not have been partakers with
them in the blood of the prophets.
31 Wherefore ye be witnesses unto yourselves,
that ye are the children of them which killed the
prophets.
32 Fill ye up then the measure of your fathers.
33 *Ye* serpents, *ye* generation of vipers, how can
ye escape the damnation of hell?
34 ¶ Wherefore, behold, I send unto you prophets,
and wise men, and scribes: and *some* of them ye
shall kill and crucify; and *some* of them shall ye
scourge in your synagogues, and persecute *them*
from city to city:

23:13–39 Jesus turned from his disciples to directly address the Pharisees. *woe*. The prophetic equivalent of a curse, repeated throughout this chapter. *hypocrites*. Play actors, here those who wear a religious mask of external religion with hearts empty of true piety, whether they know it themselves or not.

23:13 First Woe: False Teaching. *shut up the kingdom of heaven*. They used their authority as teachers to stop the people from believing the true doctrine of Christ and Scripture (16:19; Luke 11:52).

23:14 Second Woe: Use of Religion to Exploit the Poor. *devour widows' houses*. Exploit the elderly, solitary, and vulnerable for financial gain.

23:15 Third Woe: Missions without the Gospel. *compass*. Go around, travel. *proselyte*. Convert. *child of hell*. Literally, "son of hell," an idiom for a person doomed to eternal punishment (see note at 5:22).

23:16–22 Fourth Woe: Frivolous Oaths. The Pharisees saw some oaths as binding and others as not binding, making fine distinctions that allowed them to swear dishonestly while still adding deceptive weight to their words by invoking sacred objects. Christ showed their reasoning to be flawed and hypocritical, for even invoking things associated with God involves His holiness and honor (5:33–37)

23:17 *whether*. Which (v. 19).

23:23–24 Fifth Woe: Majoring in the Minors While Neglecting the Soul of Piety. *tithe*. A tenth. *weightier matters of the law*. Jesus affirmed the obligation to tithe (*these ought ye to have done*), but condemned the Pharisees for neglecting the more important things of the law, namely, love to God, true worship, inward purity of heart and life, justice (*judgment*), etc. *gnat... camel*. Legalism and hypocrisy throws everything out of proportion (7:3), placing enormous significance on minute details of obedience while neglecting massively important matters.

23:25–26 Sixth Woe: Outwardly Clean Yet Inwardly Filthy. Though insistent on various washings (15:2), their purity was merely external and ceremonial, not a purity of the heart (5:8).

23:27–28 Seventh Woe: Secret Tombs of Death. Contact with the corpses of the *dead* made a person ritually unclean (Num. 19:11–13), but the Pharisees were tombs painted white (*whited sepulchres*), outwardly religious but full of defilement and making others unclean.

23:29–32 Eighth Woe: Murderers of the Prophets. *children of them which killed the prophets*. The Pharisees, by their self-righteous and God-rejecting doctrine, were the spiritual offspring of those who resisted and killed the prophets.

23:33 *serpents... vipers*. The seed of the serpent (3:7; 12:34; Gen. 3:15), belonging to the kingdom of Satan. *hell*. See note at 5:22.

23:34 *I send*. The verbal form of the word "apostle" (10:2,5). *prophets*. People enabled by the Spirit to speak new revelations from God, as were the apostles and some others. *wise men*. Christ's ministers bring the wisdom of the Word, for Christ is the divine Wisdom (Luke 11:49). *scribes*. Men who have studied God's Word to obey it and teach it (Ezra 7:6,10). *kill*. The Pharisees would treat Christ's messengers in the same

35 That upon you may come all the righteous
blood shed upon the earth, from the blood of
righteous Abel unto the blood of Zacharias son
of Barachias, whom ye slew between the temple
and the altar.
36 Verily I say unto you, All these things shall
come upon this generation.
37 O Jerusalem, Jerusalem, *thou* that killest
the prophets, and stonest them which are sent
unto thee, how often would I have gathered thy
children together, even as a hen gathereth her
chickens under *her* wings, and ye would not!
38 Behold, your house is left unto you desolate.
39 For I say unto you, Ye shall not see me hence-
forth, till ye shall say, Blessed *is* he that cometh in
the name of the Lord.

CHAPTER 24

AND Jesus went out, and departed from the
temple: and his disciples came to *him* for to shew
him the buildings of the temple.
2 And Jesus said unto them, See ye not all these
things? verily I say unto you, There shall not be
left here one stone upon another, that shall not be
thrown down.
3 ¶ And as he sat upon the mount of Olives, the
disciples came unto him privately, saying, Tell us,
when shall these things be? and what *shall be* the
sign of thy coming, and of the end of the world?
4 And Jesus answered and said unto them, Take
heed that no man deceive you.
5 For many shall come in my name, saying, I am
Christ; and shall deceive many.
6 And ye shall hear of wars and rumours of wars:
see that ye be not troubled: for all *these things*
must come to pass, but the end is not yet.
7 For nation shall rise against nation, and king-
dom against kingdom: and there shall be famines,
and pestilences, and earthquakes, in divers places.
8 All these *are* the beginning of sorrows.
9 Then shall they deliver you up to be afflicted,
and shall kill you: and ye shall be hated of all na-
tions for my name's sake.
10 And then shall many be offended, and shall
betray one another, and shall hate one another.
11 And many false prophets shall rise, and shall
deceive many.
12 And because iniquity shall abound, the love of
many shall wax cold.
13 But he that shall endure unto the end, the
same shall be saved.
14 And this gospel of the kingdom shall be
preached in all the world for a witness unto all

---

manner as their fathers treated the Old Testament prophets (5:12).

23:35 *Abel . . . Zacharias.* By referring to the first and last martyrs of the Old Testament era, all the martyrs are in view.

23:37 *O Jerusalem, Jerusalem.* The great woes of Jesus turn into great lamentation. *as a hen gathereth her chickens.* A poignant and indicting picture of love and mercy for the lost (Ezek. 33:11; Hos. 11:8). *ye would not!* You were not willing. Though God is sovereign to save whom He chooses (11:25,27; 22:14), sinners are personally responsible and culpable for their unwillingness to repent (Ex. 10:1–4).

23:39 *Blessed is he that cometh in the name of the Lord.* Citing Ps. 118:26 (see note at 21:9). This saying could mean that most of physical Israel would not *see* the Messiah after His death and resurrection until He returned as King. Or it may mean their spiritual blindness (vv. 16–17,19,24,26) would not be lifted until the day came when the Holy Spirit would lead them to confess with faith that He is the King of Israel (2 Cor. 3:14–17). There is still hope for stubborn rebels if they turn to the Lord.

Thoughts for Personal/Family Worship: Chapter 23

The source of the Pharisees' problem rested in their pride (vv. 6–7). Pride blinds us to our sin. Pride leads us to justify ourselves before God (Luke 16:15). We think of ourselves more highly than we ought to think (Rom. 12:3). Meanwhile, we bind ourselves and those around us to traditions, ceremonies, rules that have not been expressly laid down in the Scriptures. The law, however, can only arouse sin in us and render us condemned before the tribunal of God. The gospel is the only remedy. Our unrighteousness is not as much of an obstacle to our salvation as our self-righteousness. How can we avoid the pit of being like the Pharisees?

The Olivet Discourse (24:1—25:46)

Chapter 24: *Jesus teaches on the destruction of Jerusalem and the times preceding the final judgment.*

24:1 *Jesus . . . departed from the temple.* This exit, after His denunciation of the Pharisees (ch. 23), recalls when God's glory departed from the temple because of Israel's sins (Ezek. 10).

24:2 *verily.* Truly. *not . . . one stone upon another.* The complete destruction of the temple, which took place by the Roman invasion led by Titus in AD 70.

24:3 *when shall these things be . . . what shall be the sign . . . of the end of the world?* Whether the disciples were aware or not, they asked two different questions that would pertain to two different times. Jesus' answer refers to both the destruction of the temple in Jerusalem and Jesus' second coming at a later date, which helps resolve some of questions about the prophecies given here.

24:6–8 *wars and rumours of wars . . . famines, and pestilences, and earthquakes.* The disciples are not to think the end of the age has come because they see great conflicts and disasters. *divers.* Various. *sorrows.* Birth or labor pains, an image associated with the day of the Lord (Isa. 13:6–8; 1 Thess. 5:2–3). Such troubles are not the day of the Lord, being experienced in the first century AD, but are only the *beginning* of the last days initiated by Christ's first coming (Heb. 1:1–2) and leading to His return.

24:9 *deliver you up . . . kill you.* Church history records that the majority of the apostles were martyred for their faith, except for John, who died on the island of Patmos from old age.

24:12 *wax.* Become. The last days are a period not only of worldwide evangelism (v. 14), but also increasing sin (2 Tim. 3:1–9).

24:13 *endure . . . shall be saved.* True faith perseveres, and without perseverance there is no salvation (10:22; 13:20–23; Col. 1:21–23; Heb. 3:6).

24:14 *preached in all the world.* The evangelization of *all*

nations; and then shall the end come.
15 When ye therefore shall see the abomination
of desolation, spoken of by Daniel the prophet,
stand in the holy place, (whoso readeth, let him
understand:)
16 Then let them which be in Judaea flee into the
mountains:
17 Let him which is on the housetop not come
down to take any thing out of his house:
18 Neither let him which is in the field return
back to take his clothes.
19 And woe unto them that are with child, and to
them that give suck in those days!
20 But pray ye that your flight be not in the
winter, neither on the sabbath day:
21 For then shall be great tribulation, such as was
not since the beginning of the world to this time,
no, nor ever shall be.
22 And except those days should be shortened,
there should no flesh be saved: but for the elect's
sake those days shall be shortened.
23 Then if any man shall say unto you, Lo, here *is*
Christ, or there; believe *it* not.
24 For there shall arise false Christs, and false
prophets, and shall shew great signs and wonders;
insomuch that, if *it were* possible, they shall
deceive the very elect.
25 Behold, I have told you before.
26 Wherefore if they shall say unto you, Behold,
he is in the desert; go not forth: behold, *he is* in
the secret chambers; believe *it* not.
27 For as the lightning cometh out of the east,
and shineth even unto the west; so shall also the
coming of the Son of man be.
28 For wheresoever the carcase is, there will the
eagles be gathered together.
29 ¶ Immediately after the tribulation of those
days shall the sun be darkened, and the moon
shall not give her light, and the stars shall fall
from heaven, and the powers of the heavens shall
be shaken:
30 And then shall appear the sign of the Son of
man in heaven: and then shall all the tribes of the
earth mourn, and they shall see the Son of man
coming in the clouds of heaven with power and
great glory.
31 And he shall send his angels with a great sound
of a trumpet, and they shall gather together his
elect from the four winds, from one end of heaven
to the other.
32 Now learn a parable of the fig tree; When his
branch is yet tender, and putteth forth leaves, ye
know that summer *is* nigh:
33 So likewise ye, when ye shall see all these
things, know that it is near, *even* at the doors.
34 Verily I say unto you, This generation shall not
pass, till all these things be fulfilled.
35 Heaven and earth shall pass away, but my
words shall not pass away.
36 ¶ But of that day and hour knoweth no *man*,

nations (28:19) indicates that Jesus prophesied of an extended time between the destruction of Jerusalem and judgment day. This then is presently the age when the church must pour its energy and prayers into missions.

24:15 *abomination of desolation.* An expression from the prophet *Daniel* recording the defilement of the temple (*holy place*) by the Gentiles (Dan. 9:24–27; cf. Dan. 8:13; 11:31; 12:11), partially fulfilled by Antiochus IV (d. 164 BC), but more fully in the Roman destruction of Jerusalem in AD 70, as the parallel passage in Luke's gospel confirms (Luke 21:20). Thus Christ instructs believers in Judaea to flee quickly for their lives when the Roman armies drew near (vv. 16–20).

24:17–18 *housetop.* Homes in the Ancient Near East were flat-roofed. These are images communicating the terrible urgency of escaping quickly before the Roman armies come.

24:20 *sabbath day.* Christ expected that His disciples would still be observing the fourth commandment (Ex. 20:8–11), implying its continuing validity for Christians.

24:21 *tribulation.* Trouble or distress, the experience of believers in all times (Ps. 34:19; Rom. 5:3; 12:12; Rev. 1:9). The Roman assault on Jerusalem brought *great* sorrows; according to Josephus, the Roman siege killed 1.1 million people of all ages. *such as was not since the beginning.* Perhaps an allusion to the severity of God's plagues on Egypt (Ex. 9:18,24; 10:6,14). This was God's judgment (21:41,43; 22:7; 23:37–38).

24:22 *no flesh.* An idiom meaning "no one" (Jer. 12:12; cf. Acts 2:17). *the elect.* God's chosen ones (20:16; 22:14), those whom Satan will attempt to deceive (v. 24) but whom Christ will save on the last day (v. 31).

24:23–27 Christ's disciples should not be led astray by *false Christs, and false prophets* (7:15; 2 Thess. 2:1–12; 1 John 2:18). *lightning . . . shineth.* Jesus' return in judgment will not be a secret, but will be displayed openly for all to see (v. 30).

24:28 *carcase.* Dead body, perhaps an allusion to the battle of Gog (Ezek. 39:17–20; Rev. 19:17–18).

24:29 *tribulation of those days.* The sufferings of the church will continue "until the times of the Gentiles be fulfilled" (Luke 21:24; cf. Acts 14:22). *sun be darkened . . . moon shall not give her light . . . stars shall fall . . . powers of the heavens shall be shaken.* The cosmic disruptions of the day of the Lord (e.g., Isa. 13:10; 24:23; 34:4; Ezek. 32:7).

24:30 *Son of man coming in the clouds.* Christ will come visibly in the skies to establish His kingdom with open *power* and *glory* (Dan. 7:13–14; cf. Matt. 26:64).

24:31 Christ will use His *angels* as the instruments to separate His people from the wicked and bring the *elect* from all the earth (*four winds*) to Himself in a public display (*trumpet*) of His love (13:41; 1 Thess. 4:16–17).

24:32–33 *fig tree.* The *parable* refers to Israel and God's judgment on Jerusalem for its failure to produce spiritual fruit (21:19). *nigh.* Near. Believers in Judaea must be alert for the signs of the approaching Gentile army for the destruction of Jerusalem will follow shortly (vv. 15–22).

24:34 *Verily.* Truly. *This generation.* The destruction of Jerusalem took place about forty years after Christ spoke these words.

24:35 *my words shall not pass away.* Jesus claims to speak the very words of God, equal in authority to the Old Testament Scriptures (5:18).

24:36 *that day and hour knoweth no man.* The date of the second coming of Christ is hidden to mankind until the time arrives (vv. 42–44; 25:13). Therefore, all date setting is forbidden.

no, not the angels of heaven, but my Father only.
37 But as the days of Noe *were*, so shall also the
coming of the Son of man be.
38 For as in the days that were before the flood
they were eating and drinking, marrying and
giving in marriage, until the day that Noe entered
into the ark,
39 And knew not until the flood came, and took
them all away; so shall also the coming of the Son
of man be.
40 Then shall two be in the field; the one shall be
taken, and the other left.
41 Two *women shall be* grinding at the mill; the
one shall be taken, and the other left.
42 ¶ Watch therefore: for ye know not what hour
your Lord doth come.
43 But know this, that if the goodman of the
house had known in what watch the thief would
come, he would have watched, and would not
have suffered his house to be broken up.
44 Therefore be ye also ready: for in such an hour
as ye think not the Son of man cometh.
45 Who then is a faithful and wise servant, whom
his lord hath made ruler over his household, to
give them meat in due season?
46 Blessed *is* that servant, whom his lord when he
cometh shall find so doing.
47 Verily I say unto you, That he shall make him
ruler over all his goods.
48 But and if that evil servant shall say in his
heart, My lord delayeth his coming;
49 And shall begin to smite *his* fellowservants,
and to eat and drink with the drunken;
50 The lord of that servant shall come in a day
when he looketh not for *him*, and in an hour that
he is not aware of,
51 And shall cut him asunder, and appoint *him*
his portion with the hypocrites: there shall be
weeping and gnashing of teeth.

CHAPTER 25

THEN shall the kingdom of heaven be likened
unto ten virgins, which took their lamps, and
went forth to meet the bridegroom.
2 And five of them were wise, and five *were*
foolish.
3 They that *were* foolish took their lamps, and
took no oil with them:
4 But the wise took oil in their vessels with their
lamps.
5 While the bridegroom tarried, they all slum-
bered and slept.
6 And at midnight there was a cry made, Behold,
the bridegroom cometh; go ye out to meet him.
7 Then all those virgins arose, and trimmed their
lamps.
8 And the foolish said unto the wise, Give us of
your oil; for our lamps are gone out.
9 But the wise answered, saying, *Not so*; lest there
be not enough for us and you: but go ye rather to
them that sell, and buy for yourselves.
10 And while they went to buy, the bridegroom
came; and they that were ready went in with him
to the marriage: and the door was shut.
11 Afterward came also the other virgins, saying,

24:37 *Noe*. Noah (Gen. 6–7).
24:39–40 *one shall be taken, and the other left.* Not a secret rapture of believers, for the ones taken away in this text are the wicked like those destroyed by the *flood*.
24:42–43 *goodman*. Master, head of the household. *thief.* Christ's coming will surprise the wicked and find them unprepared for the great loss they will experience (1 Thess. 5:2,4; 2 Peter 3:10; Rev. 3:3; 16:15). *broken up*. Broken into.
24:44 *be ye also ready.* Because disciples do not know when the Lord is coming again, Jesus calls them to watchfulness.
24:45–51 *faithful and wise servant*. The doctrine of Christ's coming motivates believers to live as good stewards of Christ's gifts, anticipating the return of their Lord to hold them accountable (25:14–30). *meat*. Food in general. *delayeth his coming*. Jesus taught His disciples to expect a long wait. *asunder*. Into pieces. *weeping and gnashing of teeth*. Sinners who indulge themselves rather than obeying Christ and loving people, will reap eternal damnation in hell (see note at 8:12).

Thoughts for Personal/Family Worship: Chapter 24

1. **As much as we admire beautiful buildings, even the best architecture will fall under God's judgment if it houses rebellion and unbelief toward Christ. Our only safety is in following Christ to the end. Christ did not promise it would be easy. He warned that believers would see many tribulations, including wars, national disasters, and persecutions. He said that they must stand against false teachers and false Christs. However, He promised that He will return and gather His elect safely to Himself. How can we find the strength to persevere with Christ by leaning on the hope of His second coming?**
2. **Just as surely as the Roman army destroyed Jerusalem in AD 70, so the Son of Man will return with His angels to judge the world. This will be a day of sudden destruction for the wicked, but a day of gracious reward for the faithful servants of the Lord. We cannot know when it will happen, but we must be prepared. All of us have been made stewards of something, certainly our souls, and most of us much more. Are you faithful to the Lord? Are you prepared for Christ's coming?**

Chapter 25: *Jesus teaches His disciples to be watchful concerning the final judgment. He unfolds His coming glory in the final judgment.*

25:1 *bridegroom*. Christ, the spiritual husband of the church (9:15; 22:2).
25:2 *wise . . . foolish*. Two terms often used in Scripture for those with the fear of God and those without it (Prov. 1:7; 14:16).
25:3–4 *no oil . . . took oil*. Only the wise were prepared to persevere through a long wait for the bridegroom (vv. 5–6; 24:48). *Oil* is sometimes a symbol of the Holy Spirit (Zech. 4:1–6).
25:10 *door was shut*. Judgment is decisive without any reversal.

Lord, Lord, open to us.
12 But he answered and said, Verily I say unto
you, I know you not.
13 Watch therefore, for ye know neither the day
nor the hour wherein the Son of man cometh.
14 ¶ For *the kingdom of heaven is* as a man
travelling into a far country, *who* called his own
servants, and delivered unto them his goods.
15 And unto one he gave five talents, to another
two, and to another one; to every man according to his several ability; and straightway took his
journey.
16 Then he that had received the five talents went
and traded with the same, and made *them* other
five talents.
17 And likewise he that *had received* two, he also
gained other two.
18 But he that had received one went and digged
in the earth, and hid his lord's money.
19 After a long time the lord of those servants
cometh, and reckoneth with them.
20 And so he that had received five talents came
and brought other five talents, saying, Lord, thou
deliveredst unto me five talents: behold, I have
gained beside them five talents more.
21 His lord said unto him, Well done, *thou* good
and faithful servant: thou hast been faithful over
a few things, I will make thee ruler over many
things: enter thou into the joy of thy lord.
22 He also that had received two talents came and
said, Lord, thou deliveredst unto me two talents:
behold, I have gained two other talents beside
them.
23 His lord said unto him, Well done, good and
faithful servant; thou hast been faithful over a few
things, I will make thee ruler over many things:
enter thou into the joy of thy lord.
24 Then he which had received the one talent
came and said, Lord, I knew thee that thou art an
hard man, reaping where thou hast not sown, and
gathering where thou hast not strawed:
25 And I was afraid, and went and hid thy talent
in the earth: lo, *there* thou hast *that is* thine.
26 His lord answered and said unto him, *Thou*
wicked and slothful servant, thou knewest that I
reap where I sowed not, and gather where I have
not strawed:
27 Thou oughtest therefore to have put my
money to the exchangers, and *then* at my coming I should have received mine own with usury.
28 Take therefore the talent from him, and give *it*
unto him which hath ten talents.
29 For unto every one that hath shall be given, and
he shall have abundance: but from him that hath
not shall be taken away even that which he hath.
30 And cast ye the unprofitable servant into outer
darkness: there shall be weeping and gnashing of
teeth.
31 ¶ When the Son of man shall come in his
glory, and all the holy angels with him, then shall
he sit upon the throne of his glory:
32 And before him shall be gathered all nations:
and he shall separate them one from another, as a
shepherd divideth *his* sheep from the goats:
33 And he shall set the sheep on his right hand,
but the goats on the left.
34 Then shall the King say unto them on his right
hand, Come, ye blessed of my Father, inherit the
kingdom prepared for you from the foundation
of the world:

25:11 *Lord, Lord.* The same words that Jesus earlier put in the mouths of religious hypocrites on judgment day (7:21–22).
25:12 *Verily.* Truly. *I know you not.* Christ was not intimately acquainted with them in a relationship of love and friendship (7:23; Ps. 1:6; John 10:27).
25:15 *talents.* A transliteration of a Greek word for large units of money, each the equivalent of a laborer's wages for 6,000 days or 20 years of work (18:24). They symbolize not only our skills (English "talents") but all our abilities and resources, for all is entrusted to us by God to use for His glory. *his several.* His own. In the judgment no one can excuse himself by saying God gave him more responsibility than he could handle.
25:19 The coming of the Lord is again depicted as being a *long time* away (vv. 5–6; 24:48). *reckoneth.* Settles accounts for the money they received (18:23–24).
25:21 *Well done.* The first reward of faithfulness is the Lord's praise (Rom. 2:29). *thou good and faithful servant.* The Lord uses a man's works to reveal and vindicate his character as a person transformed by God's grace (12:33–34; 15:13; Phil. 1:6; 2:13). *few things . . . ruler over many things.* Even substantial resources in this world (v. 15) are little in comparison to the rewards to be enjoyed in the kingdom. *joy of thy lord.* Christ will share His own eternal happiness with His servants.
25:22–23 The Lord gives the same praise and honor to the servant with *two talents* as to him with "five," (vv. 20–21) implying that Christ will reward not according to quantity of results but faithfulness with what He gives us.
25:24 *hard man.* This servant did not view the Lord with faith in His goodness and righteousness, but as a cruel, unreasonable, and unjust Master. Our view of God lies at the bottom of how we live and manage what God has given us, either for good or for ill. *strawed.* Scattered.
25:27 *exchangers.* Bankers. *usury.* Interest.
25:29 The unfaithful will lose not only the kingdom of God but also all the goods of this age.
25:31 *Son of man shall come in his glory.* Jesus will come again as the King who has received the incorruptible kingdom from "the Ancient of days" (Dan. 7:13–14).
25:32 *all nations.* A universal judgment, not exclusively Israel. *shepherd divideth his sheep from the goats.* At the end of the day, it was customary in the Ancient Near East to separate the *sheep* from the *goats* with a small pitch pipe or specific command.
25:33 *right hand.* The place of honor.
25:34 *inherit.* Receive as a gift from their *Father* (Gal. 4:7). *kingdom prepared for you from the foundation of the world.* Salvation is a gift of God's free and sovereign grace for the people He chose before creation (20:23; Eph. 1:4).
25:35–40 *an hungred.* Hungry (vv. 42,44). *meat.* Food of any kind (v. 42). Good works do not merit or deserve salvation in

35 For I was an hungred, and ye gave me meat: I
was thirsty, and ye gave me drink: I was a stranger,
and ye took me in:
36 Naked, and ye clothed me: I was sick, and ye
visited me: I was in prison, and ye came unto me.
37 Then shall the righteous answer him, saying,
Lord, when saw we thee an hungred, and fed *thee*?
or thirsty, and gave *thee* drink?
38 When saw we thee a stranger, and took *thee* in?
or naked, and clothed *thee*?
39 Or when saw we thee sick, or in prison, and
came unto thee?
40 And the King shall answer and say unto them,
Verily I say unto you, Inasmuch as ye have done *it*
unto one of the least of these my brethren, ye have
done *it* unto me.
41 Then shall he say also unto them on the left
hand, Depart from me, ye cursed, into everlasting
fire, prepared for the devil and his angels:
42 For I was an hungred, and ye gave me no meat:
I was thirsty, and ye gave me no drink:
43 I was a stranger, and ye took me not in: naked,
and ye clothed me not: sick, and in prison, and ye
visited me not.
44 Then shall they also answer him, saying, Lord,
when saw we thee an hungred, or athirst, or a
stranger, or naked, or sick, or in prison, and did
not minister unto thee?
45 Then shall he answer them, saying, Verily I say
unto you, Inasmuch as ye did *it* not to one of the
least of these, ye did *it* not to me.
46 And these shall go away into everlasting
punishment: but the righteous into life eternal.

CHAPTER 26

AND it came to pass, when Jesus had finished all
these sayings, he said unto his disciples,
2 Ye know that after two days is *the feast of* the
passover, and the Son of man is betrayed to be
crucified.
3 Then assembled together the chief priests, and
the scribes, and the elders of the people, unto the
palace of the high priest, who was called Caiaphas,
4 And consulted that they might take Jesus by
subtilty, and kill *him*.
5 But they said, Not on the feast *day*, lest there be
an uproar among the people.
6 ¶ Now when Jesus was in Bethany, in the house
of Simon the leper,
7 There came unto him a woman having an
alabaster box of very precious ointment, and
poured it on his head, as he sat *at meat*.
8 But when his disciples saw *it*, they had indigna-
tion, saying, To what purpose *is* this waste?
9 For this ointment might have been sold for
much, and given to the poor.
10 When Jesus understood *it*, he said unto them,
Why trouble ye the woman? for she hath wrought
a good work upon me.

---

any way, which is of grace alone (v. 34; Luke 17:10; Eph. 2:8–10), but works reveal that a person has been saved by grace and belongs to Christ's kingdom (5:20; 7:21), particularly works of mercy to believers (5:7; 10:42; 18:5; John 13:34–35; 1 John 3:10–19). *my brethren.* Christ identified with His people as their elder brother (12:48–50; Rom. 8:29). How we treat Christians is how we treat Christ (Acts 9:4).

25:41 *Depart from me.* Those who have rejected God will be rejected by Christ and forced out of all the benefits of His goodness (7:23). *cursed.* Pronounced guilty for breaking the law of God and worthy of God's anger and punishment (Deut. 28:15–19; Gal. 3:10). *everlasting fire.* Eternal suffering in hell under the wrath of God (see notes at 3:10,12).

25:46 *everlasting punishment . . . life eternal.* Both states are everlasting; neither the righteous nor the wicked will be annihilated or cease to exist, but will continue forever in the state assigned them on judgment day.

Thoughts for Personal/Family Worship: Chapter 25

1. **There is no middle category between foolish and wise, sheep and goats. We are one or the other. The parables of this chapter give us three tests of whether we are truly the Lord's people. First, are you prepared by God's Spirit to endure for a long wait before Christ returns? Second, are you actively serving Him now by taking the personal and material resources He has given you and employing them in your vocation for His glory? Third, are you responding with compassionate action to the needs of other Christians around you as members of one family in Christ? These are tests Christ will use on the judgment day, and we should judge ourselves by them now.**
2. **Christians need not fear the return of Christ, for the Son of God will come as the merciful older brother of God's children. Indeed, if we view Christ as a hard master who treats people unfairly, we must question whether we have faith in Him at all. However, true believers may sometimes view the judgment day with fear too. How can these parables give them comfort and hope?**

Jesus' Death and Resurrection (26:1—28:20)

Chapter 26: ***The plot to kill Jesus is finalized as Judas agrees to betray Him. Jesus keeps the Passover with His disciples, institutes the Lord's Supper, is arrested, and is brought to trial.***

Jesus' Feet Anointed (26:1–13)

26:1 *And it came to pass, when Jesus had finished.* A marker of the end of another major section of teaching (see note at 11:1). His teaching on the kingdom, begun in 4:17, is now completed and the gospel now turns to the narrative of Jesus' passion.

26:3 *Caiaphas.* The Jewish *high priest* (AD 18–36), at that time a political office appointed by Rome.

26:4 *subtilty.* Cunning.

26:6 *Simon the leper.* Not otherwise known.

26:7 *woman.* Mary, the sister of Lazarus (John 12:1–8). *alabaster.* Calcite mineral used as decorative stone. *very precious ointment.* Some sort of nard oil (Mark 14:3). *sat at meat.* Reclined at a meal.

26:8 *his disciples.* They were provoked and led by Judas in this criticism (John 12:4–6).

11 For ye have the poor always with you; but me
ye have not always.
12 For in that she hath poured this ointment on
my body, she did *it* for my burial.
13 Verily I say unto you, Wheresoever this gospel
shall be preached in the whole world, *there* shall
also this, that this woman hath done, be told for a
memorial of her.
14 ¶ Then one of the twelve, called Judas Iscariot,
went unto the chief priests,
15 And said *unto them*, What will ye give me, and
I will deliver him unto you? And they covenanted
with him for thirty pieces of silver.
16 And from that time he sought opportunity to
betray him.
17 ¶ Now the first *day* of the *feast of* unleavened
bread the disciples came to Jesus, saying unto
him, Where wilt thou that we prepare for thee to
eat the passover?
18 And he said, Go into the city to such a man,
and say unto him, The Master saith, My time is at
hand; I will keep the passover at thy house with
my disciples.
19 And the disciples did as Jesus had appointed
them; and they made ready the passover.
20 Now when the even was come, he sat down
with the twelve.
21 And as they did eat, he said, Verily I say unto
you, that one of you shall betray me.
22 And they were exceeding sorrowful, and
began every one of them to say unto him, Lord,
is it I?
23 And he answered and said, He that dippeth *his*
hand with me in the dish, the same shall betray
me.
24 The Son of man goeth as it is written of him:
but woe unto that man by whom the Son of man
is betrayed! it had been good for that man if he
had not been born.
25 Then Judas, which betrayed him, answered
and said, Master, is it I? He said unto him, Thou
hast said.
26 ¶ And as they were eating, Jesus took bread,
and blessed *it*, and brake *it*, and gave *it* to the
disciples, and said, Take, eat; this is my body.
27 And he took the cup, and gave thanks, and
gave *it* to them, saying, Drink ye all of it;
28 For this is my blood of the new testament,
which is shed for many for the remission of sins.
29 But I say unto you, I will not drink hence-
forth of this fruit of the vine, until that day when
I drink it new with you in my Father's kingdom.
30 And when they had sung an hymn, they went
out into the mount of Olives.
31 Then saith Jesus unto them, All ye shall
be offended because of me this night: for it is
written, I will smite the shepherd, and the sheep
of the flock shall be scattered abroad.
32 But after I am risen again, I will go before you
into Galilee.
33 Peter answered and said unto him, Though all
men shall be offended because of thee, *yet* will I
never be offended.
34 Jesus said unto him, Verily I say unto thee,

26:11 *poor always with you.* Jesus does not say that people should have no regard for the poor (25:35–36), but rather, that we should have things in proper perspective. Nothing should demand our love and affection more than Christ (10:37).

26:12 *she did it for my burial.* It was customary to anoint the body of the deceased with spices (Mark 16:1; Luke 24:1; John 19:38–40). Mary may have been one of the only ones who, having sat often at the feet of Jesus listening to his teaching (Luke 10:39), understood the need for Christ to die as a sacrifice and substitute.

26:13 *Verily.* Truly. *gospel . . . preached in the whole world.* See note at 24:14. *for a memorial of her.* To remember and honor her. She is a model of how our love for Christ should overflow in lavish devotion because He loved us and gave Himself for us.

Judas's Betrayal of Jesus (26:14–16)

26:14 *Judas Iscariot.* His covetous betrayal is sharply contrasted with the woman's extravagant love.

26:15 *thirty pieces of silver.* About four months' wages, the economic value of a slave (Ex. 21:32).

The Last Supper (26:17–29)

26:17–18 *My time is at hand.* It was the *passover* (Ex. 12:1–13), and so the Lamb of God must die to save His people from slavery to their sins and God's wrath (John 1:29; 1 Cor. 5:7; Rev. 5:6,9).

26:24 *as it is written of him.* Christ's death fulfilled Scripture, being foretold since the garden of Eden (Gen. 3:15). *woe unto that man.* God's sovereign appointment of Christ's death does not absolve him who murderously *betrayed* Christ. God's sovereignty does not negate human responsibility.

26:26–29 *bread . . . cup.* Jesus instituted the Lord's Supper, transforming the Passover meal into a remembrance of His redeeming death to be shared by His *disciples* until the *kingdom* comes (1 Cor. 10:16–17; 11:20–34). *this is my body.* The elements of the Lord's Supper are signs of Christ's death for His people, which, in conjunction with the Word, stir and confirm their faith in Him. There is no indication that Jesus intended them to see the bread as becoming or including His flesh physically, for He used the present tense (*this is*) while He stood physically before them prior to His death and resurrection. *blood of the new testament.* Christ's sacrifice is the foundation of God's gracious covenant with sinners (Jer. 31:31–34), redeeming them and binding God and His people together forever in spiritual union and communion (Ex. 24:8; Zech. 9:11; Heb. 9:15–22; 13:20). *remission.* Forgiveness. His death paid the price for their sins (20:28). *drink it new . . . in my Father's kingdom.* The results of the death of Christ will be fully applied when He comes again to make all things *new*, and so the Lord's Supper proclaims Christ's death until He comes (1 Cor. 11:26)

Jesus' Arrest (26:30–56)

26:31 *be offended.* Stumble, fall. They will abandon Him in His darkest hour (Zech. 13:7).

26:32 *go before you into Galilee.* The disciples' fall will not be final (Luke 22:32), but He will again unite with the disciples after the resurrection (28:10,16).

26:33 *I never.* Peter's pride and lack of self-knowledge

That this night, before the cock crow, thou shalt
deny me thrice.
35 Peter said unto him, Though I should die with
thee, yet will I not deny thee. Likewise also said all
the disciples.
36 ¶ Then cometh Jesus with them unto a place
called Gethsemane, and saith unto the disciples,
Sit ye here, while I go and pray yonder.
37 And he took with him Peter and the two sons
of Zebedee, and began to be sorrowful and very
heavy.
38 Then saith he unto them, My soul is exceeding
sorrowful, even unto death: tarry ye here, and
watch with me.
39 And he went a little further, and fell on his face,
and prayed, saying, O my Father, if it be possible,
let this cup pass from me: nevertheless not as I
will, but as thou *wilt*.
40 And he cometh unto the disciples, and findeth
them asleep, and saith unto Peter, What, could ye
not watch with me one hour?
41 Watch and pray, that ye enter not into temptation:
the spirit indeed *is* willing, but the flesh
is weak.
42 He went away again the second time, and
prayed, saying, O my Father, if this cup may not
pass away from me, except I drink it, thy will be
done.
43 And he came and found them asleep again: for
their eyes were heavy.
44 And he left them, and went away again, and
prayed the third time, saying the same words.
45 Then cometh he to his disciples, and saith
unto them, Sleep on now, and take *your* rest:
behold, the hour is at hand, and the Son of man is
betrayed into the hands of sinners.
46 Rise, let us be going: behold, he is at hand that
doth betray me.
47 ¶ And while he yet spake, lo, Judas, one of the
twelve, came, and with him a great multitude
with swords and staves, from the chief priests and
elders of the people.
48 Now he that betrayed him gave them a sign,
saying, Whomsoever I shall kiss, that same is he:
hold him fast.
49 And forthwith he came to Jesus, and said, Hail,
master; and kissed him.
50 And Jesus said unto him, Friend, wherefore art
thou come? Then came they, and laid hands on
Jesus, and took him.
51 And, behold, one of them which were with Jesus
stretched out *his* hand, and drew his sword,
and struck a servant of the high priest's, and
smote off his ear.
52 Then said Jesus unto him, Put up again thy
sword into his place: for all they that take the
sword shall perish with the sword.
53 Thinkest thou that I cannot now pray to my
Father, and he shall presently give me more than
twelve legions of angels?
54 But how then shall the scriptures be fulfilled,
that thus it must be?
55 In that same hour said Jesus to the multitudes,
Are ye come out as against a thief with swords and
staves for to take me? I sat daily with you teaching
in the temple, and ye laid no hold on me.
56 But all this was done, that the scriptures of the
prophets might be fulfilled. Then all the disciples
forsook him, and fled.
57 ¶ And they that had laid hold on Jesus led
him away to Caiaphas the high priest, where the
scribes and the elders were assembled.
58 But Peter followed him afar off unto the high
priest's palace, and went in, and sat with the
servants, to see the end.
59 Now the chief priests, and elders, and all the

---

led him to resist the authority of both Christ and the Old Testament (v. 31).

26:36 *Gethsemane*. Hebrew, "press for olive oil," a garden of olive trees on the Mount of Olives (v. 30; 24:3) across the brook Cedron east of Jerusalem (John 18:1). *yonder*. There.

26:37 *two sons of Zebedee*. James and John (4:21), who with *Peter* formed the inner circle of the disciples (10:2; 17:1). *sorrowful and very heavy*. The Son of God in His human nature began to suffer the crushing weight of sin.

26:38 *tarry*. Wait. *watch*. Stay awake and alert, implying prayer (vv. 36,40–41), an echo of His previous parables of waiting for the Son of man (24:42–43; 25:13).

26:39 *this cup*. A symbol for the wrath of God against sinners (Pss. 11:6; 75:8; Isa. 51:17,22; Jer. 25:15; Rev. 14:10; 16:19). Sensing the horror of God's anger against sin coming upon Him (Isa. 53:6), Jesus pled for a way of escape if any other means of saving sinners could be given (*if it be possible*). *not as I will, but as thou wilt*. Jesus saved sinners by submitting to God's will and obeying Him to the utmost (John 6:38–39; Phil. 2:8; Heb. 10:5–10).

26:41 *Watch and pray*. Two key acts in spiritual warfare (Eph. 6:18). *the spirit indeed is willing*. Even as they failed Him, Jesus graciously recognized the sincerity of their weak love for Him.

26:45 *the hour is at hand*. The consummation of His earthly ministry had arrived.

26:47 *staves*. Clubs (v. 55).

26:48–49 *kiss*. A normal greeting. *Hail, master*. "Greetings, Rabbi." Judas's hypocrisy was evident in his words and actions.

26:50 *Friend, wherefore art thou come?* Why have you come?—a probing question.

26:52 *Put up again thy sword*. Not a universal injunction for passivism (Rom. 13:4), but submission to God's will revealed in the Scriptures (vv. 54,56). *all they that take the sword shall perish with the sword*. Probably an allusion to God's law that murderers be killed (Gen. 9:6). Peter had no authority to exercise deadly force as a private individual.

26:53 *presently*. Immediately. *twelve legions*. A Roman legion was about 6,000 men. Jesus could have easily commanded 72,000 angels to come to His aid, implying that He is the Lord of hosts.

26:54 *scriptures be fulfilled*. There was a divine necessity about Christ's death (*it must be*; 16:21), for God had decreed it (Acts 2:23; 4:28) and revealed it in Scripture (vv. 24,31; 21:42; Luke 24:25–27,44).

council, sought false witness against Jesus, to put
him to death;
60 But found none: yea, though many false wit-
nesses came, *yet* found they none. At the last came
two false witnesses,
61 And said, This *fellow* said, I am able to destroy
the temple of God, and to build it in three days.
62 And the high priest arose, and said unto him,
Answerest thou nothing? what *is it which* these
witness against thee?
63 But Jesus held his peace. And the high priest
answered and said unto him, I adjure thee by the
living God, that thou tell us whether thou be the
Christ, the Son of God.
64 Jesus saith unto him, Thou hast said: never-
theless I say unto you, Hereafter shall ye see the
Son of man sitting on the right hand of power,
and coming in the clouds of heaven.
65 Then the high priest rent his clothes, saying,
He hath spoken blasphemy; what further need
have we of witnesses? behold, now ye have heard
his blasphemy.
66 What think ye? They answered and said, He is
guilty of death.
67 Then did they spit in his face, and buffeted
him; and others smote *him* with the palms of
their hands,
68 Saying, Prophesy unto us, thou Christ, Who is
he that smote thee?
69 ¶ Now Peter sat without in the palace: and a
damsel came unto him, saying, Thou also wast
with Jesus of Galilee.
70 But he denied before *them* all, saying, I know
not what thou sayest.
71 And when he was gone out into the porch, an-
other *maid* saw him, and said unto them that were
there, This *fellow* was also with Jesus of Nazareth.
72 And again he denied with an oath, I do not
know the man.
73 And after a while came unto *him* they that
stood by, and said to Peter, Surely thou also art
one of them; for thy speech bewrayeth thee.
74 Then began he to curse and to swear, *saying*,
I know not the man. And immediately the cock
crew.
75 And Peter remembered the word of Jesus,
which said unto him, Before the cock crow, thou
shalt deny me thrice. And he went out, and wept
bitterly.

CHAPTER 27

WHEN the morning was come, all the chief priests
and elders of the people took counsel against
Jesus to put him to death:
2 And when they had bound him, they led *him*
away, and delivered him to Pontius Pilate the
governor.
3 ¶ Then Judas, which had betrayed him, when
he saw that he was condemned, repented himself,

Jesus' Trial and Sentence (26:57—27:31)

26:59 *false witness.* The unjust trial of Jesus is an ironic witness to His sinlessness, for they could find nothing against Him, and to the wicked hypocrisy of mankind.

26:61 *destroy the temple . . . build it in three days.* Jesus had stated, "Destroy this temple, and in three days I will raise it up," but He spoke of His body (John 2:19–21).

26:63 *held his peace.* Jesus did not speak in self-defense, but quietly and meekly endured false accusations (27:14) in fulfillment of Scripture (Isa. 53:7). *adjure thee.* Charge you to swear solemnly.

26:64 *Thou hast said.* Christ affirmed the statement to be true (v. 25) that He is the Christ. *nevertheless.* Moreover. *Son of man sitting on the right hand of power, and coming in the clouds of heaven.* Christ claimed to be the promised Lord over all (Ps. 110:1; Dan. 7:13; cf. Matt. 16:27; 22:41–45; 24:30).

26:65 *blasphemy.* Man's sinful heart is such that he takes the most eminent truth and calls it the most eminent lie.

26:66 *guilty.* Worthy.

26:69 *without.* Outside. *damsel.* Young woman, servant girl.

26:73 *bewrayeth.* Betrays, reveals.

26:74 While Christ was confessing His identity under oath before the high council, one of His closest apostles was placing himself under oath to deny Him. The passion of Jesus reveals both the heights of His faithful love and the depths of human depravity.

26:75 *the word of Jesus.* Even in His deepest humiliation, Jesus was revealing that all things were taking place according to God's foreknowledge and plan (v. 54).

Thoughts for Personal/Family Worship: Chapter 26

1. **Christ deserves our all. Particularly, His willingness to die for sinners ought to elicit all our affection, adoration, and devotion, as it did in Mary. She is not only dedicated to an idea or a cause, but to the Person who loved her and died for her. Do you love Jesus Christ? How has His sacrificial love for His church moved you to pour out your life for Him?**
2. **Though Christ may have appeared like a helpless victim being abused by religious and civil leaders, His institution of the Lord's Supper shows that His suffering and death was not an accident or some tragedy. His death was appointed in order to accomplish redemption from sin and the full penalty it demanded. How does Christ's knowledge of what was to come and His submission to His Father's will increase your own love for Him?**

Chapter 27: ***Jesus' trials are completed. He is sentenced to death at the hands of the Romans. Judas hangs himself in ungodly remorse, and Jesus is killed and buried.***

27:2 *Pontius Pilate.* The *governor* of Judaea (AD 26–36). His name and title (prefect of Judaea) appear in a first-century inscription on the Pilate Stone, discovered in 1961. He was known to be insensitive toward the Jews and harsh in judicial matters (Luke 13:1). Though the Jewish leaders seemed to have had the authority to stone people to death (Acts 7:58), Christ would die by crucifixion, which was a Roman punishment. Also the leaders may have had legal restrictions

and brought again the thirty pieces of silver to the
chief priests and elders,
4 Saying, I have sinned in that I have betrayed the
innocent blood. And they said, What *is that* to us?
see thou *to that*.
5 And he cast down the pieces of silver in the
temple, and departed, and went and hanged
himself.
6 And the chief priests took the silver pieces,
and said, It is not lawful for to put them into the
treasury, because it is the price of blood.
7 And they took counsel, and bought with them
the potter's field, to bury strangers in.
8 Wherefore that field was called, The field of
blood, unto this day.
9 Then was fulfilled that which was spoken by
Jeremy the prophet, saying, And they took the
thirty pieces of silver, the price of him that was
valued, whom they of the children of Israel did
value;
10 And gave them for the potter's field, as the
Lord appointed me.
11 And Jesus stood before the governor: and the
governor asked him, saying, Art thou the King of
the Jews? And Jesus said unto him, Thou sayest.
12 And when he was accused of the chief priests
and elders, he answered nothing.
13 Then said Pilate unto him, Hearest thou not
how many things they witness against thee?
14 And he answered him to never a word;
insomuch that the governor marvelled greatly.
15 Now at *that* feast the governor was wont to re-
lease unto the people a prisoner, whom they would.
16 And they had then a notable prisoner, called
Barabbas.
17 Therefore when they were gathered together,
Pilate said unto them, Whom will ye that I release
unto you? Barabbas, or Jesus which is called
Christ?
18 For he knew that for envy they had delivered
him.
19 ¶ When he was set down on the judgment seat,
his wife sent unto him, saying, Have thou nothing
to do with that just man: for I have suffered many
things this day in a dream because of him.
20 But the chief priests and elders persuaded the
multitude that they should ask Barabbas, and
destroy Jesus.
21 The governor answered and said unto them,
Whether of the twain will ye that I release unto
you? They said, Barabbas.
22 Pilate saith unto them, What shall I do then
with Jesus which is called Christ? *They* all say unto
him, Let him be crucified.
23 And the governor said, Why, what evil hath
he done? But they cried out the more, saying, Let
him be crucified.
24 ¶ When Pilate saw that he could prevail
nothing, but *that* rather a tumult was made, he
took water, and washed *his* hands before the
multitude, saying, I am innocent of the blood of
this just person: see ye *to it*.
25 Then answered all the people, and said, His
blood *be* on us, and on our children.
26 ¶ Then released he Barabbas unto them: and
when he had scourged Jesus, he delivered *him* to
be crucified.
27 Then the soldiers of the governor took Jesus
into the common hall, and gathered unto him the
whole band *of soldiers*.
28 And they stripped him, and put on him a
scarlet robe.
29 ¶ And when they had platted a crown of
thorns, they put *it* upon his head, and a reed in his
right hand: and they bowed the knee before him,
and mocked him, saying, Hail, King of the Jews!
30 And they spit upon him, and took the reed,
and smote him on the head.
31 And after that they had mocked him, they
took the robe off from him, and put his own rai-
ment on him, and led him away to crucify *him*.
32 And as they came out, they found a man of

about exacting the death penalty on or near feast days. At any rate, Christ would be crucified with the approval of all in authority at the time.

27:3–4 *repented ... I have sinned.* Though Judas felt remorse, his sorrow over sin was no true repentance (2 Cor. 7:10), for he never turned back to the Lord, trusting in His mercy (Luke 15:17–19).

27:9 *Then was fulfilled.* The act of Judas hanging himself and the purchase of the field was prophesied by the prophets Zechariah (Zech. 11:12–13) and Jeremiah (*Jeremy*; Jer. 19:1–13).

27:11 *Art thou the King.* Pilate's question was meant to see if Jesus was posing a challenge to Caesar's rule. *Thou sayest.* Jesus affirmed that He is a King, though not an earthly, political king (John 18:36).

27:15 *wont.* Used, accustomed.

27:16–19 *Barabbas.* A murderer and violent rebel against civil authority (Mark 15:7; Luke 23:18–19). Rather than courageously releasing innocent Jesus in an act of justice, Pilate showed his cowardice in trying to manipulate the crowds into choosing Jesus over this wicked criminal, and ultimately giving in to the murder of a man whom he knew to be righteous (*just*).

27:21 *Whether of the twain.* Which of the two.

27:25 *His blood be on us, and on our children.* This verse has been illegitimately used to justify hatred of the Jews, ignoring the facts: Gentiles were also culpable in Christ's death, Gentiles are no better by nature than Jews, Jesus and His first disciples were all Jews, and a few weeks after Christ's crucifixion Peter held out to these Jerusalem sinners the gospel with its call to repentance and forgiveness (Acts 2:36–40; 3:14–20).

27:26 *scourged.* Flogged with a short leather cord of nine strands, which contained sharp pieces of bone or metal and lead balls tied to the end. The scourging would rip the victim's back apart exposing muscle and bone.

27:27–31 *whole band.* A Roman cohort, a unit of about 600 soldiers. *platted.* Twisted. *crown of thorns.* The Romans

Cyrene, Simon by name: him they compelled to
bear his cross.
33 And when they were come unto a place called
Golgotha, that is to say, a place of a skull,
34 ¶ They gave him vinegar to drink mingled
with gall: and when he had tasted *thereof*, he
would not drink.
35 And they crucified him, and parted his
garments, casting lots: that it might be fulfilled
which was spoken by the prophet, They parted
my garments among them, and upon my vesture
did they cast lots.
36 And sitting down they watched him there;
37 And set up over his head his accusation
written, THIS IS JESUS THE KING OF THE
JEWS.
38 Then were there two thieves crucified with
him, one on the right hand, and another on the
left.
39 ¶ And they that passed by reviled him, wag-
ging their heads,
40 And saying, Thou that destroyest the temple,
and buildest *it* in three days, save thyself. If thou
be the Son of God, come down from the cross.
41 Likewise also the chief priests mocking *him*,
with the scribes and elders, said,
42 He saved others; himself he cannot save. If
he be the King of Israel, let him now come down
from the cross, and we will believe him.
43 He trusted in God; let him deliver him now, if
he will have him: for he said, I am the Son of God.
44 The thieves also, which were crucified with
him, cast the same in his teeth.
45 Now from the sixth hour there was darkness
over all the land unto the ninth hour.
46 And about the ninth hour Jesus cried with
a loud voice, saying, Eli, Eli, lama sabachthani?
that is to say, My God, my God, why hast thou
forsaken me?
47 Some of them that stood there, when they
heard *that*, said, This *man* calleth for Elias.
48 And straightway one of them ran, and took a
spunge, and filled *it* with vinegar, and put *it* on a
reed, and gave him to drink.
49 The rest said, Let be, let us see whether Elias
will come to save him.
50 ¶ Jesus, when he had cried again with a loud
voice, yielded up the ghost.
51 And, behold, the veil of the temple was rent in
twain from the top to the bottom; and the earth
did quake, and the rocks rent;
52 And the graves were opened; and many bodies
of the saints which slept arose,
53 And came out of the graves after his resurrec-
tion, and went into the holy city, and appeared
unto many.
54 Now when the centurion, and they that were
with him, watching Jesus, saw the earthquake, and
those things that were done, they feared greatly,
saying, Truly this was the Son of God.
55 And many women were there beholding
afar off, which followed Jesus from Galilee,
ministering unto him:
56 Among which was Mary Magdalene, and Mary

---

intended it as a painful and bloody mockery of Christ's kingship, but it was a visible reminder that Christ suffered the curse of man's fall (Gen. 3:18). *Hail, King of the Jews!* They mocked Jesus as the supposed king of a conquered and humiliated people. *raiment.* Clothing, attire.

Jesus' Death and Burial (27:32–66)

27:34 *vinegar . . . mingled with gall.* Perhaps a mild sedative for those crucified, which Christ refused.

27:35 *crucified him.* A cruel and humiliating form of death while suspended on a wooden cross, said by the Roman orator Cicero to be so disgusting as not to be discussed by Roman citizens. The belongings of the crucified person went to the execution detail, who in this instance were *casting lots* to determine who received Jesus' clothes, unwittingly fulfilling Scripture (Ps. 22:18).

27:37 *accusation.* The placard (Latin *titulus*) that carried the charges. Man derides Christ here, but God glorifies His Son here, for on the cross Christ conquered (Col. 2:14–15).

27:38 *two thieves . . . with him.* He was counted among the transgressors (Isa. 53:12).

27:39–43 *reviled.* Insulted. *wagging their heads . . . He trusted in God; let him deliver him.* The mockery of the wicked fulfilled the Scriptures (Ps. 22:7), proving the very thing that they denied, that Jesus is the *King of Israel*, the Christ. *If thou be the Son of God.* The very words of Satan (4:3).

27:44 *cast the same in his teeth.* Insulted Him in the same way.

27:45 *darkness.* A sign of God's judgment (8:12; Ex. 10:21–23; Isa. 5:30; Joel 2:30–31; Amos 5:18,20; etc.). The wrath of God came upon His Son as God counted the sins of His people against Him (2 Cor. 5:21).

27:46 *why hast thou forsaken me?* Christ was suffering the divine rejection and abandonment that sinners deserve (7:23; 25:41; Jer. 7:29; 23:39), again in fulfillment of Scripture (Ps. 22:1).

27:47 *Elias.* Elijah, the bystanders' misunderstanding of Jesus' cry, "Eli" or "my God" (v. 46). They did not understand at the time what Christ was doing. He died alone.

27:50 *yielded up the ghost.* Perhaps, an idiomatic way to say that He died; not necessarily a way of showing that Jesus determined when He would die (John 10:18).

27:51 *veil of the temple.* This is the curtain that separated the holy place from the most holy place. *rent in twain.* Torn in two. The ceremonial law was abolished and the way into God's presence opened by faith in Jesus Christ (Eph. 2:14–22; Heb. 10:19–22).

27:52–53 *graves were opened . . . after his resurrection.* Christ conquered death by His death and resurrection (Heb. 2:14; Rev. 1:18). Believers in Christ have eternal life now and in the resurrection to come (John 11:25–27).

27:54 *Truly . . . the Son of God.* Christ's death is powerful to save sinners, converting even a Gentile *centurion* at His crucifixion (John 12:31–33; Rev. 5:9).

27:55 *many women.* Not all at the cross mocked Jesus; these faithful disciples watched in sorrow.

27:57 *even.* Afternoon or evening. It was important that Jesus be buried before sunset so that they would not break the Sabbath. *rich man.* Thus Christ was buried in a rich man's

the mother of James and Joses, and the mother of
Zebedee's children.
57 When the even was come, there came a rich
man of Arimathaea, named Joseph, who also
himself was Jesus' disciple:
58 He went to Pilate, and begged the body of
Jesus. Then Pilate commanded the body to be
delivered.
59 And when Joseph had taken the body, he
wrapped it in a clean linen cloth,
60 And laid it in his own new tomb, which he had
hewn out in the rock: and he rolled a great stone
to the door of the sepulchre, and departed.
61 And there was Mary Magdalene, and the other
Mary, sitting over against the sepulchre.
62 ¶ Now the next day, that followed the day of
the preparation, the chief priests and Pharisees
came together unto Pilate,
63 Saying, Sir, we remember that that deceiver
said, while he was yet alive, After three days I will
rise again.
64 Command therefore that the sepulchre be
made sure until the third day, lest his disciples
come by night, and steal him away, and say unto
the people, He is risen from the dead: so the last
error shall be worse than the first.
65 Pilate said unto them, Ye have a watch: go your
way, make *it* as sure as ye can.
66 So they went, and made the sepulchre sure,
sealing the stone, and setting a watch.

CHAPTER 28

IN the end of the sabbath, as it began to dawn to-
ward the first *day* of the week, came Mary Mag-
dalene and the other Mary to see the sepulchre.
2 And, behold, there was a great earthquake: for
the angel of the Lord descended from heaven, and
came and rolled back the stone from the door,
and sat upon it.
3 His countenance was like lightning, and his
raiment white as snow:
4 And for fear of him the keepers did shake, and
became as dead *men*.
5 And the angel answered and said unto the
women, Fear not ye: for I know that ye seek Jesus,
which was crucified.
6 He is not here: for he is risen, as he said. Come,
see the place where the Lord lay.
7 And go quickly, and tell his disciples that he is
risen from the dead; and, behold, he goeth before
you into Galilee; there shall ye see him: lo, I have
told you.
8 And they departed quickly from the sepulchre
with fear and great joy; and did run to bring his
disciples word.
9 ¶ And as they went to tell his disciples, behold,
Jesus met them, saying, All hail. And they came
and held him by the feet, and worshipped him.
10 Then said Jesus unto them, Be not afraid: go
tell my brethren that they go into Galilee, and
there shall they see me.

tomb as prophesied (Isa. 53:9).
27:60 *hewn*. Cut. *sepulchre*. Tomb.
27:64 *made sure*. Secured.
27:65 *Ye have a watch*. Or possibly, "Take a watch," referring to a group of guards.

Thoughts for Personal/Family Worship: Chapter 27

1. **Note Judas's false repentance. It was not what Paul would later call a godly sorrow, but the sorrow of the world that brings death (2 Cor. 7:10–11). Remorse over what we have done may simply be the acting of our natural conscience. True repentance involves dying to sin and rising to newness of life by God's grace at work in us. How have you experienced godly sorrow that leads to true repentance?**
2. **Christ's suffering at the hands of men was terrible. Being forsaken by His Father, however, was the worst part of Christ's sufferings. He bore the iniquity of His people and He did so as a public person, as the representative and head of all His people. He was made a curse that the blessing might flow to all who believe, both Jews and Gentiles (Gal. 3:10–14). How do Christ's sufferings in this chapter reveal what our sins deserve? How do they show the love of God?**
3. **Scripture had prophesied many aspects of Christ's sufferings. His death was an amazing confirmation of the faithfulness of God to His promises (Rom. 15:8). Nature itself testified to the great significance of this event. Yet, most people present at the time were blind to anything other than a man suffering on a cross. Has the Spirit opened your eyes to see what you deserve as you look at Christ's suffering and death? Have you seen by faith that the veil has been rent (v.51) between God and sinners, so that sinners now have access to God through Christ's blood?**

Chapter 28: *Jesus is raised from the dead. He ascends into heaven giving His disciples the Great Commission to go out and preach the gospel to all nations.*

Jesus' Resurrection and the Great Commission (28:1–20)

28:1 *first day of the week*. Emphasized by all the Gospels (Mark 16:2,9; Luke 24:1; John 20:1) as the day when the light of the risen Christ *began to dawn* on the new creation (Gen. 1:3–5; Eph. 5:14) and the new tabernacle was built (Ex. 40:2, 17; John 2:19–21), the Lord's Day when the church subsequently gathered (Acts 20:7; 1 Cor. 16:2; cf. Rev. 1:10). Jesus was in the tomb from Friday night until Sunday morning, three days according to the Jewish method of counting partial days as whole days (12:40).
28:2–3 *great earthquake . . . lightning*. Signs of God's coming in His glory (Ex. 19:16,18; Ps. 18:7,14). *rolled back the stone*. To show that the tomb was empty. *countenance*. Appearance, here similar to other biblical appearances of angels (Dan. 10:6; Acts 1:10; Rev. 10:1; 15:6). *raiment*. Clothing. *white as snow*. Reminiscent of the Ancient of days, perhaps signifying that the Son of man had received His promised glory and dominion (Dan. 7:9, 13–14; cf. Matt. 28:18).
28:4 *keepers*. Guards. Those charged to prevent any mischief at the tomb (27:65–66) found themselves utterly powerless in the presence of God's heavenly soldiers.
28:7 *he goeth before you into Galilee*. As Jesus had said before His death (26:32).
28:9 *All hail*. Literally, "Greetings." *worshipped him*. Worship belongs to God alone (4:10), but Christ accepted their

11 ¶ Now when they were going, behold, some of
the watch came into the city, and shewed unto the
chief priests all the things that were done.
12 And when they were assembled with the
elders, and had taken counsel, they gave large
money unto the soldiers,
13 Saying, Say ye, His disciples came by night,
and stole him *away* while we slept.
14 And if this come to the governor's ears, we will
persuade him, and secure you.
15 So they took the money, and did as they were
taught: and this saying is commonly reported
among the Jews until this day.

16 ¶ Then the eleven disciples went away
into Galilee, into a mountain where Jesus had
appointed them.
17 And when they saw him, they worshipped
him: but some doubted.
18 And Jesus came and spake unto them, saying,
All power is given unto me in heaven and in earth.
19 ¶ Go ye therefore, and teach all nations,
baptizing them in the name of the Father, and of
the Son, and of the Holy Ghost:
20 Teaching them to observe all things what-
soever I have commanded you: and, lo, I am with
you alway, *even* unto the end of the world. Amen.

---

adoration (14:33), for He is the Lord (vv. 17–18).

28:13 *His disciples . . . stole him.* These stories were known to be circulating in the days of Justin Martyr (c. AD 150).

28:17 *worshipped . . . some doubted.* Outward worship does not necessarily indicate inward faith, and the disciples struggled to believe that Jesus was raised from the dead (Luke 24:37; John 20:24–29).

28:18 *All power.* Fullness of authority, which Christ had already demonstrated in His teaching, miracles, forgiveness of sin, and casting out of demons (7:29; 8:8–9; 9:6–8; 10:1). *given unto me.* As the Son of God, Christ has always shared the same divine omnipotence as the Father to rule over creation (8:26–27; 11:27; John 1:1–3). However as Mediator, having faithfully obeyed the Father to the death, Christ entered into a new state of exaltation upon His resurrection from the dead (Phil. 2:8–9). The glorified God-man received authority over all earthly and heavenly beings (Ps. 110:1–4; Dan. 7:13–14,27) in order to apply salvation to the elect from every nation (Ps. 2:7–12; John 17:1–2).

28:19 *Go ye therefore.* The disciples' mission in the world rests on Jesus' authority as Lord of all (v. 18). *teach.* Or make disciples. *all nations.* The era in which God focuses His work upon physical Israel has ended (10:5–6; 15:24; 21:43), and the promise to Abraham is now being fulfilled through the Son of Abraham (1:1; Gen. 12:3; 22:18). *baptizing.* A sign and seal of the cleansing power of Christ's blood and Spirit for those who repent of sin and trust in Him (3:1–11; Acts 2:38). *Ghost.* Spirit. Like Jesus' own baptism (3:16–17), the trinitarian baptism of Christians signifies that the nature of the one and only God (singular *name*) belongs to three distinct persons who are related to each other as Father, Son, and Spirit, one of the clearest pronouncements of the Trinity in the Bible (2 Cor. 13:14).

28:20 *Teaching.* Instructing (a different Greek word than in v. 19). There is no baptizing without teaching, for the signs are grounded in the Word. *observe.* Keep, obey God's laws (19:17). Salvation does not release Christians from obedience, but frees them from sin (1:21) to obey *all* of Christ's commands. *with you alway.* Though the church's call to obey Christ's Word and to evangelize the world seems impossible, the promise of "Emmanuel" stands: God is with us in Christ (1:23; 18:20). By His Word and Spirit He will remain with believers, and empower them to fulfill all their calling. *unto the end of the world.* Christ's spiritual presence with the church militant will be replaced by His visible presence with the church triumphant when He returns in glory (13:39–43,49; 24:3,14).

Thoughts for Personal/Family Worship: Chapter 28

1. **Christ is alive. The veracity of the resurrection is well established by eyewitness accounts in the Word of God. It is not a fairy tale or myth, but a fact of history. Yet Christ is more than a fact—He is a living person who meets us by His Word and Spirit. He deserves our worship, not just the bowing of our bodies but the trust of our hearts and obedience of our lives. How do you relate to Jesus Christ on a personal level? How does His infinite authority (v. 18) appear in your life?**
2. **Christ has all authority in heaven and on earth. Neither demons nor any earthly power can stop the expansion of His kingdom. He claims people from every nation for His disciples, having bought them with His blood. He has commissioned His church to make disciples of all nations, beginning with the apostles and continuing today. His great means are the law, the gospel, and the ordinances of worship commanded in His Word. His promise is His abiding presence with His church by His Spirit. How should these truths press upon the conscience of the church its duty to reach the world with the truth of Christ? How can these truths encourage the church to do its mission with hope, confidence, and perseverance? What do these truths teach us about the methods that the church should use to faithfully fulfill its mission?**

INTRODUCTION TO THE BOOK OF
SAINT MARK

Authorship: Though this gospel does not mention its author, church history has consistently associated John Mark with this second canonical gospel. The church father Papias (c. AD 70–150) is perhaps the earliest documented reference we have to John Mark's authorship of this Gospel. Later church fathers like Justin Martyr, Irenaeus, and Eusebius all verified this early reference.

We know little about John Mark from the New Testament. He is first mentioned among those who met at his wealthy mother's home in Jerusalem with the early church (Acts 12:12–17). We know that Mark was a close associate of Paul, Barnabas, and Peter (Acts 15:37,39; Col. 4:10; 2 Tim. 4:11; Philem. 24).

The relationship between Mark and Peter is of great interest. It is reported that Mark and Peter ministered together in Rome in the late fifties or early sixties (1 Peter 5:13). Mark is thought to have learned of the earthly ministry of Jesus through Peter, though he himself may have had some associations with Jesus while he was still alive. The similarities between Peter's preaching in Acts 10:34–43 and Mark's Gospel are often cited as corroborating evidence that Mark essentially gives us Peter's record of Christ's life, death, and resurrection.

Date: The dating of Mark has posed some difficulties throughout church history. The lynchpin seems to be how one is to interpret an extra-biblical source that speaks of Mark writing his gospel after "the exodus" of Paul and Peter. While some assume that their exodus means "death" (AD 67–68), which is a real possibility, others believe it may simply refer to their leaving Rome. Early church sources defend both positions.

Irenaeus supported the view that Mark wrote his gospel after their deaths. His conclusions are defended by Papias and an extra-biblical document titled *The Anti-Marcionite Prologue*. However, Clement of Alexandria and Origen both argue that Mark wrote while Peter was still alive. The dating issue is relatively complicated.

It is probable that Mark wrote his gospel from Rome. He uses Latin terms, at times, in preference to Greek terms, while also explaining Jewish custom to his Gentile audience (Mark 3:17; 5:41; 7:11,34; etc.). In 15:21 there is a reference to Rufus, who we know to have lived in Rome and who had been a part of the church in Rome (Rom. 16:13). This places the writing of Mark sometime within the time of Peter and Mark's ministry in Rome, but this still does not resolve the dating issue. The generally accepted date has been AD 65 to 68, though some have argued for an earlier date of AD 45 to 60.

Theme: The good news of Jesus Christ, the Son of God, the Son of Man, and the Suffering Servant of the Lord, who unveils His glory in His words and works and through suffering to save people from sin.

Purpose: To call sinners to repent and believe in the powerful Son of God to save them from sin.

Synopsis: *The Contribution of Mark to Redemptive Revelation*

Mark defines his work explicitly as "gospel" (1:1), which literally translated means "good news." Whereas the Gospel of Matthew presents several large blocks of Jesus' teachings, the good news of Mark largely consists not of teaching (though see 4:1–41; 13:1–37) but of action. (For those interested in doing a comparative study of the Synoptic Gospels, throughout these study notes on Mark are cross-references to parallel passages in Matthew and Luke.) In other words, the gospel as presented in Mark is not an abstract set of principles but the history of a person and His works, a history presented and explained here as rich in meaning and significance for our faith and obedience. The narrative of Mark is fast-paced, and he frequently uses the word "immediately" (often translated in the KJV as "straightway," "forthwith," "anon," or "as soon as") to communicate the energy with which God fulfilled His divine work through His Son—this occurs about forty times, appearing in every chapter except chs. 12, 13, and 16.

John the Baptist announced the coming of Jesus as the fulfillment of prophecy and called for repentance. He baptized Jesus, who in turn would baptize believers with the Holy Spirit and with fire. Jesus was tempted by the Devil but came forth from this temptation preaching the gospel with power and performing miracles. As He showed the glory of the kingdom by teaching and healing, opposition grew. Among controversies over the Sabbath, and who is authorized to forgive sins, some accused Him of working through the power of Beelzebub, the prince of the demons. Christ proved that He is the Stronger One who has entered the strong one's house and bound him. Christ began to teach in parables, through which the distinction between insiders (disciples) and outsiders became more pronounced.

Even the disciples, however, were slow to understand. Christ's multiplying the loaves to the 5,000 and 4,000 became occasions that revealed the disciples' hardness of heart. Though Peter confessed Christ to be the Son of God, and on the Mount of Transfiguration the Father showed the glory of Christ, the disciples did not yet see that glory, especially as it involved the suffering and death of Christ. Christ entered Jerusalem hailed as the Son of David, but, mysteriously to the disciples, pronounced the end of the temple. The significance of Christ's sufferings came into view as Christ was anointed by Mary and as He instituted the Lord's Supper with His disciples. The arrest, trial, and crucifixion of Christ proceeded in rapid succession and climaxed as a Roman centurion confessed that He was indeed the Son of God (15:39). The Gospel ends with the report of the resurrection and the appearances of Christ, until we see Him seated at the right hand of God in heaven (16:19), working through His disciples as they preached and performed signs (v. 20).

Outline:

I. Introduction to Jesus' Public Ministry (1:1–13)

II. The Galilean Period: Ministry around the Sea of Galilee (1:14—5:43)
- A. The Beginning of Jesus' Preaching (1:14–15)
- B. Call of the First Disciples (1:16–20)
- C. Miracles and Preaching (1:21—2:12)
- D. Call of Levi (2:13–17)
- E. Controversies in Galilee (2:18—3:6)
- F. Followers of Jesus (3:7–19)
- G. Further Opposition (3:20–35)
- H. Teaching in Parables (4:1–41)
- I. Healing Demoniacs (5:1–20)
- J. Jesus Returns to Galilee (5:21–43)

III. The Galilean Period: Further Journeys in Galilee (6:1—9:50)
- A. Jesus Rejected at Nazareth (6:1–6)
- B. Jesus Sends out the Twelve (6:7–13)
- C. John the Baptist Beheaded (6:14–29)
- D. Feeding the Five Thousand (6:30–44)
- E. Healing in Gennesaret (6:45–56)
- F. Pharisees Accuse Jesus (7:1–23)
- G. Ministry in Tyre, Sidon, and the Decapolis (7:24—8:9)
- H. Pharisees' Challenge in Dalmanutha (8:10–12)
- I. Pharisees' Leaven (8:13–21)
- J. Healing in Bethsaida (8:22–26)
- K. Ministry in Caesarea Philippi (8:27—9:32)
- L. Return to Capernaum (9:33–50)

IV. The Judaean Period (10:1—13:37)
- A. Jesus Travels to Jerusalem (10:1–52)
- B. Triumphal Entry (11:1–26)
- C. Public Teaching and Questions (11:27—12:44)
- D. End Times (13:1–37)

V. The Passion, Death, and Resurrection of the Son of God (14:1—16:20)
- A. Plot to Kill Jesus (14:1–2)
- B. Jesus Anointed at Bethany (14:3–9)

C. Judas's Betrayal (14:10–11)
D. The Last Supper (14:12–31)
E. Jesus' Arrest (14:32–52)
F. Jesus' Trial (14:53—15:20)
G. Jesus' Death and Burial (15:21–47)
H. Jesus' Resurrection and Ascension (16:1–20)

THE GOSPEL ACCORDING TO SAINT

MARK

CHAPTER 1

THE beginning of the gospel of Jesus Christ, the
Son of God;
2 As it is written in the prophets, Behold, I send
my messenger before thy face, which shall prepare
thy way before thee.
3 The voice of one crying in the wilderness,
Prepare ye the way of the Lord, make his paths
straight.
4 John did baptize in the wilderness, and preach
the baptism of repentance for the remission of sins.
5 And there went out unto him all the land of Ju-
daea, and they of Jerusalem, and were all baptized
of him in the river of Jordan, confessing their sins.
6 And John was clothed with camel's hair, and
with a girdle of a skin about his loins; and he did
eat locusts and wild honey;
7 And preached, saying, There cometh one
mightier than I after me, the latchet of whose
shoes I am not worthy to stoop down and unloose.
8 I indeed have baptized you with water: but he
shall baptize you with the Holy Ghost.
9 And it came to pass in those days, that Jesus
came from Nazareth of Galilee, and was baptized
of John in Jordan.
10 And straightway coming up out of the water,
he saw the heavens opened, and the Spirit like a
dove descending upon him:
11 And there came a voice from heaven, *saying*,
Thou art my beloved Son, in whom I am well
pleased.
12 And immediately the Spirit driveth him into
the wilderness.
13 And he was there in the wilderness forty days,
tempted of Satan; and was with the wild beasts;
and the angels ministered unto him.

Chapter 1: ***John the Baptist prepares for Christ's coming in accordance with the prophets. Christ is baptized and tempted in the wilderness. Christ teaches and does miracles in Galilee.***

INTRODUCTION TO JESUS' PUBLIC MINISTRY (1:1–13)

1:1 *gospel.* Good news, what God has done to save His people from their sin. *Son of God.* Divine title for Jesus used often in Mark in connection to His unique relationship to the Father and His majestic Lordship over the demons (v. 11; 3:11; 5:7; 9:7; 12:6; 13:32; 14:61–62; 15:39).

1:2–6 See parallels in Matt. 3:1–6; Luke 3:1–6.

1:2–3 *written in the prophets.* John was the herald of the messianic King (Isa. 40:3; Mal. 3:1). In their context, these prophecies speak of the arrival of the Owner of the temple and prepare for the coming of *the Lord* (*Jehovah*).

1:4 *repentance.* A grace of God whereby we turn from sin to God in trust and obedience (2:17; Isa. 1:16–18; Ezek. 18:30–32). *remission.* Forgiveness.

1:5 *Jordan.* The Lord dried up this *river* so that Israel could pass through it when the people entered the Promised Land (Josh. 3:1—4:24). It was associated with Elijah (1 Kings 17:3,5; 2 Kings 2:6–7,13), and a Gentile was healed of leprosy by washing in it (2 Kings 5:10,14). *confessing their sins.* John evidently did not preach a political savior but a Savior from sin (cf. Matt. 1:21).

1:6 *camel's hair . . . eat locusts and wild honey.* John the Baptist's lifestyle of simplicity was a visual demonstration of repentance from a life of luxury (Matt. 11:8) and a statement of his continuity with Old Testament prophets (Zech. 13:4), especially Elijah (2 Kings 1:8; Mal. 4:5).

1:7–11 See parallels in Matt. 3:11–17; Luke 3:15–22.

1:7 *latchet of whose shoes.* The straps of His sandals. John preached that Christ was in an entirely different category from the prophets, far *mightier* and worthy of infinitely more honor.

1:8 *baptize you with the Holy Ghost.* God's ministers can only baptize the body *with water*, but the Lord gives the Holy Spirit (Acts 1:5; 2:38; 11:16; 1 Cor. 12:13).

1:9 *in those days.* Probably a reference to the height of John's ministry.

1:10 *straightway.* Immediately, a common term throughout Mark's Gospel. *he saw.* Not a private vision but a public manifestation of God (cf. John 1:32–34). *the Spirit . . . descending.* Anointing Jesus with power for His ministry (Isa. 11:2; 61:1). *like a dove.* A sign associated with gentleness (Matt. 10:16), sorrow (Isa. 38:14; 59:11), and new creation (Gen. 1:2; 8:10).

1:11 *my beloved Son, in whom I am well pleased.* In speaking to Jesus (*Thou*), the Father manifests Himself to be a person distinct from the Son and the Spirit, though the three are one God. The anointing of the Spirit and the Father's words indicated that Jesus is the Servant-King through whom God will establish His kingdom of justice on the earth (Ps. 2:7; Isa. 42:1).

1:12–13 See parallels in Matt. 4:1–11; Luke 4:1–13.

1:12 *Spirit driveth him into the wilderness.* As the Spirit led Israel in a wilderness where they were tested (Isa. 63:10–14; cf. Ex. 13:20–21; 16:1—17:14), and in contrast to Adam's temptation in a garden (Gen. 3:1–6). Though they failed, Jesus stood firm in obedience, showing Himself to be the last Adam and the true Israel.

1:13 *forty days.* A duration of time associated with meeting with God (Ex. 24:18; 34:28) and a testing of faith (Num. 13:25;

14 Now after that John was put in prison, Jesus came into Galilee, preaching the gospel of the kingdom of God,
15 And saying, The time is fulfilled, and the kingdom of God is at hand: repent ye, and believe the gospel.
16 Now as he walked by the sea of Galilee, he saw Simon and Andrew his brother casting a net into the sea: for they were fishers.
17 And Jesus said unto them, Come ye after me, and I will make you to become fishers of men.
18 And straightway they forsook their nets, and followed him.
19 And when he had gone a little further thence, he saw James the *son* of Zebedee, and John his brother, who also were in the ship mending their nets.
20 And straightway he called them: and they left their father Zebedee in the ship with the hired servants, and went after him.
21 And they went into Capernaum; and straightway on the sabbath day he entered into the synagogue, and taught.
22 And they were astonished at his doctrine: for he taught them as one that had authority, and not as the scribes.
23 And there was in their synagogue a man with an unclean spirit; and he cried out,
24 Saying, Let *us* alone; what have we to do with thee, thou Jesus of Nazareth? art thou come to destroy us? I know thee who thou art, the Holy One of God.
25 And Jesus rebuked him, saying, Hold thy peace, and come out of him.
26 And when the unclean spirit had torn him, and cried with a loud voice, he came out of him.
27 And they were all amazed, insomuch that they questioned among themselves, saying, What thing is this? what new doctrine *is* this? for with authority commandeth he even the unclean spirits, and they do obey him.
28 And immediately his fame spread abroad throughout all the region round about Galilee.
29 And forthwith, when they were come out of the synagogue, they entered into the house of Simon and Andrew, with James and John.
30 But Simon's wife's mother lay sick of a fever, and anon they tell him of her.
31 And he came and took her by the hand, and lifted her up; and immediately the fever left her, and she ministered unto them.
32 And at even, when the sun did set, they brought unto him all that were diseased, and them that were possessed with devils.
33 And all the city was gathered together at the door.

---

cf. Num. 14:33–34; 32:13). *wild beasts.* Perhaps another contrast with Adam in the garden (Gen. 2:19–20). *angels.* The heavenly servants of Christ (8:38; 13:27), sent also to care for His people (Heb. 1:14).

THE GALILEAN PERIOD: MINISTRY AROUND THE SEA OF GALILEE (1:14—5:43)

1:14–20 See parallels in Matt. 4:12–22; Luke 4:14–15.

The Beginning of Jesus' Preaching (1:14–15)

1:14 *John was put in prison.* John's ministry was temporary; he had to step aside for the Messiah to start His ministry (John 3:30). *kingdom of God.* God's reign among men through His Mediator by the Spirit, presently a kingdom of grace in the heart and one day a kingdom of visible glory (v. 15; 4:11,26,30; 9:1,47; 10:14–15,23–25; 12:34; 14:25; 15:43). This is the same as the "kingdom of heaven" (Matt. 4:17; 19:23).

1:15 *time is fulfilled.* With Jesus' preaching, the consummation of God's prophetic declaration concerning the coming Messiah was finally blossoming. *repent ye, and believe the gospel.* The purpose statement of the Gospel of Mark (6:12; 16:16).

Call of the First Disciples (1:16–20)

1:16 *sea of Galilee.* Also known as the sea of Tiberias or the lake of Gennesaret.

1:17 *Come ye after me.* The "gospel" (v. 15) demands following Christ in submission to His teaching, communion with His person, and imitation of His example (8:34). *I will make you . . . fishers of men.* Jesus specifically called these disciples to a new vocation, the work of preaching the gospel to gather people into the kingdom (Matt. 13:47–50).

1:19 *James . . . and John.* Their mother, Salome, may have been the sister of Mary (15:40; Matt. 27:56), making them Jesus' cousins.

1:21–28 See parallel in Luke 4:31–37.

1:21 *entered in the synagogue, and taught.* This was Jesus' custom (v. 39; 6:2). A rabbi would read a portion of Scripture and then explain what it meant with various applications (Luke 4:16–21; Acts 13:14–15; cf. Neh. 8:1–8). Christ's earthly ministry was characterized by the work of teaching (2:13; 4:1–2; 6:2,6,34; 8:31; 9:31; 10:1; 11:17; 12:14,35; 14:49).

Miracles and Preaching (1:21—2:12)

1:22 *astonished . . . one that had authority.* The *scribes* and Pharisees taught from ancient traditions, but Christ spoke as the spiritual King, whose words were marked by God's truthfulness and power (v. 27).

1:23 *unclean spirit.* Demon, a fallen angel in rebellion against God (vv. 26–27; 2 Peter 2:4).

1:24 *Holy One of God.* Another title for the Son of God (Acts 3:14). *destroy us.* The hellish forces of Satan were fully aware of Christ's majesty as Lord and Judge, and they feared Him (James 2:19).

1:25 *Hold thy peace.* Be muzzled, that is, be silent.

1:26 *torn him.* Probably not a reference to wounds but to convulsions.

1:27 *amazed.* The crowds had earlier been amazed at Jesus' words (v. 22); now they are amazed at His works, though this amazement did not prove itself to be saving faith and repentance (Luke 10:13–15).

1:29–38 See parallels in Matt. 8:14–17; Luke 4:38–43.

1:29–30 *forthwith . . . anon.* Immediately; the same Greek word translated "straightway" (vv. 10,18,20–21).

1:31 *she ministered unto them.* A demonstration of the power and completeness of Jesus' healing. It is significant that this healing occurred on the Sabbath (v. 21; 3:2).

1:32 *even.* Evening.

1:33 *all the city was gathered.* News about Jesus spread rapidly.

34 And he healed many that were sick of divers
diseases, and cast out many devils; and suffered
not the devils to speak, because they knew him.
35 And in the morning, rising up a great while
before day, he went out, and departed into a
solitary place, and there prayed.
36 And Simon and they that were with him
followed after him.
37 And when they had found him, they said unto
him, All *men* seek for thee.
38 And he said unto them, Let us go into the next
towns, that I may preach there also: for therefore
came I forth.
39 And he preached in their synagogues through-
out all Galilee, and cast out devils.
40 And there came a leper to him, beseeching
him, and kneeling down to him, and saying unto
him, If thou wilt, thou canst make me clean.
41 And Jesus, moved with compassion, put forth
his hand, and touched him, and saith unto him, I
will; be thou clean.
42 And as soon as he had spoken, immediately the
leprosy departed from him, and he was cleansed.
43 And he straitly charged him, and forthwith
sent him away;
44 And saith unto him, See thou say nothing to
any man: but go thy way, shew thyself to the priest,
and offer for thy cleansing those things which
Moses commanded, for a testimony unto them.
45 But he went out, and began to publish *it* much,
and to blaze abroad the matter, insomuch that
Jesus could no more openly enter into the city,
but was without in desert places: and they came
to him from every quarter.

CHAPTER 2

AND again he entered into Capernaum after *some*
days; and it was noised that he was in the house.
2 And straightway many were gathered together,
insomuch that there was no room to receive
them, no, not so much as about the door: and he
preached the word unto them.
3 And they come unto him, bringing one sick of
the palsy, which was borne of four.
4 And when they could not come nigh unto him
for the press, they uncovered the roof where he
was: and when they had broken *it* up, they let
down the bed wherein the sick of the palsy lay.
5 When Jesus saw their faith, he said unto the sick

1:34 *divers.* Various. *suffered not the devils.* Did not allow the demons. Jesus desires the testimony to His glory to come not from evil spirits but from the Holy Spirit (John 15:26; 16:14; 1 Tim. 3:16).

1:35 *solitary place . . . prayed.* Jesus showed His dependence upon God by devoting Himself to prayer before He went out to minister among His fellow Israelites (6:46; 14:35).

1:37–38 *All men seek for thee.* Despite the temptation to seek popularity, Christ was about His Father's will, not the will and pleasure of men (Ps. 40:8). *for therefore came I forth.* This was His purpose in coming from heaven: not to establish a large ministry in one place based on the attraction of His miracles but to *preach* the gospel in all the *towns* (v. 39).

1:39 See parallels in Matt. 4:23; Luke 4:44.

1:40–45 See parallels in Matt. 8:1–4; Luke 5:12–16.

1:40 *leper.* A person with a skin disease (not necessarily modern leprosy) that made him ritually unclean and required him to live in isolation (Lev. 13:45–46). It is remarkable that Jesus came so close to him. *beseeching.* Asking urgently. *If thou wilt, thou canst.* If Thou choosest, Thou hast the power. Only God is able to do whatever He wills (Pss. 115:3; 135:6).

1:41 *moved with compassion . . . touched him.* Jesus not only showed His power and authority over people but had tender mercy even for the most offensive and unclean.

1:42 *as soon as he had spoken.* Again, a demonstration of the power of Christ's words (vv. 22,27).

1:43 *straitly charged.* Spoke sternly, with strong emotion and vehemence.

1:44 *shew thyself to the priest.* Christ urged him to obey the ceremonial law of Moses and to be declared ritually clean by proper authority (Lev. 14:3).

1:45 *without.* Outside.

Thoughts for Personal/Family Worship: Chapter 1

1. **God is faithful to His Word. Even though the prophets had lived and died hundreds of years earlier, God's Word is living and powerful and will accomplish His pleasure. The promised messenger (John) came in due time, as did the Lord Jesus Himself. The gospel is a declaration that God is faithful to His Word and that all His promises are fulfilled in Jesus Christ. God's faithfulness calls us to be faithful to the Word as well, even when its fulfillment seems distant or even impossible. How can God's faithfulness in Christ strengthen us to be faithful?**
2. **As soon as Christ received the Spirit's anointing and the Father's commendation, He was propelled into conflict with Satan, though not by power but by temptation. Unlike Adam, Jesus remained faithful and conquered the Devil by perfect obedience (Heb. 4:15). It is not a coincidence that shortly afterward the demons were cringing before Jesus. He can save us from Satan's power because He has overcome the Devil's temptations (Heb. 2:18).**
3. **When Christ calls men into the ministry of the Word today, He still says to them, "Come ye after me, and I will make you to become fishers of men" (v. 17). No one makes himself a true minister of the Word, but when Christ calls, He equips. The duty of the called is to follow Jesus in obedience and imitation and never to forget that the goal of fishermen is to catch fish. What implications does this have for pastoral ministry?**

Chapter 2: *Christ forgives and heals a paralytic man. He calls Matthew to follow Him and declares Himself to be the great Physician of sinners and the Lord of the Sabbath.*

2:1–22 See parallels in Matt. 9:1–17; Luke 5:17–39.

2:1–2 *noised.* Heard. *in the house . . . he preached the word.* Jesus often taught in the synagogues, but He also taught outside them. *straightway.* Immediately.

2:3 *palsy.* Paralysis. *borne of four.* Carried by four men.

2:4 *nigh . . . for the press.* Near because of the crowd. *uncovered the roof.* Likely made of clay, mud, and tree branches. Digging

of the palsy, Son, thy sins be forgiven thee.
6 But there were certain of the scribes sitting
there, and reasoning in their hearts,
7 Why doth this *man* thus speak blasphemies?
who can forgive sins but God only?
8 And immediately when Jesus perceived in his
spirit that they so reasoned within themselves,
he said unto them, Why reason ye these things in
your hearts?
9 Whether is it easier to say to the sick of the
palsy, *Thy* sins be forgiven thee; or to say, Arise,
and take up thy bed, and walk?
10 But that ye may know that the Son of man
hath power on earth to forgive sins, (he saith to
the sick of the palsy,)
11 I say unto thee, Arise, and take up thy bed, and
go thy way into thine house.
12 And immediately he arose, took up the bed,
and went forth before them all; insomuch that
they were all amazed, and glorified God, saying,
We never saw it on this fashion.
13 And he went forth again by the sea side; and all
the multitude resorted unto him, and he taught
them.
14 And as he passed by, he saw Levi the *son* of
Alphaeus sitting at the receipt of custom, and said
unto him, Follow me. And he arose and followed
him.
15 And it came to pass, that, as Jesus sat at meat in
his house, many publicans and sinners sat also to-
gether with Jesus and his disciples: for there were
many, and they followed him.
16 And when the scribes and Pharisees saw him
eat with publicans and sinners, they said unto his
disciples, How is it that he eateth and drinketh
with publicans and sinners?
17 When Jesus heard *it*, he saith unto them, They
that are whole have no need of the physician, but
they that are sick: I came not to call the righteous,
but sinners to repentance.
18 And the disciples of John and of the Pharisees
used to fast: and they come and say unto him,
Why do the disciples of John and of the Pharisees
fast, but thy disciples fast not?
19 And Jesus said unto them, Can the children of
the bridechamber fast, while the bridegroom is
with them? as long as they have the bridegroom
with them, they cannot fast.
20 But the days will come, when the bridegroom
shall be taken away from them, and then shall
they fast in those days.
21 No man also seweth a piece of new cloth on
an old garment: else the new piece that filled it
up taketh away from the old, and the rent is made
worse.
22 And no man putteth new wine into old bot-
tles: else the new wine doth burst the bottles, and
the wine is spilled, and the bottles will be marred:
but new wine must be put into new bottles.
23 And it came to pass, that he went through the
corn fields on the sabbath day; and his disciples
began, as they went, to pluck the ears of corn.

---

through the roof showed their earnestness to get their friend to Jesus.

2:5 *saw their faith.* Both that of the paralytic and of his friends. *thy sins be forgiven thee.* Christ sees through our apparent needs to our deepest need. Forgiveness comes by faith in Christ (Acts 10:43).

2:7 *forgive sins but God only.* The scribes were correct (Isa. 43:25). Priests and sacrifices had no inherent power to confer forgiveness (Mic. 6:7); this ability was reserved for the Lord (Neh. 9:17; Dan. 9:9).

2:8 *reasoned within themselves . . . in your hearts.* Christ miraculously perceived their thoughts (v. 6), underscoring His supernatural insight as the Judge (1 Kings 8:39; Jer. 17:10; Rev. 2:23).

2:9 *Whether is it easier.* Which is easier. Jesus proved His sovereign authority over the spiritual realm by displaying His omnipotent power over the temporal world. God incarnate was standing in their presence.

2:10 *Son of man.* A prophetic expression for the supreme King given eternal authority (*power*) over all by God (Dan. 7:13–14), a title often used by Jesus of Himself (v. 28; 8:31,38; 9:9,12,31; 10:33,45; 13:26; 14:21,41,62).

Call of Levi (2:13–17)

2:14 *Levi.* Also called Matthew. *son of Alphaeus.* James the Lesser also had a father named Alphaeus (3:18), but they may not have been brothers. *receipt of custom.* Place where the Jewish tax collectors took money on behalf of the Roman Empire.

2:15 *sat at meat.* Reclined at a meal. *publicans.* Tax collectors who had purchased their rights to collect taxes from the Roman government. They were hated, especially in Palestine, because of their connection with Gentiles and the oppressive Roman government.

2:17 *call . . . sinners to repentance.* Christ's gospel is good news indeed for sinners, but just as healthy people will not often seek out a physician, those *righteous* in their own eyes will not depend on Christ for salvation until the Holy Spirit convicts them of sin (John 16:8).

Controversies in Galilee (2:18—3:6)

2:18 *used to fast.* Were regularly denying themselves food. The law commanded fasting only one day a year, on the Day of Atonement (Lev. 16:29), though voluntary fasts could be observed on other days (Neh. 1:4).

2:19 *children of the bridechamber.* Wedding guests or attendants of the groom. It was their responsibility to make sure the wedding was a time of celebration and feasting, not of mourning and fasting.

2:20 *bridegroom.* The Lord is the spiritual husband of Israel (Isa. 54:5; 62:5; Hos. 2:19–20). *taken away.* One of Jesus' earliest allusions to His upcoming death, likely a reference to Isa. 53:8. *shall they fast in those days.* Christ's death, and later His absence from earth, will induce His disciples to grieve and fast.

2:21–22 Sewing a *new cloth* onto an *old garment* in those days would have caused the old cloth to tear when the new cloth shrank. Old wineskins would burst with new and still fermenting wine.

2:23—3:6 See parallels in Matt. 12:1–14; Luke 6:1–11.

2:23 *pluck the ears of corn.* This was permitted by the law of God (Deut. 23:25).

24 And the Pharisees said unto him, Behold,
why do they on the sabbath day that which is not
lawful?
25 And he said unto them, Have ye never read
what David did, when he had need, and was an
hungred, he, and they that were with him?
26 How he went into the house of God in the days
of Abiathar the high priest, and did eat the shew-
bread, which is not lawful to eat but for the priests,
and gave also to them which were with him?
27 And he said unto them, The sabbath was made
for man, and not man for the sabbath:
28 Therefore the Son of man is Lord also of the
sabbath.

CHAPTER 3

AND he entered again into the synagogue; and
there was a man there which had a withered hand.
2 And they watched him, whether he would heal
him on the sabbath day; that they might accuse
him.
3 And he saith unto the man which had the
withered hand, Stand forth.
4 And he saith unto them, Is it lawful to do good
on the sabbath days, or to do evil? to save life, or
to kill? But they held their peace.
5 And when he had looked round about on them
with anger, being grieved for the hardness of their
hearts, he saith unto the man, Stretch forth thine
hand. And he stretched *it* out: and his hand was
restored whole as the other.
6 And the Pharisees went forth, and straightway
took counsel with the Herodians against him,
how they might destroy him.
7 But Jesus withdrew himself with his disciples
to the sea: and a great multitude from Galilee
followed him, and from Judaea,
8 And from Jerusalem, and from Idumaea, and
from beyond Jordan; and they about Tyre and
Sidon, a great multitude, when they had heard
what great things he did, came unto him.
9 And he spake to his disciples, that a small ship
should wait on him because of the multitude, lest
they should throng him.
10 For he had healed many; insomuch that they
pressed upon him for to touch him, as many as
had plagues.
11 And unclean spirits, when they saw him, fell
down before him, and cried, saying, Thou art the
Son of God.
12 And he straitly charged them that they should
not make him known.
13 And he goeth up into a mountain, and calleth

2:24 *not lawful.* The laws that Jesus and His disciples were breaking were man-made customs and traditions.
2:25–26 *an hungred.* Hungry. The ceremonial laws of the old covenant could be suspended when a person was in *need* (1 Sam. 21:1–6). If David could put aside the ceremonial law, how much more could the Son of Man put aside human regulations?
2:27 *sabbath was made for man.* Man was created first, and then the Sabbath was instituted for him to benefit from its holy rest (Gen. 1:26–28; 2:1–3). Jesus was not abolishing the Sabbath, for He called it a creation ordinance, but He did oppose man-made legalism that made it a burden rather than an opportunity for spiritual delight in God (Isa. 58:13–14).
2:28 *the Son of man is Lord also of the sabbath.* Jesus is Lord and Lawgiver, and He claimed the Sabbath as His day (Rev. 1:10), to be observed by all who call Him Lord.

Thoughts for Personal/Family Worship: Chapter 2

1. **Christ is the Lord of all, God in the flesh. He is the sovereign Judge who sees the faith and unbelief in the hearts of men and grants His forgiveness to the sinner who believes (vv. 5–11). He is the spiritual husband of Israel, whose presence is the joy of His people and whose absence is their greatest sorrow (vv. 19–21). He is the Lawgiver and Lord of the Sabbath, whose ordinances are authoritative and sufficient, neither to be added to nor neglected. How should the descriptions of Christ in this chapter move His people to greater love and submission to Him?**
2. **This glorious Lord took a despised sinner and tax collector into the band of His disciples. Christ loves sinners, and so He gladly ate with them, not to justify their sins but to call them to repentance and eternal life. Therefore His gospel is utterly incompatible with the legalism of self-righteous men. Why is His grace so offensive to our pride? How should we live so as to show His grace to sinners around us?**

Chapter 3: ***Jesus heals a man with a withered hand on the Sabbath. He gathers twelve apostles around Him. The Pharisees accuse Him of casting out demons by the power of Beelzebub, but Christ demolishes their accusations.***

3:1 *withered hand.* According to the Pharisaic tradition it was legal on the Sabbath to heal a man who had a life-threatening disease. Jesus again challenged the regulations of men.
3:4 *lawful to do good . . . or to do evil?* Christ's question exposed their hypocrisy, for they condemned Him for loving and serving people on the *Sabbath* but profaned the Sabbath with their hatred and murderous intent (vv. 2,6). *held their peace.* Were silent.
3:5 *anger . . . grieved for the hardness of their hearts.* Christ is a model of righteous anger against sin, as these Pharisees showed that they cared more about their religious traditions than about loving people.
3:6 *Herodians.* Supporters of Herod. *destroy him.* The first reference in Mark to the enemies of Jesus seeking His death. Jesus has already predicted His death before His enemies begin to plot it (2:20), underscoring God's sovereignty and redemptive purpose in Jesus' sufferings.

Followers of Jesus (3:7–19)

3:11 *fell down . . . Thou art the Son of God.* Even in His state of humiliation Jesus related to His Father in such a way that He possessed glory and Lordship far above all spiritual powers.
3:12 *straitly charged.* Strongly admonished. Jesus again silenced the demons, rejecting their testimony to His deity (1:34) so that it might be displayed instead by His works and words in the Spirit.
3:13–19 See parallels in Matt. 10:1–4; Luke 6:12–16.

unto him whom he would: and they came unto
him.
14 And he ordained twelve, that they should be
with him, and that he might send them forth to
preach,
15 And to have power to heal sicknesses, and to
cast out devils:
16 And Simon he surnamed Peter;
17 And James the *son* of Zebedee, and John the
brother of James; and he surnamed them Boa-
nerges, which is, The sons of thunder:
18 And Andrew, and Philip, and Bartholomew,
and Matthew, and Thomas, and James the *son*
of Alphaeus, and Thaddaeus, and Simon the
Canaanite,
19 And Judas Iscariot, which also betrayed him:
and they went into an house.
20 And the multitude cometh together again, so
that they could not so much as eat bread.
21 And when his friends heard *of it*, they went
out to lay hold on him: for they said, He is beside
himself.
22 ¶ And the scribes which came down from
Jerusalem said, He hath Beelzebub, and by the
prince of the devils casteth he out devils.
23 And he called them *unto him*, and said unto
them in parables, How can Satan cast out Satan?
24 And if a kingdom be divided against itself,
that kingdom cannot stand.
25 And if a house be divided against itself, that
house cannot stand.
26 And if Satan rise up against himself, and be
divided, he cannot stand, but hath an end.
27 No man can enter into a strong man's house,
and spoil his goods, except he will first bind the
strong man; and then he will spoil his house.
28 Verily I say unto you, All sins shall be forgiven
unto the sons of men, and blasphemies where-
with soever they shall blaspheme:
29 But he that shall blaspheme against the Holy
Ghost hath never forgiveness, but is in danger of
eternal damnation:
30 Because they said, He hath an unclean spirit.
31 ¶ There came then his brethren and his
mother, and, standing without, sent unto him,
calling him.
32 And the multitude sat about him, and they
said unto him, Behold, thy mother and thy
brethren without seek for thee.
33 And he answered them, saying, Who is my
mother, or my brethren?
34 And he looked round about on them which
sat about him, and said, Behold my mother and
my brethren!
35 For whosoever shall do the will of God, the
same is my brother, and my sister, and mother.

3:13 *up into a mountain.* Luke reports that Jesus spent the night praying there (Luke 6:12). *whom he would.* Those whom He chose.

3:14 *ordained twelve.* Jesus had spent the previous night praying on the mountain before ordaining His twelve apostles (Luke 6:12). *be with him.* Ministry springs from a close relationship with the Lord. *send them forth.* The verb form corresponding to the noun "apostle" (6:30).

3:16 *Peter.* Not a typical name in Aramaic or Greek but an indication of Peter's character and Christ's purpose for him in confessing Christ as the Son of God (Matt. 16:15–18).

3:17 *James.* The first apostle to be martyred (Acts 12:2). *John.* Likely the last apostle to die. *sons of thunder.* An idiom for their character, perhaps indicating that they were passionate (Luke 9:54).

3:18 *James the son of Alphaeus.* James; not the son of Zebedee, this James was known as "James the Lesser." *Thaddaeus.* Also known as Judas, the son of James, and in some earlier manuscripts Lebbaeus. *Canaanite.* Aramaic for "zealot"; this *Simon* was either part of the sect of the Zealots or personally zealous for the Lord.

3:19 *Judas Iscariot . . . betrayed him.* Jesus' whole ministry was lived in the shadow of the cross, and He chose Judas knowing what he would do (John 6:64,70–71).

Further Opposition (3:20–35)

3:21 *his friends.* Perhaps His family (v. 31). *lay hold . . . beside himself.* Seize Him, imagining that He was insane. Jesus was opposed not only by religious leaders but also by those closely associated with Him.

3:22–30 See parallels in Matt. 12:22–37; Luke 11:14–23.

3:22 *Beelzebub.* From 2 Kings 1:1–6,16, used here as a name for Satan, the ruler of demons (*prince of devils*).

3:23 *parables.* Metaphors often drawn from creation to both reveal and conceal divine and eternal truths (4:11–12).

3:24–26 Jesus showed how ridiculous the Pharisees' accusation was by using a *kingdom* and a family (*house*) to demonstrate that disunity brings destruction. Jesus was destroying the works of Satan, not serving him.

3:27 *bind the strong man.* Christ defeated the Devil in His first coming (1:13,24; Rev. 20:1–3; cf. Luke 10:18; John 12:31; 16:11) and is presently freeing people from his evil kingdom (*spoil his house*; Col. 1:13), though Satan is still active in the world (4:15; Rev. 12:9).

3:28 *Verily.* Truly. *blasphemies.* Speaking against. Though a heinous sin (Ex. 20:7; Lev. 24:10–16), irreverent and dishonoring speech against God can be forgiven by God's grace (1 Tim. 1:13).

3:29 *Holy Ghost.* Holy Spirit. The unforgivable sin is knowingly and boldly attributing the Spirit's works to demonic forces (v. 22); people who do this reject the Spirit's testimony to Christ and thus will never seek the Savior for forgiveness.

3:31–35 See parallels in Matt. 12:46–50; Luke 8:19–21.

3:31 *his brethren.* Probably the biological half-brothers of Jesus (6:3). *without.* Outside.

3:35 *do the will of God . . . my brother.* While not disparaging family relationships (7:9–13), Jesus stressed that God is creating a new, spiritual family bound by ties closer than blood, a common submission to the Word of God.

Thoughts for Personal/Family Worship: Chapter 3

1. **All who will live godly lives will suffer tribulation (2 Tim. 3:12). This was true for Christ and is also true for Christians. The world is not simply watching us but seeking to win us over, to destroy our faith and obedience to the Word (Mark 4:17). To them we seem insane. Indeed, the greatest persecution may come from the most religious**

CHAPTER 4

AND he began again to teach by the sea side: and
there was gathered unto him a great multitude, so
that he entered into a ship, and sat in the sea; and
the whole multitude was by the sea on the land.
2 And he taught them many things by parables,
and said unto them in his doctrine,
3 Hearken; Behold, there went out a sower to
sow:
4 And it came to pass, as he sowed, some fell by
the way side, and the fowls of the air came and
devoured it up.
5 And some fell on stony ground, where it had
not much earth; and immediately it sprang up,
because it had no depth of earth:
6 But when the sun was up, it was scorched; and
because it had no root, it withered away.
7 And some fell among thorns, and the thorns
grew up, and choked it, and it yielded no fruit.
8 And other fell on good ground, and did yield
fruit that sprang up and increased; and brought
forth, some thirty, and some sixty, and some an
hundred.
9 And he said unto them, He that hath ears to
hear, let him hear.
10 And when he was alone, they that were about
him with the twelve asked of him the parable.
11 And he said unto them, Unto you it is given
to know the mystery of the kingdom of God: but
unto them that are without, all *these* things are
done in parables:
12 That seeing they may see, and not perceive;
and hearing they may hear, and not understand;
lest at any time they should be converted, and
their sins should be forgiven them.
13 And he said unto them, Know ye not this
parable? and how then will ye know all parables?
14 ¶ The sower soweth the word.
15 And these are they by the way side, where the
word is sown; but when they have heard, Satan
cometh immediately, and taketh away the word
that was sown in their hearts.
16 And these are they likewise which are sown
on stony ground; who, when they have heard the
word, immediately receive it with gladness;
17 And have no root in themselves, and so endure
but for a time: afterward, when affliction or per-
secution ariseth for the word's sake, immediately
they are offended.
18 And these are they which are sown among
thorns; such as hear the word,
19 And the cares of this world, and the deceit-
fulness of riches, and the lusts of other things
entering in, choke the word, and it becometh
unfruitful.
20 And these are they which are sown on good
ground; such as hear the word, and receive *it*,
and bring forth fruit, some thirtyfold, some

---

people, for their religion of pride and hypocrisy comes into direct conflict with Christ's ways of love and obedience. However, in Christ God gives believers a new spiritual family, united by their obedience to God's Word. How can members of the church strengthen and encourage one another to stay faithful in persecution?

2. Apart from Christ we are enslaved to sin and Satan. We cannot stand against this strong man in our own strength. We need One stronger than the strong man. Christ's coming into the world, His obedient life, and His substitutionary death deliver captive sinners. What are signs that a person is a slave of Satan? What are signs that Jesus has set someone free?

Chapter 4: *Jesus teaches the truth of the kingdom of God through parables, both veiling and revealing His glory to the crowds.*

Teaching in Parables (4:1–41)

4:1–20 See parallels in Matt. 13:1–23; Luke 8:4–15.

4:1 *great multitude.* Large crowd (2:4,13; 3:9,20,32); the first time *great* has been used of such gatherings. *ship.* Boat, used to remove Himself a little distance from the crowd in order to teach (3:9).

4:8 *thirty, and some sixty, and some an hundred.* The work of the sower produces considerable results, even though only one of the four soils is good.

4:11 *mystery.* Not a secret knowledge reserved for a few (like pagan notions of mystery or mystery religions) but something hidden until God reveals it. Christ gave those who truly sought Him further revelation about the meaning of the parables (v. 34) but did not so bless outsiders (*them that are without*) who were merely curious or unwilling to commit themselves to Him.

4:12 *seeing . . . not perceive; and hearing . . . not understand.* Citing Isa. 6:9–10. *lest at any time they should be converted.* Jesus' use of parables both reveals and conceals. God is sovereign over the salvation of individuals, and He has decreed the salvation of some but not all (Matt. 11:25,27; John 10:26–29). Therefore the spiritual insights of the disciples do not come from their own wisdom or will but depend upon God's grace (Matt. 16:17; 1 Cor. 2:10–16).

4:14 *soweth the word.* The *sower* represents the preacher of the Word of Christ (John 4:35–38; 1 Cor. 9:11).

4:15 *Satan . . . taketh away the word.* Though defeated by Christ (3:27), the Devil still exercises much power to prevent people from understanding and believing the gospel (2 Cor. 4:4).

4:16–17 *offended.* Stumbled and fell away. Their apparent conversion (*gladness*) proves superficial (*no root*) because of the hardness of a yet unchanged heart (*stony ground*; Ezek. 36:26).

4:19 *cares of this world.* Fears about earthly things. *deceitfulness of riches.* Desire for earthly things based on the lies about what they can provide (Eph. 4:22). *lusts.* Strong desires, covetousness. *choke the word.* Worldly fear and love cloud our eyes from seeing the surpassing glory of the kingdom, thus preventing our hearts from responding to the gospel with faith and repentance.

4:20 *hear the word, and receive it.* Faith comes by hearing the preaching of the Word (Rom. 10:14–17). *fruit, some thirty-fold . . . sixty . . . hundred.* Real conversion produces a life of good works (Gal. 5:22–24; Col. 1:5–6), though in varying degrees.

sixty, and some an hundred.
21 ¶ And he said unto them, Is a candle brought
to be put under a bushel, or under a bed? and not
to be set on a candlestick?
22 For there is nothing hid, which shall not be
manifested; neither was any thing kept secret, but
that it should come abroad.
23 If any man have ears to hear, let him hear.
24 And he said unto them, Take heed what
ye hear: with what measure ye mete, it shall be
measured to you: and unto you that hear shall
more be given.
25 For he that hath, to him shall be given: and he
that hath not, from him shall be taken even that
which he hath.
26 ¶ And he said, So is the kingdom of God, as if a
man should cast seed into the ground;
27 And should sleep, and rise night and day, and
the seed should spring and grow up, he knoweth
not how.
28 For the earth bringeth forth fruit of herself;
first the blade, then the ear, after that the full corn
in the ear.
29 But when the fruit is brought forth, immedi-
ately he putteth in the sickle, because the harvest
is come.
30 ¶ And he said, Whereunto shall we liken the
kingdom of God? or with what comparison shall
we compare it?
31 *It is* like a grain of mustard seed, which, when
it is sown in the earth, is less than all the seeds that
be in the earth:
32 But when it is sown, it groweth up, and
becometh greater than all herbs, and shooteth out
great branches; so that the fowls of the air may
lodge under the shadow of it.
33 And with many such parables spake he the
word unto them, as they were able to hear *it*.
34 But without a parable spake he not unto them:
and when they were alone, he expounded all
things to his disciples.
35 And the same day, when the even was come,
he saith unto them, Let us pass over unto the other
side.
36 And when they had sent away the multitude,
they took him even as he was in the ship. And
there were also with him other little ships.
37 And there arose a great storm of wind, and the
waves beat into the ship, so that it was now full.
38 And he was in the hinder part of the ship,
asleep on a pillow: and they awake him, and say
unto him, Master, carest thou not that we perish?
39 And he arose, and rebuked the wind, and said
unto the sea, Peace, be still. And the wind ceased,
and there was a great calm.
40 And he said unto them, Why are ye so fearful?
how is it that ye have no faith?
41 And they feared exceedingly, and said one to

4:21–25 See parallel in Luke 8:16–18.
4:21 *candle . . . candlestick.* Oil lamp and a stand to put it on, an image of the light produced by the Word of God (Ps. 119:105). *bushel.* Basket. The Pharisees had hidden God's Word under their traditions and regulations, but a true disciple lets the Word shine forth in preaching and obedient living.
4:24 *Take heed.* Look, pay attention. *with what measure ye mete.* According to the measure you use to give others their portion.
4:26–28 *sleep . . . bringeth forth fruit of herself.* The preacher spreads the Word but cannot make it grow and bear fruit; only God can do that (1 Cor. 3:5–7), and His ways are beyond man's understanding (*knoweth not how*; John 3:8). *blade . . . ear . . . full corn.* The kingdom begins small but over time produces distinctive results that cannot be hidden.
4:29 *harvest.* Perhaps a reference to the judgment at the end of the age, when all those who truly belong to the kingdom will be gathered (Matt. 13:39; Rev. 14:15). The consummation of the kingdom is coming, and nothing can prevent its final growth.
4:30–34 See parallel in Matt. 13:31–32,34–35.
4:31 *mustard seed.* Considered to be one of the smallest seeds.
4:32 *fowls . . . lodge.* Birds find a home in the tree, a picture of people taking refuge under the protection and prosperity of a great king (Ezek. 17:23; 31:6; Dan. 4:11–12,20–22).
4:35–41 See parallels in Matt. 8:23–27; Luke 8:22–25.
4:35 *same day.* The day had been busy and long for Jesus, and He was weary (v. 38).
4:38 *asleep on a pillow.* As a good minister of the word, Jesus had preached the message of the kingdom and now rested (v. 27). *carest thou not that we perish?* The fact that they appeal to Christ suggests sparks of faith amid the smoke of unbelief in this cry (Matt. 8:26).
4:39 *Peace, be still . . . and there was a great calm.* Jesus is Lord over nature, possessing in His mere word the power to control creation as its Creator (Gen. 1:9; Ps. 33:6–8).
4:41 *they feared exceedingly.* After Jesus calmed the storm that had terrified them, the disciples next experienced an even greater fear with regard to Jesus, for only God can so rule the waves (Ps. 107:28–29).

Thoughts for Personal/Family Worship: Chapter 4

1. **Though the four soils represent different kinds of hearers, they also teach us about spiritual influences that resist the Word in everyone who hears it preached: Satan, sin in the heart, and the world. According to Christ's explanation of the parable (vv. 14–20), how does each influence work against a fruitful response to God's Word? How can we seek to overcome these evil influences by God's grace so that we benefit from the preaching of the Scriptures?**
2. **The two parables involving sowers have much to say to preachers of the Word (vv. 14–20,26–29). What lessons for ministers do you gather from them? How ought these lessons to humble them? How should they encourage them?**
3. **We do not read that the disciples consulted with Christ before the ship was in danger of sinking. Yet when they finally cried to Him they seemed to accuse the Lord of a lack of care. Can you see yourself in this picture? How have you responded to similar trials? How should we respond, in light of the fact that Jesus is the Lord who rules all things with His mere word?**

another, What manner of man is this, that even
the wind and the sea obey him?

CHAPTER 5

AND they came over unto the other side of the sea,
into the country of the Gadarenes.
2 And when he was come out of the ship,
immediately there met him out of the tombs a
man with an unclean spirit,
3 Who had *his* dwelling among the tombs; and
no man could bind him, no, not with chains:
4 Because that he had been often bound with
fetters and chains, and the chains had been
plucked asunder by him, and the fetters broken in
pieces: neither could any *man* tame him.
5 And always, night and day, he was in the moun-
tains, and in the tombs, crying, and cutting
himself with stones.
6 But when he saw Jesus afar off, he ran and
worshipped him,
7 And cried with a loud voice, and said, What
have I to do with thee, Jesus, *thou* Son of the
most high God? I adjure thee by God, that thou
torment me not.
8 For he said unto him, Come out of the man,
thou unclean spirit.
9 And he asked him, What *is* thy name? And he
answered, saying, My name *is* Legion: for we are
many.
10 And he besought him much that he would not
send them away out of the country.
11 Now there was there nigh unto the mountains
a great herd of swine feeding.
12 And all the devils besought him, saying, Send
us into the swine, that we may enter into them.
13 And forthwith Jesus gave them leave. And
the unclean spirits went out, and entered into
the swine: and the herd ran violently down a
steep place into the sea, (they were about two
thousand;) and were choked in the sea.
14 And they that fed the swine fled, and told *it* in
the city, and in the country. And they went out to
see what it was that was done.
15 And they come to Jesus, and see him that
was possessed with the devil, and had the legion,
sitting, and clothed, and in his right mind: and
they were afraid.
16 And they that saw *it* told them how it befell to
him that was possessed with the devil, and *also*
concerning the swine.
17 And they began to pray him to depart out of
their coasts.
18 And when he was come into the ship, he that
had been possessed with the devil prayed him
that he might be with him.
19 Howbeit Jesus suffered him not, but saith unto
him, Go home to thy friends, and tell them how
great things the Lord hath done for thee, and hath
had compassion on thee.
20 And he departed, and began to publish in
Decapolis how great things Jesus had done for
him: and all *men* did marvel.
21 And when Jesus was passed over again by ship
unto the other side, much people gathered unto
him: and he was nigh unto the sea.
22 And, behold, there cometh one of the rulers of
the synagogue, Jairus by name; and when he saw
him, he fell at his feet,
23 And besought him greatly, saying, My little

Chapter 5: *Jesus withdraws from Galilee and ministers in the surrounding region, both teaching and healing.*

Healing Demoniacs (5:1–20)

5:1–20 See parallels in Matt. 8:28–34; Luke 8:26–39.

5:1–2 *country of the Gadarenes.* Near the city of Khersa (Gersa/Kersa), where many caves in the hill were used as *tombs. ship.* Boat. *man with an unclean spirit.* A person under the influence of a demon (1:23). Matthew records that there were two men (Matt. 8:28), while Mark and Luke both mention only one man (Luke 8:27), perhaps acting as spokesman for the two.

5:4 *fetters.* Chains, shackles. *plucked asunder.* Torn apart. No human efforts could control him.

5:7 *adjure.* Place under solemn oath, perhaps echoing the language of Jewish exorcists (Acts 19:13).

5:9 *What is thy name?* Not necessary for Jesus to cast out demons (1:25); perhaps Jesus was revealing to His disciples the extent of this man's bondage and thus of Christ's power. *Legion.* Roman military unit consisting of about 6,000 soldiers.

5:10 *besought.* Asked urgently. An army of demons cowered before Jesus in desperate fear, begging in His majestic presence.

5:13 *gave them leave.* Permitted them. One soul is worth infinitely more than any number of animals.

5:16 *befell.* Happened.

5:17 *pray.* Ask urgently (same word used of the demons; vv. 10,12). *coasts.* Regions. Sadly, rather than rejoicing in the salvation of a man from demonic power and seeking to know the Lord who saved him, they desired only to avoid His presence, as the demons had.

5:18 *prayed . . . that he might be with him.* In contrast to his countrymen, he asked to follow Jesus as His disciple and enjoy communion with Him.

5:19–20 *Go home . . . and tell them.* Though Jesus forbade the man to follow Him physically, He commanded him to follow Him in ministry, becoming a witness to Christ in his homeland. *great things the Lord hath done for thee . . . great things Jesus had done for him.* The parallel shows that the man declared that Jesus is the Lord. *Decapolis.* The Ten Cities, a Gentile region to which Jesus would return (7:31).

Jesus Returns to Galilee (5:21–43)

5:21–34 See parallels in Matt. 9:18–26; Luke 8:40–56.

5:21 *passed over again.* Jesus crossed back over to the region of Capernaum.

5:22 *rulers of the synagogue.* Not all of the religious leaders were opposed to Jesus.

5:23 *that she may be healed; and . . . live.* Jairus expressed his faith in Jesus' power.

5:25–26 *issue of blood.* Such bleeding would have made her unclean and left her isolated (Lev. 15:25,33). *twelve years . . .*

daughter lieth at the point of death: *I pray thee,*
come and lay thy hands on her, that she may be
healed; and she shall live.
24 And *Jesus* went with him; and much people
followed him, and thronged him.
25 And a certain woman, which had an issue of
blood twelve years,
26 And had suffered many things of many
physicians, and had spent all that she had, and
was nothing bettered, but rather grew worse,
27 When she had heard of Jesus, came in the press
behind, and touched his garment.
28 For she said, If I may touch but his clothes, I
shall be whole.
29 And straightway the fountain of her blood
was dried up; and she felt in *her* body that she was
healed of that plague.
30 And Jesus, immediately knowing in himself
that virtue had gone out of him, turned him about
in the press, and said, Who touched my clothes?
31 And his disciples said unto him, Thou seest
the multitude thronging thee, and sayest thou,
Who touched me?
32 And he looked round about to see her that had
done this thing.
33 But the woman fearing and trembling,
knowing what was done in her, came and fell
down before him, and told him all the truth.
34 And he said unto her, Daughter, thy faith hath
made thee whole; go in peace, and be whole of
thy plague.
35 While he yet spake, there came from the ruler
of the synagogue's *house certain* which said, Thy
daughter is dead: why troublest thou the Master
any further?
36 As soon as Jesus heard the word that was
spoken, he saith unto the ruler of the synagogue,
Be not afraid, only believe.
37 And he suffered no man to follow him, save
Peter, and James, and John the brother of James.
38 And he cometh to the house of the ruler of the
synagogue, and seeth the tumult, and them that
wept and wailed greatly.
39 And when he was come in, he saith unto them,
Why make ye this ado, and weep? the damsel is
not dead, but sleepeth.
40 And they laughed him to scorn. But when he
had put them all out, he taketh the father and the
mother of the damsel, and them that were with
him, and entereth in where the damsel was lying.
41 And he took the damsel by the hand, and said
unto her, Talitha cumi; which is, being inter-
preted, Damsel, I say unto thee, arise.
42 And straightway the damsel arose, and walked;
for she was *of the age* of twelve years. And they
were astonished with a great astonishment.
43 And he charged them straitly that no man
should know it; and commanded that something
should be given her to eat.

CHAPTER 6

AND he went out from thence, and came into his
own country; and his disciples follow him.

but rather grew worse. When the power of man is insufficient, Jesus is more than able (10:27).

5:27 *press.* Crowd.

5:30 *knowing in himself.* Her healing did not take place apart from Christ's knowledge and will. *virtue.* Power. *Who touched my clothes?* Jesus took time from helping an important Jewish leader to minister to this outcast woman (7:25–30).

5:34 *thy faith hath made thee whole.* Literally, "Your faith has saved you." Christ's miracles of healing were signs of His power to heal the soul of sin and damnation through faith and repentance (2:17).

5:36 *Be not afraid, only believe.* Jesus propped up Jairus's sinking faith after the father had heard of his daughter's death, calling him to trust His divine power even in the face of a seemingly hopeless situation (Ex. 14:13; 2 Chron. 20:15).

5:37 *save.* Except.

5:38 *tumult.* Disturbance. *wept and wailed greatly.* After a death a family would often hire professional mourners to display their grief.

5:39 *this ado.* Disturbance. *damsel is not dead, but sleepeth.* Jesus was not denying the reality of the girl's death but speaking figuratively because He was about to awaken her.

5:40 *laughed him to scorn.* The professional mourners mocked him.

5:41 *Talitha cumi.* Stated in Aramaic, a language similar to Hebrew spoken in Judaea in that day, which Mark translated into Greek for his readers.

5:43 *straitly.* Strictly. *given her to eat.* After the extraordinary miracle Christ called them to return to ordinary life.

Thoughts for Personal/Family Worship: Chapter 5

1. **The Lord Jesus has the power to save from the most hopeless of situations. Whether He finds us dominated by Satan's forces in a way that no one can control, suffering from a problem no man can heal, or facing the finality of death itself, Christ is able to help us. In this age He saves sinners from the guilt and penalty of sin and from the domination of sin and Satan. In the age to come He will deliver His people from death, illness, and all misery. However, salvation is neither automatic nor universal but received by faith, as the bleeding woman shows us.**
2. **People respond in very different ways when they encounter Jesus Christ. Some, like the Gadarenes, desire only that He leave them alone, for He disturbs and terrifies them. Others, like the mourners at the dead girl's home, mock Him because His Word makes no sense to their unbelieving minds. Still others, however, like the man rescued from the legion of demons, desire to be near to Him because He alone has the power to save them, and they are eager to tell others of His saving work in their lives. How have you encountered Jesus in His Word? How have you responded?**

THE GALILEAN PERIOD: FURTHER JOURNEYS IN GALILEE (6:1—9:50)

Chapter 6: ***Jesus faces opposition from His hometown. John the Baptist is beheaded. Christ again withdraws Himself from Galilee, performing miracles and teaching.***

2 And when the sabbath day was come, he began
to teach in the synagogue: and many hearing *him*
were astonished, saying, From whence hath this
man these things? and what wisdom *is* this which
is given unto him, that even such mighty works
are wrought by his hands?
3 Is not this the carpenter, the son of Mary, the
brother of James, and Joses, and of Juda, and
Simon? and are not his sisters here with us? And
they were offended at him.
4 But Jesus said unto them, A prophet is not
without honour, but in his own country, and
among his own kin, and in his own house.
5 And he could there do no mighty work, save
that he laid his hands upon a few sick folk, and
healed *them*.
6 And he marvelled because of their unbelief.
And he went round about the villages, teaching.
7 ¶ And he called *unto him* the twelve, and began
to send them forth by two and two; and gave
them power over unclean spirits;
8 And commanded them that they should take
nothing for *their* journey, save a staff only; no
scrip, no bread, no money in *their* purse:
9 But *be* shod with sandals; and not put on two
coats.
10 And he said unto them, In what place soever
ye enter into an house, there abide till ye depart
from that place.
11 And whosoever shall not receive you, nor hear
you, when ye depart thence, shake off the dust
under your feet for a testimony against them.
Verily I say unto you, It shall be more tolerable for
Sodom and Gomorrha in the day of judgment,
than for that city.
12 And they went out, and preached that men
should repent.
13 And they cast out many devils, and anointed
with oil many that were sick, and healed *them*.
14 And king Herod heard *of him*; (for his name
was spread abroad:) and he said, That John the
Baptist was risen from the dead, and therefore
mighty works do shew forth themselves in him.
15 Others said, That it is Elias. And others said,
That it is a prophet, or as one of the prophets.
16 But when Herod heard *thereof*, he said, It is
John, whom I beheaded: he is risen from the dead.
17 For Herod himself had sent forth and laid
hold upon John, and bound him in prison for
Herodias' sake, his brother Philip's wife: for he
had married her.
18 For John had said unto Herod, It is not lawful
for thee to have thy brother's wife.
19 Therefore Herodias had a quarrel against him,
and would have killed him; but she could not:
20 For Herod feared John, knowing that he was
a just man and an holy, and observed him; and
when he heard him, he did many things, and
heard him gladly.
21 And when a convenient day was come, that
Herod on his birthday made a supper to his lords,
high captains, and chief *estates* of Galilee;
22 And when the daughter of the said Herodias
came in, and danced, and pleased Herod and
them that sat with him, the king said unto the
damsel, Ask of me whatsoever thou wilt, and I
will give *it* thee.
23 And he sware unto her, Whatsoever thou shalt
ask of me, I will give *it* thee, unto the half of my
kingdom.

Jesus Rejected at Nazareth (6:1–6)

6:1–6 See parallel in Matt. 13:53–58.
6:1 *his own country.* Nazareth, His hometown (1:9,24).
6:2 Unlike His earlier visit in Capernaum (2:1–2), people did not flock to Jesus in Nazareth, so He apparently waited to teach on the *sabbath day*, His last appearance in a *synagogue* in this gospel.
6:3 *carpenter . . . . And they were offended at him.* They could not deny His wisdom and authority, yet their earthly familiarity with Jesus caused them to disdain this preacher who had once been practicing His step-father's manual trade (Matt. 13:55).
6:4 *prophet.* The office of declaring new revelations from God by the Holy Spirit.
6:5 *could there do no mighty work.* Though capable of working miracles whenever He pleased, Christ was limited by His Father's will to use miracles to confirm faith. *save.* Except.
6:6 *villages.* Christ labored to reach the small towns, not just the cities, with the gospel (vv. 36,56). *teaching.* Jesus' primary ministry at this time (see note at 1:21).

Jesus Sends out the Twelve (6:7–13)

6:7–13 See parallels in Matt. 10:1–15; Luke 9:1–6.
6:7 *the twelve.* The apostles (v. 30), whom He had earlier chosen to be with Him (3:14). *by two and two.* As witnesses (Deut. 17:6; 19:15) and for mutual support (Eccl. 4:9–12). *power.* Authority. Christ delegated some of His spiritual authority and victory over Satan to them as His representatives.
6:8 *scrip.* Bag.
6:11 *shake off the dust.* The Jews did this when they left a Gentile nation and came into the Holy Land, a symbolic act underscoring the seriousness of despising the Word of God. *Verily.* Truly. *more tolerable for Sodom and Gomorrha.* With the hearing of the gospel comes great responsibility.
6:12 *repent.* They preached the same message as Jesus (1:15; 2:17).
6:13 *anointed with oil.* Oil was used medicinally (Isa. 1:6; Luke 10:34) and for joyful occasions (Ps 23:5; Luke 7:46) but here appears to function as a symbol of the work of God (James 5:14–15).

John the Baptist Beheaded (6:14–29)

6:14–44 See the parallels in Matt. 14:1–21; Luke 9:7–17.
6:14 *king Herod.* Herod Antipas, the son of Herod the Great. *abroad.* Over a wide area.
6:17 Herod divorced his wife, the daughter of the Nabataean king, Aretas IV, and took *his brother Philip's wife.*
6:18 *not lawful.* Prohibited by the law of God (Lev. 18:16; 20:21).
6:21 *lords, high captains, and chief estates.* Great men, commanders, and first ones—civil and military leaders.
6:22 *damsel.* Young woman, girl.

24 And she went forth, and said unto her mother,
What shall I ask? And she said, The head of John
the Baptist.
25 And she came in straightway with haste unto
the king, and asked, saying, I will that thou give me
by and by in a charger the head of John the Baptist.
26 And the king was exceeding sorry; *yet* for his
oath's sake, and for their sakes which sat with him,
he would not reject her.
27 And immediately the king sent an executioner,
and commanded his head to be brought: and he
went and beheaded him in the prison,
28 And brought his head in a charger, and gave it
to the damsel: and the damsel gave it to her mother.
29 And when his disciples heard *of it*, they came
and took up his corpse, and laid it in a tomb.
30 And the apostles gathered themselves together
unto Jesus, and told him all things, both what
they had done, and what they had taught.
31 And he said unto them, Come ye yourselves
apart into a desert place, and rest a while: for there
were many coming and going, and they had no
leisure so much as to eat.
32 And they departed into a desert place by ship
privately.
33 And the people saw them departing, and many
knew him, and ran afoot thither out of all cities,
and outwent them, and came together unto him.
34 And Jesus, when he came out, saw much people,
and was moved with compassion toward them,
because they were as sheep not having a shepherd:
and he began to teach them many things.
35 And when the day was now far spent, his
disciples came unto him, and said, This is a desert
place, and now the time *is* far passed:
36 Send them away, that they may go into the
country round about, and into the villages, and
buy themselves bread: for they have nothing to eat.
37 He answered and said unto them, Give ye
them to eat. And they say unto him, Shall we go
and buy two hundred pennyworth of bread, and
give them to eat?
38 He saith unto them, How many loaves have ye?
go and see. And when they knew, they say, Five,
and two fishes.
39 And he commanded them to make all sit down
by companies upon the green grass.
40 And they sat down in ranks, by hundreds, and
by fifties.
41 And when he had taken the five loaves and
the two fishes, he looked up to heaven, and
blessed, and brake the loaves, and gave *them* to
his disciples to set before them; and the two fishes
divided he among them all.
42 And they did all eat, and were filled.
43 And they took up twelve baskets full of the
fragments, and of the fishes.
44 And they that did eat of the loaves were about
five thousand men.
45 And straightway he constrained his disciples to
get into the ship, and to go to the other side before
unto Bethsaida, while he sent away the people.
46 And when he had sent them away, he departed
into a mountain to pray.
47 And when even was come, the ship was in the
midst of the sea, and he alone on the land.
48 And he saw them toiling in rowing; for the
wind was contrary unto them: and about the
fourth watch of the night he cometh unto them,
walking upon the sea, and would have passed by
them.
49 But when they saw him walking upon the sea,
they supposed it had been a spirit, and cried out:
50 For they all saw him, and were troubled. And
immediately he talked with them, and saith unto
them, Be of good cheer: it is I; be not afraid.

6:25 *by and by.* Right away or quickly. *charger.* Dish.
6:26 *exceeding sorry.* Not a godly sorrow leading to repentance but the sorrow of the world (2 Cor. 7:10).

Feeding the Five Thousand (6:30–44)

6:31 *desert place.* An area without many inhabitants or settlements.
6:33 *ran afoot thither.* Rushed there on foot.
6:34 *compassion.* Despite the fact that the crowds had interrupted some much needed rest and time to grieve John's death (vv. 29–31), Jesus was deeply moved with love for them in their spiritual need and so gave them the Word (*teach them many things*). *sheep not having a shepherd.* An image for people lacking the care of a good leader (1 Kings 22:17; Ezek. 34:5; Zech. 10:2).
6:37 *Give ye them to eat.* Jesus knew His disciples had no means of providing food for such a large group, and so He prompted them to seek all they needed from His all-sufficiency.
6:41 *looked up to heaven.* A common gesture of prayer.
6:42 *all . . . were filled.* Five loaves and two fish provided more than enough food for several thousand people, a sign that His grace was sufficient to enable His disciples to minister to the needs of man.
6:43 *twelve baskets.* Perhaps each of the apostles was carrying a visible reminder of His power.
6:44 *five thousand men.* Not counting women and children (Matt. 14:21).

Healing in Gennesaret (6:45–56)

6:45–56 See the parallel in Matt. 14:22–36.
6:45 *Bethsaida.* There were two towns by that name in Jesus' day, Bethsaida-Julius on the western shore and Bethsaida-Galilee near Capernaum. They came to the latter of the two.
6:46 *departed into a mountain to pray.* Though for the sake of serving the crowds Christ delayed the retreat He needed (vv. 29–34), He sought solitude to commune with His Father (1:35).
6:48 *he saw them.* Jesus' sight of them at a distance at night was supernatural. *fourth watch.* The three hours before sunrise. *would have passed by them.* Jesus was walking parallel to the boat to reveal His glory and to test His disciples' faith.
6:50 *Be of good cheer.* Have courage. *it is I.* Literally, "I am," perhaps an allusion to the name of God, *Jehovah* (Ex. 3:14), in the context of demonstrating Christ's Lordship over creation by walking on water.

51 And he went up unto them into the ship; and
the wind ceased: and they were sore amazed in
themselves beyond measure, and wondered.
52 For they considered not *the miracle* of the
loaves: for their heart was hardened.
53 And when they had passed over, they came
into the land of Gennesaret, and drew to the
shore.
54 And when they were come out of the ship,
straightway they knew him,
55 And ran through that whole region round
about, and began to carry about in beds those
that were sick, where they heard he was.
56 And whithersoever he entered, into villages, or
cities, or country, they laid the sick in the streets,
and besought him that they might touch if it were
but the border of his garment: and as many as
touched him were made whole.

CHAPTER 7

THEN came together unto him the Pharisees, and
certain of the scribes, which came from Jerusalem.
2 And when they saw some of his disciples eat
bread with defiled, that is to say, with unwashen,
hands, they found fault.
3 For the Pharisees, and all the Jews, except they
wash *their* hands oft, eat not, holding the tradition
of the elders.
4 And *when they come* from the market, except
they wash, they eat not. And many other things
there be, which they have received to hold, *as* the
washing of cups, and pots, brasen vessels, and of
tables.
5 Then the Pharisees and scribes asked him, Why
walk not thy disciples according to the tradition
of the elders, but eat bread with unwashen hands?
6 He answered and said unto them, Well hath
Esaias prophesied of you hypocrites, as it is
written, This people honoureth me with *their* lips,
but their heart is far from me.
7 Howbeit in vain do they worship me, teaching
for doctrines the commandments of men.
8 For laying aside the commandment of God, ye
hold the tradition of men, *as* the washing of pots
and cups: and many other such like things ye do.
9 And he said unto them, Full well ye reject the
commandment of God, that ye may keep your
own tradition.
10 For Moses said, Honour thy father and thy
mother; and, Whoso curseth father or mother, let
him die the death:
11 But ye say, If a man shall say to his father
or mother, *It is* Corban, that is to say, a gift, by
whatsoever thou mightest be profited by me; *he
shall be free*.
12 And ye suffer him no more to do ought for his
father or his mother;
13 Making the word of God of none effect
through your tradition, which ye have delivered:
and many such like things do ye.
14 ¶ And when he had called all the people *unto
him*, he said unto them, Hearken unto me every
one *of you*, and understand:

6:51 *sore.* Extremely.

6:52 *considered not . . . the loaves.* They should have learned the same lesson from His walking on the water as from the feeding of the 5,000; namely, that Christ is God. *heart was hardened.* The obvious message of this miracle could not penetrate the stubborn unbelief that remained in them (8:17; 16:14).

6:53 *Gennesaret.* A famous, densely populated plain along the northwestern shore of the Sea of Galilee.

Thoughts for Personal/Family Worship: Chapter 6

1. **The death of John was lamentable, though for John it marked his entrance into glory. What was infinitely more lamentable was Herod's continued life in worldly splendor, with a guilty conscience and an unrepentant heart. Who would you rather be like, the dead John or the living Herod? Why?**
2. **The disciples did not have what it took to feed thousands of people; yet Christ asked them to give food to the crowd (v. 37). Christ often asks us to do things that are impossible from our perspective so that we may learn His all-sufficiency through difficulty, faith, and prayer.**
3. **Though they followed Christ, the disciples' hearts were still so hardened (v. 52). How do you manifest hard-heartedness against the Lord despite all that God has given you in the Word and through His providence? What should you do about this?**

Chapter 7: ***Jesus again faces opposition from the religious elite. He heals a Syrophoenician woman's daughter, as well as a deaf man.***

7:1–37 See the parallel in Matt. 15:1–31.

Pharisees Accuse Jesus (7:1–23)

7:2 *with unwashen, hands.* Jesus' disciples did not ceremonially wash their hands before they ate meals as required by some Jewish traditions.

7:3–4 Mark includes this note for his non-Jewish audience.

7:5 The Pharisees and scribes recognized that the disciples broke no explicit command of God but only the *tradition*(s) of men.

7:6 *Esaias.* Isaiah (Isa. 29:13). *lips . . . heart.* An outward show of religion is the work of mere play actors (*hypocrites*); true godliness springs from inward faith, love, and obedience.

7:7 *in vain do they worship me.* God is not pleased with worship based on man's inventions and traditions but only that which He commands in His Word, with nothing added (Ex. 25:40; 39:43).

7:9–10 *commandment of God . . . your own tradition.* Religion that seeks to add man's traditions as necessary parts of serving God leads to rejecting the Word of God (Ex. 20:12; 21:17).

7:11 *Corban.* Hebrew word meaning "offering" or "something consecrated to the service of God" (cf. Lev. 1:2; Num. 7:3,13).

7:12 *suffer him no more to do ought.* Permit him no longer to do anything. They authorized people to declare their property devoted to God and yet held on to it for years, releasing them from the duty of caring for their parents.

7:14 *Hearken.* Listen.

15 There is nothing from without a man, that
entering into him can defile him: but the things
which come out of him, those are they that defile
the man.
16 If any man have ears to hear, let him hear.
17 And when he was entered into the house from
the people, his disciples asked him concerning the
parable.
18 And he saith unto them, Are ye so without
understanding also? Do ye not perceive, that
whatsoever thing from without entereth into the
man, *it* cannot defile him;
19 Because it entereth not into his heart, but into
the belly, and goeth out into the draught, purging
all meats?
20 And he said, That which cometh out of the
man, that defileth the man.
21 For from within, out of the heart of men,
proceed evil thoughts, adulteries, fornications,
murders,
22 Thefts, covetousness, wickedness, deceit,
lasciviousness, an evil eye, blasphemy, pride,
foolishness:
23 All these evil things come from within, and
defile the man.
24 ¶ And from thence he arose, and went into the
borders of Tyre and Sidon, and entered into an
house, and would have no man know *it*: but he
could not be hid.
25 For a *certain* woman, whose young daughter
had an unclean spirit, heard of him, and came
and fell at his feet:
26 The woman was a Greek, a Syrophenician by
nation; and she besought him that he would cast
forth the devil out of her daughter.
27 But Jesus said unto her, Let the children first
be filled: for it is not meet to take the children's
bread, and to cast *it* unto the dogs.
28 And she answered and said unto him, Yes,
Lord: yet the dogs under the table eat of the
children's crumbs.
29 And he said unto her, For this saying go thy
way; the devil is gone out of thy daughter.
30 And when she was come to her house, she
found the devil gone out, and her daughter laid
upon the bed.
31 ¶ And again, departing from the coasts of
Tyre and Sidon, he came unto the sea of Galilee,
through the midst of the coasts of Decapolis.
32 And they bring unto him one that was deaf,
and had an impediment in his speech; and they
beseech him to put his hand upon him.
33 And he took him aside from the multitude,
and put his fingers into his ears, and he spit, and
touched his tongue;
34 And looking up to heaven, he sighed, and saith
unto him, Ephphatha, that is, Be opened.
35 And straightway his ears were opened, and
the string of his tongue was loosed, and he spake
plain.
36 And he charged them that they should tell no
man: but the more he charged them, so much the
more a great deal they published *it*;
37 And were beyond measure astonished, saying,
He hath done all things well: he maketh both the
deaf to hear, and the dumb to speak.

7:15 *without.* Outside. *defile.* Make unclean or impure.
7:19 *draught.* Drain, sewer. *purging all meats.* Making all kinds of food to be clean. True purity is not about physical things, and God would soon release Israel from the ceremonial laws of clean and unclean after Christ had died and risen again (Acts 10:9–16; 15:5–29, Rom. 14:14; Col. 2:16–17).
7:20 *defileth.* Makes morally unclean.
7:21 *out of the heart.* Sin does not enter a person through external influences or physical uncleanness but comes from the inner corruption of fallen mankind (Gen. 6:5). The *heart* of man is stubbornly hostile to God and His truth (v. 6; 3:5; 6:52; 8:17; 10:5; 16:14; Rom. 8:7–8).
7:22 *lasciviousness.* Lustfulness.

Ministry in Tyre, Sidon, and the Decapolis (7:24—8:9)

7:24 *from thence he arose.* Jesus had just withstood the Jewish leaders and now withdrew Himself to Gentile lands (*Tyre and Sidon*), foreshadowing the gospel mission to all nations.
7:26 *Greek.* Non-Jewish (Rom. 1:16). *Syrophenician.* Of Phoenicia, a province of Syria. *besought.* Requested.
7:27 *children first.* Jesus' withdrawal from the Jews was not total rejection; they still had priority in God's plan. *meet.* Suitable. *dogs.* Often scavengers and unclean (Ex. 22:31; 2 Kings 9:36; Luke 16:21), apparently insulting language Christ used to test the woman's humility.
7:28 *yet the dogs . . . eat of the children's crumbs.* The woman's persistence shows her humility, faith in Christ as the only One who could help her, and reliance upon grace alone.
7:29–30 *devil.* Demon, evil spirit. Christ showed His power to heal at a distance by a mere word.
7:31 *coasts.* Regions. We are not told of any more teaching or miracles during this time. It is likely that Jesus traveled in relative obscurity with His disciples, teaching them as they went.
7:33–34 *fingers into his ears, and he spit.* Jesus' manner of healing differed from person to person, but it always involved His powerful word.
7:37 *deaf to hear . . . dumb to speak.* Signs that the glory of the Lord had come to Israel (Isa. 35:5–6).

Thoughts for Personal/Family Worship: Chapter 7

1. **Scripture alone is the divine rule of faith, worship, and obedience. Many people and churches follow a religion whose teachings and worship are based more upon human ideas than on the Word of God. They rarely ask, "What does God say in the Bible about this? Is this the faith and obedience that He commanded?" However, the Holy Scriptures reveal that God strongly objects to bringing Him worship that He has not required, for this does not honor His holiness (Lev. 10:1–3). Generally speaking, such man-made religion focuses upon outward acts such as following a ritual or saying a prayer, while neglecting godliness in the heart. As a result God's Word is neglected and many sins defile people from within. How can a person test his church or personal faith through application of Christ's standard of Scripture alone?**

CHAPTER 8

In those days the multitude being very great, and
having nothing to eat, Jesus called his disciples
unto him, and saith unto them,
2 I have compassion on the multitude, because
they have now been with me three days, and have
nothing to eat:
3 And if I send them away fasting to their own
houses, they will faint by the way: for divers of
them came from far.
4 And his disciples answered him, From whence
can a man satisfy these *men* with bread here in the
wilderness?
5 And he asked them, How many loaves have ye?
And they said, Seven.
6 And he commanded the people to sit down on
the ground: and he took the seven loaves, and gave
thanks, and brake, and gave to his disciples to set be-
fore *them*; and they did set *them* before the people.
7 And they had a few small fishes: and he blessed,
and commanded to set them also before *them*.
8 So they did eat, and were filled: and they took
up of the broken *meat* that was left seven baskets.
9 And they that had eaten were about four thou-
sand: and he sent them away.
10 ¶ And straightway he entered into a ship
with his disciples, and came into the parts of
Dalmanutha.
11 And the Pharisees came forth, and began to
question with him, seeking of him a sign from
heaven, tempting him.
12 And he sighed deeply in his spirit, and saith,
Why doth this generation seek after a sign? verily
I say unto you, There shall no sign be given unto
this generation.
13 And he left them, and entering into the ship
again departed to the other side.
14 ¶ Now *the disciples* had forgotten to take bread,
neither had they in the ship with them more than
one loaf.
15 And he charged them, saying, Take heed,
beware of the leaven of the Pharisees, and *of* the
leaven of Herod.
16 And they reasoned among themselves, saying,
It is because we have no bread.
17 And when Jesus knew *it*, he saith unto them,
Why reason ye, because ye have no bread? perceive
ye not yet, neither understand? have ye your heart
yet hardened?
18 Having eyes, see ye not? and having ears, hear
ye not? and do ye not remember?
19 When I brake the five loaves among five thou-
sand, how many baskets full of fragments took ye
up? They say unto him, Twelve.
20 And when the seven among four thousand,
how many baskets full of fragments took ye up?
And they said, Seven.
21 And he said unto them, How is it that ye do
not understand?
22 ¶ And he cometh to Bethsaida; and they bring
a blind man unto him, and besought him to
touch him.
23 And he took the blind man by the hand, and
led him out of the town; and when he had spit on
his eyes, and put his hands upon him, he asked
him if he saw ought.
24 And he looked up, and said, I see men as trees,
walking.
25 After that he put *his* hands again upon his eyes,
and made him look up: and he was restored, and

2. Christ's dealing with the Syro-Phoenician woman seems harsh; however, this was His way of maturing her faith. The Lord's ways with us may seem harsh too, but when we are tempted to take offense we should ask ourselves, "Am I willing to humble myself completely before the Lord? Do I believe so strongly in my need of Christ that I will keep clinging to Him even when His ways are hard? Will I submit to whatever He gives me on His terms, not my own?"

Chapter 8: ***Jesus feeds four thousand with seven loaves. He warns against the leaven of the Pharisees. He heals a blind man in two stages. Peter confesses Jesus as the Christ. Jesus predicts His coming death and resurrection.***

8:1–10 See the parallel in Matt. 15:32–39.

8:3 *divers.* Various.

8:4 *From whence.* How. The disciples seem to have forgotten the feeding of the five thousand (v. 19; 6:44).

8:8 *meat.* Food of any kind. *seven baskets.* Another large surplus of food, showing Christ's overflowing sufficiency to provide for His servants.

Pharisees Challenge in Dalmanutha (8:10–12)

8:10 *Dalmanutha.* Near the borders of Magadan (Matt. 15:39), probably on the northwestern shore of the Sea of Galilee near the southern end of the plain of Gennesaret.

8:11–21 See the parallel in Matt. 16:1–12.

8:11 *tempting.* Testing.

8:12 *sighed deeply.* An indication of His distress at their unbelief and hypocrisy. *verily.* Truly.

Pharisee's Leaven (8:13–21)

8:13 *he left them.* Jesus not only told them they would see no sign but again withdrew Himself from their presence.

8:15 *leaven.* Yeast or starter dough containing yeast. Legalistic doctrine and pride, once indulged, begin to permeate and affect everything (Gal. 5:9).

8:16–18 Even Jesus' simple illustration about leaven was not easily understood by the disciples because of their lack of spiritual perception (*see ye not… hear ye not*) and the stubborn unbelief remaining in them (3:5; 4:12; 6:52; Luke 24:25).

Healing in Bethsaida (8:22–26)

8:22 *Bethsaida.* Bethsaida-Julias on the east side of the Jordan, a village built by Philip in honor of Julia, the daughter of the emperor Augustus. Jesus likely traveled here to withdraw from the crowds and find a remote place to stay.

8:23 *led him out of the town.* It is possible that Jesus wanted the man to be concentrated on Him and not distracted by crowds (7:33). *ought.* Anything.

8:24 *I see men as trees, walking.* The uniqueness of this

saw every man clearly.
26 And he sent him away to his house, saying,
Neither go into the town, nor tell *it* to any in the
town.
27 ¶ And Jesus went out, and his disciples, into
the towns of Caesarea Philippi: and by the way he
asked his disciples, saying unto them, Whom do
men say that I am?
28 And they answered, John the Baptist: but some
say, Elias; and others, One of the prophets.
29 And he saith unto them, But whom say ye that
I am? And Peter answereth and saith unto him,
Thou art the Christ.
30 And he charged them that they should tell no
man of him.
31 And he began to teach them, that the Son of
man must suffer many things, and be rejected of
the elders, and *of* the chief priests, and scribes,
and be killed, and after three days rise again.
32 And he spake that saying openly. And Peter
took him, and began to rebuke him.
33 But when he had turned about and looked on
his disciples, he rebuked Peter, saying, Get thee be-
hind me, Satan: for thou savourest not the things
that be of God, but the things that be of men.
34 ¶ And when he had called the people *unto*
him with his disciples also, he said unto them,
Whosoever will come after me, let him deny
himself, and take up his cross, and follow me.
35 For whosoever will save his life shall lose it; but
whosoever shall lose his life for my sake and the
gospel's, the same shall save it.
36 For what shall it profit a man, if he shall gain
the whole world, and lose his own soul?
37 Or what shall a man give in exchange for his
soul?
38 Whosoever therefore shall be ashamed of me
and of my words in this adulterous and sinful
generation; of him also shall the Son of man be
ashamed, when he cometh in the glory of his
Father with the holy angels.

CHAPTER 9

AND he said unto them, Verily I say unto you, That
there be some of them that stand here, which shall

---

miracle is that Jesus intentionally performed it in stages as a sign to the disciples, whose spiritual sight was dim and distorted (v. 18). Even those with enough illumination to trust in Christ (v. 29; 2 Cor. 4:6) need further light from the Spirit to grow in their experiential knowledge of God and the gospel (Eph. 1:17–18).

Ministry in Caesarea Philippi (8:27—9:32)

8:27—9:10 See the parallels in Matt. 16:13—17:9; Luke 9:18–36.

8:27 *Caesarea Philippi.* A Roman city known for its wickedness, located twenty-five miles north of Bethsaida. Jesus traveled outside the city in the villages (*towns*). *Whom do men say that I am?* Jesus tested the disciples in light of their failure to apprehend the significance of His teachings.

8:29 *But whom say ye that I am?* All must grapple with this question. *Christ.* A title meaning "anointed," one chosen by God and empowered by the Spirit for a sacred office such as prophet, priest, or king (Ex. 28:41; 1 Sam. 16:13–14; 24:6; 1 Kings 19:16). All three offices are united in Jesus Christ (Heb. 1:1–9). Peter is the first person in this gospel to confess this title with application to Jesus (1:1).

8:30–31 *tell no man.* Though Peter answered rightly (Matt. 16:17), Jesus did not want the people stirred up by a mistaken version of the Messiah, teaching instead that He *must suffer many things* before He would *rise again* to glory. Jesus united the titles of Christ (v. 29) and *the Son of man* (see note at 2:10).

8:32 *he spake that saying openly.* Jesus was not speaking in veiled language. *began to rebuke him.* Peter's heart still contained much conceit, unbelief, and pride.

8:33 *Get thee behind me, Satan.* Peter was acting the part of an adversary of God's will, which is what the title *Satan* means. *savourest.* Sets the mind upon. Man's wisdom rejects the way of the cross but in so doing also rejects the wisdom of God (1 Cor. 1:18–25).

8:34 *take up his cross, and follow me.* The disciple must become like His Master (v. 31; Matt. 10:24–25), following Him in self-denial, earthly loss, and persecution (10:21).

8:36–37 *what shall it profit . . . what shall a man give.* The human *soul* is valuable beyond comparison, and therefore salvation must be pursued at any cost (Prov. 2:4; 3:14–15; Matt. 13:44–45).

8:38 *ashamed of me . . . in this adulterous and sinful generation.* The world will pressure Christ's disciples with its idolatrous love of earthly treasure and its hatred for God, forcing them to either reject the world and put all hope in Christ or to stand with the world and reject Christ. *when he cometh in the glory of his Father with the holy angels.* We ought to live today in light of the great day of the Lord.

Thoughts for Personal/Family Worship: Chapter 8

1. **Christ healed the blind man in two stages to show that when God converts sinners they do not see all there is to see about their own sinfulness or the glory of Christ. Sadly, even the truly saved still retain blindness and hardness in their souls, even leading us to fight against God's ways at times, especially the way of the cross that strips us of our pride and self-righteousness. Believers should pray regularly for God to give them more illumination and should learn to fight against their tendency to quarrel with God's Word.**
2. **The great determinative question we all must answer, and do answer by our life and actions, is "Who do you say that Jesus is?" It is not enough to be able to recite the views of others. You must come to an inner conviction of His identity. He is the Christ, God's Prophet anointed to replace our ignorance with the knowledge of God, Priest to take away our guilt for breaking God's law and give us a status of righteousness before Him, and King to conquer our sins and rescue us from all that would harm us. Who do you say Jesus is? Are you trusting in Him alone? Are you confessing Him before men?**

Chapter 9: ***Jesus is transfigured on the mountain. He heals a boy with a mute and deaf spirit. Once again He foretells His death and resurrection. He continues to teach his disciples about the heinous nature of sin and the cost of being a disciple.***

9:1 *Verily.* Truly. *taste of death.* A Hebrew idiom for physical

CHRISTIAN DISCIPLESHIP

In the midst of His public ministry the Lord Jesus Christ takes time in Mark 8:34 to spell out what He demands from those who wish to follow Him: "Whosoever will come after me, let him deny himself, and take up his cross, and follow me." These words are addressed to all Christians in every time and place; thus, they are still in force today.

What is a disciple? The Greek word *mathetes* means "one who learns," especially one who learns by inquiry and by use or practice of what he is taught (Abbott-Smith, *A Manual Greek-Lexicon of the New Testament*). Christ said, "Learn of me" (Matt. 11:29). All who belong to Christ must enroll in His school and learn from Him, receiving His doctrine and testimony and conforming themselves to His example of faith and godliness.

Learners need teachers. Christ has appointed teachers for His church, namely the apostles and their successors, the ministers of the Word (Acts 6:4; 1 Tim. 5:17). As servants of Christ these earthly teachers must defer to Him, and the goal of their instruction should be that Christ be formed in those under their care (Gal. 4:19): "We preach not ourselves, but Christ Jesus the Lord" (2 Cor. 4:5).

What should Christ's disciples learn? *First*, they must learn to deny themselves, to say no to self and its demands. Self-denial begins with the recognition that our problems in life result from consulting our own will, going our own way, and living for our own ends. Christ must show us that to be self-centered and self-serving is self-destructive. This cult of self is the outworking of the sinful nature with which we are born. We must turn our backs on it in order to follow Christ. Self-denial is so basic to the Christian life that Christ includes it as the third petition of His model prayer. "Thy will be done" means "Grant that we and all men may renounce our own will, and without murmuring obey Thy will, which is only good" (Heidelberg Catechism, Q. 124).

Second, disciples must learn to take up their crosses. Note the possessive pronoun. The cross indicated in this imperative is not Christ's cross but ours, the cross appointed for each of us to bear. None of us could do what Christ did for us when He went to the cross and died for our sins. Our duty is to submit to God's will for our lives as Christ did, even if the burden is heavy, the way is hard, and the end is death. Cross-bearing is grievous to us, as it was grievous to Christ. We must learn to pray as He prayed in Gethsemane, "O my Father, if this cup may not pass away from me, except I drink it, thy will be done" (Matt. 26:42).

Finally, disciples must learn to follow Christ, living by faith, walking in love, and doing good to all: "For even hereunto were ye called: because Christ also suffered for us, leaving us an example, that ye should follow in his steps" (1 Peter 2:21). To follow also means to accompany someone as a fellow traveler; as Christians, our greatest joy and privilege is to live in communion with Christ as our living Head. The psalmist Asaph knew that he was never alone in his sufferings: "I am continually with thee: thou hast holden me by my right hand. Thou shalt guide me with thy counsel, and afterward receive me to glory" (Ps. 73:23–24).

The call to discipleship is an essential part of gospel proclamation: "Go ye therefore, and make disciples of all nations." Christ's church is not merely an organization of like-minded people. Rather, as members of the body of Christ, all contribute to "the increase of the body unto the edifying of itself in love." The goal is to "grow up into him in all things, which is the head, even Christ" (Eph. 4:15–16). Disciples must grow in love for Christ and for one another, according to Christ's rule: "By this shall all men know that ye are my disciples, if ye have love one to another" (John 13:35).

not taste of death, till they have seen the kingdom
of God come with power.
2 ¶ And after six days Jesus taketh *with him* Peter,
and James, and John, and leadeth them up into an
high mountain apart by themselves: and he was
transfigured before them.
3 And his raiment became shining, exceeding
white as snow; so as no fuller on earth can white
them.
4 And there appeared unto them Elias with
Moses: and they were talking with Jesus.
5 And Peter answered and said to Jesus, Master,
it is good for us to be here: and let us make three
tabernacles; one for thee, and one for Moses, and
one for Elias.
6 For he wist not what to say; for they were sore
afraid.
7 And there was a cloud that overshadowed
them: and a voice came out of the cloud, saying,
This is my beloved Son: hear him.
8 And suddenly, when they had looked round
about, they saw no man any more, save Jesus only
with themselves.
9 And as they came down from the mountain, he
charged them that they should tell no man what
things they had seen, till the Son of man were
risen from the dead.
10 And they kept that saying with themselves,
questioning one with another what the rising
from the dead should mean.
11 ¶ And they asked him, saying, Why say the
scribes that Elias must first come?
12 And he answered and told them, Elias verily
cometh first, and restoreth all things; and how it
is written of the Son of man, that he must suffer
many things, and be set at nought.
13 But I say unto you, That Elias is indeed come,
and they have done unto him whatsoever they
listed, as it is written of him.
14 ¶ And when he came to *his* disciples, he saw
a great multitude about them, and the scribes
questioning with them.
15 And straightway all the people, when they
beheld him, were greatly amazed, and running to
him saluted him.
16 And he asked the scribes, What question ye
with them?
17 And one of the multitude answered and said,
Master, I have brought unto thee my son, which
hath a dumb spirit;
18 And wheresoever he taketh him, he teareth
him: and he foameth, and gnasheth with his teeth,
and pineth away: and I spake to thy disciples that
they should cast him out; and they could not.
19 He answereth him, and saith, O faithless gen-
eration, how long shall I be with you? how long
shall I suffer you? bring him unto me.
20 And they brought him unto him: and when he
saw him, straightway the spirit tare him; and he
fell on the ground, and wallowed foaming.
21 And he asked his father, How long is it ago
since this came unto him? And he said, Of a child.
22 And ofttimes it hath cast him into the fire, and
into the waters, to destroy him: but if thou canst
do any thing, have compassion on us, and help us.
23 Jesus said unto him, If thou canst believe, all
things *are* possible to him that believeth.
24 And straightway the father of the child cried
out, and said with tears, Lord, I believe; help thou
mine unbelief.
25 When Jesus saw that the people came running
together, he rebuked the foul spirit, saying unto
him, *Thou* dumb and deaf spirit, I charge thee,
come out of him, and enter no more into him.
26 And *the spirit* cried, and rent him sore,
and came out of him: and he was as one dead;
insomuch that many said, He is dead.
27 But Jesus took him by the hand, and lifted him
up; and he arose.
28 And when he was come into the house, his

death. *seen the kingdom of God.* The power of God's reign through Christ appeared soon after this in the transfiguration of Jesus (vv. 2–8), as well as in Christ's death, resurrection, ascension, and pouring out of the Spirit (see note at Matt. 16:28).

9:2 *high mountain.* Significant in Scripture as a place of divine revelation (Ex. 3:1; 19–20; 34:1–9; 1 Kings 18:19–20; 19:8–12; Ezek. 40:2). *transfigured.* Transformed in appearance, as Moses was in the presence of God, but with far greater glory (Ex. 34:29–35; Rev. 1:16).

9:3 *raiment.* Clothing. *fuller.* Bleacher or cleaner of cloth.

9:4 *talking with Jesus.* The three of them were discussing Jesus' upcoming death and resurrection (Luke 9:31).

9:6 *wist.* Knew. *sore.* Extremely.

9:7 *my beloved Son.* The Father affirmed Jesus' special mission and His unique relationship to Himself (1:11). *hear him.* Identifying Jesus as the Prophet promised by Moses (Deut. 18:15), whose Word we must follow if we desire to be saved (Acts 3:19–23). Peter later confirmed the historical reality of Jesus' transfiguration as an eyewitness of the event (2 Peter 1:16–18).

9:8 *save.* Except.

9:11–13 See the parallel in Matt. 17:10–13.

9:12 *Elias.* Elijah, in whose spirit John the Baptist came to preach against sin in Israel (see notes at 1:5 and 6).

9:14–32 See the parallels in Matt. 17:14–23; Luke 9:37–45.

9:15 *amazed.* Terrified.

9:17 *dumb spirit.* A demon that made him unable to speak.

9:18 *wheresoever he taketh him.* Whenever it seizes him. *pineth away.* Dries, withers, perhaps stiffens.

9:19 *how long.* Jesus, being sinless and holy, found it distressing and provoking to live among *faithless* people. *suffer.* Bear with, endure.

9:22 *if thou canst.* His faith was weak (contrast 1:40).

9:23 *If thou canst believe, all things are possible.* Jesus turns the man's statement around (v. 22), showing that it is not a question of Christ's ability, for He can do all things, but of the man's faith.

9:24 *Lord, I believe; help thou mine unbelief.* Christ has achieved His aim with the father of the boy, exposing the inward struggle in his heart and drawing him to seek help from Christ against unbelief.

disciples asked him privately, Why could not we
cast him out?
29 And he said unto them, This kind can come
forth by nothing, but by prayer and fasting.
30 ¶ And they departed thence, and passed
through Galilee; and he would not that any man
should know *it*.
31 For he taught his disciples, and said unto
them, The Son of man is delivered into the hands
of men, and they shall kill him; and after that he is
killed, he shall rise the third day.
32 But they understood not that saying, and were
afraid to ask him.
33 ¶ And he came to Capernaum: and being in
the house he asked them, What was it that ye
disputed among yourselves by the way?
34 But they held their peace: for by the way they
had disputed among themselves, who *should be*
the greatest.
35 And he sat down, and called the twelve, and
saith unto them, If any man desire to be first, *the
same* shall be last of all, and servant of all.
36 And he took a child, and set him in the midst
of them: and when he had taken him in his arms,
he said unto them,
37 Whosoever shall receive one of such children
in my name, receiveth me: and whosoever shall re-
ceive me, receiveth not me, but him that sent me.
38 ¶ And John answered him, saying, Master, we
saw one casting out devils in thy name, and he
followeth not us: and we forbad him, because he
followeth not us.
39 But Jesus said, Forbid him not: for there is no
man which shall do a miracle in my name, that
can lightly speak evil of me.
40 For he that is not against us is on our part.
41 For whosoever shall give you a cup of water to
drink in my name, because ye belong to Christ,
verily I say unto you, he shall not lose his reward.
42 And whosoever shall offend one of *these* little
ones that believe in me, it is better for him that
a millstone were hanged about his neck, and he
were cast into the sea.
43 And if thy hand offend thee, cut it off: it is
better for thee to enter into life maimed, than
having two hands to go into hell, into the fire that
never shall be quenched:
44 Where their worm dieth not, and the fire is not
quenched.
45 And if thy foot offend thee, cut it off: it is
better for thee to enter halt into life, than having
two feet to be cast into hell, into the fire that never
shall be quenched:
46 Where their worm dieth not, and the fire is not
quenched.
47 And if thine eye offend thee, pluck it out: it is
better for thee to enter into the kingdom of God
with one eye, than having two eyes to be cast into
hell fire:
48 Where their worm dieth not, and the fire is not
quenched.
49 For every one shall be salted with fire, and
every sacrifice shall be salted with salt.
50 Salt *is* good: but if the salt have lost his

9:26 *sore*. Greatly, severely.
9:29 *prayer and fasting*. Though endowed by Christ with gifts to cast out demons (6:7), the apostles still needed to depend completely on God for power. Spiritual gifts must be exercised by faith.
9:31 *Son of man . . . killed . . . rise*. See note at 8:30–31.

Return to Capernaum (9:33–50)

9:33–37 See the parallels in Matt. 18:1–5; Luke 9:46–48.
9:34 *held their peace*. Were silent.
9:35–36 *servant of all*. See 10:44–45. *he took a child*. The humility and dependence of children are a model for the disciples' faith in the Lord and participation in His kingdom, and therefore one mark of a true disciple is welcoming humble believers in Jesus Christ.
9:38–41 See the parallel in Luke 9:49–50.
9:38 *he followeth not us*. Though a professing believer in Christ (*in thy name*), this man was not directly associated with the apostles. At this point in history the church was not yet separated from the nation of Israel, and Christ's followers were scattered among the Jews, not yet gathered in churches under the oversight of the apostles.
9:41 *whosoever shall give you a cup of water*. While this may seem like a small gesture that could easily be forgotten, when given in God's name it shall be rewarded (Matt 10:42).
9:42–50 See the parallel in Matt. 18:6–9.
9:43–48 *offend*. Cause to stumble or fall. *halt*. Lame. *cut it off . . . pluck it out*. While Jesus spoke metaphorically, it is important to note the level of self-denial required to fight sin. *hell*. Greek *gehenna*, originally from the Hebrew phrase "valley of Hinnom" (see note at Jer. 19:6) used by Christ for the final and never-ending punishment of the wicked. *fire . . . not quenched*. God's anger will punish the wicked with unremitting pain (Deut. 32:22; Isa. 33:14; 34:9–10). *worm dieth not*. The wicked will experience unending death, decay, and disgrace (Isa. 66:24).
9:49 *salted with fire*. Likely represents purification through sufferings on earth. *every sacrifice . . . salted*. Old Testament offerings involved salt as a sign of covenant faithfulness (Lev. 2:13; Num. 18:19; Ezek. 43:24). Believers are living sacrifices, offered in faithfulness as their response to God's saving mercies (Rom. 12:1–2).
9:50 *Salt is good*. Salt is valuable for its pleasing flavor (Job 6:6) and action to preserve food, and also as an antiseptic (Ezek. 16:4), and so the distinctive faithfulness of believers pleases God, promotes good in the world, and restrains evil. *lost his saltness*. Salt in the ancient world was a mixture of minerals, and the sodium chloride could leach away by moisture, leaving behind useless minerals. *Have salt in yourselves*. It is useless to try to have an influence on others for good if things are not right with us, beginning with our relationships within the church (*peace one with another*).

Thoughts for Personal/Family Worship: Chapter 9

1. **There is every reason to listen to God's Son. He has now even more glory than on the Mount of Transfiguration, for now in heaven He is crowned with glory and**

saltness, wherewith will ye season it? Have salt in
yourselves, and have peace one with another.

CHAPTER 10

AND he arose from thence, and cometh into the
coasts of Judaea by the farther side of Jordan: and
the people resort unto him again; and, as he was
wont, he taught them again.
2 ¶ And the Pharisees came to him, and asked
him, Is it lawful for a man to put away *his* wife?
tempting him.
3 And he answered and said unto them, What did
Moses command you?
4 And they said, Moses suffered to write a bill of
divorcement, and to put *her* away.
5 And Jesus answered and said unto them, For
the hardness of your heart he wrote you this
precept.
6 But from the beginning of the creation God
made them male and female.
7 For this cause shall a man leave his father and
mother, and cleave to his wife;
8 And they twain shall be one flesh: so then they
are no more twain, but one flesh.
9 What therefore God hath joined together, let
not man put asunder.
10 And in the house his disciples asked him again
of the same *matter*.
11 And he saith unto them, Whosoever shall put
away his wife, and marry another, committeth
adultery against her.
12 And if a woman shall put away her husband,
and be married to another, she committeth
adultery.
13 ¶ And they brought young children to him,
that he should touch them: and *his* disciples
rebuked those that brought *them*.
14 But when Jesus saw *it*, he was much displeased,
and said unto them, Suffer the little children to
come unto me, and forbid them not: for of such
is the kingdom of God.
15 Verily I say unto you, Whosoever shall not
receive the kingdom of God as a little child, he
shall not enter therein.
16 And he took them up in his arms, put *his*
hands upon them, and blessed them.
17 ¶ And when he was gone forth into the way,
there came one running, and kneeled to him, and
asked him, Good Master, what shall I do that I
may inherit eternal life?
18 And Jesus said unto him, Why callest thou me
good? *there is* none good but one, *that is*, God.
19 Thou knowest the commandments, Do not

---

splendor. God still says of Him, "Hear him" (v. 7). He is God's appointed Prophet over the church, the Teacher who speaks through all faithful teachers of the Word. How should it change our attitude toward preaching and teaching to know that if the preacher or teacher faithfully explains and applies the Bible, the Lord Jesus Christ is personally speaking to us?

2. **Faith and unbelief wrestle for dominance in the regenerate heart (v. 24). It can seem sometimes as though unbelief will grab faith by the throat and try to strangle it. Faith, however, cries to Christ for help, which Christ is sure to give. How does the father's prayer, "Lord, I believe; help thou mine unbelief," encourage us to pray?**
3. **Having seen the glory of Christ, it is hard to believe the disciples would argue about who of them was the greatest (v. 34). Yet how prone we are as sinful human beings to boast and brag—even about spiritual experiences. We need to learn again and again the lesson of vv. 35–36.**

THE JUDEAN PERIOD (10:1—13:37)

Chapter 10: *Jesus travels to and labors in Judaea. He teaches His disciples about true greatness. He heals blind Bartimaeus.*

Jesus Travels to Jerusalem (10:1–52)

10:1–31 See the parallel in Matt. 19:1–30.

10:1 *coasts.* Regions. Mark records Jesus' final journey to Jerusalem with this short summary statement. *resort.* Gather. *wont.* Accustomed.

10:2 *tempting.* Putting Him to the test.

10:4 *suffered.* Permitted. *write a bill of divorcement.* Many of the religious elite saw this permission to be a blessing, not just a concession (Deut. 24:1).

10:5 *hardness of your heart.* While the Pharisees looked at this precept as a license to put away their wives, Jesus showed that this precept was based on man's deplorable moral character.

10:6–8 *from the beginning of the creation.* Jesus appealed to the original created order (Gen. 1:27; 2:24), indicating that He understood Gen. 1–2 to teach God's creation of mankind at the very *beginning* of His making of the world, as opposed to many years later. Based on God's creation ordinance, Jesus taught that marriage is to be only between a man and a woman (*male and female . . . man . . . wife*). *twain shall be one flesh.* The two individuals are joined in a lasting personal and sexual union.

10:9 *God hath joined together.* Marriage, though entered into by a man and a woman, is more than a social contract; it is an act of God. *asunder.* Apart.

10:11 *put away.* Divorce. Christ qualified His general prohibition against divorce with the exception of the case of sexual immorality (Matt. 5:31–32; 19:8–9).

10:14–15 *displeased.* This is no little matter to Christ and shows His love for children. *Suffer.* Permit. *of such is the kingdom.* Jesus was not teaching that all children are saved but that all who have a part in His kingdom are like children in their humility, receptiveness to authority, and simple yet profound trust in God's grace (*receive . . . as a little child*). *Verily.* Truly.

10:17 *there came one.* He was a young, rich ruler (v. 22; Luke 18:18). *running . . . kneeled . . . Good Master.* He approached Jesus with eagerness and respect.

10:18 *Why callest thou me good?* Jesus was not denying that He is good (1:11) but pressing the man to consider what truly constitutes goodness. *none good but . . . God.* God is the true standard of goodness. Goodness must come from God and God alone because of man's wicked nature.

10:19 Jesus quoted the fifth through ninth commandments

commit adultery, Do not kill, Do not steal, Do
not bear false witness, Defraud not, Honour thy
father and mother.
20 And he answered and said unto him, Master,
all these have I observed from my youth.
21 Then Jesus beholding him loved him, and said
unto him, One thing thou lackest: go thy way, sell
whatsoever thou hast, and give to the poor, and
thou shalt have treasure in heaven: and come, take
up the cross, and follow me.
22 And he was sad at that saying, and went away
grieved: for he had great possessions.
23 ¶ And Jesus looked round about, and saith
unto his disciples, How hardly shall they that have
riches enter into the kingdom of God!
24 And the disciples were astonished at his words.
But Jesus answereth again, and saith unto them,
Children, how hard is it for them that trust in
riches to enter into the kingdom of God!
25 It is easier for a camel to go through the eye
of a needle, than for a rich man to enter into the
kingdom of God.
26 And they were astonished out of measure,
saying among themselves, Who then can be saved?
27 And Jesus looking upon them saith, With men
it is impossible, but not with God: for with God
all things are possible.
28 ¶ Then Peter began to say unto him, Lo, we
have left all, and have followed thee.
29 And Jesus answered and said, Verily I say unto
you, There is no man that hath left house, or
brethren, or sisters, or father, or mother, or wife,
or children, or lands, for my sake, and the gospel's,
30 But he shall receive an hundredfold now in
this time, houses, and brethren, and sisters, and
mothers, and children, and lands, with persecu-
tions; and in the world to come eternal life.
31 But many *that are* first shall be last; and the
last first.
32 ¶ And they were in the way going up to
Jerusalem; and Jesus went before them: and they
were amazed; and as they followed, they were
afraid. And he took again the twelve, and began
to tell them what things should happen unto him,
33 *Saying*, Behold, we go up to Jerusalem; and
the Son of man shall be delivered unto the chief
priests, and unto the scribes; and they shall
condemn him to death, and shall deliver him to
the Gentiles:
34 And they shall mock him, and shall scourge
him, and shall spit upon him, and shall kill him:
and the third day he shall rise again.
35 ¶ And James and John, the sons of Zebedee,
come unto him, saying, Master, we would that
thou shouldest do for us whatsoever we shall
desire.
36 And he said unto them, What would ye that I
should do for you?
37 They said unto him, Grant unto us that we
may sit, one on thy right hand, and the other on
thy left hand, in thy glory.
38 But Jesus said unto them, Ye know not what ye
ask: can ye drink of the cup that I drink of? and
be baptized with the baptism that I am baptized
with?
39 And they said unto him, We can. And Jesus
said unto them, Ye shall indeed drink of the cup
that I drink of; and with the baptism that I am
baptized withal shall ye be baptized:
40 But to sit on my right hand and on my left
hand is not mine to give; but *it shall be given to*
them for whom it is prepared.

---

concerning man's responsibility to man (Ex. 20:12–16). *Defraud not.* Do not take things or rights from others by abuse of power or unjust legal action (Greek Septuagint of Ex. 21:10; Deut. 15:7; Mal. 3:5; also Luke 19:8; 1 Cor. 6:7–8).

10:20 *all these have I observed from my youth.* Though perhaps he had an outward conformity to the law (Phil. 3:6), he was blind to the condition of his heart (see note at 7:21).

10:21 *loved him.* Christ's response was not cold and disinterested but one of genuine concern, reflective of what God says of Himself in Hosea 11:1,3,8. *One thing thou lackest.* Christ put His finger on the man's central problem: a covetous heart. *sell whatsoever thou hast.* Not a command to all, but the believer must treasure Christ above all things (Matt. 13:44; Phil. 3:8).

10:23 *hardly.* With difficulty.

10:24 *trust in riches.* Riches are not inherently sinful, but sinners abuse wealth to feed their sense of independence, pride, and self-righteousness (Prov. 18:10–11,23; 28:11). One's hope must be in God and one's holy ambition to gain the heavenly treasure of His kingdom (v. 21; 1 Tim. 6:6–10,17–19).

10:25 *easier for a camel to go through the eye of a needle.* An impossibility, perhaps being illustrated by a popular proverb.

10:26–27 *Who then can be saved?* Since the rich were commonly regarded as blessed by God, Jesus' words seemed to make salvation impossible for any. *With men . . . impossible . . . with God all things are possible.* Christ affirmed that man's condition is so bad that no one can save or convert himself (John 6:44), but God can save anyone He chooses because of His infinite power (Jer. 32:17; Luke 1:37).

10:30 *now in this time.* The Christian's reward (Heb. 11:26) is not merely for a distant future; even in this age he receives many blessings from God's providence, including the fellowship of the church, yet mixed *with persecutions* until Christ returns with *eternal life.*

10:32–34 See the parallels in Matt. 20:17–19; Luke 18:31–34.

10:33–34 *scourge.* Whip. Jesus prophesied in explicit detail what would happen to Him at the hand of the *Gentiles* (15:15,19). God's foreknowledge of the future is perfect.

10:35–45 See the parallel in Matt. 20:20–28.

10:37 *right hand . . . left hand, in thy glory.* Places of honor and prestige in royal courts.

10:38 *drink of the cup.* A symbol of one's portion from God, whether of joy (Pss. 23:5; 116:13) or of suffering (Ps. 75:8; Isa. 51:17–23; Zech. 12:2). *baptized.* A figure of speech for Christ's sufferings, compared to sinking in deep waters (Luke 12:50; cf. Ps. 69:1–2; Jonah 2:3).

10:39 *Ye shall indeed.* Jesus did not rebuke their rashness but promised they would endure suffering. *withal.* With.

10:43–44 *minister.* Servant. *servant.* The term for a bond-

41 And when the ten heard *it*, they began to be
much displeased with James and John.
42 But Jesus called them *to him*, and saith unto
them, Ye know that they which are accounted to
rule over the Gentiles exercise lordship over them;
and their great ones exercise authority upon
them.
43 But so shall it not be among you: but
whosoever will be great among you, shall be your
minister:
44 And whosoever of you will be the chiefest,
shall be servant of all.
45 For even the Son of man came not to be
ministered unto, but to minister, and to give his
life a ransom for many.
46 ¶ And they came to Jericho: and as he went out
of Jericho with his disciples and a great number
of people, blind Bartimaeus, the son of Timaeus,
sat by the highway side begging.
47 And when he heard that it was Jesus of
Nazareth, he began to cry out, and say, Jesus, *thou*
Son of David, have mercy on me.
48 And many charged him that he should hold
his peace: but he cried the more a great deal, *Thou*
Son of David, have mercy on me.
49 And Jesus stood still, and commanded him to
be called. And they call the blind man, saying unto
him, Be of good comfort, rise; he calleth thee.
50 And he, casting away his garment, rose, and
came to Jesus.
51 And Jesus answered and said unto him, What
wilt thou that I should do unto thee? The blind
man said unto him, Lord, that I might receive my
sight.
52 And Jesus said unto him, Go thy way; thy
faith hath made thee whole. And immediately he
received his sight, and followed Jesus in the way.

CHAPTER 11

AND when they came nigh to Jerusalem, unto
Bethphage and Bethany, at the mount of Olives,
he sendeth forth two of his disciples,
2 And saith unto them, Go your way into the
village over against you: and as soon as ye be
entered into it, ye shall find a colt tied, whereon
never man sat; loose him, and bring *him*.
3 And if any man say unto you, Why do ye
this? say ye that the Lord hath need of him; and
straightway he will send him hither.

slave, a person of the lowest status in society, the position Christ took to save sinners and accomplish His Father's will (Phil. 2:8; cf. John 13:3–5).

10:45 *Son of man*. The divinely appointed King of kings (see note at 2:10). *not . . . ministered unto, but to minister*. Not served, but to serve, an amazing mission of condescension and humility for One so great. *ransom*. The price to redeem sinners from the guilt and punishment they deserve (Ex. 21:30; Ps. 130:3–4,7–8). *for many*. Literally, "in the place of many," communicating the substitution of Christ for His people under the judgment of God against sinners (Isa. 53:4–6).

10:46–52 See the parallels in Matt. 20:29–34; Luke 18:35–43.

10:46 *blind Bartimaeus*. Mark's use of the man's name (unique in the Gospels) suggests that he was likely known to the early church.

10:47 *Son of David*. A title for the Messiah, based on God's covenant with King David in which God promised to give an eternal kingdom to David's offspring (2 Sam. 7:12–16; Ps. 89:1–3,19–37).

10:48 *hold his peace*. Be quiet. The persistence of Bartimaeus despite pressure from the crowd shows the depth of his faith in Jesus.

10:49 *Be of good comfort*. Have courage.

10:50 *garment*. Here, his outer cloak.

10:51 *What wilt thou?* What do you want? *Lord*. Literally, "Rabbi."

10:52 *thy faith hath made thee whole*. Literally, "your faith has saved you." Many of Christ's miracles worked through the trust of people, a sign that spiritual salvation is by faith (2:5; 5:34).

Thoughts for Personal/Family Worship: Chapter 10

1. **Marriage is an institution of God, defined by Him at creation, formed by Him in the bond between each husband and wife, and jealously watched over by Him. For this reason marriage is to be held in high honor and neither dismissed nor distorted. How is marriage under attack in your nation? How do Christ's teachings (vv. 2–12) enable Christians to defend marriage biblically?**
2. **The human heart is by nature deceitful and self-righteous, minimizing the severity of our sins even as we outwardly may seem very religious (vv. 17–27). Our pride flatters us that we have kept God's commandments and can do what God requires to enter His kingdom. This horrible arrogance especially feeds upon riches and prosperity, falsely assuring us that God has blessed us because we are good. Christ shows us how to confront our pride: through the searching application of God's laws to the heart, by the gospel call to follow Christ, and by the declaration of human inability and divine sovereignty in salvation. People may find these truths offensive and leave grieved, but they are the method of the loving Savior (v. 21) to win people to true discipleship.**
3. **Christ asked the same question of James and John as of blind Bartimaeus: "What do you want Me to do for you?" (vv. 36,51). Their answers were markedly different. The apostles sought personal honor and glory among men, while the beggar sought mercy and healing. If Christ were to ask you this question, what would you say you most desire from Him? What would your answer show about your heart?**

Chapter 11: *Jesus enters into Jerusalem, cleanses the temple, and confronts the chief priests and scribes who challenge His authority.*

Triumphal Entry (11:1–26)

11:1–10 See the parallels in Matt. 21:1–9; Luke 19:28–40.

11:1 *Bethphage and Bethany*. Both of these villages were on the slopes of the *mount of Olives*, a ridge east of Jerusalem.

11:2 *whereon never man sat*. Animals that had never carried a burden were used for special, sacred purposes (Num. 19:2; Deut. 21:3; 1 Sam. 6:7).

11:3 *hither*. Here.

4 And they went their way, and found the colt
tied by the door without in a place where two
ways met; and they loose him.
5 And certain of them that stood there said unto
them, What do ye, loosing the colt?
6 And they said unto them even as Jesus had
commanded: and they let them go.
7 And they brought the colt to Jesus, and cast
their garments on him; and he sat upon him.
8 And many spread their garments in the way:
and others cut down branches off the trees, and
strawed *them* in the way.
9 And they that went before, and they that
followed, cried, saying, Hosanna; Blessed *is* he
that cometh in the name of the Lord:
10 Blessed *be* the kingdom of our father David,
that cometh in the name of the Lord: Hosanna in
the highest.
11 And Jesus entered into Jerusalem, and into the
temple: and when he had looked round about
upon all things, and now the eventide was come,
he went out unto Bethany with the twelve.
12 ¶ And on the morrow, when they were come
from Bethany, he was hungry:
13 And seeing a fig tree afar off having leaves, he
came, if haply he might find any thing thereon:
and when he came to it, he found nothing but
leaves; for the time of figs was not *yet*.
14 And Jesus answered and said unto it, No
man eat fruit of thee hereafter for ever. And his
disciples heard *it*.
15 ¶ And they come to Jerusalem: and Jesus went
into the temple, and began to cast out them that
sold and bought in the temple, and overthrew
the tables of the moneychangers, and the seats of
them that sold doves;
16 And would not suffer that any man should
carry *any* vessel through the temple.
17 And he taught, saying unto them, Is it not
written, My house shall be called of all nations
the house of prayer? but ye have made it a den
of thieves.
18 And the scribes and chief priests heard *it*, and
sought how they might destroy him: for they
feared him, because all the people was astonished
at his doctrine.
19 And when even was come, he went out of the
city.
20 ¶ And in the morning, as they passed by, they
saw the fig tree dried up from the roots.
21 And Peter calling to remembrance saith unto
him, Master, behold, the fig tree which thou
cursedst is withered away.
22 And Jesus answering saith unto them, Have
faith in God.
23 For verily I say unto you, That whosoever shall
say unto this mountain, Be thou removed, and be
thou cast into the sea; and shall not doubt in his
heart, but shall believe that those things which he
saith shall come to pass; he shall have whatsoever
he saith.
24 Therefore I say unto you, What things soever
ye desire, when ye pray, believe that ye receive
them, and ye shall have *them*.
25 And when ye stand praying, forgive, if ye have
ought against any: that your Father also which is

11:4 *without.* Outside.

11:7 *brought the colt . . . he sat upon him.* Christ arrived in Jerusalem in a manner that announced Himself to be the promised king (Zech. 9:9).

11:8 *strawed.* Scattered. Spreading garments on the ground was a way of honoring a new king (2 Kings 9:13).

11:9–10 *Hosanna.* Literally a prayer meaning, "Please save." The people used the words of Ps. 118:24–26, though perhaps this had become something of a religious formula. When in a few days Jesus was in the power of the Romans instead of saving Israel from the Romans, the fickle crowd's cry changed to "Crucify him" (15:13).

11:11–26 See the parallels in Matt. 21:10–22; Luke 19:45–48.

11:12 *the morrow.* The next day.

11:13–14 *leaves.* An indication that the *tree* probably had small or undeveloped figs, though spring was not the season for large, fully ripened figs (*the time of figs was not yet*). *found nothing but leaves.* The disappointing absence of fruit provided Jesus with an object lesson on hypocrisy. The *fig tree* was a symbol of Israel's prosperity (13:28; Deut. 8:8; 1 Kings 4:25; Jer. 8:13; Hos. 9:10; Zech. 3:10). God desired the fruit of righteousness (12:2; Isa. 5:7), but when Christ inspected Jerusalem and its temple He found it barren (vv. 11,15–17), despite its outward beauty (13:1), and thus pronounced divine judgment on it, symbolized by the withering of the tree.

11:15 *cast out . . . overthrew the tables.* Jesus acted as the Lord of the temple, come to purify His people's worship according to the covenant (Mal. 3:1–4). It is possible that the sellers and bankers (*moneychangers*) took more profit for their services than they had coming.

11:16 *suffer.* Permit. This verse is unique to Mark, likely referring to people walking through the court of the Gentiles as a shortcut on their way to conducting business, a form of irreverence and worldliness.

11:17 *house of prayer . . . den of thieves.* God had designed the temple as a place where people of all nations could seek His grace by repentance and prayer (1 Kings 8:28–53), but Israel was abusing its outward forms of worship as a way to cover their refusal to repent of sin (Isa. 56:7; Jer. 7:11).

11:20–26 See the parallels in Matt. 21:20–22.

11:22 *Have faith in God.* Or possibly, "Grasp hold of the faithfulness of God."

11:23 *verily.* Truly. *mountain . . . cast into the sea.* Not a literal reference to massive changes in geography but a figure of speech for prophesying of God's judgment against His enemies, here Mount Zion or Jerusalem itself (Ps. 46:2; Jer. 51:25; Zech. 4:7).

11:24 *believe that ye receive them.* Prayer should be lifted up with faith in God's generosity (James 1:6) and in unity with other believers (*ye* is plural; cf. Matt. 18:19) without division caused by a lack of forgiving each other (vv. 25–26). Such prayers generally receive what they seek from God, though this promise cannot be taken to allow man to dictate his own will over God's will and glory. In this context the promise is linked to prayers for God to overcome the enemies of His worship and kingdom.

in heaven may forgive you your trespasses.
26 But if ye do not forgive, neither will your
Father which is in heaven forgive your trespasses.
27 ¶ And they come again to Jerusalem: and as he
was walking in the temple, there come to him the
chief priests, and the scribes, and the elders,
28 And say unto him, By what authority doest
thou these things? and who gave thee this
authority to do these things?
29 And Jesus answered and said unto them, I will
also ask of you one question, and answer me, and
I will tell you by what authority I do these things.
30 The baptism of John, was *it* from heaven, or of
men? answer me.
31 And they reasoned with themselves, saying, If
we shall say, From heaven; he will say, Why then
did ye not believe him?
32 But if we shall say, Of men; they feared the
people: for all *men* counted John, that he was a
prophet indeed.
33 And they answered and said unto Jesus, We
cannot tell. And Jesus answering saith unto them,
Neither do I tell you by what authority I do these
things.

CHAPTER 12

AND he began to speak unto them by parables. A
certain man planted a vineyard, and set an hedge
about *it*, and digged *a place for* the winefat, and
built a tower, and let it out to husbandmen, and
went into a far country.
2 And at the season he sent to the husbandmen a
servant, that he might receive from the husband-
men of the fruit of the vineyard.
3 And they caught *him*, and beat him, and sent
him away empty.
4 And again he sent unto them another servant;
and at him they cast stones, and wounded *him* in
the head, and sent *him* away shamefully handled.
5 And again he sent another; and him they killed,
and many others; beating some, and killing some.
6 Having yet therefore one son, his wellbeloved,
he sent him also last unto them, saying, They will
reverence my son.
7 But those husbandmen said among themselves,
This is the heir; come, let us kill him, and the
inheritance shall be ours.
8 And they took him, and killed *him*, and cast
him out of the vineyard.
9 What shall therefore the lord of the vineyard
do? he will come and destroy the husbandmen,
and will give the vineyard unto others.
10 And have ye not read this scripture; The stone
which the builders rejected is become the head of
the corner:
11 This was the Lord's doing, and it is marvellous
in our eyes?

Public Teaching and Questions (11:27—12:44)

11:27–33 See the parallels in Matt. 21:23–27; Luke 20:1–8.
11:28 *what authority... who gave thee this authority.* The two questions posed to Jesus were meant to trap Him, since He had not been officially trained as a rabbi and had no human credentials. They would not recognize the divine testimony of His works and words.
11:33 *Neither do I tell you.* Jesus turned the tables on them, trapping them with His question because they feared man rather than loving the truth (vv. 31–32) and thus refused to answer.

Thoughts for Personal/Family Worship: Chapter 11

1. **Hypocritical religion pretends to be what it is not, but Christ will uncover it. Like a tree with many leaves yet no fruit, the religious hypocrite displays to the world many impressive activities of devotion and self-denial, but under the leaves of external religion the Lord sees that there are no fruits of Christian love for God and man, joy in the Lord, or peace by Christ's blood. The Lord Jesus is patient, but the time will come when He will judge us all. If our godliness is only a form without His underlying power, He will curse us with a supernatural word of judgment that will wither us from the roots. Search yourself by this word. Is your godliness a matter of mere leaves? What spiritual fruits is Christ producing in you?**
2. **Prayer is an instrument of immense power, for it invokes the almighty arm of God. We should take up prayer with boldness, believing it to be the weapon by which God casts down every mountain raised up against the true worship of Himself. We should pray with faith in God's goodness and generosity toward His children, and we should pray together with other believers in a spirit of love, forgiveness, and unity. How would you describe your prayer life now? How does this chapter stir you to desire a deeper prayer life?**

Chapter 12: *Jesus tells the parable of the wicked husbandmen. He teaches concerning the authority of Caesar, vindicates the doctrine of the resurrection against the Sadducees, teaches concerning the two great commandments, and teaches about the widow's mite.*

12:1–12 See the parallels in Matt. 21:33–46; Luke 20:9–19.
12:1 *vineyard.* An image for Israel (Ps. 80:8–16; Isa. 5:1–7; Jer. 2:21). *winefat.* Winepress. *husbandmen.* Tenant farmers. Nothing has been left undone in preparing this vineyard to be fruitful.
12:2–5 *servant.* One of God's messengers, the Old Testament prophets who suffered persecution from Israel.
12:6 *one son, his wellbeloved.* Jesus discreetly spoke of His unique relationship with His Father, who loves Him dearly (1:11; 9:7). *They will reverence my son.* God was not ignorant or mistaken concerning their plans against Jesus (vv. 10–11; Acts 2:23); the parable expresses the honor they should have given Christ as the Son of God (Ps. 2:7–12).
12:9 *destroy . . . give the vineyard unto others.* The kingdom will be taken from Israel as a nation and given over to believers, both Jews and Gentiles (Matt. 21:43), a reconstitution of spiritual Israel around Christ so that by union with Him it may bear much fruit (John 15:1–8).
12:10–11 *this scripture.* Citing Ps. 118:22–23 (cf. 11:9–10). *stone which the builders rejected.* God foretold Christ's rejection by the leaders centuries before Christ came. *head of the corner.* Cornerstone. Though Christ was rejected by men, God made

12 And they sought to lay hold on him, but feared
the people: for they knew that he had spoken the
parable against them: and they left him, and went
their way.
13 ¶ And they send unto him certain of the
Pharisees and of the Herodians, to catch him in
his words.
14 And when they were come, they say unto him,
Master, we know that thou art true, and carest
for no man: for thou regardest not the person of
men, but teachest the way of God in truth: Is it
lawful to give tribute to Caesar, or not?
15 Shall we give, or shall we not give? But he,
knowing their hypocrisy, said unto them, Why
tempt ye me? bring me a penny, that I may see *it*.
16 And they brought *it*. And he saith unto them,
Whose *is* this image and superscription? And they
said unto him, Caesar's.
17 And Jesus answering said unto them, Render
to Caesar the things that are Caesar's, and to God
the things that are God's. And they marvelled at
him.
18 ¶ Then come unto him the Sadducees, which
say there is no resurrection; and they asked him,
saying,
19 Master, Moses wrote unto us, If a man's
brother die, and leave *his* wife *behind him*, and
leave no children, that his brother should take his
wife, and raise up seed unto his brother.
20 Now there were seven brethren: and the first
took a wife, and dying left no seed.
21 And the second took her, and died, neither left
he any seed: and the third likewise.
22 And the seven had her, and left no seed: last of
all the woman died also.
23 In the resurrection therefore, when they shall
rise, whose wife shall she be of them? for the seven
had her to wife.
24 And Jesus answering said unto them, Do
ye not therefore err, because ye know not the
scriptures, neither the power of God?
25 For when they shall rise from the dead, they
neither marry, nor are given in marriage; but are
as the angels which are in heaven.
26 And as touching the dead, that they rise: have
ye not read in the book of Moses, how in the bush
God spake unto him, saying, I *am* the God of Abra-
ham, and the God of Isaac, and the God of Jacob?
27 He is not the God of the dead, but the God of
the living: ye therefore do greatly err.
28 ¶ And one of the scribes came, and having
heard them reasoning together, and perceiving
that he had answered them well, asked him,
Which is the first commandment of all?
29 And Jesus answered him, The first of all the
commandments *is*, Hear, O Israel; The Lord our
God is one Lord:
30 And thou shalt love the Lord thy God with all
thy heart, and with all thy soul, and with all thy
mind, and with all thy strength: this *is* the first
commandment.
31 And the second *is* like, *namely* this, Thou shalt
love thy neighbour as thyself. There is none other
commandment greater than these.
32 And the scribe said unto him, Well, Master,
thou hast said the truth: for there is one God; and
there is none other but he:
33 And to love him with all the heart, and with
all the understanding, and with all the soul, and
with all the strength, and to love *his* neighbour
as himself, is more than all whole burnt offerings
and sacrifices.

Him the foundation of His kingdom and church. *marvellous in our eyes.* An unexpected, amazing thing that only God could have planned and accomplished.

12:13–27 See the parallels in Matt. 22:15–33; Luke 20:20–40.

12:14 *thou art true.* Flattery was the bait in their trap. *tribute to Caesar.* A Roman tax that was highly unpopular; this may have implied worshiping the Emperor and led to a Jewish uprising (cf. Acts 5:37).

12:15 *Why tempt ye me?* Why do you try to trap me? *penny.* Denarius, a day's wage.

12:16 *image and superscription.* The coin bore the likeness of Tiberius and writing ascribing divinity to him.

12:17 *Render to Caesar . . . and to God.* God requires us to confer honor and pay taxes to civil government, but our total love, obedience, and worship are owed to God alone (v. 30). *they marvelled at him.* He not only thwarted the design of the Pharisees but provided a deeper understanding of the believer's relationship to the civil government (Rom. 13:1–7).

12:19 *Moses wrote unto us.* Both Jesus and His fellow Jews identified Moses as the human author of the first books of the Bible (v. 26; 1:44; 7:10; 10:3–4). The law commanded the brother of a deceased man to take his wife if the couple had been childless and to raise offspring with her (Deut. 25:5–6).

12:24–27 Jesus pointed out two problems of the Sadducees. First, they did not understand the Old Testament *Scriptures*, for they failed to recognize that God's statement to Moses, *I am the God of Abraham* (Ex. 3:6), implied that God had a continuing covenant relationship with the patriarchs even centuries after they had died. It is striking that Christ rebuked them for their ignorance of a logical inference of Scripture, not an explicit statement. Second, they did not understand God's *power*, for at the resurrection from the dead God would make earthly, sexual relationships obsolete when He gave His people glorious and heavenly bodies (*as the angels*, cf. Dan. 12:3; 1 Cor. 15:35–50).

12:28–34 See the parallel in Matt. 22:34–40.

12:29–31 Rather than setting one of the Ten Commandments above the others, Jesus taught that the love commandments summarized the entire law (Lev. 19:18; Deut. 6:4–5). *love . . . as thyself.* Self-love is not commanded but assumed to be natural to all men, for even the wicked love themselves and those who love them (Matt. 5:46–47; Luke 6:32–34). The law requires us to extend our love beyond ourselves to those whom God has placed around us (*thy neighbour*) and to engage *all* our powers and efforts to love God supremely.

12:32 *none other but he.* See Deut. 4:35; Isa. 45:21.

12:33 *to love . . . is more than all whole burnt offerings.* This scribe had learned the lesson Jesus pressed upon the

34 And when Jesus saw that he answered dis-
creetly, he said unto him, Thou art not far from
the kingdom of God. And no man after that durst
ask him *any question.*
35 ¶ And Jesus answered and said, while he taught
in the temple, How say the scribes that Christ is
the Son of David?
36 For David himself said by the Holy Ghost, The
LORD said to my Lord, Sit thou on my right hand,
till I make thine enemies thy footstool.
37 David therefore himself calleth him Lord;
and whence is he *then* his son? And the common
people heard him gladly.
38 ¶ And he said unto them in his doctrine,
Beware of the scribes, which love to go in long
clothing, and *love* salutations in the marketplaces,
39 And the chief seats in the synagogues, and the
uppermost rooms at feasts:
40 Which devour widows' houses, and for a
pretence make long prayers: these shall receive
greater damnation.
41 ¶ And Jesus sat over against the treasury,
and beheld how the people cast money into the
treasury: and many that were rich cast in much.
42 And there came a certain poor widow, and she
threw in two mites, which make a farthing.
43 And he called *unto him* his disciples, and saith
unto them, Verily I say unto you, That this poor
widow hath cast more in, than all they which have
cast into the treasury:
44 For all *they* did cast in of their abundance; but
she of her want did cast in all that she had, *even*
all her living.

CHAPTER 13

AND as he went out of the temple, one of his
disciples saith unto him, Master, see what manner

Pharisees, that eternal rituals are nothing without love (Hos. 6:6; Matt 9:13; 12:7).

12:34 *not far from the kingdom.* The difference between being outside and inside the kingdom is as great as that between death and life, bridged only by supernatural resurrection and rebirth (John 3:3; 5:24–25). However, some people outside the kingdom are closer than others, such as this man who had received sufficient enlightenment to understand God's law. *durst.* Dared.

12:35–37 See the parallels in Matt. 22:41–46; Luke 20:41–44.

12:35–36 *Holy Ghost.* The Holy Spirit. Jesus' respect for the Scriptures was such that He used its authority to prove His deity, knowing that prophets like *David* had written by the direction of the Spirit of God (2 Peter 1:20–21). *The LORD said to my Lord.* Both times *Lord* translates the same Greek word, but Jesus quoted Ps. 110:1, and in its Hebrew text the first is God's name, *Jehovah*, and the second is a title meaning "my Master." Though David was the king of Israel, he wrote of Christ as the King of kings, seated at the *right hand* of *Jehovah* to reign with Him in glory (14:62). Therefore the *Son of David*, though human, must have been far more than a man, even the Son of God. *till I make thine enemies thy footstool.* Though the leaders of Israel sought to destroy Jesus, He will reign over His enemies.

12:38–40 See the parallels in Matt. 23:1–36; Luke 20:45–47.

12:38 *long clothing.* The *tallith*, a long garment worn to show piety and scholarship. *salutations in the marketplace.* Greetings and honor from men as they journeyed through the social center of the city.

12:39 *chief seats in the synagogues.* Seats placed near the front of the synagogue close to the chest where the scrolls were kept, places of favor and honor. *uppermost rooms.* The reclining couches were reserved as a place of honor among all the guests *at feasts.*

12:41–44 See the parallel in Luke 21:1–4.

12:42 *two mites.* The smallest coin in circulation, made of copper. *farthing.* A Roman coin equivalent to one sixty-fourth of a day's labor.

12:43 *cast more in, than all they.* God's rewards will surprise us, reversing our expectations (10:31).

12:44 *of their abundance . . . all that she had.* The rich made no sacrifice in what they gave, but the poor woman sacrificed much. Jesus praises not the amount but the proportion and attitude of our giving (2 Cor. 8:5,12; 9:6–7).

Thoughts for Personal/Family Worship: Chapter 12

1. **The parable of the wicked husbandmen appears to end in tragedy with the death of the son. It is indeed a horrible sin that the nation did not honor God's Son, and we all by nature reject Christ. However, God had planned Christ's rejection as the pathway to His exaltation. Only by being killed on the cross and buried could Christ become the cornerstone of a new temple of God, a living building composed of people who rest the full weight of their souls on Christ alone to save them from sin. Christ is the King seated at God's right hand, reigning in absolute power and glory as the Son of David and the Son of God. His death has turned to triumph, and the same Holy Spirit who moved the prophets to write of Christ now moves sinners to submit to His reign. The great fruit of His reign in the heart is love—love for God above all and for our neighbor as ourselves that animates obedience to all God's commandments. How does this chapter show you the beauty and glory of King Jesus?**
2. **The foolish attempts of proud men to trap Jesus in His words only caused His divine wisdom to shine brighter. Jesus is the great Teacher, God-in-the-flesh come to reveal Himself. Sadly, the Pharisees, Herodians, and Sadducees did not benefit from His teaching because they rejected His authority. They did not come asking questions in a sincere desire to know the truth but with wicked motives. Even the scribe who was "not far from the kingdom" in his understanding of the Bible had not yet entered the kingdom by faith in Christ. The fundamental obstacle to all these men was their pride and love of human honor (vv. 38–40). Far different from them was the poor widow, who humbly gave her two mites to the Lord. Do you come to the preaching of God's Word to submit to the Lord Jesus, learn from Him, and humbly serve Him with all you are? Or do you come to argue and exalt yourself as though you were Lord?**

Chapter 13: ***Jesus teaches His disciples concerning the destruction of Jerusalem and the signs of His coming. He urges watchfulness.***

End Times (13:1–37)

13:1–37 See the parallels in Matt. 24; Luke 21.

13:1 *manner.* Sort.

of stones and what buildings *are here*!
2 And Jesus answering said unto him, Seest thou
these great buildings? there shall not be left one
stone upon another, that shall not be thrown
down.
3 And as he sat upon the mount of Olives over
against the temple, Peter and James and John and
Andrew asked him privately,
4 Tell us, when shall these things be? and what
shall be the sign when all these things shall be
fulfilled?
5 And Jesus answering them began to say, Take
heed lest any *man* deceive you:
6 For many shall come in my name, saying, I am
Christ; and shall deceive many.
7 And when ye shall hear of wars and rumours
of wars, be ye not troubled: for *such things* must
needs be; but the end *shall* not *be* yet.
8 For nation shall rise against nation, and
kingdom against kingdom: and there shall be
earthquakes in divers places, and there shall be
famines and troubles: these *are* the beginnings of
sorrows.
9 ¶ But take heed to yourselves: for they shall
deliver you up to councils; and in the synagogues
ye shall be beaten: and ye shall be brought before
rulers and kings for my sake, for a testimony
against them.
10 And the gospel must first be published among
all nations.
11 But when they shall lead *you*, and deliver you
up, take no thought beforehand what ye shall
speak, neither do ye premeditate: but whatsoever
shall be given you in that hour, that speak ye: for it
is not ye that speak, but the Holy Ghost.
12 Now the brother shall betray the brother to
death, and the father the son; and children shall
rise up against *their* parents, and shall cause them
to be put to death.
13 And ye shall be hated of all *men* for my name's
sake: but he that shall endure unto the end, the
same shall be saved.
14 ¶ But when ye shall see the abomination of
desolation, spoken of by Daniel the prophet,
standing where it ought not, (let him that readeth
understand,) then let them that be in Judaea flee
to the mountains:
15 And let him that is on the housetop not go
down into the house, neither enter *therein*, to take
any thing out of his house:
16 And let him that is in the field not turn back
again for to take up his garment.
17 But woe to them that are with child, and to
them that give suck in those days!
18 And pray ye that your flight be not in the winter.
19 For *in* those days shall be affliction, such as
was not from the beginning of the creation which
God created unto this time, neither shall be.
20 And except that the Lord had shortened those
days, no flesh should be saved: but for the elect's
sake, whom he hath chosen, he hath shortened
the days.
21 And then if any man shall say to you, Lo, here
is Christ; or, lo, *he is* there; believe *him* not:
22 For false Christs and false prophets shall rise,
and shall shew signs and wonders, to seduce, if *it*
were possible, even the elect.
23 But take ye heed: behold, I have foretold you
all things.
24 ¶ But in those days, after that tribulation, the

13:2 *not . . . one stone upon another.* Jesus' prophecy found fulfillment in AD 70 when the Roman general Titus destroyed Jerusalem and the temple.
13:4 *when shall these things be . . . all these things shall be fulfilled?* The disciples appear to be speaking about more than the destruction of the temple, though they may have believed that the temple's destruction and the day of the Lord would occur at the same time. Jesus' answer combines the distant future with the closer historical judgment, as the prophets spoke of the day of the Lord (Isa. 13:1–22).
13:5 *Take heed.* Look out, pay attention.
13:7–8 *divers.* Various. Natural disasters and international conflicts do not indicate that the day of the Lord is near but characterize this present age as creation groans under the curse of sin (Rom. 8:19–22).
13:11 *take no thought.* Do not worry. *not ye that speak, but the Holy Ghost.* As He did through the Old Testament prophets (12:36), the Holy Spirit spoke through the New Testament apostles and prophets, giving them supernatural wisdom, boldness, and inerrant truth from Christ (John 15:26–27; 16:13–15; Acts 2:4; 4:8; 9:17–20; 13:9).
13:13 *endure unto the end . . . shall be saved.* Wherever God works by His grace there will be a persevering to the end to receive ultimate salvation (Phil. 1:6; 2:12–13; Heb. 3:6).
13:14 *abomination of desolation.* The desecration of the temple in Jerusalem by Gentiles (Dan. 9:24–27; cf. Dan. 8:13; 11:31; 12:11). The disciples could expect some event that would desecrate the temple of God, likely in connection with the destruction of Jerusalem in AD 70. *let them . . . in Judaea flee.* When the Roman armies approach the city of Jerusalem, the disciples of Jesus must flee *to the mountains* for safety (Luke 21:20–21).
13:15–18 These examples communicate the great urgency of fleeing quickly.
13:19 *in those days.* The time of Jerusalem's siege and destruction. *affliction, such as was not from the beginning of creation.* Similar language as that used of the plagues on Egypt (Ex. 9:18,24; 10:6,14), communicating the terrible severity of this judgment on Israel (Jer. 30:7; Dan. 12:1). Josephus wrote that the Roman siege resulted in the deaths of over a million people of all ages and the taking captive of almost a hundred thousand (*Wars of the Jews*, 6.9.3).
13:20 *elect's sake, whom he hath chosen.* The people God chose for salvation (John 15:19; Eph. 1:4), whom Satan attempts to lead astray (v. 22) but whom Christ will bring to glory in the end (v. 27).
13:21–23 Christ here speaks of an indefinite time period when the church's faithfulness will be tested by *false Christs and false prophets* (Acts 13:6; 1 John 2:18; 4:1), which in this chapter seems to correspond to what Luke calls "the times of

sun shall be darkened, and the moon shall not
give her light,
25 And the stars of heaven shall fall, and the
powers that are in heaven shall be shaken.
26 And then shall they see the Son of man coming
in the clouds with great power and glory.
27 And then shall he send his angels, and shall
gather together his elect from the four winds,
from the uttermost part of the earth to the utter-
most part of heaven.
28 Now learn a parable of the fig tree; When her
branch is yet tender, and putteth forth leaves, ye
know that summer is near:
29 So ye in like manner, when ye shall see these
things come to pass, know that it is nigh, *even* at
the doors.
30 Verily I say unto you, that this generation shall
not pass, till all these things be done.
31 Heaven and earth shall pass away: but my
words shall not pass away.
32 ¶ But of that day and *that* hour knoweth no
man, no, not the angels which are in heaven,
neither the Son, but the Father.
33 Take ye heed, watch and pray: for ye know not
when the time is.
34 *For the Son of man is* as a man taking a far
journey, who left his house, and gave authority
to his servants, and to every man his work, and
commanded the porter to watch.
35 Watch ye therefore: for ye know not when the
master of the house cometh, at even, or at mid-
night, or at the cockcrowing, or in the morning:
36 Lest coming suddenly he find you sleeping.
37 And what I say unto you I say unto all, Watch.

CHAPTER 14

AFTER two days was *the feast of* the passover, and
of unleavened bread: and the chief priests and
the scribes sought how they might take him by

the Gentiles" after Jerusalem's fall (Luke 21:24).

13:24 *in those days.* A phrase used of the fall of Jerusalem (v. 17, cf. v. 19) but also more generically (1:9; 2:20; 8:1). In the prophetic perspective given here, events described in just a short space actually span many years.

13:25 *stars . . . fall, and the powers . . . shaken.* The prophetic language of the day of the Lord (Isa. 13:10; 24:23; 34:4).

13:26 *Son of man coming in the clouds.* As prophesied by Daniel, Christ will come from heaven with *power and glory* that is visible and public (*shall they see*) to establish His kingdom over all (Dan. 7:13–14).

13:27 *his angels.* Christ is the Lord over heaven and its angels (8:38). *gather . . . from the four winds.* The Savior will summon to Himself all His chosen and redeemed people from all nations.

13:28–29 *fig tree.* A symbol for Israel, referring to its judgment for failing to produce fruit for the Lord (11:13–14). *nigh.* Near.

13:30 *Verily.* Truly. *this generation.* The destruction of Jerusalem came about forty years after Christ had spoken these words.

13:31 *my words shall not pass away.* Christ's teachings are God's eternal and unfailing Word.

13:32 *knoweth no man.* God has kept the date of the day of the Lord secret, and anyone who claims to have calculated it is not following God's Word. *neither the Son.* Though Christ knows all things in His infinite deity, His human mind was limited, being a created intelligence; as man, He knew only what God progressively revealed to Him at various stages of His life (Luke 2:52).

13:33 *watch.* Stay awake, an image of spiritual readiness and alertness in prayer.

13:34 *watch.* Stay alert (vv. 35,37; a similar but different word from that used in v. 33).

Thoughts for Personal/Family Worship: Chapter 13

1. **Just as the Lord Jesus warned, the holy city of Jerusalem fell to the Roman legions in AD 70, experiencing a horrifying massacre in fulfillment of Christ's own words. God's judgment came and destroyed His own temple. However, God's plan had not failed. Jesus speaks in this same prophecy of the salvation of God's elect through all these tribulations. Even now God is gathering His chosen ones from among the Jews and Gentiles by bringing them to faith in Christ through the preaching of the gospel. Though the destruction of Jerusalem must have shaken first-century Jewish believers, they could rejoice that the kingdom of Christ can never be shaken. How can this comfort us if we see the church under persecution and great Christian institutions falling under God's judgment because of gross infidelity?**
2. **Jesus said that His disciples must pass through much tribulation and endure vicious persecution, even from religious leaders professing to serve God. The Christian life is one of perseverance under pressure. However, Jesus also said that believers wait for something well worth all our sorrows. Christ will come with visible power and glory to establish His kingdom. What a day of joy and vindication that will be! How can we make use of this hope to strengthen ourselves to endure to the end?**
3. **At the conclusion of His teaching Christ repeatedly called His disciples to watch, watch, watch. The biblical doctrine of Christ's second coming is not something to stimulate curiosity and speculation about a timetable of events. It is a summons to spiritual alertness and constant prayer, since we do not know when the Lord will appear. What does it mean to be spiritually sleeping? How can a Christian develop a daily discipline of watchfulness?**

THE PASSION, DEATH, AND RESURRECTION OF THE SON OF GOD (14:1—16:20)

Chapter 14: ***The religious leaders plot Jesus' death. Mary anoints Jesus for His burial. Christ institutes the Lord's Supper with His disciples, prays in the garden of Gethsemane. and is arrested and tried. Peter denies Christ.***

14:1–31 See the parallels in Matt. 26:1–35; Luke 22:1–34.

Plot to Kill Jesus (14:1–2)

14:1 *feast of the passover.* The remembrance of God's passing over of the people of Israel who had painted their doorposts with the blood of a sacrificial lamb before the exodus from Egypt (Ex. 12:1–13). *unleavened bread.* A feast celebrating Israel's exit from Egypt (Ex. 12:14–20). That great act of salvation from slavery to the idolatrous powers of evil and

craft, and put *him* to death.
2 But they said, Not on the feast *day*, lest there be
an uproar of the people.
3 ¶ And being in Bethany in the house of Simon
the leper, as he sat at meat, there came a woman
having an alabaster box of ointment of spikenard
very precious; and she brake the box, and poured
it on his head.
4 And there were some that had indignation
within themselves, and said, Why was this waste
of the ointment made?
5 For it might have been sold for more than three
hundred pence, and have been given to the poor.
And they murmured against her.
6 And Jesus said, Let her alone; why trouble ye
her? she hath wrought a good work on me.
7 For ye have the poor with you always, and
whensoever ye will ye may do them good: but me
ye have not always.
8 She hath done what she could: she is come
aforehand to anoint my body to the burying.
9 Verily I say unto you, Wheresoever this gospel
shall be preached throughout the whole world,
this also that she hath done shall be spoken of for
a memorial of her.
10 ¶ And Judas Iscariot, one of the twelve, went
unto the chief priests, to betray him unto them.
11 And when they heard *it*, they were glad, and
promised to give him money. And he sought how
he might conveniently betray him.
12 ¶ And the first day of unleavened bread, when
they killed the passover, his disciples said unto
him, Where wilt thou that we go and prepare that
thou mayest eat the passover?
13 And he sendeth forth two of his disciples, and
saith unto them, Go ye into the city, and there
shall meet you a man bearing a pitcher of water:
follow him.
14 And wheresoever he shall go in, say ye to the
goodman of the house, The Master saith, Where
is the guestchamber, where I shall eat the passover
with my disciples?
15 And he will shew you a large upper room fur-
nished *and* prepared: there make ready for us.
16 And his disciples went forth, and came into
the city, and found as he had said unto them: and
they made ready the passover.
17 And in the evening he cometh with the twelve.
18 And as they sat and did eat, Jesus said, Verily
I say unto you, One of you which eateth with me
shall betray me.
19 And they began to be sorrowful, and to say
unto him one by one, *Is* it I? and another *said, Is*
it I?
20 And he answered and said unto them, *It is* one
of the twelve, that dippeth with me in the dish.
21 The Son of man indeed goeth, as it is written
of him: but woe to that man by whom the Son of
man is betrayed! good were it for that man if he
had never been born.
22 ¶ And as they did eat, Jesus took bread, and
blessed, and brake *it*, and gave to them, and said,
Take, eat: this is my body.
23 And he took the cup, and when he had given
thanks, he gave *it* to them: and they all drank of it.
24 And he said unto them, This is my blood of

---

from God's wrath against sinners was a type of the greater redemption Christ was about to accomplish (1 Cor. 5:7).

Jesus Anointed at Bethany (14:3–9)

14:3 *Bethany.* A city close to Jerusalem. *Simon the leper.* Otherwise unknown from Scripture. *woman.* Mary, the sister of Martha and Lazarus (John 12:1–3). *sat at meat.* Reclined at a meal.

14:5 *three hundred pence.* 300 denarii, the equivalent of a year's wages for a laborer. *murmured.* Spoke angrily or sternly.

14:6 *Let her alone.* Christ forcefully defended her and commended her for her devotion to Him (*good work on me*). *wrought.* Worked.

14:7 *poor with you always.* This does not diminish generosity to the poor, to whom Christ said we must do good. However, the woman recognized a unique opportunity to show her love for Christ, who would soon die.

14:8 *anoint my body to the burying.* A traditional practice for the deceased (16:1). She was one of the few who had a spiritual understanding of Christ's predictions of His death and who responded to His self-sacrifice with overflowing love, as we should (2 Cor. 5:15). Perhaps she was unsure of whether she could do this after His death because He had said He would be seized by the civil powers (10:33).

14:9 *Verily.* Truly. *this gospel.* Wherever men proclaimed the good news of Jesus' historic life and saving work throughout the world (1:1; 16:15), this woman's extravagant devotion to Him would be remembered (*memorial*). God honors those who honor Him (1 Sam. 2:30; John 12:26).

Judas's Betrayal (14:10–11)

14:10–11 *Judas Iscariot.* Mark's Gospel sharply contrasts the woman's act of expensive devotion to Jesus (v. 5) with the betrayer's treachery to obtain *money*. Ironically, just as the woman's act has brought her honor wherever the gospel is preached, so Judas's will always be remembered to his shame.

The Last Supper (14:12–31)

14:14 *goodman.* Master, head of the household. *guestchamber.* Place for travelers to stay.

14:18 *One of you . . . shall betray me.* Jesus made it clear that He was fully aware of what was about to happen, in order to impress upon the disciples that His death was the purpose and plan of God.

14:21 *goeth, as it is written.* Every aspect of Christ's sufferings was the ordained plan of God for Him, revealed in the Holy Scriptures and necessary for Him to fulfill. *but woe to that man.* Jesus saw no tension between the sovereignty of God and human responsibility. Judas's having been foreordained to this purpose did not remove the guilt of his sin (Acts 2:23,36–38). *good . . . never been born.* The fate of the wicked is not annihilation but a punishment worse than non-existence: the fire of hell (9:43–48).

14:22–25 *Jesus took bread . . . the cup.* Using elements of the Jewish Passover meal, Jesus instituted the Lord's Supper (1 Cor. 10:16–17; 11:20–34), one of the two New Testament

the new testament, which is shed for many.
25 Verily I say unto you, I will drink no more of
the fruit of the vine, until that day that I drink it
new in the kingdom of God.
26 ¶ And when they had sung an hymn, they
went out into the mount of Olives.
27 And Jesus saith unto them, All ye shall be of-
fended because of me this night: for it is written,
I will smite the shepherd, and the sheep shall be
scattered.
28 But after that I am risen, I will go before you
into Galilee.
29 But Peter said unto him, Although all shall be
offended, yet *will* not I.
30 And Jesus saith unto him, Verily I say unto
thee, That this day, *even* in this night, before the
cock crow twice, thou shalt deny me thrice.
31 But he spake the more vehemently, If I should
die with thee, I will not deny thee in any wise.
Likewise also said they all.
32 And they came to a place which was named
Gethsemane: and he saith to his disciples, Sit ye
here, while I shall pray.
33 And he taketh with him Peter and James and
John, and began to be sore amazed, and to be very
heavy;
34 And saith unto them, My soul is exceeding
sorrowful unto death: tarry ye here, and watch.
35 And he went forward a little, and fell on the
ground, and prayed that, if it were possible, the
hour might pass from him.
36 And he said, Abba, Father, all things *are*
possible unto thee; take away this cup from me:
nevertheless not what I will, but what thou wilt.
37 And he cometh, and findeth them sleeping,
and saith unto Peter, Simon, sleepest thou?
couldest not thou watch one hour?
38 Watch ye and pray, lest ye enter into tempta-
tion. The spirit truly *is* ready, but the flesh *is* weak.
39 And again he went away, and prayed, and
spake the same words.
40 And when he returned, he found them asleep
again, (for their eyes were heavy,) neither wist
they what to answer him.
41 And he cometh the third time, and saith
unto them, Sleep on now, and take *your* rest: it is
enough, the hour is come; behold, the Son of man
is betrayed into the hands of sinners.
42 Rise up, let us go; lo, he that betrayeth me is
at hand.
43 ¶ And immediately, while he yet spake, cometh
Judas, one of the twelve, and with him a great
multitude with swords and staves, from the chief
priests and the scribes and the elders.
44 And he that betrayed him had given them a
token, saying, Whomsoever I shall kiss, that same
is he; take him, and lead *him* away safely.
45 And as soon as he was come, he goeth straight-
way to him, and saith, Master, master; and kissed
him.
46 ¶ And they laid their hands on him, and took
him.
47 And one of them that stood by drew a sword,
and smote a servant of the high priest, and cut
off his ear.
48 And Jesus answered and said unto them, Are
ye come out, as against a thief, with swords and
with staves to take me?

---

sacraments or ordinances (cf. 16:16). This sacrament is an ordinance of symbolic acts for the exercise of faith in Christ, not a miraculous giving of Christ's human body for physical consumption. It would have been unthinkable for Jews to eat and drink the physical flesh and blood of a man (John 6:52), for this would have violated the law of Moses (Lev. 3:17; 7:26–27). *this is my body.* The broken bread symbolizes Christ's obedient offering up of His body on the cross as the ransom price substituted on behalf of sinners to satisfy the demands of God's justice (10:45; Rom. 3:25–26). *This is my blood of the new testament.* The cup symbolizes Christ's submission to a sacrificial death (*blood*) as the Mediator of the new covenant, so that He would obtain and distribute the blessings of the promised inheritance (Heb. 9:15). The new covenant is the promise of the final administration of the covenant of grace whereby all spiritual blessings of transformation, communion with God, and forgiveness are effectively given to all the people of God (Jer. 31:31–34; Heb. 8:6–13). *drink it new.* The Lord's Supper looks back to the cross but also forward to the second coming.

14:26 *hymn.* A song of praise, likely composed of one or more of the Hallel Psalms (Pss. 113–118), which were customary to sing after the Passover meal.

14:27 *smite the shepherd.* Citing Zech. 13:7. *sheep shall be scattered.* Jesus predicted that His disciples would temporarily fall when He was arrested and killed.

14:28 *I will go before you into Galilee.* See 16:7.

Jesus' Arrest (14:32–52)

14:32–72 See the parallels in Matt. 26:36–75; Luke 22:39–71.

14:32 *Gethsemane.* The Aramaic means "oil press." Gethsemane was a place Jesus visited frequently throughout His ministry (John 18:2).

14:33 *sore amazed . . . very heavy.* Astonished, frightened, and distressed, almost to the point of physical death (vv. 34–35). Christ's human nature began to sense the horrible burden of sin and wrath (v. 36).

14:36 *Abba.* This is the only recorded use by Jesus of a very personal and endearing Aramaic term for God as Father. Those who are united to Christ may also pray to God as *Abba* (Rom. 8:15; Gal. 4:6). *cup.* A symbol of suffering under the anger of God against sinners (Pss. 11:6; 75:8; Isa. 51:17,22; Jer. 25:15; Rev. 14:10; 16:19). *not what I will, but what thou wilt.* Jesus shows the resignation of His human will to the Father's will. Christ saved sinners by His amazing obedience.

14:40 *wist.* Knew.

14:43 *Judas, one of the twelve.* His position as an apostle rendered his betrayal all the more evil. *great multitude with swords.* They had come prepared to take Jesus by force, as though He were a criminal supported by a band of violent men (v. 48). *staves.* Clubs or staffs of wood.

14:44 *token.* Sign. It would have been difficult in the darkness of the garden to recognize Jesus. *kiss.* A common greeting, allowing Judas to get a close enough look to distinguish

49 I was daily with you in the temple teaching,
and ye took me not: but the scriptures must be
fulfilled.
50 And they all forsook him, and fled.
51 And there followed him a certain young man,
having a linen cloth cast about *his* naked *body*;
and the young men laid hold on him:
52 And he left the linen cloth, and fled from them
naked.
53 ¶ And they led Jesus away to the high priest:
and with him were assembled all the chief priests
and the elders and the scribes.
54 And Peter followed him afar off, even into
the palace of the high priest: and he sat with the
servants, and warmed himself at the fire.
55 And the chief priests and all the council sought
for witness against Jesus to put him to death; and
found none.
56 For many bare false witness against him, but
their witness agreed not together.
57 And there arose certain, and bare false witness
against him, saying,
58 We heard him say, I will destroy this temple
that is made with hands, and within three days I
will build another made without hands.
59 But neither so did their witness agree together.
60 And the high priest stood up in the midst,
and asked Jesus, saying, Answerest thou nothing?
what *is it which* these witness against thee?
61 But he held his peace, and answered nothing.
Again the high priest asked him, and said unto
him, Art thou the Christ, the Son of the Blessed?
62 And Jesus said, I am: and ye shall see the Son
of man sitting on the right hand of power, and
coming in the clouds of heaven.
63 Then the high priest rent his clothes, and saith,
What need we any further witnesses?
64 Ye have heard the blasphemy: what think ye?
And they all condemned him to be guilty of death.
65 And some began to spit on him, and to cover
his face, and to buffet him, and to say unto him,
Prophesy: and the servants did strike him with
the palms of their hands.
66 ¶ And as Peter was beneath in the palace, there
cometh one of the maids of the high priest:
67 And when she saw Peter warming himself, she
looked upon him, and said, And thou also wast
with Jesus of Nazareth.
68 But he denied, saying, I know not, neither
understand I what thou sayest. And he went out
into the porch; and the cock crew.
69 And a maid saw him again, and began to say to
them that stood by, This is *one* of them.
70 And he denied it again. And a little after, they
that stood by said again to Peter, Surely thou art
one of them: for thou art a Galilaean, and thy
speech agreeth *thereto*.
71 But he began to curse and to swear, *saying*, I
know not this man of whom ye speak.
72 And the second time the cock crew. And Peter

Jesus from the others.

14:49 *scriptures must be fulfilled*. Even the choice of His enemies as to when and how they arrested Him fulfilled God's decree revealed in the Old Testament (vv. 21,27; 9:12; 12:10; 15:28).

14:50 *they all forsook him, and fled*. Fulfilling Jesus' earlier prophecy (v. 27).

14:52 *fled from them naked*. A picture of the shame and confusion of Jesus' followers at this time.

Jesus' Trial (14:53—15:20)

14:58 *We heard him say*. The false witnesses perverted Jesus' words, which did not threaten to destroy the temple but spoke of the resurrection of His body after His death (John 2:19–21).

14:61 *Christ, the Son*. See notes at 1:1; 8:29. *the Blessed*. God.

14:62 *I am*. Jesus affirmed His divine identity and mission, using words that may have alluded to His deity as *Jehovah* (see note at 6:50). *Son of man . . . coming in the clouds*. The supreme King, appointed by God to an eternal kingdom over all the world (Dan. 7:13–14). *sitting on the right hand of power*. Seated at the right hand of God as the Lord whose reign will conquer all (Ps. 110:1). Christ meekly endured their unjust abuse because He entrusted Himself to God (1 Peter 2:23), who would faithfully keep His promises so that one day Christ would return as the Judge to condemn His wicked judges if they did not repent of rejecting Him (Rev. 1:7).

14:64 *blasphemy*. According to the Mosaic law a crime deserving death (*guilty of death*; Lev. 24:16; 1 Kings 21:10). They condemned Him for telling the truth because they rejected Him who is the Truth.

14:66 *maid*. Servant girl (v. 69)

14:68 *crew*. Crowed.

14:70 *thy speech agreeth thereto*. His accent confirmed that he was from Galilee.

14:71 *began to curse and to swear*. Jesus confessed His identity before the council, though it would cost Him His life, but Peter put himself under oath to deny Jesus in order to save his life. The contrast between God's righteousness and man's sin could not be sharper.

14:72 *wept*. The form of the Greek verb indicates prolonged or repeated weeping, a sign that Christ's grace was winning Peter back in repentance (Luke 22:31–32).

Thoughts for Personal/Family Worship: Chapter 14

1. **Christ appears in this chapter as the sovereign Lord, walking purposefully to His death exactly as God had planned and revealed in the Bible. He knew that He would rise to rule over all the world as the promised King of kings. Yet He also appears as the submissive Servant, staggering under the weight of His burden but praying "not what I will, but what Thou wilt" to His Father. His obedience is everything to believers, because He went to the cross as their perfect Surety, paying their debts and drinking the awful cup of God's wrath against their sins. Thus in the Lord's Supper He presents Himself as the loving Savior who gave His body as a sacrifice and brings sinners into a gracious covenant with their God. How does this chapter show us that Jesus is infinitely worthy of our trust and love?**
2. **The chief priests and Judas prepared to kill Jesus. The disciples failed to prepare at all. However, Mary understood something of the beauty and preciousness of the suffering Savior and prepared by pouring out her earthly**

called to mind the word that Jesus said unto him,
Before the cock crow twice, thou shalt deny me
thrice. And when he thought thereon, he wept.

CHAPTER 15

AND straightway in the morning the chief priests
held a consultation with the elders and scribes
and the whole council, and bound Jesus, and
carried *him* away, and delivered *him* to Pilate.
2 And Pilate asked him, Art thou the King of the
Jews? And he answering said unto him, Thou
sayest *it*.
3 And the chief priests accused him of many
things: but he answered nothing.
4 And Pilate asked him again, saying, Answerest
thou nothing? behold how many things they
witness against thee.
5 But Jesus yet answered nothing; so that Pilate
marvelled.
6 Now at *that* feast he released unto them one
prisoner, whomsoever they desired.
7 And there was *one* named Barabbas, *which lay*
bound with them that had made insurrection
with him, who had committed murder in the
insurrection.
8 And the multitude crying aloud began to desire
him to do as he had ever done unto them.
9 But Pilate answered them, saying, Will ye that I
release unto you the King of the Jews?
10 For he knew that the chief priests had deliv-
ered him for envy.
11 But the chief priests moved the people, that he
should rather release Barabbas unto them.
12 And Pilate answered and said again unto
them, What will ye then that I shall do *unto him*
whom ye call the King of the Jews?
13 And they cried out again, Crucify him.
14 Then Pilate said unto them, Why, what evil
hath he done? And they cried out the more
exceedingly, Crucify him.
15 ¶ And *so* Pilate, willing to content the people,
released Barabbas unto them, and delivered Jesus,
when he had scourged *him*, to be crucified.
16 And the soldiers led him away into the hall,
called Praetorium; and they call together the
whole band.
17 And they clothed him with purple, and plat-
ted a crown of thorns, and put it about his *head*,
18 And began to salute him, Hail, King of the
Jews!
19 And they smote him on the head with a reed,
and did spit upon him, and bowing *their* knees
worshipped him.
20 And when they had mocked him, they took off
the purple from him, and put his own clothes on
him, and led him out to crucify him.
21 And they compel one Simon a Cyrenian, who
passed by, coming out of the country, the father of
Alexander and Rufus, to bear his cross.
22 And they bring him unto the place Golgotha,
which is, being interpreted, The place of a skull.
23 And they gave him to drink wine mingled with
myrrh: but he received *it* not.
24 And when they had crucified him, they parted
his garments, casting lots upon them, what every
man should take.
25 And it was the third hour, and they crucified
him.
26 And the superscription of his accusation was

treasure in love for Him (v. 9). Christ commends her good work to us so that we can learn from her example. How has Christ's sacrificial love moved you to love Him in return? How can you show that love in acts of costly devotion?

Chapter 15: *Jesus is condemned to death, dies the death of the cross, and is buried by several of His disciples.*

15:1 See the parallels in Matt. 27:1–7; Luke 23:1. *straightway in the morning.* Ancient records show that the Romans began their trials at dawn. *Pilate.* The Roman governor of the land of Judaea.
15:2–5 See the parallels in Matt. 27:11–14; Luke 23:2–5.
15:5 *answered nothing.* See Isa. 53:7.
15:6–15 See the parallels in Matt. 27:15–26; Luke 23:17–25.
15:6 *that feast.* Pilate was accustomed to releasing a prisoner to the people during Passover.
15:7 *Barabbas.* A revolutionary (*insurrection*[ist]) and robber guilty of *murder.* He likely belonged to the sect of the Zealots.
15:10 *for envy.* Pilate, in part, perceived the sinful intentions of the chief priests and therefore understood the injustice of punishing Jesus.
15:15 *released Barabbas . . . delivered Jesus.* Pilate, acting as the judge, unwittingly provided a striking illustration of the way God the Judge saves sinners: the Righteous One was condemned so that the wicked lawbreaker could go free (2 Cor. 5:21). *scourged.* Whipped, a Greek term referring to the use of the Roman flagellum, a whip of multiple leather cords with pieces of metal tied at intervals to tear open skin and muscle.
15:16–20 See the parallel in Matt. 27:27–31.
15:16 Jesus is led into the courtyard (*hall*) of the palace (*Praetorium*). *band.* A Roman cohort, a military unit of about 600 men.

Jesus' Death and Burial (15:21–47)

15:21–47 See the parallels in Matt. 27:32–61; Luke 23:26–56.
15:22 *interpreted.* Translated.
15:23 *wine mingled with myrrh.* They may have been offering him a chance to relieve the pain, but He intended to endure the wrath of God to its full extent with a clear mind.
15:24 *crucified.* The Gospels do not go into a great amount of detail regarding the procedure of crucifixion, but the suspension of the condemned on a wooden cross was extremely painful and the victim usually took a long time to die (sometimes days; v. 44), generally as a result of asphyxiation when the victim's lungs filled up with fluids that slowly suffocated him. This was a gruesome form of capital punishment that remained common until Constantine outlawed it in the fourth century. *parted his garments, casting lots.* In fulfillment of Ps. 22:18.
15:28 *scripture was fulfilled.* Citing Isa. 53:12. Christ's cruci-

written over, THE KING OF THE JEWS.
27 And with him they crucify two thieves; the one
on his right hand, and the other on his left.
28 And the scripture was fulfilled, which saith,
And he was numbered with the transgressors.
29 And they that passed by railed on him, wagging
their heads, and saying, Ah, thou that destroyest
the temple, and buildest *it* in three days,
30 Save thyself, and come down from the cross.
31 Likewise also the chief priests mocking said
among themselves with the scribes, He saved
others; himself he cannot save.
32 Let Christ the King of Israel descend now from
the cross, that we may see and believe. And they
that were crucified with him reviled him.
33 And when the sixth hour was come, there was
darkness over the whole land until the ninth hour.
34 And at the ninth hour Jesus cried with a loud
voice, saying, Eloi, Eloi, lama sabachthani? which
is, being interpreted, My God, my God, why hast
thou forsaken me?
35 And some of them that stood by, when they
heard *it*, said, Behold, he calleth Elias.
36 And one ran and filled a spunge full of vinegar,
and put *it* on a reed, and gave him to drink, saying,
Let alone; let us see whether Elias will come to take
him down.
37 And Jesus cried with a loud voice, and gave up
the ghost.
38 And the veil of the temple was rent in twain
from the top to the bottom.
39 ¶ And when the centurion, which stood over
against him, saw that he so cried out, and gave
up the ghost, he said, Truly this man was the Son
of God.
40 There were also women looking on afar off:
among whom was Mary Magdalene, and Mary the
mother of James the less and of Joses, and Salome;
41 (Who also, when he was in Galilee, followed
him, and ministered unto him;) and many other
women which came up with him unto Jerusalem.
42 ¶ And now when the even was come, because
it was the preparation, that is, the day before the
sabbath,
43 Joseph of Arimathaea, an honourable coun-
sellor, which also waited for the kingdom of God,
came, and went in boldly unto Pilate, and craved
the body of Jesus.
44 And Pilate marvelled if he were already dead:
and calling *unto him* the centurion, he asked him
whether he had been any while dead.
45 And when he knew *it* of the centurion, he gave
the body to Joseph.
46 And he bought fine linen, and took him down,

---

fixion with thieves (v. 27) publicly showed that the Righteous One was suffering the punishment of lawbreakers.

15:29 *railed.* Insulted, blasphemed. While Jesus was being crucified for His supposed blasphemy, those who condemned Him stood by blaspheming.

15:33 *darkness over the whole land.* A supernatural historical event, signifying the judgment of God resting upon Christ (Ex. 10:21–23).

15:34 *Eloi . . . sabachthani.* Christ cried out in Aramaic (5:41; 14:36). *why hast thou forsaken me?* Citing Ps. 22:1; Christ's spiritual agony was worse than the physical, for He experienced the divine rejection and desolation deserved by sinners (Jer. 7:15,29). Yet Christ remained faithful, clinging to God's covenant promises (*my God*) and hoping in the coming worldwide kingdom that would spring from His death and resurrection (Ps. 22:22–31).

15:35 *Elias.* Some standing by misunderstood Jesus' Aramaic word "Eloi" (v. 34) thinking that he was calling out to Elijah to save him.

15:37 *gave up the ghost.* An idiom for death (Job 3:11; 14:10).

15:38 *veil of the temple.* The curtain that separated the Holy Place from the Holy of Holies. *rent in twain.* Torn in two. When Christ, the living temple of God, was slain to redeem sinners, all the ceremonies of the law that pointed to Him were abolished and the way opened for believers to draw near to the Holy God (Heb. 9:1–14; 10:1,19–22).

15:39 *Son of God.* This confession from a Gentile soldier suggests that Christ's death redeems sinners from all nations and would bring them to God (Rev. 5:9–10).

15:40 *Mary Magdalene.* A woman whom Jesus had saved from seven demons (Luke 8:2).

15:42 *preparation.* Because the *Sabbath* was soon coming, the Jews needed to bury Jesus quickly before they would be lawfully forbidden from doing so.

15:43 *Joseph of Arimathaea.* A respected member of the Sanhedrin (*honourable counsellor*) who did not condone the death of Jesus (Luke 23:50–51). *boldly . . . craved.* Courageously asked. Joseph's earlier fear of revealing that he was a follower of Jesus dissipated at Jesus' death (John 19:38).

Thoughts for Personal/Family Worship: Chapter 15

1. **The cross reveals man's hatred of God. Our hostility against God is universal. Christ was rejected and reviled by religious and political leaders, Jews and Gentiles, high officials and crowds, soldiers and civilians. Our hostility against God, too, is violent and murderous. When God came to mankind in human flesh to love sinners like us, we tortured and killed Him. What reasons does this chapter give us to grieve over sin, humble ourselves, and repent?**
2. **The cross reveals God's sovereignty over man. Even as sinners committed the most horrible atrocities against the Son of God, they fulfilled the decree of God that He had announced centuries earlier by His prophets. Even as they callously gambled for His clothing, they willingly did what God had predestined them to do (cf. Acts 4:27–28). It was no accident that the cross itself proclaimed that Jesus is the King (v. 26). How does this chapter teach us to bow before God's throne and worship Christ as the King who rules over all things?**
3. **The cross reveals God's righteousness and love for sinners. Rather than damning all sinners to hell forever for their sins, God sent His Son to die. We deserve to be cast into the outer darkness, but the darkness of divine wrath came upon Him. We should be rejected forever for our rejection of God, but instead God caused Christ to become God-forsaken. God's justice for His people was satisfied in Christ, and because Christ was crucified**

and wrapped him in the linen, and laid him in
a sepulchre which was hewn out of a rock, and
rolled a stone unto the door of the sepulchre.
47 And Mary Magdalene and Mary *the mother* of
Joses beheld where he was laid.

CHAPTER 16

AND when the sabbath was past, Mary Magda-
lene, and Mary the *mother* of James, and Salome,
had bought sweet spices, that they might come
and anoint him.
2 And very early in the morning the first *day* of
the week, they came unto the sepulchre at the
rising of the sun.
3 And they said among themselves, Who shall roll
us away the stone from the door of the sepulchre?
4 And when they looked, they saw that the stone
was rolled away: for it was very great.
5 And entering into the sepulchre, they saw a
young man sitting on the right side, clothed in a
long white garment; and they were affrighted.
6 And he saith unto them, Be not affrighted: Ye
seek Jesus of Nazareth, which was crucified: he is
risen; he is not here: behold the place where they
laid him.
7 But go your way, tell his disciples and Peter that
he goeth before you into Galilee: there shall ye see
him, as he said unto you.
8 And they went out quickly, and fled from the
sepulchre; for they trembled and were amazed:
neither said they any thing to any *man*; for they
were afraid.
9 ¶ Now when *Jesus* was risen early the first *day*
of the week, he appeared first to Mary Magdalene,
out of whom he had cast seven devils.
10 *And* she went and told them that had been
with him, as they mourned and wept.
11 And they, when they had heard that he was
alive, and had been seen of her, believed not.
12 ¶ After that he appeared in another form unto
two of them, as they walked, and went into the
country.
13 And they went and told *it* unto the residue:
neither believed they them.
14 ¶ Afterward he appeared unto the eleven as
they sat at meat, and upbraided them with their
unbelief and hardness of heart, because they
believed not them which had seen him after he
was risen.
15 And he said unto them, Go ye into all the
world, and preach the gospel to every creature.
16 He that believeth and is baptized shall be
saved; but he that believeth not shall be damned.

---

believers are released from condemnation and punishment, as was Barabbas. What does this show us about the love of God? Why should it move us to trust in Christ without reservation?

Chapter 16: *Jesus rises from the dead, appears to Mary and His disciples, commissions His disciples to preach the gospel, and ascends into heaven, working now through His apostles.*

Jesus' Resurrection and Ascension (16:1–20)

16:1–11 See the parallels in Matt. 28:1–10; Luke 24:1–12.

16:2 *sepulchre.* Tomb.

16:5 *young man . . . in a long white garment.* An angel, a powerful, heavenly spirit sent from God (Matt. 28:2,5). His appearance suggests the arrival of the heavenly kingdom (8:38). *affrighted.* Terrified.

16:6 *he is risen; he is not here.* The empty tomb was a witness that Christ did not come back as a spirit but had risen physically from the dead. The body once killed on the cross and buried in the tomb was reunited with His human spirit and given eternal life, as Jesus had foretold (8:31; 10:34).

16:9–20 Some scholars doubt that these verses were originally part of Mark's Gospel because they are missing from two old Greek manuscripts and some ancient translations. However, the overwhelming majority of Greek manuscripts contain them, and church fathers as early as the second century AD bear witness to them as Scripture. Jerome (d. AD 420) was aware of these textual matters but included this section in his Latin translation of the Bible. Omitting vv. 9–20 leaves the gospel with a very sudden and harsh ending, but including them concludes it well. Both from the manuscript record and from the book itself there are weighty reasons to view these verses as part of Scripture.

16:9–14 Christ's resurrection was confirmed by His appearance to many witnesses at different times, proving that it was not a hallucination or deceit springing from a misguided individual (1 Cor. 15:4–9).

16:9 *Mary Magdalene.* See v. 1; 15:40,47. *cast seven devils.* Perhaps this appears here as a reminder that if Christ had already conquered Satan in the days of His humiliation, He had done so in a far greater way as the risen Lord.

16:12–13 *in another form.* They did not at first recognize the risen Lord (Luke 24:16). *the residue.* The rest of them. See the parallel in Luke 24:13–35.

16:14 *eleven.* The remaining apostles after Judas had betrayed Christ. *sat at meat.* Reclined at a meal. *upbraided.* Rebuked. *unbelief and hardness of heart.* The lack of spiritual perception arising from hostility to God in the heart is a theme running throughout Mark (3:5; 4:12; 6:52; 7:6,21; 8:17,33; 10:5). It warns the reader not to rest in head knowledge of the gospel but to seek the illumination of the Holy Spirit to produce heart knowledge, even after conversion (Ps. 119:18,36; Eph. 1:17–18).

16:15 *Go . . . and preach the gospel.* The risen Lord Jesus commissioned His apostles to publicly proclaim the good news of the Son of God and what He had done (Matt. 28:18–20; Luke 24:45–49; Acts 1:5–8). *every creature.* All mankind throughout creation.

16:16 *believeth and is baptized.* Salvation is by union with Christ through faith; the outward sign of this union is baptism. *believeth not shall be damned.* Note that a lack of baptism does not damn.

16:17–18 *signs . . . cast out devils . . . lay hands on the sick.* The apostles' ministry was confirmed by miracles. *speak with new tongues.* See Acts 2:3–4,11; 10:46; 19:6. *take up serpents.* See Acts 28:3–5.

16:19 *received up into heaven.* Christ physically ascended

17 And these signs shall follow them that believe;
In my name shall they cast out devils; they shall
speak with new tongues;
18 They shall take up serpents; and if they drink
any deadly thing, it shall not hurt them; they shall
lay hands on the sick, and they shall recover.
19 ¶ So then after the Lord had spoken unto
them, he was received up into heaven, and sat on
the right hand of God.
20 And they went forth, and preached every
where, the Lord working with *them*, and confirm-
ing the word with signs following. Amen.

into God's presence (Acts 1:9–11). *sat on the right hand of God.* The promise is fulfilled, and the kingdom is begun (12:36; 14:62; Ps. 110:1).

16:20 *the Lord working with them.* Jesus continued His ministry through the preaching of His disciples (Matt. 28:20) and by confirming their message with miracles (Heb. 2:3–4), as the book of Acts shows.

Thoughts for Personal/Family Worship: Chapter 16

1. **Jesus Christ died for sinners, but today He is alive. The full payment for sin has been made, and now Christ is applying the results of His redemption to the salvation of lost sinners. The living Lord reigns as King of the angels, sitting at God's right hand. His kingdom has come in heavenly glory and operates through the power of the gospel. Though we still wait for His kingdom to come in visible glory on earth, believers can rejoice. Jesus is alive! Jesus reigns! How can this give Christians hope no matter what evil they face?**
2. **Christ's final commission to the apostles has a wide scope: "to every creature" (v. 15). The apostles labored to spread the gospel to many nations, and Christianity spread in a remarkable way in its early years. However, the apostolic mandate still rests upon the church. Small and great, educated and uneducated, rich and poor, young and old, all need to hear the gospel. How is your church engaged in reaching the world with the good news?**

INTRODUCTION TO THE BOOK OF SAINT LUKE

Authorship: It is clear that the author of the Gospel of Luke and the book of Acts is the same person (1:3; Acts 1:1). Though both books are technically anonymous, both internal and external evidence suggests that the church's tradition of naming Luke, the physician, as the author is accurate.

Luke did not witness the events of Jesus' life firsthand, writing, "even as they delivered them unto us, which from the beginning were eyewitnesses, and ministers of the word" (Luke 1:2). Luke stands as an example of one who was inspired by the Holy Spirit even as he searched out the facts from eyewitness sources, a beautiful overlap of divine sovereignty and human activity.

From Acts we learn that the author was a close companion of Paul on his missionary travels, as is evident from the use of "we" in many contexts (Acts 16:10–17; 20:5–15; 21:1–18; 27:1—28:16). A number of men qualify as close companions: Mark, Demas, Jesus Justus, Epaphroditus, Epaphras, and Luke. Of these, Luke is the only obvious choice to have authored both books. Irenaeus (c. 130–200) in his book *Against Heresies* wrote that Paul and Luke were "inseparable."

The early church and early manuscripts of the New Testament ascribed the volumes of this gospel and Acts to Luke, the beloved physician. By the year AD 200 Luke was uncontested in his authorship of this gospel, and sources such as 1 and 2 Clement, Justin Martyr, the Muratorian Canon, Irenaeus, the Anti-Marcionite Prologue, Tertullian, and Eusebius all verify Luke's authorship.

Luke is mentioned three times by name in the New Testament (Col. 4:14; 2 Tim. 4:11; Philem. 24). From these brief citations and the literary style of Luke/Acts we understand that Luke was a physician, a Gentile, educated, likely wealthy, and that he remained with Paul through his arrest in Rome.

Date: The date of Luke depends largely on the date of Acts. It is almost a universal opinion that Acts was written after the Gospel of Luke. Acts was likely written in the early- to mid-60s, based primarily on the fact that there is no record of Paul's release from prison. Moreover, Acts does not record the fall of Jerusalem (AD 70).

Theme: The triune God's purpose in salvation as it unfolds in the life, death, resurrection, and ascension of Jesus Christ.

Purpose: Luke stated explicitly that his purpose in writing was "that thou mightest know the certainty of those things, wherein thou hast been instructed" (Luke 1:4); that is, to ground those catechized in the faith in a true account of the life of Jesus Christ for the confirmation of their faith and repentance.

Synopsis: *The Contribution of Luke to Redemptive Revelation*

Luke presents Jesus' ministry as the fulfillment of salvation history. Throughout the history of redemption God has been preparing the world to receive the incarnation of His Son, Jesus Christ. From the beginning of the Bible until the end of John's ministry, God was promising to fulfill his covenant plan of redemption. As Jesus began His earthly ministry and, later, His heavenly ministry (Acts), God was fulfilling these promises made since the time of Adam and Eve, including the promise made to Abraham that all nations would be blessed through Him (Luke 2:32; 7:1–10; 10:25–37; 24:47). Luke brings this out clearly in his account of Christ's person and work (3:38; 9:20–22). Luke's presentation of Jesus fulfilling salvation history focuses on His threefold office of Prophet, Priest, and King (see 1:31–33,69; 4:18,40; 5:13–14; 24:51; etc.).

Luke not only shows that Jesus is the culmination of salvation history but also that all previous revelation centered on Jesus' person and ministry. From Moses to the prophets all the biblical authors wrote and testified of Jesus. Luke shows that all revelation was about revealing Jesus to God's covenant people (24:27,44–49). In conjunction with this, he portrays Christ as the fulfillment of God's foretold (suffering) Servant, Messiah, and Prophet (4:18–19; 7:16; 9:7–9,20; 11:47–51; etc.).

Luke, as a doctor, had a particular interest in Jesus' healing ministry. Jesus' public ministry was concerned with healing the blind and setting at liberty those who had been bruised (4:18). Throughout Luke's Gospel Jesus is shown to heal the sick, exorcise evil spirits, cure various diseases, and even bring the dead back to life. Acts subsequently shows many of these miracles being carried out by the apostles in the power of the Holy Spirit given by Jesus. Jesus' miracles and healing testify to the authority He has over all things.

Luke also emphasizes Jesus' ministry to many outcasts, including the poor, sinners, and tax collectors (4:25–27; 8:1–4; 10:30–37; 18:15–17; 19:5; etc.). More than the other Gospel writers, Luke pays attention to Christ's dealings with women (e.g., 7:11–17,36–50; 8:1–3; 10:38–42; 13:11–17; 18:1–8).

Christ's ministry is carried on in the work of the Holy Spirit. Jesus was conceived of the Holy Spirit (1:35) and born through the virgin Mary. At His baptism Jesus was filled with the Holy Spirit and driven into the wilderness by the Spirit (4:1). He taught the people in the power of the Spirit (4:14) and testified to the crowds that the Spirit of the Lord had anointed Him (4:18). Jesus ended His earthly ministry in Luke charging His disciples to await the coming of the Spirit (24:49), who plays an integral role in applying the work of redemption to individual hearts (1:17; 11:13).

Outline:

- I. Prologue (1:1–4)
- II. Jesus' Early History (1:5—2:52)
  - A. John's and Jesus' Births Foretold (1:5–80)
  - B. Birth of Jesus (2:1–21)
    - 1. Jesus Is Born (2:1–7)
    - 2. Shepherds Visit Jesus (2:8–21)
  - C. Jesus' Childhood (2:22–52)
    - 1. Jesus Presented at the Temple (2:22–40)
    - 2. The Boy Jesus Teaches in the Temple (2:41–52)
- III. Jesus' Preparation for Ministry (3:1—4:13)
  - A. John Prepares the Way (3:1–22)
  - B. The Genealogy of Jesus Christ (3:23–28)
  - C. The Temptation of Jesus in the Wilderness (4:1–13)
- IV. Jesus Begins His Ministry in Galilee (4:14—9:50)
  - A. Jesus Goes Up to Galilee (4:14–15)
  - B. Jesus Rejected in Galilee (4:16–30)
  - C. Jesus in Capernaum and around Judaea (4:31–44)
  - D. Jesus Calls His First Disciples (5:1–11)
  - E. Jesus Heals a Leper and a Paralytic (5:12–26)
  - F. Jesus Calls Levi (5:27–32)
  - G. Jesus Is Questioned about Fasting (5:33–39)
  - H. Jesus Is Lord of the Sabbath (6:1–11)
    - 1. Jesus Defends His Disciples' Plucking Grain on the Sabbath (6:1–5)
    - 2. Jesus Defends a Healed Man on the Sabbath (6:6–11)
  - I. The Twelve Apostles (6:12–16)
  - J. The Beatitudes and Christ's Further Teaching (6:17–49)
  - K. Jesus Cares for a Gentile and a Woman (7:1–17)
    - 1. Jesus Heals the Centurion's Servant (7:1–10)
    - 2. Jesus Raises a Widow's Only Son (7:11–17)
  - L. John's Disciples Question Jesus (7:18–35)
  - M. Jesus Forgives a Sinful Woman (7:36–50)
  - N. Women Follow Jesus (8:1–3)
  - O. Jesus' Teaching concerning Parables (8:4–18)
  - P. Jesus' Mother and Brothers and the Will of God (8:19–21)
  - Q. Jesus Performs Four Miracles (8:22–56)

1. Jesus Calms a Storm (8:22–25)
2. Jesus Heals a Demon-possessed Man (8:26–39)
3. Jesus Heals a Woman (8:40–48)
4. Jesus Heals Jairus's Daughter (8:49–56)

R. Jesus and the Disciples (9:1–50)
1. Jesus Sends Out the Apostles (9:1–6)
2. Herod Fears Jesus (9:7–9)
3. Jesus Feeds Five Thousand (9:10–17)
4. Peter Confesses Jesus as the Christ (9:18–20)
5. Jesus Foretells His Death (9:21–22)
6. Jesus Teaches His Disciples to Suffer (9:23–27)
7. The Transfiguration of Jesus (9:28–36)
8. Jesus Heals a Boy with an Unclean Spirit (9:37–43)
9. Jesus Foretells His Death a Second Time (9:44–45)
10. Kingdom Greatness (9:46–48)
11. Kingdom Meekness (9:49–50)

V. On the Way to Jerusalem (9:51—19:27)

A. The First Stage in Jesus' Journey to Jerusalem (9:51—13:21)
1. The Samaritans Reject Jesus (9:51–56)
2. The Cost of Discipleship (9:57–62)
3. Jesus Commissions the Seventy (10:1–24)
4. Parables and Various Teachings (10:25—13:21)

B. The Second Stage in Jesus' Journey to Jerusalem (13:22—17:10)
1. The Narrow Gate (13:22–30)
2. Jesus Laments Jerusalem (13:31–35)
3. Jesus Heals a Man on the Sabbath (14:1–6)
4. Parables and Teachings (14:7—17:10)

C. The Third Stage in Jesus' Journey to Jerusalem (17:11—19:27)
1. Jesus Heals Ten Lepers (17:11–19)
2. The Coming of the Kingdom (17:20–37)
3. Parable of the Persistent Widow (18:1–8)
4. The Pharisee and the Tax Collector (18:9–14)
5. Jesus Blesses the Children (18:15–17)
6. A Rich Young Ruler (18:18–30)
7. Jesus Foretells His Death a Third Time (18:31–34)
8. Jesus Heals a Blind Man (18:35–43)
9. Jesus Brings Salvation to Zacchaeus (19:1–10)
10. Parable of the Ten Pounds (19:11–27)

VI. In Jerusalem (19:28—24:53)

A. Jesus Enters Jerusalem (19:28–48)

B. Jesus and the Authorities in Conflict (20:1—21:4)

C. Jesus Teaches concerning the End (21:5–38)

D. Jesus' Last Supper, Betrayal, and Arrest (22:1—23:56)
1. The Last Supper (22:1–46)
2. Jesus' Arrest and Death (22:47—23:56)

E. The Resurrection and Ascension of Jesus (24:1–53)
1. Jesus' Resurrection (24:1–12)
2. Appearances to Disciples (24:13–49)
3. Jesus' Ascension (24:50–53)

THE GOSPEL ACCORDING TO SAINT

LUKE

CHAPTER 1

FORASMUCH as many have taken in hand to set
forth in order a declaration of those things which
are most surely believed among us,
2 Even as they delivered them unto us, which
from the beginning were eyewitnesses, and
ministers of the word;
3 It seemed good to me also, having had perfect
understanding of all things from the very first, to
write unto thee in order, most excellent Theophilus,
4 That thou mightest know the certainty of those
things, wherein thou hast been instructed.
5 ¶ THERE was in the days of Herod, the king of
Judaea, a certain priest named Zacharias, of the
course of Abia: and his wife *was* of the daughters
of Aaron, and her name *was* Elisabeth.
6 And they were both righteous before God,
walking in all the commandments and ordi-
nances of the Lord blameless.
7 And they had no child, because that Elisabeth
was barren, and they both were *now* well stricken
in years.
8 And it came to pass, that while he executed the
priest's office before God in the order of his course,
9 According to the custom of the priest's office,
his lot was to burn incense when he went into the
temple of the Lord.
10 And the whole multitude of the people were
praying without at the time of incense.
11 And there appeared unto him an angel of the
Lord standing on the right side of the altar of in-
cense.
12 And when Zacharias saw *him*, he was troubled,
and fear fell upon him.
13 But the angel said unto him, Fear not,
Zacharias: for thy prayer is heard; and thy wife
Elisabeth shall bear thee a son, and thou shalt call
his name John.
14 And thou shalt have joy and gladness; and
many shall rejoice at his birth.
15 For he shall be great in the sight of the Lord,
and shall drink neither wine nor strong drink;
and he shall be filled with the Holy Ghost, even
from his mother's womb.
16 And many of the children of Israel shall he
turn to the Lord their God.
17 And he shall go before him in the spirit and
power of Elias, to turn the hearts of the fathers to

Chapter 1: ***After relating his purpose, Luke details early events surrounding Zacharias, Elisabeth, and Mary as God brings His Son into the world.***

PROLOGUE (1:1–4)

1:1 *Forasmuch.* Since. The preface follows the typical form of introduction found in many writings from the first century.

1:2 *delivered them unto.* Luke was delivering eyewitness testimony, not reconstructing history.

1:3 *write unto thee in order.* Luke followed the chronology of Jesus' ministry. *Theophilus.* Often thought to have helped finance Luke's endeavor, as was frequently acknowledged in this fashion in ancient times. His name means, literally, "friend of God."

1:4 Luke's purpose in writing this gospel was to give firmness and stability (*certainty*) to the faith of those who had been catechized or taught in Christianity (*instructed*; Eph. 4:12–14; Col. 2:7).

JESUS' EARLY HISTORY (1:5—2:52)

John's and Jesus' Births Foretold (1:5–80)

1:5 *days of Herod, the king of Judaea.* Herod the Great ruled over Judaea, Galilee, Perea, and Syria from 37–4 BC, having received this commission from Mark Antony. *Zacharias.* Priests would serve at the temple for two one-week appointments. *Abia.* Abijah (1 Chron. 24:10).

1:7 *well stricken in years.* Old.

1:9 *to burn incense.* A special and high favor.

1:10 *without.* Outside. The whole scene is one of devotion and worship.

1:11 *appeared unto him an angel of the Lord.* God's first special revelation in almost 400 years.

1:12 *fear fell upon him.* A common response to God's miraculous appearance (vv. 29–30; 5:8–10; Acts 5:5,11).

1:13 *thy prayer is heard.* This prayer probably included a plea for the coming of the Messiah, for which pious Jews prayed regularly.

1:14 *many shall rejoice at his birth.* John's birth was a consolation not for his parents alone but for all of Israel.

1:15 *Holy Ghost.* The Holy Spirit, who would infuse John with love for Christ (vv. 41–44) and the ability to prophesy (vv. 16–17). *from his mother's womb.* God is able to save and call sinners while they are yet infants.

1:17 *spirit and power of Elias.* John's ministry would be much like that of Elijah. His call was to turn the hearts of *the fathers to the children*, a description of the reviving work of God (Mal. 4:6).

1:18 *stricken in years.* Old.

the children, and the disobedient to the wisdom
of the just; to make ready a people prepared for
the Lord.
18 And Zacharias said unto the angel, Whereby
shall I know this? for I am an old man, and my
wife well stricken in years.
19 And the angel answering said unto him, I am
Gabriel, that stand in the presence of God; and
am sent to speak unto thee, and to shew thee these
glad tidings.
20 And, behold, thou shalt be dumb, and not able
to speak, until the day that these things shall be
performed, because thou believest not my words,
which shall be fulfilled in their season.
21 And the people waited for Zacharias, and
marvelled that he tarried so long in the temple.
22 And when he came out, he could not speak
unto them: and they perceived that he had seen a
vision in the temple: for he beckoned unto them,
and remained speechless.
23 And it came to pass, that, as soon as the days of
his ministration were accomplished, he departed
to his own house.
24 And after those days his wife Elisabeth
conceived, and hid herself five months, saying,
25 Thus hath the Lord dealt with me in the days
wherein he looked on *me*, to take away my re-
proach among men.
26 And in the sixth month the angel Gabriel
was sent from God unto a city of Galilee, named
Nazareth,
27 To a virgin espoused to a man whose name
was Joseph, of the house of David; and the vir-
gin's name *was* Mary.
28 And the angel came in unto her, and said, Hail,
thou that art highly favoured, the Lord *is* with
thee: blessed *art* thou among women.
29 And when she saw *him*, she was troubled at
his saying, and cast in her mind what manner of
salutation this should be.
30 And the angel said unto her, Fear not, Mary:
for thou hast found favour with God.
31 And, behold, thou shalt conceive in thy womb,
and bring forth a son, and shalt call his name
JESUS.
32 He shall be great, and shall be called the Son
of the Highest: and the Lord God shall give unto
him the throne of his father David:
33 And he shall reign over the house of Jacob for
ever; and of his kingdom there shall be no end.
34 Then said Mary unto the angel, How shall this
be, seeing I know not a man?
35 And the angel answered and said unto her, The
Holy Ghost shall come upon thee, and the power
of the Highest shall overshadow thee: therefore
also that holy thing which shall be born of thee
shall be called the Son of God.
36 And, behold, thy cousin Elisabeth, she hath
also conceived a son in her old age: and this is the
sixth month with her, who was called barren.
37 For with God nothing shall be impossible.
38 And Mary said, Behold the handmaid of the
Lord; be it unto me according to thy word. And
the angel departed from her.
39 And Mary arose in those days, and went into
the hill country with haste, into a city of Juda;
40 And entered into the house of Zacharias, and
saluted Elisabeth.
41 And it came to pass, that, when Elisabeth
heard the salutation of Mary, the babe leaped in
her womb; and Elisabeth was filled with the Holy
Ghost:

1:20 *dumb.* Mute, unable to speak. The angel gives Zacharias a sign by taking away his speech (Dan. 10:15).
1:24 *hid herself five months.* No reason is given, though Luke does show that she was in a state of rejoicing, not shame (v. 25).
1:26 *the sixth month.* Of Elisabeth's pregnancy.
1:27 *virgin.* Fulfillment of Isa. 7:14. *espoused.* Not like a contemporary engagement but the first step in the Jewish marital ceremony, whereby the bride legally belonged to her husband. *Joseph, of the house of David.* Joseph was a descendant of David and a rightful heir of the Davidic throne. Jesus is later known as the "Son of David" (18:38–39).
1:28 *Hail.* Greetings. *highly favoured.* One who has been given much grace by God. Just as with all sinners, Mary needed the atoning work of God in order to be restored to a favorable position with Him. Mary was not the dispenser of God's grace but a receiver. *the Lord is with thee.* Also an angel's words to Gideon (Judg. 6:12).
1:29 *troubled.* Puzzled, not at the content of the message but by the greeting of the angel.
1:30 *found favour.* Received grace (v. 28).
1:31 *conceive . . . and bring forth a son.* An allusion to the promise of Immanuel (Isa. 7:14; cf. Matt. 1:23 ["Emmanuel"]). *JESUS.* A Greek form of the Hebrew name *Joshua*, meaning, "*Jehovah* saves" (Matt. 1:21).
1:32 *Son.* Israel was God's national son (Ex. 4:22; Hos. 11:1; cf. Deut. 32:6; Isa. 63:16; Mal. 1:6; 2:10), and the royal offspring of *David* was God's Son (1 Chron. 17:13; Pss. 2:6–7,12; 89:26–27), but Christ's divine Sonship uniquely transcends that of any earthly person because He is the holy God, as is evident from His fully pleasing the Father and ruling all things by His mere word (3:22; 4:3; 8:28; 9:35; 10:22; 20:13). *the Highest.* God. *throne.* A symbol for His kingdom.
1:33 *reign . . . for ever . . . no end.* The reigns of other kings were cut short by their sin and mortality, but this King is holy and immortal (Isa. 9:6–7).
1:34 *How shall this be?* Likely not a reference to Mary doubting but to her confused state; she did not understand how such a thing could possibly happen. *know not a man.* Had never had sexual relations with a man.
1:35 *Holy Ghost shall come upon thee.* Luke emphasizes the Holy Spirit's role in the miraculous conception, like a renewal of creation (Isa. 32:15). *overshadow.* Like God's glory cloud (9:34) over the tabernacle (Ex. 40:35). Through the virginal conception (*therefore*), a fully divine person (*Son of God*; v. 32) took upon Himself a fully human nature, yet without sin (*holy*; Heb. 2:14,17; 4:15).
1:38 *handmaid.* Literally, "slave."
1:41 *filled with the Holy Ghost.* See v. 15.

42 And she spake out with a loud voice, and said, Blessed *art* thou among women, and blessed *is* the fruit of thy womb.
43 And whence *is* this to me, that the mother of my Lord should come to me?
44 For, lo, as soon as the voice of thy salutation sounded in mine ears, the babe leaped in my womb for joy.
45 And blessed *is* she that believed: for there shall be a performance of those things which were told her from the Lord.
46 And Mary said, My soul doth magnify the Lord,
47 And my spirit hath rejoiced in God my Saviour.
48 For he hath regarded the low estate of his handmaiden: for, behold, from henceforth all generations shall call me blessed.
49 For he that is mighty hath done to me great things; and holy *is* his name.
50 And his mercy *is* on them that fear him from generation to generation.
51 He hath shewed strength with his arm; he hath scattered the proud in the imagination of their hearts.
52 He hath put down the mighty from *their* seats, and exalted them of low degree.
53 He hath filled the hungry with good things; and the rich he hath sent empty away.
54 He hath holpen his servant Israel, in remembrance of *his* mercy;
55 As he spake to our fathers, to Abraham, and to his seed for ever.
56 And Mary abode with her about three months, and returned to her own house.
57 Now Elisabeth's full time came that she should be delivered; and she brought forth a son.
58 And her neighbours and her cousins heard how the Lord had shewed great mercy upon her; and they rejoiced with her.
59 And it came to pass, that on the eighth day they came to circumcise the child; and they called him Zacharias, after the name of his father.
60 And his mother answered and said, Not *so*; but he shall be called John.
61 And they said unto her, There is none of thy kindred that is called by this name.
62 And they made signs to his father, how he would have him called.
63 And he asked for a writing table, and wrote, saying, His name is John. And they marvelled all.
64 And his mouth was opened immediately, and his tongue *loosed*, and he spake, and praised God.
65 And fear came on all that dwelt round about them: and all these sayings were noised abroad throughout all the hill country of Judaea.
66 And all they that heard *them* laid *them* up in their hearts, saying, What manner of child shall this be! And the hand of the Lord was with him.
67 And his father Zacharias was filled with the Holy Ghost, and prophesied, saying,
68 Blessed *be* the Lord God of Israel; for he hath visited and redeemed his people,
69 And hath raised up an horn of salvation for us in the house of his servant David;
70 As he spake by the mouth of his holy prophets, which have been since the world began:
71 That we should be saved from our enemies, and from the hand of all that hate us;
72 To perform the mercy *promised* to our fathers, and to remember his holy covenant;
73 The oath which he sware to our father Abraham,
74 That he would grant unto us, that we being

1:43 Elisabeth confessed faith already in the person of Jesus, for she noted that Mary bore the God-man (*mother of my Lord*).
1:46–55 This song of Mary is often called the "Magnificat," which is the first word of the Latin version. Her song focuses on God's deliverance in times past, with an eye toward the imminent fulfillment of these promises. Allusions to many Old Testament Scriptures, especially to the song of Hannah (1 Sam. 2:1–10), can be identified in her praise.
1:47 *God my Saviour.* Mary spoke of God's intervention in history for the salvation of His people.
1:48 *low estate of his handmaiden.* Humble condition of His (female) servant (1 Sam. 1:11).
1:50 *mercy . . . from generation to generation.* See Ps. 103:17.
1:51 *strength with his arm.* A common expression found throughout the Old Testament (Deut. 4:34; Pss. 44:3; 89:13; Isa. 53:1), referring especially to God's mighty deliverance and salvation from trials like the exodus. Mary confessed that God is still redeeming His people with His mighty power.
1:58 *shewed great mercy.* One of the great themes of Mary's song (vv. 50,54). Luke uses this language to tie in John's birth with the preceding song and with God's work of redemption. The time of fulfillment is here, for God is fulfilling His promises of the ages. *rejoiced with her.* In partial fulfillment of v. 14.
1:59 *Zacharias, after the name of his father.* A common tradition.
1:63 *writing table.* Writing tablet. *His name is John.* In obedience to God's command (v. 13).
1:65 *noised abroad.* Widely reported.
1:67–80 Zacharias's song is often referred to as the "Benedictus," again after the first word of the Latin version. In language saturated with Old Testament imagery, he praised and prophesied of the work of God on behalf of His people through the promised Son of David, acknowledging his own son, John, as the forerunner of the Messiah.
1:69 *horn of salvation.* A common Old Testament phrase used to speak of a king's great power (Deut. 33:17; 2 Sam. 22:3; Ps. 75:4–5) and often identified with God's power. Here Zacharias speaks of the Messiah, who will come in the kingly strength of God and redeem His people from their enemies.
1:70–71 *spake by the mouth of his holy prophets.* Zacharias shows his confidence that the Old Testament prophets spoke the very words of God.
1:72–73 *his holy covenant.* God's merciful dealing with His people through Jesus Christ fulfills His solemn promises given to *Abraham* (Deut. 7:9; 1 Kings 8:23).
1:74–75 *might serve him without fear, in holiness and*

delivered out of the hand of our enemies might
serve him without fear,
75 In holiness and righteousness before him, all
the days of our life.
76 And thou, child, shalt be called the prophet of
the Highest: for thou shalt go before the face of
the Lord to prepare his ways;
77 To give knowledge of salvation unto his people
by the remission of their sins,
78 Through the tender mercy of our God; where-
by the dayspring from on high hath visited us,
79 To give light to them that sit in darkness and
in the shadow of death, to guide our feet into the
way of peace.
80 And the child grew, and waxed strong in spirit,
and was in the deserts till the day of his shewing
unto Israel.

CHAPTER 2

AND it came to pass in those days, that there went
out a decree from Caesar Augustus, that all the
world should be taxed.
2 (*And* this taxing was first made when Cyrenius
was governor of Syria.)
3 And all went to be taxed, every one into his own
city.
4 And Joseph also went up from Galilee, out of
the city of Nazareth, into Judaea, unto the city of
David, which is called Bethlehem; (because he
was of the house and lineage of David:)
5 To be taxed with Mary his espoused wife, being
great with child.
6 And so it was, that, while they were there,
the days were accomplished that she should be
delivered.
7 And she brought forth her firstborn son, and
wrapped him in swaddling clothes, and laid him
in a manger; because there was no room for them
in the inn.
8 And there were in the same country shepherds
abiding in the field, keeping watch over their flock
by night.
9 And, lo, the angel of the Lord came upon them,
and the glory of the Lord shone round about
them: and they were sore afraid.
10 And the angel said unto them, Fear not: for,
behold, I bring you good tidings of great joy,
which shall be to all people.
11 For unto you is born this day in the city of

righteousness before him. Deliverance comes with the result that God is freely worshiped and obeyed (Ex. 3:12).

1:76 *prophet . . . go before the face of the Lord to prepare his ways.* John would be the forerunner of the Lord, heralding the message of salvation that is found in Jesus (Isa. 40:3–5; Mal. 3:1).

1:77 *remission.* Forgiveness. Zechariah understood *salvation* not as an immediate political upheaval but as first and foremost spiritual deliverance from sin and its penalty.

1:78 *tender mercy.* Literally, "compassions of mercy" (7:13; 15:20); God's redemption reveals His loving character (Ex. 34:6). *dayspring.* Literally, "rising," a title signifying that Jesus is the Messiah who brings light to our darkness (v. 79; Num. 24:17; Isa. 60:1; Mal. 4:2) and possibly also alluding to Him as the promised Branch rising out of the line of David (the same word is used in the Greek Septuagint translation of Jer. 23:5; Zech. 3:8; cf. Isa. 11:1; Jer. 33:15).

Thoughts for Personal/Family Worship: Chapter 1

1. **Luke wrote this gospel so that each individual might know the certainty of the things he has been taught. Read it as the truth of God, for it is inspired by God. Read this gospel personally, as addressed to you. It is not a myth, nor is it merely interesting history. It is a true account of Jesus Christ and a message calling you to faith and repentance. How should that affect the way you read it?**
2. **Here is the announcement of the coming of a great person, so great that a mighty prophet had to go ahead of Him in the power of the Holy Spirit. This person is the Son of God, coming to rule His kingdom forever. He is also the Son of David, fulfilling all the ancient promises of God's covenants. He is holy, sinless, and devoted to God from conception. He is a shining light of truth. Yet He is full of tenderness, mercy, and forgiveness to sinners. How do the descriptions of Jesus in this chapter move you to trust Him?**
3. **This chapter contains songs and praises from Mary, Zacharias, and Elisabeth. Even John leaps in his mother's womb. Why does the coming of Jesus Christ move people to rejoice and praise God? Has the Holy Spirit produced joy in your heart because of Jesus? Why or why not?**

Chapter 2: *Christ is born in Bethlehem, presented in the temple in Jerusalem, and at twelve years old confesses to be about His Father's business, though He also subjects Himself to Mary and Joseph.*

Birth of Jesus (2:1–21)

Jesus Is Born (2:1–7)

2:1 *decree.* The Roman Emperor, *Caesar Augustus*, unwittingly carried forward God's plan of redemption when he required people to travel to their homelands to register so that taxes could be collected.

2:2 *taxing.* Registration, census.

2:4 *Bethlehem.* The hometown of David and origin of the promised King (Mic. 5:2).

2:5 *espoused wife.* The woman betrothed to him (1:27).

2:7 *swaddling clothes.* Strips of cloth. *manger.* Feeding trough for livestock, a shocking contrast to the visible glory of Caesar (v. 1). The text repeatedly draws attention to it (vv. 12,16).

Shepherds Visit Jesus (2:8–21)

2:9 *sore afraid.* Very frightened, a normal response to an angelic revelation (1:12,29).

2:10 *good tidings.* Good news, gospel. *great joy.* Luke views salvation and redemption through the lens of joy (10:17; 15:7,10; 24:52).

2:11 *city of David.* The baby was the heir of the throne of the kingdom (1:32). *Saviour.* A term for a powerful man or deity who rescues and preserves His people (1:47; Acts 5:31; 13:23). *Christ.* The man anointed by God through the Holy Spirit (4:18) as Prophet, Priest, and, especially in this context, King (v. 26; 3:15; 4:41; 9:20; 20:41; 22:67; 23:2,35,39; 24:26,46). *the Lord.* In

David a Saviour, which is Christ the Lord.
12 And this *shall be* a sign unto you; Ye shall find
the babe wrapped in swaddling clothes, lying in
a manger.
13 And suddenly there was with the angel a multi-
tude of the heavenly host praising God, and saying,
14 Glory to God in the highest, and on earth
peace, good will toward men.
15 And it came to pass, as the angels were gone
away from them into heaven, the shepherds
said one to another, Let us now go even unto
Bethlehem, and see this thing which is come to
pass, which the Lord hath made known unto us.
16 And they came with haste, and found Mary,
and Joseph, and the babe lying in a manger.
17 And when they had seen *it*, they made known
abroad the saying which was told them concern-
ing this child.
18 And all they that heard *it* wondered at those
things which were told them by the shepherds.
19 But Mary kept all these things, and pondered
them in her heart.
20 And the shepherds returned, glorifying and
praising God for all the things that they had heard
and seen, as it was told unto them.
21 And when eight days were accomplished for
the circumcising of the child, his name was called
JESUS, which was so named of the angel before
he was conceived in the womb.
22 And when the days of her purification
according to the law of Moses were accomplished,
they brought him to Jerusalem, to present *him* to
the Lord;
23 (As it is written in the law of the Lord, Every
male that openeth the womb shall be called holy
to the Lord;)
24 And to offer a sacrifice according to that which
is said in the law of the Lord, A pair of turtledoves,
or two young pigeons.
25 And, behold, there was a man in Jerusalem,
whose name *was* Simeon; and the same man *was*
just and devout, waiting for the consolation of
Israel: and the Holy Ghost was upon him.
26 And it was revealed unto him by the Holy
Ghost, that he should not see death, before he had
seen the Lord's Christ.
27 And he came by the Spirit into the temple: and
when the parents brought in the child Jesus, to do
for him after the custom of the law,
28 Then took he him up in his arms, and blessed
God, and said,
29 Lord, now lettest thou thy servant depart in
peace, according to thy word:
30 For mine eyes have seen thy salvation,
31 Which thou hast prepared before the face of
all people;
32 A light to lighten the Gentiles, and the glory of
thy people Israel.
33 And Joseph and his mother marvelled at those
things which were spoken of him.
34 And Simeon blessed them, and said unto Mary
his mother, Behold, this *child* is set for the fall
and rising again of many in Israel; and for a sign
which shall be spoken against;
35 (Yea, a sword shall pierce through thy own
soul also,) that the thoughts of many hearts may
be revealed.
36 And there was one Anna, a prophetess, the
daughter of Phanuel, of the tribe of Aser: she was
of a great age, and had lived with an husband
seven years from her virginity;
37 And she *was* a widow of about fourscore and
four years, which departed not from the temple,
but served *God* with fastings and prayers night
and day.
38 And she coming in that instant gave thanks
likewise unto the Lord, and spake of him to all
them that looked for redemption in Jerusalem.

the mouth of an angel, a title for God; a term commonly used through the Old Testament and chs. 1–2 of this gospel for the God of Israel.

2:12 *sign.* To confirm his message.

2:17 *abroad.* Over a wide area.

2:18–19 *pondered them in her heart.* Deeply reflected in an effort to search out the meaning.

Jesus' Childhood (2:22–52)

Jesus Presented at the Temple (2:22–40)

2:22–23 *present him to the Lord.* Joseph and Mary went up to Jerusalem in accordance with the Old Testament law to purify Mary and to have Jesus presented in the temple (Ex.13:2,12).

2:24 *law of the Lord.* Citing Lev. 12:8.

2:25 *Simeon.* Outside this account in the gospel of Luke, nothing is known of him.

2:26–27 The encounter between Simeon and Jesus was divinely orchestrated. It was the Holy Spirit who brought them together. The Holy Spirit was active with His people even before Pentecost.

2:30–32 *light . . . Gentiles, and the glory . . . Israel.* Christ brings God's truth, *salvation*, and gracious presence to *all* nations (Isa. 42:6; 49:6; 60:1–3).

2:34 *fall and rising again.* Language from the Old Testament prophets (Isa. 8:14–15; 28:13–16). Jesus' person and work in Israel would cause a national division. Some would be condemned through His mission, while others would be blessed through it (John 3:19–21; 2 Cor. 2:14–17).

2:35 *pierce through thy own soul.* Mary would not be spared from experiencing deep emotional turmoil throughout the life and ministry of her son. *thoughts of many hearts may be revealed.* The purpose of Jesus' coming has an inward work in view.

2:36 *prophetess.* A woman empowered by the Holy Spirit to declare new revelation from God (Ex. 15:20; Judg. 4:4; 2 Kings 22:14; Isa. 8:3). *seven years from her virginity.* Anna was married for seven years before her husband died, after which she lived as a widow.

2:37 *fourscore and four years.* Eighty-four years, having dedicated her life to the service and ministry of God in the temple.

39 And when they had performed all things
according to the law of the Lord, they returned
into Galilee, to their own city Nazareth.
40 And the child grew, and waxed strong in spirit,
filled with wisdom: and the grace of God was
upon him.
41 Now his parents went to Jerusalem every year
at the feast of the passover.
42 And when he was twelve years old, they went
up to Jerusalem after the custom of the feast.
43 And when they had fulfilled the days, as they
returned, the child Jesus tarried behind in Jeru-
salem; and Joseph and his mother knew not *of it*.
44 But they, supposing him to have been in the
company, went a day's journey; and they sought
him among *their* kinsfolk and acquaintance.
45 And when they found him not, they turned
back again to Jerusalem, seeking him.
46 And it came to pass, that after three days they
found him in the temple, sitting in the midst of
the doctors, both hearing them, and asking them
questions.
47 And all that heard him were astonished at his
understanding and answers.
48 And when they saw him, they were amazed:
and his mother said unto him, Son, why hast thou
thus dealt with us? behold, thy father and I have
sought thee sorrowing.
49 And he said unto them, How is it that ye
sought me? wist ye not that I must be about my
Father's business?
50 And they understood not the saying which he
spake unto them.
51 And he went down with them, and came to
Nazareth, and was subject unto them: but his
mother kept all these sayings in her heart.
52 And Jesus increased in wisdom and stature,
and in favour with God and man.

CHAPTER 3

Now in the fifteenth year of the reign of Tiberius
Caesar, Pontius Pilate being governor of Judaea,
and Herod being tetrarch of Galilee, and his
brother Philip tetrarch of Ituraea and of the region
of Trachonitis, and Lysanias the tetrarch of Abilene,
2 Annas and Caiaphas being the high priests, the
word of God came unto John the son of Zacharias
in the wilderness.
3 And he came into all the country about Jordan,

The Boy Jesus Teaches in the Temple (2:41–52)

2:42 *to Jerusalem after the custom of the feast.* Passover was one of three festivals each year that required the Jews to travel up to Jerusalem.
2:44 *in the company.* They often traveled in caravans comprised in large part of relatives. Joseph and Mary assumed that Jesus was with His relatives in the company. It would not be until night, when families gathered together, that they would notice He was not present with them.
2:46 *three days.* Either counted from the time they initially left Jerusalem or indicating that they searched in Jerusalem for three days. *in the temple, sitting in the midst of the doctors.* The boy Jesus was assuming the traditional role of a student. In Jesus' days the teachers (*doctors*) would sit in the midst of their students, who would be asking them questions.
2:49–50 *wist ye not.* Did you not know. *my Father's business.* Christ notes that it was necessary for Him to be about the work or in the house of His Father.
2:51 *subject unto them.* Even as a child Jesus was fulfilling the moral law of God on behalf of His people (Ex. 20:12; Rom. 8:1–4).
2:52 *wisdom and stature, and in favour with God and man.* In His human nature Christ grew mentally, physically, and spiritually. He was always completely pleasing to His heavenly Father (3:22; 9:35).

Thoughts for Personal/Family Worship: Chapter 2

1. **As we read about the birth of Christ, many focus on the shepherds and angels. Certainly there are many lessons in what we are told about them and in what they did. Most important, however, is what Christ Himself did in His birth: He came to this lost world to be a Savior. Equally important is what God the Father did in the birth of His Son. He sent His Son in order to glorify Himself in the salvation of lost and miserable sinners like these shepherds. Reflect upon how low God stooped by sending His Son in the likeness of sinful flesh and for sin (Rom. 8:3). Why was it necessary for the Lord to come in such humiliation as to lie in a manger rather than in a king's crib? What does this foreshadow about the manner in which Christ would save sinners?**
2. **When Jesus was born the angels of God sang "Glory to God in the highest," and the shepherds were glorifying and praising God for all they had heard and seen. Godly old Simeon was moved by the Holy Spirit to give public praise to God, and faithful Anna thanked the Lord and told many of the birth of the Redeemer. Why should Christ's coming move Christians to sing and praise God? If our hearts are cold and sluggish to worship, what might this reveal about us?**

JESUS' PREPARATION FOR MINISTRY (3:1—4:13)

Chapter 3: *John preaches in the wilderness the message of repentance and baptizes Christ; the chapter finishes with the genealogy of Christ.*

John Prepares the Way (3:1–22)

3:1–2 Luke places the ministries of John and Jesus within a detailed historical account. *Tiberius Caesar.* The emperor of the Roman Empire, ruling through various legates and prefects. *Pontius Pilate.* The governor or prefect of Judaea, coming to power after the son of Herod the Great, Archelaus, had been banished from the empire. *Herod . . . tetrarch.* Herod Antipas, the regional ruler over the land of *Galilee*, the second son of Herod the Great and the uncle of Herod Agrippa I (Acts 26:1). *Philip.* The third son of Herod the Great and ruler of *Ituraea* and *Trachonitis* beyond the Jordan River. *Lysanias the tetrarch of Abilene.* Mentioned in extra-biblical sources from about this time. *Annas and Caiaphas.* High priests between the years AD 6 and 36. It was into this complex governmental situation that *the word of God came unto John.*
3:3 *baptism of repentance.* John's baptism was not the sacrament that Christ later ordained (Matt. 28:18–20), though

preaching the baptism of repentance for the
remission of sins;
4 As it is written in the book of the words of Esai-
as the prophet, saying, The voice of one crying in
the wilderness, Prepare ye the way of the Lord,
make his paths straight.
5 Every valley shall be filled, and every mountain
and hill shall be brought low; and the crooked
shall be made straight, and the rough ways *shall
be* made smooth;
6 And all flesh shall see the salvation of God.
7 Then said he to the multitude that came forth
to be baptized of him, O generation of vipers,
who hath warned you to flee from the wrath to
come?
8 Bring forth therefore fruits worthy of repen-
tance, and begin not to say within yourselves,
We have Abraham to *our* father: for I say unto
you, That God is able of these stones to raise up
children unto Abraham.
9 And now also the axe is laid unto the root of
the trees: every tree therefore which bringeth not
forth good fruit is hewn down, and cast into the
fire.
10 And the people asked him, saying, What shall
we do then?
11 He answereth and saith unto them, He that
hath two coats, let him impart to him that hath
none; and he that hath meat, let him do likewise.
12 Then came also publicans to be baptized, and
said unto him, Master, what shall we do?
13 And he said unto them, Exact no more than
that which is appointed you.
14 And the soldiers likewise demanded of him,
saying, And what shall we do? And he said unto
them, Do violence to no man, neither accuse *any*
falsely; and be content with your wages.
15 And as the people were in expectation, and all
men mused in their hearts of John, whether he
were the Christ, or not;
16 John answered, saying unto *them* all, I indeed
baptize you with water; but one mightier than
I cometh, the latchet of whose shoes I am not
worthy to unloose: he shall baptize you with the
Holy Ghost and with fire:
17 Whose fan *is* in his hand, and he will throughly
purge his floor, and will gather the wheat into
his garner; but the chaff he will burn with fire
unquenchable.
18 And many other things in his exhortation
preached he unto the people.
19 But Herod the tetrarch, being reproved by him
for Herodias his brother Philip's wife, and for all
the evils which Herod had done,
20 Added yet this above all, that he shut up John
in prison.
21 Now when all the people were baptized, it
came to pass, that Jesus also being baptized, and
praying, the heaven was opened,
22 And the Holy Ghost descended in a bodily
shape like a dove upon him, and a voice came
from heaven, which said, Thou art my beloved
Son; in thee I am well pleased.
23 And Jesus himself began to be about thirty
years of age, being (as was supposed) the son of
Joseph, which was *the son* of Heli,
24 Which was *the son* of Matthat, which was *the
son* of Levi, which was *the son* of Melchi, which
was *the son* of Janna, which was *the son* of Joseph,
25 Which was *the son* of Mattathias, which was

it signified the same gospel promise, given by the prophets, of the sprinkling of clean water (Ezek. 36:25) and the washing away of sin (Zech. 13:1). *remission*. Forgiveness.

3:4–6 *Esaias*. Isaiah (Isa. 40:3–5). John preached that *the Lord* (*Jehovah* in Isaiah's prophesy) was coming in His glorious power to bring *salvation* (Luke 1:69,71,77; 19:9).

3:10–14 *What shall we do*. Repentance must engage us to change our ways with regard to specific sins; it may involve different actions, depending on our vocations.

3:11 *meat*. Food.

3:12 *publicans*. Tax collectors. John's answer implied that there is nothing inherently wrong with civil authority and taxes.

3:16 *latchet of whose shoes*. Strap of whose sandals.

3:17 *Whose fan is in his hand.* A picture of harvesting. A winnowing fork would gather up both the wheat and the chaff. The farmer would throw the wheat with the chaff into the air. The wind would blow away the lighter chaff, while the wheat would fall to the ground and later be gathered into the barn (*garner*). In the same way, Jesus' ministry is one of salvation and judgment.

3:19 John *reproved* Herod the tetrarch, first for divorcing his wife, Aretas IV of Nabatea, in order to marry his half-brother's wife Herodias; but second *for all the evils which Herod had done*, referring to his many moral failures.

3:21 This verse takes place before John was arrested by Herod (v. 20).

3:22 *Holy Ghost descended.* The Holy Spirit anointed Christ with the power for ministry (4:1,14,18). *my beloved Son . . . well pleased.* The Father expressed His love for and delight in His Son, commissioning Him for the work of God's Servant-King (Ps. 2:7; Isa. 42:1). All three persons of the Trinity appear here, showing the distinct personhood of each and yet their unity in the work of salvation (10:21).

The Genealogy of Jesus Christ (3:23–38)

3:23–38 Luke's genealogy differs from that of the Gospel of Matthew (Matt. 1:1–17), particularly in deriving Jesus' ancestry through David's son *Nathan* (v. 31; 2 Sam. 5:14; 1 Chron. 3:5; 14:4; Zech. 12:12) instead of Solomon. Some believe that Luke traces Mary's line (*Heli* would then be her father). However, Luke is likely tracing Jesus' lineage through Joseph, whom this gospel has identified as a descendant of David (1:27; 2:4). There is no reason why intermarriage in the line of David could not have resulted in both Nathan and Solomon being ancestors of Joseph. The spelling of some of these names is different from that in the Old Testament, reflecting their Greek form, as compared to the Hebrew.

3:23 *thirty years of age.* Joseph, the Aaronic priests, David, and Ezekiel all began their ministry around this age (Gen.

the son of Amos, which was *the son* of Naum,
which was *the son* of Esli, which was *the son* of
Nagge,
26 Which was *the son* of Maath, which was *the
son* of Mattathias, which was *the son* of Semei,
which was *the son* of Joseph, which was *the son*
of Juda,
27 Which was *the son* of Joanna, which was *the
son* of Rhesa, which was *the son* of Zorobabel,
which was *the son* of Salathiel, which was *the son*
of Neri,
28 Which was *the son* of Melchi, which was *the
son* of Addi, which was *the son* of Cosam, which
was *the son* of Elmodam, which was *the son* of Er,
29 Which was *the son* of Jose, which was *the son* of
Eliezer, which was *the son* of Jorim, which was *the
son* of Matthat, which was *the son* of Levi,
30 Which was *the son* of Simeon, which was *the
son* of Juda, which was *the son* of Joseph, which
was *the son* of Jonan, which was *the son* of Eliakim,
31 Which was *the son* of Melea, which was *the son*
of Menan, which was *the son* of Mattatha, which
was *the son* of Nathan, which was *the son* of David,
32 Which was *the son* of Jesse, which was *the son*
of Obed, which was *the son* of Booz, which was
the son of Salmon, which was *the son* of Naasson,
33 Which was *the son* of Aminadab, which was *the
son* of Aram, which was *the son* of Esrom, which
was *the son* of Phares, which was *the son* of Juda,
34 Which was *the son* of Jacob, which was *the son*
of Isaac, which was *the son* of Abraham, which
was *the son* of Thara, which was *the son* of Nachor,
35 Which was *the son* of Saruch, which was *the
son* of Ragau, which was *the son* of Phalec, which
was *the son* of Heber, which was *the son* of Sala,
36 Which was *the son* of Cainan, which was *the
son* of Arphaxad, which was *the son* of Sem, which
was *the son* of Noe, which was *the son* of Lamech,
37 Which was *the son* of Mathusala, which was
the son of Enoch, which was *the son* of Jared,
which was *the son* of Maleleel, which was *the son*
of Cainan,
38 Which was *the son* of Enos, which was *the son*
of Seth, which was *the son* of Adam, which was
the son of God.

CHAPTER 4

AND Jesus being full of the Holy Ghost returned
from Jordan, and was led by the Spirit into the
wilderness,
2 Being forty days tempted of the devil. And in
those days he did eat nothing: and when they
were ended, he afterward hungered.
3 And the devil said unto him, If thou be the
Son of God, command this stone that it be made
bread.
4 And Jesus answered him, saying, It is written,

41:46; Num. 4:3; 2 Sam. 5:4; Ezek. 1:1). *supposed the son of Joseph.* A reference to Jesus' virgin birth. Joseph was Jesus' father legally but not biologically (1:34–37).

3:27 *Zorobabel.* Zerubabbel, the head of the tribe of Judah when Judah returned from exile at around 539–519 BC.

3:31 *David.* Jesus is the rightful heir to the throne of Israel, as God had promised (2 Sam. 7:12).

3:33 *Juda.* Judah; a fulfillment of Jacob's prophecy (Gen. 49:10).

3:34 *Abraham.* Jesus is the promised seed of Abraham, through whom the nations will be blessed (Gen. 22:17–18).

3:36 *Noe.* Noah.

3:38 *Adam . . . the son of God.* The conclusion to Luke's genealogy implies that Adam was a real, historical person and that Jesus, the Son of God (v. 22), came not just to save Israel but as the last Adam for humankind in all the nations (Rom. 5:12,14; 1 Cor. 15:22,45) in order to conquer Satan (4:1–13) and reverse the curse of man's fall.

Thoughts for Personal/Family Worship: Chapter 3

1. **John prepared the way for Jesus by preaching repentance of sin. This is God's order of working with fallen man. Unless we recognize and acknowledge our sins, the forgiveness of sins will mean nothing to us. Repentance means that we grieve from our hearts that we have assaulted God's honor, confess our sins truly and uprightly before God, and forsake these sins, all by grace. As John pointed out to the people who came to him, repentance needs to be specific. Why is it impossible to trust in Jesus and be saved by Him without repenting of our sins?**
2. **The genealogy of Christ goes back all the way to Adam, the "son of God" (v. 38). Before we hear of this son of God, who fell into sin and misery, carrying the entire race with Him, we have already heard heaven's words concerning Christ: "Thou art my beloved Son; in thee I am well pleased" (v. 22). Having spent so long a time "in" the first Adam, lost and guilty, we must place our hope in the last Adam, righteous and beloved. Trust Jesus as the great Son of David, the King who can rule you in righteousness. Trust Jesus as the promised Son of Abraham, the Mediator of God's blessing to those under God's curse for their sins. Trust Jesus as the last Adam, who obeyed God and won everlasting life when we have all earned eternal damnation.**

Chapter 4: ***After being tempted by the Devil, Christ preaches in Nazareth, where He is rejected, after which He performs miracles and preaches the kingdom through Galilee.***

The Temptation of Jesus in the Wilderness (4:1–13)

4:1 *full of the Holy Ghost.* Empowered by the Holy Spirit for His ministry (1:15,41,67; Acts 2:4; 4:8,31; 6:3,5,8; 7:55; 9:17; 11:24; 13:9). Christ's obedience in the wilderness despite Satan's temptations stands in contrast to Adam's disobedience in the garden at the instigation of Satan (Gen. 3:1–24).

4:2 *forty days tempted.* The Devil put Christ to the test in an attempt to induce Him to fall into sin. The Greek allows for Jesus' temptation to have occurred throughout the course of the forty days, culminating in the three recorded temptations. Forty is a significant number in the history of Israel, associated with both testing and divine revelation (Ex. 24:18; 34:28; Num. 13:25; 14:33–34; 32:13).

4:3 *If thou be the Son of God.* The Devil was enticing Jesus to distrust God's love and provision.

That man shall not live by bread alone, but by
every word of God.
5 And the devil, taking him up into an high
mountain, shewed unto him all the kingdoms of
the world in a moment of time.
6 And the devil said unto him, All this power will
I give thee, and the glory of them: for that is deliv-
ered unto me; and to whomsoever I will I give it.
7 If thou therefore wilt worship me, all shall be
thine.
8 And Jesus answered and said unto him, Get
thee behind me, Satan: for it is written, Thou
shalt worship the Lord thy God, and him only
shalt thou serve.
9 And he brought him to Jerusalem, and set him
on a pinnacle of the temple, and said unto him, If
thou be the Son of God, cast thyself down from
hence:
10 For it is written, He shall give his angels charge
over thee, to keep thee:
11 And in *their* hands they shall bear thee up, lest
at any time thou dash thy foot against a stone.
12 And Jesus answering said unto him, It is said,
Thou shalt not tempt the Lord thy God.
13 And when the devil had ended all the tempta-
tion, he departed from him for a season.
14 ¶ And Jesus returned in the power of the Spirit
into Galilee: and there went out a fame of him
through all the region round about.
15 And he taught in their synagogues, being
glorified of all.
16 ¶ And he came to Nazareth, where he had
been brought up: and, as his custom was, he went
into the synagogue on the sabbath day, and stood
up for to read.
17 And there was delivered unto him the book of
the prophet Esaias. And when he had opened the
book, he found the place where it was written,
18 The Spirit of the Lord *is* upon me, because
he hath anointed me to preach the gospel to the
poor; he hath sent me to heal the brokenhearted,
to preach deliverance to the captives, and recov-
ering of sight to the blind, to set at liberty them
that are bruised,
19 To preach the acceptable year of the Lord.
20 And he closed the book, and he gave *it* again
to the minister, and sat down. And the eyes of all
them that were in the synagogue were fastened on
him.
21 And he began to say unto them, This day is
this scripture fulfilled in your ears.
22 And all bare him witness, and wondered at
the gracious words which proceeded out of his
mouth. And they said, Is not this Joseph's son?
23 And he said unto them, Ye will surely say
unto me this proverb, Physician, heal thyself:
whatsoever we have heard done in Capernaum,
do also here in thy country.
24 And he said, Verily I say unto you, No prophet
is accepted in his own country.
25 But I tell you of a truth, many widows were in
Israel in the days of Elias, when the heaven was
shut up three years and six months, when great
famine was throughout all the land;
26 But unto none of them was Elias sent, save
unto Sarepta, *a city* of Sidon, unto a woman *that*
was a widow.
27 And many lepers were in Israel in the time
of Eliseus the prophet; and none of them was
cleansed, saving Naaman the Syrian.
28 And all they in the synagogue, when they
heard these things, were filled with wrath,
29 And rose up, and thrust him out of the city,
and led him unto the brow of the hill whereon
their city was built, that they might cast him
down headlong.

4:4 *by every word of God.* Citing Deut. 8:3, Jesus used the law to combat the Devil's temptations.
4:5 *mountain.* Which one is unknown. *shewed unto him all the kingdoms of the world.* Either in a vision or else in a representative way.
4:6 *power . . . glory.* The Devil promised Jesus the reward He would in fact receive from His Father (Ps. 2:8).
4:8 *worship . . . him only.* Quoting Deut. 6:13. Worship belongs to God and God alone (Rev. 19:10).
4:9 *pinnacle.* Probably some high point in the temple area, from which the Devil suggested that Christ make a public scene.
4:10–11 The Devil tempted Jesus by quoting Scripture to him. The intensity of this temptation cannot be exxagerated. The Devil used God's promises against Jesus (Ps. 91:11–12).
4:12 *Thou shalt not tempt the Lord thy God.* Jesus again quotes from Deuteronomy (Deut. 6:16). Jesus did not need to test the Father's confirmation that He is the Son of God. Rather, He rested securely in the Father's promise.

JESUS BEGINS HIS MINISTRY IN GALILEE (4:14—9:50)

Jesus Goes Up to Galilee (4:14–15)

4:15 Jesus' normal manner of teaching was to do so in the synagogue (vv. 16,33,44; 6:6; 13:10).

Jesus Rejected in Galilee (4:16–30)

4:16 *Nazareth.* Jesus' hometown. *sabbath day.* Most of the Sabbath passages in Luke's gospel result in controversy between Jesus and the religious rulers (v. 31; 6:1–11; 13:10–17; 14:1–6).
4:18–19 *The Spirit of the Lord is upon me.* Quoting Isa. 61:1–3. This passage connects the year of Jubilee (Lev. 25:8–17) with Jesus' ministry, for His ministry was not one of bondage but of freeing and releasing captives.
4:22 The response of the crowds is twofold. Even as they marvel at Jesus' words, they also wonder about His origin. Unbelievers often react that way today.
4:23 *Physician, heal thyself.* A popular meaning, something like "Do what you say." The people of Nazareth had just heard Jesus proclaim the miracles He would perform and had likely heard reports of Jesus from Judaea. Now they wanted to witness this same work.
4:24 *Verily.* Truly.
4:25–26 *Elias.* Elijah (see 1 Kings 17). *save.* Except.
4:27 *Eliseus.* Elisha (see 2 Kings 5).
4:30 *passing through the midst.* Jesus walked away unscathed.

30 But he passing through the midst of them
went his way,
31 And came down to Capernaum, a city of Gali-
lee, and taught them on the sabbath days.
32 And they were astonished at his doctrine: for
his word was with power.
33 ¶ And in the synagogue there was a man,
which had a spirit of an unclean devil, and cried
out with a loud voice,
34 Saying, Let *us* alone; what have we to do with
thee, *thou* Jesus of Nazareth? art thou come to
destroy us? I know thee who thou art; the Holy
One of God.
35 And Jesus rebuked him, saying, Hold thy
peace, and come out of him. And when the devil
had thrown him in the midst, he came out of him,
and hurt him not.
36 And they were all amazed, and spake among
themselves, saying, What a word *is* this! for with
authority and power he commandeth the unclean
spirits, and they come out.
37 And the fame of him went out into every place
of the country round about.
38 ¶ And he arose out of the synagogue, and
entered into Simon's house. And Simon's wife's
mother was taken with a great fever; and they
besought him for her.
39 And he stood over her, and rebuked the fever;
and it left her: and immediately she arose and
ministered unto them.
40 ¶ Now when the sun was setting, all they that
had any sick with divers diseases brought them
unto him; and he laid his hands on every one of
them, and healed them.
41 And devils also came out of many, crying out,
and saying, Thou art Christ the Son of God. And
he rebuking *them* suffered them not to speak: for
they knew that he was Christ.
42 And when it was day, he departed and went
into a desert place: and the people sought him,
and came unto him, and stayed him, that he
should not depart from them.
43 And he said unto them, I must preach the
kingdom of God to other cities also: for therefore
am I sent.
44 And he preached in the synagogues of Galilee.

CHAPTER 5

AND it came to pass, that, as the people pressed
upon him to hear the word of God, he stood by
the lake of Gennesaret,
2 And saw two ships standing by the lake: but the
fishermen were gone out of them, and were wash-
ing *their* nets.
3 And he entered into one of the ships, which was
Simon's, and prayed him that he would thrust out
a little from the land. And he sat down, and taught
the people out of the ship.
4 Now when he had left speaking, he said unto
Simon, Launch out into the deep, and let down
your nets for a draught.
5 And Simon answering said unto him, Master,
we have toiled all the night, and have taken
nothing: nevertheless at thy word I will let down
the net.
6 And when they had this done, they inclosed a
great multitude of fishes: and their net brake.

Jesus in Capernaum and around Judaea (4:31–44)

4:31 *Capernaum.* A major Jewish town, located on the northwestern shore of the Sea of Galilee.
4:32 *astonished.* The people of Capernaum marveled at Jesus' words, just as the people of Nazareth had.
4:38 *Simon.* Peter. Luke records that Peter lived in Capernaum, but John states that it was Bethsaida (John 1:44). There is no contradiction here, as Bethsaida likely refers to Peter's childhood home and Capernaum to the place of his current dwelling. *besought.* Asked.
4:40 *divers.* Various, different.
4:43 *I must.* The phrase indicates a divine necessity propelling Jesus to fulfill God's plan and mission (2:49; 9:22; 13:33; 17:25; 19:5; 21:9; 22:37; 24:7,26,44,46). *preach.* The Greek verb refers specifically to preaching the gospel or good news (v. 18; 1:19; 2:10; 3:18; 7:22; 8:1; 9:6; 16:16; 20:1). Christ's calling was not to establish a settled ministry but to evangelize many cities in Israel as an itinerant preacher.
4:44 *preach.* Proclaim as a herald (vv. 18–19; 3:3; 8:1,39; 9:2; 12:3; 24:47); not the same word as in v. 43.

Thoughts for Personal/Family Worship: Chapter 4

1. **Though Christ was the Word of God incarnate, He chose to use the Word of God in Scripture to ward off the assaults of Satan. If He used the Word of God as a sword, should we presume to wage warfare without it? We need to be intimately acquainted with the Word. There is no spiritual weapon like it, and without it we are rightfully vulnerable. What are some ways in which you can use the Bible when you face temptations to sin or unbelief?**
2. **Christ's ministry on earth would be one of grace. The Spirit anointed Him to preach liberty to spiritual captives and the opening of the eyes of the blind. What do poor sinners need? How does Jesus provide them with all these things? Why is it important to recognize our need?**
3. **The miracles Christ performed were signs that showed His majesty, grace, and power. He did not come just to heal a few people so that they could be more comfortable on earth. Instead, His miracles pictured what His grace does still today: it drives back sin and Satan and restores peace and fellowship to miserable and undeserving sinners.**

Chapter 5: *Christ calls His first disciples, as well as Levi the publican, and through His teaching and miracles manifests the grace and power of the kingdom of God.*

Jesus Calls His First Disciples (5:1–11)

5:1 *Gennesaret.* The Sea of Galilee (Matt. 4:18).
5:4 *Simon.* Peter (v. 8; 4:38; 6:14). In this narrative Jesus begins to draw together His circle of apostles (v. 10). These men will play a vital role throughout Luke's gospel and Acts. *draught.* Catch of fish.
5:5 *nevertheless at thy word.* Peter trusted the word of Jesus

7 And they beckoned unto *their* partners, which
were in the other ship, that they should come and
help them. And they came, and filled both the
ships, so that they began to sink.
8 When Simon Peter saw *it*, he fell down at Jesus'
knees, saying, Depart from me; for I am a sinful
man, O Lord.
9 For he was astonished, and all that were with
him, at the draught of the fishes which they had
taken:
10 And so *was* also James, and John, the sons of
Zebedee, which were partners with Simon. And
Jesus said unto Simon, Fear not; from henceforth
thou shalt catch men.
11 And when they had brought their ships to
land, they forsook all, and followed him.
12 ¶ And it came to pass, when he was in a certain city, behold a man full of leprosy: who seeing
Jesus fell on *his* face, and besought him, saying,
Lord, if thou wilt, thou canst make me clean.
13 And he put forth *his* hand, and touched him,
saying, I will: be thou clean. And immediately the
leprosy departed from him.
14 And he charged him to tell no man: but go,
and shew thyself to the priest, and offer for thy
cleansing, according as Moses commanded, for a
testimony unto them.
15 But so much the more went there a fame
abroad of him: and great multitudes came together to hear, and to be healed by him of their
infirmities.
16 ¶ And he withdrew himself into the wilderness, and prayed.
17 And it came to pass on a certain day, as he was
teaching, that there were Pharisees and doctors of
the law sitting by, which were come out of every
town of Galilee, and Judaea, and Jerusalem: and
the power of the Lord was *present* to heal them.
18 ¶ And, behold, men brought in a bed a man
which was taken with a palsy: and they sought
means to bring him in, and to lay *him* before him.
19 And when they could not find by what *way*
they might bring him in because of the multitude,
they went upon the housetop, and let him down
through the tiling with *his* couch into the midst
before Jesus.
20 And when he saw their faith, he said unto him,
Man, thy sins are forgiven thee.
21 And the scribes and the Pharisees began to
reason, saying, Who is this which speaketh blasphemies? Who can forgive sins, but God alone?
22 But when Jesus perceived their thoughts, he
answering said unto them, What reason ye in
your hearts?
23 Whether is easier, to say, Thy sins be forgiven
thee; or to say, Rise up and walk?
24 But that ye may know that the Son of man
hath power upon earth to forgive sins, (he said
unto the sick of the palsy,) I say unto thee, Arise,
and take up thy couch, and go into thine house.
25 And immediately he rose up before them, and
took up that whereon he lay, and departed to his
own house, glorifying God.
26 And they were all amazed, and they glorified
God, and were filled with fear, saying, We have
seen strange things to day.
27 ¶ And after these things he went forth, and saw
a publican, named Levi, sitting at the receipt of
custom: and he said unto him, Follow me.
28 And he left all, rose up, and followed him.

---

more than his own experience and expertise.

5:8 *fell down at Jesus' knees.* A response of worship and confession of sin. Peter realized from the miracle that he was in the presence of the holy *Lord* of creation (Isa. 6:5).

Jesus Heals a Leper and a Paralytic (5:12–26)

5:12 *besought.* Begged, prayed. *if thou wilt, thou canst.* The Lord is able to do whatever He chooses to do, a suggestion of Christ's deity (1:37; 18:27; Gen. 18:14).

5:13 *I will.* Jesus showed His sovereign authority over this disease. *immediately.* The instantaneous healing of the man by the word and touch of the Lord displays Christ's great power.

5:14 *tell no man.* This command was given so that the leper would have time to be declared clean by a priest and *offer* the sacrifice required by the Mosaic law (Lev. 14:1–32). *testimony unto them.* Jesus desired the priests and people to know He was not overthrowing the law but fulfilling it (Matt. 5:17).

5:15 *abroad.* Over a wide area.

5:16 Throughout Luke's gospel, Jesus' times of prayer happen at significant moments in His ministry, showing His dependence upon God (3:21; 6:12; 9:18,28–29; 11:1; 22:41,44). Here Jesus was preparing to enter into a series of conflicts.

5:17 *Pharisees.* Their first appearance in this gospel. The Pharisees were one of four religious groups in first-century Judaism. They were lay separatists who took responsibility for keeping the Jews faithful to the Mosaic laws and the traditions of their fathers. *doctors of the law.* Teachers who attempted to contemporize the Mosaic law for the people of Israel. *power of the Lord was present.* Jesus works in conjunction with the Father (John 5:19–20) by the Holy Spirit (4:14; 6:19; 8:46; Acts 10:38).

5:18 *palsy.* Paralysis (v. 24).

5:20 *saw their faith.* The faith of all of them, including the paralytic. *thy sins are forgiven.* Jesus not only demonstrated His willingness and authority to heal physical diseases but indicated clearly that He also had a willingness and the authority to forgive sins. This would be the first point of conflict between Jesus and the religious elite.

5:23 *Whether.* Which. Christ would perform both, and the healing would confirm the forgiving. The Pharisees had everything upside down: rather than judging Jesus for blasphemy they should have recognized His deity.

5:24 *Son of man.* The phrase can refer to a human being in general (Ps. 8:4) or, more specifically, to the man to whom God was giving an eternal kingdom over all for the sake of God's people (Dan. 7:13–14,27). This was one of Jesus' favorite titles for Himself (6:5; 9:22,26; 17:22–30; 21:27; 22:69, etc.). *power.* Authority.

Jesus Calls Levi (5:27–32)

5:27 *publican.* Tax collector. *Levi.* Same as Matthew. *receipt of custom.* The tax office, the place of toll.

5:28 *left all.* Just as with the fishermen (v. 11), so now with

29 And Levi made him a great feast in his own
house: and there was a great company of publi-
cans and of others that sat down with them.
30 But their scribes and Pharisees murmured
against his disciples, saying, Why do ye eat and
drink with publicans and sinners?
31 And Jesus answering said unto them, They that
are whole need not a physician; but they that are
sick.
32 I came not to call the righteous, but sinners to
repentance.
33 ¶ And they said unto him, Why do the dis-
ciples of John fast often, and make prayers, and
likewise *the disciples* of the Pharisees; but thine eat
and drink?
34 And he said unto them, Can ye make the
children of the bridechamber fast, while the
bridegroom is with them?
35 But the days will come, when the bridegroom
shall be taken away from them, and then shall
they fast in those days.
36 ¶ And he spake also a parable unto them; No
man putteth a piece of a new garment upon an
old; if otherwise, then both the new maketh a
rent, and the piece that was *taken* out of the new
agreeth not with the old.
37 And no man putteth new wine into old bottles;
else the new wine will burst the bottles, and be
spilled, and the bottles shall perish.
38 But new wine must be put into new bottles;
and both are preserved.
39 No man also having drunk old *wine* straight-
way desireth new: for he saith, The old is better.

CHAPTER 6

AND it came to pass on the second sabbath after
the first, that he went through the corn fields; and
his disciples plucked the ears of corn, and did eat,
rubbing *them* in *their* hands.
2 And certain of the Pharisees said unto them,
Why do ye that which is not lawful to do on the
sabbath days?
3 And Jesus answering them said, Have ye not read
so much as this, what David did, when himself was
an hungred, and they which were with him;
4 How he went into the house of God, and did
take and eat the shewbread, and gave also to them
that were with him; which it is not lawful to eat
but for the priests alone?
5 And he said unto them, That the Son of man is
Lord also of the sabbath.

Levi; when Jesus calls His disciples they forsake all to follow him.

5:29 *The great feast* Levi threw for Jesus and His friends was meant to introduce the friends to Him. Table fellowship is often used by Luke to communicate spiritual lessons (7:36–50; 9:10–17; 10:38–42, etc.).

5:31–32 Jesus' response gets to the heart of His ministry. He has not come to help the self-righteous, who do not recognize their need, but rather the spiritually *sick* who acknowledge their need of His grace.

Jesus Is Questioned about Fasting (5:33–39)

5:34–35 *children of the bridechamber.* Wedding guests or attendants of the groom. *bridegroom.* The Lord is the spiritual husband of Israel (Isa. 54:5; 62:5; Hos. 2:19–20). Jesus implicitly identified Himself with the covenant God of Israel. His presence is the joy of His people. *days will come.* His absence gives His disciples cause to mourn and fast, whether during His death and burial or while they wait for His return from heaven.

5:36–39 *maketh a rent.* Splits it apart. *bottles.* Leather bags to hold wine. Christ would not just tweak the message of the religious elites. The message in its entirety had to come from Him.

Thoughts for Personal/Family Worship: Chapter 5

1. **This miracle of the great catch of fish so overwhelmed Peter that he felt as though he and Christ could never fit together. The truth of the gospel, however, is exactly the opposite. Though by nature there is no greater contrast than that between a holy God and an unholy sinner, for Christ's sake the holy God and the unholy sinner can indeed be reconciled, with God's glory magnified in the process. Jesus has the right to forgive sins. Have you been brought low before Jesus Christ by a sense of His holiness? Has His message of grace brought peace to your soul?**
2. **The cleansing of the leper and the healing of the paralytic reflect two important parts of the gospel purpose of Christ's coming. His grace cleanses from the pollution of sin as well as frees from the power of sin. Christ makes sinners clean and able to serve Him. He is mighty to work a full work, filling our every need by His grace and gospel.**

Chapter 6: *Christ collides with the Pharisees on the Sabbath, appoints His twelve apostles, and teaches concerning the nature of true religion.*

Jesus is Lord of the Sabbath (6:1–11)

Jesus Defends His Disciples' Plucking Grain on the Sabbath (6:1–5)

6:1 *plucked the ears.* Not stealing but authorized by the law (Deut. 23:25). *corn.* A general term for grain. *rubbing them in their hands.* This action was deemed by some as breaking Sabbath regulations.

6:3–4 *an hungred.* Hungry. *what David did.* To refute the claims of the Pharisees, Jesus refers to the example of David and his men, who, while persecuted by Saul, found refuge in his God (1 Sam. 21:1–7; 22:9–10). So too Christ and His disciples, now persecuted by the religious authorities, find refuge in God's creation. By drawing this analogy Jesus is indicating that, like David, He stands as the royal representative of the Lord's people. *shewbread.* The bread set out in the presence of God on the golden table in the tabernacle and then eaten by the priests (Lev. 24:5–9).

6:5 *Son of man.* See note at 5:24. *Lord also of the sabbath.* When accused of breaking the Sabbath, Christ did not dismiss the fourth commandment (Ex. 20:8–11) but claimed it as His own and taught how to properly observe it, implying His deity as the Lawgiver (Isa. 33:22; James 4:12) and the continuing obligation upon His disciples to observe a day of holy rest (Rev. 1:10).

6 And it came to pass also on another sabbath,
that he entered into the synagogue and taught: and
there was a man whose right hand was withered.
7 And the scribes and Pharisees watched him,
whether he would heal on the sabbath day; that
they might find an accusation against him.
8 But he knew their thoughts, and said to the
man which had the withered hand, Rise up, and
stand forth in the midst. And he arose and stood
forth.
9 Then said Jesus unto them, I will ask you one
thing; Is it lawful on the sabbath days to do good,
or to do evil? to save life, or to destroy *it*?
10 And looking round about upon them all, he
said unto the man, Stretch forth thy hand. And
he did so: and his hand was restored whole as the
other.
11 And they were filled with madness; and com-
muned one with another what they might do to
Jesus.
12 And it came to pass in those days, that he went
out into a mountain to pray, and continued all
night in prayer to God.
13 ¶ And when it was day, he called *unto him* his
disciples: and of them he chose twelve, whom also
he named apostles;
14 Simon, (whom he also named Peter,) and
Andrew his brother, James and John, Philip and
Bartholomew,
15 Matthew and Thomas, James the *son* of Al-
phaeus, and Simon called Zelotes,
16 And Judas *the brother* of James, and Judas
Iscariot, which also was the traitor.
17 ¶ And he came down with them, and stood in
the plain, and the company of his disciples, and
a great multitude of people out of all Judaea and
Jerusalem, and from the sea coast of Tyre and
Sidon, which came to hear him, and to be healed
of their diseases;
18 And they that were vexed with unclean spirits:
and they were healed.
19 And the whole multitude sought to touch him:
for there went virtue out of him, and healed *them*
all.
20 ¶ And he lifted up his eyes on his disciples, and
said, Blessed *be ye* poor: for yours is the kingdom
of God.
21 Blessed *are ye* that hunger now: for ye shall be
filled. Blessed *are ye* that weep now: for ye shall
laugh.
22 Blessed are ye, when men shall hate you, and
when they shall separate you *from their company*,
and shall reproach *you*, and cast out your name as
evil, for the Son of man's sake.
23 Rejoice ye in that day, and leap for joy: for,
behold, your reward *is* great in heaven: for in the
like manner did their fathers unto the prophets.
24 But woe unto you that are rich! for ye have
received your consolation.
25 Woe unto you that are full! for ye shall hunger.
Woe unto you that laugh now! for ye shall mourn
and weep.

Jesus Defends A Healed Man on the Sabbath (6:6–11)

6:6 *whose right hand was withered.* The man's life was not in jeopardy, and thus the urgency of Jesus' healing appears to have been undermined.

6:9 *Is it lawful.* Jesus' question showed the scribes and Pharisees where they could find their "accusation" (v. 17). The only unlawful thing Jesus did was to heal a man, doing him good, even when this was not necessary in order to save his life.

6:10 *was restored.* The man's healing indicates that God approved of Jesus' action on the Sabbath.

6:11 *what they might do to Jesus.* The contrast is sharp and ironic. Jesus was accused of the good He was doing, while the scribes and Pharisees were seeking to do Him evil. They were the ones who stood condemned on this Sabbath day.

The Twelve Apostles (6:12–16)

6:12 *continued all night in prayer to God.* Jesus is seen in Luke's gospel praying at important points in His ministry (see the note at 5:16). This night of prayer occurred before Jesus had selected the twelve apostles.

6:13 *apostles.* Literally, "sent ones," men whom Jesus chose and later sent out to represent Him with delegated authority to preach and work miracles (9:1–2).

The Beatitudes and Christ's Further Teaching (6:17–49)

6:18–19 Luke highlights the great success and fame of Jesus with the crowds. As Jesus heals the multitudes He shows that nothing is beyond the scope of His power. *virtue.* Power, not an impersonal force or energy but the wise and supernatural activity of the Holy Spirit (see note at 5:17).

6:20–26 These blessings and woes serve as a prophetic call to discipleship (Isa. 65:13–14).

6:20 *poor.* Beggars. The word refers here not merely to a socioeconomic status but to spiritual poverty in which one is in deep need of God (Pss. 9:17–18; 10:14; 14:6; 34:6; Isa. 29:19) and His grace in light of one's sin and debt before God (18:13; Isa. 66:2).

6:21 *hunger.* God's people hunger for Him and His righteousness. They are not satisfied without it. *weep.* Mourn over sin and the loss of God. *laugh.* Rejoice in God's blessing (Gen. 21:6; Ps. 126:2).

6:22 *hate . . . separate . . . reproach . . . cast out your name.* There may be an ascending order of persecution faced by Jesus' disciples. *for the Son of man's sake.* The Beatitudes of Jesus presuppose union with Himself through true faith, not primarily socioeconomic or political affliction.

6:23 *in heaven.* The blessings of which Jesus speaks are only fully consummated in the age to come. Nevertheless, it is true that based on Jesus' life, death, and resurrection disciples can have a foretaste of these blessings today. *prophets.* Jesus' disciples stand in the same line of faithful believers as the prophets.

6:24–26 The woes of judgment are coordinated or paralleled with the blessing section (Deut. 28:1—30:20).

6:24 *rich.* It is good to remember that while wealth does pose a real danger and threat to the spiritual well-being of disciples, Christ's condemnation is of a spiritual self-sufficiency that man by nature possesses which prevents him from seeing himself as he truly is (Hos. 12:8; Rev. 3:17).

6:25 *laugh.* The laughing Jesus has in mind is a jeering that

26 Woe unto you, when all men shall speak well of
you! for so did their fathers to the false prophets.
27 ¶ But I say unto you which hear, Love your
enemies, do good to them which hate you,
28 Bless them that curse you, and pray for them
which despitefully use you.
29 And unto him that smiteth thee on the *one*
cheek offer also the other; and him that taketh
away thy cloke forbid not *to take thy* coat also.
30 Give to every man that asketh of thee; and of
him that taketh away thy goods ask *them* not again.
31 And as ye would that men should do to you,
do ye also to them likewise.
32 For if ye love them which love you, what thank
have ye? for sinners also love those that love them.
33 And if ye do good to them which do good to
you, what thank have ye? for sinners also do even
the same.
34 And if ye lend *to them* of whom ye hope to re-
ceive, what thank have ye? for sinners also lend to
sinners, to receive as much again.
35 But love ye your enemies, and do good, and
lend, hoping for nothing again; and your reward
shall be great, and ye shall be the children of the
Highest: for he is kind unto the unthankful and
to the evil.
36 Be ye therefore merciful, as your Father also
is merciful.
37 Judge not, and ye shall not be judged: condemn
not, and ye shall not be condemned: forgive, and
ye shall be forgiven:
38 Give, and it shall be given unto you; good
measure, pressed down, and shaken together, and
running over, shall men give into your bosom.
For with the same measure that ye mete withal it
shall be measured to you again.
39 And he spake a parable unto them, Can the
blind lead the blind? shall they not both fall into
the ditch?
40 The disciple is not above his master: but every
one that is perfect shall be as his master.
41 And why beholdest thou the mote that is in
thy brother's eye, but perceivest not the beam that
is in thine own eye?
42 Either how canst thou say to thy brother,
Brother, let me pull out the mote that is in thine
eye, when thou thyself beholdest not the beam
that is in thine own eye? Thou hypocrite, cast out
first the beam out of thine own eye, and then shalt
thou see clearly to pull out the mote that is in thy
brother's eye.
43 For a good tree bringeth not forth corrupt fruit;
neither doth a corrupt tree bring forth good fruit.
44 For every tree is known by his own fruit. For of
thorns men do not gather figs, nor of a bramble
bush gather they grapes.
45 A good man out of the good treasure of his
heart bringeth forth that which is good; and an
evil man out of the evil treasure of his heart brin-
geth forth that which is evil: for of the abundance
of the heart his mouth speaketh.
46 ¶ And why call ye me, Lord, Lord, and do not
the things which I say?
47 Whosoever cometh to me, and heareth my
sayings, and doeth them, I will shew you to whom
he is like:
48 He is like a man which built an house, and
digged deep, and laid the foundation on a rock:
and when the flood arose, the stream beat vehe-
mently upon that house, and could not shake it:
for it was founded upon a rock.
49 But he that heareth, and doeth not, is like a
man that without a foundation built an house
upon the earth; against which the stream did beat

carries the idea of worldly ease and indifference to life based on self-satisfaction (Eccl. 2:1–2; 7:2–6). Those who rest content in their possessions and life will face an eternity of dissatisfaction and difficulties.

6:26 *speak well of you.* The picture here is of one who caters his words and message to tickling the ears of those around him (2 Tim. 4:3).

6:28 *despitefully use.* Insult, slander.

6:35 *the Highest.* God. *Children* often take on the characteristics of their fathers.

6:38 *mete withal.* Measure with.

6:41–42 These verses are about presumptuous, proud, and hypocritical judging where one man places himself above his brother, not about the discernment necessary to honor God and do good to men. *mote.* Speck of dust.

6:48 The man in this parable digs deeply until he finds the bedrock on which he needs to build.

6:49 By contrast, the second man merely builds a house, perhaps without testing Jesus' words or his own heart. Though he hears the words of Jesus, the end result is devastation.

Thoughts for Personal/Family Worship: Chapter 6

1. **Christ showed the true intention of the fourth commandment. While God forbids work on the Lord's Day, the law commands that people show mercy and do works of necessity. We need to guard against the universal human tendency to observe the letter of God's law while omitting the spirit or heart of the law (Isa. 58:13–14). How can human traditions about the Sabbath make the word of God void? Why is keeping the Sabbath under the Lordship of Christ a blessing?**
2. **Christ's teaching shows the inward and genuine nature of true religion. The great enemy of true religion is not just our natural unbelief but also our conceited pride, which makes us deceive ourselves. Has God's Spirit made you spiritually poor and hungry? Has He made you a mourner over sin and its guilt and offense against God? This is not just a one-time experience. If God has worked this in you, He keeps you near and needy at His feet in order that in Christ He might be your all and in all.**
3. **Note the commendation Jesus gives to the man who builds His house upon the rock: his house will stand in the day of trouble and distress. Though both men hear the Word of God, the wise man alone has received the grace whereby he does the Word of God. Is your life built on the bedrock of Christ—His Word, work, and worth?**

vehemently, and immediately it fell; and the ruin
of that house was great.

CHAPTER 7

NOW when he had ended all his sayings in the au-
dience of the people, he entered into Capernaum.
2 And a certain centurion's servant, who was dear
unto him, was sick, and ready to die.
3 And when he heard of Jesus, he sent unto him
the elders of the Jews, beseeching him that he
would come and heal his servant.
4 And when they came to Jesus, they besought
him instantly, saying, That he was worthy for
whom he should do this:
5 For he loveth our nation, and he hath built us
a synagogue.
6 Then Jesus went with them. And when he was
now not far from the house, the centurion sent
friends to him, saying unto him, Lord, trouble not
thyself: for I am not worthy that thou shouldest
enter under my roof:
7 Wherefore neither thought I myself worthy to
come unto thee: but say in a word, and my servant
shall be healed.
8 For I also am a man set under authority, having
under me soldiers, and I say unto one, Go, and he
goeth; and to another, Come, and he cometh; and
to my servant, Do this, and he doeth *it*.
9 When Jesus heard these things, he marvelled
at him, and turned him about, and said unto the
people that followed him, I say unto you, I have
not found so great faith, no, not in Israel.
10 And they that were sent, returning to the
house, found the servant whole that had been sick.
11 ¶ And it came to pass the day after, that he
went into a city called Nain; and many of his
disciples went with him, and much people.
12 Now when he came nigh to the gate of the city,
behold, there was a dead man carried out, the
only son of his mother, and she was a widow: and
much people of the city was with her.
13 And when the Lord saw her, he had compassion
on her, and said unto her, Weep not.
14 And he came and touched the bier: and they
that bare *him* stood still. And he said, Young man,
I say unto thee, Arise.
15 And he that was dead sat up, and began to
speak. And he delivered him to his mother.
16 And there came a fear on all: and they glori-
fied God, saying, That a great prophet is risen up
among us; and, That God hath visited his people.
17 And this rumour of him went forth through-
out all Judaea, and throughout all the region
round about.
18 And the disciples of John shewed him of all
these things.
19 ¶ And John calling *unto him* two of his disci-
ples sent *them* to Jesus, saying, Art thou he that
should come? or look we for another?
20 When the men were come unto him, they said,
John Baptist hath sent us unto thee, saying, Art
thou he that should come? or look we for another?
21 And in that same hour he cured many of *their*
infirmities and plagues, and of evil spirits; and
unto many *that were* blind he gave sight.
22 Then Jesus answering said unto them, Go your
way, and tell John what things ye have seen and
heard; how that the blind see, the lame walk, the
lepers are cleansed, the deaf hear, the dead are
raised, to the poor the gospel is preached.
23 And blessed is *he*, whosoever shall not be
offended in me.
24 ¶ And when the messengers of John were
departed, he began to speak unto the people
concerning John, What went ye out into the wil-
derness for to see? A reed shaken with the wind?
25 But what went ye out for to see? A man clothed

Chapter 7: *Christ shows His marvelous grace by healing the servant of a Gentile, raising the son of a widow, showing His merciful character to John in prison, and forgiving a sinful woman.*

Jesus Cares for a Gentile and a Woman (7:1–17)

Jesus Heals the Centurion's Servant (7:1–10)

7:2 *centurion.* One of a number of important military men who, according to the historical record, made large sums of money in the Roman legions. This centurion was not Jewish (v. 9).

7:4–5 *besought . . . instantly.* Urged earnestly. *worthy.* The elders of the Jews apparently esteemed this man for his religious zeal more than the man esteemed himself (v. 6).

7:9 *great faith.* Surprisingly, this Gentile showed more trust in and spiritual insight with regard to Christ—in his sense of unworthiness of Christ's presence (vv. 6–7) and his confidence that Christ could work miracles at a distance with a mere word—than did Israel (vv. 7–8).

Jesus Raises a Widow's Only Son (7:11–17)

7:11–17 Christ's miracle of raising to life the widow's dead son reveals His *compassion* and great power, signs that *God* Himself has *visited* mankind in the flesh.

7:11 *Nain.* A small city twenty miles from Capernaum.

7:12 *only son.* This heightens the reader's understanding of the grief of this widow.

7:14 *bier.* A stretcher-like frame that carries a body or coffin.

7:16 *great prophet.* Jesus is the One promised by Moses (Deut. 18:15).

John's Disciples Question Jesus (7:18–35)

7:19 *he that should come.* A common title for the coming Messiah. Suffering in prison (3:20), John sought from Jesus confirmation for his faith (Matt. 11:2–3).

7:21–22 *the blind see . . . to the poor the gospel is preached.* Christ allows His actions and miracles to speak for themselves, for they are the very things the prophets had foretold (Isa. 35:5–6; 61:1). Thus He puts faith into action.

7:25 *clothed in soft raiment . . . gorgeously apparelled.* Dressed in fine clothing, a sign of living in luxury (*delicately*).

in soft raiment? Behold, they which are gorgeously
apparelled, and live delicately, are in kings' courts.
26 But what went ye out for to see? A prophet? Yea,
I say unto you, and much more than a prophet.
27 This is *he*, of whom it is written, Behold, I send
my messenger before thy face, which shall prepare
thy way before thee.
28 For I say unto you, Among those that are born
of women there is not a greater prophet than John
the Baptist: but he that is least in the kingdom of
God is greater than he.
29 And all the people that heard *him*, and the
publicans, justified God, being baptized with the
baptism of John.
30 But the Pharisees and lawyers rejected the
counsel of God against themselves, being not
baptized of him.
31 ¶ And the Lord said, Whereunto then shall I
liken the men of this generation? and to what are
they like?
32 They are like unto children sitting in the mar-
ketplace, and calling one to another, and saying,
We have piped unto you, and ye have not danced;
we have mourned to you, and ye have not wept.
33 For John the Baptist came neither eating bread
nor drinking wine; and ye say, He hath a devil.
34 The Son of man is come eating and drink-
ing; and ye say, Behold a gluttonous man, and a
winebibber, a friend of publicans and sinners!
35 But wisdom is justified of all her children.
36 ¶ And one of the Pharisees desired him that he
would eat with him. And he went into the Phari-
see's house, and sat down to meat.
37 And, behold, a woman in the city, which was
a sinner, when she knew that *Jesus* sat at meat in
the Pharisee's house, brought an alabaster box of
ointment,
38 And stood at his feet behind *him* weeping, and
began to wash his feet with tears, and did wipe
them with the hairs of her head, and kissed his
feet, and anointed *them* with the ointment.
39 Now when the Pharisee which had bidden him
saw *it*, he spake within himself, saying, This man,
if he were a prophet, would have known who and
what manner of woman *this is* that toucheth him:
for she is a sinner.
40 And Jesus answering said unto him, Simon,
I have somewhat to say unto thee. And he saith,
Master, say on.
41 There was a certain creditor which had two
debtors: the one owed five hundred pence, and
the other fifty.
42 And when they had nothing to pay, he frankly
forgave them both. Tell me therefore, which of
them will love him most?
43 Simon answered and said, I suppose that *he*,
to whom he forgave most. And he said unto him,
Thou hast rightly judged.
44 And he turned to the woman, and said unto
Simon, Seest thou this woman? I entered into
thine house, thou gavest me no water for my
feet: but she hath washed my feet with tears, and
wiped *them* with the hairs of her head.
45 Thou gavest me no kiss: but this woman since
the time I came in hath not ceased to kiss my feet.
46 My head with oil thou didst not anoint: but
this woman hath anointed my feet with ointment.
47 Wherefore I say unto thee, Her sins, which are
many, are forgiven; for she loved much: but to
whom little is forgiven, *the same* loveth little.
48 And he said unto her, Thy sins are forgiven.
49 And they that sat at meat with him began to
say within themselves, Who is this that forgiveth
sins also?
50 And he said to the woman, Thy faith hath
saved thee; go in peace.

7:27 *it is written*. Citing Mal. 3:1.
7:28 *John* was an Old Testament *prophet* who served as a bridge into the time of fulfillment as the old economy of redemption was giving way to the new. With Jesus as the final Prophet and living Word from God (John 1:1,14; Heb. 1:1–2), God's people have the full revelation of divine truth until Christ returns and they no longer need new prophetic revelation. Therefore, the *least* of them has entered into *greater* spiritual privilege than even John (10:23–24).
7:29 *publicans*. Tax collectors.
7:30 *lawyers*. Not experts in civil law but scholars in the law of Moses.
7:35 *wisdom . . . her children*. Jesus identified Himself as the embodiment of divine wisdom (2:40; 11:31,49), appearing in Proverbs as a godly woman (Prov. 9:1–12). *justified*. Declared righteous or publicly vindicated. Many sinners acknowledged God's righteousness in what He did through John and His Son (v. 29).

Jesus Forgives a Sinful Woman (7:36–50)

7:36 *one of the Pharisees*. The following exchange between Jesus and the Pharisee will exemplify what Jesus has just said. This Pharisee will show that he rejects the message of Jesus and attempts to justify himself, when in actuality he is condemning himself (v. 30). The sinful woman exhibits true wisdom in embracing the message of Jesus. *sat down to meat*. Reclined to eat food.
7:41–42 Jesus showed that this woman's actions were driven by *love*, the response of believers to the forgiveness and salvation of Christ. *frankly forgave*. Literally, He "gave grace."
7:47 *for she loved much*. Jesus was not saying that this woman's forgiveness was contingent upon her love. His parable had just shown the exact opposite: her love flowed from having been forgiven much.
7:48–49 *sat at meat*. Reclined at the table. *Thy sins are forgiven*. Jesus now openly assured the woman of her forgiveness.
7:50 *Thy faith hath saved thee*. Faith is the empty hand by which we receive Christ and all His benefits.

Thoughts for Personal/Family Worship: Chapter 7

1. **Christ's power is so great that He could heal a young man near death from a distance, as well as raise another young man who was already dead. He heals the lame**

CHAPTER 8

AND it came to pass afterward, that he went
throughout every city and village, preaching and
shewing the glad tidings of the kingdom of God:
and the twelve *were* with him,
2 And certain women, which had been healed of
evil spirits and infirmities, Mary called Magda-
lene, out of whom went seven devils,
3 And Joanna the wife of Chuza Herod's steward,
and Susanna, and many others, which ministered
unto him of their substance.
4 ¶ And when much people were gathered
together, and were come to him out of every city,
he spake by a parable:
5 A sower went out to sow his seed: and as he
sowed, some fell by the way side; and it was trod-
den down, and the fowls of the air devoured it.
6 And some fell upon a rock; and as soon as it
was sprung up, it withered away, because it lacked
moisture.
7 And some fell among thorns; and the thorns
sprang up with it, and choked it.
8 And other fell on good ground, and sprang up,
and bare fruit an hundredfold. And when he had
said these things, he cried, He that hath ears to
hear, let him hear.
9 And his disciples asked him, saying, What
might this parable be?
10 And he said, Unto you it is given to know the
mysteries of the kingdom of God: but to others
in parables; that seeing they might not see, and
hearing they might not understand.
11 Now the parable is this: The seed is the word
of God.
12 Those by the way side are they that hear; then
cometh the devil, and taketh away the word out of
their hearts, lest they should believe and be saved.
13 They on the rock *are they*, which, when they
hear, receive the word with joy; and these have
no root, which for a while believe, and in time of
temptation fall away.
14 And that which fell among thorns are they,
which, when they have heard, go forth, and are
choked with cares and riches and pleasures of *this*
life, and bring no fruit to perfection.
15 But that on the good ground are they, which in
an honest and good heart, having heard the word,
keep *it*, and bring forth fruit with patience.
16 ¶ No man, when he hath lighted a candle,
covereth it with a vessel, or putteth *it* under a bed;
but setteth *it* on a candlestick, that they which
enter in may see the light.
17 For nothing is secret, that shall not be made
manifest; neither *any thing* hid, that shall not be
known and come abroad.
18 Take heed therefore how ye hear: for whoso-
ever hath, to him shall be given; and whosoever
hath not, from him shall be taken even that which
he seemeth to have.
19 ¶ Then came to him *his* mother and his
brethren, and could not come at him for the press.
20 And it was told him *by certain* which said, Thy
mother and thy brethren stand without, desiring
to see thee.

---

and gives sight to the blind. Jesus is the Lord God and the all-sufficient Savior, come to rescue sinners from their sin and misery. None need despair; all should seek grace from Christ for the healing of their souls in this age and the healing of all they are in the age to come.

2. **The woman loved Christ a great deal, as she had been forgiven much. If you do not love Christ at all you can be sure you have not tasted of His forgiveness. What a depth of sin there is in our hearts! However, the love of God is infinitely deeper. When you experience His love it becomes a fountain of love in your heart flowing to Christ and to the Father. Do you have the kind of faith in Christ that results in love for Him?**

Chapter 8: *Christ teaches in parables and continues His miracles, including stilling the storm, delivering a Gadarene from demon possession, healing a woman with an issue of blood, and raising Jairus's daughter from the dead.*

Women Follow Jesus (8:1–3)

8:1 *throughout every city and village.* Christ labored to bring the Word not only to the significant centers of population but also to small towns (9:6; 13:22). *shewing the glad tidings.* Preaching the good news.

8:3 *Herod's steward.* An administrative official in Herod's court; thus *Joanna* was a woman of some financial means (*substance*).

Jesus' Teaching concerning Parables (8:4–18)

8:4 *parable.* As Jesus was rejected by the people His teaching style became more veiled (v. 10).

8:6–8 The seed on the *rock* and *thorns* failed to produce the fruit it needed because of the soil in which it was implanted. The seed on the *good* soil was allowed to take root and bear bountiful fruit. Despite the unbelief of many, God's Word will be effective and produce a bountiful harvest. *ears to hear.* A prophetic call to listen to Jesus' words and respond rightly.

8:10 *seeing . . . not see, and hearing . . . not understand.* Those who do not follow Christ are given over to spiritual blindness, as Christ's concealing of truth in the parables indicates (Isa. 6:9).

8:12–14 Jesus expounded three reasons why the preached Word remains ineffective in the hearts of so many who hear it: the influence of the Devil to prevent faith (2 Cor. 4:4), the persistent hardness of the heart despite outward appearances of conversion (Heb. 3:12–13), and the love of this world that chokes out godliness (1 John 2:15–17).

8:15 *honest and good heart.* Mere knowledge is insufficient; a right response to Jesus requires a new heart given by God's regeneration (Jer. 31:33; Ezek. 36:26). *patience.* Endurance.

8:16 *candle.* Lamp, likely a reference to Jesus' teaching.

8:17 *nothing is secret.* The Word of Jesus not only illuminates but also exposes the thoughts and intentions of the heart (Heb. 4:13).

8:18 *Take heed . . . how ye hear.* Pay attention to how you listen to the preaching of God's Word.

8:19–20 *press.* Crowd. *without.* Outside.

21 And he answered and said unto them, My
mother and my brethren are these which hear the
word of God, and do it.
22 ¶ Now it came to pass on a certain day, that
he went into a ship with his disciples: and he said
unto them, Let us go over unto the other side of
the lake. And they launched forth.
23 But as they sailed he fell asleep: and there came
down a storm of wind on the lake; and they were
filled *with water*, and were in jeopardy.
24 And they came to him, and awoke him, saying,
Master, master, we perish. Then he arose, and re-
buked the wind and the raging of the water: and
they ceased, and there was a calm.
25 And he said unto them, Where is your faith?
And they being afraid wondered, saying one
to another, What manner of man is this! for he
commandeth even the winds and water, and they
obey him.
26 ¶ And they arrived at the country of the
Gadarenes, which is over against Galilee.
27 And when he went forth to land, there met
him out of the city a certain man, which had
devils long time, and ware no clothes, neither
abode in *any* house, but in the tombs.
28 When he saw Jesus, he cried out, and fell down
before him, and with a loud voice said, What have
I to do with thee, Jesus, *thou* Son of God most
high? I beseech thee, torment me not.
29 (For he had commanded the unclean spirit
to come out of the man. For oftentimes it had
caught him: and he was kept bound with chains
and in fetters; and he brake the bands, and was
driven of the devil into the wilderness.)
30 And Jesus asked him, saying, What is thy
name? And he said, Legion: because many devils
were entered into him.
31 And they besought him that he would not
command them to go out into the deep.
32 And there was there an herd of many swine
feeding on the mountain: and they besought him
that he would suffer them to enter into them. And
he suffered them.
33 Then went the devils out of the man, and en-
tered into the swine: and the herd ran violently
down a steep place into the lake, and were choked.
34 When they that fed *them* saw what was done,
they fled, and went and told *it* in the city and in
the country.
35 Then they went out to see what was done;
and came to Jesus, and found the man, out of
whom the devils were departed, sitting at the feet
of Jesus, clothed, and in his right mind: and they
were afraid.
36 They also which saw *it* told them by what means
he that was possessed of the devils was healed.
37 ¶ Then the whole multitude of the country
of the Gadarenes round about besought him to
depart from them; for they were taken with great
fear: and he went up into the ship, and returned
back again.
38 Now the man out of whom the devils were de-
parted besought him that he might be with him:
but Jesus sent him away, saying,
39 Return to thine own house, and shew how
great things God hath done unto thee. And he
went his way, and published throughout the whole
city how great things Jesus had done unto him.
40 And it came to pass, that, when Jesus was re-
turned, the people *gladly* received him: for they
were all waiting for him.
41 ¶ And, behold, there came a man named
Jairus, and he was a ruler of the synagogue: and
he fell down at Jesus' feet, and besought him that
he would come into his house:
42 For he had one only daughter, about twelve
years of age, and she lay a dying. But as he went
the people thronged him.

Jesus' Mother and Brothers and the Will of God (8:19–21)

8:21 *brethren.* Brothers. Union with Christ is stronger than earthly relationships, creating a family more significant and enduring than earthly families.

Jesus Performs Four Miracles (8:22–56)

Jesus Calms a Storm (8:22–25)

8:22 *the lake.* The Sea of Galilee.

8:24 *rebuked the wind . . . and there was a calm.* Only the Creator can rule the raging seas with His mere word (Gen. 1:9; Pss. 33:6–8; 107:28–29).

8:25 *Where is your faith?* The disciples had seen Jesus' works but had failed to understand the grandeur of His glory.

Jesus Heals a Demon-possessed Man (8:26–39)

8:26 *Gadarenes.* The region east of the Sea of Galilee, a thoroughfare for Roman armies and a predominantly Gentile area.

8:27 *ware.* Wore.

8:28 *Son of God most high?* This demon recognized the authority of Jesus when many others failed to do so. Even in Gentile territory Jesus retained his Lordship and authority.

8:29 *fetters.* Chains.

8:30 *Legion.* A unit in the Roman army consisting of thousands of soldiers. Jesus stood before a great host of hell's army.

8:31 *besought him.* Despite the demons' great power over the man, they could only beg Jesus not to cast them into the bottomless pit of hell (*the deep*).

8:32 *suffer.* Permit.

8:33 While Jesus did not command the death of the pigs, His release of the demons into the swine certainly shows that He values one human soul above a whole herd of animals.

8:38–39 *besought.* Asked. Remarkably, this third request was denied by Jesus, for the man would serve Him better as a witness to his own people. *great things God hath done unto thee . . . great things Jesus had done unto him.* The works of Jesus are the works of God.

Jesus Heals a Woman (8:40–48)

8:42 *thronged.* Pressed hard; literally, "choked" (v. 14).

43 ¶ And a woman having an issue of blood
twelve years, which had spent all her living upon
physicians, neither could be healed of any,
44 Came behind *him*, and touched the border of
his garment: and immediately her issue of blood
stanched.
45 And Jesus said, Who touched me? When all
denied, Peter and they that were with him said,
Master, the multitude throng thee and press *thee*,
and sayest thou, Who touched me?
46 And Jesus said, Somebody hath touched me:
for I perceive that virtue is gone out of me.
47 And when the woman saw that she was not
hid, she came trembling, and falling down before
him, she declared unto him before all the people
for what cause she had touched him, and how she
was healed immediately.
48 And he said unto her, Daughter, be of good
comfort: thy faith hath made thee whole; go in
peace.
49 ¶ While he yet spake, there cometh one from
the ruler of the synagogue's *house*, saying to him,
Thy daughter is dead; trouble not the Master.
50 But when Jesus heard *it*, he answered him, say-
ing, Fear not: believe only, and she shall be made
whole.
51 And when he came into the house, he suffered
no man to go in, save Peter, and James, and John,
and the father and the mother of the maiden.
52 And all wept, and bewailed her: but he said,
Weep not; she is not dead, but sleepeth.
53 And they laughed him to scorn, knowing that
she was dead.
54 And he put them all out, and took her by the
hand, and called, saying, Maid, arise.
55 And her spirit came again, and she arose
straightway: and he commanded to give her meat.
56 And her parents were astonished: but he
charged them that they should tell no man what
was done.

CHAPTER 9

THEN he called his twelve disciples together, and
gave them power and authority over all devils,
and to cure diseases.
2 And he sent them to preach the kingdom of
God, and to heal the sick.
3 And he said unto them, Take nothing for *your*
journey, neither staves, nor scrip, neither bread,
neither money; neither have two coats apiece.
4 And whatsoever house ye enter into, there
abide, and thence depart.
5 And whosoever will not receive you, when ye go

8:43 *issue.* Flow (v. 44). *spent all her living on physicians.* Like the demonized man (v. 29), her problem could not be solved by human wisdom or ability.
8:44 *stanched.* Stopped.
8:46 *Somebody hath touched me.* Jesus drew out the woman to make a public confession of her faith in Him and her healing by the power (*virtue*) of the Holy Spirit (4:14; 5:17; 6:19).
8:48 *Daughter.* While Jairus was seeking the healing of his daughter (v. 42), Jesus healed this His "daughter." *be of good comfort.* Have courage. *thy faith hath made thee whole; go in peace.* Literally, "your faith has saved you; go in peace," the same words spoken to the forgiven woman (7:50).

Jesus Heals Jairus's Daughter (8:49–56)

8:50 *believe only.* Even death itself cannot defeat Jesus. All that was required of Jairus was faith, the same means by which the woman received her healing.
8:51 *save.* Except.
8:52 *sleepeth.* Jesus used this term metaphorically because her death, though real, was not final (John 11:11–14).
8:53 *laughed him to scorn.* The crowds not only doubted Jesus' words but mocked Him.
8:55 *her spirit came again.* Her life returned to her body, a clear statement that she had been dead but that Christ had supernaturally raised her to life (1 Kings 17:22). *meat.* Food of any kind. Jesus likely was directing the family to return to normal life.
8:56 *tell no man.* Jesus does not desire people to focus on His miracles; it was for the cross and resurrection that He had ultimately come.

Thoughts for Personal/Family Worship: Chapter 8

1. **The parable of the sower paints a picture of four representative human hearts. Take a look at your own heart in its light. Do you find thorns, packed soil, withered plants, or fruit? However things stand, take the exhortation of v. 18 to heart: "Take heed therefore how ye hear." We must not come to the preaching of the Word expecting the preacher to do all the work. What responsibility do we have as hearers of the Word?**
2. **When Christ calmed the storm at sea He showed His great power and majesty. He did no less when He cast out the legion of demons from the Gadarene man. He healed the woman of an incurable disease and raised a girl from the dead. However, while this girl experienced resurrection she would again experience physical death. These miracles do more than show us that Jesus can heal all our physical problems (as He will do when He returns in glory). The way Luke linked the healed woman and the forgiven woman (v. 48; 7:50) reminds us that our most pressing need is for spiritual salvation. We need Christ to heal our souls, so that like the Gadarene man we may sit at His feet, clothed and in our right minds, desiring to live in His presence and willing to declare His glory to others. Why is that the greatest healing?**

Chapter 9: ***Jesus sends His disciples to preach, feeds the five thousand, announces His suffering and death, and is transfigured before three of His disciples, whereupon He casts out a demon and begins His journey to Jerusalem to suffer and die.***

Jesus and the Disciples (9:1–50)

Jesus Sends Out the Apostles (9:1–6)

9:3 *staves.* Staffs, sticks. *scrip.* Bag.
9:5 *not receive you.* If a city rejects the message of the disciples, it is as good as rejecting the message of Jesus. *shake off the very dust from your feet.* A symbolic act of separation from the unclean, warning of the coming judgment (Neh. 5:13; Acts 18:6).

out of that city, shake off the very dust from your
feet for a testimony against them.
6 And they departed, and went through the towns,
preaching the gospel, and healing every where.
7 ¶ Now Herod the tetrarch heard of all that was
done by him: and he was perplexed, because that
it was said of some, that John was risen from the
dead;
8 And of some, that Elias had appeared; and of
others, that one of the old prophets was risen
again.
9 And Herod said, John have I beheaded: but who
is this, of whom I hear such things? And he de-
sired to see him.
10 ¶ And the apostles, when they were returned,
told him all that they had done. And he took
them, and went aside privately into a desert place
belonging to the city called Bethsaida.
11 And the people, when they knew *it*, followed
him: and he received them, and spake unto them
of the kingdom of God, and healed them that had
need of healing.
12 And when the day began to wear away, then
came the twelve, and said unto him, Send the
multitude away, that they may go into the towns
and country round about, and lodge, and get
victuals: for we are here in a desert place.
13 But he said unto them, Give ye them to eat.
And they said, We have no more but five loaves
and two fishes; except we should go and buy meat
for all this people.
14 For they were about five thousand men. And
he said to his disciples, Make them sit down by
fifties in a company.
15 And they did so, and made them all sit down.
16 Then he took the five loaves and the two fishes,
and looking up to heaven, he blessed them, and
brake, and gave to the disciples to set before the
multitude.
17 And they did eat, and were all filled: and there
was taken up of fragments that remained to them
twelve baskets.
18 ¶ And it came to pass, as he was alone praying,
his disciples were with him: and he asked them,
saying, Whom say the people that I am?
19 They answering said, John the Baptist; but
some *say*, Elias; and others *say*, that one of the old
prophets is risen again.
20 He said unto them, But whom say ye that I
am? Peter answering said, The Christ of God.
21 And he straitly charged them, and com-
manded *them* to tell no man that thing;
22 Saying, The Son of man must suffer many
things, and be rejected of the elders and chief
priests and scribes, and be slain, and be raised the
third day.
23 ¶ And he said to *them* all, If any *man* will come
after me, let him deny himself, and take up his
cross daily, and follow me.
24 For whosoever will save his life shall lose it: but
whosoever will lose his life for my sake, the same
shall save it.
25 For what is a man advantaged, if he gain the
whole world, and lose himself, or be cast away?
26 For whosoever shall be ashamed of me and
of my words, of him shall the Son of man be
ashamed, when he shall come in his own glory,
and *in his* Father's, and of the holy angels.
27 But I tell you of a truth, there be some stand-
ing here, which shall not taste of death, till they
see the kingdom of God.
28 ¶ And it came to pass about an eight days after

Herod Fears Jesus (9:7–9)

9:7 *Herod the tetrarch.* See note at 3:1–2.

9:9 *desired to see him.* Herod's desire to see Christ was born not of faith but from a desire to merely witness these spectacular things.

Jesus Feeds Five Thousand (9:10–17)

9:12–13 *victuals.* Food. *Give ye them to eat.* Christ's command is instructional. They are to take His command back to Him in order that He might show Himself to be the great Provider. *meat.* Food of any kind.

9:17 *all filled.* Christ revealed that He is sufficient for the ministry of His servants to the people (2 Cor. 3:5).

Peter Confesses Jesus as the Christ (9:18–20)

9:18 *as he was alone praying.* On Jesus' prayers, see note at 5:16. This prayer came before Jesus asked His disciples to make their confession of Him.

9:20 *The Christ of God.* The Anointed One, promised and sent by God as the King and Savior (see note at 2:11).

Jesus Foretells His Death (9:21–22)

9:21–22 *straitly charged.* Strictly admonished. *tell no man.* Jesus' command of silence was to prevent the people from thinking that glory comes without suffering (24:26). *Son of man.* See the note at 5:24. *suffer.* The rejection of Christ by the leaders of Israel, His death, and His resurrection would all take place by divine necessity (*must*), fulfilling the decree of God revealed in Scripture (see the note at 4:43).

Jesus Teaches His Disciples to Suffer (9:23–27)

9:23 *take up his cross daily.* Crucifixion was a scandalously shameful death. Following Christ as His disciples requires us to put our proud and sinful desires to death and to experience the world's rejection (Gal. 5:24; 6:14). *follow me.* The Christian life is the imitation of Christ.

9:24–25 *save his life . . . lose it.* The paradox of the disciple's life. Losing all through suffering is the means for gaining all. And gaining all things, as the natural man desires, is to forfeit an eternal inheritance.

9:27 The *kingdom* appeared in glory at Christ's transfiguration and came in power after Pentecost as the nations were being converted through the ministry of the apostles. Judgment fell on Jerusalem in AD 70, within the lifetime of some of Jesus' present disciples.

The Transfiguration of Jesus (9:28–36)

9:28 *eight days after.* After Peter's grand confession of Jesus as the Son of God. *pray.* Again, before a crucial moment in Christ's ministry, He was praying (v. 18).

ANGELS

Angels are members of a great company of spiritual natures or substances, created to be ministering spirits under God. The Puritans had a high view of angels, yet they continually subordinated them to God. Ordinarily their explanation of angels was in connection with another topic or as part of an exposition of a relevant scriptural passage. Noting that many others erred in over-exalting angels, the Puritans emphasized that one must continually be guarded by a passion for both the mediation of Christ alone and the glory of God alone.

The Westminster Larger Catechism (Q. 16) says, "God created all the angels spirits, immortal, holy, excelling in knowledge, mighty in power, to execute his commandments, and to praise his name, yet subject to change." This highlights two important truths: angels have *similarities* to God, yet as creatures they possess *dissimilarities* as well.

Angels are like God in that they are invisible spirits that are impalpable—that is, they cannot be felt (Luke 24:39). Also, angels are rational, endowed with the noblest faculties of understanding and will (Eph. 3:10; cf. Ps. 103:20; Luke 15:10).

However, God is infinitely more glorious than angels (Ps. 148:13), and they are far below Him. Therefore, there are significant dissimilarities between angels and God. Angels are creatures, and therefore fully under the dominion of their Creator. God created the angels holy (cf. Matt. 25:31; Mark 8:38; Rev. 14:10), but their holiness is infinitely less than His (Rev. 15:4). Angels possess great knowledge (2 Sam. 14:20), but only God knows men's hearts (Jer. 17:10) and the future (Isa. 41:23). Angels excel in power (Ps. 103:20; Eph. 6:12; 2 Thess. 1:7; cf. Matt. 28:2–7), but only God could create the world (Isa. 40:28) and sustain its existence (Heb. 1:3). Further, only God can regenerate the soul as a new creation (Eph. 2:10). Angels were created in a high state of glory, but they were not immutable, as many fell (Jude 6).

A detailed history of angels is not readily evident in Scripture. It is clear that they were determined according to God's eternal decree. The predestination of angels lies within the secret counsel of God and therefore is largely hidden. Thus the election and reprobation of angels (cf. 1 Tim. 5:21) is to be considered parallel to that of man in some ways. However, whereas some men are chosen *unto salvation*, *from sin*, and, most importantly, *in Christ*, none of these qualifications relate to the elect angels. This is an essential distinction.

Scripture testifies that angels are created beings (Col. 1:16). The timing of their creation is difficult to ascertain, but it is certain that it was during the six-day creation of all things (cf. Job 38:7). God permitted some angels to fall from the glory of their original creation. There was thus a time when angels were confirmed in their status—either as elect angels or demons. The former were established in holiness for eternity, while the latter were confirmed in their fall. The time and manner of this confirmation is not extensively discussed in Scripture.

The elect angels today are God's servants. Their number is vast (Dan. 7:10; Matt. 26:53; Heb. 12:22). God employs this host of angels primarily in glorifying Himself and, secondarily, in serving His creation, most particularly His people.

The angels celebrate the glory of God, crying thrice "Holy!" (Isa. 6:3). The angels have worshiped God from the dawn of creation (Job 38:7) and will continue to do so throughout eternal glory (Heb. 12:22–23; Rev. 5:11–12; cf. Luke 2:13–14; 15:7,10; Heb. 1:6). Their special delight is the wonders of His gospel (1 Peter 1:12).

The angels are also busy serving the heirs of eternal life (Ps. 91:11–12; Dan. 10:13, 20; Heb. 1:14). They minister to men (Gen. 24:7; Ex. 23:23; Dan. 6:22; Luke 1:19,26; Acts 12:1–11; Heb. 1:14; Jude 9), watching over them as sentinels (2 Kings 6:17; Ps. 34:7). God commands His angels to care for His saints—but *not* to rule over them or receive worship from them. Furthermore, the popular notion of a special guardian angel for each individual believer is not scripturally supported. Rather, Scripture affirms an even more precious truth: the care of the believer is not the task of one angel only; the whole angelic host with one consent watches over the believer and his salvation (Gen. 32:1–2; 2 Kings 6:17; Luke 15:10; 16:22).

these sayings, he took Peter and John and James,
and went up into a mountain to pray.
29 And as he prayed, the fashion of his countenance was altered, and his raiment *was* white *and*
glistering.
30 And, behold, there talked with him two men,
which were Moses and Elias:
31 Who appeared in glory, and spake of his decease which he should accomplish at Jerusalem.
32 But Peter and they that were with him were
heavy with sleep: and when they were awake, they
saw his glory, and the two men that stood with
him.
33 And it came to pass, as they departed from
him, Peter said unto Jesus, Master, it is good for
us to be here: and let us make three tabernacles;
one for thee, and one for Moses, and one for Elias:
not knowing what he said.
34 While he thus spake, there came a cloud, and
overshadowed them: and they feared as they entered into the cloud.
35 And there came a voice out of the cloud,
saying, This is my beloved Son: hear him.
36 And when the voice was past, Jesus was found
alone. And they kept *it* close, and told no man in
those days any of those things which they had
seen.
37 ¶ And it came to pass, that on the next day,
when they were come down from the hill, much
people met him.
38 And, behold, a man of the company cried out,
saying, Master, I beseech thee, look upon my son:
for he is mine only child.
39 And, lo, a spirit taketh him, and he suddenly
crieth out; and it teareth him that he foameth
again, and bruising him hardly departeth from
him.
40 And I besought thy disciples to cast him out;
and they could not.
41 And Jesus answering said, O faithless and
perverse generation, how long shall I be with you,
and suffer you? Bring thy son hither.
42 And as he was yet a coming, the devil threw
him down, and tare *him*. And Jesus rebuked the
unclean spirit, and healed the child, and delivered
him again to his father.
43 ¶ And they were all amazed at the mighty
power of God. But while they wondered every
one at all things which Jesus did, he said unto his
disciples,
44 Let these sayings sink down into your ears: for
the Son of man shall be delivered into the hands
of men.
45 But they understood not this saying, and it
was hid from them, that they perceived it not: and
they feared to ask him of that saying.
46 ¶ Then there arose a reasoning among them,
which of them should be greatest.
47 And Jesus, perceiving the thought of their
heart, took a child, and set him by him,
48 And said unto them, Whosoever shall receive
this child in my name receiveth me: and whosoever shall receive me receiveth him that sent me:
for he that is least among you all, the same shall
be great.
49 ¶ And John answered and said, Master, we saw
one casting out devils in thy name; and we forbad
him, because he followeth not with us.
50 And Jesus said unto him, Forbid *him* not: for
he that is not against us is for us.

9:29 *countenance was altered.* The appearance of His face was gloriously transformed. *raiment.* Clothing. *glistering.* Shining. Christ's body was transformed so as to reveal something of His coming glory. Though Jesus must suffer (v. 22), He is still the King of Glory.

9:30 *Moses and Elias* (Elijah). Representatives of the Law and the Prophets.

9:31 *decease.* Literally, "exodus." Moses and Elijah conversed with Jesus about His death, which was the antitype of Israel's exodus from Egypt (22:1,15). The time of fulfillment had come.

9:33 *tabernacles.* Temporary shelters. Peter may have thought this was a fitting place and time to celebrate the Feast of Tabernacles, an Old Testament feast honoring God's faithfulness to the Israelites in the wilderness after the exodus (Lev. 23:34).

9:35 *hear him.* God confirmed that Jesus is the great Prophet whose words we must believe and obey if we would be saved (Deut. 18:15,19).

9:36 *Jesus was found alone.* Jesus is superior to Moses and Elijah, to the Law and the Prophets, for He is the only Savior. *kept it close.* The disciples kept this revelation to themselves. It is meant to be thought about, not paraded about in a show of arrogance.

Jesus Heals a Boy with an Unclean Spirit (9:37–43)

9:37–40 As with His baptism (3:22–23; 4:1–2), Jesus went from a revelation of glory to confront the Devil.

9:40–41 *they could not.* Luke does not elaborate on why the disciples were unable to cast out the demon, but Jesus' rebuke indicates that they lacked faith (*faithless*) to do so. *hither.* Here.

9:42 *tare.* Tore, here probably referring to convulsions.

Jesus Foretells His Death a Second Time (9:44–45)

9:44 *Let these sayings sink down into your ears.* Literally, "As for you, put into your ears these words." Jesus did not want His disciples to be caught up in marveling at His power but to soberly remember His coming sufferings (cf. Ex. 17:14).

Kingdom Greatness (9:46–48)

9:46 *reasoning.* Debate.

9:47 Jesus' response to the pride of His disciples is found in a *child*, illustrating humility and dependence (Ps. 131; Matt. 18:1–5).

9:48 *receive this child.* The manner in which one welcomes the humble disciples of Christ reveals whether or not one has faith in Christ (*receiveth me*). *least . . . shall be great.* God reverses human expectations by honoring the humble (1:52–53; 18:14).

Kingdom Meekness (9:49–50)

9:49 *followeth not with us.* This man did not physically travel with the band of disciples, and thus the disciples thought He should not be casting out demons.

9:50 The man clearly could not cast out demons aside from Christ's power working through him.

51 ¶ And it came to pass, when the time was come
that he should be received up, he stedfastly set his
face to go to Jerusalem,
52 And sent messengers before his face: and they
went, and entered into a village of the Samaritans,
to make ready for him.
53 And they did not receive him, because his face
was as though he would go to Jerusalem.
54 And when his disciples James and John saw
this, they said, Lord, wilt thou that we command
fire to come down from heaven, and consume
them, even as Elias did?
55 But he turned, and rebuked them, and said, Ye
know not what manner of spirit ye are of.
56 For the Son of man is not come to destroy
men's lives, but to save *them*. And they went to
another village.
57 ¶ And it came to pass, that, as they went in the
way, a certain *man* said unto him, Lord, I will fol-
low thee whithersoever thou goest.
58 And Jesus said unto him, Foxes have holes, and
birds of the air *have* nests; but the Son of man
hath not where to lay *his* head.
59 And he said unto another, Follow me. But
he said, Lord, suffer me first to go and bury my
father.
60 Jesus said unto him, Let the dead bury their
dead: but go thou and preach the kingdom of God.
61 And another also said, Lord, I will follow thee;
but let me first go bid them farewell, which are at
home at my house.
62 And Jesus said unto him, No man, having put
his hand to the plough, and looking back, is fit for
the kingdom of God.

CHAPTER 10

AFTER these things the Lord appointed other sev-
enty also, and sent them two and two before his
face into every city and place, whither he himself
would come.
2 Therefore said he unto them, The harvest truly
is great, but the labourers *are* few: pray ye there-
fore the Lord of the harvest, that he would send
forth labourers into his harvest.
3 Go your ways: behold, I send you forth as lambs
among wolves.
4 Carry neither purse, nor scrip, nor shoes: and
salute no man by the way.
5 And into whatsoever house ye enter, first say,
Peace *be* to this house.
6 And if the son of peace be there, your peace
shall rest upon it: if not, it shall turn to you again.
7 And in the same house remain, eating and
drinking such things as they give: for the labourer
is worthy of his hire. Go not from house to house.

ON THE WAY TO JERUSALEM (9:51—19:27)

The First Stage of Jesus' Journey to Jerusalem (9:51—13:21)

The Samaritans Reject Jesus (9:51–56)

9:51 This is an important turning point in Luke's gospel. Christ turned from His Galilean ministry and resolved to go up to Jerusalem, where He would face death. What follows is a detailed account of his journey to Jerusalem. *stedfastly set his face.* Jesus moved with great resolve, fully aware of God's divine purpose for Him (Isa. 50:6–7).

9:53 *did not receive him.* It was not only the Jews who rejected Jesus but the Samaritans as well.

The Cost of Discipleship (9:57–62)

9:57 *whithersoever.* Where.

9:59–60 *Let the dead bury their dead.* Christ was not saying that caring for one's parents is unimportant (Mark 7:9–13); He was rejecting the man's request to wait to follow Him until after his father had died and was buried. Following Christ must have higher priority than all earthly ties (14:26).

9:62 *hand to the plough, and looking back.* A picture of a man who is indecisive and unfaithful. One cannot plow a straight line unless he is looking forward.

Thoughts for Personal/Family Worship: Chapter 9

1. **Christ went to the cross to suffer and die to pay the price for sin. His disciples must also prepare to live a life of suffering and self-denial, not in order to atone for sin but to conform them to their Head and Master. In the meantime the glorious radiance of Christ, as He showed it on the Mount of Transfiguration, ought to sustain and strengthen them to meet with suffering and death. In fact, it should keep them from desiring human greatness (v. 38); rather, they are to live in this world in meekness, following Christ at whatever the cost toward true greatness in His kingdom. What is your response to the call to take up your cross and follow Jesus? Why does the life of discipleship hinge upon our answer to Christ's question in v. 20, "Whom say ye that I am?"**
2. **After the experience on the Mount of Transfiguration, Christ and the disciples seemed to leave the edges of heaven for the edges of hell as they met the demon-possessed boy, his father, and the other disciples, so powerless without their Lord (vv. 37–42). Christ's experience contained many ups and downs, and so will that of the followers of Jesus. How can we find stability in Christ so that the ups will not overly elate us and the downs not discourage us?**

Chapter 10: *Jesus sends out seventy disciples to preach and perform miracles, after which He teaches in various ways about what it means to be a true partaker of the kingdom of God.*

Jesus Commissions the Seventy (10:1–24)

10:1–11 Compare Jesus' instructions here with His previous directions to the Twelve (9:3–5). The *seventy* were not apostles but were given an itinerant ministry of working miracles and preaching (v. 9), like that of Philip the evangelist (Acts 8:5–40; 21:8).

10:1 *whither.* Where.

10:4 *scrip.* Bag. *salute.* Greet.

10:5–6 *Peace be to this house.* The way to peace and blessing lies in falling in with the kingdom of God, as revealed in the person and work of Jesus and proclaimed by His disciples. *son of peace.* A Hebrew idiom for a person who receives the gospel of peace.

10:7 *the labourer is worthy of his hire.* Cited by Paul together

8 And into whatsoever city ye enter, and they
receive you, eat such things as are set before you:
9 And heal the sick that are therein, and say unto
them, The kingdom of God is come nigh unto
you.
10 But into whatsoever city ye enter, and they
receive you not, go your ways out into the streets
of the same, and say,
11 Even the very dust of your city, which cleaveth
on us, we do wipe off against you: notwithstand-
ing be ye sure of this, that the kingdom of God is
come nigh unto you.
12 But I say unto you, that it shall be more toler-
able in that day for Sodom, than for that city.
13 Woe unto thee, Chorazin! woe unto thee,
Bethsaida! for if the mighty works had been done
in Tyre and Sidon, which have been done in you,
they had a great while ago repented, sitting in
sackcloth and ashes.
14 But it shall be more tolerable for Tyre and
Sidon at the judgment, than for you.
15 And thou, Capernaum, which art exalted to
heaven, shalt be thrust down to hell.
16 He that heareth you heareth me; and he that
despiseth you despiseth me; and he that despiseth
me despiseth him that sent me.
17 ¶ And the seventy returned again with joy,
saying, Lord, even the devils are subject unto us
through thy name.
18 And he said unto them, I beheld Satan as light-
ning fall from heaven.
19 Behold, I give unto you power to tread on ser-
pents and scorpions, and over all the power of the
enemy: and nothing shall by any means hurt you.
20 Notwithstanding in this rejoice not, that the
spirits are subject unto you; but rather rejoice,
because your names are written in heaven.
21 ¶ In that hour Jesus rejoiced in spirit, and said,
I thank thee, O Father, Lord of heaven and earth,
that thou hast hid these things from the wise and
prudent, and hast revealed them unto babes: even
so, Father; for so it seemed good in thy sight.
22 All things are delivered to me of my Father:
and no man knoweth who the Son is, but the
Father; and who the Father is, but the Son, and *he*
to whom the Son will reveal *him*.
23 ¶ And he turned him unto *his* disciples, and
said privately, Blessed *are* the eyes which see the
things that ye see:
24 For I tell you, that many prophets and kings
have desired to see those things which ye see,
and have not seen *them*; and to hear those things
which ye hear, and have not heard *them*.
25 ¶ And, behold, a certain lawyer stood up, and
tempted him, saying, Master, what shall I do to
inherit eternal life?
26 He said unto him, What is written in the law?
how readest thou?
27 And he answering said, Thou shalt love the
Lord thy God with all thy heart, and with all thy
soul, and with all thy strength, and with all thy
mind; and thy neighbour as thyself.
28 And he said unto him, Thou hast answered
right: this do, and thou shalt live.
29 But he, willing to justify himself, said unto
Jesus, And who is my neighbour?
30 And Jesus answering said, A certain *man* went
down from Jerusalem to Jericho, and fell among
thieves, which stripped him of his raiment, and
wounded *him*, and departed, leaving *him* half dead.

---

with the law of Moses, both of which he refers to as Scripture (1 Tim. 5:18). Jesus gave permission to the disciples to gain their sustenance from the preaching of the gospel and not to shrink from receiving support from others (1 Cor. 9:14).

10:13 *Tyre* and *Sidon*. Two Gentile cities.

10:14 *more tolerable*. This does not mean that *Tyre and Sidon* would escape *judgment* under the eternal wrath of God but that the condemnation against Chorazin and Bethsaida would be greater than theirs.

10:18–19 *Satan as lightning fall from heaven*. The preaching of the kingdom is God's means not only of saving His people but also of judging the powers of darkness (11:20–22). *tread on serpents*. Christ was already giving His people victory over Satan, as God had promised after the fall of man (Gen. 3:15; cf. Rom. 16:20). Though many reject the gospel, Christ is still today triumphing over Satan.

10:20 *rejoice not . . . but rather rejoice*. While spiritual gifts and success in ministry are a cause for joy, a Christian's primary and constant cause for rejoicing is that God has chosen him to be a citizen in the kingdom (*your names are written in heaven*; Isa. 4:3; Phil. 4:3).

10:21 *Jesus rejoiced*. A rare reference to the joy of Jesus during His earthly life. *in spirit*. Probably "in the Holy Spirit," the giver of all spiritual joy (Acts 13:52; Rom. 14:17; 15:13; Gal. 5:22; 1 Thess. 1:6). If so, all three members of the Trinity appear together here (3:22). *thou hast hid these things . . . revealed them*. Man is responsible for rejecting the gospel (10:12–15), but God is still sovereign, revealing Christ to whomever He pleases (v. 22; Gal. 1:15–16). *babes*. Not literal babies but the childlike disciples, unimportant and simple-minded compared to the scribes and Pharisees.

10:22 *All things are delivered to me*. The Father shares His sovereignty over the universe with the Son (John 17:2). *he to whom the Son will reveal him*. Literally, "to whomever the Son chooses to reveal." Like the Father, the Son of God is free to give or withhold the heart knowledge necessary for salvation.

Parables and Various Teachings (10:25—13:21)

10:25 *tempted*. Tested.

10:26 *What is written in the law?* Jesus affirmed the Old Testament law as the revealed will of God.

10:27 *love the Lord*. Citing Deut. 6:5. *thy neighbour as thyself*. Citing Lev. 19:18.

10:28 *this do, and thou shalt live*. Though the covenant with Israel was given in grace (Ex. 20:1–2), the moral law (absolutely considered) promises life upon perfect obedience (Lev. 18:5).

10:29 *willing to justify himself*. Desiring to vindicate himself or to show himself righteous.

10:30 *raiment*. Clothing.

31 And by chance there came down a certain
priest that way: and when he saw him, he passed
by on the other side.
32 And likewise a Levite, when he was at the
place, came and looked *on him*, and passed by on
the other side.
33 But a certain Samaritan, as he journeyed, came
where he was: and when he saw him, he had com-
passion *on him*,
34 And went to *him*, and bound up his wounds,
pouring in oil and wine, and set him on his own
beast, and brought him to an inn, and took care
of him.
35 And on the morrow when he departed, he
took out two pence, and gave *them* to the host,
and said unto him, Take care of him; and what-
soever thou spendest more, when I come again, I
will repay thee.
36 Which now of these three, thinkest thou, was
neighbour unto him that fell among the thieves?
37 And he said, He that shewed mercy on him.
Then said Jesus unto him, Go, and do thou
likewise.
38 ¶ Now it came to pass, as they went, that he
entered into a certain village: and a certain woman
named Martha received him into her house.
39 And she had a sister called Mary, which also
sat at Jesus' feet, and heard his word.
40 But Martha was cumbered about much
serving, and came to him, and said, Lord, dost
thou not care that my sister hath left me to serve
alone? bid her therefore that she help me.
41 And Jesus answered and said unto her, Martha,
Martha, thou art careful and troubled about
many things:
42 But one thing is needful: and Mary hath cho-
sen that good part, which shall not be taken away
from her.

CHAPTER 11

AND it came to pass, that, as he was praying in a
certain place, when he ceased, one of his disciples
said unto him, Lord, teach us to pray, as John also
taught his disciples.
2 And he said unto them, When ye pray, say,
Our Father which art in heaven, Hallowed be thy
name. Thy kingdom come. Thy will be done, as in
heaven, so in earth.
3 Give us day by day our daily bread.
4 And forgive us our sins; for we also forgive
every one that is indebted to us. And lead us not
into temptation; but deliver us from evil.
5 And he said unto them, Which of you shall have
a friend, and shall go unto him at midnight, and
say unto him, Friend, lend me three loaves;
6 For a friend of mine in his journey is come to
me, and I have nothing to set before him?
7 And he from within shall answer and say, Trou-
ble me not: the door is now shut, and my children
are with me in bed; I cannot rise and give thee.
8 I say unto you, Though he will not rise and give
him, because he is his friend, yet because of his
importunity he will rise and give him as many as
he needeth.
9 And I say unto you, Ask, and it shall be given

10:31–32 *priest . . . Levite.* Jesus intentionally chose the religious elite, experts in the law.
10:33 *Samaritan.* A person considered an outcast by the Jews based on nationality (John 4:9). *he had compassion.* Not from compulsion or guilt but based on love, this man had mercy on the poor, broken man—a picture of Christ's love for sinners.
10:34 The Samaritan pays meticulous attention to the man's needs, providing for him at his own personal cost.
10:35 *pence.* Denarii, each of which was worth a day's wages for a laborer.
10:40 *cumbered.* Distracted. *bid.* Tell. Martha not only was aggravated at Mary but accused Christ of wrong (*dost thou not care*).
10:41 *careful.* Anxious. *troubled.* Disturbed.
10:42 *one thing is needful.* Though loving and serving others is a crucial part of doing God's will (as the parable of the Good Samaritan declares), the greatest commandment is to love the Lord (v. 27), and service to others must not distract from communion with Him through His Word (v. 39).

Thoughts for Personal/Family Worship: Chapter 10

1. **None of us would be unimpressed if we were to see demons cast out. However, Christ admonished His disciples to recognize the true seat of joy and happiness. These states are not found in what we can do, not even in ministry to Him; rather, they are found in being the objects of what God has done and alone can do. We can discover whether our names are written in heaven only in the way of true faith and repentance. If you do not know whether you have a title to life and an inheritance among the saints, you need to repent and seek God. That is the only way to true joy.**
2. **Martha's problem was not that she was serving; it was that she was distracted by "much serving" (v. 40). It is not only bad things that keep us from true communion with Christ; it is often an excessive preoccupation, anxiety, and distractedness with good things. One thing above all is necessary, and that is to sit at the feet of Him into whose lips "grace is poured" (Ps. 45:2). How do we sit at His feet today? What can we do to make that a priority in our lives?**

Chapter 11: *Jesus teaches His disciples how to pray and warns against the hypocrisy of the Pharisees.*

11:1 As noted, Luke portrays Jesus praying at important times (see note at 5:16). It is fitting that immediately preceding His great discourse on prayer Jesus would be modeling prayer.
11:2–4 On the Lord's Prayer, see notes at Matt. 6:9–13.
11:5–8 The parable does not portray God but teaches by contrast: if this reluctant man could be persuaded to help by sheer boldness and refusal to take no for an answer (*importunity*), how much more will a gracious, loving heavenly Father hear the bold and persistent (but reverent) prayers of believers?

you; seek, and ye shall find; knock, and it shall be
opened unto you.
10 For every one that asketh receiveth; and he
that seeketh findeth; and to him that knocketh it
shall be opened.
11 If a son shall ask bread of any of you that is a
father, will he give him a stone? or if *he ask* a fish,
will he for a fish give him a serpent?
12 Or if he shall ask an egg, will he offer him a
scorpion?
13 If ye then, being evil, know how to give good
gifts unto your children: how much more shall
your heavenly Father give the Holy Spirit to them
that ask him?
14 ¶ And he was casting out a devil, and it was
dumb. And it came to pass, when the devil was gone
out, the dumb spake; and the people wondered.
15 But some of them said, He casteth out devils
through Beelzebub the chief of the devils.
16 And others, tempting *him*, sought of him a
sign from heaven.
17 But he, knowing their thoughts, said unto
them, Every kingdom divided against itself
is brought to desolation; and a house *divided*
against a house falleth.
18 If Satan also be divided against himself, how
shall his kingdom stand? because ye say that I cast
out devils through Beelzebub.
19 And if I by Beelzebub cast out devils, by whom
do your sons cast *them* out? therefore shall they
be your judges.
20 But if I with the finger of God cast out devils,
no doubt the kingdom of God is come upon you.
21 When a strong man armed keepeth his palace,
his goods are in peace:
22 But when a stronger than he shall come upon
him, and overcome him, he taketh from him all
his armour wherein he trusted, and divideth his
spoils.
23 He that is not with me is against me: and he
that gathereth not with me scattereth.
24 When the unclean spirit is gone out of a man,
he walketh through dry places, seeking rest; and
finding none, he saith, I will return unto my
house whence I came out.
25 And when he cometh, he findeth *it* swept and
garnished.
26 Then goeth he, and taketh *to him* seven other
spirits more wicked than himself; and they enter
in, and dwell there: and the last *state* of that man
is worse than the first.
27 ¶ And it came to pass, as he spake these things,
a certain woman of the company lifted up her
voice, and said unto him, Blessed *is* the womb that
bare thee, and the paps which thou hast sucked.
28 But he said, Yea rather, blessed *are* they that
hear the word of God, and keep it.
29 ¶ And when the people were gathered thick to-
gether, he began to say, This is an evil generation:
they seek a sign; and there shall no sign be given
it, but the sign of Jonas the prophet.
30 For as Jonas was a sign unto the Ninevites, so
shall also the Son of man be to this generation.
31 The queen of the south shall rise up in the
judgment with the men of this generation, and
condemn them: for she came from the utmost
parts of the earth to hear the wisdom of Solomon;
and, behold, a greater than Solomon *is* here.
32 The men of Nineve shall rise up in the judg-
ment with this generation, and shall condemn it:
for they repented at the preaching of Jonas; and,
behold, a greater than Jonas *is* here.
33 No man, when he hath lighted a candle,
putteth *it* in a secret place, neither under a bushel,
but on a candlestick, that they which come in may
see the light.
34 The light of the body is the eye: therefore when
thine eye is single, thy whole body also is full of
light; but when *thine eye* is evil, thy body also *is*
full of darkness.
35 Take heed therefore that the light which is in
thee be not darkness.
36 If thy whole body therefore *be* full of light,
having no part dark, the whole shall be full of
light, as when the bright shining of a candle doth
give thee light.

11:9 *Ask . . . seek . . . knock.* The progression from one verb to another suggests an increasing level of urgency in prayer. *given . . . find . . . opened.* A life of prayer is a life of receiving grace from God.

11:11–13 Jesus uses a comparison from lesser to great. If a sinful earthly father is willing to respond to the requests of his child, how much more is the heavenly Father willing to answer the prayers of His children? *give the Holy Spirit.* Through the Spirit disciples receive the manifold blessings of God.

11:14 *the people wondered.* Not a positive wonder, as the later division of the crowd indicates.

11:16 *tempting.* Putting Him to the test.

11:20 *finger of God.* God's power to judge His enemies (Ex. 8:19). *the kingdom of God is come.* Jesus' miracles are a sure sign that the King has come to overthrow the powers of darkness.

11:21 *strong man.* Satan, depicted as a captor who has a careful watch and armament over his own.

11:22 *a stronger than he.* Jesus has come to undo the works of the Devil and so to destroy Satan's authority over His people.

11:27 *paps.* A mother's breasts.

11:28 Even the closest physical association with Jesus is insufficient to grant blessedness. His true family is defined by spiritual unity in its obedience to God's Word (8:21).

11:33 *candle.* Oil lamp. *bushel.* Basket. *candlestick.* Stand for a lamp.

11:34 *single.* Healthy, whole. *eye is evil.* An idiom for greed (Deut. 15:9; Prov. 28:22).

11:35 *Take heed.* Consider, give careful attention.

11:36 Receiving the light of Jesus is what makes one whole. When one is spiritually whole one becomes light as well (Eph. 5:8).

37 ¶ And as he spake, a certain Pharisee besought
him to dine with him: and he went in, and sat
down to meat.
38 And when the Pharisee saw *it*, he marvelled
that he had not first washed before dinner.
39 And the Lord said unto him, Now do ye Phar-
isees make clean the outside of the cup and the
platter; but your inward part is full of ravening
and wickedness.
40 *Ye* fools, did not he that made that which is
without make that which is within also?
41 But rather give alms of such things as ye have;
and, behold, all things are clean unto you.
42 But woe unto you, Pharisees! for ye tithe mint
and rue and all manner of herbs, and pass over
judgment and the love of God: these ought ye to
have done, and not to leave the other undone.
43 Woe unto you, Pharisees! for ye love the up-
permost seats in the synagogues, and greetings in
the markets.
44 Woe unto you, scribes and Pharisees, hypo-
crites! for ye are as graves which appear not, and
the men that walk over *them* are not aware *of them*.
45 ¶ Then answered one of the lawyers, and said
unto him, Master, thus saying thou reproachest
us also.
46 And he said, Woe unto you also, *ye* lawyers! for
ye lade men with burdens grievous to be borne,
and ye yourselves touch not the burdens with one
of your fingers.
47 Woe unto you! for ye build the sepulchres of
the prophets, and your fathers killed them.
48 Truly ye bear witness that ye allow the deeds of
your fathers: for they indeed killed them, and ye
build their sepulchres.
49 Therefore also said the wisdom of God, I will
send them prophets and apostles, and *some* of
them they shall slay and persecute:
50 That the blood of all the prophets, which was
shed from the foundation of the world, may be
required of this generation;
51 From the blood of Abel unto the blood of
Zacharias, which perished between the altar
and the temple: verily I say unto you, It shall be
required of this generation.
52 Woe unto you, lawyers! for ye have taken away
the key of knowledge: ye entered not in yourselves,
and them that were entering in ye hindered.
53 And as he said these things unto them, the
scribes and the Pharisees began to urge *him*
vehemently, and to provoke him to speak of many
things:
54 Laying wait for him, and seeking to catch
something out of his mouth, that they might
accuse him.

CHAPTER 12

IN the mean time, when there were gathered
together an innumerable multitude of people,

11:37 *besought.* Asked. *sat down to meat.* Reclined at a meal.
11:38 *had not first washed before dinner.* The custom was to wash one's hands before eating to avoid ceremonial uncleanness.
11:39 *platter.* Dish. *ravening.* Greed, robbery.
11:40 *without.* Outside. God created man's body and soul and therefore requires not just the worship of the body but the adoration of the soul.
11:42 *tithe.* Give a tenth. *rue.* An herb.
11:43 *love the uppermost seats.* The Pharisees loved to be seen by men and to garner their praise. They were prideful in heart.
11:45 *lawyers.* Not experts in civil law but scholars in the law of Moses.
11:46 *lade men with burdens grievous to be borne.* Load people down with regulations they cannot keep, even as the legal experts refuse to keep the law themselves.
11:47 *sepulchres.* Tombs.
11:48 *allow.* Agree with, approve of.
11:49 *the wisdom of God.* Jesus is the divine Wisdom of whom Solomon wrote in Proverbs (v. 31), calling fools and sinners to listen and repent (Prov. 1:20–33; 8:1—9:18). *prophets and apostles.* Christ's appointed messengers (Eph. 4:11) are the messengers of wisdom, rejected by a proud and foolish world (1 Cor. 1:18—2:16).
11:50–51 *required of this generation.* By rejecting Jesus, the lawyers were bearing responsibility for the blood of the prophets. *Zacharias.* Likely the man whose martyrdom is recorded in the final book of the Hebrew Old Testament (2 Chron. 24:20–25), in contrast to *Abel* in the first (Gen. 4:1–26). Thus Jesus indicted them for the blood of every martyr in biblical history. *verily.* Truly.
11:52 *key of knowledge.* The lawyers saw themselves as defenders of God's truth and knowledge. Yet they failed to understand God's wisdom themselves and thus clouded over the truth for their hearers.
11:54 *Laying wait for him.* Jesus accused the lawyers of murdering the prophets. Before the words were out of His mouth they had already begun plotting His death, thus confirming His accusation.

Thoughts for Personal/Family Worship: Chapter 11

1. **We need to be taught how to pray because by nature we do not know. This awareness is the first step in this direction. Though the Lord's Prayer is a glorious pattern for prayer, praying itself is an exercise of faith in which believers need to learn the art of asking, seeking, and knocking (vv. 9–10). We can never truly pray unless by faith we also apprehend something of the mercy and grace of God the Father (v. 13). We especially need to ask God for more of the work of the Holy Spirit (v. 13), for the Spirit brings to believers all the blessings purchased by Christ's finished work. What is one lesson from this chapter about prayer that you want to put into practice? How will you do so?**
2. **The Devil is strong. Christ compared him to a "strong man armed" (v. 21). Thanks be to God there is "a stronger than he" (v. 22). Has He freed you? Don't rest content simply to be externally religious or, as Christ says, "swept and garnished" (v. 25). If that is you, you are exposed to grave danger (v. 26), especially when you are blinded by self-righteousness. How can we recognize the Devil's work of pride and self-righteousness in ourselves?**

insomuch that they trode one upon another, he
began to say unto his disciples first of all, Beware ye
of the leaven of the Pharisees, which is hypocrisy.
2 For there is nothing covered, that shall not be
revealed; neither hid, that shall not be known.
3 Therefore whatsoever ye have spoken in darkness
shall be heard in the light; and that which
ye have spoken in the ear in closets shall be proclaimed
upon the housetops.
4 And I say unto you my friends, Be not afraid
of them that kill the body, and after that have no
more that they can do.
5 But I will forewarn you whom ye shall fear: Fear
him, which after he hath killed hath power to cast
into hell; yea, I say unto you, Fear him.
6 Are not five sparrows sold for two farthings,
and not one of them is forgotten before God?
7 But even the very hairs of your head are all
numbered. Fear not therefore: ye are of more
value than many sparrows.
8 Also I say unto you, Whosoever shall confess
me before men, him shall the Son of man also
confess before the angels of God:
9 But he that denieth me before men shall be
denied before the angels of God.
10 And whosoever shall speak a word against the
Son of man, it shall be forgiven him: but unto him
that blasphemeth against the Holy Ghost it shall
not be forgiven.
11 And when they bring you unto the synagogues,
and *unto* magistrates, and powers, take ye
no thought how or what thing ye shall answer, or
what ye shall say:
12 For the Holy Ghost shall teach you in the same
hour what ye ought to say.
13 ¶ And one of the company said unto him,
Master, speak to my brother, that he divide the
inheritance with me.
14 And he said unto him, Man, who made me a
judge or a divider over you?
15 And he said unto them, Take heed, and beware
of covetousness: for a man's life consisteth not in
the abundance of the things which he possesseth.
16 And he spake a parable unto them, saying,
The ground of a certain rich man brought forth
plentifully:
17 And he thought within himself, saying, What
shall I do, because I have no room where to bestow
my fruits?
18 And he said, This will I do: I will pull down my
barns, and build greater; and there will I bestow
all my fruits and my goods.
19 And I will say to my soul, Soul, thou hast much
goods laid up for many years; take thine ease, eat,
drink, *and* be merry.
20 But God said unto him, *Thou* fool, this night
thy soul shall be required of thee: then whose
shall those things be, which thou hast provided?
21 So *is* he that layeth up treasure for himself, and
is not rich toward God.
22 ¶ And he said unto his disciples, Therefore I
say unto you, Take no thought for your life, what
ye shall eat; neither for the body, what ye shall
put on.
23 The life is more than meat, and the body *is*
more than raiment.
24 Consider the ravens: for they neither sow nor
reap; which neither have storehouse nor barn;
and God feedeth them: how much more are ye
better than the fowls?

Chapter 12: *Christ continues exposing the hypocritical religion of the Pharisees and teaching how best to prepare for the future.*

12:1 *leaven.* Yeast or starter dough, that is, the hypocritical religion *of the Pharisees* that worked like yeast to puff up and influence everything in and around it (1 Cor. 5:6–8).

12:3 *closets.* Private rooms.

12:6 *five sparrows.* Some of the least significant animals bought at markets. *two farthings.* Coins (Greek *assarion*), sixteen of which were the equivalent of a denarius or one day's wages for a laborer.

12:7 *hairs . . . numbered.* God's providence cares for the smallest details of our lives. *more value than many sparrows.* If God does not forget the little birds (v. 24), how much more can Christ's disciples find comfort and confidence in His care for them, people created in His image and saved by His Son?

12:10 *blasphemeth against the Holy Ghost.* Slanders the Holy Spirit. The Pharisees attributed the miracles of Jesus to the Devil (11:15; Mark 3:22–30). Such repeated and willful rejecting of the Spirit's testimony to Jesus as evil, calling the light darkness, hardens the heart against repentance so that the sinner will not seek forgiveness. Those who tremble over sin and confess it, looking to Christ for salvation, may be assured that they have not committed the unforgivable sin (Isa. 66:2; 1 John 1:7—2:2).

12:12 *the Holy Ghost shall teach you.* Christians are to take comfort in the fact that when they face persecutions and sufferings the Holy Spirit is with them (1 Peter 4:14). This promise had a special application to the apostles, to whom the Spirit gave new revelation upon which the church was built in the midst of its sufferings (John 15:18—16:15; Eph. 2:20; 3:5,13).

12:14 *who made me a judge.* Though Jesus is Lord, His office at this stage of history was not to make civil judgments on issues such as dividing an inheritance but to save and rule His people by the Word and Spirit. This man needed more than a fair ruling on financial matters; he needed an inward change.

12:19 *Soul.* Ironically, he was not thinking of the welfare of his soul but that of his physical life. *take thine ease.* Take it easy.

12:21 *rich toward God.* Seeking treasure in heaven through works of mercy (vv. 33–34; 1 Tim. 6:17–19). Those who put their comfort and hope in material possessions are enemies of God (16:13).

12:22 *Take no thought.* Do not be anxious. A man must work to provide for himself and his family (1 Thess. 4:11–12; 2 Thess. 3:10; 1 Tim. 5:8). However, we must work with faith in God's provision and from a desire for heavenly rewards, as opposed to being driven by undue love and care for earthly security and wealth.

12:23 *meat.* Food of any kind. *raiment.* Clothing.

12:24 *fowls.* Birds. God is able to care for His own, even the seemingly insignificant.

25 And which of you with taking thought can
add to his stature one cubit?
26 If ye then be not able to do that thing which is
least, why take ye thought for the rest?
27 Consider the lilies how they grow: they toil
not, they spin not; and yet I say unto you, that
Solomon in all his glory was not arrayed like one
of these.
28 If then God so clothe the grass, which is to day
in the field, and to morrow is cast into the oven;
how much more *will he clothe* you, O ye of little
faith?
29 And seek not ye what ye shall eat, or what ye
shall drink, neither be ye of doubtful mind.
30 For all these things do the nations of the world
seek after: and your Father knoweth that ye have
need of these things.
31 ¶ But rather seek ye the kingdom of God; and
all these things shall be added unto you.
32 Fear not, little flock; for it is your Father's good
pleasure to give you the kingdom.
33 Sell that ye have, and give alms; provide your-
selves bags which wax not old, a treasure in
the heavens that faileth not, where no thief ap-
proacheth, neither moth corrupteth.
34 For where your treasure is, there will your
heart be also.
35 Let your loins be girded about, and *your* lights
burning;
36 And ye yourselves like unto men that wait for
their lord, when he will return from the wedding;
that when he cometh and knocketh, they may
open unto him immediately.
37 Blessed *are* those servants, whom the lord
when he cometh shall find watching: verily I say
unto you, that he shall gird himself, and make
them to sit down to meat, and will come forth
and serve them.
38 And if he shall come in the second watch, or
come in the third watch, and find *them* so, blessed
are those servants.
39 And this know, that if the goodman of the
house had known what hour the thief would
come, he would have watched, and not have
suffered his house to be broken through.
40 Be ye therefore ready also: for the Son of man
cometh at an hour when ye think not.
41 ¶ Then Peter said unto him, Lord, speakest
thou this parable unto us, or even to all?
42 And the Lord said, Who then is that faithful
and wise steward, whom *his* lord shall make ruler
over his household, to give *them their* portion of
meat in due season?
43 Blessed *is* that servant, whom his lord when he
cometh shall find so doing.
44 Of a truth I say unto you, that he will make
him ruler over all that he hath.
45 But and if that servant say in his heart, My lord
delayeth his coming; and shall begin to beat the
menservants and maidens, and to eat and drink,
and to be drunken;
46 The lord of that servant will come in a day
when he looketh not for *him*, and at an hour when
he is not aware, and will cut him in sunder, and
will appoint him his portion with the unbelievers.
47 And that servant, which knew his lord's will,
and prepared not *himself*, neither did according
to his will, shall be beaten with many *stripes*.
48 But he that knew not, and did commit things
worthy of stripes, shall be beaten with few *stripes*.
For unto whomsoever much is given, of him
shall be much required: and to whom men have
committed much, of him they will ask the more.
49 ¶ I am come to send fire on the earth; and
what will I, if it be already kindled?
50 But I have a baptism to be baptized with; and
how am I straitened till it be accomplished!
51 Suppose ye that I am come to give peace on
earth? I tell you, Nay; but rather division:
52 For from henceforth there shall be five in one
house divided, three against two, and two against
three.
53 The father shall be divided against the son, and
the son against the father; the mother against the

12:25 *cubit*. About eighteen inches.

12:35 *loins be girded*. Dressed with a belt so that one is ready to move quickly (Ex. 12:11), an expression for being prepared for action at a moment's notice.

12:37 *watching*. Staying awake and alert. *sit down to meat*. Recline at a meal. *serve them*. The picture is that the servants are ready to welcome the master, who in turn will serve His servants.

12:38 *second watch, or . . . third watch*. The night was divided into three or four watches (Ex. 14:24; Judg. 7:19; Ps. 90:4; Matt. 14:25), so this places His return in the dead of night, communicating the difficulty of remaining faithful and alert through the long wait.

12:39 *goodman*. Master.

12:41 *us, or . . . all*. Contrasting those who are faithful to Jesus with the crowds standing around.

12:42–48 Jesus' response to Peter's question indicated that disciples are to be particularly observant but also that the coming of the Son of Man will have ramifications for the whole world. Therefore, it serves both as a prodding to the disciples and a warning to unbelievers.

12:42 *meat*. Food of any kind.

12:46 *in sunder*. In pieces.

12:47–48 *many stripes . . . few stripes*. Judgment comes upon all sinners, but with greater knowledge comes a greater responsibility to be faithful to that knowledge.

12:50 *baptism*. The divine judgment that He must endure for the sake of His people. *straitened*. Pressed upon inwardly, as a woman in childbirth. Jesus knew that His ministry would lead Him to great suffering, and in a holy zeal He anticipated the day when all things would be accomplished.

12:51 *peace . . . but rather division*. Christ makes peace between God and His people but provokes conflict between those who repent and follow Him and those who continue to

daughter, and the daughter against the mother;
the mother in law against her daughter in law, and
the daughter in law against her mother in law.
54 ¶ And he said also to the people, When ye see
a cloud rise out of the west, straightway ye say,
There cometh a shower; and so it is.
55 And when *ye see* the south wind blow, ye say,
There will be heat; and it cometh to pass.
56 *Ye* hypocrites, ye can discern the face of the sky
and of the earth; but how is it that ye do not dis-
cern this time?
57 Yea, and why even of yourselves judge ye not
what is right?
58 ¶ When thou goest with thine adversary to the
magistrate, *as thou art* in the way, give diligence
that thou mayest be delivered from him; lest he
hale thee to the judge, and the judge deliver thee
to the officer, and the officer cast thee into prison.
59 I tell thee, thou shalt not depart thence, till
thou hast paid the very last mite.

CHAPTER 13

THERE were present at that season some that told
him of the Galilaeans, whose blood Pilate had
mingled with their sacrifices.
2 And Jesus answering said unto them, Suppose
ye that these Galilaeans were sinners above all the
Galilaeans, because they suffered such things?
3 I tell you, Nay: but, except ye repent, ye shall all
likewise perish.
4 Or those eighteen, upon whom the tower in
Siloam fell, and slew them, think ye that they were
sinners above all men that dwelt in Jerusalem?
5 I tell you, Nay: but, except ye repent, ye shall all
likewise perish.
6 ¶ He spake also this parable; A certain *man* had
a fig tree planted in his vineyard; and he came and
sought fruit thereon, and found none.
7 Then said he unto the dresser of his vineyard,
Behold, these three years I come seeking fruit on
this fig tree, and find none: cut it down; why cum-
bereth it the ground?
8 And he answering said unto him, Lord, let it
alone this year also, till I shall dig about it, and
dung *it*:
9 And if it bear fruit, *well*: and if not, *then* after
that thou shalt cut it down.
10 And he was teaching in one of the synagogues
on the sabbath.
11 ¶ And, behold, there was a woman which had
a spirit of infirmity eighteen years, and was bowed
together, and could in no wise lift up *herself*.
12 And when Jesus saw her, he called *her to him*,
and said unto her, Woman, thou art loosed from
thine infirmity.

---

follow Satan (Gen. 3:15).

12:53 The division Jesus brings will sever the closest of familial relationships.

12:56 *this time?* The people had failed to understand the significance of Jesus' life and ministry.

12:58–59 Jesus uses a picture to stress the importance of discerning these days and embracing His message through faith. *hale.* Haul, drag. *mite.* Greek *lepton*, a small coin, 128 of which were equal to a denarius or a day's wages for a laborer.

Thoughts for Personal/Family Worship: Chapter 12

1. **The rich fool in the parable wanted to take it easy and just enjoy himself (v. 19). That is one of the great sins of our day and age. Many dream of a long, luxurious, and easy retirement. There is nothing wrong with enjoying the gifts God has given, provided we do not neglect the true reason we are here on the earth: to prepare for the life to come and in the meantime to steward our privileges in a God-honoring way. As long as we are able we must serve.**
2. **God's care for His people should eradicate all needless or undue worry or anxiety (vv. 22–30). Excessive worry does not necessarily mean we have no faith; as Christ said, it is at the least a sign of "little faith" (v. 28). If that is you, pray: "Lord, increase my faith." God increases faith by His Spirit when He motivates us to rest more squarely on His Word and promises. God is jealous of our allegiance and affections. Cares and concerns are so many invitations to cast our cares upon Him and find His care (1 Peter 5:7). How can Christ's teachings about the birds and flowers encourage us to trust God more?**
3. **Watchfulness is the great emphasis of Christ in vv. 31–59. Our world has invested a lot in meteorology, or predicting weather patterns. Christ tells us that it is of much greater importance to "discern this time" (v. 56) so as to be ready for Christ's return. We will never know in advance the exact day or hour, as some fear-mongers claim we might; however, we can be sure that each day we are one day closer. It refocuses us to live in light of Christ's imminent coming. How would it change your attitudes and habits to live each day watching for Christ's return?**

Chapter 13: *Christ urges repentance through the parable of the fig tree, heals a woman who has been bent over with the spirit of infirmity, and teaches about the kingdom of heaven.*

13:2 *sinners above all.* The worst sinners. A typical human response to calamity is to see those who suffer as especially guilty (John 9:1–3).

13:3 *Nay.* Jesus rejected simplistic judgments of others based upon their sufferings. *repent . . . perish.* The lesson we must learn from disasters and atrocities is that judgment is coming to all the world, and each of us must therefore turn from sin to the Lord Jesus for salvation.

13:6–9 *fig tree.* Often a symbol of the condition of Israel (21:29; Deut. 8:8; 1 Kings 4:25; Jer. 8:13; Zech. 3:10). Jesus came to His people seeking the *fruit* of godliness (Isa. 5:7), and their spiritual barrenness threatened them with judgment (Matt. 21:19). Jesus' parable vividly and memorably gives shape to the urgency of repentance (Rom. 2:4–5).

13:7 *cumbereth.* Waste.

13:11 *bowed together, and could in no wise lift up.* Bent over and unable to lift up her body. She was a picture of how the regulations of the religious leaders were burdening the people (11:46).

13:12 *thou art loosed.* You are set free from the bondage to your disease.

13 And he laid *his* hands on her: and immediately
she was made straight, and glorified God.
14 And the ruler of the synagogue answered with
indignation, because that Jesus had healed on the
sabbath day, and said unto the people, There are
six days in which men ought to work: in them
therefore come and be healed, and not on the
sabbath day.
15 The Lord then answered him, and said, *Thou*
hypocrite, doth not each one of you on the sab-
bath loose his ox or *his* ass from the stall, and lead
him away to watering?
16 And ought not this woman, being a daughter
of Abraham, whom Satan hath bound, lo, these
eighteen years, be loosed from this bond on the
sabbath day?
17 And when he had said these things, all his ad-
versaries were ashamed: and all the people rejoiced
for all the glorious things that were done by him.
18 ¶ Then said he, Unto what is the kingdom of
God like? and whereunto shall I resemble it?
19 It is like a grain of mustard seed, which a man
took, and cast into his garden; and it grew, and
waxed a great tree; and the fowls of the air lodged
in the branches of it.
20 And again he said, Whereunto shall I liken the
kingdom of God?
21 It is like leaven, which a woman took and
hid in three measures of meal, till the whole was
leavened.
22 And he went through the cities and villages,
teaching, and journeying toward Jerusalem.
23 Then said one unto him, Lord, are there few
that be saved? And he said unto them,
24 ¶ Strive to enter in at the strait gate: for many,
I say unto you, will seek to enter in, and shall not
be able.
25 When once the master of the house is risen up,
and hath shut to the door, and ye begin to stand
without, and to knock at the door, saying, Lord,
Lord, open unto us; and he shall answer and say
unto you, I know you not whence ye are:
26 Then shall ye begin to say, We have eaten and
drunk in thy presence, and thou hast taught in
our streets.
27 But he shall say, I tell you, I know you not
whence ye are; depart from me, all *ye* workers of
iniquity.
28 There shall be weeping and gnashing of teeth,
when ye shall see Abraham, and Isaac, and Jacob,
and all the prophets, in the kingdom of God, and
you *yourselves* thrust out.
29 And they shall come from the east, and *from*
the west, and from the north, and *from* the south,
and shall sit down in the kingdom of God.
30 And, behold, there are last which shall be first,
and there are first which shall be last.
31 ¶ The same day there came certain of the
Pharisees, saying unto him, Get thee out, and de-
part hence: for Herod will kill thee.
32 And he said unto them, Go ye, and tell that fox,
Behold, I cast out devils, and I do cures to day and
to morrow, and the third *day* I shall be perfected.
33 Nevertheless I must walk to day, and to mor-
row, and the *day* following: for it cannot be that a
prophet perish out of Jerusalem.

13:15–16 *on the sabbath loose his ox.* The religious elite cared more for their animals than for human beings. *daughter of Abraham.* An heir of the promise of blessing (19:9), which Jesus was fulfilling by bringing His kingdom (v. 28; 1:55,73).

13:19 *mustard seed . . . great tree.* The small beginnings of the kingdom with Jesus teaching His disciples would expand into the world. *fowls . . . lodged in the branches.* Birds found a home in the tree, an image of a prosperous kingdom giving protection and provision to its people (Dan. 4:12).

13:21 *leaven.* Yeast or starter dough. The working of leaven through dough is invisible to the human eye, but the dough is changed slowly until the whole of it has been transformed. In the same way the growth of God's kingdom is not always discernible, but it is always working to change people.

The Second Stage in Jesus' Journey to Jerusalem (13:22—17:10)

The Narrow Gate (13:22–30)

13:22 *journeying toward Jerusalem.* Jesus moved with intentionality toward the goal of His mission, His death and subsequent resurrection (9:51).

13:23–24 *few that be saved.* Jesus did not answer the question directly, but His response underlines the urgency and difficulty of salvation. *Strive.* Struggle, fight, a term sometimes used of athletes (1 Cor. 9:25; 1 Tim. 6:12; 2 Tim. 4:7). *strait.* Narrow. *many . . . will seek . . . and shall not be able.* As explained in the following parable (vv. 25–30), entrance into the *gate* does not here represent conversion but entrance into the glory and joy of the kingdom when Christ returns. Thus He was not saying that many people will sincerely desire salvation in this life but be somehow excluded, but that many will presume upon Christ's mercy, while refusing to repent (vv. 26–27), and find themselves shut out of life at the coming of Christ.

13:25 *shut to.* Shut up. *without.* Outside. *I know you not whence ye are.* I do not know where you come from; in other words, you do not belong to Me.

13:28–29 *weeping and gnashing of teeth.* Christ's expression for the suffering of hell (Matt. 8:12). *from the east . . . west . . . north . . . south.* While many will be locked out, many others will come into the *kingdom* from around the world (Rev. 7:9,14) to share the fulfillment of God's covenant with Israel (*Abraham, and Isaac, and Jacob*). *sit down.* Recline as at a meal; the kingdom is like a banquet (14:16–24).

13:30 *last . . . first.* There is a reversal of positions in the kingdom of God; we cannot depend on our religious privileges to withstand God's judgment but must humble ourselves.

Jesus Laments Jerusalem (13:31–35)

13:31 *Herod will kill thee.* Regardless of the Pharisees' motivation for issuing this warning, Jesus did not back down.

13:32 *that fox.* Jesus showed no fear of Herod. *third day.* Jesus' words imply the hope of His resurrection.

13:33 *cannot . . . perish out of Jerusalem.* Jesus went on, knowing well that His life and earthly ministry would end in Jerusalem.

34 O Jerusalem, Jerusalem, which killest the
prophets, and stonest them that are sent unto
thee; how often would I have gathered thy chil-
dren together, as a hen *doth gather* her brood
under *her* wings, and ye would not!
35 Behold, your house is left unto you desolate:
and verily I say unto you, Ye shall not see me, until
the time come when ye shall say, Blessed *is* he that
cometh in the name of the Lord.

CHAPTER 14

AND it came to pass, as he went into the house
of one of the chief Pharisees to eat bread on the
sabbath day, that they watched him.
2 And, behold, there was a certain man before
him which had the dropsy.
3 And Jesus answering spake unto the lawyers
and Pharisees, saying, Is it lawful to heal on the
sabbath day?
4 And they held their peace. And he took *him*,
and healed him, and let him go;
5 And answered them, saying, Which of you shall
have an ass or an ox fallen into a pit, and will not
straightway pull him out on the sabbath day?
6 And they could not answer him again to these
things.
7 ¶ And he put forth a parable to those which
were bidden, when he marked how they chose out
the chief rooms; saying unto them,
8 When thou art bidden of any *man* to a wed-
ding, sit not down in the highest room; lest a
more honourable man than thou be bidden of
him;
9 And he that bade thee and him come and say
to thee, Give this man place; and thou begin with
shame to take the lowest room.
10 But when thou art bidden, go and sit down
in the lowest room; that when he that bade
thee cometh, he may say unto thee, Friend, go
up higher: then shalt thou have worship in the
presence of them that sit at meat with thee.
11 For whosoever exalteth himself shall be
abased; and he that humbleth himself shall be
exalted.
12 ¶ Then said he also to him that bade him,
When thou makest a dinner or a supper, call not
thy friends, nor thy brethren, neither thy kins-
men, nor *thy* rich neighbours; lest they also bid
thee again, and a recompence be made thee.
13 But when thou makest a feast, call the poor,
the maimed, the lame, the blind:
14 And thou shalt be blessed; for they cannot
recompense thee: for thou shalt be recompensed
at the resurrection of the just.
15 ¶ And when one of them that sat at meat with

13:34 *hen . . . under her wings.* A picture of Christ's tender love for sinners. *ye would not!* You were not willing. God is sovereign in giving grace (10:21–22), but He cannot be blamed when sinners are damned; they are damned for the guilt of their own sins and refusal to repent (v. 27).
13:35 *your house is left . . . desolate.* God's judgment would fall upon Israel for their refusal to repent and follow Christ, resulting in the destruction of Jerusalem in AD 70 (21:6,20,24). *verily.* Truly. *Blessed is he.* Referencing to the coming of the King (Ps. 118:26).

Thoughts for Personal/Family Worship: Chapter 13

1. **Life is filled with uncertainties. Natural disasters and human violence can strike at any time and anywhere, and they often catch people totally unawares, leaving thousands dead within brief spans of time. The only way we can truly face the uncertainties of life is to live in repentance for our sins. Repentance is not just a decision a person makes at a given point in life but a lifetime of striving, struggling, and fighting against sin by faith in the grace of Christ. Many who hear the gospel admire Christ and presume upon His mercy but will find themselves shut out on the day of judgment. How is this especially a warning to those who regularly go to church and tend to think of themselves as better than others?**
2. **The healing of the woman from her long-term infirmity was a sign of what Christ does in the gospel for sinners. His grace releases them from the burden of their sins and the heavy load of human rules, expectations, and ceremonies. Christ is not a tyrant but full of sweet love for sinners. He is willing to save all who are willing to come to Him. He proved His will to save sinners by His determination to go to Jerusalem and die for their sins.**

What reasons does this chapter give for sinners to come to Christ and trust completely in Him?

Chapter 14: *Christ heals a man on the Sabbath and tells the parable of the marriage supper.*

Jesus Heals a Man on the Sabbath (14:1–6)

14:1 *watched him.* Attempted to catch Him doing or saying something objectionable.
14:2 *dropsy.* A sickness or condition in which fluids build up in the tissues of the body.
14:4 *held their peace.* Remained silent.
14:5 *straightway.* Immediately. Jesus argued from the lesser to the greater: since it was certainly lawful to help an endangered animal on the *Sabbath*, how much more so to do works of mercy to men (13:15).

Parables and Teachings (14:7—19:27)

14:7 *bidden.* Invited; literally, "called" (so throughout vv. 7–24). *marked.* Jesus was now the one watching them (v. 1). *chief rooms.* Places of honor at the table.
14:8–9 *sit not down in the highest room.* Do not seek the more honored place among the guests. Contrary to man's zeal for self-promotion, Jesus taught humility and service (22:26; Rom. 12:16).
14:9 *bade.* Same word as "bidden" (v. 7). *Give this man place.* Make room for him.
14:10 *have worship.* Receive honor. *sit at meat.* Recline at a meal together with others (v. 15).
14:11 *exalteth.* Lifts up. *abased.* Made low. As the preceding parable illustrates, proudly seeking glory from men leads to humiliation from God, but humbly deferring to others brings honor from God (Phil. 2:3–11; James 4:6,10).
14:15 *eat . . . in the kingdom.* It is likely that these Pharisees

him heard these things, he said unto him, Blessed
is he that shall eat bread in the kingdom of God.
16 Then said he unto him, A certain man made a
great supper, and bade many:
17 And sent his servant at supper time to say to
them that were bidden, Come; for all things are
now ready.
18 And they all with one *consent* began to make
excuse. The first said unto him, I have bought a
piece of ground, and I must needs go and see it: I
pray thee have me excused.
19 And another said, I have bought five yoke of
oxen, and I go to prove them: I pray thee have me
excused.
20 And another said, I have married a wife, and
therefore I cannot come.
21 So that servant came, and shewed his lord
these things. Then the master of the house being
angry said to his servant, Go out quickly into the
streets and lanes of the city, and bring in hither the
poor, and the maimed, and the halt, and the blind.
22 And the servant said, Lord, it is done as thou
hast commanded, and yet there is room.
23 And the lord said unto the servant, Go out
into the highways and hedges, and compel *them*
to come in, that my house may be filled.
24 For I say unto you, That none of those men
which were bidden shall taste of my supper.
25 ¶ And there went great multitudes with him:
and he turned, and said unto them,
26 If any *man* come to me, and hate not his fa-
ther, and mother, and wife, and children, and
brethren, and sisters, yea, and his own life also, he
cannot be my disciple.
27 And whosoever doth not bear his cross, and
come after me, cannot be my disciple.
28 For which of you, intending to build a tower,
sitteth not down first, and counteth the cost,
whether he have *sufficient* to finish *it*?
29 Lest haply, after he hath laid the foundation,
and is not able to finish *it*, all that behold *it* begin
to mock him,
30 Saying, This man began to build, and was not
able to finish.
31 Or what king, going to make war against an-
other king, sitteth not down first, and consulteth
whether he be able with ten thousand to meet him
that cometh against him with twenty thousand?
32 Or else, while the other is yet a great way off,
he sendeth an ambassage, and desireth conditions
of peace.
33 So likewise, whosoever he be of you that forsak-
eth not all that he hath, he cannot be my disciple.
34 ¶ Salt *is* good: but if the salt have lost his
savour, wherewith shall it be seasoned?
35 It is neither fit for the land, nor yet for the
dunghill; *but* men cast it out. He that hath ears to
hear, let him hear.

---

were mistakenly presuming their place in the end-time feast. The parable that follows rebukes the presumption of the Pharisees.

14:16 The kingdom of God is like a *great supper*, and the gospel is the call to come.

14:17–20 In accordance with ancient customs, a second invitation would be issued on the cusp of the feast. This invitation they would decline for reasons showing an infatuation with earthly things (8:14).

14:19 *prove.* Try them out, test.

14:21–23 *halt.* Lame. The new set of invitations goes out to those who cannot repay the master, who have nothing and who stand to receive only grace. These are the ones who come and feast at the dinner.

14:24 Those who initially were invited are stripped of their freedom to come to the dinner.

14:26–27 *hate . . . father . . . mother.* Jesus spoke comparatively, teaching that He must be first in our love and lives (Matt. 10:37). His unrivaled preeminence in a disciple's life might be construed as hatred by a relative. *bear His cross.* Following Jesus includes shame, rejection, death to one's pride, and perhaps even death to the body (9:23). *cannot be my disciple.* This is the cost of following Him and gaining His kingdom (repeated for emphasis).

14:28–29 *build a tower.* Following Christ is like a construction project (6:48) requiring a major investment and perseverance to ensure that it will not end in great shame. *lest haply.* Unless it should happen that.

14:31–32 *going to make war.* Following Christ is a struggle or battle against sin and Satan (13:24; Eph. 6:10–18), demanding hope that victory is in Christ (1 John 5:5). *ambassage.* Ambassadors.

14:33 *forsaketh all.* Though disciples may have and use material possessions as stewards of the Lord (1 Tim. 6:17–19), they must renounce this world as their treasure in order to hope in Christ alone.

14:34–35 *Salt.* Valuable for its pleasing flavor (*savour*), preservation of food from decay, and use as an antiseptic (Job 6:6; Ezek. 16:4). The self-denying loyalty of disciples to Christ pleases God, promotes good in the world, and restrains evil. *neither fit.* Not useful. Salt in the ancient world was a mixture of minerals, and water could leach away the sodium chloride, leaving useless minerals behind. *cast it out.* Without the distinctive character of true disciples, professing Christians will be rejected by God.

Thoughts for Personal/Family Worship: Chapter 14

1. Grace humbles a person. Instead of presuming that we are deserving of the chief places in society, it makes us ready to serve others and choose the lowest place for ourselves. Christ showed this spirit during His life, and He teaches this by His Spirit to all His people (vv. 7–9). What a day it will be when Christ will exalt all His people and say, "Friend, go up higher" (v. 10). As James writes, "Humble yourselves in the sight of the Lord, and he shall lift you up" (James 4:10). How can hope in God's reward in glory make Christians willing to serve in lowly, unrecognized ways in this life?

2. Christ said that when they heard the invitation to the kingdom "they all with one consent began to make excuse" (v. 18). Man by nature loves to weave a web of thinking that makes his rejection of Christ's call look plausible. Others make a superficial response to the gospel but fail to count the cost and excuse themselves

CHAPTER 15

THEN drew near unto him all the publicans and
sinners for to hear him.
2 And the Pharisees and scribes murmured, say-
ing, This man receiveth sinners, and eateth with
them.
3 ¶ And he spake this parable unto them, saying,
4 What man of you, having an hundred sheep, if
he lose one of them, doth not leave the ninety and
nine in the wilderness, and go after that which is
lost, until he find it?
5 And when he hath found *it*, he layeth *it* on his
shoulders, rejoicing.
6 And when he cometh home, he calleth together
his friends and neighbours, saying unto them,
Rejoice with me; for I have found my sheep which
was lost.
7 I say unto you, that likewise joy shall be in
heaven over one sinner that repenteth, more than
over ninety and nine just persons, which need no
repentance.
8 ¶ Either what woman having ten pieces of sil-
ver, if she lose one piece, doth not light a candle,
and sweep the house, and seek diligently till she
find *it*?
9 And when she hath found *it*, she calleth *her*
friends and *her* neighbours together, saying,
Rejoice with me; for I have found the piece which
I had lost.
10 Likewise, I say unto you, there is joy in the
presence of the angels of God over one sinner that
repenteth.
11 ¶ And he said, A certain man had two sons:
12 And the younger of them said to *his* father,
Father, give me the portion of goods that falleth
to me. And he divided unto them *his* living.
13 And not many days after the younger son
gathered all together, and took his journey into a
far country, and there wasted his substance with
riotous living.
14 And when he had spent all, there arose a
mighty famine in that land; and he began to be
in want.
15 And he went and joined himself to a citizen
of that country; and he sent him into his fields to
feed swine.
16 And he would fain have filled his belly with
the husks that the swine did eat: and no man gave
unto him.
17 And when he came to himself, he said, How
many hired servants of my father's have bread
enough and to spare, and I perish with hunger!
18 I will arise and go to my father, and will say
unto him, Father, I have sinned against heaven,
and before thee,
19 And am no more worthy to be called thy son:
make me as one of thy hired servants.
20 And he arose, and came to his father. But when
he was yet a great way off, his father saw him, and
had compassion, and ran, and fell on his neck,
and kissed him.
21 And the son said unto him, Father, I have
sinned against heaven, and in thy sight, and am
no more worthy to be called thy son.

---

because discipleship seems too hard. What motivates true disciples to turn from all such excuses and pursue Christ and His kingdom at any cost? How can we seek that kind of response in prayer?

Chapter 15: ***Christ is approachable to publicans and sinners, which He explains in the parable of the lost sheep, the lost coin, and the prodigal son.***

15:1 *publicans.* Tax collectors, considered by the people to be great *sinners* (19:7).

15:2 *receiveth sinners, and eateth with them.* Christ was criticized for being a friend to the worst of men, and particularly for sharing table fellowship with them (5:30; 7:34).

15:3 The singular *parable* implies that it is important to see these three scenes as closely linked together, expressing the totality of Jesus' teaching on this subject.

15:4 Jesus views sinners as lost *sheep* who have wandered from the flock of God, abandoning their Shepherd and putting themselves in great danger (Isa. 53:6; Matt. 9:36; 10:6; 15:24). *lose one.* Note the emphasis on the individual in contrast to the group (*hundred*). Christ's compassion is not about numbers but about the need of each individual sinner.

15:6 *Rejoice with me.* An implicit call to join with Jesus in delighting in God's mercy to sinners (repeated for emphasis in v. 9; cf. v. 32).

15:8 *ten pieces of silver.* Ten silver coins (Greek, *drachme*), worth ten days' wages for a laborer. *candle.* Oil lamp. *seek diligently.* The coin is totally passive in its recovery, but the woman works hard to find it, a picture of God's mighty works of sovereign grace to save those dead in sin (vv. 24,32).

15:11 The third scene of Jesus' parable uses the example of a lost son, a familial connection that serves to make the parable all the more intimate and personal.

15:12 *younger.* The younger son prematurely asks his father for his inheritance, disrespectfully treating his father as though he were already dead. *living.* Wealth.

15:13 *substance.* Property. *riotous living.* The son further disgraced his father by spending his money in reckless and loose ways.

15:14–15 *be in want.* Lack what he needed and desired. *feed swine.* A degrading occupation for any Israelite, since pigs were ceremonially unclean (Lev. 11:7; Deut. 14:8).

15:16 *would fain.* Strongly desired. *husks.* Probably the pods of a carob tree.

15:17 *came to himself.* Repentance begins with a change of mind. *bread enough and to spare.* His change involves trust in his *father's* kindness (Rom. 2:4).

15:18 *sinned against heaven, and before thee.* Repentance involves realizing that we have not only wronged people but broken God's law and dishonored Him above all (Ps. 51:4).

15:19 *no more worthy.* Repentance humbles a person, stripping away one's sense of deserving blessing while sustaining some hope of mercy (*make me one of thy hired servants*).

15:20 *compassion.* The Lord's salvation springs from His tender mercy to miserable sinners (1:78; 7:13).

22 But the father said to his servants, Bring forth
the best robe, and put *it* on him; and put a ring on
his hand, and shoes on *his* feet:
23 And bring hither the fatted calf, and kill *it*; and
let us eat, and be merry:
24 For this my son was dead, and is alive again;
he was lost, and is found. And they began to be
merry.
25 Now his elder son was in the field: and as he
came and drew nigh to the house, he heard musick and dancing.
26 And he called one of the servants, and asked
what these things meant.
27 And he said unto him, Thy brother is come;
and thy father hath killed the fatted calf, because
he hath received him safe and sound.
28 And he was angry, and would not go in: therefore came his father out, and intreated him.
29 And he answering said to *his* father, Lo, these
many years do I serve thee, neither transgressed
I at any time thy commandment: and yet thou
never gavest me a kid, that I might make merry
with my friends:
30 But as soon as this thy son was come, which
hath devoured thy living with harlots, thou hast
killed for him the fatted calf.
31 And he said unto him, Son, thou art ever with
me, and all that I have is thine.
32 It was meet that we should make merry, and
be glad: for this thy brother was dead, and is alive
again; and was lost, and is found.

CHAPTER 16

AND he said also unto his disciples, There was a
certain rich man, which had a steward; and the
same was accused unto him that he had wasted his
goods.
2 And he called him, and said unto him, How is
it that I hear this of thee? give an account of thy
stewardship; for thou mayest be no longer steward.
3 Then the steward said within himself, What
shall I do? for my lord taketh away from me the
stewardship: I cannot dig; to beg I am ashamed.
4 I am resolved what to do, that, when I am put
out of the stewardship, they may receive me into
their houses.
5 So he called every one of his lord's debtors *unto
him*, and said unto the first, How much owest
thou unto my lord?
6 And he said, An hundred measures of oil. And
he said unto him, Take thy bill, and sit down
quickly, and write fifty.
7 Then said he to another, And how much owest
thou? And he said, An hundred measures of
wheat. And he said unto him, Take thy bill, and
write fourscore.
8 And the lord commended the unjust steward,

15:23 *hither.* Here. *fatted.* Grain-fed for delicious meat.
15:24 *my son.* The father refused to take back the sinner as a servant (as though the son could earn blessing) but fully restored him. Salvation transforms God's enemies into adopted and beloved children of God (8:21; Eph. 1:5; Gal. 4:4–7). *dead . . . is alive again.* Salvation is a resurrection from spiritual death (v. 32; Ezek. 37:1–14; John 5:24–25; Eph. 2:1–10). Such a miracle should be celebrated (Eph. 1:6).
15:25 *elder son.* Just as important to this parable as is the wayward son.
15:28 *he was angry.* The Pharisees and scribes were standing outside Christ's feasting with repentant sinners, just as the older brother remains outside the feast in self-righteous outrage. *came his father out.* The father willingly left the celebration in an attempt to draw his elder son into it, again showing his merciful and compassionate spirit, just as Jesus appealed to the Pharisees.
15:32–33 *meet . . . make merry.* Fitting that we rejoice. The final words of the father in the parable are Christ's words to the Pharisees concerning why they should not criticize His grace to sinners but instead join Him (vv. 1–2).

Thoughts for Personal/Family Worship: Chapter 15

1. **Each of the three scenes of the parable shows the heart of God that beats with love till the lost sheep, coin, and son are found. There is no other cause for the salvation of lost sinners besides the love of God in Christ. John says it beautifully: "We love him, because he first loved us" (1 John 4:19). How do Christ's words show us the glory of God's love?**
2. **Like the prodigal, by our sin we have turned our back on God and taken God's gifts and used them for our own pleasure and glory. This will bring nothing but lack, misery, and unless we repent, damnation in hell forevermore. Sinner, what has following your own heart brought you? Is it not time to come to your senses and remember the goodness of God?**
3. **The attitude of our hearts to sinners being saved is a barometer of whether or not we have ourselves experienced the grace of God. The Pharisees, like the elder son, stood outside the joy and gladness, for their hearts were still closed to the grace of God. Why should the words of the father (v. 32) melt our hearts into joy over the conversion of the worst of men?**

Chapter 16: *Jesus continues His teaching on repentance in the parables of the unjust steward and the rich man and Lazarus.*

16:1 *steward.* A servant placed in authority to manage the master's property. *wasted his goods.* There are thematic and grammatical connections between this parable and the previous one (15:13). Unlike the previous parable with its two sons, however, here there is only one man, implying that all people have squandered the Lord's goods by their unfaithfulness.
16:4–7 The steward reduces the amount of debt the debtors owe to his master so that they will take care of him after he loses his job.
16:8 *done wisely.* The master's response does not clarify whether his reduction of the debts was legitimate or illegitimate, but he does commend his shrewdness. *children of light.* Literally, "sons of light," an idiom for Christ's disciples as those transformed by the light of His Word (1:79; 11:34–36), in contrast to the *children of this world* who live for present, earthly

because he had done wisely: for the children of
this world are in their generation wiser than the
children of light.
9 And I say unto you, Make to yourselves friends
of the mammon of unrighteousness; that, when
ye fail, they may receive you into everlasting
habitations.
10 He that is faithful in that which is least is faith-
ful also in much: and he that is unjust in the least
is unjust also in much.
11 If therefore ye have not been faithful in the
unrighteous mammon, who will commit to your
trust the true *riches*?
12 And if ye have not been faithful in that which
is another man's, who shall give you that which is
your own?
13 ¶ No servant can serve two masters: for either
he will hate the one, and love the other; or else
he will hold to the one, and despise the other. Ye
cannot serve God and mammon.
14 And the Pharisees also, who were covetous,
heard all these things: and they derided him.
15 And he said unto them, Ye are they which jus-
tify yourselves before men; but God knoweth
your hearts: for that which is highly esteemed
among men is abomination in the sight of God.
16 The law and the prophets *were* until John:
since that time the kingdom of God is preached,
and every man presseth into it.
17 And it is easier for heaven and earth to pass,
than one tittle of the law to fail.
18 Whosoever putteth away his wife, and marri-
eth another, committeth adultery: and whosoever
marrieth her that is put away from *her* husband
committeth adultery.
19 ¶ There was a certain rich man, which was
clothed in purple and fine linen, and fared sump-
tuously every day:
20 And there was a certain beggar named Lazarus,
which was laid at his gate, full of sores,
21 And desiring to be fed with the crumbs which
fell from the rich man's table: moreover the dogs
came and licked his sores.
22 And it came to pass, that the beggar died, and
was carried by the angels into Abraham's bosom:
the rich man also died, and was buried;
23 And in hell he lift up his eyes, being in tor-
ments, and seeth Abraham afar off, and Lazarus
in his bosom.
24 And he cried and said, Father Abraham, have
mercy on me, and send Lazarus, that he may dip
the tip of his finger in water, and cool my tongue;
for I am tormented in this flame.
25 But Abraham said, Son, remember that thou
in thy lifetime receivedst thy good things, and
likewise Lazarus evil things: but now he is com-
forted, and thou art tormented.
26 And beside all this, between us and you there
is a great gulf fixed: so that they which would pass
from hence to you cannot; neither can they pass
to us, that *would come* from thence.
27 Then he said, I pray thee therefore, father, that
thou wouldest send him to my father's house:
28 For I have five brethren; that he may testify unto
them, lest they also come into this place of torment.
29 Abraham saith unto him, They have Moses
and the prophets; let them hear them.
30 And he said, Nay, father Abraham: but if one
went unto them from the dead, they will repent.
31 And he said unto him, If they hear not Moses
and the prophets, neither will they be persuaded,
though one rose from the dead.

---

things. Ironically, Christians often lack the degree of foresight in preparing for their eternal future demonstrated by worldly people in preparing for their earthly future.

16:9 *Make . . . friends of the mammon.* Use money and possessions to serve people. *receive you into everlasting habitations.* Part of a disciple's reward will be the heavenly gratitude of other believers whom they have served in this life.

16:13 *two masters.* Jesus' disciples must have an undivided heart to *love* Him above all things (14:26,33). *mammon.* Worldly riches or wealth, here personified as a false god.

16:14 *covetous.* The Pharisees had the divided hearts Jesus had just spoken against. *derided.* Sneered, ridiculed. The Pharisees continued in their stubborn rejection of Jesus' person and work.

16:16 *presseth into it.* Yearns and strives to enter it (13:24; Matt. 11:12).

16:17 *tittle.* A small projection on some Hebrew letters. Even the smallest part of the Bible is the unchanging Word of God.

16:19 *sumptuously.* Luxuriously, extravagantly.

16:20–21 *Lazarus.* The Greek form of the Hebrew name *Eliezer,* "he whom God helps." The rich man's wickedness is evident in his utter neglect of the needy person on his doorstep.

16:22 *Abraham's bosom.* Here a figure of speech for the intermediate state of believers between death and resurrection (2 Cor. 5:8; Phil. 1:21–23; Heb. 12:23), pictured as a place of close fellowship shared by those who have the faith of Abraham.

16:24 *dip the tip of his finger.* Those in hell still long for earthly pleasures but are denied the smallest comforts as they are *tormented* by God's punishment for sin.

16:26 *great gulf fixed.* A large chasm is set. Heaven and hell cannot be bridged from one to the other in either direction.

16:28 *lest they also come into this place of torment.* It is likely that this man does not want them in hell with him, as this would only add to his own torment and suffering.

16:29–31 *Moses and the prophets.* The Old Testament is sufficient on its own to lead men to repentance and salvation by faith in Christ (v. 16; 2 Tim. 3:15).

16:31 *rose from the dead.* No miracle, not even Jesus' resurrection, to which He subtly refers here, is sufficient to convert sinners if they are not convinced by the Holy Scriptures.

Thoughts for Personal/Family Worship: Chapter 16

1. **The main lesson of the parable of the unjust steward is that we ought to wisely prepare for eternity through repentance and faith. This shrewd steward's preparation for his future, even if he did it in unjust ways, should stir us up to make provisions for our own future, since by nature we have all mismanaged our stewardship of the**

CHAPTER 17

THEN said he unto the disciples, It is impossible
but that offences will come: but woe *unto him*,
through whom they come!
2 It were better for him that a millstone were
hanged about his neck, and he cast into the sea,
than that he should offend one of these little ones.
3 ¶ Take heed to yourselves: If thy brother tres-
pass against thee, rebuke him; and if he repent,
forgive him.
4 And if he trespass against thee seven times in a
day, and seven times in a day turn again to thee,
saying, I repent; thou shalt forgive him.
5 And the apostles said unto the Lord, Increase
our faith.
6 And the Lord said, If ye had faith as a grain of
mustard seed, ye might say unto this sycamine
tree, Be thou plucked up by the root, and be thou
planted in the sea; and it should obey you.
7 But which of you, having a servant plowing or
feeding cattle, will say unto him by and by, when
he is come from the field, Go and sit down to meat?
8 And will not rather say unto him, Make ready
wherewith I may sup, and gird thyself, and serve
me, till I have eaten and drunken; and afterward
thou shalt eat and drink?
9 Doth he thank that servant because he did the
things that were commanded him? I trow not.
10 So likewise ye, when ye shall have done all
those things which are commanded you, say,
We are unprofitable servants: we have done that
which was our duty to do.
11 ¶ And it came to pass, as he went to Jerusalem,
that he passed through the midst of Samaria and
Galilee.
12 And as he entered into a certain village, there
met him ten men that were lepers, which stood
afar off:
13 And they lifted up *their* voices, and said, Jesus,
Master, have mercy on us.
14 And when he saw *them*, he said unto them, Go
shew yourselves unto the priests. And it came to
pass, that, as they went, they were cleansed.
15 And one of them, when he saw that he was
healed, turned back, and with a loud voice glori-
fied God,
16 And fell down on *his* face at his feet, giving
him thanks: and he was a Samaritan.
17 And Jesus answering said, Were there not ten
cleansed? but where *are* the nine?
18 There are not found that returned to give
glory to God, save this stranger.
19 And he said unto him, Arise, go thy way: thy
faith hath made thee whole.

---

resources God has entrusted to us, and our stewardship on earth will soon end. We must realize that we cannot serve two masters and must turn from loving money to loving God with an undivided heart. What does it mean to live every day not as our own masters but as trustees of our time, resources, privileges, and so on?

2. The parable of the rich man and Lazarus teaches us that prosperity in this life does not imply prosperity in the next, nor does difficulty in this life portend difficulty in the next. It would be better to suffer for a time here than to suffer eternally in the place of torment. The key question is how we respond to the Bible. The Scriptures are sufficient for life and godliness. They are of greater weight and authority to convince people of God's truth than if someone were once again to rise from the dead (v. 31). Do you rightly esteem the glory of the Scriptures, both the Old and the New Testaments? If you do you will live by faith in Christ, repentance of sin, and mercy toward men.

Chapter 17: *Christ teaches about forgiveness, faith, and thankfulness and explains His return.*

17:1 *offences*. Causes of stumbling and falling.
17:2 *little ones*. Christ's disciples in their childlikeness.
17:3 *Take heed*. Give attention. *If thy brother trespass*. Jesus turns from the sinning brother to the brother who has been sinned against. *rebuke him*. An act of brotherly love (Lev. 19:17–18; Prov. 27:5–6). *forgive him*. While we are not the divine Judge, we should offer personal forgiveness if a fellow believer expresses repentance for his sin (Eph. 4:32); even if he does not repent, we need to stand ready to forgive him by God's grace if he later asks for forgiveness.
17:6 *sycamine*. Mulberry or sycamore. Faith cannot perform magical tricks, but even in its weakest form it can by the Spirit's blessing accomplish amazing things for God's kingdom, as this mini-parable shows (see note at Mark 11:23).
17:7–9 *having a servant*. Forgiving one another by faith (vv. 3–6) is not going above and beyond the call of duty but is simply doing what we are called to do as servants of the Lord.
17:7 *sit down to meat*. Recline at the table to eat food of any kind.
17:9 *trow*. Think.
17:10 *unprofitable servants*. Christians should not swell up in pride over their service but should realize that obedience to the Lord is simply their *duty*, of itself meriting no praise or reward.

The Third Stage in Jesus' Journey to Jerusalem (17:11—19:27)

Jesus Heals Ten Lepers (17:11–19)

17:12 In accordance with the Old Testament law, *lepers* were outcasts (Lev. 13:45–56). Thus, these unclean men *stood afar off* from Jesus to prevent Him from becoming ceremonially unclean.
17:14 *shew yourselves unto the priests*. Lepers were required by the Mosaic law to be declared pure by the priest before they could reenter Jewish society (Lev. 14).
17:15 *glorified God*. The one leper understood that Jesus' work is of God.
17:16 *Samaritan*. A member of a people group despised by the Jews (10:33).
17:17 *where are the nine?* Many people have received healing and other benefits from Christ, but few honor Him with their gratitude (7:41–47).
17:18 *save this stranger*. Except for this foreigner.
17:19 *thy faith hath made thee whole*. Literally, "your faith has saved you," an expression used for either physical deliverance or spiritual salvation (7:50; 8:48; 18:42).

20 ¶ And when he was demanded of the Pharisees, when the kingdom of God should come, he answered them and said, The kingdom of God cometh not with observation:
21 Neither shall they say, Lo here! or, lo there! for, behold, the kingdom of God is within you.
22 And he said unto the disciples, The days will come, when ye shall desire to see one of the days of the Son of man, and ye shall not see *it*.
23 And they shall say to you, See here; or, see there: go not after *them*, nor follow *them*.
24 For as the lightning, that lighteneth out of the one *part* under heaven, shineth unto the other *part* under heaven; so shall also the Son of man be in his day.
25 But first must he suffer many things, and be rejected of this generation.
26 And as it was in the days of Noe, so shall it be also in the days of the Son of man.
27 They did eat, they drank, they married wives, they were given in marriage, until the day that Noe entered into the ark, and the flood came, and destroyed them all.
28 Likewise also as it was in the days of Lot; they did eat, they drank, they bought, they sold, they planted, they builded;
29 But the same day that Lot went out of Sodom it rained fire and brimstone from heaven, and destroyed *them* all.
30 Even thus shall it be in the day when the Son of man is revealed.
31 In that day, he which shall be upon the housetop, and his stuff in the house, let him not come down to take it away: and he that is in the field, let him likewise not return back.
32 Remember Lot's wife.
33 Whosoever shall seek to save his life shall lose it; and whosoever shall lose his life shall preserve it.
34 I tell you, in that night there shall be two *men* in one bed; the one shall be taken, and the other shall be left.
35 Two *women* shall be grinding together; the one shall be taken, and the other left.
36 Two *men* shall be in the field; the one shall be taken, and the other left.
37 And they answered and said unto him, Where, Lord? And he said unto them, Wheresoever the body *is*, thither will the eagles be gathered together.

CHAPTER 18

AND he spake a parable unto them *to this end*, that men ought always to pray, and not to faint;
2 Saying, There was in a city a judge, which feared not God, neither regarded man:
3 And there was a widow in that city; and she came unto him, saying, Avenge me of mine adversary.

The Coming of the Kingdom (17:20–37)

17:20 *not with observation.* The kingdom will not come in the pomp and flair the Pharisees are seeking.

17:21 *within you.* Though this may mean that the kingdom will be manifested among Christ's disciples, it more likely signifies that God's kingdom is initially and decisively manifest within the hearts and souls of those who are regenerated and sanctified by the Holy Spirit (John 3:3–5; Rom. 14:17).

17:22 *the days of the Son of man.* The consummation of the kingdom (v. 26), when the King will return (on this title for Jesus, see the note at 5:24).

17:26 *Noe.* Noah.

17:29 *brimstone.* Sulphur (Gen. 19:24; Deut. 29:23).

17:31 *housetop.* Homes of the time often had flat roofs that were used as a part of the home.

17:32 *Remember Lot's wife.* A warning against loving the world instead of pursuing God's grace wholeheartedly (Gen. 19:17,26).

17:37 *thither.* There. *eagles be gathered together.* Just as vultures gather to consume the prey that has been killed or has died (Ezek. 39:17; Rev. 19:17), so there will be signs showing what is going to happen.

Thoughts for Personal/Family Worship: Chapter 17

1. **Christ's disciples will reveal themselves in how they behave toward each other, rebuking each other when necessary (v. 3) but also forgiving each other (v. 4) as Christ has forgiven them. They are not in the Christian life for themselves but to serve Christ and one another. Yet they are to serve with humility, for even if we would be able to do everything right, which we never could, we would still be only "unprofitable servants" (v. 10). How can these truths help us when we begin to resent other Christians or think that the church or Christ cannot do without us?**
2. **When the one leper returned to thank Christ, He looked for the other nine who had also been healed to bring glory to Him, but they were nowhere to be found. We need more than God's help with our physical needs and problems. We need grace to make us truly grateful so we bring glory to God. Where are you when you experience a blessing from the Lord—with the one or with the nine? How can you become more grateful?**
3. **Do not presume that all will be well simply because you are among Christians. As Christ warns, "Remember Lot's wife" (v. 32). She was close to making it, but she looked back and perished because she was not prepared to lose all else in order that she might gain salvation. Her doom is a graphic image of Christ's warning: "No man, having put his hand to the plough, and looking back, is fit for the kingdom of God" (9:62). Why do people look back to the world after starting to follow Christ?**

Chapter 18: ***Christ tells parables on prayer, teaches a ruler how to attain eternal life, foretells His death and resurrection, and gives sight to a blind beggar.***

Parable of the Persistent Widow (18:1–8)

18:1 *faint.* Grow weak or discouraged.

18:2–8 The meaning of this parable is not that God begrudgingly listens to the cries of His people; rather, the unscrupulous *judge* is not a picture of God but a contrast to Him. If a proud and wicked judge will help a widow who means nothing to him based on her persistence, how much more will the righteous God answer the prayers of the people whom He chose (*elect*) in His love.

18:3 *widow.* A figure of powerlessness and vulnerability (Ex.

4 And he would not for a while: but afterward he
said within himself, Though I fear not God, nor
regard man;
5 Yet because this widow troubleth me, I will
avenge her, lest by her continual coming she
weary me.
6 And the Lord said, Hear what the unjust judge
saith.
7 And shall not God avenge his own elect, which
cry day and night unto him, though he bear long
with them?
8 I tell you that he will avenge them speedily.
Nevertheless when the Son of man cometh, shall
he find faith on the earth?
9 And he spake this parable unto certain which
trusted in themselves that they were righteous,
and despised others:
10 Two men went up into the temple to pray; the
one a Pharisee, and the other a publican.
11 The Pharisee stood and prayed thus with
himself, God, I thank thee, that I am not as other
men *are*, extortioners, unjust, adulterers, or even
as this publican.
12 I fast twice in the week, I give tithes of all that
I possess.
13 And the publican, standing afar off, would not
lift up so much as *his* eyes unto heaven, but smote
upon his breast, saying, God be merciful to me a
sinner.
14 I tell you, this man went down to his house
justified *rather* than the other: for every one that
exalteth himself shall be abased; and he that
humbleth himself shall be exalted.
15 And they brought unto him also infants, that
he would touch them: but when *his* disciples saw
it, they rebuked them.
16 But Jesus called them *unto him*, and said,
Suffer little children to come unto me, and forbid
them not: for of such is the kingdom of God.
17 Verily I say unto you, Whosoever shall not
receive the kingdom of God as a little child shall
in no wise enter therein.
18 And a certain ruler asked him, saying, Good
Master, what shall I do to inherit eternal life?
19 And Jesus said unto him, Why callest thou me
good? none *is* good, save one, *that is*, God.
20 Thou knowest the commandments, Do not
commit adultery, Do not kill, Do not steal, Do
not bear false witness, Honour thy father and thy
mother.
21 And he said, All these have I kept from my
youth up.
22 Now when Jesus heard these things, he said
unto him, Yet lackest thou one thing: sell all that
thou hast, and distribute unto the poor, and thou
shalt have treasure in heaven: and come, follow me.
23 And when he heard this, he was very sorrow-
ful: for he was very rich.
24 And when Jesus saw that he was very sorrow-
ful, he said, How hardly shall they that have riches
enter into the kingdom of God!
25 For it is easier for a camel to go through a

22:22–24). *Avenge me.* Give me justice in my legal dispute.

18:7 *though he bear long with them.* God will avenge His elect, even though He is enduring with longsuffering those who are afflicting His people.

18:8 *when the Son of man cometh.* The ultimate answer to the prayers of believers is the return of Christ (9:26; 12:40; 21:27).

The Pharisee and the Tax Collector (18:9–14)

18:9 Jesus spoke this parable to point His readers to the righteousness that is found in Him alone (Rom. 3:21–26; 2 Cor. 5:21).

18:10 *Pharisee . . . publican.* Representing the opposite extremes of religious devotion to God's law (Phil. 3:5–6) and worldly treachery; the latter was epitomized in the eyes of the people by a tax collector for Rome.

18:11 *I thank thee.* The main problem with the Pharisee's prayer was that he thought he would be able to stand before God based on his works (Pss. 130:3; 143:2). There is no note of repentance of sin.

18:13 *standing afar off . . . not lift up . . . his eyes.* Acts of humility, utterly opposite the stance of the Pharisee. *smote upon his breast.* Struck his chest, an expression of grief. *be merciful.* Literally, "be propitiated," a term for the appeasement of God's righteous anger (Ps. 78:38) effected by priests at the temple (v. 10) by the blood of a sacrifice, a type of Christ's atoning death (Heb. 2:17). *me a sinner.* His standing before God could not be based on anything within him but on grace alone (Ps. 51:1–2).

18:14 *justified.* Declared righteous by the Judge. The justification of a sinner is by grace alone through faith alone in God's provision of a sacrifice (v. 13; Rom. 3:28; Gal. 2:16). *exalteth . . . abased.* Lifts up and is made low. An essential component of saving faith is humility.

Jesus Blesses the Children (18:15–17)

18:15 *infants.* While the disciples rebuke the children, Jesus blesses them.

18:16 *Suffer.* Permit. Just as God justifies and honors the humble sinner who trusts in His grace (vv. 13–14), so Jesus welcomes *little children* because salvation belongs to those who are childlike toward God (*of such is the kingdom*).

18:17 *in no wise enter therein.* Certainly not come into it.

A Rich Young Ruler (18:18–30)

18:18 *what shall I do to inherit eternal life?* Though we might applaud this man's concern about obtaining eternal life, he is still stuck in a scheme of works, as Christ's response indicates.

18:19 *none is good.* Jesus was not denying His goodness (3:22) or deity (5:23–24; 6:5) but was confronting the ruler's inadequate understanding of who is good in the eyes of *God. save.* Except.

18:20 *Thou knowest the commandments.* Jesus quoted the fifth through ninth of the Ten Commandments (Ex. 20:12–16). He focused on the second table about man's relationship to man, perhaps because wealth often promotes selfishness.

18:22–23 *sell all that thou hast.* Jesus' response is not a requirement for all His disciples but His prescription for this man's idolatrous love of riches, as is evident in his *very sorrowful* response.

18:24 *hardly.* With difficulty. *they that have riches.* Jesus did not deny the right of Christians to make money but warned that fallen man generally abuses wealth to the destruction of

needle's eye, than for a rich man to enter into the
kingdom of God.
26 And they that heard *it* said, Who then can be
saved?
27 And he said, The things which are impossible
with men are possible with God.
28 Then Peter said, Lo, we have left all, and fol-
lowed thee.
29 And he said unto them, Verily I say unto you,
There is no man that hath left house, or parents,
or brethren, or wife, or children, for the kingdom
of God's sake,
30 Who shall not receive manifold more in
this present time, and in the world to come life
everlasting.
31 ¶ Then he took *unto him* the twelve, and said
unto them, Behold, we go up to Jerusalem, and all
things that are written by the prophets concern-
ing the Son of man shall be accomplished.
32 For he shall be delivered unto the Gentiles,
and shall be mocked, and spitefully entreated, and
spitted on:
33 And they shall scourge *him*, and put him to
death: and the third day he shall rise again.
34 And they understood none of these things:
and this saying was hid from them, neither knew
they the things which were spoken.
35 ¶ And it came to pass, that as he was come
nigh unto Jericho, a certain blind man sat by the
way side begging:
36 And hearing the multitude pass by, he asked
what it meant.
37 And they told him, that Jesus of Nazareth pass-
eth by.
38 And he cried, saying, Jesus, *thou* Son of David,
have mercy on me.
39 And they which went before rebuked him, that
he should hold his peace: but he cried so much
the more, *Thou* Son of David, have mercy on me.
40 And Jesus stood, and commanded him to be
brought unto him: and when he was come near,
he asked him,
41 Saying, What wilt thou that I shall do unto thee?
And he said, Lord, that I may receive my sight.
42 And Jesus said unto him, Receive thy sight: thy
faith hath saved thee.
43 And immediately he received his sight, and
followed him, glorifying God: and all the people,
when they saw *it*, gave praise unto God.

CHAPTER 19

AND *Jesus* entered and passed through Jericho.
2 And, behold, *there was* a man named Zac-
chaeus, which was the chief among the publicans,
and he was rich.

his soul, such as by trusting in it or growing proud because of it (Prov. 18:10–11,23; 28:11).

18:26–27 *Who then can be saved?* The disciples understood that if a blessing like money presents such an obstacle to faith and repentance, all mankind is in a desperate situation. *impossible with men . . . possible with God.* Jesus affirmed that no man is able to produce saving faith and repentance in himself (John 3:5–6; 6:44,65; Rom. 8:7) but that God is able to work the miracle of regeneration unto conversion (3:8; Acts 11:18; 13:48; 16:14).

18:29 *Verily.* Truly.

Jesus Foretells His Death a Third Time (18:31–34)

18:31 *all things . . . written by the prophets . . . shall be accomplished.* Christ's mission is the great message of Scripture (24:26–27,44–47), and God's will revealed in His Book cannot fail (16:17).

18:32–33 *spitefully entreated.* Abused, humiliated. *scourge.* Whip. *Gentiles.* The Jews were not alone in killing Christ; Gentiles were not innocent either.

Jesus Heals a Blind Man (18:35–43)

18:38–39 *Son of David.* A title of the messianic king promised in God's covenant with David (see note at 1:32).

18:42 *thy faith hath saved thee.* Even on His way to Jerusalem Jesus willingly and gladly stops to redeem people. The man's faith, a plea for mercy, was enough for him to receive the glorious blessings of salvation from Jesus. The blind man's faith is a sharp contrast to the attitude of the rich ruler, who went away sorrowful because he was unwilling to lean on Jesus for salvation.

18:43 *followed him, glorifying God.* As Jesus, the Son of David prepares to go up and enter Jerusalem, where the glory of God's kingdom awaits Him, He draws weak and helpless individuals to follow him. *glorifying . . . praise unto God.* God's mercy is for the praise of His glory (Eph. 1:6,12,14).

Thoughts for Personal/Family Worship: Chapter 18

1. **In the parable of the Pharisee and the publican, the Pharisee failed to see that he was in need of God's grace. He justified himself and did not lean on God's mercy for justification. The man was self-deceived. What a dangerous place to be! Neither did the rich young ruler lean on Christ for righteousness. He still had not come to an end of his own righteousness. It is the blind beggar who sues for mercy from the great Son of David—and receives it. His prayer is most like that of the publican (vv. 13,38). No wonder he ends up glorifying God (v. 43). Why must we repent of the ways of the Pharisee and the rich ruler and become like a blind beggar if we would be saved by Jesus Christ?**
2. **Salvation from our side is not only difficult, it is impossible. However, what a comfort and pleading ground are Christ's words: "The things which are impossible with men are possible with God" (v. 27). Christ will prove this in the next chapter with Zacchaeus (19:1–10). Why is salvation impossible for man? How does God accomplish the impossible?**

Chapter 19: ***Jesus seeks and saves the publican Zacchaeus, tells the parable of the pounds, enters Jerusalem on a donkey, cleanses the city, and weeps over it.***

Jesus Brings Salvation to Zacchaeus (19:1–10)

19:2 *chief among the publicans.* Not only did he collect taxes but he also commissioned tax collectors throughout Jericho. *he was rich.* Jesus had just warned that the salvation of the rich is humanly impossible (18:25). This brief description reveals

3 And he sought to see Jesus who he was; and could not for the press, because he was little of stature.

4 And he ran before, and climbed up into a sycomore tree to see him: for he was to pass that *way*.

5 And when Jesus came to the place, he looked up, and saw him, and said unto him, Zacchaeus, make haste, and come down; for to day I must abide at thy house.

6 And he made haste, and came down, and received him joyfully.

7 And when they saw *it*, they all murmured, saying, That he was gone to be guest with a man that is a sinner.

8 And Zacchaeus stood, and said unto the Lord; Behold, Lord, the half of my goods I give to the poor; and if I have taken any thing from any man by false accusation, I restore *him* fourfold.

9 And Jesus said unto him, This day is salvation come to this house, forsomuch as he also is a son of Abraham.

10 For the Son of man is come to seek and to save that which was lost.

11 And as they heard these things, he added and spake a parable, because he was nigh to Jerusalem, and because they thought that the kingdom of God should immediately appear.

12 He said therefore, A certain nobleman went into a far country to receive for himself a kingdom, and to return.

13 And he called his ten servants, and delivered them ten pounds, and said unto them, Occupy till I come.

14 But his citizens hated him, and sent a message after him, saying, We will not have this *man* to reign over us.

15 And it came to pass, that when he was returned, having received the kingdom, then he commanded these servants to be called unto him, to whom he had given the money, that he might know how much every man had gained by trading.

16 Then came the first, saying, Lord, thy pound hath gained ten pounds.

17 And he said unto him, Well, thou good servant: because thou hast been faithful in a very little, have thou authority over ten cities.

18 And the second came, saying, Lord, thy pound hath gained five pounds.

19 And he said likewise to him, Be thou also over five cities.

20 And another came, saying, Lord, behold, *here is* thy pound, which I have kept laid up in a napkin:

21 For I feared thee, because thou art an austere man: thou takest up that thou layedst not down, and reapest that thou didst not sow.

22 And he saith unto him, Out of thine own mouth will I judge thee, *thou* wicked servant. Thou knewest that I was an austere man, taking up that I laid not down, and reaping that I did not sow:

23 Wherefore then gavest not thou my money into the bank, that at my coming I might have required mine own with usury?

24 And he said unto them that stood by, Take from him the pound, and give *it* to him that hath ten pounds.

25 (And they said unto him, Lord, he hath ten pounds.)

26 For I say unto you, That unto every one which hath shall be given; and from him that hath not, even that he hath shall be taken away from him.

27 But those mine enemies, which would not that

---

that Zacchaeus likely overcharged people on their taxes.

19:3–4 *press.* Crowd. *climbed up into a sycomore tree.* Not a culturally accepted practice for men, but in order to see Jesus, Zacchaeus was even willing to climb a tree. Luke portrays this powerful man as childlike (*little*, 9:48; 17:2) in the simplicity and urgency of his need for Jesus.

19:5 *he looked up.* Though we are told that Zacchaeus was seeking to see Jesus, Luke records that it was Jesus who saw Zacchaeus. *must abide at thy house.* Jesus again spoke of a divine necessity to His work (see note at 4:43), here implying God's predestination of His meeting with this individual.

19:8 *half of my goods . . . fourfold.* Very costly acts of mercy and repentance, the opposite of the rich young ruler's response to Jesus (18:22–23).

19:9 *son of Abraham.* Not just his physical descendant but one who shared the faith of Abraham and thus also the inheritance of God's covenant (Rom. 4:16–18).

19:10 *Son of man.* The King (see note at 5:24). *seek and to save.* Though Zacchaeus sought Jesus (v. 3), this was because Christ was first seeking Zacchaeus. This explains why this particular rich man was able to do the impossible and be converted (18:25–27): the Lord overcame his pride and greed and instilled within him a desire for Christ and salvation. Jesus' ministry is primarily a mission of forgiveness and mercy (1:77–78).

Parable of the Ten Pounds (19:11–27)

19:11 *thought that the kingdom of God should immediately appear.* As Jesus neared Jerusalem His followers were under the notion that He would usher in the kingdom of God with a show of power against the Roman government. Jesus told the next parable in response to this confusion.

19:12 Jesus did not speak of the immediate coming of His kingdom but of His imminent death, resurrection, and ascension into heaven in order *to receive for himself a kingdom* at the Father's right hand.

19:13 *Occupy.* Trade, do business with. The lord expects his servants to realize a profit from the wealth he has entrusted to them. *ten pounds.* Each mina was worth one hundred denarii, the wages of one hundred days for a laborer.

19:16–19 *ten pounds . . . ten cities . . . five pounds . . . five cities.* The lord found two of the servants to be *good* stewards of what he had entrusted to them, though with differing degrees of profit, and rewarded each, proportionately to his work, from the great wealth of his kingdom.

19:20 *napkin.* Cloth, handkerchief.

19:21 The third servant's unfaithfulness stemmed from his lack of trust in the lord's goodness and righteousness, resulting in slavish fear.

19:23 *usury.* Interest on money lent. The lord expected at

I should reign over them, bring hither, and slay
them before me.
28 ¶ And when he had thus spoken, he went be-
fore, ascending up to Jerusalem.
29 And it came to pass, when he was come nigh to
Bethphage and Bethany, at the mount called *the
mount* of Olives, he sent two of his disciples,
30 Saying, Go ye into the village over against *you*;
in the which at your entering ye shall find a colt
tied, whereon yet never man sat: loose him, and
bring *him hither*.
31 And if any man ask you, Why do ye loose *him*?
thus shall ye say unto him, Because the Lord hath
need of him.
32 And they that were sent went their way, and
found even as he had said unto them.
33 And as they were loosing the colt, the owners
thereof said unto them, Why loose ye the colt?
34 And they said, The Lord hath need of him.
35 And they brought him to Jesus: and they cast
their garments upon the colt, and they set Jesus
thereon.
36 And as he went, they spread their clothes in
the way.
37 And when he was come nigh, even now at the
descent of the mount of Olives, the whole multi-
tude of the disciples began to rejoice and praise
God with a loud voice for all the mighty works
that they had seen;
38 Saying, Blessed *be* the King that cometh in the
name of the Lord: peace in heaven, and glory in
the highest.
39 And some of the Pharisees from among the
multitude said unto him, Master, rebuke thy
disciples.
40 And he answered and said unto them, I tell
you that, if these should hold their peace, the
stones would immediately cry out.
41 ¶ And when he was come near, he beheld the
city, and wept over it,
42 Saying, If thou hadst known, even thou, at
least in this thy day, the things *which belong* unto
thy peace! but now they are hid from thine eyes.
43 For the days shall come upon thee, that thine
enemies shall cast a trench about thee, and com-
pass thee round, and keep thee in on every side,
44 And shall lay thee even with the ground, and
thy children within thee; and they shall not leave
in thee one stone upon another; because thou
knewest not the time of thy visitation.
45 And he went into the temple, and began to cast
out them that sold therein, and them that bought;
46 Saying unto them, It is written, My house is
the house of prayer: but ye have made it a den of
thieves.
47 And he taught daily in the temple. But the
chief priests and the scribes and the chief of the
people sought to destroy him,
48 And could not find what they might do: for all
the people were very attentive to hear him.

---

least some minimal return on his investment.

19:27 The citizens are counted as *enemies* of Jesus because they refused His rule (v. 14). People owe their allegiance to Christ, though He is ascended to heaven and physically absent from earth, for He is their rightful King.

IN JERUSALEM (19:28—24:53)

Jesus Enters Jerusalem (19:28–48)

19:29 *Bethphage and Bethany.* The last two cities before travelers would enter into Jerusalem.

19:30 *colt.* This narrative fulfills Old Testament prophecy of the coming King (Zech. 9:9).

19:31–34 *the Lord hath need of him.* It is unclear whether Jesus had made these preparations beforehand or whether this took place by divine providence. Regardless, the disciples repeated the exact words Jesus had told them to say, and these words were all the owners needed to hear.

19:41 *wept over it.* Though Jerusalem appears joyful in accepting this king, Jesus knew the people's hearts and understood that they did not grasp the truth of His person and work.

19:42 *hid from thine eyes.* Spiritual blindness dooms sinners (4:18; 6:39,41; 11:34–35).

19:43–44 *compass thee round.* Surround or besiege you. Jesus foretold the destruction of Jerusalem by Titus in AD 70. *thy visitation.* The Lord their God had visited them (1:68,78; 7:16), but they had rejected Him, bringing upon themselves divine judgment through the Roman armies.

19:46 God gave Israel the temple as a place for prayerful and repentant seeking of God's grace (*house of prayer*; Isa. 56:7), but they abused ritual worship as a covering for sin (*den of thieves*; Jer. 7:11).

19:47 *taught daily.* Jesus continued His ministry in the temple despite His fast approaching death (20:1), showing what a high priority He placed upon His prophetic work (4:14–15,43–44).

19:48 The religious elite *could not find* grounds to destroy Jesus and so tried to trap Him with His own words as He spoke publicly (20:1–47).

Thoughts for Personal/Family Worship: Chapter 19

1. **A divine purpose lay behind everything Christ did. The truth must have sounded very precious to Zacchaeus when Jesus said to him, "I must abide at thy house" (v. 5). Nothing will fail of whatever Christ has planned and purposed to do for the salvation of each sinner He has chosen. How can this instill within us confidence to share the gospel with the worst of sinners?**
2. **The man who hid his pound explained, "I feared thee, because thou art an austere man" (v. 21). Sadly, this man betrayed a deficient, rebellious view of God, which he used as an excuse to live as he thought appropriate. We will act in accordance with our real view of God. How will a view of God as harsh and unfair lead us into sin? How will an experiential knowledge of His love and righteousness lead us to a life of faithfulness?**
3. **Jesus said with tears, "If thou hadst known . . . the things which belong unto thy peace!" (v. 42) Despite the welcome the people gave Christ as He entered the city, Christ saw through their actions to what they were truly about. The people by and large did not understand their need of a Savior to propitiate God's anger over their sins,**

CHAPTER 20

AND it came to pass, *that* on one of those days, as
he taught the people in the temple, and preached
the gospel, the chief priests and the scribes came
upon *him* with the elders,
2 And spake unto him, saying, Tell us, by what
authority doest thou these things? or who is he
that gave thee this authority?
3 And he answered and said unto them, I will also
ask you one thing; and answer me:
4 The baptism of John, was it from heaven, or of
men?
5 And they reasoned with themselves, saying, If
we shall say, From heaven; he will say, Why then
believed ye him not?
6 But and if we say, Of men; all the people will
stone us: for they be persuaded that John was a
prophet.
7 And they answered, that they could not tell
whence *it was*.
8 And Jesus said unto them, Neither tell I you by
what authority I do these things.
9 Then began he to speak to the people this par-
able; A certain man planted a vineyard, and let it
forth to husbandmen, and went into a far country
for a long time.
10 And at the season he sent a servant to the
husbandmen, that they should give him of the
fruit of the vineyard: but the husbandmen beat
him, and sent *him* away empty.
11 And again he sent another servant: and they
beat him also, and entreated *him* shamefully, and
sent *him* away empty.
12 And again he sent a third: and they wounded
him also, and cast *him* out.
13 Then said the lord of the vineyard, What shall
I do? I will send my beloved son: it may be they
will reverence *him* when they see him.
14 But when the husbandmen saw him, they
reasoned among themselves, saying, This is the
heir: come, let us kill him, that the inheritance
may be ours.
15 So they cast him out of the vineyard, and killed
him. What therefore shall the lord of the vineyard
do unto them?
16 He shall come and destroy these husbandmen,
and shall give the vineyard to others. And when
they heard *it*, they said, God forbid.
17 And he beheld them, and said, What is this
then that is written, The stone which the build-
ers rejected, the same is become the head of the
corner?
18 Whosoever shall fall upon that stone shall be
broken; but on whomsoever it shall fall, it will
grind him to powder.
19 ¶ And the chief priests and the scribes the
same hour sought to lay hands on him; and they
feared the people: for they perceived that he had
spoken this parable against them.
20 And they watched *him*, and sent forth spies,
which should feign themselves just men, that they
might take hold of his words, that so they might
deliver him unto the power and authority of the
governor.
21 And they asked him, saying, Master, we know
that thou sayest and teachest rightly, neither ac-
ceptest thou the person *of any*, but teachest the
way of God truly:
22 Is it lawful for us to give tribute unto Caesar,
or no?
23 But he perceived their craftiness, and said unto
them, Why tempt ye me?
24 Shew me a penny. Whose image and super-
scription hath it? They answered and said, Caesar's.

justify them before God, and consecrate them to God. Do you know the things that belong to your peace? Why do you need Jesus?

Jesus and the Authorities in Conflict (20:1—21:4)

Chapter 20: Jesus responds to the challenges He receives from the religious leaders, all the while asserting His authority as God's Son.

20:1 *taught the people . . . preached the gospel.* In spite of the growing hostility Jesus still devoted Himself to His prophetic calling to communicate the truth (19:47).

20:2–8 *by what authority.* The first attempt of Christ's enemies to trap Him in His words resulted in failure. Christ turned the question around to expose their lack of spiritual authority that arose from their hypocrisy and fear of man instead of their receiving messengers authorized by God (*from heaven*).

20:9–16 This is the first *parable* of the last section of Luke's gospel, spoken in light of the challenge to His authority and His upcoming death. It is strikingly simple, yet profound, covering Israel's whole history, including the rejection of the prophets, the rejection of Jesus, and finally the judgment.

20:9–10 *vineyard.* The people of God, from whom He seeks the fruit of righteousness (Isa. 5:1–7). *husbandmen.* Tenant farmers.

20:11 *entreated . . . shamefully.* Dishonored, humiliated.

20:13 *I will send my beloved son.* Jesus was asserting that He has a unique identity in relation to God (3:22; 9:35) and comes as One sent with authority from God to do His work.

20:14 *that the inheritance may be ours.* The murder of Jesus was motivated by a desire to escape the authority of the Lord (Ps. 2:1–3) and seize His authority for themselves (Matt. 27:18).

20:17–18 *stone which the builders rejected.* The rejection of Jesus by the religious leaders was not only condemned but prophesied (Ps. 118:22), fulfilling God's plan to make Him the cornerstone (*head of the corner*) of His work (Eph. 2:20; 1 Peter 2:6–8). *fall upon this stone . . . powder.* Christ and His kingdom will destroy those who stumble over Him in unbelief (Isa. 8:14–15; Dan. 2:34–35,44–45).

20:20–22 The second challenge to Jesus, given by *spies*, was an attempt to trap Him between the options of setting Himself against Rome's authority or provoking the hostility of His fellow Jews.

20:23 *tempt.* Put to the test.

20:24 *penny.* Denarius. The coin was stamped with the emperor's picture and titles (*image and superscription*).

25 And he said unto them, Render therefore unto
Caesar the things which be Caesar's, and unto
God the things which be God's.
26 And they could not take hold of his words be-
fore the people: and they marvelled at his answer,
and held their peace.
27 ¶ Then came to *him* certain of the Sadducees,
which deny that there is any resurrection; and
they asked him,
28 Saying, Master, Moses wrote unto us, If any
man's brother die, having a wife, and he die
without children, that his brother should take his
wife, and raise up seed unto his brother.
29 There were therefore seven brethren: and the
first took a wife, and died without children.
30 And the second took her to wife, and he died
childless.
31 And the third took her; and in like manner the
seven also: and they left no children, and died.
32 Last of all the woman died also.
33 Therefore in the resurrection whose wife of
them is she? for seven had her to wife.
34 And Jesus answering said unto them, The
children of this world marry, and are given in
marriage:
35 But they which shall be accounted worthy to
obtain that world, and the resurrection from the
dead, neither marry, nor are given in marriage:
36 Neither can they die any more: for they are
equal unto the angels; and are the children of
God, being the children of the resurrection.
37 Now that the dead are raised, even Moses
shewed at the bush, when he calleth the Lord the
God of Abraham, and the God of Isaac, and the
God of Jacob.
38 For he is not a God of the dead, but of the
living: for all live unto him.
39 ¶ Then certain of the scribes answering said,
Master, thou hast well said.
40 And after that they durst not ask him any *ques-
tion at all.*
41 And he said unto them, How say they that
Christ is David's son?
42 And David himself saith in the book of
Psalms, The LORD said unto my Lord, Sit thou on
my right hand,
43 Till I make thine enemies thy footstool.
44 David therefore calleth him Lord, how is he
then his son?
45 ¶ Then in the audience of all the people he
said unto his disciples,
46 Beware of the scribes, which desire to walk in
long robes, and love greetings in the markets, and
the highest seats in the synagogues, and the chief
rooms at feasts;
47 Which devour widows' houses, and for a shew
make long prayers: the same shall receive greater
damnation.

20:25 *Render.* Give back. *unto Caesar . . . and unto God.* Civil rulers should receive respect, taxes, and civil submission, but God should receive worship and obedience in all of life (Rom. 12:1–2; 13:1–7).

20:27–33 The third challenge came from the *Sadducees,* a party of the Jews associated with the priests (Acts 4:1; 5:17) and often opposed to the Pharisees in their beliefs (Acts 23:6–8). They attempted to trap Jesus between the options of looking foolish for holding to alleged absurdities in the doctrine of the *resurrection* or of denying a cardinal doctrine held by the Pharisees and many of the people.

20:28 *take his wife, and raise up seed.* The Old Testament institution of levirate marriage was designed to continue the name and inheritance of the deceased and to protect the widow (Deut. 25:5; Ruth 4:1–12).

20:34 *children of this world.* Literally, "sons of this age," an idiom for people living in the present age, as opposed to the future age of glory and immortality.

20:35–36 The Sadducees failed to understand the differences between this age and the one to come, when institutions of the present creation, such as marriage, would become obsolete.

20:37–38 *even Moses shewed at the bush, when he calleth.* Jesus did not quote the speech of Moses but the speech of God (Ex. 3:6), showing that He regarded Moses to be the author of Exodus. *God of Abraham . . . of the living.* The Sadducees failed to understand the implications of the Scriptures, for God's statement that He was still the God of Abraham centuries after Abraham had died implied the continuing life of the patriarchs after death and their reception of the promised inheritance at the resurrection.

20:40 *durst not.* Did not dare.

20:41–44 A final challenge now came from Christ, ultimately answering their question of His authority (v. 2) by pressing them to consider the identity of the *Christ.* King David called Him *my Lord* (Ps. 110:1–2), implying that the Son of David, though human, was also a person far greater than any man. Jesus had already been heralded as the Son of David (18:38–39), and the people rejoiced in Him as the coming king (19:38), so He was clearly asserting His own divine authority and calling men to repent of their questioning and submit to His Lordship.

20:46–47 Jesus warned against the false religiosity, pride, greed, and lack of compassion in the Pharisees. *chief rooms.* Most honored places at the table.

Thoughts for Personal/Family Worship: Chapter 20

1. **The religious leaders asked "by what authority doest thou these things?" (v. 2), but they should have asked this question of themselves. It is important to be under the proper authority, and the irony is that Christ was the perfectly obedient Son of the Father, while these religious leaders were rejecting His authority. Along with it they were rejecting God's Word, His truth, and His Son. People can seem to be religious and yet reject God's rule over them and God's Son as Lord.**
2. **Just as Jesus portrayed the landowner saying of his son "they will reverence him" (v. 13), so the Lord has every right to expect that we will worship and obey His Son. Psalm 2 directs us to "Kiss the Son, lest he be angry, and ye perish from the way. . . . Blessed are all they that put their trust in him" (Ps. 2:12). Do you reverence Christ? Do you bow to His authority in all areas of your life? Or do you question His right to rule you and rebel against His Word?**

CHAPTER 21

AND he looked up, and saw the rich men casting
their gifts into the treasury.
2 And he saw also a certain poor widow casting in
thither two mites.
3 And he said, Of a truth I say unto you, that this
poor widow hath cast in more than they all:
4 For all these have of their abundance cast in
unto the offerings of God: but she of her penury
hath cast in all the living that she had.
5 ¶ And as some spake of the temple, how it was
adorned with goodly stones and gifts, he said,
6 *As for* these things which ye behold, the days
will come, in the which there shall not be left
one stone upon another, that shall not be thrown
down.
7 And they asked him, saying, Master, but when
shall these things be? and what sign *will there be*
when these things shall come to pass?
8 And he said, Take heed that ye be not deceived:
for many shall come in my name, saying, I am
Christ; and the time draweth near: go ye not
therefore after them.
9 But when ye shall hear of wars and commo-
tions, be not terrified: for these things must first
come to pass; but the end *is* not by and by.
10 Then said he unto them, Nation shall rise
against nation, and kingdom against kingdom:
11 And great earthquakes shall be in divers places,
and famines, and pestilences; and fearful sights
and great signs shall there be from heaven.
12 But before all these, they shall lay their hands
on you, and persecute *you*, delivering *you* up to
the synagogues, and into prisons, being brought
before kings and rulers for my name's sake.
13 And it shall turn to you for a testimony.
14 Settle *it* therefore in your hearts, not to medi-
tate before what ye shall answer:
15 For I will give you a mouth and wisdom,
which all your adversaries shall not be able to
gainsay nor resist.
16 And ye shall be betrayed both by parents, and
brethren, and kinsfolks, and friends; and *some* of
you shall they cause to be put to death.
17 And ye shall be hated of all *men* for my name's
sake.
18 But there shall not an hair of your head perish.
19 In your patience possess ye your souls.
20 And when ye shall see Jerusalem compassed
with armies, then know that the desolation
thereof is nigh.
21 Then let them which are in Judaea flee to the
mountains; and let them which are in the midst
of it depart out; and let not them that are in the
countries enter thereinto.
22 For these be the days of vengeance, that all

---

3. The gospel of Christ crucified is a stumbling block or plain foolishness to the natural man. Paul asserts this in 1 Cor. 1:23. Has God enabled you to see how necessary and suitable Christ is for your sinful soul, as well as how precious and beautiful He is for every need and circumstance of your life? How poor you are if you are seeking to build on your own foundation. Submit to God. Forsake your own righteousness. Realize that everything you try apart from Christ will only condemn you, both now and forever. On the other hand, to those who believe, Christ is precious (1 Peter 2:7).

Chapter 21: ***Jesus commends the poor widow's gift to the treasury and prophesies the destruction of the temple and the end of the world, urging vigilance.***

21:2 *thither.* There. *two mites.* This was the least valuable coin (Greek, *lepton*) of the currency at this time, worth only an eighth of a farthing, less than one hundredth of a day's wages (12:6,59). To most this would have been a negligible amount.

21:3 *cast in more than they all.* Jesus weighs our giving according to the thoughts and intents of our heart and our gift's proportion to what we have left over (2 Cor. 8:5,12; 9:7), so His judgment and reward of each person's giving may surprise us (13:30).

21:4 *penury.* Poverty.

Jesus Teaches concerning the End (21:5–38)

21:5 *adorned with goodly stones and gifts.* Made beautiful with lovely stones and offerings. The second temple was exquisite, being built and refurbished from 19 BC until about AD 63.

21:8 *Take heed.* Look out, pay attention. *go ye not . . . after them.* Do not be led astray by false teachers and self-proclaimed Christs (17:23; 1 John 2:18; 4:1).

21:9 *commotions.* Instability, disorder. *the end is not by and by.* We should not look for Christ to return immediately after various *wars* and troubles, for they occur throughout this age.

21:11 *divers.* Various, different.

21:13 *turn to you for a testimony.* Persecution will result in opportunities to speak as Christ's witnesses.

21:15 *mouth and wisdom.* The ability to speak for the truth when unbelievers contradict it (*gainsay*). Jesus had just exhibited both of these characteristics against His adversaries (20:1–47). The language He uses here is reminiscent of God's promise to Moses for his prophetic work (Ex. 4:11–12). It finds direct fulfillment in the apostles and other specially gifted evangelists (Acts 4:8,13; 6:10) but also has an indirect application to the Spirit's assistance for all believers who have occasion to speak for Christ (Titus 1:9; 1 Peter 3:14–15; 4:10–11,14).

21:16–17 *hated of all men for my name's sake.* The disciple of Jesus cannot expect better treatment than Jesus himself received.

21:18 *not an hair of your head perish.* Though persecuted even to the death (v. 16), true disciples will ultimately lose nothing (8:35–37).

21:19 *patience.* Endurance by faith and hope (Rom. 2:7; 5:3; Col. 1:11). *possess ye your souls.* Though they lose earthly goods for Christ, they will gain real life by persevering in the faith (9:24).

21:20 *when ye shall see.* Jesus foretold that when the Roman *armies* surrounded (*compassed*) the city of *Jerusalem* (AD 70), this was the sign that the destruction falling on Israel was near (*nigh*). This was the *desolation* of God's holy temple after the death of the Messiah (13:35; Dan. 9:26–27; Matt. 24:15), decisively ending the priestly ceremonies of the law (Heb. 8:13).

21:21–24 The coming tribulation ushered in by the Roman

THE LORD'S SUPPER

Holy Baptism and the Lord's Supper were instituted by the Lord Jesus Christ for use in His church under the gospel. Hence, they are called "dominical sacraments," in distinction from rites later declared to be sacraments in various branches of the church, such as marriage or ordination to church office. The Eastern churches claim nine sacraments; the Western church, seven. Since the Reformation, Protestant churches acknowledge only the two instituted by Christ.

In both sacraments there are earthly elements to be consecrated, administered, and received as signs and seals of the promises of God proclaimed in the gospel. As signs, they direct our faith to the unseen realities they represent. As seals, they are a visible confirmation of the truth and certainty of the promises connected with them.

As an ordinance of Christ the Lord's Supper is a means of grace, subordinate to and dependent upon the faithful preaching of the Word. The Holy Spirit uses preaching of the Word to work faith in our hearts. He confirms or strengthens that faith through the administration of the sacraments. So Christians "grow in grace, and in the knowledge of Christ" (2 Peter 3:18) by hearing the Word with faith and receiving the sacraments in faith.

To rid the Lord's Supper of the many corruptions attached to it in the pre-Reformation church, the Reformers insisted that it be administered strictly according to the institution, command, and example of Christ. The church is to use it as He intended and to do what He did in administering it, and nothing more.

Hence, the elements are common bread and wine. They are consecrated by reading "the words of institution" (Matt. 26:26–30; 1 Cor. 11:23–29) and offering a prayer of thanksgiving for the death of Christ and all its benefits as His finished work of atonement for sin. The bread is broken and distributed to the communicants, and afterward the cup. The action of the sacrament is accompanied by the Word, in the form of an invitation to the godly to partake; a warning to the ungodly not to partake; an exposition of the meaning and right use of the sacrament; and, after communion, an exhortation to believers to profit from it and, finally, acts of praise and thanksgiving.

In the Lord's Supper believers remember Christ, His death on the cross, and all its saving benefits. *Second*, they lift up their hearts to the risen and ascended Christ in heaven, there to be nourished with His crucified body and shed blood. *Third*, through the communion of the Holy Spirit, the ties that bind them as one body in Christ are deepened and strengthened. All join in renewing their covenant with God in Christ and with one another as His church. *Finally*, the sacrament must be continued in the church until Christ comes again in glory.

Concerning the manner in which Christ is received in the sacrament, one error is to locate His presence in the elements of bread and wine, which gives rise to superstition and idolatry. The ancient church erred in regarding the Lord's Supper as a further sacrifice for sin, meant to augment or continue the work of Christ on the cross. Under the gospel, "there is no more offering for sin" (Heb. 10:18). Still others deny any presence of Christ in the Holy Supper, holding that it is only a memorial feast.

Another error is to assume that the Lord's Supper is appointed only for people who possess full assurance of salvation or lead exemplary lives of personal holiness and victory over sin. In humility, some Christians feel they are not worthy to partake. This error has been mistakenly attributed to the Puritans, but the Puritan divines at the Westminster Assembly were clearly of a different mind. They insisted that "promises are made, and this sacrament is appointed, for the relief even of weak and doubting Christians." Such a Christian "is to bewail his unbelief, and labour to have his doubts resolved; and so doing, he may and ought to come to the Lord's supper, that he may be further strengthened" (Westminster Larger Catechism, Q. 172).

things which are written may be fulfilled.
23 But woe unto them that are with child, and to
them that give suck, in those days! for there shall
be great distress in the land, and wrath upon this
people.
24 And they shall fall by the edge of the sword,
and shall be led away captive into all nations: and
Jerusalem shall be trodden down of the Gentiles,
until the times of the Gentiles be fulfilled.
25 ¶ And there shall be signs in the sun, and in
the moon, and in the stars; and upon the earth
distress of nations, with perplexity; the sea and
the waves roaring;
26 Men's hearts failing them for fear, and for
looking after those things which are coming
on the earth: for the powers of heaven shall be
shaken.
27 And then shall they see the Son of man com-
ing in a cloud with power and great glory.
28 And when these things begin to come to pass,
then look up, and lift up your heads; for your re-
demption draweth nigh.
29 And he spake to them a parable; Behold the fig
tree, and all the trees;
30 When they now shoot forth, ye see and know
of your own selves that summer is now nigh at
hand.
31 So likewise ye, when ye see these things come
to pass, know ye that the kingdom of God is nigh
at hand.
32 Verily I say unto you, This generation shall not
pass away, till all be fulfilled.
33 Heaven and earth shall pass away: but my
words shall not pass away.
34 ¶ And take heed to yourselves, lest at any time
your hearts be overcharged with surfeiting, and
drunkenness, and cares of this life, and *so* that day
come upon you unawares.
35 For as a snare shall it come on all them that
dwell on the face of the whole earth.
36 Watch ye therefore, and pray always, that
ye may be accounted worthy to escape all these
things that shall come to pass, and to stand before
the Son of man.
37 And in the day time he was teaching in the
temple; and at night he went out, and abode in
the mount that is called *the mount* of Olives.
38 And all the people came early in the morning
to him in the temple, for to hear him.

CHAPTER 22

Now the feast of unleavened bread drew nigh,
which is called the Passover.

---

army would be devastating, requiring disciples of Christ in *Judaea* to flee without delay for their lives, but it would also mark a change in God's dealing with the nations (*times of the Gentiles*).

21:25–26 Jesus subtly transitions from the destruction of Jerusalem to the end of the age, marked by the cosmic disruptions of the day of the Lord (Isa. 13:10; 24:23; 34:4).

21:27 *see the Son of man coming in a cloud.* Jesus Christ will return visibly *with power and great glory* (9:26; 17:24) to judge His enemies and reign over all things forever, as was prophesied (Dan. 7:13–14).

21:28 *redemption.* Though Christ accomplished the purchase of redemption in His first coming and death (1:68; Mark 10:45; Rom. 3:24–25; Eph. 1:7), He will complete the application of redemption at His second coming (2:38; Rom. 8:23; Eph. 1:14; 4:30). *draweth nigh.* Comes near. *lift up your heads.* Believers can rejoice at the coming of Jesus with hope, not terror.

21:29–31 *fig tree.* Often a symbol for the condition of Israel (see note at 13:6–9). The *parable* speaks of recognizing the signs that a coming event or season is near (*nigh*).

21:32 *This generation.* As we can see from Gen. 2:4; 5:1; 6:9, and so on, God's purposes are ordered according to certain generation markers. The generation of Jesus Christ is announced in Matt. 1:1, and this generation will not be replaced by another until all is complete.

21:33 *Heaven and earth shall pass away.* Christ's coming will usher in a new creation (Isa. 65:17; 2 Peter 3:13; Rev. 21:1–2). *not pass away.* Christ's *words* are eternal truth, equal in authority to the Old Testament Scriptures (16:17).

21:34–36 *take heed . . . Watch.* This parable focuses on the need for vigilance and alertness in preparation for the coming of the kingdom. *overcharged with surfeiting.* Weighed down by sickness brought on by overeating or drinking, a picture of the spiritual stupor and weakness produced by sin. *unawares.* Unexpectedly (1 Thess. 5:1–10).

21:37 *teaching in the temple.* Knowing that His death would soon end His earthly ministry of public teaching, Christ busied Himself to fulfill His prophetic calling in Israel (19:47; 20:1).

Thoughts for Personal/Family Worship: Chapter 21

1. **Little could this widow have known that her two mites would go down in history as an example, inspiration, and challenge to untold millions. Of course, without Christ discerning her heart and speaking the truth, we would never have known about her gift. What an event it will be when the triune God will unveil to the watching world on judgment day the innermost thoughts of the heart (8:17). Insofar as the Spirit has revealed your own heart to you, what will that day disclose about you?**
2. **Christ is coming again. If the desolation that fell upon Jerusalem called for fleeing without delay to safety, how much more does the judgment of the Son of Man call for us to flee without delay to Christ's saving mercy. Will judgment day find you safe in Jesus? Christ does not want people to be deceived (v. 8), but neither does He desire for believers to be terrified (v. 9). The anticipation of Christ's return should move Christians to lift up their heads with hope (v. 28). He particularly calls us to live in constant watchfulness and spiritual alertness (vv. 34–36). How does the doctrine of Christ's return affect you?**

Jesus' Last Supper, Betrayal, and Arrest (22:1—23:56)

Chapter 22: ***Under the cloud of scheming and betrayal, Jesus celebrates the Passover with His disciples and institutes the Lord's Supper, after which He prays in Gethsemane, is arrested and taken to the high priest, and is denied by Peter.***

The Last Supper (22:1–46)

22:1 *feast of unleavened bread . . . Passover.* Together they

2 And the chief priests and scribes sought how
they might kill him; for they feared the people.
3 ¶ Then entered Satan into Judas surnamed
Iscariot, being of the number of the twelve.
4 And he went his way, and communed with the
chief priests and captains, how he might betray
him unto them.
5 And they were glad, and covenanted to give
him money.
6 And he promised, and sought opportunity to
betray him unto them in the absence of the multi-
tude.
7 ¶ Then came the day of unleavened bread,
when the passover must be killed.
8 And he sent Peter and John, saying, Go and pre-
pare us the passover, that we may eat.
9 And they said unto him, Where wilt thou that
we prepare?
10 And he said unto them, Behold, when ye are
entered into the city, there shall a man meet you,
bearing a pitcher of water; follow him into the
house where he entereth in.
11 And ye shall say unto the goodman of the
house, The Master saith unto thee, Where is the
guestchamber, where I shall eat the passover with
my disciples?
12 And he shall shew you a large upper room
furnished: there make ready.
13 And they went, and found as he had said unto
them: and they made ready the passover.
14 And when the hour was come, he sat down,
and the twelve apostles with him.
15 And he said unto them, With desire I have de-
sired to eat this passover with you before I suffer:
16 For I say unto you, I will not any more eat
thereof, until it be fulfilled in the kingdom of God.
17 And he took the cup, and gave thanks, and
said, Take this, and divide *it* among yourselves:
18 For I say unto you, I will not drink of the fruit
of the vine, until the kingdom of God shall come.
19 ¶ And he took bread, and gave thanks, and
brake *it*, and gave unto them, saying, This is my
body which is given for you: this do in remem-
brance of me.
20 Likewise also the cup after supper, saying, This
cup *is* the new testament in my blood, which is
shed for you.
21 ¶ But, behold, the hand of him that betrayeth
me *is* with me on the table.
22 And truly the Son of man goeth, as it was
determined: but woe unto that man by whom he
is betrayed!
23 And they began to enquire among themselves,
which of them it was that should do this thing.
24 ¶ And there was also a strife among them,
which of them should be accounted the greatest.
25 And he said unto them, The kings of the Gen-
tiles exercise lordship over them; and they that ex-
ercise authority upon them are called benefactors.
26 But ye *shall* not *be* so: but he that is greatest
among you, let him be as the younger; and he that
is chief, as he that doth serve.
27 For whether *is* greater, he that sitteth at meat,
or he that serveth? *is* not he that sitteth at meat?
but I am among you as he that serveth.
28 Ye are they which have continued with me in
my temptations.
29 And I appoint unto you a kingdom, as my
Father hath appointed unto me;
30 That ye may eat and drink at my table in my
kingdom, and sit on thrones judging the twelve
tribes of Israel.
31 ¶ And the Lord said, Simon, Simon, behold,
Satan hath desired *to have* you, that he may sift
you as wheat:
32 But I have prayed for thee, that thy faith fail

---

commemorated the deliverance from Egypt (Ex. 12:1–20). *nigh*. Near.

22:3 *entered Satan into Judas.* Satan possessed Judas, one of the *twelve* apostles, whose close relation to Jesus highlights the pain of the betrayal even more. Not only did earthly powers rage against the Lord's Anointed (Ps. 2:1–3), but so did spiritual powers (vv. 31,53; 4:2–13; 8:12; 10:18; 11:18; 13:16).

22:4 *communed.* Talked together.

22:7 *the passover must be killed.* The lamb must be slaughtered for the Passover, and so by divine necessity the fulfillment of Jesus' ministry and His sacrifice for sins were at hand (see note at 4:43).

22:11 *goodman.* Master.

22:15 *With desire I have desired.* A strong phrase in the original Greek, conveying deep intensity of desire. In light of His coming death these words of Jesus are sweet and comforting, for Jesus was not a reluctant *Passover* lamb; instead, He delighted to do His Father's will and bring back sinners to God (Heb. 12:2).

22:16 *not any more eat.* While abrogating Passover, Jesus instituted something new in its place, the Lord's Supper, which looks forward to the day when Christ will dine with His people in the *kingdom of God* (1 Cor. 11:20,26).

22:19–20 *This is my body.* Jesus is speaking not literally but metaphorically. *remembrance.* While the Lord's Supper is certainly more than a memorial service, it is not less. *new testament in my blood.* By His death Jesus instituted the new covenant, which promises inner sanctification and covenantal knowledge of God based upon forgiveness of sins (Jer. 31:31–34). *shed for you.* Jesus speaks of His substitutionary death, the only necessary and final sacrifice to be made. Like the Passover lamb, He died so that His people might escape God's judgment and live.

22:22 *as it was determined.* The events of Christ's suffering and death were predestined by God (Acts 2:23; 4:28; 1 Peter 1:19–20). *woe unto that man.* Jesus affirmed both divine determination and human responsibility. Though Jesus' death was ordained, this does not remove the responsibility of Judas in bearing his guilt.

22:27 *whether.* Which (of the two). *sitteth at meat.* Reclines at a meal. *I am among you as he that serveth.* While the disciples argued about greatness, Jesus set an example of humility and servanthood (John 13:1–17). His death was the ultimate display of humble service (Mark 10:45; Phil. 2:3–8).

22:31 *Satan.* The Devil aimed to destroy Christ and His

not: and when thou art converted, strengthen thy
brethren.
33 And he said unto him, Lord, I am ready to go
with thee, both into prison, and to death.
34 And he said, I tell thee, Peter, the cock shall not
crow this day, before that thou shalt thrice deny
that thou knowest me.
35 And he said unto them, When I sent you with-
out purse, and scrip, and shoes, lacked ye any
thing? And they said, Nothing.
36 Then said he unto them, But now, he that hath
a purse, let him take *it*, and likewise *his* scrip: and
he that hath no sword, let him sell his garment,
and buy one.
37 For I say unto you, that this that is written
must yet be accomplished in me, And he was
reckoned among the transgressors: for the things
concerning me have an end.
38 And they said, Lord, behold, here *are* two
swords. And he said unto them, It is enough.
39 ¶ And he came out, and went, as he was wont,
to the mount of Olives; and his disciples also fol-
lowed him.
40 And when he was at the place, he said unto
them, Pray that ye enter not into temptation.
41 And he was withdrawn from them about a
stone's cast, and kneeled down, and prayed,
42 Saying, Father, if thou be willing, remove this
cup from me: nevertheless not my will, but thine,
be done.
43 And there appeared an angel unto him from
heaven, strengthening him.
44 And being in an agony he prayed more ear-
nestly: and his sweat was as it were great drops of
blood falling down to the ground.
45 And when he rose up from prayer, and was
come to his disciples, he found them sleeping for
sorrow,
46 And said unto them, Why sleep ye? rise and
pray, lest ye enter into temptation.
47 ¶ And while he yet spake, behold a multitude,
and he that was called Judas, one of the twelve, went
before them, and drew near unto Jesus to kiss him.
48 But Jesus said unto him, Judas, betrayest thou
the Son of man with a kiss?
49 When they which were about him saw what
would follow, they said unto him, Lord, shall we
smite with the sword?
50 ¶ And one of them smote the servant of the
high priest, and cut off his right ear.
51 And Jesus answered and said, Suffer ye thus
far. And he touched his ear, and healed him.
52 Then Jesus said unto the chief priests, and
captains of the temple, and the elders, which were
come to him, Be ye come out, as against a thief,
with swords and staves?
53 When I was daily with you in the temple, ye
stretched forth no hands against me: but this is
your hour, and the power of darkness.
54 ¶ Then took they him, and led *him*, and

apostles (22:3). *desired.* Demanded. *you.* The plural form refers to all the Twelve.

22:32 *prayed.* Christ preserves His people by His intercession from completely and finally falling away (Rom. 8:34; Heb. 7:25), praying for the *faith* of each individual Christian (*thee* is singular). *art converted.* Turn back—not referring to Peter's initial conversion but to his restoration following a great fall. Christ was certain that His prayer would obtain effective grace for Peter; notice Christ's reference to *when* (not if) Peter turns. *strengthen thy brethren.* Believers restored and repentant after falling into sin serve God by helping others turn to the Lord (Ps. 51:12–13).

22:33 *I am ready.* Peter saw himself as strong, failing to believe Christ's warning.

22:35–36 *scrip.* Bag. *sell his garment, and buy.* Since there was not time for the disciples to purchase weapons, it is clear that Jesus was speaking metaphorically to warn them of the coming danger.

22:37 *this that is written must yet be accomplished.* It is necessary that the predictions of the Scriptures come to complete fulfillment (*end*). Jesus died not only as a result of the sins of Satan and Judas but more fundamentally on the basis of God's will. *reckoned among the transgressors.* Counted as a lawbreaker when God placed the guilt of sinners upon the suffering Servant and punished Him in their place (Isa. 53:12).

22:38 *two swords.* The disciples misunderstood Jesus' words, thinking He spoke of a literal sword (vv. 50–51). *It is enough.* He was dismissing the disciples' thoughtless comment.

22:39 *wont.* Accustomed.

22:40 *Pray.* Luke emphasizes Jesus' example and teaching on prayer throughout his gospel, here highlighting that prayer is necessary to overcome temptation from Satan (11:4).

22:42 *cup.* Often a symbol of God's wrath (Pss. 11:6; 75:8; Isa. 51:17,22; Jer. 25:15; Zech. 12:2; Rev. 14:10; 16:19). The anticipation of suffering God's punishment for sin was a burden and anguish to Jesus, yet he willingly endured it for the sake of His people. *not my will, but thine, be done.* Christ's greatest work was His obedience to the Father unto death, even the death of the cross (Phil. 2:8).

22:43 *angel . . . strengthening him.* Though the Father willed for Christ to die, God heard Jesus' cries and supported His human nature with comfort through a heavenly spirit (Matt. 4:11).

22:44 *great drops of blood falling down to the ground.* Jesus was so anguished by the cup of wrath that He perspired blood (hematridosis), a sign of extreme stress.

22:45 *sleeping for sorrow.* Luke uses a medical word here that indicates more than physical exhaustion, implying intense pain, anguish, or sorrow.

Jesus' Arrest and Death (22:47—23:56)

22:47 *multitude.* A mob of men ready to use force to arrest Jesus. *kiss.* A common and honorable way to greet a person (7:45), though a highly ironic, hypocritical, and cold way of identifying Jesus for arrest.

22:51 *Suffer ye thus far.* Jesus stopped His disciples from using force to prevent His arrest and used His power only to heal His attacker, thus demonstrating His amazing meekness and mercy.

22:52 *staves.* Poles, staffs.

22:53 *this is your hour.* God had determined that this was to be the time when sinners would kill His Son. *power of darkness.* Satan worked in and through them (vv. 3,31; John 14:30; Acts 26:18; Eph. 6:12). Christ's passion and death constituted a

brought him into the high priest's house. And
Peter followed afar off.
55 And when they had kindled a fire in the midst
of the hall, and were set down together, Peter sat
down among them.
56 But a certain maid beheld him as he sat by the
fire, and earnestly looked upon him, and said,
This man was also with him.
57 And he denied him, saying, Woman, I know
him not.
58 And after a little while another saw him, and
said, Thou art also of them. And Peter said, Man,
I am not.
59 And about the space of one hour after another
confidently affirmed, saying, Of a truth this *fellow*
also was with him: for he is a Galilaean.
60 And Peter said, Man, I know not what thou
sayest. And immediately, while he yet spake, the
cock crew.
61 And the Lord turned, and looked upon Peter.
And Peter remembered the word of the Lord, how
he had said unto him, Before the cock crow, thou
shalt deny me thrice.
62 And Peter went out, and wept bitterly.
63 ¶ And the men that held Jesus mocked him,
and smote *him*.
64 And when they had blindfolded him, they
struck him on the face, and asked him, saying,
Prophesy, who is it that smote thee?
65 And many other things blasphemously spake
they against him.
66 ¶ And as soon as it was day, the elders of the
people and the chief priests and the scribes came
together, and led him into their council, saying,
67 Art thou the Christ? tell us. And he said unto
them, If I tell you, ye will not believe:
68 And if I also ask *you*, ye will not answer me,
nor let *me* go.
69 Hereafter shall the Son of man sit on the right
hand of the power of God.
70 Then said they all, Art thou then the Son of
God? And he said unto them, Ye say that I am.
71 And they said, What need we any further
witness? for we ourselves have heard of his own
mouth.

CHAPTER 23

AND the whole multitude of them arose, and led
him unto Pilate.
2 And they began to accuse him, saying, We
found this *fellow* perverting the nation, and for-
bidding to give tribute to Caesar, saying that he
himself is Christ a King.
3 And Pilate asked him, saying, Art thou the King
of the Jews? And he answered him and said, Thou
sayest *it*.
4 Then said Pilate to the chief priests and *to* the
people, I find no fault in this man.
5 And they were the more fierce, saying, He
stirreth up the people, teaching throughout all
Jewry, beginning from Galilee to this place.

---

conflict between spiritual kingdoms (Col. 2:15; Heb. 2:14).

22:60 *immediately.* There was no lapse of time between Peter's third denial and the crowing of the rooster. *crew.* Crowed.

22:61 *the Lord . . . word of the Lord.* The title *Lord* is significant, implying that Jesus is the Lord of heaven and earth, going to die not as a helpless victim but in total control as the Redeemer of His people.

22:62 *wept bitterly.* Peter turned in true repentance as he wept over his sin of denying the Lord.

22:63–65 *struck him on the face.* See Isa. 50:6. *Prophesy, who . . . smote thee.* The soldiers mocked Jesus' prophetic office.

22:69 *Son of man.* God's appointed King over all things forever (Dan. 7:13–14). *sit on the right hand of . . . God.* The position of supreme Lordship, reigning with God's *power* (Ps. 110:1; cf. 20:42).

22:70–71 *Ye say that I am.* This was understood by the council as a clear affirmation and valid legal testimony (*witness*). *What need we.* Why do we need. Sadly, they gave no thought about whether Jesus' testimony of Himself might have been true.

Thoughts for Personal/Family Worship: Chapter 22

1. **The Passover spoke of divine deliverance through the shedding of the blood of the sacrifice. The application of the blood of the lamb caused God's punishment of death to pass over those hidden within the house, foreshadowing Christ's work on the cross. If Christ's death is applied to us, God's wrath will pass over us, for His just wrath against sin is satisfied. How is Christ's blood applied to sinners so that they are hidden and saved in Him?**
2. **Watching and praying are key to resisting temptation (v. 46). God's people are so weak in themselves that without God's grace they cannot stand for one moment against Satan's devices. How often Satan catches them off guard, without their armor, and they look back and think, "I have not watched and prayed." Thanks be to God that Jesus did not fail here. When the Devil sifted the disciples like wheat, Christ devoted Himself to prayer and submitted His will entirely to the cup of God's wrath. As in the wilderness (4:1–11), so now in the garden Jesus is both our example to imitate and our champion who has already won the victory. How do you need to look to Him in the temptations you are facing right now?**

Chapter 23: *Condemned to death by Pilate, Christ shows Himself to Be the Savior in His suffering, death, and burial.*

23:1 *Pilate.* The governor of Judaea (3:1), appointed by the Roman emperor.

23:2 *tribute.* Tax. The court painted Jesus as a political figure advocating independence from Rome, a crime punishable by death.

23:3 *Thou sayest it.* Jesus did not deny the title of *king* but confessed it before Pilate (1 Tim. 6:13), though meaning it in a heavenly and spiritual sense (John 18:28–38).

23:4 *I find no fault.* Christ would die as a man publicly vindicated as innocent (vv. 14–15,22).

23:5 *Jewry.* The whole region known to have Jewish inhabitants.

6 When Pilate heard of Galilee, he asked whether
the man were a Galilaean.
7 And as soon as he knew that he belonged unto
Herod's jurisdiction, he sent him to Herod, who
himself also was at Jerusalem at that time.
8 ¶ And when Herod saw Jesus, he was exceed-
ing glad: for he was desirous to see him of a long
season, because he had heard many things of him;
and he hoped to have seen some miracle done by
him.
9 Then he questioned with him in many words;
but he answered him nothing.
10 And the chief priests and scribes stood and
vehemently accused him.
11 And Herod with his men of war set him at
nought, and mocked *him*, and arrayed him in a
gorgeous robe, and sent him again to Pilate.
12 ¶ And the same day Pilate and Herod were
made friends together: for before they were at en-
mity between themselves.
13 ¶ And Pilate, when he had called together the
chief priests and the rulers and the people,
14 Said unto them, Ye have brought this man
unto me, as one that perverteth the people: and,
behold, I, having examined *him* before you, have
found no fault in this man touching those things
whereof ye accuse him:
15 No, nor yet Herod: for I sent you to him; and,
lo, nothing worthy of death is done unto him.
16 I will therefore chastise him, and release *him*.
17 (For of necessity he must release one unto
them at the feast.)
18 And they cried out all at once, saying, Away
with this *man*, and release unto us Barabbas:
19 (Who for a certain sedition made in the city,
and for murder, was cast into prison.)
20 Pilate therefore, willing to release Jesus, spake
again to them.
21 But they cried, saying, Crucify *him*, crucify
him.
22 And he said unto them the third time, Why,
what evil hath he done? I have found no cause of
death in him: I will therefore chastise him, and
let *him* go.
23 And they were instant with loud voices,
requiring that he might be crucified. And the
voices of them and of the chief priests prevailed.
24 And Pilate gave sentence that it should be as
they required.
25 And he released unto them him that for sedi-
tion and murder was cast into prison, whom they
had desired; but he delivered Jesus to their will.
26 And as they led him away, they laid hold
upon one Simon, a Cyrenian, coming out of the
country, and on him they laid the cross, that he
might bear *it* after Jesus.
27 ¶ And there followed him a great company of
people, and of women, which also bewailed and
lamented him.
28 But Jesus turning unto them said, Daughters
of Jerusalem, weep not for me, but weep for your-
selves, and for your children.
29 For, behold, the days are coming, in the which
they shall say, Blessed *are* the barren, and the
wombs that never bare, and the paps which never
gave suck.
30 Then shall they begin to say to the mountains,
Fall on us; and to the hills, Cover us.
31 For if they do these things in a green tree, what
shall be done in the dry?
32 And there were also two other, malefactors, led
with him to be put to death.

23:6–7 *Galilaean . . . Herod's jurisdiction.* Herod Antipas ruled as tetrarch of Galilee (3:1).
23:8 *exceeding glad.* Herod had earlier sought to see Jesus, though with evil motives (9:7–9; 13:31).
23:9 *answered him nothing.* In Jesus' fulfilling His divine mission of redemption, He did not open His mouth to offer Himself a defense but willingly went to the cross (Isa. 53:7).
23:11 *set him at nought.* Despised Him (Isa. 53:1).
23:12 Historical records show that *Pilate and Herod* were known to be enemies (*at enmity*) but were united in their common hatred of Jesus, fulfilling the words of the psalmist, "The kings of the earth set themselves, and the rulers take counsel together, against the LORD, and against his anointed" (Ps. 2:2; cf. Acts 4:25–28).
23:14–16 Pilate's guilt certainly was not lessened by His waffling attempts to release Jesus.
23:18 *release unto us Barabbas.* It was customary for Pilate to release one prisoner to the Jews before the Passover feast (Matt. 27:15).
23:19 *sedition.* Political insurrection or uprising, the very crime of which they accused Jesus (v. 2).
23:22 *chastise.* Discipline, probably by a beating.
23:23 *instant.* Urgent.
23:25 The gross injustice of Pilate's ruling and the horrible choice of the crowd not only executed God's decree but illustrated its results, for the righteous Jesus was punished and the sinner set free.
23:26 *Cyrenian.* Cyrene is the location of modern day Tripoli in North Africa (Acts 6:9; 11:20; 13:1).
23:28 *Daughters of Jerusalem, weep . . . for your children.* God's judgment was coming upon Israel (21:20–24).
23:29 *paps which never gave suck.* A mother's breasts that never nursed a child (cf. 11:27).
23:30 *mountains, Fall on us.* A sign of desperate desire to escape God's judgment, which is worse than death (Hos. 10:8; cf. Rev. 6:16).
23:31 *green tree . . . dry.* Perhaps a contrast between Jesus as full of spiritual life (Hos. 14:8) and Israel as spiritually dead and barren (cf. Isa. 56:3).
23:32 *malefactors.* Evildoers. Jesus was dying the death of a thief. It is important to the biblical testimony that Jesus did not die a martyr's death, nor was He honored at His death or given any special privileges. In His death for His people, Jesus endured the ignominy and shame of being crucified among transgressors and as a transgressor.
23:33 *Calvary.* Luke translated the name for His readers into the Greek word meaning "skull" (cf. Mark 15:22), here rendered by the KJV translators by the word derived from the traditional

33 And when they were come to the place, which
is called Calvary, there they crucified him, and the
malefactors, one on the right hand, and the other
on the left.
34 ¶ Then said Jesus, Father, forgive them; for
they know not what they do. And they parted his
raiment, and cast lots.
35 And the people stood beholding. And the rulers also with them derided *him*, saying, He saved
others; let him save himself, if he be Christ, the
chosen of God.
36 And the soldiers also mocked him, coming to
him, and offering him vinegar,
37 And saying, If thou be the king of the Jews,
save thyself.
38 And a superscription also was written over
him in letters of Greek, and Latin, and Hebrew,
THIS IS THE KING OF THE JEWS.
39 ¶ And one of the malefactors which were
hanged railed on him, saying, If thou be Christ,
save thyself and us.
40 But the other answering rebuked him, saying,
Dost not thou fear God, seeing thou art in the
same condemnation?
41 And we indeed justly; for we receive the due
reward of our deeds: but this man hath done
nothing amiss.
42 And he said unto Jesus, Lord, remember me
when thou comest into thy kingdom.
43 And Jesus said unto him, Verily I say unto thee,
To day shalt thou be with me in paradise.
44 And it was about the sixth hour, and there was
a darkness over all the earth until the ninth hour.
45 And the sun was darkened, and the veil of the
temple was rent in the midst.
46 ¶ And when Jesus had cried with a loud voice,
he said, Father, into thy hands I commend my
spirit: and having said thus, he gave up the ghost.
47 Now when the centurion saw what was done,
he glorified God, saying, Certainly this was a righteous man.
48 And all the people that came together to that
sight, beholding the things which were done,
smote their breasts, and returned.
49 And all his acquaintance, and the women that
followed him from Galilee, stood afar off, beholding these things.
50 ¶ And, behold, *there was* a man named Joseph,
a counsellor; *and he was* a good man, and a just:
51 (The same had not consented to the counsel
and deed of them;) *he was* of Arimathaea, a city
of the Jews: who also himself waited for the
kingdom of God.
52 This *man* went unto Pilate, and begged the
body of Jesus.
53 And he took it down, and wrapped it in linen,
and laid it in a sepulchre that was hewn in stone,
wherein never man before was laid.
54 And that day was the preparation, and the
sabbath drew on.

Latin term for skull (*calvariae*).
23:34 *Father, forgive them.* Even as Jesus hung on the cross enduring the wrath of God for His people, He interceded for the transgressors (Isa. 53:12), revealing that His purpose in dying was to save sinners (19:10; 22:20). *parted his raiment, and cast lots.* Gambled to divide His clothing, a fulfillment of prophecy (Ps. 22:18).
23:35 *derided.* Sneered, scoffed.
23:38 *superscription.* A placard commonly hung above the condemned man listing the charge.
23:39 *railed.* Insulted, blasphemed.
23:40–41 The one criminal, having earlier mocked Jesus (Mark 15:32), experienced a change such that he began to *fear God*, acknowledging the justice of his own condemnation to die (*due reward of our deeds*) and the righteousness of Christ (*nothing amiss*).
23:42 *Lord.* A striking confession of Christ even as Jesus died on the cross. *remember me, when thou comest into thy kingdom.* The thief placed his trust in Christ's grace and his hope in Christ's glory, a conversion that testifies to the power of Christ's death to redeem the lost (John 12:32–33).
23:43 *Verily.* Truly. *To day.* Though just converted from a life of sin and blasphemy, this man did not have to wait until after ages of purgatory or unconsciousness but immediately upon his death joined Christ in glory. *paradise.* A word for a beautiful garden, used here of the heavenly realm where pardoned souls are gathered after death like a return to the garden of Eden (2 Cor. 12:4; Rev. 2:7; cf. Rev. 22:1–3).
23:44 *sixth hour . . . ninth hour.* Noon to 3:00 p.m. *darkness.* Associated divine judgment (Ex. 10:21–23) and the day of the Lord (Joel 2:1–2,10,31; Amos 5:18,20; 8:9; Zeph. 1:15).
23:45 *veil of the temple.* The curtain that separated the holy place from the Holy of Holies, separating even the priests and Israelites from the dwelling place of God. *rent in the midst.* Torn in the middle. As Jesus died He entered into the heavenly sanctuary and thus made a way for sinners to come into communion with God (Heb. 9:1—10:39). Through Jesus' death the physical temple became obsolete and is no longer the center of God's activity (John 4:21).
23:46 *into thy hands I commend my spirit.* Jesus demonstrated to the end His faith and piety toward God (Ps. 31:5). *gave up the ghost.* Expired, died (Job 3:11; 14:10).
23:47 *centurion.* The Gentile military commander at the execution site, observing what happened there, recognized and confessed that Jesus was *righteous. glorified God.* A strange response, even given an understanding of Christ's innocence, unless the soldier somehow understood Christ's death to be God's plan to confer mercy upon men (Rom. 15:8–9). He was the second convert at the cross (vv. 40–42).
23:50 *counsellor.* Member of the Sanhedrin or Jewish high council. *just.* Righteous, the same description used of Zacharias, Elisabeth, and Simeon (1:6; 2:25).
23:51 *waited for the kingdom of God.* Like Anna and her friends (2:38).
23:52 *begged the body of Jesus.* A bold act, identifying himself with the One condemned by the council for blasphemy and killed as a criminal.
23:53 *took it down.* In obedience to Deut. 21:22–23. *sepulchre.* Tomb. *hewn.* Shaped by cutting. Jesus' body was not buried in disgrace but in honor.
23:54 *preparation.* The day before the beginning of the Sabbath or a feast, at which time everything was prepared so

55 And the women also, which came with him
from Galilee, followed after, and beheld the sep-
ulchre, and how his body was laid.
56 And they returned, and prepared spices and
ointments; and rested the sabbath day according
to the commandment.

CHAPTER 24

NOW upon the first *day* of the week, very early
in the morning, they came unto the sepulchre,
bringing the spices which they had prepared, and
certain *others* with them.
2 And they found the stone rolled away from the
sepulchre.
3 And they entered in, and found not the body of
the Lord Jesus.
4 And it came to pass, as they were much per-
plexed thereabout, behold, two men stood by
them in shining garments:
5 And as they were afraid, and bowed down *their*
faces to the earth, they said unto them, Why seek
ye the living among the dead?
6 He is not here, but is risen: remember how he
spake unto you when he was yet in Galilee,
7 Saying, The Son of man must be delivered into
the hands of sinful men, and be crucified, and the
third day rise again.
8 And they remembered his words,
9 And returned from the sepulchre, and told all
these things unto the eleven, and to all the rest.
10 It was Mary Magdalene, and Joanna, and
Mary *the mother* of James, and other *women that
were* with them, which told these things unto the
apostles.
11 And their words seemed to them as idle tales,
and they believed them not.
12 Then arose Peter, and ran unto the sepulchre;
and stooping down, he beheld the linen clothes
laid by themselves, and departed, wondering in
himself at that which was come to pass.
13 ¶ And, behold, two of them went that same
day to a village called Emmaus, which was from
Jerusalem *about* threescore furlongs.
14 And they talked together of all these things
which had happened.
15 And it came to pass, that, while they com-
muned *together* and reasoned, Jesus himself drew
near, and went with them.
16 But their eyes were holden that they should
not know him.
17 And he said unto them, What manner of com-
munications *are* these that ye have one to another,
as ye walk, and are sad?
18 And the one of them, whose name was Cleo-
pas, answering said unto him, Art thou only a

the Jews could rest when they were required to rest.

23:55 These women would later prove to be the first witnesses of Jesus' resurrection. We have no need to doubt their testimony or conjecture that they had the wrong grave. Luke clearly states that these women had followed Joseph and knew the placement of Jesus' body.

23:56 *sabbath day according to the commandment.* The old covenant Sabbath was the seventh day of the week (Saturday), requiring the women to rest and thus to wait before anointing the body.

Thoughts for Personal/Family Worship: Chapter 23

1. **Christ's work would not have been the same if He had simply been murdered by a mob or off in some dark alley. According to the will of God and the prophecies of the Old Testament, He had to be sentenced by the official governing bodies as a criminal. Pilate, Herod, and the religious authorities all signed off on the legality of this execution, thus showing the exceeding sinfulness of mankind. None can plead innocent—including ourselves. Blinded by sin, we would have done nothing essentially different from what they did. May God humble us to see ourselves as wholly unjust, and the Son of God as gloriously just. Through it all God's justice would be executed upon His Son, in order that the elect might be freely justified. In this way God would "be just, and the justifier of him which believeth in Jesus" (Rom. 3:26). How should the cross of Jesus both humble us for our sins and afford us hope for complete forgiveness in Christ?**
2. **Calvary speaks not only of justice but also of salvation. On the cross Christ prayed for transgressors, and He saved the thief dying next to Him. The veil was rent, giving mankind access to God through the blood of the everlasting covenant. A Roman centurion, too, was saved. Thus in the darkest day of history we see the Lord Jesus doing the best works. How does the cross reveal the mystery and wonder of God's will?**

Chapter 24: *Jesus rises from the dead, gives hope to His disciples, opens their understanding regarding the Scriptures, and in their presence ascends into heaven.*

The Resurrection and Ascension of Jesus (24:1–53)

Jesus' Resurrection (24:1–12)

24:1–3 One of the greatest witnesses to the resurrection of Jesus from the dead is the empty tomb (*sepulchre*).

24:5 *Why seek ye the living among the dead?* The angels understood that God had raised Jesus from the dead, though the women, despite having been told of Jesus' resurrection, did not yet realize that Jesus was raised.

24:6 *how he spake unto you.* Everything happened just as the Lord had said (9:22), encouraging unwavering faith in His Word.

24:7–8 *must be delivered . . . crucified . . . rise again.* This chapter repeatedly uses the language of divine necessity (vv. 26,44,46), summing up a great theme of the gospel that Christ's work fulfills God's decree, which cannot fail (see note at 4:43).

24:11 *idle tales.* Nonsense or foolish talk.

24:12 The facts of the situation were verified by multiple witnesses, all of whom were slow to believe.

Appearances to Disciples (24:13–49)

24:13 *two of them.* We do not know the identity of these two individuals, though we do know that one is named Cleopas (v. 18). *threescore furlongs.* Sixty Roman *stadia*, about 7 miles or 12 kilometers.

24:16 *were holden.* Literally, "were powerfully restrained."

stranger in Jerusalem, and hast not known the
things which are come to pass there in these days?
19 And he said unto them, What things? And they
said unto him, Concerning Jesus of Nazareth,
which was a prophet mighty in deed and word
before God and all the people:
20 And how the chief priests and our rulers delivered him to be condemned to death, and have
crucified him.
21 But we trusted that it had been he which
should have redeemed Israel: and beside all this,
to day is the third day since these things were
done.
22 Yea, and certain women also of our company made us astonished, which were early at the
sepulchre;
23 And when they found not his body, they came,
saying, that they had also seen a vision of angels,
which said that he was alive.
24 And certain of them which were with us went
to the sepulchre, and found *it* even so as the
women had said: but him they saw not.
25 Then he said unto them, O fools, and slow of
heart to believe all that the prophets have spoken:
26 Ought not Christ to have suffered these things,
and to enter into his glory?
27 And beginning at Moses and all the prophets,
he expounded unto them in all the scriptures the
things concerning himself.
28 And they drew nigh unto the village, whither
they went: and he made as though he would have
gone further.
29 But they constrained him, saying, Abide with
us: for it is toward evening, and the day is far
spent. And he went in to tarry with them.
30 And it came to pass, as he sat at meat with
them, he took bread, and blessed *it*, and brake,
and gave to them.
31 And their eyes were opened, and they knew
him; and he vanished out of their sight.
32 And they said one to another, Did not our
heart burn within us, while he talked with us by
the way, and while he opened to us the scriptures?
33 And they rose up the same hour, and returned
to Jerusalem, and found the eleven gathered
together, and them that were with them,
34 Saying, The Lord is risen indeed, and hath
appeared to Simon.
35 And they told what things *were done* in the
way, and how he was known of them in breaking
of bread.
36 ¶ And as they thus spake, Jesus himself stood
in the midst of them, and saith unto them, Peace
be unto you.
37 But they were terrified and affrighted, and
supposed that they had seen a spirit.
38 And he said unto them, Why are ye troubled?
and why do thoughts arise in your hearts?
39 Behold my hands and my feet, that it is I
myself: handle me, and see; for a spirit hath not
flesh and bones, as ye see me have.
40 And when he had thus spoken, he shewed
them *his* hands and *his* feet.
41 And while they yet believed not for joy, and
wondered, he said unto them, Have ye here any
meat?
42 And they gave him a piece of a broiled fish,
and of an honeycomb.
43 And he took *it*, and did eat before them.
44 And he said unto them, These *are* the words

24:18 *only a stranger.* The sole outsider. The events surrounding Jesus' arrest and death were known publicly.
24:25–26 *O fools.* The message of *all* the Scriptures is the suffering and *glory* of the *Christ*, yet even disciples of Jesus are *slow of heart* to recognize and *believe*. The book of Acts will further draw out several important Old Testament texts that foretell the sufferings of Jesus (Deut. 18:15; Pss. 2:7; 16:8–11; 110:1; 118:1–29; Isa. 53:8).
24:26 *Ought not.* Was it not necessary (same word as "must" in v. 7).
24:27 *in all the scriptures.* Jesus reveals to the disciples the manner in which all of the Scriptures pointed to him. It is likely that Christ went through the major sections of the Hebrew Bible, showing that He is the sum and content of their message. It is important to remember that Christ is the main character of both the Old and New Testaments.
24:28 *nigh.* Near. *whither.* Where, to which place.
24:30 *sat at meat.* Reclined at a meal.
24:31 *eyes were opened.* Just as Christ opened their eyes to see how the Scriptures testified of Him (v. 27, cf. v. 45). *vanished.* Jesus' appearance was a testimony to His disciples that He lives, and yet His disappearance showed that He is Lord, going where He chooses and ministering to whomever He wills.
24:32 *our heart burn within us.* Christ's saving illumination through the *Scriptures* not only informs the mind but also ignites the affections toward God (Ps. 119:18,36–37).
24:33 *eleven gathered together.* John records that Thomas was not present when Jesus appeared the first time (John 20:24). Thus, Luke may be using official nomenclature for the apostles rather than specifying how many of them were actually present.
24:36 *as they thus spake.* Jesus appears in the midst of the disciples just as quickly as He had vanished from the sight of the two disciples. *Peace be unto you.* The normal greeting is filled with new significance because Jesus has made peace between God and sinners (2:14; 7:50; Eph. 2:13–17).
24:37 *affrighted.* Frightened.
24:38 *thoughts.* Or doubts.
24:39 *Behold my hands and my feet.* He verified that He was the risen Lord Jesus by the visible proofs of His death by crucifixion (John 20:27). *flesh and bones.* Though returned from the dead, Jesus was not a ghost (*spirit*) but had a real, living, physical body that could be touched and could consume food (Luke v. 43). Jesus' resurrected body is similar to the resurrected and glorified bodies believers will receive upon His return (1 Cor. 15:35–50; Phil. 3:20–21).
24:41 *meat.* Food of any kind.
24:44 *all things must be fulfilled.* God's decree, revealed in Scripture, cannot fail to succeed. *written in the law . . . prophets . . . psalms, concerning me.* Jesus indicated that every part of

which I spake unto you, while I was yet with
you, that all things must be fulfilled, which were
written in the law of Moses, and *in* the prophets,
and *in* the psalms, concerning me.
45 Then opened he their understanding, that
they might understand the scriptures,
46 And said unto them, Thus it is written, and
thus it behoved Christ to suffer, and to rise from
the dead the third day:
47 And that repentance and remission of sins
should be preached in his name among all na-
tions, beginning at Jerusalem.
48 And ye are witnesses of these things.
49 ¶ And, behold, I send the promise of my Fa-
ther upon you: but tarry ye in the city of Jerusa-
lem, until ye be endued with power from on high.
50 ¶ And he led them out as far as to Bethany, and
he lifted up his hands, and blessed them.
51 And it came to pass, while he blessed them, he
was parted from them, and carried up into heaven.
52 And they worshipped him, and returned to
Jerusalem with great joy:
53 And were continually in the temple, praising
and blessing God. Amen.

the Old Testament testifies of Him and His saving work.

24:45 *opened he their understanding.* As the great Prophet of the church, Christ not only reveals divine truth but by His Spirit (Acts 1:2) opens the hearts of sinners and overcomes their spiritual blindness so that they can receive that divine truth with faith and love (vv. 27,32; Acts 16:14; 2 Cor. 4:6).

24:46 *it behoved.* It was necessary for (same word as "must," vv. 7,44).

24:47 Just as the Scriptures foretold Christ's death and resurrection, they also foretell the mission of the church to preach *repentance* and forgiveness (*remission*; 3:3; Acts 2:28; 5:31) to *all nations* (Matt. 28:19). This will be the theme of Acts as the disciples go from Jerusalem to the ends of the world (Acts 1:8) proclaiming salvation in Jesus' name alone (Acts 4:12).

24:49 *endued.* Endowed. The promise of the Spirit was fulfilled on the day of Pentecost (Acts 2:1–47), fifty days after Christ's resurrection. The disciples would not preach in their own power but in the power of the Spirit freely given by Jesus in His ascended glory (Acts 1:8; 2:4,14; 4:8,31).

Jesus' Ascension (24:50–53)

24:50 *he led them out as far as to Bethany.* This scene did not occur immediately after the previous one; as Luke later tells us, Jesus taught His disciples concerning the kingdom of God for forty days after His resurrection (Acts 1:3). *lifted up his hands, and blessed them.* A priestly act, granting them the blessings obtained by His once-for-all sacrifice (Lev. 9:22).

24:51 *carried up into heaven.* Jesus was vindicated by His Father and glorified at His right hand (Acts 1:9–11; 2:32–33; cf. 1 Tim. 3:16), showing that what He taught was true and that what He had done was accepted by His Father.

24:52–53 *returned to Jerusalem.* The disciples obeyed Jesus and returned to the temple, the same place at which Luke's gospel had begun (1:9). Their dispositions had been changed from fear into the praise and worship of God.

Thoughts for Personal/Family Worship: Chapter 24

1. **God's ways are higher than man's ways and God's thoughts than man's thoughts (Isa. 55:8). These women and the other disciples were resigning themselves to live on despite a dead Jesus. If this had been the end of the story, we believers with them would be "of all men most miserable" (1 Cor. 15:19). "But now is Christ risen from the dead" (1 Cor. 15:20). His resurrection is proclaimed by the infallible Word of God, declared by angels, proven by the empty tomb, and confirmed by eyewitnesses. What difference should the resurrection of Christ make in our lives once we believe it?**
2. **What a Bible study Christ offered on the road of Emmaus: "And beginning at Moses and all the prophets, he expounded unto them in all the Scriptures the things concerning himself" (v. 27). Notice how eager Christ was to focus His disciples on the Scriptures. He could have chosen to omit this step and simply reveal Himself, but He loves the Bible and wants His people to see Him, the living Word, in the Bible, the written Word. While the Scriptures have important revelations about all sorts of issues, their primary purpose is to reveal God in the face of Jesus Christ. We must remember this always when we read the Bible. Yet we must also remember that we need Christ to open our eyes or we will not see His glory in the Bible. What are some ways in which the whole Bible reveals Christ? Why do we need to pray regularly for Christ's illumination as we read and hear the Word?**
3. **The Gospel According to Luke began with a temple scene in which Zacharias was unable to bless the people because he had been silenced after seeing an angel and doubting the message from the Lord. Luke ends his gospel once again in the temple, this time with the disciples "praising and blessing God" because the risen Christ had ascended into heaven with His hands lifted up to bless them as their ever living Priest. Though rejected by His national people, teachers, rulers, and priests, the Lord Jesus is the great Prophet, Priest, and King of His spiritual people. The Savior lives to bless His people. What reasons does this give believers to bless God? How do you need to apply those reasons to your own heart, so that by God's Spirit you too can praise the Lord?**

INTRODUCTION TO THE BOOK OF SAINT JOHN

Authorship: The author of this Gospel does not identify himself by name but only as "the disciple whom Jesus loved" (21:20,24). However, there is strong evidence that he was the apostle John, one of the sons of Zebedee. He was an eyewitness of Jesus Christ's life (1:14) and was present at the Last Supper, reclining at the meal beside Jesus (13:23). This identifies him as one of the twelve apostles (Mark 14:17). It may also imply that he was one of the apostles particularly close to Christ, whom the Gospels identify as Peter, James, and John (Mark 5:37; 9:2; 13:3; 14:33). This Gospel names other apostles at the Supper, implying that the unnamed disciple was not Thomas, Philip, or the other Judas (John 14:5,8,22). Christ chose the beloved disciple to care for His mother, Mary (19:26), another sign that he was especially close to the Lord. He is clearly distinguished from Peter (13:24; 21:20). James, the son of Zebedee, died very early (Acts 12:1–2) and so is unlikely to have written this Gospel. Though it is theoretically possible that one of the lesser known apostles wrote the Gospel, the evidence heavily favors John, the other son of Zebedee, as its author (21:2,7). This is confirmed by the testimony of later writers, such as Irenaeus (AD second century).

When we refer to the authorship of the books of the Bible we must always remind ourselves that the writers were moved by the Holy Spirit (2 Peter 1:21). God is their ultimate author. So sublime a book as the Gospel of John can only be accounted for as the fruit of divine inspiration. This is how the Bible writers are to be regarded. They were so guided and controlled by God in what they wrote that their writings are to be received by men as infallible and therefore in every way reliable.

Date: The apostle John died in the last decade of the first century AD. The exact date when he wrote this Gospel is not known, but it is probable that he composed it in the last years of his life (AD 90–100).

Theme: Jesus is the Christ, the Son of God, God-in-the-flesh sent by the Father to give eternal life to all whom the Father has given to Him.

Purpose: To call people to believe in Christ and so to have eternal life (20:30–31).

Synopsis: *The Contribution of John to Redemptive Revelation*

We refer to the first three New Testament Gospels as the Synoptic Gospels because they have much in common. (The Greek word *synopsis* means "seeing together"). John's Gospel is noticeably different from the other three, though it does not contradict them. It supplements the three Synoptic Gospels and throws wonderful light on the heavenly and glorious person of the Lord Jesus Christ.

Jesus of Nazareth is both God and man (1:1,14). He showed His glory by His miracles (2:11; 11:39–44) and by His power to rise again from the dead (10:17–18; 20:1–31). He revealed His identity by teaching that He is the Son in a unique relationship with the Father, such that they share one divine essence, power, knowledge, and life (1:18; 5:17–20,26; 10:28–30). He is the Father's eternal Word (1:1), and to see Him is to see the Father (14:9). Therefore Jesus does the works of God, such as judgment and resurrection (5:21–22), and receives worship as God (20:28), not as a rival to the Father but as the One through whom we can know and honor the Father (5:23; 14:9; 17:3).

Jesus used simple illustrations prefaced by the words "I am . . ." to teach us aspects of His grace and saving power, for example, "I am the light of the world" (8:12). Yet through such simple words He communicated profound truths. The repetition of "I am" (Greek *egō eimi*) at key points in this gospel identifies Christ with *Jehovah* (8:58), the LORD whose name means "I am" (Ex. 3:14). This phrase appears (in the Greek text) on Christ's lips at times when He was demonstrating supernatural power and knowledge (4:26; 6:20; 13:19; 18:5–6). Thus when Jesus used the "I am" phrase to declare that He is the bread of life; the light of the world; the door; the good shepherd; the resurrection and the life; the way, the truth, and the life; and the true vine (6:35; 8:12; 10:7,11; 11:25; 14:6; 15:1), He was declaring that He is the fullness of God come to fill His people in all their needs (4:14; 6:35; 7:37).

With the Father and the Son, the Holy Spirit receives a great deal of attention in this gospel. Jesus spoke of the Spirit as "another Comforter" (14:16), whose ministry would resemble Christ's and continue His work after He had returned to the Father (16:7). Jesus said that the Spirit comes from the Father "in my name" (14:26), not as an independent third party but as One who brings the things the Son received from the Father to the souls of men so that Christ is glorified (16:13–14). The Spirit acts as the Lord and Life-giver (6:63), bringing sinners to a new birth according to the Spirit's sovereign will (3:3–8), so that the wicked become worshipers who exchange worldly lusts for eternal satisfaction in God (4:10,14,23–24; 7:37–39). The Holy Spirit does this work through His Word (6:63), for He is the Spirit of truth (14:17; 15:26; 16:13). He is the witness convicting the world of its guilt (16:8–11) and the guide teaching believers the whole counsel of God (16:13). John gives us a glorious theology of the Trinity that is profoundly relevant for evangelism, worship, and the Christian life.

The triune God appears in John's gospel as a missionary God. John's remarkable teachings about God come in the context not of an abstract theological treatise but as the good news of the divine mission into a perishing world. This appears in John's use of two Greek words, both translated as "send" or "sent" (about sixty times). The Father *sent* the Son to save perishing sinners out of the world (3:16–17; 6:38–39), and the Spirit anoints and assists Christ in His work (1:32–33; 3:34). The Father and the Son *send* the Holy Spirit to reveal and glorify the Son (14:26; 15:26; 16:7). The Son also *sends* His disciples into the world to bear witness to Him by the power of the Spirit (15:26–27; 17:18; 20:21–22). Thus the mission of the church is Trinitarian and God-centered; it comes from God, is performed by God, and aims at God's glory (17:1–5,10).

Though the book contains many lofty and transcendent teachings, it also portrays Jesus in a most personal way, recording His conversations with a number of individuals. Jesus revealed Himself to an ever-widening group of people: to His early disciples (1:1–51), to the rabbi Nicodemus (3:1–16), to the Samaritan woman (4:1–54), to the man at the Pool of Bethesda (5:1–47), etc. As Christ talked with people, He made it clear that no one has eternal life except those who are born again and so have saving faith in Himself. Formal religion by itself is not pleasing to God. To profess faith without true love for Christ as God's dear Son is worthless in the end. Thus the Gospel calls for a personal response to Jesus Christ, as John stated clearly: "But these are written, that ye might believe that Jesus is the Christ, the Son of God; and that believing ye might have life through his name" (20:31).

Outline:

I. Christ, the Eternal Son of God (1:1–18)

II. Christ Reveals His Glory in His Public Ministry (1:19—12:50)
   - A. Christ's Early Ministry (1:19—4:54)
   - B. Christ Rejected by Unbelievers (5:1—6:71)
   - C. At the Feast of Tabernacles (7:1–53)
   - D. The Woman Taken in Adultery and the Light of the World (8:1–59)
   - E. The Healing of the Man Born Blind (9:1–41)
   - F. The Good Shepherd (10:1–42)
   - G. The Raising of Lazarus (11:1–57)
   - H. Conclusion to the Public Ministry (12:1–50)

III. Christ Reveals His Glory in His Passion, Death, and Resurrection (13:1—21:25)
   - A. Jesus Washes the Disciples' Feet (13:1–38)
   - B. Jesus' Upper Room Discourse and High Priestly Prayer (14:1—17:26)
   - C. Jesus' Arrest, Trial, Crucifixion, and Burial (18:1—19:42)
   - D. Jesus' Resurrection and Appearances (20:1—21:25)

THE GOSPEL ACCORDING TO SAINT

JOHN

CHAPTER 1

IN the beginning was the Word, and the Word was
with God, and the Word was God.
2 The same was in the beginning with God.
3 All things were made by him; and without him
was not any thing made that was made.
4 In him was life; and the life was the light of
men.
5 And the light shineth in darkness; and the dark-
ness comprehended it not.
6 ¶ There was a man sent from God, whose name
was John.
7 The same came for a witness, to bear witness of
the Light, that all *men* through him might believe.
8 He was not that Light, but *was sent* to bear
witness of that Light.
9 *That* was the true Light, which lighteth every
man that cometh into the world.
10 He was in the world, and the world was made
by him, and the world knew him not.
11 He came unto his own, and his own received
him not.
12 But as many as received him, to them gave he
power to become the sons of God, *even* to them
that believe on his name:
13 Which were born, not of blood, nor of the will
of the flesh, nor of the will of man, but of God.
14 And the Word was made flesh, and dwelt

Chapter 1: *The Word becomes flesh, John the Baptist declares Christ to be the Lamb of God, and Christ reveals Himself to His first disciples.*

CHRIST, THE ETERNAL SON OF GOD (1:1–18)

1:1–18 This is the prologue of John's gospel. It contains a summary of vital truths about Christ: He is God, the Creator of the world and the Source of all the true knowledge of God mankind has ever had. He is the Fountain of all saving grace, who came to earth to reveal God's saving truth to fallen mankind.

1:1 *In the beginning.* Christ is eternal, having existed already when the world was created (8:58; Gen. 1:1; Prov. 8:22–31). *Word.* Divine speech, the living expression of God's nature and character (Col. 1:15; Heb. 1:3) and thus the revealer of God and His saving purposes (v. 18; 14:9). *was with God.* He is a person distinct from the Father and in eternal relationship with Him (v. 18; 17:5,24). *was God.* He possesses one and the same deity and divine nature as the Father (10:30; Phil. 2:6) and so is the proper object of worship (20:28). The same expression (*God* without the Greek article) is often used of God the Father (v. 18; 8:54; etc.). This teaching that the Son of God is a distinct person from the Father, yet is Himself God, is a key component of the doctrine of the Trinity.

1:3 *All things . . . by him.* Christ is the Creator of the entire universe, including men and angels (v. 10; Col. 1:16–17; Heb. 1:2,10–12). This clearly implies that He was not created, for *any thing made* was created by Christ.

1:4–5 *In him was life.* He possesses the life of God and so is the giver of all life (5:26; 6:57; 11:25), possibly a reference to the Holy Spirit (6:63; 7:38–39; cf. vv. 32–33). *light.* Truth, the wisdom that exposes sin and guides in a righteous and blessed life (vv. 7–9; 3:19–21; 5:35; 8:12; 9:5; 11:9–10; 12:35–36,46). *darkness comprehended it not.* This evil world neither receives Christ's light (3:19–20) nor is able to overcome His light—the Greek verb can bear either meaning.

1:6–8 *witness.* John the Baptist was appointed by God to bear testimony to Christ as His forerunner (vv. 15,19–36). John, however, was a mere man and not the equal of Christ (v. 27). *all.* Not every individual in the world but many in Israel and elsewhere (Matt. 3:5–6).

1:9 *lighteth every man.* Christ came to bring God's truth to people of all nations (18:36–37). To "enlighten" people can mean to teach them the truth (Ps. 119:130). This refers to natural revelation, which leaves all men without excuse (Rom. 1:20). This is not a statement of universal grace, for Christ's light does not shine in the hearts of unbelievers (11:10; Matt. 6:23; Eph. 5:8).

1:10–11 *the world knew him not.* Though Jesus is the Creator come in the flesh (vv. 1–3,14), His own creation rejected Him ("know" often implies love and intimacy; 10:14). *his own, and his own.* His property and His people. The King of Israel (vv. 45,49) came to the people who had the promises of His coming, but they rejected Him.

1:12–13 *received . . . believe.* Saving faith is resting upon and receiving Christ for all that He has revealed Himself to be (*his name*). *power.* Authority, the right. *sons of God.* Literally, "children of God," beloved and adopted by the Father and given His image (11:52; 1 John 2:29—3:2,10). *born . . . of God.* The reason some trust in Christ when most do not (vv. 10–11) is that God has brought about a new birth or regeneration in them (3:1–8; Titus 3:5). Salvation does not come from being born of the right human lineage (*not of blood*), nor of man's will in his fallen condition (*will of the flesh*), nor of a parent's decision (*will of man*, or "of a husband"), but of God's grace alone.

1:14 *the Word was made flesh.* The eternal Lord (v. 1) took upon Himself human nature, body and soul, in the weakness and mortality of man's fallen condition (3:6; 6:51–56,63; 8:15; 17:2). He truly became a man, although He was without sin (Heb. 2:14; 4:15). *dwelt.* Literally, "tabernacled," for Christ is the true tabernacle or temple by whom God's *glory* dwells with

among us, (and we beheld his glory, the glory as
of the only begotten of the Father,) full of grace
and truth.
15 ¶ John bare witness of him, and cried, saying,
This was he of whom I spake, He that cometh after
me is preferred before me: for he was before me.
16 And of his fulness have all we received, and
grace for grace.
17 For the law was given by Moses, *but* grace and
truth came by Jesus Christ.
18 No man hath seen God at any time; the only
begotten Son, which is in the bosom of the Father,
he hath declared *him*.
19 ¶ And this is the record of John, when the Jews
sent priests and Levites from Jerusalem to ask
him, Who art thou?
20 And he confessed, and denied not; but con-
fessed, I am not the Christ.
21 And they asked him, What then? Art thou
Elias? And he saith, I am not. Art thou that
prophet? And he answered, No.
22 Then said they unto him, Who art thou? that
we may give an answer to them that sent us. What
sayest thou of thyself?
23 He said, I *am* the voice of one crying in the
wilderness, Make straight the way of the Lord, as
said the prophet Esaias.
24 And they which were sent were of the Phari-
sees.
25 And they asked him, and said unto him, Why
baptizest thou then, if thou be not that Christ, nor
Elias, neither that prophet?
26 John answered them, saying, I baptize with
water: but there standeth one among you, whom
ye know not;
27 He it is, who coming after me is preferred
before me, whose shoe's latchet I am not worthy
to unloose.
28 These things were done in Bethabara beyond
Jordan, where John was baptizing.
29 ¶ The next day John seeth Jesus coming unto
him, and saith, Behold the Lamb of God, which
taketh away the sin of the world.
30 This is he of whom I said, After me cometh
a man which is preferred before me: for he was
before me.
31 And I knew him not: but that he should be
made manifest to Israel, therefore am I come
baptizing with water.
32 And John bare record, saying, I saw the Spirit
descending from heaven like a dove, and it abode
upon him.
33 And I knew him not: but he that sent me to
baptize with water, the same said unto me, Upon
whom thou shalt see the Spirit descending, and
remaining on him, the same is he which baptizeth
with the Holy Ghost.
34 And I saw, and bare record that this is the Son
of God.
35 ¶ Again the next day after John stood, and two
of his disciples;
36 And looking upon Jesus as he walked, he saith,
Behold the Lamb of God!
37 And the two disciples heard him speak, and
they followed Jesus.
38 Then Jesus turned, and saw them following,

man (2:19–21; Ex. 25:8; 40:34), the fullness of deity in bodily form (Col. 2:9). *only begotten.* A term for an only or unique child (Luke 7:12; 8:42; 9:38; Heb. 11:17), used of God's Son (v. 18; 3:16,18; 1 John 4:9) in contrast to mere men and women born again and adopted into God's family (vv. 12–13) because of the unique relationship in which the Father eternally shares the whole divine nature with His Son (5:26; 6:57). *grace and truth.* Saving power and doctrine, or God's undeserved favor and faithfulness (Ex. 34:6; cf. Ex. 33:12—34:9).

1:15 *preferred before me . . . before me.* Jesus ranks far above John the Baptist because Jesus existed before John was born, although John was born first (Luke 1:57,63). John understood the truth of Christ's eternal deity.

1:17 *law . . . grace and truth.* The moral and ceremonial law, both of which prepared and called for Christ. Christ came as the Savior of lawbreakers and so is greater than *Moses*, who was merely a prophet.

1:18 *No man hath seen God.* Every revelation of God, in both the Old and New Testaments, was through the *Son* of God (8:56). *only begotten.* See note at v. 14. *in the bosom.* Close to, in a position of intimacy and fellowship with (13:23; Luke 16:22). Christ is able to reveal the Father because of His unique relationship with Him (Matt. 11:27).

CHRIST REVEALS HIS GLORY IN HIS PUBLIC MINISTRY (1:19—12:50)

Christ's Early Ministry (1:19—4:54)

1:19 *record.* Literally, "testimony."

1:21 *Elias.* Elijah (cf. Mal. 4:5–6). *that prophet.* Moses foretold that a great prophet would come; this prophecy was fulfilled in Jesus (Deut. 18:15).

1:23 *voice of one crying.* John confessed to being the forerunner spoken of by Isaiah (*Esaias*; Isa. 40:3). John the Baptist's ministry was to prepare the Jewish nation for the coming of Christ. By his powerful preaching and multiple baptisms he shook the whole of society.

1:24 *Pharisees.* A powerful religious sect of Jews at the time.

1:25 *baptizest.* John did not enter his remarkable ministry through the conventional method of the rabbinical schools, and thus his authority to baptize was challenged.

1:27 *shoe's latchet.* Sandal strap. *unloose.* Untie.

1:28 *Bethabara.* Bethany, an important place in Jesus' ministry (12:1).

1:29 *next day.* There are four successive days referred to in this passage (vv. 19,29,35,43). *Lamb of God.* Christ is the God-appointed sacrifice for the sins of all who believe in Him (v. 36; 1 Peter 1:18–20), foreshadowed in the animal sacrifices (Heb. 10:1–4). *taketh away the sin.* Atones for sin so that the sinner is forgiven (Ex. 34:7; Num. 14:18; Ps. 25:18). *of the world.* Christ's death on the cross is the only effective sacrifice for mankind, and it will save many, though not all.

1:32 *Spirit descending from heaven.* The miraculous sign at the time Jesus was baptized by John that revealed to John that Jesus was indeed the Christ (Matt. 3:16). *abode.* Remained.

1:33 *Ghost.* Spirit.

1:37 *disciples.* Followers of a master or teacher who sought to embrace His ways.

CHRIST'S INCARNATION

While pronouncing His curse on Adam and Eve because of their sin, God promised to provide them with a Savior, born among their own descendants, who would suffer at the hands of the enemy of their souls but, in the end, would crush this enemy underfoot and free them from his power (Gen. 3:15). This Savior must be "the seed of the woman," possessing a true human nature. Only as a man among men could He stand up as our champion and confront the Devil, to destroy him and all his works (1 John 3:8).

As time passed many promises were added to the first. The Savior must be "the seed of Abraham," in whom all nations would be blessed (Gen. 22:18). He must come out of Jacob as a star appears in the night sky, to rule among the nations, rising out of Israel as a scepter in the hand of God (Num. 24:17). He must be raised up from among His Israelite brothers as a prophet like Moses (Deut. 18:15–19). He must be "a priest for ever after the order of Melchizedek" (Ps. 110:4). He must descend from David and sit upon his throne to reign as King: "The LORD hath sworn in truth unto David; he will not turn from it; of the fruit of thy body I will set upon thy throne" (Ps. 132:11).

These promises affirmed that the Savior of the people of God must be a true man, one belonging to a particular nation, tribe, and family. Other promises indicated that this true Son of man would also be the Son of God: "I will declare the decree: the LORD hath said unto me, Thou art my Son; this day have I begotten thee" (Ps. 2:7); and "He shall cry unto me, Thou art my father, my God, and the rock of my salvation. Also will I make him my firstborn, higher than the kings of the earth" (Ps. 89:26–27).

Paul heralds the time when the two strands of promises found common fulfillment in the advent of Christ as the God-man: "When the fulness of time was come, God sent forth his Son, made of a woman, made under the law, to redeem them that were under the law" (Gal. 4:4–5).

John introduces the Son of God as "the Word," existing from all eternity and preexisting the creation, being "with God" as a distinct Person of the Godhead and being Himself God (John 1:1–2). He then says simply, "The Word was made flesh, and dwelt among us" (John 1:14). Theologians therefore speak of the incarnation (literally, "enfleshment") of the eternal Son of God. John adds, "And we beheld his glory, the glory as of the only begotten of the Father, full of grace and truth." John knows that every Christian is a child of God by adoption, for Christ's sake (John 1:12), but that Christ alone is the eternal and natural Son of God.

It took many centuries for the church to work out all the implications of the incarnation. In the end, orthodox theologians concluded that we must affirm equally that Christ is God and that Christ is man. To diminish one nature or the other is to end up in deadly error. These two natures exist in one Person: "Although He is God and man, yet He is not two, but one Christ" (Athanasian Creed, Art. 34).

As God, Christ is more powerful than all creatures; He drew on the power of His Godhead to sustain the burden of God's wrath. As man, He is one with those for whom He laid down His life, "in all things made like unto his brethren . . . in all points tempted like as we are, yet without sin" (Heb. 2:17; 4:15). In the same human nature that sinned, Christ made satisfaction for sin. So it was necessary that Christ be both God and man. When Christ assumed our nature from the flesh and blood of the Virgin Mary, He conferred great honor upon it. In the ascension of Christ that same human nature was taken up into heaven as a sure pledge that He will in due time take up all His children to Himself.

and saith unto them, What seek ye? They said
unto him, Rabbi, (which is to say, being inter-
preted, Master,) where dwellest thou?
39 He saith unto them, Come and see. They came
and saw where he dwelt, and abode with him that
day: for it was about the tenth hour.
40 One of the two which heard John *speak*, and
followed him, was Andrew, Simon Peter's brother.
41 He first findeth his own brother Simon, and
saith unto him, We have found the Messias, which
is, being interpreted, the Christ.
42 And he brought him to Jesus. And when Jesus
beheld him, he said, Thou art Simon the son of
Jona: thou shalt be called Cephas, which is by in-
terpretation, A stone.
43 ¶ The day following Jesus would go forth into
Galilee, and findeth Philip, and saith unto him,
Follow me.
44 Now Philip was of Bethsaida, the city of
Andrew and Peter.
45 Philip findeth Nathanael, and saith unto him,
We have found him, of whom Moses in the law,
and the prophets, did write, Jesus of Nazareth, the
son of Joseph.
46 And Nathanael said unto him, Can there any
good thing come out of Nazareth? Philip saith
unto him, Come and see.
47 Jesus saw Nathanael coming to him, and saith
of him, Behold an Israelite indeed, in whom is no
guile!
48 Nathanael saith unto him, Whence knowest
thou me? Jesus answered and said unto him,
Before that Philip called thee, when thou wast
under the fig tree, I saw thee.
49 Nathanael answered and saith unto him,
Rabbi, thou art the Son of God; thou art the King
of Israel.
50 Jesus answered and said unto him, Because I
said unto thee, I saw thee under the fig tree, believ-
est thou? thou shalt see greater things than these.
51 And he saith unto him, Verily, verily, I say unto
you, Hereafter ye shall see heaven open, and the
angels of God ascending and descending upon
the Son of man.

CHAPTER 2

AND the third day there was a marriage in Cana of
Galilee; and the mother of Jesus was there:
2 And both Jesus was called, and his disciples, to
the marriage.
3 And when they wanted wine, the mother of
Jesus saith unto him, They have no wine.
4 Jesus saith unto her, Woman, what have I to do
with thee? mine hour is not yet come.
5 His mother saith unto the servants, Whatsoever

1:38 *dwellest.* Stays, resides.
1:39 *tenth hour.* Likely reckoned after the Jewish time, 4:00 p.m.; or perhaps 10:00 a.m. according to the Roman method of reckoning.
1:41 *Messias.* The Messiah, literally, "the anointed one," which in Greek is *Christ*.
1:42 *Cephas.* Aramaic for *stone* (as Peter is Greek for "rock"). Jesus made a prophetic statement that Simon would one day be a great leader in the church (Matt. 16:16–18).
1:43 *day following.* See note at v. 29.
1:45 *Nathanael.* Likely Bartholomew (Matt. 10:3).
1:46 *Nazareth.* A lowly city. Though born in Bethlehem, Jesus was raised in Nazareth (Matt. 2:23).
1:47 *guile.* Deceit, perhaps a word play, since "Jacob" (whose name was changed to Israel; Gen. 35:10) means "deceiver" (Gen. 27:36). Nathanael was a man sincerely devoted to God, a member of the true spiritual Israel (*Israelite indeed*).
1:48–49 *under the fig tree.* Christ's supernatural vision provoked Nathanael to confess Him as the divinely sent Teacher, Ruler, and Savior (*Rabbi . . . Son of God . . . King of Israel*).
1:51 *Verily, verily.* Truly, truly, or literally, "Amen, amen," a statement of certainty. *angels of God ascending and descending.* Christ is the fulfillment of Jacob's dream of the ladder between earth and heaven (Gen. 28:12–13), the true Mediator between God and men who sends His angels to do His will. *Son of man.* The heavenly King appointed by God to rule forever over all (Dan. 7:13–14; also 3:13–14; 5:27; 6:27,53,62; 8:28; 12:23,34; 13:31).

Thoughts for Personal/Family Worship: Chapter 1

1. **When John called Jesus "the Word," he implied that Christ not only brings us a message from God but is Himself the Message. Jesus is God in the flesh, the infinite glory and grace of the Father dwelling among men in the tabernacle of a human body. Therefore, to believe in Christ is much more than trusting Him to teach us or help us; saving faith is receiving Him as our God, our very life. What difference does it make to the Christian faith that Christ is God?**
2. **John the Baptist shows us that a preacher's calling is to point away from himself to Christ and to lift the Savior high before men's eyes. A minister can do this only by having a low view of himself and a high view of Christ. A Christ-centered ministry is particularly a cross-centered ministry, focusing regularly (though not exclusively) on Christ's death as the Lamb of God. How can you pray for ministers that they would be like John in this manner?**
3. **To find Christ is the most wonderful discovery of all. It is too good to be kept to oneself. How can you become more like these early disciples who eagerly told their family and friends about Jesus?**

Chapter 2: ***This chapter reveals two major events in the life of Christ: His first miracle at the wedding in Cana in Galilee and the cleansing of the temple.***

2:1–2 Jesus' participation in a wedding feast implies His approval of *marriage* as a divine ordinance (Gen. 2:18–25; 1 Tim. 4:3–4).
2:3 *wanted.* Lacked.
2:4 *Woman, what have I to do with thee?* A gentle rebuke, implying no disrespect. *mine hour.* Christ knew that His mission was eternally ordained and that a time had been set for all of His works (4:21,23; 5:25; 7:6,8), especially His death (7:30; 8:20; 12:23,27; 13:1; 16:32; 17:1).
2:5 *Whatsoever he saith . . . do it.* Mary's advice is good for us all.

he saith unto you, do *it*.
6 And there were set there six waterpots of stone,
after the manner of the purifying of the Jews,
containing two or three firkins apiece.
7 Jesus saith unto them, Fill the waterpots with
water. And they filled them up to the brim.
8 And he saith unto them, Draw out now, and bear
unto the governor of the feast. And they bare *it*.
9 When the ruler of the feast had tasted the water
that was made wine, and knew not whence it was:
(but the servants which drew the water knew;) the
governor of the feast called the bridegroom,
10 And saith unto him, Every man at the begin-
ning doth set forth good wine; and when men
have well drunk, then that which is worse: *but*
thou hast kept the good wine until now.
11 This beginning of miracles did Jesus in Cana
of Galilee, and manifested forth his glory; and his
disciples believed on him.
12 ¶ After this he went down to Capernaum, he,
and his mother, and his brethren, and his disci-
ples: and they continued there not many days.
13 ¶ And the Jews' passover was at hand, and
Jesus went up to Jerusalem,
14 And found in the temple those that sold oxen
and sheep and doves, and the changers of money
sitting:
15 And when he had made a scourge of small
cords, he drove them all out of the temple, and the
sheep, and the oxen; and poured out the changers'
money, and overthrew the tables;
16 And said unto them that sold doves, Take
these things hence; make not my Father's house
an house of merchandise.
17 And his disciples remembered that it was
written, The zeal of thine house hath eaten me up.
18 ¶ Then answered the Jews and said unto him,
What sign shewest thou unto us, seeing that thou
doest these things?
19 Jesus answered and said unto them, Destroy
this temple, and in three days I will raise it up.
20 Then said the Jews, Forty and six years was
this temple in building, and wilt thou rear it up
in three days?
21 But he spake of the temple of his body.
22 When therefore he was risen from the dead,
his disciples remembered that he had said this
unto them; and they believed the scripture, and
the word which Jesus had said.
23 ¶ Now when he was in Jerusalem at the pass-
over, in the feast *day*, many believed in his name,
when they saw the miracles which he did.
24 But Jesus did not commit himself unto them,
because he knew all *men*,
25 And needed not that any should testify of
man: for he knew what was in man.

2:6 *waterpots.* Stone pots were used for Mosaic ceremonial cleansing. *manner.* Custom. *two or three firkins apiece.* Each pot held twenty or thirty gallons.
2:7 *filled . . . to the brim.* John emphasizes the large quantity of water.
2:8–9 *governor . . . ruler of the feast.* The chief steward of the wedding arrangements.
2:10 *at the beginning . . . good wine.* The taste of the wine was noticeably better than that served earlier, which was against custom, drawing attention to its high quality.
2:11 *beginning of miracles.* The first of the seven signs worked by Christ that this gospel reports (4:46–54; 5:1–9; 6:1–14,15–21; 9:1–7; 11:1–46), though it acknowledges that there were many others (v. 23; 20:30). One may study Christ's thirty-seven recorded miracles under these headings: (1) of nature, (2) of healing, (3) of exorcism, and (4) of raising from the dead. *manifested forth.* Showed, made visible. *his glory.* Only the Creator has the power to turn one chemical substance into another by His mere will. *believed on him.* See 20:31.
2:13 *passover.* Held annually in the month of March or April. Every male Jew of the age of twelve or over was expected to be at this important feast, which commemorated the deliverance of Israel from Egyptian bondage. The feast lasted seven days.
2:15–16 Christ cleansed the Temple at Jerusalem on two occasions, here at the beginning of His three-year ministry and later at the close of it (see Matt. 21). *scourge.* Whip.
2:16 Jesus was deeply displeased to witness a scene in His *Father's house*, which by this point more resembled a market (*house of merchandise*) than a place of worship.
2:17 Christ's disciplinary actions arise from His holy zeal for God and for God's pure worship (Ps. 69:9).
2:18 Rather than repenting of worldliness, the temple authorities sinfully challenged Jesus' action.
2:20–22 *Forty and six years.* Herod the Great had begun restoring the temple years earlier. *rear.* Raise. The physical building was but a shadow of *the temple of his body*, for God's glory was there dwelling among them as a man (1:14). *three days.* The duration of Christ's death, including Friday evening, Saturday, and Sunday morning.
2:23–25 *Many* people were impressed by Christ's powerful works, but their faith was not the fruit of a change of heart. *believed . . . when they saw the miracles.* While miracles are signs to confirm faith in Christ (v. 11), sinners tend to see them as a sign of the power to fulfill their earthly desires (6:14–15), so Jesus rebuked those seeking signs (4:48; 6:30). *he knew all men.* Christ was not deceived by their attention. He read more than their outward professions of faith; He read their hearts (Jer. 17:10).

Thoughts for Personal/Family Worship: Chapter 2

1. **Miracles performed by Christ are evidences or signs to show us that He is God. The faith of the disciples was strengthened by this first miracle, for it showed that Christ has the power of the Creator over His creation (1:3). The miracle of turning water into wine also suggests the manner in which Christ replaced the rituals of external religion (for which the water pots were used, v. 6) with abundant joy and life. Trusting in Christ means going beyond the outward form of religion and experiencing a new creation within by His power.**
2. **Carnal men invariably spoil the worship of God in one way or another. Worship must be regulated by God's holy Word. It is a sin to corrupt the public worship of God's house either by commerce or by entertainment. Worship must be reverent. Christ also shows here that**

CHAPTER 3

THERE was a man of the Pharisees, named Nico-
demus, a ruler of the Jews:
2 The same came to Jesus by night, and said unto
him, Rabbi, we know that thou art a teacher come
from God: for no man can do these miracles that
thou doest, except God be with him.
3 Jesus answered and said unto him, Verily, verily,
I say unto thee, Except a man be born again, he
cannot see the kingdom of God.
4 Nicodemus saith unto him, How can a man be
born when he is old? can he enter the second time
into his mother's womb, and be born?
5 Jesus answered, Verily, verily, I say unto thee,
Except a man be born of water and *of* the Spirit,
he cannot enter into the kingdom of God.
6 That which is born of the flesh is flesh; and that
which is born of the Spirit is spirit.
7 Marvel not that I said unto thee, Ye must be
born again.
8 The wind bloweth where it listeth, and thou
hearest the sound thereof, but canst not tell
whence it cometh, and whither it goeth: so is
every one that is born of the Spirit.
9 Nicodemus answered and said unto him, How
can these things be?
10 Jesus answered and said unto him, Art thou
a master of Israel, and knowest not these things?
11 Verily, verily, I say unto thee, We speak that
we do know, and testify that we have seen; and ye
receive not our witness.
12 If I have told you earthly things, and ye believe
not, how shall ye believe, if I tell you *of* heavenly
things?
13 And no man hath ascended up to heaven, but
he that came down from heaven, *even* the Son of
man which is in heaven.
14 ¶ And as Moses lifted up the serpent in the
wilderness, even so must the Son of man be lift-
ed up:
15 That whosoever believeth in him should not
perish, but have eternal life.
16 ¶ For God so loved the world, that he gave his
only begotten Son, that whosoever believeth in
him should not perish, but have everlasting life.
17 For God sent not his Son into the world to

---

discipline is essential to a faithful church. If Christ could cleanse the temple even in His state of humiliation on earth, how much more could He discipline His church as its exalted and glorious Lord? Why should this cause us to conduct worship with holy fear? How can we follow the Lord in His zeal for the purity of God's worship?

Chapter 3: *Jesus teaches the necessity of being born again, and John the Baptist exalts Christ.*

3:1 *Pharisees.* A religious sect among the Jews that had begun in the second century BC. Their great error was to add the authority of man-made tradition to Scripture. *Nicodemus.* A *ruler* and prominent teacher among the Jews (v. 10, 7:45–52; 19:38–39).

3:2 *by night.* Evidently to avoid being seen by other Pharisees. This event appears to have occurred in Jerusalem, and Nicodemus exhibited the kind of miracle-based faith that Jesus has just been depicted as rejecting (2:23–25). *Rabbi.* Teacher.

3:3 *Verily, verily.* See note at 1:51. *born again.* Birth represents the beginning of new life in relationship to the Father who causes the birth (1:13; James 1:17–18; 1 Peter 1:3). Though Nicodemus was highly educated in the Bible, positive toward Jesus, and very religious, he was unable to spiritually perceive the glory and reign of Christ (*cannot see the kingdom*; vv. 10,19–20) until God changed his heart (2 Cor. 4:4–6).

3:5 *born of water.* Not baptism but an allusion to Old Testament imagery of the renewing power *of the Spirit* (Isa. 44:3–5; Ezek. 36:25–27), given through the Mediator, Jesus Christ (v. 34; 1:33; 4:10; 7:37–39; Isa. 32:1–2,15; Titus 3:5–6). *cannot enter into the kingdom.* It is impossible for people to be converted and saved unless God works a miracle in their souls (6:44,65; Matt. 19:25–26).

3:6 *born of the flesh is flesh.* Fallen human nature in its sin and misery can only produce more of the same. Salvation requires a supernatural work of the Holy *Spirit* (6:63), who produces His image (*spirit*) in sinners by the new birth (1 John 2:29; 3:9; 4:7; 5:1,4,18).

3:8 *wind.* The same Greek word as *Spirit*, perhaps alluding to Ezekiel's vision of the dry bones (Ezek. 37:9,14). Like the wind, the Holy Spirit is powerful, invisible, and beyond the scope of man's control or manipulation through ritual or method; He works as He chooses (*listeth*).

3:10 *master of Israel.* Teacher of the Jewish people. Jesus' rebuke implies that His teaching on the new birth is rooted in the Old Testament, and also that Nicodemus's mind was blind to the truth despite his Pharisaic training in the Scriptures.

3:12 *earthly things . . . heavenly things.* The new birth is a basic teaching of the faith, a foundation for understanding deeper teachings.

3:13 *came down from heaven.* The language of God displaying His glory on earth (Ex. 19:11,18,20; 24:16; Neh. 9:13). *Son of man.* See note at 1:51. *which is in heaven.* Though in His human nature Christ was on earth, in His divine nature He was present in all places (1:48), including heaven. Christ's deity and majesty mean that He has infinite authority to speak on all subjects (v. 12).

3:14–15 *lifted up the serpent.* After Israel's sins had brought deadly snake bites, God instructed Moses to affix a bronze image of a snake to a pole to heal anyone looking up at it (Num. 21:4–9). This was a type or representation revealing God's decree that it was necessary (*must*) for the heavenly King (*Son of man*; v. 13) to *be lifted up* on the cross (8:28; 12:32–33) so that all who look upon Him with the spiritual sight of faith will receive *eternal life* with God.

3:16 *For.* A further explanation of vv. 14–15. *God.* The ultimate explanation for anyone's salvation is the will of the Father (6:38–40; Gal. 1:4–5; Eph. 2:4). *so loved.* The Son did not win the Father's love for sinners but came because God loved sinners, indeed loved them so much *that he gave* the most precious and costly gift imaginable, *his only begotten Son* (1 John 4:9–10; see note at 1:14). *world.* A general term for humanity, viewed not as all persons without exception in all places and times (8:26; 12:19; 14:22; 16:20) but as man in his unified rebellion against God (v. 19; 1:9–11; 7:7; 8:23; 14:17,30; 15:18–19; 16:11,20; 17:14,25), making God's sacrificial love for mankind all the more amazing (Rom. 5:6–8). *whosoever believeth.* God's purpose in sending Christ was not to save all

condemn the world; but that the world through
him might be saved.
18 ¶ He that believeth on him is not condemned:
but he that believeth not is condemned already,
because he hath not believed in the name of the
only begotten Son of God.
19 And this is the condemnation, that light is
come into the world, and men loved darkness
rather than light, because their deeds were evil.
20 For every one that doeth evil hateth the light,
neither cometh to the light, lest his deeds should
be reproved.
21 But he that doeth truth cometh to the light,
that his deeds may be made manifest, that they
are wrought in God.
22 ¶ After these things came Jesus and his disci-
ples into the land of Judaea; and there he tarried
with them, and baptized.
23 ¶ And John also was baptizing in Aenon near
to Salim, because there was much water there:
and they came, and were baptized.
24 For John was not yet cast into prison.
25 ¶ Then there arose a question between *some*
of John's disciples and the Jews about purifying.
26 And they came unto John, and said unto him,
Rabbi, he that was with thee beyond Jordan, to
whom thou barest witness, behold, the same
baptizeth, and all *men* come to him.
27 John answered and said, A man can receive
nothing, except it be given him from heaven.
28 Ye yourselves bear me witness, that I said, I am
not the Christ, but that I am sent before him.
29 He that hath the bride is the bridegroom: but
the friend of the bridegroom, which standeth and
heareth him, rejoiceth greatly because of the bride-
groom's voice: this my joy therefore is fulfilled.
30 He must increase, but I *must* decrease.
31 He that cometh from above is above all: he
that is of the earth is earthly, and speaketh of the
earth: he that cometh from heaven is above all.
32 And what he hath seen and heard, that he tes-
tifieth; and no man receiveth his testimony.
33 He that hath received his testimony hath set to
his seal that God is true.
34 For he whom God hath sent speaketh the
words of God: for God giveth not the Spirit by
measure *unto him*.
35 The Father loveth the Son, and hath given all
things into his hand.
36 He that believeth on the Son hath everlasting
life: and he that believeth not the Son shall not see
life; but the wrath of God abideth on him.

persons but to give *everlasting life* to those whom He would bring to saving faith through the new birth (vv. 3–8). Salvation from eternal ruin (*perish*) requires faith in Christ.

3:17–18 *not . . . to condemn*. Christ's first coming was not in order to judge or punish but to bring salvation. To reject Christ is to bring God's judgment upon oneself. *He that believeth . . . is not condemned*. Sinners are legally justified by the divine Judge through faith alone in Christ (Gal. 2:16).

3:19–20 God loves the *world* (v. 16), but the world hates Christ (*the light*; 1:4,9) because of its pride, self-righteousness, and love for sin. Thus God must change the heart before anyone will come to Christ in saving faith (*cometh to the light*; 6:35). *reproved*. A legal term implying conviction of wrongdoing.

3:21 *wrought in God*. Worked by God or through God's grace. No one comes to Christ apart from a prior work of God in the soul (v. 3; 6:37,44).

3:22 *tarried*. Remained or stayed for a time. Jesus *baptized* by means of His disciples (4:2).

3:25 *purifying*. Purification rites from the Mosaic law. Evidently some were displeased to think that Jesus was becoming more popular than John.

3:26 *all men come to him*. An example of *all* meaning many, though not everyone.

3:27 *except it be given him*. God's ministers are utterly dependent upon the Lord for the success of their ministry (1 Cor. 3:5–7).

3:29 *bridegroom*. Christ is the spiritual husband of the true Israel, her covenant Lord (Isa. 54:5; 62:4–5; Mark 2:19–20).

3:31–36 Christ is *above all*, for His teaching is based on what He has *seen and heard* as the Son of God in *heaven*, that is, the everlasting and infallible counsels of Almighty God. Christ has the Holy *Spirit* dwelling in Him in complete fullness (*not . . . by measure*). As the *Son* of God, Jesus is loved by the *Father* and has had all authority given to Him. To believe in Christ alone for salvation is to be sure of heaven; to reject Christ is to be under the wrath and displeasure of God.

3:33 *hath set to his seal*. Has certified or given his confirmation by believing.

3:34 *giveth not the Spirit by measure*. Christ possesses the Holy Spirit without limit to carry out the divine work of the Father (1:32–33; Isa. 11:1–2).

3:36 *wrath of God*. Many focus on the doctrine of God's love; however, God also hates sin, and His anger burns with holy hatred against all who are not yet saved by faith in Christ (Ps. 5:4–6; Rom. 1:18; 2:5,8). Therefore, we dare not presume on the love of God to excuse unbelief.

Thoughts for Personal/Family Worship: Chapter 3

1. **In the church it is not enough for leaders to be academically well trained, nor for its members to be well taught. Without the new birth men are entirely unfit for the kingdom of God. Through the new birth dead sinners are made alive, and at last they will be raised up from the dead to sit with Him in the glory of heaven. Why is the new birth absolutely necessary for salvation? Are you born again?**
2. **God's sending of His Son to save the world from condemnation is the greatest display of love in all of human history. God gave His best, His unique Son who shares His very nature, for those who hate and reject Him. Christ was lifted up on the cross to die so that guilty sinners could live forever in relationship with God. What love is this! Why should His love move sinners to trust in Him?**
3. **We must resist our ignorant and worldly tendency to boast of one minister above another. The abilities and success of each are gifts from heaven. Like John the Baptist, we should have a low view of ourselves and give our full affection and admiration to the Bridegroom. How wonderful is the marriage of the Lord to His people! How can loving Jesus as our spiritual Husband protect us from exalting mere men?**

CHAPTER 4

WHEN therefore the Lord knew how the Pharisees
had heard that Jesus made and baptized more
disciples than John,
2 (Though Jesus himself baptized not, but his
disciples,)
3 He left Judaea, and departed again into Galilee.
4 And he must needs go through Samaria.
5 Then cometh he to a city of Samaria, which is
called Sychar, near to the parcel of ground that
Jacob gave to his son Joseph.
6 Now Jacob's well was there. Jesus therefore, be-
ing wearied with *his* journey, sat thus on the well:
and it was about the sixth hour.
7 There cometh a woman of Samaria to draw
water: Jesus saith unto her, Give me to drink.
8 (For his disciples were gone away unto the city
to buy meat.)
9 Then saith the woman of Samaria unto him,
How is it that thou, being a Jew, askest drink of
me, which am a woman of Samaria? for the Jews
have no dealings with the Samaritans.
10 Jesus answered and said unto her, If thou
knewest the gift of God, and who it is that saith to
thee, Give me to drink; thou wouldest have asked
of him, and he would have given thee living water.
11 The woman saith unto him, Sir, thou hast
nothing to draw with, and the well is deep: from
whence then hast thou that living water?
12 Art thou greater than our father Jacob, which
gave us the well, and drank thereof himself, and
his children, and his cattle?
13 Jesus answered and said unto her, Whosoever
drinketh of this water shall thirst again:
14 But whosoever drinketh of the water that I
shall give him shall never thirst; but the water that
I shall give him shall be in him a well of water
springing up into everlasting life.
15 The woman saith unto him, Sir, give me this
water, that I thirst not, neither come hither to draw.
16 Jesus saith unto her, Go, call thy husband, and
come hither.
17 The woman answered and said, I have no hus-
band. Jesus said unto her, Thou hast well said, I
have no husband:
18 For thou hast had five husbands; and he
whom thou now hast is not thy husband: in that
saidst thou truly.
19 The woman saith unto him, Sir, I perceive that
thou art a prophet.
20 Our fathers worshipped in this mountain; and
ye say, that in Jerusalem is the place where men
ought to worship.
21 Jesus saith unto her, Woman, believe me, the
hour cometh, when ye shall neither in this moun-
tain, nor yet at Jerusalem, worship the Father.
22 Ye worship ye know not what: we know what
we worship: for salvation is of the Jews.
23 But the hour cometh, and now is, when the
true worshippers shall worship the Father in spirit
and in truth: for the Father seeketh such to wor-
ship him.
24 God *is* a Spirit: and they that worship him
must worship *him* in spirit and in truth.
25 The woman saith unto him, I know that
Messias cometh, which is called Christ: when he

Chapter 4: *Jesus speaks with the Samaritan woman at the well, and many Samaritans believe. Then Jesus heals a nobleman's son.*

4:1–4 Jesus travels northward from Judaea to Galilee, intentionally passing through *Samaria*, a region inhabited by people despised by strict Jews (v. 9) as being of mixed race and religion since the exile of the northern tribes (2 Kings 17:22–41).

4:5–6 *parcel.* Piece, portion. *Jacob gave to . . . Joseph.* See note at Gen. 48:22. *sixth hour.* Likely noon, the heat of the day.

4:8 *meat.* Food of any kind.

4:9 *thou, being a Jew.* Jesus' actions were culturally and religiously unacceptable to the mindset of His day, but He is not bound by men's conventions or prejudices.

4:10 *gift of God.* Jesus identified Himself as the One who gives God's spiritual blessing. *living water.* Jesus used "fresh, running water" to symbolize the overflowing life of joy found only by union with God through Christ in the Holy Spirit (7:37–39; Ps. 42:1–2; Jer. 2:13; Zech. 14:8; Rev. 21:6; 22:17; cf. Ezek. 47:1–12).

4:14 *never thirst.* Physical desires require repeated satisfaction and never fully satiate us, but Christ becomes an internal source of vitality that satisfies the heart (*in him a well of water*; Isa. 12:3) and leads to complete happiness forever (*springing up into everlasting life*; Rev. 7:15–17).

4:15 *hither.* Here (v. 16).

4:16–18 *Go, call thy husband.* Having caught her attention, He now put His finger on her conscience to reveal her sins and need of salvation.

4:19 *prophet.* She realized that He had a supernatural knowledge of her life (v. 29). Her conscience was roused, and she moved on to the level of religious conversation.

4:20 *this mountain.* Mt. Gerizim, long the site of the Samaritan temple.

4:21 *hour cometh.* Christ's coming brought about the fullness of time (Gal. 4:4), and through Him God was beginning to implement His plan to draw the nations into true worship. *nor yet at Jerusalem.* The temple and ceremonial law were passing away because the true temple had come in Christ (1:14; 2:21).

4:22 *worship ye know not what.* While the Samaritans accepted the five books of Moses, their rejection of the rest of the Old Testament caused them to worship in a manner unacceptable to God.

4:23 *worship the Father in spirit and truth.* True worship takes place when the Holy Spirit engages the human spirit with God's Word. The outward worship that largely characterized the temple of the old covenant was being replaced by the simplicity and privilege of access to the *Father* in the Spirit through faith in the Son (Eph. 2:18,21–22).

4:24 *God is a Spirit.* Or "God is spirit" (cf. 1 John 1:5; 4:8,16). God's being is not material or bound by physical location but is infinite, eternal, and personal life (Isa. 31:3).

is come, he will tell us all things.
26 Jesus saith unto her, I that speak unto thee
am *he*.
27 ¶ And upon this came his disciples, and
marvelled that he talked with the woman: yet no
man said, What seekest thou? or, Why talkest thou
with her?
28 The woman then left her waterpot, and went
her way into the city, and saith to the men,
29 Come, see a man, which told me all things that
ever I did: is not this the Christ?
30 Then they went out of the city, and came un-
to him.
31 ¶ In the mean while his disciples prayed him,
saying, Master, eat.
32 But he said unto them, I have meat to eat that
ye know not of.
33 Therefore said the disciples one to another,
Hath any man brought him *ought* to eat?
34 Jesus saith unto them, My meat is to do the
will of him that sent me, and to finish his work.
35 Say not ye, There are yet four months, and
then cometh harvest? behold, I say unto you, Lift
up your eyes, and look on the fields; for they are
white already to harvest.
36 And he that reapeth receiveth wages, and
gathereth fruit unto life eternal: that both he that
soweth and he that reapeth may rejoice together.
37 And herein is that saying true, One soweth,
and another reapeth.
38 I sent you to reap that whereon ye bestowed
no labour: other men laboured, and ye are en-
tered into their labours.
39 ¶ And many of the Samaritans of that city
believed on him for the saying of the woman,
which testified, He told me all that ever I did.
40 So when the Samaritans were come unto him,
they besought him that he would tarry with them:
and he abode there two days.
41 And many more believed because of his own
word;
42 And said unto the woman, Now we believe,
not because of thy saying: for we have heard *him*
ourselves, and know that this is indeed the Christ,
the Saviour of the world.
43 ¶ Now after two days he departed thence, and
went into Galilee.
44 For Jesus himself testified, that a prophet hath
no honour in his own country.
45 Then when he was come into Galilee, the Gali-
laeans received him, having seen all the things
that he did at Jerusalem at the feast: for they also
went unto the feast.
46 So Jesus came again into Cana of Galilee,
where he made the water wine. And there was a
certain nobleman, whose son was sick at Caper-
naum.
47 When he heard that Jesus was come out
of Judaea into Galilee, he went unto him, and
besought him that he would come down, and heal
his son: for he was at the point of death.
48 Then said Jesus unto him, Except ye see signs
and wonders, ye will not believe.
49 The nobleman saith unto him, Sir, come down
ere my child die.
50 Jesus saith unto him, Go thy way; thy son
liveth. And the man believed the word that Jesus
had spoken unto him, and he went his way.
51 And as he was now going down, his servants
met him, and told *him*, saying, Thy son liveth.
52 Then enquired he of them the hour when he
began to amend. And they said unto him, Yester-
day at the seventh hour the fever left him.
53 So the father knew that *it was* at the same hour,
in the which Jesus said unto him, Thy son liveth:
and himself believed, and his whole house.
54 This *is* again the second miracle *that* Jesus did,
when he was come out of Judaea into Galilee.

4:25–26 *Messias.* Messiah, or Christ (1:41). *I . . . am he.* Jesus openly confessed to the Samaritans that He is the promised Christ.
4:27 *marvelled.* It was a rule that a rabbi not speak with any *woman* in the street.
4:28 *left her waterpot.* She had found the true well.
4:29–30 As when the disciples of John discovered Jesus (1:41-42,45–46), the Samaritan woman quickly told her neighbors and friends about Him.
4:31 *prayed.* Asked.
4:34 His spiritual food (*meat*) was to complete His great mission on earth, which was to gather in God's elect people into His kingdom. Evangelism satisfies God's servants.
4:35–36 There is a *harvest* of souls ripe for ingathering. Those who sow gospel truth and those who gather in precious souls for God will rejoice together on the great day.
4:37–38 *One soweth.* Jesus sowed the Word among the Samaritans (vv. 41–42), and the apostles would one day reap a harvest of churches in Samaria (Acts 1:8; 8:5,14,25).
4:39–42 *Saviour of the world.* Not just of the Jews but of sinners from all nations (Rev. 5:9).
4:43–45 Jesus continued His journey northward to *Galilee* (v. 3).
4:46 *came again into Cana of Galilee.* This marks the starting point of Christ's great Galilean ministry, which was to last for about sixteen months, a period extensively recorded in the other three gospels but largely assumed in this gospel, except for the healing of the nobleman's son (vv. 46–53) and the feeding of the five thousand (6:5–14). *nobleman.* Royal officer.
4:47 *besought.* Asked.
4:48 *ye.* Plural of "you"; Christ's rebuke was not aimed specifically at the man but at the people in general, warning against faith based merely on miracles (2:23–25).
4:49 *ere.* Before.
4:50 *thy son liveth.* Christ's mere *word* was powerful to heal at a distance (v. 51; Matt. 8:8–10). Cana and Capernaum were sixteen miles apart.
4:52–53 *amend.* Change for the better. *seventh hour.* 1:00 p.m. *the same hour.* The healing of the child at the same time Jesus spoke confirmed that the healing was done at His word,

CHAPTER 5

AFTER this there was a feast of the Jews; and Jesus
went up to Jerusalem.
2 Now there is at Jerusalem by the sheep *mar-ket* a pool, which is called in the Hebrew tongue
Bethesda, having five porches.
3 In these lay a great multitude of impotent folk,
of blind, halt, withered, waiting for the moving
of the water.
4 For an angel went down at a certain season into
the pool, and troubled the water: whosoever then
first after the troubling of the water stepped in
was made whole of whatsoever disease he had.
5 And a certain man was there, which had an
infirmity thirty and eight years.
6 When Jesus saw him lie, and knew that he had
been now a long time *in that case*, he saith unto
him, Wilt thou be made whole?
7 The impotent man answered him, Sir, I have no
man, when the water is troubled, to put me into
the pool: but while I am coming, another step-peth down before me.
8 Jesus saith unto him, Rise, take up thy bed, and
walk.
9 And immediately the man was made whole,
and took up his bed, and walked: and on the same
day was the sabbath.
10 ¶ The Jews therefore said unto him that was
cured, It is the sabbath day: it is not lawful for thee
to carry *thy* bed.
11 He answered them, He that made me whole,
the same said unto me, Take up thy bed, and walk.
12 Then asked they him, What man is that which
said unto thee, Take up thy bed, and walk?
13 And he that was healed wist not who it was:
for Jesus had conveyed himself away, a multitude
being in *that* place.
14 Afterward Jesus findeth him in the temple, and
said unto him, Behold, thou art made whole: sin
no more, lest a worse thing come unto thee.
15 The man departed, and told the Jews that it
was Jesus, which had made him whole.
16 And therefore did the Jews persecute Jesus,
and sought to slay him, because he had done these
things on the sabbath day.
17 ¶ But Jesus answered them, My Father work-eth hitherto, and I work.
18 Therefore the Jews sought the more to kill
him, because he not only had broken the sabbath,
but said also that God was his Father, making
himself equal with God.
19 Then answered Jesus and said unto them,
Verily, verily, I say unto you, The Son can do
nothing of himself, but what he seeth the Father
do: for what things soever he doeth, these also
doeth the Son likewise.

---

which confirmed the faith of the father; his family and servants were also saved (*his whole house*; Acts 16:31–34).

4:54 *second miracle.* See note at 2:11.

Thoughts for Personal/Family Worship: Chapter 4

1. **The Christian should learn to turn conversations with unconverted persons to the subject of salvation, as Christ does so kindly here. Christ wisely began with physical, visible things but used them as a lead-in to God's gift and our spiritual need. In our preaching and evangelism we must strive to convince hearers that they have sinned against God. The sinner's conscience is the preacher's friend. However, a sense of sin helps no one without the knowledge of the Savior of the world. Where do you see yourself most in this chapter? The woman confronted, convicted, or converted?**
2. **Worship is unacceptable to God unless it is "in spirit and in truth" (v. 23). That means that the worshiper must be spiritually reborn and be walking in the Spirit and that the content and form of worship offered must be according to God's Word. What are some examples of worship that are not done "in spirit"? What are examples of worship not offered "in truth"?**

Christ Rejected by Unbelievers (5:1—6:71)

Chapter 5: *Jesus heals on the Sabbath, and the Jews persecute Him. Jesus gives a defense of His authority to the Jews.*

5:1 *feast of the Jews.* We do not know whether it was Passover, Pentecost, or Tabernacles.

5:2 *Bethesda.* "House of Mercy." *porches.* Covered colonnades where the sick gathered in large numbers.

5:3 *impotent.* Weak. *halt.* Crippled.

5:4 These words explain the large gathering of invalids around this pool.

5:5 *infirmity.* Weakness. *thirty and eight years.* Only an act of God could heal him of a condition so entrenched and long-term.

5:6 *Wilt thou.* Are you willing, do you wish.

5:7 *I have no man . . . another steppeth down before me.* Every man was out for himself, a display of humanity's selfish nature.

5:10 *not lawful.* The sour religionists instead of rejoicing scold him for allegedly breaking the Sabbath.

5:13 *wist not.* Did not know. *conveyed himself away.* Left without being seen.

5:14 *sin no more.* It is clear that though this man's body had been healed, his soul had not been saved. *a worse thing.* God's eternal judgment is far more horrible than thirty-eight years of severe disability (Matt. 5:29–30).

5:15 *told . . . it was Jesus.* He knowingly betrayed the Lord who had healed him to Christ's enemies.

5:16 *Jews persecute Jesus.* Here, and often elsewhere (v. 18; 7:1,11,13; etc.), the Pharisees and other leaders of Judaea, not necessarily the Jewish people as a whole.

5:17–18 *My Father.* An unprecedented way to speak of God. The Jews rightly understood it as claiming Jesus' equality with God (10:30–33). *hitherto.* Until now.

5:19 *Verily, verily.* See note at 1:51. *can do nothing of himself.* The Father and the Son are one God and have one perfect will, and yet there is order in the Trinity, such that the Father leads and the Son follows. *what things soever he doeth . . . the Son likewise.* All the works of the Trinity in creation, providence, and salvation engage all three divine persons in united action, for they share one divine power (see note at 6:65).

5:20 *sheweth him all things that himself doeth.* This implies

20 For the Father loveth the Son, and sheweth
him all things that himself doeth: and he will
shew him greater works than these, that ye may
marvel.
21 For as the Father raiseth up the dead, and
quickeneth *them*; even so the Son quickeneth
whom he will.
22 For the Father judgeth no man, but hath
committed all judgment unto the Son:
23 That all *men* should honour the Son, even as
they honour the Father. He that honoureth not
the Son honoureth not the Father which hath
sent him.
24 Verily, verily, I say unto you, He that heareth
my word, and believeth on him that sent me, hath
everlasting life, and shall not come into condem-
nation; but is passed from death unto life.
25 Verily, verily, I say unto you, The hour is com-
ing, and now is, when the dead shall hear the voice
of the Son of God: and they that hear shall live.
26 For as the Father hath life in himself; so hath
he given to the Son to have life in himself;
27 And hath given him authority to execute
judgment also, because he is the Son of man.
28 Marvel not at this: for the hour is coming, in
the which all that are in the graves shall hear his
voice,
29 And shall come forth; they that have done
good, unto the resurrection of life; and they
that have done evil, unto the resurrection of
damnation.
30 I can of mine own self do nothing: as I hear, I
judge: and my judgment is just; because I seek not
mine own will, but the will of the Father which
hath sent me.
31 If I bear witness of myself, my witness is not
true.
32 ¶ There is another that beareth witness of me;
and I know that the witness which he witnesseth
of me is true.
33 Ye sent unto John, and he bare witness unto
the truth.
34 But I receive not testimony from man: but
these things I say, that ye might be saved.
35 He was a burning and a shining light: and ye
were willing for a season to rejoice in his light.
36 ¶ But I have greater witness than *that* of John:
for the works which the Father hath given me to
finish, the same works that I do, bear witness of
me, that the Father hath sent me.
37 And the Father himself, which hath sent me,
hath borne witness of me. Ye have neither heard
his voice at any time, nor seen his shape.
38 And ye have not his word abiding in you: for
whom he hath sent, him ye believe not.
39 ¶ Search the scriptures; for in them ye think
ye have eternal life: and they are they which tes-
tify of me.
40 And ye will not come to me, that ye might have
life.
41 I receive not honour from men.
42 But I know you, that ye have not the love of
God in you.
43 I am come in my Father's name, and ye receive
me not: if another shall come in his own name,
him ye will receive.
44 How can ye believe, which receive honour one
of another, and seek not the honour that *cometh*
from God only?
45 Do not think that I will accuse you to the

---

that the Son has the infinite knowledge of God (16:30; 21:17). *greater works than these.* Christ's healings were signs that He would raise the dead (vv. 21–22), in the last day unto judgment (vv. 22–23,28–29) and in this age to spiritual life (vv. 24–25). These are the works of God.

5:21 *quickeneth.* Gives life. *whom he will.* Christ is sovereign in salvation (Matt. 11:27).

5:22–23 God *the Father* displays the divine honor of God *the Son* in appointing Him to execute the divine work of judging all men, so that people must reverence Christ.

5:24 *hath everlasting life.* The glorious life of the coming kingdom (Matt. 25:46) has already come into this world in Jesus Christ (1:4) for all who are in union with Him by faith.

5:25 *hour is coming, and now is.* Christ's coming marks the climax of God's plan. *dead . . . shall live.* Christ brings a spiritual resurrection from the dead (v. 24; Luke 15:32; Eph. 2:1,5; 1 John 3:14) through His powerful Word (*hear the voice*; cf. 11:43–44).

5:26 *life in himself.* The triune God is the "I AM" (8:58; Ex. 3:14), the self-existent One who depends on nothing outside Himself (aseity) but is His own life and so gives all life to others (1:4; 4:10,14,24; Ps. 36:8–9; Jer. 2:13; 17:13). *given to the Son to have life in himself.* God the Son possesses the same self-existence of the divine nature as the Father, yet this is from the Father, implying that the Father eternally begets or generates the person of the Son in the fullness of the divine nature (6:57).

5:28–29 *hour is coming.* Judgment day, at Christ's return. *in the graves . . . shall come forth.* The physical resurrection from the dead of the *good* and *evil* to their eternal destinies (Dan. 12:2).

5:31–39 Christ was accused of breaking the Sabbath and of falsely claiming equality with God (vv. 16,18). In response He cites various witnesses who support His testimony of Himself (v. 31), including John the Baptist (vv. 32–35, and, far greater, God the Father, who testified of His approval through Christ's miracles (vv. 36–37; see Acts 10:38) and in His Word, the Scriptures (vv. 38–39).

5:38–39 Though scholars of the *Scriptures*, they had rejected the message of the Bible (*have not his word abiding in you*) because they were blind to its most important teaching: Jesus is the Christ (*testify of me*).

5:40 *ye will not come to me.* Literally, "You are not willing to come to Me." The responsibility for man's damnation falls upon sinners because they refuse to believe.

5:43 *if another shall come in his own name.* In the coming days there were to be many false messiahs (Matt. 24:24) whom people would follow; an example is Simon Bar-Kochba (d. 135).

5:44 *How can ye believe.* It is a snare to seek the honor and praise of men.

Father: there is *one* that accuseth you, *even* Moses,
in whom ye trust.
46 For had ye believed Moses, ye would have
believed me: for he wrote of me.
47 But if ye believe not his writings, how shall ye
believe my words?

CHAPTER 6

AFTER these things Jesus went over the sea of Gali-
lee, which is *the sea* of Tiberias.
2 And a great multitude followed him, because
they saw his miracles which he did on them that
were diseased.
3 And Jesus went up into a mountain, and there
he sat with his disciples.
4 And the passover, a feast of the Jews, was nigh.
5 ¶ When Jesus then lifted up *his* eyes, and saw a
great company come unto him, he saith unto Phil-
ip, Whence shall we buy bread, that these may eat?
6 And this he said to prove him: for he himself
knew what he would do.
7 Philip answered him, Two hundred pennyworth
of bread is not sufficient for them, that every one
of them may take a little.
8 One of his disciples, Andrew, Simon Peter's
brother, saith unto him,
9 There is a lad here, which hath five barley
loaves, and two small fishes: but what are they
among so many?
10 And Jesus said, Make the men sit down. Now
there was much grass in the place. So the men sat
down, in number about five thousand.
11 And Jesus took the loaves; and when he had
given thanks, he distributed to the disciples, and
the disciples to them that were set down; and
likewise of the fishes as much as they would.
12 When they were filled, he said unto his disci-
ples, Gather up the fragments that remain, that
nothing be lost.
13 Therefore they gathered *them* together, and
filled twelve baskets with the fragments of the five
barley loaves, which remained over and above
unto them that had eaten.
14 Then those men, when they had seen the mir-
acle that Jesus did, said, This is of a truth that
prophet that should come into the world.
15 ¶ When Jesus therefore perceived that they
would come and take him by force, to make him a
king, he departed again into a mountain himself
alone.
16 And when even was *now* come, his disciples
went down unto the sea,
17 And entered into a ship, and went over the sea
toward Capernaum. And it was now dark, and
Jesus was not come to them.
18 And the sea arose by reason of a great wind
that blew.
19 So when they had rowed about five and twenty
or thirty furlongs, they see Jesus walking on the

5:45–47 These unconverted rabbis professed to respect and observe Moses' teachings. But, ironically, since they rejected Christ they would in the last days discover that Moses would be among the first to accuse them of error and sin.
5:46 *Moses . . . wrote.* Jesus affirmed that Moses was the author of the biblical books known as "The Law" (7:19; see Introduction to the Pentateuch).

Thoughts for Personal/Family Worship: Chapter 5

1. **Christ blessed the cripple before he had even asked to be healed. Yet He also issued a strong call to repentance (v. 14). Many who receive physical or material blessings from Christ do not acknowledge God in a life of repentance. How have you experienced earthly blessings from Christ? What does it mean for you to hear Christ's "Sin no more, lest a worse thing come unto thee" (v. 14)?**
2. **None will ever honor Christ rightly until they recognize that He is the eternal Son of God incarnate. From all eternity the Father, the Son, and the Holy Spirit have shared one divine nature, with one will and one power. They cooperate in a beautiful relationship as three persons in one God. Honoring the Son as God does not demean the Father, for honoring the Son is the way through which the Father desires to be honored. How can we honor the Son as the Giver of eternal life? As the Judge?**

Chapter 6: *Christ multiplies the loaves and fish, walks on the sea, and discourses on the bread of heaven. The people stumble at His teaching, but Peter confesses faith in Christ.*

6:1–15 The feeding of the five thousand occurred at the close of Christ's great Galilean ministry. It is the only miracle of Christ narrated in all four Gospels (Matt. 14:15–21; Mark 6:35–44; Luke 9:12–17).
6:1 *went over the sea.* To the eastern side of the sea of Galilee (*Tiberias*).
6:3 *went up into a mountain.* Perhaps a comparison with Moses (v. 15; see Ex. 19:2–3,20; 24:15).
6:4 *passover.* A *feast* celebrating Israel's salvation from Egypt (Ex. 12:1–51), generally commemorated around our month of April. *nigh.* Near.
6:6 *prove.* Test.
6:7 *Two hundred pennyworth.* Two hundred denarii, about eight months of wages for a laborer.
6:10 *men . . . five thousand.* In addition there were women and children (Matt. 14:21).
6:14 *that prophet that should come.* They recognized Jesus as the fulfillment of the promise of Moses (Deut. 18:15; Acts 3:22; 7:37).
6:15 *make him a king.* They intended to use Christ's power to save them from their earthly problems and satisfy their earthly desires, rather than to trust Christ to save them from sin and satisfy them with God (v. 27). *he departed.* Christ refused a kingdom of this world in order that He might instead build a spiritual kingdom upon the truth (18:36–37).
6:16 *even.* Evening.
6:17 *over the sea toward Capernaum.* Back to the western shore.
6:19 *five and twenty or thirty furlongs.* Twenty-five or thirty *stadia*, about three or three and one-half miles. *drawing nigh.* Coming near. Christ's miracle of *walking on the sea* shows His Lordship and alludes to Old Testament statements about the

sea, and drawing nigh unto the ship: and they
were afraid.
20 But he saith unto them, It is I; be not afraid.
21 Then they willingly received him into the ship:
and immediately the ship was at the land whither
they went.
22 ¶ The day following, when the people which
stood on the other side of the sea saw that there
was none other boat there, save that one whereinto his disciples were entered, and that Jesus
went not with his disciples into the boat, but *that*
his disciples were gone away alone;
23 (Howbeit there came other boats from Tiberias nigh unto the place where they did eat bread,
after that the Lord had given thanks:)
24 When the people therefore saw that Jesus was
not there, neither his disciples, they also took shipping, and came to Capernaum, seeking for Jesus.
25 And when they had found him on the other
side of the sea, they said unto him, Rabbi, when
camest thou hither?
26 Jesus answered them and said, Verily, verily, I
say unto you, Ye seek me, not because ye saw the
miracles, but because ye did eat of the loaves, and
were filled.
27 Labour not for the meat which perisheth, but
for that meat which endureth unto everlasting
life, which the Son of man shall give unto you: for
him hath God the Father sealed.
28 Then said they unto him, What shall we do,
that we might work the works of God?
29 Jesus answered and said unto them, This is
the work of God, that ye believe on him whom
he hath sent.
30 They said therefore unto him, What sign
shewest thou then, that we may see, and believe
thee? what dost thou work?
31 Our fathers did eat manna in the desert; as it is
written, He gave them bread from heaven to eat.
32 Then Jesus said unto them, Verily, verily, I say
unto you, Moses gave you not that bread from
heaven; but my Father giveth you the true bread
from heaven.
33 For the bread of God is he which cometh
down from heaven, and giveth life unto the world.
34 Then said they unto him, Lord, evermore give
us this bread.
35 And Jesus said unto them, I am the bread of
life: he that cometh to me shall never hunger; and
he that believeth on me shall never thirst.
36 But I said unto you, That ye also have seen me,
and believe not.
37 All that the Father giveth me shall come to
me; and him that cometh to me I will in no wise
cast out.
38 For I came down from heaven, not to do mine
own will, but the will of him that sent me.
39 And this is the Father's will which hath sent
me, that of all which he hath given me I should
lose nothing, but should raise it up again at the
last day.
40 And this is the will of him that sent me, that
every one which seeth the Son, and believeth on
him, may have everlasting life: and I will raise him
up at the last day.
41 The Jews then murmured at him, because
he said, I am the bread which came down from
heaven.
42 And they said, Is not this Jesus, the son of
Joseph, whose father and mother we know? how
is it then that he saith, I came down from heaven?
43 Jesus therefore answered and said unto them,
Murmur not among yourselves.
44 No man can come to me, except the Father

glory and mystery of God (Job 9:8; Ps. 77:19; Isa. 43:16).
6:21 *immediately . . . at the land.* This itself was a supernatural event, though not typically considered one of John's seven recorded miracles. *whither.* To which.
6:23 *Howbeit.* But. *nigh.* Near.
6:24 *took shipping.* Set sail.
6:25 *hither.* Here, to this place.
6:26–27 *Verily, verily.* See note at 1:51. *Son of man.* The heavenly King (vv. 53,62; see note at 1:51). Christ did not answer their question but rebuked them because their interest in Him arose from their having been well fed with earthly food, not from a hunger for God and His righteousness (Matt. 5:6).
6:28–29 *work the works of God.* If men are to serve God, their first calling is to *believe* in Christ as Savior.
6:31 *manna . . . bread from heaven.* Believing that Christ might be the prophet like Moses (v. 14), they asked Jesus to work miracles similar to those Israel had seen *in the desert* (Ex. 16; Pss. 78:24; 105:40).
6:32–35 *I am.* One of the several "I am" declarations of Christ, linking His deity (Ex. 3:14) to His sufficiency to meet every need (vv. 48,51). *true bread from heaven . . . bread of life.* The manna in the wilderness was a type or representation of Christ being the life of His people in a lifeless world. Thus Jesus is far greater than Moses. *never hunger . . . never thirst.* See note at 4:14.
6:37 *All that the Father giveth me.* Those persons whom God chose in eternity for the Son to save and whom He calls to the Son (v. 39; 10:29; 17:2,6,9,11–12,24; 18:9; cf. 15:16) by the Word and Spirit (v. 63). *shall come to me.* God's election and calling produce faith in Christ (1:12–13). *I will in no wise cast out.* Christ will never reject any sinner coming to Him in faith (Matt. 11:28).
6:38 *came down . . . to do . . . the will of him that sent me.* Christ's saving mission comes from the love and sovereign decree of the Father (3:16). The essence of Christ's work is to obey His Father's will (4:34; 5:30; 10:18; 12:49; 17:4; Gal. 1:4; Phil. 2:8), again showing the order of persons within the Trinity (5:19).
6:39 *lose nothing.* Not one person chosen, redeemed, and called in Christ will perish, but all will be saved through faith (8:30). *the last day.* The end of this age, with the resurrection and the judgment (5:28–29).
6:41 *murmured.* Even as the crowds demanded that Christ give them manna as Moses had (vv. 30–31), they acted like unbelieving Israel in the wilderness (Ex. 15:24; 16:2,7–9).
6:44 *No man can come to me.* God's grace is necessary in order to produce faith (v. 37) because sinners are spiritually

which hath sent me draw him: and I will raise him
up at the last day.
45 It is written in the prophets, And they shall be
all taught of God. Every man therefore that hath
heard, and hath learned of the Father, cometh
unto me.
46 Not that any man hath seen the Father, save he
which is of God, he hath seen the Father.
47 Verily, verily, I say unto you, He that believeth
on me hath everlasting life.
48 I am that bread of life.
49 Your fathers did eat manna in the wilderness,
and are dead.
50 This is the bread which cometh down from
heaven, that a man may eat thereof, and not die.
51 I am the living bread which came down from
heaven: if any man eat of this bread, he shall live
for ever: and the bread that I will give is my flesh,
which I will give for the life of the world.
52 The Jews therefore strove among themselves,
saying, How can this man give us *his* flesh to eat?
53 Then Jesus said unto them, Verily, verily, I say
unto you, Except ye eat the flesh of the Son of
man, and drink his blood, ye have no life in you.
54 Whoso eateth my flesh, and drinketh my
blood, hath eternal life; and I will raise him up at
the last day.
55 For my flesh is meat indeed, and my blood is
drink indeed.
56 He that eateth my flesh, and drinketh my
blood, dwelleth in me, and I in him.
57 As the living Father hath sent me, and I live
by the Father: so he that eateth me, even he shall
live by me.
58 This is that bread which came down from
heaven: not as your fathers did eat manna, and are
dead: he that eateth of this bread shall live for ever.
59 These things said he in the synagogue, as he
taught in Capernaum.
60 Many therefore of his disciples, when they had
heard *this*, said, This is an hard saying; who can
hear it?
61 When Jesus knew in himself that his disciples
murmured at it, he said unto them, Doth this
offend you?
62 *What* and if ye shall see the Son of man ascend
up where he was before?
63 It is the spirit that quickeneth; the flesh prof-
iteth nothing: the words that I speak unto you,
they are spirit, and *they* are life.
64 But there are some of you that believe not. For
Jesus knew from the beginning who they were
that believed not, and who should betray him.
65 And he said, Therefore said I unto you, that no
man can come unto me, except it were given unto
him of my Father.
66 ¶ From that *time* many of his disciples went
back, and walked no more with him.
67 Then said Jesus unto the twelve, Will ye also
go away?
68 Then Simon Peter answered him, Lord, to
whom shall we go? thou hast the words of eternal
life.
69 And we believe and are sure that thou art that
Christ, the Son of the living God.
70 Jesus answered them, Have not I chosen you
twelve, and one of you is a devil?
71 He spake of Judas Iscariot *the son* of Simon:
for he it was that should betray him, being one of
the twelve.

---

unable to trust in Christ on their own accord (v. 65; 3:3–6, 19–20; Eph. 2:1, 5). *draw*. The verb, meaning to powerfully and effectively pull (21:11; Acts 16:19; 21:30), is here applied to God's effectual call of sinners to Christ (12:32).

6:45 *all taught of God*. Citing Isa. 54:13.

6:46 *save*. Except.

6:51 *eat of this bread . . . my flesh*. By eating his flesh, Christ does not here refer to the sacrament of the Lord's Supper but to the importance of having faith in Him (v. 35). The Lord's Supper was not instituted until the night before He died, and so an allusion to it here would have been meaningless to His hearers.

6:52 *strove*. Fought.

6:53 *drink his blood*. The law of Moses prohibited consumption of the blood of animals (Lev. 7:26–27)—and much more so the blood of man—showing that this should not be taken literally.

6:57 *living Father . . . I live by the Father*. The living God.

6:59 The above discourse was not conducted in the open air by the sea (v. 25) but inside the *synagogue* at *Capernaum*.

6:60 *disciples*. Those impressed by Christ's teaching and His miracles and who followed Him for a time, not just the twelve apostles (v. 67).

6:63 *the spirit that quickeneth*. Literally, "the Spirit is the Life-giver." Man's fallen nature (*flesh*) is unable to produce saving faith (vv. 44,65; 3:6), so God the Holy Spirit creates it through the Word that He inspired (*the words . . . are spirit, and . . . life*).

6:65 *no man can come . . . given unto him of my Father*. See notes at vv. 37,44. The same work of overcoming man's hostility and drawing him to Christ is ascribed to the *Father* and to the Holy Spirit (v. 63), for the works of the Trinity are undivided (5:19).

6:68–69 Peter, by a clear profession of faith, shows that he is a genuine disciple of Christ. *words of eternal life*. True and enduring disciples look to Jesus not primarily for earthly power and provision but for the truths that lead to communion with God and heavenly glory in the age to come.

6:70–71 *chosen you twelve*. Appointed them as apostles; not a reference to election to or to salvation. *one of you is a devil*. In His divine knowledge of the human heart, the Lord Jesus already knew that *Judas* remained in Satan's kingdom and would betray Him (13:2), a statement that must have startled them and should have provoked self-examination (Matt. 26:22).

Thoughts for Personal/Family Worship: Chapter 6

1. The crowds were attracted by Christ's miracles, but not by His power to save souls. In the same way the "health and wealth" gospel attracts many but does not stress the need for true conversion. Only when men are

CHAPTER 7

AFTER these things Jesus walked in Galilee: for he
would not walk in Jewry, because the Jews sought
to kill him.
2 Now the Jews' feast of tabernacles was at hand.
3 His brethren therefore said unto him, Depart
hence, and go into Judaea, that thy disciples also
may see the works that thou doest.
4 For *there is* no man *that* doeth any thing in
secret, and he himself seeketh to be known openly.
If thou do these things, shew thyself to the world.
5 For neither did his brethren believe in him.
6 Then Jesus said unto them, My time is not yet
come: but your time is alway ready.
7 The world cannot hate you; but me it hateth, be-
cause I testify of it, that the works thereof are evil.
8 Go ye up unto this feast: I go not up yet unto
this feast; for my time is not yet full come.
9 When he had said these words unto them, he
abode *still* in Galilee.
10 ¶ But when his brethren were gone up, then
went he also up unto the feast, not openly, but as
it were in secret.
11 Then the Jews sought him at the feast, and
said, Where is he?
12 And there was much murmuring among the
people concerning him: for some said, He is a
good man: others said, Nay; but he deceiveth the
people.
13 Howbeit no man spake openly of him for fear
of the Jews.
14 ¶ Now about the midst of the feast Jesus went
up into the temple, and taught.
15 And the Jews marvelled, saying, How knoweth
this man letters, having never learned?
16 Jesus answered them, and said, My doctrine is
not mine, but his that sent me.
17 If any man will do his will, he shall know of
the doctrine, whether it be of God, or *whether* I
speak of myself.
18 He that speaketh of himself seeketh his own
glory: but he that seeketh his glory that sent him,
the same is true, and no unrighteousness is in
him.
19 Did not Moses give you the law, and *yet* none
of you keepeth the law? Why go ye about to kill
me?
20 The people answered and said, Thou hast a
devil: who goeth about to kill thee?
21 Jesus answered and said unto them, I have
done one work, and ye all marvel.
22 Moses therefore gave unto you circumcision;
(not because it is of Moses, but of the fathers;)
and ye on the sabbath day circumcise a man.
23 If a man on the sabbath day receive circumci-
sion, that the law of Moses should not be broken;
are ye angry at me, because I have made a man
every whit whole on the sabbath day?
24 Judge not according to the appearance, but
judge righteous judgment.
25 Then said some of them of Jerusalem, Is not
this he, whom they seek to kill?

---

converted do they put spiritual and heavenly values first in life. When Jesus challenged the crowds, He lost much of His visible following. Why must churches be willing to challenge men's worldliness, even if doing so may reduce their numbers?

2. **None can come to Christ for salvation but those whom God Himself draws. The truths of the gospel will always be offensive to those who are unconverted. The preacher is not at liberty to alter the truth in order to gain the favor of unbelieving sinners, as our Lord Himself here shows by His perfect example. Instead, the church must rely on the Spirit of God to do what no man can. How does this call us to fervent and regular prayer for the preaching of the Word?**

Chapter 7: *Christ goes up secretly to the Feast of Tabernacles, declares that His doctrine is from God and that He will return to God, and calls the thirsty to drink from Him.*

At the Feast of Tabernacles (7:1–53)

7:1 *Jewry*. Judaea.

7:2 *feast of tabernacles*. A celebration of dwelling in booths, commemorated around October in memory of Israel's journey from Egypt to the Promised Land.

7:3–5 *brethren.* Probably Jesus' unbelieving half-brothers (Mark 3:21), who would be converted after Jesus' resurrection (Acts 1:14). They wanted Jesus to perform miracles for all to see.

7:6 *My time*. Jesus acted based on a prophetic sense of God's plan for His life and death (vv. 8,30; see note at 2:4).

7:7 *world*. Mankind fallen away from God (see note at 3:16) and full of hatred against Christ because His teaching exposed its sin (3:19–20; 15:18,22–24). This text shows that *world* need not include every individual, since most at that time were as yet unaware of Jesus.

7:10 *not openly*. Jesus went up unannounced.

7:11–13 John uses the term *Jews* to refer to the Jewish leaders, not to the *people* as a whole. *Howbeit*. Nevertheless. *fear of the Jews*. The leaders opposed Christ and excommunicated His followers from the synagogue (12:42).

7:14–15 *midst of the feast*. It lasted a week, and halfway through Jesus started teaching publicly. *letters, having never learned?* Jesus had not been formally trained as a rabbi.

7:16–17 *not mine, but his*. Christ's teaching (*doctrine*) was given to Him by God (14:10; 17:8), not by human traditions. Instead of men's testing Christ by His human credentials, Christ's teaching tests men as to whether or not their will is submitted to God's *will*.

7:18 A sound preacher is one who aims not for the promotion of his own reputation but for the advancement of God's glory.

7:20 *goeth about*. Endeavors, tries. Many in the crowd who had come from other areas for the feast, perhaps ignorant of the leaders' hatred for Christ (v. 1; 5:15,18), accused Him of being insane based on demonic influence (*hast a devil*).

7:21 *one work*. Christ's healing of the sick man at the pool of Bethesda on the Sabbath (5:1–16).

7:23 *every whit whole*. Restored to full health.

7:25 Those in the temple crowd who lived in *Jerusalem* were

26 But, lo, he speaketh boldly, and they say nothing unto him. Do the rulers know indeed that this is the very Christ?
27 Howbeit we know this man whence he is: but when Christ cometh, no man knoweth whence he is.
28 Then cried Jesus in the temple as he taught, saying, Ye both know me, and ye know whence I am: and I am not come of myself, but he that sent me is true, whom ye know not.
29 But I know him: for I am from him, and he hath sent me.
30 Then they sought to take him: but no man laid hands on him, because his hour was not yet come.
31 And many of the people believed on him, and said, When Christ cometh, will he do more miracles than these which this *man* hath done?
32 ¶ The Pharisees heard that the people murmured such things concerning him; and the Pharisees and the chief priests sent officers to take him.
33 Then said Jesus unto them, Yet a little while am I with you, and *then* I go unto him that sent me.
34 Ye shall seek me, and shall not find *me*: and where I am, *thither* ye cannot come.
35 Then said the Jews among themselves, Whither will he go, that we shall not find him? will he go unto the dispersed among the Gentiles, and teach the Gentiles?
36 What *manner of* saying is this that he said, Ye shall seek me, and shall not find *me*: and where I am, *thither* ye cannot come?
37 In the last day, that great *day* of the feast, Jesus stood and cried, saying, If any man thirst, let him come unto me, and drink.
38 He that believeth on me, as the scripture hath said, out of his belly shall flow rivers of living water.
39 (But this spake he of the Spirit, which they that believe on him should receive: for the Holy Ghost was not yet *given*; because that Jesus was not yet glorified.)
40 ¶ Many of the people therefore, when they heard this saying, said, Of a truth this is the Prophet.
41 Others said, This is the Christ. But some said, Shall Christ come out of Galilee?
42 Hath not the scripture said, That Christ cometh of the seed of David, and out of the town of Bethlehem, where David was?
43 So there was a division among the people because of him.
44 And some of them would have taken him; but no man laid hands on him.
45 ¶ Then came the officers to the chief priests and Pharisees; and they said unto them, Why have ye not brought him?
46 The officers answered, Never man spake like this man.
47 Then answered them the Pharisees, Are ye also deceived?
48 Have any of the rulers or of the Pharisees believed on him?
49 But this people who knoweth not the law are cursed.
50 Nicodemus saith unto them, (he that came to Jesus by night, being one of them,)
51 Doth our law judge *any* man, before it hear him, and know what he doeth?

---

better informed than those from outlying places. They knew of the threat to *kill* Christ.

7:26 *lo.* An exclamation. *the very Christ.* Truly the Christ.

7:27 *whence he is.* They dismiss Christ's claims to be their Messiah on the false supposition that he was born in Nazareth.

7:30 *his hour was not yet come.* Nothing could happen in Christ's life until the divinely appointed time had arrived.

7:35 Though the crowds misunderstood Jesus' talk of going away, not only would *Gentiles* be blessed by Jesus' teaching, but so would all the ends of the world (11:52; Ps. 22:27).

7:36 *manner.* Kind, sort.

7:37–38 *If any man thirst, let him come unto me.* Christ takes up role of divine Wisdom (Prov. 1:20,23; 9:1,5) to give a glorious gospel invitation to all who hear Him (Isa. 55:1). *belly.* Inward parts, an idiom for the mind, heart, and soul. *rivers of living water.* The ceremonies of the Feast of Tabernacles included pouring out water to celebrate God's provision of water in the wilderness (Ex. 17:1–7; Num. 20:1–13). Christ used this as a picture of the life-giving power of the Holy Spirit (3:5; 4:10,14; 6:63) flowing to and through all united to Him by faith, as promised in the *scripture* (Isa. 32:1–2,15; 41:18; 43:19–21; 44:3–4; Ezek. 47:1–12). To be a true Christian is to be blessed and to be a blessing to others.

7:39 *Spirit.* The outpouring of the Holy Spirit in His fullness did not occur until Jesus had finished His work of redemption and ascended to His throne (16:7; Acts 2:32–33).

7:40–44 *out of . . . Bethlehem.* See Mic. 5:2. Wrong ideas of the place of Jesus' birth led some to reject His Messiahship.

7:46 *Never man spake.* The officers had been spellbound upon hearing Christ's sublime preaching.

7:47–49 *people who knoweth not the law.* With breathtaking arrogance the Pharisees dismissed as *cursed* by God the mass of their own countrymen who had not studied in their rabbinical schools.

7:50–53 *Nicodemus.* See 3:1–2. His fair-minded question suggests that a work of grace was progressing in his soul. If Christ's critics had taken the trouble to study the facts concerning Jesus' birthplace, they would have found it to have been Bethlehem, not *Galilee.*

Thoughts for Personal/Family Worship: Chapter 7

1. **The unbelief of Jesus' brothers sets forth the important lesson that we can be near the truth and yet lack true faith. It is a mercy that after Christ's resurrection we find Christ's brothers in the company of those who believe. How is their unbelief a warning to those growing up in Christian families and churches? How is their conversion an encouragement with regard to what God can do?**
2. **Christ still says through the gospel, "If any man thirst, let him come unto me, and drink" (v. 37). He proclaims Himself to all who hear the gospel, promising that everyone who trusts in Him will receive the eternal life**

52 They answered and said unto him, Art thou
also of Galilee? Search, and look: for out of Galilee
ariseth no prophet.
53 And every man went unto his own house.

CHAPTER 8

JESUS went unto the mount of Olives.
2 And early in the morning he came again into
the temple, and all the people came unto him; and
he sat down, and taught them.
3 And the scribes and Pharisees brought unto
him a woman taken in adultery; and when they
had set her in the midst,
4 They say unto him, Master, this woman was
taken in adultery, in the very act.
5 Now Moses in the law commanded us, that
such should be stoned: but what sayest thou?
6 This they said, tempting him, that they might
have to accuse him. But Jesus stooped down, and
with *his* finger wrote on the ground, *as though he
heard them not*.
7 So when they continued asking him, he lifted
up himself, and said unto them, He that is with-
out sin among you, let him first cast a stone at her.
8 And again he stooped down, and wrote on the
ground.
9 And they which heard *it*, being convicted by
their own conscience, went out one by one, begin-
ning at the eldest, *even* unto the last: and Jesus was
left alone, and the woman standing in the midst.
10 When Jesus had lifted up himself, and saw
none but the woman, he said unto her, Woman,
where are those thine accusers? hath no man con-
demned thee?
11 She said, No man, Lord. And Jesus said unto
her, Neither do I condemn thee: go, and sin no
more.
12 ¶ Then spake Jesus again unto them, saying,
I am the light of the world: he that followeth me
shall not walk in darkness, but shall have the light
of life.
13 The Pharisees therefore said unto him, Thou
bearest record of thyself; thy record is not true.
14 Jesus answered and said unto them, Though
I bear record of myself, *yet* my record is true: for
I know whence I came, and whither I go; but ye
cannot tell whence I come, and whither I go.
15 Ye judge after the flesh; I judge no man.
16 And yet if I judge, my judgment is true: for I
am not alone, but I and the Father that sent me.
17 It is also written in your law, that the testi-
mony of two men is true.
18 I am one that bear witness of myself, and the
Father that sent me beareth witness of me.
19 Then said they unto him, Where is thy Father?
Jesus answered, Ye neither know me, nor my
Father: if ye had known me, ye should have
known my Father also.
20 These words spake Jesus in the treasury, as he

of God's Spirit and become a means by which the Spirit overflows to others. Sadly, many people stumble over their pride and so reject Him. Others depend on hearsay about Christ and fail to seek the facts that confirm His Messiahship and deity. How have you responded to Christ's call to come to Him?

Chapter 8: ***Christ shows mercy to the woman caught in adultery, answers the Pharisees' attacks with a defense of His authority as the One sent from God, and reveals His divine authority with an "I am" statement.***

The Woman Taken in Adultery and the Light of the World (8:1–59)

8:1–11 Some scholars believe that this text (with 7:53) was not originally part of the Gospel of John. They argue that though it is present in a large number of Greek manuscripts, it is lacking in several older manuscripts, including the few Greek manuscripts extant today that are dated earlier than the fifth century. However, other compelling attestation gives every warrant for its inclusion. Jerome (d. 420) wrote that it appeared in many Greek and Latin manuscripts available to him (from the fourth century or earlier), so it does have very ancient attestation. Ambrose (d. 397) and Augustine (d. 430) indicated that the account caused offense among those fearing it would encourage adultery, a possible reason some manuscripts omit it.

8:5 *such should be stoned.* The *law* of *Moses* commanded the death of both the adulterer and the adulteress (Lev. 20:10; Deut. 22:21–22). This was a setup—allowing mob justice without a concern for due process of the law.

8:6 *tempting.* Testing. *wrote on the ground.* Perhaps a prophetic gesture warning of divine judgment (Jer. 17:13) on those who reject the fountain of living waters (7:37–38).

8:7–9 *He that is without sin.* Christ was not demanding the sinless perfection of any who would enforce judicial punishments on criminals (Rom. 13:1–4) but appealing to the *conscience* to ensure that punishment would be meted out with justice and integrity. He also challenged their wicked attempt to trap Him instead of receiving Him.

8:11 *Neither do I.* Jesus refused to meddle in civil and judicial matters (Luke 12:13–15) but in His first coming aimed to save sinners, not to *condemn* them (3:17). *go, and sin no more.* Christ, who elsewhere condemned adultery as sin (Matt. 15:19; 19:9,18), called her to repent of this and all her sins.

8:12 *I am the light of the world.* Another of Jesus' "I am" sayings. The Feast of Tabernacles (7:2) involved a ceremony of brilliant lights in remembrance of God's pillar of fire guiding Israel through the wilderness (Ex. 13:21–22; Neh. 9:12). Light is essential to sight and knowledge, and thus to life (1:4–5). Those who do not have Christ may be highly intelligent but are wandering in *darkness* as to the things of God.

8:13–14 *bearest record.* Testifies, speaks as a witness. *whence . . . whither.* From what place and to what place, here speaking of His heavenly glory.

8:15 *judge after the flesh.* Discern and decide what is true and right based on the mindset of fallen mankind, which is hostile to God (Rom. 8:7).

8:17 *written in your law.* See Num. 35:30; Deut. 17:6; 19:15.

8:19 Those who do not *know* Christ as their Savior cannot know God as their *Father.*

8:20 *treasury.* The location of several receptacles in the Court

taught in the temple: and no man laid hands on
him; for his hour was not yet come.
21 Then said Jesus again unto them, I go my way,
and ye shall seek me, and shall die in your sins:
whither I go, ye cannot come.
22 Then said the Jews, Will he kill himself? be-
cause he saith, Whither I go, ye cannot come.
23 And he said unto them, Ye are from beneath;
I am from above: ye are of this world; I am not of
this world.
24 I said therefore unto you, that ye shall die in
your sins: for if ye believe not that I am *he*, ye shall
die in your sins.
25 Then said they unto him, Who art thou? And
Jesus saith unto them, Even *the same* that I said
unto you from the beginning.
26 I have many things to say and to judge of you:
but he that sent me is true; and I speak to the
world those things which I have heard of him.
27 They understood not that he spake to them of
the Father.
28 Then said Jesus unto them, When ye have
lifted up the Son of man, then shall ye know that I
am *he*, and *that* I do nothing of myself; but as my
Father hath taught me, I speak these things.
29 And he that sent me is with me: the Father
hath not left me alone; for I do always those
things that please him.
30 As he spake these words, many believed on him.
31 Then said Jesus to those Jews which believed
on him, If ye continue in my word, *then* are ye my
disciples indeed;
32 And ye shall know the truth, and the truth
shall make you free.
33 ¶ They answered him, We be Abraham's seed,
and were never in bondage to any man: how
sayest thou, Ye shall be made free?
34 Jesus answered them, Verily, verily, I say un-
to you, Whosoever committeth sin is the servant
of sin.
35 And the servant abideth not in the house for
ever: *but* the Son abideth ever.
36 If the Son therefore shall make you free, ye
shall be free indeed.
37 I know that ye are Abraham's seed; but ye seek
to kill me, because my word hath no place in you.
38 I speak that which I have seen with my Father:
and ye do that which ye have seen with your
father.
39 They answered and said unto him, Abraham
is our father. Jesus saith unto them, If ye were
Abraham's children, ye would do the works of
Abraham.
40 But now ye seek to kill me, a man that hath
told you the truth, which I have heard of God: this
did not Abraham.
41 Ye do the deeds of your father. Then said they
to him, We be not born of fornication; we have
one Father, *even* God.
42 Jesus said unto them, If God were your Father,
ye would love me: for I proceeded forth and came
from God; neither came I of myself, but he sent me.
43 Why do ye not understand my speech? *even*
because ye cannot hear my word.
44 Ye are of *your* father the devil, and the lusts of
your father ye will do. He was a murderer from
the beginning, and abode not in the truth, be-
cause there is no truth in him. When he speaketh
a lie, he speaketh of his own: for he is a liar, and
the father of it.
45 And because I tell *you* the truth, ye believe
me not.

---

of Women into which people could deposit their gifts.

8:21 *I go my way*. Christ was shortly, after His coming death and resurrection, to return to His heavenly Father. *die in your sins.* To die in unrepentance and unbelief (v. 24) excludes a person from Christ's presence in heaven (*ye cannot come*)—a sober warning to sinners.

8:23 *beneath . . . above*. Jesus contrasted two kingdoms, the one earthly and sinful and the other heavenly and holy. Even when they dwell on earth, Christ and His people are *not of this world* (15:19; 17:14,16) but belong to the heavenly kingdom.

8:28 *lifted up the Son of man*. In His death on the cross (12:32–33).

8:29 *do always . . . please him.* Christ always perfectly obeyed the will of His *Father* and always had His full and perfect approval (v. 46; Matt. 3:17; 17:5).

8:30–32 *believed on him.* What follows shows that this is not saving faith but a mere intellectual belief without love for Christ (v. 42). *continue in my word.* True faith abides and perseveres in following Christ's teachings. *disciples indeed.* A "disciple" is a person who submits to a master or teacher in order to become like him in faith and practice (Matt. 10:24–25; cf. 13:13–16). *know the truth . . . make you free.* Real, spiritual knowledge of Christ engages the heart with faith and love so that a person experiences true freedom (17:3; Rom. 6:17).

8:33 *Abraham's seed.* The offspring descended from Abraham, but only physically (v. 39) and thus not heirs of the covenant (Gen. 12:7; 17:7; see Rom. 2:28–29; 4:12). *bondage.* Slavery.

8:34–36 *Verily, verily.* See note at 1:51. *committeth sin . . . servant of sin.* A lifestyle of unrepentant sin reveals a heart enslaved to sin. *servant abideth not in the house.* Perhaps an allusion to the expulsion of Ishmael, the son of Abraham by a slave woman, from the covenant household (Gen. 21:10), implying that the unbelieving Jews were not true children of Abraham (Gal. 4:21–31). *Son . . . make you free.* Christ alone has been sent by God to rescue people from their slavery to sin and make them children of God.

8:42 Those who are children of God *love* Jesus Christ, His Son.

8:43–45 Christ set forth the fearful condition of the unsaved. They are unable to trust and obey (*cannot hear*) His Word (6:44). They are children of the *devil*, not that Satan made them but because they bear his image and share his evil desires (*lusts*; Eph. 2:1–3). Like the evil spirit who in essence murdered the entire human race in the beginning of history (Gen. 3:1–6) and soon would murder Christ (13:2,27), unbelievers hate Christ and His people (1 John 3:12–13). Just as Satan is the *father* of lies, so they reject the truth of God's Word. Truly, unless the Son sets us free (vv. 32,36), we are in a desperate situation.

46 Which of you convinceth me of sin? And if I
say the truth, why do ye not believe me?
47 He that is of God heareth God's words: ye
therefore hear *them* not, because ye are not of God.
48 Then answered the Jews, and said unto him,
Say we not well that thou art a Samaritan, and
hast a devil?
49 Jesus answered, I have not a devil; but I hon-
our my Father, and ye do dishonour me.
50 And I seek not mine own glory: there is one
that seeketh and judgeth.
51 Verily, verily, I say unto you, If a man keep my
saying, he shall never see death.
52 Then said the Jews unto him, Now we know
that thou hast a devil. Abraham is dead, and the
prophets; and thou sayest, If a man keep my say-
ing, he shall never taste of death.
53 Art thou greater than our father Abraham,
which is dead? and the prophets are dead: whom
makest thou thyself?
54 Jesus answered, If I honour myself, my honour
is nothing: it is my Father that honoureth me; of
whom ye say, that he is your God:
55 Yet ye have not known him; but I know him:
and if I should say, I know him not, I shall be a
liar like unto you: but I know him, and keep his
saying.
56 Your father Abraham rejoiced to see my day:
and he saw *it*, and was glad.
57 Then said the Jews unto him, Thou art not yet
fifty years old, and hast thou seen Abraham?
58 Jesus said unto them, Verily, verily, I say unto
you, Before Abraham was, I am.
59 Then took they up stones to cast at him: but
Jesus hid himself, and went out of the temple, go-
ing through the midst of them, and so passed by.

CHAPTER 9

AND as *Jesus* passed by, he saw a man which was
blind from *his* birth.
2 And his disciples asked him, saying, Master,
who did sin, this man, or his parents, that he was
born blind?
3 Jesus answered, Neither hath this man sinned,
nor his parents: but that the works of God should
be made manifest in him.
4 I must work the works of him that sent me,
while it is day: the night cometh, when no man
can work.
5 As long as I am in the world, I am the light of
the world.
6 When he had thus spoken, he spat on the
ground, and made clay of the spittle, and he
anointed the eyes of the blind man with the clay,
7 And said unto him, Go, wash in the pool of Si-
loam, (which is by interpretation, Sent.) He went
his way therefore, and washed, and came seeing.

8:46 *convinceth*. Convicts. Jesus was sinless (2 Cor. 5:21; Heb. 4:15; 7:26).
8:48 To call Christ a *Samaritan* was insulting; further, to say that He had a demon was blasphemous.
8:51–52 *never see death . . . never taste of death*. Christ gives eternal life now, so that when believers die their death will not be an experience of divine judgment (11:25–26). Christ kindly mingled a gospel promise here with His answer to His critics.
8:56 *Abraham rejoiced to see my day*. The patriarch believed in the promise that Christ would come to save the world by His death (Gen. 22:8,14; cf. Gal. 3:8,16).
8:58 *Before Abraham was*. Two thousand years before Christ. By saying *I am* instead of "I was," Christ taught that He is ancient and eternal and that He is *Jehovah*, whose name means "I am" (Ex. 3:14).

Thoughts for Personal/Family Worship: Chapter 8

1. **Christ came not to condemn sinners but to save them. The worst of sinners in this life may be saved, if he will repent and trust in Christ. Rather than judging sinners in pride and hypocrisy, we should bring them to Jesus to learn of His grace. The Son is able truly and lastingly to set sinners free!**
2. **Christ did not hold back from saying hard things to sinners who were not yet broken over their sins. He stripped them of their religious presumption based on their background and upbringing. He warned them of their slavery to sin and told them they were so bad they were unable to believe in Him. He even said they were children of Satan, the image-bearers of the great murderer and liar. Why did Jesus say such things to religious people who believed in Him? Why did He not speak this way to the woman caught in adultery? Have you submitted to what God says about you?**

Chapter 9: *Jesus heals a blind man on the Sabbath. The Pharisees interrogate both the man's parents and the man himself before casting him out of the synagogue. He confesses Christ, who charges the Pharisees with spiritual blindness.*

The Healing of the Man Born Blind (9:1–41)

9:1 *blind from his birth*. An apparently hopeless condition.
9:2–3 *who did sin*. We should be careful not to draw hasty conclusions based upon the disabilities or trials that come upon people (remember Job). Our Lord made it clear that this man's blindness was not because of a sin but had been conferred on him for a different and greater reason.
9:4 *work . . . while it is day*. Jesus knew that His death (*night*) was approaching, and He, like all men, had a limited amount of time to do good on earth. He looked at the affliction of the blind man as an opportunity to be of service to God.
9:5 *light of the world*. See 1:4,9; 8:12. This statement suggests that the blindness of the man would become an illustration for the manner in which Christ illuminates the soul.
9:6–7 *spittle*. Spit, saliva, a method Christ sometimes used in healing (Mark 7:33, 8:23), a gesture ordinarily associated with shame (Num. 12:14; Deut. 25:9). The mud did nothing to heal the blindness but constituted a test of the man's obedience in washing as commanded.
9:7 *pool of Siloam*. A reservoir cut into the rock by Jerusalem (Neh. 3:15). *interpretation*. Translation (from Hebrew to Greek). *came seeing*. The healing of the blind was a distinctive sign that the Christ had come (v. 32; Matt. 11:5).

8 ¶ The neighbours therefore, and they which
before had seen him that he was blind, said, Is not
this he that sat and begged?
9 Some said, This is he: others *said*, He is like
him: *but* he said, I am *he*.
10 Therefore said they unto him, How were thine
eyes opened?
11 He answered and said, A man that is called
Jesus made clay, and anointed mine eyes, and said
unto me, Go to the pool of Siloam, and wash: and
I went and washed, and I received sight.
12 Then said they unto him, Where is he? He said,
I know not.
13 ¶ They brought to the Pharisees him that
aforetime was blind.
14 And it was the sabbath day when Jesus made
the clay, and opened his eyes.
15 Then again the Pharisees also asked him how
he had received his sight. He said unto them, He
put clay upon mine eyes, and I washed, and do see.
16 Therefore said some of the Pharisees, This
man is not of God, because he keepeth not the
sabbath day. Others said, How can a man that is a
sinner do such miracles? And there was a division
among them.
17 They say unto the blind man again, What say-
est thou of him, that he hath opened thine eyes?
He said, He is a prophet.
18 But the Jews did not believe concerning him,
that he had been blind, and received his sight,
until they called the parents of him that had
received his sight.
19 And they asked them, saying, Is this your son,
who ye say was born blind? how then doth he
now see?
20 His parents answered them and said, We know
that this is our son, and that he was born blind:
21 But by what means he now seeth, we know
not; or who hath opened his eyes, we know not:
he is of age; ask him: he shall speak for himself.
22 These *words* spake his parents, because they
feared the Jews: for the Jews had agreed already,
that if any man did confess that he was Christ, he
should be put out of the synagogue.
23 Therefore said his parents, He is of age; ask
him.
24 Then again called they the man that was blind,
and said unto him, Give God the praise: we know
that this man is a sinner.
25 He answered and said, Whether he be a sinner
or no, I know not: one thing I know, that, whereas
I was blind, now I see.
26 Then said they to him again, What did he to
thee? how opened he thine eyes?
27 He answered them, I have told you already,
and ye did not hear: wherefore would ye hear *it*
again? will ye also be his disciples?
28 Then they reviled him, and said, Thou art his
disciple; but we are Moses' disciples.
29 We know that God spake unto Moses: *as for*
this *fellow*, we know not from whence he is.
30 The man answered and said unto them, Why
herein is a marvellous thing, that ye know not from
whence he is, and *yet* he hath opened mine eyes.
31 Now we know that God heareth not sinners:
but if any man be a worshipper of God, and doeth
his will, him he heareth.
32 Since the world began was it not heard that
any man opened the eyes of one that was born
blind.
33 If this man were not of God, he could do noth-
ing.
34 They answered and said unto him, Thou wast
altogether born in sins, and dost thou teach us?
And they cast him out.
35 Jesus heard that they had cast him out; and
when he had found him, he said unto him, Dost
thou believe on the Son of God?
36 He answered and said, Who is he, Lord, that I
might believe on him?
37 And Jesus said unto him, Thou hast both seen
him, and it is he that talketh with thee.
38 And he said, Lord, I believe. And he wor-
shipped him.
39 ¶ And Jesus said, For judgment I am come into
this world, that they which see not might see; and
that they which see might be made blind.
40 And *some* of the Pharisees which were with

9:8–12 Neighbors were at a loss to explain how the man now had sight, but they served as witnesses that Christ had indeed performed a miracle.
9:13 *aforetime.* Before.
9:16 *keepeth not the sabbath day.* See 5:16. *How can . . . a sinner do such miracles?* The powerful testimony of Christ's signs caused a *division* even among the Pharisees.
9:17 The healed man courageously confessed Christ to be a *prophet*, though he did not yet recognize His deity (vv. 35–36).
9:18–23 The cowardice of the man's parents (*they feared the Jews*) is an example of those who will not confess and follow Christ because of their fear of man (5:44; 12:42–43).
9:24 *Give God the praise.* They placed him under oath (Josh. 7:19).
9:25–33 The bold testimony of the man and his refusal to be pressured into accusing Jesus of wrong is a model of faithful witness.
9:34 *cast him out.* Excommunicated him (v. 22; 12:42). The stark refusal of the Pharisees to acknowledge the plain facts before them reveals the total blindness of lost sinners (3:3).
9:35–38 Christ gave the man further teaching about His identity, and the man became an example not just of outward healing but of the inward healing of faith as He worshiped Christ as the *Son of God.*
9:39–41 Christ teaches a deep truth here. His coming has a twofold effect upon men. As the light of the world (v. 5) He enables those who are spiritually blind to see His glory by faith in the gospel (2 Cor. 4:6). On the other hand, those who think they have spiritual sight because they are religious (*ye say, We see*) are doubly blind—hampered by a Christless religion and

him heard these words, and said unto him, Are
we blind also?
41 Jesus said unto them, If ye were blind, ye
should have no sin: but now ye say, We see; there-
fore your sin remaineth.

CHAPTER 10

VERILY, verily, I say unto you, He that entereth not
by the door into the sheepfold, but climbeth up
some other way, the same is a thief and a robber.
2 But he that entereth in by the door is the shep-
herd of the sheep.
3 To him the porter openeth; and the sheep hear
his voice: and he calleth his own sheep by name,
and leadeth them out.
4 And when he putteth forth his own sheep, he
goeth before them, and the sheep follow him: for
they know his voice.
5 And a stranger will they not follow, but will flee
from him: for they know not the voice of strangers.
6 This parable spake Jesus unto them: but they
understood not what things they were which he
spake unto them.
7 Then said Jesus unto them again, Verily, verily, I
say unto you, I am the door of the sheep.
8 All that ever came before me are thieves and
robbers: but the sheep did not hear them.
9 I am the door: by me if any man enter in, he
shall be saved, and shall go in and out, and find
pasture.
10 The thief cometh not, but for to steal, and to
kill, and to destroy: I am come that they might have
life, and that they might have *it* more abundantly.
11 I am the good shepherd: the good shepherd
giveth his life for the sheep.
12 But he that is an hireling, and not the shep-
herd, whose own the sheep are not, seeth the wolf
coming, and leaveth the sheep, and fleeth: and the
wolf catcheth them, and scattereth the sheep.
13 The hireling fleeth, because he is an hireling,
and careth not for the sheep.
14 I am the good shepherd, and know my *sheep*,
and am known of mine.

---

self-righteousness (3:19). When people are ignorant of God's truth but are open to being corrected, their sinful state is less of a deterrent. Such people have hope that God may save them, but those adamant in their proud opinion that they are right are hardened in their unbelief.

Thoughts for Personal/Family Worship: Chapter 9

1. **God has given each of His servants a day to work, but the night is coming. Until the Lord returns we will all die. Therefore, let us learn to redeem the time. Even the sorrows of this fallen world are opportunities to glorify God.**
2. **Christ's Word confronts us, and there is no neutrality. We can be like the man who was healed and boldly follow the truth to worship at the feet of Jesus and confess Him before men; like his parents, who in the fear of man bowed under the intimidation of this world; or like the Pharisees, who were so blind they rejected the plain truth to cling to their own ways. Only one of these individuals or groups could see; the others were blind to the light of Christ's glory. Which do you most resemble?**

Chapter 10: *Christ declares Himself to be the door and the good shepherd and declares His unity with the Father. The bystanders seek to stone Him.*

The Good Shepherd (10:1–42)

10:1–18 Through the veiled speech of a parable about *sheep*, Christ called believers in Israel to abandon the destructive spiritual leadership of the Pharisees and priests who opposed Him and His disciples (7:32; 9:22; 11:47–50). He presented Himself as the King (*shepherd*) of the true Israel, constituted of believers from both the Jews and the nations (v. 16), the King who must die to save His people (vv. 11,15,17–18).

10:1–2 *Verily, verily.* Truly (see note at 1:51). *sheepfold.* A walled-in place of refuge for flocks, especially at night. The people of God (*sheep*) are overseen by God's appointed leaders (*shepherd*), a common picture of Israel in the Old Testament (Isa. 56:9–12; Jer. 3:15; 23:1–4; 25:32–38; Ezek. 34:1–31; Zech. 11:1–17). *thief and a robber.* Any leader who uses and harms the church, here especially the Pharisees (9:13–34, 39–41). *entereth in by the door.* All who would hold office in the church must have spiritually entered God's people through faith in Jesus Christ (who is *the door*; v. 7; see 1 Tim. 4:16).

10:3–5 *porter.* The man who keeps the door, looks after the sheep overnight, and unlocks the door of the sheepfold every morning when the shepherd comes. He knows the shepherd, as do the sheep. *calleth his own sheep by name.* The spiritual leader has a personal and loving relationship with each member of the flock under his care. *know his voice.* God's people follow the faithful preacher but reject false teachers. God's Spirit gives them discernment to recognize the truth of His Word (1 John 2:18–27; 4:1–6).

10:6 *parable.* A proverb or saying with a concealed meaning (16:25,29; not the same Greek word commonly translated "parable," as in Matt. 13:3, etc.). Being spiritually blind, many who heard this parable failed to understand it.

10:7–9 *I am the door.* Christ is the only Mediator through whom people must come to God and salvation (14:6). *All that . . . came before me.* The context is not history, for Christ affirmed the prophets (5:35,39,46), but the parable in which the shepherd comes in the morning, as opposed to *thieves and robbers* like the Pharisees (v. 1), who sneak in during the night.

10:10 *steal . . . kill . . . destroy.* The false teachers reveal their likeness to the Devil (8:44). *have life, and . . . more abundantly.* Christ and His leaders do not exploit the people but serve them for the purpose of their eternal and overflowing happiness in God (4:10,14).

10:11 *good shepherd.* A shepherd was an image commonly used of a king, both of God (Ps. 23:1; Ezek. 34:11–16) and of David (Ps. 78:70–72; Ezek. 34:23–24). As God incarnate (1:1,14) and the Son of David, Christ is the only King of the church. *giveth his life.* In a stunning exchange the King gave life to His people (v. 10) by dying in their place on the cross. The good shepherd is the Lamb of God (1:29; 13:1; 19:36).

10:12–13 *hireling.* A hired hand. The minister who is not called by God to this work but who does it only for personal gain will not love the people enough to face false teachers and persecutors (*wolf*; Matt. 7:15; 10:16; Acts 20:29).

10:14–15 *know . . . and am known.* Christ (*the good shepherd*) shares a close relationship of love with His people, a love that

15 As the Father knoweth me, even so know I the
Father: and I lay down my life for the sheep.
16 And other sheep I have, which are not of this
fold: them also I must bring, and they shall hear
my voice; and there shall be one fold, *and* one
shepherd.
17 Therefore doth my Father love me, because I
lay down my life, that I might take it again.
18 No man taketh it from me, but I lay it down
of myself. I have power to lay it down, and I have
power to take it again. This commandment have I
received of my Father.
19 ¶ There was a division therefore again among
the Jews for these sayings.
20 And many of them said, He hath a devil, and is
mad; why hear ye him?
21 Others said, These are not the words of him
that hath a devil. Can a devil open the eyes of the
blind?
22 ¶ And it was at Jerusalem the feast of the dedi-
cation, and it was winter.
23 And Jesus walked in the temple in Solomon's
porch.
24 Then came the Jews round about him, and
said unto him, How long dost thou make us to
doubt? If thou be the Christ, tell us plainly.
25 Jesus answered them, I told you, and ye
believed not: the works that I do in my Father's
name, they bear witness of me.
26 But ye believe not, because ye are not of my
sheep, as I said unto you.
27 My sheep hear my voice, and I know them,
and they follow me:
28 And I give unto them eternal life; and they
shall never perish, neither shall any *man* pluck
them out of my hand.
29 My Father, which gave *them* me, is greater than
all; and no *man* is able to pluck *them* out of my
Father's hand.
30 I and *my* Father are one.
31 Then the Jews took up stones again to stone
him.
32 Jesus answered them, Many good works have
I shewed you from my Father; for which of those
works do ye stone me?
33 The Jews answered him, saying, For a good
work we stone thee not; but for blasphemy; and
because that thou, being a man, makest thyself
God.
34 Jesus answered them, Is it not written in your
law, I said, Ye are gods?
35 If he called them gods, unto whom the word
of God came, and the scripture cannot be broken;
36 Say ye of him, whom the Father hath sancti-

---

stretches beyond head knowledge to experiential and vital knowledge (v. 27; 17:3). *As the Father knoweth me.* Christ's relationship with His people mirrors His relationship with God the Father (17:21–23). *lay down my life for the sheep.* Christ died for those He knows because the Father gave them to Him in election (v. 29), which is not for every man (v. 26). This is the doctrine of particular and effective redemption (Rom. 8:32,35; Eph. 5:25; Titus 2:14).

10:16 *other sheep.* Converts from the Gentile world. *hear my voice.* Not directly, but through the faithful preaching of Christ's Word (Eph. 2:17). *one fold.* Christ will not build two churches, for Jews and Gentiles (Eph. 2:14–15), respectively, but unites saved sinners from all nations into one church ruled by the Word of the one King (*one shepherd*; Eccl. 12:11; Ezek. 34:23; 37:24).

10:17–18 *love me, because.* The Father has loved His Son from eternity (3:35; 5:20; 17:24); this refers to God's delight in Christ's obedience (Phil. 2:8–9). *power to lay it down, and . . . take it again.* Christ did not die as a helpless victim, nor was He passive in His resurrection, but He exercised His sovereignty as God to voluntarily give His life and then rise from the dead. *commandment.* The Son's saving work is essentially an act of obedience to the Father's will (see note at 6:38).

10:19–21 *division . . . again.* See 9:16. *blind.* This whole narrative is within the context of the man healed of his blindness (9:1–51).

10:22 *feast of the dedication.* Modern Hanukkah, celebrated in December to commemorate the purification of the temple after it had been defiled by Antiochus Epiphanes in the second century BC.

10:23 *Solomon's porch.* A covered area of columns (Acts 3:11; 5:12).

10:24–25 *If thou be the Christ.* By His miracles (*works*) and teachings (*told you*) Christ had shown Himself to be their Messiah, but He had not used that term in speaking to the Jewish leaders because they were looking for a political liberator (6:15).

10:26–27 *believe not, because ye are not of my sheep.* Those who are not God's elect and redeemed people (vv. 11,29) will not trust in Christ (6:37) despite all His miracles and teachings (v. 25). God's sovereign grace must overcome our unbelief (5:40). *My sheep . . . follow me.* The defining mark of those for whom Christ died is their faith and obedience to His Word. He died for them, and they in turn live for Him (2 Cor. 5:15; Titus 2:14). *hear my voice.* The power of Christ operates through the Word of Christ to produce life (5:24–25).

10:28–29 *shall never perish.* The Greek uses a double negative for emphasis: "will certainly never be damned." *pluck.* Seize, the same verb used of the wolf (v. 12). False teaching and persecution cannot cause true believers to ultimately fall away from Christ. *my hand.* An expression for Christ's power, which preserves believers so that they in turn will persevere (6:39; Jer. 32:40). *gave them me.* Christ's sheep are His eternally elected people, chosen by the *Father* and committed to the Son for salvation through the Holy Spirit (Eph. 1:3–4; 2 Thess. 2:13–14; 2 Tim. 1:9; see note at 6:37).

10:30 *one.* The word is not masculine but neuter in Greek, implying that the Father and the Son are not one person but one in essence, eternity, power, and will (v. 38), again provoking His enemies to kill Him for claiming deity (v. 33; 5:17–23; 8:58–59).

10:34–35 *Ye are gods.* Citing Ps. 82:6, addressed to men whom God would judge for abusing their power as rulers; perhaps an implicit warning to the Jewish leaders that God would judge them if they persisted in walking in the darkness (8:12; 9:39–41; Ps. 82:5) and unjustly killed God's Son. *the word of God . . . the scripture cannot be broken.* Jesus believed and taught that the Old Testament is the infallible truth of God (Matt. 5:17–18).

fied, and sent into the world, Thou blasphemest;
because I said, I am the Son of God?
37 If I do not the works of my Father, believe
me not.
38 But if I do, though ye believe not me, believe
the works: that ye may know, and believe, that the
Father *is* in me, and I in him.
39 Therefore they sought again to take him: but
he escaped out of their hand,
40 And went away again beyond Jordan into the
place where John at first baptized; and there he
abode.
41 And many resorted unto him, and said, John
did no miracle: but all things that John spake of
this man were true.
42 And many believed on him there.

CHAPTER 11

Now a certain *man* was sick, *named* Lazarus, of
Bethany, the town of Mary and her sister Martha.
2 (It was *that* Mary which anointed the Lord with
ointment, and wiped his feet with her hair, whose
brother Lazarus was sick.)
3 Therefore his sisters sent unto him, saying,
Lord, behold, he whom thou lovest is sick.
4 When Jesus heard *that*, he said, This sickness is
not unto death, but for the glory of God, that the
Son of God might be glorified thereby.
5 Now Jesus loved Martha, and her sister, and
Lazarus.
6 When he had heard therefore that he was sick,
he abode two days still in the same place where
he was.
7 Then after that saith he to *his* disciples, Let us
go into Judaea again.
8 *His* disciples say unto him, Master, the Jews of
late sought to stone thee; and goest thou thither
again?
9 Jesus answered, Are there not twelve hours in
the day? If any man walk in the day, he stumbleth
not, because he seeth the light of this world.
10 But if a man walk in the night, he stumbleth,
because there is no light in him.
11 These things said he: and after that he saith
unto them, Our friend Lazarus sleepeth; but I go,
that I may awake him out of sleep.
12 Then said his disciples, Lord, if he sleep, he
shall do well.
13 Howbeit Jesus spake of his death: but they
thought that he had spoken of taking of rest in
sleep.
14 Then said Jesus unto them plainly, Lazarus is
dead.
15 And I am glad for your sakes that I was not
there, to the intent ye may believe; nevertheless
let us go unto him.
16 Then said Thomas, which is called Didymus,
unto his fellowdisciples, Let us also go, that we
may die with him.
17 Then when Jesus came, he found that he had
lain in the grave four days already.

10:36 *sanctified.* Set apart for sacred purposes (17:19). If it was legitimate to speak of human rulers as "gods," in a qualified sense, how much more is it right, when speaking of the *Son* who was *sent* by the Father, to call Christ "God" in an unqualified sense (1:1; 20:28)?
10:37 *works of my Father.* Miracles by divine power, a public testimony to Christ (5:36).
10:38 *the Father is in me, and I in him.* Language of union or oneness (17:21,23). Christ's miracles indicate that He shares the same divine power as the Father (14:10–11).
10:40 *abode.* Remained.
10:41 *resorted.* Came.

Thoughts for Personal/Family Worship: Chapter 10

1. **Jesus claimed to be the great Shepherd of God's people. He is the King who loves His people and cares for them intimately and individually. No one is truly a sheep in Christ's flock who does not listen to Him and follow Him. What does this parable teach us about true discipleship to Jesus?**
2. **While the image of a shepherd is comforting, Jesus used it to call people to follow Him in the midst of thieves, robbers, and fierce wolves. Indeed, Jesus is an unusual Shepherd, for He defends His flock by dying for His sheep. What spiritual dangers did Jesus describe in this parable? How can we find safety from them?**
3. **God has given to Jesus a particular people, His "sheep," to save and bring to eternal life (vv. 27–29). Christ knows them in a special way (v. 14), for He died for them in particular (vv. 11,15). They will hear His voice in Scripture and obey Him (vv. 4,16,27), and only they will believe in Him (vv. 26). He will never lose them, for the power of God keeps them safe (vv. 28–29). These verses epitomize the doctrines of election, particular redemption, effectual calling, and perseverance of the saints. How do these truths give comfort to believers? How do they encourage evangelism?**

Chapter 11: *Christ raises Lazarus, the Jews plot to kill Jesus, and Christ leaves for a region near the wilderness.*

The Raising of Lazarus (11:1–57)

11:2 *anointed . . . wiped.* See 12:1–6.
11:4 *for the glory of God.* Raising Lazarus would prove to be Christ's greatest and final sign in this gospel (2:11), revealing Him as the Life before He died and rose again (v. 25).
11:6 *two days.* Jesus deliberately waited until Lazarus was dead.
11:8 *thither.* There.
11:9 *walk in the day . . . stumbleth not.* The safe way to live is always to do as God says.
11:10 *no light in him.* Those who do not trust in Christ are in total spiritual darkness.
11:11 *sleepeth . . . awake him.* An expression for dying and being raised from the dead (vv. 13–14; Eph. 5:14).
11:15 *I am glad.* Suffering and death are worthwhile if they result in faith in Christ.
11:16 *Didymus.* Means "twin."

18 Now Bethany was nigh unto Jerusalem, about
fifteen furlongs off:
19 And many of the Jews came to Martha and
Mary, to comfort them concerning their brother.
20 Then Martha, as soon as she heard that Jesus
was coming, went and met him: but Mary sat *still*
in the house.
21 Then said Martha unto Jesus, Lord, if thou
hadst been here, my brother had not died.
22 But I know, that even now, whatsoever thou
wilt ask of God, God will give *it* thee.
23 Jesus saith unto her, Thy brother shall rise
again.
24 Martha saith unto him, I know that he shall
rise again in the resurrection at the last day.
25 Jesus said unto her, I am the resurrection, and
the life: he that believeth in me, though he were
dead, yet shall he live:
26 And whosoever liveth and believeth in me
shall never die. Believest thou this?
27 She saith unto him, Yea, Lord: I believe that
thou art the Christ, the Son of God, which should
come into the world.
28 And when she had so said, she went her way,
and called Mary her sister secretly, saying, The
Master is come, and calleth for thee.
29 As soon as she heard *that*, she arose quickly,
and came unto him.
30 Now Jesus was not yet come into the town, but
was in that place where Martha met him.
31 The Jews then which were with her in the
house, and comforted her, when they saw Mary,
that she rose up hastily and went out, followed her,
saying, She goeth unto the grave to weep there.
32 Then when Mary was come where Jesus was,
and saw him, she fell down at his feet, saying unto
him, Lord, if thou hadst been here, my brother
had not died.
33 When Jesus therefore saw her weeping, and
the Jews also weeping which came with her, he
groaned in the spirit, and was troubled,
34 And said, Where have ye laid him? They said
unto him, Lord, come and see.
35 Jesus wept.
36 Then said the Jews, Behold how he loved him!
37 And some of them said, Could not this man,
which opened the eyes of the blind, have caused
that even this man should not have died?
38 Jesus therefore again groaning in himself
cometh to the grave. It was a cave, and a stone lay
upon it.
39 Jesus said, Take ye away the stone. Martha, the
sister of him that was dead, saith unto him, Lord,
by this time he stinketh: for he hath been *dead*
four days.
40 Jesus saith unto her, Said I not unto thee, that,
if thou wouldest believe, thou shouldest see the
glory of God?
41 Then they took away the stone *from the place*
where the dead was laid. And Jesus lifted up *his*
eyes, and said, Father, I thank thee that thou hast
heard me.
42 And I knew that thou hearest me always: but
because of the people which stand by I said *it*, that
they may believe that thou hast sent me.
43 And when he thus had spoken, he cried with a
loud voice, Lazarus, come forth.
44 And he that was dead came forth, bound
hand and foot with graveclothes: and his face
was bound about with a napkin. Jesus saith unto
them, Loose him, and let him go.
45 Then many of the Jews which came to Mary,
and had seen the things which Jesus did, believed
on him.
46 But some of them went their ways to the Phar-
isees, and told them what things Jesus had done.
47 ¶ Then gathered the chief priests and the
Pharisees a council, and said, What do we? for this

11:18 *nigh.* Near. *fifteen furlongs.* About two miles.

11:24 *I know that he shall rise again.* Martha knew the doctrine of the *resurrection* from the Old Testament (Job 19:25–26; Isa. 25:7–8; 26:19; Dan. 12:2–3; Hos. 13:14).

11:25 *I am the resurrection, and the life.* Another one of Jesus' major "I am" claims to be God and Savior (6:35; 8:12,58; 10:7,11; 14:6; 15:1). Jesus not only shows the way to life (6:68) and gives life (4:10), but He is the life (1:4; 5:26; 14:6), that is, He is the glorious, immortal, eternal life of the coming age, already breaking into our world for the blessing of those united to Him (2 Tim. 1:10; 1 John 1:2). Christ's words constitute the hope of all His believing people. The last day will show how true His claim is.

11:26 *never die.* A believer will not experience death as the curse of the law against sin (1 Cor. 15:55–57) but will triumph as one alive to God even in physical death (8:51–52).

11:32 *fell down.* A sign of great honor and devotion.

11:33–35 *groaned in the spirit, and was troubled . . . Jesus wept.* Our Lord was indignant that sin had brought such sorrow into this world and shed tears of love and compassion. Though having infinite knowledge in His deity, in His humanity His knowledge was limited (*Where have ye laid him*). His humanness is a great comfort to His people, for He is touched by our troubles, remembers His own experiences, and is able to help us as a sympathetic High Priest (Heb. 4:15).

11:38 *stone lay upon it.* Usually a large slab of stone used to protect the dead body from animals entering the cave.

11:39 *stinketh.* Lazarus's body had already begun decomposing.

11:40 *see the glory of God.* The miracle will display God's power in Christ to save sinners from the misery of the fall, represented in that great enemy, death (Gen. 2:17).

11:42 *thou hearest me always.* Christ's intercession always obtains grace from God because the Son is perfectly pleasing to the Father (8:29).

11:43 *he cried with a loud voice, Lazarus, come forth.* A foreshadowing of the judgment day (5:28–29; 1 Thess. 4:16). Though the dead man had no ability to hear or obey, Christ's command contained the power to produce life and obedience and so provides a picture of conversion by grace alone (5:25; Eph. 2:1,5).

11:44 *napkin.* One of the burial garments covering Lazarus.

man doeth many miracles.

48 If we let him thus alone, all *men* will believe on him: and the Romans shall come and take away both our place and nation.

49 And one of them, *named* Caiaphas, being the high priest that same year, said unto them, Ye know nothing at all,

50 Nor consider that it is expedient for us, that one man should die for the people, and that the whole nation perish not.

51 And this spake he not of himself: but being high priest that year, he prophesied that Jesus should die for that nation;

52 And not for that nation only, but that also he should gather together in one the children of God that were scattered abroad.

53 Then from that day forth they took counsel together for to put him to death.

54 Jesus therefore walked no more openly among the Jews; but went thence unto a country near to the wilderness, into a city called Ephraim, and there continued with his disciples.

55 ¶ And the Jews' passover was nigh at hand: and many went out of the country up to Jerusalem before the passover, to purify themselves.

56 Then sought they for Jesus, and spake among themselves, as they stood in the temple, What think ye, that he will not come to the feast?

57 Now both the chief priests and the Pharisees had given a commandment, that, if any man knew where he were, he should shew *it*, that they might take him.

CHAPTER 12

THEN Jesus six days before the passover came to Bethany, where Lazarus was which had been dead, whom he raised from the dead.

2 There they made him a supper; and Martha served: but Lazarus was one of them that sat at the table with him.

3 Then took Mary a pound of ointment of spikenard, very costly, and anointed the feet of Jesus, and wiped his feet with her hair: and the house was filled with the odour of the ointment.

4 Then saith one of his disciples, Judas Iscariot, Simon's *son*, which should betray him,

5 Why was not this ointment sold for three hundred pence, and given to the poor?

6 This he said, not that he cared for the poor; but because he was a thief, and had the bag, and bare what was put therein.

7 Then said Jesus, Let her alone: against the day of my burying hath she kept this.

8 For the poor always ye have with you; but me ye have not always.

9 Much people of the Jews therefore knew that he was there: and they came not for Jesus' sake only, but that they might see Lazarus also, whom he had raised from the dead.

11:47–48 *council.* The Sanhedrin, the ruling body of Judaea. *Romans shall come.* Perhaps they thought Jesus was about to lead a popular uprising (12:19).

11:50–52 *expedient.* Better. *one man should die for the people.* The ambiguous prophecy of the high priest was meant by him to commend Christ's murder, but it unwittingly served to declare God's purpose that Christ should die as a substitute for His people. This displays God's sovereignty in accomplishing His loving plan of salvation through, not in spite of, the malice of men. *children of God.* Those who would come to trust in Christ and be adopted by God (1:12), even though many of them had not yet heard the gospel (10:16). Christ died for a particular people, God's elect scattered among the nations, and they will be saved (10:14–15,26–28). *abroad.* Over a wide area.

11:53–54 *from that day forth they took counsel.* The time of our Lord's death was drawing near (vv. 56–57).

11:55 *the Jews' passover.* Our Lord's death had to be at the time of the Passover, for He is the true Passover Lamb (1:29; 1 Cor. 5:7).

Thoughts for Personal/Family Worship: Chapter 11

1. **Since Christ's death is the death of death to all His people, they need not sorrow excessively when facing death. In the great day the voice of Jesus will raise up all believers in glory. Though believers die physically, they never die spiritually or eternally but will rise at last to meet the Lord in the air at His second coming (1 Thess. 4:13–16). How do these truths affect the way in which you will face death?**
2. **Though Christ is the infinite and living God, He is also a man with a human mind and emotions like our own. Therefore, we need not fear to approach Him but can pour out our hearts to Him and know He will sympathize with all except those who are rebellious against God. Here is a Priest who can help us in temptation. Consider that "Jesus wept" (v. 35). How does that encourage you to seek Him as the sympathizing High Priest (Heb. 4:15)?**

Chapter 12: ***Mary anoints Jesus at Bethany, Christ enters triumphantly into Jerusalem, the Greeks wish to see Jesus, and people express a mixture of unbelief and faith.***

Conclusion to the Public Ministry (12:1–50)

12:1 Here begins the last week of Jesus' ministry before his death. *Bethany.* In Judaea.

12:3 *ointment of spikenard.* Fragrant oil. This is a similar, but not identical, event to that recorded in Luke 7:36–50.

12:4 *Judas.* His ungenerous attitude reflected his unregenerate heart (6:70–71).

12:5 *pence.* A denarius, the equivalent of a day's wages for a laborer. Thus the container of ointment was worth about a year's wages, a large sum.

12:6 *thief.* His heart was ruled by greed (Matt. 26:15). *bag.* To hold money collected for the ministry.

12:7–8 *against the day of my burying.* Mary evidently believed Christ's predictions that He must die to save His people (3:14; 10:15,17–18), and the knowledge of God's love (3:16) stirred her heart to express her answering love in an act of costly devotion.

12:9 *Jews.* Evidently not the religious leaders, who hated Christ.

10 ¶ But the chief priests consulted that they
might put Lazarus also to death;
11 Because that by reason of him many of the
Jews went away, and believed on Jesus.
12 ¶ On the next day much people that were
come to the feast, when they heard that Jesus was
coming to Jerusalem,
13 Took branches of palm trees, and went forth to
meet him, and cried, Hosanna: Blessed *is* the King
of Israel that cometh in the name of the Lord.
14 And Jesus, when he had found a young ass, sat
thereon; as it is written,
15 Fear not, daughter of Sion: behold, thy King
cometh, sitting on an ass's colt.
16 These things understood not his disciples at the
first: but when Jesus was glorified, then remem-
bered they that these things were written of him,
and *that* they had done these things unto him.
17 The people therefore that was with him when
he called Lazarus out of his grave, and raised him
from the dead, bare record.
18 For this cause the people also met him, for that
they heard that he had done this miracle.
19 The Pharisees therefore said among them-
selves, Perceive ye how ye prevail nothing? behold,
the world is gone after him.
20 ¶ And there were certain Greeks among them
that came up to worship at the feast:
21 The same came therefore to Philip, which was
of Bethsaida of Galilee, and desired him, saying,
Sir, we would see Jesus.
22 Philip cometh and telleth Andrew: and again
Andrew and Philip tell Jesus.
23 ¶ And Jesus answered them, saying, The hour
is come, that the Son of man should be glorified.
24 Verily, verily, I say unto you, Except a corn
of wheat fall into the ground and die, it abideth
alone: but if it die, it bringeth forth much fruit.
25 He that loveth his life shall lose it; and he that
hateth his life in this world shall keep it unto life
eternal.
26 If any man serve me, let him follow me; and
where I am, there shall also my servant be: if any
man serve me, him will *my* Father honour.
27 Now is my soul troubled; and what shall I say?
Father, save me from this hour: but for this cause
came I unto this hour.
28 Father, glorify thy name. Then came there a
voice from heaven, *saying*, I have both glorified *it*,
and will glorify *it* again.
29 The people therefore, that stood by, and heard
it, said that it thundered: others said, An angel
spake to him.
30 Jesus answered and said, This voice came not
because of me, but for your sakes.
31 Now is the judgment of this world: now shall
the prince of this world be cast out.
32 And I, if I be lifted up from the earth, will draw
all *men* unto me.
33 This he said, signifying what death he should
die.
34 The people answered him, We have heard out
of the law that Christ abideth for ever: and how
sayest thou, The Son of man must be lifted up?
who is this Son of man?
35 Then Jesus said unto them, Yet a little while is

12:10–11 Such was the hardness of the hearts of the *chief priests* that rather than responding to Jesus' raising of Lazarus (11:1–57) with faith, they plotted to kill Lazarus.

12:12 *feast.* The Passover (v. 1). *much people.* Large crowds.

12:13 *Hosanna.* Literally, "Please save" (Ps. 118:25). *Blessed is . . . cometh in the name of the Lord.* Citing Ps. 118:26. This was one of the Hallel Psalms sung at Passover.

12:14–15 *young ass.* A sign of the coming of the humble King (Zech. 9:9).

12:16 *when Jesus was glorified.* After His death and resurrection.

12:17–18 *bare record.* Testified as witnesses. One reason for the enthusiasm of the crowds at Christ's triumphal entry was His miracle of raising *Lazarus* from the dead.

12:19 *the world is gone after him.* An example of how *world* can mean many, but not all, for it refers to crowds of Jews but not to all Jews, and certainly not the distant nations.

12:20–22 *Greeks . . . saying, Sir, we would see Jesus.* A token of the gathering of people from many nations, not just Jews, into the church through the death of Christ (v. 32).

12:23 *Jesus answered them.* Christ immediately recognized the significance of this request from Gentiles. *The hour is come.* God's appointed time for Christ to display God's glory in the death and resurrection (*be glorified*; 7:39; 13:31; 17:1,5) of God's appointed King (*Son of man*; Dan. 7:13–14) over all mankind.

12:24 *Verily, verily.* Truly (see note at 1:51). *corn.* Grain. *die . . . much fruit.* Using the illustration of a seed, Jesus taught that His death was necessary to multiply His life in many people. The crucified Christ produced a harvest of crucified Christians (Gal. 2:19–20; 5:24; 6:14).

12:25 *life in this world . . . life eternal.* The contrast between the earthly and heavenly kingdoms (8:23) is also a contrast between this age and the age to come. The Christian denies himself many pleasures and benefits in this age (*hateth his life*) because he puts his hope and seeks his treasure in Christ's kingdom (Luke 9:24–25).

12:27 *my soul troubled.* His emotions were deeply disturbed by the agonies about to come upon Him when He died for His people, but He pressed on with determination.

12:28 *glorify thy name.* The ultimate purpose of Christ's work is to make known the glory of God in all His perfections and attributes (17:1–5; Isa. 48:9,11; Phil. 1:11).

12:31 *judgment of this world.* Christ's death is a mysterious conquest of man in rebellion against God (16:33). *prince of this world.* Satan, the spiritual ruler of fallen man (8:44; 14:30; 16:11; 2 Cor. 4:4; Eph. 2:2; 6:12). *cast out.* Figurative language for Christ's decisive victory over the Devil (Col. 2:15).

12:32–33 *draw all men.* As a result of Christ's *death* on the cross (*lifted up*), the Lord Jesus will have the power and right to effectively pull (*draw*) *all* kinds of people, including Gentiles (v. 20), out of Satan's kingdom and to Himself in saving faith (see note at 6:44).

12:35–36 *Yet a little while is the light.* Christ would be with them for only two or three more days. His public ministry to the Jews was ending. *darkness.* Judgment (Jude 13). *children*

the light with you. Walk while ye have the light,
lest darkness come upon you: for he that walketh
in darkness knoweth not whither he goeth.
36 While ye have light, believe in the light, that ye
may be the children of light. These things spake
Jesus, and departed, and did hide himself from
them.
37 ¶ But though he had done so many miracles
before them, yet they believed not on him:
38 That the saying of Esaias the prophet might
be fulfilled, which he spake, Lord, who hath be-
lieved our report? and to whom hath the arm of
the Lord been revealed?
39 Therefore they could not believe, because that
Esaias said again,
40 He hath blinded their eyes, and hardened their
heart; that they should not see with *their* eyes, nor
understand with *their* heart, and be converted,
and I should heal them.
41 These things said Esaias, when he saw his
glory, and spake of him.
42 ¶ Nevertheless among the chief rulers also
many believed on him; but because of the Phari-
sees they did not confess *him*, lest they should be
put out of the synagogue:
43 For they loved the praise of men more than
the praise of God.
44 ¶ Jesus cried and said, He that believeth on me,
believeth not on me, but on him that sent me.
45 And he that seeth me seeth him that sent me.
46 I am come a light into the world, that
whosoever believeth on me should not abide in
darkness.
47 And if any man hear my words, and believe
not, I judge him not: for I came not to judge the
world, but to save the world.
48 He that rejecteth me, and receiveth not my
words, hath one that judgeth him: the word that I
have spoken, the same shall judge him in the last
day.
49 For I have not spoken of myself; but the Fa-
ther which sent me, he gave me a commandment,
what I should say, and what I should speak.
50 And I know that his commandment is life
everlasting: whatsoever I speak therefore, even as
the Father said unto me, so I speak.

CHAPTER 13

NOW before the feast of the passover, when Jesus
knew that his hour was come that he should
depart out of this world unto the Father, having
loved his own which were in the world, he loved
them unto the end.
2 And supper being ended, the devil having now
put into the heart of Judas Iscariot, Simon's *son*,
to betray him;
3 Jesus knowing that the Father had given all
things into his hands, and that he was come from
God, and went to God;
4 He riseth from supper, and laid aside his gar-
ments; and took a towel, and girded himself.
5 After that he poureth water into a bason, and
began to wash the disciples' feet, and to wipe *them*
with the towel wherewith he was girded.
6 Then cometh he to Simon Peter: and Peter saith

of light. An idiom for people characterized by their allegiance to Christ and His truth.

12:37 *many miracles . . . yet they believed not*. Miracles do not save souls.

12:38–40 *Esaias*. Isaiah (Isa. 6:10; 53:1). God had now given the bulk of the nation over to unbelief. This hardening was sent upon them as a judgment for their pride.

12:41 *Esaias . . . saw his glory*. The majestic vision of the holy Lord recorded in Isa. 6 was a revelation of the high and exalted Son of God before His incarnation. Isaiah's vision of glory is linked to the prophecy of the Suffering Servant by the words "high and lifted up" (Isa. 6:1; see note at Isa. 52:13).

12:43 *loved the praise of men*. Man's proud preoccupation with the honor he receives from other people is deadly to saving faith (5:44; Rom. 2:29).

12:44–50 These words are a summary of Christ's public teaching and preaching over the previous three years.

12:45 *he that seeth me seeth him that sent me*. The Father and the Son are one, sharing the same nature, so that the Son perfectly reveals the Father (1:18; 10:30; 14:7,9).

12:46 *light*. See 1:4–5,9; 3:19–21; 8:12; 9:5; 11:9–10.

12:47 *I came not to judge*. Christ came the first time not to judge sinners but to save them (3:17). He will return at the end of history to judge the world.

Thoughts for Personal/Family Worship: Chapter 12

1. **Those who love Christ and honor Him must expect to be critically misjudged by those who are only nominal Christians. That should not discourage them from pouring out their lives in love for the One who died for them. How can you imitate Mary's costly devotion?**
2. **The death of Christ is the most sublime of all God's works to glorify Himself. In His dying Christ has in a unique way manifested the love, justice, and wisdom of God. At the cross Satan's power was broken and the nations redeemed. The cross of Christ breaks the heart of all elect sinners and leads them to devote their lives to Him. In what way do you see God's glory in Christ crucified? How does that draw you to Christ as Savior and Lord?**

CHRIST REVEALS HIS GLORY IN HIS PASSION, DEATH, AND RESURRECTION (13:1—21:25)

Chapter 13: ***Jesus washes the disciples' feet, Judas betrays Jesus, and Jesus announces the new commandment.***

Jesus Washes the Disciples' Feet (13:1–38)

13:1 *before the feast*. Thursday night. *knew that his hour was come*. Our Lord faced the cross with complete knowledge of His coming glory and with a heart full of love toward His own dear people.

13:2 *the devil having . . . put into the heart of Judas*. The flesh-and-blood enemies of Christ were but instruments of Satan's hatred and schemes to destroy Christ (v. 27; cf. Acts 5:3).

13:4 *towel*. Christ assumed the garments and position of a common servant. *girded*. Tied around the waist.

unto him, Lord, dost thou wash my feet?
7 Jesus answered and said unto him, What I do
thou knowest not now; but thou shalt know here-
after.
8 Peter saith unto him, Thou shalt never wash my
feet. Jesus answered him, If I wash thee not, thou
hast no part with me.
9 Simon Peter saith unto him, Lord, not my feet
only, but also *my* hands and *my* head.
10 Jesus saith to him, He that is washed needeth
not save to wash *his* feet, but is clean every whit:
and ye are clean, but not all.
11 For he knew who should betray him; therefore
said he, Ye are not all clean.
12 So after he had washed their feet, and had
taken his garments, and was set down again, he
said unto them, Know ye what I have done to you?
13 Ye call me Master and Lord: and ye say well;
for *so* I am.
14 If I then, *your* Lord and Master, have washed
your feet; ye also ought to wash one another's feet.
15 For I have given you an example, that ye
should do as I have done to you.
16 Verily, verily, I say unto you, The servant is
not greater than his lord; neither he that is sent
greater than he that sent him.
17 If ye know these things, happy are ye if ye do
them.
18 ¶ I speak not of you all: I know whom I have
chosen: but that the scripture may be fulfilled, He
that eateth bread with me hath lifted up his heel
against me.
19 Now I tell you before it come, that, when it is
come to pass, ye may believe that I am *he*.
20 Verily, verily, I say unto you, He that receiveth
whomsoever I send receiveth me; and he that re-
ceiveth me receiveth him that sent me.
21 When Jesus had thus said, he was troubled in
spirit, and testified, and said, Verily, verily, I say
unto you, that one of you shall betray me.
22 Then the disciples looked one on another,
doubting of whom he spake.
23 Now there was leaning on Jesus' bosom one of
his disciples, whom Jesus loved.
24 Simon Peter therefore beckoned to him, that
he should ask who it should be of whom he spake.
25 He then lying on Jesus' breast saith unto him,
Lord, who is it?
26 Jesus answered, He it is, to whom I shall give
a sop, when I have dipped *it*. And when he had
dipped the sop, he gave *it* to Judas Iscariot, *the son*
of Simon.
27 And after the sop Satan entered into him. Then
said Jesus unto him, That thou doest, do quickly.
28 Now no man at the table knew for what intent
he spake this unto him.
29 For some *of them* thought, because Judas had
the bag, that Jesus had said unto him, Buy *those*
things that we have need of against the feast; or,
that he should give something to the poor.
30 He then having received the sop went immedi-
ately out: and it was night.
31 ¶ Therefore, when he was gone out, Jesus
said, Now is the Son of man glorified, and God is
glorified in him.
32 If God be glorified in him, God shall also
glorify him in himself, and shall straightway
glorify him.
33 Little children, yet a little while I am with
you. Ye shall seek me: and as I said unto the Jews,
Whither I go, ye cannot come; so now I say to you.
34 A new commandment I give unto you, That ye
love one another; as I have loved you, that ye also
love one another.
35 By this shall all *men* know that ye are my
disciples, if ye have love one to another.

13:8 *no part with me.* Clearly our Lord refers to this washing as a symbol of the spiritual washing that all sinners need (3:5).
13:10 *save.* Except. *every whit.* Completely. A person who has had the new birth does not need it twice, but he does need cleansing from daily sins (1 John 1:9). *not all.* Ominously, Jesus now revealed that one of the twelve disciples was graceless and unconverted.
13:12–17 Christ's self-humbling action ought to be an example to all believers (Phil. 2:3–8).
13:18 *I know whom I have chosen.* Christ knows who are, and who are not, His own elect people given to Him by the Father (10:14). Though not yet named, Judas was about to fulfill the ominous prophecy here quoted by Christ (Ps. 41:9).
13:19 *I am he.* Literally, "I am," probably an allusion to Christ's deity (8:58), which was displayed in His foreknowledge of men's sinful choices (Isa. 41:4; 43:10–13).
13:23 *leaning.* Reclining at a supper table was common practice in Jesus' day. *whom Jesus loved.* The disciple John, the author of this gospel.
13:26 *sop.* A piece of unleavened bread dipped into a dish of sauce made of different fruits.
13:27 *Satan entered into him.* Judas's refusal to repent even after Christ warned of the coming betrayal (v. 21) opened him to Satan's complete control. *do quickly.* Christ sovereignly dismissed the demonized betrayer, setting in motion the events of His arrest and death on the Passover, according to God's eternal purpose.
13:28 *no man . . . knew.* The other disciples did not suspect Judas.
13:30 *night.* A suggestion of the power of spiritual darkness at work (Luke 22:53).
13:31–32 *the Son of man glorified.* God's appointed Mediator-King was about to take His eternal kingdom over all (Dan. 7:13–14), yet through humiliation (*Now*). God conquered the world and revealed His glory by the death and exaltation of Jesus (7:39; 12:23–24,27–28; 17:1,4–5). Thus Christ's sufferings both concealed and revealed His glory. *straightway.* Immediately.
13:34–35 The highest duty of Christians is to *love one another*. This is the best mark of grace (*know that ye are my disciples*) and the surest way to impact the world (17:21,23). Though an old *commandment* (Lev. 19:18), the obligation to love each other was revealed with *new* brilliance by the example of Christ (*as I have loved you*) in His sacrifice (Eph. 5:2; 1 John 3:16–18; 4:9–11).

36 ¶ Simon Peter said unto him, Lord, whither
goest thou? Jesus answered him, Whither I go,
thou canst not follow me now; but thou shalt
follow me afterwards.
37 Peter said unto him, Lord, why cannot I fol-
low thee now? I will lay down my life for thy sake.
38 Jesus answered him, Wilt thou lay down thy
life for my sake? Verily, verily, I say unto thee,
The cock shall not crow, till thou hast denied me
thrice.

CHAPTER 14

LET not your heart be troubled: ye believe in God,
believe also in me.
2 In my Father's house are many mansions: if *it*
were not *so*, I would have told you. I go to prepare
a place for you.
3 And if I go and prepare a place for you, I will
come again, and receive you unto myself; that
where I am, *there* ye may be also.
4 And whither I go ye know, and the way ye know.
5 Thomas saith unto him, Lord, we know not
whither thou goest; and how can we know the way?
6 Jesus saith unto him, I am the way, the truth,
and the life: no man cometh unto the Father, but
by me.
7 If ye had known me, ye should have known my
Father also: and from henceforth ye know him,
and have seen him.
8 Philip saith unto him, Lord, shew us the Father,
and it sufficeth us.
9 Jesus saith unto him, Have I been so long
time with you, and yet hast thou not known me,
Philip? he that hath seen me hath seen the Father;
and how sayest thou *then*, Shew us the Father?
10 Believest thou not that I am in the Father, and
the Father in me? the words that I speak unto you
I speak not of myself: but the Father that dwelleth
in me, he doeth the works.
11 Believe me that I *am* in the Father, and the
Father in me: or else believe me for the very
works' sake.
12 Verily, verily, I say unto you, He that believeth
on me, the works that I do shall he do also; and
greater *works* than these shall he do; because I go
unto my Father.
13 And whatsoever ye shall ask in my name,
that will I do, that the Father may be glorified in
the Son.

13:36 *whither.* Where. Peter does not understand where the Lord is going. But by and by Peter will *follow* the Lord to the heavenly Father's house above (14:2; 2 Peter 1:14).

13:37–38 *I will lay down my life.* Peter has not yet learned how weak he is.

Thoughts for Personal/Family Worship: Chapter 13

1. **As Christ looked beyond the cross to the crown, which He was soon to wear, so believers should look beyond their earthly trials to the glory to be theirs at last. How can this hope empower you to humbly serve others as Christ did?**
2. **God is in control of every situation. Judas had his covetous eye on the money promised to him, but God's purpose was to save a multitude of sinners through Christ's shed blood. How profound are Peter's words in his sermon on the day of Pentecost: "Him, being delivered by the determinate counsel and foreknowledge of God, ye have taken, and by wicked hands have crucified and slain" (Acts 2:23). If God can even use a traitor to provide salvation, how are you motivated to trust Him with your trials now?**
3. **A Christian may have much to learn about his own weakness. Mercifully, God is ready to forgive all who have true faith. Peter was a true child of God, yet he fell through overconfidence; Judas was no true child of God but a hypocrite, and he went to his own place. Let every man search his own heart and ask, "Lord, is it I?"**

Jesus' Upper Room Discourse and High Priestly Prayer (14:1—17:26)

Chapter 14: ***Christ proclaims to His disciples that He is the way, the truth, and the life, after which He comforts them with the promised coming of the Holy Spirit.***

14:1 *troubled.* The same word used of Christ's own inner disturbance (12:27; 13:21). Christ shares His hope and joy with His disciples in order to sustain them (v. 27; 15:11).

14:2 *mansions.* The Greek word simply means dwelling places (v. 23), which also carries the older sense of the English word "mansions." *prepare a place.* By His sufferings and exaltation He will obtain a place for them with the Father in heaven (Heb. 6:19–20).

14:3 *come again.* Jesus spoke of His coming throughout this chapter in a variety of ways (vv. 18,23,28). *where I am . . . ye may be.* See 17:24.

14:4–5 *whither.* Where, to what place.

14:6 *I am the way, the truth, and the life.* Christ summarizes here how in Him the Lord God (*I am*) has come to mankind to be all they need for salvation. Christ Himself is the only path (*way*) by which sinners far from God can draw near to Him (1:51; 10:9) in reconciled relationship (3:36); the only knowledge (*truth*) by which those ignorant of God can receive revelation (1:1,14,18) and illumination (1:3; 8:12) so as to know Him (17:3); and the only power by which those dead in sin can be raised (*life;* 5:25–26) to live for God and with God in the Spirit (6:63; 7:37–39) both now and forever (11:25–26). This summary corresponds to Christ's offices as Priest, Prophet, and King. *no man cometh . . . but by me.* Christ is the only Mediator between God and man (1 Tim. 2:5), and faith in Christ is the necessary means of salvation (Acts 4:12; Rom. 10:13–14).

14:7 *henceforth.* From this time forward.

14:8 *sufficeth.* Is sufficient.

14:9 *he that hath seen me hath seen the Father.* Christ is the perfect image of God, for He has the same divine nature (1:1,18; 2 Cor. 4:4; Col. 1:15).

14:12 *Verily, verily.* Truly (see note at 1:51). *greater works.* A larger numbers of converts would be gathered in by the preaching of the apostles (Acts 2:41; 4:4).

14:13–14 *ask in my name.* Christ's name is shorthand for God's glory revealed in Christ through the gospel, the object of saving faith (1:12; 3:18; 12:28; 17:6,26; 20:31). To act in someone else's name is to do so as one sent or given authority

14 If ye shall ask any thing in my name, I will
do *it*.
15 ¶ If ye love me, keep my commandments.
16 And I will pray the Father, and he shall give
you another Comforter, that he may abide with
you for ever;
17 *Even* the Spirit of truth; whom the world can-
not receive, because it seeth him not, neither
knoweth him: but ye know him; for he dwelleth
with you, and shall be in you.
18 I will not leave you comfortless: I will come
to you.
19 Yet a little while, and the world seeth me no
more; but ye see me: because I live, ye shall live
also.
20 At that day ye shall know that I *am* in my
Father, and ye in me, and I in you.
21 He that hath my commandments, and keepeth
them, he it is that loveth me: and he that loveth
me shall be loved of my Father, and I will love
him, and will manifest myself to him.
22 Judas saith unto him, not Iscariot, Lord, how is
it that thou wilt manifest thyself unto us, and not
unto the world?
23 Jesus answered and said unto him, If a man
love me, he will keep my words: and my Father
will love him, and we will come unto him, and
make our abode with him.
24 He that loveth me not keepeth not my sayings:
and the word which ye hear is not mine, but the
Father's which sent me.
25 These things have I spoken unto you, being *yet*
present with you.
26 But the Comforter, *which is* the Holy Ghost,
whom the Father will send in my name, he shall
teach you all things, and bring all things to your
remembrance, whatsoever I have said unto you.
27 Peace I leave with you, my peace I give unto
you: not as the world giveth, give I unto you. Let
not your heart be troubled, neither let it be afraid.
28 Ye have heard how I said unto you, I go away,
and come *again* unto you. If ye loved me, ye
would rejoice, because I said, I go unto the Father:
for my Father is greater than I.
29 And now I have told you before it come to pass,
that, when it is come to pass, ye might believe.
30 Hereafter I will not talk much with you: for
the prince of this world cometh, and hath noth-
ing in me.
31 But that the world may know that I love the

---

by Him (v. 26; 10:25). Therefore, to pray in Jesus' name (15:16; 16:23–24,26) is to approach God through faith in Christ's person and saving work, as those to whom the Father has given the right to make our requests boldly because of His Son.

14:15 The best proof of *love* for Christ is obedience. *my commandments*. Jesus taught His disciples to obey the Ten Commandments from a heart of love (Matt. 5:17–28; 12:1–13; 15:3–9; 22:37–40).

14:16 *I will pray the Father*. The outpouring and continuing ministry of the Spirit is the fruit of Christ's work (Gal. 3:13–14), obtained by His priestly intercession. *another Comforter*. An advocate or helper (Greek, *paraklêtos*), a title for the Holy Spirit, as it is of Christ (1 John 2:2). The Spirit is depicted as teaching (v. 26), testifying to the world (15:26), and convicting the world of its wrongs (16:7–8).

14:17 *Spirit of truth*. Another title for the Holy Spirit (15:26; 16:13), emphasizing that His work is inseparable from that of Christ (v. 6) and the written Word of God (6:63). *seeth him not, neither knoweth him*. The Spirit's saving work is foreign to unbelievers, not being part of their mindset or experience; they *cannot receive* His truth until He changes them (3:3; 6:44). *be in you*. Though the Spirit is in all places (Ps. 139:7), He is uniquely present in believers as the Spirit of adoption (v. 18; Rom. 8:9,14–16).

14:18 *I will not leave you comfortless*. Literally, "I will not leave you as orphans." *I will come to you*. This refers to His coming in the Spirit (v. 17) on the day of Pentecost (Acts 2:1–47), not to His second coming (v. 3).

14:19 *a little while*. It was only a few hours before Christ would die and be buried. *world seeth me no more*. Christ would appear to many of His disciples after His resurrection (20:1—21:25), but not publicly to unbelievers. *because I live, ye shall live also*. The union of believers with Christ (v. 20) gives them the same spiritual life possessed by Christ in His human nature, a reflection of the shared life within the Trinity (5:26).

14:20 *At that day*. Pentecost and after. The ascent of Christ and the descent of the Spirit were a vindication (*ye shall know*) that God had received and was satisfied with the work of Christ. *in my Father . . . in me . . . in you*. This is the language of union and oneness.

14:21 *shall be loved . . . I will love*. God's love and benevolence are not based on anything in us but are the reason anyone is saved (3:16; 1 John 4:9–10). However, God delights in the obedience to His *commandments* His grace produces, and He shows that delight by revealing Himself (*manifest*) in a deeper way to obedient believers (Ps. 25:14).

14:22 *Judas . . . not Iscariot*. See Luke 6:16. Judas (a Greek form of Judah) was a common name among Jews.

14:23 *make our abode with him*. Just as the believer will dwell with God and Christ in the glories of heaven (*abode* is the same word as "mansions," v. 2), so the triune God already dwells in the hearts of true believers, all of whom are in a state of grace (Eph. 3:17; Col. 1:27).

14:26 *teach you all things*. Christ will continue His work (*in my name*) as the Prophet and teacher of the disciples through the Holy Spirit (16:12–14). *bring . . . to your remembrance*. The Gospel records of Christ's teachings are inspired by the Holy Spirit and thus are Holy Scripture (cf. 1 Tim. 5:18 with Luke 10:7). This promise has special reference to the apostles, whom the Spirit used to bring the gospel into all the world (20:21–23; Eph. 2:20–22; 3:5). It also has application to the Spirit's continuing work of applying the completed Scriptures to the church.

14:27 *my peace*. The inner peace Christ gives to believers is solid and comforting, even in the midst of distressing trials (16:33; 20:19,21,26; Phil. 4:7).

14:28 The disciples should be glad to think that their Master is returning to the Father in heaven. *my Father is greater than I*. In respect not to Christ's deity (5:18) but to His human nature, and also to the state of His person in the time of His humiliation, which was about to end (*go unto the Father*).

14:30 *prince of this world*. Satan (see note at 12:31). *hath nothing in me*. Christ knows that He is not guilty of that for which they seek to condemn Him.

14:31 *that the world may know*. Christ glorified the Father

Father; and as the Father gave me commandment,
even so I do. Arise, let us go hence.

CHAPTER 15

I AM the true vine, and my Father is the husband-
man.
2 Every branch in me that beareth not fruit he
taketh away: and every *branch* that beareth fruit,
he purgeth it, that it may bring forth more fruit.
3 Now ye are clean through the word which I
have spoken unto you.
4 Abide in me, and I in you. As the branch cannot
bear fruit of itself, except it abide in the vine; no
more can ye, except ye abide in me.
5 I am the vine, ye *are* the branches: He that abid-
eth in me, and I in him, the same bringeth forth
much fruit: for without me ye can do nothing.
6 If a man abide not in me, he is cast forth as a
branch, and is withered; and men gather them,
and cast *them* into the fire, and they are burned.
7 If ye abide in me, and my words abide in you,
ye shall ask what ye will, and it shall be done unto
you.
8 Herein is my Father glorified, that ye bear much
fruit; so shall ye be my disciples.
9 As the Father hath loved me, so have I loved
you: continue ye in my love.
10 If ye keep my commandments, ye shall abide
in my love; even as I have kept my Father's com-
mandments, and abide in his love.
11 These things have I spoken unto you, that my
joy might remain in you, and *that* your joy might
be full.
12 This is my commandment, That ye love one
another, as I have loved you.
13 Greater love hath no man than this, that a man
lay down his life for his friends.
14 Ye are my friends, if ye do whatsoever I com-
mand you.
15 Henceforth I call you not servants; for the
servant knoweth not what his lord doeth: but I
have called you friends; for all things that I have
heard of my Father I have made known unto you.

(12:28; 13:31) whom He loves by obeying His *commandment* even to the point of death of the cross (Phil. 2:8).

Thoughts for Personal/Family Worship: Chapter 14

1. **Just as Jesus showed His love by washing the feet of His disciples (13:1–38), so He demonstrated His great mercy by teaching them in the upper room just before He was arrested and killed (14:1—17:26). Rather than turning inward as His death approached, Christ devoted Himself all the more to serving others. Rather than demanding comfort, He disbursed it to others. How can we imitate His example?**
2. **Verse 6 is one of Christ's most loved statements, a precious distillation in just a few words of all that He is for His people. How have you known Christ as your way? Your truth? Your life? Why is He the only way to the Father?**
3. **As Jesus prepared His disciples for His departure, He repeatedly pointed them to the Divine Person who would continue Christ's ministry among them after Jesus left: the Holy Spirit. What does this chapter teach us about the Spirit's work and why we need Him?**

Chapter 15: ***Jesus tells the parable of the vine and the branches. He instructs concerning mutual love and the believer's relationship to the world.***

15:1–8 *the true vine.* The prophets depicted Israel as a vineyard or vine planted by God in order to produce the fruit of righteousness and justice that delights Him (Isa. 5:1–7; 27:2–6; cf. Ps. 80:8–16; Jer. 2:21; 6:9; Ezek. 15:1–8; 17:1–21; 19:10–11; Hos. 10:1; 14:7). In this parable Christ presents Himself as the true Israel and teaches that it is only by living union with Him that people can bear *fruit* that is pleasing to God (Gal. 5:19–24; Phil. 1:11).

15:1–2 *husbandman.* Farmer. The Father works actively in Christ and among His people to make them fruitful (5:17). *taketh away.* In judgment (v. 6). *purgeth.* Prunes, referring to that painful process of divine discipline of His children by which they grow in holiness (Heb. 12:5–13).

15:3 *clean through the word.* Believers are saved by faith in the gospel (3:15–16), through which God washes them of spiritual defilement (13:8–10; Acts 15:9; Eph. 5:26).

15:4 *Abide.* Remain, here as a *branch* clings to the *vine* and continually draws life from it. This is a picture of vital and persevering faith in Christ as one's only salvation (14:6).

15:5 *in me . . . in him.* A relationship of close union and communion. *bringeth forth much fruit . . . can do nothing.* There is no holy or fruitful life except one lived by faith in Jesus Christ. Any spiritual goodness in any man comes through Christ as the Mediator.

15:6 *cast them into the fire.* A symbol of eternal punishment (Matt. 3:10; 7:19; 13:42,50; 18:8–9). Unfruitful Christians are no Christians at all (Matt. 7:21; James 2:14,17).

15:7 *my words abide in you.* Living by faith in Christ requires the receiving of God's truth into the heart so as to change one's beliefs, affections, and behavior (8:31–32). *ask what ye will.* Answered prayer arises from knowing, loving, and praying His will revealed in Scripture (1 John 5:14).

15:8 To *bear much fruit* is the pathway to honoring God (*Herein is my Father glorified*) and finding strong assurance of salvation (*shall ye be my disciples,* 2 Peter 1:5–11).

15:9 *As the Father . . . so have I.* Amazingly, Christ's love for His people is an extension of the love within the eternal Trinity (17:23). *continue ye.* The same Greek word translated "abide" elsewhere in this chapter (see note at v. 4).

15:10–11 *keep my commandments . . . even as I have.* Obedience to Christ's moral law and imitation of Christ together constitute the way to be sure of His love (1 John 2:3–6) and to receive *joy* that is *full*—even the joy of the Son in His Father's love (*my joy*).

15:12–13 *This is my commandment.* Love is the sum of God's law (13:34; Matt. 22:37–40), the greatest of all the graces (1 Cor. 13:13), and our highest duty to our fellow Christians (1 John 3:23). *as I have loved you . . . lay down his life.* Just as spiritual life flows from union with Christ by faith in His death and resurrection (vv. 3–5), so also the spiritual life is shaped and directed by the imitation of Christ in His self-sacrifice for others (1 John 3:16–18).

15:14–15 Jesus used the affectionate term *friends,* rather than *servants,* of those who are truly His. Friends are permitted to hear family secrets that servants do not.

16 Ye have not chosen me, but I have chosen you,
and ordained you, that ye should go and bring
forth fruit, and *that* your fruit should remain: that
whatsoever ye shall ask of the Father in my name,
he may give it you.
17 These things I command you, that ye love one
another.
18 If the world hate you, ye know that it hated me
before *it hated* you.
19 If ye were of the world, the world would love
his own: but because ye are not of the world, but
I have chosen you out of the world, therefore the
world hateth you.
20 Remember the word that I said unto you, The
servant is not greater than his lord. If they have
persecuted me, they will also persecute you; if they
have kept my saying, they will keep yours also.
21 But all these things will they do unto you for
my name's sake, because they know not him that
sent me.
22 If I had not come and spoken unto them, they
had not had sin: but now they have no cloke for
their sin.
23 He that hateth me hateth my Father also.
24 If I had not done among them the works
which none other man did, they had not had sin:
but now have they both seen and hated both me
and my Father.
25 But *this cometh to pass*, that the word might be
fulfilled that is written in their law, They hated me
without a cause.
26 But when the Comforter is come, whom I will
send unto you from the Father, *even* the Spirit of
truth, which proceedeth from the Father, he shall
testify of me:
27 And ye also shall bear witness, because ye have
been with me from the beginning.

CHAPTER 16

THESE things have I spoken unto you, that ye
should not be offended.

15:16 *Ye have not chosen me.* Left to themselves, these disciples, or anyone, for that matter, would never have chosen Christ. *I have chosen you.* This does not refer to Christ's selection of men for the office of apostle; the selection to which Christ here refers takes a person out of the kingdom of sin (v. 18) and makes him fruitful in godliness (contrast 6:70). This is God's election of sinners to salvation and holiness (6:37; Eph. 1:4–5; 1 Thess. 2:13). Though the Father is the primary agent of eternal election, the Son has also elected because He too is God, and all the persons of the Trinity share one divine will (5:19–20; 10:30). *ordained.* Literally, "put," here probably in the sense of appoint. *go.* Perhaps, "go into the world," so that they can see the *fruit* of genuine discipleship and glorify the Father (v. 8; Matt. 5:14–16). Election motivates mission (2 Tim. 2:9–10).

15:18—16:4 Union with Christ makes a person fruitful for God, but it also places him in direct opposition to the wicked *world*, which hates God and Christ and so hates His people. Therefore, the disciples' participation in the true Israel alienated them from unbelieving Israel (*synagogues*; 16:2), and they were now to expect its persecution.

15:18 *world.* The human race viewed in its united hostility to God, here referring not to all people everywhere (see note at 3:16) but to those who had seen Christ's miracles and heard His preaching in Israel (vv. 22,24). *hated me.* No one is neutral to Christ or God; those who hear the gospel but are not yet converted hate and reject Him (1:10; 3:19–20; 7:7).

15:19 *not of the world.* Their citizenship is in heaven (8:23; Phil. 3:20). *chosen you out.* Christ's election of sinners results in a change of nature and allegiance so that His disciples no longer fit in with the patterns of unbelief and sin that characterize fallen mankind.

15:20 *Remember the word.* See 13:16. Christ's disciples are under Him as their Lord, and as they imitate Him (13:15) they must expect to have similar experiences of rejection.

15:21 *for my name's sake.* It is a comfort to the believer to realize that he suffers because of Christ (Matt. 5:11–12; 1 Peter 4:12–19).

15:22. Christ's ministry in Israel, like the preaching of the gospel in various nations today, removes the excuse (*cloke*) of men's ignorance and provokes their antipathy (v. 24; 3:19).

15:23 *hateth my Father also.* To hate Jesus is to hate God. No one who rejects Christ gives true worship to God, no matter how devoted he may be to his own religion.

15:25 *their law.* A general reference to the Old Testament. *They hated me without a cause.* Quoting Ps. 69:4, a psalm often cited for its prophecies of Christ (2:17; Luke 23:36; Acts 1:20; Rom. 11:9–10; 15:3). Christ did only good to mankind, but for all His love and kindness they hated and crucified Him.

15:26–27 *Comforter . . . Spirit of truth.* The Holy Spirit (14:16–17), depicted here in His witness to the world. *proceedeth.* Literally, "is going out from." The Spirit's continuous procession *from the Father* in His work of glorifying Christ has often been taken as a revelation of His eternal personal relation to the Father as His "Spirit" (by analogy to the breath of a living being, 20:22; Job 33:4; Ps. 33:6). *he shall testify of me . . . ye also shall bear witness.* The Spirit's testimony to Christ comes through the Word, exercised especially in the preaching of the risen Lord by the apostles and other faithful ministers (Acts 1:8).

Thoughts for Personal/Family Worship: Chapter 15

1. **Jesus is the Vine and Christians are the branches. Without the Lord we can do nothing pleasing to the Lord. Union and communion with Christ are crucial to a fruitful spiritual life that pleases God. By rejecting Christ the unbelieving Jews cut themselves off from their only hope of becoming what God intended Israel to be. Jews and Gentiles who trust in Christ become God's true vineyard. Are you abiding in Christ by a living faith? What fruits are you bearing that demonstrate this? How can you cultivate a deeper life of abiding in the Vine?**
2. **The history of Christianity illustrates clearly the principle that Christians should expect persecution. Why does the world hate Christ? Why does it hate the servants of Christ? In what way does this teach us our need for the Holy Spirit in order to be effective witnesses for Christ?**

Chapter 16: *Christ teaches concerning the work of the Comforter, announces His departure, and unfolds something of His Father's love.*

16:1–4 See note at 15:18—16:4. Christians need to fortify

2 They shall put you out of the synagogues: yea,
the time cometh, that whosoever killeth you will
think that he doeth God service.
3 And these things will they do unto you, because
they have not known the Father, nor me.
4 But these things have I told you, that when the
time shall come, ye may remember that I told you
of them. And these things I said not unto you at
the beginning, because I was with you.
5 But now I go my way to him that sent me; and
none of you asketh me, Whither goest thou?
6 But because I have said these things unto you,
sorrow hath filled your heart.
7 Nevertheless I tell you the truth; It is expedient
for you that I go away: for if I go not away, the
Comforter will not come unto you; but if I depart,
I will send him unto you.
8 And when he is come, he will reprove the world
of sin, and of righteousness, and of judgment:
9 Of sin, because they believe not on me;
10 Of righteousness, because I go to my Father,
and ye see me no more;
11 Of judgment, because the prince of this world
is judged.
12 I have yet many things to say unto you, but ye
cannot bear them now.
13 Howbeit when he, the Spirit of truth, is come,
he will guide you into all truth: for he shall not
speak of himself; but whatsoever he shall hear,
that shall he speak: and he will shew you things
to come.
14 He shall glorify me: for he shall receive of
mine, and shall shew *it* unto you.
15 All things that the Father hath are mine: there-
fore said I, that he shall take of mine, and shall
shew *it* unto you.
16 A little while, and ye shall not see me: and
again, a little while, and ye shall see me, because I
go to the Father.
17 Then said *some* of his disciples among them-
selves, What is this that he saith unto us, A little
while, and ye shall not see me: and again, a little
while, and ye shall see me: and, Because I go to
the Father?
18 They said therefore, What is this that he saith,
A little while? we cannot tell what he saith.
19 Now Jesus knew that they were desirous to ask
him, and said unto them, Do ye enquire among
yourselves of that I said, A little while, and ye shall
not see me: and again, a little while, and ye shall
see me?
20 Verily, verily, I say unto you, That ye shall
weep and lament, but the world shall rejoice: and
ye shall be sorrowful, but your sorrow shall be
turned into joy.
21 A woman when she is in travail hath sorrow,
because her hour is come: but as soon as she is de-
livered of the child, she remembereth no more the
anguish, for joy that a man is born into the world.
22 And ye now therefore have sorrow: but I will
see you again, and your heart shall rejoice, and
your joy no man taketh from you.
23 And in that day ye shall ask me nothing. Verily,
verily, I say unto you, Whatsoever ye shall ask the

themselves against their trials by realizing that excommunication and even death may be in their path in the time to come. Those who do not know God by faith in Christ can be so fanatically deceived that they imagine it to be their duty to murder Christians. *offended.* stumble.
16:5 *Whither.* Where, to what place.
16:7 Christ comforted them with the assurance that His going to glory would be to their advantage (*expedient*) since He would send the Holy Spirit (*Comforter;* 14:16) to come to them. *if I depart.* The Spirit would not come in His fullness until Christ was glorified at God's right hand (7:39; 13:31; Acts 2:32–33). *I will send him.* Jesus had earlier stated that the Father would send the Spirit (14:26), but Christ also says that He Himself sends the Spirit (15:26), another indication of order in the relationships in the Trinity: the Father is the first person, the Son the second (5:19), and the Spirit the third, though all are equally God.
16:8–11 Jesus here gives a description of the Holy Spirit's ministry to unbelievers (*the world*). *reprove.* Convict of wrong action or belief (3:20; 8:9,46; Titus 1:9). The Spirit reveals to men three fundamental truths: (1) their violation of God's Word (*sin*), which will damn them if they *believe not* in Christ (3:36; 5:45–46); (2) the perfect *righteousness* of the exalted Christ (*I go to my Father*), for they have rejected the only One who can save them; and (3) Christ's victory over Satan (*prince of this world is judged*; 12:31–32), which anticipates His judgment of all sinners (*the world*). This effect of the Spirit is evidenced by the apostles' preaching at Pentecost and later on by causing people to seriously consider the Word even though they had not yet been converted (Acts 2:37; 16:30; 24:25).
16:12 *many things to say.* Christ would continue His teaching through the apostles by the Spirit after His resurrection (Acts 1:1–3) and ascension (Eph. 3:5; 4:8–11), when His Spirit would give them greater spiritual illumination (v. 13; Luke 24:45).
16:13–15 *Howbeit.* But. *Spirit of truth.* See note at 14:17. *guide you.* The Holy Spirit gave the apostles the full revelation of God's will for His church (*all truth*), which is now recorded in the New Testament (14:26; 1 Cor. 2:9–13; Eph. 3:3,5,8), and continues to assist the church in understanding and applying the Holy Scriptures (Eph. 1:17). *not speak of himself . . . take of mine, and shall shew it.* The Holy Spirit does not work independently of the Father (like the Son, 12:49) but continues the Son's mission by revealing Him (*glorify me*), which is also to reveal the Father's glory (*All things that the Father hath*) in the Son (13:31–32; 17:1). This too reveals the unity and order of the persons in the Trinity (v. 7).
16:16 *not see me . . . ye shall see me.* A few short hours from this point Jesus would be dead and in the grave; three days after that He would be visibly with them once again for a time.
16:20 *Verily, verily.* Truly (see note at 1:51). Jesus explains by saying that at His crucifixion and death ungodly men would *rejoice* but that His own people would be deeply *sorrowful*; at His resurrection and ascension there would be a reversal of these emotions.
16:21 *travail.* Labor pains. *delivered of the child.* Has given birth.
16:23 *in that day . . . ask me nothing.* After the Spirit came at Pentecost they would understand the work of redemption. *ask . . . in my name.* See note at 14:13–14.

Father in my name, he will give *it* you.
24 Hitherto have ye asked nothing in my name:
ask, and ye shall receive, that your joy may be full.
25 These things have I spoken unto you in prov-
erbs: but the time cometh, when I shall no more
speak unto you in proverbs, but I shall shew you
plainly of the Father.
26 At that day ye shall ask in my name: and I say
not unto you, that I will pray the Father for you:
27 For the Father himself loveth you, because ye
have loved me, and have believed that I came out
from God.
28 I came forth from the Father, and am come
into the world: again, I leave the world, and go to
the Father.
29 His disciples said unto him, Lo, now speakest
thou plainly, and speakest no proverb.
30 Now are we sure that thou knowest all things,
and needest not that any man should ask thee: by
this we believe that thou camest forth from God.
31 Jesus answered them, Do ye now believe?
32 Behold, the hour cometh, yea, is now come,
that ye shall be scattered, every man to his own,
and shall leave me alone: and yet I am not alone,
because the Father is with me.
33 These things I have spoken unto you, that in
me ye might have peace. In the world ye shall have
tribulation: but be of good cheer; I have overcome
the world.

CHAPTER 17

THESE words spake Jesus, and lifted up his eyes to
heaven, and said, Father, the hour is come; glorify
thy Son, that thy Son also may glorify thee:
2 As thou hast given him power over all flesh, that
he should give eternal life to as many as thou hast
given him.
3 And this is life eternal, that they might know
thee the only true God, and Jesus Christ, whom
thou hast sent.
4 I have glorified thee on the earth: I have fin-
ished the work which thou gavest me to do.
5 And now, O Father, glorify thou me with thine
own self with the glory which I had with thee
before the world was.
6 I have manifested thy name unto the men
which thou gavest me out of the world: thine they

16:24 *Hitherto.* Until now.
16:25 *proverbs.* Sayings difficult to understand. *the time cometh.* The new covenant would bring more clarity of truth than the old covenant.
16:26 *I say not . . . I will pray.* Christ would continue to pray for them (14:16), but He meant that they would have personal access to *the Father* (Rom. 8:15; Eph. 2:18).
16:27 *loveth you, because.* Another example of God's love based on His delight in obedience to His commands, (14:21), not the love of His free grace that precedes all our love for Christ (3:16).
16:29 *Lo.* An interjection similar to "behold!"
16:32 *ye shall be scattered.* Though the disciples believed truly in Christ, they would, through fear of persecution (10:12), abandon Him in the moment of His need (13:38), as the Scriptures had prophesied (Zech. 13:7).
16:33 *tribulation.* Trouble, distress. *be of good cheer.* Have courage.

Thoughts for Personal/Family Worship: Chapter 16

1. **Not only are men and women perishing in their sins under the wrath of God and unable and unwilling to come to Christ, but they are strangely unaware of their desperate condition. The Spirit must awaken them to their guilt before God; the perfection of the Savior, Jesus Christ; and the reality that God's judgment on this wicked world has already begun in Christ's victory over Satan (vv. 7–11). How should this truth motivate and guide us in praying for the Spirit's help in our evangelism?**
2. **The Spirit is the Teacher of the church, bringing to us the glories of Christ so that we may see that all the fullness of the Father is in Christ for our benefit (vv. 12–15). How often do you pray for the work of the Spirit in the church of Christ? How can you be more fervent in your prayers for the Holy Spirit?**
3. **The Christian's life is a strange paradox in this world, a puzzling mixture of distress and peace, fear and courage (vv. 32–33). Why is this so? How can we grow in peace and courage by pleading the promise "I have overcome the world"?**

Chapter 17: *Christ offers up His high priestly prayer for Himself, His disciples, and all who would believe in Him through His Word.*

17:1–5 First, Christ prayed for Himself and His mission.
17:1 Jesus probably spoke this prayer while still in the upper room (18:1). *lifted up.* A gesture of reverence. *the hour is come.* The most crucial hour of all history, the climax of Christ's work (see note at 2:4). *glorify.* The highest goal of the *Father* and the *Son* (and the Spirit, 16:14) is to make known each other's glory (vv. 4–5,10,22,24; 1:14; 2:11; 7:18,39; 8:50,54; 11:4,40; 12:16,23,28; 13:31–32; 14:13; 15:8).
17:2 *power over all flesh.* Authority over all mankind in every nation. Christ is the Mediator of God's kingdom (3:35; 5:22–23; Matt. 28:18). *as many as thou hast given him.* The Son uses His kingly authority over all people in order to give complete salvation to those chosen by God (17:6,9,11–12,24; 6:37–40; 10:27–29; cf. 15:16).
17:3 *life eternal . . . know thee.* Christ confers a spiritual, experiential knowledge of God that involves communion with Himself in everlasting life. *only true God.* Not to the exclusion of *Jesus Christ,* for He too is God (1:1; 20:28), one with the Father (10:30), but to the exclusion of the deities of all other religions (Jer. 10:10–11; 1 John 5:20–21).
17:4 *I have glorified . . . finished.* Christ spoke in anticipation of His imminent and certain death on the cross (same verb as "finished" in 19:30).
17:5 *glorify thou me.* As to His divine nature Christ has always been in heaven (1:18; 3:13), but in His human nature He longed to be in glory, enjoying full communion *with* His Father. *I had . . . before the world was.* Christ's preexistence as the eternal God (8:58) with the other persons of the Trinity before the universe was created (1:1).
17:6–19 Second, Christ prayed for His present disciples, particularly the eleven apostles.
17:6 Here Christ begins to pray particularly (but not

EXPERIENTIAL KNOWLEDGE

The Reformers and Puritans loved to preach on John 17:3, "And this is life eternal, that they might know thee the only true God, and Jesus Christ, whom thou hast sent." They understood that the word "know," as used in this context, meant an intimate kind of knowledge that involved a deeply personal and abiding relationship with God in Christ Jesus. They were fond of calling this an experimental knowledge. Today we more commonly speak of it as experiential knowledge.

The term *experimental* comes from the Latin *experimentum*, meaning "trial." It is derived from the verb *experior*, meaning "to try, prove, or put to the test." That verb also can mean "to find or know by experience," thus leading to the word *experientia*, meaning "knowledge gained by experiment." John Calvin used *experiential* and *experimental* interchangeably, since both words indicate the need for measuring experienced knowledge against the touchstone of Scripture. Experiential knowledge addresses the vital matter of how a Christian *experiences* the truth of biblical doctrine in his life.

Experiential preaching seeks to explain in terms of biblical truth how matters ought to go, how they do go, and the end goal of the Christian life—eternal communion with God in glory (Rev. 21–22). It aims to apply divine truth to the whole range of the believer's personal experience, including his relationships with his family, the church, and the world around him. With the Spirit's blessing, the mission of such preaching is transforming because it accurately reflects the vital experience of the children of God (cf. Rom. 5:1–11), clearly explains the marks and fruits of saving grace necessary for a believer (Matt. 5:3–12; Gal. 5:22–23), and sets before believer and unbeliever alike their eternal futures (Rev. 21:1–9).

Experiential preaching and knowledge can be known by these four marks:

1. *It is Word- and Christ-centered.* That is, it flows out of the scriptural passage as it is expounded in accord with sound exegetical and hermeneutical principles, so as to foster true conviction of sin and true growth (John 16:7–8; Rom. 10:14; 1 Peter 2:2). The great theme and controlling contour of experiential preaching is Jesus Christ, for He is the supreme focus, prism, and goal of God's revelation (1 Cor. 2:2). Preaching must exalt Christ for awakening, justifying, sanctifying, and comforting sinners (Isa. 61:2; 1 Cor. 1:30; Eph. 5:14).
2. *It is applicatory.* Applicatory preaching is the process of riveting truth so powerfully in people that they cannot help but see how they must change and how they can be empowered to do so. It applies the text to every aspect of a listener's life, promoting, by the grace of the Spirit, a religion that is power and not mere form (2 Tim. 3:5). Robert Burns defines such knowledge as "Christianity brought home to men's business and bosoms." He goes on to say that the principle on which it rests is that "Christianity should not only be known, and understood, and believed, but also felt, and enjoyed, and practically applied."
3. *It is discriminatory.* It clearly defines the difference between a Christian and a non-Christian, opening the kingdom of heaven by offering the forgiveness of sins and eternal life to all who embrace Christ as Savior and Lord by true faith, and shutting the kingdom of heaven by proclaiming the wrath of God and His eternal condemnation upon those who are impenitent and unbelieving. If our knowledge of God is not experiential, we will perish—not because experience itself saves but because the Christ who saves sinners must be experienced personally as the foundation upon which the house of our eternal hope is built (Matt. 7:22–27; 1 Cor. 1:30).
4. *It is both realistic and idealistic.* It is realistic because it explains how matters actually go in the lives of God's people (e.g., Rom. 7:14–25), and it is idealistic because it explains how matters *ought* to go in their lives (e.g., Rom. 8). Both are essential. Telling how matters go without indicating how they should go lulls the believer to cease from pressing forward to grow in the grace and knowledge of Christ (2 Peter 3:18). On the other hand, only conveying how matters should be, as opposed to how they really are, discourages the believer from being assured that the Lord has worked in his heart.

were, and thou gavest them me; and they have
kept thy word.
7 Now they have known that all things whatso-
ever thou hast given me are of thee.
8 For I have given unto them the words which
thou gavest me; and they have received *them*, and
have known surely that I came out from thee, and
they have believed that thou didst send me.
9 I pray for them: I pray not for the world, but
for them which thou hast given me; for they are
thine.
10 And all mine are thine, and thine are mine;
and I am glorified in them.
11 And now I am no more in the world, but these
are in the world, and I come to thee. Holy Father,
keep through thine own name those whom thou
hast given me, that they may be one, as we *are*.
12 While I was with them in the world, I kept
them in thy name: those that thou gavest me I
have kept, and none of them is lost, but the son
of perdition; that the scripture might be fulfilled.
13 And now come I to thee; and these things I
speak in the world, that they might have my joy
fulfilled in themselves.
14 I have given them thy word; and the world
hath hated them, because they are not of the
world, even as I am not of the world.
15 I pray not that thou shouldest take them out
of the world, but that thou shouldest keep them
from the evil.
16 They are not of the world, even as I am not of
the world.
17 Sanctify them through thy truth: thy word is
truth.
18 As thou hast sent me into the world, even so
have I also sent them into the world.
19 And for their sakes I sanctify myself, that they
also might be sanctified through the truth.
20 Neither pray I for these alone, but for them
also which shall believe on me through their word;
21 That they all may be one; as thou, Father, *art*
in me, and I in thee, that they also may be one
in us: that the world may believe that thou hast
sent me.
22 And the glory which thou gavest me I have giv-
en them; that they may be one, even as we are one:
23 I in them, and thou in me, that they may be
made perfect in one; and that the world may
know that thou hast sent me, and hast loved
them, as thou hast loved me.
24 Father, I will that they also, whom thou hast
given me, be with me where I am; that they may

---

exclusively) for His apostles. See v. 12. *manifested thy name.* Revealed the glory of God in the gospel. *thou gavest them me; and they have kept thy word.* Election produces obedience (1 Thess. 1:4–6).

17:7–8 *believed that thou didst send me.* Saving faith receives Christ as the One appointed by God to save sinners and give them eternal life, as Peter confessed (6:68–69).

17:9 *I pray not for the world.* Though as King Christ rules over all mankind (v. 2), and as Prophet calls all people who hear the gospel to faith (7:37), as Priest He prays exclusively for the church of God's elect (Rom. 8:33–34), for they have been particularly entrusted to Him by the Father for salvation (*them which thou hast given me*) as His bride (3:29).

17:10 *all mine are thine.* Believers belong to God (Titus 2:14). Christ's words prove His equality with the Father; the two share divine authority and ownership (5:20).

17:11 *Holy Father.* A title of God found nowhere else in Scripture, appealing to His supreme majesty and compassionate love (Ps. 68:5). *keep through thine own name.* Preserve them in the faith by the gospel revelation of who God is (*name*; v. 6). *may be one.* Unified in Christ and with one another.

17:12 *none of them is lost.* Christ secured and preserved His own even as many other disciples fell away (6:66–69). *son of perdition.* Idiom for a person destined for ruin (2 Thess. 2:3,8). *scripture might be fulfilled.* The apostasy of Judas had been prophesied centuries earlier (Pss. 41:9; 55:12–14; 109:6; Zech. 11:12–13). Even the worst things that happen to Christ and His people are all predestined by God (Luke 22:22).

17:14 *world hath hated them.* See notes at 15:18—16:4.

17:15 *pray not . . . take them out of the world.* Christ does not desire for His disciples to withdraw from the world into monasteries (1 Cor. 5:9–10). *keep them from the evil.* Preserve them from being spiritually destroyed by the temptations of Satan.

17:16 *not of the world.* God's grace has taken them out of the kingdom of Satan and caused them to belong to the heavenly kingdom, as Christ does (8:23; 15:19).

17:17 *Sanctify them.* Make them holy, set them apart for sacred service. *through thy truth.* Just as God's Word is instrumental in conversion (15:3), so it is also God's means to make Christ's disciples grow in His likeness. *thy word is truth.* The Bible contains no errors but is entirely trustworthy in all that it teaches (Pss. 12:6; 19:7–9; Prov. 30:5–6).

17:18 *I also sent them.* Holiness (v. 17) overflows into missions, for the essence of obedience is loving others as Christ has loved us (15:12–13). The emphasis here is on Christ's sending of the apostles to preach His gospel to the world (20:21).

17:19 *I sanctify myself, that they also might be sanctified.* Christ set Himself apart as Priest (Ex. 28:41) in order to offer Himself as a sacrifice in obedience to His mission from the Father (10:36) to produce the holiness and mission of His church (vv. 17–18).

17:20–26 Third, Christ prayed for all future converts through the apostolic witness.

17:20 *for them also which shall believe.* From here to the end of His prayer Christ prayed for the believing church to the end of time, but still not for the world (v. 9).

17:21–23 *may be one in us.* Not a mere external unity but a unity founded upon union with Christ and God (*I in them, and thou in me*), and thus a unity of the new birth, faith, and love (Eph. 4:4–6). *as thou, Father, art in me, and I in thee.* The unity of Christians is part of the image of God, a visible picture of the unity in the Trinity (*even as we are one*). *that the world may believe . . . that the world may know.* The supernatural love that bonds Christians together is a powerful demonstration of the truth of the gospel by which God draws sinners to Christ and to His church (13:35; Acts 2:44–47). *glory . . . I have given them, that they may be one.* The foundation of Christian unity is the gospel revelation of God that He gave us through the mediation of Christ (v. 6; Eph. 4:13).

17:24 *be with me.* Christ's ultimate desire and will is that all who constitute His elect bride (*whom thou hast given me*) will enjoy the infinite *glory* and *love* of God by intimate union and

behold my glory, which thou hast given me: for
thou lovedst me before the foundation of the
world.
25 O righteous Father, the world hath not known
thee: but I have known thee, and these have
known that thou hast sent me.
26 And I have declared unto them thy name, and
will declare *it*: that the love wherewith thou hast
loved me may be in them, and I in them.

CHAPTER 18

WHEN Jesus had spoken these words, he went
forth with his disciples over the brook Cedron,
where was a garden, into the which he entered,
and his disciples.
2 And Judas also, which betrayed him, knew the
place: for Jesus ofttimes resorted thither with his
disciples.
3 Judas then, having received a band *of men* and
officers from the chief priests and Pharisees,
cometh thither with lanterns and torches and
weapons.
4 Jesus therefore, knowing all things that should
come upon him, went forth, and said unto them,
Whom seek ye?
5 They answered him, Jesus of Nazareth. Jesus
saith unto them, I am *he*. And Judas also, which
betrayed him, stood with them.
6 As soon then as he had said unto them, I am *he*,
they went backward, and fell to the ground.
7 Then asked he them again, Whom seek ye? And
they said, Jesus of Nazareth.
8 Jesus answered, I have told you that I am *he*: if
therefore ye seek me, let these go their way:
9 That the saying might be fulfilled, which he
spake, Of them which thou gavest me have I lost
none.
10 Then Simon Peter having a sword drew it, and
smote the high priest's servant, and cut off his
right ear. The servant's name was Malchus.
11 Then said Jesus unto Peter, Put up thy sword
into the sheath: the cup which my Father hath
given me, shall I not drink it?
12 Then the band and the captain and officers of
the Jews took Jesus, and bound him,
13 And led him away to Annas first; for he was fa-
ther in law to Caiaphas, which was the high priest
that same year.
14 Now Caiaphas was he, which gave counsel
to the Jews, that it was expedient that one man
should die for the people.

---

communion with His beloved Son (Rev. 22:4–5). *before the foundation*. See v. 5.

17:25–26 *righteous Father*. Another unique title of God (v. 11), emphasizing the great difference between Him and the wicked *world* that does not know Him. *I have known thee*. Christ is the sinless Son of God, and therefore God will answer His prayers (8:29; 11:22,42; Heb. 7:25–26). *will declare it*. Christ will continue His ministry as the Prophet of the church through the Holy Spirit (16:12–13). *love . . . in them, and I in them*. The truth of the gospel aims at bringing people into fellowship with God and the love shared in the Trinity.

Thoughts for Personal/Family Worship: Chapter 17

1. **This great high-priestly prayer of Christ is the consummation of the preceding discourse (14:1—16:33). We see here a sample of the intercessory work of Christ at the right hand of God. Everything Christ prays for will be granted by the heavenly Father, since Christ is the God-man whose redemptive work so greatly glorifies God. How can it encourage believers to know that Jesus is interceding with God to preserve them, unify them, and bring them to glory?**
2. **Christ's prayer for unity (v. 21) has often been used as an argument for church union irrespective of doctrine and practices. However, we must seek unity in a way that honors His prayer, "Sanctify them through thy truth: thy word is truth" (v. 17). There is no true unity without a common faith in the teachings of the inerrant Bible, along with a common life of holiness. Why are these necessary for spiritual unity?**
3. **The desire of Christ is that Christians will be with Him to gaze upon His glory forever (v. 24). "Blessed are the pure in heart: for they shall see God" (Matt. 5:8). Is this truly your desire? If so, reflect on the truth that heaven is a world of love.**

Jesus' Arrest, Trial, Crucifixion, and Burial (18:1—19:42)

Chapter 18: *Christ is betrayed and arrested and brought before Annas, Caiaphas, and Pilate. Peter denies Jesus three times in fulfillment of Jesus' prophecy, and Christ declares His kingdom before Pilate.*

18:1 *Cedron*. The Kidron Valley, the eastern boundary of Jerusalem. *garden*. Gethsemane, where Jesus agonized in prayer (Mark 14:32–42).

18:2 *resorted thither*. Met there.

18:3 *band of men*. They came armed with *weapons* in anticipation of the possibility of Jesus attempting to resist arrest.

18:5–6 *I am he*. Literally, "I am." Jesus boldly declared His identity as *Jehovah* (8:58; Ex. 3:14). *went backward, and fell*. Christ's words manifested enough of His divine glory to overcome them, showing how easily the Lord could have escaped their arrest.

18:8 *let these go*. The Shepherd protects His own dear sheep, even as He lays down His own life (10:11–12).

18:9 *I lost none*. As He had prayed (17:12), Christ preserved all of His disciples, here by not allowing them to be tempted beyond their strength.

18:10 *Malchus*. See Luke 22:50–51.

18:11 *cup . . . shall I not drink it?* Symbolic language for receiving on Himself the justice and wrath of God against sinners (Pss. 11:6; 75:8; Isa. 51:17,22; Jer. 25:15; Rev. 14:10; 16:19). *which my Father hath given me*. Christ died in love and obedience to God (10:18).

18:13–27 Jesus was *first* tried by the Jewish leaders at night, showing His rejection by the corrupt religious powers of Israel. Examination of ancient Jewish writings suggests that these leaders violated several of their own regulations in their zeal to find Jesus guilty.

18:14 *expedient that one man should die*. A reminder both that the priests had already determined to kill Jesus, regardless of the outcome of the judicial proceedings, and that this

15 ¶ And Simon Peter followed Jesus, and *so did*
another disciple: that disciple was known unto
the high priest, and went in with Jesus into the
palace of the high priest.
16 But Peter stood at the door without. Then
went out that other disciple, which was known
unto the high priest, and spake unto her that kept
the door, and brought in Peter.
17 Then saith the damsel that kept the door unto
Peter, Art not thou also *one* of this man's disci-
ples? He saith, I am not.
18 And the servants and officers stood there, who
had made a fire of coals; for it was cold: and they
warmed themselves: and Peter stood with them,
and warmed himself.
19 ¶ The high priest then asked Jesus of his dis-
ciples, and of his doctrine.
20 Jesus answered him, I spake openly to the
world; I ever taught in the synagogue, and in the
temple, whither the Jews always resort; and in
secret have I said nothing.
21 Why askest thou me? ask them which heard
me, what I have said unto them: behold, they
know what I said.
22 And when he had thus spoken, one of the
officers which stood by struck Jesus with the
palm of his hand, saying, Answerest thou the high
priest so?
23 Jesus answered him, If I have spoken evil,
bear witness of the evil: but if well, why smitest
thou me?
24 Now Annas had sent him bound unto Caia-
phas the high priest.
25 And Simon Peter stood and warmed himself.
They said therefore unto him, Art not thou also
one of his disciples? He denied *it*, and said, I am
not.
26 One of the servants of the high priest, being
his kinsman whose ear Peter cut off, saith, Did not
I see thee in the garden with him?
27 Peter then denied again: and immediately the
cock crew.
28 ¶ Then led they Jesus from Caiaphas unto
the hall of judgment: and it was early; and they
themselves went not into the judgment hall, lest
they should be defiled; but that they might eat the
passover.
29 Pilate then went out unto them, and said,
What accusation bring ye against this man?
30 They answered and said unto him, If he were
not a malefactor, we would not have delivered
him up unto thee.
31 Then said Pilate unto them, Take ye him, and
judge him according to your law. The Jews there-
fore said unto him, It is not lawful for us to put
any man to death:
32 That the saying of Jesus might be fulfilled,
which he spake, signifying what death he should
die.
33 Then Pilate entered into the judgment hall
again, and called Jesus, and said unto him, Art
thou the King of the Jews?
34 Jesus answered him, Sayest thou this thing of
thyself, or did others tell it thee of me?
35 Pilate answered, Am I a Jew? Thine own nation
and the chief priests have delivered thee unto me:
what hast thou done?
36 Jesus answered, My kingdom is not of this
world: if my kingdom were of this world, then
would my servants fight, that I should not be de-
livered to the Jews: but now is my kingdom not
from hence.
37 Pilate therefore said unto him, Art thou a king
then? Jesus answered, Thou sayest that I am a
king. To this end was I born, and for this cause
came I into the world, that I should bear witness

was the will of God for the salvation of sinners from all nations (11:49–53).

18:15 *another disciple.* Most likely John, the author of this gospel.

18:16 *without.* Outside.

18:17 *damsel.* Servant or slave girl.

18:19–20 *doctrine.* Teaching. *whither . . . resort.* Where they gather.

18:22–23 *If I have spoken evil.* Even as Christ meekly went to die, as a prophet He briefly protested the injustice of their actions (Jer. 20:1–6).

18:26 The fact that the question came from a relative (*kinsman*) of the man whose ear Peter had cut off (v. 10) highlights the danger Peter must have felt himself to be in.

18:27 *the cock crew.* The rooster crowed after Peter had denied the Lord three times (vv. 17,25), just as Jesus had foretold (13:38)—another sign of the Lord's sovereignty over His own Passion.

18:28—19:16 Christ's trials before Caiaphas and the Sanhedrin were now over, and His trial before Pilate was to begin *early* the following day, highlighting His condemnation by the unjust civil powers of the Gentiles.

18:28 *lest they . . . be defiled.* Evidence of their hypocrisy in observing the ceremonial law while arranging the murder of God's Son.

18:29 Pontius *Pilate*, the prefect of the imperial province of Judaea, was not necessarily interested in this case but was driven by his fear of unrest among the Jews.

18:30 *malefactor.* Evil-doer, criminal.

18:31 *not lawful for us to put any man to death.* It is debated whether this was on the basis of the feast or tied to some temporary political restriction.

18:32 *what death he should die.* Christ had foretold that he would be "lifted up" in death (3:14; 12:32–33) and thus not die by stoning on the part of the Jews (10:31–33; 11:8); He would die by the Roman punishment of crucifixion, a sign of bearing the curse of the broken moral law of God (Deut. 21:22–23; Gal. 3:13).

18:33–37 *Art thou the King.* Christ's reply could not be a simple yes or no. His *kingdom* is not political (*of this world*) but is spiritual (3:3–6; Rom. 14:17), for He rules His subjects not by coercive force but through their faith (*heareth my voice*) in His Word (*bear witness unto the truth*). He was not a violent political revolutionary.

unto the truth. Every one that is of the truth
heareth my voice.
38 Pilate saith unto him, What is truth? And
when he had said this, he went out again unto the
Jews, and saith unto them, I find in him no fault
at all.
39 But ye have a custom, that I should release
unto you one at the passover: will ye therefore
that I release unto you the King of the Jews?
40 Then cried they all again, saying, Not this
man, but Barabbas. Now Barabbas was a robber.

CHAPTER 19

THEN Pilate therefore took Jesus, and scourged
him.
2 And the soldiers platted a crown of thorns, and
put *it* on his head, and they put on him a purple
robe,
3 And said, Hail, King of the Jews! and they smote
him with their hands.
4 Pilate therefore went forth again, and saith
unto them, Behold, I bring him forth to you, that
ye may know that I find no fault in him.
5 Then came Jesus forth, wearing the crown of
thorns, and the purple robe. And *Pilate* saith unto
them, Behold the man!
6 When the chief priests therefore and officers
saw him, they cried out, saying, Crucify *him,*
crucify *him.* Pilate saith unto them, Take ye him,
and crucify *him*: for I find no fault in him.
7 The Jews answered him, We have a law, and by
our law he ought to die, because he made himself
the Son of God.
8 ¶ When Pilate therefore heard that saying, he
was the more afraid;
9 And went again into the judgment hall, and
saith unto Jesus, Whence art thou? But Jesus gave
him no answer.
10 Then saith Pilate unto him, Speakest thou not
unto me? knowest thou not that I have power to
crucify thee, and have power to release thee?
11 Jesus answered, Thou couldest have no power
at all against me, except it were given thee from
above: therefore he that delivered me unto thee
hath the greater sin.
12 And from thenceforth Pilate sought to release
him: but the Jews cried out, saying, If thou let this
man go, thou art not Caesar's friend: whosoever
maketh himself a king speaketh against Caesar.
13 ¶ When Pilate therefore heard that saying, he
brought Jesus forth, and sat down in the judg-
ment seat in a place that is called the Pavement,
but in the Hebrew, Gabbatha.
14 And it was the preparation of the passover,
and about the sixth hour: and he saith unto the
Jews, Behold your King!
15 But they cried out, Away with *him,* away with

18:38 *no fault at all.* Pilate gave public testimony that Jesus was innocent (19:6).

18:40 *Barabbas.* An insurrectionist, guilty of multiple crimes, including murder (Mark 15:7).

Thoughts for Personal/Family Worship: Chapter 18

1. **Christ, as the great "I am," could easily have destroyed His enemies by His divine power (v. 6). He had many powerful servants (the angels) who could have protected Him, but He did not come to be that kind of king (v. 36). Instead, His kingdom comes by preaching and believing the truth (v. 37). What does this teach us about the manner in which the church overcomes this world?**
2. **Christ was condemned to die under charges of criminal acts (v. 33; 19:12), and the one guilty of criminal acts was set free (v. 40). This teaches us two lessons, for both human sin and divine providence were at work here. First, so deep is the hatred and hardness of the hearts of fallen men that they prefer a murderer to the righteous Son of God (Acts 3:14). Second, so deep is the love of God that He sent His Son to die for the sins of His people in order that they, the guilty, would go free (3:16–17). How should these truths humble us and fill us with gratitude?**

Chapter 19: *Jesus is crucified and buried.*

19:1 *scourged.* Lashed with a whip of cords on the ends of which were sharp pieces of metal or bone, greatly damaging to the body and often leading to death.

19:2–3 *platted.* Twisted, wove. *crown of thorns.* The barbaric soldiers mocked Christ as though He were a political king, ironically placing on Him an emblem of man's fall into sin in Adam (Gen. 3:18).

19:5 *Behold the man!* Pilate probably intended little more than to draw attention from Christ's mockers to the sad figure still dressed in the bloody *crown* and *robe*, but John may be presenting Jesus as "the Man," the last Adam suffering for the sins of His people in order to reign with them as the Son of Man (6:62; 12:23–24; 13:31).

19:6 The repeated cry for His crucifixion was not started by the ordinary people but by the chief priests. *no fault in him.* See 18:38.

19:7 *the Son of God.* See Jesus' confession in Matt. 26:63–64; Mark 14:61–62.

19:8 *the more afraid.* Pilate may have wondered whether Christ was divine in some sense, especially after his wife had a disturbing dream about Him (Matt. 27:19).

19:9 *Whence art thou?* Where do you come from? *no answer.* Jesus was often silent when being accused (Mark 14:61; 15:3–5), meekly submitting to God's will and fulfilling prophecy (Isa. 53:7).

19:11 *no power . . . except it were given thee from above.* Christ reminded Pilate that all rule and authority are a gift of God (3:27), making the one who wields them accountable to God.

19:12 *thenceforth.* From that time. Christ's words and conduct appear to have moved Pilate's conscience so that he *sought to release* Jesus, but Pilate's fear of appearing disloyal or weak before *Caesar* was stronger than his conscience (5:44; 12:42–43).

19:13 *judgment seat.* To give a formal sentence. *Hebrew.* Or Aramaic, the common language of the Hebrew people at that time.

19:14 *sixth hour.* It was now about 6:00 a.m. (using Roman time). The crucifixion took place at 9:00 a.m. (Mark 15:25,33; Luke 23:44). *Behold your King!* Pilate's words mocked the Jews.

him, crucify him. Pilate saith unto them, Shall I
crucify your King? The chief priests answered, We
have no king but Caesar.
16 Then delivered he him therefore unto them
to be crucified. And they took Jesus, and led *him*
away.
17 And he bearing his cross went forth into a
place called *the place* of a skull, which is called in
the Hebrew Golgotha:
18 Where they crucified him, and two other with
him, on either side one, and Jesus in the midst.
19 ¶ And Pilate wrote a title, and put *it* on the
cross. And the writing was, JESUS OF NAZA-
RETH THE KING OF THE JEWS.
20 This title then read many of the Jews: for the
place where Jesus was crucified was nigh to the
city: and it was written in Hebrew, *and* Greek, *and*
Latin.
21 Then said the chief priests of the Jews to Pilate,
Write not, The King of the Jews; but that he said, I
am King of the Jews.
22 Pilate answered, What I have written I have
written.
23 ¶ Then the soldiers, when they had crucified
Jesus, took his garments, and made four parts, to
every soldier a part; and also *his* coat: now the coat
was without seam, woven from the top through-
out.
24 They said therefore among themselves, Let us
not rend it, but cast lots for it, whose it shall be:
that the scripture might be fulfilled, which saith,
They parted my raiment among them, and for my
vesture they did cast lots. These things therefore
the soldiers did.
25 ¶ Now there stood by the cross of Jesus his
mother, and his mother's sister, Mary the *wife* of
Cleophas, and Mary Magdalene.
26 When Jesus therefore saw his mother, and
the disciple standing by, whom he loved, he saith
unto his mother, Woman, behold thy son!
27 Then saith he to the disciple, Behold thy
mother! And from that hour that disciple took
her unto his own *home*.
28 ¶ After this, Jesus knowing that all things were
now accomplished, that the scripture might be
fulfilled, saith, I thirst.
29 Now there was set a vessel full of vinegar: and
they filled a spunge with vinegar, and put *it* upon
hyssop, and put *it* to his mouth.
30 When Jesus therefore had received the vinegar,
he said, It is finished: and he bowed his head, and
gave up the ghost.
31 The Jews therefore, because it was the prepara-
tion, that the bodies should not remain upon the
cross on the sabbath day, (for that sabbath day was
an high day,) besought Pilate that their legs might
be broken, and *that* they might be taken away.
32 Then came the soldiers, and brake the legs
of the first, and of the other which was crucified
with him.
33 But when they came to Jesus, and saw that he
was dead already, they brake not his legs:
34 But one of the soldiers with a spear pierced
his side, and forthwith came there out blood and
water.
35 And he that saw *it* bare record, and his record
is true: and he knoweth that he saith true, that ye
might believe.
36 For these things were done, that the scripture
should be fulfilled, A bone of him shall not be
broken.
37 And again another scripture saith, They shall

19:15 *Away with him.* Take him away.

19:17 *Golgotha.* Aramaic for *skull.* The place of execution was a short distance outside the city of Jerusalem.

19:19–20 *writing.* A sign displaying the formal charges in three languages, at least one of which would have been known by each person in Jerusalem during the Passover.

19:23–24 Each of the *four* soldiers would take a piece of the clothing for himself. *rend it.* Tear it. *parted my raiment.* Divided my clothes. *vesture.* Clothing. The seamless robe was given to the soldier selected randomly according to the casting of *lots* (fulfilling Ps. 22:18).

19:26–27 *behold thy son . . . Behold thy mother!* Jesus lovingly committed the care of His mother to the apostle John (*the disciple . . . whom he loved*). This may also suggest that the death of Jesus created a spiritual family (20:17; Gal. 4:4–7; cf. Matt. 12:46–50).

19:28–29 *I thirst . . . vinegar.* Another fulfillment of prophecy (Pss. 22:15; 69:21). *hyssop.* A plant associated with application of the blood of the Passover lamb (Ex. 12:22) and Jewish rituals of cleansing (Lev. 14:4,6,49–52; Num. 19:6,18; Ps. 51:7).

19:30 *It is finished.* Christ had completed the work of fulfilling God's purposes (17:4) that He had announced in Scripture (the same verb as *finished* is translated "accomplished" in v. 28). The full price is paid for the elect (10:14–15; Mark 10:45) and the wrath of God appeased toward believers (3:17,36; 18:11). *gave up the ghost.* Expired, died (Gen. 25:8). The Greek words are an unusual way to express death, literally, "He surrendered the spirit" (not the same verb as in Matt. 27:50; Mark 15:37; Luke 23:46), suggesting His voluntary laying down of His life (10:17–18).

19:31 *high day.* An important day. The Passover fell on the Sabbath. *besought.* Asked. *legs . . . broken.* The smashing of the legs with a heavy hammer, cruel as it was, had the effect of hastening death on the cross. In Latin this was termed *crucifragium.*

19:33–34 The flow of *blood and water* from His pierced side has sometimes been explained as the result of death by a rupture of the heart (cf. Ps. 69:20), but in any case it certainly confirms that He was *dead.* The *water* may also have been a visible reminder that God poured out the Spirit through the death of Christ (4:10,14; 7:37–39; Gal. 3:13–14).

19:35 *bare record.* Testified as a witness.

19:36 *A bone of him shall not be broken.* The instructions for handling the Passover lamb (Ex. 12:46; Num. 9:12). Jesus is the Lamb of God (1:29) whose death satisfied God's justice and wrath against sin (3:14–17,36), saving His people from eternal death (5:24) and bringing them out of slavery to sin and Satan (8:34,36,44; 12:31–33) into the kingdom of God by the Spirit's

look on him whom they pierced.
38 ¶ And after this Joseph of Arimathaea, being
a disciple of Jesus, but secretly for fear of the
Jews, besought Pilate that he might take away the
body of Jesus: and Pilate gave *him* leave. He came
therefore, and took the body of Jesus.
39 And there came also Nicodemus, which at the
first came to Jesus by night, and brought a mix-
ture of myrrh and aloes, about an hundred pound
weight.
40 Then took they the body of Jesus, and wound
it in linen clothes with the spices, as the manner
of the Jews is to bury.
41 Now in the place where he was crucified there
was a garden; and in the garden a new sepulchre,
wherein was never man yet laid.
42 There laid they Jesus therefore because of the
Jews' preparation *day*; for the sepulchre was nigh
at hand.

CHAPTER 20

THE first *day* of the week cometh Mary Magda-
lene early, when it was yet dark, unto the sepul-
chre, and seeth the stone taken away from the
sepulchre.
2 Then she runneth, and cometh to Simon Peter,
and to the other disciple, whom Jesus loved, and
saith unto them, They have taken away the Lord
out of the sepulchre, and we know not where they
have laid him.
3 Peter therefore went forth, and that other dis-
ciple, and came to the sepulchre.
4 So they ran both together: and the other
disciple did outrun Peter, and came first to the
sepulchre.
5 And he stooping down, *and looking in*, saw the
linen clothes lying; yet went he not in.
6 Then cometh Simon Peter following him,
and went into the sepulchre, and seeth the linen
clothes lie,
7 And the napkin, that was about his head, not
lying with the linen clothes, but wrapped together
in a place by itself.
8 Then went in also that other disciple, which
came first to the sepulchre, and he saw, and
believed.
9 For as yet they knew not the scripture, that he
must rise again from the dead.
10 Then the disciples went away again unto their
own home.
11 ¶ But Mary stood without at the sepulchre
weeping: and as she wept, she stooped down, *and*
looked into the sepulchre,
12 And seeth two angels in white sitting, the one
at the head, and the other at the feet, where the
body of Jesus had lain.
13 And they say unto her, Woman, why weep-
est thou? She saith unto them, Because they have
taken away my Lord, and I know not where they
have laid him.
14 And when she had thus said, she turned herself
back, and saw Jesus standing, and knew not that
it was Jesus.
15 Jesus saith unto her, Woman, why weepest
thou? whom seekest thou? She, supposing him to

life-giving work (3:3–5; 7:39).

19:37 *look on him whom they pierced.* Citing Zech. 12:10, a prophecy of the outpouring of the Spirit of repentance in the context of a fountain of cleansing for sin (Zech. 13:1).

19:38–40 *Joseph* (Matt. 27:57; Luke 23:50–51) and *Nicodemus* (3:1), who was now converted, attended to the burial.

19:39 *myrrh and aloes.* For the anointing of the body.

19:40 *manner.* Custom or tradition.

19:41–42 *sepulchre.* Tomb. *nigh at hand.* Near.

Thoughts for Personal/Family Worship: Chapter 19

1. **Pontius Pilate will forever be remembered for the gross miscarriage of justice he permitted in the murder of God's Son. We should never allow ourselves to be bullied into doing what in conscience we know to be wrong. Why is the fear of man so powerful as to move people to go against their conscience? How can it be overcome?**
2. **How clear it is from Christ's willingness to voluntarily undergo such horrible sufferings that He loved His Heavenly Father and also His own dear people! Even as He was dying He was caring for others, as His words to His mother show. Yet His last words, "It is finished," declare that He did not die as a helpless martyr but as the conquering King, even as the sign on the cross stated. In one sense the cross was the chariot on which the King of grace rode to victory over all that had been oppressing His own. Yet He conquered as the Lamb of God, suffering and dying to turn away God's just judgment against sinners. Why should this chapter move us to trust, love, admire, and surrender to this King of infinite grace? How does this chapter affect you?**

Jesus' Resurrection and Appearances (20:1—21:15)

Chapter 20: *Jesus rises from the dead and appears to Mary Magdalene and the disciples.*

20:1 *first day of the week.* The Lord's Day (see note at Matt. 28:1). *Mary Magdalene.* A disciple of Jesus whom He had rescued from seven demons (19:25; Mark 16:9; Luke 8:1–3). *sepulchre.* Tomb. *stone.* A large stone used to cover the entrance to the tomb.

20:2 *runneth.* Demonstrates a sense of urgency (v. 4). *They have taken.* Mary did not assume Jesus had risen but that His body has been removed by someone else.

20:5–7 *linen clothes.* The burial cloth wrapped around the body (19:40). *napkin.* A cloth for covering the face of the deceased (11:44). The orderly arrangement of the clothes was evidence in itself that the body had not been stolen.

20:8–9 The *disciple* (John) *believed* that the tomb was empty, as Mary had said; he may also have believed that Christ had risen, though he did not yet understand the significance of the resurrection as the fulfillment of God's revealed plan (*knew not the scripture*).

20:11 *without.* Outside. *weeping.* Mary loved Christ as her Savior and Lord.

20:14 *knew not that it was Jesus.* See 21:4; Luke 24:16.

be the gardener, saith unto him, Sir, if thou have
borne him hence, tell me where thou hast laid
him, and I will take him away.
16 Jesus saith unto her, Mary. She turned her-
self, and saith unto him, Rabboni; which is to say,
Master.
17 Jesus saith unto her, Touch me not; for I am not
yet ascended to my Father: but go to my brethren,
and say unto them, I ascend unto my Father, and
your Father; and *to* my God, and your God.
18 Mary Magdalene came and told the disciples
that she had seen the Lord, and *that* he had
spoken these things unto her.
19 ¶ Then the same day at evening, being the first
day of the week, when the doors were shut where
the disciples were assembled for fear of the Jews,
came Jesus and stood in the midst, and saith unto
them, Peace *be* unto you.
20 And when he had so said, he shewed unto
them *his* hands and his side. Then were the dis-
ciples glad, when they saw the Lord.
21 Then said Jesus to them again, Peace *be* unto
you: as *my* Father hath sent me, even so send I
you.
22 And when he had said this, he breathed on
them, and saith unto them, Receive ye the Holy
Ghost:
23 Whose soever sins ye remit, they are remitted
unto them; *and* whose soever *sins* ye retain, they
are retained.
24 ¶ But Thomas, one of the twelve, called Didy-
mus, was not with them when Jesus came.
25 The other disciples therefore said unto him,
We have seen the Lord. But he said unto them, Ex-
cept I shall see in his hands the print of the nails,
and put my finger into the print of the nails, and
thrust my hand into his side, I will not believe.
26 ¶ And after eight days again his disciples were
within, and Thomas with them: *then* came Jesus,
the doors being shut, and stood in the midst, and
said, Peace *be* unto you.
27 Then saith he to Thomas, Reach hither thy
finger, and behold my hands; and reach hither
thy hand, and thrust *it* into my side: and be not
faithless, but believing.
28 And Thomas answered and said unto him, My
Lord and my God.
29 Jesus saith unto him, Thomas, because thou
hast seen me, thou hast believed: blessed *are* they
that have not seen, and *yet* have believed.
30 ¶ And many other signs truly did Jesus in the
presence of his disciples, which are not written in
this book:
31 But these are written, that ye might believe

20:15 *borne him hence.* Carried him away.
20:16 *Rabboni.* Aramaic for "my teacher" (*Master*).
20:17 *Touch me not.* Do not cling to Me or try to hold on to Me. Christ had been raised with His physical body and could be touched (v. 27; Luke 24:39). *go.* Jesus chose this woman to be the first eyewitness of His resurrection (Mark 16:9). *my brethren.* Christ receives His disciples as their loving elder brother (Rom. 8:29; Heb. 2:11). *I ascend unto my Father.* Christ's resurrection was the first step of the exaltation of His human nature into the glory of heaven (17:5) as the vindicated Servant who had fulfilled the covenant (*my God*). *your Father.* Christ assured His disciples that despite their sins against Him, His death brings them into the family of God (1:12; see note at 19:26–27).
20:19 *when the doors were shut.* Christ, having been raised in the heavenly life of the Spirit (1 Cor. 15:42–49), now had bodily powers of a higher kind and could move quickly and freely, without hindrance (Luke 24:31,36; cf. Acts 8:39–40). *Peace be unto you.* The ordinary greeting is infused with new gospel meaning (v. 21) because Christ has completed the work of redemption and lives as the risen Savior (Eph. 2:16–17).
20:20 *shewed . . . his hands and his side.* The Lord confirmed the reality of His resurrection by offering irrefutable evidence, to which the apostles were witnesses (Luke 24:36–43; Acts 1:3).
20:21–23 *send I you.* Jesus commissioned the apostles, as the leaders of the church, to go forth and preach with His authority (Matt. 28:18–20; Luke 24:44–48). *breathed on them.* A prophetic action symbolizing the procession of the Spirit from the Son to the disciples in vital union with Him (14:19; 15:26; 16:7). *Receive ye the Holy Ghost.* The risen Lord made this statement in anticipation of Pentecost (Acts 2:1–47), by which they would receive power for their witness (Acts 1:8). *Whose soever sins ye remit . . . retain.* Whoever's sins you declare either forgiven or not forgiven. Men have no authority in themselves to forgive sins (Mark 2:7), but the gospel as preached and then applied in biblical church membership, and discipline promises forgiveness to all who believe in Christ, and only to them (3:17–18).
20:24 *Didymus.* Means "twin."
20:25 *nails.* Spikes used to crucify Jesus on the cross (cf. Col. 2:14). *his side.* Where the spear had pierced Him (19:34).
20:26 *after eight days.* By the inclusive method of reckoning time, this was a week later, the next Sunday (v. 1). *doors being shut . . . said, Peace.* See note at v. 19.
20:27 *hither.* Here. Christ graciously came to convince Thomas, offering him the plain evidence he had demanded.
20:28 *My Lord and my God.* Just as this gospel began by declaring that Christ is God (1:1), so it climaxes in Thomas's adoring confession of the deity of the risen Lord. Although Christ is a real man with a body and soul, He is also God.
20:29 *blessed are they.* Jesus commended those who believe His gospel without such visible evidence as that which He presented to the apostles. Faith rests ultimately not on observed miracles but in the divine testimony of God's Word (3:33; 4:42; 5:37–39).
20:30 *many other signs.* We do not have a record in the Gospels of every miracle of Christ (21:25).
20:31 *that ye might believe.* John tells us the purpose of his gospel: to proclaim *Jesus* as the incarnate Lord (*Son of God*; 1:14,18; 5:19–23) sent by God to save sinners (*Christ*; 4:42; 17:2–3), so that people might receive eternal *life* by faith in Him.

Thoughts for Personal/Family Worship: Chapter 20

1. It is absurd to argue that the resurrection of Christ was a fabrication of the disciples. They were all inclined not to believe it until compelled by the evidence of the risen Jesus. These apostles of Christ have not given us myths

that Jesus is the Christ, the Son of God; and that
believing ye might have life through his name.

CHAPTER 21

AFTER these things Jesus shewed himself again
to the disciples at the sea of Tiberias; and on this
wise shewed he *himself*.
2 There were together Simon Peter, and Thomas
called Didymus, and Nathanael of Cana in Gali-
lee, and the *sons* of Zebedee, and two other of his
disciples.
3 Simon Peter saith unto them, I go a fishing.
They say unto him, We also go with thee. They
went forth, and entered into a ship immediately;
and that night they caught nothing.
4 But when the morning was now come, Jesus
stood on the shore: but the disciples knew not
that it was Jesus.
5 Then Jesus saith unto them, Children, have ye
any meat? They answered him, No.
6 And he said unto them, Cast the net on the
right side of the ship, and ye shall find. They cast
therefore, and now they were not able to draw it
for the multitude of fishes.
7 Therefore that disciple whom Jesus loved saith
unto Peter, It is the Lord. Now when Simon Peter
heard that it was the Lord, he girt *his* fisher's coat
unto him, (for he was naked,) and did cast himself
into the sea.
8 And the other disciples came in a little ship; (for
they were not far from land, but as it were two
hundred cubits,) dragging the net with fishes.
9 As soon then as they were come to land, they
saw a fire of coals there, and fish laid thereon, and
bread.
10 Jesus saith unto them, Bring of the fish which
ye have now caught.
11 Simon Peter went up, and drew the net to land
full of great fishes, an hundred and fifty and three:
and for all there were so many, yet was not the
net broken.
12 Jesus saith unto them, Come *and* dine. And
none of the disciples durst ask him, Who art
thou? knowing that it was the Lord.
13 Jesus then cometh, and taketh bread, and
giveth them, and fish likewise.
14 This is now the third time that Jesus shewed
himself to his disciples, after that he was risen
from the dead.
15 ¶ So when they had dined, Jesus saith to
Simon Peter, Simon, *son* of Jonas, lovest thou me
more than these? He saith unto him, Yea, Lord;
thou knowest that I love thee. He saith unto him,
Feed my lambs.
16 He saith to him again the second time, Simon,
son of Jonas, lovest thou me? He saith unto him,
Yea, Lord; thou knowest that I love thee. He saith
unto him, Feed my sheep.
17 He saith unto him the third time, Simon,
son of Jonas, lovest thou me? Peter was grieved
because he said unto him the third time, Lovest
thou me? And he said unto him, Lord, thou
knowest all things; thou knowest that I love thee.
Jesus saith unto him, Feed my sheep.
18 Verily, verily, I say unto thee, When thou
wast young, thou girdedst thyself, and walkedst
whither thou wouldest: but when thou shalt

---

or legends but solid, historically reliable accounts of our Lord. Our wisdom is to believe them and to build our lives upon them. What difference would it make to you if Jesus had never risen from the dead? What does that say about your faith?

2. The resurrection appearances of Jesus pulsate with love between Him and His disciples. We see it in the rush of Peter and John to the empty tomb and in the tears of Mary Magdalene. We feel it in the pathos of Jesus' simple address to her—"Mary"—and in her devoted response—"Master." We hear it as Jesus called those who had abandoned Him "my brethren," and reminded them that God is "your Father." He appeared to them with "Peace" on His lips and gently condescended to meet Thomas in his skepticism. Thomas cried out with adoration to the Savior, "My Lord and my God." Do you know the love of the living Lord Jesus? If so, how has His love created in you an answering love for Him?

Chapter 21: *Jesus appears to seven of the disciples as they are fishing. He draws a confession of love from Peter and charges him to feed His sheep.*

21:1 *sea of Tiberias.* Sea of Galilee. *shewed.* Literally, "revealed." *this wise.* This way.

21:5 *meat.* Food of any kind.

21:7 *It is the Lord.* Peter realized that what had just happened mirrored what Jesus had done when He had first called them to discipleship and ministry (Luke 5:1–11). *girt his fisher's coat unto him.* Clothed himself in his outer garment. *naked.* Probably in at least a loincloth. Peter had been working without his normal outer garments so as to be freer in his movements.

21:8 *two hundred cubits.* About one hundred yards or ninety meters.

21:9 *fire of coals.* Christ was cooking breakfast for them, acting as a loving host (v. 13). *fish . . . bread.* The same foods mentioned in the feeding of the five thousand (6:5–13).

21:11 *an hundred and fifty and three.* This number does not seem to have any symbolic meaning, indicating simply a very large catch of fish. *not . . . broken.* Another indication of God's intervention.

21:12 *durst.* Dared.

21:15–17 Peter had three times denied his Master (18:17, 25,27) and now was required three times to affirm his love for Him, a painful (*grieved*) but gracious restoration. At the same time Christ renewed Peter's commission to shepherd (*Feed*) the flock for whom Christ had died (10:1–18; Acts 20:28; 1 Peter 5:1–2). *thou knowest all things.* Christ, in His knowledge of everything past, present, and future (omniscience, 16:30; 18:4), knew the heart of Peter (Jer. 17:10; Rev. 2:23) and so confirmed the sincerity of his love for Him.

21:18–19 *When thou wast young, thou girdedst thyself, and*

be old, thou shalt stretch forth thy hands, and
another shall gird thee, and carry *thee* whither
thou wouldest not.
19 This spake he, signifying by what death he
should glorify God. And when he had spoken
this, he saith unto him, Follow me.
20 Then Peter, turning about, seeth the disciple
whom Jesus loved following; which also leaned
on his breast at supper, and said, Lord, which is he
that betrayeth thee?
21 Peter seeing him saith to Jesus, Lord, and what
shall this man *do*?
22 Jesus saith unto him, If I will that he tarry till
I come, what *is that* to thee? follow thou me.
23 Then went this saying abroad among the
brethren, that that disciple should not die: yet
Jesus said not unto him, He shall not die; but, If I
will that he tarry till I come, what *is that* to thee?
24 This is the disciple which testifieth of these
things, and wrote these things: and we know that
his testimony is true.
25 And there are also many other things which
Jesus did, the which, if they should be written
every one, I suppose that even the world itself
could not contain the books that should be
written. Amen.

---

walkedst whither thou wouldest. When you were young, you used to dress yourself and go wherever you chose. *stretch forth thy hands.* Likely a reference to *death* by crucifixion. History records that Peter was crucified upside-down. *glorify God.* Peter's death as a faithful apostle would honor the Lord, as Christ's had (12:27–28), though in a much smaller way. *Follow me.* The call to discipleship, involving faith, obedience, and imitation of Christ (1:43; 8:12; 10:4,27; 12:26; Luke 9:23), is essential to ministry (Matt. 4:19).

21:22 *will that he tarry.* Choose that he remain. Not all of Christ's servants are required to die as martyrs, but each lives and dies according to the will of the Lord Jesus, implying His divine sovereignty over our circumstances (James 4:13–16). *follow thou me.* Christ repeated His call to discipleship (21:19). Christians must not be preoccupied with future unknowns but are to devote themselves to living for their Lord (Rom. 14:8; Phil. 1:20–21).

21:23 *went this saying abroad.* The *disciple* who wrote this gospel (v. 24) was well known in the early church. Some early Christians (*brethren*; 20:17) wrongly interpreted Jesus' statement to mean that John would *not die*, so John here corrects them.

21:24 *we know.* A confirmation from John's associates, perhaps the elders of the church at Ephesus.

21:25 *the world itself could not contain the books.* Certainly this would be the case if one were to attempt a written record of all Jesus' acts as Creator and Lord (1:3). However, we do not need to know everything *Jesus did*, for God has given us evidence enough. Our duty is to believe it and to assert, with Thomas, "My Lord and my God!"

Thoughts for Personal/Family Worship: Chapter 21

1. **The miracle of catching 153 fish, like the feeding of the five thousand, is a sign of Christ's all-sufficient power to enable the apostles (and other gospel preachers) to experience great success as fishers of men (Mark 1:17; Luke 5:10). Yet their fishing all night and catching nothing reminds us that success is not from the preacher or on his terms but subject to Christ's sovereignty. Each servant of God has a future determined by the will of Christ, in some cases a life ending in martyrdom. However, our calling is not to guess about the future but to devote ourselves to following Him by faith. What lessons are there here to encourage you to serve the Lord?**
2. **Peter's restoration plays a vital role in the conclusion to this Gospel because the risen Christ would soon ascend (20:17), having delegated the visible leadership of His people to the apostles and the elders of each church. The apostle Peter was a man broken over his sins against Christ, motivated by his love for Christ, and called to shepherd the people of Christ. Why are all these qualities essential for a minister of the gospel of Jesus Christ?**

INTRODUCTION TO THE BOOK OF ACTS

Authorship: The author of Acts is the same as that of the Gospel of Luke, as its opening words prove: "The former treatise have I made, O Theophilus, of all that Jesus began both to do and teach" (1:1). Both Luke and Acts are addressed to Theophilus (Luke 1:3). Acts refers to the "former treatise" and continues the record of the work of Jesus from heaven by His Spirit through His apostles. The Gospel of Luke ends with Jesus ascending to heaven and the disciples praising and blessing God in the temple (Luke 24:53). Acts opens with a restatement of Jesus' ascension (Acts 1:9), the same command Jesus gave to His disciples (vv. 4,12), and the promise of the coming Spirit (v. 5). Likewise, Jesus is the central character of both Luke and Acts, though in Acts Jesus works through His apostles while He is in His heavenly session at God's right hand. These connections between the ending of Luke and the beginning of Acts establish unequivocally the common themes and authorship of Luke over both his Gospel and Acts. Beyond this, the external and internal evidence points to Luke as the common author of both volumes.

We know that the author of Acts was a traveling companion of Paul because of the many "we" statements used in the later narratives (16:10–17; 20:5–15; 21:1–18; 27:1—28:16). We further know that the author was not a companion of Jesus during His earthly life (Luke 1:1–4). Thus the possibilities narrow; we do know that Luke was a traveling companion of Paul (Col. 4:14; 2 Tim. 4:11; Philem. 24). The difficulty and eloquence of the Greek in both Luke and Acts point to a well-educated author who has a knowledge of God's redemptive work throughout the Old Testament, though commentators note that there are many stylistic differences between the two books. Still Luke, a physician, fits the criterion of being such a learned and skilled author (Col. 4:14).

Likewise, external testimony is virtually unanimous in agreeing to Luke's authorship. By AD 200 Luke was the accepted author of both the Gospel and Acts. There are references throughout church history confirming this accreditation. Testimonies from Justin Martyr, the *Muratorian Canon*, Irenaeus, Clement of Alexandria, Tertullian, and Origen all reflect the early church's conviction that Luke is the author.

Date: The date of Acts is tied closely to the date of Luke. It is almost a universal opinion that Acts was written after the Gospel of Luke. It is believed that Luke was written in the early 60s, and thus Acts would have been written at a later date. It is important to note what events Luke does not include in Acts and to ask why he has left out several important historical occurrences. Looking at these criteria will help us ascertain a close approximation of the date of Acts.

Luke records Paul's preaching before Felix (ruled c. AD 52–60) and Festus (ruled c. AD 60–62) and his imprisonment in Rome, which occurred in AD 62 (28:11–31). But Luke does not record Paul's release from prison, and there is no mention of Paul's death (likely in AD 67). Likewise, Luke does not record the persecution the early Christians suffered under Emperor Nero (ruled AD 54–68) and includes no hint of the Jewish war in the late 60s. It is important to consider as well that Luke does not include the destruction of the temple in AD 70—a monumental event in both redemptive history and the life of the church. While some scholars argue that Luke left out these important events because they did not fit his purposes in writing, it seems best to conclude that Luke composed Acts somewhere in the early to mid-60s.

Theme: Christ's continuing work after His ascension to expand His church through the gospel preaching of the apostles and disciples throughout the world.

Purpose: As with the Gospel of Luke, to confirm the faith of those instructed in Christianity (Luke 1:4) and, further, to deepen that faith by tracing Christ's building of the church from Jewish Jerusalem to Gentile Rome.

Synopsis: *The Contribution of the Book of Acts to Redemptive Revelation*

Acts is important to the New Testament canon because it carries on the narrative of Jesus' work through His disciples. Acts is not so much about the work of the disciples as it is about the continuing work of Christ from His heavenly session. Acts reveals that Jesus, now seated in glory, continues His work of redemption through His Spirit and for His church. As such, the book gives us a unique glimpse into the life of the early church and the early missionary movements as the apostles took the Word of Christ to the ends of the world.

The Gospel of Luke emphasized the mighty work of God in history through the person and work of Jesus. The Gospel ended and Acts began with the ascension of Jesus to His heavenly throne. But God's mighty act of salvation did not stop with Jesus' ascension. Rather, the ascended Christ now works mightily and savingly through His church on earth. Acts is a record of Christ's continued work in and through His apostles, disciples, and people.

Central to the book of Acts is the manifestation of Christ as the glorious and exalted God over the whole world. Luke uses specific Christological titles to magnify Christ in His exaltation. Christ is the promised Lord and Christ (2:36); He is the appointed Judge of the living and the dead (10:42); He is the greater Son of David (2:30), the promised Messiah (5:42); and He is standing at the right hand of the Father (7:56). Christ's work on earth may be finished, but His work from His exalted state is not. It is in the name of Jesus that the sick are healed (3:6), and His name is the only means of salvation (4:12). It was necessary for Christ to ascend to heaven that He might carry on His ministry even while exalted in glory. Jesus' ascension to God's right hand and the subsequent coming of the Spirit serve as proofs to Jesus' claim of divinity. The Father was pleased with the work of the Son and honored the Son by sending the promised Spirit (5:30–32).

Closely related to Christ's exaltation is the connected note that Christ does not work alone. After He ascended into heaven He sent His Holy Spirit to continue the work Jesus had begun in His disciples (1:8; 2:30–36; 16:7). The Holy Spirit first fell on the disciples (2:1–4), then on the Samaritans (8:17), then on the Gentiles (10:46), and then the disciples of John (19:6). Each of these successive fallings of the Spirit is similar to the initial falling at Pentecost and shows that through Christ's ascended work by means of His Spirit the doors of salvation are equally open to *all* kinds of people to come to Him in faith. Thus the Spirit works as evidence of Christ's power through His disciples to perform signs, wonders, and miracles testifying to His heavenly commission (19:10–11).

A broader purpose is served by Acts as well, that of showing the consequences of the large-scale rejection of Jesus during His ministry and the post-Pentecost inclusion of the nations into the fold of salvation. Acts serves as a major transition in redemptive history, tracing the history of the beginnings of the early church through Paul's final days. Now, as Acts records for us, those who confess faith in Christ and are united to the church become the true possessors of God's covenantal promises. By faith even Gentiles are grafted into God's wonderful plan of redemption and salvation.

Acts 1:8 serves as an organizing principle in understanding the gospel development in the book of Acts. Jesus tells His apostles that they will be His witnesses beginning in Jerusalem and extending to Judaea, Samaria, and into the uttermost parts of the earth. As Luke composes Acts he follows this trajectory. The apostles first proclaim the message of Christ's resurrection in Jerusalem (ch. 2). Philip preaches to the Samaritans (ch. 8). An Ethiopian eunuch comes to faith in Christ (ch. 8). And Paul travels to Ephesus and other parts of Asia Minor and Europe, even bringing the message of salvation to Rome. Following this structure Luke shows us the triumph of the gospel and the power of the preached Word as it goes forth converting and turning the world upside down.

Outline:

I. The Prologue (1:1–5)
   A. Introduction to Theophilus (1:1)
   B. Summary of Jesus' Final Days on Earth (1:2–3)
   C. Jesus' Final Commands to the Disciples (1:4–5)
II. The Outpouring of the Spirit of Christ (1:6—2:13)
   A. The Ascension of Christ (1:6–11)

- B. The Praying Church (1:12–26)
- C. The Coming of the Holy Spirit (2:1–13)

III. The Increase of the Word (2:14—20:38)
- A. In Jerusalem (2:14—6:7)
  1. Peter's First Sermon (2:14–36)
  2. The First Converts Repent and Are Baptized (2:37–41)
  3. The Unity of the Early Church (2:42–47)
  4. The Healing of the Lame Beggar (3:1–26)
  5. Peter and John Arrested (4:1–22)
  6. The Church Prays for Strength (4:23–31)
  7. Unity and Discipline in the Early Church (4:32—5:11)
  8. Miracles Performed in the Early Church (5:12–16)
  9. The Apostles Suffer Persecution (5:17–42)
  10. Deacons Appointed to Help the Elders (6:1–7)
- B. In Judaea, Galilee, and Samaria (6:8—9:31)
  1. Stephen's Martyrdom (6:8—7:60)
  2. Saul's Persecution Introduced (8:1–3)
  3. Philip's Ministry (8:4–40)
  4. Saul's Conversion and Beginning of Ministry (9:1–31)
- C. In the Mediterranean (9:32—12:24)
  1. Peter Performs Two Miracles (9:32–43)
  2. Gentiles Receive the Holy Spirit (10:1—11:18)
  3. The Church in Antioch (11:19–30)
  4. James and Peter Suffer Persecution (12:1–24)
- D. In Asia (12:25—16:5)
  1. Barnabas and Saul Sent to Asia (12:25—13:3)
  2. Barnabas and Saul in Cyprus (13:4–12)
  3. Paul and Barnabas Travel to Antioch in Pisidia (13:13–52)
  4. Paul and Barnabas Travel to Iconium (14:1–7)
  5. Paul and Barnabas Travel to Lystra (14:8–23)
  6. Paul and Barnabas Return to Antioch in Syria (14:24–28)
  7. The Jerusalem Council (15:1–35)
  8. Paul and Barnabas Separate (15:36–41)
  9. Timothy Joins Paul and Silas (16:1–5)
- E. In Europe (16:6—20:38)
  1. Paul Is Called to Macedonia (16:6–10)
  2. Ministry in Philippi (16:11–40)
  3. Ministry in Thessalonica (17:1–9)
  4. Ministry in Berea (17:10–15)
  5. Ministry in Athens (17:16–34)
  6. Paul in Corinth (18:1–17)
  7. Paul Returns to Antioch (18:18–23)
  8. Apollos Speaks in Ephesus (18:24–28)
  9. Paul in Ephesus (19:1–41)
  10. Paul in Macedonia and Greece (20:1–38)

IV. Testimony before Rulers and Rome (21:1—28:31)
- A. Paul in Jerusalem (21:1—23:11)
  1. Paul Travels to Jerusalem (21:1–16)
  2. Paul and James (21:17–26)
  3. Paul's Arrest (21:27—23:11)
- B. Paul Sent to Felix (23:12—24:27)
  1. Plot to Kill Paul Uncovered (23:12–22)
  2. Paul and Felix (23:23—24:27)
- C. Paul before Leaders (25:1—26:32)
  1. Paul Appeals to Caesar (25:1–12)
  2. Festus Seeks Agrippa's Advice (25:13–27)
  3. Paul Preaches before Agrippa (26:1–32)

D. Paul Travels to Rome (27:1—28:31)
   1. Paul Sets Sail for Rome (27:1–12)
   2. Paul's Ship Is Wrecked in a Storm (27:13–44)
   3. Paul on the Island of Malta (28:1–10)
   4. Paul in Rome (28:11–31)

THE ACTS OF THE APOSTLES

CHAPTER 1

THE former treatise have I made, O Theophilus, of all that Jesus began both to do and teach,
2 Until the day in which he was taken up, after that he through the Holy Ghost had given commandments unto the apostles whom he had chosen:
3 To whom also he shewed himself alive after his passion by many infallible proofs, being seen of them forty days, and speaking of the things pertaining to the kingdom of God:
4 And, being assembled together with *them*, commanded them that they should not depart from Jerusalem, but wait for the promise of the Father, which, *saith he*, ye have heard of me.
5 For John truly baptized with water; but ye shall be baptized with the Holy Ghost not many days hence.
6 When they therefore were come together, they asked of him, saying, Lord, wilt thou at this time restore again the kingdom to Israel?
7 And he said unto them, It is not for you to know the times or the seasons, which the Father hath put in his own power.
8 But ye shall receive power, after that the Holy Ghost is come upon you: and ye shall be witnesses unto me both in Jerusalem, and in all Judaea, and in Samaria, and unto the uttermost part of the earth.
9 And when he had spoken these things, while they beheld, he was taken up; and a cloud received him out of their sight.
10 And while they looked stedfastly toward heaven as he went up, behold, two men stood by them in white apparel;
11 Which also said, Ye men of Galilee, why stand ye gazing up into heaven? this same Jesus, which is taken up from you into heaven, shall so come in like manner as ye have seen him go into heaven.
12 Then returned they unto Jerusalem from the mount called Olivet, which is from Jerusalem a sabbath day's journey.

Chapter 1: *Christ ascends into heaven after instructing the disciples to wait in Jerusalem for the Spirit; they do so, along with choosing a twelfth apostle in fulfillment of prophecy.*

THE PROLOGUE (1:1–5)

Introduction to Theophilus (1:1)

1:1 *former treatise.* Luke refers here to his Gospel. *Theophilus.* Perhaps a friend, a benefactor, or a patron of Luke. Regardless of their relationship, Luke shows a concern that Theophilus understand the truths of Jesus' person and work on earth, as well as from heaven.

Summary of Jesus' Final Days on Earth (1:2–3)

1:2 *Holy Ghost.* The Holy Spirit (so throughout Acts).

1:3 *infallible proofs.* Christ's appearances to the disciples provide unmistakable proof that the resurrection is fact, not fiction (1 Cor. 15:5–7). *forty days.* Often a time period preparatory for something else (Luke 4:2). *speaking of . . . the kingdom.* Helping His disciples understand the Scriptures' testimony to His person and work (Luke 24:45–47).

Jesus' Final Commands to the Disciples (1:4–5)

1:4 *promise of the Father.* The Holy Spirit (Joel 2:28–32; Isa. 32:15; 44:3). *ye have heard of me.* See Luke 4:18; 11:13; 12:12; John 14–16.

1:5 *John . . . baptized.* John's baptism would be surpassed by the baptism with the Holy Spirit, which was the Holy Spirit being initially poured out on the disciples as a sign and guarantee of Jesus' resurrection to the Father.

THE OUTPOURING OF THE SPIRIT OF CHRIST (1:6—2:13)

The Ascension of Christ (1:6–11)

1:6–7 *restore again the kingdom to Israel.* The kingdom promised to the son of David was coming already in Christ's heavenly reign through the preaching of the gospel (2:29–30,34; 5:30–31; 13:22–23,32–39; 15:14–17). Thus Jesus responded to the disciples' question by reminding them that they cannot *know the times* of His return (Matt. 24:36) but should focus on being gospel witnesses throughout the whole earth, by which the kingdom is built.

1:8 *witnesses unto me.* The commission Christ particularly gave those of His apostles who had personally seen His earthly ministry and resurrection (v. 22; 2:32; 3:15; 4:33; 5:32; 10:39,41; 13:31; 22:15,18; 23:11; 26:16,22; Luke 24:48); this commission is similar to Israel's calling in the Old Testament to declare God's unique glory to the nations (Isa. 43:10; 44:8). *Jerusalem . . . Judaea . . . Samaria . . . uttermost part of the earth.* This is the itinerary for preaching the gospel in Acts, which the apostles follow throughout the remainder of the book.

1:9 *cloud received him.* This lines up with the manner in which God often showed His majesty and splendor (Ex. 40:34; 1 Kings 8:10–11; Mark 13:26; Luke 9:34–36).

1:10–11 *apparel.* Clothing, garments. *in like manner.* A reference to the Son of Man coming with the clouds (Luke 21:27).

13 And when they were come in, they went up into an upper room, where abode both Peter, and James, and John, and Andrew, Philip, and Thomas, Bartholomew, and Matthew, James *the son* of Alphaeus, and Simon Zelotes, and Judas *the brother* of James.

14 These all continued with one accord in prayer and supplication, with the women, and Mary the mother of Jesus, and with his brethren.

15 ¶ And in those days Peter stood up in the midst of the disciples, and said, (the number of names together were about an hundred and twenty,)

16 Men *and* brethren, this scripture must needs have been fulfilled, which the Holy Ghost by the mouth of David spake before concerning Judas, which was guide to them that took Jesus.

17 For he was numbered with us, and had obtained part of this ministry.

18 Now this man purchased a field with the reward of iniquity; and falling headlong, he burst asunder in the midst, and all his bowels gushed out.

19 And it was known unto all the dwellers at Jerusalem; insomuch as that field is called in their proper tongue, Aceldama, that is to say, The field of blood.

20 For it is written in the book of Psalms, Let his habitation be desolate, and let no man dwell therein: and his bishoprick let another take.

21 Wherefore of these men which have companied with us all the time that the Lord Jesus went in and out among us,

22 Beginning from the baptism of John, unto that same day that he was taken up from us, must one be ordained to be a witness with us of his resurrection.

23 And they appointed two, Joseph called Barsabas, who was surnamed Justus, and Matthias.

24 And they prayed, and said, Thou, Lord, which knowest the hearts of all *men*, shew whether of these two thou hast chosen,

25 That he may take part of this ministry and apostleship, from which Judas by transgression fell, that he might go to his own place.

26 And they gave forth their lots; and the lot fell upon Matthias; and he was numbered with the eleven apostles.

The Praying Church (1:12–26)

1:13 *Peter . . . Judas.* The twelve apostles (Matt. 10:2–4; Mark 3:16–19; Luke 6:14–16). Here they are all present except Judas the traitor.

1:14 *continued with one accord.* They prayed corporately. *brethren.* Jesus' half-brothers who became followers of Jesus after His resurrection. James became a prominent leader in the church in Jerusalem, and both James and Jude wrote books of the New Testament.

1:15 *Peter stood up.* Peter had been restored after his fall (John 21) and transformed into a man of courage. *the disciples.* Those who submitted to Jesus as learners and imitators under His authority (see note at Matt. 10:24–25); even after the name "Christians" was introduced (11:26; 26:28; 1 Peter 4:16), *disciples* was still the predominant term used by Luke for the followers of Jesus Christ. *an hundred and twenty.* Luke focuses on numbers throughout the early chapters of Acts to show with what force and triumph the gospel message began converting people.

1:16 *must needs.* Necessarily. As in the Gospel of Luke (see notes at Luke 4:43; 24:7–8), Acts teaches that the *Scripture* reveals God's decree, which takes place by sovereign necessity (v. 22; 3:21; 4:12; 9:16; 14:22; 17:3; 18:21; 19:21; 23:11; 27:24,26). *the Holy Ghost by the mouth of David spake.* The author of the Bible is the Holy Spirit, who communicated through prophets (1 Peter 1:10–12; 2 Peter 1:20–21). Peter noted that the actions of Judas and his replacement as one of the twelve apostles had been prophesied (v. 20), using the Christ-centered principle of interpreting the Old Testament that Jesus had taught His disciples (Luke 24:44).

1:18 *falling headlong, he burst.* Judas hanged himself (Matt. 27:5). It is likely that Judas's body hung until the rope broke and his decaying corpse broke open (*asunder*), such that his inner organs (*bowels*) came out, a sign of dying in utter disgrace.

1:19 *proper.* Own.

1:20 *it is written.* Citing Pss. 69:25; 109:8. *habitation.* Dwelling. *bishoprick.* Office of pastoral oversight (1 Tim. 3:1).

1:21 *companied.* Accompanied. *all the time that the Lord Jesus went in and out.* An apostle had to have been an eyewitness of Jesus' ministry from John's baptism to the resurrection (10:41; Mark 1:14–20; John 1:35–51).

1:22 *ordained to be a witness.* See note at v. 8.

1:26 *lots.* Small objects commonly used in the Old Testament to determine how to act in a particular situation, not to rely on chance or to test God but to trust Him (Num. 26:55; 33:54; Josh. 20:9–10; 1 Sam. 14:41–42; Neh. 10:34; Prov. 16:33). This is the only time believers cast lots in the New Testament. After Pentecost, Acts indicates that the disciples relied on the wisdom given by the Word and the Spirit of God (see Phil. 3:15).

Thoughts for Personal/Family Worship: Chapter 1

1. **Luke refers to his Gospel as what Jesus "began both to do and teach" (v. 1). The implication is that Christ is continuing to act and teach, now as the Lord enthroned in heaven (v. 9) who works through His Spirit (v. 8). How does the knowledge that Jesus continues to act and teach in the world strengthen the faith of believers?**
2. **The disciples did not wait passively for the coming of the Spirit, doing nothing, but they devoted themselves to prayer meetings (v. 14). They loved the Scriptures as the infallible voice of God's Spirit (v. 16) and applied the Word to order the church according to God's will (v. 20). Thus they provide an example of how believers should wait for the coming of Christ: by devoting themselves to prayer, the Word, and the church, as ordered by Scripture.**
3. **Christ captured the mission of the church in the phrase "witnesses unto me" (v. 8). Witnesses do not invent their own message but faithfully declare what they know to be true. The witness of the church did not end with the apostles but must continue to the ends of the earth, for God's purpose is to bring this message concerning Christ and redemption to all nations. Only when all the elect from all tribes and tongues are brought in through the word of Christ's witnesses will the end come. How is your**

CHAPTER 2

AND when the day of Pentecost was fully come,
they were all with one accord in one place.
2 And suddenly there came a sound from heaven
as of a rushing mighty wind, and it filled all the
house where they were sitting.
3 And there appeared unto them cloven tongues
like as of fire, and it sat upon each of them.
4 And they were all filled with the Holy Ghost,
and began to speak with other tongues, as the
Spirit gave them utterance.
5 And there were dwelling at Jerusalem Jews,
devout men, out of every nation under heaven.
6 Now when this was noised abroad, the multi-
tude came together, and were confounded, because
that every man heard them speak in his own
language.
7 And they were all amazed and marvelled, say-
ing one to another, Behold, are not all these which
speak Galilaeans?
8 And how hear we every man in our own tongue,
wherein we were born?
9 Parthians, and Medes, and Elamites, and the
dwellers in Mesopotamia, and in Judaea, and
Cappadocia, in Pontus, and Asia,
10 Phrygia, and Pamphylia, in Egypt, and in the
parts of Libya about Cyrene, and strangers of
Rome, Jews and proselytes,
11 Cretes and Arabians, we do hear them speak in
our tongues the wonderful works of God.
12 And they were all amazed, and were in doubt,
saying one to another, What meaneth this?
13 Others mocking said, These men are full of
new wine.
14 ¶ But Peter, standing up with the eleven, lifted
up his voice, and said unto them, Ye men of
Judaea, and all *ye* that dwell at Jerusalem, be this
known unto you, and hearken to my words:
15 For these are not drunken, as ye suppose,
seeing it is *but* the third hour of the day.
16 But this is that which was spoken by the
prophet Joel;
17 And it shall come to pass in the last days, saith
God, I will pour out of my Spirit upon all flesh:
and your sons and your daughters shall prophesy,
and your young men shall see visions, and your
old men shall dream dreams:
18 And on my servants and on my handmaidens
I will pour out in those days of my Spirit; and they
shall prophesy:
19 And I will shew wonders in heaven above, and
signs in the earth beneath; blood, and fire, and
vapour of smoke:
20 The sun shall be turned into darkness, and the
moon into blood, before that great and notable
day of the Lord come:
21 And it shall come to pass, *that* whosoever shall
call on the name of the Lord shall be saved.

---

church engaged in this witness? If you are a Christian, how are you part of this mission?

Chapter 2: *God pours out the Holy Spirit in fulfillment of prophecy, thus empowering Peter to preach and blessing His Word with abundant conversions and daily growth of the church.*

The Coming of the Holy Spirit (2:1–13)

2:1 *Pentecost.* The Feast of Weeks, celebrated fifty days after the first Sabbath of Passover (Ex. 34:22; Deut. 16:10); also known as the "day of the firstfruits" (Num. 28:26). This was ten days after Jesus' last appearance to His disciples (1:3).

2:2 *mighty wind . . . filled all the house.* The imagery is strikingly similar to God's glory descending on the tabernacle and temple (Ex. 40:34–48; 2 Chron. 7:1–2).

2:3 *cloven.* Divided.

2:4 *filled with the Holy Ghost.* While all Christians have the Holy Spirit (Rom. 8:9), the terminology here used by Luke refers specifically to the gift of unusual power from the Spirit to serve or speak for the glory of the Lord (4:8,31; 6:3, cf. 6:5,8; 7:55; 9:17; 11:24; 13:9; Luke 1:15,41,67; 4:1). *other tongues.* Human languages, not ecstatic angelic languages or babbling (v. 6). *the Spirit gave them utterance.* The Holy Spirit empowered them to speak; this was not self-induced.

2:5 *every nation under heaven.* The Passover had drawn thousands of people from around the known world. The miracle of Pentecost signified a reversal of God's curse on the tower of Babel, which had confused and divided humanity for its pride (Gen. 11:1–9), whereas the gospel of Christ unites the nations to glorify God (v. 11; Rom. 15:5–12). Yet it was also a sign of judgment upon those who reject the gospel, as much of Israel had done (Isa. 28:11–12; 1 Cor. 14:21–22).

2:6 *noised abroad.* Widely broadcasted.

2:9–11 *Parthians, and Medes, and Elamites, and . . . Mesopotamia.* Nations east of the Euphrates River, the lands of the earliest dispersion of the Israelites under the Assyrian exile. *Judaea.* Broadly referring to the land controlled by David and Solomon's kingdoms. The other lands mentioned focus on the vast collection of peoples and nations present in Jerusalem on the day of Pentecost. *proselytes.* People in the process of converting to the faith of the Jews.

2:12–13 The miracle attracted a crowd, but the varied responses from the people showed that the miracle required explanation by the preaching of the Scriptures.

THE INCREASE OF THE WORD (2:14—20:38)

In Jerusalem (2:14—6:7)

Peter's First Sermon (2:14–36)

2:14 *hearken.* Listen. The once fearful Peter now preached in the very city that had crucified Jesus. His sermon focuses on the fulfillment of God's saving purposes through Jesus Christ.

2:15 *third hour.* 9:00 a.m. Peter defended the gift of tongues by pointing out that this was not drunkenness, confirmed by the early hour of the day.

2:17–21 Peter's first Old Testament citation comes from Joel 2:28–32, where God promised not only that He would pour out His Spirit but that He would come in judgment against man and creation.

2:21 *whosoever shall call on the name of the Lord shall be saved.* It was not necessary to become a Jewish proselyte to be saved (v. 10). Instead, all who, based on the misery of their own sin, renounce their confidence in themselves or in other powers and pray to God in Christ for salvation will be rescued

22 Ye men of Israel, hear these words; Jesus of
Nazareth, a man approved of God among you by
miracles and wonders and signs, which God did
by him in the midst of you, as ye yourselves also
know:
23 Him, being delivered by the determinate
counsel and foreknowledge of God, ye have taken,
and by wicked hands have crucified and slain:
24 Whom God hath raised up, having loosed the
pains of death: because it was not possible that he
should be holden of it.
25 For David speaketh concerning him, I foresaw
the Lord always before my face, for he is on my
right hand, that I should not be moved:
26 Therefore did my heart rejoice, and my tongue
was glad; moreover also my flesh shall rest in
hope:
27 Because thou wilt not leave my soul in hell,
neither wilt thou suffer thine Holy One to see
corruption.
28 Thou hast made known to me the ways of
life; thou shalt make me full of joy with thy
countenance.
29 Men *and* brethren, let me freely speak unto
you of the patriarch David, that he is both dead
and buried, and his sepulchre is with us unto this
day.
30 Therefore being a prophet, and knowing that
God had sworn with an oath to him, that of the
fruit of his loins, according to the flesh, he would
raise up Christ to sit on his throne;
31 He seeing this before spake of the resurrection
of Christ, that his soul was not left in hell, neither
his flesh did see corruption.
32 This Jesus hath God raised up, whereof we all
are witnesses.
33 Therefore being by the right hand of God
exalted, and having received of the Father the
promise of the Holy Ghost, he hath shed forth
this, which ye now see and hear.
34 For David is not ascended into the heavens:
but he saith himself, The LORD said unto my Lord,
Sit thou on my right hand,
35 Until I make thy foes thy footstool.
36 Therefore let all the house of Israel know as-
suredly, that God hath made that same Jesus,
whom ye have crucified, both Lord and Christ.
37 ¶ Now when they heard *this*, they were pricked
in their heart, and said unto Peter and to the rest
of the apostles, Men *and* brethren, what shall we
do?
38 Then Peter said unto them, Repent, and be
baptized every one of you in the name of Jesus
Christ for the remission of sins, and ye shall re-
ceive the gift of the Holy Ghost.
39 For the promise is unto you, and to your

---

from God's punishment and their sin (Rom. 10:13).

2:22 *a man approved of God among you by miracles.* Jesus' public ministry vindicates Him as the One sent by God with the power to save (10:38; Luke 7:20–23).

2:23 *being delivered by the determinate counsel and foreknowledge of God.* Jesus' death was the working out of God's eternal plan of redemption (see note at 1:16). Even while sinful people were persecuting and crucifying Jesus, God's hand was orchestrating the events (4:27–28).

2:24 *pains.* Like that of a woman in labor. *holden.* Held. Death swallows up and the grave is never satisfied (Prov. 30:16), but Jesus' resurrection broke the power of death, so that it has no claim on Him (Rom. 6:9).

2:25–28 The second Scripture Peter saw as fulfilled in Jesus was Ps. 16:8–11.

2:27 *hell.* The Greek term (*hades*) can refer to the punishment of the wicked after death (Luke 10:15; 16:23), but, like the Hebrew word *sheol*, it can also refer simply to death and the grave (1 Cor. 15:55). God promised not to allow (*suffer*) His *Holy One* to experience the decay (*corruption*) of remaining in the grave (13:35–36).

2:30–31 *being a prophet . . . spake of the resurrection of Christ.* David knew God's covenant to give him a descendant who would reign over his kingdom forever (*sit on his throne*; 2 Sam. 7:12–13) and was enabled by the Holy Spirit to foretell Christ's resurrection in Ps. 16.

2:32–33 *whereof we all are witnesses.* The resurrection serves as the catalyst or impetus for preaching the gospel message (1 Cor. 15:14). *Jesus . . . Father . . . Holy Ghost.* Just as at the time Christ was baptized and publicly anointed with the Holy Spirit (Luke 3:22), so also in Christ's glorification all three persons of the divine Trinity manifested themselves as the one God. *he hath shed forth this.* The pouring out of the Holy Spirit was a public display of Christ's royal power, as He is *exalted* at *the right hand of God* (v. 34; 5:31; 7:55–56).

2:34–35 Peter cited Ps. 110:1 to show Christ's supreme exaltation as *LORD* and enduring kingship until His enemies (*foes*) were destroyed, just as Jesus had used this reference to declare His divinity (Luke 20:41–44; 22:69).

2:36 *both Lord and Christ.* Both of these titles were used of Jesus while He was on earth (Luke 2:11), but after Christ finished His work on the cross the Father manifested the glory of the incarnate Son in a far greater way (Phil. 2:6–11).

The First Converts Repent and Are Baptized (2:37–41)

2:37 *pricked in their heart.* The Holy Spirit wields the Word like a knife or sword to pierce the heart with conviction of sin (John 16:8; Eph. 6:17; Heb. 4:12). *what shall we do?* Those convicted of sin are not yet saved, but they do feel their need of a Savior (16:30).

2:38 *Repent.* The call of the gospel commands sinners to turn from sin and idols out of a sense of their evil and to turn to God with trust in His grace and a resolve to obey Him (3:19; 5:31; 9:35; 11:18,21; 14:15; 17:30; 20:21; 26:20; Luke 5:32; 13:3,5; 24:47). *baptized . . . in the name of Jesus Christ.* Having said that all who call on the name of the Lord would be saved (v. 21) and identifying Jesus as Lord (v. 36), Peter now linked this promise to identifying publicly with Jesus through baptism, which does not itself save but is an external sign and seal of the Lord's promises to His people (1 Peter 3:21). His *name* is His glory revealed in the gospel (Pss. 8:1; 9:10), not just a spoken formula (19:13–17) but shorthand for the gospel or for acting by faith in the gospel (3:6; 4:18; 5:40–42; 8:12,16; 9:27,29; 10:48; 15:26; 16:18; 19:5; 21:13; 22:16). *remission.* Forgiveness. *receive . . . the Holy Ghost.* Faith unites a person to Christ so that the Spirit given to Jesus (v. 33) also indwells the believer.

children, and to all that are afar off, *even* as many
as the Lord our God shall call.
40 And with many other words did he testify and
exhort, saying, Save yourselves from this unto-
ward generation.
41 ¶ Then they that gladly received his word were
baptized: and the same day there were added *unto*
them about three thousand souls.
42 And they continued stedfastly in the apostles'
doctrine and fellowship, and in breaking of bread,
and in prayers.
43 And fear came upon every soul: and many
wonders and signs were done by the apostles.
44 And all that believed were together, and had all
things common;
45 And sold their possessions and goods, and
parted them to all *men*, as every man had need.
46 And they, continuing daily with one accord
in the temple, and breaking bread from house
to house, did eat their meat with gladness and
singleness of heart,
47 Praising God, and having favour with all the
people. And the Lord added to the church daily
such as should be saved.

CHAPTER 3

NOW Peter and John went up together into the
temple at the hour of prayer, *being* the ninth *hour*.
2 And a certain man lame from his mother's
womb was carried, whom they laid daily at the
gate of the temple which is called Beautiful, to ask
alms of them that entered into the temple;
3 Who seeing Peter and John about to go into the
temple asked an alms.
4 And Peter, fastening his eyes upon him with
John, said, Look on us.
5 And he gave heed unto them, expecting to re-
ceive something of them.
6 Then Peter said, Silver and gold have I none;
but such as I have give I thee: In the name of Jesus
Christ of Nazareth rise up and walk.
7 And he took him by the right hand, and lifted
him up: and immediately his feet and ankle bones
received strength.
8 And he leaping up stood, and walked, and
entered with them into the temple, walking, and
leaping, and praising God.
9 And all the people saw him walking and prais-
ing God:

2:39 *promise.* God's covenant (Gen. 17:7). Peter first told his hearers that this promise comes in all sincerity to them (*unto you*). If they repent they will receive the forgiveness of sins (v. 38). Secondly, it comes also to their descendants (*your children*), as in the Old Testament. Thirdly, it comes with all sincerity to people *afar off*, dispersed Jews as well as Gentiles. This promise must be preached indiscriminately, but it does not take place automatically; it must also be applied through faith by the Holy Spirit.
2:40 *untoward.* Crooked, wicked.
2:41 *added unto them about three thousand.* This is a remarkable work of the Spirit, reflecting the greater things Jesus promised that His disciples would do (John 14:12). The small initial band of 120 disciples has grown very large through the preaching of Jesus Christ. The result of Peter's first sermon shows the triumph of the gospel by the power of the Spirit of Christ.

The Unity of the Early Church (2:42–47)

2:42 *continued stedfastly.* The new converts devoted themselves to the public means of grace in submission to godly leaders. *apostles' doctrine.* Like their Lord, they gave themselves to teaching the Word (6:4). *breaking of bread.* Either the Lord's Supper or simply table fellowship (v. 46; 20:7,11; 27:35; Mark 8:6; Luke 22:19; 24:30,35; 1 Cor. 10:16). *prayers.* Literally, "the prayers," probably prayer meetings at set times. Acts emphasizes the importance of corporate prayer (1:14,24; 3:1; 6:4,6; 12:5,12; 13:2–3; 14:23; 16:13,16,25; 20:36; 21:5).
2:43 *wonders and signs.* The miracles promised to be the sign of the last days (v. 19), a confirmation of the apostles' message.
2:44–47 These verses manifest the unity the early church enjoyed through her Lord. The selling of property and sharing of goods were necessary because of the large numbers of people visiting from outside the area for the feast (vv. 1,5).
2:46 *meat.* Food of any kind.
2:47 *the Lord added to the church.* Christ is sovereign over salvation; each conversion and addition to the membership of the church is brought about by Him (11:21; 13:48).

Thoughts for Personal/Family Worship: Chapter 2

1. **The work of the Triune God is obvious at every important point of history: creation, incarnation, resurrection, and also Pentecost. Exalted by the Father (v. 33), Christ poured out His Spirit (v. 33), and the Spirit testified of Christ (v. 31) while the Lord added to the church (v. 47). Blessed be the triune God (Eph.1:3).**
2. **True repentance for sin and a crying out to God for mercy (vv. 37–38) is the only proper response to the preaching of the Word of God. Have you come before God as a sinner, seeking mercy for Christ's sake? Never doubt the power of God to convert sinners. He cut the people of Jerusalem to the heart and transformed cowardly Peter into a fearless preacher.**
3. **The church after Pentecost was marked by faithfulness, fellowship, fear, and fervency. Trace this out in verses 41 to 47 and ask whether these qualities characterize you. How can you pray regularly for these characteristics to increase in your own church?**

Chapter 3: ***Peter heals a lame beggar in the name of Christ, after which he preaches Christ and calls people to repentance.***

The Healing of the Lame Beggar (3:1–26)

3:1 The disciples continued to go to the *temple* as a place of prayer. *hour of prayer.* The temple had two designated times of daily prayer, at 9:00 a.m. and 3:00 p.m. (*ninth hour*).
3:2 *from his mother's womb.* As was common with many of Jesus' miracles, the man's helpless state is noted. He had never known full health of his body. *Beautiful.* Uncertain location, perhaps the Nicanor Gate, which was ornately decorated.
3:5 *gave heed.* Paid attention.
3:6 *In the name of Jesus.* It was by faith in Jesus' power as the resurrected Lord that the disciples had the ability to heal.
3:7 *immediately.* Not a gradual change but sudden and complete.

10 And they knew that it was he which sat for
alms at the Beautiful gate of the temple: and they
were filled with wonder and amazement at that
which had happened unto him.
11 And as the lame man which was healed held
Peter and John, all the people ran together unto
them in the porch that is called Solomon's, greatly
wondering.
12 ¶ And when Peter saw *it*, he answered unto the
people, Ye men of Israel, why marvel ye at this? or
why look ye so earnestly on us, as though by our
own power or holiness we had made this man to
walk?
13 The God of Abraham, and of Isaac, and of
Jacob, the God of our fathers, hath glorified his
Son Jesus; whom ye delivered up, and denied him
in the presence of Pilate, when he was determined
to let *him* go.
14 But ye denied the Holy One and the Just, and
desired a murderer to be granted unto you;
15 And killed the Prince of life, whom God hath
raised from the dead; whereof we are witnesses.
16 And his name through faith in his name hath
made this man strong, whom ye see and know:
yea, the faith which is by him hath given him this
perfect soundness in the presence of you all.
17 And now, brethren, I wot that through igno-
rance ye did *it*, as *did* also your rulers.
18 But those things, which God before had
shewed by the mouth of all his prophets, that
Christ should suffer, he hath so fulfilled.
19 ¶ Repent ye therefore, and be converted, that
your sins may be blotted out, when the times of
refreshing shall come from the presence of the
Lord;
20 And he shall send Jesus Christ, which before
was preached unto you:
21 Whom the heaven must receive until the
times of restitution of all things, which God hath
spoken by the mouth of all his holy prophets
since the world began.
22 For Moses truly said unto the fathers, A
prophet shall the Lord your God raise up unto
you of your brethren, like unto me; him shall ye
hear in all things whatsoever he shall say unto you.
23 And it shall come to pass, *that* every soul,
which will not hear that prophet, shall be de-
stroyed from among the people.
24 Yea, and all the prophets from Samuel and
those that follow after, as many as have spoken,
have likewise foretold of these days.
25 Ye are the children of the prophets, and of
the covenant which God made with our fathers,
saying unto Abraham, And in thy seed shall all the
kindreds of the earth be blessed.
26 Unto you first God, having raised up his Son

3:10 *they knew that it was he.* The public healing of a widely known disabled person became a testimony to the power of the resurrected Christ.

3:12 *by our own power or holiness.* Peter was quick to deflect any exaltation from himself, a mere man, instead giving glory to Christ (Gen. 41:15–16; Dan. 2:23,26–30).

3:13 *God of Abraham . . . Isaac . . . Jacob, the God of our fathers.* The Lord who keeps His covenant and saves His people (Ex. 3:6,15). *Son.* Not the usual Greek word for "son" but a term meaning child (20:12) or servant (4:25), applied to *Jesus* (v. 26; 4:27,30) perhaps as the Servant of the Lord promised by Isaiah (Isa. 42:1; 52:13, Greek Septuagint; cf. Acts 8:32–33).

3:15 *Prince.* A strong and potent word, referring to one who has paved the way or forged a path for others to follow (Heb. 2:10). *witnesses.* The apostolic commission (see note at 1:8).

3:16 *through faith in his name.* The miracle highlights faith as the means by which Christ's blessings come. Faith is the empty hand by which sinners take hold of Christ and all His benefits.

3:17 *wot.* Know.

3:18 *he hath so fulfilled.* Christ had taught them that the Old Testament Scriptures spoke of His sufferings and resurrection and that God would do what He had planned (see note at 1:16).

3:19 *Repent.* Turn from sin to God (see note at 2:38). *sins . . . blotted out.* Sin makes us guilty, and the guilt of sin must be forgiven (Ps. 51:1). *times of refreshing.* Seasons when gospel peace, rest, and joy come with power and pervasiveness as the Holy Spirit applies the blood of Christ to many (Ezek. 34:26).

3:20 *shall send Jesus Christ.* His second coming. The promise is that those who repent and have faith in Christ will enter Christ's rest.

3:21 *Whom the heaven must receive.* For now, Jesus is ascended on high and remains in heaven. *times of restitution.* When God restores *all things* by the coming of His kingdom (1:6; Isa. 65:17–18).

3:22–23 *prophet . . . like unto me.* Jesus is the great Prophet of whom *Moses* had both spoken and was a type (Lev. 23:29; Deut. 18:15,19). Our salvation hinges on whether we will listen to His teaching with faith and obedience (Luke 9:35; John 10:4,27–28).

3:25 *in thy seed . . . blessed.* Citing Gen. 22:18.

3:26 *raised up . . . to bless you.* Christ is the promised Seed of Abraham (v. 25; Matt. 1:1; Gal. 3:16) through whom God blesses the nations, and the first blessing is the gift of repentance (*turning away every one of you from his iniquities*; 5:31; 11:18).

Thoughts for Personal/Family Worship: Chapter 3

1. **Though the Bible calls Christians to show generosity to the poor, the preaching of the gospel and the transformation that it brings must always be central to the life of the church. Peter used this miracle as an opportunity to declare the power of the name of Jesus, not just to heal the sick but as the person in whom we must place our faith. It is fitting that this miracle took place at the gate called Beautiful, for it reveals the loveliness of the Savior as He takes hopeless sinners and restores them to strength, joy, and praise.**
2. **Just because God raised Christ from the dead does not mean that people are automatically saved. The gospel calls sinners to repent and be converted, so that their sins might be blotted out (v. 19). Do not rest simply on hearing the truth of the gospel, being a child of believers, or being around people who know the gospel. Apart from repentance toward God and faith in the Lord Jesus you are neither saved nor safe. Have you repented?**

Jesus, sent him to bless you, in turning away every
one of you from his iniquities.

CHAPTER 4

AND as they spake unto the people, the priests,
and the captain of the temple, and the Sadducees,
came upon them,
2 Being grieved that they taught the people, and
preached through Jesus the resurrection from the
dead.
3 And they laid hands on them, and put *them* in
hold unto the next day: for it was now eventide.
4 Howbeit many of them which heard the word
believed; and the number of the men was about
five thousand.
5 ¶ And it came to pass on the morrow, that their
rulers, and elders, and scribes,
6 And Annas the high priest, and Caiaphas, and
John, and Alexander, and as many as were of the
kindred of the high priest, were gathered together
at Jerusalem.
7 And when they had set them in the midst, they
asked, By what power, or by what name, have ye
done this?
8 Then Peter, filled with the Holy Ghost, said
unto them, Ye rulers of the people, and elders of
Israel,
9 If we this day be examined of the good deed
done to the impotent man, by what means he is
made whole;
10 Be it known unto you all, and to all the people
of Israel, that by the name of Jesus Christ of Naza-
reth, whom ye crucified, whom God raised from
the dead, *even* by him doth this man stand here
before you whole.
11 This is the stone which was set at nought of
you builders, which is become the head of the
corner.
12 Neither is there salvation in any other: for
there is none other name under heaven given
among men, whereby we must be saved.
13 ¶ Now when they saw the boldness of Peter
and John, and perceived that they were unlearned
and ignorant men, they marvelled; and they took
knowledge of them, that they had been with Jesus.
14 And beholding the man which was healed
standing with them, they could say nothing
against it.
15 But when they had commanded them to go
aside out of the council, they conferred among
themselves,
16 Saying, What shall we do to these men? for
that indeed a notable miracle hath been done by
them *is* manifest to all them that dwell in Jerusa-
lem; and we cannot deny *it*.
17 But that it spread no further among the
people, let us straitly threaten them, that they
speak henceforth to no man in this name.
18 And they called them, and commanded them
not to speak at all nor teach in the name of Jesus.
19 But Peter and John answered and said unto
them, Whether it be right in the sight of God to
hearken unto you more than unto God, judge ye.
20 For we cannot but speak the things which we
have seen and heard.
21 So when they had further threatened them,
they let them go, finding nothing how they might
punish them, because of the people: for all *men*
glorified God for that which was done.
22 For the man was above forty years old, on
whom this miracle of healing was shewed.

Chapter 4: ***The rulers of the temple arrest Peter and John because of their preaching of Christ; when Peter witnesses with power among them they let them go, warning them not to preach in Christ's name. However, with prayer for boldness and much resultant fruit they continue to do so.***

Peter and John Arrested (4:1–22)

4:1–2 *Saducees.* A Jewish sect associated with the *priests* (5:17) that denied the *resurrection from the dead* (23:8). *grieved.* Offended, angered (16:18).

4:6 *Annas* served as *high priest* from AD 6 to 14 and Caiaphas from AD 18 to 36, with Annas also retaining the title as the head of the family.

4:7 *By what power, or by what name.* The disciples had already publicly declared this (2:38; 3:12–13,16).

4:8 *filled with the Holy Ghost.* Given unusual power to serve by the Holy Spirit (see note at 2:4).

4:9 *impotent.* Weak, a reference to the crippled man (3:2).

4:10 Peter unashamedly preached the reality of Jesus' resurrection in giving them the power and authority to do and proclaim these things.

4:11 *set at nought.* Despised, rejected. Peter quoted Ps. 118:22, the same text Jesus used when confronting the people of Jerusalem over their rejection of Him (Luke 20:17). *head of the corner.* Cornerstone. Though rejected by men, Jesus was exalted by God as the foundation of His spiritual building (1 Cor. 3:11; Eph. 2:20; 1 Peter 2:6–7).

4:12 *none other . . . whereby we must be saved.* Salvation is given exclusively to those who embrace Jesus Christ by faith. There is no other way of salvation (John 14:6; 1 Tim. 2:5). *name.* See note at 2:38.

4:13 *unlearned . . . ignorant.* The apostles lacked the professional qualifications of religious teachers. *they had been with Jesus.* Their one qualification was discipleship under Jesus, their Teacher (Mark 3:14). Peter's bold witness to Christ made evident what he had once denied (Luke 22:56).

4:17 *straitly threaten.* Literally, "threaten a threat," an idiom for severely threatening. *henceforth.* From now on. *in this name.* It is the authority and power of Jesus' name that the leadership wants to restrain, but this is in vain.

4:20 *which we have seen and heard.* The apostles point out their role as witnesses in God's plan of salvation (1:8). They will not fail to carry out their divinely appointed mission.

4:22 *forty years old.* This note emphasizes the profound miracle of the healing. The man had long been in his state of despair.

23 ¶ And being let go, they went to their own
company, and reported all that the chief priests
and elders had said unto them.
24 And when they heard that, they lifted up their
voice to God with one accord, and said, Lord,
thou *art* God, which hast made heaven, and earth,
and the sea, and all that in them is:
25 Who by the mouth of thy servant David hast
said, Why did the heathen rage, and the people
imagine vain things?
26 The kings of the earth stood up, and the rulers
were gathered together against the Lord, and
against his Christ.
27 For of a truth against thy holy child Jesus,
whom thou hast anointed, both Herod, and
Pontius Pilate, with the Gentiles, and the people
of Israel, were gathered together,
28 For to do whatsoever thy hand and thy counsel
determined before to be done.
29 And now, Lord, behold their threatenings: and
grant unto thy servants, that with all boldness
they may speak thy word,
30 By stretching forth thine hand to heal; and
that signs and wonders may be done by the name
of thy holy child Jesus.
31 ¶ And when they had prayed, the place was
shaken where they were assembled together; and
they were all filled with the Holy Ghost, and they
spake the word of God with boldness.
32 And the multitude of them that believed were
of one heart and of one soul: neither said any *of*
them that ought of the things which he possessed
was his own; but they had all things common.
33 And with great power gave the apostles witness
of the resurrection of the Lord Jesus: and great
grace was upon them all.
34 Neither was there any among them that lacked:
for as many as were possessors of lands or houses
sold them, and brought the prices of the things
that were sold,
35 And laid *them* down at the apostles' feet: and
distribution was made unto every man according
as he had need.
36 And Joses, who by the apostles was surnamed
Barnabas, (which is, being interpreted, The son
of consolation,) a Levite, *and* of the country of
Cyprus,
37 Having land, sold *it*, and brought the money,
and laid *it* at the apostles' feet.

CHAPTER 5

BUT a certain man named Ananias, with Sapphira
his wife, sold a possession,
2 And kept back *part* of the price, his wife also
being privy *to it*, and brought a certain part, and
laid *it* at the apostles' feet.
3 But Peter said, Ananias, why hath Satan filled
thine heart to lie to the Holy Ghost, and to keep
back *part* of the price of the land?
4 Whiles it remained, was it not thine own? and
after it was sold, was it not in thine own power?
why hast thou conceived this thing in thine heart?
thou hast not lied unto men, but unto God.
5 And Ananias hearing these words fell down,
and gave up the ghost: and great fear came on all
them that heard these things.
6 And the young men arose, wound him up, and

The Church Prays for Strength (4:23–31)

4:25–27 Citing Ps. 2:1–2 as having been fulfilled in Jesus' sufferings and death. Both *Gentiles* and *Israel* are identified with the enemies of God and Christ. *child.* Or servant (v. 30; see note at 3:13).

4:28 *hand.* Power. *counsel.* Purpose, will. *determined before.* Predestined (Rom. 8:29–30; Eph. 1:5,11). God's announcement of the wicked opposition against His Christ a thousand years before it took place (vv. 25–26) shows that He had predestined even this for His glory.

Unity and Discipline in the Early Church (4:32—5:11)

4:32 *had all things common.* Not a forced socialism but a spiritual unity producing voluntary self-sacrifice of personal property (5:4).

4:36 *Barnabas.* A significant figure in the apostolic church (9:27; 11:22–26,30; 12:25; 13:1—15:41), whose kindness is contrasted with the greed of Ananias and Sapphira (5:1–2).

Thoughts for Personal/Family Worship: Chapter 4

1. **It is often asserted today that people can be saved apart from knowing about Jesus. Some say that explicit knowledge about Jesus is not necessary in order to be saved. Verse 12 stands in absolute contrast to this. We need to be prepared to stand and say this against the tide of relativism in our culture. Why is faith in Jesus Christ the only way to God?**
2. **The apostles quoted Psalm 2 in their prayer (vv. 25–26). They were bringing back to God His own Word. How does this help us see the connection between these two means of grace: prayer and Bible reading?**
3. **Though they responded resolutely to the intimidation of the Sanhedrin, the apostles still felt the need to pray to God to grant them "boldness." They were not content to move forward in their own strength or on the strength of past resolutions. They understood their need to draw down strength from God. Do you know this strengthening power of prayer in your life? How dependent are you on God's Spirit?**

Chapter 5: *Ananias and Sapphira bring the wrath of God upon themselves by lying to the church, and hence the Holy Spirit, while the disciples, though persecuted, are helped by God and the church grows.*

5:2 *kept back part.* The sin is not that they retained some of their private property; rather, it is that they pretended to give it all (v. 4). *privy.* Aware of their secret.

5:3–4 *Satan filled thine heart . . . why hast thou conceived this thing in thine heart.* The Devil works in sinners (Eph. 2:2; 2 Tim. 2:26), but their sin also arises from their own choices, and so they are responsible for it. *lie to the Holy Ghost . . . lied . . . unto God.* The Holy Spirit is God.

carried *him* out, and buried *him*.

7 And it was about the space of three hours after, when his wife, not knowing what was done, came in.

8 And Peter answered unto her, Tell me whether ye sold the land for so much? And she said, Yea, for so much.

9 Then Peter said unto her, How is it that ye have agreed together to tempt the Spirit of the Lord? behold, the feet of them which have buried thy husband *are* at the door, and shall carry thee out.

10 Then fell she down straightway at his feet, and yielded up the ghost: and the young men came in, and found her dead, and, carrying *her* forth, buried *her* by her husband.

11 And great fear came upon all the church, and upon as many as heard these things.

12 ¶ And by the hands of the apostles were many signs and wonders wrought among the people; (and they were all with one accord in Solomon's porch.

13 And of the rest durst no man join himself to them: but the people magnified them.

14 And believers were the more added to the Lord, multitudes both of men and women.)

15 Insomuch that they brought forth the sick into the streets, and laid *them* on beds and couches, that at the least the shadow of Peter passing by might overshadow some of them.

16 There came also a multitude *out* of the cities round about unto Jerusalem, bringing sick folks, and them which were vexed with unclean spirits: and they were healed every one.

17 ¶ Then the high priest rose up, and all they that were with him, (which is the sect of the Sadducees,) and were filled with indignation,

18 And laid their hands on the apostles, and put them in the common prison.

19 But the angel of the Lord by night opened the prison doors, and brought them forth, and said,

20 Go, stand and speak in the temple to the people all the words of this life.

21 And when they heard *that*, they entered into the temple early in the morning, and taught. But the high priest came, and they that were with him, and called the council together, and all the senate of the children of Israel, and sent to the prison to have them brought.

22 But when the officers came, and found them not in the prison, they returned, and told,

23 Saying, The prison truly found we shut with all safety, and the keepers standing without before the doors: but when we had opened, we found no man within.

24 Now when the high priest and the captain of the temple and the chief priests heard these things, they doubted of them whereunto this would grow.

25 Then came one and told them, saying, Behold, the men whom ye put in prison are standing in the temple, and teaching the people.

26 Then went the captain with the officers, and brought them without violence: for they feared the people, lest they should have been stoned.

27 And when they had brought them, they set *them* before the council: and the high priest asked them,

28 Saying, Did not we straitly command you that ye should not teach in this name? and, behold, ye have filled Jerusalem with your doctrine, and intend to bring this man's blood upon us.

29 ¶ Then Peter and the *other* apostles answered and said, We ought to obey God rather than men.

30 The God of our fathers raised up Jesus, whom ye slew and hanged on a tree.

31 Him hath God exalted with his right hand *to be* a Prince and a Saviour, for to give repentance to Israel, and forgiveness of sins.

32 And we are his witnesses of these things; and *so is* also the Holy Ghost, whom God hath given to them that obey him.

33 ¶ When they heard *that*, they were cut *to the heart*, and took counsel to slay them.

34 Then stood there up one in the council, a

5:5 *gave up the ghost.* Died, or expired (12:23).

5:11 *great fear.* God's judgment of hypocrites in the church produced a healthy reverence for His holiness and a fear of offending Him (9:31; 17:17).

Miracles Performed in the Early Church (5:12–16)

5:12 *by the hands of the apostles.* The Lord worked *signs and wonders* through the apostles to confirm their witness to the world (2:43; Heb. 2:3–4).

5:13–14 *durst no man join . . . but . . . magnified.* God's judgment on Ananias and Sapphira gave public honor to the church but also caused people to fear, preventing them from joining the church simply because it was a popular or novel thing to do. Nevertheless, large numbers *both of men and women* became *believers*.

5:15 *the shadow of Peter . . . might overshadow some.* An unprecedented event, demonstrating the mighty power of God.

The Apostles Suffer Persecution (5:17–42)

5:17–20 *filled with indignation.* The earlier council (4:18,21) that had charged Peter and John to cease speaking in Jesus' name acted again, but God intervened so that persecution could not stop the apostles' public witness to Christ (*stand and speak in the temple*).

5:23 *shut with all safety.* The guards themselves testified to the supernatural intervention of God. *without.* Outside.

5:26 The civil authorities often did use *violence* against people, but they were restrained by fear based on popular approval of the disciples (Luke 20:6,19; 22:2).

5:28 *filled Jerusalem with your doctrine.* The first stage of Jesus' commission was finding fulfillment (1:8). *bring this man's blood upon us.* The council refused to admit their guilt in crucifying Jesus.

5:30 *The God of our fathers.* Peter has not rejected his Jewish roots. The faithful God of the covenant raised Jesus from the

Pharisee, named Gamaliel, a doctor of the law,
had in reputation among all the people, and com-
manded to put the apostles forth a little space;
35 And said unto them, Ye men of Israel, take
heed to yourselves what ye intend to do as touch-
ing these men.
36 For before these days rose up Theudas, boast-
ing himself to be somebody; to whom a number
of men, about four hundred, joined themselves:
who was slain; and all, as many as obeyed him,
were scattered, and brought to nought.
37 After this man rose up Judas of Galilee in the
days of the taxing, and drew away much people
after him: he also perished; and all, *even* as many
as obeyed him, were dispersed.
38 And now I say unto you, Refrain from these
men, and let them alone: for if this counsel or this
work be of men, it will come to nought:
39 But if it be of God, ye cannot overthrow it; lest
haply ye be found even to fight against God.
40 And to him they agreed: and when they
had called the apostles, and beaten *them*, they
commanded that they should not speak in the
name of Jesus, and let them go.
41 ¶ And they departed from the presence of the
council, rejoicing that they were counted worthy
to suffer shame for his name.
42 And daily in the temple, and in every house,
they ceased not to teach and preach Jesus Christ.

CHAPTER 6

AND in those days, when the number of the disci-
ples was multiplied, there arose a murmuring of
the Grecians against the Hebrews, because their
widows were neglected in the daily ministration.
2 Then the twelve called the multitude of the
disciples *unto them*, and said, It is not reason that
we should leave the word of God, and serve tables.
3 Wherefore, brethren, look ye out among you
seven men of honest report, full of the Holy
Ghost and wisdom, whom we may appoint over
this business.
4 But we will give ourselves continually to prayer,
and to the ministry of the word.
5 ¶ And the saying pleased the whole multitude:
and they chose Stephen, a man full of faith and of
the Holy Ghost, and Philip, and Prochorus, and
Nicanor, and Timon, and Parmenas, and Nicolas
a proselyte of Antioch:

---

dead (3:13). *whom ye slew.* Peter does not shrink back from asserting the accusation that the council attempted to deny.

5:34 *Gamaliel.* The only rabbi mentioned in Acts, a prominent and highly esteemed teacher who had instructed Paul (22:3). *put the apostles forth a little space.* Prudently sent them outside for a short time so that they might confer behind closed doors.

5:36–37 *Theudas.* The identity of this man is not known with certainty, but he may have been a rebel under the reign of Herod the Great at around 4 BC. *taxing.* Census taking (c. AD 6). *nought.* Nothing (v. 38). The movements seemed significant for a while but failed.

5:38–39 *if it be of God.* Luke uses Gamaliel's logic to showcase the gospel's advance under persecution in order to confirm that God's power supported it (Phil. 1:28). *lest haply.* In case it should happen that.

5:40 *speak in the name of Jesus.* See note at 2:38.

5:41 *rejoicing . . . counted worthy to suffer.* A remarkable response, consistent with Jesus' teaching (Luke 6:22–23) but possible only by the Holy Spirit.

5:42 *daily.* The apostles lost no time in going back to diligently *teach and preach Jesus Christ*, whether in public meetings (the *temple*) or in smaller groups (*every house*).

Thoughts for Personal/Family Worship: Chapter 5

1. **Satan wages war at the level of our hearts, seeking to fill the thoughts and affections of people with greed, deceit, and hypocrisy (v. 3). Yet sinners cannot excuse themselves by saying that the Devil made them do it. Ananias and Sapphira "conceived this thing" in their hearts (v. 4). As a result God rightly judged them for putting on a false show of righteousness. How should this event teach us to fear the Lord?**
2. **The apostles preached "the words of . . . life" (v. 20). The message of the gospel is powerful, saving, and effectual when blessed by the Holy Spirit. God uses preaching to bring the spiritually dead soul to life and to increase Christ's life in the believing soul. How should this affect the way we come to read or hear the Word? How should this motivate us to speak it to others who do not yet believe?**
3. **We naturally shrink back from suffering, and nowhere does the Bible tell us to choose suffering for its own sake. However, if doing the right thing brings suffering, we should not shrink back but learn from the apostles to see our suffering as a privilege in light of God's purpose (v. 41). Why did they rejoice?**

Chapter 6: ***The apostles appoint deacons to assist them in order that the poor might receive help without diverting the apostles from their central tasks, and one of the deacons, Stephen, is falsely accused.***

Deacons Appointed to Help the Elders (6:1–7)

6:1 *Grecians . . . Hebrews.* Greek-speaking people versus Hebrew-speaking people. Most of them were either Jews or proselytes. *ministration.* Service of charity.

6:2 *twelve called the multitude of the disciples.* The apostles exercised authority in the new community, even in administrative details. *leave the word of God, and serve tables.* Though distributing food to the poor was an important ministry, the apostles would not allow it to divert them from their calling.

6:3 *men of honest report.* Men whose good reputation was confirmed by testimony. *full of the Holy Ghost and wisdom.* Even those administrating the practical ministry of the church must manifest gifts of the Holy Spirit, particularly *wisdom* (v. 10; Ex. 28:3; 31:3; 35:31; Deut. 34:9; Isa. 11:2; Luke 2:40; Eph. 1:17). *we may appoint.* The apostles take the initiative to appoint, though the people are to elect the seven individuals.

6:4 The responsibilities of apostles (and also pastors) can be summarized under two heads: *prayer* (literally, "the prayers," set times of prayer, including public meetings for prayer and worship; 1:14; 2:42; 3:1) and *the ministry of the word* (publicly and privately; 5:42; 20:20).

6 Whom they set before the apostles: and when
they had prayed, they laid *their* hands on them.
7 And the word of God increased; and the
number of the disciples multiplied in Jerusalem
greatly; and a great company of the priests were
obedient to the faith.
8 And Stephen, full of faith and power, did great
wonders and miracles among the people.
9 ¶ Then there arose certain of the synagogue,
which is called *the synagogue* of the Libertines,
and Cyrenians, and Alexandrians, and of them of
Cilicia and of Asia, disputing with Stephen.
10 And they were not able to resist the wisdom
and the spirit by which he spake.
11 Then they suborned men, which said, We have
heard him speak blasphemous words against
Moses, and *against* God.
12 And they stirred up the people, and the elders,
and the scribes, and came upon *him*, and caught
him, and brought *him* to the council,
13 And set up false witnesses, which said, This
man ceaseth not to speak blasphemous words
against this holy place, and the law:
14 For we have heard him say, that this Jesus of
Nazareth shall destroy this place, and shall change
the customs which Moses delivered us.
15 And all that sat in the council, looking sted-
fastly on him, saw his face as it had been the face
of an angel.

CHAPTER 7

THEN said the high priest, Are these things so?
2 And he said, Men, brethren, and fathers,
hearken; The God of glory appeared unto our
father Abraham, when he was in Mesopotamia,
before he dwelt in Charran,
3 And said unto him, Get thee out of thy coun-
try, and from thy kindred, and come into the land
which I shall shew thee.
4 Then came he out of the land of the Chaldaeans,
and dwelt in Charran: and from thence, when his
father was dead, he removed him into this land,
wherein ye now dwell.
5 And he gave him none inheritance in it, no, not
so much as to set his foot on: yet he promised that
he would give it to him for a possession, and to his
seed after him, when *as yet* he had no child.
6 And God spake on this wise, That his seed
should sojourn in a strange land; and that they
should bring them into bondage, and entreat
them evil four hundred years.
7 And the nation to whom they shall be in bond-
age will I judge, said God: and after that shall they
come forth, and serve me in this place.
8 And he gave him the covenant of circumcision:
and so *Abraham* begat Isaac, and circumcised him
the eighth day; and Isaac *begat* Jacob; and Jacob
begat the twelve patriarchs.
9 And the patriarchs, moved with envy, sold

6:5 *proselyte.* A Gentile converted to join Israel in worshiping the true God.
6:6 *laid their hands on them.* Symbolically, the apostles commissioned the deacons with the authority to carry out this ministry and blessed their labors with fruit.
6:7 *the word of God increased . . . multiplied.* The language of creation flourishing under God's blessing and covenant grace (Gen. 1:22,28; 8:17; 9:1,7; 35:11; 48:4). This is a summary (9:31; 12:24; 19:20), marking a transition from the earliest stage of the apostles' work in Jerusalem (5:28) to the spread of the gospel beyond Jerusalem (1:8).

In Judaea, Galilee, and Samaria (6:8—9:31)

Stephen's Martyrdom (6:8—7:60)

6:8 *Stephen.* One of the deacons (vv. 3–6). *full of faith and power.* By the Holy Spirit (vv. 3,10).
6:9 *Libertines.* Freed slaves. Up to this point in Acts, it has been only the leaders in the temple who have frowned on the work of the early Christians. Now, however, the rift between the early church and the *synagogue* begins to grow.
6:10 *resist the wisdom and the spirit.* The Lord Jesus gave His servant the power of the Holy Spirit to proclaim the gospel in such a way that no one could refute him (Luke 21:12–15).
6:11 *suborned.* Secretly brought in, here false witnesses by prior arrangement (v. 13; 1 Kings 21:10).

Thoughts for Personal/Family Worship: Chapter 6

1. **The apostles discerned the temptation we all face to be distracted from our main callings. Satan bombards us with distractions, because he knows we will be far less effective if we are preoccupied with many other things. Every Christian needs wisdom from God to discern his calling so that he can devote himself to it with dedication. Pastors in particular need humility and wisdom to delegate tasks to others.**
2. **What a mercy it was that "a great company of the priests were obedient to the faith" (v. 7). They had served and ministered in the types and shadows of the old sanctuary. But now, not only had the physical veil been torn but the spiritual veil over their hearts had also been rent, and by faith they submitted to the righteousness of God in Jesus Christ. Why was their conversion a surprise (4:1–2)? How does it demonstrate the power of Christ?**
3. **Stephen was "full of faith and of the Holy Ghost" (v. 5). Though the Holy Spirit is a gift of God, the Bible does command us to seek after the Spirit's work (Luke 11:13) and not to quench (1 Thess. 5:19) or grieve Him (Eph. 4:30). Why do we need the Spirit?**

Chapter 7: *Stephen reviews biblical history to show how God's true cause climaxes in Jesus Christ.*

7:2–50 Stephen briefly summarized the history of Israel, highlighting several types and shadows of Christ, rejected in their day and leading to Israel's rejection of God's ultimate Redeemer, Jesus Christ.
7:2 *Men, brethren, and fathers.* Stephen addressed the angry crowd with respectful titles. *hearken.* Listen. *God of glory.* A reminder that the majestic Lord over all creation cannot be confined to a temple (vv. 48–50; Ps. 29:3,9; cf. Ex. 40:34–35).
7:5 *none inheritance.* Abraham owned nothing in the land but waited upon the promise.
7:6 *seed.* Physical descendants. *sojourn in a strange land.* Dwell in a foreign country.
7:8 *covenant of circumcision.* The covenant that was signified

Joseph into Egypt: but God was with him,
10 And delivered him out of all his afflictions,
and gave him favour and wisdom in the sight of
Pharaoh king of Egypt; and he made him gover-
nor over Egypt and all his house.
11 Now there came a dearth over all the land of
Egypt and Chanaan, and great affliction: and our
fathers found no sustenance.
12 But when Jacob heard that there was corn in
Egypt, he sent out our fathers first.
13 And at the second *time* Joseph was made
known to his brethren; and Joseph's kindred was
made known unto Pharaoh.
14 Then sent Joseph, and called his father Jacob
to *him*, and all his kindred, threescore and fifteen
souls.
15 So Jacob went down into Egypt, and died, he,
and our fathers,
16 And were carried over into Sychem, and laid
in the sepulchre that Abraham bought for a sum
of money of the sons of Emmor *the father* of
Sychem.
17 But when the time of the promise drew nigh,
which God had sworn to Abraham, the people
grew and multiplied in Egypt,
18 Till another king arose, which knew not
Joseph.
19 The same dealt subtilly with our kindred, and
evil entreated our fathers, so that they cast out
their young children, to the end they might not
live.
20 In which time Moses was born, and was ex-
ceeding fair, and nourished up in his father's
house three months:
21 And when he was cast out, Pharaoh's daughter
took him up, and nourished him for her own son.
22 And Moses was learned in all the wisdom of
the Egyptians, and was mighty in words and in
deeds.
23 And when he was full forty years old, it came
into his heart to visit his brethren the children of
Israel.
24 And seeing one *of them* suffer wrong, he de-
fended *him*, and avenged him that was oppressed,
and smote the Egyptian:
25 For he supposed his brethren would have un-
derstood how that God by his hand would deliver
them: but they understood not.
26 And the next day he shewed himself unto
them as they strove, and would have set them at
one again, saying, Sirs, ye are brethren; why do ye
wrong one to another?
27 But he that did his neighbour wrong thrust
him away, saying, Who made thee a ruler and a
judge over us?
28 Wilt thou kill me, as thou diddest the Egyptian
yesterday?
29 Then fled Moses at this saying, and was a
stranger in the land of Madian, where he begat
two sons.
30 And when forty years were expired, there
appeared to him in the wilderness of mount Sina
an angel of the Lord in a flame of fire in a bush.
31 When Moses saw *it*, he wondered at the sight:
and as he drew near to behold *it*, the voice of the
Lord came unto him,
32 *Saying*, I *am* the God of thy fathers, the God
of Abraham, and the God of Isaac, and the God
of Jacob. Then Moses trembled, and durst not
behold.
33 Then said the Lord to him, Put off thy shoes
from thy feet: for the place where thou standest
is holy ground.
34 I have seen, I have seen the affliction of my
people which is in Egypt, and I have heard their
groaning, and am come down to deliver them.
And now come, I will send thee into Egypt.
35 This Moses whom they refused, saying, Who
made thee a ruler and a judge? the same did God
send *to be* a ruler and a deliverer by the hand of
the angel which appeared to him in the bush.
36 He brought them out, after that he had shewed
wonders and signs in the land of Egypt, and in the
Red sea, and in the wilderness forty years.
37 ¶ This is that Moses, which said unto the
children of Israel, A prophet shall the Lord your
God raise up unto you of your brethren, like unto
me; him shall ye hear.
38 This is he, that was in the church in the wil-
derness with the angel which spake to him in the
mount Sina, and *with* our fathers: who received
the lively oracles to give unto us:

---

and sealed by circumcision (Gen. 17). So close were the sign and the promises that they are at times interchangeable in scriptural language. *begat.* Became the father of. *Isaac . . . Jacob . . . patriarchs.* See Gen. 21:1–2; 25:26; 29:31—30:24; 35:16–18).

7:9 *patriarchs, moved with envy.* Abraham's seed proved itself sinful, rejecting His appointed leader (Gen. 37:1–36). *God was with him.* Despite Israel's sin, God's presence did not leave His chosen servant (10:38; Gen. 39:2–3,21,23).

7:17–29 See Ex. 1–2.

7:17 *promise . . . sworn to Abraham.* See vv. 6–7. *nigh.* Near.

7:19 *dealt subtilly with.* Craftily took advantage of. *evil entreated.* Mistreated.

7:30 *angel of the Lord.* Often in the Old Testament, the Lord who is sent by the Lord, the preincarnate Christ, who revealed Himself at decisive times to rescue His people (Ex. 3:1–6).

7:34 *seen the affliction of my people.* Christ is near to His people in their suffering in a personal and compassionate manner (9:4).

7:35 The people of Israel *refused* to have Moses deliver them (v. 25), just as the present generation was refusing to allow Jesus to save them.

7:37 *prophet . . . like unto me.* Moses was a type of Christ, the final Prophet (3:22; Deut. 18:15).

7:38 The *church* did not begin in ch. 2 but was present already in the *wilderness* during Israel's exodus. The Greek

39 To whom our fathers would not obey, but
thrust *him* from them, and in their hearts turned
back again into Egypt,
40 Saying unto Aaron, Make us gods to go before
us: for *as for* this Moses, which brought us out of
the land of Egypt, we wot not what is become of
him.
41 And they made a calf in those days, and offered sacrifice unto the idol, and rejoiced in the
works of their own hands.
42 Then God turned, and gave them up to
worship the host of heaven; as it is written in the
book of the prophets, O ye house of Israel, have
ye offered to me slain beasts and sacrifices *by the
space of* forty years in the wilderness?
43 Yea, ye took up the tabernacle of Moloch, and
the star of your god Remphan, figures which ye
made to worship them: and I will carry you away
beyond Babylon.
44 Our fathers had the tabernacle of witness in
the wilderness, as he had appointed, speaking
unto Moses, that he should make it according to
the fashion that he had seen.
45 Which also our fathers that came after brought
in with Jesus into the possession of the Gentiles,
whom God drave out before the face of our
fathers, unto the days of David;
46 Who found favour before God, and desired to
find a tabernacle for the God of Jacob.
47 But Solomon built him an house.
48 Howbeit the most High dwelleth not in
temples made with hands; as saith the prophet,
49 Heaven *is* my throne, and earth *is* my footstool: what house will ye build me? saith the Lord:
or what *is* the place of my rest?
50 Hath not my hand made all these things?
51 ¶ Ye stiffnecked and uncircumcised in heart
and ears, ye do always resist the Holy Ghost: as
your fathers *did*, so *do* ye.
52 Which of the prophets have not your fathers
persecuted? and they have slain them which
shewed before of the coming of the Just One;
of whom ye have been now the betrayers and
murderers:
53 Who have received the law by the disposition
of angels, and have not kept *it*.
54 ¶ When they heard these things, they were cut
to the heart, and they gnashed on him with *their*
teeth.
55 But he, being full of the Holy Ghost, looked up
stedfastly into heaven, and saw the glory of God,
and Jesus standing on the right hand of God,
56 And said, Behold, I see the heavens opened,
and the Son of man standing on the right hand
of God.
57 Then they cried out with a loud voice, and
stopped their ears, and ran upon him with one
accord,
58 And cast *him* out of the city, and stoned *him*:
and the witnesses laid down their clothes at a
young man's feet, whose name was Saul.
59 And they stoned Stephen, calling upon *God*,
and saying, Lord Jesus, receive my spirit.
60 And he kneeled down, and cried with a loud
voice, Lord, lay not this sin to their charge. And
when he had said this, he fell asleep.

word translated *church* in the New Testament is the same as that used in the Greek translation of the Old Testament for the assembly or congregation of Israel.

7:39 *turned back again into Egypt.* Just as the people in the wilderness had rejected God's leader and promised inheritance, so many of the Jews in Stephen's day were turning from Jesus to go back to the bondage of human legalism, tradition, and ceremony.

7:40–41 *wot.* Know. *Make us gods . . . a calf.* See Ex. 32.

7:42–43 *gave them up to worship the host of heaven.* Idolatry, like relying on the stars, is not only a sin but serves as God's judgment against the people who reject Him (Rom. 1:18–32). *as it is written.* Citing Amos 5:25–27.

7:44 *tabernacle of witness.* The tent of meeting, where God dwelled with His people (Ex. 25:9).

7:45–47 *Jesus.* A Greek form of the name "Joshua." *drave.* Drove. *found favour before God.* God commended David for his honorable desire to build a more permanent dwelling place (*tabernacle*) for God's presence, *but Solomon* was the king authorized to build the temple (*house*; 2 Sam. 7:1–29). Stephen was contrasting them with those to whom he was speaking here.

7:48 *dwelleth not in temples.* See 17:24; 1 Kings 8:27.

7:49–50 *Heaven is my throne.* The God of glory (v. 2) is so great that no temple can contain Him, for He created all things, and so religion is not about buildings but about humility (Isa. 66:1–2).

7:51–52 *stiffnecked and uncircumcised in heart and ears.* Stephen accused his listeners of being stubborn and rebellious against God's covenant Word, as had been Old Testament Israel (Lev. 26:41; Deut. 10:16; 30:6). *resist the Holy Ghost.* They rejected the words the Holy Spirit had given His *prophets* and apostles (2 Kings 17:13–14; Isa. 63:10) and murdered God's Righteous (*Just*) One, Jesus, thus rejecting all three Persons of the Godhead.

7:53 *disposition.* Arrangement, ordinance. *have not kept it.* Though claiming to be zealous for God's *law* (6:13–14), they broke His commandments.

7:54 *gnashed . . . teeth.* An expression for rage (Ps. 37:12).

7:55 *the glory of God.* Stephen's sermon began with "the God of glory" (v. 2), and Luke now identifies this God with the ascended and enthroned Lord *Jesus.* Thus the true temple is the presence of Christ. *right hand.* See note at 2:32–33.

7:57 *one accord.* The people, in unity with each other, rejected Stephen's message and their opportunity to repent and instead conspired together to kill him.

7:58 *Saul.* Paul is introduced for the first time as a *young man* presiding over the stoning of Stephen. Thus Stephen's martyrdom serves to connect the opening chapters of Acts with the narrative of Paul's mission.

7:59–60 *receive my spirit . . . lay not this sin to their charge.* Stephen died (*fell asleep*) in Christ-like love for his enemies and submission to God by faith in the *Lord Jesus* (Luke 23:34,46).

Thoughts for Personal/Family Worship: Chapter 7

1. Note that Stephen opens his speech saying, "The God of

CHAPTER 8

AND Saul was consenting unto his death. And at
that time there was a great persecution against
the church which was at Jerusalem; and they were
all scattered abroad throughout the regions of
Judaea and Samaria, except the apostles.
2 And devout men carried Stephen *to his burial*,
and made great lamentation over him.
3 As for Saul, he made havock of the church,
entering into every house, and haling men and
women committed *them* to prison.
4 Therefore they that were scattered abroad went
every where preaching the word.
5 Then Philip went down to the city of Samaria,
and preached Christ unto them.
6 And the people with one accord gave heed unto
those things which Philip spake, hearing and see-
ing the miracles which he did.
7 For unclean spirits, crying with loud voice,
came out of many that were possessed *with them*:
and many taken with palsies, and that were lame,
were healed.
8 And there was great joy in that city.
9 But there was a certain man, called Simon,
which beforetime in the same city used sorcery,
and bewitched the people of Samaria, giving out
that himself was some great one:
10 To whom they all gave heed, from the least to
the greatest, saying, This man is the great power
of God.
11 And to him they had regard, because that of
long time he had bewitched them with sorceries.
12 But when they believed Philip preaching the
things concerning the kingdom of God, and the
name of Jesus Christ, they were baptized, both
men and women.
13 Then Simon himself believed also: and when
he was baptized, he continued with Philip, and
wondered, beholding the miracles and signs which
were done.
14 Now when the apostles which were at Jerusa-
lem heard that Samaria had received the word of
God, they sent unto them Peter and John:
15 Who, when they were come down, prayed for
them, that they might receive the Holy Ghost:
16 (For as yet he was fallen upon none of them:
only they were baptized in the name of the Lord
Jesus.)
17 Then laid they *their* hands on them, and they
received the Holy Ghost.
18 And when Simon saw that through laying on
of the apostles' hands the Holy Ghost was given,
he offered them money,
19 Saying, Give me also this power, that on

---

glory appeared unto our father Abraham" (v. 2). Likewise his speech ends by noting that he "saw the glory of God, and Jesus standing on the right hand of God" (v. 55). Stephen's eyes have been opened to the glory of God in the face of Jesus Christ, as revealed throughout Scripture. What does it mean to read the Bible in such a way as to see God's glory in the face of Christ?

2. **Spiritual privileges do not necessarily equate to spiritual possession. Israel was privileged in many ways. When they considered this the equivalent of being God's special possession they deceived themselves, and God punished them by giving them up to idolatry (v. 42). Though they had the Word of God and the external form of His worship, they were "uncircumcised in heart and ears" (v. 51). How should this danger move us to pray for God's work within our hearts?**

Chapter 8: *Saul and others were persecuting the church so that many were forced to scatter, taking the Word wherever they went, resulting in conversions in Samaria and of a man from as far away as Ethiopia.*

Saul's Persecution Introduced (8:1–3)

8:1 *Saul.* See 7:58. *scattered.* A verb of the same root as that used for sowing seed. *abroad.* Over a wide area. God used this dispersion of the church in Jerusalem to bring the gospel to other nations (v. 4). *except the apostles.* The church's leaders stayed behind, endured the persecution, and served as the means of preserving a large church in Jerusalem (15:4; 21:20).

8:3 *made havock.* Humiliated, devastated. *haling.* Dragging. Saul was bent on destroying the church of God (9:1; 22:4; 26:9–11; 1 Cor. 15:9; Gal. 1:13).

Philip's Ministry (8:4–40)

8:5 *Philip.* Almost certainly the man appointed a deacon (6:5), not the apostle (1:13), because the apostles remained in Jerusalem (v. 1) and later sent Peter and John to the Samaritans (v. 14). *Samaria.* The Samaritans and the Jews despised each other (John 4:9). The Lord Jesus was executing the next phase of His promise about the witness of His disciples (1:8).

8:6 In Acts most of the *miracles* performed were by the apostles, but these signs confirmed the divine truth of the gospel (Mark 16:20) as it reached the Samaritans for the first time since Christ died (John 4:1–42).

8:8 *great joy.* The Greek word translated *great* appears eight times in vv. 1–13, contrasting the "great persecution," the "great lamentation" of the church (vv. 1–2), and the "great power" of Satan (v. 10) over against the "great powers" exercised by God to heal and deliver (v. 13) and the *great joy* among those who believed in Jesus. Greater is He who is in us than he who is in the world (1 John 4:4).

8:10 *gave heed.* Paid attention. *great power of God.* Simon the sorcerer performed counterfeit miracles and led people astray.

8:11 *bewitched them with sorceries.* Amazed them with magical powers or knowledge.

8:13 *Simon himself believed.* This was not true faith but temporary belief (John 6:66). *miracles and signs.* Literally, "signs and great powers."

8:14 *apostles . . . sent unto them Peter and John.* The church later sent a similar delegation to the converts in Antioch (11:22–24).

8:15–16 *that they might receive the Holy Ghost.* The first act of faith comes from the Holy Spirit (1 Cor. 12:3), but He had not yet come in His fullness and evident power (1:8). *only they were baptized.* This is plainly an irregular experience, for it does not fit Peter's promise (2:38).

8:17 *laid they their hands on them.* God normally gives the Spirit through the hearing of the gospel with faith (10:44; 11:17; 15:8–9; Gal. 3:2), but God chose to give the Spirit to the Samari-

whomsoever I lay hands, he may receive the Holy
Ghost.
20 But Peter said unto him, Thy money perish
with thee, because thou hast thought that the gift
of God may be purchased with money.
21 Thou hast neither part nor lot in this matter:
for thy heart is not right in the sight of God.
22 Repent therefore of this thy wickedness, and
pray God, if perhaps the thought of thine heart
may be forgiven thee.
23 For I perceive that thou art in the gall of bitter-
ness, and *in* the bond of iniquity.
24 Then answered Simon, and said, Pray ye to the
Lord for me, that none of these things which ye
have spoken come upon me.
25 And they, when they had testified and preached
the word of the Lord, returned to Jerusalem,
and preached the gospel in many villages of the
Samaritans.
26 And the angel of the Lord spake unto Philip,
saying, Arise, and go toward the south unto the
way that goeth down from Jerusalem unto Gaza,
which is desert.
27 And he arose and went: and, behold, a man
of Ethiopia, an eunuch of great authority under
Candace queen of the Ethiopians, who had the
charge of all her treasure, and had come to Jeru-
salem for to worship,
28 Was returning, and sitting in his chariot read
Esaias the prophet.
29 Then the Spirit said unto Philip, Go near, and
join thyself to this chariot.
30 And Philip ran thither to *him*, and heard him
read the prophet Esaias, and said, Understandest
thou what thou readest?
31 And he said, How can I, except some man
should guide me? And he desired Philip that he
would come up and sit with him.
32 The place of the scripture which he read was
this, He was led as a sheep to the slaughter; and
like a lamb dumb before his shearer, so opened he
not his mouth:
33 In his humiliation his judgment was taken
away: and who shall declare his generation? for
his life is taken from the earth.
34 And the eunuch answered Philip, and said, I
pray thee, of whom speaketh the prophet this? of
himself, or of some other man?
35 Then Philip opened his mouth, and began at
the same scripture, and preached unto him Jesus.
36 And as they went on *their* way, they came unto
a certain water: and the eunuch said, See, *here is*
water; what doth hinder me to be baptized?
37 And Philip said, If thou believest with all thine
heart, thou mayest. And he answered and said, I
believe that Jesus Christ is the Son of God.
38 And he commanded the chariot to stand still:
and they went down both into the water, both
Philip and the eunuch; and he baptized him.
39 And when they were come up out of the water,
the Spirit of the Lord caught away Philip, that the
eunuch saw him no more: and he went on his way
rejoicing.
40 But Philip was found at Azotus: and passing
through he preached in all the cities, till he came
to Caesarea.

---

tans through this means, probably to build a strong connection between the Jewish apostles and the Samaritan believers.

8:18 *offered them money.* It was not uncommon in New Testament times to offer money for a high status or ability, especially in religious cults. Paying for religious position is known today as simony.

8:24 *Pray ye to the Lord for me.* The exact intentions of Simon are not given to us. Considering the context, it is probable that Simon refused to repent.

8:25 *many villages.* The apostles sought to take the gospel to the small towns, not just the larger cities (Luke 8:1).

8:26 *angel of the Lord spake . . . Arise.* Luke compares Philip to the prophet Elijah (2 Kings 1:3; see note at v. 39).

8:27 *Ethiopia.* The land south of Egypt (also called Cush) in present day Sudan. *eunuch.* Sometimes just an official title, but likely a man rendered unable to father children and thus excluded from old covenant worship (Deut. 23:1; Isa. 56:3–5). *Candace.* A title for royalty in Ethiopia.

8:28 *read.* He had a (rare) scroll of the Scriptures. *Esaias.* Isaiah.

8:32–33 *as a sheep to the slaughter.* Citing Isa. 53:7–8, the prophecy of the Suffering Servant, another example of how the Scriptures speak of Jesus Christ (Luke 22:37; 24:44).

8:35 *preached unto him Jesus.* Proclaimed the good news about Jesus.

8:39 *the Spirit of the Lord caught away Philip.* A similar experience to that ascribed to the prophet Elijah (1 Kings 18:12; 2 Kings 2:16; see note at v. 26). *and he went on his way rejoicing.* Some scholars note that Ethiopia was seen as the outer fringes of the known world, and so the gospel was already beginning to go to the ends of the earth (1:8).

8:40 *Azotus.* The Old Testament city of Ashdod (Isa. 20:1), quite a distance from Gaza. *Caesarea.* Philip apparently settled there (21:8).

Thoughts for Personal/Family Worship: Chapter 8

1. **Many of us carry a great fear of persecution and death. The deaths of the martyrs should grieve believers (v. 2), and it is certainly not wrong to flee from persecution unless duty requires one to stay (v. 4). However, we must remember that those killed for Christ are immediately welcomed by Christ into glory (7:54–56). In fact, the persecution that people like Saul meant for evil God meant for good, to spread the gospel far and wide, even to Ethiopia. How does this chapter teach us to pray about persecution?**
2. **Though the gospel was blessed in Samaria so that many were saved, Simon shows that not every seeming conversion is real. Proper procedures of discipline must function to ensure that those who are hypocrites be unmasked and, if they refuse to repent, excluded from the membership of the church. Why can we not presume that all apparent converts are saved, even when God works powerfully in a place?**

CHAPTER 9

AND Saul, yet breathing out threatenings and
slaughter against the disciples of the Lord, went
unto the high priest,
2 And desired of him letters to Damascus to
the synagogues, that if he found any of this way,
whether they were men or women, he might
bring them bound unto Jerusalem.
3 And as he journeyed, he came near Damascus:
and suddenly there shined round about him a
light from heaven:
4 And he fell to the earth, and heard a voice saying
unto him, Saul, Saul, why persecutest thou me?
5 And he said, Who art thou, Lord? And the Lord
said, I am Jesus whom thou persecutest: *it is* hard
for thee to kick against the pricks.
6 And he trembling and astonished said, Lord,
what wilt thou have me to do? And the Lord *said*
unto him, Arise, and go into the city, and it shall
be told thee what thou must do.
7 And the men which journeyed with him stood
speechless, hearing a voice, but seeing no man.
8 And Saul arose from the earth; and when his
eyes were opened, he saw no man: but they led
him by the hand, and brought *him* into Damascus.
9 And he was three days without sight, and
neither did eat nor drink.
10 ¶ And there was a certain disciple at Damas-
cus, named Ananias; and to him said the Lord in
a vision, Ananias. And he said, Behold, I *am here*,
Lord.
11 And the Lord *said* unto him, Arise, and go into
the street which is called Straight, and enquire in
the house of Judas for *one* called Saul, of Tarsus:
for, behold, he prayeth,
12 And hath seen in a vision a man named Ana-
nias coming in, and putting *his* hand on him, that
he might receive his sight.
13 Then Ananias answered, Lord, I have heard by
many of this man, how much evil he hath done to
thy saints at Jerusalem:
14 And here he hath authority from the chief
priests to bind all that call on thy name.
15 But the Lord said unto him, Go thy way: for
he is a chosen vessel unto me, to bear my name
before the Gentiles, and kings, and the children
of Israel:
16 For I will shew him how great things he must
suffer for my name's sake.
17 And Ananias went his way, and entered into
the house; and putting his hands on him said,
Brother Saul, the Lord, *even* Jesus, that appeared
unto thee in the way as thou camest, hath sent me,
that thou mightest receive thy sight, and be filled
with the Holy Ghost.
18 And immediately there fell from his eyes as it
had been scales: and he received sight forthwith,
and arose, and was baptized.
19 And when he had received meat, he was
strengthened. Then was Saul certain days with the
disciples which were at Damascus.
20 And straightway he preached Christ in the
synagogues, that he is the Son of God.
21 But all that heard *him* were amazed, and said;
Is not this he that destroyed them which called on
this name in Jerusalem, and came hither for that
intent, that he might bring them bound unto the
chief priests?

Chapter 9: ***Christ appears to Saul of Tarsus, converts him, and shows His power by making him a preacher of the gospel with a weighty task, while Peter continues ministering near the coast.***

Saul's Conversion and Beginning of Ministry (9:1–31)

9:1 *Saul.* See 8:1–3.

9:2 *Damascus.* An ancient city of Syria, perhaps reached by the gospel through people converted at Pentecost (2:5). *way.* Road or path, an early title given to Christianity or discipleship to Jesus (16:17; 18:25–26; 19:9,23; 22:4; 24:14,22).

9:3–22 Luke includes the conversion account of Paul three times (22:3–16; 26:4–18).

9:3 *light from heaven.* Paul's conversion began with a vision of God's glory in Christ, as Stephen's life ended (7:56), also reminiscent of a prophetic commission (Isa. 6:1–13; Ezek. 1:1–28).

9:4 *Saul, Saul.* Jesus addressed him directly and emphatically. *Why persecutest thou me?* Jesus so closely identifies Himself with His people that their persecution is persecution of Jesus.

9:5–6 *Lord . . . Lord.* Saul was compelled to recognize that the *Jesus* whom they had crucified is the Lord of glory (1 Cor. 2:8). *pricks.* Goads used for driving cattle. Saul was like an animal fighting ferociously against Christ's gospel and church, but Christ brought him to his knees.

9:8–12 *three days without sight.* Saul's blindness and Christ's appearance to *Ananias* both confirmed that his experience of Jesus on the road had been real. His physical blindness may also symbolize his former spiritual blindness to the glory of Christ (2 Cor. 4:4).

9:13 *saints.* Literally, "holy ones," a reference to God's people in general (vv. 32,41; 26:10).

9:15 *chosen vessel.* God had set him apart before he was born to be a Christian and an apostle (Gal. 1:1,15). *bear my name.* Preach Christ's glory in the gospel (2 Cor. 4:5; see note at 2:38). *before the Gentiles*. Paul's personal mission fits into the overall mission of the apostles (1:8).

9:16 *how great things he must suffer.* While Saul once persecuted the church, God's call to be an apostle will result in great persecution for Saul (vv. 24,29; Eph. 3:1,13).

9:17 *Brother Saul.* Ananias trusted the word of the Lord and upon finding Saul called him by a term of endearment and communion. *filled with the Holy Ghost.* Empowered by the Holy Spirit to serve Christ (vv. 20,22; see note at 2:4).

9:19 *received meat.* Eaten food (of any kind).

9:20 *straightway he preached Christ.* Saul wasted no time in turning from his persecuting ways to proclaiming the gospel to his fellow Jews. *synagogues.* It was a custom in New Testament times for rabbis and teachers to travel to synagogues and teach the people, just as Jesus had done (Luke 4:15). *the Son of God.* He declared Jesus' divinity as the heavenly Lord (see note at Luke 1:32).

9:22 *increased the more in strength.* Not physical strength,

22 But Saul increased the more in strength, and
confounded the Jews which dwelt at Damascus,
proving that this is very Christ.
23 ¶ And after that many days were fulfilled, the
Jews took counsel to kill him:
24 But their laying await was known of Saul. And
they watched the gates day and night to kill him.
25 Then the disciples took him by night, and let
him down by the wall in a basket.
26 And when Saul was come to Jerusalem, he
assayed to join himself to the disciples: but they
were all afraid of him, and believed not that he
was a disciple.
27 But Barnabas took him, and brought *him* to
the apostles, and declared unto them how he
had seen the Lord in the way, and that he had
spoken to him, and how he had preached boldly
at Damascus in the name of Jesus.
28 And he was with them coming in and going
out at Jerusalem.
29 And he spake boldly in the name of the Lord
Jesus, and disputed against the Grecians: but they
went about to slay him.
30 *Which* when the brethren knew, they brought
him down to Caesarea, and sent him forth to
Tarsus.
31 Then had the churches rest throughout all
Judaea and Galilee and Samaria, and were edified;
and walking in the fear of the Lord, and in the
comfort of the Holy Ghost, were multiplied.
32 ¶ And it came to pass, as Peter passed through-
out all *quarters*, he came down also to the saints
which dwelt at Lydda.
33 And there he found a certain man named
Aeneas, which had kept his bed eight years, and
was sick of the palsy.
34 And Peter said unto him, Aeneas, Jesus Christ
maketh thee whole: arise, and make thy bed. And
he arose immediately.
35 And all that dwelt at Lydda and Saron saw him,
and turned to the Lord.
36 ¶ Now there was at Joppa a certain disciple
named Tabitha, which by interpretation is called
Dorcas: this woman was full of good works and
almsdeeds which she did.
37 And it came to pass in those days, that she was
sick, and died: whom when they had washed, they
laid *her* in an upper chamber.
38 And forasmuch as Lydda was nigh to Joppa,
and the disciples had heard that Peter was there,
they sent unto him two men, desiring *him* that he
would not delay to come to them.
39 Then Peter arose and went with them. When
he was come, they brought him into the upper
chamber: and all the widows stood by him weep-
ing, and shewing the coats and garments which
Dorcas made, while she was with them.
40 But Peter put them all forth, and kneeled
down, and prayed; and turning *him* to the body
said, Tabitha, arise. And she opened her eyes: and
when she saw Peter, she sat up.
41 And he gave her *his* hand, and lifted her up,
and when he had called the saints and widows,
presented her alive.
42 And it was known throughout all Joppa; and
many believed in the Lord.
43 And it came to pass, that he tarried many days
in Joppa with one Simon a tanner.

---

but intellectual and spiritual power to proclaim and defend the gospel. *very Christ.* Literally, "the Christ," a title meaning "anointed" (10:38; see note at Luke 2:11).

9:26 *assayed.* Tried, attempted.

9:27 *Barnabas.* Living up to his name, the "son of consolation" or "encouragement" (4:36–37) again showed his loving character by testifying of Saul's true conversion.

9:29 *Grecians.* Greek-speaking Jews. *to slay him.* Paul had become the target of the same wrath that had once possessed him (v. 1).

9:30 *Caesarea.* A large city, key to the continuing mission. *Tarsus.* Saul's hometown (v. 11).

9:31 *rest.* Literally, "peace," a season of stability and strength despite some ongoing persecution. *edified.* Built up, like a construction of the temple. *fear of the Lord . . . comfort of the Holy Ghost.* The triune God caused the church to flourish in godly reverence and inward strength. *multiplied.* See note at 6:7.

In the Mediterranean (9:32—12:24)

Peter Performs Two Miracles (9:32–43)

9:32 Luke transitions back again to *Peter*, a reminder that Acts is not primarily about Paul, or any individual apostle, but about Jesus' continuing work through the apostles from His exalted place of glory. *Lydda.* A Jewish town on the Mediterranean coast.

9:33 *palsy.* Paralysis.

9:34 *Jesus Christ maketh thee whole.* Peter was simply the instrument by which Jesus worked (3:12–16). *he arose immediately.* Just as Jesus' miracles were immediate and total, so too are the miracles of Acts.

9:35 *all.* Likely "many" or "all kinds" of people. *turned to the Lord.* Repentance, nothing short of a radical turn from a previous course of life to newness of life in Christ (2:38; 3:19).

9:36 *Tabitha . . . Dorcas.* "Gazelle" in Aramaic and Greek. *full of good works and almsdeeds.* A model of goodness and mercy, especially to poor widows (v. 39).

9:38 *Joppa.* About twelve miles away from Lydda. *not delay to come to them.* Their urgent seeking of Peter from that distance indicates that the miracles he performed were not common even in New Testament times.

9:39 *weeping.* Believers may appropriately grieve the death of a much loved and respected woman like Dorcas (8:2).

9:43 *tarried.* Remained.

Thoughts for Personal/Family Worship: Chapter 9

1. The same glory of Christ that greeted Stephen at his death (7:56) brought Saul to spiritual life (vv. 3–6). Christ is the beginning and the end of all His people's lives. Are you still living for your own glory, or has Christ's glory brought you to look away from yourself to Him? One test is whether you are willing to suffer, and even to die, so that others might see His glory. Paul was a chosen vessel

CHAPTER 10

THERE was a certain man in Caesarea called Cor-
nelius, a centurion of the band called the Italian
band,
2 *A* devout *man*, and one that feared God with all
his house, which gave much alms to the people,
and prayed to God alway.
3 He saw in a vision evidently about the ninth
hour of the day an angel of God coming in to
him, and saying unto him, Cornelius.
4 And when he looked on him, he was afraid, and
said, What is it, Lord? And he said unto him, Thy
prayers and thine alms are come up for a memo-
rial before God.
5 And now send men to Joppa, and call for *one*
Simon, whose surname is Peter:
6 He lodgeth with one Simon a tanner, whose
house is by the sea side: he shall tell thee what
thou oughtest to do.
7 And when the angel which spake unto
Cornelius was departed, he called two of his
household servants, and a devout soldier of them
that waited on him continually;
8 And when he had declared all *these* things unto
them, he sent them to Joppa.
9 ¶ On the morrow, as they went on their jour-
ney, and drew nigh unto the city, Peter went up
upon the housetop to pray about the sixth hour:
10 And he became very hungry, and would have
eaten: but while they made ready, he fell into a
trance,
11 And saw heaven opened, and a certain vessel
descending unto him, as it had been a great sheet
knit at the four corners, and let down to the earth:
12 Wherein were all manner of fourfooted beasts
of the earth, and wild beasts, and creeping things,
and fowls of the air.
13 And there came a voice to him, Rise, Peter; kill,
and eat.
14 But Peter said, Not so, Lord; for I have never
eaten any thing that is common or unclean.
15 And the voice *spake* unto him again the second
time, What God hath cleansed, *that* call not thou
common.
16 This was done thrice: and the vessel was re-
ceived up again into heaven.
17 Now while Peter doubted in himself what this
vision which he had seen should mean, behold,
the men which were sent from Cornelius had
made enquiry for Simon's house, and stood
before the gate,
18 And called, and asked whether Simon, which
was surnamed Peter, were lodged there.
19 ¶ While Peter thought on the vision, the Spirit

specifically marked out by God to suffer for the name of Christ (v. 16). While you may not become a martyr, how willing are you to suffer some degree of insult or anger in order to make known the glory of Jesus Christ to others?

2. **We do not know for how long Saul was kicking against the goads ("pricks," v. 5), but God was using His law in Paul's life to convict him of sin (Rom. 7:7–9), and no doubt Paul had heard the gospel from the very disciples he was persecuting. Are you kicking against God's goads, such as His Word, inner convictions of conscience, and works of providence that call you to Jesus? Why is it foolish to "kick against the pricks"?**
3. **Saul's conversion was so surprising that many doubted it could be real (v. 26). Though a period of testing is good and necessary for new converts (8:18–24), we should have high expectations of what God can do by His grace. What are the dangers of keeping true converts out of the church because of their previous lifestyles of sin?**

Gentiles Receive the Holy Spirit (10:1—11:18)

Chapter 10: *God sends Peter to preach the gospel to Cornelius, a Roman centurion, who is converted with his family and friends and receives the Holy Spirit.*

10:1 *centurion.* Officer in the Roman army. *Cornelius* is not an example of a pagan seeking God through another religion but of a Gentile already somewhat acquainted with the Scriptures of Israel.

10:2 *devout man . . . gave much alms . . . prayed to God.* Cornelius was a moral and religious Gentile man (v. 22), but he needed to be saved through hearing the gospel of Jesus Christ with faith (11:14; cf. 4:12). *feared God.* Not the inward, childlike fear in conjunction with salvation (Ps. 103:17; Jer. 32:40) but language used by the Jews for Gentiles who had not fully submitted to the old covenant laws but still honored the God of Israel (13:16,26). *house.* Household, including servants (v. 7). God was about to open the doors of salvation to the Gentiles (11:18; 14:27).

10:3 *evidently.* Plainly, clearly.

10:4 *come up for a memorial.* God remembered his *prayers* and acts of mercy to the poor (*alms*); that is, the Lord answered them (v. 31). God was not rewarding any merit in him but was leading him to find the only One who could satisfy the hunger God had planted in his heart.

10:6 *oughtest to.* Should. God did not give the gospel to Cornelius by direct revelation or through the angel but used His ordinary means of a preacher from the church (Rom. 10:14–15). By sending a Jew to preach to Gentiles He was tearing down ethnic barriers.

10:9 *housetop.* Often with a flat roof for people to use as another floor. *sixth hour.* 12:00 noon.

10:10 *trance.* A vision from the Lord.

10:11 *heaven opened.* A revelation from the presence of God (7:56; Ezek. 1:1; Luke 3:21).

10:13 *kill, and eat.* The Old Testament ceremonial law prohibited eating the meat of animals classified as ritually unclean (Lev. 11:1–47).

10:14 *Not so, Lord.* Perhaps thinking this a test, Peter expressed his devotion to God's law (Ezek. 4:14).

10:15 *What God hath cleansed.* God released His people to eat all kinds of foods as the Gentiles did (1 Tim. 4:3–5), implying the end of the whole ceremonial law and the unifying of Jew and Gentile in Christ (Eph. 2:11–22).

10:16 *thrice.* The repetition removed any doubt, a necessary emphasis for an unexpected and radically new message (vv. 17,20; cf. Gal. 2:11–16).

10:19–20 *the Spirit said.* The Holy Spirit is not a mere energy

said unto him, Behold, three men seek thee.
20 Arise therefore, and get thee down, and go
with them, doubting nothing: for I have sent
them.
21 Then Peter went down to the men which were
sent unto him from Cornelius; and said, Behold, I
am he whom ye seek: what *is* the cause wherefore
ye are come?
22 And they said, Cornelius the centurion, a
just man, and one that feareth God, and of good
report among all the nation of the Jews, was
warned from God by an holy angel to send for
thee into his house, and to hear words of thee.
23 Then called he them in, and lodged *them*. And
on the morrow Peter went away with them, and
certain brethren from Joppa accompanied him.
24 And the morrow after they entered into Caes-
area. And Cornelius waited for them, and had
called together his kinsmen and near friends.
25 And as Peter was coming in, Cornelius met
him, and fell down at his feet, and worshipped
him.
26 But Peter took him up, saying, Stand up; I
myself also am a man.
27 And as he talked with him, he went in, and
found many that were come together.
28 And he said unto them, Ye know how that it is
an unlawful thing for a man that is a Jew to keep
company, or come unto one of another nation;
but God hath shewed me that I should not call
any man common or unclean.
29 Therefore came I *unto you* without gainsaying,
as soon as I was sent for: I ask therefore for what
intent ye have sent for me?
30 And Cornelius said, Four days ago I was fast-
ing until this hour; and at the ninth hour I prayed
in my house, and, behold, a man stood before me
in bright clothing,
31 And said, Cornelius, thy prayer is heard, and
thine alms are had in remembrance in the sight
of God.
32 Send therefore to Joppa, and call hither Simon,
whose surname is Peter; he is lodged in the house
of *one* Simon a tanner by the sea side: who, when
he cometh, shall speak unto thee.
33 Immediately therefore I sent to thee; and thou
hast well done that thou art come. Now there-
fore are we all here present before God, to hear all
things that are commanded thee of God.
34 ¶ Then Peter opened *his* mouth, and said, Of a
truth I perceive that God is no respecter of persons:
35 But in every nation he that feareth him, and
worketh righteousness, is accepted with him.
36 The word which *God* sent unto the children
of Israel, preaching peace by Jesus Christ: (he is
Lord of all:)
37 That word, *I say*, ye know, which was pub-
lished throughout all Judaea, and began from
Galilee, after the baptism which John preached;
38 How God anointed Jesus of Nazareth with
the Holy Ghost and with power: who went about
doing good, and healing all that were oppressed
of the devil; for God was with him.
39 And we are witnesses of all things which he
did both in the land of the Jews, and in Jerusalem;
whom they slew and hanged on a tree:
40 Him God raised up the third day, and shewed
him openly;
41 Not to all the people, but unto witnesses
chosen before of God, *even* to us, who did eat and
drink with him after he rose from the dead.
42 And he commanded us to preach unto the
people, and to testify that it is he which was or-
dained of God *to be* the Judge of quick and dead.
43 To him give all the prophets witness, that
through his name whosoever believeth in him
shall receive remission of sins.
44 ¶ While Peter yet spake these words, the Holy

---

or force but a divine person who speaks and rules angels and men (*I have sent them*; see 5:3–4; 13:2,4).

10:24 *called together his kinsmen and near friends.* Cornelius calls together his closest associates to hear what Peter has to tell them. He is in great anticipation to learn what God is doing in, for, and through him.

10:25–26 The sight of Peter caused immense reverence in Cornelius (*worshipped*), but Peter responded with great humility, expressing his equality with the Gentile (*I myself also am a man*).

10:34 *God is no respecter of persons.* God shows no favoritism based on ethnic or social differences among people (Rom. 2:11). In a climactic moment in the book of Acts, as well as in redemptive history, the apostle publicly acknowledged that the Jews were no better off than the Gentiles, and vice versa, for all must be saved by God's grace alone (Rom. 3:22–24).

10:35 *in every nation.* God no longer focused His blessings on physical Israel (Ps. 147:19–20). *feareth him . . . righteousness.* The same terminology used of Cornelius's religion and morality (v. 22). Peter was not teaching justification by works, for forgiveness comes only by faith in Christ (v. 43), but was saying that the gospel offers salvation not just to Jews but also to God-fearing Gentiles (see note at v. 2).

10:38 *God anointed Jesus . . . with the Holy Ghost.* An explanation of the title "Christ" or "Anointed One" (Luke 2:11; 3:22; 4:18). All three persons in the Trinity were engaged in Christ's mission. *healing all.* Including some Gentiles (Mark 7:25–30; Luke 6:17; 8:26–39).

10:39–41 *witnesses of all things which he did . . . witnesses chosen before of God.* The commission of the apostles after Christ rose from the dead (1:8,22; Luke 24:48).

10:42–43 *Judge.* The gospel announces both salvation and judgment through Jesus Christ, for He is Lord (17:31). *quick.* Living. *whosoever believeth in him.* Faith in Christ is the only means of salvation for both Jews and Gentiles (1 Peter 2:6–7). Everyone who calls upon the name of the Lord will be saved (2:21). *remission.* Forgiveness, like salvation also obtained only by faith in Christ (13:38–39; 26:18; Luke 5:20).

10:44–46 *the Holy Ghost fell on all them.* The Holy Spirit came upon these Gentile believers in much the same way (*speak*

Ghost fell on all them which heard the word.
45 And they of the circumcision which believed
were astonished, as many as came with Peter,
because that on the Gentiles also was poured out
the gift of the Holy Ghost.
46 For they heard them speak with tongues, and
magnify God. Then answered Peter,
47 Can any man forbid water, that these should
not be baptized, which have received the Holy
Ghost as well as we?
48 And he commanded them to be baptized in
the name of the Lord. Then prayed they him to
tarry certain days.

CHAPTER 11

AND the apostles and brethren that were in Judaea
heard that the Gentiles had also received the word
of God.
2 And when Peter was come up to Jerusalem,
they that were of the circumcision contended
with him,
3 Saying, Thou wentest in to men uncircumcised,
and didst eat with them.
4 But Peter rehearsed *the matter* from the beginning, and expounded *it* by order unto them,
saying,
5 I was in the city of Joppa praying: and in a
trance I saw a vision, A certain vessel descend, as
it had been a great sheet, let down from heaven by
four corners; and it came even to me:
6 Upon the which when I had fastened mine eyes,
I considered, and saw fourfooted beasts of the
earth, and wild beasts, and creeping things, and
fowls of the air.
7 And I heard a voice saying unto me, Arise,
Peter; slay and eat.
8 But I said, Not so, Lord: for nothing common
or unclean hath at any time entered into my
mouth.
9 But the voice answered me again from heaven,
What God hath cleansed, *that* call not thou
common.
10 And this was done three times: and all were
drawn up again into heaven.
11 And, behold, immediately there were three
men already come unto the house where I was,
sent from Caesarea unto me.
12 And the Spirit bade me go with them, nothing
doubting. Moreover these six brethren accompanied me, and we entered into the man's house:
13 And he shewed us how he had seen an angel in
his house, which stood and said unto him, Send
men to Joppa, and call for Simon, whose surname
is Peter;
14 Who shall tell thee words, whereby thou and
all thy house shall be saved.
15 And as I began to speak, the Holy Ghost fell on
them, as on us at the beginning.
16 Then remembered I the word of the Lord, how
that he said, John indeed baptized with water; but
ye shall be baptized with the Holy Ghost.
17 Forasmuch then as God gave them the like gift
as *he did* unto us, who believed on the Lord Jesus
Christ; what was I, that I could withstand God?
18 When they heard these things, they held their

with tongues) that He did on the Jewish disciples of Jesus on the day of Pentecost (2:1–47), so that Peter and the other Jews (*they of the circumcision*) would see that Jesus had torn down the dividing wall between Israel and the nations (11:15–17; 15:7–11; Eph. 2:14).

10:47–48 *be baptized.* Just as with the Ethiopian eunuch (8:36), nothing hindered these believing Gentiles from receiving the sign of the covenant of grace (2:38–39) by which they were united to God's redemptive purposes, as unfolded in Israel's history.

Thoughts for Personal/Family Worship: Chapter 10

1. **When considering the events of this chapter we must see them all as orchestrated by the Lord. God prepared the soil (Cornelius and his family), brought the sower of the seed (Peter), and sent down the rain (the Holy Spirit) so that there might be a harvest (conversion). All the glory goes to God and not to man. God planted a sense of need in Cornelius that made him restless and discontent with a life of paganism, so that he began crying out to God in prayer. Has God awakened you to your spiritual need so that you pray for your soul and your eternal salvation? Have you embraced the gospel by the Holy Spirit?**
2. **Just as people had struggled with the idea that Saul of Tarsus had truly been saved, many would struggle with the concept that Gentiles like Cornelius could be saved. Our own prejudices are often so engrained that it takes a lot of convincing for us to believe what God has plainly said in His Word, that no sinner is too vile or wretched or far gone in sin for God to save him or her. What kind of people might you or others in your church have a hard time accepting if they were to be converted? Why?**

Chapter 11: *Peter defends his contact with Gentiles, and other Gentiles are converted along the Mediterranean coast and on some of the islands.*

11:2 *the circumcision.* Jews, especially those who observed the ceremonial law of Moses.

11:3 *eat with them.* Unaware of Peter's vision, they accused him of breaking the ceremonial law.

11:4 *rehearsed.* Reported, declared. The repetition of the story of ch. 10 emphasizes its importance and the need for the Jewish believers to see that the Lord had initiated this change.

11:12 *bade.* Told.

11:16 *remembered I the word of the Lord.* Peter not only relied on his vision and the spiritual experiences of Cornelius's household but tested these things by the teachings of Christ (1:5). Spiritual experiences can only be explained by the Word of God.

11:18 *held their peace.* Stopped arguing. *repentance unto life.* Salvation and eternal life are gained through turning from sin back to God. Repentance itself is a gift (*God . . . granted*) of God's sovereign grace through Jesus Christ (5:30; 2 Tim. 2:25).

peace, and glorified God, saying, Then hath God
also to the Gentiles granted repentance unto life.
19 ¶ Now they which were scattered abroad upon
the persecution that arose about Stephen trav-
elled as far as Phenice, and Cyprus, and Antioch,
preaching the word to none but unto the Jews only.
20 And some of them were men of Cyprus and
Cyrene, which, when they were come to Anti-
och, spake unto the Grecians, preaching the Lord
Jesus.
21 And the hand of the Lord was with them: and a
great number believed, and turned unto the Lord.
22 ¶ Then tidings of these things came unto the
ears of the church which was in Jerusalem: and
they sent forth Barnabas, that he should go as far
as Antioch.
23 Who, when he came, and had seen the grace of
God, was glad, and exhorted them all, that with
purpose of heart they would cleave unto the Lord.
24 For he was a good man, and full of the Holy
Ghost and of faith: and much people was added
unto the Lord.
25 Then departed Barnabas to Tarsus, for to seek
Saul:
26 And when he had found him, he brought him
unto Antioch. And it came to pass, that a whole
year they assembled themselves with the church,
and taught much people. And the disciples were
called Christians first in Antioch.
27 ¶ And in these days came prophets from Jeru-
salem unto Antioch.
28 And there stood up one of them named
Agabus, and signified by the Spirit that there
should be great dearth throughout all the world:
which came to pass in the days of Claudius Caesar.
29 Then the disciples, every man according to his
ability, determined to send relief unto the breth-
ren which dwelt in Judaea:
30 Which also they did, and sent it to the elders
by the hands of Barnabas and Saul.

CHAPTER 12

NOW about that time Herod the king stretched
forth *his* hands to vex certain of the church.
2 And he killed James the brother of John with
the sword.
3 And because he saw it pleased the Jews, he
proceeded further to take Peter also. (Then were
the days of unleavened bread.)

The Church in Antioch (11:19–30)

11:19 *scattered abroad.* See 8:1. *Phenice.* Phoenicia, an area on the Mediterranean coast within the land of Syria. *Cyprus.* An island south of Asia Minor. *Antioch.* A city in Asia Minor in contemporary Turkey. The *word* spread to the north of Judaea.
11:20 *Grecians.* Hellenists, those who adopted the Greek language and culture, which had greatly influenced the Roman Empire. Here the term is contrasted with "Jews only" (v. 19) and implies Gentiles.
11:21 *hand of the Lord.* God's power (Ex. 9:3; 1 Sam. 5:6) accompanied the preaching of the gospel, producing many conversions (*great number believed . . . turned*; 1 Thess. 1:4–6; 2:13).
11:22 *tidings.* News.
11:23 *seen the grace of God.* The evidence of true conversion was plain. *cleave unto the Lord.* Continue persevering in the faith (14:22).
11:25 *to Tarsus . . . seek Saul.* See 9:30.
11:27 Acts frequently speaks of the Old Testament *prophets*, the messengers of God's Word, but this is the first mention of living prophets in the New Testament era (13:1; 15:32; 21:9–10; Rom. 12:6; 1 Cor. 12:10,28–29; 14), such as Agabus (11:28); yet speaking in foreign tongues as occurred on Pentecost is linked to prophesying (2:4,17; 19:6), and Philip had some prophet-like experiences (8:26,29,39). New Testament prophets were closely associated with the apostles in laying a foundation of new revelation for the church (Luke 11:49; 1 Cor. 12:28–29; Eph. 2:20; 3:5; 4:11). With the completion of the Scriptures and the passing of the apostles, prophecy also passed away, and we must neither add to nor subtract from the Bible God has given us (Rev. 22:18–19).
11:28 *by the Spirit.* Through the prophetic gift of the Holy Spirit (2:17–18; 13:1–2; 19:6; 20:23; 21:4,11), like that of the Old Testament prophets (1:16; 28:25). *dearth.* Famine. *Claudius Caesar.* The nephew of Tiberius Caesar and Roman emperor from AD 41 to 54. Famine occurred in the first, second, fourth, ninth, and eleventh years of his reign.
11:29 *send relief unto the brethren which dwelt in Judaea.* The Gentile believers saw themselves as brothers united to the Jewish believers and so sought to help them.
11:30 *sent . . . Barnabas and Saul.* This is probably the visit Paul mentioned in Gal. 2:1–10.

Thoughts for Personal/Family Worship: Chapter 11

1. **Peter's vision did not introduce the idea of the inclusion of the Gentiles into salvation, nor did it inaugurate this change. It was prophesied in the Old Testament (Ps. 72:17–19), foretold by Jesus (Luke 24:44–47), and accomplished by His death (Eph. 2:12–15). The vision of Peter confirmed the change and prodded the church to follow Christ in evangelizing and welcoming the nations. Why are we sometimes slow to take the gospel to ethnic groups or cultures that are different from our own? Why does the Lord press us to do so?**
2. **Barnabas visited the believers in Antioch and saw "the grace of God" in the work there (v. 23). This means that he saw the results of the grace of God at work in the lives of those who had come to trust in Christ and follow Him as His disciples. The name "Christians" was first used of believers and disciples in Antioch (v. 26); the name expresses the close relationship between Christ, which means "Anointed One," and His people who share His anointing in the Holy Spirit. If we carry the name of Christian, why is it important that people be able to see the grace of Christ's Spirit in our lives?**

Chapter 12: *Herod kills James and imprisons Peter, but an angel delivers Peter, and later Herod is struck dead.*
James and Peter Suffer Persecution (12:1–24)

12:1 *Herod the king.* Herod Agrippa I (9 BC–AD 44), the grandson of Herod the Great. *vex.* Harm.
12:2 *James the brother of John.* The first apostle martyred; the son of Zebedee (Luke 5:10; 6:14), not James, Jesus' brother,

4 And when he had apprehended him, he put
him in prison, and delivered *him* to four quaterni-
ons of soldiers to keep him; intending after Easter
to bring him forth to the people.
5 Peter therefore was kept in prison: but prayer
was made without ceasing of the church unto
God for him.
6 And when Herod would have brought him
forth, the same night Peter was sleeping between
two soldiers, bound with two chains: and the
keepers before the door kept the prison.
7 And, behold, the angel of the Lord came upon
him, and a light shined in the prison: and he smote
Peter on the side, and raised him up, saying, Arise
up quickly. And his chains fell off from *his* hands.
8 And the angel said unto him, Gird thyself,
and bind on thy sandals. And so he did. And he
saith unto him, Cast thy garment about thee, and
follow me.
9 And he went out, and followed him; and wist
not that it was true which was done by the angel;
but thought he saw a vision.
10 When they were past the first and the second
ward, they came unto the iron gate that leadeth
unto the city; which opened to them of his own
accord: and they went out, and passed on through
one street; and forthwith the angel departed from
him.
11 And when Peter was come to himself, he said,
Now I know of a surety, that the Lord hath sent
his angel, and hath delivered me out of the hand
of Herod, and *from* all the expectation of the
people of the Jews.
12 And when he had considered *the thing*, he
came to the house of Mary the mother of John,
whose surname was Mark; where many were
gathered together praying.
13 And as Peter knocked at the door of the gate, a
damsel came to hearken, named Rhoda.
14 And when she knew Peter's voice, she opened
not the gate for gladness, but ran in, and told how
Peter stood before the gate.
15 And they said unto her, Thou art mad. But she
constantly affirmed that it was even so. Then said
they, It is his angel.
16 But Peter continued knocking: and when they
had opened *the door*, and saw him, they were
astonished.
17 But he, beckoning unto them with the hand
to hold their peace, declared unto them how the
Lord had brought him out of the prison. And he
said, Go shew these things unto James, and to the
brethren. And he departed, and went into another
place.
18 Now as soon as it was day, there was no small
stir among the soldiers, what was become of Peter.
19 And when Herod had sought for him, and
found him not, he examined the keepers, and
commanded that *they* should be put to death.
And he went down from Judaea to Caesarea, and
there abode.
20 ¶ And Herod was highly displeased with them
of Tyre and Sidon: but they came with one ac-
cord to him, and, having made Blastus the king's
chamberlain their friend, desired peace; because
their country was nourished by the king's *country*.
21 And upon a set day Herod, arrayed in royal
apparel, sat upon his throne, and made an oration
unto them.
22 And the people gave a shout, *saying, It is* the
voice of a god, and not of a man.
23 And immediately the angel of the Lord smote
him, because he gave not God the glory: and he
was eaten of worms, and gave up the ghost.

---

who served as a leader of the church in Jerusalem (v. 17; 15:13; 21:18).

12:4 *apprehended.* Seized. *quaternions.* Squads of four soldiers. *Easter.* Literally, "Passover."

12:5 *prayer . . . of the church.* They responded to persecution with corporate prayer (v. 12; 4:24).

12:8 *Gird thyself.* Get dressed and ready to go.

12:9 *wist not.* Did not know.

12:10 *ward.* Guard.

12:11 *of a surety.* Truly, for sure.

12:12 *John . . . Mark.* First introduced here, he would go on mission trips with Paul and Barnabas, his uncle, and later alone with Barnabas (v. 25; 13:5,13; 15:37,39; Col. 4:10; 2 Tim. 4:11; Philem. 24; 1 Peter 5:13).

12:13 *damsel came to hearken.* Girl or servant came to listen (to whomever was knocking).

12:15 *Thou art mad . . . It is his angel.* The church seems to have had little faith in God's answers to its own prayers, but God did more than they imagined.

12:19 *went down from Judaea to Caesarea, and there abode.* Acts tells us nothing of his ministry until he returned to Jerusalem (15:7).

12:20 *Herod* suffered political turmoil with *Tyre and Sidon,* two coastal cities in Phoenicia. They asked that he not remove his ports and thus hurt them financially. *chamberlain.* Chief of staff.

12:21 *apparel.* Clothing, garments. *made an oration.* We have no other record of this speech.

12:23 *gave not God the glory.* God will punish all rulers and great men who glorify themselves or idols instead of Him (Dan. 4:30–32; 5:23). *eaten of worms.* Perhaps a sign of dying under God's eternal wrath (Isa. 66:24; Mark 9:44,46,48). *gave up the ghost.* Expired, died.

12:24 *word . . . grew and multiplied.* Persecution could not stop the gospel (see note at 6:7).

In Asia (12:25—16:5)

Barnabas and Saul Sent to Asia (12:25—13:3)

12:25 *Barnabas and Saul.* The order likely indicates that Barnabas was the leader of the two until Saul grew into his ministry. *took with them John.* John Mark (see note at v. 12).

Thoughts for Personal/Family Worship: Chapter 12

1. Why James was killed and Peter was allowed to live for several more years is a divine mystery. God could have supernaturally saved both James and Peter. He showed

24 ¶ But the word of God grew and multiplied.
25 And Barnabas and Saul returned from Jeru-
salem, when they had fulfilled *their* ministry, and
took with them John, whose surname was Mark.

CHAPTER 13

Now there were in the church that was at Antioch
certain prophets and teachers; as Barnabas, and
Simeon that was called Niger, and Lucius of
Cyrene, and Manaen, which had been brought up
with Herod the tetrarch, and Saul.
2 As they ministered to the Lord, and fasted, the
Holy Ghost said, Separate me Barnabas and Saul
for the work whereunto I have called them.
3 And when they had fasted and prayed, and laid
their hands on them, they sent *them* away.
4 ¶ So they, being sent forth by the Holy Ghost,
departed unto Seleucia; and from thence they
sailed to Cyprus.
5 And when they were at Salamis, they preached
the word of God in the synagogues of the Jews:
and they had also John to *their* minister.
6 And when they had gone through the isle unto
Paphos, they found a certain sorcerer, a false
prophet, a Jew, whose name *was* Bar-jesus:
7 Which was with the deputy of the country, Ser-
gius Paulus, a prudent man; who called for Barna-
bas and Saul, and desired to hear the word of God.
8 But Elymas the sorcerer (for so is his name by
interpretation) withstood them, seeking to turn
away the deputy from the faith.
9 Then Saul, (who also *is called* Paul,) filled with
the Holy Ghost, set his eyes on him,
10 And said, O full of all subtilty and all mischief,
thou child of the devil, *thou* enemy of all righ-
teousness, wilt thou not cease to pervert the right
ways of the Lord?
11 And now, behold, the hand of the Lord *is* upon
thee, and thou shalt be blind, not seeing the sun
for a season. And immediately there fell on him a
mist and a darkness; and he went about seeking
some to lead him by the hand.
12 Then the deputy, when he saw what was done,
believed, being astonished at the doctrine of the
Lord.
13 Now when Paul and his company loosed from
Paphos, they came to Perga in Pamphylia: and
John departing from them returned to Jerusalem.
14 ¶ But when they departed from Perga, they
came to Antioch in Pisidia, and went into the
synagogue on the sabbath day, and sat down.
15 And after the reading of the law and the
prophets the rulers of the synagogue sent unto

His sovereignty in allowing Peter to do more work on earth, while James would enter Christ's presence sooner. When we are tempted to compare our circumstances in life with those of others, how can what happened to James and Peter teach us to submit to God?

2. Jesus commands His disciples to continually ask, seek, and knock for their requests, anticipating that God will hear our prayers. Thus the scene before us in this chapter is so striking: when their prayers were answered they could not believe it. Even as we pray for various requests, we should also pray, "O Lord, increase our faith."

3. Their deaths are recorded in the same chapter of the Bible, but what different deaths James and Herod experienced! In one moment James went from prison to heaven. Herod too in one moment went from his earthly glory to an everlasting prison in hell. How true it is: "Blessed are the dead which die in the Lord" (Rev. 14:13).

Chapter 13: *Paul and Barnabas begin their first missionary journey to Cyprus and then to Antioch in Pisidia, where Paul testifies at length of Christ in the synagogue.*

13:1 The list of names indicates that the prophets and teachers in Antioch were marked by ethnic diversity. Little to nothing is known of these individuals beyond Barnabas and Saul. *Herod the tetrarch.* Herod Antipas, ruler of Galilee (Luke 3:1), not the Herod in ch. 12.

13:2 *the Holy Ghost said . . . I have called them.* The Holy Spirit revealed Himself to be a divine person (an *I*, not an "it"), the Lord of the church and its mission (8:29; 10:19–20; 15:28; 16:6–7).

Barnabas and Saul in Cyprus (13:4–12)

13:4 *Cyprus.* An important island in the Mediterranean.

13:5 Like Jesus, they started their preaching in the Jewish *synagogues* (see note at 9:20). *John to their minister.* John Mark (12:12) assisted them.

13:6 *sorcerer.* Condemned in the Old Testament (Deut. 18:9–12; cf. Rev. 21:8). *Bar-jesus.* Literally, "son of Jesus"; the irony is obvious.

13:7 *deputy of the country.* Roman proconsul, a prominent and influential ruler.

13:8 *Elymas . . . withstood them.* Not just a confrontation between men but one between two spiritual powers and kingdoms (Ex. 7:10–11).

13:9 *Saul . . . also is called Paul.* From this point onward Acts refers to him by his Latin name (same as "Paulus," v. 7) instead of his Jewish name, except when referring back to his conversion. *filled with the Holy Ghost.* Given power by the Holy Spirit (see note at 2:4).

13:10 *subtilty.* Cunning. *child of the devil.* Literally, "son of the Devil," an idiom for a person characterized by satanic evil; an ironic title given that his name meant "son of Jesus."

13:11 *mist and a darkness.* Like God's plague on Egypt (Ex. 10:21–23; Ps. 105:28).

13:12 *believed, being astonished at the doctrine of the Lord.* The power of Christ overwhelmed that of Satan, but it was primarily the Word that captured the attention of Paulus.

Paul and Barnabas Travel to Antioch in Pisidia (13:13–52)

13:13 *Perga in Pamphylia.* In southern Asia Minor. *John departing from them.* John Mark's abandonment of the mission would later cause a division between Paul and Barnabas (15:37–39).

13:14 *Antioch in Pisidia.* An important civil and military city in the Roman Empire.

13:15 *reading of the law and the prophets . . . word of exhortation.* The common practice of the synagogue with a

THE HOLY SPIRIT

Our Lord Jesus Christ suffered and died to secure for His people the indwelling presence of the Holy Spirit. Like the Father and the Son, the Holy Spirit is present throughout the entirety of the universe (Ps. 139:7), He is all-seeing (John 16:13), and He is eternal (Heb. 9:14). He was involved in the creation of the universe, doing what only God can do—bringing into existence all that exists out of nothing (Gen. 1:1–2; Ps. 104:30). So He is fully God. And like the Father and the Son, He is a Person: He has a will (1 Cor. 12:11), He has knowledge (Rom. 8:27; 1 Cor. 2:11), and He has an emotional life (Eph. 4:30).

In the Old Testament era the Spirit empowered men and women for specific tasks: craftsmanship related to the place of worship (Ex. 31:2–3), leadership (Judg. 3:10), and prophecy (2 Chron. 15:1; Mic. 3:8). He inspired men during the Old Testament and New Testament periods to write Holy Scripture (2 Peter 1:21). And He saved sinners and kept them saved (Ps. 51:11).

His work in the New Testament period is intimately linked with that of the Lord Jesus. The humanity of Jesus was created by the Spirit's power (Luke 1:35). Jesus ministered in the power of the Spirit (Matt. 12:28), and by the Spirit He offered Himself to the Father as a propitiation for the sins of men and women (Heb. 9:14). And the Spirit raised Christ from the dead (Rom. 8:11; 1 Peter 3:18).

With regard to believers, the Holy Spirit first makes us aware that we were created to be spiritual beings and makes God's love real for us (Rom 5:5). So He regenerates and quickens God's elect (John 3:5–6; Titus 3:5–6). He enables us to embrace Christ as Savior and call Jesus "Lord" (1 Cor. 12:3). At conversion a believer is baptized in the Holy Spirit by Christ, uniting him with all other believers in one body (1 Cor. 12:13). The Spirit indwells believers so they are never alone (Rom. 8:9; 1 Cor. 3:16–17). He also assures believers of their salvation (Rom. 8:15–16) and keeps them secure as a seal does a letter (1 Cor. 1:21–22; Eph. 4:30).

The Spirit also gives believers the boldness to come into the presence of the awesome and almighty Maker of heaven and earth and to call him "Abba, Father" (Gal. 4:6). He calls believers to serve Christ (Acts 13:2–4). He works in the church by giving believers gifts to serve Christ's body (1 Cor. 12:7–11). He sanctifies the believer; that is, He makes the believer become more like Jesus (Gal. 5:22–24). He prays for believers (Rom. 8:26). In a word, He undergirds and empowers the entirety of our spiritual lives as believers. The apostle urges us in Gal. 5:25 that because we "live in the Spirit"—that is, since we have been given spiritual life by the Spirit—we should "also walk in the Spirit"—that is, we are to live lives characterized by genuine spirituality.

In all of these activities of the Holy Spirit in the lives of believers, there is one thing above all else He is seeking to do. There is a center to His work and ministry in the lives of Christians. We see in John 16:13–14 that on the night of His betrayal Jesus is assuring His disciples that they will not be left alone when He returns to the Father after the cross and resurrection. Jesus says He will still be present with them, but no longer via His incarnate presence; rather, He will be with them by means of His Holy Spirit. He is thus helping them understand something of the ministry of the Holy Spirit after the event we call Pentecost.

In the words "He shall glorify me" (John 16:14), Jesus sets forth for us the Holy Spirit's major new covenant role. The Spirit has been sent by God the Father to focus our attention on Christ, to kindle in our hearts an unquenchable love for Christ and for His purposes, and to enable us to reflect faithfully His person and character.

them, saying, *Ye* men *and* brethren, if ye have any
word of exhortation for the people, say on.
16 Then Paul stood up, and beckoning with *his*
hand said, Men of Israel, and ye that fear God,
give audience.
17 The God of this people of Israel chose our
fathers, and exalted the people when they dwelt as
strangers in the land of Egypt, and with an high
arm brought he them out of it.
18 And about the time of forty years suffered he
their manners in the wilderness.
19 And when he had destroyed seven nations
in the land of Chanaan, he divided their land to
them by lot.
20 And after that he gave *unto them* judges about
the space of four hundred and fifty years, until
Samuel the prophet.
21 And afterward they desired a king: and God
gave unto them Saul the son of Cis, a man of the
tribe of Benjamin, by the space of forty years.
22 And when he had removed him, he raised up
unto them David to be their king; to whom also
he gave testimony, and said, I have found David
the *son* of Jesse, a man after mine own heart,
which shall fulfil all my will.
23 Of this man's seed hath God according to *his*
promise raised unto Israel a Saviour, Jesus:
24 When John had first preached before his com-
ing the baptism of repentance to all the people of
Israel.
25 And as John fulfilled his course, he said, Whom
think ye that I am? I am not *he*. But, behold, there
cometh one after me, whose shoes of *his* feet I am
not worthy to loose.
26 Men *and* brethren, children of the stock of
Abraham, and whosoever among you feareth
God, to you is the word of this salvation sent.
27 For they that dwell at Jerusalem, and their rul-
ers, because they knew him not, nor yet the voices
of the prophets which are read every sabbath day,
they have fulfilled *them* in condemning *him*.
28 And though they found no cause of death *in
him*, yet desired they Pilate that he should be slain.
29 And when they had fulfilled all that was
written of him, they took *him* down from the tree,
and laid *him* in a sepulchre.
30 But God raised him from the dead:
31 And he was seen many days of them which
came up with him from Galilee to Jerusalem, who
are his witnesses unto the people.
32 And we declare unto you glad tidings, how that
the promise which was made unto the fathers,
33 God hath fulfilled the same unto us their
children, in that he hath raised up Jesus again; as
it is also written in the second psalm, Thou art my
Son, this day have I begotten thee.
34 And as concerning that he raised him up from
the dead, *now* no more to return to corruption, he
said on this wise, I will give you the sure mercies
of David.
35 Wherefore he saith also in another *psalm*,
Thou shalt not suffer thine Holy One to see
corruption.
36 For David, after he had served his own genera-
tion by the will of God, fell on sleep, and was laid
unto his fathers, and saw corruption:
37 But he, whom God raised again, saw no
corruption.
38 ¶ Be it known unto you therefore, men *and*
brethren, that through this man is preached unto
you the forgiveness of sins:
39 And by him all that believe are justified from
all things, from which ye could not be justified by
the law of Moses.
40 Beware therefore, lest that come upon you,
which is spoken of in the prophets;
41 Behold, ye despisers, and wonder, and perish:
for I work a work in your days, a work which ye
shall in no wise believe, though a man declare it
unto you.
42 And when the Jews were gone out of the syn-
agogue, the Gentiles besought that these words

---

visiting teacher (Luke 4:16–21).

13:16–41 This is Paul's longest recorded synagogue speech, a recounting of Israel's history with a focus on Christ. Just as the risen Lord commissioned the apostles (Luke 24:44–47), Paul preached from the Old Testament Scriptures that the Christ must die and rise again (vv. 28–31; 1 Cor. 15:3–5) for the repentance (or faith) and *forgiveness of sins* (vv. 38–39) of the nations.

13:16 *Men of Israel, and ye that fear God.* Paul called both Jews and Gentiles who reverenced the true God to listen (*give audience*), for the gospel is for all nations (v. 26; 10:34–36).

13:22 *I have found David.* Citing Ps. 89:20. *man after mine own heart.* Citing 1 Sam. 13:14.

13:23 *Of this man's seed . . . according to his promise.* See 2 Sam. 7:12–14.

13:29 *tree.* The Greek word can refer to a pole or structure made of wood, here the cross (5:30; 10:39). Christ's death in this manner indicated that, though righteous, He suffered God's curse as the substitute for lawbreakers (Deut. 21:22–23; Gal. 3:10,13). *sepulchre.* Tomb.

13:33 *second psalm.* Citing Ps. 2:7. The promise of the exaltation of God's Son to His divinely appointed throne was fulfilled in Christ's resurrection and ascension.

13:34 *sure mercies of David.* Citing Isa. 55:3.

13:35 *another psalm.* Citing Ps. 16:10 (see Peter's comments in 2:25–31).

13:36 *fell on sleep.* Died.

13:39 *all that believe are justified.* God, as the righteous Judge, declares sinners righteous if they trust in Christ, on the sole basis of Christ's obedience unto death and not on any of our works of obedience to God's *law* (Rom. 3:19–28; 5:18–19; Gal. 2:16).

13:40–41 *Beware.* The gospel includes both a promise of blessing to believers and a warning of curse against those who despise it, in accordance with the Old Testament (Hab. 1:5).

13:42 *besought.* Urged, begged.

might be preached to them the next sabbath.
43 Now when the congregation was broken up,
many of the Jews and religious proselytes followed Paul and Barnabas: who, speaking to them,
persuaded them to continue in the grace of God.
44 ¶ And the next sabbath day came almost the
whole city together to hear the word of God.
45 But when the Jews saw the multitudes, they
were filled with envy, and spake against those
things which were spoken by Paul, contradicting
and blaspheming.
46 Then Paul and Barnabas waxed bold, and said,
It was necessary that the word of God should first
have been spoken to you: but seeing ye put it from
you, and judge yourselves unworthy of everlasting
life, lo, we turn to the Gentiles.
47 For so hath the Lord commanded us, *saying*,
I have set thee to be a light of the Gentiles, that
thou shouldest be for salvation unto the ends of
the earth.
48 And when the Gentiles heard this, they were
glad, and glorified the word of the Lord: and as
many as were ordained to eternal life believed.
49 And the word of the Lord was published
throughout all the region.
50 But the Jews stirred up the devout and honourable women, and the chief men of the city, and
raised persecution against Paul and Barnabas, and
expelled them out of their coasts.
51 But they shook off the dust of their feet against
them, and came unto Iconium.
52 And the disciples were filled with joy, and with
the Holy Ghost.

CHAPTER 14

AND it came to pass in Iconium, that they went
both together into the synagogue of the Jews, and
so spake, that a great multitude both of the Jews
and also of the Greeks believed.
2 But the unbelieving Jews stirred up the Gentiles, and made their minds evil affected against
the brethren.
3 Long time therefore abode they speaking boldly
in the Lord, which gave testimony unto the word
of his grace, and granted signs and wonders to be
done by their hands.
4 But the multitude of the city was divided: and
part held with the Jews, and part with the apostles.
5 And when there was an assault made both of
the Gentiles, and also of the Jews with their rulers,
to use *them* despitefully, and to stone them,
6 They were ware of *it*, and fled unto Lystra and
Derbe, cities of Lycaonia, and unto the region that
lieth round about:
7 And there they preached the gospel.
8 ¶ And there sat a certain man at Lystra, impotent in his feet, being a cripple from his mother's
womb, who never had walked:
9 The same heard Paul speak: who stedfastly

13:45 *envy.* Literally, "jealousy." The same motive that provoked the religious leaders in Jerusalem to kill Jesus also moved the Jews in the Dispersion to discredit the gospel (17:5; Matt. 27:18).

13:46 *waxed bold.* Spoke freely and boldly. *we turn to the Gentiles.* Not a rejection of the Jewish people (14:1; Rom. 1:16; 10:1) but a concentration of their mission upon the nations (9:15).

13:47 *light of the Gentiles . . . ends of the earth.* God's promise to His Servant (Isa. 49:6), the Lord Jesus Christ (see notes at 3:13; 8:32–33). They saw God's command to Christ as applying to the apostolic mission by the church's union with Christ (Col. 1:24–25).

13:48 *glad.* Not because Israel rejected the message (Rom. 11:18) but because the gospel was for them as well. *as many as were ordained to eternal life believed.* Only those whom God has sovereignly appointed to salvation will believe the gospel (1 Thess. 1:4–5; 2 Thess. 2:13–14).

13:51 *shook off the dust of their feet.* A sign of judgment against those who rejected the gospel (Luke 10:11).

13:52 *filled with joy . . . the Holy Ghost.* Not the same term as that rendered "filled" when used of the Spirit's empowerment for service (2:4) but another Greek word (also in Eph. 5:18). The Spirit is the giver of supernatural joy in Christ (Rom. 14:17; 15:13; Gal. 5:22; 1 Thess. 1:6).

Thoughts for Personal/Family Worship: Chapter 13

1. **Though the Holy Spirit sent Paul and Barnabas to preach the gospel to the lost, the church in Antioch was the vehicle through which the Spirit set them apart for this ministry. Are you praying for missionaries and supporting them as you are able?**
2. **Paul met many enemies of the gospel on his journey, the sorcerer Bar-jesus being only one of them. Christ's promise that the gates of hell cannot prevail against the church is profoundly meaningful in the midst of such hellish conflict (Matt. 16:18). Why do we need to be filled with the power of God's Spirit to see the kingdom advance?**
3. **When they heard the stunning message of free justification by faith alone, some wanted to hear this exact message preached again on the next Sabbath (v. 42). What a blessed thing it is never to tire of the "old" gospel, to find it always new. What do we learn about the content of the gospel message from this chapter? What makes it so precious?**

Chapter 14: *Paul and Barnabas preach the gospel in southern Asia Minor, returning to Antioch to give a report.*

Paul and Barnabas Travel to Iconium (14:1–7)

14:1 *Iconium.* A ruling city for the region (in present day Turkey); little is known of its Jewish population. *into the synagogue.* As was his custom (9:20; 13:5).

14:2–4 *evil affected.* Embittered. *the city was divided.* The antithesis between the Jewish and Gentile disciples of Jesus (v. 1) and the *unbelieving Jews* was growing stronger.

14:5 *use . . . despitefully.* Abuse, humiliate.

14:6 *ware.* Aware. The disciples did not seek persecution. This is not the first time a disciple fled from prospective persecution. *Lystra and Derbe, cities of Lycaonia.* Fifty-five miles southwest of Iconium on the Imperial Road, an underdeveloped territory

beholding him, and perceiving that he had faith
to be healed,
10 Said with a loud voice, Stand upright on thy
feet. And he leaped and walked.
11 And when the people saw what Paul had done,
they lifted up their voices, saying in the speech of
Lycaonia, The gods are come down to us in the
likeness of men.
12 And they called Barnabas, Jupiter; and Paul,
Mercurius, because he was the chief speaker.
13 Then the priest of Jupiter, which was before
their city, brought oxen and garlands unto the
gates, and would have done sacrifice with the
people.
14 *Which* when the apostles, Barnabas and Paul,
heard *of*, they rent their clothes, and ran in among
the people, crying out,
15 And saying, Sirs, why do ye these things? We
also are men of like passions with you, and preach
unto you that ye should turn from these vanities
unto the living God, which made heaven, and
earth, and the sea, and all things that are therein:
16 Who in times past suffered all nations to walk
in their own ways.
17 Nevertheless he left not himself without witness, in that he did good, and gave us rain from
heaven, and fruitful seasons, filling our hearts
with food and gladness.
18 And with these sayings scarce restrained they
the people, that they had not done sacrifice unto
them.
19 ¶ And there came thither *certain* Jews from
Antioch and Iconium, who persuaded the people,
and, having stoned Paul, drew *him* out of the city,
supposing he had been dead.
20 Howbeit, as the disciples stood round about
him, he rose up, and came into the city: and the
next day he departed with Barnabas to Derbe.
21 And when they had preached the gospel to
that city, and had taught many, they returned
again to Lystra, and *to* Iconium, and Antioch,
22 Confirming the souls of the disciples, *and*
exhorting them to continue in the faith, and that
we must through much tribulation enter into the
kingdom of God.
23 And when they had ordained them elders in
every church, and had prayed with fasting, they
commended them to the Lord, on whom they
believed.
24 And after they had passed throughout Pisidia,
they came to Pamphylia.
25 And when they had preached the word in
Perga, they went down into Attalia:
26 And thence sailed to Antioch, from whence
they had been recommended to the grace of God
for the work which they fulfilled.
27 And when they were come, and had gathered
the church together, they rehearsed all that God
had done with them, and how he had opened the
door of faith unto the Gentiles.
28 And there they abode long time with the
disciples.

---

compared to the city of Iconium.

Paul and Barnabas Travel to Lystra (14:8–23)

14:8 *impotent.* Powerless, disabled.

14:9 *perceiving that he had faith to be healed.* An insight from the Lord (Luke 5:20).

14:12 *Jupiter.* Zeus, the god of thunder and the supreme deity in Greco-Roman mythology. *Mercurius.* Hermes, the divine messenger of the gods.

14:14 *apostles.* Because Barnabas is listed here as an apostle alongside Paul, it is likely that Luke is using the word in the general sense of one who is sent (John 13:16; 2 Cor. 8:23; Phil. 2:25). *rent their clothes.* Tore them, a gesture of grief.

14:15 *We also are men.* The apostles did not seek to be elevated as gods but called men to turn from useless idols (*vanities*) to serve the *living God* (1 Thess. 1:9–10). Evangelizing pagans requires not only sharing the person and work of Christ but also calling them to monotheism.

14:16–17 *suffered.* Permitted. God had not given the nations His special revelation (Ps. 147:19–20). *not . . . without witness.* God's creation and providence testify to all mankind of His goodness (Rom. 1:19–21), yet apart from the Word and Spirit none will turn to the Lord and be saved (4:12; Rom. 10:14–15).

14:20 *Derbe.* About thirty-five miles southeast of Lystra, on the edge of Galatia.

14:22–23 *Confirming the souls of the disciples.* Strengthening the Christians. This they did by two means: first, by preaching perseverance in *the faith* through trouble (*tribulation*) in the hope of the coming *kingdom*, and, second, by establishing proper structures of church leadership, particularly a plurality of qualified *elders in every church* (Phil. 1:1; 1 Tim. 3:1–7; Titus 1:5–9).

Paul and Barnabas Return to Antioch in Syria (14:24–28)

14:25 *Attalia.* A chief port of Pamphylia.

14:26 They reported back to the church in *Antioch*, where they had received their original commission to carry the gospel throughout Asia Minor (13:1–3). *recommended to the grace of God.* Entrusted the missionaries to God's help and support, probably through prayer (15:40; cf. v. 23; 20:32).

14:27 *rehearsed.* Announced. *opened the door of faith.* All glory for successful missions must go to God, for saving faith in Christ is a gift from God (2:47; 11:21), as is repentance (11:18).

Thoughts for Personal/Family Worship: Chapter 14

1. **Imagine seeing Paul when he returned to Lystra, perhaps with bruises and cuts from being stoned still visible on him from when he was last there. What would it have been like to hear this man say, "we must through much tribulation enter into the kingdom of God" (v. 22)? What might it cost a typical Christian in your land to follow Christ to the end? What has it cost you?**
2. **This section on Paul's first missionary journey (13:1—14:28) concludes with a concern for proper church order. Paul and Barnabas prayerfully led each church to appoint a group of elders to lead it. The missionaries returned to their sending church to report about God's work through them among the nations. There is a profound sense that both office-bearers in the church and missionaries from the church serve as those commissioned by the church**

CHAPTER 15

AND certain men which came down from Judaea
taught the brethren, *and said*, Except ye be cir-
cumcised after the manner of Moses, ye cannot
be saved.
2 When therefore Paul and Barnabas had no
small dissension and disputation with them, they
determined that Paul and Barnabas, and certain
other of them, should go up to Jerusalem unto the
apostles and elders about this question.
3 And being brought on their way by the church,
they passed through Phenice and Samaria, de-
claring the conversion of the Gentiles: and they
caused great joy unto all the brethren.
4 And when they were come to Jerusalem, they
were received of the church, and *of* the apostles
and elders, and they declared all things that God
had done with them.
5 But there rose up certain of the sect of the
Pharisees which believed, saying, That it was
needful to circumcise them, and to command
them to keep the law of Moses.
6 ¶ And the apostles and elders came together for
to consider of this matter.
7 And when there had been much disputing, Pe-
ter rose up, and said unto them, Men *and* breth-
ren, ye know how that a good while ago God made
choice among us, that the Gentiles by my mouth
should hear the word of the gospel, and believe.
8 And God, which knoweth the hearts, bare them
witness, giving them the Holy Ghost, even as *he
did* unto us;
9 And put no difference between us and them,
purifying their hearts by faith.
10 Now therefore why tempt ye God, to put a yoke
upon the neck of the disciples, which neither our
fathers nor we were able to bear?
11 But we believe that through the grace of the
Lord Jesus Christ we shall be saved, even as they.
12 ¶ Then all the multitude kept silence, and gave
audience to Barnabas and Paul, declaring what
miracles and wonders God had wrought among
the Gentiles by them.
13 ¶ And after they had held their peace, James
answered, saying, Men *and* brethren, hearken
unto me:
14 Simeon hath declared how God at the first did
visit the Gentiles, to take out of them a people for
his name.
15 And to this agree the words of the prophets;
as it is written,
16 After this I will return, and will build again the
tabernacle of David, which is fallen down; and I
will build again the ruins thereof, and I will set
it up:
17 That the residue of men might seek after
the Lord, and all the Gentiles, upon whom my
name is called, saith the Lord, who doeth all these
things.
18 Known unto God are all his works from the
beginning of the world.
19 Wherefore my sentence is, that we trouble not
them, which from among the Gentiles are turned
to God:

---

and upheld by its prayers. Why is the local church central to world missions?

Chapter 15: *Paul and Barnabas travel to Jerusalem, where the apostles and elders meet to deal with unrest in the churches over the issue of whether or not Gentile believers need to be circumcised, after which Paul proceeds to minister, not with Barnabas but with Silas.*

The Jerusalem Council (15:1–35)

15:2 *go up to Jerusalem.* The dating of this journey and the subsequent council has been the subject of much controversy, but it appears that Gal. 2:1 corresponds to an earlier journey (11:30) and that ch. 15 refers to a third visit to Jerusalem for Paul.

15:4 *all things that God had done.* The conversion of the Gentiles was the work of God (14:26), not the result of mere human efforts.

15:5 *needful to circumcise . . . keep the law of Moses.* The ancient ceremonies required by God in His covenants with Abraham (Gen. 17:9–10) and with the nation of Israel (as in the book of Leviticus).

15:7 *much disputing.* There were heated disputes within the church. *God made choice.* Again, the apostle deferred to God's sovereignty, here with respect to his vision leading him to Cornelius (ch. 10).

15:8 God had confirmed His will in this matter when He had sent the Holy Spirit upon the Gentiles (10:44–48; 11:15–17). *as he did unto us.* The Gentiles received the same promised Spirit, who unifies all believers in Christ under the Father (Eph. 2:18; 4:3–6).

15:9 *purifying their hearts.* Likely referring to circumcision of the heart (Deut. 30:6; Rom. 2:29). *by faith.* Trust in Christ (10:43; 11:17; 13:39), not the ceremonial rites of the old covenant, is God's means for cleansing the soul (26:18).

15:10 *yoke.* A frame placed around an animal's neck to restrain and harness it for service, as directed by its master (Gen. 27:40; Lev. 26:13; Lam. 3:27; Matt. 11:29–30; Gal. 5:1; 1 Tim. 6:1). *disciples.* Including believing Gentiles.

15:11 *through the grace of the Lord.* Salvation is a free gift and powerful work of God through the death and resurrection of the now glorified *Jesus Christ. we . . . even as they.* Peter concluded from God's manner of saving the Gentiles that Jews must be saved in the same way.

15:13 *James*, the half-brother of Jesus (Mark 6:3; Gal. 1:19; 2:9), had a prominent leadership role in the church in Jerusalem (12:17; 21:8) and acted as facilitator for the council.

15:14–17 James quoted the Old Testament (Amos 9:11–12) to show that Peter (*Simeon*) was in line with God's revelation. *residue.* Remnant. In the Gentile mission God was restoring the kingdom and house (*tabernacle*) of *David* through his offspring, Jesus Christ (2:29–36).

15:18 *Known unto God are all his works.* God's plan of redemption is eternal and does not change (Ps. 33:11; Isa. 46:10; Eph. 1:4,11; 3:11).

15:19 *my sentence is, that we trouble not them.* James declared that the *Gentiles* who repent of sin should not be burdened with keeping the ceremonial law.

20 But that we write unto them, that they abstain
from pollutions of idols, and *from* fornication,
and *from* things strangled, and *from* blood.
21 For Moses of old time hath in every city them
that preach him, being read in the synagogues
every sabbath day.
22 Then pleased it the apostles and elders, with
the whole church, to send chosen men of their
own company to Antioch with Paul and Barna-
bas; *namely*, Judas surnamed Barsabas, and Silas,
chief men among the brethren:
23 And they wrote *letters* by them after this
manner; The apostles and elders and brethren
send greeting unto the brethren which are of the
Gentiles in Antioch and Syria and Cilicia:
24 Forasmuch as we have heard, that certain
which went out from us have troubled you with
words, subverting your souls, saying, *Ye must* be
circumcised, and keep the law: to whom we gave
no *such* commandment:
25 It seemed good unto us, being assembled with
one accord, to send chosen men unto you with
our beloved Barnabas and Paul,
26 Men that have hazarded their lives for the
name of our Lord Jesus Christ.
27 We have sent therefore Judas and Silas, who
shall also tell *you* the same things by mouth.
28 For it seemed good to the Holy Ghost, and to
us, to lay upon you no greater burden than these
necessary things;
29 That ye abstain from meats offered to idols,
and from blood, and from things strangled, and
from fornication: from which if ye keep your-
selves, ye shall do well. Fare ye well.
30 So when they were dismissed, they came to
Antioch: and when they had gathered the multi-
tude together, they delivered the epistle:
31 *Which* when they had read, they rejoiced for
the consolation.
32 And Judas and Silas, being prophets also them-
selves, exhorted the brethren with many words,
and confirmed *them*.
33 And after they had tarried *there* a space, they
were let go in peace from the brethren unto the
apostles.
34 Notwithstanding it pleased Silas to abide there
still.
35 Paul also and Barnabas continued in Antioch,
teaching and preaching the word of the Lord,
with many others also.
36 ¶ And some days after Paul said unto Barna-
bas, Let us go again and visit our brethren in every
city where we have preached the word of the Lord,
and see how they do.
37 And Barnabas determined to take with them
John, whose surname was Mark.
38 But Paul thought not good to take him with
them, who departed from them from Pamphylia,
and went not with them to the work.
39 And the contention was so sharp between
them, that they departed asunder one from the
other: and so Barnabas took Mark, and sailed
unto Cyprus;
40 And Paul chose Silas, and departed, being rec-

15:20 *we write.* This list appears also in v. 29; 21:25. *pollutions of idols.* Participating in idol ceremonies or feasts. *fornication.* Sexual immorality, including sexual practices in the pagan temples. *strangled.* Some debate centers around this verb, but it likely refers to meat with the *blood* not drained from it (Gen. 9:4; Lev. 3:17; 17:10–14). Thus the first two items pertain to the most common violations by Gentiles of the first and second tables of the Ten Commandments and the latter two with food.

15:21 *Moses . . . read in the synagogues.* At least part of the reason for the restrictions listed in v. 20 appears to have been the need for the Gentiles to accommodate their Jewish brothers.

15:22 *pleased it the apostles and elders, with the whole church.* The council did not simply issue a decree from James but came to a unified understanding among the leaders and members of the church. *Judas surnamed Barsabas.* The only reference to this man in the Bible. *Silas.* A faithful disciple who later traveled much with Paul (vv. 27,32,40; 16:19; 17:4; 18:5, etc.; 2 Cor. 1:19; 1 Thess. 1:1; 2 Thess. 1:1; 1 Peter 5:12).

15:23 *Gentiles in Antioch and Syria and Cilicia.* The letter produced by the council was meant to be published to all the churches in the area.

15:24 *Forasmuch.* Since, seeing that. *subverting your souls.* Upsetting you.

15:28 *good to the Holy Ghost.* The apostles depended upon the Holy Spirit to keep them in the truth of Christ.

15:32 *prophets . . . exhorted . . . confirmed.* The gift of prophecy was not just to predict the future but to apply God's truth to men for their obedience and comfort (1 Cor. 14:3).

Paul and Barnabas Separate (15:36–41)

15:37–39 *John . . . Mark.* Barnabas's relative (Col. 4:10), who had left an earlier mission (13:13) and thus now became the occasion of a dispute between Barnabas and Paul over whether to bring him, resulting in their separating (*departed asunder*). Paul later found John Mark to be very helpful in his ministry (2 Tim. 4:11).

Thoughts for Personal/Family Worship: Chapter 15

1. **The early church had to contend not only with persecution but also with strife and division. We can learn important principles from how the church in Jerusalem responded. First, the leaders of the church met together to discuss the matter. Second, their discussion was God-centered and God-exalting; together they looked to His will and bowed to His providence. Third, they discussed the Holy Scriptures, basing their decision on the Spirit's teaching in the Word of God. Fourth, they guided their decision by the principles of salvation by grace through faith in Jesus Christ, not through bondage to human traditions or old covenant ceremonies. Fifth, no one man decreed what the church would do; though Peter and James had more authority than the others, the church sought unity of mind. How can your church put these lessons into practice in its own discussions?**
2. **Another interesting disagreement, this time of a personal nature, is recorded as being between Barnabas**

ommended by the brethren unto the grace of God.
41 And he went through Syria and Cilicia, con-
firming the churches.

CHAPTER 16

THEN came he to Derbe and Lystra: and, behold, a
certain disciple was there, named Timotheus, the
son of a certain woman, which was a Jewess, and
believed; but his father *was* a Greek:
2 Which was well reported of by the brethren that
were at Lystra and Iconium.
3 Him would Paul have to go forth with him; and
took and circumcised him because of the Jews
which were in those quarters: for they knew all
that his father was a Greek.
4 And as they went through the cities, they deliv-
ered them the decrees for to keep, that were or-
dained of the apostles and elders which were at
Jerusalem.
5 And so were the churches established in the
faith, and increased in number daily.
6 Now when they had gone throughout Phrygia
and the region of Galatia, and were forbidden of
the Holy Ghost to preach the word in Asia,
7 After they were come to Mysia, they assayed to
go into Bithynia: but the Spirit suffered them not.
8 And they passing by Mysia came down to Troas.
9 And a vision appeared to Paul in the night;
There stood a man of Macedonia, and prayed him,
saying, Come over into Macedonia, and help us.
10 And after he had seen the vision, immediately
we endeavoured to go into Macedonia, assuredly
gathering that the Lord had called us for to preach
the gospel unto them.
11 Therefore loosing from Troas, we came with a
straight course to Samothracia, and the next *day*
to Neapolis;
12 And from thence to Philippi, which is the chief
city of that part of Macedonia, *and* a colony: and
we were in that city abiding certain days.
13 And on the sabbath we went out of the city by
a river side, where prayer was wont to be made;
and we sat down, and spake unto the women
which resorted *thither*.
14 ¶ And a certain woman named Lydia, a seller
of purple, of the city of Thyatira, which wor-
shipped God, heard *us*: whose heart the Lord
opened, that she attended unto the things which
were spoken of Paul.
15 And when she was baptized, and her house-
hold, she besought *us*, saying, If ye have judged
me to be faithful to the Lord, come into my house,
and abide *there*. And she constrained us.
16 ¶ And it came to pass, as we went to prayer,
a certain damsel possessed with a spirit of divi-

and Paul (vv. 37–39). This one was solved by the two going their separate ways. Another way of looking at this was that now two teams went out, doubling the effectiveness and coverage of the mission effort. Even this conflict could not halt the work of God. Is it ever necessary for two Christians who share common beliefs nevertheless to go separate ways in ministry? Why?

Chapter 16: ***After taking Timothy into their company, Paul and Silas travel to Macedonia, where God works remarkable conversions.***

Timothy Joins Paul and Silas (16:1–5)

16:1 *Timotheus.* Timothy, a major figure in the life of Paul, as his two letters to him testify. *son of . . . a Jewess, and believed; but his father was a Greek.* Timothy was of mixed lineage, both culturally and religiously (2 Tim. 1:5; 3:14–15).

16:3 *circumcised.* Not going against the recent decision of the Jerusalem council (15:1–41), nor for religious reasons (Gal. 2:3), but for the sake of ministry to the *Jews* (1 Cor. 9:19–20).

16:4–5 *churches established . . . increased.* The *decrees* of the *Jerusalem* council proved to be a means of God's blessing the church in terms of spiritual and numerical growth.

In Europe (16:6—20:38)

Paul Is Called to Macedonia (16:6–10)

16:6 *Phrygia . . . Galatia.* Commentators disagree as to whether Luke uses these terms to refer to one province (the north Galatia view) or two (the south Galatia view), for Galatia can be understood either as a geographical region or a Roman province. Though there are arguments for and against both theories, the south Galatian view seems to better fit the overall evidence. *forbidden of the Holy Ghost.* We do not know how the Holy Spirit communicated this, but it was clearly accomplished with the sovereign plan of bringing Paul to Europe (vv. 9–10).

16:7 *Mysia.* A region located in northwest Asia Minor. *assayed.* Tried, attempted. *Bithynia.* Located northeast of Mysia. *suffered them not.* Would not permit them.

16:8 *Troas.* A coastal city on the western edge of Mysia.

16:9 *Macedonia.* In northern Greece, the ancient territory of Philip, the father of Alexander the Great. The Greeks in Paul's day thought of the Macedonians as barbarians.

16:10 *immediately we endeavoured to go.* When the Spirit finally opened a door for them to move ahead in their mission, they readily obeyed.

Ministry in Philippi (16:11–40)

16:12 *Philippi.* A central city in Macedonia, though it was not the largest or its capital. Archaeological evidence shows that it was largely a Roman city with a small Jewish population.

16:13 *by a river side.* It is not known which river. The water would have been used for ceremonial cleansing. *wont.* Accustomed. *resorted thither.* Met together.

16:14 *Lydia.* Their first evangelistic effort was directed toward a woman. *seller of purple.* An honorable and likely profitable trade. Purple dye was found either in shellfish or extracted from a certain plant. *Thyatira.* A city known for its linens (Rev. 2:18–29). *whose heart the Lord opened.* God's saving grace is necessary and effective for the conversion of each individual He saves (John 6:37,44).

16:15 *baptized.* As common throughout the book of Acts, converts are immediately baptized. *her household.* Including slaves. Lydia probably was widowed or unmarried since she is mentioned as the head of her household. *besought.* Asked urgently.

16:16 *damsel.* Young woman, servant. *divination.* Prediction by evil spirits. *soothsaying.* Professing to predict the future, a

nation met us, which brought her masters much
gain by soothsaying:
17 The same followed Paul and us, and cried, say-
ing, These men are the servants of the most high
God, which shew unto us the way of salvation.
18 And this did she many days. But Paul, being
grieved, turned and said to the spirit, I command
thee in the name of Jesus Christ to come out of
her. And he came out the same hour.
19 ¶ And when her masters saw that the hope of
their gains was gone, they caught Paul and Silas,
and drew *them* into the marketplace unto the
rulers,
20 And brought them to the magistrates, saying,
These men, being Jews, do exceedingly trouble
our city,
21 And teach customs, which are not lawful for
us to receive, neither to observe, being Romans.
22 And the multitude rose up together against
them: and the magistrates rent off their clothes,
and commanded to beat *them*.
23 And when they had laid many stripes upon
them, they cast *them* into prison, charging the
jailor to keep them safely:
24 Who, having received such a charge, thrust
them into the inner prison, and made their feet
fast in the stocks.
25 ¶ And at midnight Paul and Silas prayed, and
sang praises unto God: and the prisoners heard
them.
26 And suddenly there was a great earthquake, so
that the foundations of the prison were shaken:
and immediately all the doors were opened, and
every one's bands were loosed.
27 And the keeper of the prison awaking out of
his sleep, and seeing the prison doors open, he
drew out his sword, and would have killed him-
self, supposing that the prisoners had been fled.
28 But Paul cried with a loud voice, saying, Do
thyself no harm: for we are all here.
29 Then he called for a light, and sprang in, and
came trembling, and fell down before Paul and
Silas,
30 And brought them out, and said, Sirs, what
must I do to be saved?
31 And they said, Believe on the Lord Jesus Christ,
and thou shalt be saved, and thy house.
32 And they spake unto him the word of the
Lord, and to all that were in his house.
33 And he took them the same hour of the night,
and washed *their* stripes; and was baptized, he
and all his, straightway.
34 And when he had brought them into his
house, he set meat before them, and rejoiced,
believing in God with all his house.
35 And when it was day, the magistrates sent the
serjeants, saying, Let those men go.
36 And the keeper of the prison told this saying to
Paul, The magistrates have sent to let you go: now
therefore depart, and go in peace.
37 But Paul said unto them, They have beaten us
openly uncondemned, being Romans, and have
cast *us* into prison; and now do they thrust us out
privily? nay verily; but let them come themselves
and fetch us out.
38 And the serjeants told these words unto the
magistrates: and they feared, when they heard
that they were Romans.
39 And they came and besought them, and
brought *them* out, and desired *them* to depart out
of the city.
40 And they went out of the prison, and entered
into *the house of* Lydia: and when they had seen
the brethren, they comforted them, and departed.

---

common trade based on the belief in magical powers granted by the gods. *brought her masters much gain.* This girl was exploited by her masters for money.

16:17–18 Though the demon spoke truth regarding Paul and Silas, Paul was concerned that the people would associate the gospel of Christ with demonic powers. Satan can even come as an angel of light (2 Cor. 11:14). The apostle released the girl from the demon by speaking *in the name of Jesus Christ* (see note at 2:38), clearly showing that Christ has supreme power (Matt. 28:18) and that He is not an evil spirit but the Savior from evil spirits (8:6–7; Luke 11:15–22).

16:19 *the hope of their gains was gone.* They were more concerned about their monetary loss than about the nurture of this young slave girl or the glory of Jesus (19:23–27).

16:22–23 *rent.* Tore. *stripes.* Blows or wounds.

16:25 *prayed, and sang praises.* A remarkable act of faith and testimony to the other *prisoners.*

16:26 *great earthquake.* Earthquakes were not uncommon in this region.

16:30 *What must I do to be saved?* The singing of Paul and Silas and their commitment to not run away left an impression on this man. Recognizing his need of grace and forgiveness, he implores them for help.

16:31 *Believe on the Lord Jesus Christ.* A concise summary of the call of the gospel (13:39). *thou shalt be saved, and thy house.* The gospel promises salvation to all people who trust in Christ, whether free or slaves, adults or children, including all in the household (2:39).

16:33–34 *baptized, he and all his . . . believing in God with all his house.* Another example of the conversion and baptism of a household (v. 15; 10:44,48; 11:14; 18:8). *meat.* Food of any kind.

16:35 *serjeants.* Officers. *Let those men go.* The magistrates of the city did not come and personally release Paul and Silas but sought to release them secretly.

16:37 *openly uncondemned.* The magistrates had Paul and Silas in public view, though they had made no formal charges or conducted trial proceedings against them. *being Romans.* A Roman citizen was protected by law against beatings without trial (22:25). Paul used his Roman citizenship now, after his beating, to obtain a public declaration of innocence in order to protect the Christians he was leaving behind in Philippi. *privily.* Secretly. *verily.* Surely, truly.

16:38 *they feared.* Paul could bring formal charges against the magistrates.

16:40 *comforted them.* Remarkably, the ones who had been

CHAPTER 17

NOW when they had passed through Amphipolis
and Apollonia, they came to Thessalonica, where
was a synagogue of the Jews:
2 And Paul, as his manner was, went in unto
them, and three sabbath days reasoned with them
out of the scriptures,
3 Opening and alleging, that Christ must needs
have suffered, and risen again from the dead; and
that this Jesus, whom I preach unto you, is Christ.
4 And some of them believed, and consorted with
Paul and Silas; and of the devout Greeks a great
multitude, and of the chief women not a few.
5 ¶ But the Jews which believed not, moved with
envy, took unto them certain lewd fellows of the
baser sort, and gathered a company, and set all
the city on an uproar, and assaulted the house of
Jason, and sought to bring them out to the people.
6 And when they found them not, they drew
Jason and certain brethren unto the rulers of the
city, crying, These that have turned the world
upside down are come hither also;
7 Whom Jason hath received: and these all do
contrary to the decrees of Caesar, saying that
there is another king, *one* Jesus.
8 And they troubled the people and the rulers of
the city, when they heard these things.
9 And when they had taken security of Jason, and
of the other, they let them go.
10 ¶ And the brethren immediately sent away
Paul and Silas by night unto Berea: who coming
thither went into the synagogue of the Jews.
11 These were more noble than those in Thes-
salonica, in that they received the word with all
readiness of mind, and searched the scriptures
daily, whether those things were so.
12 Therefore many of them believed; also of
honourable women which were Greeks, and of
men, not a few.
13 But when the Jews of Thessalonica had knowl-
edge that the word of God was preached of Paul
at Berea, they came thither also, and stirred up the
people.
14 And then immediately the brethren sent away
Paul to go as it were to the sea: but Silas and
Timotheus abode there still.
15 And they that conducted Paul brought him
unto Athens: and receiving a commandment
unto Silas and Timotheus for to come to him with
all speed, they departed.
16 ¶ Now while Paul waited for them at Athens,
his spirit was stirred in him, when he saw the city
wholly given to idolatry.
17 Therefore disputed he in the synagogue with
the Jews, and with the devout persons, and in the
market daily with them that met with him.
18 Then certain philosophers of the Epicureans,
and of the Stoicks, encountered him. And some

beaten and imprisoned strengthened the other believers (2 Cor. 1:4).

Thoughts for Personal/Family Worship: Chapter 16

1. **The Holy Spirit is an integral part of the church's mission. Here we read of the Spirit both forbidding and permitting Paul and his companions to carry out their ministry (vv. 6–7). Though today we seek no revelations of the Spirit apart from the Scriptures, we do need to rely upon Him for wisdom in every decision regarding church and evangelism. Furthermore, the opening of Lydia's heart to believe (v. 14) reminds us that the preaching of the gospel depends completely on the Spirit for success in conversions. How should these realities motivate us to pray? How are you praying with regard to these matters?**
2. **With the earthquake and the outstretched sword, the conversion of the jailor was violent and forceful, but no less productive of true faith and joy (v. 34) than that of Lydia. God's actions in bringing people to Christ are different for each person, but true, saving grace always shows itself in faith and love that God Himself works in the hearts of sinners. Why is it a mistake to insist that each person's experience of conversion has exactly the same outward features?**

Chapter 17: *Paul travels with the gospel to Thessalonica, Berea, and Athens.*

Ministry in Thessalonica (17:1–9)

17:1 *Amphipolis . . . Thessalonica.* Major cities of Macedonia, the latter of which served as the home of the proconsul and was very pro-Caesar.

17:2 *manner.* Custom. *reasoned . . . out of the scriptures.* To the Jews Paul gave a well-thought-out argument about the person and work of Christ (v. 3) from the Old Testament (13:16–41).

17:3 *Opening and alleging.* Explaining and presenting.

17:4 *consorted.* Joined. *chief women.* Prominent women within society, perhaps the wives of leading men.

17:5 *lewd fellows of the baser sort.* Evil, common men. *Jason.* Mentioned only here in the New Testament (except possibly in Rom. 16:21).

17:7 *another king.* An act of treason against the emperor (*Caesar*), who was worshiped.

17:9 *taken security.* Likely a kind of bail.

Ministry in Berea (17:10–15)

17:10 *Berea.* Another city of Macedonia, not as important as Thessalonica, on the way from Thessalonica to Athens. *thither.* There.

17:11 *searched the scriptures daily.* Luke implicitly calls people to study the Bible with an open mind that is eager for the truth.

Ministry in Athens (17:16–34)

17:16 *Athens.* A renowned city, the capital of Attica, highly esteemed among the Romans. *his spirit was stirred.* Intense and burning anger against the idolatry that enslaved the multitudes because of Paul's zeal for the glory of God in Christ.

17:18 *Epicureans.* Adherents to a branch of philosophy founded by Epicurus (341–270 BC) that cared very little for talk of the gods and is often viewed as hedonism, seeing pleasure as the highest good. *Stoicks.* A branch of philosophy founded by Zeno (340–265 BC) marked by self-control in conduct and not being given over to one's passions. *babbler.* Literally, a "seed-picker," a derisive term for someone who like a bird

said, What will this babbler say? other some, He
seemeth to be a setter forth of strange gods: be-
cause he preached unto them Jesus, and the
resurrection.
19 And they took him, and brought him unto
Areopagus, saying, May we know what this new
doctrine, whereof thou speakest, *is*?
20 For thou bringest certain strange things to our
ears: we would know therefore what these things
mean.
21 (For all the Athenians and strangers which
were there spent their time in nothing else, but
either to tell, or to hear some new thing.)
22 ¶ Then Paul stood in the midst of Mars' hill,
and said, *Ye* men of Athens, I perceive that in all
things ye are too superstitious.
23 For as I passed by, and beheld your devotions,
I found an altar with this inscription, TO THE
UNKNOWN GOD. Whom therefore ye igno-
rantly worship, him declare I unto you.
24 God that made the world and all things
therein, seeing that he is Lord of heaven and
earth, dwelleth not in temples made with hands;
25 Neither is worshipped with men's hands, as
though he needed any thing, seeing he giveth to
all life, and breath, and all things;
26 And hath made of one blood all nations of
men for to dwell on all the face of the earth, and
hath determined the times before appointed, and
the bounds of their habitation;
27 That they should seek the Lord, if haply they
might feel after him, and find him, though he be
not far from every one of us:
28 For in him we live, and move, and have our
being; as certain also of your own poets have said,
For we are also his offspring.
29 Forasmuch then as we are the offspring of
God, we ought not to think that the Godhead is
like unto gold, or silver, or stone, graven by art
and man's device.
30 And the times of this ignorance God winked
at; but now commandeth all men every where to
repent:
31 Because he hath appointed a day, in the which
he will judge the world in righteousness by *that*
man whom he hath ordained; *whereof* he hath
given assurance unto all *men*, in that he hath
raised him from the dead.
32 ¶ And when they heard of the resurrection of
the dead, some mocked: and others said, We will
hear thee again of this *matter*.
33 So Paul departed from among them.
34 Howbeit certain men clave unto him, and
believed: among the which *was* Dionysius the

---

pecks at thoughts here or there but is not truly a philosopher by Greek standards. *resurrection.* Foolishness to Greeks (v. 32), who considered the physical body to be inherently against the purity of spirit.

17:19 *took him.* Either arrested or merely escorted. *Areopagus.* Mars Hill, a place where people would gather to discuss the newest philosophical ideas (v. 21), after which a council would judge whether one spoke wisdom; not unlike modern academic circles.

17:22 *stood in the midst of Mars' hill.* While legal language is not used throughout this section, Paul was informally put on trial before the council. *superstitious.* The Greek can mean either superstitious or religious. Here it signifies both based on their devotion to many idols.

17:23 *devotions.* Sacred objects or things worshiped. *TO THE UNKNOWN GOD.* In case they had missed a particular god among the many they worshiped, they had erected an altar to this "god" to make sure they were covering all their bases. Paul used this to proclaim to them the one true God, whom they had indeed neglected.

17:24–25 *God that made the world.* Addressing pagans, Paul began with the general revelation of the Creator in His creation (Ps. 19:1; Rom. 1:19–20). *Lord of heaven and earth . . . giveth to all life . . . and all things.* There is one God who is not Himself the universe but is the Owner and Sovereign over the universe (Gen. 1:1; Pss. 95:3–5; 104:1–30). *dwelleth not in temples . . . Neither . . . needed any thing.* God is infinite and independent (Ps. 50:12–13; Isa. 66:1–2; Jer. 23:23–24). Paul critiqued the crude idolatry of the common people, a point with which many philosophical Greeks and Romans would have agreed.

17:26 *made of one blood all nations.* God created man and thus has the right to rule him (Gen. 1:26). All of humanity comes from Adam (Gen. 2:4–25; 5:1–5) via Noah's family (Gen. 10), which should destroy all racism and ethnic arrogance. *determined the times . . . bounds.* God's providence controls the changing state of the nations (Dan. 2:21; 4:32).

17:27 *That they should seek the Lord.* God's creation and care of the world put man under the responsibility to worship Him, but since the fall unregenerate man refuses to honor God (Rom. 1:21–22). *haply.* Perhaps. *feel after him.* The sense of the Greek is of groping as in darkness (Deut. 28:29). Despite their philosophy the Greeks fumbled about in ignorance and foolishness (Eph. 4:17–18).

17:28 *in him we live.* God is close, not because He is everything but because He is present everywhere to powerfully sustain our existence and abilities (James 1:17). *offspring.* As a child is dependent on his father, so too humans are dependent on God, though sin has alienated man and destroyed his sonship to God (Eph. 2:12,19). *your own poets.* Citing both Epimenides and Aratus, Paul used fragments of Greek thought even as he gave Greek philosophy a devastating critique.

17:29 Paul reasoned that since God created man to be His *offspring*, and man is greater than the materials he shapes into an idol, God cannot be like the idols—a stinging rebuke of idolatry based on their darkened reasoning. *Godhead.* God's nature (Rom. 1:20; Gal. 4:8).

17:30 *winked at.* Overlooked, not that God was neutral to idolatry and false religion but that He did not destroy the Gentiles for their sins because He purposed to send them the gospel. *all men every where to repent.* The gospel places all who hear it under obligation (*commandeth*) to turn from sin and idolatry (*repent*) to God and Christ (14:15; 1 Thess. 1:9–10).

17:31 *he hath appointed a day.* Though brought into the Areopagus to be tried, Paul turned the tables to show the council that they stood in the courtroom of God, who *will judge* them. *by that man . . . raised him from the dead.* Even to pagan philosphers Paul preached the person and work of Jesus Christ (4:12).

17:34 *Howbeit.* But. *clave.* Literally, "glued," committed

Areopagite, and a woman named Damaris, and
others with them.

CHAPTER 18

AFTER these things Paul departed from Athens,
and came to Corinth;
2 And found a certain Jew named Aquila, born in
Pontus, lately come from Italy, with his wife Pris-
cilla; (because that Claudius had commanded all
Jews to depart from Rome:) and came unto them.
3 And because he was of the same craft, he abode
with them, and wrought: for by their occupation
they were tentmakers.
4 And he reasoned in the synagogue every sab-
bath, and persuaded the Jews and the Greeks.
5 And when Silas and Timotheus were come
from Macedonia, Paul was pressed in the spirit,
and testified to the Jews *that* Jesus *was* Christ.
6 And when they opposed themselves, and blas-
phemed, he shook *his* raiment, and said unto
them, Your blood *be* upon your own heads; I *am*
clean: from henceforth I will go unto the Gentiles.
7 ¶ And he departed thence, and entered into
a certain *man's* house, named Justus, *one* that
worshipped God, whose house joined hard to the
synagogue.
8 And Crispus, the chief ruler of the synagogue,
believed on the Lord with all his house; and many
of the Corinthians hearing believed, and were
baptized.
9 Then spake the Lord to Paul in the night by a
vision, Be not afraid, but speak, and hold not thy
peace:
10 For I am with thee, and no man shall set on thee
to hurt thee: for I have much people in this city.
11 And he continued *there* a year and six months,
teaching the word of God among them.
12 ¶ And when Gallio was the deputy of Achaia,
the Jews made insurrection with one accord
against Paul, and brought him to the judgment
seat,
13 Saying, This *fellow* persuadeth men to worship
God contrary to the law.
14 And when Paul was now about to open *his*
mouth, Gallio said unto the Jews, If it were a
matter of wrong or wicked lewdness, O *ye* Jews,
reason would that I should bear with you:
15 But if it be a question of words and names, and
of your law, look ye *to it*; for I will be no judge of
such *matters*.
16 And he drave them from the judgment seat.
17 Then all the Greeks took Sosthenes, the chief
ruler of the synagogue, and beat *him* before the

themselves. *Areopagite.* A member of the council.

Thoughts for Personal/Family Worship: Chapter 17

1. **The Bereans serve as a good example of men and women who love truth and the Scriptures. After hearing the preaching and teaching of the apostles, they "received the word with all readiness of mind, and searched the scriptures daily, whether those things were so" (v. 11). So often we fall into a passive kind of sitting under the teaching and preaching of the Word. The Bereans are commended for their eagerness to search the Scriptures and discover the truth of the apostles' teaching. How can we imitate them?**
2. **Paul's preaching to those who knew the Scriptures (v. 2) and those steeped in worldly philosophy (vv. 16–31), respectively, was different. However, Paul's message in the Areopagus has sometimes been misapplied, as though Paul were using this opportunity to build bridges of common beliefs between Christianity and different religions and philosophies. On the contrary, Paul's message was as sharp as ever, exposing sin, idolatry, and ignorance; declaring the glory of the true God and Savior; and calling men to repent now or face the judgment. What can we learn from him for speaking about our faith to people outside the church?**

Chapter 18: *Paul brings the gospel to Corinth and Ephesus.*

Paul in Corinth (18:1–17)

18:1 *Corinth.* A prominent city in Greece on the sea, west of Athens, an administrative center for the province of Achaia and point of connection for the eastern and western Mediterranean Sea.

18:2 *Aquila . . . with his wife Priscilla.* Paul called them elsewhere his "helpers in Christ Jesus" (Rom. 16:3). *Claudius.* The Roman emperor. *commanded all Jews to depart from Rome.* Likely a reference to the ejection of those who had disturbed Rome in AD 49.

18:4 *reasoned in the synagogue.* See 17:2,10–11.

18:5 *pressed in the spirit.* Compelled by the Holy Spirit to magnify *Jesus* to the Jews.

18:6 *raiment.* Clothing. Shaking the dust from his garment was a sign of his innocence of their blood (20:26–27) but judgment upon them (Neh. 5:13; cf. 13:51; Luke 9:5). *henceforth.* From this time onward.

18:7 *joined hard.* Was attached.

18:8 *Crispus.* See 1 Cor. 1:14. *chief ruler of the synagogue.* Some Jews were still converting under Paul's preaching. *believed . . . with all his house . . . baptized.* On the evangelization, conversion, and baptism of households, see notes at 16:31, 33–34.

18:9–10 *hold not thy peace.* Do not be silent. *I am with thee.* The strength and consolation of all the church in its mission (Matt. 18:20). *set on.* Attack. *I have much people in this city.* Though they were not yet converted, *the Lord* Jesus knew His chosen sheep whom He had redeemed and made sure they heard the gospel through His servant (13:48; John 10:14–16).

18:12 *deputy.* The Roman proconsul, *Gallio,* was known to be concerned about justice and inquired diligently into civil cases. *made insurrection with one accord.* Stood together in opposition to. *judgment seat.* God's providence again brought His witness to speak before authorities (Luke 21:12–15).

18:13 *contrary to the law.* Probably an accusation of breaking Roman law by opposing Caesar.

18:14–15 *question of words and names.* He saw it as a matter of nuanced religious definitions, not a crime (*lewdness*) against the state, part of Luke's apologetic against official persecution (23:29; 25:18–19).

18:16 *drave.* Drove.

judgment seat. And Gallio cared for none of those
things.
18 ¶ And Paul *after this* tarried *there* yet a good
while, and then took his leave of the brethren, and
sailed thence into Syria, and with him Priscilla
and Aquila; having shorn *his* head in Cenchrea:
for he had a vow.
19 And he came to Ephesus, and left them there:
but he himself entered into the synagogue, and
reasoned with the Jews.
20 When they desired *him* to tarry longer time
with them, he consented not;
21 But bade them farewell, saying, I must by all
means keep this feast that cometh in Jerusalem:
but I will return again unto you, if God will. And
he sailed from Ephesus.
22 And when he had landed at Caesarea, and
gone up, and saluted the church, he went down
to Antioch.
23 And after he had spent some time *there*, he de-
parted, and went over *all* the country of Galatia and
Phrygia in order, strengthening all the disciples.
24 ¶ And a certain Jew named Apollos, born at
Alexandria, an eloquent man, *and* mighty in the
scriptures, came to Ephesus.
25 This man was instructed in the way of the
Lord; and being fervent in the spirit, he spake and
taught diligently the things of the Lord, knowing
only the baptism of John.
26 And he began to speak boldly in the syna-
gogue: whom when Aquila and Priscilla had
heard, they took him unto *them*, and expounded
unto him the way of God more perfectly.
27 And when he was disposed to pass into Achaia,
the brethren wrote, exhorting the disciples to
receive him: who, when he was come, helped
them much which had believed through grace:
28 For he mightily convinced the Jews, *and that*
publickly, shewing by the scriptures that Jesus was
Christ.

CHAPTER 19

AND it came to pass, that, while Apollos was at
Corinth, Paul having passed through the up-
per coasts came to Ephesus: and finding certain
disciples,
2 He said unto them, Have ye received the Holy
Ghost since ye believed? And they said unto him,
We have not so much as heard whether there be
any Holy Ghost.
3 And he said unto them, Unto what then were
ye baptized? And they said, Unto John's baptism.
4 Then said Paul, John verily baptized with the
baptism of repentance, saying unto the people,
that they should believe on him which should
come after him, that is, on Christ Jesus.
5 When they heard *this*, they were baptized in the
name of the Lord Jesus.
6 And when Paul had laid *his* hands upon them,

18:17 *Sosthenes.* Possibly converted at some point in time (1 Cor. 1:1). *Gallio cared for none of those things.* This proconsul was sadly unconcerned about the mob violence in his court.

Paul Returns to Antioch (18:18–23)

18:18 *shorn his head.* Cut his hair. *he had a vow.* Paul had sworn an oath, perhaps a Nazarite vow (Num. 6:18,21).

18:19 *Ephesus.* The capital city of the Roman province of Asia (western Turkey), located on a major trade route and home to the great temple of Artemis.

18:21 *bade . . . farewell.* Dismissed, said goodbye. *this feast.* The Passover. Paul did not go for religious worship (Gal. 4:10; Col. 2:16–17) but to preach the Lamb of God (1 Cor. 5:7).

Apollos Speaks in Ephesus (18:24–28)

18:24–25 *Apollos.* Our first introduction to the gifted Jewish preacher (19:1; 1 Cor. 3:4; Titus 3:13). *mighty in the scriptures.* Powerful in his ability to understand and preach the Bible, though he lacked the full New Testament revelation of Christ (*knowing only the baptism of John*).

18:26 *way of God.* A name for the Christian faith and discipleship to Jesus Christ (9:2). *more perfectly.* Great preachers can still learn much from other godly men and women.

18:27 *believed through grace.* Faith is a gift of God, worked in the heart by the Spirit (16:14).

Thoughts for Personal/Family Worship: Chapter 18

1. **Even Paul could feel afraid (v. 9). Christ encouraged Paul during the difficult early stage of his time in Corinth. He was working hard making tents for a living (v. 3), and his witness was opposed (v. 6). However, God's works are known to Him from all eternity. He tells Paul that He has "much people" in this city (v. 10). That did not mean that there had been many converts to this point but that Christ had claimed them as His own by the decree of election. They still needed the preaching of the gospel so that they might come to faith and repentance and thereby confirm their election from God (1 Thess. 1:3–6). How does the truth that God has chosen many sinners for salvation encourage evangelism?**
2. **Apollos was "mighty in the scriptures" (v. 24). No doubt that meant that by the Spirit's grace he loved the Bible, studied it carefully, and could teach it well (Ezra 7:10). It was like a sword that he used to defend the truth, attack strongholds of unbelief, and set the prisoners free. His response to Aquila and Priscilla shows that he was still humble, teachable, and eager to grow in his knowledge (v. 26). How can we imitate his example?**

Chapter 19: ***Paul brings the gospel to Ephesus, laboring there for some years with such fruit that his success occasioned an uproar among the silversmiths.***

Paul in Ephesus (19:1–41)

19:1 *Ephesus.* See note at 18:19.

19:2–3 *John's baptism.* Similar to and perhaps because of Apollos (18:25). John did preach about the Spirit (Luke 3:16), making their ignorance puzzling (*whether there be any Holy Ghost*), unless the issue was that they did not know the Spirit had been poured out (cf. John 7:39).

19:4 *verily.* Truly.

19:5 *baptized in the name of Lord Jesus.* Not a formula of words (baptism was done in the triune name, Matt. 28:19), but

the Holy Ghost came on them; and they spake
with tongues, and prophesied.
7 And all the men were about twelve.
8 And he went into the synagogue, and spake
boldly for the space of three months, disputing
and persuading the things concerning the king-
dom of God.
9 But when divers were hardened, and believed
not, but spake evil of that way before the multitude,
he departed from them, and separated the disci-
ples, disputing daily in the school of one Tyrannus.
10 And this continued by the space of two years;
so that all they which dwelt in Asia heard the word
of the Lord Jesus, both Jews and Greeks.
11 And God wrought special miracles by the
hands of Paul:
12 So that from his body were brought unto the
sick handkerchiefs or aprons, and the diseases
departed from them, and the evil spirits went out
of them.
13 ¶ Then certain of the vagabond Jews, exorcists,
took upon them to call over them which had evil
spirits the name of the Lord Jesus, saying, We
adjure you by Jesus whom Paul preacheth.
14 And there were seven sons of *one* Sceva, a Jew,
and chief of the priests, which did so.
15 And the evil spirit answered and said, Jesus I
know, and Paul I know; but who are ye?
16 And the man in whom the evil spirit was
leaped on them, and overcame them, and pre-
vailed against them, so that they fled out of that
house naked and wounded.
17 And this was known to all the Jews and Greeks
also dwelling at Ephesus; and fear fell on them all,
and the name of the Lord Jesus was magnified.
18 And many that believed came, and confessed,
and shewed their deeds.
19 Many of them also which used curious arts
brought their books together, and burned them
before all *men*: and they counted the price of
them, and found *it* fifty thousand *pieces* of silver.
20 So mightily grew the word of God and
prevailed.
21 ¶ After these things were ended, Paul purposed
in the spirit, when he had passed through
Macedonia and Achaia, to go to Jerusalem, saying,
After I have been there, I must also see Rome.
22 So he sent into Macedonia two of them that
ministered unto him, Timotheus and Erastus; but
he himself stayed in Asia for a season.
23 And the same time there arose no small stir
about that way.
24 For a certain *man* named Demetrius, a sil-
versmith, which made silver shrines for Diana,
brought no small gain unto the craftsmen;
25 Whom he called together with the workmen
of like occupation, and said, Sirs, ye know that by
this craft we have our wealth.
26 Moreover ye see and hear, that not alone at Eph-
esus, but almost throughout all Asia, this Paul hath
persuaded and turned away much people, saying
that they be no gods, which are made with hands:
27 So that not only this our craft is in danger to
be set at nought; but also that the temple of the
great goddess Diana should be despised, and her
magnificence should be destroyed, whom all Asia
and the world worshippeth.
28 And when they heard *these sayings*, they were
full of wrath, and cried out, saying, Great *is* Diana
of the Ephesians.
29 And the whole city was filled with confusion:
and having caught Gaius and Aristarchus, men
of Macedonia, Paul's companions in travel, they
rushed with one accord into the theatre.
30 And when Paul would have entered in unto
the people, the disciples suffered him not.

---

as a sign of salvation through faith in Christ (see note at 2:38). The baptism of John was superseded by Christian baptism.

19:6 *spake with tongues, and prophesied.* The third and last occurrence of these phenomena in this book (2:4; 10:46) and the first under Paul's ministry. This may signify that the new covenant fullness of the Spirit is received only by faith in Christ.

19:9 *divers.* Various. *separated the disciples.* Paul did not remove the disciples of Jesus from the Jewish synagogue until public opposition disturbed them.

19:10 *all . . . which dwelt in Asia.* Ephesus became a center for the Gentile mission in that province.

19:13 *vagabond . . . exorcists.* Men who traveled around casting out demons (Luke 11:19). *adjure.* Bind by invoking the name of a spiritual power in an oath (Greek, *orkizō*, root of "exorcist" or Greek, *exorkistês*). They attempted to produce a miracle by invoking the *name of the Lord Jesus* but did so not by faith or commission from Christ but only imitating what others did (*whom Paul preacheth*).

19:14 *chief of the priests.* Perhaps of the high priestly clan, if not himself the high priest.

19:17 *the name of the Lord Jesus was magnified.* The humiliation of the sons of Sceva shows that Christ is not a power to be manipulated by magic but the Lord to be trusted and obeyed.

19:19 *curious arts.* Magic, sorcery. Ephesus was known for its magical arts used to invoke the help of spiritual powers (Eph. 1:21; 6:12). *fifty thousand pieces of silver.* A massive sacrifice, marking the great repentance of the Ephesians.

19:20 *mightily grew . . . and prevailed.* See note at 6:7.

19:21 *in the spirit.* Possibly by the Holy Spirit. This is the first announcement of Paul's intention to travel to *Jerusalem* and *Rome* (20:16,22; Rom. 15:23–25), which will dominate the latter portion of the book (21:1—28:31).

19:24 *Diana.* Greek, "Artemis," the goddess of fertility and death, whose large temple was located in Ephesus (v. 27). *no small gain unto the craftsmen.* The gospel threatened a large sector of the economy in Ephesus, the making and selling of idols. The intertwining of human society with sin and idolatry implies that the gospel will disrupt the existing evil order.

19:25–28 *by this craft we have our wealth . . . Great is Diana of the Ephesians.* Other motives, such as greed, may underlie religious fervor and persecution of converts to Christianity. *set at nought.* Come into contempt.

19:29 *theatre.* A place where the whole city could meet.

31 And certain of the chief of Asia, which were
his friends, sent unto him, desiring *him* that he
would not adventure himself into the theatre.
32 Some therefore cried one thing, and some an-
other: for the assembly was confused; and the more
part knew not wherefore they were come together.
33 And they drew Alexander out of the multitude,
the Jews putting him forward. And Alexander
beckoned with the hand, and would have made
his defence unto the people.
34 But when they knew that he was a Jew, all with
one voice about the space of two hours cried out,
Great *is* Diana of the Ephesians.
35 And when the townclerk had appeased the peo-
ple, he said, *Ye* men of Ephesus, what man is there
that knoweth not how that the city of the Ephe-
sians is a worshipper of the great goddess Diana,
and of the *image* which fell down from Jupiter?
36 Seeing then that these things cannot be spoken
against, ye ought to be quiet, and to do nothing
rashly.
37 For ye have brought hither these men, which
are neither robbers of churches, nor yet blas-
phemers of your goddess.
38 Wherefore if Demetrius, and the craftsmen
which are with him, have a matter against any
man, the law is open, and there are deputies: let
them implead one another.
39 But if ye enquire any thing concerning other
matters, it shall be determined in a lawful assembly.
40 For we are in danger to be called in question
for this day's uproar, there being no cause whereby
we may give an account of this concourse.
41 And when he had thus spoken, he dismissed
the assembly.

CHAPTER 20

AND after the uproar was ceased, Paul called
unto *him* the disciples, and embraced *them*, and
departed for to go into Macedonia.
2 And when he had gone over those parts, and
had given them much exhortation, he came into
Greece,
3 And *there* abode three months. And when the
Jews laid wait for him, as he was about to sail into
Syria, he purposed to return through Macedonia.
4 And there accompanied him into Asia Sopater
of Berea; and of the Thessalonians, Aristarchus
and Secundus; and Gaius of Derbe, and Timo-
theus; and of Asia, Tychicus and Trophimus.
5 These going before tarried for us at Troas.
6 And we sailed away from Philippi after the
days of unleavened bread, and came unto them
to Troas in five days; where we abode seven days.
7 And upon the first *day* of the week, when the
disciples came together to break bread, Paul
preached unto them, ready to depart on the mor-
row; and continued his speech until midnight.
8 And there were many lights in the upper

19:30–31 *suffered him not.* Did not permit him. *certain of the chief of Asia.* Some of the Asiarchs, high-ranking officers in the Roman province of Asia. *adventure.* Risk. Christians must be wise in how they respond to the great dangers of persecution (Matt. 10:16).

19:35 *townclerk.* An official responsible for keeping track of the temple funds throughout the city. *image which fell down from Jupiter.* Literally, "the God-fallen," an object revered in Ephesus because of a legend that it had fallen from Zeus.

19:38 *law.* Legal court. *deputies.* Roman proconsuls. *implead.* Bring legal charges.

19:40 *called in question . . . uproar.* Luke implicitly reminds the people that mob action against Christians could lead to civil penalties. *concourse.* Crowd.

Thoughts for Personal/Family Worship: Chapter 19

1. **The advance of the gospel faces many obstacles and enemies. There is incomplete knowledge, a situation in which people know enough to call themselves disciples but lack a full understanding of the gospel and thus also lack spiritual power. There is hardness of heart, whereby the very people one expects to welcome the gospel force the church to separate from them. There is magic and sorcery, which may even try to use "Jesus" as another spiritual force to invoke without knowing the Lord. There is idolatry so deeply embedded in society that it drives the economy. There is persecution that can threaten the lives of Christians with violent mobs. Nevertheless we read, "So mightily grew the word of God and prevailed" (v. 20). God's Word carries God's power to accomplish God's purposes. How can that encourage those who preach and teach the Bible?**
2. **Materialism is a false god that must be renounced if we are to follow Christ. For the Ephesians, repentance required destroying books of sorcery that had cost an enormous amount of money (v. 19), but the Christians took the loss in order to honor Christ. On the other hand, the love of money turned the silversmiths into violent enemies of the church, even though they pretended to act in religious zeal (vv. 25–31). What place does money hold in your heart relative to Christ? How do you know?**

Chapter 20: *Paul travels to Macedonia, Troas, and finally to Miletus, to which he calls the elders from Ephesus, whom he charges one final time.*

Paul in Macedonia and Greece (20:1–38)

20:1–2 *Macedonia.* See note at 16:9. *Greece.* Achaia and the Aegean coast.

20:3 *three months.* As commentators note, in either AD 55–56 or 56–57.

20:4 The men's names suggest that many of them were Greek.

20:5 *tarried.* Waited. *Troas.* Located along the eastern Aegean coast, northwest of Ephesus (2 Cor. 2:12). There is a span of seven weeks between here and Paul's arrival in Jerusalem in 21:17.

20:7 This is the first mention in Acts of Christians gathering on *the first day of the week* to hear the Word *preached.* All four Gospels emphasize that this was the day when Christ rose from the dead (Matt. 28:1; Mark 16:2, 9; Luke 24:1; John 20:1), and thus it became the day set apart by the apostles for public

chamber, where they were gathered together.
9 And there sat in a window a certain young man
named Eutychus, being fallen into a deep sleep:
and as Paul was long preaching, he sunk down
with sleep, and fell down from the third loft, and
was taken up dead.
10 And Paul went down, and fell on him, and
embracing *him* said, Trouble not yourselves; for
his life is in him.
11 When he therefore was come up again, and
had broken bread, and eaten, and talked a long
while, even till break of day, so he departed.
12 And they brought the young man alive, and
were not a little comforted.
13 ¶ And we went before to ship, and sailed unto
Assos, there intending to take in Paul: for so had
he appointed, minding himself to go afoot.
14 And when he met with us at Assos, we took
him in, and came to Mitylene.
15 And we sailed thence, and came the next *day*
over against Chios; and the next *day* we arrived
at Samos, and tarried at Trogyllium; and the next
day we came to Miletus.
16 For Paul had determined to sail by Ephesus,
because he would not spend the time in Asia: for
he hasted, if it were possible for him, to be at Jeru-
salem the day of Pentecost.
17 ¶ And from Miletus he sent to Ephesus, and
called the elders of the church.
18 And when they were come to him, he said
unto them, Ye know, from the first day that I came
into Asia, after what manner I have been with you
at all seasons,
19 Serving the Lord with all humility of mind,
and with many tears, and temptations, which
befell me by the lying in wait of the Jews:
20 *And* how I kept back nothing that was prof-
itable *unto you*, but have shewed you, and have
taught you publickly, and from house to house,
21 Testifying both to the Jews, and also to the
Greeks, repentance toward God, and faith toward
our Lord Jesus Christ.
22 And now, behold, I go bound in the spirit unto
Jerusalem, not knowing the things that shall befall
me there:
23 Save that the Holy Ghost witnesseth in every
city, saying that bonds and afflictions abide me.
24 But none of these things move me, neither
count I my life dear unto myself, so that I might
finish my course with joy, and the ministry, which
I have received of the Lord Jesus, to testify the
gospel of the grace of God.
25 And now, behold, I know that ye all, among
whom I have gone preaching the kingdom of
God, shall see my face no more.
26 Wherefore I take you to record this day, that I
am pure from the blood of all *men*.
27 For I have not shunned to declare unto you all
the counsel of God.
28 ¶ Take heed therefore unto yourselves, and to
all the flock, over the which the Holy Ghost hath
made you overseers, to feed the church of God,
which he hath purchased with his own blood.
29 For I know this, that after my departing shall
grievous wolves enter in among you, not sparing
the flock.

---

worship (1 Cor. 16:1–2) as the Christian Sabbath or Lord's Day (Rev. 1:10). *break bread.* See note at 2:42. *on the morrow.* The next day.

20:9 *third loft.* The third floor of the building, thus the deadly fall.

20:10 *Trouble not yourselves.* The same word appears in Christ's mouth just before He raised a young girl from the dead (Mark. 5:39). *fell . . . embracing him.* Elijah and Elisha also embraced the dead children God was about to raise up through them (1 Kings 17:21; 2 Kings 4:34). Like the prophets, Paul was a servant of the Lord.

20:14–15 The account records the ship's travels at it stops at many port cities along the Aegean and Mediterranean Seas. *Miletus.* About a day's journey from Ephesus.

20:16 *hasted.* Went quickly. *day of Pentecost.* See v. 6; 18:21.

20:17 *elders of the church.* Paul had established a group of elders in each church he had planted (14:23). These same officers are called "overseers" and charged to pastor God's flock (v. 28; 1 Peter 5:1–2)

20:20 *publickly, and from house to house.* The ministry of the Word requires both preaching in public and teaching and exhorting smaller groups in private settings.

20:21 *repentance toward God, and faith toward our Lord Jesus Christ.* This was the essential message of Paul's ministry, the call of the gospel of Christ (Mark 1:15).

20:22–23 *bound in the spirit.* Possibly "under necessity or obligation by the Spirit." Paul was under a solemn burden to go to *Jerusalem* and suffer according to God's will. *befall.* Happen. *Save.* Except. *the Holy Ghost witnesseth.* The Holy Spirit testifies, probably through the words of prophets (21:10–11).

20:24 Paul's primary duty and passion, more important than *life* itself, were to finish his duty as a faithful witness (*testify*) to the good news (*gospel*) of how God freely and powerfully saves undeserving sinners through Jesus Christ (*grace*).

20:26 *pure from the blood of all men.* He had been a faithful watchman, warning sinners of the judgment to come (18:6; Ezek. 33:1–9).

20:27 *all the counsel of God.* God's entire will or sovereign plan, as revealed in Christ (2:23; 4:28; Eph. 1:11). The faithful ministry must teach all the major doctrines of God's Word: law and gospel, divine sovereignty and human responsibility, heaven and hell, etc.

20:28 *Take heed . . . unto yourselves.* Elders must watch their life and doctrine carefully, for they influence many (1 Tim. 4:16). *the Holy Ghost hath made you.* Though people appoint elders, the Holy Spirit rules over this process when it is conducted by prayer and the Word. *overseers.* Sometimes translated "bishop" (Phil. 1:1; 1 Tim. 3:2; Titus 1:7; 1 Peter 2:25), a title communicating the authority of elders that is delegated to them by God. *feed.* Pastor, care for the *flock* as a shepherd (Eph. 4:11; 1 Peter 5:2). *which he hath purchased with his own blood.* God in His divine nature does not have blood and cannot die (John 4:24; 1 Tim. 1:17). However, God the Son took upon Himself a human nature so that He might bleed and die to redeem sinners (Phil 2:6–8).

20:29–31 An important role of an overseer, as Paul modeled,

30 Also of your own selves shall men arise, speak-
ing perverse things, to draw away disciples after
them.
31 Therefore watch, and remember, that by the
space of three years I ceased not to warn every one
night and day with tears.
32 And now, brethren, I commend you to God,
and to the word of his grace, which is able to build
you up, and to give you an inheritance among all
them which are sanctified.
33 I have coveted no man's silver, or gold, or
apparel.
34 Yea, ye yourselves know, that these hands have
ministered unto my necessities, and to them that
were with me.
35 I have shewed you all things, how that so
labouring ye ought to support the weak, and to
remember the words of the Lord Jesus, how he
said, It is more blessed to give than to receive.
36 ¶ And when he had thus spoken, he kneeled
down, and prayed with them all.
37 And they all wept sore, and fell on Paul's neck,
and kissed him,
38 Sorrowing most of all for the words which he
spake, that they should see his face no more. And
they accompanied him unto the ship.

CHAPTER 21

AND it came to pass, that after we were gotten
from them, and had launched, we came with a
straight course unto Coos, and the *day* following
unto Rhodes, and from thence unto Patara:
2 And finding a ship sailing over unto Phenicia,
we went aboard, and set forth.
3 Now when we had discovered Cyprus, we left
it on the left hand, and sailed into Syria, and
landed at Tyre: for there the ship was to unlade her
burden.
4 And finding disciples, we tarried there seven
days: who said to Paul through the Spirit, that he
should not go up to Jerusalem.
5 And when we had accomplished those days, we
departed and went our way; and they all brought
us on our way, with wives and children, till *we
were* out of the city: and we kneeled down on the
shore, and prayed.
6 And when we had taken our leave one of an-
other, we took ship; and they returned home again.
7 And when we had finished *our* course from
Tyre, we came to Ptolemais, and saluted the
brethren, and abode with them one day.
8 And the next *day* we that were of Paul's com-
pany departed, and came unto Caesarea: and we
entered into the house of Philip the evangelist,
which was *one* of the seven; and abode with him.
9 And the same man had four daughters, virgins,
which did prophesy.
10 And as we tarried *there* many days, there came
down from Judaea a certain prophet, named
Agabus.
11 And when he was come unto us, he took Paul's

is to watch out carefully for false teachers who may rise up even among the eldership of the church.

20:32 *commend you to God, and to the word of his grace.* God's servants perform ministry by the power and truth He supplies through the Word and Spirit (2 Cor. 3:3–6; 4:1–2).

20:33–35 *coveted no man's silver.* Church leaders ought not to be lovers of money, lest they fail to remain faithful to Jesus' command. *apparel.* Clothing, garments.

20:37 *wept sore.* Literally, "there was strong weeping." This heart-rending scene reminds us that elders should be bound together in strong friendship and affection for one another.

Thoughts for Personal/Family Worship: Chapter 20

1. **Paul's ministry did not hold back anything that would truly profit his people (v. 20). He imparted to them the whole counsel of God (v. 27), from beginning to end, for all God's truth is profitable (2 Tim. 3:16). He did not skip over difficult doctrines or hard sayings, nor did he leave out sweet comforts and encouraging exhortations. We may be tempted to be imbalanced and to avoid certain teachings of Scripture, but this comes from pride and self-love instead of serving in love for God and our neighbor. In contrast, Paul did not love his own life but gave his complete devotion to being faithful to the Word. How is he an example for pastors and teachers? How is he an example for us all?**
2. **Paul was concerned about "grievous wolves" entering the flock and not sparing it (v. 29). Though God will save His elect from damnation, and Christ will preserve His church on earth, local congregations and even groups of churches can be ruined by false teaching. Therefore we must guard against it and encourage our elders to do the same. Why is it difficult to oppose false teachers? Why is it crucial?**

TESTIMONY BEFORE RULERS AND ROME (21:1—28:31)

Paul in Jerusalem (21:1—23:11)

Chapter 21: *With suffering looming, Paul arrives in Jerusalem, where in the temple precincts he is met with an uproar and is whisked away by a Roman military contingent, but not without first being allowed to address the people.*

Paul Travels to Jerusalem (21:1–16)

21:1 *were gotten.* Pulled away.

21:3 *discovered.* Come in view of.

21:4 *through the Spirit.* Paul would not have disobeyed the Holy Spirit; evidently the Spirit revealed to prophets that danger waited in Jerusalem, and they assumed that he therefore *should not go.*

21:5 *kneeled . . . prayed.* As with the Ephesian elders (20:36).

21:8 *Philip . . . one of the seven.* See 6:1–6; 8:8–40.

21:9 *four daughters, virgins, which did prophesy.* The gift of prophecy to women was a sign that God's Spirit was poured out on all God's people (2:17–18; cf. 1 Cor. 11:5).

21:10–11 *prophet, named Agabus.* See 11:27–28. *girdle.* Belt. *bound his own hands.* Symbolic actions were also performed by prophets in the Old Testament (Jer. 27:2; Ezek. 4:1). *Thus saith the Holy Ghost.* The formula used to introduce speech from the Lord, *Jehovah* (Ex. 5:1), implying that the Holy Spirit

girdle, and bound his own hands and feet, and
said, Thus saith the Holy Ghost, So shall the Jews
at Jerusalem bind the man that owneth this gir-
dle, and shall deliver *him* into the hands of the
Gentiles.
12 And when we heard these things, both we, and
they of that place, besought him not to go up to
Jerusalem.
13 Then Paul answered, What mean ye to weep
and to break mine heart? for I am ready not to be
bound only, but also to die at Jerusalem for the
name of the Lord Jesus.
14 And when he would not be persuaded, we
ceased, saying, The will of the Lord be done.
15 And after those days we took up our carriages,
and went up to Jerusalem.
16 There went with us also *certain* of the disciples
of Caesarea, and brought with them one Mnason
of Cyprus, an old disciple, with whom we should
lodge.
17 And when we were come to Jerusalem, the
brethren received us gladly.
18 And the *day* following Paul went in with us
unto James; and all the elders were present.
19 And when he had saluted them, he declared
particularly what things God had wrought among
the Gentiles by his ministry.
20 And when they heard *it*, they glorified the
Lord, and said unto him, Thou seest, brother, how
many thousands of Jews there are which believe;
and they are all zealous of the law:
21 And they are informed of thee, that thou
teachest all the Jews which are among the Gentiles
to forsake Moses, saying that they ought not to
circumcise *their* children, neither to walk after the
customs.
22 What is it therefore? the multitude must needs
come together: for they will hear that thou art
come.
23 Do therefore this that we say to thee: We have
four men which have a vow on them;
24 Them take, and purify thyself with them, and
be at charges with them, that they may shave
their heads: and all may know that those things,
whereof they were informed concerning thee, are
nothing; but *that* thou thyself also walkest or-
derly, and keepest the law.
25 As touching the Gentiles which believe, we
have written *and* concluded that they observe no
such thing, save only that they keep themselves
from *things* offered to idols, and from blood, and
from strangled, and from fornication.
26 Then Paul took the men, and the next day
purifying himself with them entered into the
temple, to signify the accomplishment of the days
of purification, until that an offering should be
offered for every one of them.
27 And when the seven days were almost ended,
the Jews which were of Asia, when they saw him
in the temple, stirred up all the people, and laid
hands on him,
28 Crying out, Men of Israel, help: This is the
man, that teacheth all *men* every where against
the people, and the law, and this place: and fur-
ther brought Greeks also into the temple, and
hath polluted this holy place.
29 (For they had seen before with him in the city
Trophimus an Ephesian, whom they supposed
that Paul had brought into the temple.)
30 And all the city was moved, and the people
ran together: and they took Paul, and drew him
out of the temple: and forthwith the doors were
shut.
31 And as they went about to kill him, tidings
came unto the chief captain of the band, that all
Jerusalem was in an uproar.
32 Who immediately took soldiers and centuri-
ons, and ran down unto them: and when they
saw the chief captain and the soldiers, they left
beating of Paul.

---

is God (5:3–4) and that New Testament prophecy was equal to Old Testament prophecy in its divine authority. *bind . . . deliver.* Paul later used almost these identical words to describe what happened in Jerusalem—"delivered prisoner" or "bound" (28:17), confirming that this was the word of God and that Agabus was a true prophet (Deut. 18:20–22).

21:12–13 *both we, and they . . . besought him.* All of Paul's companions exhorted him not to go, but although he was deeply moved he was prepared even to *die* for Christ's glory in the gospel (*name*), for this was His calling (20:24).

21:14 *The will of the Lord be done.* God's will determines all things, and we must live in constant submission to Him, trusting Him with the future (18:21; Rom. 1:10; 1 Cor. 4:19).

21:15 *took up our carriages.* Packed up our possessions.

Paul and James (21:17–26)

21:18 *James.* See note at 15:13.

21:19 *saluted.* Greeted. *he declared.* Another missionary report to the church (14:27; 15:3–4). *wrought.* Worked.

21:20 *thousands . . . which believe.* The evangelistic work among the *Jews* was not useless.

21:21 *thou teachest all the Jews . . . . to forsake Moses.* The earlier council had decided that the believing Gentiles were not bound to keep the law (15:1–41). The issue here was whether the believing Jews dispersed among the Gentiles should keep the law.

21:23–24 *be at charges with them.* Pay the expenses associated with their offerings. *shave their heads.* See note at 18:18.

21:25 *save.* Except. They reiterated the decision of the council (15:19–20,28–29).

Paul's Arrest (21:27—23:11)

21:28 *polluted this holy place.* There were several courts within the temple precincts, and the Gentiles were allowed only in the outermost court so that they would not defile the holy places with uncleanness.

21:30 *moved.* Excited, stirred up. *drew.* Forcefully dragged. *forthwith.* Immediately.

21:31 *tidings.* News. *chief captain of the band.* Commander of the Roman cohort, a unit of several hundred soldiers.

33 Then the chief captain came near, and took
him, and commanded *him* to be bound with two
chains; and demanded who he was, and what he
had done.
34 And some cried one thing, some another,
among the multitude: and when he could not
know the certainty for the tumult, he com-
manded him to be carried into the castle.
35 And when he came upon the stairs, so it was,
that he was borne of the soldiers for the violence
of the people.
36 For the multitude of the people followed after,
crying, Away with him.
37 And as Paul was to be led into the castle, he
said unto the chief captain, May I speak unto
thee? Who said, Canst thou speak Greek?
38 Art not thou that Egyptian, which before
these days madest an uproar, and leddest out
into the wilderness four thousand men that were
murderers?
39 But Paul said, I am a man *which am* a Jew of
Tarsus, *a city* in Cilicia, a citizen of no mean city:
and, I beseech thee, suffer me to speak unto the
people.
40 And when he had given him licence, Paul
stood on the stairs, and beckoned with the hand
unto the people. And when there was made a
great silence, he spake unto *them* in the Hebrew
tongue, saying,

CHAPTER 22

MEN, brethren, and fathers, hear ye my defence
which I make now unto you.
2 (And when they heard that he spake in the
Hebrew tongue to them, they kept the more
silence: and he saith,)
3 I am verily a man *which am* a Jew, born in
Tarsus, *a city* in Cilicia, yet brought up in this city
at the feet of Gamaliel, *and* taught according to
the perfect manner of the law of the fathers, and
was zealous toward God, as ye all are this day.
4 And I persecuted this way unto the death, bind-
ing and delivering into prisons both men and
women.
5 As also the high priest doth bear me witness,
and all the estate of the elders: from whom also
I received letters unto the brethren, and went to
Damascus, to bring them which were there bound
unto Jerusalem, for to be punished.
6 And it came to pass, that, as I made my journey,
and was come nigh unto Damascus about noon,
suddenly there shone from heaven a great light
round about me.
7 And I fell unto the ground, and heard a voice say-
ing unto me, Saul, Saul, why persecutest thou me?
8 And I answered, Who art thou, Lord? And he
said unto me, I am Jesus of Nazareth, whom thou
persecutest.
9 And they that were with me saw indeed the
light, and were afraid; but they heard not the
voice of him that spake to me.
10 And I said, What shall I do, Lord? And the
Lord said unto me, Arise, and go into Damascus;
and there it shall be told thee of all things which
are appointed for thee to do.
11 And when I could not see for the glory of that
light, being led by the hand of them that were
with me, I came into Damascus.
12 And one Ananias, a devout man according to

21:32 *left*. Stopped.
21:33 The Romans *bound* Paul after the Jews had seized him. Thus the prophecy is fulfilled just a week after Paul entered Jerusalem (v. 11).
21:39 *beseech*. Request. *suffer*. Permit.
21:40 *given him licence*. Permitted him. *Hebrew tongue*. Language of the Jews, at that time Aramaic. This was likely an attempt to show the Jews that he was not abandoning his heritage or the ways of Judaism (22:2).

Thoughts for Personal/Family Worship: Chapter 21

1. **What a beautiful prayer meeting on the shore (v. 5). Do you think the children, at least the older ones, ever forgot kneeling there with the apostle Paul as he was heading to Jerusalem to suffer for the gospel's sake? Why is it good to send off friends with prayer?**
2. **Mnason of Cyprus, known as "an old disciple," opened his house to Paul (v. 16). What are the blessings of following Christ for a long time into old age? They must have enjoyed sweet fellowship in Mnason's home. What blessings does it bring to show hospitality to traveling missionaries and pastors?**
3. **As in the riot in Ephesus (19:29–41), the mob in Jerusalem was full of confusion (vv. 30–34), acting rashly in violence on the basis of false information (vv. 28–29). Why is it foolish to join an angry mob? What is a better alternative for addressing wrongs?**

Chapter 22: *Paul defends his gospel ministry to his fellow Jews, telling of his conversion and commission; still, they shut him down.*

22:1 *brethren, and fathers*. Paul respectfully addressed those who had just been beating him.
22:2 *Hebrew tongue*. See note at 21:40.
22:3 *verily*. Truly. *manner*. Custom, habit. *Gamaliel*. See 5:34.
22:4–21 Paul recounted his conversion story in many of the same details found in ch. 9.
22:5 *estate of the elders*. Literally, "the presbytery," the eldership or council of leaders (1 Tim. 4:14). *bound unto Jerusalem*. Ironically, Paul had sought to bring others bound to Jerusalem, but now he has brought himself to Jerusalem to be bound.
22:6 *nigh*. Near. *noon*. He was not dreaming or asleep, it being the middle of the day.
22:9 *saw . . . light . . . heard not the voice*. Earlier Paul had said that they were "hearing a voice, but seeing no man" (9:7). It appears that they perceived light and sound but did not have the distinct experience of Christ's glory and understanding of His words that Paul did.
22:12 *devout man according to the law*. Christians honored the Old Testament Scriptures.

the law, having a good report of all the Jews which
dwelt *there*,
13 Came unto me, and stood, and said unto me,
Brother Saul, receive thy sight. And the same hour
I looked up upon him.
14 And he said, The God of our fathers hath
chosen thee, that thou shouldest know his will,
and see that Just One, and shouldest hear the
voice of his mouth.
15 For thou shalt be his witness unto all men of
what thou hast seen and heard.
16 And now why tarriest thou? arise, and be
baptized, and wash away thy sins, calling on the
name of the Lord.
17 And it came to pass, that, when I was come
again to Jerusalem, even while I prayed in the
temple, I was in a trance;
18 And saw him saying unto me, Make haste, and
get thee quickly out of Jerusalem: for they will not
receive thy testimony concerning me.
19 And I said, Lord, they know that I imprisoned
and beat in every synagogue them that believed
on thee:
20 And when the blood of thy martyr Stephen
was shed, I also was standing by, and consenting
unto his death, and kept the raiment of them that
slew him.
21 And he said unto me, Depart: for I will send
thee far hence unto the Gentiles.
22 And they gave him audience unto this word,
and *then* lifted up their voices, and said, Away
with such a *fellow* from the earth: for it is not fit
that he should live.
23 And as they cried out, and cast off *their* clothes,
and threw dust into the air,
24 The chief captain commanded him to be
brought into the castle, and bade that he should
be examined by scourging; that he might know
wherefore they cried so against him.
25 And as they bound him with thongs, Paul
said unto the centurion that stood by, Is it lawful
for you to scourge a man that is a Roman, and
uncondemned?
26 When the centurion heard *that*, he went and
told the chief captain, saying, Take heed what
thou doest: for this man is a Roman.
27 Then the chief captain came, and said unto
him, Tell me, art thou a Roman? He said, Yea.
28 And the chief captain answered, With a great
sum obtained I this freedom. And Paul said, But
I was *free* born.
29 Then straightway they departed from him
which should have examined him: and the chief
captain also was afraid, after he knew that he was
a Roman, and because he had bound him.
30 On the morrow, because he would have
known the certainty wherefore he was accused
of the Jews, he loosed him from *his* bands, and
commanded the chief priests and all their council
to appear, and brought Paul down, and set him
before them.

CHAPTER 23

AND Paul, earnestly beholding the council, said,
Men *and* brethren, I have lived in all good con-
science before God until this day.
2 And the high priest Ananias commanded them
that stood by him to smite him on the mouth.
3 Then said Paul unto him, God shall smite thee,

22:14 *God of our fathers.* Paul's ministry is in continuity with God's plan of redemption begun in the Old Testament, as promised in the ancient covenants. *Just One.* Christ, the Righteous (3:14; 7:52).
22:16 *tarriest.* Wait. *be baptized, and wash away thy sins, calling on the name of the Lord.* Baptism is a sign of cleansing from guilt and sin, but spiritual washing takes place through faith in the gospel of Christ and prayer for salvation (2:21; 15:9; 1 Peter 3:21).
22:17–21 *trance.* This is the first time we hear of this vision.
22:20 *martyr.* Literally, "witness" (Greek *martus*), a term used elsewhere in Acts in a positive sense only of the apostles (see note at 1:8). *raiment.* Clothing.
22:22 The crowd listened (*gave him audience*) until Paul spoke of God favoring the Gentiles, and then reacted violently as though he had committed blasphemy (Luke 4:24–30).
22:24 *bade.* Said. *scourging.* Worse than the whipping Paul had earlier received (16:22), this sometimes deadly punishment involved beating with a long leather band to which metal shards, stone, or bone were attached.
22:25 *thongs.* Leather straps. *Roman.* Paul again invoked his imperial citizenship to protest unjust punishment (16:37–39). Good laws protect Christians from persecution.
22:29 *straightway.* Immediately.
22:30 *On the morrow.* The next day.

Thoughts for Personal/Family Worship: Chapter 22

1. **When God converts us, even if we are in a crowd, it is as though He leads us apart and speaks to us personally. His words enter our mind and hearts in a way that may leave others untouched and cold. Conversion is God's sovereign work in the individual soul. It glorifies Him for us to reflect upon our conversions, whether dramatic or quiet, and to tell others of the work of our Savior. Has God saved you? If so, how does your conversion manifest the glory of His sovereign grace?**
2. **Paul loved those who were his people according to the flesh. He would have died for his fellow Jews if this would have saved them (Rom. 9:1–3). Even after they unjustly seized him and beat him he did not curse them but lovingly told them about the Savior of both Jew and Gentile. Do you have a burden for those who do not know Christ? What can you do with that burden?**

Chapter 23: ***Paul testifies before the Sanhedrin and escapes a plot on his life by being moved to Caesarea in the custody of Felix.***

23:1 *good conscience before God.* Christians should seek to live in the peace of careful obedience to all God's laws, confessing their sins and resting in Christ for forgiveness (24:16;

thou whited wall: for sittest thou to judge me
after the law, and commandest me to be smitten
contrary to the law?
4 And they that stood by said, Revilest thou God's
high priest?
5 Then said Paul, I wist not, brethren, that he was
the high priest: for it is written, Thou shalt not
speak evil of the ruler of thy people.
6 But when Paul perceived that the one part were
Sadducees, and the other Pharisees, he cried out
in the council, Men *and* brethren, I am a Pharisee,
the son of a Pharisee: of the hope and resurrec-
tion of the dead I am called in question.
7 And when he had so said, there arose a dissen-
sion between the Pharisees and the Sadducees:
and the multitude was divided.
8 For the Sadducees say that there is no resurrec-
tion, neither angel, nor spirit: but the Pharisees
confess both.
9 And there arose a great cry: and the scribes
that were of the Pharisees' part arose, and strove,
saying, We find no evil in this man: but if a spirit
or an angel hath spoken to him, let us not fight
against God.
10 And when there arose a great dissension, the
chief captain, fearing lest Paul should have been
pulled in pieces of them, commanded the soldiers
to go down, and to take him by force from among
them, and to bring *him* into the castle.
11 And the night following the Lord stood by
him, and said, Be of good cheer, Paul: for as thou
hast testified of me in Jerusalem, so must thou
bear witness also at Rome.
12 And when it was day, certain of the Jews band-
ed together, and bound themselves under a curse,
saying that they would neither eat nor drink till
they had killed Paul.
13 And they were more than forty which had
made this conspiracy.
14 And they came to the chief priests and elders,
and said, We have bound ourselves under a great
curse, that we will eat nothing until we have slain
Paul.
15 Now therefore ye with the council signify to
the chief captain that he bring him down unto
you to morrow, as though ye would enquire
something more perfectly concerning him: and
we, or ever he come near, are ready to kill him.
16 And when Paul's sister's son heard of their
lying in wait, he went and entered into the castle,
and told Paul.
17 Then Paul called one of the centurions unto
him, and said, Bring this young man unto the chief
captain: for he hath a certain thing to tell him.
18 So he took him, and brought *him* to the chief
captain, and said, Paul the prisoner called me
unto *him*, and prayed me to bring this young man
unto thee, who hath something to say unto thee.
19 Then the chief captain took him by the hand,
and went *with him* aside privately, and asked *him*,
What is that thou hast to tell me?
20 And he said, The Jews have agreed to desire
thee that thou wouldest bring down Paul to
morrow into the council, as though they would
enquire somewhat of him more perfectly.
21 But do not thou yield unto them: for there
lie in wait for him of them more than forty men,
which have bound themselves with an oath, that
they will neither eat nor drink till they have killed
him: and now are they ready, looking for a prom-
ise from thee.
22 So the chief captain *then* let the young man
depart, and charged *him*, *See thou* tell no man that
thou hast shewed these things to me.
23 And he called unto *him* two centurions,
saying, Make ready two hundred soldiers to go to
Caesarea, and horsemen threescore and ten, and
spearmen two hundred, at the third hour of the
night;
24 And provide *them* beasts, that they may set Paul
on, and bring *him* safe unto Felix the governor.
25 And he wrote a letter after this manner:

Rom. 2:15; 2 Cor. 1:12; 1 Tim. 1:5; Heb. 9:14; 1 John 1:5–10).

23:3 *whited.* White-washed, a figure of speech for superficial, hypocritical religion (Matt. 23:27).

23:5 *I wist not.* I did not know, perhaps due to poor eyesight (Gal. 1:13–15). *not speak evil of the ruler.* Paul showed respect for authority, even ungodly authority (Ex. 22:28; cf. Titus 3:1–2).

23:6 *I am a Pharisee.* See Phil. 3:5.

23:9 *not fight against God.* Similar advice to that given by Gamaliel, also a Pharisee (5:39; cf. 11:17).

23:11 *Be of good cheer.* Have courage. *must thou bear witness also at Rome.* The *Lord* Jesus revealed to Paul that a divine necessity (see note at 1:16) would bring him to the capital of the empire (27:24), just as Jesus had gone by divine necessity to Jerusalem (Luke 9:22). The same decree that sent Jesus to the cross now sends the witnesses of Jesus into the heart of the pagan world to preach the gospel, as the Scriptures had foretold (Luke 24:44–47).

Paul Sent to Felix (23:12—24:27)

Plot to Kill Paul Uncovered (23:12–22)

23:16 *Paul's sister's son heard.* Paul had family in Jerusalem, and God's providence arranged for his nephew to save him from certain death.

Paul and Felix (23:23—24:27)

23:23 God's secret providence again acted so that Paul, an accused prisoner, received a large military escort to ensure his safety. *threescore and ten.* Seventy.

23:24 *Felix the governor.* Marcus Antonius Felix, a former slave appointed by emperor Claudius as procurator of Judaea (ruled AD 52/53–59/60) but later losing his position because he failed to deal with the violent uprising of the Jews.

23:25–30 The inclusion of Claudius's *letter* reminds the reader that Luke had researched the historical sources (Luke 1:1–3). It emphasizes that Paul was accused on religious grounds, not of crimes against the state (18:15), an important

26 Claudius Lysias unto the most excellent governor Felix *sendeth* greeting.
27 This man was taken of the Jews, and should have been killed of them: then came I with an army, and rescued him, having understood that he was a Roman.
28 And when I would have known the cause wherefore they accused him, I brought him forth into their council:
29 Whom I perceived to be accused of questions of their law, but to have nothing laid to his charge worthy of death or of bonds.
30 And when it was told me how that the Jews laid wait for the man, I sent straightway to thee, and gave commandment to his accusers also to say before thee what *they had* against him. Farewell.
31 Then the soldiers, as it was commanded them, took Paul, and brought *him* by night to Antipatris.
32 On the morrow they left the horsemen to go with him, and returned to the castle:
33 Who, when they came to Caesarea, and delivered the epistle to the governor, presented Paul also before him.
34 And when the governor had read *the letter*, he asked of what province he was. And when he understood that *he was* of Cilicia;
35 I will hear thee, said he, when thine accusers are also come. And he commanded him to be kept in Herod's judgment hall.

CHAPTER 24

AND after five days Ananias the high priest descended with the elders, and *with* a certain orator *named* Tertullus, who informed the governor against Paul.
2 And when he was called forth, Tertullus began to accuse *him*, saying, Seeing that by thee we enjoy great quietness, and that very worthy deeds are done unto this nation by thy providence,
3 We accept *it* always, and in all places, most noble Felix, with all thankfulness.
4 Notwithstanding, that I be not further tedious unto thee, I pray thee that thou wouldest hear us of thy clemency a few words.
5 For we have found this man *a* pestilent *fellow*, and a mover of sedition among all the Jews throughout the world, and a ringleader of the sect of the Nazarenes:
6 Who also hath gone about to profane the temple: whom we took, and would have judged according to our law.
7 But the chief captain Lysias came *upon us*, and with great violence took *him* away out of our hands,
8 Commanding his accusers to come unto thee: by examining of whom thyself mayest take knowledge of all these things, whereof we accuse him.
9 And the Jews also assented, saying that these things were so.
10 Then Paul, after that the governor had beckoned unto him to speak, answered, Forasmuch as I know that thou hast been of many years a judge unto this nation, I do the more cheerfully answer for myself:
11 Because that thou mayest understand, that there are yet but twelve days since I went up to Jerusalem for to worship.
12 And they neither found me in the temple disputing with any man, neither raising up the people, neither in the synagogues, nor in the city:
13 Neither can they prove the things whereof they now accuse me.
14 But this I confess unto thee, that after the way which they call heresy, so worship I the God of my fathers, believing all things which are written in the law and in the prophets:

defense for Christians in the empire.

Thoughts for Personal/Family Worship: Chapter 23

1. **Paul was in prison for the hope of Israel. Already a Pharisee, he had believed there was such a thing as a resurrection, though he did not believe that Christ had been raised until He appeared to him on the road to Damascus. It was then that he came to understand that Christ fulfilled Old Testament prophecy and that Jesus Himself was the hope of Israel. Jeremiah called God Himself "the hope of Israel" (Jer. 14:8; 17:13), and when Paul met Christ he lost all hope in himself and saw Christ as his only hope. Why is the future resurrection that Christ will bring the center of the hope of believers?**
2. **Christ appeared to Paul to assure him that he would testify not only in Jerusalem but also in Rome (v. 11). Paul's work was not yet done. Even though people plotted his death day and night, Christ's Word could not be undone. God predestined not only the sufferings of His Son to purchase redemption but also the success of His servants to proclaim redemption so that the nations would believe. While we do not know God's specific decree for our future, how can recognizing His sovereignty give us confidence in serving Him?**

Chapter 24: ***The case against Paul is argued in front of Felix; though Paul defends himself and the gospel with an effect that causes Felix to tremble, Felix leaves Paul in prison in the hope of a bribe.***

24:1 *orator.* Professional spokesman, probably trained in the Greek rhetorical arts.
24:2–3 *by thy providence.* Because of your foresight and planning. *Tertullus* began by flattering Felix, probably in an effort to get him to take the side of the Jews.
24:4 *clemency.* Kindness, patience.
24:5 *pestilent fellow.* A plague. *mover of sedition.* One who stirs uprisings. *Nazarenes.* So named because Jesus was from Nazareth (2:22; 22:8).
24:6 *profane the temple.* The same false charge made earlier (21:28–29).
24:7 *great violence.* Much force, perhaps a reference to a large group of soldiers (21:32).
24:14 *God of my fathers.* Paul declared the strong continuity

15 And have hope toward God, which they them-
selves also allow, that there shall be a resurrection
of the dead, both of the just and unjust.
16 And herein do I exercise myself, to have always
a conscience void of offence toward God, and
toward men.
17 Now after many years I came to bring alms to
my nation, and offerings.
18 Whereupon certain Jews from Asia found me
purified in the temple, neither with multitude,
nor with tumult.
19 Who ought to have been here before thee, and
object, if they had ought against me.
20 Or else let these same *here* say, if they have
found any evil doing in me, while I stood before
the council,
21 Except it be for this one voice, that I cried
standing among them, Touching the resurrection
of the dead I am called in question by you this
day.
22 And when Felix heard these things, having
more perfect knowledge of *that* way, he deferred
them, and said, When Lysias the chief captain
shall come down, I will know the uttermost of
your matter.
23 And he commanded a centurion to keep Paul,
and to let *him* have liberty, and that he should
forbid none of his acquaintance to minister or
come unto him.
24 And after certain days, when Felix came with
his wife Drusilla, which was a Jewess, he sent for
Paul, and heard him concerning the faith in Christ.
25 And as he reasoned of righteousness, temper-
ance, and judgment to come, Felix trembled, and
answered, Go thy way for this time; when I have a
convenient season, I will call for thee.
26 He hoped also that money should have been
given him of Paul, that he might loose him:
wherefore he sent for him the oftener, and com-
muned with him.
27 But after two years Porcius Festus came into
Felix' room: and Felix, willing to shew the Jews a
pleasure, left Paul bound.

CHAPTER 25

NOW when Festus was come into the province,
after three days he ascended from Caesarea to
Jerusalem.
2 Then the high priest and the chief of the Jews
informed him against Paul, and besought him,
3 And desired favour against him, that he would
send for him to Jerusalem, laying wait in the way
to kill him.
4 But Festus answered, that Paul should be kept
at Caesarea, and that he himself would depart
shortly *thither*.
5 Let them therefore, said he, which among you
are able, go down with *me*, and accuse this man, if
there be any wickedness in him.
6 And when he had tarried among them more
than ten days, he went down unto Caesarea; and

between the Old Testament (*all things . . . . written in the law and . . . prophets*) and Christian doctrine.

24:15 *resurrection . . . of the just and unjust*. See Dan. 12:2.

24:16 *conscience void of offence*. No inward sense of guilt from sin that has been cleansed by repentance and forgiveness.

24:17 *bring alms to my nation*. He came to Jerusalem with the intention of helping the poor of his nation, not destroying it.

24:22 *that way*. A name for discipleship of Jesus or Christianity (9:2). *know the uttermost of your matter*. Thoroughly examine your case.

24:23 *liberty*. Paul was merely under house arrest and was permitted visitors (28:30).

24:24 *Drusilla*. Felix's third wife (he was her second husband). The daughter of Herod Agrippa I and sister to Agrippa II, at this time she was about eighteen years old. She was a Jew and perhaps Felix hoped she might have some insight into Paul's words.

24:25 *temperance*. Self-control. *trembled*. Given Felix's sexual sin (v. 24) and love of bribes (v. 26), Paul's teaching on moral accountability with God alarmed Felix.

24:26 *loose*. Free. *wherefore*. Therefore. *communed*. Spent time with, talked together.

24:27 *Porcius Festus*. Roman procurator of Judaea (ruled c. AD 59–62). *came into Felix' room*. Replaced Felix, who lost his position because he failed to deal adequately with a Jewish uprising.

Thoughts for Personal/Family Worship: Chapter 24

1. **Paul held before all his hearers the truth of the resurrection of the dead, "both of the just and unjust" (v. 15). It is a solemn truth that we will rise again, and all souls that ever lived will be in one or the other group: righteous or wicked. Felix trembled when he heard of "righteousness, temperance, and judgment to come" (v. 25), but he did not repent. Why is it not enough to feel guilt over sin and fear over the judgment day? What did Felix lack in order to be saved?**
2. **One reason Paul could speak so boldly and freely before all men when Felix trembled before God was that Paul's mindset was "to have always a conscience void of offence toward God, and toward men" (v. 16). Proverbs 28:1 says, "The wicked flee when no man pursueth: but the righteous are bold as a lion." Obviously Paul was a sinner, but he sought daily cleansing for his sins and grace to live righteously and holily by grace. Why does living with a clear conscience give courage? How can we do this?**

Paul before Leaders (25:1—26:32)

Chapter 25: ***Again the case against Paul is made, now in front of Festus, ending with Paul's appeal to Caesar, while Paul has an opportunity to explain the gospel to Festus, along with King Agrippa and Bernice.***

Paul Appeals to Caesar (25:1–12)

25:2 *besought*. Urged.

25:4 *thither*. There, to that place.

25:6 *tarried*. Waited. *judgment seat*. Acts frequently depicts apostles and disciples being dragged into formal and informal court situations where they faithfully witness to Jesus and His resurrection.

the next day sitting on the judgment seat com-
manded Paul to be brought.
7 And when he was come, the Jews which came
down from Jerusalem stood round about, and
laid many and grievous complaints against Paul,
which they could not prove.
8 While he answered for himself, Neither against
the law of the Jews, neither against the temple, nor
yet against Caesar, have I offended any thing at all.
9 But Festus, willing to do the Jews a pleasure,
answered Paul, and said, Wilt thou go up to
Jerusalem, and there be judged of these things
before me?
10 Then said Paul, I stand at Caesar's judgment
seat, where I ought to be judged: to the Jews have
I done no wrong, as thou very well knowest.
11 For if I be an offender, or have committed any
thing worthy of death, I refuse not to die: but
if there be none of these things whereof these
accuse me, no man may deliver me unto them. I
appeal unto Caesar.
12 Then Festus, when he had conferred with
the council, answered, Hast thou appealed unto
Caesar? unto Caesar shalt thou go.
13 And after certain days king Agrippa and
Bernice came unto Caesarea to salute Festus.
14 And when they had been there many days,
Festus declared Paul's cause unto the king, saying,
There is a certain man left in bonds by Felix:
15 About whom, when I was at Jerusalem, the
chief priests and the elders of the Jews informed
me, desiring *to have* judgment against him.
16 To whom I answered, It is not the manner of
the Romans to deliver any man to die, before that
he which is accused have the accusers face to face,
and have licence to answer for himself concerning
the crime laid against him.
17 Therefore, when they were come hither,
without any delay on the morrow I sat on the
judgment seat, and commanded the man to be
brought forth.
18 Against whom when the accusers stood up,
they brought none accusation of such things as
I supposed:
19 But had certain questions against him of their
own superstition, and of one Jesus, which was
dead, whom Paul affirmed to be alive.
20 And because I doubted of such manner of
questions, I asked *him* whether he would go to
Jerusalem, and there be judged of these matters.
21 But when Paul had appealed to be reserved
unto the hearing of Augustus, I commanded him
to be kept till I might send him to Caesar.
22 Then Agrippa said unto Festus, I would also
hear the man myself. To morrow, said he, thou
shalt hear him.
23 And on the morrow, when Agrippa was come,
and Bernice, with great pomp, and was entered
into the place of hearing, with the chief captains,
and principal men of the city, at Festus' com-
mandment Paul was brought forth.
24 And Festus said, King Agrippa, and all men
which are here present with us, ye see this man,
about whom all the multitude of the Jews have
dealt with me, both at Jerusalem, and *also* here,
crying that he ought not to live any longer.
25 But when I found that he had committed
nothing worthy of death, and that he himself hath
appealed to Augustus, I have determined to send
him.
26 Of whom I have no certain thing to write unto
my lord. Wherefore I have brought him forth
before you, and specially before thee, O king
Agrippa, that, after examination had, I might have
somewhat to write.
27 For it seemeth to me unreasonable to send a
prisoner, and not withal to signify the crimes *laid*
against him.

25:7 *which they could not prove.* Two years had not given them enough evidence to convict Paul.

25:11 *I appeal unto Caesar.* Paul petitioned for his case to be judged by the highest imperial authority in Rome, not only to avoid murder by the unbelieving Jews (v. 3) but also to press on to fulfill the will of Christ for his ministry (19:21; 23:11).

Festus Seeks Agrippa's Advice (25:13–27)

25:13 *king Agrippa and Bernice.* Herod Agrippa II and his sister Bernice; she was about a year younger than he. He was partly Jewish but a loyal and trusted governor for Rome, respected as an expert in Jewish matters (26:3). She was a sister of Drusilla (24:24), lived with Agrippa, married several times, and became a mistress to the emperor. *salute.* Greet.

25:16 *manner.* Custom, habit.

25:18 *none accusation of such things as I supposed.* Festus found no well-founded charges against Paul.

25:20 *manner.* Kind, sort.

25:21 *Augustus.* Another title for Caesar.

25:23 *pomp.* Showy appearance.

25:26 *no certain thing to write unto my lord.* Usually accompanying a prisoner to Rome was a sheet of charges against him to help inform Caesar of the situation, but Festus had no formal charges and was at a loss as to how to send Paul to the emperor.

25:27 *withal.* Also, likewise.

Thoughts for Personal/Family Worship: Chapter 25

1. **Though Paul was in prison for the sake of the gospel, the Word of God was not bound. Paul's sorrows became doorways for the gospel to come to rulers and judges. Though they came in great pomp and show of their power and wealth, they were desperately needy sinners who would soon face death, after which would come judgment. When persecution brings God's people before rulers and judges, let us remember that the Lord Jesus rules over all for the sake of spreading the gospel to all people. How should this change the way we view our trials? In what way should it make us alert for evangelistic opportunities?**
2. **Paul's accusers had many and grievous complaints against Paul, but "they could not prove" them (v. 7).**

CHAPTER 26

THEN Agrippa said unto Paul, Thou art permitted
to speak for thyself. Then Paul stretched forth the
hand, and answered for himself:
2 I think myself happy, king Agrippa, because
I shall answer for myself this day before thee
touching all the things whereof I am accused of
the Jews:
3 Especially *because I know* thee to be expert in all
customs and questions which are among the Jews:
wherefore I beseech thee to hear me patiently.
4 My manner of life from my youth, which was
at the first among mine own nation at Jerusalem,
know all the Jews;
5 Which knew me from the beginning, if they
would testify, that after the most straitest sect of
our religion I lived a Pharisee.
6 And now I stand and am judged for the hope of
the promise made of God unto our fathers:
7 Unto which *promise* our twelve tribes, instantly
serving *God* day and night, hope to come. For
which hope's sake, king Agrippa, I am accused of
the Jews.
8 Why should it be thought a thing incredible
with you, that God should raise the dead?
9 I verily thought with myself, that I ought to
do many things contrary to the name of Jesus of
Nazareth.
10 Which thing I also did in Jerusalem: and
many of the saints did I shut up in prison, having
received authority from the chief priests; and
when they were put to death, I gave my voice
against *them*.
11 And I punished them oft in every synagogue,
and compelled *them* to blaspheme; and being
exceedingly mad against them, I persecuted *them*
even unto strange cities.
12 Whereupon as I went to Damascus with au-
thority and commission from the chief priests,
13 At midday, O king, I saw in the way a light
from heaven, above the brightness of the sun,
shining round about me and them which jour-
neyed with me.
14 And when we were all fallen to the earth, I
heard a voice speaking unto me, and saying in the
Hebrew tongue, Saul, Saul, why persecutest thou
me? *it is* hard for thee to kick against the pricks.
15 And I said, Who art thou, Lord? And he said, I
am Jesus whom thou persecutest.
16 But rise, and stand upon thy feet: for I have
appeared unto thee for this purpose, to make
thee a minister and a witness both of these things
which thou hast seen, and of those things in the
which I will appear unto thee;
17 Delivering thee from the people, and *from* the
Gentiles, unto whom now I send thee,
18 To open their eyes, *and* to turn *them* from
darkness to light, and *from* the power of Satan
unto God, that they may receive forgiveness of
sins, and inheritance among them which are
sanctified by faith that is in me.
19 Whereupon, O king Agrippa, I was not disobe-
dient unto the heavenly vision:
20 But shewed first unto them of Damascus, and
at Jerusalem, and throughout all the coasts of
Judaea, and *then* to the Gentiles, that they should
repent and turn to God, and do works meet for
repentance.
21 For these causes the Jews caught me in the
temple, and went about to kill *me*.

Christ's faithful servants mirror the righteousness of their Lord, although imperfectly, and thus even the world must admit that they have done nothing worthy of the persecution they endure. If you were brought to trial before men, could they find you guilty of no other crime than being a faithful Christian?

Chapter 26: *Paul preaches before Festus, King Agrippa, and Bernice.*

Paul Preaches before Agrippa (26:1–32)

26:3 *expert in all customs and questions.* Paul highlights here that Agrippa is truly learned in Jewish affairs, customs, and theology. Paul will recount his conversion story, showing once again the unity and continuity the Christian faith has with the faith of the fathers.

26:4–18 The third time Paul's conversion is recounted (9:1–22; 22:1–21).

26:5 *straitest sect of our religion.* Strictest religious group (Gal. 1:13–14; Phil. 3:4–6).

26:6 *hope of the promise made of God unto our fathers.* The resurrection of the dead (v. 8). Paul defended himself by showing that he had not invented a new religion but was following the ancient faith of the Jews in the promises of Holy Scripture (v. 22; 24:14–15).

26:7 *instantly serving.* Earnestly worshiping.

26:9 *verily.* Truly. *do many things contrary.* Ironically, this Pharisaic defender of the resurrection fought against the Risen One. *name of Jesus.* His glory, revealed in the gospel (see note at 2:38).

26:11 *strange.* Foreign.

26:14 *Hebrew tongue.* Language spoken by the Jews, at that time Aramaic. *against the pricks.* Against the cattle goads (see note at 9:5–6).

26:16 *witness.* A key term used of apostles in this book (1:8).

26:17 Jesus commissioned Paul to proclaim the gospel to the Jews and the *Gentiles*.

26:18 *open their eyes.* Give sight instead of blindness (Isa. 35:5; 42:7), a work of God's saving illumination (2 Cor. 4:4–6). *turn . . . receive.* Conversion involves repentance from sin to God and *faith* in Christ (11:21; 20:21). *darkness to light.* The Lord saves a person by moving him from one kingdom (*power*) to another so that we no longer serve *Satan* through our sins and idols but instead worship and serve *God* (Col. 1:13). *forgiveness . . . sanctified.* Salvation gives rise to distinct but inseparable graces: justification and sanctification, that is, a new status of righteousness in God's sight (13:39) and a new heart to love righteousness and exercise self-control (24:25).

26:20 *meet for.* Suited to, reflective of.

26:21 *For these causes.* The only thing he was guilty of was

22 Having therefore obtained help of God, I con-
tinue unto this day, witnessing both to small and
great, saying none other things than those which
the prophets and Moses did say should come:
23 That Christ should suffer, *and* that he should
be the first that should rise from the dead, and
should shew light unto the people, and to the
Gentiles.
24 And as he thus spake for himself, Festus said
with a loud voice, Paul, thou art beside thyself;
much learning doth make thee mad.
25 But he said, I am not mad, most noble Festus;
but speak forth the words of truth and soberness.
26 For the king knoweth of these things, before
whom also I speak freely: for I am persuaded that
none of these things are hidden from him; for this
thing was not done in a corner.
27 King Agrippa, believest thou the prophets? I
know that thou believest.
28 Then Agrippa said unto Paul, Almost thou
persuadest me to be a Christian.
29 And Paul said, I would to God, that not only
thou, but also all that hear me this day, were both
almost, and altogether such as I am, except these
bonds.
30 And when he had thus spoken, the king rose
up, and the governor, and Bernice, and they that
sat with them:
31 And when they were gone aside, they talked
between themselves, saying, This man doeth
nothing worthy of death or of bonds.
32 Then said Agrippa unto Festus, This man
might have been set at liberty, if he had not ap-
pealed unto Caesar.

CHAPTER 27

AND when it was determined that we should sail
into Italy, they delivered Paul and certain other
prisoners unto *one* named Julius, a centurion of
Augustus' band.
2 And entering into a ship of Adramyttium, we
launched, meaning to sail by the coasts of Asia;
one Aristarchus, a Macedonian of Thessalonica,
being with us.
3 And the next *day* we touched at Sidon. And
Julius courteously entreated Paul, and gave *him*
liberty to go unto his friends to refresh himself.
4 And when we had launched from thence, we
sailed under Cyprus, because the winds were
contrary.
5 And when we had sailed over the sea of Cilicia
and Pamphylia, we came to Myra, *a city* of Lycia.
6 And there the centurion found a ship of Alex-
andria sailing into Italy; and he put us therein.
7 And when we had sailed slowly many days,
and scarce were come over against Cnidus, the
wind not suffering us, we sailed under Crete, over
against Salmone;
8 And, hardly passing it, came unto a place which

preaching the gospel.

26:22–23 Paul taught that Christ's death and resurrection constitute the same message as the Old Testament (*prophets and Moses*), just as Jesus had taught (Luke 24:44–48).

26:24 *beside thyself . . . mad.* The Greeks and Romans were accustomed to many gods and religions, but the message of the gospel is insane foolishness to the world (17:32; 1 Cor. 1:18,22–24).

26:25 *truth and soberness.* Paul's words are the exact opposite of insanity.

26:26 *not done in a corner.* Jesus' death and resurrection were not secret or private but published throughout the area (Luke 24:18–22).

26:27 *believest thou the prophets.* Paul confronted Agrippa, who was schooled in the Old Testament, with this clear choice between believing the gospel and rejecting the Hebrew Bible.

26:28 *Almost thou persuadest me to be a Christian.* Some have taken Agrippa's words to be mocking, but Paul's response (v. 29) makes it is more likely that Agrippa felt the compelling force of Paul's gospel presentation but gave an evasive answer.

26:29 *I would to God.* A prayer, expressed as a wish from the heart of a loving gospel preacher, who in love for all people desires each to be not just *almost* but *altogether* a Christian.

26:31 *nothing worthy of death.* Again, Luke vindicates Christianity from charges of being a threat to the government. These are the same words used by Pilate of Jesus (Luke 23:15).

Thoughts for Personal/Family Worship: Chapter 26

1. **Verse 18 gives us a short but rich summary of the true conversion Christ works through the preaching of the gospel. What does this verse teach us about the nature of conversion? What does it teach about its happy effects?**
2. **Agrippa knew much about the Scriptures (v. 3), being an expert in all sorts of matters relating to the Jews. He is said to have believed the prophets (v. 27), which means he must have given intellectual assent to the Bible. Nevertheless, he would not bow under the Christ of the Scriptures. Yet he said, "Almost thou persuadest me" (v. 28). He remained tragically blind, unrepentantly clinging to sin and remaining a part of the kingdom of Satan (v. 18). "Almost Christians" end up in hell. Only those who submit entirely to the righteousness of God in Christ, abandoning all hope of being saved by any other means, will be saved. What might it look like to be an "almost Christian" today? What does this text say to such people?**

Paul Travels to Rome (27:1—28:31)

Chapter 27: *With other prisoners, Paul sails toward Rome, but the vessel is shipwrecked, occasioning further testimony of Paul's Master, Jesus Christ.*

Paul Sets Sail for Rome (27:1–12)

27:1 *band.* Cohort, a unit of the Roman army.

27:3 *courteously entreated.* Treated kindly.

27:6 *Alexandria.* Located in Egypt, the supplier of much of the grain to the Roman Empire. Paul was likely on a grain ship traveling up to Rome.

27:7–8 *suffering.* Allowing. *nigh whereunto.* Near to which. *hardly.* With difficulty.

27:9 *sailing was now dangerous.* Typically sailors docked from

is called The fair havens; nigh whereunto was the
city *of* Lasea.
9 Now when much time was spent, and when
sailing was now dangerous, because the fast was
now already past, Paul admonished *them*,
10 And said unto them, Sirs, I perceive that this
voyage will be with hurt and much damage, not
only of the lading and ship, but also of our lives.
11 Nevertheless the centurion believed the master
and the owner of the ship, more than those things
which were spoken by Paul.
12 And because the haven was not commodi-
ous to winter in, the more part advised to depart
thence also, if by any means they might attain to
Phenice, *and there* to winter; *which is* an haven of
Crete, and lieth toward the south west and north
west.
13 And when the south wind blew softly, suppos-
ing that they had obtained *their* purpose, loosing
thence, they sailed close by Crete.
14 But not long after there arose against it a
tempestuous wind, called Euroclydon.
15 And when the ship was caught, and could not
bear up into the wind, we let *her* drive.
16 And running under a certain island which is
called Clauda, we had much work to come by the
boat:
17 Which when they had taken up, they used
helps, undergirding the ship; and, fearing lest they
should fall into the quicksands, strake sail, and so
were driven.
18 And we being exceedingly tossed with a tem-
pest, the next *day* they lightened the ship;
19 And the third *day* we cast out with our own
hands the tackling of the ship.
20 And when neither sun nor stars in many days
appeared, and no small tempest lay on *us*, all hope
that we should be saved was then taken away.
21 But after long abstinence Paul stood forth in
the midst of them, and said, Sirs, ye should have
hearkened unto me, and not have loosed from
Crete, and to have gained this harm and loss.
22 And now I exhort you to be of good cheer: for
there shall be no loss of *any man's* life among you,
but of the ship.
23 For there stood by me this night the angel of
God, whose I am, and whom I serve,
24 Saying, Fear not, Paul; thou must be brought
before Caesar: and, lo, God hath given thee all
them that sail with thee.
25 Wherefore, sirs, be of good cheer: for I believe
God, that it shall be even as it was told me.
26 Howbeit we must be cast upon a certain island.
27 But when the fourteenth night was come,
as we were driven up and down in Adria, about
midnight the shipmen deemed that they drew
near to some country;
28 And sounded, and found *it* twenty fathoms:
and when they had gone a little further, they
sounded again, and found *it* fifteen fathoms.
29 Then fearing lest we should have fallen upon
rocks, they cast four anchors out of the stern, and
wished for the day.
30 And as the shipmen were about to flee out of
the ship, when they had let down the boat into the
sea, under colour as though they would have cast
anchors out of the foreship,
31 Paul said to the centurion and to the soldiers,
Except these abide in the ship, ye cannot be saved.
32 Then the soldiers cut off the ropes of the boat,
and let her fall off.
33 And while the day was coming on, Paul
besought *them* all to take meat, saying, This day
is the fourteenth day that ye have tarried and
continued fasting, having taken nothing.
34 Wherefore I pray you to take *some* meat: for
this is for your health: for there shall not an hair
fall from the head of any of you.

---

mid-September to mid-March. *the fast.* The Day of Atonement on the Jewish calendar.

27:10 *lading*. Load, cargo.

27:12 *Phenice*. Phoenicia.

Paul's Ship Is Wrecked in a Storm (27:13–44)

27:14 *Euroclydon.* A compound word taken from both Greek and Latin and referring to a northeastern wind of great strength.

27:15 *we let her drive*. The men no longer had control of the ship.

27:17 *used helps, undergirding the ship.* Attempted to secure the planks of the ship with ropes so that it would not fall apart in the wind. *strake sail*. Literally, "let down the gear."

27:18–19 *lightened the ship*. Threw out its load so it would not sink.

27:20 *neither sun nor stars in many days appeared.* It was impossible to navigate.

27:21 *long abstinence*. They had not eaten for some time. *hearkened*. Obeyed. *loosed*. Launched.

27:22 *be of good cheer*. Be encouraged or in good spirits. *no loss of . . . life*. Astounding words to men on board a ship lost in a stormy sea and running out of food.

27:24 *must be brought before Caesar*. The divine necessity of God's decree guaranteed that Paul would take the gospel to Rome (1:16; 23:11). *given thee all*. Perhaps in answer to his prayers.

27:25 *I believe God*. Paul's confidence was not mere positive thinking but faith in God's trustworthiness and promise.

27:27 *Adria*. Adriatic Sea.

27:28 *fathoms*. Each about six feet in length.

27:30 *under colour*. Pretending. *foreship*. Bow or front of the ship.

27:31 *Except these abide . . . ye cannot be saved.* Though God's promise to preserve their lives could not fail, God would save them through means like the sailors' help or eating food (v. 34), so they must be faithful to preserve and use the means God was giving them.

27:33 *besought*. Urged. *meat*. Food of any kind.

27:34 *not an hair fall*. An idiom for complete safety (1 Sam. 14:45; 2 Sam. 14:11; 1 Kings 1:52; Luke 21:18).

35 And when he had thus spoken, he took bread,
and gave thanks to God in presence of them all:
and when he had broken *it*, he began to eat.
36 Then were they all of good cheer, and they also
took *some* meat.
37 And we were in all in the ship two hundred
threescore and sixteen souls.
38 And when they had eaten enough, they light-
ened the ship, and cast out the wheat into the sea.
39 And when it was day, they knew not the land:
but they discovered a certain creek with a shore,
into the which they were minded, if it were
possible, to thrust in the ship.
40 And when they had taken up the anchors, they
committed *themselves* unto the sea, and loosed
the rudder bands, and hoised up the mainsail to
the wind, and made toward shore.
41 And falling into a place where two seas met,
they ran the ship aground; and the forepart stuck
fast, and remained unmoveable, but the hinder
part was broken with the violence of the waves.
42 And the soldiers' counsel was to kill the prison-
ers, lest any of them should swim out, and escape.
43 But the centurion, willing to save Paul, kept
them from *their* purpose; and commanded that
they which could swim should cast *themselves*
first *into the sea*, and get to land:
44 And the rest, some on boards, and some on
broken pieces of the ship. And so it came to pass,
that they escaped all safe to land.

CHAPTER 28

AND when they were escaped, then they knew that
the island was called Melita.
2 And the barbarous people shewed us no little
kindness: for they kindled a fire, and received
us every one, because of the present rain, and
because of the cold.
3 And when Paul had gathered a bundle of sticks,
and laid *them* on the fire, there came a viper out
of the heat, and fastened on his hand.
4 And when the barbarians saw the *venomous*
beast hang on his hand, they said among them-
selves, No doubt this man is a murderer, whom,
though he hath escaped the sea, yet vengeance
suffereth not to live.
5 And he shook off the beast into the fire, and felt
no harm.
6 Howbeit they looked when he should have
swollen, or fallen down dead suddenly: but after
they had looked a great while, and saw no harm
come to him, they changed their minds, and said
that he was a god.

27:36 *good cheer.* Encouraged (v. 22). *meat.* Food of any kind. The men trusted Paul's prophecy and followed his instructions to eat some food to preserve their health and strength.
27:37 *two hundred threescore and sixteen souls.* 276 people. God's providence has again used Paul's sufferings to bring his witness to people, here a captive audience of hundreds.
27:38 *cast out the wheat into the sea.* Throwing out the cargo showed their hopelessness of preserving anything beyond their lives.
27:39 *discovered.* Came in view.
27:40 *hoised.* Hoisted.
27:41 *forepart . . . hinder part.* The prow (front) and stern (back) of the ship.
27:42–43 *soldier's counsel . . . But the centurion.* A near calamity for Paul, but God's providence rules over the wills of men in order to accomplish His will (4:27–28).
27:44 *all safe to land.* The tense narrative is over and the Lord has proved faithful (v. 24), not only to Paul but to the soldiers, prisoners, and passengers with him, a testimony to His kindness.

Thoughts for Personal/Family Worship: Chapter 27

1. **We need to be careful not to draw conclusions from providence. "Fair weather" providences do not mean that it is always good to move ahead as we plan. Nor do "stormy" providences necessarily mean we are doomed to fail. Our faith and duty must not take their direction from the shifting winds of providence but from the unchanging promises of God. Why is it dangerous to take today's providence as tomorrow's promise?**
2. **On this ship Paul was strikingly unlike Jonah, the Old Testament prophet who was following the path of disobedience. In that situation the sailors almost lost their lives because of him (Jonah 1:6); now the sailors are saved because of Paul (v. 24). Jonah hid, sleeping, below deck until the pagan sailors roused him, but Paul gave leadership and encouragement through his words and prayers. When trials come, how are we tempted to be like Jonah? How ought we to be like Paul?**
3. **The church of Christ sometimes seems doomed to sink beneath the waves of her troubles, but the Lord Jesus still rules the seas. Paul's troubles in the ship seemed to threaten his mission to Rome but instead proved to be an opportunity to demonstrate God's power and love to 276 people in a way they would never forget. How can that encourage the church in her mission to the world?**

Chapter 28: *Faithful to His promise, the Lord brings Paul safely to Rome, where the apostle preaches the gospel to Jews and Gentiles in the center of the pagan Empire.*

Paul on the Island of Malta (28:1–10)

28:1 *Melita.* Modern day Malta, located south of Italy.
28:2 *barbarous.* Not influenced by Greek culture (so also, "barbarians," v. 4). *shewed us no little kindness.* Though they were social outcasts according to Roman thought, they extended great hospitality to Paul and the other people with him.
28:3 *Paul had gathered a bundle of sticks.* The apostle did not lord his position over others but humbly served others, willing to do the most menial of tasks so long as they did not conflict with his calling to preach the gospel.
28:4 *vengeance suffereth not to live.* The goddess Justice did not allow him to survive.
28:5 *felt no harm.* A miracle validating that he was a messenger of Christ (Mark 16:18) and perhaps also a sign that the gospel will not be stopped by Satan (Gen. 3:14–15; Rom. 16:20).
28:6 *said that he was a god.* As in Lystra (14:11), the miracle was misinterpreted by their pagan mindset to indicate that Paul was divine. Miracles need explanation by the Word.

7 In the same quarters were possessions of the
chief man of the island, whose name was Publius;
who received us, and lodged us three days
courteously.
8 And it came to pass, that the father of Publius
lay sick of a fever and of a bloody flux: to whom
Paul entered in, and prayed, and laid his hands on
him, and healed him.
9 So when this was done, others also, which had
diseases in the island, came, and were healed:
10 Who also honoured us with many honours;
and when we departed, they laded *us* with such
things as were necessary.
11 And after three months we departed in a ship
of Alexandria, which had wintered in the isle,
whose sign was Castor and Pollux.
12 And landing at Syracuse, we tarried *there* three
days.
13 And from thence we fetched a compass, and
came to Rhegium: and after one day the south
wind blew, and we came the next day to Puteoli:
14 Where we found brethren, and were desired
to tarry with them seven days: and so we went
toward Rome.
15 And from thence, when the brethren heard of
us, they came to meet us as far as Appii forum,
and The three taverns: whom when Paul saw, he
thanked God, and took courage.
16 And when we came to Rome, the centurion
delivered the prisoners to the captain of the
guard: but Paul was suffered to dwell by himself
with a soldier that kept him.
17 And it came to pass, that after three days Paul
called the chief of the Jews together: and when
they were come together, he said unto them, Men
and brethren, though I have committed nothing
against the people, or customs of our fathers, yet
was I delivered prisoner from Jerusalem into the
hands of the Romans.
18 Who, when they had examined me, would
have let *me* go, because there was no cause of
death in me.
19 But when the Jews spake against *it*, I was con-
strained to appeal unto Caesar; not that I had
ought to accuse my nation of.
20 For this cause therefore have I called for you,
to see *you*, and to speak with *you*: because that for
the hope of Israel I am bound with this chain.
21 And they said unto him, We neither received
letters out of Judaea concerning thee, neither any
of the brethren that came shewed or spake any
harm of thee.
22 But we desire to hear of thee what thou think-
est: for as concerning this sect, we know that every
where it is spoken against.
23 And when they had appointed him a day, there
came many to him into *his* lodging; to whom he
expounded and testified the kingdom of God,
persuading them concerning Jesus, both out of
the law of Moses, and *out of* the prophets, from
morning till evening.
24 And some believed the things which were
spoken, and some believed not.
25 And when they agreed not among themselves,
they departed, after that Paul had spoken one
word, Well spake the Holy Ghost by Esaias the
prophet unto our fathers,
26 Saying, Go unto this people, and say, Hearing
ye shall hear, and shall not understand; and seeing
ye shall see, and not perceive:

28:7 *chief man*. It was not uncommon for Paul in his missionary travels to approach leaders with the gospel (13:7).
28:8 *bloody flux*. Flow of blood, dysentery. *laid his hands on him, and healed him*. Paul heals Publius's father and brings the message of salvation in Christ to the island of Melita.
28:10 *laded*. Loaded.

Paul in Rome (28:11–31)

28:11 *Castor and Pollux*. The patron gods of sailors, whose images were placed on ships in the hope of good luck. In the light of ch. 27, a reminder that the world trusts in dead and powerless idols instead of in the living God who rules the seas and all things (17:24).
28:13 *fetched a compass*. Went around, turned around. This is not a reference to magnetic navigational compasses, which had not yet been invented.
28:14 *found brethren*. Christians were already in Italy, a reminder that the book of Acts does not tell us all the early missionary endeavors of the disciples.
28:15 *Appii forum*. The Forum of Appius, a town in Italy forty-three miles southeast of Rome. *The three taverns*. Further down the Appian Way toward Rome.
28:16 *suffered to dwell by himself*. Allowed to live under house arrest (v. 30).
28:17 *called the chief of the Jews*. Though forced to go to Rome, at least humanly speaking, by the Jews of Jerusalem, still Paul desired to evangelize his countrymen in Rome.
28:23–31 Luke wraps up the book with some of the key themes of his Gospel and Acts: preaching the gospel of Jesus Christ from the Old Testament (v. 23); the mixed response to the gospel of its hearers (v. 24); God's sovereignty over the human response to the gospel (vv. 25–27); the sending of the gospel of salvation to the Gentiles even as many, though not all, Jews rejected it (vv. 28–29); and the faithfulness of God's witnesses in preaching Christ even in the midst of persecution (vv. 30–31).
28:25–27 *Esaias*. Isaiah (Isa. 6:9–10; cf. Mark 4:12; John 12:40).
28:30–31 *two whole years*. Luke does not include Paul's trial before Caesar or his remaining life and martyrdom. This reminds the reader that the book of Acts is not primarily about Paul or any of the apostles but about the mighty works of *the Lord Jesus Christ* to take His witnesses to every part of the world (1:8), including the greatest city of the Roman Empire.

Thoughts for Personal/Family Worship: Chapter 28

The Gospel of Luke started in rural Judaea, after the emperor had compelled the people to register for taxes, unwittingly bringing the unborn Christ to the place where the Scriptures had foretold His birth. The book of Acts ends in the heart of the Roman Empire, with God's

27 For the heart of this people is waxed gross, and
their ears are dull of hearing, and their eyes have
they closed; lest they should see with *their* eyes,
and hear with *their* ears, and understand with
their heart, and should be converted, and I should
heal them.
28 Be it known therefore unto you, that the
salvation of God is sent unto the Gentiles, and
that they will hear it.
29 And when he had said these words, the Jews
departed, and had great reasoning among themselves.
30 And Paul dwelt two whole years in his own
hired house, and received all that came in unto
him,
31 Preaching the kingdom of God, and teaching
those things which concern the Lord Jesus Christ,
with all confidence, no man forbidding him.

servant boldly preaching Christ and His kingdom in the city of Caesar. From beginning to end the writings of Luke testify that God is fulfilling His decree concerning the Savior. Nothing could stop the complete accomplishment of redemption by Christ's death and resurrection, and nothing can stop the preaching of the gospel to all nations—not even a poisonous snake bite on a missionary's hand. It is not pagan gods or luck that rules over this world but the triune God. This does not permit us to be foolish or fail to use God's appointed means, but it does teach us to serve Christ with confidence. How does the closing scene of Acts encourage you about the future of the kingdom of Jesus Christ? What is your standing in relationship to Christ and His kingdom?

INTRODUCTION TO THE EPISTLES

Counting the book of Revelation (which is a kind of epistle to the seven churches of Asia Minor), the epistles comprise more than forty percent of the New Testament. This is all the more remarkable because the Old Testament has no books that are epistles, and only a few contain epistles, such as Jeremiah's letter to the captives (Jer. 29). No doubt part of the reason for the letters of the New Testament is the fact that the Roman Empire had a well-functioning postal system, and a sensible way to reach the congregations spread throughout the Mediterranean region was by mail, especially for the apostle Paul, who found himself in prison for long periods of time.

The epistles of the New Testament represent the personal and direct character whereby Christ speaks to His people through His apostles. The endearing way in which most of the epistles begin with greetings and end with blessings suggests the close communion between Christ and His churches. Paul even draws a practical point concerning the medium of letters, saying that the lives of true Christians are to be read by all as reflecting the will of Christ: "Ye are our epistle written in our hearts, known and read of all men: forasmuch as ye are manifestly declared to be the epistle of Christ ministered by us, written not with ink, but with the Spirit of the living God; not in tables of stone, but in fleshly tables of the heart" (2 Cor. 3:2–3).

Paul's correspondence heads up the whole section of epistles in the New Testament. Both from Acts and from the epistles themselves, we learn that Paul was not a stand-apart leader but operated as the leader of a mission team. He was constantly naming, commending, and greeting associates. It is likely that Paul retained copies of the letters he wrote. This was common even for relatively unimportant correspondence.

Paul's mission plan had a definite urban orientation. The cities shared a common language, as well as common customs. Nearly every city had a center for Jews from the Dispersion, synagogues, or prayer houses.

Within Paul's urban focus, great attention was given to the basic unit of Greco-Roman society—the household. This consisted of immediate family as well as slaves, freedmen, servants and laborers, and sometimes even business associates and tenants. The master had authority over all members of his household, as well as obligations and legal responsibilities. A "house" where a large household had its residence did not have private residences but large houses with shops at the front and living quarters in the back. Often there would be workshops and living quarters for dependents and visitors. In this vein Paul refers to the "house of Stephanus," "Chloe's houshold," "Caesar's house," etc. Paul used this picture of a household for the close relation God's people enjoy as brothers and sisters of one Lord and Master, God, for the sake of Christ, the Heir of all (Eph. 2:19; Gal. 6:10; 1 Tim. 5:8).

Paul and the other authors of the epistles identified themselves as apostle, elders, or servants of Jesus Christ. The term "apostle" suggests one who has been sent on a mission. Christ Himself was the "Apostle" (Heb. 3:1; cf. Mark 9:37). These apostles became founders of the New Testament churches (Eph. 2:20; 4:11). Paul was "the last " of the apostles (1 Cor. 15:11), yet this "last" apostle was apportioned a great terrain of ministry—the Gentile world (Gal. 2:7-9). During his ministry his apostleship was questioned (cf. 1 Cor. 9:1) and opposed (2 Cor. 11:13,23) by self-proclaimed apostles.

Especially recently, many scholars have claimed that a number of the epistles were not written by those whose names are mentioned as authors. This is referred to as a pseudonymous writing. These scholars usually argue that it was culturally acceptable and understood at the time to pretend to write as someone else. This, however, is a biblically unacceptable point of view. The Scriptures make much of the truthfulness of God (Titus 1:2) and of those who speak on God's behalf (Rom. 9:1; Gal. 1:20). Moreover, the church of God cannot just accept the testimony of anyone, especially someone who was pretending to be someone else. The Bible stresses the importance of the apostles as those upon whom the church has been built (Eph. 2:20). They were eyewitnesses of the things of which they spoke. Obviously, some who wrote parts of the New Testament worked with the apostles (such as Luke and Mark) and wrote on their behalf. However, we never see any of them pretending to be anything they are not. Thus, to apply the notion of pseudonymity to any part of the New Testament is both fallacious and dangerous.

The great theme holding all the epistles together is Christ and the salvation He has accomplished and is applying in His people. These people are the church of God, chosen unto everlasting life, whom God saves by calling, justifying, sanctifying, and glorifying for the sake of Christ's work of dying and rising on their behalf. Christ fulfills all of salvation history, for it finds its culmination in Him. In Him all the promises of God as sure—yea and amen (2 Cor. 1:20). He is the Seed of Abraham (Gal. 3:16) and was the Rock in the wilderness (1 Cor. 10:4). He is the Passover of His people (1 Cor. 5:7), and as the New Adam His resurrection guarantees theirs (1 Cor. 15:40ff.). He is the author and finisher of the faith (Heb. 12:2), the chief Shepherd of the sheep (1 Peter 5:4), and the Lamb slain from before the foundation of the world (Rev. 5:6; 13:8).

The relationship between Christ and His people is central in a number of Paul's important letters, including Romans, Corinthians, Ephesians, and Philippians. God has created one new man in Jesus Christ (Eph. 2:15). The moral life of a Christian consists in putting on Christ (Rom. 13:14; Eph. 4:25-5:2; Col. 3:5-17). Christian husbands are to love their wives as Christ loved the church (Eph. 5:25), and Christian wives are to submit to their husbands as the church does to Christ. The Christian life as a whole is contained in the truth of "learning Christ" (Eph. 4:20). Everything needs to be done in the name of the Lord Jesus (Col. 3:17).

Christ delivers from the curse of the law, having Himself become a curse (Gal. 3:10). He apprehends sinners to save them from a life of pursuing their own righteousness. He gives them the new ambition of gaining Christ and knowing Christ (Phil. 3:9-11). This is so distinct from a life dedicated to food laws that those who are seeking to establish a righteousness of their own find that Christ cannot profit them (Gal. 1:6-7; 5:2). Instead, Christians are dead to the law in order that they might live in union with Christ, and His life is their life.

Christ's return is an important subject throughout the epistles (e.g., 1 Thess. 1:10; 2 Thess. 2; 2 Peter 3; James 5:8–9; the whole of Revelation). When Christ returns, He will be glorified with the saints (2 Thess. 1:10). Believers are those who wait for His coming (2 Thess. 3:5). His first coming has dealt with the principalities and powers that kept the nations away from the gospel (Eph. 1:21). Meanwhile, the fashion of this world is passing away (1 Cor. 7:31). His future coming gives urgency to gospel preaching (2 Cor. 5:10). To believe in Christ means escaping the wrath to come (1Thess. 1:10; 5:9; 2 Thess. 2:13). The return of Christ will not happen without events that fulfill God's plan (2 Thess. 2:1–10), but in the end Christ will destroy all other forces. His coming with the saints and for the saints is a cause for comfort, as is the fact that believers who die, sleep in Christ (1 Thess. 4:14–18).

INTRODUCTION TO THE BOOK OF ROMANS

Authorship: The epistle was written by Paul, the apostle (1:1).

Date: The apostle Paul appears to have written this letter from Corinth or its vicinity. This can be deduced from the references to Cenchrea (16:1), which was the port of Corinth, and to Gaius (16:23), who is also mentioned as a member of the Corinthian Church (1 Cor. 1:14). The reference to Erastus (also in Rom. 16:23) is consistent with the Corinthian connection in 2 Tim. 4:20. Paul stayed in Greece (probably largely in Corinth) for three months (Acts 20:2–3) on his way to Jerusalem with the collection from the Gentile churches for the poor saints there. Paul viewed this gift as extremely important, not only because the Jerusalem Christians had need of it but also because of its immense significance in cementing the unity between the Jewish and Gentile segments of the church. He makes reference to it in this epistle (Rom. 15:23–28). This would place the probable date of the writing of the epistle to the Romans at approximately AD 57 or 58.

Theme: Salvation by grace alone, especially justification by faith alone and the imputation of the righteousness of Jesus Christ to all who believe.

Purpose: To ground the believer's faith upon God's righteousness imputed through Christ alone, for the glory of God alone and for the unity of the church.

Synopsis: *The Contribution of Romans to Redemptive Revelation*

The letter declares the apostle's intention to visit Rome and provides in advance a systematic treatment (1:1—8:39) of the gospel that he preaches and has been "separated unto" (1:1) as an apostle to the Gentiles. It stresses the unity of Jew and Gentile through this one gospel given by God to both (1:16; 3:9,29–30; 4:16; 10:19–21; 11:30–31; 15:6; etc.). The letter also gives practical direction as to the proper fruit of faith in Christ in various aspects of the Christian life (12:1—15:21). In God's goodness we have been given in this epistle the most systematic and extended demonstration of the true doctrine of the gospel anywhere in the inerrant Word of God. It is not surprising that God has used this part of His Word when bringing about rediscovery of the true gospel in history, particularly at the time of the Reformation.

The Church at Rome

We have no solid evidence of what means God had used to bring the church at Rome into existence. There is no reason to think that the apostle Peter had been to Rome prior to this time. Perhaps the most plausible explanation is that converts from Pentecost had gone to Rome. Other Christians may have immigrated from elsewhere and joined themselves to this church at the heart of the Empire. Without doubt there was a constant stream of travelers to and from Rome.

It becomes clear that there were both Jews and Gentiles in this church. The apostle addresses both directly (2:17; 11:13); he refers to his "kinsmen" (16:7,11) yet magnifies his office as an apostle to the Gentiles and to the church and his intention to visit (1:5,13). He was acquainted with some of its members (16:3–15, suggesting that the membership of the Roman church was predominantly Gentile.

The Use of the Word "Justification" in Romans

It is of great importance in understanding this majestic epistle that we get a clear grasp of what the term "justification" means in its usage by the apostle Paul. We can say the following:

1. Justification is an act of God. "It is God that justifieth" (8:33). God is the ultimate Judge, beyond whom there is no appeal.
2. Justification is God declaring guilty sinners righteous. He "justifieth the ungodly" (4:5). "Justification" is used as a legal term and is the opposite of condemnation (8:34).
3. God does not justify all the ungodly. He is "just, and the justifier of him which believeth in Jesus" (3:26).
4. God justifies believing sinners by imputing to them ("crediting to" or "reckoning to" their account) the righteousness of Jesus Christ (4:25; 8:34). This includes Christ's righteousness in both His passive obedience (suffering the wrath of God in the place of sinners) and His active obedience (keeping God's law on their behalf). See note at 5:18–19. It is this righteousness of Christ that is referred to by the phrase "righteousness of God" (1:17; 3:22; 10:3), as revealed in the gospel.
5. Faith is not an alternative righteousness but the sole instrument of justification. God justifies believing sinners, "not by imputing faith itself, the act of believing, or any other evangelical obedience, to them as their righteousness; but by imputing the obedience and satisfaction of Christ unto them, they receiving and resting on him and his righteousness by faith; which faith they have not of themselves; it is the gift of God" (Westminster Confession of Faith, 11.1).

Justification and Sanctification

Keeping a clear distinction between these two biblical terms is important to understanding the book of Romans and the biblical gospel. Justification relates to God declaring the sinner righteous. It refers to a legal standing, the removal of the guilt of sin and the constituting of the sinner as righteous before God. Justification is available to believers on account of Christ's imputed righteousness.

Sanctification relates not to being *declared* righteous but to being made righteous. It means being separated to God or being made holy. It addresses not the guilt of sin but the actual presence, pollution, and practice of sin. It has in view an imparted, as opposed to an imputed, righteousness in Christ.

This distinction explains why, for example, the Westminster Shorter Catechism (Q.33 and 35) speaks of justification as an "act of God" and sanctification as a "work of God." Justification is something God declares about His people, whereas sanctification is something He does to His people. Chapter 6 of Romans shows that the justified man is invariably a changed man. He has been and is continuously being sanctified. Nevertheless, though both these blessings (justification and sanctification) are bestowed by Christ upon His people (and never only one without the other), they are two different gifts, and the distinction between them must not be blurred. Holiness of life is the evidence of true faith in Christ, but it is by faith alone, through the imputation of Christ's merits alone, that we are justified (3:21,28; 4:6; etc.).

Roman Catholicism historically has failed to distinguish between justification and sanctification. Although the Roman Catholic Church asserts that Christ's righteousness merits our justification, nevertheless it pronounces a curse on anyone who claims that Christ's righteousness is actually declared to be ours. In this view justification is both the forgiveness of sins and the renewal of the soul. Thus justification is by means of the sanctifying process in this life and continued in the next as necessary. This is contrary to the biblical doctrine of justification so clearly presented in Paul's epistle to the Romans.

The stand taken by Martin Luther by the grace of God in the Protestant Reformation of the sixteenth century has not become redundant. The Lord who spoke by the prophets and in these last days by His Son (Heb. 1:1–2) has also given us apostolic epistles to expound the meaning of Christ's redeeming work and to elucidate the doctrine of salvation. The epistle to the Romans is central to that culmination of God's revelation to men.

Outline: I. Introduction (1:1–17)

- A. Greeting (1:1–7)
- B. Declaration of Resolve to Visit (1:8–15)
- C. Summary of the Gospel That Paul Preaches (1:16–17)

II. The Doctrine of the Gospel (1:18—8:39)

- A. Gospel Basics (1:18—3:31)
  1. The Gentiles Are Sinners (1:18–32)

2. The Jews Are Sinners (2:1—3:8)
3. All Have Sinned (3:9–20)
4. The Only Hope Is God's Righteousness Provided in Christ (3:21–31)

B. Old Testament Confirmation (4:1–25)
1. Abraham and Justification (4:1–5)
2. David and Justification (4:6–8)
3. Justification Independent of Circumcision (4:9–12)
4. Promise and Law (4:13–17)
5. Abraham's Faith to Be Followed (4:18–25)

C. The Blessedness and Safety of the Justified (5:1–11)
D. Justification in Christ as Sure as Condemnation in Adam (5:12–21)
E. The Forgiven Man Is Being Made Holy (6:1–23)
F. The Gospel and the Law (7:1–25)
1. The Believer's Changed Relationship to the Law (7:1–6)
2. The Law Exposes Sin and the Need for Christ (7:7–13)
3. The Believer Loves But Still Breaks God's Law (7:14–25)

G. Benefits Accompanying Justification in This Life and the Next (8:1–39)
1. Deliverance from Sin (8:1–11)
2. The Privileges of Adoption (8:12–17)
3. The Full Inheritance and Its Earnest (8:18–27)
4. The Certainty of Triumph in Christ (8:28–39)

III. Israel and the Gospel (9:1—11:36)
A. Israel's Unbelief No Objection to the Gospel (9:1–33)
1. The Apostle's Sorrow (9:1–5)
2. God Never Promised the Salvation of All Israelites (9:6–9)
3. God's Sovereign Prerogative of Election (9:10–18)
4. Twofold Effect of the Gospel (9:19–33)

B. Israel's Failure to Submit to the Righteousness of God (10:1–21)
C. Israel's Rejection Neither Total Nor Final (11:1–36)

IV. The Response of Real Holiness (12:1—15:33)
A. Devotion to the Lord Shown in the Church and in Our Conduct to All (12:1–21)
B. Duty to the Civil Magistrate and to Our Neighbor (13:1–14)
C. Using Our Knowledge Lovingly (14:1–23)
D. Unity of the Body (15:1–33)
1. Christ's Example (15:1–7)
2. Unity of Jew and Gentile in Christ's Body (15:8–13)
3. Paul's Ministry to the United Body (15:14–33)

V. Conclusion (16:1–27)
A. Paul's Greetings (16:1–16)
B. Final Warnings (16:17–20)
C. Greetings from Particular Brothers at Corinth (16:21–23)
D. Doxology (16:25–27)

THE EPISTLE OF PAUL THE APOSTLE TO THE

ROMANS

CHAPTER 1

PAUL, a servant of Jesus Christ, called *to be* an
apostle, separated unto the gospel of God,
2 (Which he had promised afore by his prophets
in the holy scriptures,)
3 Concerning his Son Jesus Christ our Lord,
which was made of the seed of David according
to the flesh;
4 And declared *to be* the Son of God with power,
according to the spirit of holiness, by the resur-
rection from the dead:
5 By whom we have received grace and apostle-
ship, for obedience to the faith among all nations,
for his name:
6 Among whom are ye also the called of Jesus
Christ:
7 To all that be in Rome, beloved of God, called
to be saints: Grace to you and peace from God our
Father, and the Lord Jesus Christ.
8 First, I thank my God through Jesus Christ for
you all, that your faith is spoken of throughout
the whole world.
9 For God is my witness, whom I serve with my
spirit in the gospel of his Son, that without ceas-
ing I make mention of you always in my prayers;
10 Making request, if by any means now at length
I might have a prosperous journey by the will of
God to come unto you.
11 For I long to see you, that I may impart unto
you some spiritual gift, to the end ye may be es-
tablished;
12 That is, that I may be comforted together with
you by the mutual faith both of you and me.
13 Now I would not have you ignorant, brethren,
that oftentimes I purposed to come unto you,
(but was let hitherto,) that I might have some fruit
among you also, even as among other Gentiles.
14 I am debtor both to the Greeks, and to the
Barbarians; both to the wise, and to the unwise.
15 So, as much as in me is, I am ready to preach

Chapter 1: *The apostle greets his readers at Rome, declaring his apostolic calling and his desire to visit them. He summarizes the true gospel and then, surveying first the Gentile world, begins his argument that all are sinners and in need of this gospel.*

INTRODUCTION (1:1–17)

Greeting (1:1–7)

1:1 *servant of Jesus Christ.* Paul is using the Old Testament language of a servant of the Lord (*Jehovah*) and applying it to Christ as *Jehovah*. *gospel of God.* The source of his message is God.

1:2 *afore.* Before, previously. The gospel Paul preaches is no novelty but a fulfillment of prophecy.

1:3–4 Paul presents the leading figure of the gospel. Jesus Christ, always the Son of God, became a man as the *seed of David* and so was and continues to be God and man in two distinct natures, yet one person forever. *with power.* Not "powerfully declared" but declared to be the "powerful Son of God," having all power in heaven and on earth (Matt. 28:18). All His claims were vindicated by the resurrection. *spirit of holiness.* The Holy Spirit, by whose agency Christ was raised from the dead (8:11) and whom Christ, as the exalted King, can and does send forth (John 14:16; Acts 2:33).

1:5 *obedience to the faith.* God requires faith (16:26; 2 Thess. 1:8; 1 Peter 4:17), meaning submission to the gospel (6:17). Unbelief is a sin (Mark 6:6; John 16:9; Heb. 3:12). Our natural inability to believe does not diminish our obligation to do so.

1:6–7 *called.* God's effectual call, which actually brings a sinner to faith (8:30; 9:11), not merely the outward call of the gospel from which it is distinguished (1 Cor. 1:23–24).

Declaration of Resolve to Visit (1:8–15)

1:8 In thanking God for their faith Paul acknowledges that faith is the gift of God (Eph. 2:8). He includes in his address those he does not yet know.

1:9–12 *God is my witness.* Paul's lawful use of an oath (9:1; 2 Cor. 1:23; 11:31; Gal. 1:20; 1 Thess. 2:5). *by the will of God.* His will of purpose or decree (Dan. 4:35; Eph. 1:11) rather than of precept (Matt. 7:21; 12:50). *spiritual gift.* Some take this to refer to those miraculous gifts the Lord conveyed through the apostles, but it may simply refer to his desire that the Lord would strengthen them in the faith through his ministry among them.

1:13–14 *let.* Hindered. *debtor.* God had placed upon him an obligation to preach the gospel to them. *Greeks.* Not only those of Greece itself but all who were Greek in language and culture. *Barbarians.* Those peoples outside the sphere of Greek cultural influence. These two classes matched up with the *wise* and *unwise* from the standpoint of those who had imbibed the refinement of Greek learning and culture, as the Romans had to a considerable extent.

1:15 He declares his readiness to preach in Rome. Delay in doing so had been on account of providential circumstances, not reluctance on his part.

the gospel to you that are at Rome also.
16 For I am not ashamed of the gospel of Christ:
for it is the power of God unto salvation to every
one that believeth; to the Jew first, and also to the
Greek.
17 For therein is the righteousness of God
revealed from faith to faith: as it is written, The
just shall live by faith.
18 For the wrath of God is revealed from heaven
against all ungodliness and unrighteousness of
men, who hold the truth in unrighteousness;
19 Because that which may be known of God is
manifest in them; for God hath shewed *it* unto
them.
20 For the invisible things of him from the
creation of the world are clearly seen, being
understood by the things that are made, *even*
his eternal power and Godhead; so that they are
without excuse:
21 Because that, when they knew God, they
glorified *him* not as God, neither were thankful;
but became vain in their imaginations, and their
foolish heart was darkened.
22 Professing themselves to be wise, they became
fools,
23 And changed the glory of the uncorruptible
God into an image made like to corruptible man,
and to birds, and fourfooted beasts, and creeping
things.
24 Wherefore God also gave them up to unclean-
ness through the lusts of their own hearts, to
dishonour their own bodies between themselves:
25 Who changed the truth of God into a lie, and
worshipped and served the creature more than
the Creator, who is blessed for ever. Amen.
26 For this cause God gave them up unto vile
affections: for even their women did change the
natural use into that which is against nature:
27 And likewise also the men, leaving the natural
use of the woman, burned in their lust one
toward another; men with men working that
which is unseemly, and receiving in themselves
that recompence of their error which was meet.
28 And even as they did not like to retain God in
their knowledge, God gave them over to a reprobate
mind, to do those things which are not convenient;

Summary of the Gospel That Paul Preaches (1:16–17)

1:16–17 The apostle's reasoning is clear if we keep in mind the use of the word "for" (Greek, *gar*), which appears four times in vv. 16–18, an emphasis often lost in many paraphrase-type translations.

1:16 He is not ashamed of the gospel because it is true and it is through belief in the gospel alone that God manifests His power in saving sinners. Apostolic Christianity is exclusive. *to the Jew first, and also to the Greek.* Israel constituted the Old Testament church, the members of whom must now hear the message of the risen Christ (Acts 1:4,8; 3:25–26; 13:46). Those who received the message remained in the continuing church, while other branches were broken off (11:17; Matt. 21:43). But the priority of the Jew was not exclusive. The Greek-speaking Gentile world must hear as well. The term *Greek* is used here not in distinction from the barbarians (v. 14) but as indicating that the gospel was to be preached to the Gentile world by reference to that part of it to which many of the Roman Christians belonged.

1:17 The gospel of Christ is the power of God unto salvation because in that gospel God reveals His own provided and approved righteousness, which is imputed to all who believe. *righteousness of God.* Not simply God's attribute of righteousness but Christ's righteousness worked out through His perfect life and atoning death. *from faith to faith.* Not "by faith from first to last"; this righteousness is imputed (1) through faith, and (2) it is imputed to those very individuals who have this faith, not to anyone else. Habakkuk 2:4 provides Old Testament confirmation, teaching not only that the righteous have faith but that faith, which ensures their safety in a day when God's judgment was falling upon Judah by means of Babylon, must also ensure peace with God forever.

THE DOCTRINE OF THE GOSPEL (1:18—8:39)

Gospel Basics (1:18—3:31)

The Gentiles Are Sinners (1:18–32)

1:18 The reason all stand in need of this God-provided righteousness revealed in the gospel is that all men are sinners and so are liable to the wrath of God. *ungodliness.* Sins committed directly against God, that is to say, transgressions against the "first table" of God's law, lead to all others. *hold.* Possibly the idea is of "holding down" but certainly the thought of having truth but utterly misusing it.

1:19–22 Ungodliness at its source is described. *that which may be known of God* (v. 19) is contrasted with the "righteousness of God" revealed in the gospel. General revelation shown in God's works does not teach men the way of salvation. But these works do show something "to them", even *invisible things* (v. 20) about God that could be known all along from the foundation (*creation*) *of the world* and that are evident from *the things that are made.* His *eternal power* (singled out by contrast to the ridiculous notions of deity found in idolatry and described later on) and *Godhead* (all of His glorious attributes displayed in creation; Ps.19:1–6) are here named. Idolatry is inexcusable because of the display of God's glory in creation. Since the fall of man into sin, man's heart is antagonistic to the true God as He has revealed Himself (8:7). The light is rejected. According to Scripture, sin is rooted in the foolishness that comes from rejecting God (vv. 21–22).

1:23–25 Idolatry is the outworking of enmity against the true God. It entails the hideous exchange of a right view of God's glory for the concept of a god who is like a finite creature. Note the contrast between the *uncorruptible* God and *corruptible* man and things (v. 23). Verse 24 anticipates the fuller explanation in vv. 26–28. The truth from God and about God is exchanged (*changed*) for a lie, and worship is offered to a mere *creature* rather than to God, who is *blessed for ever* (v. 25). *Amen* is the believing response of those who heartily acknowledge where true worship should be directed.

1:26–28 Consequences among men for rejecting the knowledge of God. *natural . . . against nature.* Notice that the apostle does not say contrary to the "sexual orientation" of the individual but contrary to God's created order of male and female (Gen. 1:27–28; 2:24), which is of universal application.

1:26 *vile.* Disgusting.

1:27 *unseemly.* Shameful and bringing dire consequences, even in this life. *meet.* Suitable, fit.

1:28 *reprobate mind.* A mind void of judgment, unable to see

29 Being filled with all unrighteousness, forni-
cation, wickedness, covetousness, maliciousness;
full of envy, murder, debate, deceit, malignity;
whisperers,
30 Backbiters, haters of God, despiteful, proud,
boasters, inventors of evil things, disobedient to
parents,
31 Without understanding, covenantbreakers,
without natural affection, implacable, unmerciful:
32 Who knowing the judgment of God, that they
which commit such things are worthy of death,
not only do the same, but have pleasure in them
that do them.

CHAPTER 2

THEREFORE thou art inexcusable, O man, who-
soever thou art that judgest: for wherein thou
judgest another, thou condemnest thyself; for
thou that judgest doest the same things.
2 But we are sure that the judgment of God is
according to truth against them which commit
such things.
3 And thinkest thou this, O man, that judgest
them which do such things, and doest the same,
that thou shalt escape the judgment of God?
4 Or despisest thou the riches of his goodness and
forbearance and longsuffering; not knowing that
the goodness of God leadeth thee to repentance?
5 But after thy hardness and impenitent heart
treasurest up unto thyself wrath against the day of
wrath and revelation of the righteous judgment
of God;
6 Who will render to every man according to his
deeds:
7 To them who by patient continuance in well
doing seek for glory and honour and immortal-
ity, eternal life:
8 But unto them that are contentious, and do not
obey the truth, but obey unrighteousness, indig-
nation and wrath,
9 Tribulation and anguish, upon every soul of
man that doeth evil, of the Jew first, and also of
the Gentile;
10 But glory, honour, and peace, to every man
that worketh good, to the Jew first, and also to the
Gentile:
11 For there is no respect of persons with God.

---

what once it did. *not convenient*. Not fitting.

1:29–32 A list of accompanying sins.

1:29 *debate*. Strife. *malignity*. Deep-seated hatred, great malice.

1:30 *Backbiters*. Slanderers. *despiteful*. Contemptuous.

1:31–32 *covenantbreakers*. Breakers of sworn promises. *knowing the judgment of God*. They know in their consciences (2:14–15) that God's sentence of eternal death (6:23) is upon these things, yet they still love these sins, both for themselves and for others.

Thoughts for Personal/Family Worship: Chapter 1

1. **All true ministers of Christ are separated unto the gospel (v. 1), and the church must devote itself to the preaching of the good news. Do not be ashamed of the gospel (v. 16), nor of its doctrinal content (6:17). There is no gospel without the announcement of God's gift of righteousness through faith in Jesus Christ (v. 17) and the realities of sin and God's wrath (v. 18; 1 John 4:10). The church must declare both His love and justice.**
2. **If men do not love God, they will not love their neighbor (v. 18). Ungodliness and unrighteousness go together. Those who give away God in exchange for idols will find that God gives them over to many sins, including homosexual lusts and practices. When God gives a people over to sin (vv. 24,26,28), it is as though they are blinded at noonday. How is that spiritual and moral blindness evident in the world around you today?**
3. **Before Paul explains in detail the good news of salvation, he details the guilt and misery of sin. Why must we know God's justice and wrath against sin if we are ever to know the saving mercy of Jesus Christ? How does this gospel of justice against sin and grace to sinners promote true gratitude and enduring love for God?**

The Jews Are Sinners (2:1—3:8)

Chapter 2: ***Having shown that the Gentiles are all sinners, the apostle turns to the Jews and shows that they are all sinners too (a theme continuing to 3:8).***

2:1 The Jews *judg*[ed] the Gentiles as though they themselves were innocent, but this was far from the case. In condemning the Gentiles they condemned themselves, since the sins listed in 1:29–31 were found abundantly among the Jews as well as the Gentiles.

2:2–3 *thinkest thou . . . thou shalt escape?* There is no escape from the judgment of God, who judges without exception according to truth.

2:4 Privilege does not prevent guilt but rather increases it. *goodness of God*. His favor and kindness (Luke 6:35). This goodness should lead to *repentance*, though it does not do so except as the Holy Spirit changes the heart and will.

2:5 *impenitent*. Unrepentant. *treasur*[ing] *up*. Building up like water behind a dam. *revelation of the righteous judgment*. The open manifestation of the just *wrath* of God, no longer restrained by His patience. Outside of Christ, far from building up merit before God we only amass guilt and punishment from God.

2:6 *render . . . according to his deeds*. This refers to the distinction between the saved and the unsaved, considered in their contrasting manner of life; it is not a mere restatement of the covenant of works. The wicked will be punished both on account of their works and according to them. The righteous, on the other hand, will be rewarded, not on account of their works but according to them, all of which, of course, are owing to Christ. All is of grace.

2:7–11 These verses give us a description of two kinds of persons. The one is a believer (vv. 7,10) whose whose faith is evident from his life as he does "press toward the mark" of holiness (Phil. 3:14) without which no man shall see the Lord (Heb. 12:14). The other is an unrepentant sinner who continues to argue with God and does not obey the gospel; he will reap the just deserts of his sin. Both of these outcomes apply to Jew and Gentile alike (v. 11).

2:12–16 Paul considers how having or not having the

12 For as many as have sinned without law shall
also perish without law: and as many as have
sinned in the law shall be judged by the law;
13 (For not the hearers of the law *are* just before
God, but the doers of the law shall be justified.
14 For when the Gentiles, which have not the law,
do by nature the things contained in the law, these,
having not the law, are a law unto themselves:
15 Which shew the work of the law written in
their hearts, their conscience also bearing witness,
and *their* thoughts the mean while accusing or
else excusing one another;)
16 In the day when God shall judge the secrets of
men by Jesus Christ according to my gospel.
17 Behold, thou art called a Jew, and restest in the
law, and makest thy boast of God,
18 And knowest *his* will, and approvest the things
that are more excellent, being instructed out of
the law;
19 And art confident that thou thyself art a guide
of the blind, a light of them which are in darkness,
20 An instructor of the foolish, a teacher of babes,
which hast the form of knowledge and of the
truth in the law.
21 Thou therefore which teachest another,
teachest thou not thyself? thou that preachest a
man should not steal, dost thou steal?
22 Thou that sayest a man should not commit
adultery, dost thou commit adultery? thou that
abhorrest idols, dost thou commit sacrilege?
23 Thou that makest thy boast of the law, through
breaking the law dishonourest thou God?
24 For the name of God is blasphemed among
the Gentiles through you, as it is written.
25 For circumcision verily profiteth, if thou keep
the law: but if thou be a breaker of the law, thy
circumcision is made uncircumcision.
26 Therefore if the uncircumcision keep the righ-
teousness of the law, shall not his uncircumcision
be counted for circumcision?
27 And shall not uncircumcision which is by
nature, if it fulfil the law, judge thee, who by the
letter and circumcision dost transgress the law?
28 For he is not a Jew, which is one outwardly;
neither *is that* circumcision, which is outward in
the flesh:
29 But he *is* a Jew, which is one inwardly; and
circumcision *is that* of the heart, in the spirit, *and*

Scriptures will affect the individual on judgment day.

2:12–14 Both unbelievers who have been given the written *law* of God and those who have not still *perish*. It is not that people are innocent until the Word of God comes to them. Those having been exposed to the written law of God are guiltier (Luke 12:47–48), and they will be judged on the basis of that written law, since possession of the law does not justify. Yet those who do not have the law in written form are not without the law in every respect (v. 14). Their constitution as human beings created in God's image means that they have a sense of right and wrong (however blunted) in the "conscience" (v. 15). For this reason sin is restrained, and in some outward respects they do *the things contained in the law* (though not out of love for God, 1:21; 8:7). *law unto themselves*. Not in the colloquial sense, but they are so constituted as to be the very means of bringing God's law to themselves.

2:15 *work of the law written in their hearts*. Not the law itself, written in the regenerate heart by the Spirit so that people love and obey God (v. 29), but its *work*, which shows itself in their recognizing that some things are right and others wrong. *one another*. A reference either to the thoughts themselves and the inner workings and struggles of conscience, or to the Gentiles among themselves.

2:16 *In the day when*. Links back to vv. 5–12, further describing the judgment as being pronounced by *Jesus Christ* (14:10) and as extending to the *secrets of men*, not merely externals.

2:17–24 Here Paul treats false Jewish grounds for confidence before God. These verses show what men can do while still being lovers of sin and not lovers of God.

2:17 *Jew*. A name first mentioned in 2 Kings 16:6; it was used initially of those who dwelt in Judah and then of the Israelites generally, and the name had become a matter of great pride. *restest in the law*. They relied upon their knowledge of and conformity to the law. They construed God's bestowment of many privileges as a reason to assume that God must be pleased with them and so made their *boast of God* by using His name as a vehicle of pride (in contrast to Ps. 34:2, where David gloried in the greatness of the Lord).

2:18 They approved many of the outward requirements of the law.

2:19–20 They considered themselves well qualified to teach others the outward *form* of the law, while all the while actually breaking that law, even their own external form of it.

2:22 *sacrilege*. This may refer to the withholding of tithes (Mal. 1:6–8), or it may mean more simply that there were those who would disapprove of pagan idolatry while not balking at the stealing of pagan idols for personal gain while claiming a moral superiority at the same time (Acts 19:37).

2:24 *as it is written*. Citing Isa. 52:5 (Greek).

2:25–29 The outward sign of *circumcision* can exist without the inner reality signified, and vice versa.

2:25–26 *circumcision*. The Old Testament sign of the covenant of grace. It pointed to the saving blessings that sinners who belong to Christ actually have in Him, both now and in the future. It was a sign of being united to the Lord (Gen. 17:7–11), the new birth (Deut. 30:6), repentance and faith (Deut. 10:16; Jer. 4:4), and justification and forgiveness of sins (4:11). A true believer manifests something of the holiness of heart and life that is defined by God's law (8:4). One can have the sign without any of the holiness that marks a child of God, while another can be a true believer, as evidenced by holiness of life, and yet not have the sign.

2:27–29 The Jew may have had both the sign of circumcision and the Scriptures (*letter*) from his youth, but the Gentile who hears and believes the gospel and begins to serve the Lord from the heart, as the law teaches, will *judge* or bear witness against the unbelieving Jew (Matt. 12:41–42). The contrast in vv. 28–29 is between the man with the outward religious forms and the written law (*letter*) and the truly born-again man who has the life-giving Spirit writing the law upon His heart (Jer. 31:33; 2 Cor. 3:3).

Thoughts for Personal/Family Worship: Chapter 2

1. The unbelieving Jews convinced themselves that they were not really sinners in God's sight by comparing themselves to Gentiles. Do you try to evade the reality of

not in the letter; whose praise *is* not of men, but
of God.

CHAPTER 3

WHAT advantage then hath the Jew? or what
profit *is there* of circumcision?
2 Much every way: chiefly, because that unto
them were committed the oracles of God.
3 For what if some did not believe? shall their
unbelief make the faith of God without effect?
4 God forbid: yea, let God be true, but every
man a liar; as it is written, That thou mightest be
justified in thy sayings, and mightest overcome
when thou art judged.
5 But if our unrighteousness commend the righ-
teousness of God, what shall we say? *Is* God unrigh-
teous who taketh vengeance? (I speak as a man)
6 God forbid: for then how shall God judge the
world?
7 For if the truth of God hath more abounded
through my lie unto his glory; why yet am I also
judged as a sinner?
8 And not *rather*, (as we be slanderously reported,
and as some affirm that we say,) Let us do evil,
that good may come? whose damnation is just.
9 What then? are we better *than they*? No, in no
wise: for we have before proved both Jews and
Gentiles, that they are all under sin;
10 As it is written, There is none righteous, no,
not one:
11 There is none that understandeth, there is
none that seeketh after God.
12 They are all gone out of the way, they are
together become unprofitable; there is none that
doeth good, no, not one.
13 Their throat *is* an open sepulchre; with their
tongues they have used deceit; the poison of asps
is under their lips:
14 Whose mouth *is* full of cursing and bitterness:
15 Their feet *are* swift to shed blood:
16 Destruction and misery *are* in their ways:
17 And the way of peace have they not known:
18 There is no fear of God before their eyes.
19 Now we know that what things soever the law
saith, it saith to them who are under the law: that
every mouth may be stopped, and all the world
may become guilty before God.

---

your guilt before God by comparing yourself with others rather than by assessing yourself against the standard of God's law? Why does this kind of comparison fail to excuse our sins?

2. **Those who do not hear the gospel are still condemned as guilty sinners (v. 12). Otherwise, the preaching of the gospel would be best avoided, as exposure to it would risk making innocent people guilty. The evangelistic imperative rests on the fact that all who are without Christ are lost, and "how shall they believe in him of whom they have not heard?" (10:14). How should this motivate Christians to spread the gospel?**
3. **The Lord will judge the "secrets of men" (v. 16), even what is hidden from those closest to us. Having a Bible and knowing its contents, while good, is not enough (vv. 17–18). People may think highly of us and praise our devotion to God, but that devotion is meaningless unless God sees evidence of His saving work in our hearts (v. 29; see John 5:44). How should these truths drive us to seek Christ?**

Chapter 3: ***After completing the section on the guilt of the Jews as well as the Gentiles (vv. 1–8), the apostle comes to the conclusion that all men are sinners and stand in need of the imputation of God's provided righteousness in Christ.***

3:1–8 *let God be true.* God is the standard of truth, and Christians believe that God is always right.

3:1–2 *Much every way.* The Jews had real privileges but were misusing the majority of them at that time (9:4–5). First among these was their possessing the *oracles of God*, the words uttered by the mouth of God, that is, Holy Scripture.

3:3–4 The unbelief of men does not affect God's faithfulness (*faith of God*). *thou mightest be justified.* The repentant believer declares God to be righteous even though that means condemning himself (Ps. 51:4).

3:5 An objection is envisioned, probably from unbelieving Jews. Some may have set forth a distorted gospel by claiming that salvation by grace through Christ meant that it did not matter how they lived. And some Jews may even have seized upon this to allege that the gospel promoted lawlessness. The argument is that if unbelief serves to highlight God's truthfulness by contrast, how can that unbelief (and the falsehood flowing from it) be counted as sin and judged by God? *I speak as a man.* This is human logic.

3:6 The fact that God orders all sin to His own glory does not remove His prerogative to *judge* all—and Paul regarded it as inconceivable that God would not judge.

3:7–8 *Let us do evil, that good may come.* The false argument is given in expanded form, and the full wicked conclusion is spelled out and condemned as a distortion of the apostle's doctrine, attacking the very authority of God.

All Have Sinned (3:9–20)

3:9 *all under sin.* Under its dominion (5:21; 6:14; see note at 5:17).

3:10–12 A quotation from Pss. 14:1–3; 53:1–3, using the Greek translation of the Old Testament known as the Septuagint. The two psalms are largely identical except that in Ps. 14 the name "Jehovah" (LORD) is used, perhaps with respect to the wicked in Israel, whereas in Ps. 53 "Elohim" (God) replaces it, perhaps to speak of Israel's pagan enemies. This double reference is fitting, as the apostle is showing that Jew and Gentile are both under sin.

3:11 The mind is darkened (1:21–22), and the will is in bondage to sin (6:20).

3:12 Man's inner depravity is shown in his practice.

3:13–18 Paul quotes from Pss. 5:9; 10:7; 140:3; Isa. 59:7–8; and Ps. 36:1 (in that order), describing man's deadly corruption in every area of life, including speech (*tongues*), actions (*feet*), and perspective (*eyes*). *fear of God.* Man lacks the beginning of wisdom (Prov. 9:10), and from this failure to reverence God's majesty flow all the disorders of human society (1:21–32).

3:19 The *law* speaks to *all*, whether or not men have the Scriptures (2:14–15), and it condemns all. This should stop every mouth now and will do so at the judgment.

20 Therefore by the deeds of the law there shall
no flesh be justified in his sight: for by the law *is*
the knowledge of sin.
21 But now the righteousness of God without the
law is manifested, being witnessed by the law and
the prophets;
22 Even the righteousness of God *which is* by
faith of Jesus Christ unto all and upon all them
that believe: for there is no difference:
23 For all have sinned, and come short of the
glory of God;
24 Being justified freely by his grace through the
redemption that is in Christ Jesus:
25 Whom God hath set forth *to be* a propitiation
through faith in his blood, to declare his righ-
teousness for the remission of sins that are past,
through the forbearance of God;
26 To declare, *I say*, at this time his righteousness:
that he might be just, and the justifier of him
which believeth in Jesus.
27 Where *is* boasting then? It is excluded. By what
law? of works? Nay: but by the law of faith.
28 Therefore we conclude that a man is justified
by faith without the deeds of the law.
29 *Is he* the God of the Jews only? *is he* not also of
the Gentiles? Yes, of the Gentiles also:
30 Seeing *it is* one God, which shall justify the
circumcision by faith, and uncircumcision
through faith.
31 Do we then make void the law through faith?
God forbid: yea, we establish the law.

CHAPTER 4

WHAT shall we say then that Abraham our father,
as pertaining to the flesh, hath found?

3:20 There is no hope of earning acceptance with God by trying to keep God's law. What the law does do, when correctly understood, is expose our sin as in a mirror (*by the law is the knowledge of sin*).

The Only Hope Is God's Righteousness Provided in Christ (3:21–31)

3:21 *righteousness of God.* Not simply God's attribute of righteousness but His righteousness provided in Christ and imputed to all who believe (1:17; 2 Cor. 5:21). *without the law.* Apart from personal attempts to keep God's law. *being witnessed.* The same gospel to which the Old Testament testified (1:2).

3:22 *faith of Jesus Christ.* Trust in Jesus Christ. *no difference.* Between Jew and Gentile in terms of condemnation and need for Christ.

3:23 *glory.* The reflection of God's character that ought to be found in us.

3:24 *Being.* Jewish and Gentile believers. *justified.* Declared righteous by God, the Judge (Introduction: Synopsis). *grace.* Favor to the undeserving (in fact, the hell-deserving). *redemption.* Buying back or paying a ransom (Mark 10:45) to release from bondage. Christ paid the debt, not to Satan or to any creature but to the justice of God (vv. 25–26).

3:25 *propitiation.* Renderings such as "atoning sacrifice" or "expiation," though expressive of biblical truth, are inadequate as a translation of the Greek *hilasterion*, since the term implies the removal of God's wrath (1:18; 2:5,8). *in his blood.* By Christ's suffering in body and soul unto death. *through faith.* God intends the propitiation for believers in all ages and applies it to them instrumentally by their trust in God through Christ (4:24–25). *remission.* Not the typical word for forgiveness, but rather "overlooking" in His forbearance. Men may often have misinterpreted God's delay in punishing sin, yet Christ's substitutionary death on the cross demonstrates that He does punish sin.

3:26 God's attribute of righteousness is now demonstrated; He shows Himself to be just by nature in the way He redeems sinners by requiring that His righteous law be satisfied in Christ's obedience and death (Gal. 3:10,13; 4:4). He is "a just God and a Saviour" (Isa. 45:21; see Pss. 85:10–11; 98:2; 1 John.1:9). The gospel shows God as He is in His character, attributes, and glory (1 Tim. 1:11).

3:27 *Law* is used here in the sense of "system of justification." The way God saves excludes all human pride (1 Cor. 1:27–31; Eph. 2:8).

3:29 The phrase *God of* is the language of God's covenant in Christ (Gen. 17:7; Ps. 95:7; Ezek. 36:27–28; Hos. 2:23; Matt. 22:31–32; John 20:17; 2 Cor. 6:16; Rev. 21:3,7; etc.).

3:30 *circumcision . . . uncircumcision.* Jews and Gentiles. The prepositions *by* and *through* are both used elsewhere (e.g., v. 25; 5:1). The argument is for sameness, not difference.

3:31 The law is established because Christ fulfilled it perfectly and bore its penalty, and believers, and only believers, begin to truly keep it (8:3–4).

Thoughts for Personal/Family Worship: Chapter 3

1. **No amount of human consensus can overturn the truth of God (v. 4). The final appeal for Christians is not any national court or international convention, or the court of public opinion, but the Word of God. Also, the false conclusions of others do not justify rejection of the truth (v. 5). The truth of the Bible must be believed. Sinners will always want a gospel that allows them to continue in sin (v. 8), but the apostle Paul draws out the unbeliever from every false refuge, whether trust in a name (v. 17), in ordinances (v. 15), or in false reasoning (vv. 5–8). Have you given up all your excuses and arguments and submitted to God's Word as your ulimate authority?**
2. **Christ is the object of our faith; our own believing cannot be. We must look outside ourselves to Christ (v. 22). The Old Testament testifies that we must look to Christ (v. 21). Our only hope of righteousness is not in our works of obeying God's law (v. 20) but in Christ's work of redeeming sinners at the cost of His precious blood (vv. 24–25). Christ alone can satisfy God's justice directed against sinners and appease His righteous wrath against those who dishonor Him (vv. 25–26). Anyone, Jew or Gentile, who trusts in Christ alone is declared righteous by the supreme Judge (vv. 22,30). Thus the Lord says to all who hear the gospel, "Behold me, behold me" (Isa. 65:1). Have you cast aside your self-righteousness and received and rested upon Christ as your only righteousness before God?**

Chapter 4: *We are now given Old Testament confirmation that the doctrine of justification by faith is no novelty.*

Old Testament Confirmation (4:1–25)

Abraham and Justification (4:1–5)

4:1–3 Did *Abraham* have grounds for boasting that he was

CHRIST'S SATISFACTION OF GOD'S JUSTICE

No promise of the gospel is more basic or precious than the forgiveness of sins. When our sins rise up against us, we sink under the weight of conviction, knowing the justice of the charges laid against us. We long to know that God will show us mercy and take our guilt away.

But how can a just God forgive sins? He cannot deny Himself, and therefore He cannot allow sin to go unpunished. Sin incurs a terrible kind of moral and spiritual debt. The sinner has withheld from God the love and obedience that are His due as our Creator. As a result, the sinner is held hostage to God's justice and must perish under God's wrath unless that moral and spiritual debt is fully repaid or satisfied.

This view of sin loomed large in Christ's thought. He inserted it into His model prayer as the fifth petition: "Forgive us our debts" (Matt. 6:12). He saw the people He came to save as dying under the weight of the debt they had incurred by sinning against God. He came into the world "to give his life a ransom for many" (Matt. 20:28), that is, to make satisfaction, to repay the debt in full, and thereby to secure the debtors' release or deliverance from punishment.

Paul works these ideas out in a compelling way in Romans 3:24–25. He has shown that "all have sinned, and come short of the glory of God" (v. 23). But he adds that believers have been "justified freely by his grace through the redemption that is in Christ Jesus" (v. 24). *Redemption* means "release effected by payment of a ransom."

But Paul is not finished. Why is Christ's death a ransom for many? It is because God has "set forth" or fore-ordained His incarnate Son to be "a propitiation through faith in his blood" (v. 25). A propitiation is a sin offering that takes into account not only the guilt of sin but also the wrath of God against us because of our sin. God's wrath is His justice aroused and on the move.

The fury of God's wrath can be quenched only when the demands of His justice are satisfied or paid in full. Paul declares that God has provided such a satisfaction by sending His own Son to die on the cross. In this way God can be just and, at the same time, "the justifier of him which believeth in Jesus" (v. 26). Mercy need no longer be restrained by justice; justice need not be denied for mercy's sake.

In other words, God has punished sin in His beloved Son, Jesus Christ, with the bitter and shameful death on the cross. As the payment of a ransom, the righteousness of Christ is accepted as a satisfaction for the sinner's debt, acquitting him of all guilt. As a propitiation, His righteousness covers our sin and delivers us from God's wrath and judgment. We can receive and apply to ourselves this righteousness and satisfaction in no other way than by Spirit-worked faith in Christ. "He is our peace" (Eph. 2:14).

Such was the doctrine of Christ and His apostles. Sadly, more recent generations have professed to be embarrassed by what they deem to be the "barbaric theory" of blood atonement. In fact, what has changed is their view of sin: How could mere human frailties and mistakes incur divine wrath? Would not a God of love overlook such trifles? Viewed in this light, the death of Christ seems quite literally to be overkill on God's part.

Christ anticipated such a development by instituting the sacraments of holy baptism and the Lord's Supper to direct our faith to His sacrifice on the cross as the only ground of our salvation. The one is a sign of the washing away of sins by His blood; the other is a showing forth of Christ's death until He comes again. The sacraments seal to our hearts the promise of redemption through His blood and the forgiveness of sins.

2 For if Abraham were justified by works, he hath
whereof to glory; but not before God.
3 For what saith the scripture? Abraham be-
lieved God, and it was counted unto him for
righteousness.
4 Now to him that worketh is the reward not
reckoned of grace, but of debt.
5 But to him that worketh not, but believeth
on him that justifieth the ungodly, his faith is
counted for righteousness.
6 Even as David also describeth the blessedness
of the man, unto whom God imputeth righteous-
ness without works,
7 *Saying*, Blessed *are* they whose iniquities are
forgiven, and whose sins are covered.
8 Blessed *is* the man to whom the Lord will not
impute sin.
9 *Cometh* this blessedness then upon the circum-
cision *only*, or upon the uncircumcision also? for
we say that faith was reckoned to Abraham for
righteousness.
10 How was it then reckoned? when he was
in circumcision, or in uncircumcision? Not in
circumcision, but in uncircumcision.
11 And he received the sign of circumcision, a
seal of the righteousness of the faith which *he
had yet* being uncircumcised: that he might be
the father of all them that believe, though they
be not circumcised; that righteousness might be
imputed unto them also:
12 And the father of circumcision to them
who are not of the circumcision only, but who
also walk in the steps of that faith of our father
Abraham, which *he had* being *yet* uncircumcised.
13 For the promise, that he should be the heir
of the world, *was* not to Abraham, or to his seed,
through the law, but through the righteousness
of faith.
14 For if they which are of the law *be* heirs, faith is
made void, and the promise made of none effect:
15 Because the law worketh wrath: for where no
law is, *there is* no transgression.
16 Therefore *it is* of faith, that *it might be* by
grace; to the end the promise might be sure to all
the seed; not to that only which is of the law, but
to that also which is of the faith of Abraham; who
is the father of us all,
17 (As it is written, I have made thee a father of
many nations,) before him whom he believed,
even God, who quickeneth the dead, and calleth
those things which be not as though they were.
18 Who against hope believed in hope, that he
might become the father of many nations, ac-
cording to that which was spoken, So shall thy
seed be.
19 And being not weak in faith, he considered
not his own body now dead, when he was about
an hundred years old, neither yet the deadness of
Sara's womb:
20 He staggered not at the promise of God
through unbelief; but was strong in faith, giving
glory to God;
21 And being fully persuaded that, what he had
promised, he was able also to perform.

---

justified by works? No, *not before God* the righteous Judge, who declared him justified by faith (Gen. 15:6). *counted . . . for righteousness*. Abraham's faith was not his righteousness or merit before God, for even his faith was imperfect (Gen. 12:8–13; 20:1–2). His faith in God's promise was the instrument by which he received the righteousness of God in Christ (3:22).

4:4–5 *grace . . . debt*. Justification by works would mean that God gives the wages due for work accomplished, whereas justification by faith entails God showing kindness to the undeserving. Faith is not a meritorious alternative to works but the instrument by which Christ's meritorious righteousness is imputed or credited (*reckoned . . . counted*) to a sinner.

David and Justification (4:6–8)

4:6–8 A quotation from Ps. 32:1–2 to show, as an accessory argument, that *David* also was justified by faith, before Paul returns to considering Abraham.

Justification Independent of Circumcision (4:9–12)

4:9–12 Abraham was pronounced justified before he was circumcised. He received circumcision as an adult believer (Gen. 17:24), unlike, for example, Isaac (Gen. 21:4).

4:11–12 *seal*. A sign given by God as an assurance of the promises of forgiveness through the promised Christ. Abraham is the *father of all* believers, whether or not they are circumcised, that is, not in the sense that they imitate his reliance upon God's promise (*walk in the steps of that faith of our father*).

Promise and Law (4:13–17)

4:13 The *promise* was not fulfilled on the basis of personal keeping of the *law* but was given so that sinners like Abraham would be justified through faith in Christ. *heir of the world*. The promise of the land to Abraham's seed (Gen. 17:4–8). It was not automatically fulfilled to the physical seed (Num. 14:30; Heb. 4:2); only the believing seed had any title to it (though the two groups are not perfectly separated in this world). A purified remnant would return (Ezek. 36:25–28). The words for "land" and "earth" are the same in both the Hebrew and the Greek. As a place where Israel was to enjoy settled fellowship with the Lord, the land of Canaan was an imperfect shadow of the new heaven and the new earth, which are part of the inheritance of all God's people in all generations (Rom. 8:19–23; Ps. 37:3,9; Matt. 5:5; 2 Peter 3:10–13).

4:14 *faith is made void*. We cannot embrace promises of mercy for sinners if we are seeking to be justified through the merit of personal works of obeying the law.

4:15 For sinners, the *law* can only expose guilt and liability to God's *wrath*. There could be *no transgression* if there were *no law*.

4:16 *of the law*. The administration of the law of Moses under the Jewish theocracy. We must be true children of Abraham by following him in trusting God's promises.

Abraham's Faith to Be Followed (4:18–25)

4:18 *against hope*. In the face of circumstances (v. 19), suggesting that confident expectation was foolish. *believed in hope*. Abraham trusted the word of the omnipotent God.

4:20–21 *staggered not*. He did not doubt God's Word or His ability to fulfill it.

22 And therefore it was imputed to him for righ-
teousness.
23 Now it was not written for his sake alone, that
it was imputed to him;
24 But for us also, to whom it shall be imputed, if
we believe on him that raised up Jesus our Lord
from the dead;
25 Who was delivered for our offences, and was
raised again for our justification.

CHAPTER 5

THEREFORE being justified by faith, we have peace
with God through our Lord Jesus Christ:
2 By whom also we have access by faith into this
grace wherein we stand, and rejoice in hope of the
glory of God.
3 And not only *so*, but we glory in tribulations
also: knowing that tribulation worketh patience;
4 And patience, experience; and experience, hope:
5 And hope maketh not ashamed; because the
love of God is shed abroad in our hearts by the
Holy Ghost which is given unto us.
6 For when we were yet without strength, in due
time Christ died for the ungodly.
7 For scarcely for a righteous man will one die: yet
peradventure for a good man some would even
dare to die.
8 But God commendeth his love toward us, in
that, while we were yet sinners, Christ died for us.
9 Much more then, being now justified by his
blood, we shall be saved from wrath through him.
10 For if, when we were enemies, we were recon-
ciled to God by the death of his Son, much more,
being reconciled, we shall be saved by his life.
11 And not only *so*, but we also joy in God
through our Lord Jesus Christ, by whom we have
now received the atonement.
12 Wherefore, as by one man sin entered into
the world, and death by sin; and so death passed
upon all men, for that all have sinned:
13 (For until the law sin was in the world: but sin
is not imputed when there is no law.
14 Nevertheless death reigned from Adam to

4:22 *imputed to him for righteousness.* See v. 3.
4:23–25 We must follow Abraham in believing that God will save us if we believe His promises about Christ's death and resurrection. Through Christ's complete work of atonement He forgives and declares righteous all who believe. He is faithful (1 John 1:9).

Thoughts for Personal/Family Worship: Chapter 4

1. **Abraham believed the gospel (John 8:56; Gal. 3:8,17), as did Moses (Heb. 11:24–26) and David (Ps. 32). There has only been one way of salvation for any sinner since the fall of man in the garden of Eden (Gen. 3:15), and there will be only this one way until the end of the world (Rev. 22:17). Only in Christ is there acceptance with God. We must trust in the one Seed, Jesus Christ, in whom many of Abraham's literal seed and sinners from all nations are blessed (Gal. 3:16).**
2. **Even the greatness of your sins does not exclude you from the promise of mercy. God justifies the ungodly (v. 5) who trust in Christ. You must not "stagger" at the promise of God. Do not say "I do not know whom to believe" because you should know. You must believe God (2 Tim. 1:12). Take your great sins to God and seek forgiveness in Christ. Tell Him your great need, as David did:, "For thy name's sake, O LORD, pardon mine iniquity; for it is great" (Ps. 25:11). He has purposed to make Himself known as the God of grace (9:23; Eph. 3:9–10). Why do sinners sometimes shrink back from trusting Christ? How can this chapter encourage them to come without delay?**
3. **Believing glorifies God (v. 20) by acknowledging His power and truthfulness: He can and will perform what He has promised in accordance with His love for His people and His justice in accepting them for Christ's sake. Honor God by trusting Him.**

Chapter 5: *This chapter shows us both the certainty of justification and some blessings that accompanies it.*

The Blessedness and Safety of the Justified (5:1–11)

5:1 *peace with God.* The objective removal of hostility between God and believers because Christ has borne the wrath of God against their sins (3:25).
5:2 *grace.* The undeserved blessing of justification. *hope.* Sure expectation, not something tentative. *glory of God.* The revelation of God's glory in Christ and its reflection in believers once they have been conformed to Christ's glorified humanity (8:17–18,29).
5:3–4 The chain of blessing through *tribulations* (troubles): *patience* (endurance), *experience* (the result of being proven, having stood the test), and then back to *hope.* We glory in tribulations because they serve ultimately to strengthen that hope in which we glory.
5:5 *hope maketh not ashamed.* Hope will not disappoint us because it rests upon that love of which we are assured by the pouring out of the Holy Spirit (15:30; Titus 3:3–4; 1 John 4:12–13).
5:6–8 The greatness of God's love contrasts infinitely with even the noblest acts of love that are possible for the natural man, for it is revealed in the voluntary death of the best, Jesus Christ, for the worst (Gal. 2:20; Eph. 5:25; 1 John 4:9–10).
5:7 *peradventure.* Perhaps.
5:9–10 Paul moves from the present reality to a certain future. Being *justified* in the present *by his blood* (summing up the benefit of Christ's atoning sufferings), believers can be sure of safety from the *wrath* to come. When we were God's enemies we were *reconciled* (restored from wrath to a relationship of friendship); now the future is sure because of our living Savior's endless intercession on our behalf (8:34; Heb. 7:24–25).
5:11 Not only is the future secure, but we exult and rejoice (*joy*) in God now because we already have reconciliation (*atonement*) in Christ.

Justification in Christ as Sure as Condemnation in Adam (5:12–21)

5:12 *Death* entered the human race and became universal through one historical figure, Adam (Gen. 2:1—3:24), as the guilt of his first transgression was imputed to all descending from him by ordinary generation (Gen. 5:1–3).
5:13–14 Since everyone dies, everyone is shown to be guilty because death comes from sin (6:23; Gen. 2:17). Even between *Adam* and *Moses* (through whom the written law was given),

Moses, even over them that had not sinned after
the similitude of Adam's transgression, who is the
figure of him that was to come.
15 But not as the offence, so also *is* the free gift.
For if through the offence of one many be dead,
much more the grace of God, and the gift by
grace, *which is* by one man, Jesus Christ, hath
abounded unto many.
16 And not as *it was* by one that sinned, *so is* the
gift: for the judgment *was* by one to condemna-
tion, but the free gift *is* of many offences unto
justification.
17 For if by one man's offence death reigned by
one; much more they which receive abundance of
grace and of the gift of righteousness shall reign
in life by one, Jesus Christ.)
18 Therefore as by the offence of one *judgment*
came upon all men to condemnation; even so by
the righteousness of one *the free gift came* upon all
men unto justification of life.
19 For as by one man's disobedience many were
made sinners, so by the obedience of one shall
many be made righteous.
20 Moreover the law entered, that the offence
might abound. But where sin abounded, grace
did much more abound:
21 That as sin hath reigned unto death, even so
might grace reign through righteousness unto
eternal life by Jesus Christ our Lord.

CHAPTER 6

WHAT shall we say then? Shall we continue in sin,
that grace may abound?
2 God forbid. How shall we, that are dead to sin,
live any longer therein?

---

everyone died. So law, sin, and guilt existed (4:15) even among those who had not sinned in the same way (*similitude*) as Adam, that is, against a verbally revealed command (*transgression*). Indeed, in the case of newborns dying in infancy, they have not committed personal transgression at all, yet death demonstrates guilt: the guilt of Adam's first sin imputed to them. This presupposes that Adam represented all mankind in a legal arrangement before God, often called the covenant of works. *figure*. A type. Adam foreshadowed Christ, who represents His people in the covenant of grace.

5:15–17 Here Paul provides both a parallel and a contrast between Adam and Christ, Adam representing mankind and Christ representing His people. *Much more* indicates that believers are more blessed in Christ even than Adam was before he sinned (1 Cor. 15:47–49).

5:15 The *one* transgressed God's law (*offence*) and brought death upon those he represented, while the other brought the *gift* of saving *grace*.

5:16 The *one* sin brought *condemnation* to all (Adam's sin passed along not only sin but also the guilt of his transgression), but the *many offences* were graciously removed by *justification* through God's *free gift* of Christ's righteousness.

5:17 *Death reigned* by the sin of *one* man, but *Jesus Christ* not only gives life but causes His people to *reign in life*, that is, to share in His kingdom of eternal life (2 Tim. 2:12). The language of "reigning" (v. 21; 6:12; cf. 3:9; 6:9,14; 7:1; 14:9) implies two kingdoms (14:17; Col. 1:13). The first is the one where sin and death rule over fallen man; but God's kingdom is coming and already starting in Christ in the kingdom of grace.

5:18–19 Paul summarizes the whole argument linking up with v. 12, since all of the material between has simply expanded the detail of the contrast (hence, the parentheses in the KJV). The parallel is between *one* Adam and *one* Christ, both acting on behalf of others as though there have been no other men in the history of the world (1 Cor. 15:45,47). The contrasts are between *offence* and *righteousness* and between *condemnation* and *justification.* Verse 19 makes further contrasts between *disobedience* and *obedience* and between *made sinners* and *made righteous.* These latter terms are used in the sense of legal standing rather than pollution or sanctification (see Introduction: Synopsis).

5:20–21 The giving of the written law only increased guilt (4:15; 7:8), but God's saving grace overcomes all of this for His people. Sin prevailed (*reigned*) in bringing death; so grace prevails to the extent that it brings eternal life through Christ.

Thoughts for Personal/Family Worship: Chapter 5

1. **Do you have peace with God (v. 1)? This is not a question of your feelings but of your objective standing before God. Only when you have been forgiven and declared righteous through faith in Christ can you experience "the peace of God, which passeth all understanding" (Phil. 4:7).**
2. **Glorying in tribulations is no easy thing, even for a strong believer. We must take to heart the truth of God's providential government over all of our circumstances and trust His wisdom, power, and promised grace, which ensure that all things work for our good. Only then will we be able to accept that those things that seem to harm us are actually still sent for our good (2 Cor. 12:7–10). We must also rest our hearts upon the righteousness of God in Christ. Why is a sense of peace with God necessary in order for us to glory in trials?**
3. **Christianity is not just a set of principles for living but a claim about history. This chapter presupposes that Adam was a literal and historical individual. Gen. 1:1—3:24 must be understood that way if we are to make sense of Rom. 5. We see, also, the importance of the virgin birth. Christ was not, in His human nature, descended from Adam by ordinary generation, and so the guilt of Adam's first transgression was not imputed to Him under the covenant of works. This means that, as the perfectly guiltless Mediator of the covenant of grace, He can act as the substitute for His people. (2 Cor. 5:21). Why do the faith and hope of Christians stand or fall on the historical reality of these two persons, Adam and Christ?**

Chapter 6: *The forgiven man has undergone a radical change by which he is being made holy. He will not abuse the doctrine of justification by faith in order to excuse an ungodly life.*

The Forgiven Man Is Being Made Holy (6:1–23)

6:1–4 Justification is not the change of man's moral nature, but every justified man is a changed man (Titus 3:4–7).

6:1 *continue in sin*. This is the cherished desire of the unregenerate: if salvation is of grace and justification is by faith, I can go on sinning and still class myself as a justified believer (3:8; James 2:14).

6:2 Paul provides the answer: *God forbid*. No truly regenerate

3 Know ye not, that so many of us as were baptized
into Jesus Christ were baptized into his death?
4 Therefore we are buried with him by baptism
into death: that like as Christ was raised up from
the dead by the glory of the Father, even so we
also should walk in newness of life.
5 For if we have been planted together in the like-
ness of his death, we shall be also *in the likeness* of
his resurrection:
6 Knowing this, that our old man is crucified
with *him*, that the body of sin might be destroyed,
that henceforth we should not serve sin.
7 For he that is dead is freed from sin.
8 Now if we be dead with Christ, we believe that
we shall also live with him:
9 Knowing that Christ being raised from the dead
dieth no more; death hath no more dominion
over him.
10 For in that he died, he died unto sin once: but
in that he liveth, he liveth unto God.
11 Likewise reckon ye also yourselves to be dead
indeed unto sin, but alive unto God through Jesus
Christ our Lord.
12 Let not sin therefore reign in your mortal
body, that ye should obey it in the lusts thereof.
13 Neither yield ye your members *as* instruments
of unrighteousness unto sin: but yield yourselves
unto God, as those that are alive from the dead,
and your members *as* instruments of righteous-
ness unto God.
14 For sin shall not have dominion over you: for
ye are not under the law, but under grace.
15 What then? shall we sin, because we are not
under the law, but under grace? God forbid.
16 Know ye not, that to whom ye yield yourselves
servants to obey, his servants ye are to whom ye
obey; whether of sin unto death, or of obedience
unto righteousness?
17 But God be thanked, that ye were the servants
of sin, but ye have obeyed from the heart that
form of doctrine which was delivered you.
18 Being then made free from sin, ye became the
servants of righteousness.
19 I speak after the manner of men because of the
infirmity of your flesh: for as ye have yielded your
members servants to uncleanness and to iniquity
unto iniquity; even so now yield your members
servants to righteousness unto holiness.
20 For when ye were the servants of sin, ye were
free from righteousness.

---

and believing man will say any such thing. The change that has taken place ensures this.

6:3–4 *baptized into.* A sign of being brought into lasting union with Christ (1 Cor. 1:13; 10:1–2; 12:13) and thus of sharing in His death, burial, and resurrection (2 Cor. 5:14–15; Gal. 2:20; 5:24; 6:14; Eph. 2:5–6; Col. 2:20; 3:1). *by the glory of the Father.* The glorious attributes of God were displayed in raising Christ from the dead. There must be, therefore, a death (of the sin-dominated man) and the raising of a new man in Christ to the glory of God.

6:5–11 Union with Christ and the radical break with sin.

6:5 *planted together.* The Greek word conveys the idea of a common source, here stressing the sharing of death and resurrection between Christ and His people. The term *likeness,* however, indicates that this is by way of analogy rather than physical correspondence.

6:6 *our old man.* Not our sinful nature in general but the unregenerate and sin-dominated man (1 John 3:6–9). This passage does not teach Christian perfection in this life. *body of sin.* The physical body (v. 12), not as the location of sin but as being at the disposal of sin.

6:7 *freed.* A judicial term. We are released from the prison or bond service of sin.

6:8 *if . . . dead . . . also live.* Freedom from sin comes in conjunction with new life toward God.

6:9 *no more dominion.* The saving change is as irreversible and unrepeatable as the death and resurrection of Christ (v. 14).

6:10–11 *dead . . . unto sin.* Just as Christ died once and for all as the substitute bearing the penalty for sin, and then rose in freedom and glory, so also believers must by faith in Christ consider (*reckon*) themselves radically separated (*dead indeed unto*) sin and given a new identity and a disposition for God to be acknowledged as central and supreme in all of existence (*alive unto God*).

6:12–14 Paul exhorts believers to live like freed men. Believers are under new management and must follow this through in practice. The body is *mortal* on account of sin but is not itself the location of sin. Nevertheless, sin is worked out through the various faculties of the body. The members of the body must, therefore, be enlisted in the service of King Jesus as *instruments* (weapons) *of righteousness.*

6:14 *under the law.* Ruled by the strict demands of the law for perfect obedience as the basis of our standing before God, subject to its threats to condemn and curse all who break the least commandment (Gal. 3:10), and yet given no gracious power to overcome sin or atone for it, as in the covenant of works (Gen. 2:16–17). *under grace.* Ruled by God's love in Christ, who has perfectly atoned for sin and gives power to fight and overcome it. See also 7:1–6.

6:15–18 True freedom is enjoyed in serving God.

6:15–16 Those committed to serving sin are the *servants* of sin, and that leads to *death* (in its fullest sense, 2:8–9). The justified man is also set free from the tyranny of sin.

6:17 *God be thanked . . . ye have obeyed.* Man's submission to the Word in faith is a gift of God, and all glory must go to Him (1:8; Col. 1:3–4; 1 Thess. 1:2–5). *form of doctrine.* The Word of God brings us an authoritative set of teachings we must believe in order to be saved.

6:18 *free from sin . . . servants of righteousness.* When God enables people to believe the gospel, He liberates them from the bondage of sin and brings them under His mastery. They cannot, therefore, go on simply serving their old master.

6:19–23 *manner.* Custom, habit. In these verses Paul enjoins consistency in the right thing.

6:19 *after the manner of men.* An illustration from human life that does not fully correspond in all points to the matter in hand but helps us grasp the point because of the effect of sin upon our understanding. *infirmity of your flesh.* Our weakness and inability by nature since the fall of Adam. *as ye have yielded . . . even so now yield.* We should aim to be as consistent in pursuing holiness as we were in pursuing sin before we were called by grace.

6:21–22 There was no *fruit* (benefit) in past sin, but only present shame. Moreover, uninterrupted sin leads to *death.* In

21 What fruit had ye then in those things whereof
ye are now ashamed? for the end of those things
is death.
22 But now being made free from sin, and
become servants to God, ye have your fruit unto
holiness, and the end everlasting life.
23 For the wages of sin *is* death; but the gift of
God *is* eternal life through Jesus Christ our Lord.

CHAPTER 7

KNOW ye not, brethren, (for I speak to them that
know the law,) how that the law hath dominion
over a man as long as he liveth?
2 For the woman which hath an husband is
bound by the law to *her* husband so long as he
liveth; but if the husband be dead, she is loosed
from the law of *her* husband.
3 So then if, while *her* husband liveth, she be
married to another man, she shall be called an
adulteress: but if her husband be dead, she is free
from that law; so that she is no adulteress, though
she be married to another man.
4 Wherefore, my brethren, ye also are become
dead to the law by the body of Christ; that ye
should be married to another, *even* to him who is
raised from the dead, that we should bring forth
fruit unto God.
5 For when we were in the flesh, the motions of
sins, which were by the law, did work in our mem-
bers to bring forth fruit unto death.
6 But now we are delivered from the law, that
being dead wherein we were held; that we should
serve in newness of spirit, and not *in* the oldness
of the letter.
7 What shall we say then? *Is* the law sin? God
forbid. Nay, I had not known sin, but by the law:
for I had not known lust, except the law had said,
Thou shalt not covet.
8 But sin, taking occasion by the commandment,
wrought in me all manner of concupiscence. For
without the law sin *was* dead.

---

contrast, the fruit of becoming a servant of God is holiness and everlasting life.

6:23 The contrast is not only between sin and holiness and death and life but also between *wages* and *gift* (3:24; 4:4; 5:15,17; Eph. 2:8–9). The former is deserved, while the latter is undeserved, though freely bestowed through the mediation of Christ.

Thoughts for Personal/Family Worship: Chapter 6

1. **People often love to talk about the privileges of God's children, but they may neglect to realize that union with Christ means that we have died and risen with Him. This must show itself in our lives. Though justification is entirely through faith, true faith brings the effects of Christ's cross into our lives to crucify the old man. How then can believers continue comfortably in sin? His resurrection overflows by the Spirit into each of those for whom He died and brings to life a person who loves God. How then can believers fail to live for Him? How is a person who claims to be one with Christ and yet lives for sin and is dead toward God a stark contradiction?**
2. **We all serve someone (v. 16). If it is the world, the flesh, and the Devil, the idea that this is true freedom is an illusion. Sinners are in fact slaves of their own thoughts and desires (Titus 3:3). However, salvation in Christ does not set us free to live for ourselves, for this is the very slavery we must escape. When God joins a sinner to Christ, that sinner becomes a willing slave of Christ to do His righteous will. Serving Christ is true freedom (John 8:36). Why is this so? Are you a slave of Christ?**

Chapter 7: ***Paul speaks to the believer's relationship to the law of God and leads on to the question of when and whether the believer will ever be totally free from the pollution and practice of sin.***

The Gospel and the Law (7:1–25)

The Believer's Changed Relationship to the Law (7:1–6)

7:1 *law.* The whole law given by Moses, including the permanent moral law summed up in the Ten Commandments. *law hath dominion.* The law rules people with its demands for complete obedience and threats of punishment as long as they are under the covenant of works. The apostle returns to the thought of 6:14 and explains what it means to be not under the law but under grace.

7:2–3 The marriage illustration is used to show that only the intervention of death (*be dead*) can sever the bond of the law and allow remarriage.

7:4 *body of Christ.* Christ's suffering and crucifixion as an atonement for sin. *dead to the law.* The law is not dead, for it remains the definition of sin and righteousness even for the believer. Still, there has been a death that removes from the life of the believer the former relationship of dominion under the law. We are now married to Christ. Only now, in Christ, do we begin to *bring forth fruit unto God.* The law tells us what is sinful, but it cannot eradicate the love of sin.

7:5 *in the flesh.* In the state of nature without saving grace. *motions.* Impulses. *by the law.* Sin is so strong that the law does not curtail it, but in response to the law sin stirs itself up all the more (vv. 8,11,13). *members.* Parts and faculties of a human being.

7:6 *delivered from the law.* Saved by Christ's grace from the condemnation of the law. *law, that being dead wherein we were held.* Better "being dead to that by which we were held." Believers died, not the law. *newness of spirit . . . letter.* The Holy Spirit in contrast to only the written law (2:29; 2 Cor. 3:3,6; cf. Rom. 8:2–3).

The Law Exposes Sin and the Need for Christ (7:7–13)

7:7–13 Far from our still being married to the law, as though we could merit acceptance with God by our attempts to keep it, the first right use of the law is to show us our sin and need of Christ.

7:7–8 Paul recoils in horror at the idea that our break with the law as a ground of righteousness means that there is something wrong with the law (vv. 12,14). Rather, the law exposes our sin and need of Christ (3:20). *lust . . . covet.* The tenth commandment (Ex. 20:17) showed him the sinfulness of his desires. *Concupiscence* is the same Greek word as "covetousness" and refers to sinful desire. *sin was dead.* Sin was comparatively dormant until its prohibition in the law of God actually made it more attractive to a rebellious nature.

9 For I was alive without the law once: but when
the commandment came, sin revived, and I died.
10 And the commandment, which *was ordained*
to life, I found *to be* unto death.
11 For sin, taking occasion by the command-
ment, deceived me, and by it slew *me*.
12 Wherefore the law *is* holy, and the command-
ment holy, and just, and good.
13 Was then that which is good made death unto
me? God forbid. But sin, that it might appear
sin, working death in me by that which is good;
that sin by the commandment might become
exceeding sinful.
14 For we know that the law is spiritual: but I am
carnal, sold under sin.
15 For that which I do I allow not: for what I
would, that do I not; but what I hate, that do I.
16 If then I do that which I would not, I consent
unto the law that *it is* good.
17 Now then it is no more I that do it, but sin that
dwelleth in me.
18 For I know that in me (that is, in my flesh,)
dwelleth no good thing: for to will is present
with me; but *how* to perform that which is good I
find not.
19 For the good that I would I do not: but the evil
which I would not, that I do.
20 Now if I do that I would not, it is no more I
that do it, but sin that dwelleth in me.
21 I find then a law, that, when I would do good,
evil is present with me.
22 For I delight in the law of God after the inward
man:
23 But I see another law in my members, war-
ring against the law of my mind, and bringing
me into captivity to the law of sin which is in my
members.
24 O wretched man that I am! who shall deliver
me from the body of this death?
25 I thank God through Jesus Christ our Lord. So
then with the mind I myself serve the law of God;
but with the flesh the law of sin.

7:9 *alive*. Complacently hopeful of attaining to works righteousness. *the commandment came*. To the conscience by the convicting power of the Holy Spirit. *revived*. Was stirred to more vigorous exercise.
7:10 *ordained to life*. It originally regulated unfallen Adam's path of righteousness so that he might remain in a state of life in Paradise (Gen. 2:9,16–17; 3:22). *unto death*. The occasion of greater sin.
7:11 His sinful nature *deceived* him into thinking that he could have life through the commandment, when it actually led to greater sin and guilt.
7:12–13 *holy, and just, and good*. There is no defect in God's law (Pss. 19:7–11; 119:137–138), but such was Paul's sinful nature that, when presented with that holy law, it was aroused to greater and more manifest sinful activity.

The Believer Loves But Still Breaks God's Law (7:14–25)

7:14 *spiritual . . . carnal*. The contrast between that which is produced by the Holy Spirit and man's fallen nature, the remains of which the apostle still has within him. Sin does still reside in Paul as a believer (vv. 17,20; see 1 Cor. 3:1–3; Gal. 5:17). *sold under sin*. The verb is not active, as in Ahab's giving himself wholeheartedly to evil (1 Kings 21:20,25), but is passive, fitting a believer's desire not to sin and his continuous struggle against sin.
7:15 *allow*. Know, in the sense of approve. *would*. Choose as an act of will (the same verb appears through vv. 16–21); the primary inclination of the believer's will is toward what is good, but he is divided and frustrated by his remaining sin. *hate*. Even when a believer sins, he reacts against it with hatred. The unregenerate man does not hate his sin as offensive to God but only hates its effects and the sense of guilt and fear it brings to his conscience (2:15; Acts 24:25).
7:16–17 *I*. The Greek here is emphatic. Whereas the unregenerate man's "I" is fully engaged in sin, this is not the case with the regenerate (*no more I*).
7:18 *that is, in my flesh*. Though he is the person sinning, Paul refers not to an unqualified *me* but to something else present within him that is alien to his identity in Christ.
7:19–21 Paul expresses more than a fear-motivated attempt at self-reformation. There is in his heart an engagement toward holiness and an opposition to the sin he commits.
7:22 *delight in the law of God*. Like the psalmist, he genuinely loves God's Word (Ps. 119:16,24,35,47,70,77,92,143), even as he grieves over his sins (Ps. 119:174–176). *inward man*. His truest self and deepest motivation, in contrast to those of hypocrites (2:28–29).
7:23 *another law . . . warring*. Sin is an active and aggressive principle within him (Gal. 5:17; 1 Peter 2:11) that he can never fully escape (*captivity*).
7:24 *who shall deliver me*. The regenerate but imperfect saint cries out in misery (*wretched*, Matt. 5:3–6), and Paul's answer begins in v. 25 and continues throughout the next chapter. *body of this death*. The body as the vehicle of sin.
7:25 *with the mind I myself serve the law*. He is a glad and willing slave of righteousness (the verb *serve* echoes the servant-master language of 6:1–23).

Thoughts for Personal/Family Worship: Chapter 7

1. **The law reveals to us our sin and therefore our need for Christ, the Savior of sinners (v. 7; Mark 10:17–21; John 4:16–18; Acts 2:36–37). Conviction of sin alone is not conversion to Christ. The holy law can be like sunshine on a stagnant pond that makes it stink even worse than before (vv. 8–13). Felix trembled but was not converted (Acts 24:25). Nevertheless, there can be no trusting in Christ to save us if we are oblivious to the sin from which we must be saved. How has God's law uncovered your sin? How has it helped you to see your need of Christ?**
2. **If we are in Christ, the battle is not over but the victory is sure (v. 25). He has purchased our sanctification and glorification, as well as our justification (8:1–39). However, we cannot ignore the experiential struggle in the Christian's soul between what is ideal and what is actual. Godly believers are often deeply frustrated over their lack of conformity to God's holy commands. While they need to be encouraged to press on in the battle, they also need to be comforted with the truth that this is the normal experience of believers on earth. How might losing sight of this truth lead to deep discouragement? How might it lead to hypocrisy and superficiality in the church?**

CHAPTER 8

THERE *is* therefore now no condemnation to them
which are in Christ Jesus, who walk not after the
flesh, but after the Spirit.
2 For the law of the Spirit of life in Christ Jesus
hath made me free from the law of sin and death.
3 For what the law could not do, in that it was
weak through the flesh, God sending his own
Son in the likeness of sinful flesh, and for sin,
condemned sin in the flesh:
4 That the righteousness of the law might be
fulfilled in us, who walk not after the flesh, but
after the Spirit.
5 For they that are after the flesh do mind the
things of the flesh; but they that are after the
Spirit the things of the Spirit.
6 For to be carnally minded *is* death; but to be
spiritually minded *is* life and peace.
7 Because the carnal mind *is* enmity against God:
for it is not subject to the law of God, neither
indeed can be.
8 So then they that are in the flesh cannot please
God.
9 But ye are not in the flesh, but in the Spirit, if
so be that the Spirit of God dwell in you. Now if
any man have not the Spirit of Christ, he is none
of his.
10 And if Christ *be* in you, the body *is* dead
because of sin; but the Spirit *is* life because of
righteousness.
11 But if the Spirit of him that raised up Jesus
from the dead dwell in you, he that raised up
Christ from the dead shall also quicken your
mortal bodies by his Spirit that dwelleth in you.
12 Therefore, brethren, we are debtors, not to the
flesh, to live after the flesh.
13 For if ye live after the flesh, ye shall die: but if
ye through the Spirit do mortify the deeds of the
body, ye shall live.
14 For as many as are led by the Spirit of God,
they are the sons of God.
15 For ye have not received the spirit of bondage
again to fear; but ye have received the Spirit of
adoption, whereby we cry, Abba, Father.
16 The Spirit itself beareth witness with our
spirit, that we are the children of God:
17 And if children, then heirs; heirs of God, and
joint-heirs with Christ; if so be that we suffer with
him, that we may be also glorified together.
18 For I reckon that the sufferings of this present

Chapter 8: *This chapter gives us a wonderful description of the benefits accompanying justification, both in this life and in the next.*

Benefits Accompanying Justification in This Life and the Next (8:1–39)

Deliverance from Sin (8:1–11)

8:1 *no condemnation.* We are taken back to the subject of justification (3:21—5:11) because Christ's bearing of the guilt of sin paves the way for deliverance from that corruption of our whole nature which the guilt of Adam's first transgression brought upon us under the judgment of God (5:12). Justification and sanctification must go together; Christ has purchased both for His people. *in Christ Jesus.* This is the answer to the question in 7:24, having begun in 7:25 with the words "I thank God through Jesus Christ our Lord."

8:2 *law of the Spirit of life.* The justified sinner has the Holy Spirit within him (v. 9), bringing a new principle of spiritual vitality toward God that delivers him from the principle of sin (7:23).

8:3–4 *law could not do.* The law can show us our sin (3:20; 7:7) but can neither enable us to stop committing those sins nor atone for sin because in spite of all attempts to keep the law we are fallen and sinful men (*flesh*). *likeness of sinful flesh.* Without ceasing to be God, Christ became like us in all areas except for our sin (Heb. 4:15; 7:26). *for sin.* To bear its guilt as a sacrifice to God (3:24–25). *condemned sin in the flesh.* Christ destroyed the power of sin by bearing its guilt. The result of His atoning work is a people who, under the direction and quickening of the Holy Spirit, begin to keep the law of God from the heart, since that law is still the divine definition of holiness.

8:5–6 There are only two categories: those who live according to man's fallen nature and those who are indwelt by the *Spirit. carnally.* In a fleshly manner. *death . . . life and peace.* Death and life are not only the future destinies of men but their present spiritual conditions (Eph. 2:1,5).

8:7 *carnal mind is enmity against God.* The mindset of fallen man is hatred of God (John 3:19–20; 15:18,23), a futile war indeed (Ps. 2). *neither… can be.* It is impossible for those without the Spirit to obey God's commandments from the heart, for even when outwardly obedient they remain enemies of God (Rom. 5:10; Col. 1:21).

8:9 *But ye.* In stark contrast to the wicked (vv. 7–8). *not in the flesh.* Not in the same kingdom as the wicked, and thus not ruled by sin. *but in the Spirit.* The Holy Spirit gives them the freedom and power to submit with delight to God's law (7:22,25) and thus to please God as obedient sons (v. 14). Everyone who belongs to Christ has this Spirit. *Spirit of God . . . Spirit of Christ.* The Holy Spirit proceeds from both the Father and the Son in the Trinity, coming from the Father through the mediation of Christ (John 14:26; 16:7; Titus 3:5–6).

8:10–11 Though sin has brought death to their bodies (*mortal*), the Holy Spirit will bring life, applying the power of Christ's resurrection (1:4; 1 Cor. 15:22,44–45).

The Privileges of Adoption (8:12–17)

8:12–14 A description of living as the sons of God. Believers owe nothing to the *flesh* (fallen human nature) but are *led by the Spirit* in a life of killing sin, as it expresses itself through the body. Sin is any breach of God's law (1 John 3:4). *mortify.* Kill.

8:15 The *spirit of bondage* may refer to the Holy Spirit in His work of convicting of sin through the law (John 16:8; cf. Gal. 4:24). Believers have now received Him as the *Spirit of adoption* who gives them boldness to approach God as their *Father*. *Abba.* Aramaic for "father" (Mark 14:36; Gal. 4:6).

8:16 The Spirit's *witness with our spirit* is not direct revelation but His enabling believers to see themselves as children of God in the light of the Word. The pronoun *itself* is neuter because *spirit* is a neuter noun in Greek. The personality of the Holy Spirit is clear, however (v. 27; John 14:16–17,26; 16:13).

The Full Inheritance and Its Earnest (8:18–27)

8:18 Having spoken of being glorified with Christ (v. 17), Paul

ADOPTION

Adoption is the gracious act of God whereby He chooses us, calls us to Himself, and gives us the privileges and blessings of being His children. God has a fatherly nature—His plans for His family are expansive. Though mankind lost the status and privileges of sonship in his tragic fall in Paradise, adoption translates the believer out of a miserable estate into a happy union with God.

Adoption is triune in nature: God the Father chose His children before the foundation of the world (Rom. 8:28–29; Eph. 1:5,11; 1 Thess. 1:4; 1 Peter 2:9); God the Son earned the blessings by which we become children of God (1 John 4:10); and God the Holy Spirit changes our nature by regeneration, so that we move from being children of wrath to children of God (1 John 2:29; 3:9).

Adoption brings relationship changes. *First*, the relationship with God is changed, as He is now "Abba, Father" (Rom. 8:15). Thus, the child of God declares, as Christ did, "I seek not mine own will, but the will of the Father" (John 5:30). The believer's life is controlled by the conviction that God is now his Father (Matt. 7:11; cf. Matt. 6:9). This is his comfort in all aspects of life (Matt. 6:32; John 14:1–2; James 1:16–18).

Second, our relationship to the world is changed. It is now a troubled one (1 John 3:1). Further, it is one that the believer continually strives to put to death, because even though he lives in the world he must not be "of" it (John 15:19; 17:16; Rom. 12:2; cf. Ex. 23:32–33; Judg. 2:1–2; 2 Cor. 6:17–18; Phil. 1:27; James 1:27; 4:4).

Third, our relationship to the family of God is changed, for the child of God has many brothers and sisters in Christ (1 John 3:14–18). As the believer is united to God in Christ, so he is united to all other people of God (John 17:21). Thus, adoption brings with it a communion of saints (Ps. 133:1; Rom. 12:4–5; 1 Cor. 12:12–31; 1 Thess. 5:11).

Moreover, adoption includes two precious benefits: a blessed status and wondrous privileges. God's adopted children share a status similar to the very Son of God (cf. Hos. 1:10; Rom. 9:26; 2 Cor. 6:18), who is their Elder Brother (Heb. 2:11). This means that they enjoy the same love from God that exists between the Father and His Son (John 17:23; cf. Jer. 31:3; 1 John 3:1). Thus, God declares of the believer what He says of His Son: "This is my beloved" (Matt. 3:17).

Furthermore, the child of God receives manifold privileges. He receives the Spirit of adoption (Rom. 8:15), is changed into the likeness of Christ (Rom. 8:29; 2 Cor. 3:18), is chastened for sanctification (Heb. 12:6–7), is comforted by God's filial love and pity (Ps. 103:13), is preserved from falling (Jude 24), and is provided all things necessary for life (Matt. 7:7–11; James 1:17).

Beyond all this, the believer enjoys the privileges of the only begotten Son Himself. This brings with it acceptance (Eph. 1:6), communion (2 Cor. 13:14), life (John 1:12–13; 1 John 3:1–3), and an eternal inheritance (Rom. 8:17). Adoption, under Roman law, was a legal act by which a man chose someone outside the family to be an heir to his inheritance. This inheritance was divided; yet, though there are countless heirs of Christ, each believer receives the full and entire inheritance of God.

These privileges bring the responsibility of joyful service to the Father. This includes childlike, reverential love for the Father; submission to the Father in all His providences; obedience and imitation of the Father; and love for the Father's children. As a child rejoices in pleasing his father, so the believer searches the smiles and frowns of God to guide his conduct in life.

From being a child of the Devil to becoming a child of God; from a child of wrath to the object of God's favor; from a child of condemnation to an heir of all the promises and a possessor of all blessings; from the greatest misery to the highest felicity—adoption is a stupendous wonder. The prodigal has nothing by which to move God to adopt him. Further, there is much in him to discourage the adoption; yet God delights to become his Father in Christ by the Spirit.

time *are* not worthy *to be compared* with the glory
which shall be revealed in us.
19 For the earnest expectation of the creature
waiteth for the manifestation of the sons of God.
20 For the creature was made subject to vanity,
not willingly, but by reason of him who hath
subjected *the same* in hope,
21 Because the creature itself also shall be
delivered from the bondage of corruption into
the glorious liberty of the children of God.
22 For we know that the whole creation groaneth
and travaileth in pain together until now.
23 And not only *they*, but ourselves also, which
have the firstfruits of the Spirit, even we ourselves
groan within ourselves, waiting for the adoption,
to wit, the redemption of our body.
24 For we are saved by hope: but hope that is seen
is not hope: for what a man seeth, why doth he
yet hope for?
25 But if we hope for that we see not, *then* do we
with patience wait for *it*.
26 Likewise the Spirit also helpeth our infirmi-
ties: for we know not what we should pray for as
we ought: but the Spirit itself maketh intercession
for us with groanings which cannot be uttered.
27 And he that searcheth the hearts knoweth
what *is* the mind of the Spirit, because he maketh
intercession for the saints according to *the will*
of God.
28 And we know that all things work together for
good to them that love God, to them who are the
called according to *his* purpose.
29 For whom he did foreknow, he also did
predestinate *to be* conformed to the image of his
Son, that he might be the firstborn among many
brethren.
30 Moreover whom he did predestinate, them he
also called: and whom he called, them he also justi-
fied: and whom he justified, them he also glorified.
31 What shall we then say to these things? If God
be for us, who *can be* against us?
32 He that spared not his own Son, but delivered
him up for us all, how shall he not with him also
freely give us all things?
33 Who shall lay any thing to the charge of God's
elect? *It is* God that justifieth.
34 Who *is* he that condemneth? *It is* Christ that
died, yea rather, that is risen again, who is even at
the right hand of God, who also maketh interces-
sion for us.
35 Who shall separate us from the love of Christ?
shall tribulation, or distress, or persecution, or

---

now compares the sufferings characteristic of the present age to the eternal *glory* of that which is to come.

8:19 The whole creation (*creature*) awaits glorious renovation when *the sons of God* are manifested in their resurrection bodies.

8:20–22 The creation is personified as groaning under the curse brought on by sin and waiting for the transformation at the last day, the day when the bodies of the redeemed will be glorified (Acts 3:21; 2 Peter 3:12–13). *vanity*. The idea of life as a vapor and, apart from the renewing work of God, full of distress and frustration (Gen. 3:17–19). *hope*. The plan of God that the creation will not remain under the curse.

8:23 Christians have the beginnings of the new creation within them by the indwelling of the Holy *Spirit*. They *groan* for the full inheritance that includes the resurrection body. This is called the *adoption* because it is the fullest enjoyment of the privileges of the children of God. *firstfruits of the Spirit*. The Holy Spirit within us is the guarantee that the new creation will be completed (2 Cor. 1:22; Eph. 1:13–14; 4:30). *to wit*. That is.

8:24 *by hope*. Possibly "in hope." Hope is the sure expectation of unseen future good arising from faith in the divine testimony.

8:26 *maketh intercession*. Acts as an advocate, who both speaks for his client and instructs him how to speak. In the first sense Christ is our advocate (v. 34), but in the second it is the Holy Spirit. The *groanings* He causes in us are not irrational but cannot be fully expressed in words (2 Cor. 9:15; 1 Peter 1:8). God the Father regards and approves of those desires the Spirit produces in us as in accord with His will (v. 27).

The Certainty of Triumph in Christ (8:28–39)

8:28 The climax of the certainty of the full bestowal of all the benefits of salvation upon believers is now reached with the consideration that not only does God govern *all things* but He does so in their best interests (1 Cor. 3:21–23).

8:29 *foreknow*. Not equivalent to "know about beforehand," since this would be true of all things. Paul is not talking about some unspecified thing (such as foreseen faith) that is known but about persons. Knowing a person is a common biblical expression for loving that person (Jer. 1:5; Hos. 13:5; Amos 3:2; Matt. 1:24–25; Luke 1:34; Gal. 4:9). *brethren*. See Matt. 28:10; Heb. 2:12.

8:30 Known as the "golden chain," this verse presents the unfailing sequence of God's saving acts, bound together such that the same group of people experiences every step. *did predestinate*. God set apart the people He chose from before the foundation of the world to receive salvation and eternal glory (9:23; Eph. 1:4–5,11). *also called*. God gives the gospel and the Spirit to all of His elect (1:6–7; Gal. 1:15–16; 1 Thess. 2:13–14). *also justified*. He declares them all righteous by faith in Christ (3:21–24), which implies that their calling is effective to produce faith. *also glorified*. God will bring all of His elect into His eternal glory and the presence and image of Christ (2:7,10; 5:2; 8:17–18,21,29; 9:23); He has already begun leading them from glory to glory in their sanctification (2 Cor. 3:18).

8:31–32 God giving His Son is the supreme display of love (5:6–8). If He has already given Him, God will surely not withhold anything that is truly in our best interest (Ps. 84:11).

8:33–34 *It is God that justifieth*. God's verdict is final. There is no appeal court beyond Him, either for us or for our accusers. Christ's work ensures that all of the elect will be justified, though this blessing is not bestowed until they are effectually called (v. 30). *justifieth . . . condemneth*. Justification is the legal opposite of condemnation, and its basis is the atoning death, resurrection, and intercession of our Lord Jesus Christ. *right hand of God*. As supreme Lord over all (Ps. 110:1). *maketh intercession*. Though Christ finished the work of purchasing redemption, He continues that of applying redemption by interceding for His elect until everyone for whom He died receives all of the benefits He has purchased for them (Heb. 7:24–25; 1 John 2:1).

8:35–39 *tribulation*. Trouble. Persecution is normal and to

famine, or nakedness, or peril, or sword?
36 As it is written, For thy sake we are killed all
the day long; we are accounted as sheep for the
slaughter.
37 Nay, in all these things we are more than con-
querors through him that loved us.
38 For I am persuaded, that neither death, nor
life, nor angels, nor principalities, nor powers, nor
things present, nor things to come,
39 Nor height, nor depth, nor any other creature,
shall be able to separate us from the love of God,
which is in Christ Jesus our Lord.

CHAPTER 9

I SAY the truth in Christ, I lie not, my conscience
also bearing me witness in the Holy Ghost,
2 That I have great heaviness and continual
sorrow in my heart.
3 For I could wish that myself were accursed
from Christ for my brethren, my kinsmen accord-
ing to the flesh:
4 Who are Israelites; to whom *pertaineth* the
adoption, and the glory, and the covenants, and
the giving of the law, and the service *of God*, and
the promises;
5 Whose *are* the fathers, and of whom as con-
cerning the flesh Christ *came*, who is over all, God
blessed for ever. Amen.
6 Not as though the word of God hath taken
none effect. For they *are* not all Israel, which are
of Israel:
7 Neither, because they are the seed of Abraham,
are they all children: but, In Isaac shall thy seed
be called.
8 That is, They which are the children of the
flesh, these *are* not the children of God: but the
children of the promise are counted for the seed.
9 For this *is* the word of promise, At this time will
I come, and Sara shall have a son.
10 And not only *this*; but when Rebecca also had
conceived by one, *even* by our father Isaac;
11 (For *the children* being not yet born, neither
having done any good or evil, that the purpose

---

be expected (Ps. 44:22; see Phil. 1:29; 2 Tim. 3:12), but we are *more than conquerors*, because we not only get through the trouble, but it is all ordered for our good.

8:38–39 The list covers all dimensions of time and space, as well as angels and demons (*principalities*) and all created *powers*. The "love of Christ" (v. 35) is now the *love of God* through Christ, for it is the love of the triune God, including the "Spirit" (v. 27).

Thoughts for Personal/Family Worship: Chapter 8

1. **Knowing the law, on its own, will not eradicate the love for sin (v. 3). Walking in the Spirit, however, is not some mystical experience; rather, this occurs when the Spirit of God fills our hearts with loving gratitude to God for His love in Christ and we express that by fulfilling God's law (v. 4). As children of a good Father, believers realize that sin never does them any good (v. 13) but that the ways of God are life and peace (v. 6). All their lives are in His loving hands, and He will bring His adopted children to the glory of His Son (vv. 28–29). How do these truths motivate you to love and obey God?**
2. **To call God "Father" (v. 15) is an immense privilege. The divine love behind this word is breathtaking. God did not spare His only begotten Son but gave Him up so that sinners thereby might have God. God adopted His enemies as His children, and He gives them His Spirit to stir them to call Him Abba, or Father. Why are we so reluctant to draw near to Him? How can Rom. 8 encourage us to be more faithful and fervent in prayer?**

ISRAEL AND THE GOSPEL (9:1—11:36)

Chapter 9: *Beginning his treatment of Israel and the gospel, Paul shows that Israel's unbelief constitutes no objection to the gospel's truthfulness.*

Israel's Unbelief No Objection to the Gospel (9:1–33)

The Apostle's Sorrow (9:1–5)

9:1–3 The apostle describes his great and continuous sorrow concerning his fellow Israelites' rejection of the true gospel, reflecting a benevolent love patterned after God's (Matt. 5:43–48; Luke 6:35–36).

9:3 *I could wish*. Not an actual prayer, these words express the intensity of his compassion; he could contemplate going to hell for their salvation, although this would be impossible.

9:4–5 An abundance of privilege belongs to the Jews. *Israelites*. Israel, "the prince of God" (Gen. 32:28), was their forebear. *adoption*. See Ex. 4:22; Jer. 31:9. *glory*. God's visible presence with His church (Ex. 24:16–17; 1 Kings 8:10–11). *covenants*. Various administrations of God's covenant revealed to Abraham (Gen. 17), Moses (Ex. 20), and David (Ps. 89:19–28). *service of God*. Divine worship (Heb. 9:1,6). *promises*. Of Christ (John 8:56; Gal. 3:8,16). *Christ*. As regards His human nature, Jesus was born among them. Paul's intention of showing the greatness of the Israelites' privilege confirms the rendering in our Bibles that Christ is *God blessed for ever*, the incarnate Lord (1 Tim. 3:16).

God Never Promised the Salvation of All Israelites (9:6–9)

9:6–9 God's Word has not failed because God had never promised that every Israelite would be saved. God always distinguished *Isaac* from Ishmael—both were natural children of Abraham, but only one was a child of promise, as God promised that he would be an heir of salvation (Gen. 21:12).

God's Sovereign Prerogative of Election (9:10–18)

9:10–13 The second example of *Esau* and *Jacob* shows even more clearly God's absolute right to choose who shall be saved. Both boys had the same mother, as well as the same father, and Esau, not Jacob, was the firstborn twin. Neither had done anything when God's purpose concerning them was revealed. Therefore God's sovereign election was entirely based on His good pleasure and unearned by any merit. The idea of foreseen good works or faith does not even enter the apostle's thinking. God knows the future because He has planned it, including who will be the heirs of salvation and who will not. There is no such thing as foreknowledge independent of foreordination. God foresees what He will do (Ps. 135:6; Dan. 4:34–35; Acts 15:18; Eph. 1:11). The quotation from Mal. 1:2–3 (Rom. 9:13) refers to God's decree in relation to the two nations, but the general blessing of Israel as a nation (rather than Edom) stems from God's purpose with regard to the two individual men and

of God according to election might stand, not of
works, but of him that calleth;)
12 It was said unto her, The elder shall serve the
younger.
13 As it is written, Jacob have I loved, but Esau
have I hated.
14 What shall we say then? *Is there* unrighteous-
ness with God? God forbid.
15 For he saith to Moses, I will have mercy on
whom I will have mercy, and I will have compas-
sion on whom I will have compassion.
16 So then *it is* not of him that willeth, nor of him
that runneth, but of God that sheweth mercy.
17 For the scripture saith unto Pharaoh, Even
for this same purpose have I raised thee up, that I
might shew my power in thee, and that my name
might be declared throughout all the earth.
18 Therefore hath he mercy on whom he will
have mercy, and whom he will he hardeneth.
19 Thou wilt say then unto me, Why doth he yet
find fault? For who hath resisted his will?
20 Nay but, O man, who art thou that repliest
against God? Shall the thing formed say to him
that formed *it*, Why hast thou made me thus?
21 Hath not the potter power over the clay, of the
same lump to make one vessel unto honour, and
another unto dishonour?
22 *What* if God, willing to shew *his* wrath, and to
make his power known, endured with much long-
suffering the vessels of wrath fitted to destruction:
23 And that he might make known the riches of
his glory on the vessels of mercy, which he had
afore prepared unto glory,
24 Even us, whom he hath called, not of the Jews
only, but also of the Gentiles?
25 As he saith also in Osee, I will call them my
people, which were not my people; and her
beloved, which was not beloved.
26 And it shall come to pass, *that* in the place
where it was said unto them, Ye *are* not my
people; there shall they be called the children of
the living God.
27 Esaias also crieth concerning Israel, Though
the number of the children of Israel be as the sand
of the sea, a remnant shall be saved:
28 For he will finish the work, and cut *it* short in
righteousness: because a short work will the Lord
make upon the earth.
29 And as Esaias said before, Except the Lord
of Sabaoth had left us a seed, we had been as
Sodoma, and been made like unto Gomorrha.
30 What shall we say then? That the Gentiles,
which followed not after righteousness, have
attained to righteousness, even the righteousness
which is of faith.
31 But Israel, which followed after the law of
righteousness, hath not attained to the law of
righteousness.
32 Wherefore? Because *they sought it* not by faith,
but as it were by the works of the law. For they

---

cannot be separated from it.

9:14 *unrighteousness with God.* What God does is, by definition, righteous.

9:15 God asserts His absolute right to show *mercy* as He pleases (Ex. 33:19).

9:16 *not of him that willeth . . . runneth.* Man has no independent ability to choose or obtain salvation, and God is under no obligation to bestow *mercy* upon man.

9:17–18 *scripture saith.* God's speaking is equated with Scripture's speaking. The example of *Pharaoh* shows that God exercises His right not to show mercy (Ex. 9:16). God raised up Pharaoh on the historical scene to show His power in Pharaoh's judgment. God hardened Pharaoh's heart (Ex. 4:21; 7:3; 9:12), and God is therefore sovereign over the will of man, either to show mercy or to harden.

Twofold Effect of the Gospel (9:19–33)

9:19–20 *who art thou.* Man answers to God, not the other way around.

9:21–23 A *potter* can make of one *lump* of *clay* vessels for very different uses (Isa. 29:15–16; 45:9; 64:8; Jer. 18:1–6). So God can make from one fallen mankind some vessels to demonstrate His *power* and justice in their condemnation and others *vessels of mercy* to display His mercy in their salvation. *afore.* Before.

9:24 *Even us.* The believer can be assured that he is one of God's elect by knowing that he has been effectually *called* and that this is due to his having been chosen in Christ before the foundation of the world (8:30; 2 Peter 1:10).

9:25–29 *Osee . . . Esaias.* Citing Isa. 1:9; 10:22–23 and Hos. 1:10; 2:23 to show God's sovereignty in appointing many Gentiles in the New Testament age to salvation, whereas there were times when the number of believing Jews was small enough to be called a remnant. *Sabaoth.* Hosts (in the title "the Lord of hosts"), one of the few untranslated Hebrew words in the Greek New Testament (possibly assimilated into the Greek language).

9:30–33 Paul refers again to *Gentiles* outside the sphere of special revelation. Whatever concern they had for right and wrong, they did not pursue acceptance with God in response to His revelation. Now they have attained to that acceptance by their hearts being opened to the gospel of justification by faith in Jesus Christ as it has been preached to them. Meanwhile, Israel, by responding to divine revelation through attempting to keep the law, has not attained to righteousness (Isa. 8:14; 28:16; see 1 Peter 2:6–10), as had been planned by God (9:21–23).

Thoughts for Personal/Family Worship: Chapter 9

1. **The strength of Paul's expression of compassion for the lost (vv. 1–3) may startle us; it should. We are to love our neighbor as ourselves. If we care about not going to hell ourselves, how can we be indifferent to our neighbor being on the broad road that leads to destruction? How does this challenge you to pray and to take action?**
2. **God is absolutely sovereign over the will of men. Even sinful acts, though God does not condone them (nor is He the author of sin), are included in the plan of God (Gen. 50:20; 2 Sam. 16:9–11; 2 Chron. 18:20–22; Ps. 76:10). Even the fact that the holy angels did not fall is based on God's sovereign election (1 Tim. 5:21). We should believe the doctrine of God's sovereign predestination**

stumbled at that stumblingstone;
33 As it is written, Behold, I lay in Sion a stum-
blingstone and rock of offence: and whosoever
believeth on him shall not be ashamed.

CHAPTER 10

BRETHREN, my heart's desire and prayer to God
for Israel is, that they might be saved.
2 For I bear them record that they have a zeal of
God, but not according to knowledge.
3 For they being ignorant of God's righteousness,
and going about to establish their own righteous-
ness, have not submitted themselves unto the
righteousness of God.
4 For Christ *is* the end of the law for righteous-
ness to every one that believeth.
5 For Moses describeth the righteousness which
is of the law, That the man which doeth those
things shall live by them.
6 But the righteousness which is of faith speaketh
on this wise, Say not in thine heart, Who shall
ascend into heaven? (that is, to bring Christ down
from above:)
7 Or, Who shall descend into the deep? (that is, to
bring up Christ again from the dead.)
8 But what saith it? The word is nigh thee, *even* in
thy mouth, and in thy heart: that is, the word of
faith, which we preach;
9 That if thou shalt confess with thy mouth the
Lord Jesus, and shalt believe in thine heart that
God hath raised him from the dead, thou shalt
be saved.
10 For with the heart man believeth unto righ-
teousness; and with the mouth confession is
made unto salvation.
11 For the scripture saith, Whosoever believeth
on him shall not be ashamed.
12 For there is no difference between the Jew and
the Greek: for the same Lord over all is rich unto
all that call upon him.
13 For whosoever shall call upon the name of the
Lord shall be saved.
14 How then shall they call on him in whom they
have not believed? and how shall they believe in
him of whom they have not heard? and how shall
they hear without a preacher?
15 And how shall they preach, except they be
sent? as it is written, How beautiful are the feet of
them that preach the gospel of peace, and bring
glad tidings of good things!
16 But they have not all obeyed the gospel. For
Esaias saith, Lord, who hath believed our report?
17 So then faith *cometh* by hearing, and hearing
by the word of God.
18 But I say, Have they not heard? Yes verily, their
sound went into all the earth, and their words
unto the ends of the world.
19 But I say, Did not Israel know? First Moses saith,
I will provoke you to jealousy by *them that are* no
people, *and* by a foolish nation I will anger you.
20 But Esaias is very bold, and saith, I was found

---

on the testimony of Holy Scripture (9:12–13,15,17). It is not incompatible with evangelistic concern (vv. 1–3), however difficult it may seem to reconcile the two. How can trusting that God is in control give us confidence and freedom to faithfully proclaim the gospel?

3. We should not try to guess whom, among the unconverted, are God's elect. "Front-runners" can remain unregenerate, whereas "unpromising candidates" may come to faith in Christ (vv. 30–31). How should this encourage us to preach the gospel to all kinds of people?

Chapter 10: *The apostle to the Gentiles looks at Israel's failure to submit to the righteousness of God.*

Israel's Failure to Submit to the Righteousness of God (10:1–21)

10:1 Israel's numerous privileges (9:4–5) do not alter the fact that they are not *saved* without faith in Christ.

10:2 *zeal . . . not according to knowledge.* Their religious fervor and knowledge of the content of Scripture still fell short of true *knowledge* (Greek, *epignosis*) of God and Christ by the enlightenment of the Holy Spirit (2 Cor. 3:14–17).

10:3–4 The result is that they sought to make themselves righteous by keeping the *law* instead of embracing God's *righteousness* provided in Christ (1:17; 3:22).

10:5 *doeth those things shall live.* Paul does not indicate that Lev.18:5 taught a works salvation. This would be contrary to his use of Deuteronomy in the next verse. Eternal life and holiness go together (6:22), but the law on its own confers neither (8:3).

10:6–8 The apostle paraphrases Deut. 30:12–14 to show that we do not have to do the work of Christ as redeemer or revealer; rather, all that we need is in the gospel that has been preached to us.

10:9–11 Faith is essential (Isa. 28:16). Only those who *believe* receive Christ's imputed *righteousness. Confession* of faith is an inevitable fruit of faith (Matt. 10:32–33).

10:12–13 There is only one Way for all, but it is real for *all* who call upon Him (Joel 2:32). *Lord.* Identifying Christ as *Jehovah* ("the Lord" in Joel).

10:14–15 The *gospel* is necessary, for without the truth of special revelation (now in Scripture) there can be no faith and no salvation. Hence the preciousness of the preaching of the gospel (Isa. 52:7).

10:16–17 As vital as is the preaching of God's Word, it does not produce faith in all who hear it. This was largely disbelieved by Israel, both in the past and in Paul's day (Isa. 53:1).

10:18 General revelation in creation and providence is universal (Ps. 19:4). This is a precursor of the spread of the special revelation spoken of in the second half of that psalm (15:20–21; Matt. 24:14).

10:19 Israel had been told that, as they had worshiped non-gods, so the Lord would gather a non-people to be His own in order to provoke them to jealousy (Deut. 32:21).

10:20–21 Isaiah 65:1–2 is applied to the present unbelief of the bulk of the Jews and the ingathering of the Gentiles (Acts 13:44–48). *gainsaying.* Obstinate.

Thoughts for Personal/Family Worship: Chapter 10

1. Paul's prayer (v. 1) indicates both his belief that

of them that sought me not; I was made manifest
unto them that asked not after me.
21 But to Israel he saith, All day long I have
stretched forth my hands unto a disobedient and
gainsaying people.

CHAPTER 11

I SAY then, Hath God cast away his people? God
forbid. For I also am an Israelite, of the seed of
Abraham, *of* the tribe of Benjamin.
2 God hath not cast away his people which he
foreknew. Wot ye not what the scripture saith of
Elias? how he maketh intercession to God against
Israel, saying,
3 Lord, they have killed thy prophets, and digged
down thine altars; and I am left alone, and they
seek my life.
4 But what saith the answer of God unto him? I
have reserved to myself seven thousand men, who
have not bowed the knee to *the image of* Baal.
5 Even so then at this present time also there is a
remnant according to the election of grace.
6 And if by grace, then *is it* no more of works:
otherwise grace is no more grace. But if *it be* of
works, then is it no more grace: otherwise work
is no more work.
7 What then? Israel hath not obtained that which
he seeketh for; but the election hath obtained it,
and the rest were blinded
8 (According as it is written, God hath given
them the spirit of slumber, eyes that they should
not see, and ears that they should not hear;) unto
this day.
9 And David saith, Let their table be made a
snare, and a trap, and a stumblingblock, and a
recompence unto them:
10 Let their eyes be darkened, that they may not
see, and bow down their back alway.
11 I say then, Have they stumbled that they
should fall? God forbid: but *rather* through their
fall salvation *is come* unto the Gentiles, for to
provoke them to jealousy.
12 Now if the fall of them *be* the riches of the
world, and the diminishing of them the riches of
the Gentiles; how much more their fulness?
13 For I speak to you Gentiles, inasmuch as I am
the apostle of the Gentiles, I magnify mine office:

salvation is in God's hands and his compassion toward the unbelieving. There is no contradiction here (Acts 26:29). Nor are there valid excuses for unbelief (vv. 6–9). You have a Bible in your hand to read. It is your duty to believe. And there is within it every encouragement to trust Christ. He is rich (v. 12) to all who do believe, bestowing upon them such great mercies as forgiveness of sin, peace with God, and the hope of glory for all who do so (Ps. 86:5). How should this encourage evangelism? How should this impress upon all who hear the gospel their need to trust in Christ?

2. The preaching of the gospel is vital as the means appointed by the sovereign God for the ingathering of His elect (vv. 13–15). We have no divine authorization from Scripture to believe that people dying without the knowledge of God's Word will be saved by some other means (Acts 4:12). Sinners must believe in Christ in order to be saved, and they must hear the gospel in order to believe. How should this motivate churches and seminaries to train and send out laborers to preach the gospel everywhere on earth? How can you help?

Chapter 11: ***There has often been only a remnant in Israel who believe, but always at least that. In due time there will be more—a fullness of Israel grafted into the church.***

Israel's Rejection Neither Total Nor Final (11:1–36)

11:1 Paul himself is an example of the fact that God has not completely rejected ethnic Israel.

11:2–4 *foreknew.* Nationally elected and loved (Amos 3:2). *Elias.* Elijah. Even when Israel constituted the visible church of God, there were times when the genuinely godly were only a remnant—but there again, there was always such a remnant (1 Kings 19:10,14,18).

11:5–6 *remnant according to the election.* Even now, within the nation God had of old elected, there are elect individuals who have been brought to faith in Christ. This is due to God's sovereign grace—his *grace* alone to the ill-deserving, not because of any superiority in them compared with those not elected.

11:7 Israel as a whole has not obtained righteousness before God, but an elect remnant has; the rest were *blinded,* an act of divine sovereignty (9:18) as God's just judgment for their sins (1:21,28; 2 Thess. 2:11–12).

11:8 The Scriptures teach the doctrine of reprobation, that is, that God decreed not to save some sinners but instead to harden them (citing in combination Deut. 29:4 and Isa. 29:10 in such a way as to emphasize the action of God).

11:9–10 *David saith.* Paul looks beyond David and the kingdom of God as represented by him to Christ, the Son of David, and the vindication of God in Him (Ps. 69:22–23). *table.* Normally for their benefit, made something harmful as a recompense for their wickedness. *darkened.* Blinded to the truth. *bow down.* Possibly in fear or grief.

11:11 *that they should fall.* The fall of Israel was not the end of the matter but the occasion for the gathering of large numbers of Gentiles into the kingdom (Matt. 8:11). This in turn was intended by God to *provoke* Israel to *jealousy* (v. 14; 10:19).

11:12 The apostle is still contrasting ethnic Israel with the *Gentiles* (vv. 12–14), or *world* (v. 15). The *fall* of Israel is not a reference to the unbelief of many in all previous generations but to their specific, large-scale apostasy in the present. *diminishing . . . fulness.* The contrast is not parallel but sequential. This apostasy was instrumental in Christ's redeeming work (Acts 2:23) and in the spread of the gospel to the Gentiles (Acts 8:4; 11:19–20; 13:45–47). The *fulness,* therefore, is the comparative bulk of Israel who will come to believe on a similar scale to their present unbelief. The *much more* is best understood as a greater display of the gospel blessing than was occasioned by their apostasy.

11:13–15 Paul's ministry to the Gentiles still had Israel's interests at heart, since Gentile church growth provokes Israel to copy the Gentiles in turning to Christ. *life from the dead.* A great revival of spiritual life—the same sequence of thought as in v. 12.

14 If by any means I may provoke to emulation
them which are my flesh, and might save some
of them.
15 For if the casting away of them *be* the
reconciling of the world, what *shall* the receiving
of them be, but life from the dead?
16 For if the firstfruit *be* holy, the lump *is* also
holy: and if the root *be* holy, so *are* the branches.
17 And if some of the branches be broken off,
and thou, being a wild olive tree, wert graffed in
among them, and with them partakest of the root
and fatness of the olive tree;
18 Boast not against the branches. But if thou
boast, thou bearest not the root, but the root thee.
19 Thou wilt say then, The branches were broken
off, that I might be graffed in.
20 Well; because of unbelief they were broken off,
and thou standest by faith. Be not highminded,
but fear:
21 For if God spared not the natural branches,
take heed lest he also spare not thee.
22 Behold therefore the goodness and severity
of God: on them which fell, severity; but toward
thee, goodness, if thou continue in *his* goodness:
otherwise thou also shalt be cut off.
23 And they also, if they abide not still in unbe-
lief, shall be graffed in: for God is able to graff
them in again.
24 For if thou wert cut out of the olive tree which
is wild by nature, and wert graffed contrary to
nature into a good olive tree: how much more
shall these, which be the natural *branches*, be
graffed into their own olive tree?
25 For I would not, brethren, that ye should be
ignorant of this mystery, lest ye should be wise
in your own conceits; that blindness in part
is happened to Israel, until the fulness of the
Gentiles be come in.
26 And so all Israel shall be saved: as it is written,
There shall come out of Sion the Deliverer, and
shall turn away ungodliness from Jacob:
27 For this *is* my covenant unto them, when I
shall take away their sins.
28 As concerning the gospel, *they are* enemies for
your sakes: but as touching the election, *they are*
beloved for the fathers' sakes.
29 For the gifts and calling of God *are* without
repentance.
30 For as ye in times past have not believed God,
yet have now obtained mercy through their
unbelief:
31 Even so have these also now not believed, that
through your mercy they also may obtain mercy.
32 For God hath concluded them all in unbelief,
that he might have mercy upon all.
33 O the depth of the riches both of the wisdom
and knowledge of God! how unsearchable *are* his
judgments, and his ways past finding out!
34 For who hath known the mind of the Lord? or
who hath been his counsellor?
35 Or who hath first given to him, and it shall be
recompensed unto him again?
36 For of him, and through him, and to him, *are*
all things: to whom *be* glory for ever. Amen.

11:16–24 The visible church through both Testaments is represented as an *olive tree,* branches of which are broken off by God on the basis of unbelief. The tree is rooted in the Hebrew patriarchs but continues today among Jewish believers in Christ, along with Gentile believers who have been grafted in (*graffed*) by their union with Christ.
11:16 The first batch of the dough was given to the Lord for the consecration of the lump (Num. 15:17–21). Likewise, the patriarchs (Abraham, Isaac, and Jacob) were separated from the world so that Israel as a whole could be set apart in the saving purpose of God.
11:17 *branches be broken off.* The majority of the Jews refused to submit to Christ and His apostles and therefore were removed from the visible church (Matt. 21:43), particularly when God ended the ceremonial law and replaced it with the new covenant ordinances of worship, such as baptism and the Lord's Supper. *wert graffed.* Were grafted. Gentiles, though formerly outsiders, were joined to the visible church (Eph. 2:11–12,19). *fatness.* Health.
11:18 *Boast not.* The fact that the Gentiles have been brought into a church that was not Gentile in its roots, but of the Israelite patriarchs, ought to keep them all from ethnic pride.
11:19–22 Since the tree is only the visible church, Gentiles within it should be humbled by the fact that they too will be *broken off* if they are not true believers in Christ. *highminded.* Puffed up with pride.
11:23–26 The gathering of Israel into the church is not just a possibility (v. 23) or even a probability (v. 24) but a promised certainty (vv. 25–26).
11:25–26 *mystery.* God's plan of salvation in Christ, unknowable except by revelation from God (16:25). The term is used of all aspects of Christ's redeeming work and its application by the Holy Spirit (1 Cor. 15:51; Eph. 5:32; 1 Tim. 3:16), including the interaction between Jew and Gentile (Eph. 3:3–6; Col. 1:25–27). *conceits.* Proud ideas. *fulness of the Gentiles.* When the ingathering of the Gentiles reaches a high point (cf. Matt. 24:14; Luke 21:24) and the provocation of Israel, therefore, also reaches its height (vv. 11,14; 10:19).
11:26–27 *all Israel.* Used of all God's people in Gal. 6:16 but due to the opposite context better understood as large numbers of people from ethnic Israel, according to the contrast in this chapter between Israel and the Gentiles. *as it is written.* The greater efficacy of the new covenant administration will lead to the ingathering of ethnic Israel back into the church, as Israel's general pattern of covenant breaking is changed to a general pattern of knowing the Lord (Isa. 59:20; Jer. 31:34; see Heb. 8:8–13).
11:28–29 Though God largely casts away the Jews so that the gospel blessing might come to the Gentiles, their national election to prominence in the church was promised irrevocably to the fathers, and so the further positive interaction with the believing Gentiles is sure.
11:32 *concluded.* Closed up.
11:33–36 Paul gives the only appropriate response to the wonders of grace that he has set forth: adoring God for His wise decrees, independent planning (Isa. 40:13), and absolute sovereignty in showing mercy (Job 41:11). *of him, and through him, and to him.* Everything has its origin in God the Creator;

CHAPTER 12

I BESEECH you therefore, brethren, by the mercies
of God, that ye present your bodies a living
sacrifice, holy, acceptable unto God, *which is* your
reasonable service.
2 And be not conformed to this world: but be ye
transformed by the renewing of your mind, that
ye may prove what *is* that good, and acceptable,
and perfect, will of God.
3 For I say, through the grace given unto me,
to every man that is among you, not to think *of
himself* more highly than he ought to think; but
to think soberly, according as God hath dealt to
every man the measure of faith.
4 For as we have many members in one body, and
all members have not the same office:
5 So we, *being* many, are one body in Christ, and
every one members one of another.
6 Having then gifts differing according to the
grace that is given to us, whether prophecy, *let us
prophesy* according to the proportion of faith;
7 Or ministry, *let us wait* on *our* ministering: or
he that teacheth, on teaching;
8 Or he that exhorteth, on exhortation: he that
giveth, *let him do it* with simplicity; he that ruleth,
with diligence; he that sheweth mercy, with
cheerfulness.
9 *Let* love be without dissimulation. Abhor that
which is evil; cleave to that which is good.
10 *Be* kindly affectioned one to another with
brotherly love; in honour preferring one another;
11 Not slothful in business; fervent in spirit;
serving the Lord;
12 Rejoicing in hope; patient in tribulation;
continuing instant in prayer;
13 Distributing to the necessity of saints; given to
hospitality.
14 Bless them which persecute you: bless, and
curse not.
15 Rejoice with them that do rejoice, and weep
with them that weep.
16 *Be* of the same mind one toward another.
Mind not high things, but condescend to men of
low estate. Be not wise in your own conceits.
17 Recompense to no man evil for evil. Provide
things honest in the sight of all men.
18 If it be possible, as much as lieth in you, live
peaceably with all men.

---

is directed by God, the Lord of all things; and will display His *glory* as the ultimate purpose of all things.

Thoughts for Personal/Family Worship: Chapter 11

1. **The apostle treats David's prayer for God's punishment on the wicked (Ps. 69:22–23) as the Word of God (vv. 9–10) as surely as the prophecies of Christ's sufferings in that Psalm (Ps. 69:9,20–21), and so should we. We should read and sing such psalms without embarrassment. If we have a problem with them, the problem lies in our minds and hearts, not in the Word of God.**
2. **The gospel has come to us in our various nations, but it was not always so (Acts 14:16). We should be thankful to God, for He did not owe us the gospel! When was the last time you thanked God that you have heard the good news? How can the last four verses of this chapter help you to worship God for His saving plans?**
3. **Though Christians debate God's future plans for the physical descendants of Abraham, Isaac, and Jacob (v. 25), we should all join Paul in praying for their conversion (10:1). Let us devote ourselves to praying "that the kingdom of sin and Satan may be destroyed, the gospel propagated throughout the world, the Jews called, the fullness of the Gentiles brought in . . . that Christ would rule in our hearts here, and hasten the time of his second coming, and our reigning with him forever . . ." (Westminster Larger Catechism, A.191). Do you pray for these things? If not, why not?**

THE RESPONSE OF REAL HOLINESS (12:1—15:33)

Chapter 12: ***This chapter begins to tell us the response of true holiness that should follow the glorious truths that have been unfolded.***

Devotion to the Lord Shown in the Church and in Our Conduct to All (12:1–21)

12:1 *beseech.* Exhort, urge. *therefore.* In gratitude for *the mercies of God* (Ps. 116:12), just described in this glorious gospel of Christ (1:18—11:36). *your bodies.* Once the instruments of sin, but now to be employed for God in holiness (6:13). *living sacrifice.* As those reconciled to God and given close access to Him by Christ's sacrifice (5:1,10–11), believers are now to live as priests, constantly presenting their whole lives in God's presence as offerings for God's pleasure (1 Peter 2:5). *reasonable service.* Conscious obedience for the glory of God.

12:2 *will of God.* The standard aimed at, which makes us different from the *world.* This is the preceptive (Matt. 7:21), not the decretive will of God (Eph. 1:11). See note at Rom. 1:9–12.

12:3–5 Humility, realism, and diligence about our gifts for use in the body are necessary. Each gift is to be exercised as being God-given, and we are to accept it with trust in the Lord for the continued grace to use it (*the measure of faith*).

12:6–8 *prophecy.* A temporary gift of occasional infallible speaking of God's word. Prophets are usually listed between apostles and teachers (1 Cor. 12:28; Eph. 4:11). This gift was to be used to the extent that the prophet was assured he had the word of the Lord to give and so could speak in faith. *ministry.* The word from which we derive "deacon." *teaching . . . exhortation.* The work of expounding and applying the Scriptures. *giveth . . . with simplicity.* Use your wealth to bless others with straightforward motive and without show. *mercy, with cheerfulness.* Visiting the sick and needy with a sweet disposition that does not make them feel like a nuisance (2 Cor. 9:7).

12:9 *dissimulation.* Pretense or hypocrisy. *Abhor.* Hate, reject.

12:11 *business.* Activity in general; here our role in the church, whatever it is.

12:12 *instant.* Urgent.

12:14–15 God-centered humility and love will change the way we react to our enemies, as well as giving us gladness in others' welfare and sympathy for the afflicted (Prov. 17:5).

12:16 *same mind one toward another.* A mutual love for one another, without discord. *Mind not high things.* Do not set your minds on position and honor, but mingle freely with the lowly. *conceits.* Proud ideas.

12:17–18 *Recompense.* Pay back. *Provide things honest.* Show things that are honorable.

19 Dearly beloved, avenge not yourselves, but
rather give place unto wrath: for it is written,
Vengeance *is* mine; I will repay, saith the Lord.
20 Therefore if thine enemy hunger, feed him;
if he thirst, give him drink: for in so doing thou
shalt heap coals of fire on his head.
21 Be not overcome of evil, but overcome evil
with good.

CHAPTER 13

LET every soul be subject unto the higher powers.
For there is no power but of God: the powers that
be are ordained of God.
2 Whosoever therefore resisteth the power,
resisteth the ordinance of God: and they that
resist shall receive to themselves damnation.
3 For rulers are not a terror to good works, but
to the evil. Wilt thou then not be afraid of the
power? do that which is good, and thou shalt have
praise of the same:
4 For he is the minister of God to thee for good.
But if thou do that which is evil, be afraid; for he
beareth not the sword in vain: for he is the minis-
ter of God, a revenger to *execute* wrath upon him
that doeth evil.
5 Wherefore *ye* must needs be subject, not only
for wrath, but also for conscience sake.
6 For for this cause pay ye tribute also: for they
are God's ministers, attending continually upon
this very thing.
7 Render therefore to all their dues: tribute to
whom tribute *is due*; custom to whom custom;
fear to whom fear; honour to whom honour.
8 Owe no man any thing, but to love one another;
for he that loveth another hath fulfilled the law.
9 For this, Thou shalt not commit adultery, Thou
shalt not kill, Thou shalt not steal, Thou shalt
not bear false witness, Thou shalt not covet; and
if *there be* any other commandment, it is briefly
comprehended in this saying, namely, Thou shalt
love thy neighbour as thyself.
10 Love worketh no ill to his neighbour: therefore
love *is* the fulfilling of the law.
11 And that, knowing the time, that now *it is* high
time to awake out of sleep: for now *is* our salva-
tion nearer than when we believed.
12 The night is far spent, the day is at hand: let us
therefore cast off the works of darkness, and let us
put on the armour of light.
13 Let us walk honestly, as in the day; not in
rioting and drunkenness, not in chambering and

12:19 *give place unto wrath*. Acknowledge and rest content that God is the one to punish the evildoer, not us. *Vengeance is mine*. God is the Judge with the authority to punish sin (Deut. 32:35), since all sin is ultimately against Him (Ps. 51:4).
12:20–21 *heap coals*. Not increase his punishment from God, but inflame his conscience with acts of love, in the hope that he will repent and thus be *overcome* with *good* (Prov. 25:21–22).

Thoughts for Personal/Family Worship: Chapter 12

1. **When we have experienced something of the misery of our sin, along with the deliverance given in Jesus Christ, our hearts will respond with the love of true gratitude. This is the practical fruit of the gospel: "What shall I render unto the LORD for all his benefits toward me?" (Ps. 116:12). Rather than yearning to fit in with the world, we are to devote the whole of our lives, mind and body, to learning and doing God's will. How can the Christian live as a priest, offering every day as a sacrifice to God?**
2. **Real love must express itself in service. For this cause God gave various spiritual gifts to empower His people to serve. However, rather than waiting with anxiety until we know what our gifts are, God calls us to give ourselves to the life of a servant of God, cheerfully and fervently caring for each other. How are you serving?**
3. **The key to combating vengefulness is to know our place before God. He is the Judge, not us. When people wrong us, let us remember that it is not about our honor but about the glory of God. How can the Lord's statement "Vengeance is mine; I will repay" (v. 19) set us free from any impulse to take personal vengeance in word or deed?**

Chapter 13: *This chapter deals with our duty to the civil authorities and to our neighbor as part of our service to Christ.*

Duty to the Civil Magistrate and to Our Neighbor (13:1–14)

13:1–2 *higher powers*. The civil rulers; at the time the emperor and officers of the Roman Empire. *ordained of God*. Instituted and authorized by Him, not merely coming about in His providence. Thus submission to God requires submitting to the civil authorities (1 Peter 2:13–14). *damnation*. Judgment in this world by civil penalty.
13:3–4 Paul states the divine purpose and duty of a ruler as God's servant (*minister*), namely to give *praise* to the *good* and punishment to the *evil*. Since the latter can refer only to that which a civil ruler is competent to judge, it must be understood as sin exressed in outward criminal acts. *sword*. The use of deadly force to punish or defend against evil (Gen. 9:6; Acts 25:11). *execute wrath*. The ruler inflicts a measure of God's judgment against sin (12:19).
13:5 Submission to civil authority should be a matter of pleasing God (*conscience*), not mere fear of punishment for an infraction.
13:6–7 *tribute . . . custom*. Tax. Tax or benefit fraud is not for the Christian. Also, we should treat public officers with due *honour* (Acts 23:1; 1 Peter 2:17).
13:8 *Owe no man any thing*. Borrowing is legitimate (Ex. 22:25; Ps. 37:26; Matt. 5:42; Luke 6:35), but refusal to repay is not.
13:9–10 The Ten Commandments (Ex. 20:1–17) are of abiding authority (Eph. 6:2), expounding the implications of the general command to love our neighbor as ourselves (Lev. 19:18; Mark 12:31).
13:11–12 *awake*. The dawning day of Christ should arouse us from spiritual stupor (1 Thess. 5:6–7). *salvation*. Used here of its completion in resurrection glory. *night is far spent*. The last days began with the first coming of Christ (Acts 2:16–17; 1 Cor. 10:11; Heb. 1:1–2; 1 John 2:18;). *armour of light*. The life of God's kingdom that comes to us through Christ, engaging us in fierce battle with the kingdom of darkness (2 Cor. 6:7; 10:4; Eph. 6:10–18; 1 Thess. 5:8).

wantonness, not in strife and envying.
14 But put ye on the Lord Jesus Christ, and
make not provision for the flesh, to *fulfil* the lusts
thereof.

CHAPTER 14

HIM that is weak in the faith receive ye, *but* not to
doubtful disputations.
2 For one believeth that he may eat all things:
another, who is weak, eateth herbs.
3 Let not him that eateth despise him that eateth
not; and let not him which eateth not judge him
that eateth: for God hath received him.
4 Who art thou that judgest another man's ser-
vant? to his own master he standeth or falleth.
Yea, he shall be holden up: for God is able to make
him stand.
5 One man esteemeth one day above another:
another esteemeth every day *alike*. Let every man
be fully persuaded in his own mind.
6 He that regardeth the day, regardeth *it* unto the
Lord; and he that regardeth not the day, to the
Lord he doth not regard *it*. He that eateth, eateth
to the Lord, for he giveth God thanks; and he that
eateth not, to the Lord he eateth not, and giveth
God thanks.
7 For none of us liveth to himself, and no man
dieth to himself.
8 For whether we live, we live unto the Lord; and
whether we die, we die unto the Lord: whether we
live therefore, or die, we are the Lord's.
9 For to this end Christ both died, and rose, and
revived, that he might be Lord both of the dead
and living.
10 But why dost thou judge thy brother? or why
dost thou set at nought thy brother? for we shall
all stand before the judgment seat of Christ.
11 For it is written, *As* I live, saith the Lord, every
knee shall bow to me, and every tongue shall con-
fess to God.
12 So then every one of us shall give account of
himself to God.
13 Let us not therefore judge one another any
more: but judge this rather, that no man put
a stumblingblock or an occasion to fall in *his*
brother's way.
14 I know, and am persuaded by the Lord Jesus,
that *there is* nothing unclean of itself: but to him
that esteemeth any thing to be unclean, to him *it*
is unclean.
15 But if thy brother be grieved with *thy* meat,
now walkest thou not charitably. Destroy not him
with thy meat, for whom Christ died.

13:13 *chambering.* Sexual immorality. *wantonness.* Debauchery.
13:14 *put ye on . . . Christ.* Live in communion and fellowship with Christ, with whom God has united us (Gal. 3:27; Eph. 4:24; Col. 3:10,12), so that He is our armor (v. 12). *make not provision for the flesh.* Do not make plans to satisfy evil thoughts or desires.

Thoughts for Personal/Family Worship: Chapter 13

1. **Our duty to civil authority should be determined by God-given biblical principle, not by the degree of our fear of getting caught in an infraction (v. 5). Though people around us may neither give honor to authority nor exercise authority in an honorable way, Christians must be people who conscientiously honor authority because they honor God. What would that have meant for Christians in pagan Rome? What about for you?**
2. **We need God's law to tell us how to love (vv. 8–10). There is no conflict between law and love. Love is a command, and the Ten Commandments show us in greater detail what that means. The Old Testament taught love, even to our enemies (Ex. 23:4–5). There is no difference in moral standards between the testaments, though the same standard is more fully revealed in the New Testament.**

Chapter 14: *This chapter deals with our duty to the weaker brother and our obligation to use our knowledge lovingly.*

Using Our Knowledge Lovingly (14:1–23)

14:1 *Him that is weak in the faith.* Not a heretic but a brother, and not a brother with a weakness for a particular sin but one who has a weakness of conscience causing him to think that something lawful is actually sinful. He is to be received authentically, not merely provisionally and conditionally, even while we try to reason him out of his position (*doubtful disputations*).
14:2–3 The first example: eating only vegetables (*herbs*), perhaps an issue for Jews who still regarded themselves as bound by the Old Testament dietary laws and who could observe them in pagan Rome only by avoiding meat altogether. Man-made rules must not be imposed upon the church; instead, we must bear with people who are overly scrupulous.
14:4 We are not to take Christ's place as though the brother is ultimately accountable to us. His perceived error of judgment does not result in dismissal from Christ's service. *holden up.* Held up. Christ is able to sustain him in his walk with Himself.
14:5–6 A second example: honoring special days, probably the ceremonial holy days of the old covenant, once appointed by God but canceled in Christ (Gal. 4:10; Col. 2:16–17). While this could include some ceremonial elements of the Mosaic Sabbath observance, the Sabbath itself is a creation ordinance and therefore has abiding moral force (Gen. 2:1–3; Ex. 20:11; Rev. 1:10). Paul's words here cannot mean that Christians are under no obligation to observe any sacred days, for then his words about food (vv. 14–23) would imply that Christians are under no obligation to observe a sacred use of food, as in the Lord's Supper.
14:7–8 We are the Lord's possession, an obligation that extends even to glorifying God in our death (Acts 7:59–60; Phil. 1:20; Heb. 11:21–22).
14:9 *died, and rose . . . that he might be Lord.* Since Christ's saving work aimed at His exaltation, to usurp His place by judging other Christians is a practical denial of the gospel.
14:10–12 *judgment seat of Christ . . . the Lord . . . God.* Paul's use of Isa. 45:23 assumes that Christ is *Jehovah* ("the LORD" and "God" in Isa. 45:21–25), the Judge of all (Phil. 2:9–11).
14:13 Our use of legitimate things can still be a *stumblingblock* to the weak, causing them to sin (v. 23). Things legitimate under the first table of the law should not be used contrary to love to our neighbor.

16 Let not then your good be evil spoken of:
17 For the kingdom of God is not meat and
drink; but righteousness, and peace, and joy in
the Holy Ghost.
18 For he that in these things serveth Christ *is*
acceptable to God, and approved of men.
19 Let us therefore follow after the things which
make for peace, and things wherewith one may
edify another.
20 For meat destroy not the work of God. All
things indeed *are* pure; but *it is* evil for that man
who eateth with offence.
21 *It is* good neither to eat flesh, nor to drink wine,
nor *any thing* whereby thy brother stumbleth, or
is offended, or is made weak.
22 Hast thou faith? have *it* to thyself before God.
Happy *is* he that condemneth not himself in that
thing which he alloweth.
23 And he that doubteth is damned if he eat,
because *he eateth* not of faith: for whatsoever *is*
not of faith is sin.

CHAPTER 15

WE then that are strong ought to bear the infirmi-
ties of the weak, and not to please ourselves.
2 Let every one of us please *his* neighbour for *his*
good to edification.
3 For even Christ pleased not himself; but, as it is
written, The reproaches of them that reproached
thee fell on me.
4 For whatsoever things were written aforetime
were written for our learning, that we through
patience and comfort of the scriptures might have
hope.
5 Now the God of patience and consolation grant
you to be likeminded one toward another accord-
ing to Christ Jesus:
6 That ye may with one mind *and* one mouth
glorify God, even the Father of our Lord Jesus
Christ.
7 Wherefore receive ye one another, as Christ also
received us to the glory of God.
8 Now I say that Jesus Christ was a minister of the

14:14–15 *nothing unclean.* No food in and of itself is essentially sinful (Acts 10:15; 1 Tim. 4:4). *to him that esteemeth . . . it is unclean.* It is wrong to force people to act against their conscience even when they are mistaken.
14:15 *meat.* Food of any kind (vv. 17,20). *walkest thou not charitably.* You are not acting in love. *Destroy.* The word can refer to losses short of eternal damnation (Mark 9:41; 1 Cor. 10:9) and in this context refers to causing someone else to sin. Alternatively, it could refer to the tendency of the action, not the actual result.
14:16 *good.* The liberty of the strong to enjoy God's creation should not be made a cause of criticism by its inappropriate use.
14:17 *kingdom of God.* Though Christ's kingdom has not yet come in open glory, it has already arrived in the holiness of God's people, though not in rules about mere externals (*meat and drink*) but by the inward graces of the Holy Spirit (*Ghost*).
14:18 *in these things.* The promotion of the things mentioned in the previous verse.
14:19–20 The last clause begins to explain why it is so important to avoid pressuring the weak (even by our practice) into doing what they are not convinced is lawful.
14:21 *flesh.* Meat (a different Greek word from that used in vv. 15,17,20).
14:23 When a brother does what is lawful but believes it is not, he sins in motive, even though not outwardly. He does not act out of love to Christ, in *faith*, or in confidence that he is pleasing the Lord. *damned.* Used here of the disapproval of God (as well as of the conscience), not of eternal judgment. The strong are to avoid sinning by a wrong use of what is, in itself, lawful (v. 22).

Thoughts for Personal/Family Worship: Chapter 14

1. **We should rebuke blatant sin and rebellion (Lev. 19:17) but exercise restraint and gentleness toward those young in the faith and those who need encouragement in the ways of the Lord, rather than condemning them for every defect arising from ignorance or a misguided conscience. This is not a compromising of holiness but an exercise of it, for the essence of holiness is love. What kinds of issues does the church face today where some are bound by conscience in matters not commanded in Scripture, while others are free? How should they bear with each other in mutual love and respect?**
2. **We should never disturb the peace of the church except over a matter of real and vital principle (v. 19). Rather than crusading for our own views in matters of minor importance, we should be zealous for peace. We should also seek greater illumination of our brother's minds and consciences through prayer and the Word, for coercing people into conformity without real conviction is a hollow victory. In what ways does this principle require a great deal of patience toward other Christians?**

Chapter 15: *The unity of the body of Christ is to be earnestly sought because of Christ's mission, God's purpose, and Paul's own ministry to both Jew and Gentile.*

Unity of the Body (15:1–33)

Christ's Example (15:1–7)

15:1–2 *strong . . . weak.* Those who have a faith strong in its apprehension of our freedom of Christ, and those who are weak in that freedom and thus bound in conscience by various unnecessary scruples (14:1). Our unity-seeking love for the weaker brother is to be shown to the whole church of God. *edification.* Building up in spiritual life.
15:3 *as it is written.* Citing Ps. 69:9. *reproached thee.* Dishonored God.
15:4–5 *aforetime.* Beforehand. *patience.* Endurance, perseverance. *consolation.* Same word translated as *comfort. scriptures.* The Old Testament (along with the New Testament) is God's Word and so is spiritually profitable to afford strength and *hope* to believers (2 Tim. 3:16).
15:6 *one mind and one mouth.* Unity of faith and love leads to unity in worship, despite all the ethnic and cultural differences that can divide the church.
15:7 Christ received us as sinners to the glory of God's grace (Luke 15:2), so we ought to openheartedly receive imperfect saints.

Unity of Jew and Gentile in Christ's Body (15:8–13)

15:8 *minister of the circumcision.* Servant to the Jews. Christ glorified God's faithfulness (*truth*) by coming in accordance

circumcision for the truth of God, to confirm the
promises *made* unto the fathers:
9 And that the Gentiles might glorify God for *his*
mercy; as it is written, For this cause I will con-
fess to thee among the Gentiles, and sing unto thy
name.
10 And again he saith, Rejoice, ye Gentiles, with
his people.
11 And again, Praise the Lord, all ye Gentiles; and
laud him, all ye people.
12 And again, Esaias saith, There shall be a root
of Jesse, and he that shall rise to reign over the
Gentiles; in him shall the Gentiles trust.
13 Now the God of hope fill you with all joy and
peace in believing, that ye may abound in hope,
through the power of the Holy Ghost.
14 And I myself also am persuaded of you, my
brethren, that ye also are full of goodness, filled
with all knowledge, able also to admonish one
another.
15 Nevertheless, brethren, I have written the
more boldly unto you in some sort, as putting
you in mind, because of the grace that is given to
me of God,
16 That I should be the minister of Jesus Christ
to the Gentiles, ministering the gospel of God,
that the offering up of the Gentiles might be
acceptable, being sanctified by the Holy Ghost.
17 I have therefore whereof I may glory through
Jesus Christ in those things which pertain to God.
18 For I will not dare to speak of any of those
things which Christ hath not wrought by me, to
make the Gentiles obedient, by word and deed,
19 Through mighty signs and wonders, by
the power of the Spirit of God; so that from
Jerusalem, and round about unto Illyricum, I
have fully preached the gospel of Christ.
20 Yea, so have I strived to preach the gospel, not
where Christ was named, lest I should build upon
another man's foundation:
21 But as it is written, To whom he was not
spoken of, they shall see: and they that have not
heard shall understand.
22 For which cause also I have been much hin-
dered from coming to you.
23 But now having no more place in these parts,
and having a great desire these many years to
come unto you;
24 Whensoever I take my journey into Spain, I
will come to you: for I trust to see you in my jour-
ney, and to be brought on my way thitherward
by you, if first I be somewhat filled with your
company.
25 But now I go unto Jerusalem to minister unto
the saints.
26 For it hath pleased them of Macedonia and
Achaia to make a certain contribution for the
poor saints which are at Jerusalem.
27 It hath pleased them verily; and their debtors
they are. For if the Gentiles have been made
partakers of their spiritual things, their duty is
also to minister unto them in carnal things.

---

with the covenant *promises* of God. All of the promised covenant blessings to Abraham were through the one promised Seed, Christ (Gal. 3:16).

15:9 *glorify God for his mercy*. Christ came so that the nations (*Gentiles*) would praise God for His amazing grace in including them in His covenant grace promised to Israel (Ps. 18:49).

15:10–12 *he saith*. Citing Deut. 32:43; Ps. 117:1; Isa. 11:10. *laud*. Praise. *Esaias*. Isaiah.

15:13 Christian *hope* is not a bare belief in the head but an experiential reality in the heart, produced by the Holy Spirit (*Ghost*) through faith exercised in God's promises and vitally related to *joy* and *peace*. Therefore we should pray for it, as Paul's wish here implies.

Paul's Ministry to the United Body (15:14–33)

15:14–33 This marks the beginning of Paul's conclusion with an explanation of his boldness in the letter, but it is also relevant to the unity of this largely Gentile church because he explains that he, a Jew, has seen God's blessing among the Gentiles.

15:14–16 Despite thinking well of his readers, he is bold in exhorting them on the basis of his calling (*grace*) as an apostle to the Gentiles.

15:18 *wrought*. Worked. The apostle's ministry was actually the work of *Christ* through him.

15:19 *signs and wonders*. The apostles were empowered by Christ to work miracles to confirm the new revelation they brought (2 Cor. 12:12). *Illyricum*. Region between Italy and Greece.

15:20 *not where Christ was named*. Paul's apostolic commission was to take the gospel to peoples yet unreached by it, as is the calling of missionaries today, for apart from the preaching of the gospel no one can be saved (10:13–15).

15:21 *as it is written*. The preaching of the gospel to the nations fulfills the prophecy of God's Servant (Isa. 52:15).

15:24 *brought on my way thitherward*. Sent out or helped on my journey there.

15:25–28 He can now come to them, but it must be via *Jerusalem* so that he can convey the gift from the Gentile churches to the church there. This gift was of great importance to the apostle Paul, not only because of the need in Jerusalem but also as cementing the unity between the Jewish and Gentile segments of the church (2 Cor. 8:1—9:15). The Gentiles had been brought into the *spiritual* riches that had to this point been largely confined to the Jews. It was fitting, therefore, that the Gentiles should share their earthly goods with their Jewish brothers (*carnal things*).

15:27 *verily*. Truly.

Thoughts for Personal/Family Worship: Chapter 15

1. **The attitude that says "It's my life; I'll please myself" is ungodly and inconsistent with a sense of dependence upon and gratitude to the Lord Jesus Christ (vv. 1–3). It is also contradictory to the mission of Christ, for He came to unite all nations in the praise of God for His faithfulness and mercy. Why is selfishness so divisive to the church and so destructive to its calling?**
2. **Emotion is part of Christian experience (v. 13). Feeling does not determine truth, but it is involved in a right**

28 When therefore I have performed this, and
have sealed to them this fruit, I will come by you
into Spain.
29 And I am sure that, when I come unto you,
I shall come in the fulness of the blessing of the
gospel of Christ.
30 Now I beseech you, brethren, for the Lord
Jesus Christ's sake, and for the love of the Spirit,
that ye strive together with me in *your* prayers to
God for me;
31 That I may be delivered from them that do
not believe in Judaea; and that my service which *I
have* for Jerusalem may be accepted of the saints;
32 That I may come unto you with joy by the will
of God, and may with you be refreshed.
33 Now the God of peace *be* with you all. Amen.

CHAPTER 16

I COMMEND unto you Phebe our sister, which is a
servant of the church which is at Cenchrea:
2 That ye receive her in the Lord, as becometh
saints, and that ye assist her in whatsoever
business she hath need of you: for she hath been a
succourer of many, and of myself also.
3 Greet Priscilla and Aquila my helpers in Christ
Jesus:
4 Who have for my life laid down their own
necks: unto whom not only I give thanks, but also
all the churches of the Gentiles.
5 Likewise *greet* the church that is in their house.
Salute my wellbeloved Epaenetus, who is the first-
fruits of Achaia unto Christ.
6 Greet Mary, who bestowed much labour on us.
7 Salute Andronicus and Junia, my kinsmen, and
my fellowprisoners, who are of note among the
apostles, who also were in Christ before me.
8 Greet Amplias my beloved in the Lord.
9 Salute Urbane, our helper in Christ, and Stachys
my beloved.
10 Salute Apelles approved in Christ. Salute them
which are of Aristobulus' *household*.
11 Salute Herodion my kinsman. Greet them that
be of the *household* of Narcissus, which are in the
Lord.
12 Salute Tryphena and Tryphosa, who labour
in the Lord. Salute the beloved Persis, which la-
boured much in the Lord.
13 Salute Rufus chosen in the Lord, and his
mother and mine.
14 Salute Asyncritus, Phlegon, Hermas, Patrobas,
Hermes, and the brethren which are with them.
15 Salute Philologus, and Julia, Nereus, and his
sister, and Olympas, and all the saints which are
with them.
16 Salute one another with an holy kiss. The
churches of Christ salute you.
17 Now I beseech you, brethren, mark them
which cause divisions and offences contrary to
the doctrine which ye have learned; and avoid
them.
18 For they that are such serve not our Lord Jesus

reaction to truth. The Christian has distinctive sorrows over sin (2 Cor. 7:9–10) and joys in God (5:11) that come from believing. How can Christians cultivate a biblical emotional life? What role does the Holy Spirit play?

3. Paul's heart beat to bring the gospel to those who had never heard the name of Jesus. Though a remarkably gifted theologian and preacher, his calling did not allow him to settle in to a stable school or church but propelled him outward to the nations. Not everyone has such a calling, but the church as a whole still has a responsibility to preach the gospel to all creation. How are you praying for and supporting those called to bring the gospel?

Chapter 16: *Paul closes with a commendation of Phebe, specific greetings, final warnings, greetings from the brothers at Corinth, and a doxology.*

CONCLUSION (16:1–27)

Paul's Greetings (16:1–16)

16:1–2 *Phebe*. A pagan name, though she was now a follower of the Lord Jesus of outstanding godliness and exemplary hospitality. There are no grounds here for any office of deaconess, as the Greek word *diakonos* (servant) can be used generically or officially, just as can the word *presbuteros* (elder). The deacons of the church were evidently men (Acts 6:3–6; 1 Tim. 3:12). *Cenchrea* was the eastern harbor of Corinth. Possibly Phebe was the bearer of the letter.

16:3–5 *Priscilla and Aquila*. An exemplary couple, always mentioned positively (Acts 18:2–3; 1 Cor. 16:19; 2 Tim. 4:19).

16:6 *labour*. Toil (v. 12).

16:7–11 *kinsmen*. May signify fellow Jews (9:3), though only six people are described as such in this chapter (see v. 21), so they could be actual relatives. *Junia*. Could be male or female. *Narcissus*. An individual of this name is believed to have been martyred at the beginning of Nero's reign. It is his family who are here greeted.

16:12 *Tryphena and Tryphosa*. Possibly sisters.

16:13 *Rufus*. Possibly the one mentioned in Mark 15:21; if so, his salvation is not traced to his outward proximity to Christ on earth but to God's sovereign election.

16:16 *Salute*. Greet. The *kiss*, an ordinary greeting (Ex. 4:27; 18:7; Luke 7:45), was to be holy, not hypocritical (2 Sam. 20:9–10; Prov. 27:6; Luke 22:48).

Final Warnings (16:17–20)

16:17 False teachers who cause division by novel and unsound doctrine are to be *mark*(ed). Their office in the church (if one is held) should not make us oblivious to this possibility. The distinction between truth and error must be applied.

16:18–19 He would have them to be *wise* in following truth and *simple*, or inexperienced, in following lies.

16:20 Christ's triumph over *Satan* (Gen. 3:15) is applied to the redeemed as joint heirs with Christ and therefore as more than conquerors through Him.

Greetings from Particular Brothers at Corinth (16:21–23)

16:21–23 *Timotheus*. Timothy. *Tertius*. The secretary writing down Paul's words (1 Cor. 16:21; Gal. 6:11; Col. 4:18; 2 Thess. 3:17). *Gaius*. Mentioned in 1 Cor. 1:14; possibly the same as Justus in Acts 18:7, as an individual having more than one

Christ, but their own belly; and by good words
and fair speeches deceive the hearts of the simple.
19 For your obedience is come abroad unto all
men. I am glad therefore on your behalf: but yet I
would have you wise unto that which is good, and
simple concerning evil.
20 And the God of peace shall bruise Satan under
your feet shortly. The grace of our Lord Jesus
Christ *be* with you. Amen.
21 Timotheus my workfellow, and Lucius, and
Jason, and Sosipater, my kinsmen, salute you.
22 I Tertius, who wrote *this* epistle, salute you in
the Lord.
23 Gaius mine host, and of the whole church,
saluteth you. Erastus the chamberlain of the city
saluteth you, and Quartus a brother.
24 The grace of our Lord Jesus Christ *be* with you
all. Amen.
25 Now to him that is of power to stablish you according to my gospel, and the preaching of Jesus
Christ, according to the revelation of the mystery,
which was kept secret since the world began,
26 But now is made manifest, and by the scriptures of the prophets, according to the commandment of the everlasting God, made known to all
nations for the obedience of faith:
27 To God only wise, *be* glory through Jesus
Christ for ever. Amen.

name was common. *chamberlain*. Manager or steward, here the city treasurer.

Doxology (16:25–27)

16:25–27 The gospel begins in eternity in the mind and purpose of God. It is unknown to man unless revealed (*mystery*; 11:25), and it was revealed in Israel, but only at this point had those Old Testament *Scriptures* been spread among the nations. Only in the days of the early church had the truth of their fulfillment in Christ been made known among all nations by God's appointed messengers at His command and with the demand of the *obedience of faith* (1:5).

Thoughts for Personal/Family Worship: Chapter 16

1. **The closing chapter of Romans reminds us that the church does not consist only of the great leaders like Paul but of many people serving in their own unique capacities. We find a great example in Priscilla and Aquila (vv. 3–5), who are always found at full stretch for the cause of the gospel. How can we follow in their faith? If Paul had mentioned you in this chapter, how might he have described you?**
2. **Heretics are not to be trifled with (vv. 17–19). Christian love does not condone letting the wolves loose among the flock. "Avoid them" (v. 17). If more Christians did this, there would be greater unity among those who do love the Lord and His truth. Why is heresy so destructive?**
3. **The gospel begins in the mind of God and is revealed to men, not deduced by them. It is God who sends it freely to sinners, whose accountability it is to receive it. If we have been privileged to hear this joyful sound and Spirit-enabled to believe in Christ, we are blessed indeed. God's glorious attributes, such as His eternity and wisdom (vv. 26–27), shine through in the gospel. Take some time to praise God for the glorious gospel of Christ revealed in this great epistle.**

Whether therefore ye eat or drink or whatsoever ye do do all to the glory of God

1 CORINTHIANS 10:31

INTRODUCTION TO THE BOOK OF 1 CORINTHIANS

Authorship: The apostle Paul identifies himself as the author (1:1), and there is no compelling reason to doubt the claim. The vocabulary, theology, and personal information all point to the legitimacy of Pauline authorship.

Date: Paul wrote the letter while at Ephesus before the celebration of Pentecost (16:8). He planted the church in Corinth in AD 51 and stayed in the city for "a good while" (Acts 18:18). The next year he went on to Ephesus where he stayed for almost three years. During the latter part of his time in Ephesus he wrote 1 Corinthians, placing the date in the spring of either AD 54 or 55.

Theme: Boasting or glorying in God, which promotes unity in the body as well as purity in both doctrine and behavior.

Purpose: (1) To respond to a letter from the Corinthian believers asking questions on various topics (marriage and divorce, food offered to idols, decorum in public worship, spiritual gifts, and the collection), and (2) to address the troubling reports he heard from those of Chloe's household informing him of the divisions that existed within the church and threatened the unity of the body and, therefore, brought reproach to God's glory.

Synopsis: *The Contribution of 1 Corinthians to Redemptive Revelation*

After Paul endured beatings in Philippi (Acts 16) and scorn in Athens (Acts 17), he traveled to Corinth (Acts 18) "in weakness, and in fear, and in much trembling" (1 Cor. 2:3). He began preaching in the synagogue every Sabbath (Acts 18:4) and after opposition from the Jews he turned his focus to preaching the gospel to the Gentiles. Despite the discouragement of the opposition, Paul saw fruit from the preaching of the gospel. Crispus, the chief ruler of the synagogue, believed on Christ and many Corinthians heard and believed. Paul received greater confidence and encouragement directly from the Lord, who exhorted the apostle not to be afraid, but to speak, "for I am with thee, and no man shall set on thee to hurt thee: for I have much people in this city" (Acts 18:10). Paul remained in Corinth for eighteen months teaching them. Apollos ministered in Corinth after Paul had gone on to Ephesus. Certainly because of the time Paul spent, as well as the ministry of Apollos and even Peter, Paul expected the Corinthian believers to be more mature in their walk with God than was evidenced by the reports and questions that came to him (as seen in the letter's repeated refrain, "know ye not?" [1 Cor. 3:16; 5:6; 6:2–3,9,15–16,19; 9:13,24]).

Given the nature of the sordid behavior for which Paul must confront the Corinthian believers, the letter surprisingly begins with numerable commendations and thanksgiving to God for the grace shown to the church at Corinth. Paul identifies them as the church of God, sanctified in Christ, and called to be saints (1:2). This greeting sets the basis for how Paul will confront them throughout the book. They are God's church, set apart by God in Christ to be saints. Therefore, they are to live as God's people, as gospel people. Rather than boasting in themselves, they are to boast in God (1:31; 3:21; 4:7). They are not to live for themselves but for God's glory in all things (10:31), and for the good of others with love governing all their words, thoughts, and actions (ch. 13). In the opening greetings and thanksgiving Paul genuinely praises God for the work of grace in them and urges them to continue to pursue Christ so that they might be blameless in the day of the Lord Jesus Christ (1:8).

After the opening verses Paul immediately draws focus onto the report he has heard, namely, that of divisions in the church (1:18—6:20). There were those in the church who were

COR
GAL
EPH

encouraging a party spirit, rallying around Paul, Apollos, Cephas (Peter), and even a party that claimed to be of Christ. Given that these men preached the same gospel and their teachings were not antithetical one to another, the nature of the party spirit was not theological, but one of personality. Paul objects to the disunity by enumerating the glories of the gospel of Jesus Christ. Though foolish, offensive, and weak from man's natural perspective, the gospel is the wisdom and power of God and it is through the preaching of the cross that God has demonstrated His glory. Paul builds his argument to its culminating point by announcing that believers are by God in union with Christ, who of God was made unto us wisdom, that is, our righteousness, sanctification, and redemption (1:30). Jesus Christ is everything to and for the believer with the result that all glory is due to God alone. A divisive party spirit is antithetical to the gospel of Jesus Christ. Paul goes on to show that the nature of gospel ministry (chs. 3–4) also eradicates the acceptability of having a party spirit.

Not only was there a divisive spirit among the church, there was also immorality so odious that the Gentiles did not even name it (ch. 5). What was so grieving to Paul was not merely the fact that one within the church would be involved in an illicit relation with his father's wife (5:1), but that the church tolerated it! He exhorts them to deal with the sin and deliver such a one over to Satan and he rebukes them for glorying in the sin itself. Again, the gospel forms the basis of Paul's argumentation. Christ is our Passover (5:7). In Christ all things are new. The old is to be put away and believers are not to be holding on to the former things of malice and wickedness, but rather, are to live in sincerity and truth (5:8). In Christ they are sanctified, set apart. Therefore, they are to live accordingly.

Next, Paul addresses the report that there were scandalous litigations between church members (ch. 6). The Corinthians boasted in themselves about how spiritual they were. Yet, they could not even resolve differences between themselves. They took their differences before the unbelievers to find resolution (6:6). Paul encourages them that it is better to accept the wrong and the loss than it is to bring reproach to Christ's name (6:7).

Chapters 7–16 form the second major division of the book. In these chapters Paul addresses issues raised by the Corinthian church. Chapter 7 focuses on the subject of marriage and divorce. Chapters 8–10 touch upon food offered to idols and how to deal with fellow church members whose consciences vary on these matters. Paul provides a personal illustration in ch. 9, showing the difference between rights and liberty. As an apostle he has the right to receive remuneration for his labors, but for the sake of his testimony and for the usefulness of his ministry he has the liberty to refuse it. Chapter 11 focuses on decorum in public worship with respect to gender distinctions and the Lord's Supper. Chapters 12–14 provide the most detailed treatment of the spiritual gifts in the New Testament, which Paul frames around love for the brethren and orderly worship. While much of the focus in this letter focuses on purity of life, we see in ch. 15 that Christians are to be pure in doctrine as well. Paul's in-depth treatment of the resurrection of Christ and of believers highlights the point that belief is a matter of morality and motivation for the Christian life (15:58). Finally, Paul addresses the matter of the collection for the saints. He closes his letter by mentioning his travel plans and final exhortations to stand fast in the faith (16:13).

Paul's first letter addresses many issues that are relevant for the church today and he wisely shows believers how to apply the gospel to the everyday circumstances of life.

Outline: I. Introduction (1:1–9)
- A. Greeting (1:1–3)
- B. Thanksgiving (1:4–9)

II. Solutions to Problems Reported (1:10—6:20)
- A. The Problem of Division (1:10—4:21)
  1. Divisions in the Church (1:10–17)
  2. The Gospel of Christ Resolves Division (1:18—3:4)
  3. The Nature of Gospel Ministry Resolves Division (3:5—4:21)
- B. The Problems of Scandalous Sins (5:1—6:20)
  1. Failure to Discipline Sin (5:1–13)
  2. Litigation between Church Members (6:1–8)
  3. Sin, the Kingdom, and Salvation (6:9–11)
  4. Sexual Promiscuity (6:12–20)

III. Answers to Questions from Corinthian Church (7:1—16:4)
- A. Concerning Marriage, Divorce, the Unmarried, and Widows (7:1–40)

- B. Concerning Conscience regarding Meat Offered to Idols (8:1—11:1)
  - 1. Importance of Conscience (8:1–13)
  - 2. Personal Illustration from Apostolic Rights (9:1–27)
  - 3. Warnings against Idolatry and Call to Glorify God (10:1—11:1)
- C. Concerning Decorum in Public Worship (11:2–34)
  - 1. Headship and Headcoverings (11:2–16)
  - 2. Behavior at the Lord's Supper (11:17–34)
- D. Concerning the Spiritual Gifts (12:1—14:40)
  - 1. Unity in Diversity in the One Body (12:1–31)
  - 2. Preeminence of Love (13:1–13)
  - 3. Prophecy and Tongues, Decency and Order (14:1–40)
- E. Concerning the Resurrection (15:1–58)
- F. Concerning the Collection (16:1–4)

IV. Conclusion (16:5–24)

- A. Paul's Travel Plans (16:5–12)
- B. Concluding Exhortations (16:13–18)
- C. Final Greetings (16:19–24)

THE FIRST EPISTLE OF PAUL THE APOSTLE TO THE

CORINTHIANS

CHAPTER 1

PAUL, called *to be* an apostle of Jesus Christ
through the will of God, and Sosthenes *our*
brother,
2 Unto the church of God which is at Corinth, to
them that are sanctified in Christ Jesus, called *to
be* saints, with all that in every place call upon the
name of Jesus Christ our Lord, both theirs and
ours:
3 Grace *be* unto you, and peace, from God our
Father, and *from* the Lord Jesus Christ.
4 I thank my God always on your behalf, for the
grace of God which is given you by Jesus Christ;
5 That in every thing ye are enriched by him, in
all utterance, and *in* all knowledge;
6 Even as the testimony of Christ was confirmed
in you:
7 So that ye come behind in no gift; waiting for
the coming of our Lord Jesus Christ:
8 Who shall also confirm you unto the end, *that
ye may be* blameless in the day of our Lord Jesus
Christ.
9 God *is* faithful, by whom ye were called unto
the fellowship of his Son Jesus Christ our Lord.
10 Now I beseech you, brethren, by the name of
our Lord Jesus Christ, that ye all speak the same
thing, and *that* there be no divisions among you;
but *that* ye be perfectly joined together in the
same mind and in the same judgment.
11 For it hath been declared unto me of you, my
brethren, by them *which are of the house* of Chloe,
that there are contentions among you.
12 Now this I say, that every one of you saith, I
am of Paul; and I of Apollos; and I of Cephas; and
I of Christ.
13 Is Christ divided? was Paul crucified for you?
or were ye baptized in the name of Paul?
14 I thank God that I baptized none of you, but
Crispus and Gaius;
15 Lest any should say that I had baptized in mine
own name.
16 And I baptized also the household of Steph-
anas: besides, I know not whether I baptized any
other.

Chapter 1: *Paul greets the church at Corinth and addresses the problem of division reported to him from the brethren of the household of Chloe.*

INTRODUCTION (1:1–9)

Greeting (1:1–3)

1:1 Paul was not writing to the Corinthians with some kind of pretended authority, but as an apostle according to God's will.
1:2 *sanctified in Christ Jesus.* Paul speaks here objectively of professing believers at Corinth. *called to be saints.* The church of God's people, who are holy ones. This reality that is theirs in Christ is to be demonstrated in the way they live.

Thanksgiving (1:4–9)

1:5 *ye are enriched by him.* All of their blessings are a result of God's grace to them. Therefore, they have no room for pride or self-boasting. In various places in the letter Paul will rebuke them for being puffed up and proud (4:6–8). *in all utterance, and in all knowledge.* Speaking and knowing are two areas where the Corinthian believers were proud (8:1–3; 13:2; 14).
1:8 *Who shall also confirm you unto the end.* God has set them apart in Christ Jesus and will continue His work of grace unto the end when there will be blamelessness. Though the Corinthians were not demonstrating holiness in every area, God would not fail in His work of redemption (Phil. 1:6).

SOLUTIONS TO PROBLEMS REPORTED (1:10—6:20)

The Problem of Division (1:10—4:21)

Divisions in the Church (1:10–17)

1:10 *Now* transitions to the topic of divisions. Paul introduces the issue of division, calling them to be unified and to speak, or agree on, the same thing. This is further described by the phrase *be perfectly joined together in the same mind and in the same judgment.*
1:12 Paul describes the particular division he has in mind. There were factions within the church following certain leaders: there was a Paul faction, an Apollos faction, a Cephas (Peter) faction, and a faction that seemed to be more pompous than the rest by claiming to be of Christ. These factions were not theological in nature given that each one taught the same gospel. All believers belong to Christ (3:22–23), so He should not be claimed as just another party. Paul, Apollos, and Cephas are servants for Christ's sake (3:5–9; 4:1–2).
1:13 *Is Christ divided?* All believers are united to Christ (v. 2). To be divided into factions contradicts the very nature of the church that has many members but is one body. The obvious answer to the question, along with the next two (*was Paul crucified for you?* and *were ye baptized in the name of Paul?*), is No! These questions highlight the absurdity of a selfish, party spirit within the church. Paul did not encourage the party

17 For Christ sent me not to baptize, but to
preach the gospel: not with wisdom of words, lest
the cross of Christ should be made of none effect.
18 For the preaching of the cross is to them that
perish foolishness; but unto us which are saved it
is the power of God.
19 For it is written, I will destroy the wisdom of
the wise, and will bring to nothing the under-
standing of the prudent.
20 Where *is* the wise? where *is* the scribe? where
is the disputer of this world? hath not God made
foolish the wisdom of this world?
21 For after that in the wisdom of God the world
by wisdom knew not God, it pleased God by the
foolishness of preaching to save them that believe.
22 For the Jews require a sign, and the Greeks
seek after wisdom:
23 But we preach Christ crucified, unto the Jews a
stumblingblock, and unto the Greeks foolishness;
24 But unto them which are called, both Jews and
Greeks, Christ the power of God, and the wisdom
of God.
25 Because the foolishness of God is wiser than
men; and the weakness of God is stronger than men.
26 For ye see your calling, brethren, how that not
many wise men after the flesh, not many mighty,
not many noble, *are called*:
27 But God hath chosen the foolish things of the
world to confound the wise; and God hath chosen
the weak things of the world to confound the
things which are mighty;
28 And base things of the world, and things which
are despised, hath God chosen, *yea*, and things
which are not, to bring to nought things that are:
29 That no flesh should glory in his presence.
30 But of him are ye in Christ Jesus, who of God
is made unto us wisdom, and righteousness, and
sanctification, and redemption:
31 That, according as it is written, He that glori-
eth, let him glory in the Lord.

CHAPTER 2

AND I, brethren, when I came to you, came not
with excellency of speech or of wisdom, declaring
unto you the testimony of God.
2 For I determined not to know any thing among
you, save Jesus Christ, and him crucified.

---

spirit, even among those who supported him.

1:17 *preach the gospel.* Paul announces what his role was in the founding of the Corinthian church. He was the messenger, heralding the gospel. *not with wisdom of words.* Paul introduces the idea of wisdom, which will be a critical part of his discussion from 1:17—2:16, contrasting God's wisdom with man's wisdom. The phrase *wisdom of words* refers to a kind of rhetoric and persuasion that characterized the Greek orators. Paul preached the good news of God's salvation through the cross of Christ in plain speech, not in a manner that manipulated or impressed his hearers. Here the message of the cross is set against the wisdom of words.

The Gospel of Christ Resolves Division (1:18—3:4)

1:18 *preaching of the cross.* Literally, "the word of the cross." Paul again highlights the opposite nature of his apostolic message from the wisdom of words. The focus is not on the act of preaching, but the content, namely, the message of the cross. Unbelievers view the gospel as foolishness, but to believers the word of the cross is God's power (Rom. 1:16).

1:19 *For it is written.* Paul cites Isa. 29:14 to show that God destroys the supposed wisdom of the world. The context of Isaiah attributes this wisdom to Israel who drew near with their mouth and honored God with their lips. This is a strong warning to the church in Corinth, who professed Christ, that being enamored with worldly wisdom never ends well.

1:21 *foolishness of preaching.* What the world considers foolishness is the very thing that saves them that believe. That is God's wisdom at work and it is according to His will or pleasure.

1:22 *Jews require a sign.* The Gospels show the Jews persistently requesting a sign or miracle from Christ, which He refused to give since they refused to believe the miracles that He did perform. *Greeks seek after wisdom.* The cultured Greeks sought after that which fit within their framework of wisdom and sophistication. That God would take on flesh and die for the guilty was the height of absurdity to them.

1:23 *stumblingblock.* A crucified Messiah was counterintuitive to what the Jews expected and, therefore, it was an offense. *foolishness.* To the Greeks the message of the cross made no sense.

1:24 God calls both Jews and Greeks, and His call effectively removes their blindness so that they see that the message of the cross is powerful and wise (2 Cor. 4:4–6).

1:26–29 *For ye see.* To consider, to look at with understanding. Believers do well to look at their calling because it magnifies the grace of God in saving sinners. God chooses *foolish things, weak things, base* (lowly) *things, despised* things, and *things which are not* in order to accomplish His saving purpose. All of this is to the end *that no flesh should glory in his presence.* The message of the cross magnifies the glory of God alone.

1:30 *who of God is made unto us.* The Father unites sinners to Christ by His call (v. 24) so that they share in His blessings. *wisdom.* All wisdom is found in Christ, who is our wisdom. Wisdom in Scripture is ability and skill. The wisdom that Christ is for us is explained by these words: all that we need to be right before God (*righteousness*), to be holy in this life (*sanctification*), and to see full salvation (*redemption*) is found in Christ Jesus.

Thoughts for Personal/Family Worship: Chapter 1

1. **Meditate upon God's objective act of setting you apart in Christ Jesus. If you have been sanctified in Christ, what are the ramifications and implications of that reality for your daily life, family life, and church life?**
2. **Are you consistently finding hope and satisfaction in the gospel of Christ's life, death, and resurrection? What are warning signs that someone is being taken up with or enamored by the wisdom of this world?**
3. **We are all boasters. Paul does not rebuke the Corinthian church for boasting or glorying, but for boasting and glorying in the wrong thing. Do you consciously boast in God's saving work and His grace in sending His own Son to the cross, or are you glorying in your own talents, gifts, and graces?**

Chapter 2: *Paul illustrates the wisdom and power of God's gospel through his ministry among them, highlighting the necessity of the Holy Spirit's work*

THE CALLING OF GOD

How does God bring sinners to Himself? The Bible says that He calls them. One New Testament description of Christians appears in 1 Corinthians 1:24: "them which are called," or, more simply translated, "the called," that is, those called or summoned by God into the grace and life found only through faith in Jesus Christ. Using the same term, Paul assures us, "All things work together for good to them that love God, to them who are the called according to his purpose" (Rom. 8:28).

One of the first instances of God calling a sinner is found in Genesis 11. A man named Abram (later changed to Abraham), born in Ur of the Chaldees, goes along with his father Terah and his household when Terah leaves Ur to settle in the land of Canaan. Why do these ancient Chaldeans pull up stakes and set out to relocate six hundred miles away, at the other end of the Fertile Crescent? Genesis 12:1 begins to tell us: "Now the LORD had said unto Abram, Get thee out of thy country, and from thy kindred, and from thy father's house, unto a land that I will shew thee." The command to leave Ur and seek a new country is accompanied by promises of blessing upon Abram, blessing upon his family, and, through him, blessing for all families of the earth.

God had revealed Himself to a pagan idolater, speaking to him with such compelling authority that Abram could do nothing but trust and obey. The fruit of Abram's newfound faith in the one true God was obedience to His command: "By faith Abraham, when he was called to go out into a place which he should after receive for an inheritance, obeyed; and he went out not knowing whither he went" (Heb. 11:8).

Throughout Scripture we see God continuing to call sinners. He speaks a word of command, often to someone who previously did not know or acknowledge Him as God and who lived in ignorance, unbelief, and lawless disobedience. The call is presented as an invitation, but with God an invitation is always a command, cast in the imperative mood, however graciously it is expressed. Christ Himself issues such a call and command, saying, "Come unto me, all ye that labour and are heavy laden, and I will give you rest" (Matt. 11:28). The word of command is seamlessly joined to the gracious promise.

Today God calls sinners to faith in Christ and repentance from sin through the preaching of the gospel. The church has been given the task of proclaiming that gospel to all nations, inviting and urging all who hear to come to Christ by faith so as to obtain forgiveness of sins and everlasting life. So compelling is the command, so gracious and appealing the invitation, that one can only stand amazed that so few respond and so many turn a deaf ear.

The Bible's solution to this problem is the doctrine of gracious, unconditional election. Out of the sinful mass of mankind some people have been chosen or ordained by God to eternal life, while others have been passed by and allowed to go on as they are and choose to be, as unbelievers and unrepentant sinners. Aside from God's call, there is no difference between the elect and the reprobate; all are sinners. Election is not a matter of mental capacity, moral rectitude, religious aptitude, or racial superiority: "All have sinned, and come short of the glory of God" (Rom. 3:23).

God's election serves His great purpose to glorify His Son as the Savior of sinners. The elect were given by the Father to the Son (John 6:37). Christ embraced them as His own and laid down His life to save them (John 10:11–15). By His Word and Holy Spirit He draws them to Himself, enlightening their minds and renewing their hearts and wills, enabling them to believe the gospel promise and turn from sin to serve Him in loving, thankful obedience.

The Bible declares, "Many are called, but few are chosen" (Matt. 22:14). In the vocabulary of the Westminster divines, all those who hear the gospel are called, but only some are called effectually (Westminster Confession of Faith, ch. 10). The outward call of the gospel must be accompanied by an inward work of divine grace in the hearts of the elect.

3 And I was with you in weakness, and in fear,
and in much trembling.
4 And my speech and my preaching *was* not with
enticing words of man's wisdom, but in demon-
stration of the Spirit and of power:
5 That your faith should not stand in the wisdom
of men, but in the power of God.
6 Howbeit we speak wisdom among them that
are perfect: yet not the wisdom of this world, nor
of the princes of this world, that come to nought:
7 But we speak the wisdom of God in a mystery,
even the hidden *wisdom*, which God ordained
before the world unto our glory:
8 Which none of the princes of this world knew:
for had they known *it*, they would not have cruci-
fied the Lord of glory.
9 But as it is written, Eye hath not seen, nor ear
heard, neither have entered into the heart of man,
the things which God hath prepared for them that
love him.
10 But God hath revealed *them* unto us by his
Spirit: for the Spirit searcheth all things, yea, the
deep things of God.
11 For what man knoweth the things of a man, save
the spirit of man which is in him? even so the things
of God knoweth no man, but the Spirit of God.
12 Now we have received, not the spirit of the
world, but the spirit which is of God; that we might
know the things that are freely given to us of God.
13 Which things also we speak, not in the words
which man's wisdom teacheth, but which the
Holy Ghost teacheth; comparing spiritual things
with spiritual.
14 But the natural man receiveth not the things
of the Spirit of God: for they are foolishness unto
him: neither can he know *them*, because they are
spiritually discerned.
15 But he that is spiritual judgeth all things, yet he
himself is judged of no man.
16 For who hath known the mind of the Lord,
that he may instruct him? But we have the mind
of Christ.

CHAPTER 3

AND I, brethren, could not speak unto you as unto
spiritual, but as unto carnal, *even* as unto babes
in Christ.
2 I have fed you with milk, and not with meat:
for hitherto ye were not able *to bear it*, neither yet
now are ye able.
3 For ye are yet carnal: for whereas *there is* among
you envying, and strife, and divisions, are ye not
carnal, and walk as men?
4 For while one saith, I am of Paul; and another, I
am of Apollos; are ye not carnal?
5 Who then is Paul, and who *is* Apollos, but min-
isters by whom ye believed, even as the Lord gave
to every man?
6 I have planted, Apollos watered; but God gave
the increase.
7 So then neither is he that planteth any thing,

to enable human beings to discern the true nature of spiritual things.

2:1 *when I came to you.* See Acts 18:1–17 for the record of Paul's entrance to Corinth.

2:2–5 *save.* Except. *Jesus Christ, and him crucified.* Paul's sole desire entering into Corinth was to preach the message of the cross. It was not his desire to impress them with eloquence or sophisticated speech, lest their faith rest (*stand*) in his abilities as a speaker (*the wisdom of men*). Rather, he preached the gospel and depended on the Spirit for his hearers to experience the power of God.

2:6 *wisdom.* Refers to the wisdom of God, the message of the cross. *perfect.* Mature or spiritual.

2:7 *mystery.* That which is unknown apart from God revealing it. The gospel was God's hidden plan before the world began. In time He has revealed it, most clearly in Jesus Christ who was made for us to be wisdom (Eph. 3:3; Col. 1:26).

2:9–11 The gospel cannot be perceived by human beings apart from the illuminating grace of the Holy Spirit.

2:13 *comparing spiritual things with spiritual.* Literally, "comparing spiritual in spiritual." The context suggests that Paul is saying he speaks according to the Holy Spirit's teaching, that is, spiritual ideas with spiritual words. The things (*truth*) we preach, we preach not with men's words, but with the Spirit's words.

2:14 *natural man.* Man in his fallen state, as opposed to spiritual man.

Thoughts for Personal/Family Worship: Chapter 2

1. **This chapter teaches the necessity of the Holy Spirit's work in illuminating you to discern the gospel. If you are a believer in Christ, why should that truth motivate you to praise God?**
2. **Paul says that those who have received the Spirit are able to judge all things. Do you live daily in the awareness that the Spirit guides you? How can you evaluate all things in the light of the Spirit's ministry in your life?**
3. **Pray for the help of the Holy Spirit each time you open the Word, asking for guidance as you meditate on the Word, both personally and with family.**

Chapter 3: ***Paul addresses the nature of gospel ministry that builds the church, rebuking immature, divisive, and worldly thinking.***

3:1 *spiritual, but as unto carnal.* The Corinthian believers were spiritual because they had received the Holy Spirit. However, they were acting carnally, being driven by fleshly desires, and immature, as babes. This would certainly be a shock to them, as they perceived themselves to be mature spiritual people.

3:2 *hitherto.* Until now.

3:3 *yet carnal.* Paul justifies his claim that they are acting carnally by describing their behavior: envying, strife, and divisions. These things are not to characterize Christians.

The Nature of Gospel Ministry Resolves Division (3:5—4:21)

3:6 *planted . . . watered . . . increase.* Paul uses agricultural imagery to highlight the foolishness of developing factions around ministers. Any lasting success in ministry is God's doing. Therefore, He receives the glory.

neither he that watereth; but God that giveth the
increase.
8 Now he that planteth and he that watereth are
one: and every man shall receive his own reward
according to his own labour.
9 For we are labourers together with God: ye are
God's husbandry, *ye are* God's building.
10 According to the grace of God which is given
unto me, as a wise masterbuilder, I have laid the
foundation, and another buildeth thereon. But let
every man take heed how he buildeth thereupon.
11 For other foundation can no man lay than that
is laid, which is Jesus Christ.
12 Now if any man build upon this foundation
gold, silver, precious stones, wood, hay, stubble;
13 Every man's work shall be made manifest: for
the day shall declare it, because it shall be revealed
by fire; and the fire shall try every man's work of
what sort it is.
14 If any man's work abide which he hath built
thereupon, he shall receive a reward.
15 If any man's work shall be burned, he shall
suffer loss: but he himself shall be saved; yet so
as by fire.
16 Know ye not that ye are the temple of God,
and *that* the Spirit of God dwelleth in you?
17 If any man defile the temple of God, him shall
God destroy; for the temple of God is holy, which
temple ye are.
18 Let no man deceive himself. If any man among
you seemeth to be wise in this world, let him
become a fool, that he may be wise.
19 For the wisdom of this world is foolishness
with God. For it is written, He taketh the wise in
their own craftiness.
20 And again, The Lord knoweth the thoughts of
the wise, that they are vain.
21 Therefore let no man glory in men. For all
things are yours;
22 Whether Paul, or Apollos, or Cephas, or the
world, or life, or death, or things present, or things
to come; all are yours;
23 And ye are Christ's; and Christ *is* God's.

CHAPTER 4

LET a man so account of us, as of the ministers of
Christ, and stewards of the mysteries of God.
2 Moreover it is required in stewards, that a man
be found faithful.
3 But with me it is a very small thing that I should
be judged of you, or of man's judgment: yea, I
judge not mine own self.
4 For I know nothing by myself; yet am I not

3:9 *we are labourers together with God.* Literally, "we are fellow workers of God." Paul and Apollos are co-laborers in one ministry under God (v. 8). *ye are God's building.* Paul transitions from agricultural imagery (*husbandry*, that is farming) to architectural imagery (*building*). The imagery continues the element of partnership in the first metaphor, but here Paul will add the element of how one builds in the ministry.
3:10 *I have laid the foundation.* Paul's apostolic role in the founding of the church in Corinth. *another buildeth thereon.* Apollos continued the work that Paul started. Paul laid the foundation and Apollos builds the structure. These two works are not contrary one to another, but complementary.
3:11 *foundation.* The only true foundation is Jesus Christ. He appeals to the very message he wanted the Corinthians to know, Jesus Christ and Him crucified (2:2).
3:12–15 Paul addresses church leaders directly regarding how they build upon the foundation (although there is application for anyone who serves in the church). One can build upon the foundation with perishable materials: *wood, hay*, and *stubble.* Or one can build with imperishable materials: *gold, silver*, and *precious stones.* Every ministry will be evaluated because it *shall be revealed by fire.* The minister who builds according to God's Word will receive reward. *he himself shall be saved; yet so as by fire.* Though the leader who builds unwisely will suffer loss, if he is a true believer, his salvation is not lost.
3:16–17 *ye are the temple of God.* "Ye" is plural. The church corporately is the temple of God. The Spirit dwells in the church. If any man defile the temple of God, him shall God destroy. It is no small thing to trifle with the church of God.
3:18–20 Paul brings his arguments regarding the nature of the church ministry back to the contrast between worldly wisdom and true wisdom. If a believer is to be truly wise, he must be willing to be a fool according to the world (v. 18). Paul again cites the Old Testament (Job 5:13; Ps. 94:11) to remind them that God *taketh* (or catches) *the wise in their own craftiness,* and views their wisdom to be *vain.*
3:21–23 *all things are yours.* In Christ, all things belong to believers. It is folly to boast in one thing when all belong to you. God gave the church in Corinth Paul, Apollos, and Cephas for their benefit, not for them to create divisive factions. *ye are Christ's.* They belong to Christ, all of them, and so envying and strife should be cast away. *Christ is God's.* Being in Christ they have access to the source of all things, God Himself.

Thoughts for Personal/Family Worship: Chapter 3

1. **How do you view your minister? Do you pray for the minister(s) that God has given to you?**
2. **Talk through the significance of what it means that all things belong to believers in Christ (v. 22) and how that corrects worldly notions of entitlement.**
3. **If believers are the temple of God corporately, how should we live our lives? Pursuing holiness does not just benefit individuals, but has a corporate effect.**

Chapter 4: ***To resist divisions in the church, Paul identifies ministers as stewards, and calls the church to repudiate pride since all things come from God.***

4:1 *Let a man so account of us.* Let people regard or consider us. *ministers.* Servants working for and under the authority of Christ. *stewards.* Servants entrusted with someone else's possession. *mysteries of God.* God's revelation, including but not limited to the gospel.
4:2 *be found faithful.* The measure of a steward is not eloquence, craftiness, or ability, but faithfulness.
4:3 *it is a very small thing that I should be judged of you.* Paul was more conscious of and concerned for God's evaluation of him that he considered it of very little consequence that

hereby justified: but he that judgeth me is the Lord.
5 Therefore judge nothing before the time, until
the Lord come, who both will bring to light
the hidden things of darkness, and will make
manifest the counsels of the hearts: and then shall
every man have praise of God.
6 And these things, brethren, I have in a figure
transferred to myself and *to* Apollos for your
sakes; that ye might learn in us not to think *of men*
above that which is written, that no one of you be
puffed up for one against another.
7 For who maketh thee to differ *from another*?
and what hast thou that thou didst not receive?
now if thou didst receive *it*, why dost thou glory,
as if thou hadst not received *it*?
8 Now ye are full, now ye are rich, ye have reigned
as kings without us: and I would to God ye did
reign, that we also might reign with you.
9 For I think that God hath set forth us the apostles
last, as it were appointed to death: for we are made a
spectacle unto the world, and to angels, and to men.
10 We *are* fools for Christ's sake, but ye *are* wise
in Christ; we *are* weak, but ye *are* strong; ye *are*
honourable, but we *are* despised.
11 Even unto this present hour we both hunger,
and thirst, and are naked, and are buffeted, and
have no certain dwellingplace;
12 And labour, working with our own hands: be-
ing reviled, we bless; being persecuted, we suffer it:
13 Being defamed, we intreat: we are made as the
filth of the world, *and are* the offscouring of all
things unto this day.
14 I write not these things to shame you, but as
my beloved sons I warn *you*.
15 For though ye have ten thousand instructors in
Christ, yet *have ye* not many fathers: for in Christ
Jesus I have begotten you through the gospel.
16 Wherefore I beseech you, be ye followers of me.
17 For this cause have I sent unto you Timotheus,
who is my beloved son, and faithful in the Lord,
who shall bring you into remembrance of my
ways which be in Christ, as I teach every where in
every church.
18 Now some are puffed up, as though I would
not come to you.
19 But I will come to you shortly, if the Lord will,
and will know, not the speech of them which are
puffed up, but the power.
20 For the kingdom of God *is* not in word, but
in power.
21 What will ye? shall I come unto you with a rod,
or in love, and *in* the spirit of meekness?

CHAPTER 5

IT is reported commonly *that there is* fornica-
tion among you, and such fornication as is not
so much as named among the Gentiles, that one
should have his father's wife.
2 And ye are puffed up, and have not rather
mourned, that he that hath done this deed might
be taken away from among you.
3 For I verily, as absent in body, but present in
spirit, have judged already, as though I were pres-
ent, *concerning* him that hath so done this deed,
4 In the name of our Lord Jesus Christ, when
ye are gathered together, and my spirit, with the
power of our Lord Jesus Christ,

---

the Corinthian church was judging him. *or of man's judgment.* Literally, "man's day." The thought is of a human court.

4:4 *For I know nothing by myself.* Paul knew nothing against himself that would conclude he was unfaithful.

4:7 *who maketh thee to differ from another.* Who makes you different from someone else? Paul shows that glorying in self contradicts the reality that all we are and have come from God.

4:8 *Now ye are full, now ye are rich.* The Corinthians proudly thought they had reached ultimate status of reigning as kings—without Paul, Apollos, Cephas, etc.! *I would to God ye did reign, that we also might reign with you.* Paul expresses his desire that they would wait for him to catch up to them!

4:9–13 Paul describes the reality of life in the present age. While the Corinthians viewed themselves to have already arrived, Paul points to present suffering that he faces as an apostle having been *made a spectacle* (public show) *unto the world.* While the Corinthians consider themselves to be wise, strong, and honorable, Paul says he and his fellow laborers were *fools for Christ's sake . . . weak,* and *despised.*

4:14–15 *as my beloved sons.* Paul loved the Corinthians enough to warn them. He considered them his children in the faith. *not many fathers.* The church boasted in spiritual guides like Apollos and Cephas. Yet Paul reminded them that they only had one father. He says that in Christ he had begotten them through the gospel. They ought, therefore, to listen to his fatherly admonishing for their own benefit.

4:18 *Now some are puffed up.* Some proudly thought Paul was talking boastfully but would not actually come and visit them.

Thoughts for Personal/Family Worship: Chapter 4

1. **Consider your daily need of grace to grow in godliness. Learn from Paul's warning to the Corinthian church that we will not ever be at a place in this life where we can say, "I have finally arrived spiritually." What reminders have you had lately that you have not yet arrived?**
2. **Consider in your mind and with your family that all you and they have and are comes from God, and praise Him for His goodness and kindness.**

The Problems of Scandalous Sins (5:1—6:20)

Chapter 5: ***Paul confronts the sexual immorality present in the church and exhorts the church to take action.***

Failure to Discipline Sin (5:1–13)

5:1 *fornication . . . have his father's wife.* Sexual relations with his stepmother. This was such an extraordinary sin that the pagan Gentiles would not even tolerate it.

5:2 *And ye are puffed up.* What seems to be even more shocking to Paul than the sin itself was the arrogance of the church in not dealing with the sin.

5:3–5 *verily.* Truly. These verses are actually one lengthy sentence, addressing Paul's judgment (v. 3), Christ's authority

5 To deliver such an one unto Satan for the de-
struction of the flesh, that the spirit may be saved
in the day of the Lord Jesus.
6 Your glorying *is* not good. Know ye not that a
little leaven leaveneth the whole lump?
7 Purge out therefore the old leaven, that ye may
be a new lump, as ye are unleavened. For even
Christ our passover is sacrificed for us:
8 Therefore let us keep the feast, not with old
leaven, neither with the leaven of malice and
wickedness; but with the unleavened *bread* of
sincerity and truth.
9 I wrote unto you in an epistle not to company
with fornicators:
10 Yet not altogether with the fornicators of this
world, or with the covetous, or extortioners, or
with idolaters; for then must ye needs go out of
the world.
11 But now I have written unto you not to keep
company, if any man that is called a brother be a
fornicator, or covetous, or an idolater, or a railer,
or a drunkard, or an extortioner; with such an
one no not to eat.
12 For what have I to do to judge them also that
are without? do not ye judge them that are within?
13 But them that are without God judgeth.
Therefore put away from among yourselves that
wicked person.

CHAPTER 6

DARE any of you, having a matter against another,
go to law before the unjust, and not before the
saints?
2 Do ye not know that the saints shall judge the
world? and if the world shall be judged by you, are
ye unworthy to judge the smallest matters?
3 Know ye not that we shall judge angels? how
much more things that pertain to this life?
4 If then ye have judgments of things pertain-
ing to this life, set them to judge who are least
esteemed in the church.
5 I speak to your shame. Is it so, that there is not
a wise man among you? no, not one that shall be
able to judge between his brethren?
6 But brother goeth to law with brother, and that
before the unbelievers.
7 Now therefore there is utterly a fault among

(v. 4), and the church's action (v. 5). *absent in body, but present in spirit, have judged already.* Even though Paul was not physically with them, he judged the fornication to be contrary to God's will, and directed the church in taking action. All disciplinary action is done in the name of the Lord Jesus Christ, the church's ultimate authority. *deliver such an one unto Satan.* Excommunication of an unrepentant sinner from the fellowship of the church community (Matt. 18:17). The expelled sinner finds himself in Satan's realm, having been removed from the ordinary means of grace. *for the destruction of the flesh.* A difficult phrase, either referring to the sinful corruption of man, or the physical body, which often suffers from the consequences of sin. *that the spirit may be saved.* The goal of discipline, even excommunication, is always repentance and restoration.

5:6 *Your glorying is not good.* Paul returns to address the response of the church to the sin of fornication. *Know ye not.* Though boasting in their maturity, they acted in ignorance of what they should know from God's law. *a little leaven leaveneth the whole lump.* Only a small amount of yeast can influence a large amount of new dough, just as a little sin affects the whole body of believers.

5:7 *Purge out . . . the old leaven.* The church is to purge out all kinds of evil and behavior characteristic of the former life apart from Christ. *ye may be a new lump.* New creation in Christ (2 Cor. 5:17). Christ, our Passover Lamb, is sacrificed for us. Christ is the fulfillment of the Old Testament Passover rite (Ex. 12). The Jews removed all the old yeast (*leaven*) and consumed unleavened bread for a week. Christians are unleavened, having been sanctified in Christ (1:2). When He died for sin He put an end to sin (15:3; 2 Cor. 5:15). Christians are to live in light of that reality.

5:8 Christians figuratively keep the feast by living holy lives in sincerity and truth.

5:9 *I wrote unto you.* Paul had communicated with the Corinthian church in a letter prior to 1 Corinthians.

5:11–13 Paul clarifies what he said earlier about expelling a sinner from fellowship, noting that he had in mind those who professed to be a Christian, yet continued in sinful behavior. Those *without*, or outside of the church, he leaves to God to judge. *railer.* Abusive person.

Thoughts for Personal/Family Worship: Chapter 5

1. **Consider the sobering effects of sin. What are some examples of how sin not only affects the one who commits the sin, but also those who are connected to him/her, both family and church?**
2. **Meditate on the guilt-removing and life-transforming work of Christ's sacrifice. He is the true Passover, or Deliverer from bondage. If you are in Christ, things are fundamentally different. This reality ought to be remembered daily and depended upon experientially.**

Chapter 6: *Paul continues to address the subject of immorality, as well as professing believers bringing cases against other professing believers before unjust and unbelieving judges.*

Litigation between Church Members (6:1–8)

6:1 *matter against another.* Paul's concern with believers going before unjust and unbelieving judges does not extend to criminal matters; rather, it is regarding civil matters where one brother has wronged another (v. 7). Believers are to handle their own matters within the church (5:12).

6:2–3 *Know ye not.* Rebuke for what they should already know (see Introduction: Synopsis). *the saints shall judge the world.* When the kingdom is consummated, God's people will participate with Christ in judging unbelievers and the angels. Why then would they appeal to unbelievers in this life to judge between Christians?

6:4 *judgments of things pertaining to this life.* Lawsuits in everyday matters, common things having to do with life. *least esteemed in the church.* Could be interpreted either as a statement about those within the Christian church, or more likely, as sarcasm, asking why they go to pagans, those who are least esteemed by the church.

6:6 This is a summary of the problem; one brother is going to

you, because ye go to law one with another. Why do ye not rather take wrong? why do ye not rather *suffer yourselves to* be defrauded?
8 Nay, ye do wrong, and defraud, and that *your* brethren.
9 Know ye not that the unrighteous shall not inherit the kingdom of God? Be not deceived: neither fornicators, nor idolaters, nor adulterers, nor effeminate, nor abusers of themselves with mankind,
10 Nor thieves, nor covetous, nor drunkards, nor revilers, nor extortioners, shall inherit the kingdom of God.
11 And such were some of you: but ye are washed, but ye are sanctified, but ye are justified in the name of the Lord Jesus, and by the Spirit of our God.
12 All things are lawful unto me, but all things are not expedient: all things are lawful for me, but I will not be brought under the power of any.
13 Meats for the belly, and the belly for meats: but God shall destroy both it and them. Now the body *is* not for fornication, but for the Lord; and the Lord for the body.
14 And God hath both raised up the Lord, and will also raise up us by his own power.
15 Know ye not that your bodies are the members of Christ? shall I then take the members of Christ, and make *them* the members of an harlot? God forbid.
16 What? know ye not that he which is joined to an harlot is one body? for two, saith he, shall be one flesh.
17 But he that is joined unto the Lord is one spirit.
18 Flee fornication. Every sin that a man doeth is without the body; but he that committeth fornication sinneth against his own body.
19 What? know ye not that your body is the temple of the Holy Ghost *which is* in you, which ye have of God, and ye are not your own?
20 For ye are bought with a price: therefore glorify God in your body, and in your spirit, which are God's.

CHAPTER 7

NOW concerning the things whereof ye wrote unto me: *It is* good for a man not to touch a woman.

---

law against another and so dishonoring the Lord in the eyes of unbelievers.

6:7 *take wrong . . . be defrauded.* One problem that manifested itself in various ways in the Corinthian church was petty pride. Here Paul calls the believers to be more willing to suffer wrong for the sake of the body than to see an injustice righted immediately and ruin the testimony of the church. He has already reminded them of Judgment Day, when all wrongs will be made right after all is said and done. This therefore is not a tolerance for injustice, but Christian patience and hope.

6:8 Even if a Christian feels he has been wronged by a brother, taking a brother to court before unbelievers is a scandal that does wrong to the unity of the body.

Sin, the Kingdom, and Salvation (6:9–11)

6:9–10 Paul makes a stark contrast between pagans and the church to highlight the scandals addressed in chs. 5–6, and to call professing believers to repentance over sin. *unrighteous.* Those who do not turn from sin to God in Christ. *shall not inherit the kingdom.* Will have no place in God's glory when Christ returns, but will suffer God's wrath (Matt. 25:34,41; Eph. 5:5–6). *fornicators.* Sexually immoral. *effeminate, nor abusers of themselves with mankind.* Passive and active participants in homosexual sex. *revilers.* Verbally abusive person (same word as "railer," 5:11).

6:11 Paul reminds the Corinthian church again who they are in Christ and by the Spirit. *washed.* Cleansed from sin (Ps. 51:2,7). *sanctified.* Made holy and sacred by God's holiness in Christ (1:2). *justified.* Declared righteous by God with respect to the law (Rom. 2:13; 3:19–26). They must be who they are, not what they used to be.

Sexual Promiscuity (6:12–20)

6:12 *All things are lawful unto me.* Paul cites this slogan twice in this verse and twice in 10:23. The Corinthians were repeating this in justification for their twisting of Christian liberty into license for sin, particularly in matters of a sexual nature. Christian liberty is limited by the moral law, and also by what is profitable (*expedient*) and what does not bring one under the control (*power*) of anything, for Christians are not their own, but were bought by the Lord (vv. 19–20).

6:13–14 *Meats* (food) *for the belly, and the belly for meats.* Another slogan the Corinthians used to justify sexual sin. *God shall destroy.* This world will pass away, and sin will fall under judgment. *the body is . . . for the Lord.* Union with Christ makes the Christian's body a sacred object, destined for resurrection and glory (ch. 15).

6:15–17 Paul again draws their attention to their union with Christ by the Holy Spirit (*one spirit*) and its ethical ramifications. As a result, their bodies are the members of Christ. It is unthinkable, then, to join the members of Christ to a prostitute (*harlot*). The Corinthians seemed to think that what they did in their body did not affect their spiritual state, but in fact sexual sins contradict their union with Christ.

6:18 *Flee fornication.* Like Joseph fleeing Potiphar's wife (Gen. 39:12). Flee is in the present tense. Believers are to be vigilant daily in consciously fleeing from sexual temptations in its many forms. Other sins are done outside the body. However, when one commits fornication he sins against his own body.

6:19 *your body is the temple of the Holy Ghost.* "Your body" is singular (compare with 3:16, "ye are the temple of God"). The Holy Spirit indwells each believer as His holy place: the theological basis behind the command to flee sexual immorality. *ye are not your own.* We do not claim ownership of our own bodies. We are to be wise stewards of the bodies we have been given (stewardship is an important element in Paul's discussion of a faithful ministry in 4:1).

Thoughts for Personal/Family Worship: Chapter 6

1. If there has been a wrong done, how do you pursue reconciliation with another believer in your church or another member in your family?

2. How does the believer's union with Christ affect his or her daily living? Chapter 6 works out in detail the relationship between doctrine and practice. Paul draws the reader's attention to objective truths, or indicatives: you have been washed, you have been sanctified, you have been justified, your bodies are members of Christ, and your

2 Nevertheless, *to avoid* fornication, let every
man have his own wife, and let every woman have
her own husband.
3 Let the husband render unto the wife due be-
nevolence: and likewise also the wife unto the
husband.
4 The wife hath not power of her own body, but
the husband: and likewise also the husband hath
not power of his own body, but the wife.
5 Defraud ye not one the other, except *it be* with
consent for a time, that ye may give yourselves to
fasting and prayer; and come together again, that
Satan tempt you not for your incontinency.
6 But I speak this by permission, *and* not of
commandment.
7 For I would that all men were even as I myself.
But every man hath his proper gift of God, one
after this manner, and another after that.
8 I say therefore to the unmarried and widows, It
is good for them if they abide even as I.
9 But if they cannot contain, let them marry: for
it is better to marry than to burn.
10 And unto the married I command, *yet* not I,
but the Lord, Let not the wife depart from *her*
husband:
11 But and if she depart, let her remain unmar-
ried, or be reconciled to *her* husband: and let not
the husband put away *his* wife.
12 But to the rest speak I, not the Lord: If any
brother hath a wife that believeth not, and she be
pleased to dwell with him, let him not put her away.
13 And the woman which hath an husband that
believeth not, and if he be pleased to dwell with
her, let her not leave him.
14 For the unbelieving husband is sanctified by
the wife, and the unbelieving wife is sanctified by
the husband: else were your children unclean; but
now are they holy.
15 But if the unbelieving depart, let him depart.
A brother or a sister is not under bondage in such
cases: but God hath called us to peace.
16 For what knowest thou, O wife, whether thou
shalt save *thy* husband? or how knowest thou, O
man, whether thou shalt save *thy* wife?
17 But as God hath distributed to every man, as
the Lord hath called every one, so let him walk.
And so ordain I in all churches.
18 Is any man called being circumcised? let
him not become uncircumcised. Is any called in
uncircumcision? let him not be circumcised.
19 Circumcision is nothing, and uncircumci-
sion is nothing, but the keeping of the command-
ments of God.
20 Let every man abide in the same calling
wherein he was called.
21 Art thou called *being* a servant? care not for

body is the temple of the Holy Ghost. He then gives a command: flee fornication. What is the relationship between what you are in Christ and the importance of purity?

ANSWERS TO QUESTIONS FROM CORINTHIAN CHURCH (7:1—16:4)

Chapter 7: *Paul addresses questions from the Corinthian congregation, beginning with that of marriage, divorce, and contentment with one's current status.*

Concerning Marriage, Divorce, the Unmarried, and Widows (7:1–40)

7:1 *Now concerning.* Paul addresses the issues raised by their correspondence with him (v. 25; 8:1; 12:1; 16:1). *It is good for a man not to touch a woman.* Paul repeats a phrase used by some within the Corinthian church who took a stand that Christians abstain from marriage and even sexual activity within marriage. He does not intend to show that marriage is wrong (1 Tim. 4:3). Rather, he teaches spouses how to live selflessly in marriage (vv. 2–5), and why singleness might be preferred given one's present circumstances (vv. 25–40).

7:2 *Nevertheless.* While singleness might be preferred in some cases, Paul addresses here the wisdom of marriage. *to avoid fornication.* Marriage is a God-given safeguard against immorality. To guard against sin, let every man have relations with his own wife and every woman with her own husband.

7:3 *render . . . due benevolence.* Each spouse is to perform their duties of sexual love to the other, rather than claiming their own rights.

7:4 *power of . . . body.* Husband and wife do not coexist independently; they exist as one flesh (Gen. 2:24) and share their bodies to serve each other.

7:5 *Defraud ye not one the other.* Each spouse is not to deprive the other of marital intimacy. The phrase from v. 1, "it is good for a man not to touch a woman," does not apply to marriage. *except it be with consent for a time.* Paul acknowledges that there will be times of abstinence within marriage, but notes that it is with consent, that is, both spouses agree to it. The abstinence is not permanent, but for a specified time. He gives reasons for such abstaining: *fasting and prayer.* And Paul repeats one purpose of returning to regular intimacy, namely, *that Satan tempt you not for your incontinency* (lack of self-control).

7:6 *But I speak this by permission.* Paul's concession here is linked directly to what precedes in v. 5. He is not conceding that marriage is good; for marriage was instituted by God as good. He is conceding that there may be a time for temporary abstinence in marriage; he is not commanding it.

7:7–9 Paul encourages contentment with one's present calling, pointing to himself as an example. Yet, if one is not able to remain in such a state of singleness without being able to control (*contain*) his sexual desires, Paul repeats his point, *it is better to marry* (v. 2).

7:10–16 Paul instructs the married to remain in their position. Marriage is intended to be permanent.

7:10 *not I, but the Lord.* Paul reiterates Christ's express command for the permanency of marriage (Matt. 5:32; 19:3–9; Mark 10:2–12; Luke 16:18).

7:12–16 Paul addresses marriage with one believing and one unbelieving spouse.

7:12 *speak I, not the Lord.* Paul is not advising something contrary to Christ's teaching, but addressing a situation that Christ did not specifically address. Paul encourages the believer to remain in the marriage and seek peace. *not put her away.* If the unbelieving spouse is pleased to remain in the marriage, then the believer should not divorce her.

7:14 *sanctified.* The home of a believer is set apart as for blessing before God, even the unbelieving spouse and children.

it: but if thou mayest be made free, use *it* rather.
22 For he that is called in the Lord, *being* a
servant, is the Lord's freeman: likewise also he
that is called, *being* free, is Christ's servant.
23 Ye are bought with a price; be not ye the
servants of men.
24 Brethren, let every man, wherein he is called,
therein abide with God.
25 Now concerning virgins I have no commandment of the Lord: yet I give my judgment, as
one that hath obtained mercy of the Lord to be
faithful.
26 I suppose therefore that this is good for the present distress, *I say*, that *it is* good for a man so to be.
27 Art thou bound unto a wife? seek not to be
loosed. Art thou loosed from a wife? seek not a
wife.
28 But and if thou marry, thou hast not sinned;
and if a virgin marry, she hath not sinned.
Nevertheless such shall have trouble in the flesh:
but I spare you.
29 But this I say, brethren, the time *is* short: it
remaineth, that both they that have wives be as
though they had none;
30 And they that weep, as though they wept not;
and they that rejoice, as though they rejoiced not;
and they that buy, as though they possessed not;
31 And they that use this world, as not abusing *it*:
for the fashion of this world passeth away.
32 But I would have you without carefulness.
He that is unmarried careth for the things that
belong to the Lord, how he may please the Lord:
33 But he that is married careth for the things
that are of the world, how he may please *his* wife.
34 There is difference *also* between a wife and a virgin. The unmarried woman careth for the things of
the Lord, that she may be holy both in body and in
spirit: but she that is married careth for the things
of the world, how she may please *her* husband.
35 And this I speak for your own profit; not that
I may cast a snare upon you, but for that which
is comely, and that ye may attend upon the Lord
without distraction.
36 But if any man think that he behaveth himself
uncomely toward his virgin, if she pass the flower
of *her* age, and need so require, let him do what he
will, he sinneth not: let them marry.
37 Nevertheless he that standeth stedfast in his
heart, having no necessity, but hath power over
his own will, and hath so decreed in his heart that
he will keep his virgin, doeth well.
38 So then he that giveth *her* in marriage doeth
well; but he that giveth *her* not in marriage doeth
better.
39 The wife is bound by the law as long as her
husband liveth; but if her husband be dead, she
is at liberty to be married to whom she will; only
in the Lord.
40 But she is happier if she so abide, after my judgment: and I think also that I have the Spirit of God.

CHAPTER 8

NOW as touching things offered unto idols, we
know that we all have knowledge. Knowledge
puffeth up, but charity edifieth.

7:15 *let him depart.* If the unbelieving spouse is not willing to remain, the believing husband or wife is to let the unbelieving spouse depart. Again, the Christian is to pursue peace always.
7:17–24 God calls people to Himself who find themselves in various circumstances of life. Paul exhorts them not to seek another calling once God converts them (v. 20). What matters is obeying God's commands (v. 18). If a servant, don't concern yourself with it, but pursue freedom if it is available. The point Paul is making is that if God called you while married, don't seek to be unmarried. *wherein he is called, therein abide.* Remain in the calling in which you were called (v. 24).
7:25–40 Paul addresses the unmarried and the widows.
7:25 *Now concerning virgins.* Though debated, most likely females of marriageable age who have not been married. The Corinthian slogan of "it is good for a man not to touch a woman" (v. 1) suggests that they encouraged others not to marry. *no commandment of the Lord . . . my judgment.* Paul again addresses a specific issue that is not directly mentioned by Christ, speaking by the authority given him by God's mercy.
7:26 *present distress.* Most likely the persecution that Christians faced for their faith (15:30–31), a practical reason why single persons might refrain from marriage.
7:28 *if thou marry, thou hast not sinned . . . Nevertheless such shall have trouble in the flesh.* Paul acknowledges that circumstances factor in the determination of what one ought to do. While the decision to marry even in the present distress is not sin, it still will present its own difficulties because of the difficult circumstances.
7:32–35 *carefulness.* Anxiety. Singleness provides opportunity for the believer to give undivided devotion to the Lord. Paul is not against marriage, but he does speak honestly about the necessary concerns spouses may add to temporal matters.
7:36–37 *uncomely.* In an inappropriate manner. *pass the flower of her age.* Past marriageable age with reference to the virgin. In v. 37, Paul says if the man is able to stand firm and have power over his will, he does well not to marry.
7:39–40 Paul summarizes his argument. Marriage is permanent. If one spouse dies, there is liberty for the widow(er) to marry. *only in the Lord.* A single Christian must marry in the Lord, that is, a believer. Paul's comment does not contradict his earlier statements regarding a marriage between one believing spouse and an unbeliever.

Thoughts for Personal/Family Worship: Chapter 7

1. **The grace of Christian contentment pervades Paul's entire argument. Are you enjoying contentment in your current calling? If single, are you content? If married, are you contentedly relating to your spouse in selfless ways?**
2. **God's providential orchestration of your circumstances is His will for you. How do you factor in God's providence in your decision-making process?**

Concerning Conscience regarding Meat Offered to Idols (8:1—11:1)

2 And if any man think that he knoweth any thing,
he knoweth nothing yet as he ought to know.
3 But if any man love God, the same is known
of him.
4 As concerning therefore the eating of those
things that are offered in sacrifice unto idols, we
know that an idol *is* nothing in the world, and
that *there is* none other God but one.
5 For though there be that are called gods,
whether in heaven or in earth, (as there be gods
many, and lords many,)
6 But to us *there is but* one God, the Father, of
whom *are* all things, and we in him; and one Lord
Jesus Christ, by whom *are* all things, and we by him.
7 Howbeit *there is* not in every man that knowl-
edge: for some with conscience of the idol unto
this hour eat *it* as a thing offered unto an idol; and
their conscience being weak is defiled.
8 But meat commendeth us not to God: for
neither, if we eat, are we the better; neither, if we
eat not, are we the worse.
9 But take heed lest by any means this liberty of
yours become a stumblingblock to them that are
weak.
10 For if any man see thee which hast knowledge
sit at meat in the idol's temple, shall not the con-
science of him which is weak be emboldened to
eat those things which are offered to idols;
11 And through thy knowledge shall the weak
brother perish, for whom Christ died?
12 But when ye sin so against the brethren, and
wound their weak conscience, ye sin against
Christ.
13 Wherefore, if meat make my brother to offend,
I will eat no flesh while the world standeth, lest I
make my brother to offend.

CHAPTER 9

AM I not an apostle? am I not free? have I not seen
Jesus Christ our Lord? are not ye my work in the
Lord?
2 If I be not an apostle unto others, yet doubtless
I am to you: for the seal of mine apostleship are
ye in the Lord.
3 Mine answer to them that do examine me is this,
4 Have we not power to eat and to drink?
5 Have we not power to lead about a sister, a wife,
as well as other apostles, and *as* the brethren of
the Lord, and Cephas?
6 Or I only and Barnabas, have not we power to
forbear working?
7 Who goeth a warfare any time at his own
charges? who planteth a vineyard, and eateth not
of the fruit thereof? or who feedeth a flock, and
eateth not of the milk of the flock?
8 Say I these things as a man? or saith not the law
the same also?

Chapter 8: *Paul introduces the second subject raised from the Corinthian's letter, food offered to idols.*

Importance of Conscience (8:1–13)

8:1 *we all have knowledge.* The Corinthian church boasted in the knowledge they believed they had. Paul notes that knowledge alone fills men with pride (*puffeth up*), maintaining that there must also be love which builds up (*charity edifieth*).
8:4–5 *we know that an idol is nothing . . . and that there is none other God but one.* Scripture is clear that false gods are no gods at all (Ps. 96:5).
8:6 There is only one true God, who made all things for His glory (Rom. 11:36). The words "God" and "Lord" are both used in the Old Testament as divine titles for the Creator (Gen. 1–2), so Paul indicates the full deity of both the Father and His Son, our Lord Jesus Christ (Rom. 9:5; Phil. 2:6; Col. 2:9). Since there is only one God, the Father and Son share one divine essence (John 10:30). However, Paul distinguishes between the persons in the Trinity: the Father is first in order (*of whom*) and He shares all His divine works with His Son (*by whom*, John 5:17–20).
8:7 *Howbeit.* But. *there is not in every man that knowledge.* Evidently some Christians in Corinth had consciences that could not grasp the nothingness of idols. Their weak conscience would not permit them to eat food offered to an idol.
8:8 *meat.* Food of any kind. *commendeth us not to God.* A believer is not more holy, or better, if he eats. Nor is a believer worse if he does not eat.
8:9–10 Since meat does not commend a believer to God and the believer's actions must be governed by both knowledge and love, a Christian should be willing to set aside liberty for the sake of a weaker brother or sister. *stumblingblock.* Obstacle that causes one to trip or sin. *emboldened to eat.* One with a weaker conscience is moved against his conscience to eat because of the act of one who is strong.
8:11–12 *perish.* Paul is not saying that a weaker brother can lose his salvation. Yet, the stronger believer must be concerned not to wound the conscience of a weaker brother. To cause another believer to sin, or to wound another's conscience is to sin against Christ.
8:13 *make . . . to offend.* Cause to sin. Paul, motivated by love, announces that he would rather set aside a liberty permanently rather than cause another to sin.

Thoughts for Personal/Family Worship: Chapter 8

1. **How do you view Christian liberty? As something that you have to do? Do you couple your knowledge regarding liberties with love for the brethren?**
2. **If Christ died for the believer with a weak conscience, how should we view such a person? The reality of the atonement ought to govern and dictate how believers view each other.**
3. **Consider all that you know by God's grace. Why is it important that your knowledge be coupled with love?**

Chapter 9: *Paul uses a personal illustration on the importance of setting aside his rights for a greater purpose.*

Personal Illustration from Apostolic Rights (9:1–27)

9:1 *have I not seen Jesus Christ our Lord.* Paul validates his claim of apostleship. *are not ye my work in the Lord.* The evidence of Paul's apostolic ministry among them is the Corinthian church itself.
9:3–5 *them that do examine me.* There were members of the Corinthian church that questioned Paul's authority. *power.*

9 For it is written in the law of Moses, Thou shalt
not muzzle the mouth of the ox that treadeth out
the corn. Doth God take care for oxen?
10 Or saith he *it* altogether for our sakes? For
our sakes, no doubt, *this* is written: that he that
ploweth should plow in hope; and that he that
thresheth in hope should be partaker of his hope.
11 If we have sown unto you spiritual things, *is it*
a great thing if we shall reap your carnal things?
12 If others be partakers of *this* power over you,
are not we rather? Nevertheless we have not used
this power; but suffer all things, lest we should
hinder the gospel of Christ.
13 Do ye not know that they which minister
about holy things live *of the things* of the temple?
and they which wait at the altar are partakers with
the altar?
14 Even so hath the Lord ordained that they
which preach the gospel should live of the gospel.
15 But I have used none of these things: neither
have I written these things, that it should be so
done unto me: for *it were* better for me to die,
than that any man should make my glorying void.
16 For though I preach the gospel, I have nothing
to glory of: for necessity is laid upon me; yea, woe
is unto me, if I preach not the gospel!
17 For if I do this thing willingly, I have a reward:
but if against my will, a dispensation *of the gospel*
is committed unto me.
18 What is my reward then? *Verily* that, when
I preach the gospel, I may make the gospel of
Christ without charge, that I abuse not my power
in the gospel.
19 For though I be free from all *men*, yet have I
made myself servant unto all, that I might gain
the more.
20 And unto the Jews I became as a Jew, that I
might gain the Jews; to them that are under the
law, as under the law, that I might gain them that
are under the law;
21 To them that are without law, as without law,
(being not without law to God, but under the law
to Christ,) that I might gain them that are with-
out law.
22 To the weak became I as weak, that I might
gain the weak: I am made all things to all *men*,
that I might by all means save some.
23 And this I do for the gospel's sake, that I might
be partaker thereof with *you*.
24 Know ye not that they which run in a race run
all, but one receiveth the prize? So run, that ye
may obtain.
25 And every man that striveth for the mastery is
temperate in all things. Now they *do it* to obtain a
corruptible crown; but we an incorruptible.
26 I therefore so run, not as uncertainly; so fight
I, not as one that beateth the air:
27 But I keep under my body, and bring *it* into

Paul had rights or liberties as an apostle. The example he gives is marriage. Cephas, or Peter, was married. This is an important comment from the apostle for those who claim the necessity of clerical celibacy.

9:6–7 *have not we power to forbear working.* A minister has the right to be paid by the people to whom he ministers. Paul had the right to receive support from the Corinthian church, but he supported himself as a tentmaker (Acts 18:3). He cites examples from military and agricultural life to support his claim.

9:8–11 Paul further supports his argument by noting that not only secular law suggests the same, but Old Testament law as well (Deut. 25:4; cf. 1 Tim. 5:18). He *that ploweth* should do so with hope, or expectation, of reward. Paul remarks that he has sown to them spiritual things. How great of a thing is it, then, to be rewarded with temporal things for the care of his body?

9:12 *we have not used this power.* The apostle interjects here with a statement that foreshadows his conclusion, which will be stated fully in v. 15. Paul did not demand his right to receive support that the gospel of Christ not be hindered.

9:13 He provides more Old Testament evidence to support his argument that he has a right to be supported (Lev. 6:16,26; 7:6). *live.* Literally, "to feed."

9:15–16 *I have used none of these things.* Paul has cataloged several arguments to conclusively demonstrate his right to receive support. Yet, he set his rights aside for the sake of preaching the gospel. He did not want to be accused of preaching for money, nor could it be said that he preached for any reason other than the will of God.

9:17 *willingly.* Paul was not coerced to set aside his right. If so, that would make his argument null and void. He willingly set aside his liberty. *dispensation.* Paul describes his ministry as one of a stewardship (4:1).

9:18 *Verily.* Truly.

9:20–22 *I became as a Jew.* When ministering to Jews, Paul adopted Jewish customs that he did not consider to be essential for the sake of preaching the gospel. *to them that are under the law.* When ministering to Gentiles, Paul lived as one without the law. Lest he be confused as disregarding God's moral law and justifying sin, he adds *being not without law to God, but under the law to Christ.* Paul makes a distinction between the Jewish rituals and the enduring moral law (7:19). *To the weak.* In ministering to those who were weak, Paul took care not to harm the conscience. This last example certainly would have been understood in the Corinthian church as this serves as an illustration of how the strong and the weak are to live at peace in the church, even regarding food offered to idols (8:9–13).

9:23 *this I do for the gospel's sake.* For Paul, the gospel is more important than his own rights and liberties. This is to be true of all believers.

9:24–27 After Paul concludes his argument from a personal illustration, he introduces an illustration from Greek athletics.

9:24 *So run, that ye may obtain.* Paul uses the illustration to picture the Christian life as a race. He encourages believers to run with the focus and determination that a runner implements in competition. A Christian is to live life with the end goal in mind.

9:25 *every man that striveth for the mastery is temperate.* The competitor is described as one who strives or fights. The contestant does not take the race lightly. The athlete takes training seriously, even depriving self of excess. Christians, like athletes, are to exercise self-control, keeping the goal in mind.

9:26 *not as one that beateth the air.* A boxer maximizes energy

subjection: lest that by any means, when I have
preached to others, I myself should be a castaway.

CHAPTER 10

MOREOVER, brethren, I would not that ye should
be ignorant, how that all our fathers were under
the cloud, and all passed through the sea;
2 And were all baptized unto Moses in the cloud
and in the sea;
3 And did all eat the same spiritual meat;
4 And did all drink the same spiritual drink: for
they drank of that spiritual Rock that followed
them: and that Rock was Christ.
5 But with many of them God was not well
pleased: for they were overthrown in the wilder-
ness.
6 Now these things were our examples, to the
intent we should not lust after evil things, as they
also lusted.
7 Neither be ye idolaters, as *were* some of them;
as it is written, The people sat down to eat and
drink, and rose up to play.
8 Neither let us commit fornication, as some of
them committed, and fell in one day three and
twenty thousand.
9 Neither let us tempt Christ, as some of them
also tempted, and were destroyed of serpents.
10 Neither murmur ye, as some of them also
murmured, and were destroyed of the destroyer.
11 Now all these things happened unto them for
ensamples: and they are written for our admoni-
tion, upon whom the ends of the world are come.
12 Wherefore let him that thinketh he standeth
take heed lest he fall.
13 There hath no temptation taken you but such
as is common to man: but God *is* faithful, who
will not suffer you to be tempted above that ye are
able; but will with the temptation also make a way
to escape, that ye may be able to bear *it*.
14 Wherefore, my dearly beloved, flee from
idolatry.
15 I speak as to wise men; judge ye what I say.
16 The cup of blessing which we bless, is it not
the communion of the blood of Christ? The
bread which we break, is it not the communion

---

by landing punches on the target, not aimlessly punching the air. Paul seeks to maximize his ministry opportunities, seeing many people come to Christ through his preaching.

9:27 *keep under my body.* To give oneself a black eye. Paul inverts the boxing image and says his opponent is himself. He exercises self-denial and self-discipline, both to advance the gospel and for his own ultimate salvation (Phil. 2:12–13; 3:8–14). *castaway.* Tested and rejected as worthless. Without self-denial, there is no following Christ to gain eternal life (Luke 9:23–26).

Thoughts for Personal/Family Worship: Chapter 9

1. **Do you love your liberties more than you love your brothers? Paul openly acknowledged the liberties and rights he had as an apostle and minister of the gospel. Yet, he was willing to set his liberties aside for the sake of something greater, the gospel of Jesus Christ.**
2. **Are you running the Christian race? If so, how does the Christian race play itself out in your life and in the lives of your family? How are you showing that the gospel of Jesus Christ reigns supreme in your affections as you seek to run the race before you?**

Warnings against Idolatry and Call to Glorify God (10:1—11:1)

Chapter 10: *Paul warns the Corinthians of the peril of idolatry, reminding them of Israel's history, and concludes with counsel on matters of conscience.*

10:1–5 Paul issues a warning from history to show that not all who experience benefits finish well. Rather than introduce a completely new topic, the example of Israel's history logically follows what he previously said regarding running well to obtain the prize. Notice the five "alls" in the first four verses. Israel, the people of God, all experienced incredible privileges, yet with many of them God was not pleased.

10:1 *our fathers.* Paul highlights the continuity between Israel as the people of God and the church (made of both Jews and Greeks) as the people of God.

10:2 *all baptized unto Moses.* God delivered Israel by leading them out of Egypt through Moses and parting the Red Sea (Ex. 12–14). Their passage through the waters is compared to Christian baptism, by which members of the church are identified with Christ.

10:3–5 *spiritual meat* (food) . . . *spiritual drink.* The provision of manna and water in the wilderness (Ex. 16–17) is compared to the Lord's Supper (v. 16). *Rock.* The stone cliff which Moses struck to get water for Israel (Ex. 17:6). *followed them.* The Lord is called the Rock of Israel (Deut. 32:4). Paul identified Him with Christ before His incarnation. *But with many of them God was not well pleased.* Likewise, being baptized and participating in the Lord's Supper does not guarantee eternal life.

10:6 *examples.* Literally, "types."

10:7 *The people sat down to eat and drink.* When worshiping the golden calf (Ex. 32:6). Some of the Corinthians considered it their liberty not only to eat meat offered to idols, but also to do so in a pagan temple.

10:11 *Now all these things happened unto them for ensamples.* Paul repeats the sentiment of v. 6, that all these events of Israel's history happened as ensamples, or examples, or types for believers later.

10:12 *thinketh he standeth take heed lest he fall.* Some in the Corinthian church were puffed up with pride. All Christians, especially those who believe they are strong, ought not to rely on self. Self-reliance and self-confidence end with a great fall.

10:13 Paul encourages Christians in two ways regarding temptations: (1) *God is faithful* and *will not suffer* (literally, "to let" or "to permit") believers to be tempted above what they can endure, and (2) God demonstrates His faithfulness by providing a way of escape. God is sovereign over the weight of temptation and the escape from temptation. A Christian has only himself to blame when he sins.

10:14 *flee from idolatry.* Paul succinctly drives home his concern for the Corinthian church. While idols in themselves are nothing because there is one true God (8:4–6), participation in pagan feasts is something, namely, idolatry. Christians are not to have anything to do with idolatry.

10:16 *cup of blessing . . . bread which we break.* Paul mentions

of the body of Christ?
17 For we *being* many are one bread, *and* one
body: for we are all partakers of that one bread.
18 Behold Israel after the flesh: are not they which
eat of the sacrifices partakers of the altar?
19 What say I then? that the idol is any thing, or
that which is offered in sacrifice to idols is any
thing?
20 But *I say*, that the things which the Gentiles
sacrifice, they sacrifice to devils, and not to God:
and I would not that ye should have fellowship
with devils.
21 Ye cannot drink the cup of the Lord, and the
cup of devils: ye cannot be partakers of the Lord's
table, and of the table of devils.
22 Do we provoke the Lord to jealousy? are we
stronger than he?
23 All things are lawful for me, but all things are
not expedient: all things are lawful for me, but all
things edify not.
24 Let no man seek his own, but every man an-
other's *wealth*.
25 Whatsoever is sold in the shambles, *that* eat,
asking no question for conscience sake:
26 For the earth *is* the Lord's, and the fulness
thereof.
27 If any of them that believe not bid you *to a feast*,
and ye be disposed to go; whatsoever is set before
you, eat, asking no question for conscience sake.
28 But if any man say unto you, This is offered
in sacrifice unto idols, eat not for his sake that
shewed it, and for conscience sake: for the earth *is*
the Lord's, and the fulness thereof:
29 Conscience, I say, not thine own, but of the
other: for why is my liberty judged of another
man's conscience?
30 For if I by grace be a partaker, why am I evil
spoken of for that for which I give thanks?
31 Whether therefore ye eat, or drink, or whatso-
ever ye do, do all to the glory of God.
32 Give none offence, neither to the Jews, nor to
the Gentiles, nor to the church of God:
33 Even as I please all *men* in all *things*, not
seeking mine own profit, but the *profit* of many,
that they may be saved.

CHAPTER 11

BE ye followers of me, even as I also *am* of Christ.
2 Now I praise you, brethren, that ye remember
me in all things, and keep the ordinances, as I
delivered *them* to you.
3 But I would have you know, that the head of
every man is Christ; and the head of the woman *is*
the man; and the head of Christ *is* God.
4 Every man praying or prophesying, having *his*
head covered, dishonoureth his head.
5 But every woman that prayeth or prophesieth

---

the Lord's Supper to show that participating in a religious meal involves more than just partaking of the elements of the meal. When a believer partakes of the bread and the wine there is a very real fellowship and association (*communion*) with Jesus Christ.

10:18 *partakers.* From the same root as "communion" (v. 16). Israelites were sharers or partners with the altar. Participating and sharing in a meal was not new to the Lord's Supper, but consistent with the Old Testament sacrifices.

10:20–21 *they sacrifice to devils.* The spiritual beings behind empty idols are to be rejected. A Christian cannot participate in the table of the Lord and the table of devils.

10:23 *All things are lawful for me.* Paul repeats the common phrase (6:12). *expedient.* Profitable. *edify.* Build up, strengthen.

10:25 *shambles.* Meat market. Paul instructs the Corinthians that they do not need to ask the detailed questions about meat purchased at the market.

10:27 *set before you.* Just as believers do not need to investigate at the meat market, so they ought to eat what is placed before them in another's home without asking questions.

10:28 *This is offered in sacrifice unto idols.* Yet, if the host tells them outright the food was used in idol worship, then it is best and wise for the Christian to refrain from eating. In these three situations (vv. 25,27–28), Paul encourages discernment, wisdom, and love for the sake of another's conscience.

10:31 *do all to the glory of God.* The exercise of rights and liberties is never more important than God's glory. If God's glory is at stake even in eating and drinking, then Christians do well to factor God's glory into everything they do.

10:32–33 *not seeking mine own profit.* God's glory is the ultimate factor in matters of liberty, and the good of the brethren is next in importance.

Thoughts for Personal/Family Worship: Chapter 10

1. **Paul applies the Old Testament history to our lives to show the importance of persevering in the faith. It is not enough to experience the external benefits of the visible church. There must be the experiential application of God's grace in the soul. Reflect on how a spiritual privilege is not the same as a spiritual possession.**
2. **Paul encourages discernment (determining the spiritual profit of a thing) and love (determining whether something builds up) in deciding questions relating to liberty. How does this work itself out in your life and in the life of your family? How does God's glory and others' good play into the exercise of what you do and do not do?**

Chapter 11: *Paul addresses various ordinances within the context of public worship.*

Concerning Decorum in Public Worship (11:2–34)

Headship and Headcoverings (11:2–16)

11:3 Paul addresses three relationships: Christ and man, man and woman, and God and Christ. *head.* Authority. As Christ is the servant-leader of the man, so the husband is the head of the wife (Eph. 5:22–23). *Christ.* Messianic title of Jesus; the focus here is on distinction of role or function, and not that of essence. Just as the Son of God, as Mediator, submitted Himself to the will of the Father, so the wife should submit to the husband, and the husband to Christ. The structure of these relationships forms the basis for the argument that follows.

11:4 *praying or prophesying.* Acts done in public worship. *head covered.* Literally, "down from the head." If a man participates in corporate worship by praying or prophesying with his

with *her* head uncovered dishonoureth her head:
for that is even all one as if she were shaven.
6 For if the woman be not covered, let her also
be shorn: but if it be a shame for a woman to be
shorn or shaven, let her be covered.
7 For a man indeed ought not to cover *his* head,
forasmuch as he is the image and glory of God:
but the woman is the glory of the man.
8 For the man is not of the woman; but the
woman of the man.
9 Neither was the man created for the woman;
but the woman for the man.
10 For this cause ought the woman to have power
on *her* head because of the angels.
11 Nevertheless neither is the man without the
woman, neither the woman without the man, in
the Lord.
12 For as the woman *is* of the man, even so *is* the
man also by the woman; but all things of God.
13 Judge in yourselves: is it comely that a woman
pray unto God uncovered?
14 Doth not even nature itself teach you, that, if a
man have long hair, it is a shame unto him?
15 But if a woman have long hair, it is a glory to
her: for *her* hair is given her for a covering.
16 But if any man seem to be contentious, we have
no such custom, neither the churches of God.
17 Now in this that I declare *unto you* I praise *you*
not, that ye come together not for the better, but
for the worse.
18 For first of all, when ye come together in the
church, I hear that there be divisions among you;
and I partly believe it.
19 For there must be also heresies among you,
that they which are approved may be made mani-
fest among you.
20 When ye come together therefore into one
place, *this* is not to eat the Lord's supper.
21 For in eating every one taketh before *other* his
own supper: and one is hungry, and another is
drunken.
22 What? have ye not houses to eat and to drink
in? or despise ye the church of God, and shame
them that have not? What shall I say to you? shall
I praise you in this? I praise *you* not.
23 For I have received of the Lord that which also
I delivered unto you, That the Lord Jesus the *same*
night in which he was betrayed took bread:
24 And when he had given thanks, he brake
it, and said, Take, eat: this is my body, which is
broken for you: this do in remembrance of me.
25 After the same manner also *he took* the cup,
when he had supped, saying, This cup is the new
testament in my blood: this do ye, as oft as ye
drink *it*, in remembrance of me.
26 For as often as ye eat this bread, and drink this
cup, ye do shew the Lord's death till he come.
27 Wherefore whosoever shall eat this bread, and
drink *this* cup of the Lord, unworthily, shall be
guilty of the body and blood of the Lord.
28 But let a man examine himself, and so let him
eat of *that* bread, and drink of *that* cup.
29 For he that eateth and drinketh unworthily,
eateth and drinketh damnation to himself, not
discerning the Lord's body.
30 For this cause many *are* weak and sickly

head covered, he shames and dishonors his head and his Lord.

11:5–6 The woman dishonors her husband (*her head*) in worship by having her head uncovered. The shame would have been akin to having her hair shaven.

11:7–9 *forasmuch.* Since. Women were also made in the image of God (Gen. 1:27). Paul's point is on the order of creation. Man was created first, and then woman was created for the man (Gen. 2:7,21–23). Therefore, man reflects God's glory and the woman reflects man's glory. By man having his head uncovered and by woman having her head covered, all glory points to God in public worship.

11:10 *power.* Authority. The woman is to have the symbol or sign of authority on her head. *because of the angels.* Angels were witnesses of creation (Job 38:4,7) and are witnesses of God's wisdom in the church (Eph. 3:10). They would observe the dishonoring of God's created authority structure in the Corinthian church.

11:11 *Nevertheless.* Lest Paul be misunderstood to be saying that the woman is of less worth, he highlights the mutual dependency of male and female.

11:14–15 *Doth not even nature.* After arguing from creation, Paul argues from what is known in the natural order. God has made men and women to be different, and hair is one distinguishing marker between them.

11:16 The behavior of the Corinthian church quarreled with the universal custom (*practice*) of the churches, that the men were to worship with their heads uncovered and the women with their heads covered.

Behavior at the Lord's Supper (11:17–34)

11:17–34 Paul turns to another ordinance in public worship, the church's behavior at the Lord's Supper.

11:19 *heresies.* Literally, "factions."

11:20 *is not to eat the Lord's supper.* The factions present in the church were such a scandal that their coming together to eat could hardly be viewed as the Lord's Supper. Fellowship with the Lord and with one another is an essential element of the Lord's Supper. Their division turned the supper from being the Lord's into a troubling imitation.

11:21–22 These verses show the disunity that existed in the Corinthian church. How sad it was that even around the most special feast of the Christian church there were believers who acted in complete disregard of their brothers. The wealthy gave little to no consideration for the poor.

11:23–26 Paul records the institution of the Lord's Supper (Luke 22:19–20), which he received of the Lord Himself. In the institution and administration of the Lord's Supper, Christians see three perspectives of time converge. By eating and drinking in faith the Christian experiences in the present (*this do*) the benefits of Christ's atoning work in the past (*in remembrance of me*) and anticipates the blessed hope of Christ's return (*till he come*).

11:27 *unworthily.* Eating and drinking in a careless manner without due regard to its significance as a pointer to the sacrificed body and blood of the Lord, and a holy means of fellowship with Him (10:16).

among you, and many sleep.
31 For if we would judge ourselves, we should not
be judged.
32 But when we are judged, we are chastened of
the Lord, that we should not be condemned with
the world.
33 Wherefore, my brethren, when ye come to-
gether to eat, tarry one for another.
34 And if any man hunger, let him eat at home;
that ye come not together unto condemnation.
And the rest will I set in order when I come.

CHAPTER 12

NOW concerning spiritual *gifts*, brethren, I would
not have you ignorant.
2 Ye know that ye were Gentiles, carried away
unto these dumb idols, even as ye were led.
3 Wherefore I give you to understand, that no
man speaking by the Spirit of God calleth Jesus
accursed: and *that* no man can say that Jesus is the
Lord, but by the Holy Ghost.
4 Now there are diversities of gifts, but the same
Spirit.
5 And there are differences of administrations,
but the same Lord.
6 And there are diversities of operations, but it is
the same God which worketh all in all.
7 But the manifestation of the Spirit is given to
every man to profit withal.
8 For to one is given by the Spirit the word of
wisdom; to another the word of knowledge by
the same Spirit;
9 To another faith by the same Spirit; to another
the gifts of healing by the same Spirit;
10 To another the working of miracles; to an-
other prophecy; to another discerning of spirits;
to another *divers* kinds of tongues; to another the
interpretation of tongues:
11 But all these worketh that one and the selfsame
Spirit, dividing to every man severally as he will.
12 For as the body is one, and hath many mem-
bers, and all the members of that one body, being
many, are one body: so also *is* Christ.
13 For by one Spirit are we all baptized into one
body, whether *we be* Jews or Gentiles, whether *we
be* bond or free; and have been all made to drink
into one Spirit.
14 For the body is not one member, but many.
15 If the foot shall say, Because I am not the hand,
I am not of the body; is it therefore not of the
body?

11:29 *damnation.* Judgment, but not necessarily eternal condemnation (v. 32). *not discerning the Lord's body.* Either the body of the Lord, or the body of believers with a focus on unity. This statement of receiving the Lord's Supper unworthily is closely linked to v. 27, and it seems best to take the Lord's body as a shortened form of the phrase "body and blood of the Lord" (v. 27).

11:31 *if we would judge ourselves, we should not be judged.* Christians can be preserved from God's disciplinary judgment (vv. 30,32) by eating and drinking with discernment, which involves proper self-examination.

Thoughts for Personal/Family Worship: Chapter 11

1. **When you come to the house of God for corporate worship, how you conduct yourself matters. Paul argues for proper decorum in public worship according to His created order. When you enter the house of God for worship, how should you act in a way that honors the glory and will of the Lord?**
2. **God has blessed His people with wonderful tokens of His love such as the Lord's Supper. Here Christians celebrate the union they have with Christ and with one another in Christ. This is a time for self-examination, and therefore a serious time. It is a sign and seal of Christ's atoning work by which the believer is nourished and strengthened in his faith in God's promises.**

Concerning the Spiritual Gifts (12:1—14:40)

Chapter 12: *Paul addresses the proper understanding and use of the spiritual gifts.*

Unity in Diversity in the One Body (12:1–31)

12:2–3 *ye were Gentiles, carried away unto these dumb idols.* The Corinthian church is not to think of spiritual gifts like its former pagan superstitions. Paul wants them now to be led by the Spirit (*Holy Ghost*) who never dishonors Christ, and who alone can enable us to trust Jesus as Lord, which is essential for salvation (Rom. 10:9).

12:4–6 Paul provides a Trinitarian understanding of the spiritual gifts. There are a variety of gifts that originate from the one, true, and triune God. This emphasizes the unity-in-diversity theme of the chapter. It also shows the ignorance of placing one gift, tongues, in a place of superiority. *administrations.* Ministries.

12:7 *manifestation of the Spirit is given to every man.* God gives His Spirit to every believer. *to profit withal.* For what is helpful (same word as "expedient," 6:12; 10:23).

12:8–10 Paul provides a partial list of the spiritual gifts, reflective of the various kinds of gifts that serve the benefit of the body. *word of wisdom.* The spiritual ability to apply God's truth to specific situations. *word of knowledge.* The spiritual ability to understand and clearly explain biblical truth. *tongues . . . interpretation of tongues.* The supernatural ability to speak and understand languages not otherwise known (14:2; Acts 2:4–6). Tongues and interpretation functioned similarly to prophecy because both are revelatory speech gifts (Acts 2:16–18; 19:6). Therefore they, like the gift of the apostles, were foundational to the church and no longer part of its experience (Eph. 2:20).

12:11 *dividing . . . as he will.* The distribution of gifts is according to the sovereign will of God. Christians are not to boast in self or in the fact that they have one gift over another. *severally.* Separately.

12:12–13 *the body is one.* Unity among believers is not secured by making all believers the same. Unity is secured among the many because all believers are in Christ. Though there is diversity in gifts by the Spirit, by one Spirit all believers are baptized in one body.

12:14–17 Paul illustrates the importance of each diverse member for the unity of the one body by drawing attention to the human body. The body needs the foot, the hand, the ear, the eye, and the nose in order to properly function. Each member contributes to the health of the whole.

16 And if the ear shall say, Because I am not the
eye, I am not of the body; is it therefore not of
the body?
17 If the whole body *were* an eye, where *were* the
hearing? If the whole *were* hearing, where *were*
the smelling?
18 But now hath God set the members every one
of them in the body, as it hath pleased him.
19 And if they were all one member, where *were*
the body?
20 But now *are they* many members, yet but one
body.
21 And the eye cannot say unto the hand, I have
no need of thee: nor again the head to the feet, I
have no need of you.
22 Nay, much more those members of the body,
which seem to be more feeble, are necessary:
23 And those *members* of the body, which we
think to be less honourable, upon these we bestow
more abundant honour; and our uncomely *parts*
have more abundant comeliness.
24 For our comely *parts* have no need: but God
hath tempered the body together, having given
more abundant honour to that *part* which lacked:
25 That there should be no schism in the body;
but *that* the members should have the same care
one for another.
26 And whether one member suffer, all the mem-
bers suffer with it; or one member be honoured,
all the members rejoice with it.
27 Now ye are the body of Christ, and members
in particular.
28 And God hath set some in the church, first
apostles, secondarily prophets, thirdly teachers,
after that miracles, then gifts of healings, helps,
governments, diversities of tongues.
29 *Are* all apostles? *are* all prophets? *are* all teach-
ers? *are* all workers of miracles?
30 Have all the gifts of healing? do all speak with
tongues? do all interpret?
31 But covet earnestly the best gifts: and yet shew
I unto you a more excellent way.

CHAPTER 13

THOUGH I speak with the tongues of men and
of angels, and have not charity, I am become *as*
sounding brass, or a tinkling cymbal.
2 And though I have *the gift of* prophecy, and
understand all mysteries, and all knowledge; and
though I have all faith, so that I could remove
mountains, and have not charity, I am nothing.
3 And though I bestow all my goods to feed *the
poor*, and though I give my body to be burned,
and have not charity, it profiteth me nothing.
4 Charity suffereth long, *and* is kind; charity
envieth not; charity vaunteth not itself, is not
puffed up,
5 Doth not behave itself unseemly, seeketh not
her own, is not easily provoked, thinketh no evil;
6 Rejoiceth not in iniquity, but rejoiceth in the
truth;
7 Beareth all things, believeth all things, hopeth
all things, endureth all things.

12:18–20 The importance of diversity.

12:25 The purpose of such diversity is that there be no divisions (*schism*) in the body. This appears to be counterintuitive until Christians realize that unity is not uniformity. The sovereign, all-wise God intends diversity for the goal of unity.

12:29–30 If believers were all apostles, or all prophets, or all teachers, or all miracle workers, etc., then the body would not function properly. It is important to note here, along with the following encouragement to strive for the best gifts, that Paul places the gift of tongues last.

12:31 *covet earnestly the best gifts.* Paul encourages them to strive fervently for the greater gifts, those that edify the whole body.

Thoughts for Personal/Family Worship: Chapter 12

1. **God graciously gives gifts to each of His children. He sovereignly decides who receives what gift and how many. Often Christians become discouraged because they do not have the same gift as someone else. Others can become proud because of the gifts that they have as though they earned it. God's sovereign giving of gifts should evoke praise and thanksgiving rather than discouragement, and instill humility because the gifts were *granted according to God's will* and not the receiver's merit. When considering your gift, do so with a God-centered perspective rather than a self-centered one.**
2. **Paul highlights the unity of the church in his discussion of the spiritual gifts. He describes this unity by reminding believers that when one suffers, all suffer. And when one is honored, all rejoice. In many ways, it is easier to suffer alongside another who is suffering. It is not always easy to rejoice when another is honored. What is your response when someone else is honored and you feel overlooked? Are you able to rejoice with them? How can we dissipate envying and jealousy in our churches and in our homes?**

Chapter 13: *Paul exhorts all believers to demonstrate love in the exercise of their spiritual gifts.*

Preeminence of Love (13:1–13)

13:1–3 *charity.* Love. Paul shows that love is essential in the exercise of spiritual gifts. Love must be a part of all that we say (v. 1), all that we know (v. 2), and all that we do (v. 3). Without love, everything is vain. He begins with the gift of tongues, most likely because some within the church had elevated that gift above all others and were not exercising it with love for the brethren.

13:4–7 Paul describes love in various ways and actions. *suffereth long.* Patient. *vaunteth not itself.* Does not brag or parade itself. *puffed up.* Conceited, proud, arrogant. *Doth not behave itself unseemly.* Behave disgracefully or rudely. *thinketh no evil.* Does not keep or consider a record of wrongs.

13:8 Love is permanent. Love will not fall down or collapse. Prophecy will pass away, and tongues will cease. *knowledge.* The spiritual gift of knowledge (12:8).

13:9–10 The word *perfect* is opposite of *in part,* and thus

8 Charity never faileth: but whether *there be*
prophecies, they shall fail; whether *there be*
tongues, they shall cease; whether *there be* knowl-
edge, it shall vanish away.
9 For we know in part, and we prophesy in part.
10 But when that which is perfect is come, then
that which is in part shall be done away.
11 When I was a child, I spake as a child, I under-
stood as a child, I thought as a child: but when I
became a man, I put away childish things.
12 For now we see through a glass, darkly; but
then face to face: now I know in part; but then
shall I know even as also I am known.
13 And now abideth faith, hope, charity, these
three; but the greatest of these *is* charity.

CHAPTER 14

FOLLOW after charity, and desire spiritual *gifts*, but
rather that ye may prophesy.
2 For he that speaketh in an *unknown* tongue
speaketh not unto men, but unto God: for no
man understandeth *him*; howbeit in the spirit he
speaketh mysteries.
3 But he that prophesieth speaketh unto men *to*
edification, and exhortation, and comfort.
4 He that speaketh in an *unknown* tongue edifi-
eth himself; but he that prophesieth edifieth the
church.
5 I would that ye all spake with tongues, but
rather that ye prophesied: for greater *is* he that
prophesieth than he that speaketh with tongues,
except he interpret, that the church may receive
edifying.
6 Now, brethren, if I come unto you speaking
with tongues, what shall I profit you, except I shall
speak to you either by revelation, or by knowl-
edge, or by prophesying, or by doctrine?
7 And even things without life giving sound,
whether pipe or harp, except they give a distinc-
tion in the sounds, how shall it be known what is
piped or harped?
8 For if the trumpet give an uncertain sound,
who shall prepare himself to the battle?
9 So likewise ye, except ye utter by the tongue
words easy to be understood, how shall it be known
what is spoken? for ye shall speak into the air.
10 There are, it may be, so many kinds of voices
in the world, and none of them *is* without
signification.
11 Therefore if I know not the meaning of the
voice, I shall be unto him that speaketh a barbarian,
and he that speaketh *shall be* a barbarian unto me.
12 Even so ye, forasmuch as ye are zealous
of spiritual *gifts*, seek that ye may excel to the
edifying of the church.
13 Wherefore let him that speaketh in an *un-
known* tongue pray that he may interpret.
14 For if I pray in an *unknown* tongue, my spirit
prayeth, but my understanding is unfruitful.
15 What is it then? I will pray with the spirit, and
I will pray with the understanding also: I will sing
with the spirit, and I will sing with the under-
standing also.
16 Else when thou shalt bless with the spirit, how
shall he that occupieth the room of the unlearned
say Amen at thy giving of thanks, seeing he
understandeth not what thou sayest?
17 For thou verily givest thanks well, but the
other is not edified.

---

refers to when believers experience full redemption at the consummation in the new heaven and new earth when believers have come into full maturity.

13:12 *now I know in part; but then shall I know.* Paul again sets the present age against the future. Now Christians know in partial knowledge, but then Christians will know in perfect knowledge.

Thoughts for Personal/Family Worship: Chapter 13

1. **Love is to govern all of our motives. Examine whether all you say, know, and do is governed by love. What sins against love do you need to confess?**
2. **Paul describes love in various action verbs. It has often been said that we can replace the word "charity" with the name "Christ" and see more clearly God's grace to us in His Son. Christ acts toward us in all these ways. It is only through Christ that you will ever be able to have and show true love.**

Chapter 14: *Paul focuses on the spiritual gifts of prophecy and tongues.*

Prophecy and Tongues, Decency and Order (14:1–40)

14:1 *Follow after charity.* Paul links the previous chapter to his direct focus on prophecy and tongues by encouraging the Corinthian believers to pursue love.

14:2 *unknown tongue.* The word unknown is added by the translators. Literally, "he who speaks in tongues." On tongues see note at 12:8–10. *no man understandeth.* Not even the one speaking understands without an interpreter (vv. 13–14).

14:3 *prophesieth.* Paul contrasts tongues and prophecy. To prophesy is to speak the message of God clearly to the hearers in a language that is understood. The result is threefold: building up spiritually (*edification*), pressing people to believe and obey (*exhortation*), and bringing them to peace and joy in Christ (*comfort*).

14:5 *I would that ye all spake with tongues.* Paul does not want to be misunderstood to be devaluing the gift of tongues. He is focusing on the greater and more direct benefit of prophecy because all understand.

14:6–19 Paul argues that tongues without interpretation do not edify and would be as though one is merely just speaking into the air (v. 9).

14:11 *barbarian.* Foreigner; one who speaks unintelligibly to another.

14:12 *forasmuch.* Since. *seek that ye may excel to the edifying of the church.* Paul returns to the corporate benefit of gifts, again showing that the purpose is for the body as a whole and not self. Christians should pursue the gifts that have the greatest benefit.

14:17 *verily.* Truly.

18 I thank my God, I speak with tongues more
than ye all:
19 Yet in the church I had rather speak five words
with my understanding, that *by my voice* I might
teach others also, than ten thousand words in an
unknown tongue.
20 Brethren, be not children in understanding:
howbeit in malice be ye children, but in under-
standing be men.
21 In the law it is written, With *men of* other
tongues and other lips will I speak unto this
people; and yet for all that will they not hear me,
saith the Lord.
22 Wherefore tongues are for a sign, not to them
that believe, but to them that believe not: but
prophesying *serveth* not for them that believe not,
but for them which believe.
23 If therefore the whole church be come together
into one place, and all speak with tongues,
and there come in *those that are* unlearned, or
unbelievers, will they not say that ye are mad?
24 But if all prophesy, and there come in one that
believeth not, or *one* unlearned, he is convinced
of all, he is judged of all:
25 And thus are the secrets of his heart made man-
ifest; and so falling down on *his* face he will wor-
ship God, and report that God is in you of a truth.
26 How is it then, brethren? when ye come to-
gether, every one of you hath a psalm, hath a
doctrine, hath a tongue, hath a revelation, hath an
interpretation. Let all things be done unto edifying.
27 If any man speak in an *unknown* tongue, *let
it be* by two, or at the most *by* three, and *that* by
course; and let one interpret.
28 But if there be no interpreter, let him keep si-
lence in the church; and let him speak to himself,
and to God.
29 Let the prophets speak two or three, and let the
other judge.
30 If *any thing* be revealed to another that sitteth
by, let the first hold his peace.
31 For ye may all prophesy one by one, that all
may learn, and all may be comforted.
32 And the spirits of the prophets are subject to
the prophets.
33 For God is not *the author* of confusion, but of
peace, as in all churches of the saints.
34 Let your women keep silence in the churches:
for it is not permitted unto them to speak; but
they are commanded to be under obedience, as
also saith the law.
35 And if they will learn any thing, let them ask
their husbands at home: for it is a shame for
women to speak in the church.
36 What? came the word of God out from you? or
came it unto you only?
37 If any man think himself to be a prophet, or
spiritual, let him acknowledge that the things that I
write unto you are the commandments of the Lord.
38 But if any man be ignorant, let him be ignorant.
39 Wherefore, brethren, covet to prophesy, and
forbid not to speak with tongues.
40 Let all things be done decently and in order.

CHAPTER 15

MOREOVER, brethren, I declare unto you the gos-
pel which I preached unto you, which also ye have
received, and wherein ye stand;
2 By which also ye are saved, if ye keep in memory
what I preached unto you, unless ye have believed
in vain.
3 For I delivered unto you first of all that which
I also received, how that Christ died for our sins

14:18–19 *I speak with tongues more than ye all.* Paul does not present his views on the greater benefit of prophecy over tongues to the body out of jealousy or envy because he does not have the gift of tongues. Rather, he has the gift of tongues. Yet, he would rather speak even just five words and be understood.
14:20 He encourages them to be mature in their understanding and not to become childish. But (*howbeit*) they are to be like children in their understanding of wickedness (*malice*).
14:21 *the law.* The whole Old Testament. *it is written.* See Isa. 28:11–12. Israel refused to listen to God's Word in a language that was understandable to them. Therefore, God sent a word of judgment that came via the language of the Assyrians which they did not understand.
14:22 *Wherefore.* Therefore. He applies the Isaiah citation to argue that tongues are a sign to unbelievers that has a confirming effect of hardening them in their unbelief.
14:27 *let it be by two, or at the most by three.* Paul instructs the church to practice tongues in an orderly fashion. *that by course.* Speak in turn, not all at one time.
14:34–35 Let your women keep silence in the churches. Paul does not contradict his words in 11:5. His context here is leading the worship in an orderly fashion, and women were not to stand in judgment on prophecies or interrupt the worship.

Thoughts for Personal/Family Worship: Chapter 14

1. **Within the context of prophecy and tongues, Paul highlights the importance of decent and orderly worship. When the church gathers in God's presence, believers are to engage in worship seriously and reverently. How do Paul's exhortations in this chapter teach you how to frame your focus when you enter into God's house?**
2. **As you consider your spiritual gifts, is your focus more on the gift from a self-centered perspective or from the perspective of love for the brethren and desire to edify, encourage, and build up the brethren? How can you put your gifts into practice in a way that glorifies God and edifies the body?**

Chapter 15: *Paul details the importance of the resurrection of Christ and the subsequent certainty of the believer's resurrection.*

Concerning the Resurrection (15:1–58)

15:2 *in vain.* Without effect. Paul used three different words for *vain* in vv. 2,10,17.

according to the scriptures;
4 And that he was buried, and that he rose again
the third day according to the scriptures:
5 And that he was seen of Cephas, then of the
twelve:
6 After that, he was seen of above five hundred
brethren at once; of whom the greater part re-
main unto this present, but some are fallen asleep.
7 After that, he was seen of James; then of all the
apostles.
8 And last of all he was seen of me also, as of one
born out of due time.
9 For I am the least of the apostles, that am not
meet to be called an apostle, because I persecuted
the church of God.
10 But by the grace of God I am what I am: and
his grace which *was bestowed* upon me was not in
vain; but I laboured more abundantly than they all:
yet not I, but the grace of God which was with me.
11 Therefore whether *it were* I or they, so we
preach, and so ye believed.
12 Now if Christ be preached that he rose from
the dead, how say some among you that there is
no resurrection of the dead?
13 But if there be no resurrection of the dead,
then is Christ not risen:
14 And if Christ be not risen, then *is* our preach-
ing vain, and your faith *is* also vain.
15 Yea, and we are found false witnesses of God;
because we have testified of God that he raised up
Christ: whom he raised not up, if so be that the
dead rise not.
16 For if the dead rise not, then is not Christ raised:
17 And if Christ be not raised, your faith *is* vain;
ye are yet in your sins.
18 Then they also which are fallen asleep in
Christ are perished.
19 If in this life only we have hope in Christ, we
are of all men most miserable.
20 But now is Christ risen from the dead, *and*
become the firstfruits of them that slept.
21 For since by man *came* death, by man *came*
also the resurrection of the dead.
22 For as in Adam all die, even so in Christ shall
all be made alive.
23 But every man in his own order: Christ the
firstfruits; afterward they that are Christ's at his
coming.
24 Then *cometh* the end, when he shall have
delivered up the kingdom to God, even the
Father; when he shall have put down all rule and
all authority and power.
25 For he must reign, till he hath put all enemies
under his feet.
26 The last enemy *that* shall be destroyed *is* death.
27 For he hath put all things under his feet. But
when he saith all things are put under *him, it is*
manifest that he is excepted, which did put all
things under him.
28 And when all things shall be subdued unto
him, then shall the Son also himself be subject
unto him that put all things under him, that God
may be all in all.
29 Else what shall they do which are baptized for
the dead, if the dead rise not at all? why are they
then baptized for the dead?
30 And why stand we in jeopardy every hour?
31 I protest by your rejoicing which I have in
Christ Jesus our Lord, I die daily.
32 If after the manner of men I have fought with
beasts at Ephesus, what advantageth it me, if the
dead rise not? let us eat and drink; for to morrow
we die.
33 Be not deceived: evil communications corrupt
good manners.
34 Awake to righteousness, and sin not; for some
have not the knowledge of God: I speak *this* to
your shame.

15:3 *first of all.* First in priority and importance.
15:3–6. Paul summarizes the gospel by pointing to two historical facts: the death of Christ for our sins and His resurrection. Each fact of the gospel is said to be according to the Scriptures. The word of the cross originates with God; it is God's wisdom (1:17–25). Also, each fact of the gospel is verified by two supporting realities: He was buried and He was seen by Peter (*Cephas*) and over five hundred others.
15:8 *seen of me also.* A prerequisite for the call of an apostle (9:1). *one born out of due time.* Premature birth or stillborn. Paul witnessed the resurrected Christ after all the others listed previously, and as one involved in the persecution of the church after the ascension of Christ.
15:10 *vain.* Without success.
15:17 *vain.* Fruitless, useless. *ye are yet in your sins.* Christ died for our sins as the substitute for sinners (v. 3). Christ's resurrection as the surety of His people shows that His sacrifice for sin was accepted by God and powerful to take away our sins. If Christ is not raised, then His death is not effective to save sinners.
15:19 *If in this life only we have hope in Christ.* Because Christ is raised, He is our hope not only in this life, but also in the next.
15:20 *firstfruits.* The firstfruits anticipate the harvest that follows. Christ's resurrection guarantees that the resurrection of believers will certainly follow.
15:22 *in Adam . . . in Christ.* Paul sees all humanity in relation to their federal head. Either we are in Adam, and therefore fallen and under the curse, or we are in Christ and therefore a partaker of life.
15:25–26 *he must reign.* Christ is presently reigning and will continue to reign until all enemies are under His feet (Gen. 3:15; Ps. 110:1), ultimately including death itself.
15:28 *then shall the Son also himself be subject unto him.* Paul is speaking of the Son in His mediatorial role and function, not His essence, power, and glory which are equal to the Father (8:6).
15:29 *baptized for the dead.* A difficult phrase; perhaps a sarcastic reference to a practice Paul did not approve of, or maybe an abbreviated reference to being baptized in hope of the resurrection of the dead (cf. Rom. 6:3–5).
15:30–34 Paul points to the resurrection as the reason why he is able to endure the prospect of death on a daily basis for the sake of the gospel. He knows that he will be raised.

CHRIST'S RESURRECTION AND OURS

Considering Christ's resurrection, there are three points to be expressed: *first*, the necessity of the resurrection; *second*, the significant characteristics of the resurrection; and *third*, the uses of the resurrection for comforting the child of God.

Christ's resurrection was necessary for three reasons. *First*, His resurrection evidenced a complete victory over death. For believers, the resurrection confirms that Christ's whole obedience was a work both of perfect satisfaction, destroying death, and of a meritorious nature, earning life. *Second*, Christ's resurrection was demanded by virtue of His divine nature as the Son of God. He is the Author of life itself; for this reason it was neither fitting nor possible for Him to be overcome by death. Thus, it was imperative that Christ rise from death to life. *Third*, Christ's resurrection confirmed that His priestly work consisted of two parts. One was to make satisfaction for sin by sacrificing Himself on the cross. The other was to apply the virtue of this sacrifice to every believer. Therefore, Christ rose to perform this second part of His priesthood for His people.

Christ's resurrection had significant characteristics. *First*, He rose as a public person, standing in place of His people not only in death but also in resurrection. Consequently, when Christ rose the whole church rose in Him (Eph. 2:6). *Second*, Christ by His own power raised Himself from the dead (John 2:19; 10:18). This demonstrated that He was not only man but also true God. Further, this exhibited Christ's power to raise also His church from death to life. *Third*, Christ rose again with an earthquake. This was to prove that He had lost no power by death, that He still remained the absolute Lord of heaven and earth, before whom the earth still trembled.

Fourth, Christ's death and resurrection were accompanied by other wonders as well. For example, Matthew 27:52–53 declares that graves were opened and that many were raised. This occurred in order that the church might know that there is a renewing and quickening virtue in the resurrection of Christ, whereby He is able to raise those who are dead in sin to newness of life. This signifies the order of it all: Christ arose, then the saints after Him; thus, He is the firstborn of the dead, with many to follow Him in rising (Col. 1:18).

This flows into the uses of the resurrection in comforting the child of God. These comforts are three. *First*, Christ's resurrection effects the justification of all who believe in Him (Rom. 4:25). Indeed, life was the very wage He was sent to earn (Isa. 32:17); therefore, having been reconciled by His death, we shall much more be saved by His life (Rom. 5:10). *Second*, the resurrection of Christ is the notable means by which God works sanctification (Rom. 6:4–5; 1 Peter 1:3). As Christ by the power of His Godhead freed His manhood from death and from the guilt of our sins, so does Christ free the believer from the corruption of nature in which he lies dead—all so that he may live unto God (Rom. 14:8).

Third, the resurrection of Christ discloses the church's resurrection. He that raised Christ from the dead "shall also quicken your mortal bodies" (Rom. 8:11). This is why Christ is called the firstfruits of the dead (1 Cor. 15:20). His resurrection is a pledge and assurance of the resurrection of the church. He is the head of His church; therefore, all His members must follow after Christ in their time. The godly rise by the power of Christ their Redeemer, who raises them up so that they may be partakers of the benefits of His death (Heb. 3:14)—to enjoy both in body and soul the kingdom of heaven that He has so dearly bought for them. The godly rise as Christ by the virtue of Christ's own resurrection. They rise, as He did, unto eternal glory.

—adapted from William Perkins, "Christ's Resurrection," in *An Exposition of the Symbole or Creed of the Apostles*

35 But some *man* will say, How are the dead
raised up? and with what body do they come?
36 *Thou* fool, that which thou sowest is not
quickened, except it die:
37 And that which thou sowest, thou sowest not
that body that shall be, but bare grain, it may
chance of wheat, or of some other *grain*:
38 But God giveth it a body as it hath pleased
him, and to every seed his own body.
39 All flesh *is* not the same flesh: but *there is*
one *kind of* flesh of men, another flesh of beasts,
another of fishes, *and* another of birds.
40 *There are* also celestial bodies, and bodies
terrestrial: but the glory of the celestial *is* one, and
the *glory* of the terrestrial *is* another.
41 *There is* one glory of the sun, and another
glory of the moon, and another glory of the stars:
for *one* star differeth from *another* star in glory.
42 So also *is* the resurrection of the dead. It is
sown in corruption; it is raised in incorruption:
43 It is sown in dishonour; it is raised in glory: it
is sown in weakness; it is raised in power:
44 It is sown a natural body; it is raised a spiri-
tual body. There is a natural body, and there is a
spiritual body.
45 And so it is written, The first man Adam was
made a living soul; the last Adam *was made* a
quickening spirit.
46 Howbeit that *was* not first which is spiritual,
but that which is natural; and afterward that
which is spiritual.
47 The first man *is* of the earth, earthy: the second
man *is* the Lord from heaven.
48 As *is* the earthy, such *are* they also that are
earthy: and as *is* the heavenly, such *are* they also
that are heavenly.
49 And as we have borne the image of the earthy,
we shall also bear the image of the heavenly.
50 Now this I say, brethren, that flesh and blood
cannot inherit the kingdom of God; neither doth
corruption inherit incorruption.
51 Behold, I shew you a mystery; We shall not all
sleep, but we shall all be changed,
52 In a moment, in the twinkling of an eye, at the
last trump: for the trumpet shall sound, and the
dead shall be raised incorruptible, and we shall be
changed.
53 For this corruptible must put on incorruption,
and this mortal *must* put on immortality.
54 So when this corruptible shall have put on in-
corruption, and this mortal shall have put on im-
mortality, then shall be brought to pass the saying
that is written, Death is swallowed up in victory.
55 O death, where *is* thy sting? O grave, where *is*
thy victory?
56 The sting of death *is* sin; and the strength of
sin *is* the law.
57 But thanks *be* to God, which giveth us the
victory through our Lord Jesus Christ.
58 Therefore, my beloved brethren, be ye stedfast,
unmoveable, always abounding in the work of the
Lord, forasmuch as ye know that your labour is
not in vain in the Lord.

CHAPTER 16

NOW concerning the collection for the saints, as I
have given order to the churches of Galatia, even
so do ye.
2 Upon the first *day* of the week let every one of
you lay by him in store, as *God* hath prospered
him, that there be no gatherings when I come.

15:35–49 Paul discusses the nature of the resurrection body.
15:37–44 *God giveth it a body as it hath pleased him.* God is sovereign and gives a body that is specific for its environment. *All flesh is not the same flesh.* In God's wisdom fish have bodies for water, and birds have bodies for the air. So, in the resurrection, the resurrected body of believers is a body fit for eternity with God: it is immortal, glorious, and powerful by the work of the Spirit (*spiritual*).
15:43 *dishonour.* A state of shame, humiliation.
15:45 *The first man Adam . . . the last Adam.* Those in the first Adam are living beings, but those in the last Adam, that is Christ, are made alive with eternal life. The contrast is between merely living and *quickening* (life-giving).
15:58 *Therefore, my beloved brethren, be ye stedfast.* Paul concludes the discussion of the resurrection with a word of encouragement. Because Jesus was raised and believers will one day be raised, Christians ought to stand firm because what is done for God in this life will be richly rewarded in glory. *forasmuch.* Since.

Thoughts for Personal/Family Worship: Chapter 15

1. **The New Testament writers often pointed believers to the hope of the resurrection. The reality of Christ's bodily resurrection assures them that God the Father accepted the sacrifice made by God the Son. Because Jesus Christ was raised, dear believer, you can know with certainty that sin no longer holds dominion over you. The risen Lord reigns and rules over all, and all things have been put under His feet. How can you make sure you don't live as those who are "of all men most miserable" (v. 19)?**
2. **Because Jesus was raised and all those in Him will one day receive a body like His glorified body, your labors are not in vain. Consider how this truth should motivate you as you live before God each day in all the various spheres of service God has called you to: in the home, in the church, in the workplace.**

Chapter 16: *Paul addresses the matter of the collection for the saints, and then gives closing exhortations and final greetings.*

Concerning the Collection (16:1–4)

16:1 *Now concerning.* Paul considers the final topic addressed to him in the letter from the Corinthians. *collection for the saints.* Paul appealed to the Christian churches to send monetary aid to the poor believers in Jerusalem (Acts 11:28–29; 24:17; Rom. 15:25–26; 2 Cor. 8–9; Gal. 2:10).
16:2 *lay by him in store.* Put something aside. *gatherings.* Collections. This implies that each church would collect these

3 And when I come, whomsoever ye shall ap-
prove by *your* letters, them will I send to bring
your liberality unto Jerusalem.
4 And if it be meet that I go also, they shall go
with me.
5 Now I will come unto you, when I shall pass
through Macedonia: for I do pass through
Macedonia.
6 And it may be that I will abide, yea, and winter
with you, that ye may bring me on my journey
whithersoever I go.
7 For I will not see you now by the way; but I
trust to tarry a while with you, if the Lord permit.
8 But I will tarry at Ephesus until Pentecost.
9 For a great door and effectual is opened unto
me, and *there are* many adversaries.
10 Now if Timotheus come, see that he may be
with you without fear: for he worketh the work of
the Lord, as I also *do*.
11 Let no man therefore despise him: but conduct
him forth in peace, that he may come unto me:
for I look for him with the brethren.
12 As touching *our* brother Apollos, I greatly de-
sired him to come unto you with the brethren:
but his will was not at all to come at this time; but
he will come when he shall have convenient time.
13 Watch ye, stand fast in the faith, quit you like
men, be strong.
14 Let all your things be done with charity.
15 I beseech you, brethren, (ye know the house of
Stephanas, that it is the firstfruits of Achaia, and
that they have addicted themselves to the minis-
try of the saints,)
16 That ye submit yourselves unto such, and to
every one that helpeth with *us*, and laboureth.
17 I am glad of the coming of Stephanas and
Fortunatus and Achaicus: for that which was
lacking on your part they have supplied.
18 For they have refreshed my spirit and yours:
therefore acknowledge ye them that are such.
19 The churches of Asia salute you. Aquila and
Priscilla salute you much in the Lord, with the
church that is in their house.
20 All the brethren greet you. Greet ye one
another with an holy kiss.
21 The salutation of *me* Paul with mine own hand.
22 If any man love not the Lord Jesus Christ, let
him be Anathema Maran-atha.
23 The grace of our Lord Jesus Christ *be* with you.
24 My love *be* with you all in Christ Jesus. Amen.

---

gifts on the first day of the week so that all would be ready upon his arrival. Giving was considered an act of worship (Phil. 4:18; Heb. 13:16). Since this was Paul's directive to the churches of Galatia too (v. 1), the church as a whole was evidently meeting for Sabbath worship on the first day (Acts 20:7), called the "Lord's day" (Rev. 1:10) because Christ rose on it (Matt. 28:1; Mark 16:2; Luke 24:1; John 20:1) and Christ declared Himself Lord of the Sabbath (Mark 2:28).

16:3 *whomsoever ye shall approve.* Lest there be any suspicion surrounding Paul's handling and delivering of the money, he requested that they choose someone to deliver the collection to the saints in Jerusalem.

16:4 *if it be meet.* If it is worthwhile, fitting, or proper, then Paul would go with them to make the delivery.

CONCLUSION (16:5–24)

Paul's Travel Plans (16:5–12)

16:8 *Pentecost.* Feast of harvest seven weeks following Passover, often in mid-May, early June. This time of the year would be more favorable to travel.

Concluding Exhortations (16:13–18)

16:13 *quit you like men.* Behave yourself like men, be courageous.

16:16 *submit yourselves unto such, and to every one that helpeth . . . and laboureth.* Paul reminds the church that they are to submit to the leadership and he uses language that again calls to mind the unity that the leaders have as helpers in the work. This serves as a reminder to the Corinthians that the party spirit is divisive.

Final Greetings (16:19–24)

16:20 *holy kiss.* Common act to communicate friendship between believers.

16:21 *of me Paul.* Paul often used secretaries to write his letters, but he desires the Corinthians to know that he is writing the final greeting with *mine own hand.*

16:22 *Anathema.* Let him be cursed (12:3). Paul closes with a biting curse upon those who do not love the Lord but cause harm to His church (3:17). *Maran-atha.* Aramaic expression with various nuances: (1) our Lord has come, (2) our Lord is coming, and (3) our Lord, come (Rev. 22:20). The third option fits best as those who love the Lord eagerly await His coming (2 Tim. 4:8).

16:24 *My love be with you all.* Paul wrote hard words to the Corinthians concerning very serious matters, so he closes with an assuring word of his love for them.

Thoughts for Personal/Family Worship: Chapter 16

1. **The collection for the saints in Jerusalem reminds us that the church of Jesus Christ is one church. Throughout the book Paul focuses on unity within the local church. It is not just the local church that is to be one, but also the universal, visible church. While it is not possible to meet every need of every believer in the world, Christians ought to have a broader vision of the kingdom of God on earth and seek to help in any way they are able. In what ways can you and your family meet needs outside your own local church?**
2. **The words "Anathema" and "Maran-atha" (v. 22) bring us to the very edge of eternity. Ask yourself which word applies to you. The great line of division is between those who love Christ and those who do not. Believer, Christ bore your curse and now you long for His coming. Unbeliever, the curse is still resting upon you. You need to repent and seek Christ or He will appear as your justly condemning Judge.**

INTRODUCTION TO THE BOOK OF 2 CORINTHIANS

Authorship: The apostle Paul claims to be the author (1:1), and there is no evidence to dispute this claim. The only section in the letter to come under dispute is 6:14—7:1. The objections to Pauline authorship on this section are not substantial enough to cast doubt. Second Corinthians is clearly one of the most personal of all Paul's letters and, therefore, there is no reason to question the legitimacy of Paul's authorship.

Date: Paul wrote from Macedonia (7:5; 8:1; 9:2) about a year after writing 1 Corinthians, placing the timing of the letter in AD 56.

Theme: The nature of new covenant ministry: by the power of the Spirit, with present suffering, and for future glory.

Purpose: To defend Paul's ministry and message. Paul's ministry came under severe attack from two main vantage points. *First*, his message was viewed to be insufficient, and *second*, his ministry was characterized by weakness and suffering. While his opponents appear to be embarrassed by the apostle's suffering and subsequently reject Paul's ministry, Paul shows that suffering is a crucial part of advancing the glory of God. This is a book to which not only gospel ministers, but all Christians, can go to find encouragement and perspective in the midst of the difficulties of criticism, inadequacy, and insufficiency. Rather than give a false sense of self-worth, Paul bluntly affirms the insufficiency of any new covenant minister, but Christians may rejoice because their sufficiency is of God in all areas of life.

Synopsis: *The Contribution of 2 Corinthians to Redemptive Revelation*

The book begins with an opening salutation that is common in letters of Paul's day (1:1–2). As he did in 1 Corinthians, he reminds the church that he is an apostle according to God's will. His apostleship has been called into question and they considered Paul an embarrassment given the many evidences of weakness and suffering he endured. The Corinthian church continued to be enamored with evidences of success and triumph in ministry. Paul did not appear to be a Spirit-empowered success story. Despite the personal attacks Paul received, he offers thanksgiving to God, the Father of mercies, and the God of all comfort (1:3). He thanks the church for their prayers during times of persecution (v. 11).

Following the introductory elements of the letter, Paul immediately addresses his travel plans and why his plans changed (1:12—2:13). Some in the church accused Paul of vacillating in his travel plans, announcing his plans and then changing them without cause. He explains that his desire was to be a benefit to them (2:15), yet he decided not to come rather than cause such grief as he did in his prior visit (vv. 1–4). He chose instead to write them and tell them how much he loved them (v. 4).

Paul then turns his attention to a defense of his ministry (2:14—7:16). New covenant ministry in this present age does not always appear to be triumphant, but is often characterized by suffering. Some Corinthians often confused the future benefits of the kingdom with the present. Paul wrote that sufferings and trials do not contradict God's will in the present. God chose weak and earthen vessels to communicate His gospel so that it would be unmistakably clear that the power of the gospel is of God and not of ministers (4:7). The present weakness and trials are not the final story. The light affliction is but for a moment and believers look forward to a far greater, eternal weight of glory (v. 17). Holding together "the already" dimension of redemption along with the "not yet" blessings of redemption gives balance to Christians and ministers as they experience difficulties and trials in this present age. Within his discussion of the ministry, Paul unfolds the superiority of new covenant ministry by comparing it to the ministry of the old covenant (ch. 3). The glory of the new covenant ministry resides in the person of Jesus Christ, who has come and fulfilled His redemptive work. Christ is everything in this new covenant ministry. Christ's love motivates the minister to endure trials, even rejection. The reality that Christ died and rose again compelled Paul to preach reconciliation (5:11–21).

Paul encourages the Corinthian church to complete the giving that was begun earlier for the saints in Jerusalem (chs. 8–9). He tells them that the Macedonians have given generously despite their own trial of afflictions and poverty (8:1–5). Paul instructs the church regarding the manner in which it ought to give. Each person should purpose in his heart to give not out of guilt or necessity, or even grudgingly, but cheerfully (9:7). All generous giving is in grateful response to God's unspeakable gift (v. 15).

Paul's tone shifts in chs. 10–13. In this section he addresses his opponents directly, sharply challenging them. Some condemned Paul for being bold in his letters and weak when present (ch. 10). They boasted in themselves and compared themselves to others, seeking to show their own superiority (vv. 12–18). Paul turns the table on his opponents and requests that they bear with him as he engages in the folly of boasting (11:1). Paul's boast is different than theirs. He boasts in his weakness, because it is in weakness that God's strength is on display. Paul would rather glory in his infirmities in order that the power of Christ would rest on him (12:9–11). He brings his point home by telling them that he is willing to spend and be spent for their sakes because he loves them, even if it means they love him less (v. 15). He closes his letter with final exhortations, a warm demonstration of love, and a gracious doxology.

Outline:

I. Introduction (1:1–11)
  A. Greetings (1:1–2)
  B. Blessings to God for Comfort in Afflictions (1:3–11)
II. Defense of Travel Plans (1:12—2:13)
  A. Defense of Personal Integrity (1:12–24)
  B. Defense of Changed Plans (2:1–13)
III. Defense of Ministry (2:14—7:16)
  A. Message of Christ: Savor of Death and Life (2:14–17)
  B. People as Paul's Letter of Recommendation (3:1–6)
  C. The Greater Glory of New Covenant Ministry (3:7–18)
  D. The Message of Christ, the Light of the Gospel (4:1–6)
  E. The Treasure of the Gospel in Earthen Vessels (4:7–15)
  F. The Hope of Future Glory (4:16—5:10)
  G. The Ministry of Reconciliation (5:11–21)
  H. The Credentials of a Genuine Servant of God (6:1–13)
  I. An Appeal to Refuse Fellowship with Unbelievers (6:14—7:1)
  J. Final Exhortation and Rejoicing at Repentance (7:2–16)
IV. The Collection (8:1—9:15)
  A. Grace Given to Churches of Macedonia (8:1–5)
  B. Instruction to Complete the Gifts Begun (8:6–15)
  C. Commendation of Titus (8:16–24)
  D. Exhortations to Be Ready for the Collection (9:1–5)
  E. Importance of Cheerful Giving (9:6–15)
V. Rebuke to Opponents in Preparation for His Visit (10:1—13:10)
  A. Defense of Authority and Rebuke of Opponents (10:1–7)
  B. Opposition to Foolish Boasting and Comparisons (10:8–18)
  C. Apostolic Boasting (11:1–33)
  D. Boasting in Weakness So That Christ's Power Is Seen (12:1–10)
  E. Paul Provides Signs of a True Apostle (12:11–18)
  F. Conclusion of Defense with Concerns and Warnings (12:19—13:10)
VI. Conclusion (13:11–14)
  A. Final Greetings (13:11–13)
  B. Final Benediction (13:14)

THE SECOND EPISTLE OF PAUL THE APOSTLE TO THE

CORINTHIANS

CHAPTER 1

PAUL, an apostle of Jesus Christ by the will of God,
and Timothy *our* brother, unto the church of God
which is at Corinth, with all the saints which are
in all Achaia:
2 Grace *be* to you and peace from God our Father,
and *from* the Lord Jesus Christ.
3 Blessed *be* God, even the Father of our Lord
Jesus Christ, the Father of mercies, and the God
of all comfort;
4 Who comforteth us in all our tribulation, that
we may be able to comfort them which are in any
trouble, by the comfort wherewith we ourselves
are comforted of God.
5 For as the sufferings of Christ abound in us, so
our consolation also aboundeth by Christ.
6 And whether we be afflicted, *it is* for your
consolation and salvation, which is effectual in
the enduring of the same sufferings which we also
suffer: or whether we be comforted, *it is* for your
consolation and salvation.
7 And our hope of you *is* stedfast, knowing, that
as ye are partakers of the sufferings, so *shall ye be*
also of the consolation.
8 For we would not, brethren, have you ignorant
of our trouble which came to us in Asia, that we
were pressed out of measure, above strength,
insomuch that we despaired even of life:
9 But we had the sentence of death in ourselves,
that we should not trust in ourselves, but in God
which raiseth the dead:
10 Who delivered us from so great a death, and
doth deliver: in whom we trust that he will yet
deliver *us*;
11 Ye also helping together by prayer for us, that
for the gift *bestowed* upon us by the means of
many persons thanks may be given by many on
our behalf.
12 For our rejoicing is this, the testimony of our
conscience, that in simplicity and godly sincerity,
not with fleshly wisdom, but by the grace of God,
we have had our conversation in the world, and
more abundantly to you-ward.
13 For we write none other things unto you, than

Chapter 1: *Paul greets the church of God at Corinth, blesses the God of all comfort who delivers from affliction, and defends his change of travel plans.*

INTRODUCTION (1:1–11)

Greetings (1:1–2)

1:1 *apostle . . . will of God.* See notes at Eph. 1:1; 3:4–5. Opponents in the Corinthian church questioned Paul's credibility, authority, and ministry, but he reminds them that God is the One who called him to be an apostle of Jesus Christ.

1:2 *Grace . . . peace.* Common greetings in Paul's letters. *Grace.* God's purpose to save sinners. *peace.* Relationship believers have with God and others as a result of grace.

Blessings to God for Comfort in Afflictions (1:3–11)

1:3 *Blessed be God.* Praise be to God. *comfort.* God encourages His people in the midst of their affliction so that they find in God the strength needed to endure.

1:4 *that we may be able to comfort.* Believers who experience the comfort of God in their afflictions are able to extend consolation and encouragement to others.

1:5 *the sufferings of Christ.* Believers in union with Christ share in His sufferings, not His sacrificial, atoning suffering, but the sufferings that come for the gospel's sake. *so our consolation also aboundeth.* As the suffering abounds so does the consolation.

1:6–7 *it is for your consolation and salvation.* Paul viewed all of his sufferings as well as all of his comforts as being for the good of those to whom he preached the gospel. Those who advance the gospel and those who embrace the gospel share in both suffering and consolation.

1:9 *we had the sentence of death in ourselves, that we should not trust in ourselves.* Paul often found himself in situations where death seemed the only result. In these times his trust was in the God who raises the dead.

1:10 *Who delivered us from so great a death . . . doth deliver . . . will yet deliver.* Paul's hope is in God who is the deliverer. He experienced God's deliverance in the past, continues to experience it in the present, and expects it in the future.

1:11 *by prayer for us.* Paul's hope and confidence rested in God. Yet, he grasps the importance of prayer within God's sovereign purposes.

DEFENSE OF TRAVEL PLANS (1:12—2:13)

Defense of Personal Integrity (1:12–24)

1:12 *rejoicing.* The reason for or object of boasting. Paul is able to boast, or rejoice, because his conscience is clear in that he did not act in a fickle manner as some accused him of acting. This boast is not self-centered, for he points to *the grace of God* as the ultimate reason for his simplicity and sincerity. *fleshly wisdom.* Worldly wisdom. *had our conversation.*

what ye read or acknowledge; and I trust ye shall
acknowledge even to the end;
14 As also ye have acknowledged us in part, that
we are your rejoicing, even as ye also *are* ours in
the day of the Lord Jesus.
15 And in this confidence I was minded to come
unto you before, that ye might have a second
benefit;
16 And to pass by you into Macedonia, and to
come again out of Macedonia unto you, and of
you to be brought on my way toward Judaea.
17 When I therefore was thus minded, did I use
lightness? or the things that I purpose, do I pur-
pose according to the flesh, that with me there
should be yea yea, and nay nay?
18 But *as* God *is* true, our word toward you was
not yea and nay.
19 For the Son of God, Jesus Christ, who was
preached among you by us, *even* by me and
Silvanus and Timotheus, was not yea and nay, but
in him was yea.
20 For all the promises of God in him *are* yea, and
in him Amen, unto the glory of God by us.
21 Now he which stablisheth us with you in
Christ, and hath anointed us, *is* God;
22 Who hath also sealed us, and given the earnest
of the Spirit in our hearts.
23 Moreover I call God for a record upon my soul,
that to spare you I came not as yet unto Corinth.
24 Not for that we have dominion over your faith,
but are helpers of your joy: for by faith ye stand.

CHAPTER 2

BUT I determined this with myself, that I would
not come again to you in heaviness.
2 For if I make you sorry, who is he then that
maketh me glad, but the same which is made sorry
by me?
3 And I wrote this same unto you, lest, when I
came, I should have sorrow from them of whom
I ought to rejoice; having confidence in you all,
that my joy is *the joy* of you all.
4 For out of much affliction and anguish of heart
I wrote unto you with many tears; not that ye
should be grieved, but that ye might know the
love which I have more abundantly unto you.
5 But if any have caused grief, he hath not grieved
me, but in part: that I may not overcharge you all.
6 Sufficient to such a man *is* this punishment,

Conducted ourselves. *to you-ward*. Toward you.

1:13 *For we write none other things unto you, than what ye read*. He is as forthright and honest in his letters as he is in his actions and decisions.

1:15 *a second benefit*. Literally, "a second grace."

1:17–18 *use lightness*. Changed plans lightly. He did not make decisions according to the ways of the world (*according to the flesh*). His words and actions can be counted as trustworthy. *yea . . . nay*. Yes and no. His yes means yes and his no means no (Matt. 5:37). Just as *God is true*, so Paul can be counted trustworthy.

1:20 *in him are yea*. The gospel announces that all God's *promises* are fulfilled in Christ. *Amen . . . by us*. Believers affirm God's faithfulness in Christ (John 3:33).

1:22 *sealed us*. Preserved and ensured full salvation. *earnest*. Pledge or down payment of redemption. See notes at Eph. 1:13–14.

1:23 *call God for a record upon my soul*. Call God as a witness, implying that God will bring a curse if he fails to tell the truth.

1:24 *have dominion*. Be tyrannical or dictatorial. His desire is that he might help the Corinthians. If he had come as planned, his visit would have been counterproductive.

Thoughts for Personal/Family Worship: Chapter 1

1. **When you put your trials—past and present—next to what Paul says here, can you see any purpose, comfort, or mercy in your affliction?**
2. **One result of experiencing the comfort of God is that you are able to provide comfort to others in their trials. Enduring trials and experiencing God's comfort should make you more sensitive to the afflictions of those around you. Do you know someone suffering as you once did? How can you help?**
3. **Paul defended his travel plans to those in Corinth. The assumptions made against Paul are shocking. Instead of thinking the best—that there would be some legitimate reason to move the apostle to change his plans—some accused him of being fickle, untrustworthy, and worldly. This should cause us to pause and evaluate how quickly we also assume the worst. Are you more prone to think the worst or the best of others?**

Chapter 2: *Paul continues his defense of changed travel plans, and begins his defense of his ministry and message.*

Defense of Changed Plans (2:1–13)

2:1 *heaviness*. Grief. Paul felt it was more important not to go to them again with such painful business. He cared for them more than a planned itinerary.

2:2 *if I make you sorry, who is he then that maketh me glad*. Disciplining these erring, professing believers does not make Paul glad.

2:3 *I wrote this same unto you*. Instructions for dealing with the professing Christian who was in sin (1 Cor. 5). It was his hope that they would act immediately, so that by the time he arrived he could rejoice with them at the repentance and restoration of the individual.

2:4 Paul reveals his emotions. It was not his desire that they *be grieved*, but to see repentance and restoration. He was overcome with *tears* and desired that they know that love for them moved him to write such a letter.

2:5 *overcharge*. Burden or weigh down. The structure of this sentence in the Greek is difficult. The idea is that the one who has caused sorrow in the church has not grieved Paul as much as the sinner who has grieved the church itself.

2:6–8 *Sufficient to such a man is this punishment*. The measures taken to discipline are enough. Paul encourages the church to rally around the repentant sinner with forgiveness and *comfort*, lest the individual be overcome with sorrow.

2:10 *I forgive also*. Paul notes that what they decided he approves.

2:11 Undue harshness and failure to extend forgiveness to

which *was inflicted* of many.
7 So that contrariwise ye *ought* rather to forgive
him, and comfort *him*, lest perhaps such a one
should be swallowed up with overmuch sorrow.
8 Wherefore I beseech you that ye would confirm
your love toward him.
9 For to this end also did I write, that I might
know the proof of you, whether ye be obedient
in all things.
10 To whom ye forgive any thing, I *forgive* also:
for if I forgave any thing, to whom I forgave *it*,
for your sakes *forgave I it* in the person of Christ;
11 Lest Satan should get an advantage of us: for
we are not ignorant of his devices.
12 Furthermore, when I came to Troas to *preach*
Christ's gospel, and a door was opened unto me
of the Lord,
13 I had no rest in my spirit, because I found not
Titus my brother: but taking my leave of them, I
went from thence into Macedonia.
14 Now thanks *be* unto God, which always causeth
us to triumph in Christ, and maketh manifest
the savour of his knowledge by us in every place.
15 For we are unto God a sweet savour of Christ,
in them that are saved, and in them that perish:
16 To the one *we are* the savour of death unto
death; and to the other the savour of life unto life.
And who *is* sufficient for these things?
17 For we are not as many, which corrupt the
word of God: but as of sincerity, but as of God, in
the sight of God speak we in Christ.

CHAPTER 3

Do we begin again to commend ourselves? or
need we, as some *others*, epistles of commendation
to you, or *letters* of commendation from you?
2 Ye are our epistle written in our hearts, known
and read of all men:
3 *Forasmuch as ye are* manifestly declared to be
the epistle of Christ ministered by us, written not
with ink, but with the Spirit of the living God; not
in tables of stone, but in fleshy tables of the heart.
4 And such trust have we through Christ to
God-ward:
5 Not that we are sufficient of ourselves to think
any thing as of ourselves; but our sufficiency *is* of
God;
6 Who also hath made us able ministers of the
new testament; not of the letter, but of the spirit:
for the letter killeth, but the spirit giveth life.
7 But if the ministration of death, written *and*

---

the penitent plays into Satan's schemes (*devices*) to cause disruption and division in the church.

2:12–13 *no rest in my spirit.* Paul waited for Titus to receive a report about Corinth, and when Titus could not be found, Paul was anxious for the well-being of the church. *taking my leave of them.* Even though Paul saw much fruit of the gospel in Troas his love for the Corinthians was greater.

DEFENSE OF MINISTRY (2:14—7:16)

Message of Christ: Savor of Death and Life (2:14–17)

2:14 *thanks be unto God.* Despite Paul's frequent suffering, God was giving victory. *triumph.* Military word for the triumphal procession upon return from victory. *savour.* Aroma. *his knowledge.* The knowledge of Christ, revealed in the gospel.

2:15 *sweet savour.* Pleasant fragrance (not the same word as *savour* in vv. 14,16). Both terms are used together of God's pleasure in a sacrifice (Eph. 5:2; Phil. 4:18). God delights in His Son and His saving work, and so He also delights in gospel ministry even if people reject Christ. *saved.* Greek present tense, "are being saved" by faith in Christ. *perish.* Also present tense, "are being ruined" by unbelief and sin.

2:16 *savour of death.* The gospel of Christ crucified stinks of death to unbelievers, who find it foolish and offensive (1 Cor. 1:23). *savour of life.* Believers find the same gospel to be a sweet fragrance of the divine Savior (1 Cor. 1:24). *unto death . . . unto life.* The gospel either hardens and confirms sinners in spiritual death or raises and renews them to eternal life. *who is sufficient for these things?* Not any man, but God (2 Cor. 3:4–6).

2:17 *corrupt.* Deal deceitfully or peddle it. Paul handled the Word of God with sincerity, whereas his opponents peddled it for their own purposes. A distinguishing mark of a genuine minister is how he handles the Word of God.

Thoughts for Personal/Family Worship: Chapter 2

1. **Discipline is necessary for the restoration of an erring brother or sister and for the purity of the church. Paul encourages Christians to use discernment and a balance between confrontation and forgiveness. He reminds us that Satan is always looking for an advantage. How do you respond to sin that you see in yourself, in others at church, and in your family members?**
2. **The message of the gospel is an aroma to all who hear its proclamation. To those who embrace the gospel, it is a sweet fragrance of life unto life. To those who reject it, the gospel is a stench of death unto death. Where do you stand in relation to its message?**

Chapter 3: *Paul counts the Corinthian church as his letter of recommendation and describes his ministry as a ministry of the new covenant, which is superior to the old covenant ministry.*

People as Paul's Letter of Recommendation (3:1–6)

3:1 *letters of commendation.* A common way of introducing oneself during this period. Paul was not opposed to letters of commendation in all circumstances, but was exasperated that they demanded them from their spiritual father who planted the church. Their conscience should bear witness to his genuineness as God's servant (5:11).

3:2 *Ye are our epistle written in our hearts.* The proof and legitimacy of Paul's ministry was the success of the gospel in Corinth.

3:3 *Forasmuch as.* Seeing that. *epistle of Christ ministered by us.* Christ worked grace by *the Spirit* through the apostle as the instrument. *not in tables of stone, but in fleshy tables of the heart.* The new covenant promise (Jer. 31:33).

3:4 *to God-ward.* Toward God.

3:5 *our sufficiency is of God.* Paul answers the question he raised in 2:16. Paul's confidence in ministry rests not upon himself, but in God who is able to save sinners.

The Greater Glory of New Covenant Ministry (3:7–18)

engraven in stones, was glorious, so that the
children of Israel could not stedfastly behold the
face of Moses for the glory of his countenance;
which *glory* was to be done away:
8 How shall not the ministration of the spirit be
rather glorious?
9 For if the ministration of condemnation *be*
glory, much more doth the ministration of righ-
teousness exceed in glory.
10 For even that which was made glorious had no
glory in this respect, by reason of the glory that
excelleth.
11 For if that which is done away *was* glorious,
much more that which remaineth *is* glorious.
12 Seeing then that we have such hope, we use
great plainness of speech:
13 And not as Moses, *which* put a vail over his
face, that the children of Israel could not sted-
fastly look to the end of that which is abolished:
14 But their minds were blinded: for until this
day remaineth the same vail untaken away in the
reading of the old testament; which *vail* is done
away in Christ.
15 But even unto this day, when Moses is read,
the vail is upon their heart.
16 Nevertheless when it shall turn to the Lord, the
vail shall be taken away.
17 Now the Lord is that Spirit: and where the
Spirit of the Lord *is*, there *is* liberty.
18 But we all, with open face beholding as in a
glass the glory of the Lord, are changed into the
same image from glory to glory, *even* as by the
Spirit of the Lord.

CHAPTER 4

THEREFORE seeing we have this ministry, as we
have received mercy, we faint not;
2 But have renounced the hidden things of dis-
honesty, not walking in craftiness, nor handling
the word of God deceitfully; but by manifesta-
tion of the truth commending ourselves to every
man's conscience in the sight of God.
3 But if our gospel be hid, it is hid to them that
are lost:
4 In whom the god of this world hath blinded the

3:7 *ministration of death.* God saved sinners in the Old Testament (Rom. 4:3,6), but the law cannot impart life (Gal. 3:21). *glorious.* The law still enjoyed a measure of glory, evidenced in the fact that the children of Israel could not look directly into the face of Moses (Ex. 34:29–35).
3:8–11 *the ministration of the spirit be rather glorious?* If the ministry of death enjoyed glory, then the ministry of the Spirit is much more glorious because it brings righteousness and is more permanent. The old covenant was glorious, but it was a temporary pointer to the perfect Mediator. Now Christ has accomplished redemption and been given a ministry with a more permanent glory (*which remaineth*).
3:12 *Seeing then that we have such hope.* Paul's confidence is in God, who is sufficient to change the hearts of his hearers by the Spirit. Therefore, Paul preached boldly with frank teaching of the gospel (*plainness of speech*), not having to conceal anything.
3:13 *Moses* did not enjoy the same boldness and confidence that Paul now claims, but *put a vail over his face* so that the Israelites would not see the glory that was temporary and would soon pass away (*abolished*).
3:14–15 *But their minds were blinded.* Israelites could not see that the old covenant was temporary. Paul notes that the same is the case *even unto this day, when Moses is read, the vail is upon their heart.* When Moses came down from the mount the veil covered his face. Now a veil covers the heart of those who hear but do not turn to the Lord (4:3–4).
3:16 *when it shall turn to the Lord, the vail shall be taken away.* Paul uses language similar to v. 14. When God brings a person to Himself and grants faith, the eyes are opened to see the beauty of the Lord Jesus Christ, so that the Spirit writes upon a now soft heart (v. 3).
3:17 *Now the Lord is that Spirit . . . the Spirit of the Lord.* Paul highlights the involvement of the Trinity in redemption without confusing the persons of the Trinity. New covenant ministry emphasizes the Father, the Son, and the Holy Spirit. *liberty.* Freedom. Believers are no longer under the bondage of the law. They are in Christ and the Spirit writes the law of God on their hearts and leads them in a life that is pleasing to God.
3:18 *But we all.* Not only Jewish believers but Gentile believers also. *with open face.* Not veiled like Moses. *beholding . . . the glory of the Lord.* As Christians gaze upon the glory of the Lord in the mirror (*glass*) of the gospel they *are changed into the same image.* The Reformers and those who followed them spoke of the double benefit of Christ: (1) justification and (2) transformation. As Christians experience their union with Christ and behold Him by faith they are transformed into His image. *from glory to glory.* Transformation is ongoing by means of progressive sanctification. *as by the Spirit of the Lord.* God works this transformation in the lives of believers through the ministry of the Holy Spirit.

Thoughts for Personal/Family Worship: Chapter 3

1. **Paul's attention to the superiority of the new covenant glory comes to a climax by celebrating the reality that all those who believe can behold Jesus Christ with uncovered faces. This is a remarkable and amazing benefit. Paul says that there are those even today that still read Moses with veiled hearts. One can perform religious duties and even be identified with the church, but there must be faith in order to see Christ as He is. Do you have faith to see the spiritual glory of Christ? What does it mean to experience this saving privilege?**
2. **The great freedom of the gospel is the access a believer has to gaze upon Christ by faith through the help of the Spirit. The result of this gaze is greater conformity to the image of Jesus Christ. People become like what they gaze upon or see. How does this motivate you to diligently use the ordinary means of grace such as preaching? What should we pray as we prepare to worship with the church?**

Chapter 4: ***Paul describes his message in opposition to the message of false teachers and writes that God chose to give the treasure of the gospel to earthen vessels. Paul places present suffering in ministry within the context of future glory.***

minds of them which believe not, lest the light of
the glorious gospel of Christ, who is the image of
God, should shine unto them.
5 For we preach not ourselves, but Christ Jesus the
Lord; and ourselves your servants for Jesus' sake.
6 For God, who commanded the light to shine
out of darkness, hath shined in our hearts, to *give*
the light of the knowledge of the glory of God in
the face of Jesus Christ.
7 But we have this treasure in earthen vessels, that
the excellency of the power may be of God, and
not of us.
8 *We are* troubled on every side, yet not dis-
tressed; *we are* perplexed, but not in despair;
9 Persecuted, but not forsaken; cast down, but
not destroyed;
10 Always bearing about in the body the dying of
the Lord Jesus, that the life also of Jesus might be
made manifest in our body.
11 For we which live are alway delivered unto
death for Jesus' sake, that the life also of Jesus
might be made manifest in our mortal flesh.
12 So then death worketh in us, but life in you.
13 We having the same spirit of faith, according
as it is written, I believed, and therefore have I
spoken; we also believe, and therefore speak;
14 Knowing that he which raised up the Lord
Jesus shall raise up us also by Jesus, and shall
present *us* with you.
15 For all things *are* for your sakes, that the abun-
dant grace might through the thanksgiving of
many redound to the glory of God.
16 For which cause we faint not; but though
our outward man perish, yet the inward *man* is
renewed day by day.
17 For our light affliction, which is but for a mo-
ment, worketh for us a far more exceeding *and*
eternal weight of glory;
18 While we look not at the things which are seen,
but at the things which are not seen: for the things
which are seen *are* temporal; but the things which
are not seen *are* eternal.

The Message of Christ, the Light of the Gospel (4:1–6)

4:1 *Therefore*. The nature of new covenant ministry (ch. 3) is the reason why he does not lose heart and become discouraged (*faint*).
4:2 In contrast to his opponents, Paul does not tamper with the Word of God in a deceitful, crafty, or false manner, but is plain and true. Thus he commends himself as a true servant of God to everyone, including God Himself.
4:3 *if our gospel be hid*. Veiled to those who reject it (3:15).
4:4 *the god of this world*. Satan's influence on unbelievers blinds their minds. *Lest the light . . . should shine unto them.* God opens the eyes of the blind. Though Satan has control, he cannot thwart God's saving will. Christ, who is *the image of God*, radiates light and glory in the gospel (Rom. 8:29; Col. 1:15; Heb. 1:3).
4:5 *we preach not ourselves.* Paul's message stands opposite to his opponents, whose message was self-centered. His message centered on *Christ Jesus the Lord*.
4:6 *God . . . hath shined in our hearts.* Just as God commanded the light to shine out of darkness at creation by the power of His voice (Gen. 1:3), so He commands the gospel to shine in the hearts of sinners with sovereign and irresistible life. *knowledge of the glory of God in the face of Jesus Christ.* To know God is to see Christ. To see God's glory is to see the face of Jesus Christ (John 14:9).

The Treasure of the Gospel in Earthen Vessels (4:7–15)

4:7 *this treasure.* The gospel ministry and the message of the knowledge of God in the face of Jesus Christ. *earthen vessels.* Clay vessels, the weakness of man, which the Corinthians consider to be embarrassing. This is God's intent so that all glory may be His.
4:8–10 Paul describes the weakness and afflictions he faces, yet notes that these do not lead to despair. *bearing about in the body the dying of the Lord Jesus.* Paul often links his suffering to the suffering of Jesus Christ (Rom. 8:36; 1 Cor. 4:9; 15:31; 2 Cor. 11:23; Gal. 6:17; Phil. 3:10).
4:12 *death worketh in us.* The suffering Paul endures for the sake of the gospel leads to spiritual *life* in others as the Spirit opens their minds to the gospel.
4:15 *all things are for your sakes.* Paul reiterates that he is willing to endure hardship for the benefit of others. *redound.* Overflow. Paul is not presenting his endurance of hardships in such a way that would cause others to praise him, but rejoices that his sufferings lead others who have received abundant grace to give God all the glory. For Paul, God's glory is ultimate (1 Cor. 10:31).

The Hope of Future Glory (4:16—5:10)

4:16 *outward man.* Body. *inward man.* Soul. Despite the perishing of the body, the Christian may find his spirit refreshed and strengthened by the grace of God.
4:17 *light affliction.* Surprising given his many sufferings (11:16–33), but explained in that God was working a far greater, *eternal weight of glory* in them, namely, being transformed into the likeness of Jesus Christ (3:18). The exaltation of Christ follows His humiliation (Phil. 2:6–11), and this pattern governs Paul's perspective of his own suffering.
4:18 The key to Paul's perspective is that in the midst of his suffering, he focuses on the *eternal* things, those things that are invisible to the physical eye (5:7).

Thoughts for Personal/Family Worship: Chapter 4

1. **God is sovereign in salvation. Through the preaching of the gospel (general call) God commands the light of the glorious gospel of Christ to shine in the hearts of some hearers (effectual call). Have you experienced the gospel in your heart, or do you continue to have your eyes blinded by Satan? Experiencing the light of the gospel brings you to the knowledge of the glory of God in the face of Jesus Christ.**
2. **The Bible teaches about different kinds of suffering. There is suffering because of sin (David and Bathsheba). There is suffering because of someone else's sin (Achan). There is suffering because of righteousness' sake (Paul). There is suffering when the cause is not immediately discernible (Job). Paul's words here apply most directly to the latter two kinds of suffering. The only way to consider real and deep affliction as light is to see them compared to the weight of eternal glory. As you go through hardships in your life, seek God's grace to suffer well and to have an eternal perspective, focusing on those things that are not seen and are eternal.**

CHAPTER 5

FOR we know that if our earthly house of *this*
tabernacle were dissolved, we have a building of
God, an house not made with hands, eternal in
the heavens.
2 For in this we groan, earnestly desiring to
be clothed upon with our house which is from
heaven:
3 If so be that being clothed we shall not be found
naked.
4 For we that are in *this* tabernacle do groan,
being burdened: not for that we would be un-
clothed, but clothed upon, that mortality might
be swallowed up of life.
5 Now he that hath wrought us for the selfsame
thing *is* God, who also hath given unto us the ear-
nest of the Spirit.
6 Therefore *we are* always confident, knowing
that, whilst we are at home in the body, we are
absent from the Lord:
7 (For we walk by faith, not by sight:)
8 We are confident, *I say*, and willing rather to be
absent from the body, and to be present with the
Lord.
9 Wherefore we labour, that, whether present or
absent, we may be accepted of him.
10 For we must all appear before the judgment
seat of Christ; that every one may receive the
things *done* in *his* body, according to that he hath
done, whether *it be* good or bad.
11 Knowing therefore the terror of the Lord, we
persuade men; but we are made manifest unto
God; and I trust also are made manifest in your
consciences.
12 For we commend not ourselves again unto
you, but give you occasion to glory on our behalf,
that ye may have somewhat to *answer* them which
glory in appearance, and not in heart.
13 For whether we be beside ourselves, *it is* to
God: or whether we be sober, *it is* for your cause.
14 For the love of Christ constraineth us; because
we thus judge, that if one died for all, then were
all dead:
15 And *that* he died for all, that they which live
should not henceforth live unto themselves, but
unto him which died for them, and rose again.
16 Wherefore henceforth know we no man after
the flesh: yea, though we have known Christ after
the flesh, yet now henceforth know we *him* no
more.
17 Therefore if any man *be* in Christ, *he is* a new
creature: old things are passed away; behold, all
things are become new.
18 And all things *are* of God, who hath reconciled
us to himself by Jesus Christ, and hath given to us
the ministry of reconciliation;
19 To wit, that God was in Christ, reconciling the
world unto himself, not imputing their trespasses
unto them; and hath committed unto us the word
of reconciliation.

Chapter 5: *Paul describes the eternal home of believers and the ministry of reconciliation.*

5:1 *earthly house of this tabernacle.* Earthly tent, the temporal body. *dissolved.* Died. *a building of God, an house not made with hands.* The permanent, eternal body believers will receive in the future.

5:2 The present body with its frailties brings forth groaning and anticipation for the resurrection body.

5:3 *found naked.* Believers at death, though present with the Lord, still wait until the soul is reunited with the glorified body.

5:5 *earnest of the Spirit.* The Holy Spirit has been given as the guarantee of redemption and glorification (1:22).

5:6–7 *Therefore we are always confident.* Paul's confidence remained intact even in the midst of suffering because he lived *by faith* and *not by sight*.

5:10 *For we must all appear before the judgment seat of Christ.* The judgment that evaluates deeds done in this life (in the *body*). Christians are not under condemnation (Rom. 8:1), nor is salvation by works (Rom. 3:28); but actions have consequences, and believers will receive rewards (1 Cor. 3:14). Paul's conscience is clear before God. This future judgment is a warning to his opponents who threaten the purity of Christ's church.

The Ministry of Reconciliation (5:11–21)

5:11 *the terror of the Lord.* The fear of the Lord, living in a deep awareness of who God is and with God at the center of all their thoughts, even the reality of standing before Christ's judgment seat. Because Paul knows the fear of the Lord, he will *persuade men* in preaching the gospel. *manifest unto God.* God knows all things, including motives, actions, and thoughts. Paul wishes the Corinthian people could know him as God knows him.

5:12 *we commend not ourselves again unto you.* Paul's desire was not to focus on himself, but to provide an answer to those who continued to doubt his ministry.

5:13 *beside ourselves . . . or whether we be sober.* Some considered Paul to be insane, possibly because of his testimony to revelations and visions (12:1). Paul responds that he does everything for God's glory and the good of others.

5:14 *the love of Christ.* Christ's love for His people. The context focuses on what Christ has done for His people in dying and rising again. Christ's love for him compels (*constraineth*) him to serve.

5:15 *that he died for all.* The *all* are defined by *they which live* spiritually because of Christ's death. All those for whom He died will not *live unto themselves*, but unto Christ.

5:16 *after the flesh.* According to human standards. *though we have known Christ after the flesh.* From a worldly perspective Christ is rejected and discarded. *yet now henceforth know we him no more.* Once Christ presented Himself to Paul on the Damascus road the apostle Paul knew Christ for who He really is, the Son of God (Acts 9:5,20).

5:17 *in Christ.* Union with Christ changes everything because the coming of Christ changed everything by His suffering, death, resurrection, and ascension. All those who are in Him enjoy life in the new creation (*new creature*), under the new covenant (ch. 3).

5:18–20 *all things are of God.* God planned redemption. *reconciled.* This highlights the animosity between God and man because of mankind's rebellion, and the peace worked by God through the death and resurrection of Christ (Rom.

20 Now then we are ambassadors for Christ, as
though God did beseech *you* by us: we pray *you* in
Christ's stead, be ye reconciled to God.
21 For he hath made him *to be* sin for us, who
knew no sin; that we might be made the righteousness of God in him.

CHAPTER 6

WE then, *as* workers together *with him*, beseech *you*
also that ye receive not the grace of God in vain.
2 (For he saith, I have heard thee in a time accepted, and in the day of salvation have I succoured
thee: behold, now *is* the accepted time; behold,
now *is* the day of salvation.)
3 Giving no offence in any thing, that the ministry be not blamed:
4 But in all *things* approving ourselves as the
ministers of God, in much patience, in afflictions,
in necessities, in distresses,
5 In stripes, in imprisonments, in tumults, in
labours, in watchings, in fastings;
6 By pureness, by knowledge, by longsuffering, by
kindness, by the Holy Ghost, by love unfeigned,
7 By the word of truth, by the power of God, by
the armour of righteousness on the right hand
and on the left,
8 By honour and dishonour, by evil report and
good report: as deceivers, and *yet* true;
9 As unknown, and *yet* well known; as dying,
and, behold, we live; as chastened, and not killed;
10 As sorrowful, yet alway rejoicing; as poor, yet
making many rich; as having nothing, and *yet*
possessing all things.
11 O *ye* Corinthians, our mouth is open unto
you, our heart is enlarged.
12 Ye are not straitened in us, but ye are straitened
in your own bowels.
13 Now for a recompence in the same, (I speak as
unto *my* children,) be ye also enlarged.
14 Be ye not unequally yoked together with unbelievers: for what fellowship hath righteousness
with unrighteousness? and what communion
hath light with darkness?
15 And what concord hath Christ with Belial? or
what part hath he that believeth with an infidel?
16 And what agreement hath the temple of God
with idols? for ye are the temple of the living God;
as God hath said, I will dwell in them, and walk
in *them*; and I will be their God, and they shall be
my people.
17 Wherefore come out from among them, and
be ye separate, saith the Lord, and touch not the
unclean *thing*; and I will receive you,

5:10; Eph. 2:14,16). *To wit.* That is. *imputing.* Counting, like an accountant reckoning financial debts and obligations (Rom. 4:4–8). *beseech.* Appeal, urge, exhort. *pray you in Christ's stead.* I request or beg you as Christ's representative. Amazingly, the glorious Lord appeals to poor, wicked sinners to turn to Him. Ministers must represent Christ in their earnest appeals for men to come to Him.

5:21 *he hath made him to be sin for us, who knew no sin.* God charged His Son, Jesus Christ, the sinless one, with the sin of His people, so that Christ was counted a sinner. *that we might be made the righteousness of God in him.* God counts sinners as righteous in union with Christ—the great exchange of the gospel. Christ took our sin and we by grace through faith receive His righteousness (double imputation).

Thoughts for Personal/Family Worship: Chapter 5

1. **Meditate on the future realities of the gospel. Have you learned by grace to groan to be clothed with a glorified body? Take time to consider and meditate upon all that awaits the children of God. If you have the Spirit, all this is yours in earnest already.**
2. **Chapter 5 closes with one of the most succinctly stated summaries of the gospel. God made Christ to be sin for His people. Sinners receive the righteousness of Christ by faith. Have you rested in the gospel? Do you know experientially what it is to be counted as righteous in God's eyes? If so, celebrate the reconciliation that is found in Christ. If you have received that reconciliation, like Paul, how can you help others to be reconciled to Him?**

Chapter 6: *Paul presents credentials of a genuine minister and warns the church not to be entangled with the fellowship of unbelievers.*

The Credentials of a Genuine Servant of God (6:1–13)

6:1 *in vain.* For no good purpose. This is a warning not to heed the false teachers nor to turn away from the grace they have been given.

6:2 Paul cites Isa. 49:8. Paul's point is to call his hearers to faith and repentance as Isaiah did to his hearers. *behold, now is the day of salvation.* Christ's coming has brought in the new era (5:17); the fulfillment of all that is promised has arrived. There is no better time to embrace the gospel than now since it has arrived in fullness.

6:4–10 Paul characterizes the various qualifications of a genuine minister. He describes pressures and afflictions that come from every side (vv. 4–5), the divine provision that the Holy Spirit (*Holy Ghost*) grants to ministers (vv. 6–7), and triumph over difficulties and attacks (vv. 8–10).

6:11 *our mouth is opened unto you, our heart is enlarged.* Paul says that he has spoken freely to them and has opened his heart to them letting them know his emotions.

6:12 *Ye are not straitened in us.* There is much room for them in his heart. *ye are straitened in your own bowels.* The Corinthian church has not made room for Paul in their emotions.

6:13 *Now for a recompense in the same.* Paul has accepted them and he calls for them to receive him in the same way, to open their hearts toward him.

An Appeal to Refuse Fellowship with Unbelievers (6:14—7:1)

6:14–15 *Be ye not unequally yoked together with unbelievers.* The Corinthian church has been stingy in receiving Paul, yet open in being influenced by and accepting wicked and false teachers. They should not be wrongly matched in their associations. *Belial.* Satan.

6:16 *ye are the temple of the living God.* The church is the dwelling place of God, and therefore, preservation of purity is of vital importance (1 Cor. 3:16). *I will dwell in them.* The heart of the covenantal promise: God will be their God and they will be His people.

18 And will be a Father unto you, and ye shall be
my sons and daughters, saith the Lord Almighty.

CHAPTER 7

HAVING therefore these promises, dearly beloved,
let us cleanse ourselves from all filthiness of the
flesh and spirit, perfecting holiness in the fear of
God.
2 Receive us; we have wronged no man, we have
corrupted no man, we have defrauded no man.
3 I speak not *this* to condemn *you*: for I have said
before, that ye are in our hearts to die and live
with *you*.
4 Great *is* my boldness of speech toward you,
great *is* my glorying of you: I am filled with com-
fort, I am exceeding joyful in all our tribulation.
5 For, when we were come into Macedonia, our
flesh had no rest, but we were troubled on every
side; without *were* fightings, within *were* fears.
6 Nevertheless God, that comforteth those that
are cast down, comforted us by the coming of
Titus;
7 And not by his coming only, but by the conso-
lation wherewith he was comforted in you, when
he told us your earnest desire, your mourning,
your fervent mind toward me; so that I rejoiced
the more.
8 For though I made you sorry with a letter, I do
not repent, though I did repent: for I perceive that
the same epistle hath made you sorry, though *it*
were but for a season.
9 Now I rejoice, not that ye were made sorry, but
that ye sorrowed to repentance: for ye were made
sorry after a godly manner, that ye might receive
damage by us in nothing.
10 For godly sorrow worketh repentance to
salvation not to be repented of: but the sorrow of
the world worketh death.
11 For behold this selfsame thing, that ye
sorrowed after a godly sort, what carefulness it
wrought in you, yea, *what* clearing of yourselves,
yea, *what* indignation, yea, *what* fear, yea, *what*
vehement desire, yea, *what* zeal, yea, *what* revenge!
In all *things* ye have approved yourselves to be
clear in this matter.
12 Wherefore, though I wrote unto you, *I did it*
not for his cause that had done the wrong, nor for
his cause that suffered wrong, but that our care for
you in the sight of God might appear unto you.
13 Therefore we were comforted in your comfort:
yea, and exceedingly the more joyed we for the joy
of Titus, because his spirit was refreshed by you
all.
14 For if I have boasted any thing to him of you,
I am not ashamed; but as we spake all things to

6:17–18 *Wherefore.* Therefore. *come out from among them.* After Paul makes his case against fellowshiping with unbelievers, he issues a call to separate from them. Paul cites Isa. 52:11–12 and uses Old Testament covenantal language to describe God's fatherly relationship to His church (Isa. 43:6; Hos. 1:10).

Thoughts for Personal/Family Worship: Chapter 6

1. **This chapter addresses the qualifications of a genuine ministry in contrast to a false ministry. How can the truths presented here instruct you in praying for your minister and other church officers in personal and family times of prayer?**
2. **Associations matter to God. Because you have received reconciliation with God it is contradictory to remain in close association with unbelievers and have your life influenced by your former way of life. In what ways should Christians give careful attention to their associations?**

Chapter 7: *Paul exhorts the Corinthian church to receive his ministry.*

7:1 *Having therefore these promises.* The promises set forth in the preceding verses have ethical implications. *let us cleanse ourselves.* Though sanctification is a work of God's grace, the believer has a responsibility in sanctification to actively pursue holiness because of the promises of God. *from all filthiness of the flesh and spirit.* The pollution that affects the entire being, both body and soul.

Final Exhortation and Rejoicing at Repentance (7:2–16)

7:2 *Receive us.* After Paul focuses on the negative side of separation from unbelievers, he appeals to the church to positively embrace him and his ministry.

7:3 *ye are in our hearts to die and live with you.* Paul's deep affection for the Corinthian church will endure through life and death.

7:5 *For, when we were come into Macedonia.* Paul returns to his emotions first expressed in 2:13. *without.* Outside.

7:6–9 Paul recounts his joy at Titus coming to him as well as the joy he felt when Titus reported to him of the genuine repentance in the church.

7:10 One can be sorry for getting caught, but this alone is not "after a godly manner" (v. 9). Godly sorrow leads to genuine repentance, which is a turning away from sin unto Christ with a sincere desire to do what is pleasing to God. *repentance to salvation not to be repented of.* Genuine repentance that leads to salvation is not to be regretted.

7:11 *selfsame.* Same. *godly sort.* Godly manner. *carefulness.* Eagerness. *vehement desire.* Strong longing. *In all things ye have approved yourselves to be clear in this matter.* The repentant response of the church to Paul's letter affirms that they are truly God's people.

7:12 *our care for you.* The purpose of Paul's confrontation of the sin in Corinth was not limited to dealing with only the offender but was out of love for the church of Jesus Christ and to preserve its unity and purity. The ultimate purpose is to please God (*in the sight of God*).

7:13–16 Paul returns to his interaction with Titus and tells the church that he is comforted by them and joyful at their ministry to Titus and warm reception of him. He is not ashamed of the boasting he made on their behalf to Titus, because his words proved to be true by their response to confrontation.

Thoughts for Personal/Family Worship: Chapter 7

1. **How Christians live matters to God. In the Bible there are many motivations for pursuing holiness. Gratitude for**

you in truth, even so our boasting, which *I made* before Titus, is found a truth.
15 And his inward affection is more abundant toward you, whilst he remembereth the obedience of you all, how with fear and trembling ye received him.
16 I rejoice therefore that I have confidence in you in all *things*.

CHAPTER 8

MOREOVER, brethren, we do you to wit of the grace of God bestowed on the churches of Macedonia;
2 How that in a great trial of affliction the abundance of their joy and their deep poverty abounded unto the riches of their liberality.
3 For to *their* power, I bear record, yea, and beyond *their* power *they were* willing of themselves;
4 Praying us with much intreaty that we would receive the gift, and *take upon us* the fellowship of the ministering to the saints.
5 And *this they did*, not as we hoped, but first gave their own selves to the Lord, and unto us by the will of God.
6 Insomuch that we desired Titus, that as he had begun, so he would also finish in you the same grace also.
7 Therefore, as ye abound in every *thing, in* faith, and utterance, and knowledge, and *in* all diligence, and *in* your love to us, *see* that ye abound in this grace also.
8 I speak not by commandment, but by occasion of the forwardness of others, and to prove the sincerity of your love.
9 For ye know the grace of our Lord Jesus Christ, that, though he was rich, yet for your sakes he became poor, that ye through his poverty might be rich.
10 And herein I give *my* advice: for this is expedient for you, who have begun before, not only to do, but also to be forward a year ago.
11 Now therefore perform the doing *of it*; that as *there was* a readiness to will, so *there may be* a performance also out of that which ye have.
12 For if there be first a willing mind, *it is* accepted according to that a man hath, *and* not according to that he hath not.
13 For *I mean* not that other men be eased, and ye burdened:
14 But by an equality, *that* now at this time your abundance *may be a supply* for their want, that their abundance also may be *a supply* for your want: that there may be equality:
15 As it is written, He that *had gathered* much had nothing over; and he that *had gathered* little had no lack.

God's grace is a chief motivation. So are the promises of God. Paul appeals to God's covenantal promise to be your God and to receive you as His sons and daughters. Being a child of God ought to affect and influence your behavior. Children often look and act like their parents. How do things stand with you?

2. **When sin is confronted in your life, do you experience a sorrow for getting caught, or is there a sorrow for offending God that leads to repentance? The Christian life is one of perpetual repentance. There should be constant turning from sin unto Christ. Are you grateful that God granted you repentance to seek Him for grace to lead a life pleasing to Him? While dealing with sin is hard, a repentance that leads to salvation is never to be regretted.**

THE COLLECTION (8:1—9:15)

Chapter 8: *Paul addresses the collection for the saints in Jerusalem.*

Grace Given to Churches of Macedonia (8:1–5)

8:1 *we do you to wit.* We want to make known to you. *grace of God.* Christian generosity comes from the work of God's grace upon the soul (1 Chron. 29:17–18).
8:2 *riches of their liberality.* They gave generously.
8:3 *willing of themselves.* Not under pressure, but freely of their own will.
8:4 *Praying us with much intreaty.* Despite their own affliction and poverty, they pleaded with the apostle to be able to participate in the collection for the saints.
8:5 *not as we hoped.* They participated beyond what Paul had expected. *first.* In priority, not chronology. The Macedonians saw their giving primarily as an act of worship to the Lord (Phil. 4:18; Heb. 13:16).

Instruction to Complete the Gifts Begun (8:6–15)

8:6 Titus addressed the gift at his visit in Corinth, and he is instructed to encourage them in seeing the collection finalized.
8:7 *as ye abound in every thing.* Paul points to clear evidences of grace in the Corinthian church (1 Cor. 1:4–5) and motivates them to abound in the giving of monetary help as well.
8:8 *I speak not by commandment.* Giving ought to be voluntary. *forwardness.* Earnestness and diligence of others in giving. *to prove.* To test or try.
8:9 *For ye know the grace of our Lord Jesus Christ.* God's grace to believers ought to move them to be gracious to others; in this case, it ought to move them to give to others' needs. *though he was rich, yet for your sakes he became poor.* As the eternal Son of God, Christ enjoyed divine status, but He took on humiliation with the incarnation (Phil. 2:6–8). *that ye through his poverty might be rich.* Christ suffered and died for the salvation of sinners to give them spiritual blessings (not mere temporal wealth). Given all that Christ has done in salvation, it is not too much to expect Christians to help others in need.
8:10 *expedient.* For your benefit. *forward a year ago.* Paul advises them to make good on their promise and desire to help, which they expressed earlier.
8:12 *a willing mind . . . accepted according to that a man hath.* Paul does not stipulate an exact amount each person is to give. The giver must have a willingness to give and should give according to what he is able to give.
8:13–14 *not that other men be eased, and ye burdened: But by an equality.* Fairness in the gathering of funds for the saints, not to enrich some at others' expense, but to care for all.
8:15 *As it is written.* Citing Ex. 16:18. *nothing over.* Not too much. Just as God did when He fed His people with manna in the wilderness, He supplies each man's needs.

16 But thanks *be* to God, which put the same ear-
nest care into the heart of Titus for you.
17 For indeed he accepted the exhortation; but
being more forward, of his own accord he went
unto you.
18 And we have sent with him the brother, whose
praise *is* in the gospel throughout all the churches;
19 And not *that* only, but who was also chosen
of the churches to travel with us with this grace,
which is administered by us to the glory of the
same Lord, and *declaration of* your ready mind:
20 Avoiding this, that no man should blame us in
this abundance which is administered by us:
21 Providing for honest things, not only in the
sight of the Lord, but also in the sight of men.
22 And we have sent with them our brother,
whom we have oftentimes proved diligent in
many things, but now much more diligent, upon
the great confidence which *I have* in you.
23 Whether *any do enquire* of Titus, *he is* my
partner and fellowhelper concerning you: or our
brethren *be enquired of, they are* the messengers of
the churches, *and* the glory of Christ.
24 Wherefore shew ye to them, and before the
churches, the proof of your love, and of our
boasting on your behalf.

CHAPTER 9

FOR as touching the ministering to the saints, it is
superfluous for me to write to you:
2 For I know the forwardness of your mind, for
which I boast of you to them of Macedonia, that
Achaia was ready a year ago; and your zeal hath
provoked very many.
3 Yet have I sent the brethren, lest our boasting of
you should be in vain in this behalf; that, as I said,
ye may be ready:
4 Lest haply if they of Macedonia come with me,
and find you unprepared, we (that we say not,
ye) should be ashamed in this same confident
boasting.
5 Therefore I thought it necessary to exhort the
brethren, that they would go before unto you, and
make up beforehand your bounty, whereof ye had
notice before, that the same might be ready, as *a*
matter of bounty, and not as *of* covetousness.
6 But this *I say*, He which soweth sparingly shall
reap also sparingly; and he which soweth bounti-
fully shall reap also bountifully.
7 Every man according as he purposeth in his
heart, *so let him give*; not grudgingly, or of neces-
sity: for God loveth a cheerful giver.
8 And God *is* able to make all grace abound
toward you; that ye, always having all sufficiency
in all *things*, may abound to every good work:
9 (As it is written, He hath dispersed abroad;
he hath given to the poor: his righteousness
remaineth for ever.
10 Now he that ministereth seed to the sower
both minister bread for *your* food, and multiply
your seed sown, and increase the fruits of your
righteousness;)
11 Being enriched in every thing to all bountiful-

Commendation of Titus (8:16–24)

8:16 *But thanks be to God, which put the same earnest care.* Paul offers thanks to God for Titus's love for the saints in Corinth, which they should imitate in loving others.

8:18 *the brother.* Though the original readers of this letter would know of whom Paul writes, the brother's identity is not known today with any certainty.

8:19 *grace.* Gift. *to the glory of the same Lord.* The ultimate goal of all giving.

8:20–22 *that no man should blame us.* Paul does everything to remain above reproach in the collecting and delivering of the gift for the saints. *honest.* Honorable. He takes with him trusted men so that all walk in integrity *not only in the sight of the Lord, but also in the sight of men.*

8:23 *messengers of the churches, and the glory of Christ.* The men chosen were men of credibility and an honor to Christ. *enquired.* Inquired, asked about.

Thoughts for Personal/Family Worship: Chapter 8

1. **The truth of the gospel ought to motivate us at many levels. To think how Christ gave of Himself (v. 9) should make us ready to give of ourselves and our possessions. How should this motivate your giving?**
2. **Paul takes great care to remain above reproach in the matter of the collection. He knows that there might be some in Corinth suspicious of how Paul was handling the monetary funds. Instead of dismissing such suspicions as unfounded, he goes the extra mile to take precautions. How should this example direct you?**

Chapter 9: *Paul encourages the church to be ready for the collection and instructs them in the importance of cheerful giving.*

Exhortations to Be Ready for the Collection (9:1–5)

9:1 *For as touching.* Concerning the collection of money for the poor believers in Judea. *superfluous.* Not necessary.

9:2 *forwardness of your mind.* Zeal or readiness.

9:4 *haply.* Perhaps.

9:5 *make up beforehand.* Prepare in advance. *bounty.* Literally, "blessing," the gift.

Importance of Cheerful Giving (9:6–15)

9:7 *Every man according as he purposeth in his heart.* Paul does not demand a specific percentage of one's income, but urges voluntary giving. *not grudgingly, or of necessity.* Christians should not feel forced into giving, nor should they give while still desiring to hold on to their money. *cheerful.* Joyful, glad, not angry. God delights in cheerful giving, and that alone should motivate Christians to give cheerfully.

9:8 *grace abound . . . abound to every good work.* God's grace is the cause of all goodness in Christians (8:1), and God overflows with enough grace to make us extremely generous while still having enough (*sufficiency*) for ourselves.

9:9 *As it is written.* Citing Ps. 112:9. *dispersed.* Scattered. *abroad.* Over a wide area.

ness, which causeth through us thanksgiving to
God.
12 For the administration of this service not only
supplieth the want of the saints, but is abundant
also by many thanksgivings unto God;
13 Whiles by the experiment of this ministration
they glorify God for your professed subjection
unto the gospel of Christ, and for *your* liberal dis-
tribution unto them, and unto all *men*;
14 And by their prayer for you, which long after
you for the exceeding grace of God in you.
15 Thanks *be* unto God for his unspeakable gift.

CHAPTER 10

NOW I Paul myself beseech you by the meekness
and gentleness of Christ, who in presence *am* base
among you, but being absent am bold toward you:
2 But I beseech *you*, that I may not be bold when
I am present with that confidence, wherewith I
think to be bold against some, which think of us
as if we walked according to the flesh.
3 For though we walk in the flesh, we do not war
after the flesh:
4 (For the weapons of our warfare *are* not carnal,
but mighty through God to the pulling down of
strong holds;)
5 Casting down imaginations, and every high
thing that exalteth itself against the knowledge of
God, and bringing into captivity every thought to
the obedience of Christ;
6 And having in a readiness to revenge all disobe-
dience, when your obedience is fulfilled.
7 Do ye look on things after the outward
appearance? If any man trust to himself that he is
Christ's, let him of himself think this again, that,
as he *is* Christ's, even so *are* we Christ's.
8 For though I should boast somewhat more of
our authority, which the Lord hath given us for
edification, and not for your destruction, I should
not be ashamed:
9 That I may not seem as if I would terrify you
by letters.
10 For *his* letters, say they, *are* weighty and
powerful; but *his* bodily presence *is* weak, and *his*
speech contemptible.
11 Let such an one think this, that, such as we are
in word by letters when we are absent, such *will*

9:10 *ministereth.* Supplies. *fruits of your righteousness.* Spiritual harvest produced by righteous acts of mercy (Heb. 12:11; James 3:18).

9:11 *bountifulness.* Generosity. The one who gives cheerfully will find that God provides sufficiently in all things. God's provision then turns into thanksgiving to God for all He does.

9:12 Cheerful giving has a twofold consequence: (1) it meets the temporal needs (*the want*) of those who receive the gift, and (2) it leads to joyful thanksgiving to God, which is the ultimate goal of all actions, to give God the glory.

9:13 *experiment of this ministration.* Experience and approval of this service.

9:15 *Thanks be unto God.* God's grace produces good works for God's praise. *his unspeakable gift.* His indescribable gift of grace in His Son, Jesus Christ (8:9). Paul never lost his wonder that God would send His Son for His people and for how Christ changes people's lives.

Thoughts for Personal/Family Worship: Chapter 9

1. **Take time to praise God for the privilege to give. If you have children, teach them by precept and example that giving is in response to God's gifts. In times of corporate worship, be mindful that the time devoted to giving is to be an act of worship not an intermission to worship.**
2. **Paul concludes his discussion on the collection with a prayer of praise to God for His indescribable gift. One of the remarkable characteristics of the apostle Paul is that he sees Christ in and behind everything. Pray to God for such a view of Christ—both His person and work—and that you never lose the wonder of God's grace in giving His only begotten Son. Thanks be unto God for His unspeakable gift!**

REBUKE TO OPPONENTS IN PREPARATION FOR HIS VISIT (10:1—13:10)

Chapter 10: *Paul defends his authority, chides his opponents, and rejects foolish boasting and foolish comparisons.*

Defense of Authority and Rebuke of Opponents (10:1–7)

10:1 *Now.* Introduces a new subject. *I Paul myself.* Emphatic personal pronoun. Paul's tone changes to one of defense in the final chapters of this letter. He turns his attention to dealing directly with those who are opposed to him and threatening the church. *beseech.* Appeal. *meekness and gentleness of Christ.* He asserted his apostolic authority in a Christlike manner of patience and kindness. His opponents accused him of being a mere show: *bold* and strong in letters but weak and despicable (*base*) in person (v. 10).

10:3 *we do not war after the flesh.* Though Paul lives in the physical world, the pressing battle is spiritual.

10:4–5 *weapons of our warfare are not carnal.* Because the battle is spiritual, the weapons are not swords and spears, nor human wisdom and tricks (2:17; 1 Cor. 2:4), but the Word, prayer, and the power of the Spirit (6:6–7). *mighty through God to the pulling down of strong holds.* God's power works through God's means to overcome all of Satan's devices: worldly strategies, philosophies, and everything set up to reign in God's place.

10:6 *readiness to revenge.* Ready to enact judgment against disobedience. *fulfilled.* Complete. He expects that the church will display obedience by not siding with the false teachers and gives them time to repent before he disciplines the disobedient.

Opposition to Foolish Boasting and Comparisons (10:8–18)

10:8–10 *somewhat more.* Excessively. Paul notes that if he boasted it would be to boast in the authority the Lord gave him. However, the authority he has is not intended to be used for *destruction* but for building up (*edification*). Paul does not assert his authority in such a way since that would give his opponents opportunity to continue pointing at his apparent boldness in letters but weakness in person. He summarizes their accusation in vv. 9–10.

10:11 *such as we are in word by letters . . . such will we be also in deed when we are present.* He conducts himself with

we be also in deed when we are present.
12 For we dare not make ourselves of the number,
or compare ourselves with some that commend
themselves: but they measuring themselves by
themselves, and comparing themselves among
themselves, are not wise.
13 But we will not boast of things without *our*
measure, but according to the measure of the rule
which God hath distributed to us, a measure to
reach even unto you.
14 For we stretch not ourselves beyond *our*
measure, as though we reached not unto you: for
we are come as far as to you also in *preaching* the
gospel of Christ:
15 Not boasting of things without *our* measure,
that is, of other men's labours; but having hope,
when your faith is increased, that we shall be
enlarged by you according to our rule abundantly,
16 To preach the gospel in the *regions* beyond
you, *and* not to boast in another man's line of
things made ready to our hand.
17 But he that glorieth, let him glory in the Lord.
18 For not he that commendeth himself is ap-
proved, but whom the Lord commendeth.

CHAPTER 11

WOULD to God ye could bear with me a little in
my folly: and indeed bear with me.
2 For I am jealous over you with godly jealousy:
for I have espoused you to one husband, that I
may present *you as* a chaste virgin to Christ.
3 But I fear, lest by any means, as the serpent
beguiled Eve through his subtilty, so your minds
should be corrupted from the simplicity that is
in Christ.
4 For if he that cometh preacheth another Jesus,
whom we have not preached, or *if* ye receive an-
other spirit, which ye have not received, or another
gospel, which ye have not accepted, ye might well
bear with *him*.
5 For I suppose I was not a whit behind the very
chiefest apostles.
6 But though *I be* rude in speech, yet not in
knowledge; but we have been throughly made
manifest among you in all things.
7 Have I committed an offence in abasing myself
that ye might be exalted, because I have preached
to you the gospel of God freely?
8 I robbed other churches, taking wages *of them*,
to do you service.
9 And when I was present with you, and wanted,
I was chargeable to no man: for that which was
lacking to me the brethren which came from
Macedonia supplied: and in all *things* I have kept
myself from being burdensome unto you, and *so*
will I keep *myself*.
10 As the truth of Christ is in me, no man shall

integrity and consistency (1:18).
10:12 He shames his opponents for their constant pursuit of honor in comparison to other men, and sarcastically says he *dare not* count himself in the *number* of such great ones.
10:13–14 *measure of the rule.* Extent of the ministry which God assigned him.
10:15 *Not boasting of things without our measure.* Paul does not boast in someone else's ministry. He was the minister that brought the gospel to Corinth. *when your faith is increased.* When they mature in spirituality, they will love and honor Paul appropriately (*we shall be enlarged*).
10:16 *not to boast in another man's line of things.* Paul's ministry is to preach the gospel where it has not been preached, not to invade in someone else's ministry as his opponents are doing to his ministry in Corinth.
10:17 See Jer. 9:23–24; 1 Cor. 1:31.
10:18 *but whom the Lord commendeth.* God's judgment, not man's praise, matters most (Rom. 2:29; 1 Cor. 4:3–4). Paul is confident that the Lord approves of his ministry.

Thoughts for Personal/Family Worship: Chapter 10

1. **We live in a day not much different from Paul's day in Corinth. It is easy to evaluate ministers by their charisma and appearance. Yet what matters is God's call in their life. How do you view your minister? Do you love him and pray for him, or do you compare him with leaders or preachers who are more well-known?**
2. **Paul reminds his readers of the real battle that is waged in this life (vv. 3–5). Give attention to your life and seek after the weapons that through God's might are able to bring every thought captive to the obedience of Jesus Christ. How can you use the spiritual weapons of the Word, prayer, and the ministry of the Spirit to overthrow the imaginations and high things that are against the knowledge of God?**

Apostolic Boasting (11:1–33)

Chapter 11: *Paul provides an explanation for his boasting, even asking his readers to bear with him in his folly as he boasts in his sufferings.*

11:1 *Would to God.* Oh that! *bear with me a little in my folly.* Paul expresses discomfort in boasting, even considering it foolish. He asks his readers to put up with him as he boasts.
11:2 *For.* The reason it was necessary to boast. *godly jealousy.* Jealousy from God, a zeal for the well-being and purity of those God loves. *espoused you to one husband.* As a father (1 Cor. 4:15) who introduced them to Christ, their husband (Eph. 5:25). *chaste.* Pure.
11:3 Just as Satan deceived (*beguiled*) the first woman with subtlety and cunning (*subtilty*) by directing her away from God's Word (Gen. 3:1–6), so the false teachers tempt the church away from God. *simplicity.* Sincerity or undivided devotion. *in Christ.* Toward Christ.
11:4 *For.* The means by which the church could turn away from sincerity to Christ. False teachers preach lies about the person (*another Jesus*) and work (*another gospel*) of Christ, and so impart another mindset and attitude (*another spirit*) than that of the Spirit of Christ.
11:5 *not a whit.* Not in anything. *chiefest apostles.* Paul is probably referring to these supposed apostles who acted as if they were some kind of superapostles.
11:6 *rude in speech.* Not trained as a speaker, a complaint

stop me of this boasting in the regions of Achaia.
11 Wherefore? because I love you not? God
knoweth.
12 But what I do, that I will do, that I may cut off
occasion from them which desire occasion; that
wherein they glory, they may be found even as we.
13 For such *are* false apostles, deceitful workers,
transforming themselves into the apostles of Christ.
14 And no marvel; for Satan himself is transformed into an angel of light.
15 Therefore *it is* no great thing if his ministers
also be transformed as the ministers of righteousness; whose end shall be according to their works.
16 I say again, Let no man think me a fool; if
otherwise, yet as a fool receive me, that I may
boast myself a little.
17 That which I speak, I speak *it* not after the
Lord, but as it were foolishly, in this confidence
of boasting.
18 Seeing that many glory after the flesh, I will
glory also.
19 For ye suffer fools gladly, seeing ye *yourselves*
are wise.
20 For ye suffer, if a man bring you into bondage,
if a man devour *you*, if a man take *of you*, if a man
exalt himself, if a man smite you on the face.
21 I speak as concerning reproach, as though we
had been weak. Howbeit whereinsoever any is
bold, (I speak foolishly,) I am bold also.
22 Are they Hebrews? so *am* I. Are they Israelites?
so *am* I. Are they the seed of Abraham? so *am* I.
23 Are they ministers of Christ? (I speak as a
fool) I *am* more; in labours more abundant, in
stripes above measure, in prisons more frequent,
in deaths oft.
24 Of the Jews five times received I forty *stripes*
save one.
25 Thrice was I beaten with rods, once was I
stoned, thrice I suffered shipwreck, a night and a
day I have been in the deep;
26 *In* journeyings often, *in* perils of waters, *in*
perils of robbers, *in* perils by *mine own* countrymen, *in* perils by the heathen, *in* perils in the city,
in perils in the wilderness, *in* perils in the sea, *in*
perils among false brethren;
27 In weariness and painfulness, in watchings
often, in hunger and thirst, in fastings often, in
cold and nakedness.
28 Beside those things that are without, that
which cometh upon me daily, the care of all the
churches.
29 Who is weak, and I am not weak? who is offended, and I burn not?
30 If I must needs glory, I will glory of the things
which concern mine infirmities.
31 The God and Father of our Lord Jesus Christ,
which is blessed for evermore, knoweth that I lie not.
32 In Damascus the governor under Aretas the

against Paul (10:10). *yet not in knowledge*. Paul refused to use the manipulative tricks of some Greek orators, but taught true spiritual knowledge of Christ (2:14,17).

11:7 *abasing*. Humbling. *freely*. Without payment.

11:8–9 *I robbed other churches . . . to do you service*. Speaking sarcastically of the voluntary support from other churches, in order to shame the Corinthian opponents.

11:11–12 *that I may cut off occasion from them which desire occasion*. Some were looking for ways to criticize Paul. The apostle chose to cut off any opportunity for criticism by not receiving financial support from the Corinthian church.

11:13–14 Paul describes the evil and deceptive character of false teachers. *And no marvel*. He expresses no shock at their character as they are just like *Satan himself*, who is deceptive.

11:15 False teachers may temporarily appear to be genuine, but are servants of Satan (*his ministers*), and they will be judged *according to their works*.

11:16 Paul reiterates his discomfort in boasting about himself.

11:17 *I speak it not after the Lord*. Paul continues to speak under divine inspiration, but such self-boasting is out of character as an apostle of Jesus Christ. Yet, his boasting is done in order to advance Christ in Corinth.

11:18 *I will glory also*. Paul again explains his self-boasting. If his opponents get to do it with such apparent success, then he ought to be afforded the same privilege.

11:20 These are descriptions of the false teachers. They arrogantly demean the Corinthian church, yet some in the church allow (*suffer*) such bondage, rejecting the affection and love of the apostle.

11:22–27 Paul catalogs his pedigree and his sufferings, drawing attention to the fact that he endured hardships and imminent death for the sake of the gospel. All of these hardships are set against the earlier description of the false teachers who ministered for self-interest and prosperity. *forty stripes save one*. Forty lashes minus one (Deut. 25:3). *painfulness*. Labor.

11:28 *Beside those things that are without*. Apart from extra things, or apart from (the just mentioned) external hardships. *the care of all the churches*. Paul cared deeply for all the churches that he planted and their spiritual progress weighed heavily upon him. The inner burden he carried for so many believers cannot be estimated.

11:29–30 *weak . . . and I burn not?* He expresses solidarity and support for the one who has stumbled, pointing to the indignation he feels toward the one who caused the believer to sin—a pastor who sympathizes with the experiences of ordinary Christians.

11:32 *apprehend*. Lay hold of, seize.

Thoughts for Personal/Family Worship: Chapter 11

1. The character and subtlety of false teachers should keep Christians watchful and discerning. The best way to identify the threats of the false teachers is to be convinced of the truthfulness of the gospel and to be single-mindedly devoted to Christ (v. 3). Failing to remain devoted to Christ can make a believer susceptible to the subtle attacks of Satan, the deceiver. How can you be vigilant and jealous to protect your exclusive devotion to Jesus Christ?

2. Paul boasted in his sufferings and in his weakness. Let Paul's boasting cause you to reflect on your own trials and afflictions. He was willing to endure hardships and even face death. It is only as you are captivated by Christ and certain of His love for you that you will have

king kept the city of the Damascenes with a gar-
rison, desirous to apprehend me:
33 And through a window in a basket was I let
down by the wall, and escaped his hands.

CHAPTER 12

IT is not expedient for me doubtless to glory. I will
come to visions and revelations of the Lord.
2 I knew a man in Christ above fourteen years
ago, (whether in the body, I cannot tell; or whether
out of the body, I cannot tell: God knoweth;) such
an one caught up to the third heaven.
3 And I knew such a man, (whether in the body,
or out of the body, I cannot tell: God knoweth;)
4 How that he was caught up into paradise, and
heard unspeakable words, which it is not lawful
for a man to utter.
5 Of such an one will I glory: yet of myself I will
not glory, but in mine infirmities.
6 For though I would desire to glory, I shall not
be a fool; for I will say the truth: but *now* I forbear,
lest any man should think of me above that which
he seeth me *to be*, or *that* he heareth of me.
7 And lest I should be exalted above measure
through the abundance of the revelations, there
was given to me a thorn in the flesh, the messen-
ger of Satan to buffet me, lest I should be exalted
above measure.
8 For this thing I besought the Lord thrice, that it
might depart from me.
9 And he said unto me, My grace is sufficient for
thee: for my strength is made perfect in weakness.
Most gladly therefore will I rather glory in my infir-
mities, that the power of Christ may rest upon me.
10 Therefore I take pleasure in infirmities, in
reproaches, in necessities, in persecutions, in
distresses for Christ's sake: for when I am weak,
then am I strong.
11 I am become a fool in glorying; ye have com-
pelled me: for I ought to have been commended of
you: for in nothing am I behind the very chiefest
apostles, though I be nothing.
12 Truly the signs of an apostle were wrought
among you in all patience, in signs, and wonders,
and mighty deeds.
13 For what is it wherein ye were inferior to other
churches, except *it be* that I myself was not bur-
densome to you? forgive me this wrong.
14 Behold, the third time I am ready to come to
you; and I will not be burdensome to you: for I seek
not yours, but you: for the children ought not to lay
up for the parents, but the parents for the children.
15 And I will very gladly spend and be spent for
you; though the more abundantly I love you, the
less I be loved.
16 But be it so, I did not burden you: neverthe-
less, being crafty, I caught you with guile.
17 Did I make a gain of you by any of them whom
I sent unto you?
18 I desired Titus, and with *him* I sent a brother.
Did Titus make a gain of you? walked we not in

a framework by which to view your own trials properly. Reflect on what it means to be singularly devoted to Christ, even in the midst of trying circumstances.

Chapter 12: *Paul boasts in his weakness and in God's sufficient grace. He identifies signs of the true apostle and shares his concerns and warnings with his readers.*

Boasting in Weakness So That Christ's Power Is Seen (12:1–10)

12:1 *expedient*. Profitable. Paul moves the topic of his boasting from his ministerial experiences of hardship in ch. 11 to *visions and revelations* received from the Lord.

12:2 *I knew a man in Christ.* Paul is speaking of himself. *whether in the body . . . or whether out of the body.* Paul does not know whether it was a vision or he was physically transported. *caught up to the third heaven.* Taken up to heaven, God's dwelling place.

12:4 *paradise*. Enclosed garden; same place as third heaven (v. 3; Luke 22:43), portrayed like the garden of Eden (Rev. 2:7). *unspeakable.* Not able to be repeated.

12:5 *infirmities*. Weaknesses.

12:7 *lest I should be exalted.* Visions could lead to pride, so God humbled Paul. *thorn in the flesh*. Meaning is debated; possibly a disease of the body (*flesh*). *messenger of Satan.* This *thorn* was used by Satan to torment the apostle. *buffet.* Literally, "to strike with the fist."

12:8 *besought the Lord thrice*. Prayed three times.

12:9 *is sufficient*. Present tense; God will always provide the necessary grace for His afflicted people. *Most gladly.* Paul received an answer from God and was satisfied, though God did not remove the thorn. *that the power of Christ may rest upon me.* Paul would rather endure the thorn if it meant experiencing Christ's power and making Christ known to all.

Paul Provides Signs of a True Apostle (12:11–18)

12:11 *I am become a fool in glorying.* Paul's discomfort in boasting is evident, but the behavior of some in listening to the false teachers compelled him to do so. *for I ought to have been commended of you.* The church should have defended Paul against the charges and claims of the false teachers. *in nothing am I behind the very chiefest apostles.* He once more calls his opponents superapostles, but he is a genuine apostle, called by the will of God (1:1), though *nothing* in himself.

12:12 Paul's genuine apostleship was manifested by his acts among them, both of persevering *patience* and supernatural power.

12:14 *I will not be burdensome to you.* Paul plans on visiting them a third time and still he will not expect or demand payment from them. *Parents* do not expect small *children* to provide for them. Paul does not seek their possessions, but the people themselves.

12:15 *though the more abundantly I love you, the less I be loved.* They misunderstood his loving service for weakness, but he was willing to love them despite it all.

12:16–18 *nevertheless, being crafty, I caught you with guile.* Some accused Paul of deceiving them by taking some of the collection for himself. He denies this by asking whether he gained anything from those whom he sent or whether *Titus* made a profit. Mentioning *Titus* was important since the

the same spirit? *walked we* not in the same steps?
19 Again, think ye that we excuse ourselves unto
you? we speak before God in Christ: but *we do* all
things, dearly beloved, for your edifying.
20 For I fear, lest, when I come, I shall not find
you such as I would, and *that* I shall be found
unto you such as ye would not: lest *there be*
debates, envyings, wraths, strifes, backbitings,
whisperings, swellings, tumults:
21 *And* lest, when I come again, my God will
humble me among you, and *that* I shall bewail
many which have sinned already, and have not
repented of the uncleanness and fornication and
lasciviousness which they have committed.

CHAPTER 13

THIS *is* the third *time* I am coming to you. In the
mouth of two or three witnesses shall every word
be established.
2 I told you before, and foretell you, as if I were
present, the second time; and being absent now I
write to them which heretofore have sinned, and
to all other, that, if I come again, I will not spare:
3 Since ye seek a proof of Christ speaking in me,
which to you-ward is not weak, but is mighty in
you.
4 For though he was crucified through weakness,
yet he liveth by the power of God. For we also are
weak in him, but we shall live with him by the
power of God toward you.
5 Examine yourselves, whether ye be in the faith;
prove your own selves. Know ye not your own
selves, how that Jesus Christ is in you, except ye
be reprobates?
6 But I trust that ye shall know that we are not
reprobates.
7 Now I pray to God that ye do no evil; not that
we should appear approved, but that ye should do
that which is honest, though we be as reprobates.
8 For we can do nothing against the truth, but
for the truth.
9 For we are glad, when we are weak, and ye are
strong: and this also we wish, *even* your perfection.
10 Therefore I write these things being absent, lest
being present I should use sharpness, according

---

congregation trusted him. Paul found it shocking they would trust *Titus* (7:13–15) but not the one who sent *Titus*.

Conclusion of Defense with Concerns and Warnings (12:19—13:10)

12:19 *excuse*. Defend. Paul's great concern was not his own honor, but strengthening (*edifying*) the congregation. *we speak before God in Christ*. Paul, like all people, is ultimately accountable to God (5:10), who knows that he acted by God's grace through his union with Christ (1:18–23).

12:20 Paul feared returning to Corinth and finding the same disobedience. There is a parallel in this verse: Paul fears finding them as he does not wish (*not . . . as I would*), and if so, they will find him as they do not wish (*as ye would not*), strong to discipline. *envyings, wraths, strifes*. The plural indicates several displays of these sins. *swellings*. Pride.

12:21 *humble me among you*. It would humiliate Paul to find the church he planted still unrepentant over gross sins, yet Paul's covenant Lord (*my God*) remains in control (1 Cor. 3:7). *bewail*. Mourn. *lasciviousness*. Indecent and filthy behavior.

Thoughts for Personal/Family Worship: Chapter 12

1. **With one hand God gives thorns to His children, but with the other He gives sufficient grace. Whatever affliction or trial you may be enduring presently, dear believer, be sure to recognize God's sufficient supply of grace as well. Satan may intend to torment you through this thorn, but God means it for your good and His glory. What trials are you facing now? What does it mean to boast in your weaknesses, so that Christ's power may be seen?**
2. **Paul's love to the Corinthians was simply amazing. He could write in v. 19, "we do all things, dearly beloved, for your edifying." By the Spirit's grace, what means can you use so that you could come closer to being able to say this, as a husband and wife to each other and as parents to your children?**

Chapter 13: ***Paul issues warnings and gives final greetings to the church.***

13:1 *two or three witnesses*. Needed for discipline (Deut. 19:15; Matt. 18:16). Paul is coming a third time, and he will take action if there is no repentance.

13:2 *heretofore*. Before, previously. *I will not spare*. Paul will hold nothing back during his next visit if the disobedience persists.

13:3 *to you-ward*. Toward you.

13:4 *though he was crucified through weakness, yet he liveth by the power of God*. Present weakness does not discount God's presence and power, for this was Christ's experience. The cross demonstrated the power of God in bringing salvation through shame and weakness (1 Cor. 1:22–24). In union with Christ, believers are also *weak*, but share in Christ's resurrection power even now (1:9; 4:10–11).

13:5 *Examine*. Test.

13:7 *honest*. Honorable. *as reprobates*. Rejected as counterfeit by the false teachers.

13:9 *your perfection*. Paul's great concern was for their spiritual maturity.

CONCLUSION (13:11–14)

Final Greetings (13:11–13)

13:11 *Be perfect*. Be mature.

13:12 *holy kiss*. Common expression of affection and kindness.

Final Benediction (13:14)

13:14 Paul closes with a Trinitarian benediction to his readers. *communion*. Fellowship, the relationship of shared life between God and His people, and between Christians in the church by the Spirit (1 Cor. 6:17; Eph. 4:4; 1 John 1:3).

Thoughts for Personal/Family Worship: Chapter 13

1. **Paul closes his letter with a solemn exhortation to examine oneself. He has been scrutinized and forced into a position where he must defend his claim as an apostle of Christ. He asks his readers to scrutinize themselves. It is not enough to be associated with the church of Jesus Christ. You must examine yourself whether you**

to the power which the Lord hath given me to
edification, and not to destruction.
11 Finally, brethren, farewell. Be perfect, be of
good comfort, be of one mind, live in peace; and
the God of love and peace shall be with you.
12 Greet one another with an holy kiss.
13 All the saints salute you.
14 The grace of the Lord Jesus Christ, and the
love of God, and the communion of the Holy
Ghost, *be* with you all. Amen.

are in Christ or not. What are the marks of a true believer in Christ?

2. All the spiritual blessings you receive come from the love of God the Father, who planned salvation before time began. All blessings come through the grace of Jesus Christ, the Mediator, who died to purchase redemption and rose again to apply it to His people. And all blessings are shared within the church by the Holy Spirit. Have you experienced the grace of Christ, the love of the Father, and the communion of the Holy Spirit? If so, then meditate upon these blessings and pray for God to increase your enjoyment of Him. If not, then turn from your sin in genuine repentance and turn to Christ in faith.

INTRODUCTION TO THE BOOK OF GALATIANS

Authorship: Pauline authorship of Galatians is clearly stated (1:1–2; 5:2). Furthermore, it has been advocated and defended throughout church history. The earliest writings of various church fathers (e.g., Clement of Rome, Ignatius, Polycarp, Justin Martyr) contain frequent references to Galatians and to Paul's authorship. Pauline authorship has been almost universally maintained. No convincing arguments have been produced by those who have denied it.

Date: The date of Galatians has been intensely debated. Though some advocate a later date (AD 57–58), the earlier date (AD 48–49) is preferable. *First*, in 2:1–10 Paul refers to a visit to Jerusalem, when he met with certain men who were leaders. While some see this visit corresponding to the Jerusalem Council (Acts 15:1–4), it is more likely that this visit was for the famine relief visit to Jerusalem (11:30), which occurred approximately AD 47. This indicates that the epistle was written sometime after Paul's first missionary journey that preceded the Jerusalem Council. *Second*, while some argue that "at the first" in Gal. 4:13 refers to Paul's second missionary journey (Acts 16:6), this is not necessary as the Greek could simply indicate "previously." It is therefore probable that Paul is referring to his visit to South Galatia (14:21), which occurred before the Jerusalem Council. *Third*, the epistle was written soon after the conversion of the Galatians (Gal. 1:6). Paul was amazed, not only at the fact that the Galatians were moving away from the Lord, but that they were moving away "so soon." In light of these facts, it is preferable to assign an early date of AD 48–49 for the composition of Galatians.

Likewise, who these Galatians were to whom Paul is writing has also been vigorously debated. The letter is addressed to "the churches of Galatia" (1:2) and the "Galatians" (3:1). The contention is whether this is a territorial or ethnic identification. Ethnically, Galatia would refer to the territory where the Gauls or Celts dwelt after their invasion of Central Europe in 278 BC. If Paul is addressing the ethnic people, the letter would be addressed to the cities of Ancyra, Pessinus, and Tavium—the northern Galatia territory. If Paul is addressing the territory, it is the Roman province of Galatia, which would indicate the cities in southern Galatia of Antioch of Pisidia, Iconium, Lystra, and Derbe. We know that Paul visited these cities in his first missionary journey.

While the arguments are complex, it is probable that Paul is addressing the southern Galatians and therefore Galatia should be understood as a territory. This is likely for several reasons. *First*, Paul knew the readers personally (1:8; 4:11–15,19). *Second*, the route listed in Acts 16:6 and 18:23 appears to be through south Galatia. *Third*, Paul typically used the Roman designation of provinces. *Fourth*, Galatia contributed to the relief fund (1 Cor. 16:1), with persons from South Galatia accompanying the transport of the gift (Acts 20:4). *Fifth*, Barnabas is mentioned three times in Galatians (Gal. 2:1,9,13), intimating that the readers knew Barnabas. Barnabas, however, only journeyed with Paul on his first missionary journey. For these reasons, it is likely that Paul is addressing those in south Galatia.

Theme: Salvation is by the free grace of God received through faith in the righteousness of Christ apart from any works of the law.

Purpose: *First*, to emphasize again the very heart of the gospel, justification by faith alone in Christ's righteousness apart from the works of the law. *Second*, to call the Galatian Christians to prove the reality of their spirituality through living by faith in Christ, a life in which the fruit of the Spirit would abound. *Third*, to destroy the message of the Judaizers by showing that it was a false gospel.

Synopsis: *The Contribution of Galatians to Redemptive Revelation*

The writing of this letter was occasioned by the insidious influence that was being exerted upon the Galatian churches by the dangerous teaching of the Judaizers. They were arguing that to be truly saved, one who professed faith in Christ also had to submit to circumcision and indeed to the entire Jewish ceremonial law. This was the heresy that the Jerusalem Council would later address (Acts 15), though it would continue to trouble the churches.

With apostolic authority (1:1,11–12) and loving directness (v. 6; 4:12–20), Paul sets forth the exclusive claims of the gospel against any mixture of law and gospel in justification. Even if an angel of light taught any other thing than the gospel of God which Paul had brought, to leave the gospel would bring a curse (1:8–9; 3:10), from which Christ delivers all those who believe (3:13–14). By faith we are united to Christ, his death and resurrection (2:19–20; 5:24). The giving of the Mosaic law had neither undone the doctrine of justification by faith alone as was seen in Abraham, the father of the faithful (3:7–9,15–18), but rather served as a schoolmaster to bring to Christ (vv. 19–25). Those who have believed will prove the genuineness of their faith through living by faith in Christ (2:20), thus living a life that shows the fruit of the Spirit (5:22–24; 6:8). There is no other way of acceptance with God apart from the cross of Christ and faith in His merit (2:16,21; 6:14).

Outline:

- I. Introduction (1:1–5)
- II. Defense of Paul's Apostleship (1:6—2:21)
  - A. Paul's Gospel Is True (1:6–10)
  - B. Paul's Calling to the Gospel (1:11–24)
    - 1. Christ Revealed in Paul (1:11–17)
    - 2. Paul's Early Ministry (1:18–24)
  - C. Paul's Confirmation by the Apostles (2:1–10)
  - D. Paul's Conflict with Peter (2:11–21)
    - 1. Paul Opposed Peter (2:11–14)
    - 2. Christ's Death Effectual in Paul (2:15–21)
- III. Proclamation of Justification (3:1—5:12)
  - A. Receiving the Spirit by Faith (3:1–6)
  - B. Justification by Faith Alone (3:7–29)
    - 1. Scriptural Verification (3:7–14)
    - 2. Human Example (3:15–18)
    - 3. Law and Faith (3:19–29)
  - C. Sonship Is by Faith (4:1–7)
  - D. Blessings Come by Faith (4:8–31)
  - E. Endurance through Faith (5:1–12)
- IV. Revelation of Life in the Spirit (5:13—6:10)
  - A. Walking by the Spirit (5:13–26)
  - B. Serving One Another (6:1–10)
- V. Closing (6:11–18)

THE EPISTLE OF PAUL THE APOSTLE TO THE

GALATIANS

CHAPTER 1

PAUL, an apostle, (not of men, neither by man, but
by Jesus Christ, and God the Father, who raised
him from the dead;)
2 And all the brethren which are with me, unto
the churches of Galatia:
3 Grace *be* to you and peace from God the Father,
and *from* our Lord Jesus Christ,
4 Who gave himself for our sins, that he might
deliver us from this present evil world, according
to the will of God and our Father:
5 To whom *be* glory for ever and ever. Amen.
6 I marvel that ye are so soon removed from him
that called you into the grace of Christ unto an-
other gospel:
7 Which is not another; but there be some that
trouble you, and would pervert the gospel of
Christ.
8 But though we, or an angel from heaven,
preach any other gospel unto you than that which
we have preached unto you, let him be accursed.
9 As we said before, so say I now again, If any
man preach any other gospel unto you than that
ye have received, let him be accursed.
10 For do I now persuade men, or God? or do
I seek to please men? for if I yet pleased men, I
should not be the servant of Christ.
11 But I certify you, brethren, that the gospel
which was preached of me is not after man.
12 For I neither received it of man, neither was
I taught *it*, but by the revelation of Jesus Christ.
13 For ye have heard of my conversation in time
past in the Jews' religion, how that beyond mea-
sure I persecuted the church of God, and wasted it:
14 And profited in the Jews' religion above many
my equals in mine own nation, being more
exceedingly zealous of the traditions of my fathers.
15 But when it pleased God, who separated me
from my mother's womb, and called *me* by his
grace,

Chapter 1: ***Paul commences his defense of justification by grace through faith alone by presenting his personal testimony. He was the living proof that the Judaism he had once espoused was a hopeless and damning error.***

INTRODUCTION (1:1–5)

1:1 *Paul, an apostle, (not of men . . . but by Jesus Christ).* An assertion of the immediate divine origin of his apostleship and of the gospel he preached (v. 12).

1:2 *And all the brethren . . . with me.* Colleagues in service but by extension those in agreement with his doctrine. *Galatia.* Likely the cities in southern Galatia (see Introduction: Date).

1:3 *Grace . . . and peace.* Though sharp in his tone throughout the epistle Paul desires the Galatians to enjoy gospel blessings. Salvation and growth come from *the Father* and *Jesus Christ*, implying that both are God, one divine Savior.

1:4 *gave himself.* Christ's death was a voluntary self-sacrifice (John 10:17–18; Eph. 5:2). *world.* Or age. *according to the will of God.* Christ's redemptive work was according to the divine will (Eph. 1:5,9,11), thus the false gospel must be denounced and the true gospel defended.

1:5 *for ever and ever.* Literally, "the ages of the ages." Salvation is for God's *glory* (Rom. 9:23; 11:36; Eph. 1:6; 3:21).

DEFENSE OF PAUL'S APOSTLESHIP (1:6—2:21)

Paul's Gospel Is True (1:6–10)

1:6 *marvel.* Be amazed, in a negative way. *another gospel.* Another of a different kind; thus different altogether from the true gospel. Paul does not mean that there are other ways of salvation.

1:7 *Which is not another.* Not another of the same kind; thus not the same at all as the gospel Paul preached. *pervert.* To change into an opposite form, thus a perversion.

1:8 *though we.* Literally, "even if we" signifying a hypothetical situation. *accursed.* "Anathema," a declaration of eternal judgment.

1:9 *If any man preach any other gospel.* The Judaizers were preaching a false gospel. *received.* Paul shows the relationship one has to the gospel. It is merely one of receiving God's Word, not inventing, manipulating, or designing (1 Cor. 15:3).

1:10 *do I now persuade . . . please men?* The severe tones already employed indicate that Paul was not a people pleaser as his enemies alleged. *persuade.* Literally, "move the heart."

Paul's Calling to the Gospel (1:11–24)

Christ Revealed in Paul (1:11–17)

1:11 *certify.* Literally, "make known."

1:12 *by the revelation of Jesus Christ.* A revelation given by Christ to Paul through the Spirit (1 Cor. 2:12–13; Eph. 3:5).

1:13 *conversation.* Conduct. *the Jews' religion.* Translation of one word meaning "Judaism," hence the term "Judaizer."

1:14 *profited.* Hewn out a path in order to advance. *traditions of my fathers.* Likely the law and different explanations of the law that unnecessarily bound men's consciences.

1:15 *separated.* Marked off by bounds. *from my mother's*

16 To reveal his Son in me, that I might preach
him among the heathen; immediately I conferred
not with flesh and blood:
17 Neither went I up to Jerusalem to them which
were apostles before me; but I went into Arabia,
and returned again unto Damascus.
18 Then after three years I went up to Jerusalem
to see Peter, and abode with him fifteen days.
19 But other of the apostles saw I none, save
James the Lord's brother.
20 Now the things which I write unto you,
behold, before God, I lie not.
21 Afterwards I came into the regions of Syria
and Cilicia;
22 And was unknown by face unto the churches
of Judaea which were in Christ:
23 But they had heard only, That he which per-
secuted us in times past now preacheth the faith
which once he destroyed.
24 And they glorified God in me.

CHAPTER 2

THEN fourteen years after I went up again to
Jerusalem with Barnabas, and took Titus with *me*
also.
2 And I went up by revelation, and commu-
nicated unto them that gospel which I preach
among the Gentiles, but privately to them which
were of reputation, lest by any means I should
run, or had run, in vain.
3 But neither Titus, who was with me, being a
Greek, was compelled to be circumcised:
4 And that because of false brethren unawares
brought in, who came in privily to spy out our
liberty which we have in Christ Jesus, that they
might bring us into bondage:
5 To whom we gave place by subjection, no, not
for an hour; that the truth of the gospel might
continue with you.
6 But of these who seemed to be somewhat,
(whatsoever they were, it maketh no matter to

womb. An act of predestination (Jer. 1:5). God chose whom He would save and when He would convert them before they were born (Rom. 9:11; Eph. 1:4,11; 2 Thess. 2:13; 2 Tim. 1:9).
1:16 *To reveal his Son in me.* The inward revelation of Christ (Acts 9:15; 2 Cor. 4:6). *conferred not with flesh and blood.* Did not consult with men.
1:17 *apostles before me.* The other apostles who temporally preceded Paul in the office; he was no less an apostle than they (1 Cor. 9:1; 15:8). *Arabia.* Acts does not record Paul's time in Arabia, though *Damascus* is mentioned (Acts 9:19–25).

Paul's Early Ministry (1:18–24)

1:18 *Then after three years.* Three years from the time of his conversion. *abode.* Stayed for a time.
1:19 *save.* Except. *James the Lord's brother.* Leading figure in the Jerusalem church (Acts 15:13–21; 21:18–25), who with Peter gave acceptance to Paul and his message.
1:20 *behold, before God, I lie not.* A solemn affirmation of veracity.
1:21 *the regions of Syria and Cilicia.* Two Roman provinces. Paul moved to these areas due to attempts on his life (Acts 9:26–30). Thus he had no further contact with apostles and other church leaders. The book of Acts records little of the events during this time.
1:22 *unknown by face.* The Judean churches had never seen Paul.
1:23 *they had heard only.* From their fellow believers in Jerusalem, who had been persecuted by Paul, the Judean churches had heard of the wonderful transformation in his life.
1:24 *they glorified God in me.* Those formerly persecuted by him now rejoiced in his ministry, a fact that would have been a devastating rebuttal of the Judaizers.

Thoughts for Personal/Family Worship: Chapter 1

1. **The surest protection from the false gospel is a fresh and clear reminder of the true gospel. This Paul does in his opening greeting in vv. 3–5, in which he gives a succinct summary of the victorious deliverance that flows from Christ's atoning sacrifice. Meditate on this true gospel, and praise God for it.**
2. **There can be no compromise with those who pervert the gospel of Christ. Paul not only brands the false gospel as a perversion of the true; he also by inspiration reveals that those who promote another gospel will be damned. Thus there can be no fellowship with such men. Why is separation from preachers of a false gospel absolutely imperative?**
3. **The conversion of those who were formerly opponents of the gospel brings great glory to the Lord. Paul, the former blasphemer and persecutor, goes into much detail to show the reality of his conversion so that the very people he had persecuted glorified God for the change they saw in him. For what enemies of the gospel are you praying?**

Chapter 2: ***Having asserted the divine origin of the gospel he proclaimed, Paul proceeds to show that it stands on its own merit and does not require human validation.***

Paul's Confirmation by the Apostles (2:1–10)

2:1 *Then fourteen years after.* Fourteen years after his conversion or his first visit to Jerusalem (1:18). The chronology is uncertain.
2:2 *I went up by revelation.* Divine revelation corroborating the commission given to him and Barnabas by the church in Antioch (Acts 11:27–30). *communicated.* Laid before. *them which were of reputation.* Other apostles elevated by the Judaizers in an attempt to disparage Paul's apostleship (see also vv. 6,9).
2:3 *neither Titus . . . was compelled to be circumcised.* Not forced by the other apostles as the Judaizers wanted. The leaders at Jerusalem held to the same gospel as Paul (Acts 15:10,19). *Greek.* Gentile. Thus the circumcision requirement was not necessary by a unified testimony.
2:4 *unawares brought in.* To intrude stealthily. *privily.* Same word denoting stealth, though evil intent is involved. *our liberty.* Spiritual freedom *in Christ* (see note at 5:1).
2:5 *subjection.* Brought into obedience. *no, not for an hour.* Figurative use of *hour* signifying at no time whatsoever.
2:6 *God accepteth no man's person.* God does not show partiality based on human status (Deut. 10:17; 2 Chron. 19:7; Rom. 2:11; Eph. 6:9). *in conference added nothing to me.* Literally, "conferred nothing to me." The esteemed apostles added nothing to Paul's message.
2:7 *contrariwise.* On the contrary. *the gospel of the uncircumcision was committed unto me.* Paul was entrusted to preach

me: God accepteth no man's person:) for they
who seemed *to be somewhat* in conference added
nothing to me:
7 But contrariwise, when they saw that the gospel
of the uncircumcision was committed unto me,
as *the gospel* of the circumcision *was* unto Peter;
8 (For he that wrought effectually in Peter to the
apostleship of the circumcision, the same was
mighty in me toward the Gentiles:)
9 And when James, Cephas, and John, who
seemed to be pillars, perceived the grace that was
given unto me, they gave to me and Barnabas the
right hands of fellowship; that we *should go* unto
the heathen, and they unto the circumcision.
10 Only *they would* that we should remember the
poor; the same which I also was forward to do.
11 But when Peter was come to Antioch, I with-
stood him to the face, because he was to be
blamed.
12 For before that certain came from James, he
did eat with the Gentiles: but when they were
come, he withdrew and separated himself, fearing
them which were of the circumcision.
13 And the other Jews dissembled likewise with
him; insomuch that Barnabas also was carried
away with their dissimulation.
14 But when I saw that they walked not uprightly
according to the truth of the gospel, I said unto
Peter before *them* all, If thou, being a Jew, livest
after the manner of Gentiles, and not as do the
Jews, why compellest thou the Gentiles to live as
do the Jews?
15 We *who are* Jews by nature, and not sinners of
the Gentiles,
16 Knowing that a man is not justified by the
works of the law, but by the faith of Jesus Christ,
even we have believed in Jesus Christ, that we
might be justified by the faith of Christ, and not
by the works of the law: for by the works of the
law shall no flesh be justified.
17 But if, while we seek to be justified by Christ,
we ourselves also are found sinners, *is* therefore
Christ the minister of sin? God forbid.
18 For if I build again the things which I de-
stroyed, I make myself a transgressor.
19 For I through the law am dead to the law, that
I might live unto God.
20 I am crucified with Christ: nevertheless I live;
yet not I, but Christ liveth in me: and the life which
I now live in the flesh I live by the faith of the Son
of God, who loved me, and gave himself for me.
21 I do not frustrate the grace of God: for if
righteousness *come* by the law, then Christ is dead
in vain.

---

the gospel to the Gentiles. *as the gospel of the circumcision was unto Peter.* Literally, "just as Peter of the circumcision." Paul and Peter preached the same gospel, though commissioned to speak to different people.
2:8 *wrought.* Worked. *wrought effectually in Peter . . . was mighty in me.* Same word in the original Greek denoting an equality of honor.
2:9 *perceived the grace that was given unto me.* Paul's apostleship was recognized by the leading apostles. *gave . . . the right hands of fellowship.* Signified the conclusion of a matter and the establishment of an agreement. There was unity between Paul and the apostles. *heathen.* Gentiles.
2:10 *they would.* They desired or commanded, not in the Greek. *forward.* Eager.

Paul's Conflict with Peter (2:11–21)

Paul Opposed Peter (2:11–14)

2:11 *withstood.* Stood against or opposed. *blamed.* The original word signifies self-condemned.
2:12 *from James.* Likely not sent or commissioned by James. *fearing.* Likely indicating intimidation.
2:13 *dissembled . . . dissimulation.* Acted hypocritically . . . hypocrisy.
2:14 *walked . . . uprightly.* Literally, "to straight-foot"; here used negatively to indicate the failure to walk a straight line. *after the manner of Gentiles.* Live like a Gentile. *compellest.* Force (see v. 3). *to live as do the Jews.* Literally, "to Judaize."

Christ's Death Effectual in Paul (2:15–21)

2:15 *by nature.* By birth or descent.
2:16 *justified.* Declared righteous by God, as by a judge in a court of law (Deut. 25:1; 1 Kings 8:32). *by the faith of Jesus Christ . . . by the faith of Christ.* Faith that has Christ as its object of trust. God counts sinners righteous simply by their faith in Christ, not any of their good *works* (Phil. 3:9), because their sins were counted against Christ on the cross, and His righteousness is credited to them (Rom. 3:23–26; 4:4–5; 5:18–19; 2 Cor. 5:21).
2:17 *Christ the minister of sin?* If (as the Judaizers asserted) faith alone in Christ alone does not save, then men are left in their sin. Thus Christ, in that sense, would become the servant or the promoter of sin. *God forbid.* Literally, "Let it not be," a very forceful idiom.
2:18 *destroyed.* Threw down.
2:19 *through the law . . . dead to the law.* Through Christ's perfect obedience to the law the believer is delivered from the law's demand for personal obedience in order to be justified. *live unto God.* Live by union with Christ in His resurrection (Rom. 6:4–5,11).
2:20 *crucified with Christ.* United with Christ in His death (5:24; Rom. 6:6). *the life which I now live in the flesh.* The believer's earthly life. *live by the faith.* Daily rely upon the Christ as revealed in the promises of God for wisdom, righteousness before God, increasing holiness, and ultimate redemption from all evil (cf. 1 Cor. 1:30). *loved me, and gave himself for me.* Christ's death was motivated by a love for particular persons chosen by God to be His true church (Eph. 1:4; 5:25).
2:21 *frustrate.* Reject or throw away.

Thoughts for Personal/Family Worship: Chapter 2

1. **The Christian should make every effort to remove all doubts about his or her profession of the gospel. Paul knew that his enemies had slandered him before his fellow apostles; thus when he went to Jerusalem he carefully showed them that he believed and preached the same gospel as they did. It is always good to remove all suspicion from our names, if possible, remembering that it is only in Christ that believers are justified.**
2. **Sometimes even the rebuking of a fellow believer is**

JUSTIFICATION BY FAITH ALONE

In Galatians 2:16 Paul cuts to the very heart of what it means to be a Christian: "Even we have believed in Jesus Christ, that we might be justified by the faith of Christ, and not by works of the law." Paul is citing the greatest of all the promises of God. He promises to pardon the sins of all who truly believe in Jesus Christ alone for salvation, freeing them from all guilt, and to impute to them the perfect righteousness of Christ as a covering for all their remaining infirmities and indwelling sin. As justified people, they are righteous in Christ before God and heirs of eternal life.

This doctrine is as old as the Bible. Abram "believed in the LORD; and he counted it to him for righteousness" (Gen. 15:6). David declares: "Blessed is he whose transgression is forgiven, whose sin is covered. Blessed is the man unto whom the LORD imputeth not iniquity" (Ps. 32:1–2). Isaiah records God's promise that "By his knowledge shall my righteous servant justify many, for he shall bear their iniquities" (Isa. 53:11). And God's Word to Habakkuk is "The just shall live by faith" (Hab. 2:4).

Preaching to the Jews of Antioch, Paul proclaims Jesus as the Son of God, crucified, dead, and buried, but raised from the dead by God as Israel's Savior in fulfillment of the promise made to their fathers: "Through this man is preached unto you the forgiveness of sins: and by him, all that believe are justified from all things, from which you could not be justified by the law of Moses" (Acts 13:38,39). This doctrine was taught by all the apostles, but it fell to Paul to expound it at length in his epistles.

In the centuries that followed the Christian church came to equate justification with sanctification, holding that a sinner had to pursue justification by adhering to a stern regimen of penance, aided by infusions of grace through the sacraments. The goal was not so much justification as purgation, or cleansing from sin. Acknowledging that achievement of this goal in this life lay beyond the abilities of most people—in reality, of course, *all* people—the pre-Reformation church extended the path of penance and purgation into the next life. It reduced forgiveness to a commodity in the form of ecclesiastical pardons or "indulgences," which were offered for sale by special agents known as "pardoners."

One such agent, Johann Tetzel (1465–1519), could be heard to cry, "As soon as the coin in the moneybox rings, the soul from Purgatory springs!" In 1517 Martin Luther responded with his Ninety-Five Theses, assailing the system of penance and the sale of pardons. Luther went on to reassert the biblical doctrine of justification by faith in Christ alone as the rallying cry of the Reformation.

Justification is the free gift of God to all who believe in Jesus Christ as the only Savior, finding in Him all things necessary for their salvation. It asks nothing from us but faith, it extends to every sin except the sin of unbelief, and it depends entirely upon who Christ is and what He has done, and on nothing at all in us.

Some see a contradiction between Paul and James on justification by faith apart from works. The fact is that James is asking a question about faith, not about justification (James 2:14). The faith that justifies is no dead faith but is always accompanied by graces such as self-denial, repentance, and thankfulness to God, and it always produces fruit in the form of good works done in conformity to God's law and for His glory. Paul agrees with James that a faith without such graces and fruits is a dead faith that cannot justify the sinner. The works of Abraham and Rahab show that theirs was the living, active, justifying faith of true Christians. "For in Jesus Christ neither circumcision availeth anything, nor uncircumcision; but faith which worketh by love" (Gal. 5:6).

CHAPTER 3

O FOOLISH Galatians, who hath bewitched you,
that ye should not obey the truth, before whose
eyes Jesus Christ hath been evidently set forth,
crucified among you?
2 This only would I learn of you, Received ye the
Spirit by the works of the law, or by the hearing
of faith?
3 Are ye so foolish? having begun in the Spirit,
are ye now made perfect by the flesh?
4 Have ye suffered so many things in vain? if *it be*
yet in vain.
5 He therefore that ministereth to you the Spirit,
and worketh miracles among you, *doeth he it* by
the works of the law, or by the hearing of faith?
6 Even as Abraham believed God, and it was
accounted to him for righteousness.
7 Know ye therefore that they which are of faith,
the same are the children of Abraham.
8 And the scripture, foreseeing that God would
justify the heathen through faith, preached before
the gospel unto Abraham, *saying*, In thee shall all
nations be blessed.
9 So then they which be of faith are blessed with
faithful Abraham.
10 For as many as are of the works of the law are
under the curse: for it is written, Cursed *is* every
one that continueth not in all things which are
written in the book of the law to do them.
11 But that no man is justified by the law in the
sight of God, *it is* evident: for, The just shall live
by faith.
12 And the law is not of faith: but, The man that
doeth them shall live in them.
13 Christ hath redeemed us from the curse of the
law, being made a curse for us: for it is written,
Cursed *is* every one that hangeth on a tree:
14 That the blessing of Abraham might come on
the Gentiles through Jesus Christ; that we might
receive the promise of the Spirit through faith.
15 Brethren, I speak after the manner of men;
Though *it be* but a man's covenant, yet *if it be* con-
firmed, no man disannulleth, or addeth thereto.
16 Now to Abraham and his seed were the prom-
ises made. He saith not, And to seeds, as of many;
but as of one, And to thy seed, which is Christ.
17 And this I say, *that* the covenant, that was con-
firmed before of God in Christ, the law, which was
four hundred and thirty years after, cannot disan-
nul, that it should make the promise of none effect.

necessary in order to defend the gospel. At Antioch Paul had to withstand Peter because his action in separating from the Gentiles endangered the truth of justification through Christ alone. But Peter did not resent the rebuke, later referring to Paul as a "beloved brother" (2 Peter 3:15). Do you welcome correction and reproof as David did (Ps. 141:5)?

3. **Believers live the Christian life in the same manner as they commence it. This is Paul's triumphant assertion in v. 20. The believer is in union with Christ and by faith draws from Him all that is needed to live the life of the believer in a sinful world. Reflect on the all-powerful and ever-fresh gospel of Christ's death for sinners.**

PROCLAMATION OF JUSTIFICATION (3:1—5:12)

Chapter 3: *Paul proceeds to show that both the experience of the Galatians and of Scripture bears testimony to the truth of the gospel.*

Receiving the Spirit by Faith (3:1–6)

3:1 *foolish.* Thoughtless (v. 3; Luke 24:25). *bewitched.* Misled or deceived. *set forth.* Literally, "written before," "placarded" or "displayed." *crucified among you.* They had heard or read such faithful gospel preaching that it was as if they had seen Christ on the cross.

3:2 *Received ye the Spirit.* The reference is to the time of their conversion. *by the works of the law, or by the hearing of faith?* Reception of the Spirit could only be by faith (v. 14).

3:3 *are ye now made perfect.* Literally, "being perfected," signifying attaining maturity.

3:4 *in vain.* To no purpose. *if it be yet in vain.* Hint that Paul had not given up hope altogether.

3:5 *ministereth.* Gives. *ministereth . . . worketh.* These words in the original language indicate an ongoing ministry.

3:6 *Even as.* That is, as is recorded in Scripture (Gen. 15:6). *accounted.* Imputed or reckoned to one's account.

Justification by Faith Alone (3:7–29)

Scriptural Verification (3:7–14)

3:7 *children of Abraham.* Literally, "sons" in the spiritual sense (v. 29; Rom. 4:11).

3:8 *foreseeing.* Seeing beforehand. This personal action is ascribed to the Scripture due to its divine author, the God who sees the future. *heathen.* Gentiles.

3:9 *faithful Abraham.* Believing Abraham, referring to Abraham's personal, subjective faith.

3:10 *curse . . . Cursed.* Both intensive forms signifying the most terrible consequence of trusting in works.

3:11 *no man is justified by the law.* Proven by the quotation from Habakkuk which says that "the just shall live by his faith" (Hab. 2:4).

3:12 *the law is not of faith.* That is, reliance upon the law is the opposite of faith (Lev. 18:5).

3:13 *redeemed.* Bought out of, often used in reference to the purchase of a slave. *the curse of the law.* The law's penalty for any failure to conform is eternal death. *being made a curse.* An accursed one (Deut. 21:23).

3:14 *the blessing of Abraham.* The blessing he received was the promise of the Spirit.

Human Example (3:15–18)

3:15 *a man's covenant.* A binding agreement between men (Gen. 21:27–32). *confirmed.* Ratified or put into effect. *disannulleth.* To set aside as being of no value or to negate. The meaning refers to when a covenant is made: once the covenant is put into effect, it cannot be changed.

3:16 *seed.* Collective noun but applied here to one person, Christ. Paul is not contradicting the meaning of Scripture, but giving it according to the Old Testament understanding of a federal head who represents a people.

3:17 *confirmed before.* The translation of one word in the original signifying to ratify beforehand. *four hundred and thirty years.* The law came 430 years after God established his

18 For if the inheritance *be* of the law, *it is* no
more of promise: but God gave *it* to Abraham by
promise.
19 Wherefore then *serveth* the law? It was added
because of transgressions, till the seed should
come to whom the promise was made; *and it was*
ordained by angels in the hand of a mediator.
20 Now a mediator is not *a mediator* of one, but
God is one.
21 *Is* the law then against the promises of God?
God forbid: for if there had been a law given
which could have given life, verily righteousness
should have been by the law.
22 But the scripture hath concluded all under sin,
that the promise by faith of Jesus Christ might be
given to them that believe.
23 But before faith came, we were kept under the
law, shut up unto the faith which should afterwards be revealed.
24 Wherefore the law was our schoolmaster *to
bring us* unto Christ, that we might be justified
by faith.
25 But after that faith is come, we are no longer
under a schoolmaster.
26 For ye are all the children of God by faith in
Christ Jesus.
27 For as many of you as have been baptized into
Christ have put on Christ.
28 There is neither Jew nor Greek, there is neither
bond nor free, there is neither male nor female:
for ye are all one in Christ Jesus.
29 And if ye *be* Christ's, then are ye Abraham's
seed, and heirs according to the promise.

CHAPTER 4

NOW I say, *That* the heir, as long as he is a child,
differeth nothing from a servant, though he be
lord of all;
2 But is under tutors and governors until the
time appointed of the father.
3 Even so we, when we were children, were in
bondage under the elements of the world:
4 But when the fulness of the time was come,

covenant with Abraham (see note at Ex. 12:40). *none effect.* Nullified or left idle. God cannot break His covenant oath (Heb. 6:13–18).

3:18 *the inheritance.* A lot, an inherited possession freely granted by promise, showing that salvation is not on the basis of works (Rom. 4:13–16).

Law and Faith (3:19–29)

3:19 *because of transgressions.* The law was formally given at Sinai for the purpose of convicting of sin (Rom. 3:19–20), not to replace the covenant of grace, but to assist it, thus leading sinners to Christ (v. 24). *ordained.* Appointed. *by angels.* Literally, "through angels" (Deut. 33:2; Ps. 68:17).

3:20 *a mediator.* Greek literally reads, "the Mediator"—only referring to Christ for there never has been any other sufficient and effectual Mediator between God and sinners (1 Tim. 2:5). *is not a mediator of one.* Literally, "is not of one"; that is, Christ as the Mediator mediates both law and promise, the issues under scrutiny in the context. *but God is one.* The one and same God is in view in both the case of the promise and the law. Therefore, Paul is teaching that since both the law and the promise were given through Christ the Mediator, there is no disagreement between them.

3:21 *Is the law then against the promises.* Reiteration of the previous thought—the law and the promises (the gospel) are not in conflict but in harmony (Rom. 3:21,31). *which could have given life.* Inferring that the purpose of the law was not to give life. Thus justification is not by the law.

3:22 *concluded.* Literally, "shut up" (v. 23) or "inclosed" (Luke 5:6). *all under sin.* Under its power and penalty so as to be unable to give the obedience the law requires in order to be justified.

3:23 *kept.* Like a military guard. *under the law.* The law as broken through sin holds the sinner as guilty and liable to judgment (4:4–5,21; 5:18; Rom. 3:19; 6:14–15). *shut up unto the faith.* Enclosed so as to be convinced that the gospel is the only remedy.

3:24 *schoolmaster.* Literally, "a leader of children," signifying the strict disciplines of the law (vv. 22–23) like a servant watching over minor children (4:1–3).

3:25 *after that faith is come . . . no longer under a schoolmaster.* Saving faith delivers from the law's demand for perfect obedience in order to be justified.

3:27 *baptized into Christ.* Symbolic term denoting union with Christ, which is pictured in baptism (Rom. 6:3–4; 1 Cor. 12:12–13). *have put on.* Greek signifies being clothed (Rom. 13:12,14; Eph. 4:24; 6:11,14; Col. 3:10,12; 1 Thess. 5:8), thus used metaphorically here of being united with Christ and covered with Christ's righteous merit.

3:28 *all one in Christ Jesus.* Union with Christ creates spiritual equality among all believers (Col. 3:11).

3:29 *Abraham's seed.* All who are in union with Christ are the spiritual seed of Abraham. *heirs.* Those who obtain a lot or portion (v. 18). *according to the promise.* Of the gospel.

Thoughts for Personal/Family Worship: Chapter 3

1. **It is imperative to guard against all that would take away our confidence in Christ alone in the Christian life. Spiritual growth and maturity are never enhanced by reliance on the efforts of the flesh. How can Christians drift away from complete dependence on Christ?**
2. **The penalty of the law is its dreadful curse—the sentence of death. Thus, for sinners to be freed from that curse and to be justified before the law that demands it, Christ became a curse for them! Let no child of God ever forget what Christ endured.**
3. **No sinner is ever justified by the law, but not because there is any fault in the law. The fault lies in the sinner; namely, in his inability to give the perfect obedience the law requires. But the inflexible demands of the law cause it to become a means of bringing the sinner to faith in Christ's perfect obedience by which the law was satisfied. Are you resting in Christ alone for acceptance with God?**

Chapter 4: ***Paul continues to emphasize the central truth that justification is not by the works of the law.***

Sonship Is by Faith (4:1–7)

4:1 *child.* One who is yet a minor. *servant.* Slave. *though he be*

God sent forth his Son, made of a woman, made
under the law,
5 To redeem them that were under the law, that
we might receive the adoption of sons.
6 And because ye are sons, God hath sent forth
the Spirit of his Son into your hearts, crying,
Abba, Father.
7 Wherefore thou art no more a servant, but a son;
and if a son, then an heir of God through Christ.
8 Howbeit then, when ye knew not God, ye did
service unto them which by nature are no gods.
9 But now, after that ye have known God, or
rather are known of God, how turn ye again to
the weak and beggarly elements, whereunto ye
desire again to be in bondage?
10 Ye observe days, and months, and times, and
years.
11 I am afraid of you, lest I have bestowed upon
you labour in vain.
12 Brethren, I beseech you, be as I *am*; for I *am* as
ye *are*: ye have not injured me at all.
13 Ye know how through infirmity of the flesh I
preached the gospel unto you at the first.
14 And my temptation which was in my flesh ye
despised not, nor rejected; but received me as an
angel of God, *even* as Christ Jesus.
15 Where is then the blessedness ye spake of? for
I bear you record, that, if *it had been* possible, ye
would have plucked out your own eyes, and have
given them to me.
16 Am I therefore become your enemy, because I
tell you the truth?
17 They zealously affect you, *but* not well; yea,
they would exclude you, that ye might affect them.
18 But *it is* good to be zealously affected always
in *a* good *thing*, and not only when I am present
with you.
19 My little children, of whom I travail in birth
again until Christ be formed in you,
20 I desire to be present with you now, and to
change my voice; for I stand in doubt of you.
21 Tell me, ye that desire to be under the law, do
ye not hear the law?
22 For it is written, that Abraham had two sons,
the one by a bondmaid, the other by a freewoman.
23 But he *who was* of the bondwoman was born
after the flesh; but he of the freewoman *was* by
promise.

---

lord of all. That is, legal heir or owner of everything.

4:2 *tutors.* Signifies one entrusted with care, a guardian (cf. 3:24). *governors.* Those who rule a house, senior servants. *time appointed.* Time set beforehand.

4:3 *in bondage.* Enslaved. *elements of the world.* Or "worldly elements," the original word for *element* signifying an elementary teaching; here religious teaching whether Jewish or Gentile.

4:4 *fulness of the time . . . sent forth his Son.* Implying that Christ already existed as God's Son before He became human (John 1:1,14; 3:17; 10:36). Word for *time* signifies a period of time, thus the phrase describes the close of that period. *made of a woman.* The verb can mean, "to be born," signifying Christ's real humanity.

4:5 *To redeem.* To ransom or set free (3:13; cf. 1 Cor. 6:20; Rev. 5:9). *adoption.* The word is used only by Paul and signifies "to place as a son" in one's family (Rom. 8:15,23; 9:4; Eph. 1:5).

4:6 *the Spirit of his Son.* A title of the Spirit signifying adoption. *Abba.* Aramaic for "father," an expression of childlike trust and intimacy with the Father (Mark 14:36; Rom. 8:15).

Blessings Come by Faith (4:8–31)

4:8 *ye did service.* You served. *by nature are no gods.* Heathen idols, not deities at all, being but the invention of man's fallen mind. God has a distinct *nature* from all other beings (Isa. 40:18,25; Jer. 10:6).

4:9 *ye have known God.* That is, have come to know Him, which is eternal life (John 17:3). *known of God.* Literally, "by God," stressing divine sovereignty in salvation (1 Cor. 8:3). *how turn ye.* How do you turn back. *to the weak and beggarly elements.* Impoverished Judaistic rituals, which were powerless to justify.

4:10 *observe.* Literally, "to keep closely," thus intense observation. *days, and months, and times, and years.* The cycle of Jewish rituals (Lev. 23; 25; Col. 2:16).

4:11 *lest.* Literally, "lest somehow," denoting pessimism but designed to rouse them to repentance. *bestowed . . . in vain.* Paul's work among them had been to no effect.

4:12 *beseech.* Beg earnestly. *not injured me.* The reference is to his initial visit to Galatia when he enjoyed great harmony with the people.

4:13 *infirmity of the flesh.* Bodily weakness or illness, perhaps something about his eyes (v. 15).

4:14 *temptation . . . in my flesh.* Paul's illness. *despised.* Treated with contempt. *rejected.* Literally, "spat out." Whatever the nature of his illness it could have brought this kind of treatment but had not. *received me as an angel . . . even as Christ.* As if Paul's voice had been that of an angel or even Christ Himself (Matt. 10:40).

4:15 *blessedness.* Happiness. *plucked out your own eyes.* Indicative of the esteem in which Paul had been held by the Galatians.

4:16 *Am I . . . your enemy.* A question designed to prove that he was their friend.

4:17 *zealously affect you.* Have a warm interest in someone. *but not well.* Not for the right purpose. *exclude you.* Shut out or isolate from all other influences. *that ye might affect them.* Same word as *zealously affect*; thus the goal of the Judaizers was to gain the support of the Galatians by isolating them from Paul.

4:18 *it is good to be zealously affected . . . in a good thing.* A reminder to the Galatians that they had been rightly warm toward him. *and not only when I am present with you.* Their warm interest had not been maintained toward Paul or the gospel.

4:19 *travail in birth.* Have labor pains (v. 27). *formed.* Signifies an inward change into Christ's likeness (cf. Rom. 8:29; Col. 1:27–28).

4:20 *to change my voice.* To alter the mode of speaking. *stand in doubt.* Literally, "to be without a way," thus to be in perplexity.

4:21 *under the law.* As a way to justification. *do ye not hear the law?* The *law* in another sense, namely the Pentateuch from which he proceeds to quote.

4:22 *bondmaid.* Word indicates a young female servant. *freewoman.* One who is free, akin to the word "liberty" (5:1).

4:23 *born after the flesh.* Ishmael's birth was the product

24 Which things are an allegory: for these are the
two covenants; the one from the mount Sinai,
which gendereth to bondage, which is Agar.
25 For this Agar is mount Sinai in Arabia, and
answereth to Jerusalem which now is, and is in
bondage with her children.
26 But Jerusalem which is above is free, which is
the mother of us all.
27 For it is written, Rejoice, *thou* barren that
bearest not; break forth and cry, thou that
travailest not: for the desolate hath many more
children than she which hath an husband.
28 Now we, brethren, as Isaac was, are the chil-
dren of promise.
29 But as then he that was born after the flesh
persecuted him *that was born* after the Spirit, even
so *it is* now.
30 Nevertheless what saith the scripture? Cast out
the bondwoman and her son: for the son of the
bondwoman shall not be heir with the son of the
freewoman.
31 So then, brethren, we are not children of the
bondwoman, but of the free.

CHAPTER 5

STAND fast therefore in the liberty wherewith
Christ hath made us free, and be not entangled
again with the yoke of bondage.
2 Behold, I Paul say unto you, that if ye be
circumcised, Christ shall profit you nothing.
3 For I testify again to every man that is circum-
cised, that he is a debtor to do the whole law.
4 Christ is become of no effect unto you, whoso-
ever of you are justified by the law; ye are fallen
from grace.
5 For we through the Spirit wait for the hope of
righteousness by faith.
6 For in Jesus Christ neither circumcision avail-
eth any thing, nor uncircumcision; but faith
which worketh by love.
7 Ye did run well; who did hinder you that ye
should not obey the truth?
8 This persuasion *cometh* not of him that calleth
you.
9 A little leaven leaveneth the whole lump.
10 I have confidence in you through the Lord,
that ye will be none otherwise minded: but he

of the natural power of procreation (Gen. 16). *he of the freewoman was by promise.* Isaac's birth was the result of faith in God's promise (Gen. 15; 17; 21; Heb. 11:11).

4:24 *allegory.* The word signifies giving a meaning other than the strictly literal. *these are the two covenants.* They are representatives of two covenants. *gendereth.* To beget. *which is Agar.* Paul applies Hagar to the bondage of justification by the law.

4:25 *answereth to.* Literally, "is in the same row"; thus it corresponds. *Jerusalem which now is.* Jerusalem of Paul's day, representing the Judaism that rejected Christ.

4:26 *Jerusalem . . . above.* Heaven, the divine source of salvation and all blessing (Heb. 12:22–24; Rev. 21:1—22:5). *the mother of us all.* That is, of Jew and Gentile both.

4:27 *For it is written.* A predictive promise from Isa. 54:1 to show that fruitfulness follows barrenness as in the case of Sarah. *travailest not.* Not feel labor pains. *desolate.* Barren.

4:28 *the children of promise.* The status of all who are Christ's (Rom. 9:8).

4:29 *persecuted.* Pursued. *even so it is now.* Ishmael's persecution of Isaac was a portrayal of the unregenerate persecuting the regenerate with continual strife.

4:30 *Cast out the bondwoman and her son.* The physical expulsion of Hagar and Ishmael from Abraham's house underlines that works and grace cannot dwell together (Gen. 21:10–14).

4:31 *not . . . of the bondwoman, but of the free.* All believers of all time are the spiritual offspring of God's grace (3:29).

Thoughts for Personal/Family Worship: Chapter 4

1. **Christ's first coming was an astounding miracle, for it was the appearance of the God-man. God sent forth His Son—there is His deity. He was made of a woman—there is His humanity. But the two natures are united in the one person; thus, He is the God-man. Great is the mystery of redemption! Let's dwell on this truth: "God was manifest in the flesh" (1 Tim. 3:16).**
2. **We must agonize over those who are endangered by another gospel. Paul had labored hard and suffered much to see the Galatians converted to Christ. But he was prepared to go through labor pains again to see them recovered from the soul-destroying message of the Judaizers. Let us labor by grace to see those who are deluded cast aside the lie. Whom do you know in this position? How are you laboring for them?**
3. **It is vital for the Christian to know the Scriptures. Note Paul's use of the Word of God as he reasons with the Galatians: "Do ye not hear the law?" (v. 21); "For it is written" (v. 22); "Nevertheless what saith the scripture?" (v. 30). Is Scripture the only compass to which you turn daily?**

Chapter 5: *Paul commences his application of the doctrine of justification in terms of the liberty from sin that the truth produces in the believer's experience.*

Endurance through Faith (5:1–12)

5:1 *Stand fast therefore.* Continual perseverance against the Judaizers. *in the liberty wherewith Christ hath made us free.* That is, by means of gospel liberty the believer is enabled to stand fast (John 8:32–36; Rom. 6:17–23; 7:3–4; 8:2,21; 1 Cor. 7:22; 9:1,19–23; 2 Cor. 3:17). *yoke of bondage.* Brought under oppression by a different form of spiritual slavery.

5:2 *Christ shall profit you nothing.* The terrible result of the yoke of bondage—all gospel blessing forfeited.

5:3 *a debtor to do the whole law.* Submission to circumcision would bring an obligation to obey the entire law, moral and ceremonial (Rom. 2:25).

5:4 *Christ is . . . of no effect unto you.* Reiteration of v. 2—forfeiture of gospel blessings. *fallen from grace.* Fallen away from the system of gospel grace.

5:5 *through the Spirit.* By reliance upon the Spirit. *wait for the hope of righteousness.* The ultimate outcome of justification by Christ's righteousness; namely, public acquittal at Christ's return (2 Tim. 4:8).

5:6 *For in Jesus Christ.* The words mean "in relation to Christ." *neither circumcision . . . nor uncircumcision.* See 6:15; 1 Cor. 7:19; Col. 3:11. *faith . . . worketh by love.* Faith's reality is proved by other graces such as love.

that troubleth you shall bear his judgment, who-
soever he be.
11 And I, brethren, if I yet preach circumcision,
why do I yet suffer persecution? then is the offence
of the cross ceased.
12 I would they were even cut off which trouble
you.
13 For, brethren, ye have been called unto liberty;
only *use* not liberty for an occasion to the flesh,
but by love serve one another.
14 For all the law is fulfilled in one word, *even* in
this; Thou shalt love thy neighbour as thyself.
15 But if ye bite and devour one another, take
heed that ye be not consumed one of another.
16 *This* I say then, Walk in the Spirit, and ye shall
not fulfil the lust of the flesh.
17 For the flesh lusteth against the Spirit, and the
Spirit against the flesh: and these are contrary the
one to the other: so that ye cannot do the things
that ye would.
18 But if ye be led of the Spirit, ye are not under
the law.
19 Now the works of the flesh are manifest, which
are *these*; Adultery, fornication, uncleanness,
lasciviousness,
20 Idolatry, witchcraft, hatred, variance, emula-
tions, wrath, strife, seditions, heresies,
21 Envyings, murders, drunkenness, revellings,
and such like: of the which I tell you before, as I
have also told *you* in time past, that they which do
such things shall not inherit the kingdom of God.
22 But the fruit of the Spirit is love, joy, peace,
longsuffering, gentleness, goodness, faith,
23 Meekness, temperance: against such there is
no law.
24 And they that are Christ's have crucified the

5:7 *Ye did run well.* Metaphorical term taken from a foot race (2:2; 1 Cor. 9:24–27; Heb. 12:1). *hinder.* Cut in on the runner so as to push him back. *obey.* Original word denotes obedience resulting from persuasion.

5:8 *This persuasion.* The Judaistic teaching that threatened to win them over.

5:9 *A little leaven leaveneth the whole lump.* A proverbial expression revealing the infiltrating power of false teaching (Matt. 16:6,11–12; 1 Cor. 5:6).

5:10 *I have confidence.* I am persuaded. *through the Lord.* Literally, "in the Lord"; Paul was confident that those united to Christ would receive his correction and turn from heresy (Rom. 15:14; 2 Thess. 3:4). *none otherwise minded.* Not thinking differently. *troubleth you.* Throws you into confusion. *shall bear his judgment.* Will come under the divine penalty (1:8–9).

5:11 *why do I yet suffer persecution?* The fact that he suffered persecution disproved the allegation that Paul preached circumcision as needful. *offence.* Stumbling block or something that causes opposition.

5:12 *cut off.* Excommunicated.

REVELATION OF LIFE IN THE SPIRIT (5:13—6:10)

Walking by the Spirit (5:13–26)

5:13 *called unto liberty.* Called to freedom from salvation by works and from the ceremonial law. *occasion to the flesh.* Opportunity for sin. *by love serve one another.* Spiritual freedom enables believers to serve one another.

5:14 *fulfilled.* Signifies complete obedience.

5:15 *bite . . . devour . . . consumed.* Strong words denoting an entire process of wounding, eating, and destroying.

5:16 *Walk in the Spirit.* Christian behavior must be controlled by the Spirit (Rom. 8:6–16). *lust.* Strong desire. *the flesh.* Sin in fallen human nature.

5:17 *the flesh lusteth against the Spirit, and the Spirit against the flesh.* The spiritual battle experienced in the heart of the believer. *contrary.* Opposed. *so that ye cannot do the things that ye would.* The words illustrate the result of this inward struggle (Rom. 7:14–25).

5:18 *led of the Spirit.* Better, "led by the Spirit" in growing sanctification. *ye are not under the law.* That is, the leading of the Spirit indicates freedom from the law's curse (Rom. 6:14; 8:1–4).

5:19 *the works of the flesh.* The various operations of sin in human nature. *manifest.* Open, visible. *Adultery.* Unlawful physical relations with another's spouse (Ex. 20:14). *fornication.* Unlawful physical relations (1 Cor. 6:12–18). *uncleanness.* Sexual impurity (Rom. 1:24). *lasciviousness.* Lack of self-control in moral matters (Rom. 13:13; 1 Peter 4:3).

5:20 *Idolatry.* Possession of an image of a divine being, or worship through an image (Ex. 20:4–6). *witchcraft.* Sorcery involving the use of drugs (Deut. 18:10). *variance.* Fighting and contention (1 Cor. 3:3). *emulations.* Jealousy (James 3:13–16). *wrath.* Outburst of anger (Eph. 4:31). *strife.* Selfish ambition (Phil. 2:3–4). *seditions.* Divisions (1 Cor. 3:4). *heresies.* Self-willed opinions that lead to the formation of sects (Acts 24:14; 2 Peter 2:1).

5:21 *Envyings.* Feelings of displeasure upon seeing the prosperity of others. *revellings.* Carousing and intoxication (Rom. 13:13). *and such like.* The list given is representative not exhaustive. *of the which I tell you before.* That is, beforehand. *shall not inherit the kingdom of God.* While no sinner can enter God's kingdom by religious works yet he will certainly shut himself out by evil works (1 Cor. 6:9–11; Eph. 5:5–6).

5:22 *fruit of the Spirit.* The singular *fruit* denotes that the fruit of the Spirit is an indivisible whole possessed in varying degrees by every believer. *love.* The word signifies the highest form of love—spiritual love (Rom. 5:8). *peace.* Inward serenity and harmony in relationships (Rom. 5:1; Eph. 2:14–15). *longsuffering.* Literally, "long of temper," signifying patience (Eph. 4:2). *gentleness.* Inward kindness (Eph. 2:7). *goodness.* Outward actions that are meant to help others.

5:23 *Meekness.* Humility and gentleness (2 Tim. 2:25). *temperance.* Self-control (1 Cor. 9:25). *against such there is no law.* An encouragement to the believer to manifest these graces.

5:24 *Christ's.* Literally, "of the Christ"; hence in union with Christ. *have crucified the flesh with the affections and lusts.* Union with Christ produces death to the flesh and its works (2:19; Rom. 6:1–3).

5:25 *If we live in the Spirit.* The source of spiritual life is in the Spirit (John 6:63; Rom. 8:10). *walk.* The Greek word (not the same as in v. 16) means "walk in line," thus by walking in line with the Spirit the believer walks contrary to the flesh.

5:26 *desirous of vain glory.* One word in the original signifying empty boasting. *provoking.* Literally, "calling forth," thus to incite to a contest. *envying.* Word signifies a feeling of displeasure due to witnessing the prosperity of others.

Thoughts for Personal/Family Worship: Chapter 5

1. The Christian's liberty in Christ is the means whereby he stands fast against all that would enslave. The goal

flesh with the affections and lusts.
25 If we live in the Spirit, let us also walk in the
Spirit.
26 Let us not be desirous of vain glory, provoking
one another, envying one another.

CHAPTER 6

BRETHREN, if a man be overtaken in a fault, ye
which are spiritual, restore such an one in the
spirit of meekness; considering thyself, lest thou
also be tempted.
2 Bear ye one another's burdens, and so fulfil the
law of Christ.
3 For if a man think himself to be something,
when he is nothing, he deceiveth himself.
4 But let every man prove his own work, and then
shall he have rejoicing in himself alone, and not
in another.
5 For every man shall bear his own burden.
6 Let him that is taught in the word communi-
cate unto him that teacheth in all good things.
7 Be not deceived; God is not mocked: for
whatsoever a man soweth, that shall he also reap.
8 For he that soweth to his flesh shall of the flesh
reap corruption; but he that soweth to the Spirit
shall of the Spirit reap life everlasting.
9 And let us not be weary in well doing: for in due
season we shall reap, if we faint not.
10 As we have therefore opportunity, let us do
good unto all *men*, especially unto them who are
of the household of faith.
11 Ye see how large a letter I have written unto
you with mine own hand.
12 As many as desire to make a fair shew in the
flesh, they constrain you to be circumcised; only
lest they should suffer persecution for the cross
of Christ.
13 For neither they themselves who are circum-
cised keep the law; but desire to have you circum-

of the Enemy is to bring the believer into spiritual bondage, thereby robbing the soul of enjoyment in Christ. But his defense is the very liberty he has in Christ. Christ sets believers free from the law's demand for perfect obedience by giving that perfect obedience on our behalf, forming the basis for their justification and thus the basis for standing fast against all that would enslave. Do you know this struggle personally? To whom do you look for defense and liberty?

2. **Christian liberty is freedom from sin and condemnation to serve Christ. Some teach that the believer's liberty in Christ is freedom from God's moral law as a direction for how to live, thus granting freedom to indulge fleshly appetites. This antinomian heresy must be resisted vigorously. The liberty to which we have been called is not license to sin but freedom to obey Christ and do His will. Why is it the Christian's liberty to serve others in love?**
3. **The justified man produces true holiness because he has the Holy Spirit within. Justification is always followed by sanctification; and sanctification is by the Spirit, not by the law. The Spirit is God's gift to the Christian on the basis of the merit of Christ. By the Spirit's work in the heart the believer is made holy, demonstrated by the fruit that the Spirit produces. Why is it crucial that we remember that sanctification is by grace alone?**

Chapter 6: *Paul continues with his application of the doctrine of justification in terms of the conquest of the flesh.*

Serving One Another (6:1–10)

6:1 *overtaken in a fault.* Caught by sin due to being off guard. *restore.* To restore to a previous position of usefulness. *meekness.* See note at 5:23.

6:2 *Bear ye one another's burdens.* Share the load. *the law of Christ.* The commandments of God taken up under the Lordship of Christ (Matt. 5:17–48; 12:8; 1 Cor. 9:21), especially the principle of love for fellow believers (5:14; John 13:34; Rom. 13:8–10).

6:3 *think himself to be something.* Overconfidence in self as a consequence of not finding in oneself the faults of others.

6:4 *prove.* Put to the test (Rom. 12:3). *rejoicing in himself alone, and not in another.* That is, rejoicing in what the Lord has done in his life, not rejoicing simply because of the absence of faults seen in others.

6:5 *every man shall bear his own burden.* Each person is accountable for his faults and cannot shift the responsibility to another.

6:6 *taught in.* The Greek word is the root from which we get our word "to catechize." *communicate . . . in all good things.* Students should share their friendship and physical resources with their teachers (1 Cor. 9:11–14).

6:7 *Be not deceived.* Do not allow yourself to be led astray (1 Cor. 6:9; 15:33; Eph. 5:6). *mocked.* Sneered at or scorned. It is no light thing to mock at God (Isa. 37:23,36–38)—which all sin does.

6:8 *soweth to his flesh.* Gives time and energy to satisfy sinful desires. *reap corruption.* The noun corruption is akin to the verb that means "to destroy by means of corrupting," so to reap corruption signifies destruction in contrast with *life everlasting.*

6:9 *weary.* Faint or lose heart. *well doing.* Good works. *in due season.* Signifies a time divinely appointed.

6:10 *household.* The company of the redeemed who embrace the *faith* of the gospel is one spiritual family (Eph. 2:19; 1 Tim. 3:15), and all believers are brothers and sisters under one Father (1:1–2).

CLOSING (6:11–18)

6:11 *how large a letter.* The word for "letter" is plural and refers to the characters of the alphabet. Paul's handwriting was large.

6:12 *to make a fair shew.* Literally, "to be good of face," here a metaphor for the Judaizers' outward display of religious zeal. *constrain.* Compel or force. *the cross of Christ.* That which was so precious to Paul, the Judaizers did not consider worth suffering for.

6:13 *glory in your flesh.* The objective of the Judaizers—to glory or boast—had they been able to have the Galatians submit to circumcision.

6:14 *God forbid.* The third use of this term in the epistle (2:17; 3:21). All the believer's boasting must be in God's work through Jesus Christ (1 Cor. 1:29–31).

6:15 *availeth any thing.* Literally, "is of any force." *new creature.* In Christ, believers are being recreated after the image of God (2 Cor. 5:17; Eph. 2:10; Col. 3:10–11).

6:16 *walk.* Live in conformity to (same word as in 5:25). *rule.*

cised, that they may glory in your flesh.
14 But God forbid that I should glory, save in the
cross of our Lord Jesus Christ, by whom the world
is crucified unto me, and I unto the world.
15 For in Christ Jesus neither circumcision avail-
eth any thing, nor uncircumcision, but a new
creature.
16 And as many as walk according to this rule,
peace *be* on them, and mercy, and upon the Israel
of God.
17 From henceforth let no man trouble me: for I
bear in my body the marks of the Lord Jesus.
18 Brethren, the grace of our Lord Jesus Christ *be*
with your spirit. Amen.

Principle. *the Israel of God.* Signifying the full company of God's people from both Jews and Gentiles (3:28–29).
6:17 *trouble.* Plural noun signifying the many distractions that Paul had suffered due to the departure from truth by the Galatian churches. *marks.* Literally, "stigmata," the reference being to the scars on Paul's body received through persecution for Christ's sake (2 Cor. 11:24–25).
6:18 *Brethren.* A closing reminder of the apostle's love for the Galatians, though they had erred so grievously.

Thoughts for Personal/Family Worship: Chapter 6

1. A ministry of restoration can only be exercised by believers who are spiritually strong. Paul's injunction is that those who are spiritual are to restore the one who is caught off guard and falls into sin. The inference is that the ministry of restoration can only be exercised by believers who themselves are on their guard. One of the marks of spiritual strength is a cautiousness so as to avoid every pit that Satan digs, into which the careless will fall (Jude 23). Should this not move us to pray earnestly that we might be kept from falling?
2. Spiritual increase will come at God's appointed time. Paul states that "in due season we shall reap" (v. 9). The word for "season" refers to a fixed or appointed time, signifying that the Lord has times appointed when spiritual reaping will take place. It is such a truth that actually is the means of keeping us from fainting and growing weary in the lengthy times of sowing the spiritual seed. Ultimately our "harvest time" is Christ's coming. How can you rest more in God's appointed time for all things?
3. The one matter in which the believer may rightfully boast is the work of Christ. Paul repudiates all thoughts of glorying or boasting in anything except "the cross," the finished work of Christ. In that work no man had any part, for Christ alone was qualified to make satisfaction for sin. Therefore, in the work of the cross the believer may boast without sinning. What is it about the cross that excites the Christian to rejoice, exalt, and praise the Lord?

FOR *By Grace* ARE YE SAVED THROUGH FAITH *&* THAT NOT OF YOURSELVES IT IS *The Gift* OF GOD

EPHESIANS 2:8

INTRODUCTION TO THE BOOK OF EPHESIANS

Authorship: No one in the early church questioned that Paul wrote this epistle. However, some modern scholars argue that another author wrote in Paul's name. They say: (1) Ephesians has a different style and vocabulary than Paul's letters. (2) Ephesians goes beyond Paul's theology in its view of church and marriage, and fails to include his characteristic emphasis on Christ's future coming. (3) Ephesians is somewhat similar to Colossians, thus proving that it was written by someone imitating Paul's style. (4) Another author could have used Paul's name in order to honor him, employing a pseudonymous style acceptable among early Christians.

In response to these arguments, we can say that: (1) An author can be quite versatile in his style and vocabulary as he writes on different occasions. Writings as short as the New Testament epistles do not give us a large enough sample of an author's writings to draw fine lines about distinctive style and vocabulary. (2) No single epistle of Paul captures all of his teachings, so we should not be surprised that Ephesians adds some insights to what we find in his other writings, while not contradicting them. Nor does it neglect Paul's great themes. For example, this epistle says much about the hope of Christ's coming (1:10–11,14,18; 2:7; 4:4,10,13,30; 5:5–6,27; 6:8). (3) The similarities of Ephesians to Colossians are fascinating, but can be explained by the same author addressing two churches in different situations. (4) Impersonating an apostle was not acceptable in the early church. Both Tertullian and Serapion of Antioch bore witness that the church rejected writings falsely claiming to be written by apostles.

The epistle itself testifies that it was written by "Paul, an apostle of Jesus Christ" (1:1). In the midst of the epistle, the author refers to himself as "I Paul, the prisoner of Jesus Christ" (3:1). He also writes of his supernatural calling as an apostle to the Gentiles (vv. 5–8). If the author was not the apostle Paul, then he was guilty of gross deception. Indeed, he would be a hypocrite of the worst kind, for he urged the Ephesians to put away lying and speak the truth (4:25). Such accusations are unworthy of this noble epistle. On the contrary, Ephesians bears the marks of being divine revelation, the Word of the God who cannot lie (Rom. 3:4; Titus 1:2). Therefore we have every reason to accept it for what it claims to be: the epistle of the apostle Paul.

Date: Paul said that he wrote as a prisoner in chains (3:1; 4:1; 6:20). Paul was imprisoned many times (2 Cor. 11:23), but his major imprisonments took place in Caesarea from AD 57–59 (Acts 23:33; 24:27), and in Rome from AD 60–62 (Acts 28:30). Tradition holds that he wrote this epistle from Rome. It seems likely that Ephesians was written during the same imprisonment as Colossians, since they have similar messages; both speak of his imprisonment (Col. 4:3,10,18), and both were delivered by Tychicus (Eph. 6:21; Col. 4:7).

Theme: God's riches of grace in Christ for His body.

Purpose: To teach believers about the glorious riches which belong to them by their union to the crucified and resurrected Lord Jesus, and to call them to walk worthy of their privileges by vital church membership, lifelong repentance, well-ordered households, and spiritual combat against the Devil. Unlike some epistles, Paul does not address any specific spiritual dangers threatening the church. Instead, he writes to strengthen a healthy church. If we may deduce Paul's purpose from his prayers for the church, then he wrote to the Ephesians in order to lead them into a richer experiential knowledge of their Savior in the context of their everyday lives in a fallen world.

Synopsis: *The Contribution of Ephesians to Redemptive Revelation*

Ephesians presents theology as doxology, that is, the truth of God for the worship of God. It is a book resounding with praise for the riches of God in Christ. His death (1:7; 2:13–16; 5:2,25) and exaltation (1:20–22; 2:5–6; 4:8–10) are the means to salvation for all those united to Him. In Him believers have every spiritual blessing (1:3), riches of grace (vv. 7,18; 3:8) overflowing from God's great love for His people (2:5). Paul strains language to express the inexpressible glory of God (1:19; 2:7; 3:20), which comes through Christ in fullness (1:23; 3:17; 4:10,13; 5:18). God's riches for His people consist particularly of the Holy Spirit in all His gifts and fruit (1:13–14,17; 2:18,22; 3:5,16; 4:3–4,30; 5:9,18; 6:17–18). The book is profoundly shaped by the doctrine of the Trinity, as Father, Son, and Holy Spirit operate in harmony to save a people for God's glory.

Thus Ephesians has much to say about the church, the body, and the bride of Jesus Christ (1:1,18,23; 2:19–22; 3:6,15,21; 4:4–16; 5:23,25–27,29–32; 6:18). They are nothing less than the temple of the living God and the showcase of God's glory. As a people of amazing privilege, they have a high calling to fulfill (4:1). This calling places ethical obligations upon every dimension of life, as Paul makes clear in the second half of the epistle. The body must be united in love and the saints must be holy in conduct (chs. 4–5). The church must be a light exposing the corruptions of the world (5:7–14) and a spiritual army standing in righteousness against the demonic forces of evil (6:10–18).

This strong moral thrust finds its footing in the doctrines of salvation by grace alone (1–2). Though Christians were once as the rest of the world, dead in sin, dwelling in spiritual darkness, and doomed to suffer God's wrath (2:1–3; 4:17–19; 5:5–6), God has given His people forgiveness and life, a life shaped and energized by the gospel of Jesus Christ. They are the people in union with Christ, and this union, expressed in the frequent "in him" or "with him," is central to Paul's message. It is the "mystery of the gospel" (6:19), that is, the secret truth planned by God in eternity and now revealed. The mystery is that God is joining people from all nations to His Son in order to enjoy His redemptive love and share in His exaltation as head over all things (1:9–10; 3:3–6,9; 5:29–32). Thus, Ephesians reveals the riches of God's grace in Christ to Christ's body, the elect from Jew and Gentile. It is a book of salvation by grace alone, in Christ alone, for the glory of God alone.

Outline:

I. Greetings: Grace and Peace (1:1–2)

II. The Doctrine of God's Grace in Christ for His Body (1:3—3:21)
- A. The Praise of God's Grace in Christ (1:3–14)
- B. The Power of God's Grace in the Risen Lord (1:15—2:10)
- C. The Peace of God's Grace in the Crucified Lord (2:11–22)
- D. The Purpose of God's Grace Revealed in Christ (3:1–21)

III. The Calling to Walk as the Body of Christ (4:1—6:22)
- A. Walk Worthy as One Body (4:1–16)
- B. Walk in the New Man, Not in the Old Ways of Sin (4:17—5:14)
- C. Walk in God's Wisdom for Relationships (5:15—6:9)
- D. Walk in the Lord's Armor for Spiritual Warfare (6:10–22)

IV. Concluding Blessing: Peace and Grace (6:23–24)

THE EPISTLE OF PAUL THE APOSTLE TO THE EPHESIANS

CHAPTER 1

PAUL, an apostle of Jesus Christ by the will of
God, to the saints which are at Ephesus, and to
the faithful in Christ Jesus:
2 Grace *be* to you, and peace, from God our
Father, and *from* the Lord Jesus Christ.
3 Blessed *be* the God and Father of our Lord
Jesus Christ, who hath blessed us with all spiritual
blessings in heavenly *places* in Christ:
4 According as he hath chosen us in him before
the foundation of the world, that we should be
holy and without blame before him in love:
5 Having predestinated us unto the adoption of
children by Jesus Christ to himself, according to
the good pleasure of his will,
6 To the praise of the glory of his grace, wherein
he hath made us accepted in the beloved.
7 In whom we have redemption through his
blood, the forgiveness of sins, according to the
riches of his grace;
8 Wherein he hath abounded toward us in all
wisdom and prudence;
9 Having made known unto us the mystery of his
will, according to his good pleasure which he hath
purposed in himself:
10 That in the dispensation of the fulness of
times he might gather together in one all things
in Christ, both which are in heaven, and which
are on earth; *even* in him:
11 In whom also we have obtained an inheritance,
being predestinated according to the purpose of
him who worketh all things after the counsel of
his own will:
12 That we should be to the praise of his glory,
who first trusted in Christ.
13 In whom ye also *trusted*, after that ye heard
the word of truth, the gospel of your salvation: in
whom also after that ye believed, ye were sealed
with that holy Spirit of promise,
14 Which is the earnest of our inheritance until

Chapter 1: ***Paul greets the saints, exults in the grace of the triune God, and prays for greater illumination for God's people to know Him better.***

GREETINGS: GRACE AND PEACE (1:1–2)

1:1 By God's sovereign *will*, Christ sent Paul as an *apostle*, an eyewitness of the risen Lord, authorized by Him to work miracles and proclaim the Word revealed directly to him by God (3:4–5; Matt. 10:1–8; 1 Cor. 9:1; Gal. 1:12). All God's people are *saints*, made holy by grace.

1:2 *Grace*. God's loving purpose and power to save sinners and bring them to Himself. *peace*. Not just a feeling of safety, but relationships of harmony with God, oneself, and other people.

THE DOCTRINE OF GOD'S GRACE IN CHRIST FOR HIS BODY (1:3—3:21)

The Praise of God's Grace in Christ (1:3–14)

1:3 *Blessed*. We worship the triune God because of His grace to us. *God and Father of our Lord Jesus Christ*. A title of covenant relationship, like "the God of Abraham." *in Christ*. Through our union with Christ, who is already exalted *in heavenly places* (v. 20). *spiritual*. By the Holy Spirit.

1:4 Before we chose God, He chose us. *in him*. God made Christ our representative in the covenant. *that we should be holy*. God's election produces holiness, not hypocrisy (2 Thess. 2:13).

1:5 *adoption*. Gift of the status of sons to outsiders. Predestination arises from God's fatherly love. *according to the good pleasure of his will*. Not based on anything in us, but only because of His love (Deut. 7:7–8; Rom. 9:11–13).

1:6 *praise of the glory of his grace*. God's incomparable glory shining in His saving grace, moves His people to worship Him. *beloved*. Christ is God's beloved Son (Matt. 17:5).

1:7–8 *redemption*. Gift of freedom by the payment of a ransom price (Ex. 21:30), the sacrificial death (*blood*) of Christ (Mark 10:45). Christ redeemed elect sinners by satisfying God's justice (Rom. 3:24–26). God's forgiveness is not stingy, but *hath abounded* in *the riches of his grace*.

1:9 *mystery*. Secret known only to God and those to whom He reveals it (3:3–5; Matt. 13:11). The gospel reveals God's eternal plan that centers upon Christ (v. 10; 3:11).

1:10 *dispensation*. Economy, administration, organized plan. *gather together in one all things*. Sum up the entire universe under Christ as its risen and ruling head (vv. 20–22).

1:11 *obtained an inheritance*. Given the right to enjoy God's kingdom as God's adopted sons (vv. 14,18; 5:5; Rom. 8:17). *worketh all things*. God's providence controls every event according to His plan (*counsel*) so that His elect will be saved and enter glory (Rom. 8:28–30).

1:12 Believers exist for *the praise of his glory* (Isa. 43:7,21).

1:13–14 Salvation ordained by the Father and purchased by the Son is applied by the Holy Spirit. Literally, "hearing the word of truth . . . and believing, you were sealed." Legal documents were authorized by the impression of a seal upon wax.

the redemption of the purchased possession, unto
the praise of his glory.
15 Wherefore I also, after I heard of your faith in
the Lord Jesus, and love unto all the saints,
16 Cease not to give thanks for you, making
mention of you in my prayers;
17 That the God of our Lord Jesus Christ, the
Father of glory, may give unto you the spirit of
wisdom and revelation in the knowledge of him:
18 The eyes of your understanding being
enlightened; that ye may know what is the hope
of his calling, and what the riches of the glory of
his inheritance in the saints,
19 And what *is* the exceeding greatness of his
power to us-ward who believe, according to the
working of his mighty power,
20 Which he wrought in Christ, when he raised
him from the dead, and set *him* at his own right
hand in the heavenly *places*,
21 Far above all principality, and power, and
might, and dominion, and every name that is
named, not only in this world, but also in that
which is to come:
22 And hath put all *things* under his feet, and gave
him *to be* the head over all *things* to the church,
23 Which is his body, the fulness of him that
filleth all in all.

CHAPTER 2

AND you *hath he quickened*, who were dead in
trespasses and sins;
2 Wherein in time past ye walked according to
the course of this world, according to the prince
of the power of the air, the spirit that now work-
eth in the children of disobedience:
3 Among whom also we all had our conversation
in times past in the lusts of our flesh, fulfilling the
desires of the flesh and of the mind; and were by
nature the children of wrath, even as others.
4 But God, who is rich in mercy, for his great love
wherewith he loved us,

The Spirit impresses the gospel on the heart so that we give our Amen to God's promises and are marked as His people (2 Cor. 1:19–22; 3:3). *Spirit of promise*. Spirit promised by the prophets (Isa. 44:3; Ezek. 36:27; Joel 2:28). *earnest*. Down payment, a legally binding pledge of full possession in the future. *until the redemption*. Until Christ's purchased people enjoy total freedom (Rom. 8:21–23).

The Power of God's Grace in the Risen Lord (1:15—2:10)

1:15–16 We should thank God for *faith* and *love* because they are His gifts.

1:17 Paul calls upon the Trinity so that believers would know their Savior better. *the spirit of wisdom and revelation in the knowledge of him*. The Holy Spirit gives wisdom (Isa. 11:2) and reveals truth (1 Cor. 2:10–12) so that believers increase in the experiential knowledge of God.

1:18 *enlightened*. Believers need more spiritual light in their minds and hearts (Ps. 119:18), so they appreciate the *riches* of God's grace. *hope of his calling*. Future glory to which God calls us.

1:19 *believe, according to the working of his mighty power*. God creates faith by applying the divine power of Christ's resurrection to His elect (1:20; 2:5; 2 Cor. 4:6; 1 Peter 1:3).

1:20 God's power comes to us *in Christ*, through our union with Him in His resurrection. *at his own right hand*. The position of Lordship above all kings and angels (Ps. 110:1; Heb. 1:13).

1:21 *every name that is named*. Ephesus was full of idolatry and magic that invoked cosmic powers by name (Acts 19:11–20,27,35). Christ is infinitely greater than all spirits, good or evil.

1:22 *put all things under his feet*. Quoting Ps. 8:6. Christ, the exalted God-man, restores mankind even higher than our former dignity by ruling as *the head over* all creation (Heb. 2:5–10).

1:23 The church is *his body*, joined to Christ by the Spirit (1 Cor. 12:12–13). *the fulness of him that filleth all in all*. Christ is filling His church with His Spirit in order to fill all creation with the glory of the Lord (3:19; 4:10; 5:18).

Thoughts for Personal/Family Worship: Chapter 1

1. **The doctrine of election calls us to Christ. All of election's blessings are in Him. We dare not wait to come to Christ until we first somehow discover that we are elect. John Calvin said that the way to know that God elected us is by believing in Jesus Christ alone for salvation.**
2. **Election empowers holiness. Since God chose "that we should be holy" (v. 4), we must never isolate election from obeying God's laws. Those who say they can sin freely because they are elect have rejected the God who elects sinners unto holiness. Believers can pursue holiness confident that God's decree will give us all we need in Christ to attain it.**
3. **Grace fuels heartfelt praise. If your heart is sluggish in the aim for which we were made, it is the amazing grace of the triune God to sinners that you need most of all. Meditate on this chapter, and then make sure you take time to seek His face and sing His praises.**
4. **The gospel whets our appetite for God. Take Paul's prayer in this chapter and make it into your prayer for yourself and other believers. Stir up your heart with the glory of God's grace to desire to know Him better. Pray fervently for the Spirit of wisdom and revelation to give you more illumination about the riches of Jesus Christ.**

Chapter 2: ***Paul teaches the saints to remember who they once were and how God saved them in Christ so that they might marvel at God's grace to them.***

2:1 *quickened*. Made alive. *dead in trespasses and sins*. Like a corpse, unable to do any spiritual good, and unclean and offensive in God's sight (Rom. 8:6–8). Not just lacking life but an enemy to God's life (4:18).

2:2–3 *prince of the power of the air*. Satan, the invisible ruler of the world since our fall (2 Cor. 4:4; Rev. 12:9). *children of disobedience*. People characterized by disobedience. *conversation*. Conduct or lifestyle. *children of wrath*. People liable to suffer God's anger (5:6). All people outside of Christ are ruled by Satan, motivated by selfishness, and cursed by God.

2:4–5 *by grace ye are saved*. We are saved *sola gratia*, by grace alone. Saving grace is motivated only by God's magnificent *mercy* and *love*, not any worthiness in us (Titus 3:5). Salvation comes from God's power, not by any good decision or act of ours, for it is a supernatural resurrection from the dead by

5 Even when we were dead in sins, hath quick-
ened us together with Christ, (by grace ye are
saved;)
6 And hath raised *us* up together, and made *us* sit
together in heavenly *places* in Christ Jesus:
7 That in the ages to come he might shew the
exceeding riches of his grace in *his* kindness
toward us through Christ Jesus.
8 For by grace are ye saved through faith; and
that not of yourselves: *it is* the gift of God:
9 Not of works, lest any man should boast.
10 For we are his workmanship, created in Christ
Jesus unto good works, which God hath before
ordained that we should walk in them.
11 Wherefore remember, that ye *being* in time
past Gentiles in the flesh, who are called Uncir-
cumcision by that which is called the Circumci-
sion in the flesh made by hands;
12 That at that time ye were without Christ, being
aliens from the commonwealth of Israel, and
strangers from the covenants of promise, having
no hope, and without God in the world:
13 But now in Christ Jesus ye who sometimes
were far off are made nigh by the blood of Christ.
14 For he is our peace, who hath made both one,
and hath broken down the middle wall of parti-
tion *between us*;
15 Having abolished in his flesh the enmity, *even*
the law of commandments *contained* in ordi-
nances; for to make in himself of twain one new
man, *so* making peace;
16 And that he might reconcile both unto God
in one body by the cross, having slain the enmity
thereby:
17 And came and preached peace to you which
were afar off, and to them that were nigh.
18 For through him we both have access by one
Spirit unto the Father.
19 Now therefore ye are no more strangers and
foreigners, but fellowcitizens with the saints, and
of the household of God;
20 And are built upon the foundation of the
apostles and prophets, Jesus Christ himself being
the chief corner *stone*;
21 In whom all the building fitly framed together
groweth unto an holy temple in the Lord:

---

union with Christ (*quickened us together with Christ*).

2:6–7 The believer's union *in* and *through Christ Jesus* implies that he already shares Christ's exaltation *in heavenly places* and one day will experience that glory (1:3,20; Rev. 3:21). *shew the exceeding riches of his grace in his kindness*. God will glorify Himself by showering love upon His people forever.

2:8–9 Salvation *by grace* is received only *through faith* in Christ, and *not of works* as if one could have any merit (Rom. 3:28; Gal. 2:16). *it is the gift of God*. Since believers were once dead in sin (v. 1), both faith and the blessings it receives must come from God. *lest any man should boast*. To reserve all glory for God alone (1 Cor. 1:31).

2:10 God's grace changes people so that they do the *good works* to which God predestined them (1:4). *created in Christ Jesus*. The risen Lord was the first to rise from the dead with a resurrected body (Col. 1:18), and those united to Him are new creations (2 Cor. 5:17).

The Peace of God's Grace in the Crucified Lord (2:11–22)

2:11 *remember*. Meditate on your former condition to stimulate love for the Savior. *called the Circumcision in the flesh made by hands*. Mere externals are not true religion (Rom. 2:28).

2:12 *aliens*. Foreigners outside God's covenant people. *without God*. Non-Christian Gentiles worship many gods, but have no relationship with the only true God (1 Cor. 8:5–6; 10:20).

2:13 *sometimes*. At one time. *far off*. Not the distance of location, but of broken relationship and alienation. *made nigh*. Brought near to God in reconciled relationship by union with Christ and His sacrifice (*blood*).

2:14–16 *peace*. Harmony in relationships, with the well-being it brings. Christ became "our peace" when He *made both* Jews and Gentiles, who were two (*twain*), into *one*, united with each other and reconciled to God *by the cross*. Christ's death *abolished . . . the law*, not in its moral directions (6:2), but in its ceremonial rules such as circumcision and temple worship (vv. 11,21) that divided Jews from Gentiles. He also abolished the law in its divine curse against sinners so as to bring them near to God (vv. 13,18; Gal. 3:10,13). *one new man*. Mankind created anew (v. 10) in the last Adam (1 Cor. 15:45).

2:17 *preached peace to you which were afar off*. See Isa. 57:19. Jesus never visited Ephesus, but in His Spirit the risen Lord speaks wherever the gospel is preached (John 10:16).

2:18 A directory for trinitarian, evangelical corporate worship. We together draw near *unto the Father* in prayer and praise *through* Jesus Christ, enjoying God's presence *by one Spirit*.

2:19 *Now therefore*. Paul completes the contrast begun in v. 12. Gentiles once *strangers and foreigners* are now *fellowcitizens* in Israel and members *of the household* under God's promises. Christ has constituted a new Israel in fulfillment of the covenant of grace (Gal. 3:29; 6:16).

2:20 On *apostles*, see note at 1:1. *Prophets* are gifted by the Spirit to receive and declare new revelations from God (Deut. 18:20–22; 1 Cor. 14:29–31). The *apostles and prophets* are the *foundation* because they proclaimed the truths now written as the New Testament (see note at 3:4–5). Christ is *the chief corner stone* for all depends upon Him (Isa. 28:16).

2:21–22 God's *holy temple* is no longer a building in Jerusalem but a people who assemble for worship in many locations (1 Peter 2:5–6). Union with Christ (*In whom . . . in the Lord*) holds the building together. Members *are builded together* in love (4:16). God dwells with them and works in them *through the Spirit* (1 Cor. 3:16).

Thoughts for Personal/Family Worship: Chapter 2

1. **The gospel demands humility. What reason do true Christians have to boast? We were dead in sin and distant from God. Satan ruled us, and God's wrath burned against us. If we have spiritual life, it is entirely due to God's grace in Christ. Why then do we look down on others? Who makes us to differ? Let us prostrate ourselves before the Lord Jesus, give all glory to God, and learn the meekness of the dove-like Spirit.**
2. **Believers are richer than kings. They are joined with none other than Jesus Christ, seated with Him in heavenly places. They are re-created with the risen Christ as their Adam. God will show how great He is by pouring out kindness upon them for all eternity. All of this is by grace through the great sufferings of Christ on the cross. If we**

22 In whom ye also are builded together for an
habitation of God through the Spirit.

CHAPTER 3

FOR this cause I Paul, the prisoner of Jesus Christ
for you Gentiles,
2 If ye have heard of the dispensation of the grace
of God which is given me to you-ward:
3 How that by revelation he made known unto
me the mystery; (as I wrote afore in few words,
4 Whereby, when ye read, ye may understand my
knowledge in the mystery of Christ)
5 Which in other ages was not made known unto
the sons of men, as it is now revealed unto his
holy apostles and prophets by the Spirit;
6 That the Gentiles should be fellowheirs, and of
the same body, and partakers of his promise in
Christ by the gospel:
7 Whereof I was made a minister, according to
the gift of the grace of God given unto me by the
effectual working of his power.
8 Unto me, who am less than the least of all saints,
is this grace given, that I should preach among the
Gentiles the unsearchable riches of Christ;
9 And to make all *men* see what *is* the fellow-
ship of the mystery, which from the beginning of
the world hath been hid in God, who created all
things by Jesus Christ:
10 To the intent that now unto the principalities
and powers in heavenly *places* might be known by
the church the manifold wisdom of God,
11 According to the eternal purpose which he
purposed in Christ Jesus our Lord:
12 In whom we have boldness and access with
confidence by the faith of him.
13 Wherefore I desire that ye faint not at my
tribulations for you, which is your glory.
14 For this cause I bow my knees unto the Father
of our Lord Jesus Christ,
15 Of whom the whole family in heaven and
earth is named,
16 That he would grant you, according to the
riches of his glory, to be strengthened with might
by his Spirit in the inner man;
17 That Christ may dwell in your hearts by faith;
that ye, being rooted and grounded in love,
18 May be able to comprehend with all saints what

---

are truly saved, we should bless God and sing His praises all our lives.

3. **All nations are one at the foot of the cross. Despite our tendency to exalt ourselves and judge others based on race or culture, all believers are one and Christ is all. Let us therefore repent of our arrogance and welcome one another.**
4. **There is no sweeter place on earth than the gathered church. She is the temple of the living God, the dwelling place of His Spirit. Love the church. Serve the church. Stop complaining about the church. She is still under construction—as are her members.**

Chapter 3: *Paul explains how his suffering arises from his calling as God's special messenger, and prays for God to fill believers with Christ's love.*

The Purpose of God's Grace Revealed in Christ (3:1–21)

3:1 Paul begins a sentence here but breaks it off to resume it later (v. 14 or 4:1). *prisoner of Jesus Christ*. He was a prisoner of the Roman Empire, but Christ is Lord over suffering saints and wicked sinners.

3:2–3 Paul interrupts himself to write about his apostolic office. His suffering was no tragedy, but part of God's stewardship entrusted to him (*dispensation*), a gift he did not deserve (*grace*). *by revelation*. God directly revealed to Paul the *mystery* (see note at 1:9) of Christ (Gal. 1:11–12). Christianity is built upon divine revelation, preserved as the Holy Scriptures. *afore*. A little before.

3:4–5 God gave new revelation *by the Spirit* to a group Paul called the *holy apostles and prophets*. In the New Testament church, these are two distinct offices (4:11) that God used to lay a foundation of revealed truth (2:20). Paul was the last apostle appointed as an eyewitness of the risen Christ (1 Cor. 9:1–2; 15:9). After the apostles died, new revelation ceased and is no longer needed because the church has the Holy Scriptures.

3:6 The Old Testament reveals Christ (Rom. 1:2; 16:25). But God revealed to the apostles the mystery that believing Gentiles would be *fellowheirs* in Israel by union with Christ as His *body*.

3:7 *minister*. Here a servant of the gospel of God. On *the effectual working of his power* to call Paul, see Acts 9; Gal. 1:11–17.

3:8 *less than the least of all saints*. Not less in knowledge, gifts, authority, or integrity, but less because of his past sins of ignorance (1 Tim. 1:13–15) and present heart sins against knowledge (Rom. 7:7,17,23). *unsearchable*. Beyond our ability to comprehend (1:7,19; 2:7; 3:19).

3:9 *fellowship*. Communication.

3:10–11 *manifold*. Literally, "plentifully multicolored," with great abundance of variety. *purposed*. Performed. God created the world with this *eternal purpose*: to reveal His complex *wisdom* to the angelic *powers* by uniting many nations *in Christ*. The angels learn about God's glory as He saves the *church* through Jesus Christ (1 Cor. 4:9; 1 Peter 1:12).

3:12 *access*. Close and confident friendship with God the Father (2:18). God's plan is to display His glory by lavishing His love upon His multiethnic spiritual family in Christ (1:3–6; 2:7).

3:13 The *tribulations* of Christ's servants are God's plan to bring the elect to enjoy eternal *glory* (2 Tim. 2:10). Therefore, the suffering of ministers should not discourage the church.

3:14–15 *For this cause*. Repeated from v. 1, possibly resuming the thought Paul started there. *bow my knees*. Posture of reverence (Rom. 14:11). Confident access to the Father does not make the fear of God obsolete (2 Cor. 6:18—7:1). *the whole family*. Or "every clan," perhaps declaring that He is the Father of all His worshipers among the nations (Pss. 22:27; 96:7).

3:16–17 Paul asked the heavenly King to share His *riches* and *glory* with His adopted children. But he did not request health and wealth, but inward strengthening *by his Spirit*. The Spirit strengthens *faith*, by which *Christ* is present in the heart or inner man (Gal. 2:20). This makes believers strong and stable (*rooted and grounded*) in their assurance of God's *love*.

3:18–19 *the breadth, and length, and depth, and height*. The infinite *fulness of God* which *passeth knowledge* (Job 11:7–9). God gave believers Himself as their covenant God in Christ, so Paul asks the triune God that they *might be filled* with

is the breadth, and length, and depth, and height;
19 And to know the love of Christ, which passeth
knowledge, that ye might be filled with all the
fulness of God.
20 Now unto him that is able to do exceeding
abundantly above all that we ask or think, accord-
ing to the power that worketh in us,
21 Unto him *be* glory in the church by Christ
Jesus throughout all ages, world without end.
Amen.

CHAPTER 4

I THEREFORE, the prisoner of the Lord, beseech
you that ye walk worthy of the vocation where-
with ye are called,
2 With all lowliness and meekness, with longsuf-
fering, forbearing one another in love;
3 Endeavouring to keep the unity of the Spirit in
the bond of peace.
4 *There is* one body, and one Spirit, even as ye are
called in one hope of your calling;
5 One Lord, one faith, one baptism,
6 One God and Father of all, who *is* above all, and
through all, and in you all.
7 But unto every one of us is given grace accord-
ing to the measure of the gift of Christ.
8 Wherefore he saith, When he ascended up on
high, he led captivity captive, and gave gifts unto
men.
9 (Now that he ascended, what is it but that he
also descended first into the lower parts of the
earth?
10 He that descended is the same also that
ascended up far above all heavens, that he might
fill all things.)
11 And he gave some, apostles; and some, proph-
ets; and some, evangelists; and some, pastors and
teachers;
12 For the perfecting of the saints, for the work
of the ministry, for the edifying of the body of
Christ:
13 Till we all come in the unity of the faith, and
of the knowledge of the Son of God, unto a

---

experiential knowledge of Him (1:16–19). He particularly asked for them to know *the love of Christ*, for God displays His glory most excellently in Christ's grace for us (Rom. 3:26; 5:8; 1 Cor. 1:23–24).

3:20–21 The ultimate purpose of God's infinite *power that worketh* in every member of *the church* is His *glory* forever in *Christ Jesus*.

Thoughts for Personal/Family Worship: Chapter 3

1. **Don't take the Bible or preaching for granted. It is an amazing gift of grace that God would reveal Christ to us. We never would have known the mystery of the gospel, but God has given it to us through the apostles and prophets so that His people might know His love. Furthermore, God's servants have suffered greatly through the ages to proclaim Christ's riches to the nations. Treasure the Word, read it often, and thank God for it.**
2. **In Christ believers have boldness and access with confidence to the Father. Do you experience that freedom in your prayers? The Father welcomes sinners into His presence with joy when they come in Jesus' name. God desires that His children pray with absolute confidence that He will be good to them (Luke 11:13).**
3. **Pray for great spiritual blessings for believers. God has given every blessing to us in the exalted Christ. The Spirit has already done a supernatural work of resurrection in everyone who now believes. Yet there is more of God's fullness for us to know. God is able to do far more than we can ask or imagine. John Newton said, "Thou art coming to a King; large petitions with thee bring; for His grace and power are such, none can ever ask too much." Begin by taking Paul's prayer in this chapter and praying it for your church.**

THE CALLING TO WALK AS THE BODY OF CHRIST (4:1—6:22)

Chapter 4: ***Paul exhorts Christians to live worthy of their calling as Christ's body, and begins to admonish them to put off sin and put on Christ.***

Walk Worthy as One Body (4:1–16)

4:1 *therefore.* Doctrine in chs. 1–3 leads to practice in chs. 4–6. *the prisoner of the Lord.* Perhaps resuming the thought of 3:1. *beseech.* Urge or exhort. *walk.* Conduct yourself in daily attitude and actions. *vocation.* God's effectual calling of the elect through the gospel (2 Thess. 2:13–14). The Spirit powerfully calls sinners so that they trust Christ (1 Cor. 1:24; 2:4), and follow Him into holiness and glory (Rom. 8:29–30; 1 Thess. 2:12; 4:7; 5:23–24; Rev. 17:14). Given the privileges of grace, believers must *walk worthy* of their calling, not in the sense of deserving it (2 Tim. 1:9), but worthy in the sense of conduct fitting to the gospel (Luke 3:8).

4:2–3 *all lowliness.* Humility in every relationship and situation. *longsuffering.* Patience. *forbearing.* Enduring pain and annoyance with self-control. *Endeavouring.* Making effort.

4:4–6 The church must keep unity because we are really *one* in God the *Father*, the *Lord* Jesus, and the Holy *Spirit*. *hope of your calling.* See 1:18. *Father of all.* In context, of all believers.

4:7 *grace.* Here not salvation, but the gift of power to serve God (3:8; 1 Peter 4:10). *according to the measure.* God gave each believer ability according to His will (1 Cor. 12:11,18).

4:8 Paul quoted Ps. 68, which speaks of God's victory for Israel, and applied it to Christ, who is God. *gave gifts.* Psalm 68:18 says, "received gifts" but also says God "giveth strength and power unto his people" (v. 35). Paul thus summarized the psalm.

4:9 *ascended.* Christ went up into heaven (1:20). *descended.* Before ascending, Christ *first* came down to earth to be a man and save sinners (John 3:13–16). *lower parts of the earth.* Not hell, but death and the tomb (Ps. 63:9–10).

4:10 *fill all things.* Christ shares His victory with us so that, as each church member uses his spiritual gifts (v. 7), Christ's kingdom is filling the earth (1:23; Ps. 72:8,19).

4:11–12 These offices of proclaiming the Word are the gifts of the ascended Christ to His church. On *apostles* and *prophets*, see notes at 1:1; 2:20; 3:4–5. *evangelists.* Rare word used only of two men in the New Testament (Acts 21:8; 2 Tim. 4:5). Scripture only gives directions for appointing the fourth group (*pastors and teachers*) listed here (1 Tim. 3:1–7; Titus 1:5–9), the ordinary ministry defined by shepherding (*pastors*) and instructing (*teachers*). This is the labor of the elders of the church (Acts 14:23; 20:17,28).

perfect man, unto the measure of the stature of
the fulness of Christ:
14 That we *henceforth* be no more children, tossed
to and fro, and carried about with every wind
of doctrine, by the sleight of men, *and* cunning
craftiness, whereby they lie in wait to deceive;
15 But speaking the truth in love, may grow up into
him in all things, which is the head, *even* Christ:
16 From whom the whole body fitly joined
together and compacted by that which every joint
supplieth, according to the effectual working in
the measure of every part, maketh increase of the
body unto the edifying of itself in love.
17 This I say therefore, and testify in the Lord,
that ye henceforth walk not as other Gentiles
walk, in the vanity of their mind,
18 Having the understanding darkened, being
alienated from the life of God through the igno-
rance that is in them, because of the blindness of
their heart:
19 Who being past feeling have given themselves
over unto lasciviousness, to work all uncleanness
with greediness.
20 But ye have not so learned Christ;
21 If so be that ye have heard him, and have been
taught by him, as the truth is in Jesus:
22 That ye put off concerning the former conver-
sation the old man, which is corrupt according to
the deceitful lusts;
23 And be renewed in the spirit of your mind;
24 And that ye put on the new man, which after
God is created in righteousness and true holiness.
25 Wherefore putting away lying, speak every man
truth with his neighbour: for we are members one
of another.
26 Be ye angry, and sin not: let not the sun go
down upon your wrath:
27 Neither give place to the devil.
28 Let him that stole steal no more: but rather
let him labour, working with *his* hands the thing

4:13–14 *children.* Immature in the faith. *a perfect man.* The Greek is specifically masculine and singular, pointing to Christ, the last Adam. The goal of pastoral ministry is that every member (*we all*) of the church reaches a full *stature*, or maturity in *the Son of God* and likeness to Him. This gives the church *unity*, maturity, and stability to resist false *doctrine*. *sleight.* Deceitfulness.

4:15–16 *compacted.* Bound together. The church must use both biblical *truth* and *love* in its pursuit of Christ. As its mighty *head* (1:21–22), He gives growth (*increase*) to the body. Christ works by the Word (v. 11) and also through the friendships by which members are *joined together* and the *working* of *every part* of the body in active service (1 Cor. 12:12–19).

Walk in the New Man, Not in the Old Ways of Sin (4:17—5:14)

4:17 *walk.* See note at v. 1. *Gentiles.* Unbelievers outside of Israel. *vanity.* Futility, uselessness. Though believers once acted like the world, they must no longer follow its worthless thinking.

4:18 *alienated from the life of God.* Hating the holy life God gives through Christ's resurrection (2:5; Col. 1:21). *ignorance.* Not knowing God (2:12; 1 Thess. 4:5). *blindness.* Hardness or stubbornness. The root cause of mankind's foolishness is a stubborn refusal to know God (Rom. 1:20–21).

4:19 *past feeling.* Callous to sin and guilt (Prov. 10:23; Rom. 1:32). *lasciviousness.* Sexual wantonness (Rom. 1:24–27). *greediness.* Lust for either more pleasure or more possessions.

4:20–21 *learned Christ.* Received the Word about Christ. *the truth is in Jesus.* Believing the gospel unites us to Christ (1:13), including the holiness of His human nature (*Jesus*). The gospel message calls us to repent of sin and follow Christ in obeying God's will (Acts 26:20).

4:22–24 *old man . . . new man.* Not just an individual's past and present, but the old humanity in Adam and the new creation of mankind in Christ (2:10,16). *holiness.* Probably covenantal piety and devotion to God (Pss. 4:3; 50:5). The pattern of repentance is twofold (Col. 3:9–10): (1) to *put off* sin both in outward conduct (*conversation*) and its inward lies and evil desires (*deceitful lusts*), and (2) to *put on* the image of God (*after God*) by renewing the *mind* through truth (v. 24). In the next verses Paul applies the *put off–put on* pattern to the moral law.

4:25 *Wherefore.* Therefore. *speak every man truth with his neighbour.* Quoting Zech. 8:16. See the ninth commandment (Ex. 20:16). *members.* Christians are parts of the same body (v. 16).

4:26–27 *Be ye angry, and sin not.* Quoting Ps. 4:4. This is not a command to get angry (v. 31), but a warning not to let anger move you to sin (Matt. 5:22). *let not the sun go down.* Turn that very day (Deut. 24:15) from anger to mercy. *devil.* Literally, "slanderer." *give place.* Sinful anger gives Satan a foothold in the heart.

4:28 See the eighth commandment (Ex. 20:15). Christians must not only put off theft, but also put on hard work, doing good (2 Thess. 3:12–13), and giving generously to the needy.

4:29 *corrupt communication.* Literally, "rotten talk." *edifying.* Literally, "building up of the need" (v. 16). This requires listening (Prov. 18:13) and speaking the truth in love (v. 15) about Christ's *grace*.

4:30 *Grieve* implies that the Spirit is a person with emotions. The words *holy Spirit of God* (only here in the Bible) and the quotation of Isa. 63:10 suggest His fearsome majesty and judgments against sin (Acts 5:3–5). *sealed unto the day of redemption.* Marked by the Spirit as belonging to God until total freedom arrives (1:13–14). The Spirit gives joy and hope (Rom. 15:13; Gal. 5:22). If a believer persists in sin, the Spirit will wither his comfort (Pss. 32:4–5; 51:11–12).

4:31–32 Believers must *put away* all selfish and bitter anger and put on the forgiveness, tender compassion, and love that the Father shows them *for Christ's sake*.

Thoughts for Personal/Family Worship: Chapter 4

1. **Doctrine demands action, and a living faith produces works. It is presumptuous to rest in our knowledge about God if we do not walk in a manner fitting to that knowledge. Even the demons believe, and tremble. The first response the gospel requires is humility. Those who believe the doctrines of grace should of all people be most humble. Therefore, let us examine ourselves, grieve over pride, pray for humility, and meditate on the gospel.**
2. **The life of the church revolves around Christ. Our unity springs from our union with God through Christ. Our abilities to serve flow from Christ's victory. Knowing Him and being like Him are our maturity and stability. He is the head from whom all members and relationships in the body draw life. Therefore, pray often for your church that Christ would be central in its worship and fellowship.**
3. **Repentance is fundamental to the Christian life. Turning from sin toward the Lord is the ABC of the faith from**

which is good, that he may have to give to him
that needeth.
29 Let no corrupt communication proceed out of
your mouth, but that which is good to the use of edifying, that it may minister grace unto the hearers.
30 And grieve not the holy Spirit of God, whereby
ye are sealed unto the day of redemption.
31 Let all bitterness, and wrath, and anger, and
clamour, and evil speaking, be put away from you,
with all malice:
32 And be ye kind one to another, tenderhearted,
forgiving one another, even as God for Christ's
sake hath forgiven you.

CHAPTER 5

Be ye therefore followers of God, as dear children;
2 And walk in love, as Christ also hath loved us,
and hath given himself for us an offering and a
sacrifice to God for a sweetsmelling savour.
3 But fornication, and all uncleanness, or covet-
ousness, let it not be once named among you, as
becometh saints;
4 Neither filthiness, nor foolish talking, nor
jesting, which are not convenient: but rather
giving of thanks.
5 For this ye know, that no whoremonger, nor
unclean person, nor covetous man, who is an
idolater, hath any inheritance in the kingdom of
Christ and of God.
6 Let no man deceive you with vain words: for
because of these things cometh the wrath of God
upon the children of disobedience.
7 Be not ye therefore partakers with them.
8 For ye were sometimes darkness, but now *are ye*
light in the Lord: walk as children of light:
9 (For the fruit of the Spirit *is* in all goodness and
righteousness and truth;)
10 Proving what is acceptable unto the Lord.
11 And have no fellowship with the unfruitful
works of darkness, but rather reprove *them.*
12 For it is a shame even to speak of those things
which are done of them in secret.
13 But all things that are reproved are made
manifest by the light: for whatsoever doth make
manifest is light.
14 Wherefore he saith, Awake thou that sleepest,
and arise from the dead, and Christ shall give thee
light.
15 See then that ye walk circumspectly, not as
fools, but as wise,
16 Redeeming the time, because the days are evil.
17 Wherefore be ye not unwise, but understand-
ing what the will of the Lord *is.*

---

which we never graduate. All Christians must continually put off sin and put on the image of Christ. Repentance is specific, and so the Bible's commandments address specific areas of life. Of the commands in this chapter, what is one area where you need to repent? What must you put off? Put on?

Chapter 5: ***Paul continues to exhort believers to put off sin and put on holiness, and explains their calling to be light in the world and to follow God's wisdom in relationships.***

5:1 Knowing He loves them *as dear children*, they are set free to imitate Him (4:32; Col. 3:12).

5:2 *hath given himself.* So Christians should give themselves away to love others. *offering and a sacrifice.* Price to appease God's holy anger (Heb. 10:5,10). *sweetsmelling savour.* Pleasing to God for His devotion and obedience. People cannot ransom themselves from sin, but they do sacrifice themselves to reach people with the gospel—and God is pleased (Phil. 4:18).

5:3–4 *fornication.* Sexual activity outside of marriage. *uncleanness.* Sexual sin. *covetousness.* Greed. *filthiness.* Obscene or shameful talk. *jesting.* Humor cleverly hinting at sexual matters—see the seventh and tenth commandments (Ex. 20:14,17). Lustful or greedy talk is unfit (*not convenient*) for God's holy people (*saints*). Instead, they should use God's good gifts with *thanks* to God (1 Tim. 4:4).

5:5–6 *whoremonger.* Fornicator, person having sex outside marriage. He who lives for pleasure or possessions is *an idolater,* for whatever masters you is your god (Matt. 6:24; Phil. 3:19). All such persons will be shut out of *the kingdom* and will suffer *the wrath of God* (Gal. 5:19–21; Rev. 21:8). *Let no man deceive you* (1 Cor. 6:9–10; Gal. 6:7). Satan always tries to deceive people that God will not punish sin (Gen. 3:5). *children of disobedience.* See note at 2:2–3.

5:7 *partakers with them.* God's people are not to share with sinners in their lust, greed, and disobedience.

5:8 *sometimes.* At one time; once. While unconverted, they were once not only in the darkness, but they *were . . . darkness.* But union with Christ (*in the Lord*) changed them into light.

5:9 The light is explained as *all goodness and righteousness and truth.* The "children of light" (v. 8) are people shining with God's light (Isa. 60:1–3), in *the fruit of the Spirit* (Gal. 5:22).

5:10 *Proving.* Testing to discern God's will (Rom. 12:2). Those who walk as "children of light" (v. 8) make it their ambition to please the Lord, not the world (2 Cor. 5:9; Gal. 1:10).

5:11 *have no fellowship.* Do not participate. *unfruitful.* Sin does no good (4:17), unlike the fruit God produces in believers. *reprove.* Expose their evil by bringing the light of Christ to them.

5:12 *a shame even to speak.* Even talking about sin is distasteful (vv. 3–4) and should be avoided except insofar as is necessary. Cultivate wise innocence (Matt. 10:16; Rom. 16:19).

5:13 May be translated: "but all things exposed by the light are visible, for everything made visible is light." Overcome the darkness of evil by shining the light of God's goodness.

5:14 Perhaps a song based on Scriptures (Isa. 9:2; 26:19; 60:1). Through the gospel call, God raises sinners to life in *Christ* (2:5), so that His *light* shines in them (v. 8; 2 Cor. 3:18; 4:6). If God's children walk in holiness (v. 9), they help to bring people from darkness to light by the gospel (Acts 26:18).

Walk in God's Wisdom for Relationships (5:15—6:9)

5:15 *walk circumspectly.* Paul exhorts them to walk worthy of their calling (4:1) in a wise and careful lifestyle, particularly in the local church (vv. 18–21) and the home (5:22—6:9).

5:16 *Redeeming.* Buying up each opportunity (*time*) as at a market or auction before it is lost. *days are evil.* Stay alert, there is a war against the forces of evil (6:12–13).

5:17 *unwise.* Not lack of intelligence, but lack of biblical wisdom. *understanding what the will of the Lord is.* Christians

18 And be not drunk with wine, wherein is ex-
cess; but be filled with the Spirit;
19 Speaking to yourselves in psalms and hymns
and spiritual songs, singing and making melody
in your heart to the Lord;
20 Giving thanks always for all things unto God
and the Father in the name of our Lord Jesus
Christ;
21 Submitting yourselves one to another in the
fear of God.
22 Wives, submit yourselves unto your own hus-
bands, as unto the Lord.
23 For the husband is the head of the wife, even
as Christ is the head of the church: and he is the
saviour of the body.
24 Therefore as the church is subject unto Christ,
so *let* the wives *be* to their own husbands in every
thing.
25 Husbands, love your wives, even as Christ also
loved the church, and gave himself for it;
26 That he might sanctify and cleanse it with the
washing of water by the word,
27 That he might present it to himself a glori-
ous church, not having spot, or wrinkle, or any
such thing; but that it should be holy and without
blemish.
28 So ought men to love their wives as their own
bodies. He that loveth his wife loveth himself.
29 For no man ever yet hated his own flesh; but
nourisheth and cherisheth it, even as the Lord the
church:
30 For we are members of his body, of his flesh,
and of his bones.
31 For this cause shall a man leave his father and
mother, and shall be joined unto his wife, and
they two shall be one flesh.
32 This is a great mystery: but I speak concerning
Christ and the church.
33 Nevertheless let every one of you in particular
so love his wife even as himself; and the wife *see*
that she reverence *her* husband.

CHAPTER 6

CHILDREN, obey your parents in the Lord: for this
is right.

must always be learners, students of Christ (Matt. 11:29; 17:5).

5:18 Intoxication with *wine* or other drugs aims at happiness but results in a foolish, wasted, and shameful life (*excess*, Prov. 23:29–35), not careful wisdom (vv. 15–16). Being *filled with the Spirit* results in obedience, faith, wisdom, and joy (Luke 4:1; Acts 6:3,5; 7:55; 11:24; 13:52). The present imperative form of the verb *be filled* implies a continual duty. It is a daily drinking deeply of Christ through faith in the word of Christ (3:17,19; John 7:37–39; Col. 3:16).

5:19–20 The church should sing *psalms and hymns and spiritual songs*, terms most often used of the biblical psalms. The church's worship should be trinitarian, empowered by the Spirit (v. 18) to sing to the *Lord* Jesus and to give *thanks* to *the Father* through *our Lord Jesus Christ* (2:18).

5:21 *Submitting yourselves.* Voluntarily subjecting yourselves to honor and to obey proper authority. *one to another.* Not everyone to everyone (Matt. 24:10; Mark 4:41), but as appropriate in each relationship, which Paul explains further (5:22—6:9). *in the fear of God.* Submission to authority is motivated by love for God's majesty, and so limited by God's law. This means submission to another cannot ever be a license to disobey God's commandments.

5:22 *Wives, submit.* The first application of the principle of Spirit-filled submission to authority (v. 21). *your own husbands.* Not to all men generally. *as unto the Lord.* Serve and obey Christ.

5:23–24 *head.* Authority (2 Sam. 22:44). *as the church is subject unto Christ.* A wife should obey her husband's leadership as the church obeys its *head*, and depend on her husband's care as the church depends on its *saviour*. *in every thing.* In every area of life, yet limited by God's laws.

5:25–27 *as Christ also loved the church.* A husband should give his special love exclusively to one woman as Christ loved *the church*, sacrifice his resources for her as Christ *gave himself*, and labor for her holiness as Christ aimed to *sanctify* His people. *washing of water by the word.* Spiritual purification by the Holy Spirit through the Word of Christ (Titus 3:5–6), symbolized once in washings (Lev. 14:8; 15:13) and now baptism (Acts 22:16). The Son's death has the same goal as the Father's election: that the elect become *holy and without blemish* (1:4).

5:28–30 *as their own bodies.* A husband ought to be as attentive and sympathetic to his wife as to the needs and feelings of his own body, for she is a part of him (v. 31). *nourisheth.* Provides what is needed to live and flourish. *cherisheth.* Protects from danger and harm. *we are members of his body.* Believers are joined to Christ in a living bond by His Spirit (1 Cor. 6:17; Col. 1:18; 2:19).

5:31–32 *one flesh.* Husband and wife are joined together by God in a lasting union (Matt. 19:5–6). Paul quotes Gen. 2:24 about Adam and his wife, but surprisingly applies it to *Christ and the church.* Adam was a type of Christ (Rom. 5:14), and marriage is a picture of the believer's union to Christ.

5:33 *let every one of you in particular.* Each person must make particular application of God's Word to his own case. *reverence.* Wives are to show respect and honor to their husband as their head (v. 23).

Thoughts for Personal/Family Worship: Chapter 5

1. **Christians must not be like the world. Too often the church wants to blend in, either to avoid persecution or to attract new members. But how can light blend into darkness—without ceasing to be light? Our mission requires that we be different. The most effective outreach program consists of producing people who radiate goodness, righteousness, and truth. Such Christians by their very lives convict sinners, validate God's law and judgment, and confirm the power of the gospel.**
2. **Pray for the Spirit to fill your church. Ask God to make your congregation a people who daily go to Christ and drink deeply of the intoxicating joy of the Holy Spirit. Seek the Spirit's grace for heartfelt singing of the psalms, profound thanksgiving to the Father through Christ, and humble submission to authority in the home, church, and state.**
3. **Marriage exists to show the glory of Christ. It is not a social contract formed when and how we please. It is not just a convenience for satisfying our desires. It is God's display case for the beautiful relationship between Christ and the church. Husbands and wives have a high**

2 Honour thy father and mother; (which is the
first commandment with promise;)
3 That it may be well with thee, and thou mayest
live long on the earth.
4 And, ye fathers, provoke not your children to
wrath: but bring them up in the nurture and
admonition of the Lord.
5 Servants, be obedient to them that are *your*
masters according to the flesh, with fear and trem-
bling, in singleness of your heart, as unto Christ;
6 Not with eyeservice, as menpleasers; but as the
servants of Christ, doing the will of God from the
heart;
7 With good will doing service, as to the Lord,
and not to men:
8 Knowing that whatsoever good thing any man
doeth, the same shall he receive of the Lord,
whether *he be* bond or free.
9 And, ye masters, do the same things unto them,
forbearing threatening: knowing that your Mas-
ter also is in heaven; neither is there respect of
persons with him.
10 Finally, my brethren, be strong in the Lord,
and in the power of his might.
11 Put on the whole armour of God, that ye may
be able to stand against the wiles of the devil.
12 For we wrestle not against flesh and blood, but
against principalities, against powers, against the
rulers of the darkness of this world, against spiri-
tual wickedness in high *places*.
13 Wherefore take unto you the whole armour of
God, that ye may be able to withstand in the evil
day, and having done all, to stand.
14 Stand therefore, having your loins girt about
with truth, and having on the breastplate of
righteousness;
15 And your feet shod with the preparation of the
gospel of peace;
16 Above all, taking the shield of faith, wherewith
ye shall be able to quench all the fiery darts of the
wicked.
17 And take the helmet of salvation, and the
sword of the Spirit, which is the word of God:
18 Praying always with all prayer and supplication

calling. Commit yourself to serve your spouse as God commands in His Word—whether your marriage is sweet or sorrowful.

Chapter 6: ***Paul concludes his description of wisdom in the household and calls believers to stand against the Devil with the full equipment Christ provides.***

6:1 Submission (5:21) is now applied to the parent-child relationship. *Children* are addressed as responsible individuals who must willingly obey. *in the Lord*. By Christ's grace and for His glory.

6:2–3 *Honour.* Quoting the fifth commandment (Deut. 5:16). Though Christ abolished the law in its ceremonies and condemnation (2:15), the Ten Commandments still direct Christians in obedience to the Lord (1 Cor. 7:19; 9:21). *promise*. Rebellion against authority brings danger and God's wrath (Prov. 20:20; 30:17); honoring authority brings His blessing (Prov. 1:7–8; 3:1–4).

6:4 *fathers*. The father bears primary responsibility as head of the household (5:23). *nurture*. Training and discipline. *admonition*. Teaching with appeals for action (1 Thess. 2:11–12).

6:5–9 *Servants . . . masters*. Not the same as the enslavement of Africans in America. Slavery was not a matter of race, for slaves were of various races and colors. In cities of the Roman Empire 20–30 percent of the population consisted of slaves. A typical household included father, mother, children, and slaves. Slavery was the legal status of being bound to serve a master, but the work of slaves varied from field labor to serving as doctors, teachers, and accountants. Some slaves saved money and bought their freedom. Paul is not condoning slavery but commenting on a social institution of his day.

6:5–7 *fear and trembling*. Sensing the dangerous consequences of laziness. *singleness*. Sincerely committed to do a good job. *eyeservice*. Working hard only when someone is watching. *as the servants of Christ*. Cheerfully doing all to please the Lord (Col. 3:23).

6:8 All good work will *receive of the Lord* its due reward (Matt. 25:21; Mark 9:41; 2 Cor. 5:10).

6:9 *masters, do the same things unto them*. Give them the same justice and reward as the Lord (same Greek word as *masters*) does His servants (Col. 4:1). *forbearing*. Desisting from, leaving off. *neither is there respect of persons*. The Lord will judge all people, and He plays no favorites (Rom. 2:11; Col. 3:24–25).

Walk in the Lord's Armor for Spiritual Warfare (6:10–22)

6:10 *be strong*. Be courageous for God (Deut. 31:6). Christianity demands courage; the fearful go to hell (Rev. 21:8). *the power of his might*. Drawing on Christ's strength as Lord (1:19–20).

6:11–13 *Put on*. Same word used in 4:24. *Put on* the character of Christ by faith and repentance. *whole armour of God*. Putting on Christ (Rom. 13:12–14), a believer puts on the very armor of the Divine Warrior (Isa. 59:15–20). *wiles of the devil*. Satan's crafty tactics (4:14). Christians need divine armor because their battle is not against weak mankind (*flesh and blood*), but a vast army of powerful, evil, invisible spirits who control the unsaved world (2:2; Mark 5:9; Rev. 12:9). Clothed with Christ's power, Christians are *able to withstand* all the forces of the Devil.

6:14 Meditation on the *truth* of the Bible, like a belt that ties up a loose robe (*loins girt about*), makes one's mind ready for action (Luke 12:35,40; 1 Peter 1:13). Doing *righteousness* (4:24; 5:9) protects one's soul from the wounds of sin as a *breastplate* protects the heart and lungs.

6:15 Renewing one's faith in *the gospel of peace*, like putting on a soldier's boots (*feet shod*), gives one firm footing to face Satan so one does not slip into fear, guilt, and spiritual bondage.

6:16 Satan tempts God's people with burning arrows (*fiery darts*) that aim to ignite and consume their souls with deceitful desires. *Faith* in God's promises is like a large Roman *shield* (4 ft. by 2.5 ft.), which covers the body; it can overcome *all* temptations (1 John 2:14; 5:4–5).

6:17 The hope of one's future *salvation* from all evils (1 Thess. 5:8–9) protects one's mind like a *helmet* from being stunned or broken. Christians can strike back at Satan's kingdom by speaking *the word of God*, which is like the short, nimble, and sharp Roman *sword*. It has the power of the *Spirit* to pierce the heart (Heb. 4:12), for it is the Word of Christ the Prophet (Isa. 49:2).

6:18 *Praying always . . . all prayer . . . all perseverance . . . all saints*. Prayer is the universal weapon of warfare, needed at all times. *in the Spirit*. The Spirit directs prayers through the Word

in the Spirit, and watching thereunto with all
perseverance and supplication for all saints;
19 And for me, that utterance may be given unto
me, that I may open my mouth boldly, to make
known the mystery of the gospel,
20 For which I am an ambassador in bonds: that
therein I may speak boldly, as I ought to speak.
21 But that ye also may know my affairs, *and*
how I do, Tychicus, a beloved brother and faithful
minister in the Lord, shall make known to you all
things:
22 Whom I have sent unto you for the same
purpose, that ye might know our affairs, and *that*
he might comfort your hearts.
23 Peace *be* to the brethren, and love with faith,
from God the Father and the Lord Jesus Christ.
24 Grace *be* with all them that love our Lord Jesus
Christ in sincerity. Amen.

(v. 17) so that Christians experience bold and joyful access to the Father through the Son (2:18; 3:12; 5:18–20).

6:19–20 *mystery of the gospel.* See notes at 1:9; 3:2–3. *ambassador in bonds.* Paradoxically, Paul was both the authorized representative of the Lord (2 Cor. 5:20), and a prisoner of men. Believers must pray for preachers (Rom. 15:30; Col. 4:3–4), especially that they would preach the gospel *boldly* by the Holy Spirit (Acts 4:8; 6:5,10).

6:21–22 *that ye also may know . . . that ye might know.* Churches need reports from missionaries to inform their prayers and to encourage (*comfort*) them by news of perseverance and progress (2 Cor. 1:3–11). For such reports to be credible, they must be brought by *a beloved brother and faithful minister.*

CONCLUDING BLESSING: PEACE AND GRACE (6:23–24)

6:23–24 *Peace* is a typical Jewish blessing (*shalom*). Just as Paul opens his letter with grace and peace, so he closes by blessing them with yet more—a deeper experience of Christ. Grace belongs only to those who *love our Lord Jesus Christ*, for all others are God's accursed enemies (1 Cor. 16:22). *in sincerity.* Or perhaps, "with immortality," that is, undying love.

Thoughts for Personal/Family Worship: Chapter 6

1. **Paul's instructions for parenting are surprisingly simple. On the one hand, this is because the hardest thing about being a father or mother is doing what you know that you should do: be kind and just, not angry and unfair; train and discipline your children consistently; teach them the Word of God. On the other hand, Paul's few words to fathers stand upon two broad bases. First, the book of Proverbs offers a wealth of wisdom for training children. Second, the rest of Eph. 4–6 reminds us that successful parenting requires us to walk worthy of our calling in every area of life: church, daily repentance, avoiding worldliness, and marriages of love and respect. If we are faithful in these four areas, we have laid a solid foundation for raising our children.**
2. **No Christian is a spiritual civilian. We are all soldiers on the front lines. Therefore we must live in a state of battle readiness, always alert for our enemy. Believers, however, need not live in bondage to fear. Christ is our armor, and He is sufficient to overcome a legion of fallen angels. Let us therefore make walking with Christ our lifestyle, by meditating on the truth, doing what is right, resting on Christ's blood for peace of conscience, trusting God's promises, hoping in total salvation, speaking God's Word, and praying always for ourselves, other Christians, and the preachers of the gospel. By God's grace in Christ, we can overcome the Evil One.**

SPIRITUAL WARFARE

The Christian life is not a playground; it is a spiritual battlefield. It is one where the forces of darkness are arrayed against us seeking to do us great harm. The Puritan, William Gurnall, said that this war is so serious it makes the cruelest battle between armies of men to seem like a child's game. Sometimes we can forget this; other times we can make too much of it. The apostle Paul would not have us to fall into either extreme. In Eph. 6 he gives us a proper balance to spiritual warfare so that we neither *underestimate it nor overestimate it*. How we think about this spiritual battle is critical to how we fight it. This classic passage gives us a biblical framework for spiritual warfare. It provides us a perspective that can dramatically shape our daily lives, showing us how to engage rightly in this great conflict.

As believers, our first step in successfully waging spiritual warfare is recognizing our weakness and the Lord's great strength. Self-sufficiency is a killer in this battle; dependence on Christ is crucial. Ephesians 6:10–20 repeatedly reminds us of our insufficiency for this fight. We need strength (v. 10), weaponry (vv. 11,14–17), and lines of communication with our Savior for aid (vv. 18–20). These means are external to us. Without them, we have inadequate strength to stand against principalities, powers, the rulers of the darkness, and spiritual hosts of wickedness. Left to ourselves we would soon crumble in the heat of battle. We are simply deficient for the task. However, God loves His people and never leaves us defenseless.

Throughout the rest of this section Paul calls us to "put on the whole armour of God" and describes each piece of the armor (vv. 11–17; cf. Rom. 13:12; 2 Cor. 6:7; 10:4–5; 1 Thess. 5:8). As Christians, we need the whole armor because our enemy is a relentless foe. If Satan and his minions cannot wound us in one place, they will target another: if not the head, then the heart; if not the conscience, then the emotions. Since Satan and his cohorts attack us in a variety of ways, God provides a variety of defenses sufficient to withstand any assault they might throw at us. Every piece of armor is another way of putting on Christ (Rom. 13:12,14). William Gurnall said, "What is this armour? By armour is meant Christ. Till Christ be put on, the creature is unarmed."

The apostle also calls us to *stand* (vv. 11,13,14). The Christian is a man of war, and as a good soldier of the Lord Jesus Christ, he is to maintain his spiritual position throughout life. The verb "stand" means "to hold one's position continually." It suggests a soldier firm and steady while under fierce attack. Thus, Paul is calling us to put on the full armor of God so that the Devil will not gain one inch in our lives or lead us off course. In sum, we are to hold fast the solid ground that Jesus has already won us in our lives. It is clear then from Paul's language that the Christian life is not intended to be one of defeat in which the Devil is constantly having his way with us. While we might lose some battles with Satan at times, the believer is ultimately the winner because He who is in him is greater than he who is in the world (1 John 4:4).

Lastly, Paul calls us to pray (v. 18). Prayer is not an additional piece of the armor but the means by which each piece is effectively employed. No doubt, Paul mentions prayer last for the sake of emphasis. The passage that begins with "be strong in the Lord" (v. 10) ends with "praying always with all prayer and supplication" (v. 18). Prayer is the critical component of our warfare, reinforcing each piece of our armor. The armor of God does not consist of literal pieces we can put on; rather, it consists of spiritual truths that the Christian appropriates through prayer. Christians must daily put on each piece with prayer, calling on our great Commander-in-Chief for fresh supplies of grace and help for combat.

I CAN DO *All Things* THROUGH CHRIST WHICH STRENGTHENETH *Me*

PHILIPPIANS 4:13

INTRODUCTION TO THE BOOK OF PHILIPPIANS

Authorship: Paul wrote the epistle to the Philippians (1:1). The apostle ministered to the church in Philippi and was familiar with the believers there (Acts 16:12; 20:1–6). The epistle contains many personal references to the apostle, such as his stay in prison (Phil. 1:12–26), his personal interaction with Epaphroditus (2:25–30), and his personal testimony (3:4–7). The apostle's authorship is beyond doubt and has not been seriously questioned from the early church to the present day.

Date: The date of Paul's epistle depends on which imprisonment he was enduring while he wrote Philippians. There are three main views: Ephesus, Caesarea, and Rome. Given that there is no definitive evidence supporting Paul's being imprisoned in Ephesus this view is the least likely. He was in prison in Caesarea (AD 57–59), but Paul's comments about the palace (1:13) and his statement about the possibility of impending death (vv. 20–26) do not seem to fit as well with Caesarea as they do with Rome. The traditional view sees Paul writing to the believers in Philippi during the latter end of his Roman imprisonment around AD 61 or 62.

Theme: Paul writes to encourage the believers to joyfully persevere in the gospel in spite of present difficulties and trying circumstances, expressing confidence that the God who began a good work in them will complete it (1:6).

Purpose: To encourage faithful believers and spur them on to further humility, unity, joy, and peace by an undistracted pursuit of Christ and His likeness.

Synopsis: *The Contribution of Philippians to Redemptive Revelation*
Epaphroditus's return to Philippi occasioned the writing of Philippians as Paul corresponded with the Christians in Philippi through him (2:25). Throughout the letter, Paul expresses his love for them and his continued prayers on their behalf (1:3–8; 4:10). As Paul wrote, he was imprisoned and wrote to inform the Philippians of his present situation, that his chains have been for the advancement of the gospel (1:12–18). In light of the sufferings that God ordains for His church (v. 29), Paul encourages the church to Christlike unity and humility (1:27—2:18) and warns of the false teachers who threaten the purity of the gospel by calling the Philippians to return to Judaism (3:1–21).

Paul highly commended this faithful church, and called them to make it their highest ambition to know Christ better and be more like Him, for He is our joy and peace. Several themes contribute to this great river of blessedness. *First*, Paul assures them of his love for them and his continued prayers to God on their behalf (1:3–8). *Second*, he writes to them concerning his present situation in prison. He reminds those who possibly misunderstood his choices that led to his imprisonment that what has taken place has been for the advancement of the gospel (vv. 12–18). *Third*, Paul encourages the church to strive for unity and harmony in the midst of their own difficulties and trials, pointing them to the ultimate example of humility and selflessness, Jesus Christ (1:27—2:18). *Fourth*, Paul warns the church of false teachers who threaten the purity of the gospel by returning to Judaism, exhorting the believers to continue pursuing Christ and following the pattern set by the apostle himself (3:1–21). *Fifth*, Paul expresses thanks to the church for their gift to him (4:10) and exhorts them to receive Epaphroditus with gladness and to hold him in high regard (2:25–30).

Philippians reminds Christians that though they often find themselves in difficult circumstances, this should not make them call God's love and care into question. Rather, trials are used to further the witness of the gospel and to mature Christians in their faith and sanctification.

Paul reminds the Philippian believers that God has not only given the gift of faith but also the gift of suffering for His sake (1:29). Paul applies this to his own circumstances in prison and to the circumstances of the believers to whom he is writing. Even though trials often tempt believers to become divided, Paul encourages them to embrace suffering and give themselves to selfless, Christlike living. While life on the timeline between the work of grace begun and the work of grace completed is often hard, Paul expresses confidence that God's grace will sustain them (v. 6). Paul also encourages believers that regardless of life's difficulties, joy ought to characterize Christians. Neither joy nor contentment are rooted in circumstances, either good or bad, but in Jesus Christ. In order to lead Christians to greater Christlikeness, Paul pens one of the most beautiful statements of Christology (2:6–11). If Christ, who is God, joyfully and humbly took on humanity to give Himself in death for others, then we, too, can esteem others better than ourselves as we press on toward the mark of the high calling of God in Christ Jesus.

Outline:

I. Introduction (1:1–11)

II. Paul's Rejoicing in Present Circumstances (1:12–26)
- A. Gospel Advancement through Imprisonment (1:12–13)
- B. Gospel Advancement through Preaching Christ (1:14–18)
- C. Living and Dying Is Viewed as Gaining Christ (1:19–26)

III. Paul's Exhortations to the Church (1:27—2:18)
- A. Live a Life Consistent with the Gospel of Christ (1:27–30)
- B. Live in Humble, Selfless Unity with the Body of Christ (2:1–11)
- C. Live as Lights in a Dark World (2:12–18)

IV. Paul's Report Concerning Timothy and Epaphroditus (2:19–30)

V. Paul's Warnings (3:1–21)
- A. Paul's Warning against Judaizers (3:1–11)
- B. Paul's Personal Testimony of Advancing in the Gospel (3:12–16)
- C. Paul's Warning against Lawlessness (3:17–21)

VI. Paul's Concluding Exhortations and Thanksgiving (4:1–23)

THE EPISTLE OF PAUL THE APOSTLE TO THE

PHILIPPIANS

CHAPTER 1

PAUL and Timotheus, the servants of Jesus Christ,
to all the saints in Christ Jesus which are at
Philippi, with the bishops and deacons:
2 Grace *be* unto you, and peace, from God our
Father, and *from* the Lord Jesus Christ.
3 I thank my God upon every remembrance of
you,
4 Always in every prayer of mine for you all
making request with joy,
5 For your fellowship in the gospel from the first
day until now;
6 Being confident of this very thing, that he which
hath begun a good work in you will perform *it*
until the day of Jesus Christ:
7 Even as it is meet for me to think this of you all,
because I have you in my heart; inasmuch as both
in my bonds, and in the defence and confirma-
tion of the gospel, ye all are partakers of my grace.
8 For God is my record, how greatly I long after
you all in the bowels of Jesus Christ.
9 And this I pray, that your love may abound yet
more and more in knowledge and *in* all judgment;
10 That ye may approve things that are excellent;
that ye may be sincere and without offence till the
day of Christ;

Chapter 1: *Paul greets the church in Philippi and expresses thankfulness to God for them, interceding to God on their behalf. Paul provides an update on his present circumstances, encouraging those concerned not to worry because what has happened to him is for the advancement of the gospel.*

INTRODUCTION (1:1–11)

1:1 *Paul and Timotheus, the servants of Jesus Christ.* Instead of appealing to his apostolic authority, Paul, the author, highlights that he and Timothy, his co-laborer, are humble slaves of Jesus Christ. Humble service is a necessary Christian disposition, and an important theme in the book. *Philippi.* This city was located in Macedonia and founded by Philip II of Macedon (358–336 BC). It was part of the Roman Empire and laid upon the main route (*Via Egnatia*) between Rome and the east. *bishops.* Elders, namely, the spiritual overseers. *deacons.* Those who serve the physical needs of the congregation.

1:3 *I thank my God.* Paul recognizes God as the ultimate source of all blessings and to whom all thanks is properly due. *upon every remembrance of you.* Every time Paul remembered the Philippian believers, he thanked God.

1:4 Paul presents a glimpse of his *prayer* life in stating that his thanksgiving to God for the saints is expressed regularly (*always*). *making request.* Petition is also a regular part of Paul's prayer. *with joy.* This is the first of over a dozen occurrences of the word group for "joy." Because of the transforming power of the gospel of Jesus Christ and the ministry of the Holy Spirit, joy characterizes the life of the believer despite the experience of difficult circumstances. Even while in prison, Paul joyfully prays for other believers who, themselves, are suffering.

1:5 *your fellowship.* Much of Philippians is marked by a desire for the unity of the church. Paul's initial thanksgiving is for unity that the Philippians share with him in the ministry of the gospel. *from the first day until now.* The immediate cause for Paul's joyful thanksgiving and prayer is the consistent fellowship in the gospel the Philippian believers have demonstrated from the time the gospel reached them to the present day.

1:6 *Being confident of this very thing, that he . . . will perform it until the day of Jesus Christ.* Paul not only expresses joy at God's grace in their lives up to the present time, but also expresses confidence that the God who saved them will complete the work of salvation. Despite the present circumstances, Paul is confident that they will persevere by God's grace to full salvation.

1:7 *meet for me.* It is right for me to think this of you. *I have you in my heart.* Paul has great affection for the saints in Philippi (4:1). *partakers.* Again Paul sounds the note of unity with fellow believers. The Philippian Christians maintained fellowship with Paul both in his bonds and in the defense of the gospel. *my grace.* Paul is not crediting himself as the originator of grace but noting that his fellow brothers are partakers of the same grace that he is partaking of in Christ Jesus.

1:8 *God is my record.* Paul calls on God as his witness to testify to the truth of what he is saying. *bowels of Jesus Christ.* Paul deeply longs after them with great compassion empowered by the affection that Jesus Christ has for them. Throughout the Gospels, Jesus is often said to have compassion on sinners (Matt. 9:36). Paul longs for the saints because Jesus Christ displays deep affection for the saints.

1:9 *this I pray.* Paul now transitions in his prayer from thanksgiving to intercession for the saints in Philippi. *love may abound yet more and more.* Believers are to always be growing in their love for God and for others. Believers do not reach a point in this life where they cannot grow more in love. *in knowledge and in all judgment.* Love grows where truth and discernment in Christ grow. The love Paul commends to the Philippians is not an aimless, groundless, or merely emotional love, but a love that is rooted in the gospel and Christian maturity.

1:10 *approve things that are excellent.* Be able to discern what

11 Being filled with the fruits of righteousness,
which are by Jesus Christ, unto the glory and
praise of God.
12 But I would ye should understand, brethren,
that the things *which happened* unto me have
fallen out rather unto the furtherance of the
gospel;
13 So that my bonds in Christ are manifest in all
the palace, and in all other *places*;
14 And many of the brethren in the Lord, waxing
confident by my bonds, are much more bold to
speak the word without fear.
15 Some indeed preach Christ even of envy and
strife; and some also of good will:
16 The one preach Christ of contention, not sin-
cerely, supposing to add affliction to my bonds:
17 But the other of love, knowing that I am set for
the defence of the gospel.
18 What then? notwithstanding, every way,
whether in pretence, or in truth, Christ is
preached; and I therein do rejoice, yea, and will
rejoice.
19 For I know that this shall turn to my salvation
through your prayer, and the supply of the Spirit
of Jesus Christ,
20 According to my earnest expectation and *my*
hope, that in nothing I shall be ashamed, but *that*
with all boldness, as always, *so* now also Christ
shall be magnified in my body, whether *it be* by
life, or by death.
21 For to me to live *is* Christ, and to die *is* gain.
22 But if I live in the flesh, this *is* the fruit of my
labour: yet what I shall choose I wot not.
23 For I am in a strait betwixt two, having a
desire to depart, and to be with Christ; which is
far better:

---

is the best. Love cultivates discernment and discernment cultivates love. *that ye may be sincere and without offence.* Abounding in love in both knowledge and discernment leads to lives that are pure and without blame. The believer is to use discernment to live in a manner that is pleasing to God.

1:11 *Being filled with the fruits of righteousness, which are by Jesus Christ.* The believer united to Christ is not only declared to be righteous (justification), but they cultivate holiness and righteousness in their lives (sanctification). Paul encourages believers to pursue the righteousness that is by Jesus Christ. *unto the glory and praise of God.* A believer's holiness is to redound to doxological praise (Matt. 5:16).

PAUL'S REJOICING IN PRESENT CIRCUMSTANCES (1:12–26)

Gospel Advancement through Imprisonment (1:12–13)

1:12 *have fallen out.* His present circumstances have happened for the advancement of the gospel. His imprisonment did not stunt the advancement of the gospel.

Gospel Advancement through Preaching Christ (1:14–18)

1:14 *waxing confident.* Growing, or increasing, in their confidence to speak more boldly.

1:15 Paul's imprisonment motivated some to preach the gospel with *envy* and others of *good will.* The content of the message was *Christ*, the motivations of the messengers differed.

1:16 *preach Christ of contention … supposing to add affliction to my bonds.* There were some who selfishly and insincerely preached Christ to get at Paul and add to his sufferings.

1:18 *Christ is preached; and I therein do rejoice.* Since Paul sees himself as a slave of Christ, he was concerned only that his Master be exalted. It was of little concern to him that others preached to add to his suffering if by it Christ and the gospel of Christ was advanced. Paul's comforts mattered little when the most excellent thing of the gospel is at stake.

Living and Dying Is Viewed as Gaining Christ (1:19–26)

1:19 *this shall turn to my salvation.* Paul did not view his present suffering as a thing to prevent his full salvation. Part of the answer to the first question in The Heidelberg Catechism expresses Paul's sentiment, "that everything must fit his purpose for my salvation" (Q.1). *through your prayer, and the supply of the Spirit of Jesus Christ.* Paul greatly appreciated the intercession of the saints for him and depended upon the supply of grace from the Holy Spirit.

1:20 Paul's greatest concern in either life or death was magnifying Christ, his Master.

1:21–26 *to live is Christ, and to die is gain.* So great and personal was Paul's experience of Christ that he wanted to live only if he could exalt the Savior, and viewed dying to be gain because it meant he could be with Christ, which he considered to be far better. Paul considered living worthwhile only if his life contributed to the furtherance and joy of the faith of those at Philippi. *wot not.* Know not.

PAUL'S EXHORTATIONS TO THE CHURCH (1:27—2:18)

Live a Life Consistent with the Gospel of Christ (1:27–30)

1:27 *conversation.* Conduct; literally, "citizenship." *as it becometh.* As is fitting. Paul moves from providing an update of his personal circumstances to exhorting the church to live in a manner that is worthy of *the gospel of Christ.* He encourages them to unity and to be of *one mind striving together for the faith of the gospel*, rather than striving against one another in the midst of their difficult circumstances.

1:28 *in nothing terrified by your adversaries.* Do not be frightened or intimidated by your adversaries. The fearless striving for the gospel in the midst of persecution is a *token*, or sign, to them that the enemies of God will be destroyed and the followers of God will be saved.

1:29 *not only to believe on him, but also to suffer for his sake.* There is no question that belief in Jesus Christ, the Son of God, is a gift. Paul goes on to say that suffering for Christ's sake is also a gift. In order for believers to endure with joy, Paul reminds them that it is a privilege to suffer for the sake of Christ.

1:30 Paul uses himself as an example of how to joyfully suffer for Christ's sake.

Thoughts for Personal/Family Worship: Chapter 1

1. **It is easy to enter the place of prayer mindlessly, falling prey to vain repetitions. Sometimes we struggle with knowing what to pray for or how to shape our prayers. Paul's prayer in the opening section of this chapter models for us a biblically informed prayer. Prayer is to be a part of the regular rhythm of a Christian's life. Prayer expresses itself in thanksgiving to God and in intercession for others. Paul does not merely make general requests of blessing, but specifically prays that God would work in the Christians' lives and grow them in love for the purpose of knowing how to live in this world.**
2. **What do you live for? Is the fame of Christ's name more important to you, or is comfort and ease of life? Paul's life was so wrapped up in Christ and the gospel that he**

24 Nevertheless to abide in the flesh *is* more
needful for you.
25 And having this confidence, I know that I shall
abide and continue with you all for your further-
ance and joy of faith;
26 That your rejoicing may be more abundant in
Jesus Christ for me by my coming to you again.
27 Only let your conversation be as it becometh
the gospel of Christ: that whether I come and see
you, or else be absent, I may hear of your affairs,
that ye stand fast in one spirit, with one mind
striving together for the faith of the gospel;
28 And in nothing terrified by your adversaries:
which is to them an evident token of perdition,
but to you of salvation, and that of God.
29 For unto you it is given in the behalf of Christ,
not only to believe on him, but also to suffer for
his sake;
30 Having the same conflict which ye saw in me,
and now hear *to be* in me.

CHAPTER 2

If *there be* therefore any consolation in Christ, if
any comfort of love, if any fellowship of the Spirit,
if any bowels and mercies,
2 Fulfil ye my joy, that ye be likeminded, having
the same love, *being* of one accord, of one mind.
3 *Let* nothing *be done* through strife or vainglory;
but in lowliness of mind let each esteem other
better than themselves.
4 Look not every man on his own things, but
every man also on the things of others.
5 Let this mind be in you, which was also in
Christ Jesus:
6 Who, being in the form of God, thought it not
robbery to be equal with God:
7 But made himself of no reputation, and took
upon him the form of a servant, and was made in
the likeness of men:
8 And being found in fashion as a man, he hum-
bled himself, and became obedient unto death,
even the death of the cross.
9 Wherefore God also hath highly exalted him,
and given him a name which is above every name:
10 That at the name of Jesus every knee should
bow, of *things* in heaven, and *things* in earth, and
things under the earth;
11 And *that* every tongue should confess that
Jesus Christ *is* Lord, to the glory of God the Father.
12 Wherefore, my beloved, as ye have always
obeyed, not as in my presence only, but now
much more in my absence, work out your own
salvation with fear and trembling.

---

wanted nothing more than to see the gospel advance, even if it meant that others sought to add to his affliction. When life's circumstances get difficult, it is easy to become focused on self and how to minimize discomfort. But Paul encourages us to remain firm and live in a way that is worthy of the gospel.

Chapter 2: *Paul exhorts the church to unity, selflessness, and humility, having the mind of Christ in order to shine as lights in the dark world.*

Live in Humble, Selfless Unity with the Body of Christ (2:1–11)

2:1–4 Paul continues the theme of unity that he began in the preceding verses by implementing four *if* clauses that highlight the reality that pursuing unity with the body of Christ flows from union with Christ. The four "if" clauses introduce the purpose of Paul's exhortation: to *fulfill ye my joy* by being *likeminded, having the same love, being of one accord*; to do nothing *through strife or vainglory*, that is, boastfulness; and to *esteem others better* than self, looking *on the things of others*. *consolation*. Encouragement. *bowels*. Affections.

2:5 *Let this mind be in you.* Paul points to Christ as the greatest example of selflessness. Verse 5 introduces a beautiful and rich Christological hymn, showing that deep theology is deeply practical. Believers are to have the same mind, or attitude, as Christ in dealing with others. This verse reminds us that the exhortations in vv. 1–4 can be summarized by the phrase "be like Christ."

2:6 What makes Jesus Christ the supreme example of selfless humility is that He, prior to His birth, existed in *the form of God*. To have the *form* of something is to have the essence of the thing. Jesus Christ, being in essence God, did not view equality with God as something to be stolen, robbed, or snatched because He already had it.

2:7 *made himself of no reputation.* Literally, "emptied Himself." Christ did not set aside His deity. Rather the force of the text highlights the humility of Christ. Here we are brought face-to-face with the miracle and wonder of the incarnation. The eternal Son of God, who did not view equality with God something to be grasped, in mercy took hold of the *form*, or essence, of man as a *servant*.

2:8 *humbled himself.* Christ's great act of humiliation that Paul highlights is the voluntary submission of Christ to the Father's will that led to Christ's death on the cross. The greatest need humanity has is to be reconciled to God. Jesus Christ selflessly and humbly did what was necessary to meet the needs of others, namely, to die on the cross as the sin-bearer. Paul's message to the saints is to have the same mindset as Christ.

2:9–11 Paul continues his teaching about Christ by reminding the saints that Christ was *exalted*. The pathway to exaltation is marked by suffering and just as Christ was glorified and exalted after His suffering, so too will God's children. *Wherefore God.* God the Father exalted His Son because the Son's suffering was successful and the result is salvation for all those given to Christ and the glory of God the Father.

Live as Lights in a Dark World (2:12–18)

2:12 *work out your own salvation with fear and trembling.* Paul returns to his exhortations to the church. The church in Philippi had a good reputation of obedience and Paul encourages them to give even greater care to obedience. To *work out* salvation does not mean to work one's own regeneration or justification, for God works these by His grace alone (Rom. 3:24; Eph. 2:1–10; Titus 3:4–7). However, Christians must put energy into the outworking of their sanctification to grow in obedience. *fear and trembling.* These words demonstrate the care and seriousness the believer is to give to obedience. Believers are to work out, or manifest, obedience in selfless humility with caution and awareness of the importance of unity.

13 For it is God which worketh in you both to
will and to do of *his* good pleasure.
14 Do all things without murmurings and
disputings:
15 That ye may be blameless and harmless, the
sons of God, without rebuke, in the midst of a
crooked and perverse nation, among whom ye
shine as lights in the world;
16 Holding forth the word of life; that I may re-
joice in the day of Christ, that I have not run in
vain, neither laboured in vain.
17 Yea, and if I be offered upon the sacrifice and
service of your faith, I joy, and rejoice with you all.
18 For the same cause also do ye joy, and rejoice
with me.
19 But I trust in the Lord Jesus to send Timotheus
shortly unto you, that I also may be of good
comfort, when I know your state.
20 For I have no man likeminded, who will natu-
rally care for your state.
21 For all seek their own, not the things which are
Jesus Christ's.
22 But ye know the proof of him, that, as a son
with the father, he hath served with me in the
gospel.
23 Him therefore I hope to send presently, so
soon as I shall see how it will go with me.
24 But I trust in the Lord that I also myself shall
come shortly.
25 Yet I supposed it necessary to send to you
Epaphroditus, my brother, and companion in la-
bour, and fellowsoldier, but your messenger, and
he that ministered to my wants.
26 For he longed after you all, and was full of
heaviness, because that ye had heard that he had
been sick.
27 For indeed he was sick nigh unto death: but
God had mercy on him; and not on him only, but
on me also, lest I should have sorrow upon sorrow.
28 I sent him therefore the more carefully, that,
when ye see him again, ye may rejoice, and that I
may be the less sorrowful.
29 Receive him therefore in the Lord with all
gladness; and hold such in reputation:
30 Because for the work of Christ he was nigh
unto death, not regarding his life, to supply your
lack of service toward me.

CHAPTER 3

FINALLY, my brethren, rejoice in the Lord. To
write the same things to you, to me indeed *is* not
grievous, but for you *it is* safe.
2 Beware of dogs, beware of evil workers, beware
of the concision.
3 For we are the circumcision, which worship
God in the spirit, and rejoice in Christ Jesus, and
have no confidence in the flesh.

2:13 *For it is God which worketh.* The great hope and encouragement to the believer is that he is not left to himself, but is energized to obey by God. *to will and to do.* God works in His children the willing and the doing of His good pleasure. It is the responsibility of the believer to obey God. And God graciously works in and empowers the believer to obey Him. While we are active in sanctification, it is God's work.

2:14 *Do all things without murmurings.* Few things disrupt unity and discourage like-mindedness than does griping and arguments (*disputings*).

2:15 *That ye may be blameless.* The testimony of the church is at stake in unity and like-mindedness. A body of believers at odds with each other brings accusations and charges from a watching world. *crooked and perverse.* These are the descriptions of the culture that surround the church. Believers are to remain distinct from such perversions and *shine as lights in the world.*

2:17 *if I be offered.* Paul alludes to his imprisonment and possible martyrdom with Old Testament sacrificial language. In a similar sentiment as 1:2–26, Paul is willing to die, or be poured out like a drink offering, in connection to the sacrifice and service that he is calling the Philippian believers to make.

2:18 *joy, and rejoice.* Though the Christian life is often one of sacrifice, there is to be joy and rejoicing.

PAUL'S REPORT CONCERNING TIMOTHY AND EPAPHRODITUS (2:19–30)

2:19–24 Paul writes about his desire to send Timothy (*Timotheus*) to Philippi. Paul viewed Timothy as his own *son* and knew no one so *likeminded*, or dear to him, as was Timothy. Timothy enjoyed a good reputation among the believers there. Paul expresses his desire to come to them shortly.

2:25–30 Paul writes as well to commend *Epaphroditus* to them, stating that though he is returning sooner than expected he indeed ministered to Paul. Paul encourages them to receive Epaphroditus with *gladness* and with honor because he almost died (*nigh unto death*) for the work of Christ in order to serve Paul on the behalf of the Philippian church. *hold such in reputation.* Honor such people.

Thoughts for Personal/Family Worship: Chapter 2

1. **Meditate on the wonder of the incarnation of the Son of God. Consider the humiliation of Christ in His birth, life, and death. Praise God the Father for the gift of the Son, who willingly submitted Himself to die the shameful death of the cross to redeem unworthy sinners.**
2. **Christ deserves our all. Consider the commands in vv. 3–5,12–16 and think practically about what they call you to. How did Timothy (vv. 19–24) and Epaphroditus (vv. 25–30) model obedience to these commands?**

Chapter 3: ***Paul warns against two kinds of false teaching: one that encourages trust in works righteousness, and another that encourages worldliness. He gives himself as an example of the necessity to forsake self-righteousness and seek the righteousness which is of God by faith.***

PAUL'S WARNINGS (3:1–21)

Paul's Warnings against Judaizers (3:1–11)

3:1 *To write the same things to you.* Paul reminds them that the things he is about to write by way of warning is that which they have already heard. That he repeats is not grieving to Paul, since what he is about to say is for their safety, or security.

4 Though I might also have confidence in the
flesh. If any other man thinketh that he hath
whereof he might trust in the flesh, I more:
5 Circumcised the eighth day, of the stock of
Israel, *of* the tribe of Benjamin, an Hebrew of the
Hebrews; as touching the law, a Pharisee;
6 Concerning zeal, persecuting the church; touch-
ing the righteousness which is in the law, blameless.
7 But what things were gain to me, those I counted
loss for Christ.
8 Yea doubtless, and I count all things *but* loss for
the excellency of the knowledge of Christ Jesus
my Lord: for whom I have suffered the loss of all
things, and do count them *but* dung, that I may
win Christ,
9 And be found in him, not having mine own
righteousness, which is of the law, but that which
is through the faith of Christ, the righteousness
which is of God by faith:
10 That I may know him, and the power of his
resurrection, and the fellowship of his sufferings,
being made conformable unto his death;
11 If by any means I might attain unto the resur-
rection of the dead.
12 Not as though I had already attained, either
were already perfect: but I follow after, if that I
may apprehend that for which also I am appre-
hended of Christ Jesus.
13 Brethren, I count not myself to have appre-
hended: but *this* one thing *I do*, forgetting those
things which are behind, and reaching forth unto
those things which are before,
14 I press toward the mark for the prize of the
high calling of God in Christ Jesus.
15 Let us therefore, as many as be perfect, be
thus minded: and if in any thing ye be otherwise
minded, God shall reveal even this unto you.
16 Nevertheless, whereto we have already attained,
let us walk by the same rule, let us mind the same
thing.
17 Brethren, be followers together of me, and
mark them which walk so as ye have us for an
ensample.
18 (For many walk, of whom I have told you
often, and now tell you even weeping, *that they
are* the enemies of the cross of Christ:
19 Whose end *is* destruction, whose God *is their*
belly, and *whose* glory *is* in their shame, who mind
earthly things.)
20 For our conversation is in heaven; from
whence also we look for the Saviour, the Lord
Jesus Christ:

He will mention again in v. 18 that these matters have been told to them often.

3:2 *Beware.* Paul warns against Judaizers, using three terms to describe them. *dogs.* A derogatory term used in Paul's day. Often used by Jews toward Gentiles, but Paul uses the term to refer to the Judaizers. *evil workers.* Those who do evil. *concision.* Literally, "mutilation." Those who require circumcision for salvation.

3:3 The Judaizers argued that physical circumcision saved, but Paul here describes true believers as *the circumcision*, the true people of God. True believers are those who: (1) *worship God in the spirit*, (2) *rejoice in Christ Jesus*, and (3) *have no confidence in the flesh.*

3:4–7 Paul makes the case that if one wanted to boast in the flesh, he had the greatest pedigree to do so. He was *circumcised the eighth day* according to Gen. 17:12; he could boast in knowing what *tribe* he was from (*Benjamin*); concerning the *law,* he was a *Pharisee* who gave attention to obedience; he had great *zeal*, demonstrated in his unmixed focus to persecute the church; *touching the righteousness which is in the law,* Paul testified that he followed it with precision and was *blameless*. All these things that Paul could have boasted in for personal gain or spiritual advantage, he considered to be worthless when Christ is considered to be gain.

3:8 *count them but dung.* Paul considers any item of self-righteousness to be refuse, worthless rubbish. Anything that impedes the knowledge of Christ, even self-righteousness, is to be cast aside.

3:9 *not having mine own righteousness.* What Paul could have boasted of in no way could be considered righteousness. Obedience to the law does not make one righteous before God. *but that which is through the faith of Christ, the righteousness which is of God by faith.* Righteousness does not come by works of the law. Rather, Paul says, righteousness comes by faith in Christ. Faith is the instrument that receives and Christ is the object of faith. And this righteousness is from God. This righteousness of God is given to all those who are *found in him*, to all those in union with Christ.

3:10 *That I may know him.* Nothing was more important to Paul than knowing Jesus Christ, more and more. *and the power of his resurrection.* Remarkably, the power that the believer is able to know and experience in his life is the power that raised Jesus from the dead (Eph. 1:19–20). Knowing Christ in a personal way also means that the believer will experience suffering. Whether it be Paul's present circumstances in prison or the trials of the Philippian believers, Paul reminds them that to know Christ is to suffer. But it also means to know resurrection power.

Paul's Personal Testimony of Advancing in the Gospel (3:12–16)

3:12 *Not as though I had already attained.* Full salvation is not attained in this life, but only at glorification. Believers do not get to a point in life where there is no more need to pursue Christ. Paul is encouraging perseverance in the hope that the work begun will be completed at the day of Christ (1:6). *apprehend.* Take hold of.

3:14 *the mark.* The goal or objective. *the prize.* Paul seeks *the prize* of full salvation which is eternal life with Jesus Christ.

3:15 *perfect.* Not moral perfection, but maturity.

3:16 *same rule.* The way of obedience already communicated to them.

Paul's Warning against Lawlessness (3:17–21)

3:17 *mark them.* Paul exhorts the saints to deliberately observe and imitate those who have walked in a manner worthy of the gospel. *ensample.* Example.

3:18–19 Believers are not only to beware of those who encourage boasting in self-righteousness, but they are also to beware of those who live for the pleasure of this world. *whose God is their belly.* Idolatry of self leads to indulgence of physical desires.

3:20 Believers are not to live for the pleasures of this world

21 Who shall change our vile body, that it may be
fashioned like unto his glorious body, according
to the working whereby he is able even to subdue
all things unto himself.

CHAPTER 4

THEREFORE, my brethren dearly beloved and
longed for, my joy and crown, so stand fast in the
Lord, *my* dearly beloved.
2 I beseech Euodias, and beseech Syntyche, that
they be of the same mind in the Lord.
3 And I intreat thee also, true yokefellow, help
those women which laboured with me in the
gospel, with Clement also, and *with* other my fel-
lowlabourers, whose names *are* in the book of life.
4 Rejoice in the Lord alway: *and* again I say,
Rejoice.
5 Let your moderation be known unto all men.
The Lord *is* at hand.
6 Be careful for nothing; but in every thing by
prayer and supplication with thanksgiving let
your requests be made known unto God.
7 And the peace of God, which passeth all un-
derstanding, shall keep your hearts and minds
through Christ Jesus.
8 Finally, brethren, whatsoever things are true,
whatsoever things *are* honest, whatsoever things
are just, whatsoever things *are* pure, whatsoever
things *are* lovely, whatsoever things *are* of good
report; if *there be* any virtue, and if *there be* any
praise, think on these things.
9 Those things, which ye have both learned, and
received, and heard, and seen in me, do: and the
God of peace shall be with you.
10 But I rejoiced in the Lord greatly, that now at
the last your care of me hath flourished again;
wherein ye were also careful, but ye lacked
opportunity.
11 Not that I speak in respect of want: for I have
learned, in whatsoever state I am, *therewith* to be
content.
12 I know both how to be abased, and I know
how to abound: every where and in all things I am
instructed both to be full and to be hungry, both
to abound and to suffer need.
13 I can do all things through Christ which
strengtheneth me.
14 Notwithstanding ye have well done, that ye did
communicate with my affliction.
15 Now ye Philippians know also, that in the
beginning of the gospel, when I departed from
Macedonia, no church communicated with me as
concerning giving and receiving, but ye only.
16 For even in Thessalonica ye sent once and
again unto my necessity.

---

because their *conversation*, or literally, "citizenship," is in *heaven*. This world is temporary.

3:21 *Who shall change our vile body.* The hope of the saints is the arrival of Jesus Christ from above. *vile.* Lowly. At the sight of Christ believers will become like Him and receive glorified bodies and full salvation.

Thoughts for Personal/Family Worship: Chapter 3

1. **In what ways are you tempted to boast in your accomplishments? Are you actively pursuing an experiential knowledge of Christ? The Christian life is one of growth. Paul uses the language of a race (v. 14) and he highlights the importance of constantly making Christ the prize after which he runs.**
2. **Paul reminds believers that their citizenship is in heaven, where Jesus Christ is and where we are to look. He tells them that when Jesus Christ arrives they will be changed into their glorified bodies. That happens in an instant. If seeing Christ physically changes you in a moment, then you should recognize that seeing Christ now spiritually changes you progressively. This is progressive sanctification. How do you seek to daily gaze on Christ and lead others to do the same?**

Chapter 4: *Paul offers final exhortations to steadfastness, unity, and joyful faith.*

PAUL'S CONCLUDING EXHORTATIONS AND THANKSGIVING (4:1–23)

4:1 *so stand fast.* In light of all that he has written he encourages the saints again to remain firm.

4:2–3 *Euodias* and *Syntyche*. These two women were co-laborers with Paul in the gospel. But something came between them and led to strife. Paul encourages them to be of one mind, to live in accordance with the unity and Christlikeness to which he has called all the saints. *true yokefellow.* Paul appeals to an unnamed individual to help the two women to unity.

4:5 *moderation.* Gentleness and forbearance.

4:6 *Be careful for nothing.* Do not have anxiety. Rather, bring your concerns to the Lord in prayer.

4:7 *peace of God.* God gives peace to those who bring their cares to Him. *which passeth all understanding.* Given certain circumstances in life, anxiety makes sense. However, God is able to grant peace in the presence of suffering that transcends human understanding.

4:8 *think on these things.* The Christian is to intentionally give attention and meditation to those things that are *true*, *honest*, *just*, *pure*, *lovely*, and honorable (*of good report*).

4:10–20 Paul addresses the gift the Philippian believers sent to him and offers thanks to them, as well as using the opportunity to address the nature of contentment.

4:11 *Not that I speak in respect of want.* While Paul is grateful for their gift, he wants them to know that his joyful contentment is not tied to material things.

4:12 Paul notes that contentment is to be learned in seasons of prosperity *(abound)* and in seasons of poverty *(be abased)*. Contentment is a matter of the heart and not found in circumstances.

4:13 *all things through Christ.* Christ is the key to contentment. For a believer, whether there is prosperity or poverty, there is always Christ. The believer can live in all kinds of circumstances with contentment because of the sufficiency of Jesus Christ.

4:14 *Notwithstanding.* Though Paul did not need their gift to be content, he reminds them that he is grateful. *communicate.* To connect or share with him in his affliction.

4:15–16 Paul recounts their previous acts of generosity.

17 Not because I desire a gift: but I desire fruit
that may abound to your account.
18 But I have all, and abound: I am full, having
received of Epaphroditus the things *which were*
sent from you, an odour of a sweet smell, a
sacrifice acceptable, wellpleasing to God.
19 But my God shall supply all your need according
to his riches in glory by Christ Jesus
20 Now unto God and our Father *be* glory for
ever and ever. Amen.
21 Salute every saint in Christ Jesus. The brethren
which are with me greet you.
22 All the saints salute you, chiefly they that are of
Caesar's household.
23 The grace of our Lord Jesus Christ *be* with you
all. Amen.

4:18 Paul rejoices more in the spirit of the gifts to him by the saints than he does in the gift itself. He sees their kindness to him as that which is *wellpleasing to God*.
4:19 *shall supply all your need.* Whatever needs the saints have Paul is confident that God will meet them.
4:20–23 Paul concludes his letter with a doxology and final greetings. *All the saints.* Though believers are scattered geographically, there is a unity in Christ.

Thoughts for Personal/Family Worship: Chapter 4

1. **How do you handle the concerns of life? Is prayer to God a first or last option? Paul, like Peter, encourages us to cast all those things that cause anxiety upon the Lord in prayer. What is true about God that encourages believers to pray? Why should we add thanksgiving to our supplications?**
2. **Contentment is a battle. It is easy to think that we will achieve it if only our circumstances change. Yet, Paul says that he had to learn contentment even when he was abounding. Jesus Christ is the prize of the believer. All things, either poverty or prosperity, cannot compare to knowing and having Christ. Extol Christ in your life and in your home in a manner that clearly demonstrates He is the key to contentment.**

CHRIST'S STATES

Theologians in the Reformed tradition have long differentiated Christ's incarnation into two states, based on Philippians 2:6–11: His state of humiliation (vv. 6–8) and His state of exaltation (vv. 9–11).

Christ's Humiliation

Jesus Christ's earthly ministry was a display of divine humility. In every aspect of that ministry we see the humble Jesus—from his expectant mother being forced to give birth to Him in a stable for animals since there was no room for her and her husband in the inn (Luke 2:7) to His burial in the grave of another (Matt. 27:57–60). He was raised in humble circumstances—His mother's husband, Joseph, was a carpenter, not a man of influence or wealth according to this world's standards (Matt. 13:55).

After a life of doing good, healing the sick, and preaching the gospel (Mark 1:14–15; Acts 10:38), He was arrested by Jewish and Roman authorities, though He was innocent of any wrongdoing (Matt. 27:4,19; John 18:38). Those closest to Him, His disciples, abandoned Him, Peter denied that he knew Him, and Judas Iscariot betrayed Him (Mark 14:50,66–71). He who was "the Truth" and a flawless lover of God was accused of being a blasphemer (Mark 14:61–64). He was spat upon by members of the Jewish temple guard (Mark 14:65; Luke 22:63–65; 23:11) and suffered shamefully at the hands of Roman imperial soldiers, being scourged and mocked (Matt. 27:26–31; Mark 15:15–20; John 19:1–3). He was stripped of all His clothing and put to death with nothing to cover His nakedness (Mark 15:24; Luke 23:34; John 19:23–24). His was the most shameful and painful death known to the Romans, crucifixion (John 19:16–18; Heb. 12:2). Even as the peerless Son of God died, bystanders and an unrepentant brigand, who was being crucified alongside Him, mocked Him (Matt. 27:38–44; Mark 15:29–32; Luke 23:35–39). And the Author of life, who had raised the dead, was buried in the tomb of Joseph of Arimathaea (John 19:38–42; 1 Cor. 15:4).

Most horrific of all, however, was the sense of abandonment by His heavenly Father that flooded the soul of Jesus as He died (Matt. 27:46; Mark 15:34), for in His death He bore and experienced for His elect the hellish wrath they deserved (1 Cor. 15:3; 2 Cor. 5:21; Heb. 9:11–14, 28; 1 Peter 2:24; 1 John 2:2; Rev. 1:5).

Christ's Exaltation

The psalmist had predicted that God would not allow the soul of His Holy One to stay in the grave (Ps. 16:10; Acts 2:24–31), for neither death nor Satan had any claim on Him. And so God the Father, by the Holy Spirit, raised Jesus from the dead on the third day after His death (Matt. 28:6–7; Mark 16:6; Luke 24:13–43; John 20:1–29; Acts 2:32; Rom 8:11), and He was seen on various occasions by His apostles and a select band of disciples for a period of forty days, during which time he taught them about the kingdom of God (Matt. 28:9,16–20; Luke 24; John 20–21; Acts 1:3–8; 1 Cor. 15:4–8). This was the beginning of His exaltation.

Following His resurrection He ascended to heaven (Luke 24:50–51; Acts 1:9–11; Eph. 4:8), where He remains seated on the right hand of God the Father (Acts 2:33–34; Col. 3:1; Heb. 1:3; 8:1; 10:12; 1 Peter 3:22), the place of absolute power and authority. He was given glory and honor among the citizens of heaven, angels and glorified saints (Heb. 1:6), and declared to be Lord over all (Acts 2:36; 5:30–31; Phil. 2:11; 1 Peter 3:22).

In time Christ's lordship will be acknowledged by all of humanity, for He is coming back to make this vale of tears and sinful ruin a kingdom of love and righteousness in which He will rule with His Father forever; "of his kingdom there will be no end" (Luke 1:33).

INTRODUCTION TO THE BOOK OF COLOSSIANS

Authorship: The apostle Paul identifies himself as the author, along with Timothy, who possibly served as his scribe in writing (1:1). The letter contains a first person reference in v. 23 and closes with the words, "The salutation by the hand of me, Paul" (4:18). While some scholars have cast doubt on Pauline authorship because of stylistic and theological differences, their arguments are not convincing. While some of the style and language are specific to the Colossian situation, there is much in the letter that fits Paul's other writings. Regarding the theology of the book, while the specifics of the threat of a worldly "philosophy" (2:8) are unique to the church in Colosse, Paul's emphasis on a high Christology and the centrality of the gospel to combat such a threat is in keeping with the theology of Paul's other letters. There is little reason to doubt the authenticity of Pauline authorship.

Colossians is considered one of the Prison Epistles (4:3,18) and it is believed that Paul wrote this while imprisoned in Rome. This fits with Paul's references to Aristarchus and Luke (4:10,14; see also Acts 27:2).

Date: Paul wrote the letter from prison in Rome around AD 61 or 62.

Theme: The supremacy of Christ over all things.

Purpose: To ground and settle the Colossians in the knowledge of Christ against error.

Synopsis: *The Contribution of Colossians to Redemptive Revelation*

Though Paul did not plant the church in Colosse or visit the believers there, he cared deeply for the church and received reports regarding the church's health. Upon hearing that false teachers threatened the purity of the gospel of free grace, Paul responded with a letter. Though there are certainly difficulties in grasping a full understanding of the threat the Colossian believers' faced, it is clear that it demanded adherence to external rites, that it was according to men and contrary to Christ (2:8,20–21). Paul responds by reminding the church that Jesus Christ is supreme over all creation and over the new creation (the church). Therefore, anything that detracts from the supremacy of Christ is to be repudiated. Paul intercedes for them and encourages them, that rather than becoming pulled away from the faith that they learned from Epaphras (1:7), they will continue to grow in and be filled with the knowledge of God's will in all wisdom and spiritual understanding (v. 9).

The Christian life becomes visible in everyday life; it is distinct from the world. There must be a change in the heart, though, before there is change in one's life. The Colossian believers faced a teaching that following certain external rules would make a person more spiritual (2:21). This teaching was contrary to the gospel of Christ and resulted in a form of religion that, while it may have appeared to be wise and humble (v. 23), actually threatened the sufficiency of the gospel. Because of this threat, Paul wrote to the Colossians to encourage them to continue in the faith of Christ that they initially received (v. 6). Instead of following after man-made wisdom, believers should continue to pursue Christ, in whom are hid all the treasures of wisdom and knowledge (v. 3).

Therefore, the greatest antidote to external religion is a clearer vision of the person and work of Jesus Christ (1:15–22). Seeing Christ, in whom the fullness of the Godhead dwelt bodily (v. 19; 2:9), is utterly transforming. Paul highlights this in his prayer and works it out in greater detail in chs. 2–3. Knowing God's will, grasping one's union with Christ in his death and resurrection, and fixing one's mind on things above where Christ is leads to Christlikeness, which is the goal of sanctification (3:10). Because Christ is sufficient for both justification and sanctification, the Christian should not shortchange himself by conforming merely to external forms of religion. All that he has and needs is found in Christ. Paul is quick to remind them that relying solely on Christ and living in light of the resurrection does not lead to licentiousness. Rather, those in Christ, as the elect of God, are holy and live holy lives (3:12—4:1). Reading Colossians and grasping its message brings the believer into a deeper and greater experience of the blessings found in Jesus Christ, the visible image of the invisible God.

Outline:

I. Introduction (1:1–14)
  A. Greetings (1:1–2)
  B. Thanksgiving (1:3–8)
  C. Prayer (1:9–14)
II. Glorying in the Supremacy of Christ (1:15–23)
  A. Supremacy of Christ over Creation (1:15–17)
  B. Supremacy of Christ over the New Creation (1:18)
  C. Supremacy of Christ in the Work of Redemption (1:19–23)
III. Paul's Ministry and Conflict for the Colossian Believers (1:24—2:7)
  A. Paul's Ministry of Preaching the Mystery of God (1:24–29)
  B. Paul's Concern for the Colossian Believers (2:1–7)
IV. Paul's Warning of and Solution to False Teaching (2:8–23)
  A. Summary of False Teaching (2:8)
  B. Sufficiency of Christ's Death and Resurrection (2:9–15)
  C. False Teaching Described in Greater Detail (2:16–23)
V. Paul's Description of the Christian Life (3:1—4:6)
  A. Foundation of the Christian Life Wrapped Up in Christ (3:1–4)
  B. The Mortification of Sin (3:5–11)
  C. The Putting On of Holiness (3:12–17)
  D. Description of the Christian Life in the Household (3:18—4:1)
  E. The Christian's Prayer Life (4:2–4)
  F. The Christian's Life before the World (4:5–6)
VI. Final Words (4:7–18)
  A. Comments regarding Paul's Companions (4:7–14)
  B. Final Greetings to the Brethren and the Benediction (4:15–18)

THE EPISTLE OF PAUL THE APOSTLE TO THE

COLOSSIANS

CHAPTER 1

PAUL, an apostle of Jesus Christ by the will of God,
and Timotheus *our* brother,
2 To the saints and faithful brethren in Christ
which are at Colosse: Grace *be* unto you, and
peace, from God our Father and the Lord Jesus
Christ.
3 We give thanks to God and the Father of our
Lord Jesus Christ, praying always for you,
4 Since we heard of your faith in Christ Jesus, and
of the love *which ye have* to all the saints,
5 For the hope which is laid up for you in heaven,
whereof ye heard before in the word of the truth
of the gospel;
6 Which is come unto you, as *it is* in all the world;
and bringeth forth fruit, as *it doth* also in you,
since the day ye heard *of it*, and knew the grace of
God in truth:
7 As ye also learned of Epaphras our dear fel-
lowservant, who is for you a faithful minister of
Christ;
8 Who also declared unto us your love in the
Spirit.
9 For this cause we also, since the day we heard *it*,
do not cease to pray for you, and to desire that ye
might be filled with the knowledge of his will in
all wisdom and spiritual understanding;
10 That ye might walk worthy of the Lord unto
all pleasing, being fruitful in every good work,
and increasing in the knowledge of God;
11 Strengthened with all might, according to his
glorious power, unto all patience and longsuffer-
ing with joyfulness;
12 Giving thanks unto the Father, which hath
made us meet to be partakers of the inheritance
of the saints in light:

Chapter 1: ***Paul greets the believers of Colosse and gives thanks to God the Father for their faith and intercedes for them. Paul focuses on the supremacy of Christ over the created order and in redemption.***

INTRODUCTION (1:1–14)

Greetings (1:1–2)

1:1 *Paul* identifies himself as the author and mentions *Timotheus* (Timothy) his son in the faith (1 Tim. 1:2).

1:2 *the saints.* A common designation Paul uses to address the church.

Thanksgiving (1:3–8)

1:3 *give thanks to God and the Father.* Paul frequently expresses his love for the brethren by offering thanksgiving to God for them. In doing so, he aims at two things: 1) to direct thanksgiving to God as the ultimate source of blessing, and 2) to encourage the believers for whom he is thankful. *praying always for you.* Paul's thoughts toward the Colossians and subsequent prayers for them were repetitive, not a one-time act.

1:4–5 Paul points to their *faith* in Christ, *love* for the brethren, and *hope* of full salvation as the reason why he thanks God—his summary of the Christian life (1 Cor. 13:13). *whereof.* Of which.

1:5 *word of the truth of the gospel.* The word of truth is the gospel (see Eph. 1:13; James 1:18).

1:6 *as it is in all the world.* The gospel successfully came to Colosse as evidenced by their faith, love, and hope. But the gospel is not limited to one place. By the time of Paul's letter the gospel had spread from all Jerusalem, Judea, and Samaria and was being spread throughout the whole world according to Christ's commission (Acts 1:8).

1:7 *Epaphras,* a native of Colosse (4:12), brought the gospel and planted the church in the city. Paul recognizes him as a *fellowservant* in the gospel. *minister.* Literally, "servant."

1:8 *love in the Spirit.* Love by the Holy Spirit. Love is a vital part of the fruit of the Holy Spirit (Gal. 5:22).

Prayer (1:9–14)

1:9–14 Paul transitions from thanksgiving to intercession, writing the saints in Colossae precisely how he prays for them. Paul's prayers for the specific churches contain themes that are worked out in his letters. He does not pray abstractly for churches, but specifically for what they need in the particular circumstances in which they find themselves.

1:9 *filled with the knowledge of his will.* The only way to combat the false teaching and the vain philosophy that threatened the health of the church is to be filled with the knowledge of God's will. God's will is not something to be known only by an elite few. But it is revealed and is to be known by all the saints. The knowledge of God's will is over against the knowledge promised by the false teachers. *In all wisdom and spiritual understanding* highlights the practical use of and spiritual discernment of the knowledge of God's will. Knowing God's will manifests itself properly in the ability to apply it to life's situations.

1:10 *That ye might walk worthy.* The ultimate evidence of knowing God's will is living in a manner that is pleasing to God. *unto all pleasing.* While the temptation to please others faces believers at every turn, it is the chief aim of Christians to please God.

13 Who hath delivered us from the power of
darkness, and hath translated *us* into the king-
dom of his dear Son:
14 In whom we have redemption through his
blood, *even* the forgiveness of sins:
15 Who is the image of the invisible God, the
firstborn of every creature:
16 For by him were all things created, that are in
heaven, and that are in earth, visible and invisible,
whether *they be* thrones, or dominions, or princi-
palities, or powers: all things were created by him,
and for him:
17 And he is before all things, and by him all
things consist.
18 And he is the head of the body, the church:
who is the beginning, the firstborn from the dead;
that in all *things* he might have the preeminence.
19 For it pleased *the Father* that in him should all
fulness dwell;
20 And, having made peace through the blood of
his cross, by him to reconcile all things unto him-
self; by him, *I say*, whether *they be* things in earth,
or things in heaven.
21 And you, that were sometime alienated and
enemies in *your* mind by wicked works, yet now
hath he reconciled
22 In the body of his flesh through death, to pre-
sent you holy and unblameable and unreproveable
in his sight:
23 If ye continue in the faith grounded and
settled, and *be* not moved away from the hope of
the gospel, which ye have heard, *and* which was
preached to every creature which is under heaven;
whereof I Paul am made a minister;
24 Who now rejoice in my sufferings for you, and
fill up that which is behind of the afflictions of
Christ in my flesh for his body's sake, which is the
church:
25 Whereof I am made a minister, according to
the dispensation of God which is given to me for
you, to fulfil the word of God;
26 *Even* the mystery which hath been hid from
ages and from generations, but now is made
manifest to his saints:
27 To whom God would make known what *is*
the riches of the glory of this mystery among the
Gentiles; which is Christ in you, the hope of glory:
28 Whom we preach, warning every man, and
teaching every man in all wisdom; that we may
present every man perfect in Christ Jesus:
29 Whereunto I also labour, striving according to
his working, which worketh in me mightily.

1:11 *Strengthened with all might.* Paul does not exhort Christians to live holy lives pleasing to the Lord without assuring them that God gives the strength *according to his glorious power, unto all patience and longsuffering with joyfulness.* Paul does not leave the believer in doubt as to the end result of experiencing this power. It manifests itself in patient endurance and longsuffering. The former is often used with reference to circumstances and the latter with people. Christians, by God's glorious power, are strengthened to endure hardships and show patience toward others.

1:12 *made us meet.* Made us sufficient or qualified us.

1:13 *translated.* Transferred. When God redeems a sinner He transfers them from the power of darkness to the kingdom of His Son, Jesus Christ.

GLORYING IN THE SUPREMACY OF CHRIST (1:15–23)

Supremacy of Christ over Creation (1:15–17)

1:15 *image of the invisible God.* Jesus Christ, true God of true God, is here called the representation of God. God, who is invisible, is now seen in the person of Jesus. While human beings are made in the image of God (Gen. 1:27), Paul says here that Jesus Christ *is* the exact image of God. The focus here is on the revelatory character of Jesus Christ. It is this image that believers are renewed after in their sanctification (3:10). *firstborn.* While firstborn can sometimes refer to temporal order, here Paul highlights preeminent status (Ps. 89:27). *of every creature.* This phrase is subordinate to "firstborn." Christ is supreme over all creation.

1:16 *by him, and for him.* The reason for his supremacy over creation is because Christ is the agent of (*by*) and the goal of (*for*) creation.

1:17 *by him all things consist.* Literally, "in him all things are held together." Christ is not only supreme over creation because He is the agent and goal of creation, but also because He sustains creation (Heb. 1:2–3).

Supremacy of Christ over the New Creation (1:18)

1:18 *head of the body, the church.* Paul now demonstrates Christ's supremacy in redemption, noting Christ's authority and headship over the church, the new creation. *firstborn from the dead.* Christ's resurrection is the guarantee of resurrection for all the saints (1 Cor. 15:20–22). *that in all things he might have the preeminence.* The end result of Christ's work of redemption is His unmistaken supremacy.

Supremacy of Christ in the Work of Redemption (1:19–23)

1:19 *all fulness.* All the glory and majesty of God dwells in Jesus (2:9).

1:20 *peace through the blood of his cross.* Christ reconciles sinners to God by virtue of His life and atoning death. That Christ who is supreme over creation and over the new creation would suffer and die for rebellious creatures magnifies the grace and mercy of the triune God.

1:21 *alienated and enemies.* Sin alienates human beings from God (Rom. 8:7). However, Christ's death and resurrection reconcile sinners and they are restored to peace with God.

1:22 *to present you holy and unblameable and unreproveable.* Such is the power of Christ's work in redemption that He not only restores peace by reconciling sinners to God, He transforms them in order to present them as holy and without blame and without reproof (Eph. 5:25–27).

1:23 *If ye continue in the faith.* Christ secures salvation for all those who place their faith in Him. Believers need, however, to persevere in that faith and not be moved away from the hope of the gospel. The Colossian believers heard teachings that tempted them to move away from or past Christ. Paul calls them to remain committed and rooted in the faith of Jesus Christ.

PAUL'S MINISTRY AND CONFLICT FOR THE COLOSSIAN BELIEVERS (1:24—2:7)

Paul's Ministry of Preaching the Mystery of God (1:24–29)

CHAPTER 2

FOR I would that ye knew what great conflict I
have for you, and *for* them at Laodicea, and *for* as
many as have not seen my face in the flesh;
2 That their hearts might be comforted, being
knit together in love, and unto all riches of
the full assurance of understanding, to the
acknowledgement of the mystery of God, and of
the Father, and of Christ;
3 In whom are hid all the treasures of wisdom
and knowledge.
4 And this I say, lest any man should beguile you
with enticing words.
5 For though I be absent in the flesh, yet am I
with you in the spirit, joying and beholding your
order, and the stedfastness of your faith in Christ.
6 As ye have therefore received Christ Jesus the
Lord, *so* walk ye in him:
7 Rooted and built up in him, and stablished
in the faith, as ye have been taught, abounding
therein with thanksgiving.
8 Beware lest any man spoil you through philos-
ophy and vain deceit, after the tradition of men,
after the rudiments of the world, and not after
Christ.
9 For in him dwelleth all the fulness of the God-
head bodily.
10 And ye are complete in him, which is the head
of all principality and power:
11 In whom also ye are circumcised with the cir-
cumcision made without hands, in putting off the
body of the sins of the flesh by the circumcision
of Christ:
12 Buried with him in baptism, wherein also ye
are risen with *him* through the faith of the opera-
tion of God, who hath raised him from the dead.
13 And you, being dead in your sins and
the uncircumcision of your flesh, hath he

1:24 *fill up that which is behind of the afflictions of Christ.* Paul has already shown that Christ's sacrifice is sufficient and supreme. He does not imply that he needs to add to the atoning sufferings of Christ. Rather, he is referring to the suffering of God's people in the latter days. Christ told His followers that they would suffer for the sake of the gospel. Paul rejoiced that he was able to share in suffering for the sake of the gospel (Phil. 3:10).

1:26–27 Paul uses the word *mystery* to describe a truth that is known only by the revelation of God, hidden *from ages and from generations.* While there has always been a universal aspect of the Abrahamic promise (Gen. 12:2; 22:18), the full display of God's purposes in salvation was not clearly seen until the arrival of Christ and His subsequent death and resurrection. The content of the mystery of the gospel that is now fully revealed is described in v. 27, namely, that the Gentiles enjoy full participation among the people of God. All those trusting in Christ enjoy His covenantal presence, namely, *Christ in you.*
1:28 *perfect.* Mature.

Thoughts for Personal/Family Worship: Chapter 1

1. **Give attention to the great wonder of the incarnation. Meditate upon the supremacy of Christ in His person as the agent, sustainer, and goal of creation, considering that this person would take on flesh to redeem you from your sins. What are some reasons why Christ's incarnation would make you praise God?**
2. **Paul prays that the believers at Colosse might be filled with the knowledge of God. He prays that they might "walk worthy of the Lord unto all pleasing." Believers tend to think of God's will as that which only deals with future plans. Yet Paul writes about God's will as informing our lives in the present, how we may live before God, being fruitful in every good work.**

Chapter 2: ***Paul opposes false teaching and argues for the supremacy of Christ over worldly philosophies, vain deceits, and the traditions of men.***

Paul's Concern for the Colossian Believers (2:1–7)

2:1 *conflict.* Struggle.
2:3 *In whom are hid.* Wisdom and knowledge can be found in Christ. He holds all these treasures in Himself. To know Christ is to have wisdom and knowledge.
2:4 *beguile.* Deceive.
2:5 *Order* and *stedfastness* are military terms. Paul rejoices that he has beheld their disciplined efforts in standing for the faith.
2:6 Paul encourages them to remain walking in the teaching they first received.

PAUL'S WARNING OF AND SOLUTION TO FALSE TEACHING (2:8–23)

Summary of False Teaching (2:8)

2:8 *spoil.* Literally, "capture, take captive." Some sought to capture the Colossian believers through the means of *philosophy and vain deceit*, or empty deceptions. The term *philosophy* in Paul's day was more broad than today. It was used to describe a particular school or system of thought. The kind of philosophy and vain deceit that threatened the Colossians is described by the preposition *after*, used three times. This philosophy was *after the tradition of men.* This contrasts with the faith first received which was from God. *after the rudiments of the world.* Literally, "fundamental components of the world," referring either to the spirits of the world, or, more likely in this context, the world's principles and rules. The church was being tempted to adhere to certain rules (vv. 16,20–23) if they wanted to be spiritually full. *not after Christ.* The chief problem of all the problems with the vain and empty philosophy was that it was contrary to Christ.

Sufficiency of Christ's Death and Resurrection (2:9–15)

2:9 *Godhead bodily.* Christ is fully God made visible in the flesh (John 1:18). Paul again reminds the believers that true knowledge and wisdom are to be found in Christ alone (1 Cor. 1:30).
2:10 *complete in him.* Everything that a believer needs is found in Christ, and a believer is complete in union with Christ. *head of all principality and power.* Since Christ is supreme over all things, it is utter folly to seek fullness in anything other than Him.
2:11 *circumcision.* Paul addresses the rite of circumcision and focuses on its spiritual significance, giving the true meaning of the rite. In Christ, the sins of the flesh have been cut off.
2:12 *baptism.* Paul now shows the spiritual significance of baptism, linking baptism and circumcision. The essence of both rites is Christ. The believer who is circumcised in Christ (v. 11) is also buried with Him in baptism. Baptism points to the washing away of sins. Being risen with Christ through faith

quickened together with him, having forgiven you all trespasses;
14 Blotting out the handwriting of ordinances that was against us, which was contrary to us, and took it out of the way, nailing it to his cross;
15 *And* having spoiled principalities and powers, he made a shew of them openly, triumphing over them in it.
16 Let no man therefore judge you in meat, or in drink, or in respect of an holyday, or of the new moon, or of the sabbath *days*:
17 Which are a shadow of things to come; but the body *is* of Christ.
18 Let no man beguile you of your reward in a voluntary humility and worshipping of angels, intruding into those things which he hath not seen, vainly puffed up by his fleshly mind,
19 And not holding the Head, from which all the body by joints and bands having nourishment ministered, and knit together, increaseth with the increase of God.
20 Wherefore if ye be dead with Christ from the rudiments of the world, why, as though living in the world, are ye subject to ordinances,
21 (Touch not; taste not; handle not;
22 Which all are to perish with the using;) after the commandments and doctrines of men?
23 Which things have indeed a shew of wisdom in will worship, and humility, and neglecting of the body; not in any honour to the satisfying of the flesh.

CHAPTER 3

IF ye then be risen with Christ, seek those things which are above, where Christ sitteth on the right hand of God.
2 Set your affection on things above, not on things on the earth.
3 For ye are dead, and your life is hid with Christ in God.
4 When Christ, *who is* our life, shall appear, then shall ye also appear with him in glory.
5 Mortify therefore your members which are

---

shows that sin no longer reigns and has dominion.
2:13 The result of being circumcised in Christ and buried with Him in baptism is forgiveness.
2:14 *handwriting of ordinances.* Literally, "handwritten record of debts." The debt against an individual accrued by sin (Rom. 3:23) is wiped out and obliterated. *against us.* The debt condemns the sinner. *nailing it to his cross.* Christ, however, graciously and lovingly took the debt that was against sinners and nailed it to the cross. In His sacrificial, substitutionary death, Christ paid the penalty of sin and canceled the debt.
2:15 *spoiled principalities and powers.* Christ's death conquered spiritual powers of evil (Heb. 2:14–15). *made a shew of them openly.* Christ's death was a public showing of the defeat of Satan and the powers of evil, exposing and disgracing them before all.

False Teaching Described in Greater Detail (2:16–23)

2:16–17 *Let no man therefore.* Given what Christ has done as the One who is supreme over creation and redemption, let no man judge regarding the observance of those things that are but a shadow. Paul's argument leads to this conclusion, namely, that Christ is the substance of all these things.
2:18 *Let no man beguile you.* Let no man rob you or condemn you. *humility*. False teachers often demonstrate a humility that encourages a following. *vainly puffed up.* This humility, however, is betrayed by an arrogance that claims a knowledge enjoyed by only a few.
2:19 *not holding the Head.* That their philosophy is not after Christ (v. 8) is revealed in terms as not holding to the Head, which is Christ. Their teaching is detached from Christ. *bands.* Ligaments. *having nourishment.* Only those things that are connected to Christ can be supported. Christians find their nourishment and growth only in union to Jesus Christ.
2:20–23 *if ye be dead with Christ from the rudiments of the world.* Since Christians have died with Christ and therefore been freed from obeying rules in an effort to please Him, why then live in a way that subjects one to self-effort. Do not live in subjection to those things from which Christ set you free (John 8:36). *shew of wisdom in will worship, and humility.* Relying on external religion and obedience to man-made rules may appear to be wise and spiritually mature. *not in any honour to the satisfying of the flesh.* While it appears to be wise, it cannot defeat the sinful longings of the flesh. You cannot curtail sin with asceticism.

Thoughts for Personal/Family Worship: Chapter 2

1. **In Christ are all the treasures of wisdom and knowledge. Yet, we so often seek guidance for life outside of Christ. Whether it be self-help tips or the latest marketing fad, we can be tempted to find quick solutions to life's problems outside of Christ. Give yourself, by grace, to a perpetual pursuit of experiencing Christ and living in the enjoyment of being united to Him.**
2. **How ought you to view your standards of conduct? When Paul says that external things do not conquer the indulgences of the flesh, is he advocating the repudiation of all standards? Consider the sufficiency of Christ's death and resurrection to sanctify, along with the motivation of the standards set forth, personally and for family.**

Chapter 3: *Seeking Christ, who is above, leads to genuine holiness and the defeat of the flesh.*

PAUL'S DESCRIPTION OF THE CHRISTIAN LIFE (3:1—4:6)

Foundation of the Christian Life Wrapped Up in Christ (3:1–4)

3:1 *If ye then be risen with Christ.* Those who have been risen with Christ (2:12,20) can pursue those things which are above. *those things.* This refers to the substance of Paul's prayer in ch. 1: knowledge of God's will, wisdom and spiritual understanding, strength according to God's glorious power, etc.
3:2 *Set your affection.* Set your mind upon, to think upon.
3:3 *your life is hid.* This phrase has the idea of life being hidden, secure, or safe in Christ. Paul has exhorted the believers not to be deceived or judged by others. Now he encourages them that they, having died in Christ, are alive and secure in Christ.

The Mortification of Sin (3:5–11)

3:5 *Mortify therefore your members.* The solution to the legalism Paul warns Christians of in 2:20–23 is not antinomianism

upon the earth; fornication, uncleanness, inordi-
nate affection, evil concupiscence, and covetous-
ness, which is idolatry:
6 For which things' sake the wrath of God cometh
on the children of disobedience:
7 In the which ye also walked some time, when
ye lived in them.
8 But now ye also put off all these; anger, wrath,
malice, blasphemy, filthy communication out of
your mouth.
9 Lie not one to another, seeing that ye have put
off the old man with his deeds;
10 And have put on the new *man*, which is re-
newed in knowledge after the image of him that
created him:
11 Where there is neither Greek nor Jew, circum-
cision nor uncircumcision, Barbarian, Scythian,
bond *nor* free: but Christ *is* all, and in all.
12 Put on therefore, as the elect of God, holy and
beloved, bowels of mercies, kindness, humbleness
of mind, meekness, longsuffering;
13 Forbearing one another, and forgiving one
another, if any man have a quarrel against any:
even as Christ forgave you, so also *do* ye.
14 And above all these things *put on* charity,
which is the bond of perfectness.
15 And let the peace of God rule in your hearts,
to the which also ye are called in one body; and
be ye thankful.
16 Let the word of Christ dwell in you richly in all
wisdom; teaching and admonishing one another
in psalms and hymns and spiritual songs, singing
with grace in your hearts to the Lord.
17 And whatsoever ye do in word or deed, *do* all
in the name of the Lord Jesus, giving thanks to
God and the Father by him.
18 Wives, submit yourselves unto your own
husbands, as it is fit in the Lord.
19 Husbands, love *your* wives, and be not bitter
against them.
20 Children, obey *your* parents in all things: for
this is well pleasing unto the Lord.
21 Fathers, provoke not your children *to anger*,
lest they be discouraged.
22 Servants, obey in all things *your* masters
according to the flesh; not with eyeservice, as men-
pleasers; but in singleness of heart, fearing God:
23 And whatsoever ye do, do *it* heartily, as to the
Lord, and not unto men;
24 Knowing that of the Lord ye shall receive the
reward of the inheritance: for ye serve the Lord
Christ.

---

or a license to sin. Rather, in Christ the believer is able and expected to put to death (Rom. 8:13) the deeds of the flesh. Being dead to sin and alive in Christ, Christians are to live in a way that is in accordance to God's will, not the evil deeds of the former life outside of Christ.

3:6 *which things' sake.* The believer's life is not to be characterized by those things the wrath of God is against (v. 5; Rom. 1:18–32).

3:10 *new man.* Christians are new creatures. They are now identified by their union with Christ. *image of him that created him.* Paul has already identified Christ as the image of the invisible God and the agent of creation (1:15). He now applies those realities to the believer's salvation. A Christian is a new man in Christ. He is being renewed in the image of Christ. Holiness is not adhering to man-made rules, but conformity to and renewal in the image of Christ.

3:11 In Christ there is unity among the people of God. Whereas the vain philosophy of the false teachers divided and promoted various levels of spirituality, there is a genuine Christian equality in Christ.

The Putting On of Holiness (3:12–17)

3:12–17 *the elect of God, holy, and beloved.* Knowing that God lovingly chose them and set them apart for Himself transforms the way they live toward others and encourages unity among the body of Christ. *bowels of mercies.* Deep compassion.

3:16 *psalms and hymns and spiritual songs.* Three common terms used to describe the parts of the Old Testament Psalms.

3:17 *do all in the name of the Lord Jesus.* Paul highlights one of the primary motivations of the Christian life. Believers are not to live for the praise or affirmation of man, but all their deeds and words are to be for Christ, with a heart of gratitude to God.

Description of the Christian Life in the Household (3:18—4:1)

3:18 *as it is fit in the Lord.* The wife's submission to her husband is in obedience to the Lord. It is in compliance to the God-given roles unique to man and woman.

3:19 *Husbands, love your wives.* The husband's leadership is exercised and demonstrated in his love for his wife (Eph. 5:25). *be not bitter.* The husband is not to be harsh toward his wife.

3:20 *this is well pleasing unto the Lord.* Paul cites the fifth commandment, exhorting children to obey their parents. In doing so, God is pleased. Children and parents do well to recognize this authority structure. The child's obedience to parents is obedience to God. God is ultimate in these exhortations. The husband is under God's authority as evidenced in the wife's submission being fit in the Lord and the child's obedience being pleasing to the Lord.

3:21 *lest they be discouraged.* Fathers are the authority in the home. However, the fathers are not to be overbearing in a way that causes the child to be discouraged, or lose heart.

3:22—4:1 Paul addresses the relationship between master and slave. Servants were to work diligently with a singular focus on pleasing God. Masters were to treat servants justly, remembering that they are under God, the Master in heaven. Paul is not necessarily condoning slavery, but he is teaching the moral implications of the gospel on individuals within present day societal institutions.

Thoughts for Personal/Family Worship: Chapter 3

1. **Believers are risen with Christ and exhorted to fix their minds on things above. Do you give attention to this focus in your personal walk and in your family? Do you find strength (1:11) to mortify and put off sin in God's power? Perhaps you are frustrated seeking to mortify sin in your own strength. What does living according to 3:12–16 look like in your personal interactions and in your family life?**
2. **Notice the manifold grace of the Holy Spirit (vv. 12–15), with which we are commanded to clothe ourselves. Reflect practically on what this calls you to do or perhaps change in your life.**
3. **Talk through the responsibilities of husband, wife, father, mother, and children with the whole family present**

25 But he that doeth wrong shall receive for the
wrong which he hath done: and there is no re-
spect of persons.

CHAPTER 4

MASTERS, give unto *your* servants that which is
just and equal; knowing that ye also have a Master
in heaven.
2 Continue in prayer, and watch in the same with
thanksgiving;
3 Withal praying also for us, that God would
open unto us a door of utterance, to speak the
mystery of Christ, for which I am also in bonds:
4 That I may make it manifest, as I ought to
speak.
5 Walk in wisdom toward them that are without,
redeeming the time.
6 Let your speech *be* alway with grace, seasoned
with salt, that ye may know how ye ought to an-
swer every man.
7 All my state shall Tychicus declare unto you,
who is a beloved brother, and a faithful minister
and fellowservant in the Lord:
8 Whom I have sent unto you for the same
purpose, that he might know your estate, and
comfort your hearts;
9 With Onesimus, a faithful and beloved brother,
who is *one* of you. They shall make known unto
you all things which *are done* here.
10 Aristarchus my fellowprisoner saluteth you,
and Marcus, sister's son to Barnabas, (touching
whom ye received commandments: if he come
unto you, receive him;)
11 And Jesus, which is called Justus, who are of
the circumcision. These only *are my* fellowwork-
ers unto the kingdom of God, which have been a
comfort unto me.
12 Epaphras, who is *one* of you, a servant of
Christ, saluteth you, always labouring fervently
for you in prayers, that ye may stand perfect and
complete in all the will of God.
13 For I bear him record, that he hath a great zeal
for you, and them *that are* in Laodicea, and them
in Hierapolis.
14 Luke, the beloved physician, and Demas, greet
you.
15 Salute the brethren which are in Laodicea, and
Nymphas, and the church which is in his house.
16 And when this epistle is read among you,
cause that it be read also in the church of the
Laodiceans; and that ye likewise read the *epistle*
from Laodicea.
17 And say to Archippus, Take heed to the min-
istry which thou hast received in the Lord, that
thou fulfill it.
18 The salutation by the hand of me, Paul.
Remember my bonds. Grace *be* with you. Amen.

(vv. 18–25). Consider that each relationship is lived under God, before whom all relationships are accountable.

Chapter 4: *Paul offers final exhortations and greetings.*

The Christian's Prayer Life (4:2–4)

4:2 *Continue in prayer.* For the Christian, prayer is absolutely vital. Believers ought to give heed to their prayers, seeking to guard and to protect the duty of prayer so as not to neglect it but to continue in it. *watch in the same.* Prayer should be thoughtful and intentional.

4:3–4 Paul requests the believers to intercede for him for effectiveness in the spread of the gospel.

The Christian's Life before the World (4:5–6)

4:5–6 Paul exhorts the believers to live wisely with regard to those outside the believing community. There is a watching world and it is necessary that Christians live and speak in a way that is glorifying to God.

FINAL WORDS (4:7–18)

Comments regarding Paul's Companions (4:7–14)

4:9 *Onesimus.* Philemon's slave converted to Jesus Christ under Paul's ministry.

4:10 *Marcus.* Paul's mention of Mark (Marcus) informs that there had been full restoration between the two (Acts 15:36–39; see 2 Tim. 4:11).

4:11 *of the circumcision.* Aristarchus, Marcus, and Jesus, who is called *Justus* are Jewish Christians (Acts 27:2).

Final Greetings to the Brethren and the Benediction (4:15–18)

4:16 *when this epistle is read among you.* Paul intended his letters to be read to the churches collectively. *epistle from Laodicea.* Some have suggested this letter to be the same as Paul's epistle to the Ephesians, but it is difficult to know with certainty.

4:18 *by the hand of me, Paul.* Paul writes the final salutation with his own hand. Timothy (1:1) may have served as his secretary in writing the letter, but here Paul writes himself.

Thoughts for Personal/Family Worship: Chapter 4

1. **Prayer is vital for the Christian life. Prayer ought to be thoughtful. It involves thanksgiving and intercession. It is easy to neglect thanksgiving, but believers have so much for which they ought to praise God. Believers ought also to remember to intercede for others, especially as it relates to the advancement of the gospel. Teach your family to pray regularly, thoughtfully, thankfully, and missionally.**
2. **What does it mean to make your speech around unbelievers "seasoned with salt" (v. 6)? What unbelievers do you talk to? How can you bring grace and salt into your conversations with them?**

THE IMAGE OF GOD

What makes man unique among God's creatures? Scripture reveals that God had a definite purpose when He reached the summit of His creative labors: "God said, Let us make man in our image, after our likeness. . . . So God created man in his own image, in the image of God created he them" (Gen. 1:26–27). Note that man is made *in* God's image, not *as* God's image. There is something in man's constitution that reflects the being and character of God, just as the image in a mirror is the reflection of the one looking into it. So we must look for the image of God in man.

As God's Son Christ alone is "the brightness of his glory and the express image of his person" (Heb. 1:3). This image must be inwardly seen, or perceived by faith: "God, who commanded the light to shine out of darkness, hath shined in our hearts, to give the light of the knowledge of the glory of God in the face of Jesus Christ" (2 Cor. 4:6). John says, "We beheld his glory, the glory of the only begotten of the Father. . . . No man hath seen God at any time; the only begotten Son, which is in the bosom of the Father, he hath declared him" (John 1:14,18).

The human body must be excluded from the image of God in man. God is "a most pure Spirit, invisible, without body, parts, or passions" (Westminster Confession of Faith, 2.1). Nothing physical or visible about man can be part of the image of the invisible, spiritual God. It was crude paganism for Michelangelo to portray the Creator on the ceiling of the Sistine Chapel as a muscular European male with long white hair and a flowing white beard. Man's present body is "of the earth, earthy" (1 Cor. 15:4), taken from the dust of the ground and suited to life on this earth, and nowhere else.

However, when God breathed "the breath of life" into this earthen vessel, "man became a living soul" (Gen. 2:7). There is a human soul, an inward aspect to man's constitution, "the hidden man of the heart" (1 Peter 3:4). The image of God is found in these "inward parts" of man (Ps. 51:6). The New Testament discerns three elements in this image: righteousness, holiness, and knowledge (Eph. 4:24; Col. 3:10).

The phrase "true holiness" (Eph. 4:24) can also be translated as "holiness of truth." The phrase can be extended to include "righteousness." In other words, Paul says that our Creator is renewing His image in us by imparting knowledge of the truth, and that He is using that knowledge to make us righteous or just in our dealings with others and holy in our walk with God.

When man fell into sin, knowledge gave way to ignorance, righteousness to iniquity, and holiness to ungodliness. The Creator had made man "a little lower than the angels" and had crowned him "with glory and honor" (Ps. 8:5), but man by his own act cast himself down into sin, guilt, misery, and shame and cast away his glorious, honorable crown. The good news of the gospel is that fallen man can be cleansed from sin, renewed by grace, and restored to honor.

This renewal proceeds along three lines in a particular order. *First*, we must acquire knowledge of the truth, which is imparted through the preaching of the Word. James directs us to "receive with meekness the engrafted word, which is able to save your souls" (James 1:21); the Word is "engrafted" when it is firmly transplanted into the good soil of a believing heart. In light of this knowledge we must begin to do the will of God, dealing justly with our brothers in Christ and our fellow human beings in general (Ps. 15:1,2). Finally, in thankfulness, we must consecrate ourselves, soul and body, to serving God with loving reverence and godly fear (Rom. 12:1, Heb. 12:28). The ultimate goal is for every Christian to be conformed to the image of Christ, "that he might be the firstborn among many brethren" (Rom. 8:29).

IN

Every Thing

GIVE THANKS

FOR THIS IS

The Will

OF **GOD** IN

Christ Jesus

CONCERNING YOU

1 THESSALONIANS 5:18

INTRODUCTION TO THE BOOK OF 1 THESSALONIANS

Authorship: Paul's authorship of 1 Thessalonians was widely accepted in the early church. Church fathers such as Irenaeus (c. AD 130–200), Clement of Alexandria (c. AD 150–215), and Tertullian (c. AD 160–225) all acknowledged Pauline authorship of 1 Thessalonians. Until the mid-nineteenth century, Pauline authorship was almost unanimously agreed upon. Thessalonica was an important port city in Macedonia and was situated along the *Via Egnatia*, which served as the main Roman road near Asia Minor. Greeks, Romans, and Jews all lived in Thessalonica and idolatry ran rampant throughout the city. Paul had brought the gospel to the people of Thessalonica while on his second missionary journey, along with Silas and Timothy, his missionary colleagues. The events connected with this missionary outreach to Thessalonica are recorded in Acts 17:1–10. At Thessalonica Paul had preached first to the Jews. But they had rejected Paul's evidence to show that Jesus is their Messiah. Wonderfully, however, a large number of Greeks had come to saving faith in Christ. But persecution and civil disturbance had resulted and the Christian converts sent Paul and Silas away by night for their safety. The missionaries then came to Berea, where young Timothy joined them. Now, understandably, Paul was concerned for the converts in Thessalonica. But Timothy was able to report to him that these converts were standing fast in the faith.

Date: It is commonly believed that Paul wrote 1 Thessalonians after Timothy arrived in Corinth, where Paul spent a number of months (AD 51–52). It is likely that Paul wrote this epistle around AD 52.

Theme: Endure suffering.

Purpose: To encourage believers with the hope of Christ's return.

Synopsis: *The Contribution of 1 Thessalonians to Redemptive Revelation*

This epistle is written to make clear to the young church at Thessalonica, Paul's affectionate and heartfelt concern for their spiritual and moral well-being. In the course of his address to them he gives them assurance of their "election of God" (1:4), his appreciation of their evangelistic zeal (v. 8), his gratitude that many have received the gospel as from God (2:13), and many tokens of his love and prayerful concern (3:9–10). In the course of his letter he takes care to vindicate his own motives as a genuine servant of God (2:1–10) and he explains the sad state of the Jewish nation on that date, since they were exposed to the message of the gospel (vv. 14–16). Two clear notes which he weaves into his epistle also are: (1) the great importance to the believer of holiness (4:1–8); and (2) the need to watch and pray so that we may not be "asleep" when our blessed Savior comes to judge the whole world in righteousness (5:1–8). The epistle is notable for the numerous basic exhortations with which it ends (v. 16–22).

This epistle reflects the joy and relief of Paul upon hearing that the Thessalonian believers were standing firm: "For now we live, if ye stand fast in the Lord" (3:8). The apostle does not give detailed theological teaching in this letter, although he does give comforting instruction on the state of believers after death, and of the happiness awaiting believers at the second coming of Christ (4:13–18).

Outline:

I. Greetings (1:1)

II. Paul's Response to the Good Report Concerning the Thessalonians (1:2—3:13)
- A. Grounds for Believing the Faith of His Readers Is Genuine (1:2–10)
- B. Paul's Tenderness, Affection, Sincerity, and Propriety toward Them (2:1–13)
- C. The Sad Condition of the Persecutors (2:14–16)
- D. Paul's Comfort Because They Were Steadfast in Their Faith (2:17—3:10)
- E. Paul's Affectionate Prayer for Them and His Wish to See Them Soon (3:11–13)

III. Paul's Exhortations to the Thessalonian Believers (4:1—5:28)
- A. The Need for Christians to Be Holy (4:1–12)
- B. The Second Coming of Christ (4:13—5:11)
- C. Various Exhortations (5:12–22)
- D. Closing Prayer, Greeting, and Benediction (5:23–28)

THE FIRST EPISTLE OF PAUL THE APOSTLE TO THE

THESSALONIANS

CHAPTER 1

PAUL, and Silvanus, and Timotheus, unto the
church of the Thessalonians *which is* in God the
Father and *in* the Lord Jesus Christ: Grace *be* unto
you, and peace, from God our Father, and the
Lord Jesus Christ.
2 We give thanks to God always for you all,
making mention of you in our prayers;
3 Remembering without ceasing your work of
faith, and labour of love, and patience of hope in
our Lord Jesus Christ, in the sight of God and our
Father;
4 Knowing, brethren beloved, your election of
God.
5 For our gospel came not unto you in word only,
but also in power, and in the Holy Ghost, and in
much assurance; as ye know what manner of men
we were among you for your sake.
6 And ye became followers of us, and of the Lord,
having received the word in much affliction, with
joy of the Holy Ghost:
7 So that ye were ensamples to all that believe in
Macedonia and Achaia.
8 For from you sounded out the word of the
Lord not only in Macedonia and Achaia, but also
in every place your faith to God-ward is spread
abroad; so that we need not to speak any thing.
9 For they themselves shew of us what manner of
entering in we had unto you, and how ye turned
to God from idols to serve the living and true
God;
10 And to wait for his Son from heaven, whom he

Chapter 1: ***Paul expresses his joy as he calls to mind the evidences of a genuine spiritual change in the lives of his readers since they heard Paul's preaching of the gospel to them. He associates this epistle with his fellow laborers who have been with him in this great missionary outreach to northern Greece—Silas and young Timothy. To give the Thessalonians encouragement, Paul informs them that they are clearly among the elect (v. 4), whom God has eternally chosen in Christ.***

GREETINGS (1:1)

1:1 *Paul.* Apostle to the Gentiles. *Silvanus.* Also called Silas, a distinguished member of the church in Jerusalem. When Paul parted with Barnabas over John Mark, Paul chose Silas as his companion in missionary work. *Timotheus.* Or Timothy, son of a Jewish mother and a Gentile father. Timothy was marked out for special service by a divine prophecy (1 Tim. 1:18; 4:16). *The church of the Thessalonians* was only very recently formed, during the visit to that city of Paul, Silas, and Timothy on Paul's second missionary journey (shortly after AD 50). *the church . . . which is in God the Father and in the Lord Jesus Christ.* All true churches are united to God the Father and to Christ by spiritual union and communion.

PAUL'S RESPONSE TO THE GOOD REPORT CONCERNING THE THESSALONIANS (1:2—3:13)

Grounds for Believing the Faith of His Readers Is Genuine (1:2–10)

1:2 Paul, rather than praising the Thessalonians, encourages them by telling them that he *thanks* God for them and also remembers them in his *prayers.*

1:3 The three virtues here are the fruit of the gift of the new birth by the Holy Spirit: *faith, love,* and *hope.* These graces are never inactive, but bring forth God-honoring activity in the soul. Faith produces *work,* love incites to *labour,* and hope teaches us *patience.*

1:4 *election.* God predestines His people to salvation and glory by choosing them in Christ before the beginning of the world. He makes His election infallibly effective in each of His elect people during the course of their life in this world, so that they receive grace to believe the gospel of Christ when they hear it. This is how Paul explains to them the ultimate cause of faith and repentance.

1:5 Paul explains how God's election works: (1) the gospel did not come to these Thessalonian believers *in word only;* (2) but was accompanied by the *power* of the Holy Spirit (*Holy Ghost*); (3) the effect of which was that they were given an inward *assurance* that the gospel is true. Along with this assurance was their realization that Paul was a man of God, bringing the message of heaven to them that they might be eternally saved.

1:6 When people are genuinely converted, they become sincere disciples of those whose gospel message they have received. Two very conflicting experiences must follow them in this life, *affliction* and *joy* inspired by the Holy Spirit.

1:7 *ensamples.* Examples. Christians are examples to other Christians. *Macedonia* was in northern Greece; *Achaia,* in southern Greece. Paul's second missionary journey took him from Philippi in the north to Athens and Corinth in the south (Acts 17:16,18).

1:8 The people of Thessalonica had a consistent and sound faith so that reports of them *spread abroad.*

1:9 *ye turned to God.* The central change in conversion is a new appreciation of God and of the claims of God on one's life.

raised from the dead, *even* Jesus, which delivered
us from the wrath to come.

CHAPTER 2

FOR yourselves, brethren, know our entrance in
unto you, that it was not in vain:
2 But even after that we had suffered before, and
were shamefully entreated, as ye know, at Philippi,
we were bold in our God to speak unto you the
gospel of God with much contention.
3 For our exhortation *was* not of deceit, nor of
uncleanness, nor in guile:
4 But as we were allowed of God to be put in trust
with the gospel, even so we speak; not as pleasing
men, but God, which trieth our hearts.
5 For neither at any time used we flattering
words, as ye know, nor a cloke of covetousness;
God *is* witness:
6 Nor of men sought we glory, neither of you,
nor *yet* of others, when we might have been bur-
densome, as the apostles of Christ.
7 But we were gentle among you, even as a nurse
cherisheth her children:
8 So being affectionately desirous of you, we were
willing to have imparted unto you, not the gospel
of God only, but also our own souls, because ye
were dear unto us.
9 For ye remember, brethren, our labour and
travail: for labouring night and day, because we
would not be chargeable unto any of you, we
preached unto you the gospel of God.
10 Ye *are* witnesses, and God *also*, how holily and
justly and unblameably we behaved ourselves
among you that believe:
11 As ye know how we exhorted and comforted
and charged every one of you, as a father *doth* his
children,
12 That ye would walk worthy of God, who hath
called you unto his kingdom and glory.
13 For this cause also thank we God without
ceasing, because, when ye received the word of
God which ye heard of us, ye received *it* not *as*
the word of men, but as it is in truth, the word of

True religion is not a mere creed but a new lifestyle of which God Himself is the center.

1:10 The sincere believer is content to suffer many evils in this life since he is persuaded that Christ will return. The guarantee of Christ's second coming is His resurrection (1 Cor. 15). The Greek word translated *delivered* is in the present tense. Christ has by His blessed death atoned for sins; when He returns at the end of time He will rescue His people from all sorrow and misery. He is delivering His people by His heavenly intercession and by the supplies of daily grace.

Thoughts for Personal/Family Worship: Chapter 1

1. **When we understand the Bible's teachings aright, we see that coming by faith to Christ could never happen as a result of our own free will. True faith is God-given and therefore, if we are believers, we should thank God that He has given us the ability to come to Jesus and to believe in Him, as Paul here shows (v. 4).**
2. **It cannot be too strongly noted that the only evidence of a person's being one of God's elect is when they live a godly life and so bring forth the fruits of righteousness. Election makes men saints, not mere religious talkers, or learned hypocrites, or adherents to some religious group.**

Chapter 2: *Paul, as a minister to the Thessalonians, expresses his deep affection for his hearers. When the gospel is believed, Paul rejoices. When it is rejected, he sorrows. Paul's joy is to hear of his people's progress in grace. The joy, in spite of all Satan's malice, will be consummated at last when Christ returns.*

Paul's Tenderness, Affection, Sincerity, and Propriety toward Them (2:1–13)

2:1–13 Here Paul makes clear that his motives in preaching to them were sincere and not driven by self-interest. This is an important section since it teaches all Christians to examine their motives.

2:1 *entrance in unto you.* Coming to you. Paul's ministry among the Thessalonians was not *vain*, even as the fruit of his ministry helped to verify.

2:2 *entreated.* Treated. He has recently come to them from the neighboring city of *Philippi*, where he and Silas had suffered very rough and unworthy treatment. Such treatment made Paul *bold.*

2:3 Paul says he is free from these three evils: *deceit*, by which men preach a false gospel; *uncleanness*, by which some religious leaders bring disgrace on themselves; and *guile*, by which some speak sweet words with an ulterior motive.

2:4 In the last resort a man's true character is best seen in this light: does he aim to please men, or God?

2:5 Paul reveals the purity of his preaching. *flattering words.* Words that seek to unduly puff people up. *cloke.* Cloak, an outward show to cover inner evil. *covetousness.* Seeking for greedy gain and profit, being a lover of material possessions or wealth.

2:6 Moreover, he has not sought *glory*, which is human praise to enhance his own reputation, nor has he loaded his disciples with *burdensome* expenses, so making his ministry a means to get rich.

2:7 Paul had not been troublesome but extremely tender with his young converts.

2:8 *imparted unto you . . . our own souls.* Paul and his colleagues were willing to lose their life to bring the gospel to the Thessalonians. *dear unto us.* Paul had great love for the Thessalonians.

2:9 With God-given zeal for their good, Paul had worked *night and day* to avoid being in any way burdensome to these young converts.

2:10 His conduct was in every way above reproach and the people of Thessalonica were *witnesses* with *God* concerning Paul's purity.

2:11 *exhorted and comforted and charged.* Paul's words were affectionately spoken as a *father* speaks to his children.

2:12 *walk worthy of God.* The Christian life consists of daily conduct fitting and honoring to our Lord. Christians are called to participate in Christ's *kingdom* and His *glory*.

2:13 Nothing is to be preached but what is consistent with the Bible, which alone is God's holy and infallible Word. The duty of the congregation is to receive God's Word into their hearts and minds. The effect will be a gradual alteration

God, which effectually worketh also in you that
believe.
14 For ye, brethren, became followers of the
churches of God which in Judæa are in Christ
Jesus: for ye also have suffered like things of your
own countrymen, even as they *have* of the Jews:
15 Who both killed the Lord Jesus, and their own
prophets, and have persecuted us; and they please
not God, and are contrary to all men:
16 Forbidding us to speak to the Gentiles that
they might be saved, to fill up their sins alway: for
the wrath is come upon them to the uttermost.
17 But we, brethren, being taken from you for a
short time in presence, not in heart, endeavoured
the more abundantly to see your face with great
desire.
18 Wherefore we would have come unto you,
even I Paul, once and again; but Satan hindered us.
19 For what *is* our hope, or joy, or crown of re-
joicing? *Are* not even ye in the presence of our
Lord Jesus Christ at his coming?
20 For ye are our glory and joy.

CHAPTER 3

WHEREFORE when we could no longer forbear, we
thought it good to be left at Athens alone;
2 And sent Timotheus, our brother, and minister
of God, and our fellowlabourer in the gospel
of Christ, to establish you, and to comfort you
concerning your faith:
3 That no man should be moved by these afflic-
tions: for yourselves know that we are appointed
thereunto.
4 For verily, when we were with you, we told you
before that we should suffer tribulation; even as it
came to pass, and ye know.
5 For this cause, when I could no longer forbear,
I sent to know your faith, lest by some means the
tempter have tempted you, and our labour be in
vain.
6 But now when Timotheus came from you unto
us, and brought us good tidings of your faith and
charity, and that ye have good remembrance of
us always, desiring greatly to see us, as we also *to
see* you:

---

for good in their lives, because God's Word is both true and powerful.

The Sad Condition of the Persecutors (2:14–16)

2:14–16 In this section Paul explains the sad truth to them that unbelievers, whether Jews or Gentiles, are opposed to the truth of God. He explains this at great length in Rom. 9–11, where he shows that the Jews, the Old Testament people of God, have for a time fallen into unbelief, until at some future date God removes the veil from their heart (2 Cor. 3:15–16), and the Jewish people are grafted into the church again (Rom. 11:23–27).

2:14 As the Christians in *Judaea* were being persecuted by the unbelieving *Jews*, so now were the Thessalonians being persecuted by their unbelieving *countrymen*. Unbelief in all nations produces the same dead fruit of unkindness and enmity.

2:15 Unbelief produces enmity against the Lord's people, even as it resulted in the death of *the Lord Jesus* and the *prophets* before them. Persecution ought to be expected. *contrary to all men.* The unbelieving Jews refused to allow the gospel to be openly preached to the Gentiles.

2:16 Sadly, unbelief was now moving the Jews who were living in Greece to attempt to stop the preaching of the gospel, by which the Gentiles could be saved. The anger of God against the wicked was shortly to reach a terrible climax, either in this world, or in the world to come.

Paul's Comfort Because They Were Steadfast in Their Faith (2:17—3:10)

2:17–20 Here Paul assures the believers in Thessalonica that he longs to see them face-to-face, though he has not been able to do so thus far, in spite of repeated attempts.

2:17 Christian love draws *brethren* together.

2:18 *Satan hindered* many a noble desire on the part of God's people, but is ultimately subservient to the power and authority of Christ.

2:19–20 Godly preachers long for the good of their congregations and look forward to eternal happiness with them and with Christ Himself at His second coming.

Thoughts for Personal/Family Worship: Chapter 2

1. **Contrary to what we often think, affliction produces greater confidence and boldness in the people of God (v. 2). If it is viewed rightly, affliction takes our confidence away from ourselves and other people, and settles it on the gospel and God alone.**
2. **Tenderness for the Lord's people is one of the characteristics of a spiritual preacher. Paul uses the pictures of a nurse (v. 7) and a father (v. 11). How do both kinds of love form a good soil for spiritual growth?**

Chapter 3: *Paul, being unable to go himself to see the Thessalonian believers, explains that he sent Timothy to see them instead. He movingly explains how Timothy's report of their steadfastness in the faith had brought him deep comfort. So much of Paul's life is bound up with theirs that he prays for them day and night. He yearns to see them, urges them to show love one to another and to look forward to the day when they will be perfectly holy and blameless.*

3:1–10 Though Paul had to be away from the Thessalonian believers in their trial of suffering he was profoundly concerned for them all the time. The good report which Timothy brought back of their steadfast faith gave exquisite comfort to the apostle, whose longing and constant prayer was for their good.

3:1 *We* here is an epistolary plural, meaning Paul is politely referring to himself.

3:2 Paul's affection for Timothy, who was many years his junior, is an example to older believers as to how to think of their younger brothers and sisters.

3:3–4 Suffering sometimes moves people to become less earnest in their Christian faith. But suffering is *appointed* by God for His people to share in the sufferings of Christ (Col. 1:24). Paul says that Christians *should suffer tribulation* in this world and should not be surprised by this experience. *verily*. Truly.

3:5 Paul expresses genuine concern and interest in the *faith* of the Christians at Thessalonica in case *the tempter*, that is Satan, had *tempted* them and they had fallen from the faith. Paul's ministerial aim was to cultivate faith lest his *labour be in vain*.

3:6 Paul's fear had been in vain. The Thessalonian believers, as Timothy reported to him in Athens, were full of *faith* in the gospel and *charity* (love).

7 Therefore, brethren, we were comforted over
you in all our affliction and distress by your faith:
8 For now we live, if ye stand fast in the Lord.
9 For what thanks can we render to God again
for you, for all the joy wherewith we joy for your
sakes before our God;
10 Night and day praying exceedingly that we
might see your face, and might perfect that which
is lacking in your faith?
11 Now God himself and our Father, and our
Lord Jesus Christ, direct our way unto you.
12 And the Lord make you to increase and
abound in love one toward another, and toward
all *men*, even as we *do* toward you:
13 To the end he may stablish your hearts
unblameable in holiness before God, even our
Father, at the coming of our Lord Jesus Christ
with all his saints.

CHAPTER 4

FURTHERMORE then we beseech you, brethren,
and exhort *you* by the Lord Jesus, that as ye have
received of us how ye ought to walk and to please
God, *so* ye would abound more and more.
2 For ye know what commandments we gave you
by the Lord Jesus.
3 For this is the will of God, *even* your sanctifica-
tion, that ye should abstain from fornication:
4 That every one of you should know how to
possess his vessel in sanctification and honour;
5 Not in the lust of concupiscence, even as the
Gentiles which know not God:
6 That no *man* go beyond and defraud his
brother in *any* matter: because that the Lord *is* the
avenger of all such, as we also have forewarned
you and testified.
7 For God hath not called us unto uncleanness,
but unto holiness.
8 He therefore that despiseth, despiseth not man,
but God, who hath also given unto us his holy
Spirit.
9 But as touching brotherly love ye need not that
I write unto you: for ye yourselves are taught of
God to love one another.
10 And indeed ye do it toward all the brethren
which are in all Macedonia: but we beseech you,
brethren, that ye increase more and more;
11 And that ye study to be quiet, and to do your
own business, and to work with your own hands,
as we commanded you;
12 That ye may walk honestly toward them that
are without, and *that* ye may have lack of nothing.
13 But I would not have you to be ignorant,

3:7–8 Paul's ministry was wrapped up in the life of the Thessalonian believers and his encouragement was dependent on their response.

3:9–10 Paul hears and rejoices in the report of the Thessalonian believers and expresses his *thanks* to God.

Paul's Affectionate Prayer for Them and His Wish to See Them Soon (3:11–13)

3:11–13 Once again Paul prays for the good of the Thessalonian believers that God would *increase* their *love* and that they would be *unblameable in holiness before God.* Despite the good report, the Thessalonians can still grow in grace.

Thoughts for Personal/Family Worship: Chapter 3

1. **People in the pew do not always understand how great a burden their ministers carry day and night for their eternal good. Spend a little time praying for your ministers and elders that God would give them patience, endurance, and wisdom in shepherding the flock of Christ.**
2. **It is an encouraging thing for Christians to meditate on the return of Christ and the grace and glory He will usher in. Believers must always have one eye on the great day when our Lord will return and His people will be eternally at peace. At the same time, we must not forget that we live in this world and thus must await the return of Christ.**

PAUL'S EXHORTATIONS TO THE THESSALONIAN BELIEVERS (4:1—5:28)

Chapter 4: ***Two main subjects are handled here by the apostle: (1) The great importance of holiness in the life of a Christian (vv. 1–12); and (2) the comfort we are entitled to have over the blessed dead, who are safe with Christ in death and who will be honored by Him at His second coming (vv. 13–18).***

The Need for Christians to Be Holy (4:1–12)

4:1–12 The proper behavior for Christians is to study to be obedient to God's holy will. This means, negatively, to avoid lust and sensual pleasure; and, positively, to love our neighbor as ourselves.

4:1 The Christian life is one of continual growth in grace and sanctification. Conversion is the beginning of the Christian life and Christians are to *abound more and more.* The Christian life is a *walk* (see note at 2:12).

4:2 The Christian is not saved by keeping God's *commandments*, but he is to keep them out of duty and gratitude to God.

4:3 Justification is a one time act where God declares an individual to be righteous. *Sanctification* is a work and process. It includes both abstaining from sin and living a holy life.

4:4 *Possess his vessel* is a reference to the body, which the believer should keep clean of sexual misconduct of all kinds.

4:5 *concupiscence.* Strong desire driven by lust. It begins in the heart when the eye sees some unlawful pleasure and seeks by crafty means to enjoy it.

4:6 Christians must not *defraud* their fellow believers in anything. If they do, God will avenge the ones who were defrauded.

4:8–9 He who *despiseth* a fellow Christian *despiseth* God. The *Holy Spirit* has been given to believers that they might dwell in *brotherly love*.

4:11–12 The work ethic of the gospel is that Christians are to live *quiet* and tend to their own *business* while working with their own *hands*. Christianity does not alleviate a Christian from living a normal life of work and private dealings. *without.* Outside (the church).

The Second Coming of Christ (4:13—5:11)

4:13–18 Paul reveals how Christians who have died ought to be regarded when Christ returns.

4:13 *ignorant.* Not knowing or naïve. This ignorance of men's state after death is a great source of discouragement for many people. There is no need to fall into excessive grief

brethren, concerning them which are asleep, that
ye sorrow not, even as others which have no hope.
14 For if we believe that Jesus died and rose again,
even so them also which sleep in Jesus will God
bring with him.
15 For this we say unto you by the word of the
Lord, that we which are alive *and* remain unto the
coming of the Lord shall not prevent them which
are asleep.
16 For the Lord himself shall descend from
heaven with a shout, with the voice of the archan-
gel, and with the trump of God: and the dead in
Christ shall rise first:
17 Then we which are alive *and* remain shall be
caught up together with them in the clouds, to
meet the Lord in the air: and so shall we ever be
with the Lord.
18 Wherefore comfort one another with these
words.

CHAPTER 5

BUT of the times and the seasons, brethren, ye
have no need that I write unto you.
2 For yourselves know perfectly that the day of
the Lord so cometh as a thief in the night.
3 For when they shall say, Peace and safety; then
sudden destruction cometh upon them, as travail
upon a woman with child; and they shall not
escape.
4 But ye, brethren, are not in darkness, that that
day should overtake you as a thief.
5 Ye are all the children of light, and the chil-
dren of the day: we are not of the night, nor of
darkness.
6 Therefore let us not sleep, as *do* others; but let
us watch and be sober.
7 For they that sleep sleep in the night; and they
that be drunken are drunken in the night.
8 But let us, who are of the day, be sober, putting
on the breastplate of faith and love; and for an
helmet, the hope of salvation.
9 For God hath not appointed us to wrath, but to
obtain salvation by our Lord Jesus Christ,
10 Who died for us, that, whether we wake or
sleep, we should live together with him.
11 Wherefore comfort yourselves together, and
edify one another, even as also ye do.
12 And we beseech you, brethren, to know them
which labour among you, and are over you in the
Lord, and admonish you;
13 And to esteem them very highly in love
for their work's sake. *And* be at peace among
yourselves.
14 Now we exhort you, brethren, warn them that
are unruly, comfort the feebleminded, support

when a believer dies, though grief is inevitable, the nature of mortality, and a consequence of sin (Acts 8:2).

4:14 Death for the godly is like *sleep* because their bodies await the resurrection while their souls are well and in heaven with Christ. At the second coming of Christ, the blessed dead will receive their bodies back in a renewed and glorified state (1 Cor. 15:42–44,51–57).

4:15 With the *coming of the Lord* believers who *are asleep* will be at no disadvantage compared with those who *remain*, or are alive. The living will not go into glory ahead of those who have experienced death. *prevent*. Go before.

4:16 Christ's return will be supernatural, public, awesome, and visible—not a secret or quiet event. *trump*. Trumpet call.

4:17 There will be an order: (1) resurrected believers will ascend first; (2) then believers who have not entered into a state of death will ascend next. In this way all Christians will together *meet the Lord in the air* and will *ever be with the Lord*.

4:18 Christ's bodily descent and the future resurrection of believers is a source of *comfort* for the church, and believers are commanded to *comfort* one another *with these words*.

Thoughts for Personal/Family Worship: Chapter 4

1. **Sanctification involves careful obedience to the Ten Commandments, a number of which are addressed in this chapter. When we are saved by grace, we do not leave behind the commandments of God. On the contrary, we find the power to keep them in love.**
2. **Believers sorrow when their Christian brothers and sisters die, but their sorrow is mingled with comfort to know they shall soon be with them again forever, when Christ returns. When you look back on the deaths of loved ones, or look forward to future deaths, keep one eye on Christ's coming, and you will find comfort.**

Chapter 5: ***There are two parts to this chapter: (1) Further teaching on the second coming (vv. 1–11); (2) a variety of exhortations and the final greeting at the end of the epistle (vv. 12–28).***

5:1–2 *of the times and the seasons*. Referring to the coming of Christ and the resurrection of the dead. *as a thief in the night*. Christ's coming will be sudden and public though there are "signs of the times" (Matt. 16:3; Mark 13).

5:3 Christ's sudden coming will bring in a *sudden destruction* of the unbelieving of this world, who *shall not escape*. *travail*. Childbirth.

5:4–6 During their lives, believers are prepared for the coming of Christ, being enlightened by God to know and believe His Word of warning. Christians are to live each day so as not to be ashamed when the trumpet of God's judgment finally sounds. *watch and be sober*. Believers are to earnestly yet patiently wait for Christ's coming.

5:7 The unbelievers of this world *sleep* (spiritually and morally), living, as they characteristically do, in a condition of men who are dead to God and unaware of the punishment to be visited on them for their sinful ways.

5:8–11 On the other hand, believers should live filled with faith, hope, and love since they are saved by Christ's blood and are therefore fitted for heaven, whether they live or die (Phil. 1:20–21).

Various Exhortations (5:12–22)

5:12–13 *we beseech you*. This is Paul's final exhortation in this closing chapter of the epistle. His words mean that church members should highly value (*know*) those who *labour among* them—faithful elders and deacons.

5:14 The *brethren* are to work and function in such a manner that those struggling Christians ought to be borne up with

the weak, be patient toward all *men.*
15 See that none render evil for evil unto any
man; but ever follow that which is good, both
among yourselves, and to all *men.*
16 Rejoice evermore.
17 Pray without ceasing.
18 In every thing give thanks: for this is the will of
God in Christ Jesus concerning you.
19 Quench not the Spirit.
20 Despise not prophesyings.
21 Prove all things; hold fast that which is good.
22 Abstain from all appearance of evil.
23 And the very God of peace sanctify you
wholly; and *I pray God* your whole spirit and soul
and body be preserved blameless unto the coming
of our Lord Jesus Christ.
24 Faithful *is* he that calleth you, who also will do
it.
25 Brethren, pray for us.
26 Greet all the brethren with an holy kiss.
27 I charge you by the Lord that this epistle be
read unto all the holy brethren.
28 The grace of our Lord Jesus Christ *be* with you.
Amen.

---

patience and meekness. *Warn . . . comfort . . . support . . . be patient.* Different struggles and weaknesses deserve different responses from a faithful congregation. *unruly.* Disorderly.

5:15 Even toward *all men* believers are to conduct themselves in a goodly manner.

5:16 *Rejoice.* Joy is a fruit of the Spirit, and rejoicing is a duty of the believer.

5:17 *without ceasing.* This does not mean believers are to be in a constant state of prayer, but rather that in every circumstance and personal disposition, Christians are to *pray.*

5:18 *In every thing give thanks.* One does not wish for sufferings and difficulties, but the command is to give thanks *in* every situation that they encounter.

5:19 *Quench.* Stop or extinguish. Christians must not discourage their ministers by failing to value their preaching; and they ought not, through neglect or carelessness, to allow their own God-given gift of prayer, or edifying conversation, or zeal, to decline for want of spirituality.

5:20 *Prophesyings* refer to expositions of God's Word in preaching.

5:21 *Prove.* Discriminate between what is sound and unsound doctrine and practice. *hold fast.* Listen to, obey, or cherish those things that are good.

5:22 *appearance of evil.* The believer is to keep away from anything that has the hint or scent of sin in it.

Closing Prayer, Greeting, and Benediction (5:23–28)

5:23 *spirit and soul and body.* The total constitution of man. This is a way of speaking in which every faculty and every aspect of your being should be seen to be in view. *Soul* and *spirit* are not different elements but essentially refer to the same thing.

5:24 God will bring all His saints to a state of perfect holiness at last.

5:25 *pray for us.* Even Paul valued people's prayers.

5:26 *holy kiss.* This form of greeting is not required, but shows a common greeting of Paul's day as a means of welcoming the *brethren*, all people in the congregation.

5:27 *charge.* Put under oath, solemnly require. *be read unto all the holy brethren.* Paul's epistles were often to be shared and read to the different congregations. The reading and studying of God's Word is valuable for the Lord's people.

Thoughts for Personal/Family Worship: Chapter 5

1. **Believers have the sure and blessed hope of heaven forever. Therefore, seek by God's grace to live for the glory of our great Lord and Savior. Do not be seduced by the glitter and glamor of this world, for God will take it away in a moment.**
2. **The unconverted are like men who are asleep on an express train soon to plunge into an ocean of fire and misery. Should they not be warned and told of the God who sent His Son to die for lost sinners? Let us speak the gospel to our family and neighbors, and support the gospel preaching of our ministers and missionaries with encouragement, prayer, and financial gifts.**
3. **God is in this life sanctifying His people through His Word of truth. Therefore let us be those who value the Bible as our greatest earthly treasure.**

INTRODUCTION TO THE BOOK OF

2 THESSALONIANS

Authorship: The author of this epistle identifies himself as Paul (1:1; 3:17). The early church and biblical scholarship throughout most of history have held to its Pauline authorship. Some modern scholars have argued that 1 and 2 Thessalonians present different theological perspectives on the end times, and therefore Paul wrote the first but not the second epistle. Some scholars also identify the "man of sin" (2:3) with the legend of the return of Nero from the dead (*Nero redivivus*), which arose after Paul had died. Neither of these arguments warrants the conclusion that Paul is not the author. *First*, the teachings of both epistles on the coming of Christ are quite compatible. *Second*, the idea of an antichrist goes back at least to the prophet Daniel (Dan. 11:36). It would be remarkably hypocritical for the author to write severely against deception and lies (2 Thess. 2:3,9–12) and to commend "the love of the truth" (v. 10) if he were presenting himself under a false name. The best reading of the epistle is that it was written by "Paul," the apostle closely associated with Silvanus (or Silas) and Timotheus (or Timothy) (1:1; Acts 15:40; 16:1–3; 2 Cor. 1:1,19)—the same three persons mentioned in the opening of 1 Thessalonians.

Date: Though a few scholars have argued that 2 Thessalonians came before what we call 1 Thessalonians, they have no definitive proof. Paul writes of an "epistle" he previously sent to this church (2:15), which most likely refers to 1 Thessalonians. It appears that 2 Thessalonians was written several months after 1 Thessalonians (see Introduction to 1 Thessalonians), during Paul's second missionary journey. He probably wrote from Corinth where Silas and Timothy had joined him (Acts 18:1,5).

Theme: The coming judgment against those who persecute the glorious saints of Christ.

Purpose: To balance the expectations in the church about the end times, revealing that Christ's coming has not yet happened, but when it does, He will come with judgment and glory.

Synopsis: *The Contribution of 2 Thessalonians to Redemptive Revelation*

This is a short epistle but it contains very important teaching, both theological and practical. Its burden is to correct a misunderstanding that had evidently been reported to Paul as having harmfully influenced the faith of the Thessalonian believers. The error Paul corrects is the mistaken idea that Christ's second coming was just moments away (2:1). Before Christ returns, he says, there must be revealed a notable enemy of God on the stage of history called "that man of sin" (v. 3). Evidently some of the church members at Thessalonica had been so influenced by the expectation of an immediate coming of Christ that they were not working to support themselves and their families. Paul denounces this as utterly immoral. He lays down the healthy principle that if any do not work, neither should they eat (v. 10). If a church member does not work, he is choosing to starve. Then he should be judged "disorderly" (v. 11). Such persons should be made to feel "ashamed" (v. 14).

Outline:

I. Salutation: Grace and Peace (1:1–2)
II. Courage for Suffering Saints (1:3–12)
  A. Thanksgiving for Faith, Love, and Endurance (1:3–4)
  B. Judgment on Persecutors and Glory for Saints (1:5–10)
  C. Prayer for Power and Glory (1:11–12)
III. Correction of Mistaken End-Times Expectations (2:1–12)

   - A. The False Report of the Day of Christ (2:1–2)
   - B. The Rise and Destruction of the Man of Sin (2:3–12)

IV. Confidence in Salvation and Call to Prayer (2:13—3:5)

   - A. Thanksgiving and Exhortation to Elect Saints (2:13–15)
   - B. Prayer for Comfort and Strength (2:16–17)
   - C. Request for Prayer for the Mission (3:1–2)
   - D. Assurance and Prayer for Endurance (3:3–5)
   - E. Command to Discipline Disorderly Brothers (3:6–15)

V. Farewell: Peace and Grace (3:16–18)

THE SECOND EPISTLE OF PAUL THE APOSTLE TO THE

THESSALONIANS

CHAPTER 1

PAUL, and Silvanus, and Timotheus, unto the
church of the Thessalonians in God our Father
and the Lord Jesus Christ:
2 Grace unto you, and peace, from God our
Father and the Lord Jesus Christ.
3 We are bound to thank God always for you,
brethren, as it is meet, because that your faith
groweth exceedingly, and the charity of every one
of you all toward each other aboundeth;
4 So that we ourselves glory in you in the
churches of God for your patience and faith in all
your persecutions and tribulations that ye endure:
5 *Which is* a manifest token of the righteous
judgment of God, that ye may be counted worthy
of the kingdom of God, for which ye also suffer:
6 Seeing *it is* a righteous thing with God to rec-
ompense tribulation to them that trouble you;
7 And to you who are troubled rest with us, when
the Lord Jesus shall be revealed from heaven with
his mighty angels,
8 In flaming fire taking vengeance on them that
know not God, and that obey not the gospel of
our Lord Jesus Christ:
9 Who shall be punished with everlasting
destruction from the presence of the Lord, and
from the glory of his power;
10 When he shall come to be glorified in his

Chapter 1: ***God's people experience persecution in this life and it is their duty to be steadfast. Paul reminds them that God's vengeance will be heavy on all who mistreat His people. Christians are to have their eyes focused on that day when their Savior will return. Meanwhile they are to seek to live lives that are to the glory of God here and now in this present life.***

SALUTATION: GRACE AND PEACE (1:1–2)

1:1 *Paul, and Silvanus, and Timotheus*. The apostle Paul and his beloved colleagues Silas (Acts 15:22–40; 16:25,29; 17:10–15; 18:5; 2 Cor. 1:19; 1 Thess. 1:1), and Timothy (Acts 16:1; 17:14–15; 18:5; 19:22; 20:4). *in God our Father and the Lord Jesus Christ*. The *church* is in spiritual union with the Father and Son (1 John 1:3).

1:2 *Grace . . . and peace*. Paul's usual greeting to a church, wishing believers a growing experience of God's undeserved kindness (*grace*) and harmony in relationship with God and each other (*peace*). The blessings of salvation come from both the *Father* and *Christ*, for both possess full deity. Verses 1–2 are almost identical in Greek to 1 Thess. 1:1.

COURAGE FOR SUFFERING SAINTS (1:3–12)

Thanksgiving for Faith, Love, and Endurance (1:3–4)

1:3 *bound*. It is our obligation and duty to thank God for His grace in His people, for He is the author of both conversion and perseverance (2:13–14; 1 Thess. 1:3–5; 2:13; 5:23–24). *brethren*. Brothers in Christ (including Christian women and girls). *meet*. Fitting. *charity*. Love. Faith, love, and enduring hope (v. 4) are three primary fruits of true Christianity (1 Cor. 13:13; Gal. 5:5–6; Eph. 1:15,18; Col. 1:4–5; 1 Thess. 1:3; 5:8; 2 Tim. 1:12–13).

1:4 *glory*. Boast. *tribulations*. Pressures, troubles (Acts 14:22). *patience*. Endurance under difficulty. Paul encouraged these suffering saints, whose exemplary conduct under persecution is an inspiring model for all other *churches* (1 Thess. 1:6–7).

Judgment on Persecutors and Glory for Saints (1:5–10)

1:5 *manifest token*. Their endurance of persecution and perseverance in faith (v. 4) was visible evidence or proof that God, the *righteous* Judge, counted them righteous and would vindicate them and punish their persecutors (Phil. 1:28). Their courage showed God was with them. *counted worthy*. Honored as true citizens of God's *kingdom* (Luke 20:35; 21:36; Acts 5:41).

1:6–7 *recompense tribulation*. Pay back with painful trouble, an act of divine justice (*righteous thing with God*) when He avenges His people (Rom. 2:6–11; 12:19). *rest*. The freedom from sorrow that Christ will give the whole church (*with us*) when He returns (Isa. 25:8). *revealed from heaven*. His glory will appear visibly in the sky (Matt. 24:30; Acts 1:9–11). This is the hope of the church (1 Cor. 1:7; 1 Peter 1:5,7; 4:13; 5:1). *his mighty angels*. The heavenly servants of Christ who will execute His divine judgment (Matt. 13:39,41,49; 16:27; 24:31; 25:31).

1:8 *flaming fire*. Image of the powerful anger of God the Judge, inflicting pain on the wicked (Deut. 32:22; Isa. 66:15; Dan. 7:9–10; Matt. 13:42,50; 25:41). *them that know not God*. The pagan Gentiles (Jer. 10:25; 1 Cor. 1:21; Gal. 4:8; 1 Thess. 4:5). *obey not the gospel*. The gospel requires submission to the Word of God (Rom. 1:5; 6:17).

1:9 *destruction*. Not annihilation, but ruin or desolation (1 Cor. 5:5; cf. Ezek. 6:14; 14:16, Greek Septuagint translation). The punishment of the wicked will be *everlasting*, conscious suffering in hell (Matt. 25:46; Rev. 14:11). *from the presence of the Lord, and from the glory of his power*. Paul cited Isa. 2:10,19,21 (from the Greek Septuagint), implying that Christ is the Lord God.

1:10 *glorified in his saints*. Worshiped by His people as their glory and joy, as He is in heaven (Ps. 89:5–7,15–17). *admired*. Marveled; believers will be amazed at Christ's majesty. *that day*. The day of the Lord (Isa. 2:11–12,17), when Christ returns to judge (2:2; Rom. 2:5,16; 13:12; 1 Cor. 1:8; 3:13; 5:5; 2 Cor. 1:14;

saints, and to be admired in all them that believe
(because our testimony among you was believed)
in that day.
11 Wherefore also we pray always for you, that
our God would count you worthy of *this* calling,
and fulfil all the good pleasure of *his* goodness,
and the work of faith with power:
12 That the name of our Lord Jesus Christ may be
glorified in you, and ye in him, according to the
grace of our God and the Lord Jesus Christ.

CHAPTER 2

NOW we beseech you, brethren, by the coming
of our Lord Jesus Christ, and *by* our gathering
together unto him,
2 That ye be not soon shaken in mind, or be trou-
bled, neither by spirit, nor by word, nor by letter
as from us, as that the day of Christ is at hand.
3 Let no man deceive you by any means: for *that*
day shall not come, except there come a falling
away first, and that man of sin be revealed, the
son of perdition;
4 Who opposeth and exalteth himself above all
that is called God, or that is worshipped; so that
he as God sitteth in the temple of God, shewing
himself that he is God.
5 Remember ye not, that, when I was yet with
you, I told you these things?
6 And now ye know what withholdeth that he
might be revealed in his time.
7 For the mystery of iniquity doth already work:
only he who now letteth *will let*, until he be taken
out of the way.
8 And then shall that Wicked be revealed, whom
the Lord shall consume with the spirit of his
mouth, and shall destroy with the brightness of
his coming:
9 *Even him*, whose coming is after the working of
Satan with all power and signs and lying wonders,

Eph. 4:30; Phil. 1:6,10; 2:16; 1 Thess. 5:1–8; 2 Tim. 1:12,18; 4:8).

Prayer for Power and Glory (1:11–12)

1:11–12 *Wherefore also we pray.* The proper response to news of persecution is prayer for the persecuted church, but prayer driven by hope in Christ's coming to judge. *count you worthy.* Honor you (1 Tim. 5:17; Heb. 3:3), similar verb as that used in v. 5. *calling.* God's call that saves sinners and brings them to glory (2:14; 1 Thess. 2:12). *fulfil all the good pleasure of his goodness.* Use His *power* to bring every good purpose in their souls to produce many good works (*his* is not in the Greek). *work of faith.* The obedient service produced through their trust in Christ (1 Thess. 1:3). God is at work in the believer during this life even in the midst of persecutions, sanctifying him and so preparing him for future glory with Christ. *glorified in you.* See note at v. 10. *ye in him.* Christians will be glorified with Christ, sharing in His resurrection immortality and splendor (Rom. 8:17–18; 1 Cor. 15:42–57; Phil. 3:20–21)

Thoughts for Personal/Family Worship: Chapter 1

1. **The best Christians are sometimes those who are suffering the worst persecution. We should pray daily for our brothers and sisters in lands that are hostile to the gospel. Use missionary newsletters, websites, maps, and other tools to pray intelligently for the persecuted church.**
2. **We are not to avenge ourselves on those who do us harm, but we are ever to keep in mind the truth that God will take vengeance on those who do us any injury because of our faith. This is the key to freedom from bitterness: trusting that God's justice will prevail. How have you suffered for Christ? How does this truth help you?**
3. **It is not a kindness in our preaching to the unconverted, to keep from them the fearful reality of hell, with its "flaming fire" (v. 8) and its "everlasting destruction" (v. 9). Pray for preachers that they would boldly preach both law and gospel, both hell and heaven.**

Chapter 2: ***The coming Man of Sin will do great harm to those deceived by his false religion, but he cannot deceive God's elect, whom God saves by the Word and Spirit.***

CORRECTION OF MISTAKEN END-TIMES EXPECTATIONS (2:1–12)

The False Report of the Day of Christ (2:1–2)

2:1 *beseech.* Ask, request. *coming.* Greek *parousia*, a key term used for the return of Christ (v. 8; Matt. 24:3,27,37,39; 1 Cor. 15:23; 1 Thess. 2:19; 3:13; 4:15; 5:23; James 5:7–8; 2 Peter 1:16; 3:4,12; 1 John 2:28). *our gathering together unto him.* Christ used the same verbal root to refer to the gathering of the elect to Him at His return (Matt. 24:31; Mark 13:27).

2:2 *letter as from us.* The church should reject letters falsely pretending to be from apostles. *day of Christ.* See note at 1:10. False teaching had confused the church into thinking that the day of the Lord was already present or at least about to begin (*is at hand*).

The Rise and Destruction of the Man of Sin (2:3–12)

2:3 *except there come . . . first.* Certain events would arise on the stage of history prior to the second coming and the gathering of the church to Christ (v. 1). *falling away.* Apostasy in the visible church, mass abandonment of truth and godliness (Matt. 24:10–13). *man of sin.* Semitic expression for a man who epitomizes sin (cf. 1 Sam. 25:25). Other texts warn of "false christs" and "antichrists" as present and future dangers (Matt. 24:24; 1 John 2:18,22; 4:3; 2 John 7). *revealed.* An implicit comparison to Christ's revelation in glory (1:7; also vv. 6,8). *son of perdition.* Person doomed to eternal destruction (John 17:12).

2:4 *exalteth himself.* The public enemy of the Lord who seeks to take His place (Dan. 7:25; 11:36–37). *as God sitteth in the temple.* He will defile religion with his idolatry and rule it with usurped authority, as Antiochus Epiphanes (d. 164 BC) did to the temple in Jerusalem (Dan. 8:11–12,25). The church is the new covenant temple (1 Cor. 3:16; 2 Cor. 6:16; Eph. 2:21).

2:6 *what withholdeth.* In Paul's day a power stood in the way of the Man of Sin so that his appearance would be delayed until God's time came for him. This power is described with a neuter word (*what*) here, but with the masculine (*he*) in v. 7.

2:7 *mystery of iniquity.* Principle of rebellion against God's law presently active in the world (Rom. 8:7; 1 John 3:4,8), but not yet revealed (*mystery*) in its full significance. *letteth . . . let.* Hinders . . . hinder—same word as "withholdeth" (v. 6).

2:8 *that Wicked.* The lawless one, the "man of sin" (v. 3). *consume with the spirit of his mouth.* He will be destroyed by Christ at His second coming with His word of judgment (Isa. 11:4). *brightness.* Or, "appearing" (1 Tim. 6:14; 2 Tim. 1:10; 4:1,8; Titus 2:13). *coming.* See note at v. 1.

10 And with all deceivableness of unrighteous-
ness in them that perish; because they received
not the love of the truth, that they might be saved.
11 And for this cause God shall send them strong
delusion, that they should believe a lie:
12 That they all might be damned who believed
not the truth, but had pleasure in unrighteousness.
13 But we are bound to give thanks alway to God
for you, brethren beloved of the Lord, because
God hath from the beginning chosen you to
salvation through sanctification of the Spirit and
belief of the truth:
14 Whereunto he called you by our gospel, to the
obtaining of the glory of our Lord Jesus Christ.
15 Therefore, brethren, stand fast, and hold the
traditions which ye have been taught, whether by
word, or our epistle.
16 Now our Lord Jesus Christ himself, and God,
even our Father, which hath loved us, and hath
given *us* everlasting consolation and good hope
through grace,
17 Comfort your hearts, and stablish you in every
good word and work.

CHAPTER 3

FINALLY, brethren, pray for us, that the word of
the Lord may have *free* course, and be glorified,
even as *it is* with you:
2 And that we may be delivered from unreason-
able and wicked men: for all *men* have not faith.
3 But the Lord is faithful, who shall stablish you,
and keep *you* from evil.
4 And we have confidence in the Lord touching

2:9 *whose coming*. Another implicit comparison to Christ (same word as in vv. 1,8). *all power and signs and lying wonders*. The Man of Sin will be empowered by Satan and attested by many apparent miracles.

2:10 *deceivableness of unrighteousness*. Deception characterized by injustice or sin. *them that perish*. Lost sinners already being ruined by sin and unbelief (1 Cor. 1:18; 2 Cor. 4:3) and headed for eternal destruction (1:9). People without sincere *love* for the *truth* of God's Word will be swept away by the lies of the Man of Sin.

2:11–12 *God shall send them strong delusion*. God cannot lie (Num. 23:19; Titus 1:2), but the Lord has the authority and power to abandon sinners to the lies of Satan as a just judgment for their sins (cf. Rom. 1:24,26,28; 11:7–10). *pleasure in unrighteousness*. The opposite of love for the truth (v. 10; 1 Cor. 13:6).

CONFIDENCE IN SALVATION AND CALL TO PRAYER (2:13—3:5)

Thanksgiving and Exhortation to Elect Saints (2:13–15)

2:13–14 Genuine Christians will be safe from the Man of Sin's delusions because of divine grace. *bound to give thanks*. See note at 1:3. *beloved of the Lord*. The objects of God's special, redeeming love (v. 16; Rom. 1:7; Gal. 2:20; Eph. 5:25). *from the beginning chosen*. God eternally chose whom He would save (Eph. 1:4). *through sanctification . . . truth*. God saves His elect by calling them powerfully by the *Spirit* and the *gospel*, so that sinners become believers, holy to the Lord (Rom. 8:29–30; 9:11,15,18,23; 1 Cor. 1:2,9,22–31). Their calling ultimately will bring them into *the glory of our Lord Jesus Christ* when He returns (see notes at 1:11–12).

2:15 The only *traditions* we are to hold are the apostolic traditions found in the Bible (3:6; 1 Cor. 11:2). No other tradition must determine the teaching or practice of the church (Mark 7:1–13; Gal. 1:14; Col. 2:8).

Prayer for Comfort and Strength (2:16–17)

2:16–17 *everlasting consolation*. The comfort given to Christ's suffering, persecuted people by the *hope* of Christ's return (Rom. 15:4; 1 Thess. 4:13–18; Heb. 6:18). The experience of spiritual hope and the power it gives for Christians to persevere in biblical truth (*word*) and obedience (*work*) are gifts of God's grace and therefore should be sought in prayer (Heb. 13:20–21).

Thoughts for Personal/Family Worship: Chapter 2

1. Gregory the Great (d. AD 604) said that anyone who claims to be the Universal Priest over all the church is the precursor of the Antichrist. Many Christians, including John Wycliffe, Martin Luther, John Calvin, and the authors of the Westminster Confession of Faith, have understood the "man of sin" to be the Pope of Rome. Other Christians expect a future antichrist to arise. However we interpret this text, we must certainly reject anyone who seeks to take a place of authority in the church that belongs only to the Lord. Christ alone has supreme authority to teach the church its doctrines, laws, and worship. Christ alone is the Mediator who atones for sin by His once-for-all sacrifice. Christ alone has the power of the Spirit to make the means of grace effective to save sinners. Take no part in a church that makes a man into Christ's substitute. Is there anyone or anything that is distracting you from Christ?

2. The only alternative to being swept up in the worship of men is salvation by the sovereign grace of God. Wherever we see people exercising faith in Christ and practical holiness, let us give thanks to God for choosing and calling them to Christ. If God has saved you, thank Him every day. If you cannot say that you know you belong to Christ, do not keep rejecting the love of the truth, or God could give you over to delusion. Turn from your sins and cry out in prayer to Christ even now to save you.

Chapter 3: ***Paul gives a number of exhortations to pray for the missionaries of the cross, to be obedient to apostolic teaching, to avoid disorderly church members, to be diligent in daily work, and to rebuke such professing Christians as would not obey the teaching given them.***

Request for Prayer for the Mission (3:1–2)

3:1–2 Christians have a responsibility to *pray* regularly for preachers of the Word, especially those that bring the gospel to people who have not heard it before (Rom. 15:30; Eph. 6:19–20; Col. 4:2–3), that the gospel would succeed in converting sinners, and preachers would be protected from dangerous opponents. *have free course, and be glorified*. The Greek paints the picture of a runner who wins a race and receives a crown of honor, an image of the gospel going out with power and being received as the Word of God, as it did with the Thessalonians (1 Thess. 1:5–6; 2:13).

Assurance and Prayer for Endurance (3:3–5)

3:3–4 *the Lord is faithful*. Paul's *confidence* in Christians rests

ELECTION

Election is God's decree whereby, of His own free will, He has predestined certain men to salvation to the praise of the glory of His name (Eph. 1:4–6; 1 Thess. 5:9). Far from being a tangential doctrine, election is the golden thread that runs through the whole Christian system. Moreover, election is the friend of sinners—and therefore a most blessed doctrine.

Election is God's positive choice, by His sheer sovereignty and out of His grace, to love some for salvation (Rom. 9:13–26; 1 Thess. 5:9). God's election is in no way universal or general, for God did not ordain all mankind to be reconciled to Himself. Rather, those whom He foreknew He predestined (Rom. 8:29). Here *foreknew* is used in the sense of choosing or ordaining people (1 Peter 1:2; cf. Rom. 11:2). Because many have wrongly attributed divine knowledge of man's future faith as causative of God's decree, it is essential to note that God's wise foreknowledge is both free and *logically* (in contrast to *temporally*) secondary to His willful ordination. Before the foundation of the world God singled out and appointed some to salvation (2 Thess. 2:13). He did not appoint those whom He foreknew would be conformed to Christ; rather, those whom He foreknew (*favorably chose*) He predestined to be conformed to His own image.

Jesus Christ is the whole foundation of election. Christ was called of His Father from all eternity to perform the work of salvation for His people (Heb. 5:5; 7:22; 13:20). In electing to perform the work of salvation, Christ is not subordinate to the Father with regard to the decree itself since He has decreed all things with the Father (John 15:16); rather, He became subordinate in its execution through His servanthood and humiliation (1 Peter 1:20).

Election can never be separated from Christ, as the elect have this status only in Christ. Furthermore, election is so closely linked to Christ that, in order to understand the true nature of election itself, one must look to the ordaining of the Mediator (Isa. 42:1; Heb. 9:15). This is why any who struggle with understanding this doctrine must be brought to view election particularly *in Christ*, for in Him are all those who are chosen of God (Eph. 1:4). The believer is chosen in Christ as His own inheritance (Deut. 32:9; Ps. 2:8; Heb. 12:2; cf. John 6:39; 17:16; Eph. 1:11; 1 Peter 2:6,9).

The covenant of grace is the means of election. This is God's contract with His people in Christ regarding life eternal. In this covenant God freely promises Christ to His people, who receive Christ's benefits upon repentant faith (Ezek. 36:25–27; Hos. 2:18–20; Mal. 3:1).

The degrees of execution are the working out of election in the life of the believer. These are the steps by which God puts into action His eternal love (cf. Acts 13:48). For those whom God has elected to inherit eternal life, He has also ordained the subordinate means whereby, in steps, they attain their ordained end (Eph. 1:4–5; 2 Thess. 2:13; cf. John 6:37; Eph. 2:8–9). Without these steps, by which God puts into action His eternal love, salvation would be unobtainable (Rom. 8:29–30). Broadly speaking, these steps are known as effectual calling, regeneration, justification, sanctification, and glorification. Thus, salvation worked out experientially in the soul of the believer is inseparable from sovereign election in Christ.

Sadly, some view election as a stumbling block to coming to Christ by faith. Unfortunately, their worry is not first "Do I have Christ?" but rather "Am I elect?" Based on this skewed perspective such people have viewed election through a convoluted lens. It must be recognized that election is impossible to ascertain apart from the prior receiving of salvation by faith, upon which, in conjunction with the resultant works, election is made sure (cf. 2 Peter 1:10). Furthermore, since Christ declares to all sinners, "Repent and believe, and you will be saved," there need not be a question of one's status other than that of *sinner*. *Thirsty* sinners (Isa. 55:1); *willing* sinners (Rev. 22:17); *heavy-laden* sinners (Matt. 11:28); *adulterous* sinners (Jer. 3:1); *lost* sinners (Luke 19:10); and, yes, even the *chief of sinners* (1 Tim. 1:15)—to all the Lord declares, "Unto you, O men, I call; and my voice is to the sons of men" (Prov. 8:4). Therefore, as the Lord is not willing that any should perish, but that all should come to repentance, "Repent ye and believe the gospel" (Mark 1:15).

—adapted from William Perkins, *A Golden Chaine*, chs. 15, 31, 35—38, 48

you, that ye both do and will do the things which
we command you.
5 And the Lord direct your hearts into the love of
God, and into the patient waiting for Christ.
6 Now we command you, brethren, in the name
of our Lord Jesus Christ, that ye withdraw your-
selves from every brother that walketh disorderly,
and not after the tradition which he received of us.
7 For yourselves know how ye ought to follow us:
for we behaved not ourselves disorderly among you;
8 Neither did we eat any man's bread for nought;
but wrought with labour and travail night and
day, that we might not be chargeable to any of you:
9 Not because we have not power, but to make
ourselves an ensample unto you to follow us.
10 For even when we were with you, this we
commanded you, that if any would not work,
neither should he eat.
11 For we hear that there are some which walk
among you disorderly, working not at all, but are
busybodies.
12 Now them that are such we command and
exhort by our Lord Jesus Christ, that with
quietness they work, and eat their own bread.
13 But ye, brethren, be not weary in well doing.
14 And if any man obey not our word by this
epistle, note that man, and have no company with
him, that he may be ashamed.
15 Yet count *him* not as an enemy, but admonish
him as a brother.
16 Now the Lord of peace himself give you peace
always by all means. The Lord *be* with you all.
17 The salutation of Paul with mine own hand,
which is the token in every epistle: so I write.
18 The grace of our Lord Jesus Christ *be* with you
all. Amen.

---

upon their union with Christ (*in the Lord*) and the trustworthiness of God, who will save to the end all whom He has chosen and called (Rom. 8:30; 1 Cor. 1:8–9; Phil. 1:6; 1 Thess. 5:23–24). *keep you from evil*. Not prevent all suffering (1:3–4), but save and preserve them from the dominion of sin and deception (John 17:11–12,15; 2 Tim. 4:18). *Evil* could also be translated, "the evil one" (Satan).

3:5 *direct your hearts*. God is the source of every good thing in the hearts of men (1 Chron. 29:18–19). Paul's prayerful wish was that God would focus their minds and faith upon His sovereign, free *love* for them (2:13,16), and upon the "patience of Christ," who is the model for all Christians in His humility and suffering of persecution (Phil. 2:5–8; Heb. 12:1–3; 1 Peter 2:21–24).

Command to Discipline Disorderly Brothers (3:6–15)

3:6 *in the name of our Lord Jesus Christ*. As Christ's authorized representative. *walketh disorderly*. Conducts himself without self-discipline (vv. 7,11,14), particularly those who do not devote themselves to a life of quiet and diligent labor in their earthly vocations (vv. 8,10–12; 1 Thess. 4:11–12; 5:14). *withdraw yourselves*. After warning them with the Word (v. 14), exclude persistent sinners from the fellowship of the church until they repent (v. 14; Matt. 18:15–20; 1 Cor. 5; 2 Cor. 2:5–11). *tradition*. See note at 2:15.

3:8 *nought*. Nothing. *wrought*. Worked. *travail*. Toil, hard work.

3:9 *ensample*. Example.

3:11 *busybodies*. People who meddle in things that do not pertain to them instead of being busy with their own proper work.

3:13 The Christians in Thessalonica were not only to work for a living, but even more they were to not grow *weary in well doing*, that is good works toward one's neighbor (Eph. 4:28).

3:15 *admonish him as a brother*. The motive of church discipline is love, and the purpose is to restore people to the ways of Christ (Gal. 6:1–2).

FAREWELL: PEACE AND GRACE (3:16–18)

3:16–18 *peace . . . grace*. See note at 1:2. Paul gives a concluding benediction and asserts his authorship of the letter by writing *with mine own hand* (1 Cor. 16:21; Gal. 6:11; Col. 4:18; Philem. 19).

Thoughts for Personal/Family Worship: Chapter 3

1. **Bad doctrine leads to bad practice. Fanatical views of the imminence of Christ's second coming can lead to a host of errors, including failing to obey the injunctions of God in personal, family, and public life. We do not know the day when Christ will return, and we must live as faithful servants every day, ready to meet the Master. Whether or not you work for a paycheck, what "jobs" has the Lord assigned to you? Why is it important for the Lord's honor and your good that you work hard at them?**
2. **When professing Christians behave badly, it is sometimes our duty to withdraw ourselves from them (v. 6), to refuse to have fellowship with them (v. 14), and to give them a brotherly admonition (v. 15). Breaking fellowship with professing believers is a solemn act of the church, and should not be done lightly or without the leadership of the church's elders. However, when done rightly, the Holy Spirit can use it to turn backsliding Christians back to Christ and to awaken hypocrites in the church to their need of salvation.**

FOR THERE IS

ONE GOD

AND

One Mediator

BETWEEN

GOD & MEN

THE MAN

Christ Jesus

1 TIMOTHY 2:5

INTRODUCTION TO THE BOOK OF
1 TIMOTHY

Authorship: According to the salutation we find in 1:1, the author of 1 Timothy is the apostle Paul. Paul attests to the fact that he used to be "a blasphemer, and a persecutor" (v. 13), but that the grace of God "was exceeding abundant" (v. 14) and that Christ Jesus placed him "in the ministry" (v. 12)—all things we know of Paul's life. The early church unanimously held to Pauline authorship for this epistle.

The addressee is Timothy. Since it is addressed to an individual and not a whole church, and deals with issues relating to the character and conduct of a minister, it has become known as a pastoral epistle (along with 2 Timothy and Titus). Timothy was one of the best known of Paul's companions and fellow-laborers (Acts 16:1–3; 19:22; 1 Cor. 4:17; 2 Cor. 1:1; Phil. 1:1; etc.). We know from the biblical record that Timothy was much younger than Paul (1 Tim. 4:12). He had been an elder in Ephesus continuing the work of Paul throughout Asia Minor of building up the church (cf. Rom. 15:19). Timothy's mother was Jewish and his father was a Greek—which meant that Timothy was both raised in the Scriptures and had a high status in society (Acts 16:1). He was one of Paul's converts, as Paul called him his "own son in the faith" (1 Tim. 1:2).

Timothy was a resident and probably a native of Lystra, one of the cities Paul visited during his first missionary journey (Acts 14:6). Later Paul refers to the things he suffered in Lystra, saying that Timothy is fully aware of what he endured (2 Tim. 3:10–11). Apparently Timothy's mother, Eunice, and his grandmother Lois had first come to faith and subsequently Timothy did also.

At the time of Paul's second missionary journey, and upon revisiting Lystra (Acts 16:1), Paul requested Timothy to become one of his associates. Since Timothy was the son of a Jewish woman, and realizing the need for him to gain access to the Jews, Paul circumcised Timothy (Acts 16:3). Timothy was sent on assignments to organize churches and preach the gospel. To the very end of his life Paul was greatly comforted by Timothy (2 Tim. 4:9,21).

Date: Scholars agree that the circumstances mentioned in the two epistles of Paul to Timothy do not fit any scenario in the book of Acts. This leads us to conclude that these two epistles were written at a later date, after Paul had been released from his two-year imprisonment at Rome. The book of Acts ends with Paul undergoing house arrest. During that time he was free to do his work, receive visitors, and preach the gospel.

The personal circumstances of Paul, as reflected in 1 Timothy, were different. He was in Macedonia and had requested Timothy to remain in Ephesus (1:3). In 2 Timothy, Paul was back in prison and had been forsaken. Only Luke was with him (2 Tim. 4:11). Paul felt, at that time, as though death was staring him in the face.

All this suggests that Paul was released from his first imprisonment at Rome, allowing him to conduct missionary travels. After being arrested a second time and brought to Rome, he was, according to church history, put on trial and finally executed (AD 67). The conclusion is drawn that 1 Timothy was written some time after his first imprisonment and probably from Macedonia (perhaps Philippi).

Theme: Contending for the Christian faith and establishing the Christian church.

Purpose: Paul wrote to encourage Timothy to remain faithful to the gospel and to organize the church according to the apostolic pattern for the church.

Synopsis: *The Contribution of 1 Timothy to Redemptive Revelation*

Paul encourages Timothy, young and timid as he appears to have been at this time, to fulfill his ministry with boldness and perseverance. Timothy must stand fast in the face of difficulties. There are dangers from within the church as well as from without. A dangerous group of Judaizers were attempting to impose Jewish legalism upon the newly founded church (1:9), militating against the doctrine of free grace. There were heretics who were promoting "doctrines of devils," that espoused a philosophical dualism (4:1). This dualism apparently taught that there were two supreme beings, one working for the good and the other working for evil. Paul instructs Timothy to lift up the one, only, and supreme Creator God. Satan is a mere fallen creature who, though bent on ruin and deformed by pride (3:6), is subject to God.

Timothy must likewise resist those who teach doctrines underestimating the value of the body and denying the physical resurrection of the dead. Such forbid marriage and emphasize abstention from certain foods (4:3). As a minister in Ephesus, Timothy must oppose all these different heresies and promote the "sound doctrine" (1:10).

Paul also shows Timothy how the church ought to be properly organized. Some of the apostles were already being taken away by death. Paul explains here to Timothy directions for public worship (ch. 2) and how the churches should be organized (ch. 3) after the oversight of the apostles was no longer available other than in their divinely written testimony.

Outline:

I. Salutation (1:1–2)

II. The Purity of the Gospel (1:3–20)
- A. Warning against Heretics Promoting Jewish Legalism (1:3–11)
- B. The Proclamation of the Gospel Entrusted to Paul (1:12–17)
- C. Timothy Encouraged to Be Faithful to the Gospel (1:18–20)

III. Ordinances and Worship (2:1—3:16)
- A. Direction for Prayer by Men in Worship Services (2:1–8)
- B. Women Are to Pray Along Silently (2:9–15)
- C. Qualifications for Elders (3:1–7)
- D. Qualifications for Deacons (3:8–13)
- E. Calling of the Church to Uphold Truth (3:14–16)

IV. Practical Encouragements for Ministers (4:1—6:16)
- A. Warning against Heresies Still to Come (4:1–5)
- B. Timothy Called to Be a Godly Example (4:6–16)
- C. How to Admonish Church Members (5:1–2)
- D. How to Counsel Widows (5:3–16)
- E. How to Counsel Elders (5:17–25)
- F. How to Counsel Slaves (6:1–2)
- G. Godliness Is Great Gain (6:3–10)
- H. Encouragement to Timothy to Be Faithful (6:11–16)

V. Final Exhortations (6:17–21)
- A. How to Counsel the Rich (6:17–19)
- B. Final Encouragement to Timothy to Be Faithful (6:20–21)

THE FIRST EPISTLE OF PAUL THE APOSTLE TO
TIMOTHY

CHAPTER 1

PAUL, an apostle of Jesus Christ by the commandment of God our Saviour, and Lord Jesus Christ, *which is* our hope;
2 Unto Timothy, *my* own son in the faith: Grace, mercy, *and* peace, from God our Father and Jesus Christ our Lord.
3 As I besought thee to abide still at Ephesus, when I went into Macedonia, that thou mightest charge some that they teach no other doctrine,
4 Neither give heed to fables and endless genealogies, which minister questions, rather than godly edifying which is in faith: *so do.*
5 Now the end of the commandment is charity out of a pure heart, and *of* a good conscience, and *of* faith unfeigned:
6 From which some having swerved have turned aside unto vain jangling;
7 Desiring to be teachers of the law; understanding neither what they say, nor whereof they affirm.
8 But we know that the law *is* good, if a man use it lawfully;
9 Knowing this, that the law is not made for a righteous man, but for the lawless and disobedient, for the ungodly and for sinners, for unholy and profane, for murderers of fathers and murderers of mothers, for manslayers,
10 For whoremongers, for them that defile themselves with mankind, for menstealers, for liars, for perjured persons, and if there be any other thing that is contrary to sound doctrine;
11 According to the glorious gospel of the blessed God, which was committed to my trust.
12 And I thank Christ Jesus our Lord, who hath enabled me, for that he counted me faithful, putting me into the ministry;

Chapter 1: ***Paul reminds Timothy that he left him at Ephesus to take care of the local church and to be watchful that no doctrine contrary to the gospel of Jesus Christ be tolerated. The false teachers claim that they are teachers of the law. Therefore Paul shows what the God-given purpose of the law is. Paul explains his own former errors regarding the law of God but asserts that Christ has shown him mercy. Now the gospel of Christ has been entrusted to his care, affording him abundant reason to praise and to thank God.***

SALUTATION (1:1–2)

1:1 Paul stresses the apostleship given him by the resurrected Christ. In secular Greek an apostle was someone who was dispatched as an envoy on behalf of others. Paul is an envoy of Christ, clothed with His authority to reveal the will of Christ in matters of life and doctrine of the church. Apostles were personally chosen, called, and sent forth by Christ, being equipped by Him and having been eyewitnesses to Christ, and set up for the founding of the church (Eph. 2:20). Though Paul did not see Christ in his earthly ministry, God specially chose Paul (Acts 9:4–6; 18:9–10; 23:11; 27:23; 1 Cor. 11:23; Gal.1:11–12,16–17).

1:2 *my own son in the faith.* The term used here denotes tender love. The apostle had been the means in God's hand to bring forth spiritual life in Timothy and affectionately considers him a spiritual child. This love is reciprocated in Timothy's life by his deep filial respect for Paul.

THE PURITY OF THE GOSPEL (1:3–20)

Warning against Heretics Promoting Jewish Legalism (1:3–11)

1:3 Paul reminds Timothy that he, traveling into Macedonia, had left Timothy at Ephesus. However, such an event is not found in the book of Acts, which probably means this happened after Acts 28.

1:4 Timothy is warned not to give heed to *fables.* The Jews were fond of constructing *genealogies* of their Jewish ancestors, adding details and events to their pedigree, which had no value for spiritual edification.

1:5 The Jews elevated the law as a means to merit salvation, but Paul explains that the aim of the law is to work out three matters in the hearts of those, who have been reconciled to God by faith: *pure love* (*charity*), *a good conscience*, and sincere (*unfeigned*) *faith.*

1:6–7 *vain jangling.* Foolish talking. Timothy must contend with false brethren, who view themselves to be *teachers of the law.* They do not understand the aim of the law and attempt to impose God's law upon people's lives as a yoke which no man has been able to keep (Acts 15:10).

1:9–10 Here Paul renders a list of sinful actions that are rebuked by the law. *profane.* Unholy, ungodly men, who despise the holy revelation of God. Another of these sinful categories is those who *defile themselves with mankind.* These are men who abuse their bodies with other men. This is an indirect reference to all homosexual activities, committed by male or female, as sin in the light of God's law.

1:11 *the glorious gospel of the blessed God.* Man must keep God's laws because they are good, but at the same time this gospel shows us that man is unable to do so. This exposes man's sinful depravity, but matches the gospel that "Christ Jesus came into the world to save sinners" (v. 15). This gospel

13 Who was before a blasphemer, and a persecu-
tor, and injurious: but I obtained mercy, because I
did *it* ignorantly in unbelief.
14 And the grace of our Lord was exceeding abun-
dant with faith and love which is in Christ Jesus.
15 This *is* a faithful saying, and worthy of all
acceptation, that Christ Jesus came into the world
to save sinners; of whom I am chief.
16 Howbeit for this cause I obtained mercy, that
in me first Jesus Christ might shew forth all long-
suffering, for a pattern to them which should
hereafter believe on him to life everlasting.
17 Now unto the King eternal, immortal, invis-
ible, the only wise God, *be* honour and glory for
ever and ever. Amen.
18 This charge I commit unto thee, son Timothy,
according to the prophecies which went before
on thee, that thou by them mightest war a good
warfare;
19 Holding faith, and a good conscience; which
some having put away concerning faith have
made shipwreck;
20 Of whom is Hymenæus and Alexander; whom
I have delivered unto Satan, that they may learn
not to blaspheme.

CHAPTER 2

I EXHORT therefore, that, first of all, supplications,
prayers, intercessions, *and* giving of thanks, be
made for all men;
2 For kings, and *for* all that are in authority;
that we may lead a quiet and peaceable life in all
godliness and honesty.

---

is glorious because it displays the blessed attributes of God, such as His righteousness, justice, love, and mercy. God is the blessed God, for He is absolute perfection, the supreme goodness and truth, and the fountain of all love and life. The glorious gospel flows forth from this blessed God.

The Proclamation of the Gospel Entrusted to Paul (1:12–17)

1:12 When the Lord considered Paul *faithful* we must realize that this was not some faithfulness God foreknew in Paul and that therefore God chose him as an apostle, but that God enabled Paul to be faithful, strengthening him in the calling God gave him (1 Cor. 7:25).

1:13 Paul used to be a *blasphemer*, persecuting the church of Christ. But he did this all *ignorantly in unbelief* not to excuse himself from being guilty, for in vv. 15–16 he confesses to be a great sinner. But being ignorant of the truth of Christ, he did not sin against the Holy Ghost (Matt. 12:31; 1 John 5:6–17), and therefore his awful sins could still be forgiven.

1:15 Paul calls himself here the *chief* of sinners. He means to say that he is the worst sinner, because he ferociously persecuted the children of God. Every child of God, being aware of the sinful inclinations of his own heart, will likewise humble himself before God and his fellow brethren with a similar confession (Gen. 18:27; Ps. 86:1; Luke 5:8; Phil. 2:3).

1:16 God saved Paul, showing him mercy. God glorified His marvelous grace, setting him as an example of His mercy.

Timothy Encouraged to Be Faithful to the Gospel (1:18–20)

1:19 Timothy is exhorted to have a *good conscience*. Timothy and all who labor in God's service should strive to live uprightly and to teach faithfully according to God's Word.

1:20 Paul states that he has delivered two false brethren to Satan, by excommunication from the church (see Matt. 18:15ff.; 1 Cor. 5:5).

Thoughts for Personal/Family Worship: Chapter 1

1. **Note Paul's reference to "God our Saviour" in v. 1. Paul uses this designation also in 1 Tim. 2:3 and 4:10. The Son of God merited salvation for His people, dying on the cross and rising on the third day. But the source of salvation rests in God, the Father. Paul frequently ascribes man's salvation to God (Rom. 8:32; 1 Cor. 1:21; Eph. 2:4–5; etc.). Verse 15 beautifully mentions Christ's saving work. To be saved means also that God gives man the richest blessings: to declare that man is righteous in the sight of God (Isa. 1:18; Rom. 3:24), is placed in the freedom of God's children (Rom. 8:2; 2 Cor. 3:17; Gal. 5:1), and receives everlasting life (John 11:25–26; Eph. 2:5; Rev. 22:5).**
2. **Note also Paul's reference in v. 1 to the "Lord Jesus Christ . . . our hope." He is not only the One who gives hope, but Christ Himself is the hope of His people. He is the *foundaton* of Christian hope, for Christ earned that hope when He laid down His life as a ransom for sin. This is a source of unspeakable comfort. Christ is also the *door* of hope. One enters into a life of hope through Him. He is the only access to God. We, unworthy guilty sinners, can only have access to God through Christ. Christ is also the *life* of hope. One can only live in true hope through Christ. Without it there is no comfort or perspective for the future.**
3. **Verse 8 speaks of the law of God, which is good and is to be used lawfully. How do we use the law lawfully? There are various uses of the law. It functions as a restraint, working in people's consciences and keeping them from committing certain sins (Rom. 2:15). The law of God reveals to us our sins (3:20), which need to be washed in the blood of Christ. Finally, the law is also a guide to lead us through life (Ps. 19:8; 119:98; Rom. 7:22).**

Chapter 2: ***Paul commands Timothy to ensure that public prayer is offered in the midst of the congregation for all kinds of people, including the civil authorities. Such prayer will promote the proclamation of the gospel. Men are called to conduct public prayer in meekness without contention. The women are called to be modest in conduct, as well as in their clothing. They are not to usurp authority over men but should be willing to be taught in subjection. The motivation for this order between men and women is found in the creation order: Adam was first created and then Eve as a helpmeet for him.***

ORDINANCES AND WORSHIP (2:1—3:16)

Direction for Prayer by Men in Worship Services (2:1–8)

2:1 This exhortation, while also giving direction for personal prayer, is primarily focused on how to conduct public prayer. Paul supplies four different words for prayer, each having a distinct meaning. *Supplications* are humble petitions to be delivered from certain needs which are keenly felt, such as afflictions, sicknesses, and spiritual needs. *Prayers* are requests laid before God to receive His assistance and blessing in our

3 For this *is* good and acceptable in the sight of
God our Saviour;
4 Who will have all men to be saved, and to come
unto the knowledge of the truth.
5 For *there is* one God, and one mediator between
God and men, the man Christ Jesus;
6 Who gave himself a ransom for all, to be
testified in due time.
7 Whereunto I am ordained a preacher, and an
apostle, (I speak the truth in Christ, *and* lie not;) a
teacher of the Gentiles in faith and verity.
8 I will therefore that men pray every where, lift-
ing up holy hands, without wrath and doubting.
9 In like manner also, that women adorn them-
selves in modest apparel, with shamefacedness
and sobriety; not with broided hair, or gold, or
pearls, or costly array;
10 But (which becometh women professing
godliness) with good works.
11 Let the woman learn in silence with all
subjection.
12 But I suffer not a woman to teach, nor to
usurp authority over the man, but to be in silence.
13 For Adam was first formed, then Eve.
14 And Adam was not deceived, but the woman
being deceived was in the transgression.
15 Notwithstanding she shall be saved in child-
bearing, if they continue in faith and charity and
holiness with sobriety.

CHAPTER 3

THIS *is* a true saying, If a man desire the office of
a bishop, he desireth a good work.

particular circumstances. *Intercessions* are petitions in which we plead in the interest of other people, laying their needs and hardships before the Lord. *Giving of thanks* is rendering gratitude to God for all His benefits received directly from Him or by means of other people. These petitions are to be made for all people. The word *all* implies here not every human being personally, but all kinds of people (Matt. 4:23; Luke 11:42; Rom. 5:18; 1 Cor. 15:22; Titus 2:11).

2:2 The church should pray for civil authorities, that there might be peace, law, and order so that the proclamation of the gospel may have its course and not be hindered by turmoil and civil unrest. For then Christians will be able to live quiet lives in *godliness* and *honesty*. *Godliness* refers to a life of honoring God, as commanded in the first table of the law, while the word *honesty* refers to conduct toward our neighbor, as prescribed in the second table of the law.

2:4 God *will have all men to be saved*. The word *will* here refers not to a decree of God to save every man, for then all men would be saved because God does all that is pleasing to Him (Ps. 115:3; Rom. 9:18; Eph. 1:11). But God saves men from every nation, social rank, and ethnicity. Another possible interpretation is that *will* refers to His revealed will, which is, as He says elsewhere, that all men should repent (Acts 17:30).

2:5–6 Prayer must be lifted up for all kinds of people, because there is only *one God* of all men. Redemption is also in one person, *the man Christ Jesus*, which is not a denial of the divine nature of Christ. Paul asserts that clearly such as in 3:16 and Acts 20:28. The emphasis here is upon the fact that Christ as a human being supplied the ransom and therefore He is most fitting to be the substitute before God on behalf of all people. This truth must be *testified in due time* implying that this gospel must be preached and proclaimed (Acts 17:30; Rom. 1:6–17; Gal. 4:4).

2:8 Men are called to pray *every where*. This is in contrast to the Jewish ceremonial law where prayer was mostly connected to the temple, while now under the gospel, prayers may be offered in all places (Mal. 1:11; John 4:21). But these men must be upright and honest, not oppressing the innocent. This uplifting of *holy hands* is intended to be in contrast to the external ceremonial washing of hands as practiced by the Jews.

Women Are to Pray Along Silently (2:9–15)

2:9 *shamefacedness*. Inner modesty. The apostle admonishes the women regarding their clothing (*apparel*). They should neither be sloppy nor extravagant, but *modest*. The apostle is not forbidding the mere braiding of hair, but braiding combined with an ostentatious display of gold and pearls, which betrays vanity and excess.

2:12 During public worship women should not teach men, but be willing to be taught in subjection by men (1 Cor. 14:34). Women are called to instruct their children at home as Solomon's mother did (Prov. 31:1).

2:15 This does not mean that women will be saved by means of *childbearing*, but that women, although they suffer in childbearing as a result of the transgression in Paradise (v. 14), may still be saved in the way of faith, through Christ, the Mediator, who was born of a woman, and born under the law (Gal. 4:4). Such true faith will evidence itself in love (*charity*), sobriety, and holiness.

Thoughts for Personal/Family Worship: Chapter 2

1. **Notice Paul's emphasis on prayer. Christian prayer has a tremendous impact upon the surrounding environment. God answers prayer. The apostle often stresses the importance of prayer, requesting prayer for himself and for the work in God's kingdom (Eph. 6:18–19; Heb. 13:18). In Acts 6:4 the apostles testify that they should give themselves to prayer. In Acts 12:5 the church prayed without ceasing for Peter who had been put in prison. The Lord Jesus stresses the importance of personal and corporate prayer (Matt. 6:6; 7:7–8; Mark 9:25). Let us pray for individuals by name, asking for God's grace upon their lives.**
2. **Let us realize the basic truth that there is one Mediator between God and men (v. 5). This counts for all men everywhere. It is only in Christ that man can be reconciled to God. That is because Jesus Christ paid the ransom. He gave Himself as a payment for sin. Outside of Christ there is no reconciliation and no propitiation. This is why no one other than Christ can ever mediate between God and man. As God, Christ was able to endure the eternal wrath of God. As man, Christ fulfilled the law perfectly for His people. Now in Christ, men can come to God in faith, and this faith does not put to shame.**

Chapter 3: ***The apostle instructs Timothy regarding the qualifications of office bearers. He warns against vices that would impede their functioning in the office. We see a total of nine positive and five negative requirements (vv. 2–12). Paul's aim is that Timothy must understand how office bearers and their wives are to function and how individual members are to behave themselves in the church of Christ, recognizing***

2 A bishop then must be blameless, the husband
of one wife, vigilant, sober, of good behaviour,
given to hospitality, apt to teach;
3 Not given to wine, no striker, not greedy of filthy
lucre; but patient, not a brawler, not covetous;
4 One that ruleth well his own house, having his
children in subjection with all gravity;
5 (For if a man know not how to rule his own
house, how shall he take care of the church of
God?)
6 Not a novice, lest being lifted up with pride he
fall into the condemnation of the devil.
7 Moreover he must have a good report of them
which are without; lest he fall into reproach and
the snare of the devil.
8 Likewise *must* the deacons *be* grave, not dou-
bletongued, not given to much wine, not greedy
of filthy lucre;
9 Holding the mystery of the faith in a pure
conscience.
10 And let these also first be proved; then let them
use the office of a deacon, being *found* blameless.
11 Even so *must their* wives *be* grave, not slander-
ers, sober, faithful in all things.
12 Let the deacons be the husbands of one wife,
ruling their children and their own houses well.
13 For they that have used the office of a deacon
well purchase to themselves a good degree, and
great boldness in the faith which is in Christ Jesus.
14 These things write I unto thee, hoping to come
unto thee shortly:
15 But if I tarry long, that thou mayest know how
thou oughtest to behave thyself in the house of
God, which is the church of the living God, the
pillar and ground of the truth.
16 And without controversy great is the mystery
of godliness: God was manifest in the flesh,
justified in the Spirit, seen of angels, preached
unto the Gentiles, believed on in the world,
received up into glory.

its sacredness and calling to be a standard bearer of the truth in this world.

Qualifications for Elders (3:1–7)

3:1 The Greek word translated here as *bishop* means "one who has oversight." This term designates all elders and pastors. It is very certain that those who aspire to such a position desire a *good work*. However, this desire must be based upon biblical grounds and not on one's own subjective will. Proper means must be used to qualify oneself for such a work, along with subjecting oneself to the judgment of the church and waiting for a formal call to this office. No one may impose himself upon the church.

3:2 The apostle describes various qualifications for the office of *bishop*. He must be *blameless*, which means "beyond reproach," and if married, may only have *one wife* (v. 12). Furthermore the office bearer must be honest, *sober* minded, and able to *teach* others.

3:3 *striker*. Quarrelsome or abusive person. *filthy lucre*. Ill-gotten gain. *brawler*. Contentious person. The apostle suggests characteristics which would disqualify someone from the office. He is not to be one who drinks much wine (given unto drunkenness), since this leads to all kinds of other sins (Prov. 23:29–35). An office bearer should never be motivated by love of money (Titus 1:7; 1 Peter 5:2).

3:4–5 Paul shows that godly leadership begins in the home and with one's own family. If a man cannot oversee his own family, he cannot oversee the family of God (see v. 12).

3:6 *novice*. Literally, "newly planted," referring to one who recently came to faith or joined himself to the congregation. The danger is that he would assume to have great wisdom, above others, if he were to be appointed as an office bearer so soon. He would then be prone to fall into the sin of pride, the same snare *the devil* fell into when he, assuming much wisdom, revolted against God (John 8:44; 2 Peter 2:4; Jude 6; Rev.12:7–8).

3:7 *without*. Outside.

Qualifications for Deacons (3:8–13)

3:8 *doubletongued*. Foolish and unstable in speech. *filthy lucre*. Ill-gotten gain. The office of the deacon is different than the office of bishop. While bishops serve as the ruling officers of the church, deacons are delegated to take care of the practical needs of the church (Acts 6). Those who are unreliable in their speech would cause offense in the congregation because of lack of trustworthiness.

3:9 The *mystery of the faith* refers to godliness, which cannot be comprehended by nature but must be revealed by God's Holy Spirit (1 Cor. 2:6–7).

3:10 *proved*. Tested.

3:11 The apostle here supplies requirements for the wives of deacons. Women are not office bearers, but Paul instructs them that they should be *faithful in all things*. The wife of an office bearer is held to a high standard in all areas of life.

3:13 *purchase to themselves a good degree*. Acquire, as it were, a measure of dignity or honor.

Calling of the Church to Uphold Truth (3:14–16)

3:15 The *church* is called to be the *pillar and ground of the truth*. It is the church's calling to hold forth the truth and confess it freely, over against all deceit and heresy.

3:16 This confession summarizes the truth and portrays it succinctly for the world and for all men to know. Christ is said to have been *justified in the Spirit*. This can also be translated as "justified through the Spirit," meaning that by the divine power of the Holy Spirit, Christ arose from the dead. Thereby God proved that He was just and innocent, although He was condemned as if He were a criminal (Rom. 1:1–4).

Thoughts for Personal/Family Worship: Chapter 3

1. **Paul describes here the requirements of an office bearer. The reference to the office as a "good work" in v. 1 shows that Paul has a high regard for the office. This implies that it is an excellent and honorable work. Nevertheless we know from early church history that in those days serving in the office was also a sacrifice. Repeatedly persecution would rage with painful consequences. False teachers did their utmost to undermine the truth. The cares of the congregation were many (2 Cor. 11:27–28). Still today, serving in the office is a sacrifice. There is the sacrifice of our time, ease, and energy. At times there will be suffering because of hardships and ill-spoken words against the office bearer. At times one's name will even be slandered for the sake of being faithful to one's calling. But let it then be realized, that it is still a "good work" worthy of performing.**
2. **One of the qualifications Paul gives for an overseer**

CHAPTER 4

Now the Spirit speaketh expressly, that in the latter
times some shall depart from the faith, giving heed
to seducing spirits, and doctrines of devils;
2 Speaking lies in hypocrisy; having their con-
science seared with a hot iron;
3 Forbidding to marry, *and commanding* to
abstain from meats, which God hath created to be
received with thanksgiving of them which believe
and know the truth.
4 For every creature of God *is* good, and nothing
to be refused, if it be received with thanksgiving:
5 For it is sanctified by the word of God and prayer.
6 If thou put the brethren in remembrance of
these things, thou shalt be a good minister of Jesus
Christ, nourished up in the words of faith and of
good doctrine, whereunto thou hast attained.
7 But refuse profane and old wives' fables, and
exercise thyself *rather* unto godliness.
8 For bodily exercise profiteth little: but godliness
is profitable unto all things, having promise of the
life that now is, and of that which is to come.
9 This *is* a faithful saying and worthy of all
acceptation.
10 For therefore we both labour and suffer re-
proach, because we trust in the living God, who
is the Saviour of all men, specially of those that
believe.
11 These things command and teach.
12 Let no man despise thy youth; but be thou an
example of the believers, in word, in conversation,
in charity, in spirit, in faith, in purity.
13 Till I come, give attendance to reading, to
exhortation, to doctrine.

---

is that he must be "blameless" (v. 2). We understand that to mean that he is to be beyond reproach and to have a good name both within and beyond the church. However, let us also realize that at heart no office bearer is "blameless" for all have sinned and come short of the glory of God (Rom. 3:23). Therefore ultimately the office bearer can only be "blameless" in Christ. Christ justifies and cleanses from sin. Every office bearer has reason to consider himself unworthy and not beyond reproach. Without undermining the need to be godly in one's conduct, let us also realize that every office bearer needs to be clothed with the righteousness of Christ. This is the only way he can be truly blameless.

3. **It seems that within churches pastors are often under attack. The Evil One will try to render a pastor's work useless by leading him to fall into sin, for if the pastor falls, many in the congregation will stumble with him and the church will be in disarray. This is true not only for the pastors but also for the elders and the deacons. They are called to have oversight of the flock and therefore they must first have oversight over themselves in the privacy of their own homes and lives. This fact ought to stir up congregants to pray for those who are office bearers over them and to be cautious lest they unduly grumble (Num. 12).**

PRACTICAL ENCOURAGEMENTS FOR MINISTERS (4:1—6:16)

Chapter 4: ***The apostle warns Timothy to realize that heresies will be forthcoming. Therefore, he should be faithful in expounding true doctrine and unmasking heresies. Such leadership will greatly benefit the church. In order for Timothy to demonstrate his ability as a minister, Paul urges him to be sober minded, exercising himself to godliness. Timothy's hope should be in the Lord, especially as he suffers reproach for Christ's sake. He is exhorted to equip himself by further study of doctrine. He may not neglect the gifts the Lord has granted him and should keep a close self-watch. In that way Timothy will save himself as well as those who hear him.***

Warning against Heresies Still to Come (4:1–5)

4:1 The expression *latter times* is not necessarily to be taken as the last few years immediately prior to the second coming of Christ, but may refer to subsequent or coming days. Timothy is warned that days are coming in which dangerous heresies will be proclaimed, threatening the church. As a result some will *depart from the faith*, which is to be understood as forsaking the doctrines of God's Word, the content of faith. They will follow deceivers, false teachers, who are instigated by Satan to promote these dangerous errors.

4:2–3 Paul provides a description of these false teachers. They adhere to a kind of philosophical dualism between good and evil and between body and spirit and teach that redemption is gained through spiritual knowledge. The negative views of the body led them to forbid marriage. Paul describes the content of their teaching as *speaking lies in hypocrisy*. These false teachers give the impression that they subject their bodies to a difficult life and thus gain a higher degree of holiness. However, in reality they talk piously to cover up their own arrogance or immorality. By persisting in sin, they have silenced their conscience to the extent that they have become callous. Their teaching contradicts the good things that God has created. *meats*. Food of any kind.

4:4–5 *Every creature* (creation) *of God is good* and there are no prohibitions concerning certain foods applicable to Christians (Acts 10:15; 15:20–21; 1 Cor. 10:25–26). Food and drink are viewed as gifts of God, to be consecrated by *thanksgiving* and *prayer*, while God extends His blessing upon His own gifts. In this way also eating and drinking are done to the glory of God (1 Cor. 10:31).

Timothy Called to Be a Godly Example (4:6–16)

4:7 Timothy, having been encouraged to be faithful in sound doctrine, is now warned against *old wives' fables*. Paul does not clarify what these fables were, though they were likely known. He tells Timothy not to be caught up in these frivolous discussions (1:4).

4:8 The expression *bodily exercise* can refer either to physical exercise performed by an athlete or to the extravagant asceticism referred to earlier. Given the context, the latter appears more appropriate so Paul is saying that asceticism *profiteth little* (Col. 2:23). In contrast to this, *exercise* to *godliness is profitable unto all things*.

4:10 The *living God* is referred to here as *the Saviour of all men*. The word *Saviour* sounds confusing, since we know that God is only the Savior of His people (John 3:18,36). This term for Savior refers more generally to God as the Protector and Sustainer of all life (Ps. 36:6; 145:16; Acts 17:28).

4:12 *conversation*. Conduct. *charity*. Love. Timothy's young age made him susceptible to be looked down upon. Paul

14 Neglect not the gift that is in thee, which was
given thee by prophecy, with the laying on of the
hands of the presbytery.
15 Meditate upon these things; give thyself wholly
to them; that thy profiting may appear to all.
16 Take heed unto thyself, and unto the doctrine;
continue in them: for in doing this thou shalt
both save thyself, and them that hear thee.

CHAPTER 5

REBUKE not an elder, but intreat *him* as a father;
and the younger men as brethren;
2 The elder women as mothers; the younger as
sisters, with all purity.
3 Honour widows that are widows indeed.
4 But if any widow have children or nephews, let
them learn first to shew piety at home, and to re-
quite their parents: for that is good and acceptable
before God.
5 Now she that is a widow indeed, and desolate,
trusteth in God, and continueth in supplications
and prayers night and day.
6 But she that liveth in pleasure is dead while she
liveth.
7 And these things give in charge, that they may
be blameless.
8 But if any provide not for his own, and specially
for those of his own house, he hath denied the
faith, and is worse than an infidel.
9 Let not a widow be taken into the number
under threescore years old, having been the wife
of one man,
10 Well reported of for good works; if she have
brought up children, if she have lodged strangers,
if she have washed the saints' feet, if she have re-
lieved the afflicted, if she have diligently followed
every good work.
11 But the younger widows refuse: for when they
have begun to wax wanton against Christ, they
will marry;
12 Having damnation, because they have cast off
their first faith.
13 And withal they learn *to be* idle, wandering
about from house to house; and not only idle,
but tattlers also and busybodies, speaking things
which they ought not.
14 I will therefore that the younger women
marry, bear children, guide the house, give none
occasion to the adversary to speak reproachfully.

shows that maturity is not necessarily an issue of age but of spiritual progress and integrity.

4:13 Timothy is encouraged to *give attendance to reading* the Scriptures. That the Scriptures are meant is clear from the context, for Paul connects this reading to *exhortation* and *doctrine*, which are based on the Scriptures.

4:14 Paul recognizes that the Lord has endowed Timothy with rich gifts that ought not to be despised by the congregation nor by Timothy. It is Timothy's responsibility to cultivate these gifts so that he may grow in the grace of the Lord and gain more insight and so that others may observe this growth in him (v. 15). The growth in grace commended here is not to receive honor of men, but to gain their respect through his demeanor of godliness.

Thoughts for Personal/Family Worship: Chapter 4

1. **Paul encourages Timothy to exercise himself "unto godliness" (v. 7). One's fruitfulness in the service of the Lord depends on it. It promotes an increase in the knowledge of sin and of the necessity and preciousness of Christ. This exercise as such will remain hidden but the effects of it will be public. It is the calling and the duty of God's children to be diligent in reading the Scriptures, and in seeking the Lord in personal private prayer. Meditating on the mysteries of godliness as revealed to us in God's Word, and praying over this will cultivate a rich fruit in the life of a Christian. If one wishes to experience more of the love of Christ and be led deeper into a life of communion with Christ, one will need to have daily secret spiritual exercises. For "thy Father which seeth in secret shall reward thee openly" (Matt. 6:6).**
2. **Paul encourages Timothy to read the Scriptures with attention (v. 13). If we are to be godly in this crooked world, we will need to diligently read the Scriptures and meditate on their doctrines, making applications to daily life in the way of pointed exhortations. Without it, our lives and worship will suffer detrimentally.**

Chapter 5: ***Paul gives Timothy directions on how to deal with certain groups of people within the congregation. He points out the duties of the younger men and women as well as the duties of the older men and women. He focuses his attention on the elderly and explains the proper care that must be given to them and especially to the widows. He shows how widows can be a blessing within the congregation. He gives further exhortations on how Timothy should conduct himself toward the elders of the church.***

How to Admonish Church Members (5:1–2)

5:1–2 Paul implies that although Timothy is still young, there will be times when he, as a minister of the gospel, will have to rebuke those in his congregation. Paul gives general guidelines as to how Timothy is to correct people of different ages and maturity levels. The underlying principle is that Timothy ought to rebuke in a gracious and respectful manner.

How to Counsel Widows (5:3–16)

5:3–6 Paul exhorts Timothy to give proper care to *widows*. He is especially concerned with those who do not have *children* and cannot count on support from other sources. Paul contrasts two attitudes of widows, one of prayerful dependence on God for their needs, and the other displaying a life of luxury and ease. The former is commended while the latter is rebuked.

5:8 *house*. Household. Paul exhorts Christians to care for their *own*. Those who fail to care for those God has entrusted into their care are worse than an *infidel*, as even unbelievers can display natural care and affection for the members of their family.

5:9–10 Paul describes the work and service that widows can perform in the congregation. There are, however, certain qualifications that must be met. In the early church these widows were not office bearers but still had a semiofficial status in the congregation and could be called upon to render services to the needy.

5:11–14 Younger widows are to be excluded from this more or less official capacity of serving as widows, for they may wish

15 For some are already turned aside after Satan.
16 If any man or woman that believeth have
widows, let them relieve them, and let not the
church be charged; that it may relieve them that
are widows indeed.
17 Let the elders that rule well be counted worthy
of double honour, especially they who labour in
the word and doctrine.
18 For the scripture saith, Thou shalt not muzzle
the ox that treadeth out the corn. And, The
labourer *is* worthy of his reward.
19 Against an elder receive not an accusation, but
before two or three witnesses.
20 Them that sin rebuke before all, that others
also may fear.
21 I charge *thee* before God, and the Lord Jesus
Christ, and the elect angels, that thou observe
these things without preferring one before another, doing nothing by partiality.
22 Lay hands suddenly on no man, neither be
partaker of other men's sins: keep thyself pure.
23 Drink no longer water, but use a little wine for
thy stomach's sake and thine often infirmities.
24 Some men's sins are open beforehand, going
before to judgment; and some *men* they follow
after.
25 Likewise also the good works *of some* are
manifest beforehand; and they that are otherwise
cannot be hid.

CHAPTER 6

LET as many servants as are under the yoke count
their own masters worthy of all honour, that the
name of God and *his* doctrine be not blasphemed.
2 And they that have believing masters, let them
not despise *them*, because they are brethren; but
rather do *them* service, because they are faithful
and beloved, partakers of the benefit. These
things teach and exhort.
3 If any man teach otherwise, and consent not
to wholesome words, *even* the words of our

to remarry. Paul has nothing against the widows remarrying, and even encourages them to do so (v. 14), but if they did so after they had been appointed to serve in the congregation, they would thereby forsake their calling and become unfaithful. Therefore Paul encourages the younger widows to remarry and to devote their energy to caring for their families.

5:13 *withal*. Also.

5:15 This refers to younger widows who, having forsaken their commitment to care for the needy, have been rebuked and put to shame. In response they have turned away from following Christ and reverted back to sinful lives.

How to Counsel Elders (5:17–25)

5:17 In v. 1 Paul used *presbuteros* ("elder") to refer to older men. Here, Paul refers to those office bearers who care for the souls of the congregation. This text shows us that there were two kinds of *elders* in the early Christian church. Some were overseers while others labored in preaching and teaching. These latter office bearers should receive *double*, ("greater"), *honour* due to their work.

5:19–20 The work of an elder sometimes provokes offense and leads people to accuse them without warrant. Therefore Timothy has to be very careful about accepting accusations against elders. He may only do so if there are *two or three witnesses*. If there are credible accusations against an elder, then admonitions need to be made *before all*, to show the sanctity of the office to all and to instill *fear* in the other elders.

5:21 *partiality*. Prejudice. Because ultimately God is judge, Timothy may not be partial and may not show favoritism in his dealings with people but should be honest and sincere.

5:22 Paul provides some practical admonitions to Timothy. He should not ordain men to the office (*lay hands*) unless they have been duly proved and have shown that they are competent in doctrine and their daily walk of life.

5:24–25 Some men are unfit for the office because of sins that are clearly demonstrated in their life, while others manifest certain sins after they have been installed to the office. Likewise there are those who exhibit good works in advance, while others have good works that initially appear to be hidden but will be clearly manifested as originating from God. The implication is that Timothy must use proper prudence and caution in installing men to the office.

Thoughts for Personal/Family Worship: Chapter 5

1. **Paul instructs Timothy how to deal with various age categories in the congregation. He refers to fathers, mothers, younger men, and women. This shows the importance of family life. In our society indifference toward family members is increasing. The church ought to reflect brotherly love, mutual respect, and an attitude of esteeming the other higher than oneself. In this way the church will be a witness in this world of Christian love and faithfulness.**
2. **Timothy is called to assess people's lives. In this regard the fruits will show who people are. We cannot judge the inward attitude, but may only listen to the testimony and observe the outward walk of life. It may be that we will see that much is lacking in our congregation. The church needs to strike a balance between showing forbearance to weak members, while encouraging improvement and publicly admonishing sin. All this must be accompanied with urgent prayer for the outpouring of God's Spirit in the midst of the congregation.**

Chapter 6: ***Practical admonitions and encouragements to maintain proper order between servants and masters, to promote true meekness and godliness within the congregation, to avoid love of money, to fight the good fight of faith, realizing the future wealth to be given to all God's children, and to hold fast to the true apostolic doctrine of salvation.***

How to Counsel Slaves (6:1–2)

6:1–2 *Servants* or slaves are called to show proper obedience to their *masters*, to avoid criticism that the Christian doctrine would be the cause of rebellion and disobedience. The expression *partakers of the benefit* can refer to Christian masters, who together with their Christian slaves, are recipients of the saving grace of God and are called to be good to one another, showing kindness and due benevolence. Paul does not condone slavery, but speaks of how Christianity ought to affect this social institution.

Lord Jesus Christ, and to the doctrine which is
according to godliness;
4 He is proud, knowing nothing, but doting
about questions and strifes of words, whereof
cometh envy, strife, railings, evil surmisings,
5 Perverse disputings of men of corrupt minds,
and destitute of the truth, supposing that gain is
godliness: from such withdraw thyself.
6 But godliness with contentment is great gain.
7 For we brought nothing into *this* world, *and it*
is certain we can carry nothing out.
8 And having food and raiment let us be there-
with content.
9 But they that will be rich fall into temptation and
a snare, and *into* many foolish and hurtful lusts,
which drown men in destruction and perdition.
10 For the love of money is the root of all evil:
which while some coveted after, they have erred
from the faith, and pierced themselves through
with many sorrows.
11 But thou, O man of God, flee these things; and
follow after righteousness, godliness, faith, love,
patience, meekness.
12 Fight the good fight of faith, lay hold on
eternal life, whereunto thou art also called, and
hast professed a good profession before many
witnesses.
13 I give thee charge in the sight of God, who
quickeneth all things, and *before* Christ Jesus, who
before Pontius Pilate witnessed a good confession;
14 That thou keep *this* commandment without
spot, unrebukeable, until the appearing of our
Lord Jesus Christ:
15 Which in his times he shall shew, *who is* the
blessed and only Potentate, the King of kings, and
Lord of lords;
16 Who only hath immortality, dwelling in the
light which no man can approach unto; whom no
man hath seen, nor can see: to whom *be* honour
and power everlasting. Amen.
17 Charge them that are rich in this world, that
they be not highminded, nor trust in uncertain
riches, but in the living God, who giveth us richly
all things to enjoy;
18 That they do good, that they be rich in good
works, ready to distribute, willing to communicate;
19 Laying up in store for themselves a good foun-
dation against the time to come, that they may lay
hold on eternal life.
20 O Timothy, keep that which is committed to
thy trust, avoiding profane *and* vain babblings,
and oppositions of science falsely so called:
21 Which some professing have erred concerning
the faith. Grace *be* with thee. Amen.

Godliness Is Great Gain (6:3–10)

6:3–5 *doting*. Literally, "like a diseased person hankering after or harping on little issues." *railings*. Abusive behaviors. *evil surmisings*. Bad suspicions. *perverse disputings*. Meddlesome activities. Again, Timothy is exhorted to be faithful to the apostolic doctrine contrary to the heretics who are characterized by pride and tend to focus on discussions regarding *words*, which lead to *strife*, instead of godliness. They are motivated by desire to receive honor and material gain rather than by godly contentment. Timothy must keep his distance from such people.

6:6–10 *Contentment* implies that the Christian may know that he will always have enough in the Lord. Love of money will cause one to deviate from the faith and to pierce himself with many *sorrows*. The same can also be said of pride and sinful lusts. These lie at the *root of all evil*. *raiment*. Clothing.

Encouragement to Timothy to Be Faithful (6:11–16)

6:11 A *man of God* is one who is governed by the Holy Spirit and shows the fruit of the Spirit.

6:12 The Christian life, especially for office bearers, is a struggle. The expression *lay hold on eternal life* is imagery taken from the arenas where the runners would exert themselves to win the race and then reach out with their hands to grasp the prize set before them.

6:13 *quickeneth*. Brings to life. This refers to the fact that God is the source of all life and also maintains life (Acts 17:25).

6:15 *Potentate*. Mighty One. At His appointed time, God will reveal the Lord Jesus to judge the living and the dead.

6:16 God is all glorious and dwells in a light of immaculate purity. No one can see Him, as He is a Spirit and is invisible (John 1:18; 1 Tim. 1:17; 1 John 4:20).

6:17 *highminded*. Proud.

FINAL EXHORTATIONS (6:17–21)

How to Counsel the Rich (6:17–19)

6:18–19 *willing to communicate*. Ready to share. The generosity of the rich does not merit eternal life, but is a fruit of faith, which God is willing to reward by grace alone for Christ's sake.

Final Encouragement to Timothy to Be Faithful (6:20–21)

6:20 The sound doctrine of God's Word has been entrusted as a pledge, or deposit, into Timothy's hand, and he has the responsibility to guard, proclaim, and teach it, especially against false teachers. He must avoid wasting time on the insanities of false teachings but positively proclaim the truth.

6:21 *Grace* is God's undeserved favor in Christ revealed toward people, who are unworthy in themselves. This grace transforms their hearts and lives, and leads them to be forever in glory.

Thoughts for Personal/Family Worship: Chapter 6

1. **Paul gives directions for slaves and masters. As such Paul does not outlaw slavery, but provides a framework within which masters and their slaves must operate on the basis of mutual respect, love, and trust. Thereby in reality the institution of slavery is undermined. In our days slave trade is forbidden, but pride, antagonism against other people, races, and those of a different social status, as well as foreigners, is deeply ingrained in the human heart. Paul points out to us the Christian attitude of love, respect, and care toward all other people.**
2. **This passage also teaches us the need not to be attached to the material blessings of this world. This world is transient. Only the salvation of the Lord Jesus Christ remains forever. We may be grateful for the many blessings of this world and use them, but at the same time realize the needs of others, alleviating them where we can. Let us use this life as a preparation for eternal life.**

INTRODUCTION TO THE BOOK OF
2 TIMOTHY

Authorship: According to the salutation, Paul wrote the epistle of 2 Timothy (1:1) with the apostolic authority he received from Christ, being sent by God (v. 11). The author relates the struggle of his personal circumstances: he was in prison and had already been on trial (4:16). He knew that his death was imminent (v. 6), and he had "fought a good fight" and finished his course (v. 7). Early church testimonies of those adhering to the orthodox faith are unanimous in stating that the apostle Paul was the author of 2 Timothy. Church leaders at the end of the first century quote from 2 Timothy, which shows that this epistle has apostolic authority.

Like 1 Timothy, this epistle was written "To Timothy, my dearly beloved son" (1:2). Timothy played an important role in the early church and was very special to Paul. He was Paul's spiritual son, probably converted during Paul's first missionary journey. Leaving his native Lystra, he accompanied Paul on his second and third missionary journeys. Paul also sent him to give direction to local churches. He seems to have been a timid person, in need of encouragement (vv. 7–8; 2:1–6).

Date: Scholars agree that the circumstances mentioned in 1 and 2 Timothy do not reflect any particular scenario in the book of Acts. This leads us to conclude that these two epistles were written at a later date, after Paul had been released from his two-year imprisonment at Rome. Shortly before his imprisonment Paul had been in Troas (4:13), a major city in the northwest of Asia Minor, on the coast of Mysia. Because Paul left his cloak there, it can be assumed that he was there in the summer, and as he desired Timothy to come to him before the winter, we may also assume that Paul has not been in prison for a long time and that it is now fall of that same year. Paul's first imprisonment was a house arrest (Acts 28). This second imprisonment was of a different nature. Paul felt forsaken (2 Tim. 4:16) and Onesiphorus had to search "very diligently" to find out where he was imprisoned (1:17). Historians estimate that Paul was put to death around AD 67. However, the chronology of the closing events of Paul's life is too obscure to be certain what year he wrote this epistle.

Theme: Encouragement in the ministry against hardships and false doctrines.

Purpose: Paul writes to encourage Timothy to remain faithful, even as Paul has, in the ministry that has been entrusted to him, that he too might receive the crown of glory.

Synopsis: *The Contribution of 2 Timothy to Redemptive Revelation*
There appear to be similarities between the two letters written to Timothy. In both, Timothy is encouraged to be strong, to organize church life, and to be alert for false teachers. Although both epistles aim at encouraging Timothy to be faithful to the Lord, however, there are profound differences. The first letter has a more objective and business-like tone, dealing with various issues of organizing and protecting church life. The second is more personal; it is the spiritual legacy of a dying friend and brother in the Lord. Paul longs for Timothy's presence, repeatedly asking him to come and visit him in his imprisonment (4:9,21).

Outline:

I. Salutations and Thanksgiving (1:1–5)
  A. Address of the Epistle (1:1–2)
  B. Thanksgiving to God for Timothy's Faith (1:3–5)
II. Encouragements and Exhortations (1:6—2:13)
  A. Exhortation to Grasp Courage and Not to Be Ashamed of Truth (1:6–11)
  B. Admonition to Hold Fast the Truth (1:12–18)
  C. Encouragement to Endure Hardship in the Ministry (2:1–13)
III. Warnings and Exhortations to Encourage Perseverance (2:14—4:5)
  A. Warnings against Heretics, False Doctrine, and Other Sins (2:14–26)
  B. Warning against Falling Away in the Last Days (3:1–9)
  C. Exhortation to Stand Firm on the Word of God (3:10–17)
  D. Exhortation to Preach the Word of God (4:1–5)
IV. Closing Remarks (4:6–22)
  A. Paul's Testimony Regarding His Death and Living Hope (4:6–8)
  B. Personal Greetings (4:9–21)
  C. Final Benediction (4:22)

THE SECOND EPISTLE OF PAUL THE APOSTLE TO TIMOTHY

CHAPTER 1

PAUL, an apostle of Jesus Christ by the will of God,
according to the promise of life which is in Christ
Jesus,
2 To Timothy, *my* dearly beloved son: Grace,
mercy, *and* peace, from God the Father and Christ
Jesus our Lord.
3 I thank God, whom I serve from *my* forefathers
with pure conscience, that without ceasing I have
remembrance of thee in my prayers night and day;
4 Greatly desiring to see thee, being mindful of
thy tears, that I may be filled with joy;
5 When I call to remembrance the unfeigned
faith that is in thee, which dwelt first in thy grand-
mother Lois, and thy mother Eunice; and I am
persuaded that in thee also.
6 Wherefore I put thee in remembrance that
thou stir up the gift of God, which is in thee by
the putting on of my hands.
7 For God hath not given us the spirit of fear; but
of power, and of love, and of a sound mind.
8 Be not thou therefore ashamed of the testi-
mony of our Lord, nor of me his prisoner: but
be thou partaker of the afflictions of the gospel
according to the power of God;
9 Who hath saved us, and called *us* with an holy
calling, not according to our works, but according
to his own purpose and grace, which was given us
in Christ Jesus before the world began,
10 But is now made manifest by the appearing
of our Saviour Jesus Christ, who hath abolished
death, and hath brought life and immortality to
light through the gospel:
11 Whereunto I am appointed a preacher, and an
apostle, and a teacher of the Gentiles.
12 For the which cause I also suffer these things:
nevertheless I am not ashamed: for I know whom
I have believed, and am persuaded that he is able
to keep that which I have committed unto him
against that day.
13 Hold fast the form of sound words, which
thou hast heard of me, in faith and love which is
in Christ Jesus.
14 That good thing which was committed unto

Chapter 1: ***The apostle expresses his love to Timothy, encouraging him to be faithful and strong to fulfill the calling God has given him. He also urges Timothy not to fear possible suffering and to be careful to hold on to the doctrine entrusted to him. Paul notes that some have forsaken him, while others have remained faithful to him.***

SALUTATIONS AND THANKSGIVING (1:1–5)

Address of the Epistle (1:1–2)

1:1–2 Paul is an apostle *according to the promise of life*. This means that he has been assigned the task of preaching the gospel of Jesus Christ, containing the promise that all who believe in Christ shall gain everlasting life. Timothy is Paul's *son*—Paul's spiritual son, nurtured by the gospel, and Paul was lovingly and fatherly disposed toward Timothy as reflected in the expression *my dearly beloved son*.

Thanksgiving to God for Timothy's Faith (1:3–5)

1:3 Paul serves God with *pure conscience* being purified by the Holy Spirit and the blood of Christ. This pure conscience must refer to the time after Paul's conversion, although according to his own reasoning he to some extent had a pure conscience before his conversion (Acts 23:1; 1 Tim. 1:13).

ENCOURAGEMENTS AND EXHORTATIONS (1:6—2:13)

Exhortation to Grasp Courage and Not to Be Ashamed of Truth (1:6–11)

1:6 *stir up the gift of God*. The illustration of a fire that is glowing, but ready to go out, and needs to be revived by blowing. Timothy must revitalize the gift of the Holy Spirit bestowed upon him through prayer, study of the Scriptures, and diligently attending to the calling the Lord gives him.

1:7 *power*. Strength and diligence of heart to fulfill one's calling in spite of animosity and hardships.

1:8 Timothy is called to partake of the *afflictions of the gospel*. As such, he must prepare himself for the hardships that come with believing, preaching, and living the Word of God. But all this must be done *according to the power of God* showing that the strength and grace of God are working in his heart.

1:9–11 Paul gives a short declaration of the gospel and his and Timothy's call to preach this gospel.

Admonition to Hold Fast the Truth (1:12–18)

1:12 In spite of all his sufferings (v. 8) Paul is not *ashamed* because he knows that his calling into the ministry is guarded by God and will remain unaffected by what he suffers.

1:13–14 Paul puts forward the triune God: the Father has entrusted him with the ministry of Jesus Christ and he is kept by the power of the Holy Spirit (*Holy Ghost*).

thee keep by the Holy Ghost which dwelleth in us.
15 This thou knowest, that all they which are
in Asia be turned away from me; of whom are
Phygellus and Hermogenes.
16 The Lord give mercy unto the house of One-
siphorus; for he oft refreshed me, and was not
ashamed of my chain:
17 But, when he was in Rome, he sought me out
very diligently, and found *me*.
18 The Lord grant unto him that he may find
mercy of the Lord in that day: and in how many
things he ministered unto me at Ephesus, thou
knowest very well.

CHAPTER 2

THOU therefore, my son, be strong in the grace
that is in Christ Jesus.
2 And the things that thou hast heard of me
among many witnesses, the same commit thou
to faithful men, who shall be able to teach others
also.
3 Thou therefore endure hardness, as a good
soldier of Jesus Christ.
4 No man that warreth entangleth himself with
the affairs of *this* life; that he may please him who
hath chosen him to be a soldier.
5 And if a man also strive for masteries, *yet* is he
not crowned, except he strive lawfully.
6 The husbandman that laboureth must be first
partaker of the fruits.
7 Consider what I say; and the Lord give thee
understanding in all things.
8 Remember that Jesus Christ of the seed of David
was raised from the dead according to my gospel:
9 Wherein I suffer trouble, as an evil doer, *even*
unto bonds; but the word of God is not bound.
10 Therefore I endure all things for the elect's
sakes, that they may also obtain the salvation
which is in Christ Jesus with eternal glory.
11 *It is* a faithful saying: For if we be dead with
him, we shall also live with *him*:
12 If we suffer, we shall also reign with *him*: if we
deny *him*, he also will deny us:
13 If we believe not, *yet* he abideth faithful: he
cannot deny himself.
14 Of these things put *them* in remembrance,
charging *them* before the Lord that they strive not
about words to no profit, *but* to the subverting of
the hearers.

1:16–18 Paul prays here twice that God will extend mercy to the house of Onesiphorus, for all the relief given to Paul.

Thoughts for Personal/Family Worship: Chapter 1

1. **Paul reminds Timothy of the deeds of the Lord in the past. He speaks of the faith of Timothy's mother and grandmother and reminds him of the faith Timothy had shown in the past. This is all to encourage Timothy to persevere in the calling God has given him. It is encouraging for spiritual life to meditate on the deeds of the Lord in our own lives as well as the lives of loved ones (Ps. 77:11–12).**
2. **Note how the apostle prays for Timothy day and night. Paul had a high regard for prayer. We see this sprinkled throughout his epistles. Every time he prays, he thinks of Timothy. Paul prayed much, for he believed in God who answers prayer. He realized that God sovereignly incorporates the prayers of His people in His dealings with mankind.**

Chapter 2: *Exhortations to promote the proclamation of the gospel. Timothy is encouraged to entrust the preaching of the gospel to others who will be faithful. He should demonstrate willingness to suffer for the sake of the gospel as a soldier of Jesus Christ, remembering His resurrection as a pivotal doctrine. He should deny himself, forbearing opposition, while realizing that Christ is faithful. Therefore Timothy should flee youthful lusts and everything that may hinder the preaching of God's Word.*

Encouragement to Endure Hardship in the Ministry (2:1–13)

2:1 To *be strong in the grace that is in Christ* implies that Timothy is exhorted to seek the strength of the Lord to be enabled to labor faithfully in his ministry despite suffering and afflictions.

2:3 Timothy is involved in spiritual warfare and is comparable to a *soldier* on the battlefield. Soldiers must be willing to bear every possible hardship and discomfort and be willing to engage in any struggle set before them (1 Tim. 1:18; 2 Cor. 10:3–4).

2:4 Soldiers called to engage the enemy may not waste their time and efforts on mundane matters as farming, trading, or earning a living, but must be vigilant and ready to fight. Likewise a faithful minister of Christ should not be engaged in mundane affairs but be faithful and diligent in fulfilling his God-given calling so as to please Him who called him (2 Cor. 5:9).

2:5 *strive for masteries*. Compete in athletic games.

2:6 *husbandman*. Farmer. In order for the farmer to enjoy the fruits of the field, he must first cultivate, seed, and harvest. Only after such labor will he be able to receive the fruit. Likewise the ministers of the gospel will first have to labor diligently before they can enjoy the fruit.

2:7 Paul prays that the Lord would enlighten Timothy, so that he would have *understanding* in matters that relate to his salvation and official work as minister of the gospel (1 Cor. 2:14).

2:8 The doctrine of the resurrection is the cornerstone of the Christian faith and is the clear validation of the forgiveness of sins and eternal life for all who believe in Christ (1 Cor. 15:14). *my gospel*. Paul has been clear that the gospel has been entrusted to him by God.

2:10 Paul exhibits here much love for God's elect. For their sake he is willing to endure hardship and suffering, especially if by means of his example of suffering for the gospel they may be strengthened in the faith.

2:11–13 God's children who suffer for the sake of Christ will also live and reign forever with Christ. God is faithful both in His promise of salvation and judgment. He cannot do anything that would contradict His perfect nature. *Faithful saying* means that what he is now saying is truly valid and sure (1 Tim. 1:15; 3:1; 4:9; Titus 3:8).

15 Study to shew thyself approved unto God, a
workman that needeth not to be ashamed, rightly
dividing the word of truth.
16 But shun profane *and* vain babblings: for they
will increase unto more ungodliness.
17 And their word will eat as doth a canker: of
whom is Hymenæus and Philetus;
18 Who concerning the truth have erred, saying
that the resurrection is past already; and over-
throw the faith of some.
19 Nevertheless the foundation of God standeth
sure, having this seal, The Lord knoweth them
that are his. And, Let every one that nameth the
name of Christ depart from iniquity.
20 But in a great house there are not only vessels
of gold and of silver, but also of wood and of earth;
and some to honour, and some to dishonour.
21 If a man therefore purge himself from these,
he shall be a vessel unto honour, sanctified, and
meet for the master's use, *and* prepared unto
every good work.
22 Flee also youthful lusts: but follow righteous-
ness, faith, charity, peace, with them that call on
the Lord out of a pure heart.
23 But foolish and unlearned questions avoid,
knowing that they do gender strifes.
24 And the servant of the Lord must not strive;
but be gentle unto all *men*, apt to teach, patient,
25 In meekness instructing those that oppose
themselves; if God peradventure will give them
repentance to the acknowledging of the truth;
26 And *that* they may recover themselves out of
the snare of the devil, who are taken captive by
him at his will.

CHAPTER 3

THIS know also, that in the last days perilous
times shall come.
2 For men shall be lovers of their own selves, cov-
etous, boasters, proud, blasphemers, disobedient
to parents, unthankful, unholy,

WARNINGS AND EXHORTATIONS TO ENCOURAGE PERSEVERANCE (2:14—4:5)

Warnings against Heretics, False Doctrine, and Other Sins (2:14–26)

2:15 Timothy must be diligent in his labors so as not to be ashamed because of any impurity or disorderliness. *Rightly dividing the word of truth* is imagery taken from either the temple priests who had to divide the sacrificial animals according to the Mosaic precepts or from a steward of a household, called to divide the food and allocate to every member of the household his fitting portion.

2:16–18 *vain babblings.* Empty words that have no spiritual content though proclaimed loudly, and serve no other purpose than to cause confusion, leading unstable people away from the faith. *canker.* Gangrene, a devastating infection unless it is thoroughly rooted out.

2:19–21 *sure.* Firm. *meet.* Suitable. In spite of people being deceived by false teachers, God's firm *foundation* of His immutable election to salvation remains sure. The *seal* is a reference to the book of life (Rev. 20:12; 22:10) showing that God knows His own. They will be saved, but this salvation will be manifested in the way of their abstaining from iniquity. The illustration is used of a *great house* containing precious *vessels*, as well as vessels for daily use. The visible church of Christ contains the elect children of God as well as the reprobate, who lack true saving faith. Believers are to purge themselves of iniquity, and then it will be apparent that they belong to the elect children of God and are prepared to perform *every good work* the Lord calls them to do (Eph. 2:10).

2:22 *charity.* Love.

2:23 *gender.* Produce.

2:25–26 *peradventure.* Perhaps. God Himself needs to lead sinners to *repentance* and to awaken them from their deception, as Satan keeps men in bondage to do *his will.*

Thoughts for Personal/Family Worship: Chapter 2

1. **Paul encourages Timothy in v. 3 to endure difficulty as a good soldier of Jesus Christ. To some extent hardships and difficulties will be the share of all who are called to be a witness of the Lord Jesus Christ. Timothy, as a minister of the gospel, had to reckon with these hardships and not be surprised when they occur. Likewise now all office bearers must count on hardships in their official work. But also God's children, as they are called to be witnesses of the Lord Jesus Christ, must reckon with scorn, tribulation, and other hardships as they witness from the Word of God.**
2. **Timothy must strive lawfully (v. 5). What does this mean? An office bearer should be honest and upright. He may not be proud or strive for glory from men. He should not be discouraged by hardships. He should not waste his energy. He should not consider himself to be indispensable. He should be willing to share the work with others and not promote himself. He must submit himself to proper church oversight, especially regarding the preaching of God's Word. He must show willingness to learn from others.**
3. **In v. 25 the purpose of all pastoral work toward those that oppose the gospel is stated. The word used there in the original is stronger than repentance. It is conversion, which implies a total change in mental and moral outlook on life. It leads to a radical change of one's attitude and conduct. Such change is not the fruit of man's persuasion but is always worked by God's Spirit, as a gift of God. Let us be humble when we know this change of life. Let our need for conversion drive us to hope in the Lord. Be careful not to grieve God's Spirit but in humility expect His working in your life.**

Chapter 3: ***Paul warns Timothy against false teachers who will arise in the last days, seducing people. He exhorts Timothy to turn away from such heretics and to follow Paul's example in bearing hardships and to realize that all who live godly in Christ Jesus will suffer such afflictions. Finally, Paul exhorts Timothy to be faithful to the doctrine of God's Word, pointing out to him how excellent and suitable the Word of God is.***

Warning against Falling Away in the Last Days (3:1–9)

3:1–5 *last days.* The present era ushered in by the coming of Christ in the flesh and the outpouring of the Holy Spirit at Pentecost, and ending with the second coming of Christ (Isa.

3 Without natural affection, trucebreakers, false
accusers, incontinent, fierce, despisers of those
that are good,
4 Traitors, heady, highminded, lovers of pleasures
more than lovers of God;
5 Having a form of godliness, but denying the
power thereof: from such turn away.
6 For of this sort are they which creep into
houses, and lead captive silly women laden with
sins, led away with divers lusts,
7 Ever learning, and never able to come to the
knowledge of the truth.
8 Now as Jannes and Jambres withstood Moses,
so do these also resist the truth: men of corrupt
minds, reprobate concerning the faith.
9 But they shall proceed no further: for their folly
shall be manifest unto all *men*, as theirs also was.
10 But thou hast fully known my doctrine, man-
ner of life, purpose, faith, longsuffering, charity,
patience,
11 Persecutions, afflictions, which came unto
me at Antioch, at Iconium, at Lystra; what per-
secutions I endured: but out of *them* all the Lord
delivered me.
12 Yea, and all that will live godly in Christ Jesus
shall suffer persecution.
13 But evil men and seducers shall wax worse and
worse, deceiving, and being deceived.
14 But continue thou in the things which thou
hast learned and hast been assured of, knowing of
whom thou hast learned *them*;
15 And that from a child thou hast known the holy
scriptures, which are able to make thee wise unto
salvation through faith which is in Christ Jesus.
16 All scripture *is* given by inspiration of God,
and *is* profitable for doctrine, for reproof, for
correction, for instruction in righteousness:
17 That the man of God may be perfect, throughly
furnished unto all good works.

CHAPTER 4

I CHARGE *thee* therefore before God, and the Lord
Jesus Christ, who shall judge the quick and the
dead at his appearing and his kingdom;
2 Preach the word; be instant in season, out of
season; reprove, rebuke, exhort with all longsuf-
fering and doctrine.

2:2; Mic. 4:1; Acts 2:17; Heb. 1:2). *incontinent.* Unruly or unrestrained and indulging in pleasures of life. *heady.* Reckless, plunging into all kinds of wickedness with little or no restraint. Such people will not be told what to do. *highminded.* Blinded with conceit. *form of godliness.* Resemblance of piety that is not true piety, lacking true love to God. *from such turn away.* Timothy must withdraw himself from such people.

3:6–7 *silly.* Foolish. *laden.* Loaded. *divers.* Various. They visit people's homes and especially try to impose themselves upon women. Throughout his epistles the apostle gives many examples of godly women who are strong in the faith, but there are also women who tend to be easily led astray and false teachers will especially focus on these, who are weak-minded, sinful, easily swayed, and will therefore never be able to acknowledge the truth as proclaimed in the gospel.

3:8–9 According to Jewish tradition, *Jannes and Jambres* are names of Egyptian wizards who opposed Moses. *reprobate concerning the faith.* They will imitate faith, proclaiming that they are teachers of piety, while in reality they are of a corrupt mind.

Exhortation to Stand Firm on the Word of God (3:10–17)

3:10–11 Paul recognizes that Timothy has followed Paul's example of godliness and willingness to suffer. The apostle gives examples of suffering he endured in Asia, which took place before Timothy accompanied Paul (Acts 13–14). *charity.* Love.

3:15–17 *scriptures.* Primarily the Old Testament, though it is also appropriate to extend this to the divinely inspired New Testament. *given by inspiration of God.* Breathed out by God's Spirit, who is the Spirit of truth and has led the authors infallibly in all truth (John 16:13; 2 Peter 1:20–21). *furnished.* Outfitted.

Thoughts for Personal/Family Worship: Chapter 3

1. **In v. 8 mention is made of two Egyptian magicians whose names, until now, have not been mentioned in the Bible. God has seen fit to give us their names here. This fact should remind us that God remembers each person's individual name, thoughts, and actions. Though all of humanity forget us, God remembers still. Judgment day will reveal many things history has forgotten. Let us therefore seek to be well-grounded in Scripture as the cornerstone of faith.**
2. **In v. 12 the apostle teaches that all who wish to live godly in Christ will suffer forms of hardship, suffering, and even persecution. They may be despised or even ostracized for the sake of the gospel. All those who wish to live godly should realize this and prepare themselves mentally in advance for such events, so as not to be shocked when they actually take place. By the Spirit's grace, they will then be able to endure such hardships and remain faithful to the Lord.**

Chapter 4: ***Again the apostle encourages Timothy earnestly to be faithful to the calling the Lord has given him, especially in light of the evil that men will devise against the Lord and His Word. Timothy should be prepared even to suffer oppression when he preaches the gospel. Paul furthermore explains that he himself will shortly be put to death but that he is greatly comforted by the glorious future the Lord has in store for all who love Him. He asks Timothy to come to him soon and informs him about his personal circumstances, especially about the trial to which he has been subjected. Paul expresses confidence that the Lord will not forsake Timothy and ends his letter with personal greetings.***

Exhortation to Preach the Word of God (4:1–5)

4:1–5 *quick.* Living. Paul admonishes Timothy to fulfill his duties as a preacher of the gospel and to be devoted to his God-given calling despite suffering and persecution. Paul exhorts Timothy five times to proclaim the gospel, because the Lord Jesus will return to judge the living and the dead. *instant in season, out of season.* Ready to preach at every possible

3 For the time will come when they will not
endure sound doctrine; but after their own lusts
shall they heap to themselves teachers, having
itching ears;
4 And they shall turn away *their* ears from the
truth, and shall be turned unto fables.
5 But watch thou in all things, endure afflictions,
do the work of an evangelist, make full proof of
thy ministry.
6 For I am now ready to be offered, and the time
of my departure is at hand.
7 I have fought a good fight, I have finished *my*
course, I have kept the faith:
8 Henceforth there is laid up for me a crown
of righteousness, which the Lord, the righteous
judge, shall give me at that day: and not to me only,
but unto all them also that love his appearing.
9 Do thy diligence to come shortly unto me:
10 For Demas hath forsaken me, having loved
this present world, and is departed unto Thessa-
lonica; Crescens to Galatia, Titus unto Dalmatia.
11 Only Luke is with me. Take Mark, and bring
him with thee: for he is profitable to me for the
ministry.
12 And Tychicus have I sent to Ephesus.
13 The cloke that I left at Troas with Carpus, when
thou comest, bring *with thee*, and the books, *but*
especially the parchments.
14 Alexander the coppersmith did me much evil:
the Lord reward him according to his works:
15 Of whom be thou ware also; for he hath greatly
withstood our words.
16 At my first answer no man stood with me, but
all *men* forsook me: *I pray God* that it may not be
laid to their charge.
17 Notwithstanding the Lord stood with me, and
strengthened me; that by me the preaching might
be fully known, and *that* all the Gentiles might
hear: and I was delivered out of the mouth of the
lion.
18 And the Lord shall deliver me from every evil
work, and will preserve *me* unto his heavenly king-
dom: to whom *be* glory for ever and ever. Amen.
19 Salute Prisca and Aquila, and the household of
Onesiphorus.
20 Erastus abode at Corinth: but Trophimus have
I left at Miletum sick.
21 Do thy diligence to come before winter. Eu-
bulus greeteth thee, and Pudens, and Linus, and
Claudia, and all the brethren.
22 The Lord Jesus Christ *be* with thy spirit. Grace
be with you. Amen.

---

opportunity, not letting his own personal inconvenience hinder him. Further, he must *reprove* and *rebuke* those who oppose the truth. Christian doctrine must be clear, for days are coming in which people will oppose *sound doctrine. itching ears*. Yearning for novelties instead of sound doctrine. *full proof of thy ministry*. So faithful that all will be convinced that he is a messenger of God, speaking the truth.

CLOSING REMARKS (4:6–22)

Paul's Testimony Regarding His Death and Living Hope (4:6–8)

4:6–8 *Offered* means that Paul will be put to death as an offering. Verse 7 compares Paul's life to a *fight* in an arena that ends with a prize. Paul rejoices that saving faith is still active in his life and that he has remained faithful to his calling as an apostle, by God's grace (Rom. 3:23–24; Eph. 2:8; Phil. 1:29; 1 Tim. 1:14). *crown of righteousness*. Eternal life—the reward of God.

Personal Greetings (4:9–21)

4:10 *Demas* was a former associate of Paul's who had deserted him (Col. 4:14; Philem. 24).
4:11 Paul expresses joy in *Mark*, who was once at the center of a serious dissension between Paul and Barnabas (Acts 15:39), but is now again of great value to Paul in his ministry.
4:13 *books*. Papyrus rolls. *parchments*. Thin animal skins, made ready for writing; likely Old Testament scrolls, first used in Pergamos, from which our word parchment is derived.
4:14–15 *be thou ware*. Be wary, alert. The evil committed by *Alexander* was rejecting and slandering the true doctrine of God. Paul invokes a curse against him, not out of a desire for revenge but moved by the Holy Spirit to desire God's honor and as a manifestation of His just punishment. Paul was not acting alone, for Alexander had withstood multiple exhortations and warnings.
4:16 *first answer*. Paul gave a first account for emperor Nero and all his helpers had neglected to stand with him, although he apparently exempts Luke (v. 11) from such conduct. Paul prays for them since they did this out of weakness and not out of spite.
4:17–18 For now Paul was delivered from the *mouth of the lion*, implying that he had been delivered from death. Paul is convinced that the Lord will ultimately keep him from every malicious assault by leading him to eternal life.
4:19 For *Prisca* and *Aquila* see Acts 18:2 and Rom. 16:3.
4:20 *Erastus* is also mentioned in Acts 19:22 and Rom. 16:23. For *Trophimus* see Acts 20:4 and 21:29.

Final Benediction (4:22)

Thoughts for Personal/Family Worship: Chapter 4

1. **In v. 2 we read that Paul desires Timothy to emphasize doctrine in his teaching. Today doctrine is not viewed as useful and people generally prefer "practical preaching." But a church without doctrine is like a house without a structure, or a building without a foundation. The church of the Lord Jesus Christ needs to be instructed in the doctrines of God's Word. Therefore preaching should contain a major focus on the fundamental Christian doctrines, such as those found in the Heidelberg Catechism or the Westminster Shorter Catechism. Parents should instruct their children in these truths.**
2. **In v. 8 we read of the reward the Lord has set in store for all those who love Him. God's people are called to meditate on the future blessings the Lord shall give to His own. One moment in glory will make all the struggles on earth worthwhile. In the midst of trials and hardships, this is a great impetus to continue the struggle, knowing that their heavenly reward is firm and sure. The future glory of God's people is grounded in Christ's resurrection. The outpouring of the Holy Ghost is a down payment of the full blessing, which is still to come.**

LOOKING FOR THAT

Blessed

HOPE

&

THE GLORIOUS

Appearing

OF THE

GREAT

God

AND OUR

SAVIOUR

Jesus Christ

TITUS 2:13

INTRODUCTION TO THE BOOK OF TITUS

Authorship: Irenaeus in the second century AD ascribed this letter to Paul. Against this, some scholars have argued that the epistles to Titus and Timothy could not have been written by Paul because: (1) their vocabulary and style differ from Paul's other letters, (2) they present a more formal and organized view of the church than Paul held, and (3) early Christians welcomed pseudonymous letters written in the name of a famous leader as an honor to him, not as a form of deceit.

In response, we make the following points: (1) An epistle's style varies according to the author's situation, the person or group to whom he writes, and the scribe to whom he dictates the letter (Rom. 16:22; 1 Cor. 16:21; 2 Thess. 3:17). (2) These epistles do not contradict Paul's view of the church. He organized churches under the oversight of elders and with the ministry of deacons (Acts 14:23; 20:17,28; Phil. 1:1). (3) Although some ancient apocalyptic writings, sermons, and histories were pseudonymous, it is not true that ancient Christians wrote and welcomed letters under false names. Paul warned against letters falsely claiming to be from him (2 Thess. 2:2), and early church leaders such as Tertullian (c. AD 160–c. 225) and Serapion (d. AD 211) condemned writings that falsely bore the names of apostles. It would be the worse hypocrisy for this author to pretend to be Paul while declaring the "truth" from God who "cannot lie," and warning against "deceivers" (1:1–2,10).

In the end, we return to the claims of the Bible itself. The author identifies himself as Paul (1:1), refers to Titus as his "own son" in the faith (v. 4), and references how Paul left him in Crete with specific instructions (v. 5). He speaks of his plan to stay the winter at Nicopolis, and urges Titus to visit him there if possible (3:12). Thus this book presents itself as a personal epistle from the apostle to a dear friend and coworker in ministry.

Date: Perhaps about the same time as 1 Timothy, around AD 62–64, between Paul's first imprisonment at Rome (AD 62) and his imprisonment and execution there (AD 64–67).

Theme: The church should be established through solid leadership and a sober lifestyle of godliness produced by the sound doctrines of election, redemption, and regeneration.

Purpose: To encourage a pastor in leading the church to overcome false teaching and mankind's inherent tendency to disorder and wickedness.

Synopsis: *The Contribution of TItus to Redemptive Revelation*

Titus was the man Paul looked to for the most difficult assignments, such as completing the reformation of doctrine and life in the church at Corinth (2 Cor. 2:12–13; 7:6–7,13–15; 8:6,16–17,23–24; 12:18). The church in Crete, a large Mediterranean island south of the Greek mainland, faced a number of challenges. False teachers sought to divide the church's members with Jewish legalism and traditions (1:10,14; 3:9–10), perhaps combined with Greek philosophical speculations. The cultural sins characteristic of the Cretans (1:12) still tugged at their hearts.

In response, Paul directed Titus to deploy godly and well-taught elders in every city and town (1:5–9). The main core of the epistle then instructs Titus to call the church to a life of sobriety and good works grounded in the sound doctrine of Christ (2:1—3:11). This epistle is a textbook, of sorts, of the doctrines of grace, covering eternal election unto faith (1:1–2), salvation by grace alone (2:11; 3:4), particular redemption unto holiness by Christ's death (2:14), human depravity (3:3), regeneration by the Holy Spirit through Christ (3:5–7), and Christ's coming in glory to bless His redeemed (2:13).

These doctrines are not taught in a merely academic way, but as the spiritual foundation and living root of godliness, "the things which become sound doctrine" (2:1). Thus Paul wove together doctrine and exhortations to self-control, submissiveness to proper authority, and zeal for good works (vv. 2–10,12,14–15; 3:1—2,8). The apostle believed that doctrine encourages rather than discourages godliness.

Outline:

I. Greetings from an Apostle for the Faith of God's Elect (1:1–4)

II. Good and Bad Leaders in the Local Church (1:5–16)
   - A. Charge to Appoint Qualified Elders (1:5–9)
   - B. Warning against False Teachers (1:10–16)

III. Godliness Formed by the Doctrines of Grace (2:1—3:11)
   - A. Instructions for a Sober Life in Various Social Groups (2:1–10)
   - B. Redemption by Christ for Good Works (2:11–14)
   - C. Exhortations to Sound Doctrine and Meekness (2:15—3:2)
   - D. Regeneration by the Holy Spirit for Good Works (3:3–7)
   - E. Teaching for Good Works and Avoiding Heresy (3:8–11)

IV. Grace and Personal Directions (3:12–15)

THE EPISTLE OF PAUL THE APOSTLE TO TITUS

CHAPTER 1

PAUL, a servant of God, and an apostle of Jesus
Christ, according to the faith of God's elect, and
the acknowledging of the truth which is after
godliness;
2 In hope of eternal life, which God, that cannot
lie, promised before the world began;
3 But hath in due times manifested his word
through preaching, which is committed unto
me according to the commandment of God our
Saviour;
4 To Titus, *mine* own son after the common faith:
Grace, mercy, *and* peace, from God the Father
and the Lord Jesus Christ our Saviour.
5 For this cause left I thee in Crete, that thou
shouldest set in order the things that are wanting,
and ordain elders in every city, as I had appointed
thee:
6 If any be blameless, the husband of one wife,
having faithful children not accused of riot or
unruly.
7 For a bishop must be blameless, as the steward
of God; not selfwilled, not soon angry, not given
to wine, no striker, not given to filthy lucre;
8 But a lover of hospitality, a lover of good men,
sober, just, holy, temperate;
9 Holding fast the faithful word as he hath been
taught, that he may be able by sound doctrine
both to exhort and to convince the gainsayers.
10 For there are many unruly and vain talkers
and deceivers, specially they of the circumcision:
11 Whose mouths must be stopped, who subvert
whole houses, teaching things which they ought
not, for filthy lucre's sake.
12 One of themselves, *even* a prophet of their
own, said, The Cretians *are* alway liars, evil beasts,
slow bellies.
13 This witness is true. Wherefore rebuke them

Chapter 1: ***Paul greets Titus, and directs him to appoint elders in every place in order to oppose the wickedness of false teachers.***

GREETINGS FROM AN APOSTLE FOR THE FAITH OF GOD'S ELECT (1:1–4)

1:1–3 *servant of God.* Slave under the divine Master. *apostle.* Messenger sent by *Jesus Christ* with authority to speak and write His Word (Gal. 1:1,12; Eph. 2:20—3:5). *faith of God's elect.* Faith given to those chosen by God (Acts 13:48). *acknowledging of the truth which is after godliness.* Biblical knowledge that agrees with and promotes reverence, love, and hope toward *God our Saviour* (2:1; 1 Tim. 6:3). This teaching was *promised before the world began* in a covenant between the Father, Son, and Holy Spirit, but was plainly revealed (*manifested*) in the gospel which Christ *committed* to Paul (2 Tim. 1:9–10). The Bible is absolutely certain, the *word* of the *God that cannot lie* (Num. 23:19).

1:4 *mine own son.* Titus was converted by Paul's preaching, so Paul was his spiritual father (1 Cor. 4:15; 1 Tim. 1:2). *Grace, mercy, and peace.* Blessing for the needy, help for the hurting, and restored harmony for the alienated.

GOOD AND BAD LEADERS IN THE LOCAL CHURCH (1:5–16)

Charge to Appoint Qualified Elders (1:5–9)

1:5 *left I thee.* Paul had to depart before completely organizing the churches. *Crete.* Island in the Mediterranean Sea, one hundred sixty miles long and on average about twenty miles wide. *elders.* Officers charged to shepherd the church for Christ (1 Peter 5:1–4).

1:6 *If any be.* Elders must meet these qualifications (1 Tim. 3:1–7). *blameless.* With no charge of wrongdoing against them. *the husband of one wife.* A one-woman man. *not accused of riot or unruly.* Not wild or rebellious.

1:7 *bishop.* Overseer, another term for "elder" (Acts 20:17,28). *steward.* Servant entrusted with authority. *selfwilled.* Arrogant. *striker.* Violent. *filthy lucre.* Money obtained by fraud, theft, or abuse of office.

1:8 *sober.* Clear-thinking and self-controlled. *lover of good men.* Literally, "lover of good." *holy.* Devoted to God. *temperate.* Disciplined.

1:9 *Holding fast.* Clinging. *faithful word.* Trustworthy message (v. 2). *sound doctrine.* Teaching for a healthy spiritual life (v. 13; 2:1–2; 1 Tim. 1:10; 6:3; 2 Tim. 1:13; 4:3). *gainsayers.* Persons who contradict God's Word.

Warning against False Teachers (1:10–16)

1:10–11 *For.* One reason a church needs good elders is to protect it from false and wicked teachers. *unruly.* Rebellious. *vain.* Empty. *circumcision.* Jews. *subvert whole houses.* Overthrow entire families. *for filthy lucre's sake.* To get rich.

1:12 Paul quoted the Cretan poet Epimenides, revered among the Greeks as a sage and *prophet*, who declared that *The Cretians* were habitual *liars*, had the morals of animals, and were lazy gluttons (*slow bellies*). All are sinners (3:3), and each nation has its own characteristic sins.

1:13 *sound in the faith.* Healthy in their understanding and belief in true doctrine, with the implication that they live by faith.

sharply, that they may be sound in the faith;
14 Not giving heed to Jewish fables, and com-
mandments of men, that turn from the truth.
15 Unto the pure all things *are* pure: but unto
them that are defiled and unbelieving *is* nothing
pure; but even their mind and conscience is
defiled.
16 They profess that they know God; but in works
they deny *him*, being abominable, and disobedi-
ent, and unto every good work reprobate.

CHAPTER 2

BUT speak thou the things which become sound
doctrine:
2 That the aged men be sober, grave, temperate,
sound in faith, in charity, in patience.
3 The aged women likewise, that *they be* in be-
haviour as becometh holiness, not false accusers,
not given to much wine, teachers of good things;
4 That they may teach the young women to be so-
ber, to love their husbands, to love their children,
5 *To be* discreet, chaste, keepers at home, good,
obedient to their own husbands, that the word of
God be not blasphemed.
6 Young men likewise exhort to be sober minded.
7 In all things shewing thyself a pattern of good
works: in doctrine *shewing* uncorruptness,
gravity, sincerity,
8 Sound speech, that cannot be condemned; that
he that is of the contrary part may be ashamed,
having no evil thing to say of you.
9 *Exhort* servants to be obedient unto their own
masters, *and* to please *them* well in all *things*; not
answering again;
10 Not purloining, but shewing all good fidelity;
that they may adorn the doctrine of God our
Saviour in all things.
11 For the grace of God that bringeth salvation
hath appeared to all men,
12 Teaching us that, denying ungodliness and
worldly lusts, we should live soberly, righteously,
and godly, in this present world;
13 Looking for that blessed hope, and the glorious

1:14 *Not giving heed.* Paying no attention. *Jewish fables.* Stories and folklore added to the Bible. *commandments of men.* Traditions that bind consciences (Matt. 15:9).

1:15 Concern for ritual purity blinded them to the need for inner purity (Matt. 23:23–26). Those who are *pure* in heart (1 Tim. 1:5; 2 Tim. 2:22) by faith in Christ (Acts 15:9) can enjoy in purity *all things* created by God (1 Tim. 4:1–5). Those *defiled* by their *unbelieving* hearts sin even when using God's good gifts (Mark 7:20–23).

1:16 *abominable.* Detestable. *unto every good work reprobate.* Tested and found totally rejectable, unable to do anything that might please God (Rom. 8:8).

Thoughts for Personal/Family Worship: Chapter 1

1. **What does Paul mean when he describes himself as both "a servant of God and an apostle of Jesus Christ"? In what way is this combination of titles unusual?**
2. **Paul stresses that church members should be concerned about what kind of men are nominated to hold office in the church as ministers, elders, or deacons. What traits of character or habits of life should we look for and value in such men?**
3. **Errors in doctrine or morals are serious, particularly in the lives of office bearers, who must set an example for the entire church. What kinds of people are vulnerable to the appeals of false teachers who would divide the church? How can we protect ourselves and our families from such persons?**

GODLINESS FORMED BY THE DOCTRINES OF GRACE (2:1—3:11)

Chapter 2: ***The faithful minister must exhort the church to live in wisdom, self-control, and godliness by faith in the crucified and coming Savior.***

Instructions for a Sober Life in Various Social Groups (2:1–10)

2:1 *But.* In contrast to the false teachers (1:10–16). *things which become sound doctrine.* The faithful preacher must tell the church to embrace traits of character and habits of life that fit the wholesome truths of God so that the gospel is honored (vv. 5,8,10).

2:2 *aged.* Old. *sober.* Thinking clearly and living carefully. *grave.* Honorable. *temperate.* Same word as "sober" in 1:8 (see note there). *sound.* Receiving healthy doctrine produces healthy living (v. 1). *charity.* Love.

2:3 *aged.* Old. *as becometh holiness.* Reverent, living always in God's sacred presence (Gen. 17:1). *false accusers.* Literally, "devils," accusers of the brethren (Rev. 12:10). *given to much wine.* Enslaved to alcohol.

2:4–5 *teach . . . to be sober.* Train in wisdom and self-control. *young.* In the ancient world, the term covered children and adults through about forty years of age. *discreet.* Same word as "temperate" (v. 2) and "sober" (see note at 1:8). *keepers at home.* Workers in the home; not an absolute limitation but the focus of a wife's duties (Prov. 31:10–31). *obedient.* Submitting to his authority (Eph. 5:22–24). *blasphemed.* Spoken of as evil.

2:6 *be sober minded.* Young men must control their thoughts and actions by wisdom (same root as "sober" in 1:8; see note there).

2:7–8 Titus must be a model (*pattern*) for others, especially the young men (v. 6), for he was a minister of the Word (*in doctrine*). *uncorruptness.* Not corrupted by false doctrine or evil motives, in contrast to false teachers (1 Tim. 6:5; 2 Tim. 3:8). *gravity.* Seriousness that shows dignity and wins respect. *Sound speech.* Healthy teaching. Such qualities take away from the enemies of the gospel any real reason to accuse God's servant of *evil*.

2:9–10 *servants.* Slaves (see notes at Eph. 6:5–9). *be obedient.* Submit with honor and obedience, sincerely desiring to work with excellence to *please* their *masters*. *not answering again.* Not talking back and arguing. *purloining.* Stealing. *fidelity.* Faithfulness. *adorn the doctrine.* Show people the beauty of God in the gospel.

Redemption by Christ for Good Works (2:11–14)

2:11–12 *For.* The motivation for the sober, righteous, godly life comes from the doctrines of *the grace of God*. Grace empowers holiness. *appeared.* Entered history visibly in Jesus Christ (3:4; 2 Tim. 1:10). *all men.* Not every person, for many do not know the gospel (Rom. 10:14,17), but all kinds of people, old and young, male and female, slave and free (vv. 2–10).

appearing of the great God and our Saviour Jesus Christ;
14 Who gave himself for us, that he might redeem
us from all iniquity, and purify unto himself a
peculiar people, zealous of good works.
15 These things speak, and exhort, and rebuke
with all authority. Let no man despise thee.

CHAPTER 3

PUT them in mind to be subject to principalities
and powers, to obey magistrates, to be ready to
every good work,
2 To speak evil of no man, to be no brawlers, *but*
gentle, shewing all meekness unto all men.
3 For we ourselves also were sometimes foolish,
disobedient, deceived, serving divers lusts and
pleasures, living in malice and envy, hateful, *and*
hating one another.
4 But after that the kindness and love of God our
Saviour toward man appeared,
5 Not by works of righteousness which we have
done, but according to his mercy he saved us, by
the washing of regeneration, and renewing of the
Holy Ghost;
6 Which he shed on us abundantly through Jesus
Christ our Saviour;
7 That being justified by his grace, we should be
made heirs according to the hope of eternal life.
8 *This is* a faithful saying, and these things I will
that thou affirm constantly, that they which have
believed in God might be careful to maintain
good works. These things are good and profitable
unto men.
9 But avoid foolish questions, and genealogies,
and contentions, and strivings about the law; for
they are unprofitable and vain.
10 A man that is an heretick after the first and

Teaching. Training, like a father instructs, encourages, and disciplines his children. *this present world*. The age of sin and misery since the fall (Gal. 1:4).

2:13 *Looking*. Waiting. One way the doctrines of grace motivate holiness is by the confident *hope* of enjoying God's glory. *blessed*. Bringing happiness. *appearing*. Just as Christ "appeared" once in "grace" (v. 11), so He will appear in glory. *the great God and our Saviour*. Better, "our great God and Savior," both applying to *Jesus Christ* (Isa. 9:6; John 1:1; 20:28; Heb. 1:8; 2 Peter 1:1). Christ is our God, glory, and hope.

2:14 *gave himself*. Voluntary gift of highest love and infinite value. *for us*. Substituting Himself for sinners under God's judgment (Gal. 3:13). *redeem*. Pay the ransom price (Mark 10:45) to release lawbreakers from *all* guilt and punishment (Ex. 21:30; Ps. 130:8), resulting in their justification (Isa. 53:11; Rom. 3:24). *purify*. Cleanse from sin (Ezek. 37:23) to walk with God in holiness (1 John 1:7), resulting in their sanctification. *unto himself a peculiar people*. Redemption aimed at a particular, chosen people (1:1; Eph. 1:4,7; 5:25), taking them to be God's special treasure in covenant relationship with Him (Ex. 19:5; 23:22; Deut. 7:6; 14:2). *zealous of good works*. An eager desire to deny yourself, obey God, and serve people is an effect and evidence of Christ dying for you (2 Cor. 5:15). He who fully satisfied the wrath of God for all our sins with His precious blood is the same Christ who by His Holy Spirit makes us sincerely willing and ready henceforth to live unto Him.

Exhortations to Sound Doctrine and Meekness (2:15—3:2)

2:15 *exhort*. Press the truth and its implications for life upon his hearers. *rebuke*. Expose and confront sin. *all authority*. Serve as the representative of the King of kings with love, faith, purity, boldness, and endurance so that people will not *despise* him (1 Tim. 4:12).

Thoughts for Personal/Family Worship: Chapter 2

1. **What are some of "the things which become sound doctrine" (v. 1)? How can we acquire them? Who is "a pattern of good works" (v. 7) for you? In what ways does your life "adorn the doctrine of God our Savior" (v. 10)? Why does it matter?**
2. **People today are beset with addictions of many kinds (alcoholism, drug abuse, overeating, pornography, etc.). Why is sobriety and sober-mindedness important for the Christian? How can we achieve it and maintain it?**
3. **What does "the grace of God" (v. 11) teach us to believe and to hope for? What does it teach about the duty required of believers? Why did Christ give Himself for His people? Why are they called His "peculiar people" (v. 14)? How do you live in the world as one who belongs to Christ?**

Chapter 3: *The faithful minister should call the church to live in humility and submission to authority, remembering their salvation by grace alone.*

3:1–2 In addition to godliness in private life (2:1–10) and toward church leaders (2:15), Christians also must be zealous for good works in society. They must give due honor and obedience (*be subject*) to government officials (*principalities and powers . . . magistrates*) as proper authorities (Rom. 13:1). *no brawlers, but gentle*. Not quick to fight, but promoting peace. *all meekness unto all men*. Humble love in every situation you face with every kind of person.

Regeneration by the Holy Spirit for Good Works (3:3–7)

3:3 *For*. Paul again grounded godliness on the doctrines of grace (2:11). Christian humility (vv. 1–2) flows from knowing the previous depravity of one's mindset, desires, and relationships. *sometimes*. Formerly. *serving*. As a slave. *divers*. Various.

3:4 Christian kindness flows from knowing God's saving kindness (Eph. 4:32—5:2). *appeared*. In Jesus Christ (see note at 2:11–12).

3:5–6 *Not by works*. Salvation is by God's grace alone without human merit (Rom. 3:28—4:8; Gal. 2:16; 3:10–14; Eph. 2:8–9; Phil. 3:9; 2 Tim. 1:9). *washing*. Cleansing from sin, pictured in baptism (Acts 22:16) but purchased by Christ (2:14) and performed by the Holy Spirit (*Holy Ghost*, Ezek. 36:25–27; 37:14,23). *regeneration*. Literally, "genesis again," a spiritual rebirth (John 3:3) or new creation (Matt. 19:28; Eph. 2:10). *shed . . . abundantly*. Poured out like a river (Isa. 32:2,15; 43:19–20; 44:3). *through Jesus Christ*. The Mediator of all saving grace (1 Tim. 2:5).

3:7 *being justified*. The Spirit produces faith in Christ (1 Cor. 12:3), and God declares believers legally righteous by faith alone (Rom. 4:5) because of Christ (2 Cor. 5:21), not our works (v. 5). Justification gives believers the right to inherit *eternal life* with God.

REGENERATION

A striking parallel exists between the beginning of physical life and the beginning of spiritual life. In the first creation, Adam had no physical life until he received the special breath of God. The molded dirt may have resembled Adam's eventual appearance, but it was just a lifeless sculpture until God breathed into it. As a lifeless shape, the first man could contribute nothing to his becoming alive. But when God breathed into the lifeless form, man became alive, and he lived as proof of his having received the principle of life.

Significantly, the Scripture refers to the beginning of spiritual life in terms of creation (2 Cor. 5:17; Gal. 6:15; Eph. 2:10). In the initial process of natural creation, man was insensible to the physical world without the life-imparting breath of God; so in spiritual creation, man remains dead to anything spiritual without the life-imparting Spirit of God (1 Cor. 2:14). In a most tragic sense, every sinner is dead to paradise. Just as Adam required God's breath for physical life, every sinner requires a gracious and special intervention of God to bring him to spiritual life. Consequently, the Scripture speaks of God's making dead sinners alive (Eph. 2:4–5; Col. 2:13). Adam made no contribution to his becoming alive; neither does the sinner aid God in becoming spiritually alive. Creation is always the unique, exclusive work of God.

This component of the gospel that concerns the beginning of spiritual life is *regeneration*. Regeneration refers to the implantation of the principle of spiritual life into the sinner's soul, which results in an instantaneous, radical, and obvious change of nature affecting the whole governing disposition of life. The prophet Ezekiel explained regeneration in terms of God's giving the sinner a new heart and a new spirit (Ezek. 36:26). The heart refers to man's mind, emotions, and will. The spirit refers to the impulses that direct and regulate the desires, thoughts, and conduct of life. The prophet's description of the old heart as stony portrays an inward nature that is cold, unfeeling, and hard. A petrified heart is utterly dead, incapable of functioning. It is a graphic image of the helpless condition of the sinner, void of any spiritual life or responsiveness. In regeneration, God graciously turns the heart of stone into viable flesh that responds to spiritual stimuli. This regeneration creates a revolutionary change in the way the sinner thinks, what he desires, and how he chooses to live. He has a new nature that is capable of spiritual activity. One moment the sinner was dead, the next he is alive. Regeneration is the application of spiritual life that awakens the sinner from the stupor of spiritual death, enabling him to see, to understand, and to receive Christ as He is offered freely in the gospel: regeneration enables saving faith and repentance. This work of the Holy Spirit is mysterious, irresistible, and effectual. When the Spirit of God implants the principle of life within the soul, the regenerated soul will evidence the vital signs of spiritual life.

Man's spiritual death and inability are answered by God's gracious provision in the atoning death and resurrection of His Son, the Lord Jesus Christ. It is only because of Christ and together with Christ that dead sinners can live. Although the Scripture uses various images to describe the essence of regeneration (e.g., circumcision, Deut. 30:6; resurrection, Eph. 2:5–6; creation, Eph. 2:10; spiritual baptism, 1 Cor. 12:13; new covenant, Jer. 31:33), perhaps the most expressive is that of the new birth (John 1:12–13; Titus 3:5; 1 Peter 1:3, 23; 1 John 2:29; 3:9; 4:7; 5:1, 4, 18).

Four important truths emerge from Christ's exposition of the new birth to Nicodemus. First, the new birth is necessary for salvation (John 3:3). Second, the Holy Spirit is the agent of the new birth (vv. 5, 6). Third, the new birth is based in God's love and purchased by Christ's death (v. 16). Fourth, the evidence of the new birth is saving faith and good works (vv. 18–21), just as breathing is the indication and not the cause of life. Regeneration is the impetus to faith. Truly, "ye must be born again."

second admonition reject;
11 Knowing that he that is such is subverted, and
sinneth, being condemned of himself.
12 When I shall send Artemas unto thee, or Tych-
icus, be diligent to come unto me to Nicopolis: for
I have determined there to winter.
13 Bring Zenas the lawyer and Apollos on their
journey diligently, that nothing be wanting unto
them.
14 And let ours also learn to maintain good works
for necessary uses, that they be not unfruitful.
15 All that are with me salute thee. Greet them
that love us in the faith. Grace *be* with you all.
Amen.

Teaching for Good Works and Avoiding Heresy (3:8–11)

3:8 *faithful saying*. Trustworthy teaching (1 Tim. 1:15; 4:9; 2 Tim. 2:11). *I will*. I desire. The preacher must *constantly* teach the *profitable* doctrines of sin, grace, regeneration, and justification (vv. 3–7), and exhort believers to respond to them with *good works*.

3:9 *genealogies*. Lists of Jewish ancestors (1:14), misused by false teachers (1 Tim. 1:4). *contentions, and strivings*. Fights and quarrels. *the law*. The law of Moses.

3:10–11 *heretick*. A person who forsakes true doctrines, teaches his own doctrine, and draws people away after his false teaching (Gal. 5:20; cf. Acts 20:30). *first and second admonition* (see Matt. 18:15–20). *reject*. Exclude from the church. *subverted*. Twisted.

GRACE AND PERSONAL DIRECTIONS (3:12–15)

3:12–13 Though a single man, Paul was never a solitary man, traveling with coworkers such as *Tychicus*, a dear brother and faithful minister (Acts 20:4; Eph. 6:21; Col. 4:7; 2 Tim. 4:12). *Nicopolis*. City on west coast of southern Macedonia. *Apollos*. Perhaps the Jew from Alexandria who was a great Christian preacher (Acts 18:24—19:1).

3:14 *ours*. Our people, the church. *maintain good works*. Same phrase used in v. 8, ending the letter with the same great emphasis on practical Christianity. *necessary uses*. Urgent needs.

3:15 *salute*. Greet. *Grace be with you all*. May all the church experience more undeserved blessings of the Spirit from the Father and the Son (1:4). *Amen*. Yes, truly.

Thoughts for Personal/Family Worship: Chapter 3

1. **Christians owe duty and obedience to the civil magistrate. What are the limits of this duty?**
2. **Are the sins of Christians more serious or less serious than the sins of unbelievers? Why?**
3. **What does it mean "to be ready to every good work" (v. 1)? Why should we show "all meekness unto all men" (v. 2)? Why must we still do good works? Do our good works have any part in our salvation? Why does Paul say that God's people are justified and made heirs according to the hope of eternal life, by God's grace imparted to us through Christ? What does this truth imply for our daily lives?**
4. **Paul warns us that there is a danger of taking up questions and topics that have little or nothing to do with the gospel's essential truths. What does he mean when he says that such questions and topics are "unprofitable and vain" (v. 9)? How do heretics condemn themselves?**

Grace
TO YOU
&
PEACE
FROM
God Our
FATHER
AND
The Lord
JESUS
Christ

PHILEMON 1:3

INTRODUCTION TO THE BOOK OF PHILEMON

Authorship: Paul and Timothy (v. 1), but primarily Paul (vv. 9,19).

Date: AD 60–62, being written from prison (vv. 1,9) and sent with Tychicus, who also carried the epistle to the Colossians (Col. 4:7–9), and Onesimus.

Theme: Brotherly love and forgiveness in Christ.

Purpose: To urge Philemon to warmly receive back his runaway slave, Onesimus.

Synopsis: *The Contribution of Philemon to Redemptive Revelation*

This letter, the shortest of Paul's epistles, was addressed to Philemon, a Christian hosting the church of Colosse in his home (v. 2). Onesimus was a slave (v. 16). Slavery in the Roman Empire was not a matter of race, for slaves came from various races and colors. Slaves comprised between a fifth and a third of the population of the cities. Slavery legally bound a person to serve a master. Their work varied from laboring in the fields to serving as doctors, teachers, and accountants. Some slaves saved money and bought their freedom. Paul called Philemon to not punish Onesimus for the financial loss he caused his master when he ran away but to welcome him home as a brother in Christ.

This epistle shows a warm fraternal spirit, as the great apostle chose not to command by right but instead to appeal by love (vv. 8–9). It also shows how the gospel and Christian love undermined the social divisions that supported slavery by making master and slave into brothers (v. 16).

Outline:

I. Greeting (vv. 1–3)
II. Thanksgiving and Prayer (vv. 4–7)
III. Appeal for Onesimus (vv. 8–20)
   A. Appeal from Paul's Heart (vv. 8–11)
   B. Call to Receive the Slave as a Brother (vv. 12–17)
   C. Offer to Pay for Philemon's Loss (vv. 18–20)
IV. Closing (vv. 21–25)

THE EPISTLE OF PAUL THE APOSTLE TO

PHILEMON

PAUL, a prisoner of Jesus Christ, and Timothy our
brother, unto Philemon our dearly beloved, and
fellowlabourer,
2 And to *our* beloved Apphia, and Archippus our
fellowsoldier, and to the church in thy house:
3 Grace to you, and peace, from God our Father
and the Lord Jesus Christ.
4 I thank my God, making mention of thee al-
ways in my prayers,
5 Hearing of thy love and faith, which thou hast
toward the Lord Jesus, and toward all saints;
6 That the communication of thy faith may
become effectual by the acknowledging of every
good thing which is in you in Christ Jesus.
7 For we have great joy and consolation in thy
love, because the bowels of the saints are refreshed
by thee, brother.
8 Wherefore, though I might be much bold in
Christ to enjoin thee that which is convenient,
9 Yet for love's sake I rather beseech *thee*, being
such an one as Paul the aged, and now also a
prisoner of Jesus Christ.
10 I beseech thee for my son Onesimus, whom I
have begotten in my bonds:
11 Which in time past was to thee unprofitable,
but now profitable to thee and to me:
12 Whom I have sent again: thou therefore
receive him, that is, mine own bowels:
13 Whom I would have retained with me, that in
thy stead he might have ministered unto me in
the bonds of the gospel:
14 But without thy mind would I do nothing;
that thy benefit should not be as it were of neces-
sity, but willingly.
15 For perhaps he therefore departed for a season,
that thou shouldest receive him for ever;

GREETING (vv. 1–3)

1 *prisoner of Jesus Christ*. Suffering imprisonment for the gospel, and under the sovereign hand of the Lord. *fellowlabourer*. Coworker for God's kingdom (Col. 4:11).

2 *Apphia*. Perhaps Philemon's wife. *Archippus*. Possibly his son. *fellowsoldier*. Comrade in the army of Christ (Phil. 2:25; 2 Tim. 2:3). *church in thy house*. Early churches did not have buildings and often met in private houses (Rom. 16:5; 1 Cor. 16:19; Col. 4:15).

3 *Grace*. Undeserved blessing on the needy. *peace*. Restored, harmonious relationships. These spiritual blessings come from both *God our Father* and *Christ*, God the Son.

THANKSGIVING AND PRAYER (vv. 4–7)

4–5 Paul prayed often and faithfully for the saints, mingling thanksgiving with petition (Phil. 4:6; 1 Thess. 5:17–18). He thanked God for their *love* for other believers and *faith* in *the Lord Jesus*, for these are the effects of saving grace (Eph. 1:15; Col. 1:4; 1 Thess. 1:2–5).

6 *That*. This is Paul's prayer for them. *communication*. Sharing, partnership, or fellowship, whether of the gospel or possessions. *effectual*. Effective. *acknowledging*. Knowledge. Christians often know what they have in Christ better when they share it with others.

7 Paul thanked God for them with *great joy* and comfort. *bowels*. Hearts, pictured here as the place of deep feelings. *saints*. All believers in Christ (1 Cor. 1:2).

APPEAL FOR ONESIMUS (vv. 8–20)

Appeal from Paul's Heart (vv. 8–11)

8–10 *Wherefore*. Therefore. *much bold in Christ*. Having more than enough authority and freedom in Christ. *enjoin*. Command. *convenient*. Proper, fitting. *beseech*. Appeal, ask with urgency. *the aged*. The old man. Rather than demand Philemon's obedience, the apostle appealed to him on the basis of brotherly love. *my son . . . begotten*. Referring to Onesimus's conversion (1 Cor. 4:15) after he met Paul in prison (*in my bonds*).

11 *unprofitable . . . now profitable*. Paul made a pun on the name Onesimus (meaning "profitable"). Though once a bad slave, now he is a blessing to his fellow believers. According to some church traditions, he may later have become bishop of Ephesus.

Call to Receive the Slave as a Brother (vv. 12–17)

12 *receive*. Here meaning "welcome, accept" (v. 17; Rom. 14:1,3; 15:7). *mine own bowels*. "My heart"; Paul had deep love, sympathy, and tender affection for Onesimus.

13 *retained*. Kept. *in thy stead*. In your place, caring for Paul as Philemon would. *ministered*. Served. Christ made the rebellious slave into a willing servant. *bonds*. Chains.

14 *without thy mind*. Without your consent. Paul sent Onesimus back so that Philemon could choose *willingly* to release him to serve Paul.

15 *receive*. Have, possess; not the same word used in vv. 12, 17. Paul called Philemon to view his temporary, earthly loss (*for a season*) in light of the eternal salvation of Onesimus, by which he gained him *for ever*.

16 *servant*. Slave. *brother*. Onesimus now has the same position as Philemon in the family of God (v. 7), thus transforming

16 Not now as a servant, but above a servant, a
brother beloved, specially to me, but how much
more unto thee, both in the flesh, and in the Lord?
17 If thou count me therefore a partner, receive
him as myself.
18 If he hath wronged thee, or oweth *thee* ought,
put that on mine account;
19 I Paul have written *it* with mine own hand, I
will repay *it*: albeit I do not say to thee how thou
owest unto me even thine own self besides.
20 Yea, brother, let me have joy of thee in the
Lord: refresh my bowels in the Lord.
21 Having confidence in thy obedience I wrote
unto thee, knowing that thou wilt also do more
than I say.
22 But withal prepare me also a lodging: for I
trust that through your prayers I shall be given
unto you.
23 There salute thee Epaphras, my fellowprisoner
in Christ Jesus;
24 Marcus, Aristarchus, Demas, Lucas, my
fellowlabourers.
25 The grace of our Lord Jesus Christ *be* with
your spirit. Amen.

---

their relationship. *in the flesh*. As fellow human beings. *in the Lord*. United by one Spirit to the same Lord Jesus Christ (Eph. 4:4–5).

17 *partner*. One sharing fellowship (same root as "communication," v. 6). *as myself*. Amazingly, this Christian master should receive his converted slave like an apostle. Though Christians have different offices and vocations, they are equal (Gal. 3:28).

Offer to Pay for Philemon's Loss (vv. 18–20)

18 *oweth thee ought*. Owe you anything by loss of his services or theft. *mine account*. Paul offered to compensate Philemon rather than have Onesimus liable for his crimes.

19 *written it with mine own hand*. Perhaps taking the pen from the scribe to whom he was dictating the letter to write this promise himself. *thou owest . . . thine own self*. Philemon had been saved through Paul's preaching, and so owed him more than money could pay.

20 *Yea*. Yes. *refresh my bowels*. Same words used in v. 7 (see note there). Philemon must now extend to his slave the same love he shows all the saints, to Paul's great joy.

CLOSING (vv. 21–25)

21–22 *thou wilt*. You will. *more than I say*. Perhaps emancipating him from slavery, or sending him back to continue to serve Paul. *withal*. At the same time. *lodging*. Hospitality, here a guest room (Acts 28:23). *given unto you*. Paul expected the sovereign, gracious God to answer the prayers of the church (plural *your* and *you*) for his release.

23–24 *salute*. Greet. *Epaphras*. The minister of the church in Colosse (Col. 1:7; 4:12). *Marcus*. Mark (2 Tim. 4:11). *Aristarchus*. A member of the missionary team from Thessalonica (Acts 19:29; 20:4; 27:2). *Demas* later fell away (2 Tim. 4:10). *Lucas*. Luke, physician and faithful coworker of Paul (v. 11). These names also appear in Col. 4:10,12,14, confirming that this letter accompanied the epistle to the Colossians.

25 *grace*. See note at v. 3. *with your spirit*. Though God's grace will glorify the bodies of believers, presently it works in their souls (Gal. 6:18; 2 Tim. 4:22). *Amen*. Yes, surely.

Thoughts for Personal/Family Worship

1. **How does Paul relate faith and love? How do you give joy and comfort to your fellow believers? What does our belief in "the communion of the body of Christ" (see 1 Cor. 10) require of us as Christians?**
2. **Would you be willing to pay the medical debts of a fellow Christian so that he or she could be free of such a burden? Would you be willing to forgive such a debt owed to you?**
3. **What is true Christian obedience? Why are mutual service and hospitality duties for all Christians? What does this say about the nature of the church as a society or body? How can you fulfill these duties?**

COMMUNION OF THE SAINTS

Article 9 of the Apostles' Creed states: "I believe one holy catholic Christian church: the communion of saints." The first treasure of the church is the bond that believers have with one another. This communion of saints—constituted of all true believers who are justified in Christ by the Spirit (Rom. 12:13; 1 Cor. 1:2; 6:11)—is twofold. *First*, it is the common right that we have to Christ and His gifts (1 John 1:3). *Second*, it is a calling to use our spiritual and temporal gifts among fellow believers (1 Cor. 12:13; Phil. 2:1–2).

This community is *one*; that is, though it has many parts and members, it is but one body (1 Cor. 12:12). This unity consists, *first*, of the unity of faith and, *second*, of the unity of the Spirit. Therefore, we are told to endeavor to "keep the unity of the Spirit in the bond of peace" (Eph. 4:3–6). The foundation for this unity is knowing Jesus Christ, the Head of the body, who joins all the parts of the body to one another (Col. 3:14–15).

This community is *holy* for three reasons. *First*, the church is separate from the unbelieving and godless world (Acts 2:40; 2 Cor. 6:17; 1 Peter 2:9). *Second*, the church is holy because the perfect holiness of Christ has been imputed to her (John 17:19; 1 Cor. 1:30). *Third*, the church strives after greater holiness because she has been cleansed by the washing of the Word (1 Peter 1:15).

This community is *catholic*, or *universal*. It consists of those in every place who call upon the name of Christ (1 Cor. 1:2; cf. Titus 1:4; 2 Peter 1:1). This community has existed from the beginning of the world and will remain forever.

This community is *Christian*, called by the name of Christ, her Bridegroom (John 3:29). Just as a wife takes the name of her husband (Gen. 2:23), so the church takes the name of Christ.

This community is called the *church*, the assembly of all believers (2 Peter 1:1). This church is sometimes called *militant*, composed of all believers on earth; sometimes *triumphant*, consisting of those saints already in glory; sometimes *visible*, the assembly of all believers who profess true faith, though intermixed with unbelievers (Matt. 13:38); sometimes *invisible*, made up of only the elect (1 Peter 1:2); sometimes *universal*, formed of all believers in every time, place, and nation; and sometimes *individual*, or spanning a local congregation.

Regarding this communion of saints, the individual believer must examine himself in several matters. *First*, he must ask whether he truly loves the brotherhood, the assembly and fellowship of believers. Belonging to the body, the believer should have a particular affection and fondness for all other members of the family (1 John 3:14). Therefore, the believer does not forsake the assembly (Heb. 10:25), whether in the public assembly of worship (Ps. 27:4) or in everyday association with believers (Ps. 16:3; Acts 2:46).

Second, the believer must ask whether he wholeheartedly strives after holiness. If he is a true member of the church and is sanctified by the blood of Christ, this should be proven by his life conduct (Heb. 12:14; 1 Peter 1:15; cf. Acts 8:21).

Third, he must examine himself to see whether he loves Christ with all his heart. Two marks prove this love: obedience (John 14:21) and longing for Christ (Rev. 22:17).

Fourth, the believer must use his talents, both his spiritual and temporal gifts, with a willing heart for the benefit of fellow believers. From this use of gifts on the part of each believer, the whole body is fitly joined together (Eph. 4:16) as each member performs his proper function without envy or spite (1 Cor. 12:16–22). In short, if the believer is a member of the body, he should do nothing through strife or self-promotion, but in lowliness of mind (Phil. 2:3).

—adapted from Godefridus Udemans, *The Practice of Faith, Hope, and Love*, ch. 13

INTRODUCTION TO THE BOOK OF

HEBREWS

Authorship: The author of Hebrews is never explicitly mentioned throughout the whole of Hebrews. Church history has been far from unanimous on the authorship of Hebrews. The early church proposed a variety of different authors. The early church father Tertullian argued that Barnabas, sometime companion of Paul, authored this book. Irenaeus and Hippolytus likewise defended a view of non-Pauline authorship. Following Jerome and Augustine, Pauline authorship was assumed by most biblical scholars. The Council of Nicea recognized the canonical status of Hebrews partly based on accrediting its authorship to Paul. The medieval church, following Nicea, largely approved of Paul's authorship, and Thomas Aquinas defended Pauline authorship. In the time of the Reformation, the view that Paul was not the author resurfaced through the influential works of Erasmus, Luther, and Calvin—Calvin preferring either Luke or Clement of Rome as the author. On the other hand, the Belgic Confession of Faith (AD 1561) endorses Pauline authorship, and the Puritan John Owen argued extensively for Pauline authorship.

By and large, modern scholarship has dismissed Pauline authorship for stylistic reasons and matters of theological emphasis. Various candidates for authorship have been proposed, including Apollos, Priscilla, and Luke. None of these proposals are without problems. In favor of Pauline authorship is the fact that when God revealed to Paul his mission, it included, besides "Gentiles, and kings," also "the children of Israel" (Acts 9:15), and the audience of this letter to the Hebrews would fit this well. In conjunction with this, Peter wrote to those of the dispersion (likely Jews; see 1 Peter 1:1) that "Paul . . . hath written unto you" (2 Peter 3:15). This does not fit any other book as well as the epistle to the Hebrews. Nevertheless, unlike the vast majority of other epistles of the New Testament, God has not seen fit to specify the author of this epistle. Not knowing the human authorship of this epistle with certainty should not hinder us from embracing the truths set forth in this great epistle as indispensable for faith.

Date and Destination: There are a couple of considerations that point to a date prior to AD 70, when Jerusalem was destroyed by the Roman armies. The author of Hebrews, when referring to the temple service, uses the Greek present tense. While this is not a definitive argument because the Greek present tense does not necessarily mean an action occurring in the present time, it is notable that the author assumes the temple sacrifices are still being offered (10:2). A second point that directs us to a date prior to AD 70 is that the author of Hebrews is silent concerning the destruction of the temple. While some argue that the atrocity of the temple's destruction may have already settled in the minds of readers, this is not convincing because of the emphasis the author places on the temple and sacrifices.

Another clue given in the book of Hebrews is the author's mention of the suffering and persecution that his readers have and are experiencing (10:32–34). Scholars have not come to consistent agreement on when this suffering occurred. Some note it may be the expulsion of Jews from Rome in AD 49 (Acts 18:2). Others attribute this suffering to the persecution under Nero in AD 64. The author of Hebrews does note that his readers have not resisted sin to the point of bloodshed, which may mean they have not endured the persecution of Nero (Heb. 12:4). However, the author's references to a previous persecution may look back to the events of AD 49 (11:26; 13:13), thus placing this work in the AD 60s. It is difficult to be definitive regarding the date as this largely depends on the provenance and destination.

The title of the book "to the Hebrews" points in the direction of a Jewish audience. Some believe these Jews dwelt within Palestine, though the evidence points to Jews living outside of Palestine. In addition, the author makes great use of the Old Testament Scriptures, institutions, and ceremonies. This would easily imply that the readers were familiar with the Old Testament religion, though perhaps more familiar with the Greek rather than the Hebrew language. Finally, there is a brief note in 13:24 ("They of Italy salute you"), though it is debated whether these people "of Italy" were traveling outside of Italy and wishing to greet those in Italy or whether they were in Italy and wishing to greet those outside of Italy.

Theme: The supremacy of Christ over all things and the fullness of God's redemption in Him.

Purpose: To exhort his readers not to draw back, but to stand firm in the faith in the midst of the trials they are enduring.

Synopsis: *The Contribution of Hebrews to Redemptive Revelation*

Hebrews is written to exalt the person and work (especially the priestly work) of Jesus Christ over the types and shadows administered under the Mosaic covenant (5:11–14). In this way the author is making a grand exhortation (13:22; see also 2:1–4; 3:12; 5:11–14; 12:12–17) that because Christians have a High Priest who is seated at the right hand of the Father in heaven (1:1–4; 8:1) and who has made full atonement for sin (1:3; 9:28), they *cannot* go back to the external forms of Judaism and its worship (3:1–6; 6:1–3; 12:25–29) without apostatizing from the faith.

Hebrews begins by exalting Christ as the full and final revelation from God to His people (1:1–4) and as the Mediator of the new covenant (8:6)—the culmination of God's saving work in history (1:1). Because the Hebrews were being tempted by a form of Judaism, which was presumably beckoning the people to revert to the Mosaic ceremonies, the author presents a skillful argument against external religion, and constantly invokes the content and imagery of the Old Testament.

The author calls forth testimony of important Old Testament characters: Moses (3:1–6), Joshua (4:8 [see study note]), Melchisedec (7:1–10), Aaron (5:1), and the Levites (7:11; 9:25); and events: creation (2:5–8), the exodus (3:7–11), and God's appearance at Mt. Sinai (12:18–25). Each time, the author underscores the superiority of Christ over all previous administrations (7:7; 10:19–22). In this way the essence and character of faith plays a significant role throughout Hebrews as the author draws the eyes of his readers away from Mosaic ceremonies and points them forward to Christ's person and work (11:1–2; 12:1–3). Simultaneously, the people of God are seen, in their suffering (10:34), to be a wandering and exiled people (4:9) in pursuit of the great and glorious heavenly city (11:10). The trajectory of the author's argument is that his congregation would see Christ in glory as he lays out the theological and practical steps that the people of God must endure in order to share in His perfect glory (13:13).

Outline:

- I. The Superiority of Christ (1:1—4:16)
  - A. Prologue (1:1–3)
  - B. Christ Superior to Angels Yet Made Like His Brethren (1:4—2:18)
  - C. Christ Ushers In a Greater Rest (3:1—4:16)
- II. The Priesthood of Christ (5:1—10:18)
  - A. Christ Our High Priest Is the Object of Our Confession (5:1—6:20)
  - B. Christ Is a Priest According to Melchisedec (7:1–7:28)
  - C. Christ Mediates a Better Covenant (8:1—10:18)
- III. The Application of Christ (10:19—13:25)
  - A. A Call to True Christian Experience (10:19–39)
  - B. Encouragements to True Faith (11:1—12:17)
  - C. A View of the Unshakable Kingdom (12:18–29)
  - D. Final Directives for Godly Living (13:1–25)

THE EPISTLE OF PAUL THE APOSTLE TO THE HEBREWS

CHAPTER 1

GOD, who at sundry times and in divers manners
spake in time past unto the fathers by the prophets,
2 Hath in these last days spoken unto us by *his*
Son, whom he hath appointed heir of all things,
by whom also he made the worlds;
3 Who being the brightness of *his* glory, and the
express image of his person, and upholding all
things by the word of his power, when he had by
himself purged our sins, sat down on the right
hand of the Majesty on high;
4 Being made so much better than the angels, as
he hath by inheritance obtained a more excellent
name than they.
5 For unto which of the angels said he at any time,
Thou art my Son, this day have I begotten thee?
And again, I will be to him a Father, and he shall
be to me a Son?
6 And again, when he bringeth in the firstbegot-
ten into the world, he saith, And let all the angels
of God worship him.
7 And of the angels he saith, Who maketh his
angels spirits, and his ministers a flame of fire.
8 But unto the Son *he saith*, Thy throne, O God, *is*
for ever and ever: a sceptre of righteousness *is* the
sceptre of thy kingdom.
9 Thou hast loved righteousness, and hated iniq-
uity; therefore God, *even* thy God, hath anointed
thee with the oil of gladness above thy fellows.
10 And, Thou, Lord, in the beginning hast laid
the foundation of the earth; and the heavens are
the works of thine hands:
11 They shall perish; but thou remainest; and
they all shall wax old as doth a garment;
12 And as a vesture shalt thou fold them up, and
they shall be changed: but thou art the same, and
thy years shall not fail.
13 But to which of the angels said he at any time,

THE SUPERIORITY OF CHRIST (1:1—4:16)

Chapter 1: *The author begins his epistle by exalting Christ above the angels.*

Prologue (1:1–3)

1:1 *God.* Old Testament revelation, though spoken through a variety of means, originated in God. *at sundry.* Various. *divers manners.* Different ways. God's revelation in the Old Testament spanned several thousand years and was given in a variety of forms.

1:2 *last days.* Everything after Christ's resurrection and ascension are the last days. *Son.* Refers to Christ's divine status as the only begotten Son (John 3:16). *heir of all things.* The Son inherited everything on account of His work of redemption (Ps. 2:8; Phil. 2:9–11). *worlds.* Literally, "ages." The Son, along with the whole Trinity, created this world and the world to come (Eph. 1:21).

1:3 *brightness of his glory.* Unequivocally divine, true God in every way (Col. 1:15). *express image.* Like a kingly seal being imprinted in wax. *upholding all things.* The Son providentially governs all of creation *by the word of his power* and is bringing history to a final and glorious end or purpose. *purged our sins.* Made atonement for our sins—Christ's priestly work. *sat down on the right hand of the Majesty on high.* Citing Ps. 110:1. Christ has completed His work and now sits enthroned over all things, having received a mediatorial glory.

Christ Superior to Angels Yet Made Like His Brethren (1:4—2:18)

1:4 *obtained a more excellent name.* At Christ's ascension to glory, He inherited a name that was above every name. He is the final Word of God to humanity and surpasses the revelation given by angels.

1:5 *Thou art my Son.* Citing Ps. 2:8. *begotten thee.* Christ was not created by the Father but He was eternally begotten. *again.* Citing 2 Sam. 7:14 concerning the Davidic covenant. The relationship between the *Father* and *Son* is one of great familial love, intimacy, and union.

1:6 *when he bringeth.* Likely a reference to Christ's ascension into glory (Ps. 89:27; see also Deut. 6:10; 11:20; 31:20), though some take it to refer to the incarnation, which also was an instance of great angelic worship (Luke 2:13–14). *world.* Not the typical Greek word referring to the present world but to the world to come (2:5). *all the angels of God worship him.* Not a direct quotation but likely alludes to Deut. 32:43 or Ps. 97:7.

1:7 Citing Ps. 104:4. The Old Testament was revealed through angels, yet angels only served (*ministers*), they were not lords of the covenant.

1:8 Citing Ps. 45:6–7. This messianic psalm exalts the Davidic throne. *for ever and ever.* Christ's kingdom is an eternal kingdom and not transient in nature as the ministration of the angels (Acts 15:16).

1:10 Citing Ps. 102:25–27.

1:12 *but thou art the same.* Christ is superior to all of creation, for creation will grow old and perish; yet Christ remains forever.

1:13 *But to which of the angels.* Citing Ps. 110. *Sit on my right hand.* The Son is given the place of preeminence in the

Sit on my right hand, until I make thine enemies
thy footstool?
14 Are they not all ministering spirits, sent forth to
minister for them who shall be heirs of salvation?

CHAPTER 2

THEREFORE we ought to give the more earnest
heed to the things which we have heard, lest at
any time we should let *them* slip.
2 For if the word spoken by angels was stedfast,
and every transgression and disobedience re-
ceived a just recompence of reward;
3 How shall we escape, if we neglect so great
salvation; which at the first began to be spoken
by the Lord, and was confirmed unto us by them
that heard *him*;
4 God also bearing *them* witness, both with signs
and wonders, and with divers miracles, and gifts
of the Holy Ghost, according to his own will?
5 For unto the angels hath he not put in subjec-
tion the world to come, whereof we speak.
6 But one in a certain place testified, saying, What
is man, that thou art mindful of him? or the son
of man, that thou visitest him?
7 Thou madest him a little lower than the angels;
thou crownedst him with glory and honour, and
didst set him over the works of thy hands:
8 Thou hast put all things in subjection under
his feet. For in that he put all in subjection under
him, he left nothing *that is* not put under him.
But now we see not yet all things put under him.
9 But we see Jesus, who was made a little lower
than the angels for the suffering of death, crowned
with glory and honour; that he by the grace of
God should taste death for every man.
10 For it became him, for whom *are* all things,
and by whom *are* all things, in bringing many
sons unto glory, to make the captain of their
salvation perfect through sufferings.

---

glorious kingdom of God. *thine enemies thy footstool.* God promises to subdue Christ's enemies whether in salvation or judgment.

1:14 The angels not only serve Christ, but they also serve (*minister*) those who inherit *salvation* from Christ. There is no going back to the Mosaic administration. Christ ushers in a far greater revelation and redemption than seen in the Old Testament.

Thought for Personal/Family Worship: Chapter 1

1. **The author opens vv. 1–4 with at least seven descriptions of who the Son (Jesus Christ) is. Trace them and reflect on the manifold glory of this opening. There is none other who can satisfy our deepest needs or longings. These are God's final words spoken to humanity; why are they such great words?**
2. **The author continues in vv. 5–14 by citing seven Old Testament passages that are for the most part direct speech from the Father to the Son. Reflect with awe and humility on the privilege of listening in on the Father's speech to His Son.**
3. **Reflect on the privilege believers have that angels serve them on their path toward full salvation. What reasons does this give God's children for gratitude, confidence, peace, and hope?**

Chapter 2: *Believers must pay heed to the Word lest they drift away. Christ endured His suffering to bring many sons to glory and to subject all of creation to Himself, giving His brothers the victory.*

2:1 *Therefore.* Because of 1:1–14. This final word deserves our utmost attention (*earnest heed*). *let them slip.* Like a boat not securely moored that drifts into danger.

2:2 *word spoken by angels.* Those who rejected the revelation and redemption mediated by angels received a just judgment (*a just recompence of reward*). *every transgression and disobedience.* All sins deserve death (Rom. 3:23).

2:3 *escape.* Avoid coming under God's wrath. *neglect.* Willful rejection of what God has revealed in the *salvation* proclaimed in Christ. *first began.* The words first came to men by *the Lord,* Jesus Christ in His earthly ministry. The apostles *confirmed* the teachings of Christ.

2:4 *signs and wonders.* The apostles in the early church confirmed the message of Christ after His ascension through miracles (Mark 16:20). *divers.* Various. These miracles authenticated the message of Christ in the early church. *according to his own will.* These miracles were only performed as God allowed.

2:5 *subjection the world to come.* The world order brought in by Jesus Christ.

2:6 *a certain place.* Psalm 8, which exposits the glory of man as created by God in such a way that it prophesies of Christ's coming. *son of man.* Mankind created in God's image (Gen. 1:26–28), not the divine title of Christ. *visitest him.* Likely a reference to God communing with man, ultimately displayed in Jesus Christ, both human and divine.

2:7 *madest him a little lower than the angels.* It likely means that man was placed in a probationary period where he was not permitted access to the glory of God like the angels. *crownedst him with glory and honour.* The image of God is knowledge, righteousness, and holiness. *over the works of thy hands.* Man was to have dominion over all the creatures.

2:8 *all things.* Man was to rule over all things and put all things in *subjection*. *But now we see not yet all things put under him.* Man is not in his created position of glory and dominion because of his fall. He is now subject to death as a result of sin.

2:9 *But we see Jesus.* By faith, believers are focused on the one and only Man, Jesus, the Savior, who in His life, death, and resurrection, successfully subdued all of creation to Himself. It is both necessary and beautiful when a spiritual sight of Christ displaces our focus on visible things. *for the suffering of death.* Christ not only had to subdue creation, but He also had to suffer in the place of man because man failed to remain obedient and sinned. The word *taste* does not at all minimize Christ's agony, but highlights the real contact Christ made with death. Death is now swallowed up in victory (1 Cor. 15:54). *for every man.* All kinds of people, not every individual.

2:10 This serves as a map of the road of glory. *many sons.* Believers have a derived sonship in Christ. *captain of their salvation.* Christ leads His people into the salvation He has secured. *perfect.* Complete and entire. Christ's *suffering* was the means of completing the work the Father had given to Him.

2:11 *he that sanctifieth and they who are sanctified.* Christ and His people. *are all of one.* There is corporate solidarity or unity between Christ and His people. *not ashamed.* Christ willingly

11 For both he that sanctifieth and they who are
sanctified *are* all of one: for which cause he is not
ashamed to call them brethren,
12 Saying, I will declare thy name unto my breth-
ren, in the midst of the church will I sing praise
unto thee.
13 And again, I will put my trust in him. And
again, Behold I and the children which God hath
given me.
14 Forasmuch then as the children are partakers
of flesh and blood, he also himself likewise took
part of the same; that through death he might
destroy him that had the power of death, that is,
the devil;
15 And deliver them who through fear of death
were all their lifetime subject to bondage.
16 For verily he took not on *him the nature of*
angels; but he took on *him* the seed of Abraham.
17 Wherefore in all things it behoved him to be
made like unto *his* brethren, that he might be a
merciful and faithful high priest in things *pertain-*
ing to God, to make reconciliation for the sins of
the people.
18 For in that he himself hath suffered being
tempted, he is able to succour them that are tempted.

CHAPTER 3

WHEREFORE, holy brethren, partakers of the
heavenly calling, consider the Apostle and High
Priest of our profession, Christ Jesus;
2 Who was faithful to him that appointed him, as
also Moses *was faithful* in all his house.
3 For this *man* was counted worthy of more glory
than Moses, inasmuch as he who hath builded the
house hath more honour than the house.
4 For every house is builded by some *man*; but he
that built all things *is* God.
5 And Moses verily *was* faithful in all his house,
as a servant, for a testimony of those things which
were to be spoken after;
6 But Christ as a son over his own house; whose

---

identifies Himself with and takes to Himself sinners as His *brethren.*

2:12 *Saying.* Citing Ps. 22:22 (Matt. 27:46).

2:13 *And again.* Citing either Ps. 18:2 or Isa. 8:17. *Behold I and the children.* Citing Isa. 8:18. Those in Christ belong to the remnant of Israel.

2:14 *Forasmuch then as.* Seeing that. *children are partakers of flesh and blood.* Christ partook of the *same* flesh and blood. That is, Christ became man for the purpose of redeeming man by fulfilling his obligations to God's law. *destroy . . . the devil.* Christ conquered Satan on the cross and refuses to allow him to charge any sin against God's elect (Zech. 3:2; Col. 2:15). *power of death.* In the fall, Satan subdued man through sin and ruled over him.

2:15 *deliver them.* When Christ subdued Satan, it was an act of deliverance for Christ's children. *through fear of death.* Though some live entirely blind to death, many apart from Christ live out their lives tormented by the inescapable reality of death.

2:16 *verily.* Truly. Christ did not assume the *nature of angels*, but He *took on him* the nature of the *seed of Abraham*, that is a human nature. *took on him.* Christ took hold of His people for the purpose of redeeming them (Isa. 41:8–10). *seed of Abraham.* Children of faith and not biological descendants of Abraham.

2:17 *in all things.* Christ not only took on flesh and blood, but subjected Himself to the law of God and to the frailty and weakness of humanity for the purpose of redeeming them. Christ was fully human and able to sympathize with our weaknesses and frailties. *behoved.* Was necessary for. *merciful and faithful high priest.* Being made like His brethren Christ is able to relate to them and extend mercy to them (1 Sam. 2:35; Ps. 145). *make reconciliation.* Propitiate or appease the wrath of God by satisfying divine justice with payment *for the sins of the people* (Rom. 3:25–26).

2:18 *hath suffered being tempted.* The author intertwines the suffering of Christ and temptation. In being tempted like His brothers, Christ is able to help (*succour*) those in temptation, as the Hebrews clearly were (1 Chron. 12:18).

Thoughts for Personal/Family Worship: Chapter 2

1. **Paying close attention to the Word of God is hard in these days filled with distraction and superficiality. Yet the judgment that awaits those who fail to take heed to God's final word in Christ is greater than the judgment that came upon rebels in the Old Testament. Why is it impossible to escape God's wrath if we neglect this great salvation?**
2. **What depth of mercy that Christ joyfully stands with His brothers (v. 11)! He not only grants them the name of brothers, but also the experience of His brothers, especially in trials.**
3. **Chapter 2 closes by speaking of how we have a merciful and faithful High Priest (vv. 17–18). Both of these descriptions of our High Priest are needed. If Christ were not merciful, sinners could have no confidence in coming to God. If Christ were not faithful, believers would not have a continued boldness to come before God.**

Christ Ushers In a Greater Rest (3:1—4:16)

Chapter 3: ***This is an exposition from Ps. 95:7–11 where God warns His people not to be deceived and hardened by sin so that they fail to enter into God's rest.***

3:1 *holy brethren.* Solidarity with Christ is not only one of brotherhood, but it sanctifies those united to Him. Jesus "took part" (2:14) in flesh and blood so they could become fellow heirs and *partakers* with Christ. *heavenly calling.* The calling to sonship comes from heaven. Christ is only called an *Apostle* here—one sent by God (John 17:3). *High Priest of our profession.* The One we confess as our Mediator with God.

3:2 *faithful.* Jesus' faithfulness to God is not contrasted with Moses' unfaithfulness but rather to the position of Jesus compared to Moses. *in.* Moses was a part of the house of God as a servant.

3:3 *this man.* Jesus. *builded the house.* Jesus builds the house of God, He does not merely serve in it.

3:5–6 *Moses* was a *servant*, but *Christ* is the *son*. Moses was *in* the house, but Christ is *over* the house.

3:5 *verily.* Truly. *for a testimony.* The revelation that came through Moses was to point forward to Christ who would fully reveal the gospel.

3:6 *whose house are we.* The people of Israel were considered the house of God (Ex. 16:31; Hos. 8:1; 1 Tim. 3:15). Hebrews

house are we, if we hold fast the confidence and
the rejoicing of the hope firm unto the end.
7 Wherefore (as the Holy Ghost saith, To day if ye
will hear his voice,
8 Harden not your hearts, as in the provocation,
in the day of temptation in the wilderness:
9 When your fathers tempted me, proved me,
and saw my works forty years.
10 Wherefore I was grieved with that generation,
and said, They do alway err in *their* heart; and
they have not known my ways.
11 So I sware in my wrath, They shall not enter
into my rest.)
12 Take heed, brethren, lest there be in any of you
an evil heart of unbelief, in departing from the
living God.
13 But exhort one another daily, while it is called
To day; lest any of you be hardened through the
deceitfulness of sin.
14 For we are made partakers of Christ, if we hold
the beginning of our confidence stedfast unto the
end;
15 While it is said, To day if ye will hear his voice,
harden not your hearts, as in the provocation.
16 For some, when they had heard, did provoke:
howbeit not all that came out of Egypt by Moses.
17 But with whom was he grieved forty years? *was*
it not with them that had sinned, whose carcases
fell in the wilderness?
18 And to whom sware he that they should not
enter into his rest, but to them that believed not?
19 So we see that they could not enter in because
of unbelief.

CHAPTER 4

LET us therefore fear, lest, a promise being left *us*
of entering into his rest, any of you should seem
to come short of it.
2 For unto us was the gospel preached, as well as

shows that New Testament believers have continuity with God's redemption plan of the Old Testament. *if we hold fast the confidence and the rejoicing of the hope.* The wilderness Israelites failed to keep their confidence and rejoicing and therefore they fell in the wilderness. The Hebrew Christians are not to fail like the Israelites. *firm unto the end.* It is one thing to start well, another to finish well. Hebrews does not deny that God's true people will actually persevere by grace, but stresses the need to press on, lest one's faith show itself as having been something other than true faith.

3:7–11 Citing Ps. 95:7–11. The people of Israel spied out the Promised Land and returned with a bad report (Num. 13). God disciplined the Israelites and prevented them from entering into the land. This citation places readers in the position of Old Testament Israel standing on the border of the Promised Land. Hardness of heart needs to be detected, dragged into the light, and evicted by the Spirit's grace.

3:7 *Holy Ghost saith.* Psalm 95 was penned by the psalmist, but is credited to the Holy Spirit. All Scripture is God-breathed, yet penned by human agents (2 Tim. 3:16). *To day.* The urgency of the gospel is that today is the day of salvation. *if ye will hear his voice.* The voice of God speaks clearly in creation, providence, and the Scriptures (1:1–4).

3:8 *Harden not.* An allusion to the stubbornness and rebellion of Israel (Ex. 17; Num. 14:26–35). God's words need to be received in faith, not in unbelief. *your hearts.* God desires the allegiance of the inward man and not just outward allegiance. *as in the provocation.* The rebellion in the wilderness. *day of temptation.* Both the day of salvation and the day of temptation.

3:9 *saw my works forty years.* The day of provocation is not one single day, but covers the forty years of Israel's wilderness wandering. They continually rejected and despised the revelation of God. *works.* Acts of redemption and salvation (Deut. 8:4,14–16).

3:11 The wilderness generation was not permitted to *enter* into the Promised Land because of their disobedience. The land symbolized the *rest* of God where the people had been planted and established. Many of those who did *enter* the land did not partake of God's *rest*, and many were exiled from the land because of their unbelief. All this should be a warning to those who profess faith, also today.

3:12 *Take heed.* A common refrain in the book of Hebrews is to listen carefully (2:1–4). All sins come from a *heart of unbelief* and distrust in the promises of God. *living God.* The people died in the wilderness because they departed from Him who promised life. God's rest is life.

3:13 *But exhort one another daily.* A corporate necessity rests on a congregation's shoulder to admonish one another to remain faithful to God. *deceitfulness of sin.* Sin can never deliver what it promises.

3:14 *partakers of Christ.* The author is referring to true union with Christ, He being the head, His church His body. *beginning of our confidence stedfast unto the end.* Most likely the author is referring to Christ as the *beginning*, the chief and principal part of the Christian's confidence. True believers will hold tenaciously to Him.

3:15 *provocation*. Rebellion.

3:16 *not all that came.* Not everyone who experienced God's salvation out of Egypt was permitted to enter into the Promised Land. *heard.* Hearing the gospel is not sufficient for salvation; hearing must be mixed with faith (Rom. 10:14ff).

3:17–19 *sinned . . . unbelief.* Just as faith is the mother grace of all other graces; unbelief is the source of all other sins. The historical citation from Ps. 95 is used because the Hebrew Christians are seen in an analogous relationship to the Israelites.

Thoughts for Personal/Family Worship: Chapter 3

1. **Verse 6 suggests an important question: Are you a part of the household of faith?**
2. **Believers have a corporate responsibility to exhort and encourage one another daily. Too often we live isolated lives. How might you help and encourage those around you?**
3. **Hebrews warns against the "deceitfulness of sin" (v. 13). We often fail to remember that sin is deceitful. When we begin to see by grace how deceitful, how wretched, how awful sin really is, we learn to look to God alone to renew our minds after knowledge, righteousness, and holiness that we might discern the exceeding depravity of sin.**

Chapter 4: ***In light of the far greater rest to be had in Christ, the author stirs his readers to seek to enter that rest.***

4:1 *promise being left us.* While many Israelites failed to enter, there is still a promise of rest held out. The Promised Land was

unto them: but the word preached did not profit
them, not being mixed with faith in them that
heard *it*.
3 For we which have believed do enter into rest,
as he said, As I have sworn in my wrath, if they
shall enter into my rest: although the works were
finished from the foundation of the world.
4 For he spake in a certain place of the seventh
day on this wise, And God did rest the seventh day
from all his works.
5 And in this *place* again, If they shall enter into
my rest.
6 Seeing therefore it remaineth that some must en-
ter therein, and they to whom it was first preached
entered not in because of unbelief:
7 Again, he limiteth a certain day, saying in David,
To day, after so long a time; as it is said, To day if
ye will hear his voice, harden not your hearts.
8 For if Jesus had given them rest, then would he
not afterward have spoken of another day.
9 There remaineth therefore a rest to the people
of God.
10 For he that is entered into his rest, he also hath
ceased from his own works, as God *did* from his.
11 Let us labour therefore to enter into that rest,
lest any man fall after the same example of unbelief.
12 For the word of God *is* quick, and powerful,
and sharper than any twoedged sword, piercing
even to the dividing asunder of soul and spirit,
and of the joints and marrow, and *is* a discerner of
the thoughts and intents of the heart.
13 Neither is there any creature that is not manifest
in his sight: but all things *are* naked and opened
unto the eyes of him with whom we have to do.
14 Seeing then that we have a great high priest,
that is passed into the heavens, Jesus the Son of
God, let us hold fast *our* profession.
15 For we have not an high priest which cannot be
touched with the feeling of our infirmities; but was
in all points tempted like as *we are*, *yet* without sin.
16 Let us therefore come boldly unto the throne
of grace, that we may obtain mercy, and find grace
to help in time of need.

CHAPTER 5

FOR every high priest taken from among men is
ordained for men in things *pertaining* to God,

not the final rest of God. *come short of it.* Fail to enter.

4:2 *unto us was the gospel preached, as well as unto them.* The gospel was not for New Testament believers alone but was the sum and substance of the Old Testament message as well. *not being mixed with faith.* They did not receive the gospel in faith and therefore the good news *did not profit them*.

4:3 *rest.* The original Greek uses two words in this chapter that are both translated as rest. The most frequent word refers to "a place of rest" (*katapausis*). The other word for *rest* (v. 9) is literally, "Sabbatism" (*sabbatismos*), which is understood by some as a "state of rest," or by others, as "the keeping of Sabbath." *works were finished from the foundation of the world.* God's rest stretches back to creation (Gen. 2:2).

4:4 *God did rest.* God's rest after creation points forward to the ultimate rest reserved for His people. In God's *rest*, believers will *rest* in Him and He will *rest* in His love (Zeph. 3:17).

4:5 There is a connection between the *rest* of Ps. 95 and Gen. 2:2. The rest properly belongs to God and comes from Him.

4:8 *Jesus.* Joshua. A type of Christ, Joshua was unable to lead the people into the ultimate rest of God. *another day.* The promise is still open for believers to enter into God's rest.

4:9 *There remaineth therefore a rest to the people of God.* This word for rest in the original is *sabbatismos* (see note at v. 3).

4:10 *For he that is entered.* Likely a reference to believers, not Christ directly.

4:11 *lest any man fall after the same example of unbelief.* Failing to believe the gospel results in a greater condemnation than experienced by Israel in Kadesh (Num. 14).

4:12 *quick.* Living. *twoedged sword.* Cuts in both directions. God's Word speaks deliverance to God's people, but destruction to those who oppose God. *asunder.* Apart. *soul and spirit.* Probably natural life and spiritual life. The Word of God can reach where we find it difficult to discern.

4:13 *opened unto the eyes of him.* Completely overpowered and vulnerable before God. *with whom we have to do.* To whom we must give account.

4:14–16 Contrasting the vivid warnings of vv. 12–13, believers are reminded that there is a way open to the throne of grace.

4:14 *a great high priest, that is passed into the heavens.* The priests who bore the ark led the people into the Promised Land (Josh. 3). Christ the High Priest has led His people into the heavenly rest. *profession.* See 3:1. Christ as priest will be the focus of the proceeding chapters.

4:15 *we have not an high priest which cannot be touched.* The double negative underscores Christ's exceeding sympathy. *touched.* Strong, mother-like empathy for people. *in all points.* Throughout the span of Jesus' life He was tempted in every way that man was tempted. *yet without sin.* Christ's temptations did not lead Him to sin. Some might imagine that a fellow sinner might be able to sympathize more. However, Christ endured temptation in a far greater measure than any sinner because we fall so quickly, but with Him the Devil pulled out all the stops, but still failed.

4:16 In light of God's searching and revealing Word that exposes all of the inadequacies and sinfulness of sinners, the author encourages his readers to *come boldly unto the throne of grace.* The Greek for boldness indicates openness and freedom. Judgment by God's Word is not the final answer.

Thoughts for Personal/Family Worship: Chapter 4

1. **Hebrews says that Israel had the gospel preached to them but it did not profit them because their hearing was not combined with faith. The gospel was preached through types and shadows and the redeeming acts of God throughout Israel's history. However, we have even greater privileges and a great degree of responsibility as a result.**
2. **The word "rest" has a lot of significance for our restless world and restless souls. What makes us so restless? What kind of comfort lies in the fact that God speaks of "my rest" (vv. 3,5)?**
3. **Far from being just an exalted Sovereign who is far removed from our situation, struggles, and trials, Christ has a tender heart for His people, especially in their afflictions and temptations. Do you know this throne as a throne of grace in your life? What is meant by this**

that he may offer both gifts and sacrifices for sins:
2 Who can have compassion on the ignorant,
and on them that are out of the way; for that he
himself also is compassed with infirmity.
3 And by reason hereof he ought, as for the
people, so also for himself, to offer for sins.
4 And no man taketh this honour unto himself,
but he that is called of God, as *was* Aaron.
5 So also Christ glorified not himself to be made
an high priest; but he that said unto him, Thou
art my Son, to day have I begotten thee.
6 As he saith also in another *place*, Thou *art* a
priest for ever after the order of Melchisedec.
7 Who in the days of his flesh, when he had
offered up prayers and supplications with strong
crying and tears unto him that was able to save
him from death, and was heard in that he feared;
8 Though he were a Son, yet learned he obedi-
ence by the things which he suffered;
9 And being made perfect, he became the author
of eternal salvation unto all them that obey him;
10 Called of God an high priest after the order of
Melchisedec.
11 Of whom we have many things to say, and
hard to be uttered, seeing ye are dull of hearing.
12 For when for the time ye ought to be teachers, ye
have need that one teach you again which *be* the first
principles of the oracles of God; and are become
such as have need of milk, and not of strong meat.
13 For every one that useth milk *is* unskilful in
the word of righteousness: for he is a babe.
14 But strong meat belongeth to them that are of
full age, *even* those who by reason of use have their
senses exercised to discern both good and evil.

"boldness"? Is it the same as "presumption"? What is the difference?

THE PRIESTHOOD OF CHRIST (5:1—10:18)

Christ Our High Priest Is the Object of Our Confession (5:1—6:20)

The main body of Hebrews is made up of two detailed arguments (5:1—7:28; 8:1—10:18). This first section shows that God's Son is a greater high priest than the Levitical priesthood under Aaron in the Old Testament. The author's chief concerns will be to defend how and why Christ is a high priest.

Chapter 5: ***Christ's high priesthood is supremely glorious in that God appointed Him to this task and He faithfully carried out His ministry in His suffering and death. The chapter closes with a warning against immaturity.***

5:1 *taken from among men ... in things pertaining to God.* Every high priest was a mediator between God and men. The priests' role in the Old Testament was to be Israel's representatives in the presence of God (Ex. 28:1,29). The work of the priest was to offer *gifts and sacrifices* to God and to make intercession, all as God commanded.

5:2 *compassion.* High priests could have compassion because they were subject to the same weakness as those they ministered to. *ignorant.* Those who sin without knowing what they do (Lev. 4:2; 5:15–16; Num. 15:22–31; Deut. 17:12). Under the old covenant there was no sacrifice for those who knowingly sinned (Num. 15:29–30). *them that are out of the way.* Those who wander or are deceived from the correct path (3:10). *compassed.* Surrounded.

5:3 *he ought . . . to offer for sins.* The high priest did not condemn sin but offered sacrifices on behalf of sins. Taken from among men, high priests needed to sacrifice for their own sins (Lev. 16:6,11,15–17).

5:4 *no man taketh this honour unto himself.* High priests were appointed by God (Num. 17), though in the time of the second temple, the priesthood was sold and bought by political powers.

5:5–6 Citing Ps. 2:7; 110:1. Christ's sonship and priesthood are closely connected. As God's King and Priest, Christ was the fulfillment of Old Testament prophecy (Zech. 6:9–15).

5:5 *So also Christ glorified not himself.* Christ was appointed as a priest by God. *Thou art my Son.* Christ's priesthood is closely connected to His sonship and so is divine.

5:6 The exalted Son is also the exalted priest over His people in fulfillment of Old Testament prophecy.

5:7 *in the days of his flesh.* During the whole of His life, but especially the suffering at the end of His life and perhaps specifically His prayer in Gethsemane (Matt. 26:36–46; Mark 14:32–42; Luke 22:40–46). *offered up.* Priests offered the blood of animals; Christ offers up Himself in prayers. *strong crying and tears.* Christ has wrestled in prayer and is able to sympathize with His people. *and was heard.* Jesus was not heard in the sense that He evaded death, but was heard in the sense that the Father would give Him ultimate victory over death in the resurrection. *in that he feared.* His whole posture before, during, and after prayer was that of trust in and reverence for His Father.

5:8–9 *which he suffered.* Jesus experienced true suffering. This is what qualifies Him to be a high priest and have compassion on His people. *perfect.* Not moral perfection but the idea of maturity or completion of a mission (2:10). *the author of eternal salvation.* Christ has a perpetual priesthood that secures a perpetual salvation for His people. *obey him.* Obedience is not a prerequisite to salvation, but it is the fruit of genuine salvation.

5:10 *Called of God.* God has spoken directly to Christ and appointed Him to this position. *Melchisedec.* See Gen. 14; Ps. 110. Christ was not after the *order* of Aaron because He was from the tribe of Judah.

5:11 *Of whom we have many things to say.* Likely referring to Christ and Melchisedec. *dull of hearing.* The emphasis placed on hearing throughout Hebrews now turns to an admonishment against the readers.

5:12 *first principles of the oracles of God.* The beginning principles of the truth of the Word of God. *milk, and not of strong meat.* Symbols of immaturity and maturity (1 Cor. 3:2).

5:13 *unskilful.* Inexperienced and lacking wisdom. *word of righteousness.* The Scriptures.

5:14 *use.* Habit. *to discern both good and evil.* Maturity is not an issue of age but discerning good and evil and practicing that which is good.

Thoughts for Personal/Family Worship: Chapter 5

1. **Christ learned obedience through what he suffered (v. 8). Though Christ was never disobedient to His Father, He learned from the inside out, as man, what it meant to obey His Father even at great cost to Himself. If sinless Christ had to suffer to learn obedience, what does this teach us about why God's children must suffer?**
2. **Christian maturity ought to be the aim, not an optional luxury of every Christian (vv. 11–14). Just as children often**

CHAPTER 6

THEREFORE leaving the principles of the doctrine
of Christ, let us go on unto perfection; not lay-
ing again the foundation of repentance from dead
works, and of faith toward God,
2 Of the doctrine of baptisms, and of laying on
of hands, and of resurrection of the dead, and of
eternal judgment.
3 And this will we do, if God permit.
4 For *it is* impossible for those who were once
enlightened, and have tasted of the heavenly gift,
and were made partakers of the Holy Ghost,
5 And have tasted the good word of God, and the
powers of the world to come,
6 If they shall fall away, to renew them again unto
repentance; seeing they crucify to themselves the
Son of God afresh, and put *him* to an open shame.
7 For the earth which drinketh in the rain that
cometh oft upon it, and bringeth forth herbs
meet for them by whom it is dressed, receiveth
blessing from God:
8 But that which beareth thorns and briers *is*
rejected, and *is* nigh unto cursing; whose end *is*
to be burned.
9 But, beloved, we are persuaded better things of
you, and things that accompany salvation, though
we thus speak.
10 For God *is* not unrighteous to forget your
work and labour of love, which ye have shewed
toward his name, in that ye have ministered to the
saints, and do minister.
11 And we desire that every one of you do shew
the same diligence to the full assurance of hope
unto the end:
12 That ye be not slothful, but followers of them
who through faith and patience inherit the
promises.
13 For when God made promise to Abraham,

can't wait to grow up and will often try to do things to demonstrate that they are grown up, believers must set aside childish things and press on in the Word and life of faith.

Chapter 6: ***The readers are cautioned against experiencing so much and yet falling short of God's salvation. The people of God must persevere to the end.***

6:1–3 These verses contain six doctrines in three groups of two.

6:1 *leaving.* The transition here is an attempt to stir the readers up to move beyond the basic teachings (*the principles of the doctrine of Christ*) on to maturity (*perfection*; 1 Cor. 2:6). *repentance from dead works.* Turning from sin to God. *faith toward God.* Trust based on knowledge of God's Word.

6:2 *doctrine of baptisms.* Either Jewish ceremonial rites, or more likely, Christian baptism (Acts 8:12–17; 10:44–48; 19:6; 1 Cor. 12:13). *laying on of hands.* Rite linked to appointment to an office (Acts 6:6; 13:3; 1 Tim. 4:14; 5:22; 2 Tim. 1:6). *resurrection of the dead.* Resurrection is rooted in the Old Testament (Job 19:25–26) but developed more thoroughly in the New Testament (1 Cor. 15). *eternal judgment.* The movement begins with faith and repentance, is communicated through the ministry of the church, and is consummated in the resurrection and the judgment that is to follow.

6:3 *this will we do.* The chapters to follow will do this.

6:4–8 These verses have caused a considerable amount of disagreement. Some argue that true believers can lose their salvation, which contradicts other passages (John 10:28–29). Some think that this "falling away" is hypothetical and could not happen. However, such a view robs these warnings of their force. The epistle is addressed to those who profess faith in Christ, and among them there are those who do not have true faith and thus, unless they are at some point truly converted, will fall away. The Old Testament background, particularly Israel's rebellion at Kadesh (Num. 14), proves that the author is describing those who mix with the true people of God, have many experiences that seem to replicate those of the true people of God, and yet fall short of the true knowledge of Christ. We ought to examine ourselves whether we are truly in the faith (2 Cor. 13:5).

6:4 *once enlightened.* The Greek word here recalls the Spirit's guidance of the people in the exodus through the pillar of fire (Ex. 13:21; Neh. 9:12). *tasted of the heavenly gift.* The manna God provided in the wilderness was known as the heavenly food (Ex. 16:4; Neh. 9:15; Ps. 105:40). *partakers of the Holy Ghost.* Balaam and Saul show that people can partake of the Holy Spirit in an outward way, without having His saving grace (Num. 24:2; 1 Sam. 10:6; 11:6).

6:5 *tasted.* Experienced. *the good word of God.* This is likely a reference to the preached gospel that the wilderness generation had preached to them, and yet they failed to obey (Josh. 21:45; 23:15). *powers of the world to come.* In the time of the exodus, both word and power were combined in delivering the people of Israel out of the hand of the Egyptians (Ex. 3:18–20; 4:28–30; Neh. 9:10–17). The same was true in the days of the apostles as salvation came with words and miracles (2:1–4).

6:6 *If they shall fall away.* Not merely a hypothetical warning. Like Israel failed to persevere and enter into the Promised Land, there are those who mix with the people of God who will be missing from the wedding supper of the Lamb. *to renew them again unto repentance.* Who among the wilderness generation was renewed to repentance after they turned away from the common operations of the Spirit? *seeing they crucify to themselves the Son of God afresh.* Just as those who knowingly rejected God's redemptive acts in the wilderness. *open shame.* Humiliation (Matt. 1:19; Col. 2:15). Those who apostatize try to humiliate Christ who is seated in God's eternal glory.

6:7–8 See Deut. 11:11–17,26–28, which speak of the curses to come upon those who are disobedient.

6:7 *For.* This clarifies the warning passage (vv. 4–6). *the earth which drinketh in the rain that cometh oft upon it.* Compare Deut. 11:11,14, where the Israelites were preparing to enter into the Promised Land that is described as drinking in the rain. *bringeth forth herbs meet* (suitable) *for them by whom it is dressed* (farmed), *receiveth blessing from God.* Blessing stands in opposition to the curse (v. 8).

6:8 *But that which beareth thorns and briers is rejected, and is nigh unto cursing.* Likely a reference to Gen. 3:17–18. *nigh unto cursing.* See Deut. 32:35. Both the Israelites in the wilderness and the readers of Hebrews were standing at pivotal crossroads. The agricultural metaphor clarifies the seriousness of the warning of ch. 6.

6:9 *beloved.* After such a harsh warning of exhortation, the author again refers to his brothers as beloved. *better things.* See 1:4; 7:19,22; 8:6; 9:23; 12:24.

6:12 *slothful.* Same word used of their dullness in hearing in 5:11. *them who through faith and patience inherit the promises.* The faithful throughout the ages.

6:13–20 The author has shown his readers that they were

because he could swear by no greater, he sware
by himself,
14 Saying, Surely blessing I will bless thee, and
multiplying I will multiply thee.
15 And so, after he had patiently endured, he
obtained the promise.
16 For men verily swear by the greater: and an oath
for confirmation *is* to them an end of all strife.
17 Wherein God, willing more abundantly to
shew unto the heirs of promise the immutability
of his counsel, confirmed *it* by an oath:
18 That by two immutable things, in which *it was*
impossible for God to lie, we might have a strong
consolation, who have fled for refuge to lay hold
upon the hope set before us:
19 Which *hope* we have as an anchor of the soul,
both sure and stedfast, and which entereth into
that within the veil;
20 Whither the forerunner is for us entered, *even*
Jesus, made an high priest for ever after the order
of Melchisedec.

CHAPTER 7

FOR this Melchisedec, king of Salem, priest of
the most high God, who met Abraham returning
from the slaughter of the kings, and blessed him;
2 To whom also Abraham gave a tenth part of all;
first being by interpretation King of righteous-
ness, and after that also King of Salem, which is,
King of peace;
3 Without father, without mother, without
descent, having neither beginning of days, nor
end of life; but made like unto the Son of God;
abideth a priest continually.
4 Now consider how great this man *was*, unto
whom even the patriarch Abraham gave the tenth
of the spoils.
5 And verily they that are of the sons of Levi, who
receive the office of the priesthood, have a com-
mandment to take tithes of the people according
to the law, that is, of their brethren, though they
come out of the loins of Abraham:
6 But he whose descent is not counted from them

---

in the same place spiritually as the Israelites in the wilderness (3:7—4:13). He exhorted them to not apostatize from following Christ in the wilderness (vv. 4–8). Those who would prove faithful would be blessed but those who were unfaithful would be cursed (vv. 9–12). The author now develops his argument by showing the steadfast faithfulness of the Lord in keeping His covenantal promises. The faithfulness of God is the pivotal hope of a people who know their inward tendency toward unfaithfulness.

6:13–14 God made this *promise to Abraham* when he willingly offered up Isaac to be sacrificed (Gen. 22:17). *he could swear by no greater.* He could swear by nothing higher than Himself.

6:15 *patiently endured.* Abraham endured despite overwhelming pressures to give up.

6:16–17 *confirmed it by an oath.* God's covenant promises rest on His very person and nature.

6:16 *verily.* Truly.

6:18 *immutable.* Unchangeable. *to lay hold upon the hope.* In the Old Testament, certain people fled to the cities of refuge or, if possible, laid hold of the horns of the altar, so the believer has in God an immutable ground for pardon and hope.

6:19 *an anchor of the soul.* The believer's connection with Christ, now on the throne of God, gives the believer the confidence he or she needs in the face of the tumult around as well as within them. *entereth into . . . the veil.* The high priest would enter once a year behind the veil into the most holy place to approach the mercyseat (9:24; 10:19–21).

6:20 *made an high priest for ever after the order of Melchisedec.* The author reintroduces Melchisedec and picks up his earlier statements regarding the priest. The immutable oath of God is first seen for believers and now to God's divine oath to Jesus.

Thoughts for Personal/Family Worship: Chapter 6

1. **In many quarters of the professing church, apostasy is in full swing. Some change the definition of faith to adjust to this reality; others claim that true believers can lose their salvation. However, the Word of God is clear that many can have the appearance of faith, who are not inwardly changed. Let us examine ourselves whether we have simply the form of religion or the true power of it.**
2. **Patience is not easy for any, also not for believers. Yet, without it we will not know the rich blessing God gives to those who in patience possess their souls. How can we take hold of the hope set before us? How does this anchor hold us in the midst of the storms of spiritual life (vv. 18–20)?**
3. **Christ is called the "forerunner" of His people (v. 20), having gone behind the curtain of God's dwelling. This imagery comes from the Old Testament tabernacle, where the actual throne room of God was located in the Holy of holies. How does this picture help explain the boldness believers ought to have in approaching the throne of grace (4:16)?**

Chapter 7: *Christ is a priest after the order of Melchisedec, not Levi. Thus His salvation is far superior to that displayed in the Old Testament ceremonies.*

Christ Is a Priest According to Melchisedec (7:1–28)

7:1–3 These verses form one sentence with many qualifying clauses. The main idea is that Christ is a divine priest and remains a priest perpetually. The author draws the reader's attention back to Gen. 14, which plays an important role in understanding Melchisedec's priestly role.

7:1 *Salem.* The Jebusite city of Jerusalem before David conquered it. *most high God.* According to Gen. 14, Melchisedec was not of Abrahamic descent; yet, he was still a priest of God (Ps. 110:4). *blessed him.* A significant role for Melchisedec as a priest (Gen. 14:18–20).

7:2 *first being by interpretation.* The meaning of Melchisedec is "the king of righteousness." *King of Salem.* The name *Salem* contains the same Hebrew root for "peace."

7:3 *Without father . . . nor end of life.* Melchisedec's lineage is not recorded in Genesis, a book of genealogies. Nor did Genesis record his birth or death, as it often does major figures. In this way, from a literary perspective, Melchisedec is portrayed as similar to *the Son of God*, an eternal person.

7:4–10 Having shown that Melchisedec's priesthood is eternal, and thus Christ's priesthood is according to His human and divine natures, the author turns to consider the subordination of the Levitical priesthood to Melchisedec's priesthood. The Levitical priesthood is only according to the flesh, and thus was necessary for Christ's priesthood to be after a different order.

THE OFFICES OF CHRIST

Christ undertook His office, or station, in order to obtain salvation for His people (1 Tim. 1:15). Both the *calling* and the *components* of His office are worthy to be considered. The *calling* is an action of God the Father, whereby He bound His willing Son to His office by an eternal covenant (Ps. 110:4; Isa. 53:10; Luke 22:22; Acts 4:28; Heb. 5:4,6; 7:24). This involved choosing the ends (Isa. 42:1), foreordaining the means (1 Peter 1:20), and sending the Son (John 3:17).

There are three *components* to Christ's office (variously referred to as three separate offices). *First*, Christ holds the office of *Prophet* (Deut. 18:15). By this component He reveals perfectly the whole will of God. This office has various names: Christ is a Teacher (Matt. 23:7), the Apostle of our confession (Heb. 3:1), the Angel of the Covenant (Mal. 3:1), the Word of God (John 1:1), the very Wisdom of God (1 Cor. 1:24), and the Treasure of wisdom and understanding (Col. 2:3).

In order to be the perfect Prophet, Christ had to be both God and man. It was necessary for Him to be God in order to perfectly understand and minister the will of God (John 1:18; 3:13; 1 Cor. 2:11,16). If He had not been man, He could not have properly declared this will to men by His own person (Heb. 1:1).

Second, Christ holds the office of *Priest*. His priesthood is after the order of Melchizedek (Heb. 7:17) and therefore is indestructible (Heb. 7:16); stable and perfect (Heb. 7:18–19); eternal (Heb. 7:24); and perpetual, leaving no room or need for other priests (Heb. 7:24–25).

In the execution of His priestly office Christ is the Priest, the sacrifice, and the altar. He is our Priest in both of His natures (Heb. 5:6). He *was* the sacrifice principally in His human nature; the Scriptures attribute His sacrifice primarily to His body (Col. 1:22; Heb. 13:12; 1 Peter 2:24) and blood (Col. 1:20). However, this sacrifice became effectual because of Christ's divine nature as the very Son of God (Acts 20:28; Rom. 8:3)—which is understood properly according to the idea of the altar (Heb. 9:14; 13:10,12,15). The function of the altar is to sanctify the offering, granting it dignity beyond itself (Matt. 23:17). Herein is demonstrated the reason Christ as Priest had to be both God and man: if He were not man, He could not have atoned for men; if He were not God, the sacrifice would not have been sufficient.

Third, Christ holds the office of *King* (cf. Deut. 17:14–20). His kingdom is variously called the kingdom *of God*, the kingdom *of peace and glory*, the kingdom *of light and glory*, the kingdom *of heaven*, and *the world to come*. In His kingdom Christ's rule is His power to dispense and administer with force and authority all things pertaining to the salvation of men (Ps. 2:6; Dan. 2:44; Luke 4:36). This kingship is universal; that is, it encompasses all ages, being eternal (Dan. 2:44; 7:14; Matt. 22:43–45). Christ's rule is over all men (Dan. 7:14; Rev. 17:14)—and even over all of the world and its creatures (Eph. 1:21,22). Christ governs both man's outward and his inward activity (Rom. 14:17), dispensing either everlasting life or death (Rev. 1:18). For the heirs of the kingdom Christ as King brings the greatest peace and the most perfect joy (Isa. 9:6; Eph. 2:16; Heb. 7:2). Again, it is necessary that Christ be King both as God and as man: as man, in order that He might be the spiritual King of our souls, dispensing eternal life and death; as God, that He might be the Ruler of the same nature as His body.

The threefold office of Christ announces three truths. *First*, it identifies the state of man and how it is remedied in Christ. Man suffers under ignorance, which is resolved by the prophecy of Christ; dwells in alienation from God (this fellowship is restored by the priestly work of Christ); and possesses no power to live in a holy manner (this lack is rectified by the kingship of Christ). *Second*, Christ's threefold office reveals the manner in which salvation is brought to bear upon man. It is preached by His prophecy; obtained by His priesthood; and applied by His kingship. *Finally*, the threefold office exposes that salvation is accomplished by Christ. Christ first taught others the will of God, then offered Himself, and finally entered to rule in His kingdom.

—adapted from William Ames, *The Marrow of Theology*, 1.19

received tithes of Abraham, and blessed him that
had the promises.
7 And without all contradiction the less is blessed
of the better.
8 And here men that die receive tithes; but there
he *receiveth them*, of whom it is witnessed that he
liveth.
9 And as I may so say, Levi also, who receiveth
tithes, payed tithes in Abraham.
10 For he was yet in the loins of his father, when
Melchisedec met him.
11 If therefore perfection were by the Levitical
priesthood, (for under it the people received the
law,) what further need *was there* that another
priest should rise after the order of Melchisedec,
and not be called after the order of Aaron?
12 For the priesthood being changed, there is
made of necessity a change also of the law.
13 For he of whom these things are spoken
pertaineth to another tribe, of which no man gave
attendance at the altar.
14 For *it is* evident that our Lord sprang out of
Juda; of which tribe Moses spake nothing con-
cerning priesthood.
15 And it is yet far more evident: for that after the
similitude of Melchisedec there ariseth another
priest,
16 Who is made, not after the law of a carnal
commandment, but after the power of an endless
life.
17 For he testifieth, Thou *art* a priest for ever after
the order of Melchisedec.
18 For there is verily a disannulling of the com-
mandment going before for the weakness and
unprofitableness thereof.
19 For the law made nothing perfect, but the
bringing in of a better hope *did*; by the which we
draw nigh unto God.
20 And inasmuch as not without an oath *he was
made priest*:
21 (For those priests were made without an oath;
but this with an oath by him that said unto him,
The Lord sware and will not repent, Thou *art* a
priest for ever after the order of Melchisedec:)
22 By so much was Jesus made a surety of a better
testament.
23 And they truly were many priests, because
they were not suffered to continue by reason of
death:
24 But this *man*, because he continueth ever, hath
an unchangeable priesthood.
25 Wherefore he is able also to save them to the
uttermost that come unto God by him, seeing he
ever liveth to make intercession for them.
26 For such an high priest became us, *who is* holy,
harmless, undefiled, separate from sinners, and

7:4 Abraham's high tribute to Melchisedec reveals *how great this man was. tenth.* A tithe or tenth part of belongings or wealth.
7:5 *verily.* Truly. *sons of Levi.* The genealogical principle that the Levitical priesthood depended on one's relationship to Levi. *have a commandment to take tithes of the people according to the law.* The law provided for the provisions of the Levites, but they were only permitted to collect a tithe from *their brethren.* Christ is far more than a brother because He is over the house of God (3:1–6).
7:6 *descent is not counted from them.* Genealogies were of the utmost importance to the Levites. *blessed him that had the promises.* Abraham was to bless the nations (Gen. 12:3) but he was blessed by Melchisedec. Christ is the source of all blessing.
7:9–10 According to a genealogical principle, Levites were present in Abraham when Abraham paid a tithe to Melchisedec. The Levites, who were descendants of Abraham, could not arise above Abraham's status in the house of God.
7:12 *priesthood being changed.* See Ps. 110:4. *law.* Ceremonial law.
7:13 *he of whom these things are spoken.* A reference to Christ, who came after the order of Melchisedec. *pertaineth.* Belongs.
7:15–17 The positive implications of the comparison between Christ and Melchisedec.
7:15 *far more evident.* Even more clear that perfection was not possible under the Levitical priesthood. *for that after the similitude.* Since according to the likeness or pattern set by *Melchisedec*.
7:16 *carnal commandment.* The Levitical priesthood was based on fleshly descent, and with fleshly ordinances. *power of an endless life.* Both eternal duration and powerful application are needed for an effective priesthood.
7:18–19 *verily.* Truly. *disannulling.* Canceling by God, the Giver of the law. *weakness and unprofitableness.* The law here is linked to the insufficiency of the Aaronic priesthood. *law made nothing perfect.* The types and shadows of the ceremonial law were not effective in themselves to bring men near (*nigh*) to God; only in as much as they pointed to Christ were they sufficient. *better hope.* Christ's priesthood, the object of our hope (6:18–20).
7:20–28 Christ has a superior priesthood in order to show that a change in the law has occurred, and Christ has ushered in a better covenant.
7:20–21 *not without an oath.* God appointed the Levites as priests by His divine word. Christ's priesthood was far greater, for He was made a Priest by a divine oath. *The Lord sware and will not repent.* Citing Ps. 110:4. An allusion to God's revoking of the priesthood of Eli and his sons (1 Sam. 2:30).
7:22 *surety.* Legal term for a person bound to perform the obligations of another (Prov. 6:1–2). The oath makes Christ a surety of a *better* covenant (*testament*). The author will soon discuss the greatness of the new covenant (ch. 8).
7:23 *suffered.* Allowed. The earthly priests did not have a perpetual ministry, because *death* ended their priesthood.
7:24 Christ received an incorruptible life, namely in His resurrection, and thus His priesthood *continueth* forever. *unchangeable.* God's faithfulness is the foundation of the unchangeableness of the priesthood—to change this oath, the death of God would be necessary.
7:25 *able . . . to save them.* Not a mere possibility but a reality. Christ is mighty to save. *to the uttermost.* Christ fully and finally saves His people to all eternity. Perfection has come through Christ. *come unto God by him.* In and for the sake of Christ, sinners can come into the very presence of God. *ever liveth to make intercession.* Christ's work continues even now and forever as effective intercession on behalf of His people.
7:26 *high priest became us.* Christ is suitable and fitting for

made higher than the heavens;
27 Who needeth not daily, as those high priests,
to offer up sacrifice, first for his own sins, and
then for the people's: for this he did once, when
he offered up himself.
28 For the law maketh men high priests which
have infirmity; but the word of the oath, which
was since the law, *maketh* the Son, who is conse-
crated for evermore.

CHAPTER 8

NOW of the things which we have spoken *this is*
the sum: We have such an high priest, who is set
on the right hand of the throne of the Majesty in
the heavens;
2 A minister of the sanctuary, and of the true
tabernacle, which the Lord pitched, and not man.
3 For every high priest is ordained to offer gifts
and sacrifices: wherefore *it is* of necessity that this
man have somewhat also to offer.
4 For if he were on earth, he should not be a
priest, seeing that there are priests that offer gifts
according to the law:
5 Who serve unto the example and shadow of
heavenly things, as Moses was admonished of
God when he was about to make the tabernacle:
for, See, saith he, *that* thou make all things accord-
ing to the pattern shewed to thee in the mount.
6 But now hath he obtained a more excellent
ministry, by how much also he is the mediator
of a better covenant, which was established upon
better promises.
7 For if that first *covenant* had been faultless, then
should no place have been sought for the second.
8 For finding fault with them, he saith, Behold,
the days come, saith the Lord, when I will make
a new covenant with the house of Israel and with
the house of Judah:
9 Not according to the covenant that I made
with their fathers in the day when I took them by
the hand to lead them out of the land of Egypt;
because they continued not in my covenant, and I
regarded them not, saith the Lord.

His people. *holy.* Purity and devotedness to God. *harmless.* Not touched by any defection or evil, but is perfectly morally qualified to serve as His people's priest. *undefiled.* Christ's moral integrity. *separate from sinners, and made higher than the heavens.* Morally separated from sinners and physically lifted up above this corrupt world.

7:27 Unlike the Levitical priests, Christ has no need to offer sacrifices for His own sin (Lev. 16:6–10). *for this he did once.* The finality of Christ's sacrifice plays a prominent role in the author's understanding of Christ's sacrifice (9:12,26,28; 10:10). *offered up himself.* Christ was active in His role of being sacrificed (John 10:18).

7:28 *infirmity.* Weakness. The *word of the oath* stands in contrast to the *law* and guarantees a better priest who remains a priest forever.

Thoughts for Personal/Family Worship: Chapter 7

1. **Here as elsewhere the author exalts Christ and shows His magnificent superiority over anything else. Why is focusing on the excellency of Christ such a great medicine for all discouragement and for drawing back from temptation?**
2. **Imagine for a moment what it must have been like for Abraham, fresh from battle, to receive God's blessing through Melchisedec. Think now of Christ blessing His people after He Himself fought the ultimate battle on their behalf.**
3. **Reflect on the truth of v. 25. From what can the power of Christ not save? Where can the power of Christ not reach? When can the power of Christ not intervene for good?**

Christ Mediates a Better Covenant (8:1—10:18)

Chapter 8: ***The new covenant, revealed in Jer. 31:31–34, is held forth to be superior to the old covenant in every way imaginable.***

8:1 *which we have spoken this is the sum.* A summary of the message of Hebrews thus far. *We have such an high priest.* Explains how and why Christ is a king-priest who has returned to the glory of God.

8:2 *A minister of the sanctuary . . . true tabernacle.* Christ's priesthood in the heavens surpasses the typical tabernacle/temple at which the Levitical priests served. *Lord pitched.* The true tabernacle is in heaven and was not built by man but by the hand of God Himself.

8:3 Every high priest was required to *offer* something to God. Christ offered up Himself to God on behalf of the sins of His people.

8:4 *For if he were on earth.* The exaltation of Christ to heaven qualifies Him for a different priesthood. *there are priests that offer gifts according to the law.* Christ's priesthood, if it had remained on earth, would have been a priesthood that was not sufficiently greater than the Levitical priesthood.

8:5 *example and shadow of heavenly things.* Priests served a temporary and typological ministry. *according to the pattern shewed to thee in the mount.* See Ex. 25:40. The Old Testament witnesses to the surpassing greatness of Christ, for He is the substance of the shadowy mystery of the priesthood.

8:6 *more excellent ministry.* The form in which it is ministered. *mediator.* He mediates as a surety (7:22). *better promises.* There were promises under the old covenant, but Christ brings a new covenant where the promises of the old covenant are given a new form, though the substance remains the same.

8:7 *faultless.* God did not make a mistake, but intentionally made the old covenant unable to take away the people's sin. Those saved under the old covenant were saved by looking to Christ, who was to bring in the new (*second*) covenant.

8:8–13 A lengthy citation of Jer. 31:31–34, a climactic moment in Israel and Judah's history as God promises restoration from the exile. Having brought his audience through the wilderness, the author now brings his readers to Mt. Sinai.

8:8 The people were at *fault*, for they broke the covenant and the Levitical priesthood was not sufficient to deal with their sin. The *new covenant* is a renewed covenant, not brand-new however in its substance. *house of Israel and with the house of Judah.* Not the national houses of Israel and Judah but a spiritual house of those who by faith are of the seed of Abraham (Gal. 3:28–29).

8:9 *took them by the hand.* Same Greek word used earlier of Christ taking on the flesh of His brothers (2:16). *because*

10 For this *is* the covenant that I will make with
the house of Israel after those days, saith the Lord;
I will put my laws into their mind, and write them
in their hearts: and I will be to them a God, and
they shall be to me a people:
11 And they shall not teach every man his neigh-
bour, and every man his brother, saying, Know
the Lord: for all shall know me, from the least to
the greatest.
12 For I will be merciful to their unrighteousness,
and their sins and their iniquities will I remember
no more.
13 In that he saith, A new *covenant*, he hath made
the first old. Now that which decayeth and waxeth
old *is* ready to vanish away.

CHAPTER 9

THEN verily the first *covenant* had also ordinances
of divine service, and a worldly sanctuary.
2 For there was a tabernacle made; the first,
wherein *was* the candlestick, and the table, and
the shewbread; which is called the sanctuary.
3 And after the second veil, the tabernacle which
is called the Holiest of all;
4 Which had the golden censer, and the ark of the
covenant overlaid round about with gold, wherein
was the golden pot that had manna, and Aaron's
rod that budded, and the tables of the covenant;
5 And over it the cherubims of glory shadow-
ing the mercyseat; of which we cannot now speak
particularly.
6 Now when these things were thus ordained,
the priests went always into the first tabernacle,
accomplishing the service *of God*.
7 But into the second *went* the high priest alone
once every year, not without blood, which he of-
fered for himself, and *for* the errors of the people:
8 The Holy Ghost this signifying, that the way
into the holiest of all was not yet made manifest,

---

they continued not in my covenant. A continual and sustained breaking of the covenant.

8:10 *I will put my laws into their mind, and write them in their hearts.* This refers to an internalization of the law. *I will be to them a God.* Standard covenantal formula from the Old Testament applied to the church of the New Testament (Gen. 17:7; Ex. 6:7; Lev. 26:12; Ps. 50:7; Jer. 7:23). There is continuity of substance between the old and new covenants.

8:11 *they shall not teach.* Though God has ordained preachers and teachers under the new covenant (Eph. 4:11), all the new covenant people of God have an experiential knowledge of the Lord by the Holy Spirit's work through the Word (John 17:3; 1 John 2:3–4,13,27).

8:12 *their sins and their iniquities will I remember no more.* There will no longer be any need to offer anything for sins because Christ has finally and fully offered Himself and atoned for sins.

8:13 *decayeth and waxeth old.* Wears out and grows old. The new covenant supersedes the old covenant by establishing the better promises. The form of the administration of the covenant has changed, not the substance.

Thoughts for Personal/Family Worship: Chapter 8

1. **Believers have their High Priest sitting upon the throne. Dear Christian, you have omnipotence and compassion coming together based on Christ's finished work. What an encouragement this should be to you who are reconciled to God through the blood of His Son!**
2. **Christ is not only supreme; He is also sufficient. Christ is the only Mediator and Surety of the new covenant. Those who seek God's favor and grace must seek it in the person and work of Jesus Christ, not in rituals and rites of religion, or the sin-stained labor of their own hands.**

Chapter 9: *Christ has entered into the heavenly Holy of Holies with His blood, providing a way for people to come to God with boldness.*

9:1–7 Much of this section describes various parts of the Old Testament ministry of the priests in the tabernacle. Christ's ministry is better.

9:1 *ordinances of divine service.* Refers to the designs of the sanctuary in the tabernacle and the activities of ritual worship. *worldly sanctuary.* The tabernacle Moses constructed.

9:2 *tabernacle.* This is used rather than temple because of the wilderness themes throughout Hebrews (chs. 3–4). The tabernacle and the temple kept the same basic design. It was comprised of an outer court where individuals would gather. Then there were the outer and inner sanctuaries. The outer sanctuary was accessible only to the Levites, and the inner sanctuary to the high priest who could only enter on the Day of Atonement. *the first.* The first sanctuary or holy place in the tabernacle. *candlestick.* Placed in the south side of the tabernacle (Ex. 26:35). *table, and the shewbread.* The table with the holy bread of the priests, which stood at the north side of the outer sanctuary (Ex. 25:23–30; 26:35). These articles of furniture had typological significance pointing to the person and work of Christ.

9:3 *second veil.* There were two curtains in the tabernacle, one separating the court from the holy place and the second, the holy place from the most holy place (Ex. 26:31–35). *tabernacle.* Holy of Holies (*Holiest of all*).

9:4 *golden censer.* The altar of incense was placed just outside of the Holy of Holies (Ex. 25:16,21; Deut. 10:1–2) and might be reckoned as belonging more properly to the second sanctuary. *ark of the covenant.* Most important piece of furniture in the tabernacle because it contained the mercyseat where the blood of the atonement was sprinkled once a year (Ex. 25:10–16). *manna.* The bread that God miraculously provided for Israel in the wilderness showing His steadfast faithfulness (Ex. 16). *Aaron's rod.* Aaron was designated as the chosen head of the priestly line when his rod budded (Num. 17:1–11). *tables of the covenant.* Tablets containing the Ten Commandments (Deut. 9:9).

9:5 *cherubims of glory.* God's glory rested over these angelic beings symbolizing God's dwelling among His people. *mercyseat.* The covering of the ark of the covenant where blood was sprinkled (Ex. 25:22). The mercyseat represented the way of access to God (Num. 7:89), and God's forgiveness of His people (Lev. 16:14–17). *cannot now speak particularly.* The instruments and furniture though important and typological could not be further developed here.

9:6 *Priests* would enter into the holy place (*first tabernacle*) daily. *accomplishing the service of God.* These priests were faithful in their daily ministrations. The point of comparison is not that Jesus was faithful and the priests were not, but how

while as the first tabernacle was yet standing:
9 Which *was* a figure for the time then present, in
which were offered both gifts and sacrifices, that
could not make him that did the service perfect,
as pertaining to the conscience;
10 *Which stood* only in meats and drinks, and
divers washings, and carnal ordinances, imposed
on them until the time of reformation.
11 But Christ being come an high priest of good
things to come, by a greater and more perfect
tabernacle, not made with hands, that is to say,
not of this building;
12 Neither by the blood of goats and calves, but
by his own blood he entered in once into the holy
place, having obtained eternal redemption *for us.*
13 For if the blood of bulls and of goats, and the
ashes of an heifer sprinkling the unclean, sanctifi-
eth to the purifying of the flesh:
14 How much more shall the blood of Christ,
who through the eternal Spirit offered himself
without spot to God, purge your conscience from
dead works to serve the living God?
15 And for this cause he is the mediator of the
new testament, that by means of death, for the
redemption of the transgressions *that were* under
the first testament, they which are called might
receive the promise of eternal inheritance.
16 For where a testament *is,* there must also of
necessity be the death of the testator.
17 For a testament *is* of force after men are dead:
otherwise it is of no strength at all while the tes-
tator liveth.
18 Whereupon neither the first *testament* was
dedicated without blood.
19 For when Moses had spoken every precept to
all the people according to the law, he took the
blood of calves and of goats, with water, and
scarlet wool, and hyssop, and sprinkled both the
book, and all the people,
20 Saying, This *is* the blood of the testament
which God hath enjoined unto you.
21 Moreover he sprinkled with blood both the
tabernacle, and all the vessels of the ministry.
22 And almost all things are by the law purged

---

far Christ's priesthood would reach.

9:7 *the second.* The Holy of Holies. *once every year.* Day of Atonement (Lev. 16). *for himself, and for . . . the people.* The high priest had to offer blood for his own sins and the sins of others (5:1–3; 7:27).

9:8 *The Holy Ghost this signifying.* The Holy Spirit designed the rituals to show that the earthly tabernacle was just a type or picture of true salvation. *way into the holiest of all was not yet made manifest.* The tabernacle and priestly ordinances were not able to give perfect access to God in the Holy of Holies. The tabernacle veiled the people from unbroken communion with God.

9:9 *figure.* Same Greek word as "parable." The tabernacle is a comparison of something, namely the heavenly tabernacle. *time then present.* The translation likely refers to the time in which these types were being used. *as pertaining to the conscience.* The sacrifices of the priests could not cleanse the conscience but were merely an outward cleansing.

9:10 *Which stood only in meats* (food) *and drinks, and divers* (various) *washings, and carnal* (outward, not inward) *ordinances.* The whole Old Testament system was ineffectual to bring the people to perfection. It served only a temporary function, and pointed forward to a time when great change and renewal (*reformation*) would be administered.

9:11–14 Christ's blood accomplishes what the blood of bulls and goats could not.

9:11–12 *But Christ.* A comparison between the ceremonial aspects of the old covenant and Christ's works, described in Levitical terms. *good things to come.* Likely to be understood in both the present time and a future time (v. 15). *by a greater and more perfect tabernacle.* Christ entered the heavenly sanctuary (7:26; 8:2) to bring His people into the presence of God (2:10). *this building.* The earthly tabernacle. *eternal redemption.* Christ's sacrifice only needed to be offered up once, not continually or daily. *for us.* Christ's death was for His people, that is, for their benefit and in their place.

9:13–14 The author lays out the implications of Christ's sacrifice for believers. The priestly sacrifices cleansed only the *flesh.* Christ's death (*blood*) cleanses (*purge*) the conscience, laden with the guilt of sins as it is (vv. 9,14; 10:2,22; 13:8). By virtue of Christ's divine nature (*eternal Spirit*), His sacrifice was a spiritual sacrifice and is therefore effective. Christ was the perfect (*without spot*) Lamb of sacrifice (Ex. 29:1; Lev. 1:3; Num. 6:14). *dead works.* Any works we might seek to perform to gain acceptance with God are defiled by sin like a dead body. Through Christ's sacrifice, believers are able to offer themselves as living sacrifices (Rom. 12:1), and thus enabled *to serve the living God.*

9:15–22 Christ perfects the mediation between God and His people.

9:15 *And for this cause.* Christ's work (described in vv. 11–14), shows Him to be the *mediator* of the new covenant (*new testament*). *for the redemption of the transgressions.* That is, all sins past and present committed by the people for whom He died. Even sins committed under the old covenant (*first testament*) were not forgiven by the blood of bulls and goats, but in advance, by virtue of what Christ's sacrifice was sure to accomplish. Those effectually *called* by the gospel already *receive* the benefits of *the promise,* though they still wait for their *eternal inheritance.*

9:16 *testament.* The Greek word *diatheke* commonly means "covenant," and translates the Hebrew word for covenant, *berith*. However, the author is bringing in the added significance of a firm and settled *testament,* being effectual only upon the death of the One who makes it. *necessity.* Christ's death was required so that He could pass on His inheritance to His brothers.

9:17 *is of force after men are dead.* Once the testator has died, there is no way to annul the testament, rendering it absolute.

9:18 *Whereupon.* Therefore, drawing a conclusion from vv. 16–17. *first testament.* The Mosaic covenant was instituted with blood because there was a self-malediction curse incorporated with the covenant. *dedicated.* Inaugurated. The old covenant was inaugurated by the blood of animals.

9:19 *For when Moses had spoken.* An allusion to Ex. 24:3–8. *sprinkled both the book, and all the people.* Everything under the old covenant was ceremonially purified with blood.

9:20 *which God hath enjoined unto you.* God commanded perfect obedience from the people in the Mosaic covenant (Lev. 18:5).

with blood; and without shedding of blood is no
remission.
23 *It was* therefore necessary that the patterns
of things in the heavens should be purified with
these; but the heavenly things themselves with
better sacrifices than these.
24 For Christ is not entered into the holy places
made with hands, *which are* the figures of the
true; but into heaven itself, now to appear in the
presence of God for us:
25 Nor yet that he should offer himself often, as
the high priest entereth into the holy place every
year with blood of others;
26 For then must he often have suffered since the
foundation of the world: but now once in the end
of the world hath he appeared to put away sin by
the sacrifice of himself.
27 And as it is appointed unto men once to die,
but after this the judgment:
28 So Christ was once offered to bear the sins
of many; and unto them that look for him shall
he appear the second time without sin unto
salvation.

CHAPTER 10

FOR the law having a shadow of good things to
come, *and* not the very image of the things, can
never with those sacrifices which they offered
year by year continually make the comers there-
unto perfect.
2 For then would they not have ceased to be of-
fered? because that the worshippers once purged
should have had no more conscience of sins.
3 But in those *sacrifices there is* a remembrance
again *made* of sins every year.
4 For *it is* not possible that the blood of bulls and
of goats should take away sins.
5 Wherefore when he cometh into the world, he
saith, Sacrifice and offering thou wouldest not,
but a body hast thou prepared me:
6 In burnt offerings and *sacrifices* for sin thou
hast had no pleasure.
7 Then said I, Lo, I come (in the volume of the
book it is written of me,) to do thy will, O God.
8 Above when he said, Sacrifice and offering and
burnt offerings and *offering* for sin thou wouldest
not, neither hadst pleasure *therein*; which are

9:22 *remission.* Forgiveness.
9:23 *the heavenly things themselves.* Not that heaven was unclean, but the bringing of guilty sinners into the holy places would defile them unless they were *purified* with Christ's blood.
9:24 Why cling to a brick and mortar building if Christ is in *heaven itself*? Christ only needs to *appear in the presence of God* on behalf of His people and it is more than enough.
9:26 *For then must he often have suffered.* Christ's death is only once. *in the end of the world.* Not a reference to the temporal end of history, but the perfection of the ages. History moves toward a definite goal and Christ is moving His people to this goal. *put away.* Remove or cancel.
9:27 *And as it is appointed unto men once to die.* The nature of death is such that it is inescapable. Death precedes judgment, which follows immediately after death.
9:28 *to bear the sins of many.* An allusion to Isa. 53:4, emphasizing substitution. *shall he appear the second time without sin unto salvation.* When He returns with the clouds, He will not appear bearing the sins of His people in order to die again, but to bring His final salvation in.

Thoughts for Personal/Family Worship: Chapter 9

1. **When Christ died on Calvary, the veil of the temple was rent from top to bottom (Matt. 27:51). God was signifying that the ordinances were to be done away with. Still today, we often let our thoughts go no further than what we can see—buildings, people, ministers, etc. However, our thoughts should be on Christ in the heavenly sanctuary, as He is there with His own blood.**
2. **The sacrifices of the Old Testament pointed forward to Christ, but they could not themselves internally cleanse people. What David prayed for in Ps. 51:7, Christ alone can do through His sacrifice. Has Christ's blood been applied to your conscience? Do you still rely on dead works to please God?**
3. **There are some who imagine that God gives second chances to people after they die to flee to Christ. Yet v. 27 is clear that it has been appointed to man to die once and then the judgment. As uncertain as our life is, this truth should make us very sober.**

Chapter 10: *Christ's sacrifice is the one and only sacrifice. Believers everywhere should live in light of this one final sacrifice.*

10:1 *For the law having a shadow of good things to come.* Specifically the laws centering on the sacrificial institutions of the old covenant (8:5; Col. 2:17). *very image.* Christ is the fulfillment of the sacrifices. *make the comers thereunto perfect.* Christ's sacrifice was perfect and by virtue of it, God's people need not look anywhere else for perfection.
10:2–4 The sacrifices served to be a continual reminder (*remembrance*) of sin before the people and God as often as they were made. *not possible that the blood of bulls and of goats should take away sins.* Christ's blood forever cleanses the conscience of sin (8:12; Jer. 31:31–34).
10:5 *cometh into the world.* Christ's incarnation. *but a body.* Citing Ps. 40:6. The Hebrew text of the psalm has "ear," where the Greek translation of the Old Testament has "body." Either word points to the submission of Christ's human nature to God. Psalm 40:6 is a reference to obedience to the law, particularly as Israel was commanded to "hear" God and be obedient (Deut. 6:4). *Sacrifice and offering thou wouldest not.* Though God prescribed sacrifices and offerings in the old covenant, these were only necessary because of sin. If there had been obedience, there would not have been a need for sacrifices and offerings. *hast thou prepared me.* God prepared a body for Christ.
10:6 *hast had no pleasure.* When presented in a God-ordained way, sacrifices were a fragrant aroma to God. Thus this statement is intended comparatively: sacrifices and offerings were secondary to true, proper, and perpetual obedience.
10:7 *Then said I.* Citing Ps. 40:7–8. *volume.* Scroll. *to do thy will, O God.* Christ was truly, properly, and perpetually obedient to God (John 6:38).
10:9 *taketh away the first.* A reference to the Levitical sacri-

offered by the law;
9 Then said he, Lo, I come to do thy will, O God.
He taketh away the first, that he may establish the
second.
10 By the which will we are sanctified through the
offering of the body of Jesus Christ once *for all.*
11 And every priest standeth daily ministering
and offering oftentimes the same sacrifices, which
can never take away sins:
12 But this man, after he had offered one sacri-
fice for sins for ever, sat down on the right hand
of God;
13 From henceforth expecting till his enemies be
made his footstool.
14 For by one offering he hath perfected for ever
them that are sanctified.
15 *Whereof* the Holy Ghost also is a witness to us:
for after that he had said before,
16 This *is* the covenant that I will make with them
after those days, saith the Lord, I will put my laws
into their hearts, and in their minds will I write
them;
17 And their sins and iniquities will I remember
no more.
18 Now where remission of these *is, there is* no
more offering for sin.
19 Having therefore, brethren, boldness to enter
into the holiest by the blood of Jesus,
20 By a new and living way, which he hath con-
secrated for us, through the veil, that is to say, his
flesh;
21 And *having* an high priest over the house of
God;
22 Let us draw near with a true heart in full
assurance of faith, having our hearts sprinkled
from an evil conscience, and our bodies washed
with pure water.
23 Let us hold fast the profession of *our* faith with-
out wavering; (for he *is* faithful that promised;)
24 And let us consider one another to provoke
unto love and to good works:
25 Not forsaking the assembling of ourselves
together, as the manner of some *is;* but exhorting
one another: and so much the more, as ye see the
day approaching.
26 For if we sin wilfully after that we have received
the knowledge of the truth, there remaineth no
more sacrifice for sins,
27 But a certain fearful looking for of judgment
and fiery indignation, which shall devour the
adversaries.
28 He that despised Moses' law died without
mercy under two or three witnesses:
29 Of how much sorer punishment, suppose ye,

fices. *establish the second.* Christ's obedience that He offered to God.

10:10 *the which will.* Whose will, that is, God's will. *we are sanctified.* The emphasis here is only the consecration Christ's work effects for His people (2:11). *through the offering of the body.* Christ's incarnation was for the purpose of His atonement. *once for all.* Christ's sacrifice was final.

10:11–13 *And every priest standeth daily ministering.* The Old Testament priests stood (Deut. 18:5); of Christ we read that He *sat down* (1:3).

10:15 *Holy Ghost.* The author is not inventing new arguments to substantiate the life and death of Christ but is witnessing in conjunction with the Holy Spirit.

10:16–18 Another citation of Jer. 31:33–34. The focus is on the internalization of the law and the forgiveness (*remission*) of sins. The "perfection" of the new covenant is that God has provided a full and final remedy for the sins of His people so that *there is no more offering for sin.*

THE APPLICATION OF CHRIST (10:19—13:25)

A Call to True Christian Experience (10:19–39)

10:19 *boldness.* Open access to approach God. *blood of Jesus.* What was open only to the high priests in the old covenant is now opened to all believers through faith in Christ's death.

10:20 *consecrated.* Only used twice in the New Testament (9:18). Christ has opened a way that was previously shut or of limited access. Thus there is *a new and living way.* The *veil* distanced God from people; by the suffering and death of Christ's *flesh* this veil is removed.

10:21 *over the house of God.* See 3:1–6.

10:22 *Let us draw near.* The first of several exhortations in this section. *true heart.* Heart characterized by sincerity. *full assurance of faith.* Complete reliance upon God (6:11). *having our hearts sprinkled.* This qualifies believers to approach God because their hearts have been cleansed with *pure water* (Ex. 24:3–8).

10:23 *Let us hold fast.* Let us retain (2:1–4). This is the second exhortation. *without wavering.* Dedicated and committed to the Lord in all things. Our motivation to hold firmly to our confession of Christ is that God is *faithful* and will be faithful to what He has *promised.*

10:24 *let us consider.* Third exhortation. There is an organic relationship between the work of Christ, individual salvation, and the existence of the corporate body, the church. *provoke.* Stimulate and motivate other Christians to *good works*, by our prayers, teaching, and example.

10:25 *forsaking.* This language suggests that rejecting God Himself is close at hand (Deut. 28:20; 1 Sam. 8:8). *the assembling.* The local gathering of the church. Forsaking God's people risks forsaking the Lord Himself. *manner.* Custom or habit. *exhorting one another.* Continual encouraging of the Lord's people. *the day approaching.* Judgment day, which is coming nearer every day.

10:26–39 The following section is a detailed exhortation not to forsake Christ by apostatizing, but instead to endure in the face of trials, tribulations, and sufferings.

10:26 *For if we sin wilfully.* From the context we can learn that the author means "the sin of apostasy" (3:12; 6:1–8; 10:27–31). *after that we have received the knowledge of the truth.* Having made some profession upon instruction (1 Tim. 2:4; 4:3; 2 Tim. 2:25; 3:7). *there remaineth no more sacrifice for sins.* Those who apostatize from the blood of Christ have left themselves with no further remedy for sins.

10:27 The judgment against apostasy is similar to what awaited the sons of Korah (Num. 16:35; 26:10).

10:28 *two or three witnesses.* See Deut. 13:6–11; 17:2–7.

10:29 *sorer.* Worse. The next phrases do not denote three separate sins, but three aspects of the one sin of apostasy.

shall he be thought worthy, who hath trodden
under foot the Son of God, and hath counted
the blood of the covenant, wherewith he was
sanctified, an unholy thing, and hath done despite
unto the Spirit of grace?
30 For we know him that hath said, Vengeance
belongeth unto me, I will recompense, saith the
Lord. And again, The Lord shall judge his people.
31 *It is* a fearful thing to fall into the hands of the
living God.
32 But call to remembrance the former days, in
which, after ye were illuminated, ye endured a
great fight of afflictions;
33 Partly, whilst ye were made a gazingstock both
by reproaches and afflictions; and partly, whilst ye
became companions of them that were so used.
34 For ye had compassion of me in my bonds,
and took joyfully the spoiling of your goods,
knowing in yourselves that ye have in heaven a
better and an enduring substance.
35 Cast not away therefore your confidence,
which hath great recompence of reward.
36 For ye have need of patience, that, after ye
have done the will of God, ye might receive the
promise.
37 For yet a little while, and he that shall come
will come, and will not tarry.
38 Now the just shall live by faith: but if *any man*
draw back, my soul shall have no pleasure in him.
39 But we are not of them who draw back unto
perdition; but of them that believe to the saving
of the soul.

CHAPTER 11

NOW faith is the substance of things hoped for,
the evidence of things not seen.
2 For by it the elders obtained a good report.
3 Through faith we understand that the worlds
were framed by the word of God, so that things
which are seen were not made of things which do
appear.
4 By faith Abel offered unto God a more excellent
sacrifice than Cain, by which he obtained witness

---

trodden under foot the Son of God. To apostatize from Christ is an attempt to detract from His exaltation over His enemies (1:13), a major theme of Hebrews. *blood of the covenant . . . an unholy thing.* The precious blood of Christ is accounted to be nothing special. Apostates have contempt (*done despite*) for the Holy *Spirit*, who comes in the preaching of *grace*. Apostates despise the whole Trinity.

10:30–31 *For we know him that hath said.* Citing Deut. 32:35–36.

10:32 *after ye were illuminated.* Reference to their initial knowledge of the truth (6:4). *ye endured a great fight of afflictions.* Terms of strong military action. There is no retreat in this battle; Christians are by grace to hold their ground.

10:33–34 A description of the suffering the Hebrew Christians were experiencing. *gazingstock.* A spectacle open to ridicule. *knowing in yourselves.* God had assured them by His word of promise and by His work in their hearts (Rom. 8:15–17). They were able to endure in previous trials because they knew that *in heaven* they had *a better and an enduring* treasure (*substance*).

10:35 *confidence.* Same Greek word used for boldness (v. 19; 4:14). *which hath great . . . reward.* Confidence is a sure promise of the heavenly inheritance they have. Confidence does not merely point to the reward, but contains the reward.

10:37 *little while.* Citing Isa. 26:20. The waiting is not yet over and the people have a great need to persevere, though Christ will not *tarry* in His coming. *shall come.* A reference to the second coming.

10:38 *Now the just shall live by faith.* Citing Hab. 2:4. The author prepares for ch. 11 by introducing the doctrine of faith here.

10:39 *of them that believe.* Positive statement to encourage the people to persevere. Much like the "better things" (6:9), the author expresses confidence that his readers will persevere to the salvation of their souls.

Thoughts for Personal/Family Worship: Chapter 10

1. In the Old Testament, the people imagined that they could do what they wanted and just keep the sacrifices going to appease God. Through the prophets, God made clear that sacrifices by themselves, without hearts that love and obey God, are abhorrent to Him (vv. 5–6). Many today look at the sacrifice of Christ in a similar way, as an insurance policy for heaven, all the while living for themselves. Why won't that work? Consider vv. 26–27.

2. Typically, we don't like it when human authorities are angry with us. Consider in this light v. 31. Why is it a fearful thing to fall into the hands of an angry God?

3. "Ye have need of patience" (v. 36). How can the past times of suffering encourage God's people going forward (vv. 32–34)? How have your past trials strengthened your hope and endurance?

Encouragements to True Faith (11:1—12:17)

Chapter 11: ***A great cloud of witnesses from the Old Testament proves that the Old Testament economy was never intended to be itself the fullness of God's revelation or redemption.***

11:1–40 This section does not interrupt the flow of his argument here in ch. 11. In fact, setting the definition of faith as he does in vv. 1–2, the author proves from a chorus of Old Testament witnesses the folly of going back to the Old Testament ordinances, as the Hebrews were tempted to do.

11:1 *faith.* Faith sees the heavenly realities that the author has been speaking about and makes believers live in a way that testifies to their reality. *substance.* This word is used elsewhere in Hebrews for "confidence" (3:14). Confident trust in the Word of God grants the believer the essence of what God promises. *things hoped for.* Heavenly realities in Christ. *evidence.* Demonstration, a legal term. Faith in God's Word provides evidence and assurance in the heart of those things that are not seen.

11:2 *elders.* Old Testament believers. *obtained a good report.* The Old Testament marks out for us the report of their faith and hope wrought in them and for them.

11:3 The temporal and material is not the ultimate reality, but the *worlds* were created *by the word of God*, showing the preeminence of God's Word. *things which are seen were not made of things which do appear.* God's invisible word brings

that he was righteous, God testifying of his gifts:
and by it he being dead yet speaketh.
5 By faith Enoch was translated that he should
not see death; and was not found, because God
had translated him: for before his translation he
had this testimony, that he pleased God.
6 But without faith *it is* impossible to please *him*:
for he that cometh to God must believe that he is,
and *that* he is a rewarder of them that diligently
seek him.
7 By faith Noah, being warned of God of things
not seen as yet, moved with fear, prepared an
ark to the saving of his house; by the which he
condemned the world, and became heir of the
righteousness which is by faith.
8 By faith Abraham, when he was called to go out
into a place which he should after receive for an
inheritance, obeyed; and he went out, not know-
ing whither he went.
9 By faith he sojourned in the land of promise, as
in a strange country, dwelling in tabernacles with
Isaac and Jacob, the heirs with him of the same
promise:
10 For he looked for a city which hath founda-
tions, whose builder and maker *is* God.
11 Through faith also Sara herself received
strength to conceive seed, and was delivered of a
child when she was past age, because she judged
him faithful who had promised.
12 Therefore sprang there even of one, and him
as good as dead, *so many* as the stars of the sky
in multitude, and as the sand which is by the sea
shore innumerable.
13 These all died in faith, not having received
the promises, but having seen them afar off, and
were persuaded of *them*, and embraced *them*, and
confessed that they were strangers and pilgrims
on the earth.
14 For they that say such things declare plainly
that they seek a country.
15 And truly, if they had been mindful of that
country from whence they came out, they might
have had opportunity to have returned.
16 But now they desire a better *country*, that is,
an heavenly: wherefore God is not ashamed to be
called their God: for he hath prepared for them
a city.
17 By faith Abraham, when he was tried, offered
up Isaac: and he that had received the promises
offered up his only begotten *son*,
18 Of whom it was said, That in Isaac shall thy
seed be called:
19 Accounting that God *was* able to raise *him* up,
even from the dead; from whence also he received
him in a figure.
20 By faith Isaac blessed Jacob and Esau concern-
ing things to come.
21 By faith Jacob, when he was a dying, blessed

---

things into being (Gen. 1:3; Ps. 33:6), both at creation and ever since then (1:3).

11:4 Each action in this chapter is described as done *by faith. Abel.* Hebrews traces the reality of faith back to the beginning of creation. *offered unto God.* Without faith it is impossible to please God (v. 6), and this principle was at work with Abel's sacrifice. *he obtained witness.* Even Abel received the declaration of righteousness by his faith. *by it.* The sacrifice offered by faith still speaks today. The word of faith transcends time.

11:5 *Enoch.* See Gen. 5:24. *translated.* Taken to heaven. Enoch did not die.

11:6 *without faith it is impossible.* Faith is necessary to please God (Rom. 14:23). *must believe that he is.* Belief in God is at the base of it all (Ex. 3:14). Without it, there is no proper object of faith. *he is a rewarder.* This is the character and nature of God. *seek him.* Rest and dwell with God.

11:7 *Noah.* See Gen. 6–9. *being warned of God of things not seen as yet.* God promised to send a flood to wipe out the world. Even until the day Noah entered the ark, the world scorned him because this was an unseen reality. Noah, however, lived by faith that God's judgment was coming upon the people as he promised. *by the which he condemned the world.* Noah's building of the ark echoed God's condemnation of the world to judgment. *and became heir of the righteousness which is by faith.* By his faith Noah became an heir of an eternal inheritance by his faith.

11:9 *sojourned in the land of promise.* Canaan was not the fulfillment of the promise. *sojourned.* Abraham was a stranger even in Canaan. *strange.* Foreign. *tabernacles.* Tents. *heirs with him of the same promise.* All the patriarchs shared in the same promised inheritance. God had promised, and thus, God would fulfill His word.

11:10 *whose builder and maker is God.* The realization of the promised inheritance was not earthly Canaan but an eternal city. Abraham testified to this reality.

11:11 *seed.* Offspring. *was delivered of a child.* Had a baby.

11:12 *sprang there even of one . . . innumerable.* From one man came a host of people. *him as good as dead.* From a human perspective, Abraham was beyond normal childbearing age and the author metaphorically sees him as dead.

11:13 *These all died in faith.* The patriarchs could not receive the inheritance apart from the remainder of the people of God (v. 40). *having seen them afar off.* Abraham's place was early in redemptive history. *persuaded.* Confidence that God would fulfill all that He had spoken. *confessed.* They were not pilgrims and strangers by default but by a confession of faith.

11:14–15 *they seek a country.* Not a homeland that could be traveled to in this life because if it was, *they might have had opportunity to have returned.* All believers are to seek the heavenly homeland.

11:16 *not ashamed to be called their God.* God identifies Himself as the God of strangers and pilgrims. Their longing and journeying could only be satisfied in the city that God *prepared for them.*

11:17–19 *offered up Isaac.* Abraham was called to sacrifice the promised heir (Gen. 22). *in Isaac shall thy seed be called.* Abraham received Isaac back from the dead, so to speak, and confirms the eternality of the promise. Abraham was *accounting that God was able to raise him up.* Abraham believed against the temporal sight of his eyes.

11:20 *Isaac blessed Jacob and Esau.* Isaac blessed Jacob despite the fact that Esau was the natural inheritor of the blessing. He foresaw the ways in which God would bless Jacob *concerning things to come.*

both the sons of Joseph; and worshipped, *leaning*
upon the top of his staff.
22 By faith Joseph, when he died, made mention
of the departing of the children of Israel; and gave
commandment concerning his bones.
23 By faith Moses, when he was born, was hid
three months of his parents, because they saw *he*
was a proper child; and they were not afraid of the
king's commandment.
24 By faith Moses, when he was come to years, re-
fused to be called the son of Pharaoh's daughter;
25 Choosing rather to suffer affliction with the
people of God, than to enjoy the pleasures of sin
for a season;
26 Esteeming the reproach of Christ greater
riches than the treasures in Egypt: for he had re-
spect unto the recompence of the reward.
27 By faith he forsook Egypt, not fearing the
wrath of the king: for he endured, as seeing him
who is invisible.
28 Through faith he kept the passover, and the
sprinkling of blood, lest he that destroyed the
firstborn should touch them.
29 By faith they passed through the Red sea as by
dry *land*: which the Egyptians assaying to do were
drowned.
30 By faith the walls of Jericho fell down, after
they were compassed about seven days.
31 By faith the harlot Rahab perished not with
them that believed not, when she had received the
spies with peace.
32 And what shall I more say? for the time would
fail me to tell of Gedeon, and *of* Barak, and *of*
Samson, and *of* Jephthae; *of* David also, and
Samuel, and *of* the prophets:
33 Who through faith subdued kingdoms,
wrought righteousness, obtained promises,
stopped the mouths of lions,
34 Quenched the violence of fire, escaped the
edge of the sword, out of weakness were made
strong, waxed valiant in fight, turned to flight the
armies of the aliens.
35 Women received their dead raised to life again:
and others were tortured, not accepting deliver-
ance; that they might obtain a better resurrection:
36 And others had trial of *cruel* mockings
and scourgings, yea, moreover of bonds and
imprisonment:
37 They were stoned, they were sawn asunder,
were tempted, were slain with the sword: they
wandered about in sheepskins and goatskins;
being destitute, afflicted, tormented;
38 (Of whom the world was not worthy:) they
wandered in deserts, and *in* mountains, and *in*

11:21 *Jacob, when he was a dying.* Jacob blessed the sons of Joseph (Ephraim and Manasseh), granting to Joseph the double portion, but at the same time reversing the order of the firstborn and lastborn (Gen. 47:1–22).

11:22 *Joseph . . . made mention of the departing of the children of Israel.* Joseph, living in Egypt, proclaimed God's promised faithfulness of again bringing His people back into the land of promise. Joseph sought for his bones to be brought back into the Promised Land.

11:23 *saw he was a proper child.* They believed that if God, who forms human life in the womb, gave Moses life and health, who was Pharaoh to take it away?

11:24 *come to years.* Became a mature adult. *refused to be called the son of Pharaoh's daughter.* Moses' slaying of the Egyptian and fleeing to Midian was a decisive rejection of his Egyptian inheritance to seek the greater inheritance of God's people (Ex. 2:11–15).

11:25 *Choosing rather to suffer affliction.* Moses, like Abraham, ought to convict those who are tempted to apostatize instead of suffering persecution. Moses had the opportunity to enjoy the *pleasures of sin* and to remain among the prosperous Egyptians, but he chose to suffer affliction and persecution rather than to return to Egypt.

11:26 *reproach of Christ.* All the suffering of God's people is organically linked to Christ's suffering (Isa. 63:9). *recompence of the reward.* Moses had sufficient revelation to understand the great reward of being accounted among the suffering people of God.

11:27 *forsook Egypt.* Moses leading the people out of Egypt during the exodus. *for he endured.* Moses persevered. *as seeing him who is invisible.* Moses acted in light of Him, whom he had seen with eyes of faith, though He is otherwise invisible.

11:28 *Through faith he kept the passover.* Even keeping the Passover was an act of faith, for there was nothing other than the words of God to go on. Moses saw the reality to which the Passover pointed.

11:29 *passed through the Red sea.* A decisive victory for the people of Israel over the Egyptians and God's greatest act of redemption to its date, a type of the greater deliverance to be done in Christ. The Israelites passed through the Red Sea *by faith. assaying.* Attempting.

11:30 *Jericho.* The destruction of Jericho (Josh. 6) marked Israel's first entrance into the Promised Land after forty years of wandering in the desert. Jericho, however, fell *by faith* showing that even the entrance into the land was a type of the heavenly inheritance. *compassed.* Surrounded.

11:31 *Rahab.* The prostitute of Jericho who hid the Israelites spies. Though she was a Gentile, she understood that the land belonged to Israel (Josh. 2:9). By faith Rahab saw the reality of God despite her lowly estate and showed it when *she had received the spies with peace.*

11:32 Included here are a number of famous and well-known biblical examples. The overarching point is that the communal witness of the entire Old Testament from the days of Abel to the days of the prophets was marked by faith.

11:33–35 Every victory was obtained through faith by those who participated, knowing that this victory was not the consummation of God's promises.

11:35 *might obtain a better resurrection.* A better resurrection than the women who *received their dead.* They looked forward to the final resurrection.

11:36–37 They persevered in the face of the temporary defeats they suffered. It is like the three friends of Daniel said, as they were about to be thrown into the furnace: If God chooses not to deliver us, we will still not serve your gods (see Dan. 3:18). *asunder.* Into two.

11:38 *Of whom the world was not worthy.* When the world rejects believers it considers *not worthy* to live, it is instead

dens and caves of the earth.
39 And these all, having obtained a good report
through faith, received not the promise:
40 God having provided some better thing for us,
that they without us should not be made perfect.

CHAPTER 12

WHEREFORE seeing we also are compassed about
with so great a cloud of witnesses, let us lay aside
every weight, and the sin which doth so easily
beset *us*, and let us run with patience the race that
is set before us,
2 Looking unto Jesus the author and finisher of
our faith; who for the joy that was set before him
endured the cross, despising the shame, and is
set down at the right hand of the throne of God.
3 For consider him that endured such contradic-
tion of sinners against himself, lest ye be wearied
and faint in your minds.
4 Ye have not yet resisted unto blood, striving
against sin.
5 And ye have forgotten the exhortation which
speaketh unto you as unto children, My son, de-
spise not thou the chastening of the Lord, nor
faint when thou art rebuked of him:
6 For whom the Lord loveth he chasteneth, and
scourgeth every son whom he receiveth.
7 If ye endure chastening, God dealeth with you
as with sons; for what son is he whom the father
chasteneth not?
8 But if ye be without chastisement, whereof all

the world that is *not worthy* of having these saints among it. *wandered.* They were pilgrims and strangers on earth despite their privileged position in God's purposes.

11:39 *having obtained a good report.* Those who died in faith received a good witness or testimony, presumably, from God Himself. This testimony continues to speak *through faith* that the substance of God's promise was not yet present in the Old Testament.

11:40 *they without us should not be made perfect.* God's wisdom ordained that all His people would share together in the fulfillment of His promises. *made perfect.* There could be no final perfection in the glorified state for the Old Testament believers without the realities that would unfold in and among the New Testament believers.

Thoughts for Personal/Family Worship: Chapter 11

1. **These heroes of faith are more than moral examples. They lived in light of a faith that would for the most part unfold beyond their lifetimes. Think of what Enoch, Abraham, Moses, and Rahab might say to you in your particular struggle right now.**
2. **How is the doctrine of creation (v. 3) a great encouragement to faith?**
3. **Verses 36–38 prove to us that faith in Christ does not free us from life's difficulties but often leads us into the heart of troubles. As a result the world may judge us as unworthy. Compare whom the world thinks of as worthy ones, and of whom God says "the world was not worthy" (v. 38). Whose verdict matters more to us?**

Chapter 12: ***The author opens with the doctrine of sonship as seen in discipline and climaxes his rhetorical argument by showing the superiority of New Testament worship over the ceremony of Old Testament worship.***

12:1–4 The opening section of ch. 12 connects closely with ch. 11. The focus of these verses is centered on Jesus and His relationship to the faith of the Old Testament saints.

12:1 *Wherefore.* Consequently, strong conjunction connecting chs. 11–12. *cloud of witnesses.* This cloud of witnesses is not primarily given for moral encouragement, but serves like witnesses in a courtroom to God's redemptive purposes. *sin which doth so easily beset us.* Especially the sins of unbelief and apostasy. The *race* is *set* before believers, shows that God determines this race.

12:2 *Jesus.* Jesus is not a final example of faith, but *the author and finisher of our faith.* Jesus' relationship to faith is qualitatively different than the heroes of the Old Testament. Whereas each Old Testament example apprehended the promise of God through faith, Christ was the captain, content, and consummator of it all. *author.* Same word used in 2:10 for "captain." *finisher.* A cognate word of the Greek *telos* which, here, shows that faith finds its focus and basis in Jesus. *joy that was set before him.* The suffering of the cross was endured because it led to His enthronement *at the right hand of the throne of God*, the ultimate joy.

12:3 *consider him.* Christ ought to be the object of our thoughts and desires, especially when we think we are suffering greatly. Considering Christ in suffering will keep us from self-pity and self-preoccupation, and will help us draw strength from His suffering. *such contradiction.* He was opposed not only by this world's power, but the religious people of the day, as well as His own followers, including Peter. *wearied and faint in your minds.* To be faint in our minds drains strength from every part of us.

12:4 The author puts their resistance into perspective, encouraging them to be prepared for more, if need be. The life of a Christian is no longer his or her own. They have *not yet resisted unto blood*, though the Author and Finisher of their faith did.

12:5–17 These verses focus on parallel themes of suffering, sonship, discipline, inheritance, and the exhortation for faith. The background of these verses lies in Deut. 8 where Moses reminds the people of God's loving discipline of them in their forty years of wilderness wandering. As God led Israel, His son, out of Egypt (Ex. 4:23–24), He lovingly disciplined them through their wilderness wandering.

12:5 *forgotten the exhortation which speaketh unto you as unto children.* Hebrews admonishes the readers for having forgotten the exhortation (2:1–4), which is a citation from Prov. 3:11–12. In it a father exhorts his son in the way of the Lord (Prov. 1:8). Here the author develops the application of "son" which has only been briefly mentioned beforehand (2:17–18). *despise not thou the chastening of the Lord.* Suffering is not a sign of God's wrath, but a sign of fatherly love. *nor faint when thou art rebuked.* The word "rebuke" is stronger than the *chastening* of God.

12:6 *whom the Lord loveth.* God loves those He is chastening as a father loves a son. God is dealing with suffering believers in the same way He dealt with His Son, who is the founder of their faith. *scourgeth.* Strongest verb used of God's discipline, also used of the sufferings of Christ and His apostles (Matt. 10:17; 20:19).

12:7 *If ye endure.* If you quietly and patiently bear these

are partakers, then are ye bastards, and not sons.
9 Furthermore we have had fathers of our flesh
which corrected *us*, and we gave *them* reverence:
shall we not much rather be in subjection unto
the Father of spirits, and live?
10 For they verily for a few days chastened *us* after
their own pleasure; but he for *our* profit, that *we*
might be partakers of his holiness.
11 Now no chastening for the present seemeth to
be joyous, but grievous: nevertheless afterward it
yieldeth the peaceable fruit of righteousness unto
them which are exercised thereby.
12 Wherefore lift up the hands which hang down,
and the feeble knees;
13 And make straight paths for your feet, lest that
which is lame be turned out of the way; but let it
rather be healed.
14 Follow peace with all *men*, and holiness, with-
out which no man shall see the Lord:
15 Looking diligently lest any man fail of the
grace of God; lest any root of bitterness spring-
ing up trouble *you*, and thereby many be defiled;
16 Lest there *be* any fornicator, or profane per-
son, as Esau, who for one morsel of meat sold his
birthright.
17 For ye know how that afterward, when he
would have inherited the blessing, he was rejected:
for he found no place of repentance, though he
sought it carefully with tears.
18 For ye are not come unto the mount that
might be touched, and that burned with fire, nor
unto blackness, and darkness, and tempest,
19 And the sound of a trumpet, and the voice of
words; which *voice* they that heard intreated that
the word should not be spoken to them any more:
20 (For they could not endure that which was
commanded, And if so much as a beast touch the
mountain, it shall be stoned, or thrust through
with a dart:
21 And so terrible was the sight, *that* Moses said,
I exceedingly fear and quake:)
22 But ye are come unto mount Sion, and unto

afflictions, this itself is already evidence that God is bestowing grace that only His children know. *as with sons.* Through Christ, believers are adopted as sons of God.

12:8 *be without chastisement.* There is danger in not being chastised by God, for he who lacks discipline lacks sonship. *all are partakers.* All legitimate children partake of discipline.

12:9 The author uses a human analogy to show the worship his readers ought to have for God their Father. *Father of spirits.* Designated here because it refers to God as the God of the living and has sovereign control over all things (Num. 16:22). *and live.* Being disciplined by the Father will lead to life because He is over all life.

12:10 *verily.* Truly. Earthly fathers discipline their children *after their own pleasure.* Human fathers can be overbearing, shortsighted, and often driven by what is convenient for them. This verse does not condone sadistic or unnecessarily harsh discipline. *but he for our profit.* God's discipline is far superior to human discipline, always aiming at His children's participation in the *holiness* of God (2:10).

12:11 Discipline is not *joyous* to endure; yet, if we seek to learn and profit from it, it will yield fruit for Christ's sake.

12:12–13 See Prov. 4:26; Isa. 35:3–4. Isaiah 35 is set within the context of the promise of God's gospel salvation coming after the chastening of the exile.

12:14 *Follow . . . holiness, without which no man shall see the Lord.* Those who are disciplined are directed to pursue gospel holiness, which is absolutely necessary if we wish to see God at the last.

12:15 *Looking diligently.* Great care in light of present sufferings is to ensure that those who suffer do not fall short of the *grace of God. root of bitterness . . . thereby many be defiled.* An allusion to Deut. 29:18–19, where Moses warns Israel on the edge of the Promised Land against any among them who turn from God to idols.

12:16 *fornicator, or profane person, as Esau.* The Old Testament makes no explicit mention of Esau's sexual immorality, though his marriage with Canaanite women does not speak in his favor (Gen. 26:35). Idolatry was often connected with sexual immorality (Num. 25:1–3; Hos. 4:14). *profane.* Opposite of holy (Lev. 10:10). *morsel of meat.* Some food. The *birthright* was the blessing of the father, which normally went to the eldest child, who would receive a greater portion than his siblings. Esau cherished present circumstances and earthly desires over his future inheritance (Gen. 25:29–34; 27:1–40).

12:17 Esau was *rejected* as the heir of the blessing. He did not come to the place of true *repentance*, as David and others did. Esau did weep *tears*, and regretted certain things, but ultimately refused to turn from sin to God. All this is a warning not to play fast and loose with spiritual privileges.

A View of the Unshakable Kingdom (12:18–29)

12:18–29 The exhortation here is similar to Moses' final speech in Deuteronomy as the people prepared to enter Canaan. The goal of the author in this section, though not explicitly stated, is to bring God's people to worship, even as the angels worshiped Christ when He came into His glory (1:6).

12:18–24 The author shows that there can be no return to Sinai because the people have left that far behind with all its external drudgeries and terrifying theophany. To return to Sinai would be a return to dread, not to reconciliation with God, which Christ's blood alone accomplished.

12:18 *For ye are not come.* Hebrews contrasts the heavenly Jerusalem with the earthly Sinai to compare the old covenant with the new covenant (Jer. 31:31–34). The Mosaic covenant had a strictness and bondage about it compared to a glory and boldness belonging to the new covenant. *unto the mount that might be touched.* Mt. Sinai had a physicality that the Hebrews seemed to be hankering after. However, when it was touched by so much as an animal, the consequence was disastrous (v. 20). *darkness.* Though the Israelites saw much, God was still veiled from their vision. *burned with fire.* Indication of God's presence on the mount (Ex. 19:18; Deut. 4:24; Isa. 30:33).

12:19 *sound of a trumpet.* The trumpet alerted the people (Ex. 19:16). *voice.* The people heard but did not see God. In Christ, believers both hear and see God (1:1–4). *the word should not be spoken to them.* The people could not bear to hear the unmediated voice of God (Ex. 20:19).

12:20 God commanded that anything which touched the mountain would be killed (Ex. 19:12–13).

12:21 *I exceedingly fear.* Moses did fear the wrath of God after the golden calf incident (Deut. 9:19). God's revelation of Himself was a revelation of great holiness.

the city of the living God, the heavenly Jerusalem,
and to an innumerable company of angels,
23 To the general assembly and church of the
firstborn, which are written in heaven, and to
God the Judge of all, and to the spirits of just men
made perfect,
24 And to Jesus the mediator of the new covenant,
and to the blood of sprinkling, that speaketh bet-
ter things than *that of* Abel.
25 See that ye refuse not him that speaketh. For if
they escaped not who refused him that spake on
earth, much more *shall not* we *escape*, if we turn
away from him that *speaketh* from heaven:
26 Whose voice then shook the earth: but now he
hath promised, saying, Yet once more I shake not
the earth only, but also heaven.
27 And this *word*, Yet once more, signifieth the
removing of those things that are shaken, as of
things that are made, that those things which
cannot be shaken may remain.
28 Wherefore we receiving a kingdom which
cannot be moved, let us have grace, whereby we
may serve God acceptably with reverence and
godly fear:
29 For our God *is* a consuming fire.

CHAPTER 13

LET brotherly love continue.
2 Be not forgetful to entertain strangers: for
thereby some have entertained angels unawares.
3 Remember them that are in bonds, as bound

12:22 *But ye are come.* Picks up again from the train of thought started in v. 18. *mount Sion.* Mt. Zion, the location of Jerusalem and the temple. There Solomon replaced the temporary tabernacle service with the great temple service, symbolic of the far greater service of God in Jesus Christ (Isa. 59:20; Zech. 9:9). *heavenly Jerusalem.* The comparison is between earthly Sinai and the heavenly Zion, for Christ sits on a heavenly throne. *innumerable company of angels.* Countless angels are seen dwelling with the heavenly Zion (Deut. 33:2).

12:23 *general assembly.* The Greek word here is used nowhere else in the New Testament and carries the meaning of a festive or joyous assembly, whether of angels or men. Sinai was a place of dread and Zion is a joyful festival. *church of the firstborn.* Those who are in Christ (1:6). *God the Judge of all.* Deuteronomy concludes with a note of God's judgment and blessing for God's people. In a similar way, the New Testament church stands before God's judgment seat to receive blessing or curse. *the spirits of just men made perfect.* All those for whom Christ died and who upon their death come to their eternal inheritance in glory, yet wait for their resurrection.

12:24 *And to Jesus the mediator.* Jesus was the Mediator of the new covenant. *blood of sprinkling.* Christ sprinkled His blood on the heavenly mercyseat. Christ's blood bridges the heavenly and temporal age. *that speaketh.* Probably God is speaking through the blood of Christ.

12:25 *refuse not him.* This is a strong word that is associated with apostatizing from God's revelation and likely alludes to the golden calf incident (Ex. 32:34–35). *spake on earth.* Those who heard God from Mt. Sinai were held accountable to the word God spoke. *speaketh from heaven.* God's word in Christ is God's final word to humanity, for Christ is the heavenly prophet.

12:26 *Whose voice then shook the earth.* A reference to the theophany on Mt. Sinai when God's word caused the earth to shake. *he hath promised.* Citing Hag. 2:6 where God promises a shaking or judging of the nations to bring God's glory and kingdom.

12:27 *removing of those things that are shaken.* Removal of the ungodly. *which cannot be shaken may remain.* Those who are connected to God's kingdom and united to God through Christ cannot be shaken.

12:28 *we receiving a kingdom which cannot be moved.* Those who are united to Christ will inherit the kingdom that Christ Himself received (1:2). *let us have grace.* Let us obtain by grace that spirit of thankfulness whereby we might offer worship pleasing to God (*serve God acceptably*). Salvation gathers a people for the service of worship (Ex. 7:16). *reverence and godly fear.* New Testament believers must remember that God's nature does not change.

12:29 *For our God is a consuming fire.* Citing Deut. 4:24. Those who heed His voice come to Him and thankfully worship Him for what He has revealed in Christ. But this does not mean that New Testament believers have an overfamiliarity with God, for if slighted, He will show Himself a consuming fire.

Thoughts for Personal/Family Worship: Chapter 12

1. **Christ endured His sufferings for the joy set before Him. The present sufferings of Christians do not outweigh the grace, glory, and joy of what they will receive with Christ's coming.**
2. **The author turns the argument believers often make regarding suffering on its head. When undergoing suffering, they often imagine that if God loved them, they would not be going through suffering. He shows how the suffering they endure is precisely proof of God's love, provided they are instructed by the chastisement. What are some ways in which believers might ensure that the suffering, though grievous, will profit them (v. 11)?**
3. **Who and what is at the pinnacle of Christian worship and why (v. 24)?**

Chapter 13: *Believers are exhorted to a Christ-centered life that accords with the supremacy of Christ.*

Final Directives for Godly Living (13:1–25)

13:1–6 There are six exhortations grouped by twos. These exhortations promote solidarity and unity in the church (10:24; 12:15). These verses show how Christians ought to relate together within the assembly.

13:1 *brotherly love.* Despite being regarded as the garbage of the world, the church is called to live in love. *continue.* They were already loving each other and exhorted to continue doing so.

13:2 *entertain strangers.* Showing hospitality to those who belong to the household of faith and yet are unknown to the Hebrew Christians. *angels.* Can mean "messengers," though may mean heavenly beings (Gen. 18:2–8; 19:1–3). Hospitality can have unexpected rewards.

13:3 *them that are in bonds.* Christians should know themselves to be in solidarity to those who are in prison for their faith. *suffer adversity.* Believers relate with those who are experiencing mistreatment because they too are subject to the same weakness.

with them; *and* them which suffer adversity, as
being yourselves also in the body.
4 Marriage *is* honourable in all, and the bed un-
defiled: but whoremongers and adulterers God
will judge.
5 *Let your* conversation *be* without covetousness;
and be content with such things as ye have: for he
hath said, I will never leave thee, nor forsake thee.
6 So that we may boldly say, The Lord *is* my helper,
and I will not fear what man shall do unto me.
7 Remember them which have the rule over you,
who have spoken unto you the word of God:
whose faith follow, considering the end of *their*
conversation.
8 Jesus Christ the same yesterday, and to day, and
for ever.
9 Be not carried about with divers and strange
doctrines. For *it is* a good thing that the heart be
established with grace; not with meats, which have
not profited them that have been occupied therein.
10 We have an altar, whereof they have no right to
eat which serve the tabernacle.
11 For the bodies of those beasts, whose blood is
brought into the sanctuary by the high priest for
sin, are burned without the camp.
12 Wherefore Jesus also, that he might sanctify
the people with his own blood, suffered without
the gate.
13 Let us go forth therefore unto him without the
camp, bearing his reproach.
14 For here have we no continuing city, but we
seek one to come.
15 By him therefore let us offer the sacrifice of
praise to God continually, that is, the fruit of *our*
lips giving thanks to his name.
16 But to do good and to communicate forget
not: for with such sacrifices God is well pleased.
17 Obey them that have the rule over you, and
submit yourselves: for they watch for your souls,
as they that must give account, that they may
do it with joy, and not with grief: for that *is*
unprofitable for you.
18 Pray for us: for we trust we have a good
conscience, in all things willing to live honestly.
19 But I beseech *you* the rather to do this, that I
may be restored to you the sooner.

13:4 *Marriage is honourable in all.* The gospel does not undermine the creation ordinances. Just because God's people know a close bond in the gospel, does not mean the marriage bond should suffer in any way. *bed undefiled.* Christians should not in any way deprecate marital intimacy that is chaste and proper. Those, however, who abuse this gift outside of marriage are never safe.

13:5 *conversation.* Conduct. The lack of contentment with our present possessions is a sign that we are not trusting God's all-sufficiency. *I will never leave thee.* God spoke this promise a number of times, but significantly to Joshua as he was about to enter into the Promised Land (Josh. 1:5).

13:6 *boldly.* Believers are encouraged to confess the Lord's help with Ps. 118:6 on their lips.

13:7 *Remember them.* Some of them have passed away, perhaps having been martyred. *spoken unto you the word of God.* God's activity through His Word comes through ministers and missionaries who proclaim His Word (2:3). *the end of their conversation.* The result of godly conduct is blessed.

13:8 Believers have the assurance that *Christ,* whose work and person has been celebrated in detail throughout this letter, has a glorious immutability and constancy as Mediator through all the ups and downs that might await them.

13:9 *divers and strange doctrines.* Hebrews does not define the content of these false teachings, but they stand in opposition to Christ's steadfastness. *heart.* Refers back to the new covenant (Jer. 31:31–34). *meats.* Food of any kind. This a reference to the Mosaic covenant and meats associated with the sacrificial system (9:10).

13:10–11 *an altar.* Christ. *they.* The priests who minister the rites of the old covenant. *no right.* God can only have one altar; thus, those who insist on the altar that Christ replaced have no right to Christ. The *bodies* of sacrificed animals were cast outside (*without*) the camp, as unclean and unholy.

13:12 Christ's suffering outside the gate removes the uncleanness of His people and renders them consecrated (*sanctify*) to God. Christ suffered outside (*without*) the gate of Jerusalem, and as High Priest entered the heavenly sanctuary, leaving the old temple as nothing more than an empty shell.

13:13 *go forth therefore unto him.* The Hebrews should not aim for acceptance from those who rejected their Lord. Instead, they are called to partake of His *reproach,* because Christ has gone first (11:26). *without the camp.* For a time, Moses was required to pitch the tent of the Lord outside the camp because the Israelites had rejected God and His presence (Ex. 33:7).

13:14 *no continuing city.* While the temple in Jerusalem once typified the rest of Israel (1 Chron. 22:9–10), no place in this world can represent what God is bringing to His people. The author dismisses the whole Old Testament worship system and points the readers to *seek* the city that is yet *to come.*

13:15 *By him . . . offer the sacrifice of praise to God.* The abolishment of the Old Testament ceremonial laws did not abrogate the need for sacrifices, but it changed the definition of sacrifice. Animals were no longer to be killed but individuals were to offer the sacrifices of the praises of their *lips* (Isa. 57:19; Hos. 14:2).

13:16 *to communicate forget not.* Do not neglect to share your life and possessions with others. Believers are to love God (v. 15) and others, the summation of the two tables of the Law. *God is well pleased.* Good works are sacrifices truly delightful to God (Phil. 4:18).

13:17 *submit yourselves.* To the leaders who are following the path of those who have died (v. 7). *for they watch for your souls.* Church leaders are to guard diligently those who are under their care. *must give account.* Leaders are responsible to Christ for the souls they oversee. *unprofitable.* This is a different Greek word than what was found in v. 9 and means "a lack of advantage."

13:18–19 Prayer is needed. *us.* The author and those with him. The *conscience* is cleansed by the sacrifice of Christ (9:11–28). *restored to you the sooner.* The author himself was likely suffering and being persecuted.

13:20 *God of peace.* He is the author of peace. *brought again from the dead our Lord Jesus, that great shepherd.* Christ is the One greater than Moses (Isa. 63:11), by whom God led His people out of bondage. Christ's death, resurrection, and ascension were an exodus (Luke 9:31) and entrance into the promised rest. Hebrews ends where it began: the glory of Christ.

13:21 *Make you perfect.* Furnished or equipped. *through*

20 Now the God of peace, that brought again
from the dead our Lord Jesus, that great shepherd
of the sheep, through the blood of the everlasting
covenant,
21 Make you perfect in every good work to do his
will, working in you that which is wellpleasing in
his sight, through Jesus Christ; to whom *be* glory
for ever and ever. Amen.
22 And I beseech you, brethren, suffer the word
of exhortation: for I have written a letter unto you
in few words.
23 Know ye that *our* brother Timothy is set at lib-
erty; with whom, if he come shortly, I will see you.
24 Salute all them that have the rule over you, and
all the saints. They of Italy salute you.
25 Grace *be* with you all. Amen.

Jesus Christ. Believers are dependent on Christ who was obedient to God.

13:22 *suffer the word.* Receive patiently and fully. *exhortation.* Letter of encouragement and summation.

13:23 *Timothy.* Companion of Paul (see 1 Tim. 1:1–3; 2 Tim. 1:1–2). *set at liberty.* From prison, though the nature of the author's imprisonment is unknown to us today.

13:24–25 *Salute all them that have the rule.* Greet the local leaders of the congregation. *Italy.* Either written from Italy, or referring to those from Italy but presently away from home.

Thoughts for Personal/Family Worship: Chapter 13

1. The glory of Christ exhibited throughout this epistle does not remove the mundane things of life. Rather it beautifies and magnifies such things as marriage, respect for elders, and hospitality (vv. 1–6).
2. It goes against our flesh to be excluded and despised. Yet, there is no greater riches than to be united with Christ, even if it be without [outside] the camp" (v. 13). How are Christians in your circumstances sometimes treated as outsiders? How might you be tempted to compromise your faith to avoid this rejection?
3. Christ's blood does not just atone for sin; it consecrates for service. Christ is the Mediator of equipping grace. Turn vv. 20–21 into a prayer for yourself, your family, and your church.

Every
GOOD GIFT
AND EVERY
Perfect Gift
IS FROM
ABOVE
AND
Cometh Down
FROM THE
FATHER
OF *Lights*

JAMES 1:17

INTRODUCTION TO THE BOOK OF JAMES

Author: The author of the book of James simply identifies himself as, "James, a servant of God and of the Lord Jesus Christ" (1:1). While there are upwards of six different people named James in the New Testament, we can be rather sure that James the half brother of Jesus is the author of this book (Mark 6:3; Gal. 1:19). *First*, James was one of the pillars of the church, and held a prominent role in Jerusalem; lacking further specification, early readers would have assumed "James" would have been *this* James. *Second*, scholars have examined the sentence structure and words spoken by James in Acts 15:13–21 and that of the epistle and have found striking similarity. *Third*, due to the contents of this book, it is clear that James was written at an early date, but also by a date when persecution, suffering, and oppression were widespread in the early church. This fits what we know about James, the brother of Christ. *Finally*, church history has well documented that James the half brother of Jesus authored this book at an early date.

What do we know about James? During Christ's ministry on earth, James and Christ's other half brothers did not believe in Christ (John 7:5). After His resurrection, Christ made a special appearance to James (1 Cor. 15:7), which may have marked the turning point for him. Afterward, we find him in prayer with the believing followers of Christ (Acts 1:14). It is worth noting that nowhere in this letter does James highlight his physical relationship to Christ. Instead, he is content to refer to himself as "a servant of God and of the Lord Jesus Christ" (James 1:1).

Date: There are many who consider James to be a very early Christian document, perhaps the first book written in the New Testament canon. As already pointed out, by the time James wrote his epistle, Christianity had been established long enough for there to be not only persecution and suffering, but also oppression of some in the church by others in the church. At the same time, James does not refer to the Jerusalem Council (AD 48 or 49). The influx of Gentiles into the church caused some major tension in the early church. However, this tension is absent from the epistle of James. Thus, it was probably written somewhere in the early to mid-40s.

Theme: The difference between pure and vain religion.

Purpose: To expose the myth that the Christian life is not costly, while encouraging true believers to live in close fellowship with the Lord.

Synopsis: *The Contribution of James to Redemptive Revelation*
James shows how times of testing are good at showing whether our religion is true or false.

1. True religion comes down from God and is established in the heart by spiritual regeneration (1:17). Carnal religion springs from the heart, which brings forth sin, and sin brings forth death (v. 15).
2. True religion arises from "the engrafted word," which saves the soul (v. 21). Carnal religion proceeds from "the wrath of man" (v. 20).
3. True religion, when tested, is patient, constant, and God-glorifying (vv. 2–18). Vain religion wavers, is unstable in everything, and fades away (vv. 2–18).
4. True religion is faith working by love (2:14–26). It keeps itself unspotted from the world (1:27), respects not persons (2:1–3), bridles the tongue (3:5–12), humbles itself before God (4:8–10), relies on God (vv. 13–17), and is fervent in prayer (5:13–20). On the other hand, vain religion does not work (2:4–26), promotes envying (3:13–18), lusts (4:1–12), and is indulgent (5:5).

5. True religion has its perfect work (1:4) and leads to peace (3:18) and precious fruits unto the coming again of the Lord (5:7). Carnal religion will be judged without mercy (2:13), and will fall into condemnation (5:12).
6. True religion saves from death (v. 20) and will lift the humble believer up (4:10). Carnal religion will lead to death (5:20) along with the Devil and his hosts (4:7).

Outline:

I. Address of the Epistle (1:1)
II. The Tests of True Religion (1:2–27)
  A. The Benefits of a Tried Faith (1:2–8)
  B. Two Tests: Poverty and Temptation (1:9–15)
  C. True Religion Distinguished from False (1:16–27)
III. The Demonstration of True Religion (2:1–26)
  A. A Case against Favoritism (2:1–13)
  B. A Case for True Faith (2:14–26)
IV. The Subtlety of Sin (3:1–18)
  A. Sin in Speaking (3:1–12)
  B. The Sin of Striving (3:13–18)
V. A Call to Humility (4:1–17)
  A. The Problem: Pride (4:1–3)
  B. Humility before God (4:4–10)
  C. Humility regarding Others (4:11–12)
  D. Humility regarding the Future (4:13–17)
VI. Life in Light of the End (5:1–20)
  A. A Warning to the Rich (5:1–6)
  B. An Encouragement to Patience (5:7–11)
  C. The Value of Prayer (5:12–20)

THE GENERAL EPISTLE OF

JAMES

CHAPTER 1

JAMES, a servant of God and of the Lord Jesus
Christ, to the twelve tribes which are scattered
abroad, greeting.
2 My brethren, count it all joy when ye fall into
divers temptations;
3 Knowing *this*, that the trying of your faith
worketh patience.
4 But let patience have *her* perfect work, that ye
may be perfect and entire, wanting nothing.
5 If any of you lack wisdom, let him ask of God,
that giveth to all *men* liberally, and upbraideth
not; and it shall be given him.
6 But let him ask in faith, nothing wavering. For
he that wavereth is like a wave of the sea driven
with the wind and tossed.
7 For let not that man think that he shall receive
any thing of the Lord.
8 A double minded man *is* unstable in all his ways.
9 Let the brother of low degree rejoice in that he
is exalted:
10 But the rich, in that he is made low: because as
the flower of the grass he shall pass away.
11 For the sun is no sooner risen with a burning
heat, but it withereth the grass, and the flower
thereof falleth, and the grace of the fashion of it
perisheth: so also shall the rich man fade away in
his ways.
12 Blessed *is* the man that endureth temptation:
for when he is tried, he shall receive the crown of
life, which the Lord hath promised to them that
love him.
13 Let no man say when he is tempted, I am
tempted of God: for God cannot be tempted with
evil, neither tempteth he any man:
14 But every man is tempted, when he is drawn

Chapter 1: *James greets the twelve tribes. He explains God's aim with trials. He calls for patience and steadfastness. He clarifies how temptation works and calls for true, Word-centered religion.*

ADDRESS OF THE EPISTLE (1:1)

1:1 *James.* The half brother of Jesus and the prominent leader of the church in Jerusalem. *servant.* The slave under a *Lord* or master. *twelve tribes.* Israel, particularly the early church of Christ which was largely Hebrew. *scattered abroad.* Dispersed, as Israel was in its exile (Deut. 28:25; 30:4; Neh. 1:9) and the church was by persecution (Acts 8:1).

THE TESTS OF TRUE RELIGION (1:2–27)

The Benefits of a Tried Faith (1:2–8)

1:2–3 *My brethren.* The family relationship that comes through faith in Christ. He is speaking to them on the basis of their profession, which may or may not be true, as James emphasizes (e.g., v. 26). *divers temptations.* Various trials. Believers are to respond to trials with *joy*, not because of the pain of the trials, but because of what God works through them (Rom. 5:3–5).

1:4 *perfect.* Complete or entire. *wanting.* Lacking.

1:5 Trials can have a way of clouding spiritual understanding and driving believers out of themselves to seek *wisdom* from God (3:13–18). *liberally.* Generously. *upbraideth not.* Does not scold (Matt. 7:11).

1:6 *nothing wavering.* Without doubting. Though doubt can be and often is present in the lives of true Christians (Mark 9:24), yet they should never be content with it in their lives, but seek to root it out of their hearts through the aid of the Spirit of God.

1:8 *double minded.* Literally, "double-heartedness," the opposite of "wholeheartedness" or "single-mindedness." It is the disposition that pulled a person in two directions instead of turning decisively from this world and its gods toward the Lord (1 Kings 18:21).

Two Tests: Poverty and Temptation (1:9–15)

1:9 *low degree.* Poor or of low standing. *exalted.* The gospel raises people up in Christ. It gives them the spiritual standing of princes (Ps. 113:7–8).

1:10–11 Christianity does not artificially distribute wealth, but it teaches that Christians, whether poor or *rich* are brothers in the Lord, of equal standing, having an inheritance incorruptible in Christ, and treasures in Him in heaven. Thus the believer to whom God has given prosperity has cause to rejoice, for Christ has delivered him from the lie that the world teaches that his riches constitute his real value. In the body of Christ, rich and poor are brothers, there to aid and assist each other. *flower of the grass.* See Isa. 40:6; 1 Peter 1:24. *grace of the fashion of it.* Its beautiful or comely form. *fade away in his ways.* Just as plain grass and flowers both wither away in the end, so too, the rich are not better in death than the poor, for none take anything with them.

1:12 *Blessed.* Truly happy (Matt. 5:3–10). *crown of life.* Not a royal diadem, but the athletic crown given to victorious champions.

1:13–14 *no man say.* It seems that some of James's readers were finding fault with God. When we are overwhelmed

away of his own lust, and enticed.
15 Then when lust hath conceived, it bringeth
forth sin: and sin, when it is finished, bringeth
forth death.
16 Do not err, my beloved brethren.
17 Every good gift and every perfect gift is from
above, and cometh down from the Father of
lights, with whom is no variableness, neither
shadow of turning.
18 Of his own will begat he us with the word of
truth, that we should be a kind of firstfruits of his
creatures.
19 Wherefore, my beloved brethren, let every
man be swift to hear, slow to speak, slow to wrath:
20 For the wrath of man worketh not the righ-
teousness of God.
21 Wherefore lay apart all filthiness and superflu-
ity of naughtiness, and receive with meekness the
engrafted word, which is able to save your souls.
22 But be ye doers of the word, and not hearers
only, deceiving your own selves.
23 For if any be a hearer of the word, and not a
doer, he is like unto a man beholding his natural
face in a glass:
24 For he beholdeth himself, and goeth his way,
and straightway forgetteth what manner of man
he was.
25 But whoso looketh into the perfect law of
liberty, and continueth *therein*, he being not a
forgetful hearer, but a doer of the work, this man
shall be blessed in his deed.
26 If any man among you seem to be religious,
and bridleth not his tongue, but deceiveth his
own heart, this man's religion *is* vain.
27 Pure religion and undefiled before God and
the Father is this, To visit the fatherless and
widows in their affliction, *and* to keep himself
unspotted from the world.

---

by trials, our hearts can quickly blame God, either secretly or openly. Though it is true that God tests people (Gen. 22:1), God does not tempt as the Devil does, so as to make us sin. God's tests are always done with the aim of purifying or sanctifying His people. When we fall into temptation, it is through our *own lust*, or sinful desire, that we are led astray. God is not the author of sin.

1:15 *Sin* begins within, in our hearts and wills, and only then comes to expression in our lives. Those who imagine that their body makes them *sin* are turning James's progression around. The root of all *sin* lies in the heart of man (Gen. 6:5; Mark 7:21–23).

True Religion Distinguished from False (1:16–27)

1:16 Man is prone to error. He needs constantly to be warned against it.

1:17 *Father of lights*. God created light, including all the shining lights in the sky (Gen. 1:3,14–18). Every *gift* comes from God, including regeneration, which is in view here (v. 18).

1:18 *begat*. Unlike our lust that conceives and brings forth sin, God's will brings into being a people after His image through *the word of truth* (1 Peter 1:23), energized by His Spirit (John 3:5–6,8). *firstfruits*. In Israel's sacrificial system, the first produce of the land was considered devoted to the Lord, since He claimed them (Deut. 26:10; cf. Rom. 8:23). *creatures*. Creations.

1:20 *wrath of man*. There is righteous anger (Mark 3:5; John 2:13–17); however, man's passions being what they are, we must mortify and subdue our anger because we are easily blinded so that we justify ourselves while judging other people's motives (Eph. 4:26,31).

1:21 *lay apart*. Set aside, or put things off like filthy garments (Eph. 4:22; 1 Peter 2:1). *filthiness*. Impurity, including all obscene talk, impure desires, and shameful practices (Eph. 5:4). *superfluity of naughtiness*. The abundance of wickedness. Sinful desires always expand and increase more and more, unless put to death in Christ. *engrafted*. Implanted. When the Word takes hold of a person it is as if it is engrafted, or rooted, into their very being (Luke 8:11–15; 1 John 3:9).

1:22 *deceiving your own selves*. James shows the seriousness of the sin of merely hearing the Word and failing to obey the Word.

1:23–24 *glass*. Mirror. God's Word is like a mirror, which if natural men and women look into it, they see something of what they look like by nature; however, since it does not sink into their mind and hearts, they quickly forget. *manner*. Kind.

1:25 *law of liberty*. God's will expressed in all His Word, and summarized in love and the Ten Commandments (2:8,11–12). The law brings liberty when we rigorously examine ourselves by its standards, honestly face who we are by nature, embrace the gospel (1:21) of forgiveness by Christ's blood and renewal by Christ's Spirit, and then set our hearts to walk in obedience (Pss. 19:7–11; 119:45; Rom. 8:1–4).

1:26 The proper result of true *religion* will be the exercise of caution that the words we speak are as God dictates they should be (3:2–3). *vain*. Empty, useless.

1:27 *fatherless and widows*. The lonely and poor who have no protector, the special objects of God's compassion (Deut. 10:17–18; 27:19; Pss. 10:14–18; 68:5–6). This verse is not the sum total of what God requires from us, but outward marks of whether or not love has become the principle that has conquered our hearts (1 John 4:11–16).

Thoughts for Personal/Family Worship: Chapter 1

1. **Trials for Christians are not a matter of if, but "when" (v. 2). Despite what some teach and many imagine, Christians are not promised an exemption from trials. We can, however, face these trials with joy, if we know that God has designed them for our good (Rom. 8:28,32) and as a means of refining us. Christ endured His greatest trial, the cross, because of the joy that was set before him (Heb. 12:2–3). What trials are you facing? How can you count them as joy?**
2. **We must learn to hate deception and love the truth (vv. 16, 18,21–22). In a day and age when skepticism is considered virtuous and agnosticism humble, we need to remember that God has revealed His truth in His Word. By the truth lost sinners are born again, by the truth they are saved, and by the truth they live in true happiness and freedom. Therefore, let us receive the truth with meekness.**
3. **James warns against worldly Christianity (v. 26). Carnal religion has no problem immersing itself in the world, which contaminates with its impurities. On the other hand, the believer seeks, by the grace of God, "to keep himself unspotted from the world" (v. 27). The Christian's affections should be rather with those who are in need,**

CHAPTER 2

My brethren, have not the faith of our Lord Jesus
Christ, *the Lord* of glory, with respect of persons.
2 For if there come unto your assembly a man
with a gold ring, in goodly apparel, and there
come in also a poor man in vile raiment;
3 And ye have respect to him that weareth the
gay clothing, and say unto him, Sit thou here in a
good place; and say to the poor, Stand thou there,
or sit here under my footstool:
4 Are ye not then partial in yourselves, and are
become judges of evil thoughts?
5 Hearken, my beloved brethren, Hath not God
chosen the poor of this world rich in faith, and
heirs of the kingdom which he hath promised to
them that love him?
6 But ye have despised the poor. Do not rich men
oppress you, and draw you before the judgment
seats?
7 Do not they blaspheme that worthy name by
the which ye are called?
8 If ye fulfil the royal law according to the scrip-
ture, Thou shalt love thy neighbour as thyself, ye
do well:
9 But if ye have respect to persons, ye commit sin,
and are convinced of the law as transgressors.
10 For whosoever shall keep the whole law, and
yet offend in one *point*, he is guilty of all.
11 For he that said, Do not commit adultery, said
also, Do not kill. Now if thou commit no adultery,
yet if thou kill, thou art become a transgressor of
the law.
12 So speak ye, and so do, as they that shall be
judged by the law of liberty.
13 For he shall have judgment without mercy,
that hath shewed no mercy; and mercy rejoiceth
against judgment.
14 What *doth it* profit, my brethren, though a
man say he hath faith, and have not works? can
faith save him?
15 If a brother or sister be naked, and destitute
of daily food,
16 And one of you say unto them, Depart in
peace, be *ye* warmed and filled; notwithstanding
ye give them not those things which are needful to
the body; what *doth it* profit?
17 Even so faith, if it hath not works, is dead, be-
ing alone.
18 Yea, a man may say, Thou hast faith, and I have
works: shew me thy faith without thy works, and I
will shew thee my faith by my works.
19 Thou believest that there is one God; thou
doest well: the devils also believe, and tremble.
20 But wilt thou know, O vain man, that faith
without works is dead?
21 Was not Abraham our father justified by

---

such as widows and orphans, than with the sinful pleasures the world offers, which only defile.

Chapter 2: ***James warns against favoritism as sin against the law of God. He stresses the need for true faith, proving from the positive examples of Abraham and Rahab that faith without works is dead.***

THE DEMONSTRATION OF TRUE RELIGION (2:1–26)

A Case against Favoritism (2:1–13)

2:1 *the Lord of glory*. Though Christ was despised and rejected on earth, He is God's Son and now reigns as the glorious King (1 Cor. 2:8; cf. Ps. 24:7–10). Thus, we should not through favoritism (*respect of persons*) despise people for how they appear on earth. We never know what glory they might have in heaven.

2:2 *goodly apparel*. Fancy clothing. *vile raiment*. Filthy clothing.

2:3 *gay clothing*. Fancy clothing (same words as "goodly apparel," v. 2)

2:4 *partial*. Prejudiced; showing favoritism. *judges*. Like corrupt judges, you have made a judgment call that has been improperly influenced by evil thoughts, whether you are conscious of them or not.

2:5 In His election of sinners to eternal life (2 Thess. 2:13), God has in many cases not *chosen* the great people of this world, but often *the poor* (Matt. 11:25; 1 Cor. 1:27–29; cf. Deut. 7:7). *rich in faith*. God highly prizes faith, Himself being the author of it.

2:8 *royal law*. Law of the divine King (v. 1; 4:12; Isa. 33:22); same as the law of liberty (1:25; 2:12).

2:9 *respect to persons*. Not a reference to honor, but favoritism. You certainly cannot claim the law on your side, if you act with partiality (Lev. 19:15; Deut. 10:17). *convinced*. Convicted.

2:10–11 *offend in one point*. The commandments are so interconnected, proceeding from the one God who commands all (*he that said*), that breaking one commandment is tantamount to breaking them all.

2:12 *law of liberty*. See note at 1:25. This is summarized in the Ten Commandments (v. 11). Those who know God's law will be judged by it (Rom. 2:12).

2:13 Partiality is like sitting in the judgment seat over others in a way that goes entirely against God's law. We ought to love others as ourselves and show *mercy* to those in misery. If you judge people with *no mercy* now, God will judge you *without mercy* (Matt. 18:23–35). *mercy rejoiceth against judgment*. Those made merciful by God's grace will receive mercy from Him (Matt. 5:7) and can look forward to judgment day with hope (Matt. 25:34–40).

A Case for True Faith (2:14–26)

2:14 *can faith save him?* That is, can an empty profession of faith save someone?

2:16 Mere talk with no action evidences a vain and hypocritical religion (1 John 3:17–18).

2:17 *being alone*. Sinners are justified by faith alone (Gal. 2:16), and yet the faith by which they are justified is never alone, but is accompanied by works of love (Gal. 5:6).

2:18 James gives his readers something, in direct speech, they could use against people who purport to believe, and yet lack true faith: "You have a profession of faith, and I have works (together with faith). Now, show me please your faith without works, and I will show you my faith by my works."

2:19 Merely assenting to propositional truths, as important and necessary as these are, will not help a person (1 Cor. 8:1; 13:2). Even the demons (*devils*) believe and *tremble* as well, which is more than many people do.

2:21 *justified by works*. The word *justified* here does not mean

works, when he had offered Isaac his son upon
the altar?
22 Seest thou how faith wrought with his works,
and by works was faith made perfect?
23 And the scripture was fulfilled which saith,
Abraham believed God, and it was imputed unto
him for righteousness: and he was called the
Friend of God.
24 Ye see then how that by works a man is justified, and not by faith only.
25 Likewise also was not Rahab the harlot justified by works, when she had received the messengers, and had sent *them* out another way?
26 For as the body without the spirit is dead, so
faith without works is dead also.

CHAPTER 3

My brethren, be not many masters, knowing that
we shall receive the greater condemnation.
2 For in many things we offend all. If any man
offend not in word, the same *is* a perfect man, *and*
able also to bridle the whole body.
3 Behold, we put bits in the horses' mouths, that
they may obey us; and we turn about their whole
body.
4 Behold also the ships, which though *they be* so
great, and *are* driven of fierce winds, yet are they
turned about with a very small helm, whithersoever the governor listeth.
5 Even so the tongue is a little member, and
boasteth great things. Behold, how great a matter
a little fire kindleth!
6 And the tongue *is* a fire, a world of iniquity: so
is the tongue among our members, that it defileth
the whole body, and setteth on fire the course of
nature; and it is set on fire of hell.
7 For every kind of beasts, and of birds, and of
serpents, and of things in the sea, is tamed, and
hath been tamed of mankind:
8 But the tongue can no man tame; *it is* an unruly
evil, full of deadly poison.

"declared righteous by God the Judge" (Deut. 25:1; Rom. 3:26), but "demonstrated to be righteous" (Luke 10:29; Rom. 3:4). *offered Isaac*. God commanded this sacrifice to test Abraham but stopped him before he killed his son (Gen. 22).

2:22 *perfect*. Showed itself in glorious fullness (2 Cor. 12:9).

2:23 Abraham had already been counted (*imputed*) righteous by faith (Gen. 15:6), but when he offered Isaac upon the altar (Gen. 22), Abraham's faith proved itself publicly, and thus his earlier justification with God was *fulfilled* or seen to be true in its perfect fullness. *Friend of God*. Abraham had a vital and personal relationship with God (2 Chron. 20:7; Isa. 41:8; cf. John 15:15), being reconciled to Him by His grace in Christ (2 Cor. 5:18–21).

2:24 *not by faith only*. James was not disagreeing with Paul's doctrine of justification by faith (Rom. 3:23–26; Gal. 2:16), but was using his terms differently. Paul spoke of true, saving faith, but James of a mere profession of faith. Paul spoke about being counted righteous before God, but James of faith proving itself true before others by the works that follow upon true faith.

2:25 *Rahab the harlot*. A Gentile convert in the line of Christ (Josh. 2:1–21; 6:17,23–25; Matt. 1:5; Heb. 11:31). Lest anyone might think that Abraham was such a unique case that we could never attain to, James refers also to Rahab, on the surface such a contrast to Abraham but also a person of true faith.

2:26 A *body* that does not move, breathe, or do anything is not alive, but is a corpse. So too, a profession of *faith* that does not show itself in works is dead.

Thoughts for Personal/Family Worship: Chapter 2

1. **How subtle and terrible sin is! Many of us by ourselves would not see how serious of a sin partiality or prejudice is. Even committing the smallest sin, incurs the guilt of breaking the whole law of God. We should never make light of our sin, but say with David: "For thy name's sake, O LORD, pardon mine iniquity; for it is great" (Ps. 25:11).**
2. **In the middle of a very convicting chapter, James proclaims the glory of God's free grace, that God made a sovereign choice to save sinners (v. 5). God has chosen the foolish, the weak, the base, and the despised things of the world, an idolater like Abraham and an outcast like Rahab. In such light, no one is too sinful to be saved. Whom might you think is the most wicked person you know? Pray for that person's conversion.**
3. **Just as money can be genuine or counterfeit, so too faith can be the real thing or just an imitation of the real thing. Works cannot justify us before God, but they can and will demonstrate the genuineness of faith to the world. Martin Luther described it this way: "Oh, it is a living, busy, active, mighty thing, this faith; and so it is impossible for it not to do good works incessantly. It does not ask whether there are good works to do, but before the question rises; it has already done them, and is always at the doing of them. He who does not these works is a faithless man. He gropes and looks about after faith and good works, and knows neither what faith is nor what good works are, though he talks and talks, with many words, about faith and good works." Which kind of person are you?**

Chapter 3: ***James warns against sins of the tongue. He proves that true wisdom shows itself not in striving but in a meek and peaceable spirit.***

THE SUBTLETY OF SIN (3:1–18)

Sin in Speaking (3:1–12)

3:1 *masters*. Teachers (John 3:10). *greater condemnation*. Not necessarily damnation, but greater responsibility before God for their authority and influence.

3:2 *we offend all*. We all stumble. By including himself, James shows continued knowledge of his sin, even after grace (Eccl. 7:20). *perfect*. Complete, not sinless. Controlling one's tongue is a key part of exercising self-control (*bridle*) in one's whole life (1:26).

3:4 *governor*. Captain on a ship. *listeth*. Desires or wills.

3:5 *tongue*. Representing our talk. *matter*. Literally, "wood."

3:6 *the course of nature*. Literally, "wheel of existence," picturing life as a wheel that turns around and around. *set on fire of hell*. Tempted by Satan, Adam fell, and in him we all fell. By nature we follow the dictates and example of Satan (v. 15; John 8:44), including sinful speech.

3:9 James goes on to show the inconsistency of the tongue, using word pictures to make his point more clear. *similitude of*

9 Therewith bless we God, even the Father; and
therewith curse we men, which are made after the
similitude of God.
10 Out of the same mouth proceedeth blessing
and cursing. My brethren, these things ought not
so to be.
11 Doth a fountain send forth at the same place
sweet *water* and bitter?
12 Can the fig tree, my brethren, bear olive
berries? either a vine, figs? so *can* no fountain
both yield salt water and fresh.
13 Who *is* a wise man and endued with knowl-
edge among you? let him shew out of a good con-
versation his works with meekness of wisdom.
14 But if ye have bitter envying and strife in your
hearts, glory not, and lie not against the truth.
15 This wisdom descendeth not from above, but
is earthly, sensual, devilish.
16 For where envying and strife *is*, there *is* confu-
sion and every evil work.
17 But the wisdom that is from above is first pure,
then peaceable, gentle, *and* easy to be intreated,
full of mercy and good fruits, without partiality,
and without hypocrisy.
18 And the fruit of righteousness is sown in peace
of them that make peace.

CHAPTER 4

FROM whence *come* wars and fightings among
you? *come they* not hence, *even* of your lusts that
war in your members?
2 Ye lust, and have not: ye kill, and desire to have,
and cannot obtain: ye fight and war, yet ye have
not, because ye ask not.
3 Ye ask, and receive not, because ye ask amiss,
that ye may consume *it* upon your lusts.
4 Ye adulterers and adulteresses, know ye not that
the friendship of the world is enmity with God?
whosoever therefore will be a friend of the world
is the enemy of God.
5 Do ye think that the scripture saith in vain, The
spirit that dwelleth in us lusteth to envy?
6 But he giveth more grace. Wherefore he saith,
God resisteth the proud, but giveth grace unto the
humble.
7 Submit yourselves therefore to God. Resist the
devil, and he will flee from you.

God. The likeness of God (Gen. 1:26–27).

3:10–12 Our speech is full of contradictions: *blessing and cursing*. Where in nature do you find a fountain that sends forth *sweet* and *bitter* water *at the same place*, or a *fig tree* that bears olives?

The Sin of Striving (3:13–18)

3:13 *endued*. Endowed. *conversation*. Behavior. Having indicted sinful speech, James goes on to tell his readers what true heavenly *wisdom* is, and how it is contrary to the sins mentioned throughout his book.

3:14 James is addressing the *strife* that was going on among his readers (1:19; 4:1).

3:15 There is an apparent *wisdom*, but in time, it shows itself to be its exact opposite, namely, folly, *devilish*, that is deriving from Satan himself, and subtle like he is (Gen. 3:1).

3:17 *wisdom that is from above*. Spiritual wisdom is the gift of God (1:5,17), granted through His Word and Spirit (Prov. 1:20–23; 2:6). Its characteristics are opposed to the angry attitude that speaks rashly (1:19–20).

3:18 Our tongues should be used, not to stir up strife and sin, but to bring *peace* (Matt. 5:9). Gospel ministers sow a gospel of peace, and God brings forth the fruit of righteousness.

Thoughts for Personal/Family Worship: Chapter 3

1. **Small things show a lot about us. Like a skillful physician, James has tested our eyes for favoritism (2:1–13). Now he takes a close look at what our tongue tells us. What comes out of our mouths reveals what is in our hearts, and what will happen to us on judgment day (Matt. 12:33–37). If you took stock of what your tongue produces over the course of a week, what would you learn about the health of your inner being?**
2. **We cannot by ourselves tame our tongue (v. 8). We need God to pardon us, and renew us entirely. The so-called wisdom of man cannot help us. Only true wisdom can, the wisdom not found on earth but that comes down from heaven above. This wisdom comes from Christ, who through His Spirit and Word renews fallen image bearers after His own image, and imparts to them a pure wisdom. How can we fill our minds and mouths with His wisdom?**

Chapter 4: *James calls his readers to repentance from worldliness. He speaks against slander. Regarding the future, he urges a spirit of dependence, not presumption.*

A CALL TO HUMILITY (4:1–17)

The Problem: Pride (4:1–3)

4:1 *wars and fightings*. A reference, probably, to verbal battles. Though the Greek can mean "physical wars," it is best seen in the context of the preceding chapter on the tongue.

4:2 *lust*. Desire evil things. *ye kill… fight… war*. Strong words to show how evil strife is within the church (Matt. 5:21–22). *ye have not, because ye ask not*. God stands ready to answer our prayers, particularly for His wisdom (1:5).

4:3 Though some among them did *ask*, James says that their prayers were asked with wrong motives. It is sometimes a mercy that God does not answer all our prayers. *lusts*. Sinful desires.

Humility before God (4:4–10)

4:4 *adulterers and adulteresses*. Though perhaps some among the readers were literally committing adultery, James's main point is that the church was worldly-minded. Since she was to be the bride of Christ, her love for the world was spiritual adultery (Jer. 3:8–9; Hos. 2:5,8; 2 Cor. 11:2). *enmity with God*. There is no neutral ground (Luke 11:23).

4:5 *the scripture saith*. A summary of many places in the Bible. Interpreters take this verse in different ways, either as speaking of the corrupt human *spirit* that is in man, which is the source of *envy*, or of the Holy Spirit, who jealously opposes the worldliness that still remains a natural tendency in believers (Gal. 5:17). Both are certainly in line with Scripture. In this context, it seems more fitting that it refers to the jealousy of God over His people (Ex. 20:5; 34:14; Ezek. 16:42).

4:6 *he saith*. See Prov. 3:34 (cf. Ps. 138:6).

8 Draw nigh to God, and he will draw nigh to
you. Cleanse *your* hands, *ye* sinners; and purify
your hearts, *ye* double minded.
9 Be afflicted, and mourn, and weep: let your
laughter be turned to mourning, and *your* joy to
heaviness.
10 Humble yourselves in the sight of the Lord,
and he shall lift you up.
11 Speak not evil one of another, brethren. He
that speaketh evil of *his* brother, and judgeth his
brother, speaketh evil of the law, and judgeth the
law: but if thou judge the law, thou art not a doer
of the law, but a judge.
12 There is one lawgiver, who is able to save and
to destroy: who art thou that judgest another?
13 Go to now, ye that say, To day or to morrow we
will go into such a city, and continue there a year,
and buy and sell, and get gain:
14 Whereas ye know not what *shall be* on the mor-
row. For what *is* your life? It is even a vapour, that
appeareth for a little time, and then vanisheth away.
15 For that ye *ought* to say, If the Lord will, we
shall live, and do this, or that.
16 But now ye rejoice in your boastings: all such
rejoicing is evil.
17 Therefore to him that knoweth to do good,
and doeth *it* not, to him it is sin.

CHAPTER 5

Go to now, *ye* rich men, weep and howl for your
miseries that shall come upon *you*.
2 Your riches are corrupted, and your garments
are motheaten.
3 Your gold and silver is cankered; and the rust of
them shall be a witness against you, and shall eat
your flesh as it were fire. Ye have heaped treasure
together for the last days.
4 Behold, the hire of the labourers who have
reaped down your fields, which is of you kept back
by fraud, crieth: and the cries of them which have
reaped are entered into the ears of the Lord of
sabaoth.
5 Ye have lived in pleasure on the earth, and been
wanton; ye have nourished your hearts, as in a day
of slaughter.
6 Ye have condemned *and* killed the just; *and* he
doth not resist you.
7 Be patient therefore, brethren, unto the coming
of the Lord. Behold, the husbandman waiteth for

4:8 *Draw nigh to God.* Draw near to Him; not implying that man takes the first step in salvation, but depicting a Spirit-worked response to God's Word. *Cleanse your hands . . . purify your hearts.* Repentance of sin both internal and external (Ps. 24:3–4). *double minded.* See 1:8.
4:9 *mourn, and weep.* In line with the Old Testament prophets, James calls a compromised people to heartfelt repentance (Joel 2:12–13).

Humility regarding Others (4:11–12)

4:11 *brethren.* James makes a transition into this section by returning to this term (1:2,16; 2:1; 3:1; etc.).
4:12 *one lawgiver.* The one King and Judge (Isa. 33:22). *who art thou that judgest another?* James is not condemning all forms of discernment in relation to other people, but proud criticism and speaking evil (v. 11; Matt. 7:1–6,15–20).

Humility regarding the Future (4:13–17)

4:14 *the morrow.* Tomorrow. *vapour.* Life is fleeting (Eccl. 2:11; cf. Ps. 103:15–16).
4:15 *If the Lord will.* God's will determines all things, including the details of our future (Acts 18:21; Rom. 1:10; 15:32; 1 Cor. 4:19; 16:7; Heb. 6:3; 1 Peter 3:17). Thus boasting is foolish and wrong.
4:17 James highlights the connection of knowing with doing (1:22). We sin not only by commission but also omission.

Thoughts for Personal/Family Worship: Chapter 4

1. **Often in our minds, people are big and God is small. We strive with others, while we depend little on God. How grateful we should be when God unmasks this as sin in our lives. Pray to see the fights and conflicts in your life as tools in His hand. Then confess to God any spiritual adultery of your heart.**
2. **James admonishes his readers to weep (vv. 9–10). While James is not saying that all forms of joy and laughter are wrong, he is saying that there is an important and prominent place for genuine, heartfelt repentance over all our sins. The Psalmist says, "A broken and a contrite heart, O God, thou wilt not despise" (Ps. 51:17; see also 2 Cor. 7: 10). Have you learned the grace of repentance?**
3. **Our attitude toward the future is a good barometer of our heart. When you think of later today, tomorrow, next year, and so on, is your disposition one that says, "I will" or "If it is the Lord's will"? How will faith in God's providence affect your plans? Your prayers?**

Chapter 5: ***James warns the wicked of the coming judgment. He comforts the faithful, and instructs them to wait patiently for Christ's return. He calls for true soul care within the churches and fervent prayer for conversions.***

LIFE IN LIGHT OF THE END (5:1–20)

A Warning to the Rich (5:1–6)

5:1 *Go to now.* Come now, an urgent call to repent from a worldly lifestyle. *weep and howl.* A dramatic call to repentance in light of an otherwise destructive end.
5:2 *motheaten.* This world is passing away, but the treasures of Christ remain forever (Matt. 6:19).
5:3 *cankered.* Corrupted, or tarnished. Even gold and silver will perish when Christ returns (1 Peter 1:7; 2 Peter 3:10–13).
5:4 James calls us to witness the unjust treatment of the laborers (Ex. 22:21–27; Lev. 19:13). *Lord of sabaoth.* A Hebrew name for God, meaning the "Lord of the hosts of heaven." Almighty God hears the cries of the poor and is hostile against wicked oppressors.
5:5 *been wanton.* Indulged oneself in luxuries, a damnable sin when combined with neglect of the poor (Luke 16:19–24).
5:6 *condemned and killed the just.* Though this may be meant literally (2:6), in line with James's potent style it may be figurative (4:2). Certainly, it shows their behavior as absolutely reprehensible.

the precious fruit of the earth, and hath long pa-
tience for it, until he receive the early and latter rain.
8 Be ye also patient; stablish your hearts: for the
coming of the Lord draweth nigh.
9 Grudge not one against another, brethren, lest
ye be condemned: behold, the judge standeth
before the door.
10 Take, my brethren, the prophets, who have
spoken in the name of the Lord, for an example
of suffering affliction, and of patience.
11 Behold, we count them happy which endure.
Ye have heard of the patience of Job, and have
seen the end of the Lord; that the Lord is very piti-
ful, and of tender mercy.
12 But above all things, my brethren, swear not,
neither by heaven, neither by the earth, neither by
any other oath: but let your yea be yea; and *your*
nay, nay; lest ye fall into condemnation.
13 Is any among you afflicted? let him pray. Is any
merry? let him sing psalms.
14 Is any sick among you? let him call for the
elders of the church; and let them pray over him,
anointing him with oil in the name of the Lord:
15 And the prayer of faith shall save the sick, and
the Lord shall raise him up; and if he have com-
mitted sins, they shall be forgiven him.
16 Confess *your* faults one to another, and pray one
for another, that ye may be healed. The effectual
fervent prayer of a righteous man availeth much.
17 Elias was a man subject to like passions as we
are, and he prayed earnestly that it might not
rain: and it rained not on the earth by the space of
three years and six months.
18 And he prayed again, and the heaven gave rain,
and the earth brought forth her fruit.
19 Brethren, if any of you do err from the truth,
and one convert him;
20 Let him know, that he which converteth the
sinner from the error of his way shall save a soul
from death, and shall hide a multitude of sins.

An Encouragement to Patience (5:7–11)

5:7 *brethren.* Again James transitions to another topic with a direct reference to his audience (4:11). *husbandman.* Farmer. *early and latter rain.* In Palestine it rains heavily between October and November and again in March and April. The first was an indication that the fields were ready to be planted, the latter, that the fields were ready to be harvested.
5:8 *stablish.* Settle.
5:9 *Grudge not.* Do not whine or complain.
5:10 *the prophets.* Such as Jeremiah, who suffered much (Jer. 9:1; 20:2; 32:2; 36:20–32; 37:15–16; 38:6). *example.* Old Testament examples encourage Christians both positively and negatively (1 Cor. 10:6).
5:11 *the patience of Job.* Better, "the endurance of Job"; though he wrestled with questions and bitterness, Job persevered in trusting the Lord through his remarkable troubles. *very pitiful.* Literally, "many-compassionate," rich in mercy to those in misery.

The Value of Prayer (5:12–20)

5:12 *swear not.* Do not use unnecessary oaths (Matt. 5:33–37). It is not easy to see the relationship of this verse to the preceding or following verses, but it may be that James moved from rebuking the irreverent invoking of God's name in oaths to the godly calling upon Him in prayer and praise.
5:13 James here covers all of spiritual experience, from the depths to the heights. The book of Psalms, including both prayers and praises, is a most suitable outlet for the entire range of spiritual experience.
5:14 *elders.* Not older people, but the group of men holding the office of elder in each church (Acts 14:23; 1 Peter 5:1). *anointing him with oil.* This may encourage the use of ordinary medicines such as oil (Luke 10:34), or the words may be a figure of speech for the soothing effect of love and prayer (Ps. 133:1–2). There is no basis to see this as a sacrament to impart spiritual grace to the dying.
5:15 *the prayer of faith shall save.* Not reciting a formula or praying out of custom or superstition, but praying with trust in God's character and promises (1:5–8; 4:2–3). In the context of this epistle, the implicit condition of this promise is, "if the Lord will" (4:15). *if he have committed sins, they shall be forgiven him.* While the Bible does not teach that all illnesses stem from sin (John 9:3), some illnesses are the consequence of sin (1 Cor. 11:29–32).
5:16 *Confess your faults one to another.* Not all sins, but those things whereby we have injured or wronged each other (Matt. 18:15). *pray one for another.* James now says the whole church can pray for healing. *that ye may be healed.* James speaks now of both physical as well as spiritual health. *effectual.* Working powerfully. *availeth much.* Has much strength.
5:17–18 *Elias.* Elijah, a prophet in Israel (1 Kings 17—2 Kings 2). He clearly was a man of extraordinary character and usefulness, but he was a man without pedigree and with similar emotions (*passions*) as all of us (1 Kings 19:4). His prayers exemplify the power of the prayer of faith because he called upon God to fulfill the words of His covenant for His glory, and God did remarkable things (see notes at 1 Kings 17:1; 18:42–45).
5:19 *one convert him.* God usually uses instruments in His hand to convert people.
5:20 *save a soul from death.* This has been one of the aims of James in this book.

Thoughts for Personal/Family Worship: Chapter 5

1. **Christ's second coming is closer today than when James wrote these words. If Christ came today, would He find you living like vv. 8–9 instruct us to live?**
2. **The church is a place where we should be able to bring our needs, petitions, joys, as well as our care and concern for others. Elders and ministers are particularly charged with the care of souls. James particularly highlights their calling to the ministry of prayer. However, he calls all Christians to a life of continual prayer and praise (v. 13). How can you cultivate the practice of petition and thanksgiving in God's presence throughout your day?**
3. **Conversion involves saving a soul from death and hiding a multitude of sins (v. 20). Do you know this grace yourself? If not, you are still in your sins and heading toward death. Seek God's mercy in Jesus Christ. If you are converted, you will love to see others converted as well. Pray and seek for awakening and revival wherever God has placed you.**

CHRIST'S COMING IN GLORY

The early Christian confession called the Nicene Creed states, as a core tenet of the church's faith, that Jesus Christ "will come again in glory to judge the living and the dead." Those who drew up this creed were right to affirm the glorious reality of Christ's second coming. It forms an important part of the apostolic faith and is intimately tied to Christ's first coming. It brings all of Christ's work in His first coming to a glorious fulfillment. Paul summed up this faith in his first letter to the believers in Thessalonica, saying, "Ye turned to God from idols to serve the living and true God; and to wait for his Son from heaven, whom he raised from the dead, even Jesus, which delivered us from the wrath to come" (1 Thess. 1:9–10). Paul ties the Thessalonians' faith to concrete actions: turning from the idols of this world, serving the living God in this world, and waiting for the return of the risen Christ, whose death delivered His people from the wrath to come. And Christ's work in His first coming—His death and resurrection and His deliverance of sinners from idolatry—is neatly tied to His second coming.

A variety of events must occur before the second coming of Christ. The gospel must be preached to all of the nations (Matt. 24:14). There will be false messiahs, wars, and rumors of war (Matt. 24:4–6). There will be earthquakes and pestilence, persecution and apostasy (Matt. 24:7–11). There will be a remarkable time of revival among God's ancient people, the Jews; the hardening of heart that is part of their present experience will end, and significant numbers of Jews will turn to their Messiah, Jesus (Rom. 11:7–8,25–26). Then, when Christ returns, His coming will be visible to all who are living on the earth at the time (Matt. 24:27; Rev. 1:7). Just as His ascension into heaven was seen by the human eye, so His return to earth will be visible (Acts 1:11). And, like His first advent, it will be heralded by angels (Matt. 24:31; 1 Cor. 15:52; 1 Thess. 4:16).

For His people Christ's second coming will be a time of glory and tremendous rejoicing, a time when their salvation will be completed in the resurrection of their glorified bodies. It will be the realization of their hearts' desire, for from that time forward they will ever be with their Lord, Savior, and heavenly Friend in the city of His people (John 14:1–3; Col. 3:4; 1 Thess. 4:17; Heb. 9:28; Rev. 22:12–14). When this glorious event takes place, Christ will also reward His people (Matt. 16:27–28; 2 Cor. 5:9–10). But for the wicked, those who have no love for the truth, the return of Christ will be a time of horror and unending despair and judgment; He will come as their Judge (Rev. 1:7; 22:12,15). The second-century Christian theologian Irenaeus rightly taught that the Son's advent purpose will be to judge all people and to separate believers from unbelievers.

Since Jesus and His apostles taught this truth, nearly two thousand years of historical events have transpired, causing some to think that our Lord's prophetic utterance about His coming back to this world was misguided. It is striking to realize that such an attitude is nearly as old as this primary element of apostolic teaching. Peter tells us that there were scoffers already in his day, people who laughed at the idea of the second coming and asked, "Where is the promise of his coming?" (2 Peter 3:3–4). Peter's response was to observe that even as there were some in Noah's day who scoffed at his preaching about the end of their civilization, so there are mockers who scorn preaching about the second coming. Yet even as the waters of the flood surely came and swept away all of Noah's world, so the Lord will return to bring a swift end to humanity's history and usher in eternity (2 Peter 3:10–13). Meanwhile, we can be convinced that the "delay" in Christ's return is to allow all of the elect to hear the gospel and come to repentance.

INTRODUCTION TO THE BOOK OF
1 PETER

Authorship: The author of this epistle was Simon Peter (1:1), the well-known and loved disciple of Christ, of whom we read in the Gospels and in the Acts of the Apostles. Both church history and internal evidence (5:1) within the epistle provide very strong evidence that 1 Peter was written by the apostle of Jesus. Evidently Peter's words were written down by Silvanus (or Silas), who was a traveling companion of Paul for some time (Acts 15:40) and, here, acted as Peter's scribe or amanuensis (1 Peter 5:12). That Peter was likely writing with an amanuensis may account for the more complex Greek that some suggest a lowly fisherman could not have written. The use of an amanuensis was not an uncommon feature of either New Testament material or other writings of the first century.

Date: Peter is believed to have died in AD 67 in the persecutions of Nero, being hung upside down on a cross. We know from historical sources that persecution arising from anti-Christian sentiments grew strong in Rome around AD 64 during the reign of Nero (AD 54–68). Peter makes references to "Babylon" (5:13), which is likely a veiled reference to Rome. In view of the references to persecution and suffering in this epistle, it would seem probable that Peter wrote this letter to give comfort to suffering believers between the time of intense Christian suffering and his own death.

Theme: Hope through Christ in the midst of suffering.

Purpose: To encourage Christians to persevere in their suffering by setting before them the hope of grace reserved for them, as well as the glory of Jesus Christ.

Synopsis: *The Contribution of 1 Peter to Redemptive Revelation*
Peter begins his epistle by lifting before the eyes of his readers the glorious privileges that they have through the gospel of Christ. The church was in the midst of facing present and future trials, afflictions, and struggles. Peter reminds Christians that they are not alone because they are following in Christ's suffering, and therefore, that Christian suffering needs to be held within the context of God's love for His people, which began before the foundation of the world and will continue into glory. Christians suffer precisely because they are "strangers" and sojourners in this world. Christians experience suffering because they do not belong to this world and are to live lives that are contrary to the standards and ideals of this world; they are suffering for righteousness's sake (3:14). The Christian's time in this world is to be marked by cultivating a life of holiness (1:15), growing in grace and knowledge of God (2:2), shunning the "fleshly lusts, which war against the soul" (v. 11), and prayerfully awaiting "the end of all things" (4:7). In all their suffering, Christians are not to be "ashamed" but may confidently "commit the keeping" of their soul to God, "as unto a faithful Creator" (v. 19).

In this way Peter pursues his objective of pointing on the one hand to our glorious privileges and on the other hand to our duties as pilgrims, as husbands and wives, as sufferers for Christ's sake, as objects of this world's criticism and scorn—and yet, through it all, as heirs of glory. Every chapter, having looked at one problem or another of the believer's life in this world, ends with some vital uplifting truth. Chapter 1 ends with the inspiration of God's Word; ch. 2 with our soul's safety in Christ's care; ch. 3 with the reminder that Christ is now ascended with universal authority over all angels, as well as over all human authorities; ch. 4 with our souls in the care of a faithful Creator; and ch. 5 with the prayer that God will, after we have suffered a while in this world, make us perfect and bring us into his "eternal glory" (v. 10). The overall message is, "Look up!"

Outline:

- I. Salutation (1:1–2)
- II. Christian Characteristics (1:3—2:10)
  - A. A Christian's Living Hope (1:3–12)
  - B. A Christian's Holiness (1:13–25)
  - C. A Christian's Sure Foundation (2:1–10)
- III. Christian Duties in the World (2:11—4:11)
  - A. Being Sojourners (2:11–12)
  - B. Submission to Earthly Authorities (2:13–25)
  - C. Submission in Marriage (3:1–7)
  - D. Submission in Suffering (3:8–22)
  - E. Submission to One Another (4:1–11)
- IV. Christian Responsibility in the Church (4:12—5:11)
  - A. Enduring Suffering Together (4:12–19)
  - B. Shepherding the Flock (5:1–4)
  - C. Living in Humility and Hope (5:5–11)
- V. Conclusion (5:12–14)

THE FIRST EPISTLE GENERAL OF
PETER

CHAPTER 1

PETER, an apostle of Jesus Christ, to the strangers
scattered throughout Pontus, Galatia, Cappado-
cia, Asia, and Bithynia,
2 Elect according to the foreknowledge of God
the Father, through sanctification of the Spirit,
unto obedience and sprinkling of the blood
of Jesus Christ: Grace unto you, and peace, be
multiplied.
3 Blessed *be* the God and Father of our Lord Jesus
Christ, which according to his abundant mercy
hath begotten us again unto a lively hope by the
resurrection of Jesus Christ from the dead,
4 To an inheritance incorruptible, and undefiled,
and that fadeth not away, reserved in heaven for
you,
5 Who are kept by the power of God through
faith unto salvation ready to be revealed in the
last time.
6 Wherein ye greatly rejoice, though now for a
season, if need be, ye are in heaviness through
manifold temptations:
7 That the trial of your faith, being much more
precious than of gold that perisheth, though it be
tried with fire, might be found unto praise and
honour and glory at the appearing of Jesus Christ:
8 Whom having not seen, ye love; in whom,
though now ye see *him* not, yet believing, ye
rejoice with joy unspeakable and full of glory:
9 Receiving the end of your faith, *even* the salva-
tion of *your* souls.
10 Of which salvation the prophets have enquired
and searched diligently, who prophesied of the
grace *that should come* unto you:
11 Searching what, or what manner of time the
Spirit of Christ which was in them did signify,
when it testified beforehand the sufferings of
Christ, and the glory that should follow.
12 Unto whom it was revealed, that not unto
themselves, but unto us they did minister the

Chapter 1: *Peter first lifts our eyes to see the high privileges of believers, then comes down to earth to take account of the believer's sufferings and brings before us motivations to consciously aim at holiness.*

SALUTATION (1:1–2)

1:1 The office of apostleship was not necessarily restricted to twelve apostles (Acts 1:26), though the office was invested with a degree of authority that other Christian offices were not. *Peter* was called mainly to preach to Jews, Paul mainly to Gentiles. *strangers scattered.* Christians who were scattered in various countries in the Middle East.

1:2 *foreknowledge.* Not a mere knowing beforehand but an act of choice on God's part whereby He decreed eternally that those whom He has chosen should come to a state of grace and, at last, of glory (Rom. 8:28–30). Those whom He has so predestinated are called His elect. All three persons of the Godhead are active in salvation: (1) the Father chooses who are to be saved; (2) the Son sheds His blood to redeem them; (3) the Holy Spirit applies the work of Christ to them by giving them a renewed nature. *sanctification.* Consecration or being set apart.

CHRISTIAN CHARACTERISTICS (1:3—2:10)

A Christian's Living Hope (1:3–12)

1:3 *begotten us again.* Caused us to be born again (John 3:1–8; Titus 3:3–5). *lively.* Living.

1:4–5 *Heaven* is *reserved* for the believer; and the believer is preserved until he reaches heaven. Both of these preservations are based on *the power of God.*

1:6–7 *rejoice.* Believers rejoice in their privileges, but for a little while they face *manifold temptations*, or various kinds of trials. *more precious than of gold . . . though it be tried.* Gold is refined by being thrust into a fiery furnace, where the dross is burned away. True faith must be similarly tried and tested and refined to determine its genuineness (Matt. 13:18–23). *season.* A time. *appearing.* Christ's second coming.

1:8–9 In the present time, believers know Christ but do not yet see him (John 20:29; 2 Cor. 5:7). But *faith* will one day become sight (John 17:24).

1:10 *prophets.* Old Testament prophets. *enquired.* Earnestly searched out.

1:11 *what manner of time.* The Greek is ambiguous, though it likely refers to the circumstances leading to Christ's *sufferings*. The greatness of salvation is enhanced because the Old Testament prophets ministered to New Testament believers. *the glory that should follow.* Christ's resurrection, ascension, and sitting at the right hand of God (v. 21; 3:22; 4:13; 5:1; Luke 24:26). *Spirit of Christ.* See Rom. 8:9. The Spirit who revealed these things to the Old Testament prophets is the same Spirit revealing the gospel to Christians (1 Cor. 2:12).

1:12 *unto us.* Strong continuity between the Old and New Testaments. *to look.* Literally, "to peer into from without." Angels marvel at the privileges of redeemed sinners. In Christ

things, which are now reported unto you by them
that have preached the gospel unto you with the
Holy Ghost sent down from heaven; which things
the angels desire to look into.
13 Wherefore gird up the loins of your mind, be
sober, and hope to the end for the grace that is to be
brought unto you at the revelation of Jesus Christ;
14 As obedient children, not fashioning your-
selves according to the former lusts in your
ignorance:
15 But as he which hath called you is holy, so be
ye holy in all manner of conversation;
16 Because it is written, Be ye holy; for I am holy.
17 And if ye call on the Father, who without re-
spect of persons judgeth according to every man's
work, pass the time of your sojourning *here* in fear:
18 Forasmuch as ye know that ye were not re-
deemed with corruptible things, *as* silver and
gold, from your vain conversation *received* by
tradition from your fathers;
19 But with the precious blood of Christ, as of a
lamb without blemish and without spot:
20 Who verily was foreordained before the foun-
dation of the world, but was manifest in these last
times for you,
21 Who by him do believe in God, that raised
him up from the dead, and gave him glory; that
your faith and hope might be in God.
22 Seeing ye have purified your souls in obeying
the truth through the Spirit unto unfeigned love
of the brethren, *see that ye* love one another with
a pure heart fervently:
23 Being born again, not of corruptible seed, but
of incorruptible, by the word of God, which liveth
and abideth for ever.
24 For all flesh *is* as grass, and all the glory of man
as the flower of grass. The grass withereth, and the
flower thereof falleth away:
25 But the word of the Lord endureth for ever.
And this is the word which by the gospel is
preached unto you.

CHAPTER 2

WHEREFORE laying aside all malice, and all guile,
and hypocrisies, and envies, and all evil speakings,
2 As newborn babes, desire the sincere milk of
the word, that ye may grow thereby:
3 If so be ye have tasted that the Lord *is* gracious.
4 To whom coming, *as unto* a living stone,

believers are raised above angels in privilege and status. *Holy Ghost.* Holy Spirit.

A Christian's Holiness (1:13–25)

1:13 Privilege brings responsibility. *gird up the loins.* Prepare oneself and be equipped for the present task (Ex. 12:11; Luke 12:35–36). *sober.* Self-controlled. *hope to the end.* Though Christians currently suffer and face persecutions, their hope lies in the future with Christ's glorious and gracious coming.

1:14 The great duty of *obedient children* is to turn their back on the old, worldly lifestyle and, since God is holy, to cultivate holiness (Lev. 20:26). *fashioning.* Forming, molding, or conforming.

1:15 *conversation.* Life, behavior.

1:16 See Lev. 19:2. God's holiness is now expressed in unity and conformity to Christ.

1:17 *respect of persons.* God judges impartially (Deut. 10:17). *pass.* Live. *sojourning.* Wandering or pilgrimage (Eph. 2:19; Heb. 11:9).

1:18 *Forasmuch as.* Since, because. Faith must be mixed with a healthy fear of displeasing the Father. This is all the more stressed as Peter shows that redemption was purchased not *with corruptible things* but with the "precious blood of Christ" (v. 19). *from your vain conversation.* Christian holiness is living in a manner that is contrary to the way in which the world lives.

1:19 *precious.* Of high value. *without blemish.* Sacrificial lambs needed to be perfect for Old Testament sacrifices; how much more did Christ (Ex. 29:1; Lev. 22:18–21)?

1:20 *verily.* Truly. Christ's death and resurrection to glory were ordained by God before time began but made visible (*manifest*) for the good of Peter's readers. *last times.* Refers to the end times. Christ's life, death, and resurrection inaugurated the final age of redemptive history (Acts 2:17; Heb. 1:2).

1:22–23 *obeying the truth.* The purification is also a consecration. Believers are set apart in their obedience (v. 1). *unfeigned.* Sincere. Christians ought to abound in love for one another since they are all converted through the same divine act of regeneration and by means of God's inspired Word (James 1:21) and belong to the family of God. *born again.* See 1 Peter 1:3. Those who have been born by the imperishable seed of God's Word have God's character—namely love toward one another.

1:24–25 *flesh.* Those born of the corruptible seed. All the generations of mankind quickly pass and are gone. But the believer's hope is grounded in God's Word, which will never pass away (Isa. 40:6–8; James 1:10–11).

Thoughts for Personal/Family Worship: Chapter 1

1. **The struggle believers wage against sin is not because of anything in us but because of God's gracious plan in choosing whom He would save before the foundation of the world in eternity past. This is a great comfort to believers of all ages and reminds us that our struggle is not ours alone but rests in the sovereign and omnipotent plan of God (vv. 1–5). How can knowing God chose them encourage suffering believers?**
2. **Sometimes it is difficult to face the many trials and temptations of life. Peter tells us that the testing of our faith is so that it might be refined in the furnace of affliction. Much as gold is required to be heated and pressed and burned, so too must faith be tested. Yet the end result is that it proves itself true and genuine and precious (vv. 6–11).**
3. **Holiness and serious Christian living are not popular in this world, but they are our duty, required by God. God's demand that our lives be holy is not a stifling and burdensome requirement of His people. But it is the gracious and loving call of God to His children to share in His holiness. In obeying, we show ourselves to be acting like our Father, who Himself is holy (vv. 12–25).**

Chapter 2: *The believer must live a new kind of life.*

A Christian's Sure Foundation (2:1–10)

2:1 *malice.* As used here, a vice that destroys fellowship. *guile.*

disallowed indeed of men, but chosen of God,
and precious,
5 Ye also, as lively stones, are built up a spiritual
house, an holy priesthood, to offer up spiritual
sacrifices, acceptable to God by Jesus Christ.
6 Wherefore also it is contained in the scripture,
Behold, I lay in Sion a chief corner stone, elect,
precious: and he that believeth on him shall not
be confounded.
7 Unto you therefore which believe *he is* precious:
but unto them which be disobedient, the stone
which the builders disallowed, the same is made
the head of the corner,
8 And a stone of stumbling, and a rock of offence,
even to them which stumble at the word, being
disobedient: whereunto also they were appointed.
9 But ye *are* a chosen generation, a royal priest-
hood, an holy nation, a peculiar people; that ye
should shew forth the praises of him who hath
called you out of darkness into his marvellous
light:
10 Which in time past *were* not a people, but *are*
now the people of God: which had not obtained
mercy, but now have obtained mercy.
11 Dearly beloved, I beseech *you* as strangers and
pilgrims, abstain from fleshly lusts, which war
against the soul;
12 Having your conversation honest among the
Gentiles: that, whereas they speak against you as
evildoers, they may by *your* good works, which they
shall behold, glorify God in the day of visitation.
13 Submit yourselves to every ordinance of man
for the Lord's sake: whether it be to the king, as
supreme;
14 Or unto governors, as unto them that are sent
by him for the punishment of evildoers, and for
the praise of them that do well.
15 For so is the will of God, that with well doing
ye may put to silence the ignorance of foolish men:
16 As free, and not using *your* liberty for a cloke
of maliciousness, but as the servants of God.
17 Honour all *men*. Love the brotherhood. Fear
God. Honour the king.
18 Servants, *be* subject to *your* masters with all
fear; not only to the good and gentle, but also to
the froward.
19 For this *is* thankworthy, if a man for conscience
toward God endure grief, suffering wrongfully.
20 For what glory *is it*, if, when ye be buffeted for
your faults, ye shall take it patiently? but if, when
ye do well, and suffer *for it*, ye take it patiently, this
is acceptable with God.
21 For even hereunto were ye called: because
Christ also suffered for us, leaving us an example,
that ye should follow his steps:
22 Who did no sin, neither was guile found in his
mouth:
23 Who, when he was reviled, reviled not again;
when he suffered, he threatened not; but commit-
ted *himself* to him that judgeth righteously:
24 Who his own self bare our sins in his own
body on the tree, that we, being dead to sins,
should live unto righteousness: by whose stripes
ye were healed.

Deceit. *evil speakings.* Slander, defamation.

2:2 Believers are to lay aside their former way of life and *desire* the Word of God. *sincere milk.* Not a sign of immaturity but of complete nourishment. *word.* Refers to the Scriptures. *grow thereby.* The Scriptures are not only the seed of regeneration (1:23) but also food for the newborn soul.

2:3 See Ps. 34:8. God's goodness allures people to Himself.

2:4–5 *disallowed.* Rejected after inspection. Christ suffered (Ps. 118:22), though precious to God, and Christians should expect to suffer. *spiritual house.* The people of God are the temple of God (1 Cor. 3:16–17; 2 Cor. 6:16). *holy priesthood.* See Ex. 19:6.

2:6 *contained in the scripture.* See Isa. 28:16. *elect, precious.* Jesus Christ was precious to God, and in His death and resurrection God was carrying out His eternal purposes (1 Peter 1:19–20) of glorifying Christ in the heavenly places.

2:7–8 See Ps. 118:22; Isa. 8:14. *which believe.* Those who believe in Christ shall not be ashamed. But those who are *disobedient* stumble and fall *at the word* of Christ (1 Cor. 1:18–30).

2:9–10 Peter applies titles used of Israel to Christians (Ex. 19:5–6; Deut. 4:20; 7:6; Isa. 43:20–21). *chosen generation.* Connects them with Christ (vv. 4,6). *peculiar people.* A treasured people. *were not a people, but are now the people of God.* Alludes back to Hos. 1:6,9–10; 2:23. Peter uses exilic language to refer to God electing His people.

CHRISTIAN DUTIES IN THE WORLD (2:11—4:11)

Being Sojourners (2:11–12)

2:11 *strangers and pilgrims.* Outsiders to the world (Eph. 2:19; Heb. 11:13). *war against the soul.* Common metaphor (2 Cor. 10:3–4; 1 Tim. 1:18), though it is important to note that Peter emphasizes Christians' war with *fleshly lusts* (Gal. 5:17).

2:12 *glorify God.* See Matt. 5:16. *day of visitation.* Either a reference to the Spirit's conviction upon the soul or to the final judgment (Isa. 10:3). But as initial salvation influences final judgment, both may be in view.

Submission to Earthly Authorities (2:13–25)

2:13–16 The gospel does not permit Christians to go against human governments unless those governments make laws against God (Acts 5:29; Rom. 13).

2:16 *As free.* In one sense, Christians are free from all people. But in another sense, Christians are bound to serve all people. *cloke of maliciousness.* Cover-up for evil.

2:17–18 We should give to men that which is due to them. *froward.* Literally, "crooked" or "bent."

2:19 *thankworthy.* Literally, "grace." God is pleased.

2:20 *buffeted.* Beaten.

2:21 *example.* Christ set a precedent for Christians enduring suffering (Luke 9:22–23; Phil. 2:5–11).

2:22 *guile.* Deceit. Peter cited Isa. 53:9.

2:23 *committed.* Greek may denote a continual committing.

2:24–25 *tree.* The cross, a sign of dying under God's curse (Deut. 21:22–23; Acts 5:30; Gal. 3:13) as Christ carried the punishment (*bare our sins*) deserved by His people (Isa. 53:4). *dead to sins . . . live unto righteousness.* Christ's death saves those united to Him not only from the penalty of sin but also

THE CHURCH

"Glorious things are spoken of thee, O city of God" (Ps. 87:3). "City of God" is one of many biblical metaphors for the church. It expresses the safety of this community, enclosed by high walls and shut in by stout gates, and points to her exalted status as the dwelling place of God among men. What glorious things are spoken of this city? *First*, her unique place in the eternal love and purposes of God; *second*, the rights and privileges God accords to her members in the covenant of grace; *third*, the promises God has made to provide her with every good thing and avert from her all evil or turn it to her profit; and *finally*, the prophecies God has given regarding her planting and flourishing in the earth and her final glory in Christ.

The word *church* is used 112 times in the English Bible to translate the Greek word *ekklesia*, meaning "that which is called out" or "assembly." But the English word derives from another Greek word used only twice in the New Testament, *kuriakos*, an adjective used to characterize something as "belonging to the Lord," whether it be the Lord's Supper (1 Cor. 11:20) or the Christian Sabbath as "the Lord's day" (Rev. 1:10). In our usage it is applied to the body of those who belong to the Lord, to their assemblies for public worship, and to the places where they meet. Hence, Christians are said *to be* the church, *to go to* church, and *to meet in* a church.

Beyond these basic meanings, there is a doctrine of the church ("ecclesiology") running through all of Scripture. The church first appears by implication in Genesis 4:26, and then more directly in the households of the patriarchs. From these small beginnings it grows into a nation of twelve tribes and families too numerous to count, persisting for many generations down to the coming of Christ. Under the gospel its borders are extended to the ends of the earth, so that it becomes the company of those redeemed to God by the blood of Christ "out of every kindred, and tongue, and people, and nation" (Rev. 5:9).

In 1 Peter 2 the apostle draws on this biblical ecclesiology to show that all that was true of the church under the law is true of the church under the gospel, but to a more exalted degree. For example, the earthly temple made by human hands has been replaced with a "spiritual house" built from "lively stones." The church under the law had a priesthood; under the gospel, the whole church is a "royal priesthood." Under the law, members of the church offered animal sacrifices to God; under the gospel, these physical sacrifices have given place to "spiritual sacrifices, acceptable to God by Jesus Christ."

Peter roots the church of both testaments in the eternal decree of God, predestining and electing her members to everlasting life and glory in Christ. Hence, the church is a "chosen generation," a reference to the adoption of her members as the sons and daughters of God in consequence of their eternal election in Christ, who is the "chief corner stone" of the church as the true temple of God.

Peter is as zealous as Paul to assure Gentile believers of their full incorporation into God's "holy nation" and "peculiar people" (cf. Eph. 2:11–22). So there is continuity between the church under the law and the church under the gospel. The only differences are the replacement of inferior physical, earthly, and temporal things with things spiritual, heavenly, and eternal and the extension of the rights and privileges of the few to many others (1 Peter 2:10).

Christianity is often reduced to a personal relationship with Christ. But everyone who belongs to Christ is bound to join himself to the church and to unite in her profession of the true religion. It is God's will that we receive the means of grace dispensed by her ministers and live under the government and care of elders whom Christ has appointed to feed His sheep (1 Peter 5:1–4). Great blessing is promised to those who love the church and pray for her peace and well-being (Ps. 122:6–9).

25 For ye were as sheep going astray; but are now
returned unto the Shepherd and Bishop of your
souls.

CHAPTER 3

LIKEWISE, ye wives, *be* in subjection to your own
husbands; that, if any obey not the word, they also
may without the word be won by the conversa-
tion of the wives;
2 While they behold your chaste conversation
coupled with fear.
3 Whose adorning let it not be that outward
adorning of plaiting the hair, and of wearing of
gold, or of putting on of apparel;
4 But *let it be* the hidden man of the heart, in that
which is not corruptible, *even the ornament* of a
meek and quiet spirit, which is in the sight of God
of great price.
5 For after this manner in the old time the
holy women also, who trusted in God, adorned
themselves, being in subjection unto their own
husbands:
6 Even as Sara obeyed Abraham, calling him lord:
whose daughters ye are, as long as ye do well, and
are not afraid with any amazement.
7 Likewise, ye husbands, dwell with *them*
according to knowledge, giving honour unto the
wife, as unto the weaker vessel, and as being heirs
together of the grace of life; that your prayers be
not hindered.
8 Finally, *be ye* all of one mind, having compas-
sion one of another, love as brethren, *be* pitiful, *be*
courteous:
9 Not rendering evil for evil, or railing for railing:
but contrariwise blessing; knowing that ye are
thereunto called, that ye should inherit a blessing.
10 For he that will love life, and see good days, let
him refrain his tongue from evil, and his lips that
they speak no guile:
11 Let him eschew evil, and do good; let him seek
peace, and ensue it.
12 For the eyes of the Lord *are* over the righteous,
and his ears *are open* unto their prayers: but the
face of the Lord *is* against them that do evil.
13 And who *is* he that will harm you, if ye be
followers of that which is good?
14 But and if ye suffer for righteousness' sake,
happy *are ye*: and be not afraid of their terror,
neither be troubled;
15 But sanctify the Lord God in your hearts: and
be ready always to *give* an answer to every man
that asketh you a reason of the hope that is in you
with meekness and fear:
16 Having a good conscience; that, whereas they
speak evil of you, as of evildoers, they may be

from its power so that they now live unto God (Rom. 6:1–4). *by whose stripes ye were healed.* By Christ's wounds believers are healed of guilt, sin, and ultimately of all misery (Isa. 53:5). *Bishop.* Overseer.

Thoughts for Personal/Family Worship: Chapter 2

1. **There is no middle ground between Christ and holiness, on the one side, and the world and sin on the other. Yet the world's lies of wisdom, wealth, and pleasure can pose a real temptation for the Christian. It takes effort and concentration on a believer's part, as well as the grace of God, to reject the habits of his past life (vv. 1–3). But we must remember that no one can be indifferent to Christ. Either they will reverence Him or else they will reject His claims and His teaching (vv. 7–8).**
2. **Christ overcame the world by love and endurance of suffering, and so do Christians. The best way to silence critics of the gospel is to be full of good works. When a Christian is known only for his kindness, love, grace, and mercy, the world will try in vain to condemn him, and his righteous deeds will point unbelievers to the glory of God (vv. 11–20). When the Christian is called to go through suffering for his faith he should remind himself that he is only following in Christ's steps (vv. 21–25). How can that comfort the believer and give him endurance?**

Chapter 3: *Both in the home and in the wider world there is always a right way to live.*

Submission in Marriage (3:1–7)

3:1–2 The wife who has an unbelieving husband should seek to win her husband to Christ by her godly living, which Peter speaks of here as being submissive to him. *Subjection* is not a license for the husband to lord his authority over his wife, but neither is it a term of pure passivity on her part.

3:3 *adorning.* The beauty of the Christian woman should be in the godliness of her life rather than in her expensive clothes or adornments. *plaiting.* Elegantly braiding. *putting on.* Dressing.

3:4 *hidden man of the heart.* Idiom for internal disposition.

3:6 *Sara* and all the faithful women of the Old Testament behaved in this way and gave proper respect to their husbands, as God's Word requires. *lord.* In Greek, means "master," which was a designation of respect. *amazement.* Literally, "fear."

3:7 *knowledge.* All due respect. *weaker vessel.* This is not a derogatory term but refers to God's created order of humanity. *being heirs together.* Husbands and wives are to live together because they are joint heirs of eternal glory. *prayers be not hindered.* Not dwelling in mutual respect can cause the prayers of individuals to be hindered. God holds unity in the family in very high regard.

Submission in Suffering (3:8–22)

3:8 *be ye all of one mind.* Peter calls Christians to dwell in unity with others. Not only is unity found in the home, it is also found in other interactions.

3:9 *railing.* Harsh or discourteous or insulting language. *contrariwise.* Rather.

3:11 *eschew.* Turn away from. *ensue.* Pursue.

3:12 To do what is right is to have God's *eyes* directed toward one and to have His *ears* tuned into them. This is a way of promising that those who do good will receive the approbation of God. To do wrong is to have God's opposition.

3:13–16 Those who do right have nothing to fear because God is on their side (Isa. 8:12–13).

3:15 *sanctify.* Set apart. Christ is to be valued in the heart as Lord. *be ready.* Rather than fearing persecutors, Christians

ashamed that falsely accuse your good conversa-
tion in Christ.
17 For *it is* better, if the will of God be so, that ye
suffer for well doing, than for evil doing.
18 For Christ also hath once suffered for sins, the
just for the unjust, that he might bring us to God,
being put to death in the flesh, but quickened by
the Spirit:
19 By which also he went and preached unto the
spirits in prison;
20 Which sometime were disobedient, when once
the longsuffering of God waited in the days of
Noah, while the ark was a preparing, wherein few,
that is, eight souls were saved by water.
21 The like figure whereunto *even* baptism doth
also now save us (not the putting away of the filth
of the flesh, but the answer of a good conscience
toward God,) by the resurrection of Jesus Christ:
22 Who is gone into heaven, and is on the right
hand of God; angels and authorities and powers
being made subject unto him.

CHAPTER 4

FORASMUCH then as Christ hath suffered for us in
the flesh, arm yourselves likewise with the same
mind: for he that hath suffered in the flesh hath
ceased from sin;
2 That he no longer should live the rest of *his*
time in the flesh to the lusts of men, but to the
will of God.
3 For the time past of *our* life may suffice us to
have wrought the will of the Gentiles, when we
walked in lasciviousness, lusts, excess of wine, rev-
ellings, banquetings, and abominable idolatries:
4 Wherein they think it strange that ye run not
with *them* to the same excess of riot, speaking evil
of *you*:
5 Who shall give account to him that is ready to
judge the quick and the dead.
6 For for this cause was the gospel preached also
to them that are dead, that they might be judged
according to men in the flesh, but live according
to God in the spirit.

---

should defend their beliefs to unbelievers.

3:18 *once.* Christ's work of purchasing redemption is finished; no other sacrifice is needed (Heb. 10:10–12). *just for the unjust.* The righteous Christ substituted Himself in the place of the unrighteous and *suffered* for their *sins* (2 Cor. 5:21). *that he might bring us to God.* The goal of Christ's saving work is to bring sinners into union and communion with God (2:5,9). *quickened.* Made alive.

3:19–20 These words are sometimes understood to teach that Christ, after dying on the cross, descended into hell for three days. But Christ's soul upon death entered into heaven, or paradise, as He said to the penitent thief (Luke 23:43). Peter's words should be interpreted as follows: Christ, by His Holy Spirit (v. 18; 1:10–11) speaking through *Noah* at the time before the flood, *preached* to the godless people of that day (2 Peter 2:5). They did not listen to Noah's inspired preaching, so their bodies were killed in the flood and their *spirits* are today all in hell, which is God's *prison* for those who die in unbelief. Water destroyed the wicked, yet the *eight* persons (*souls*) in Noah's family were *saved by water* from this evil world (Gen. 6–9).

3:21 *figure.* Literally, "antitype," the counterpart to a type or foreshadowing in the Old Testament of Christ and His kingdom (Rom. 5:14); here of baptism. *save us.* Peter here makes clear that it is not a mere ritual that saves (1 Cor. 10:1–2). Water can at most wash away the *filth* of the body. *answer of a good conscience toward God.* Calling upon God by faith for Him to forgive us of sin and declare us righteous. *by the resurrection.* Union with Christ in His resurrection, outwardly signified in baptism, is the effective means of salvation (1:3,21; Eph. 2:5–6).

3:22 Christ, being raised up and ascended, now has the highest honor, being raised to God's right hand. All created beings are subject to His absolute authority.

Thoughts for Personal/Family Worship: Chapter 3

1. **The world idolizes physical beauty, but those who are wise prefer godliness in the heart (vv. 1–4). It is good to teach our children, even at a young age, that the beauty to admire in another is the inward beauty of a heart submissive to God.**
2. **It is biblical to teach that the man is the head of the home (1 Cor. 11:3; Eph. 5:23). He must not abuse his authority but pair it with a Christlike spirit of self-sacrifice (Eph. 5:25–29). Peter admonishes husbands here to live with their wives in understanding. Submission need not be a negative thing when properly carried out (vv. 5–9).**
3. **Pilgrims who are on a journey are to have their lives characterized by a heavenly standard. Christians ought not be concerned with winning the approval of a worldly standard on which they have turned their back. Rather, Christians ought to be concerned to do what pleases God, and therefore to have His blessing (vv. 10–17).**
4. **The Bible nowhere teaches that we are automatically saved by the sacraments of baptism and the Lord's Supper. On the contrary, in order to be saved we must be born again, as Christ teaches (John 3:1–8). But the sacraments have their own place in church life as seals and confirmations of the promises of God (vv. 18–22).**

Chapter 4: *Christ suffered in this world, and so will believers. Put sin out of your life and wait patiently for the judgment day.*

Submission to One Another (4:1–11)

4:1 *suffered in the flesh* appears to be Peter's equivalent to Paul's expression "crucified with Christ" (Gal. 2:20). *ceased from sin.* Likely means that the suffering breaks patterns of sin because Christ, who has died, has delivered His people.

4:2 *flesh to the lusts.* A believer's life is not defined by sin but defined by doing the *will of God*.

4:3–5 Believers once lived for carnal pleasures, being children of wrath (Eph. 2:3). But when one is converted, the previous way of life becomes a shame and reproach, something to be fought against and put to death. The world often scoffs at such an unworldly lifestyle, but Peter is clear that God is *ready to judge the quick and the dead.*

4:3 *time past of our life.* Meaning that there was plenty of opportunity to sin before one was converted. *wrought.* Worked. *lasciviousness.* Sensuality. *banquetings.* Drinking parties.

4:4 *excess of riot.* Exceeding or overflowing wickedness.

4:6 *dead.* Likely a reference to those who are now physically dead, though when they were alive they had the *gospel preached* to them. *judged according to men.* The world judged

7 But the end of all things is at hand: be ye there-
fore sober, and watch unto prayer.
8 And above all things have fervent charity
among yourselves: for charity shall cover the
multitude of sins.
9 Use hospitality one to another without
grudging.
10 As every man hath received the gift, *even so*
minister the same one to another, as good stew-
ards of the manifold grace of God.
11 If any man speak, *let him speak* as the oracles
of God; if any man minister, *let him do it* as of the
ability which God giveth: that God in all things
may be glorified through Jesus Christ, to whom
be praise and dominion for ever and ever. Amen.
12 Beloved, think it not strange concerning the
fiery trial which is to try you, as though some
strange thing happened unto you:
13 But rejoice, inasmuch as ye are partakers of
Christ's sufferings; that, when his glory shall be
revealed, ye may be glad also with exceeding joy.
14 If ye be reproached for the name of Christ,
happy *are ye*; for the spirit of glory and of God
resteth upon you: on their part he is evil spoken
of, but on your part he is glorified.
15 But let none of you suffer as a murderer, or *as*
a thief, or *as* an evildoer, or as a busybody in other
men's matters.
16 Yet if *any man suffer* as a Christian, let him
not be ashamed; but let him glorify God on this
behalf.
17 For the time *is come* that judgment must begin
at the house of God: and if *it* first *begin* at us, what
shall the end *be* of them that obey not the gospel
of God?
18 And if the righteous scarcely be saved, where
shall the ungodly and the sinner appear?
19 Wherefore let them that suffer according to
the will of God commit the keeping of their souls
to him in well doing, as unto a faithful Creator.

CHAPTER 5

THE elders which are among you I exhort, who
am also an elder, and a witness of the sufferings of
Christ, and also a partaker of the glory that shall
be revealed:
2 Feed the flock of God which is among you, tak-
ing the oversight *thereof*, not by constraint, but
willingly; not for filthy lucre, but of a ready mind;
3 Neither as being lords over *God's* heritage, but
being ensamples to the flock.

believers by outward appearances (*flesh*). *but live according to God.* God knows His people and will vindicate them on judgment day.

4:7 *watch.* Be self-controlled and alert. The day of judgment is not far off (Matt. 25).

4:8 *charity.* Love, which ought to characterize the relationships of believers. Love renders one quick to forgive others who have sinned against us (Prov. 10:12; 1 Cor. 13:7).

4:9 *grudging.* Grumbling or complaining.

4:10–11 Every believer has received a *gift* of God's empowering *grace* (Eph. 4:7) to build up the church that God *may be glorified through Jesus Christ.* Those who teach (*speak*) must teach the Word revealed by God (*oracles*). Those who serve (*minister*) must do so by God's strength.

CHRISTIAN RESPONSIBILITY IN THE CHURCH (4:12—5:11)

Enduring Suffering Together (4:12–19)

4:12–13 If Christ, the Son of God, had to suffer in this world, it is not surprising that His followers are called to suffer. Yet, this suffering can be the cause of great joy because it is a fellowship and sharing in the sufferings of Christ (2 Cor. 1:5; Phil. 3:10; Col. 1:24) for His glory (John 21:19; Phil. 1:20).

4:14 *reproached.* Insulted, taunted. *spirit of glory and of God.* The Holy Spirit, who will glorify suffering believers with the glory of Christ when He returns (v. 13).

4:15–16 It is no shame to suffer for doing what is right. *busybody.* One of those who needlessly concern themselves with other people's affairs. *on this behalf.* Because of this.

4:17–19 Peter's conclusion is that if believers, who are justified, saved, and children of God, must experience trials and suffering in this life, what can the ungodly expect on judgment day but suffering and the reproaches of God?

Thoughts for Personal/Family Worship: Chapter 4

1. **The difference made in anyone who is born again is that rebirth reverses his whole moral outlook. He now loves what before he hated and now hates what before he loved. So great a change is made in one who is truly converted that it may amaze his friends and neighbors (vv. 1–6). Has God changed you on the inside? How?**
2. **If God has given us a gift to edify our fellow believers, we ought not to neglect it but use it. However, we must never attempt to serve God by following and teaching our own wisdom in place of His Word. And we would be fools to try to minister in our own strength instead of in the strength God supplies by His Spirit. This is the way to glorify God, for serving by the Word and Spirit is serving by faith in Christ (vv. 7–11).**
3. **Worldly men have little conception of what awaits them in the day of death when they must appear before the holy God. On the other hand, those who believe in God's holiness and the judgment day should not be surprised when God sends fiery trials to purify them, including the fire of persecution. Instead, let Christians live so that if men attack them, it will not be for their sins but for their sincere obedience to God (vv. 12–19).**

Chapter 5: ***Even in days of persecution the church must press on with the task of feeding men's souls, and teaching believers the duties that belong to all God's people.***

Shepherding the Flock (5:1–4)

5:1 *witness of the sufferings.* Perhaps a reference to Christ's earthly sufferings. *partaker of the glory.* An anticipation of Christ's glory that will be revealed for the joy of the faithful (vv. 10–11; 1:7,11,21; 4:13).

5:2 *Feed the flock.* Shepherding imagery was common throughout the Old Testament (Ps. 23; Isa. 40:11; Jer. 23:1–4). Ministers are to do their God-given work of preaching in a right spirit and without covetous motives. *filthy lucre.* Economic profit.

5:3 *lords.* Masters. Elders are not to be dictators. *heritage.* God's

4 And when the chief Shepherd shall appear, ye
shall receive a crown of glory that fadeth not away.
5 Likewise, ye younger, submit yourselves unto
the elder. Yea, all *of you* be subject one to another,
and be clothed with humility: for God resisteth
the proud, and giveth grace to the humble.
6 Humble yourselves therefore under the mighty
hand of God, that he may exalt you in due time:
7 Casting all your care upon him; for he careth
for you.
8 Be sober, be vigilant; because your adversary
the devil, as a roaring lion, walketh about, seeking
whom he may devour:
9 Whom resist stedfast in the faith, knowing that
the same afflictions are accomplished in your
brethren that are in the world.
10 But the God of all grace, who hath called us
unto his eternal glory by Christ Jesus, after that ye
have suffered a while, make you perfect, stablish,
strengthen, settle *you*.
11 To him *be* glory and dominion for ever and
ever. Amen.
12 By Silvanus, a faithful brother unto you,
as I suppose, I have written briefly, exhorting,
and testifying that this is the true grace of God
wherein ye stand.
13 The *church that is* at Babylon, elected together
with *you*, saluteth you; and *so doth* Marcus my son.
14 Greet ye one another with a kiss of charity.
Peace *be* with you all that are in Christ Jesus. Amen.

---

lot or portion. The church remains the Lord's people. *ensamples.* Examples. *flock.* Church of God.

5:4 Their reward will come when Christ Himself comes.

Living in Humility and Hope (5:5–11)

5:5–6 A believer's life is to be characterized by humility in every aspect (Prov. 3:34).

5:7 Prayer is the epitome of dependence and humility. Believers have a remedy for all anxiety, and that is to petition the Lord in prayer.

5:8–9 Satan will do all the mischief he can throughout the church of Christ. Peter depicts him as a ravenous *lion*, showing his readers not to relax their vigilance. Believers are to be strengthened by remembering that they do not bear their suffering alone but that many other believers in other places are suffering also.

5:10–11 The great and glorious God, who has eternally chosen individuals to the privileges of being His people, will complete the work. He *called* them into a state of *grace*, in which they suffer for *a while*, and will establish them in a state of *glory* forever (Rom. 8:30; 1 Thess. 2:12; 2 Thess. 2:13–14; 2 Peter 1:2–3).

CONCLUSION (5:12–14)

5:12 *Silvanus.* Silas, Peter's scribe or amanuensis.

5:13 *Babylon.* Here likely refers to Rome (Rev. 17:5,18). *saluteth.* Greets. *Marcus.* John Mark.

5:14 A *kiss* was a common greeting in the Ancient Near East (Gen. 29:13; Ex. 18:7; Prov. 27:6; Luke 7:45) and was a sign of holy love (*charity*) between disciples of the Lord (Rom. 16:16; 1 Cor. 16:20; 2 Cor. 13:12; 1 Thess. 5:26).

Thoughts for Personal/Family Worship: Chapter 5

1. **Those who bear an office or position of authority in God's church must be careful not to become "lords over God's heritage" (v. 3). Wherever there are positions of authority, the sinful heart is tempted to be puffed up with pride and self-centeredness. On the other hand, it is easy for leaders to lose their eagerness and readiness to serve in anticipation of Christ's reward (vv.1–4). How can knowing that Christ will return in glory help leaders to guard themselves from both arrogance and laziness?**
2. **Augustine once said that if he were asked the most important three qualities of the Christian life, he would say "Humility, humility, humility." God hates pride and wars against it, but tenderly cares for the humble in all their anxieties (vv. 5–7). How can we clothe ourselves in humility every day?**

INTRODUCTION TO THE BOOK OF 2 PETER

Authorship: The author of this epistle is Simon Peter, the disciple and apostle of the Lord Jesus Christ. Many scholars have expressed either difficulty with or flat out rejection of the Petrine authorship of 2 Peter. They argue: (1) this epistle uses very different language than 1 Peter, including many Greek words used nowhere else in Scripture; (2) it was written after Paul's letters were recognized as Scripture and collected (2 Peter 3:15–16); (3) it looks back to the apostles and early Christians as a previous generation that has already died (vv. 2,4); (4) an apostle would never have copied the writing of another writer, as, some argue, 2 Peter does with Jude.

In reply to these arguments, we may say: (1) Peter may have written his epistles with different secretaries (1 Peter 5:12), who, under the inspiration of the Holy Spirit (2 Peter 1:20–21), could have significantly shaped the style of each letter; (2) the reference to Paul and putting "all his epistles" on the same level as "the other scriptures" (3:15–16) implies only that the author knew of some epistles from Paul, and recognized, as Paul did, that the apostolic writings are the authoritative Word of God (v. 2; 1 Cor. 2:13; 14:37; 2 Thess. 3:14); (3) "the fathers" who had died are not the apostolic generation, but previous generations of Israelites extending back to the patriarchs (see note at 2 Peter 3:4).

As to the relationship between 2 Peter 2–3 and Jude (argument 4), it is not clear which was the original, or if both draw from another source. Though similar, they are far from exact copies in the Greek text. In any case, the apostles could have either arrived at similar thoughts independently or felt free to draw upon materials that were true and trustworthy. We observe similar parallels between portions of Kings, Chronicles, Isaiah, and Jeremiah, and between the Gospels. Therefore the arguments against Peter's authorship are not convincing.

The epistle clearly testifies that Peter is the author. (1) The author wrote as "Simon Peter, a servant and an apostle of Jesus Christ" (1:1). (2) He was a witness to Christ's transfiguration (vv. 16–18). (3) He was familiar with the epistles of Paul, whom he refers affectionately to as "our beloved brother" (3:15). (4) He was obviously very familiar with the Old Testament. (5) He informs us that this is his "second epistle" (v. 1). Unlike other (apocryphal) writings falsely bearing Peter's name, this epistle teaches no false doctrine. The church has long accepted it as an authentic writing of the apostle, recognizing the divinely inspired quality of its words.

Date: Dating the epistle depends on Peter's remark of his coming martyrdom (1:14–15). Church tradition indicates that Peter was killed under the reign of Emperor Nero, being crucified upside down. Therefore, 2 Peter was written near the end of Peter's life (c. AD 64–67). Second Peter was likely written from Rome even as his first epistle was ("Babylon," 1 Peter 5:13). It is probable that the recipients of 2 Peter, though not identified, were the same as those of his first epistle (2 Peter 3:1)—elect Christians who were living in Asia Minor (1 Peter 1:1–2).

Theme: The necessity of spiritual growth and the danger of false teaching.

Purpose: To call Christians to persevere and flourish in apostolic Christianity, and to warn them of the deceptive nature of false teachers who had crept in to lead the people of God astray.

Synopsis: *The Contribution of 2 Peter to Redemptive Revelation*

Peter summed up the twin message of this epistle in its last two verses: beware of being led astray by sinful and false teachers (3:17; expounded in chs. 2–3), and grow in the grace and knowledge of the Lord (3:18; expounded in ch. 1). He had evidently heard that false teachers had infiltrated the churches and were spreading their harmful influence among the Lord's people. Wishing to put his readers on guard against theological error propagated by false prophets and false teachers (2:1), Peter warns them against their errors. The false doctrines of these men centered on the denial of the judgment. Peter not only defends the judgment, but pronounces fearful judgment upon all false teachers. Peter manifests a zeal for truth, exhorting his readers to believe nothing but the inspired Word of God, which he calls "a light that shineth in a dark place" (1:19). The way of guarding against such heresies is to revel in the Scriptures, which alone are sufficient to reveal to us the true nature of God. They also reveal what God requires from man and promises to him, both of which will be fulfilled in the day of the Lord. Thus Peter urges God's people on to full maturity and to due diligence in regard to one's salvation.

Outline:

I. Salutation (1:1)

II. Encouragement to Press On in the Christian Faith (1:2–21)
   - A. Blessing of Increasing Grace through God's Promises (1:2–4)
   - B. Call to Grow in Every Grace unto Assurance (1:5–11)
   - C. Reminder in View of Peter's Imminent Death (1:12–15)
   - D. Testimony to Christ's Transfiguration Glory (1:16–18)
   - E. The Illuminating and Sure Word of Scripture (1:19–21)

III. Warning against False Teachers (2:1—3:16)
   - A. Description of False Teachers (2:1–3)
   - B. Illustrations of Their Destruction (2:4–9)
   - C. Corruption of False Teachers (2:10–22)
   - D. Exhortation to Remember Prophetic and Apostolic Teaching (3:1–2)
   - E. Objection of the Scoffers against Christ's Coming (3:3–9)
   - F. Expectation of the Day of the Lord (3:10–13)
   - G. Application by Diligence and Faithfulness to Scripture (3:14–16)

IV. Concluding Command to Avoid Error and Grow in Grace (3:17–18)

THE SECOND EPISTLE GENERAL OF PETER

CHAPTER 1

SIMON Peter, a servant and an apostle of Jesus
Christ, to them that have obtained like precious
faith with us through the righteousness of God
and our Saviour Jesus Christ:
2 Grace and peace be multiplied unto you
through the knowledge of God, and of Jesus our
Lord,
3 According as his divine power hath given unto
us all things that *pertain* unto life and godliness,
through the knowledge of him that hath called us
to glory and virtue:
4 Whereby are given unto us exceeding great and
precious promises: that by these ye might be partakers of the divine nature, having escaped the
corruption that is in the world through lust.
5 And beside this, giving all diligence, add to your
faith virtue; and to virtue knowledge;
6 And to knowledge temperance; and to temperance patience; and to patience godliness;
7 And to godliness brotherly kindness; and to
brotherly kindness charity.
8 For if these things be in you, and abound, they
make *you that ye shall* neither *be* barren nor unfruitful in the knowledge of our Lord Jesus Christ.
9 But he that lacketh these things is blind, and
cannot see afar off, and hath forgotten that he was
purged from his old sins.
10 Wherefore the rather, brethren, give diligence
to make your calling and election sure: for if ye do
these things, ye shall never fall:
11 For so an entrance shall be ministered unto

Chapter 1: *God has given Christians abundant grace through His promises in Christ, and so they must strive to grow in grace, motivated by Christ's majesty and the certainty of His Word.*

SALUTATION (1:1)

1:1 *Simon.* Greek, *Simeon*, Peter's Hebrew name (Acts 15:14). *obtained.* Received by lot or appointment (Luke 1:9; John 19:24; Acts 1:17). Saving faith is a gift of God through the obedience and death (*righteousness*) of the Savior. *like precious faith with us.* The faith of every believer is as much a treasure as the faith of the apostles, for it joins them to Christ and His precious blood (1 Peter 1:7–9,19). *God and our Saviour Jesus Christ.* Literally, "our God and Savior, Jesus Christ," describing one divine person—the same Greek phrase appears in v. 11, but with "Lord" in place of "God." Christ is Lord and God (John 1:1; 20:28; Rom. 9:5).

ENCOURAGEMENT TO PRESS ON IN THE CHRISTIAN FAITH (1:2–21)

Blessing of Increasing Grace through God's Promises (1:2–4)

1:2 Salvation and spiritual growth both come through *the knowledge of God* in the gospel, a theme running through the epistle (vv. 3,5–6,8,20; 2:20–21; 3:3,18; cf. John 17:3; 2 Cor. 4:6; Phil. 3:8; Col. 1:9–10; 3:10).

1:3 *all things that pertain unto life and godliness.* The false teachers cannot add anything to what God has revealed in Christ. *called us to glory and virtue.* God's *power* and Word effectively summon sinners into the radiance of His majesty and excellence (1 Peter 2:9; 5:10).

1:4 *precious promises.* The means by which God imparts "faith" (v. 1), life, and "godliness" (v. 3), including the promise of Christ's coming (3:4,13). *partakers of the divine nature.* Not that men become God, but that He makes them into His children with His image and likeness by the power of His call (1 Peter 1:15–16). *lust.* Selfish love drives worldliness (1 John 2:15–16).

Call to Grow in Every Grace unto Assurance (1:5–11)

1:5–7 *add to your faith . . . charity.* These are not seven sequential steps, but aspects of spiritual growth to be pursued by every believer. *virtue.* Moral excellence, like God (v. 3). *temperance.* Self-control. *patience.* Endurance. *godliness.* Piety or reverence and love toward God. *brotherly kindness.* Affection within the family of God (1 Peter 1:22). *charity.* Love (1 Peter 4:8), probably placed last in the list for emphasis as the core of true holiness. Christians have the duty to grow in spiritual disciplines and holy conduct in every way.

1:8 God gives *the knowledge of our Lord Jesus Christ* in the promises of the gospel (vv. 2–3) not for it to be *barren* or *unfruitful* in its hearers, but to produce real and growing holiness (Mark 4:20; John 15:7–8).

1:9 *cannot see afar off.* Lack of spiritual growth results in loss of spiritual discernment (Heb. 5:11–14), including loss of assurance that one has been cleansed (*purged*) from sin.

1:10 *give diligence to make . . . sure.* The believer has a responsibility to work to become more holy (Phil. 2:12), so that he may enjoy assurance of his salvation. *your calling.* Your having been brought out of darkness into God's light by His Word and power (v. 3; 1 Cor. 1:22–24). *election.* Your having been chosen by God for salvation (Rom. 9:11; 11:5–7; Eph. 1:4; 1 Peter 1:2; 2:9). *ye shall never fall.* Christians may have a well-grounded assurance that they will never finally fall away from Christ (Jer. 32:40; John 10:28).

1:11 *ministered.* Supplied. *abundantly.* Richly. The Christian

you abundantly into the everlasting kingdom of
our Lord and Saviour Jesus Christ.
12 Wherefore I will not be negligent to put you
always in remembrance of these things, though
ye know *them*, and be established in the present
truth.
13 Yea, I think it meet, as long as I am in this
tabernacle, to stir you up by putting *you* in re-
membrance;
14 Knowing that shortly I must put off *this* my
tabernacle, even as our Lord Jesus Christ hath
shewed me.
15 Moreover I will endeavour that ye may be able
after my decease to have these things always in
remembrance.
16 For we have not followed cunningly devised
fables, when we made known unto you the power
and coming of our Lord Jesus Christ, but were
eyewitnesses of his majesty.
17 For he received from God the Father honour
and glory, when there came such a voice to him
from the excellent glory, This is my beloved Son,
in whom I am well pleased.
18 And this voice which came from heaven we
heard, when we were with him in the holy mount.
19 We have also a more sure word of prophecy;
whereunto ye do well that ye take heed, as unto
a light that shineth in a dark place, until the day
dawn, and the day star arise in your hearts:
20 Knowing this first, that no prophecy of the
scripture is of any private interpretation.
21 For the prophecy came not in old time by the
will of man: but holy men of God spake *as they
were* moved by the Holy Ghost.

CHAPTER 2

BUT there were false prophets also among the people, even as there shall be false teachers among you, who privily shall bring in damnable heresies,

---

who works at becoming more mature will receive a rich reward in Christ's kingdom as a gift of God's fatherly grace (Matt. 6:4,6,18–21,33).

Reminder in View of Peter's Imminent Death (1:12–15)

1:12 It can be profitable to remind believers of what they already know.

1:13 *meet.* Fitting, appropriate. *tabernacle.* Tent, metaphor for his body.

1:14 *shortly I must put off this my tabernacle.* He would die soon. *Christ hath shewed me.* The risen Lord predicted that Peter would die as a martyr for God's glory (John 21:18–19), and so he did (see *The First Epistle of Clement to the Corinthians*, ch. 5).

1:15 Knowing that he will soon be gone (cf. 2 Tim. 4:6–8), he established his readers in the truths he handed down to them so that when he died they would keep them *in remembrance.*

Testimony to Christ's Transfiguration Glory (1:16–18)

1:16 *cunningly devised fables.* Stories or myths cleverly invented by religious teachers (1 Tim. 1:4; 4:7; 2 Tim. 4:4; Titus 1:14). *eyewitnesses.* Christianity is grounded in Christ's acts in real history, to which the apostles testified as witnesses (Luke 24:48; Acts 1:8,21–22; 1 Peter 5:1).

1:17–18 See the Gospel accounts of Christ's transfiguration (Matt. 17:1–9; Mark 9:2–10; Luke 9:28–36). Peter saw the *glory* of God in Christ, a foretaste of the kingdom to which God calls all believers (v. 3; Mark 9:1).

The Illuminating and Sure Word of Scripture (1:19–21)

1:19 *more sure word.* The Bible is even more certain than first-hand experience of Christ's glory (vv. 16–18); the testimony of God is more reliable than the witness of our own senses. *whereunto . . . take heed.* Pay attention to it. *light that shineth.* Though some parts of the Bible are difficult to understand (3:16), its main teachings are not dark and cloudy, but are a clear light to guide our way (Ps. 119:105). *day dawn.* Christ's future coming (Mal. 4:2).

1:20–21 *the scripture.* The written Word of God (3:16; 2 Tim. 3:16). *not . . . by the will of man.* Though the human writers were engaged with body and soul in producing Scripture, they were not its ultimate source. *moved by the Holy Ghost.* Carried along by the Holy Spirit, the divine author of the Bible (2 Sam. 23:2; Neh. 9:30; Eph. 3:5; 1 Peter 1:11), so that its every word is of God and therefore without error and spiritually profitable (Prov. 30:5–6; 2 Tim. 3:16).

Thoughts for Personal/Family Worship: Chapter 1

1. **Sanctification, unlike justification, is a lifelong process. To bear fruit believers must give all diligence to add every virtue to the knowledge they possess. The diligent Christian will by his life enjoy confirmation of his election in this life. The biblical doctrine of election does not promote laziness, but holiness. John Calvin said, "Purity of life is not improperly called the evidence and proof of election." After this life the faithful believer will enjoy a royal reception when he gets home to glory. In what areas of sanctification do you especially need to grow? Has spiritual growth in the past confirmed your sense that you belong to Christ and are headed for glory? If so, how? If not, why not?**
2. **The faithful teaching and life of those who have discipled us will be remembered with love long after they have gone home (Heb. 13:7). We should all seek to leave behind a legacy of truth. Will you be remembered as one who faithfully shared with others the truths of Scripture?**
3. **The record of Christ's life and miracles is no fabled invention but is absolutely reliable and solid truth. The world is a dark place, full of idolatry, vain philosophy, and crime, but the Bible is the one sure light that points out the path to heaven. Read it and love it.**

WARNING AGAINST FALSE TEACHERS (2:1—3:16)

Chapter 2: *False religious teachers pose an extremely dangerous influence to the beliefs and morality of the church and must be rejected.*

Description of False Teachers (2:1–3)

2:1 *false prophets . . . false teachers.* New Testament believers are to expect false teachers to arise, just as false prophets arose in Old Testament days (Matt. 7:15; Acts 20:29–30). *privily.* Secretly. *damnable heresies.* False and divisive teachings. Not all doctrinal error destroys the soul, but some teachings so undermine the teachings and practice of true Christianity

even denying the Lord that bought them, and
bring upon themselves swift destruction.
2 And many shall follow their pernicious ways;
by reason of whom the way of truth shall be evil
spoken of.
3 And through covetousness shall they with
feigned words make merchandise of you: whose
judgment now of a long time lingereth not, and
their damnation slumbereth not.
4 For if God spared not the angels that sinned,
but cast *them* down to hell, and delivered *them*
into chains of darkness, to be reserved unto
judgment;
5 And spared not the old world, but saved Noah
the eighth *person*, a preacher of righteousness,
bringing in the flood upon the world of the
ungodly;
6 And turning the cities of Sodom and Gomorrha
into ashes condemned *them* with an overthrow,
making *them* an ensample unto those that after
should live ungodly;
7 And delivered just Lot, vexed with the filthy
conversation of the wicked:
8 (For that righteous man dwelling among them,
in seeing and hearing, vexed *his* righteous soul
from day to day with *their* unlawful deeds;)
9 The Lord knoweth how to deliver the godly out
of temptations, and to reserve the unjust unto the
day of judgment to be punished:
10 But chiefly them that walk after the flesh in
the lust of uncleanness, and despise government.
Presumptuous *are they*, selfwilled, they are not
afraid to speak evil of dignities.
11 Whereas angels, which are greater in power
and might, bring not railing accusation against
them before the Lord.
12 But these, as natural brute beasts, made to be
taken and destroyed, speak evil of the things that
they understand not; and shall utterly perish in
their own corruption;
13 And shall receive the reward of unrighteous-
ness, *as* they that count it pleasure to riot in the
day time. Spots *they are* and blemishes, sporting
themselves with their own deceivings while they
feast with you;
14 Having eyes full of adultery, and that can-
not cease from sin; beguiling unstable souls: an
heart they have exercised with covetous practices;
cursed children:
15 Which have forsaken the right way, and are
gone astray, following the way of Balaam *the son*
of Bosor, who loved the wages of unrighteousness;
16 But was rebuked for his iniquity: the dumb ass
speaking with man's voice forbad the madness of
the prophet.
17 These are wells without water, clouds that are
carried with a tempest; to whom the mist of dark-
ness is reserved for ever.

---

that they lead many people to eternal punishment in hell (v. 2). *denying the Lord*. Not the word used of the "Lord" Jesus (1:2,8,11,14,16), but a term for God as supreme "master" (Acts 4:24). They professed to be slaves of God, but their wicked lives denied him (Titus 1:16). The parallels of this verse with Jude 4–5 suggest that it points to the Israelites being *bought* by God's redemption of the nation from Egypt and from their later exile, only to turn against Him (Deut. 32:6; Ps. 74:2; Isa. 52:3–4).

2:2 *pernicious*. Same Greek word translated "damnable" (v. 1), "destruction" (v. 1; 3:16), "damnation" (2:3), and "perdition" (3:7); the verbal form is "perish" (vv. 6,9). The word does not mean annihilation but "being lost or ruined" (Matt. 9:17), and refers here to the punishment in hell (Matt. 5:29; 10:28) awaiting the false teachers and their followers. *evil spoken of*. God's name was blasphemed and His Word dishonored among the Gentiles because of sin among His professing people (1 Peter 2:12; cf. 2 Sam. 12:14; Isa. 52:5).

2:3 *feigned words*. Language shaped so as to deceive. *make merchandise*. Buy and sell (James 4:13), here a figure of speech for using people to satisfy one's greed (*covetousness*). *lingereth not . . . slumbereth not*. God's justice against them is alert and active even now.

Illustrations of Their Destruction (2:4–9)

2:4 *For if God spared not*. Peter piled up examples from the Old Testament (vv. 4–9) to prove that the Lord will certainly judge the false teachers but save the righteous. *hell*. Not the usual Greek term for hell, but "Tartarus" or "the abyss" (Luke 8:31; Rev. 9:1–2,11; 20:1–3), where the *angels that sinned* await final *judgment* (Jude 6).

2:5 *Noah*. See Gen. 6–9. *the eighth person*. One of eight in the ark. *preacher of righteousness*. See note at 1 Peter 3:19–20.

2:6–8 *Sodom and Gomorrha*. See Gen. 19; compare Jude 7. *ensample*. Example. *just*. Same word as *righteous*. *vexed with the filthy conversation*. Grieved to exhaustion by their lawless, sensual behavior. *vexed his righteous soul*. Tormented his heart, for he loved God (two different Greek words are both translated *vexed* in vv. 7–8).

2:9 God will severely punish the wicked, and deliver the righteous out of danger. Both the judgment of the false teachers and the salvation of believers are certain.

Corruption of False Teachers (2:10–22)

2:10–17 Compare Jude 8–13.

2:10–11 *despise government*. Refuse to honor and submit to authority. *dignities*. Literally, "glories," probably a reference to *angels*, whether holy or fallen (v. 4). *railing accusation*. Literally, "blasphemous judgment." Even angels show more humility than these arrogant teachers of error (Jude 9).

2:12 *brute beasts*. Living creatures without rational minds, like livestock raised for slaughter.

2:13 *riot . . . sporting*. To revel/revelling in physical pleasures (Luke 7:25; James 5:5).

2:14 *that cannot cease from sin*. That have no self-restraint. *beguiling*. Enticing, alluring (v. 18). *exercised with covetous practices*. Trained in greed. *cursed children*. Literally, "children of a curse," a Semitic expression for people cursed by God (cf. Eph. 2:3).

2:15–16 *Balaam*. A false prophet with one eye on material gain for himself (Num. 22–24). *dumb ass*. Donkey, ordinarily unable to speak. *forbad*. Prevented, hindered.

2:17 *wells without water*. Promising life but empty (Jer. 2:13). *tempest*. Storm wind. *mist*. Gloom. Hell is described as a place

18 For when they speak great swelling *words* of vanity, they allure through the lusts of the flesh, *through much* wantonness, those that were clean escaped from them who live in error.

19 While they promise them liberty, they themselves are the servants of corruption: for of whom a man is overcome, of the same is he brought in bondage.

20 For if after they have escaped the pollutions of the world through the knowledge of the Lord and Saviour Jesus Christ, they are again entangled therein, and overcome, the latter end is worse with them than the beginning.

21 For it had been better for them not to have known the way of righteousness, than, after they have known *it*, to turn from the holy commandment delivered unto them.

22 But it is happened unto them according to the true proverb, The dog *is* turned to his own vomit again; and the sow that was washed to her wallowing in the mire.

CHAPTER 3

THIS second epistle, beloved, I now write unto you; in *both* which I stir up your pure minds by way of remembrance:

2 That ye may be mindful of the words which

of *darkness* (Matt. 8:12; 22:13; 25:30; Jude 13).

2:18 *great swelling words of vanity.* Their arrogance is like a huge balloon, bulging in size but empty of anything but air. Compare Jude 16. *wantonness.* Sensuality (v. 7). *were clean escaped.* Or escaped for a little while.

2:19 *servants . . . brought in bondage.* Slaves . . . enslaved to sin (Rom. 6:16–17; Titus 3:3).

2:20–21 *pollutions.* Uncleanness or contamination (v. 10). *the knowledge of the Lord.* The Word of God, including both law ("holy commandment," 3:2) and gospel (*Saviour*). *latter end is worse.* Unrepentant backsliders are in the end more culpable than those who never made any profession of Christianity in the first place.

2:22 *the true proverb.* See Prov. 26:11. *dog . . . sow.* Both unclean animals in the old covenant, and thus pictures of the wicked (Matt. 7:6). The return of these people to their former wicked lifestyle shows that though they had knowledge of the Lord, their nature was never changed by the power of God's grace (1:2–4) beyond external reformation. A *washed* pig remains a pig.

Thoughts for Personal/Family Worship: Chapter 2

1. **History bears eloquent testimony to the truth of what Peter here says concerning the danger of teachers of false religion. Yet in this age of so-called tolerance, Christians are often afraid to exercise discernment and to speak against heresy. Our silence is wrong, because all error corrupts, and errors against the foundations of the faith destroy souls forever. What damnable heresies presently endanger the Christian church? Pray for boldness for yourself and preachers to speak against them for the sake of precious souls.**
2. **The Old Testament proves repeatedly that God will destroy the wicked, especially those who lead others into wickedness like the false prophets. In their arrogance and boasting, they may appear successful and happy. However, unregenerate preachers are walking on a tightrope, and if they do not repent and find salvation, they will plunge at last into the fire of hell. We must remind ourselves of the danger into which we put ourselves if we listen to them. Regardless of the popularity of a preacher or teacher, do not give him a voice in your life, family, or church unless he speaks the truth of the Word of God and lives that truth with integrity.**

Chapter 3: ***Christians must hold on to the teachings of the prophets and apostles, especially the hope of Christ's return, regardless of how the skeptics may mock.***

Exhortation to Remember Prophetic and Apostolic Teaching (3:1–2)

3:1 *second epistle.* His first epistle was certainly 1 Peter, implying he wrote to the same people again. *beloved.* Loved by Peter and the Lord (vv. 8,14–15,17; 1 Peter 2:9–11). *pure.* Sincere.

3:2 *prophets . . . apostles.* The divinely inspired messengers in the Old and New Testaments.

Objection of the Scoffers against Christ's Coming (3:3–9)

3:3 *last days.* Time period between Christ's first and second comings (Acts 2:17; Heb. 1:2; James 5:3), characterized by false teachers (1 John 2:18). *scoffers.* Proud mockers who scorn the godly (Pss. 1:1; 119:51; Prov. 21:24), an apt term for the false teachers (2:10,18). Compare Jude 17–19.

3:4 *his coming.* The appearing of the Lord Jesus with glory (Matt. 24:3,27–31). *the fathers.* Previous generations of Israelites (Acts 3:13,22,25; Rom. 9:5; 1 Cor. 10:1; Heb. 1:1). *fell asleep.* Died (1 Kings 2:10). The argument of the scoffers was that centuries had passed since *the beginning of the creation* without the judgment and glory predicted by the prophets (cf. Jude 14–16). It is not clear whether they spiritualized these predicted events (2 Tim. 2:18) or blatantly denied them. Some strands of Greek philosophy taught that the world is eternal; Greek thought in general separated the spiritual from the physical and God from the material world.

3:5–6 *the earth standing out of the water.* God gathered the waters into seas so that the dry land appeared (Gen. 1:9–10). The scoffers intentionally overlooked (*willingly are ignorant*) the creation of the world *by the word of God* (Ps. 33:6), and its destruction by the worldwide flood (2:5), which show that God is Lord of history and can interrupt its ordinary course as He pleases.

3:7 *kept in store, reserved.* Stored up and guarded (2:4,9). *against the day.* Until the day. *perdition.* Destruction or ruin (2:1). The same powerful *word* by which God created the universe is just as active today as God preserves the universe and carries it according to His plan to the appointed consummation at judgment (Heb. 1:3). *fire.* See note at vv. 10–12.

3:8 *one day . . . as a thousand years, and a thousand years as one day.* God is never rushed, late, or impatiently waiting. The eternal God is not limited by time in any way (Job 10:5; 36:26; Pss. 90:4; 93:2; Isa. 57:15). He is Lord of time, and we must wait on Him (Pss. 31:15; 37:7).

3:9 *slack.* Late. *longsuffering to us-ward.* Patient with us. *not willing that any should perish, but that all should come to repentance.* The *any* and *all* are defined by the word *us*, which in this context consists of God's elect who obtain saving faith (1:1; 1 Peter 1:2). God is not willing that even one of His chosen people (Matt. 18:14; John 6:39) should *perish* with the

were spoken before by the holy prophets, and of
the commandment of us the apostles of the Lord
and Saviour:
3 Knowing this first, that there shall come in the
last days scoffers, walking after their own lusts,
4 And saying, Where is the promise of his coming?
for since the fathers fell asleep, all things continue
as *they were* from the beginning of the creation.
5 For this they willingly are ignorant of, that by
the word of God the heavens were of old, and the
earth standing out of the water and in the water:
6 Whereby the world that then was, being over-
flowed with water, perished:
7 But the heavens and the earth, which are now,
by the same word are kept in store, reserved unto
fire against the day of judgment and perdition of
ungodly men.
8 But, beloved, be not ignorant of this one thing,
that one day *is* with the Lord as a thousand years,
and a thousand years as one day.
9 The Lord is not slack concerning his promise,
as some men count slackness; but is longsuffering
to us-ward, not willing that any should perish, but
that all should come to repentance.
10 But the day of the Lord will come as a thief in
the night; in the which the heavens shall pass away
with a great noise, and the elements shall melt
with fervent heat, the earth also and the works
that are therein shall be burned up.
11 *Seeing* then *that* all these things shall be dis-
solved, what manner *of persons* ought ye to be in
all holy conversation and godliness,
12 Looking for and hasting unto the coming of
the day of God, wherein the heavens being on fire
shall be dissolved, and the elements shall melt
with fervent heat?
13 Nevertheless we, according to his promise,
look for new heavens and a new earth, wherein
dwelleth righteousness.
14 Wherefore, beloved, seeing that ye look for
such things, be diligent that ye may be found of
him in peace, without spot, and blameless.
15 And account *that* the longsuffering of our
Lord *is* salvation; even as our beloved brother
Paul also according to the wisdom given unto him
hath written unto you;
16 As also in all *his* epistles, speaking in them of
these things; in which are some things hard to be

---

false teachers and their followers in hell (see note at 2:2). He mercifully waits until by His grace all His elect have *come to repentance* (Acts 5:31; 11:18), and pursue His kingdom (v. 15).

Expectation of the Day of the Lord (3:10–13)

3:10–12 *day of the Lord*. The Lord's coming to judge and to save (Isa. 2:12; 13:6; Joel 2:31). *as a thief in the night*. Unexpectedly breaking in upon the wicked (Matt. 24:43–44; 1 Thess. 5:2,4). *the heavens shall pass away . . . the earth also*. Christ's coming will disrupt this world marred by the curse upon man's sin (Gen. 3:17), destruction through *fire* (Ps. 97:1–6; Isa. 34:4; Nah. 1:5) by which creation *shall be dissolved* (Ps. 102:26; Isa. 34:4; Heb. 12:26–27; Rev. 6:12–14; 20:11). This calls us to hope in (*looking for*) and eagerly seek (*hasting unto*) His kingdom in righteous conduct (*conversation*) and reverence and love to God (*godliness*, see notes at 1:5–7,11).

3:13 The destruction of this world will not be the end of creation, but its regeneration (Isa. 51:3; Matt. 19:28; Acts 3:20–21; Rom. 8:19–21) into a *new heavens and a new earth* (Isa. 65:17; 66:22; Rev. 21:1). This world has become the home of sin, but the new world will be pure and holy, the dwelling of *righteousness* (Isa. 1:26; 32:16).

Application by Diligence and Faithfulness to Scripture (3:14–16)

3:14 *Wherefore*. Therefore. Peter applied the doctrine of the day of the Lord to Christian living. The phrase *ye look . . . be diligent* is very similar in Greek to "looking for and hasting unto" (v. 12), linking the two. With the command to *be diligent*, he also returns to his opening exhortation to pursue spiritual growth (1:10), now reinforced by a glorious vision of the future.

3:15–16 *account*. Consider. *the longsuffering of our Lord is salvation*. Peter echoes v. 9, confirming that God's patience and will that none should perish pertains to the believers he was calling to persevere in hope of the day of the Lord. *wisdom given unto him*. Paul wrote as God revealed the truth to him (1 Cor. 2:12–13; Gal. 1:12). Peter regarded Paul's letters (*epistles*) as on the same level as *the other scriptures*—the Word of God (1:20–21). *they that are unlearned and unstable wrest*. The false teachers, who did not have true and solid spiritual understanding, twisted and distorted some difficult statements in Paul's letters to support their heresy.

CONCLUDING COMMAND TO AVOID ERROR AND GROW IN GRACE (3:17–18)

3:17–18 Peter ended his epistle by summarizing its two main points. First, God's *beloved* people must be watchful (*beware*) against false and lawless teachings (*the error of the wicked*), so that they persevere, established and stable in the faith (*stedfastness*, cf. 1:12; 1 Peter 5:10), as he exhorted them in chs. 2–3. Second, they must not be stagnant, but *grow in grace* and *knowledge* of Christ, as he exhorted them in ch. 1, so that Christ will receive *glory* as their *Saviour*. The doxology to Christ (*To him be glory . . . for ever*) implies that He is God, eternally equal to the Father in honor (1 Peter 4:11).

Thoughts for Personal/Family Worship: Chapter 3

1. **The warning of Peter about scoffers is fulfilled in our own day in that many have been seduced away from the Christian faith by the theory of evolution and skepticism regarding the worldwide flood. Just as Christians in the early church were tempted to compromise and distort aspects of biblical truth to fit into Jewish traditions and Greek philosophies, so too Christians today are tempted to do the same to fit our faith into modern and postmodern philosophies. Removing Christianity from the realms of real history and science destroys the faith. It is for the well-being of our own soul and that of our fellow believers that we reject all theories about the origin and destiny of the world which conflict with biblical teaching. How do you encounter this pressure, and how can you arm yourself against it?**
2. **The day of the Lord is coming. The elements will burn in the fire of God's judgment, and a new creation will arise where righteousness dwells and sin has no place. Nothing will last except Christ and obedience to His**

understood, which they that are unlearned and
unstable wrest, as *they do* also the other scrip-
tures, unto their own destruction.
17 Ye therefore, beloved, seeing ye know *these*
things before, beware lest ye also, being led away
with the error of the wicked, fall from your own
stedfastness.
18 But grow in grace, and *in* the knowledge of
our Lord and Saviour Jesus Christ. To him *be*
glory both now and for ever. Amen.

Word. On the one hand, this calls us to forcefully reject all heresies, removing false teachers from the church. On the other hand, this demands that we seek first the kingdom of God and His righteousness, making it our great priority to gain and grow in our knowledge of Christ and likeness to Him. Standing against doctrinal error and running after spiritual growth are not options, much less distractions, for the Christian. They are of the very essence of being a people who hope in Christ alone. How could you better live in light of eternity?

INTRODUCTION TO THE BOOK OF 1 JOHN

Authorship: The text of this epistle does not bear the author's name, nor greetings common to the epistles, yet it is evidently the work of the apostle John. He claims to be an eyewitness of Christ, preaching to others the Savior he saw, touched, and heard (1:1–3; 4:14). He declares a message which he received from God (1:5). He writes as a spiritual father, addressing all his readers affectionately as "my little children" (2:1), just as the apostle Paul did (Gal. 4:19). He writes with great authority, for to refuse to listen to him shows that a person does not know God (1 John 4:6). Thus the author places himself in the circle of the apostles, men appointed by Christ to be His witnesses and authoritative spokesmen. The style and vocabulary of this epistle are remarkably similar to those of the gospel of John, which is why we may conclude that John is the author of this epistle as well. Polycarp (d. c. AD 155), a student of John, cites this epistle, and Irenaeus (d. AD 202), a student of Polycarp, attributes it to the apostle John.

Date: Uncertain; if written after the gospel of John, then perhaps AD 85–95. Clement of Rome appears to cite the book around AD 96.

Theme: Personal assurance of genuine salvation.

Purpose: To clarify the difference between those who belong to God and those who belong to this world so that the church may enjoy peace and joy in Christ.

Synopsis: *The Contribution of 1 John to Redemptive Revelation*

John does not name a church or region to which he writes. With Peter, the apostle to the Jews, John was a pillar of the church in Jerusalem (Acts 3:1; 4:13,19; 8:14; Gal. 2:8–9). Tradition locates his ministry in Ephesus after the destruction of Jerusalem in AD 70. It may be that he wrote predominantly to Jewish believers, for he says they had known God's commandment "from the beginning," a time frame reaching back to Genesis (1 John 1:1; 2:7,13–14; 3:8,11–12).

John's epistle addresses a situation where false teachers denied that the man Jesus was the Christ (2:22; 4:1–3; John 1:14). In Greek thinking, a spiritual being such as Christ could not become flesh. This may be the heresy of Docetism, which taught that Christ appeared human but in fact was a spirit. The false teachers may also have taught an early form of Gnosticism, for Irenaeus said that John wrote his gospel against the heresy of Cerinthus, who claimed that the Christ-Spirit came upon Jesus at baptism but left prior to the crucifixion. Such a divorce of spirit and body often implied that the acts of the body do not affect spiritual life; thus John stresses righteous conduct to counteract these false teachings. Though at first working in the church, the false teachers eventually broke away to form their own movement (1 John 2:18–19). This disruption in the church no doubt shook the confidence of the remaining believers.

John responded to this crisis by writing a pastoral letter that drew a simple yet profound picture of the difference between the children of God and the people of this world. The letter contains a series of stark contrasts: life versus death (1:1–2; 2:25; 3:14–16; 5:11–13,16–17,20), light versus darkness (1:5–7; 2:8–11), truth versus lies (1:6,8; 2:4,8,21–22,27; 3:7,18–19; 4:1,6; 5:6,20), righteousness and keeping God's commandments versus sin (2:3–4,7–8,29; 3:3–10,22–24; 4:21—5:3), and love versus hate (2:9–11; 3:10–18,23; 4:7–12,16–21; 5:1–3).

John's message centers on God's nature as light and love (1:5; 4:8,16), revealed in the person and work of His Son. Jesus is both the Son of God and God Himself (5:20). He came in the flesh, as a real man who could be seen and touched (1:1; 4:2). The Father sent His Son into the world to give life to sinners (1:2; 4:9,14; 5:11–12), though the world hates God (3:13; 4:10). With Christ's incarnation, God's light shone into the darkness (2:8), and His love was displayed (4:9). Christ brought a message about God (1:5) and exemplified that message in His own sinless life (2:1,6,29; 3:5,7). He died as the propitiation for sins (2:2; 4:10) to make His people completely clean and forgiven (1:7,9; 2:12), and now He lives to intercede for His people as their heavenly Advocate when they sin (v. 1). He causes blind sinners to know the true God (5:20) as the Spirit bears witness within them so they know the truth of Christ (2:20,27; 4:2,6; 5:6,10). Christ has power to conquer the Devil and destroy sin in those united to Himself by faith (3:5–9; 5:5) as the Spirit dwells in them (3:24; 4:12–13). One day, Christ will come in glory so that the wicked will be ashamed (2:28) and God's children will see Him as He is (3:2).

John uses three expressions—"born of God," "abiding in him," and "knowing him"—to describe how God applies the work of Christ to the individual sinner. In the new birth, God produces a new nature inclined to faith, love, and righteous activity (2:29; 3:8–9; 4:7; 5:1,4,18). The implanting of gospel truth in the regenerated soul causes him to no longer deny his sinfulness but confess his sins to God (1:8–10). God the Father makes him into His child and a stranger to this world (3:1), which is ruled by the Devil (vv. 9–10).

The Christian life is a life of "abiding"—entering and remaining in spiritual union with Jesus Christ (2:6,10,17). His Word and the anointing of the Spirit abide within the soul (vv. 14,24,27; 3:9) so that he dwells in union with God (4:15–16). God's life and love abide in the believer, transforming his soul (2:28–29; 3:6,15,17,24; 4:11–13). The believer abides in the true church (2:19), and enjoys fellowship with God, Christ, and all who walk in the light (1:3,7).

However, God's child still sins (1:8—2:1) and possesses a varying degree of maturity (2:12–14). He must resist the alluring idols of this world and live for eternity (vv. 15–17; 5:21), purifying himself of sin (3:3), and following in the self-denying, others-serving footsteps of Jesus (2:6; 3:18). Only when Christ returns will the Christian reach total Christlikeness (v. 2).

Abiding in Him is not merely a mystical experience; it also involves spiritual knowledge. John repeatedly writes of "knowing" the Lord in a way unique to believers (2:3–4,13–14,29; 3:1,6; 4:6,7–8; 5:20). This knowledge includes doctrinal understanding and discernment (2:18,20–21; 3:2,5,15–16; 4:2,6,16; 5:18,20), and yet it is an experiential knowledge with practical results (2:3–4; 3:6; 4:7–8). Spiritual knowledge culminates in personal assurance that we know God and are united with Him in Christ (2:3,5,28–29; 3:14–15,19,24; 4:13; 5:2,13,15,19–20).

Thus John presents a vivid picture of authentic Christianity so that believers can know they are the children of God, united to His Son, and possessors of life—to their great joy (1:4; 5:13).

Outline: John's first epistle is difficult to outline because of his fluid and cyclic style. At least a dozen different outlines have been proposed by scholars. The following outline notes a cycle in the first main section of two contrasts and then a promise, repeated four times (1:5—3:24). The second section focuses on exhortations and motives (4:1—5:17). Both sections end on a note of confidence or boldness toward God in prayer (3:21; 5:14).

I. Incarnation of the Word of Life (1:1–4)
II. Contrast between God's True Children and the World (1:5—3:24)
  A. Walking with God in Gospel Forgiveness (1:5—2:2)
    1. Contrast: Fellowship with Light or Darkness (1:5–7)
    2. Contrast: Confession of Sin or Self-Deception (1:8–10)
    3. Promise of Christ's Propitiation and Intercession (2:1–2)
  B. Obeying God's Law of Love in Gospel Privileges (2:3–14)
    1. Contrast: Obedience or Disobedience to His Commandments (2:3–6)
    2. Contrast: Love in the Light or Hate in the Darkness (2:7–11)
    3. Promises to Children, Young Men, and Fathers (2:12–14)
  C. Resisting Temptation in Gospel Hope (2:15—3:3)
    1. Contrast: Love of the Father or Love of the World (2:15–17)
    2. Contrast: Christ-Centered Truth or Anti-Christian Lies (2:18–27)
    3. Promise of His Coming for God's Children (2:28—3:3)
  D. Doing Righteousness and Love with Gospel Boldness (3:4–24)
    1. Contrast: Righteousness by Christ or Sin by the Devil (3:4–10)
    2. Contrast: Love and Life or Hatred and Death (3:11–18)
    3. Promise of Confidence toward God (3:19–24)

- III. Exhortations and Motives to Abide in God's Truth and Love (4:1—5:17)
  - A. Do Not Trust False Prophets (4:1–6)
  - B. Love One Another (4:7—5:3)
    1. God's Love in God's Son (4:7–10)
    2. God's Love in God's Children (4:11–21)
    3. Loving Brothers and Obeying God (5:1–3)
  - C. Hold Onto the Witness to Christ by Faith (5:4–13)
  - D. Pray with Confidence for Each Other (5:14–17)
- IV. Conclusion (5:18–21)
  - A. Knowledge Is in Christ (5:18–20)
  - B. Watch against Idols (5:21)

THE FIRST EPISTLE GENERAL OF

JOHN

CHAPTER 1

THAT which was from the beginning, which we
have heard, which we have seen with our eyes,
which we have looked upon, and our hands have
handled, of the Word of life;
2 (For the life was manifested, and we have seen
it, and bear witness, and shew unto you that
eternal life, which was with the Father, and was
manifested unto us;)
3 That which we have seen and heard declare we
unto you, that ye also may have fellowship with
us: and truly our fellowship *is* with the Father, and
with his Son Jesus Christ.
4 And these things write we unto you, that your
joy may be full.
5 This then is the message which we have heard
of him, and declare unto you, that God is light,
and in him is no darkness at all.
6 If we say that we have fellowship with him, and
walk in darkness, we lie, and do not the truth:
7 But if we walk in the light, as he is in the light, we
have fellowship one with another, and the blood
of Jesus Christ his Son cleanseth us from all sin.
8 If we say that we have no sin, we deceive our-
selves, and the truth is not in us.
9 If we confess our sins, he is faithful and just
to forgive us *our* sins, and to cleanse us from all
unrighteousness.
10 If we say that we have not sinned, we make
him a liar, and his word is not in us.

Chapter 1: *The Father sent His living Word to us to reveal His light, and true religion consists of walking in the light, though it exposes our sins.*

INCARNATION OF THE WORD OF LIFE (1:1–4)

1:1 The *Word* that was *from the beginning* is God's eternal Son (Gen. 1:1; John 1:1). *heard . . . seen . . . handled*. The Word became flesh, a man in body and soul (4:2; John 1:14).
1:2 *with the Father*. In the eternal Trinity (John 1:2,18; 17:5). *seen . . . bear witness*. The author testifies as an eyewitness of Him who is *life* (John 1:4; 14:6). *manifested*. Appeared.
1:3 *fellowship*. Spiritual oneness with God and the church (John 17:21–23). The basis of fellowship is the apostolic teaching (*declare we unto you*) about the incarnate Word of life. *Son*. His deity and distinct personality from the Father. *Jesus*. His humanity and mission, a human name meaning "the Lord saves." *Christ*. His office, "anointed" (Luke 4:18; Acts 10:38) like God's prophets, priests, and kings (Ex. 29:7; 1 Sam. 16:13; Ps. 105:15).
1:4 *joy*. The result of fellowship and goal of the gospel (Luke 2:10; John 15:11; 16:22).

CONTRAST BETWEEN GOD'S TRUE CHILDREN AND THE WORLD (1:5—3:24)

Walking with God in Gospel Forgiveness (1:5—2:2)

Contrast: Fellowship with Light or Darkness (1:5–7)

1:5 *message . . . heard of him*. Teaching of Christ (v. 3), who revealed *God* (John 17:2–3,6,26). *light . . . darkness*. Righteousness, goodness, and truth versus sin, evil, and lies. *God is light*. His nature is absolute and infinite righteousness (Deut. 32:4). See also 4:8; John 4:24. *no darkness at all*. Greek double negative for emphasis.
1:6 *walk*. Our regular, daily pattern of conduct (present tense). *we lie*. It is hypocrisy to claim we walk with God while living in unrepentant sin.
1:7 *walk in the light*. Obeying His truth as it reveals, exposes, and directs (John 3:21; 8:12). *blood . . . cleanseth*. Old Testament image of the sacrifice of *Christ*, both human (*Jesus*) and divine (*his Son*), that atones for *all sin* (Lev. 16:18–19,30) so that repentant sinners are counted clean and have *fellowship* with the church, no longer shut out of God's holy presence (Num. 5:1–4).

Contrast: Confession of Sin or Self-Deception (1:8–10)

1:8 *deceive ourselves*. Choose blindness rather than face corruption and guilt (John 3:19–20; 9:39–41). *truth is not in us*. The gospel has not penetrated the heart.
1:9 *confess*. Openly acknowledge (John 9:22). *faithful*. God's promise *to forgive* is sure (Ps. 32:1). *just*. Christ's death satisfied God's justice so as *to cleanse* guilt (v. 7; 2:2; Heb. 9:14).
1:10 *him a liar*. To contradict God's testimony is to insult God's truthfulness (5:10), as Satan did (Gen. 3:1–5). *word is not in us*. See v. 8.

Thoughts for Personal/Family Worship: Chapter 1

1. It was stunning and virtually inconceivable to the ancient Greek mind that the divine Word would become a physical man we could see and touch. It should be stunning to us today that the Lord Jesus would take our lowly nature to His glorious person. Life has come to us in a way we can relate to, with gentleness and sympathy for our weaknesses. Consider these truths and spend some time praising God for what He did for sinners. How can Christians who lack joy in Christ acquire more genuine joy? What role does the Holy Spirit play in helping true believers experience fullness of joy?

CHAPTER 2

MY little children, these things write I unto you,
that ye sin not. And if any man sin, we have an advocate with the Father, Jesus Christ the righteous:
2 And he is the propitiation for our sins: and not
for ours only, but also for *the sins of* the whole world.
3 And hereby we do know that we know him, if
we keep his commandments.
4 He that saith, I know him, and keepeth not his
commandments, is a liar, and the truth is not in him.
5 But whoso keepeth his word, in him verily is
the love of God perfected: hereby know we that we are in him.
6 He that saith he abideth in him ought himself
also so to walk, even as he walked.
7 Brethren, I write no new commandment unto
you, but an old commandment which ye had from the beginning. The old commandment is the word which ye have heard from the beginning.
8 Again, a new commandment I write unto you,
which thing is true in him and in you: because the darkness is past, and the true light now shineth.
9 He that saith he is in the light, and hateth his
brother, is in darkness even until now.
10 He that loveth his brother abideth in the light,
and there is none occasion of stumbling in him.
11 But he that hateth his brother is in darkness, and walketh in darkness, and knoweth not whither he goeth, because that darkness hath blinded his eyes.
12 I write unto you, little children, because your
sins are forgiven you for his name's sake.
13 I write unto you, fathers, because ye have
known him *that is* from the beginning. I write unto you, young men, because ye have overcome the wicked one. I write unto you, little children, because ye have known the Father.
14 I have written unto you, fathers, because ye
have known him *that is* from the beginning. I have written unto you, young men, because ye are strong, and the word of God abideth in you, and ye have overcome the wicked one.
15 Love not the world, neither the things *that are*
in the world. If any man love the world, the love of the Father is not in him.
16 For all that *is* in the world, the lust of the flesh,
and the lust of the eyes, and the pride of life, is not of the Father, but is of the world.
17 And the world passeth away, and the lust

---

2. A relationship with the righteous God cannot coexist happily with sin. We must not call ourselves Christians and walk in the darkness; we must walk in the light, allowing Christ to expose our sin, wash us clean, and lead us in His ways. How often do you confess your sins to God? How are you using the Word to help you to see, hate, and forsake sin?

Chapter 2: *Standing upon Christ's atoning work, true Christians walk in obedience and love as they enjoy the privileges of God's children at every stage of the Christian life.*

Promise of Christ's Propitiation and Intercession (2:1–2)

2:1 *My little children.* John wrote with fatherly authority and affection (1 Thess. 2:11). *that ye sin not.* Forgiveness (1:9) does not promote sin (Ps. 130:4). *advocate.* Friend who speaks for you before a judge. *the righteous.* Christ's perfect obedience (3:5) is the basis of God's acceptance of believers (Isa. 53:11).

2:2 *propitiation.* Sacrifice (1:7) appeasing God's righteous anger against sinners (4:10; Rom. 3:25). *not for ours only.* Not limited to an ethnic group such as the Jews (John 10:16; 11:51–52; Rev. 5:9). *the whole world.* Many, but not every person (see "world" in 5:19; Rom. 1:8; Col. 1:6).

Obeying God's Law of Love in Gospel Privileges (2:3–14)

Contrast: Obedience or Disobedience to His Commandments (2:3–6)

2:3 *hereby.* By this. Assurance of salvation is possible when people *know* God (v. 13) such that they obey His *commandments* (Jer. 22:16).

2:4 *truth is not in him.* See note at 1:8.

2:5 *whoso.* Whoever. *verily.* Truly. *perfected.* Reaches its goal of producing people who obey God (4:12). *hereby.* By this. *in him.* In union with Christ by the Spirit.

2:6 *abideth in him.* Lives in union with Christ. *walk.* See note at 1:6. *as he walked.* Union with Christ results in likeness to Him.

Contrast: Love in the Light or Hate in the Darkness (2:7–11)

2:7–8 *ye had from the beginning.* Perhaps addressing Jews regarding the Old Testament. The *old commandment* of love (Lev. 19:18) became *new* when Christ came and displayed God's love in His death (4:9–10; John 13:34). In Him, the new era of *light* has already dawned (Isa. 60:1; Mal. 4:2; John 1:9; Rom. 13:12). *is past.* Literally, "is passing away" (present tense, see v. 17).

2:9 Hatred of fellow Christians reveals hypocrisy (4:20; John 15:18).

2:10 *none occasion of stumbling.* No cause of sin and harm to himself or others.

2:11 *whither.* Where he goes—to destruction (Prov. 4:18–19; Jer. 23:12; John 11:10; 12:35).

Promises to Children, Young Men, and Fathers (2:12–14)

2:12–14 John assures new converts (*little children*) of their justification in Christ and adoption by *the Father*; mature and aging believers (*fathers*) of their relationship with the unchanging, eternal God; and believers striving for holiness (*young men*) of their victory over the Devil (*the wicked one*). *forgiven . . . known . . . overcome.* Greek perfect tense: being in an established state. *for his name's sake.* Because of Him alone, and so for His glory alone (1:7; 2:1–2). *have known* (three times). Believers in Christ do not need a new knowledge offered by false teachers.

Resisting Temptation in Gospel Hope (2:15—3:3)

Contrast: Love of the Father or Love of the World (2:15–17)

2:15 *the world.* We must love people but not the present age (v. 17; John 12:25); the world is the Devil's kingdom (4:4; John 16:11) of hatred against God (3:1; John 8:23; 14:17; 15:18).

2:16 *lust of the flesh . . . of the eyes.* Strong desires to please the body and to possess visible treasures (Luke 8:14). *pride of life.* Boasting in one's acts and resources.

2:17 *passeth away.* Already falling under Christ's judgment

thereof: but he that doeth the will of God abideth
for ever.
18 Little children, it is the last time: and as ye
have heard that antichrist shall come, even now
are there many antichrists; whereby we know that
it is the last time.
19 They went out from us, but they were not of
us; for if they had been of us, they would *no doubt*
have continued with us: but *they went out*, that they
might be made manifest that they were not all of us.
20 But ye have an unction from the Holy One,
and ye know all things.
21 I have not written unto you because ye know
not the truth, but because ye know it, and that no
lie is of the truth.
22 Who is a liar but he that denieth that Jesus
is the Christ? He is antichrist, that denieth the
Father and the Son.
23 Whosoever denieth the Son, the same hath not
the Father: *[but] he that acknowledgeth the Son
hath the Father also*.
24 Let that therefore abide in you, which ye have
heard from the beginning. If that which ye have
heard from the beginning shall remain in you, ye
also shall continue in the Son, and in the Father.
25 And this is the promise that he hath promised
us, *even* eternal life.
26 These *things* have I written unto you concerning them that seduce you.
27 But the anointing which ye have received of
him abideth in you, and ye need not that any man
teach you: but as the same anointing teacheth you
of all things, and is truth, and is no lie, and even as
it hath taught you, ye shall abide in him.
28 And now, little children, abide in him; that,
when he shall appear, we may have confidence,
and not be ashamed before him at his coming.
29 If ye know that he is righteous, ye know that
every one that doeth righteousness is born of him.

CHAPTER 3

BEHOLD, what manner of love the Father hath
bestowed upon us, that we should be called the
sons of God: therefore the world knoweth us not,
because it knew him not.
2 Beloved, now are we the sons of God, and
it doth not yet appear what we shall be: but we

(v. 8; John 12:31). *thereof.* Of it. *abideth for ever.* A member of the eternal kingdom (Isa. 9:7; 40:8).

Contrast: Christ-Centered Truth or Anti-Christian Lies (2:18–27)

2:18 *the last time.* Final period of this age between Christ's first and second coming (Acts 2:17; Heb. 1:2). *antichrist shall come.* One yet in John's future who attempts to take Christ's office or position (2 Thess. 2:3–4). *many antichrists.* False teachers who usurp Christ's office as the true teacher (v. 22; 4:3; Matt. 24:24; 2 John 7). *whereby.* By which.

2:19 *from us . . . not of us.* Once part of the true church, but having rejected it and departed from it, they show that they never truly belonged. The elect persevere with the church. *made manifest.* Plainly shown.

2:20 *unction.* Anointing (Greek *chrisma*) by the Spirit, with Christ (Greek *christos*, "anointed"; see note at 1:3) to *know* God's truth, in contrast to the antichrists (Greek *antichristoi*).

2:22 False teachers reject *Jesus* as God's *Christ*, His anointed Prophet, Priest, and King, probably because they denied that a physical man could be the spiritual Lord (4:3; 2 John 7).

2:23 *Whosoever.* Everyone who. It is impossible to know God without trusting and confessing Jesus Christ (John 14:6; Rom. 10:9).

2:24 *which ye have heard.* The ancient revelation of Christ in Scripture (John 5:39). *abide in . . . continue in.* Remain in spiritual union.

2:26 *seduce.* Lead astray.

2:27 *anointing.* Same word as "unction" (v. 20). Anointed with Christ's Spirit, they are subordinate prophets, priests, and kings (Acts 2:18; Rev. 1:6). *need not that any man teach you.* The new covenant promise (Isa. 54:13; Jer. 31:34; John 6:45). *anointing teacheth you of all things.* The ministry of the Spirit of truth, promised by Christ (John 16:13).

Promise of His Coming for God's Children (2:28—3:3)

2:28 *abide in him.* Stay joined to God by clinging to Christ as the Bible reveals Him (v. 24; John 15:5–7). *he shall appear.* Christ's *coming* in visible glory (3:2) on judgment day (4:17). *ashamed.* The destiny of the wicked, not those who trust in Christ (Ps. 25:2–3; 31:1,17).

2:29 *born of him.* A new spiritual beginning caused by God (3:9; 4:7; 5:1,4,18; John 1:13; 3:1–8), creating a new heart in God's *righteous* image inclined to do *righteousness* (Ezek. 36:26–27).

Thoughts for Personal/Family Worship: Chapter 2

1. **Sometimes when we take our children to a park, we pay for their admission and their hands get stamped to show that their admission price has been paid. John explains the stamp that marks those who truly know God: they obey God's laws, love God's people, and receive God's doctrines. They should remember, however, that these marks did not pay for their admission to the kingdom; only the death and intercession of God's righteous Son does so. How can the marks and payment of salvation guide a person doubting his salvation?**
2. **Why is it important to fight against sin? How can we go on fighting against sin without becoming discouraged by our numerous failures? What comfort do true believers find in Jesus' work as their advocate when they do sin and repent of it?**
3. **God's people have the anointing of the Spirit to teach them the truth. Their faith does not depend on human testimony or secret knowledge from a special teacher, but on God's Spirit speaking through God's Word (1 Cor. 2:1–5). However, God's Spirit does work through Bible teachers (John 21:15; Eph. 4:11). How should we give due respect and attention to teachers without giving them the place of the Spirit?**

Chapter 3: ***Christian hope motivates purity, and true spiritual life produces righteousness and love in God's children, so that they may have confidence in their prayers to God.***

3:1 *manner.* Kind. *bestowed.* Given. *sons.* Literally, "children"

know that, when he shall appear, we shall be like
him; for we shall see him as he is.
3 And every man that hath this hope in him pu-
rifieth himself, even as he is pure.
4 Whosoever committeth sin transgresseth also
the law: for sin is the transgression of the law.
5 And ye know that he was manifested to take
away our sins; and in him is no sin.
6 Whosoever abideth in him sinneth not: who-
soever sinneth hath not seen him, neither known
him.
7 Little children, let no man deceive you: he that
doeth righteousness is righteous, even as he is
righteous.
8 He that committeth sin is of the devil; for the
devil sinneth from the beginning. For this pur-
pose the Son of God was manifested, that he
might destroy the works of the devil.
9 Whosoever is born of God doth not commit
sin; for his seed remaineth in him: and he cannot
sin, because he is born of God.
10 In this the children of God are manifest, and
the children of the devil: whosoever doeth not
righteousness is not of God, neither he that loveth
not his brother.
11 For this is the message that ye heard from the
beginning, that we should love one another.
12 Not as Cain, *who* was of that wicked one, and
slew his brother. And wherefore slew he him?
Because his own works were evil, and his brother's
righteous.
13 Marvel not, my brethren, if the world hate you.
14 We know that we have passed from death unto
life, because we love the brethren. He that loveth
not *his* brother abideth in death.
15 Whosoever hateth his brother is a murderer:
and ye know that no murderer hath eternal life
abiding in him.
16 Hereby perceive we the love *of God*, because he
laid down his life for us: and we ought to lay down
our lives for the brethren.
17 But whoso hath this world's good, and seeth
his brother have need, and shutteth up his bowels
of compassion from him, how dwelleth the love of
God in him?
18 My little children, let us not love in word, nei-
ther in tongue; but in deed and in truth.
19 And hereby we know that we are of the truth,
and shall assure our hearts before him.
20 For if our heart condemn us, God is greater
than our heart, and knoweth all things.
21 Beloved, if our heart condemn us not, *then*
have we confidence toward God.
22 And whatsoever we ask, we receive of him,
because we keep his commandments, and do
those things that are pleasing in his sight.
23 And this is his commandment, That we should
believe on the name of his Son Jesus Christ, and

(v. 2). Adoption by God (John 1:12) is an astonishing gift from the extraordinary *love* of the *Father* (Eph. 1:4–6), but God's children are strangers to *the world*.

3:2 *doth not yet appear*. The blessedness of God's children is still hidden (Rom. 8:18–25), but when Christ *shall appear*, their vision of His glory (John 17:24) will transform them into the same image (Rom. 8:29; 1 Cor. 15:42–49).

3:3 Christian *hope* includes love and reverence for the coming Christ, and thus striving to be *pure* in expectation of His appearing in glory (2:28; Titus 2:12–13).

Doing Righteousness and Love with Gospel Boldness (3:4–24)

Contrast: Righteousness by Christ or Sin by the Devil (3:4–10)

3:4 *Whosoever*. Everyone who. *transgression of the law*. Lawlessness, or rebellion against God's law (Rom. 8:7), either doing what it forbids or not doing what it requires.

3:5 *was manifested*. Appeared on earth. *take away our sins*. By His propitiation (2:2; Ps. 103:12; John 1:29; Heb. 10:4) and personal righteousness (*in him is no sin*, see 2:1).

3:6 *Whosoever*. Everyone who. *sinneth*. Greek present tense: continuing in constant sin without repentance. *seen him*. The spiritual sight of His glory transforms (2 Cor. 3:18; 4:6; 3 John 11).

3:8 *the devil sinneth from the beginning*. See Gen. 3:1–5; John 8:44; Rev. 12:9. Christ came to *destroy* sin. He is the seed of Eve (Gen. 3:15) who conquered *the devil* (John 12:31; 16:11).

3:9 *born of God*. See note at 2:29. *his seed*. Christ's kingdom is planted in the soul in the new birth through the Word (Matt. 13:3,32,38; 1 Peter 1:23), so that the person's nature changes and he *cannot* continue in a lifestyle of habitual *sin* (present tense), though he still sins (1:8–10).

3:10 *manifest*. Clearly seen. *children of the devil*. The "seed" of the serpent, people made by God but ruled by Satan (Gen. 3:15; John 8:44). *whosoever*. Everyone who.

Contrast: Love and Life or Hatred and Death (3:11–18)

3:11 On the ancient law of love, see note at 2:7–8.

3:12 *of that wicked one*. A child of the Devil. *slew*. Violently killed (Gen. 4:8). *wherefore*. Why. *Because his own works were evil, and his brother's righteous*. See John 3:19–20; 7:7; 15:22,24.

3:13 *Marvel not*. Do not be amazed. See John 15:18–19; 16:1–4; 17:14.

3:14 The new birth is a spiritual resurrection *from death unto life* through Christ (John 5:24–26; Eph. 2:5), evident through the *love* it produces (4:7).

3:15 *Whosoever*. Everyone who. See Matt. 5:21–22; Rev. 21:8; 22:15.

3:16 *Hereby perceive we*. By this we have come to know. *and we ought to*. Believers are obligated to imitate Christ's love (John 15:12–13; Eph. 4:32—5:2).

3:17 *whoso*. The one who. *this world's good*. Physical resources. *shutteth up his bowels*. Refuses to extend sympathy and mercy from his heart. *dwelleth . . . in him*. See 4:12.

3:18 *deed*. Work. Love must be more than talk; it leads to faithful action (cf. James 2:15–16).

Promise of Confidence toward God (3:19–24)

3:19 *hereby*. By this. *of the truth*. People who believe and obey Christ's Word (John 18:37). Believers who love others in self-denying action (vv. 14,16–18) may have a settled assurance that they are saved (2:3). *before him*. In God's presence.

3:20 *if our heart condemn us*. Believers may experience guilt and fear (4:18), but they can trust that God's love (v. 16) *is greater*, and He knows their sincere love (John 21:17).

3:21 *confidence*. Boldness to draw near to the Father.

3:22 *whatsoever*. What. Forgiven and sanctified in Christ (1:7;

love one another, as he gave us commandment.
24 And he that keepeth his commandments
dwelleth in him, and he in him. And hereby we
know that he abideth in us, by the Spirit which he
hath given us.

CHAPTER 4

BELOVED, believe not every spirit, but try the spir-
its whether they are of God: because many false
prophets are gone out into the world.
2 Hereby know ye the Spirit of God: Every spirit
that confesseth that Jesus Christ is come in the
flesh is of God:
3 And every spirit that confesseth not that Jesus
Christ is come in the flesh is not of God: and this
is that *spirit* of antichrist, whereof ye have heard
that it should come; and even now already is it in
the world.
4 Ye are of God, little children, and have over-
come them: because greater is he that is in you,
than he that is in the world.
5 They are of the world: therefore speak they of
the world, and the world heareth them.
6 We are of God: he that knoweth God heareth
us; he that is not of God heareth not us. Hereby
know we the spirit of truth, and the spirit of error.
7 Beloved, let us love one another: for love is of
God; and every one that loveth is born of God,
and knoweth God.
8 He that loveth not knoweth not God; for God
is love.
9 In this was manifested the love of God toward
us, because that God sent his only begotten Son
into the world, that we might live through him.
10 Herein is love, not that we loved God, but that
he loved us, and sent his Son *to be* the propitiation
for our sins.
11 Beloved, if God so loved us, we ought also to
love one another.
12 No man hath seen God at any time. If we love
one another, God dwelleth in us, and his love is
perfected in us.
13 Hereby know we that we dwell in him, and he
in us, because he hath given us of his Spirit.
14 And we have seen and do testify that the Father
sent the Son *to be* the Saviour of the world.
15 Whosoever shall confess that Jesus is the Son
of God, God dwelleth in him, and he in God.
16 And we have known and believed the love that

2:1–2; 3:5,8), the works of believers are *pleasing* to God, and the Father answers their prayers (5:14).

3:23 God's will is summed up by faith in Christ and love for people (John 6:29; 13:34). *name*. The revealed glory of Christ's person and work.

3:24 *dwelleth in him*. Abides in him. *hereby*. By this. The *Spirit* of God gives assurance by producing His fruit and giving the spiritual insight to recognize His work in the soul (Rom. 8:9,13–16; Gal. 5:22–23).

Thoughts for Personal/Family Worship: Chapter 3

1. **This chapter contrasts God's children and the world in terms of righteousness versus sin, love versus hatred, and life versus death. How would you summarize the difference between a true Christian and an unsaved person? Where do you stand?**
2. **If we are true believers, how does a proper understanding of the doctrine of adoption impact our relationship with God as our Father (v. 1)? With the world (v. 1)? With the future (v. 2)? With ourselves (v. 3)? With the family of believers (vv. 14–18)?**
3. **If you are born of God, then God has given you promises. When Christ comes, you will gaze into His glory without shame and be made like Him. You can have confidence toward God right now because the Spirit is working in your life. Do you have a right to claim these promises? Which of these promises is most precious to you now, and why?**

EXHORTATIONS AND MOTIVES TO ABIDE IN GOD'S TRUTH AND LOVE (4:1—5:17)

Chapter 4: ***Having distinguished between God's children and the world, John now calls the church to reject false teachers and to love one another as a sign of union with God in Christ.***

Do Not Trust False Prophets (4:1–6)

4:1 *spirits*. Spiritual powers operating in people (*prophets*) who claimed an extraordinary gift to speak divine revelations; in that time of new revelation, the apostolic church had to test (*try*) whether they were from God (1 Cor. 14:29–31; Eph. 2:20; 3:4–5; 1 Thess. 5:19–22).

4:2 *Hereby*. By this. True teaching by the Spirit declares the incarnate person (*come in the flesh*) and office (*Christ*) of the Savior (*Jesus*; see notes at 1:3; 2:22).

4:3 *spirit of antichrist*. Satan (see note at 2:18). *whereof*. Of which.

4:4 *Ye are of God*. The church belongs to God's kingdom. *he that is in you*. God (vv. 12,16; 3:24). *he that is in the world*. The Devil (3:8; 5:19).

4:5 *They are of the world*. The false prophets belong to Satan's kingdom. *speak they of the world*. They teach from the world's deceptive, lustful, and proud mindset (2:15–17).

4:6 *We are of God*. The apostles were sent by God. *heareth us*. How people receive the teachings of the apostles reveals whether they belong to *God* (John 13:20). *Hereby*. By this.

Love One Another (4:7—5:3)

God's Love in God's Son (4:7–10)

4:7 *every one that loveth is born of God*. The world has selfish love (2:15–16; Matt. 5:46–47; 7:9–11; Eph. 5:29), but Christlike love (3:16) is a supernatural gift and sign of salvation.

4:8 *God is love*. God's essence is pure and infinite love (Ex. 34:6). God is also spirit and light (1:5; John 4:24), so divine love is not physical attraction or tolerance for sin.

4:9 *was manifested*. Appeared, became visible. *sent*. On a mission to do His Father's will (John 4:34; 6:29,38; 17:3–4). *only begotten Son*. God's only Son by nature not adoption (John 1:1,14,18), and uniquely precious to Him like Isaac was to Abraham (Gen. 22:2,12).

4:10 *Herein*. In this. "God so loved" (v. 11) people who hated Him and provoked His anger that He sacrificed His Son (John 3:16,20,36) to satisfy His justice and pacify His anger (*propitiation*, see note at 2:2).

God hath to us. God is love; and he that dwelleth
in love dwelleth in God, and God in him.
17 Herein is our love made perfect, that we may
have boldness in the day of judgment: because as
he is, so are we in this world.
18 There is no fear in love; but perfect love
casteth out fear: because fear hath torment. He
that feareth is not made perfect in love.
19 We love him, because he first loved us.
20 If a man say, I love God, and hateth his brother,
he is a liar: for he that loveth not his brother
whom he hath seen, how can he love God whom
he hath not seen?
21 And this commandment have we from him,
That he who loveth God love his brother also.

CHAPTER 5

WHOSOEVER believeth that Jesus is the Christ is
born of God: and every one that loveth him that
begat loveth him also that is begotten of him.
2 By this we know that we love the children of God,
when we love God, and keep his commandments.
3 For this is the love of God, that we keep his
commandments: and his commandments are not
grievous.
4 For whatsoever is born of God overcometh the
world: and this is the victory that overcometh the
world, *even* our faith.
5 Who is he that overcometh the world, but he
that believeth that Jesus is the Son of God?
6 This is he that came by water and blood, *even*
Jesus Christ; not by water only, but by water and
blood. And it is the Spirit that beareth witness,
because the Spirit is truth.
7 For there are three that bear record in heaven,
the Father, the Word, and the Holy Ghost: and
these three are one.
8 And there are three that bear witness in earth,
the Spirit, and the water, and the blood: and these
three agree in one.
9 If we receive the witness of men, the witness
of God is greater: for this is the witness of God
which he hath testified of his Son.

God's Love in God's Children (4:11–21)

4:11 *we ought also*. The gospel obligates the saved to imitate their Savior (see note at 3:16).

4:12 *seen God*. God's essence is invisible (v. 20; John 1:18; 1 Tim. 1:17; Heb. 11:27). *love is perfected*. God's love, always perfect in Him, reaches its perfect goal when it unites God and man to become visible in God's human image (vv. 17–18; 2:5; Gen. 1:26; Col. 1:15; 3:10).

4:13 *Hereby*. By this. *dwell*. Same word as "abide." *of his Spirit*. A measure of the Spirit's work of love and faith, by which Christians *know* they are one with God (3:24).

4:14 *we have seen and do testify*. The eyewitness testimony of the apostles (1:2). *Saviour of the world*. Not just Jews, but sinners of all nations (John 4:40–42).

4:15 *Whosoever*. The one who. See 2:23.

4:16 *love . . . to us*. Or, love "in us." They can experience His love (Rom. 5:5). *dwelleth*. Abides.

4:17 *our love made perfect*. Literally, "the love has been fulfilled with us." God's love in Christ (vv. 9,16) makes people like Christ (*as he is*) to some degree even now (*in this world*) so that they have confident hope for *the day of judgment*.

4:18 *casteth out fear*. Love goes hand in hand with the fear of reverence toward God (Ps. 33:18; 103:11; 130:4). But God's love drives out the fear of future divine punishment (*torment*; v. 17; 2:28; Matt. 25:46). *not made perfect*. Not reached maturity in assurance of God's love.

4:19 Our love is born of His grace (v. 7).

4:20 *If a man say . . . liar*. See 1:6; 2:4.

4:21 See 3:11; Matt. 22:35–40.

Thoughts for Personal/Family Worship: Chapter 4

1. **What false teachers present themselves to us today in person or through media? How can you recognize them? (See v. 2; Deut. 13:1–3; Matt. 7:15–20; Acts 17:10–12; Gal. 1:8–9; 1 Tim. 4:1–5.) How should you respond? How do the differences between those who are of the world and those who are of God affect your daily life and relationships? Should it affect you and your family more? In what ways?**
2. **God is love; as the Puritans said, Christ is love covered over with flesh. The Christian life is the indwelling of God's love in men, women, and children. Christ's coming aims to produce peace and joy in His beloved, not terror. How prominent is love in your view of God? Is His love hidden behind His majesty or wrath? How can you meditate more on His love? How can you grow in your own practice of Christlike love?**

Chapter 5: *The children of God have true, spiritual knowledge of God, by which they can stand together against the world for the true faith.*

Loving Brothers and Obeying God (5:1–3)

5:1 *Whosoever*. Everyone who. *believeth*. Believing (present tense) results from having been *born of God* (perfect tense; John 1:12–13; 3:3). It is impossible to love the Father (*him that begat*) without loving all believers, for they are His children in His image (*begotten of him*).

5:2–3 To *love* people requires obeying God's *commandments*. Law directs love. *not grievous*. Not a painful burden. Love delights in God's law (Ps. 1:2; 119:97; John 14:15).

Hold Onto the Witness to Christ by Faith (5:4–13)

5:4–5 Everything God produces in the new birth (*whatsoever is born of God*) conquers (*overcometh*) the Devil's power, for God comes to reign in the soul (4:4) through *faith* in the Word (2:14). Believers still suffer and sin, but they conquer because *faith* unites them to the incarnate *Son of God* who suffered but overcame the world by the cross (John 16:11,33; Rev. 5:5,9; 17:14).

5:6 *water and blood*. Christ's baptism (John 1:32–34) and death (1:7). *beareth witness*. Testifies.

5:7 *bear record*. Testify (same word as "bear witness," vv. 6,8). *Word*. Christ (1:1–2). *Holy Ghost*. Holy Spirit. *three are one*. See Deut. 6:4; Matt. 28:19; John 10:30; 14:10–11; 17:21–23.

5:8 *three that bear witness*. The Father testified at Christ's baptism (Mark 1:11). Christ's death testified of fulfilling the Old Testament (John 19:35–37). The Spirit testifies to Christ through the apostolic word (John 15:26–27; 16:7–15). *agree in one*. All confirm that Jesus is God's Son.

5:9 *witness of God*. The divine testimony of the Word and the

10 He that believeth on the Son of God hath the
witness in himself: he that believeth not God hath
made him a liar; because he believeth not the
record that God gave of his Son.
11 And this is the record, that God hath given to
us eternal life, and this life is in his Son.
12 He that hath the Son hath life; *and* he that hath
not the Son of God hath not life.
13 These things have I written unto you that
believe on the name of the Son of God; that ye
may know that ye have eternal life, and that ye
may believe on the name of the Son of God.
14 And this is the confidence that we have in him,
that, if we ask any thing according to his will, he
heareth us:
15 And if we know that he hear us, whatsoever we
ask, we know that we have the petitions that we
desired of him.
16 If any man see his brother sin a sin *which is* not
unto death, he shall ask, and he shall give him life
for them that sin not unto death. There is a sin
unto death: I do not say that he shall pray for it.
17 All unrighteousness is sin: and there is a sin
not unto death.
18 We know that whosoever is born of God sin-
neth not; but he that is begotten of God keepeth
himself, and that wicked one toucheth him not.
19 *And* we know that we are of God, and the
whole world lieth in wickedness.
20 And we know that the Son of God is come,
and hath given us an understanding, that we may
know him that is true, and we are in him that is
true, *even* in his Son Jesus Christ. This is the true
God, and eternal life.
21 Little children, keep yourselves from idols.
Amen.

Spirit is the authoritative and sufficient basis for saving faith in Christ (1 Cor. 2:1–5).

5:10–11 *witness in himself.* The Spirit testifies within the heart (2:27). *record.* Testimony. *life is in his Son.* A summary of the gospel.

5:12 Without *the Son* there is no *life* (John 14:6). The gospel excludes all other religions (2:23; 2 John 9), demanding faith in Christ alone.

5:13 *written . . . that ye may know that ye have eternal life.* The main purpose of this epistle is for believers to rejoice (1:4) in knowing they have life in God through Christ (vv. 2,19–20; 2:3,5,28–29; 3:14–15,19,24; 4:13). *that ye may believe.* See John 20:31.

Pray with Confidence for Each Other (5:14–17)

5:14–15 *confidence . . . in him.* Boldness toward God (3:21). God revealed much of *his will* in the law (2:17) and gospel (John 6:38–40) to direct His children in confident prayer (John 15:7).

5:16–17 Believers should pray for God to give spiritual renewal (*life*) to someone observed in a pattern of disobedience (present tense *sin*). John gives no encouragement to pray for false teachers who, after experiencing the gospel and the church (2:19), become enemies of Christ, cutting themselves off from life (*sin unto death*; Gal. 1:9; Heb. 6:4–6).

CONCLUSION (5:18–21)

Knowledge Is in Christ (5:18–20)

5:18–20 These three verses conclude John's teaching with three assertions of what *we know*.

5:18 *whosoever.* Everyone who. *sinneth not.* See notes at 3:6,9. *begotten.* Either the child of God guards *himself* (v. 21; 3:3) or (another reading) the only *begotten* Son guards him. *wicked one.* The Evil One, Satan (see 2:13–14). *toucheth.* Holds or harms (4:4; Ps. 105:15).

5:19 *of God.* In God's kingdom. *whole world.* Not every person, but all people not born of God. *lieth in wickedness.* Are part of the kingdom of the Evil One (3:8,10).

5:20 *given us an understanding.* By His Word (1:5) and Spirit (2:20). *Jesus Christ* is not only the revealer of God, but He is also *the true God, and eternal life* (1:2; John 1:1,4; 20:28).

Watch against Idols (5:21)

5:21 *keep.* Watch over and guard. *idols.* Images of gods (Ex. 20:4–6), or any thing or idea that takes the place of the true God in our lives (v. 20; 2:15–16; Matt. 6:24; Rom. 1:23; Col. 3:5).

Thoughts for Personal/Family Worship: Chapter 5

1. **Christ is the teacher of His people by His Word and Spirit. He gives us the truth and convinces us of its validity by divine and authoritative testimony in the Word and in the heart. The triune God is Himself the witness to this truth. Therefore, we should submit to the Bible and receive all that it says, regardless of what men may say.**
2. **Consider what it means to "overcometh the world" (vv. 4–5). Why is it necessary to engage in spiritual warfare in order to overcome the world? In what ways can we rise above the world's way of thinking and resist worldly peer pressure? Who gives us the power to do that? Offer an example from your own life of overcoming the world by the Spirit's grace.**
3. **God wants His children to know that they have life. He does not delight in slavish fear among believers, but in their assurance. Based on what you have read in this book, how can someone have assurance of being God's child? How can one grow in that assurance?**

ASSURANCE OF SALVATION

Scripture commands us, "Examine yourselves, whether ye be in the faith; prove your own selves. Know ye not your own selves, how that Jesus Christ is in you, except ye be reprobates?" (2 Cor. 13:5). We need a practical, experiential, and well-tested knowledge of our spiritual condition. Christ pressed this question upon His hearers in His parables (Matt. 7:24–27; 13:1–9,18–23; 25:1–13). John gives us tests by which a Christian can know with assurance that they are saved by Christ, particularly obedience and love (1 John 2:3–5; 3:10,14).

What is assurance? Assurance is a joyous, strong certainty of one's present and future salvation. We must not confuse assurance and presumption, which is a delusion based on self-love, self-righteousness, and self-flattery (Prov. 16:2). We must also be careful not to confuse faith and assurance. One may have justifying faith without assurance. Assurance is an effect of faith or grows out of faith (Eph. 3:12). Faith is a direct act of the soul toward Christ, taking Him and clinging to Him. Assurance is a reflective act of the soul, perceiving of one's own faith by the power of the Holy Spirit.

It is possible for a Christian to have an assurance of his salvation. We see in Scripture that God's people have enjoyed it. David called God his God and thanked Him for forgiving his sins (Ps. 31:14; 32:1). Paul showed his assurance, and based it not on a special revelation from God but on grounds that belong to all the people of God (Rom. 8:31–39). The Christian may have certainty and assurance because the promises of God are yes and amen in Christ (2 Cor. 1:20), and the Spirit of God who renews the heart can also bear witness that we are children of God (Rom. 8:16).

There are signs of grace by which a man may know whether he is in a state of grace or not. A man who lives in the habit of unrepentant sins should be assured that he is presently in a damnable condition, and will be so as long as he lives that way (Gal. 5:19–21). God's sanctifying grace produces a supernatural life within us. It is the infused principle of a holy life, a new creation produced by regeneration (2 Cor. 5:17; 2 Peter 1:4). The Bible commends seeking assurance when it gives us descriptions of the characteristics of true saving grace in distinction from counterfeits (Matt. 5:3–10). Scripture commands us to make our calling and election sure (2 Peter 1:10). We have examples of godly believers who used their graces as comforting signs of God's love to them (2 Kings 20:3; Neh. 13:14,22; 2 Cor. 1:12; 2 Tim. 4:7–8). Our Savior lays down the principle that "the tree is known by his fruit" (Matt. 12:33).

Therefore, examine your life for the signs of God's saving grace with wisdom and caution. Do not demand sinless perfection of yourself (1 John 1:8). Also, do not require great spiritual maturity as proof of conversion. On the other hand, do not make signs of grace out of qualities that unbelievers can have, like receiving baptism and the Lord's Supper, having right doctrinal beliefs, and exercising great ability in Christian service. Test yourself by the true standard, the Word of God (Ps. 119:105).

As you look for evidences of saving grace, never forget to keep looking to Christ alone as your peace with God and basis of your salvation. Deal honestly with yourself, and fight against self-love and self-flattery. If your soul is full of darkness and despair, do not be quick to judge yourself but wait until you can think more clearly. While you examine yourself, pray to God for His Spirit to enlighten your eyes. If you discover that you are not saved, do not delay until you see more signs of grace in yourself, but trust Christ immediately to save you without any worthiness on your part. If the Spirit of God does show you evidences that you are saved, do not resist Him in unbelief, but submit to Him and glorify Him as the Spirit of adoption (Rom. 8:15).

—Adapted from Anthony Burgess (d. 1664), *Spiritual Refining*

AND THIS IS

LOVE

THAT WE WALK

After His

COMMANDMENTS

THIS IS

The

COMMANDMENT

THAT AS YE HAVE

HEARD

FROM THE

Beginning

YE

SHOULD

WALK

IN IT

2 JOHN 1:6

INTRODUCTION TO THE BOOK OF

2 JOHN

Authorship: The author identifies himself simply as "the elder," but the style and teachings of this epistle link it (and the third epistle) closely to John's first epistle (see Introduction to 1 John). An apostle could refer to himself as an elder, for Peter did so (1 Peter 5:1). Irenaeus (d. AD 202) quotes 2 John and ascribes it to John, the disciple of the Lord. Thus we may conclude that it was written by the apostle John.

Date: Uncertain. This epistle appears to address the same crisis as 1 John (v. 7; 1 John 2:18–27) and thus may have been written around the same time, perhaps AD 85–95.

Theme: The importance of love and truth for the church of the elect.

Purpose: To lovingly exhort a church and its members to watch that they continue in love and the truth of Christ though false teachers have appeared.

Synopsis: *The Contribution of 2 John to Redemptive Revelation*

John's second letter addresses "the elect lady and her children," which, given that Israel (Isa. 52:2), the church (Rev. 21:9), and ancient cities (Isa. 47:1) were often addressed as women, likely refers to a church and its members. He shows them that the Christian life consists of both truth and love (2 John 3). God's truth commands us to love one another (v. 5), and enters the soul to produce that love (v. 1). Love makes Christian leaders rejoice to hear that people are faithfully living in submission to the truth (v. 4). Love especially moves Christians to rejoice in being together with other faithful people (v. 12). Yet, John warns, love does not encourage us to welcome every teacher, but to remain faithful to the ancient truth revealed by God (v. 6). Churches must discern those who fundamentally reject God's truth about Christ (v. 7), staying alert for they threaten their eternal well-being (v. 8). Teachers who do not receive the truth of Christ are outsiders to God and His church, and should receive no welcome or encouragement from the people of God (vv. 10–11).

Outline:

I. Greetings in Truth and Love (vv. 1–3)
II. Commendation for Walking in Love (vv. 4–6)
III. Warning against False Teachers (vv. 7–11)
IV. Conclusion and Greetings (vv. 12–13)

THE SECOND EPISTLE GENERAL OF

JOHN

THE elder unto the elect lady and her children,
whom I love in the truth; and not I only, but also
all they that have known the truth;
2 For the truth's sake, which dwelleth in us, and
shall be with us for ever.
3 Grace be with you, mercy, *and* peace, from God
the Father, and from the Lord Jesus Christ, the
Son of the Father, in truth and love.
4 I rejoiced greatly that I found of thy children
walking in truth, as we have received a command-
ment from the Father.
5 And now I beseech thee, lady, not as though I
wrote a new commandment unto thee, but that
which we had from the beginning, that we love
one another.
6 And this is love, that we walk after his command-
ments. This is the commandment, That, as ye have
heard from the beginning, ye should walk in it.
7 For many deceivers are entered into the world,
who confess not that Jesus Christ is come in the
flesh. This is a deceiver and an antichrist.
8 Look to yourselves, that we lose not those things
which we have wrought, but that we receive a full
reward.
9 Whosoever transgresseth, and abideth not in
the doctrine of Christ, hath not God. He that
abideth in the doctrine of Christ, he hath both
the Father and the Son.
10 If there come any unto you, and bring not this
doctrine, receive him not into *your* house, neither
bid him God speed:
11 For he that biddeth him God speed is partaker

GREETINGS IN TRUTH AND LOVE (vv. 1–3)

1 *elect.* Chosen by God (John 17:2,6; Rev. 17:14). *lady and her children.* Most likely a metaphor for a church and its members. *love in the truth . . . known the truth.* The Word of God (1 John 1:8,10) creates a bond of love among all who believe and obey it (1 Peter 1:22–23).

2 *For the truth's sake.* Because of the Word. *dwelleth in us.* Is received permanently in the heart (John 8:31–32; 15:7; 1 John 2:14). *with us for ever.* Eternal, unchanging truth (John 10:35).

3 *Grace.* Undeserved blessing for the needy. *mercy.* Help for the suffering. *peace.* Restored relationships of harmony with God and people. Salvation and spiritual growth come from both *the Father* and *the Son*, implying that both are fully God. *in truth and love.* Spiritual blessings come through knowing and believing biblical teachings and practicing them in Christian love.

COMMENDATION FOR WALKING IN LOVE (vv. 4–6)

4 *rejoiced greatly.* The faithfulness of Christians is the joy of Christian ministers. *found of.* Discovered or learned. *walking in truth.* Living in faith and obedience to the Word.

5 *beseech.* Ask. *not . . . new . . . from the beginning.* The ancient law of love (Lev. 19:18; 1 John 2:7).

6 *walk after his commandments.* Conduct ourselves according to God's laws. Love is not contrary to obedience to the law, but is fulfilled in it (John 14:15; Rom. 13:8–10; 1 John 5:2–3).

WARNING AGAINST FALSE TEACHERS (vv. 7–11)

7 *deceivers . . . antichrist.* False teachers opposing Christ (1 John 2:18,22; 4:3). *Christ.* The office of the Savior as God's anointed Prophet, Priest, and King. *in the flesh.* Incarnate as a man.

8 *Look.* Watch. *wrought.* Worked or accomplished. Church members must be alert or false teaching may ensnare them and rob them of eternal *reward* gained by faithfully supporting the proclamation of the gospel (John 4:36).

9 *Whosoever.* Everyone who. *transgresseth, and abideth not.* Steps outside of and leaves behind. *doctrine of Christ.* Teaching about Christ's person and work. Rejecting the gospel is not an alternative form of spirituality, but a life without God (*hath not God*, 1 John 2:22–23; 5:11–12).

10–11 Christians should refuse even basic hospitality to teachers of heresy. This does not refer to confused believers or unbelieving neighbors, but to people intentionally seeking to spread heresy (Rom. 16:17; Gal. 1:8–9; Titus 3:10). *bid him God speed.* Literally, "says to him, 'Rejoice'"; speaks to him a greeting. To speak a blessing on a false teacher is to become a partner (*partaker*) with him in *evil*. This may refer to the official blessing of a church on a visiting missionary.

CONCLUSION AND GREETINGS (vv. 12–13)

12 *paper.* Probably a sheet of papyrus, made of fiber from papyrus reeds. *that our joy may be full.* Those who love each other desire personal, *face to face* meetings, not just letters.

13 *children of thy elect sister.* Perhaps members of another local church (see note at v. 1).

Thoughts for Personal/Family Worship

1. **Truth and love are closely related to each other. What are the consequences of having truth without love? Love without truth? What does it mean to love someone "in the truth" (v. 1)? How can we improve the balance of truth and love in our relationships at home, at church, at school, and in society?**
2. **The truth of Christ creates love in the family of God. Why is this so? Why is it that those who trust in God's truth**

of his evil deeds.
12 Having many things to write unto you, I
would not *write* with paper and ink: but I trust
to come unto you, and speak face to face, that our
joy may be full.
13 The children of thy elect sister greet thee. Amen.

find themselves attracted to each other and desiring to serve one another?

3. Christians must give no approval or support to false teachers. Those who seek to publicly promote lies contrary to fundamental truths about Christ are not misguided brothers but deadly enemies. Christians should love them, pray for them, and try to show them their errors. But believers should not offer them the least encouragement or hospitality, for this gives false teachers an open door to spread their soul-damning errors.

I HAVE NO

GREATER

JOY

THAN

To Hear

THAT

MY

CHILDREN

WALK IN

Truth

3 JOHN 1:4

INTRODUCTION TO THE BOOK OF 3 JOHN

Authorship: The apostle John. See Introduction to 2 John: Authorship.

Date: Uncertain; probably late in the first century.

Theme: Love for the truth; and support for true Christian teachers.

Purpose: To encourage love among brothers and service to traveling missionaries.

Synopsis: *The Contribution of 3 John to Redemptive Revelation*

John wrote this letter to a faithful Christian man about whom we know little except his name, Gaius. This common Latin name belonged to other men in the New Testament (Acts 19:29; 20:4; Rom. 16:23; 1 Cor. 1:14)—and to more than one Roman dictator. The Gaius whom John loved was no dictator. John calls him "beloved" four times in this short epistle (3 John 1,2,5,11), a lavish reminder of his pleasure in Gaius's faithfulness. He is a model of soul prosperity (v. 2) by the power of God's truth (vv. 3–4), producing the fruit of love and missionary support (vv. 5–8).

In contrast stands Diotrephes, a leader in a local church. Whereas true servants of the Lord seek the glory of His name through the gospel (v. 7), Diotrephes sought his own glory (v. 9). It does not appear that he was a heretic, for John makes no mention of false doctrine here. Yet despite his orthodoxy the truth had not entered his heart, and his proud and divisive conduct implied that he did not belong to God (v. 11). He slandered the broader church and refused to allow anyone in his congregation to welcome missionaries as they traveled through the area (v. 10).

Where John's second epistle warns against welcoming false teachers, the third gives a balancing exhortation for believers to warmly receive and help preachers who seek the glory of Christ and to maintain fellowship with other congregations.

Outline:

I. Greeting: Love in the Truth (v. 1)
II. Blessing and Joy in Gaius (vv. 2–4)
III. Commendation for Caring for Missionaries (vv. 5–8)
IV. Warning against Diotrephes (vv. 9–11)
V. Conclusion and Greeting (vv. 12–14)

THE THIRD EPISTLE GENERAL OF

JOHN

THE elder unto the wellbeloved Gaius, whom I
love in the truth.
2 Beloved, I wish above all things that thou may-
est prosper and be in health, even as thy soul
prospereth.
3 For I rejoiced greatly, when the brethren came
and testified of the truth that is in thee, even as
thou walkest in the truth.
4 I have no greater joy than to hear that my chil-
dren walk in truth.
5 Beloved, thou doest faithfully whatsoever thou
doest to the brethren, and to strangers;
6 Which have borne witness of thy charity before
the church: whom if thou bring forward on their
journey after a godly sort, thou shalt do well:
7 Because that for his name's sake they went
forth, taking nothing of the Gentiles.
8 We therefore ought to receive such, that we
might be fellowhelpers to the truth.
9 I wrote unto the church: but Diotrephes, who
loveth to have the preeminence among them,
receiveth us not.
10 Wherefore, if I come, I will remember his deeds
which he doeth, prating against us with malicious
words: and not content therewith, neither doth he
himself receive the brethren, and forbiddeth them

GREETING: LOVE IN THE TRUTH (v. 1)

1 *wellbeloved*. Loved, same Greek word as "beloved" (vv. 2, 5,11). *love in the truth*. Love as a fellow follower of God's Word (see note at 2 John 1).

2 *wish*. Pray. *even as thy soul prospereth*. The most important prosperity is the flourishing of the soul in union with Christ (Mark 8:36; Phil. 3:8).

BLESSING AND JOY IN GAIUS (vv. 2–4)

3 *I rejoiced greatly . . . walkest in the truth*. See note at 2 John 4. *brethren*. Brothers in God's family. *truth that is in thee*. God's Word planted in the heart with power (John 5:38; 1 Thess. 2:13; 1 John 2:14; 2 John 2).

4 *my children*. Christians, whom John addressed as a spiritual father (1 John 2:1). It is the *joy* of God's servants to see people transformed by biblical *truth* (Phil. 4:1; 1 Thess. 2:19–20).

COMMENDATION FOR CARING FOR MISSIONARIES (vv. 5–8)

5 *whatsoever*. Whatever. Gaius *faithfully* served visiting Christians (*brethren*), even though they were *strangers* to him—a model of hospitality (Heb. 13:2; 1 Peter 4:9).

6 *borne witness*. Testified. *charity*. Love. *bring forward*. Send out with assistance (Rom. 15:24; 1 Cor. 16:6,11). *after a godly sort*. In a way worthy of God and glorifying to God.

7 *for his name's sake*. To glorify God by preaching the gospel of Christ—the highest motive for missions (John 12:28; Acts 9:15–16; Rom. 1:5; Phil. 1:18,20). *taking nothing*. Not seeking payment from the people they evangelized, relying instead upon the generosity of believers.

8 *fellowhelpers to the truth*. Christians who give hospitality and support to missionaries are coworkers with them for the spreading of the Word of God (Phil. 1:5,7; 4:15–19).

WARNING AGAINST DIOTREPHES (vv. 9–11)

9 *I wrote unto the church*. This letter was not preserved. *loveth to have the preeminence*. Loves to have first place, which belongs to Christ (Col. 1:18). *receiveth us not*. His pride led him to cut off relations with the apostle's church and ignore the apostle's authority.

10 *Wherefore*. For this reason. *remember his deeds*. Implement church discipline. *prating*. Speaking nonsense. *therewith*. With that. *casteth them out*. Like a dictator over his kingdom, he isolated the church and excommunicated those who welcomed other believers.

11 *follow not*. Do not imitate. *of God*. Belongs to God's kingdom (1 John 4:4; 5:19). *hath not seen God*. Lacks the spiritual knowledge of God that makes the soul like God (see note at 1 John 3:6).

CONCLUSION AND GREETING (vv. 12–14)

12 *Demetrius*. Possibly the carrier of this letter. *hath good report*. Has been testified to. *and of the truth itself*. The gospel itself testifies of the character of a true believer, the qualities that Demetrius clearly had. *bear record*. Testify. *our record is true*. See John 21:24.

13–14 *pen*. Reed with cut tip dipped in ink for writing. *not with ink . . . speak face to face*. See note at 2 John 12. *salute*. Greet. Some translations separate the words from *Peace* onward into a separate verse (v. 15). Verse divisions were not inspired by God but added centuries later.

Thoughts for Personal/Family Worship

1. **How is Gaius a good example for us to follow? What does it mean to "walk in truth" (v. 4)? How could we and our families walk in the truth more effectively?**
2. **William Carey, pioneer missionary to India, once compared missions to descending into a deep mine to recover treasures, and said, "I will go down, but you must hold the ropes." Missionaries need the support of other Christians. This epistle makes it clear that they need not only financial assistance, but also love and hospitality. How are you sharing your resources, love, and home**

that would, and casteth *them* out of the church.
11 Beloved, follow not that which is evil, but that
which is good. He that doeth good is of God: but
he that doeth evil hath not seen God.
12 Demetrius hath good report of all *men*, and of
the truth itself: yea, and we *also* bear record; and
ye know that our record is true.
13 I had many things to write, but I will not with
ink and pen write unto thee:
14 But I trust I shall shortly see thee, and we shall
speak face to face. Peace *be* to thee. *Our* friends
salute thee. Greet the friends by name.

to strengthen those who go out to the nations for the Lord's sake?

3. It is easy to point the finger at arrogant leaders like Diotrephes who try to take Christ's place, but we must begin with our own pride. John Newton said, "I have read of many wicked popes, but the worst pope I ever met is Pope Self." How do you see Diotrephes's pride operating in yourself? How can you combat it? Demetrius was spoken well of by all men (v. 12). What would those who know us best say about our love for the truth and for hospitality? What would our non-Christian neighbors say?

WORLD MISSIONS

The apostle John commended missions when he wrote, "for his name's sake they went forth, taking nothing of the Gentiles" (3 John 7). These ministers go forth to preach the gospel and propagate Christianity. They go forth to convert the nations. This is an excellent service, for they went forth for God and for His name's sake. The principal aim of all ministers of the gospel should be to gather and build up a people for the glory and honor of the Lord.

However, others who are not called to preach may contribute to the progress of this work. Churches and all who love the cause of Christ should work together to support the propagation of true religion in nations dominated by false religion. We must have large hearts that are willing to share our resources beyond our private circles (Phil. 4:14–16). Then we are "fellow–helpers to the truth," as we earnestly desire, pray for, and contribute our help in the propagation of the gospel in the world (3 John 8).

When Christ preached the gospel of the kingdom, He visited not only the great and wealthy cities, but the poor, obscure villages (Matt. 9:35). The souls of those who are least in the world are as precious to Christ, and should be to us, as the souls of those who are greatest. The Lord Jesus is moved with compassion for people (v. 36), not merely because of their temporal and physical problems, but especially for their spiritual needs. He sees their ignorance and carelessness though they will soon perish. Christ is a very compassionate friend to precious souls. It was mercy to souls that brought Him from heaven to earth, and then to the cross. Like sheep without a shepherd, the nations have no spiritual king to guide them faithfully to God (v. 36; cf. 1 Kings 22:17). No creature has more of a tendency to go astray than a sheep, and becomes more helpless when it wanders. Sinners are lost sheep, and false teachers fleece the sheep rather than feeding them (Jer. 23:1–8; Ezek. 34).

Therefore the Lord stirs up His disciples to pray for laborers to bring in the spiritual harvest (Matt. 9:38). There is a great deal of work to be done, multitudes of people who need instruction from the Word of God. It is God's work to send out laborers. Christ makes ministers (Eph. 4:11). All who love Christ and souls should show it by their earnest prayers to God, that He would send more skillful, faithful, wise, and hard-working preachers. It is a good sign that God is about to give a special mercy when He stirs up His people to go to the throne of grace (Ps. 10:17). Just as Christ called His disciples to pray and then sent them out to preach (Matt. 9:38—10:8), so too God's preachers must pray, "Here am I; send me" (Isa. 6:8), and also pray that God would send others.

The risen Christ has commissioned His servants, saying, "All power is given unto me in heaven and in earth. Go ye therefore, and teach all nations, baptizing them in the name of the Father, and of the Son, and of the Holy Ghost: Teaching them to observe all things whatsoever I have commanded you: and, lo, I am with you alway, even unto the end of the world. Amen" (Matt. 28:18–20). Christ has universal dominion as the Mediator (John 17:2). He purchased it (Rom. 14:10), and now He is taking possession of it (Ps. 2:8). He commissioned first His apostles, and then their successors, the ministers of the gospel in all nations to the end of the world. Salvation by Christ must be offered to all, and none excluded except those who exclude themselves by their refusal to believe and repent.

Christ the Mediator is setting up a kingdom; bring the nations to be His subjects. Christ is setting up a school; bring the nations to be His students. Christ is raising up an army of truth and love to war against the powers of darkness; enlist the nations to serve under His banner. Conquer the nations for Christ, so that they may be truly happy!

—Adapted from Matthew Henry, *Commentary* on 3 John 7; Matt. 9:35–38; 28:18–20

INTRODUCTION TO THE BOOK OF

JUDE

Author: The letter was written by Jude, the "brother of James" (v. 1). While the name *Jude* (Hebrew: *Judah*, Greek: *Judas*) was very common (Luke 6:16), scholarship identifies this particular Jude as Jesus' half brother. The James mentioned in Jude 1 is most likely the well-known leader of the church in Jerusalem (Acts 15:13) who was another half brother of Jesus (Gal. 1:19; cf. Matt. 13:55; Mark 6:3; James 1:1). Jude's greeting and teaching are similar to James's, and Jude does not include himself within the original group of apostles (Jude 17–18).

Date: Jude wrote this letter between AD 55–80, most likely in the mid-60s. Church historian Eusebius records that Jude and his son had already died by AD 81. Jude seems to have been written after many of the original apostles had died (v. 17) but no mention is made of the destruction of Jerusalem (AD 70). Many scholars think that Jude was dependent on and thus written after 2 Peter (c. AD 64–67), since vv. 4–18 are somewhat parallel to 2 Peter 2:1—3:3 (see notes there). However, it is not clear which epistle, if either, was copied by the other (see Introduction to 2 Peter).

Theme: The importance of standing for the faith against false teachers.

Purpose: To encourage believers to "earnestly contend for the faith" (v. 3) by recognizing the character of false teachers and responding to their errors with perseverance in the truth and compassionate action to those endangered by heresy.

Synopsis: *The Contribution of Jude to Redemptive Revelation*

The letter of Jude encourages believers to "contend for the faith" (v. 3) and keep themselves "in the love of God" (v. 21). Jude warns against false teachers who corrupt the gospel and deny "our Lord Jesus Christ" (v. 4), comparing them with Old Testament examples and describing them with sharp admonitions and vivid word pictures (vv. 5–16). Jude urges believers to keep themselves from falling away and to "have compassion" on others who are in danger (vv. 22–23). The letter begins and ends with comforting truths concerning God's preservation of believers, closing with a beautiful doxology to "our Saviour" who "is able to keep you from falling" (vv. 24–25).

Theologically, Jude primarily focuses on describing false teachers and the Christian response to them (cf. 2 Thess. 2:10; 2 Peter 2:1–22; 1 John 2:18–23). The book teaches the twin doctrines of God's preservation (Jude 1–2,24–25) and the believer's need to persevere (vv. 17–23). It also teaches the doctrine of God—especially His sovereign authority in the face of rebellion, His pending judgment of ungodliness, and His triune character (vv. 20–21). Jude also forms a basis for Christian apologetics.

Key themes of the book include:

1. Faithful Christians must remember the apostolic word (vv. 17–19), keep themselves in sound doctrine (vv. 20–21), and have compassion on the lost (vv. 22–23) in order to persevere in the faith.
2. False teachers can be identified by their denial of Christ's Lordship (unbelief, v. 4) and their immoral character (ungodliness, vv. 4–16).
3. Confessing the sovereign authority of God (vv. 5–16) and striving for personal growth in the Christian graces (vv. 3,20–23) are antidotes against false teaching.

4. The Lord will judge false teachers and punish all rebellion at the coming judgment day (vv. 5–16).
5. Christ will keep His people from apostasy and present them without sin to God (vv. 24–25).

Outline:

I. Greeting (vv. 1–2)
II. Purpose (vv. 3–4)
III. Warning (vv. 5–16)
IV. Instructions (vv. 17–23)
V. Doxology (vv. 24–25)

THE GENERAL EPISTLE OF

JUDE

JUDE, the servant of Jesus Christ, and brother of
James, to them that are sanctified by God the
Father, and preserved in Jesus Christ, *and* called:
2 Mercy unto you, and peace, and love, be
multiplied.
3 Beloved, when I gave all diligence to write unto
you of the common salvation, it was needful for
me to write unto you, and exhort *you* that ye
should earnestly contend for the faith which was
once delivered unto the saints.
4 For there are certain men crept in unawares,
who were before of old ordained to this condemnation, ungodly men, turning the grace of our
God into lasciviousness, and denying the only
Lord God, and our Lord Jesus Christ.
5 I will therefore put you in remembrance,
though ye once knew this, how that the Lord,
having saved the people out of the land of Egypt,
afterward destroyed them that believed not.
6 And the angels which kept not their first estate,
but left their own habitation, he hath reserved
in everlasting chains under darkness unto the
judgment of the great day.
7 Even as Sodom and Gomorrha, and the cities
about them in like manner, giving themselves
over to fornication, and going after strange
flesh, are set forth for an example, suffering the
vengeance of eternal fire.
8 Likewise also these *filthy* dreamers defile the
flesh, despise dominion, and speak evil of dignities.
9 Yet Michael the archangel, when contending
with the devil he disputed about the body of
Moses, durst not bring against him a railing accusation, but said, The Lord rebuke thee.
10 But these speak evil of those things which they
know not: but what they know naturally, as brute

GREETING (vv. 1–2)

1 *the servant of Jesus Christ.* Humbly introducing himself as a bond servant of Jesus Christ, though he was also His half brother. *sanctified . . . preserved . . . called.* Set apart as holy, kept safe, and summoned by God's Word—the first of many triplets in this letter. God's preservation by Christ's keeping is Jude's source of comfort in the face of apostasy.

2 *Mercy . . . peace . . . love.* The second triplet. *be multiplied.* Jude's prayer for the increase of Christian graces is similar to the greeting in Peter's letters (1 Peter 1:2; 2 Peter 1:2).

PURPOSE (vv. 3–4)

3 *gave all diligence.* Was eager. *common salvation.* Salvation shared by all believers in Christ. Though he had wanted to write about a happier subject, he felt the necessity and duty as a faithful church leader of taking the less desirable task. *earnestly contend.* Exert intense effort by striving to gain or keep something (Luke 13:24; 1 Tim. 6:12; 2 Tim. 4:7). It does not mean to be contentious. Jude's concern is for the safety of believers, so his exhortation is that believers persevere in the faith. The warning examples that follow (vv. 5–16) strengthen his instructions to persevere (vv. 17–23).

4 *crept in unawares.* Slipped in undetected (Gal. 2:4). The covert entrance of false teachers into the church is the reason for Jude's earnest appeal. See the parallel in 2 Peter 2:1. *before of old ordained to this condemnation.* Literally, "in ancient times have been written of beforehand for this judgment"; predestined in God's decree to damnation for their sins (Rom. 9:22; 1 Peter 2:8). Even false teachers are part of God's predetermined plan (Deut. 13:1–3). *lasciviousness.* Lustfulness, sexual immorality. These false teachers taught *grace* as if it were permission for immorality, possibly a fatal distortion of the gospel preached by Paul (Rom. 3:8; 6:1–2; 2 Peter 3:15–16).

WARNING (vv. 5–16)

5 *put you in remembrance.* Jude gives three reminders of how God has punished apostates in the past (vv. 5–7). *people out of the land of Egypt.* God destroyed many Israelites for their unbelief and blasphemy even after they had experienced physical deliverance from Egypt (Num. 14:29; Ps. 95:7–11; Heb. 3:18).

6 *the angels which kept not their first estate.* Some angels rebelled against God's authority by refusing to stay within the position God ordained for them (*kept not their first estate, but left their own habitation*). God now guards them for the final judgment (2 Peter 2:4).

7 *fornication.* Sexual immorality. *going after strange flesh.* Pursued homosexual relationships (Gen. 19:5). The people of *Sodom and Gomorrha* are an example of the punishment of *eternal fire* coming upon all ungodly people (Gen. 19; Luke 17:29; 2 Peter 2:6).

8 *dreamers.* They spoke ignorantly about imagined unrealities (cf. Col. 2:18) and remained ungrounded in the truth (vv. 18–20). On vv. 8–13, see the parallel in 2 Peter 2:10–17.

9 *Michael.* One of the chief angels (*archangel*), a spiritual prince who stands for God's people (Dan. 10:13,21; 12:1; 1 Thess. 4:16; Rev. 12:7). *body of Moses.* He died outside of the land of Canaan, and was buried, but not by a man (Deut. 34:5–6). *durst not.* Was not so bold. *The Lord rebuke thee.* Called upon God to silence Satan, the accuser of God's people (Zech. 3:1–5). If Michael did not speak proudly against the Devil,

beasts, in those things they corrupt themselves.
11 Woe unto them! for they have gone in the
way of Cain, and ran greedily after the error of
Balaam for reward, and perished in the gainsay-
ing of Core.
12 These are spots in your feasts of charity, when
they feast with you, feeding themselves without
fear: clouds *they are* without water, carried about
of winds; trees whose fruit withereth, without
fruit, twice dead, plucked up by the roots;
13 Raging waves of the sea, foaming out their
own shame; wandering stars, to whom is reserved
the blackness of darkness for ever.
14 And Enoch also, the seventh from Adam,
prophesied of these, saying, Behold, the Lord
cometh with ten thousands of his saints,
15 To execute judgment upon all, and to
convince all that are ungodly among them of all
their ungodly deeds which they have ungodly
committed, and of all their hard *speeches* which
ungodly sinners have spoken against him.
16 These are murmurers, complainers, walking
after their own lusts; and their mouth speaketh
great swelling *words*, having men's persons in
admiration because of advantage.
17 But, beloved, remember ye the words which
were spoken before of the apostles of our Lord
Jesus Christ;
18 How that they told you there should be mock-
ers in the last time, who should walk after their
own ungodly lusts.
19 These be they who separate themselves, sen-
sual, having not the Spirit.
20 But ye, beloved, building up yourselves on
your most holy faith, praying in the Holy Ghost,
21 Keep yourselves in the love of God, looking for

---

much more should mere men not speak proudly about things beyond our knowledge or authority (Ps. 131:1).

11 *way of Cain . . . error of Balaam . . . gainsaying of Core.* Three more examples from the Old Testament of rebellions punished by God: Cain's sin (Gen. 4:5–8), Balaam's greed (Num. 22; 2 Peter 2:15), and Korah's rebellion (Num. 16:1; 26:9).

12–13 *spots.* Could be translated as hidden "reefs" that destroy ships. *feasts of charity.* Love feasts, either the Lord's Supper or fellowship meals (Acts 2:46; 1 Cor. 11:17–34). *clouds . . . without water . . . trees whose fruit withereth.* Empty promises made by those who are aimless, useless, ungrounded, and dead. *Raging waves.* A commotion that produces nothing but restlessness, instability, and foam (Isa. 57:20; Eph. 4:14). *wandering stars.* Comets that may astonish observers for a time but soon fade in the darkness of the sky.

14–15 *Enoch.* See Gen. 5:21–24; Luke 3:37–38. *prophesied.* Spoke words given by the Holy Spirit (2 Peter 1:20–21). Jude was guided by the Holy Spirit to quote and validate his prophecy as it was preserved in Jewish tradition. *ten thousands of his saints.* A vast army of holy ones, probably angels (Deut. 33:2; Ps. 68:17; Dan. 7:10; Zech. 14:5; Rev. 5:11; 19:14). *convince.* Rebuke. As early as the *seventh* generation from creation, the Lord had revealed the coming of judgment day, but fools still dismiss it.

16 *having men's persons in admiration because of advantage.* Showing favoritism for personal gain, like a judge who takes bribes (Deut. 10:17; 2 Chron. 19:6–7). See the parallel to this verse in 2 Peter 2:18.

INSTRUCTIONS (vv. 17–23)

17–23 This section contains three sets of instructions to the readers on the proper response to false teaching (vv. 17–19, 20–21,22–23).

17–19 *Remember* the apostolic teaching found in Scripture, including the warning of false and wicked teachers who scoff at the truth (*mockers*, see the parallel in 2 Peter 3:3). Apostasy should not surprise us (Acts 20:28–32). *separate themselves.* Divide the church. *sensual.* Natural, having to do with things of this world (1 Cor. 2:14; 15:44,46; James 3:15). *having not the Spirit.* Not indwelt by the Holy Spirit (Rom. 8:9).

20–21 *Keep yourselves in the love of God.* Protect yourself from anything that would draw you away from God the Father, trusting that in His love He has sanctified you and is preserving you (vv. 1,24). How to do this is succinctly explained with three participles. *building up yourselves on your most holy faith.* Growing in understanding and love of the truths given us by God (v. 3)—the opposite of following false teaching (v. 18). *praying in the Holy Ghost.* Regularly talking with the Father by the knowledge and assurance given by the Spirit through Christ (Eph. 6:18; cf. Gal. 4:6)—the opposite of being devoid of the Spirit (v. 19). *looking for the mercy of our Lord Jesus Christ.* Anticipating with great hope the grace to be experienced when the Lord returns to give us *eternal life* in its full glory (2 Tim. 1:18)—the opposite of living for this world (v. 18). Note how these verses reflect the Trinity; knowing God as Father, Son, and Holy Spirit is extremely practical in Christian spirituality (Eph. 2:18; 3:14–17).

22–23 *Have compassion* on people who are in spiritual danger, and *save* them if possible from the *fire* of hell (v. 7). Contending for the faith (v. 3) requires us to have compassion for the lost, especially for those in the church in danger of apostasy. *making a difference.* Could be understood as "contending" (v. 9; Acts 11:2), "exercising discernment" (Matt. 16:3; 1 Cor. 11:29), or "those who waver in doubt," the persons on whom we must have compassion (Matt. 21:21; James 1:6). *hating even the garment spotted by the flesh.* Old Testament language for avoiding ceremonial contamination (Lev. 15:17), here applied to the care needed to avoid becoming polluted by the error or sin of others (1 Cor. 10:14; 2 Cor. 6:17).

DOXOLOGY (vv. 24–25)

24 Jude concludes with a grand statement of praise to God for His preserving grace (cf. Rom. 16:25–27). *him that is able to keep . . . and to present.* God will exercise His infinite power to preserve His people through all temptations (v. 1; John 6:39; 10:28–29; 17:12) and bring them to enjoy Him forever *with exceeding joy* (Pss. 16:11; 43:4). *his glory.* The intense brightness of His holiness (1 Tim. 6:16).

25 Jude's doxology concludes with a final triplet of praises: *glory and majesty.* God's honor and infinite greatness. *dominion and power.* God's sovereign and unbounded authority. *both now and ever.* The infinite extent of God's glory through all ages. Our faith acknowledges who God is and bows before Him in worship.

Thoughts for Personal/Family Worship

1. **Contending for the faith does not begin with a direct attack against error but rather with a lifestyle of godliness built on biblical truth. Personal piety is the best protection against ungodliness. The holiness of the whole church is more important than public action**

the mercy of our Lord Jesus Christ unto eternal life.
22 And of some have compassion, making a difference:
23 And others save with fear, pulling *them* out of the fire; hating even the garment spotted by the flesh.
24 Now unto him that is able to keep you from falling, and to present *you* faultless before the presence of his glory with exceeding joy,
25 To the only wise God our Saviour, *be* glory and majesty, dominion and power, both now and ever. Amen.

---

against error. Showing compassion to the perishing should come after we are grounded in the most holy faith and when we are actively avoiding all associations with error that tarnish our witness. How can you grow in both godliness and compassion without compromise?

2. **Realize that false teachers are still in the church among the saints today. Note that Jude describes people who are presently in the church, not people who have already left the church. There will always be hypocrisy, ungodliness, and even apostate people among the gathering of believers. The church, especially its elders, should be prepared to confront error in its midst and to expel those who refuse to repent. How can you best guard yourself against false teachers?**
3. **Receive spiritual encouragement from God's preservation of both His church corporately and His people individually. As God delivered His people in the past, so He continues to keep His church in the present and future. Likewise, God preserves each believer individually. Though there are many causes for stumbling, believers are graciously kept from apostasy since Christ is both able and willing to keep them. God preserves His people so that they will both keep and contend for the faith. Do you feel your need for His preserving power today? Turn vv. 24–25 into a prayer for yourself and your loved ones for faith and perseverance to the glory of God.**

Holy
HOLY HOLY
LORD GOD
Almighty
WHICH WAS
AND
IS & IS
TO COME

REVELATION 4:8

INTRODUCTION TO THE BOOK OF REVELATION

Authorship: The author identifies himself as "John" (1:1,4,9; 21:2; 22:8), a "servant" or slave of Jesus Christ (1:1) and "brother" and "companion in tribulation" to his readers. The name John was common among first-century Jews (Matt. 3:1; Acts 4:6; 12:12), being a form of the Hebrew name *Johanan*, meaning, "the Lord is gracious" (2 Kings 25:23; 1 Chron. 3:15; Jer. 40:8, etc.).

Various scholars have argued that this John is not the apostle known to us in the Gospels and Acts. Some reasons given for this view are: (1) Eusebius wrote (c. AD 325) that an early writer named Papias spoke of two Johns, one the apostle and the other John the elder (cf. 2 John 1; 3 John 1). (2) Revelation is an apocalyptic writing, and such were commonly presented under the pseudonym (false name) of a famous person of a previous age. (3) The Greek grammar of Revelation is much rougher than that of the Gospel of John or the epistles of John.

In reply, we may observe: (1) We know little of Papias, having only fragments of his writings quoted by Irenaeus and Eusebius. Even if this is the correct interpretation of his words (which some scholars dispute), Papias does not say anything directly about the authorship of Revelation. (2) Revelation does not fit the pattern of Jewish apocalyptic books written under the pseudonym of a figure from a previous age because the apostle John was a person of the same era when Revelation was written. Revelation follows the pattern of a prophetic apocalyptic such as Daniel, which identifies its true author (see the Introduction to Daniel). (3) It is possible that John used a secretary who influenced his style in the Gospel of John and his epistles. It may also be that John's grammar in Revelation was affected by the harsh conditions he had endured.

A strong argument may be made that John the apostle wrote Revelation. (1) The author identified himself simply as "John" when addressing Christians in seven locations in Asia Minor (1:11). This implies that he was well known in the churches and needed no title. (2) Scholars note the Semitic style of the Greek and the many allusions to the Old Testament that imply that the writer was a Jew from Palestine. (3) He claimed to be the writer of a "prophecy" (1:3; 22:7–8) by supernatural revelation from Jesus Christ (1:1; 22:16), a message of divine authority (2:18–19) binding whole churches (v. 7), thus placing himself on the level of the prophets and apostles. (4) He used expressions also found in the Gospel of John, such as identifying Christ as "the Word" (John 1:1; Rev. 19:13) and "the Lamb" (John 1:29; Rev. 5:6), and offering the water of life to those who thirst (John 7:37; Rev. 22:17). (5) Justin Martyr (writing c. AD 155), identified the author of Revelation as the apostle John, and later writers in the second century, such as Irenaeus, Tertullian, and Clement of Alexandria, agreed. Therefore, we conclude that the author of Revelation is the apostle John, the son of Zebedee and brother of James.

Date: John wrote during a period of persecution against Christians, being banished to the island of Patmos (1:9). Two main dates have been proposed, one shortly after the fire of Rome in the reign of Emperor Nero (AD 64), and another just after the end of the reign of Emperor Domitian (AD 95). Most scholars over the last century have favored the later date.

Theme: The victory of Jesus Christ over the powers of evil.

Purpose: To strengthen Christ's churches facing persecution and temptation in this world.

Major Problem of Interpretation:

General Approaches to Revelation's Symbolism

The Apocalypse, or book of Revelation, is a book of symbols and has evoked very different interpretations, depending on how one approaches it. The *preterist* approach interprets the book almost entirely in reference to the events of John's time in the first century AD. Thus Revelation is taken to be a book about past events in the Roman Empire, except perhaps for the last chapters. The *historicist* approach reads Revelation as a chart of church history, tracing the works of Christ from His first coming through His return and the challenges to the true church from such movements as the Roman papacy and Islam. The *futurist* approach is almost the opposite of the *preterist*, seeing Revelation as a timeline of future events in the years just before Christ comes in glory. The *idealist* approach understands John's vision to reveal general spiritual principles that are always true and are not limited to a particular event in history.

Each view has weaknesses. Both the preterist and idealist approaches tend to neglect Revelation's strong expectation of Christ's total victory over evil at His future, glorious coming in human history. The historicist and futurist approaches tend to arbitrarily assign fulfillment of Revelation's symbols to events that would have meant nothing to John's original audience, whether European politics or modern technology and warfare.

However, each view also has strengths from which we can learn. With the preterists, we should interpret the symbols of Revelation according to the first-century historical and cultural context, that is to say in light of the church's persecution in the Roman Empire. With the historicists, we should recognize that cataclysmic symbols in Scripture may be at least partially fulfilled in the ordinary events of history. With the futurists, we must see Revelation presenting us with a hope that is to be ultimately fulfilled only in the second coming of Christ. And with the idealists, we gain much by recognizing that John unveils principles of spiritual warfare that guide the church through the centuries until her Lord returns.

Therefore, the best interpretation of Revelation arises from an *eclectic* approach that brings together insights from all four viewpoints. This fits with the use of symbolic language and stories in other parts of Scripture. The parables of our Lord give us examples of symbolic teaching that may be fulfilled in ordinary historical events in the near future (Matt. 21:33–46) or Christ's coming in glory (25:14–30). Other parables simply describe spiritual truths applicable to many periods of time (Mark 4:1–9; Luke 10:30–37). Symbols of cataclysmic events sometimes represent ordinary human victories in Scripture (Ps. 18).

One must be cautious in interpreting such a symbolic book. The Bible sometimes uses elaborate imagery where the message is not found in each detail so much as in the whole picture (Ezek. 16). Even the language of Christ coming to judge may not always refer to the second coming so much as to His providence in history (Rev. 2:5,16,22–23; 3:3). Numbers in Revelation often have symbolic value; one sees many instances of seven (for perfection, Gen. 2:1–3), ten (for completeness, Job 19:3; Eccl. 7:19), twelve (for God's people, Gen. 49:28; Matt. 10:2), and their fractions (3 ½) and multiples (twenty-four, a thousand, 12,000, and 144,000). Other numbers without much symbolic value such as five, eight, nine, and eleven rarely appear.

One key to interpreting Revelation is to understand its symbols by comparing them to similar images in the Old Testament. Revelation presents the climax of the hopes presented by the prophets and therefore draws heavily upon their language. The study notes that follow provide a multitude of cross-references to Old Testament texts that significantly illuminate the message of Revelation. Another key to Revelation is to remember that its aim is always to exalt the Lord Jesus Christ, for He is the hope offered in the whole Bible.

Questions of Genre

The interpretation of Revelation is also complicated by the fact that it is a blend of three genres or literary styles. (1) It is *prophecy* (1:3; 10:11; 22:7,10,18–19). Though we often think of prophecy as prediction, most biblical prophecy consists of exhortation and comfort (1 Cor. 14:3), calling people to covenant faithfulness to the Lord in light of His faithfulness to His promises and threats. This prophecy revolves around calling people to persevere in glorifying God and the Lamb (Rev. 4–5) instead of any man or idol. It is a prophetic call to follow Jesus to the end, "for the testimony of Jesus is the spirit of prophecy" (Rev. 19:10).

(2) Revelation, almost by definition, is *apocalyptic*. (The Greek word for "revelation" in Rev. 1:1 is *apokalupsis*.) The book comes in the form of symbolic visions somewhat similar to writings of

various Jewish authors between 200 BC–AD 100 describing the battle and ultimate victory of God against evil. However, the apocalyptic form of Revelation is rooted most directly in the divinely inspired dreams and visions found in the book of Daniel. We may also see something of a precedent in the dreams associated with the patriarch Joseph (Gen. 37:5–11; 40:5–19; 41:1–32).

In such visions, the Lord reveals the secrets of His future dealings with the nations of the world (Gen. 40:8; 41:16,25,28; Dan. 2:19–23,28). God also unveils a heavenly world of angelic activity and messages (4:13; 7:16; 8:13,16–17; 9:21; 10:5–6,12–14,20–21; 12:1). He makes known His sovereign control over earthly events to bring His kingdom for His people (Gen. 41:32; Dan. 2:37,44; 4:17,25; 7:13–14,22,27; 9:24–27). All of these elements appear in Revelation. Whereas Jewish apocalyptic literature was pessimistic as the remnant passively waited until the final cataclysm, Revelation is optimistic, for believers are already now overcoming by the blood of the Lamb (Rev. 12:11), and the gospel is saving many people from every nation (7:9,14). As a result, Revelation calls the church to active perseverance in its costly witness to Christ (1:2,9,13; 6:9; 11:3,7; 12:11,17; 17:6; 19:10; 20:4), who is the Faithful Witness (1:5; 3:14; 22:16–20).

(3) Revelation is an *epistle* or letter. Like Paul's epistles, it begins with an identification of its author and intended recipients and a blessing of "grace" and "peace" from God (1:1–5), and it ends with a blessing of "grace" (22:21). It addresses seven actual churches located near Ephesus in western Asia Minor (modern Turkey). Like Jeremiah's prophetic letter to the exiles in Babylon (Jer. 29:1–23), it brings the word of the Lord to a specific group of people and addresses their conditions (Rev. 2–3). Therefore, though Revelation is a message for all Christians of all ages, its contents must be understood in a manner relevant to those churches in their historical and cultural situation. It is a personal book, written for suffering saints (1:9) and intended to be read in the churches for their blessing (v. 3).

Structure and Flow

Some interpreters read the book of Revelation as a continuous story presented in chronological order, almost as if it were a graphic novel or an historical documentary in video form. However, Revelation presents itself in the form of cycles, often appearing in lists of seven: seven churches, seven seals, seven trumpets, and seven bowls.

One way that the cycles are evident is that Revelation repeatedly takes the reader to the return of Christ. Consider how the following visions are parallel to each other.

- The opening of the sixth seal brings cosmic disturbances, a massive earthquake that overthrows every mountain and island, the rolling up of the heavens like a scroll, and terror at the coming wrath of the Lord Jesus (6:12–17).
- The seventh trumpet heralds the coming of God's reign to this world and judgment day for the righteous and the wicked (11:15–19).
- The seventh bowl brings a hailstorm and earthquake that destroys the cities and every island and mountain (like the sixth seal) as God causes Babylon to drink the cup of His wrath (16:17–21). The events of this bowl match Ezekiel's vision of God's judgment against Gog (Ezek. 38:2,18–22). They are also preceded in the vision by the gathering of world powers for "the battle [or war] of that great day of God Almighty" (Rev. 16:14).
- The vision of Christ coming on the white horse also alludes to the vision of Ezekiel against Gog with its invitation for birds to feast on the bodies of all His enemies (Rev. 19:17–18; Ezek. 39:1,11,17–20). This allusion to the judgment on Gog, together with the gathering of the world's armies "to make war against him that sat on the horse" (Rev. 19:19), parallels this vision with the seventh bowl.
- Revelation explicitly names the "Gog and Magog" of Ezekiel when the nations gather for battle after the "thousand years" (20:7–8), referring to the same battle as in the seventh bowl and the vision of Christ on the white horse. The same Greek phrase, literally, "to gather them for war," is used of Satan's activity in both the sixth seal and the rebellion after the thousand years (16:14; 20:8). Just as in the sixth seal and the seventh bowl, God's presence causes "the earth and the heaven [to flee] away" (v. 11). Like the seventh trumpet, judgment day arrives (vv. 12–13).

The strong parallels between these events indicate that Revelation is structured in cycles. After the introduction and initial messages to the seven churches (chs. 1–3), each cycle describes from a different perspective the church's conflict and ultimate victory at Christ's return. The outline below reflects these seven major cycles.

The Millennium

The millennium ("thousand years") of ch. 20 has been interpreted in widely different ways. The *premillennial* view holds that Christ will return before (*pre-*) He will institute a golden age of peace lasting until a final rebellion and judgment day. Dispensationalists understand this period to revolve around the elevation of physical Israel over the nations. The *postmillennial* view holds that Christ will return after (*post-*) the church has enjoyed a golden age of success in missions and transforming society. The *amillennial* view holds that the millennium does not (*a-*) refer to a physical kingdom in the future but symbolizes the spiritual kingdom of God present now in the church's missionary advance and heavenly reign, even as it suffers persecution and waits for Christ's return and judgment day. All these views have advocates among evangelical Christians.

With all due respect to Christians who hold differing views, the notes at ch. 20 present an amillennial interpretation, supported by the following reasons:

- The New Testament teaches that God's promises to Israel have already begun to come true in a spiritual, international kingdom and will yet be fulfilled in ultimate glory, not in a nationalistic, earthly reign (Matt. 12:28; Luke 17:20–21; John 18:36–37; Acts 15:13–18; Rom. 2:28–29; 4:16; 14:17; Gal. 3:28–29; 4:26; Heb. 12:22–24,28).
- Scripture indicates that Christ's coming in glory, the resurrection of both the righteous and the wicked, judgment day, and the end of this age all take place together in history, as opposed to being dispersed over a thousand years (Dan. 12:2; Matt. 13:39–43; 16:27; 24:29–31; 25:31–46; John 5:28–29; Acts 24:15; 1 Thess. 4:13—5:11).
- The premillennial view would mingle together earthly people and a kingdom in this fallen world with the presence of the heavenly Lord and His glorified, resurrected people—an apparently incompatible mixture (1 Cor. 15:42–44,50).
- The postmillennial view pictures this age as a time of growing righteousness and peace, but the Bible forecasts growing sin in society and trouble for the church (Matt. 24:7–12, 21–24; 2 Thess. 2:1–12; 2 Tim. 3:1–3).
- Revelation is a book of symbolic visions, and therefore one must interpret the numbers (thousand) and images (binding with a chain and sealing in a pit) of ch. 20 in a similar manner to the symbols used elsewhere in the book. This is not inconsistent with a literal interpretation of God's Word but a recognition that parts of the Scriptures communicate with metaphors and symbols.
- Revelation follows a cyclic structure, repeatedly bringing the reader at the end of each cycle to the return of Christ (see Structure and Flow, above). Chapter 19 ends the cycle of the conquest of Babylon (Rev. 17–19) with the victorious return of Christ. Chapter 20, like ch. 12, steps back to consider the whole era between Christ's first and second comings before moving ahead to symbolically reveal judgment day and eternity.
- The picture of Satan being bound and sealed in the abyss in the present time is sometimes objected to because he remains active in the world. However, other Scriptures use just as absolute language to testify to Christ's conquest of the Devil at His first coming. As a result of Christ's death, "now shall the prince of this world be cast out" (John 12:31); he is "judged" (16:11). Christ came to "bind" him (Matt. 12:29) and has "spoiled" him (Col. 2:15), having died in order to "destroy him" (Heb. 2:14). Such absolute language does not mean that Satan no longer has any influence, but it does teach that Christ's victory is complete and that the Devil cannot stop the Lord Jesus from saving lost sinners among the nations.

For more details, see the specific study notes at Rev. 20:1–3; 4–6; 7–10.

Synopsis: *The Contribution of Revelation to Redemptive Revelation*

The message of Revelation is rich and complex, but we may summarize it with four key words that appear through the book: *throne*, *Lamb*, *testimony*, and *overcome*, representing the themes of kingdom, Christ, gospel proclamation, and perseverance.

First, Revelation announces the kingdom or reign of God (1:9; 11:15,17; 12:10; 19:6). It presents history as two kingdoms at war (11:7; 12:7,17; 13:7; 16:14; 20:8), a battle over who has the authority and power to reign. The Greek word for *throne* (sometimes translated "seat" in the KJV) appears about four dozen times in Revelation, more than in any other book in the Bible. Evil powers sit on thrones as they claim sovereignty and use their strength to propagate evil in the world. Satan's throne on earth threatens the church with suffering and martyrdom (2:13), and he shares his demonic power with the wicked rulers of mankind (13:2). But the throne that dominates the perspective of Revelation is the throne of God, who is called simply "Him that sat on the throne" (4:2–6,9–10; 5:1,7,13; 6:16; 7:10,15; 11:16; 19:4; 20:11; 21:5). In other words, by nature God reigns with absolute power. His decree (5:1) will prevail to punish His enemies with His wrath (6:16) and overthrow the thrones of evil (16:10). Satan's forces have only limited power granted to them by God (9:1,4–5), and even in their rebellion they do His sovereign will (17:17). God is also sovereign in judgment. He is the Judge who will summon all mankind, living and dead, before His throne to give an account for their works (20:11–12).

God's sovereignty is sweet to the saints. God's throne is the source of saving grace for His people (1:4) and a sign of Christ's saving power and victory (7:17; 12:5). Remarkably, God's throne becomes a symbol of His sharing His power and reign with the saints by their union with Christ (3:21). Even now the people of God are enthroned in heaven (4:4; 11:16; 20:4). His reigning power guarantees that He will bring all His own into the blessings of the new creation (21:5). The symbol of a river flowing from a throne shows that God's very reign over His people will be their life and joy. To be ruled by Him who sits on the throne is no curse, but salvation from the curse (22:3). Therefore, the throne of God is the symbolic focal point of the glad worship of the saints and angels (4:9–11; 5:11–14; 7:9–12,15; 14:3; 19:4; 22:3).

Second, at the center of Revelation stands the Lord Jesus Christ as the Mediator of salvation and judgment from the enthroned God. Revelation adorns Christ with many titles and symbols of majesty (especially chs. 1,19), but He is preeminently the *Lamb* (twenty-seven times in Revelation). This image of His priestly self-sacrifice (5:6) grounds salvation in Christ's redeeming death for our sins ("blood," 5:9; 7:14; 12:11; cf. 1:5). His violent death like a lamb fulfilled God's eternal decree of salvation for His elect people (13:8; 21:27). To them He is betrothed, and they await the wedding and marriage feast of the Lamb (19:7,9; 21:9), an image of His love for the church and union with it.

Yet this title of Lamb is associated not just with His death but also with His victory, power, and glory (5:6; 7:10,17; 14:1; 17:14). It even appears in the striking phrase "the wrath of the Lamb" (6:16; cf. 14:10). Over a quarter of the references to the Lamb (seven times) appear in the glorious depiction of the new Jerusalem (21:9,14,22,23,27; 22:1,3; cf. 7:17). There He is the church's heavenly husband, eternal temple, radiant light, sovereign king, fountain of life, and blessed vision of glory. In eternity Christ will be everything to believers, and all because He died like a lamb to take away their sins.

Third, God calls the church to serve and suffer as prophetic witnesses to Christ in the world. The language of *testimony*, including words such as *testify* and *witness* (sometimes translated "martyr"), appears sixteen times in Revelation. The background of this idea lies in Isaiah, where the Lord conducts a court case against the nations and calls His people as witnesses that He alone is the Lord and Savior (Isa. 43:9–13). The Word of God is "the testimony of Jesus Christ" (Rev. 1:2,9; 12:17; cf. 19:10; 20:4), and Christ is the preeminent "faithful witness" (1:5; 3:14; cf. 22:16,20) whom believers imitate even to the point of death (2:13; 6:9; 12:11; 17:6; 20:4). Holding to the testimony of Jesus and obeying the laws of God are defining marks of the true church (12:17). The church's prophet-like ministry engages divine power and yet earthly sufferings (11:3,7). Thus Revelation is a book of missions and martyrdom.

Fourth, the main thrust of Revelation's message is to call the church to persevere in its faith, obedience, and mission by its confident expectation of Christ's coming. This theme appears prominently in the use of the word *overcome* (also translated "conquer," "prevail," or "gotten the victory") seventeen times in Revelation. Again Christ is central to this theme, for He alone has overcome such that He is worthy to execute God's decree and bring salvation and judgment (5:5). Even now He is conquering the world, riding forth into the nations as the divine Warrior to bring truth and righteousness through the gospel (6:2).

By their union with Christ in God's eternal election and their effectual calling, the faithful share in Christ's victory (17:14). The Devil and his evil servants overcome the church physically (11:7; 13:7), but believers overcome the world spiritually by clinging to the gospel testimony and taking up their crosses (12:11), sharing in the suffering of the Lion who overcame by dying as the Lamb (5:5–6). Therefore, the church can persevere in joyful hope, knowing that those who overcome the world through faith in Christ will also share in all the delights of the new creation (2:7,11,17,26; 3:5,12,21)—the pleasures of childlike intimacy with the covenant God (21:7). The visions of Revelation are very practical, giving experiential comfort and endurance for spiritual warriors fleeing the city of destruction and fighting their way to the celestial city.

Outline: I. The Son of Man and the Seven Churches (1:1—3:22)

- A. Greetings, Blessing, and Doxology (1:1–8)
- B. Vision of the Glorious Son of Man (1:9–20)
- C. Messages for the Churches (2:1—3:22)
  1. To the Church of Ephesus (2:1–7)
  2. To the Church of Smyrna (2:8–11)
  3. To the Church of Pergamos (2:12–17)
  4. To the Church of Thyatira (2:18–29)
  5. To the Church of Sardis (3:1–6)
  6. To the Church of Philadelphia (3:7–13)
  7. To the Church of Laodicea (3:14–22)

II. The Lamb and the Seven Seals of God's Scroll (4:1—8:1)

- A. Heavenly Vision of God on the Throne (4:1–11)
- B. The Scroll and the Lamb that Was Slain (5:1–14)
- C. The Opening of the Six Seals (6:1–17)
- D. Visions of the Sealed, Washed, and Victorious Church (7:1–17)
- E. The Seventh Seal: Silence (8:1)

III. The Seven Trumpets (8:2—11:19)

- A. The Saints' Prayers and the First Four Trumpets (8:2–13)
- B. The First Two Woes: The Fifth and Sixth Trumpets (9:1–21)
- C. The Mighty Angel and the Little Scroll (10:1–11)
- D. The Two Witnesses (11:1–14)
- E. The Seventh Trumpet: The Kingdom and the Judgment (11:15–19)

IV. The War with the Dragon (12:1—14:20)

- A. The Woman, the Child, and the Dragon (12:1–17)
- B. The Beast with Seven Heads (13:1–10)
- C. The Beast with Horns Like a Lamb (13:11–18)
- D. The Lamb and the Redeemed (14:1–5)
- E. Three Angels of Gospel and Judgment (14:6–13)
- F. The Two Harvests (14:14–20)

V. The Seven Bowls of Wrath (15:1—16:21)

- A. The Heavenly Temple Full of Worship and Wrath (15:1–8)
- B. The Seven Bowls of Wrath Poured Out (16:1–21)

VI. The Fall of Babylon the Whore (17:1—19:21)

- A. The Vision of the Whore (17:1–18)
- B. The Fall of the City (18:1–24)
- C. The Worship of God (19:1–10)
- D. The King on the White Horse (19:11–21)

VII. The Victory of Jerusalem the Bride (20:1—22:21)

- A. The Binding of Satan, the Last Battle, and the Judgment (20:1–15)
- B. The Promise of All Things New (21:1–8)
- C. The Vision of the Bride-City (21:9—22:5)
- D. Concluding Promises, Warnings, and Grace (22:6–21)

THE REVELATION OF SAINT JOHN THE DIVINE

CHAPTER 1

THE Revelation of Jesus Christ, which God gave
unto him, to shew unto his servants things which
must shortly come to pass; and he sent and signi-
fied *it* by his angel unto his servant John:
2 Who bare record of the word of God, and of the
testimony of Jesus Christ, and of all things that
he saw.
3 Blessed *is* he that readeth, and they that hear
the words of this prophecy, and keep those things
which are written therein: for the time *is* at hand.
4 John to the seven churches which are in Asia:
Grace *be* unto you, and peace, from him which is,
and which was, and which is to come; and from
the seven Spirits which are before his throne;
5 And from Jesus Christ, *who is* the faithful
witness, *and* the first begotten of the dead, and
the prince of the kings of the earth. Unto him that
loved us, and washed us from our sins in his own
blood,
6 And hath made us kings and priests unto God
and his Father; to him *be* glory and dominion for
ever and ever. Amen.
7 Behold, he cometh with clouds; and every eye
shall see him, and they *also* which pierced him:
and all kindreds of the earth shall wail because of
him. Even so, Amen.
8 I am Alpha and Omega, the beginning and the
ending, saith the Lord, which is, and which was,
and which is to come, the Almighty.
9 I John, who also am your brother, and
companion in tribulation, and in the kingdom
and patience of Jesus Christ, was in the isle that
is called Patmos, for the word of God, and for the
testimony of Jesus Christ.
10 I was in the Spirit on the Lord's day, and heard
behind me a great voice, as of a trumpet,
11 Saying, I am Alpha and Omega, the first and
the last: and, What thou seest, write in a book,
and send *it* unto the seven churches which are in

THE SON OF MAN AND THE SEVEN CHURCHES (1:1—3:22)

Chapter 1: ***John greets seven churches of Asia Minor and describes his vision of the risen and glorified Lord Jesus Christ.***

Greetings, Blessing, and Doxology (1:1–8)

1:1 *Revelation.* Previously hidden truths about *Christ*, given by *God* the Father (John 14:24) for Christ to make known. *shew.* Show. *his servants.* God's willing slaves (7:3; 19:5). *shortly come to pass.* Revelation had immediate relevance for John's early readers as they faced persecution such as that under Domitian. *signified.* Made known by signs, through an *angel* (22:16).
1:2 *bare record.* Testified.
1:3 *therein.* In it. Scripture reading blesses the church (1 Tim. 4:13). *the time is at hand.* The last days have begun (Acts 2:17; see note at v. 9); Christ may return anytime (Matt. 24:42; James 5:9).
1:4 *Asia.* Province in western Turkey. *Grace* and *peace* come from each person in the Trinity, for all are one God. *him which is, and which was, and which is to come.* The eternal "I AM" (Ex. 3:14; John 8:58). *seven Spirits.* The Holy Spirit, described in the sevenfold perfection of His graces upon Christ (3:1; 5:6; Isa. 11:2). No mere angel is the source of grace. *before his throne.* Shining like light (4:5) and flowing like living water (22:1–2) from the King to His people.
1:5 *faithful witness.* Ultimate Prophet; model of testimony to God's glory at any cost (2:13; Isa. 43:10; 55:4; John 3:32; 18:37). *first begotten.* Firstborn, the preeminent Son raised from the dead (Ps. 89:26–27; Col. 1:18). *prince of the kings.* Ruler over the kings, supreme King over all emperors. *Unto him.* Beginning of a doxology to Christ (vv. 5–6). *washed us from our sins in his own blood.* Priest and sacrifice (Heb. 9:13–14), who cleansed His people from the guilt of their sins (Ps. 51:1–9; 1 Cor. 6:9).
1:6 *kings and priests.* Sharing Christ's anointing and privilege (5:10; 20:6), as promised to Israel and fulfilled in the new covenant (Ex. 19:6; 1 Peter 2:9). *to him be glory.* Christ is worthy of our worship, for He is the Redeemer (5:9,12).
1:7 *cometh with clouds.* See Dan. 7:13; Matt. 24:30; 26:64. *kindreds.* Clans or tribes. *pierced him . . . wail.* In grief over their sins against Christ (Zech. 12:10).
1:8 *Alpha and Omega.* First and last letters of the Greek alphabet; thus the first cause and ultimate purpose of all things (Col. 1:16). *Almighty.* Majestic ruler of all (Job 37:22–24).

Vision of the Glorious Son of Man (1:9–20)

1:9 *tribulation.* Trouble or distress, in Greek, *the tribulation*; the great conflict of the last days having already started in John's time (Dan. 12:1; 1 John 2:18). *Patmos.* A small, hilly island (*isle*) off the western coast of Asia Minor, about fifty miles from Ephesus. The island hosted a military garrison, a place for athletic competitions, and a temple to Artemis.
1:10 *in the Spirit.* Either worshiping and praying in the power of the Holy Spirit (John 4:23–24; Eph. 2:18; 6:18; Jude 20) or, more likely, caught up by the Spirit in a vision (4:2; 17:3; 21:10; Ezek. 37:1). *the Lord's day.* The first day of the week when the Lord rose (John 20:1) and the churches gather for worship

Asia; unto Ephesus, and unto Smyrna, and unto
Pergamos, and unto Thyatira, and unto Sardis,
and unto Philadelphia, and unto Laodicea.
12 And I turned to see the voice that spake
with me. And being turned, I saw seven golden
candlesticks;
13 And in the midst of the seven candlesticks *one*
like unto the Son of man, clothed with a garment
down to the foot, and girt about the paps with a
golden girdle.
14 His head and *his* hairs *were* white like wool, as
white as snow; and his eyes *were* as a flame of fire;
15 And his feet like unto fine brass, as if they
burned in a furnace; and his voice as the sound
of many waters.
16 And he had in his right hand seven stars: and
out of his mouth went a sharp twoedged sword:
and his countenance *was* as the sun shineth in his
strength.
17 And when I saw him, I fell at his feet as dead.
And he laid his right hand upon me, saying unto
me, Fear not; I am the first and the last:
18 *I am* he that liveth, and was dead; and, behold,
I am alive for evermore, Amen; and have the keys
of hell and of death.
19 Write the things which thou hast seen, and the
things which are, and the things which shall be
hereafter;
20 The mystery of the seven stars which thou
sawest in my right hand, and the seven golden
candlesticks. The seven stars are the angels of the
seven churches: and the seven candlesticks which
thou sawest are the seven churches.

CHAPTER 2

UNTO the angel of the church of Ephesus write;
These things saith he that holdeth the seven stars
in his right hand, who walketh in the midst of the
seven golden candlesticks;
2 I know thy works, and thy labour, and thy
patience, and how thou canst not bear them
which are evil: and thou hast tried them which
say they are apostles, and are not, and hast found
them liars:
3 And hast borne, and hast patience, and for my
name's sake hast laboured, and hast not fainted.
4 Nevertheless I have *somewhat* against thee,
because thou hast left thy first love.
5 Remember therefore from whence thou art
fallen, and repent, and do the first works; or else I
will come unto thee quickly, and will remove thy

(Acts 20:7; 1 Cor. 16:1–2)—the new covenant Sabbath (Mark 2:28).

1:11 *Ephesus . . . Laodicea.* Seven cities in Asia Minor, named in the order a messenger would reach them starting from the coast and traveling in a clockwise loop.

1:12–16 This vision is not a physical description of Christ but a composite of Old Testament symbols representing His glory (*countenance* or face *was as the sun shineth*; Mal. 4:2) as (a) the great High Priest serving God among the golden oil lamps (*candlesticks*) in God's temple (Ex. 25:31); (b) the mighty King to whom the Father has given all authority, an everlasting kingdom (*Son of man*; Dan. 7:13–14), and power to judge with perfect insight into the souls of men (*eyes . . . as a flame of fire*; 2:18,23; 19:12); (c) the eternal God, the "Ancient of Days" (*hairs . . . white like wool, as white as snow*; Dan. 7:9); (d) the heavenly Messenger (*girt about the paps* [or chest] *with a golden girdle*; Dan. 10:5–6,11), whose words (*mouth*) powerfully pierce the soul and destroy His enemies (*sharp twoedged sword*; 2:16; 19:15; Isa. 11:4; 49:2; Heb. 4:12). Jesus Christ is the incomparable Lord!

1:17 *fell at his feet.* Overwhelmed by supernatural glory (Ezek. 1:28; Dan. 8:17–18). *Fear not.* Christ comes with gentleness and grace for His servants. *first and the last.* Christ is the "Alpha and Omega" (see note at v. 8).

1:18 Believers can trust Christ when they face death because the risen Lord has authority (*the keys*; Isa. 22:22) over death.

1:19 *hereafter.* After these things. This may outline the order of the visions: *the things which thou hast seen* (ch. 1), *things which are, and the things which shall be* (chs. 2–22).

1:20 *mystery.* Secret that is unknown until revealed. *angels.* Literally, "messengers," here human teachers (Mal. 2:7) in *churches*, not heavenly beings. Christ is Lord (*in my right hand*) over preachers (Eph. 4:11). *candlesticks.* The *churches* are part of the temple, and Christ cares for them, as the priest tended the lampstands (Lev. 24:1–4) with the oil of His Spirit (Zech. 4:1–7).

Thoughts for Personal/Family Worship: Chapter 1

1. **Even writing while exiled on an island, John erupts into the praise of the triune God. What is his secret? He has experienced grace from the Father, the Son, and the Holy Spirit and longs for more for himself and other Christians. He is still amazed at the power of the blood of Jesus Christ. Are you? How can this chapter motivate you to praise the Lord even in the middle of trouble and persecution?**
2. **The Lord Jesus is stunningly glorious. John knew Jesus and talked with Him after His resurrection, but even a symbolic vision of Christ's glory put John on the ground. What about Christ fills you with awe? What about Christ comforts you?**

Messages for the Churches (2:1—3:22)

Chapter 2: *The Lord Jesus speaks as King of the churches, praising their faithfulness, rebuking their sins, and promising reward to those who overcome.*

To the Church of Ephesus (2:1–7)

2:1 Christ, the great High Priest, is present and active (*walketh*) in His churches (*candlesticks*; see notes at 1:12–16,20). He addresses the multiple teachers in each church (Acts 14:23; 20:17) collectively under the singular *angel*—God's "messenger." *Ephesus.* Major city of 600,000 people, home of the large temple of Artemis or Diana.

2:2–3 *know thy works.* The Lord has total knowledge of His people (John 21:17). *tried.* Tested. *borne.* Endured. Christ praises the church for its diligence, discernment, and doctrinal purity.

2:4–5 *somewhat.* Something. *first love.* The fervent love they once had (Matt. 24:12) that had motivated their earlier activity

candlestick out of his place, except thou repent.
6 But this thou hast, that thou hatest the deeds of
the Nicolaitans, which I also hate.
7 He that hath an ear, let him hear what the Spirit
saith unto the churches; To him that overcometh
will I give to eat of the tree of life, which is in the
midst of the paradise of God.
8 And unto the angel of the church in Smyrna
write; These things saith the first and the last,
which was dead, and is alive;
9 I know thy works, and tribulation, and poverty,
(but thou art rich) and *I know* the blasphemy of
them which say they are Jews, and are not, but *are*
the synagogue of Satan.
10 Fear none of those things which thou shalt
suffer: behold, the devil shall cast *some* of you
into prison, that ye may be tried; and ye shall have
tribulation ten days: be thou faithful unto death,
and I will give thee a crown of life.
11 He that hath an ear, let him hear what the
Spirit saith unto the churches; He that overcom-
eth shall not be hurt of the second death.
12 And to the angel of the church in Pergamos
write; These things saith he which hath the sharp
sword with two edges;
13 I know thy works, and where thou dwellest,
even where Satan's seat *is*: and thou holdest fast my
name, and hast not denied my faith, even in those
days wherein Antipas *was* my faithful martyr, who
was slain among you, where Satan dwelleth.
14 But I have a few things against thee, because
thou hast there them that hold the doctrine of
Balaam, who taught Balac to cast a stumbling-
block before the children of Israel, to eat things
sacrificed unto idols, and to commit fornication.
15 So hast thou also them that hold the doctrine
of the Nicolaitans, which thing I hate.
16 Repent; or else I will come unto thee quickly,
and will fight against them with the sword of my
mouth.
17 He that hath an ear, let him hear what the
Spirit saith unto the churches; To him that over-
cometh will I give to eat of the hidden manna,
and will give him a white stone, and in the stone a
new name written, which no man knoweth saving
he that receiveth *it*.

(*first works;* 2:19). *whence.* Where. Service and doctrine without love are worthless (1 Cor. 13:1–3). *I will come.* Christ's works of salvation and judgment in history are a kind of "coming" foreshadowing His return (vv. 16,23; 3:20). *remove thy candlestick.* Christians cannot lose their salvation (John 10:28), but churches can lose the Spirit's illumination in the means of grace (4:5; see note at 1:20) and even die spiritually (3:1).

2:6 *Nicolaitans.* Heretical group of unknown teachings, unless it was the same as those teaching "the doctrine of Balaam" (see note at vv. 14–15).

2:7 *He that hath an ear.* The one to whom God has granted the spiritual ability to understand the truth (Deut. 29:4; Isa. 6:9–10; Matt. 13:9–17). *Spirit saith.* The Holy Spirit speaks in all the Scriptures (14:13; 22:17; 2 Tim. 3:16; Heb. 3:7; 9:8; 10:15), addressing not just each church here but all *the churches. overcometh.* Everyone born again unto faith in Christ fights and overcomes sin in this world by Christ's victory on the cross (5:5–10; 12:11; 17:14; 1 John 5:4–5). *tree of life.* Heaven is like a return to the garden of Eden (*paradise;* 22:2,14; Gen. 2:8–9; 3:22; Luke 23:43; 2 Cor. 12:4). This stands in contrast to the goddess Artemis, symbolized by a fruitful tree; only Christ is the tree of life.

To the Church of Smyrna (2:8–11)

2:8 *angel.* See note at v. 1. *Smyrna.* Flourishing city (modern Izmir) with a harbor, home of a large Jewish community. *the first and the last.* Christ is the eternal Lord (1:8,17), whose love outlasts our sufferings (Ps. 103:17). *was dead, and is alive.* Because of His resurrection believers need not fear death (v. 10; 1:18).

2:9–10 *know.* See note at vv. 2–3. *tribulation.* Trouble, distress. *but thou art rich.* With invisible, spiritual, eternal riches in Christ (Eph. 1:18; 3:8; Col. 1:27; James 2:5), in contrast to earthly wealth (3:17). *blasphemy.* Probably slander against the Christians. *synagogue of Satan.* Not true, godly Jews (Rom. 2:28–29), but servants of the *devil* (John 8:31–44), who rules all unbelievers and especially persecutors (12:9–11). *tried.* Tested. *crown.* The victor's wreath given to God's spiritual athletes as the reward of grace to those who persevere (*faithful unto death*), consisting of eternal *life* (1 Cor. 9:25; Phil. 4:1; 1 Thess. 2:19; 2 Tim. 4:8; James 1:12; 1 Peter 5:4).

2:11 *ear . . . Spirit . . . overcometh.* See note at v. 7. *second death.* Fire of hell (20:6,14; 21:8).

To the Church of Pergamos (2:12–17)

2:12 *angel.* See note at v. 1. *Pergamos.* Capital of Asia Minor, 55 miles north of Smyrna, with a large library and magnificent temples to Greek gods. *which hath the sharp sword.* Whose Word is powerful to save and judge (see note at 1:12–16).

2:13 *know.* See note at vv. 2–3. *Satan's seat.* His "throne" or power, perhaps alluding to the 117 ft. by 110 ft. altar depicting the victory of Zeus and the Olympian gods against the giants; or possibly the worship of the emperor, for which Pergamos was the center in Asia Minor. *my faith.* Faith in Me (Christ). *martyr.* Witness. The Greek word (*martus*) later came to imply a witness who suffers and dies for his testimony to Christ (11:3,7; 12:11; 17:6).

2:14–15. After God prevented *Balaam* from cursing Israel at the invitation of *Balac* (Balak, king of Moab; Num. 22–24; Josh. 24:9), Balaam advised the king to seduce Israel into immorality (*fornication*) and idolatry (Num. 25:1–18; 31:16). The church tolerated similar false teachers, who enticed Christians to participate in idolatrous activities involving meals and sexual sin. It is not clear whether this was the error of the *Nicolaitans* or if they taught a different heresy.

2:16 *I will come.* See note at vv. 4–5. *sword.* God threatened Balaam with His angel's sword and later killed him with the sword of the Israelites (Num. 22:23,31; 31:8). Christ would judge the heretics if the church did not *repent.*

2:17 *ear . . . Spirit . . . overcometh.* See note at v. 7. *hidden manna.* Christ, the heavenly food of believers (John 6:31–35). *white stone.* For a verdict of innocence, or an invitation to a feast (19:7–9). *new name.* A new identity in God's love and glory (Isa. 62:2–4) coming from an intimate knowledge of God (3:12; 14:1; 22:4) reserved only for the redeemed (*no man knoweth;* 14:3). Names written on people or things signify identity, ownership, and spiritual oneness (3:12; 13:1,17; 14:1,11; 15:2; 17:3,5; 19:12,16; 21:12,14; 22:4).

18 And unto the angel of the church in Thyatira
write; These things saith the Son of God, who
hath his eyes like unto a flame of fire, and his feet
are like fine brass;
19 I know thy works, and charity, and service, and
faith, and thy patience, and thy works; and the last
to be more than the first.
20 Notwithstanding I have a few things against
thee, because thou sufferest that woman Jezebel,
which calleth herself a prophetess, to teach and to
seduce my servants to commit fornication, and to
eat things sacrificed unto idols.
21 And I gave her space to repent of her fornication; and she repented not.
22 Behold, I will cast her into a bed, and them
that commit adultery with her into great tribulation, except they repent of their deeds.
23 And I will kill her children with death; and
all the churches shall know that I am he which
searcheth the reins and hearts: and I will give unto
every one of you according to your works.
24 But unto you I say, and unto the rest in Thyatira, as many as have not this doctrine, and which
have not known the depths of Satan, as they
speak; I will put upon you none other burden.
25 But that which ye have *already* hold fast till I
come.
26 And he that overcometh, and keepeth my
works unto the end, to him will I give power over
the nations:
27 And he shall rule them with a rod of iron;
as the vessels of a potter shall they be broken to
shivers: even as I received of my Father.
28 And I will give him the morning star.
29 He that hath an ear, let him hear what the
Spirit saith unto the churches.

CHAPTER 3

AND unto the angel of the church in Sardis write;
These things saith he that hath the seven Spirits of
God, and the seven stars; I know thy works, that
thou hast a name that thou livest, and art dead.
2 Be watchful, and strengthen the things which
remain, that are ready to die: for I have not found
thy works perfect before God.

To the Church of Thyatira (2:18–29)

2:18 *angel.* See note at 2:1. *Thyatira.* Small city 40 miles southeast of Pergamos, dominated by trade guilds, each with its own patron god. *Son of God.* The divine King (Ps. 2:6–8), only here in Revelation; the chief god of Thyatira was Apollo, son of Zeus. *eyes.* For judgment (see note at 1:12–16).

2:19 *know.* See note at vv. 2–3. *charity.* Love. *the last to be more than the first.* The church had increased in these spiritual fruits (contrast vv. 4–5).

2:20 *Notwithstanding.* But. *sufferest.* Permits. *Jezebel.* Symbolic name, alluding to the murderous and idolatrous wife of King Ahab (1 Kings 16:31; 18:1—19:2; 21:5–25). She lived by the spirit of Babylon, the great whore (ch. 17). *prophetess.* She claimed the inspiration of God to speak new revelations. *fornication . . . idols.* See note at vv. 14–15. Workers in various trades would suffer if they did not participate in the idolatrous feasts of the trade guilds.

2:21 *space.* Time. Christ had rebuked her already, perhaps through the witness of the godly.

2:22 *cast her into a bed.* Make her sick and weak.

2:23 *children.* Followers. *reins.* Literally, "kidneys," figurative for the mind or soul. Men cannot fully discern the *hearts* of people, but Christ, being God, knows all and so can judge rightly (Jer. 17:9–10). Already the Lord Jesus judges in His providence *according to your works*, an anticipation of judgment day (20:13).

2:24 *depths.* Perhaps deep teachings or secret knowledge (Rom. 11:33; 1 Cor. 2:10), or perhaps participation in demonic and idolatrous rituals (1 Cor. 10:20) as a way to deeper spirituality or to demonstrate their so-called freedom and power in Christ.

2:25 *hold fast.* Grip, hang on, remain faithful. *till I come.* Waiting for His judgment on this Jezebel, and ultimately for His return.

2:26 *overcometh.* See note at v. 7. *my works.* The works Christ commands. *power.* Authority, right to rule.

2:27 *broken to shivers.* Shattered, crushed. The quotation from Ps. 2:9 indicates that they will share in the reign and judgment of the Son of God (Dan. 7:22; 1 Cor. 6:2–3).

2:28 *morning star.* Christ, the radiant king (22:16; Num. 24:17; 2 Peter 1:16–19).

2:29 *ear . . . Spirit.* See note at v. 7.

Thoughts for Personal/Family Worship: Chapter 2

1. **The message to the church in Ephesus warns us of the danger of dead orthodoxy, being careful in doctrine and faithful in service while our love grows cold. Those who love the truth must make sure they love God and love people all the more, for these are Christ's great commands. Why is it easy to grow complacent with mere head knowledge?**
2. **The message to the church in Smyrna encourages us that if men reject us, imprison us, and even kill us for being faithful witnesses to the truth, Christ will raise us from the dead, praise us for our faithfulness, rescue us from the flames of hell, and honor us with eternal life. How does this motivate boldness for the Lord?**
3. **The message to the church in Pergamos calls us to be watchful, for Christians can be faithful in resisting Satan in one direction (such as persecution) but let him in the back door in another direction (such as false doctrine). Never assume that faithfulness in one area is faithfulness in all. What does full-orbed faithfulness to Christ mean?**
4. **The message to the church in Thyatira exhorts us to remember that Christ is the Judge who sees into every secret place and heart. If we play with the idols and pleasures of this world, setting our heart upon them, He will punish us severely. On the other hand, if by grace we obey Him out of gratitude for His salvation, we will reign with Him as kings! What does Christ see when He looks into your heart and life?**

Chapter 3: ***The Lord of the churches warns the hypocritical, encourages the persecuted, and rebukes the self-satisfied.***

To the Church of Sardis (3:1–6)

3 Remember therefore how thou hast received
and heard, and hold fast, and repent. If there-
fore thou shalt not watch, I will come on thee as
a thief, and thou shalt not know what hour I will
come upon thee.
4 Thou hast a few names even in Sardis which
have not defiled their garments; and they shall
walk with me in white: for they are worthy.
5 He that overcometh, the same shall be clothed
in white raiment; and I will not blot out his name
out of the book of life, but I will confess his name
before my Father, and before his angels.
6 He that hath an ear, let him hear what the Spirit
saith unto the churches.
7 And to the angel of the church in Philadel-
phia write; These things saith he that is holy, he
that is true, he that hath the key of David, he that
openeth, and no man shutteth; and shutteth, and
no man openeth;
8 I know thy works: behold, I have set before thee
an open door, and no man can shut it: for thou
hast a little strength, and hast kept my word, and
hast not denied my name.
9 Behold, I will make them of the synagogue of
Satan, which say they are Jews, and are not, but do
lie; behold, I will make them to come and worship
before thy feet, and to know that I have loved thee.
10 Because thou hast kept the word of my pa-
tience, I also will keep thee from the hour of
temptation, which shall come upon all the world,
to try them that dwell upon the earth.
11 Behold, I come quickly: hold that fast which
thou hast, that no man take thy crown.
12 Him that overcometh will I make a pillar in
the temple of my God, and he shall go no more
out: and I will write upon him the name of my
God, and the name of the city of my God, *which
is* new Jerusalem, which cometh down out of
heaven from my God: and *I will write upon him*
my new name.
13 He that hath an ear, let him hear what the
Spirit saith unto the churches.
14 And unto the angel of the church of the
Laodiceans write; These things saith the Amen,
the faithful and true witness, the beginning of the
creation of God;
15 I know thy works, that thou art neither cold
nor hot: I would thou wert cold or hot.

3:1 *angel.* See note at 2:1. *Sardis.* City thirty miles southeast of Thyatira, former capital of the kingdom of Lydia, now in decline. *hath the seven Spirits of God, and the seven stars.* Lord of the manifold graces of the Holy Spirit, and King of the church's ministers (see notes at 1:4,20). *know.* See note at 2:2–3. *name.* Reputation. *dead.* Lacking the mindset given by the Spirit (Rom. 8:5–6).

3:2–3 *Be watchful.* Sardis was surrounded by cliffs and felt secure but was conquered twice due to a failure to keep watch. The church was in the same danger. *not found thy works perfect before God.* Their service was unfinished and incomplete—not pleasing to God though it impressed men (v. 1). *Remember . . . hold fast.* The church must return to gospel principles it *received* when first started. *come on thee as a thief . . . not know what hour.* Christ's coming involves temporal judgments (2:5) but refers ultimately to His return in glory (Matt. 24:42–43).

3:4–5 *defiled their garments.* Uncleanness, a symbol of sin (Jude 23). *overcometh.* See note at 2:7. *White* clothing (*raiment*), worn for festive occasions (Eccl. 9:7–8) is a sign of heavenly glory (Dan. 7:9; Matt. 17:2; 28:3) obtained by the blood and righteousness of Christ (7:9,14; 19:8). *blot out his name.* When a person's name was removed from a city's register for a crime, he lost his citizenship. Though Christians may lose their status in this world, Christ will never take away their citizenship in heaven. *book of life.* God's eternal record of all who will overcome by Christ's blood (13:8; 17:8; 20:12,15; 21:27; 22:19). *confess his name.* On judgment day (Matt. 10:32; 16:27; Luke 9:26).

3:6 *ear . . . Spirit.* See note at 2:7.

To the Church of Philadelphia (3:7–13)

3:7 *angel.* See note at 2:1. *Philadelphia.* City twenty miles southeast of Sardis, on an important trade route. *holy . . . true.* The just Judge (6:10). *key of David.* Sovereign authority over God's kingdom (Isa. 22:22), as the promised son of David (5:5; 22:16).

3:8 *know.* See note at 2:2–3. *open door.* Either entrance into His heavenly kingdom (v. 12; 4:1) or opportunity for effective witness (Acts 14:27; 1 Cor. 16:9; 2 Cor. 2:12; Col. 4:3). *little strength.* Weak but faithful, this church receives nothing but encouragement from Christ.

3:9 *synagogue of Satan.* See note at 2:9–10. *worship before thy feet.* Bow down and honor them as those *loved* by Christ (Isa. 45:14; 49:23; 60:14).

3:10 *word of my patience.* My message about endurance. *keep thee from.* Not by removing them from the world but by protecting them in it (same expression as in John 17:15). *hour of temptation . . . to try.* Time of testing. God sends judgments on the wicked to call them to repent (9:20–21; 16:9–11), but He is with His people (9:4; Isa. 43:2). *them that dwell upon the earth.* The wicked, who are in Satan's kingdom, persecute the godly and will fall under God's wrath if they do not believe the gospel (6:10; 8:13; 11:10; 12:12; 13:8,12,14; 14:6; 17:2,8).

3:11 *come quickly.* See notes at vv. 2–3; 2:4–5,16. *crown.* Reward of grace (see note at 2:9–10).

3:12 *overcometh.* See note at 2:7. *pillar in the temple.* Though rejected by the Jewish synagogue (v. 9), he will have a permanent and prominent place in God's holy presence (Isa. 56:4–5). *write upon him the name.* The public honor (Isa. 65:15) of belonging to the covenant *God*, citizenship in His *city*, and union with Christ (14:1; 22:4; see note at 2:17). *new Jerusalem.* The heavenly, eternal home of Christ and His people (21:1—22:5; Isa. 65:17–18; Gal. 4:26; Heb. 12:22).

3:13 *ear . . . Spirit.* See note at 2:7.

To the Church of Laodicea (3:14–22)

3:14 *angel.* See note at 2:1. *Laodiceans.* Inhabitants of a city forty miles southeast of Philadelphia, in communication with the church at Colosse (Col. 2:1; 4:13–16). *Amen.* Truth; the "God of truth" (Isa. 65:16) keeps all His promises in Christ (1 Cor. 1:20). *faithful and true witness.* See note at 1:5. *beginning of the creation.* Variously interpreted as the Creator of the world (1:8; John 1:3; Col. 1:16), ruler of the creation (1:5; Col. 1:15), or firstborn of the new creation (1:5; Isa. 65:17; Col. 1:18). Christ was not created (John 1:1–3).

3:15–16 *know.* See note at 2:2–3. This is the only church for

16 So then because thou art lukewarm, and
neither cold nor hot, I will spue thee out of my
mouth.
17 Because thou sayest, I am rich, and increased
with goods, and have need of nothing; and know-
est not that thou art wretched, and miserable, and
poor, and blind, and naked:
18 I counsel thee to buy of me gold tried in the
fire, that thou mayest be rich; and white raiment,
that thou mayest be clothed, and *that* the shame
of thy nakedness do not appear; and anoint thine
eyes with eyesalve, that thou mayest see.
19 As many as I love, I rebuke and chasten: be
zealous therefore, and repent.
20 Behold, I stand at the door, and knock: if any
man hear my voice, and open the door, I will come
in to him, and will sup with him, and he with me.
21 To him that overcometh will I grant to sit with
me in my throne, even as I also overcame, and am
set down with my Father in his throne.
22 He that hath an ear, let him hear what the
Spirit saith unto the churches.

CHAPTER 4

AFTER this I looked, and, behold, a door *was*
opened in heaven: and the first voice which I
heard *was* as it were of a trumpet talking with me;
which said, Come up hither, and I will shew thee
things which must be hereafter.
2 And immediately I was in the spirit: and, be-
hold, a throne was set in heaven, and *one* sat on
the throne.
3 And he that sat was to look upon like a jasper
and a sardine stone: and *there was* a rainbow round
about the throne, in sight like unto an emerald.
4 And round about the throne *were* four and
twenty seats: and upon the seats I saw four and
twenty elders sitting, clothed in white raiment;
and they had on their heads crowns of gold.
5 And out of the throne proceeded lightnings
and thunderings and voices: and *there were* seven
lamps of fire burning before the throne, which are
the seven Spirits of God.
6 And before the throne *there was* a sea of glass
like unto crystal: and in the midst of the throne,

---

which Christ had no praise. *neither cold nor hot*. Cold water at Colosse (ten miles southeast of Laodicea) refreshed the drinker, and the hot springs at Hierapolis (six miles north) soothed the bather, but the *lukewarm* water carried five miles by aqueducts to Laodicea did neither. *I would thou wert cold or hot*. I wish you were cold or hot—not cold in love, but pleasing to Christ like cold drinking water or hot bathing water. *spue*. Vomit, throw up; a sign of disgust.

3:17–18 This church disgusted Christ because of its proud self-sufficiency (*I am rich*). Just as its city was famous for wealth, textiles, and eye medicine, the church did not feel its need for the King's riches of holiness (*gold tried in the fire*; 2:9; Zech. 13:9; Mal. 3:3), the Priest's imputed righteousness (*white raiment*; Zech. 3:3–4; see note at vv. 4–5), and the Prophet's illumination of the mind by the Spirit (*anoint . . . eyesalve*). *buy of me*. Ironically, offered without cost (22:17; Isa. 55:1) to those who have no spiritual power or merit (*poor, and blind, and naked*).

3:19–20 *chasten*. Discipline. *knock*. The loving Lord and Husband is outside, appealing to the sleeping church (Song 5:2) to turn back to Him (*repent*) with all their hearts (*be zealous*). *any man*. Each individual is called to respond. *sup*. Eat a meal, a sign of friendship and fellowship.

3:21 *overcometh*. See note at 2:7. *sit with me in my throne*. Symbol of sharing His reign in the kingdom of God, the true power, honor, and riches yet awaiting believers (2:26–27).

3:22 *ear . . . Spirit*. See note at 2:7.

Thoughts for Personal/Family Worship: Chapter 3

1. **The message to the church in Sardis warns us that a church may be full of activity but in reality be dead. Christians must keep watch not just over the outward ministry but over the fruit of the Spirit. What are some early signs of deadness in a church?**
2. **The message to the church in Philadelphia encourages small and weak churches that persevere in their faithfulness and witness to Christ. The Lord does not rebuke them for their weakness but promises them victory. What promises encourage you to persevere?**
3. **The message to the church in Laodicea rebukes churches that are proud and do not depend on Christ. They think that they are strong, but Christ finds them disgusting! Yet He still calls them back to Himself. How does Christ knock at the door of a church?**

THE LAMB AND THE SEVEN SEALS OF GOD'S SCROLL (4:1—8:1)

Chapter 4: *John is caught up in a symbolic vision of God on His throne, surrounded by angels and exalted in the worship of heaven.*

Heavenly Vision of God on the Throne (4:1–11)

4:1 This begins the second visionary cycle in Revelation (4:1—8:1), shifting the focus from earth to heavenly realities. *door was opened in heaven*. Symbol of a revelation of divine secrets (19:11; Ezek. 1:1; Matt. 3:16; John 1:51; Acts 7:56; 10:11). *first voice . . . trumpet*. Voice of the Lord Jesus (1:10–13). *hither*. To this place. *hereafter*. After this (Dan. 2:28–29).

4:2 *in the spirit*. Seeing a vision by the Holy Spirit (see note at 1:10). John did not have a physical sight of heaven's unspeakable glories (2 Cor. 12:4; 1 Tim. 6:16) but a symbolic vision that draws from Isa. 6 and Ezek. 1. *throne*. Key word in Revelation (over 40 times), a symbol of God's power and authority as King (1 Kings 22:19; Pss. 11:4; 103:19; Isa. 6:1; 66:1; Ezek. 1:26).

4:3–7 The vision of the throne reveals that the King is (a) beautiful, rich, and valuable like precious stones (*jasper*, *sardine* or red carnelian, and *emerald*); (b) gracious to sinners and faithful to His covenants (*rainbow*; Gen. 9:12–17); (c) dwelling with His victorious old covenant and new covenant people (twelve plus twelve *elders*; 21:12,14) in His holy temple (*lamps*, *sea*, *lion*, and *calf* or young ox; 1 Kings 7:23–25,29,36,49,51); (d) judging according to His fearsome power and righteous law (*lightnings and thunderings* like Mt. Sinai; Ex. 19–20); (e) shining out in the witness of the churches by the Holy Spirit (*seven lamps . . . seven Spirits*; see notes at 1:4,20); and (f) attended by servants representing all the powers (*lion, calf, man, eagle*) and wisdom (*full of eyes*) of heaven and earth (5:13; Ezek. 1:10). What a glorious King!

4:4 *seats*. Same word as *throne*. *raiment*. Clothing.

4:6 *beasts*. Literally, "living ones"; not the same word as "beast" or wild animal (6:8; 11:7).

and round about the throne, *were* four beasts full
of eyes before and behind.
7 And the first beast *was* like a lion, and the second
beast like a calf, and the third beast had a face as a
man, and the fourth beast *was* like a flying eagle.
8 And the four beasts had each of them six wings
about *him*; and *they were* full of eyes within: and
they rest not day and night, saying, Holy, holy,
holy, Lord God Almighty, which was, and is, and
is to come.
9 And when those beasts give glory and honour
and thanks to him that sat on the throne, who
liveth for ever and ever,
10 The four and twenty elders fall down before
him that sat on the throne, and worship him that
liveth for ever and ever, and cast their crowns
before the throne, saying,
11 Thou art worthy, O Lord, to receive glory and
honour and power: for thou hast created all things,
and for thy pleasure they are and were created.

CHAPTER 5

AND I saw in the right hand of him that sat on the
throne a book written within and on the backside,
sealed with seven seals.
2 And I saw a strong angel proclaiming with a
loud voice, Who is worthy to open the book, and
to loose the seals thereof?
3 And no man in heaven, nor in earth, neither
under the earth, was able to open the book,
neither to look thereon.
4 And I wept much, because no man was found
worthy to open and to read the book, neither to
look thereon.
5 And one of the elders saith unto me, Weep not:
behold, the Lion of the tribe of Juda, the Root of
David, hath prevailed to open the book, and to
loose the seven seals thereof.
6 And I beheld, and, lo, in the midst of the throne
and of the four beasts, and in the midst of the
elders, stood a Lamb as it had been slain, having
seven horns and seven eyes, which are the seven
Spirits of God sent forth into all the earth.
7 And he came and took the book out of the right
hand of him that sat upon the throne.
8 And when he had taken the book, the four
beasts and four *and* twenty elders fell down before
the Lamb, having every one of them harps, and
golden vials full of odours, which are the prayers
of saints.
9 And they sung a new song, saying, Thou art

4:8–11 The glory of the King on the *throne* calls angels and men to worship Him for His nature and works. Heavenly worship, a model for earthly worship, is: (a) praising God continuously and unceasingly (*they rest not day and night*); (b) glorying in God's absolute holiness, including His sovereign power (*Lord God Almighty*; see note at 1:8) and eternal being (*which was, and is, and is to come*; see note at 1:4; *who liveth for ever and ever*); (c) humbling and subjecting themselves before God's throne (*fall down before him*; see 7:11; 11:16; 19:4) and glorifying Him for their salvation and victory (*cast their crowns before the throne*; see note at 2:10); (d) giving God His rights as universal emperor (the Roman emperor was greeted with the words *Thou art worthy*) because He *created all things* and they owe their past and continuing existence to His will (*for thy pleasure*; Prov. 16:4). Before such a God all men are as nothing (Isa. 40:17).

4:8 *holy*. Sacred, excellent, and supreme above all in every way (Ex. 15:11; 1 Sam. 2:2; Isa. 6:1–3; 40:25). Repetition indicates superior quality, and threefold repetition superlative excellence.

Thoughts for Personal/Family Worship: Chapter 4

1. **Behind the symbols of ch. 4 stands a God of unparalleled glory. That He revealed Himself through the image of a "throne" shows that despite our modern emphasis on choice, equality, and freedom, God wants to be known as the King. Imagine yourself standing before His throne. How would His glory affect you? Why?**
2. **The conflict between the church and the world boils down to this: "Who or what will you worship?" This is the great question of Revelation. What does this chapter teach us about what it means to worship God, and what motivates the worship of God?**

Chapter 5: *The Lamb appears before heaven's throne as the only One worthy to execute God's decree of salvation through judgment for His glory.*

The Scroll and the Lamb that Was Slain (5:1–14)

5:1 *book written within and on the backside*. A book (or scroll) symbolizing the heavenly King's comprehensive decree of judgment and mercy (Ezek. 2:9—3:3). *sealed*. Held shut by seven wax or clay seals, not yet being revealed or realized (Isa. 29:11; Dan. 8:26; 12:4). Sevenfold sealing was done in Roman law of a last will and testament of inheritance through death (Heb. 9:15–17).

5:2–4 *loose*. Break. *thereon*. On it. Ability to open the scroll depends not on power but on being *worthy* in personal righteousness and honor. *no man* (literally, "no one") *in heaven, nor in earth, neither under the earth*. Comprehensive expression for all creation (v. 13; Ex. 20:4; Phil. 2:10). No angel, human being, or other creature is qualified to bring salvation (Isa. 59:16)—John *wept much* at the horrible prospect that God's purpose to glorify Himself in salvation might fail.

5:5–7 The execution of God's decree and the victory of His people depend solely on One who is the mighty king (*Lion*) descended from Judah (*Juda*; Gen. 49:8–12) and *David* (Ps. 89:1–4). He has conquered this world (*prevailed*, same word as "overcome"; 2:7; John 16:33), springing up like a branch from a *root* after the line of David was cut off in the exile (Isa. 11:1). Yet shockingly, the triumphant One is also the suffering servant who *had been slain* as a sacrifice in the place of sinners (*Lamb*; Gen. 22:8,13). He took their guilt on Himself in order to rescue them from God's wrath by His blood and set them free as their true Passover (Ex. 12:1–13; Isa. 53:6–7; John 1:29; 1 Cor. 5:7). He now reigns over *all the earth* with perfect power (*seven horns*) and wisdom (*seven eyes*; Zech. 3:9; 4:10) by the anointing of the Holy Spirit (*seven Spirits of God*; see note at 1:4).

5:8–10 Just as God's creation of all things and sovereignty over them evoked worship (4:1–11), so Christ's redemption

worthy to take the book, and to open the seals
thereof: for thou wast slain, and hast redeemed
us to God by thy blood out of every kindred, and
tongue, and people, and nation;
10 And hast made us unto our God kings and
priests: and we shall reign on the earth.
11 And I beheld, and I heard the voice of many
angels round about the throne and the beasts
and the elders: and the number of them was ten
thousand times ten thousand, and thousands of
thousands;
12 Saying with a loud voice, Worthy is the Lamb
that was slain to receive power, and riches, and
wisdom, and strength, and honour, and glory,
and blessing.
13 And every creature which is in heaven, and on
the earth, and under the earth, and such as are in
the sea, and all that are in them, heard I saying,
Blessing, and honour, and glory, and power, *be*
unto him that sitteth upon the throne, and unto
the Lamb for ever and ever.
14 And the four beasts said, Amen. And the four
and twenty elders fell down and worshipped him
that liveth for ever and ever.

CHAPTER 6

AND I saw when the Lamb opened one of the
seals, and I heard, as it were the noise of thunder,
one of the four beasts saying, Come and see.
2 And I saw, and behold a white horse: and he
that sat on him had a bow; and a crown was given
unto him: and he went forth conquering, and to
conquer.
3 And when he had opened the second seal, I
heard the second beast say, Come and see.
4 And there went out another horse *that was* red:
and *power* was given to him that sat thereon to
take peace from the earth, and that they should
kill one another: and there was given unto him a
great sword.
5 And when he had opened the third seal, I heard
the third beast say, Come and see. And I beheld,
and lo a black horse; and he that sat on him had a
pair of balances in his hand.
6 And I heard a voice in the midst of the four
beasts say, A measure of wheat for a penny, and
three measures of barley for a penny; and *see* thou
hurt not the oil and the wine.
7 And when he had opened the fourth seal, I heard
the voice of the fourth beast say, Come and see.
8 And I looked, and behold a pale horse: and
his name that sat on him was Death, and Hell
followed with him. And power was given unto
them over the fourth part of the earth, to kill with
sword, and with hunger, and with death, and with
the beasts of the earth.
9 And when he had opened the fifth seal, I saw

---

and victory call forth *new* subjection (*fell down before*), praises (symbolized by *harps* or lyres used by Levites; 1 Chron. 15:16), and *prayers* for complete salvation (symbolized by *vials full of odours* or bowls of incense burned by priests; 8:3; Ps. 141:2). The Redeemer is honored as the conqueror and emperor over all (*worthy*; see note at 4:8–11), for His sacrificial death (*blood*) has purchased (*redeemed*) some people from every ethnic (*kindred*), linguistic (*tongue*), and cultural group on earth so that they will share in His victory and *reign* (20:4) and His adoring access to the Father (*kings and priests*; see notes at 1:5–6).

5:11–14 The circle of worship broadens to include many millions of *angels* and everything God created (*every creature*). Just as no one in all creation was worthy to implement God's decree (vv. 2–4), so all creation now worships the crucified Lord Jesus because He is worthy. Christ's receiving worship alongside *him that sitteth upon the throne* shows that Christ is God (19:10).

Thoughts for Personal/Family Worship: Chapter 5

1. **Christ alone has executed God's plan at the cost of His own blood. He alone is worthy. He is the Lion who conquered, and yet He is the Lamb who was slaughtered for sinners. The only way to share in God's victory and kingdom is by trusting in Christ alone. Faith in Christ alone says to Him, "Thou alone art worthy of my trust." By God's grace, do you trust Him?**
2. **Without Christ, we have cause for nothing but weeping, but with Christ we have reason for nothing but worship. If the angels sing of His worthiness, how much more should sinful men, women, and children bought by His blood give Him their submission, praise, and prayer? How does your life show adoration for Christ? How could you adore Him even more?**

Chapter 6: *The Lamb opens six seals of the scroll of God's decree, releasing the birth pains of the world and cosmic disturbances before the coming of His wrath.*

The Opening of the Six Seals (6:1–17)

6:1–2 First seal. *the Lamb opened*. The crucified Lord reigns over world history. *beasts*. See note at 4:6. The four horsemen symbolize forces at work in the world under God's sovereignty (Zech. 1:8–10; 6:1–5) and include the sorrows predicted by Christ before His return (Matt. 24:4–14). The sequence in the symbolic vision does not imply that one necessarily comes after another. *white horse: and he that sat on him*. Christ rides forth as the warrior-king, working in the world for truth and righteousness by His Word (19:11; Ps. 45:1–5; Matt. 24:14).

6:3–4 Second seal. *horse that was red*. The forces of war resulting in death (Matt. 24:6). *thereon*. On it. *peace . . . sword*. Perhaps also a reference to violent persecution (Matt. 10:34).

6:5–6 Third seal. *black horse*. The economic forces producing poverty. *balances*. Used for weighing in buying and selling, and for rationing food during famine (Lev. 26:26; Ezek. 4:16). *measure*. About a quart. *penny*. Denarius, a day's wages for a laborer. These prices are inflated to about a dozen times the norm, so that ordinary families can barely avoid starvation (Matt. 24:7).

6:7–8 Fourth seal. *pale horse*. Literally, "green horse," like something rotting or molding (Lev. 13:49; 14:37)—the forces of *Death*. This seal summarizes the effects of the previous two, war (*sword*) and famine (*hunger*), and adds disease (likely meaning of *with death*) and wild animals (*beasts*). These

under the altar the souls of them that were slain
for the word of God, and for the testimony which
they held:
10 And they cried with a loud voice, saying, How
long, O Lord, holy and true, dost thou not judge
and avenge our blood on them that dwell on the
earth?
11 And white robes were given unto every one
of them; and it was said unto them, that they
should rest yet for a little season, until their fel-
lowservants also and their brethren, that should
be killed as they *were*, should be fulfilled.
12 And I beheld when he had opened the sixth
seal, and, lo, there was a great earthquake; and
the sun became black as sackcloth of hair, and the
moon became as blood;
13 And the stars of heaven fell unto the earth,
even as a fig tree casteth her untimely figs, when
she is shaken of a mighty wind.
14 And the heaven departed as a scroll when it is
rolled together; and every mountain and island
were moved out of their places.
15 And the kings of the earth, and the great men,
and the rich men, and the chief captains, and the
mighty men, and every bondman, and every free
man, hid themselves in the dens and in the rocks
of the mountains;
16 And said to the mountains and rocks, Fall on
us, and hide us from the face of him that sitteth
on the throne, and from the wrath of the Lamb:
17 For the great day of his wrath is come; and
who shall be able to stand?

CHAPTER 7

AND after these things I saw four angels standing
on the four corners of the earth, holding the four
winds of the earth, that the wind should not blow
on the earth, nor on the sea, nor on any tree.
2 And I saw another angel ascending from the
east, having the seal of the living God: and he
cried with a loud voice to the four angels, to
whom it was given to hurt the earth and the sea,
3 Saying, Hurt not the earth, neither the sea, nor
the trees, till we have sealed the servants of our
God in their foreheads.
4 And I heard the number of them which were
sealed: *and there were* sealed an hundred *and* forty
and four thousand of all the tribes of the children
of Israel.
5 Of the tribe of Juda *were* sealed twelve thou-
sand. Of the tribe of Reuben *were* sealed twelve
thousand. Of the tribe of Gad *were* sealed twelve
thousand.

---

sorrows match the curses of the old covenant upon lawbreakers, leading up to Israel's exile (Lev. 26:14–26; Ezek. 14:21). Like those curses, they call mankind to repent before the final judgment falls.

6:9–11 Fifth seal. Though Christ is victorious (v. 2; 5:5), the age prior to His return is a time of persecution (Matt. 24:9–10). Many of His servants must, like the Lamb, be *slain* (same word as in 5:6), not for redemption but for witness (*testimony*). As the incense rose from the golden *altar* in the temple (9:13; Ex. 30:1–9), so their prayers rise like incense to the Lord (5:8; 8:3–5), calling for timely justice (*judge and avenge*) against the wicked (19:2; Ps. 79). They must wait until the group of martyrs reaches its full number (*be fulfilled*)—God is sovereign over persecution (Acts 9:15–16; Phil. 1:29; 1 Thess. 3:3). The *souls* of the martyrs already enjoy refreshment (*rest*; 14:13), victory, and glory (20:4) in Christ (*white robes*; 3:4–5; 7:9,14).

6:12–17 Sixth seal. This seal brings us to the threshold of the return of Christ (see Introduction: Major Problems of Interpretation: Structure and Flow). Cosmic disruption comes on the day of the Lord (*the great day of his wrath*; Zeph. 1:14–15; 2:2–3) as God's glory appears and overwhelms this fallen world in an act of uncreation (Ps. 102:26; Isa. 13:9–13; 24:19–23; 34:4; Jer. 4:23–28; Joel 1:15; 2:10,30–31; 3:15–16; Hag. 2:6–7) at Christ's coming with glory (Matt. 24:29–31). When the Lord is about to open the scroll (ch. 5), the heavens roll up *as a scroll* as the old order comes to an end and the new creation arrives (21:1,5).

6:15–17 The day of the Lord is a day of terror for the wicked (Amos 5:18–20; Mal. 3:5; 4:5), when all sinners from the greatest *kings* to the lowest slave (*bondman*) will hide from the glory of the Lord (Isa. 2:19,21) and prefer to be crushed to death rather than face *the wrath of the Lamb*. This symbolic language is sometimes applied to historical judgments (Hos. 10:8; Luke 23:30) but ultimately points to Christ's return, for His wrath is worse than death.

Thoughts for Personal/Family Worship: Chapter 6

1. **Every century since Christ's coming has trembled under the ravages of wars, famines, diseases, and violent persecution. Yet we should not fear. Christ rules over all. The gospel will reach every nation. Those who die in Christ already enjoy glory. What events shake the world today? How does faith in Christ equip us to meet them?**
2. **The words "the wrath of the Lamb" (v. 16) should amaze us with the evil of sin, that it provokes the loving Savior to burning anger. Thomas Boston said, "To be condemned by Him, who came to save sinners, must be double damnation. But thus it will be. The Lamb of God shall roar, as a lion, against them." Let us not trifle with the Lamb of God. Let us pray for grace that we and our families and churches may repent now.**

Chapter 7: *The sequence of the seven seals pauses for an interlude, where God reveals the protection, victory, and peace of the redeemed with the Lamb.*

Visions of the Sealed, Washed, and Victorious Church (7:1–17)

7:1–3 The frightening vision of the day of the Lord's wrath (6:12–17) is balanced by a comforting, symbolic vision of the protection of each individual marked by God's seal as belonging to Him (9:4; Ex. 13:9; Ezek. 9:4–5; 2 Cor. 1:22; Eph. 1:13; 4:30). God seals them with His own character (14:1). The Lord prevents His wrath (*the wind*; 6:13; Ps. 1:4; Ezek. 13:13; Nah. 1:2–3) from harming those who fear and obey Him, including John and his fellow Christians (*servants of our God*; 1:1). This safety guards believers in all the earth (*four corners*).

7:4 *hundred and forty and four thousand*. That is, 144,000 (12 x 12 x 10 x 10 x 10), symbolizing the fullness of God's redeemed people (14:1–5), the spiritual *Israel* of all believers in

6 Of the tribe of Aser *were* sealed twelve thousand. Of the tribe of Nepthalim *were* sealed twelve thousand. Of the tribe of Manasses *were* sealed twelve thousand.
7 Of the tribe of Simeon *were* sealed twelve thousand. Of the tribe of Levi *were* sealed twelve thousand. Of the tribe of Issachar *were* sealed twelve thousand.
8 Of the tribe of Zabulon *were* sealed twelve thousand. Of the tribe of Joseph *were* sealed twelve thousand. Of the tribe of Benjamin *were* sealed twelve thousand.
9 After this I beheld, and, lo, a great multitude, which no man could number, of all nations, and kindreds, and people, and tongues, stood before the throne, and before the Lamb, clothed with white robes, and palms in their hands;
10 And cried with a loud voice, saying, Salvation to our God which sitteth upon the throne, and unto the Lamb.
11 And all the angels stood round about the throne, and *about* the elders and the four beasts, and fell before the throne on their faces, and worshipped God,
12 Saying, Amen: Blessing, and glory, and wisdom, and thanksgiving, and honour, and power, and might, *be* unto our God for ever and ever. Amen.
13 And one of the elders answered, saying unto me, What are these which are arrayed in white robes? and whence came they?
14 And I said unto him, Sir, thou knowest. And he said to me, These are they which came out of great tribulation, and have washed their robes, and made them white in the blood of the Lamb.
15 Therefore are they before the throne of God, and serve him day and night in his temple: and he that sitteth on the throne shall dwell among them.
16 They shall hunger no more, neither thirst any more; neither shall the sun light on them, nor any heat.
17 For the Lamb which is in the midst of the throne shall feed them, and shall lead them unto living fountains of waters: and God shall wipe away all tears from their eyes.

CHAPTER 8

AND when he had opened the seventh seal, there was silence in heaven about the space of half an hour.
2 And I saw the seven angels which stood before

Christ. The Jew-Gentile distinction is abolished in the new covenant (Rom. 2:29; 4:11–12,16; Gal. 3:28–29; 6:16; Eph. 2:15,19).

7:5–8 *Juda.* Judah. *Aser.* Asher. *Nepthalim.* Naphtali. *Manasses.* Manasseh. *Zabulon.* Zebulun. The differences reflect Greek spellings of Hebrew names. Judah, the tribe of Christ, is listed first instead of Reuben. The tribes of Ephraim and Dan are omitted. Both *Joseph* and Manasseh are mentioned as distinct tribes though their descendants overlap, their being father and son. These aspects of the vision confirm it to be a symbol and not a literal counting of ethnic Jews.

7:9–14 The second vision of the interlude (vv. 9–17) pictures the redeemed (5:9) in God's kingdom (*before the throne*). They worship God and Christ as those who have experienced *salvation* symbolized in terms of a second exodus: by *the blood of the Lamb* of Passover (Ex. 12:3–7,13) and with the celebration of the Feast of Tabernacles (*palms*; Lev. 23:40–43; Zech. 14:16). The vision overflows with optimism in the success of the gospel, for there are more people than anyone can count from all clans (*kindreds*) and languages (*tongues*). This is the fulfillment of God's promises to Abraham (Gen. 12:3; 15:5; 17:4). They passed through much distress (*tribulation*; 2:9–10; John 16:33; Acts 14:22; 1 Thess. 1:6), and now they stand in victory and glory (*arrayed* or clothed in *white robes*; see note at 3:4–5). The *great tribulation*, an expression for severe trouble (2:22; Neh. 9:37, LXX; Acts 7:11, Greek), has the definite article in the Greek and refers to the period ranging from John's time (see note at 1:9) to Christ's coming (Matt. 24:21,29).

7:15–17 The glorified servants of God enjoy God's intimate presence like priests *in his temple* (1:5; 5:10; 20:6), joining in the continual worship of heaven (*day and night*; 4:8). The King on *the throne* will *dwell among them* (literally, "set his tabernacle over them"; Ezek. 37:26–28), and His presence will be their protection, healing, and satisfaction (21:3–4; Ps. 121:6; Isa. 4:6; 25:8; 32:1–2; 49:9–10). Christ will do this through the work of the Spirit (*living fountains of waters*; 22:1,17; John 4:14; 7:37–39) that He purchased by His death for their sins (*the Lamb*; 5:9; Gal. 3:13–14). The Lord is their shepherd (*feed* is literally, "care as a shepherd"), and they will dwell with Him (Ps. 23).

Thoughts for Personal/Family Worship: Chapter 7

1. **The coming wrath of God will terrify the disobedient, but believers in Christ need not fear judgment day. God has sealed each one who belongs to Him. He knows each by name. Not one of those whom Christ redeemed by His blood shall perish under God's anger. They are His beloved Israel. Children of God, do not fear, but have boldness!**
2. **The Christian life is one of many troubles and much opposition. However, when believers arrive in God's kingdom, it shall all be worth it. Are you a true believer? If so, as you consider the promises of this chapter, which promise do you find particularly sweet? Why? Memorize that promise, and take it with you, meditating on it over the coming day.**

Chapter 8: ***The seventh seal is broken, and the first four of seven angels sound their trumpets in a new cycle of visions.***

The Seventh Seal: Silence (8:1)

8:1 *seventh seal.* This should be viewed in connection to visions of the throne, the scroll, and the Lamb (chs. 4–7), not what follows (ch. 8). The temporary quiet of this seal stands in contrast to the songs of praise (chs. 4–5), cries of the martyrs, shaking of creation, and screaming of sinners (6:12–17). With the last seal God's judgment has come and all is in *silence*, a prophetic symbol of awe before God's majesty (Ps. 46:10; Isa. 23:2; Hab. 2:20; Zeph. 1:7; Zech. 2:13).

THE SEVEN TRUMPETS (8:2—11:19)

God; and to them were given seven trumpets.
3 And another angel came and stood at the altar,
having a golden censer; and there was given unto
him much incense, that he should offer *it* with the
prayers of all saints upon the golden altar which
was before the throne.
4 And the smoke of the incense, *which came* with
the prayers of the saints, ascended up before God
out of the angel's hand.
5 And the angel took the censer, and filled it with
fire of the altar, and cast *it* into the earth: and
there were voices, and thunderings, and light-
nings, and an earthquake.
6 And the seven angels which had the seven
trumpets prepared themselves to sound.
7 The first angel sounded, and there followed hail
and fire mingled with blood, and they were cast
upon the earth: and the third part of trees was
burnt up, and all green grass was burnt up.
8 And the second angel sounded, and as it were a
great mountain burning with fire was cast into the
sea: and the third part of the sea became blood;
9 And the third part of the creatures which were
in the sea, and had life, died; and the third part of
the ships were destroyed.
10 And the third angel sounded, and there fell a
great star from heaven, burning as it were a lamp,
and it fell upon the third part of the rivers, and
upon the fountains of waters;
11 And the name of the star is called Wormwood:
and the third part of the waters became worm-
wood; and many men died of the waters, because
they were made bitter.
12 And the fourth angel sounded, and the third
part of the sun was smitten, and the third part
of the moon, and the third part of the stars; so
as the third part of them was darkened, and the
day shone not for a third part of it, and the night
likewise.
13 And I beheld, and heard an angel flying
through the midst of heaven, saying with a loud
voice, Woe, woe, woe, to the inhabiters of the
earth by reason of the other voices of the trumpet
of the three angels, which are yet to sound!

CHAPTER 9

AND the fifth angel sounded, and I saw a star fall
from heaven unto the earth: and to him was given
the key of the bottomless pit.
2 And he opened the bottomless pit; and there
arose a smoke out of the pit, as the smoke of a
great furnace; and the sun and the air were dark-
ened by reason of the smoke of the pit.
3 And there came out of the smoke locusts upon
the earth: and unto them was given power, as the
scorpions of the earth have power.
4 And it was commanded them that they should

The Saints' Prayers and the First Four Trumpets (8:2–13)

8:2–5 The seven trumpets form a new cycle in Revelation's visions, like the seven churches (chs. 1–3) and the seven seals (4:1—8:1). In the opening scene in heaven, the seven trumpets answer *the prayers of all saints* for salvation and justice (5:8; 6:9–11). Their prayers come to God through Christ's priestly work of blood atonement (temple symbolism of the *altar*; Ex. 30:10) and intercession (burning *incense* in the *censer*; Lev. 16:12; Num. 16:46–48). God hears their prayers and sends His holy wrath (*fire of the altar*; Lev. 9:24—10:3) upon the wicked, judging them according to His law (*thunderings, and lightnings* as on Mt. Sinai; Ex. 19:16; 20:1–18).

8:6–12 The first four trumpets. Images such as these should be interpreted according to Old Testament events and symbolic language. Picking up the second exodus theme (see note at 7:9–14), these judgments allude to the plagues on Egypt (*hail, fire, blood* in bodies of water, pollution of drinking water, *darkened* skies; Ex. 7:17–18; 9:18,24; 10:21; Ps. 78:44–50). They are more intense than the fourth seal, destroying a *third* of the world instead of a quarter (6:8). Yet these judgments are partial, not total, in destruction. Storm images can symbolize historical judgments against nations (Ps. 18:11–14; Isa. 28:1–3; 30:30–31). The fall of a *mountain* into the *sea* is a symbol of national calamity (Ps. 46:2). Blowing trumpets, casting down mountains, and throwing a rock into the sea are images of the overthrow of Babylon (18:21; Jer. 51:25–29,63–64). Forcing people to drink bitterness (*wormwood*) signifies bitter experiences like invasion, defeat, and exile (Jer. 8:14–16; 9:15–16; 23:15; Lam. 3:15,19). Sun and moon struck (*smitten*) with darkness can be a sign of conquest by a foreign power (Ezek. 32:2,7–8,11). Therefore these trumpets symbolize natural and political disasters throughout this age that display God's sovereignty over creation, supremacy over man's idols, and wrath against sin.

8:13 *Woe.* Cry of doom. *inhabiters of the earth.* Wicked (see note at 3:10).

Thoughts for Personal/Family Worship: Chapter 8

1. **God answers prayer. By the work of Jesus Christ, our High Priest, the prayers of believers rise to God like pleasing incense. Dear believer, be encouraged to pray and not give up. Realize, however, that the ultimate answer to all our prayers is Christ's coming (Luke 18:1–8). For He is our life, and in Him all God's promises are fulfilled to His people. When you pray, hope in Christ.**
2. **In every age the Lord has sent disasters. In 2004 a tsunami killed 230,000 people in one day. In the mid-fourteenth century the Black Death killed over 100 million people in Europe and Asia. About 60 million people died in World War II. When such horrible disasters come, the Lord Jesus teaches us to repent of sin, for a judgment is coming in which all unrepentant sinners will perish (Luke 13:1–5).**

Chapter 9: ***The angels sound the fifth and sixth trumpets, unleashing demonic powers of sorrow and death upon the wicked.***

The First Two Woes: The Fifth and Sixth Trumpets (9:1–21)

9:1–11 The fifth trumpet. Even worse than the natural and political disasters pictured in the first four trumpets are the powers of spiritual evil symbolized here in a vision

not hurt the grass of the earth, neither any green
thing, neither any tree; but only those men which
have not the seal of God in their foreheads.
5 And to them it was given that they should not
kill them, but that they should be tormented five
months: and their torment *was* as the torment of
a scorpion, when he striketh a man.
6 And in those days shall men seek death, and
shall not find it; and shall desire to die, and death
shall flee from them.
7 And the shapes of the locusts *were* like unto
horses prepared unto battle; and on their heads
were as it were crowns like gold, and their faces
were as the faces of men.
8 And they had hair as the hair of women, and
their teeth were as *the teeth* of lions.
9 And they had breastplates, as it were breast-
plates of iron; and the sound of their wings *was*
as the sound of chariots of many horses running
to battle.
10 And they had tails like unto scorpions, and
there were stings in their tails: and their power
was to hurt men five months.
11 And they had a king over them, *which is* the
angel of the bottomless pit, whose name in the
Hebrew tongue *is* Abaddon, but in the Greek
tongue hath *his* name Apollyon.
12 One woe is past; *and*, behold, there come two
woes more hereafter.
13 And the sixth angel sounded, and I heard
a voice from the four horns of the golden altar
which is before God,
14 Saying to the sixth angel which had the trum-
pet, Loose the four angels which are bound in the
great river Euphrates.
15 And the four angels were loosed, which were
prepared for an hour, and a day, and a month, and
a year, for to slay the third part of men.
16 And the number of the army of the horse-
men *were* two hundred thousand thousand: and I
heard the number of them.
17 And thus I saw the horses in the vision, and
them that sat on them, having breastplates of
fire, and of jacinth, and brimstone: and the heads
of the horses *were* as the heads of lions; and
out of their mouths issued fire and smoke and
brimstone.
18 By these three was the third part of men
killed, by the fire, and by the smoke, and by the
brimstone, which issued out of their mouths.
19 For their power is in their mouth, and in their
tails: for their tails *were* like unto serpents, and
had heads, and with them they do hurt.
20 And the rest of the men which were not killed by

---

based on Joel 1–2. These powers are led by Satan, the *angel* (v. 11) that has fallen *from heaven* (v. 1; 12:7–9; Isa. 14:12) and become the murderer of mankind (John 8:44). *Abaddon* is Hebrew for "destruction." *Apollyon* is Greek for "destroyer" and may refer ironically to the false god Apollo, called *Parnopius* (literally, "of locusts"). God consigned the fallen angels to the abyss (*bottomless pit*; 11:7; 17:8; 20:1–3; same Greek word as in Luke 8:31) until judgment day (Jude 6). But God grants Satan a measure of power to rule his evil kingdom (*to him was given the key*; see note at 1:18). Like God's plague of *locusts* on Egypt (Ex. 10:1–20), these powers are God's judgment upon wicked men and are subject to His sovereign purposes (*unto them was given power*; v. 3). They are the demons of Satan (*scorpions*; Luke 10:17–19), like a locust swarm of vast numbers that darkens the world (v. 2; Ex. 10:15; Joel 1:4; 2:10). Like the angelic worshipers of God (4:6–8), so these evil spirits are symbolically depicted as composites of human and animal features. They entice men with pleasure (*hair of women*) and success (*crowns like gold*; 4:4) but in fact wage war against humanity (*horses prepared unto battle*, *breastplates*, *chariots*; Joel 2:4–5). As scorpions *torment* men (most scorpion stings are not lethal but intensely painful), so the Devil's forces bring great psychological and spiritual miseries, so much so that people often prefer death to life, though often unwilling to kill themselves (v. 6; Job 3:20–21). God grants a limited time for demons to infest this earth (12:12; Nah. 3:17; *five months* is perhaps the lifespan of a locust or the season when they are prevalent). Christ prevents Satan from harming those who belong to Him as His spiritual Israel (*the seal of God in their foreheads*; v. 4; 7:3–4), for they overcome the Devil (12:10–11). Like Joel's vision of locusts, this vision calls sinners to turn from Satan to the Lord in repentance (Joel 2:12).

9:12 *hereafter*. After these things.

9:13–19 The sixth trumpet. The *army of horsemen* at the *river Euphrates* that are somewhat like *serpents* uses the symbolism of Jeremiah's prophecy that God would use Babylon to judge Egypt (Jer. 46:1–4,22). The *Euphrates* River also marked the edge of the Roman Empire, beyond which lurked dreaded invaders from the Parthian Empire. *Fire*, *smoke*, and sulfur (*brimstone*) are symbols of destruction from God (14:10; 19:20; 20:10; 21:8), reminiscent of the overthrow of Sodom and Gomorrah (Gen. 19:24,28; Luke 17:29). The message is that God uses warring nations to punish the wicked with His wrath. However, here the horsemen are spiritual powers, evil *angels* (v. 14) leading a vast host of demons pictured as terrifying mixtures of dangerous creatures ("horses," v. 17; "lions," v. 17; *serpents*, v. 19) as in the previous vision (vv. 7–10). They are linked to the demonic locusts in that they use their *tails* to *hurt* men (same Greek words as in v. 10). Man's greatest enemy is not the army of a foreign nation but evil spirits (Eph. 6:12) arrayed in an innumerable host (Jer. 46:23). *Two hundred thousand thousand* is, literally, "two myriads of myriads" (v. 16; cf. 5:11). Thus the powers behind the wars that devour millions of people ("the third part of men"; v. 15) are revealed to be the demons of Satan. They bring war and death especially by their lies (*their mouths*; vv. 17–19; 13:5–6; contrast 1:16). Yet the demons are merely God's executioners (1 Kings 22:19–22). The Lord of heaven controls them all ("voice from . . . the golden altar"; v. 13), and has ordained for each event its precise time (*hour, day, month, year*; v. 15). The principle of the sixth seal may climax in a particular, final conflict at the end of the age when Satan gathers mankind to war against Christ to their own destruction (see notes at 16:12–16).

9:17 *jacinth*. The color blue, like sapphire.

9:20–21 *fornication*. Sexual immorality. Such is the blindness and stubbornness of mankind that suffering, war, and death do not move people to repent of their sins and turn back to

these plagues yet repented not of the works of their
hands, that they should not worship devils, and
idols of gold, and silver, and brass, and stone, and
of wood: which neither can see, nor hear, nor walk:
21 Neither repented they of their murders, nor
of their sorceries, nor of their fornication, nor of
their thefts.

CHAPTER 10

AND I saw another mighty angel come down from
heaven, clothed with a cloud: and a rainbow *was*
upon his head, and his face *was* as it were the sun,
and his feet as pillars of fire:
2 And he had in his hand a little book open: and
he set his right foot upon the sea, and *his* left *foot*
on the earth,
3 And cried with a loud voice, as *when* a lion
roareth: and when he had cried, seven thunders
uttered their voices.
4 And when the seven thunders had uttered their
voices, I was about to write: and I heard a voice from
heaven saying unto me, Seal up those things which
the seven thunders uttered, and write them not.
5 And the angel which I saw stand upon the sea
and upon the earth lifted up his hand to heaven,
6 And sware by him that liveth for ever and ever,
who created heaven, and the things that therein
are, and the earth, and the things that therein are,
and the sea, and the things which are therein, that
there should be time no longer:
7 But in the days of the voice of the seventh angel,
when he shall begin to sound, the mystery of God
should be finished, as he hath declared to his
servants the prophets.
8 And the voice which I heard from heaven
spake unto me again, and said, Go *and* take the
little book which is open in the hand of the angel
which standeth upon the sea and upon the earth.
9 And I went unto the angel, and said unto him,
Give me the little book. And he said unto me,
Take *it*, and eat it up; and it shall make thy belly
bitter, but it shall be in thy mouth sweet as honey.
10 And I took the little book out of the angel's
hand, and ate it up; and it was in my mouth sweet
as honey: and as soon as I had eaten it, my belly
was bitter.
11 And he said unto me, Thou must prophesy
again before many peoples, and nations, and
tongues, and kings.

---

the true God (16:9,11,21). The great irony of their foolishness is that through their *idols* they *worship* the very *devils* that destroy them (13:4). This demonstrates the justice of God in their damnation.

Thoughts for Personal/Family Worship: Chapter 9

1. **If only people could see the demons behind the so-called pleasures and privileges of this world, they would shrink back and cry out in horror. Behind the beautiful hair of the seductress or the gleaming gold crown of the conqueror is a locust with the teeth of lions and the sting of scorpions. Pray for God to enable you to see the evil of sin, not just in its consequences but also in its hatred against God, so that you might thoroughly repent of sin.**
2. **Though God authorizes governments to use deadly force to protect the righteous and punish the wicked (Rom. 13:1–4), it remains true that most warfare is a devilish business. Pray for peace, that your nation would not be given over to the horrors of warfare. Pray too for those who serve in the armed forces, that they would not fall into the bloodlust and corruption that Satan too easily introduces into the most just of military causes.**
3. **Though wars and disasters may bring temporary surges of attendance at worship services and prayer meetings, often people quickly slide back into their sins. Why does mankind so stubbornly cling to its idols and sins? What is wrong with us?**

Chapter 10: *The series of trumpets pauses before the seventh, and in the interlude John has visions of a mighty angel and a bittersweet scroll.*

The Mighty Angel and the Little Scroll (10:1–11)

10:1–7 Just as there was a pause between the sixth and seventh seals (7:1–17), so there is an interlude between the sixth and seventh trumpets (10:1—11:14). The *mighty angel* symbolically represents Christ (*face* like *the sun*; 1:16), the reigning and returning Son of Man (*with a cloud*; v. 1; 14:14; Dan. 7:13; Mark 13:26; 14:62). The word *angel* (or "messenger"; 1:20) does not identify Christ as a created spirit, for the Angel of the Lord in the Old Testament is God (Gen. 16:7–14; Ex. 3:1–6; Judg. 13:17–23). He possesses God's covenantal glory (*rainbow*; 4:3) and manifests God's gracious presence with His people (*pillars of fire*; Ex. 13:21–22; 14:24; Neh. 9:12,19). He executes God's decree by His redeeming work (*in his hand a little book* or scroll; 5:5–10). The King declares the wrath of God (*seven thunders*; 8:5; 11:19; 16:18; Ps. 29:3–7), for Christ has overcome (*lion*; 5:5) and will judge in anger (*roareth*; Prov. 19:12; 20:2; Isa. 31:4; Amos 3:4–8). He claims the entire world as His inheritance (*foot upon the sea . . . on the earth*), for God *created* the universe (*heaven . . . earth . . . and the sea*) and everything in it (*things which are therein*). When *the seventh angel* sounds his trumpet, Christ's kingdom will come (11:15–19), and that without further delay (*time no longer*; literally, "no further duration"). The vision symbolically shows the absolute certainty of His promise by His swearing an oath (*sware*)—God swears by God (Heb. 6:13). Yet although God has revealed parts of His decree (symbolized in the seven seals, seven trumpets, and seven bowls), parts remain hidden and are not for us to know (*Seal up . . . the seven thunders*; Dan. 12:4–9; cf. Deut. 29:29).

10:8–11 Just as Revelation opened by saying that Christ gave John His revelation (1:1), so here the angel gives John a *book* (or scroll) revealing God's purposes of redemption and destruction for all the world (*many peoples, and nations, and tongues, and kings*; 5:9; 7:9; 11:9; 14:6; 17:15). Yet it is not a revelation of God's whole plan but only a summary of it (*little book* is a diminutive form of the word used in 5:1 for the "book" of seven seals). As with the prophecy of Ezekiel (Ezek. 2:8–3:3), the apostle must not merely *take* the book but also receive it into his heart by faith (*eat it up*; Isa. 55:1–3). The Word of God is delightful to believers (Ps. 1:2), as *sweet as honey* (Ps. 19:10; 119:103; Prov. 16:24; 24:13–14). Yet the Word is also *bitter* for

CHAPTER 11

AND there was given me a reed like unto a rod:
and the angel stood, saying, Rise, and measure
the temple of God, and the altar, and them that
worship therein.
2 But the court which is without the temple leave
out, and measure it not; for it is given unto the
Gentiles: and the holy city shall they tread under
foot forty *and* two months.
3 And I will give *power* unto my two witnesses,
and they shall prophesy a thousand two hundred
and threescore days, clothed in sackcloth.
4 These are the two olive trees, and the two
candlesticks standing before the God of the earth.
5 And if any man will hurt them, fire proceedeth
out of their mouth, and devoureth their enemies:
and if any man will hurt them, he must in this
manner be killed.
6 These have power to shut heaven, that it rain
not in the days of their prophecy: and have power
over waters to turn them to blood, and to smite
the earth with all plagues, as often as they will.
7 And when they shall have finished their
testimony, the beast that ascendeth out of the
bottomless pit shall make war against them, and
shall overcome them, and kill them.
8 And their dead bodies *shall lie* in the street of
the great city, which spiritually is called Sodom
and Egypt, where also our Lord was crucified.
9 And they of the people and kindreds and
tongues and nations shall see their dead bodies
three days and an half, and shall not suffer their
dead bodies to be put in graves.
10 And they that dwell upon the earth shall re-
joice over them, and make merry, and shall send
gifts one to another; because these two prophets
tormented them that dwelt on the earth.
11 And after three days and an half the Spirit of
life from God entered into them, and they stood
upon their feet; and great fear fell upon them
which saw them.
12 And they heard a great voice from heaven
saying unto them, Come up hither. And they as-
cended up to heaven in a cloud; and their enemies
beheld them.
13 And the same hour was there a great earth-
quake, and the tenth part of the city fell, and in
the earthquake were slain of men seven thousand:

---

it speaks against sin, bringing isolation and persecution to believers in this world (Jer. 15:15–21).

Thoughts for Personal/Family Worship: Chapter 10

1. **Though demonic powers rage and ruin mankind (9:1–21), Jesus is Lord. Believers in Christ need not fear the Devil. As Martin Luther said, "The prince of darkness grim, we tremble not for him. His rage we can endure, for lo, his doom is sure." Christ's kingdom cannot fail, for His work of accomplishing redemption is already finished. How much then should we desire and delight to be part of His kingdom! Jesus will reign forever.**
2. **The Bible is a bittersweet book for believers. On the one hand, its righteous laws and trustworthy promises are sweeter than honey to those who receive them. On the other hand, it calls us into the bitterness of loneliness and persecution in the world. How are you experiencing the sweetness of the Word in your life? Its bitterness?**

Chapter 11: *John has a vision of two witnesses who prophesy faithfully unto death, and then sees the angel blow the seventh and ultimate trumpet.*

The Two Witnesses (11:1–14)

11:1–2 The second vision in the interlude between the sixth and seventh trumpets (10:1—11:14) presents the church in the world. The new covenant *temple* on earth is no building but the church of believers in union with Christ (1:20; 1 Cor. 3:16; 2 Cor. 6:16; Eph. 2:19–22). Measuring the temple symbolizes God's protection, presence, and purifying of His people (21:15; Ezek. 40–44; esp. 40:3; 43:1–9; 44:4,9–10; Zech. 2:1–5). Though sustained inwardly by the Spirit as God's sanctuary (Ezek. 37:14,26–28), the church suffers outwardly (*without*) from its enemies (*tread under foot*; Isa. 63:18; Dan. 8:13) until Christ comes. Revelation, like Daniel, refers to this time period with the symbolic number of half of seven years, enumerated in various ways, such as 1260 days (vv. 2–3; 12:6,14; 13:5; Dan. 7:25; 9:27; 12:7,11–12). This was the duration of the famine called down by Elijah (Luke 4:25; James 5:17), the abomination of desolation by Antiochus Epiphanes (167–164 BC; Dan. 11:31), and the war leading to the destruction of Jerusalem (AD 66–70; Luke 21:20–24). Revelation applies it symbolically to the world's attacks upon God's spiritual temple while the church witnesses prophetically (vv. 3–10).

11:3–6 In the midst of persecution, the church testifies as *witnesses* of Jesus Christ (1:5; 2:13), the lampstands (*candlesticks*) shining in God's temple (1:20; 2:5). *Two witnesses* were required for legal conviction of guilt (Deut. 19:15). The symbolic miracles refer to Moses (*plagues* like turning *waters* into *blood*; Ex. 7–11) and Elijah (*shut heaven, that it rain not*; 1 Kings 17:1). They show that the church stands with the persecuted prophets (18:24; Matt. 5:12; 23:34–35), just as John the Baptist was a new Elijah though working no miracles (Mal. 4:5; Matt. 11:14; Luke 1:17). Even without miracles, the preaching of the Word is as powerful as *fire* to devour God's enemies (Jer. 5:14; 20:9; 23:29), for the church is anointed with the Spirit (*olive trees* and *candlesticks*; Zech. 4:1–6). Yet its posture is one of grief and repentance (*sackcloth*; Dan. 9:3–5).

11:7–13 The church in union with Christ is depicted as sharing in the sufferings and resurrection of its *crucified* Lord. The forces of Satan (*the beast*; 13:1) persecute and *kill* God's people (v. 7; Dan. 7:21,25). The wicked appear prosperous but will fall under God's wrath as He saves His people (*Sodom and Egypt*; Gen. 13:10; 19:16,24; Jude 5,7). In this vision, unbelieving Jerusalem merges with Babylon (*the great city*; 14:8; 16:19; 17:18; 18:10,16,18–19,21) as a symbol of the wicked world, including all nations (*people and kindreds and tongues and nations*). The persecution will intensify for a brief period (compare *three days and an half* to the symbolic three-and-a-half years) when the church's mission is done at the end of the age (*when they shall have finished their testimony*; Matt. 24:14). The world celebrates a festival of victory over its enemies (*make merry, and shall send gifts*; Est. 9:22). But God will raise His slain witnesses from the dead by His *Spirit* (Rom. 8:11) and call them up (*Come up hither*) to meet Christ in the air (*cloud*; Matt. 24:30–31; 1 Thess. 4:16–17). Christ will terrify the wicked

and the remnant were affrighted, and gave glory
to the God of heaven.
14 The second woe is past; *and*, behold, the third
woe cometh quickly.
15 And the seventh angel sounded; and there were
great voices in heaven, saying, The kingdoms of this
world are become *the kingdoms* of our Lord, and of
his Christ; and he shall reign for ever and ever.
16 And the four and twenty elders, which sat
before God on their seats, fell upon their faces,
and worshipped God,
17 Saying, We give thee thanks, O Lord God
Almighty, which art, and wast, and art to come;
because thou hast taken to thee thy great power,
and hast reigned.
18 And the nations were angry, and thy wrath is
come, and the time of the dead, that they should
be judged, and that thou shouldest give reward
unto thy servants the prophets, and to the saints,
and them that fear thy name, small and great; and
shouldest destroy them which destroy the earth.
19 And the temple of God was opened in heaven,
and there was seen in his temple the ark of his tes-
tament: and there were lightnings, and voices, and
thunderings, and an earthquake, and great hail.

CHAPTER 12

AND there appeared a great wonder in heaven; a
woman clothed with the sun, and the moon un-
der her feet, and upon her head a crown of twelve
stars:
2 And she being with child cried, travailing in
birth, and pained to be delivered.
3 And there appeared another wonder in heaven;
and behold a great red dragon, having seven heads
and ten horns, and seven crowns upon his heads.
4 And his tail drew the third part of the stars of
heaven, and did cast them to the earth: and the
dragon stood before the woman which was ready
to be delivered, for to devour her child as soon as
it was born.
5 And she brought forth a man child, who was to
rule all nations with a rod of iron: and her child
was caught up unto God, and *to* his throne.
6 And the woman fled into the wilderness, where
she hath a place prepared of God, that they should
feed her there a thousand two hundred *and* three-
score days.
7 And there was war in heaven: Michael and his
angels fought against the dragon; and the dragon
fought and his angels,

(*affrighted*), and compel men to give *glory* to *God* (Phil. 2:11).

11:14 Regarding the last three trumpets as the first woe, *second woe*, and *third woe*, see 8:13; 9:12.

The Seventh Trumpet: The Kingdom and Judgment (11:15–19)

11:15–19 Upon the sounding of the seventh trumpet, God's kingdom comes without further delay (10:6–7). This is another indication that Revelation consists of cycles that repeatedly bring the reader to the end of the age. The kingdom of *Christ* will sweep away *the kingdoms of this world*, not by human activity but by God's *power* to *reign for ever* (Ex. 15:18; Dan. 2:34–35,44). He is eternal Lord of the present, past, and future (*art, and wast, and art to come*: is, and was, and is coming; 1:4,8; 4:8). God's *wrath* will come to devastate (*earthquake, hail*; 16:17–21) the *nations* that raged against His Christ (Ps. 2:1–6) and abused His creation with violence (*destroy* [or corrupt] *the earth*; 19:2; Jer. 51:25). He will raise *the dead* to judgment (Dan. 12:2; John 5:28–29). His *reward* (22:12) will bless His people for their faithful witness (*prophets*), holy obedience (*saints* or holy ones), and reverent worship (*fear thy name*). God will openly display His glory (*temple of God was opened*) in Christ (*the ark* of propitiation and communion with God; Ex. 25:22; Lev. 16:15). For this, God's victorious people of all times (*four and twenty elders*; see note at 4:3–7) will worship Him with enthusiasm (*great voices in heaven*).

Thoughts for Personal/Family Worship: Chapter 11

1. **The church can witness to the world with great confidence in God's power and presence with us. Yet there is a cost to witnessing, sometimes to the point of shedding our blood for Christ. How can you grow in your boldness and courage to speak up for the Lord?**
2. **Judgment day is coming. The kingdoms of this world are living on borrowed time, and Christ will return to reclaim His world from the wicked. This is the great hope of His people. The Lord Jesus will not forget their service to Him but will reward His faithful servants richly in His everlasting kingdom. Be encouraged, dear believer; serve the Lord with zeal, and begin the business of heaven now by worshiping God with holy fear.**

THE WAR WITH THE DRAGON (12:1—14:20)

Chapter 12: *A new cycle of visions begins with a view of the cosmic conflict between the dragon and God's angels, church, and Son.*

The Woman, the Child, and the Dragon (12:1–17)

12:1–6 Having concluded the cycle of the seven trumpets leading up to judgment day (chs. 8–11), Revelation starts a new cycle of symbolic visions. The *woman* is the church (Isa. 54:1–5), encompassing God's people both under the old covenant (*sun, moon, twelve stars*; Gen. 37:9–10; Song 6:10) and the new covenant (witnesses to Jesus Christ; v. 17). Her labor pains represent her sorrows (*travailing in birth*; Isa. 26:17; 66:7–10; John 16:21) as she waits for the Christ to come and reign (Mic. 5:2–4). Satan, the fallen angel behind the serpent of Eden (v. 9), appears as a large *dragon*, symbolizing his spiritual domination of earthly kingdoms (*seven heads* and *ten horns*; 17:9–13) and persecution of the godly as by the wicked Antiochus Epiphanes (*drew* or dragged down *the stars of heaven*; Dan. 8:10; cf. Gen. 15:5). The Devil attempted to destroy Jesus (*man child*), but He triumphed and ascended to reign as the anointed warrior-king (*rod of iron*; 2:27; 19:15; Ps. 2:9) over God's kingdom (*his throne*; 3:21; Ps. 110:1). The church on earth is sojourning and suffering (like Israel in the *wilderness*; vv. 6,14) but is still under God's care. That the *thousand two hundred and threescore* (1260) *days* begin with Christ's ascension shows the number to be figurative for this whole age (see note at 11:1–2).

12:7–12 The *war* of the angels symbolizes the effect of Christ's exaltation upon Satan and his forces. Satan's defeat relates especially to his work as *the accuser of our brethren* in the court of *heaven* (Job 1:6–11; 2:5; Zech. 3:1–5). The Greek

8 And prevailed not; neither was their place found
any more in heaven.
9 And the great dragon was cast out, that old ser-
pent, called the Devil, and Satan, which deceiveth
the whole world: he was cast out into the earth,
and his angels were cast out with him.
10 And I heard a loud voice saying in heaven, Now
is come salvation, and strength, and the kingdom
of our God, and the power of his Christ: for the
accuser of our brethren is cast down, which ac-
cused them before our God day and night.
11 And they overcame him by the blood of the
Lamb, and by the word of their testimony; and
they loved not their lives unto the death.
12 Therefore rejoice, *ye* heavens, and ye that dwell
in them. Woe to the inhabiters of the earth and
of the sea! for the devil is come down unto you,
having great wrath, because he knoweth that he
hath but a short time.
13 And when the dragon saw that he was cast
unto the earth, he persecuted the woman which
brought forth the man *child*.
14 And to the woman were given two wings of a
great eagle, that she might fly into the wilderness,
into her place, where she is nourished for a time,
and times, and half a time, from the face of the
serpent.
15 And the serpent cast out of his mouth water as
a flood after the woman, that he might cause her
to be carried away of the flood.
16 And the earth helped the woman, and the
earth opened her mouth, and swallowed up the
flood which the dragon cast out of his mouth.
17 And the dragon was wroth with the woman,
and went to make war with the remnant of her
seed, which keep the commandments of God, and
have the testimony of Jesus Christ.

CHAPTER 13

AND I stood upon the sand of the sea, and saw a
beast rise up out of the sea, having seven heads
and ten horns, and upon his horns ten crowns,
and upon his heads the name of blasphemy.
2 And the beast which I saw was like unto a leop-
ard, and his feet were as *the feet* of a bear, and his
mouth as the mouth of a lion: and the dragon gave
him his power, and his seat, and great authority.

---

word *accused* means "brought legal charges against them." Both the Hebrew word *Satan* and the Greek word translated "Devil" mean accuser or enemy who speaks evil. Christ's atoning death (*the blood of the Lamb*) redeemed His people from sin (1:5; 5:9; 7:14), and His presence in heaven (v. 5) answers all charges against them (Rom. 8:33–34; 1 John 2:1). The archangel *Michael* was assigned to fight the demons on behalf of God's people (Dan. 10:13,21; 12:1; Jude 9) and thus leads the holy *angels* as God's instruments to implement the results of Christ's victory. Satan continues to rage on earth (*great wrath*) and control people with his lies (present tense *deceiveth*) as he did in the garden (*that old serpent*; Gen. 3:1), but now he is in retreat before the armies of the Lamb (17:14), and *he knoweth that he hath but a short time*. Christ has taken up His *kingdom* and *power* and has bound the Devil and *cast* him out (20:1–3; Matt. 12:28–29; John 12:31; 16:11). He leads the church to conquer the Devil (*overcame him*; see note at 2:7) and destroy his kingdom (*neither was their place found*; Dan. 2:35,44). Satan's symbolic fall from heaven is realized as the church proclaims the gospel (*the word of their testimony*; Luke 10:1,10,17–19) and endures suffering and death for His name (*loved not their lives unto the death*; 2:10; 6:9; Matt. 24:9–14).

12:13–17 This part of the vision takes the woman's flight mentioned briefly earlier (v. 6) and expands it with imagery of a new exodus. There she experiences the Lord's salvation like Israel from Egypt (*wings* of an *eagle*; Ex. 19:4) and provision as with manna (*nourished* in the *wilderness*; cf. 2:17) during the designated time of trouble (*a time, and times, and half a time*; 11:2). Satan persecutes the church on earth, the *serpent* attacking the spiritual offspring (*seed*) of the woman (Gen. 3:14–15; Gal. 4:26–29). The Devil is enraged (*wroth*) against God's obedient witnesses. Like a huge sea *serpent* (Isa. 27:1), an image that alludes to Egypt (Ps. 74:13–14; Isa. 51:9), Satan spews out a river (*flood*), an image used of persecutors (Pss. 18:4,16; 66:1–4,14–15) and an attacking army (Isa. 8:5–8; Jer. 46:7–8; 47:2). However, just as God destroyed the army of Egypt at the Red Sea, so He destroys Satan's servants who attack the church, including the wicked in its ranks (*earth opened her mouth, and swallowed*; Ex. 15:12; Num. 16:30–32).

Thoughts for Personal/Family Worship: Chapter 12

1. **Believers must learn to read the history of Israel as a type of their own spiritual history in Jesus Christ. The Old Testament is for our encouragement and instruction (Rom. 15:4). For example, it teaches Christians to see themselves in the midst of a great exodus, experiencing God's salvation and testing in the wilderness. Another way the Old Testament helps Christians is by giving us the background for understanding the New Testament, including the book of Revelation. Treasure the whole Bible, and study it.**
2. **Christians fight in an invisible war against Satan. The church's enemy aims at nothing less than its total destruction and condemnation. Therefore Christians must be vigilant and prepared to suffer. They must cling to Jesus Christ and His shed blood as the only solution to the guilt of their sins. They must never let go of their gospel witness but trust that God will use the persecutions they face to glorify Himself and build His church. How does ch. 12 encourage you to stay in the fight for Christ?**

Chapter 13: ***The dragon, frustrated by his inability to destroy Christ or His church, employs two great beasts to further his war against the godly.***

The Beast with Seven Heads (13:1–10)

13:1–4 The first means by which Satan consolidates his kingdom on earth is political empires, symbolized in a *beast* like a combination of fierce animals representing various empires in Daniel's vision (*leopard, bear, lion*; Dan. 7:1–6,17). The beast represents not one ruler or kingdom but a principle behind all ungodly civil authorities. These murderous civil powers are like Satan (*seven heads and ten horns*; 12:3), for they receive their *power* and kingdom (*seat*, literally, "throne") from the Devil (*dragon*). The relationship between the dragon and the

3 And I saw one of his heads as it were wounded
to death; and his deadly wound was healed: and
all the world wondered after the beast.
4 And they worshipped the dragon which gave
power unto the beast: and they worshipped the
beast, saying, Who *is* like unto the beast? who is
able to make war with him?
5 And there was given unto him a mouth speak-
ing great things and blasphemies; and power was
given unto him to continue forty *and* two months.
6 And he opened his mouth in blasphemy against
God, to blaspheme his name, and his tabernacle,
and them that dwell in heaven.
7 And it was given unto him to make war with the
saints, and to overcome them: and power was giv-
en him over all kindreds, and tongues, and nations.
8 And all that dwell upon the earth shall worship
him, whose names are not written in the book of
life of the Lamb slain from the foundation of the
world.
9 If any man have an ear, let him hear.
10 He that leadeth into captivity shall go into
captivity: he that killeth with the sword must be
killed with the sword. Here is the patience and the
faith of the saints.
11 And I beheld another beast coming up out of
the earth; and he had two horns like a lamb, and
he spake as a dragon.
12 And he exerciseth all the power of the first
beast before him, and causeth the earth and them
which dwell therein to worship the first beast,
whose deadly wound was healed.
13 And he doeth great wonders, so that he maketh
fire come down from heaven on the earth in the
sight of men,
14 And deceiveth them that dwell on the earth by
the means of those miracles which he had power
to do in the sight of the beast; saying to them
that dwell on the earth, that they should make
an image to the beast, which had the wound by a
sword, and did live.
15 And he had power to give life unto the image
of the beast, that the image of the beast should
both speak, and cause that as many as would not
worship the image of the beast should be killed.
16 And he causeth all, both small and great, rich

---

first beast is thus a perverse imitation of God the Father and His Son. The symbolism of the beast's *death* and resurrection presents it as a false Christ and may point to the satanic resurgence at the end of the age (11:7; 20:7). *Wounded* is the same Greek word as "slain," used of the Lamb (5:6,9,12). These authorities demand divine honors (*name of blasphemy*) and are *worshipped* by their subjects, especially for their military power (*who is able to make war with him?*) and recovery after deadly defeats (v. 14). Various Roman emperors were given titles such as Son of God, Savior, and Lord and God. Emperor worship was prominent in Asia Minor, where the seven churches were located. The same pattern has appeared in Egypt, China, Japan, and many other nations, even in modern, secular cultures.

13:5–8 Drawing from the prophecy of Daniel (Dan. 7:8,20–21, 25; 8:9–12,22–25; 11:36–39), the beast is described as a tyrant who persecutes God's people (11:7), opposes true religion, and receives the worship of men (2 Thess. 2:3–12) during the appointed time of the church's troubles (*forty and two months*; see note at 11:1–2). In part this alludes to Antiochus IV (c. 215–164 BC). This king, called Epiphanes or "God manifest," desecrated the temple in Jerusalem with pagan worship, tried to convert the Jews to Greek culture, and fought against the Maccabean rebels for the last three-and-a-half years of his life. The spirit behind Antiochus pervades *all kindreds, and tongues, and nations*, for the world tends to deify its rulers. This is only the case, however, for those individuals (*names*) not chosen by God from eternity for redemption in Christ (*written in the book of life of the Lamb slain from the foundation of the world*; 17:8,14), implying that the people elected and called by God overcome this idolatry. Believers honor the government (Rom. 13:1–7) but refuse to worship it or trust it as the Savior.

13:9–10 The Holy Spirit interrupts the vision to call the churches to persevere. *have an ear.* See note at 2:7. *he that killeth . . . must be killed.* Justice assures us that God will punish the murderer (Gen. 9:6; Matt. 26:52).

The Beast with Horns Like a Lamb (13:11–18)

13:11–15 The second beast mimics Christ (*like a lamb*) but teaches the lies of the Devil (*spake as a dragon*). The first beast is a royal/political antichrist, and the second is a priestly/prophetic antichrist (Matt. 24:24; 1 John 2:18). The symbol of making *fire come down from heaven* alludes to the ministry of Elijah (1 Kings 18:38; 2 Kings 1:10,12), identifying this beast with false prophets (16:13; 19:20; 20:10; cf. 2:20) in competition with the prophetic witness of the true church (11:3,6). False prophets may use *miracles* to awe men into adoration, whether by demons or trickery (Ex. 7:11,22; 8:7; Deut. 13:1; Matt. 24:24; Acts 8:9–11; 13:6; 2 Thess. 2:9). Mechanisms, sorcery, and ventriloquism can make statues seem to come to *life*. False religion often serves as a tool of the state (*power of the first beast*) for its glorification (*to worship the first beast*). It also violently persecutes those who refuse to give absolute allegiance to the state and its ideals (Dan. 3:14–15). A sixteen-foot tall statue of Emperor Domitian (reigned AD 81–96) stood in a temple in Ephesus. Under Emperor Trajan (reigned AD 98–117), refusal to offer worship to an image of the emperor was a capital crime.

13:16–18 Just as the righteous belong to God and escape His wrath, symbolized by a seal or mark on their *foreheads* (7:3; 9:4; 14:1), so the wicked belong to this world system and escape its persecution, symbolized by receiving the *mark* of the first *beast*. Cultures marginalize believers and cut them off from economic opportunities (*no man might buy or sell*) because they will not give total allegiance to the state and participate in its idolatry. Most explanations of the number of the beast use the Jewish system of *gematria* to calculate 666 (*Six hundred threescore and six*) by the sum of the values of the letters of a name. However, in Revelation numbers symbolize principles, not names. The number could refer to the economic power of an idolatrous king, being Solomon's annual revenue of gold (1 Kings 10:14; cf. 11:5–7), but in a book dominated by sevens (representing completeness), 666 likely shows that evil tyrants fall short of divine perfection despite their aspirations to be gods, having merely *the number of a man*.

Thoughts for Personal/Family Worship: Chapter 13

1. Satan has long wedded political tyranny with false religion to rule the world. Believers of all ages have suffered

and poor, free and bond, to receive a mark in their
right hand, or in their foreheads:
17 And that no man might buy or sell, save he
that had the mark, or the name of the beast, or
the number of his name.
18 Here is wisdom. Let him that hath under-
standing count the number of the beast: for it is
the number of a man; and his number *is* Six hun-
dred threescore *and* six.

CHAPTER 14

AND I looked, and, lo, a Lamb stood on the mount
Sion, and with him an hundred forty *and* four
thousand, having his Father's name written in
their foreheads.
2 And I heard a voice from heaven, as the voice of
many waters, and as the voice of a great thunder:
and I heard the voice of harpers harping with
their harps:
3 And they sung as it were a new song before
the throne, and before the four beasts, and the
elders: and no man could learn that song but
the hundred *and* forty *and* four thousand, which
were redeemed from the earth.
4 These are they which were not defiled with
women; for they are virgins. These are they which
follow the Lamb whithersoever he goeth. These
were redeemed from among men, *being* the first-
fruits unto God and to the Lamb.
5 And in their mouth was found no guile: for
they are without fault before the throne of God.
6 And I saw another angel fly in the midst of
heaven, having the everlasting gospel to preach
unto them that dwell on the earth, and to every
nation, and kindred, and tongue, and people,
7 Saying with a loud voice, Fear God, and give
glory to him; for the hour of his judgment is
come: and worship him that made heaven, and
earth, and the sea, and the fountains of waters.
8 And there followed another angel, saying,
Babylon is fallen, is fallen, that great city, because
she made all nations drink of the wine of the
wrath of her fornication.
9 And the third angel followed them, saying with
a loud voice, If any man worship the beast and his
image, and receive *his* mark in his forehead, or in
his hand,
10 The same shall drink of the wine of the wrath
of God, which is poured out without mixture into
the cup of his indignation; and he shall be tor-
mented with fire and brimstone in the presence of
the holy angels, and in the presence of the Lamb:
11 And the smoke of their torment ascendeth up
for ever and ever: and they have no rest day nor
night, who worship the beast and his image, and
whosoever receiveth the mark of his name.
12 Here is the patience of the saints: here *are* they

under such unholy alliances of persecuting powers, whether under Babylon, the Roman emperors, Muslim governments, Roman Catholic princes and the Papacy, the Stuart kings of seventeenth-century England, or Nazi and Communist totalitarian states in the twentieth century. Though differing widely in ideology, all such powers display the Devil's methodology: use violence and economic penalties to unify people around a common idolatry. How do you see this principle operating today?

2. What makes it so hard to resist the pressure to conform to this world? How can the church equip Christians to face such persecution with courage, hope, and love?

Chapter 14: ***This cycle of visions concludes with a view of the triumph of the redeemed and warnings of the coming day of judgment.***

The Lamb and the Redeemed (14:1–5)

14:1–5 In contrast to the evil world depicted in the two beasts (13:1–18), the next vision portrays those *redeemed* by the blood of the *Lamb* (5:9–10). They are the spiritual Israel (*an hundred forty and four thousand*; 7:4), dwelling in the new Jerusalem (*mount Sion* or Zion; 21:10; Heb. 12:22), a symbol of Christ's kingdom (Ps. 2:6; Isa. 24:23). They belong to the *Father* and bear His likeness (*name written in their foreheads*; 7:3). By the grace of Christ they reject the spiritual "fornication" of the world's idolatry (v. 8) and devote themselves to Christ as His pure Bride (*virgins*; 21:2,9; 2 Cor. 11:2). Though surrounded by lies, they imitate Christ in His suffering obedience (*follow the Lamb whithersoever* [wherever] *he goeth*; Luke 9:23), and like Him their mouths speak truth, not deceit (*guile*), even as they are persecuted (Isa. 53:9). Their experience of being *redeemed* by Christ draws from them a thunderous *song* of praise to God like Levites in the heavenly temple (*harps*; see note at 5:8–10).

Three Angels of Gospel and Judgment (14:6–13)

14:6–7 The first *angel* represents the message that the church must *preach . . . to every nation* (Matt. 24:14; 28:19). Just as the redeemed sing to their Savior (v. 3), so the church's message may be summarized by the command to *worship* God, the Creator of all (Acts 14:15). In its broadest sense, worship means to *fear God, and give glory to him* with all one's life (15:4). This is not the whole content of the *gospel*, which centers on Christ, but it is a sum of its call to repentance.

14:8 The church also bears witness that this world, symbolized as the *city* of *Babylon* (chs. 17–18), in contrast to Jerusalem (14:1; chs. 21–22), will fall under God's judgment for its idolatry (*fornication*; Ezek. 16:15–34), and its intoxicating passion (*wine*) will end.

14:9–11 The *third angel* represents the church's testimony to the eternal wrath of God against those who belong to this world and *worship* its idols. Presently God gives many good things to the wicked (Matt. 5:45; Acts 14:17; Rom. 2:4), but in hell God will cause them to experience His anger without a drop of mercy (*without mixture*; cf. Luke 16:24–25). Hell is not the absence of God but *the presence* of the wrath *of the Lamb* (6:16), symbolized by a *cup* (Pss. 11:6; 75:8; Isa. 51:17,22–23; Jer. 25:15–17,27–28) and eternal fire, smoke, and sulfur (*brimstone*; Gen. 19:24,28; Ps. 11:6; Isa. 30:33; 34:9–10; Ezek. 38:22; Dan. 7:9–11). The wicked face *torment* in hell (18:7,10,15; Matt. 25:30) that is continuous and unceasing, just as the saints rejoice in God's glory forever (*no rest day nor night*; 4:8; Matt. 25:41,46).

14:12–13 The previous warnings motivate the endurance

HELL

Hell is the place of eternal judgment (Matt. 5:29; Luke 12:5; 16:23). Further, it is the *only* place of eternal torment, as opposed to the extra-scriptural idea of purgatory (cf. 1 Cor. 3:12–14; 2 Cor. 5:6, 8; Phil. 1:23; Heb. 1:3; 1 John 1:7). Scripture readily affirms the existence of hell (Matt. 23:33; Luke 16:19–31; 2 Peter 2:3–4) and notes that it is the place where the bodies and souls of men are afflicted. Hell has many names that underline its nature. It is described as an unquenchable fire (Luke 3:17), a furnace of fire (Matt. 13:42; cf. Dan. 3:21–22), a lake of fire (Rev. 19:20), eternal fire (Jude 7), outer darkness (Matt. 22:13), the blackness of darkness forever (Jude 13), and chains of darkness (2 Peter 2:4).

Some object to preaching and teaching on the doctrine of hell, supposing that its teaching is the antithesis of the New Testament emphasis on Christ's message of the gospel. However, all protest is laid aside when it is noted that the doctrine of hell is more clearly set forth in the New Testament than in the Old and that, further, it is found most often on the lips of Christ Himself. Furthermore, an understanding of the continual torment of body and soul in hell is meant to startle the drowsy consciences of those unbelievers yet living (Matt. 10:28; 2 Cor. 5:11). Instilling a biblical fear of hell is therefore necessary and useful.

Two realities demand this awful judgment for the unbeliever. *First*, hell is necessary because of the filthiness of sin against the infinite and holy God. It is mandatory that a proportionate punishment be executed according to God's justice. *Second*, hell is required because Christ did not satisfy the justice of God for the wicked, who must themselves bear the full wrath of God in hell.

This tormenting wrath of God in hell has two qualities. *First*, the judgment is an eternal deprivation. The presence of God (Matt. 25:41); the company of saints and angels (Matt. 22:13; 24:41); the blessedness of heaven (Luke 16:23); the mercy of God and Christ, and the godly with them (Prov. 1:26); and all hope for recovery forever (Matt. 3:12; 25:46; 2 Thess. 1:9; Jude 7; cf. Isa. 33:14; 66:24; Luke 12:59)—all are shut out by the gates of hell. Through eternity the ungodly become increasingly more and more impoverished in hell.

Second, there is a multitude of ways in which the damned are made more miserable as the wrath of the holy God is exercised in its fullest degree. This suffering is eternally augmented by: the *universality* of torments affecting the wicked in body and soul; the *extremity* of torments that can neither be quenched nor tolerated; the *continuity* of torments, having no cessation or intermission; the *society* of torments, those with whom the wicked suffer; the *quality* of torments, a misery devoid of all comfort and pleasure; the *cruelty* of torments at the hands of the Devil and his demons; and the *eternity* of torments that will forever be heaped upon the wicked.

At these things the unbeliever ought to fear and tremble so that he might be brought to repent and believe. Further, all men—and believers in particular—are thereby called to forsake the sins that lead to hell (Matt. 10:22–23; 23:14–15; Mark 12:40; Luke 12:47–48; Rom. 2:5; Heb. 13:4; 2 Peter 2:9–10). A glimpse of hell could only produce the desertion of all ungodliness. Additionally, the doctrine of hell brings the believer's heart to rest more sweetly in the glories of heaven. When the bitterness of hell is recognized, the joys of heaven become of even greater value.

—adapted from Christopher Love, *Heaven's Glory, Hell's Terror*

that keep the commandments of God, and the
faith of Jesus.
13 And I heard a voice from heaven saying unto
me, Write, Blessed *are* the dead which die in the
Lord from henceforth: Yea, saith the Spirit, that
they may rest from their labours; and their works
do follow them.
14 And I looked, and behold a white cloud, and
upon the cloud *one* sat like unto the Son of man,
having on his head a golden crown, and in his
hand a sharp sickle.
15 And another angel came out of the temple,
crying with a loud voice to him that sat on the
cloud, Thrust in thy sickle, and reap: for the time
is come for thee to reap; for the harvest of the
earth is ripe.
16 And he that sat on the cloud thrust in his sickle
on the earth; and the earth was reaped.
17 And another angel came out of the temple
which is in heaven, he also having a sharp sickle.
18 And another angel came out from the altar,
which had power over fire; and cried with a loud
cry to him that had the sharp sickle, saying, Thrust
in thy sharp sickle, and gather the clusters of the
vine of the earth; for her grapes are fully ripe.
19 And the angel thrust in his sickle into the
earth, and gathered the vine of the earth, and cast
it into the great winepress of the wrath of God.
20 And the winepress was trodden without the
city, and blood came out of the winepress, even
unto the horse bridles, by the space of a thousand
and six hundred furlongs.

CHAPTER 15

AND I saw another sign in heaven, great and
marvellous, seven angels having the seven last
plagues; for in them is filled up the wrath of God.
2 And I saw as it were a sea of glass mingled with
fire: and them that had gotten the victory over the
beast, and over his image, and over his mark, *and*
over the number of his name, stand on the sea of
glass, having the harps of God.
3 And they sing the song of Moses the servant of
God, and the song of the Lamb, saying, Great and
marvellous *are* thy works, Lord God Almighty;
just and true *are* thy ways, thou King of saints.
4 Who shall not fear thee, O Lord, and glorify thy

---

of God's people (*patience of the saints*) in obedience and *faith* (1 John 3:23–24). The damned have no rest (v. 10), but from now on to eternity (*from henceforth*) those united to Christ (*in the Lord*) when they *die* enter into a *blessed* experience of *rest* in heaven (6:11; Isa. 57:1–2,20–21; Heb. 4:10), and on judgment day they will receive rewards for their obedience (*their works do follow them*; 1 Tim. 5:24–25).

The Two Harvests (14:14–20)

14:14–16 Like the visionary cycles of the seals and trumpets, this cycle also concludes with judgment day, symbolized in a *harvest* (Matt. 3:12; 13:39). Christ appears victoriously (*golden crown*) to rule forever over all the nations (*cloud, Son of man*; 1:7; Dan. 7:13–14). The Father determined that the time is right for His Son to come and judge (*out of the temple, crying . . . the time is come*; Mark 13:32). The Son judges according to His Father's will (John 5:30). It is the day of the Lord both for the wicked and the godly (*ripe, sickle*; Joel 3:12–17).

14:17–20 A second harvest, this time of *grapes*, emphasizes that the wicked will be crushed (*trodden* or trampled) by the anger of God (*winepress of the wrath of God*; 19:15; Isa. 63:1–3; Lam. 1:15). It will fall upon all outside of God's covenant people (*without the city*; 22:14–15). The flood of *blood* symbolizes Christ's war (*horse*; 19:11,14) against the vast number of His enemies from every nation (vv. 17–18). The distance 1600 *furlongs* (184 miles) is the length of Israel from north to south; the number (4 x 4 x 10 x 10) may symbolize the fullness (ten) of peoples from the whole world (four; 7:1; 20:8). It would take the death of all humanity to make a river of blood 184 miles long, 5 feet deep, and 250 feet wide.

Thoughts for Personal/Family Worship: Chapter 14

1. **How beautiful is the Bride of Christ! In the midst of a world of oppression, lies, and idolatry, the true church is salt and light. Though hindered by remaining sin, the godly take up their crosses, deny themselves, and follow Christ. They are devoted to Him and reject the spiritual adultery of the world. Do you belong to this church? This is not just a question of official membership, though that is important. According to this chapter, what are the marks of true, spiritual membership in the church of Jesus Christ?**
2. **Unrepentant sinners will suffer in hell forever. The Bible does not teach the annihilation of the wicked in hell. That would be a mercy that is denied them. Instead, they must experience the anger of God for their sins in torment forever. How should this motivate Christians to be faithful witnesses of the gospel?**
3. **This world will not go on forever as it is. Judgment day is coming. Right now each of us is like a seed planted in the earth, developing and producing fruit either good or bad, but one day the time for harvest will arrive. Live every day with your eye on judgment day.**

THE SEVEN BOWLS OF WRATH (15:1—16:21)

Chapter 15: *The seven bowls of wrath are introduced by a vision of heavenly worship and the opening of the heavenly temple.*

The Heavenly Temple Full of Worship and Wrath (15:1–8)

15:1–4 A new cycle of sevens symbolically presents the judgments that will fulfill God's righteous purpose to punish His enemies (*in them is filled up the wrath of God*). The vision returns to the heavenly temple (4:1–11), where believers appear as those who overcame this world (*gotten the victory*; 12:11), have been washed clean in God's sight (*sea*; 4:6; 1 Kings 7:23–26; cf. Ex. 30:17–21), and praise the Lord (*harps*; 5:8). The *fire* in the sea represents God's holy wrath against sinners (8:5). The saints *fear* and *glorify* God (14:7) for His *works* of salvation through judgment (*the song of Moses*; Ex. 15:1–19), because His works reveal His majesty (*great and marvellous*), sovereign power (*Lord God Almighty*; see note at 1:8), righteousness and faithfulness (*just and true*), and incomparable excellence above all others (*thou only art holy*; Ex. 15:11). Worship fuels missions, for it declares God's worthiness that all may honor

name? for *thou* only *art* holy: for all nations shall come and worship before thee; for thy judgments are made manifest.
5 And after that I looked, and, behold, the temple of the tabernacle of the testimony in heaven was opened:
6 And the seven angels came out of the temple, having the seven plagues, clothed in pure and white linen, and having their breasts girded with golden girdles.
7 And one of the four beasts gave unto the seven angels seven golden vials full of the wrath of God, who liveth for ever and ever.
8 And the temple was filled with smoke from the glory of God, and from his power; and no man was able to enter into the temple, till the seven plagues of the seven angels were fulfilled.

CHAPTER 16

AND I heard a great voice out of the temple saying to the seven angels, Go your ways, and pour out the vials of the wrath of God upon the earth.
2 And the first went, and poured out his vial upon the earth; and there fell a noisome and grievous sore upon the men which had the mark of the beast, and *upon* them which worshipped his image.
3 And the second angel poured out his vial upon the sea; and it became as the blood of a dead *man*: and every living soul died in the sea.
4 And the third angel poured out his vial upon the rivers and fountains of waters; and they became blood.
5 And I heard the angel of the waters say, Thou art righteous, O Lord, which art, and wast, and shalt be, because thou hast judged thus.
6 For they have shed the blood of saints and prophets, and thou hast given them blood to drink; for they are worthy.
7 And I heard another out of the altar say, Even so, Lord God Almighty, true and righteous *are* thy judgments.
8 And the fourth angel poured out his vial upon the sun; and power was given unto him to scorch men with fire.

Him ("Who would not fear thee, O King of nations?" Jer. 10:7), and it anticipates the worldwide victory of His saving work through Jesus Christ (*all nations shall come and worship before thee*; Ps. 86:9–10; cf. 5:9–10; Ps. 22:27).

15:5–8 The bowls (*vials*) given to *seven angels* symbolize how God will pour out His *wrath* in answer to the prayers (like incense in bowls; 5:8) of Christians for justice (6:10; 8:3–5). The angels appear as righteous (*pure and white*; 19:8) messengers from heaven representing Christ (*breasts girded with golden girdles*; 1:13; Dan. 10:5). God's wrath will come with a public revelation of His *glory* (*temple . . . opened . . . filled with smoke*; 11:19; Ex. 40:34–35; 1 Kings 8:10–11).

Thoughts for Personal/Family Worship: Chapter 15

1. **God's judgments on the wicked will move the righteous to praise Him. This does not come from a vengeful or bloodthirsty spirit. Rather, the godly see the beauty of God's attributes in His works of judgment, and this moves them to worship Him. How do you respond to the descriptions of divine judgment in the Bible? What kind of heart do we need to praise God for His judgment?**
2. **Worship and missions are intimately related. Missions aim to see God create new worshipers, while worship declares God's worthiness of the praises of all people. Ironically, sometimes people set the two against each other: one group in the church promotes worship and neglects evangelism, while another group does the opposite. Why can we never be faithful worshipers without missions? Why must missions be grounded in worship?**

Chapter 16: ***The angels pour out the seven bowls of wrath upon the followers of the beast and its kingdom, but men only curse God rather than repenting.***

The Seven Bowls of Wrath Poured Out (16:1–21)

16:1 The full *wrath of God* is symbolized in bowls (*vials*) given to *seven angels* to *pour out* on the world (15:1). The seven bowls resemble the seven trumpets, especially the second (sea to blood; 8:8–9), third (poisoning of drinking water; 8:10–11), fifth (darkness and pain; 9:1–5), sixth (armies at the Euphrates; 9:13–16), and seventh (hail and earthquake; 11:15–19) in each series. But whereas the trumpets destroy a third of their targets, the bowls strike all. Therefore, as the trumpets symbolize calamities through history that announce God's wrath, so the bowls indicate that God's wrath will culminate in total disaster for all the wicked. The sequence of bowls need not indicate that one follows another in time, but their rapid succession without interlude suggests that the day of the Lord will come with sudden destruction (1 Thess. 5:2–3).

16:2–7 The first three bowls. With images drawn from the first plague (*blood*) and sixth plague (*sore;* v. 2) on Egypt (Ex. 7:17–18; 9:8–10), these bowls symbolize God's judgments on idolaters (*men which had the mark of the beast . . . worshipped his image*) to humiliate them (Ex. 9:11) and inflict horrible pain (*noisome and grievous*). God's wrath will show that He is *righteous*, in contrast to the persecutors of his *saints* who deserve only punishment (*they are worthy*; cf. 4:11; 5:9,12); He is eternal, in contrast to this world, which is passing away (*art, and wast, and shalt be*; see notes at 11:15–19), and He is sovereign (*Lord God Almighty*). This revelation of God's attributes on judgment day will move the citizens of heaven (*altar*) to praise Him (15:2–4).

16:8–11 The fourth and fifth bowls. The fourth bowl does not allude to a plague on Egypt and reverses the normal judgment imagery of darkness (v. 10; 6:12; 8:12; 9:2). The glory of Christ shines like the *sun* (1:16; 10:1; 21:23; 22:5). His coming will *scorch* sinners as with *fire* (2 Thess. 1:7–8) when He brings God's wrath upon them (Deut. 28:22–23; 32:22,24), even as He shelters His people (7:16). The *darkness* of the fifth bowl, like the ninth Egyptian plague (Ex. 10:21–23), signifies the day of the Lord against the *kingdom* of Satan and his servants (Isa. 13:9–10; 24:21–23; Joel 2:31). Though God's wrath moves the godly to worship Him (15:3–4), it does not change the stubborn determination of sinners to worship idols (*they repented not*; 9:20–21); they cursed God (*blasphemed*) in impotent pain (*gnawed their tongues;* Matt. 8:12; 25:30). Their *darkness* is within them (Eph. 5:8), a blindness and refusal to *give* God *glory* (Rom. 1:21).

9 And men were scorched with great heat, and
blasphemed the name of God, which hath power
over these plagues: and they repented not to give
him glory.
10 And the fifth angel poured out his vial upon
the seat of the beast; and his kingdom was full of
darkness; and they gnawed their tongues for pain,
11 And blasphemed the God of heaven because
of their pains and their sores, and repented not
of their deeds.
12 And the sixth angel poured out his vial upon
the great river Euphrates; and the water thereof
was dried up, that the way of the kings of the east
might be prepared.
13 And I saw three unclean spirits like frogs *come*
out of the mouth of the dragon, and out of the
mouth of the beast, and out of the mouth of the
false prophet.
14 For they are the spirits of devils, working
miracles, *which* go forth unto the kings of the
earth and of the whole world, to gather them to
the battle of that great day of God Almighty.
15 Behold, I come as a thief. Blessed *is* he that
watcheth, and keepeth his garments, lest he walk
naked, and they see his shame.
16 And he gathered them together into a place
called in the Hebrew tongue Armageddon.
17 And the seventh angel poured out his vial into
the air; and there came a great voice out of the tem-
ple of heaven, from the throne, saying, It is done.
18 And there were voices, and thunders, and
lightnings; and there was a great earthquake, such
as was not since men were upon the earth, so
mighty an earthquake, *and* so great.
19 And the great city was divided into three
parts, and the cities of the nations fell: and great
Babylon came in remembrance before God, to
give unto her the cup of the wine of the fierceness
of his wrath.
20 And every island fled away, and the mountains
were not found.
21 And there fell upon men a great hail out of
heaven, *every stone* about the weight of a talent:
and men blasphemed God because of the plague
of the hail; for the plague thereof was exceeding
great.

CHAPTER 17

AND there came one of the seven angels which
had the seven vials, and talked with me, saying
unto me, Come hither; I will shew unto thee the

16:12–16 The sixth bowl. This collage of symbols points to the supernatural victory of God's people over this persecuting world. The drying up of the *water* of a *river* refers to the destruction of Babylon and the salvation of exiled Israel (Isa. 44:26–28; Jer. 50:34–38), just as God once dried up the Jordan River for Israel to invade Canaan (Josh. 3:16–17; 5:1). The *kings* from *the east* represent Christ's forces that will destroy Satan's world system, like the Parthian threat to Rome from beyond the *Euphrates* (see note at 9:13–19), and Cyrus, the king "from the east" who conquered Babylon and decreed Israel's return to the land (Isa. 41:2; 44:28; 45:1; 46:11). In response to this threat, Satan and his political and religious servants (*dragon*, *beast*, and *false prophet*; ch. 12–13) employ their lies (*mouth*) and *miracles* (13:13–15) to rally *the whole world* to war against Christ and His church (17:14; 20:7–9). Satan's ability to deceive mankind is God's plague (*frogs*; Ex. 8:2) upon unbelievers (2 Thess. 2:11–12). *Armageddon* (hill or city of Megiddo) is not the location of a future military battle but a symbol of the church's victory against the world, just as God gave Israel victory at Megiddo against the Canaanites (Judg. 4:13–15; 5:19). The spiritual war will climax at the return of Jesus Christ (*great day of God Almighty*). The vision is interrupted (13:9–10) by a word from Christ that He will come unexpectedly (*as a thief*; 3:3; Matt. 24:43; 1 Thess. 5:1–4; 2 Peter 3:10), which calls for vigilance (*watcheth*) and perseverance in hope and holiness (*keepeth his garments*; 3:4–5; 1 John 2:28—3:3).
16:17–21 The seventh bowl. Like the seventh seal (8:1) and the seventh trumpet (11:15), the seventh in this series also brings the reader to the end of this age (*It is done*; 21:6). The manifest glory of God disrupts the created world (*great earthquake . . . every island fled away . . . mountains were not found*; 6:12–14; 11:19; 20:11; Hag. 2:6–7). Judgment falls from heaven like a horrific storm (Ps. 18:11–14) from the Lawgiver (*thunders, lightnings*; Ex. 19–20) with supernatural power, symbolized by hailstones (9:18; Josh. 10:11) of enormous weight (*a talent* ranged from 45 to 130 pounds—an extremely large hailstone of modern times weighed two pounds). The events of this bowl match Ezekiel's vision of God's judgment against Gog, the attacker of His people (Ezek. 38:18–22). The wicked world, symbolized by *the great city* of *Babylon* (chs. 17–18), is called to account for its sins (*remembrance;* 18:5; Jer. 14:10) and is shattered by God's *wrath*, but still hates God.

Thoughts for Personal/Family Worship: Chapter 16

1. **God's wrath is like a dammed up river. A dam holds back a great volume of water, allowing sometimes a small stream and sometimes a larger flow as the sluice gates are opened and closed. Right now God is expressing His wrath against sin (Rom. 1:18) but holds back most of it. However, behind the dam of His patience a vast reservoir of wrath is being stored up, and one day God will flood the world with His anger (Rom. 2:5). The worst disasters of history cannot compare to the firestorm of judgment that will come upon the wicked. How can you be prepared to escape that wrath?**
2. **The church appears to be surrounded by a worldwide army of unbelievers and sin. How should the expectation of judgment shape a Christian's view of the world? How can the truths of this chapter motivate a believer to be spiritually alert and not to give up?**

THE FALL OF BABYLON THE WHORE (17:1—19:21)

Chapter 17: ***A new cycle of visions opens with a symbolic view of the world like a great prostitute named Babylon, supported by the satanic beast and the rulers of this world.***

The Vision of the Whore (17:1–18)

17:1–6 An angel calls John with the same Greek word (*Come hither* or here) that later introduces the Bride of Christ (21:9).

judgment of the great whore that sitteth upon
many waters:
2 With whom the kings of the earth have com-
mitted fornication, and the inhabitants of the
earth have been made drunk with the wine of her
fornication.
3 So he carried me away in the spirit into the
wilderness: and I saw a woman sit upon a scarlet
coloured beast, full of names of blasphemy,
having seven heads and ten horns.
4 And the woman was arrayed in purple and
scarlet colour, and decked with gold and pre-
cious stones and pearls, having a golden cup in
her hand full of abominations and filthiness of
her fornication:
5 And upon her forehead *was* a name writ-
ten, MYSTERY, BABYLON THE GREAT, THE
MOTHER OF HARLOTS AND ABOMINA-
TIONS OF THE EARTH.
6 And I saw the woman drunken with the blood
of the saints, and with the blood of the martyrs of
Jesus: and when I saw her, I wondered with great
admiration.
7 And the angel said unto me, Wherefore didst
thou marvel? I will tell thee the mystery of the
woman, and of the beast that carrieth her, which
hath the seven heads and ten horns.
8 The beast that thou sawest was, and is not; and
shall ascend out of the bottomless pit, and go
into perdition: and they that dwell on the earth
shall wonder, whose names were not written in
the book of life from the foundation of the world,
when they behold the beast that was, and is not,
and yet is.
9 And here *is* the mind which hath wisdom. The
seven heads are seven mountains, on which the
woman sitteth.
10 And there are seven kings: five are fallen, and
one is, *and* the other is not yet come; and when he
cometh, he must continue a short space.
11 And the beast that was, and is not, even he
is the eighth, and is of the seven, and goeth into
perdition.
12 And the ten horns which thou sawest are ten
kings, which have received no kingdom as yet; but
receive power as kings one hour with the beast.
13 These have one mind, and shall give their
power and strength unto the beast.
14 These shall make war with the Lamb, and
the Lamb shall overcome them: for he is Lord of
lords, and King of kings: and they that are with
him *are* called, and chosen, and faithful.
15 And he saith unto me, The waters which thou
sawest, where the whore sitteth, are peoples, and

God's church and the world are symbolized by contrasting women and cities (chs. 12, 21). The *wine*, *gold*, and sexual immorality (*fornication*) of the *great whore* represent how the world seduces people to pursue the intoxicating pleasures and riches of false gods (Deut. 31:16; Ezek. 16:15–26) while disregarding the true God (Matt. 6:24; Col. 3:5; 1 John 2:15–17). *Babylon* was long associated with pride and self-sufficiency (Gen. 11:1–9; Isa. 47:1,8; Dan. 4:30). The *many waters* on which the whore sits communicate her greatness, just as Babylon used the Euphrates River and its canals for military defense and economic trade (Jer. 51:12–13; cf. note at vv. 15–18). Yet behind the glitter and glamor of the world is horrible ugliness. She dwells not in a garden or palace but in the *wilderness*, a place of loneliness, hunger, danger, and temptation (12:6,14; Deut. 8:2,15–16; Pss. 78:19; 107:4–5). She rides the seven-headed *beast* (13:1); tyranny and oppression feed the lusts of the wicked. She intoxicates people not with sweet wine but with disgusting moral filth (*abominations and filthiness*) and violence (*blood*). When the world cannot seduce Christians from holiness (*saints* are, literally, "holy ones"), it will try to murder them and silence their testimony (*martyrs* are, literally, "witnesses"). The vision of this horrible woman astonished John (*great admiration*).

17:7–14 The *angel* now interprets the symbols of the vision (Dan. 7:16; 8:15–16), for it is a secret that God has revealed (*mystery*; Eph. 3:9). The evil political and military powers through the ages (*beast*; 13:1–2,4) grasp after eternal dominion like God but will pass away (contrast the beast that *was, and is not; and shall ascend* with God "which is, and which was, and which is to come"; 1:8). The apparent resurrection of worldly power after various defeats and disasters in history (*was, and is not, and yet is*) leads the wicked to stand in awe of it (13:3–4) because they belong to Satan's kingdom (*dwell on the earth*; see note at 3:10) and are not chosen by God for salvation (*names were not written in the book of life*). Spiritual discernment comes only from sovereign grace. The *seven mountains* point to Rome, built on seven hills, as a prime example of worldly power. Various schemes attempt to identify the *kings* with specific emperors. The point is that after various kingdoms have passed away (*seven kings*) a new manifestation of the beast will arise with demonic power (*ascend out of the bottomless pit*; 11:7; 20:1–3). For a *short* time (*one hour*) it will engage its allies (*ten kings*) to *make war* against Christ and His church at the end of the age (11:7–10; 20:7–9). Christ will destroy this resurrected satanic power (*go into perdition* or ruin; 2 Thess. 2:1–12). The crucified Redeemer (*Lamb*) leads His people in His blood-bought victory (5:5,8–9) with sovereign power (*Lord of lords, and King of kings*; 1:5) according to the graces of election, effectual calling, and persevering faith (*called, and chosen, and faithful*; 2 Thess. 2:13–15).

17:15–18 The *waters* on which the *whore* sits (v. 1) show that the strength of the world system is its domination of every people group on earth (*peoples, multitudes, nations, tongues*). The wicked who rule this world (*ten horns*; v. 3; 13:1) rejoice for a time in its pleasures (v. 2) but then turn violently against them like a man who uses a prostitute but then discards her in disgust. The shaming of the whore echoes God's judgment against Jerusalem (*desolate and naked*; Ezek. 16:35–41; 23:22–30) for worshiping idols and trusting in men (Ezek. 16:15–34; 23:1–21). God rules over the *hearts* of the wicked (Prov. 21:1) to accomplish *His will* and fulfill His *words* (Dan. 4:34). He causes seducers to perish like Jezebel at the hands of violent men (*eat her flesh*; 2 Kings 9:36), for they entice members of His church into idolatry (2:20; 1 Kings 16:31; 18:19) and persecute the faithful (2 Kings 9:7). Dissatisfied by their lusts, men give themselves to the pursuit of raw power and in so doing destroy their pleasures and surrender themselves completely to Satan, their true master (*give their kingdom unto the beast*).

multitudes, and nations, and tongues.
16 And the ten horns which thou sawest upon the
beast, these shall hate the whore, and shall make
her desolate and naked, and shall eat her flesh,
and burn her with fire.
17 For God hath put in their hearts to fulfil his
will, and to agree, and give their kingdom unto
the beast, until the words of God shall be fulfilled.
18 And the woman which thou sawest is that
great city, which reigneth over the kings of the
earth.

CHAPTER 18

AND after these things I saw another angel come
down from heaven, having great power; and the
earth was lightened with his glory.
2 And he cried mightily with a strong voice, say-
ing, Babylon the great is fallen, is fallen, and is
become the habitation of devils, and the hold of
every foul spirit, and a cage of every unclean and
hateful bird.
3 For all nations have drunk of the wine of the
wrath of her fornication, and the kings of the
earth have committed fornication with her, and
the merchants of the earth are waxed rich through
the abundance of her delicacies.
4 And I heard another voice from heaven, say-
ing, Come out of her, my people, that ye be not
partakers of her sins, and that ye receive not of
her plagues.
5 For her sins have reached unto heaven, and
God hath remembered her iniquities.
6 Reward her even as she rewarded you, and
double unto her double according to her works:
in the cup which she hath filled fill to her double.
7 How much she hath glorified herself, and lived
deliciously, so much torment and sorrow give her:
for she saith in her heart, I sit a queen, and am no
widow, and shall see no sorrow.
8 Therefore shall her plagues come in one day,
death, and mourning, and famine; and she shall
be utterly burned with fire: for strong *is* the Lord
God who judgeth her.
9 And the kings of the earth, who have commit-
ted fornication and lived deliciously with her,
shall bewail her, and lament for her, when they
shall see the smoke of her burning,
10 Standing afar off for the fear of her torment,
saying, Alas, alas, that great city Babylon, that
mighty city! for in one hour is thy judgment come.
11 And the merchants of the earth shall weep and
mourn over her; for no man buyeth their mer-
chandise any more:
12 The merchandise of gold, and silver, and
precious stones, and of pearls, and fine linen, and
purple, and silk, and scarlet, and all thyine wood,
and all manner vessels of ivory, and all manner

This general truth may find special fulfillment when the resurgence of satanic power consolidates its political and military forces (*ten horns*, as it is used in v. 12). The world symbolized by a *woman* is also represented by *that great city* of Babylon, which the next chapter describes in more detail.

Thoughts for Personal/Family Worship: Chapter 17

1. **Ever since the Fall the world has been a whore. Like Potiphar's wife, the world comes to us with siren calls to pleasure, but if we reject her, she becomes our most bitter accuser. Thus it manipulates men with pleasure and pain. How is the world seeking to manipulate you?**
2. **The way to overcome the enticements of the world is through God's sovereign grace alone. Only those chosen by God, redeemed by the Lamb, and called by the Spirit will be faithful. Will-power cannot succeed. Human wisdom will fail. Rely upon Christ alone.**

Chapter 18: ***In a vision complementary to the previous chapter, the seductive world system is symbolized as a great city from which people must flee before it is destroyed by fire.***

The Fall of the City (18:1–24)

18:1–3 An angel comes with brilliant light, a sign of God's presence returning with *great power* to His earthly temple, the suffering church (*earth was lightened with his glory*; Ezek. 43:2). God's judgment is compared to the fall of ancient *Babylon* with its idols (Isa. 21:9). Presently, like a city full of sinful pleasures (*fornication*), wealth (*waxed rich*), and luxuries (*delicacies*), the abode of mankind will become as desolate as a ghost town, a home (*habitation*) only to wild creatures (Isa. 13:19–22; Jer. 50:39–40). God will turn Satan's amusement park into a prison (*hold, cage*) for sinners (*unclean*) and demons (*devils*).

18:4–8 The expectation of God's coming prompts the call for spiritual separation from participation in the world's *sins* (2 Cor. 6:17; Eph. 5:5–14), for God will save His redeemed people exiled on earth (*Come out of her*; Isa. 48:20; 52:10–12) and send His wrath upon spiritual Babylon (Jer. 51:6,45) for its towering guilt (*reached unto heaven*; Jer. 51:9). He will avenge its persecution of His people (*Reward her even as she rewarded you*; Ps. 137:8; Jer. 50:15,24). His punishment will come in the righteous equity (*double*, or equivalent amount; Jer. 16:18) of justice and wrath (*according to her works: in the cup*; Jer. 25:14–15). He will judge it for its arrogance (*I sit a queen, and am no widow*; Isa. 47:5–11) with a decisive and powerful intervention (*in one day . . . utterly burned*).

18:9–19 The end of the world's wealth and pleasure is symbolized by the *burning* of a great port city while those who enjoyed its services (*kings*) and profited from them (*merchants, shipmaster*) cry out loud in grief (*mourn, bewail*; James 5:1–6) as at the destruction of Tyre (Ezek. 26–27). The various goods listed are a study in the objects of materialism, including living luxuriously (*deliciously*) with *gold, silver*, gemstones, expensive clothing, fragrant wood (*thyine*), quality building materials, spices, incense (*odours*), food, livestock—all manner of wealth (*costliness*) and fine and splendid (*dainty and goodly*) possessions, even the evil of human trafficking (*slaves, and souls of men*; literally, "bodies and souls of men"). The Lord will ruin this system of greed and lust fulfillment and leave the wicked desolate (*come to nought*). The rising *smoke* (vv. 9,18) and *torment* (vv. 7,10,15) of the city imply that the reality behind this symbol continues in hell without end (14:11; 19:3). The damned will grieve forever because God removes all good

vessels of most precious wood, and of brass, and
iron, and marble,
13 And cinnamon, and odours, and ointments,
and frankincense, and wine, and oil, and fine
flour, and wheat, and beasts, and sheep, and
horses, and chariots, and slaves, and souls of men.
14 And the fruits that thy soul lusted after are
departed from thee, and all things which were
dainty and goodly are departed from thee, and
thou shalt find them no more at all.
15 The merchants of these things, which were
made rich by her, shall stand afar off for the fear
of her torment, weeping and wailing,
16 And saying, Alas, alas, that great city, that was
clothed in fine linen, and purple, and scarlet, and
decked with gold, and precious stones, and pearls!
17 For in one hour so great riches is come to
nought. And every shipmaster, and all the company in ships, and sailors, and as many as trade by
sea, stood afar off,
18 And cried when they saw the smoke of her burning, saying, What *city is* like unto this great city!
19 And they cast dust on their heads, and cried,
weeping and wailing, saying, Alas, alas, that great
city, wherein were made rich all that had ships in
the sea by reason of her costliness! for in one hour
is she made desolate.
20 Rejoice over her, *thou* heaven, and *ye* holy
apostles and prophets; for God hath avenged you
on her.
21 And a mighty angel took up a stone like a great
millstone, and cast *it* into the sea, saying, Thus
with violence shall that great city Babylon be
thrown down, and shall be found no more at all.
22 And the voice of harpers, and musicians, and
of pipers, and trumpeters, shall be heard no more
at all in thee; and no craftsman, of whatsoever
craft *he be*, shall be found any more in thee; and
the sound of a millstone shall be heard no more
at all in thee;
23 And the light of a candle shall shine no more
at all in thee; and the voice of the bridegroom and
of the bride shall be heard no more at all in thee:
for thy merchants were the great men of the earth;
for by thy sorceries were all nations deceived.
24 And in her was found the blood of prophets,
and of saints, and of all that were slain upon the
earth.

CHAPTER 19

AND after these things I heard a great voice of
much people in heaven, saying, Alleluia; Salvation, and glory, and honour, and power, unto the
Lord our God:
2 For true and righteous *are* his judgments: for
he hath judged the great whore, which did corrupt the earth with her fornication, and hath
avenged the blood of his servants at her hand.
3 And again they said, Alleluia. And her smoke
rose up for ever and ever.
4 And the four and twenty elders and the four
beasts fell down and worshipped God that sat on
the throne, saying, Amen; Alleluia.

from their experience (Isa. 65:13–14; Luke 6:24–26; 16:24–25), and so even their former treasures will become part of their torment (James 5:3) as they remember and long for them.

18:20 The spectacle of the world's ruin calls the citizens of *heaven* to *rejoice* (19:1–6) in God's demolition of the system that persecuted and murdered them (Jer. 51:48–49) for their preaching of the truth (*apostles and prophets*). God's vengeance (*avenged*) is not sinful revenge but the exercise of justice against those who wronged His people (6:10; 19:2).

18:21–24 The casting of a stone *into the sea* symbolizes the dramatic and final fall of the world into destruction (Ex. 15:4–5; Jer. 51:63–64; cf. 8:12). The end of music, artistry (*craftsman*), food production (*millstone*), artificial light (*candle*, or oil lamp), and celebrations (*bridegroom, bride*) represents the death of all human joy by God's curse upon lawbreakers (Isa. 24:5–9; Jer. 25:10). God will do this as His punishment for the world's pride (*thy merchants were the great men of the earth*; Isa. 23:8–9), demonic spirituality (*thy sorceries*; Isa. 47:9), and violence (*blood*), especially violence against the church (*saints*; 16:6; 17:6).

Thoughts for Personal/Family Worship: Chapter 18

1. **Hope in Christ's return motivates separation. Separation from the world does not mean physical removal, for the world is within us in our evil desires and pride (1 John 2:16). We cannot hide in monasteries or Christian ghettos. However, separation demands that we refuse to participate in the world's sins, idolatrous worship, and heart-corrupting influences. Are you separated from the world in this sense?**
2. **The pleasures of sinners will end and never begin again. Their party will end and their game will be over. God will take from them every good gift, for they have abused them and dishonored Him. Do not envy the wicked; in due time their foot will slip. Live for lasting pleasure: the joy and glory of the Lord.**

Chapter 19: ***This cycle of visions culminates in the praise of God for judging the whore and a vision of the Warrior riding on the white horse to destroy the wicked.***

The Worship of God (19:1–10)

19:1–6 The call to "rejoice over" fallen Babylon (18:20) is answered by a vast crowd of the redeemed in heaven (*much people*, v. 1, is identical in Greek to *great multitude*, v. 6; 7:9). The judgment of the wicked evokes a fourfold *Alleluia* (Hebrew, "Praise ye the Lord"; Ps. 104:35; cf. Pss. 105–150; only here in the New Testament). This remarkable chorus of praise draws together aspects of the worship of God and the Lamb found throughout Revelation (4:9–11; 5:12–13; 7:10–12; 11:15–18; 14:2–3; 15:2–4). Judgment calls forth worship because it accomplishes the *salvation* of God's people from evil, displays God's righteousness (*true and righteous*) and power (*omnipotent*, same word as "Almighty"; 1:8), brings justice against persecutors (*avenged the blood of his servants*; 6:10) through everlasting punishment (*smoke rose up for ever*; 14:11), and

5 And a voice came out of the throne, saying,
Praise our God, all ye his servants, and ye that fear
him, both small and great.
6 And I heard as it were the voice of a great
multitude, and as the voice of many waters, and as
the voice of mighty thunderings, saying, Alleluia:
for the Lord God omnipotent reigneth.
7 Let us be glad and rejoice, and give honour to
him: for the marriage of the Lamb is come, and
his wife hath made herself ready.
8 And to her was granted that she should be
arrayed in fine linen, clean and white: for the fine
linen is the righteousness of saints.
9 And he saith unto me, Write, Blessed *are* they
which are called unto the marriage supper of the
Lamb. And he saith unto me, These are the true
sayings of God.
10 And I fell at his feet to worship him. And he
said unto me, See *thou do it* not: I am thy fel-
lowservant, and of thy brethren that have the
testimony of Jesus: worship God: for the testi-
mony of Jesus is the spirit of prophecy.
11 And I saw heaven opened, and behold a
white horse; and he that sat upon him *was* called
Faithful and True, and in righteousness he doth
judge and make war.
12 His eyes *were* as a flame of fire, and on his head
were many crowns; and he had a name written,
that no man knew, but he himself.
13 And he *was* clothed with a vesture dipped in
blood: and his name is called The Word of God.
14 And the armies *which were* in heaven followed
him upon white horses, clothed in fine linen,
white and clean.
15 And out of his mouth goeth a sharp sword,
that with it he should smite the nations: and he
shall rule them with a rod of iron: and he treadeth
the winepress of the fierceness and wrath of
Almighty God.
16 And he hath on *his* vesture and on his thigh
a name written, KING OF KINGS, AND LORD
OF LORDS.
17 And I saw an angel standing in the sun; and he
cried with a loud voice, saying to all the fowls that
fly in the midst of heaven, Come and gather your-
selves together unto the supper of the great God;
18 That ye may eat the flesh of kings, and the
flesh of captains, and the flesh of mighty men,

establishes His kingdom (*reigneth*; Ex. 15:18; Ps. 146:10).

19:7–9 Revelation contrasts the world and the church like two women. The "whore" has been judged (v. 2). Now the faithful woman is taken in *marriage* by her Husband, who died to redeem her (*the Lamb*; 5:9). Redemption is a love story (Isa. 54:4–8; Hos. 3:1–5), the covenant is a vow of betrothal (Hos. 2:19–20), salvation is a wedding dress (Isa. 61:10), and the kingdom is a wedding feast (*marriage supper*; Matt. 22:1–14). She *hath made herself ready* for the feast through works of obedience (*righteousness*, literally, "righteous acts"). These works are entirely of God's grace through Christ (*to her was granted*; 1:5; 7:14; 17:14; Eph. 2:10). Grace justifies, transforms, and preserves her until she is presented to her Lord in radiant beauty for His delight (*fine linen, clean and white*; 3:4–5; Ps. 45:11; Eph. 5:25–27). Believers can rest with absolute confidence upon this promise (*the true sayings of God*; 21:5; 22:6).

19:10 Subject to frailty and sin, overwhelmed by the visions, and perhaps confusing the angel with a vision of Christ, John tried to *worship* the angel but was rebuked (22:8–9). Holy angels do not glorify themselves but Christ. God's servants must *worship God* alone (Acts 10:25–26; 14:13–15).

The King on the White Horse (19:11–21)

19:11–16 The Christ who is already conquering through the gospel now comes in glory (*behold a white horse; and him that sat upon him*; 6:2). He appears with many titles and symbols: (a) the trustworthy Witness (*Faithful and True*; 3:14) and the all-knowing Judge (*eyes . . . flame of fire*; 1:14; 2:18,23); (b) the Spirit-anointed Warrior-King (*in righteousness he doth judge*; Ps. 72:1–2; Isa. 11:1–4), the Commander of the *armies* of *heaven*; (c) the Son of God come to strike down (*smite*) the rebels and take the nations as His inheritance (*rule them with a rod of iron*; 2:26–27; 12:5; Ps. 2:7–9); (d) the Lord who alone can save the redeemed by destroying their enemies (*vesture* or robe *dipped in blood, winepress of the fierceness and wrath*; 14:19; Isa. 63:1–6); (e) the eternal *Word of God*, the living and perfect revelation of His Father (John 1:1,14), who conquers His enemies with a mere word (*out of his mouth goeth a sharp sword*; 1:16; Isa. 49:2); (f) the sovereign God above all human emperors (*KING OF KINGS, AND LORD OF LORDS*; 17:14; Deut. 10:17; Ps. 136:2–3; Dan. 2:47; 4:47 [LXX]; 1 Tim. 6:15). His glory is beyond our highest knowledge and praise (*name . . . no man knew*; Gen. 32:29; Judg. 13:18; Neh. 9:5; Ps. 145:3).

19:17–21 In horrible contrast to the wedding feast (v. 9), an *angel* summons a great host of birds (*all the fowls*) to *eat the flesh* of the wicked. This vision draws upon the symbolism of the slaughtered *armies* of Gog, the enemy of Israel whom the Lord destroys for the glory of His great name (Ezek. 39:1,4,7,17–22,25; see notes at 16:17–21; 20:7–10). To have one's dead body exposed to scavengers (cf. Matt. 24:28) is a sign of dying under the curse of God's covenant (Deut. 28:15, 26; Jer. 16:4; 34:18–20). The age-long conflict (*war*; 12:17; 17:14) between Christ (*upon the horse*) and the wicked powers (*the beast*) culminates in the final rise of the satanic world power and its supernatural defeat (see notes at 11:7–13; 16:12–16) by Christ's mighty word (*slain with the sword . . . out of his mouth*; v. 15; 1:16). Not only the leaders, but *all* sinners, even the slaves (*bond*) will fall under Christ's doom (6:15–17), just as all the slaves of the Lord will join in the joyful celebration of His victory (*both small and great*; vv. 5,18). Rather than triumphing, the wicked authorities (*beast*; 13:1–8) and heretical teachers (*false prophet*; 13:11–18) of this world will be damned to hell (*lake of fire burning with brimstone* or sulfur; 20:10,14–15; 21:8; see note at 14:9–11).

Thoughts for Personal/Family Worship: Chapter 19

1. **Just as a bride prepares for her wedding day, so Christians should prepare for Christ's return. How can you be ready? First, you must be justified by Christ's obedience. When God gives faith in Christ to a sinner, He joins that sinner to the Lord Jesus and imputes to him Christ's perfect righteousness. Second, you must be sanctified by Christ's Spirit. The same Spirit who gives a person faith also dwells in his heart, producing growing holiness. The person whom God justifies and sanctifies is dressed**

and the flesh of horses, and of them that sit on
them, and the flesh of all *men, both* free and bond,
both small and great.
19 And I saw the beast, and the kings of the earth,
and their armies, gathered together to make war
against him that sat on the horse, and against his
army.
20 And the beast was taken, and with him the
false prophet that wrought miracles before him,
with which he deceived them that had received
the mark of the beast, and them that worshipped
his image. These both were cast alive into a lake of
fire burning with brimstone.
21 And the remnant were slain with the sword
of him that sat upon the horse, which *sword*
proceeded out of his mouth: and all the fowls
were filled with their flesh.

CHAPTER 20

AND I saw an angel come down from heaven,
having the key of the bottomless pit and a great
chain in his hand.
2 And he laid hold on the dragon, that old ser-
pent, which is the Devil, and Satan, and bound
him a thousand years,
3 And cast him into the bottomless pit, and shut
him up, and set a seal upon him, that he should
deceive the nations no more, till the thousand
years should be fulfilled: and after that he must be
loosed a little season.
4 And I saw thrones, and they sat upon them,
and judgment was given unto them: and *I saw* the
souls of them that were beheaded for the witness
of Jesus, and for the word of God, and which had
not worshipped the beast, neither his image, nei-
ther had received *his* mark upon their foreheads,
or in their hands; and they lived and reigned with
Christ a thousand years.
5 But the rest of the dead lived not again until
the thousand years were finished. This *is* the first
resurrection.
6 Blessed and holy *is* he that hath part in the first
resurrection: on such the second death hath no
power, but they shall be priests of God and of
Christ, and shall reign with him a thousand years.
7 And when the thousand years are expired,
Satan shall be loosed out of his prison,

for the wedding. Are you ready?

2. Sin may seem harmless or fun today, but in reality every sin is an act of treason and war against God. All who have fought against the Lord will be stunned and horrified when their holy enemy appears in the skies. Their defeat will be total, for He is powerful. Their damnation will be just, for He is righteous. Repent now, turning from your idols to the living God, before God sends His Son in holy wrath.

THE VICTORY OF JERUSALEM THE BRIDE (20:1—22:21)

Chapter 20: ***The final cycle of Revelation's visions begins with a depiction of the binding of Satan, the final war, and judgment day.***

The Binding of Satan, the Last Battle, and the Judgment (20:1–15)

20:1–3 The seventh and final cycle of Revelation begins with a symbolic overview of God's kingdom in this present age (*thousand years*; on the various approaches to the millennium, see Introduction to Revelation). The number *thousand* symbolizes fullness (10 x 10 x 10, cf. 5:11; 7:4; 14:1; 21:16). The phrase *the dragon, that old serpent, which is the Devil, and Satan* links this vision to the defeat of Satan at Christ's exaltation to heaven (12:9; see note at 12:7–12). The Lord Jesus *bound* Satan and brought God's kingdom at His first coming (Matt. 12:28–29; cf. Isa. 24:21–23). Risen from the dead, Christ has authority over the forces of death (*key*; 1:18). He has judged and now limits Satan's forces (*chain*; 2 Peter 2:4; Jude 6) according to God's holy purposes (see notes at 9:1–11). His victory over Satan is as decisive and complete as if the Devil were dead and buried (*shut him up . . . seal*; Matt. 27:66; cf. Dan. 6:17). Other Scriptures also testify to Christ's finished and absolute conquest (5:5; Luke 10:18; John 12:31; 16:11; Col. 2:15; Heb. 2:14). Such absolute language, however, does not mean that demonic influence has ceased on earth (13:14) but that Satan cannot overcome the elect redeemed by the Lamb (v. 8; 17:14). In this context, Satan's binding implies two things. First, the Devil can no longer keep the Gentiles outside of Israel in total spiritual darkness (*deceive the nations no more*), because Christ is gathering His redeemed people through the gospel (5:9; John 12:31–33). Second, the Devil cannot so mobilize the world against the church as to destroy it (12:15–16), though he will be briefly permitted one last great attack at the end of the age (*loosed a little season*; cf. vv. 7–10).

20:4–6 God's mediatorial kingdom (*thrones, judgment was given unto them*; Ps. 122:5; Dan. 7:9,22; Luke 22:30) has already come in its spiritual reality to His people (John 18:36–37; Rom. 14:17; Eph. 1:19–21; Col. 1:12–13). They who possess the kingdom are already *blessed* by God (Matt. 5:3; cf. 1:3; 14:13; 16:15; 19:9; 22:7,14). Even now God's people, symbolized in an earlier vision by the twenty-four elders, are crowned and enthroned in God's heavenly presence (4:4; "seats" is literally, *thrones*; cf. Eph. 2:6). In this world they suffer and are murdered by the wicked rulers of the world (*beast*; 13:1–18) for their refusal to participate in its idolatry. Yet those faithful unto death still *lived* (2:10) as *priests* (Isa. 61:6) and kings (*reigned*) because of Christ's death for them (1:6; 5:10) and the Spirit's work in them (cf. the spiritual resurrection in Ezek. 37:1–14). Just as the *second death* is the ultimate punishment of hellfire (v. 14) after the (first) death of the body, so the *first resurrection* is a gift of spiritual life before the (second) resurrection of the body (vv. 12–13). A spiritual resurrection precedes the physical resurrection, as Christ taught (John 5:24–29), for believers are united to Him who is the resurrection and the life—even after they die (John 11:25–26; Col. 3:1–4; cf. Matt. 22:21–32). So they have victory already and may courageously face murderous persecutors.

20:7–10 At the end of this age (*thousand years*), when the church has completed its mission, the Lord will grant the Devil a short time (v. 3) to rally the wicked to attack God's people (2 Thess. 2:1–11; see notes at 11:7–13; 16:12–16). The sequence of chs. 20–21 corresponds to Ezekiel's visions of the spiritual resurrection of Israel and its unification under the Davidic king in the new covenant (vv. 4–6; Ezek. 36–37), the attack of an international enemy against God's peaceful

8 And shall go out to deceive the nations which
are in the four quarters of the earth, Gog and Ma-
gog, to gather them together to battle: the number
of whom *is* as the sand of the sea.
9 And they went up on the breadth of the earth,
and compassed the camp of the saints about, and
the beloved city: and fire came down from God
out of heaven, and devoured them.
10 And the devil that deceived them was cast into
the lake of fire and brimstone, where the beast
and the false prophet *are*, and shall be tormented
day and night for ever and ever.
11 And I saw a great white throne, and him that
sat on it, from whose face the earth and the heaven
fled away; and there was found no place for them.
12 And I saw the dead, small and great, stand
before God; and the books were opened: and
another book was opened, which is *the book* of
life: and the dead were judged out of those things
which were written in the books, according to
their works.
13 And the sea gave up the dead which were in it;
and death and hell delivered up the dead which
were in them: and they were judged every man
according to their works.
14 And death and hell were cast into the lake of
fire. This is the second death.
15 And whosoever was not found written in the
book of life was cast into the lake of fire.

CHAPTER 21

AND I saw a new heaven and a new earth: for the
first heaven and the first earth were passed away;
and there was no more sea.
2 And I John saw the holy city, new Jerusalem,
coming down from God out of heaven, prepared
as a bride adorned for her husband.
3 And I heard a great voice out of heaven saying,
Behold, the tabernacle of God *is* with men, and he
will dwell with them, and they shall be his people,
and God himself shall be with them, *and be* their
God.
4 And God shall wipe away all tears from their

people (*Gog*; vv. 7–9; Ezek. 38–39), and the return of God's glory returning to a new temple (ch. 21; Ezek. 40–48). That attack is summarized here and has also appeared in previous cycles of Revelation (see notes at 16:17–21; 19:17–21). This does not refer to an actual military battle but uses warfare as an image for persecution (12:17) against the church, symbolized as Israel in the wilderness of testing (a holy *camp*; Ex. 14:19–20; Deut. 23:14; cf. 12:6,14) and as Jerusalem (*beloved city*; Ps. 87:2–3; Isa. 66:10) surrounded (*compassed*) by enemies from all nations (*four quarters of the earth*). The church will be overwhelmed by the number of her enemies (*sand of the sea*; Josh. 11:4; Judg. 7:12; 1 Sam. 13:5) threatening to extinguish God's promises to the patriarchs (Gen. 22:17; 32:12; 1 Kings 4:20), but when Christ returns supernatural judgment will save the church and destroy its enemies to the glory of God (*fire . . . from God*; 2 Kings 1:10–14; Ezek. 38:22–23; 39:6; 2 Thess. 1:6–10; 2:8). Just as wicked rulers and false teachers (*the beast and the false prophet*) will be damned to hell (19:20), so too Satan ("dragon"; v. 2) will be condemned to everlasting pain (*tormented day and night for ever and ever*; 14:11; 19:3).

20:11–15 God the Creator and supreme King (*throne, and him that sat on it*; 4:2–3,9–10; 19:4) appears, and His glorious presence (*face*) dissolves this old creation (*the earth and the heaven fled away*; 6:14; Ps. 102:26; Isa. 34:4; 2 Peter 3:10,12), making way for the new (21:1,5). God will raise all mankind (*small and great*) from *the dead*, and death with all its minions (*the sea* and *death and hell*; 1:18) will be conquered and destroyed (Isa. 25:8; Hos. 13:14; 1 Cor. 15:22–26,54–55). The Lord will judge all people *according to their works*, not because salvation is by works (Eph. 2:8–9) but because salvation produces works (v. 10). Therefore works demonstrate whether or not a person was chosen and redeemed by God (*book of life*; vv. 12,15; 3:5; 13:8; 17:8; 21:27; cf. Eph. 1:4; 1 Thess. 1:2–10; 2 Thess. 2:13). Everyone not saved by God's grace will be *cast into the lake of fire*, a symbol of the total ruin and endless suffering of God's enemies (vv. 10,14–15; 19:20; 21:8; Isa. 30:33; 34:9–10). The glory of the saved is described in the next two chapters.

Thoughts for Personal/Family Worship: Chapter 20

1. **Though the church suffers and struggles on earth, Christ's kingdom has come. Satan was defeated once and for all at the cross and empty tomb. Christians today live in the paradox that they are conquering Satan spiritually, even as he seems to conquer them physically. The worst thing that this world can do to us—death—is our entrance into the heavenly reign of the saints. Therefore, let us neither fear for the church nor for our own future if we belong to Christ. Jesus reigns.**
2. **Christians should not expect the nations to get better and better, until Christ's coming scarcely causes a ripple in the pool of an already good world. Christ's return will be a cataclysmic reversal of all this world has known. Revelation warns that at the end of the age lawlessness and rebellion against God will grow to towering heights. How can Christians prepare themselves with a hope that is realistic, idealistic, and optimistic?**
3. **Judgment day will demonstrate the truth of the statement, "By their fruits ye shall know them" (Matt. 7:20). What do your works, considered as a whole, say about who you are? Do they certify that you are a genuine believer in Christ, saved by His blood?**

Chapter 21: *The future of the church is described symbolically through a vision of a new creation and a beautiful city.*

The Promise of All Things New (21:1–8)

21:1–4 God's coming in glory disrupts the old creation (20:11), not to annihilate it but to regenerate and glorify it (Matt. 19:28; Acts 3:21; Rom. 8:21) as a new creation (*new heaven and a new earth*; Isa. 65:17; 66:22; 2 Peter 3:13). The new creation centers around a people re-created (2 Cor. 4:6; 5:17; Eph. 2:10,15) by their union with Christ (*bride*; v. 9; 22:17; cf. 19:7–9). They will rejoice in His presence and kingdom (*the holy city, new Jerusalem*; Isa. 65:18–19) without any evil to trouble their joy (*no more sea*; 13:1; 17:1; 20:8,13; Isa. 51:10–11). Married to Christ, they enjoy the promised, mutual, covenant relationship with the Lord (*his people . . . their God*; Hos. 2:19–20,23; cf. Gen. 17:7; Lev. 26:12; Jer. 31:1, 33; Zech. 8:8), symbolized in the *tabernacle* where God dwelt with

HEAVEN

Heaven is the dwelling place of God and the seat of His kingdom, high above all the kingdoms of this world (1 Kings 8:30; Isa. 66:1; Matt. 25:34; Acts 14:22; 2 Cor. 12:2). It is the place of His glorious presence forever and the eternal home of believers. Heaven is both privative and positive—the former, as a place free from all misery; the latter, as a place where all divine blessings are savored. Heaven is a paradise (Luke 23:43); an eternal habitation (Luke 16:9; John 14:2; 2 Cor. 5:1); a city to come (Heb. 13:14); a glorious inheritance (Col. 1:12); a place of joy (Ps. 16:11); and, above all else, a world of love.

The triune God, the fountain of love (1 John 4:8), renders heaven a world of love. There dwells God the Father, the Father of love, who so loved the world as to sacrifice His only begotten Son. There dwells Christ, the Prince of love, who so loved the world that He shed His blood and poured out His soul unto death for men. There dwells the Holy Spirit, the Spirit of divine love, in whom the very essence of God, as it were, flows out and is breathed forth in love, and by whose immediate influence all holy love is shed abroad in the hearts of all the saints. In heaven this infinite fountain of love—this eternal Three in One—is opened without any obstacle to hinder its access, flowing forever in beams as light from the sun.

God's heavenly love is lavished upon lovely objects. Heaven is where love is not confined, for it flows out in innumerable streams toward all the saints and angels of glory. There is no odious, unlovely, or polluted person or thing to be seen there (Rev. 21:27). Nothing will offend even the most refined taste or the gentlest eye. The Father of the family is lovely, and so are all His children; the Head of the body is lovely, and so are all the members.

Christ loves all His saints in heaven. His love flows out to His whole church and to every individual member of it. Truly, heaven is not heaven without Christ. He is the very heaven of heaven. Moreover, the saints themselves not only will receive this love of Christ but will themselves love. They will love God for His own sake and each other for God's sake. In heaven there will be no remaining enmity, distaste, coldness, or deadness of heart toward God and Christ. As the saints will love God with inconceivable fervor and to the utmost of their capacity, so they will know that He has loved them from all eternity, still loves them, and will continue to love them forever.

The saints will love each other. There will be nothing external in heaven to keep its inhabitants at a distance from each other or to hinder their most perfect enjoyment of each other's love. In heaven all will be united in close and intimate relationships. They will all be as brothers, for all will be one society, or rather one family, and all members of the household of God. There will be the infant, who lived only a few days, whom we have lost below, through grace to be found above; there will be the Christian father, mother, wife, child, and friend with whom we will renew the holy fellowship of the saints.

What a haven of rest to enter, after having passed through the storms and tempests of this world, in which pride, selfishness, envy, malice, scorn, contempt, contention, and vice are as waves of a restless ocean, always rolling and often dashed about in violence and fury. There "they shall hunger no more, neither thirst any more; neither shall the sun light on them, nor any heat. For the Lamb which is in the midst of the throne shall feed them, and lead them to living fountains of waters, and God shall wipe away all tears from their eyes" (Rev. 7:16–17). May the believer long earnestly for this eternal state of blessedness, where he shall see his Redeemer with his very eyes, and see no other, for Christ will be all-consuming for him.

—adapted from Jonathan Edwards, "Heaven Is a World of Love," in *Charity and Its Fruits*

eyes; and there shall be no more death, neither
sorrow, nor crying, neither shall there be any
more pain: for the former things are passed away.
5 And he that sat upon the throne said, Behold, I
make all things new. And he said unto me, Write:
for these words are true and faithful.
6 And he said unto me, It is done. I am Alpha
and Omega, the beginning and the end. I will
give unto him that is athirst of the fountain of the
water of life freely.
7 He that overcometh shall inherit all things; and
I will be his God, and he shall be my son.
8 But the fearful, and unbelieving, and the abom-
inable, and murderers, and whoremongers, and
sorcerers, and idolaters, and all liars, shall have
their part in the lake which burneth with fire and
brimstone: which is the second death.
9 And there came unto me one of the seven an-
gels which had the seven vials full of the seven last
plagues, and talked with me, saying, Come hither,
I will shew thee the bride, the Lamb's wife.
10 And he carried me away in the spirit to a great
and high mountain, and shewed me that great
city, the holy Jerusalem, descending out of heaven
from God,
11 Having the glory of God: and her light *was*
like unto a stone most precious, even like a jasper
stone, clear as crystal;
12 And had a wall great and high, *and* had twelve
gates, and at the gates twelve angels, and names
written thereon, which are *the names* of the twelve
tribes of the children of Israel:
13 On the east three gates; on the north three
gates; on the south three gates; and on the west
three gates.
14 And the wall of the city had twelve founda-
tions, and in them the names of the twelve apos-
tles of the Lamb.
15 And he that talked with me had a golden reed
to measure the city, and the gates thereof, and the
wall thereof.
16 And the city lieth foursquare, and the length is
as large as the breadth: and he measured the city
with the reed, twelve thousand furlongs. The length
and the breadth and the height of it are equal.
17 And he measured the wall thereof, an hundred
and forty *and* four cubits, *according to* the mea-
sure of a man, that is, of the angel.
18 And the building of the wall of it was *of* jasper:
and the city *was* pure gold, like unto clear glass.
19 And the foundations of the wall of the city
were garnished with all manner of precious
stones. The first foundation *was* jasper; the sec-
ond, sapphire; the third, a chalcedony; the fourth,
an emerald;
20 The fifth, sardonyx; the sixth, sardius; the

Israel (13:6; 15:5; Ex. 29:42–46; Ezek. 37:27). His presence will comfort them and end all evil (*wipe away all tears*; Isa. 25:8; 35:1–2,10, 65:19).

21:5–8 God's promise of a new creation (*all things new*; Isa. 43:19) is backed by His sovereignty (*throne*; 4:1–11) over the universe that He created and guides to His glory (*Alpha and Omega*; 1:8) and His trustworthiness to do what He promised in Christ (*true and faithful*; 3:14; 19:11; 22:6). When Christ returns, God's decree of salvation and judgment will be fulfilled (*It is done*, same word as in 16:17) through the eternal life (*water*) given to His people, as opposed to eternal death (*fire*) to sinners. On the one hand, God offers the free gift (Isa. 55:1–2) of eternal life in the all-satisfying enjoyment of Himself (*fountain of the water of life*; 7:17; 22:1; Jer. 2:13; John 4:14). This belongs to each one who trusts in Christ and loves Him and His people with persevering faith and love (*overcometh*; 2:7,19,25–27). To him belongs the promise of covenant relationship (v. 3), restated in terms of adoption into God's royal family (*his God . . . my son*; 2 Sam. 7:14; Ps. 89:26–27) to reign over the new creation (*inherit all things*; Rom. 8:17; Gal. 4:7). On the other hand, God threatens horrifying, eternal punishment (*lake which burneth*; see note at 20:11–15) against sinners of all kinds (*abominable* means "disgusting"; *whoremonger* means "sexually immoral"), especially those who do not overcome this world by faith and endurance (*fearful* and *unbelieving*).

The Vision of the Bride-City (21:9—22:5)

21:9–11 The future glory of the church is inseparable from the pouring out of God's wrath on the wicked (*vials* or bowls; 15:1,7), for the fall of the persecuting whore (*Come hither* or here, *carried me away in the spirit*; 17:1,3) makes way for the glorification of the *bride*. The church in union with Christ (*the Lamb's wife*; Eph. 5:25–32) is symbolized by the heavenly *city* (20:9; on architecture as a symbol for people, see note at 3:12). The church will be purified by grace (*holy Jerusalem*; Isa. 1:25–27; 52:1) and exalted (*high mountain*) to share in the *light* of *the glory of God* (Isa. 2:2,5; 60:1–3; Ezek. 40:2; 43:2–5). Created to be God's image bearers (Gen. 1:26), redeemed men and women will become perfect reflectors of God's glory, as *clear* gems (*jasper*, a generic Greek term for precious stones; 4:3) sparkle in the sunlight (vv. 18,21,23).

21:12–14 The symbolic architecture reveals that the full number (*twelve* seven times, including the four sets of *three gates*) of God's people of the Old Testament (*Israel*) and the New Testament (*apostles*) will live in the security of God's protection (*wall*; Ps. 48:12–14; Isa. 26:1), for He will be there with them forever (*gates . . . names of the twelve tribes*; Ezek. 48:30–35).

21:15–17 The symbolic measurements (Ezek. 40:3) continue to repeat the number representing God's people, multiplied in their fullness (12,000 or 12 x 10 x 10 x 10, and 144 or 12 x 12). The majesty of the church of God will dwarf that of any earthly city or nation, being symbolized as a perfect cube; if one edge were placed on Rome, its other side would rest on Jerusalem, and its top would be several times higher than the orbit of modern space stations (*twelve thousand furlongs* is about 1380 miles). As before (v. 12), its safety is represented by a massive wall (144 *cubits* or 216 feet in height).

21:18–21 The abundance of precious metal and stones symbolizes the immense riches of blessing God will shower upon His servants for all eternity (Isa. 54:11–12; 60:17; Eph. 2:7; 3:8). The allusions to the Old Testament priestly garments and the Holy of Holies symbolize how the whole church will serve as priests (1:6; 5:10; 20:6) in God's most holy presence (Zech. 14:20–21; Heb. 10:19–22). Note the city's cubic shape (v. 16), angelic guardians (v. 12), engraving with the names

seventh, chrysolite; the eighth, beryl; the ninth, a
topaz; the tenth, a chrysoprasus; the eleventh, a
jacinth; the twelfth, an amethyst.
21 And the twelve gates *were* twelve pearls; every
several gate was of one pearl: and the street of the
city *was* pure gold, as it were transparent glass.
22 And I saw no temple therein: for the Lord God
Almighty and the Lamb are the temple of it.
23 And the city had no need of the sun, neither of
the moon, to shine in it: for the glory of God did
lighten it, and the Lamb *is* the light thereof.
24 And the nations of them which are saved shall
walk in the light of it: and the kings of the earth
do bring their glory and honour into it.
25 And the gates of it shall not be shut at all by
day: for there shall be no night there.
26 And they shall bring the glory and honour of
the nations into it.
27 And there shall in no wise enter into it any
thing that defileth, neither *whatsoever* worketh
abomination, or *maketh* a lie: but they which are
written in the Lamb's book of life.

CHAPTER 22

AND he shewed me a pure river of water of life,
clear as crystal, proceeding out of the throne of
God and of the Lamb.
2 In the midst of the street of it, and on either
side of the river, *was there* the tree of life, which
bare twelve *manner of* fruits, *and* yielded her fruit
every month: and the leaves of the tree *were* for
the healing of the nations.
3 And there shall be no more curse: but the
throne of God and of the Lamb shall be in it; and
his servants shall serve him:
4 And they shall see his face; and his name *shall
be* in their foreheads.
5 And there shall be no night there; and they
need no candle, neither light of the sun; for the

of the tribes of Israel (v. 12), and construction of *pure gold* and twelve gemstones (Ex. 28:6–21; 1 Kings 6:19–23). All the beauty of the glorified church will be God's glory (v. 23) shining through people in the new creation (*transparent glass*; see note at vv. 9–11).

21:22–23 In the old creation, God blessed mankind through the means of religious life (*temple*) and natural life (*sun, moon*), but in the new creation such means will become unnecessary, for God will be all in all to the redeemed (Isa. 60:19–20). Yet God's invisible essence will always be known in and through the incarnate Lord Jesus (*the Lamb*; cf. 1:16; John 1:18; Col. 1:15; Heb. 1:3). Therefore the glory that fills heaven will be the warm radiance of God's redeeming love in Jesus Christ. As Jonathan Edwards said, heaven is "a world of love."

21:24–27 The glorified church will include the ethnic diversity of *the nations* (5:9). Like an ideal city, it will enjoy the best of human culture (*glory and honour of the nations*; Isa. 60:3–11; 61:6)—food, music, fellowship, relational harmony, etc. Yet it will not face any of the dangers of earthly cities (*gates of it shall not be shut . . . no night there*) nor their corruptions (*any thing that defileth*), for it will consist entirely of those chosen and redeemed by God (*written in the Lamb's book of life*; see note at 20:11–15). The presence of *the kings of the earth* is surprising, for previously in Revelation they were the idolatrous enemies of Christ and His people (6:15; 16:14; 17:2,18; 18:3,9; 19:19). Their appearance in the new Jerusalem proclaims the triumph of God's sovereign grace and pardoning mercy to the worst of sinners.

Thoughts for Personal/Family Worship: Chapter 21

1. **God's purpose is not to rob His people of good things by their self-denial and afflictions but to give His people the best things, the treasures that will last. He will make all things new, not just the minds and spirits of believers but also their bodies and the world in which they live. All the glory of mankind in this fallen world is but a small shadow of the splendor that awaits those who trust in the Lord. Therefore, Christian, rejoice!**
2. **The glory that shines in all the delights of heaven is the glory of God in Christ. The Lord is the sweetness, beauty, pleasure, and treasure of His kingdom. Heaven holds nothing for those who do not love God for His own sake. Those who do not delight in the Lord and holiness would be repulsed by heaven if they could go there. Do you love Jesus Christ and His holiness? What are some signs of a true love for God that can assure believers that God is preparing them for eternity with Him?**

Chapter 22: ***The vision of the glorified church concludes with a return to paradise, and Revelation ends with blessings and admonitions.***

22:1–2 The symbolic vision of the church's future happiness shifts (*and he shewed me*; 21:10) to portray open access within the city (*the street*) to a new garden of Eden, the Paradise where God placed the first man (*river . . . tree of life*; Gen. 2:7–10). The church will enjoy not only the culture of a city but also the country pleasures of an orchard by a stream. The *tree* represents eternal *life* (Gen. 3:22), satisfying happiness (Prov. 3:18; 13:12), delightful variety (a different crop of *fruit every month*) reflecting the diversity of God's people (*twelve*), and complete restoration from all damage to body and soul (*healing of the nations*; Ps. 103:3; Isa. 53:5; 57:19). Noticeably absent from the new garden are the Tree of the Knowledge of Good and Evil and the serpent (Gen. 2:17; 3:1), for testing, temptation, and sin will be abolished for all time, together with the "curse" (v. 3) that came because of man's fall (Gen. 3:17; 4:11). God's reigning presence (*throne*) will constantly overflow with *life* to His people like a *pure river* of the *water of life* (v. 17; 7:17; 21:6; Ezek. 47:1–12; Zech. 14:8–9)—a symbol of delighting in God (Pss. 1:2–3; 36:8; 46:4–5) through graces of the Holy Spirit (Isa. 32:2,15; 35:6; 43:19–21; 44:3–5; John 7:37–39). That the water shines like the city (21:11) with God's light (*clear as crystal* here is literally, "bright" or "radiant as crystal") implies that the Spirit moves the heart to rejoice by communicating an experiential sense (Ps. 34:8) of God's glory in Christ (John 16:14–15; 2 Cor. 3:17–18; 4:6). Therefore the church will have personal fellowship with all three Persons of the triune God (1:4–5).

22:3–5 The communion of redeemed humanity with God (vv. 1–2) is the fruition of the mutual covenant relationship (21:3). God will rule them as their God (*throne*), and they will give Him their adoration as His people (*serve* means "to worship," like priests in a temple; 7:15). God will grant them intimate knowledge of Himself and fellowship with Him (*see his face*; Ps. 17:15; 1 Cor. 13:12; 1 John 3:2), and they will reflect back His image as His people (*name*; 14:1) while they serve Him as holy priests (*in*

Lord God giveth them light: and they shall reign
for ever and ever.
6 And he said unto me, These sayings *are* faithful
and true: and the Lord God of the holy prophets
sent his angel to shew unto his servants the things
which must shortly be done.
7 Behold, I come quickly: blessed *is* he that
keepeth the sayings of the prophecy of this book.
8 And I John saw these things, and heard *them*.
And when I had heard and seen, I fell down to
worship before the feet of the angel which shewed
me these things.
9 Then saith he unto me, See *thou do it* not: for
I am thy fellowservant, and of thy brethren the
prophets, and of them which keep the sayings of
this book: worship God.
10 And he saith unto me, Seal not the sayings of
the prophecy of this book: for the time is at hand.
11 He that is unjust, let him be unjust still: and he
which is filthy, let him be filthy still: and he that is
righteous, let him be righteous still: and he that is
holy, let him be holy still.
12 And, behold, I come quickly; and my reward *is*
with me, to give every man according as his work
shall be.
13 I am Alpha and Omega, the beginning and the
end, the first and the last.
14 Blessed *are* they that do his commandments,
that they may have right to the tree of life, and
may enter in through the gates into the city.
15 For without *are* dogs, and sorcerers, and
whoremongers, and murderers, and idolaters,
and whosoever loveth and maketh a lie.
16 I Jesus have sent mine angel to testify unto you
these things in the churches. I am the root and
the offspring of David, *and* the bright and morn-
ing star.
17 And the Spirit and the bride say, Come. And

their foreheads; Ex. 28:36–38) and everlasting kings (*reign for ever and ever*; 1:6; 5:10, 20:6; Dan. 7:27). Thus God's purpose for Israel will be fulfilled in the whole church of God (Ex. 19:6; Isa. 61:6; 1 Peter 2:9). This destiny of glory revolves around the person and work of Jesus Christ (*the Lamb* appears seven times in 21:9—22:5), just as the Father and Christ appear here as one God. The Father and Christ share one kingdom (*throne* [singular] *of God and of the Lamb*; 3:21), the Spirit's blessings ("river"; 22:1) flow from them both, both receive the worship of the godly (*serve him* [singular]), and both are the object of the blessed vision of the saints (*see his* [singular] *face*)—implying that Christ is also fully God. The glorification of the church is intertwined with Christ's glorification as our crucified and exalted Lord. The incarnate Son will always be the Mediator of God's blessings (Eph. 2:7) and the centerpiece of God's display of His glory (John 17:1, 24; Phil. 2:11).

Concluding Promises, Warnings, and Grace (22:6–21)

22:6–7 *shortly*. The visions of Revelation have immediate relevance, for they describe the spiritual war presently being waged between the church and the world (1:1). *quickly*. Though the time is uncertain, Christ's return will be sudden (16:15). *blessed*. See 1:3.

22:8–9 See 19:10. *worship God*. Since Christ receives worship (1:5–6; 5:9–14), this is a strong indication that Christ is God, in an entirely different category from an *angel* (Heb. 1:6).

22:10–11. The visions do not refer merely to events in the distant future (*Seal not*; Dan. 8:26; 12:4,9), and therefore Revelation should be publicly read in the churches (1:3). The sinner (*unjust, filthy*) will refuse to repent (9:20; 16:9,11; Dan. 12:10) apart from God's grace (2 Tim. 2:25), even if outwardly part of the church (Ezek. 3:27), but the *righteous* will listen and persevere because God gave them spiritual ears to hear (see note at 2:7).

22:12–16 Christ speaks at the end of the book (*I come quickly ... I Jesus*), just as He spoke at its beginning (1:10–13). He asserts His deity and equality with the Father. He is the coming Judge (*my reward is with me*; Isa. 40:10; 62:11), identified with the God on the throne who will call *every man* to account for *his work* (20:11–13; cf. 2:23). He is the eternal Lord of creation (*Alpha and Omega*, used of God in v. 6; 1:8), the sovereign *Jehovah* proclaimed by the prophets (*first and the last*; Isa. 41:4; 44:6). He is also a man descended from *David* in His human nature (Matt. 1:1; Rom. 1:3), whose coming to reign as King signals the dawning of a new age of glory (*morning star*; Num. 24:17; cf. Dan. 12:3). The Lord Jesus declares the seventh and last beatitude (*blessed*) in Revelation (vv. 7,14; 1:3; 14:13; 16:15; 19:9; 20:6), promising that His obedient servants will enjoy eternal life (*tree of life*; v. 2) and citizenship in His kingdom (*enter in through the gates into the city*; Isa. 26:2; 62:10). However, He warns that He will shut outside (*without*) unrepentant sinners (21:8,27) and unbelievers (*dogs* symbolize those who reject the gospel and persecute the righteous; Ps. 59:1,6,14; Matt. 7:6; Phil. 3:2).

22:17 The Holy *Spirit* uses the hope of ultimate salvation and judgment to move the church (*bride*) both to pray for Christ's coming and to call needy sinners (*athirst*; Isa. 55:1; John 6:35; 7:37) to receive eternal life in Christ *freely* (21:6). *whosoever will*. Literally, "the one who chooses." Conversion involves the human will, for God's grace changes the will (Ezek. 36:26; John 6:37,44) so that the sinner unwilling to believe becomes willing (Ps. 110:3).

22:18–19 *add ... take away*. Revelation is not just a human book but the words of the Father, the Son, and the Holy Spirit (1:1–2; 2:7; 19:9). Receiving the Scriptures as the true Word of God (v. 6; 21:5) is essential to eternal life, for salvation is by faith (John 5:24; 6:63,68; Rom. 10:9,17; 1 Thess. 2:13; 2 Tim. 3:15–16; 1 John 4:6). Disregard of the Word brings God's wrath (Deut. 29:19–20; cf. Jer. 36). The whole Bible must have unrivaled authority as the only divine rule of faith and obedience (Prov. 30:6; Jer. 26:2). False prophets lead to false worship (Deut. 4:2–3; 13:1–4). Teachings that go beyond Scripture, by either adding to it or subtracting from it, do not have the authority to bind the conscience or to excuse disobedience to the Bible (Matt. 15:3,6,9; Col. 2:8). Such teachings will ultimately reap total destruction (the *plagues*).

22:20 The central message of the book is that Christ will *come*; this is the hope of His people.

22:21 The book closes in a manner typical of a New Testament epistle (2 Thess. 3:18), just as it opened (1:4). This book of perplexing, symbolic visions aims at communicating *the grace of our Lord Jesus Christ* to its readers—the aim of the whole Bible.

Thoughts for Personal/Family Worship: Chapter 22

1. **The Bible is a book like no other, for it is the Word of God. Therefore, every word is faithful and true. To believe and obey the Bible is the path of blessing. It stands unique**

let him that heareth say, Come. And let him that
is athirst come. And whosoever will, let him take
the water of life freely.
18 For I testify unto every man that heareth the
words of the prophecy of this book, If any man
shall add unto these things, God shall add unto
him the plagues that are written in this book:
19 And if any man shall take away from the words
of the book of this prophecy, God shall take away
his part out of the book of life, and out of the holy
city, and *from* the things which are written in this
book.
20 He which testifieth these things saith, Surely I
come quickly. Amen. Even so, come, Lord Jesus.
21 The grace of our Lord Jesus Christ *be* with you
all. Amen.

in its authority, and we must never place any human tradition or philosophy on equal standing with it, or set aside any part of it because it offends our way of thinking. How does a Christian show with his life that he has received the Bible as the Word of God?

2. **The great theme of Scripture is the Lord Jesus Christ, fully God and fully man. His grace is the only salvation for sinners. His death like a lamb for the sins of His people is the only righteousness fallen men can have before God. His resurrection and future coming are the only hope of the world. God's Son will bring His people into happiness beyond their greatest expectations, for He will bring them into the eternal enjoyment of infinite good: the triune God. All three of the primary Christian graces—faith, hope, and love—focus upon Jesus Christ. Do you trust, hope in, and love God's Son? If not, call out to God even now to save you. If you do know Christ and His salvation, then use each day to seek grace to grow deeper in faith, hope, and love for Christ, as you prepare for the day of the Lord.**

SURELY I

Come

QUICKLY

Amen

EVEN SO

COME

Lord Jesus

REVELATION 22:20

STUDY HELPS

The BEATITUDES

Blessed are the poor in spirit:
for theirs is the kingdom of heaven.

Blessed are they that mourn:
for they shall be comforted.

Blessed are the meek:
for they shall inherit the earth.

Blessed are they which do hunger and thirst after righteousness:
for they shall be filled.

Blessed are the merciful:
for they shall obtain mercy.

Blessed are the pure in heart:
for they shall see God.

Blessed are the peacemakers:
for they shall be called the children of God.

Blessed are they which are persecuted for righteousness' sake:
for theirs is the kingdom of heaven.

Blessed are ye, when men shall revile you, and persecute you, and shall say all manner of evil against you falsely, for my sake. Rejoice, and be exceeding glad:
for great is your reward in heaven: for so persecuted they the prophets which were before you.

MATTHEW 5:3-12

How to Live AS A CHRISTIAN

COME

UNTO *Me*

ALL YE THAT

LABOUR

AND ARE

Heavy Laden

AND I WILL

Give You

REST

MATTHEW 11:28

COMING TO CHRIST

Since the fall of man into sin, the great question has been: "How can sinners be brought back to God?" God drove Adam and Eve out of Paradise for their sins, but through Christ we can return to God and Paradise (Rev. 22:1–2). John therefore testifies, "And the Spirit and the bride say, Come. And let him that heareth say, Come. And let him that is athirst come. And whosoever will, let him take the water of life freely" (v. 17). Man was sent away from God, but now he is brought to God through Jesus Christ. The question that remains is: *How do you and I come to Christ?*

What does it mean to come to Christ? Mistaken views abound, such as making a decision for Christ in their own strength, raising their hands during silent prayer, reciting the sinner's prayer, walking forward during an altar call, getting baptized, taking the Lord's Supper, mentally agreeing to certain truths, having mystical experiences, or seeing miracles.

Coming to Christ begins with God's call. God commands all who hear the gospel to repent and trust in Christ. The gospel presents Christ to men for their salvation. Paul said, "But we preach Christ crucified. . . . Christ the power of God, and the wisdom of God" (1 Cor. 1:23–24). The death and resurrection of the Son of God are powerful to save sinners. Christ says, "Come unto me all ye that labor and are heavy laden, and I will give you rest" (Matt. 11:28). When someone refuses to come to Him, all blame rests upon the sinner. Jesus said, "Ye will not come to me, that ye might have life" (John 5:40).

However, God does more than make a universal call. He also makes an effective call that draws sinners to Christ. The Lord Jesus said, "All that the Father giveth me shall come to me; and him that cometh to me I will in no wise cast out." (John 6:37). We are so blind and dead in sin (Eph. 2:1; 2 Cor. 4:4) that we cannot come and will not come, but with God all things are possible (Matt. 19:26; John 6:44; Eph. 2:5).

We come to Christ when we are drawn actively to Him by faith as He offers Himself to sinners in the gospel through the power of the Holy Spirit. Such faith involves *self-renunciation* as we see we have no righteousness of our own (Phil. 3:9), *reliance* as we rest upon Christ's person and shed blood upon the cross (Rom. 3:25), and *appropriation* as we receive Christ and apply Him as the great medicine for all our spiritual needs (John 1:12). We can only come to Christ to save us from sin if we see ourselves as sinners, breakers of God's holy law who deserve judgment (Rom. 3:19–20).

By the Spirit's grace, have you turned in faith to Christ as He is offered in the gospel as your only hope for salvation? This is a sure sign of coming to Him! If this is so, give glory to God, for apart from the Holy Spirit no one can come to Christ (1 Cor. 12:3). The Spirit gives life, and the flesh profits nothing (John 6:63). Praise the Father that His Spirit has blessed you with faith in Jesus Christ.

If you have not come to Christ, then why not? Let no obstacle hinder you. Read the Bible and listen to preaching that testifies of Christ. Don't let friends lead you astray. Do not let the sins of people in church keep you back from eternal life. If you have not already, learn the basics of Christianity through a good catechism. Do not persist in unbelief or harden you heart. Stop loving this world. Quit clinging to your sins. Don't be a fool and think that God would never damn you. On the other hand, do not be so proud as to think that your sins are greater than the grace of Christ. Christ can save the worst of sinners. Do not delay. Humble yourself today, and call upon the name of the Lord Jesus. He is rich to save all who come to Him.

UNITED WITH CHRIST

Union with Christ is undoubtedly one of the most extraordinary blessings and privileges of every Christian. That union is forged by the Holy Spirit in the hour of regeneration when He cuts a sinner off from Adam and grafts him into Christ. The Spirit then establishes a spiritual union between Christ and the sinner—a union that is unbreakable, irreversible, and eternal.

In so doing, the Holy Spirit reestablishes a covenantal relationship between God and sinners that once existed between God and Adam prior to the Fall. Though the essence of this union is identical to this original covenantal union, one difference is significant: the covenant bond between God and Adam proved to be breakable because it was established externally from God's being. But when the Holy Spirit unites a sinner to Christ, the bond is internal to God's being. It lies within the second Person of the Godhead, the Lord Jesus Christ. When a sinner is united to Christ, he is thereby united to the triune God with a covenantal bond that cannot be severed to all eternity. As impossible as it is to sever the divine and human natures of Christ, so the covenantal bond between God and His people, established in Christ, can never be dissolved. Paul could therefore write boldly to believers that nothing "shall be able to separate us from the love of God, which is in Christ Jesus our Lord" (Rom. 8:39).

All of this is implied when we say that believers are united to Christ by faith. However, this glorious objective truth must also become an experiential reality for us if we are to enjoy its blessed benefits. Objectively, this union is established in the hour of regeneration, but this union with Christ is subjectively established and maintained by the exercise of faith. Only by faith can the believer become conscious of this union and enjoy its benefits.

Though from God's side this union is uninterrupted, from the believer's side the awareness and enjoyment of this union is very much contingent upon the exercise of faith. The more a believer exercises faith, the more he will enjoy the reality and comfort of being united to Christ. Enjoying this union is therefore directly proportionate to our believing appropriation of it. In John 15, Christ lovingly urges His people to abide in Him, saying, "Abide in me, and I in you.... I am the vine, ye are the branches: he that abideth in me, and I in him, the same bringeth forth much fruit" (John 15:4–5). Christ makes it abundantly clear that He desires believers to live in the full awareness and comfort of this union. It is therefore essential that believers exercise faith in the Lord Jesus Christ and His finished work each day afresh. There will be times that such faith is exercised when we are not engaged emotionally—and thus even in the absence of the sweet and tender frames God's children so much enjoy. At such moments we do not feel united to Christ, but by faith we embrace the truth that nevertheless we are united to Christ. What a blessing when we increasingly live by faith and not by feeling! "Faith is the substance of things hoped for, the evidence of things not seen" (Heb. 11:1).

Do you know whether you are united to this precious Christ? If you are, you will be irresistibly drawn to Christ, embrace Him by faith, be progressively conformed to Him, and be increasingly assured of your union with Him. If this in some measure is descriptive of your life, continue coming to and abiding in Christ. In so doing, you will increasingly enjoy your objective union with Christ and the more you will understand what Paul means when he writes, "There is therefore now no condemnation to them which are in Christ Jesus" (Rom. 8:1).

EXPERIENCING JUSTIFICATION AND ADOPTION

John Calvin once said that justification is the main hinge on which religion turns. According to him, "justified by faith is he who, excluded from the righteousness of works, grasps the righteousness of Christ through faith, and clothed in it, appears in God's sight not as a sinner but as a righteous man." We find echoes of this definition of justification in Lord's Day 23 of the Heidelberg Catechism when it speaks of God imputing "to me the perfect satisfaction, righteousness and holiness of Christ;…as if I never had had, nor committed any sin,…as if I had fully accomplished all that obedience which Christ has accomplished for me."

Yet, glorious as the doctrine of justification is, there is another, related doctrine, which is even more glorious: those who are justified by faith are also adopted by God as members of His family. Why is this a greater blessing than the one flowing from justification? Adoption brings us into an even richer relationship with God than justification. Justification has to do with our legal relationship to God. In justification, God as Judge declares the sinner who believes in Christ free from the demands of the law because those demands have been met by another Surety. In adoption, however, God is not only our pacified Judge but our reconciled Father. This is the supreme good of the Christian religion. "Behold," says John the apostle, "what manner of love the Father has bestowed on us, that we should be called the sons of God" (1 John 3:1).

Why is this superior blessing not experienced more often in its richness by us? Why do not more believers enjoy the privileges of sonship as they should? Why do so many feel constrained to say with John Newton:

> 'Tis a point I long to know;
> Oft it causes anxious thought;
> Do I love the Lord or no;
> Am I His or am I not?

There are valid reasons for such laments. All God's people have times when fears and doubts beset them. When they realize who and what they are before a holy God, they can find it difficult to appropriate such great blessings to themselves. There are many who possess the essential marks of grace and yet often hesitate to say, "Abba, Father!" They may believe that Christ is their only Hope and Refuge and there are times "when peace like a river attends [their] way," but they can also go through periods when they do not have the full assurance of their sonship as they wish.

Am I describing your case? Do you often lack boldness to approach God with full assurance as your Father? So what do you do? You must learn to fix your mind on this truth: children of God are adopted through grace, for Christ's sake. Our sonship grows out of Christ's Sonship! It is based on what He has done to earn the blessing of sonship for us. He was rejected by God for a time and so deprived of His Father's love that He cried out, "My God"—not my Father, but my God—"why hast thou forsaken me?" He did this in order "that we might be accepted of God and never be forsaken of Him" (Form for Administration of the Lord's Supper).

How marvelous is God's way of salvation! Does not your heart burn within you when you hear these wonderful truths of the Word of God (Luke 24:32)? Are you still afraid to call God your Father, even if you cannot deny that you believe on His Son? Your Father wants you to call Him by His rightful name. When the prodigal son returned to his father's house with a repentant heart, he was no doubt afraid that he would find the door to that house closed. Having sinned against heaven and his father, he could not expect to be received as a son. But his father had other plans for him. Picture the scene: the father running toward his long-lost son, followed by a hearty embrace and ardent kiss, then the best robe, the ring, the shoes, and the feast—and all for a son who had been dead but was alive again.

GROWING IN
SANCTIFICATION

It is safe to say that the major concern the apostles had for the lives of those under their care was that they should live holy lives (1 Thess. 5:23; 1 Peter 1:15; 1 John 1:5–6). Sanctification is so critical that professing believers who have no desire for it reveal the dangerous state of their soul, for without holiness no one will see the Lord (Heb. 12:14).

To know how to live a sanctified life, therefore, must be a top priority for the Christian. How are we sanctified?

First, we must know and trust in the triune God who saves people from sin. Sanctification is, very simply, to grow in the likeness of our God and Father. By conforming to the image of Christ, we inevitably become more like God. One must begin by trusting Christ's finished work on the cross whereby His people are saved and made able to be sanctified. Without His life and death, there would be no justification and therefore no sanctification. The Holy Spirit indwells and sanctifies us by making us alive, giving us a heart for the things of God, applying the Word to our hearts, and creating His fruit in our lives. Without the triune God, we would all be relinquished to our natural state of being dead in our sins and trespasses, in the grips of a threefold enemy: Satan, the world, and indwelling sin (Eph. 2:1–2).

Second, we must trust that God has given us, in His Word and specifically in the Ten Commandments, all we need to know about holiness. The Bible contains what we must repent of as well as what we must obey—what we must stop doing, thinking, and feeling, and what we must begin doing, thinking, and feeling (Isa. 1:16–17; Rom. 13:12; Eph. 4:22, 24).

Third, we must be assured that God has given all the power necessary for sanctification to take place in the life of His children. In Ephesians 1:16–20, Paul prays that they would know God, have hope, know the riches of the glory of their inheritance, and know the exceeding greatness of God's power toward believers. Then he proceeds to explain that this mighty power is the very power with which Jesus was raised from the dead and "set him at his own right hand in the heavenly places" (Eph. 1:17–20).

Fourth, we must guard against two great errors regarding sanctification: legalism and liberalism. Legalism seeks to add the merit of our works to Christ and the wisdom of our rules to God's Word, but in so doing it loses Christ, freedom, hope, obedience, grace, and love (Gal. 5:1–7). Liberalism twists our freedom in Christ into an opportunity for sin, leading to sexual immorality, false worship, strife in relationships, and lack of self-control (Gal. 5:13, 19–21).

Finally, we must be crucifying the flesh and living in the Spirit (Gal. 5:24–25). Crucifying the flesh is actively putting off sin and developing a greater and greater hatred of sin. Sin seeks to do nothing else but destroy any likeness of Christ. Therefore repentance is an ongoing grace—always confessing, praying for forgiveness, and turning from sin. Living in the Spirit is growing in holiness. It is to become more and more like Christ. The fruit of the Spirit are graces diametrically opposite to the works of the flesh (Gal. 5:22–23). Love would exterminate adultery, hatred, strife, and envy. Temperance is a powerful weapon against uncleanness, drunkenness, and revelings; meekness against murders; peace against seditions, and goodness against wrath. These are graces that do not originate in the human heart. They are a direct consequence of the indwelling of the Spirit. Christians are recipients of grace, yet fully responsible to obey the command to trust the Lord and make use of the means of grace in order to have such fruit produced in abundance in our lives.

Thus, we can understand our dire need of the triune God, His holy Word, and His powerful hand, that He may graciously lead us in the grace of sanctification, keeping us far from the dangerous rocks of legalism and precipices of liberalism—all to God's glory.

ASSURED AND PERSEVERING

The fruits of genuine assurance and perseverance are sorely lacking among Christians today. The fruits of assurance and perseverance—diligent use of the means of grace, heartfelt obedience to God's will, desire for fellowship with Him, yearning for His glory and heaven, love for the church, and intercession for revival—all appear to be waning. We desperately need rich, doctrinal thinking about assurance and perseverance coupled with vibrant, sanctified living.

What is "assurance of faith" and what is "perseverance of the saints" and how do we obtain them? How do assurance and perseverance assist each other in the Christian life?

Assurance of faith is the conviction that, by God's grace, I belong to Christ, have received full pardon for all sins, and will inherit eternal life (1 John 5:11–13). If I have true assurance, I not only believe in Christ for salvation but also know that I believe. Such assurance includes freedom from guilt, joy in God, and a sense of belonging to the family of God. Assurance is also dynamic, varying according to conditions, capable of growing in force and fruitfulness.

Assurance is obtained (1) by clinging to the promises of God (2 Cor. 7:1), (2) by the Spirit's confirmation of the marks and fruits of grace within us (1 John 4:7, 13), (3) by the direct testimony of the Spirit witnessing with our spirit that we are the children of God (Rom. 8:16), and (4) by resting in God's outstanding track record of faithfulness toward us (1 Thess. 5:23–24).

What is the perseverance of the saints? We first must ask, who are the saints? Many would extend "eternal security" to all baptized persons, or to all who have made decisions for Christ at evangelistic meetings. Scripture speaks only of the perseverance of *saints* (Jer. 32:40; Rom. 8:30, 37–39; Phil. 1:1, 6), defined as those "whom God calls, according to his purpose, to the communion of his Son, our Lord Jesus Christ, and regenerates by the Holy Spirit" (Canons of Dort, Fifth Head, Art. 1). By the preserving work of the triune God (1 Cor. 1:2, 8–9), such people will persevere in true faith and in the works that proceed from faith, so long as they continue in the world.

Some theologians want to speak of the *preservation* of the saints, rather than *perseverance*. These two notions are closely related, but not the same. The preserving activity of God undergirds the saints' perseverance. He keeps them in the faith, preserves them from straying, and ultimately perfects them (1 Peter 1:5; Jude 24). We may be confident that God will finish the work of grace He has begun in us (Ps. 138:8; Phil. 1:6; Heb. 12:2). Believers are preserved through Christ's intercession (Luke 22:32; John 17:5) and the ministry of the Holy Spirit (John 14:16; 1 John 2:27).

Perseverance itself, however, is the saints' lifelong activity: confessing Christ as Savior (Rom. 10:9), bringing forth the fruits of grace (John 15:16), enduring to the end (Matt. 10:22; Heb. 10:28, 29). True believers persevere in the "things that accompany salvation" (Heb. 6:9). God does not deal with them "as unaccountable automatons, but as moral agents," says A. W. Pink; believers are active in sanctification (Phil. 2:12). They keep themselves from sin (1 John 5:18). They keep themselves in the love of God (Jude 21). They run with patience the race that is set before them (Heb. 12:1). That is how they persevere, and they are aided in this by the Holy Spirit.

How are assurance and perseverance related? Assurance helps the believer persevere, *first*, by encouraging him to rest on God's grace in Christ and His promises in the gospel; and *second*, by presenting these as a powerful motive for Christian living. Perseverance opens the way for assurance. If a man does not believe in the perseverance of the saints, he cannot be sure he is going to heaven. He may know he is in a state of grace, but he has no way of knowing whether or not he will continue in that state. Thus assurance is wedded to the doctrine of perseverance. Those who persist in doing the works that spring from faith will usually attain high levels of assurance over a period of time.

WORSHIP AND THE MEANS OF
GRACE

When Christians assemble for worship on the Lord's Day, they participate in what is by far the most meaningful and consequential activity in the body of Christ. Worship is the highest calling of the believer. It is the center jewel on the crown of Christian discipleship. It is the verdant pasture in which Christ Jesus, the Good Shepherd, feeds and nourishes His sheep. Worship is the dynamic spiritual context in which the powers of the age to come break forth into this present evil age (Heb. 6:5; Gal. 1:4). Indeed, through the means of Word, sacraments, and prayer God is glorified and His children through faith gratefully receive the benefits of redemption in Christ (Westminster Larger Catechism, Q. 154). Therefore, it is paramount that we understand and devote ourselves to corporate worship on the Lord's Day.

The early Christians made public worship a priority in their lives. Luke reports that "they devoted themselves to the apostles' teaching and the fellowship, to the breaking of bread and the prayers" (Acts 2:42). Notice the definite article preceding each action; this indicates that this was public worship. And what constitutes worship in the nascent days of the church? The Word of God, the sacraments, and prayer (cf. Matt. 28:18–20).

The faithful reading and preaching of God's Word are essential to biblical worship. Paul writes to Timothy, "Till I come, give attendance to reading, to exhortation, to doctrine" (1 Tim. 4:13). Later he charges Timothy to "preach the word; be instant in season, out of season; reprove, rebuke, exhort with all longsuffering and doctrine" (2 Tim. 4:2). All pastors and churches are called to do the same—without exception. The bride of Christ hears the voice of her beloved in worship when His living Word is read, and especially when it is preached (Rom. 10:17; Heb. 4:12). The Bible is the sure Word that we do well to pay attention to until Christ's return (2 Pet. 1:19–21; 1 Tim. 3:16–17).

The question is, dear believer, are you listening? Are you attending Lord's Day worship with a humble and teachable heart? Puritan George Swinnock commented that "all in the church may hear the Word of Christ, but few hear Christ in the Word." Nothing glorifies God more than when His dependent children gather together under the public ministry of the Word in order to hear, believe, and delight in His sublime attributes, loving promises, and fatherly commands. Moreover, nothing provides greater spiritual blessing for Christ's church (cf. Westminster Larger Catechism, Q. 155).

The sacraments of baptism and the Lord's Supper are also integral to biblical worship. They are signs and seals of God's covenant promises fulfilled in Christ. The waters of baptism represent Christ's cleansing blood and the regeneration of the Holy Spirit (Acts 22:16; Titus 3:5), and the bread and the wine of communion signify the broken body and shed blood of Christ—the sinless Lamb who bore God's wrath in our place (Matt. 26:26–28). Through these visible signs and seals, the Holy Spirit powerfully assures us that God "grants us freely the remission of sin and life eternal for the sake of that one sacrifice of Christ accomplished on the cross" (Heidelberg Catechism, Q. 66).

God creates and nourishes faith through the preaching of the Word, and He confirms it in the sacraments. Prayer, the third non-negotiable of biblical worship, is the church's humble and grateful response to the gospel (Ps. 103:1–5). Led by the minister or elders, prayer in worship is the church's heartfelt response (spoken or sung) to the sovereign majesty and grace of God.

Lord's Day worship is no ordinary activity. In an extraordinary way, biblical worship both glorifies God and sanctifies the believer. Therefore, on the divinely appointed "market day of the soul," faithfully attend worship with a ready heart and expectant faith (Heb. 10:25). Come with a heart that is eager and willing to exalt the name of the Lord and to joyfully receive all the spiritual benefits that your heavenly Father offers you in Christ.

FELLOWSHIP WITH BELIEVERS

John writes, "But if we walk in the light, as he is in the light, we have fellowship one with another" (1 John 1:3). Fellowship with other believers is a rich privilege and an important responsibility. Without it, our life would no doubt be very lonely and oppressive. Our fall into sin has cut us off from fellowship with God and godly fellowship with others; before God's work of grace in our hearts, we instead have "fellowship with the unfruitful works of darkness" (Eph. 5:11). But if in sovereign mercy God has engrafted you into His Son, you have begun to enjoy fellowship with Him and, through Him, with others.

The Bible frequently encourages and directs believers to fellowship. From this we can learn that God highly prizes the exercise of this grace for the comfort and growth of faith. Reflect on the following practical ways in which the Bible instructs believers to enjoy fellowship with each other:

1. *By assembling with one another.* This is the chief way Christians can enjoy fellowship. It's humbling to think that God has to warn us not to forsake such assemblies (Heb. 10:25). If Christians are providentially hindered from participating in corporate worship for a long time, it can be a great burden. Think of how sadness filled David's heart when he was remembering the day when he could go to the house of the Lord (Ps. 42:4).
2. *By cultivating and displaying a gracious spirit towards each other.* We cannot properly fellowship with each other when we are proud and self-centered. The Lord instructs us to show humility, gentleness, and patience towards each other (Eph. 4:1–3; 5:21). This often goes against our nature, but a gracious spirit is conducive to fellowship.
3. *By holy conversation with each other.* Christians from the past seem to have been better at this than we in our busy and digitally-oriented society. Bunyan's *Pilgrim's Progress* shows many instances in which Christian was helped by spiritual conversations with fellow-travelers to the Celestial City. God promises rich blessings upon those who cultivate such spiritually-minded fellowship (Mal. 3:16–17).
4. *By singing with each other.* Singing can greatly aid the fellowship of kindred minds (Col. 3:16). This happens in corporate worship, family worship, or just informal gatherings.
5. *By avoiding fellowship with unrighteousness.* Fellowship with ungodly people is a sure way to undermine fellowship between believers. Believers cannot afford to change like chameleons depending on whose company they are in. The Bible warns believers not to fellowship with the ungodly (Ps. 1:1; Eph. 5:11; 2 Cor. 6:1–17).
6. *By celebrating the Lord's Supper.* The Lord's Supper serves a number of purposes. An important one is that believers would be united in brotherly love through the Spirit (1 Cor. 10:17).
7. *By encouraging and helping each other.* We should see times of difficulty as special calls to fellowship with each other. Scripture tells us that if one member of the body of Christ suffers, everyone else should feel it and seek to help as able (1 Cor. 12:26–27; Rom. 12:15). Sometimes this will mean a word of encouragement or sympathy. Other times, contributing tangible help and resources is a beautiful expression of fellowship (2 Cor. 9:12–14).
8. *By praying for each other.* Can people still fellowship with each other when they are not physically together? On his many journeys and during imprisonment, Paul still enjoyed fellowship through prayer and thanksgiving for others (2 Cor. 1:11; Eph. 6:18). In a similar vein, Christians are called to cultivate fellowship with those who are persecuted by remembering them in prayer (Heb. 13:3).

Are you united to Christ? You cannot enjoy true fellowship with any of Christ's people without being united to Christ. If you are a child of God but are lax in your fellowship with other believers, examine what the cause might be. Are you humble, patient, and longing to serve others? Do you cultivate spiritual friendships? Do you use the means of grace prayerfully with a desire to be used for the good of others? In these times when the love of many is waxing cold, may God grow believers to exercise and enjoy deeper fellowship with Him and with each other.

HOW WE REGARD

OURSELVES

Right thinking about the gospel produces right living in the gospel. Vibrant Christianity does not exist in a mental vacuum; we must think right about God, about Christ, and about ourselves. In many ways, what we think about ourselves is the link between what we know to be true about the gospel and how we apply that to daily life. Simply said, how we regard ourselves is crucial to our sanctification, which is the effect of the gospel in our daily experience. The sad truth is that in our battle against sin we are too often our own worst enemy. The battle tends to rage most fiercely inside.

Romans 6 is a high-water text regarding the theology and procedure of sanctification. Significantly, Paul outlines three crucial steps in the process: what to know, what to reckon, and how to behave. We are to know our union with Christ both in terms of His death and resurrection; union with Christ is our source of life (vv. 3–10). We are to behave by not letting sin rule and not yielding to sin's dominion (vv. 12–13). What we are to reckon puts the two together: "reckon ye also yourselves to be dead indeed unto sin, but alive unto God through Jesus Christ our Lord" (v. 11). Self-perception or how we view ourselves flows from what we know and leads to how we behave. Right thinking produces right living.

The verb "to reckon" is most suggestive. Our English word "logic" comes from this word, and the Greek verb means "to take into account," "to consider," or "to regard" something as true. The word emphasizes the vital appropriation of what is believed. What the Christian is to reckon is the same thing he is to believe: deadness to sin through union with Christ (v. 8). We must acknowledge the personal relevance of the truth. We must consider ourselves to be in experience what we are positionally and legally in Christ. The believer must never lose sight or thought of what he is and what he has in the Lord Jesus Christ.

Most remarkable is the fact that this word "reckon," so crucial to the process of sanctification, occurs also in connection with the doctrine of justification (Rom. 4:3–4). However, there is one difference. In justification, God is the subject of the verb. He looks at the merits of Christ's atonement and considers (reckons) the sinner who believes in Christ to be legally free from sin, no longer liable to penalty or condemnation, and positively clothed in the robe of Christ's righteousness. In sanctification, the saint is the subject of the verb. We look at the same merits of Christ's atonement and consider (reckon) ourselves to be free from the dominion of sin. Compare closely what we know about Christ in verses 9–10 (His irreversible resurrection, His emancipation from death, His living unto God) with what we are to reckon to ourselves (our death to sin and life unto God). What is true about Christ, we claim for ourselves. In other words, we are to regard ourselves the same way God regards us: in Christ.

How we see ourselves, then, is nothing more than thinking about the gospel and living in its reality. In Christ, we are united to both His death and His resurrection (v. 5). Regarding ourselves as God regards us means that we must factor into our constant experience the knowledge that when Christ died, we died. We must factor into our experience the purpose of the crucifixion: to put to death the "old man" with its bent to sin. We must factor into our experience the new life that we have in Christ with its bent toward holiness that frees us from having to sin.

To regard ourselves in union with Christ is the secret to sanctification and victory over sin. Sin loses its appeal in the shadow of the cross. How can it be attractive when we realize that sin is the reason Christ died for us and that we died with Him? We certainly are not to think more highly of ourselves than we ought to think, but we are to think "as God hath dealt to every man the measure of faith" (Rom. 12:3). It is by that faith that we see ourselves in Christ. That is right thinking.

LOVE TO GOD

Deuteronomy 6:4–5 says, "Hear, O Israel: The LORD our God is one LORD: and thou shalt love the LORD thy God with all thine heart, and with all thy soul, and with all thy might." Our Lord and great Prophet told us that this is the first and greatest commandment (Mark 12:29). Deuteronomy 6 calls us to turn from all other gods and give sole allegiance to the Lord, because He is the "one" God, and "there is none else" (Deut. 4:39). Love moves us to cling to Him for He is our life (Deut. 30:20). Augustine said, "Thou hast made us for Thyself, and our heart is restless until it rests in Thee."

Love God with all that you are. Some people view love only as a good feeling someone gives you. Others think that love is a mere choice of the will, gutting it of affection. Scripture makes it clear that love cannot be limited to a particular part of man, but must rule all of man's inner life and outer activity: "with all thine heart, and with all thy soul, and with all thy might." The "heart" and "soul" refer to thoughts, emotions, motives, and will. The term "might" is normally the adverb, "very," but as a noun means force or energy. To love God is to keep His commandments (Deut. 5:10; 7:9).

Love starts in the heart and mind but leads to action; it makes us like Josiah, eager and busy serving God (2 Kings 23:25). Wilhelmus à Brakel writes, "Love is the sweet motion of the heart toward God—infused into the hearts of believers by the Holy Spirit—whereby they, by virtue of union with Him and in view of His perfections, delight themselves in God, and in a joyous embrace of His will, fully surrender themselves to His service."

The key word of the commandment is "all." God requires nothing less than the complete devotion to Him of every motion of your body and soul. It is not enough to put God on your list, or even to make Him the top priority on your list. God must own the list, and be written on every line. Augustine wrote, "He loves Thee too little, who loves anything together with Thee, which he loves not for Thy sake."

How humbling is this law! Calvin said, "The perfection which is here required shows with sufficient clearness how far we are from the thorough obedience to the law." We love ourselves, but the best of Christians loves God imperfectly, and the wicked hate Him.

How can we love God with all our hearts?

First, grasp hold of the gospel of "the Lord thy God" (Deut. 6:5). Do not try to love an absolute God, considered merely as a Creator and Lawgiver. Love Him as the God of the covenant, the God of salvation. His love shines supremely in the death of Christ for our sins (Rom. 5:8), and our love is but a Spirit-worked response to His glorious grace (1 John 4:9–10, 13, 19). The law commands love, but only the gospel of Jesus Christ produces love. Brakel says, "Believers on earth love Him, their hearts go out after Him, and He is the focal point of the passions of their love. . . . All their asking, crying, and weeping is for Jesus."

Second, meditate much on Scripture so that "these words" will be "in thine heart" (Deut. 6:6). Each day repeat to yourself truth you read in the Bible or heard from the preacher of the Word—and preach it to yourself until it stirs your heart to love. Treasure up God's words in your heart as the divine medicine to the lies and seduction of the gods of this world (Deut. 11:16–18).

Third, "teach" the Word to "your children" in family worship (Deut. 6:7). The term "teach" here has the root meaning of sharpen: we must not let the Word touch the surface of our family's life but penetrate through pointed application. Read the Bible with your family each day, discuss its meaning and application, and then talk about it all day long.

The best way to love God with all your might is to bring the Word of Christ into all your life through the means of grace being blessed to you by the Holy Spirit.

THE FEAR OF GOD

There are scores of verses in the Bible calling on us to fear God and instructing us what this fear of God is (for example, Deut. 31:12; Pss. 33:8; 111:10; Prov. 23:17). This is true in both Testaments; there is no warrant to think the fear of God is an Old Testament idea, no longer applicable (for example, Matt. 10:28; Luke 1:50; Phil. 2:12; Rev. 19:5). Essentially, to fear God means to reverence, love, trust, and live for God alone. It's the whole of true religion (Eccl. 12:13). John Brown of Haddington captured the fear of God in these words: "The happiness of Christians is in the love of God, and the light of his countenance is their life. It matters little to them that the world frowns on them, if he smiles; and it matters little to them that the world smiles, if he frowns."

We were created in such a way that we had the proper fear of God in our hearts. In our fall, however, we sought to cast off that fear of God, though there are remnants of it in our consciences. Many fallen sinners still have a certain dread and apprehension of God, especially when they find God coming against them in temporal judgments. None of this of itself is saving, however. Romans 3:18 makes clear that by nature there is no true fear of God before our eyes. The fear of the Lord is a gift of God from out of His gracious covenant (Jer. 32:39–40). The Holy Spirit works in the hearts of sinners to instill the fear of God, to bring it into exercise, and nurture it (Ps. 86:11). This fear of the Lord is "clean, enduring forever" (Ps. 19:9).

Do you know this fear of God? To truly fear God, *first* of all, means you will respect and reverence Him as the holy God (Isa. 8:15). God is God and we are not. This should be ample reason for the true fear of Him. Also, He has revealed Himself both in creation and in His Word as all-wise, all-powerful, holy, just, and good. He ought to be held in utmost reverence because of who He is and how He has revealed Himself. Every blade of grass is a call for us to fear God. Every breath we breathe increases our responsibility to fear Him rightly.

To truly fear God, *secondly*, means you will worship Him as He has instructed us to do (Pss. 5:7; 89:7; Heb. 12:28). We should not pretend that we know of ourselves how to fear Him. He has not, however, left us in the dark as to how to do that. The Bible instructs us clearly and precisely how to approach Him.

To truly fear God, *thirdly*, means you will hate and flee from sin. Proverbs 8:13 explains: "The fear of the LORD is to hate evil: pride, and arrogancy, and the evil way, and the froward mouth, do I hate."

To truly fear God, *fourthly*, means you will live out of the forgiveness of sins opened up in the gospel of Christ. Psalm 130:4 says, "But there is forgiveness with thee, that thou mayest be feared." This is not a single experience; as Paul instructs, it involves seeking cleansing again and again. "Having therefore these promises, dearly beloved, let us cleanse ourselves from all filthiness of the flesh and spirit, perfecting holiness in the fear of God" (2 Cor. 7:1).

To truly fear God, fifthly, means you are spoiled and ruined for this world, as Noah was. We read that Noah, "moved with fear, prepared an ark to the saving of his house; by the which he condemned the world, and became heir of the righteousness which is by faith" (Heb. 11:7).

To truly fear God, sixthly, means you will long to commune with others who fear Him (Mal. 3:16). Additionally, you want to see the fear of God spread to the coming generations and throughout the world (Ps. 34:11; Josh. 4:24).

To truly fear God, *lastly*, means you always desire to know God better. The fear of the Lord is the beginning of wisdom (Prov. 1:7). But when we fear God rightly we will never feel we have enough of that knowledge (Prov. 2:5).

LIVING BY THE TEN COMMANDMENTS

Are the Ten Commandments still relevant for the life of the Christian? Obviously there is considerable discussion about this very point in Christian circles. We remember however that Christ said He did not come to abolish the law but to fulfill it (Matt. 5:17), and He said that with the moral law exemplified in the Ten Commandments especially in mind (Matt. 5:21, 27). The better we understand the law the more we will love and serve our Savior. The Ten Commandments teach us something of Christ (Luke 24:27).

First, for Christians, the Ten Commandments reveal the extent of Christ's atonement for us. The Bible teaches that the Lord Jesus died for our sins (1 Cor. 15:3). If we neglect God's law, we might think that we do not have many sins at all, falsely believing then that Christ's death was not really that necessary. However, when we realize the full implications of the law (Matt. 5:17–48), we then understand more clearly what Christ endured for us on the cross (Rom. 3:20, 25). Christ died for all our sins, suffering the full penalty that our guilt deserved. Therefore, the more clearly we understand the Ten Commandments, the more grateful we will truly be to God for our deliverance through Christ's death.

Second, the more we understand God's law, the more clearly we view the full extent of Christ's perfect obedience. The Bible assures us that although the Lord Jesus was "made under the law" (Gal. 4:4), He "fulfilled all righteousness" (Matt. 3:15), and "did no sin" (1 Peter 2:22). As you consider the Ten Commandments in their perfection, consider Christ as the perfect Law-keeper. He is the One who lived in perfect obedience to God's holy law. Every action of our Lord Jesus was perfect in accordance with that law: no thought our Lord Jesus had ever contradicted the law of God; every word He spoke was the perfect word of God. Such was the perfection of Christ.

Third, the law teaches us the perfect righteousness that is imputed to us (Rom. 5:18–19). If we are joined to Him by saving faith, then God regards us as if we kept the whole law. Thus the law of God shows us the perfect righteousness we have in Christ. Upon our faith in the Lord Jesus, our transgressions of the law are laid upon Him—and He atones for those sins by His suffering and death. But also by faith in Him, His perfect obedience of the law is imputed to us—so perfectly that God looks upon us as cloaked in the perfection of Christ! The Heidelberg Catechism says it beautifully in answering, "How art thou righteous before God?" by stating: "God, without any merit of mine, but only out of mere grace, grants and imputes to me, the perfect satisfaction, righteousness and holiness of Christ; even so, as if I never had had, nor committed any sin: yea, as if I had fully accomplished all that obedience which Christ has accomplished for me" (Q. 60).

Fourth, the law teaches us the moral beauty of Christ being formed in us—the goal towards which Christians must strive in their sanctification. Paul teaches us that the Ten Commandments illuminate what love means, and are fulfilled when we truly love each other (Rom. 13:8–10). Then, just a few verses later, he writes, "But put ye on the Lord Jesus Christ, and make not provision for the flesh, to fulfil the lusts thereof." Therefore, we put on Christ more and more when, looking to Him by faith, we obey God's law and grow more like Him.

When you hear the Ten Commandments, think of the Lord Jesus Christ. Think of your transgressions of the law and how Christ atoned for them. That will give you a grateful heart towards Him! Think of the perfection of Christ as He lived perfectly in accordance with the Ten Commandments and imputed His righteousness to you by faith. And consider the practical holiness that Christ works in you as He dwells in your heart by the Holy Spirit. This will make you realize that Christ is your all in all!

GODLY CONTENTMENT

Paul writes in Philippians 4:11b, "I have learned, in whatsoever state I am, therewith to be content." Is this not the Christian's distinct calling and wonderful privilege, that is, to have and to demonstrate true contentment in life? See, for example, Hebrews 13:5, 1 Timothy 6:6, Philippians 4:6–7, and Psalm 37:4. Do you know and glow with Christian contentment in life?

Christian contentment is not only "an embracing of the providence of God," as one put it, but even more fundamentally, an embracing of the God of providence. Wilhelmus à Brakel states in his helpful chapter on this subject that contentment "is not a mental determination to keep ourselves satisfied, but a disposition of the soul . . . . The stronger faith is, the greater the contentment with the will of God will also be." Contentment is not to be found in having favorable circumstances and many possessions, but it is found in the triune God alone, by living in union and communion with Christ and in obedience and service before the Lord (Ps. 23).

The lie of Satan as told in Genesis 3 and replayed in history ever since is that contentment can be found apart from God. Have you seen through this deception of the devil for yourself? This ungodly world is experiencing the miseries of countless forms of discontentment and fading dreams, living in rebellion and unbelief before God (Isa. 57:20–21). Confessing Christians should shine forth the gracious fruit of peaceful contentment in our restless world of rampant murmurings (Phil. 2:14–15). Do you let your light shine with the grace of contentment even in dark and difficult circumstances?

Christian contentment is learned as we genuinely and constantly look to Christ, the Savior of sinners, in Spirit-worked repentance and faith, and so discover what a graciously complete and completely gracious Savior Jesus is (Col. 2:9–10). As Brakel put it, "If you have the all-sufficient One as your salvation, are you then still in need of anything else? Is He not better to you than a thousand worlds? . . . Therefore, speak and practice what the godly did. 'The LORD is my portion, saith my soul; therefore will I hope in Him' (Lam. 3:24)."

Jeremiah Burroughs wrote similarly in his classic, *The Rare Jewel of Christian Contentment*: "A Christian finds satisfaction in every circumstance by getting strength from another, by going out of himself to Jesus Christ, by his faith acting upon Christ and bringing the strength of Jesus Christ into his own soul, he is thereby enabled to bear whatever God lays on him, by the strength that he finds from Jesus Christ."

Do you affirm and demonstrate that while looking to Christ and abiding in Him and His Word under the ministry of the Holy Spirit there is no reason for any discontentment whatsoever, but only for true and growing contentment? The Good Shepherd calls His people to confess "my cup runneth over" in praise and honor to our triune God and in anticipation of heaven to come. Are you demonstrating this holy, happy contentment at home, school, church, and work? What areas in your life can you grow in by having and showing Christian contentment?

To move us from discontentment to contentment, the Savior calls to us, "Open thy mouth wide, and I will fill it. . . . He should have fed them also with the finest of the wheat: and with honey out of the rock should I have satisfied thee" (Ps. 81:10b, 16).

Praise God who will lead His people in endless and everlasting contentment! All honor to Him, our Savior God, from whom all blessings flow—including real contentment! Consider what Paul says in 1 Timothy 6:6: "But godliness with contentment is great gain." Are you enrolled in the school of Christ for the gift and prize of Christian contentment? The "God of all comfort" (2 Cor. 1:3) still welcomes more students, in and through Jesus Christ. "For ye know the grace of our Lord Jesus Christ, that though he was rich, yet for your sakes he became poor, that ye through his poverty might be rich" (2 Cor. 8:9).

SELF-DENIAL

Self-denial is one of the defining elements of the followers of Christ. The Lord Jesus states in Luke 9:23, "If any man will come after me, let him deny himself, and take up his cross daily, and follow me." Self-denial is an absolute requirement: if there is no self-denial, there is no following Christ. Since self-denial is so important, it is vital we know what it really is and how to do it.

What is Christian self-denial? Christ demands denying anything in our lives that opposes full faith in and obedience to His Word. As Thomas Watson points out, there are times when a Christian must deny his appetites, his ease, his finances, even his life. Yet what is the core of self-denial? The great Scottish preachers Ebenezer Erskine and James Fisher give a simple and accurate description of self-denial in their *Assembly's Shorter Catechism Explained*. They describe self-denial as giving up three things in particular.

The *first* thing to be given up is self-wisdom. We give up self-wisdom "when we are made to see our own depraved reason to be but folly, when compared with the wisdom of God revealed in his word (1 Cor. 3:19)."

The *second* thing to be given up is self-will. Self-will is given up "when God's will of precept becomes the sole rule of our heart and life (Ps. 119:105) and His will of providence is cheerfully acquiesced in as the best for us (Rom. 8:28)."

The *third* thing to be given up is self-righteousness. In giving up self-righteousness, "we submit to the righteousness of God, or found our plea for eternal life wholly and entirely upon the meritorious obedience and satisfaction of Christ, as our surety, in our room and stead (Phil. 3:8–9)."

How do we practice self-denial? Three truths are helpful to remember as we strive by God's grace to deny ourselves, giving up self-wisdom, self-will, and self-righteousness.

First, we find help when we remember we only deny ourselves by the Spirit's power. By His regenerating power, the Spirit shows us the foolishness of our own wisdom and lack of righteousness (Rom. 8:7; 2 Cor. 5:17; Col. 3:10). He reveals our wisdom to be in the person and work of Christ Jesus (Job 33; 1 Cor. 1:24; Heb. 1:1–3). He works in us the desire to deny ourselves (Phil. 2:13) and applies the righteousness of Christ to us (Rom. 3:21–26; Gal. 5:5). When we are tempted to despair at our failure to deny ourselves, we have the sure strength of the Spirit of Christ to encourage us.

Second, we find help in prayer. Prayer demands we give up self-wisdom, self-will, and self-righteousness. Praying to "our Father which art in heaven," confessing His name to be "hallowed," and asking Him to "lead us not into temptation, but deliver us from evil" requires that we set aside our wisdom and trust His. Further, there is no room for self-will when we ask "thy will be done on earth as it is in heaven," and when we confess "thine is the kingdom, and the power, and the glory forever." *Lastly*, it is impossible to be self-righteous when truly asking "forgive us our debts as we forgive our debtors" (Matt. 6:9–13). When you are struggling with self-denial, particularly with a sin you struggle with habitually, pray; God will answer your prayer and you will be strengthened by His wisdom, His will, and His righteousness.

Third, if we would deny ourselves, we must focus on Christ. It is hard to do any difficult task if we forget the reason why we are doing it. The same principle is true for self-denial. We will have no strength if we are not "looking unto Jesus the author and finisher of our faith" (Heb. 12:2). Further, our Lord says in John 15:4, "Abide in me, and I in you. As the branch cannot bear fruit of itself, except it abide in the vine; no more can ye, except ye abide in me," and in John 15:5, "without me ye can do nothing." We must never forget that Jesus calls us to deny ourselves in the context of following Him: "If any man will come after me, let him deny himself" (Luke 9:23).

HUMILITY

I had a college friend who would occasionally say, tongue-in-cheek, "I am the most humble person I know." Though we knew that he wasn't serious when he said it, it shows how elusive true humility is, for we can so easily become proud of our humility. Yet humility is not optional for the Christian. The Lord Jesus said, "Blessed are the poor in spirit: for theirs is the kingdom of heaven" (Matt. 5:3). He warned, "Except ye be converted, and become as little children, ye shall not enter into the kingdom of heaven" (Matt. 18:3). The Puritan Richard Baxter wrote, "Humility is not a mere ornament of a Christian, but an essential part of the new creature. It is a contradiction in terms to be a Christian, and not be humble."

What is humility? A humble person knows his place before God, willingly carries out his calling toward others, and has an accurate estimate of himself.

Humility is *embracing our proper place before God.* In 1 Peter 5:6, we see that we must humble ourselves before the mighty hand of God. The same truth is communicated in Mark 10:35–45, where the disciples were striving for greatness before God and Christ gives a much-needed lesson in humility. At the beginning of his *Institutes of the Christian Religion*, John Calvin wrote, "Indeed, our very poverty better discloses the infinitude of benefits reposing in God. The miserable ruin, into which the rebellion of the first man cast us, especially compels us to look upward. Thus, not only will we, in fasting and hungering, seek thence what we lack; but, in being aroused by fear, we shall learn humility." Later, Calvin heartily affirms the words of Augustine: "If you ask me concerning the precepts of the Christian religion, first, second, third, and always I would answer, 'Humility.'"

Humility is also *dealing faithfully with and carrying out our calling well toward others.* Christ establishes this in Matthew 22:39 with His declaration of the second great commandment, "Thou shalt love thy neighbor as thyself." The humble person will do what he can for the greater good of others; he will put forth his best efforts to benefit those around him. Jesus displays the perfect example of humility in the act of washing the feet of His disciples in John 13. He took the form of a *servant* in order to humble Himself and save others (Phil. 2:7–8). When we obediently do what we are called to do with satisfaction, joy, and purpose we are displaying Christ-like humility. A. W. Tozer said, "It is doubtful whether God can bless a man greatly until He has hurt him deeply"—and we could change the word "hurt" to "humbled." C. H. Spurgeon summarized the first two aspects of humility when he wrote, "Humility makes us ready to be blessed by the God of all grace, and fits us to deal efficiently with our fellow-men."

Lastly, humility is *accurately knowing ourselves*. This is brought out in Romans 12:3, "For I say, through the grace given me, to every man that is among you, not to think of himself more highly than he ought to think." Calvin often emphasized the link between humility and self-knowledge. Without humility, self-knowledge serves pride but with humility self-knowledge is most blessed. Humility smites our hearts in the awareness of our misery and lack. It also submits to God's word of grace and salvation in His Son (Isa. 66:2). Finally, humility thrives in those disciplined by the Spirit to embark on this life of suffering and vale of tears in the anticipation of heavenly glory.

Here are some helps for humility:

1. *Hear*—recover a sense of the glory and majesty of hearing God's Word preached or read. The hearing and reading of God's Word is the chief way God works humility and we manifest it.
2. *Gather*—humility enriches fellowship and fellowship encourages humility. Too often the company we keep fuels our pride; gathering with those who are lonely or in distress can teach us humility.
3. *Suffer*—submit to God's hand in sickness, afflictions, trials, and persecution. Do not seek the removal of these things until you have learned well your weakness and leaned hard on God's strength.

HOW WE KILL PRIDE

One can hardly imagine a more difficult activity than to kill pride, particularly in ourselves. This is so, not because there is any lack of it in us, but because pride blinds us to its own existence. Pride blinds us to pride.

Pride is the wellspring of all other sins. It was the first sin that begat all other. Its prevalence is so endemic to the human condition, that it is easy to become desensitized to its presence. But it exists every time we do or think or say anything contrary to God's Word or omit anything expected of us by the living God. How so? Because whenever we sin in any way, whether by omission or commission, we in effect exalt our will above God's. This is pride. Every sin is a manifestation of pride.

Though pride is common, it is an abomination. Pride in the heart is sin (Prov. 21:4). God hates pride (Prov. 6:17; 8:13). He will surely punish the proud (Prov. 15:25; 16:5). The day of the Lord is against all the proud, for the Lord alone will be exalted (Isa. 2:11–12).

How do we kill this beast in others? We do it with patience, compassion, and love. Patience because we ourselves are full of it. Compassion because we know how hateful this sin is to God and how dreadful a person's condition before Him is when caught in pride's clutches. Love because we want to see the other person conformed to God's image, which is the very opposite of pride.

How do we kill pride in ourselves? By several means.

First, we need to frequently consider the cross of Jesus Christ. Why? Because that is the best place to see the true and wretched value of that which opposes God's will. The spiritually and physically pummeled Savior died there because of our pride. A fresh, believing sight of Jesus Christ and Him crucified is a truly divine medicine against pride.

Second, we need the help of others. Having considered the blinding tendency of pride, we note that God often uses others to point out pride in us. We kill our pride by listening to their rebukes. The problem here, of course, is that our pride makes us resistant to receiving hearty counsel from others. And few of us have friends who love us enough to speak the truth in love when we need to hear it. So prayer is needed, in the moment, for the grace and humility to accept what others see, even if we don't see it ourselves.

Third, we need the help of God. It is hard to maintain pride when spending considerable time with the Almighty. Prayerlessness stokes pride; prayer has a quenching tendency.

Fourth, we need to give sober thought to the warnings of Scripture that pride brings horrible consequences. Consider these statements:

- *"When pride cometh, then cometh shame: but with the lowly is wisdom" (Prov. 11:2).*
- *"Pride goeth before destruction, and an haughty spirit before a fall. Better it is to be of an humble spirit with the lowly, than to divide the spoil with the proud" (Prov. 16:18–19).*
- *"A man's pride shall bring him low: but honour shall uphold the humble in spirit" (Prov. 29:23).*

Our pride not only hurts us but also harms others. Pride makes us arrogant mockers towards other people (Prov. 21:24). The proud person stirs up fights and conflicts (Prov. 13:10; 28:25).

Finally, let us consider well Paul's reminder to the Corinthians, "Who maketh thee to differ from another? and what hast thou that thou didst not receive? now if thou didst receive it, why dost thou glory, as if thou hadst not received it?" (1 Cor. 4:7–8). Whatever our abilities, our attainments, our acquisitions—all are gifts. Paul's motto should be our practice: "God forbid that I should glory, save in the cross of our Lord Jesus Christ, by whom the world is crucified unto me, and I unto the world" (Gal. 6:14).

We must have no tolerance for pride. We do not correct a venomous snake; we behead it. Pride, like a fire revived, needs to be stamped out lest we be consumed in the conflagration. Hasten the day, Lord, when pride will be extinguished once and forever!

COPING WITH CRITICISM

No one likes criticism. Christians with sensitive consciences may find criticism even more difficult to handle. Here are nine ways to help you cope with it.

First, consider criticism inevitable. If you're living as a Christian in a hostile world that hates what you believe, you can't escape criticism. Jesus said that the world will hate us even as it hated Him (John 15:18; 1 John 3:1). He added in Luke 6:26, "Woe unto you, when all men shall speak well of you."

Second, consider the source. Though you should take every criticism seriously, it is still wise to ask yourself: who is criticizing me? Is my critic a friend or a foe, a mature believer or a hardened unbeliever, a highly critical individual, or perhaps a fringe member of the church? If your critic is someone known for wisdom, you should encourage his or her constructive evaluation.

Third, consider timing and prayer. The physical setting, timing, and situation out of which criticism comes may help you determine whether the criticism is helpful. As a general rule, don't respond to criticism for at least twenty-four hours to allow yourself time to pray, think, and get counsel.

Fourth, consider yourself. The Holy Spirit uses our critics to keep us from exalting ourselves. So let yourself be vulnerable. Don't be afraid to say, "I was wrong; will you forgive me?" Be grateful that you can learn valuable truths from your critics. Some of our best friends are those who disagree with us lovingly, openly, and intelligently. "Faithful are the wounds of a friend" (Prov. 27:6).

Fifth, consider the content. Ask yourself honestly: What are my critics saying that might help me improve myself? Is there a kernel of truth in this particular criticism that, if changes are made, will make me more godly? If critics say something constructive, absorb it, confess your fault, take the lead in self-criticism, ask for forgiveness wholeheartedly, make changes for the better, and move on. If the critics offer nothing constructive, be kind and polite, and move on. Either way, move on—don't harbor internal bitterness. Fight God's battles, not your own, and you will discover that He will fight yours (Rom. 12:19).

Sixth, consider Scripture. Memorize and meditate upon texts such as Ephesians 6:10, "Be strong in the Lord, and in the power of his might," as well as Romans 12:10: "Be kindly affectioned one to another with brotherly love." When critics attack and you can't understand God's ways, trust Jesus' words in John 13:7, "What I do thou knowest not now; but thou shalt know hereafter."

Seventh, consider Christ. Above all, look to Jesus in the face of mounting criticism. Hebrews 12:3 advises, "Consider him that endured such contradiction of sinners against himself." Peter is more detailed: "Christ also suffered for us, leaving us an example, that ye should follow his steps: who did no sin, neither was guile found in his mouth; who, when he was reviled, reviled not again; when he suffered, he threatened not; but committed himself to him that judgeth righteously" (1 Peter 2:21–23).

Eighth, consider love. Love your critic. Seek to understand him. Thank him for coming directly to you with his criticism. Be willing to forgive any injury done to you. Pray for your critic, and if possible, pray with your critic—with integrity and humility. Put away anything that inhibits love. As Peter writes, "Laying aside all malice, and all guile, and hypocrisies, and envies, and all evil speakings" (1 Peter 2:1). When you do this, you will discover that your own wounds will heal more rapidly.

Ninth, consider eternity. Remember, all criticism for us as true believers is temporary. Our faithful Savior will be waiting for us on the other side of Jordan. He will wipe away every tear from our eye and will prove to be the Friend who sticks closer than a brother. All wrongs will be made right. There our believing critics will embrace us, and we them. We will understand that all the criticism we received here below was used in the hands of our Potter to prepare us for Immanuel's land. We will see fully that all criticisms were but a light affliction compared to the weight of glory that awaited us.

ENDURING AFFLICTION

The psalmist says, "Many are the afflictions of the righteous: but the LORD delivereth him out of them all" (Ps. 34:19). God does not distinguish His people from unbelievers by exempting them from affliction. He distinguishes them by causing all things—even their afflictions—to work out for their spiritual good and eternal deliverance (Rom. 8:28). But how should we respond to afflictions in order to best assure that we properly submit to Him in times of affliction? Think of not only persecution, but also grief, an accident, physical sickness, depression, unemployment, a strained family relationship, abuse, or any other hardship. Any of these can trouble our souls and we might ask, "Why?"

God has His sovereign purpose for everything. Whatever *God* is doing, it is better for us to ask submissively: "Lord, what must *I* do? How should I respond so that this works for my good and Thy honor?"

The Bible's answer is not an extensive "how-to" list that taps into man's inner potential, but simply says, "by faith." Faith directs us to entrust ourselves to God. Faith is exercised in a variety of ways, but every proper response to affliction is rooted in faith.

This is best illustrated by Hebrews 11. Hebrew Christians faced all kinds of afflictions in a hostile culture. To encourage them to persevere as Christians, the apostle pointed to Old Testament saints as examples. Here we find a wide spectrum of afflictions. We can only list a few samples:

- *How could Enoch endure living in such wicked times just before the Flood (Heb. 11:5)? How can you spiritually survive in the wicked culture of our godless society? The same way Enoch did. Faith in God must be a living part of your daily walk. If God is for you, what can man do to you (Rom. 8:31)?*
- *How could Abram leave his homeland, not knowing where the Lord was leading him (Heb. 11:8)? Is God taking you down an unfamiliar path? How can you avoid anxiety? As Abram did: by faith in the Lord who "leads you in the way you should go" (Isa. 48:17).*
- *How could Moses' parents obey God rather than Pharaoh's wicked command (Heb. 11:23)? How can we stand up against the immoral trends of our infant-killing culture and obey God rather than man? Only by faith in the Lord who is the sovereign King of kings.*
- *How could Moses choose to "suffer affliction with God's people" and resist the temptation of Egypt's treasures and pleasures (Heb. 11:25)? The same way Joseph ran from a seductress. By faith in the Lord, whose name they did not forget in Egypt (Gen. 39:9). By faith they valued the "reproach of Christ" more than Egypt's treasures and pleasures and saw "him who is invisible" (Heb. 11:27).*

Hebrews 11 also mentions that believers faced other dangers (Heb. 11:27–30). They "stopped the mouth of lions, quenched the violence of fire…" (Heb. 11:33ff). How? These believers had no super powers (James 5:17). It was simply by faith. Not that faith itself is a "magical potion" for physical or even psychological strength. While humanly weak, faith connected their soul to Christ (2 Cor. 12:10). For His Son's sake, God puts all things under Christ's feet for their good (Eph. 1:22). He also renews and sanctifies believers, preparing and preserving them for glory. Faith unites them to the Victorious One (1 John 5:4–5). Therefore they can endure "all things through Christ" (Phil. 4:13).

If you are afflicted but still an unbeliever, then you are in great danger. Your temporal affliction is a prelude to eternal affliction. Your affliction calls you to repent and believe. For the believer, affliction is also a call to persevere in faith. Do not stumble in unbelief at your struggle. "Is any among you afflicted? Let him pray" (James 5:13). Call upon the Lord in the day of your trouble (Ps. 50:15). Believer, remember that Christ also "was oppressed and afflicted" (Isa. 53:7). Continue "looking unto Jesus the author and finisher of our faith; who for the joy that was set before him endured the cross" (Heb. 12:2). The best way to cope with affliction is by faith in Christ, who exchanged His cross for a crown.

SPIRITUAL DESERTION

The opening verse of Psalm 130, "Out of the depths have I cried to Thee, O God," vividly portrays the gut-wrenching cry emanating from a soul deep-stricken with a loss of its sense of God's presence. John Owen confessed to a young man who was seeking counsel from him that for twenty years he had preached of the one Mediator between God and man without possessing experiential knowledge of what he was proclaiming—until, as he says, "I was brought to the mouth of the grave, and under which my soul was oppressed with horror and darkness."

This is the soul malady known as spiritual desertion and is a cross known only to the child of God. It refers to the depths into which our sovereign God at times, and according to His good pleasure, allows His people to plunge headlong (Ps. 88). However profound these depths may be, they are not the depths of hell draped with the mist of darkness; there is in them no malice, condemnation, or wrath. Sink as the regenerate soul may into unfathomable depths of dread darkness, it ever finds the Rock of Ages beneath. The unregenerate indeed know of these depths but not in the manner of God's children. It brings them no nearer to God and even serves to drive them further from God (Rev. 16:9).

The question, however, that arises deep within the heart of every believer is, "Why have I fallen into this God-forsaken pit? Has God finally rejected me and turned His face?" There is an acute loss of the sense of God's love in which the soul had previously delighted (Rom. 8:15; 1 Peter 1:8). But rest assured it is God who, in His fatherly way, sends and governs these abandonments.

The most common cause for this soul distress arises from the existence, power, and ever-deceiving remnants of indwelling sin in the regenerate. The believer may and must have the abiding assurance that once the Holy Spirit renews the soul in the cleansing from sin, he is a new creature in Christ. But the same Holy Spirit never uproots the principle and root of sin from his heart; it will remain as a plague to the end (Rom. 7:24). We stand painfully amazed as the plough of the Spirit tears through new areas of corruption within the heart, revealing once more the depths of corruption contained therein. You who have fled to Christ for refuge, never imagine that your warfare is over.

Then there are also those outbreaks of sin appearing as the fruit of sin's baneful presence within, bringing with them the grievous consequence of conscious loss of communion with God. This can be the experience of even the most mature believer (Ps. 51). Who can fully describe the depth of sorrow occasioned by the awareness of willful departure from the Lord, such as Peter when he went out and "wept bitterly"?

Times of perceived spiritual desertion also come upon those who are plunged into mental affliction. Many gracious souls have been immersed in the dread night of depression where no light is visible on any side. Octavius Winslow wrote, "Through many a dark, starless night the spiritual voyager ploughs through the ocean to the desired haven where he would be." And then, because mind and body are so intimately connected, so too the onset of debilitating physical illness can bring an intense season of night upon the soul.

Yet if ever there is a place where the gentleness and sympathy of Christ is abundantly present, it is beside the one who is suffering mental torment and intense physical affliction (Isa. 42:3). With great patience and concern, He draws near to His own who have been plunged into the dark hole of melancholy. He remembers that we are but dust, and from no heart in the entire universe does such loving compassion, tenderness, and sympathy flow as that from the heart of Christ (Ps. 103:13–14).

Isaiah 50:10 gives this counsel, "Who is among you that feareth the Lord, that obeyeth the voice of his servant, that walketh in darkness, and hath no light? Let him trust in the name of the Lord, and stay upon his God." In the darkness, walk by faith and not by sight.

FLEEING WORLDLINESS

Worldliness is when I absorb and embrace a way of thinking and living that is not submissive to God but is instead contrary to God. Worldliness is what the apostle John calls "the lust of the flesh, and the lust of the eyes, and the pride of life" (1 John 2:16). In our experiences in life, we are always meeting worldly thinking and worldly influence and worldly pressure. This worldliness aims to access our own souls and, sadly, too often gets in.

The Bible teaches us to flee worldliness. To flee means to run away as far as possible and fast as possible. John writes to Christians, "Love not the world" (1 John 2:15). Paul urges in Romans 12:2, "Be not conformed to this world." What both mean is that we are to live in such a way that we reject all sinful ways of thinking and living influenced by the devil. That is to flee worldliness.

So how do we do that?

In the *first* place, let us seek to be renewed in our minds. Paul writes in Romans 12:2, "And be not conformed to this world; but be ye transformed by the renewing of your mind." If we are not going to be conformed to this world but truly transformed, then we have to experience mind renewal through exposure to and absorption of God's Word, all blessed to us by the Holy Spirit. If we would flee worldliness, how diligent we should be in careful and prayerful reading and hearing of Scripture.

Already this point can be a test for us. If we are not getting new minds, very likely we are very worldly. Let us start with this basic, most fundamental point: "by the renewing of your mind." So open the Bible. Read it with attention and prayer. Listen to it preached. Think over it constantly and discuss it with others. That's the start.

In the *second* place, to flee worldliness, let us commit to doing God's will. John writes about this in 1 John 2. He makes the key point in verse 17 that "the world passeth away, and the lust thereof." And then John says, "he that doeth the will of God abideth for ever." John is contrasting those who love the world with those who do not love it. Those who do not love it are those who do God's will. It is both a mark of the godly and the way to godliness. When we engage in joyful, thankful obedience to the Lord, then we find the world has no power over us.

This too is a test. Do you aim to do God's commandments? Won't this help you to flee worldliness?

There is a *third* point to consider. John talks about the love of the Father. He writes in 1 John 2:15, "Love not the world, neither the things that are in the world. If any man love the world, the love of the Father is not in him." If you love the world, you don't love the Father. And that means that you don't know His love and you don't show Him love. But if you know the Father's love shed abroad in your heart through the Holy Spirit, and also show Him love, how can you love the world? To use the form of the text but changing the words, "If any man love the Father, the love of the world is not in him." It just can't be!

So this too is a test. Maybe it's the ultimate test. You cannot flee worldliness unless you love the Father. But then, how can Christians not love the Father? Is He not "the Father of mercies and God of all comfort" (2 Cor. 1:3), especially through His own beloved Son, Jesus Christ? And is He not all this even to undeserving sinners like us? Therefore, let us not love the world. What can it do for us? And besides, it is passing away (1 John 2:17). Let us not love the world, but let us love the all-beautiful Father, together with His all-glorious Son, and the ever-blessed Holy Spirit. Let us love the triune God—really love Him, by the Spirit's grace. That is the way to flee worldliness.

FIGHTING AGAINST
BACKSLIDING

Backsliding is a season of increasing sin and decreasing obedience in those who profess to be Christians. Not every sin is backsliding. Christians must sadly expect their lives to consist of a continual cycle of sinning and repenting of sin by faith in Christ crucified (1 John 1:9—2:2). In backsliding, however, this cycle of repentance is largely broken and spiritual ground is lost. The longer we persist in backsliding, the less right we have to claim to be true Christians (1 John 2:3–4), for repentance is of the essence of true Christianity (Acts 2:38; 20:21).

Backsliding from Christ is thus a serious matter. It dishonors God, disregards Christ as Savior, grieves the Spirit, tramples God's law underfoot, and abuses the gospel. And it is a sin as common as it is terrible. God laments in Hosea 11:7 that His people are "bent"—that is, prone—to backslide from Him. The propensity to sin resides in all of our hearts, as does a deep desire to avoid repentance. Little wonder, then, that God warns us so often in Hosea, Jeremiah, and other prophets to abhor and fight against backsliding.

Backsliding usually begins when believers let themselves drift from God, His Word, and His ways. We then slip away gradually, sometimes imperceptibly. One weakness leads to another. Most commonly, backsliding begins with coldness in prayer and then moves to indifference under the Word. Inner corruptions then multiply. The world is loved more and fellow believers are loved less. Man-centered hopes soon replace God-centered desires.

Backsliding reaps bitter results. It injures God's holy and worthy name. It makes us spiritually numb so that our consciences become desensitized, and it results in the church's overall decay.

So how do we fight against this abominable sin—a sin that is so unworthy of our Lord?

First, we must return to the Lord and stop running from Him. We must heed Hosea 14:1, "Return unto the LORD thy God, for thou hast fallen by thine iniquity." We must repent by recognizing our sinful condition, remembering our past obedience, searching out our sin, grieving over it, confessing it, and fleeing from it.

Second, we must pursue righteousness by returning to Christ Jesus. To that end, we must return to a diligent use of the means of grace. That means returning seriously to the Bible. Attend diligently to sound preaching of it. Read it privately every day. Share regular devotions in your family. Memorize and meditate on key verses. Engage in a serious Bible study with one or more friends.

It also means returning diligently to prayer, even when you do not feel like it. Hosea 14:2 says: "Take with you words and turn to the LORD: say unto him, Take away all iniquity, and receive us graciously." Pray the Scriptures back to God. Attend and pray at prayer meetings. Pray with close friends. Pray daily in and with your family. Pray for the Holy Spirit to restore the weeks, months, or perhaps even years, that the locusts have eaten (Joel 2:25).

Read solid, sound Christian literature that will do your soul good. As you read, pray much for grace—justifying grace, sanctifying grace, adopting grace, reviving grace, strengthening grace, reviving grace, and sovereign grace.

Buttress your reading by journaling and/or finding an accountability partner. Two good spiritually minded friends will do you more good than ten or twenty friends who may be Christians but with whom you cannot communicate from heart to heart.

Above all, take refuge to Christ Jesus every day—yes, ten times a day. Flee to Him as your Savior and Lord, your righteousness and strength, your justification and sanctification, your praying and thanking High Priest, and your able and wise Physician. Let Him be your all-in-all.

Don't rest until you are in your old way of communion with Christ again. And be assured, He will receive you back. He is a Savior of second chances; He delights to forgive even seventy times seven.

Come back home to your approachable Savior who loves to receive penitent sinners. Welcome home penitent, backsliding prodigal—welcome home in Christ to the Father's arms, lips, words, and tears of mercy (Luke 15:20–24). Your God and Savior delights in mercy (Micah 7:18). By the Spirit's grace, believe this amazing truth, embrace it, and live it out.

FAMILY WORSHIP

In today's churches, many young people become nominal members with mere notional faith or abandon evangelical truth for unbiblical doctrine and modes of worship. One major reason for this failure is the lack of emphasis upon family worship.

Joshua 24:14–15 says, "Now therefore fear the LORD, and serve him in sincerity and in truth: and put away the gods which your fathers served on the other side of the flood, and in Egypt; and serve ye the LORD. And if it seem evil unto you to serve the LORD, choose you this day whom ye will serve; whether the gods which your fathers served that were on the other side of the flood, or the gods of the Amorites, in whose land ye dwell: but as for me and my house, we will serve the LORD."

Notice three things in this text: *first*, Joshua did not make worship or service to the living God optional; *second*, Joshua enforces the service of God in families with his own example; and *third*, the word *serve* in verse 15 is an inclusive word, which is translated as *worship* many times in Scripture. Surely every God-fearing husband, father, and pastor must say with Joshua: "As for me and my household, we will serve the Lord. We will seek the Lord, worship Him, and pray to Him as a family. We will read His Word, replete with instructions, and reinforce its teachings in our family."

Given the importance of family worship as a potent force in winning untold millions to gospel truth throughout the ages, we ought not be surprised that God requires heads of households do all they can to lead their families in worshiping the living God. Our families owe their allegiance to God. God has placed us in a position of authority to guide our children in the way of the Lord (Eph. 6:4). Clothed with holy authority, we owe to our children prophetical teaching, priestly intercession, and royal guidance.

Heads of households, we must implement family worship in the home. God requires that we worship Him not only privately as individuals, but publicly as members of the covenant body and community, and socially as families. Here are some suggestions to help you establish God-honoring family worship in your homes.

According to Scripture, God should be served in special acts of worship in families today in the following three ways:

(1) *Daily instruction in the Word of God.* God should be worshiped by daily reading and instruction from His Word. Have a plan, account for special occasions, involve the family, and encourage private Bible reading and study. Through questions and answers, parents and children are to daily interact with each other about sacred truth (Deut. 6:6–7). For biblical instruction, strive to be plain in meaning, pure in doctrine, relevant in application, and affectionate in manner. Be sure to require attention.

(2) *Daily prayer to the throne of God.* Jeremiah 10:25 says, "Pour out thy fury upon the heathen that know thee not, and upon the families that call not on thy name." As Thomas Brooks said, "A family without prayer is like a house without a roof, open and exposed to all the storms of heaven." For praying, be short, be simple without being shallow, be direct, be natural yet solemn, and strive for variety.

(3) *Daily singing the praise of God.* Psalm 118:15 says, "The voice of rejoicing and salvation is in the tabernacles [or homes] of the righteous: the right hand of the LORD doeth valiantly." That is a clear reference to singing. The psalmist says this sound *is* (not simply *ought to be*) in the tents of the righteous. We advise that you sing doctrinally pure songs, sing Psalms first and foremost without neglecting sound hymns, sing simple songs if you have young children, and sing heartily and with feeling.

Some people object to regular times of family worship. Don't indulge excuses to avoid family worship. Let us remember that God often uses the restoration of family worship to usher in church revival. As goes the home, so goes the church. Family worship is a most decisive factor in how the home goes.

BEING A CHRIST-LIKE HUSBAND

Few men appreciate long articles on how to behave—especially as to how we ought to treat our wives, so here, based on Ephesians 5, are our duties summed up in terms of their pattern and their practice.

Christ is our pattern. Our basic precept for marriage is, "Husbands, love your wives, even as Christ also loved the church" (Eph. 5:25a). Following Christ's pattern of loving His bride, each of us is to love his wife in these ways:

1. *Absolutely*. Christ gives "Himself" for His bride—His total self (v. 25). He holds nothing back. That is obvious from what He has done (think of Calvary), is doing (think of His constant intercession in heaven), and will do (think of His Second Coming). So we too are called to radical, absolute giving of ourselves to our wives in authentic love.
2. *Realistically and purposely*. Christ goes on loving the church, despite her spots and wrinkles, so that He can present her perfect to His Father in the Great Day (vv. 26–27). Our love must be both realistic (remembering our wives are sinners just like us) and purposeful (aiming for their holiness).
3. *Sacrificially*. Christ nourishes and cherishes His bride at His own expense (vv. 28–29). So ought we husbands treat our wives at our own expense with the same care that we treat our bodies. If you get something in your eye, you give it immediate, tender care. Do you treat your wife with that same care when she is hurting?

How should we practice this pattern?

Show great *interest* in your wife as a person. Care about her. Ask her how her day went and how the kids behaved today. Ask her about her dreams, fears, and frustrations. Learn to listen so that she opens up the more.

Pray for your wife privately and with her. Lay out her needs before God. Be earnest in praying for her spiritual growth, and for relief in physical and emotional difficulties. Let her feel your strength and your tenderness on her behalf at God's throne of grace.

Love your wife *lavishly*. Love her as she is—faults included. Please her (1 Cor. 7:33). Respect and honor her, and treat her tenderly (1 Peter 3:7). Tell her every day how much you love her. Shower her with affection. Cherish her as God's special gift to you.

Heap *praise* on her. Tell her how beautiful and wonderful she is in your eyes. Be intimate, specific, creative, and repetitive in your compliments. Compliment her kindness, her smile, her dress, her hair, and a thousand other things. Compliment her with affection in your voice, with love in your eyes, and with arms of embrace. Praise her in the presence of others (Prov. 31:28). Never allow the children to speak disrespectfully about her.

Learn what your wife *enjoys*. Does she enjoy walking together? Walk with her. Eating out? Take her out. Learn to love what she loves as much as possible. Cultivate shared friendship and interests. The more you find to do in common, usually the better your marriage will be.

Provide your wife with biblical, tender, clear *servant leadership*, not ruthless authoritarianism. Following Christ as your pattern, delight in serving her (Matt. 20:25–26). Be the spiritual leader of your wife and children. Be the father-shepherd, a gentle giant in the home.

Never forget the differences between men and women; become an expert in knowing and responding to the way your wife is. Never allow any relationship to take priority over your friendship with your wife. Never criticize her over small things; as for big things, do it with great tenderness and love, at the right time, and in the right setting. Never compare your wife unfavorably to other people, or criticize her in front of other people. Never fail to give your wife sufficient freedom so that she can strive to be her own kind of a Proverbs 31 woman. Do not smother her or try to control her personality. Never stop being a courteous gentleman.

In conclusion, remember this: if both you and your wife put God first, each other second, and yourselves third, you will be guaranteed a truly blessed marriage.

BEING A GODLY WIFE

God's perfect plan for families includes the creation of men and women as well as how they are to relate to one another. We were created perfect; sadly, sin changed that. But God, in His mercy, gave us marriage, a jewel out of Paradise (Gen. 2:18–25). The husband's call to love, nourish, and give himself for his bride, as Christ does for the church, is complemented by the wife's call to respect and submit to him. Together, they are a team. He is the head of the home, providing and protecting (Eph. 5:23). She is at his side, the hub of the wheel in the home. The details vary, but God's plan is timeless. We discard it at our own peril, but when we follow it, we will be blessed.

Zeroing in on the role of a godly wife, the first blessing comes when we submit with contentment to this plan, trusting God's wisdom (Prov. 3:5–6), standing strong against the feminists' drumbeat which says this is degrading, choosing rather to be in God's will, and expecting more blessings.

The godly wife is blessed when she loves God the most of all, and His Word is written on her heart and manifested in her life. She fights the sin that still lives in her by spending time alone with God in prayer and reading (Eph. 6:17–18). Her walk and her talk are light on a hill and salt of the earth. Walking with Him enables her to walk in harmony with her husband.

The godly wife is blessed when she is faithful to her husband. She wholeheartedly gives him her love, affection, commitment, and attention (Titus 2:4). Giving in to temptation is not an option, in spite of his diminishing muscles, increasing girth, gray hair, and their humdrum life. She doesn't look for a new recipe, but spices up the ingredients she has by pouring her energy into her relationship with her husband.

To the single woman who wishes to be a godly wife: pray and choose wisely. Marry a man you are able to respect, not one who is foolish, selfish, angry, or immature. Marry a godly man who loves you for your whole person. Spurgeon advised us to keep our eyes wide open before marriage, and half closed after. So the married woman should focus on her husband's positive characteristics and minimize his irritating idiosyncrasies (Prov. 10:12; 1 Peter 4:8). Isn't that how we wish to be thought of?

Respect your husband (Eph. 5:33). Your respect for your husband begins in your heart and flows out in your tone of voice, facial expressions, affection (or lack of it), and words. He craves your appreciation for his work and acknowledgement of his gifts. Just as he naturally flexes his biceps when you tuck your hand in above his elbow, so he naturally flexes the characteristics you praise.

Enter his world by asking about his day. Keep connected. Discuss the inner thoughts and feelings of your hearts, of natural and spiritual things. Keep romance and intimacy alive. Continue to date. Keep yourself as healthy and attractive as possible. And always be affectionate. Nurture your marriage; it is precious.

The godly wife is also blessed when she submits to her husband (Eph. 5:22, 24). The husband and wife team could be compared to the president and vice-president of a corporation that specializes in servant leadership. They are persons of equal value, as are children and employees, but someone has to be in charge. Husband and wife ought to be best friends who make decisions together for the good of the family. When they can't agree, the husband has the final word (Eph. 5:23).

Some men are difficult to respect and submit to; their wives have the challenging task of rising above their behavior and taking the high road of obeying God (1 Peter 3:1–2). Such a wife is not a doormat, she may not enable or approve sin, but she exercises tough love. She will need to pray for fortitude. She hopes and prays he will be sanctified by her example (1 Cor. 7:10–17).

Blessings will follow the godly wife when she follows God's plan for marriage, and those around her will be blessed as well.

SHOWING

HOSPITALITY

In Genesis 18, Abraham is sitting in his tent and sees three strangers approaching. He runs to meet them, asking them to stay for a meal. He then hurries to prepare food while they wait for him. In the end, Abraham discovers that his guests are the Lord Himself and two angels. Hebrews 13:2 says, "Be not forgetful to entertain strangers: for thereby some have entertained angels unawares." Abraham's actions here, informed by the rest of Scripture, provide a pattern for our own practice of hospitality.

First, Christian hospitality is welcoming strangers into our homes so that we can minister to them, whether unbelievers or believers. Having friends and family into our homes is not hospitality—that is fellowship, which of course should play a major role in our lives as well. But biblically, hospitality is kindness to strangers; that is what the word means, and that is what we see God's people doing throughout the Bible (see Gen. 19:1–3; Josh. 2:4; Ruth 2:8–10; Judges 19:20; Acts 16:15, 34). Abraham did not know who these men were when they sat down. When is the last time you invited someone you had just met or someone you didn't really know into your home? That was the last time you practiced hospitality.

Second, Christian hospitality is sacrificial. Abraham puts more than twenty liters of flour and a whole calf into the meal—valuable commodities in the ancient Near East! Though he was a rich man, this hospitality still cost him something. Hospitality will cost us as well, whether in time, money, effort, or in some other way. Are you willing to trust God's provision for us to obey His command to practice hospitality?

Third, Christian hospitality is inconvenient. Though it will not likely mean that we have to kill, clean, and cook a cow, hospitality will involve work, which husband, wife, and children should engage in together. It usually involves arranging schedules, planning and making a meal, keeping up conversation, cleaning up, and dying to self as we love others. Hospitality is not convenient, but it is something that God calls us to do. If that is so, we should do it willingly like Abraham, for God loves the cheerful giver. Can we practice hospitality without grumbling (1 Peter 4:9)?

Fourth, Christian hospitality brings blessing. Scripture links obedience with spiritual blessing. This is as true for hospitality as it is for other biblical commands. It blesses those who are ministered to, and it blesses those who are ministering. Hebrews 13:2 encourages us to practice hospitality by reminding us of Abraham's experience; he entertained angels unawares! Calvin comments, "If someone will object that entertaining angels is an unusual occurrence, I have a ready answer, in the fact that we receive not only angels, but Christ himself, when we receive the poor in his name. If we do it to the least of these brethren, we have done it unto him." Do you believe that God will bless your hospitality for eternal good?

Hospitality is not a gift that God gives to just some of His people. It is true that it is a quality highlighted in the character necessary for an elder (1 Tim. 3:2; Titus 1:8). However, it is also a command for every Christian—regardless of giftedness, social status, economic privilege, or attitude. Romans 12:13 says that believers must be "distributing to the necessity of saints; given to hospitality." When done in love to God and love to our neighbor, it is a delight to God and blessed by Him—and will bless the stranger. Practicing hospitality is the best way to develop ability and cultivate a thankful obedience to the Bible's hospitality commands.

If you are a Christian, God has graciously brought you into reconciled fellowship with Himself after welcoming you through the gospel of His only begotten Son. The day is coming when He will welcome you into His heavenly home, although you were a stranger and enemy. How can you show the love of Christ to strangers in your life today?

RAISING CHILDREN IN THE LORD

Children are gifts from God (Ps. 127:3–5). The Lord entrusts them to us with the responsibility to care for them and to raise them in His ways. Ephesians 6:4 says, "And, ye fathers, provoke not your children to wrath: but bring them up in the nurture and admonition of the Lord." God gives both father and mother authority over their children (Ex. 20:12; Eph. 6:1–2). They are called to work as a team, with the father as the head of the household (Eph. 5:23), and the wife as his helper in the home (Gen. 2:18; Titus 2:5). They must exercise that authority to love, serve, strengthen, and prepare their children, not to discourage them (Col. 3:21).

Raising children begins before pregnancy, with prayers for future generations (Gen. 25:21). When a baby is conceived, husbands should tenderly care for their wives, and wives for their own bodies, knowing that in so doing they care for a person whom God is forming in the womb (Ps. 139:13–14).

Father and mother should start to labor to bring their children to Jesus, who delights to bless children (Matt. 19:13–15). God has provided powerful means by which parents may raise their children in the Lord. We have already noted *praying for your children*.

Another means is *teaching the Bible to your children*. One of the great purposes of the Bible is to equip fathers and mothers to teach their families to hope in the Lord and keep His commandments (Ps. 78:5–7). For this reason, parents must also make sure their children learn to read well, so that they can understand the Bible, catechisms, and other helpful books. A key time for teaching your children in addition to worship with the church is regular family worship in the home (see the article on this topic earlier in this section). However, parents should fill all of life with conversations about God's Word and how it applies (Deut. 6:6–7).

A *third* means of bringing your children to Jesus is *disciplining them in love*. Since sin entered into the human race (Rom. 5:12), proud rebellion clings to our hearts, but firm correction will drive it out (Prov. 22:15). The Bible calls this "the rod," referring to spanking. Contrary to popular belief, physical discipline administered to correct disobedience is not an act of abuse or hatred—rather, it is a necessary act of love (Prov. 13:24). By God's grace, the pain of a spanking teaches children lessons about the consequences of sin that can ultimately save their souls (Prov. 23:13–14)—especially when coupled with teaching about God's forgiveness and power in Christ. Failure to discipline one's children will bring shame and grief to parents (Prov. 29:15; 1 Sam. 2:22–36). However, angry parents who discipline in rage only create angry children and a home full of strife (Prov. 15:1, 18; 22:24–25; Eph. 6:4). Wait to discipline until by prayer you can do it with a spirit that is under control (Prov. 16:32). The motive of discipline is love, and its goal is to train a child in righteousness for his own good (Heb. 12:6, 10).

A *fourth* means of raising your children in the Lord is *offering wise counsel*. This becomes especially important as your children grow older. They face many difficult decisions about what car to purchase, what vocation to pursue, whom to marry, etc. Parents have valuable experience and insight to share. Even when mom and dad are old, their children should still listen to them (Prov. 23:22). If you have won the respect and friendship of your children over the years, their hearts will be open to hear you (Prov. 23:26).

Lastly, God has given parents the means of *living as a godly example*. Example is extremely powerful. People who do not practice what they preach only produce more hell-bound hypocrites (Matt. 23:3, 18). However, those who live in sincere godliness can say, "Those things, which ye have both learned, and received, and heard, and seen in me, do: and the God of peace shall be with you" (Phil. 4:9). There is no greater legacy to leave your child than the memories of a father and mother transformed by Christ.

BEING A CHRISTIAN
GRANDPARENT

Grandparenting brings both privilege and responsibility. Though Scripture uses the word "grandmother" only once, namely, for Lois, the grandmother of Timothy (2 Tim. 1:5), God does tell us in His Word what He expects from grandparents. Their lives can bless generations to come.

We grandparent already before becoming grandparents. The way we raise our children affects our grandchildren more than anything else we may do. Initially, parents may not look beyond their own children, but God does. The Old Testament is filled with references to "generations to come," "the third and fourth generation," and "children's children." God works through the generations and instructs parents to raise their children in the fear of His name (Ps. 78:1–8).

We grandparent by praising God for grandchildren and praying for them. As prospective grandparents, my wife and I felt a deep sense of wonder regarding the continuity of our family and the presence of the Lord in our lives. We rejoiced that God was crowning the marriages of our children with the gift of children of their own, and grandchildren to us. A deep awareness of the responsibilities of both parents and grandparents and the potential pitfalls drove us to prayer.

It is said of Philip Henry, father of Matthew Henry: "He had, in eight years' time, twenty-four grandchildren; some by each of his children; concerning whom he would often bless God. . . . He thus writes, 'I have now seen my children's children; let me also see peace upon Israel; and then I will say, Lord, now lettest thou thy servant depart.' Some were much affected with it, when he baptized two of his grandchildren together at Chester, publicly, and preached on Genesis 33:5: They are the children which God hath given thy servant."

We grandparent by being examples of the fear of God in our lives. My wife and I distinctly remember our own grandparents witnessing their faith through prayer, reading, and singing of psalms, and encouraging and teaching us in turn. Paul speaks in such a way of Timothy's grandmother Lois and his mother Eunice, referring to their "unfeigned faith" (faith without a hint of falsehood). A hypocrite has a basic disconnect between his mouth and his heart, and children are often best at sensing, even if not articulating this. Lois and Eunice taught Timothy the Scriptures, despite the fact that Timothy's own father remained a Gentile. Knowing the real significance of the Holy Scriptures for your own heart and life, you will wish your children and grandchildren to come under the same Word of God. None of us can open hearts. The Holy Spirit can bring them to the Teacher, who is able to make them wise unto salvation (2 Tim. 3:15).

We grandparent by building relationships with our grandchildren. We need to get to know each grandchild and relate to him at his own level. The Bible commands parents to teach their children "along life's way" (Deut. 6:7). We need to gain the trust of each grandchild. Young children enjoy telling and showing us their discoveries, and we can tell them of our own discoveries in the light of God's Word and faithfulness. May the Lord grant that these things may stay with them until they are grandparents themselves and, with His blessing, may be passed along by them to their own grandchildren.

We grandparent by reinforcing the long-range vision of the Scriptures for our grandchildren. There is a wonderful scene in the Bible of Jacob blessing his grandchildren, Ephraim and Manasseh (Gen. 47:9–22). Notice how lovingly Joseph sought the blessing of a godly grandparent over his own children. Jacob expressed this blessing in ways that no doubt left a mark on Ephraim and Manasseh and down through their lines of descent. Grandparents have traversed more hills and valleys of life than parents, and their experience of the Lord's faithfulness can help encourage, challenge, and motivate a longer-range vision.

May the Lord overcome our grandparenting shortcomings and give us grace to grandparent faithfully and fruitfully.

HONORING YOUR PARENTS

Imagine as a ten-year-old seeing your three-year-old baby sister trying to open a jar of rat poison. She really wants the "candies" inside! You quickly take the jar out of her hands and put it up on a high shelf out of her reach. She is very upset and cries. She thinks you are really mean for not letting her eat some of the "candy" she found. But you are older and you know better. You know that if she ate the rat poison pellets there would be serious consequences; she would become very sick or maybe even die.

Obeying your parents can be like this at times. Sometimes, as children, your parents tell you that you cannot do something that you really want to do, or they take away something that you want to have. You are upset, and maybe even think that your parents are cruel. But your parents are older and more experienced than you are. They see dangers and potential for harm in what you want to do or to have. Trust and obey your parents. Respect the father and mother that God has given to you. They know you better and love you more than any other adult in the whole world. Obey your parents promptly, willingly, out of a spirit of love and respect; not simply because you must. God sees your heart, your will.

The Fifth Commandment says, "Honour thy father and thy mother, that thy days may be long upon the land which the Lord thy God giveth thee" (Ex. 20:12). Paul likewise wrote, "Children, obey your parents in all things: for this is pleasing unto the Lord" (Col. 3:20).

Obeying and respecting your parents can become even more challenging when you become a teenager. Why? The lines of responsibility between parents and children cross during the teen years. When you were born, your parents did virtually everything for you. They fed you, clothed you, and changed your diapers. Now as you mature into a young adult, you enter a time of transition. You increasingly make more decisions: how to spend your time, where to drive once you have your license, how to deal with a friend who has wronged you, how to spend your money, and whether to apply for a job or not. You increasingly become the decision-maker and your parents step back to let you mature into adulthood.

Two challenges often present themselves during this time of transition.

1. *Teens tend to overestimate their own abilities and want too much independency too quickly.* Many teens are over-confident because they have not yet experienced very much of life's realities and consequences yet. In other words, teens may want to play with and eat "poison pellets" of temptation and sin because they do not see the dangerous consequences and think confidently, "I know how to take care of myself."
2. *Parents tend to resist and give too little independence too slowly to their teen-aged children.* This resistance to "let go" arises from parents' deep love and concern for their children's safety and welfare, and their sense of accountability before God.

As a teen, how can you help your parents confidently give you more independence and freedom? By building trust. The more your parents trust you, the easier it will be for them to agree to your requests and to grant you more freedom to do things on your own. How can you build trust with your parents?

- *Be honest with them, even when you have done wrong.*
- *Ask for their permission to do things or when a change of plans occurs.*
- *Show your love for them.*
- *Communicate with them; readily share with them and be a good listener.*
- *Try to understand them, thinking about their God-given responsibility and their deep love for you and your welfare.*
- *Pray for them, even that God would help their weaknesses and faults.*
- *Trust your parents; willingly respect and obey them.*
- *Trust that the Lord Jesus can help you to do this; pray much to God for this.*

When doing this, by God's grace, you will be blessed as children, as teenagers, all the days of your life on earth, and even eternally! Trust that God's Word and promises are true.

SERVING GOD AT WORK

The Ten Commandments teach us, "Six days shalt thou labour and do all thy work…. For in six days the LORD made heaven and earth (Ex. 20:9, 11). Our daily work reflects who we are: image-bearers of a God who spends His days working. "The works of the Lord are great," writes the psalmist. They are "honourable… glorious… made… to be remembered" (Ps. 111:3–4). His infinity limits the comparisons between His work and ours. Still, His self-revelation in Scripture shows Him busy with creation, providence, and redemption. God is not passive, simply receiving the praise and accolades that His work deserves; that has its place, but not at the expense of the work He does and expects of His creatures.

The Christian road to work has two ditches. The "work is a necessary evil" ditch contains elements of truth. Work is necessary. "If any would not work, neither should he eat" (2 Thess. 3:10). It also has been warped by the fall. "Cursed is the ground for thy sake," God told Adam in Eden, "in the sweat of thy face shalt thou eat bread" (Gen. 3:17, 19). Thorns and thistles that accompany work are not only physical ones but include the workplace politics, the unjust selfishness that takes advantage of others, and the tedium that is part of every job.

The "worship is more important than work" ditch also is based on truth. To minimize "the necessary evil," some spend as little time as possible working, preferring more spiritual activities. The monastic impulse is expressed not only in historical religious orders but also in current attitudes. Here, work has no spiritual value and is valued only for its completion. Yet there is some truth here. "Seek ye first the kingdom of God, and his righteousness, and all these things shall be added unto you" (Luke 12:33) establishes a clear priority that in our day often is forgotten. Our six days of labor, if not understood in the context of the seventh day of rest in which God is worshipped for His goodness and what He has made, inevitably leads to idolatry.

In these ditches, work is devalued, but the Christian road to work puts it in its God-ordained place. A Christian works in the context of the hopeful groanings of Romans 8. As we carry out our God-given vocations, stewarding the unique gifts He has provided us in the context where His providence has placed us, we experience the "bondage of corruption." But we also recognize that it is through carrying out our calling that we participate in the great story of history which leads from the garden of Genesis 2 to the great city of Revelation 21, in which nations and kings will walk (v. 24). The Christian hope will have physical expression when in our redeemed bodies (Rom. 8:23) we will carry out our vocations perfectly.

Solomon captures something of this "now but not yet" perspective of work, noting that man should "enjoy the good of all his labour, it is the gift of God" (Eccl. 3:13). We receive this gift in a context of life's vanity, recognizing that our calling is to "fear God and keep his commandments" (also the commandment to work) and acknowledging that "God shall bring every work into judgment" (Eccl. 12:13–14).

Those who have been crucified with Christ live in the flesh, Christ living in them (Gal. 2:20). Here is comfort, also for our work. It is Christ's perfect obedience, earned in part in His father's carpenter shop but also in His ministry vocation, that is the evidence that will be considered. Christ's obedience will be judged as being perfect. His blood will cover the penalty for our imperfections, also our workplace sins. And so the Christian goes to work with joy, knowing that He serves and worships a God who also works.

- *How does your work utilize the gifts you have been given as an image-bearer of God?*
- *What are the particular idolatries you are tempted to in your specific work context?*
- *How does living in the flesh but with Christ in us come to expression in our work?*
- *How might thinking about the work we will do in the new earth inspire us for our calling today?*

HOW TO SPEND

LEISURE TIME

Most people never have enough leisure time. They view work as a necessary evil to earn enough money to do what they want to do in their free time. They live for their evenings, weekends, and vacations. The recreation and entertainment industries love these people. Then there are others who feel guilty when they are not working. After all, God's Word says we are to "labour" six days and redeem every moment (Ex. 20:9; Eph. 5:16). Where are you in the spectrum between these poles? Neither of these extremes is biblical. Work is not a necessary evil but a God-given calling (Gen. 2:15); leisure time is not from the evil one, but a God-given gift (Eccl. 3:13; 5:18–19; 9:9).

One purpose for leisure time is to be refreshed physically, mentally, and spiritually. That is why God gave us a weekly day of rest, to begin to know Him. While on earth, the Lord Jesus knew He and His disciples needed additional times of rest. After becoming wearied by ministry and receiving the disturbing news of John the Baptist's death, He said to His disciples, "come ye yourselves apart… and rest a while" (Mark 6:31). Times of rest better equip us to work. As the Puritans said, the one who doesn't take time to rest is like the harvester who doesn't pause to sharpen his scythe and ends up being less productive.

Another purpose for leisure time is to strengthen bonds with others. God pronounced His blessing on the God-fearing people who took time to speak "often one to another" (Mal. 3:16). Bonds of family, friends, and church can be strengthened and others blessed in our free time.

Another purpose is the enjoyment of God's gifts (1 Tim. 6:17b). God shows His glory in the wonderful variety and exquisite beauty of His creation. He gives food, marriage, and other things for us to enjoy in thankfulness to Him (1 Tim. 4:4–5).

These purposes ought to govern our activities. Guard against things that conflict with them. Selfishness is one danger. Free time is often considered "my time" in which I am free to do whatever I want (Luke 12:16–21), as if God's call to love Him above all and my neighbor as myself doesn't apply during those hours. So use your free time to benefit others.

Another danger is letting time-wasters consume time without profit. Recreation and sports give exercise and teach teamwork, but when they become an obsession they rob time as our idols. Social media, internet surfing, computer games, and online entertainment easily devour spare minutes and even hours. Take spare moments to seek the things above in the midst of a busy day, maybe with the help of an app on your device or book beside your chair.

What we do when we do not "have to do" anything often betrays the priorities and preferences of our hearts. Haven't you found that your greatest problem in your use of time is your heart? What reason we have to confess to God our sin! How we need the cleansing blood of Christ and the righteous covering of the Savior, who always redeemed the time He received to work and rest. Let us seek His enlivening grace to lead us to set our affections on the things above and to give us true love to others.

God's grace enables us to enjoy His gifts with thankfulness to Him, redeem leisure time, and delight in the greatest recreation of all. The Puritan Isaac Ambrose wrote, "Contemplation is soul-recreation." He then proceeded to write a large volume (recommended reading!) entitled *Looking Unto Jesus*. As important as other uses of leisure time are, the most blessed activity involves seeking and delighting in the Lord. That is why God gave a weekly day of rest. Though we may not consider the Sabbath "leisure time," it is "time when one is not working." Guard that day, devote it to spiritual exercises, treasure the means of grace God gives on it, and seek rest in Christ. His grace makes this weekly day of rest the highlight of "leisure time" and will affect how you spend your spare moments and free days.

WITNESSING FOR CHRIST

Christians are called to be witnesses of Christ in a sinful world. This calling is established by Christ's own command (Acts 1:8) as well as by the example of the post-Pentecost church. All saved sinners desire to share the gospel with others. But more than just an *activity* (e.g., evangelism), our new identity as believers includes *being* witnesses of Christ. We are witnesses at all times, even when we are not engaged in evangelism or other missional activities.

The word *witness* is a legal term. It designates a person who has a personal knowledge of an important reality and who is willing to make public testimony to the truth of that reality. To witness about something means to consistently profess its truth and give evidence that verifies this profession. Thus Christians are witnesses of Christ. They have a personal, experiential knowledge of Christ. They publicly testify of Christ's Lordship and gospel before all peoples. Their words and lifestyle—when living by grace—are verifiable evidence of the truth.

How should we live as witnesses? Christ set the perfect pattern for us, and then sent His Spirit to fill and equip us for this task. We, like Timothy, are to follow Christ's example: "I give thee charge in the sight of God… and before Christ Jesus, who before Pontius Pilate witnessed a good confession that thou keep this commandment without spot, unrebukeable" (1 Tim. 6:13–14).

Truth was on trial during the time of Pontius Pilate. Truth Incarnate stood before this Gentile judge. The evidence of Christ's life demanded a verdict, and the clear testimony was His innocence and His divinity. Truth was also on trial in the larger courtroom of the Jewish people and before all nations (cf. Isa. 43:8–12). Christ is "the Faithful Witness" (Rev. 1:5) who witnessed a "good confession." Likewise, every believer is called to faithful living in a way that is without reproach amid this sinful world (Matt. 5:16; Phil. 2:14–16; 1 Peter 2:12). As our Lord has been the Faithful Witness, so we are called to be His faithful witnesses.

How should we faithfully witness of Christ? A concise answer is impossible since most of the New Testament was written with the primary intent of instructing believers how to live as witnesses. But in short, living as a Christian witness means following Christ by displaying His character in this sinful world while declaring the truth of the gospel. Note the following practical considerations.

First, our witness is in the presence of the Father. Paul charges Timothy "in the sight of God" and, likewise, Christ promises to acknowledge faithful witnesses before the Father in heaven (Matt. 10:32). We often are tempted to evaluate our lives and activities by the judgment of others. It is easy to forget that our witness is, first of all, in the sight of God.

Second, our witness is before a world opposed to Christ and His truth. Be prepared to be misjudged and even mistreated, as was Christ, "who, when he was reviled, reviled not again; when he suffered, he threatened not; but committed himself to him that judgeth righteously" (1 Peter 2:23).

Third, we are to witness with loving conviction. Many people are headed heedlessly to an eternal hell. We must love them enough to be socially and politically incorrect, warning them of their spiritual danger and pointing them to Christ. We who have personally experienced the reality of gospel transformation cannot but share this peace and joy with others (1 John 1:3–4).

Fourth, we are to witness with dignity, humility, and confidence in Christ who is Truth. Think of Christ standing on trial before a wicked judge and devious religious leaders. Reflect on His regal dignity and the gentle majesty in which He displayed righteous living. Consider His gracious meekness and humility (Phil. 2:5–8). Here stands the King of the universe being mocked by wicked men; but He had willingly condescended in order to testify of God's amazing love to save sinners. Be encouraged by His quiet confidence. Truth was not determined by the outcome of Pilate's judgment; Christ was and is and will always be the Truth, and soon every tongue will confess it.

DEFENDING OUR FAITH

"Defending the faith" is one definition of apologetics. However, defending the faith is not an academic exercise so much as the responsibility of every Christian. It is to be lived, not just studied. How? We read in 1 Peter 3:15, "But sanctify the Lord God in your hearts: and be ready always to give an answer to every man that asketh you a reason of the hope that is in you with meekness and fear."

First, we defend our faith when we honor the Lord in our hearts. We must fear and honor the Lord more than we fear and honor people or ideas. The Word of the Lord matters more than the words of men and women. The Bible says, "the word of the Lord endureth for ever" (1 Peter 1:25). When the gospel of our Lord changes our lives and then our relationships and communities, we are defending our faith. As William Edgar has pointed out, apologetics is relevant every day not because of our insights into our culture, but because of the good news of the gospel, which is always fresh and powerful. Living in obedience to Scripture is then living in defense of our faith.

Second, we can live defending our faith by living with hope. Peter, while writing to a persecuted and dispersed people, assumed Christians would be living with such hope that people would ask them how and why. Today this hope is contrary to the self-help and despair that most of the world lives with, because this hope is not in human change. This hope is certain faith in the revelation and resurrection of Jesus Christ, which brings with it the promise of a great inheritance. Christians can exult, "Blessed be the God and Father of our Lord Jesus Christ, which according to his abundant mercy hath begotten us again unto a lively hope by the resurrection of Jesus Christ from the dead" (1 Peter 1:3). This hope is central to what it means to live as a Christian.

Third, we live defending our faith when we are ready to give an answer. It may be answering those whom we engage in conversation, or more particularly, those who ask us why we have hope. We often think this will require much study and understanding of philosophy, culture, and other religions, and this knowledge is possible and helpful. But you do not need that before you begin defending your faith; Peter says be ready to give an answer for your hope, not your knowledge (1 Peter 1:13)! But are we living in conversation with others? Are we using creation, morality, desire, beauty, relationships, parenting, and eternity as topics of conversation with others where our hope (as informed by Scripture) can shine through? Are you ready to answer the questions: What do you believe? Why do you believe that?

Fourth, we defend our faith when we live with meekness and fear, or with gentleness and respect. As we defend ourselves, it is easy to begin to attack others. There may be a place for going on the offensive against ideas (2 Cor. 10:5), but we must remember we are not defending ourselves; we are defending the hope that we have in Christ. This must be done with winsomeness, a respectful attitude, and a good conscience. We must put away all malice, deceit, hypocrisy, envy, and all slander (1 Peter 2:1), even in the context of persecution and hatred. However, it is how we must live as we defend our faith (1 Peter 2:13–19). "For it is better...that ye suffer for well doing, than for evil doing" (1 Peter 3:17).

For all four of these, we need the gift of the Holy Spirit *in us* so we can honor the Lord and live with hope (Rom. 15:13), as well as having Him *work through us* so that we can properly live and defend our faith (John 15:26). So, as you consider how you should defend the faith, think about your own life rather than others: Is your life honoring the Lord? Is your life shining with hope? Is your life ready to engage others? Is your life lived with gentleness and respect?

FACING SICKNESS AND DEATH

Man is not naturally inclined to face sickness and death well. The unbeliever lives for the here and now, and this life is everything to him. He dreams of a life free of illness and adversity, even free of death. His life consists of the pursuit of happiness, and he would want to live here forever if that were attainable. The ungodly therefore respond in anger and bitterness when illness and/or death interrupts their pursuit of a vain happiness that so often eludes them.

If only it were true that Christians were free of such sinful emotions and such a sinful response to illness and death. When serious illness and the possibility of death suddenly intrude our lives, such a struggle arises in our hearts. The flesh can rear its ugly head when the prospect of chronic or terminal illness dramatically alters the course of our lives.

Such an unbecoming reaction to divinely sent affliction will, however, be a matter of grief to the believer, as it is the desire of his renewed inner man to surrender fully to the providential leadings of his heavenly Father. How intense the prayerful struggle to surrender wholeheartedly to a God who in His sovereign wisdom is slaying me in order to accomplish His purpose in my life!

And yet such wholehearted surrender alone will enable us to face the reality of illness or the inescapable prospect of death. Such surrender enabled Job to say that he would still trust the God who was slaying him and had thrust him into the furnace of affliction. "Though he slay me, yet will I trust in him" (Job 13:5). The grace of God prevailed mightily in a man who, on another occasion, cursed the day he was born.

Clearly, only the sustaining grace of God can enable us to face sickness and death as a Christian—that is, as someone who trusts his heavenly Father and the unfailing promises of His Word. We must learn to make use of these promises when serious trials become our portion. Only by appropriating God's precious covenantal promises will we be able to rise above our circumstances and trust our heavenly Father when nothing appears to make any sense. We must learn to judge God by His Word rather than our feelings and circumstances.

Such unwavering trust enabled Paul and Silas to sing God's praises when they found themselves in abysmal circumstances (Acts 16:22–24). Such trust enabled countless believers throughout the ages to remain steadfast during seasons of great trial. Christ wanted to teach His disciples this great lesson when He came to them in a raging storm. He first calmed their hearts by speaking to them before silencing the storm. His objective was to teach them (and us!) that in the midst of grievous trials, they should first consider His Word rather than circumstances.

What are some of the promises we can prayerfully appropriate when facing sickness or death?

- *"Can a woman forget her sucking child, that she should not have compassion on the son of her womb? Yea, they may forget, yet will I not forget thee" (Isa. 49:15). Even when God leads us in ways that are far beyond our understanding, God cannot forget His own. His eye will always be upon those who fear Him.*
- *"We know that all things work together for good to them that love God, to them who are the called according to his purpose" (Rom. 8:28). Even through sickness and death, God is working things together for the spiritual good of those who love Him, conforming them to the image of His Son (v. 29).*

This is only a small sample of the many promises our heavenly Father wants us to appropriate by faith. What a blessing when God's grace enables us to say with the psalmist, "What time I am afraid, I will trust in thee. In God I will praise his word, in God I have put my trust" (Ps. 56:3–4)! Only by faith (a gracious gift of God) can we face sickness and death and echo the words of Psalm 112:7: "[I] shall not be afraid of evil tidings: [my] heart is fixed, trusting in the Lord."

LIVING POSITIVELY

We live in an increasingly negative culture in which it's easy to be dragged down with all the discouraging and depressing events that flood our hearts and overwhelm our minds. However, the apostle Paul calls us to enjoy God's peace in the midst of the storm by feeding our minds on an alternative media diet. He writes: "Finally, brethren, whatsoever things are true, whatsoever things are honest, whatsoever things are just, whatsoever things are pure, whatsoever things are lovely, whatsoever things are of good report; if there be any virtue, and if there be any praise, think on these things" (Phil. 4:8).

This is not an argument for unrealistic isolation from the bad news that inevitably fills a fallen world. No, this is a warrant, even a demand, that in our media choices we choose *a deliberate imbalance* in favor of what is inspirational and wholesome, instead of the current imbalance on the side of what is dispiriting and gross. Paul's "Food Pyramid" for a healthy media diet contains six main categories:

1. *True Not False:* Avoid listening to lies, misrepresentation, imbalance, and distortion, on both the left and the right of the political spectrum. Beware of journalists who spend most of their time exposing the lies of "the other team." Instead, seek out the most truthful, balanced, and fair reporting. Feast on truth, wherever it appears and whoever is speaking it. Surround yourself with truth-tellers rather than muck-spreaders.
2. *Noble Not Base:* The media tends to publicize the vile and sordid side of life. Their reporters and resources are focused on the seedy cesspools of our society. "Don't do this to yourself!" appealed Paul. Trash the base and nourish the noble in your life. Noble means "majestic, awe-inspiring, worthy, and elevating": seek out media that elevate the heroic, that inspire awe, and that generate worship.
3. *Right Not Wrong:* When Paul says we should think about what is "just," he means what conforms to God's law and standards—right conduct in all of life. Paul urges us to seek out and celebrate right behavior, courageous actions, hardworking parents, loving fathers, devoted mothers, respectful children, happy families, gentle caregivers, honest employees, fair bosses, etc.
4. *Pure Not Filthy:* When was the last time you saw a film that celebrated Christian marriage or portrayed a normal functioning family? Immorality, abuse, fighting, and murder rule the day. Take the steps to move the spotlight to happy and godly relationships, long and faithful marriages, etc. Rejoice over the many godly young people who do not use porn, who do not dress immodestly, who keep their hearts with all diligence, and who keep themselves pure for marriage.
5. *Beautiful Not Ugly:* "Whatsoever things are lovely" describes what is attractive and winsome, words and actions that compel admiration and affection. In a day when many of us live among steel and concrete boxes of varying sizes and shapes, it's often very difficult to locate beauty in our immediate surroundings. We need to get out of the city, see the stunning mountains, savor the fragrance of the forest, taste the thrill of fresh and healthy produce, and listen to the exquisite birdsong. Find ways to increase your intake of beauty through your various senses.
6. *Praising Not Complaining:* Paul was saying, "Focus on what is constructive rather than destructive." Feast on whatever makes people exclaim "Well done!" rather than what makes you and others say, "That's terrible." As you drive with your family, do you suggest topics that will show people in a good light or in a bad light? Do you tell stories that will make your hearers praise God and others or in a way that will make people doubt God and condemn others?

As Paul puts it in his summary of these six criteria, "If there be any virtue, and if there be any praise, think on these things" (v. 8). This was not just a theory for Paul; he could appeal to their memory of him: "Those things, which ye have both learned, and received, and heard, and seen in me, do: and the God of peace shall be with you" (Phil. 4:9). He says, if you think like I think and do what I do, you will replace fear, anxiety, depression, and worry with divine peace.

LIVING FOR
GOD'S GLORY

What a lofty goal this is! What could be higher? Yet this is the chief end of everyone who has ever lived. God deserves all glory due to His name (Ps. 29:2). He says it Himself: "This people have I formed for myself, they shall shew forth my praise" (Isa. 43:21). The happiest beings are the angels and glorified saints in heaven, who glorify God eternally. Paul put it this way: "Ye are redeemed with a price, therefore glorify God in your body, and in your spirit" (1 Cor. 6:20).

First, we must *be redeemed by Christ*. By nature, we come short of the glory of God; in fact, we are enemies of it (Rom. 1:21–23; 3:23). We deserve everlasting shame because we have not glorified God rightly. We must be redeemed. Our service to sin must end, and Christ's blood and righteousness must be applied to set us free from the penalty and power of sin (Gal. 3:13–14; 5:24). He lived a perfect life that glorified God without fail; He paid the full ransom price on Calvary. Are you redeemed by His precious blood? Without this great Redeemer, you are lost and will never attain the purpose for which you were made.

Second, we must *glorify God in our bodies*. Many in the Corinthian church were returning to their former fleshly sins. The body is not for fornication (1 Cor. 6:13), but for the Lord. "Know ye not that your body is the temple of the Holy Ghost?" (1 Cor. 6:19). There is a great dignity to our bodies. They are not a garbage dump. They are temples of the Holy Ghost. Therefore glorify God in your body.

Let us use our eyes rightly, as Jesus did, who was filled with compassion as He looked on the multitude. Let our ears turn away from the voices of the world and use them to listen to God's Word and the advice of the godly, even if it is reproof. Let us use our lips not for gossip, but to pray, to speak of the Lord Jesus, and to speak comfort to the downcast. Let us use our hands not to steal, but to work diligently, and to give for the good of others (Eph. 4:28). Let us use our feet to go to the house of God, to walk in His ways, and to follow the Lord Jesus in His footsteps (1 Peter 2:21).

Third, we must *glorify God in our spirit*. Let us think high thoughts of God, read His Word, and submit to His will. Let us trust in Him, as was said of Abram: "he was strong in faith . . . giving glory to God" (Rom. 4:20). Let us give glory to God by confessing our sins, as David acknowledging his sin and justifying God (Ps. 51. Let us give glory to God by a life of holiness, being made conformable to His Son, denying ourselves, and taking up our cross. Let us give glory to God by being thankful, as the leper who returned to Jesus to render thanks to Him (Luke 17:18). This is our reasonable service, isn't it (Rom. 12:1)?

He has bought you with His precious blood, so glorify Him in your body and in your soul. How sad when common activities like eating and drinking remain only common activities. That is how they lived in Noah's days, swallowing it all down without honoring the Giver of these gifts. But Paul says that the children of God should be marked by doing everything to His glory (1 Cor. 10:31).

The secret? The favorable presence of God. That was the secret to Joseph's life of glorifying God in trying times. He was far from his parents, far from the Promised Land, but the Lord was not far from him. God was with him (Gen. 39:2). He experienced the communion and nearness of the Lord. Can we do with less?

Let us look to the Savior from God who could say, "I have glorified thee on the earth: I have finished the work which thou gavest me to do" (John 17:4). He gives His Spirit in answer to your prayer: "Help me thy will to do."

Twenty Centuries OF CHURCH HISTORY

AND

He Said

UNTO THEM

GO YE INTO

ALL

The World

&

PREACH

The Gospel

TO EVERY CREATURE

HE THAT

Believeth

AND IS

BAPTIZED

SHALL

Be Saved

MARK 16:15-16

The FIRST CENTURY

APOSTOLIC FOUNDATIONS

Church history is important for Christians. First, it continues the history of God's faithful dealings with His people found in Holy Scripture and records the ongoing life and work of Christ in our world. Second, we are commanded to "remember all the way which the Lord thy God led thee" (Deut. 8:2) and make it known to our children (Ps. 78:5–6). Third, church history helps to illuminate and clarify what we believe, providing a context for evaluating our beliefs and practices, according the teaching of the church of all the ages. Fourth, it is a safeguard against error; there are no new heresies, it seems, only old ones masquerading as new. Finally, it gives us mentors and heroes, guides to follow as they followed Christ. In doing so, it promotes spiritual maturation and heartfelt supplication to God to reform and revive His church.

This introduction to church history—one page for each century—was drawn from Sinclair Ferguson's pulpit ministry, then revised by Michael Haykin, Coleman Ford, Ray Lanning, and others. Given the brevity of these articles, the reader will understand that hundreds of important names and events in church history must be omitted. What is recorded will shed light on how Christ has gathered His church, by His Word and Spirit, over the past two thousand years, despite the sins and errors of many theologians and churches. Soli Deo gloria!

The first century of church history divides roughly into three periods. In the first, our Lord Jesus, through His ministry, began to fulfill the great promise of Matthew 16:18, "I will build my church." Jesus came into the world to die as the Savior of His people and to build His church. He lived and served, did His mighty works, gave us His teachings and commandments, died, and rose again from the dead that He might fulfill His promise.

The key text for the second third of the first century is Acts 1:8. Jesus told His disciples that they would be His witnesses, "both in Jerusalem, and in all Judaea, and in Samaria, and unto the uttermost part of the earth." As Acts takes us through the next twenty to thirty years, it records how that promise of Jesus was fulfilled.

First, Christ poured out His Holy Spirit on the apostles and those others gathered in Jerusalem on the Day of Pentecost. In time, they spread throughout the ancient world, preaching the gospel everywhere. In Acts 2, we learn that listening to Peter's sermon were Jews and proselytes from many parts of the ancient world, who took their faith back to their homelands.

Next, Luke reports that Philip the evangelist went down to Samaria. The Samaritans "believed Philip" (Acts 8:12), and Samaria received the Word of God.

Finally, the gospel burst upon the Gentile world through the preaching of Peter (Acts 10–11), and since then, notwithstanding setbacks, has never stopped in its progress to the ends of the earth. We know of Peter's subsequent ministry among the churches in what we now call Turkey (Asia Minor) and farther east in Iraq (Babylon). We know of Paul's ministry in Antioch, then in Turkey and on into Europe. In the last chapter of Acts, Luke records the day Paul came to Rome (Acts 28:16), seat of the far-flung Roman Empire. We know much less about the other apostles, but some of them traveled great distances to preach Christ. Thomas is remembered as the apostle to Persia and India. There is a famous denomination in India called the Mar Toma Church, the St. Thomas Church, which traces its origins back to the preaching of Thomas in the Indian state of Kerala.

Those apostolic believers also began to experience what would become the hallmark of the final third of the first century. As the church of Jesus Christ is built on earth, it faces opposition and often violent persecution. Beginning in the last part of the first century, in the mid-60s, the Emperor Nero turned upon Christians. Rome had burned in a great conflagration. To fend off accusations against himself—for he had sometimes mused out loud about leveling Rome, rebuilding it in marble, and renaming it after himself—Nero blamed the Christians, and a number of believers were martyred in Rome. Some were crucified and some were sewn into the skins of dead animals to be savaged to death by wild dogs.

An early Christian historian named Tertullian wrote in his *Apology*, his defense of the Christian faith, "The blood of the martyrs is the seed of the church," that is, a blessed means whereby Christ plants and grows His church.

The SECOND CENTURY

THE CHURCH OF MARTYRS AND CONFESSORS

Matthew 16:18 is an important text in the New Testament. The words of Jesus indicate in no uncertain terms that wherever Christ builds His church, there will be powerful opposition to what He is doing, but "the gates of hell shall not prevail against it." Joseph Alexander explains "the gates of hell" as "a strong figure for death, or destruction. . . . *Gates* has been variously explained to mean the entrance, the defenses, the military force and the judicial power." In other words, Christ promised to build His church in defiance of the enmity and destructive power of death itself.

In the second century of the Christian church, this opposition took two forms. The first was that of *blatant persecution*. There was a human strategy, undoubtedly with a diabolical intent behind it, to destroy the church by destroying its members. Paradoxically, one of the ways in which Jesus Christ has built His church down through the centuries is through the death and testimony of Christian martyrs, as Tertullian observed. In the first century, the Christian church was sheltered to some degree under Judaism, which Rome tolerated as a legal religion. But it became abundantly clear in the early second century that there was a gulf between Jews and Christians. The people of the ancient world spoke about two races of men—Jews and Gentiles. In the second century, they began to speak about three—Jews, Gentiles, and Christians.

Roman law began to accord divine honors to the emperor. Christians, confessing that Jesus is Lord of all, refused to acknowledge the divine lordship of Caesar, and so were guilty of a capital offense. Men and women, boys and girls were slain for their faith in Jesus. One of the most famous, an old man named Polycarp, declared to the authorities: "I have served Jesus Christ these eighty and six years. He has done me no harm; why should I deny Him now?" The Romans burned him.

A second form of opposition to the building of the church in the second century was *false teaching*. In the second century, the Greco-Roman world was dominated by a dualistic philosophy that regarded the spiritual realm as pure and good, but saw matter as inherently evil. It wasn't long before that philosophy started to distort the message of the Christian gospel in some very basic ways.

First, if spirit is good and matter is bad, then as an eternal and good Spirit, God could not have created the evil material world. It must have been created by some lesser kind of deity, which the false teachers called the demiurge. So the teaching of Scripture began to be eroded: the eternal God was not Maker of heaven and earth. Second, the eternal Son of God could never have become man—that is, taken upon Himself our flesh-and-blood human nature. Therefore, the incarnation was simply the Son presenting only the appearance of humanity. A third implication was denial of the resurrection of the body. Why would God resurrect the body, since, being material, it is inherently bad? At such points, the Christian faith was under attack from this false philosophy.

The church's response was to formulate confessions of the true faith in ways that highlighted that the one true and living God did indeed make heaven and earth and is the Father of our Lord Jesus Christ. These confessions also made it clear that Jesus Christ is both fully God and fully man. The Second Person of the Godhead took upon Himself a full humanity. The martyr Ignatius of Antioch tied together the ways in which the church responded to both persecution and false teaching when he said, "If Christ be not fully human and if he did not really die, why am I suffering for the gospel and prepared to die for it?"

So in the second century, Christian martyrdom confirmed the truth of the gospel, and the production of the ecumenical creeds began.

The THIRD CENTURY

PERSECUTION AND HERESY: ORIGEN AND TERTULLIAN

How should we respond to persecution and to false teaching? This was the great question facing the third-century church. Theologians who became known as "the Christian apologists" sought to answer this question. The word *apologist* or *apology* relates to 1 Peter 3:15, where Peter says we must be ready to give a "reason" (Greek: *apologia*) for the hope of the gospel that is in us. From the second century, apologists such as Justin Martyr defended the truth of the Christian gospel by expounding Scripture and refuting false accusations regarding the Christian faith. The church also responded to false teaching by quarrying out the true teaching of the Bible.

Two noteworthy figures help us understand how Christ was building the church, yet also show how even the best of Christ's servants stumble and fall. The first of these was Origen. One of the leading thinkers and apologists of the third century, Origen exercised his ministry in the great Egyptian city of Alexandria. At age eighteen, he began to teach in the theological academy of Alexandria. Through his various writings, Origen made important contributions to the understanding of Scripture, not all of which were positive. Being influenced by the Greek philosophical tradition derived from Plato, Origen tended to posit a dichotomy between heavenly things (good) and earthly things (bad). He also believed that there were many layers of meaning in the biblical text, sometimes to the neglect of a plain and literal reading. His method of interpretation would have a profound effect on the way in which Christians would read and understand the Bible.

A second individual who had an enormous influence on the church in the third century was a North African named Tertullian. Born into a pagan family, Tertullian was converted to Christianity later in life. In his ministry, Tertullian wrestled with two important things. First, he confronted the false teaching called *modalism*, an error concerning the persons of the Trinity. Modalists teach that there is one God who has appeared in different ways, or modes—as Father, Son, or Holy Spirit—thus confounding or confusing the persons of the Godhead by denying any real distinction between or among them. This teaching rejects everything Scripture has to say about the communion God enjoys within Himself as Father, Son, and Holy Spirit. Also, it denies the reality of what the Bible has to say about the person and work of our Lord Jesus Christ as the God-man. Tertullian vehemently fought against modalism and, as far as we know, was the first person in church history to use the word *Trinity*.

Tertullian's second problem was the growing moral indifference of professing Christians. Even though people were still being martyred for their faith, Tertullian perceived that unreserved consecration to Jesus Christ was beginning to disappear. He joined a charismatic sect outside the church known as the Montanists, rigorists and ascetics interested in new revelations and prophecies. He felt he had found in the Montanists what he had been looking for in the church at large. Though a zealous defender of the faith, Tertullian tended to divide the Word of God from the Spirit of God, and the Spirit from the Word. He did not grasp the principle so evident in the way Jesus Himself lived His life in obedience to God in the Spirit's power—that to do so, a believer must constantly submit to the teaching God has given in Scripture. A very important lesson arises from the third-century church: we should never separate the Spirit of God from the Word of God, or the Word of God from our dependence on the Spirit of God. If men of ability and dedication such as Origen and Tertullian found it a tremendous challenge to grasp and apply this principle, we too must take care to study and apply the Scriptures under the Holy Spirit's guidance and illumination.

The FOURTH CENTURY

THE BEGINNINGS OF THE CHRISTIAN EMPIRE

The fourth century began with a storm of persecution from without and a time of decay within the visible church. The persecution came from the Roman emperor, Diocletian. He sought to restore stability and peace to the Roman Empire, and was convinced that peace must involve a renewed commitment to the gods of ancient Rome. Diocletian was determined to destroy anything that stood in his way, particularly the Christian church. He sought to destroy places where Christians met, their Scriptures, their leaders, and Christians in general. Diocletian launched an empire-wide persecution. By God's grace, Christians stood firm in the face of such opposition.

At the same time, some Christians were disturbed by an increasing sense of ease and comfort within the church. Standards of Christian living fell as many professed the faith but did not live it. The response of some Christians was to retreat from the temptations of the world and to go into the desert to live solitary lives of prayer, contemplation, and self-denial. These early monastics, despite all their self-discipline, should remind us that Christ has called us not to separate from the world, but to live as witnesses to Christ in the world (1 Cor. 5:10).

Both these influences—an emperor bent on destroying the faith and Christians fed up with a culture not taking the faith seriously enough—had the potential to destroy the witness of the church.

At least three significant events took place in the fourth century. The first was the apparent conversion of the Emperor Constantine. After the famous Battle of Milvian Bridge in 312, he claimed to have seen a vision of the *chi rho* symbol or *labarum*—a monogram using the first two Greek letters in the title *Christ*—and heard a voice say, "In this sign, conquer!" Consequently, when he won the battle, he attributed his victory to Jesus Christ. Immediately he began to relax laws against Christians. Believers were now free to worship Christ without fear of persecution. Christianity became the preferred religion of the empire. Though Constantine did much to help the church, he ultimately hindered it by blurring the distinction between a citizen of this world and a citizen of the world to come.

The second major event was the Council of Nicaea in 325. This council helped clarify what it means for Jesus to be both God and man. An early fourth-century church leader named Arius claimed that Jesus was really a being created by God the Father (Arianism), saying, "There was a time when the Son was not." But the New Testament teaches that Christ is both the Son of God and the Son of Man. If He were not so, He could not reconcile us to God and bring us into God's presence. As a finite creature, His death would not have had infinite power to save us from the infinite guilt of sin against the infinite majesty of God. Fourth-century theologian Athanasius argued for the New Testament view of Christ as the God-man. Thanks to Athanasius, among others, the doctrinal formula produced by the Council of Nicaea, the Nicene Creed, grounded the church in the New Testament view of the person and work of Jesus Christ.

The third great event was the conversion of Augustine of Hippo. A man of great intelligence, his life is documented in his *Confessions*. After a long career in "the pleasures of sin" and as a devotee of a sect known as Manichaeism, Augustine was converted to Christianity when, under deep conviction of sin, he heard a child's voice say, "Take up and read." Seeing an open copy of Paul's Epistles nearby, he took up the book and read the first passage on which his eyes fell (Rom. 13:13–14). He felt as if God were speaking directly to him. Augustine did exactly what the text said. He "put on the Lord Jesus Christ" by faith, receiving and resting upon Him for salvation, and was baptized in 387. Augustine's theological legacy can scarcely be exaggerated. Reformed Christians are especially indebted to him; Calvinism is sometimes called Augustinianism. He was a great and influential Christian thinker, yet had it not been for the influence of his mentor, Ambrose; the prayer life of his mother, Monica; and the convicting words of Scripture, we might never have known of him. Such is the grace of God and the power of His Word!

The FIFTH CENTURY

THE CITY OF GOD AND THE CITY OF MAN

The life of Augustine encompassed two important events in the fifth century. First, barbarian tribes swept into Italy and sacked the city of Rome in 410 and in 455. Rome's reign of power over the nations was broken. One response to this tragedy was to blame the Christians. Augustine responded in his famous book *The City of God.* He argued that from the beginning of history, fallen man has been building his "city" or kingdom over against God. Any kingdom not grounded on the kingdom of God is bound to be transient. The only lasting city or kingdom is the one God is building in Jesus Christ, which Augustine identified with the church. To those who wished to lay blame for the destruction of the great city of Rome at the feet of Christians, he declared: "This is no surprise to us, to see the kingdoms of men rising and the kingdoms of men falling, because our commitment is not to eternal Rome. Our commitment is to Jesus Christ and exclusively to the kingdom He is building." There are two kingdoms, yet only the kingdom of God and His Son, Jesus Christ, will last forever.

Augustine was also involved in the second important event in the life of the church in the fifth century—the Pelagian controversy. The British monk Pelagius, while reading Augustine's famous autobiography, was struck by this prayer: "Grant what Thou commandest, and then command what Thou wilt." In other words, fallen man is utterly dependent upon God's grace for salvation. No one, for example, can practice the self-control or continence God commands unless God gives him grace to do so. These words made Pelagius quite uncomfortable. He believed in a "pull yourself up by your own bootstraps" gospel, in which human beings can amend their lives and be saved by their own efforts.

This great theological controversy engulfed the church. To refute Pelagianism, Augustine had to expound the great Pauline doctrines of grace, such as original sin, fallen man's total depravity and inability to save himself, the efficacy of the atoning death of Christ, and the necessity of faith in Him for salvation. The enormous biblical learning and perseverance of Augustine won the day against Pelagius's teaching in the church.

During this same time, another Briton, Patrick, burdened with concern for the lost and called by God to preach the gospel, demonstrated exemplary missionary zeal. When he was sixteen years old, the family farm was raided by Irish pirates. Patrick was kidnapped, taken to Ireland, and sold into slavery, laboring as a herdsman in County Mayo. During those years as a slave, God opened Patrick's heart, and he yielded his life to Christ. In his early twenties, he escaped and made his way home, where he devoted himself to the life of holiness by becoming a monk.

Feeling called in a vision to return to Ireland, Patrick labored there for the gospel from 432 to 461. His life and work as "the Apostle of the Irish" stand as a testimony to the way God calls certain men and women, even some from obscurity and slavery, to do His will. Through various experiences, God molds their passions and desires, then directs them in some singular way to become Christ's servants. The history of Christianity is adorned with accounts of those who have become signal servants of God from backgrounds of total obscurity.

From these portraits, we learn how important it is to not rely on the kingdom of man. The only lasting kingdom is the kingdom of Jesus Christ. It teaches us that salvation is not by our own accomplishments, but by grace alone through faith in Jesus Christ. It also teaches us that God is at work even in the most adverse circumstances, and can use the most unlikely people to accomplish His saving work among the nations.

The SIXTH CENTURY

JUSTINIAN, BENEDICT, & THE CONVERSION OF THE SCOTS

The sixth century witnessed renewed greatness for the Roman Empire under the reign of Justinian I from 527 to 565. He restored large parts of the empire lost to barbarians in North Africa and Italy. His codification of Roman law became the foundation of legal systems in many European countries. Justinian built many churches, including Holy Wisdom (*Hagia Sophia*) Basilica in Constantinople, considered the greatest church in Christendom. As a defender of orthodoxy, Justinian dealt a blow to paganism by closing the schools of the philosophers in Athens, persecuted Montanists as heretics, and sought to reconcile Monophysites to the orthodox faith.

Monasticism flourished under the leadership of Benedict, whose life mirrors the history of this movement in the life and work of the Western church. Benedict withdrew from life in Rome to live as a hermit, but others came to live with him as disciples. Around 525 Benedict relocated his community to Monte Cassino and wrote his famous "Holy Rule" for the government, worship, and daily work of the monks under his charge. He is remembered as "the patriarch of Monasticism."

We turn now to Scotland in the sixth century. By the standards of continental Europe, Scotland was regarded as a barbaric and uncivilized land. The area was controlled by four warring tribes. First there were the Picts, or the "painted ones," as the Romans called them; they inhabited large tracts of Scotland, living largely north of the River Forth. Then there were the Angles, who lived between the River Forth and the River Humber. Also, there were in the west the Britons, making Dumbarton their central place of activity and ruling over the region of Strathclyde. Finally there were the Scots, who originally came from Ireland, invading Scotland at the beginning of the sixth century. The country was characterized by total paganism, and the Druids acted as the pagan priests of the land. The country was desperately in need of the power of the gospel. It soon came to Scotland through the tireless work of two individuals.

One of them was Ninian. Most scholars believe he lived in the sixth century and labored in southwest Scotland in the area of Whithorn. Living in obscurity, Ninian gathered a small number of men around him and created a monastic community. By replicating this little community, he sought to evangelize the Picts, accomplishing his task with considerable success.

This pattern of planting Christians where no Christian witness existed was pioneered by Ninian and popularized by Columba, an Irish monastic from the region of Donegal. Columba came to the little island of Iona off the west coast of Scotland, and there he established a small monastery. This group devoted themselves to prayer, to the study of Scripture, and to providing for one another, and eventually grew into a community of well over a hundred. From Iona, Columba began his challenging task of evangelizing the rest of Scotland. Cell groups of disciples were planted throughout different parts of the country, waging spiritual warfare with paganism and demonstrating what it meant to live out the gospel in community.

By the witness of Ninian, Columba, and other, less-known individuals, many of the diverse peoples of Scotland came to know Jesus Christ. Two things stand out about these men. To historians, Ninian is an obscure figure with little to no background or claim to fame. Perhaps the only reason why the name of Ninian endures in Scotland is his ministry to evangelize the Picts. Faithful service is often unnoticed by men but it never remains unnoticed by God. Another lesson we learn from both Ninian and Columba is that the power of the gospel is demonstrated not only through preaching and teaching, but through the transformed Christian community. In the pattern of the New Testament, cell groups went out to be the local church in order to demonstrate Christ's grace to transform lives. Though there are various theological points where Ninian and Columba strayed from Scripture, many churches and denominations today can learn from them that grace-filled interaction between Christians will draw unbelievers to see that there is something supernaturally wonderful about Jesus Christ's kingdom.

The SEVENTH CENTURY

GREGORY THE GREAT AND THE RISE OF ISLAM

Two figures are particularly significant for the history of the church in the seventh century. The first figure is Gregory the Great. The son of a wealthy and influential Italian family, Gregory decided to follow a monastic path rather than the family tradition of public service. He eventually became the bishop of Rome. Gregory was a man of considerable organizational ability and significant vision. His times were constantly filled with turmoil, as ownership or control of Rome often went to the highest bidder or the barbarian group with the most might. Gregory sought to bring the entire world into the faith by sending bands of monks and evangelists to baptize and place the name of Christ over the nations. Rulers and kings were successfully won to the church. Nations at large were baptized into the faith. The church, so it seemed, was beginning to reign not only spiritually but also with earthly powers among the nations. But the Christian faith that was produced was like "the form of godliness" without the power of it (2 Tim. 3:5). Gregory's vision produced a kind of nominal Christianity with which the church continues to struggle to this day.

The other person who was infamously significant was Mohammed. Born in the late sixth century, Mohammed suffered from various strange illnesses, including what may have been epilepsy. He was untutored, uneducated, and possibly even illiterate. When he was a young man, he married a woman some fifteen years older than himself, the widow of a rich merchant, and became a trader. As he traded, he met Jews and Christians, and began to listen to what they professed to believe. The Christians he met were likely unorthodox or even gnostic groups—those who professed faith in Christ, but whose theology and practice deviated at key points from the faith of the historic church.

When he was older, Mohammed claimed to have several visions. The first of those visions was of the archangel Gabriel, who Mohammed believed was calling him to be the prophet of God. Responding to that vision, he began to teach what would become the foundational tenets of Islam. At first, in Mecca, he found very little response. Then, in 622, he fled to Medina, where he began to gather large numbers of followers. Within ten years, he had gathered as many as fifty thousand followers. By the turn of the century, within eighty years of Mohammed's original vision, Islam began to sweep through the Middle East. It saw success in North Africa, often through sheer brutality. But its advance ground to a halt in Spain. In the end, those who claimed to follow Allah and his prophet Mohammad conquered nearly half of the Roman Empire. The historic Christian communities of the Near East and North Africa were either destroyed or reduced to the status of despised and oppressed minorities.

Mohammed denied the deity of Christ and denied that Christ Himself died on the cross. He taught that salvation does not come through someone else's work on a person's behalf, but through a self-willed submission to Allah. In Islam, salvation knows nothing of God's grace in Christ or of the substitutionary atonement, of Christ bearing the sins of man and offering them assurance of salvation. Islam was and remains a manmade religion because it can never offer what only God can offer in and through Jesus Christ—that is, mercy, grace, and salvation for fallen, sinful human beings.

So what was the church doing when Islam was on the rise? One of the most famous gatherings of churchmen that took place in the last third of the seventh century was the Synod of Whitby, which met in England in 664. It was a gathering of bishops wrestling with the "significant" issues of their time: the shape of the tonsure worn by priests and monks, and the date of Easter. This historical example shows how sometimes the church can completely forget its mission. While there is a time and season for everything, the church must not forget what matters most: it must remain clear and steadfast on the Great Commission, not just claiming land and nations for earthly gain, but proclaiming the gospel to a lost and dying world.

The EIGHTH CENTURY

THE ICONOCLASTIC CONTROVERSY

Students of church history need to understand the two dominant languages and traditions present within the ancient church. In the Western church, the church that tended to center around Rome, the primary language for writing and worship was Latin. In the East, the primary language of the church was Greek. These languages symbolize the different ways in which these two church traditions developed. As the Roman Empire disintegrated, these traditions lost contact with each other and developed in separate ways.

An eighth-century controversy demonstrating the differences between these traditions was the disagreement over the use of icons in the worship of God. Icons are depictions of Jesus, Mary, the saints, and sometimes the persons of the Trinity, among others, and came to have particular significance in the Eastern church. Those in favor of icons argued that pictures were necessary as "books to the laity," that is, for communicating biblical truth to the illiterate and uneducated, and for helping to focus worship in the proper direction. The object of worship was not the image or icon, but the person, divine or human, it represented.

However, many began to think that icons were channels through which Christ was speaking to them and through which God was blessing them. Christians in the East would kneel before them, perhaps would kiss them as holy objects, and on occasion would light candles or burn incense before them as an expression of their desire that through the intercession of the person depicted by the icon, the heavenly Father would hear their prayers.

These practices caused a great division in the eighth-century church between *iconodules* (literally, "servants of icons") and *iconoclasts* (literally, "breakers of icons"). The controversy came to a climax in 787 at the Second Council of Nicaea. The church eventually acceded to the use of icons, insisting they not be worshiped but used only for instruction and veneration, that is, only for giving honor to the one depicted. Throughout the centuries, however, the line often became blurred as images were accorded an ever more important place in public worship and private devotion. By contrast, the making of such images, as well as worshiping or serving them, was forbidden by God in the second commandment. Yet men always attempt to be wiser than God, it seems.

Reflecting on the iconoclastic controversy, Protestants should remember the biblical "images" or "visual aids" we have been given to help us understand the gospel. The New Testament witness affords the church two—baptism and the Lord's Supper. Throughout the New Testament, Christians are encouraged to continually reflect on the significance of these two sacraments, "wherein, by sensible signs, Christ and the benefits of the New Covenant are represented, sealed, and applied to believers" (Westminster Shorter Catechism, Q. 92). Although we must be justly critical of the use of icons in the church, we also ought to be critical of ourselves for paying so little attention to the "sensible signs" that Jesus has given to us.

Though synods and councils may be preoccupied with internal disputes, in every century of the church there are those whose eyes are turned outward to see the great need of the world. Two such people from the eighth century exemplify this outward gaze. The first is Boniface, remembered as "the Apostle of the Germans." Born at the end of the seventh century in Crediton, Devon, he gave himself to the service of Christ and the church, spending his life evangelizing various parts of the world, including Frisia, Thuringia, and Bavaria. Boniface often found himself in the midst of pagan cultures, yet he stood against them with the power of the gospel. He was eventually martyred for Christ in the year 754.

The other example from the eighth century is Olopan or Alopan. The Sigan-Fu stone, discovered in northwest China in the early seventeenth century by Roman Catholic missionaries, recorded the advent of Christianity in China from 150 years prior to the time of its inscription, circa 780. It recounted the work of Olopan, an Assyrian missionary who had come from Syria to China to preach the gospel. By the eighth century, Chinese emperors were persecuting Christians and extinguishing the flame of the gospel in China. To their astonishment, the missionaries who discovered the Sigan-Fu stone one thousand years later learned what people in the seventh and eighth centuries had been willing to do and to sacrifice for Jesus Christ in China.

The NINTH CENTURY

STRUGGLE FOR POWER: RATRAMNUS & GOTTSCHALK

One of the great tension points of the ninth century was a clause in the Nicene Creed. The inclusion of this clause in the text of the creed would eventually lead to a great division between the Western church and the churches of the East.

In some ways, it was a theological difference, a difference in understanding the relationship of the Spirit to the Father and Son. But it was also part of a power struggle in the worldwide visible church and between two of its leaders: the pope, or bishop of Rome, Nicholas, a man of considerable organizational skills, and the theologian and preacher Photios, the patriarch of Constantinople. In other words, the dispute over the creed became a battleground in the long campaign to establish the supremacy of the pope over all Christendom.

In the midst of this controversy, Pope Nicholas appealed to what scholars refer to as the Pseudo-Isidorean Decretals. These documents gave the bishop of Rome supreme authority over the ecumenical or worldwide church. They were certainly not written by Isidore of Seville, but were fabricated by an unknown source at a much later period. Patriarch Photios objected to these assertions, as did all the other patriarchs and bishops of the Eastern churches.

Despite this conflict over the claims of the papacy, individual figures were arising in the church with a great zeal to see Christ's kingdom extended. In the mid-ninth century, two brothers from Thessalonica, Cyril and Methodius, set out to spread the gospel to the region that would later become Russia. Today they are often called "the Apostles of the Slavs." They devised the Cyrillic alphabet in order to translate the Scriptures and the church's liturgy into Slavonic, as essential tools for preaching Christ to the Slavic nations of Eastern Europe. They were able to evangelize the entire region around the Black Sea. The presence of Christian churches in many of these places today can be traced back to their evangelistic work.

Another significant theologian from the ninth century worth mentioning is Ratramnus of Corbie, who wrote in opposition to his fellow monastic Paschasius Radbertus, who propounded transubstantiation, the notion that the consecration of the communion bread and wine changed these earthly elements into the flesh and blood of Christ. Ratramnus also defended predestination, though he was not as zealous in this as was Gottschalk.

Born in Saxony, Gottschalk was given over by his parents to be a servant in the church. Gottschalk became fascinated by Augustine's writings. Augustine had emphasized that we are not just spiritually sick, but are, as Paul says in Ephesians 2, dead in trespasses and sins. Gottschalk began to reflect on God's grace in electing some to salvation. But he also observed that many leaders in the church were teaching salvation by works righteousness. Gottschalk argued that we need to grasp that salvation, which we receive through faith, is a gift that God planned to bestow upon us before we were born. Like Augustine before him, Gottschalk left no place for any individual contribution in gaining righteousness before God. Our faith and works are merely reflections of the salvation we have received, not a contributing factor to it.

Though he preached salvation by grace alone, Gottschalk sometimes presented his case in an unwise manner. He was passionate about double predestination, that is, the doctrine that God has assigned some to eternal life as well as many to eternal punishment. His passionate preaching led eventually to his condemnation as a heretic. He was deposed from his ministry and imprisoned for twenty years. Gottschalk challenged the condemnation and requested that he be allowed to undergo a trial by ordeal to reveal whether or not he was truly a heretic. He strongly believed he would be vindicated as a preacher of biblical truth.

Though Gottschalk was not as temperate as he should have been, he was right about our contribution to salvation. The moment we begin to think that we contribute something to our salvation, it ceases to be the salvation of grace taught in the New Testament. The church should honor Gottschalk's memory despite his human frailties. We should also continue to educate ourselves about missionaries such as Cyril and Methodius, and remember that the quest for power and recognition, demonstrated by Pope Nicholas, ultimately detracts from the mission and witness of the church.

The TENTH CENTURY

"THE DARK AGES"

We sometimes say that history repeats itself. At the end of the first millennium, the situation of the church was much the same as we face today. In the tenth century, the church was in decline theologically though not culturally and politically. We call this period "the Dark Ages," and in some ways, the description is accurate. Once-strong empires and kingdoms were beginning to crumble. The balance of power was shifting toward the church and territorial boundaries were shifting as well.

Another similarity is the nominal Christianity of the tenth century. Part of this nominalism resulted from the struggle for power and influence outside the church, which led to neglect of cultivating faith on the inside. The power gains of the church tended to corrupt the church and her leaders. Educational standards fell, and many of those who ministered God's Word were altogether ignorant of it. An ignorant ministry could not arrest the inherent decay in society with the power of the gospel. New political powers from the north (the Vikings or Norsemen) and the south and east (Muslims) swept in, challenging the worldly power of the church. The church responded with little to no spiritual direction for its members.

One exception came from a group of monastics at Cluny in eastern France. These Benedictine monks, seeing the spiritual decline all around, devoted themselves to the study of Scripture, the worship of God, simplicity of Christian living, and various other spiritual disciplines. They recognized that by and large, the members of the church had lost their zeal to know the Lord and live in devotion to Him. Leaders of the church had become worldly-minded and disinterested in spiritual matters. The Cluniac reform began as one of the more spiritual efforts of the Middle Ages, but the movement would itself suffer decay and yield to temptations to worldliness, requiring yet another reform in the following centuries.

In the last years of the tenth century, Christianity extended its reach into Russia with the baptism of Prince Vladimir and his twelve sons at Kiev in 988. Vladimir embraced Christianity upon receiving the reports of envoys sent to Constantinople. They gave a positive account of the faith and worship of that great city, and were impressed by the splendor of Justinian's Holy Wisdom Basilica. The pioneering work of Cyril and Methodius among the southern Slavs had prepared the way by furnishing a liturgy and a body of Christian literature in Slavonic. Most of the people of Kiev followed their prince's example, and thousands were baptized in the Dnieper River. From such beginnings sprang the Russian Orthodox Church.

The close of the first millennium of the Christian era found the church in a position of cultural dominance, at least within the boundaries of the Roman Empire. The church also had had no small measure of success in surviving barbarian invasions and converting the invaders.

As the empire was divided and began to retreat in the face of the invading barbarians, the church was likewise divided, East and West. The Eastern church lived under the protection of the Roman emperors, who now reigned in Constantinople. She enjoyed imperial patronage, but also suffered much from imperial interference in her affairs. The Western church had to stand alone, filling the vacuum left behind as the seat of empire shifted to the East. The popes of Rome were in a position to take power into their own hands, and they did so, with no one to call them to account. Large parts of Italy were ruled by the popes, who owned huge tracts of land, using the revenues of those lands to fund their campaigns to dominate both the worldwide church and the rulers of the many kingdoms and principalities under their sway.

Today's world is not much different from that of the tenth century. The church continues to be confronted with paganism, as well as with temptations to worldly success. While some denounce the tenth century as "the Dark Ages," we must recognize that our contemporary society demonstrates a moral and spiritual darkness, and the church is challenged to respond with the light of the gospel. Sometimes the church stands by and lets her witness be muted by worldly concerns. Rather, the church should perpetually increase in the knowledge of God's Word, be strengthened by the worship of God, and give itself to the simplicities of day-by-day devotion to Jesus Christ. By living for Christ and proclaiming the gospel, we can shine a much-needed light in the darkness.

The ELEVENTH CENTURY

THE GREAT SCHISM; ANSELM OF CANTERBURY

The eleventh century still found the church in a dark place, though glimmers of light continued to shine through. One of its darkest events, usually referred to as the Great Schism, took place in 1054. The de facto division between the Latin-speaking Western church and the Greek-speaking churches of the East was made absolute and irreconcilable. The pope of Rome and the patriarch of Constantinople excommunicated each other, and the bodies of churches under the authority of each were arrayed against each other as hostile camps. The unity of the visible church was broken, and remains broken down to our time.

The disagreement centered on the addition of the *filioque* (that is, "and from the Son') clause to the Nicene Creed. In the fifth century, Western scholars, under the influence of Augustine, had begun to look afresh at the Scriptures regarding the relationship of the Spirit to the Father and the Son. They came to the conclusion that the Scriptures teach that the Holy Spirit proceeds not only from the Father, but also from the Son. Therefore, from the fifth century onward, the Western Church had added the *filioque* clause to the relevant article of the Nicene Creed, giving it the form in which it has come down to us today: "I believe in the Holy Ghost, the Lord and Giver of life; who proceedeth from the Father and the Son."

The Eastern churches took issue and appealed to the original formulation of the Council of Nicaea, arguing that the Latin-speaking Western church did not have authority to alter a formula adopted by an ecumenical council. But behind this concern was the objection of the Eastern churches to the Western claim that the pope was the supreme bishop of the worldwide church and the "vicar" or representative of Jesus Christ on earth.

One glimmer of light during this dark time was Anselm of Canterbury, a gifted intellectual and a man of considerable spiritual and moral courage. Anselm promoted his famous ontological argument for the existence of God and served the church by providing thoughtful theological argumentation and philosophical analysis regarding the existence and nature of God.

Anselm's *Cur Deus Homo*, or *Why Did God Become Man?* plumbed the depths of the atonement of Jesus Christ and the purposes of God that stood behind it. He argued that God's justice requires Him to punish sins committed against His infinite majesty with everlasting punishment of the sinner, in body and soul. As sinners, our only hope is to find a mediator and deliverer who is very man and perfectly righteous, and therefore able to satisfy for our sins; but also very God, more powerful than all creatures, and therefore able to sustain the burden of God's wrath and obtain righteousness and eternal life for us. Our Lord Jesus Christ, who is "very God and very man," is the Savior God has provided for us.

During this time, many within the church recognized the corruption bred by the close relationship between church and state. From the time of Constantine, kings had claimed the right to appoint bishops for the churches under their rule, and they naturally chose men who favored their policies and helped them curry favor with the people. Beginning in the eleventh century, a series of popes began to challenge the authority of monarchs in this practice. The conflict became known as the Investiture Controversy, so named because the kings who appointed the bishops invested them with titles, possessions, and other temporal rights, as well as the symbols of their office, including a gold staff, or crosier, and a gold ring. Pope Gregory VII responded by asserting the power of the church to elect bishops and translate them (move them from one see to another). The pope also asserted his power over the Holy Roman emperor, citing the coronation of Charlemagne in the ninth century as a precedent. The conflict would continue into the twelfth century, finally ending with the pope securing most of the power for which he and his predecessors had contended.

This result encouraged the popes to involve themselves more and more in secular affairs and to exercise an ever-greater measure of political and even military might, at ever greater financial cost to the church. The popes became the first geo-politicians, and burdened themselves with the perpetual need to raise funds by any means, fair or foul. Worldly-minded popes had little concern for the spiritual well-being of the church, and little or no interest in her true calling and mission in the world.

The TWELFTH CENTURY

THE CRUSADES, ABELARD, LOMBARD, & THE WALDENSES

As the eleventh century gave place to the twelfth, the church began to reap the bitter fruits of the Great Schism of 1054. Signs of division continued to appear across the landscape. One consequence of this division was the unfortunate series of Christian military campaigns known as the Crusades. These expeditions, incited by the pope and backed by various kingdoms of the West, sought to combat the threat of Islam and retake Jerusalem and the "Holy Land" of Palestine.

The First Crusade began in the last few years of the eleventh century, and subsequent crusades were launched throughout the twelfth century. The Second Crusade (1145–1149) was incited by the famous monk Bernard of Clairvaux, who declared: "Pagans must not be slain if they may by other means be prevented from oppressing the faithful. However, it is better they should be put to death than that the rod of the wicked should rest on the lot of the righteous. The righteous fear no sin in killing the enemy of Christ. Christ's soldier can securely kill and more safely die. When he dies, it profits him; when he slays, it profits Christ." Rather than relying on the spiritual weapons of faith, love, prayer, evangelism, and good works, the church looked to political, military, and financial might to answer the threat of Islam.

It was thought that the only language the Islamic forces would understand was the language they themselves spoke—the language of violence. The Crusaders failed to understand that Christ enjoins His people to speak a different language. Our means and ends should be those of Jesus. Ours should be a language of humility and love in the name of Christ, not violence, slaughter, and retribution.

Regrettably, the Crusaders did not distinguish Eastern Christians and Jews from their Muslim overlords, and so they, too, were assailed with fire and sword. In the end, the Crusades failed to achieve their announced objectives. They are a dark stain on the Christian church.

One noteworthy figure from the twelfth century was Peter Abelard, perhaps more famous for his love affair with Heloise than for his theology. He was, however, one of the most influential theologians of his day. He taught a substantially different view of the atonement than Anselm, asserting that man is saved by the extraordinary demonstration of God's love in Jesus Christ. Such a demonstration should overwhelm us and cause us to respond to God in faith. But Abelard failed to see that what is amazing about the love of God is the fact that "while we were yet sinners, Christ died for us" (Rom. 5:8). Scripture connects love and propitiation: "Herein is love, not that we loved God, but that he loved us, and sent his Son to be the propitiation for our sins" (1 John 4:10). If Christ's death is not a satisfaction for sin, then it is reduced to an extravagant gesture on God's part.

Also worthy of mention is Peter Lombard, author of *The Sentences,* a compilation of quotations from church fathers on various facets of theology. From the twelfth to the sixteenth centuries, students of theology were often required to write an exposition and commentary on Lombard's *Sentences*. Lombard's method was characteristic of the times, when theological discussion and debate consisted largely of appeals to decrees of councils, opinions of ancient writers, and doctrines of men.

Noteworthy in twelfth-century France was the origin of the Waldenses and the Waldensian movement, founded by Peter Waldo, who preached in Lyons (1170–1176) and gathered followers known as "poor men" because they stressed poverty and simplicity of life. The Waldenses objected to many of the errors and corrupt practices of the Western church later targeted by the Reformers in the sixteenth century. They soon spread beyond France after being placed under a papal ban in 1184. They endured many centuries of bitter persecution, but have continued down to our time as part of the evangelical family of churches.

Many lessons can be learned from this period. One prime lesson is that when the agenda of the world becomes the agenda of the church, the church's true calling is cast aside. Although the church of the twelfth century fell into this error, its light was not extinguished. God did not leave Himself without a witness. Christ did not forsake His church, even in the darkest of ages. Ultimately, we need to remind ourselves to bow at the feet of Jesus, who is our teacher, follow His agenda, and live a gospel-centered lifestyle as witnesses to the world.

The THIRTEENTH CENTURY

FRANCIS OF ASSISI AND THOMAS AQUINAS

A significant symbol of the spiritual condition of the Christian church at the end of the twelfth century is the capture of Jerusalem by Saladin in 1187. Then too, the Crusades of the eleventh and twelfth centuries—which continued throughout most of the thirteenth century as well—underline for Christians today just how far the church had strayed from Christ's gospel. The church preached bloodshed as a way of defending relics and sacred places of the Christian faith. To be spiritual was to fight. The transformative teaching of the gospel had fallen into decay.

However, there were groups and individuals in the thirteenth century who were concerned with refocusing the church on the teaching of Christ and the apostles. Consequently, the thirteenth century became known for its Western religious orders.

The Roman Catholics continued to ascribe an important role to the monastic orders of the Benedictines, Cistercians, and Premonstratensians. Many of the Mendicant Orders, which focused primarily on preaching, pastoral ministry, and poverty, were founded in this century. The four Mendicant Orders recognized by the Second Council of Lyon are the Order of Preachers (Dominicans), founded in 1215 by Dominic de Guzman; the Hermits of St. Augustine (Augustinians), founded in 1256 by communities that followed the Rule of St. Augustine; the Order of Mount Carmel (Carmelites), which came to Europe in the thirteenth century; and the Friars Minor (Franciscans), founded in 1209 by Francis of Assisi.

Francis was one of the most influential people among those who wanted to purge the church of the power of the sword. He was born just about the time of the fall of Jerusalem. Francis began his adult life as a soldier, but when he heard a sermon from Matthew 10 that explained how Jesus sent out His disciples to proclaim the kingdom without dependence on earthly goods, he was radically transformed. He gave himself to a life of simplicity and a great concern for preaching repentance as the way into the kingdom of the Lord Jesus Christ. Though he imbibed many of the serious theological errors of Roman Catholicism, Francis sought to point the church back to a simplicity of lifestyle.

Another important figure arose in the thirteenth century—Thomas Aquinas, a Dominican who is often regarded as one of the church's great scholastic thinkers. Scholasticism had its origins in attempts to reconcile the philosophy of ancient classical philosophers with medieval Christian theology. Though it never became a philosophy or theology in itself, it played an important role as a tool and method for learning that underscores the importance of dialectical reasoning. One of scholasticism's main purposes was to answer questions and resolve apparent contradictions.

Born in 1224, Thomas was by nature quiet and shy. Based on these traits and his substantial physical proportions, others referred to him as "the dumb ox." Soon after he entered a Dominican monastery, Thomas's theological acumen became evident. Thomas's mentor, Albertus Magnus, recognizing his intellectual potential, scolded the other monks for taunting him and famously stated, "This dumb ox will fill the world with his bellowing." Albertus Magnus was himself an accomplished philosopher and theologian, and provided considerable guidance to Thomas.

Aquinas produced two major works, *Summa Contra Gentiles* and his *Summa Theologica*. The first was a defense of the Christian faith against paganism. He was concerned to use his powerful intellect to help Christians spread the gospel where it was not known. *Summa Theologica*, or *The Sum of Theology*, was a detailed analysis of the content of the Christian faith. One of Thomas's leading principles was that philosophy should be employed as the handmaiden of theology; that is, the tools of philosophy should be put to work in the exposition and defense of theological truth.

Aquinas is noteworthy for his defense of the literal sense of Scripture as the primary and authoritative sense. But ultimately, Thomas accepted the authority of the church. He was content to expound and defend the received teachings and practices of the church, whether they accorded with Scripture or not. One critic said that Thomas's system of doctrine and ethics was "merely an echo of the doctrinal teaching of the church." As able as Thomas was in many respects and as sincere as many of the monks no doubt were, later reformers would come to see the theological problems associated with Thomas's Semi-Pelagianism and the practical problems of the Western religious orders.

The FOURTEENTH CENTURY

THE CHURCH'S BABYLONIAN CAPTIVITY & JOHN WYCLIFFE

Sadly, the church hierarchy continued to pursue worldly power in the fourteenth century. The popes persisted in their bid for dominance in political affairs. While the church must be in the world, working to bring about change and draw people to Christ, we are never to be of the world. The church should not thirst for power or seek to assert its authority through political means. In the fourteenth century, the ambitions of popes and kings embroiled the church in ecclesiastical civil war.

Pope Boniface VIII involved himself in numerous political dealings to give the papacy more autonomy and authority. On the other hand, Philip IV, king of France from 1285 to 1314, sought to take advantage of family ties to Italian nobles to enhance his power over the French clergy. Measures by Boniface to secure the church against political interference enflamed the opposition of Philip and his allies.

Boniface died in 1303. His successor, Benedict XI, was not long on the papal throne when he, too, died. Rumors circulated that he had been poisoned. Clement V, Benedict's successor, was a French cleric elected with the help of French funds, a pope who would certainly be more sympathetic to Philip IV's exercise of authority over the French church. Soon after, Clement decided to relocate the papacy from Rome to Avignon in France. The French monarchs effectively owned the pope and controlled the church for seventy years. This was certainly a case in which the mission of the church was turned upside down to serve worldly interests.

The Italian poet Petrarch called this subversion of the papacy the "Babylonish captivity of the church," alluding to the Babylonian exile of the Jews in the sixth century BC. He also decried Avignon as the immoral "sewer of the world." Dante Alighieri, author of *The Divine Comedy*, placed Pope Boniface VIII in the Eighth Circle of Hell, among the simoniacs (those who practiced simony, that is, who sold offices of the church to the highest bidder).

Catherine of Siena, a notable Catholic mystic and nun, appealed to Pope Gregory XI in 1376 regarding the "sins" of Avignon. Based on her appeal, Gregory returned to Rome in order to restore the papacy there, but he died a year later. Conflict regarding the election of his successor in Rome led to the Papal Schism of the early fifteenth century. When Urban VI was chosen to succeed Gregory, disaffected clerics withdrew to Avignon and elected Clement VII. Rival popes reigned in Rome and at Avignon from 1378 to 1429.

A noteworthy luminary in this period was John Wycliffe. One of his teachers, Thomas Bradwardine, championed orthodoxy against Pelagianism and came as close as any forerunner of the Reformation to embracing the doctrine of justification by faith alone. An outstanding scholar, Wycliffe was the master of Balliol College in Oxford. He became concerned about the low spiritual state of the visible church. His concern led him back to the basic principle that Holy Scripture should be the church's rule of faith and practice.

In 1382, Wycliffe translated the Latin Bible into the English of his day so that the people might have the Word of God in their own language. His translation has influenced all succeeding English versions of the Bible. His followers, the Lollards, stressed the primacy of preaching, denied transubstantiation, questioned the papacy, and influenced later men and movements, including John Huss and the Reformation. Often cited to answer charges in church courts, Wycliffe refused to be silenced and went on with his work. After his death, the Council of Constance excommunicated him posthumously in 1415 and had his remains disinterred, burned, and cast into a river.

From Wycliffe's life, we learn the importance of getting the Word of God into the hands of the people. Despite the fact that the church's hierarchy was beset with ambitions for earthy power, some were focused on helping people know God's Word and be transformed by the gospel. Because of this conviction, Wycliffe is often referred to as "the morning star of the Reformation." Today we must see that the church exists to bring light to the world, and we must be willing to separate earthly power and gain from the mission of the church. The church accomplishes her mission by the power of the Holy Spirit, not by the might of kings or political leaders.

The FIFTEENTH CENTURY

THE RENAISSANCE, HUSS, SAVONAROLA, & GROOTE

The fifteenth century was the age of the European Renaissance, an extraordinary rebirth in social life, the arts, and intellectual activity under the banner *ad fontes* ("back to the sources" or "to the fountains"). As part of a general quest to recover the lost riches of classical antiquity, scholars began to go behind the received Latin translation of the Scriptures to study the original Hebrew and Greek texts, to discover more accurately what the New Testament itself said about the Christian faith. Two men of the fifteenth century exemplify this renewed enthusiasm for searching the Scriptures

The first was Jan Huss. Born in 1373, Huss came from Bohemia, today's Czech Republic. As a young man, he became rector at the University of Prague. He began to study the writings of men who were going back to Scripture, especially those of John Wycliffe. Huss soon realized that the teaching of the New Testament was at odds with the teachings of the church of his day. He asked himself how there could be such a dramatic difference between the faith proclaimed in the Scriptures and the faith demonstrated in the church. When he began to preach about these concerns, he met with considerable opposition. He was excommunicated and urged to repudiate his writings while on trial. His answer was that if his opponents could show him from the New Testament where he had gone wrong in his writings, he would repudiate them immediately. His challenge was received with indignation, but went unanswered. Huss was burned at the stake as a supposed enemy of the faith.

The second man was Girolamo Savonarola, a Dominican monk in Florence, Italy. Savonarola labored in his preaching until he had gained a reputation as a profound expositor of Scripture. People daily crowded the cathedral in Florence to listen to his preaching. Those listening were often convicted by the power of the gospel. Transformation soon followed, demonstrating the power of the preached Word.

Savonarola's success as a preacher, however, did not escape the eye of the ecclesiastical authorities. To silence Savonarola, the pope offered him promotion to high office, but he declined. He soon found himself rejected at every turn. Local leaders stirred up resistance against him. He was arrested, imprisoned, and tortured by the Inquisition. Like Huss before him, Savonarola was burned to death for the biblical message that he refused to recant.

Mention also should be made of Gerard Groote. In the Netherlands in the late fourteenth century, Groote organized a religious community called the Brethren of the Common Life, which stressed a return to Bible reading, meditation, and the pursuit of holiness. Members adopted a simple, self-supporting lifestyle, living from a common fund, and often earned their livelihood through copying manuscripts. Thomas à Kempis, Desiderius Erasmus, and Martin Luther were influenced by this movement in various degrees.

The Renaissance was a prelude to and preparation for the Reformation. Nothing was more important to the Reformation than the recovery of the biblical languages of Hebrew and Greek. The times were ripe for a reexamination of the teachings and practices of the church in the light of Scripture. At long last, men had solid ground on which to stand as believers and a powerful weapon to employ in combatting the errors and abuses of the church. Faith was no longer understood as unquestioning assent to whatever the church taught, but as knowledge of what God has said in His Word, confidence in its truth and trustworthiness, and submission to its supreme authority for faith and life.

Because many were faithful to what they read in the New Testament, the biblical gospel began to reemerge. Both Huss and Savonarola recognized that after their deaths, the church would experience the much-needed renewal that we call the Reformation. (Huss famously predicted that if they burned "this goose (that is, himself), God would send a swan (which proved to be Luther). Through the Reformation the gospel of the New Testament would be fully rediscovered and preached throughout the world. As we see in these examples in the fifteenth century, it is impossible to hold back the gospel once people rediscover the truth and power of God's Word.

The SIXTEENTH CENTURY

LUTHER, CALVIN, AND THE REFORMATION

The sixteenth century, the beginning of the modern age, is one of the greatest watershed moments in all history, for it witnessed the unfolding of the Protestant Reformation. Benefiting from the biblical scholarship of the Renaissance, the recovery of classical learning, and the zeal of faithful servants in the late fifteenth and early sixteenth centuries, the Reformation was the greatest revival of the Christian church since Pentecost.

Chief among the Reformers was Martin Luther. Born in Northern Germany in 1483, Luther was a bright learner sent by his father to study law at the local university. He was very much the product of medieval spirituality and theology. This theology, with a heavy emphasis on the judgment of God and man's need to achieve salvation from that judgment by doing penance, receiving the sacraments, and doing good works, led him to perpetual doubt regarding his salvation.

One day, Luther was knocked off his horse while traveling and was injured; on another occasion, he was terrified by a thunderstorm. He vowed to become a monk.

As a monk, Luther was troubled by his perceived lack of righteousness despite intense self-discipline and growing knowledge of the Bible. He soon became a Bible lecturer at the local university. He found a troubling text in Romans 1:16–17, about the righteousness of God revealed from heaven. He was terrified of the righteousness of God, seeing it only as God's righteous wrath against sin. But after further study, he came to see that the righteousness Paul had in mind is the righteousness of Jesus Christ that God offers to us as a free gift, to be received by faith. Luther felt the chains of guilt and shame fall away as he grasped this fundamental truth of the gospel for the first time.

In those years, the pope, raising funds to build a new St. Peter's Basilica in Rome, franchised the sale of indulgences or pardons. People could purchase indulgences, which promised deliverance for their deceased loved ones from the rigors of purgatory. In Luther's part of Germany, the commission to sell these pardons went to a Dominican monk, Johan Tetzel, who set about selling them with the zeal of a fishmonger.

Luther, convicted by the immorality of this practice, decided to take action. On October 31, 1517, he nailed his *Ninety-Five Theses* to the castle church door in Wittenberg. These theses, written in Latin, were intended for discussion among scholars and monks in the university. Much of what he wrote was an explanation of the truth of the gospel and a condemnation of the church for failing to believe it and to preach it. Though it was never Luther's intention, soon the *Ninety-Five Theses* were translated into almost every language in Europe. Like wildfire, the message of justification by faith in Jesus Christ alone spread across the continent. Luther was tried, his teaching was condemned, and he was excommunicated. Concerned friends shielded Luther from danger, however, and he set about the task of translating the Bible into German. In the years that followed, the Reformation took hold in many parts of Europe, and almost always it began with the writings of Luther.

Luther's influence spread and many other Reformers arose to carry on the work. John Calvin of France did the work of ten men in the compass of a relatively short life. At the heart of his life and work was the task of exegeting Scripture, to which he devoted himself day by day. Yet no aspect of life and society went untouched by Calvin's influence. Not only theology, worship, church polity, and missions, but also education, government, economics, industry, and social work all bear the imprint of Calvin's thought. Consequently, some say that Calvin wielded greater influence over our history and culture than any other individual in the last millennium or since the close of the New Testament canon.

Other Reformers included Philip Melanchthon in Germany, Ulrich Zwingli and Heinrich Bullinger in Switzerland, Peter Martyr Vermigli in Italy, John Knox in Scotland, and Thomas Cranmer in England. Much has been written about these individuals and many others who contributed to the Protestant Reformation. Believers today are indebted to their work and testimony. Though not without faults and failures, Christians in the days of the Reformation were bursting with the power and the energy of the gospel. This energy would continue to spread in the years following the Reformation.

The SEVENTEENTH CENTURY

REFORMING THE CHURCH IN ENGLAND

Reformation came to England during the reign of Henry VIII (r. 1509–1547), but not until the reign of his daughter Elizabeth I (r. 1558–1603) did it gain a firm footing. Elizabeth put England firmly in the Protestant camp, but soon it became clear that Elizabeth wanted a church that was, as Robert Walton writes, "Calvinistic in theology, Erastian in church order and government, and largely mediaeval in liturgy." Those who sought further reformation of the national church were derided as Puritans. Many had lived in Geneva or the Netherlands as refugees during the reign of Queen Mary (r. 1553–1558), and they looked on the churches of those lands as models for England. Elizabeth's *via media* ("middle way") fell far short of their idea of what a Reformed church ought to be.

Initially, Puritan concerns centered on reforming the church's liturgy. They objected to ceremonies such as the signing of the cross in baptism or kneeling to receive the Lord's Supper. Later, as Elizabeth's bishops stood in their way, they began to advocate Presbyterian church polity. More radical elements argued for congregationalism. Some despaired of reforming the Church of England from within and separated from it.

While differing on church polity, the Puritans—who included such notables as William Perkins, Matthew Henry, John Owen, Thomas Goodwin, John Bunyan, John Flavel, and Thomas Watson—were united by a concern to maintain faithful preaching of the gospel and teach sound doctrine; to promote true conversion, personal faith, and practical godliness; and to bring God's Word to bear on all aspects of life, as individuals, in families, and in the nation at large. In short, doctrinally, Puritanism was a kind of vigorous Calvinism; experientially, it was warm and contagious; evangelistically, it was aggressive, yet tender; ecclesiastically, it was theocentric and worshipful; and politically, it aimed to be scriptural and balanced.

When James VI of Scotland came to the English throne following the death of Elizabeth in 1603, Puritan hopes for a reformed national church were renewed. But as James I of England, he renounced his Presbyterian upbringing in favor of an episcopal establishment that would strengthen his hold on power. He crushed the hopes of the Puritans, though he sanctioned a new translation of the Scriptures—the King James Version, produced in 1611.

Theologically, the Puritans and their opponents had largely agreed on issues relating to soteriology, for nearly all of them were Calvinists. But in the 1620s, when Charles I came to power, he began to appoint Arminians to high positions in the Church of England.

Puritan theologians were unsparing in their criticism of Arminianism. But Archbishop William Laud, preferred by Charles I, sought to promote Arminian theology as well as to enhance the ceremonial aspects of public worship so offensive to the Puritans. Drastic measures were used to secure conformity to the Book of Common Prayer and to silence or punish dissent. Finally, Charles alienated Scottish Presbyterians when he tried to impose a version of the English liturgy on the Church of Scotland. The Presbyterians of Scotland and the Puritans of England united in determination to resist such tyranny. The result was civil war in England and Scotland, pitting forces loyal to the king against the army of Parliament, commanded by Oliver Cromwell, often hailed as the greatest Englishman of his century. Charles lost his throne and his life in 1649. For a time, it seemed that the Puritans had triumphed. The high-water mark of Puritanism was the Westminster Assembly of Divines, which met from 1643 to 1652.

But by 1662, the tide had turned and the monarchy was restored. Under Charles II, new measures were taken to secure conformity and crush dissent. Two thousand Puritan ministers were ejected from their pulpits in the Church of England. The authorities hounded them, suppressed them as ministers, and jailed them as criminals. For decades in Scotland, the crown waged war against the Presbyterians who had covenanted to maintain the Reformed faith, worship, and order of their national church, even to the death.

Though English Puritanism faded by the end of the seventeenth century, its impact on the Scottish Covenanters, the Dutch Further Reformation, New England Puritanism, and German Pietism was profound. That legacy continues today through the remarkable resurgence of Puritan literature that has transpired in the last fifty years—approximately eight hundred reprinted volumes.

The EIGHTEENTH CENTURY

THE GREAT AWAKENING

By the eighteenth century, Christian Europe had wearied of constant religious strife and bloodshed. Intellectuals embraced the Enlightenment ideal of reason as the ultimate authority. Theology was made subject to philosophy. Deism taught that God created the world, subjected it to natural law, and let nature take its course. This was not the personal God of the Bible; deism was a rejection of revelation in the name of reason. Rationalism prevailed in the eighteenth century and continues to influence theology today.

The Christian pulpit was subverted by the new theology. The gospel ("the power of God unto salvation") was supplanted by a message of thoughtful moderation and good deeds. This powerless substitute had little appeal to the masses. They were left to sink down in unbelief, drunkenness, fornication, gambling, and worse. The church became irrelevant to many people, highborn and low. No one would have guessed that a great revival was at hand.

The revival first appeared in Wales. In the early 1730s, two men who were to lead the revival in Wales—Howell Harris and Daniel Rowland—were converted. By 1750, their preaching and godliness, and that of others, had brought about the creation of 433 religious societies. These societies, whose members called themselves Calvinistic Methodists, set the tone and character of Christianity in Wales for two centuries. All the early Calvinistic Methodist leaders were convinced of the necessity of the Holy Spirit's power and anointing on their ministries.

The year 1735 also saw the conversion of George Whitefield, the leading preacher of the revival on both sides of the Atlantic. In 1732, Whitefield met John Wesley and his brother Charles, who belonged to a religious society known to history as "the Holy Club." Devout Anglicans, these men set out to pursue holiness by a rigorous discipline or method, and thus were decried as "Methodists." The Wesley brothers also became luminaries of the evangelical revival in England.

German Pietists known as the Moravians deeply influenced John Wesley. The Moravians were led by Nicolaus von Zinzendorf. Influenced by the warm piety of Jacob Spener, Zinzendorf gathered a group of like-minded believers yearning for a more experiential faith than that of the lifeless Lutheranism of eighteenth-century Germany. Their missionary efforts throughout the world in the eighteenth century were renowned.

Wesley was finally converted at a Moravian meeting in Aldersgate Street, London, in 1738. The preface to Martin Luther's commentary on Romans was read aloud, and Wesley felt his heart "strangely warmed" as he listened to Luther's account of the change God works in the heart through faith. Then and there he obtained assurance of salvation and forgiveness of sins. Heralded as "the new birth," this experiential emphasis became the warp and woof of the Great Awakening and the evangelical preaching of Whitefield, Wesley, and others of the era.

Revival also broke out among the sons of the Puritans in New England. Jonathan Edwards wrote an account of the marvelous awakening taking place in his Massachusetts congregation. In the early years of his pastorate in Northampton, his people were outwardly orthodox, but showed few signs of inward religion. In the early 1730s, Edwards observed a growing sensitivity toward sin. In a town of about twelve hundred people, Edwards reckoned that some three hundred were saved in about six months. At the revival's height in 1735, about thirty people a week professed conversion. Soon revival was breaking out in all the colonies. Estimates of those converted in New England alone, where the population was around a quarter of a million people, ranged from twenty-five thousand to fifty thousand.

This revival also included concentrated mission efforts among the Native Americans. Following in the footsteps of John Eliot, men such as David Brainerd and, later, Edwards himself set out to evangelize the native peoples of the New World. Though these efforts produced mixed results, Brainerd's spiritual diary continues to be an inspiration to missionaries today.

What this fallen world needs is not reason, but the saving grace that transforms people for Christ. The guiding lights of the Great Awakening demonstrated this fact. The evangelistic fervor of the Great Awakening produced a significant missionary expansion that aimed at reaching the whole world for Christ. It also produced a piety focused on conversion and growth in grace through knowing God's Word. We do well to honor and continue that legacy today.

The NINETEENTH CENTURY

BEGINNINGS OF MODERN THEOLOGY & KINGDOM BUILDERS

Two German philosophers cast a long shadow over the church during the nineteenth century: Immanuel Kant and Friedrich Schleiermacher. Both profoundly influenced modern theology. Kant argued that it is impossible for us to have immediate knowledge of God. Part of his philosophy posited that since all of our knowledge is gained by sense experience, it is not possible for us to have immediate knowledge of anything that lies behind sense experience. We can know the world we live in, but when it comes to that which transcends the physical world, as God does, we can have no knowledge at all. On this basis, Kant rejected both the natural theology of the rationalists and the experiential religion of the pietists.

Schleiermacher was a philosopher who served as a minister in the church. He perceived a general despising of Christianity in Europe, as something out of touch with modern sensibilities. Schleiermacher was concerned with salvaging the Christian faith. *On Religion: Speeches to Its Cultured Despisers* was his response to this perception. Schleiermacher redefined the nature of faith, how one should relate to God, and the person and work of Jesus Christ. He defined religion as the feeling of dependence on God. Jesus, he said, was a model to strive after, and the church was only a community of individuals sharing a common experience. He jettisoned orthodox Christian doctrine for experience.

Though different in their approaches, these men were very similar in their conclusions. They agreed that God is, at best, a product of our experience. Experience trumped revealed truth. Both reason and revelation were divorced from faith, and faith itself was reduced to a feeling. As a result, many today no longer believe in an objective knowledge of God.

The work of God went forward, however, in two great revivals, the Second Great Awakening at the beginning of the century in the United States and the Revival of 1859 on both sides of the Atlantic, not to mention lesser revivals in various places. The church awakened once more to her true calling—to preach the gospel to the ends of the earth. Missionaries went out from many parts of Europe and North America to build God's kingdom in Africa, Asia, and Latin America.

One of these kingdom builders was William Carey. He was a cobbler by trade. God gripped his heart and gave him a vision for evangelizing the world. He went to India in 1793 as a cobbler. Within five years, he had learned Sanskrit and translated the whole Bible into Bengali. By the end of his life, he had supervised translations of the Bible into thirty-six languages and helped launch the great missionary movement of the nineteenth century. Another great missionary from this period was Henry Martyn, who translated the New Testament into Hindustani, Arabic, and Persian, giving his life for the spread of the gospel of Jesus Christ. Others included Robert Moffat, David Livingstone, John Paton, Andrew Gordon, and Hudson Taylor. These were days of great expansion of the British Empire, and in that context, God sent His servants out to the ends of the earth.

The revival of the church and her missionary enterprise was encouraged by the pulpit ministry of gifted preachers such as Charles Spurgeon, whose sermons have been read perhaps by more people than those of any other preacher in church history. Then, too, the gospel fanned out through America and beyond through the influence of Princeton Seminary, under the aegis of devout scholars such as Archibald Alexander, Samuel Miller, and Charles Hodge, who schooled generations of faithful gospel ministers in Reformed truth.

All of these men, and multitudes more, brought God's Word and the knowledge of God in Jesus Christ to the ends of the earth. The contempt of "cultured despisers" takes nothing away from the power and truth of God's Word. God demonstrated His wisdom in that, even as people in Europe began despising the gospel, He was already preparing to go somewhere else. Surely we should pray that God would use us to continue that work of the gospel proclamation in the world today.

The TWENTIETH CENTURY

THE AGE OF PARADOXES

The twentieth century was a time of great paradoxes, as the church fell into decline in some parts of the world, but grew and flourished in others. In the first two decades, many in the West envisioned the triumph of Christianity in a golden age of peace and progress for the human race, but this vision died in the carnage and destruction of two world wars.

Rationalistic Modernism assailed the trustworthiness of Holy Scripture, sending great denominations into swift decline, as "the battle for the Bible" beset them. At the same time, Pentecostalism appeared as a tiny offshoot of Methodism and grew into a significant third force in Christendom, augmented by the charismatic movement of the 1970s. The Reformed faith was eclipsed in the early decades of the century, but since 1960, has recovered on both sides of the Atlantic, extending its reach to many parts of the developing world.

As decadent Western churches retreated from missionary work, under pressure of declining memberships and shrinking revenue, the newly planted churches of Africa and Asia grew apace. Communism waged a long and brutal campaign to destroy Christianity in the name of materialism and atheism, but failed, falling into the dustbin of history. There is a vibrant church in Russia today, and more Christians in China than in any other nation in the world. The church in the West has declined in faith and numbers, poisoned by Modernism, battered by secularism, and emasculated by worldliness. But God has continued to send forth His Word to the ends of the earth, bringing people to Himself through Christ, planting churches everywhere, and building His kingdom in the hearts of His redeemed people.

The twentieth century was hard on the churches in Europe and North America. At the beginning of the century, in many places, nearly everyone went to church as a matter of course. The rejection of evangelical theology and biblical Calvinism was regarded as a necessary adjustment to changing times; few could see that it would end with the "Death of God" theology of the 1960s. For a time, the deceptive "Neo-Orthodoxy" of Karl Barth promised to save the church from sterile, destructive Modernism, only to disappoint all but its most zealous exponents. In the wake of the two world wars, thousands gave up churchgoing in Britain, the Netherlands, and elsewhere in Europe. Churchgoing increased in the United States during the 1950s, only to fall off sharply in the 1960s, though it remained considerably higher than in Europe.

There were exceptions to the general rule. Evangelicals belatedly realized that their denominations had been hijacked by Modernism and began to protest in the name of the "fundamentals" of the faith. For better or worse, "Fundamentalism" became a force in American church life. To stem the tide of unbelief, mass evangelistic campaigns were organized in urban centers, led by Billy Sunday and, later, Billy Graham. Movements to recover the historic Reformed faith were led by able men such as J. Gresham Machen, founder of Westminster Seminary and the Orthodox Presbyterian Church. In Britain, D. Martyn Lloyd-Jones drew large congregations to London's Westminster Chapel, and through his influence, the Banner of Truth Trust began to republish outstanding but long-forgotten works of Reformed and Puritan theology.

Meanwhile, the younger churches of the developing Third World, planted by missionaries in the nineteenth century, began to flourish. In Latin America, Pentecostalism succeeded in breaking the iron grip of Roman Catholicism and drew many thousands into its ranks. Presbyterian and Reformed churches were planted in the Caribbean islands, as well as in Central and South America. In Asia, there came to be Christians of many kinds in China, a thriving if sometimes discordant family of Presbyterian churches in Korea, and significant numbers of Reformed churches in India, Pakistan, Sri Lanka, and elsewhere. As for Africa, huge numbers of Christians adhered to churches of all kinds, often coming into conflict with the forces of Islam spreading down from the north.

In the Middle East, historic Christian populations are shrinking under persecution at the hands of militant Islamists. The clash with Islam continues in Pakistan, Indonesia, and elsewhere in the world. But the record of church history teaches us to hold fast to Christ, assured that He is with us always, even to the end of the world. He will build up His church and kingdom to all generations.

CREEDS *and Confessions*

Apostles' Creed

Nicene Creed

Athanasian Creed

Belgic Confession

Heidelberg Catechism

Canons of Dort

Westminster Confession

Westminster
Shorter Catechism

Westminster
Larger Catechism

I BELIEVE
in God
THE FATHER
Almighty
MAKER OF
HEAVEN
&
EARTH

APOSTLES' CREED

APOSTLES' CREED

The Apostles' Creed owes its name to the fact that it summarizes the essential content of the apostolic faith; hence it has been rightly called "the apostolic confession of faith." It sets forth the apostles' core New Testament teachings, as has been well-said, "in sublime simplicity, in unsurpassable brevity, in beautiful order, and with liturgical solemnity." The assumption that the twelve apostles were joint authors of this creed has no historical foundation. Bearing a Trinitarian framework, the Apostles' Creed affirms faith in the saving acts of the triune God and centers upon Christ's mediatorial work.

In its simplest form the Apostles' Creed (*symbolicum apostolicum*) dates from the early part of the second century and grew out of a need to instruct catechumens preparing for baptism. Its present form developed over several centuries in the Western church and was probably not finalized before the sixth century. The Apostles' Creed was commonly used as a guide for establishing the fundamental articles of the Christian faith deemed necessary for salvation and as a defense against various heresies (especially Ebionites, Marcionites, Gnostics, and Docetists). In the eighth century it was appropriated as an official confession with ecclesiastical authority. The Reformers frequently incorporated the Apostles' Creed into their worship and liturgy. More than any other Christian creed, it may justly be called an ecumenical symbol of faith, for until the present day it is the most widely used confessional statement in the Western church. Consequently, it has frequently been denominated, "the twelve articles of our undoubted, catholic Christian faith."

I. I believe in God the Father, Almighty, Maker of heaven and earth;
II. And in Jesus Christ, His only begotten Son, our Lord;
III. Who was conceived by the Holy Ghost, born of the Virgin Mary;
IV. Suffered under Pontius Pilate; was crucified, dead and buried;
He descended into hell;
V. The third day He rose again from the dead;
VI. He ascended into heaven, and sitteth at the right hand of God the Father Almighty;
VII. From thence He shall come to judge the quick and the dead;
VIII. I believe in the Holy Ghost;
IX. I believe an holy catholic church; the communion of saints;
X. The forgiveness of sins;
XI. The resurrection of the body;
XII. And the life everlasting. Amen.

&

IN

One Lord

JESUS CHRIST

THE

ONLY-BEGOTTEN

SON OF

God

NICENE CREED

NICENE CREED

The Nicene Creed, also known as the Nicene-Constantinopolitan Creed (*symbolum Nicaeno-Constantinopolitanum*), is a statement of the orthodox faith of the early Christian church in opposition to certain heresies, especially Arianism. These heresies which disturbed the church during the fourth and fifth centuries concerned the doctrine of the Trinity and of the Person of Christ. Hence the Nicene Creed provides a more detailed affirmation of the divinity of Christ and the Holy Spirit than does the Apostles' Creed.

Both Greek (Eastern) and Latin (Western) churches held this creed in honor, making this the only Christian creed which can claim universal recognition. Nevertheless, a significant division soon developed: The Western church insisted on the inclusion of the phrase "and the Son" (known as the *filioque*) in the article on the procession of the Holy Spirit. This doctrinal distinction ultimately became a prime cause for the permanent division of Christendom in 1054 into Eastern and Western churches. Until today the Eastern churches reject the *filioque* and maintain the doctrine of "single procession," that is, that the Holy Spirit proceeds only from the Father, while most Western churches continue to uphold "double procession," that is, that the Holy Spirit proceeds from both the Father and the Son.

The Nicene Creed as we know it today is to be distinguished from the creed promulgated by the Council of Nicaea in 325. Though the roots of the Nicene Creed lay in this council, significant changes and additions were probably made by the Council of Constantinople in 381. Our present Nicene Creed was accepted as a definitive statement at the Council of Chalcedon in 451, although the *filioque* phrase was not added until 589 at the Synod of Toledo. Nevertheless, its substance portrays an accurate and majestic formulation of the Nicene faith.

I believe in one God, the Father Almighty,
Maker of heaven and earth, and of all things visible and invisible.
And in one Lord Jesus Christ, the only-begotten Son of God,
begotten of the Father before all worlds;
God of God, Light of Light, very God of very God;
begotten, not made,
being of one substance with the Father, by whom all things were made.
Who, for us men for our salvation, came down from heaven,
and was incarnate by the Holy Spirit of the virgin Mary,
and was made man;
and was crucified also for us under Pontius Pilate;
He suffered and was buried;
and the third day He rose again, according to the Scriptures;
and ascended into heaven, and sitteth on the right hand of the Father;
and He shall come again, with glory, to judge the quick and the dead;
whose kingdom shall have no end.
And I believe in the Holy Ghost, the Lord and Giver of life;
who proceedeth from the Father and the Son;
who with the Father and the Son together is worshipped and glorified;
who spake by the prophets.
And I believe one holy catholic and apostolic Church.
I acknowledge one baptism for the remission of sins;
and I look for the resurrection of the dead,
and the life of the world to come. Amen.

SO

The Father

IS GOD

The Son

IS GOD

AND THE

Holy Spirit

IS GOD

ATHANASIAN CREED

ATHANASIAN CREED

The Athanasian Creed (also called *Quicunque vult* after its opening Latin words) is the third creed widely used in Western Christendom. It is named after Athanasius (293–373), a renowned defender of the orthodox doctrine of the Trinity and of the deity of Christ. Although Athanasius did not write this creed, the name persists because until the seventeenth century it was commonly ascribed to him. The Athanasian Creed dates from the fifth century and is of Latin (Western) origin. It did not appear in completed form until the eighth century. Its author is unknown.

The Athanasian Creed opens and concludes with statements asserting that belief in the truths it contains is necessary to salvation. The bulk of the creed consists of two parts, the first setting forth the orthodox doctrine of the Trinity (3–28), and the second dealing chiefly with the incarnation and the union of the two natures of Christ in one divine person (29–43). More explicit than the Apostles' and the Nicene Creeds, the Athanasian Creed remains, as has been well-said, "a superb compendium of Trinitarian and Christological theology and offers itself as a ready outline for catechetical purposes in keeping with its original intent."

---

(1) Whosoever will be saved, before all things
it is necessary that he hold the catholic faith;
(2) Which faith except every one do keep whole and undefiled,
without doubt he shall perish everlastingly.

(3) And the catholic faith is this:
That we worship one God in Trinity,
and Trinity in Unity;
(4) Neither confounding the Persons
nor dividing the substance.
(5) For there is one Person of the Father, another of the Son,
and another of the Holy Spirit.
(6) But the Godhead of the Father, of the Son,
and of the Holy Spirit is all one,
the glory equal, the majesty coeternal.
(7) Such as the Father is, such is the Son, and such is the Holy Spirit.
(8) The Father uncreate, the Son uncreate,
and the Holy Spirit uncreate.
(9) The Father incomprehensible, the Son incomprehensible,
and the Holy Spirit incomprehensible.
(10) The Father eternal, the Son eternal,
and the Holy Spirit eternal.
(11) And yet they are not three eternals, but one eternal.
(12) As also there are not three uncreated
nor three incomprehensibles,
but one uncreated and one incomprehensible.
(13) So likewise the Father is almighty, the Son almighty,
and the Holy Spirit almighty.
(14) And yet they are not three almighties, but one almighty.
(15) So the Father is God, the Son is God,
and the Holy Spirit is God;
(16) And yet they are not three Gods, but one God.
(17) So likewise the Father is Lord, the Son Lord,
and the Holy Spirit Lord;
(18) And yet they are not three Lords, but one Lord.
(19) For like as we are compelled by the Christian verity

to acknowledge every Person by himself to be God and Lord;
(20) So are we forbidden by the catholic religion to say,
there are three Gods or three Lords.
(21) The Father is made of none,
neither created nor begotten.
(22) The Son is of the Father alone;
not made nor created, but begotten.
(23) The Holy Spirit is of the Father and of the Son;
neither made, nor created, nor begotten, but proceeding.
(24) So there is one Father, not three Fathers;
one Son, not three Sons;
one Holy Spirit, not three Holy Spirits.
(25) And in this Trinity none is afore or after another;
none is greater or less than another.
(26) But the whole three Persons are coeternal and coequal.
(27) So that in all things, as aforesaid, the Unity in Trinity
and the Trinity in Unity is to be worshipped.
(28) He therefore that will be saved must thus think of the Trinity.

(29) Furthermore it is necessary to everlasting salvation
that he also believe rightly the incarnation
of our Lord Jesus Christ.
(30) For the right faith is that we believe and confess
that our Lord Jesus Christ, the Son of God, is God and man.
(31) God of the substance of the Father, begotten before the worlds;
and man of substance of His mother, born in the world.
(32) Perfect God and perfect man,
of a reasonable soul and human flesh subsisting.
(33) Equal to the Father as touching His Godhead,
and inferior to the Father as touching His manhood.
(34) Who although He is God and man,
yet He is not two, but one Christ.
(35) One, not by conversion of the Godhead into flesh,
but by taking of that manhood into God.
(36) One altogether, not by confusion of substance,
but by unity of Person.
(37) For as the reasonable soul and flesh is one man,
so God and man is one Christ;
(38) Who suffered for our salvation, descended into hell,
rose again the third day from the dead;
(39) He ascended into heaven,
He sitteth on the right hand of the Father, God, Almighty;
(40) From thence He shall come to judge the quick and the dead.
(41) At whose coming all men shall rise again with their bodies;
(42) and shall give account of their own works.
(43) And they that have done good shall go into life everlasting
and they that have done evil into everlasting fire.

(44) This is the catholic faith, which except a man believe faithfully
he cannot be saved.

Belgic CONFESSION

Revised in the National Synod, held at Dordrecht, in the Years 1618 and 1619.

The oldest of the doctrinal standards of the Reformed Churches of the Netherlands is the Confession of Faith, most commonly known as the Belgic Confession, following the seventeenth-century Latin designation *Confessio Belgica*. "Belgica" referred to the Lowlands or the whole of the Netherlands, both north and south, which today is divided into the Netherlands and Belgium. Variant names for the Belgic Confession include the Walloon Confession and the Netherlands Confession.

The Confession's chief author was Guido de Brès (1522–1567), a godly itinerant pastor of Reformed persuasion. During the sixteenth century the Reformed churches in the Netherlands were exposed to severe persecution through Philip II of Spain, an ally of the Roman Catholic Church. As an apology for the persecuted band of Reformed believers in the Lowlands who formed the so-called churches under the cross, de Brès prepared this confession in French in 1561. De Brès was most likely assisted by his fellow pastors who, together with himself, desired to prove to their persecutors that the adherents of the Reformed faith were not rebels as was charged, but law-abiding citizens who professed only biblical doctrines. The Confession was written as an independent composition, though it was modeled after the Gallic Confession, a 1559 French Reformed confession, which in turn was dependent upon Calvin's design. Basically, the Confession follows what has become known as the traditional doctrinal order of the six loci of Reformed systematic theology—the doctrines concerning God (theology proper, articles 1–11), man (anthropology, articles 12–15), Christ (Christology, articles 16–21), salvation (soteriology, articles 22–26), the church (ecclesiology, articles 27–35), and the last things (eschatology, article 37). Article 36 addresses the theocratic nature of civil government. Despite following an objective doctrinal order, the Confession breathes a warmly experiential and personal spirit, facilitated by its repeated use of the pronoun "we."

The following year, 1562, a copy was sent to King Philip II together with an address in which the petitioners declared that they were ready to obey the government in all lawful things, but that they would "offer their backs to stripes, their tongues to knives, their mouths to gags, and their whole bodies to the fire, well knowing that those who follow Christ must take His cross and deny themselves" rather than deny the truth expressed in this Confession. Neither the Confession nor the petition, however, bore the desired fruit of toleration for Protestants with the Spanish authorities. Five years later de Brès himself became one martyr among thousands who sealed his faith with blood. Nevertheless his work has and will continue to endure through this remarkable doctrinal standard which still stands as a priceless symbolical statement of Reformed doctrine.

The Belgic Confession was readily received by Reformed churches in the Netherlands after its early translation into Dutch in 1562. In 1566 it was revised by the Synod of Antwerp. Subsequently it was regularly adopted by national Dutch Synods held during the last three decades of the sixteenth century. After a further revision of the text, the Synod of Dort (1618–1619) adopted it as one of the doctrinal standards to which all office-bearers in the Reformed churches were required to subscribe.

ARTICLE 1

There Is One Only God

We all believe with the heart, and confess with the mouth, that there is one only simple[1] and spiritual[2] Being, which we call God; and that He is eternal,[3] incomprehensible,[4] invisible,[5] immutable,[6] infinite,[7] almighty, perfectly wise,[8] just,[9] good,[10] and the overflowing fountain of all good.[11]

[1] Eph. 4:6; Deut. 6:4; 1 Tim. 2:5; 1 Cor. 8:6 [2] John 4:24 [3] Isa. 40:28 [4] Rom. 11:33 [5] Rom. 1:20 [6] Mal. 3:6 [7] Isa. 44:6 [8] 1 Tim. 1:17 [9] Jer. 12:1 [10] Matt. 19:17 [11] James. 1:17; 1 Chron. 29:10–12

ARTICLE 2

By What Means God is Made Known Unto Us

We know Him by two means: first, by the creation, preservation, and government of the universe;[1] which is before our eyes as a most elegant book, wherein all creatures, great and small, are as so many characters leading us to contemplate *the invisible things of God*, namely, *His eternal power and divinity*, as the apostle Paul saith (Rom. 1:20). All which things are sufficient to convince men, and leave them without excuse.

Secondly, He makes Himself more clearly and fully known to us by His holy and divine Word;[2] that is to say, as far as is necessary for us to know in this life, to His glory and our salvation.

[1] Ps. 19:2; Eph. 4:6 [2] Ps. 19:8; 1 Cor. 12:6

ARTICLE 3

The Written Word of God

We confess that this Word of God was not sent nor delivered by the will of man, but that *holy men of God spake as they were moved by the Holy Ghost*, as the apostle Peter saith.[1] And that afterwards God, from a special care which He has for us and our salvation, commanded His servants, the prophets[2] and apostles,[3] to commit His revealed Word to writing; and He Himself wrote with His own finger the two tables of the law.[4] Therefore we call such writings holy and divine Scriptures.

[1] 2 Peter 1:21 [2] Ex. 24:4; Ps. 102:19; Hab. 2:2 [3] 2 Tim. 3:16; Rev. 1:11 [4] Ex. 31:18

ARTICLE 4

Canonical Books of the Holy Scriptures

We believe that the Holy Scriptures are contained in two books, namely, the Old and New Testaments, which are canonical, against which nothing can be alleged. These are thus named in the Church of God.

The books of the Old Testament are: the five books of Moses, namely, Genesis, Exodus, Leviticus, Numbers, Deuteronomy; the books of Joshua, Judges, Ruth, the two books of Samuel, the two of the Kings, two books of the Chronicles, commonly called Paralipomenon, the first of Ezra, Nehemiah, Esther, Job, the Psalms of David, the three books of Solomon, namely, the Proverbs, Ecclesiastes, and the Song of Songs; the four great prophets, Isaiah, Jeremiah, Ezekiel, and Daniel; and the twelve lesser prophets, namely, Hosea, Joel, Amos, Obadiah, Jonah, Micah, Nahum, Habakkuk, Zephaniah, Haggai, Zechariah, and Malachi.

Those of the New Testament are: the four Evangelists, namely, Matthew, Mark, Luke, and John; the Acts of the Apostles; the fourteen epistles of the apostle Paul, namely, one to the Romans, two to the Corinthians, one to the Galatians, one to the Ephesians, one to the Philippians, one to the Colossians, two to the Thessalonians, two to Timothy, one to Titus, one to Philemon, and one to the Hebrews; the seven epistles of the other apostles, namely, one of James, two of Peter, three of John, one of Jude; and the Revelation of the apostle John.

ARTICLE 5

From Whence the Holy Scriptures Derive Their Dignity and Authority

We receive all these books, and these only, as holy and canonical, for the regulation, foundation, and confirmation of our faith; believing without any doubt all things contained in them, not so much because the Church receives and approves them as such, but more especially because the Holy Ghost witnesseth in our hearts that they are from God, whereof they carry the evidence in themselves. For the very blind are able to perceive that the things foretold in them are fulfilling.

ARTICLE 6

The Difference Between the Canonical and Apocryphal Books

We distinguish these sacred books from the apocryphal, viz., the third and fourth book of Esdras, the books of Tobias, Judith, Wisdom, Jesus Syrach, Baruch, the appendix to the book of Esther, the Song of the Three Children in the Furnace, the History of Susannah, of Bell and the Dragon, the Prayer of Manasses, and the two books of the Maccabees. All of which the Church may read and take instruction from, so far as they agree with the canonical books; but they are far from having such power and efficacy as that we may from their testimony confirm any point of faith or of the Christian religion; much less to detract from the authority of the other sacred books.

ARTICLE 7

The Sufficiency of the Holy Scriptures to be the Only Rule of Faith

We believe that those Holy Scriptures fully contain the will of God, and that whatsoever man ought to believe unto salvation is sufficiently taught therein.[1] For since the whole manner of worship which God requires of us is written in them at large, it is unlawful for any one, though an apostle, to teach otherwise[2] than we are now taught in the Holy Scriptures: *nay, though it were an angel from heaven,* as the apostle Paul saith.[3] For since it is forbidden *to add unto or take away any thing from the Word of God,*[4] it doth thereby evidently appear that the doctrine thereof is most perfect and complete in all respects.

Neither do we consider of equal value any writing of men, however holy these men may have been, with those divine Scriptures;[5] nor ought we to consider custom, or the great multitude, or antiquity, or succession of times and persons, or councils, decrees, or statutes, as of equal value with the truth of God,[6] for the truth is above all; for all men are of themselves liars,[7] and more vain than vanity itself. Therefore we reject with all our hearts whatsoever doth not agree with this infallible rule[8] which the apostles have taught us, saying, *Try the spirits whether they are of God.*[9] Likewise, *If there come any unto you, and bring not this doctrine, receive him not into your house.*[10]

[1] Rom. 15:4; John 4:25; 2 Tim. 3:15–17; 1 Peter 1:1; Prov. 30:5; Rev. 22:18; John 15:15; Acts 2:27 [2] 1 Peter 4:11; 1 Cor.15:2–3; 2 Tim. 3:14; 1 Tim. 1:3; 2 John 10 [3] Gal. 1:8–9; 1 Cor. 15:2; Acts 26:22; Rom. 15:4; 1 Peter 4:11; 2 Tim. 3:14 [4] Deut. 12:32; Prov. 30:6; Rev. 22:18; John 4:25 [5] Matt. 15:3; 17:5; Mark 7:7; Isa. 1:12; 1 Cor. 2:4 [6] Isa. 1:12; Rom. 3:4; 2 Tim. 4:3–4 [7] Ps. 62:10 [8] Gal. 6:16; 1 Cor. 3:11; 2 Thess. 2:2 [9] 1 John 4:1 [10] 2 John 10

ARTICLE 8

God is One in Essence, Yet Distinguished in Three Persons

According to this truth and this Word of God, we believe in one only God, who is one single essence,[1] in which are three persons,[2] really, truly, and eternally distinct, according to their incommunicable properties; namely, the Father, and the Son, and the Holy Ghost.[3] The Father is the cause, origin, and beginning of all things, visible and invisible;[4] the Son is the word,[5] wisdom,[6] and image of the Father;[7] the Holy Ghost is the eternal power and might,[8] proceeding from the Father and the Son.[9] Nevertheless God is not by this distinction divided into three, since the Holy Scriptures teach us that the Father, and the Son, and the Holy Ghost have each His personality, distinguished by their properties; but in such wise that these three persons are but one only God. Hence then, it is evident that the Father is not the Son, nor the Son the Father, and likewise the Holy Ghost is neither the Father nor the Son. Nevertheless these persons thus distinguished are not divided nor intermixed; for the Father hath not assumed the flesh, nor hath the Holy Ghost, but the Son only.[10] The Father hath never been without His Son, or without His Holy Ghost. For they are all three coeternal and coessential. There is neither first nor last; for they are all three one, in truth, in power, in goodness, and in mercy.

[1] Isa. 43:10 [2] 1 John 5:7; Heb. 1:3 [3] Matt. 28:19 [4] 1 Cor. 8:6; Col. 1:16 [5] John 1:1,2; Rev. 19:13; Prov. 8:12 [6] Prov. 8:12, 22 [7] Col. 1:15; Heb. 1:3 [8] Matt. 12:28 [9] John 15:26; Gal. 4:6 [10] Phil. 2:6, 7; Gal. 4:4; John 1:14

ARTICLE 9

The Proof of the Foregoing Article of the Trinity of Persons in One God

All this we know, as well from the testimonies of Holy Writ as from their operations, and chiefly by those we feel in ourselves. The testimonies of the Holy Scriptures that teach us to believe this Holy Trinity are written in many places of the Old Testament, which are not so necessary to enumerate as to choose them out with discretion and judgment. In Genesis 1:26, 27, God saith: *Let us make man in our image, after our likeness, etc.*[1] *So God created man in His own image, male and female created He them.* And Genesis 3:22: *Behold, the man is become as one of us.*[2] From this saying, *Let us make man in our image*, it appears that there are more persons than one in the Godhead; and when He saith *God created*, He signifies the unity. It is true He doth not say how many persons there are, but that which appears to us somewhat obscure in the Old Testament is very plain in the New.

For when our Lord was baptized in Jordan,[3] the voice of the Father was heard, saying, *This is My beloved Son:* the Son was seen in the water, and the Holy Ghost appeared in the shape of a dove. This form is also instituted by Christ in the baptism of all believers. *Baptize all nations, in the name of the Father and of the Son, and of the Holy Ghost.*[4] In the Gospel of Luke the angel Gabriel thus addressed Mary, the mother of our Lord: *The Holy Ghost shall come upon thee, and the power of the Highest shall overshadow thee, therefore also that holy thing which shall be born of thee shall be called the Son of God.*[5] Likewise, *The grace of our Lord Jesus Christ, and the love of God, and the communion of the Holy Ghost be with you.*[6] And, *There are three that bear record in heaven, the Father, the Word, and the Holy Ghost, and these three are one.*[7] In all which places we are fully taught that there are three persons in one only divine essence. And although this doctrine far surpasses all human understanding, nevertheless we now believe it by means of the Word of God, but expect hereafter to enjoy the perfect knowledge and benefit thereof in heaven.[8]

Moreover, we must observe the particular offices and operations of these three persons towards us. The Father is called our Creator by His power;[9] the Son is our Savior and Redeemer by His blood;[10] the Holy Ghost is our Sanctifier by His dwelling in our hearts.[11]

This doctrine of the Holy Trinity hath always been defended and maintained by the true Church since the times of the apostles to this very day, against the Jews, Mohammedans, and some false Christians and heretics, as Marcion, Manes, Praxeas, Sabellius, Samosatenus, Arius, and such like, who have been justly condemned by the orthodox fathers.

Therefore, in this point we do willingly receive the three creeds, namely, that of the Apostles, of Nice, and of Athanasius; likewise that which, conformable thereunto, is agreed upon by the ancient fathers.

[1] Gen. 1:26, 27 [2] Gen. 3:22 [3] Matt. 3:16–17 [4] Matt. 28:19 [5] Luke 1:35 [6] 2 Cor. 13:13 [7] 1 John 5:7 [8] Ps. 45:8; Isa. 61:1 [9] Eccl. 12:3; Mal. 2:10; 1 Peter 1:2 [10] 1 Peter 1:2; 1 John 1:7; 4:14 [11] 1 Cor. 6:11; 1 Peter 1:2; Gal. 4:6; Titus 3:5; Rom. 8:9; John 14:16

ARTICLE 10

Jesus Christ is True and Eternal God

We believe that Jesus Christ, according to His divine nature, is the only begotten Son of God,[1] begotten from eternity,[2] not made nor created (for then He would be a creature), but coessential[3] and coeternal[4] with the Father, *the express image of His person, and the brightness of His glory*,[5] equal unto Him in all things.[6] He is the Son of God, not only from the time that He assumed our nature, but from all eternity,[7] as these testimonies, when compared together, teach us. Moses saith that *God created the world*;[8] and John saith that *all things were made by that Word*, which he calleth God.[9] And the apostle saith that *God made the worlds by His Son;*[10] likewise, that *God created all things by Jesus Christ.*[11] Therefore it must needs follow that He—who is called God, the Word, the Son, and Jesus Christ—did exist at that time when all things were created by Him.[12] Therefore the prophet Micah saith: *His goings forth have been from of old, from everlasting.*[13] And the apostle: *He hath neither beginning of days nor end of life.*[14] He therefore is that true, eternal, and almighty God, whom we invoke, worship, and serve.

[1] John 1:18, 49 [2] John 1:14; Col. 1:15 [3] John 10:30; Phil. 2:6 [4] John 1:2; 17:5; Rev. 1:8 [5] Heb. 1:3 [6] Phil. 2:6 [7] John 8:23, 58; 9:35–37; Acts 8:37; Rom. 9:5 [8] Gen. 1:1 [9] John 1:3 [10] Heb. 1:2 [11] Col. 1:16 [12] Col. 1:16 [13] Mic. 5:2 [14] Heb. 7:3

ARTICLE 11

The Holy Ghost is True and Eternal God

We believe and confess also that the Holy Ghost from eternity proceeds from the Father[1] and Son,[2] and therefore is neither made, created, nor begotten, but only proceedeth from both; who in order is the third person of the Holy Trinity, of one and the same essence, majesty, and glory with the Father and the Son; and therefore is the true and eternal God, as the Holy Scriptures teach us.[3]

[1] Ps. 33:6, 17; John 14:16 [2] Gal. 4:6; Rom. 8:9; John 15:26 [3] Gen. 1:2; Isa. 48:16; 61:1; Acts 5:3–4; 28:25; 1 Cor. 3:16; 6:19; Ps. 139:7

ARTICLE 12

The Creation

We believe that the Father, by the Word, that is, by His Son,[1] created of nothing the heaven, the earth, and all creatures as it seemed good unto Him, giving unto every creature its being, shape, form, and several offices to serve its Creator; that He doth also still uphold and govern them by His eternal providence and infinite power[2] for the service of mankind,[3] to the end that man may serve his God.[4]

He also created the angels good,[5] to be His messengers[6] and to serve His elect;[7] some of whom are fallen from that excellency in which God created them into everlasting perdition[8] and the others have, by the grace of God,[9] remained steadfast and continued in their primitive state. The devils and evil spirits are so depraved that they are enemies of God and every good thing, to the utmost of their power,[10] as murderers watching to ruin the Church and every member thereof, and by their wicked strategems to destroy all;[11] and are therefore, by their own wickedness, adjudged to eternal damnation, daily expecting their horrible torments.[12] Therefore we reject and abhor the error of the Sadducees who deny the existence of spirits and angels,[13] and also that of the Manichees who assert that the devils have their origin of themselves, and that they are wicked of their own nature, without having been corrupted.

[1] Gen. 1:1; Isa. 40:26; Heb. 3:4; Rev. 4:11; 1 Cor. 8:6; John 1:3; Col. 1:16 [2] Heb. 1:3; Ps. 104:10; Acts 17:25 [3] 1 Tim. 4:3–4; Gen. 1:29–30; 9:2–3; Ps. 104:14–15 [4] 1 Cor. 3:22; 6:20; Matt. 4:10 [5] Col. 1:16 [6] Ps. 103:20; 34:8; 148:2 [7] Heb. 1:14; Ps. 34:8 [8] John 8:44; 2 Peter 2:4; Luke 8:31; Jude 6 [9] Matt. 25:31 [10] 1 Peter 5:8; Job 1:7 [11] Gen. 3:1; Matt. 13:25; 2 Cor. 2:11; 11:3, 14 [12] Matt. 25:41; Luke 8:30, 31 [13] Acts 23:8

ARTICLE 13

Divine Providence

We believe that the same God, after He had created all things, did not forsake them, nor give them up to fortune or chance, but that He rules and governs them according to His holy will,[1] so that nothing happens in this world without His appointment;[2] nevertheless, God neither is the author of, nor can be charged with, the sins which are committed. For His power and goodness are so great and incomprehensible, that He orders and executes His work in the most excellent and just manner, even then when devils and wicked men act unjustly.[3] And as to what He doth surpassing human understanding, we will not curiously inquire into it further than our capacity will admit of; but with the greatest humility and reverence adore the righteous judgments of God which are hid from us,[4] contenting ourselves that we are disciples of Christ to learn only those things which He has revealed to us in His Word without transgressing these limits.

This doctrine affords us unspeakable consolation, since we are taught thereby that nothing can befall us by chance, but by the direction of our most gracious and heavenly Father, who watches over us with a paternal care, keeping all creatures so under His power[5] that not a hair of our head (for they are all numbered), nor a sparrow, can fall to the ground without the will of our Father,[6] in whom we do entirely trust; being persuaded that He so restrains the devil and all our enemies that, without His will and permission, they cannot hurt us. And therefore we reject that damnable error of the Epicureans, who say that God regards nothing, but leaves all things to chance.

[1] John 5:17; Heb. 1:3; Prov. 16:4; Ps. 104:9, etc.; Ps. 139:2, etc. [2] James 4:15; Job 1:21; 1 Kings 22:20; Acts 4:28; 1 Sam. 2:25; Ps. 115:3; 45:7; Amos 3:6; Deut. 19:5; Prov. 21:1; Ps. 105:25; Isa. 10:5–7; 2 Thess. 2:11; Ezek. 14:9; Rom. 1:28; Gen. 45:8; 1:20; 2 Sam. 16:10; Gen. 27:20; Ps. 75:7–8; Isa. 45:7; Prov. 16:4; Lam. 3:37–38; 1 Kings 22:34, 38; Ex. 21:13 [3] Matt. 8:31, 32; John 3:8 [4] Rom. 11:33–34 [5] Matt. 8:31; Job 1:12; 2:6 [6] Matt. 10:29–30

ARTICLE 14

The Creation and Fall of Man, and His Incapacity to Perform What is Truly Good

We believe that God created man out of the dust of the earth, and made and formed him after His own image and likeness,[1] good, righteous, and holy, capable in all things to will agreeably to the will of God.[2] But being in honor he understood it not, neither knew his excellency,[3] but willfully subjected himself to sin, and consequently to death and the curse, giving ear to the words of the devil.[4] For the commandment of life which he had received,[5] he transgressed; and by sin separated himself from God[6] who was his true life, having corrupted his whole nature,[7] whereby he made himself liable to corporal and spiritual death.[8] And being thus become wicked, perverse, and corrupt in all his ways, he hath lost all his excellent gifts which he had received from God[9] and only retained a few remains thereof,[10] which, however, are sufficient to leave man without excuse;[11] for all the light which is in us is changed into darkness,[12] as the Scriptures teach us, saying: *The light shineth in darkness, and the darkness comprehendeth*[13] *it not*; where St. John calleth men darkness.

Therefore we reject all that is taught repugnant to this concerning the free will of man, since man is but a slave to sin[14] and has nothing of himself unless it is given him from heaven.[15] For who may presume to boast that he of himself can do any good, since Christ saith, *No man can come to Me, except the Father which hath sent Me draw him?*[16] *Who will glory in his own will, who understands that to be carnally minded is enmity against God?*[17] Who can speak of his knowledge, since *the natural man receiveth not the things of the Spirit of God?*[18] In short, who dare suggest any thought, since he knows that *we are not sufficient of ourselves to think any thing as of ourselves, but that our sufficiency is of God?*[19] And therefore what the apostle saith ought justly to be held sure and firm, that *God worketh in us both to will and to do of His good pleasure.*[20] For there is no will nor understanding conformable to the divine will and understanding but what Christ hath wrought in man, which He teaches us when He saith, *Without Me ye can do nothing.*[21]

[1] Gen. 1:26; Eccl. 7:29; Eph. 4:24 [2] Gen. 1:31; Eph. 4:24 [3] Ps. 49:20; Isa. 59:2 [4] Gen. 3:6, 17 [5] Gen. 1:3, 7 [6] Isa. 59:2 [7] Eph. 4:18 [8] Rom.. 5:12; Gen. 2:17; 3:19 [9] Rom. 3:10 [10] Acts 14:16–17; 17:27 [11] Rom. 1:20, 21; Acts 17:27 [12] Eph. 5:8; Matt. 6:23 [13] John 1:5 [14] Isa. 26:12; Ps. 94:11; John 8:34; Rom. 6:17; 7:5, 17 [15] John 3:27; Isa. 26:12 [16] John 3:27; 6:44, 65 [17] Rom. 8:7 [18] 1 Cor. 2:14; Ps. 94:11 [19] 2 Cor. 3:5 [20] Phil. 2:13 [21] John 15:5

ARTICLE 15

Original Sin

We believe that through the disobedience of Adam original sin is extended to all mankind,[1] which is a corruption of the whole nature and an hereditary disease, wherewith infants themselves are infected even in their mother's womb,[2] and which produceth in man all sorts of sin, being in him as a root thereof;[3] and therefore is so vile and abominable in the sight of God that it is sufficient to condemn all mankind.[4] Nor is it by any means abolished or done away by baptism; since sin always issues forth from this woeful source as water from a fountain; notwithstanding it is not imputed to the children of God unto condemnation, but by His grace and mercy is forgiven them. Not that they should rest securely in sin, but that a sense of this corruption should make believers often to sigh, desiring to be delivered from this body of death.[5] Wherefore we reject the error of the Pelagians, who assert that sin proceeds only from imitation.

[1] Rom. 5:12, 13; Ps. 51:7; Rom. 3:10; Gen. 6:3; John 3:6; Job 14:4 [2] Isa. 48:8; Rom. 5:14 [3] Gal. 5:19; Rom. 7:8, 10, 13, 17–18, 20, 23 [4] Eph. 2:3, 5 [5] Rom. 7:18, 24

ARTICLE 16

Eternal Election

We believe that all the posterity of Adam, being thus fallen into perdition and ruin by the sin of our first parents, God then did manifest Himself such as He is; that is to say, *merciful and just:*[1] *merciful*, since He delivers and preserves from this perdition all whom He, in His eternal and unchangeable counsel, of mere goodness hath elected in Christ Jesus our Lord, without any respect to their works;[2] *just*, in leaving others in the fall and perdition wherein they have involved themselves.[3]

[1] Rom. 9:18,22–23; 3:12 [2] Rom. 9:15–16; 11:32; Eph. 2:8–10; Ps. 100:3; 1 John 4:10; Deut. 32:8; 1 Sam. 12:22; Ps. 115:5; Mal. 1:2; 2 Tim. 1:9; Rom. 8:29; 9:11, 21; 11:5–6; Eph. 1:4; Titus 3:4–5; Acts 2:47; 13:48; 2 Tim. 2:19–20; 1 Peter 1:2; John 6:27; 15:16; 17:9 [3] Rom. 9:17, 18; 2 Tim. 2:20

ARTICLE 17

The Recovery of Fallen Man

We believe that our most gracious God, in His admirable wisdom and goodness, seeing that man had thus thrown himself into temporal and spiritual death, and made himself wholly miserable, was pleased to seek and comfort him when he trembling[1] fled from His presence, promising him that He would give His Son, who should *be made of a woman, to bruise the head of the serpent*, and would make him happy.[2]

[1] Gen. 3:8–9, 19; Isa. 65:1–2 [2] Heb. 2:14; Gen. 22:18; Isa. 7:14; John 7:42; 2 Tim. 2:8; Heb. 7:14; Gen. 3:15; Gal. 4:4

ARTICLE 18

The Incarnation of Jesus Christ

We confess, therefore, that God did fulfill the promise which He made to the fathers by the mouth of His holy prophets[1] when He sent into the world, at the time appointed by Him, His own only-begotten and eternal Son, *who took upon Him the form of a servant, and became like unto man,*[2] really assuming the true human nature, with all its infirmities, sin excepted,[3] being conceived in the womb of the blessed Virgin Mary, by the power of the Holy Ghost, without the means of man;[4] and did not only assume human nature as to the body, but also a true human soul,[5] that He might be a real man. For since the soul was lost as well as the body, it was necessary that He should take both upon him, to save both. Therefore we confess (in opposition to the heresy of the Anabaptists, who deny that Christ assumed human flesh of His mother) that Christ is become *a partaker of the flesh and blood of the children;*[6] that He is a *fruit of the loins of David* after the flesh;[7] *made of the seed of David according to the flesh;*[8] a *fruit of the womb* of the Virgin Mary;[9] *made of a woman;*[10] a *branch* of David;[11] a shoot of *the root of Jesse;*[12] *sprung from the tribe of Judah;*[13] *descended from the Jews according to the flesh:*[14] *of the seed of Abraham, since He took on Him the seed of Abraham,*[15] *and became like unto His brethren in all things, sin excepted;*[16] *so that in truth He is our Immanuel*, that is to say, *God with us.*[17]

[1] Isa. 11:1; Luke 1:55; Gen. 26:4; 2 Sam. 7:12; Ps. 132:11; Acts 13:23 [2] 1 Tim. 2:5; 3:16; Phil. 2:7 [3] Heb. 2:14–15; 4:15 [4] Luke 1:31, 34–35 [5] Matt. 26:38; John 12:27 [6] Heb. 2:14 [7] Acts 2:30 [8] Ps. 132:11; Rom. 1:3 [9] Luke 1:42 [10] Gal. 4:4 [11] Jer. 33:15 [12] Isa. 11:1 [13] Heb. 7:14 [14] Rom. 9:5 [15] Gen. 22:18; 2 Sam. 7:12; Matt. 1:1; Gal. 3:16 [16] Heb. 2:15–17 [17] Isa. 7:14; Matt. 1:23

ARTICLE 19

The Union and Distinction of the Two Natures in the Person of Christ

We believe that by this conception the person of the Son is inseparably united and connected with the human nature, so that there are not two Sons of God, nor two persons, but two natures united in one single person; yet that each nature retains its own distinct properties. As then the divine nature hath always remained uncreated, without beginning of days or end of life,[1] filling heaven and earth, so also hath the human nature not lost its properties, but remained a creature, having beginning of days, being a finite nature, and retaining all the properties of a real body.[2] And though He hath by His resurrection given immortality to the same, nevertheless He hath not changed the reality of His human nature, forasmuch as our salvation and resurrection also depend on the reality of His body.

But these two natures are so closely united in one person that they were not separated even by His death. Therefore that which He, when dying, commended into the hands of His Father, was a real human spirit, departing from His body.[3] But in the meantime the divine nature always remained united with the human, even when He lay in the grave; and the Godhead did not cease to be in Him, any more than it did when He was an infant, though it did not so clearly manifest itself for a while. Wherefore we confess that He is *very God* and *very man*: very God by His power to conquer death, and very man that He might die for us according to the infirmity of His flesh.

[1] Heb. 7:3 [2] 1 Cor. 15:13, 21; Phil. 3:21; Matt. 26:11; Acts 1:2, 11; 3:21; Luke 24:39; John 20:25, 27 [3] Luke 23:46; Matt. 27:50

ARTICLE 20

God Hath Manifested His Justice and Mercy in Christ

We believe that God, who is perfectly merciful and just, sent His Son to assume that nature in which the disobedience was committed, to make satisfaction in the same and to bear the punishment of sin by His most bitter passion and death.[1] God therefore manifested His justice against His Son when He laid our iniquities[2] upon Him and poured forth His mercy and goodness on us, who were guilty and worthy of damnation, out of mere and perfect love, giving His Son unto death for us and raising Him for our justification,[3] that through Him we might obtain immortality and life eternal.

[1] Heb. 2:14; Rom. 8:3, 32–33 [2] Isa. 53:6; John 1:29; 1 John 4:9 [3] Rom. 4:25

ARTICLE 21

The Satisfaction of Christ, Our Only High Priest, For Us

We believe that Jesus Christ is ordained with an oath to be an everlasting High Priest after the order of Melchizedek,[1] and that He hath presented Himself in our behalf before the Father to appease His wrath by His full satisfaction,[2] by offering Himself on the tree of the cross, and pouring out His precious blood to purge away our sins, as the prophets had foretold. For it is written, *He was wounded for our transgressions, He was bruised for our iniquities: the chastisement of our peace was upon Him, and with His stripes we are healed. He was brought as a lamb to the slaughter, and numbered with the transgressors;*[3] and condemned by Pontius Pilate as a malefactor, though he had first declared Him innocent.[4] Therefore, *He restored that which He took not away,*[5] and *suffered the just for the unjust,*[6] as well in His body as in His soul, feeling the terrible punishment which our sins had merited; insomuch that *His sweat became like unto drops of blood falling on the ground.*[7] He called out, *My God, My God, why hast Thou forsaken Me?*[8] and hath suffered all this for the remission of our sins.

Wherefore we justly say with the apostle Paul, *that we know nothing but Jesus Christ, and Him crucified;*[9] *we count all things but loss and dung for the excellency of the knowledge of Christ Jesus our Lord,*[10] in whose wounds we find all manner of consolation. Neither is it necessary to seek or invent any other means of being reconciled to God than this only sacrifice, once offered, by which believers are made perfect forever.[11] This is also the reason why He was called by the angel of God, *Jesus*, that is to say, *Savior*, because He should save His people from their sins.[12]

[1] Ps. 110:4; Heb. 5:10 [2] Col. 1:14; Rom. 5:8–9; Col. 2:14; Heb. 2:17; 9:14; Rom. 3:24; 8:2; John 15:3; Acts 2:24; 13:28; John 3:16; 1 Tim. 2:6 [3] Isa. 53:5, 7, 12 [4] Luke 23:22, 24; Acts 13:28; Ps. 22:16; John 18:38; Ps. 69:5; 1 Peter 3:18 [5] Ps. 69:5 [6] 1 Peter 3:18 [7] Luke 22:44 [8] Ps. 22:2; Matt. 27:46 [9] 1 Cor. 2:2 [10] Phil. 3:8 [11] Heb. 9:25–26; 10:14 [12] Matt. 1:21; Acts 4:12

ARTICLE 22

Our Justification Through Faith in Jesus Christ

We believe that to attain the true knowledge of this great mystery the Holy Ghost kindleth in our hearts an upright faith, which embraces Jesus Christ with all His merits, appropriates Him,[1] and seeks nothing more besides Him.[2] For it must needs follow, either that all things which are requisite to our salvation are not in Jesus Christ, or if all things are in Him, that then those who possess Jesus Christ through faith have complete salvation in Him.[3] Therefore, for any to assert that Christ is not sufficient, but that something more is required besides Him, would be too gross a blasphemy; for hence it would follow that Christ was but half a Savior.

Therefore we justly say with Paul, *that we are justified by faith alone*, or *by faith without works.*[4] However, to speak more clearly, we do not mean that faith itself justifies us, for it is only an instrument with which we embrace Christ our Righteousness. But Jesus Christ, imputing to us all His merits and so many holy works which He hath done for us and in our stead, is our Righteousness.[5] And faith is an instrument that keeps us in communion with Him in all His benefits, which, when they become ours, are more than sufficient to acquit us of our sins.

[1] Eph. 3:16–17; Ps. 51:13; Eph. 1:17–18; 1 Cor. 2:12 [2] 1 Cor. 2:2; Acts 4:12; Gal. 2:21; Jer. 23:6; 1 Cor. 1:30; Jer. 31:10 [3] Matt. 1:21; Rom. 3:27; 8:1, 33 [4] Rom. 3:27; Gal. 2:6; 1 Peter 1:4–5; Rom. 10:4 [5] Jer. 23:6; 1 Cor. 1:30; 2 Tim. 1:2; Luke 1:77; Rom. 3:24–25; 4:5; Ps. 32:1–2; Phil. 3:9; Titus 3:5; 2 Tim. 1:9

ARTICLE 23

Wherein Our Justification Before God Consists

We believe that our salvation consists in the remission of our sins for Jesus Christ's sake, and that therein our righteousness before God is implied; as David and Paul teach us, declaring this to be the happiness of man, that God imputes righteousness to him without works.[1] And the same apostle saith, that *we are justified freely by His grace, through the redemption which is in Jesus Christ.*[2]

And therefore we always hold fast this foundation, ascribing all the glory to God,[3] humbling ourselves before Him, and acknowledging ourselves to be such as we really are, without presuming to trust in any thing in ourselves or in any merit of ours,[4] relying and resting upon the obedience of Christ crucified alone,[5] which becomes ours when we believe in Him.[6] This is sufficient to cover all our iniquities and to give us confidence in approaching to God;[7] freeing the conscience of fear, terror, and dread, without following the example of our first father, Adam, who, trembling, attempted to cover himself with fig leaves.[8] And verily, if we should appear before God relying on ourselves or on any other creature, though ever so little, we should, alas! be consumed.[9] And therefore every one must pray with David: *O Lord, enter not into judgment with Thy servant: for in Thy sight shall no man living be justified.*[10]

[1] Luke 1:77; Col. 1:14; Ps. 32:1–2; Rom. 4:6–7 [2] Rom. 3:23–24; Acts 4:12 [3] Ps. 115:1; 1 Cor. 4:7; Rom. 4:2 [4] 1 Cor. 4:7; Rom. 4:2; 1 Cor. 1:29, 31 [5] Rom. 5:19 [6] Heb. 11:6–7; Eph. 2:8; 2 Cor. 5:19; 1 Tim. 2:6 [7] Rom. 5:1; Eph. 3:12; 1 John 2:1 [8] Gen. 3:7 [9] Isa. 33:14; Deut. 27:26; James 2:10 [10] Ps. 130:3; Matt. 18:23–26; Ps. 143:2; Luke 16:15

ARTICLE 24

Man's Sanctification and Good Works

We believe that this true faith, being wrought in man by the hearing of the Word of God and the operation of the Holy Ghost,[1] doth regenerate and make him a new man, causing him to live a new life[2] and freeing him from the bondage of sin.[3] Therefore it is so far from being true that this justifying faith makes men remiss in a pious and holy life,[4] that on the contrary without it they would never do anything out of love to God, but only out of self-love or fear of damnation. Therefore it is impossible that this holy faith can be unfruitful in man; for we do not speak of a vain faith,[5] but of such a faith as is called in Scripture a faith that worketh by love,[6] which excites man to the practice of those works which God has commanded in His Word. Which works, as they proceed from the good root of faith, are good and acceptable in the sight of God, forasmuch as they are all sanctified by His grace; howbeit they are of no account towards our justification.[7] For it is by faith in Christ that we are justified, even before we do good works;[8] otherwise they could not be good works, any more than the fruit of a tree can be good before the tree itself is good.[9]

Therefore we do good works, but not to merit by them (for what can we merit?)—nay, we are beholden to God for the good works we do and not He to us,[10] *since it is He that worketh in us both to will and to do of His good pleasure.*[11] Let us therefore attend to what is written: *When ye shall have done all those things which are commanded you, say we are unprofitable servants: we have done that which was our duty to do.*[12]

In the meantime we do not deny that God rewards our good works, but it is through His grace that He crowns His gifts.[13] Moreover, though we do good works, we do not found our salvation upon them;[14] for we can do no work but what is polluted by our flesh, and also punishable;[15] and although we could perform such works, still the remembrance of one sin is sufficient to make God reject them. Thus, then, we would always be in doubt, tossed to and fro without any certainty, and our poor consciences would be continually vexed if they relied not on the merits of the suffering and death of our Savior.[16]

[1] 1 Peter 1:23; Rom. 10:17; John 5:24 [2] 1 Thess. 1:5; Rom. 8:15; John 6:29; Col. 2:12; Phil. 1:1, 29; Eph. 2:8 [3] Acts 15:9; Rom. 6:4, 22; Titus 2:12; John 8:36 [4] Titus 2:12 [5] Titus 3:8; John 15:5; Heb. 11:6; 1 Tim. 1:5 [6] 1 Tim. 1:5; Gal. 5:6; Titus 3:8 [7] 2 Tim. 1:9; Rom. 9:32; Titus 3:5 [8] Rom. 4:4; Gen. 4:4 [9] Heb. 11:6; Rom. 14:23; Gen. 4:4; Matt. 7:17 [10] 1 Cor. 4:7; Isa. 26:12; Gal. 3:5; 1 Thess. 2:13 [11] Phil. 2:13 [12] Luke 17:10 [13] Matt. 10:42; 25:34–35; Rev. 3:12, 21; Rom. 2:6; Rev. 2:11; 2 John 8; Rom. 11:6 [14] Eph. 2:9–10 [15] Isa. 64:6 [16] Isa. 28:16; Rom. 10:11; Hab. 2:4

ARTICLE 25

The Abolishing of the Ceremonial Law

We believe that the ceremonies and figures of the law ceased at the coming of Christ[1] and that all the shadows are accomplished, so that the use of them must be abolished among Christians;[2] yet the truth and substance of them remain with us in Jesus Christ, in whom they have their completion. In the meantime we still use the testimonies taken out of the law and the prophets, to confirm us in the doctrine of the gospel,[3] and to regulate our life in all honesty to the glory of God, according to His will.

[1] Rom. 10:4 [2] Gal. 5:2–4; 3:1; 4:10–11; Col. 2:16–1 [3] 2 Peter 1:19

ARTICLE 26

Christ's Intercession

We believe that we have no access unto God but alone through the only Mediator and Advocate, Jesus Christ the righteous,[1] who therefore became man, having united in one person the divine and human natures, that we men might have access to the divine Majesty, which access would otherwise be barred against us. But this Mediator, whom the Father hath appointed between Him and us, ought in no wise affright us by His majesty, or cause us to seek another according to our fancy.[2] For there is no creature, either in heaven or on earth, who loveth us more than Jesus Christ;[3] *who, though He was in the form of God, yet made Himself of no reputation, and took upon Him the form of a man and of a servant for us,*[4] *and was made like unto His brethren in all things.* If, then, we should seek for another mediator who would be well affected towards us, whom could we find who loved us more than He who laid down His life for us, even when we were His enemies?[5] And if we seek for one who hath power and majesty, who is there that hath so much of both as *He who sits at the right hand of His Father*, and who hath *all power in heaven and on earth*?[6] And who will sooner be heard than the own well-beloved Son of God?

Therefore it was only through distrust that this practice of dishonoring instead of honoring the saints was introduced, doing that which they never have done nor required, but have, on the contrary, steadfastly rejected, according to their bounden duty, as appears by their writings.[7] Neither must we plead here our unworthiness; for the meaning is not that we should offer our prayers to God on account of our own worthiness, but only on account of the excellency and worthiness of the Lord Jesus Christ,[8] whose righteousness is become ours by faith.

Therefore the apostle, to remove this foolish fear or rather distrust, from us, justly saith that *Jesus Christ was made like unto His brethren in all things, that He might be a merciful and faithful High Priest, to make reconciliation for the sins of the people. For in that He Himself hath suffered, being tempted, He is able to succor them that are tempted.*[9] And further to encourage us, he adds: *Seeing, then, that we have a great High Priest that is passed into the heavens, Jesus the Son of God, let us hold fast our profession. For we have not a High Priest which cannot be touched with the feeling of our infirmities; but was in all points tempted like as we are, yet without sin. Let us therefore come boldly unto the throne of grace, that we may obtain mercy, and find grace to help in time of need.*[10] The same apostle saith: *Having boldness to enter into the holiest by the blood of Jesus, let us draw near with a true heart in full assurance of faith,* etc.[11] Likewise, *Christ hath an unchangeable priesthood, wherefore He is able also to save them to the uttermost that come unto God by Him, seeing He ever liveth to make intercession for them.*[12]

What more can be required? since Christ Himself saith: *I am the way, and the truth, and the life; no man cometh unto the Father but by Me.*[13] To what purpose should we then seek another advocate,[14] since it hath pleased God to give us His own Son as our Advocate?[15] Let us not forsake Him to take another, or rather to seek after another, without ever being able to find Him; for God well knew, when He gave Him to us, that we were sinners.

Therefore, according to the command of Christ, we call upon the heavenly Father through Jesus Christ our only Mediator, as we are taught in the Lord's Prayer;[16] being assured that whatever we ask of the Father in His Name will be granted us.[17]

[1] 1 Tim. 2:5; 1 John 2:1; Rom. 8:33 [2] Hosea. 13:9; Jer. 2:13, 3 [3] John 10:11; 1 John 4:10; Rom. 5:8; Eph. 3:19; John 15:1 [4] Phil. 2:7 [5] Rom. 5:8 [6] Mark 16:19; Col. 3:1; Rom. 8:33; Matt. 11:27; 28:18 [7] Acts 10:26; 14:15 [8] Dan. 9:17–18; John 16:23; Eph. 3:12; Acts 4:12; 1 Cor. 1:31; Eph. 2:18 [9] Heb. 2:17,18 [10] Heb. 4:14–16 [11] Heb. 10:19, 22 [12] Heb. 7:24, 25 [13] John 14:6 [14] Ps. 44:21 [15] 1 Tim. 2:5; 1 John 2:1; Rom. 8:33 [16] Luke 11:2 [17] John 4:17; 16:23; 14:13

ARTICLE 27

The Catholic Christian Church

We believe and profess one catholic or universal Church,[1] which is a holy congregation of true Christian believers, all expecting their salvation in Jesus Christ, being washed by His blood, sanctified and sealed by the Holy Ghost.

This Church hath been from the beginning of the world and will be to the end thereof,[2] which is evident from this, that Christ is an eternal king, which, without subjects He cannot be.[3] And this holy Church is preserved or supported by God against the rage of the whole world;[4] though she sometimes (for a while) appears very small, and in the eyes of men, to be reduced to nothing,[5] as during the perilous reign of Ahab when nevertheless *the Lord reserved unto Him seven thousand men, who had not bowed their knees to Baal.*[6]

Furthermore, this holy Church is not confined, bound, or limited to a certain place or to certain persons, but is spread and dispersed over the whole world; and yet is joined and united with heart and will,[7] by the power of faith, in one and the same spirit.[8]

[1] Isa. 2:2; Ps. 46:5; 102:14; Jer. 31:36 [2] Matt. 28:20; 2 Sam. 7:16 [3] Luke 1:32–33; Ps. 89:37–38; 110:2–4 [4] Matt. 16:18; John 16:33; Gen. 22:17; 2 Tim. 2:19 [5] Luke 12:32; Isa. 1:9; Rev. 12:6, 14; Luke 17:21; Matt. 16:18 [6] Rom. 12:4; 11:2, 4; 1 Kings 19:18; Isa. 1:9; Rom. 9:29 [7] Acts 4:32 [8] Eph. 4:3–4

ARTICLE 28

Every One is Bound to Join Himself to the True Church

We believe, since this holy congregation is an assembly of those who are saved and out of it there is no salvation,[1] that no person of whatsoever state or condition he may be ought to withdraw himself to live in a separate state from it;[2] but that all men are in duty bound to join and unite themselves with it, maintaining the unity of the Church;[3] submitting themselves to the doctrine and discipline thereof; bowing their necks under the yoke of Jesus Christ;[4] and as mutual members of the same body,[5] serving to the edification of the brethren, according to the talents God has given them.

And that this may be the more effectually observed, it is the duty of all believers, according to the Word of God, to separate themselves from those who do not belong to the Church,[6] and to join themselves to this congregation wheresoever God hath established it,[7] even though the magistrates and edicts of princes be against it; yea, though they should suffer death or any other corporal punishment.[8] Therefore all those who separate themselves from the same or do not join themselves to it, act contrary to the ordinance of God.

[1] 1 Peter 3:20; Joel 2:32 [2] Acts 2:40; Isa. 52:11 [3] Ps. 22:23; Eph. 4:3, 12; Heb. 2:12 [4] Ps. 2:10–12; Matt. 11:29 [5] Eph. 4:12, 16; 1 Cor. 12:12, etc. [6] Acts 2:40; Isa. 52:11; 2 Cor. 6:17; Rev. 18:4 [7] Matt. 12:30; 24:28; Isa. 49:22; Rev. 17:14 [8] Dan. 3:17–18; 6:8–10; Rev. 14:14; Acts 4:17, 19; 17:7; 18:13

ARTICLE 29

The Marks of the True Church, and Wherein She Differs From the False Church

We believe that we ought diligently and circumspectly to discern from the Word of God which is the true Church, since all sects which are in the world assume to themselves the name of the Church. But we speak here not of hypocrites, who are mixed in the Church with the good, yet are not of the Church, though externally in it;[1] but we say that the body and communion of the true Church must be distinguished from all sects who call themselves the Church.

The marks by which the true Church is known are these: if the pure doctrine of the gospel is preached therein;[2] if she maintains the pure administration of the sacraments as instituted by Christ;[3] if church discipline is exercised in punishing of sin;[4] in short, if all things are managed according to the pure Word of God, all things contrary thereto rejected,[5] and Jesus Christ acknowledged as the only Head of the Church.[6] Hereby the true Church may certainly be known, from which no man has a right to separate himself.

With respect to those who are members of the Church, they may be known by the marks of Christians, namely, by faith;[7] and when they have received Jesus Christ the only Savior,[8] they avoid sin, follow after righteousness,[9] love the true God and their neighbor, neither turn aside to the right or left, and crucify the flesh with the works thereof.[10] But this is not to be understood as if there did not remain in them great infirmities; but they fight against them through the Spirit all the days of their life,[11] continually taking their refuge in the blood, death, passion, and obedience of our Lord Jesus Christ, *in whom they have remission of sins through faith in Him*.[12]

As for the false Church, she ascribes more power and authority to herself and her ordinances than to the Word of God,[13] and will not submit herself to the yoke of Christ.[14] Neither does she administer the sacraments as appointed by Christ in His Word, but adds to and takes from them as she thinks proper; she relieth more upon men than upon Christ; and persecutes those who live holily according to the Word of God,[15] and rebuke her for her errors, covetousness, and idolatry.[16] These two Churches are easily known and distinguished from each other.

[1] Matt. 13:22; 2 Tim. 2:18–20; Rom. 9:6 [2] John 10:27; Eph. 2:20; Acts 17:11–12; Col. 1:23; John 8:47 [3] Matt. 28:19; Luke 22:19; 1 Cor. 11:23 [4] Matt. 18:15–18; 2 Thess. 3:14–15 [5] Matt. 28:2; Gal. 1:6–8 [6] Eph. 1:22–23; John 10:4–5, 14 [7] Eph. 1:13; John 17:20 [8] 1 John 4:2 [9] 1 John 3:8–10 [10] Rom. 6:2; Gal. 5:24 [11] Rom. 7:6, 17; Gal. 5:17 [12] Col. 1:14 [13] Col. 2:18–19 [14] Ps. 2:3 [15] Rev. 12:4; John 16:2 [16] Rev. 17:3, 4, 6

ARTICLE 30

The Government of and Offices in the Church

We believe that this true Church must be governed by the spiritual policy which our Lord hath taught us in His Word— namely, that there must be ministers or pastors to preach the Word of God, and to administer the sacraments;[1] also elders and deacons, who, together with the pastors, form the council of the Church;[2] that by these means the true religion may be preserved, and the true doctrine everywhere propagated, likewise transgressors punished and restrained by spiritual means;[3] also that the poor and distressed may be relieved and comforted, according to their necessities. By these means everything will be carried on in the Church with good order and decency, when faithful men are chosen according to the rule prescribed by St. Paul in his epistle to Timothy.[4]

[1] Eph. 4:11; 1 Cor. 4:1–2; 2 Cor. 5:20; John 20:23; Acts 26:17–18; Luke 10:16 [2] Acts 6:3; 14:23 [3] Matt. 18:17; 1 Cor. 5:4–5 [4] 1 Tim. 3:1; Titus 1:5

ARTICLE 31

The Ministers, Elders, and Deacons

We believe that the ministers of God's Word,[1] and the elders and deacons,[2] ought to be chosen to their respective offices by a lawful election of the Church, with calling upon the name of the Lord, and in that order which the Word of God teacheth. Therefore every one must take heed not to intrude himself by indecent means, but is bound to wait till it shall please God to call him,[3] that he may have testimony of his calling, and be certain and assured that it is of the Lord.

As for the ministers of God's Word, they have equally the same power and authority wheresoever they are, as they are all ministers of Christ,[4] the only universal Bishop and the only Head of the Church.[5]

Moreover, that this holy ordinance of God may not be violated or slighted, we say that every one ought to esteem the ministers of God's Word and the elders of the Church very highly for their work's sake, and be at peace with them without murmuring, strife, or contention,[6] as much as possible.

[1] 1 Tim. 5:22 [2] Acts 6:3 [3] Jer. 23:21; Heb. 5:4; Acts 1:23; 13:2 [4] 1 Cor. 4:1; 3:9; 2 Cor. 5:20; Acts 26:16–17 [5] 1 Peter 2:25; 5:4; Isa. 61:1; Eph. 1:22; Col. 1:18 [6] 1 Thess. 5:12, 13; 1 Tim. 5:17; Heb. 13:17

ARTICLE 32

The Order and Discipline of the Church

In the meantime we believe, though it is useful and beneficial, that those who are rulers of the Church institute and establish certain ordinances among themselves for maintaining the body of the Church; yet they ought studiously to take care that they do not depart from those things which Christ, our only Master, hath instituted.[1] And therefore, we reject all human inventions, and all laws which man would introduce into the worship of God, thereby to bind and compel the conscience in any manner whatever.[2]

Therefore we admit only of that which tends to nourish and preserve concord and unity, and to keep all men in obedience to God. For this purpose excommunication or church discipline is requisite, with the several circumstances belonging to it, according to the Word of God.[3]

[1] Col. 2:6–7 [2] 1 Cor. 7:23; Matt. 15:9; Isa. 29:13; Gal. 5:1; Rom. 16:17–18 [3] Matt. 18:17; 1 Cor. 5:5; 1 Tim. 1:20

ARTICLE 33

The Sacraments

We believe that our gracious God, on account of our weakness and infirmities, hath ordained the sacraments for us, thereby to seal unto us His promises,[1] and to be pledges of the good will and grace of God toward us, and also to nourish and strengthen our faith, which He hath joined to the Word of the gospel, the better to present to our senses both that which He signifies to us by His Word, and that which He works inwardly in our hearts, thereby assuring and confirming in us the salvation which He imparts to us. For they are visible signs and seals of an inward and invisible thing, by means whereof God worketh in us by the power of the Holy Ghost. Therefore the signs are not in vain or insignificant, so as to deceive us. For Jesus Christ is the true object presented by them, without whom they would be of no moment.[2]

Moreover, we are satisfied with the number of sacraments which Christ our Lord hath instituted, which are two only, namely, the sacrament of baptism and the Holy Supper of our Lord Jesus Christ.[3]

[1] Rom. 4:11; Gen. 9:13; 17:11 [2] Col. 2:11, 17; 1 Cor. 5:7 [3] Matt. 26:36; 28:19

ARTICLE 34

Holy Baptism

We believe and confess that Jesus Christ, who is the end of the law,[1] hath made an end, by the shedding of His blood, of all other sheddings of blood which men could or would make as a propitiation or satisfaction for sin; and that He, having abolished circumcision, which was done with blood, hath instituted the sacrament of baptism[2] instead thereof, by which we are received into the Church of God, and separated from all other people and strange religions, that we may wholly belong to Him whose ensign and banner we bear, and which serves as a testimony unto us that He will forever be our gracious God and Father.

Therefore He has commanded all those who are His to be baptized with pure water, *in the name of the Father, and of the Son, and of the Holy Ghost*,[3] thereby signifying to us, that as water washeth away the filth of the body, when poured upon it, and is seen on the body of the baptized, when sprinkled upon him, so doth the blood of Christ, by the power of the Holy Ghost, internally sprinkle the soul, cleanse it from its sins, and regenerate us from children of wrath unto children of God.[4] Not that this is effected by the external water, but by the sprinkling of the precious blood of the Son of God,[5] who is our Red Sea, through which we must pass to escape the tyranny of Pharaoh, that is, the devil, and to enter into the spiritual land of Canaan.

Therefore the ministers on their part administer the sacrament and that which is visible,[6] but our Lord giveth that which is signified by the sacrament, namely, the gifts and invisible grace; washing, cleansing, and purging our souls of all filth and unrighteousness;[7] renewing our hearts and filling them with all comfort; giving unto us a true assurance of His fatherly goodness; putting on us the new man, and putting off the old man with all his deeds.[8]

Therefore we believe that every man who is earnestly studious of obtaining life eternal ought to be but once baptized with this only baptism, without ever repeating the same,[9] since we cannot be born twice. Neither doth this baptism only avail us at the time when the water is poured upon us and received by us, but also through the whole course of our life.[10]

Therefore we detest the error of the Anabaptists, who are not content with the one only baptism they have once received, and moreover condemn the baptism of the infants of believers, whom we believe ought to be baptized and sealed with the sign of the covenant,[11] as the children in Israel formerly were circumcised[12] upon the same promises which are made unto our children. And indeed, Christ shed His blood no less for the washing of the children of the faithful than for adult persons;[13] and therefore, they ought to receive the sign and sacrament of that which Christ hath done for them; as the Lord commanded in the law, that they should be made partakers of the sacrament of Christ's suffering and death shortly after they were born, by offering for them a lamb, which was a sacrament of Jesus Christ.[14] Moreover, what circumcision was to the Jews, that baptism is to our children. And for this reason Paul calls baptism the *circumcision of Christ.*[15]

[1] Rom. 10:4 [2] Col. 2:11; 1 Peter 3:21; 1 Cor. 10:2 [3] Matt. 28:19 [4] 1 Cor. 6:11; Titus 3:5; Heb. 9:14; 1 John 1:7; Rev. 1:6 [5] John 19:34 [6] Matt. 3:11; 1 Cor. 3:5, 7; Rom. 6:3 [7] Eph. 5:26; Acts 22:16; 1 Peter 3:21 [8] Gal. 3:27; 1 Cor. 12:13; Eph. 4:22–24 [9] Mark 16:16; Matt. 28:19; Eph. 4:5; Heb. 6:2 [10] Acts 2:38; 8:16 [11] Matt. 19:14; 1 Cor. 7:14 [12] Gen. 17:11–12 [13] Col. 2:11–12 [14] John 1:29; Lev. 12:6 [15] Col. 2:11

ARTICLE 35

The Holy Supper of Our Lord Jesus Christ

We believe and confess that our Savior Jesus Christ did ordain and institute the sacrament of the Holy Supper[1] to nourish and support those whom He hath already regenerated and incorporated into His family, which is His Church.

Now those who are regenerated have in them a twofold life:[2] the one corporal and temporal, which they have from the first birth and is common to all men; the other spiritual and heavenly, which is given them in their second birth,[3] which is effected by the word of the gospel[4] in the communion of the body of Christ; and this life is not common, but is peculiar to God's elect.[5] In like manner God hath given us, for the support of the bodily and earthly life, earthly and common bread which is subservient thereto and is common to all men, even as life itself. But for the support of the spiritual and heavenly life which believers have, He hath sent a living bread which descended from heaven, namely, Jesus Christ,[6] who nourishes and strengthens the spiritual life of believers when they eat Him, that is to say, when they apply and receive Him by faith in the Spirit.[7]

Christ, that He might represent unto us this spiritual and heavenly bread, hath instituted an earthly and visible bread as a sacrament of His body, and wine as a sacrament of His blood,[8] to testify by them unto us that as certainly as we receive and hold this sacrament in our hands, and eat and drink the same with our mouths, by which our life is afterwards nourished, we also do as certainly receive by faith (which is the hand and mouth of our soul) the true body and blood of Christ our only Savior in our souls, for the support of our spiritual life.[9]

Now as it is certain and beyond all doubt that Jesus Christ hath not enjoined to us the use of His sacraments in vain, so He works in us all that He represents to us by these holy signs, though the manner surpasses our understanding and cannot be comprehended by us, as the operations of the Holy Ghost are hidden and incomprehensible. In the meantime we err not when we say that what is eaten and drunk by us is the proper and natural body and the proper blood of Christ.[10] But the manner of our partaking of the same is not by the mouth, but by the

Spirit through faith. Thus, then, though Christ always sits at the right hand of His Father in the heavens,[11] yet doth He not therefore cease to make us partakers of Himself by faith. This feast is a spiritual table at which Christ communicates Himself with all His benefits to us, and gives us there to enjoy both Himself and the merits of His sufferings and death,[12] nourishing, strengthening, and comforting our poor comfortless souls by the eating of His flesh, quickening and refreshing them by the drinking of His blood.[13]

Further, though the sacraments are connected with the thing signified, nevertheless both are not received by all men; the ungodly indeed receives the sacrament to his condemnation,[14] but he doth not receive the truth of the sacrament. As Judas and Simon the sorcerer, both indeed received the sacrament, but not Christ who was signified by it, of whom believers only are made partakers.

Lastly, we receive this holy sacrament in the assembly of the people of God with humility and reverence,[15] keeping up among us a holy remembrance of the death of Christ our Savior with thanksgiving, making there confession of our faith and of the Christian religion. Therefore no one ought to come to this table without having previously rightly examined himself; lest by eating of this bread and drinking of this cup he eat and drink judgment to himself. [16] In a word, we are excited by the use of this holy sacrament to a fervent love towards God and our neighbor.

Therefore we reject all mixtures and damnable inventions which men have added unto and blended with the sacraments as profanations of them, and affirm that we ought to rest satisfied with the ordinance which Christ and His apostles have taught us, and that we must speak of them in the same manner as they have spoken.

---

[1] Matt. 26:26; Mark 14:22; Luke 22:19; 1 Cor. 11:23–25 [2] John 3:6 [3] John 3:5 [4] John 5:23, 25 [5] 1 John 5:12; John 10:28 [6] John 6:32–33, 51 [7] John 6:63 [8] Mark 6:26 [9] 1 Cor.. 10:16–17; Eph. 3:17; John 6:35 [10] John 6:55–56; 1 Cor. 10:16 [11] Acts 3:21; Mark 16:19; Matt. 26:11 [12] Matt. 26:26, etc.; Luke 22:19–20; 1 Cor. 10:2–4 [13] Isa. 55:2; Rom. 8:22–23 [14] 1 Cor. 11:29; 2 Cor. 6:14–15; 1 Cor. 2:14 [15] Acts 2:42; 20:7 [16] 1 Cor. 11:27–28

ARTICLE 36

The Magistrates

We believe that our gracious God, because of the depravity of mankind, hath appointed kings, princes, and magistrates,[1] willing that the world should be governed by certain laws and policies; to the end that the dissoluteness of men might be restrained, and all things carried on among them with good order and decency. For this purpose He hath invested the magistracy with the sword, *for the punishment of evil doers, and for the praise of them that do well.* And their office is not only to have regard unto and watch for the welfare of the civil state, but also that they protect the sacred ministry, and thus may remove and prevent all idolatry and false worship;[2] that the kingdom of antichrist may be thus destroyed and the kingdom of Christ promoted. They must, therefore, countenance the preaching of the word of the gospel everywhere, that God may be honored and worshipped by every one, as He commands in His Word. Moreover, it is the bounden duty of every one, of what state, quality, or condition soever he may be, to subject himself to the magistrates;[3] to pay tribute,[4] to show due honor and respect to them, and to obey them in all things which are not repugnant to the Word of God;[5] to supplicate for them in their prayers, that God may rule and guide them in all their ways, and that we may lead a quiet and peaceable life in all godliness and honesty.[6] Wherefore we detest the error of the Anabaptists and other seditious people, and in general all those who reject the higher powers and magistrates, and would subvert justice,[7] introduce a community of goods, and confound that decency and good order which God hath established among men.[8]

---

[1] Ex. 18:20, etc.; Rom. 13:1; Prov. 8:15; Jer. 21:12; 22:2–3; Ps. 82:1, 6; 101:2; Deut. 1:15–16; 16:18; 17:15; Dan. 2:21, 37; 5:18 [2] Isa. 49:23, 25; 1 Kings 15:12; 2 Kings 23:2–4 [3] Titus 3:1; Rom. 13:1 [4] Mark 12:17; Matt. 17:24 [5] Acts 4:17–19; 5:29; Hosea 5:11 [6] Jer. 29:7; 1 Tim. 2:1–2 [7] 2 Peter 2:10 [8] Jude 8, 10

ARTICLE 37

The Last Judgment

Finally, we believe according to the Word of God, when the time appointed by the Lord (which is unknown to all creatures)[1] is come, and the number of the elect complete, that our Lord

Jesus Christ will come from heaven, corporally and visibly, as He ascended,[2] with great glory and majesty to declare Himself Judge of the quick and the dead,[3] burning this old world with fire and flame to cleanse it.[4] And then all men will personally appear before this great Judge, both men and women, and children, that have been from the beginning of the world to the end thereof,[5] being summoned by the voice of the archangel and by the sound of the trumpet of God.[6] For all the dead shall be raised out of the earth, and their souls joined and united with their proper bodies in which they formerly lived.[7] As for those who shall then be living, they shall not die as the others, but be changed in the twinkling of an eye, and from corruptible become incorruptible.[8]

Then the books (that is to say, the consciences) shall be opened, and the dead judged according to what they shall have done in this world, whether it be good or evil.[9] Nay, all men shall give an account of every idle word they have spoken, which the world only counts amusement and jest;[10] and then the secrets and hypocrisy of men shall be disclosed and laid open before all.[11]

And, therefore, the consideration of this judgment is justly terrible and dreadful to the wicked and ungodly,[12] but most desirable and comfortable to the righteous and the elect; because then their full deliverance shall be perfected, and there they shall receive the fruits of their labor and trouble which they have borne.[13] Their innocence shall be known to all, and they shall see the terrible vengeance which God shall execute on the wicked,[14] who most cruelly persecuted, oppressed, and tormented them in this world;[15] and who shall be convicted by the testimony of their own consciences,[16] and, being immortal, shall be tormented in that everlasting fire[17] which is prepared for the devil and his angels.[18]

But on the contrary, the faithful and elect shall be crowned with glory and honor;[19] and the Son of God will confess their names before God His Father and His elect angels;[20] all tears shall be wiped from their eyes;[21] and their cause, which is now condemned by many judges and magistrates as heretical and impious, will then be known to be the cause of the Son of God.[22] And for a gracious reward, the Lord will cause them to possess such a glory as never entered into the heart of man to conceive.[23]

Therefore we expect that great day with a most ardent desire, to the end that we may fully enjoy the promises of God in Christ Jesus our Lord.[24] Amen.

Even so, come, Lord Jesus (Rev. 22:20).

---

[1] Matt. 24:36; 25:13; 1 Thess. 5:1–2; Rev. 6:11; Acts 1:7; 2 Peter 3:10 [2] Acts 1:11 [3] 2 Thess. 1:7–8; Acts 17:31; Matt. 24:30; 25:31; Jude 15; 1 Peter 4:5; 2 Tim. 4:1 [4] 2 Peter 3:7, 10; 2 Thess. 1:8 [5] Rev. 20:12–13; Acts 17:31; Heb. 6:2; 9:27; 2 Cor. 5:10; Rom. 14:10 [6] 1 Cor. 15:42; Rev. 20:12–13; 1 Thess. 4:16 [7] John 5:28–29; 6:54; Dan. 12:2; Job 19:26–27 [8] 1 Cor. 15:51–53 [9] Rev. 20:12–13; 1 Cor. 4:5; Rom. 14:11–12; Job 34:11; John 5:24; Dan. 12:2; Ps. 62:12; Matt. 11:22; 23:33; John 5:29; Rom. 2:5–6; 2 Cor. 5:10; Heb. 6:2; 9:27 [10] Rom. 2:5; Jude 15; Matt. 12:36 [11] 1 Cor. 4:5; Rom. 2:1–2, 16; Matt. 7:1–2 [12] Rev. 6:15–16; Heb. 10:27 [13] Luke 21:28; 1 John 3:2; 4:17; Rev. 14:7; 2 Thess. 1:5–7; Luke 14:14 [14] Dan. 7:26 [15] Matt. 25:46; 2 Thess. 1:6–8; Mal. 4:3 [16] Rom. 2:15 [17] Rev. 21:8; 2 Peter 2:9 [18] Mal. 4:1; Matt. 25:41 [19] Matt. 25:34; 13:43 [20] Matt. 10:32 [21] Isa. 25:8; Rev. 21:4 [22] Isa. 66:5 [23] Isa. 64:4; 1 Cor. 2:9 [24] Heb. 10:36–38

The HEIDELBERG Catechism

METHOD OF INSTRUCTION IN THE CHRISTIAN RELIGION AS THE SAME IS TAUGHT IN THE REFORMED CHURCHES AND SCHOOLS IN HOLLAND AND IN AMERICA

The Heidelberg Catechism received its name from being composed in Heidelberg at the request of Elector Frederick III (1516–1576), ruler of the Palatinate, an influential German province. To secure harmony in Protestant teaching and to facilitate the establishment of the Reformed faith in his province, this pious prince commissioned Zacharias Ursinus (1534–1583), twenty-eight years of age and professor of theology at the Heidelberg University, and Caspar Olevianus (1536–1587), twenty-six years old and Frederick's court preacher, to prepare a Reformed catechism for instructing the youth and guiding pastors and teachers. Of these two young and learned divines, Ursinus bore the primary responsibility for the Catechism's material content, while Olevianus was more involved in final composition and editing. Blessed by the Spirit, "the learning of Ursinus and the eloquence of Olevianus are reflected in the final product—a catechism of unusual power and beauty, an acknowledged masterpiece." Further, Frederick indicates that many others, including the theological faculty and the chief officers of the Palatinate church, provided assistance in perfecting its final reading.

After the Catechism was approved by a Heidelberg Synod in January 1563, three additional German editions, each with small additions, as well as a Latin translation, were published the same year in Heidelberg. The fourth edition is regarded as the official text of the Catechism and is used as a basis for the English translation printed on the following pages.

When the first edition of the Heidelberg Catechism appeared, the German Bible had not yet been divided into verses. Consequently, Scripture passages listed in the margin included only book and chapter. Moreover, the Catechism's questions were not numbered. A Latin translation soon rectified these problems by including verse references and numbering the questions. Moreover, the Catechism was also soon divided into fifty-two sections so that one section—referred to as "Lord's Day"—could be expounded each Sunday of the year.

In this present edition the more than 700 textual references are recorded here for good reason. The Catechism contains more prooftexts than other catechisms of its day because its authors wanted it to be "an echo of the Bible." These prooftexts were to be regarded as an important part of the Catechism, as noted in Frederick's original preface: "The Scripture proof by which the faith of the children is confirmed are such only as have been selected with great pains from the divinely inspired Scriptures."

The Heidelberg Catechism's 129 questions and answers are divided into three parts patterned after the book of Romans. After a moving introduction related to the true believer's comfort, questions 3–11 consider the experience of sin and misery (Romans 1–3:20); questions 12–85 are concerned with redemption in Christ and faith (Romans 3:21–11:36), incorporating a lengthy exposition of the Apostles' Creed and the sacraments; and questions 86–129 stress true gratitude for God's deliverance (Romans 12–16), primarily through a consideration of the Ten Commandments and the Lord's Prayer. One of the Catechism's precious distinctives is its presentation of doctrines with clarity and warm piety in an experiential, practical manner. It is more subjective than objective, more spiritual than dogmatical. It is not surprising that the Catechism, so personal and devotional throughout as exemplified in its use of singular pronouns, has been called "the book of comfort" for God's people.

The Catechism was translated already in 1563 into Dutch by Petrus Dathenus and was published in his rhymed Psalter in 1566. Its personal style and experiential content soon won the love of God's people also in the Netherlands. Already that same year Peter Gabriel set a pattern for Dutch ministers by expounding the Catechism every Sunday afternoon to his Amsterdam congregation. Moreover, the Catechism was approved by the Synods of Wesel (1568), Embden (1571), Dort (1578), the Hague (1586), as well as the great Synod of Dort (1618–1619), which officially adopted it as the second of the Three Forms of Unity and made its weekly exposition by the ministers obligatory.

The Catechism has been translated into all European and dozens of Asiatic and African languages. It is thought to have been circulated more widely than any other book "except the Bible, *The Imitation of Christ*, and *Pilgrim's Progress*." Diffused with the Spirit's unction, soundly Calvinistic, yet moderate in tone and irenic in spirit, this precious "book of comfort" remains one of the most widely used and warmly praised catechisms of the Reformation period.

LORD'S DAY 1

Question 1: What is thy only comfort in life and death?

Answer: That I with body and soul, both in life and death,[1] am not my own,[2] but belong unto my faithful Savior Jesus Christ;[3] who, with His precious blood,[4] hath fully satisfied for all my sins,[5] and delivered me from all the power of the devil;[6] and so preserves me[7] that without the will of my heavenly Father, not a hair can fall from my head;[8] yea, that all things must be subservient to my salvation,[9] and therefore, by His Holy Spirit, He also assures me of eternal life,[10] and makes me sincerely willing and ready, henceforth, to live unto Him.[11]

Question 2: How many things are necessary for thee to know, that thou, enjoying this comfort, mayest live and die happily?

Answer: Three;[12] the first, how great my sins and miseries are;[13] the second, how I may be delivered from all my sins and miseries;[14] the third, how I shall express my gratitude to God for such deliverance.[15]

[1] 1 Cor. 6:19–20 [2] Rom. 14:7–9 [3] 1 Cor. 3:23 [4] 1 Pet. 1:18–19 [5] John 1:7 [6] 1 John 3:8 [7] John 6:39 [8] Luke 21:18 [9] Rom. 8:28 [10] 2 Cor. 1:22 [11] Rom. 8:14 [12] Luke 24:47 [13] 1 Cor. 6:10–11 [14] John 17:3 [15] Eph. 5:8–10

THE FIRST PART — OF THE MISERY OF MAN

LORD'S DAY 2

Question 3: Whence knowest thou thy misery?

Answer: Out of the law of God.[1]

Question 4: What doth the law of God require of us?

Answer: Christ teaches us that briefly, Matthew 22:37–40, "Thou shalt love the Lord thy God with all thy heart, with all thy soul, and with all thy mind, and with all thy strength. This is the first and the great commandment; and the second is like unto it, Thou shalt love thy neighbor as thyself. On these two commandments hang all the law and the prophets."[2]

Question 5: Canst thou keep all these things perfectly?

Answer: In no wise;[3] for I am prone by nature to hate God and my neighbor.[4]

[1] Rom. 3:20 [2] Luke 10:27 [3] Rom. 3:10; John 1:8 [4] Rom. 8:7; Titus 3:3

LORD'S DAY 3

Question 6. Did God then create man so wicked and perverse?

Answer: By no means; but God created man good,[1] and after His own image, in true righteousness and holiness,[2] that he might rightly know God his Creator, heartily love Him and live with Him in eternal happiness to glorify and praise Him.[3]

Question 7: Whence then proceeds this depravity of human nature?

Answer: From the fall and disobedience of our first parents, Adam and Eve, in Paradise;[4] hence our nature is become so corrupt that we are all conceived and born in sin.[5]

Question 8: Are we then so corrupt that we are wholly incapable of doing any good, and inclined to all wickedness?

Answer: Indeed we are,[6] except we are regenerated by the Spirit of God.[7]

[1] Gen. 1:31 [2] Gen. 1:26–27; Col. 3:10; Eph. 4:24 [3] Eph. 1:6; 1 Cor. 6:20 [4] Gen. 3:6; Rom. 5:12, 18–19 [5] Ps. 51:5; Gen. 5:3 [6] Gen. 6:5; Job 14:4; Job 15:14, 16 [7] John 3:5; Eph. 2:5

LORD'S DAY 4

Question 9: Doth not God then do injustice to man, by requiring from him in His law that which he cannot perform?

Answer: Not at all;[1] for God made man capable of performing it;[2] but man, by the instigation of the devil,[3] and his own wilful disobedience, deprived himself and all his posterity of those divine gifts.[4]

Question 10: Will God suffer such disobedience and rebellion to go unpunished?

Answer: By no means; but is terribly displeased[5] with our original as well as actual sins; and will punish them in His just judgment temporally and eternally,[6] as He hath declared, "Cursed is every one that continueth not in all things, which are written in the book of the law, to do them."[7]

Question 11: Is not God then also merciful?

Answer: God is indeed merciful,[8] but also just; therefore His justice requires[9] that sin which is committed against the most high majesty of God be also punished with extreme,[10] that is, with everlasting punishment of body and soul.[11]

[1] Eccl. 7:29 [2] John 8:44; 2 Cor. 11:3 [3] Gen. 3:4, 7 [4] Rom. 5:12 [5] Ps. 5:5 [6] Rom. 1:18; Deut. 28:15; Heb. 9:27 [7] Deut. 27:26; Gal. 3:10 [8] Ex. 34:6 [9] Ex. 20:5; Job 34:10–11 [10] Ps. 5:5–6 [11] Gen. 2:17; Rom. 6:23

THE SECOND PART—OF MAN'S DELIVERANCE

LORD'S DAY 5

Question 12: Since then, by the righteous judgment of God, we deserve temporal and eternal punishment, is there no way by which we may escape that punishment, and be again received into favor?

Answer: God will have His justice satisfied,[1] and therefore we must make this full satisfaction, either by ourselves or by another.[2]

Question 13: Can we ourselves then make this satisfaction?

Answer: By no means;[3] but on the contrary we daily increase our debt.[4]

Question 14: Can there be found anywhere one, who is a mere creature, able to satisfy for us?

Answer: None; for, first, God will not punish any other creature for the sin which man hath committed;[5] and further, no mere creature can sustain the burden of God's eternal wrath against sin, so as to deliver others from it.[6]

Question 15: What sort of a mediator and deliverer then must we seek for?

Answer: For one who is very man,[7] and perfectly righteous; and yet more powerful than all creatures; that is, one who is also very God.[8]

[1] Ex. 20:5 [2] Deut. 24:16; 2 Cor. 5:14–15 [3] Job 9:2–3; Job 15:14–16 [4] Matt. 6:12 [5] Ezek. 18:20 [6] Rev. 5:3; Ps. 49:8–9 [7] 1 Cor. 15:21; Rom. 8:3 [8] Rom. 9:5; Isa. 7:14

LORD'S DAY 6

Question 16: Why must he be very man, and also perfectly righteous?

Answer: Because the justice of God requires that the same human nature which hath sinned, should likewise make satisfaction for sin;[1] and one, who is himself a sinner, cannot satisfy for others.[2]

Question 17: Why must He in one person be also very God?

Answer: That He might by the power of His Godhead sustain in His human nature the burden of God's wrath;[3] and might obtain for, and restore to us, righteousness and life.[4]

Question 18: Who then is that Mediator, who is in one person both very God, and a real righteous man?

Answer: Our Lord Jesus Christ,[5] "who of God is made unto us wisdom, and righteousness, and sanctification, and redemption."[6]

Question 19: Whence knowest thou this?

Answer: From the holy gospel, which God Himself first revealed in Paradise;[7] and afterwards published by the patriarchs and prophets,[8] and represented by the sacrifices and other ceremonies of the law;[9] and lastly, has fulfilled it by His only begotten Son.[10]

[1] Rom. 5:12, 15 [2] 1 Pet. 3:18; Isa. 53:11 [3] 1 Pet. 3:18; Acts 2:24; Isa. 53:8 [4] 1 John 1:2; Jer. 23:6; 2 Tim. 1:10; John 6:51 [5] Matt. 1:23; 1 Tim. 3:16; Luke 2:11 [6] 1 Cor. 1:30 [7] Gen. 3:15 [8] Gen. 22:17–18; Gen. 28:14; Rom. 1:2; Heb. 1:1; John 5:46 [9] Heb. 10:7–8 [10] Rom. 10:4; Heb. 13:8

LORD'S DAY 7

Question 20: Are all men then, as they perished in Adam, saved by Christ?

Answer: No; only those who are ingrafted into Him,[1] and receive all His benefits, by a true faith.[2]

Question 21: What is true faith?

Answer: True faith is not only a certain knowledge, whereby I hold for truth all that God has revealed to us in His Word,[3] but also an assured confidence,[4] which the Holy Ghost[5] works by the gospel in my heart,[6] that not only to others, but to me also, remission of sin,[7] everlasting righteousness and salvation[8] are freely given by God, merely of grace, only for the sake of Christ's merits.[9]

Question 22: What is then necessary for a Christian to believe?

Answer: All things promised us in the gospel,[10] which the articles of our catholic undoubted Christian faith briefly teach us.

Question 23: What are these articles?

Answer:

I. I believe in God the Father, Almighty, Maker of heaven and earth;
II. And in Jesus Christ, His only begotten Son, our Lord;
III. Who was conceived by the Holy Ghost, born of the Virgin Mary;
IV. Suffered under Pontius Pilate; was crucified, dead, and buried; He descended into hell;
V. The third day He arose again from the dead;
VI. He ascended into heaven, and sitteth at the right hand of God the Father Almighty;
VII. From thence He shall come to judge the quick and the dead;
VIII. I believe in the Holy Ghost;
IX. I believe an holy catholic church; the communion of saints;
X. The forgiveness of sins;
XI. The resurrection of the body;
XII. And the life everlasting. Amen.

[1] Matt. 1:21; Isa. 53:11 [2] John 1:12–13; Rom. 11:20; Heb. 10:39 [3] John 6:69; John 17:3; Heb. 11:3, 6 [4] Eph. 3:12 [5] Rom. 4:16, 20–21; Heb. 11:1; Eph. 3:12; Rom. 1:16; 1 Cor. 1:21; Acts 16:14; Matt. 16:17; John 3:5 [6] Rom. 10:14, 17; Matt. 9:2 [7] Rom. 5:1 [8] Gal. 2:20 [9] Rom. 3:24–26 [10] John 20:31; Matt. 28:19–20

LORD'S DAY 8

Question 24: How are these articles divided?
Answer: Into three parts; the first is of God the Father and our creation;[1] the second, of God the Son and our redemption;[2] the third, of God the Holy Ghost and our sanctification.[3]

Question 25: Since there is but one only divine essence,[4] why speakest thou of Father, Son, and Holy Ghost?
Answer: Because God hath so revealed Himself in His Word,[5] that these three distinct persons are the one only true and eternal God.

[1] Gen. 1 [2] 1 Pet. 1:18–19 [3] 1 Pet. 1:21–22 [4] Deut. 6:4 [5] Gen. 1:26; Isa. 61:1; John 14:16–17; 1 John 5:7; John 1:13; Matt. 28:19; 2 Cor. 13:14

OF GOD THE FATHER

LORD'S DAY 9

Question 26: What believest thou when thou sayest, "I believe in God the Father, Almighty, Maker of heaven and earth?"
Answer: That the eternal Father of our Lord Jesus Christ (who of nothing made heaven and earth, with all that is in them;[1] who likewise upholds and governs the same by His eternal counsel and providence)[2] is for the sake of Christ His Son, my God and my Father; on whom I rely so entirely, that I have no doubt but He will provide me with all things necessary for soul and body;[3] and further, that He will make whatever evils He sends upon me, in this valley of tears, turn out to my advantage;[4] for He is able to do it, being Almighty God,[5] and willing, being a faithful Father.[6]

[1] Gen. 1 and 2; Ps. 33:6 [2] Ps. 115:3; Matt. 10:29; Heb. 1:3; John 5:17; Rom. 8:15–16; Gal. 4:5–6; Eph. 1:5; 1 John 3:1 [4] Ps. 55:22; Matt. 6:26 [5] Rom. 8:28; Rom. 4:21 [6] Rom. 10:12; Matt. 6:26; Matt. 7:9–11

LORD'S DAY 10

Question 27: What dost thou mean by the providence of God?
Answer: The almighty and everywhere present power of God;[1] whereby, as it were by His hand, He upholds and governs heaven, earth, and all creatures;[2] so that herbs and grass, rain and drought,[3] fruitful and barren years, meat and drink,[4] health and sickness,[5] riches and poverty,[6] yea, and all things come, not by chance, but by His fatherly hand.[7]

Question 28: What advantage is it to us to know that God has created, and by His providence doth still uphold all things?
Answer: That we may be patient in adversity;[8] thankful in prosperity;[9] and that in all things, which may hereafter befall us, we place our firm trust in our faithful God and Father,[10] that nothing shall separate us from His love;[11] since all creatures are so in His hand, that without His will they cannot so much as move.[12]

[1] Acts 17:25–28 [2] Heb. 1:3 [3] Jer. 5:24 [4] Acts 14:17 [5] John 9:3 [6] Prov. 22:2; Job 1:21 [7] Matt. 10:29–30; Eph. 1:11 [8] Rom. 5:3; Ps. 39:10 [9] Deut. 8:10 1; 1 Thes. 5:18 [10] Rom. 5:3–6 [11] Rom. 8:38–39 [12] Job 1:12; Job 2:6; Matt. 8:31; Isa. 10:15

OF GOD THE SON

LORD'S DAY 11

Question 29: Why is the Son of God called Jesus, that is, a Savior?
Answer: Because He saveth us, and delivereth us from our sins;[1] and likewise, because we ought not to seek, neither can find salvation in any other.[2]

Question 30: Do such then believe in Jesus the only Savior, who seek their salvation and welfare of saints, of themselves, or anywhere else?
Answer: They do not; for though they boast of Him in words, yet in deeds they deny Jesus the only deliverer and Savior;[3] for one of these two things must be true, that either Jesus is not a complete Savior or that they, who by a true faith receive this Savior, must find all things in Him necessary to their salvation.[4]

[1] Matt. 1:21 [2] Acts 4:12 [3] 1 Cor. 1:13, 31; Gal. 5:4 [4] Col. 2:20; Isa. 9:6–7; Col. 1:19–20

LORD'S DAY 12

Question 31: Why is He called Christ, that is, anointed?
Answer: Because He is ordained of God the Father, and anointed with the Holy Ghost,[1] to be our chief Prophet and Teacher,[2] who has fully revealed to us the secret counsel and will of God concerning our redemption; and to be our only High Priest, who by the one sacrifice of His body, has redeemed us,[3] and makes continual intercession with the Father for us;[4] and also to be our eternal King,[5] who governs us by His word and Spirit, and who defends and preserves us[6] in the enjoyment of that salvation He has purchased for us.

Question 32: But why art thou called a Christian?
Answer: Because I am a member of Christ by faith,[7] and thus am partaker of His anointing;[8] that so I may confess His name,[9] and present myself a living sacrifice of thankfulness to Him;[10] and also that with a free and good conscience I may fight against sin and Satan in this life,[11] and afterwards reign with Him eternally, over all creatures.[12]

[1] Heb. 1:9 [2] Deut. 18:18; Acts 3:22; John 1:18; John 15:15; Matt. 11:27 [3] Ps. 110:4; Heb. 7:21; Heb. 10:14 [4] Rom. 8:34 [5] Ps. 2:6; Luke 1:33 [6] Matt. 28:18; John 10:28 [7] 1 Cor. 6:15 [8] 1 John 2:27; Joel 2:28 [9] Matt. 10:32 [10] Rom. 12:1 [11] Eph. 6:11–12; 1 Tim. 1:18–19 [12] 2 Tim. 2:12

LORD'S DAY 13

Question 33: Why is Christ called the only begotten Son of God, since we are also the children of God?
Answer: Because Christ alone is the eternal and natural Son of God;[1] but we are children adopted of God, by grace, for His sake.[2]

Question 34: Wherefore callest thou Him our Lord?
Answer: Because He hath redeemed us, both soul and body, from all our sins, not with gold or silver, but with His precious blood, and hath delivered us from all the power of the devil; and thus hath made us His own property.[3]

[1] John 1:1; Heb. 1:2 [2] Rom. 8:15–17; Eph. 1:5–6 [3] 1 Pet. 1:18–19; 1 Cor. 6:20

LORD'S DAY 14

Question 35: What is the meaning of these words —"He was conceived by the Holy Ghost, born of the Virgin Mary"?
Answer: That God's eternal Son, who is,[1] and continueth true and eternal God,[2] took upon Him the very nature of man, of the flesh and blood of the Virgin Mary,[3] by the operation of the Holy Ghost;[4] that He might also be the true seed of David,[5] like unto His brethren in all things, sin excepted.[6]

Question 36: What profit dost thou receive by Christ's holy conception and nativity?
Answer: That He is our Mediator,[7] and with His innocence and perfect holiness, covers in the sight of God, my sins,[8] wherein I was conceived and brought forth.

[1] John 1:1; Col. 1:15; Ps. 2:7 [2] Rom. 9:5; 1 John 5:20 [3] John 1:14; Gal. 4:4 [4] Matt. 1:18; Luke 1:35 [5] Ps. 132:2; Acts 2:30; Rom. 1:3 [6] Phil. 2:7; Heb. 4:15 [7] Heb. 2:16–17 [8] Ps. 32:1; 1 Cor. 1:30; Rom. 8:34

LORD'S DAY 15

Question 37: What dost thou understand by the words, "He suffered"?
Answer: That He, all the time that He lived on earth, but especially at the end of His life, sustained in body and soul[1] the wrath of God against the sins of all mankind; that so by His passion, as the only propitiatory sacrifice,[2] He might redeem our body and soul from everlasting damnation, and obtain for us the favor of God, righteousness, and eternal life.

Question 38: Why did He suffer under Pontius Pilate as judge?
Answer: That He, being innocent, and yet condemned by a temporal judge,[3] might thereby free us from the severe judgment of God to which we were exposed.[4]

Question 39: Is there anything more in His being crucified than if He had died some other death?
Answer: Yes, there is; for thereby I am assured, that He took on Him the curse which lay upon me; for the death of the cross was accursed of God.[5]

[1] 1 Pet. 2:24; Isa. 53:12 [2] 1 John 2:2; Rom. 3:25 [3] Luke 23:14; John 19:4; Ps. 69:4 [4] Gal. 3:13–14 [5] Deut. 21:23; Gal. 3:13

LORD'S DAY 16

Question 40: Why was it necessary for Christ to humble Himself even unto death?
Answer: Because with respect to the justice and truth of God, satisfaction for our sins could be made no otherwise[1] than by the death of the Son of God.[2]

Question 41: Why was He also "buried"?
Answer: Thereby to prove that He was really dead.[3]

Question 42: Since then Christ died for us, why must we also die?
Answer: Our death is not a satisfaction for our sins, but only an abolishing of sin, and a passage into eternal life.[4]

Question 43: What further benefit do we receive from the sacrifice and death of Christ on the cross?
Answer: That by virtue thereof our old man is crucified, dead and buried with Him;[5] that so the corrupt inclinations of the flesh may no more reign in us,[6] but that we may offer ourselves unto Him a sacrifice of thanksgiving.[7]

Question 44: Why is there added, "He descended into hell"?
Answer: That in my greatest temptations, I may be assured, and wholly comfort myself in this, that my Lord Jesus Christ, by His inexpressible anguish, pains, terrors, and hellish agonies, in which He was plunged during all His sufferings, but especially on the cross, hath delivered me from the anguish and torments of hell.[8]

[1] Gen. 2:17 [2] Heb. 2:9–10; Phil. 2:8 [3] Acts 13:29; Mark 15:43, 46 [4] John 5:24; Phil. 1:23 [5] Rom. 6:6, 7 [6] Rom. 6:12 [7] Rom. 12:1
[8] Isa. 53:10 [9] Matt. 27:46

LORD'S DAY 17

Question 45: What doth the resurrection of Christ profit us?
Answer: First, by His resurrection He has overcome death, that He might make us partakers of that righteousness which He had purchased for us by His death;[1] secondly, we are also by His power raised up to a new life;[2] and lastly, the resurrection of Christ is a sure pledge of our blessed resurrection.[3]

[1] 1 Cor. 15:16 [2] Rom. 6:4; Col. 3:1 [3] 1 Cor. 15; Rom. 8:11

LORD'S DAY 18

Question 46: How dost thou understand these words, "He ascended into heaven"?
Answer: That Christ, in sight of His disciples, was taken up from earth into heaven;[1] and that He continues there for our interest[2] until He comes again to judge the quick and the dead.

Question 47: Is not Christ then with us even to the end of the world, as He hath promised?
Answer: Christ is very man and very God; with respect to His human nature, He is no more on earth;[3] but with respect to His Godhead, majesty, grace and Spirit, He is at no time absent from us.

Question 48: But if His human nature is not present, wherever His Godhead is, are not then these two natures in Christ separated from one another?
Answer: Not at all, for since the Godhead is illimitable and omnipresent,[4] it must necessarily follow that the same is beyond the limits of the human nature He assumed,[5] and yet is nevertheless in this human nature, and remains personally united to it.

Question 49: Of what advantage to us is Christ's ascension into heaven?
Answer: First, that He is our Advocate in the presence of His Father in heaven;[6] secondly, that we have our flesh in heaven as a sure pledge that He, as the head, will also take up to Himself, us, His members;[7] thirdly, that He sends us His Spirit as an earnest,[8] by whose power we "seek the things which are above, where Christ sitteth on the right hand of God," and not things on earth.[9]

---

[1] Acts 1:9; Mark 16:19 [2] Heb. 4:14; Rom. 8:34; Eph. 4:10 [3] Acts 3:21; John 3:13; John 16:28; Matt. 28:20 [4] Acts 7:49; Matt. 24:30 [5] Matt. 28:20; John 16:28; John 17:11; John 3:13 [6] Heb. 9:24; 1 John 2:2; Rom. 8:34 [7] John 14:2; Eph. 2:6 [8] John 14:16; 2 Cor. 1:22; 2 Cor. 5:5 [9] Col. 3:1; Phil. 3:20

LORD'S DAY 19

Question 50: Why is it added, "and sitteth at the right hand of God"?
Answer: Because Christ is ascended into heaven for this end, that He might appear as head of His church,[1] by whom the Father governs all things.[2]

Question 51: What profit is this glory of Christ, our Head, unto us?
Answer: First, that by His Holy Spirit He pours out heavenly graces upon us His members;[3] and then that by His power He defends and preserves us against all enemies.[4]

Question 52: What comfort is it to thee that "Christ shall come again to judge the quick and the dead"?
Answer: That in all my sorrows and persecutions, with uplifted head I look for the very same person, who before offered Himself for my sake to the tribunal of God, and has removed all curse from me, to come as judge from heaven;[5] who shall cast all His and my enemies into everlasting condemnation,[6] but shall translate me with all His chosen ones to Himself, into heavenly joys and glory.[7]

---

[1] Eph. 1:20–22; Col. 1:18 [2] Matt. 28:18; John 5:22 [3] Eph. 4:8 [4] Ps. 2:9; John 10:28 [5] Luke 21:28; Rom. 8:23–24; 1 Thes. 4:16 [6] 2 Thes. 1:6–9; Matt. 25:41 [7] Matt. 25:34

OF GOD THE HOLY GHOST

LORD'S DAY 20

Question 53: What dost thou believe concerning the Holy Ghost?
Answer: First, that He is true and coeternal God with the Father and the Son;[1] secondly, that He is also given me,[2] to make me by a true faith, partaker of Christ and all His benefits,[3] that He may comfort me[4] and abide with me for ever.[5]

---

[1] Gen. 1:2; Isa. 48:16; 1 Cor. 3:16 [2] Matt. 28:19; 2 Cor. 1:22 [3] Gal. 3:14; 1 Pet. 1:2 [4] Acts 9:31 [5] John 14:16; 1 Pet. 4:14

LORD'S DAY 21

Question 54: What believest thou concerning the "holy catholic church" of Christ?
Answer: That the Son of God[1] from the beginning to the end of the world,[2] gathers,[3] defends, and preserves to Himself[4] by His Spirit and Word,[5] out of the whole human race,[6] a Church chosen to everlasting life,[7] agreeing in true faith; and that I am and for ever shall remain, a living member thereof.[8]

Question 55: What do you understand by "the communion of saints"?
Answer: First, that all and every one who believes, being members of Christ, are in common, partakers of Him, and of all His riches and gifts;[9] secondly, that every one must know it to be his duty, readily and cheerfully to employ his gifts, for the advantage and salvation of other members.[10]

Question 56: What believest thou concerning "the forgiveness of sins"?
Answer: That God, for the sake of Christ's satisfaction,[11] will no more remember my sins, neither my corrupt nature, against which I have to struggle all my life long; but will graciously impute to me the righteousness of Christ,[12] that I may never be condemned before the tribunal of God.[13]

[1] John 10:11 [2] Gen. 26:4 [3] Rom. 9:24; Eph. 1:10 [4] John 10:16 [5] Isa. 59:21 [6] Deut. 10:14–15 [7] Acts 13:48 [8] 1 Cor. 1:8–9; Rom. 8:35 [9] John 1:3–4; Rom. 8:32; 1 Cor. 12:13 [10] 1 Cor. 13:5; Phil. 2:4–6 [11] 1 John 2:2; 2 Cor. 5:19, 21 [12] Jer. 31:34; Ps. 103:3–4, 10–11; Rom. 8:1–3 [13] John 3:18

LORD'S DAY 22

Question 57: What comfort doth the "resurrection of the body" afford thee?
Answer: That not only my soul after this life shall be immediately taken up to Christ its Head;[1] but also, that this my body, being raised by the power of Christ, shall be reunited with my soul, and made like unto the glorious body of Christ.[2]

Question 58: What comfort takest thou from the article of "life everlasting"?
Answer: That since I now feel in my heart the beginning of eternal joy,[3] after this life I shall inherit perfect salvation,[4] which "eye hath not seen, nor ear heard, neither have entered into the heart of man" to conceive,[5] and that, to praise God therein for ever.

[1] Luke 23:43; Phil. 1:23 [2] 1 Cor. 15:53; Job 19:25–26 [3] 2 Cor. 5:2–3, 6; Rom. 14:17 [4] Ps. 16:11 [5] 1 Cor. 2:9

LORD'S DAY 23

Question 59: But what doth it profit thee now that thou believest all this?
Answer: That I am righteous in Christ, before God, and an heir of eternal life.[1]

Question 60: How art thou righteous before God?
Answer: Only by a true faith in Jesus Christ;[2] so that, though my conscience accuse me, that I have grossly transgressed all the commandments of God, and kept none of them,[3] and am still inclined to all evil;[4] notwithstanding, God, without any merit of mine,[5] but only of mere grace,[6] grants[7] and imputes to me[8] the perfect satisfaction, righteousness and holiness of Christ;[9] even so, as if I never had had, nor committed any sin; yea, as if I had fully accomplished all that obedience which Christ has accomplished for me,[10] inasmuch as I embrace such benefit with a believing heart.[11]

Question 61: Why sayest thou that thou art righteous by faith only?
Answer: Not that I am acceptable to God, on account of the worthiness of my faith,[12] but because only the satisfaction, righteousness, and holiness of Christ, is my righteousness before God;[13] and that I cannot receive and apply the same to myself any other way than by faith only.[14]

[1] Rom. 5:1; Rom. 1:17; John 3:36 [2] Rom. 3:22; Gal. 2:16; Eph. 2:8–9 [3] Rom. 3:9 [4] Rom. 7:23 [5] Rom. 3:24 [6] Titus 3:5; Eph. 2:8–9 [7] Rom. 4:4–5; 2 Cor. 5:19 [8] 1 John 2:1 [9] Rom. 3:24–25 [10] 2 Cor. 5:21 [11] Rom. 3:28; John 3:18 [12] Ps. 16:2; Eph. 2:8–9 [13] 1 Cor. 1:30; 1 Cor. 2:2 [14] 1 John 5:10

LORD'S DAY 24

Question 62: But why cannot our good works be the whole or part of our righteousness before God?
Answer: Because that the righteousness, which can be approved of before the tribunal of God, must be absolutely perfect, and in all respects conformable to the divine law;[1] and also, that our best works in this life are all imperfect and defiled with sin.[2]

Question 63: What! Do not our good works merit, which yet God will reward in this and in a future life?
Answer: This reward is not of merit, but of grace.[3]

Question 64: But doth not this doctrine make men careless and profane?
Answer: By no means: for it is impossible that those, who are implanted into Christ by a true faith, should not bring forth fruits of thankfulness.[4]

---

[1] Gal. 3:10; Deut. 27:26 [2] Isa. 64:6 [3] Luke 17:10 [4] Matt. 7:17–18; John 15:5

OF THE SACRAMENTS

LORD'S DAY 25

Question 65: Since then we are made partakers of Christ and all His benefits by faith only, whence doth this faith proceed?
Answer: From the Holy Ghost, who works faith[1] in our hearts by the preaching of the gospel, and confirms it by the use of the sacraments.[2]

Question 66: What are the sacraments?
Answer: The sacraments are holy visible signs and seals, appointed of God for this end, that by the use thereof He may the more fully declare and seal to us the promise of the gospel, namely, that He grants us freely the remission of sin and life eternal for the sake of that one sacrifice of Christ accomplished on the cross.[3]

Question 67: Are both Word and sacraments, then, ordained and appointed for this end, that they may direct our faith to the sacrifice of Jesus Christ on the cross as the only ground of our salvation?
Answer: Yes, indeed, for the Holy Ghost teaches us in the gospel, and assures us by the sacraments, that the whole of our salvation depends upon that one sacrifice of Christ which He offered for us on the cross.[4]

Question 68: How many sacraments has Christ instituted in the new covenant, or testament?
Answer: Two, namely, holy baptism and the holy supper.[5]

---

[1] Eph. 2:8; Eph. 6:23; Phil. 1:29 [2] Matt. 28:19; Rom. 4:11 [3] Gen. 17:11; Rom. 4:11; Lev. 6:25; Acts 22:16; Acts 2:38; Matt. 26:28 [4] Rom. 6:3; Gal. 3:27 [5] 1 Cor. 10:2–4

OF HOLY BAPTISM

LORD'S DAY 26

Question 69: How art thou admonished and assured by holy baptism that the one sacrifice of Christ upon the cross is of real advantage to thee?
Answer: Thus: That Christ appointed this external washing with water,[1] adding thereto this promise,[2] that I am as certainly washed by His blood and Spirit from all the pollution of my soul, that is, from all my sins,[3] as I am washed externally with water, by which the filthiness of the body is commonly washed away.

Question 70: What is it to be washed with the blood and Spirit of Christ?
Answer: It is to receive of God the remission of sins freely, for the sake of Christ's blood which He shed for us by His sacrifice upon the cross;[4] and also to be renewed by the Holy Ghost, and sanctified to be members of Christ, that so we may more and more die unto sin, and lead holy and unblamable lives.[5]

Question 71: Where has Christ promised us, that He will as certainly wash us by His blood and Spirit, as we are washed with the water of baptism?
Answer: In the institution of baptism, which is thus expressed: "Go ye therefore, and teach all nations, baptizing them in the name of the Father, and of the Son, and of the Holy Ghost";[6] "He that believeth and is baptized, shall be saved; but he that believeth not shall be damned."[7] This promise is also repeated, where the Scripture calls baptism the washing of regeneration[8] and the washing away of sins.[9]

[1] Matt. 28:19; Acts 2:38 [2] Mark 16:16; Matt. 3:11; Rom. 6:3 [3] Mark 1:4; Luke 3:3 [4] Heb. 12:24; 1 Pet. 1:2 [5] John 1:33; Rom. 6:4; Col. 2:11 [6] Matt. 28:19 [7] Mark 16:16 [8] Titus 3:5 [9] Acts 22:16

LORD'S DAY 27

Question 72: Is then the external baptism with water the washing away of sin itself?
Answer: Not at all; for the blood of Jesus Christ only,[1] and the Holy Ghost cleanse us from all sin.[2]

Question 73: Why then doth the Holy Ghost call baptism "the washing of regeneration" and the "washing away of sins"?
Answer: God speaks thus not without great cause, to wit, not only thereby to teach us that as the filth of the body is purged away by water, so our sins are removed by the blood and Spirit of Jesus Christ;[3] but especially that by this divine pledge and sign He may assure us that we are spiritually cleansed from our sins as really as we are externally washed with water.[4]

Question 74: Are infants also to be baptized?
Answer: Yes, for since they, as well as the adult, are included in the covenant[5] and church of God;[6] and since redemption from sin[7] by the blood of Christ, and the Holy Ghost, the author of faith, is promised to them[8] no less than to the adult; they must therefore by baptism, as a sign of the covenant, be also admitted into the Christian church, and be distinguished from the children of unbelievers[9] as was done in the old covenant or testament by circumcision,[10] instead of which baptism is instituted in the new covenant.[11]

[1] Matt. 3:11; 1 Pet. 3:21 [2] 1 John 1:7; 1 Cor. 6:11 [3] Rev. 1:5; 1 Cor. 6:11 [4] Mark 16:16; Gal. 3:27 [5] Gen. 17:7; Acts 2:39 [6] 1 Cor. 7:14; Joel 2:16 [7] Matt. 19:14 [8] Luke 1:14–15; Ps. 22:10; Acts 2:39 [9] Acts 10:47; 1 Cor. 12:13; 1 Cor. 7:14 [10] Gen. 17:14 [11] Col. 2:11–13

OF THE HOLY SUPPER OF OUR LORD JESUS CHRIST

LORD'S DAY 28

Question 75: How art thou admonished and assured in the Lord's Supper that thou art a partaker of that one sacrifice of Christ, accomplished on the cross, and of all His benefits?
Answer: Thus: That Christ has commanded me and all believers to eat of this broken bread and to drink of this cup in remembrance of Him, adding these promises:[1] first, that His body was offered and broken on the cross for me, and His blood shed for me, as certainly as I see with my eyes the bread of the Lord broken for me and the cup communicated to me; and further, that He feeds and nourishes my soul to everlasting life, with His crucified body and shed blood, as assuredly as I receive from the hands of the minister, and taste with my mouth the bread and cup of the Lord, as certain signs of the body and blood of Christ.

Question 76: What is it then to eat the crucified body, and drink the shed blood of Christ?
Answer: It is not only to embrace with a believing heart all the sufferings and death of Christ, and thereby to obtain the pardon of sin and life eternal;[2] but also, besides that, to become more and more united to His sacred body, by the Holy Ghost, who dwells both in Christ and in us;[3] so that we, though Christ is in heaven[4] and we on earth, are notwithstanding "flesh of His flesh, and bone of His bone";[5] and that we live, and are governed forever by one spirit, as members of the same body are by one soul.[6]

Question 77: Where has Christ promised that He will as certainly feed and nourish believers with His body and blood, as they eat of this broken bread, and drink of this cup?
Answer: In the institution of the supper, which is thus expressed: "The Lord Jesus the same night in which he was betrayed took bread: and when he had given thanks, he brake it, and said, Take, eat: this is my body, which is broken for you; this do in remembrance of me.[7] After the same manner also he took the cup, when he had supped, saying, This cup is the new testament in my blood;[8] this do ye, as often as ye drink it, in remembrance of me. For, as often as ye eat this bread, and drink this cup, ye do show the Lord's death till he come."[9]

This promise is repeated by the holy apostle Paul, where he says: "The cup of blessing which we bless, is it not the communion of the blood of Christ? The bread which we break, is it not the communion of the body of Christ? For we, being many, are one bread and one body: for we are all partakers of that one bread."[10]

---

[1] Matt. 26:26–28; Mark 14:22–24; Luke 22:19–20; 1 Cor. 10:16–17; 1 Cor. 11:23–25 [2] John 6:35, 40, 47–48, 50–51, 53–54 [3] John 6:55–56 [4] Acts 3:21; Acts 1:9–11; 1 Cor. 11:26 [5] Eph. 5:29–32; 1 Cor. 6:15, 17, 19; 1 John 3:24 [6] John 6:56–58; Eph. 4:15–16 [7] 1 Cor. 11:23; Matt. 26:26; Mark 14:22; Luke 22:19 [8] Ex. 24:8; Heb. 9:20 [9] Ex. 13:9; 1 Cor. 11:26 [10] 1 Cor. 10:16–17

LORD'S DAY 29

Question 78: Do then the bread and wine become the very body and blood of Christ?
Answer: Not at all; but as the water in baptism is not changed into the blood of Christ, neither is the washing away of sin itself, being only the sign and confirmation thereof appointed of God;[1] so the bread in the Lord's Supper is not changed into the very body of Christ,[2] though agreeably to the nature and properties of sacraments,[3] it is called the body of Christ Jesus.

Question 79: Why then doth Christ call the bread His body, and the cup His blood, or the new covenant in His blood; and Paul, the "communion of the body and blood of Christ"?
Answer: Christ speaks thus not without great reason, namely, not only thereby to teach us that as bread and wine support this temporal life, so His crucified body and shed blood are the true meat and drink whereby our souls are fed to eternal life;[4] but more especially by these visible signs and pledges to assure us that we are as really partakers of His true body and blood (by the operation of the Holy Ghost) as we receive by the mouths of our bodies these holy signs in remembrance of Him;[5] and that all His sufferings and obedience are as certainly ours, as if we had in our own persons suffered and made satisfaction for our sins to God.[6]

---

[1] 1 Cor. 10:1–4; 1 Pet. 3:21; John 6:35, 62–63 [2] 1 Cor. 10:16; 1 Cor. 11:20 [3] Gen. 17:10–11, 14; Ex. 12:26–27, 43, 48; Acts 7:8; Matt. 26:26; Mark 14:24 [4] John 6:51, 55–56 [5] 1 Cor. 10:16–17; 1 Cor. 11:26–28 [6] Rom. 5:9, 18–19; Rom. 8:4

LORD'S DAY 30

Question 80: What difference is there between the Lord's Supper and the popish Mass?
Answer: The Lord's Supper testifies to us that we have a full pardon of all sin by the only sacrifice of Jesus Christ, which He Himself has once accomplished on the cross;[1] and that we by the Holy Ghost are ingrafted into Christ,[2] who, according to His human nature is now not on earth, but in heaven, at the right hand of God His Father,[3] and will there be worshipped by us[4]— but the Mass teaches that the living and dead have not the pardon of sins through the sufferings of Christ, unless Christ is also daily offered for them by the priests; and further, that Christ is bodily under the form of bread and wine, and therefore is to be worshipped in them; so that the Mass, at bottom, is nothing else than a denial of the one sacrifice and sufferings of Jesus Christ, and an accursed idolatry.[5]

Question 81: For whom is the Lord's Supper instituted?
Answer: For those who are truly sorrowful for their sins,[6] and yet trust that these are forgiven them for the sake of Christ; and that their remaining infirmities are covered by His passion and death;[7] and who also earnestly desire to have their faith more and more strengthened, and their lives more holy;[8] but hypocrites, and such as turn not to God with sincere hearts, eat and drink judgment to themselves.[9]

Question 82: Are they also to be admitted to this supper, who, by confession and life, declare themselves unbelieving and ungodly?
Answer: No; for by this, the covenant of God would be profaned and His wrath kindled against the whole congregation;[10] therefore it is the duty of the Christian church, according to the appointment of Christ and His apostles, to exclude such persons[11] by the keys of the kingdom of heaven till they show amendment of life.

---

[1] Heb. 7:27; Heb. 9:12, 26; Matt. 26:28; Luke 22:19–20; 2 Cor. 5:21 [2] 1 Cor. 12:13 [3] Heb. 1:3; Heb. 8:1 [4] John 4:21–23; Col. 3:1; Phil. 3:20; Luke 24:52–53; Acts 7:55 [5] Isa. 1:11, 14; Matt. 15:9; Col. 2:22–23; Jer. 2:13 [6] Matt. 5:3, 6; Luke 7:37–38; Luke 15:18–19 [7] Ps. 103:3 [8] Ps. 116:12–14; 1 Pet. 2:11–12 [9] 1 Cor. 10:20; 1 Cor. 11:28; Titus 1:16; Ps. 50:15–16 [10] 1 Cor. 10:21; 1 Cor. 11:30–31; Isa. 1:11, 13; Jer. 7:21; Ps. 50:16, 22 [11] Matt. 18:17–18

LORD'S DAY 31

Question 83: What are the keys of the kingdom of heaven?[1]
Answer: The preaching of the holy gospel, and Christian discipline,[2] or excommunication out of the Christian church;[3] by these two, the kingdom of heaven is opened to believers and shut against unbelievers.

Question 84: How is the kingdom of heaven opened and shut by the preaching of the holy gospel?
Answer: Thus: when according to the command of Christ[4] it is declared and publicly testified to all and every believer, that, whenever they receive the promise of the gospel by a true faith,[5] all their sins are really forgiven them of God for the sake of Christ's merits; and on the contrary, when it is declared and testified to all unbelievers, and such as do not sincerely repent, that they stand exposed to the wrath of God and eternal condemnation,[6] so long as they are unconverted;[7] according to which testimony of the gospel, God will judge them both in this and in the life to come.

Question 85: How is the kingdom of heaven shut and opened by Christian discipline?
Answer: Thus: when according to the command of Christ,[8] those, who under the name of Christians, maintain doctrines or practices inconsistent therewith,[9] and will not, after having been often brotherly admonished, renounce their errors and wicked course of life, are complained of to the church or to those[10] who are thereunto appointed by the church;[11] and if they despise their admonition, are by them forbidden the use of the sacraments;[12] whereby they are excluded from the Christian church and by God Himself from the kingdom of Christ; and when they promise and show real amendment, are again received as members of Christ and His church.[13]

---

[1] Matt. 16:19 [2] John 20:23 [3] Matt. 18:15–18 [4] Matt. 28:19 [5] John 3:18, 36; Mark 16:16 [6] 2 Thes. 1:7–9 [7] John 20:21–23; Matt. 16:19; Rom. 2:2, 13–17 [8] Matt. 18:15 [9] 1 Cor. 5:12 [10] Matt. 18:15–18 [11] Rom. 12:7–9; 1 Cor. 12:28; 1 Tim. 5:17; 2 Thes. 3:14 [12] Matt. 18:17; 1 Cor. 5:3–5 [13] 2 Cor. 2:6–8, 10–11; Luke 15:18

THE THIRD PART — OF THANKFULNESS

LORD'S DAY 32

Question 86: Since then we are delivered from our misery, merely of grace, through Christ, without any merit of ours, why must we still do good works?
Answer: Because Christ, having redeemed and delivered us by His blood, also renews us by His Holy Spirit after His own image; that so we may testify, by the whole of our conduct, our gratitude to God for His blessings,[1] and that He may be praised by us;[2] also, that every one may be

assured in himself of his faith by the fruits thereof;[3] and that by our godly conversation others may be gained to Christ.[4]

Question 87: Cannot they then be saved, who, continuing in their wicked and ungrateful lives, are not converted to God?
Answer: By no means; for the Holy Scripture declares that no unchaste person, idolator, adulterer, thief, covetous man, drunkard, slanderer, robber, or any such like, shall inherit the kingdom of God.[5]

---

[1] 1 Cor. 6:19–20; Rom. 6:13; Rom. 12:1–2; 1 Pet. 2:5, 9–10 [2] Matt. 5:16; 1 Pet. 2:12 [3] 2 Pet. 1:10; Gal. 5:6, 24 [4] 1 Pet. 3:1–2; Matt. 5:16; Rom. 14:19 [5] 1 Cor. 6:9–10; Eph. 5:5–6; 1 John 3:14–15; Gal. 5:21

LORD'S DAY 33

Question 88: Of how many parts doth the true conversion of man consist?
Answer: Of two parts: of the mortification of the old, and the quickening of the new man.[1]

Question 89: What is the mortification of the old man?
Answer: It is a sincere sorrow of heart that we have provoked God by our sins, and more and more to hate and flee from them.[2]

Question 90: What is the quickening of the new man?
Answer: It is a sincere joy of heart in God, through Christ,[3] and with love and delight to live according to the will of God in all good works.[4]

Question 91: But what are good works?
Answer: Only those which proceed from a true faith,[5] are performed according to the law of God,[6] and to His glory;[7] and not such as are founded on our imaginations or the institutions of men.[8]

---

[1] Rom. 6:4–6; Eph. 4:22–23; Col. 3:5; 1 Cor. 5:7 [2] Ps. 51:3, 8, 17; Luke 15:18; Rom. 8:13; Joel 1:12–13 [3] Rom. 5:1–2; Rom. 14:17; Isa. 57:15 [4] Rom. 6:10–11; 1 Pet. 4:2; Gal. 2:20 [5] Rom. 14:23 [6] 1 Sam. 15:22; Eph. 2:2, 10 [7] 1 Cor. 10:31 [8] Deut. 12:32; Ezek. 20:18; Matt. 15:9

LORD'S DAY 34

Question 92: What is the law of God?
Answer: God spake all these words (Ex. 20:1–17; Deut. 5:6–21), saying, I am the LORD thy God, which have brought thee out of the land of Egypt, out of the house of bondage.

I. Thou shalt have no other gods before Me.

II. Thou shalt not make unto thee any graven image, or any likeness of any thing that is in heaven above, or that is in the earth beneath, or that is in the water under the earth: thou shalt not bow down thyself to them, nor serve them; for I the LORD thy God am a jealous God, visiting the iniquity of the fathers upon the children unto the third and fourth generation of them that hate Me; and shewing mercy unto thousands of them that love Me, and keep My commandments.

III. Thou shalt not take the name of the LORD thy God in vain; for the LORD will not hold him guiltless that taketh His name in vain.

IV. Remember the Sabbath day, to keep it holy. Six days shalt thou labour and do all thy work: but the seventh day is the Sabbath of the LORD thy God: in it thou shalt not do any work, thou, nor thy son, nor thy daughter, thy manservant, nor thy maidservant, nor thy cattle, nor thy stranger that is within thy gates: for in six days the LORD made heaven and earth, the sea, and all that in them is, and rested the seventh day: wherefore the LORD blessed the Sabbath day, and hallowed it.

V. Honour thy father and thy mother: that thy days may be long upon the land which the LORD thy God giveth thee.

VI. Thou shalt not kill.

VII. Thou shalt not commit adultery.

VIII. Thou shalt not steal.

IX. Thou shalt not bear false witness against thy neighbour.

X. Thou shalt not covet thy neighbour's house, thou shalt not covet thy neighbour's wife, nor his manservant, nor his maidservant, nor his ox, nor his ass, nor any thing that is thy neighbour's.

Question 93: How are these commandments divided?
Answer: Into two tables;[1] the first of which teaches us how we must behave towards God; the second, what duties we owe to our neighbor.[2]

Question 94: What doth God enjoin in the first commandment?
Answer: That I, as sincerely as I desire the salvation of my own soul, avoid and flee from all idolatry,[3] sorcery, soothsaying, superstition,[4] invocation of saints, or any other creatures;[5] and learn rightly to know the only true God;[6] trust in Him alone;[7] with humility and patience[8] submit to Him;[9] expect all good things from Him only;[10] love,[11] fear,[12] and glorify[13] Him with my whole heart; so that I renounce and forsake all creatures,[14] rather than commit even the least thing contrary to His will.[15]

Question 95: What is idolatry?
Answer: Idolatry is, instead of, or besides that one true God who has manifested Himself in His word, to contrive, or have any other object, in which men place their trust.[16]

[1] Ex. 34:28–29 [2] Deut. 4:13; Deut. 10:3–4 [3] 1 Cor. 6:9–10; 1 Cor. 10:7, 14; Deut. 18:10–12 [5] Matt. 4:10; Rev. 19:10 [6] John 17:3 [7] Jer. 17:5, 7 [8] Heb. 10:36; Col. 1:11; Rom. 5:3–4; Phil. 2:14 [9] 1 Pet. 5:5–6 [10] Ps. 104:27; Isa. 45:7; James 1:17 [11] Deut. 6:5; Matt. 22:37 [12] Deut. 6:5; Matt. 10:28 [13] Matt. 4:10 [14] Matt. 5:29–30; Acts 5:29; Matt. 10:37 [15] Matt. 5:19 [16] 2 Chron. 16:12; Phil. 3:18–19; Gal. 4:8; Eph. 2:12

LORD'S DAY 35

Question 96: What doth God require in the second commandment?
Answer: That we in no wise represent God by images,[1] nor worship Him in any other way than He has commanded in His Word.[2]

Question 97: Are images then not at all to be made?
Answer: God neither can, nor may be represented by any means.[3] But as to creatures, though they may be represented, yet God forbids to make, or have any resemblance of them, either in order to worship them or to serve God by them.[4]

Question 98: But may not images be tolerated in the churches as books to the laity?
Answer: No, for we must not pretend to be wiser than God, who will have His people taught, not by dumb images,[5] but by the lively preaching of His Word.[6]

[1] Deut. 4:15; Isa. 40:18; Rom. 1:23; Acts 17:29 [2] 1 Sam. 15:23; Deut. 12:30 [3] Deut. 4:15–16; Isa. 46:5; Rom. 1:23 [4] Ex. 23:24; Ex. 34:13–14; Numb. 33:52; Deut. 7:5 [5] 2 Tim. 3:16; 2 Pet. 1:19 [6] Jer. 10:1; Hab. 2:18–19

LORD'S DAY 36

Question 99: What is required in the third commandment?
Answer: That we, not only by cursing[1] or perjury, but also by rash swearing,[2] must not profane or abuse the name of God; nor by silence or connivance be partakers of these horrible sins in others; and, briefly, that we use the holy name of God[3] no otherwise than with fear and reverence, so that He may be rightly confessed[4] and worshipped by us,[5] and be glorified in all our words and works.

Question 100: Is then the profaning of God's Name by swearing and cursing so heinous a sin that His wrath is kindled against those who do not endeavor, as much as in them lies, to prevent and forbid such cursing and swearing?
Answer: It undoubtedly is, for there is no sin greater or more provoking to God than the profaning of His Name;[6] and therefore He has commanded this sin to be punished with death.[7]

[1] Lev. 24:11; Lev. 19:12; Matt. 5:37; Lev. 5:4 [2] Isa. 45:23–24 [3] Matt. 10:32 [4] 1 Tim. 2:8 [5] 1 Cor. 3:16–17 [6] Lev. 5: [7] Lev. 24:15

LORD'S DAY 37

Question 101: May we then swear religiously by the name of God?
Answer: Yes, either when the magistrates demand it of the subjects or when necessity requires us thereby to confirm fidelity and truth to the glory of God and the safety of our neighbor;[1] for such an oath is founded on God's Word,[2] and therefore was justly used by the saints, both in the Old and New Testament.[3]

Question 102: May we also swear by saints or any other creatures?
Answer: No; for a lawful oath is calling upon God as the only one who knows the heart, that He will bear witness to the truth and punish me if I swear falsely;[4] which honor is due to no creature.[5]

[1] Ex. 22:11; Neh. 13:25 [2] Deut. 6:13; Heb. 6:16 [3] Gen. 21:24; Josh. 9:15, 19; 1 Sam. 24:22; 2 Cor. 1:23; Rom. 1:9 [4] 2 Cor. 1:23 [5] Matt. 5:34–35

LORD'S DAY 38

Question 103: What doth God require in the fourth commandment?
Answer: First, that the ministry of the gospel and the schools be maintained;[1] and that I, especially on the Sabbath, that is, on the day of rest,[2] diligently frequent the church of God[3] to hear His word, to use the sacraments,[4] publicly to call upon the Lord,[5] and contribute to the relief of the poor,[6] as becomes a Christian. Secondly, that all the days of my life I cease from my evil works, and yield myself to the Lord, to work by His Holy Spirit in me; and thus begin in this life the eternal Sabbath.[7]

---

[1] Deut. 12:19; Titus 1:5; 1 Tim. 3:14–15; 1 Cor. 9:11; 2 Tim. 2:2; 1 Tim. 3:15 [2] Lev. 23:3 [3] Acts 2:42, 46; 1 Cor. 14:19, 29, 31 [4] 1 Cor. 11:33 [5] 1 Tim. 2:1 [6] 1 Cor. 16:2 [7] Isa. 66:23

LORD'S DAY 39

Question 104: What doth God require in the fifth commandment?
Answer: That I show all honor, love and fidelity, to my father and mother and all in authority over me, and submit myself to their good instruction and correction, with due obedience;[1] and also patiently bear with their weaknesses and infirmities,[2] since it pleases God to govern us by their hand.[3]

---

[1] Eph. 6:1–2; Col. 3:18, 20; Eph. 5:22; Rom. 1:31 [2] Prov. 23:22 [3] Eph. 6:5–6; Col. 3:19, 21; Rom. 13:1–8; Matt. 22:21

LORD'S DAY 40

Question 105: What doth God require in the sixth commandment?
Answer: That neither in thoughts, nor words, nor gestures, much less in deeds, I dishonor, hate, wound, or kill my neighbor, by myself or by another;[1] but that I lay aside all desire of revenge;[2] also, that I hurt not myself, nor wilfully expose myself to any danger.[3] Wherefore also the magistrate is armed with the sword to prevent murder.[4]

Question 106: But this commandment seems only to speak of murder?
Answer: In forbidding murder, God teaches us that He abhors the causes thereof, such as envy,[5] hatred,[6] anger, and desire of revenge; and that He accounts all these as murder.[7]

Question 107: But is it enough that we do not kill any man in the manner mentioned above?
Answer: No, for when God forbids envy, hatred, and anger, He commands us to love our neighbor as ourselves;[8] to show patience,[9] peace, meekness,[10] mercy,[11] and all kindness towards him, and prevent his hurt as much as in us lies;[12] and that we do good, even to our enemies.[13]

---

[1] Matt. 5:21–22; Prov. 12:18; Matt. 26:52 [2] Eph. 4:26; Rom. 12:19; Matt. 5:39–40 [3] Matt. 4:5–7; Col. 2:23 [4] Gen. 9:6; Matt. 26:52; Rom. 13:4 [5] James 1:20; Gal. 5:20 [6] Rom. 1:29; 1 John 2:9 [7] 1 John 3:15 [8] Matt. 22:39; Matt. 7:12 [9] Rom. 12:10 [10] Eph. 4:2; Gal. 6:1–2; Matt. 5:5; Rom. 12:18 [11] Ex. 23:5 [12] Matt. 5:45 [13] Rom. 12:20

LORD'S DAY 41

Question 108: What doth the seventh commandment teach us?
Answer: That all uncleanness is accursed of God;[1] and that therefore we must with all our hearts detest the same,[2] and live chastely and temperately,[3] whether in holy wedlock or in single life.[4]

Question 109: Doth God forbid in this commandment only adultery and such like gross sins?
Answer: Since both our body and soul are temples of the Holy Ghost, He commands us to preserve them pure and holy; therefore He forbids all unchaste actions, gestures,[5] words, thoughts, desires,[6] and whatever can entice men thereto.[7]

[1] Lev. 18:27 [2] Deut. 29:20–23 [3] 1 Thes. 4:3–4 [4] Heb. 13:4; 1 Cor. 7:4–9 [5] Eph. 5:3 1; Cor. 6:18 [6] Matt. 5:28 [7] Eph. 5:18; 1 Cor. 15:33

LORD'S DAY 42

Question 110: What doth God forbid in the eighth commandment?
Answer: God forbids not only those thefts[1] and robberies[2] which are punishable by the magistrate; but He comprehends under the name of theft all wicked tricks and devices, whereby we design to appropriate to ourselves the goods which belong to our neighbor;[3] whether it be by force, or under the appearance of right, as by unjust weights,[4] ells, measures,[5] fraudulent merchandise, false coins, usury,[6] or by any other way forbidden by God; as also all covetousness,[7] all abuse and waste of His gifts.

Question 111: But what doth God require in this commandment?
Answer: That I promote the advantage of my neighbor in every instance I can or may, and deal with him as I desire to be dealt with by others;[8] further also that I faithfully labor, so that I may be able to relieve the needy.[9]

[1] 1 Cor. 6:10 [2] 1 Cor. 5:10 [3] Luke 3:14; 1 Thes. 4:6 [4] Prov. 11:1 [5] Ezek. 45:9–11; Deut. 25:13 [6] Ps. 15:5; Luke 6:35 [7] 1 Cor. 6:10 [8] Matt. 7:12 [9] Prov. 5:16; Eph. 4:28

LORD'S DAY 43

Question 112: What is required in the ninth commandment?
Answer: That I bear false witness against no man[1] nor falsify any man's words;[2] that I be no backbiter nor slanderer;[3] that I do not judge, nor join in condemning any man rashly or unheard;[4] but that I avoid all sorts of lies and deceit,[5] as the proper works of the devil,[6] unless I would bring down upon me the heavy wrath of God; likewise, that in judgment and all other dealings I love the truth, speak it uprightly and confess it;[7] also that I defend and promote, as much as I am able, the honor and good character of my neighbor.[8]

[1] Prov. 19:5, 9; Prov. 21:28 [2] Ps. 15:3 [3] Rom. 1:29–30 [4] Matt. 7:1; Luke 6:37 [5] Lev. 19:11 [6] Prov. 12:22; Prov. 13:5 [7] 1 Cor. 13:6; Eph. 4:25 [8] 1 Pet. 4:8

LORD'S DAY 44

Question 113: What doth the tenth commandment require of us?
Answer: That even the smallest inclination or thought contrary to any of God's commandments never rise in our hearts; but that at all times we hate all sin with our whole heart, and delight in all righteousness.[1]

Question 114: But can those who are converted to God perfectly keep these commandments?
Answer: No, but even the holiest men, while in this life, have only a small beginning of this obedience;[2] yet so, that with a sincere resolution they begin to live, not only according to some, but all the commandments of God.[3]

Question 115: Why will God then have the ten commandments so strictly preached, since no man in this life can keep them?

Answer: First, that all our lifetime we may learn more and more to know our sinful nature,[4] and thus become the more earnest in seeking the remission of sin and righteousness in Christ;[5] likewise, that we constantly endeavor and pray to God for the grace of the Holy Spirit, that we may become more and more conformable to the image of God, till we arrive at the perfection proposed to us in a life to come.[6]

[1] Rom. 7:7 [2] Rom. 7:14 [3] Rom. 7:22, 15; James 3:2 [4] 1 John 1:9; Rom. 3:20; Rom. 5:13; Rom. 7:7 [5] Rom. 7:24 [6] 1 Cor. 9:24; Phil. 3:12–14

OF PRAYER

LORD'S DAY 45

Question 116: Why is prayer necessary for Christians?

Answer: Because it is the chief part of thankfulness which God requires of us;[1] and also, because God will give His grace and Holy Spirit to those only, who with sincere desires continually ask them of Him, and are thankful for them.[2]

Question 117: What are the requisites of that prayer which is acceptable to God and which He will hear?

Answer: First, that we from the heart pray to the one true God only, who hath manifested Himself in His Word,[3] for all things He hath commanded us to ask of Him;[4] secondly, that we rightly and thoroughly know our need and misery, that so we may deeply humble ourselves in the presence of His divine majesty;[5] thirdly, that we be fully persuaded that He, notwithstanding that we are unworthy of it,[6] will, for the sake of Christ our Lord, certainly hear our prayer,[7] as He has promised us in His Word.[8]

Question 118: What hath God commanded us to ask of Him?

Answer: All things necessary for soul and body,[9] which Christ our Lord has comprised in that prayer He Himself has taught us.[10]

Question 119: What are the words of that prayer?

Answer: Our Father which art in heaven, hallowed be Thy name. Thy kingdom come. Thy will be done in earth, as it is in heaven. Give us this day our daily bread. And forgive us our debts, as we forgive our debtors. And lead us not into temptation, but deliver us from evil: for Thine is the kingdom, and the power, and the glory, for ever. Amen.

[1] Ps. 50:14–15 [2] Matt. 7:7; Luke 11:9, 13; Matt. 13:12; Ps. 50:15 [3] John 4:22–23 [4] Rom. 8:26; 1 John 5:14 [5] John 4:23–24; Ps. 145:18 [6] 2 Chron. 20:12 [7] Ps. 2:11; Ps. 34:18–19; Isa. 66:2 [8] Rom. 10:13; Rom. 8:15–16; James 1:6; John 14:13; Dan. 9:17–18; Matt. 7:8; Ps. 143:1 [9] James 1:17; Matt. 6:33 [10] Matt. 6:9–10; Luke 11:2

LORD'S DAY 46

Question 120: Why hath Christ commanded us to address God thus: "Our Father"?

Answer: That immediately, in the very beginning of our prayer, He might excite in us a childlike reverence for and confidence in God, which are the foundation of our prayer, namely, that God is become our Father in Christ,[1] and will much less deny us what we ask of Him in true faith than our parents will refuse us earthly things.[2]

Question 121: Why is it here added, "which art in heaven"?

Answer: Lest we should form any earthly conceptions of God's heavenly majesty,[3] and that we may expect from His almighty power all things necessary for soul and body.[4]

[1] Matt. 6:9 [2] Matt. 7:9–11; Luke 11:11; Isa. 49:15 [3] Jer. 23:24 [4] Acts 17:24; Rom. 10:12

LORD'S DAY 47

Question 122: Which is the first petition?
Answer: "Hallowed be Thy name";[1] that is, grant us, first, rightly to know Thee,[2] and to sanctify, glorify and praise Thee in all Thy works, in which Thy power, wisdom, goodness, justice, mercy and truth, are clearly displayed;[3] and further also, that we may so order and direct our whole lives, our thoughts, words and actions, that Thy Name may never be blasphemed, but rather honored and praised on our account.[4]

[1] Matt. 6:9 [2] John 17:3; Jer. 9:23–24; Matt. 16:17; James 1:5 [3] Ps. 119:137–138; Luke 1:46; Ps. 145:8–9 [4] Ps. 115:1; Ps. 71:8

LORD'S DAY 48

Question 123: Which is the second petition?
Answer: "Thy kingdom come";[1] that is, rule us so by Thy Word and Spirit, that we may submit ourselves more and more to Thee;[2] preserve and increase Thy church;[3] destroy the works of the devil,[4] and all violence which would exalt itself against Thee; and also, all wicked counsels devised against Thy holy Word; till the full perfection of Thy kingdom take place,[5] wherein Thou shalt be all in all.[6]

[1] Matt. 6:10 [2] Ps. 119:5 [3] Ps. 51:18 [4] 1 John 3:8; Rom. 16:20 [5] Rev. 22:17, 20 [6] 1 Cor. 15:15, 28

LORD'S DAY 49

Question 124: Which is the third petition?
Answer: "Thy will be done in earth as it is in heaven";[1] that is, grant that we and all men may renounce our own will,[2] and without murmuring obey Thy will,[3] which is only good; that so every one may attend to and perform the duties of his station and calling[4] as willingly and faithfully as the angels do in heaven.[5]

[1] Matt. 6:10 [2] Matt. 16:24; Titus 2:12 [3] Luke 22:42 [4] 1 Cor. 7:24; Eph. 4:1 [5] Ps. 103:20

LORD'S DAY 50

Question 125: Which is the fourth petition?
Answer: "Give us this day our daily bread";[1] that is, be pleased to provide us with all things necessary for the body,[2] that we may thereby acknowledge Thee to be the only fountain of all good,[3] and that neither our care nor industry, nor even Thy gifts, can profit us without Thy blessing;[4] and therefore that we may withdraw our trust from all creatures and place it alone in Thee.[5]

[1] Matt. 6:11 [2] Ps. 145:15; Matt. 6:25 [3] Acts 17:25; Acts 14:17 [4] 1 Cor. 15:58; Deut. 8:3; Ps. 127:1–2 [5] Ps. 62:11; Ps. 55:22

LORD'S DAY 51

Question 126: Which is the fifth petition?
Answer: "And forgive us our debts as we forgive our debtors";[1] that is, be pleased for the sake of Christ's blood, not to impute to us poor sinners our transgressions, nor that depravity which always cleaves to us;[2] even as we feel this evidence of Thy grace in us, that it is our firm resolution from the heart to forgive our neighbor.[3]

[1] Matt. 6:12 [2] Ps. 51:1; 1 John 2:1–2 [3] Matt. 6:14–15

LORD'S DAY 52

Question 127: Which is the sixth petition?
Answer: "And lead us not into temptation, but deliver us from evil";[1] that is, since we are so weak in ourselves that we cannot stand a moment;[2] and besides this, since our mortal enemies, the

devil,[3] the world,[4] and our own flesh,[5] cease not to assault us, do Thou therefore preserve and strengthen us by the power of Thy Holy Spirit, that we may not be overcome in this spiritual warfare, but constantly and strenuously may resist our foes[6] till at last we obtain a complete victory.[7]

Question 128: How dost thou conclude thy prayer?
Answer: "For thine is the kingdom, and the power, and the glory, for ever";[8] that is, all these we ask of Thee, because Thou, being our King and almighty, art willing and able to give us all good;[9] and all this we pray for, that thereby not we, but Thy holy Name, may be glorified for ever.[10]

Question 129: What doth the word "Amen" signify?
Answer: "Amen" signifies it shall truly and certainly be, for my prayer is more assuredly heard of God than I feel in my heart that I desire these things of Him.[11]

---

[1] Matt. 6:13 [2] Rom. 8:26; Ps. 103:14 [3] 1 Pet. 5:8 [4] Eph. 6:12; John 15:19 [5] Rom. 7:23; Gal. 5:17 [6] Matt. 26:41; Mark 13:33 [7] 1 Thes. 3:13; 1 Thes. 5:23 [8] Matt. 6:13 [9] Rom. 10:12; 2 Pet. 2:9 [10] John 14:13; Ps. 115:1; Phil. 4:20 [11] 2 Cor. 1:20; 2 Tim. 2:13

THE CANONS OF DORT

RATIFIED IN THE NATIONAL SYNOD OF THE REFORMED CHURCH

Held at Dordrecht in the years 1618 and 1619

The Decision of the Synod of Dort on the Five Main Points of Doctrine in Dispute in the Netherlands is popularly known as the Canons of Dort (or the Five Articles Against the Remonstrants). It consists of statements of doctrine adopted by the great Synod of Dort which met in the city of Dordrecht in 1618–1619. Although this was a national Synod of the Reformed Churches of the Netherlands, it had an international character, since it was composed not only of sixty-two Dutch delegates, but also of twenty-seven foreign delegates representing eight countries.

The Synod of Dort was held in order to settle a serious controversy in the Dutch churches initiated by the rise of Arminianism. Jacob Arminius (1560–1609), a theological professor at Leiden University, departed from the Reformed faith on a number of important points. After Arminius's death, forty-three of his ministerial followers drafted and presented their heretical views to the States General of the Netherlands on five of these points in the Remonstrance of 1610. In this document and even more explicitly in later writings, the Arminians, who came to be called "Remonstrants," taught (1) election based on foreseen faith, (2) the universal merits of Christ, (3) the free will of man due to only partial depravity, (4) the resistibility of grace, and (5) the possibility of a lapse from grace. They desired the Reformed church's doctrinal standards to be revised and their own minority views to be protected by the government. The Arminian-Calvinism conflict became so severe that it led the Netherlands to the brink of civil war. Finally in 1617 the States General voted four to three to call a national Synod to address Arminianism.

The Synod held 154 formal sessions over a period of seven months (November 1618 to May 1619). Thirteen Remonstrant theologians, led by Simon Episcopius, used various tactics to delay the work of Synod and to divide the delegates — tactics which proved to be unsuccessful. Under the leadership of Johannes Bogerman, the Remonstrants were dismissed. The Synod then developed the Canons which thoroughly rejected the Remonstrance of 1610 and scripturally set forth the Reformed doctrine on these debated points, now popularly called "the five points of Calvinism": unconditional election, limited atonement, total depravity, irresistible grace, and the perseverance of saints. Though these points do not embrace the full scope of Calvinism and are better regarded as Calvinism's five answers to the five errors of Arminianism, they certainly lie at the heart of the Reformed faith, particularly Reformed soteriology, for they flow out of the principle of absolute divine sovereignty. They may be summarized as follows: (1) Unconditional election and faith are sovereign gifts of God. (2) While the death of Christ is abundantly sufficient to expiate the sins of the whole world, its saving efficacy is limited to the elect. (3,4) All are so totally depraved and corrupted by sin that they cannot effect any part of their salvation; in sovereign grace God irresistibly calls and regenerates the elect to newness of life. (5) Those thus saved God graciously preserves so that they persevere until the end, even though they may be troubled by many infirmities as they seek to make their calling and election sure. Simply stated, we may say that the subject matter of the Canons is: sovereign grace conceived, sovereign grace merited, sovereign grace needed and applied, and sovereign grace preserved.

Although in form the Canons have only four sections, we speak properly of five points or heads of doctrine because the Canons were structured to correspond to the five articles of the 1610 Remonstrance. The third and fourth sections were purposely combined into one since the Dortian divines considered them inseparable, and hence are designated as "Head of Doctrine 3/4."

The Canons have a special character because of their original purpose as a judicial decision on the doctrinal points in dispute during the Arminian controversy. The original preface called them a "judgment, in which both the true view, agreeing with God's Word, concerning the aforesaid five points of doctrine is explained, and the false view, disagreeing with God's Word, is rejected." The Canons also have a limited character in that they do not cover the whole range of doctrine, but focus on the five points of doctrine in dispute. Each of the main heads consists of a positive and a negative part, the former being an exposition of the Reformed doctrine on the subject, the latter a repudiation of corresponding Arminian errors (see italicized parts below). In all, the Canons contain fifty-nine articles of exposition and thirty-four repudiations of error.

The Canons form a remarkably scriptural and balanced document on the specific doctrines expounded. They are unique in being the sole Form of Unity composed by an ecclesiastical assembly and in representing a consensus of all the Reformed churches of their day. Both Dutch and foreign delegates without exception affixed their signatures to the Canons, whether of supralapsarian or infralapsarian persuasion. A service of thanksgiving was held upon the Canons' completion to acknowledge the Lord for preserving the doctrine of sovereign grace among the Reformed churches.

FIRST HEAD OF DOCTRINE

Of Divine Predestination

ARTICLE 1

As all men have sinned in Adam, lie under the curse, and are deserving of eternal death, God would have done no injustice by leaving them all to perish, and delivering them over to condemnation on account of sin, according to the words of the apostle, "that every mouth may be stopped, and all the world may become guilty before God" (Rom. 3:19). And verse 23: "For all have sinned, and come short of the glory of God." And Romans 6:23: "For the wages of sin is death."

ARTICLE 2

But in this the love of God was manifested, that He sent His only begotten Son into the world, that whosoever believeth on Him should not perish, but have everlasting life. "In this was manifested the love of God toward us, because that God sent His only begotten Son into the world, that we might live through Him" (1 John 4:9). "For God so loved the world, that He gave His only begotten Son, that whosoever believeth in Him should not perish, but have everlasting life" (John 3:16).

ARTICLE 3

And that men may be brought to believe, God mercifully sends the messengers of these most joyful tidings to whom He will and at what time He pleaseth; by whose ministry men are called to repentance and faith in Christ crucified. "How then shall they call on Him in whom they have not believed? and how shall they believe in Him of whom they have not heard? and how shall they hear without a preacher? And how shall they preach, except they be sent?" (Rom. 10:14–15).

ARTICLE 4

The wrath of God abideth upon those who believe not this gospel. But such as receive it, and embrace Jesus the Savior by a true and living faith, are by Him delivered from the wrath of God and from destruction, and have the gift of eternal life conferred upon them.

ARTICLE 5

The cause or guilt of this unbelief, as well as of all other sins, is no wise in God, but in man himself; whereas faith in Jesus Christ and salvation through Him is the free gift of God, as it is written: "For by grace are ye saved through faith; and that not of yourselves: it is the gift of

God" (Eph. 2:8). "For unto you it is given in the behalf of Christ, not only to believe on Him," etc. (Phil. 1:29).

ARTICLE 6

That some receive the gift of faith from God and others do not receive it proceeds from God's eternal decree, for "known unto God are all his works from the beginning of the world" (Acts 15:18). "Who worketh all things after the counsel of his own will" (Eph. 1:11). According to which decree, He graciously softens the hearts of the elect, however obstinate, and inclines them to believe, while He leaves the non-elect in His just judgment to their own wickedness and obduracy. And herein is especially displayed the profound, the merciful, and at the same time the righteous discrimination between men, equally involved in ruin; or that decree of election and reprobation revealed in the Word of God, which though men of perverse, impure and unstable minds wrest to their own destruction, yet to holy and pious souls affords unspeakable consolation.

ARTICLE 7

Election is the unchangeable purpose of God, whereby, before the foundation of the world, He hath out of mere grace, according to the sovereign good pleasure of His own will, chosen, from the whole human race, which had fallen through their own fault from their primitive state of rectitude into sin and destruction, a certain number of persons to redemption in Christ, whom He from eternity appointed the Mediator and Head of the elect, and the foundation of salvation.

This elect number, though by nature neither better nor more deserving than others, but with them involved in one common misery, God hath decreed to give to Christ, to be saved by Him, and effectually to call and draw them to His communion by His Word and Spirit, to bestow upon them true faith, justification and sanctification; and having powerfully preserved them in the fellowship of His Son, finally, to glorify them for the demonstration of His mercy and for the praise of His glorious grace, as it is written: "According as he hath chosen us in him before the foundation of the world, that we should be holy and without blame before him in love: having predestinated us unto the adoption of children by Jesus Christ to himself, according to the good pleasure of his will, to the praise of the glory of his grace, wherein he hath made us accepted in the beloved" (Eph. 1:4–6). And elsewhere: "Whom he did predestinate, them he also called: and whom he called, them he also justified: and whom he justified them he also glorified" (Rom. 8:30).

ARTICLE 8

There are not various decrees of election, but one and the same decree respecting all those who shall be saved, both under the Old and New Testament; since the Scripture declares the good pleasure, purpose and counsel of the divine will to be one, according to which He hath chosen us from eternity, both to grace and glory, to salvation and the way of salvation, which He hath ordained that we should walk therein.

ARTICLE 9

This election was not founded upon foreseen faith, and the obedience of faith, holiness, or any other good quality or disposition in man, as the prerequisite, cause or condition on which it depended; but men are chosen to faith and to the obedience of faith, holiness, etc.; therefore election is the fountain of every saving good, from which proceeds faith, holiness, and the other gifts of salvation, and finally eternal life itself, as its fruits and effects, according to that of the apostle: "He hath chosen us [not because we were but] that we should be holy, and without blame, before him in love" (Eph. 1:4).

ARTICLE 10

The good pleasure of God is the sole cause of this gracious election, which doth not consist herein, that out of all possible qualities and actions of men God has chosen some as a condition of salvation; but that He was pleased out of the common mass of sinners to adopt some certain persons as a peculiar people to Himself, as it is written, "For the children being not yet born, neither having done any good or evil," etc., it was said (namely to Rebecca): "The elder shall serve the younger. As it is written, Jacob have I loved, but Esau have I hated" (Rom. 9:11-13). "And as many as were ordained to eternal life believed" (Acts 13:48).

ARTICLE 11

And as God Himself is most wise, unchangeable, omniscient and omnipotent, so the election made by Him can neither be interrupted nor changed, recalled or annulled; neither can the elect be cast away, nor their number diminished.

ARTICLE 12

The elect in due time, though in various degrees and in different measures, attain the assurance of this their eternal and unchangeable election, not by inquisitively prying into the secret and deep things of God, but by observing in themselves, with a spiritual joy and holy pleasure, the infallible fruits of election pointed out in the Word of God — such as a true faith in Christ, filial fear, a godly sorrow for sin, a hungering and thirsting after righteousness, etc.

ARTICLE 13

The sense and certainty of this election afford to the children of God additional matter for daily humiliation before Him, for adoring the depth of His mercies, for cleansing themselves, and rendering grateful returns of ardent love to Him, who first manifested so great love towards them. The consideration of this doctrine of election is so far from encouraging remissness in the observance of the divine commands or from sinking men in carnal security, that these, in the just judgment of God, are the usual effects of rash presumption or of idle and wanton trifling with the grace of election in those who refuse to walk in the ways of the elect.

ARTICLE 14

As the doctrine of divine election by the most wise counsel of God was declared by the prophets, by Christ Himself, and by the apostles, and is clearly revealed in the Scriptures, both of the Old and New Testament, so it is still to be published in due time and place in the Church of God, for which it was peculiarly designed, provided it be done with reverence, in the spirit of discretion and piety, for the glory of God's most holy Name, and for enlivening and comforting His people, without vainly attempting to investigate the secret ways of the Most High. "For I have not shunned to declare unto you all the counsel of God" (Acts 20:27); "O the depth of the riches both of the wisdom and knowledge of God! how unsearchable are his judgments, and his ways past finding out! For who hath known the mind of the Lord? or who hath been his counsellor?" (Rom. 11:33–34); "For I say, through the grace given unto me, to every man that is among you, not to think of himself more highly than he ought to think; but to think soberly, according as God hath dealt to every man the measure of faith" (Rom. 12:3); "Wherein God, willing more abundantly to shew unto the heirs of promise the immutability of his counsel, confirmed it by an oath: that by two immutable things, in which it was impossible for God to lie, we might have a strong consolation, who have fled for refuge to lay hold upon the hope set before us" (Heb. 6:17–18).

ARTICLE 15

What peculiarly tends to illustrate and recommend to us the eternal and unmerited grace of election, is the express testimony of sacred Scripture that not all, but some only are elected, while others are passed by in the eternal decree; whom God, out of His sovereign, most just, irreprehensible and unchangeable good pleasure, hath decreed to leave in the common misery into which they have wilfully plunged themselves, and not to bestow upon them saving faith and the grace of conversion; but permitting them in His just judgment to follow their own ways, at last for the declaration of His justice, to condemn and perish them forever, not only on account of their unbelief, but also for all their other sins. And this is the decree of reprobation which by no means makes God the author of sin (the very thought of which is blasphemy), but declares Him to be an awful, irreprehensible, and righteous Judge and avenger thereof.

ARTICLE 16

Those who do not yet experience a lively faith in Christ, an assured confidence of soul, peace of conscience, an earnest endeavor after filial obedience, and glorying in God through Christ, efficaciously wrought in them, and do nevertheless persist in the use of the means which God hath appointed for working these graces in us, ought not to be alarmed at the mention of reprobation, nor to rank themselves among the reprobate, but diligently to persevere in the use of means, and with ardent desires devoutly and humbly to wait for a season of richer grace. Much less cause have they to be terrified by the doctrine of reprobation, who, though they seriously desire to be turned to God, to please Him only, and to be delivered from the body of death, cannot yet reach that measure of holiness and faith to which they aspire; since a merciful God has promised that He will not quench the smoking flax nor break the bruised reed. But this doctrine is justly terrible to those, who, regardless of God and of the Savior Jesus Christ, have wholly given themselves up to the cares of the world and the pleasures of the flesh, so long as they are not seriously converted to God.

ARTICLE 17

Since we are to judge of the will of God from His Word which testifies that the children of believers are holy, not by nature, but in virtue of the covenant of grace, in which they, together with the parents, are comprehended, godly parents have no reason to doubt of the election and salvation of their children whom it pleaseth God to call out of this life in their infancy.

ARTICLE 18

To those who murmur at the free grace of election and just severity of reprobation, we answer with the apostle: "Nay but, O man, who art thou that repliest against God?" (Rom. 9:20), and quote the language of our Savior: "Is it not lawful for me to do what I will with mine own?" (Matt. 20:15). And therefore with holy adoration of these mysteries, we exclaim in the words of the apostle: "O the depth of the riches both of the wisdom and knowledge of God! how unsearchable are his judgments, and his ways past finding out! For who hath known the mind of the Lord? or who hath been his counsellor? Or who hath first given to him, and it shall be recompensed unto him again? For of him, and through him, and to him, are all things: to whom be glory for ever. Amen" (Rom. 11:33–36).

The true doctrine concerning election and rejection having been explained, the Synod **rejects** the errors of those who teach:

REJECTION 1

That the will of God to save those who would believe and would persevere in faith and in the obedience of faith, is the whole and entire decree of election unto salvation, and that nothing else concerning this decree has been revealed in God's Word.

For these deceive the simple and plainly contradict the Scriptures which declare that God will not only save those who will believe, but that He has also from eternity chosen certain particular persons to whom above others He in time will grant both faith in Christ and perseverance, as it is written: "I have manifested thy name unto the men which thou gavest me out of the world" (John 17:6). "And as many as were ordained to eternal life believed" (Acts 13:48). And: "According as he hath chosen us in him before the foundation of the world, that we should be holy and without blame before him in love" (Eph. 1:4).

REJECTION 2

That there are various kinds of election of God unto eternal life: the one general and indefinite, the other particular and definite; and that the latter in turn is either incomplete, revocable, nondecisive and conditional, or complete, irrevocable, decisive and absolute. Likewise: that there is one election unto faith and another unto salvation, so that election can be unto justifying faith without being a decisive election unto salvation.

For this is a fancy of men's minds, invented regardless of the Scriptures, whereby the doctrine of election is corrupted, and this golden chain of our salvation is broken: "Moreover whom he did predestinate, them he also called: and whom he called, them he also justified: and whom he justified, them he also glorified" (Rom. 8:30).

REJECTION 3

That the good pleasure and purpose of God, of which Scripture makes mention in the doctrine of election, does not consist in this, that God chose certain persons rather than others, but in this, that He chose out of all possible conditions (among which are also the works of the law), or out of the whole order of things, the act of faith which from its very nature is undeserving, as well as its incomplete obedience, as a condition of salvation, and that He would graciously consider this in itself as a complete obedience and count it worthy of the reward of eternal life.

For by this injurious error the pleasure of God and the merits of Christ are made of none effect, and men are drawn away by useless questions from the truth of gracious justification and from the simplicity of Scripture, and this declaration of the apostle is charged as untrue: "Who hath saved us, and called us with an holy calling, not according to our works, but according to his own purpose and grace, which was given us in Christ Jesus before the world began" (2 Tim. 1:9).

REJECTION 4

That in the election unto faith this condition is beforehand demanded, namely, that man should use the light of nature aright, be pious, humble, meek, and fit for eternal life, as if on these things election were in any way dependent.

For this savors of the teaching of Pelagius, and is opposed to the doctrine of the apostle, when he writes: "Among whom also we all had our conversation in times past in the lusts of our flesh, fulfilling the desires of the flesh and of the mind; and were by nature the children of wrath, even as others. But God, who is rich in mercy, for his great love wherewith he loved us, even when we were dead in sins, hath quickened us together with Christ, (by grace ye are saved;) and hath raised us up together, and made us sit together in heavenly places in Christ Jesus: that in the ages to come he might show the exceeding riches of his grace in his kindness toward us through Christ Jesus. For by grace are ye saved through faith; and that not of yourselves: it is the gift of God: not of works, lest any man should boast" (Eph. 2:3–9).

REJECTION 5

That the incomplete and non-decisive election of particular persons to salvation occurred because of a foreseen faith, conversion, holiness, godliness, which either began or continued for some time; but that the complete and decisive election occurred because of foreseen perseverance unto the end in faith, conversion, holiness and godliness; and that this is the gracious and evangelical worthiness for the sake of which he who is chosen is more worthy than he who is not chosen; and that therefore faith, the obedience of faith, holiness, godliness and perseverance are not fruits of the unchangeable election unto glory, but are conditions, which, being required beforehand, were foreseen as being met by those who will be fully elected, and are causes without which the unchangeable election to glory does not occur.

This is repugnant to the entire Scripture which constantly inculcates this and similar declarations: Election is not out of works, but of him that calleth. "That the purpose of God according to election might stand, not of works, but of him that calleth" (Rom. 9:11). "And as many as were ordained to eternal life believed" (Acts 13:48). "He hath chosen us in him before the foundation of the world, that we should be holy" (Eph. 1:4). "Ye have not chosen me, but I have chosen you" (John 15:16). "But if it be of works, then is it no more grace" (Rom. 11:6). "Herein is love, not that we loved God, but that he loved us, and sent his Son" (1 John 4:10).

REJECTION 6

That not every election unto salvation is unchangeable, but that some of the elect, any decree of God notwithstanding, can yet perish and do indeed perish.

By which gross error they make God to be changeable, and destroy the comfort which the godly obtain out of the firmness of their election, and contradict the Holy Scripture which teaches that the elect cannot be led astray: "Insomuch that, if it were possible, they shall deceive the very elect" (Matt. 24:24); that Christ does not lose those whom the Father gave Him: "And this is the Father's will which hath sent me, that of all which he hath given me I should lose nothing" (John 6:39); and that God hath also glorified those whom he foreordained, called and justified: "Moreover whom he did predestinate, them he also called: and whom he called, them he also justified: and whom he justified, them he also glorified" (Rom. 8:30).

REJECTION 7

That there is in this life no fruit and no consciousness of the unchangeable election to glory, nor any certainty, except that which depends on a changeable and uncertain condition.

For not only is it absurd to speak of an uncertain certainty, but also contrary to the experience of the saints, who by virtue of the consciousness of their election rejoice with the apostle and praise this favor of God, Ephesians 1; who according to Christ's admonition rejoice with His disciples that their names are written in heaven, "but rather rejoice, because your names are written in heaven" (Luke 10:20); who also place the consciousness of their election over against the fiery darts of the devil, asking: "Who shall lay any thing to the charge of God's elect?" (Rom. 8:33).

REJECTION 8

That God, simply by virtue of His righteous will, did not decide either to leave anyone in the fall of Adam and in the common state of sin and condemnation, or to pass anyone by in the communication of grace which is necessary for faith and conversion.

For this is firmly decreed: "Therefore hath he mercy on whom he will have mercy, and whom he will he hardeneth" (Rom. 9:18). And also this: "It is given unto you to know the mysteries of the kingdom of heaven, but to them it is not given" (Matt. 13:11). Likewise: "I thank thee, O Father, Lord of heaven and earth, because thou hast hid these things from the wise and prudent, and hast revealed them unto babes. Even so, Father: for so it seemed good in thy sight" (Matt. 11:25–26).

REJECTION 9

That the reason why God sends the gospel to one people rather than to another is not merely and solely the good pleasure of God, but rather the fact that one people is better and worthier than another to whom the gospel is not communicated.

For this Moses denies, addressing the people of Israel as follows: "Behold, the heaven and the heaven of heavens is the LORD's thy God, the earth also, with all that therein is. Only the LORD had a delight in thy fathers to love them, and he chose their seed after them, even you above all people, as it is this day" (Deut. 10:14–15). And Christ said: "Woe unto thee, Chorazin! woe unto thee, Bethsaida! for if the mighty works, which were done in you, had been done in Tyre and Sidon, they would have repented long ago in sackcloth and ashes" (Matt. 11:21).

SECOND HEAD OF DOCTRINE
Of the Death of Christ and the Redemption of Men Thereby

ARTICLE 1

God is not only supremely merciful, but also supremely just. And His justice requires (as He hath revealed Himself in His Word), that our sins committed against His infinite majesty should be punished, not only with temporal, but with eternal punishment, both in body and soul; which we cannot escape unless satisfaction be made to the justice of God.

ARTICLE 2

Since therefore we are unable to make that satisfaction in our own persons or to deliver ourselves from the wrath of God, He hath been pleased in His infinite mercy to give His only begotten Son, for our surety, who was made sin, and became a curse for us and in our stead, that He might make satisfaction to divine justice on our behalf.

ARTICLE 3

The death of the Son of God is the only and most perfect sacrifice and satisfaction for sin, and is of infinite worth and value, abundantly sufficient to expiate the sins of the whole world.

ARTICLE 4

This death derives its infinite value and dignity from these considerations because the person who submitted to it was not only really man and perfectly holy, but also the only begotten Son of God, of the same eternal and infinite essence with the Father and the Holy Spirit, which qualifications were necessary to constitute Him a Savior for us; and because it was attended with a sense of the wrath and curse of God due to us for sin.

ARTICLE 5
Moreover, the promise of the gospel is, that whosoever believeth in Christ crucified, shall not perish, but have everlasting life. This promise, together with the command to repent and believe, ought to be declared and published to all nations, and to all persons promiscuously and without distinction, to whom God out of His good pleasure sends the gospel.

ARTICLE 6
And whereas many who are called by the gospel do not repent nor believe in Christ, but perish in unbelief, this is not owing to any defect or insufficiency in the sacrifice offered by Christ upon the cross, but is wholly to be imputed to themselves.

ARTICLE 7
But as many as truly believe, and are delivered and saved from sin and destruction through the death of Christ, are indebted for this benefit solely to the grace of God, given them in Christ from everlasting, and not to any merit of their own.

ARTICLE 8
For this was the sovereign counsel, and most gracious will and purpose of God the Father, that the quickening and saving efficacy of the most precious death of His Son should extend to all the elect, for bestowing upon them alone the gift of justifying faith, thereby to bring them infallibly to salvation: that is, it was the will of God, that Christ by the blood of the cross, whereby He confirmed the new covenant, should effectually redeem out of every people, tribe, nation, and language, all those, and those only, who were from eternity chosen to salvation and given to Him by the Father; that He should confer upon them faith, which together with all the other saving gifts of the Holy Spirit, He purchased for them by His death; should purge them from all sin, both original and actual, whether committed before or after believing; and having faithfully preserved them even to the end, should at last bring them free from every spot and blemish to the enjoyment of glory in His own presence forever.

ARTICLE 9
This purpose proceeding from everlasting love towards the elect has from the beginning of the world to this day been powerfully accomplished, and will henceforward still continue to be accomplished, notwithstanding all the ineffectual opposition of the gates of hell, so that the elect in due time may be gathered together into one, and that there never may be wanting a church composed of believers, the foundation of which is laid in the blood of Christ, which may steadfastly love and faithfully serve Him as their Savior, who as a bridegroom for his bride, laid down His life for them upon the cross, and which may celebrate His praises here and through all eternity.

The true doctrine (concerning redemption) having been explained, the Synod **rejects** the errors of those who teach:

REJECTION 1
That God the Father has ordained His Son to the death of the cross without a certain and definite decree to save any, so that the necessity, profitableness and worth of what Christ merited by His death might have existed, and might remain in all its parts complete, perfect and intact, even if the merited redemption had never in fact been applied to any person.

For this doctrine tends to the despising of the wisdom of the Father and of the merits of Jesus Christ, and is contrary to Scripture. For thus saith our Savior: "I lay down my life for the sheep, and I know them" (John 10:15, 27). And the prophet Isaiah saith concerning the Savior: "When thou shalt make his soul an offering for sin, he shall see his seed, he shall prolong his days, and the pleasure of the LORD shall prosper in his hand" (Is. 53:10). Finally, this contradicts the article of faith according to which we believe the catholic Christian church.

REJECTION 2
That it was not the purpose of the death of Christ that He should confirm the new covenant of grace through His blood, but only that He should acquire for the Father the mere right to establish with man such a covenant as He might please, whether of grace or of works.

For this is repugnant to Scripture which teaches that Christ has become the Surety and Mediator of a better, that is, the new covenant, and that a testament is of force where death has occurred. "By so much was Jesus made a surety of a better testament" (Heb. 7:22); "And for this cause he is the Mediator of the new testament, that by means of death, for the redemption of the transgressions that were under the first testament, they which are called might receive the promise of eternal inheritance"; "For a testament is of force after men are dead: otherwise it is of no strength at all while the testator liveth" (Heb. 9:15, 17).

REJECTION 3

That Christ by His satisfaction merited neither salvation itself for anyone, nor faith, whereby this satisfaction of Christ unto salvation is effectually appropriated; but that He merited for the Father only the authority or the perfect will to deal again with man, and to prescribe new conditions as He might desire, obedience to which, however, depended on the free will of man, so that it therefore might have come to pass that either none or all should fulfill these conditions.

For these adjudge too contemptuously of the death of Christ, do in no wise acknowledge the most important fruit or benefit thereby gained, and bring again out of hell the Pelagian error.

REJECTION 4

That the new covenant of grace, which God the Father, through the mediation of the death of Christ, made with man, does not herein consist that we by faith, inasmuch as it accepts the merits of Christ, are justified before God and saved, but in the fact that God having revoked the demand of perfect obedience of faith, regards faith itself and the obedience of faith, although imperfect, as the perfect obedience of the law, and does esteem it worthy of the reward of eternal life through grace.

For these contradict the Scriptures: "Being justified freely by his grace through the redemption that is in Christ Jesus: whom God hath set forth to be a propitiation through faith in his blood" (Rom. 3:24–25). And these proclaim, as did the wicked Socinus, a new and strange justification of man before God against the consensus of the whole church.

REJECTION 5

That all men have been accepted unto the state of reconciliation and unto the grace of the covenant, so that no one is worthy of condemnation on account of original sin, and that no one shall be condemned because of it, but that all are free from the guilt of original sin.

For this opinion is repugnant to Scripture which teaches that we are by nature children of wrath (Eph. 2:3).

REJECTION 6

The use of the difference between meriting and appropriating, to the end that they may instill into the minds of the imprudent and inexperienced this teaching that God, as far as He is concerned, has been minded of applying to all equally the benefits gained by the death of Christ; but that, while some obtain the pardon of sin and eternal life, and others do not, this difference depends on their own free will, which joins itself to the grace that is offered without exception, and that it is not dependent on the special gift of mercy, which powerfully works in them, that they rather than others should appropriate unto themselves this grace.

For these, while they feign that they present this distinction in a sound sense, seek to instill into the people the destructive poison of the Pelagian errors.

REJECTION 7

That Christ neither could die, needed to die, nor did die for those whom God loved in the highest degree and elected to eternal life, and did not die for these, since these do not need the death of Christ.

For they contradict the apostle, who declares: "the Son of God, who loved me, and gave himself for me" (Gal. 2:20). Likewise: "Who shall lay any thing to the charge of God's elect? It is God that justifieth. Who is he that condemneth? It is Christ that died" (Rom. 8:33–34), namely, for them; and the Savior who says: "I lay down my life for the sheep" (John 10:15). And: "This is my commandment, That ye love one another, as I have loved you. Greater love hath no man than this, that a man lay down his life for his friends" (John 15:12–13).

THIRD AND FOURTH HEADS OF DOCTRINE
Of the Corruption of Man, His Conversion to God, and the Manner Thereof

ARTICLE 1
Man was originally formed after the image of God. His understanding was adorned with a true and saving knowledge of his Creator and of spiritual things; his heart and will were upright; all his affections pure; and the whole man was holy; but revolting from God by the instigation of the devil, and abusing the freedom of his own will, he forfeited these excellent gifts; and on the contrary entailed on himself blindness of mind, horrible darkness, vanity and perverseness of judgment, became wicked, rebellious, and obdurate in heart and will, and impure in his affections.

ARTICLE 2
Man after the fall begat children in his own likeness. A corrupt stock produced a corrupt offspring. Hence all the posterity of Adam, Christ only excepted, have derived corruption from their original parent, not by imitation, as the Pelagians of old asserted, but by the propagation of a vicious nature.

ARTICLE 3
Therefore all men are conceived in sin, and by nature children of wrath, incapable of saving good, prone to evil, dead in sin, and in bondage thereto, and without the regenerating grace of the Holy Spirit, they are neither able nor willing to return to God, to reform the depravity of their nature, or to dispose themselves to reformation.

ARTICLE 4
There remain, however, in man since the fall, the glimmerings of natural light, whereby he retains some knowledge of God, of natural things, and of the differences between good and evil, and discovers some regard for virtue, good order in society, and for maintaining an orderly external deportment. But so far is this light of nature from being sufficient to bring him to a saving knowledge of God and to true conversion, that he is incapable of using it aright even in things natural and civil. Nay, further, this light, such as it is, man in various ways renders wholly polluted and holds it in unrighteousness, by doing which he becomes inexcusable before God.

ARTICLE 5
In the same light are we to consider the law of the decalogue, delivered by God to His peculiar people the Jews by the hands of Moses. For though it discovers the greatness of sin, and more and more convinces man thereof, yet as it neither points out a remedy nor imparts strength to extricate him from misery, and thus being weak through the flesh leaves the transgressor under the curse, man cannot by this law obtain saving grace.

ARTICLE 6
What therefore neither the light of nature, nor the law could do, that God performs by the operation of the Holy Spirit through the Word or ministry of reconciliation, which is the glad tidings concerning the Messiah, by means whereof it hath pleased God to save such as believe, as well under the Old, as under the New Testament.

ARTICLE 7
This mystery of His will God discovered to but a small number under the Old Testament; under the New (the distinction between various peoples having been removed), He reveals Himself to many without any distinction of people. The cause of this dispensation is not to be ascribed to the superior worth of one nation above another, nor to their making a better use of the light of nature, but results wholly from the sovereign good pleasure and unmerited love of God. Hence they, to whom so great and so gracious a blessing is communicated above their desert, or rather notwithstanding their demerits, are bound to acknowledge it with humble and grateful hearts, and with the apostle to adore, not curiously to pry into the severity and justice of God's judgments displayed to others, to whom this grace is not given.

ARTICLE 8
As many as are called by the gospel are unfeignedly called. For God hath most earnestly and truly declared in His Word what will be acceptable to Him; namely, that all who are called, should comply with the invitation. He, moreover, seriously promises eternal life and rest to as many as shall come to Him and believe on Him.

ARTICLE 9
It is not the fault of the gospel nor of Christ, offered therein, nor of God, who calls men by the gospel and confers upon them various gifts, that those who are called by the ministry of the Word refuse to come and be converted. The fault lies in themselves, some of whom when called, regardless of their danger, reject the word of life; others, though they receive it, suffer it not to make a lasting impression on their heart; therefore, their joy, arising only from a temporary faith, soon vanishes and they fall away; while others choke the seed of the Word by perplexing cares and the pleasures of this world, and produce no fruit. This our Savior teaches in the parable of the sower (Matt. 13).

ARTICLE 10
But that others who are called by the gospel obey the call and are converted is not to be ascribed to the proper exercise of free will, whereby one distinguishes himself above others, equally furnished with grace sufficient for faith and conversions as the proud heresy of Pelagius maintains; but it must be wholly ascribed to God, who as He has chosen His own from eternity in Christ, so He confers upon them faith and repentance, rescues them from the power of darkness, and translates them into the kingdom of His own Son, that they may show forth the praises of Him who hath called them out of darkness into His marvelous light; and may glory not in themselves, but in the Lord according to the testimony of the apostles in various places.

ARTICLE 11
But when God accomplishes His good pleasure in the elect or works in them true conversion, He not only causes the gospel to be externally preached to them and powerfully illuminates their mind by His Holy Spirit, that they may rightly understand and discern the things of the Spirit of God; but by the efficacy of the same regenerating Spirit, pervades the inmost recesses of the man; He opens the closed, and softens the hardened heart, and circumcises that which was uncircumcised, infuses new qualities into the will, which though heretofore dead, He quickens; from being evil, disobedient, and refractory, He renders it good, obedient, and pliable; actuates and strengthens it, that like a good tree, it may bring forth the fruits of good actions.

ARTICLE 12
And this is the regeneration so highly celebrated in Scripture and denominated a new creation: a resurrection from the dead, a making alive, which God works in us without our aid. But this is in no wise effected merely by the external preaching of the gospel, by moral suasion, or such a mode of operation, that after God has performed His part, it still remains in the power of man to be regenerated or not, to be converted or to continue unconverted; but it is evidently a supernatural work, most powerful, and at the same time most delightful, astonishing, mysterious, and ineffable; not inferior in efficacy to creation or the resurrection from the dead, as the Scripture inspired by the author of this work declares; so that all in whose heart God works in this marvelous manner are certainly, infallibly, and effectually regenerated, and do actually believe. Whereupon the will thus renewed is not only actuated and influenced by God, but in consequence of this influence, becomes itself active. Wherefore also, man is himself rightly said to believe and repent, by virtue of that grace received.

ARTICLE 13
The manner of this operation cannot be fully comprehended by believers in this life. Notwithstanding which, they rest satisfied with knowing and experiencing that by this grace of God they are enabled to believe with the heart, and love their Savior.

ARTICLE 14
Faith is therefore to be considered as the gift of God, not on account of its being offered by God to man, to be accepted or rejected at his pleasure; but because it is in reality conferred,

breathed, and infused into him; or even because God bestows the power or ability to believe, and then expects that man should by the exercise of his own free will, consent to the terms of salvation and actually believe in Christ; but because He who works in man both to will and to do, and indeed all things in all, produces both the will to believe and the act of believing also.

ARTICLE 15
God is under no obligation to confer this grace upon any; for how can He be indebted to man, who had no previous gifts to bestow, as a foundation for such recompense? Nay, who has nothing of his own but sin and falsehood? He therefore who becomes the subject of this grace, owes eternal gratitude to God, and gives Him thanks forever. Whoever is not made partaker thereof, is either altogether regardless of these spiritual gifts and satisfied with his own condition, or is in no apprehension of danger and vainly boasts the possession of that which he has not. With respect to those who make an external profession of faith and live regular lives, we are bound, after the example of the apostle, to judge and speak of them in the most favorable manner. For the secret recesses of the heart are unknown to us. And as to others, who have not yet been called, it is our duty to pray for them to God, who calls the things that are not, as if they were. But we are in no wise to conduct ourselves towards them with haughtiness, as if we had made ourselves to differ.

ARTICLE 16
But as man by the fall did not cease to be a creature endowed with understanding and will, nor did sin which pervaded the whole race of mankind deprive him of the human nature, but brought upon him depravity and spiritual death; so also this grace of regeneration does not treat men as senseless stocks and blocks, nor takes away their will and its properties, neither does violence thereto; but spiritually quickens, heals, corrects, and at the same time sweetly and powerfully bends it; that where carnal rebellion and resistance formerly prevailed, a ready and sincere spiritual obedience begins to reign, in which the true and spiritual restoration and freedom of our will consist. Wherefore unless the admirable Author of every good work wrought in us, man could have no hope of recovering from his fall by his own free will, by the abuse of which, in a state of innocence, he plunged himself into ruin.

ARTICLE 17
As the almighty operation of God, whereby He prolongs and supports this our natural life, does not exclude, but requires the use of means, by which God of His infinite mercy and goodness hath chosen to exert His influence, so also the beforementioned supernatural operation of God, by which we are regenerated, in no wise excludes or subverts the use of the gospel, which the most wise God has ordained to be the seed of regeneration and food of the soul. Wherefore, as the apostles, and teachers who succeeded them, piously instructed the people concerning this grace of God, to His glory, and the abasement of all pride, and in the meantime, however, neglected not to keep them by the sacred precepts of the gospel in the exercise of the Word, sacraments and discipline; so even to this day, be it far from either instructors or instructed to presume to tempt God in the church by separating what He of His good pleasure hath most intimately joined together. For grace is conferred by means of admonitions; and the more readily we perform our duty, the more eminent usually is this blessing of God working in us, and the more directly is His work advanced; to whom alone all the glory both of means, and of their saving fruit and efficacy is forever due. Amen.

The true doctrine (concerning corruption and conversion) having been explained, the Synod **rejects** the errors of those who teach:

REJECTION 1
That it cannot properly be said that original sin in itself suffices to condemn the whole human race or to deserve temporal and eternal punishment.

For these contradict the apostle, who declares: "Wherefore, as by one man sin entered into the world, and death by sin; and so death passed upon all men, for that all have sinned" (Rom. 5:12). And: "The judgment was by one to condemnation" (Rom. 5:16). And: "The wages of sin is death" (Rom. 6:23).

REJECTION 2

That the spiritual gifts or the good qualities and virtues, such as goodness, holiness, righteousness, could not belong to the will of man when he was first created, and that these, therefore, could not have been separated therefrom in the fall.

For such is contrary to the description of the image of God which the apostle gives in Ephesians 4:24, where he declares that it consists in righteousness and holiness, which undoubtedly belong to the will.

REJECTION 3

That in spiritual death the spiritual gifts are not separate from the will of man, since the will in itself has never been corrupted, but only hindered through the darkness of the understanding and the irregularity of the affections; and that, these hindrances having been removed, the will can then bring into operation its native powers, that is, that the will of itself is able to will and to choose, or not to will and not to choose, all manner of good which may be presented to it.

This is an innovation and an error, and tends to elevate the powers of the free will, contrary to the declaration of the prophet: "The heart is deceitful above all things, and desperately wicked" (Jer. 17:9); and of the apostle: "Among whom (sons of disobedience) also we all had our conversation in times past in the lusts of our flesh, fulfilling the desires of the flesh and of the mind" (Eph. 2:3).

REJECTION 4

That the unregenerate man is not really nor utterly dead in sin, nor destitute of all powers unto spiritual good, but that he can yet hunger and thirst after righteousness and life, and offer the sacrifice of a contrite and broken spirit, which is pleasing to God.

For these are contrary to the express testimony of Scripture. "Who were dead in trespasses and sins"; "Even when we were dead in sins" (Eph. 2:1, 5); and: "every imagination of the thoughts of his heart was only evil continually" (Gen. 6:5); "for the imagination of man's heart is evil from his youth" (Gen. 8:21).

Moreover, to hunger and thirst after deliverance from misery, and after life, and to offer unto God the sacrifice of a broken spirit, is peculiar to the regenerate and those that are called blessed. "Create in me a clean heart, O God; and renew a right spirit within me"; "Then shalt thou be pleased with the sacrifices of righteousness, with burnt offering and whole burnt offering: then shall they offer bullocks upon thine altar" (Ps. 51:10, 19); "Blessed are they which do hunger and thirst after righteousness: for they shall be filled" (Matt. 5:6).

REJECTION 5

That the corrupt and natural man can so well use the common grace (by which they understand the light of nature), or the gifts still left him after the fall, that he can gradually gain by their good use a greater, namely, the evangelical or saving grace and salvation itself. And that in this way God on His part shows Himself ready to reveal Christ unto all men, since He applies to all sufficiently and efficiently the means necessary to conversion.

For the experience of all ages and the Scriptures do both testify that this is untrue. "He sheweth his word unto Jacob, his statutes and His judgments unto Israel. He hath not dealt so with any nation: and as for his judgments, they have not known them" (Ps. 147:19, 20). "Who in times past suffered all nations to walk in their own ways" (Acts 14:16). And: "Now when they (Paul and his companions) had gone throughout Phrygia and the region of Galatia, and were forbidden of the Holy Ghost to preach the word in Asia, after they were come to Mysia, they assayed to go into Bithynia: but the Spirit suffered them not" (Acts 16:6, 7).

REJECTION 6

That in the true conversion of man no new qualities, powers or gifts can be infused by God into the will, and that therefore faith through which we are first converted, and because of which we are called believers, is not a quality or gift infused by God, but only an act of man, and that it cannot be said to be a gift, except in respect of the power to attain to this faith.

For thereby they contradict the Holy Scriptures which declare that God infuses new qualities of faith, of obedience, and of the consciousness of His love into our hearts: "I will put my law in their inward parts, and write it in their hearts" (Jer. 31:33). And: "I will pour water upon him that is thirsty, and floods upon the dry ground: I will pour my Spirit upon thy seed" (Is. 44:3).

And: "the love of God is shed abroad in our hearts by the Holy Ghost which is given unto us" (Rom. 5:5). This is also repugnant to the continuous practice of the Church, which prays by the mouth of the prophet thus: "turn thou me, and I shall be turned" (Jer. 31:18).

REJECTION 7

That the grace whereby we are converted to God is only a gentle advising, or (as others explain it), that this is the noblest manner of working in the conversion of man, and that this manner of working, which consists in advising, is most in harmony with man's nature; and that there is no reason why this advising grace alone should not be sufficient to make the natural man spiritual, indeed, that God does not produce the consent of the will except through this manner of advising; and that the power of the divine working, whereby it surpasses the working of Satan, consists in this, that God promises eternal, while Satan promises only temporal goods.

But this is altogether Pelagian and contrary to the whole Scripture which, besides this, teaches yet another and far more powerful and divine manner of the Holy Spirit's working in the conversion of man, as in Ezekiel: "A new heart also will I give you, and a new spirit will I put within you: and I will take away the stony heart out of your flesh, and I will give you an heart of flesh" (Ezek. 36:26).

REJECTION 8

That God in the regeneration of man does not use such powers of His omnipotence as potently and infallibly bend man's will to faith and conversion; but that all the works of grace having been accomplished, which God employs to convert man, man may yet so resist God and the Holy Spirit when God intends man's regeneration and wills to regenerate him, and indeed that man often does so resist that he prevents entirely his regeneration, and that it therefore remains in man's power to be regenerated or not.

For this is nothing less than the denial of all the efficiency of God's grace in our conversion, and the subjecting of the working of the Almighty God to the will of man, which is contrary to the apostles, who teach: "who believe, according to the working of his mighty power" (Eph. 1:19). And: "That our God would...fulfil all the good pleasure of his goodness, and the work of faith with power" (2 Thess. 1:11). And: "According as his divine power hath given unto us all things that pertain unto life and godliness" (2 Pet. 1:3).

REJECTION 9

That grace and free will are partial causes, which together work the beginning of conversion, and that grace, in order of working, does not precede the working of the will; that is, that God does not efficiently help the will of man unto conversion until the will of man moves and determines to do this.

For the ancient Church has long ago condemned this doctrine of the Pelagians according to the words of the apostle: "So then it is not of him that willeth, nor of him that runneth, but of God that sheweth mercy" (Rom. 9:16). Likewise: "For who maketh thee to differ from another? and what hast thou that thou didst not receive?" (1 Cor. 4:7). And: "For it is God which worketh in you both to will and to do of his good pleasure" (Phil. 2:13).

FIFTH HEAD OF DOCTRINE

Of the Perseverance of the Saints

ARTICLE 1

Whom God calls, according to His purpose, to the communion of His Son, our Lord Jesus Christ, and regenerates by the Holy Spirit, He delivers also from the dominion and slavery of sin in this life; though not altogether from the body of sin and from the infirmities of the flesh, so long as they continue in this world.

ARTICLE 2

Hence spring daily sins of infirmity, and hence spots adhere to the best works of the saints, which furnish them with constant matter for humiliation before God, and flying for refuge to Christ crucified; for mortifying the flesh more and more by the spirit of prayer, and by holy exercises of piety; and for pressing forward to the goal of perfection, till being at length delivered from this body of death, they are brought to reign with the Lamb of God in heaven.

ARTICLE 3

By reason of these remains of indwelling sin, and the temptations of sin and of the world, those who are converted could not persevere in a state of grace if left to their own strength. But God is faithful, who having conferred grace, mercifully confirms and powerfully preserves them therein, even to the end.

ARTICLE 4

Although the weakness of the flesh cannot prevail against the power of God, who confirms and preserves true believers in a state of grace, yet converts are not always so influenced and actuated by the Spirit of God, as not in some particular instances sinfully to deviate from the guidance of divine grace, so as to be seduced by, and comply with the lusts of the flesh; they must, therefore, be constant in watching and prayer that they be not led into temptation. When these are neglected, they are not only liable to be drawn into great and heinous sins by Satan, the world and the flesh, but sometimes by the righteous permission of God actually fall into these evils. This the lamentable fall of David, Peter, and other saints described in Holy Scripture demonstrates.

ARTICLE 5

By such enormous sins, however, they very highly offend God, incur a deadly guilt, grieve the Holy Spirit, interrupt the exercise of faith, very grievously wound their consciences, and sometimes lose the sense of God's favor for a time, until on their returning into the right way of serious repentance, the light of God's fatherly countenance again shines upon them.

ARTICLE 6

But God, who is rich in mercy, according to His unchangeable purpose of election, does not wholly withdraw the Holy Spirit from His own people, even in their melancholy falls; nor suffers them to proceed so far as to lose the grace of adoption, and forfeit the state of justification, or to commit the sin unto death; nor does He permit them to be totally deserted, and to plunge themselves into everlasting destruction.

ARTICLE 7

For in the first place, in these falls He preserves in them the incorruptible seed of regeneration from perishing or being totally lost; and again, by His Word and Spirit, certainly and effectually renews them to repentance, to a sincere and godly sorrow for their sins, that they may seek and obtain remission in the blood of the Mediator, may again experience the favor of a reconciled God, through faith adore His mercies, and henceforward more diligently work out their own salvation with fear and trembling.

ARTICLE 8

Thus, it is not in consequence of their own merits or strength, but of God's free mercy, that they do not totally fall from faith and grace, nor continue and perish finally in their backslidings; which, with respect to themselves, is not only possible, but would undoubtedly happen; but with respect to God, it is utterly impossible, since His counsel cannot be changed nor His promise fail, neither can the call according to His purpose be revoked, nor the merit, intercession and preservation of Christ be rendered ineffectual, nor the sealing of the Holy Spirit be frustrated or obliterated.

ARTICLE 9

Of this preservation of the elect to salvation and of their perseverance in the faith, true believers for themselves may and do obtain assurance according to the measure of their faith, whereby they arrive at the certain persuasion that they ever will continue true and living members of the church; and that they experience forgiveness of sins, and will at last inherit eternal life.

ARTICLE 10

This assurance, however, is not produced by any peculiar revelation contrary to, or independent of the Word of God; but springs from faith in God's promises, which He has most abundantly revealed in His Word for our comfort; from the testimony of the Holy Spirit witnessing with our spirit that we are children and heirs of God (Rom. 8:16); and lastly, from a serious and holy desire to preserve a good conscience and to perform good works. And if the elect of God were deprived of this solid comfort that they shall finally obtain the victory and of this infallible pledge or earnest of eternal glory, they would be of all men the most miserable.

ARTICLE 11
The Scripture moreover testifies that believers in this life have to struggle with various carnal doubts and that under grievous temptations they are not always sensible of this full assurance of faith and certainty of persevering. But God, who is the Father of all consolation, does not suffer them to be tempted above that they are able, but will with the temptation also make a way to escape that they may be able to bear it (1 Cor. 10:13), and by the Holy Spirit again inspires them with the comfortable assurance of persevering.

ARTICLE 12
This certainty of perseverance, however, is so far from exciting in believers a spirit of pride or of rendering them carnally secure, that on the contrary, it is the real source of humility, filial reverence, true piety, patience in every tribulation, fervent prayers, constancy in suffering, and in confessing the truth, and of solid rejoicing in God; so that the consideration of this benefit should serve as an incentive to the serious and constant practice of gratitude and good works, as appears from the testimonies of Scripture and the examples of the saints.

ARTICLE 13
Neither does renewed confidence of persevering produce licentiousness or a disregard to piety in those who are recovering from backsliding; but it renders them much more careful and solicitous to continue in the ways of the Lord, which He hath ordained, that they who walk therein may maintain an assurance of persevering, lest by abusing His fatherly kindness, God should turn away His gracious countenance from them, to behold which is to the godly dearer than life, the withdrawing whereof is more bitter than death, and they in consequence hereof should fall into more grievous torments of conscience.

ARTICLE 14
And as it hath pleased God, by the preaching of the gospel, to begin this work of grace in us, so He preserves, continues, and perfects it by the hearing and reading of His Word, by meditation thereon, and by the exhortations, threatenings, and promises thereof, as well as by the use of the sacraments.

ARTICLE 15
The carnal mind is unable to comprehend this doctrine of the perseverance of the saints and the certainty thereof, which God hath most abundantly revealed in His Word, for the glory of His Name, and the consolation of pious souls, and which He impresses upon the hearts of the faithful. Satan abhors it; the world ridicules it; the ignorant and hypocrite abuse, and heretics oppose it; but the spouse of Christ hath always most tenderly loved and constantly defended it as an inestimable treasure; and God, against whom neither counsel nor strength can prevail, will dispose her to continue this conduct to the end. Now, to this one God, Father, Son, and Holy Spirit, be honor and glory forever. Amen.

The true doctrine (concerning perseverance) having been explained, the Synod **rejects** the errors of those who teach:

REJECTION 1
That the perseverance of the true believers is not a fruit of election or a gift of God gained by the death of Christ, but a condition of the new covenant, which (as they declare) man before his decisive election and justification must fulfill through his free will.

For the Holy Scripture testifies that this follows out of election, and is given the elect in virtue of the death, the resurrection and intercession of Christ: "but the election hath obtained it, and the rest were blinded" (Rom. 11:7). Likewise: "He that spared not his own Son, but delivered him up for us all, how shall he not with him also freely give us all things? Who shall lay any thing to the charge of God's elect? It is God that justifieth. Who is he that condemneth? It is Christ that died, yea rather, that is risen again, who is even at the right hand of God, who also maketh intercession for us. Who shall separate us from the love of Christ?" (Rom. 8:32–35).

REJECTION 2

That God does indeed provide the believer with sufficient powers to persevere and is ever ready to preserve these in him, if he will do his duty; but that though all things which are necessary to persevere in faith and which God will use to preserve faith are made use of, it even then ever depends on the pleasure of the will whether it will persevere or not.

For this idea contains an outspoken Pelagianism, and while it would make men free, it makes them robbers of God's honor, contrary to the prevailing agreement of the evangelical doctrine, which takes from man all cause of boasting and ascribes all the praise for this favor to the grace of God alone; and contrary to the apostle, who declares that it is God "who shall also confirm you unto the end, that ye may be blameless in the day of our Lord Jesus Christ" (1 Cor. 1:8).

REJECTION 3

That the true believers and regenerate not only can fall from justifying faith and likewise from grace and salvation wholly and to the end, but indeed often do fall from this and are lost forever.

For this conception makes powerless the grace, justification, regeneration, and continued keeping by Christ, contrary to the expressed words of the apostle Paul: "That, while we were yet sinners, Christ died for us. Much more then, being now justified by his blood, we shall be saved from wrath through him" (Rom. 5:8, 9). And contrary to the apostle John: "Whosoever is born of God doth not commit sin; for his seed remaineth in him: and he cannot sin, because he is born of God" (1 John 3:9). And also contrary to the words of Jesus Christ: "I give unto them eternal life; and they shall never perish, neither shall any man pluck them out of my hand. My Father, which gave them me, is greater than all; and no man is able to pluck them out of my Father's hand" (John 10:28, 29).

REJECTION 4

That true believers and regenerate can sin the sin unto death or against the Holy Spirit.

Since the same apostle John, after having spoken in the fifth chapter of his first epistle, verses 16 and 17, of those who sin unto death and having forbidden to pray for them, immediately adds to this in verse 18: "We know that whosoever is born of God sinneth not (meaning a sin of that character); but he that is begotten of God keepeth himself, and that wicked one toucheth him not" (1 John 5:18).

REJECTION 5

That without a special revelation we can have no certainty of future perseverance in this life.

For by this doctrine the sure comfort of the true believers is taken away in this life and the doubts of the papist are again introduced into the church, while the Holy Scriptures constantly deduce this assurance, not from a special and extraordinary revelation, but from the marks proper to the children of God and from the constant promises of God. So especially the apostle Paul: "Nor any other creature, shall be able to separate us from the love of God, which is in Christ Jesus our Lord" (Rom. 8:39). And John declares: "And he that keepeth his commandments dwelleth in him, and he in him. And hereby we know that he abideth in us, by the Spirit which he hath given us" (1 John 3:24).

REJECTION 6

That the doctrine of the certainty of perseverance and of salvation from its own character and nature is a cause of indolence and is injurious to godliness, good morals, prayers and other holy exercises, but that on the contrary it is praiseworthy to doubt.

For these show that they do not know the power of divine grace and the working of the indwelling Holy Spirit. And they contradict the apostle John, who teaches the opposite with express words in his first epistle: "Beloved, now are we the sons of God, and it doth not yet appear what we shall be: but we know that, when he shall appear, we shall be like him; for we shall see him as he is. And every man that hath this hope in him purifieth himself, even as he is pure" (1 John 3:2–3). Furthermore, these are contradicted by the example of the saints, both of the Old and the New Testament, who though they were assured of their perseverance and salvation, were nevertheless constant in prayers and other exercises of godliness.

REJECTION 7

That the faith of those who believe for a time does not differ from justifying and saving faith except only in duration.

For Christ Himself, in Matthew 13:20, Luke 8:13, and in other places, evidently notes, besides this duration, a threefold difference between those who believe only for a time and true believers, when He declares that the former receive the seed in stony ground, but the latter in the good ground or heart; that the former are without root, but the latter have a firm root; that the former are without fruit, but that the latter bring forth their fruit in various measure with constancy and steadfastness.

REJECTION 8

That it is not absurd that one having lost his first regeneration, is again and even often born anew.

For these deny by this doctrine the incorruptibleness of the seed of God, whereby we are born again, contrary to the testimony of the apostle Peter: "Being born again, not of corruptible seed, but of incorruptible" (1 Peter 1:23).

REJECTION 9

That Christ has in no place prayed that believers should infallibly continue in faith.

For they contradict Christ Himself, who says: "I have prayed for thee (Simon), that thy faith fail not" (Luke 22:32); and the evangelist John, who declares that Christ has not prayed for the apostles only, but also for those who through their word would believe: "Holy Father, keep through thine own name those whom thou hast given me," and: "I pray not that thou shouldest take them out of the world, but that thou shouldest keep them from the evil"; "Neither pray I for these alone, but for them also which shall believe on me through their word" (John 17:11, 15, 20).

CONCLUSION

And this is the perspicuous, simple, and ingenuous declaration of the orthodox doctrine respecting the five articles which have been controverted in the Belgic churches, and the rejection of the errors with which they have for some time been troubled. This doctrine the Synod judges to be drawn from the Word of God and to be agreeable to the confessions of the Reformed churches. Whence it clearly appears that some whom such conduct by no means became, have violated all truth, equity, and charity, in wishing to persuade the public:

"That the doctrine of the Reformed churches concerning predestination, and the points annexed to it, by its own genius and necessary tendency, leads off the minds of men from all piety and religion; that it is an opiate administered by the flesh and the devil, and the stronghold of Satan, where he lies in wait for all; and from which he wounds multitudes, and mortally strikes through many with the darts both of despair and security; that it makes God the author of sin, unjust, tyrannical, hypocritical; that it is nothing more than interpolated Stoicism, Manicheism, Libertinism, Turcism; that it renders men carnally secure, since they are persuaded by it that nothing can hinder the salvation of the elect, let them live as they please; and therefore, that they may safely perpetrate every species of the most atrocious crimes; and that if the reprobate should even perform truly all the works of the saints, their obedience would not in the least contribute to their salvation; that the same doctrine teaches that God, by a mere arbitrary act of His will, without the least respect or view to any sin, has predestinated the greatest part of the world to eternal damnation; and has created them for this very purpose; that in the same manner in which the election is the fountain and the cause of faith and good works, reprobation is the cause of unbelief and impiety; that many children of the faithful are torn guiltless from their mothers' breasts and tyrannically plunged into hell; so that neither baptism nor the prayers of the Church at their baptism, can at all profit by them"; and many other things of the same kind which the Reformed Churches not only do not acknowledge, but even detest with their whole soul. Wherefore, this Synod of Dort, in the name of the Lord, conjures as many as piously call upon the name of our Savior Jesus Christ, to judge of the faith of the Reformed Churches not from the calumnies, which on every side are heaped

upon it; nor from the private expressions of a few among ancient and modern teachers, often dishonestly quoted or corrupted and wrested to a meaning quite foreign to their intention; but from the public confessions of the Churches themselves and from the declaration of the orthodox doctrine, confirmed by the unanimous consent of all and each of the members of the whole Synod. Moreover, the Synod warns calumniators themselves to consider the terrible judgment of God which awaits them for bearing false witness against the confessions of so many churches, for distressing the consciences of the weak, and for laboring to render suspect the society of the truly faithful. Finally, this Synod exhorts all their brethren in the gospel of Christ to conduct themselves piously and religiously in handling this doctrine, both in the universities and churches; to direct it, as well in discourse as in writing, to the glory of the divine Name, to holiness of life, and to the consolation of afflicted souls; to regulate, by the Scripture, according to the analogy of faith, not only their sentiments, but also their language; and to abstain from all those phrases which exceed the limits necessary to be observed in ascertaining the genuine sense of the holy Scriptures, and may furnish insolent sophists with a just pretext for violently assailing or even vilifying the doctrine of the Reformed churches.

May Jesus Christ, the Son of God, who, seated at the Father's right hand, gives gifts to men, sanctify us in the truth, bring to the truth those who err, shut the mouths of the calumniators of sound doctrine, and endue the faithful minister of His Word with the spirit of wisdom and discretion, that all their discourses may tend to the glory of God and the edification of those who hear them. Amen.

That this is our faith and decision we certify by subscribing our names.

Here follow the names, not only of President, Assistant President, and Secretaries of the Synod, and of the Professors of Theology in the Dutch Churches, but of all the Members who were deputed to the Synod as the Representatives of their respective Churches, that is, of the Delegates from Great Britain, the Electoral Palatinate, Hessia, Switzerland, Wetteraw, The Republic and Church of Geneva, The Republic and Church of Bremen, The Republic and Church of Emden, The Duchy of Gelderland and of Zutphen, South Holland, North Holland, Zeeland, The Province of Utrecht, Friesland, Transylvania, The State of Groningen and Omland, Drent, The French Churches.

ALL *Scripture* IS GIVEN BY INSPIRATION *of God* TO BE THE RULE OF *Faith* AND *Life*

WESTMINSTER CONFESSION

WESTMINSTER
CONFESSION OF FAITH (1647)

The Confession of Faith produced by the Westminster divines has undoubtedly been one of the most influential documents of the post-Reformation period of the Christian church. A carefully worded exposition of seventeenth-century Reformed theology, the calmness of its sentences largely hides the tempestuousness of the political backcloth against which it was written.

The Westminster Assembly was convened in 1643 after years of tension between Charles I and his increasingly Puritan Parliament. Meeting under the chairmanship of the learned William Twisse against the king's express wishes, its original vision was to effect closer uniformity of faith and practice throughout his realm. The original task of the delegates was to revise the Thirty-Nine Articles of the Church of England, but following the signing of the Solemn League and Covenant, this developed into the more specific and exacting task of framing theological and ecclesiastical formulas that would bring the Church of England into conformity with the doctrine and practice of the Presbyterian church of Scotland.

Ministerial delegates from the Kirk (who declined to become members of the Assembly) were ecclesiastical statesman Alexander Henderson, the high Calvinistic theologian and exponent of Reformed piety Samuel Rutherford, the extraordinarily gifted young George Gillespie, and the fascinating Robert Baillie (in whose *Letters and Journals* we find snapshots of the Assembly's activities and personalities). For all practical purposes these Scottish delegates constituted the most powerful group among those who gathered in the Chapel of Henry VII and later in the Jerusalem Chamber at Westminster Abbey, London, during the years of discussion and debate from 1643 to 1649.

The various documents composed by the Assembly proceeded through a process of committee work in the afternoons, followed by plenary discussion on the floor of the Assembly in the mornings, with regular additional gatherings for worship, fast days, and the like. The end result was that the divines produced one of the truly monumental documents of church history, which has instructed, directed, and profoundly influenced Presbyterian churches worldwide ever since.

The Westminster Confession of Faith represents a high point in the development of federal theology, and its inner dynamic is powerfully covenantal. Divided into thirty-three chapters, it carefully covers the whole range of Christian doctrine, beginning with Scripture as the source of knowledge of divine things (following the First and Second Helvetic Confessions, the Formula of Concord, and the Irish Articles). It continues with an exposition of God and His decrees, creation, providence, and the fall (II–VI) before turning to expound the covenant of grace, the work of Christ, and, at length, the application of redemption (X–XVIII). Careful attention is given under various chapter headings to questions of law and liberty, as well as to the doctrine of the church and sacraments (XXV–XXIX) and the last things (XXXII–XXXIII).

While the confession was composed by disciplined theological minds, it also displays the influence of men with deep pastoral, experiential, and preaching experience. It is an outstanding expression of classical Puritan Reformed theology framed for the needs of the people of God.

Chapter I: Of the Holy Scripture

1. Although the light of nature and the works of creation and providence do so far manifest the goodness, wisdom, and power of God, as to leave men unexcusable;[a] yet are they not sufficient to give that knowledge of God, and of His will, which is necessary unto salvation.[b] Therefore it pleased the Lord, at sundry times, and in divers manners, to reveal Himself, and to declare that His will unto His Church;[c] and afterwards, for the better preserving and propagating of the truth, and for the more sure establishment and comfort of the Church against the corruption of the flesh, and the malice of Satan and of the world, to commit the same wholly unto writing:[d]

which maketh the Holy Scripture to be most necessary;[e] those former ways of God's revealing His will unto His people being now ceased.[f]

[a] Rom. 2:14–15. Rom. 1:19–20. Ps. 19:1–3. Rom. 1:32 with Rom. 2:1. [b] 1 Cor. 1:21. 1 Cor. 2:13–14. [c] Heb. 1:1. [d] Prov. 22:19–21. Luke 1:3–4. Rom. 15:4. Matt. 4:4, 7, 10. Isa. 8:19–20. [e] 2 Tim. 3:15. 2 Peter 1:19. [f] Heb. 1:1–2.

2. Under the name of Holy Scripture, or the Word of God written, are now contained all the books of the Old and New Testament, which are these: Of the Old Testament:

Genesis
Exodus
Leviticus
Numbers
Deuteronomy
Joshua
Judges
Ruth
I Samuel
II Samuel
I Kings
II Kings
I Chronicles
II Chronicles
Ezra
Nehemiah
Esther
Job
Psalms
Proverbs
Ecclesiastes
The Song of Songs
Isaiah
Jeremiah
Lamentations
Ezekiel
Daniel
Hosea
Joel
Amos
Obadiah
Jonah
Micah
Nahum
Habakkuk
Zephaniah
Haggai
Zechariah
Malachi

Of the New Testament:

The Gospels, according to Matthew
Mark
Luke
John
The Acts of the Apostles
Paul's Epistles, to the Romans
Corinthians I
Corinthians II
Galatians
Ephesians
Philippians
Colossians
Thessalonians I
Thessalonians II
To Timothy I
To Timothy II
To Titus
To Philemon
The Epistle to the Hebrews
The Epistle of James
The first and second Epistles of Peter
The first, second and third Epistles of John
The Epistle of Jude
The Revelation of John

All which are given by inspiration of God, to be the rule of faith and life.[g]

[g] Luke 16:29, 31. Eph. 2:20. Rev. 22:18–19. 2 Tim. 3:16.

3. The books commonly called Apocrypha, not being of divine inspiration, are no part of the canon of the Scripture; and therefore are of no authority in the Church of God, nor to be any otherwise approved, or made use of, than other human writings.[h]

[h] Luke 24:27, 44. Rom. 3:2. 2 Peter 1:21.

4. The authority of the Holy Scripture, for which it ought to be believed and obeyed, dependeth not upon the testimony of any man, or Church; but wholly upon God (who is truth itself) the author thereof: and therefore it is to be received because it is the Word of God.[i]

[i] 2 Peter 1:19, 21. 2 Tim. 3:16. 1 John 5:9. 1 Thess. 2:13.

5. We may be moved and induced by the testimony of the Church to a high and reverent esteem of the Holy Scripture.[k] And the heavenliness of the matter, the efficacy of the doctrine, the majesty of the style, the consent of all the parts, the scope of the whole (which is, to give all glory to God), the full discovery it makes of the only way of man's salvation, the many other incomparable excellencies, and the entire perfection thereof, are arguments whereby it doth abundantly evidence itself to be the Word of God: yet notwithstanding, our full persuasion and assurance of the infallible truth and divine authority thereof, is from the inward work of the Holy Spirit bearing witness by and with the Word in our hearts.[l]

[k] 1 Tim. 3:15. [l] 1 John 2:20, 27. John 16:13–14. 1 Cor. 2:10–12. Isa. 59:21.

6. The whole counsel of God concerning all things necessary for His own glory, man's salvation, faith, and life, is either expressly set down in Scripture, or by good and necessary consequence may be deduced from Scripture: unto which nothing at any time is to be added, whether by new revelations of the Spirit, or traditions of men.[m] Nevertheless we acknowledge the inward illumination of the Spirit of God to be necessary for the saving understanding of such things as are revealed in the Word:[n] and that there are some circumstances concerning the worship of God, and government of the Church, common to human actions and societies, which are to be ordered by the light of nature and Christian prudence, according to the general rules of the Word, which are always to be observed.[o]

[m] 2 Tim. 3:15–17. Gal. 1:8–9. 2 Thess. 2:2. [n] John 6:45. 1 Cor. 2:9–12. [o] 1 Cor. 11:13–14. 1 Cor. 14:26, 40.

7. All things in Scripture are not alike plain in themselves, nor alike clear unto all:[p] yet those things which are necessary to be known, believed, and observed for salvation, are so clearly propounded and opened in some place of Scripture or other, that not only the learned, but the unlearned, in a due use of the ordinary means, may attain unto a sufficient understanding of them.[q]

[p] 2 Peter 3:16. [q] Ps. 119:105, 130.

8. The Old Testament in Hebrew (which was the native language of the people of God of old), and the New Testament in Greek (which at the time of the writing of it was most generally known to the nations), being immediately inspired by God, and by His singular care and providence kept pure in all ages, are therefore authentical;[r] so as, in all controversies of religion, the Church is finally to appeal unto them.[s] But, because these original tongues are not known to all the people of God, who have right unto, and interest in the Scriptures, and are commanded, in the fear of God, to read and search them,[t] therefore they are to be translated into the vulgar language of every nation unto which they come,[u] that the Word of God dwelling plentifully in all, they may worship Him in an acceptable manner;[w] and, through patience and comfort of the Scriptures, may have hope.[x]

[r] Matt. 5:1. [s] Isa. 8:20. Acts 15:15. John 5:39, 46. [t] John 5:39. [u] 1 Cor. 14:6, 9, 11–12, 24, 27–28. [w] Col. 3:16. [x] Rom. 15:4.

9. The infallible rule of interpretation of Scripture is the Scripture itself: and therefore, when there is a question about the true and full sense of any Scripture (which is not manifold, but one) it must be searched and known by other places that speak more clearly.[y]

[y] 2 Peter 1:20–21. Acts 15:15–16.

10. The supreme judge by which all controversies of religion are to be determined, and all decrees of councils, opinions of ancient writers, doctrines of men, and private spirits, are to be examined; and in whose sentence we are to rest; can be no other but the Holy Spirit speaking in the Scripture.[z]

[z] Matt. 22:29, 31. Eph. 2:20 with Acts 28:25.

Chapter II: Of God, and of the Holy Trinity

1. There is but one only,[a] living, and true God:[b] who is infinite in being and perfection,[c] a most pure spirit,[d] invisible,[e] without body, parts,[f] or passions,[g] immutable,[h] immense,[i] eternal,[k] incomprehensible,[l] almighty,[m] most wise,[n] most holy,[o] most free,[p] most absolute,[q] working all things according to the counsel of His own immutable and most righteous will,[r] for His own glory;[s] most loving,[t] gracious, merciful, long-suffering, abundant in goodness and truth, forgiving iniquity, transgression, and sin;[u] the rewarder of them that diligently seek Him;[w] and withal, most just and terrible in His judgments,[x] hating all sin,[y] and who will by no means clear the guilty.[z]

[a] Deut. 6:4. 1 Cor. 8:4, 6. [b] 1 Thess. 1:9. Jer. 10:10. [c] Job 11:7–9. Job 26:14. [d] John 4:24. [e] 1 Tim. 1:17. [f] Deut. 4:15–16. John 4:24 with Luke 24:39. [g] Acts 14:11, 15. [h] James 1:17. Mal. 3:6. [i] 1 Kings 8:27. Jer. 23:23–24. [k] Ps. 90:2. 1 Tim. 1:17. [l] Ps. 145:3. [m] Gen. 17:1. Rev. 4:8. [n] Rom. 16:27. [o] Isa. 6:3. Rev. 4:8. [p] Ps. 115:3. [q] Ex. 3:14. [r] Eph. 1:11. [s] Prov. 16:4. [s] Rom. 11:36. [t] 1 John 4:8, 16. [u] Ex. 34:6–7. [w] Heb. 11:6. [x] Neh. 9:32–33. [y] Ps. 5:5–6. [z] Nah. 1:2–3. Ex. 34:7.

2. God hath all life,[a] glory,[b] goodness,[c] blessedness,[d] in and of Himself; and is alone in and unto Himself all-sufficient, not standing in need of any creatures which He hath made,[e] nor deriving any glory from them,[f] but only manifesting His own glory in, by, unto, and upon them: He is the alone fountain of all being, of whom, through whom, and to whom are all things;[g] and hath most sovereign dominion over them, to do by them, for them, or upon them whatsoever Himself pleaseth.[h] In His sight all things are open and manifest;[i] His knowledge is infinite, infallible, and independent upon the creature,[k] so as nothing is to Him contingent, or uncertain.[l] He is most holy in all His counsels, in all His works, and in all His commands.[m] To Him is due from angels and men, and every other creature, whatsoever worship, service, or obedience He is pleased to require of them.[n]

[a] John 5:26. [b] Acts 7:2. [c] Ps. 119:68. [d] 1 Tim. 6:15. Rom. 9:5. [e] Acts 17:24–25. [f] Job 22:2–3. [g] Rom. 11:36. [h] Rev. 4:11. [h] 1 Tim. 6:15. Dan. 4:25, 35. [i] Heb. 4:13. [k] Rom. 11:33–34. Ps. 147:5. [l] Acts 15:18. Ezek. 11:5. [m] Ps. 145:17. Rom. 7:12. [n] Rev. 5:12–14.

3. In the unity of the Godhead there be three persons, of one substance, power, and eternity: God the Father, God the Son, and God the Holy Ghost.[o] The Father is of none, neither begotten, nor proceeding: the Son is eternally begotten of the Father:[p] the Holy Ghost eternally proceeding from the Father and the Son.[q]

[o] 1 John 5:7. Matt. 3:16–17. Matt. 28:19. 2 Cor. 13:14. [p] John 1:14, 18. [q] John 15:26. Gal. 4:6.

Chapter III: Of God's Eternal Decree

1. God from all eternity did, by the most wise and holy counsel of His own will, freely, and unchangeably ordain whatsoever comes to pass:[a] yet so, as thereby neither is God the author of sin,[b] nor is violence offered to the will of the creatures, nor is the liberty or contingency of second causes taken away, but rather established.[c]

[a] Eph. 1:11. Rom. 11:33. Heb. 6:17. Rom. 9:15, 18. [b] James 1:13, 17. 1 John 1:5. [c] Acts 2:23. Matt. 17:12. Acts 4:27–28. John 19:11. Prov. 16:33.

2. Although God knows whatsoever may or can come to pass upon all supposed conditions,[d] yet hath He not decreed anything because He foresaw it as future, or as that which would come to pass upon such conditions.[e]

[d] Acts 15:18. 1 Sam. 23:11–12. Matt. 11:21, 23. [e] Rom. 9:11, 13, 16, 18.

3. By the decree of God, for the manifestation of His glory, some men and angels[f] are predestinated unto everlasting life, and others fore-ordained to everlasting death.[g]

[f] 1 Tim. 5:21. Matt. 25:41. [g] Rom. 9:22–23. Eph. 1:5–6. Prov. 16:4.

4. These angels and men, thus predestinated and fore-ordained, are particularly and unchangeably designed, and their number is so certain and definite, that it cannot be either increased or diminished.[h]

[h] 2 Tim. 2:19. John 13:18.

5. Those of mankind that are predestinated unto life, God, before the foundation of the world was laid, according to His eternal and immutable purpose, and the secret counsel and good pleasure of His will, hath chosen, in Christ, unto everlasting glory,[i] out of His mere free grace and love, without any foresight of faith or good works, or perseverance in either of them, or any other thing in the creature, as conditions, or causes moving Him thereunto:[k] and all to the praise of His glorious grace.[l]

[i] Eph. 1:4, 9, 11. Rom. 8:30. 2 Tim. 1:9. 1 Thess. 5:9. [k] Rom. 9:11, 13, 16. Eph. 1:4, 9. [l] Eph. 1:6, 12.

6. As God hath appointed the elect unto glory, so hath He, by the eternal and most free purpose of His will, fore-ordained all the means thereunto.[m] Wherefore they who are elected, being fallen in Adam, are redeemed by Christ,[n] are effectually called unto faith in Christ by His Spirit working in due season, are justified, adopted, sanctified,[o] and kept by His power through

faith unto salvation.[p] Neither are any other redeemed by Christ, effectually called, justified, adopted, sanctified, and saved, but the elect only.[q]

[m] 1 Peter 1:2. Eph. 1:4–5. Eph. 2:10. 2 Thess. 2:13. [n] 1 Thess. 5:9–10. Titus 2:14. [o] Rom. 8:30. Eph. 1:5. 2 Thess. 2:13. [p] 1 Peter 1:5. [q] John 17:9. Rom. 8:28–39. John 6:64–65. John10:26. John 8:47. 1 John 2:19.

7. The rest of mankind God was pleased, according to the unsearchable counsel of His own will, whereby He extendeth or withholdeth mercy, as He pleaseth, for the glory of His sovereign power over His creatures, to pass by; and to ordain them to dishonor and wrath, for their sin, to the praise of His glorious justice.[r]

[r] Matt. 11:25–26. Rom. 9:17–18, 21–22. 2 Tim. 2:19–20. Jude 4. 1 Peter 2:8.

8. The doctrine of this high mystery of predestination is to be handled with special prudence and care,[s] that men attending the will of God revealed in His Word, and yielding obedience thereunto, may, from the certainty of their effectual vocation, be assured of their eternal election.[t] So shall this doctrine afford matter of praise, reverence, and admiration of God,[u] and of humility, diligence, and abundant consolation to all that sincerely obey the Gospel.[w]

[s] Rom. 9:20. Rom. 11:33. Deut. 29:29. [t] 2 Peter 1:10. [u] Eph. 1:6. Rom. 11:33. [w] Rom. 11:5–6, 20. 2 Peter 1:10. Rom. 8:33. Luke 10:20.

Chapter IV: Of Creation

1. It pleased God the Father, Son, and Holy Ghost,[a] for the manifestation of the glory of His eternal power, wisdom, and goodness,[b] in the beginning, to create, or make of nothing, the world, and all things therein whether visible or invisible, in the space of six days; and all very good.[c]

[a] Heb. 1:2. John 1:2–3. Gen. 1:2. Job 26:13. Job 33:4. [b] Rom. 1:20. Jer. 10:12. Ps. 104:24. Ps. 33:5–6. [c] Gen. 1:1–31. Heb. 11:3. Col. 1:16. Acts 17:24.

2. After God had made all other creatures, He created man, male and female,[d] with reasonable and immortal souls,[e] endued with knowledge, righteousness, and true holiness, after His own image;[f] having the law of God written in their hearts,[g] and power to fulfil it:[h] and yet under a possibility of transgressing, being left to the liberty of their own will, which was subject unto change.[i] Beside this law written in their hearts, they received a command, not to eat of the tree of the knowledge of good and evil, which while they kept, they were happy in their communion with God,[k] and had dominion over the creatures.[l]

[d] Gen. 1:27. [e] Gen. 2:7 with Eccles. 12:7 and Luke 23:43 and Matt. 10:28. [f] Gen. 1:26. Col. 3:10. Eph. 4:24. [g] Rom. 2:14–15. [h] Eccles. 7:29. [i] Gen. 3:6. Eccles. 7:29. [k] Gen. 2:17. Gen. 3:8–11, 23. [l] Gen. 1:26, 28.

Chapter V: Of Providence

1. God the great Creator of all things doth uphold,[a] direct, dispose, and govern all creatures, actions, and things,[b] from the greatest even to the least,[c] by His most wise and holy providence,[d] according to His infallible fore-knowledge,[e] and the free and immutable counsel of His own will,[f] to the praise of the glory of His wisdom, power, justice, goodness, and mercy.[g]

[a] Heb. 1:3. [b] Dan. 4:34–35. Ps. 135:6. Acts 17:25–26, 28. Job 38–41. [c] Matt. 10:29–31. [d] Prov. 15:3. Ps. 104:24. Ps. 145:17. [e] Acts 15:18. Ps. 94:8–11. [f] Eph. 1:11. Ps. 33:10–11. [g] Isa. 63:14. Eph. 3:10. Rom. 9:17. Gen. 45:7. Ps. 145:7.

2. Although, in relation to the fore-knowledge and decree of God, the first Cause, all things come to pass immutably, and infallibly:[h] yet, by the same providence, He ordereth them to fall out, according to the nature of second causes, either necessarily, freely, or contingently.[i]

[h] Acts 2:23. [i] Gen. 8:22. Jer. 31:35. Ex. 21:13 with Deut. 19:5. 1 Kings 22:28, 34. Isa. 10:6–7.

3. God in His ordinary providence maketh use of means,[k] yet is free to work without,[l] above,[m] and against them at His pleasure.[n]

[k] Acts 27:31, 44. Isa. 55:10–11. Hosea 2:21–22. [l] Hosea 1:7. Matt. 4:4. Job 34:20. [m] Rom. 4:19–21. [n] 2 Kings 6:6. Dan. 3:27.

4. The almighty power, unsearchable wisdom, and infinite goodness of God so far manifest themselves in His providence, that it extendeth itself even to the first fall, and all other sins of angels and men;[o] and that not by a bare permission,[p] but such as hath joined with it a most wise and powerful bounding,[q] and otherwise ordering and governing of them, in a manifold dispensation, to His own holy ends;[r] yet so, as the sinfulness thereof proceedeth only from the creature, and not from God, who, being most holy and righteous, neither is, nor can be, the author or approver of sin.[s]

[o] Rom. 11:32–34. 2 Sam. 24:1 with 1 Chron. 21:1. 1 Kings 22:22–23. 1 Chron. 10:4, 13–14. 2 Sam. 16:10. Acts 2:23. Acts 4:27–28. [p] Acts 14:16. [q] Ps. 76:10. 2 Kings 19:28. [r] Gen. 50:20. Isa. 10:6–7, 12. [s] James 1:13–14, 17. 1 John 2:16. Ps. 50:21.

5. The most wise, righteous, and gracious God doth oftentimes leave for a season His own children to manifold temptations, and the corruption of their own hearts, to chastise them for their former sins, or to discover unto them the hidden strength of corruption, and deceitfulness of their hearts, that they may be humbled;[t] and, to raise them to a more close and constant dependence for their support upon Himself, and to make them more watchful against all future occasions of sin, and for sundry other just and holy ends.[u]

[t] 2 Chron. 32:25–26, 31. 2 Sam. 24:1. [u] 2 Cor. 12:7–9. Ps. 73 throughout. Ps. 77:1–12. Mark 14:66–72 with John 21:15–17.

6. As for those wicked and ungodly men whom God, as a righteous Judge, for former sins doth blind and harden,[w] from them He not only withholdeth His grace, whereby they might have been enlightened in their understandings, and wrought upon in their hearts;[x] but sometimes also withdraweth the gifts which they had,[y] and exposeth them to such objects as their corruption makes occasions of sin;[z] and, withal, gives them over to their own lusts, the temptations of the world, and the power of Satan:[a] whereby it comes to pass that they harden themselves, even under those means which God useth for the softening of others.[b]

[w] Rom. 1:24, 26, 28. Rom. 11:7–8. [x] Deut. 29:4. [y] Matt. 13:12. Matt. 25:29. [z] Deut. 2:30. 2 Kings 8:12–13. [a] Ps. 81:11–12. 2 Thess. 2:10–12. [b] Ex. 7:3 with Ex. 8:15, 32. 2 Cor. 2:15–16. Isa. 8:14. 1 Peter 2:7–8. Isa. 6:9–10 with Acts 28:26–27.

7. As the providence of God doth in general reach to all creatures, so after a most special manner it taketh care of His Church, and disposeth all things to the good thereof.[c]

[c] 1 Tim. 4:10. Amos 9:8–9. Rom. 8:28. Isa. 43:3–5, 14.

Chapter VI: Of the Fall of Man, of Sin, and of the Punishment thereof

1. Our first parents, being seduced by the subtilty and temptation of Satan, sinned in eating the forbidden fruit.[a] This their sin God was pleased, according to His wise and holy counsel, to permit, having purposed to order it to His own glory.[b]

[a] Gen. 3:13. 2 Cor. 11:3. [b] Rom. 11:32.

2. By this sin they fell from their original righteousness and communion with God,[c] and so became dead in sin,[d] and wholly defiled in all the faculties and parts of soul and body.[e]

[c] Gen. 3:6–8. Eccles. 7:29. Rom. 3:23. [d] Gen. 2:17. Eph. 2:1. [e] Titus 1:15. Gen. 6:5. Jer. 17:9. Rom. 3:10–19.

3. They being the root of all mankind, the guilt of this sin was imputed,[f] and the same death in sin and corrupted nature conveyed, to all their posterity descending from them by ordinary generation.[g]

[f] Gen. 1:27–28 and Gen. 2:16–17 and Acts 17:26 with Rom. 5:12, 15–19 and 1 Cor. 15:21–22, 49. [g] Ps. 51:5. Gen. 5:3. Job 14:4. Job 15:14.

4. From this original corruption, whereby we are utterly indisposed, disabled, and made opposite to all good,[h] and wholly inclined to all evil,[i] do proceed all actual transgressions.[k]

[h] Rom. 5:6. Rom. 8:7. Rom. 7:18. Col. 1:21. [i] Gen. 6:5. Gen. 8:21. Rom. 3:10–12. [k] James 1:14–15. Eph. 2:2–3. Matt. 15:19.

5. This corruption of nature, during this life, doth remain in those that are regenerated;[l] and although it be, through Christ, pardoned, and mortified, yet both itself and all the motions thereof are truly and properly sin.[m]

[l] 1 John 1:8, 10. Rom. 7:14, 17–18, 23. James 3:2. Prov. 20:9. Eccles. 7:20. [m] Rom. 7:5, 7–8, 25. Gal. 5:17.

6. Every sin, both original and actual, being a transgression of the righteous law of God, and contrary thereunto,[n] doth, in its own nature, bring guilt upon the sinner;[o] whereby he is bound over to the wrath of God,[p] and curse of the law,[q] and so made subject to death,[r] with all miseries spiritual,[s] temporal,[t] and eternal.[u]

[n] 1 John 3:4. [o] Rom. 2:15. Rom. 3:9, 19. [p] Eph. 2:3. [q] Gal. 3:10. [r] Rom. 6:23. [s] Eph. 4:18. [t] Rom. 8:20. Lam. 3:39. [u] Matt. 25:41. 2 Thess. 1:9.

Chapter VII: Of God's Covenant with Man

1. The distance between God and the creature is so great, that although reasonable creatures do owe obedience unto Him as their Creator, yet they could never have any fruition of Him as their blessedness and reward, but by some voluntary condescension on God's part, which He hath been pleased to express by way of covenant.[a]

[a] Isa. 40:13–17. Job 9:32–33. 1 Sam. 2:25. Ps. 113:5–6. Ps. 100:2–3. Job 22:2–3. Job 35:7–8. Luke 17:10. Acts 17:24–25.

2. The first covenant made with man was a covenant of works,[b] wherein life was promised to Adam, and in him to his posterity,[c] upon condition of perfect and personal obedience.[d]

[b] Gal. 3:12. [c] Rom. 10:5. Rom. 5:12–20. [d] Gen. 2:17. Gal. 3:10.

3. Man by his fall having made himself incapable of life by that covenant, the Lord was pleased to make a second,[e] commonly called the covenant of grace; wherein He freely offereth unto sinners life and salvation by Jesus Christ, requiring of them faith in Him that they may be saved,[f] and promising to give unto all those that are ordained unto life His Holy Spirit, to make them willing and able to believe.[g]

[e] Gal. 3:21. Rom. 8:3. Rom. 3:20–21. Gen. 3:15. Isa. 42:6. [f] Mark 16:15–16. John 3:16. Rom. 10:6, 9. Gal. 3:11. [g] Ezek. 36:26–27. John 6:44–45.

4. This covenant of grace is frequently set forth in Scripture by the name of a Testament, in reference to the death of Jesus Christ the Testator, and to the everlasting inheritance, with all things belonging to it, therein bequeathed.[h]

[h] Heb. 9:15–17. Heb. 7:22. Luke 22:20. 1 Cor. 11:25.

5. This covenant was differently administered in the time of the law, and in the time of the gospel:[i] under the law, it was administered by promises, prophecies, sacrifices, circumcision, the paschal lamb, and other types and ordinances delivered to the people of the Jews, all fore-signifying Christ to come:[k] which were, for that time, sufficient and efficacious, through the operation of the Spirit, to instruct and build up the elect in faith in the promised Messiah,[l] by whom they had full remission of sins, and eternal salvation; and is called, the Old Testament.[m]

[i] 2 Cor. 3:6–9. [k] Heb. 8–10. Rom. 4:11. Col. 2:11–12. 1 Cor. 5:7. [l] 1 Cor. 10:1–4. Heb. 11:13. John 8:56. [m] Gal. 3:7–9, 14.

6. Under the gospel, when Christ, the substance,[n] was exhibited, the ordinances in which this covenant is dispensed are the preaching of the Word, and the administration of the sacraments of Baptism and the Lord's Supper:[o] which, though fewer in number, and administered with more simplicity, and less outward glory; yet, in them, it is held forth in more fulness, evidence, and spiritual efficacy,[p] to all nations, both Jews and Gentiles;[q] and is called the New Testament.[r] There are not therefore two covenants of grace, differing in substance, but one and the same, under various dispensations.[s]

[n] Col. 2:17. [o] Matt. 28:19–20. 1 Cor. 11:23–25. [p] Heb. 12:22–28. Jer. 31:33–34. [q] Matt. 28:19. Eph. 2:15–19. [r] Luke 22:20. [s] Gal. 3:14, 16. Rom. 3:21–23, 30. Ps. 32:1 with Rom. 4:3, 6, 16–17, 23–24. Heb. 13:8. Acts 15:11.

Chapter VIII: Of Christ the Mediator

1. It pleased God, in His eternal purpose, to choose and ordain the Lord Jesus, His only begotten Son, to be the Mediator between God and man;[a] the Prophet,[b] Priest,[c] and King,[d] the Head and Savior of His Church,[e] the Heir of all things,[f] and Judge of the world:[g] unto whom He did from all eternity give a people, to be His seed,[h] and to be by Him in time redeemed, called, justified, sanctified, and glorified.[i]

[a] Isa. 42:1. Peter 1:19–20. John 3:16. 1 Tim. 2:5. [b] Acts 3:22. [c] Heb. 5:5–6. [d] Ps. 2:6. Luke 1:33. [e] Eph. 5:23. [f] Heb. 1:2. [g] Acts 17:31. [h] John 17:6. Ps. 22:30. Isa. 53:10. [i] 1 Tim. 2:6. Isa. 55:4–5. 1 Cor. 1:30.

2. The Son of God, the second person in the Trinity, being very and eternal God, of one substance and equal with the Father, did, when the fulness of time was come, take upon Him man's nature,[k] with all the essential properties and common infirmities thereof, yet without sin:[l] being conceived by the power of the Holy Ghost, in the womb of the virgin Mary, of her substance.[m] So that two whole, perfect, and distinct natures, the Godhead and the manhood, were inseparably joined together in one person, without conversion, composition, or confusion.[n] Which person is very God, and very man, yet one Christ, the only Mediator between God and man.[o]

[k] John 1:1, 14. 1 John 5:20. Phil. 2:6. Gal. 4:4. [l] Heb. 2:14, 16–17. Heb. 4:15. [m] Luke 1:27, 31, 35. Gal. 4:4. [n] Luke 1:35. Col. 2:9. Rom. 9:5. 1 Peter 3:18. 1 Tim. 3:16. [o] Rom. 1:3–4. 1 Tim. 2:5.

3. The Lord Jesus, in His human nature thus united to the divine, was sanctified and anointed with the Holy Spirit, above measure,[p] having in Him all the treasures of wisdom and knowledge;[q] in whom it pleased the Father that all fulness should dwell;[r] to the end that, being holy, harmless, undefiled, and full of grace and truth,[s] He might be thoroughly furnished to execute the office of a mediator and surety.[t] Which office He took not unto Himself, but was thereunto called by His Father,[u] who put all power and judgment into His hand, and gave Him commandment to execute the same.[w]

[p] Ps. 45:7. John 3:34. [q] Col. 2:3. [r] Col. 1:19. [s] Heb. 7:26. John 1:14. [t] Acts 10:38. Heb. 12:24. Heb. 7:22. [u] Heb. 5:4–5. [w] John 5:22, 27. Matt. 28:18. Acts 2:36.

4. This office the Lord Jesus did most willingly undertake;[x] which that He might discharge, He was made under the law,[y] and did perfectly fulfil it,[z] endured most grievous torments immediately in His soul,[a] and most painful sufferings in His body;[b] was crucified, and died;[c] was buried, and remained under the power of death; yet saw no corruption.[d] On the third day He arose from the dead,[e] with the same body in which He suffered,[f] with which also he ascended into heaven, and there sitteth at the right hand of His Father,[g] making intercession,[h] and shall return to judge men and angels at the end of the world.[i]

[x] Ps. 40:7–8 with Heb. 10:5–10. John 10:18. Phil. 2:8. [y] Gal. 4:4. [z] Matt. 3:15. Matt. 5:17. [a] Matt. 26:37–38. Luke 22:44. Matt. 27:46. [b] Matt. 26–27. [c] Phil. 2:8. [d] Acts 2:23–24, 27. Acts 13:37. Rom. 6:9. [e] 1 Cor. 15:3–4. [f] John 20:25, 27. [g] Mark 16:19. [h] Rom. 8:34. Heb. 9:24. Heb. 7:25. [i] Rom. 14:9–10. Acts 1:11. Acts 10:42. Matt. 13:40–42. Jude 6. 2 Peter 2:4.

5. The Lord Jesus, by His perfect obedience, and sacrifice of Himself, which He, through the eternal Spirit, once offered up unto God, hath fully satisfied the justice of His Father;[k] and purchased, not only reconciliation, but an everlasting inheritance in the kingdom of heaven, for all those whom the Father hath given unto Him.[l]

[k] Rom. 5:19. Heb. 9:14, 16. Heb. 10:14. Eph. 5:2. Rom. 3:25–26. [l] Dan. 9:24, 26. Col. 1:19–20. Eph. 1:11, 14. John 17:2. Heb. 9:12, 15.

6. Although the work of redemption was not actually wrought by Christ till after His incarnation, yet the virtue, efficacy, and benefits thereof were communicated unto the elect in all ages successively from the beginning of the world, in and by those promises, types, and sacrifices, wherein He was revealed and signified to be the seed of the woman which should bruise the serpent's head; and the Lamb slain from the beginning of the world: being yesterday and today the same, and for ever.[m]

[m] Gal. 4:4–5. Gen. 3:15. Rev. 13:8. Heb. 13:8.

7. Christ, in the work of mediation, acteth according to both natures, by each nature doing that which is proper to itself:[n] yet, by reason of the unity of the person, that which is proper

to one nature, is sometimes in Scripture attributed to the person denominated by the other nature.[o]

[n] Heb. 9:14. 1 Peter 3:18. [o] Acts 20:28. John 3:13. 1 John 3:16.

8. To all those for whom Christ hath purchased redemption, He doth certainly and effectually apply and communicate the same,[p] making intercession for them,[q] and revealing unto them, in and by the Word, the mysteries of salvation,[r] effectually persuading them by His Spirit to believe and obey, and governing their hearts by His Word and Spirit,[s] overcoming all their enemies by His almighty power and wisdom, in such manner, and ways, as are most consonant to His wonderful and unsearchable dispensation.[t]

[p] John 6:37, 39. John 10:15–16. [q] 1 John 2:1–2. Rom. 8:34. [r] John 15:13, 15. Eph. 1:7–9. [r] John 17:6. [s] John 14:16. Heb. 12:2. 2 Cor. 4:13. Rom. 8:9, 14. Rom. 15:18–19. John 17:17. [t] Ps. 110:1. 1 Cor. 15:25–26. Mal. 4:2–3. Col. 2:15.

Chapter IX: Of Free Will

1. God hath endued the will of man with that natural liberty, that it is neither forced, nor by any absolute necessity of nature determined to good or evil.[a]

[a] Matt. 17:12. James 1:14. Deut. 30:19.

2. Man, in his state of innocency, had freedom and power to will and to do that which was good, and well pleasing to God;[b] but yet mutably, so that he might fall from it.[c]

[b] Eccles. 7:29. Gen. 1:26. [c] Gen. 2:16–17. Gen. 3:6.

3. Man, by his fall into a state of sin, hath wholly lost all ability of will to any spiritual good accompanying salvation:[d] so as, a natural man, being altogether averse from that good,[e] and dead in sin,[f] is not able, by his own strength, to convert himself, or to prepare himself thereunto.[g]

[d] Rom. 5:6. Rom. 8:7. John 15:5. [e] Rom. 3:10, 12. [f] Eph. 2:1, 5. Col. 2:13. [g] John 6:44, 65. Eph. 2:2–5. 1 Cor. 2:14. Titus 3:3–5.

4. When God converts a sinner, and translates him into the state of grace, He freeth him from his natural bondage under sin;[h] and, by His grace alone, enables him freely to will and to do that which is spiritually good;[i] yet so, as that by reason of his remaining corruption, he doth not perfectly, nor only, will that which is good, but doth also will that which is evil.[k]

[h] Col. 1:13. John 8:34, 36. [i] Phil. 2:13. Rom. 6:18, 22. [k] Gal. 5:17. Rom. 7:15, 18–19, 21, 23.

5. The will of man is made perfectly and immutably free to good alone, in the state of glory only.[l]

[l] Eph. 4:13. Heb. 12:23. 1 John 3:2. Jude 24.

Chapter X: Of Effectual Calling

1. All those whom God hath predestinated unto life, and those only, He is pleased in His appointed and accepted time effectually to call,[a] by His Word and Spirit,[b] out of that state of sin and death, in which they are by nature, to grace and salvation by Jesus Christ;[c] enlightening their minds spiritually and savingly to understand the things of God;[d] taking away their heart of stone, and giving unto them an heart of flesh;[e] renewing their wills, and by His almighty power determining them to that which is good,[f] and effectually drawing them to Jesus Christ:[g] yet so, as they come most freely, being made willing by His grace.[h]

[a] Rom. 8:30. Rom. 11:7. Eph. 1:10–11. [b] 2 Thess. 2:13–14. 2 Cor. 3:3, 6. [c] Rom. 8:2. Eph. 2:1–5. 2 Tim. 1:9–10. [d] Acts 26:18. 1 Cor. 2:10, 12. Eph. 1:17–18. [e] Ezek. 36:26. [f] Ezek. 11:19. Phil. 2:13. Deut. 30:6. Ezek. 36:27. [g] Eph. 1:19. John 6:44–45. [h] Song of Sol. 1:4. Ps. 110:3. John 6:37. Rom. 6:16–18.

2. This effectual call is of God's free and special grace alone, not from anything at all foreseen in man,[i] who is altogether passive therein, until being quickened and renewed by the Holy Spirit,[k] he is thereby enabled to answer this call, and to embrace the grace offered and conveyed in it.[l]

[i] 2 Tim. 1:9. Titus 3:4–5. Eph. 2:4–5, 8–9. Rom. 9:11. [k] 1 Cor. 2:14. Rom. 8:7. Eph. 2:5. [l] John 6:37. Ezek. 36:27. John 5:25.

3. Elect infants, dying in infancy, are regenerated, and saved by Christ through the Spirit,[m] who worketh when, and where, and how He pleaseth:[n] so also, are all other elect persons who are uncapable of being outwardly called by the ministry of the Word.[o]

[m] Luke 18:15–16 and Acts 2:38–39 and John 3:3, 5 and 1 John 5:12 and Rom. 8:9 compared. [n] John 3:8. [o] 1 John 5:12. Acts 4:12.

4. Others, not elected, although they may be called by the ministry of the Word,[p] and may have some common operations of the Spirit,[q] yet they never truly come unto Christ, and therefore cannot be saved:[r] much less can men, not professing the Christian religion, be saved in any other way whatsoever, be they never so diligent to frame their lives according to the light of nature, and the law of that religion they do profess.[s] And, to assert and maintain that they may, is very pernicious, and to be detested.[t]

[p] Matt. 22:14. [q] Matt. 7:22. Matt. 13:20–21. Heb. 6:4–5. [r] John 6:64–66. John 8:24. [s] Acts 4:12. John 14:6. Eph. 2:12. John 4:22. John 17:3. [t] 2 John 9–11. 1 Cor. 16:22. Gal. 1:6–8.

Chapter XI: Of Justification

1. Those whom God effectually calleth, He also freely justifieth:[a] not by infusing righteousness into them, but by pardoning their sins, and by accounting and accepting their persons as righteous; not for anything wrought in them, or done by them, but for Christ's sake alone; nor by imputing faith itself, the act of believing, or any other evangelical obedience to them, as their righteousness, but by imputing the obedience and satisfaction of Christ unto them,[b] they receiving and resting on Him and His righteousness by faith; which faith they have not of themselves, it is the gift of God.[c]

[a] Rom. 8:30. Rom. 3:24. [b] Rom. 4:5–8. 2 Cor. 5:19, 21. Rom. 3:22, 24–25, 27–28. Titus 3:5, 7. Eph. 1:7. Jer. 23:6. 1 Cor. 1:30–31. Rom. 5:17–19. [c] Acts 10:43. Gal. 2:16. Phil. 3:9. Acts 13:38–39. Eph. 2:7–8.

2. Faith, thus receiving and resting on Christ and His righteousness, is the alone instrument of justification;[d] yet is it not alone in the person justified, but is ever accompanied with all other saving graces, and is no dead faith, but worketh by love.[e]

[d] John 1:12. Rom. 3:28. Rom. 5:1. [e] James 2:17, 22, 26. Gal. 5:6.

3. Christ, by His obedience and death, did fully discharge the debt of all those that are thus justified, and did make a proper, real, and full satisfaction to His Father's justice in their behalf.[f] Yet, inasmuch as He was given by the Father for them;[g] and His obedience and satisfaction accepted in their stead;[h] and both freely, not for anything in them; their justification is only of free grace;[i] that both the exact justice, and rich grace of God, might be glorified in the justification of sinners.[k]

[f] Rom. 5:8–10, 19. 1 Tim. 2:5–6. Heb. 10:10, 14. Dan. 9:24, 26. Isa. 53:4–6, 10–12. [g] Rom. 8:32. [h] 2 Cor. 5:21. Matt. 3:17. Eph. 5:2. [i] Rom. 3:24. Eph. 1:7. [k] Rom. 3:26. Eph. 2:7.

4. God did, from all eternity, decree to justify all the elect,[l] and Christ did, in the fulness of time, die for their sins, and rise again for their justification:[m] nevertheless, they are not justified, until the Holy Spirit doth, in due time, actually apply Christ unto them.[n]

[l] Gal. 3:8. 1 Peter 1:2, 19–20. Rom. 8:30. [m] Gal. 4:4. 1 Tim. 2:6. Rom. 4:25. [n] Col. 1:21–22. Gal. 2:16. Titus 3:3–7.

5. God doth continue to forgive the sins of those that are justified:[o] and, although they can never fall from the state of justification;[p] yet they may, by their sins, fall under God's fatherly displeasure, and not have the light of His countenance restored unto them, until they humble themselves, confess their sins, beg pardon, and renew their faith and repentance.[q]

[o] Matt. 6:12. 1 John 1:7, 9. 1 John 2:1–2. [p] Luke 22:32. John 10:28. Heb. 10:14. [q] Ps. 89:31–33. Ps. 51:7–12. Ps. 32:5. Matt. 26:75. 1 Cor. 11:30, 32. Luke 1:20.

6. The justification of believers under the Old Testament was, in all these respects, one and the same with the justification of believers under the New Testament.[r]

[r] Gal. 3:9, 13–14. Rom. 4:22–24. Heb. 13:8.

Chapter XII: Of Adoption

1. All those that are justified, God vouchsafeth, in and for His only Son Jesus Christ, to make partakers of the grace of adoption:[a] by which they are taken into the number, and enjoy the liberties and privileges of the children of God,[b] have His name put upon them,[c] receive the spirit of adoption,[d] have access to the throne of grace with boldness,[e] are enabled to cry, Abba, Father,[f] are pitied,[g] protected,[h] provided for,[i] and chastened by Him as by a Father;[k] yet never cast off,[l] but sealed to the day of redemption,[m] and inherit the promises,[n] as heirs of everlasting salvation.[o]

[a] Eph. 1:5. [b] Gal. 4:4–5. Rom. 8:17. John 1:12. [c] Jer. 14:9. 2 Cor. 6:18. Rev. 3:12. [d] Rom. 8:15. [e] Eph. 3:12. Rom. 5:2. [f] Gal. 4:6. [g] Ps. 103:13. [h] Prov. 14:26. [i] Matt. 6:30, 32. 1 Peter 5:7. [k] Heb. 12:6. [l] Lam. 3:31. [m] Eph. 4:30. [n] Heb. 6:12. [o] 1 Peter 1:3–4. Heb. 1:14.

Chapter XIII: Of Sanctification

1. They who are effectually called and regenerated, having a new heart and a new spirit created in them, are further sanctified, really and personally, through the virtue of Christ's death and resurrection,[a] by His Word and Spirit dwelling in them:[b] the dominion of the whole body of sin is destroyed,[c] and the several lusts thereof are more and more weakened and mortified;[d] and they more and more quickened and strengthened in all saving graces,[e] to the practice of true holiness, without which no man shall see the Lord.[f]

[a] 1 Cor. 6:11. Acts 20:32. Phil. 3:10. Rom. 6:5–6. [b] John 17:17. Eph. 5:26. 2 Thess. 2:13. [c] Rom. 6:6, 14. [d] Gal. 5:24. Rom. 8:13. [e] Col. 1:11. Eph. 3:16–19. [f] 2 Cor. 7:1. Heb. 12:14.

2. This sanctification is throughout, in the whole man;[g] yet imperfect in this life, there abiding still some remnants of corruption in every part:[h] whence ariseth a continual and irreconcilable war; the flesh lusting against the Spirit, and the Spirit against the flesh.[i]

[g] 1 Thess. 5:23. [h] 1 John 1:10. Rom. 7:18, 23. Phil. 3:12. [i] Gal. 5:17. 1 Peter 2:11.

3. In which war, although the remaining corruption, for a time, may much prevail;[k] yet through the continual supply of strength from the sanctifying Spirit of Christ, the regenerate part doth overcome;[l] and so, the saints grow in grace,[m] perfecting holiness in the fear of God.[n]

[k] Rom. 7:23. [l] Rom. 6:14. 1 John 5:4. Eph. 4:15–16. [m] 2 Peter 3:18. 2 Cor. 3:18. [n] 2 Cor. 7:1.

Chapter XIV: Of Saving Faith

1. The grace of faith, whereby the elect are enabled to believe to the saving of their souls,[a] is the work of the Spirit of Christ in their hearts;[b] and is ordinarily wrought by the ministry of the Word:[c] by which also, and by the administration of the sacraments, and prayer, it is increased and strengthened.[d]

[a] Heb. 10:39. [b] 2 Cor. 4:13. Eph. 1:17–19. Eph. 2:8. [c] Rom. 10:14, 17. [d] 1 Peter 2:2. Acts 20:32. Rom. 4:11. Luke 17:5. Rom. 1:16–17.

2. By this faith, a Christian believeth to be true whatsoever is revealed in the Word, for the authority of God Himself speaking therein;[e] and acteth differently upon that which each particular passage thereof containeth; yielding obedience to the commands,[f] trembling at the threatenings,[g] and embracing the promises of God for this life, and that which is to come.[h] But the principal acts of saving faith are accepting, receiving, and resting upon Christ alone for justification, sanctification, and eternal life, by virtue of the covenant of grace.[i]

[e] John 4:42. 1 Thess. 2:13. 1 John 5:10. Acts 24:14. [f] Rom. 16:26. [g] Isa. 66:2. [h] Heb. 11:13. 1 Tim. 4:8. [i] John 1:12. Acts 16:31. Gal. 2:20. Acts 15:11.

3. This faith is different in degrees, weak or strong;[k] may be often and many ways assailed, and weakened, but gets the victory;[l] growing up in many to the attainment of a full assurance through Christ,[m] who is both the author and finisher of our faith.[n]

[k] Heb. 5:13–14. Rom. 4:19–20. Matt. 6:30. Matt. 8:10. [l] Luke 22:31–32. Eph. 6:16. 1 John 5:4–5. [m] Heb. 6:11–12. Heb. 10:22. Col. 2:2. [n] Heb. 12:2.

Chapter XV: Of Repentance unto Life

1. Repentance unto life is an evangelical grace,[a] the doctrine whereof is to be preached by every minister of the Gospel, as well as that of faith in Christ.[b]

[a] Zech. 12:10. Acts 11:18. [b] Luke 24:47. Mark 1:15. Acts 20:21.

2. By it, a sinner, out of the sight and sense not only of the danger, but also of the filthiness and odiousness of his sins, as contrary to the holy nature and righteous law of God; and upon the apprehension of his mercy in Christ to such as are penitent, so grieves for, and hates his sins, as to turn from them all unto God,[c] purposing and endeavouring to walk with Him in all the ways of His commandments.[d]

[c] Ezek. 18:30–31. Ezek. 36:31. Isa. 30:22. Ps. 51:4. Jer. 31:18–19. Joel 2:12–13. [c] Amos 5:15. Ps. 119:128. 2 Cor. 7:11.
[d] Ps. 119:6, 59, 106. Luke 1:6. 2 Kings 23:25.

3. Although repentance be not to be rested in, as any satisfaction for sin, or any cause of the pardon thereof,[e] which is the act of God's free grace in Christ;[f] yet is it of such necessity to all sinners, that none may expect pardon without it.[g]

[e] Ezek. 36:31–32. Ezek. 16:61–63. [f] Hosea 14:2, 4. Rom. 3:24. Eph. 1:7. [g] Luke 13:3, 5. Acts 17:30–31.

4. As there is no sin so small, but it deserves damnation;[h] so there is no sin so great, that it can bring damnation upon those who truly repent.[i]

[h] Rom. 6:23. Rom. 5:12. Matt. 12:36. [i] Isa. 55:7. Rom. 8:1. Isa. 1:16, 18.

5. Men ought not to content themselves with a general repentance, but it is every man's duty to endeavour to repent of his particular sins, particularly.[k]

[k] Ps. 19:13. Luke 19:8. 1 Tim. 1:13, 15.

6. As every man is bound to make private confession of his sins to God, praying for the pardon thereof;[l] upon which, and the forsaking of them, he shall find mercy:[m] so, he that scandalizeth his brother, or the Church of Christ, ought to be willing, by a private or public confession, and sorrow for his sin, to declare his repentance to those that are offended,[n] who are thereupon to be reconciled to him, and in love to receive him.[o]

[l] Ps. 51:4–5, 7, 9, 14. Ps. 32:5–6. [m] Prov. 28:13. 1 John 1:9. [n] James 5:16. Luke 17:3–4. Josh. 7:19. Ps. 51 throughout.
[o] 2 Cor. 2:8.

Chapter XVI: Of Good Works

1. Good works are only such as God hath commanded in His holy Word,[a] and not such as, without the warrant thereof, are devised by men, out of blind zeal, or upon any pretence of good intention.[b]

[a] Micah 6:8. Rom. 12:2. Heb. 13:21. [b] Matt. 15:9. Isa. 29:13. 1 Peter 1:18. Rom. 10:2. John 16:2. 1 Sam. 15:21–23.

2. These good works, done in obedience to God's commandments, are the fruits and evidences of a true and lively faith:[c] and by them believers manifest their thankfulness,[d] strengthen their assurance,[e] edify their brethren,[f] adorn the profession of the Gospel,[g] stop the mouths of the adversaries,[h] and glorify God,[i] whose workmanship they are, created in Christ Jesus thereunto;[k] that, having their fruit unto holiness, they may have the end, eternal life.[l]

[c] James 2:18, 22. [d] Ps. 116:12–13. 1 Peter 2:9. [e] 1 John 2:3, 5. 2 Peter 1:5–10. [f] 2 Cor. 9:2. Matt. 5:16. [g] Titus 2:5, 9–12. 1 Tim. 6:1. [h] 1 Peter 2:15. [i] 1 Peter 2:12. Phil. 1:11. John 15:8. [k] Eph. 2:10. [l] Rom. 6:22.

3. Their ability to do good works is not at all of themselves, but wholly from the Spirit of Christ.[m] And that they may be enabled thereunto, besides the graces they have already received, there is required an actual influence of the same Holy Spirit, to work in them to will and to do of His good pleasure:[n] yet are they not hereupon to grow negligent, as if they were not

bound to perform any duty, unless upon a special motion of the Spirit; but they ought to be diligent in stirring up the grace of God that is in them.[o]

[m]John 15:4–5. Ezek. 36:26–27. [n]Phil. 2:13. Phil. 4:13. 2 Cor. 3:5. [o]Phil. 2:12. Heb. 6:11–12. 2 Peter 1:3, 5, 10–11. Isa. 64:7. 2 Tim. 1:6. Acts 26:6–7. Jude 20–21.

4. They, who in their obedience attain to the greatest height which is possibly in this life, are so far from being able to supererogate, and to do more than God requires, as that they fall short of much which in duty they are bound to do.[p]

[p]Luke 17:10. Neh. 13:22. Job 9:2–3. Gal. 5:17.

5. We cannot, by our best works, merit pardon of sin, or eternal life at the hand of God, by reason of the great disproportion that is between them and the glory to come; and the infinite distance that is between us and God, whom, by them, we can neither profit, nor satisfy for the debt of our former sins,[q] but when we have done all we can, we have done but our duty, and are unprofitable servants;[r] and because, as they are good, they proceed from His Spirit;[s] and as they are wrought by us, they are defiled, and mixed with so much weakness and imperfection, that they cannot endure the severity of God's judgment.[t]

[q]Rom. 3:20. Rom. 4:2, 4, 6. Eph. 2:8–9. Titus 3:5–7. Rom. 8:18. Ps. 16:2. Job 22:2–3. Job 35:7–8. [r]Luke 17:10. [s]Gal. 5:22–23. [t]Isa. 64:6. Gal. 5:17. [t]Rom. 7:15, 18. Ps. 143:2. Ps. 130:3.

6. Yet notwithstanding, the persons of believers being accepted through Christ, their good works also are accepted in Him,[u] not as though they were in this life wholly unblameable and unreproveable in God's sight;[w] but that He, looking upon them in His Son, is pleased to accept and reward that which is sincere, although accompanied with many weaknesses and imperfections.[x]

[u]Eph. 1:6. 1 Peter 2:5. Ex. 28:38. Gen. 4:4 with Heb. 11:4. [w]Job 9:20. Ps. 143:2. [x]Heb. 13:20–21. 2 Cor. 8:12. Heb. 6:10. Matt. 25:21, 23.

7. Works done by unregenerate men, although, for the matter of them, they may be things which God commands, and of good use both to themselves and others:[y] yet, because they proceed not from a heart purified by faith;[z] nor are done in a right manner according to the Word;[a] nor to a right end, the glory of God;[b] they are therefore sinful, and cannot please God, or make a man meet to receive grace from God.[c] And yet, their neglect of them is more sinful, and displeasing unto God.[d]

[y]2 Kings 10:30–31. 1 Kings 21:27, 29. Phil. 1:15–16, 18. [z]Gen. 4:5 with Heb. 11:4. Heb. 11:6. [a]1 Cor. 13:3. Isa. 1:12. [b]Matt. 6:2, 5, 16. [c]Hag. 2:14. Titus 1:15. Amos 5:21–22. Hosea 1:4. Rom. 9:16. Titus 3:15. [d]Ps. 14:4. Ps. 36:3. Job 21:14–15. Matt. 25:41–43, 45. Matt. 23:23.

Chapter XVII: Of the Perseverance of the Saints

1. They, whom God hath accepted in His Beloved, effectually called, and sanctified by His Spirit, can neither totally, nor finally, fall away from the state of grace: but shall certainly persevere therein to the end, and be eternally saved.[a]

[a]Phil. 1:6. 2 Peter 1:10. John 10:28–29. 1 John 3:9. 1 Peter 1:5, 9.

2. This perseverance of the saints depends not upon their own free will, but upon the immutability of the decree of election flowing from the free and unchangeable love of God the Father;[b] upon the efficacy of the merit and intercession of Jesus Christ;[c] the abiding of the Spirit, and of the seed of God within them;[d] and the nature of the covenant of grace:[e] from all which ariseth also the certainty and infallibility thereof.[f]

[b]2 Tim. 2:18–19. Jer. 31:3. [c]Heb. 10:10, 14. Heb. 13:20–21. Heb. 9:12–15. [c]Rom. 8:33–39. [c]John 17:11, 24. Luke 22:32. Heb. 7:25. [d]John 14:16–17. [d]1 John 2:27. 1 John 3:9. [e]Jer. 32:40. [f]John 10:28. 2 Thess. 3:3. 1 John 2:19.

3. Nevertheless, they may, through the temptations of Satan and of the world, the prevalency of corruption remaining in them, and the neglect of the means of their preservation, fall into grievous sins;[g] and, for a time, continue therein:[h] whereby they incur God's displeasure,[i] and

grieve His Holy Spirit,[k] come to be deprived of some measure of their graces and comforts,[l] have their hearts hardened,[m] and their consciences wounded,[n] hurt and scandalize others,[o] and bring temporal judgments upon themselves.[p]

[g] Matt. 26:70, 72, 74. [h] Ps. 51 (title) and Ps. 51:14. [i] Isa. 64:5, 7, 9. 2 Sam. 11:27. [k] Eph. 4:30. [l] Ps. 51:8, 10, 12. Rev. 2:4. Song of Sol. 5:2–4, 6. [m] Isa. 63:17. Mark 6:52. Mark 16:14. [n] Ps. 32:3–4. Ps. 51:8. [o] 2 Sam. 12:14. [p] Ps. 89:31–32. 1 Cor. 11:32.

Chapter XVIII: Of the Assurance of Grace and Salvation

1. Although hypocrites and other unregenerate men may vainly deceive themselves with false hopes, and carnal presumptions of being in the favour of God, and estate of salvation;[a] which hope of theirs shall perish:[b] yet such as truly believe in the Lord Jesus, and love Him in sincerity, endeavouring to walk in all good conscience before Him, may, in this life, be certainly assured that they are in the state of grace,[c] and may rejoice in the hope of the glory of God, which hope shall never make them ashamed.[d]

[a] Job 8:13–14. Micah 3:11. Deut. 29:19. John 8:41. [b] Matt. 7:22–23. [c] 1 John 2:3. 1 John 3:14, 18–19, 21, 24. 1 John 5:13. [d] Rom. 5:2, 5.

2. This certainty is not a bare conjectural and probable persuasion, grounded upon a fallible hope;[e] but an infallible assurance of faith, founded upon the divine truth of the promises of salvation,[f] the inward evidence of those graces unto which these promises are made,[g] the testimony of the Spirit of adoption witnessing with our spirits that we are the children of God:[h] which Spirit is the earnest of our inheritance, whereby we are sealed to the day of redemption.[i]

[e] Heb. 6:11, 19. [f] Heb. 6:17–18. [g] 2 Peter 1:4–5, 10–11. 1 John 2:3. 1 John 3:14. 2 Cor. 1:12. [h] Rom. 8:15–16. [i] Eph. 1:13–14. Eph. 4:30. 2 Cor. 1:21–22.

3. This infallible assurance doth not so belong to the essence of faith, but that a true believer may wait long, and conflict with many difficulties before he be partaker of it:[k] yet, being enabled by the Spirit to know the things which are freely given him of God, he may without extraordinary revelation, in the right use of ordinary means, attain thereunto.[l] And therefore it is the duty of everyone to give all diligence to make his calling and election sure;[m] that thereby his heart may be enlarged in peace and joy in the Holy Ghost, in love and thankfulness to God, and in strength and cheerfulness in the duties of obedience, the proper fruits of this assurance:[n] so far is it from inclining men to looseness.[o]

[k] 1 John 5:13. Isa. 50:10. Mark 9:24. Ps. 88 throughout. Ps. 77:1–12. [l] 1 Cor. 2:12. 1 John 4:13. Heb. 6:11–12. Eph. 3:17–19. [m] 2 Peter 1:10. [n] Rom. 5:1–2, 5. Rom. 14:17. Rom. 15:13. Eph. 1:3–4. Ps. 4:6–7. Ps. 119:32. [o] 1 John 2:1–2. Rom. 6:1–2. Titus 2:11–12, 14. 2 Cor. 7:1. Rom. 8:1, 12. 1 John 3:2–3. Ps. 130:4. 1 John 1:6–7.

4. True believers may have the assurance of their salvation divers ways shaken, diminished, and intermitted; as, by negligence in preserving of it, by falling into some special sin, which woundeth the conscience and grieveth the Spirit; by some sudden or vehement temptation, by God's withdrawing the light of His countenance, and suffering even such as fear Him to walk in darkness and to have no light:[p] yet are they never so utterly destitute of that seed of God, and life of faith, that love of Christ and the brethren, that sincerity of heart, and conscience of duty, out of which, by the operation of the Spirit, this assurance may, in due time, be revived;[q] and by the which, in the mean time, they are supported from utter despair.[r]

[p] Song of Sol. 5:2–3, 6. Ps. 51:8, 12, 14. Eph. 4:30–31. Ps. 77:1–10. Matt. 26:69–72. Ps. 31:22. Ps. 88 throughout. Isa. 50:10. [q] 1 John 3:9. Luke 22:32. Job 13:15. Ps. 73:15. Ps. 51:8, 12. Isa. 50:10. [r] Micah 7:7–9. Jer. 32:40. Isa. 54:7–10. [r] Ps. 22:1. Ps. 88 throughout.

Chapter XIX: Of the Law of God

1. God gave to Adam a law, as a covenant of works, by which He bound him and all his posterity to personal, entire, exact, and perpetual obedience; promised life upon the fulfilling, and threatened death upon the breach of it: and endued him with power and ability to keep it.[a]

[a] Gen. 1:26–27 with Gen. 2:17. Rom. 2:14–15. Rom. 10:5. Rom. 5:12, 19. Gal. 3:10, 12. Eccles. 7:29. Job 28:28.

2. This law, after his fall, continued to be a perfect rule of righteousness, and, as such, was delivered by God upon Mount Sinai, in ten commandments, and written in two tables:[b] the four first commandments containing our duty towards God; and the other six our duty to man.[c]

[b] James 1:25. James 2:8, 10–12. Rom. 13:8–9. Deut. 5:32. Deut. 10:4. Ex. 34:1. [c] Matt. 22:37–40.

3. Beside this law, commonly called moral, God was pleased to give to the people of Israel, as a church under age, ceremonial laws, containing several typical ordinances, partly of worship, prefiguring Christ, His graces, actions, sufferings, and benefits;[d] and partly holding forth divers instructions of moral duties.[e] All which ceremonial laws are now abrogated, under the New Testament.[f]

[d] Heb. 9. Heb. 10:1. Gal. 4:1–3. Col. 2:17. [e] 1 Cor. 5:7. 2 Cor. 6:17. Jude 23. [f] Col. 2:14, 16–17. Dan. 9:27. Eph. 2:15–16.

4. To them also, as a body politic, He gave sundry judicial laws, which expired together with the State of that people; not obliging any other now, further than the general equity thereof may require.[g]

[g] Ex. 21. Ex. 22:1–29. Gen. 49:10 with 1 Peter 2:13–14. Matt. 5:17 with Matt. 5:38–39. 1 Cor. 9:8–10.

5. The moral law doth for ever bind all, as well justified persons as others, to the obedience thereof;[h] and that, not only in regard of the matter contained in it, but also in respect of the authority of God the Creator, who gave it:[i] neither doth Christ, in the Gospel, any way dissolve, but much strengthen this obligation.[k]

[h] Rom. 13:8–10. Eph. 6:2. 1 John 2:3–4, 7–8. [i] James 2:10–11. [k] Matt. 5:17–19. James 2:8. Rom. 3:31.

6. Although true believers be not under the law, as a covenant of works, to be thereby justified or condemned;[l] yet is it of great use to them, as well as to others; in that, as a rule of life informing them of the will of God, and their duty, it directs, and binds them to walk accordingly;[m] discovering also the sinful pollutions of their nature, hearts, and lives;[n] so as, examining themselves thereby, they may come to further conviction of, humiliation for, and hatred against sin;[o] together with a clearer sight of the need they have of Christ, and the perfection of His obedience.[p] It is likewise of use to the regenerate, to restrain their corruptions, in that it forbids sin:[q] and the threatenings of it serve to show what even their sins deserve; and what afflictions, in this life, they may expect for them, although freed from the curse thereof threatened in the law.[r] The promises of it, in like manner, show them God's approbation of obedience, and what blessings they may expect upon the performance thereof;[s] although not as due to them by the law, as a covenant of works.[t] So as, a man's doing good, and refraining from evil, because the law encourageth to the one, and deterreth from the other, is no evidence of his being under the law; and not under grace.[u]

[l] Rom. 6:14. Gal. 2:16. Gal. 3:13. Gal. 4:4–5. Acts 13:39. Rom. 8:1. [m] Rom. 7:12, 22, 25. Ps. 119:4–6. 1 Cor. 7:19. Gal. 5:14, 16, 18–23. [n] Rom. 7:7. Rom. 3:20. [o] James 1:23–25. Rom. 7:9, 14, 24. [p] Gal. 3:24. Rom. 7:24–25. Rom. 8:3–4. [q] James 2:11. Ps. 119:101, 104, 128. [r] Ezra 9:13–14. Ps. 89:30–34. [s] Lev. 26:1–14 with 2 Cor. 6:16. Eph. 6:2–3. Ps. 37:11 with Matt. 5:5. Ps. 19:11. [t] Gal. 2:16. Luke 17:10. [u] Rom. 6:12, 14. 1 Peter 3:8–12 with Ps. 34:12–16. Heb. 12:28–29.

7. Neither are the forementioned uses of the law contrary to the grace of the Gospel, but do sweetly comply with it;[w] the Spirit of Christ subduing and enabling the will of man to do that, freely and cheerfully, which the will of God, revealed in the law, requireth to be done.[x]

[w] Gal. 3:21. [x] Ezek. 36:27. Heb. 8:10 with Jer. 31:33.

Chapter XX: Of Christian Liberty, and Liberty of Conscience

1. The liberty which Christ hath purchased for believers under the Gospel consists in their freedom from the guilt of sin, the condemning wrath of God, the curse of the moral law;[a] and, in their being delivered from this present evil world, bondage to Satan, and dominion of sin;[b] from the evil of afflictions, the sting of death, the victory of the grave, and everlasting damnation;[c] as also, in their free access to God,[d] and their yielding obedience unto Him, not out of slavish fear, but a child-like love and willing mind.[e] All which were common also to believers under the law.[f] But, under the New Testament, the liberty of Christians is further enlarged, in

their freedom from the yoke of the ceremonial law, to which the Jewish Church was subjected;[g] and in greater boldness of access to the throne of grace,[h] and in fuller communications of the free Spirit of God, than believers under the law did ordinarily partake of.[i]

[a]Titus 2:14. 1 Thess. 1:10. Gal. 3:13. [b]Gal. 1:4. Col. 1:13. Acts 26:18. Rom. 6:14. [c]Rom. 8:28. Ps. 119:71. 1 Cor. 15:54–57. Rom. 8:1. [d]Rom. 5:1–2. [e]Rom. 8:14–15. 1 John 4:18. [f]Gal. 3:9, 14. [g]Gal. 4:1–3, 6–7. Gal. 5:1. Acts 15:10–11. [h]Heb. 4:14, 16. Heb. 10:19–22. [i]John 7:38–39. 2 Cor. 3:13, 17–18.

2. God alone is Lord of the conscience,[k] and hath left it free from the doctrines and commandments of men, which are in any thing contrary to His Word; or beside it, if matters of faith or worship.[l] So that, to believe such doctrines, or to obey such commands, out of conscience, is to betray true liberty of conscience:[m] and the requiring of an implicit faith, and an absolute and blind obedience is to destroy liberty of conscience, and reason also.[n]

[k]James 4:12. Rom. 14:4. [l]Acts 4:19. Acts 5:29. 1 Cor. 7:23. Matt. 23:8–10. 2 Cor. 1:24. Matt. 15:9. [m]Col. 2:20, 22–23. Gal. 1:10. Gal. 2:4–5. Gal. 5:1. [n]Rom. 10:17. Rom. 14:23. Isa. 8:20. Acts 17:11. John 4:22. Hosea 5:11. Rev. 13:12, 16–17. Jer. 8:9.

3. They who, upon pretence of Christian liberty, do practise any sin, or cherish any lust, do thereby destroy the end of Christian liberty, which is, that being delivered out of the hands of our enemies, we might serve the Lord, without fear, in holiness and righteousness before Him, all the days of our life.[o]

[o]Gal. 5:13. 1 Peter 2:16. 2 Peter 2:19. John 8:34. Luke 1:74–75.

4. And because the powers which God hath ordained, and the liberty which Christ hath purchased, are not intended by God to destroy, but mutually to uphold and preserve one another; they who, upon pretence of Christian liberty, shall oppose any lawful power, or the lawful exercise of it, whether it be civil or ecclesiastical, resist the ordinance of God.[p] And, for their publishing of such opinions, or maintaining of such practices, as are contrary to the light of nature, or to the known principles of Christianity, whether concerning faith, worship, or conversation; or, to the power of godliness; or, such erroneous opinions or practices, as either in their own nature, or in the manner of publishing or maintaining them, are destructive to the external peace and order which Christ hath established in the Church, they may lawfully be called to account, and proceeded against by the censures of the Church,[q] and by the power of the civil magistrate.[r]

[p]Matt. 12:25. 1 Peter 2:13–14, 16. Rom. 13:1–8. Heb. 13:17. [q]Rom. 1:32 with 1 Cor. 5:1, 5, 11, 13. 2 John 10, 11 and 2 Thess. 3:14 and 1 Tim. 6:3–5 and Titus 1:10–11, 13 and Titus 3:10 with Matt. 18:15–17. 1 Tim. 1:19–20. Rev. 2:2, 14–15, 20. Rev. 3:9. [r]Deut. 13:6–12. Rom. 13:3–4 with 2 John 10, 11. Ezra 7:23, 25–28. Rev. 17:12, 16–17. Neh. 13:15, 17, 21–22, 25, 30. 2 Kings 23:5–6, 9, 20–21. 2 Chron. 34:33. 2 Chron. 15:12–13, 16. Dan. 3:29. 1 Tim. 2:2. Isa. 49:23. Zech. 13:2–3.

Chapter XXI: Of Religious Worship, and the Sabbath Day

1. The light of nature showeth that there is a God, who hath lordship and sovereignty over all, is good, and doth good unto all, and is therefore to be feared, loved, praised, called upon, trusted in, and served, with all the heart, and with all the soul, and with all the might.[a] But the acceptable way of worshipping the true God is instituted by Himself, and so limited by His own revealed will, that He may not be worshipped according to the imaginations and devices of men, or the suggestions of Satan, under any visible representation, or any other way not prescribed in the holy Scripture.[b]

[a]Rom. 1:20. Acts 17:24. Ps. 119:68. Jer. 10:7. Ps. 31:23. Ps. 18:3. Rom. 10:12. Ps. 62:8. Josh. 24:14. Mark 12:33. [b]Deut. 12:32. Matt. 15:9. Acts 17:25. Matt. 4:9–10. Deut. 4:15–20. Ex. 20:4–6. Col. 2:23.

2. Religious worship is to be given to God, the Father, Son, and Holy Ghost; and to Him alone;[c] not to angels, saints, or any other creature:[d] and since the fall, not without a Mediator; nor in the mediation of any other but of Christ alone.[e]

[c]Matt. 4:10 with John 5:23 and 2 Cor. 13:14. [d]Col. 2:18. Rev. 19:10. Rom. 1:25. [e]John 14:6. 1 Tim. 2:5. Eph. 2:18. Col. 3:17.

3. Prayer, with thanksgiving, being one special part of religious worship,[f] is by God required of all men:[g] and that it may be accepted, it is to be made in the name of the Son,[h] by the help

of His Spirit,[i] according to His will,[k] with understanding, reverence, humility, fervency, faith, love, and perseverance;[l] and, if vocal, in a known tongue.[m]

[f]Phil. 4:6. [g]Ps. 65:2. [h]John 14:13–14. 1 Peter 2:5. [i]Rom. 8:26. [k]1 John 5:14. [l]Ps. 47:7. Eccles. 5:1–2. Heb. 12:28. Gen. 18:27. James 5:16. James 1:6–7. Mark 11:24. Matt. 6:12, 14–15. Col. 4:2. Eph. 6:18. [m]1 Cor. 14:14.

4. Prayer is to be made for things lawful,[n] and for all sorts of men living, or that shall live hereafter:[o] but not for the dead,[p] nor for those of whom it may be known that they have sinned the sin unto death.[q]

[n]1 John 5:14. [o]1 Tim. 2:1–2. John 17:20. 2 Sam. 7:29. Ruth 4:12. [p]2 Sam. 12:21–23 with Luke 16:25–26. Rev. 14:13. [q]1 John 5:16.

5. The reading of the Scriptures with godly fear;[r] the sound preaching[s] and conscionable hearing of the Word, in obedience unto God, with understanding, faith, and reverence;[t] singing of psalms with grace in the heart;[u] as also, the due administration and worthy receiving of the sacraments instituted by Christ; are all parts of the ordinary religious worship of God:[w] beside religious oaths,[x] vows,[y] solemn fastings,[z] and thanksgivings, upon special occasions,[a] which are, in their several times and seasons, to be used in a holy and religious manner.[b]

[r]Acts 15:21. Rev. 1:3. [s]2 Tim. 4:2. [t]James 1:22. Acts 10:33. Matt. 13:19. Heb. 4:2. Isa. 66:2. [u]Col. 3:16. Eph. 5:19. James 5:13. [w]Matt. 28:19. 1 Cor. 11:23–29. Acts 2:42. [x]Deut. 6:13 with Neh. 10:29. [y]Isa. 19:21 with Eccles. 5:4–5. [z]Joel 2:12. Esther 4:16. Matt. 9:15. 1 Cor. 7:5. [a]Ps. 107 throughout. Esther 9:22. [b]Heb. 12:28.

6. Neither prayer, nor any other part of religious worship, is now under the Gospel either tied unto, or made more acceptable by any place in which it is performed, or towards which it is directed:[c] but God is to be worshipped everywhere,[d] in spirit and truth;[e] as in private families[f] daily,[g] and in secret each one by himself;[h] so, more solemnly, in the public assemblies, which are not carelessly or wilfully to be neglected, or forsaken, when God, by His Word or providence, calleth thereunto.[i]

[c]John 4:21. [d]Mal. 1:11. 1 Tim. 2:8. [e]John 4:23–24. [f]Jer. 10:25. Deut. 6:6–7. Job 1:5. 2 Sam. 6:18, 20. 1 Peter 3:7. Acts 10:2. [g]Matt. 6:11. [h]Matt. 6:6. Eph. 6:18. [i]Isa. 56:6–7. Heb. 10:25. Prov. 1:20–21, 24. Prov. 8:34. Acts 13:42. Luke 4:16. Acts 2:42.

7. As it is the law of nature, that, in general, a due proportion of time be set apart for the worship of God; so, in His Word, by a positive, moral, and perpetual commandment, binding all men, in all ages, He hath particularly appointed one day in seven, for a Sabbath, to be kept holy unto Him:[k] which, from the beginning of the world to the resurrection of Christ, was the last day of the week; and, from the resurrection of Christ, was changed into the first day of the week,[l] which, in Scripture, is called the Lord's Day,[m] and is to be continued to the end of the world, as the Christian Sabbath.[n]

[k]Ex. 20:8, 10–11. Isa. 56:2, 4, 6–7. [l]Gen. 2:2–3. 1 Cor. 16:1–2. Acts 20:7. [m]Rev. 1:10. [n]Ex. 20:8, 10 with Matt. 5:17–18.

8. This Sabbath is then kept holy unto the Lord, when men, after a due preparing of their hearts, and ordering of their common affairs beforehand, do not only observe an holy rest, all the day, from their own works, words, and thoughts about their worldly employments, and recreations,[o] but also are taken up the whole time in the public and private exercises of His worship, and in the duties of necessity and mercy.[p]

[o]Ex. 20:8. Ex. 16:23, 25–26, 29–30. Ex. 31:15–17. [o]Isa. 58:13. Neh. 13:15–19, 21–22. [p]Isa. 58:13. Matt. 12:1–13

Chapter XXII: Of Lawful Oaths and Vows

1. A lawful oath is a part of religious worship,[a] wherein, upon just occasion, the person swearing solemnly calleth God to witness what he asserteth, or promiseth; and to judge him according to the truth or falsehood of what he sweareth.[b]

[a]Deut. 10:20. [b]Ex. 20:7. Lev. 19:12. 2 Cor. 1:23. 2 Chron. 6:22–23.

2. The name of God only is that by which men ought to swear; and therein it is to be used with all holy fear and reverence.[c] Therefore, to swear vainly or rashly, by that glorious and dreadful Name; or, to swear at all by any other thing, is sinful, and to be abhorred.[d] Yet, as in matters of

weight and moment, an oath is warranted by the Word of God, under the New Testament, as well as under the Old;[e] so a lawful oath, being imposed by lawful authority, in such matters ought to be taken.[f]

[c]Deut. 6:13. [d]Ex. 20:7. Jer. 5:7. Matt. 5:34, 37. James 5:12. [e]Heb. 6:16. 2 Cor. 1:23. Isa. 65:16. [f]1 Kings 8:31. Neh. 13:25. Ezra 10:5.

3. Whosoever taketh an oath ought duly to consider the weightiness of so solemn an act; and therein to avouch nothing, but what he is fully persuaded is the truth.[g] Neither may any man bind himself by oath to anything but what is good and just, and what he believeth so to be, and what he is able and resolved to perform.[h] Yet is it a sin to refuse an oath touching anything that is good and just, being imposed by lawful authority.[i]

[g]Ex. 20:7. Jer. 4:2. [h]Gen. 24:2–3, 5–6, 8–9. [i]Num. 5:19, 21. Neh. 5:12. Ex. 22:7–11.

4. An oath is to be taken in the plain and common sense of the words, without equivocation, or mental reservation.[k] It cannot oblige to sin: but in anything not sinful, being taken, it binds to performance, although to a man's own hurt.[l] Nor is it to be violated, although made to heretics, or infidels.[m]

[k]Jer. 4:2. Ps. 24:4. [l]1 Sam. 25:22, 32–34. Ps. 15:4. [m]Ezek. 17:16, 18–19. Josh. 9:18–19 with 2 Sam. 21:1.

5. A vow is of the like nature with a promissory oath, and ought to be made with the like religious care, and to be performed with the like faithfulness.[n]

[n]Isa. 19:21. Eccles. 5:4–6. Ps. 61:8. Ps. 66:13–14.

6. It is not to be made to any creature, but to God alone:[o] and, that it may be accepted, it is to be made voluntarily, out of faith, and conscience of duty, in way of thankfulness for mercy received, or for the obtaining of what we want; whereby we more strictly bind ourselves to necessary duties; or to other things, so far and so long as they may fitly conduce thereunto.[p]

[o]Ps. 76:11. Jer. 44:25–26. [p]Deut. 23:21–23. Ps. 50:14. Gen. 28:20–22. 1 Sam. 1:11. Ps. 66:13–14. Ps. 132:2–5.

7. No man may vow to do anything forbidden in the Word of God, or what would hinder any duty therein commanded, or which is not in his own power, and for the performance whereof he hath no promise of ability from God.[q] In which respects, Popish monastical vows of perpetual single life, professed poverty, and regular obedience, are so far from being degrees of higher perfection, that they are superstitious and sinful snares, in which no Christian may entangle himself.[r]

[q]Acts 23:12, 14. Mark 6:26. Num. 30:5, 8, 12–13. [r]Matt. 19:11–12. 1 Cor. 7:2, 9. Eph. 4:28. 1 Peter 4:2. 1 Cor. 7:23.

Chapter XXIII: Of the Civil Magistrate

1. God, the supreme Lord and King of all the world, hath ordained civil magistrates, to be, under Him, over the people, for His own glory, and the public good: and, to this end, hath armed them with the power of the sword, for the defence and encouragement of them that are good, and for the punishment of evil doers.[a]

[a]Rom. 13:1–4. 1 Peter 2:13–14.

2. It is lawful for Christians to accept and execute the office of a magistrate, when called thereunto;[b] in the managing whereof, as they ought especially to maintain piety, justice, and peace, according to the wholesome laws of each commonwealth;[c] so for that end, they may lawfully now, under the New Testament, wage war, upon just and necessary occasion.[d]

[b]Prov. 8:15–16. Rom. 13:1–2, 4. [c]Ps. 2:10–12. 1 Tim. 2:2. Ps. 82:3–4. 2 Sam. 23:3. 1 Peter 2:13. [d]Luke 3:14. Rom. 13:4. Matt. 8:9–10. Acts 10:1–2. Rev. 17:14, 16.

3. The civil magistrate may not assume to himself the administration of the Word and sacraments, or the power of the keys of the kingdom of heaven:[e] yet he hath authority, and it is his duty, to take order, that unity and peace be preserved in the Church, that the truth of God

be kept pure and entire; that all blasphemies and heresies be suppressed; all corruptions and abuses in worship and discipline prevented or reformed; and all the ordinances of God duly settled, administered, and observed.[f] For the better effecting whereof, he hath power to call synods, to be present at them, and to provide that whatsoever is transacted in them be according to the mind of God.[g]

[e] 2 Chron. 26:18 with Matt. 18:17 and Matt. 16:19. 1 Cor. 12:28–29. Eph. 4:11–12. 1 Cor. 4:1–2. Rom. 10:15. Heb. 5:4. [f] Isa. 49:23. Ps. 122:9. Ezra 7:23, 25–28. Lev. 24:16. Deut. 13:5–6, 12. 2 Kings 18:4. 1 Chron. 13:1–9. 2 Kings 23:1–26. 2 Chron. 34:33. 2 Chron. 15:12–13. [g] 2 Chron. 19:8–11. 2 Chron. 29–30. Matt. 2:4–5.

4. It is the duty of people to pray for magistrates,[h] to honor their persons,[i] to pay them tribute and other dues,[k] to obey their lawful commands, and to be subject to their authority, for conscience' sake.[l] Infidelity, or difference in religion, doth not make void the magistrates' just and legal authority, nor free the people from their due obedience to them:[m] from which ecclesiastical persons are not exempted;[n] much less hath the Pope any power and jurisdiction over them in their dominions, or over any of their people; and, least of all, to deprive them of their dominions, or lives, if he shall judge them to be heretics, or upon any other pretence whatsoever.[o]

[h] 1 Tim. 2:1–2. [i] 1 Peter 2:17. [k] Rom. 13:6–7. [l] Rom. 13:5. Titus 3:1. [m] 1 Peter 2:13–14, 16. [n] Rom. 13:1. 1 Kings 2:35. Acts 25:9–11. 2 Peter 2:1, 10–11. Jude 8–11. [o] 2 Thess. 2:4. Rev. 13:15–17.

Chapter XXIV: Of Marriage and Divorce

1. Marriage is to be between one man and one woman: neither is it lawful for any man to have more than one wife, nor for any woman to have more than one husband; at the same time.[a]

[a] Gen. 2:24. Matt. 19:5–6. Prov. 2:17.

2. Marriage was ordained for the mutual help of husband and wife,[b] for the increase of mankind with a legitimate issue, and of the Church with an holy seed;[c] and for preventing of uncleanness.[d]

[b] Gen. 2:18. [c] Mal. 2:15. [d] 1 Cor. 7:2, 9.

3. It is lawful for all sorts of people to marry, who are able with judgment to give their consent.[e] Yet it is the duty of Christians to marry only in the Lord:[f] and therefore such as profess the true reformed religion should not marry with infidels, papists, or other idolaters: neither should such as are godly be unequally yoked, by marrying with such as are notoriously wicked in their life, or maintain damnable heresies.[g]

[e] Heb. 13:4. 1 Tim. 4:3. 1 Cor. 7:36–38. Gen. 24:57–58. [f] 1 Cor. 7:39. [g] Gen. 34:14. Ex. 34:16. Deut. 7:3–4. 1 Kings 11:4. Neh. 13:25–27. Mal. 2:11–12. 2 Cor. 6:14.

4. Marriage ought not to be within the degrees of consanguinity or affinity forbidden in the Word;[h] nor can such incestuous marriages ever be made lawful by any law of man or consent of parties, so as those persons may live together as man and wife.[i] The man may not marry any of his wife's kindred nearer in blood than he may of his own; nor the woman of her husband's kindred nearer in blood than of her own.[k]

[h] Lev. 18. 1 Cor. 5:1. Amos 2:7. [i] Mark 6:18. Lev. 18:24–28. [k] Lev. 20:19–21.

5. Adultery or fornication committed after a contract, being detected before marriage, giveth just occasion to the innocent party to dissolve that contract.[l] In the case of adultery after marriage, it is lawful for the innocent party to sue out a divorce: and, after the divorce,[m] to marry another, as if the offending party were dead.[n]

5 [l] Matt. 1:18–20. [m] Matt. 5:31–32. [n] Matt. 19:9. Rom. 7:2–3. [o] Matt. 19:8–9. 1 Cor. 7:15. Matt. 19:6.

6. Although the corruption of man be such as is apt to study arguments unduly to put asunder those whom God hath joined together in marriage: yet nothing but adultery, or such wilful desertion as can no way be remedied by the Church or civil magistrate, is cause sufficient of dissolving the bond of marriage:[o] wherein, a public and orderly course of proceeding is to be

observed; and the persons concerned in it not left to their own wills and discretion, in their own case.[p]

[p] Deut. 24:1–4.

Chapter XXV: Of the Church

1. The catholic or universal Church which is invisible, consists of the whole number of the elect, that have been, are, or shall be gathered into one, under Christ the Head thereof; and is the spouse, the body, the fulness of Him that filleth all in all.[a]

[a] Eph. 1:10, 22–23. Eph. 5:23, 27, 32. Col. 1:18.

2. The visible Church, which is also catholic or universal under the Gospel (not confined to one nation as before under the law), consists of all those throughout the world that profess the true religion;[b] and of their children:[c] and is the kingdom of the Lord Jesus Christ,[d] the house and family of God,[e] out of which there is no ordinary possibility of salvation.[f]

[b] 1 Cor. 1:2. 1 Cor. 12:12–13. Ps. 2:8. Rev. 7:9. Rom. 15:9–12. [c] 1 Cor. 7:14. Acts 2:39. Ezek. 16:20–21. Rom. 11:16. Gen. 3:15. Gen. 17:7. [d] Matt. 13:47. Isa. 9:7. [e] Eph. 2:19. Eph. 3:15. [f] Acts 2:47.

3. Unto this catholic visible Church Christ hath given the ministry, oracles, and ordinances of God, for the gathering and perfecting of the saints, in this life, to the end of the world: and doth by His own presence and Spirit, according to His promise, make them effectual thereunto.[g]

[g] 1 Cor. 12:28. Eph. 4:11–13. Matt. 28:19–20. Isa. 59:21.

4. This catholic Church hath been sometimes more, sometimes less visible.[h] And particular Churches, which are members thereof, are more or less pure, according as the doctrine of the Gospel is taught and embraced, ordinances administered, and public worship performed more or less purely in them.[i]

[h] Rom. 11:3–4. Rev. 12:6, 14. [i] Rev. 2 and 3. 1 Cor. 5:6–7.

5. The purest Churches under heaven are subject both to mixture and error:[k] and some have so degenerated, as to become no Churches of Christ, but synagogues of Satan.[l] Nevertheless, there shall be always a Church on earth, to worship God according to His will.[m]

[k] 1 Cor. 13:12. Rev. 2 and 3. Matt. 13:24–30, 47. [l] Rev. 18:2. Rom. 11:18–22. [m] Matt. 16:18. Ps. 72:17. Ps. 102:28. Matt. 28:19–20.

6. There is no other head of the Church, but the Lord Jesus Christ;[n] nor can the Pope of Rome, in any sense, be head thereof; but is that Antichrist, that man of sin, and son of perdition, that exalteth himself, in the Church, against Christ and all that is called God.[o]

[n] Col. 1:18. Eph. 1:22. [o] Matt. 23:8–10. 2 Thess. 2:3–4, 8–9. Rev. 13:6.

Chapter XXVI: Of the Communion of Saints

1. All saints, that are united to Jesus Christ their Head by His Spirit and by faith, have fellowship with Him in His graces, sufferings, death, resurrection, and glory:[a] and, being united to one another in love, they have communion in each other's gifts and graces,[b] and are obliged to the performance of such duties, public and private, as do conduce to their mutual good, both in the inward and outward man.[c]

[a] 1 John 1:3. Eph. 3:16–19. John 1:16. Eph. 2:5–6. Phil. 3:10. Rom. 6:5–6. 2 Tim. 2:12. [b] Eph. 4:15–16. 1 Cor. 12:7. 1 Cor. 3:21–23. Col. 2:19. [c] 1 Thess. 5:11, 14. Rom. 1:11–12, 14. 1 John 3:16–18. Gal. 6:10.

2. Saints by profession are bound to maintain a holy fellowship and communion in the worship of God; and in performing such other spiritual services as tend to their mutual edification;[d] as also in relieving each other in outward things, according to their several abilities, and

necessities. Which communion, as God offereth opportunity, is to be extended unto all those who, in every place, call upon the name of the Lord Jesus.[e]

[d] Heb. 10:24–25. Acts 2:42, 46. Isa. 2:3. 1 Cor. 11:20. [e] Acts 2:44–45. 1 John 3:17. 2 Cor. 8 and 9. Acts 11:29–30.

3. This communion, which the saints have with Christ, doth not make them, in any wise, partakers of the substance of His Godhead; or to be equal with Christ, in any respect: either of which to affirm is impious and blasphemous.[f] Nor doth their communion one with another, as saints, take away, or infringe the title or propriety which each man hath in his goods and possessions.[g]

[f] Col. 1:18–19. 1 Cor. 8:6. Isa. 42:8. 1 Tim. 6:15–16. Ps. 45:7 with Heb. 1:8–9. [g] Ex. 20:15. Eph. 4:28. Acts 5:4.

Chapter XXVII: Of the Sacraments

1. Sacraments are holy signs and seals of the covenant of grace,[a] immediately instituted by God,[b] to represent Christ and His benefits; and to confirm our interest in Him;[c] as also, to put a visible difference between those that belong unto the Church, and the rest of the world;[d] and solemnly to engage them to the service of God in Christ, according to His Word.[e]

[a] Rom. 4:11. Gen. 17:7, 10. [b] Matt. 28:19. 1 Cor. 11:23. [c] 1 Cor. 10:16. 1 Cor. 11:25–26. Gal. 3:17. [d] Rom. 15:8. Ex. 12:48. Gen. 34:14. [e] Rom. 6:3–4. 1 Cor. 10:16, 21.

2. There is in every sacrament a spiritual relation, or sacramental union, between the sign and the thing signified: whence it comes to pass, that the names and effects of the one are attributed to the other.[f]

[f] Gen. 17:10. Matt. 26:27–28. Titus 3:5.

3. The grace which is exhibited in or by the sacraments rightly used, is not conferred by any power in them: neither doth the efficacy of a sacrament depend upon the piety or intention of him that doth administer it:[g] but upon the work of the Spirit,[h] and the word of institution, which contains, together with a precept authorizing the use thereof, a promise of benefit to worthy receivers.[i]

[g] Rom. 2:28–29. 1 Peter 3:21. [h] Matt. 3:11. 1 Cor. 12:13. [i] Matt. 26:27–28. Matt. 28:19–20.

4. There be only two sacraments ordained by Christ our Lord in the Gospel; that is to say, Baptism and the Supper of the Lord: neither of which may be dispensed by any but by a minister of the Word lawfully ordained.[k]

[k] Matt. 28:19. 1 Cor. 11:20, 23. 1 Cor. 4:1. Heb. 5:4.

5. The sacraments of the Old Testament, in regard of the spiritual things thereby signified and exhibited, were, for substance, the same with those of the New.[l]

[l] 1 Cor. 10:1–4.

Chapter XXVIII: Of Baptism

1. Baptism is a sacrament of the New Testament, ordained by Jesus Christ,[a] not only for the solemn admission of the party baptized into the visible Church;[b] but also, to be unto him a sign and seal of the covenant of grace,[c] of his ingrafting into Christ,[d] of regeneration,[e] of remission of sins,[f] and of his giving up unto God through Jesus Christ, to walk in newness of life.[g] Which sacrament is, by Christ's own appointment, to be continued in His Church until the end of the world.[h]

[a] Matt. 28:19. [b] 1 Cor. 12:13. [c] Rom. 4:11 with Col. 2:11–12. [d] Gal. 3:27. Rom. 6:5. [e] Titus 3:5. [f] Mark 1:4. [g] Rom. 6:3–4. [h] Matt. 28:19, 20.

2. The outward element to be used in this sacrament is water, wherewith the party is to be baptized, in the name of the Father, and of the Son, and of the Holy Ghost, by a minister of the Gospel, lawfully called thereunto.[i]

[i] Matt. 3:11. John 1:33. Matt. 28:19–20.

3. Dipping of the person into the water is not necessary: but Baptism is rightly administered by pouring or sprinkling water upon the person.[k]

[k] Heb. 9:10, 19–22. Acts 2:41. Acts 16:33. Mark 7:4.

4. Not only those that do actually profess faith in and obedience unto Christ,[l] but also the infants of one or both believing parents, are to be baptized.[m]

[l] Mark 16:15–16. Acts 8:37–38. [m] Gen. 17:7, 9–10 with Gal. 3:9, 14 and Col. 2:11–12 and Acts 2:38–39 and Rom. 4:11–12. 1 Cor. 7:14. Matt. 28:19. Mark 10:13–16. Luke 18:15.

5. Although it be a great sin to contemn or neglect this ordinance,[n] yet grace and salvation are not so inseparably annexed unto it, as that no person can be regenerated or saved without it;[o] or, that all that are baptized are undoubtedly regenerated.[p]

[n] Luke 7:30 with Ex. 4:24–26. [o] Rom. 4:11. Acts 10:2, 4, 22, 31, 45, 47. [p] Acts 8:13, 23.

6. The efficacy of Baptism is not tied to that moment of time wherein it is administered;[q] yet notwithstanding, by the right use of this ordinance, the grace promised is not only offered, but really exhibited and conferred, by the Holy Ghost, to such (whether of age or infants) as that grace belongeth unto, according to the counsel of God's own will, in His appointed time.[r]

[q] John 3:5, 8. [r] Gal. 3:27. Titus 3:5. Eph. 5:25–26. Acts 2:38, 41.

7. The sacrament of Baptism is but once to be administered unto any person.[s]

[s] Titus 3:5.

Chapter XXIX: Of the Lord's Supper

1. Our Lord Jesus, in the night wherein He was betrayed, instituted the sacrament of His body and blood, called the Lord's Supper, to be observed in His Church, unto the end of the world, for the perpetual remembrance of the sacrifice of Himself in His death; the sealing all benefits thereof unto true believers, their spiritual nourishment and growth in Him, their further engagement in and to all duties which they owe unto Him; and to be a bond and pledge of their communion with Him, and with each other, as members of His mystical body.[a]

[a] 1 Cor. 11:23–26. 1 Cor. 10:16–17, 21. 1 Cor. 12:13.

2. In this sacrament, Christ is not offered up to His Father; nor any real sacrifice made at all for remission of sins of the quick or dead;[b] but only a commemoration of that one offering up of Himself, by Himself, upon the cross, once for all: and a spiritual oblation of all possible praise unto God for the same:[c] so that the Popish sacrifice of the mass (as they call it) is most abominably injurious to Christ's one, only sacrifice, the alone propitiation for all the sins of his elect.[d]

[b] Heb. 9:22, 25–26, 28. [c] 1 Cor. 11:24–26. Matt. 26:26–27. [d] Heb. 7:23–24; 27. Heb. 10:11–12, 14, 18.

3. The Lord Jesus hath, in this ordinance, appointed His ministers to declare His word of institution to the people; to pray, and bless the elements of bread and wine, and thereby to set them apart from a common to a holy use; and to take and break the bread, to take the cup, and (they communicating also themselves) to give both to the communicants;[e] but to none who are not then present in the congregation.[f]

[e] Matt. 26:26–28 and Mark 14:22–24 and Luke 22:19–20 with 1 Cor. 11:23–26. [f] Acts 20:7. 1 Cor. 11:20.

4. Private masses, or receiving this sacrament by a priest or any other alone;[g] as likewise, the denial of the cup to the people,[h] worshipping the elements, the lifting them up or carrying them about for adoration, and the reserving them for any pretended religious use; are all contrary to the nature of this sacrament, and to the institution of Christ.[i]

[g] 1 Cor. 10:16. [h] Mark 14:23. 1 Cor. 11:25–29. [i] Matt. 15:9.

5. The outward elements in this sacrament, duly set apart to the uses ordained by Christ, have such relation to Him crucified, as that, truly, yet sacramentally only, they are sometimes called by the name of the things they represent, to wit, the body and blood of Christ;[k] albeit in substance and nature they still remain truly and only bread and wine, as they were before.[l]

[k] Matt. 26:26–28. [l] 1 Cor. 11:26–28. Matt. 26:29.

6. That doctrine which maintains a change of the substance of bread and wine into the substance of Christ's body and blood (commonly called transubstantiation) by consecration of a priest, or by any other way, is repugnant, not to Scripture alone, but even to common sense and reason; overthroweth the nature of the sacrament, and hath been, and is the cause of manifold superstitions; yea, of gross idolatries.[m]

[m] Acts 3:21 with 1 Cor. 11:24–26. Luke 24:6, 39.

7. Worthy receivers outwardly partaking of the visible elements in this sacrament,[n] do then also, inwardly by faith, really and indeed, yet not carnally and corporally, but spiritually, receive and feed upon Christ crucified, and all benefits of His death: the body and blood of Christ being then, not corporally or carnally, in, with, or under the bread and wine; yet, as really, but spiritually, present to the faith of believers in that ordinance, as the elements themselves are to their outward senses.[o]

[n] 1 Cor. 11:28. [o] 1 Cor. 10:16.

8. Although ignorant and wicked men receive the outward elements in this sacrament: yet they receive not the thing signified thereby, but by their unworthy coming thereunto are guilty of the body and blood of the Lord to their own damnation. Wherefore, all ignorant and ungodly persons, as they are unfit to enjoy communion with Him, so are they unworthy of the Lord's table; and cannot, without great sin against Christ while they remain such, partake of these holy mysteries,[p] or be admitted thereunto.[q]

[p] 1 Cor. 11:27–29. 2 Cor. 6:14–16. [q] 1 Cor. 5:6–7, 13. 2 Thess. 3:6, 14–15. Matt. 7:6.

Chapter XXX: Of Church Censures

1. The Lord Jesus, as King and Head of His Church, hath therein appointed a government, in the hand of Church officers, distinct from the civil magistrate.[a]

[a] Isa. 9:6–7. 1 Tim. 5:17. 1 Thess. 5:12. Acts 20:17, 28. Heb. 13:7, 17, 24. 1 Cor. 12:28. Matt. 28:18–20.

2. To these officers, the keys of the kingdom of heaven are committed: by virtue whereof, they have power respectively to retain, and remit sins; to shut that kingdom against the impenitent, both by the Word and censures; and to open it unto penitent sinners, by the ministry of the Gospel, and by absolution from censures, as occasion shall require.[b]

[b] Matt. 16:19. Matt. 18:17–18. John 20:21–23. 2 Cor. 2:6–8.

3. Church censures are necessary, for the reclaiming and gaining of offending brethren, for deterring of others from the like offences, for purging out of that leaven which might infect the whole lump, for vindicating the honor of Christ, and the holy profession of the Gospel, and for preventing the wrath of God, which might justly fall upon the Church, if they should suffer His covenant and the seals thereof to be profaned by notorious and obstinate offenders.[c]

[c] 1 Cor. 5. 1 Tim. 5:20. Matt. 7:6. 1 Tim. 1:20. 1 Cor. 11:27–34 with Jude 23.

4. For the better attaining of these ends, the officers of the Church are to proceed by admonition; suspension from the sacrament of the Lord's Supper for a season; and by excommunication from the Church; according to the nature of the crime, and demerit of the person.[d]

[d] 1 Thess. 5:12. 2 Thess. 3:6, 14–15. 1 Cor. 5:4–5; 13. Matt. 18:17. Titus 3:10.

Chapter XXXI: Of Synods and Councils

1. For the better government, and further edification of the Church, there ought to be such assemblies as are commonly called synods or councils.[a]

[a] Acts 15:2, 4, 6.

2. As magistrates may lawfully call a synod of ministers, and other fit persons, to consult and advise with, about matters of religion;[b] so, if magistrates be open enemies to the Church, the ministers of Christ of themselves, by virtue of their office, or they, with other fit persons, upon delegation from their Churches, may meet together in such assemblies.[c]

[b] Isa. 49:23. 1 Tim. 2:1–2. 2 Chron. 19:8–11. 2 Chron. 29 and 30. Matt. 2:4–5. Prov. 11:14. [c] Acts 15:2, 4, 22, 23, 25.

3. It belongeth to synods and councils, ministerially to determine controversies of faith and cases of conscience, to set down rules and directions for the better ordering of the public worship of God, and government of His Church; to receive complaints in cases of maladministration, and authoritatively to determine the same: which decrees and determinations, if consonant to the Word of God, are to be received with reverence and submission; not only for their agreement with the Word, but also for the power whereby they are made, as being an ordinance of God appointed thereunto in His Word.[d]

[d] Acts 15:15, 19, 24, 27–31. Acts 16:4. Matt. 18:17–20.

4. All synods or councils, since the Apostles' times, whether general or particular, may err; and many have erred. Therefore they are not to be made the rule of faith or practice; but to be used as a help in both.[e]

[e] Eph. 2:20. Acts 17:11. 1 Cor. 2:5. 2 Cor. 1:24.

5. Synods and councils are to handle, or conclude, nothing, but that which is ecclesiastical: and are not to intermeddle with civil affairs which concern the commonwealth; unless by way of humble petition, in cases extraordinary; or by way of advice, for satisfaction of conscience, if they be thereunto required by the civil magistrate.[f]

[f] Luke 12:13–14. John 18:36.

Chapter XXXII: Of the State of Men after Death, and of the Resurrection of the Dead

1. The bodies of men, after death, return to dust and see corruption:[a] but their souls (which neither die nor sleep) having an immortal subsistence, immediately return to God who gave them:[b] the souls of the righteous, being then made perfect in holiness, are received into the highest heavens, where they behold the face of God, in light and glory, waiting for the full redemption of their bodies.[c] And the souls of the wicked are cast into hell, where they remain in torments and utter darkness, reserved to the judgment of the great day.[d] Beside these two places, for souls separated from their bodies, the Scripture acknowledgeth none.

[a] Gen. 3:19. Acts 13:36. [b] Luke 23:43. Eccles. 12:7. [c] Heb. 12:23. 2 Cor. 5:1, 6, 8. Phil. 1:23 with Acts 3:21 and Eph. 4:10.
[d] Luke 16:23–24. Acts 1:25. Jude 6–7. 1 Peter 3:19.

2. At the last day, such as are found alive shall not die, but be changed:[e] and all the dead shall be raised up, with the selfsame bodies and none other, although with different qualities, which shall be united again to their souls for ever.[f]

[e] 1 Thess. 4:17. 1 Cor. 15:51–52. [f] Job 19:26–27. 1 Cor. 15:42–44.

3. The bodies of the unjust shall, by the power of Christ, be raised to dishonor: the bodies of the just, by His Spirit, unto honor; and be made conformable to His own glorious body.[g]

[g] Acts 24:15. John 5:28–29. 1 Cor. 15:43. Phil. 3:21.

Chapter XXXIII: Of the Last Judgment

1. God hath appointed a day, wherein He will judge the world in righteousness, by Jesus Christ,[a] to whom all power and judgment is given of the Father.[b] In which day, not only the apostate angels shall be judged,[c] but likewise all persons that have lived upon earth shall appear before the tribunal of Christ, to give an account of their thoughts, words, and deeds; and to receive according to what they have done in the body, whether good or evil.[d]

[a] Acts 17:31. [b] John 5:22, 27. [c] 1 Cor. 6:3. Jude 6. 2 Peter 2:4. [d] 2 Cor. 5:10. Eccles. 12:14. Rom. 2:16. Rom. 14:10, 12. Matt. 12:36–37.

2. The end of God's appointing this day is for the manifestation of the glory of His mercy, in the eternal salvation of the elect; and of His justice, in the damnation of the reprobate who are wicked and disobedient. For then shall the righteous go into everlasting life, and receive that fullness of joy and refreshing, which shall come from the presence of the Lord: but the wicked, who know not God, and obey not the Gospel of Jesus Christ, shall be cast into eternal torments, and be punished with everlasting destruction from the presence of the Lord, and from the glory of His power.[e]

[e] Matt. 25:31–46. Rom. 2:5–6. Rom. 9:22–23. Matt. 25:21. Acts 3:19. 2 Thess. 1:7–10.

3. As Christ would have us to be certainly persuaded that there shall be a day of judgment, both to deter all men from sin, and for the greater consolation of the godly in their adversity:[f] so will He have that day unknown to men, that they may shake off all carnal security, and be always watchful, because they know not at what hour the Lord will come; and may be ever prepared to say, Come, Lord Jesus, come quickly, Amen.[g]

[f] 2 Peter 3:11, 14. 2 Cor. 5:10–11. 2 Thess. 1:5–7. Luke 21:27–28. Rom. 8:23–25. [g] Matt. 24:36, 42–44. Mark 13:35–37. Luke 12:35–36. Rev. 22:20.

MAN'S *Chief End* IS TO GLORIFY *God* AND TO *Enjoy Him* FOR EVER

WESTMINSTER SHORTER CATECHISM

WESTMINSTER

SHORTER CATECHISM (1647)

The Westminster Assembly produced two catechisms. The shorter of these contains 107 questions to which, generally speaking, single-sentence answers are formulated, although occasionally a more detailed response is given. The pattern followed is broadly that of the Confession of Faith, but here the theological definitions given are compact and concise.

The most notable and famous feature of the Catechism is the brilliance of its first question and answer: "What is the chief end of man? Man's chief end is to glorify God, and to enjoy him for ever." But equally important, if less often recognized, is its stress that this is to be accomplished by conformity to the Word and will of God. Hence careful attention is given to the exposition of the Decalogue (Q. 41–81). Far from being an indication of actual or incipient legalism, the Westminster divines themselves regarded this as an essential lesson in Christian living. For them the knowledge of God's will lay largely in living for Christ in the power of the Spirit in order to fulfill the will of the heavenly Father revealed in Scripture.

QUESTION 1. What is the chief end of man?
ANSWER. Man's chief end is to glorify God, and to enjoy him for ever. 1 Cor. 10:31; Rom. 11:36; Ps. 73:25–28.

Q. 2. What rule hath God given to direct us how we may glorify and enjoy him?
A. The Word of God, which is contained in the Scriptures of the Old and New Testaments, is the only rule to direct us how we may glorify and enjoy him. 2 Tim. 3:16; Eph. 2:20; 1 John 1:3–4.

Q. 3. What do the Scriptures principally teach?
A. The Scriptures principally teach, what man is to believe concerning God, and what duty God requires of man. 2 Tim. 1:13; 2 Tim. 3:16.

Q. 4. What is God?
A. God is a Spirit, infinite, eternal, and unchangeable, in his being, wisdom, power, holiness, justice, goodness, and truth. John 4:24; Job 11:7–9; Ps. 90:2; Jas. 1:17; Ex. 3:14; Ps. 147:5; Rev. 4:8; Rev. 15:4; Ex. 34:6–7.

Q. 5. Are there more Gods than one?
A. There is but one only, the living and true God. Deut. 6:4; Jer. 10:10.

Q. 6. How many persons are there in the Godhead?
A. There are three persons in the Godhead; the Father, the Son, and the Holy Ghost; and these three are one God, the same in substance, equal in power and glory. 1 John 5:7; Matt. 28:19.

Q. 7. What are the decrees of God?
A. The decrees of God are, his eternal purpose, according to the counsel of his will, whereby, for his own glory, he hath foreordained whatsoever comes to pass. Eph. 1:4, 11; Rom. 9:22–23.

Q. 8. How doth God execute his decrees?
A. God executeth his decrees in the works of creation and providence.

Q. 9. What is the work of creation?
A. The work of creation is, God's making all things of nothing, by the word of his power, in the space of six days, and all very good. Gen. 1; Heb. 11:3.

Q. 10. How did God create man?
A. God created man male and female, after his own image, in knowledge, righteousness, and holiness, with dominion over the creatures. Gen. 1:26–28; Col. 3:10; Eph. 4:24.

Q. 11. What are God's works of providence?
A. God's works of providence are, his most holy, wise, and powerful preserving and governing all his creatures, and all their actions. Ps. 145:17; Ps. 104:24; Isa. 28:29; Heb. 1:3; Ps. 103:19; Matt. 10:29–31.

Q. 12. What special act of providence did God exercise toward man in the estate wherein he was created?
A. When God had created man, he entered into a covenant of life with him, upon condition of perfect obedience; forbidding him to eat of the tree of the knowledge of good and evil, upon the pain of death. Gal. 3:12; Gen. 2:17.

Q. 13. Did our first parents continue in the estate wherein they were created?
A. Our first parents, being left to the freedom of their own will, fell from the estate wherein they were created, by sinning against God. Gen. 3:6–8, 13; Eccl. 7:29.

Q. 14. What is sin?
A. Sin is any want of conformity unto, or transgression of, the law of God. 1 John 3:4.

Q. 15. What was the sin whereby our first parents fell from the estate wherein they were created?
A. The sin whereby our first parents fell from the estate wherein they were created, was their eating the forbidden fruit. Gen. 3:6, 12.

Q. 16. Did all mankind fall in Adam's first transgression?
A. The covenant being made with Adam, not only for himself, but for his posterity; all mankind, descending from him by ordinary generation, sinned in him, and fell with him in his first transgression. Gen. 2:16–17; Rom. 5:12; 1 Cor. 15:21–22.

Q. 17. Into what estate did the fall bring mankind?
A. The fall brought mankind into an estate of sin and misery. Rom. 5:12.

Q. 18. Wherein consists the sinfulness of that estate whereinto man fell?
A. The sinfulness of that estate whereinto man fell, consists in the guilt of Adam's first sin, the want of original righteousness, and the corruption of his whole nature, which is commonly called original sin; together with all actual transgressions which proceed from it. Rom. 5:10–20; Eph. 2:1–3; Jas. 1:14–15; Matt. 15:19.

Q. 19. What is the misery of that estate whereinto man fell?
A. All mankind, by their fall, lost communion with God, are under his wrath and curse, and so made liable to all miseries in this life, to death itself, and to the pains of hell for ever. Gen. 3:8, 10, 24; Eph. 2:2–3; Gal. 3:10; Lam. 3:39; Rom. 6:23; Matt. 25:41, 46.

Q. 20. Did God leave all mankind to perish in the estate of sin and misery?
A. God having, out of his mere good pleasure, from all eternity, elected some to everlasting life, did enter into a covenant of grace, to deliver them out of the estate of sin and misery, and to bring them into an estate of salvation by a Redeemer. Eph. 1:4; Rom. 3:20–22; Gal. 3:21–22.

Q. 21. Who is the Redeemer of God's elect?
A. The only Redeemer of God's elect is the Lord Jesus Christ, who, being the eternal Son of God, became man, and so was, and continueth to be, God and man in two distinct natures, and one person, for ever. 1 Tim. 2:5–6; John 1:14; Gal. 4:4; Rom. 9:5; Luke 1:35; Col. 2:9; Heb. 7:24–25.

Q. 22. How did Christ, being the Son of God, become man?
A. Christ, the Son of God, became man, by taking to himself a true body and a reasonable soul, being conceived by the power of the Holy Ghost, in the womb of the Virgin Mary, and born of her, yet without sin. Heb. 2:14, 16; Heb. 10:5; Matt. 26:38; Luke 1:27, 31, 35, 42; Gal. 4:4; Heb. 4:15; Heb. 7:26.

Q. 23. What offices doth Christ execute as our Redeemer?
A. Christ, as our Redeemer, executeth the offices of a prophet, of a priest, and of a king, both in his estate of humiliation and exaltation. Acts 3:21–22; Heb. 12:25 with 2 Cor. 13:3; Heb. 5:5–7; Heb. 7:25; Ps. 2:6; Isa. 9:6–7; Matt. 21:5; Ps. 2:8–11.

Q. 24. How doth Christ execute the office of a prophet?
A. Christ executeth the office of a prophet, in revealing to us, by his Word and Spirit, the will of God for our salvation. John 1:18; 1 Pet. 1:10–12; John 15:15; John 20:31.

Q. 25. How doth Christ execute the office of a priest?
A. Christ executeth the office of a priest, in his once offering up of himself a sacrifice to satisfy divine justice and reconcile us to God, and in making continual intercession for us. Heb. 9:14, 28; Heb. 2:17; Heb. 7:24–25.

Q. 26. How doth Christ execute the office of a king?
A. Christ executeth the office of a king, in subduing us to himself, in ruling and defending us, and in restraining and conquering all his and our enemies. Acts 15:14–16; Isa. 33:22; Isa. 32:1–2; 1 Cor. 15:25.

Q. 27. Wherein did Christ's humiliation consist?
A. Christ's humiliation consisted in his being born, and that in a low condition, made under the law, undergoing the miseries of this life, the wrath of God, and the cursed death of the cross; in being buried, and continuing under the power of death for a time. Luke 2:7; Gal. 4:4; Heb. 12:2–3; Isa. 53:2–3; Luke 22:44; Matt. 27:46; Phil. 2: 8; 1 Cor. 15:3–4; Acts 2:24–27, 31.

Q. 28. Wherein consisteth Christ's exaltation?
A. Christ's exaltation consisteth in his rising again from the dead on the third day, in ascending up into heaven, in sitting at the right hand of God the Father, and in coming to judge the world at the last day. 1 Cor. 15:4; Mark 16:19; Eph. 1:20; Acts 1:11; Acts 17:31.

Q. 29. How are we made partakers of the redemption purchased by Christ?
A. We are made partakers of the redemption purchased by Christ, by the effectual application of it to us by his Holy Spirit. John 1:11–12; Titus 3:5–6.

Q. 30. How doth the Spirit apply to us the redemption purchased by Christ?
A. The Spirit applieth to us the redemption purchased by Christ, by working faith in us, and thereby uniting us to Christ in our effectual calling. Eph. 1:13–14; John 6:37, 39; Eph. 2:8; Eph. 3:17; 1 Cor. 1:9.

Q. 31. What is effectual calling?
A. Effectual calling is the work of God's Spirit, whereby convincing us of our sin and misery, enlightening our minds in the knowledge of Christ, and renewing our wills, he doth persuade and enable us to embrace Jesus Christ, freely offered to us in the gospel. 2 Tim. 1:9; 2 Thess. 2:13–14; Acts 2:37; Acts 26:18; Ezek. 36:26–27; John 6: 44–45; Phil. 2:13.

Q. 32. What benefits do they that are effectually called partake of in this life?
A. They that are effectually called do in this life partake of justification, adoption, sanctification, and the several benefits which, in this life, do either accompany or flow from them. Rom. 8:30; Eph. 1:5; 1 Cor. 1:26, 30.

Q. 33. What is justification?
A. Justification is an act of God's free grace, wherein he pardoneth all our sins, and accepteth us as righteous in his sight, only for the righteousness of Christ imputed to us, and received by faith alone. Rom. 3:24–25; Rom. 4:6–8; 2 Cor. 5:19, 21; Rom. 5:17–19; Gal. 2:16; Phil. 3:9.

Q. 34. What is adoption?
A. Adoption is an act of God's free grace, whereby we are received into the number, and have a right to all the privileges, of the sons of God. 1 John 3:1; John 1:12; Rom. 8:17.

Q. 35. What is sanctification?
A. Sanctification is the work of God's free grace, whereby we are renewed in the whole man after the image of God, and are enabled more and more to die unto sin, and live unto righteousness. 2 Thess. 2:13; Eph. 4:23–24; Rom. 6:4, 6; Rom. 8:1.

Q. 36. What are the benefits which in this life do accompany or flow from justification, adoption, and sanctification?
A. The benefits which in this life do accompany or flow from justification, adoption, and sanctification, are, assurance of God's love, peace of conscience, joy in the Holy Ghost, increase of grace, and perseverance therein to the end. Rom. 5:1–2, 5; Rom. 14:17; Prov. 4:18; 1 John 5:13; 1 Pet. 1:5.

Q. 37. What benefits do believers receive from Christ at death?
A. The souls of believers are, at their death, made perfect in holiness, and do immediately pass into glory; and their bodies, being still united to Christ, do rest in their graves until the resurrection. Heb. 12:23; 2 Cor. 5:1, 6, 8; Phil. 1:23; Luke 23:43; 1 Thess. 4:14; Isa. 57:2; Job 19:26–27.

Q. 38. What benefits do believers receive from Christ at the resurrection?
A. At the resurrection, believers, being raised up to glory, shall be openly acknowledged and acquitted in the day of judgment, and made perfectly blessed in the full enjoying of God to all eternity. 1 Cor. 15:43; Matt. 25:23; Matt. 10:32; 1 John 3:2; 1 Cor. 13:12; 1 Thess. 4: 17–18.

Q. 39. What is the duty which God requireth of man?
A. The duty which God requireth of man, is obedience to his revealed will. Mic. 6:8; 1 Sam. 15:22.

Q. 40. What did God at first reveal to man for the rule of his obedience?
A. The rule which God at first revealed to man for his obedience, was the moral law. Rom. 2:14–15; Rom. 10:5.

Q. 41. Where is the moral law summarily comprehended?
A. The moral law is summarily comprehended in the ten commandments. Deut. 10:4; Matt. 19:17.

Q. 42. What is the sum of the ten commandments?
A. The sum of the ten commandments is, to love the Lord our God, with all our heart, with all our soul, with all our strength, and with all our mind; and our neighbor as ourselves. Matt. 22:37–40.

Q. 43. What is the preface to the ten commandments?
A. The preface to the ten commandments is in these words, I am the Lord thy God, which have brought thee out of the land of Egypt, out of the house of bondage. Ex. 20:2.

Q. 44. What doth the preface to the ten commandments teach us?
A. The preface to the ten commandments teacheth us, that because God is the Lord, and our God, and Redeemer, therefore we are bound to keep all his commandments. Luke 1:74–75; 1 Pet. 1:15–19.

Q. 45. Which is the first commandment?
A. The first commandment is, Thou shalt have no other gods before me. Ex. 20:3.

Q. 46. What is required in the first commandment?
A. The first commandment requireth us to know and acknowledge God to be the only true God, and our God, and to worship and glorify him accordingly. 1 Chron. 28:9; Deut. 26:17; Matt. 4:10; Ps. 29:2.

Q. 47. What is forbidden in the first commandment?
A. The first commandment forbiddeth the denying, or not worshipping and glorifying, the true God as God, and our God; and the giving of that worship and glory to any other, which is due to him alone. Ps. 14:1; Rom. 1:21; Ps. 81:10–11; Rom. 1:25–26.

Q. 48. What are we specially taught by these words, "before me," in the first commandment?
A. These words, "before me," in the first commandment teach us, that God, who seeth all things, taketh notice of, and is much displeased with, the sin of having any other God. Ezek. 8:5–18; Ps. 44:20–21.

Q. 49. Which is the second commandment?
A. The second commandment is, Thou shalt not make unto thee any graven image, or any likeness of anything that is in heaven above, or that is in the earth beneath, or that is in the water under the earth; thou shalt not bow down thyself to them, nor serve them; for I the Lord thy God am a jealous God, visiting the iniquity of the fathers upon the children unto the third and fourth generation of them that hate me: and showing mercy unto thousands of them that love me, and keep my commandments. Ex. 20:4–6.

Q. 50. What is required in the second commandment?
A. The second commandment requireth the receiving, observing, and keeping pure and entire, all such religious worship and ordinances as God hath appointed in his Word. Deut. 32:46; Matt. 28:20; Acts 2:42.

Q. 51. What is forbidden in the second commandment?
A. The second commandment forbiddeth the worshipping of God by images, or any other way not appointed in his Word. Deut. 4:15–19; Ex. 32:5, 8; Deut. 12:31–32.

Q. 52. What are the reasons annexed to the second commandment?
A. The reasons annexed to the second commandment are, God's sovereignty over us, his propriety in us, and the zeal he hath to his own worship. Ps. 95:2–3, 6; Ps. 45:11; Ex. 34:13–14.

Q. 53. Which is the third commandment?
A. The third commandment is, Thou shalt not take the name of the Lord thy God in vain: for the Lord will not hold him guiltless that taketh his name in vain. Ex. 20:7.

Q. 54. What is required in the third commandment?
A. The third commandment requireth the holy and reverent use of God's names, titles, attributes, ordinances, word, and works. Matt. 6:9; Deut. 28:58; Ps. 68:4; Rev. 15:3–4; Mal. 1:11, 14; Ps. 138:1–2; Job 36:24.

Q. 55. What is forbidden in the third commandment?
A. The third commandment forbiddeth all profaning or abusing of anything whereby God maketh himself known. Mal. 1:6–7, 12; Mal. 2:2; Mal. 3:14.

Q. 56. What is the reason annexed to the third commandment?
A. The reason annexed to the third commandment is, that however the breakers of this commandment may escape punishment from men, yet the Lord our God will not suffer them to escape his righteous judgment. 1 Sam. 2:12, 17, 22, 29; 1 Sam. 3:13; Deut. 28:58–59.

Q. 57. Which is the fourth commandment?
A. The fourth commandment is, Remember the Sabbath day, to keep it holy. Six days shalt thou labor, and do all thy work: but the seventh day is the Sabbath of the Lord thy God: in it thou shalt not do any work, thou, nor thy son, nor thy daughter, thy man–servant, nor thy maid–servant, nor thy cattle, nor thy stranger that is within thy gates: for in six days the Lord made heaven and earth, the sea, and all that in them is, and rested the seventh day: wherefore the Lord blessed the Sabbath–day, and hallowed it. Ex. 20:8–11.

Q. 58. What is required in the fourth commandment?
A. The fourth commandment requireth the keeping holy to God such set times as he hath appointed in his Word; expressly one whole day in seven, to be a holy Sabbath to himself. Deut. 5:12–14.

Q. 59. Which day of the seven hath God appointed to be the weekly Sabbath?
A. From the beginning of the world to the resurrection of Christ, God appointed the seventh day of the week to be the weekly Sabbath; and the first day of the week, ever since, to continue to the end of the world, which is the Christian Sabbath. Gen. 2:2–3; 1 Cor. 16:1–2; Acts 20:7.

Q. 60. How is the Sabbath to be sanctified?
A. The Sabbath is to be sanctified by a holy resting all that day, even from such worldly employments and recreations as are lawful on other days; and spending the whole time in the public and private exercises of God's worship, except so much as is to be taken up in the works of necessity and mercy. Ex. 20:8, 10; Ex. 16:25–28; Neh. 13:15–19, 21–22; Luke 4:16; Acts 20:7; Ps. 92 title; Isa. 66:23; Matt. 12:1–13.

Q. 61. What is forbidden in the fourth commandment?
A. The fourth commandment forbiddeth the omission, or careless performance, of the duties required, and the profaning the day by idleness, or doing that which is in itself sinful, or by unnecessary thoughts, words, or works, about our worldly employments or recreations. Ezek. 22:26; Amos 8:5; Mal. 1:13; Acts 20:7, 9; Ezek. 23:38; Jer. 17:24–26; Isa. 58:13.

Q. 62. What are the reasons annexed to the fourth commandment?
A. The reasons annexed to the fourth commandment are, God's allowing us six days of the week for our own employments, his challenging a special propriety in the seventh, his own example, and his blessing the Sabbath day. Ex. 20:9, 11.

Q. 63. Which is the fifth commandment?
A. The fifth commandment is, Honor thy father and thy mother: that thy days may be long upon the land which the Lord thy God giveth thee. Ex. 20:12.

Q. 64. What is required in the fifth commandment?
A. The fifth commandment requireth the preserving the honor, and performing the duties, belonging to every one in their several places and relations, as superiors, inferiors, or equals. Eph. 5:21; 1 Pet. 2:17; Rom. 12:10.

Q. 65. What is forbidden in the fifth commandment?
A. The fifth commandment forbiddeth the neglecting of, or doing anything against, the honor and duty which belongeth to every one in their several places and relations. Matt. 15:4–6; Ezek. 34:2–4; Rom. 13:8.

Q. 66. What is the reason annexed to the fifth commandment?
A. The reason annexed to the fifth commandment is, a promise of long life and prosperity (as far as it shall serve for God's glory, and their own good) to all such as keep this commandment. Deut. 5:16; Eph. 6:2–3.

Q. 67. Which is the sixth commandment?
A. The sixth commandment is, Thou shalt not kill. Ex. 20:13.

Q. 68. What is required in the sixth commandment?
A. The sixth commandment requireth all lawful endeavours to preserve our own life, and the life of others. Eph. 5:28–29; 1 Kings 18:4.

Q. 69. What is forbidden in the sixth commandment?
A. The sixth commandment forbiddeth the taking away of our own life, or the life of our neighbor unjustly, or whatsoever tendeth thereunto. Acts 16:28; Gen. 9:6.

Q. 70. What is the seventh commandment?
A. The seventh commandment is, Thou shalt not commit adultery. Ex. 20:14.

Q. 71. What is required in the seventh commandment?
A. The seventh commandment requireth the preservation of our own and our neighbor's chastity, in heart, speech, and behaviour. 1 Cor. 7:2–3, 5, 34, 36; Col. 4:6; 1 Pet. 3:2.

Q. 72. What is forbidden in the seventh commandment?
A. The seventh commandment forbiddeth all unchaste thoughts, words, and actions. Matt. 15:19; Matt. 5:28; Eph. 5:3–4.

Q. 73. Which is the eighth commandment?
A. The eighth commandment is, Thou shalt not steal. Ex. 20:15.

Q. 74. What is required in the eighth commandment?
A. The eighth commandment requireth the lawful procuring and furthering the wealth and outward estate of ourselves and others. Gen. 30:30; 1 Tim. 5:8; Lev. 25:35; Deut. 22:1–5; Ex. 23:4–5; Gen. 47:14, 20.

Q. 75. What is forbidden in the eighth commandment?
A. The eighth commandment forbiddeth whatsoever doth, or may, unjustly hinder our own, or our neighbor's, wealth, or outward estate. Prov. 21:17; Prov. 23:20–21; Prov. 28:19; Eph. 4:28.

Q. 76. Which is the ninth commandment?
A. The ninth commandment is, Thou shalt not bear false witness against thy neighbor. Ex. 20:16.

Q. 77. What is required in the ninth commandment?
A. The ninth commandment requireth the maintaining and promoting of truth between man and man, and of our own and our neighbor's good name, especially in witness bearing. Zech. 8:16; 3 John 1:12; Prov. 14:5, 25.

Q. 78. What is forbidden in the ninth commandment?
A. The ninth commandment forbiddeth whatsoever is prejudicial to truth, or injurious to our own or our neighbor's good name. 1 Sam. 17:28; Lev. 19:16; Ps. 15:3.

Q. 79. Which is the tenth commandment?
A. The tenth commandment is, Thou shalt not covet thy neighbor's house, thou shalt not covet thy neighbor's wife, nor his manservant, nor his maidservant, nor his ox, nor his ass, nor anything that is thy neighbor's. Ex. 20:17.

Q. 80. What is required in the tenth commandment?
A. The tenth commandment requireth full contentment with our own condition, with a right and charitable frame of spirit toward our neighbor, and all that is his. Heb. 13:5; 1 Tim. 6:6; Job 31:29; Rom. 12:15; 1 Tim. 1:5; 1 Cor. 13:4–7.

Q. 81. What is forbidden in the tenth commandment?
A. The tenth commandment forbiddeth all discontentment with our own estate, envying or grieving at the good of our neighbor, and all inordinate motions and affections to anything that is his. 1 Kings 21:4; Esther 5:13; 1 Cor. 10:10; Gal. 5:26; Jas. 3:14, 16; Rom. 7:7–8; Rom. 13:9; Deut. 5:21.

Q. 82. Is any man able perfectly to keep the commandments of God?
A. No mere man since the fall is able in this life perfectly to keep the commandments of God, but doth daily break them in thought, word, and deed. Eccl. 7:20; 1 John 1:8, 10; Gal. 5:17; Gen. 6:5; Gen. 8:21; Rom. 3:9–21; Jas. 3:2–13.

Q. 83. Are all transgressions of the law equally heinous?
A. Some sins in themselves, and by reason of several aggravations, are more heinous in the sight of God than others. Ezek. 8:6, 13, 15; 1 John 5:16; Ps. 78:17, 32, 56.

Q. 84. What doth every sin deserve?
A. Every sin deserveth God's wrath and curse, both in this life, and that which is to come. Eph. 5:6; Gal. 3:10; Lam. 3:39; Matt. 25:41.

Q. 85. What doth God require of us, that we may escape his wrath and curse, due to us for sin?
A. To escape the wrath and curse of God, due to us for sin, God requireth of us faith in Jesus Christ, repentance unto life, with the diligent use of all the outward means whereby Christ communicateth to us the benefits of redemption. Acts 20:21; Prov. 2:1–5; Prov. 8:33–36; Isa. 55:3.

Q. 86. What is faith in Jesus Christ?
A. Faith in Jesus Christ is a saving grace, whereby we receive and rest upon him alone for salvation, as he is offered to us in the gospel. Heb. 10:39; John 1:12; Isa. 26:3–4; Phil. 3:9; Gal. 2:16.

Q. 87. What is repentance unto life?
A. Repentance unto life is a saving grace, whereby a sinner, out of a true sense of his sin, and apprehension of the mercy of God in Christ, doth, with grief and hatred of his sin, turn from it unto God, with full purpose of, and endeavor after, new obedience. Acts 11:18; Acts 2:37–38; Joel 2:12; Jer. 3:22; Jer. 31:18–19; Ezek. 36:31; 2 Cor. 7:11; Isa. 1:16–17.

Q. 88. What are the outward and ordinary means whereby Christ communicateth to us the benefits of redemption?
A. The outward and ordinary means whereby Christ communicateth to us the benefits of redemption are, his ordinances, especially the Word, Sacraments, and prayer; all which are made effectual to the elect for salvation. Matt. 28:19–20; Acts 2:42, 46–47.

Q. 89. How is the Word made effectual to salvation?
A. The Spirit of God maketh the reading, but especially the preaching, of the Word, an effectual means of convincing and converting sinners, and of building them up in holiness and comfort through faith unto salvation. Neh. 8:8; 1 Cor. 14:24–25; Acts 26:18; Ps. 19:8; Acts 20:32; Rom. 15:4; 2 Tim. 3:15–17; Rom. 10:13–17; Rom. 1:16.

Q. 90. How is the Word to be read and heard, that it may become effectual to salvation?
A. That the Word may become effectual to salvation, we must attend thereunto with diligence, preparation, and prayer; receive it with faith and love, lay it up in our hearts, and practice it in our lives. Prov. 8:34; 1 Pet. 2:1–2; Ps. 119:18; Heb. 4:2; 2 Thess. 2:10; Ps. 119:11; Luke 8:15; Jas. 1:25.

Q. 91. How do the Sacraments become effectual means of salvation?
A. The Sacraments become effectual means of salvation, not from any virtue in them, or in him that doth administer them; but only by the blessing of Christ, and the working of his Spirit in them that by faith receive them. 1 Pet. 3:21; Matt. 3:11; 1 Cor. 3:6–7; 1 Cor. 12:13.

Q. 92. What is a Sacrament?
A. A Sacrament is a holy ordinance instituted by Christ; wherein, by sensible signs, Christ and the benefits of the new covenant are represented, sealed, and applied to believers. Gen. 17:7, 10; Ex. 12; 1 Cor. 11:23, 26.

Q. 93. Which are the Sacraments of the New Testament?
A. The Sacraments of the New Testament are Baptism, and the Lord's Supper. Matt. 28:19; Matt. 26:26–28.

Q. 94. What is Baptism?
A. Baptism is a Sacrament, wherein the washing with water, in the name of the Father, and of the Son, and of the Holy Ghost, doth signify and seal our ingrafting into Christ, and partaking of the benefits of the covenant of grace, and our engagement to be the Lord's. Matt. 28:19; Rom. 6:4; Gal. 3:27.

Q. 95. To whom is Baptism to be administered?
A. Baptism is not to be administered to any that are out of the visible Church, till they profess their faith in Christ, and obedience to him; but the infants of such as are members of the visible Church are to be baptized. Acts 8:36–37; Acts 2:38–39; Gen. 17:10 with Col. 2:11–12; 1 Cor. 7:14.

Q. 96. What is the Lord's Supper?
A. The Lord's Supper is a Sacrament, wherein, by giving and receiving bread and wine, according to Christ's appointment, his death is showed forth; and the worthy receivers are, not after a corporal and carnal manner, but by faith, made partakers of his body and blood, with all his benefits, to their spiritual nourishment and growth in grace. 1 Cor. 11:23–26; 1 Cor. 10:16.

Q. 97. What is required to the worthy receiving of the Lord's Supper?
A. It is required of them that would worthily partake of the Lord's Supper, that they examine themselves, of their knowledge to discern the Lord's body, of their faith to feed upon him, of their repentance, love, and new obedience; lest, coming unworthily, they eat and drink judgment to themselves. 1 Cor. 11:28–29; 2 Cor. 13:5; 1 Cor. 11:31; 1 Cor. 10:16–17; 1 Cor. 5:7–8.

Q. 98. What is prayer?
A. Prayer is an offering up of our desires unto God, for things agreeable to his will, in the name of Christ, with confession of our sins, and thankful acknowledgment of his mercies. Ps. 62:8; 1 John 5:14; John 16:23; Ps. 32:5–6; Dan. 9:4; Phil. 4:6.

Q. 99. What rule hath God given for our direction in prayer?
A. The whole Word of God is of use to direct us in prayer, but the special rule of direction is that form of prayer which Christ taught his disciples, commonly called, The Lord's Prayer. 1 John 5:14; Matt. 6:9–13 with Luke 11:2–4.

Q. 100. What doth the preface of the Lord's Prayer teach us?
A. The preface of the Lord's Prayer, which is, "Our Father which art in heaven," teacheth us to draw near to God with all holy reverence and confidence, as children to a father, able and ready to help us; and that we should pray with and for others. Matt. 6:9; Rom. 8:15; Luke 11:13; Acts 12:5; 1 Tim. 2:1–2.

Q. 101. What do we pray for in the first petition?
A. In the first petition, which is, "Hallowed be thy name," we pray, that God would enable us, and others, to glorify him in all that whereby he maketh himself known, and that he would dispose all things to his own glory. Matt. 6:9; Ps. 67; 2–3; Ps. 83.

Q. 102. What do we pray for in the second petition?
A. In the second petition, which is, "Thy kingdom come," we pray, that Satan's kingdom may be destroyed; and that the kingdom of grace may be advanced, ourselves and others brought into it, and kept in it; and that the kingdom of glory may be hastened. Matt. 6:10; Ps. 68:1, 18; Rev. 12:10–11; 2 Thess. 3:1; Rom. 10:1; John 17:9, 20; Rev. 22:20.

Q. 103. What do we pray for in the third petition?
A. In the third petition, which is, "Thy will be done in earth as it is in heaven," we pray, that God, by his grace, would make us able and willing to know, obey, and submit to his will in all things, as the angels do in heaven. Matt. 6:10; Ps. 67; Ps. 119:36; Matt. 26:39; 2 Sam. 15:25; Job 1:21; Ps. 103: 20–21.

Q. 104. What do we pray for in the fourth petition?
A. In the fourth petition, which is, "Give us this day our daily bread," we pray, that of God's free gift we may receive a competent portion of the good things of this life, and enjoy his blessing with them. Matt. 6:11; Prov. 30:8–9; Gen. 28:20; 1 Tim. 4:4–5.

Q. 105. What do we pray for in the fifth petition?
A. In the fifth petition, which is, "And forgive us our debts, as we forgive our debtors," we pray, that God, for Christ's sake, would freely pardon all our sins; which we are the rather encouraged

to ask, because by his grace we are enabled from the heart to forgive others. Matt. 6:12; Ps. 51:1–2, 7, 9; Dan. 9:17–19; Luke 11:4; Matt. 18:35.

Q. 106. What do we pray for in the sixth petition?
A. In the sixth petition, which is, "And lead us not into temptation, but deliver us from evil," we pray, that God would either keep us from being tempted to sin, or support and deliver us when we are tempted. Matt. 6:12; Matt. 26:41; 2 Cor. 12:7–8.

Q. 107. What doth the conclusion of the Lord's Prayer teach us?
A. The conclusion of the Lord's Prayer, which is, "For thine is the kingdom, and the power, and the glory, for ever. Amen," teacheth us to take our encouragement in prayer from God only, and in our prayers to praise him, ascribing kingdom, power, and glory to him; and in testimony of our desire and assurance to be heard, we say, Amen. Matt. 6:13; Dan. 9:4–9, 16–19; 1 Chron. 29:10–13; 1 Cor. 14:16; Rev. 22:20–21.

WESTMINSTER

LARGER CATECHISM (1648)

The Larger Catechism shares the theology and many of the characteristics of the Shorter Catechism, its better known companion, but covers more ground in greater detail. It contains 196 questions and answers. The usefulness of the Larger Catechism lies less in its memorizability than in its value as a teaching aid framed in the catechetical form. The Larger Catechism serves well as a useful guidebook for teaching doctrinal themes.

Following five opening questions indicating that it is from Scripture that we learn who God is, how we may know Him and what He requires, questions 6–90 teach us what we are to believe about Him. Questions 91–196 spell out the duties of the Christian life.

As is the case with the Shorter Catechism, this emphasis on the obedience of the Christian is set within a strong context of God's grace in Christ. The divines set out to provide a well-structured guide to applying the Word of God in the practical context of everyday life.

QUESTION 1. What is the chief and highest end of man?
ANSWER. Man's chief and highest end is to glorify God, and fully to enjoy him for ever. Rom. 11:36; 1 Cor. 10:31; Ps. 73:24–28; John 17:21–23.

Q. 2. How doth it appear that there is a God?
A. The very light of nature in man, and the works of God, declare plainly that there is a God; but his Word and Spirit only, do sufficiently and effectually reveal him unto men for their salvation. Rom. 1:19–20; Ps. 19:1–3; Acts 17:28; 1 Cor. 2:9–10; 2 Tim. 3:15–17; Isa. 59:21.

Q. 3. What is the Word of God?
A. The Holy Scriptures of the Old and New Testaments are the Word of God, the only rule of faith and obedience. 2 Tim. 3:16; 2 Peter 1:19–21; Eph. 2:20; Rev. 22:18–19; Isa. 8:20; Luke 16:29, 31; Gal. 1:8–9; 2 Tim. 3:15–16.

Q. 4. How doth it appear that the Scriptures are the Word of God?
A. The Scriptures manifest themselves to be the Word of God, by their majesty and purity; by the consent of all the parts, and the scope of the whole, which is to give all glory to God; by their light and power to convince and convert sinners, to comfort and build up believers unto salvation: but the Spirit of God bearing witness by and with the Scriptures in the heart of man, is alone able fully to persuade it that they are the very Word of God. Hos. 8:12; 1 Cor. 2:6–7, 13; Ps. 119:18, 129; Ps. 12:6; Ps. 119:140; Acts 10:43; Acts 26:22; Rom. 3:19, 27; Acts 18:28; Heb. 4:12; Jas. 1:18; Ps. 19:7–9; Rom. 15: 4; Acts 20:32; John 16:13–14; 1 John 2:20, 27; John 20:31.

Q. 5. What do the Scriptures principally teach?
A. The Scriptures principally teach, what man is to believe concerning God, and what duty God requires of man. 2 Tim. 1:13.

WHAT MAN OUGHT TO BELIEVE CONCERNING GOD

Q. 6. What do the Scriptures make known of God?
A. The Scriptures make known what God is, the persons in the Godhead, his decrees, and the execution of his decrees. Heb. 11:6; 1 John 5:7; Acts 15:14–15, 18; Acts 4:27–28.

Q. 7. What is God?
A. God is a Spirit, in and of himself infinite in being, glory, blessedness, and perfection; all–sufficient, eternal, unchangeable, incomprehensible, everywhere present, almighty, knowing all things, most wise, most holy, most just, most merciful and gracious, long–suffering, and

abundant in goodness and truth. John 4:24; Ex. 3:14; Job 11:7–9; Acts 7:2; 1 Tim. 6:15; Matt. 5:48; Gen. 17:1; Ps. 90:2; Mal. 3:6; Jas. 1:17; 1 Kings 8:27; Ps. 139:1–13; Rev. 4:8; Heb. 4:13; Ps. 147:5; Rom. 16:27; Isa. 6:3; Rev. 15:4; Deut. 32:4; Ex. 34:6.

Q. 8. Are there more Gods than one?
A. There is but one only, the living and true God. Deut. 6:4; 1 Cor. 8:4, 6; Jer. 10:10.

Q. 9. How many persons are there in the Godhead?
A. There be three persons in the Godhead, the Father, the Son, and the Holy Ghost: and these three are one true, eternal God, the same in substance, equal in power and glory; although distinguished by their personal properties. 1 John 5:7; Matt. 3:16–17; Matt. 28:19; 2 Cor. 13:14; John 10:30.

Q. 10. What are the personal properties of the three persons in the Godhead?
A. It is proper to the Father to beget the Son, and to the Son to be begotten of the Father, and to the Holy Ghost to proceed from the Father and the Son from all eternity. Heb. 1:5–6, 8; John 1:14, 18; John 15:26; Gal. 4:6.

Q. 11. How doth it appear that the Son and the Holy Ghost are God equal with the Father?
A. The Scriptures manifest that the Son and the Holy Ghost are God equal with the Father, ascribing unto them such names, attributes, works, and worship, as are proper to God only. Isa. 6:3, 5, 8; John 12:41; Acts 28:25; 1 John 5:20; Acts 5:3–4; John 1:1; Isa. 9: 6; John 2:24–25; 1 Cor. 2:10–11; Col. 1:16; Gen. 1:2; Matt. 28:19; 2 Cor. 13:14.

Q. 12. What are the decrees of God?
A. God's decrees are the wise, free, and holy acts of the counsel of his will, whereby, from all eternity, he hath, for his own glory, unchangeably fore–ordained whatsoever comes to pass in time, especially concerning angels and men. Eph. 1:11; Rom. 11:33; Rom. 9:14–15, 18; Eph. 1:4, 11; Rom. 9:22–23; Ps. 33:11.

Q. 13. What hath God especially decreed concerning angels and men?
A. God, by an eternal and immutable decree, out of his mere love, for the praise of his glorious grace, to be manifested in due time, hath elected some angels to glory; and in Christ hath chosen some men to eternal life, and the means thereof: and also according to his sovereign power, and the unsearchable counsel of his own will, (whereby he extendeth or withholdeth favor as he pleaseth), hath passed by, and fore–ordained the rest to dishonor and wrath, to be for their sin inflicted, to the praise of the glory of his justice. 1 Tim. 5:21; Eph. 1:4–6; 2 Thess. 2:13–14; Rom. 9:17–18, 21–22; Matt. 11:25–26; 2 Tim. 2:20; Jude 1:4; 1 Peter 2:8.

Q. 14. How doth God execute his decrees?
A. God executeth his decrees in the works of creation and providence, according to his infallible fore–knowledge, and the free and immutable counsel of his own will. Eph. 1:11.

Q. 15. What is the work of creation?
A. The work of creation is that wherein God did in the beginning, by the word of his power, make of nothing the world, and all things therein, for himself, within the space of six days, and all very good. Gen. 1; Heb. 11:3; Prov. 16:4.

Q. 16. How did God create angels?
A. God created all the angels spirits, immortal, holy, excelling in knowledge, mighty in power, to execute his commandments, and to praise his name, yet subject to change. Col. 1:16; Ps. 104:4; Matt. 22:30; Matt. 25:31; 2 Sam. 14:17; Matt. 24:36; 2 Thess. 1:7; Ps. 103:20–21; 2 Peter 2:4.

Q. 17. How did God create man?
A. After God had made all other creatures, he created man, male and female; formed the body of the man of the dust of the ground, and the woman of the rib of the man; endued them with living, reasonable, and immortal souls; made them after his own image, in knowledge, righteousness and holiness, having the law of God written in their hearts and power to fulfill

it, with dominion over the creatures; yet subject to fall. Gen. 1:27; Gen. 2:7; Gen. 2:22; Gen. 2:7; Job 35:11; Eccl. 12:7; Matt. 10:28; Luke 23:43; Gen. 1:27; Col. 3:10; Eph. 4:24; Rom. 2:14–15; Eccl. 7:29; Gen. 1: 28; Gen. 3:6; Eccl. 7:29.

Q. 18. What are God's works of providence?
A. God's works of providence are his most holy, wise, and powerful preserving, and governing all his creatures; ordering them, and all their actions, to his own glory. Ps. 145:17; Ps. 104:24; Isa. 28:29; Heb. 1:3; Ps. 103:19; Matt. 10:29–31; Gen. 45:7; Rom. 11:36; Isa. 63:14.

Q. 19. What is God's providence toward the angels?
A. God by his providence permitted some of the angels, willfully and irrecoverably, to fall into sin and damnation, limiting and ordering that, and all their sins, to his own glory; and established the rest in holiness and happiness; employing them all, at his pleasure, in the administrations of his power, mercy, and justice. Jude 1:6; 2 Peter 2:4; Heb. 2:16; John 8:44; Job 1:12; Matt. 8:31; 1 Tim. 5:21; Mark 8:38; Heb. 12:22; Ps. 104:4; 2 Kings 19:35; Heb. 1:14.

Q. 20. What was the providence of God toward man in the estate in which he was created?
A. The providence of God toward man in the estate in which he was created, was the placing him in paradise, appointing him to dress it, giving him liberty to eat of the fruit of the earth; putting the creatures under his dominion, and ordaining marriage for his help; affording him communion with Himself; instituting the Sabbath; entering into a covenant of life with him, upon condition of personal, perfect, and perpetual obedience, of which the tree of life was a pledge; and forbidding to eat of the tree of knowledge of good and evil, upon the pain of death. Gen. 2:8, 15–16; Gen. 1:28; Gen. 2:18; Gen. 1:26–29; Gen. 3:8; Gen. 2:3; Gal. 3:12; Rom. 10:5; Gen. 2:9, 17.

Q. 21. Did man continue in that estate wherein God at first created him?
A. Our first parents being left to the freedom of their own will, through the temptation of Satan, transgressed the commandment of God, in eating the forbidden fruit, and thereby fell from the estate of innocency wherein they were created. Gen. 3:6–8, 13; Eccl. 7:29; 2 Cor. 11:3.

Q. 22. Did all mankind fall in that first transgression?
A. The covenant being made with Adam, as a public person, not for himself only, but for his posterity; all mankind descending from him by ordinary generation, sinned in him, and fell with him in that first transgression. Acts 17:26; Gen. 2:16–17; Rom. 5:12–20; 1 Cor. 15:21–22.

Q. 23. Into what estate did the fall bring mankind?
A. The fall brought mankind into an estate of sin and misery. Rom. 5:12; Rom. 3:23.

Q. 24. What is sin?
A. Sin is any want of conformity unto, or transgression of, any law of God, given as a rule to the reasonable creature. 1 John 3:4; Gal. 3:10, 12.

Q. 25. Wherein consisteth the sinfulness of that estate whereinto man fell?
A. The sinfulness of that estate whereinto man fell, consisteth in the guilt of Adam's first sin, the want of that righteousness wherein he was created, and the corruption of his nature, whereby he is utterly indisposed, disabled, and made opposite unto all that is spiritually good, and wholly inclined to all evil, and that continually; which is commonly called Original Sin, and from which do proceed all actual transgressions. Rom. 5:12, 19; Rom. 3:10–19; Eph. 2:1–3; Rom. 5:6; Rom. 8:7–8; Gen. 6:5; Jas. 1:14–15; Matt. 15:19.

Q. 26. How is original sin conveyed from our first parents unto their posterity?
A. Original sin is conveyed from our first parents unto their posterity by natural generation, so as all that proceed from them in that way are conceived and born in sin. Ps. 51:5; Job 14:4; Job 15:14; John 3:6.

Q. 27. What misery did the fall bring upon mankind?
A. The fall brought upon mankind the loss of communion with God, his displeasure and curse; so as we are by nature children of wrath, bond slaves to Satan, and justly liable to all

punishments in this world and that which is to come. Gen. 3:8, 10, 24; Eph. 2:2–3; 2 Tim. 2:26; Gen. 2:17; Lam. 3:39; Rom. 6:23; Matt. 25:41, 46; Jude 7.

Q. 28. What are the punishments of sin in this world?
A. The punishments of sin in this world, are either inward, as blindness of mind, a reprobate sense, strong delusions, hardness of heart, horror of conscience, and vile affections: or outward, as the curse of God upon the creatures for our sake; and all other evils that befall us in our bodies, names, estates, relations, and employments; together with death itself. Eph. 4:18; Rom. 1:28; 2 Thess. 2:11; Rom. 2:5; Isa. 33:14; Gen. 4:13; Matt. 27: 4; Rom. 1:26; Gen. 3:17; Deut. 28:15–68; Rom. 6:21, 23.

Q. 29. What are the punishments of sin in the world to come?
A. The punishments of sin in the world to come, are everlasting separation from the comfortable presence of God, and most grievous torments in soul and body, without intermission, in hell–fire for ever. 2 Thess. 1:9; Mark 9:43–44, 46, 48; Luke 16:24.

Q. 30. Doth God leave all mankind to perish in the estate of sin and misery?
A. God doth not leave all men to perish in the estate of sin and misery, into which they fell by the breach of the first covenant, commonly called the Covenant of Works; but of his mere love and mercy delivereth his elect out of it, and bringeth them into an estate of salvation by the second covenant, commonly called the Covenant of Grace. 1 Thess. 5:9; Gal. 3:10, 12; Titus 3:4–7; Gal. 3:21; Rom. 3:20–22.

Q. 31. With whom was the covenant of grace made?
A. The covenant of grace was made with Christ as the second Adam, and in him with all the elect as his seed. Gal. 3:16; Rom. 5:15–21; Isa. 53:10–11.

Q. 32. How is the grace of God manifested in the second covenant?
A. The grace of God is manifested in the second covenant, in that he freely provideth and offereth to sinners a Mediator, and life and salvation by him; and, requiring faith as the condition to interest them in him, promiseth and giveth his Holy Spirit to all his elect, to work in them that faith, with all other saving graces; and to enable them unto all holy obedience, as the evidence of the truth of their faith and thankfulness to God, and as the way which he hath appointed them to salvation. Gen. 3:15; Isa. 42:6; John 6:27; 1 John 5:11–12; John 3:16; John 1:12; Prov. 1:23; 2 Cor. 4:13; Gal. 5:22–23; Ezek. 36:27; Jas. 2:18, 22; 2 Cor. 5:14–15; Eph. 2:10.

Q. 33. Was the covenant of grace always administered after one and the same manner?
A. The covenant of grace was not always administered after the same manner, but the administrations of it under the Old Testament were different from those under the New. 2 Cor. 3:6–9.

Q. 34. How was the covenant of grace administered under the Old Testament?
A. The covenant of grace was administered under the Old Testament, by promises, prophecies, sacrifices, circumcision, the passover, and other types and ordinances, which did all fore–signify Christ then to come, and were for that time sufficient to build up the elect in faith in the promised Messiah, by whom they then had full remission of sin, and eternal salvation. Rom. 15:8; Acts 3:20, 24; Heb. 10:1; Rom. 4:11; 1 Cor. 5:7; Heb. 8–10, 11:13; Gal. 3:7–9, 14.

Q. 35. How is the covenant of grace administered under the New Testament?
A. Under the New Testament, when Christ the substance was exhibited, the same covenant of grace was and still is to be administered in the preaching of the Word, and the administration of the sacraments of baptism and the Lord's supper; in which grace and salvation are held forth in more fullness, evidence, and efficacy, to all nations. Mark 16:15; Matt. 28:19–20; 1 Cor. 11:23–25; 2 Cor. 3:6–18; Heb. 8:6, 10, 11; Matt. 28:19.

Q. 36. Who is the Mediator of the covenant of grace?
A. The only Mediator of the covenant of grace is the Lord Jesus Christ, who, being the eternal Son of God, of one substance and equal with the Father, in the fullness of time became man, and so was and continues to be God and man, in two entire distinct natures, and one person,

forever. 1 Tim. 2:5; John 1:1, 14; John 10:30; Phil. 2:6; Gal. 4:4; Luke 1:35; Rom. 9:5; Col. 2:9; Heb. 7:24–25.

Q. 37. How did Christ, being the Son of God, become man?
A. Christ the Son of God became man, by taking to himself a true body, and a reasonable soul, being conceived by the power of the Holy Ghost in the womb of the Virgin Mary, of her substance, and born of her, yet without sin. John 1:14; Matt. 26:38; Luke 1:27, 31, 35, 42; Gal. 4:4; Heb. 4:15; Heb. 7:26.

Q. 38. Why was it requisite that the Mediator should be God?
A. It was requisite that the Mediator should be God, that he might sustain and keep the human nature from sinking under the infinite wrath of God, and the power of death; give worth and efficacy to his sufferings, obedience and intercession; and to satisfy God's justice, procure his favor, purchase a peculiar people, give his Spirit to them, conquer all their enemies, and bring them to everlasting salvation. Acts 2:24–25; Rom. 1:4; Rom. 4:25; Heb. 9:14; Acts 20:28; Heb. 9:14; Heb. 7: 25–28; Rom. 3:24–26; Eph. 1:6; Matt. 3:17; Titus 2:13–14; Gal. 4:6; Luke 1:68–69, 71, 74; Heb. 5:8–9; Heb. 9:11–15.

Q. 39. Why was it requisite that the Mediator should be man?
A. It was requisite that the Mediator should be man, that he might advance our nature, perform obedience to the law, suffer and make intercession for us in our nature, have a fellow-feeling of our infirmities; that we might receive the adoption of sons, and have comfort and access with boldness unto the throne of grace. Heb. 2:16; Gal. 4:4; Heb. 2:14; Heb. 7:24–25; Heb. 4:15; Gal. 4:5; Heb. 4:16.

Q. 40. Why was it requisite that the Mediator should be God and man in one person?
A. It was requisite that the Mediator, who was to reconcile God and man, should himself be both God and man, and this in one person, that the proper works of each nature might be accepted of God for us, and relied on by us, as the works of the whole person. Matt. 1:21, 23; Matt. 3:17; Heb. 9:14; 1 Peter 2:6.

Q. 41. Why was our Mediator called Jesus?
A. Our Mediator was called Jesus, because he saveth his people from their sins. Matt. 1:21.

Q. 42. Why was our Mediator called Christ?
A. Our Mediator was called Christ, because he was anointed with the Holy Ghost above measure; and so set apart, and fully furnished with all authority and ability, to execute the offices of prophet, priest, and king of his Church, in the estate both of his humiliation and exaltation. John 3:34; Ps. 45:7; John 6:27; Matt. 28:18–20; Acts 3:21–22; Luke 4:18, 21; Heb. 5:5–7; Heb. 4:14–15; Ps. 2:6; Matt. 21:5; Isa. 9:6–7; Phil. 2:8–11.

Q. 43. How doth Christ execute the office of a prophet?
A. Christ executeth the office of a prophet, in his revealing to the Church in all ages, by his Spirit and Word, in divers ways of administration, the whole will of God, in all things concerning their edification and salvation. John 1:18; 1 Peter 1:10–12; Heb. 1:1–2; John 15:15; Acts 20:32; Eph. 4:11–13; John 20:31.

Q. 44. How doth Christ execute the office of a priest?
A. Christ executeth the office of a priest, in his once offering himself a sacrifice without spot to God, to be a reconciliation for the sins of his people; and in making continual intercession for them. Heb. 9:14, 28; Heb. 2:17; Heb. 7:25.

Q. 45. How doth Christ execute the office of a king?
A. Christ executeth the office of a king, in calling out of the world a people to himself, and giving them officers, laws, and censures, by which he visibly governs them; in bestowing saving grace upon his elect, rewarding their obedience, and correcting them for their sins, preserving and supporting them under all their temptations and sufferings, restraining and overcoming all their enemies, and powerfully ordering all things for his own glory and their good: and also in

taking vengeance on the rest, who know not God, and obey not the gospel. Acts 15:14–16; Isa. 55:4–5; Gen 49:10; Ps. 110:3; Eph. 4:11–12; 1 Cor. 12:28; Isa. 33:22; Matt. 18:17–18; 1 Cor. 5:4–5; Acts 5:31; Rev. 22:12; Rev. 2:10; Rev. 3:19; Isa. 63:9; 1 Cor. 15:25; Ps. 110:1–7; Rom. 14:10–11; Rom. 8:28; 2 Thess. 1: 8–9; Ps. 2:8–9.

Q. 46. What was the estate of Christ's humiliation?
A. The estate of Christ's humiliation was that low condition, wherein he, for our sakes, emptying himself of his glory, took upon him the form of a servant, in his conception and birth, life, death, and after his death, until his resurrection. Phil. 2:6–8; Luke 1:31; 2 Cor. 8:9; Acts 2:24.

Q. 47. How did Christ humble himself in his conception and birth?
A. Christ humbled himself in his conception and birth, in that, being from all eternity the Son of God, in the bosom of the Father, he was pleased in the fullness of time to become the son of man, made of a woman of low estate, and to be born of her; with divers circumstances of more than ordinary abasement. John 1:14, 18; Gal. 4:4; Luke 2:7.

Q. 48. How did Christ humble himself in his life?
A. Christ humbled himself in his life, by subjecting himself to the law, which he perfectly fulfilled; and by conflicting with the indignities of the world, temptations of Satan, and infirmities in his flesh, whether common to the nature of man, or particularly accompanying that his low condition. Gal. 4:4; Matt. 5:17; Rom. 5:19; Ps. 22:6; Heb. 12:2–3; Matt. 4:1–12; Luke 4:13; Heb. 2:17–18; Heb. 4:15; Isa. 52:13–14.

Q. 49. How did Christ humble himself in his death?
A. Christ humbled himself in his death, in that having been betrayed by Judas, forsaken by his disciples, scorned and rejected by the world, condemned by Pilate, and tormented by his persecutors; having also conflicted with the terrors of death, and the powers of darkness, felt and borne the weight of God's wrath, he laid down his life an offering for sin, enduring the painful, shameful, and cursed death of the cross. Matt. 27:4; Matt. 26:56; Isa. 53:2–3; Matt. 27:26–50; John 19:34; Luke 22:44; Matt. 27:46; Isa. 53:10; Phil. 2:8; Heb. 12:2; Gal. 3:13.

Q. 50. Wherein consisted Christ's humiliation after his death?
A. Christ's humiliation after his death consisted in his being buried; and continuing in the state of the dead and under the power of death till the third day, which hath been otherwise expressed in these words, He descended into hell. 1 Cor. 15:3–4; Ps. 16:10; Acts 2:24–27, 31; Rom. 6:9; Matt. 12:40.

Q. 51. What was the estate of Christ's exaltation?
A. The estate of Christ's exaltation comprehendeth his resurrection, ascension, sitting at the right hand of the Father, and his coming again to judge the world. 1 Cor. 15:4; Mark 16:19; Eph. 1:20; Acts 1:11; Acts 17:31.

Q. 52. How was Christ exalted in his resurrection?
A. Christ was exalted in his resurrection, in that, not having seen corruption in death (of which it was not possible for him to be held) and having the very same body in which he suffered, with the essential properties thereof (but without mortality and other common infirmities belonging to this life) really united to his soul, he rose again from the dead the third day by his own power; whereby he declared himself to be the Son of God, to have satisfied divine justice, to have vanquished death, and him that had the power of it, and to be Lord of quick and dead: all which he did as a public person, the head of his church, for their justification, quickening in grace, support against enemies, and to assure them of their resurrection from the dead at the last day. Acts 2:24, 27; Luke 24:39; Rom. 6:9; Rev. 1:18; John 10:18; Rom. 1:4; Rom. 8:34; Heb. 2:14; Rom. 14:9; 1 Cor. 15:21–22; Eph. 1:20, 22–23; Col. 1:18; Rom. 4:25; Eph. 2:1, 5–6; Col. 2:12; 1 Cor. 15:25–27; 1 Cor. 15:20.

Q. 53. How was Christ exalted in his ascension?
A. Christ was exalted in his ascension, in that having after his resurrection often appeared unto and conversed with his apostles, speaking to them of the things pertaining to the kingdom

of God, and giving them commission to preach the gospel to all nations, forty days after his resurrection, he, in our nature and as our head, triumphing over enemies, visibly went up into the highest heavens, there to receive gifts for men, to raise up our affections thither, and to prepare a place for us, where himself is and shall continue till his second coming at the end of the world. Acts 1:2–3; Matt. 28:19–20; Heb. 6:20; Eph. 4:8; Acts 1:9–11; Eph. 4:10; Ps. 68:18; Col. 3:1–2; John 14:3; Acts 3:21.

Q. 54. How is Christ exalted in his sitting at the right hand of God?
A. Christ is exalted in his sitting at the right hand of God, in that as God man he is advanced to the highest favor with God the Father, with all fullness of joy, glory, and power over all things in heaven and earth; and doth gather and defend his Church, and subdue their enemies; furnisheth his ministers and people with gifts and graces, and maketh intercession for them. Phil. 2:9; Acts 2:28; Ps. 16:11; John 17:5; Eph. 1:22; 1 Peter 3:22; Eph. 4:10–12; Ps. 110:1; Rom. 8:34.

Q. 55. How doth Christ make intercession?
A. Christ maketh intercession, by his appearing in our nature continually before the Father in heaven, in the merit of his obedience and sacrifice on earth, declaring his will to have it applied to all believers; answering all accusations against them, and procuring for them quiet of conscience, notwithstanding daily failings, access with boldness to the throne of grace, and acceptance of their persons and services. Heb. 9:12, 24; Heb. 1:3; John 3:16; John 17:9, 20, 24; Rom. 8:33–34; Rom. 5:1–2; 1 John 2:1–2; Heb. 4:16; Eph. 1:6; 1 Peter 2:5.

Q. 56. How is Christ to be exalted in his coming again to judge the world?
A. Christ is to be exalted in his coming again to judge the world, in that he, who was unjustly judged and condemned by wicked men, shall come again at the last day in great power, and in the full manifestation of his own glory and of his Father's, with all his holy angels, with a shout, with the voice of the archangel, and with the trumpet of God, to judge the world in righteousness. Acts 3:14–15; Matt. 24:30; Luke 9:26; Matt. 25:31; 1 Thess. 4:16; Acts 17:31.

Q. 57. What benefits hath Christ procured by his mediation?
A. Christ by his mediation hath procured redemption, with all other benefits of the covenant of grace. Heb. 9:12; 2 Cor. 1:20.

Q. 58 How do we come to be made partakers of the benefits which Christ hath procured?
A. We are made partakers of the benefits which Christ hath procured by the application of them unto us, which is the work especially of God the Holy Ghost. John 1:11–12; Titus 3:5–6.

Q. 59. Who are made partakers of redemption through Christ?
A. Redemption is certainly applied, and effectually communicated, to all those for whom Christ hath purchased it; who are in time by the Holy Ghost enabled to believe in Christ according to the gospel. Eph. 1:13–14; John 6:37, 39; John 10:15–16; Eph. 2:8; 2 Cor. 4:13.

Q. 60. Can they who have never heard of the gospel, and so know not Jesus Christ, nor believe in him, be saved by their living according to the light of nature?
A. They who, having never heard the gospel, know not Jesus Christ, and believe not in him, cannot be saved, be they never so diligent to frame their lives according to the light of nature, or the laws of that religion which they profess; neither is there salvation in any other, but in Christ alone, who is the Saviour only of his body the Church. Rom. 10:14; 2 Thess. 1:8–9; Eph. 2:12; John 1:10–12; John 8:24; Mark 16:16; 1 Cor. 1:20–24; John 4:22; Rom. 9:31–32; Phil. 3:4–9; Acts 4:12; Eph. 5:23.

Q. 61. Are all they saved who hear the gospel, and live in the Church?
A. All that hear the gospel, and live in the visible Church, are not saved; but only they who are true members of the Church invisible. John 12:38–40; Rom. 9:6; Matt. 22:14; Matt. 7:21; Rom. 11:7.

Q. 62. What is the visible Church?
A. The visible Church is a society made up of all such as in all ages and places of the world do profess the true religion, and of their children. 1 Cor. 1:2; 1 Cor. 12:13; Rom. 15:9–12; Rev. 7:9;

Ps. 2:8; Ps. 22:27–31; Ps. 45: 17; Matt. 28:19–20; Isa. 59:21; 1 Cor. 7:14; Acts 2:39; Rom. 11:16; Gen. 17:7.

Q. 63. What are the special privileges of the visible Church?
A. The visible Church hath the privilege of being under God's special care and government; of being protected and preserved in all ages, notwithstanding the opposition of all enemies; and of enjoying the communion of saints, the ordinary means of salvation, and offers of grace by Christ to all the members of it in the ministry of the gospel, testifying, that whosoever believes in him shall be saved, and excluding none that will come unto him. Isa. 4:5–6; 1 Tim. 4:10; Ps. 115:1–18; Isa. 31:4–5; Zech. 12:2–4,8–9; Acts 2:39, 42; Ps. 147:19–20; Rom. 9:4; Eph. 4:11–12; Mark 16:15–16; John 6:37.

Q. 64. What is the invisible Church?
A. The invisible Church is the whole number of the elect, that have been, are, or shall be gathered into one under Christ the head. Eph. 1:10, 22–23; John 10:16; John 11:52.

Q. 65. What special benefits do the members of the invisible Church enjoy by Christ?
A. The members of the invisible Church, by Christ, enjoy union and communion with him in grace and glory. John 17:21; Eph. 2:5–6; John 17:24.

Q. 66. What is that union which the elect have with Christ?
A. The union which the elect have with Christ is the work of God's grace, whereby they are spiritually and mystically, yet really and inseparably, joined to Christ as their head and husband; which is done in their effectual calling. Eph. 1:22; Eph. 2:6–8; 1 Cor. 6:17; John 10:28; Eph. 5:23, 30; 1 Peter 5:10; 1 Cor. 1:9.

Q. 67. What is effectual calling?
A. Effectual calling is the work of God's almighty power and grace, whereby (out of his free and special love to his elect, and from nothing in them moving him thereunto) he doth, in his accepted time, invite and draw them to Jesus Christ, by his Word and Spirit; savingly enlightening their minds, renewing and powerfully determining their wills, so as they (although in themselves dead in sin) are hereby made willing and able freely to answer his call, and to accept and embrace the grace offered and conveyed therein. John 5:25; Eph. 1:18–20; 2 Tim. 1:8–9; Titus 3:4–5; Eph. 2:4–5, 7–9; Rom. 9:11; 2 Cor. 5:20, 2 Cor. 6:1–2; John 6:44; 2 Thess. 2:13–14; Acts 26:18; 1 Cor. 2:10, 12; Ezek. 11:19; Ezek. 36:26–27; John 6:45; Eph. 2:5; Phil. 2:13; Deut. 30:6.

Q. 68. Are the elect only effectually called?
A. All the elect, and they only, are effectually called; although others may be, and often are, outwardly called by the ministry of the Word, and have some common operations of the Spirit; who, for their willful neglect and contempt of the grace offered to them, being justly left in their unbelief, do never truly come to Jesus Christ. Acts 13:48; Matt. 22:14; Matt. 7:22; Matt. 13:20–21; Heb. 6:4–6; John 12:38–40; Acts 28:25–27; John 6:64–65; Ps. 81:11–12.

Q. 69. What is the communion in grace, which the members of the invisible Church have with Christ?
A. The communion in grace, which the members of the invisible Church have with Christ, is their partaking of the virtue of his mediation, in their justification, adoption, sanctification, and whatever else in this life manifests their union with him. Rom. 8:30; Eph. 1:5; 1 Cor. 1:30.

Q. 70. What is justification?
A. Justification is an act of God's free grace unto sinners, in which he pardoneth all their sins, accepteth and accounteth their persons righteous in his sight; not for any thing wrought in them, or done by them, but only for the perfect obedience and full satisfaction of Christ, by God imputed to them, and received by faith alone. Rom. 3:22, 24–25; Rom. 4:5; 2 Cor. 5:19, 21; Rom. 3:22, 24–25, 27–28; Titus 3: 5, 7; Eph. 1:7; Rom. 5:17–19; Rom. 4:6–8; Acts 10:43; Gal. 2:16; Phil. 3:9.

Q. 71. How is justification an act of God's free grace?
A. Although Christ, by his obedience and death, did make a proper, real and full satisfaction to God's justice in the behalf of them that are justified; yet in as much as God accepteth the

satisfaction from a surety, which he might have demanded of them, and did provide this surety, his own only Son, imputing his righteousness to them, and requiring nothing of them for their justification but faith, which also is his gift, their justification is to them of free grace. Rom. 5:8–10, 19; 1 Tim. 2:5–6; Heb. 10:10; Matt. 20:28; Dan. 9:24, 26; Isa. 53: 4–6; Isa. 53:10–12; Heb. 7:22; Rom. 8:32; 1 Peter 1:18–19; 2 Cor. 5:21; Rom. 3: 24–25; Eph. 2:8; Eph. 1:7.

Q. 72. What is justifying faith?
A. Justifying faith is a saving grace, wrought in the heart of a sinner, by the Spirit and Word of God, whereby he, being convinced of his sin and misery, and of the disability in himself and all other creatures to recover him out of his lost condition, not only assenteth to the truth of the promise of the gospel, but receiveth and resteth upon Christ and his righteousness therein held forth, for pardon of sin, and for the accepting and accounting of his person righteous in the sight of God for salvation. Heb. 10:39; 2 Cor. 4:13; Eph. 1:17–19; Rom. 10:14, 17; Acts 2:37; Acts 16:30; John 16:8–9; Rom. 5:6; Eph. 2:1; Acts 4:12; Eph. 1:13; John 1:12; Acts 16:31; Acts 10:43; Phil. 3:9; Acts 15:11.

Q. 73. How doth faith justify a sinner in the sight of God?
A. Faith justifies a sinner in the sight of God, not because of those other graces which do always accompany it, or of good works that are the fruits of it, nor as if the grace of faith, or any act thereof, were imputed to him for his justification; but only as it is an instrument by which he receiveth and applieth Christ and his righteousness. Gal. 3:11; Rom. 3:28; Rom. 4:5; Rom. 10:10; John 1:12; Phil. 3:9; Gal. 2:16.

Q. 74. What is adoption?
A. Adoption is an act of the free grace of God, in and for his only Son Jesus Christ, whereby all those that are justified are received into the number of his children, have his name put upon them, the Spirit of his Son given to them, are under his fatherly care and dispensations, admitted to all the liberties and privileges of the sons of God, made heirs of all the promises, and fellow–heirs with Christ in glory. 1 John 3:1; Eph. 1:5; Gal. 4:4–5; John 1:12; 2 Cor. 6:18; Rev. 3:12; Gal. 4:6; Ps. 103:13; Prov. 14:26; Matt. 6:32; Heb. 6:12; Rom. 8:17.

Q. 75. What is sanctification?
A. Sanctification is a work of God's grace, whereby they whom God hath before the foundation of the world chosen to be holy, are in time through the powerful operation of his Spirit, applying the death and resurrection of Christ unto them, renewed in their whole man after the image of God; having the seeds of repentance unto life, and all other saving graces, put into their hearts, and those graces so stirred up, increased, and strengthened, as that they more and more die unto sin and rise unto newness of life. Eph. 1:4; 1 Cor. 6:11; 2 Thess. 2:13; Rom. 6:4–6; Eph. 4:23–24; Acts 11:18; 1 John 3:9; Jude 1:20; Heb. 6:11–12; Eph. 3:16–19; Col. 1:10–11; Rom. 6:4, 6, 14; Gal. 5:24.

Q. 76. What is repentance unto life?
A. Repentance unto life is a saving grace, wrought in the heart of a sinner by the Spirit and word of God, whereby, out of the sight and sense, not only of the danger, but also of the filthiness and odiousness of his sins, and upon the apprehension of God's mercy in Christ to such as are penitent, he so grieves for and hates his sins, as that he turns from them all to God, purposing and endeavouring constantly to walk with him in all the ways of new obedience. 2 Tim. 2:25; Zech. 12:10; Acts 11:18, 20–21; Ezek. 18:28, 30, 32; Luke 15:17–18; Hos. 2:6–7; Ezek. 36:31; Isa. 30:22; Joel 2:12–13; Jer. 31:18–19; 2 Cor. 7:11; Acts 26: 18; Ezek. 14:6; 1 Kings 8:47–48; Ps. 119:6, 59, 128; Luke 1:6; 2 Kings 23:25.

Q. 77. Wherein do justification and sanctification differ?
A. Although sanctification be inseparably joined with justification, yet they differ, in that God in justification imputeth the righteousness of Christ; in sanctification his Spirit infuseth grace, and enableth to the exercise thereof; in the former, sin is pardoned; in the other, it is subdued; the one doth equally free all believers from the revenging wrath of God, and that perfectly in this life, that they never fall into condemnation; the other is neither equal in all, nor in this life perfect in any, but growing up to perfection. 1 Cor. 6:11; 1 Cor. 1:30; Rom. 4:6, 8; Ezek. 36:27;

Rom. 3:24–25; Rom. 6:6, 14; Rom. 8:33–34; 1 John 2:12–14; Heb. 5:12–14; 1 John 1:8, 10; 2 Cor. 7:1; Phil. 3:12–14.

Q. 78. Whence ariseth the imperfection of sanctification in believers?
A. The imperfection of sanctification in believers ariseth from the remnants of sin abiding in every part of them, and the perpetual lustings of the flesh against the spirit; whereby they are often foiled with temptations, and fall into many sins, are hindered in all their spiritual services, and their best works are imperfect and defiled in the sight of God. Rom. 7:18, 23; Mark 14:66–72; Gal. 2:11–12; Heb. 12:1; Isa. 64:6; Ex. 28:38.

Q. 79. May not true believers, by reason of their imperfections, and the many temptations and sins they are overtaken with, fall away from the state of grace?
A. True believers, by reason of the unchangeable love of God, and his decree and covenant to give them perseverance, their inseparable union with Christ, his continual intercession for them, and the Spirit and seed of God abiding in them, can neither totally nor finally fall away from the state of grace, but are kept by the power of God through faith unto salvation. Jer. 31:3; 2 Tim. 2:19; Heb. 13:20–21; 2 Sam. 23:5; 1 Cor. 1:8–9; Heb. 7:25; Luke 22:32; 1 John 3:9; 1 John 2:27; Jer. 32:40; John 10:28; 1 Peter 1:5.

Q. 80. Can true believers be infallibly assured that they are in the estate of grace, and that they shall persevere therein unto salvation?
A. Such as truly believe in Christ, and endeavor to walk in all good conscience before him, may, without extraordinary revelation, by faith grounded upon the truth of God's promises, and by the Spirit enabling them to discern in themselves those graces to which the promises of life are made, and bearing witness with their spirits that they are the children of God, be infallibly assured that they are in the estate of grace and shall persevere therein unto salvation. 1 John 2:3; 1 Cor. 2:12; 1 John 3:14, 18–19, 21, 24; 1 John 4:13, 16; Heb. 6:11–12; Rom. 8:16; 1 John 5:13.

Q. 81. Are all true believers at all times assured of their present being in the estate of grace, and that they shall be saved?
A. Assurance of grace and salvation not being of the essence of faith, true believers may wait long before they obtain it; and, after the enjoyment thereof, may have it weakened and intermitted, through manifold distempers, sins, temptations, and desertions; yet are they never left without such a presence and support of the Spirit of God, as keeps them from sinking into utter despair. Eph. 1:13; Isa. 1:10; Ps. 88:1–18; Ps. 77:1–12; Song of Sol. 5:2–3, 6; Ps. 51:8, 12; Ps. 31:22; Ps. 22:1; 1 John 3:9; Job 13:15; Ps. 73:15, 23; Isa. 54:7–10.

Q. 82. What is the communion in glory which the members of the invisible Church have with Christ?
A. The communion in glory which the members of the invisible Church have with Christ, is in this life, immediately after death, and at last perfected at the resurrection and day of judgment. 2 Cor. 3:18; Luke 23:43; 1 Thess. 4:17.

Q. 83. What is the communion in glory with Christ which the members of the invisible Church enjoy in this life?
A. The members of the invisible Church have communicated to them in this life the first-fruits of glory with Christ, as they are members of him their head, and so in him are interested in that glory which he is fully possessed of; and, as an earnest thereof, enjoy the sense of God's love, peace of conscience, joy in the Holy Ghost, and hope of glory; as, on the contrary, sense of God's revenging wrath, horror of conscience, and a fearful expectation of judgment, are to the wicked the beginning of their torments which they shall endure after death. Eph.2:6; Rom. 5:5 with 2 Cor. 1:22; Rom. 5:1–2; Rom. 14:17; Gen. 4:13; Matt. 27:4; Heb. 10:27; Rom. 2:9; Mark 9:44.

Q. 84. Shall all men die?
A. Death being threatened as the wages of sin, it is appointed unto all men once to die; for that all have sinned. Rom. 6:23; Heb. 9:27; Rom. 5:12.

Q. 85. Death, being the wages of sin, why are not the righteous delivered from death, seeing all their sins are forgiven in Christ?
A. The righteous shall be delivered from death itself at the last day, and even in death are delivered from the sting and curse of it; so that, although they die, yet it is out of God's love, to free them perfectly from sin and misery, and to make them capable of further communion with Christ in glory, which they then enter upon. 1 Cor. 15:26, 55–57; Heb. 2:15; Isa. 57:1–2; 2 Kings 22:20; Rev. 14:13; Eph. 5: 27; Luke 23:43; Phil. 1:23.

Q. 86. What is the communion in glory with Christ, which the members of the invisible Church enjoy immediately after death?
A. The communion in glory with Christ, which the members of the invisible Church enjoy immediately after death, is, in that their souls are then made perfect in holiness, and received into the highest heavens, where they behold the face of God in light and glory; waiting for the full redemption of their bodies, which even in death continue united to Christ, and rest in their graves, as in their beds, till at the last day they be again united with their souls. Whereas the souls of the wicked are at their death cast into hell, where they remain in torments and utter darkness; and their bodies kept in their graves, as in their prisons, until the resurrection and judgment of the great day. Heb. 12:23; 2 Cor. 5:1, 6, 8; Phil. 1:23; Acts 3:21; Eph. 4:10; 1 John 3:2; 1 Cor. 13:12; Rom. 8:23; Ps. 16:9; 1 Thess. 4:14; Isa. 57:2; Job 19:26–27; Luke 16: 23–24; Acts 1:25; Jude 6–7.

Q. 87. What are we to believe concerning the resurrection?
A. We are to believe, that, at the last day, there shall be a general resurrection of the dead, both of the just and unjust: when they that are then found alive shall in a moment be changed; and the selfsame bodies of the dead which are laid in the grave, being then again united to their souls for ever, shall be raised up by the power of Christ. The bodies of the just, by the Spirit of Christ, and by virtue of his resurrection as their head, shall be raised in power, spiritual, incorruptible, and made like to his glorious body; and the bodies of the wicked shall be raised up in dishonor by him, as an offended judge. Acts 24:15; 1 Cor. 15:51–53; 1 Thess. 4:15–17; John 5:28–29; 1 Cor. 15:21–23, 42–44; Phil. 3:21; John 5:27–29; Matt. 25:33.

Q. 88. What shall immediately follow after the resurrection?
A. Immediately after the resurrection shall follow the general and final judgment of angels and men; the day and hour whereof no man knoweth, that all may watch and pray, and be ever ready for the coming of the Lord. 2 Peter 2:4; Jude 6–7, 14–15; Matt. 25:46; Matt. 24:36, 42, 44; Luke 21:35–36.

Q. 89. What shall be done to the wicked at the day of judgment?
A. At the day of judgment, the wicked shall be set on Christ's left hand, and, upon clear evidence and full conviction of their own consciences, shall have the fearful but just sentence of condemnation pronounced against them; and thereupon shall be cast out from the favorable presence of God, and the glorious fellowship with Christ, his saints, and all his holy angels, into hell, to be punished with unspeakable torments both of body and soul, with the devil and his angels for ever. Matt. 25:33; Rom. 2:15–16; Matt. 25:41–43; Luke 16:26; 2 Thess. 1:8–9.

Q. 90. What shall be done to the righteous at the day of judgment?
A. At the day of judgment, the righteous, being caught up to Christ in the clouds, shall be set on his right hand, and there openly acknowledged and acquitted, shall join with him in the judging of reprobate angels and men, and shall be received into heaven, where they shall be fully and for ever freed from all sin and misery; filled with inconceivable joys, made perfectly holy and happy both in body and soul, in the company of innumerable saints and holy angels, but especially in the immediate vision and fruition of God the Father, of our Lord Jesus Christ, and of the Holy Spirit, to all eternity. And this is the perfect and full communion, which the members of the invisible Church shall enjoy with Christ in glory, at the resurrection and day of judgment. 1 Thess. 4:17; Matt. 25:33; Matt. 10:32; 1 Cor. 6:2–3; Matt. 25:34, 46; Eph. 5: 27; Rev. 14:13; Ps. 16:11; Heb. 12:22–23; 1 John 3:2; 1 Cor. 13:12; 1 Thess. 4:17–18.

HAVING SEEN WHAT THE SCRIPTURES PRINCIPALLY TEACH US TO BELIEVE CONCERNING GOD, IT FOLLOWS TO CONSIDER WHAT THEY REQUIRE AS THE DUTY OF MAN

Q. 91. What is the duty which God requireth of man?
A. The duty which God requireth of man is obedience to his revealed will. Rom. 12:1–2; Mic. 6:8; 1 Sam. 15:22.

Q. 92. What did God at first reveal unto man as the rule of his obedience?
A. The rule of obedience revealed to Adam in the estate of innocence, and to all mankind in him, beside a special command not to eat of the fruit of the tree of the knowledge of good and evil, was the moral law. Gen. 1:26–27; Rom. 2:14–15; Rom. 10:5; Gen. 2:17.

Q. 93. What is the moral law?
A. The moral law is the declaration of the will of God to mankind, directing and bonding every one to personal, perfect, and perpetual conformity and obedience thereunto, in the frame and disposition of the whole man, soul and body, and in performance of all those duties of holiness and righteousness which he oweth to God and man: promising life upon the fulfilling, and threatening death upon the breach of it. Deut. 5:1–3, 31, 33; Luke 10:26–27; Gal. 3:10; 1 Thess. 5:23; Luke 1:75; Acts 24:16; Rom. 10:5; Gal. 3:10, 12.

Q. 94. Is there any use of the moral law to man since the fall?
A. Although no man, since the fall, can attain to righteousness and life by the moral law; yet there is great use thereof, as well common to all men, as peculiar either to the unregenerate, or the regenerate. Rom. 8:3; Gal. 2:16; 1 Tim. 1:8.

Q. 95. Of what use is the moral law to all men?
A. The moral law is of use to all men, to inform them of the holy nature and will of God, and of their duty, binding them to walk accordingly; to convince them of their disability to keep it, and of the sinful pollution of their nature, hearts, and lives; to humble them in the sense of their sin and misery, and thereby help them to a clearer sight of the need they have of Christ, and of the perfection of his obedience. Lev. 11:44–45; Lev. 20:7–8; Rom. 7:12; Mic. 6:8; Jas. 2:10–11; Ps. 19:11–12; Rom. 3:20; Rom. 7:7; Rom. 3:9, 23; Gal. 3:21–22; Rom. 10:4.

Q. 96. What particular use is there of the moral law to unregenerate men?
A. The moral law is of use to unregenerate men, to awaken their consciences to flee from wrath to come, and to drive them to Christ; or, upon their continuance in the estate and way of sin, to leave them inexcusable, and under the curse thereof. 1 Tim. 1:9–10; Gal. 3:24; Rom. 1:20; Rom. 2:15; Gal. 3:10.

Q. 97. What special use is there of the moral law to the regenerate?
A. Although they that are regenerate, and believe in Christ, be delivered from the moral law as a covenant of works, so as thereby they are neither justified nor condemned: yet, beside the general uses thereof common to them with all men, it is of special use to show them how much they are bound to Christ for his fulfilling it, and enduring the curse thereof in their stead and for their good; and thereby to provoke them to more thankfulness, and to express the same in their greater care to conform themselves thereunto as the rule of their obedience. Rom. 6:14; Rom. 7:4, 6; Gal. 4:4–5; Rom. 3:20; Gal. 5:23; Rom. 8:1; Rom. 7: 24–25; Gal. 3:13–14; Rom. 8:3–4; Luke 1:68–69, 74–75; Col. 1:12–14; Rom. 7:22; Rom. 12:2; Titus 2:11–14.

Q. 98. Where is the moral law summarily comprehended?
A. The moral law is summarily comprehended in the ten commandments, which were delivered by the voice of God upon mount Sinai, and written by him in two tables of stone; and are recorded in the twentieth chapter of Exodus. The four first commandments containing our duty to God, and the other six our duty to man. Deut. 10:4; Ex. 34:1–4; Matt. 22:37–40.

Q. 99. What rules are to be observed for the right understanding of the ten commandments?
A. For the right understanding of the ten commandments, these rules are to be observed: 1. That the law is perfect, and bindeth every one to full conformity in the whole man unto the righteousness thereof, and unto entire obedience for ever; so as to require the utmost perfection of every duty, and to forbid the least degree of every sin. 2. That it is spiritual, and so reacheth the understanding, will, affections, and all other powers of the soul; as well as words, works, and gestures. 3. That one and the same thing, in divers respects, is required or forbidden in several commandments. 4. That as, where a duty is commanded, the contrary sin is forbidden; and, where a sin is forbidden the contrary duty is commanded: so, where a promise is annexed, the contrary threatening is included; and, where a threatening is annexed, the contrary promise is included. 5. That what God forbids, is at no time to be done; what he commands, is always our duty; and yet every particular duty is not to be done at all times. 6. That under one sin or duty, all of the same kind are forbidden or commanded; together with all the causes, means, occasions, and appearances thereof, and provocations thereunto. 7. That what is forbidden or commanded to ourselves, we are bound, according to our places, to endeavor that it may be avoided or performed by others, according to the duty of their places. 8. That in what is commanded to others, we are bound, according to our places and callings, to be helpful to them; and to take heed of partaking with others in what is forbidden them. Ps. 19:7; Jas. 2:10; Matt. 5:21–22; Rom. 7:14; Deut. 6:5; Matt. 22:37–39; Matt. 5: 27–28, 33–34, 37–39, 43–44; Col. 3:5; Amos 8:5; Prov. 1:19; 1 Tim. 6:10; Isa. 58:13; Deut. 6:13; Matt. 4:9–10; Matt. 15:4–6; Matt. 5:21–24; Eph. 4:28; Ex. 20:12; Prov. 30:17; Jer. 18:7–8; Ex. 20:7; Ps. 15:1, 4–5; Ps. 24:4–5; Job 13:7–8; Rom. 3:8; Job 36:21; Heb. 11:25; Deut. 4:8–9; Matt. 12:7, Matt. 5:21–22, 27–28; Matt. 15:4–6; Heb. 10:24–25; 1 Thess. 5:22; Jude 1:23; Gal. 5:26; Col. 3:21; Ex. 20:10; Lev. 19:17; Gen. 18:19; Josh. 24:15: Deut. 6:6–7; 2 Cor. 1:24; 1 Tim. 5:22; Eph. 5:11.

Q. 100. What special things are we to consider in the ten commandments?
A. We are to consider in the ten commandments, the preface, the substance of the commandments themselves, and the several reasons annexed to some of them the more to enforce them. No references.

Q. 101. What is the preface to the ten commandments?
A. The preface to the ten commandments is contained in these words, I am the Lord thy God, which have brought thee out of the land of Egypt, out of the house of bondage. Wherein God manifesteth his sovereignty, as being Jehovah, the eternal, immutable, and almighty God; having his being in and of himself, and giving being to all his words and works: and that he is a God in covenant, as with Israel of old, so with all his people; who, as he brought them out of their bondage in Egypt, so he delivereth us from our spiritual thraldom: and that therefore we are bound to take him for our God alone, and to keep all his commandments. Ex. 20:2; Isa. 44:6; Ex. 3:14; Ex. 6:3; Acts 17:24, 28; Gen. 17:7; Rom. 3:29; Luke 1:74–75; 1 Peter 1:15–18; Lev. 18:30; Lev. 19:37.

Q. 102. What is the sum of the four commandments which contain our duty to God?
A. The sum of the four commandments containing our duty to God, is, to love the Lord our God with all our heart, and with all our soul, and with all our strength, and with all our mind. Luke 10:27.

Q. 103. Which is the first commandment?
A. The first commandment is, Thou shalt have no other gods before me. Ex. 20:3.

Q. 104. What are the duties required in the first commandment?
A. The duties required in the first commandment are, the knowing and acknowledging of God to be the only true God, and our God; and to worship and glorify him accordingly, by thinking, meditating, remembering, highly esteeming, honoring, adoring, choosing, loving, desiring, fearing of him; believing him; trusting, hoping, delighting, rejoicing in him; being zealous for him; calling upon him; giving all praise and thanks, and yielding all obedience and submission to him with the whole man; being careful in all things to please him, and sorrowful when in anything he is offended; and walking humbly with him. 1 Chron. 28:9; Deut. 26:17; Isa. 43:10; Jer. 14:22; Ps. 95:6–7; Matt. 4:10; Ps. 29:2; Mal. 3:16; Ps. 63:6; Eccl. 12:1; Ps. 71:19; Mal. 1:6; Isa. 45:23;

Josh. 24:15, 22; Deut. 6:5; Ps. 73:25; Isa. 8:13; Ex. 14:31; Isa. 26:4; Ps. 130:7; Ps. 37:4; Ps. 32:11; Rom. 12:11; Num. 25:11; Phil. 4:6; Jer. 7:23; Jas 4:7; 1 John 3:22; Jer. 31:18; Ps. 119:136; Mic. 6:8.

Q. 105. What are the sins forbidden in the first commandment?
A. The sins forbidden in the first commandment are atheism, in denying, or not having a God; idolatry, in having or worshiping more gods than one, or any with, or instead of the true God; the not having and avouching him for God, and our God; the omission or neglect of any thing due to him, required in this commandment; ignorance, forgetfulness, misapprehensions, false opinions, unworthy and wicked thoughts of him; bold and curious searching into his secrets; all profaneness, hatred of God; self–love, self–seeking, and all other inordinate and immoderate setting of our mind, will, or affections upon other things, and taking them off from him in whole or in part; vain credulity, unbelief, heresy, misbelief, distrust, despair, incorrigibleness, and insensibleness under judgments; hardness of heart; pride; presumption; carnal security; tempting of God; using unlawful means, and trusting in lawful means; carnal delights and joys; corrupt, blind, and indiscreet zeal; lukewarmness, and deadness in the things of God; estranging ourselves, and apostatizing from God; praying, or giving any religious worship, to saints, angels, or any other creatures; all compacts and consulting with the devil, and hearkening to his suggestions; making men the lords of our faith and conscience; slighting and despising God and his commands; resisting and grieving of his Spirit, discontent and impatience at his dispensations, charging him foolishly for the evils he inflicts on us; and ascribing the praise of any good we either are, have, or can do, to fortune, idols, ourselves, or any other creature. Ps. 14:1; Eph. 2:12; Jer. 2:27–28; 1 Thess. 1:9; Ps. 81:11; Isa. 43:22–24; Jer. 4: 22; Hos. 4:1, 6; Jer. 2:32; Acts 17:23, 29; Isa. 40:18; Ps. 50:21; Deut. 29:29; Titus 1:16; Heb. 12:16; Rom. 1:30; 2 Tim. 3:2; Phil. 2:21; 1 John 2:15–16; 1 Sam. 2: 29; Col. 3:2, 5; 1 John 4:1; Heb. 3:12; Gal. 5:20; Titus 3:10; Acts 26:9; Ps. 78:22; Gen. 4:13; Jer. 5:3; Isa. 42:25; Rom. 2:5; Jer. 13:15; Ps. 19:13; Zeph. 1:12; Matt. 4:7; Rom. 3:8; Jer. 17:5; 2 Tim. 3:4; Gal. 4:17; John 16:2; Rom. 10:2; Luke 9: 54–55; Rev. 3:16; Rev. 3:1; Ezek. 14:5; Isa. 1:4–5; Rom. 10:13–14; Hos. 4:12; Acts 10:25–26; Rev. 19:10; Matt. 4:10; Col. 2:18; Rom. 1:25; Lev. 20:6; 1 Sam. 28:7, 11; 1 Chron. 10:13–14; Acts 5:3; 2 Cor. 1:24; Matt. 23:9; Deut. 32:15; 2 Sam. 12: 9; Prov. 13:13; Acts 7:51; Eph. 4:30; Ps. 73:2–3, 13–15, 22; Job 1:22; 1 Sam. 6: 7–9; Dan. 5:23; Deut. 8:17; Dan. 4:30; Hab. 1:16.

Q. 106. What are we especially taught by these words (before me) in the first commandment?
A. These words (before me) or before my face, in the first commandment teach, us that God who seeth all things, taketh special notice of, and is much displeased with, the sin of having any other god; that so it may be an argument to dissuade from it, and to aggravate it as a most impudent provocation; as also to persuade us to do as in his sight, whatever we do in his service. Ezek.. 8:5–18; Ps. 44:20–21; 1 Chron. 28:9.

Q. 107. Which is the second commandment?
A. The second commandment is, Thou shalt not make unto thee any graven image, or any likeness of anything that is in heaven above, or that is in the earth beneath, or that is in the water under the earth: thou shalt not bow down thyself to them, nor serve them: for I the Lord thy God am a jealous God, visiting the iniquity of the fathers upon the children, unto the third and fourth generation of them that hate me; and showing mercy unto thousands of them that love me, and keep my commandments. Ex. 20:4–6.

Q. 108. What are the duties required in the second commandment?
A. The duties required in the second commandment are, the receiving, observing, and keeping pure and entire, all such religious worship and ordinances as God hath instituted in his Word; particularly prayer and thanksgiving in the name of Christ; the reading, preaching, and hearing of the Word; the administration and receiving of the sacraments; church government and discipline; the ministry and maintenance thereof; religious fasting; swearing by the name of God, and vowing unto him: as also the disapproving, detesting, opposing, all false worship; and, according to each one's place and calling, removing it, and all monuments of idolatry. Deut. 32:46–47; Matt. 28:20; Acts 2:42; 1 Tim. 6:13–14; Phil. 4:6; Eph. 5:20; Deut. 17:18–19; Acts 15:21; 2 Tim. 4:2; Jas. 1:21–22: Acts 10:33; Matt. 28:19; 1 Cor. 11:23–30; Matt. 18:15–17; Matt. 16:19; 1 Cor. 5:1–13; 1 Cor. 12:28; Eph. 4: 11–12; 1 Tim. 5:17–18; 1 Cor. 9:7–15; Joel 2:12–13; 1 Cor. 7:5; Deut. 6:13; Isa. 19: 21; Ps. 76:11; Acts 17:16–17; Ps. 16:4; Deut. 7:5; Isa. 30:22.

Q. 109. What are the sins forbidden in the second commandment?
A. The sins forbidden in the second commandment are, all devising, counselling, commanding, using, and anywise approving, any religious worship not instituted by God himself; tolerating a false religion; the making any representation of God, of all, or of any of the three Persons, either inwardly in our mind, or outwardly in any kind of image or likeness of any creature whatsoever; all worshiping of it, or God in it or by it; the making of any representation of feigned deities, and all worship of them, or service belonging to them; all superstitious devices, corrupting the worship of God, adding to it, or taking from it, whether invented and taken up of ourselves, or received by tradition from others, though under the title of antiquity, custom, devotion, good intent, or any other pretence whatsoever; simony; sacrilege; all neglect, contempt, hindering, and opposing the worship and ordinances which God hath appointed. Num. 15:39; Deut. 13:6–8; Hos. 5:11; Mic. 6:16; 1 Kings 11:33; 1 Kings 12: 33; Deut. 12:30–32; Deut. 13:6–12; Zech. 13:2–3; Rev. 2:2, 14–15, 20; Rev. 17:12, 16–17; Deut. 4:15–19; Acts 17:29; Rom. 1:21–23, 25; Dan. 3:18; Gal. 4:8; Ex. 32: 5; Ex. 32:8; 1 Kings 18:26, 28; Isa. 65:11; Acts 17:22; Col. 2:21–23; Mal. 1:7–8, 14; Deut. 4:2; Ps. 106:39; Matt. 15:9; 1 Peter 1:18; Jer. 44:17; Isa. 65:3–5; Gal. 1: 13–14; 1 Sam. 13:11–12; 1 Sam. 15:21; Acts 8:18; Rom. 2:22; Mal. 3:8; Ex. 4:24–26; Matt. 22:5; Mal. 1:7, 13; Matt. 23:13; Acts 13:44–45; 1 Thess. 2:15–16.

Q. 110. What are the reasons annexed to the second commandment, the more to enforce it?
A. The reasons annexed to the second commandment, the more to enforce it, contained in these words, For I the Lord thy God am a jealous God, visiting the iniquity of the fathers upon the children unto the third and fourth generation of them that hate me; and showing mercy unto thousands of them that love me, and keep my commandments; are, besides God's sovereignty over us, and propriety in us, his fervent zeal for his own worship, and his revengeful indignation against all false worship, as being a spiritual whoredom; accounting the breakers of this commandment such as hate him, and threatening to punish them into divers generations; and esteeming the observers of it such as love him and keep his commandments, and promising mercy to them unto many generations. Ex. 20:5–6; Ps. 45:11; Rev. 15:3–4; Ex. 34:13–14; 1 Cor. 10:20–22; Jer. 7:18–20; Ezek. 16:26–27; Deut. 32:16–20; Hos. 2:2–4; Deut. 5:29.

Q. 111. Which is the third commandment?
A. The third commandment is, Thou shalt not take the name of the Lord thy God in vain: for the Lord will not hold him guiltless that taketh his name in vain. Ex. 20:7.

Q. 112. What is required in the third commandment?
A. The third commandment requires, that the name of God, his titles, attributes, ordinances, the word, sacraments, prayer, oaths, vows, lots, his works, and whatsoever else there is whereby he makes himself known, be holily and reverently used in thought, meditation, word, and writing; by an holy profession, and answerable conversation, to the glory of God, and the good of ourselves and others. Matt. 6:9; Deut. 28:58; Ps. 29:2; Ps. 68:4; Rev. 15:3–4; Mal. 1:14; Eccl. 5:1; Ps. 138:2; 1 Cor. 11:24–25, 28–29; 1 Tim. 2:8; Jer. 4:2; Eccl. 5:2, 4–6; Acts 1:24, 26; Job 36:24; Mal. 3:16; Ps. 8:1, 3–4, 9; Col. 3:17; Ps. 105:2, 5; Ps. 102:18; 1 Peter 3:15; Mic. 4:5; Phil. 1:27; 1 Cor. 10:31; Jer. 32:39; 1 Peter 2:12.

Q. 113. What are the sins forbidden in the third commandment?
A. The sins forbidden in the third commandment are, the not using of God's name as is required; and the abuse of it in an ignorant, vain, irreverent, profane, superstitious, or wicked mentioning or otherwise using his titles, attributes, ordinances, or works, by blasphemy, perjury; all sinful cursings, oaths, vows, and lots; violating of our oaths and vows, if lawful; and fulfilling them, if of things unlawful; murmuring and quarreling at, curious prying into, and misapplying of God's decrees and providences; misinterpreting, misapplying, or any way perverting the Word, or any part of it, to profane jests, curious or unprofitable questions, vain janglings, or the maintaining of false doctrines; abusing it, the creatures, or any thing contained under the name of God, to charms, or sinful lusts and practices; the maligning, scorning, reviling, or any wise opposing of God's truth, grace, and ways; making profession of religion in hypocrisy, or for sinister ends; being ashamed of it, or a shame to it, by unconformable, unwise, unfruitful and offensive walking, or backsliding from it. Mal. 2:2; Acts 17:23; Prov. 30:9; Mal. 1:6–7, 12; Mal. 3:14; 1 Sam. 4:3–5; Jer. 7:4, 9–10, 14, 31; Col. 2:20–22; 2 Kings 18:30, 35; Ex. 5:2; Ps. 139:20;

Ps. 50:16–17; Isa. 5:12; 2 Kings 19:22; Lev. 24:11; Zech. 5:4; Zech. 8:17; 1 Sam. 17:43; 2 Sam. 16:5; Jer. 5:7; Jer. 23:10; Deut. 23:18; Acts 23:12, 14; Esther 3:7; Esther 9:24; Ps. 22:18; Ps. 24:4; Ezek. 17:16, 18–19; Mark 6:26; 1 Sam. 25:22, 32–34; Rom. 9:14, 19–20; Deut. 29:29; Rom. 3:5, 7; Rom. 6:1–2; Eccl. 8:11; Eccl. 9:3; Ps. 39:1–13; Matt. 5:21–28; Ezek. 13:22; 2 Peter 3:16; Matt. 22:24–31; Isa. 22:13; Jer. 23:34, 36, 38; 1 Tim. 1:4, 6–7; 1 Tim. 6:4–5, 20; 2 Tim. 4:3–4; Rom. 13:13–14; 1 Kings 21:9–10; Jude 1:4: Acts 13:45; 1 John 3:12; Ps. 1:1; 2 Peter 3:3; 1 Peter 4:4; Acts 13:45–46, 50; Acts 4:18; Acts 19:9; 1 Thess. 2:16; Heb. 10:29; 2 Tim. 3:5; Matt. 23:14; Matt. 6:1–2, 5, 16; Mark 8:38; Ps. 73:14–15; 1 Cor. 6:5–6; Eph. 5:15–17; Isa. 5:4; 2 Peter 1:8–9; Rom. 2:23–24; Gal. 3:1, 3; Heb. 6:6; 2 Tim. 2:14; Titus 3:9; Deut. 18:10–14; Acts 19:13.

Q. 114. What reasons are annexed to the third commandment?
A. The reasons annexed to the third commandment, in these words, "The Lord thy God," and "for the Lord will not hold him guiltless that taketh his name in vain" are, because he is the Lord and our God, therefore his name is not to be profaned or any way abused by us; especially because he will be so far from acquitting and sparing the transgressors of this commandment, as that he will not suffer them to escape his righteous judgment, albeit many such escape the censures and punishments of men. Ex. 20:7; Lev. 19:12; Ezek. 36:21–23; Deut. 28:58–59; Zech. 5:2–4; 1 Sam. 2:12, 17, 22, 24; 1 Sam. 3:13.

Q. 115. What is the fourth commandment?
A. The fourth commandment is, Remember the sabbath–day, to keep it holy. Six days shalt thou labor, and do all thy work; but the seventh day is the sabbath of the Lord thy God: in it thou shalt not do any work, thou, nor thy son, nor thy daughter, thy man–servant, nor thy maid–servant, nor thy cattle, nor thy stranger that is within thy gates. For in six days the Lord made heaven and earth, the sea, and all that in them is, and rested the seventh day: wherefore the Lord blessed the sabbath–day and hallowed it. Ex. 20:8–11.

Q. 116. What is required in the fourth commandment?
A. The fourth commandment requireth of all men the sanctifying or keeping holy to God such set times as he hath appointed in his word, expressly one whole day in seven; which was the seventh from the beginning of the world to the resurrection of Christ, and the first day of the week ever since, and so to continue to the end of the world; which is the Christian sabbath, and in the New Testament called The Lord's Day. Deut. 5:12–14; Gen. 2:2–3; 1 Cor. 16:1–2; Acts 20:7; Matt. 5:17–18; Isa. 56:2, 4, 6–7; Rev. 1:10.

Q. 117. How is the sabbath or the Lord's day to be sanctified?
A. The sabbath or Lord's day is to be sanctified by an holy resting all the day, not only from such works as are at all times sinful, but even from such worldly employments and recreations as are on other days lawful; and making it our delight to spend the whole time (except so much of it as is to be taken up in works of necessity and mercy) in the public and private exercises of God's worship: and, to that end, we are to prepare our hearts, and with such foresight, diligence, and moderation, to dispose, and seasonably to despatch our worldly business, that we may be the more free and fit for the duties of that day. Ex. 20:8, 10; Ex. 16:25–28; Neh. 13:15–22; Jer. 17:21–22; Matt. 12:1–13; Isa. 58: 13; Luke 4:16; Acts 20:7; 1 Cor. 16:1–2; Ps. 92 title; Isa. 66:23; Lev. 23:3; Ex. 20: 8; Luke 23:54, 56; Ex. 16:22, 25–26, 29; Neh. 13:19.

Q. 118. Why is the charge of keeping the sabbath more specially directed to governors of families and other superiors?
A. The charge of keeping the sabbath is more specially directed to governors of families and other superiors, because they are bound not only to keep it themselves, but to see that it be observed by all those that are under their charge; and because they are prone ofttimes to hinder them by employments of their own. Ex. 20:10; Josh. 24:15; Neh. 13:15, 17; Jer. 17:20–22; Ex. 23:12.

Q. 119. What are the sins forbidden in the fourth commandment?
A. The sins forbidden in the fourth commandment are, all omissions of the duties required, all careless, negligent, and unprofitable performing of them, and being weary of them; all profaning the day by idleness, and doing that which is in itself sinful; and by all needless works,

words, and thoughts, about our worldly employments and recreations. Ezek 22:26; Acts 20:7, 9; Ezek. 33:30–32; Amos 8:5; Mal. 1:13; Ezek. 23:38; Jer. 17:24, 27; Isa. 58:13.

Q. 120. What are the reasons annexed to the fourth commandment, the more to enforce it?
A. The reasons annexed to the fourth commandment, the more to enforce it, are taken from the equity of it, God allowing us six days of seven for our own affairs, and reserving but one for himself, in these words, six days shalt thou labor and do all thy work: from God's challenging a special propriety in that day, the seventh day is the sabbath of the Lord thy God: from the example of God, who in six days made heaven and earth, the sea, and all that in them is, and rested the seventh day: and from that blessing which God put upon that day, not only in sanctifying it to be a day for his service, but in ordaining it to be a means of blessing to us in our sanctifying it, wherefore the Lord blessed the sabbath–day and hallowed it. Ex. 20:9; Ex. 20:10; Ex. 20:11.

Q. 121. Why is the word remember set in the beginning of the fourth commandment?
A. The word remember is set in the beginning of the fourth commandment, partly, because of the great benefit of remembering it, we being thereby helped in our preparation to keep it; and, in keeping it, better to keep all the rest of the commandments, and to continue a thankful remembrance of the two great benefits of creation and redemption, which contain a short abridgement of religion; and partly, because we are very ready to forget it, for that there is less light of nature for it, and yet it restraineth our natural liberty in things at other times lawful; that it cometh but once in seven days, and many worldly businesses come between, and too often take off our minds from thinking of it, either to prepare for it, or to sanctify it; and that Satan with his instruments much labor to blot out the glory, and even the memory of it, to bring in all irreligion and impiety. Ex. 20:8; Ex. 16:23; Luke 23:54, 56; Mark 15:42; Neh. 13:19; Ps. 92 title, 13–14; Ezek. 20:12, 19–20; Gen. 2:2–3; Ps. 118:22, 24; Acts 4:10–11; Rev. 1:10; Ezek. 22:26; Neh. 9:14; Ex. 34:21; Deut. 5:14–15; Amos 8:5; Lam. 1:7; Jer. 17:21–23; Neh. 13:15–23.

Q. 122. What is the sum of the six commandments which contain our duty to man?
A. The sum of the six commandments which contain our duty to man, is, to love our neighbor as ourselves, and to do to others what we would have them to do to us. Matt. 22:39; Matt. 7:12.

Q. 123. Which is the fifth commandment?
A. The fifth commandment is, Honor thy father and thy mother: that thy days may be long upon the land which the Lord thy God giveth thee. Ex. 20:12.

Q. 124. Who are meant by father and mother in the fifth commandment?
A. By father and mother, in the fifth commandment, are meant, not only natural parents, but all superiors in age and gifts; and especially such as, by God's ordinance, are over us in place of authority, whether in family, church, or commonwealth. Prov. 23:22, 25: Eph. 6:1–2; 1 Tim. 5:1–2; Gen. 4:20–22; Gen. 45:8; 2 Kings 5:13; 2 Kings 2:12; 2 Kings 13:14; Gal. 4:19; Isa. 49:23.

Q. 125. Why are superiors styled father and mother?
A. Superiors are styled father and mother, both to teach them in all duties towards their inferiors, like natural parents, to express love and tenderness to them, according to their several relations; and to work inferiors to a greater willingness and cheerfulness in performing their duties to their superiors, as to their parents. Eph. 6:4; 2 Cor. 12:14; 1 Thess. 2:7–8, 11; Num. 11:11–12; 1 Cor. 4:14–16; 2 Kings 5:13.

Q. 126. What is the general scope of the fifth commandment?
A. The general scope of the fifth commandment is the performance of those duties which we mutually owe in our several relations, as inferiors, superiors, or equals. Eph. 5:21; 1 Peter 2:17; Rom. 12:10.

Q. 127. What is the honor that inferiors owe to their superiors?
A. The honor which inferiors owe to their superiors is, all due reverence in heart, word, and behavior; prayer and thanksgiving for them; imitation of their virtues and graces; willing obedience to their lawful commands and counsels; due submission to their corrections; fidelity to, defence and maintenance of their persons and authority, according to their several ranks,

and the nature of their places; bearing with their infirmities, and covering them in love, that so they may be an honor to them and to their government. Mal. 1:6; Lev. 19:3; Prov. 31:28; 1 Peter 3:6; Lev. 19:32; 1 Kings 2:19; 1 Tim. 2: 1–2; Heb. 13:7; Phil. 3:17; Eph. 6:1–2, 5–7; 1 Peter 2:13–14; Rom. 13:1–5; Heb. 13: 17; Prov. 4:3–4; Prov. 23:22; Ex. 18:19, 24; Heb. 12:9; 1 Peter 2:18–20; Titus 2: 9–10; 1 Sam. 26:15–16; 2 Sam. 18:3; Esther 6:2; Matt. 22:21; Rom. 13:6–7; 1 Tim. 5:17–18; Gal. 6:6; Gen. 45:11; Gen. 47:12; 1 Peter 2:18; Prov. 23:22; Gen. 9:23; Ps. 127:3–5; Prov. 31:23.

Q. 128. What are the sins of inferiors against their superiors?
A. The sins of inferiors against their superiors are, all neglect of the duties required toward them; envying at, contempt of, and rebellion against, their persons and places, in their lawful counsels, commands, and corrections; cursing, mocking, and all such refractory and scandalous carriage, as proves a shame and dishonor to them and their government. Matt. 15:4–6; Num. 11:28–29; 1 Sam. 8:7; Isa. 3:5; 2 Sam. 15:1–12; Ex. 21: 15; 1 Sam. 10:27; 1 Sam. 2:25; Deut. 21:18–21; Prov. 30:11, 17; Prov. 19:26.

Q. 129. What is required of superiors towards their inferiors?
A. It is required of superiors, according to that power they receive from God, and that relation wherein they stand, to love, pray for, and bless their inferiors; to instruct, counsel and admonish them; countenancing, commending, and rewarding such as do well; and discountenancing, reproving, and chastising such as do ill; protecting, and providing for them all things necessary for soul and body: and, by grave, wise, holy, and exemplary carriage, to procure glory to God, honor to themselves, and so to preserve that authority which God hath put upon them. Col. 3:19; Titus 2:4; 1 Sam. 12:23; Job 1:5; 1 Kings 8:55–56; Heb. 7:7; Gen. 49:28; Deut. 6:6–7; Eph. 6:4; 1 Peter 3:7; 1 Peter 2:14; Rom. 13:3; Esther 6:3; Rom. 13:3–4; Prov. 29:15; 1 Peter 2:14; Job 29:12–17; Isa. 1:10, 17; Eph. 6:4; 1 Tim. 5: 8; 1 Tim. 4:12; Titus 2:3–5; 1 Kings 3:28; Titus 2:15.

Q. 130. What are the sins of superiors?
A. The sins of superiors are, besides the neglect of the duties required of them, an inordinate seeking of themselves, their own glory, ease, profit, or pleasure; commanding things unlawful, or not in the power of inferiors to perform; counseling, encouraging, or favoring them in that which is evil; dissuading, discouraging, or discountenancing them in that which is good; correcting them unduly; careless exposing, or leaving them to wrong, temptation, and danger; provoking them to wrath; or in any way dishonoring themselves, or lessening their authority, by an unjust, indiscreet, rigorous, or remiss behavior. Ezek. 34:2–4; Phil. 2:21; John 5:44; John 7:18; Isa. 56:10–11; Deut. 17:17; Dan. 3:4–6; Acts 4:17–18; Ex. 5:10–18; Matt. 23:2, 4; Matt. 14:8; Mark 6:24; 2 Sam. 13: 28; 1 Sam. 3:13; John 7:46–49; Col. 3:21; Ex. 5:17; 1 Peter 2:18–20; Heb. 12:10; Deut. 25:3; Gen. 38:11, 26; Acts 18:17; Eph. 6:4; Gen. 9:21; 1 Kings 12:13–16; 1 Kings 1:6; 1 Sam. 2:29–31.

Q. 131. What are the duties of equals?
A. The duties of equals are, to regard the dignity and worth of each other, in giving honor to go one before another; and to rejoice in each other's gifts and advancement, as their own. 1 Peter 2:17; Rom. 12:10; Rom. 12:15–16; Phil. 2:3–4.

Q. 132. What are the sins of equals?
A. The sins of equals are, besides the neglect of the duties required, the undervaluing of the worth, envying the gifts, grieving at the advancement or prosperity one of another; and usurping pre–eminence one over another. Rom. 13:8; 2 Tim. 3:3; Acts 7:9; Gal. 5:26; Num. 12:2; Esther 6:12–13; 3 John 1:9; Luke 22:24.

Q. 133. What is the reason annexed to the fifth commandment, the more to enforce it?
A. The reason annexed to the fifth commandment in these words, "that thy days may be long upon the land which the Lord thy God giveth thee," is an express promise of long life and prosperity, as far as it shall serve for God's glory and their own good, to all such as keep this commandment. Ex. 20:12; Deut. 5:16; 1 Kings 8:25; Eph. 6:2–3.

Q. 134. Which is the sixth commandment?
A. The sixth commandment is, Thou shalt not kill. Ex. 20:13.

Q. 135. What are the duties required in the sixth commandment?
A. The duties required in the sixth commandment are, all careful studies, and lawful endeavours, to preserve the life of ourselves and others by resisting all thoughts and purposes, subduing all passions, and avoiding all occasions, temptations, and practices, which tend to the unjust taking away the life of any; by just defence thereof against violence, patient bearing of the hand of God, quietness of mind, cheerfulness of spirit; a sober use of meat, drink, physic, sleep, labor, and recreation; by charitable thoughts, love, compassion, meekness, gentleness, kindness; peaceable, mild, and courteous speeches and behavior: forbearance, readiness to be reconciled, patient bearing and forgiving of injuries, and requiting good for evil; comforting and succoring the distressed, and protecting and defending the innocent. Eph. 5:28–29; 1 Kings 18:4; Jer. 26:15–16; Acts 23:12, 16–17, 21, 27; Eph. 4: 26–27; 2 Sam. 2:22; Deut. 22:8; Matt. 4:6–7; Prov. 1:10–11, 15–16; 1 Sam. 24:12; 1 Sam. 26:9–11; Gen. 37:21–22; Ps. 82:4; Prov. 24:11–12; 1 Sam. 14:45; Jas. 5:7–11; Heb. 12:9; 1 Thess. 4:11; 1 Peter 3:3–4; Ps. 37:8–11; Prov. 17:22; Prov. 25:16, 27; 1 Tim. 5:23; Isa. 38:21; Ps. 127:2; Eccl. 5:12; 2 Thess. 3:10, 12; Prov. 16:26; Eccl. 3:4, 11; 1 Sam. 19:4–5; 1 Sam. 22:13–14; Rom. 13:10; Luke 10:33–34; Col. 3:12–13; Jas. 3:17; 1 Peter 3:8–11; Prov. 15:1; Judg. 8:1–3; Matt. 5:24; Eph. 4:2, 32; Rom. 12:17, 20–21; 1 Thess. 5:14; Job 31:19–20; Matt. 25:35–36; Prov. 31:8–9.

Q. 136. What are the sins forbidden in the sixth commandment?
A. The sins forbidden in the sixth commandment are, all taking away the life of ourselves, or of others, except in case of public justice, lawful war, or necessary defence; the neglecting or withdrawing the lawful and necessary means of preservation of life; sinful anger, hatred, envy, desire of revenge; all excessive passions, distracting cares; immoderate use of meat, drink, labor, and recreations; provoking words; oppression, quarreling, striking, wounding, and whatsoever else tends to the destruction of the life of any. Acts 16:28; Gen. 9:6; Num. 35:31, 33; Jer. 48:10; Deut. 20:1–20; Ex. 22:2–3; Matt. 25:42–43; Jas. 2:15–16; Eccl. 6:1–2; Matt. 5:22; 1 John 3:15; Lev. 19:17; Prov. 14:30; Rom. 12:19; Eph. 4:31; Matt. 6:31, 34; Luke 21:34; Rom. 13:13; Eccl. 12:12; Eccl. 2:22–23; Isa. 5:12; Prov. 15:1; Prov. 12:18; Ezek. 18:18; Ex. 1:14; Gal. 5:15; Prov. 23:29; Num. 35:16–18, 21; Ex. 21:18–36.

Q. 137. Which is the seventh commandment?
A. The seventh commandment is, Thou shalt not commit adultery. Ex. 20:14.

Q. 138. What are the duties required in the seventh commandment?
A. The duties required in the seventh commandment are, chastity in body, mind, affections, words, and behavior; and the preservation of it in ourselves and others; watchfulness over the eyes and all the senses; temperance, keeping of chaste company, modesty in apparel; marriage by those that have not the gift of continency, conjugal love, and cohabitation; diligent labor in all our callings; shunning all occasions of uncleanness, and resisting temptations thereunto. 1 Thess. 4:4; Job 31:1; 1 Cor. 7:34; Col. 4:6; 1 Peter 3:2; 1 Cor. 7:2, 35–36; Job 31:1; Acts 24:24–25; Prov. 2:16–20; 1 Tim. 2:9; 1 Cor. 7:2, 9; Prov. 5:19–20; 1 Peter 3:7; Prov. 31:11, 27–28; Prov. 5:8; Gen. 39:8–10.

Q. 139. What are the sins forbidden in the seventh commandment?
A. The sins forbidden in the seventh commandment, besides the neglect of the duties required, are, adultery, fornication, rape, incest, sodomy, and all unnatural lusts; all unclean imaginations, thoughts, purposes, and affections; all corrupt or filthy communications, or listening thereunto; wanton looks; impudent or light behavior; immodest apparel; prohibiting of lawful, and dispensing with unlawful marriages; allowing, tolerating, keeping of stews, and resorting to them; entangling vows of single life; undue delay of marriage; having more wives or husbands than one at the same time; unjust divorce or desertion; idleness, gluttony, drunkenness, unchaste company; lascivious songs, books, pictures, dancing, stage plays; all other provocations to, or acts of uncleanness, either in ourselves or others. Prov. 5:7; Heb. 13:4; Gal. 5:19; 2 Sam. 13:14; 1 Cor. 5:1; Rom. 1:24, 26–27; Lev. 20:15–16; Matt. 5:28; Matt. 15:19; Col. 3:5; Eph. 5:3–4; Prov. 7:5, 21–22; Isa. 3:16; 2 Peter 2:14; Prov. 7:10, 13; 1 Tim. 4:3; Lev. 18:1–21; Mark 6:18; Mal. 2: 11–12; 1 Kings 15:12; 2 Kings 23:7; Deut. 23:17–18; Lev. 19:29; Jer. 5:7; Prov. 7:24–27; Matt. 19:10–11; 1 Cor. 7:7–9; Gen. 38:26; Mal. 2:14–15; Matt. 19:5; Mal. 2:16; Matt. 5:32; 1 Cor. 7:12–13; Ezek. 16:49; Prov. 23:30–33; Gen. 39:10; Prov. 5:8; Eph. 5:4; Ezek. 23:14–16; Isa. 23:15–17; Isa. 3:16; Mark 6:22; Rom. 13:13; 1 Peter 4:3; 2 Kings 9:30; Jer. 4:30; Ezek. 23:40.

Q. 140. Which is the eighth commandment?

A. The eighth commandment is, Thou shalt not steal. Ex. 20:15.

Q. 141. What are the duties required in the eighth commandment?

A. The duties required in the eighth commandment are, truth, faithfulness, and justice in contracts and commerce between man and man; rendering to every one his due; restitution of goods unlawfully detained from the right owners thereof; giving and lending freely, according to our abilities, and the necessities of others; moderation of our judgments, wills, and affections, concerning worldly goods; a provident care and study to get, keep, use, and dispose of those things which are necessary and convenient for the sustentation of our nature, and suitable to our condition; a lawful calling, and diligence in it; frugality; avoiding unnecessary law–suits, and suretyship, or other like engagements; and an endeavor, by all just and lawful means, to procure, preserve, and further the wealth and outward estate of others, as well as our own. Ps. 15:2, 4; Zech. 7:4, 10; Zech. 8:16–17; Rom. 13:7; Lev. 6:2–5; Luke 19:8; Luke 6:30, 38; 1 John 3:17; Eph. 4:28; Gal. 6:10; 1 Tim. 6:6–9; Gal. 6:14; 1 Tim. 5:8; Prov. 27:23–27; Eccl. 2:24; Eccl. 3:12–13; 1 Tim. 6:17–18; Isa. 38:1; Matt. 11: 8; 1 Cor. 7:20; Gen. 2:15; Gen. 3:19; Eph. 4:28; Prov. 10:4; John 6:12; Prov. 21: 20; 1 Cor. 6:1–9; Prov. 6:1–6; Prov. 11:15; Lev. 25:35; Deut. 22:1–4; Ex. 23:4–5; Gen. 47:14, 20; Phil. 2:4; Matt. 22:39.

Q. 142. What are the sins forbidden in the eighth commandment?

A. The sins forbidden in the eighth commandment, besides the neglect of the duties required, are, theft, robbery, man–stealing, and receiving any thing that is stolen; fraudulent dealing; false weights and measures; removing landmarks; injustice and unfaithfulness in contracts between man and man, or in matters of trust; oppression; extortion; usury; bribery; vexatious lawsuits; unjust inclosures and depopulations; engrossing commodities to enhance the price, unlawful callings, and all other unjust or sinful ways of taking or withholding from our neighbor what belongs to him, or of enriching ourselves; covetousness; inordinate prizing and affecting worldly goods; distrustful and distracting cares and studies in getting, keeping, and using them; envying at the prosperity of others; as likewise idleness, prodigality, wasteful gaming; and all others ways whereby we do unduly prejudice our own outward estate, and defrauding ourselves of the due use and comfort of that estate which God hath given us. Jas. 2:15–16; 1 John 3:17; Eph. 4:28; Ps. 62:10; 1 Tim. 1:10; Prov. 29:24; Ps. 50:18; 1 Thess. 4:6; Prov. 11:1; Prov. 20:10; Deut. 19:14; Prov. 23:10; Amos 8:5; Ps. 37:21; Luke 16:10–12; Ezek. 22:29; Lev. 25:17; Matt. 23:25; Ezek. 22:12; Ps. 15:5; Job 15:34; 1 Cor. 6:6–8; Prov. 3:29–30; Isa. 5:8; Mic. 2:2; Prov. 11:26; Acts 19:19, 24–25; Job 20:19; Jas. 5:4; Prov. 21:6; Luke 12:15; 1 Tim. 6:5; Col. 3:2; Prov. 23:5; Ps. 62:10; Matt. 6:25, 31, 34; Eccl. 5:12; Ps. 73:3; Ps. 37:1, 7; 2 Thess. 3:11; Prov. 18:9; Prov. 21:17; Prov. 23:20–21; Prov. 28:19; Eccl. 4:8; Eccl. 6:2; 1 Tim. 5:8.

Q. 143. Which the ninth commandment?

A. The ninth commandment is, Thou shalt not bear false witness against thy neighbor. Ex. 20:16.

Q. 144. What are the duties required in the ninth commandment?

A. The duties required in the ninth commandment are, the preserving and promoting of truth between man and man, and the good name of our neighbor, as well as our own: appearing and standing for the truth; and from the heart, sincerely, freely, clearly, and fully, speaking the truth, and only the truth, in matters of judgment and justice, and in all other things whatsoever; a charitable esteem of our neighbors; loving, desiring, and rejoicing in their good name; sorrowing for, and covering of their infirmities; freely acknowledging of their gifts and graces, defending their innocency; a ready receiving of good report, and unwillingness to admit of an evil report, concerning them; discouraging tale–bearers, flatterers, and slanderers; love and care of our own good name, and defending it when need requireth; keeping of lawful promises; study and practising of whatsoever things are true, honest, lovely, and of good report. Zech. 8:16; 3 John 1:12; Prov. 31:8–9; Ps. 15:2; 2 Chron. 19:9; 1 Sam. 19:4–5; Josh. 7:19; 2 Sam. 14:18–20; Lev. 19:15; Prov. 14:5, 25; 2 Cor. 1:17–18; Eph. 4: 25; Heb. 6:9; 1 Cor. 13:7; Rom. 1:8; 2 John 1:4; 3 John 1:3–4; 1 Cor. 1:4–5, 7; 2 Tim. 1:4–5; 1 Sam. 22:14; 1 Cor. 13:6–7; Ps. 15:3; Prov. 25:23; Prov. 26:24–25; Ps. 101:5; Prov. 22:1; John 8:49; Ps. 15:4; Phil. 4:8; 2 Cor. 2:4; 2 Cor. 12: 21; Prov. 17:9; 1 Peter 4:8.

Q. 145. What are the sins forbidden in the ninth commandment?
A. The sins forbidden in the ninth commandment are, all prejudicing the truth, and the good name of our neighbors, as well as our own, especially in public judicature; giving false evidence; suborning false witnesses; wittingly appearing and pleading for an evil cause; out–facing and overbearing the truth; passing unjust sentence; calling evil good, and good evil; rewarding the wicked according to the work of the righteous, and the righteous according to the work of the wicked; forgery; concealing the truth; undue silence in a just cause, and holding our peace when iniquity calleth for either a reproof from ourselves, or complaint to others; speaking the truth unseasonably, or maliciously to a wrong end, or perverting it to a wrong meaning, or in doubtful and equivocal expressions, to the prejudice of truth or justice; speaking untruth, lying, slandering, backbiting, detracting, tale–bearing, whispering, scoffing, reviling, rash, harsh, and partial censuring; misconstructing intentions, words, and actions; flattering, vain–glorious boasting, thinking or speaking too highly or too meanly of ourselves or others; denying the gifts and graces of God; aggravating smaller faults; hiding, excusing, or extenuating of sins, when called to a free confession; unnecessary discovering of infirmities; raising false rumours, receiving and countenancing evil reports, and stopping our ears against just defence; evil suspicion; envying or grieving at the deserved credit of any, endeavouring or desiring to impair it, rejoicing in their disgrace and infamy; scornful contempt; fond admiration; breach of lawful promises; neglecting such things as are of good report; and practicing or not avoiding ourselves, or not hindering what we can in others, such things as procure an ill name. 1 Sam. 17:28; 2 Sam.16:3; 2 Sam. 1:9–10, 15–16; Lev. 19:15; Hab. 1:4; Prov. 19:5; Prov. 6:16, 19; Acts 6:13; Jer. 9:3, 5; Acts 24:2, 5; Ps. 12:3–4; Ps. 52:1–4; Prov. 17:15; 1 Kings 21:9–14; Isa. 5:23; Ps.119:69; Luke 19:8; Luke 16:5–7; Lev. 5:1; Deut. 13:8; Acts 5:3, 8–9; 2 Tim. 4:16; 1 Kings 1:6; Lev. 19:17; Isa. 59:4; Prov. 29:11; 1 Sam. 22:9–10; Ps. 52:1–5; Ps. 56:5; John 2:19; Matt. 26:60–61; Gen. 3:5; Gen. 26: 7, 9; Isa. 59:13; Lev. 19:11; Col. 3:9; Ps. 50:20; Ps. 15:3; Jas. 4:11; Jer. 38:4; Lev. 19:16; Rom. 1:29–30: Gen. 21:9; Gal. 4:29; 1 Cor. 6:10; Matt. 7:1; Acts 28:4; Gen. 38:24; Rom. 2:1; Neh. 6:6–8; Rom. 3:8; Ps. 69:10; 1 Sam. 1:13–15; 2 Sam. 10:3; Ps. 12:2–3; 2 Tim. 3:2; Luke 18:9, 11; Rom. 12:16; 1 Cor. 4:6; Acts 12:22; Ex. 4: 10–14; Job 27:5–6; Job 4:6; Matt. 7:3–5; Prov. 28:13; Prov. 30:20; Gen. 3:12–13; Jer. 2:35; 2 Kings 5:25; Gen. 4:9; Gen. 9:22; Prov. 25:9–10; Ex. 23:1; Prov. 29:12; Acts 7:56–57; Job 31:13–14; 1 Cor. 13:5; 1 Tim. 6:4; Num. 11:29; Matt. 21:15; Ezra 4:12–13; Jer. 48:27; Ps. 35:15–16, 21; Matt. 27:28–29; Jude 1:16; Acts 12:22; Rom. 1:31; 2 Tim. 3:3; 1 Sam. 2:24; 2 Sam. 13:12–13; Prov. 5:8–9; Prov. 6:33.

Q. 146. Which is the tenth commandment?
A. The tenth commandment is, Thou shalt not covet thy neighbor's house, thou shalt not covet thy neighbor's wife, nor his man–servant, nor his maid–servant, nor his ox, nor his ass, nor any thing that is thy neighbor's. Ex. 20:17.

Q. 147. What are the duties required in the tenth commandment?
A. The duties required in the tenth commandment are, such a full contentment with our own condition, and such a charitable frame of the whole soul toward our neighbor, as that all our inward motions and affections touching him, tend unto, and further all that good which is his. Heb. 13:5; 1 Tim. 6:6; Job 31:29; Rom. 12:15; Ps. 122:7–9; 1 Tim. 1:5; Esther 10:3; 1 Cor. 13:4–7.

Q. 148. What are the sins forbidden in the tenth commandment?
A. The sins forbidden in the tenth commandment are, discontentment with our own estate; envying, and grieving at the good of our neighbor, together with all inordinate motions and affections to anything that is his. 1 Kings 21:4; Esther 5:13; 1 Cor. 10:10; Gal. 5:26; Jas. 3:14, 16; Ps. 112:9–10; Neh. 2:10; Rom. 7:7–8; Rom. 13:9; Col. 3:5; Deut. 5:21.

Q. 149. Is any man able perfectly to keep the commandments of God?
A. No man is able, either of himself, or by any grace received in this life, perfectly to keep the commandments of God; but doth daily break them in thought, word, and deed. Jas. 3:2; John 15:5; Rom. 8:3; Eccl. 7:20; 1 John 1:8, 10; Gal. 5:17; Rom. 7: 18–19; Gen. 6:5; Gen. 8:21; Rom. 3:9–19; Jas. 3:2–13.

Q. 150. Are all transgressions of the law of God equally heinous in themselves, and in the sight of God?

A. All transgressions of the law of God are not equally heinous; but some sins in themselves, and by reason of several aggravations, are more heinous in the sight of God than others. John 19:11; Ezek. 8:6, 13, 15; 1 John 5:16; Ps. 78:17, 32, 56.

Q. 151. What are those aggravations that make some sins more heinous than others?

A. Sins receive their aggravations, 1. From the persons offending: if they be of riper age, greater experience or grace, eminent for profession, gifts, place, office, guides to others, and whose example is likely to be followed by others. 2. From the parties offended: if immediately against God, his attributes, and worship; against Christ, and his grace; the Holy Spirit, his witness, and workings; against superiors, men of eminency, and such as we stand especially related and engaged unto; against any of the saints, particularly weak brethren, the souls of them or any other, and the common good of all or many. 3. From the nature and quality of the offence: if it be against the express letter of the law, break many commandments, contain in it many sins: if not only conceived in the heart, but break forth in words and actions, scandalize others, and admit of no reparation: if against means, mercies, judgments, light of nature, conviction of conscience, public or private admonition, censures of the church, civil punishments; and our prayers, purposes, promises, vows, covenants, and engagements to God or men: if done deliberately, wilfully, presumptuously, impudently, boastingly, maliciously, frequently, obstinately, with delight, continuance, or relapsing after repentance. 4. From circumstances of time and place: if on the Lord's day, or other times of divine worship; or immediately before or after these, or other helps to prevent or remedy such miscarriages: if in public, or in the presence of others, who are thereby likely to be provoked or defiled. Jer. 2:8; Job 32:7, 9; Eccl. 4:13; 1 Kings 11:4, 9; 2 Sam. 12:14; 1 Cor. 5:1; Jas. 4:17; Luke 12:47–48; Jer. 5:4–5; 2 Sam. 12:7–9; Ezek. 8:11–12; Rom. 2:17–24; Gal. 2:11–14; Matt. 21:38–39; 1 Sam. 2:25; Acts 5:4; Ps. 51:4; Rom. 2:4; Mal. 1:8, 14; Heb. 2:2–3; Heb. 12:25; Heb. 10:29; Matt. 12:31–32; Eph. 4:30; Heb. 6:4–6; Jude 1:8; Num. 12:8–9; Isa. 3:5; Prov. 30:17; 2 Cor. 12:15; Ps. 55:12–15; Zeph. 2:8, 10–11; Matt. 18:6; 1 Cor. 6:8; Rev. 17:6; 1 Cor. 8:11–12; Rom. 14:13, 15, 21; Ezek. 13:19; 1 Cor. 8:12; Rev. 18:12–13; Matt. 23:15; 1 Thess. 2:15–16; Josh. 22:20; Prov. 6:30–33; Ezra 9:10–12; 1 Kings 11:9–10; Col. 3:5; 1 Tim. 6:10; Prov. 5:8–12; Prov. 6:32–33; Josh. 7:21; Jas. 1:14–15; Matt. 5:22; Mic. 2:1; Matt. 18:7; Rom. 2:23–24; Deut. 22:22, 28–29; Prov. 6:32–35; Matt. 11:21–24; John 15:22; Isa. 1:3; Deut. 32:6; Amos 4:8–11; Jer. 5:3; Rom. 1:26–27; Rom. 1:32; Dan. 5:22; Titus 3:10–11; Prov. 29:1; Titus 3:10; Matt. 18:17; Prov. 27:22: Prov. 23:35; Ps. 78:34–37; Jer. 2: 20; Jer. 42:5–6, 20, 21; Eccl. 5:4–6; Prov. 20:25; Lev. 26:25; Prov. 2:17; Ezek. 17: 18–19; Ps. 36:4; Jer. 6:16; Num. 15:30; Ex. 21:14; Jer. 3:3; Prov. 7:13; Ps. 52:1; 3 John 1:10; Num. 14:22; Zech. 7:11–12; Prov. 2:14; Isa. 57:17; Jer. 34:8–11; 2 Peter 2:20–22; 2 Kings 5:26; Jer. 7:10; Isa. 26:10; Ezek. 23:37–39; Isa. 58:3–5; Num. 25: 6–7; 1 Cor. 11:20–21; Jer. 7:8–10; Prov. 7:14–15; John 13:27, 30; Ezra 9:13–14; 2 Sam. 16:22; 1 Sam. 2:22–24.

Q. 152. What doth every sin deserve at the hands of God?

A. Every sin, even the least, being against the sovereignty, goodness, and holiness of God, and against his righteous law, deserveth his wrath and curse, both in this life, and that which is to come; and cannot be expiated but by the blood of Christ. Jas. 2:10–11; Ex. 20:1–2; Hab. 1:13; Lev. 10:3; Lev. 11:44–45; 1 John 3:4; Rom. 7:12; Eph. 5:6; Gal. 3:10; Lam. 3:39; Deut. 28:15–68; Matt. 25:41; Heb. 9:22; 1 Peter 1:18–19.

Q. 153. What doth God require of us, that we may escape his wrath and curse due to us by reason of the transgression of the law?

A. That we may escape the wrath and curse of God due to us by reason of the transgression of the law, he requireth of us repentance toward God, and faith toward our Lord Jesus Christ, and the diligent use of the outward means whereby Christ communicates to us the benefits of his mediation. Acts 20:21; Matt. 3:7–8; Luke 13:3, 5; Acts 16:30–31; John 3:16, 18; Prov. 2:1–5; Prov. 8:33–36.

Q. 154. What are the outward means whereby Christ communicates to us the benefits of his mediation?

A. The outward and ordinary means whereby Christ communicates to his church the benefits of his mediation, are all his ordinances; especially the Word, Sacraments, and prayer: all which are made effectual to the elect for their salvation. Matt. 28:19–20; Acts 2:42, 46–47.

Q. 155. How is the Word made effectual to salvation?
A. The Spirit of God maketh the reading, but especially the preaching of the Word, an effectual means of enlightening, convincing, and humbling sinners; of driving them out of themselves, and drawing them unto Christ; of conforming them to his image, and subduing them to his will; of strengthening them against temptations and corruptions; of building them up in grace, and establishing their hearts in holiness and comfort through faith unto salvation. Neh. 8:8; Acts 26:18; Ps. 19:8; 1 Cor. 14:24–25; 2 Chron. 34:18–19, 26–28; Acts 2:37, 41; Acts 8:27–39; 2 Cor. 3:18; 2 Cor. 10:4–6; Rom. 6:17; Matt. 4:4, 7, 10; Eph. 6:16–17; Ps. 19:11; 1 Cor. 10:11; Acts 20:32; 2 Tim. 3:15–17; Rom. 16:25; 1 Thess. 3:2, 10–11, 13; Rom. 15:4; Rom. 10:13–17; Rom. 1:16.

Q. 156. Is the Word of God to be read by all?
A. Although all are not to be permitted to read the Word publicly to the congregation, yet all sorts of people are bound to read it apart by themselves, and with their families: to which end, the holy Scriptures are to be translated out of the original into vulgar languages. Deut. 31:9, 11–13; Neh. 8:2–3; Neh. 9:3–5; Deut. 17:19; Rev. 1:3; John 5:39; Isa. 34:16; Deut. 6:6–9; Gen. 18:17, 19; Ps. 78:5–7; 1 Cor. 14:6, 9, 11–12, 15–16, 24, 27–28.

Q. 157. How is the Word of God to be read?
A. The holy Scriptures are to be read with an high and reverent esteem of them; with a firm persuasion that they are the very Word of God; and that he only can enable us to understand them; with desire to know, believe, and obey, the will of God revealed in them; with diligence, and attention to the matter and scope of them; with meditation, application, self–denial, and prayer. Ps. 19:10; Neh. 8:3–10; Ex. 24:7; 2 Chron. 34:27; Isa. 66:2; 2 Peter 1:19–21; Luke 24:45; 2 Cor. 3:13–16; Deut. 17:19–20; Acts 17:11; Acts 8:30, 34; Luke 10:26–28; Ps. 1:2; Ps. 119:97; 2 Chron. 34:21; Prov. 3:5; Deut. 33:3; Prov. 2:1–6; Ps.119: 18; Neh. 8:6, 8.

Q. 158. By whom is the Word of God to be preached?
A. The Word of God is to be preached only by such as are sufficiently gifted, and also duly approved and called to that office. 1 Tim. 3:2, 6; Eph. 4:8–11; Hos. 4:6; Mal. 2:7; 2 Cor. 3:6; Jer. 14:15; Rom. 10: 15; Heb. 5:4; 1 Cor. 12:28–29; 1 Tim. 3:10; 1 Tim. 4:14; 1 Tim. 5:22.

Q. 159. How is the Word of God to be preached by those that are called thereunto?
A. They that are called to labor in the ministry of the Word are to preach sound doctrine, diligently, in season, and out of season; plainly, not in the enticing words of man's wisdom but in demonstration of the Spirit, and of power; faithfully, making known the whole counsel of God; wisely, applying themselves to the necessities and capacities of the hearers; zealously, with fervent love to God and the souls of his people; sincerely, aiming at his glory, and their conversion, edification, and salvation. Titus 2:1, 8; Acts 18:25; 2 Tim. 4:2; 1 Cor. 14:19; 1 Cor. 2:4; Jer. 23:28; 1 Cor. 4:1–2; Acts 20:27; Col. 1:28; 2 Tim. 2:15; 1 Cor. 3:2; Heb. 5:12–14; Luke 12:42; Acts 18:25; 2 Cor. 5:13–14; Phil. 1:15–17; Col. 4:12; 2 Cor. 12:15; 2 Cor. 2:17; 2 Cor. 4:2; 1 Thess. 2:4–6; John 7:18; 1 Cor. 9:19–22; 2 Cor. 12:19; Eph. 4:12; 1 Tim. 4:16; Acts 26:16–18.

Q. 160. What is required of those that hear the Word preached?
A. It is required of those that hear the Word preached, that they attend upon it with diligence, preparation, and prayer; examine what they hear by the Scriptures; receive the truth with faith, love, meekness, and readiness of mind, as the Word of God; meditate, and confer of it; hide it in their hearts, and bring forth the fruit of it in their lives. Prov. 8:34; 1 Peter 2:1–2; Luke 8:18; Ps. 119:18; Eph. 6:18–19; Acts 17:11; Heb. 4:2; 2 Thess. 2:10; Jas. 1:21; Acts 17:11; 1 Thess. 2:13; Luke 9:44; Heb. 2:1; Luke 24:14; Deut. 6:6–7; Prov. 2:1; Ps.119:11; Luke 8:15; Jas. 1:25.

Q. 161. How do the Sacraments become effectual means of salvation?
A. The Sacraments become effectual means of salvation, not by any power in themselves, or any virtue derived from the piety or intention of him by whom they are administered; but only by the working of the Holy Ghost, and the blessing of Christ by whom they are instituted. 1 Peter 3:21; Acts 8:13, 23; 1 Cor. 3:6–7; 1 Cor. 12:13.

Q. 162. What is a Sacrament?
A. A Sacrament is an holy ordinance instituted by Christ in his Church, to signify, seal, and exhibit unto those that are within the covenant of grace, the benefits of his mediation; to strengthen and increase their faith, and all other graces; to oblige them to obedience; to testify and cherish their love and communion one with another; and to distinguish them from those that are without. Gen. 17:7, 10; Ex. 12:1–51; Matt. 28:19; Matt. 26:26–28; Rom. 4:11; 1 Cor. 11: 24–25; Rom. 15:8; Ex. 12:48; Acts 2:38; 1 Cor. 10:16; Rom. 4:11; Gal. 3:27; Rom. 6:3– 4; 1 Cor. 10:21; Eph. 4:2–5; 1 Cor. 12:13; Eph. 2:11; Gen. 34:14.

Q. 163. What are the parts of a Sacrament?
A. The parts of a Sacrament are two: the one, an outward and sensible sign used according to Christ's own appointment; the other, an inward and spiritual grace thereby signified. Matt. 3:11; 1 Peter 3:21; Rom. 2:28–29.

Q. 164. How many Sacraments hath Christ instituted in his Church under the New Testament?
A. Under the New Testament Christ hath instituted in his Church only two Sacraments, Baptism and the Lord's Supper. Matt. 28:19; 1 Cor. 11:20, 23; Matt. 26:26–28.

Q. 165. What is Baptism?
A. Baptism is a Sacrament of the New Testament, wherein Christ hath ordained the washing with water in the name of the Father, and of the Son, and of the Holy Ghost, to be a sign and seal of ingrafting into himself, of remission of sins by his blood, and regeneration by his Spirit; of adoption, and resurrection unto everlasting life; and whereby the parties baptized are solemnly admitted into the visible Church, and enter into an open and professed engagement to be wholly and only the Lord's. Matt. 28:19; 2 Cor. 11:20, 23; Matt. 26:26–28; Matt. 5:26; Gal. 3:26–27; 1 Cor. 15:29; Rom. 6:5; 1 Cor. 12:13; Rom. 6:4.

Q. 166. Unto whom is Baptism to be administered?
A. Baptism is not to be administered to any that are out of the visible Church, and so strangers from the covenant of promise, till they profess their faith in Christ, and obedience to him; but infants descended from parents, either both or but one of them professing faith in Christ, and obedience to him, are in that respect, within the covenant, and to be baptized. Acts 8:36–37; Acts 2:38; Gen. 17:7, 9; Gal. 3:9, 14; Col. 2:11–12; Acts 2:38–39; Rom. 4:11–12; 1 Cor. 7:14; Matt. 28:19; Luke 18:15–16; Rom. 11:16.

Q. 167. How is our Baptism to be improved by us?
A. The needful but much neglected duty of improving our Baptism, is to be performed by us all our life long, especially in the time of temptation, and when we are present at the administration of it to others, by serious and thankful consideration of the nature of it, and of the ends for which Christ instituted it, the privileges and benefits conferred and sealed thereby, and our solemn vow made therein; by being humbled for our sinful defilement, our falling short of, and walking contrary to, the grace of the Baptism and our engagements; by growing up to assurance of pardon of sin, and of all other blessings sealed to us in that Sacrament; by drawing strength from the death and resurrection of Christ, into whom we are baptized, for the mortifying of sin, and quickening of grace; and by endeavoring to live by faith, to have our conversation in holiness and righteousness, as those that have therein given up their names to Christ; and to walk in brotherly love, as being baptized by the same Spirit into one body. Col. 2:11–12; Rom. 6:4, 6, 11; Rom. 6:3–5; 1 Cor. 1:11–13; Rom. 6:2–3; Rom. 4:11–12; 1 Peter 3:21; Rom. 6:3–5; Gal. 3:26–27; Rom. 6:22; Acts 2:38; 1 Cor. 12:13, 25–27.

Q. 168. What is the Lord's Supper?
A. The Lord's Supper is a Sacrament of the New Testament, wherein, by giving and receiving bread and wine according to the appointment of Jesus Christ, his death is shewed forth; and they that worthily communicate feed upon his body and blood, to their spiritual nourishment and growth in grace; have their union and communion with him confirmed; testify and renew their thankfulness, and engagement to God, and their mutual love and fellowship each with other, as members of the same mystical body. Luke 22:20; Matt. 26:26–28; 1 Cor. 11:23–26; 1 Cor. 10:16; 1 Cor. 11:24; 1 Cor. 10:14–16, 21; 1 Cor. 10:17.

Q. 169. How hath Christ appointed bread and wine to be given and received in the Sacrament of the Lord's Supper?
A. Christ hath appointed the ministers of his Word, in the administration of this Sacrament of the Lord's Supper, to set apart the bread and wine from common use, by the word of institution, thanksgiving, and prayer; to take and break the bread, and to give both the bread and the wine to the communicants: who are, by the same appointment, to take and eat the bread, and to drink the wine, in thankful remembrance that the body of Christ was broken and given, and his blood shed, for them. 1 Cor. 11:23–24; Matt. 26:26–28; Mark 14:22–24; Luke 22:19–20.

Q. 170. How do they that worthily communicate in the Lord's Supper feed upon the body and blood of Christ therein?
A. As the body and blood of Christ are not corporally or carnally present in, with, or under the bread and wine in the Lord's Supper; and yet are spiritually present to the faith of the receiver, no less truly and really than the elements themselves are to their outward senses; so they that worthily communicate in the Sacrament of the Lord's Supper, do therein feed upon the body and blood of Christ, not after a corporal or carnal, but in a spiritual manner; yet truly and really, while by faith they receive and apply unto themselves Christ crucified, and all the benefits of his death. Acts 3:21; Matt. 26:26, 28; 1 Cor. 11:24–29; 1 Cor. 10:16.

Q. 171. How are they that receive the Sacrament of the Lord's Supper to prepare themselves before they come unto it?
A. They that receive the Sacrament of the Lord's Supper, are, before they come, to prepare themselves thereunto, by examining themselves of their being in Christ; of their sins and wants; of the truth and measure of their knowledge, faith, repentance, love to God and the brethren, charity to all men, forgiving those that have done them wrong; of their desires after Christ, and of their new obedience; and by renewing the exercise of these graces, by serious meditation, and fervent prayer. 1 Cor. 11:28; 2 Cor. 13:5; 1 Cor. 5:7; Ex. 12:15; 1 Cor. 11:29; 2 Cor. 13:5; Matt. 26:28; Zech. 12:10; 1 Cor. 11:31; 1 Cor. 10:16–17; Acts 2:46–47; 1 Cor. 5:8; 1 Cor. 11:18, 20; Matt. 5:23–24; Isa. 55:1; John 7:37; 1 Cor. 5:7–8; 1 Cor. 11:25–26, 28; Heb. 10:21–22, 24; Ps. 26:6; 1 Cor. 11:24–25; 2 Chron. 30:18–19; Matt. 26:26.

Q. 172. May one who doubteth of his being in Christ, or of his due preparation, come to the Lord's Supper?
A. One who doubteth of his being in Christ, or of his due preparation to the Sacrament of the Lord's Supper, may have true interest in Christ, though he be not yet assured thereof; and in God's account hath it, if he be duly affected with the apprehension of the want of it, and unfeignedly desires to be found in Christ, and to depart from iniquity: in which case (because promises are made, and this Sacrament is appointed, for the relief even of weak and doubting Christians) he is to bewail his unbelief, and labor to have his doubts resolved; and, so doing, he may and ought to come to the Lord's Supper, that he may be further strengthened. Isa. 1:10; 1 John 5:13; Ps. 88:1–18; Ps. 77:1–12; Jonah 2:4, 7; Isa. 54:7–10; Matt. 5:3–4; Ps. 31:22; Ps. 73:13, 22–23; Phil. 3:8–9; Ps. 10:17; Ps. 42:1–2, 5, 11; 2 Tim. 2:19; Isa. 1:10; Ps. 66:18–20; Isa. 40:11, 29, 31; Matt. 11:28; Matt. 12:20; Matt. 26:28; Mark 9:24; Acts 2:37; Acts 16:30; Rom. 4:11; 1 Cor. 11:28.

Q. 173. May any who profess the faith, and desire to come to the Lord's Supper, be kept from it?
A. Such as are found to be ignorant or scandalous, notwithstanding their profession of the faith, and desire to come to the Lord's Supper, may and ought to be kept from that Sacrament, by the power which Christ hath left in his Church, until they receive instruction, and manifest their reformation. 1 Cor. 11:27–34; Matt. 7:6; 1 Cor. 5:1–13; Jude 23; 1 Tim. 5:22; 2 Cor. 2:7.

Q. 174. What is required of them that receive the Sacrament of the Lord's Supper in the time of the administration of it?
A. It is required of them that receive the Sacrament of the Lord's Supper, that, during the time of the administration of it, with all holy reverence and attention they wait upon God in that ordinance, diligently observe the sacramental elements and actions, heedfully discern the Lord's body, and affectionately meditate on his death and sufferings, and thereby stir up themselves to a vigorous exercise of their graces; in judging themselves and sorrowing for sin; in earnest hungering and thirsting after Christ, feeding on him by faith, receiving of his fulness, trusting in his

merits, rejoicing in his love, giving thanks for his grace; in renewing of their covenant with God, and love to all the saints. Lev. 10:3; Heb. 12:28; Ps. 5:7; 1 Cor. 11:17, 26–27; Ex. 24:8; Matt. 26:28; 1 Cor. 11:29; Luke 22:19; 1 Cor. 11:26; 1 Cor. 10:3–5, 11, 14; 1 Cor. 11:31; Zech. 12:10; Rev. 22:17; John 6:35; John 1:16; Phil. 3:9; Ps. 63:4–5; 2 Chron. 30:21; Ps. 22:26; Jer. 1:5; Ps. 1:5; Acts 2:42.

Q. 175. What is the duty of Christians, after they have received the Sacrament of the Lord's Supper?
A. The duty of Christians, after they have received the Sacrament of the Lord's Supper, is seriously to consider how they have behaved themselves therein, and with what success; if they find quickening and comfort, to bless God for it, beg the continuance of it, watch against relapses, fulfill their vows, and encourage themselves to a frequent attendance on that ordinance: but if they find no present benefit, more exactly to review their preparation to, and carriage at, the Sacrament; in both which, if they can approve themselves to God and their own consciences, they are to wait for the fruit of it in due time: but, if they see that they have failed in either, they are to be humbled, and to attend upon it afterward with more care and diligence. Ps. 28:7; Ps. 85:8; 1 Cor. 11:17, 30–31; 2 Chron. 30:21–23, 25–26; Acts 2:42, 46–47; Ps. 36:10; Song of Sol. 3:4; 1 Chron. 29:18; 1 Cor. 10:3–5, 12; Ps. 1:14; 1 Cor. 11:25–26; Acts 2:42, 46; Song of Sol. 5:1–6; Eccl. 5:1–6; Ps. 73:1–2; Ps. 42:5, 8; Ps. 43:3–5; 2 Chron. 30:18–19; Isa. 1:16, 18; 2 Cor. 7:11; 1 Chron. 15:12–14.

Q. 176. Wherein do the Sacraments of Baptism and the Lord's Supper agree?
A. The Sacraments of Baptism and the Lord's Supper agree, in that the author of both is God; the spiritual part of both is Christ and his benefits; both are seals of the same covenant, are to be dispensed by ministers of the gospel and by none other; and to be continued in the Church of Christ until his second coming. Matt. 28:19; 1 Cor. 11:23; Rom. 6:3–4; 1 Cor. 10:16; Rom. 4:11; Col. 2:12; Matt. 26:27–28; John 1:33; Matt. 28:19; 1 Cor. 11:23; 1 Cor. 4:1; Heb. 5:4; Matt. 28: 19–20; 1 Cor. 11:26.

Q. 177. Wherein do the Sacraments of Baptism and the Lord's Supper differ?
A. The Sacraments of Baptism and the Lord's Supper differ, in that Baptism is to be administered but once, with water, to be a sign and seal of our regeneration and ingrafting into Christ, and that even to infants; whereas the Lord's Supper is to be administered often, in the elements of bread and wine, to represent and exhibit Christ as spiritual nourishment to the soul, and to confirm our continuance and growth in him, and that only to such as are of years and ability to examine themselves. Matt. 3:11; Titus 3:5; Gal. 3:27; Gen. 17:7, 9; Acts 2:38–39; 1 Cor. 7:14; 1 Cor. 11:23–26; 1 Cor. 10:16; 1 Cor. 11:28–29.

Q. 178. What is prayer?
A. Prayer is an offering up of our desires unto God, in the name of Christ, by the help of his Spirit; with confession of our sins, and thankful acknowledgment of his mercies. Ps. 62:8; John 16:23; Rom. 8:26; Ps. 32:5–6; Dan. 9:4; Phil. 4:6.

Q. 179. Are we to pray unto God only?
A. God only being able to search the hearts, hear the requests, pardon the sins, and fulfill the desires of all; and only to be believed in, and worshiped with religious worship; prayer, which is a special part thereof, is to be made by all to him alone, and to none other. 1 Kings 8:39; Acts 1:24; Rom. 8:27; Ps. 65:2; Mic. 7:18; Ps. 145:18–19; Rom. 10:14; Matt. 4:10; 1 Cor. 1:2; Ps. 50:15; Rom. 10:14.

Q. 180. What is it to pray in the name of Christ?
A. To pray in the name of Christ is, in obedience to his command, and in confidence on his promises, to ask mercy for his sake; not by bare mentioning of his name, but by drawing our encouragement to pray, and our boldness, strength, and hope of acceptance in prayer, from Christ and his mediation. John 14:13–14; John 16:24; Dan. 9:17; Matt. 7:21; Heb. 4:14–16; 1 John 5:13–15.

Q. 181. Why are we to pray in the name of Christ?
A. The sinfulness of man, and his distance from God by reason thereof, being so great, as that we can have no access into his presence without a mediator; and there being none in heaven

or earth appointed to, or fit for, that glorious work but Christ alone, we are to pray in no other name but his only. John 14:6; Isa. 59:2; Eph. 3:12; John 6:27; Heb. 7:25–27; 1 Tim. 2:5; Col. 3: 17; Heb. 13:15.

Q. 182. How doth the Spirit help us to pray?
A. We not knowing what to pray for as we ought, the Spirit helpeth our infirmities, by enabling us to understand both for whom, and what, and how prayer is to be made; and by working and quickening in our hearts (although not in all persons, nor at all times, in the same measure) those apprehensions, affections, and graces, which are requisite for the right performance of that duty. Rom. 8:26–27; Ps. 10:17; Zech. 12:10.

Q. 183. For whom are we to pray?
A. We are to pray for the whole church of Christ upon earth; for magistrates and ministers; for ourselves, our brethren, yea, our enemies; and for all sorts of men living, or that shall live hereafter; but not for the dead, nor for those that are known to have sinned the sin unto death. Eph. 6:18; Ps. 28:9; 1 Tim. 2:1–2; Col. 4:3; Gen. 32:11; Jas. 5:16; Matt. 5: 44; 1 Tim. 2:1–2; John 17:20; 2 Sam. 7:29; 2 Sam. 12:21–23; 1 John 5:16.

Q. 184. For what things are we to pray?
A. We are to pray for all things tending to the glory of God, the welfare of the church, our own or others' good; but not for any thing that is unlawful. Matt. 6:9; Ps. 51:18; Ps. 122:6; Matt. 7:11; Ps. 125:4; 1 John 5:14.

Q. 185. How are we to pray?
A. We are to pray with an awful apprehension of the majesty of God, and deep sense of our unworthiness, necessities, and sins; with penitent, thankful, and enlarged hearts; with understanding, faith, sincerity, fervency, love, and perseverance, waiting upon him, with humble submission to his will. Eccl. 5:1; Gen. 18:27: Gen. 32:10; Luke 15:17–19; Luke 18:13–14; Ps. 51:17; Phil. 4:6; 1 Sam. 1:15; 1 Sam. 2:1; 1 Cor. 14:15; Mark 11:24; Jas. 1:6; Ps. 145:18; Ps. 17:1; Jas. 5:16; 1 Tim. 2:8; Eph. 6:18; Mic. 7:7; Matt. 26:39.

Q. 186. What rule hath God given for our direction in the duty of prayer?
A. The whole Word of God is of use to direct us in the duty of prayer; but the special rule of direction is that form of prayer which our Saviour Christ taught his disciples, commonly called, The Lord's Prayer. 1 John 5:14; Matt. 6:9–13; Luke 11:2–4.

Q. 187. How is the Lord's Prayer to be used?
A. The Lord's Prayer is not only for direction, as a pattern, according to which we are to make other prayers; but may also be used as a prayer, so that it be done with understanding, faith, reverence, and other graces necessary to the right performance of the duty of prayer. Matt. 6:9; Luke 11:2.

Q. 188. Of how many parts doth the Lord's prayer consist?
A. The Lord's prayer consists of three parts; a preface, petitions, and a conclusion.

Q. 189. What doth the preface of the Lord's prayer teach us?
A. The preface of the Lord's prayer (contained in these words, "Our Father which art in heaven,") teacheth us, when we pray, to draw near to God with confidence of his fatherly goodness, and our interest therein; with reverence, and all other child–like dispositions, heavenly affections, and due apprehensions of his sovereign power, majesty, and gracious condescension: as also, to pray with and for others. Matt. 6:9; Luke 11:13; Rom. 8:15; Isa. 64:9; Ps. 123:1; Lam. 3:41; Isa. 63:15–16; Neh. 1:4–6; Acts 12:5.

Q. 190. What do we pray for in the first petition?
A. In the first petition (which is, "Hallowed be thy name,") acknowledging the utter inability and indisposition that is in ourselves and all men to honor God aright, we pray, that God would by his grace enable and include us and others to know, to acknowledge, and highly to esteem him, his titles, attributes, ordinances, word, works, and whatsoever he is pleased to make himself

known by; and to glorify him in thought, word, and deed: that he would prevent and remove atheism, ignorance, idolatry, profaneness, and whatsoever is dishonorable to him; and by his overruling providence, direct and dispose of all things to his own glory. Matt. 6:9; 2 Cor. 3:5; Ps. 51:15: Ps. 67:2–3; Ps. 83:18; Ps. 86:10–13, 15; 2 Thess. 3:1; Ps. 147:19–20; Ps. 138:1–3; 2 Cor. 2:14–15; Ps. 145:1–21: Ps. 8; Ps. 103:1; Ps. 19:14; Phil. 1:9, 11; Ps. 67:1–4; Eph. 1:17–18; Ps. 97:7; Ps. 74:18, 22–23; 2 Kings 19:15–16; 2 Chron. 20:6, 10–12; Ps. 83:1–18; Ps. 140:4–8.

Q. 191. What do we pray for in the second petition?
A. In the second petition, (which is, "thy Kingdom come,") acknowledging ourselves and all mankind to be by nature under the dominion of sin and Satan, we pray that the kingdom of sin and Satan may be destroyed, the gospel propagated throughout the world, the Jews called, the fulness of the Gentiles brought in; the church furnished with all gospel officers and ordinances, purged from corruption, countenanced and maintained by the civil magistrates; that the ordinances of Christ may be purely dispensed, and made effectual to the converting of those that are yet in their sins, and the confirming, comforting, and building up those that are already converted: that Christ would rule in our hearts here, and hasten the time of his second coming, and our reigning with him for ever: and that he would be pleased so to exercise the kingdom of his power in all the world, as may best conduce to these ends. Matt. 6:10; Eph. 2:2–3; Ps. 68:1, 18; Rev. 12:10–11; 2 Thess. 3:1; Rom. 10:1; John 17:9, 20; Rom. 11:25–26; Ps. 67:1–7; Matt. 9:38; 2 Thess. 3:1; Mal. 1:11; Zeph. 3: 9; 1 Tim. 2:1–2; Acts 4:29–30; Eph. 3:14–20; Rev. 22:20; Isa. 64:1–2; Rev. 4:8–11; Eph. 6:18–20; Rom. 15:29–30, 32; 2 Thess. 1:11; 2 Thess. 2:16–17.

Q. 192. What do we pray for in the third petition?
A. In the third petition, (which is, "Thy will be done in earth, as it is in heaven,") acknowledging that by nature we and all men are not only utterly unable and unwilling to know and do the will of God, but prone to rebel against his word, to repine and murmur against his providence, and wholly inclined to do the will of the flesh, and of the devil: we pray, that God would by his Spirit take away from ourselves and others all blindness, weakness, indisposedness, and perverseness of heart; and by his grace make us able and willing to know, do, and submit to his will in all things, with the like humility, cheerfulness, faithfulness, diligence, zeal, sincerity, and constancy, as the angels do in heaven. Matt. 6:10; Rom. 7:18; Job 21:14; 1 Cor. 2:14; Rom. 8:7; Ex. 17:7; Num. 14:2; Eph. 2:2; Eph. 1:17–18; Eph. 3:16; Matt. 26:40–41; Jer. 31:18–19; Ps. 119:1, 8, 35– 36; Acts 21:14; Mic. 6:8; Ps. 100:2; Job 1:21; 2 Sam. 15:25–26; Isa. 38:3; Ps. 119: 4–5; Rom. 12:11; Ps. 119:80; Ps. 119:112; Isa. 6:2–3; Ps. 103:20–21; Matt. 18:10.

Q. 193. What do we pray for in the fourth petition?
A. In the fourth petition, (which is, "Give us this day our daily bread,") acknowledging, that in Adam, and by our own sin, we have forfeited our right to all the outward blessings of this life, and deserve to be wholly deprived of them by God, and to have them cursed to us in the use of them; and that neither they of themselves are able to sustain us, nor we to merit, or by our own industry to procure them; but prone to desire, get, and use them unlawfully: we pray for ourselves and others, that both they and we, waiting upon the providence of God from day to day in the use of lawful means, may of his free gift, and as to his fatherly wisdom shall seem best, enjoy a competent portion of them, and have the same continued and blessed unto us in our holy and comfortable use of them, and contentment in them; and be kept from all things that are contrary to our temporal support and comfort. Matt. 6:11; Gen. 2:17; Gen. 3:17; Rom. 8:20–22; Jer. 5:25; Deut. 28:15–68; Deut. 8:3; Gen. 32:10; Deut. 8:17–18; Jer. 6:13; Mark 7:21–22; Hos. 12:7; Jas. 4: 3; Gen. 43:12–14; Gen. 28:20; Eph. 4:28; 2 Thess. 3:11–12; Phil. 4:6; 1 Tim. 4: 3–5; 1 Tim. 6:6–8; Prov. 30:8–9.

Q. 194. What do we pray for in the fifth petition?
A. In the fifth petition, (which is, "Forgive us our debts, as we forgive our debtors,") acknowledging, that we and all others are guilty both of original and actual sin, and thereby become debtors to the justice of God; and that neither we, nor any other creature, can make the least satisfaction of that debt: we pray for ourselves and others, that God of his free grace would, through the obedience and satisfaction of Christ, apprehended and applied by faith, acquit us both from the guilt and punishment of sin, accept us in his Beloved, continue his favour and grace to us, pardon our daily failings, and fill us with peace and joy, in giving us daily more and

more assurance of forgiveness; which we are the rather emboldened to ask, and encouraged to expect, when we have this testimony in ourselves, that we from the heart forgive others their offences. Matt. 6:12; Rom. 3:9–22; Matt. 18:24–25; Ps. 130:3–4; Rom. 3:24–26; Heb. 9:22; Eph. 1:6–7; 2 Peter 1:2; Hos. 14:2; Jer. 14:7; Rom. 15:13; Ps. 51:7–10, 12; Luke 11: 4; Matt. 6:14–15; Matt. 18:35.

Q. 195. What do we pray for in the sixth petition?
A. In the sixth petition, (which is, "And lead us not into temptation, but deliver us from evil,") acknowledging that the most wise, righteous, and gracious God, for divers holy and just ends, may so order things that we may be assaulted, foiled, and for a time led captive by temptations; that Satan, the world, and the flesh, are ready powerfully to draw us aside and ensnare us; and that we, even after the pardon of our sins, by reason of our corruption, weakness, and want of watchfulness, are not only subject to be tempted, and forward to expose ourselves unto temptations; but also of ourselves unable and unwilling to resist them, to recover out of them, and to improve them; and worthy to be left under the power of them: we pray, that God would so overrule the world and all in it, subdue the flesh, and restrain Satan, order all things, bestow and bless all means of grace, and quicken us to watchfulness in the use of them, that we and all his people may by his providence be kept from being tempted to sin; or, if tempted, that by his Spirit we may be powerfully supported and enabled to stand in the hour of temptation; or when fallen, raised again and recovered out of it, and have a sanctified use and improvement thereof: that our sanctification and salvation may be perfected, Satan trodden under our feet, and we fully freed from sin, temptation, and all evil for ever. Matt. 6:13; 2 Chron. 32:31; 1 Chron. 21:1; Luke 21:34; Mark 4:19; Jas. 1:14; Gal. 5:17; Matt. 26:41; Matt. 26:69–72; Gal. 2:11–14; 2 Chron. 18:3; 2 Chron. 19: 2; Rom. 7:23–24; 1 Chron. 21:1–4; 2 Chron. 16:7–10; Ps. 81:11–12; John 17:15; Ps. 51:10; Ps. 119:133; 2 Cor. 12:7–8; 1 Cor. 10:12–13; Heb. 13:20–21; Matt. 26: 41; Ps. 19:13; Eph. 3:14–17; 1 Thess. 3:13; Jude 1:24; Ps. 51:12; 1 Peter 5:8–10; 2 Cor. 13:7, 9; Rom. 16:20; Zech. 3:2; Luke 12:31–32; John 17:15; 1 Thess. 5:23.

Q. 196. What doth the conclusion of the Lord's Prayer teach us?
A. The conclusion of the Lord's Prayer, (which is, "For thine is the kingdom, and the power, and the glory, for ever. Amen.") teacheth us to enforce our petitions with arguments, which are to be taken, not from any worthiness in ourselves, or in any other creature, but from God: and with our prayers to join praises, ascribing to God alone eternal sovereignty, omnipotency, and glorious excellency; in regard whereof, as he is able and willing to help us, so we by faith are emboldened to plead with him that he would, and quietly to rely upon him, that he will fulfill our requests. And, to testify this our desire and assurance, we say, Amen. Matt. 6:13; Rom. 15:30; Dan. 9:4, 7–9, 16–19; Phil. 4:6; 1 Chron. 29:10–13; Eph. 3:20–21; Luke 11:13; 2 Chron. 20:6, 11; 2 Chron. 14:11; 1 Cor. 14:16; Rev. 22:20– 21.

BUT HIS

DELIGHT

IS IN

The Law

OF

THE LORD

AND IN

His Law

DOTH HE

MEDITATE

Day

AND *Night*

PSALM 1:2

Read

THE BIBLE

IN A YEAR

All
SCRIPTURE
IS GIVEN BY INSPIRATION
of God
AND IS PROFITABLE FOR
DOCTRINE
FOR
Reproof
FOR
CORRECTION
FOR
Instruction
IN RIGHTEOUSNESS

2 TIMOTHY 3:16

READ THE BIBLE *in a year*

ROBERT MURRAY M'CHEYNE'S READING PLAN

Robert Murray M`Cheyne (1813–1843) wrote his famous *Calendar for Reading Though the Word of God in a Year* in 1842 for his own church at St. Peter's in Dundee, Scotland. Reprinted below, this calendar suggests reading four portions (usually four chapters) of Scripture each day—two for family worship (morning and evening), and two for private reading (morning and evening). In the course of a year, the entire Bible will be read at least once, with the Psalms and New Testament being read twice. The center column contains the day of the month. The first two columns contain the chapters to be read in the family. The two last columns contain the portions to be read privately.

M`Cheyne's goal was that his entire congregation would be reading the same portions each day so that they could converse more freely together about what they were reading, and that the pastor might also make reference to, or expound upon, these chapters in his preaching. He also hoped that families would discuss their private and family worship readings at mealtimes. In this way, he wrote, "the sweet bond of Christian love and unity will be strengthened. We shall often be led to think of those dear brothers and sisters in the Lord, who agree to join with us in reading these portions. We shall more often be led to agree on earth, touching something we shall ask of God. We shall pray over the same promises, mourn over the same confessions, praise God in the same songs, and be nourished by the same words of eternal life."

JANUARY

Family Worship		Date	Private Reading	
Genesis 1	Matthew 1	1st	Ezra 1	Acts 1
Genesis 2	Matthew 2	2nd	Ezra 2	Acts 2
Genesis 3	Matthew 3	3rd	Ezra 3	Acts 3
Genesis 4	Matthew 4	4th	Ezra 4	Acts 4
Genesis 5	Matthew 5	5th	Ezra 5	Acts 5
Genesis 6	Matthew 6	6th	Ezra 6	Acts 6
Genesis 7	Matthew 7	7th	Ezra 7	Acts 7
Genesis 8	Matthew 8	8th	Ezra 8	Acts 8
Genesis 9-10	Matthew 9	9th	Ezra 9	Acts 9
Genesis 11	Matthew 10	10th	Ezra 10	Acts 10
Genesis 12	Matthew 11	11th	Nehemiah 1	Acts 11
Genesis 13	Matthew 12	12th	Nehemiah 2	Acts 12
Genesis 14	Matthew 13	13th	Nehemiah 3	Acts 13
Genesis 15	Matthew 14	14th	Nehemiah 4	Acts 14
Genesis 16	Matthew 15	15th	Nehemiah 5	Acts 15
Genesis 17	Matthew 16	16th	Nehemiah 6	Acts 16
Genesis 18	Matthew 17	17th	Nehemiah 7	Acts 17
Genesis 19	Matthew 18	18th	Nehemiah 8	Acts 18
Genesis 20	Matthew 19	19th	Nehemiah 9	Acts 19
Genesis 21	Matthew 20	20th	Nehemiah 10	Acts 20
Genesis 22	Matthew 21	21st	Nehemiah 11	Acts 21
Genesis 23	Matthew 22	22nd	Nehemiah 12	Acts 22

Genesis 24	Matthew 23	23rd	Nehemiah 13	Acts 23
Genesis 25	Matthew 24	24th	Esther 1	Acts 24
Genesis 26	Matthew 25	25th	Esther 2	Acts 25
Genesis 27	Matthew 26	26th	Esther 3	Acts 26
Genesis 28	Matthew 27	27th	Esther 4	Acts 27
Genesis 29	Matthew 28	28th	Esther 5	Acts 28
Genesis 30	Mark 1	29th	Esther 6	Romans 1
Genesis 31	Mark 2	30th	Esther 7	Romans 2
Genesis 32	Mark 3	31st	Esther 8	Romans 3

FEBRUARY

Family Worship		Date	Private Reading	
Genesis 33	Mark 4	1st	Esther 9-10	Romans 4
Genesis 34	Mark 5	2nd	Job 1	Romans 5
Genesis 35-36	Mark 6	3rd	Job 2	Romans 6
Genesis 37	Mark 7	4th	Job 3	Romans 7
Genesis 38	Mark 8	5th	Job 4	Romans 8
Genesis 39	Mark 9	6th	Job 5	Romans 9
Genesis 40	Mark 10	7th	Job 6	Romans 10
Genesis 41	Mark 11	8th	Job 7	Romans 11
Genesis 42	Mark 12	9th	Job 8	Romans 12
Genesis 43	Mark 13	10th	Job 9	Romans 13
Genesis 44	Mark 14	11th	Job 10	Romans 14
Genesis 45	Mark 15	12th	Job 11	Romans 15
Genesis 46	Mark 16	13th	Job 12	Romans 16
Genesis 47	Luke 1:1-38	14th	Job 13	1 Corinthians 1
Genesis 48	Luke 1:39ff	15th	Job 14	1 Corinthians 2
Genesis 49	Luke 2	16th	Job 15	1 Corinthians 3
Genesis 50	Luke 3	17th	Job 16-17	1 Corinthians 4
Exodus 1	Luke 4	18th	Job 18	1 Corinthians 5
Exodus 2	Luke 5	19th	Job 19	1 Corinthians 6
Exodus 3	Luke 6	20th	Job 20	1 Corinthians 7
Exodus 4	Luke 7	21st	Job 21	1 Corinthians 8
Exodus 5	Luke 8	22nd	Job 22	1 Corinthians 9
Exodus 6	Luke 9	23rd	Job 23	1 Corinthians 10
Exodus 7	Luke 10	24th	Job 24	1 Corinthians 11
Exodus 8	Luke 11	25th	Job 25-26	1 Corinthians 12
Exodus 9	Luke 12	26th	Job 27	1 Corinthians 13
Exodus 10	Luke 13	27th	Job 28	1 Corinthians 14
Exodus 11-12:21	Luke 14	28th	Job 29	1 Corinthians 15

MARCH

Family Worship		Date	Private Reading	
Exodus 12:22ff	Luke 15	1st	Job 30	1 Corinthians 16
Exodus 13	Luke 16	2nd	Job 31	2 Corinthians 1

Exodus 14	Luke 17	3rd	Job 32	2 Corinthians 2
Exodus 15	Luke 18	4th	Job 33	2 Corinthians 3
Exodus 16	Luke 19	5th	Job 34	2 Corinthians 4
Exodus 17	Luke 20	6th	Job 35	2 Corinthians 5
Exodus 18	Luke 21	7th	Job 36	2 Corinthians 6
Exodus 19	Luke 22	8th	Job 37	2 Corinthians 7
Exodus 20	Luke 23	9th	Job 38	2 Corinthians 8
Exodus 21	Luke 24	10th	Job 39	2 Corinthians 9
Exodus 22	John 1	11th	Job 40	2 Corinthians 10
Exodus 23	John 2	12th	Job 41	2 Corinthians 11
Exodus 24	John 3	13th	Job 42	2 Corinthians 12
Exodus 25	John 4	14th	Proverbs 1	2 Corinthians 13
Exodus 26	John 5	15th	Proverbs 2	Galatians 1
Exodus 27	John 6	16th	Proverbs 3	Galatians 2
Exodus 28	John 7	17th	Proverbs 4	Galatians 3
Exodus 29	John 8	18th	Proverbs 5	Galatians 4
Exodus 30	John 9	19th	Proverbs 6	Galatians 5
Exodus 31	John 10	20th	Proverbs 7	Galatians 6
Exodus 32	John 11	21st	Proverbs 8	Ephesians 1
Exodus 33	John 12	22nd	Proverbs 9	Ephesians 2
Exodus 34	John 13	23rd	Proverbs 10	Ephesians 3
Exodus 35	John 14	24th	Proverbs 11	Ephesians 4
Exodus 36	John 15	25th	Proverbs 12	Ephesians 5
Exodus 37	John 16	26th	Proverbs 13	Ephesians 6
Exodus 38	John 17	27th	Proverbs 14	Philippians 1
Exodus 39	John 18	28th	Proverbs 15	Philippians 2
Exodus 40	John 19	29th	Proverbs 16	Philippians 3
Leviticus 1	John 20	30th	Proverbs 17	Philippians 4
Leviticus 2-3	John 21	31st	Proverbs 18	Colossians 1

APRIL

Family Worship		Date	Private Reading	
Leviticus 4	Psalms 1-2	1st	Proverbs 19	Colossians 2
Leviticus 5	Psalms 3-4	2nd	Proverbs 20	Colossians 3
Leviticus 6	Psalms 5-6	3rd	Proverbs 21	Colossians 4
Leviticus 7	Psalms 7-8	4th	Proverbs 22	1 Thessalonians 1
Leviticus 8	Psalm 9	5th	Proverbs 23	1 Thessalonians 2
Leviticus 9	Psalm 10	6th	Proverbs 24	1 Thessalonians 3
Leviticus 10	Psalms 11-12	7th	Proverbs 25	1 Thessalonians 4
Leviticus 11-12	Psalms 13-14	8th	Proverbs 26	1 Thessalonians 5
Leviticus 13	Psalms 15-16	9th	Proverbs 27	2 Thessalonians 1
Leviticus 14	Psalm 17	10th	Proverbs 28	2 Thessalonians 2
Leviticus 15	Psalm 18	11th	Proverbs 29	2 Thessalonians 3
Leviticus 16	Psalm 19	12th	Proverbs 30	1 Timothy 1
Leviticus 17	Psalms 20-21	13th	Proverbs 31	1 Timothy 2
Leviticus 18	Psalm 22	14th	Ecclesiastes 1	1 Timothy 3
Leviticus 19	Psalms 23-24	15th	Ecclesiastes 2	1 Timothy 4
Leviticus 20	Psalm 25	16th	Ecclesiastes 3	1 Timothy 5

Leviticus 21	Psalms 26-27	17th	Ecclesiastes 4	1 Timothy 6
Leviticus 22	Psalms 28-29	18th	Ecclesiastes 5	2 Timothy 1
Leviticus 23	Psalm 30	19th	Ecclesiastes 6	2 Timothy 2
Leviticus 24	Psalm 31	20th	Ecclesiastes 7	2 Timothy 3
Leviticus 25	Psalm 32	21st	Ecclesiastes 8	2 Timothy 4
Leviticus 26	Psalm 33	22nd	Ecclesiastes 9	Titus 1
Leviticus 27	Psalm 34	23rd	Ecclesiastes 10	Titus 2
Numbers 1	Psalm 35	24th	Ecclesiastes 11	Titus 3
Numbers 2	Psalm 36	25th	Ecclesiastes 12	Philemon 1
Numbers 3	Psalm 37	26th	Song of Solomon 1	Hebrews 1
Numbers 4	Psalm 38	27th	Song of Solomon 2	Hebrews 2
Numbers 5	Psalm 39	28th	Song of Solomon 3	Hebrews 3
Numbers 6	Psalms 40-41	29th	Song of Solomon 4	Hebrews 4
Numbers 7	Psalms 42-43	30th	Song of Solomon 5	Hebrews 5

MAY

Family Worship		Date	Private Reading	
Numbers 8	Psalm 44	1st	Song of Solomon 6	Hebrews 6
Numbers 9	Psalm 45	2nd	Song of Solomon 7	Hebrews 7
Numbers 10	Psalms 46-47	3rd	Song of Solomon 8	Hebrews 8
Numbers 11	Psalm 48	4th	Isaiah 1	Hebrews 9
Numbers 12-13	Psalm 49	5th	Isaiah 2	Hebrews 10
Numbers 14	Psalm 50	6th	Isaiah 3-4	Hebrews 11
Numbers 15	Psalm 51	7th	Isaiah 5	Hebrews 12
Numbers 16	Psalms 52-54	8th	Isaiah 6	Hebrews 13
Numbers 17-18	Psalm 55	9th	Isaiah 7	James 1
Numbers 19	Psalms 56-57	10th	Isaiah 8-9:7	James 2
Numbers 20	Psalms 58-59	11th	Isaiah 9:8-10:4	James 3
Numbers 21	Psalms 60-61	12th	Isaiah 10:5ff	James 4
Numbers 22	Psalms 62-63	13th	Isaiah 11-12	James 5
Numbers 23	Psalms 64-65	14th	Isaiah 13	1 Peter 1
Numbers 24	Psalms 66-67	15th	Isaiah 14	1 Peter 2
Numbers 25	Psalm 68	16th	Isaiah 15	1 Peter 3
Numbers 26	Psalm 69	17th	Isaiah 16	1 Peter 4
Numbers 27	Psalms 70-71	18th	Isaiah 17-18	1 Peter 5
Numbers 28	Psalm 72	19th	Isaiah 19-20	2 Peter 1
Numbers 29	Psalm 73	20th	Isaiah 21	2 Peter 2
Numbers 30	Psalm 74	21st	Isaiah 22	2 Peter 3
Numbers 31	Psalms 75-76	22nd	Isaiah 23	1 John 1
Numbers 32	Psalm 77	23rd	Isaiah 24	1 John 2
Numbers 33	Psalm 78:1-37	24th	Isaiah 25	1 John 3
Numbers 34	Psalm 78:38ff	25th	Isaiah 26	1 John 4
Numbers 35	Psalm 79	26th	Isaiah 27	1 John 5
Numbers 36	Psalm 80	27th	Isaiah 28	2 John 1
Deuteronomy 1	Psalms 81-82	28th	Isaiah 29	3 John 1
Deuteronomy 2	Psalms 83-84	29th	Isaiah 30	Jude 1
Deuteronomy 3	Psalm 85	30th	Isaiah 31	Revelation 1
Deuteronomy 4	Psalms 86-87	31st	Isaiah 32	Revelation 2

JUNE

Family Worship		Date	Private Reading	
Deuteronomy 5	Psalm 88	1st	Isaiah 33	Revelation 3
Deuteronomy 6	Psalm 89	2nd	Isaiah 34	Revelation 4
Deuteronomy 7	Psalm 90	3rd	Isaiah 35	Revelation 5
Deuteronomy 8	Psalm 91	4th	Isaiah 36	Revelation 6
Deuteronomy 9	Psalms 92-93	5th	Isaiah 37	Revelation 7
Deuteronomy 10	Psalm 94	6th	Isaiah 38	Revelation 8
Deuteronomy 11	Psalms 95-96	7th	Isaiah 39	Revelation 9
Deuteronomy 12	Psalms 97-98	8th	Isaiah 40	Revelation 10
Deuteronomy 13-14	Psalms 99-101	9th	Isaiah 41	Revelation 11
Deuteronomy 15	Psalm 102	10th	Isaiah 42	Revelation 12
Deuteronomy 16	Psalm 103	11th	Isaiah 43	Revelation 13
Deuteronomy 17	Psalm 104	12th	Isaiah 44	Revelation 14
Deuteronomy 18	Psalm 105	13th	Isaiah 45	Revelation 15
Deuteronomy 19	Psalm 106	14th	Isaiah 46	Revelation 16
Deuteronomy 20	Psalm 107	15th	Isaiah 47	Revelation 17
Deuteronomy 21	Psalms 108-109	16th	Isaiah 48	Revelation 18
Deuteronomy 22	Psalms 110-111	17th	Isaiah 49	Revelation 19
Deuteronomy 23	Psalms 112-113	18th	Isaiah 50	Revelation 20
Deuteronomy 24	Psalms 114-115	19th	Isaiah 51	Revelation 21
Deuteronomy 25	Psalm 116	20th	Isaiah 52	Revelation 22
Deuteronomy 26	Psalms 117-118	21st	Isaiah 53	Matthew 1
Deuteronomy 27-28:19	Psalm 119:1-24	22nd	Isaiah 54	Matthew 2
Deuteronomy 28:20ff	Psalm 119:25-48	23rd	Isaiah 55	Matthew 3
Deuteronomy 29	Psalm 119:49-72	24th	Isaiah 56	Matthew 4
Deuteronomy 30	Psalm 119:73-96	25th	Isaiah 57	Matthew 5
Deuteronomy 31	Psalm 119:97-120	26th	Isaiah 58	Matthew 6
Deuteronomy 32	Psalm 119:121-144	27th	Isaiah 59	Matthew 7
Deuteronomy 33-34	Psalm 119:145-176	28th	Isaiah 60	Matthew 8
Joshua 1	Psalms 120-122	29th	Isaiah 61	Matthew 9
Joshua 2	Psalms 123-125	30th	Isaiah 62	Matthew 10

JULY

Family Worship		Date	Private Reading	
Joshua 3	Psalms 126-128	1st	Isaiah 63	Matthew 11
Joshua 4	Psalms 129-131	2nd	Isaiah 64	Matthew 12
Joshua 5-6:5	Psalms 132-134	3rd	Isaiah 65	Matthew 13
Joshua 6:6ff	Psalms 135-136	4th	Isaiah 66	Matthew 14
Joshua 7	Psalms 137-138	5th	Jeremiah 1	Matthew 15
Joshua 8	Psalm 139	6th	Jeremiah 2	Matthew 16
Joshua 9	Psalms 140-141	7th	Jeremiah 3	Matthew 17
Joshua 10	Psalms 142-143	8th	Jeremiah 4	Matthew 18
Joshua 11	Psalm 144	9th	Jeremiah 5	Matthew 19
Joshua 12-13	Psalm 145	10th	Jeremiah 6	Matthew 20
Joshua 14-15	Psalms 146-147	11th	Jeremiah 7	Matthew 21

Joshua 16-17	Psalm 148	12th	Jeremiah 8	Matthew 22
Joshua 18-19	Psalms 149-150	13th	Jeremiah 9	Matthew 23
Joshua 20-21	Acts 1	14th	Jeremiah 10	Matthew 24
Joshua 22	Acts 2	15th	Jeremiah 11	Matthew 25
Joshua 23	Acts 3	16th	Jeremiah 12	Matthew 26
Joshua 24	Acts 4	17th	Jeremiah 13	Matthew 27
Judges 1	Acts 5	18th	Jeremiah 14	Matthew 28
Judges 2	Acts 6	19th	Jeremiah 15	Mark 1
Judges 3	Acts 7	20th	Jeremiah 16	Mark 2
Judges 4	Acts 8	21st	Jeremiah 17	Mark 3
Judges 5	Acts 9	22nd	Jeremiah 18	Mark 4
Judges 6	Acts 10	23rd	Jeremiah 19	Mark 5
Judges 7	Acts 11	24th	Jeremiah 20	Mark 6
Judges 8	Acts 12	25th	Jeremiah 21	Mark 7
Judges 9	Acts 13	26th	Jeremiah 22	Mark 8
Judges 10-11:11	Acts 14	27th	Jeremiah 23	Mark 9
Judges 11:12ff	Acts 15	28th	Jeremiah 24	Mark 10
Judges 12	Acts 16	29th	Jeremiah 25	Mark 11
Judges 13	Acts 17	30th	Jeremiah 26	Mark 12
Judges 14	Acts 18	31st	Jeremiah 27	Mark 13

AUGUST

Family Worship		Date	Private Reading	
Judges 15	Acts 19	1st	Jeremiah 28	Mark 14
Judges 16	Acts 20	2nd	Jeremiah 29	Mark 15
Judges 17	Acts 21	3rd	Jeremiah 30-31	Mark 16
Judges 18	Acts 22	4th	Jeremiah 32	Psalms 1-2
Judges 19	Acts 23	5th	Jeremiah 33	Psalms 3-4
Judges 20	Acts 24	6th	Jeremiah 34	Psalms 5-6
Judges 21	Acts 25	7th	Jeremiah 35	Psalms 7-8
Ruth 1	Acts 26	8th	Jeremiah 36 & 45	Psalm 9
Ruth 2	Acts 27	9th	Jeremiah 37	Psalm 10
Ruth 3-4	Acts 28	10th	Jeremiah 38	Psalms 11-12
1 Samuel 1	Romans 1	11th	Jeremiah 39	Psalms 13-14
1 Samuel 2	Romans 2	12th	Jeremiah 40	Psalms 15-16
1 Samuel 3	Romans 3	13th	Jeremiah 41	Psalm 17
1 Samuel 4	Romans 4	14th	Jeremiah 42	Psalm 18
1 Samuel 5-6	Romans 5	15th	Jeremiah 43	Psalm 19
1 Samuel 7-8	Romans 6	16th	Jeremiah 44	Psalms 20-21
1 Samuel 9	Romans 7	17th	Jeremiah 46	Psalm 22
1 Samuel 10	Romans 8	18th	Jeremiah 47	Psalms 23-24
1 Samuel 11	Romans 9	19th	Jeremiah 48	Psalm 25
1 Samuel 12	Romans 10	20th	Jeremiah 49	Psalms 26-27
1 Samuel 13	Romans 11	21st	Jeremiah 50	Psalms 28-29
1 Samuel 14	Romans 12	22nd	Jeremiah 51	Psalm 30
1 Samuel 15	Romans 13	23rd	Jeremiah 52	Psalm 31
1 Samuel 16	Romans 14	24th	Lamentations 1	Psalm 32
1 Samuel 17	Romans 15	25th	Lamentations 2	Psalm 33

1 Samuel 18	Romans 16	26th	Lamentations 3	Psalm 34
1 Samuel 19	1 Corinthians 1	27th	Lamentations 4	Psalm 35
1 Samuel 20	1 Corinthians 2	28th	Lamentations 5	Psalm 36
1 Samuel 21-22	1 Corinthians 3	29th	Ezekiel 1	Psalm 37
1 Samuel 23	1 Corinthians 4	30th	Ezekiel 2	Psalm 38
1 Samuel 24	1 Corinthians 5	31st	Ezekiel 3	Psalm 39

SEPTEMBER

Family Worship		Date	Private Reading	
1 Samuel 25	1 Corinthians 6	1st	Ezekiel 4	Psalms 40-41
1 Samuel 26	1 Corinthians 7	2nd	Ezekiel 5	Psalms 42-43
1 Samuel 27	1 Corinthians 8	3rd	Ezekiel 6	Psalm 44
1 Samuel 28	1 Corinthians 9	4th	Ezekiel 7	Psalm 45
1 Samuel 29-30	1 Corinthians 10	5th	Ezekiel 8	Psalms 46-47
1 Samuel 31	1 Corinthians 11	6th	Ezekiel 9	Psalm 48
2 Samuel 1	1 Corinthians 12	7th	Ezekiel 10	Psalm 49
2 Samuel 2	1 Corinthians 13	8th	Ezekiel 11	Psalm 50
2 Samuel 3	1 Corinthians 14	9th	Ezekiel 12	Psalm 51
2 Samuel 4-5	1 Corinthians 15	10th	Ezekiel 13	Psalms 52-54
2 Samuel 6	1 Corinthians 16	11th	Ezekiel 14	Psalm 55
2 Samuel 7	2 Corinthians 1	12th	Ezekiel 15	Psalms 56-57
2 Samuel 8-9	2 Corinthians 2	13th	Ezekiel 16	Psalms 58-59
2 Samuel 10	2 Corinthians 3	14th	Ezekiel 17	Psalms 60-61
2 Samuel 11	2 Corinthians 4	15th	Ezekiel 18	Psalms 62-63
2 Samuel 12	2 Corinthians 5	16th	Ezekiel 19	Psalms 64-65
2 Samuel 13	2 Corinthians 6	17th	Ezekiel 20	Psalms 66-67
2 Samuel 14	2 Corinthians 7	18th	Ezekiel 21	Psalm 68
2 Samuel 15	2 Corinthians 8	19th	Ezekiel 22	Psalm 69
2 Samuel 16	2 Corinthians 9	20th	Ezekiel 23	Psalms 70-71
2 Samuel 17	2 Corinthians 10	21st	Ezekiel 24	Psalm 72
2 Samuel 18	2 Corinthians 11	22nd	Ezekiel 25	Psalm 73
2 Samuel 19	2 Corinthians 12	23rd	Ezekiel 26	Psalm 74
2 Samuel 20	2 Corinthians 13	24th	Ezekiel 27	Psalms 75-76
2 Samuel 21	Galatians 1	25th	Ezekiel 28	Psalm 77
2 Samuel 22	Galatians 2	26th	Ezekiel 29	Psalm 78:1-37
2 Samuel 23	Galatians 3	27th	Ezekiel 30	Psalm 78:38ff
2 Samuel 24	Galatians 4	28th	Ezekiel 31	Psalm 79
1 Kings 1	Galatians 5	29th	Ezekiel 32	Psalm 80
1 Kings 2	Galatians 6	30th	Ezekiel 33	Psalms 81-82

OCTOBER

Family Worship		Date	Private Reading	
1 Kings 3	Ephesians 1	1st	Ezekiel 34	Psalms 83-84
1 Kings 4-5	Ephesians 2	2nd	Ezekiel 35	Psalm 85
1 Kings 6	Ephesians 3	3rd	Ezekiel 36	Psalm 86

1 Kings 7	Ephesians 4	4th	Ezekiel 37	Psalms 87-88
1 Kings 8	Ephesians 5	5th	Ezekiel 38	Psalm 89
1 Kings 9	Ephesians 6	6th	Ezekiel 39	Psalm 90
1 Kings 10	Philippians 1	7th	Ezekiel 40	Psalm 91
1 Kings 11	Philippians 2	8th	Ezekiel 41	Psalms 92-93
1 Kings 12	Philippians 3	9th	Ezekiel 42	Psalm 94
1 Kings 13	Philippians 4	10th	Ezekiel 43	Psalms 95-96
1 Kings 14	Colossians 1	11th	Ezekiel 44	Psalms 97-98
1 Kings 15	Colossians 2	12th	Ezekiel 45	Psalms 99-101
1 Kings 16	Colossians 3	13th	Ezekiel 46	Psalm 102
1 Kings 17	Colossians 4	14th	Ezekiel 47	Psalm 103
1 Kings 18	1 Thessalonians 1	15th	Ezekiel 48	Psalm 104
1 Kings 19	1 Thessalonians 2	16th	Daniel 1	Psalm 105
1 Kings 20	1 Thessalonians 3	17th	Daniel 2	Psalm 106
1 Kings 21	1 Thessalonians 4	18th	Daniel 3	Psalm 107
1 Kings 22	1 Thessalonians 5	19th	Daniel 4	Psalms 108-109
2 Kings 1	2 Thessalonians 1	20th	Daniel 5	Psalms 110-111
2 Kings 2	2 Thessalonians 2	21st	Daniel 6	Psalms 112-113
2 Kings 3	2 Thessalonians 3	22nd	Daniel 7	Psalms 114-115
2 Kings 4	1 Timothy 1	23rd	Daniel 8	Psalm 116
2 Kings 5	1 Timothy 2	24th	Daniel 9	Psalms 117-118
2 Kings 6	1 Timothy 3	25th	Daniel 10	Psalm 119:1-24
2 Kings 7	1 Timothy 4	26th	Daniel 11	Psalm 119:25-48
2 Kings 8	1 Timothy 5	27th	Daniel 12	Psalm 119:49-72
2 Kings 9	1 Timothy 6	28th	Hosea 1	Psalm 119:73-96
2 Kings 10	2 Timothy 1	29th	Hosea 2	Psalm 119:97-120
2 Kings 11-12	2 Timothy 2	30th	Hosea 3-4	Psalm 119:121-144
2 Kings 13	2 Timothy 3	31st	Hosea 5-6	Psalm 119:145-176

NOVEMBER

Family Worship		Date	Private Reading	
2 Kings 14	2 Timothy 4	1st	Hosea 7	Psalms 120-122
2 Kings 15	Titus 1	2nd	Hosea 8	Psalms 123-125
2 Kings 16	Titus 2	3rd	Hosea 9	Psalms 126-128
2 Kings 17	Titus 3	4th	Hosea 10	Psalms 129-131
2 Kings 18	Philemon 1	5th	Hosea 11	Psalms 132-134
2 Kings 19	Hebrews 1	6th	Hosea 12	Psalms 135-136
2 Kings 20	Hebrews 2	7th	Hosea 13	Psalms 137-138
2 Kings 21	Hebrews 3	8th	Hosea 14	Psalm 139
2 Kings 22	Hebrews 4	9th	Joel 1	Psalms 140-141
2 Kings 23	Hebrews 5	10th	Joel 2	Psalm 142
2 Kings 24	Hebrews 6	11th	Joel 3	Psalm 143
2 Kings 25	Hebrews 7	12th	Amos 1	Psalm 144
1 Chronicles 1-2	Hebrews 8	13th	Amos 2	Psalm 145
1 Chronicles 3-4	Hebrews 9	14th	Amos 3	Psalms 146-147
1 Chronicles 5-6	Hebrews 10	15th	Amos 4	Psalms 148-150
1 Chronicles 7-8	Hebrews 11	16th	Amos 5	Luke 1:1-38
1 Chronicles 9-10	Hebrews 12	17th	Amos 6	Luke 1:39ff

1 Chronicles 11-12	Hebrews 13	18th	Amos 7	Luke 2
1 Chronicles 13-14	James 1	19th	Amos 8	Luke 3
1 Chronicles 15	James 2	20th	Amos 9	Luke 4
1 Chronicles 16	James 3	21st	Obadiah 1	Luke 5
1 Chronicles 17	James 4	22nd	Jonah 1	Luke 6
1 Chronicles 18	James 5	23rd	Jonah 2	Luke 7
1 Chronicles 19-20	1 Peter 1	24th	Jonah 3	Luke 8
1 Chronicles 21	1 Peter 2	25th	Jonah 4	Luke 9
1 Chronicles 22	1 Peter 3	26th	Micah 1	Luke 10
1 Chronicles 23	1 Peter 4	27th	Micah 2	Luke 11
1 Chronicles 24-25	1 Peter 5	28th	Micah 3	Luke 12
1 Chronicles 26-27	2 Peter 1	29th	Micah 4	Luke 13
1 Chronicles 28	2 Peter 2	30th	Micah 5	Luke 14

DECEMBER

Family Worship		Date	Private Reading	
1 Chronicles 29	2 Peter 3	1st	Micah 6	Luke 15
2 Chronicles 1	1 John 1	2nd	Micah 7	Luke 16
2 Chronicles 2	1 John 2	3rd	Nahum 1	Luke 17
2 Chronicles 3-4	1 John 3	4th	Nahum 2	Luke 18
2 Chronicles 5-6:11	1 John 4	5th	Nahum 3	Luke 19
2 Chronicles 6:12ff	1 John 5	6th	Habakkuk 1	Luke 20
2 Chronicles 7	2 John 1	7th	Habakkuk 2	Luke 21
2 Chronicles 8	3 John 1	8th	Habakkuk 3	Luke 22
2 Chronicles 9	Jude 1	9th	Zephaniah 1	Luke 23
2 Chronicles 10	Revelation 1	10th	Zephaniah 2	Luke 24
2 Chronicles 11-12	Revelation 2	11th	Zephaniah 3	John 1
2 Chronicles 13	Revelation 3	12th	Haggai 1	John 2
2 Chronicles 14-15	Revelation 4	13th	Haggai 2	John 3
2 Chronicles 16	Revelation 5	14th	Zechariah 1	John 4
2 Chronicles 17	Revelation 6	15th	Zechariah 2	John 5
2 Chronicles 18	Revelation 7	16th	Zechariah 3	John 6
2 Chronicles 19-20	Revelation 8	17th	Zechariah 4	John 7
2 Chronicles 21	Revelation 9	18th	Zechariah 5	John 8
2 Chronicles 22-23	Revelation 10	19th	Zechariah 6	John 9
2 Chronicles 24	Revelation 11	20th	Zechariah 7	John 10
2 Chronicles 25	Revelation 12	21st	Zechariah 8	John 11
2 Chronicles 26	Revelation 13	22nd	Zechariah 9	John 12
2 Chronicles 27-28	Revelation 14	23rd	Zechariah 10	John 13
2 Chronicles 29	Revelation 15	24th	Zechariah 11	John 14
2 Chronicles 30	Revelation 16	25th	Zechariah 12-13:1	John 15
2 Chronicles 31	Revelation 17	26th	Zechariah 13:2ff	John 16
2 Chronicles 32	Revelation 18	27th	Zechariah 14	John 17
2 Chronicles 33	Revelation 19	28th	Malachi 1	John 18
2 Chronicles 34	Revelation 20	29th	Malachi 2	John 19
2 Chronicles 35	Revelation 21	30th	Malachi 3	John 20
2 Chronicles 36	Revelation 22	31st	Malachi 4	John 21

MONEY, WEIGHTS, & MEASURES
Concordance

TABLES OF WEIGHTS AND MEASURES USED IN THE HOLY SCRIPTURES

Note: all measures are only given the approximate equivalent in modern measures.

OLD TESTAMENT WEIGHTS

Type of Weight	Equivalent Old Testament Measure	Approx. Equivalent Imperial Measure	Approx. Equivalent Metric Measure	Biblical References
Bekah	10 gerahs; half-shekel	0.22 oz	6.2 g	Ex. 38:26
Dram	Heb. adarkon lit., handful darics, drachmae	0.31 oz	8.8 g	1Ch. 29:7; Ezr. 2:69, 8.27; Ne. 7.70-72
Gerah	$\frac{1}{20}$ of a shekel	0.022 oz	0.62 g	Ex. 30:13; Le. 27:25; Nu. 3:47, 18:16; Eze. 45:12
Pound	Heb. mnah 300 shekels	6.6 lb	3 kg	1Ki. 10:17; Ezr. 2:69; Ne. 7:71,72
Shekel	20 gerahs 2 bekahs	0.44 oz	12.4 g	Ge. 23:15,16; Ex. 21:32
Shekel of the sanctuary		0.5 oz	14.2 g	Ex. 38:24,25; Le. 27:3-7; Nu. 7:13,14, 18:16
Shekel after the king's weight		The exact weight is unknown; if standard, the entire weight would be about 6 lb or 2.7 kg		2Sa. 14:26
Talent	Heb. kikar 3,000 shekels	66 lb	30 kg	Ex. 25:39, 37:24, 38:24,25; 1Ki. 9:14,28; 2Ki. 5:5,22,23

OLD TESTAMENT LENGTHS

Type of Length	Equivalent Old Testament Measure	Approx. Equivalent Imperial Measure	Approx. Equivalent Metric Measure	Biblical References
Cubit of a man (ordinary cubit)*	Heb. ammah from elbow to fingertip; 2 spans	17.5 in	445 mm	Ge. 6:15,16; Ex. 26:28,13,16; 2Ki. 14:13; Eze. 41:1-5; Da. 3:1
Royal cubit (cubit plus handbreadth)	2 spans and 1 handbreadth	20.5 in	521 mm	2Ch. 3:3; Eze. 40:5

OLD TESTAMENT LENGTHS (continued)

Type of Length	Equivalent Old Testament Measure	Approx. Equivalent Imperial Measure	Approx. Equivalent Metric Measure	Biblical References
Handbreadth	Heb. tophach width at base of hand; 4 digits	3 in	76 mm	Ex. 37:12; 2Ch. 4:5; Ps. 39:5
Reed	Heb. qaneh 6 cubits	105 in	2.67 m	Eze. 40:3,5,6,7,8, 41:8, 42:16-19
Span	Heb. zereth width across outstretched hand; 3 handbreadths	9 in	229 mm	Ex. 28:16, 39:9; 1Sa. 17:4; Is. 40:12; La. 2:20

*The cubit mentioned in Ju. 3:16 is gomed, a different Hebrew word, and is probably shorter than an ordinary cubit.

OLD TESTAMENT LIQUID MEASURES

Type of Liquid Measure	Equivalent Old Testament Measure	Approx. Equivalent Imperial Measure	Approx. Equivalent Metric Measure	Biblical References
Bath	6 hins	9 gal	34 l	1Ki. 7:26,38; 2Ch. 2:10, 4:5; Ezr. 7:22; Is. 5:10; Eze. 45:10,11,14
Hin	12 logs	1.5 gal	5.7 l	Ex. 29:40, 30:24; Le. 19:36; Nu. 15:7; Eze. 46:5
Homer	10 baths	90 gal	340 l	Eze. 45:11,14
Log		Just under 1 pt	0.5 l	Le. 14:10,12,15,21,24

OLD TESTAMENT DRY MEASURES

Type of Dry Measure	Equivalent Old Testament Measure	Approx. Equivalent Imperial Measure	Approx. Equivalent Metric Measure	Biblical References
Cab	4 logs	3.5 pt	2 l	2Ki. 6:25
Ephah	10 omers	0.95 bu	34 l	Ex. 16:36; Le. 5:11, 6:20, 19:36; Nu. 5:15, 28:5; Ru. 2:17
Homer	10 ephahs	9.5 bu	340 l	Le. 27:16; Nu. 11:32; Is. 5:10; Eze. 45:11,13; Ho. 3:2
Measure	Heb. seah 6 cabs	20 pt	11 l	2Ki. 7:1,16,18
Omer	7 logs $\frac{1}{10}$ of an ephah	6.5 pt	3.6 l	Ex. 16:16,18,32,33,36

OLD TESTAMENT MONEY

Type of Money	Hebrew Name used	Biblical References
piece of money*	Heb. qsitah (qsitah is rendered "pieces of silver" in Jos. 24:32)	Ge. 33:19; Job 42:11
piece of silver*	Heb. keseph (a different Hebrew word, qsitah, used in Jos. 24:32)	Ge. 20:16
shekel	Heb. shekel	Ex. 30:15; Le. 5:15
talent	In the Old Testament, generally a disk of a precious metal (gold, silver, etc.) weighing one talent	

*also listed in the New Testament Money table

OLD TESTAMENT TIME

Unit of Time	Name of Division	Time Covered by Division	Biblical References
Watch	middle watch	10:00 pm to 2:00 am	Ju. 7:19
	morning watch	2:00 am to 6:00 am	Ex. 14:24

NEW TESTAMENT WEIGHTS

Type of Weight	Equivalent New Testament Measure	Approx. Equivalent Imperial Measure	Approx. Equivalent Metric Measure	Biblical References
Pound	Gr. litra	12 oz	340 g	Jn. 12:3, 19:39
Talent	Gr. talanton	75 lb	34 kg	Re. 16:21

NEW TESTAMENT LENGTHS

Type of Length	Equivalent New Testament Measure	Approx. Equivalent Imperial Measure	Approx. Equivalent Metric Measure	Biblical References
Cubit	Gr. pechus from elbow to fingertip; 2 spans	18 in	450 mm	Mat. 6:27; Lu. 12:25
Fathom	Gr. orguia	6 ft	1.83 m	Ac. 27:28
Furlong	Gr. stadion	660 ft	200 m	Lu. 24:13; Jn. 6:19, 11:18; Re. 14:20, 21:16
Mile	Gr. milion Roman mile	4,986 ft 0.944 modern mi	1,520 m	Mat. 5:41

NEW TESTAMENT LIQUID MEASURES

Type of Liquid Measure	Equivalent New Testament Measure	Approx. Equivalent Imperial Measure	Approx. Equivalent Metric Measure	Biblical References
Firkin	Gr. metretes Heb. bath	9 gal	34 l	Jn. 2:6

NEW TESTAMENT DRY MEASURES

Type of Dry Measure	Equivalent New Testament Measure	Approx. Equivalent Imperial Measure	Approx. Equivalent Metric Measure	Biblical References
Bushel	Gr. modios	2 dry gal	8.8 l	Mat. 4:21, 5:15; Lu. 11:33

NEW TESTAMENT MONEY

Type of Money	Greek Name used	Biblical References
Drachme	Gr. drachme a day's wage	Lu. 15:8
Farthing	Gr. kodrantes 2 of the mites in Mar. 12:42; 2 lepta	Mat. 5:26
Gold	Gr. chrusos	Mat. 10:9; Ac. 3:6, 20:33; Ja. 5:3; 1Pe. 1:18
Farthing	Gr. assarion 8 lepta	Mat. 10:29; Lu. 12:6
Mite	Gr. lepton 0.5 of a kodrantes or farthing	Mar. 12:42; Lu. 12:59, 21:2
Pence	Gr. denaria each penny 16 assaria; a day's wage; 16 of the farthings in Mat. 10:29	Mat. 18:28; Mar. 14:5; Lu. 7:41; Jn. 12:5
Penny	Gr. denarion 16 assaria; a day's wage	Mat. 20:2,9,10,13, 22:19; Mar. 6:37, 12:15; Lu. 20:24; Jn. 6:7; Re. 6:6
Piece of money*	Gr. stater a NT shekel; 4 days' wages	Mat. 17:27
Piece of silver*	Gr. argurion (a different Greek word, drachme, is used in Lu. 15:8)	Mat. 27:3
Pound	Gr. mina 100 denaria;100 of the pennies in Mat. 20:2	Lu. 19:13,16,18, 20,24,25
Talent	Gr. talanton 60 mina; 60 of the pounds in Lu. 19:13	Mat. 18:24, 25:15, 16,20,22,24,25,28
Tribute	Gr. didrachmon a NT half-shekel; 2 days' wages	Mat. 17:24, 22:19

Note. Since inflation continually changes the equivalent value of modern currencies, the current rate of exchange of the first century has been used rather than the current minimum wage. To compare the current earning power equivalent, one simply needs to consider a current daily wage.

*also listed in the Old Testament Money table

NEW TESTAMENT TIME

Unit of Time	Name of Division	Time Covered by Division	Biblical References
Watch	first watch	6:00 pm to 9:00 pm	not mentioned
	second watch	9:00 pm to midnight	Lu. 12:38
	third watch	midnight to 3:00 am	Lu. 12:38
	fourth watch	3:00 am to 6:00 am	Mat. 14:25

OLD AND NEW TESTAMENT CONCORDANCE

AARON
called for Moses and *A* — Ex. 8:8
prophetess, the sister of *A* — Ex. 15:20
And *A* shall burn thereon — Ex. 30:7
A shall make an atonement — Ex. 30:10
Speak unto *A* thy brother — Lev. 16:2
when *A* and his sons — Num. 4:15
to Moses, and to *A* — Num. 13:26
LORD spake unto *A* — Num. 18:20

ABOMINATION
every *a* to the LORD — Deut. 12:31
Chemosh, the *a* of Moab — 1 Kin. 11:7
incense is an *a* unto — Is. 1:13
whatsoever worketh *a* — Rev. 21:27

ABOMINATIONS
and with all thine *a* — Ezek. 5:11
committed in all their *a* — Ezek. 6:9
thee for all thine *a* — Ezek. 7:8
man cast away the *a* — Ezek. 20:8
overspreading of *a* — Dan. 9:27

ABRAHAM
A fell upon his face — Gen. 17:17
I sware unto *A* thy — Gen. 26:3
LORD God of *A* thy father — Gen. 28:13
father, the God of *A* — Ex. 3:6
fathers, the God of *A* — Ex. 3:15
Remember *A*, Isaac — Ex. 32:13
the seed of *A*, Isaac — Jer. 33:26
unto our father *A* — Acts 7:2

AFRAID
Egypt, which thou wast *a* — Deut. 28:60
fear not, nor be *a* — Deut. 31:6
not *a*, neither be thou — Josh. 1:9
whom shall I be *a* — Ps. 27:1
trust, and not be *a* — Is. 12:2
And they shall be *a* — Is. 13:8

ALTAR
there builded he an *a* — Gen. 12:7
there he builded an *a* — Gen. 12:8
and built there an *a* — Gen. 13:18
horns of the *a* of sweet — Lev. 4:7
his fat upon the *a* — Lev. 4:26
mine *a*, to burn incense — 1 Sam. 2:28
accepted upon mine *a* — Is. 56:7
the porch and the *a* — Ezek. 8:16

ANGEL
a of his presence saved — Is. 63:9
And the *a* answered — Luke 1:35
unto the *a* of the church — Rev. 3:1
to the *a* of the church — Rev. 3:7
unto the *a* of the church — Rev. 3:14
The first *a* sounded — Rev. 8:7
And the seventh *a* sounded — Rev. 11:15
Jesus have sent mine *a* — Rev. 22:16

ANGELS
Father with his *a* — Matt. 16:27
the devil and his *a* — Matt. 25:41
Spirit, seen of *a* — 1 Tim. 3:16
innumerable company of *a* — Heb. 12:22
presence of the holy *a* — Rev. 14:10

ANGER
overthrew in his *a* — Deut. 29:23
have provoked me to *a* — Deut. 32:21
a of the LORD was hot — Judg. 2:14
to provoke him to *a* — 2 Kin. 17:17
the *a* of the LORD kindled — Is. 5:25
to accomplish my *a* — Ezek. 20:8
merciful, slow to *a* — Joel 2:13
retaineth not his *a* — Mic. 7:18

ANOINTED
horn of oil, and *a* — 1 Sam. 16:13
God, thy God, hath *a* — Ps. 45:7
LORD to his *a*, to Cyrus — Is. 45:1
LORD hath *a* me to preach — Is. 61:1

APPEARED
the LORD *a* unto Abram — Gen. 12:7
the LORD *a* to Abram — Gen. 17:1
And the LORD *a* unto — Gen. 18:1
The God of glory *a* — Acts 7:2

APPOINTED
the time *a* I will return — Gen. 18:14
thee, in the time *a* — Ex. 23:15
a feasts my soul hateth — Is. 1:14
Son, whom he hath *a* — Heb. 1:2

ARISE
after thee shall any *a* — 1 Kin. 3:12
Kings shall see and *a* — Is. 49:7
trouble they will say, *A* — Jer. 2:27
a, and be baptized — Acts 22:16

ARK
upon the *a* of the testimony — Ex. 25:22
which is upon the *a* — Lev. 16:2
his face before the *a* — Josh. 7:6
fear, prepared an *a* — Heb. 11:7

ARM
greatness of thine *a* — Ex. 15:16
the lambs with his *a* — Is. 40:11
made bare his holy *a* — Is. 52:10
and stretched out *a* — Jer. 32:17

ASHAMED
said, O my God, I am *a* — Ezra 9:6

a and brought to confusion Ps. 35:26
not be ***a*** that wait Is. 49:23
not thou therefore ***a*** 2 Tim. 1:8
nevertheless I am not ***a*** 2 Tim. 1:12

ASSYRIA
Tiglathpileser king of ***A*** 2 Kin. 15:29
Hoshea the king of ***A*** 2 Kin. 17:6
king of ***A*** sent Tartan 2 Kin. 18:17
shall be left, from ***A*** Is. 11:11
perish in the land of ***A*** Is. 27:13

BABYLON
out to the king of ***B*** 2 Kin. 24:12
B, and the king's mother 2 Kin. 24:15
and brought him to ***B*** 2 Chr. 36:10
Go ye forth of ***B***, flee Is. 48:20
Nebuchad-rezzar king of ***B*** Jer. 21:7
hand of the king of ***B*** Jer. 21:10
Nebuchad-rezzar the king of ***B*** Jer. 25:9
the king of ***B*** slew Jer. 39:6

BARE
The LORD hath made ***b*** Is. 52:10
and he ***b*** the sin of Is. 53:12
he ***b*** them, and carried Is. 63:9
tree of life, which ***b*** Rev. 22:2

BEAR
shalt not avenge, nor ***b*** Lev. 19:18
Kohath shall come to ***b*** Num. 4:15
which she shall ***b*** Deut. 28:57
conceive, and ***b*** a son Is. 7:14
he shall ***b*** their iniquities Is. 53:11
falsely, and the priests ***b*** Jer. 5:31
vessel unto me, to ***b*** Acts 9:15
b witness, and shew 1 John 1:2

BEAST
Egypt, both man and ***b*** Ex. 12:12
night, who worship the ***b*** Rev. 14:11
And the ***b*** was taken Rev. 19:20
not worshipped the ***b*** Rev. 20:4
b and the false prophet Rev. 20:10

BEASTS
drank, and their ***b*** Num. 20:11
air, and unto the ***b*** Deut. 28:26
the wild ***b*** of the islands Is. 13:22
idols were upon the ***b*** Is. 46:1
heaven, and for the ***b*** Jer. 7:33
heaven, and for the ***b*** Jer. 16:4
b, and in the midst Rev. 5:6

BEGINNING
all nations, ***b*** at Jerusalem Luke 24:47
murderer from the ***b*** John 8:44
b, which we have heard 1 John 1:1
Alpha and Omega, the ***b*** Rev. 1:8

BLESS
b thee, and make thy Gen. 12:2
b them that ***b*** thee Gen. 12:3
blessing I will ***b*** thee Gen. 22:17
thee, and will ***b*** thee Gen. 26:3
b all the work of thine Deut. 28:12

BLESSED
of the earth be ***b*** Gen. 12:3
of the earth be ***b*** Gen. 22:18
of the earth be ***b*** Gen. 26:4
LORD thy God hath ***b*** Deut. 12:7
right hand, Come, ye ***b*** Matt. 25:34
B be the Lord God of Luke 1:68
b hope, and the glorious Titus 2:13
B is the man that endureth James 1:12

BLOOD
Whoso sheddeth man's ***b*** Gen. 9:6
shall put some of the ***b*** Lev. 4:7
hands are full of ***b*** Is. 1:15
LORD is filled with ***b*** Is. 34:6
and the moon into ***b*** Joel 2:31
purchased with his own ***b*** Acts 20:28
shall the ***b*** of Christ Heb. 9:14
sins in his own ***b*** Rev. 1:5

BODY
the fruit of thy ***b*** Deut. 28:18
fruit of thine own ***b*** Deut. 28:53
transgression, the fruit of my ***b*** Mic. 6:7
them which kill the ***b*** Matt. 10:28
baptized into one ***b*** 1 Cor. 12:13
things done in his ***b*** 2 Cor. 5:10
the head of the ***b*** Col. 1:18
our sins in his own ***b*** 1 Pet. 2:24

BOOK
this ***b***, that thou mayest Deut. 28:58
found written in the ***b*** Dan. 12:1
seest, write in a ***b*** Rev. 1:11
b of life, but I will Rev. 3:5
b of life of the Lamb Rev. 13:8

BORN
Shall a child be ***b*** Gen. 17:17
be a stranger, or ***b*** Ex. 12:19
Behold, a son shall be ***b*** 1 Chr. 22:9
unto us a child is ***b*** Is. 9:6
thing which shall be ***b*** Luke 1:35
man which am a Jew, ***b*** Acts 22:3

BOW
Thou shalt not ***b*** down Ex. 20:5
shall ***b*** down to thee Is. 49:23
Lud, that draw the ***b*** Is. 66:19
appearance of the ***b*** Ezek. 1:28

BREAD
face shalt thou eat ***b*** Gen. 3:19
fire, and unleavened ***b*** Ex. 12:8
ye eat unleavened ***b*** Ex. 12:15
feast of unleavened ***b*** Ex. 23:15
eat ***b***, nor drink water Ex. 34:28
be on the ***b*** for a memorial Lev. 24:7
feast of unleavened ***b*** Deut. 16:16
eat of my ***b***, hath lifted Ps. 41:9

BREAK
Thou shalt ***b*** them with Ps. 2:9
b down the wall thereof Is. 5:5
wilderness shall waters ***b*** Is. 35:6
and ***b*** forth into singing Is. 49:13
pluck up, and to ***b*** Jer. 31:28
b in pieces and consume Dan. 2:44

BRETHREN
the midst of his ***b*** 1 Sam. 16:13
of these my ***b***, ye have Matt. 25:40
firstborn among many ***b*** Rom. 8:29

beseech you therefore, ***b*** **Rom. 12:1**
we command you, ***b*** **2 Thess. 3:6**
Wherefore, my beloved ***b*** **James 1:19**
b, Hath not God chosen **James 2:5**
unfeigned love of the ***b*** **1 Pet. 1:22**

BROKEN
And the city was ***b*** **2 Kin. 25:4**
thou hast ***b*** the yoke **Is. 9:4**
withered, they shall be ***b*** **Is. 27:11**
out cisterns, ***b*** cisterns **Jer. 2:13**
time I have ***b*** thy yoke **Jer. 2:20**
daughter of my people is ***b*** **Jer. 14:17**
confounded, Merodach is ***b*** **Jer. 50:2**
captives, because I am ***b*** **Ezek. 6:9**

BROTHER
evil toward his ***b*** **Deut. 28:54**
made Zedekiah his ***b*** **2 Chr. 36:10**
trust ye not in any ***b*** **Jer. 9:4**
and every man his ***b*** **Jer. 31:34**
he did pursue his ***b*** **Amos 1:11**
is angry with his ***b*** **Matt. 5:22**
Zelotes, and Judas the ***b*** **Acts 1:13**
b that walketh disorderly **2 Thess. 3:6**

BROUGHT
he ***b*** him forth abroad **Gen. 15:5**
thy God, which have ***b*** **Ex. 20:2**
gods, O Israel, which ***b*** **1 Kin. 12:28**
Nebuchadnezzar sent, and ***b*** **2 Chr. 36:10**
b upon them the king **2 Chr. 36:17**
he is ***b*** as a lamb to **Is. 53:7**
And he ***b*** me into the **Ezek. 8:16**
city in Cilicia, yet ***b*** **Acts 22:3**

BUILD
thou shalt ***b*** an house **Deut. 28:30**
He shall ***b*** an house **2 Sam. 7:13**
Solomon ***b*** an high place **1 Kin. 11:7**
to throw down, to ***b*** **Jer. 1:10**
restore and to ***b*** Jerusalem **Dan. 9:25**

BUILT
b for Pharaoh treasure **Ex. 1:11**
also ***b*** them high places **1 Kin. 14:23**
the street shall be ***b*** **Dan. 9:25**
b houses of hewn stone **Amos 5:11**
are ***b*** upon the foundation **Eph. 2:20**
lively stones, are ***b*** **1 Pet. 2:5**

BULLOCK
hath sinned, a young ***b*** **Lev. 4:3**
the blood of the ***b*** **Lev. 4:7**
the skin of the ***b*** **Lev. 4:11**
whole ***b*** shall he carry **Lev. 4:12**

BURN
morning ye shall ***b*** **Ex. 12:10**
are poured out, and ***b*** **Lev. 4:12**
children of Israel did ***b*** **2 Kin. 18:4**
and it shall ***b***, and **Jer. 7:20**
Babylon, and he shall ***b*** **Jer. 21:10**
Chaldeans, and they shall ***b*** **Jer. 38:18**
own mouth, to ***b*** incense **Jer. 44:17**
cometh, that shall ***b*** **Mal. 4:1**

BURNED
thou shalt not be ***b*** **Is. 43:2**
Chaldeans ***b*** the king's **Jer. 39:8**

And ***b*** the house of **Jer. 52:13**
earth is ***b*** at his presence **Nah. 1:5**
brass, as if they ***b*** **Rev. 1:15**

BURNT
altar of the ***b*** offering **Lev. 4:7**
out shall he be ***b*** **Lev. 4:12**
bring your ***b*** offerings **Deut. 12:6**
your ***b*** offerings, and **Deut. 12:11**
great delight in ***b*** **1 Sam. 15:22**
And he ***b*** the house **2 Kin. 25:9**
their ***b*** offerings and **Is. 56:7**
your ***b*** offerings are **Jer. 6:20**

CALL
I ***c*** heaven and earth **Deut. 4:26**
c upon me in the day **Ps. 50:15**
them that ***c*** upon thee **Ps. 86:5**
c upon me, but I will **Prov. 1:28**
a son, and shall ***c*** **Is. 7:14**
the city that men ***c*** **Lam. 2:15**
c on my name, and I **Zech. 13:9**
son, and thou shalt ***c*** **Matt. 1:21**

CALLED
be ***c*** Wonderful, Counsellor **Is. 9:6**
mine house shall be ***c*** **Is. 56:7**
be ***c*** trees of righteousness **Is. 61:3**
c, THE LORD OUR RIGHTEOUSNESS **Jer. 23:6**
c the Son of the Highest **Luke 1:32**
Rome, beloved of God, ***c*** **Rom. 1:7**
praises of him who hath ***c*** **1 Pet. 2:9**
ye are thereunto ***c*** **1 Pet. 3:9**

CAPTAIN
anointed thee to be ***c*** **1 Sam. 10:1**
Abner the son of Ner, ***c*** **2 Sam. 2:8**
Abner the son of Ner, ***c*** **1 Kin. 2:32**
And the ***c*** of the guard **2 Kin. 25:18**
rebellion appointed a ***c*** **Neh. 9:17**

CAPTIVITY
into ***c*** unto Sihon king **Num. 21:29**
they shall go into ***c*** **Deut. 28:41**
those carried he into ***c*** **2 Kin. 24:15**
cause to return the ***c*** **Jer. 33:11**
as are for ***c*** to ***c*** **Jer. 43:11**
into ***c*** with his priests **Jer. 48:7**
c of my people of Israel **Amos 9:14**

CARRIED
c them captive to Assyria **2 Kin. 15:29**
Samaria, and ***c*** Israel **2 Kin. 17:6**
And he ***c*** out thence **2 Kin. 24:13**
And he ***c*** away Jehoiachin **2 Kin. 24:15**
borne our griefs, and ***c*** **Is. 53:4**
he bare them, and ***c*** **Is. 63:9**

CAST
thine olive shall ***c*** **Deut. 28:40**
forsake him, he will ***c*** **1 Chr. 28:9**
thee, and ***c*** thy law **Neh. 9:26**
man ***c*** away the abominations **Ezek. 20:8**
shall they ***c*** out devils **Mark 16:17**
c alive into a lake **Rev. 19:20**
deceived them was ***c*** **Rev. 20:10**
death and hell were ***c*** **Rev. 20:14**

CHALDEANS
flee ye from the ***C*** **Is. 48:20**

CONGREGATION
c of Israel shall kill **Ex. 12:6**
tabernacle of the *c* **Lev. 4:7**
tabernacle of the *c* **Num. 4:15**
wroth with all the *c* **Num. 16:22**
abundantly, and the *c* **Num. 20:11**
whole *c* of the children **Josh. 18:1**
and the *c* was gathered **Judg. 20:1**
the mount of the *c* **Is. 14:13**

CONSUMED
thee, until he have *c* **Deut. 28:21**
thou hast *c* them, but **Jer. 5:3**
shall be *c* by the sword **Jer. 16:4**
c in the midst of thee **Ezek. 5:12**

COUNSEL
priest, who shall ask *c* **Num. 27:21**
Ahithophel saw that his *c* **2 Sam. 17:23**
king took *c*, and made **1 Kin. 12:28**
Great in *c*, and mighty **Jer. 32:19**
is *c* perished from **Jer. 49:7**
things after the *c* **Eph. 1:11**

COUNTRY
cane from a far *c* **Jer. 6:20**
out of the north *c* **Jer. 23:8**
sacrifice in the north *c* **Jer. 46:10**
inhabited places of the *c* **Ezek. 34:13**
Levite, and of the *c* **Acts 4:36**

COVENANT
day the LORD made a *c* **Gen. 15:18**
will establish my *c* **Gen. 17:7**
keep my *c*, then ye **Ex. 19:5**
thou shalt make no *c* **Deut. 7:2**
remembered for them his *c* **Ps. 106:45**
make an everlasting *c* **Is. 55:3**
the *c* that I will make **Jer. 31:33**
of the *c*, whom ye delight **Mal. 3:1**

CURSE
I will not again *c* **Gen. 8:21**
that bless thee, and *c* **Gen. 12:3**
proverb, a taunt and a *c* **Jer. 24:9**
reproach, a waste, and a *c* **Jer. 49:13**
redeemed us from the *c* **Gal. 3:13**

CURSED
C shalt thou be in **Deut. 28:16**
C shall be thy basket **Deut. 28:17**
C shalt thou be when **Deut. 28:19**
Depart from me, ye *c* **Matt. 25:41**

DARKNESS
blind gropeth in *d* **Deut. 28:29**
the land, behold *d* **Is. 5:30**
shall be turned into *d* **Joel 2:31**
to turn them from *d* **Acts 26:18**
hidden things of *d* **1 Cor. 4:5**
called you out of *d* **1 Pet. 2:9**

DAUGHTER
thy son, nor thy *d* **Ex. 20:10**
thy *d* thou shalt not **Deut. 7:3**
wife Jezebel the *d* **1 Kin. 16:31**
make his son or his *d* **2 Kin. 23:10**
virgin *d* of my people **Jer. 14:17**
head at the *d* of Jerusalem **Lam. 2:15**
Rejoice greatly, O *d* **Zech. 9:9**
D, be of good comfort **Matt. 9:22**

DAUGHTERS
escaped, and his *d* **Num. 21:29**
Thy sons and thy *d* **Deut. 28:32**
shalt beget sons and *d* **Deut. 28:41**
sons and of thy *d* **Deut. 28:53**
their sons and their *d* **2 Kin. 17:17**
your sons and your *d* **Joel 2:28**

DAVID
D from that day forward **1 Sam. 16:13**
upon the throne of *D* **Is. 9:7**
sure mercies of *D* **Is. 55:3**
I will raise unto *D* **Jer. 23:5**
LORD their God, and *D* **Hos. 3:5**
upon the house of *D* **Zech. 12:10**
throne of his father *D* **Luke 1:32**
hath the key of *D* **Rev. 3:7**

DAY
d the LORD made a covenant **Gen. 15:18**
first *d* ye shall put **Ex. 12:15**
seventh *d* is the sabbath **Ex. 20:10**
d have I begotten thee **Ps. 2:7**
call upon me in the *d* **Ps. 50:15**
to pass in that *d* **Is. 11:11**
I have this *d* set thee **Jer. 1:10**
behold, the *d* cometh **Mal. 4:1**

DAYS
d shall ye eat unleavened **Ex. 12:15**
that thy *d* may be long **Ex. 20:12**
thee all the *d* of thy **Josh. 1:5**
And when thy *d* be fulfilled **2 Sam. 7:12**
shall prolong his *d* **Is. 53:10**
d come, saith the LORD **Jer. 23:5**
d Judah shall be saved **Jer. 23:6**
in the *d* of these kings **Dan. 2:44**

DEAD
supposing he had been *d* **Acts 14:19**
conscience from *d* works **Heb. 9:14**
the *d* our Lord Jesus **Heb. 13:20**
Christ from the *d*. **1 Pet. 1:3**
begotten of the *d* **Rev. 1:5**
fell at his feet as *d* **Rev. 1:17**
liveth, and was *d* **Rev. 1:18**
livest, and art *d* **Rev. 3:1**

DEATH
out his soul unto *d* **Is. 53:12**
loosed the pains of *d* **Acts 2:24**
wages of sin is *d* **Rom. 6:23**
d he might destroy **Heb. 2:14**
God, being put to *d* **1 Pet. 3:18**
keys of hell and of *d* **Rev. 1:18**
d and hell were cast **Rev. 20:14**
which is the second *d* **Rev. 21:8**

DEFILED
after wizards, to be *d* **Lev. 19:31**
And he *d* Topheth, which **2 Kin. 23:10**
sanctuary, they have *d* **Ps. 74:7**
thou hast *d* my sanctuary **Ezek. 5:11**

DELIVER
I am come down to *d* **Ex. 3:8**
LORD thy God shall *d* **Deut. 7:2**

can ***d*** out of my hand — **Deut. 32:39**
d thee, and thou shalt — **Ps. 50:15**
have I no power to ***d*** — **Is. 50:2**
LORD, I will ***d*** Zedekiah — **Jer. 21:7**
And I will ***d*** them to — **Jer. 24:9**
midst of Babylon, and ***d*** — **Jer. 51:6**

DELIVERED
against Israel, and he ***d*** — **Judg. 2:14**
children of Israel, who ***d*** — **Judg. 3:9**
and the LORD ***d*** Chushanrishathaim — **Judg. 3:10**
people shall be ***d*** — **Dan. 12:1**
All things are ***d*** unto — **Matt. 11:27**
d him to Pontius Pilate — **Matt. 27:2**
being ***d*** by the determinate — **Acts 2:23**
Who was ***d*** for our offences — **Rom. 4:25**

DEPART
sceptre shall not ***d*** — **Gen. 49:10**
my mercy shall not ***d*** — **2 Sam. 7:15**
on the left hand, ***D*** — **Matt. 25:41**
d out of this world — **John 13:1**

DESOLATE
your land shall be ***d*** — **Lev. 26:33**
cry in their ***d*** houses — **Is. 13:22**
any more be termed ***D*** — **Is. 62:4**
to make thy land ***d*** — **Jer. 4:7**
make their land ***d*** — **Jer. 18:16**
and I will make it ***d*** — **Ezek. 25:13**
he shall make it ***d*** — **Dan. 9:27**

DESTROY
them, and utterly ***d*** — **Deut. 7:2**
rejoice over you to ***d*** — **Deut. 28:63**
d in all my holy mountain — **Is. 11:9**
pull down, and to ***d*** — **Jer. 1:10**
and will utterly ***d*** — **Jer. 25:9**
shed blood, and to ***d*** — **Ezek. 22:27**
come shall ***d*** the city — **Dan. 9:26**
through death he might ***d*** — **Heb. 2:14**

DESTROYED
shall utterly be ***d*** — **Deut. 4:26**
d, and until thou perish — **Deut. 28:20**
thee, until thou be ***d*** — **Deut. 28:24**
neck, until he have ***d*** — **Deut. 28:48**
land, until thou be ***d*** — **Deut. 28:51**
which shall never be ***d*** — **Dan. 2:44**

DESTRUCTION
into the pit of ***d*** — **Ps. 55:23**
raise up a cry of ***d*** — **Is. 15:5**
the earth, for the ***d*** — **Lam. 2:11**
then sudden ***d*** cometh — **1 Thess. 5:3**

DIE
that he ***d*** not — **Lev. 16:2**
thing, lest they ***d*** — **Num. 4:15**
surely ***d*** in the wilderness — **Num. 26:65**
thou diest, will I ***d*** — **Ruth 1:17**
a man that shall ***d*** — **Is. 51:12**
d of grievous deaths — **Jer. 16:4**
part of thee shall ***d*** — **Ezek. 5:12**
it, though he shall ***d*** — **Ezek. 12:13**

DIED
but Er and Onan ***d*** in — **Gen. 46:12**
the king of Egypt ***d*** — **Ex. 2:23**
devoured them, and they ***d*** — **Lev. 10:2**
hanged himself, and ***d*** — **2 Sam. 17:23**
These all ***d*** in faith — **Heb. 11:13**

DOOR
on the upper ***d*** post — **Ex. 12:7**
offering, which is at the ***d*** — **Lev. 4:7**
three keepers of the ***d*** — **2 Kin. 25:18**
Jerusalem, to the ***d*** — **Ezek. 8:3**
and, behold, at the ***d*** — **Ezek. 8:16**

DRINK
that the people may ***d*** — **Ex. 17:6**
eat bread, nor ***d*** water — **Ex. 34:28**
but shalt neither ***d*** — **Deut. 28:39**
a mocker, strong ***d*** — **Prov. 20:1**
and through strong ***d*** — **Is. 28:7**
plant vineyards, and ***d*** — **Amos 9:14**
been all made to ***d*** — **1 Cor. 12:13**
shall ***d*** of the wine — **Rev. 14:10**

DUST
formed man of the ***d*** — **Gen. 2:7**
for ***d*** thou art, and — **Gen. 3:19**
seed shall be as the ***d*** — **Gen. 28:14**
land powder and ***d*** — **Deut. 28:24**
earth, and lick up the ***d*** — **Is. 49:23**

DWELL
sware to make you ***d*** — **Num. 14:30**
cause his name to ***d*** — **Deut. 12:11**
and thou shalt not ***d*** — **Deut. 28:30**
I ***d*** in the high and — **Is. 57:15**
Israel shall ***d*** safely — **Jer. 23:6**
ye shall ***d*** in the land — **Jer. 35:15**
shall ***d*** in the land — **Ezek. 37:25**
that ***d*** upon the earth — **Rev. 13:8**

DWELT
came unto Haran, and ***d*** — **Gen. 11:31**
and Israel ***d*** in all — **Num. 21:25**
and ***d*** among the people — **Judg. 1:16**
it be ***d*** in from generation — **Is. 13:20**
your fathers have ***d*** — **Ezek. 37:25**
was made flesh, and ***d*** — **John 1:14**

EAR
and give ***e***, O earth — **Is. 1:2**
Incline your ***e***, and — **Is. 55:3**
not inclined your ***e*** — **Jer. 35:15**
He that hath an ***e*** — **Rev. 2:7**

EARS
fat, and make their ***e*** — **Is. 6:10**
they cry in mine ***e*** — **Ezek. 8:18**
uncircumcised in heart and ***e*** — **Acts 7:51**
e of the Lord of sabaoth — **James 5:4**

EARTH
for all the ***e*** is mine — **Ex. 19:5**
the face of the ***e*** — **Deut. 7:6**
kingdoms of the ***e*** — **Deut. 28:25**
end of the ***e***, as swift — **Deut. 28:49**
the one end of the ***e*** — **Deut. 28:64**
unto the end of the ***e*** — **Is. 49:6**
and justice in the ***e*** — **Jer. 23:5**
in heaven and in ***e*** — **Matt. 28:18**

EAST
west, and to the ***e*** — **Gen. 28:14**
back by a strong ***e*** — **Ex. 14:21**
children of the ***e*** — **Judg. 6:3**

thy seed from the ***e*** Is. 43:5
faces toward the ***e*** Ezek. 8:16

EAT
thy face shalt thou ***e*** Gen. 3:19
they shall ***e*** the flesh Ex. 12:8
days shall ye ***e*** unleavened Ex. 12:15
And there ye shall ***e*** Deut. 12:7
thou knowest not ***e*** Deut. 28:33
e the fruit of thy Deut. 28:51
e of my bread, hath Ps. 41:9
overcometh will I give to ***e*** Rev. 2:7

EDOM
put garrisons in ***E*** 2 Sam. 8:14
E in the day of Jerusalem Ps. 137:7
E, thus saith the LORD Jer. 49:7
the mighty men of ***E*** Jer. 49:22
transgressions of ***E*** Amos 1:11

EGYPTIANS
the hand of the ***E*** Ex. 3:8
the ***E***, and I will rid Ex. 6:6
the burdens of the ***E*** Ex. 6:7
E may know that I am Ex. 14:4
brought upon the ***E*** Ex. 15:26

ELDERS
sight of the ***e*** of Israel Ex. 17:6
unto the seventy ***e*** Num. 11:25
e of Israel, and put Josh. 7:6
the ***e*** and chief priests Matt. 16:21
had ordained them ***e*** Acts 14:23
midst of the ***e***, stood Rev. 5:6

END
ingathering, which is in the ***e*** Ex. 23:16
sons have made an ***e*** Num. 4:15
from the ***e*** of the earth Deut. 28:49
people, from the one ***e*** Deut. 28:64
be no ***e***, upon the throne Is. 9:7
salvation unto the ***e*** Is. 49:6
transgression, and to make an ***e*** Dan. 9:24
there shall be no ***e*** Luke 1:33

ENEMIES
the gate of his ***e*** Gen. 22:17
slain before your ***e*** Lev. 26:17
smitten before thine ***e*** Deut. 28:25
thou serve thine ***e*** Deut. 28:48
e for bondmen and bondwomen Deut. 28:68
hands of their ***e*** round Judg. 2:14
I make thine ***e*** thy Ps. 110:1
the hand of their ***e*** Jer. 21:7

ENEMY
straitness, wherewith thine ***e*** Deut. 28:57
turned to be their ***e*** Is. 63:10
desolate, because the ***e*** Lam. 1:16
hath caused thine ***e*** Lam. 2:17

ENTER
And ***e*** not into judgment Ps. 143:2
these things, and to ***e*** Luke 24:26
much tribulation ***e*** Acts 14:22
shall in no wise ***e*** Rev. 21:27

ESCAPE
will send those that ***e*** Is. 66:19
and thou shalt not ***e*** Jer. 38:18

e of you shall remember Ezek. 6:9
and they shall not ***e*** 1 Thess. 5:3

ETERNAL
King ***e***, immortal, invisible 1 Tim. 1:17
the ***e*** Spirit offered Heb. 9:14
shew unto you that ***e*** 1 John 1:2
true God, and ***e*** life 1 John 5:20

EVERLASTING
Canaan, for an ***e*** possession Gen. 17:8
mighty God, The ***e*** Father Is. 9:6
I will make an ***e*** covenant Is. 55:3
living God, and an ***e*** Jer. 10:10
iniquity, and to bring in ***e*** Dan. 9:24
from of old, from ***e*** Mic. 5:2
ye cursed, into ***e*** fire Matt. 25:41
perish, but have ***e*** John 3:16

EVIL
of man's heart is ***e*** Gen. 8:21
to do ***e*** in the sight 2 Kin. 17:17
God, and eschewed ***e*** Job 1:1
against this city for ***e*** Jer. 21:10
repenteth him of the ***e*** Joel 2:13
none ***e*** can come upon Mic. 3:11
sprinkled from an ***e*** Heb. 10:22
rendering ***e*** for ***e*** 1 Pet. 3:9

EYE
very delicate, his ***e*** Deut. 28:54
and tenderness, her ***e*** Deut. 28:56
mine ***e*** shall weep sore Jer. 13:17
mine ***e*** shall not spare Ezek. 8:18
and every ***e*** shall see Rev. 1:7

EYES
gift doth blind the ***e*** Deut. 16:19
his ***e*** behold, his eyelids Ps. 11:4
I will hide mine ***e*** Is. 1:15
heavy, and shut their ***e*** Is. 6:10
LORD, are not thine ***e*** Jer. 5:3
Riblah before his ***e*** Jer. 39:6
To open their ***e***, and Acts 26:18
e, which we have looked 1 John 1:1

FACE
thy ***f*** shalt thou eat Gen. 3:19
And I will set my ***f*** Lev. 26:17
upon the ***f*** of the earth Deut. 7:6
to thee with their ***f*** Is. 49:23
I hid not my ***f*** from Is. 50:6
as dung upon the ***f*** Jer. 16:4
For I have set my ***f*** Jer. 21:10
f, and I heard a voice Ezek. 1:28

FAITH
continue in the ***f*** Acts 14:22
repentance toward God, and ***f*** Acts 20:21
are sanctified by ***f*** Acts 26:18
ye continue in the ***f*** Col. 1:23
full assurance of ***f*** Heb. 10:22
By ***f*** Noah, being warned Heb. 11:7
finisher of our ***f*** Heb. 12:2
this world rich in ***f*** James 2:5

FALL
Fear and dread shall ***f*** Ex. 15:16
shall ***f*** when none pursueth Lev. 26:36
Your carcases shall ***f*** Num. 14:29

their host shall *f* Is. 34:4
f by the sword round Ezek. 5:12
And the slain shall *f* Ezek. 6:7
they of Dedan shall *f* Ezek. 25:13
and the stars shall *f* Matt. 24:29

FALSE
a *f* vision and divination Jer. 14:14
adulterers, and against *f* Mal. 3:5
because many *f* prophets 1 John 4:1
f prophet that wrought Rev. 19:20
beast and the *f* prophet Rev. 20:10

FAMINE
for the *f*, to the *f* Jer. 15:2
the sword, and by *f* Jer. 16:4
sword, and from the *f* Jer. 21:7
pestilence, and with *f* Ezek. 5:12

FAT
that ye eat neither *f* Lev. 3:17
But Jeshurun waxed *f* Deut. 32:15
hearken than the *f* 1 Sam. 15:22
heart of this people *f* Is. 6:10
blood, it is made *f* Is. 34:6

FATHER
F, The Prince of Peace Is. 9:6
the glory of his *F* Matt. 16:27
the *F*, and of the Son Matt. 28:19
throne of his *f* David Luke 1:32
begotten of the *F* John 1:14
of the *F*, he hath declared John 1:18
Ye are of your *f* the John 8:44
cometh unto the *F* John 14:6

FATHERS
the iniquity of the *f* Ex. 20:5
neither thou nor thy *f* Deut. 28:36
neither thou nor thy *f* Deut. 28:64
shalt sleep with thy *f* 2 Sam. 7:12
LORD God of their *f* 2 Chr. 36:15
shall be thy nursing *f* Is. 49:23
servant, wherein your *f* Ezek. 37:25
of the law of the *f* Acts 22:3

FEAR
F and dread shall fall Ex. 15:16
that thou mayest *f* Deut. 28:58
F thou not Is. 41:10
F not, thou worm Jacob Is. 41:14
and shall *f* the LORD Hos. 3:5
and *f* not me, saith Mal. 3:5
moved with *f*, prepared Heb. 11:7
me, saying unto me, *F* Rev. 1:17

FEAST
ye shall keep it a *f* Ex. 12:14
Thou shalt keep the *f* Ex. 23:15
f of harvest, the firstfruits Ex. 23:16
f of unleavened bread Deut. 16:16

FEED
He shall *f* his flock Is. 40:11
their own land, and *f* Ezek. 34:13
f them, even my servant Ezek. 34:23
f the church of God Acts 20:28

FEET
his *f*, until Shiloh Gen. 49:10
your shoes on your *f* Ex. 12:11

f, and toward her children Deut. 28:57
the dust of thy *f* Is. 49:23
darkness, and before your *f* Jer. 13:16
city at the *f* of Gamaliel Acts 22:3
Satan under your *f* Rom. 16:20
him, I fell at his *f* Rev. 1:17

FELL
they *f* upon their faces Num. 16:22
his clothes, and *f* Josh. 7:6
when I saw it, I *f* Ezek. 1:28
and *f* on his face Matt. 26:39
when I saw him, I *f* Rev. 1:17
cities of the nations *f* Rev. 16:19

FIELD
hast sown in the *f* Ex. 23:16
the trees of the *f* Lev. 26:4
shalt thou be in the *f* Deut. 28:16
the *f*, and shalt gather Deut. 28:38
of the fuller's *f* 2 Kin. 18:17
the trees of the *f* Jer. 7:20

FILLED
f Jerusalem with innocent 2 Kin. 24:4
then the house was *f* 2 Chr. 5:13
sword of the LORD is *f* Is. 34:6
f with the Holy Ghost Luke 1:15
f with the Holy Ghost Acts 2:4
f with envy, and spake Acts 13:45
but be *f* with the Spirit Eph. 5:18

FIRE
night, roast with *f* Ex. 12:8
pass through the *f* Lev. 18:21
pass through the *f* 2 Kin. 17:17
part through the *f* Zech. 13:9
everlasting *f*, prepared Matt. 25:41
be tormented with *f* Rev. 14:10
alive into a lake of *f* Rev. 19:20
which burneth with *f* Rev. 21:8

FIRSTBORN
f in the land of Egypt Ex. 12:12
the *f*, whatsoever openeth Ex. 13:2
bitterness for his *f* Zech. 12:10
the *f* among many brethren Rom. 8:29

FLEE
and ye shall *f* when Lev. 26:17
them, and *f* seven ways Deut. 28:25
f unto Zoar, an heifer Is. 15:5
of Babylon, *f* ye from Is. 48:20

FLESH
eat the *f* in that night Ex. 12:8
f, shall one man sin Num. 16:22
of the *f* of his children Deut. 28:55
spirit upon all *f* Joel 2:28
the Word was made *f* John 1:14
manifest in the *f* 1 Tim. 3:16
to death in the *f* 1 Pet. 3:18
the filth of the *f* 1 Pet. 3:21

FLOCK
f of Jethro his father Ex. 3:1
leadest Joseph like a *f* Ps. 80:1
feed his *f* like a shepherd Is. 40:11
yourselves, and to all the *f* Acts 20:28

FOUND
leaven ***f*** in your houses Ex. 12:19
seek him, he will be ***f*** 1 Chr. 28:9
seek him, he will be ***f*** 2 Chr. 15:2
he could not be ***f*** Ps. 37:36
gladness shall be ***f*** Is. 51:3
f written in the book Dan. 12:1
f in fashion as a man Phil. 2:8
f written in the book Rev. 20:15

FRUIT
The ***f*** of thy land Deut. 28:33
olive shall cast his ***f*** Deut. 28:40
eat the ***f*** of thy cattle Deut. 28:51
thou shalt eat the ***f*** Deut. 28:53
they shall eat the ***f*** Is. 3:10
to the ***f*** of his doings Jer. 17:10
to the ***f*** of his doings Jer. 32:19
and bringeth forth ***f*** Col. 1:6

FULL
f line to keep alive 2 Sam. 8:2
O Lord, art a God ***f*** Ps. 86:15
hands are ***f*** of blood Is. 1:15
earth is ***f*** of his glory Is. 6:3
the earth shall be ***f*** Is. 11:9
f of grace and truth John 1:14
I am ***f***, having received Phil. 4:18
a true heart in ***f*** assurance Heb. 10:22

FURY
LORD the cup of his ***f*** Is. 51:17
will I also deal in ***f*** Ezek. 8:18
will pour out my ***f*** Ezek. 20:8
would pour out my ***f*** Ezek. 20:13
his ***f*** is poured out Nah. 1:6

GATE
shall possess the ***g*** Gen. 22:17
the ***g*** between two walls 2 Kin. 25:4
builded the sheep ***g*** Neh. 3:1
above the ***g*** of Ephraim Neh. 12:39
door of the inner ***g*** Ezek. 8:3

GATES
that is within thy ***g*** Ex. 20:10
stranger that is in thy ***g*** Deut. 14:21
thy ***g***, until thy high Deut. 28:52
thee in all thy ***g*** Deut. 28:55
distress thee in thy ***g*** Deut. 28:57
him the two leaved ***g*** Is. 45:1

GATHER
vineyard, and shalt not ***g*** Deut. 28:30
field, and shalt ***g*** Deut. 28:38
wine, nor ***g*** the grapes Deut. 28:39
outcasts of Israel, and ***g*** Is. 11:12
he shall ***g*** the lambs Is. 40:11
captivity, and I will ***g*** Jer. 29:14
g the shields Jer. 51:11
from the people, and ***g*** Ezek. 34:13

GATHERED
year, when thou hast ***g*** Ex. 23:16
Sihon ***g*** all his people Num. 21:23
congregation was ***g*** Judg. 20:1
g out the stones thereof Is. 5:2
nations shall be ***g*** Jer. 3:17
children of Israel be ***g*** Hos. 1:11

GAVE
And he ***g*** unto Moses Ex. 31:18
he ***g*** them all into 2 Chr. 36:17
I ***g*** my back to the Is. 50:6
Hamath, where he ***g*** Jer. 39:5
received him, to them ***g*** John 1:12
the world, that he ***g*** John 3:16
tongues, as the Spirit ***g*** Acts 2:4
Who ***g*** himself for us Titus 2:14

GENERATIONS
after thee in their ***g*** Gen. 17:7
throughout your ***g*** Ex. 12:14
commandments to a thousand ***g*** Deut. 7:9
ancient days, in the ***g*** Is. 51:9

GENTILES
judgment to the ***G*** Is. 42:1
the ***G***, that thou mayest Is. 49:6
destroyer of the ***G*** Jer. 4:7
before the ***G***, and kings Acts 9:15
hath God also to the ***G*** Acts 11:18
whether we be Jews or ***G*** 1 Cor. 12:13
preached unto the ***G*** 1 Tim. 3:16
is given unto the ***G*** Rev. 11:2

GHOST
and of the Holy ***G*** Matt. 28:19
Holy ***G***, whom the Father John 14:26
after that the Holy ***G*** Acts 1:8
filled with the Holy ***G*** Acts 2:4
gift of the Holy ***G*** Acts 2:38
Nazareth with the Holy ***G*** Acts 10:38
the Holy ***G*** hath made Acts 20:28
renewing of the Holy ***G*** Titus 3:5

GIVE
Unto thy seed will I ***g*** Gen. 12:7
And I will ***g*** unto thee Gen. 17:8
Lord himself shall ***g*** Is. 7:14
I will also ***g*** thee Is. 49:6
the reins, even to ***g*** Jer. 17:10
to ***g*** his life a ransom Matt. 20:28
the Lord God shall ***g*** Luke 1:32
I ***g*** to eat of the tree Rev. 2:7

GIVETH
LORD thy God ***g*** thee Ex. 20:12
LORD thy God ***g*** thee Deut. 4:40
g breath unto the people Is. 42:5
g wisdom unto the wise Dan. 2:21
killeth, but the spirit ***g*** 2 Cor. 3:6
the living God, who ***g*** 1 Tim. 6:17
that ***g*** to all men liberally James 1:5

GLORY
the LORD, and shalt ***g*** Is. 41:16
the likeness of the ***g*** Ezek. 1:28
in the ***g*** of his Father Matt. 16:27
beheld his ***g***, the ***g*** John 1:14
to whom be ***g*** for ever Rom. 11:36
God, be honour and ***g*** 1 Tim. 1:17
received up into ***g*** 1 Tim. 3:16
brightness of his ***g*** Heb. 1:3

GOD
for I the LORD thy ***G*** Ex. 20:5
LORD your ***G*** shall choose Deut. 12:5
the messengers of ***G*** 2 Chr. 36:16

Counsellor, The mighty ***G*** — **Is. 9:6**
Spirit of the Lord ***G*** — **Is. 61:1**
No man hath seen ***G*** — **John 1:18**
G so loved the world — **John 3:16**
and a sacrifice to ***G*** — **Eph. 5:2**

GODS
g of Egypt I will execute — **Ex. 12:12**
LORD, among the ***g*** — **Ex. 15:11**
your God is God of ***g*** — **Deut. 10:17**
thou serve other ***g*** — **Deut. 28:36**
shalt serve other ***g*** — **Deut. 28:64**
behold thy ***g***, O Israel — **1 Kin. 12:28**
worshipped other ***g*** — **Jer. 22:9**
after other ***g*** to serve — **Jer. 35:15**

GOLD
linen, and put a ***g*** — **Gen. 41:42**
made two calves of ***g*** — **1 Kin. 12:28**
g which Solomon king — **2 Kin. 24:13**
silver and their ***g*** — **Is. 60:9**
the carbuncle, and ***g*** — **Ezek. 28:13**
and have a chain of ***g*** — **Dan. 5:7**
gods of silver, and ***g*** — **Dan. 5:23**
will try them as ***g*** — **Zech. 13:9**

GOOD
land unto a ***g*** land — **Ex. 3:8**
shall he not make it ***g*** — **Num. 23:19**
anointed me to preach ***g*** — **Is. 61:1**
for ***g***, saith the LORD — **Jer. 21:10**
thee, O man, what is ***g*** — **Mic. 6:8**
people, zealous of ***g*** — **Titus 2:14**
g gift and every perfect — **James 1:17**
the answer of a ***g*** conscience — **1 Pet. 3:21**

GOSPEL
and preaching the ***g*** — **Matt. 4:23**
separated unto the ***g*** — **Rom. 1:1**
my spirit in the ***g*** — **Rom. 1:9**
to my ***g***, and the preaching — **Rom. 16:25**
light of the glorious ***g*** — **2 Cor. 4:4**
g, which ye have heard — **Col. 1:23**

GRACE
Jerusalem, the spirit of ***g*** — **Zech. 12:10**
full of ***g*** and truth — **John 1:14**
G to you and peace — **Rom. 1:7**
the ***g*** of our Lord Jesus — **2 Cor. 8:9**
The ***g*** of the Lord Jesus — **2 Cor. 13:14**
and knew the ***g*** of God — **Col. 1:6**
G unto you, and peace — **1 Pet. 1:2**
G be unto you, and — **Rev. 1:4**

GREAT
make of thee a ***g*** nation — **Gen. 12:2**
Egypt unto the ***g*** river — **Gen. 15:18**
lords, a ***g*** God, a mighty — **Deut. 10:17**
portion with the ***g*** — **Is. 53:12**
anger, and of ***g*** kindness — **Joel 2:13**
g, and shall be called — **Luke 1:32**
without controversy ***g*** — **1 Tim. 3:16**
the ***g*** God and our Saviour — **Titus 2:13**

GROUND
the dust of the ***g*** — **Gen. 2:7**
return unto the ***g*** — **Gen. 3:19**
not again curse the ***g*** — **Gen. 8:21**
thy name to the ***g*** — **Ps. 74:7**
floods upon the dry ***g*** — **Is. 44:3**
root out of a dry ***g*** — **Is. 53:2**
the fruit of the ***g*** — **Jer. 7:20**

HAND
deliver them out of the ***h*** — **Ex. 3:8**
a timbrel in her ***h*** — **Ex. 15:20**
h, until I make thine — **Ps. 110:1**
shall prosper in his ***h*** — **Is. 53:10**
I will turn mine ***h*** — **Zech. 13:7**
right ***h***, Come, ye blessed — **Matt. 25:34**
on the left ***h***, Depart — **Matt. 25:41**
right ***h*** of the Majesty — **Heb. 1:3**

HANDS
delivered them into the ***h*** — **Judg. 2:14**
the work of thy ***h*** — **Ps. 102:25**
h, I will hide mine — **Is. 1:15**
the reward of his ***h*** — **Is. 3:11**
planting, the work of my ***h*** — **Is. 60:21**
pass by clap their ***h*** — **Lam. 2:15**
looked upon, and our ***h*** — **1 John 1:1**
foreheads, or in their ***h*** — **Rev. 20:4**

HAST
thou ***h*** obeyed my voice — **Gen. 22:18**
which thou ***h*** purchased — **Ex. 15:16**
labours, which thou ***h*** — **Ex. 23:16**
doings, whereby thou ***h*** — **Deut. 28:20**
h drunk at the hand — **Is. 51:17**
thou ***h*** stricken them — **Jer. 5:3**
behold, thou ***h*** made — **Jer. 32:17**
saith unto him, Thou ***h*** — **Matt. 26:64**

HEAD
bruise thy ***h***, and thou — **Gen. 3:15**
thy ***h*** shall be brass — **Deut. 28:23**
unto the top of thy ***h*** — **Deut. 28:35**
the ***h***, and thou shalt — **Deut. 28:44**
poured it upon his ***h*** — **1 Sam. 10:1**
lip, they shake the ***h*** — **Ps. 22:7**
astonished, and wag his ***h*** — **Jer. 18:16**
hiss and wag their ***h*** — **Lam. 2:15**

HEAR
him, ***H*** ye me, Asa — **2 Chr. 15:2**
prayers, I will not ***h*** — **Is. 1:15**
with their eyes, and ***h*** — **Is. 6:10**
h, and your soul shall — **Is. 55:3**
voice, yet will I not ***h*** — **Ezek. 8:18**
name, and I will ***h*** — **Zech. 13:9**
h ye him — **Matt. 17:5**
hath an ear, let him ***h*** — **Rev. 2:7**

HEARD
h their cry by reason — **Ex. 3:7**
they ***h*** that the LORD — **Ex. 4:31**
the LORD, and he ***h*** — **Ps. 120:1**
have not ***h*** my fame — **Is. 66:19**
face, and I ***h*** a voice — **Ezek. 1:28**
When they ***h*** these things — **Acts 11:18**
gospel, which ye have ***h*** — **Col. 1:23**
beginning, which we have ***h*** — **1 John 1:1**

HEARKEN
thou wilt diligently ***h*** — **Ex. 15:26**
if thou wilt not ***h*** — **Deut. 28:15**
h than the fat of rams — **1 Sam. 15:22**
deceive you, neither ***h*** — **Jer. 29:8**

me, and would not ***h*** Ezek. 20:8
H, my beloved brethren James 2:5

HEART
with gladness of ***h*** Deut. 28:47
LORD looketh on the ***h*** 1 Sam. 16:7
him with a perfect ***h*** 1 Chr. 28:9
h of this people fat Is. 6:10
and to revive the ***h*** Is. 57:15
deceit of their ***h*** Jer. 14:14
LORD search the ***h*** Jer. 17:10
And rend your ***h***, and Joel 2:13

HEARTS
faintness into their ***h*** Lev. 26:36
LORD with all your ***h*** 1 Sam. 7:3
LORD searcheth all ***h*** 1 Chr. 28:9
write it in their ***h*** Jer. 31:33
counsels of the ***h*** 1 Cor. 4:5
stablish your ***h*** unblameable 1 Thess. 3:13
faith, having our ***h*** Heb. 10:22

HEATHEN
scatter you among the ***h*** Lev. 26:33
number among the ***h*** Deut. 4:27
shall give thee the ***h*** Ps. 2:8
didst drive out the ***h*** Ps. 44:2
hast cast out the ***h*** Ps. 80:8
polluted before the ***h*** Ezek. 20:9
h, which ye have profaned Ezek. 36:23
the ***h***, saith the LORD Mal. 1:11

HEAVEN
the stars of the ***h*** Gen. 22:17
Lord's throne is in ***h*** Ps. 11:4
for the fowls of ***h*** Jer. 16:4
God of ***h*** set up a kingdom Dan. 2:44
lo a voice from ***h*** Matt. 3:17
in the clouds of ***h*** Matt. 26:64
me in ***h*** and in earth Matt. 28:18
God out of ***h***, prepared Rev. 21:2

HEAVENS
h are the work of thy Ps. 102:25
Hear, O ***h***, and give Is. 1:2
darkened in the ***h*** thereof Is. 5:30
dissolved, and the ***h*** Is. 34:4
that created the ***h*** Is. 42:5
stretcheth forth the ***h*** Is. 44:24
lo, the ***h*** were opened Matt. 3:16
the powers of the ***h*** Matt. 24:29

HID
I ***h*** not my face from Is. 50:6
h as it were our faces Is. 53:3
wrath I ***h*** my face from Is. 54:8
are not ***h*** from my face Jer. 16:17

HIDE
h it not from me Josh. 7:19
apple of the eye, ***h*** Ps. 17:8
hands, I will ***h*** mine Is. 1:15
will even ***h*** his face Mic. 3:4

HIGH
Solomon build an ***h*** 1 Kin. 11:7
salvation, and my ***h*** Ps. 18:2
JEHOVAH, art the most ***h*** Ps. 83:18
to Dibon, the ***h*** places Is. 15:2
saith the ***h*** and lofty Is. 57:15

Mind not ***h*** things Rom. 12:16
of the Majesty on ***h*** Heb. 1:3
we have not an ***h*** priest Heb. 4:15

HOLD
trembling shall take ***h*** Ex. 15:15
h not thy peace at Ps. 39:12
sorrows shall take ***h*** Is. 13:8
cisterns, that can ***h*** Jer. 2:13
I cannot ***h*** my peace Jer. 4:19
take ***h*** of your fathers Zech. 1:6
h the doctrine of Balaam Rev. 2:14

HOLY
priests, and an ***h*** nation Ex. 19:6
For thou art an ***h*** people Deut. 7:6
set my king upon my ***h*** Ps. 2:6
Son, and of the ***H*** Ghost Matt. 28:19
filled with the ***H*** Ghost Acts 2:4
receive the gift of the ***H*** Acts 2:38
the ***H*** Ghost hath made Acts 20:28
royal priesthood, an ***h*** 1 Pet. 2:9

HONOUR
H thy father and thy Ex. 20:12
with their lips do ***h*** Is. 29:13
only wise God, be ***h*** 1 Tim. 1:17
be ***h*** and power everlasting 1 Tim. 6:16
crowned with glory and ***h*** Heb. 2:9

HOPE
promise, having no ***h*** Eph. 2:12
moved away from the ***h*** Col. 1:23
love, and patience of ***h*** 1 Thess. 1:3
In ***h*** of eternal life Titus 1:2
for that blessed ***h*** Titus 2:13

HORSES
shall not multiply ***h*** Deut. 17:16
chariots, and some in ***h*** Ps. 20:7
stay on ***h***, and trust Is. 31:1
Their ***h*** also are swifter Hab. 1:8

HOST
said, This is God's ***h*** Gen. 32:2
and upon all his ***h*** Ex. 14:4
the ***h*** of heaven, shouldest Deut. 4:19
h of heaven, and served 2 Kin. 17:16
Hezekiah with a great ***h*** 2 Kin. 18:17
And all the ***h*** of heaven Is. 34:4

HOSTS
zeal of the LORD of ***h*** Is. 9:7
redeemer the LORD of ***h*** Is. 44:6
saith the LORD of ***h*** Jer. 49:7
saith the LORD of ***h*** Zech. 13:7
messenger of the LORD of ***h*** Mal. 2:7
saith the LORD of ***h*** Mal. 3:1
saith the LORD of ***h*** Mal. 3:5
saith the LORD of ***h*** Mal. 4:1

HOUR
whole from that ***h*** Matt. 9:22
him, because his ***h*** John 7:30
Jesus knew that his ***h*** John 13:1
h was there a great Rev. 11:13

HOUSE
Egypt, out of the ***h*** Ex. 20:2
He shall build an ***h*** 2 Sam. 7:13
thine ***h*** and thy kingdom 2 Sam. 7:16

treasures of the *h* 2 Kin. 24:13
mountain of the LORD's *h* Is. 2:2
will make with the *h* Jer. 31:33
will pour upon the *h* Zech. 12:10
shall reign over the *h* Luke 1:33

HOUSES
leaven out of your *h* Ex. 12:15
house, and all the *h* 2 Kin. 25:9
desolate *h*, and dragons Is. 13:22
and all the *h* of Jerusalem Jer. 52:13

HUNDRED
him that is an *h* years Gen. 17:17
upward, for six *h* thousand Ex. 38:26
you shall chase an *h* Lev. 26:8
h horsemen, and twenty 2 Sam. 8:4
Obadiah took an *h* prophets 1 Kin. 18:4
two *h* and ninety days Dan. 12:11

IDOLS
Nebo stoopeth, their *i* Is. 46:1
her *i* are confounded Jer. 50:2
whoring after their *i* Ezek. 6:9
forsake the *i* of Egypt Ezek. 20:8
your *i*, will I cleanse Ezek. 36:25
in sacrifice unto *i* 1 Cor. 8:4
temple of God with *i* 2 Cor. 6:16

IMAGE
i of God made he man Gen. 9:6
i of God, should shine 2 Cor. 4:4
glory, and the express *i* Heb. 1:3
i, and whosoever receiveth Rev. 14:11
that worshipped his *i* Rev. 19:20

INCENSE
the altar of sweet *i* Lev. 4:7
of Israel did burn *i* 2 Kin. 18:4
cometh there to me *i* Jer. 6:20
own mouth, to burn *i* Jer. 44:17
place *i* shall be offered Mal. 1:11

INHABITANTS
will deliver the *i* Ex. 23:31
have withdrawn the *i* Deut. 13:13
the *i* of the land faint Josh. 2:9
i of Dor and her towns Josh. 17:11
Tishbite, who was of the *i* 1 Kin. 17:1
land, and against the *i* Jer. 25:9
David, and upon the *i* Zech. 12:10

INHERITANCE
is the lot of his *i* Deut. 32:9
captain over his *i* 1 Sam. 10:1
heathen for thine *i* Ps. 2:8
an *i* unto your fathers Jer. 3:18
is the rod of his *i* Jer. 10:16
forgiveness of sins, and *i* Acts 26:18
have obtained an *i* Eph. 1:11

INIQUITY
God, visiting the *i* Ex. 20:5
truth and without *i* Deut. 32:4
commit *i*, I will chasten 2 Sam. 7:14
hath laid on him the *i* Is. 53:6
i, and I will remember Jer. 31:34
reconciliation for *i* Dan. 9:24
thee, that pardoneth *i* Mic. 7:18
redeem us from all *i* Titus 2:14

ISAAC
father, and the God of *I* Gen. 28:13
Abraham, the God of *I* Ex. 3:15
Remember Abraham, *I* Ex. 32:13
seed of Abraham, *I* Jer. 33:26

ISRAEL
be cut off from *I* Ex. 12:15
the children of *I* Ex. 19:6
from reigning over *I* 1 Sam. 16:1
behold thy gods, O *I* 1 Kin. 12:28
LORD the King of *I* Is. 44:6
the preserved of *I* Is. 49:6
and *I* shall dwell safely Jer. 23:6
is to be ruler in *I* Mic. 5:2

JACOB
And *J* called the name Gen. 32:30
And *J* rent his clothes Gen. 37:34
house of the God of *J* Is. 2:3
Fear not, thou worm *J* Is. 41:14
redeemed his servant *J* Is. 48:20
up the tribes of *J* Is. 49:6
I have given unto *J* Ezek. 37:25
over the house of *J* Luke 1:33

JERUSALEM
you to go up to *J* 1 Kin. 12:28
beautiful garments, O *J* Is. 52:1
all the houses of *J* Jer. 52:13
shout, O daughter of *J* Zech. 9:9
J, the spirit of grace Zech. 12:10
go unto *J*, and suffer Matt. 16:21
nations, beginning at *J* Luke 24:47
holy city, new *J*, coming Rev. 21:2

JESUS
J went about all Galilee Matt. 4:23
And *J* came and spake Matt. 28:18
J saith unto him, I John 14:6
J Christ for the remission Acts 2:38
Father, and the Lord *J* Rom. 1:7
are ye in Christ *J* 1 Cor. 1:30
God and our Saviour *J* Titus 2:13
And from *J* Christ Rev. 1:5

JEWS
J, came Jesus and stood John 20:19
the *J* saw the multitudes Acts 13:45
came thither certain *J* Acts 14:19
J that Jesus was Christ Acts 18:5
Testifying both to the *J* Acts 20:21
body, whether we be *J* 1 Cor. 12:13

JOHN
day *J* seeth Jesus coming John 1:29
Peter, and James, and *J* Acts 1:13
J to the seven churches Rev. 1:4
I *J* saw the holy city Rev. 21:2

JOSEPH
drew and lifted up *J* Gen. 37:28
the LORD was with *J* Gen. 39:2
And *J* was the governor Gen. 42:6
thou that leadest *J* Ps. 80:1

JOSHUA
and *J* the son of Nun Num. 14:30
And *J* rent his clothes Josh. 7:6
commandment of the LORD to *J* Josh. 15:13

to *J* the son of Josedech — Hag. 1:1
Hear now, O *J* the high — Zech. 3:8

JOY
for situation, the *j* — Ps. 48:2
rejoice even with *j* — Is. 35:2
j and gladness shall — Is. 51:3
ashes, the oil of *j* — Is. 61:3
The voice of *j*, and — Jer. 33:11
perfection of beauty, The *j* — Lam. 2:15
the *j* that was set — Heb. 12:2

JUDAH
And the sons of *J* — Gen. 46:12
not depart from *J* — Gen. 49:10
Jehoiachin the king of *J* — 2 Kin. 24:12
me, Asa, and all *J* — 2 Chr. 15:2
Zedekiah king of *J* — Jer. 21:7
days *J* shall be saved — Jer. 23:6
all the nobles of *J* — Jer. 39:6
the thousands of *J* — Mic. 5:2

JUDGE
the *J* of all the earth — Gen. 18:25
LORD shall *j* his people — Deut. 32:36
cometh to *j* the earth — Ps. 96:13
relieve the oppressed, *j* — Is. 1:17
they *j* not the fatherless — Is. 1:23
j the poor, and reprove — Is. 11:4
The heads thereof *j* — Mic. 3:11
Therefore *j* nothing — 1 Cor. 4:5

JUDGMENT
Egypt I will execute *j* — Ex. 12:12
shalt not wrest *j* — Deut. 16:19
all his ways are *j* — Deut. 32:4
establish it with *j* — Is. 9:7
shall bring forth *j* — Is. 42:1
prison and from *j* — Is. 53:8
execute *j* and justice — Jer. 23:5
come near to you to *j* — Mal. 3:5

JUDGMENTS
arm, and with great *j* — Ex. 6:6
statutes, and my *j* — Lev. 18:5
sinned against thy *j* — Neh. 9:29
they despised my *j* — Ezek. 20:13
walk in my *j*, and observe — Ezek. 37:24
j, and his ways past — Rom. 11:33

KING
bring thee, and thy *k* — Deut. 28:36
the *k* took counsel — 1 Kin. 12:28
Yet have I set my *k* — Ps. 2:6
saith the LORD the *K* — Is. 44:6
righteous Branch, and a *K* — Jer. 23:5
k of Babylon, my servant — Jer. 25:9
behold, thy *K* cometh — Zech. 9:9
Then shall the *K* say — Matt. 25:34

KINGDOM
be unto me a *k* of priests — Ex. 19:6
will establish his *k* — 2 Sam. 7:12
the throne of his *k* — 2 Sam. 7:13
David, and upon his *k* — Is. 9:7
heaven set up a *k* — Dan. 2:44
the gospel of the *k* — Matt. 4:23
Father, inherit the *k* — Matt. 25:34
and of his *k* there — Luke 1:33

KINGS
loose the loins of *k* — Is. 45:1
servant of rulers, *K* — Is. 49:7
k shall be thy nursing — Is. 49:23
k of the land of Uz — Jer. 25:20
the days of these *k* — Dan. 2:44
the Gentiles, and *k* — Acts 9:15
the prince of the *k* — Rev. 1:5
lords, and King of *k* — Rev. 17:14

KNEW
thee in the belly I *k* — Jer. 1:5
passover, when Jesus *k* — John 13:1
be sin for us, who *k* — 2 Cor. 5:21
k the grace of God — Col. 1:6

KNOWETH
the proud he *k* afar — Ps. 138:6
and no man *k* the Son — Matt. 11:27
walketh in darkness *k* — John 12:35
him not, neither *k* — John 14:17
written, which no man *k* — Rev. 2:17

KNOWLEDGE
shall be full of the *k* — Is. 11:9
by his *k* shall my righteous — Is. 53:11
unto the wise, and *k* — Dan. 2:21
lips should keep *k* — Mal. 2:7
wisdom and *k* of God — Rom. 11:33
mysteries, and all *k* — 1 Cor. 13:2

LAID
Dibon, and we have *l* — Num. 21:30
hast thou *l* the foundation — Ps. 102:25
for it is *l* waste — Is. 23:1
and the LORD hath *l* — Is. 53:6
thy cities shall be *l* — Jer. 4:7
had prayed, they *l* — Acts 6:6
Henceforth there is *l* — 2 Tim. 4:8
he *l* his right hand — Rev. 1:17

LAMB
he is brought as a *l* — Is. 53:7
saith, Behold the *L* — John 1:29
L which is in the midst — Rev. 7:17
book of life of the *L* — Rev. 13:8
presence of the *L* — Rev. 14:10
make war with the *L* — Rev. 17:14

LAND
will I give this *l* — Gen. 12:7
have I given this *l* — Gen. 15:18
l unto a good *l* and — Ex. 3:8
brought thee out of the *l* — Ex. 20:2
l which the LORD thy — Ex. 20:12
The fruit of thy *l* — Deut. 28:33
thee up out of the *l* — 1 Kin. 12:28
them against this *l* — Jer. 25:9

LAW
Jethro his father in *l* — Ex. 3:1
the words of this *l* — Deut. 28:58
l, which Moses my servant — Josh. 1:7
the *l*, and the word — Is. 2:3
LORD, I will put my *l* — Jer. 31:33
seek the *l* at his mouth — Mal. 2:7
perfect manner of the *l* — Acts 22:3
woman, made under the *l* — Gal. 4:4

LAY
that I may *l* my hand Ex. 7:4
flesh, and fasted, and *l* 1 Kin. 21:27
And I will *l* it waste Is. 5:6
l their hand upon Edom Is. 11:14
Lord God, Behold, I *l* Is. 28:16
pray thee, come and *l* Mark 5:23
and I *l* down my life John 10:15

LIE
man, that he should *l* Num. 23:19
another man shall *l* Deut. 28:30
and I *l* even among Ps. 57:4
speaketh a *l*, he speaketh John 8:44
God, that cannot *l* Titus 1:2
abomination, or maketh a *l* Rev. 21:27

LIFE
nostrils the breath of *l* Gen. 2:7
the days of thy *l* Josh. 1:5
minister, and to give his *l* Matt. 20:28
have everlasting *l* John 3:16
the truth, and the *l* John 14:6
the spirit giveth *l* 2 Cor. 3:6
(For the *l* was manifested 1 John 1:2
eat of the tree of *l* Rev. 2:7

LIFT
thou *l* up thine eyes Deut. 4:19
ashamed and blush to *l* Ezra 9:6
he will *l* up an ensign Is. 5:26
L up your eyes to the Is. 51:6
aloud, spare not, *l* Is. 58:1

LIFTED
And Lot *l* up his eyes Gen. 13:10
Moses *l* up his hand Num. 20:11
they *l* up their voice 2 Chr. 5:13
of my bread, hath *l* Ps. 41:9
every one that is *l* Is. 2:12
and the spirit *l* me Ezek. 8:3
Because thine heart is *l* Ezek. 28:2

LIGHT
l thing that thou shouldest Is. 49:6
shall not give her *l* Matt. 24:29
life was the *l* of men John 1:4
from darkness to *l* Acts 26:18
bring to *l* the hidden 1 Cor. 4:5
l of the glorious gospel 2 Cor. 4:4
immortality, dwelling in the *l* 1 Tim. 6:16
into his marvellous *l* 1 Pet. 2:9

LIVE
man do, he shall *l* Lev. 18:5
man do, he shall *l* Neh. 9:29
deceitful men shall not *l* Ps. 55:23
your soul shall *l* Is. 55:3
as I *l*, saith the Lord Ezek. 5:11
do, he shall even *l* Ezek. 20:13
Syriack, O king, *l* Dan. 2:4
as I *l*, saith the Lord Zeph. 2:9

LIVING
man became a *l* soul Gen. 2:7
every thing l, as I Gen. 8:21
sight shall no man *l* Ps. 143:2
the land of the *l* Is. 53:8
the fountain of *l* waters Jer. 2:13
true God, he is the *l* Jer. 10:10

present your bodies a *l* Rom. 12:1
works to serve the *l* Heb. 9:14

LONG
that thy days may be *l* Ex. 20:12
them all the day *l* Deut. 28:32
great plagues, and of *l* Deut. 28:59
How *l* wilt thou mourn 1 Sam. 16:1
said I, Lord, how *l* Is. 6:11
How *l*, O Lord, holy Rev. 6:10

LORD
L appeared unto Abram Gen. 12:7
day the *L* made a covenant Gen. 15:18
for I the *L* thy God Ex. 20:5
L your God shall choose Deut. 12:5
L shall scatter thee Deut. 28:64
zeal of the *L* of hosts Is. 9:7
saith the *L*, that I Jer. 23:5
called, THE *L* OUR RIGHTEOUSNESS Jer. 23:6

LOVE
thou shalt *l* thy neighbour Lev. 19:18
his *l* and in his pity Is. 63:9
and my people *l* to Jer. 5:31
justly, and to *l* mercy Mic. 6:8
And walk in *l*, as Christ Eph. 5:2
promised to them that *l* James 1:12
promised to them that *l* James 2:5
is *l*, not that we loved 1 John 4:10

LOVED
For God so *l* the world John 3:16
Christ also hath *l* Eph. 5:2
love, not that we *l* 1 John 4:10
that *l* us, and washed Rev. 1:5

MADE
day the Lord *m* a covenant Gen. 15:18
and *m* the sea dry land Ex. 14:21
forsook God which *m* Deut. 32:15
m two calves of gold 1 Kin. 12:28
sin of many, and *m* Is. 53:12
the Word was *m* flesh John 1:14
the Holy Ghost hath *m* Acts 20:28
Jesus, who of God is *m* 1 Cor. 1:30

MAKE
shall he not *m* it good Num. 23:19
thou shalt *m* no covenant Deut. 7:2
I *m* thine enemies thy Ps. 110:1
yea, when ye *m* many Is. 1:15
thou shalt *m* his soul Is. 53:10
and I will *m* an everlasting Is. 55:3
destroy them, and *m* Jer. 25:9
to *m* an end of sins Dan. 9:24

MAKETH
He *m* wars to cease Ps. 46:9
m the clouds his chariot Ps. 104:3
wise son *m* a glad father Prov. 10:1
Lord that *m* all things Is. 44:24
worketh abomination, or *m* Rev. 21:27

MAN
God is not a *m*, that Num. 23:19
any *m* be able to stand Josh. 1:5
even to give every *m* Jer. 17:10
shepherd, and against the *m* Zech. 13:7
For the Son of *m* shall Matt. 16:27

Even as the Son of *m* Matt. 20:28
No *m* hath seen God John 1:18
m cometh unto the Father John 14:6

MANNER
m, to slay the righteous Gen. 18:25
any *m* of creeping thing Lev. 11:44
eateth any *m* of blood Lev. 17:10
kingdom, and healing all *m* Matt. 4:23
perfect *m* of the law Acts 22:3
bare twelve *m* of fruits Rev. 22:2

MAYEST
thou *m* prolong thy Deut. 4:40
book, that thou *m* fear Deut. 28:58
courageous, that thou *m* Josh. 1:7
Gentiles, that thou *m* Is. 49:6

MEAT
remnant of the *m* offering Lev. 2:3
theirs, every *m* offering Num. 18:9
carcase shall be *m* Deut. 28:26
this people shall be *m* Jer. 7:33
carcases shall be *m* Jer. 16:4
bodies shall be for *m* Jer. 34:20

MEN
with the rod of *m* 2 Sam. 7:14
the children of *m* Ps. 11:4
m may know that thou Ps. 83:18
worm Jacob, and ye *m* Is. 41:14
and rejected of *m* Is. 53:3
houses of the great *m* Jer. 52:13
the city that *m* call Lam. 2:15
old *m* shall dream dreams Joel 2:28

MERCY
thee from above the *m* Ex. 25:22
with them, nor shew *m* Deut. 7:2
and plenteous in *m* Ps. 86:15
them shall have *m* Prov. 28:13
and he will have *m* Is. 55:7
have pity, nor have *m* Jer. 21:7
justly, and to love *m* Mic. 6:8
he delighteth in *m* Mic. 7:18

MIDST
anointed him in the *m* 1 Sam. 16:13
were torn in the *m* Is. 5:25
diviners, that be in the *m* Jer. 29:8
be consumed in the *m* Ezek. 5:12
shall fall in the *m* Ezek. 6:7
m of the land of Egypt Ezek. 20:8
princes in the *m* thereof Ezek. 22:27
life, which is in the *m* Rev. 2:7

MIGHTY
a *m* hand, and redeemed Deut. 7:8
lords, a great God, a *m* Deut. 10:17
all the *m* men of valour 2 Kin. 24:14
officers, and the *m* 2 Kin. 24:15
Wonderful, Counsellor, The *m* Is. 9:6
let the *m* man glory Jer. 9:23
Great in counsel, and *m* Jer. 32:19
heart of the *m* men Jer. 49:22

MINE
all the earth is *m* Ex. 19:5
Yea, *m* own familiar Ps. 41:9
hands, I will hide *m* Is. 1:15
m elect, in whom my Is. 42:1
transgressions for *m* Is. 43:25
accepted upon *m* altar Is. 56:7
m eye shall not spare Ezek. 8:18
and I will turn *m* hand Zech. 13:7

MINISTER
ministered unto, but to *m* Matt. 20:28
I Paul am made a *m* Col. 1:23
spirits, sent forth to *m* Heb. 1:14
if any man *m*, let him 1 Pet. 4:11

MOAB
mighty men of *M*, trembling Ex. 15:15
hath consumed Ar of *M* Num. 21:28
Woe to thee, *M* Num. 21:29
he smote *M*, and measured 2 Sam. 8:2
the abomination of *M* 1 Kin. 11:7
M shall howl over Nebo Is. 15:2
shall cry out for *M* Is. 15:5
of Israel, Surely *M* Zeph. 2:9

MONTH
day of the same *m* Ex. 12:6
first *m*, on the fourteenth Ex. 12:18
appointed of the *m* Ex. 23:15
Observe the *m* of Abib Deut. 16:1
king, in the sixth *m* Hag. 1:1
her fruit every *m* Rev. 22:2

MOON
the sun, and the *m* Deut. 4:19
going forth, and the *m* Is. 13:10
darkness, and the *m* Joel 2:31
darkened, and the *m* Matt. 24:29

MORNING
remain until the *m* Ex. 12:10
third day in the *m* Ex. 19:16
sweet incense every *m* Ex. 30:7
night until the *m* Lev. 19:13
In the *m* thou shalt Deut. 28:67
he wakeneth *m* by *m* Is. 50:4
the bright and *m* star Rev. 22:16

MOSES
Now *M* kept the flock Ex. 3:1
And *M* stretched out Ex. 14:21
M did so in the sight Ex. 17:6
And he gave unto *M* Ex. 31:18
M lifted up his hand Num. 20:11
I was with *M*, so I Josh. 1:5
law, which *M* my servant Josh. 1:7
offer the gift that *M* Matt. 8:4

MOTHER
thy father and thy *m* Ex. 20:12
Babylon, he, and his *m* 2 Kin. 24:12
Babylon, and the king's *m* 2 Kin. 24:15
heaviness of his *m* Prov. 10:1
thy father and thy *m* Matt. 19:19
women, and Mary the *m* Acts 1:14

MOUNT
thick cloud upon the *m* Ex. 19:16
upon *m* Sinai, two tables Ex. 31:18
shined forth from *m* Deut. 33:2
whole earth, is *m* Zion Ps. 48:2
sit also upon the *m* Is. 14:13
LORD in the holy *m* Is. 27:13

in *m* Zion from henceforth Mic. 4:7
ye are come unto *m* Heb. 12:22

MOUNTAIN
m of God, even to Horeb Ex. 3:1
m of the LORD's house Is. 2:2
to the *m* of the LORD Is. 2:3
destroy in all my holy *m* Is. 11:9
bring to my holy *m* Is. 56:7
in Zion, my holy *m* Joel 3:17

MOUNTAINS
Before the *m* were brought Ps. 90:2
in the top of the *m* Is. 2:2
singing, ye *m*, O forest Is. 44:23
into singing, O *m* Is. 49:13
stumble upon the dark *m* Jer. 13:16
feed them upon the *m* Ezek. 34:13
The *m* quake at him Nah. 1:5
that I could remove *m* 1 Cor. 13:2

MOUTH
with the rod of his *m* Is. 11:4
m, and with their lips Is. 29:13
he opened not his *m* Is. 53:7
own *m*, to burn incense Jer. 44:17
m they shew much love Ezek. 33:31
the trumpet to thy *m* Hos. 8:1
seek the law at his *m* Mal. 2:7
m went a sharp twoedged Rev. 1:16

MULTITUDE
stars of heaven for *m* Deut. 28:62
the sea shore in *m* 1 Sam. 13:5
gone with the *m*, I Ps. 42:4
m of thy tender mercies Ps. 51:1
to the *m* of his mercies Ps. 106:45
m, and take her spoil Ezek. 29:19
man is mad, for the *m* Hos. 9:7

NATION
of thee a great *n* Gen. 12:2
priests, and an holy *n* Ex. 19:6
a *n* which thou knowest Deut. 28:33
over thee, unto a *n* Deut. 28:36
LORD shall bring a *n* Deut. 28:49
A *n* of fierce countenance Deut. 28:50
n abhorreth, to a servant Is. 49:7
priesthood, an holy *n* 1 Pet. 2:9

NATIONS
n of the earth be blessed Gen. 22:18
byword, among all *n* Deut. 28:37
n shalt thou find no Deut. 28:65
the kindreds of the *n* Ps. 22:27
and all *n* shall flow Is. 2:2
set thee over the *n* Jer. 1:10
all these *n* round about Jer. 25:9
and teach all *n*, baptizing Matt. 28:19

NEIGHBOUR
thou shalt love thy *n* Lev. 19:18
hath given it to a *n* 1 Sam. 15:28
his *n*, and trust ye Jer. 9:4
more every man his *n* Jer. 31:34

NIGHT
flesh in that *n*, roast Ex. 12:8
land of Egypt this *n* Ex. 12:12
east wind all that *n* Ex. 14:21
men of war fled by *n* 2 Kin. 25:4
run down with tears *n* Jer. 14:17
came to Jesus by *n* John 3:2
no rest day nor *n* Rev. 14:11
tormented day and *n* Rev. 20:10

NORTH
the sides of the *n* Ps. 48:2
the sides of the *n* Is. 14:13
the *n*, saith the LORD Jer. 25:9
looketh toward the *n* Ezek. 8:3

NUMBER
if thou be able to *n* Gen. 15:5
n, from twenty years Num. 14:29
shall be left few in *n* Deut. 4:27
shall be left few in *n* Deut. 28:62
marvellous things without *n* Job 5:9

OFFER
But ye shall *o* an offering Lev. 23:8
Seven days ye shall *o* Lev. 23:36
children of Israel *o* Num. 18:19
fire which ye shall *o* Num. 28:3
O unto God thanksgiving Ps. 50:14
Sheba and Seba shall *o* Ps. 72:10
priest, and *o* the gift Matt. 8:4
holy priesthood, to *o* 1 Pet. 2:5

OFFERED
incense shall be *o* Mal. 1:11
those things that are *o* 1 Cor. 8:4
without blood, which he *o* Heb. 9:7
the eternal Spirit *o* Heb. 9:14

OFFERING
shekel shall be the *o* Ex. 30:13
altar of the burnt *o* Lev. 4:7
even an *o* made by fire Lev. 24:7
is the *o* made by fire Num. 28:3
tithes, and the heave *o* Deut. 12:11
make his soul an *o* Is. 53:10
name, and a pure *o* Mal. 1:11
for us an *o* and a sacrifice Eph. 5:2

OFFERINGS
heave *o* of the holy Num. 18:19
bring your burnt *o* Deut. 12:6
burnt *o*, and your sacrifices Deut. 12:11
delight in burnt *o* 1 Sam. 15:22
burnt *o* and their sacrifices Is. 56:7
burnt *o* are not acceptable Jer. 6:20
to pour out drink *o* Jer. 44:17

OIL
thyself with the *o* Deut. 28:40
either corn, wine, or *o* Deut. 28:51
Samuel took a vial of *o* 1 Sam. 10:1
thine horn with *o* 1 Sam. 16:1
horn of *o*, and anointed 1 Sam. 16:13
anointed thee with the *o* Ps. 45:7
beauty for ashes, the *o* Is. 61:3

OPEN
LORD shall *o* unto thee Deut. 28:12
loins of kings, to *o* Is. 45:1
for thine eyes are *o* Jer. 32:19
To *o* their eyes, and Acts 26:18

OPENED
afflicted, yet he *o* Is. 53:7

and the books were ***o*** Dan. 7:10
the heavens were ***o*** Matt. 3:16
Then Peter ***o*** his mouth Acts 10:34
temple of God was ***o*** Rev. 11:19

PART
p of thee shall die Ezek. 5:12
will bring the third ***p*** Zech. 13:9
unto the uttermost ***p*** Acts 1:8
now I know in ***p*** 1 Cor. 13:12
their ***p*** in the lake Rev. 21:8

PASS
For I will ***p*** through Ex. 12:12
let any of thy seed ***p*** Lev. 18:21
to ***p***, if thou wilt Deut. 28:15
their daughters to ***p*** 2 Kin. 17:17
to ***p*** in the last days Is. 2:2
come to ***p*** in that day Is. 11:11
p by clap their hands Lam. 2:15
p afterward, that I Joel 2:28

PASSED
And the LORD ***p*** by before Ex. 34:6
and the people ***p*** over Josh. 3:16
he ***p*** away, and, lo Ps. 37:36
old things are ***p*** away 2 Cor. 5:17

PAUL
P and Barnabas waxed Acts 13:46
having stoned ***P***, drew Acts 14:19
Macedonia, ***P*** was pressed Acts 18:5
P, a servant of Jesus Rom. 1:1
whereof I ***P*** am made Col. 1:23

PEACE
Father, The Prince of ***P*** Is. 9:6
his government and ***p*** Is. 9:7
chastisement of our ***p*** Is. 53:5
held their ***p***, and glorified Acts 11:18
p from God our Father Rom. 1:7
Follow ***p*** with all men Heb. 12:14
Grace unto you, and ***p*** 1 Pet. 1:2
be unto you, and ***p*** Rev. 1:4

PEOPLE
gathering of the ***p*** Gen. 49:10
unto me above all ***p*** Ex. 19:5
thou art an holy ***p*** Deut. 7:6
scatter thee among all ***p*** Deut. 28:64
arose against his ***p*** 2 Chr. 36:16
disease among the ***p*** Matt. 4:23
a peculiar ***p***, zealous Titus 2:14
nation, a peculiar ***p*** 1 Pet. 2:9

PERFECT
me, and be thou ***p*** Gen. 17:1
Rock, his work is ***p*** Deut. 32:4
serve him with a ***p*** 1 Chr. 28:9
man was ***p*** and upright Job 1:1
good gift and every ***p*** James 1:17

PERISH
shall soon utterly ***p*** Deut. 4:26
destroyed, and until thou ***p*** Deut. 28:20
thee until thou ***p*** Deut. 28:22
be angry, and ye ***p*** Ps. 2:12
not ***p***, but have everlasting John 3:16

PHARAOH
P took off his ring Gen. 41:42
they built for ***P*** treasure Ex. 1:11
P, which I have put Ex. 4:21
P also called the wise Ex. 7:11
hand of ***P*** king of Egypt Deut. 7:8
wise counsellors of ***P*** Is. 19:11

PHILISTINES
unto the sea of the ***P*** Ex. 23:31
five lords of the ***P*** Josh. 13:3
the hand of the ***P*** 1 Sam. 7:3
the land of the ***P*** Jer. 25:20

PIECES
groves, and brake in ***p*** 2 Kin. 18:4
house, and cut in ***p*** 2 Kin. 24:13
shalt dash them in ***p*** Ps. 2:9
Merodach is broken in ***p*** Jer. 50:2
break in ***p*** and consume Dan. 2:44
shall be dashed in ***p*** Hos. 13:16

PIT
the ***p***, and sold Joseph Gen. 37:28
go down into the ***p*** Ps. 28:1
into the ***p*** of destruction Ps. 55:23
the sides of the ***p*** Is. 14:15

PLACE
unto the ***p*** of the Canaanites Ex. 3:8
the ***p*** which the LORD Deut. 12:5
be a ***p*** which the LORD Deut. 12:11
LORD thy God in the ***p*** Deut. 16:16
Solomon build an high ***p*** 1 Kin. 11:7
on his dwelling ***p*** 2 Chr. 36:15
the high and holy ***p*** Is. 57:15
his ***p*** to make thy land Jer. 4:7

PLACES
lords of the high ***p*** Num. 21:28
ride on the high ***p*** Deut. 32:13
Dibon, the high ***p*** Is. 15:2
comfort all her waste ***p*** Is. 51:3
shall weep in secret ***p*** Jer. 13:17
p whither I shall drive Jer. 24:9
all the inhabited ***p*** Ezek. 34:13
wickedness in high ***p*** Eph. 6:12

PLAIN
and beheld all the ***p*** Gen. 13:10
p, even the salt sea Josh. 3:16
the way toward the ***p*** 2 Kin. 25:4
a ***p*** from Geba to Rimmon Zech. 14:10

POOR
hath pity upon the ***p*** Prov. 19:17
judge the ***p***, and reprove Is. 11:4
strength to the ***p*** Is. 25:4
children, and of the ***p*** Jer. 40:7
treading is upon the ***p*** Amos 5:11
the gospel to the ***p*** Luke 4:18
sakes he became ***p*** 2 Cor. 8:9
not God chosen the ***p*** James 2:5

POSSESS
and thy seed shall ***p*** Gen. 22:17
go over Jordan to ***p*** Deut. 4:26
whither thou goest to ***p*** Deut. 28:21
whither thou goest to ***p*** Deut. 28:63

POUR
shall ***p*** all the blood — **Lev. 4:7**
For I will ***p*** water — **Is. 44:3**
afterward, that I will ***p*** — **Joel 2:28**
I will ***p*** upon the house — **Zech. 12:10**

POURED
where the ashes are ***p*** — **Lev. 4:12**
vial of oil, and ***p*** — **1 Sam. 10:1**
he hath ***p*** out his soul — **Is. 53:12**
of God, which is ***p*** — **Rev. 14:10**

POWER
or have I no ***p*** to deliver — **Is. 50:2**
hand of ***p***, and coming — **Matt. 26:64**
them, saying, All ***p*** — **Matt. 28:18**
ye shall receive ***p*** — **Acts 1:8**
p of Satan unto God — **Acts 26:18**
that is of ***p*** to stablish — **Rom. 16:25**
be honour and ***p*** everlasting — **1 Tim. 6:16**
the word of his ***p*** — **Heb. 1:3**

PRAISE
voice of joy and ***p*** — **Ps. 42:4**
mourning, the garment of ***p*** — **Is. 61:3**
P the LORD of hosts — **Jer. 33:11**
whose ***p*** is not of men — **Rom. 2:29**
man have ***p*** of God — **1 Cor. 4:5**
sacrifice of ***p*** to God — **Heb. 13:15**
Christ, to whom be ***p*** — **1 Pet. 4:11**

PRAY
a little water, I ***p*** — **Gen. 18:4**
Achan, My son, give, I ***p*** — **Josh. 7:19**
LORD thy God, and ***p*** — **1 Kin. 13:6**
said, I ***p*** thee, O LORD — **Jon. 4:2**
and I ***p*** God your whole — **1 Thess. 5:23**
say that he shall ***p*** — **1 John 5:16**

PRAYER
the ***p*** which thy servant — **1 Kin. 8:29**
Hear my ***p***, O LORD — **Ps. 39:12**
joyful in my house of ***p*** — **Is. 56:7**
Praying always with all ***p*** — **Eph. 6:18**

PRESENCE
be moved at his ***p*** — **Is. 19:1**
angel of his ***p*** saved — **Is. 63:9**
burned at his ***p***, yea — **Nah. 1:5**
the ***p*** of the holy angels — **Rev. 14:10**

PRIEST
father in law, the ***p*** — **Ex. 3:1**
And the ***p*** shall put — **Lev. 4:7**
the ***p*** and the prophet — **Is. 28:7**
the ***p***, the son of Buzi — **Ezek. 1:3**
Josedech, the high ***p*** — **Hag. 1:1**
shew thyself to the ***p*** — **Matt. 8:4**
have not an high ***p*** — **Heb. 4:15**
second went the high ***p*** — **Heb. 9:7**

PRIESTS
of ***p***, and an holy nation — **Ex. 19:6**
Abiathar, were the ***p*** — **2 Sam. 8:17**
places, and made ***p*** — **1 Kin. 12:31**
and the ***p*** bear rule — **Jer. 5:31**
captivity with his ***p*** — **Jer. 48:7**
Her ***p*** have violated — **Ezek. 22:26**
reward, and the ***p*** thereof — **Mic. 3:11**
elders and chief ***p*** — **Matt. 16:21**

PRINCE
everlasting Father, The ***P*** — **Is. 9:6**
David shall be their ***p*** — **Ezek. 37:25**
the people of the ***p*** — **Dan. 9:26**
the dead, and the ***p*** — **Rev. 1:5**

PRINCES
servants, and his ***p*** — **2 Kin. 24:12**
Jerusalem, and all the ***p*** — **2 Kin. 24:14**
Thy ***p*** are rebellious — **Is. 1:23**
shall see and arise, ***p*** — **Is. 49:7**
king of Babylon's ***p*** — **Jer. 38:18**
his priests and his ***p*** — **Jer. 48:7**
p in the midst thereof — **Ezek. 22:27**

PROPHESY
The prophets ***p*** falsely — **Jer. 5:31**
The prophets ***p*** lies — **Jer. 14:14**
Wherefore dost thou ***p*** — **Jer. 32:3**
daughters shall ***p*** — **Joel 2:28**

PROPHET
be a ***p*** among you, I — **Num. 12:6**
called a ***P*** was beforetime — **1 Sam. 9:9**
the priest and the ***p*** — **Is. 28:7**
p is a fool, the spiritual — **Hos. 9:7**
LORD by Haggai the ***p*** — **Hag. 1:1**
send you Elijah the ***p*** — **Mal. 4:5**
the false ***p*** that wrought — **Rev. 19:20**
beast and the false ***p*** — **Rev. 20:10**

PROPHETS
and misused his ***p*** — **2 Chr. 36:16**
backs, and slew thy ***p*** — **Neh. 9:26**
The ***p*** prophesy falsely — **Jer. 5:31**
The ***p*** prophesy lies — **Jer. 14:14**
your ***p*** and your diviners — **Jer. 29:8**
servants the ***p***, rising — **Jer. 35:15**
hire, and the ***p*** thereof — **Mic. 3:11**
my servants the ***p*** — **Zech. 1:6**

PURE
a row, upon the ***p*** table — **Lev. 24:6**
thou shalt put ***p*** frankincense — **Lev. 24:7**
my name, and a ***p*** offering — **Mal. 1:11**
bodies washed with ***p*** — **Heb. 10:22**

RAISED
the LORD hath ***r*** up — **Jer. 51:11**
be killed, and be ***r*** — **Matt. 16:21**
Whom God hath ***r*** up — **Acts 2:24**
offences, and was ***r*** — **Rom. 4:25**

RECEIVE
have refused to ***r*** correction — **Jer. 5:3**
But ye shall ***r*** power — **Acts 1:8**
sins, and ye shall ***r*** — **Acts 2:38**
r forgiveness of sins — **Acts 26:18**
one may ***r*** the things — **2 Cor. 5:10**
r the crown of life — **James 1:12**

RECEIVED
he was ***r*** up into heaven — **Mark 16:19**
as ***r*** him, to them gave — **John 1:12**
tradition which he ***r*** — **2 Thess. 3:6**
world, ***r*** up into glory — **1 Tim. 3:16**
r the mark of the beast — **Rev. 19:20**
image, neither had ***r*** — **Rev. 20:4**

REDEEMED
mighty hand, and ***r*** — **Deut. 7:8**

SAINTS
ten thousands of *s* Deut. 33:2
the people of the *s* Dan. 7:27
God, called to be *s* Rom. 1:7
supplication for all *s* Eph. 6:18
Christ with all his *s* 1 Thess. 3:13

SAKE
any more for man's *s* Gen. 8:21
transgressions for mine own *s* Is. 43:25
Christ's *s* hath forgiven Eph. 4:32
flesh for his body's *s* Col. 1:24

SALVATION
the Rock of his *s* Deut. 32:15
my *s*, and my high tower Ps. 18:2
Behold, God is my *s* Is. 12:2
and rejoice in his *s* Is. 25:9
thou mayest be my *s* Is. 49:6
garments of *s*, he hath Is. 61:10
just, and having *s* Zech. 9:9
shall be heirs of *s* Heb. 1:14

SANCTIFIED
I *s* thee, and I ordained Jer. 1:5
when I shall be *s* Ezek. 36:23
which are *s* by faith Acts 26:18
washed, but ye are *s* 1 Cor. 6:11

SANCTIFY
S unto me all the firstborn Ex. 13:2
ye shall therefore *s* Lev. 11:44
And I will *s* my great Ezek. 36:23
he might *s* and cleanse Eph. 5:26

SANCTUARY
the shekel of the *s* Ex. 30:13
of covering the *s* Num. 4:15
the house of their *s* 2 Chr. 36:17
cast fire into thy *s* Ps. 74:7
the city and the *s* Dan. 9:26

SAT
of the LORD, and *s* Ezek. 20:1
into heaven, and *s* Mark 16:19
purged our sins, *s* Heb. 1:3
thrones, and they *s* Rev. 20:4

SAUL
wilt thou mourn for *S* 1 Sam. 16:1
it from *S*, whom I put 2 Sam. 7:15
As for *S*, he made havock Acts 8:3
the tetrarch, and *S* Acts 13:1

SAVE
dwell therein, *s* Caleb Num. 14:30
no man shall *s* thee Deut. 28:29
remained, *s* the poorest 2 Kin. 24:14
did their own arm *s* Ps. 44:3
him, and he will *s* Is. 25:9
he shall *s* his people Matt. 1:21
any man the Father, *s* Matt. 11:27
baptism doth also now *s* 1 Pet. 3:21

SAVED
and we shall be *s* Ps. 80:7
angel of his presence *s* Is. 63:9
days Judah shall be *s* Jer. 23:6
the end shall be *s* Matt. 10:22
through him might be *s* John 3:17
according to his mercy he *s* Titus 3:5

SCATTERED
out his arrows, and *s* Ps. 18:14
Israel is a *s* sheep Jer. 50:17
the sheep shall be *s* Zech. 13:7
were *s* abroad, as sheep Matt. 9:36

SEA
the fish of the *s* Gen. 1:26
is upon the *s* shore Gen. 22:17
his hand over the *s* Ex. 14:21
heaven and earth, the *s* Ex. 20:11
the *s* of the plain Josh. 3:16
waters cover the *s* Is. 11:9
the islands of the *s* Is. 11:11
I dry up the *s*, I make Is. 50:2

SEED
woman, and between thy *s* Gen. 3:15
Unto thy *s* will I give Gen. 12:7
Unto thy *s* have I given Gen. 15:18
thee, and to thy *s* Gen. 17:8
will multiply thy *s* Gen. 22:17
let any of thy *s* pass Lev. 18:21
I will set up thy *s* 2 Sam. 7:12
his *s*, he shall prolong Is. 53:10

SEEK
ye *s*, and thither thou Deut. 12:5
if thou *s* him, he will 1 Chr. 28:9
and if ye *s* him, he 2 Chr. 15:2
s judgment, relieve Is. 1:17
Israel return, and *s* Hos. 3:5
s the law at his mouth Mal. 2:7
the Lord, whom ye *s* Mal. 3:1
s ye first the kingdom Matt. 6:33

SEND
LORD shall *s* upon thee Deut. 28:20
which the LORD shall *s* Deut. 28:48
I will *s* thee to Jesse 1 Sam. 16:1
Behold, I will *s* and Jer. 25:9
Behold, I will *s* my Mal. 3:1
whom the Father will *s* John 14:26
come, whom I will *s* John 15:26
write in a book, and *s* Rev. 1:11

SERVANT
law, which Moses my *s* Josh. 1:7
Behold my *s*, whom I Is. 42:1
hath redeemed his *s* Is. 48:20
thou shouldest be my *s* Is. 49:6
nation abhorreth, to a *s* Is. 49:7
my righteous *s* justify Is. 53:11
king of Babylon, my *s* Jer. 25:9
Paul, a *s* of Jesus Rom. 1:1

SERVANTS
his *s*, when he seeth Deut. 32:36
Moabites became David's *s* 2 Sam. 8:2
Edom became David's *s* 2 Sam. 8:14
which he spake by his *s* 2 Kin. 24:2
mother, and his *s* 2 Kin. 24:12
of Judah, and his *s* Jer. 21:7
s the prophets, rising Jer. 35:15
which I commanded my *s* Zech. 1:6

SERVE
thyself to them, nor *s* Ex. 20:5
worship them, and *s* Deut. 4:19
there shalt thou *s* Deut. 28:36

shalt thou *s* thine	Deut. 28:48
there thou shalt *s*	Deut. 28:64
of thy father, and *s*	1 Chr. 28:9
my witness, whom I *s*	Rom. 1:9
from dead works to *s*	Heb. 9:14

SET

the camp is to *s* forward	Num. 4:15
thou shalt *s* over thee	Deut. 28:36
thy fathers, I will *s*	2 Sam. 7:12
Yet have I *s* my king	Ps. 2:6
Lord shall *s* his hand	Is. 11:11
I have this day *s* thee	Jer. 1:10
the God of heaven *s*	Dan. 2:44
the joy that was *s*	Heb. 12:2

SEVENTH

day until the *s* day	Ex. 12:15
the *s* day is the sabbath	Ex. 20:10
and rested the *s* day	Ex. 20:11
And the *s* angel sounded	Rev. 11:15

SHADOW

yea, in the *s* of thy	Ps. 57:1
from the storm, a *s*	Is. 25:4
dry place, as the *s*	Is. 32:2
variableness, neither *s*	James 1:17

SHAME

them be clothed with *s*	Ps. 35:26
uncovered, to the *s*	Is. 20:4
face from *s* and spitting	Is. 50:6
cross, despising the *s*	Heb. 12:2

SHED

shall his blood be *s*	Gen. 9:6
ravening the prey, to *s*	Ezek. 22:27
testament, which is *s*	Matt. 26:28
Holy Ghost, he hath *s*	Acts 2:33

SHEEP

thy *s* shall be given	Deut. 28:31
or flocks of thy *s*	Deut. 28:51
his people, and the *s*	Ps. 100:3
like *s* have gone astray	Is. 53:6
slaughter, and as a *s*	Is. 53:7
shepherd, and the *s*	Zech. 13:7
scattered abroad, as *s*	Matt. 9:36
shepherd of the *s*	Heb. 13:20

SHEPHERD

his flock like a *s*	Is. 40:11
I will set up one *s*	Ezek. 34:23
all shall have one *s*	Ezek. 37:24
sword, against my *s*	Zech. 13:7

SHEW

covenant with them, nor *s*	Deut. 7:2
s favour to the young	Deut. 28:50
mouth they *s* much love	Ezek. 33:31
dream, and we will *s*	Dan. 2:4
but go thy way, *s* thyself	Matt. 8:4
forth began Jesus to *s*	Matt. 16:21
that ye should *s* forth	1 Pet. 2:9
bear witness, and *s*	1 John 1:2

SHUT

is none *s* up, or left	Deut. 32:36
s up and left in Israel	1 Kin. 14:10
their ears heavy, and *s*	Is. 6:10
gates shall not be *s*	Is. 45:1

SIDE

strike it on the two *s*	Ex. 12:7
Hinnom unto the south *s*	Josh. 15:8
many, fear on every *s*	Jer. 20:10
either *s* of the river	Rev. 22:2

SIGHT

Moses did so in the *s*	Ex. 17:6
shalt be mad for the *s*	Deut. 28:34
the *s* of thine eyes	Deut. 28:67
wickedness in the *s*	1 Kin. 21:25
s of the LORD, to provoke	2 Kin. 17:17
in thy *s* shall no man	Ps. 143:2
and recovering of *s*	Luke 4:18
Jesus Christ, in the *s*	1 Thess. 1:3

SIGN

be upon thee for a *s*	Deut. 28:46
shall give you a *s*	Is. 7:14
And I will set a *s*	Is. 66:19
s of the Son of man	Matt. 24:30

SILVER

twenty pieces of *s*	Gen. 37:28
sons from far, their *s*	Is. 60:9
praised the gods of *s*	Dan. 5:23
over with gold and *s*	Hab. 2:19
their *s* nor their gold	Zeph. 1:18
will refine them as *s*	Zech. 13:9
and purifier of *s*	Mal. 3:3

SIN

transgression and *s*	Ex. 34:7
man *s*, and wilt thou	Num. 16:22
an offering for *s*	Is. 53:10
and he bare the *s* of	Is. 53:12
will remember their *s*	Jer. 31:34
which taketh away the *s*	John 1:29
hath made him to be *s*	2 Cor. 5:21
are, yet without *s*	Heb. 4:15

SINNED

hath *s*, a young bullock	Lev. 4:3
your sins which ye *s*	Deut. 9:18
but *s* against thy judgments	Neh. 9:29
God, because we have *s*	Dan. 9:11

SINS

that covereth his *s*	Prov. 28:13
your *s* be as scarlet	Is. 1:18
not remember thy *s*	Is. 43:25
to make an end of *s*	Dan. 9:24
s, and ye shall receive	Acts 2:38
purged our *s*, sat down	Heb. 1:3
once suffered for *s*	1 Pet. 3:18
washed us from our *s*	Rev. 1:5

SIT

unto my Lord, *S* thou	Ps. 110:1
I will *s* also upon	Is. 14:13
said, I am a God, I *s*	Ezek. 28:2
cometh, and they *s*	Ezek. 33:31

SLAIN

you, and ye shall be *s*	Lev. 26:17
and the *s* of the LORD	Is. 66:16
And the *s* shall fall	Ezek. 6:7
life of the Lamb *s*	Rev. 13:8

SLAY

manner, to *s* the righteous	Gen. 18:25

innocent and righteous *s* **Ex. 23:7**
his lips shall he *s* **Is. 11:4**
he shall *s* the dragon **Is. 27:1**

SLEW
s the sons of Zedekiah **2 Kin. 25:7**
who *s* their young men **2 Chr. 36:17**
backs, and *s* thy prophets **Neh. 9:26**
the king of Babylon *s* **Jer. 39:6**

SMITE
this night, and will *s* **Ex. 12:12**
thou shalt *s* them **Deut. 7:2**
The LORD will *s* thee **Deut. 28:27**
he shall *s* the earth **Is. 11:4**
s the shepherd, and **Zech. 13:7**

SMOTE
his rod he *s* the rock **Num. 20:11**
And Israel *s* him with **Num. 21:24**
he *s* Moab, and measured **2 Sam. 8:2**
David *s* also Hadadezer **2 Sam. 8:3**
And *s* all the firstborn **Ps. 78:51**
s him with the palms **Matt. 26:67**

SOLOMON
time *S* held a feast **1 Kin. 8:65**
S build an high place **1 Kin. 11:7**
vessels of gold which *S* **2 Kin. 24:13**
And thou, *S* my son **1 Chr. 28:9**
The proverbs of *S* **Prov. 10:1**

SON
neither the *s* of man **Num. 23:19**
conceive, and bear a *s* **Is. 7:14**
is born, unto us a *s* **Is. 9:6**
For the *S* of man shall **Matt. 16:27**
Father, and of the *S* **Matt. 28:19**
shall be called the *S* **Luke 1:32**
the only begotten *S* **John 1:18**
begotten *S*, that whosoever **John 3:16**

SONS
And the *s* of Judah **Gen. 46:12**
s have made an end **Num. 4:15**
Thy *s* and thy daughters **Deut. 28:32**
Thou shalt beget *s* **Deut. 28:41**
a king among his *s* **1 Sam. 16:1**
they caused their *s* **2 Kin. 17:17**
Babylon slew the *s* **Jer. 39:6**
your *s* and your daughters **Joel 2:28**

SOUL
became a living *s* **Gen. 2:7**
seventh day, that *s* **Ex. 12:15**
elect, in whom my *s* **Is. 42:1**
thou shalt make his *s* **Is. 53:10**
the travail of his *s* **Is. 53:11**
hath poured out his *s* **Is. 53:12**
hear, and your *s* shall **Is. 55:3**
rejoice in the LORD, my *s* **Is. 61:10**

SOULS
blood, and to destroy *s* **Ezek. 22:27**
find rest unto your *s* **Matt. 11:29**
Confirming the *s* of **Acts 14:22**
and I saw the *s* of **Rev. 20:4**

SPIRIT
I have put my *s* upon **Is. 42:1**
The *S* of the Lord GOD **Is. 61:1**
will pour out my *s* **Joel 2:28**
s of grace and of supplications **Zech. 12:10**
tongues, as the *S* gave **Acts 2:4**
justified in the *S* **1 Tim. 3:16**
quickened by the *S* **1 Pet. 3:18**
hear what the *S* saith **Rev. 2:7**

STAND
Behold, I will *s* before **Ex. 17:6**
any man be able to *s* **Josh. 1:5**
could not any longer *s* **Judg. 2:14**
liveth, before whom I *s* **1 Kin. 17:1**
Jesse, which shall *s* **Is. 11:10**
awake, *s* up, O Jerusalem **Is. 51:17**
kingdoms, and it shall *s* **Dan. 2:44**
time shall Michael *s* **Dan. 12:1**

STARS
heaven, and tell the *s* **Gen. 15:5**
multiply thy seed as the *s* **Gen. 22:17**
to multiply as the *s* **Gen. 26:4**
s shall fall from heaven **Matt. 24:29**

STATUTES
keep my *s*, and my judgments **Lev. 18:5**
his *s*, and his commandments **Deut. 4:40**
s which I command thee **Deut. 28:15**
walked not in my *s* **Ezek. 20:13**
judgments, and observe my *s* **Ezek. 37:24**
and my *s*, which I commanded **Zech. 1:6**

STONE
be as still as a *s* **Ex. 15:16**
testimony, tables of *s* **Ex. 31:18**
other gods, wood and *s* **Deut. 28:36**
known, even wood and *s* **Deut. 28:64**
The *s* which the builders **Ps. 118:22**
a *s*, a tried *s*, a precious **Is. 28:16**
the chief corner *s* **Eph. 2:20**
And a *s* of stumbling **1 Pet. 2:8**

STONES
hail *s* and coals of **Ps. 18:13**
s thereof, and planted **Is. 5:2**
committed adultery with *s* **Jer. 3:9**
these *s* be made bread **Matt. 4:3**
as lively *s*, are built **1 Pet. 2:5**

STOOD
behold, the LORD *s* **Gen. 28:13**
from above *s* and rose **Josh. 3:16**
spake to the men that *s* **1 Sam. 17:26**
came and *s* by the conduit **2 Kin. 18:17**
s still in the prison **Neh. 12:39**
times ten thousand *s* **Dan. 7:10**
Jews, came Jesus and *s* **John 20:19**
midst of the elders, *s* **Rev. 5:6**

STRANGER
wherein thou art a *s* **Gen. 17:8**
s, or born in the land **Ex. 12:19**
thy cattle, nor thy *s* **Ex. 20:10**
s that is within thee **Deut. 28:43**
for I am a *s* with thee **Ps. 39:12**
that turn aside the *s* **Mal. 3:5**

STRENGTH
by *s* of hand the LORD **Ex. 13:3**
By *s* of hand the LORD **Ex. 13:14**

s, in whom I will trust Ps. 18:2
the LORD is the *s* of Ps. 27:1
made not God his *s* Ps. 52:7
LORD JEHOVAH is my *s* Is. 12:2
put on thy *s*, O Zion Is. 52:1
sun shineth in his *s* Rev. 1:16

STRONG
back by a *s* east wind Ex. 14:21
children of Ammon was *s* Num. 21:24
s and of a good courage Deut. 31:6
thou *s* and very courageous Josh. 1:7
Wine is a mocker, *s* Prov. 20:1
wine, and through *s* Is. 28:7
because they are very *s* Is. 31:1
the spoil with the *s* Is. 53:12

SUN
when thou seest the *s* Deut. 4:19
the *s* shall be darkened Is. 13:10
they worshipped the *s* Ezek. 8:16
the *s* and the moon Joel 2:10
The *s* shall be turned Joel 2:31
the rising of the *s* Mal. 1:11
those days shall the *s* Matt. 24:29

SURELY
LORD said, I have *s* Ex. 3:7
s be a snare unto thee Ex. 23:33
s die in the wilderness Num. 26:65
S the princes of Zoan Is. 19:11
S he hath borne our Is. 53:4
S the least of the Jer. 49:20
S, because thou hast Ezek. 5:11
God of Israel, *S* Moab Zeph. 2:9

SWEET
LORD smelled a *s* savour Gen. 8:21
horns of the altar of *s* Lev. 4:7
Sheba, and the *s* cane Jer. 6:20
an odour of a *s* smell Phil. 4:18

SWORD
the edge of the *s* Num. 21:24
burning, and with the *s* Deut. 28:22
young men with the *s* 2 Chr. 36:17
s of the LORD is filled Is. 34:6
consumed by the *s* Jer. 16:4
pestilence, from the *s* Jer. 21:7
fall by the *s* round Ezek. 5:12
Awake, O *s*, against Zech. 13:7

TABERNACLE
in the *t* of the congregation Lev. 4:7
the court of the *t* Lev. 6:16
Aaron went into the *t* Lev. 9:23
And I will set my *t* Lev. 26:11
pitch round about the *t* Num. 1:53
of Kohath in the *t* Num. 4:15
tarried long upon the *t* Num. 9:19
Shiloh, and set up the *t* Josh. 18:1

TEACH
will *t* us of his ways Is. 2:3
t no more every man Jer. 31:34
the priests thereof *t* Mic. 3:11
t all nations, baptizing Matt. 28:19
shall *t* you all things John 14:26

TEMPLE
Israel had made in the *t* 2 Kin. 24:13
LORD is in his holy *t* Ps. 11:4
vengeance of his *t* Jer. 51:11
at the door of the *t* Ezek. 8:16
suddenly come to his *t* Mal. 3:1
agreement hath the *t* 2 Cor. 6:16
t leave out, and measure Rev. 11:2

TEN
covenant, the *t* commandments Ex. 34:28
t thousands of saints Deut. 33:2
men of valour, even *t* 2 Kin. 24:14
t thousand times *t* Dan. 7:10

THINE
thou settest *t* hand Deut. 28:20
smitten before *t* enemies Deut. 28:25
shalt thou serve *t* Deut. 28:48
fill *t* horn with oil 1 Sam. 16:1
t house and thy kingdom 2 Sam. 7:16
I make *t* enemies thy Ps. 110:1
blessing upon *t* offspring Is. 44:3
O LORD, are not *t* eyes Jer. 5:3

THOUSAND
put ten *t* to flight Lev. 26:8
commandments to a *t* Deut. 7:9
a *t*, and two put ten Deut. 32:30
Syrians of Zoba, twenty *t* 2 Sam. 10:6
valour, even ten *t* 2 Kin. 24:14
t thousands ministered Dan. 7:10
reigned with Christ a *t* Rev. 20:4

THRONE
will stablish the *t* 2 Sam. 7:13
thy *t* shall be established 2 Sam. 7:16
temple, the LORD's *t* Ps. 11:4
Thy *t*, O God, is for Ps. 45:6
no end, upon the *t* Is. 9:7
t of his father David Luke 1:32
hand of the *t* of God Heb. 12:2
which are before his *t* Rev. 1:4

TIME
the *t* appointed I will Gen. 18:14
commanded thee, in the *t* Ex. 23:15
t to recover the remnant Is. 11:11
t shall Michael stand Dan. 12:1
t forth began Jesus Matt. 16:21
seen God at any *t* John 1:18
the *t*, until the Lord 1 Cor. 4:5
the fulness of the *t* Gal. 4:4

TIMES
Three *t* in a year shall Deut. 16:16
fire, and observed *t* 2 Kin. 21:6
And he changeth the *t* Dan. 2:21
ten thousand *t* ten Dan. 7:10
to change *t* and laws Dan. 7:25
even in troublous *t* Dan. 9:25
a time, *t*, and an half Dan. 12:7

TONGUE
t thou shalt not understand Deut. 28:49
t cleaveth to my jaws Ps. 22:15
their *t* a sharp sword Ps. 57:4
the *t* of the dumb sing Is. 35:6

also *w* in my judgments	Ezek. 37:24
w humbly with thy God	Mic. 6:8
ordained that we should *w*	Eph. 2:10
And *w* in love, as Christ	Eph. 5:2

WALL	
pisseth against the *w*	1 Kin. 14:10
break down the *w* thereof	Is. 5:5
storm against the *w*	Is. 25:4
built again, and the *w*	Dan. 9:25
her a *w* of fire round	Zech. 2:5

WAR	
and went out to *w*	Judg. 3:10
men of *w* fled by night	2 Kin. 25:4
the end of the *w* desolations	Dan. 9:26
fleshly lusts, which *w*	1 Pet. 2:11
make *w* with the Lamb	Rev. 17:14

WATER	
there shall come *w*	Ex. 17:6
the *w* under the earth	Ex. 20:4
For I will pour *w* upon	Is. 44:3
w, and dieth for thirst	Is. 50:2
that can hold no *w*	Jer. 2:13
baptize you with *w*	Matt. 3:11
whosoever drinketh of the *w*	John 4:14
washed with pure *w*	Heb. 10:22

WATERS	
dry land, and the *w*	Ex. 14:21
That the *w* which came	Josh. 3:16
chambers in the *w*	Ps. 104:3
LORD, as the *w* cover	Is. 11:9
w break out, and streams	Is. 35:6
fountain of living *w*	Jer. 2:13
upon the *w* of the river	Dan. 12:7
living fountains of *w*	Rev. 7:17

WAYS	
them, and flee seven *w*	Deut. 28:25
not prosper in thy *w*	Deut. 28:29
for all his *w* are judgment	Deut. 32:4
teach us of his *w*	Is. 2:3
according to his *w*	Jer. 17:10
w of the sons of men	Jer. 32:19
according to our *w*	Zech. 1:6
and his *w* past finding	Rom. 11:33

WHEREFORE	
W say unto the children	Ex. 6:6
w the LORD blessed	Ex. 20:11
W now let the fear	2 Chr. 19:7
W the Lord said, Forasmuch	Is. 29:13
W, when I came, was	Is. 50:2
W, as I live, saith	Ezek. 5:11
W, my beloved brethren	James 1:19
W gird up the loins	1 Pet. 1:13

WHEREWITH	
the straitness, *w* thine	Deut. 28:53
the straitness, *w* thine	Deut. 28:55
siege and straitness, *w*	Deut. 28:57
fear of thine heart *w*	Deut. 28:67

WICKED	
righteous with the *w*	Gen. 18:25
not justify the *w*	Ex. 23:7
Woe unto the *w*	Is. 3:11
shall he slay the *w*	Is. 11:4
his grave with the *w*	Is. 53:9
Let the *w* forsake his	Is. 55:7
doth the way of the *w*	Jer. 12:1
by *w* hands have crucified	Acts 2:23

WICKEDNESS	
of the *w* of thy doings	Deut. 28:20
sell himself to work *w*	1 Kin. 21:25
righteousness, and hatest *w*	Ps. 45:7
strengthened himself in his *w*	Ps. 52:7
spiritual *w* in high	Eph. 6:12

WIFE	
his son Abram's *w*	Gen. 11:31
God said, Sarah thy *w*	Gen. 17:19
shalt betroth a *w*	Deut. 28:30
brother, and toward the *w*	Deut. 28:54
to *w* Jezebel the daughter	1 Kin. 16:31
Jezebel his *w* stirred	1 Kin. 21:25
about a sister, a *w*	1 Cor. 9:5
husband of one *w*, vigilant	1 Tim. 3:2

WILDERNESS	
shall fall in this *w*	Num. 14:29
Israel into the *w*	Num. 21:23
forty years in the *w*	Deut. 8:2
w shall waters break	Is. 35:6
make the rivers a *w*	Is. 50:2
make her *w* like Eden	Is. 51:3
against me in the *w*	Ezek. 20:13
against them in the *w*	Ezek. 20:21

WILT	
man sin, and *w* thou	Num. 16:22
to pass, if thou *w*	Deut. 28:15
If thou *w* not observe	Deut. 28:58
How long *w* thou mourn	1 Sam. 16:1
But if thou *w* not go	Jer. 38:18

WIND	
by a strong east *w*	Ex. 14:21
the wings of the *w*	Ps. 104:3
hiding place from the *w*	Is. 32:2
fan them, and the *w*	Is. 41:16

WINE	
w, nor gather the grapes	Deut. 28:39
thee either corn, *w*	Deut. 28:51
W is a mocker, strong	Prov. 20:1
have erred through *w*	Is. 28:7
vineyards, and drink the *w*	Amos 9:14
be not drunk with *w*	Eph. 5:18
angry, not given to *w*	Titus 1:7
w of the wrath of God	Rev. 14:10

WISDOM	
man glory in his *w*	Jer. 9:23
Is *w* no more in Teman	Jer. 49:7
giveth *w* unto the wise	Dan. 2:21
riches both of the *w*	Rom. 11:33
is made unto us *w*	1 Cor. 1:30
any of you lack *w*	James 1:5

WISE	
gift blindeth the *w*	Ex. 23:8
the eyes of the *w*	Deut. 16:19
thee a *w* and an understanding	1 Kin. 3:12
deceived thereby is not *w*	Prov. 20:1

YOUNG

hath sinned, a ***y*** bullock	**Lev. 4:3**
shew favour to the ***y***	**Deut. 28:50**
her ***y*** one that cometh	**Deut. 28:57**
Chaldees, who slew their ***y***	**2 Chr. 36:17**
Ethiopians captives, ***y***	**Is. 20:4**
those that are with ***y***	**Is. 40:11**
dream dreams, your ***y***	**Joel 2:28**
forest, as a ***y*** lion	**Mic. 5:8**

ZEDEKIAH

the LORD, and made ***Z***	**2 Chr. 36:10**
I will deliver ***Z*** king	**Jer. 21:7**
overtook ***Z*** in the plains	**Jer. 39:5**
slew the sons of ***Z***	**Jer. 39:6**

GO YE
Therefore
& TEACH
ALL NATIONS
Baptizing
THEM
IN THE NAME OF
The Father
AND OF
THE SON
AND OF THE
Holy Ghost

MATTHEW 28:19

ACKNOWLEDGMENTS

The production of a study Bible requires the dedicated efforts of a large team of people, and this one is no exception. Reformation Heritage Books would like to express its appreciation to the many people who gave their time, talents, financial support, and prayers to this project. We would especially like to thank the following contributors of notes: Geoff Banister, Charles Barrett, Michael Barrett, Joel Beeke, Gerald Bilkes, Brian DeVries, Ian Goligher, John Greer, Jerrold Lewis, Alan Macgregor, Andy McIntosh, Pooyan Mehrshahi, Colin Mercer, Gerald Procee, Maurice Roberts, David Silversides, John Thackway, and Malcolm Watts. Thanks, too, to Sinclair Ferguson for allowing us to edit his short talks on church history and print them here, to Christopher Coldwell for supplying the text for the Westminster Confession of Faith, as well as to dozens of contributors who have written other articles throughout this study Bible, both interspersed within the text and in the Christian living section. We express our gratitude to the Study Bible Board, to the staff of Credo Communications and Trinitarian Bible Society, and to various copyeditors and proofreaders. And finally, in addition to our staff, we owe a large debt of gratitude to our general editor, Joel Beeke, and his teaching assistant, Paul Smalley, together with Michael Barrett as Old Testament Editor and Gerald Bilkes as New Testament Editor for the countless hours they dedicated to this task as a labor of love.

NOTES

NOTES

NOTES

NOTES

NOTES

NOTES

NOTES

NOTES

NOTES

NOTES

NOTES

MAPS

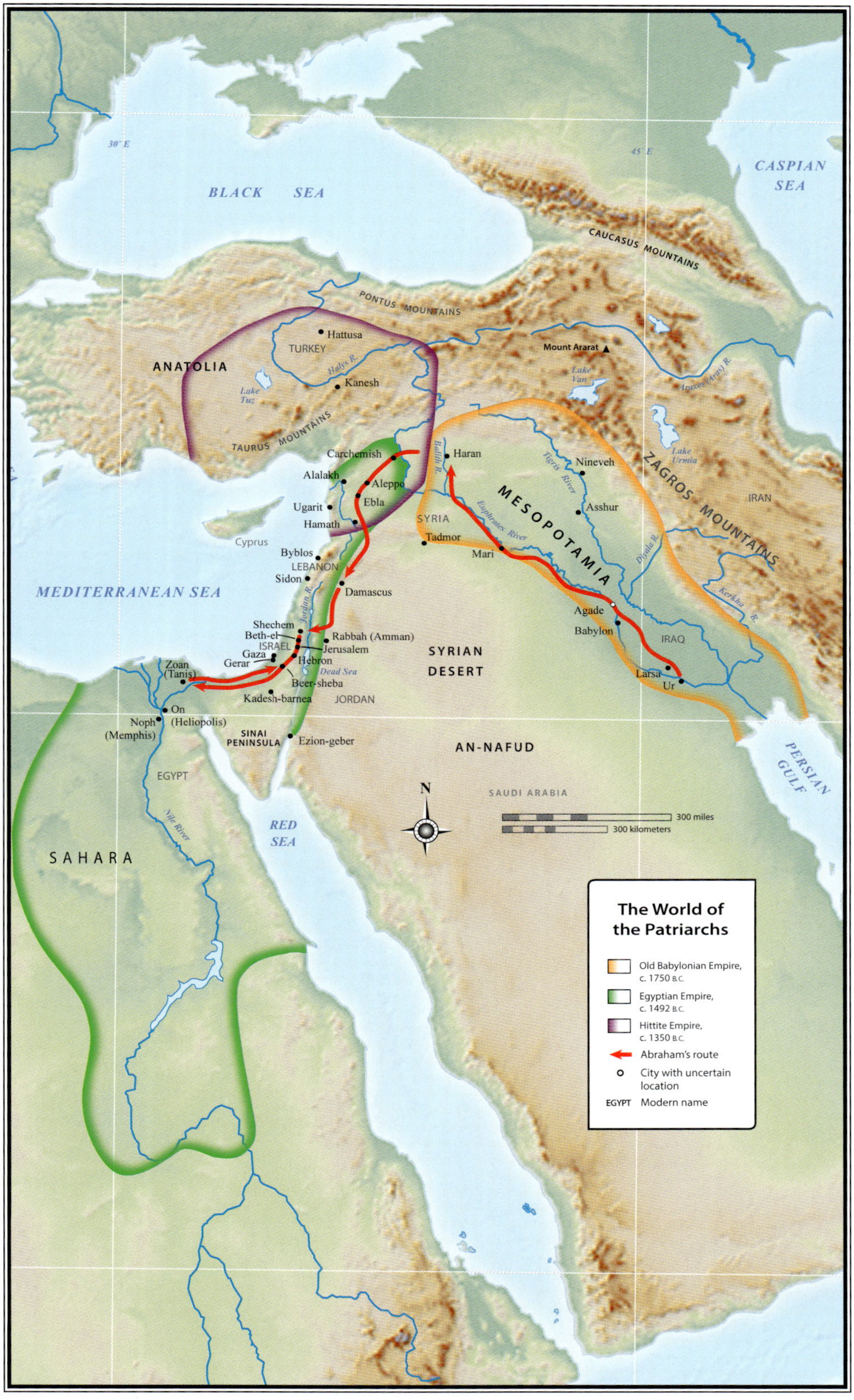

The World of the Patriarchs
Old Babylonian Empire, c. 1750 B.C.
Egyptian Empire, c. 1492 B.C.
Hittite Empire, c. 1350 B.C.
Abraham's route
City with uncertain location
EGYPT Modern name
BLACK SEA
CASPIAN SEA
30° E
45° E
CAUCASUS MOUNTAINS
PONTUS MOUNTAINS
Hattusa
TURKEY
ANATOLIA
Halys R.
Kanesh
Lake Tuz
TAURUS MOUNTAINS
Mount Ararat
Lake Van
Araxes (Aras) R.
Lake Urmia
ZAGROS MOUNTAINS
IRAN
Carchemish
Haran
Balikh R.
Nineveh
Tigris River
Alalakh
Aleppo
Ebla
Ugarit
Hamath
MESOPOTAMIA
Asshur
SYRIA
Euphrates River
Tadmor
Mari
Cyprus
Byblos
LEBANON
Sidon
Damascus
Diyala R.
Kerkha R.
MEDITERRANEAN SEA
Jordan R.
Agade
Babylon
IRAQ
Shechem
Beth-el
ISRAEL
Rabbah (Amman)
Jerusalem
Gaza
Gerar
Hebron
Dead Sea
Zoan (Tanis)
Beer-sheba
Kadesh-barnea
JORDAN
SYRIAN DESERT
Larsa
Ur
On (Heliopolis)
Noph (Memphis)
SINAI PENINSULA
Ezion-geber
AN-NAFUD
PERSIAN GULF
EGYPT
SAUDI ARABIA
N
300 miles
300 kilometers
Nile River
RED SEA
SAHARA

The Exodus from Egypt
Traditional route
Alternate routes of Red Sea crossing
City
City with uncertain location
Mountain
50 miles
50 kilometers
MEDITERRANEAN SEA
RED SEA
32° E
34° E
32° N
30° N
28° N
N
Sea of Galilee
Jordan R.
Dead Sea
AMMON
Mount Nebo
CANAAN
MOAB
EDOM
MIDIAN
Kadesh-barnea
WILDERNESS OF ZIN
Zoar
Punon
WILDERNESS OF PARAN
Ezion-geber
SINAI
WILDERNESS OF SIN
Rephidim
Mount Sinai (Jebel Musa)
Gulf of Aqaba
Gulf of Suez
Sile
Raamses
GOSHEN
Succoth
Pithom
Lake Timsah
Great Bitter Lake
Little Bitter Lake
EGYPT
On (Heliopolis)
Noph (Memphis)
Nile River

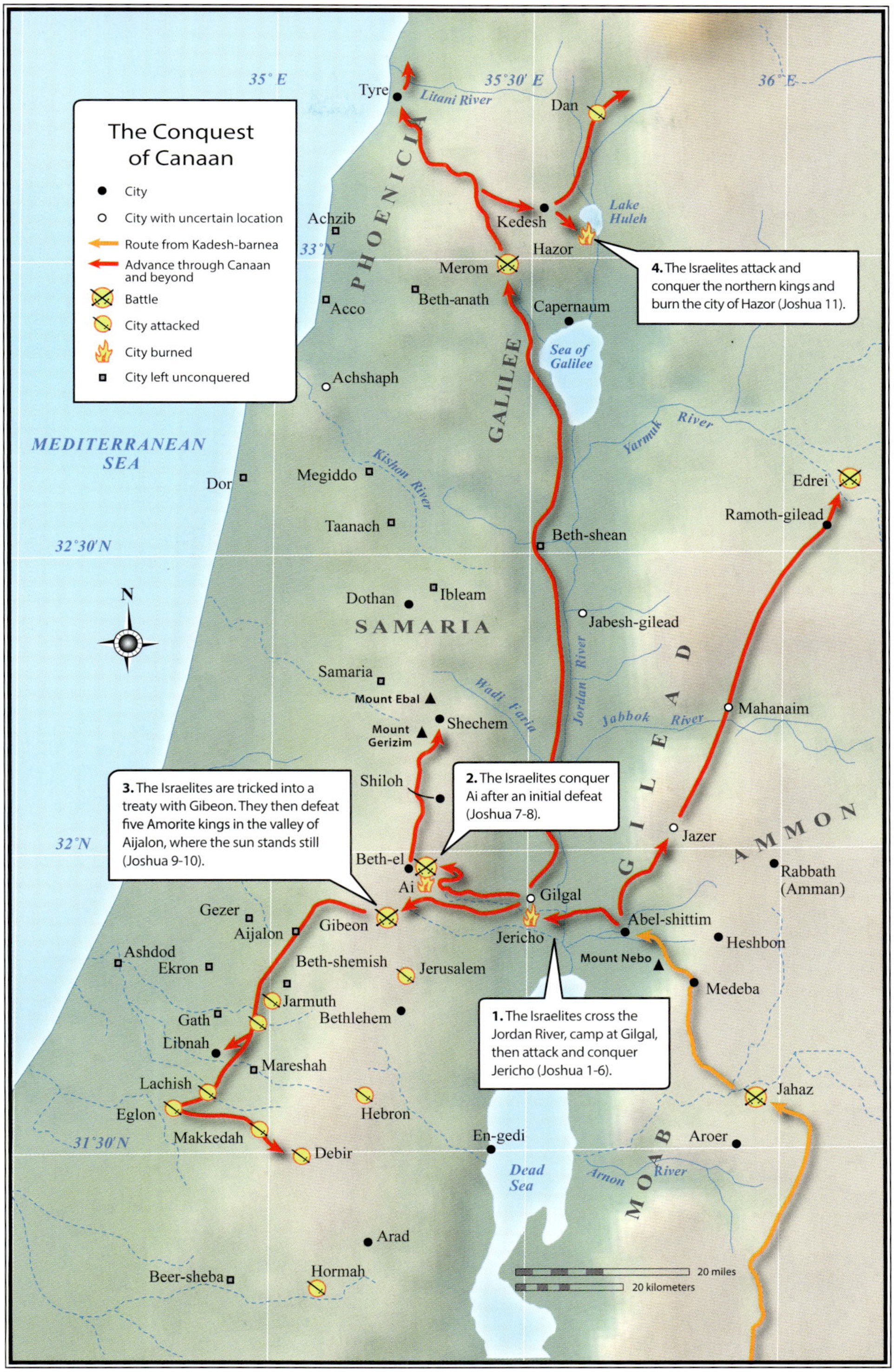

The Conquest of Canaan
City
City with uncertain location
Route from Kadesh-barnea
Advance through Canaan and beyond
Battle
City attacked
City burned
City left unconquered
35° E
35°30′ E
36° E
33°N
32°30′N
32°N
31°30′N
MEDITERRANEAN SEA
PHOENICIA
GALILEE
SAMARIA
GILEAD
AMMON
MOAB
Tyre
Litani River
Dan
Kedesh
Lake Huleh
Hazor
Achzib
Merom
Acco
Beth-anath
Capernaum
Sea of Galilee
Achshaph
Yarmuk River
Kishon River
Dor
Megiddo
Taanach
Edrei
Ramoth-gilead
Beth-shean
Dothan
Ibleam
Jabesh-gilead
Jordan River
Samaria
Wadi Faria
Mount Ebal
Mount Gerizim
Shechem
Jabbok River
Mahanaim
Shiloh
Jazer
Beth-el
Ai
Gilgal
Rabbath (Amman)
Gezer
Aijalon
Gibeon
Jericho
Abel-shittim
Heshbon
Ashdod
Ekron
Beth-shemish
Jerusalem
Mount Nebo
Medeba
Jarmuth
Gath
Bethlehem
Libnah
Mareshah
Lachish
Eglon
Hebron
Jahaz
Makkedah
Debir
En-gedi
Aroer
Dead Sea
Arnon River
Arad
Beer-sheba
Hormah
20 miles
20 kilometers
N
1. The Israelites cross the Jordan River, camp at Gilgal, then attack and conquer Jericho (Joshua 1-6).
2. The Israelites conquer Ai after an initial defeat (Joshua 7-8).
3. The Israelites are tricked into a treaty with Gibeon. They then defeat five Amorite kings in the valley of Aijalon, where the sun stands still (Joshua 9-10).
4. The Israelites attack and conquer the northern kings and burn the city of Hazor (Joshua 11).

The Allotments to the Twelve Tribes
City
City of refuge
City with uncertain location
34° 30′ E
35° E
35° 30′ E
36° E
33°N
32°30′N
32°N
31°30′N
31°N
MEDITERRANEAN SEA
N
Litani River
Tyre
Ijon
Dan
ARAM (Syria)
ASHER
NAPHTALI
Rehob
Abdon
Kedesh
Lake Huleh
Hazor
Merom
EAST MANASSEH
Mishal
Nahalal
Rimmon
Helkath
ZEBULUN
Sea of Galilee
Hammath
Golan
Ashtaroth
Daberath
Yarmuk River
Jokneam
Megiddo
Dor
Kishon River
ISSACHAR
Jarmuth
Edrei
Taanach
Beth-shean
Ramoth-gilead
Ibleam
Jabesh-gilead
WEST MANASSEH
Samaria
Mount Ebal
Shechem
Mount Gerizim
Wadi Faria
Jordan River
Jabbok River
Mahanaim
Gath-rimmon
Joppa
Shiloh
EPHRAIM
GAD
Jazer
AMMON
Rabbah (Amman)
DAN
Eltekah
Beth-horon
Gezer
Bethel
Gibeon
Gilgal
Geba
Jericho
Gibbethon
Aijalon
BENJAMIN
Abel-shittim
Heshbon
Mount Nebo
Bezer
Beth-shemesh
Jerusalem
Medeba
Bethlehem
Ashkelon
Libnah
REUBEN
Lachish
Hebron
Dead Sea
Eglon
Jahaz
Gaza
JUDAH
Juttah
Aroer
Debir
En-gedi
Eshtemoa
Arnon River
Gerar
Ashan
Beer-sheba
Hormah
MOAB
SIMEON
20 miles
20 kilometers
Zered Brook
EDOM

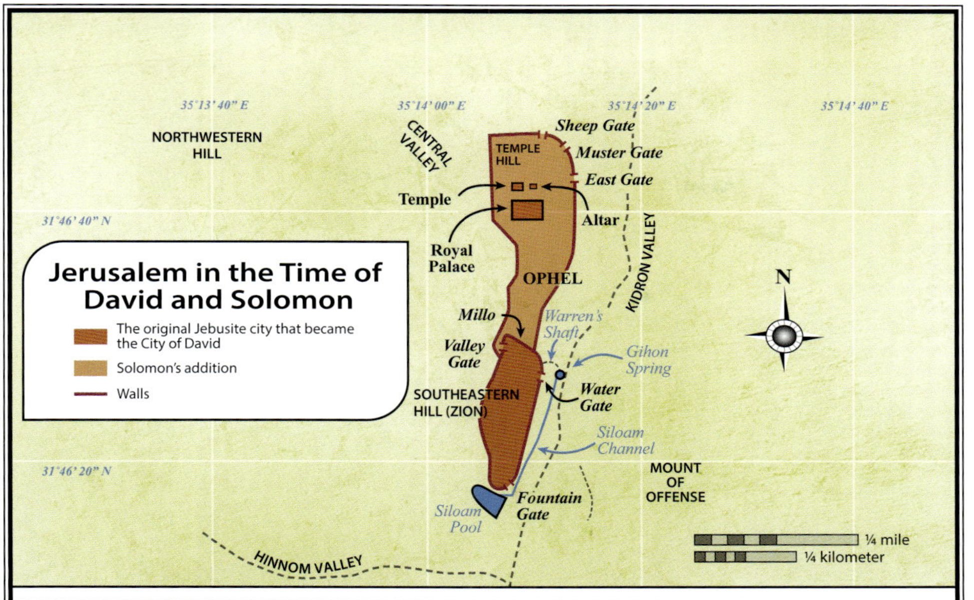

Jerusalem in the Time of David and Solomon
The original Jebusite city that became the City of David
Solomon's addition
Walls
35°13' 40" E
35°14' 00" E
35°14' 20" E
35°14' 40" E
31°46' 40" N
31°46' 20" N
NORTHWESTERN HILL
CENTRAL VALLEY
TEMPLE HILL
Sheep Gate
Muster Gate
East Gate
Temple
Altar
Royal Palace
OPHEL
KIDRON VALLEY
Millo
Warren's Shaft
Valley Gate
Gihon Spring
Water Gate
SOUTHEASTERN HILL (ZION)
Siloam Channel
MOUNT OF OFFENSE
Fountain Gate
Siloam Pool
HINNOM VALLEY
N
¼ mile
¼ kilometer

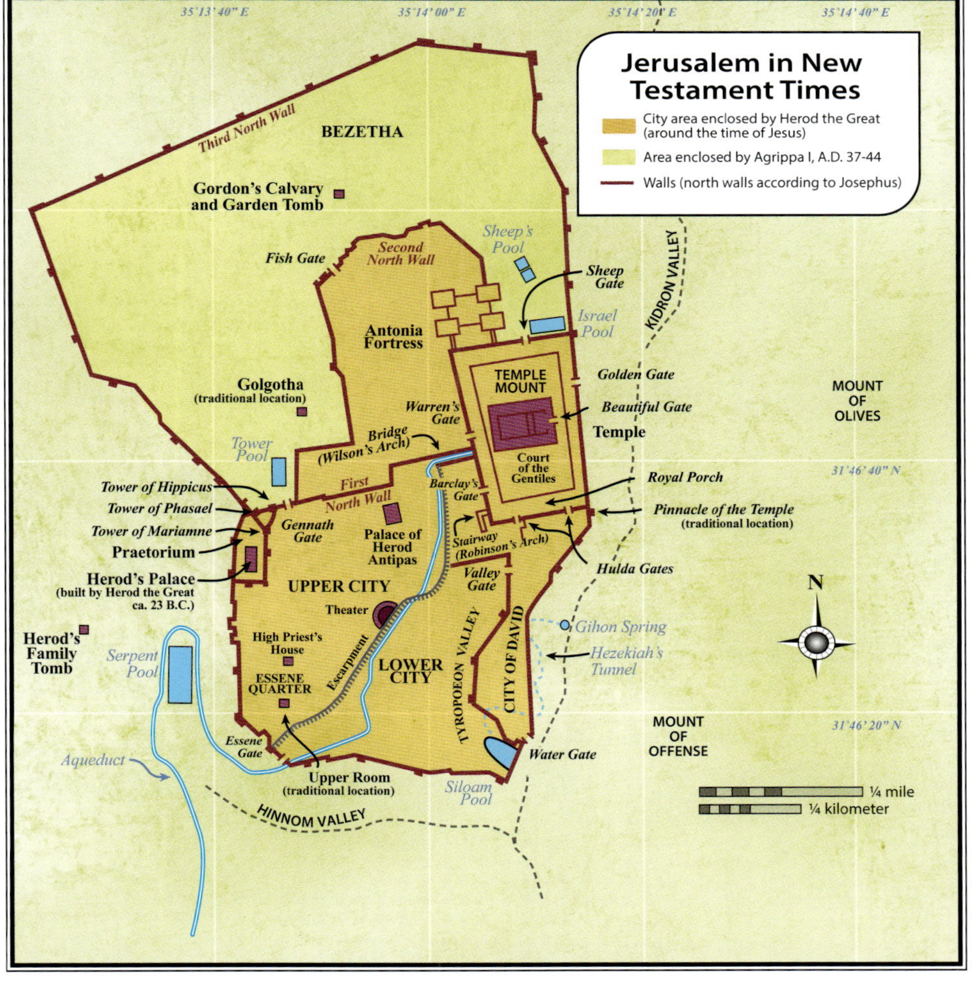

Jerusalem in New Testament Times
City area enclosed by Herod the Great (around the time of Jesus)
Area enclosed by Agrippa I, A.D. 37-44
Walls (north walls according to Josephus)
35°13' 40" E
35°14' 00" E
35°14' 20" E
35°14' 40" E
31°46' 40" N
31°46' 20" N
Third North Wall
BEZETHA
Gordon's Calvary and Garden Tomb
Fish Gate
Second North Wall
Sheep's Pool
Sheep Gate
KIDRON VALLEY
Israel Pool
Antonia Fortress
TEMPLE MOUNT
Golden Gate
MOUNT OF OLIVES
Golgotha (traditional location)
Warren's Gate
Beautiful Gate
Temple
Bridge (Wilson's Arch)
Tower Pool
Court of the Gentiles
Royal Porch
Tower of Hippicus
First North Wall
Barclay's Gate
Tower of Phasael
Pinnacle of the Temple (traditional location)
Tower of Mariamne
Gennath Gate
Palace of Herod Antipas
Stairway (Robinson's Arch)
Praetorium
Hulda Gates
Herod's Palace (built by Herod the Great ca. 23 B.C.)
Valley Gate
UPPER CITY
Theater
Gihon Spring
Herod's Family Tomb
High Priest's House
Escarpment
Hezekiah's Tunnel
Serpent Pool
LOWER CITY
TYROPOEON VALLEY
CITY OF DAVID
ESSENE QUARTER
MOUNT OF OFFENSE
Essene Gate
Water Gate
Aqueduct
Upper Room (traditional location)
Siloam Pool
HINNOM VALLEY
N
¼ mile
¼ kilometer

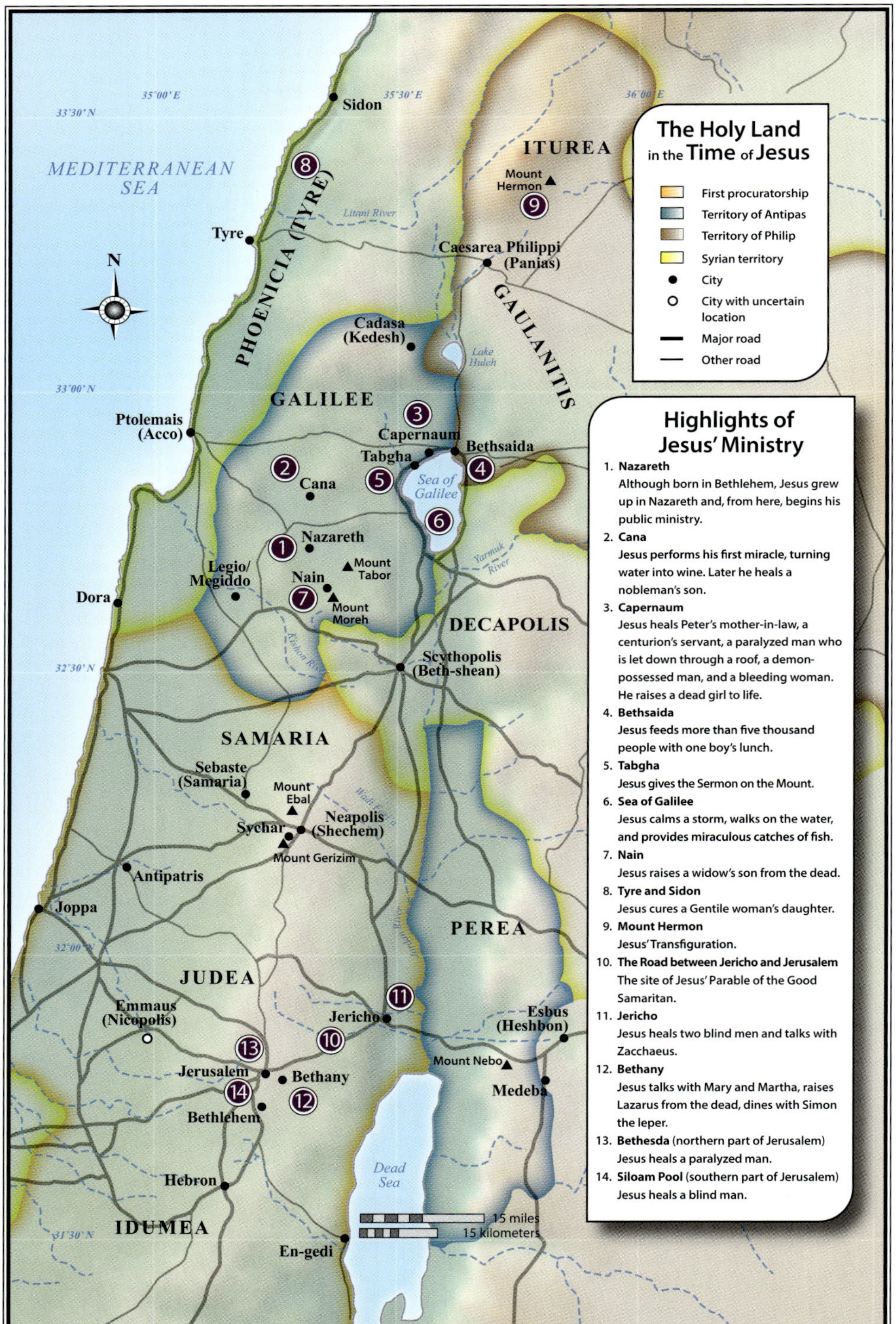
The Holy Land
in the Time of Jesus
First procuratorship
Territory of Antipas
Territory of Philip
Syrian territory
City
City with uncertain location
Major road
Other road
Highlights of Jesus' Ministry
1. Nazareth
Although born in Bethlehem, Jesus grew up in Nazareth and, from here, begins his public ministry.
2. Cana
Jesus performs his first miracle, turning water into wine. Later he heals a nobleman's son.
3. Capernaum
Jesus heals Peter's mother-in-law, a centurion's servant, a paralyzed man who is let down through a roof, a demon-possessed man, and a bleeding woman. He raises a dead girl to life.
4. Bethsaida
Jesus feeds more than five thousand people with one boy's lunch.
5. Tabgha
Jesus gives the Sermon on the Mount.
6. Sea of Galilee
Jesus calms a storm, walks on the water, and provides miraculous catches of fish.
7. Nain
Jesus raises a widow's son from the dead.
8. Tyre and Sidon
Jesus cures a Gentile woman's daughter.
9. Mount Hermon
Jesus' Transfiguration.
10. The Road between Jericho and Jerusalem
The site of Jesus' Parable of the Good Samaritan.
11. Jericho
Jesus heals two blind men and talks with Zacchaeus.
12. Bethany
Jesus talks with Mary and Martha, raises Lazarus from the dead, dines with Simon the leper.
13. Bethesda (northern part of Jerusalem)
Jesus heals a paralyzed man.
14. Siloam Pool (southern part of Jerusalem)
Jesus heals a blind man.
MEDITERRANEAN SEA
N
35°00′E
35°30′E
36°00′E
33°30′N
33°00′N
32°30′N
32°00′N
31°30′N
Sidon
Tyre
PHOENICIA (TYRE)
ITUREA
Mount Hermon
Litani River
Caesarea Philippi (Panias)
GAULANITIS
Cadasa (Kedesh)
Lake Huleh
GALILEE
Ptolemais (Acco)
Capernaum
Bethsaida
Tabgha
Sea of Galilee
Cana
Nazareth
Mount Tabor
Legio/ Megiddo
Nain
Mount Moreh
Dora
Yarmuk River
Kishon River
DECAPOLIS
Scythopolis (Beth-shean)
SAMARIA
Sebaste (Samaria)
Mount Ebal
Wadi Far'a
Neapolis (Shechem)
Sychar
Mount Gerizim
Antipatris
Joppa
PEREA
JUDEA
Emmaus (Nicopolis)
Jericho
Esbus (Heshbon)
Mount Nebo
Jerusalem
Bethany
Medeba
Bethlehem
Dead Sea
Hebron
IDUMEA
En-gedi
15 miles
15 kilometers

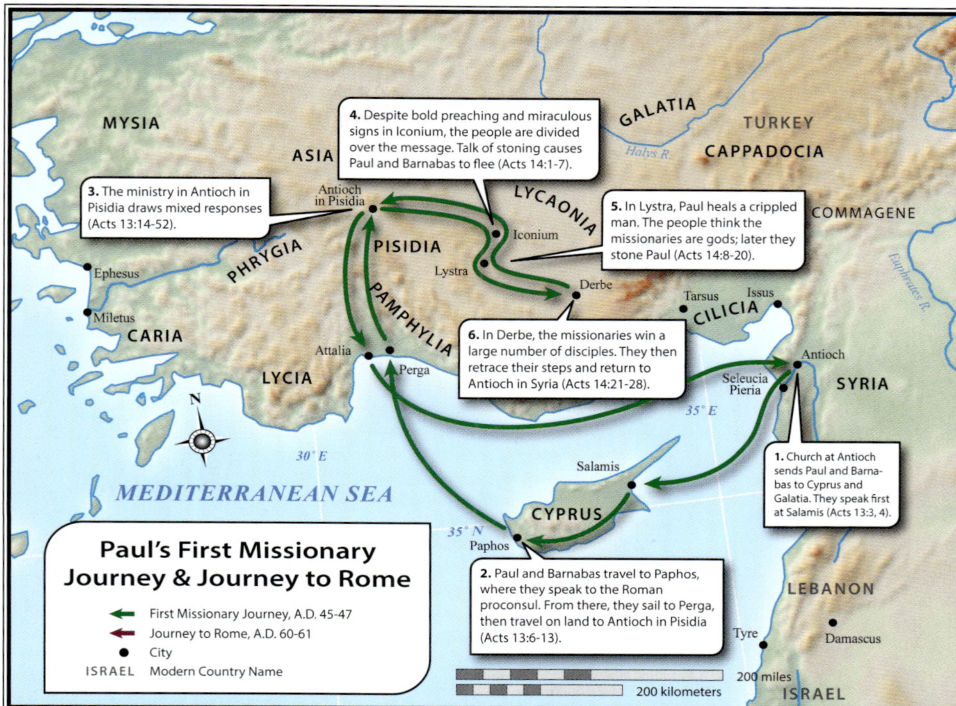
Paul's First Missionary Journey & Journey to Rome
First Missionary Journey, A.D. 45-47
Journey to Rome, A.D. 60-61
City
ISRAEL Modern Country Name
MYSIA
ASIA
GALATIA
TURKEY
CAPPADOCIA
LYCAONIA
COMMAGENE
PHRYGIA
PISIDIA
PAMPHYLIA
CILICIA
CARIA
LYCIA
SYRIA
CYPRUS
LEBANON
ISRAEL
MEDITERRANEAN SEA
Halys R.
Euphrates R.
Antioch in Pisidia
Iconium
Lystra
Derbe
Tarsus
Issus
Ephesus
Miletus
Attalia
Perga
Antioch
Seleucia Pieria
Salamis
Paphos
Tyre
Damascus
30° E
35° E
35° N
N
200 miles
200 kilometers
1. Church at Antioch sends Paul and Barnabas to Cyprus and Galatia. They speak first at Salamis (Acts 13:3, 4).
2. Paul and Barnabas travel to Paphos, where they speak to the Roman proconsul. From there, they sail to Perga, then travel on land to Antioch in Pisidia (Acts 13:6-13).
3. The ministry in Antioch in Pisidia draws mixed responses (Acts 13:14-52).
4. Despite bold preaching and miraculous signs in Iconium, the people are divided over the message. Talk of stoning causes Paul and Barnabas to flee (Acts 14:1-7).
5. In Lystra, Paul heals a crippled man. The people think the missionaries are gods; later they stone Paul (Acts 14:8-20).
6. In Derbe, the missionaries win a large number of disciples. They then retrace their steps and return to Antioch in Syria (Acts 14:21-28).

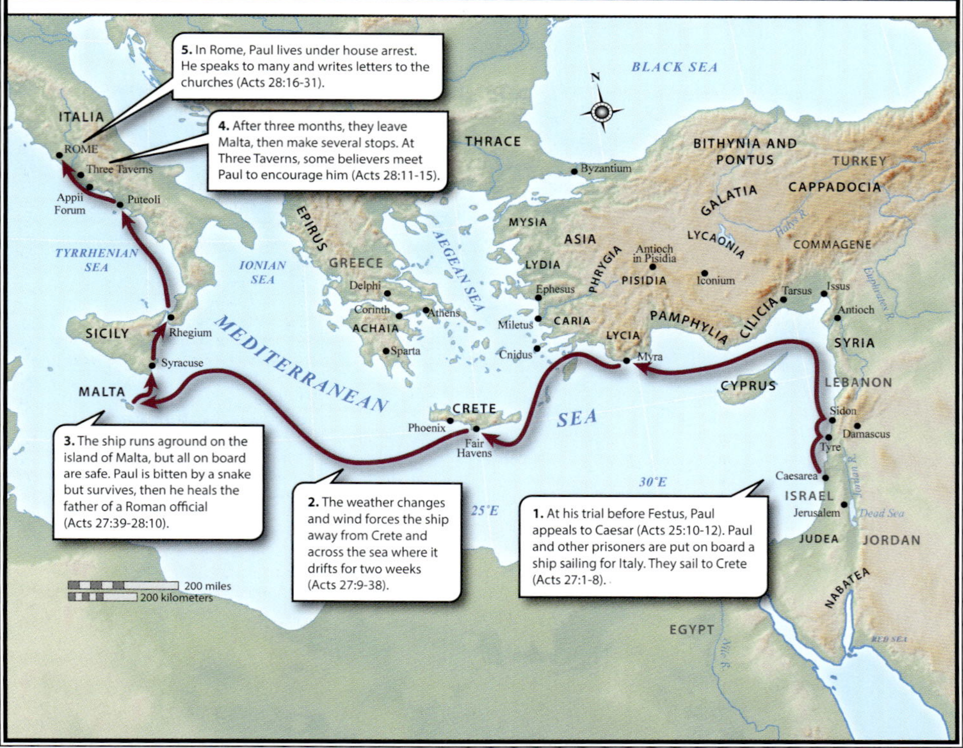
BLACK SEA
ITALIA
ROME
Three Taverns
Appii Forum
Puteoli
TYRRHENIAN SEA
IONIAN SEA
SICILY
Rhegium
Syracuse
MALTA
EPIRUS
GREECE
Delphi
Corinth
Athens
ACHAIA
Sparta
AEGEAN SEA
THRACE
Byzantium
MYSIA
ASIA
LYDIA
PHRYGIA
Ephesus
Miletus
CARIA
Cnidus
LYCIA
Myra
PISIDIA
Antioch in Pisidia
Iconium
PAMPHYLIA
CILICIA
Tarsus
Issus
Antioch
BITHYNIA AND PONTUS
GALATIA
LYCAONIA
CAPPADOCIA
TURKEY
COMMAGENE
Halys R.
Euphrates R.
SYRIA
CYPRUS
LEBANON
Sidon
Damascus
Tyre
Caesarea
ISRAEL
Jerusalem
Dead Sea
Jordan R.
JUDEA
JORDAN
NABATEA
EGYPT
Nile R.
RED SEA
MEDITERRANEAN SEA
CRETE
Phoenix
Fair Havens
25°E
30°E
N
200 miles
200 kilometers
1. At his trial before Festus, Paul appeals to Caesar (Acts 25:10-12). Paul and other prisoners are put on board a ship sailing for Italy. They sail to Crete (Acts 27:1-8).
2. The weather changes and wind forces the ship away from Crete and across the sea where it drifts for two weeks (Acts 27:9-38).
3. The ship runs aground on the island of Malta, but all on board are safe. Paul is bitten by a snake but survives, then he heals the father of a Roman official (Acts 27:39-28:10).
4. After three months, they leave Malta, then make several stops. At Three Taverns, some believers meet Paul to encourage him (Acts 28:11-15).
5. In Rome, Paul lives under house arrest. He speaks to many and writes letters to the churches (Acts 28:16-31).